DICTIONARY OF WOMEN WORLDWIDE:

25,000 Women through the Ages

DICTIONARY OF WOMEN WORLDWIDE:

25,000 Women through the Ages

Volume 1
A-L

Anne Commire, Editor
Deborah Klezmer, Associate Editor

YORKIN PUBLICATIONS

THOMSON

GALE

Detroit • New York • San Francisco • New Haven, Conn. • Waterville, Maine • London • Munich

Dictionary of Women Worldwide: 25,000 Women through the Ages

Yorkin Publications Staff
Anne Commire, *Editor*
Deborah Klezmer, *Associate Editor*
Eileen O'Pasek, *Editorial Assistant*
Chetna Chopra, Jennifer Jue-Steuck, Bronwyn Law-Viljoen, Catherine Powers, Elizabeth Renaud, Andy Smith, Mary Staub, *Contributors*

Project Editor
Margaret Mazurkiewicz

Editorial Support Services
Emmanuel T. Barrido, Luann Brennan

Rights Acquisitions Management
Jackie Jones, Kim Smilay

Imaging
Lezlie Light, Christine O'Bryan

Composition
Evi Seoud

Product Design
Jennifer Wahi

Manufacturing
Rita Wimberley

LIBRARY OF CONGRESS CATALOGING-IN-PUBLICATION DATA

Dictionary of women worldwide : 25,000 women through the ages / Anne Commire, editor ; Deborah Klezmer, associate editor.
   p. cm.
      Includes bibliographical references.
      ISBN 0-7876-7585-7 (set hardcover : alk. paper) –
      ISBN 0-7876-7676-4 (vol 1 : alk. paper) –
      ISBN 0-7876-7677-2 (vol 2 : alk. paper) –
      ISBN 1-4144-1861-2 (vol 3 : alk. paper)
      1. Women–Biography–Dictionaries.
      I. Commire, Anne. II. Klezmer, Deborah.

CT3202.D53 2006
920.72–dc22

2006008290

British Library Cataloguing-in-Publication Data
A catalogue record for this book is available from the British Library

This title is also available as an e-book
ISBN 0-7876-9394-4
Contact your Thompson Gale sales representative for ordering information.

Printed in the United States of America
10 9 8 7 6 5 4 3 2

CONTENTS

INTRODUCTION

The idea for *Dictionary of Women Worldwide* (*DWW*) began while we were editing the 17-volume set of reference books entitled *Women in World History* (*WIWH*). While frequently turning to dictionaries for help, we were startled by the paucity of women included. In one oft-used biographical dictionary under 5% were women. Other biographical dictionaries had the same or less. It soon became clear that as long as women's entries had to compete with each other for the small percentage of pages set aside for them in traditional dictionaries, these sources were nearly useless to readers looking for a more balanced view of history.

And did those women included in conventional biographical dictionaries get short shrift? Let us approximate the ways. In one recent edition, Abigail Adams was allotted around 25 words, Rosa Bonheur, Empress Theodora, Hypatia, Charlotte Corday, Aspasia, Berthe Morisot, Anna Comnena, between 30 and 40, Mary Cassatt, Dorothea Dix and Anne Boleyn, around 50, Teresa of Avila, 75, and Rosa Luxemburg, 80. As for the men: Halsford Mackinder was allotted around 80 words, Charles Parry, Vincas Kreve and August Kotzebue, over 100, Gebhard Blucher, over 200, Charles I, over 400, Oliver Cromwell, over 600, and Napoleon, over 900. Richard Milhous Nixon, well over 400, was a great deal longer than Indira Gandhi, around 100, Empress Maria Theresa, around 125, Catherine II the Great, around 150, Queen Victoria, around 250, and Elizabeth I, 350.

Dictionary of Women Worldwide is a single source for researching women of any time period and any field of endeavor. It can answer a question quickly, saving users an afternoon slog on the Internet. Since the advent of the Web, conventional wisdom would have us believe that the women in *DWW* can be found quickly and easily in cyberspace. Would that were true; it would certainly have made our job easier. To make the most of the Internet, name variations, correct spellings, dates and personal information are vital. Being multilingual also helps. As well, the Internet has a kind of now-you-see-it-now-you-don't quality. Sites that were there yesterday, loaded with information, vanish like vapor. (Remember those in-depth personal accounts of athletes for the Sydney Olympics? Gone now.) "The average lifespan of a Web page today is 100 days," noted Brewster Kahle of the Internet Archive in San Francisco in 2003. Our goal was to produce a work that would allow the user to verify facts, answer ready reference questions, and begin to research a woman in less time than it takes to log on.

Because of the subject matter, the entries for *DWW* had to be longer than those found in a standard dictionary. For women, the personal is indeed the political. Who the king married is not traditionally required; who the queen married is. In an entry for Eleanor Dulles, listing her brother is essential. In an entry for John Foster Dulles, listing his sister is annoyingly optional. Names of husbands are also important; these are names that the women often went by in public and private life (e.g., Mrs. John Drew). More often than not, after time-consuming sleuthing, we only found a death date for an entrant after uncovering one or all of her married names. We also came across numerous duplicate entries in other biographical dictionaries, women who were listed under two different names, because without personal information it was impossible to see the duplication.

Realizing the influence that such name variations have had in fracturing women's historical identities was one of the greatest lessons we learned while editing *Women in World History*. The genealogical charts we produced for that work are also included in this volume for reasons best explained in the following excerpt from the introduction of *WIWH*. The excerpt addresses two of the most difficult challenges involved in an undertaking like *Dictionary of Women Worldwide*: sorting out and cross-referencing the myriad names given to historical women and naming the nameless.

Throughout the ages, fathers and sons have been scrupulously documented in historical records; for mothers and daughters, birth and death dates are often unknown and approximated. Many cultures do not even count daughters as children. The king's daughter was often treated with the same indifference as the daughter of a tavern owner. But, like certain Soviet leaders who made an art form of airbrushing discredited colleagues from the photographic record, history has occasionally left in a hand or an elbow by mistake. We encountered one historic tome that solemnly noted: "Ariadne was a 5th-century Byzantine empress and daughter of the childless Leo I." Leo had no sons. Records of Eliza Lynch, a major figure in the cultural and political development of Paraguay, scrupulously list her children with dictator Francisco Solano López: "Jan (b. 1855); Enrique (b. 1858); Federico (b. 1860); Carlos (b. 1861); Leopoldo (b. 1862); Miguel (b. 1866); and three daughters, names unknown."

For expediency, historians have eliminated what they perceive to be the secondary storyline. When a woman is known to exist historically, she has often been the casualty of streamlining. The secret to good writing is brevity. "The Holy Roman emperor Otto I arranged a marriage for his son Otto II to a Byzantine empress" is much more readable than "Empress Adelaide of Burgundy and Holy Roman emperor Otto I arranged a marriage for their son Otto II to Theophano, a Byzantine empress."

In the world's text, women have been relegated to common nouns (the queen, the princess, the sister of Charles IV, the duchess of Carlisle) and possessive pronouns ("and his daughter," "and his mother," "and his wife"). In many accounts that chronicle the early years of the 20th century, this phrase appears: "The 1914 assassination of Archduke Franz Ferdinand and his wife led directly to World War I." (Worse, in most reports Archduchess Sophie Chotek's death goes unmentioned; Franz Ferdinand dies alone.) Michael Collins storms the barricade during the Easter rising, and Michael Collins is named; Constance Markievicz and Winifred Carney storm the same barricade, and they are referred to as "two women activists." The often-used phrase "Einstein and his wife" (he had two) evokes an image of a disheveled genius and a drab, faceless woman when, in fact, Mileva Einstein-Marić did the computations for his theory of relativity.

We were determined not to leave a mother, wife, duchess or daughter unturned. Take Ingeborg. Our morning would start simply enough; then we would read: "After his marriage at Amiens, on August 14, 1193, Philip II Augustus, king of France, took a sudden aversion to his 18-year-old Danish bride and sought a divorce." Well, there it was. Obviously, by her marriage to Philip II Augustus, the Danish bride was a queen of France, but who was she? From one source, we learned that she was on good terms with the ensuing French kings; from another, that she lived peacefully, gaining a reputation for kindness. From a third, that she died highly esteemed but, as in the previous sources, nameless, either in 1237 or 1238. Within an hour, we had her name: Ingeborg. By mid-morning, we learned that Ingeborg was the daughter of Waldemar I the Great, king of Denmark. No mother mentioned. Now we had a nameless Danish queen, and a barely named French one.

To give complete and accurate information on Ingeborg, we needed her mother, but while pouring through Palle Lauring's *A History of Denmark*, we read in passing that Philip Augustus "had threatened to cast off his first wife." Another ball in the air. Now we had a nameless Danish queen, one barely named daughter, and an unnamed first wife. By noon, we had uncovered Isabella, first wife of Philip and daughter of Baldwin V, count of Hainault. No mother mentioned. Unfortunately, we had also uncovered a third wife, known only as the mother of Philip Hurepel. Now we had the aforementioned twosome, a newly named first wife, and an unknown third. By mid-afternoon, we gleaned that the mother of Philip Hurepel was named Agnes; she was also the mother of the nonessential Marie. By late afternoon, we had a headache. The results of our day's exploration can be found under the names Agnes of Meran (d. 1201), Ingeborg (c. 1176-1237/38), Isabella of Hainault (1170-1190), and Marie of France (1198-c. 1223). As far as we were able to ascertain, Ingeborg's mother was either Sophie of Russia or Richezza of Poland. No one knows for sure. These were not idle chases. Often the woman off-handedly referred to as the "queen-regent" or "queen mother" turned out to be someone of major import, like Catherine de Medici or Eleanor of Aquitaine. A towering stack of books would eventually straighten out these problems, but the quantity needed will not be found in a small library collection.

The majority of the time, when we did find the woman for whom we were looking, she didn't have one name; she had five or six. Unlike most men whose various names have been sifted down over time to one or two, Holy Roman Empress Agnes of Poitou strolls through the history books as Agnes of Aquitaine, Agnes of Guienne, Agnes of Bavaria, or Agnes of Germany. The dowager empress of China, in her various transliterations, is known as Cixi or Tz'u-hsi, Tse-Hi, Tsu-Hsi, Tze Hsi, Tzu Hsi, Tsze Hsi An, Yehonala, Xiaoqin Xian Huanghou, Xi Taihou, Nala Taihou, Lao Fuoye, or Imperial Concubine Yi. Running down these names easily added years to the project, but we had no choice. Otherwise, the same woman would be scattered throughout our series as Yolande of Brienne on page 29, Jolanta on page 403, and Isabella II of Jerusalem on page 1602.

Name changes that accompany marriage added to the difficulty. Women from outside Russia took on Russian names when they married tsars; one minute they're Sophia Augusta Frederika, princess of Anhalt-Zerbst, the next minute they're Catherine II the Great. East Germany's Christa Rothenburger won the Olympic gold medal in speedskating in 1984. In 1992, she won the silver medal as Christa Luding. In some books, Alice Guy Blache can be found under B; in others, Alice Guy-Blache is found under G. Then there's the longtime bugbear: Mrs. John D. Rockefeller. Which one? Mrs. John D. the 1st, the 3rd, or junior? So often, the dreaded, "the philanthropist, Mrs. Reid," stopped us cold. Is that Mrs. Ogden Mills Reid or Mrs. Whitelaw Reid?

We were not alone in our exasperation. "How are you listing Etta Palm?," queried one of our French historians about an assignment: "As *Palm, Etta Aelders? Palm Aelders, Etta?* or Palm d'Aelders, Etta? My best sources call her Etta Palm d'Aelders, but I'll put her under Palm because she's more widely known to English audiences as Etta Palm. Whew! You'd think there would be more uniformity in these matters."

Researching the lives of Roman women in Republican times was also daunting. Free Roman men had three or four names: the praenomen or given name, the nomen or family name, and sometimes the cognomen or distinguishing name: thus, Gaius Julius Caesar. The women,

however, were given only one name, the feminine form of the family name. That is why the daughters of Julius Caesar and his sister are all named Julia. Only Julia. Historians have taken to qualifiers like Julia Minor and Julia Major, but it has not solved the problem. Five of the Julias can be found in *Women in World History* [and *Dictionary of Women Worldwide*], as well as all eight Cleopatras (Cleopatra VII is the famous one), five Arsinoes, seven sisters Bonaparte, seven Beatrice d'Estes, numerous Euphrosynes, Eurydices, Eudocias, Theopanos, Theodoras, Zoes, Faustinas, and Flavias, many Sforzas and Viscontis, and all 35 women named Medici.

Eventually, we picked up speed. With the material we had accumulated, we could begin to answer our own questions more readily and find the women more quickly. Out of necessity, we were using Women in *World History* as a primary reference source, long before it was completed.

We were also using our charts. Women are rarely included on existing genealogies. A Chinese journalist recalled being handed a copy of her family tree which stretched back 3,000 years. "Not one woman was included on the tree," she noted, "not a mother, a sister, a daughter, a wife." For expediency, women have been left off charts which, while following the male line, are difficult enough to read without adding a cadre of women. When women do appear because of their regal status, usually only their sons are noted on the ancestral line below. In one case, a son was included who had died at age six, while his surviving sister, who had become queen of a neighboring country, was missing.

Determined to come up with an easy-to-use cast list, we set about giving one name to each woman on the world stage as she made her entrances and exits throughout the series. In order to do this, we needed to make our own charts, settle on a name for the subject, and add dates if known. Without identifying dates, five Margarets of Austria all look alike. Thought was given to imposing a rational system on the names, but problems outweighed the advantages. One commonly used data base made a stab at it by changing all Catherines to Katherine. Thus, they had Katherine the Great. Whenever possible, we have tried to use the name by which the subject has been most clearly identified in historical contexts. In so doing, the inconsistencies arise. A Spanish historian might call a queen Isabella; an English historian might call the same queen Elizabeth; a French and German historian, Elisabeth; a Russian historian, Elizaveta.

If the women were difficult for us to locate without knowing the exact name used, we knew the task would be even more difficult for our readers. For this reason, we offer many avenues to find the women sought: by the charts, by indexing, by cross-referencing of collective name variants (*Rejcka. Variant of Ryksa.*), by cross-referencing of name variations within the entries (*Gonzaga, Eleanor [1534-1594]. See Eleanora of Austria.*), and by cross-referencing of titles (*Pembroke, countess of. See Clifford Anne [1590-1676].*).

We began to rely so heavily on our genealogical charts—all 85 of them—that we decided to put them in the front of Volume I [in both *WIWH* and *DWW*], alphabetized by country. If a woman is bolded on the chart, she appears in her own entry under the name given. Sometimes her sketch will just be personal data, but as Rutger's Kay Vandergrift notes: "The first step for those who are the 'others' in traditional history is to prove their very existence."

We envisioned a series heavily focused on international women, many of whom were enormously important, even revered in their own countries, though seldom known in the United States. Most books in the U.S. cover only American women; by so doing, they isolate women's accomplishments to the last 200 years and neglect about 3,000 years of women's history. An international emphasis, however, did not prove easy. Since much of the information and many of the primary sources we needed for our research were not available in

English, we asked professors to undertake translations. More than 300 contributors, from over 20 nations, participated in the *WIWH* project [and their contributions are reflected in *DWW*].

Readers will inevitably find omissions and inequities in length. We invite suggestions for inclusion in every area from our readers. We have also spent years checking our facts. Nonetheless, because women have been ignored historically, the record is replete with inaccuracies which have been given widespread circulation. Thus, there will be errors in these volumes. We welcome suggestions and corrections.

Anne Commire
Deborah Klezmer

GENEALOGICAL CHARTS

Designed to show the relation of ancestors to descendants, the following genealogical charts are family trees that begin with the original rulers on the highest branch. From this extends a lower branch that shows their children and those whom their children married (when known). The next branch shows their children's children and corresponding spouses (when known), and so on.

Charts are grouped alphabetically by country, and headings for each country are located at the top of every chart. Each chart displays a House Title, which identifies the name of the ruling house.

The following symbols and abbreviations are used:

| indicates the descent of children

= indicates marriage, liaison, or other intimate relationship

⋮ indicates illegitimate descent of children

m. indicates marriage

(1) indicates first wife or husband

(2) indicates second wife or husband

(3) indicates third wife or husband (etc.)

(illeg.) illegitimate

Women whose names appear in bold on the charts have entries in the *Dictionary of Women Worldwide* as well as *Women in World History* series.

CHARTS

GENEALOGICAL CHARTS

The House of Saxe-Coburg
(1831–)

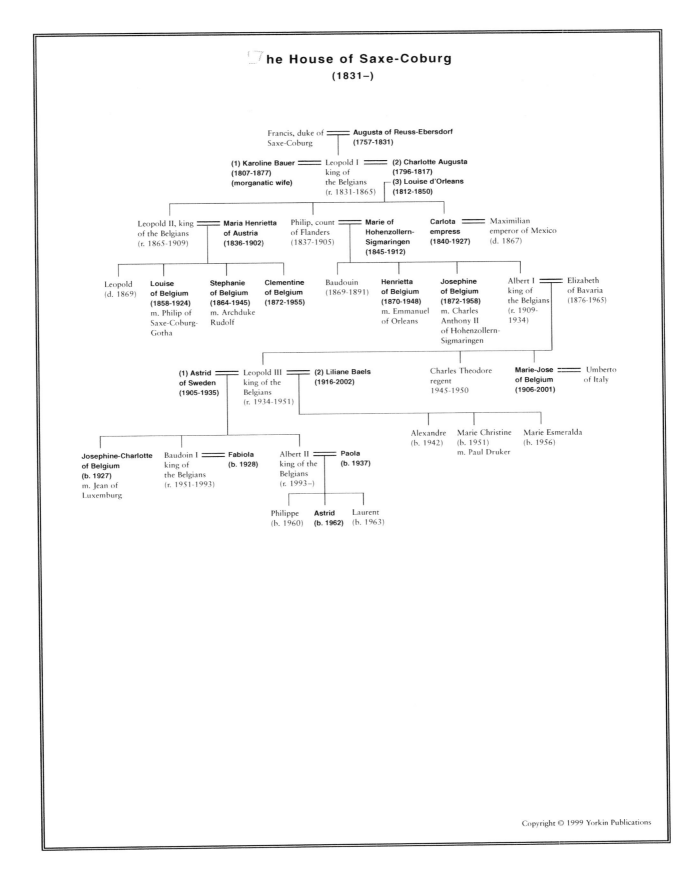

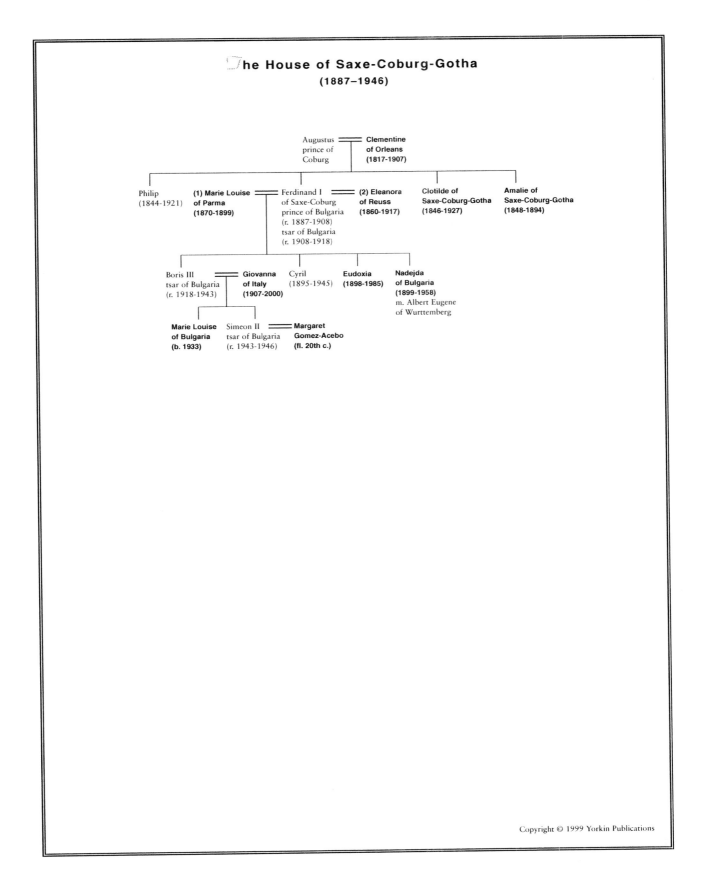

The House of Saxe-Coburg-Gotha
(1887–1946)

Augustus prince of Coburg ═══ Clementine of Orleans (1817-1907)

Philip (1844-1921)

(1) **Marie Louise of Parma (1870-1899)** ═══ Ferdinand I of Saxe-Coburg prince of Bulgaria (r. 1887-1908) tsar of Bulgaria (r. 1908-1918) ═══ **(2) Eleanora of Reuss (1860-1917)**

Clotilde of Saxe-Coburg-Gotha (1846-1927)

Amalie of Saxe-Coburg-Gotha (1848-1894)

Boris III tsar of Bulgaria (r. 1918-1943) ═══ **Giovanna of Italy (1907-2000)**

Cyril (1895-1945)

Eudoxia (1898-1985)

Nadejda of Bulgaria (1899-1958) m. Albert Eugene of Wurttemberg

Marie Louise of Bulgaria (b. 1933)

Simeon II tsar of Bulgaria (r. 1943-1946) ═══ **Margaret Gomez-Acebo (fl. 20th c.)**

Empresses & Emperors of Byzantium

REIGN	EMPRESS OR EMPEROR	SPOUSE
306-337	Constantine I the Great	Fausta (d. 324)
337-361	Constantius II	Galla (fl. 320)
		Eusebia of Macedonia (fl. 300 CE)
		Faustina of Antioch
361-363	Julian	Helena (c. 320-?)
363-364	Jovian	Charito
364-378	Valens	Albia Domnica
379-395	Theodosius I the Spaniard	Flaccilla (fl. 370-400)
395-408	Arcadius	Eudocia of Byzantium (r. 400-404)
408-450	Theodosius II the Calligrapher	Eudocia (c. 400-460)
	Pulcheria (c. 398-453) sister of and joint ruler with emperor Theodosius II	
450-457	Marcian	Pulcheria (c. 398-453)
457-474	Leo I	Verina (fl. 437-483)
474	Leo II	
474-491	Zeno the Isaurian	Ariadne (fl. 457-515)
491-518	Anastasius I [Anastasios I]	Ariadne (fl. 457-515)
518-527	Justin I [Flavius Justinus]	Lupicinia-Euphemia (d. 523)
527-565	Justinian I, the Great	Theodora (c. 500-548)
565-578	Justin II [Flavius Justinus]	Sophia (c. 525-after 600)
	administered affairs of empire jointly with Tiberius II Constantine	
578-582	Tiberius II Constantine	Ino-Anastasia
582-602	Maurice Tiberius [Mauritius]	Constantina (fl. 582-602)
602-610	Phocas I [Phokas I]	Leontia (fl. 602-610)
610-641	Heraclius I [Herakleios I] of Carthage	Fabia-Eudocia (fl. 600s)
		Martina
641	Heraclonas-Constantine	Gregoria-Anastasia
641	Heraclonas II [Heracleon; Heraklonas]	unmarried
641-668	Constantine III [Constans II]	Fausta (fl. 600s)
668-685	Constantine IV [Pogonatus]	Anastasia (fl. 600s)
685-695 and		
705-711	Justinian II Rhinotmetos	Eudocia (fl. 700s)
		Theodora of the Khazars (fl. 700s)
695-698	Leontius II [Leontios]	unknown
698-705	Tiberius III Apsimar	unknown
711-713	Philippikos Vardan [Philippicus]	unknown
713-715	Anastasius II Artemius	Irene (fl. 700s)
715-717	Theodosius III	unknown
717-741	Leo III the Iconoclast	Maria (fl. 700s)
741-775	Constantine V [Kopronymus]	Irene of the Khazars (d. 750?)
		Maria (fl. 700s)
		Eudocia (fl. 700s)
775-780	Leo IV the Khazar	Irene of Athens (c. 752-803)
780-797	Constantine VI [Porphyrogenitus]	Maria of Amnia (fl. 782)
		Theodote (fl. 795)
780-790	Irene of Athens (c. 752-803) regent and co-emperor	
792-797	Irene of Athens (c. 752-803) co-emperor	
797-802	Irene of Athens (c. 752-803)	
802-811	Nicephorus I	unknown
811	Stauracius [Stavrakios]	Theophano of Athens
811-813	Michael I Rhangabé	Prokopia (fl. 800s)
813-820	Leo V Gnuni the Armenian	Barca-Theodosia
820-829	Michael II of Amorion	Thecla (fl. 800s)
		Euphrosyne (fl. 800s)
829-842	Theophilos I [Theophilus]	Theodora the Blessed (fl. 842-856)
842-867	Michael III the Drunkard	Eudocia Decapolita (fl. 800s)
842-866	Bardas	
867	Theophilus II	
867-886	Basil I the Macedonian	Maria of Macedonia
		Eudocia Ingerina (fl. 800s)
886-912	Leo VI the Wise	St. Theophano (866-893)
		Zoe Zautzina (c. 870-c. 899)
		Eudocia Baiane (d. 902)
		Zoe Carbopsina (c. 890-920)
912-913	Alexander [III]	unknown
913-959	Constantine VII Porphyrogenetos	Helena Lekapena (c. 920-961)
919-944	Romanus I Lecapenus	Theodora (early 900s)
959-963	Romanus II	Bertha-Eudocia the Frank
		Theophano (c. 940-?)
963-969	Nicephoros II Phocas	Theophano (c. 940-?)
969-976	John I Tzimisces	Theodora (late 900s)
976-1025	Basil II the Bulgar Slayer	unmarried
1025-1028	Constantine VIII	Helena of Alypia

REIGN	EMPRESS OR EMPEROR	SPOUSE
1028-1050	**Zöe Porphyrogenita (980-1050)**	Romanus III Argyrus
1028-1034	**Zöe Porphyrogenita (980-1050)**	(co-emperor) Romanus III Argyrus
1034-1041	**Zöe Porphyrogenita (980-1050)**	Michael IV Paphlagonian
1041-1042	Michael V Kalaphates	unknown (probably unmarried)
1042-1050	**Zöe Porphyrogenita (980-1050)**	(co-emperor) Constantine IX Monomachus
1050-1056	**Theodora Porphyrogenita (c. 989-1056)**	unmarried
1056-1057	Michael VI Bringas	unknown
1057-1059	Isaac I Comnenus	**Catherine of Bulgaria (fl. 1050)**
1059-1067	Constantine X Ducas	**Eudocia Macrembolitissa (1021-1096)**
1067	**Eudocia Macrembolitissa (1021-1096)**	
1068-1071	Romanus IV Diogenes	**Eudocia Macrembolitissa (1021-1096)**
1071-1078	Michael VII Ducas	**Maria of Alania (fl. 1070-1081)**
1078-1081	Nicephorus III Botaneiates	Verdenia
		Maria of Alania (fl. 1070-1081)
1081-1118	Alexius I Comnenus [Alexios I Komnenos]	**Irene Ducas (c. 1066-1133)**
1118-1143	John II Comnenus	**Priska-Irene of Hungary (c. 1085-1133)**
1143-1180	Manuel I Comnenus	**Bertha-Irene of Sulzbach (d. 1161)**
		Marie of Antioch (fl. 1180-1183)
1180-1183	Alexius II Comnenus	**Agnes-Anne of France (b. 1171)**
1183-1185	Andronicus I Comnenus	**Agnes-Anne of France (b. 1171)**
1185-1195	Isaac II Angelus [Angelos-Comnenus]	**Margaret-Mary of Hungary (c. 1177-?)**
1195-1203	Alexius III Angelus	**Euphrosyne (d. 1203)**
1203-1204	Isaac II Angelus [restored]	
1203-1204	Alexius IV Angelus	unmarried
1204	Alexius V Ducas Mourtzouphlos	**Eudocia Angelina (fl. 1204)**

In April 1204, when Crusaders and Venetians attacked the imperial palace in Constantinople, thousands were killed and the emperor, Alexius V, fled. The conquerors crowned a Latin emperor, Baldwin of Flanders. Shortly after, a young Byzantine noble, Theodore Lascaris, organized a government-in-exile 40 miles away across the Straits of Nicaea. These Nicaean emperors—Theodore and his successors—are considered by some to have continued the Byzantine line.

Nicaean emperors

REIGN	EMPEROR	SPOUSE
1204-1222	Theodore I Lascaris	**Anna Angelina (d. 1210?)**
		Philippa of Lesser Armenia
		Marie de Courtenay (fl. 1215)
1222-1254	John III Ducas Vatatzes	**Irene Lascaris (fl. 1222-1235)**
		Constance-Anna of Hohenstaufen
1254-1258	Theodore II Lascaris	**Helen Asen of Bulgaria (d. 1255?)**
1258-1261	John IV Lascaris	unmarried
1261-1282	Michael VIII Paleologus [Palaiologos]	**Theodora Ducas (fl. 1200s)**
1282-1328	Andronicus II Paleologus	**Anna of Hungary (d. around 1284)**
		Irene of Montferrat (fl. 1300)
1328-1341	Andronicus III Paleologus	**Irene of Brunswick (fl. 1300s)**
		Anne of Savoy (c. 1320-1353)
1341-1347	John V Paleologus	**Helena Cantacuzene (fl. 1340s)**
1347-1354	John VI Cantacuzene [Kantakouzenos]	**Irene Asen**
1355-1391	John V Paleologus (restored)	**Helena Cantacuzene (fl. 1340s)**
1376-1379	Andronicus IV Paleologus	**Maria-Kyratza Asen**
1390	John VII Paleologus	**Eugenia Gattilusi**
1391-1425	Manuel II Paleologus	**Helena Dragas (fl. 1400)**
1425-1448	John VIII Paleologus	**Anna of Moscow (1393-1417)**
		Sophie of Montferrat
		Maria of Trebizond (d. 1439)
1448-1453	Constantine XI Paleologus	**Magdalena-Theodora Tocco**
		Caterina Gattilusi

The Byzantine empire—an empire that had endured for over 1,000 years—ceased to exist on May 29, 1453, when the Turks "scaled the walls."

Latin emperors (in Constantinople)

REIGN	EMPEROR	SPOUSE
1204-1205	Baldwin I of Constantinople	**Marie of Champagne (c. 1180-1203)**
	(also known as Baldwin IX; count of Flanders & Hainault)	
1205-1216	Henry	
1216-1217	Peter de Courtenay	**Yolande of Courtenay (d. 1219)**
1218-1228	Robert de Courtenay	
1228-1261	Baldwin II of Constantinople	

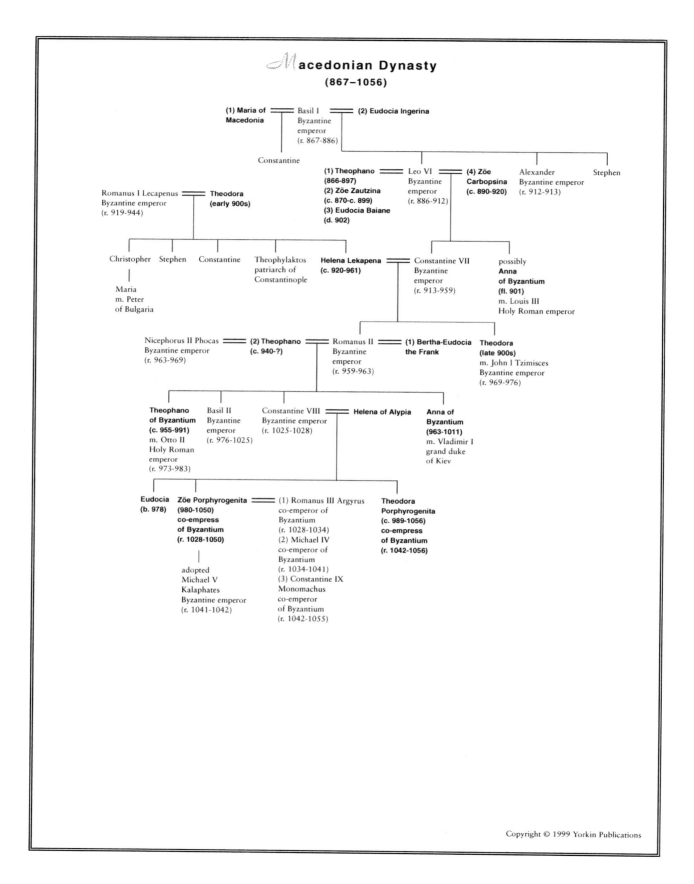

ℳacedonian Dynasty
(867–1056)

(1) Maria of Macedonia ══ Basil I Byzantine emperor (r. 867-886) ══ **(2) Eudocia Ingerina**

Constantine

(1) Theophano (866-897) (2) Zöe Zautzina (c. 870-c. 899) (3) Eudocia Baiane (d. 902) ══ Leo VI Byzantine emperor (r. 886-912) ══ **(4) Zöe Carbopsina (c. 890-920)**

Alexander Byzantine emperor (r. 912-913)

Stephen

Romanus I Lecapenus Byzantine emperor (r. 919-944) ══ **Theodora (early 900s)**

Christopher

Stephen

Constantine

Theophylaktos patriarch of Constantinople

Helena Lekapena (c. 920-961) ══ Constantine VII Byzantine emperor (r. 913-959)

possibly **Anna of Byzantium (fl. 901)** m. Louis III Holy Roman emperor

Maria m. Peter of Bulgaria

Nicephorus II Phocas Byzantine emperor (r. 963-969) ══ **(2) Theophano (c. 940-?)** ══ Romanus II Byzantine emperor (r. 959-963) ══ **(1) Bertha-Eudocia the Frank**

Theodora (late 900s) m. John I Tzimisces Byzantine emperor (r. 969-976)

Theophano of Byzantium (c. 955-991) m. Otto II Holy Roman emperor (r. 973-983)

Basil II Byzantine emperor (r. 976-1025)

Constantine VIII Byzantine emperor (r. 1025-1028) ══ **Helena of Alypia**

Anna of Byzantium (963-1011) m. Vladimir I grand duke of Kiev

Eudocia (b. 978)

Zöe Porphyrogenita (980-1050) co-empress of Byzantium (r. 1028-1050) ══ (1) Romanus III Argyrus co-emperor of Byzantium (r. 1028-1034) (2) Michael IV co-emperor of Byzantium (r. 1034-1041) (3) Constantine IX Monomachus co-emperor of Byzantium (r. 1042-1055)

Theodora Porphyrogenita (c. 989-1056) co-empress of Byzantium (r. 1042-1056)

adopted Michael V Kalaphates Byzantine emperor (r. 1041-1042)

The Comneni & Angeli
(1057–1204)

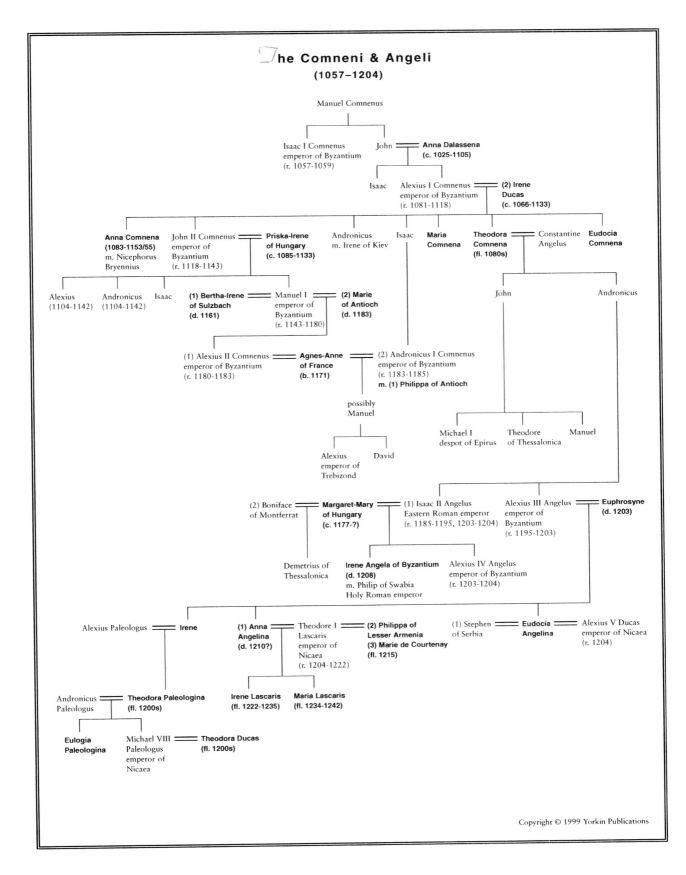

Manuel Comnenus

Isaac I Comnenus emperor of Byzantium (r. 1057-1059)

John — **Anna Dalassena (c. 1025-1105)**

Isaac

Alexius I Comnenus emperor of Byzantium (r. 1081-1118) — **(2) Irene Ducas (c. 1066-1133)**

Anna Comnena (1083-1153/55) m. Nicephorus Bryennius

John II Comnenus emperor of Byzantium (r. 1118-1143) — **Priska-Irene of Hungary (c. 1085-1133)**

Andronicus m. Irene of Kiev

Isaac

Maria Comnena

Theodora Comnena (fl. 1080s) — Constantine Angelus

Eudocia Comnena

Alexius (1104-1142)

Andronicus (1104-1142)

Isaac

(1) Bertha-Irene of Sulzbach (d. 1161) — Manuel I emperor of Byzantium (r. 1143-1180) — **(2) Marie of Antioch (d. 1183)**

John

Andronicus

(1) Alexius II Comnenus emperor of Byzantium (r. 1180-1183) — **Agnes-Anne of France (b. 1171)** — (2) Andronicus I Comnenus emperor of Byzantium (r. 1183-1185) **m. (1) Philippa of Antioch**

possibly Manuel

Alexius emperor of Trebizond

David

Michael I despot of Epirus

Theodore of Thessalonica

Manuel

(2) Boniface of Montferrat — **Margaret-Mary of Hungary (c. 1177-?)** — (1) Isaac II Angelus Eastern Roman emperor (r. 1185-1195, 1203-1204)

Alexius III Angelus emperor of Byzantium (r. 1195-1203) — **Euphrosyne (d. 1203)**

Demetrius of Thessalonica

Irene Angela of Byzantium (d. 1208) m. Philip of Swabia Holy Roman emperor

Alexius IV Angelus emperor of Byzantium (r. 1203-1204)

Alexius Paleologus — Irene

(1) Anna Angelina (d. 1210?) — Theodore I Lascaris emperor of Nicaea (r. 1204-1222) — **(2) Philippa of Lesser Armenia (3) Marie de Courtenay (fl. 1215)**

(1) Stephen of Serbia — **Eudocia Angelina** — Alexius V Ducas emperor of Nicaea (r. 1204)

Andronicus Paleologus — **Theodora Paleologina (fl. 1200s)**

Irene Lascaris (fl. 1222-1235)

Maria Lascaris (fl. 1234-1242)

Eulogia Paleologina

Michael VIII Paleologus emperor of Nicaea — **Theodora Ducas (fl. 1200s)**

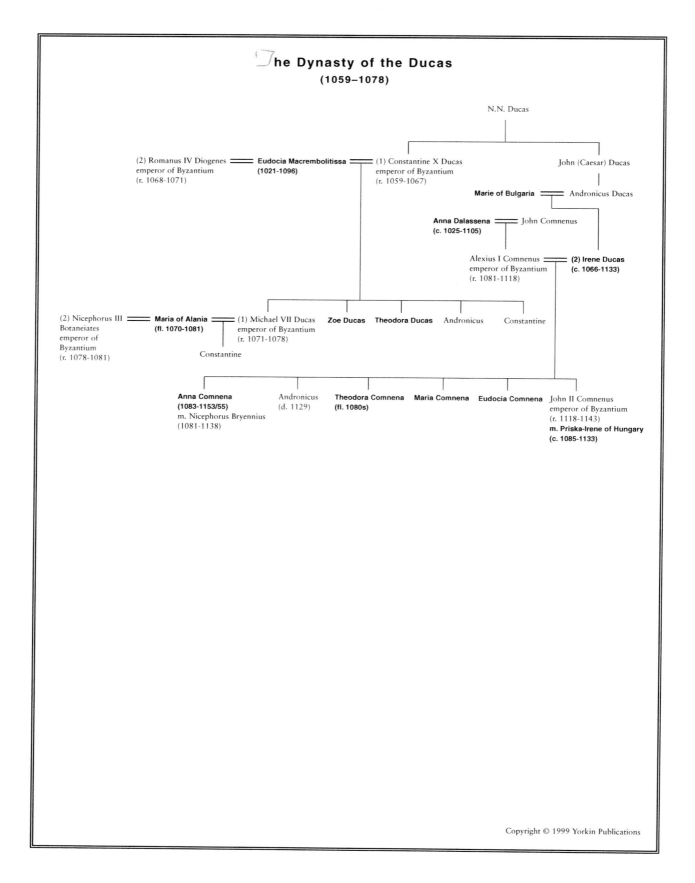

The Dynasty of the Ducas
(1059–1078)

N.N. Ducas

(2) Romanus IV Diogenes
emperor of Byzantium
(r. 1068-1071)
═══ **Eudocia Macrembolitissa**
(1021-1096) ═══
(1) Constantine X Ducas
emperor of Byzantium
(r. 1059-1067)

John (Caesar) Ducas

Marie of Bulgaria ═══ Andronicus Ducas

Anna Dalassena
(c. 1025-1105) ═══ John Comnenus

Alexius I Comnenus
emperor of Byzantium
(r. 1081-1118) ═══ **(2) Irene Ducas**
(c. 1066-1133)

(2) Nicephorus III
Botaneiates
emperor of
Byzantium
(r. 1078-1081) ═══ **Maria of Alania**
(fl. 1070-1081) ═══ (1) Michael VII Ducas
emperor of Byzantium
(r. 1071-1078)

Constantine

Zoe Ducas   **Theodora Ducas**   Andronicus   Constantine

Anna Comnena
(1083-1153/55)
m. Nicephorus Bryennius
(1081-1138)

Andronicus
(d. 1129)

Theodora Comnena
(fl. 1080s)

Maria Comnena

Eudocia Comnena

John II Comnenus
emperor of Byzantium
(r. 1118-1143)
m. Priska-Irene of Hungary
(c. 1085-1133)

The Dynasty of the Lascarids
(1204–1261)

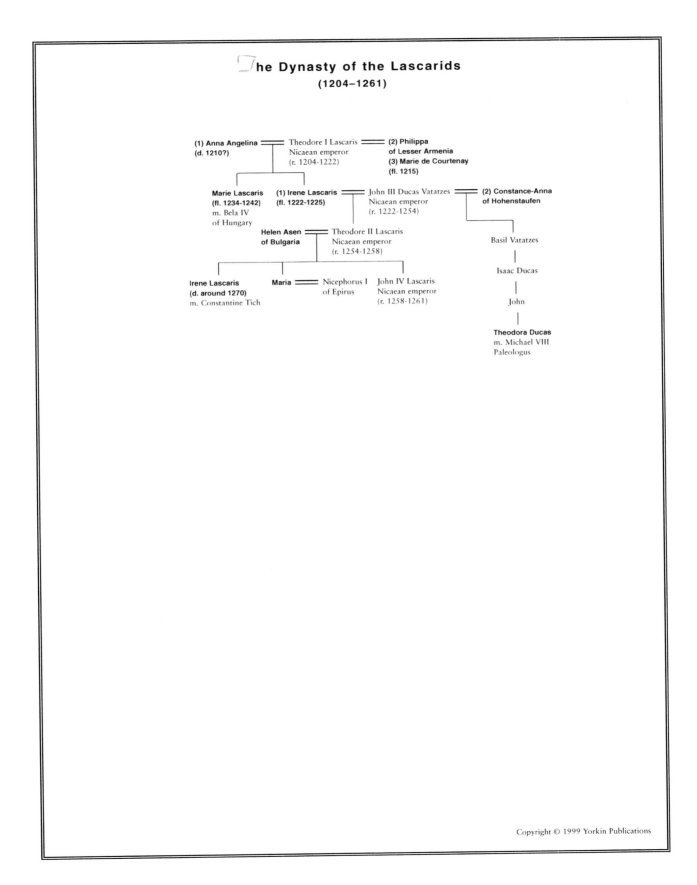

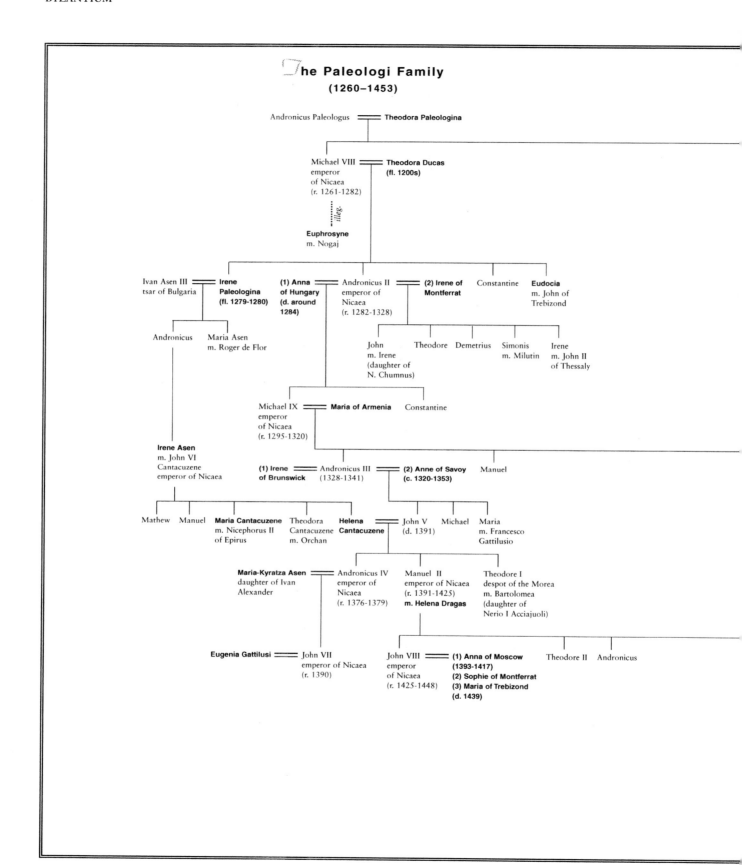

The Paleologi Family
(1260–1453)

Andronicus Paleologus ══ **Theodora Paleologina**

Michael VIII ══ **Theodora Ducas**
emperor **(fl. 1200s)**
of Nicaea
(r. 1261-1282)

illeg.

Euphrosyne
m. Nogaj

Ivan Asen III ══ **Irene**   **(1) Anna** ══ Andronicus II ══ **(2) Irene of**   Constantine   **Eudocia**
tsar of Bulgaria   **Paleologina**   **of Hungary**   emperor of   **Montferrat**   m. John of
               (fl. 1279-1280)   **(d. around**   Nicaea   Trebizond
                                 1284)   (r. 1282-1328)

Andronicus   Maria Asen   John   Theodore   Demetrius   Simonis   Irene
            m. Roger de Flor   m. Irene   m. Milutin   m. John II
                              (daughter of   of Thessaly
                              N. Chumnus)

                     Michael IX ══ **Maria of Armenia**   Constantine
                     emperor
                     of Nicaea
                     (r. 1295-1320)

Irene Asen   **(1) Irene** ══ Andronicus III ══ **(2) Anne of Savoy**   Manuel
m. John VI   **of Brunswick**   (1328-1341)   **(c. 1320-1353)**
Cantacuzene
emperor of Nicaea

Mathew   Manuel   **Maria Cantacuzene**   Theodora   **Helena** ══ John V   Michael   Maria
                  m. Nicephorus II   Cantacuzene   **Cantacuzene**   (d. 1391)   m. Francesco
                  of Epirus   m. Orchan   Gattilusio

Maria-Kyratza Asen ══ Andronicus IV   Manuel II   Theodore I
daughter of Ivan   emperor of   emperor of Nicaea   despot of the Morea
Alexander   Nicaea   (r. 1391-1425)   m. Bartolomea
                    (r. 1376-1379)   **m. Helena Dragas**   (daughter of
                                               Nerio I Acciajuoli)

Eugenia Gattilusi ══ John VII   John VIII ══ **(1) Anna of Moscow**   Theodore II   Andronicus
                   emperor of Nicaea   emperor   **(1393-1417)**
                   (r. 1390)   of Nicaea   **(2) Sophie of Montferrat**
                               (r. 1425-1448)   **(3) Maria of Trebizond**
                                           (d. 1439)

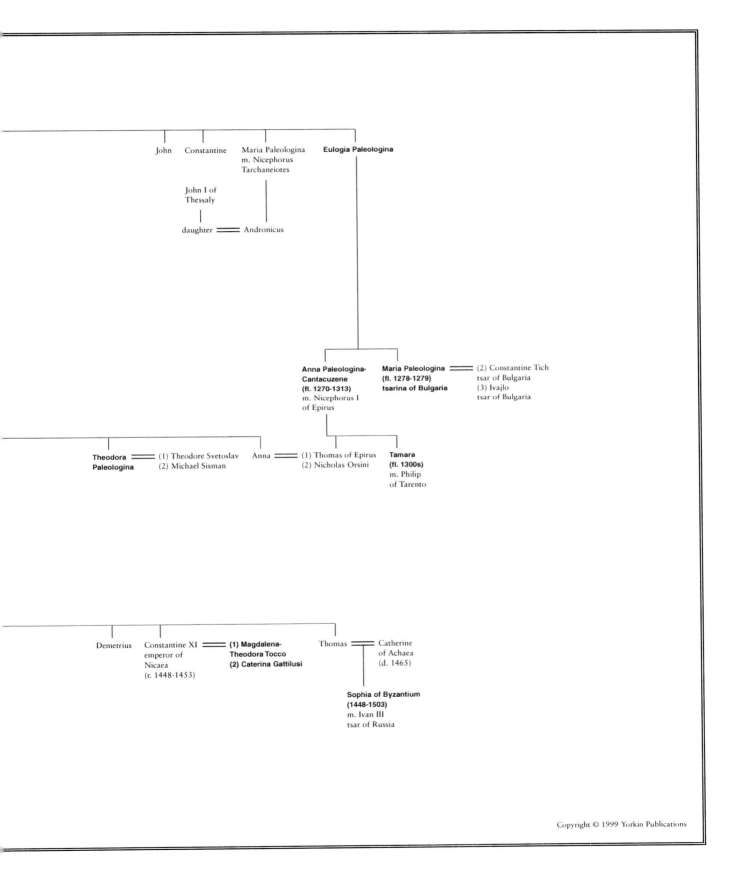

John   Constantine   Maria Paleologina   **Eulogia Paleologina**
                       m. Nicephorus
                       Tarchaneiotes

John I of
Thessaly

daughter ═══ Andronicus

Anna Paleologina-   **Maria Paleologina** ═══ (2) Constantine Tich
Cantacuzene   **(fl. 1278-1279)**   tsar of Bulgaria
(fl. 1270-1313)   **tsarina of Bulgaria**   (3) Ivajlo
m. Nicephorus I   tsar of Bulgaria
of Epirus

Theodora ═══ (1) Theodore Svetoslav   Anna ═══ (1) Thomas of Epirus   **Tamara**
Paleologina   (2) Michael Sisman   (2) Nicholas Orsini   **(fl. 1300s)**
                                                                        m. Philip
                                                                        of Tarento

Demetrius   Constantine XI ═══ **(1) Magdalena-**   Thomas ═══ Catherine
             emperor of   **Theodora Tocco**   of Achaea
             Nicaea   **(2) Caterina Gattilusi**   (d. 1465)
             (r. 1448-1453)

                                 Sophia of Byzantium
                                 (1448-1503)
                                 m. Ivan III
                                 tsar of Russia

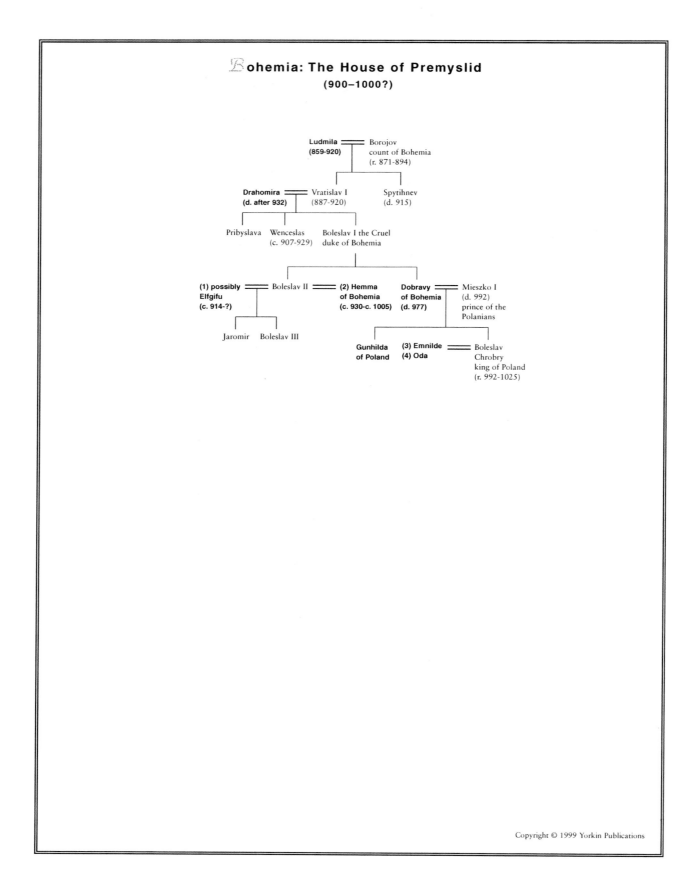

Bohemia: The House of Premyslid
(900–1000?)

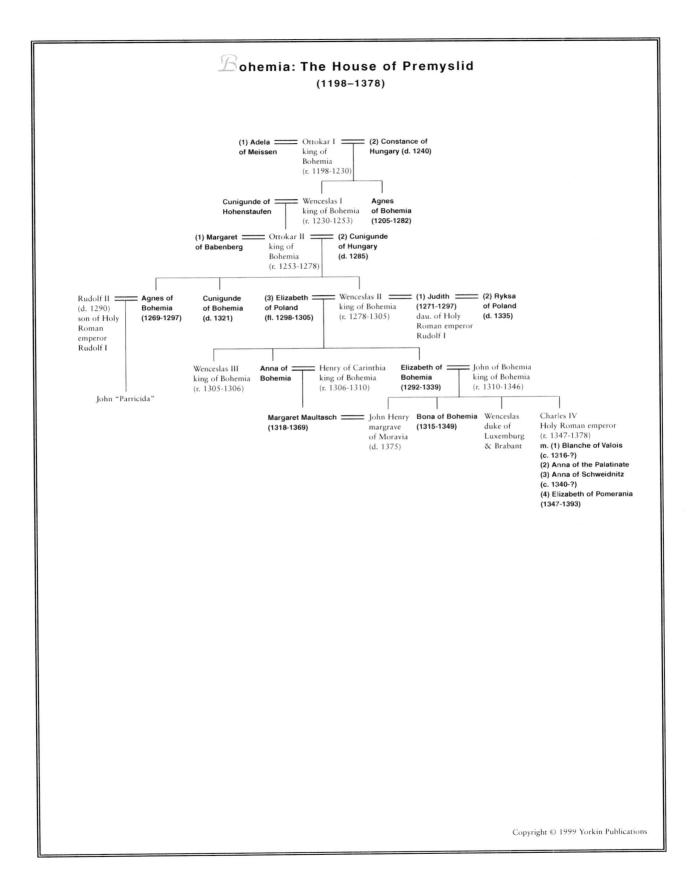

Bohemia: The House of Premyslid
(1198–1378)

(1) Adela of Meissen ══ Ottokar I king of Bohemia (r. 1198-1230) ══ **(2) Constance of Hungary (d. 1240)**

Cunigunde of Hohenstaufen ══ Wenceslas I king of Bohemia (r. 1230-1253)   **Agnes of Bohemia (1205-1282)**

(1) Margaret of Babenberg ══ Ottokar II king of Bohemia (r. 1253-1278) ══ **(2) Cunigunde of Hungary (d. 1285)**

Rudolf II (d. 1290) son of Holy Roman emperor Rudolf I ══ **Agnes of Bohemia (1269-1297)**   Cunigunde of Bohemia (d. 1321)   **(3) Elizabeth of Poland (fl. 1298-1305)** ══ Wenceslas II king of Bohemia (r. 1278-1305) ══ **(1) Judith (1271-1297)** dau. of Holy Roman emperor Rudolf I   **(2) Ryksa of Poland (d. 1335)**

John "Parricida"

Wenceslas III king of Bohemia (r. 1305-1306)   **Anna of Bohemia** ══ Henry of Carinthia king of Bohemia (r. 1306-1310)   **Elizabeth of Bohemia (1292-1339)** ══ John of Bohemia king of Bohemia (r. 1310-1346)

Margaret Maultasch (1318-1369) ══ John Henry margrave of Moravia (d. 1375)   **Bona of Bohemia (1315-1349)**   Wenceslas duke of Luxemburg & Brabant   Charles IV Holy Roman emperor (r. 1347-1378) **m. (1) Blanche of Valois (c. 1316-?) (2) Anna of the Palatinate (3) Anna of Schweidnitz (c. 1340-?) (4) Elizabeth of Pomerania (1347-1393)**

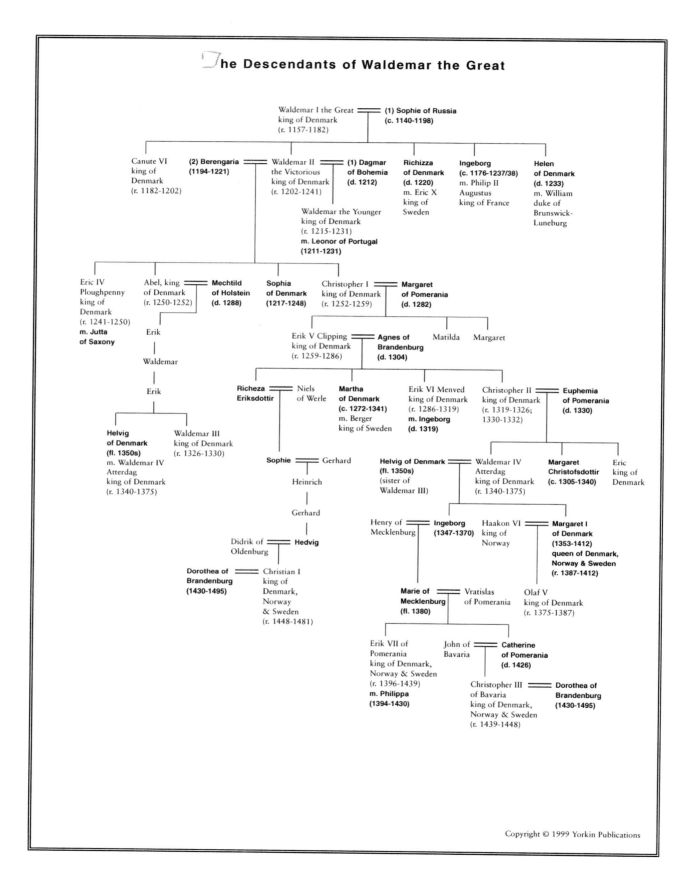

The Descendants of Waldemar the Great

Waldemar I the Great
king of Denmark
(r. 1157-1182)
═══ **(1) Sophie of Russia
(c. 1140-1198)**

Canute VI
king of
Denmark
(r. 1182-1202)

**(2) Berengaria
(1194-1221)** ═══ Waldemar II
the Victorious
king of Denmark
(r. 1202-1241) ═══ **(1) Dagmar
of Bohemia
(d. 1212)**

**Richizza
of Denmark
(d. 1220)**
m. Eric X
king of
Sweden

**Ingeborg
(c. 1176-1237/38)**
m. Philip II
Augustus
king of France

**Helen
of Denmark
(d. 1233)**
m. William
duke of
Brunswick-
Luneburg

Waldemar the Younger
king of Denmark
(r. 1215-1231)
**m. Leonor of Portugal
(1211-1231)**

Eric IV
Ploughpenny
king of
Denmark
(r. 1241-1250)
**m. Jutta
of Saxony**

Abel, king
of Denmark
(r. 1250-1252) ═══ **Mechtild
of Holstein
(d. 1288)**

**Sophia
of Denmark
(1217-1248)**

Christopher I
king of Denmark
(r. 1252-1259) ═══ **Margaret
of Pomerania
(d. 1282)**

Erik

Waldemar

Erik

Erik V Clipping
king of Denmark
(r. 1259-1286) ═══ **Agnes of
Brandenburg
(d. 1304)**

Matilda   Margaret

**Richeza
Eriksdottir** ═══ Niels
of Werle

**Martha
of Denmark
(c. 1272-1341)**
m. Berger
king of Sweden

Erik VI Menved
king of Denmark
(r. 1286-1319)
**m. Ingeborg
(d. 1319)**

Christopher II
king of Denmark
(r. 1319-1326;
1330-1332) ═══ **Euphemia
of Pomerania
(d. 1330)**

**Helvig
of Denmark
(fl. 1350s)**
m. Waldemar IV
Atterdag
king of Denmark
(r. 1340-1375)

Waldemar III
king of Denmark
(r. 1326-1330)

Sophie ═══ Gerhard

Heinrich

Gerhard

**Helvig of Denmark
(fl. 1350s)**
(sister of
Waldemar III) ═══ Waldemar IV
Atterdag
king of Denmark
(r. 1340-1375)

**Margaret
Christofsdottir
(c. 1305-1340)**

Eric
king of
Denmark

Didrik of
Oldenburg ═══ **Hedvig**

Henry of
Mecklenburg ═══ **Ingeborg
(1347-1370)**

Haakon VI
king of
Norway ═══ **Margaret I
of Denmark
(1353-1412)
queen of Denmark,
Norway & Sweden
(r. 1387-1412)**

**Dorothea of
Brandenburg
(1430-1495)** ═══ Christian I
king of
Denmark,
Norway
& Sweden
(r. 1448-1481)

**Marie of
Mecklenburg
(fl. 1380)** ═══ Vratislas
of Pomerania

Olaf V
king of Denmark
(r. 1375-1387)

Erik VII of
Pomerania
king of Denmark,
Norway & Sweden
(r. 1396-1439)
**m. Philippa
(1394-1430)**

John of
Bavaria ═══ **Catherine
of Pomerania
(d. 1426)**

Christopher III
of Bavaria
king of Denmark,
Norway & Sweden
(r. 1439-1448) ═══ **Dorothea of
Brandenburg
(1430-1495)**

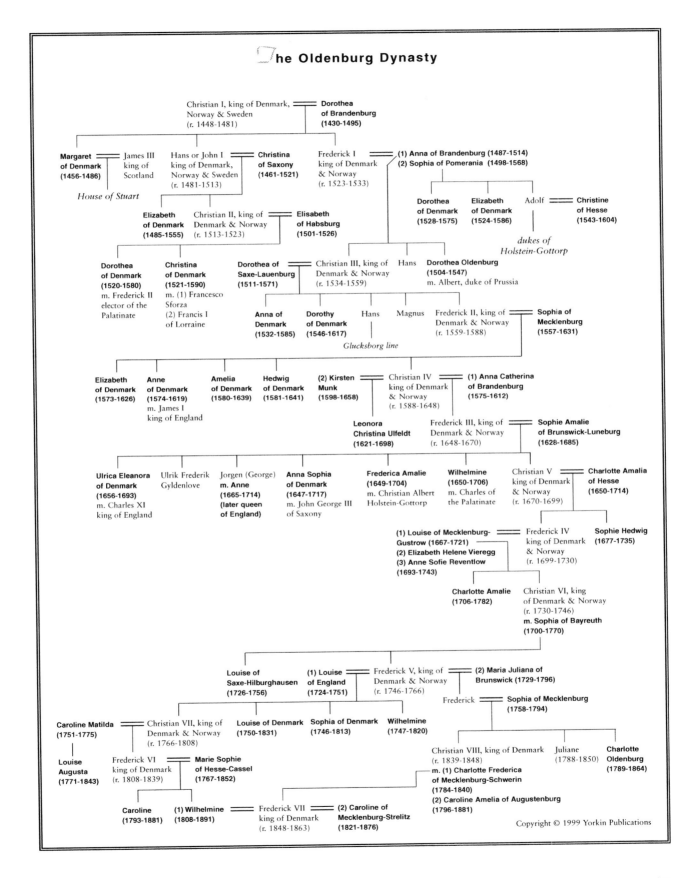

The Oldenburg Dynasty

Christian I, king of Denmark, Norway & Sweden (r. 1448-1481) ═══ Dorothea of Brandenburg (1430-1495)

Margaret of Denmark (1456-1486) ═══ James III king of Scotland

House of Stuart

Hans or John I king of Denmark, Norway & Sweden (r. 1481-1513) ═══ Christina of Saxony (1461-1521)

Frederick I king of Denmark & Norway (r. 1523-1533) ═══ (1) Anna of Brandenburg (1487-1514) / (2) Sophia of Pomerania (1498-1568)

Dorothea of Denmark (1528-1575)

Elizabeth of Denmark (1524-1586)

Adolf ═══ Christine of Hesse (1543-1604)

dukes of Holstein-Gottorp

Elizabeth of Denmark (1485-1555)

Christian II, king of Denmark & Norway (r. 1513-1523) ═══ Elisabeth of Habsburg (1501-1526)

Dorothea of Denmark (1520-1580) m. Frederick II elector of the Palatinate

Christina of Denmark (1521-1590) m. (1) Francesco Sforza (2) Francis I of Lorraine

Dorothea of Saxe-Lauenburg (1511-1571) ═══ Christian III, king of Denmark & Norway (r. 1534-1559)

Hans

Dorothea Oldenburg (1504-1547) m. Albert, duke of Prussia

Anna of Denmark (1532-1585)

Dorothy of Denmark (1546-1617)

Hans

Magnus

Frederick II, king of Denmark & Norway (r. 1559-1588) ═══ Sophia of Mecklenburg (1557-1631)

Glucksborg line

Elizabeth of Denmark (1573-1626)

Anne of Denmark (1574-1619) m. James I king of England

Amelia of Denmark (1580-1639)

Hedwig of Denmark (1581-1641)

(2) Kirsten Munk (1598-1658) ═══ Christian IV king of Denmark & Norway (r. 1588-1648) ═══ (1) Anna Catherina of Brandenburg (1575-1612)

Leonora Christina Ulfeldt (1621-1698)

Frederick III, king of Denmark & Norway (r. 1648-1670) ═══ Sophie Amalie of Brunswick-Luneburg (1628-1685)

Ulrica Eleanora of Denmark (1656-1693) m. Charles XI king of England

Ulrik Frederik Gyldenlove

Jorgen (George) m. Anne (1665-1714) (later queen of England)

Anna Sophia of Denmark (1647-1717) m. John George III of Saxony

Frederica Amalie (1649-1704) m. Christian Albert Holstein-Gottorp

Wilhelmine (1650-1706) m. Charles of the Palatinate

Christian V king of Denmark & Norway (r. 1670-1699) ═══ Charlotte Amalia of Hesse (1650-1714)

(1) Louise of Mecklenburg-Gustrow (1667-1721) / (2) Elizabeth Helene Vieregg / (3) Anne Sofie Reventlow (1693-1743) ═══ Frederick IV king of Denmark & Norway (r. 1699-1730)

Sophie Hedwig (1677-1735)

Charlotte Amalie (1706-1782)

Christian VI, king of Denmark & Norway (r. 1730-1746) m. Sophia of Bayreuth (1700-1770)

Louise of Saxe-Hilburghausen (1726-1756)

(1) Louise of England (1724-1751) ═══ Frederick V, king of Denmark & Norway (r. 1746-1766) ═══ (2) Maria Juliana of Brunswick (1729-1796)

Frederick ═══ Sophia of Mecklenburg (1758-1794)

Caroline Matilda (1751-1775) ═══ Christian VII, king of Denmark & Norway (r. 1766-1808)

Louise Augusta (1771-1843)

Frederick VI king of Denmark (r. 1808-1839) ═══ Marie Sophie of Hesse-Cassel (1767-1852)

Louise of Denmark (1750-1831)

Sophia of Denmark (1746-1813)

Wilhelmine (1747-1820)

Christian VIII, king of Denmark (r. 1839-1848) m. (1) Charlotte Frederica of Mecklenburg-Schwerin (1784-1840) (2) Caroline Amelia of Augustenburg (1796-1881)

Juliane (1788-1850)

Charlotte Oldenburg (1789-1864)

Caroline (1793-1881)

(1) Wilhelmine (1808-1891) ═══ Frederick VII king of Denmark (r. 1848-1863) ═══ (2) Caroline of Mecklenburg-Strelitz (1821-1876)

Copyright © 1999 Yorkin Publications

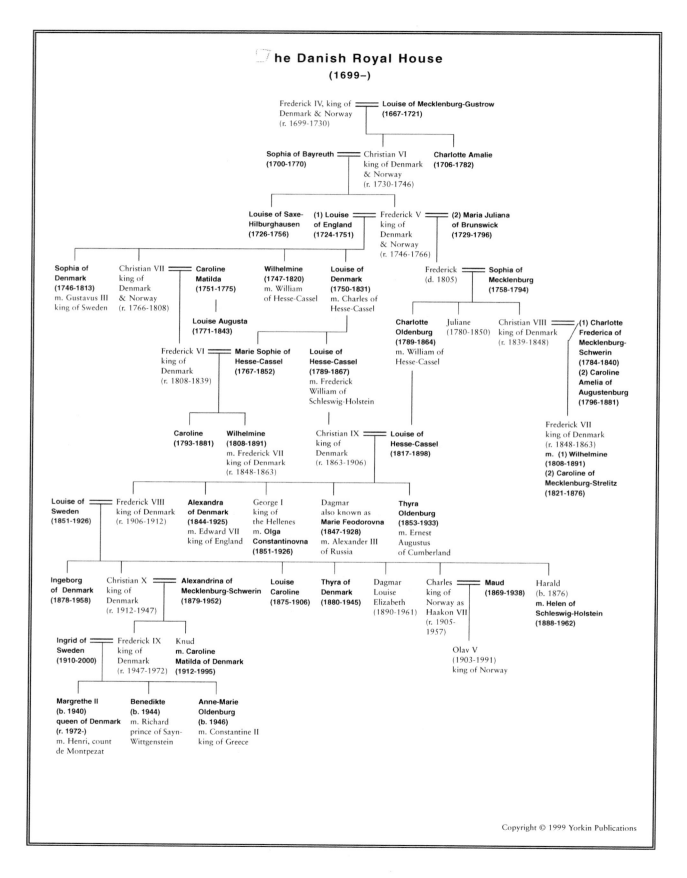

The Danish Royal House
(1699–)

Frederick IV, king of Denmark & Norway (r. 1699-1730) === Louise of Mecklenburg-Gustrow (1667-1721)

Sophia of Bayreuth (1700-1770) === Christian VI king of Denmark & Norway (r. 1730-1746)   Charlotte Amalie (1706-1782)

Louise of Saxe-Hilburghausen (1726-1756)   (1) Louise of England (1724-1751) === Frederick V king of Denmark & Norway (r. 1746-1766) === (2) Maria Juliana of Brunswick (1729-1796)

Sophia of Denmark (1746-1813) m. Gustavus III king of Sweden

Christian VII king of Denmark & Norway (r. 1766-1808) === Caroline Matilda (1751-1775)

Wilhelmine (1747-1820) m. William of Hesse-Cassel

Louise of Denmark (1750-1831) m. Charles of Hesse-Cassel

Frederick (d. 1805) === Sophia of Mecklenburg (1758-1794)

Louise Augusta (1771-1843)

Charlotte Oldenburg (1789-1864) m. William of Hesse-Cassel

Juliane (1780-1850)

Christian VIII king of Denmark (r. 1839-1848) === (1) Charlotte Frederica of Mecklenburg-Schwerin (1784-1840) (2) Caroline Amelia of Augustenburg (1796-1881)

Frederick VI king of Denmark (r. 1808-1839) === Marie Sophie of Hesse-Cassel (1767-1852)

Louise of Hesse-Cassel (1789-1867) m. Frederick William of Schleswig-Holstein

Caroline (1793-1881)

Wilhelmine (1808-1891) m. Frederick VII king of Denmark (r. 1848-1863)

Christian IX king of Denmark (r. 1863-1906) === Louise of Hesse-Cassel (1817-1898)

Frederick VII king of Denmark (r. 1848-1863) m. (1) Wilhelmine (1808-1891) (2) Caroline of Mecklenburg-Strelitz (1821-1876)

Louise of Sweden (1851-1926) === Frederick VIII king of Denmark (r. 1906-1912)

Alexandra of Denmark (1844-1925) m. Edward VII king of England

George I king of the Hellenes m. Olga Constantinovna (1851-1926)

Dagmar also known as Marie Feodorovna (1847-1928) m. Alexander III of Russia

Thyra Oldenburg (1853-1933) m. Ernest Augustus of Cumberland

Ingeborg of Denmark (1878-1958)

Christian X king of Denmark (r. 1912-1947) === Alexandrina of Mecklenburg-Schwerin (1879-1952)

Louise Caroline (1875-1906)

Thyra of Denmark (1880-1945)

Dagmar Louise Elizabeth (1890-1961)

Charles king of Norway as Haakon VII (r. 1905-1957) === Maud (1869-1938)

Harald (b. 1876) m. Helen of Schleswig-Holstein (1888-1962)

Ingrid of Sweden (1910-2000) === Frederick IX king of Denmark (r. 1947-1972)

Knud m. Caroline Matilda of Denmark (1912-1995)

Olav V (1903-1991) king of Norway

Margrethe II (b. 1940) queen of Denmark (r. 1972-) m. Henri, count de Montpezat

Benedikte (b. 1944) m. Richard prince of Sayn-Wittgenstein

Anne-Marie Oldenburg (b. 1946) m. Constantine II king of Greece

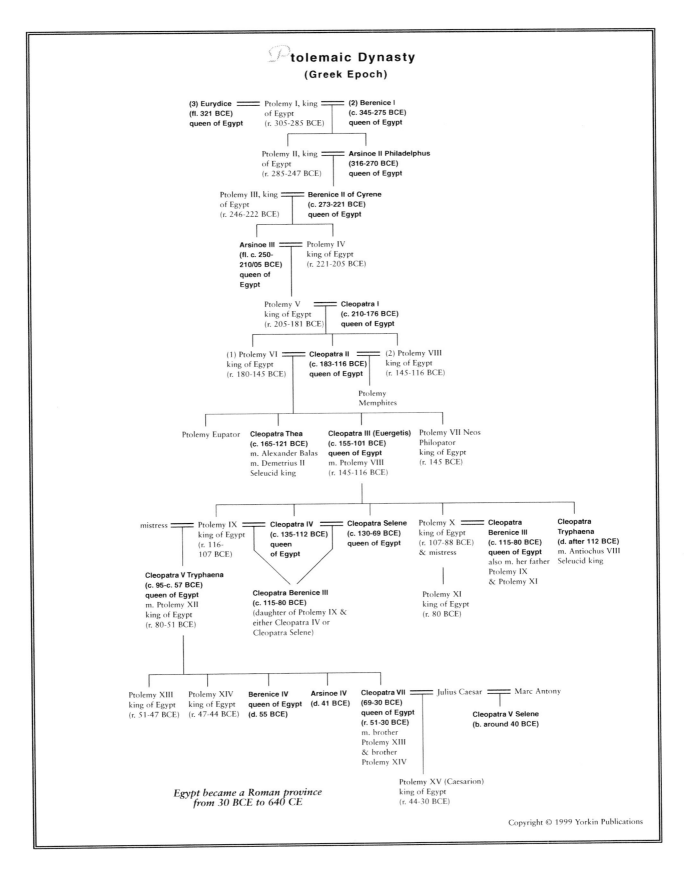

Ptolemaic Dynasty
(Greek Epoch)

(3) Eurydice (fl. 321 BCE) queen of Egypt ══ Ptolemy I, king of Egypt (r. 305-285 BCE) ══ **(2) Berenice I (c. 345-275 BCE) queen of Egypt**

Ptolemy II, king of Egypt (r. 285-247 BCE) ══ **Arsinoe II Philadelphus (316-270 BCE) queen of Egypt**

Ptolemy III, king of Egypt (r. 246-222 BCE) ══ **Berenice II of Cyrene (c. 273-221 BCE) queen of Egypt**

Arsinoe III (fl. c. 250-210/05 BCE) queen of Egypt ══ Ptolemy IV king of Egypt (r. 221-205 BCE)

Ptolemy V king of Egypt (r. 205-181 BCE) ══ **Cleopatra I (c. 210-176 BCE) queen of Egypt**

(1) Ptolemy VI king of Egypt (r. 180-145 BCE) ══ **Cleopatra II (c. 183-116 BCE) queen of Egypt** ══ (2) Ptolemy VIII king of Egypt (r. 145-116 BCE)

Ptolemy Memphites

Ptolemy Eupator   **Cleopatra Thea (c. 165-121 BCE) m. Alexander Balas m. Demetrius II Seleucid king**   **Cleopatra III (Euergetis) (c. 155-101 BCE) queen of Egypt m. Ptolemy VIII (r. 145-116 BCE)**   Ptolemy VII Neos Philopator king of Egypt (r. 145 BCE)

mistress ══ Ptolemy IX king of Egypt (r. 116-107 BCE)   **Cleopatra IV (c. 135-112 BCE) queen of Egypt**   **Cleopatra Selene (c. 130-69 BCE) queen of Egypt**   Ptolemy X king of Egypt (r. 107-88 BCE) & mistress ══ **Cleopatra Berenice III (c. 115-80 BCE) queen of Egypt also m. her father Ptolemy IX & Ptolemy XI**   **Cleopatra Tryphaena (d. after 112 BCE) m. Antiochus VIII Seleucid king**

Cleopatra V Tryphaena (c. 95-c. 57 BCE) queen of Egypt m. Ptolemy XII king of Egypt (r. 80-51 BCE)

Cleopatra Berenice III (c. 115-80 BCE) (daughter of Ptolemy IX & either Cleopatra IV or Cleopatra Selene)

Ptolemy XI king of Egypt (r. 80 BCE)

Ptolemy XIII king of Egypt (r. 51-47 BCE)   Ptolemy XIV king of Egypt (r. 47-44 BCE)   **Berenice IV queen of Egypt (d. 55 BCE)**   **Arsinoe IV (d. 41 BCE)**   **Cleopatra VII (69-30 BCE) queen of Egypt (r. 51-30 BCE) m. brother Ptolemy XIII & brother Ptolemy XIV** ══ Julius Caesar ══ Marc Antony

Cleopatra V Selene (b. around 40 BCE)

Ptolemy XV (Caesarion) king of Egypt (r. 44-30 BCE)

Egypt became a Roman province from 30 BCE to 640 CE

Copyright © 1999 Yorkin Publications

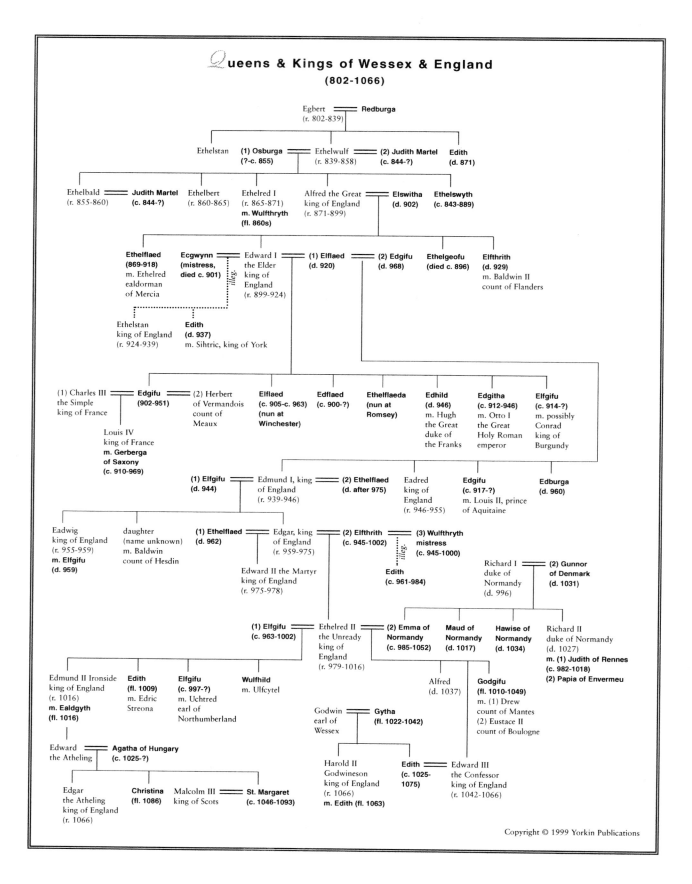

Queens & Kings of Wessex & England
(802-1066)

Egbert (r. 802-839) — Redburga

Ethelstan | (1) Osburga (?-c. 855) — Ethelwulf (r. 839-858) — (2) Judith Martel (c. 844-?) | Edith (d. 871)

Ethelbald (r. 855-860) — Judith Martel (c. 844-?) | Ethelbert (r. 860-865) | Ethelred I (r. 865-871) m. Wulfthryth (fl. 860s) | Alfred the Great king of England (r. 871-899) — Elswitha (d. 902) | Ethelswyth (c. 843-889)

Ethelflaed (869-918) m. Ethelred ealdorman of Mercia | Ecgwynn (mistress, died c. 901) — illeg. — Edward I the Elder king of England (r. 899-924) — (1) Elflaed (d. 920) — (2) Edgifu (d. 968) | Ethelgeofu (died c. 896) | Elfthrith (d. 929) m. Baldwin II count of Flanders

Ethelstan king of England (r. 924-939) | Edith (d. 937) m. Sihtric, king of York

(1) Charles III the Simple king of France — Edgifu (902-951) — (2) Herbert of Vermandois count of Meaux | Elflaed (c. 905-c. 963) (nun at Winchester) | Edflaed (c. 900-?) | Ethelflaeda (nun at Romsey) | Edhild (d. 946) m. Hugh the Great duke of the Franks | Edgitha (c. 912-946) m. Otto I the Great Holy Roman emperor | Elfgifu (c. 914-?) m. possibly Conrad king of Burgundy

Louis IV king of France m. Gerberga of Saxony (c. 910-969)

(1) Elfgifu (d. 944) — Edmund I, king of England (r. 939-946) — (2) Ethelflaed (d. after 975) | Eadred king of England (r. 946-955) | Edgifu (c. 917-?) m. Louis II, prince of Aquitaine | Edburga (d. 960)

Eadwig king of England (r. 955-959) m. Elfgifu (d. 959) | daughter (name unknown) m. Baldwin count of Hesdin | (1) Ethelflaed (d. 962) — Edgar, king of England (r. 959-975) — (2) Elfthrith (c. 945-1002) — (3) Wulfthryth mistress (c. 945-1000) | Richard I duke of Normandy (d. 996) — (2) Gunnor of Denmark (d. 1031)

Edward II the Martyr king of England (r. 975-978) | Edith (c. 961-984)

(1) Elfgifu (c. 963-1002) — Ethelred II the Unready king of England (r. 979-1016) — (2) Emma of Normandy (c. 985-1052) | Maud of Normandy (d. 1017) | Hawise of Normandy (d. 1034) | Richard II duke of Normandy (d. 1027) m. (1) Judith of Rennes (c. 982-1018) (2) Papia of Envermeu

Edmund II Ironside king of England (r. 1016) m. Ealdgyth (fl. 1016) | Edith (fl. 1009) m. Edric Streona | Elfgifu (c. 997-?) m. Uchtred earl of Northumberland | Wulfhild m. Ulfcytel | Alfred (d. 1037) | Godgifu (fl. 1010-1049) m. (1) Drew count of Mantes (2) Eustace II count of Boulogne

Edward the Atheling — Agatha of Hungary (c. 1025-?) | Godwin earl of Wessex — Gytha (fl. 1022-1042)

Edgar the Atheling king of England (r. 1066) | Christina (fl. 1086) | Malcolm III king of Scots — St. Margaret (c. 1046-1093) | Harold II Godwineson king of England (r. 1066) m. Edith (fl. 1063) | Edith (c. 1025-1075) — Edward III the Confessor king of England (r. 1042-1066)

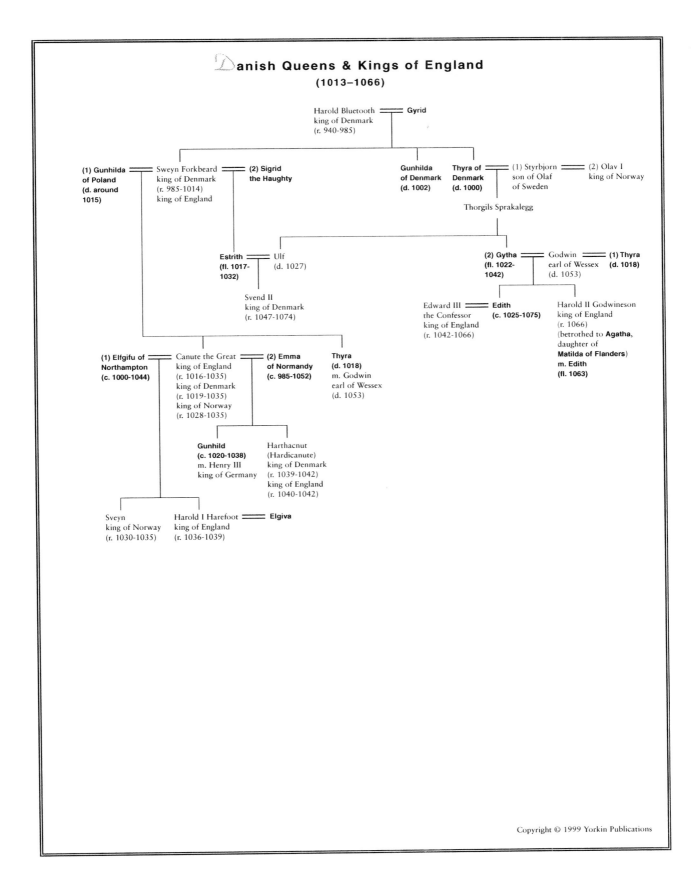

Danish Queens & Kings of England
(1013–1066)

Harold Bluetooth ══ Gyrid
king of Denmark
(r. 940-985)

(1) Gunhilda ══ Sweyn Forkbeard ══ **(2) Sigrid**
of Poland   king of Denmark   **the Haughty**
(d. around   (r. 985-1014)
1015)   king of England

Gunhilda   **Thyra of** ══ (1) Styrbjorn ══ (2) Olav I
of Denmark   **Denmark**   son of Olaf   king of Norway
(d. 1002)   **(d. 1000)**   of Sweden

Thorgils Sprakalegg

Estrith ══ Ulf
(fl. 1017-   (d. 1027)
1032)

(2) Gytha ══ Godwin ══ **(1) Thyra**
(fl. 1022-   earl of Wessex   **(d. 1018)**
1042)   (d. 1053)

Svend II
king of Denmark
(r. 1047-1074)

Edward III ══ **Edith**   Harold II Godwineson
the Confessor   **(c. 1025-1075)**   king of England
king of England   (r. 1066)
(r. 1042-1066)   (betrothed to **Agatha**,
    daughter of
    Matilda of Flanders)
    m. Edith
    (fl. 1063)

(1) Elfgifu of ══ Canute the Great ══ **(2) Emma**   Thyra
Northampton   king of England   **of Normandy**   **(d. 1018)**
(c. 1000-1044)   (r. 1016-1035)   **(c. 985-1052)**   m. Godwin
   king of Denmark   earl of Wessex
   (r. 1019-1035)   (d. 1053)
   king of Norway
   (r. 1028-1035)

Gunhild   Harthacnut
(c. 1020-1038)   (Hardicanute)
m. Henry III   king of Denmark
king of Germany   (r. 1039-1042)
    king of England
    (r. 1040-1042)

Sveyn   Harold I Harefoot ══ **Elgiva**
king of Norway   king of England
(r. 1030-1035)   (r. 1036-1039)

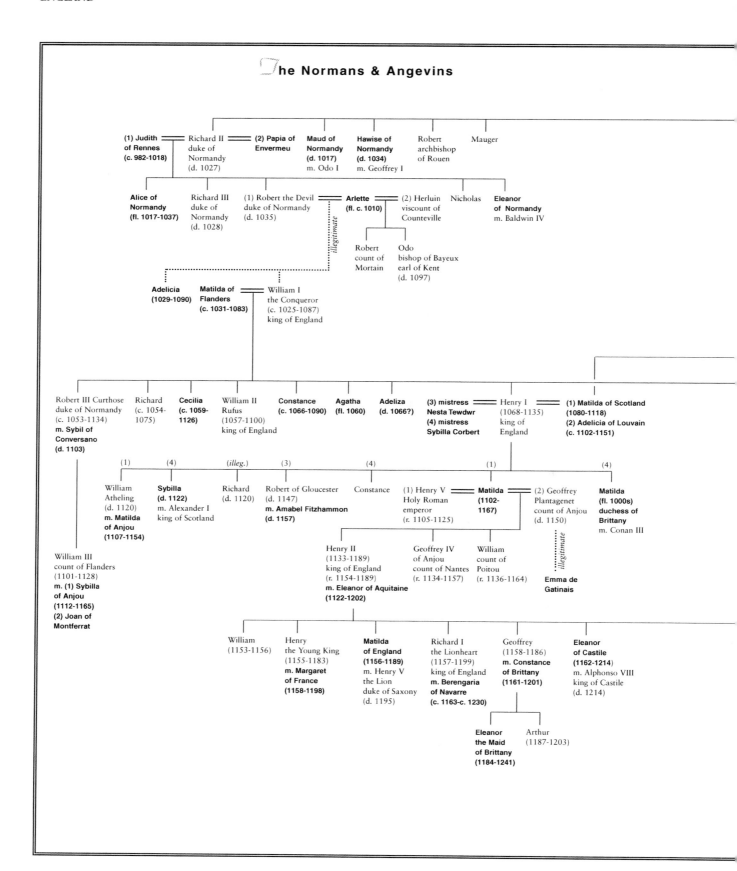

The Normans & Angevins

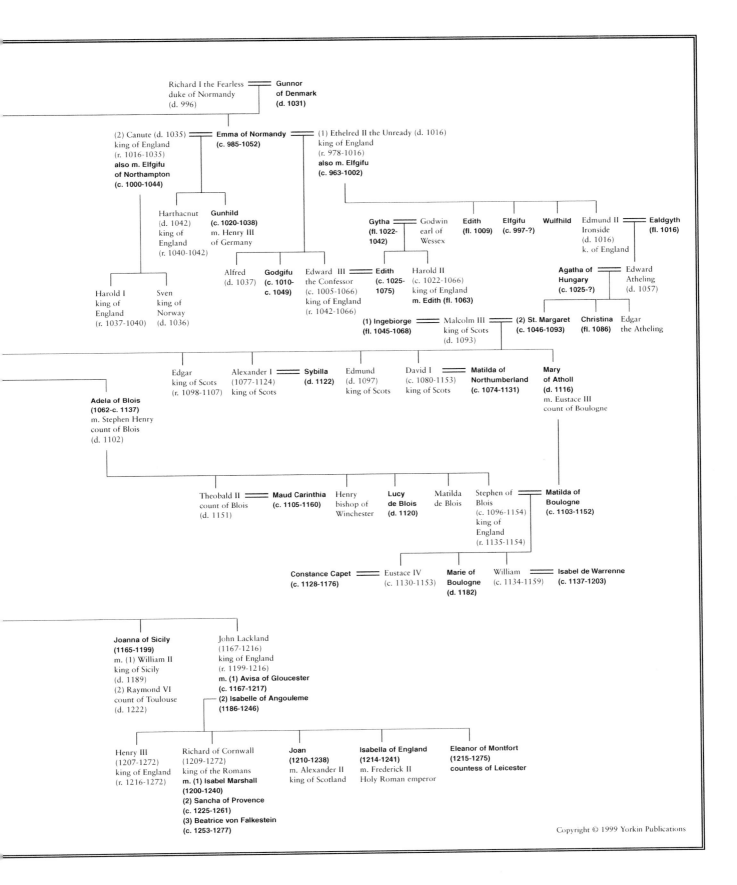

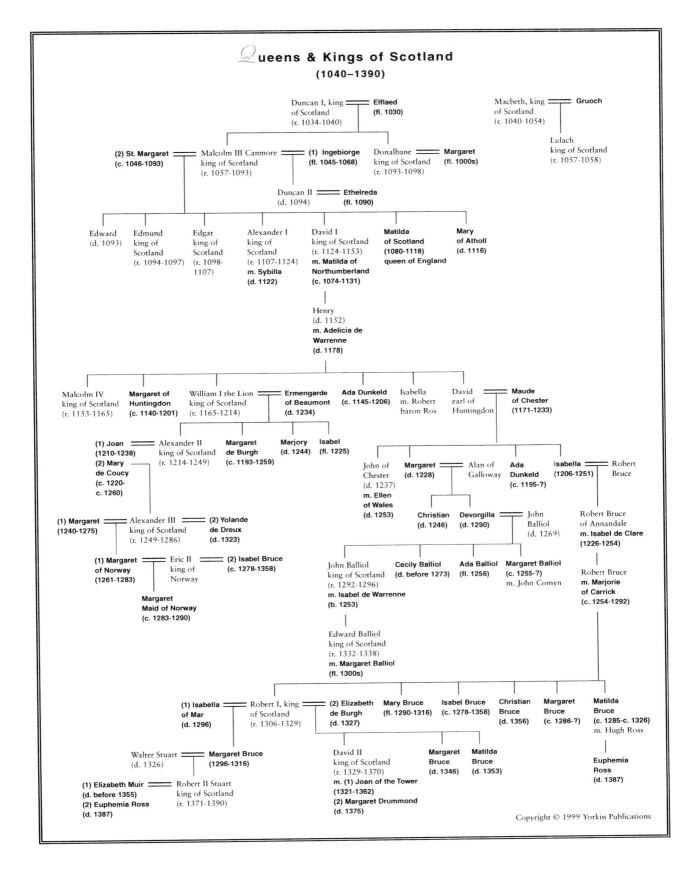

Queens & Kings of Scotland

(1040–1390)

Duncan I, king of Scotland (r. 1034-1040) ══ **Elflaed** (fl. 1030)

Macbeth, king of Scotland (r. 1040-1054) ══ **Gruoch**

Lulach king of Scotland (r. 1057-1058)

(2) St. Margaret (c. 1046-1093) ══ Malcolm III Canmore king of Scotland (r. 1057-1093) ══ **(1) Ingebiorge** (fl. 1045-1068) ── Donalbane king of Scotland (r. 1093-1098) ══ **Margaret** (fl. 1000s)

Duncan II (d. 1094) ══ **Ethelreda** (fl. 1090)

Edward (d. 1093) — Edmund king of Scotland (r. 1094-1097) — Edgar king of Scotland (r. 1098-1107) — Alexander I king of Scotland (r. 1107-1124) **m. Sybilla** (d. 1122) — David I king of Scotland (r. 1124-1153) **m. Matilda of Northumberland** (c. 1074-1131) — **Matilda of Scotland** (1080-1118) queen of England — **Mary of Atholl** (d. 1116)

Henry (d. 1152) **m. Adelicia de Warrenne** (d. 1178)

Malcolm IV king of Scotland (r. 1153-1165) — **Margaret of Huntingdon** (c. 1140-1201) — William I the Lion king of Scotland (r. 1165-1214) ══ **Ermengarde of Beaumont** (d. 1234) — **Ada Dunkeld** (c. 1145-1206) — **Isabella** m. Robert baron Ros — David earl of Huntingdon ══ **Maude of Chester** (1171-1233)

(1) Joan (1210-1238) ══ Alexander II king of Scotland (r. 1214-1249) — **Margaret de Burgh** (c. 1193-1259) — **Marjory** (d. 1244) — **Isabel** (fl. 1225)
(2) Mary de Coucy (c. 1220-c. 1260)

John of Chester (d. 1237) **m. Ellen of Wales** (d. 1253) — **Margaret** (d. 1228) ══ Alan of Galloway ── **Ada Dunkeld** (c. 1195-?) — **Isabella** (1206-1251) ══ **Robert Bruce**

Christian (d. 1246) — Devorgilla (d. 1290) ══ John Balliol (d. 1269)

Robert Bruce of Annandale **m. Isabel de Clare** (1226-1254)

(1) Margaret (1240-1275) ══ Alexander III king of Scotland (r. 1249-1286) ══ **(2) Yolande de Dreux** (d. 1323)

John Balliol king of Scotland (r. 1292-1296) **m. Isabel de Warrenne** (b. 1253) — **Cecily Balliol** (d. before 1273) — **Ada Balliol** (fl. 1256) — **Margaret Balliol** (c. 1255-?) m. John Comyn

Robert Bruce **m. Marjorie of Carrick** (c. 1254-1292)

(1) Margaret of Norway (1261-1283) ══ Eric II king of Norway ══ **(2) Isabel Bruce** (c. 1278-1358)

Margaret Maid of Norway (c. 1283-1290)

Edward Balliol king of Scotland (r. 1332-1338) **m. Margaret Balliol** (fl. 1300s)

(1) Isabella of Mar (d. 1296) ══ Robert I, king of Scotland (r. 1306-1329) ══ **(2) Elizabeth de Burgh** (d. 1327) — **Mary Bruce** (fl. 1290-1316) — **Isabel Bruce** (c. 1278-1358) — **Christian Bruce** (d. 1356) — **Margaret Bruce** (c. 1286-?) — **Matilda Bruce** (c. 1285-c. 1326) m. Hugh Ross

Walter Stuart (d. 1326) ══ **Margaret Bruce** (1296-1316) — David II king of Scotland (r. 1329-1370) **m. (1) Joan of the Tower** (1321-1362) **(2) Margaret Drummond** (d. 1375) — **Margaret Bruce** (d. 1346) — **Matilda Bruce** (d. 1353)

Euphemia Ross (d. 1387)

(1) Elizabeth Muir (d. before 1355) ══ Robert II Stuart king of Scotland (r. 1371-1390)
(2) Euphemia Ross (d. 1387)

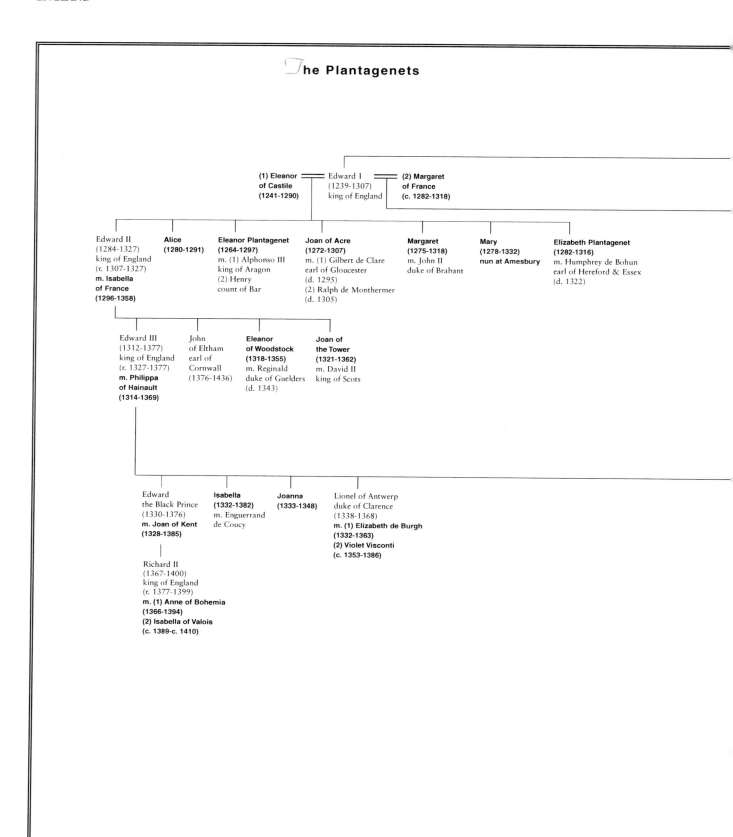

The Plantagenets

(1) Eleanor of Castile (1241-1290) ══ Edward I (1239-1307) king of England ══ **(2) Margaret of France (c. 1282-1318)**

Edward II (1284-1327) king of England (r. 1307-1327) **m. Isabella of France (1296-1358)**

Alice (1280-1291)

Eleanor Plantagenet (1264-1297) m. (1) Alphonso III king of Aragon (2) Henry count of Bar

Joan of Acre (1272-1307) m. (1) Gilbert de Clare earl of Gloucester (d. 1295) (2) Ralph de Monthermer (d. 1305)

Margaret (1275-1318) m. John II duke of Brabant

Mary (1278-1332) nun at Amesbury

Elizabeth Plantagenet (1282-1316) m. Humphrey de Bohun earl of Hereford & Essex (d. 1322)

Edward III (1312-1377) king of England (r. 1327-1377) **m. Philippa of Hainault (1314-1369)**

John of Eltham earl of Cornwall (1376-1436)

Eleanor of Woodstock (1318-1355) m. Reginald duke of Guelders (d. 1343)

Joan of the Tower (1321-1362) m. David II king of Scots

Edward the Black Prince (1330-1376) **m. Joan of Kent (1328-1385)**

Isabella (1332-1382) m. Enguerrand de Coucy

Joanna (1333-1348)

Lionel of Antwerp duke of Clarence (1338-1368) **m. (1) Elizabeth de Burgh (1332-1363) (2) Violet Visconti (c. 1353-1386)**

Richard II (1367-1400) king of England (r. 1377-1399) **m. (1) Anne of Bohemia (1366-1394) (2) Isabella of Valois (c. 1389-c. 1410)**

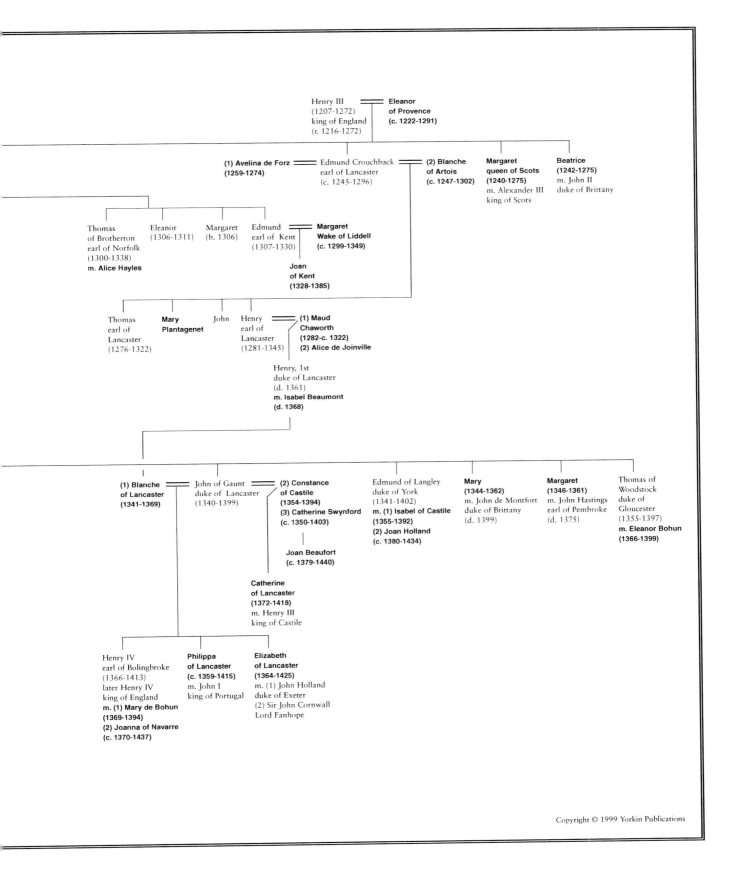

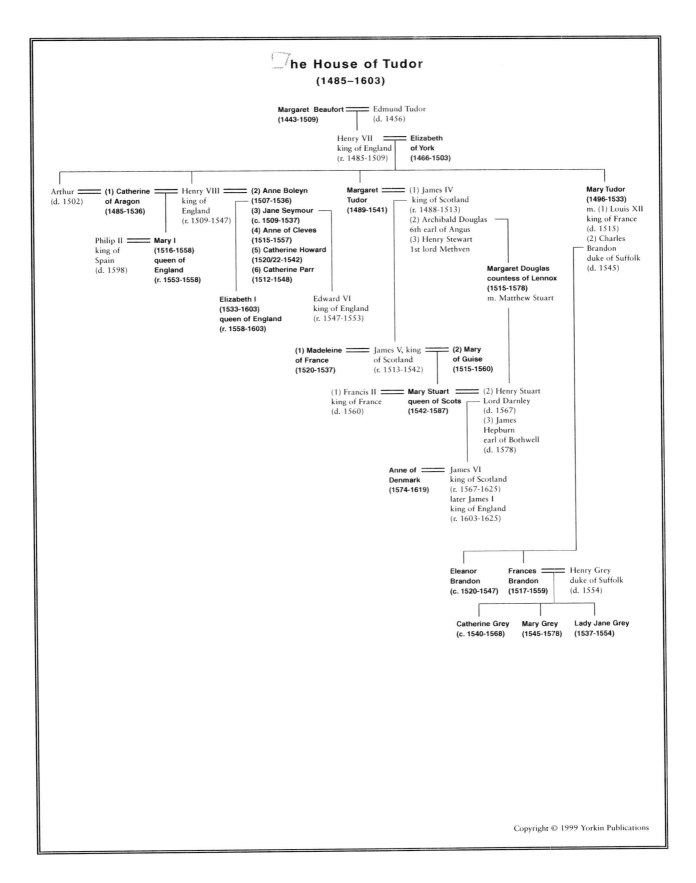

The House of Tudor
(1485–1603)

Margaret Beaufort (1443-1509) ═══ Edmund Tudor (d. 1456)

Henry VII king of England (r. 1485-1509) ═══ Elizabeth of York (1466-1503)

Arthur (d. 1502) ═══ (1) Catherine of Aragon (1485-1536) ═══ Henry VIII king of England (r. 1509-1547) ═══ (2) Anne Boleyn (1507-1536) (3) Jane Seymour (c. 1509-1537) (4) Anne of Cleves (1515-1557) (5) Catherine Howard (1520/22-1542) (6) Catherine Parr (1512-1548)

Margaret Tudor (1489-1541) ═══ (1) James IV king of Scotland (r. 1488-1513) (2) Archibald Douglas 6th earl of Angus (3) Henry Stewart 1st lord Methven

Mary Tudor (1496-1533) m. (1) Louis XII king of France (d. 1515) (2) Charles Brandon duke of Suffolk (d. 1545)

Philip II king of Spain (d. 1598) ═══ Mary I (1516-1558) queen of England (r. 1553-1558)

Margaret Douglas countess of Lennox (1515-1578) m. Matthew Stuart

Elizabeth I (1533-1603) queen of England (r. 1558-1603)

Edward VI king of England (r. 1547-1553)

(1) Madeleine of France (1520-1537) ═══ James V, king of Scotland (r. 1513-1542) ═══ (2) Mary of Guise (1515-1560)

(1) Francis II king of France (d. 1560) ═══ Mary Stuart queen of Scots (1542-1587) ═══ (2) Henry Stuart Lord Darnley (d. 1567) (3) James Hepburn earl of Bothwell (d. 1578)

Anne of Denmark (1574-1619) ═══ James VI king of Scotland (r. 1567-1625) later James I king of England (r. 1603-1625)

Eleanor Brandon (c. 1520-1547)

Frances Brandon (1517-1559) ═══ Henry Grey duke of Suffolk (d. 1554)

Catherine Grey (c. 1540-1568)

Mary Grey (1545-1578)

Lady Jane Grey (1537-1554)

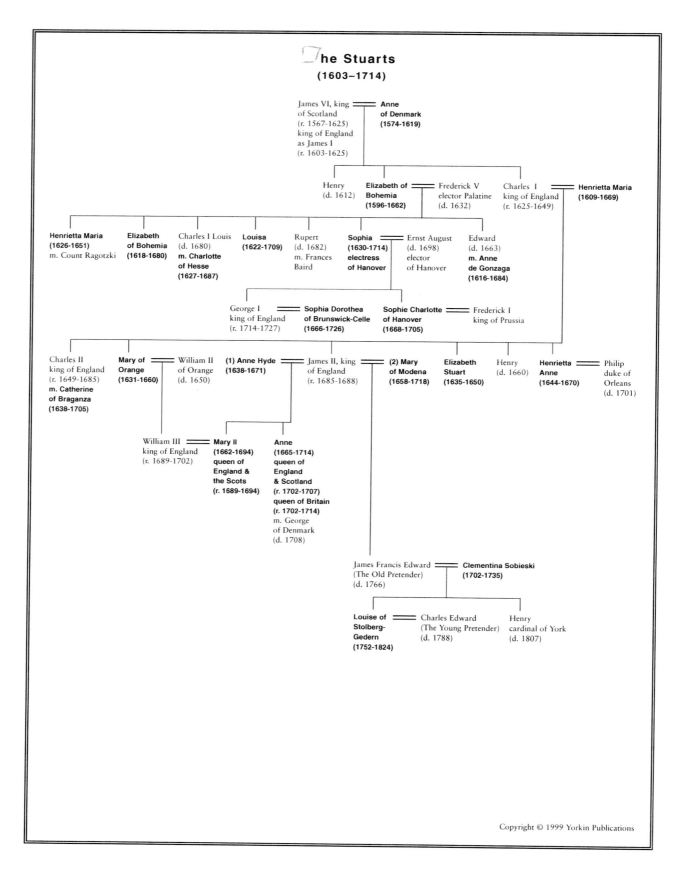

The Stuarts
(1603–1714)

James VI, king of Scotland (r. 1567-1625) king of England as James I (r. 1603-1625) === **Anne of Denmark (1574-1619)**

Henry (d. 1612)

Elizabeth of Bohemia (1596-1662) === Frederick V elector Palatine (d. 1632)

Charles I king of England (r. 1625-1649) === **Henrietta Maria (1609-1669)**

Henrietta Maria (1626-1651) m. Count Ragotzki

Elizabeth of Bohemia (1618-1680)

Charles I Louis (d. 1680) **m. Charlotte of Hesse (1627-1687)**

Louisa (1622-1709)

Rupert (d. 1682) m. Frances Baird

Sophia (1630-1714) electress of Hanover === Ernst August (d. 1698) elector of Hanover

Edward (d. 1663) **m. Anne de Gonzaga (1616-1684)**

George I king of England (r. 1714-1727) === **Sophia Dorothea of Brunswick-Celle (1666-1726)**

Sophie Charlotte of Hanover (1668-1705) === Frederick I king of Prussia

Charles II king of England (r. 1649-1685) **m. Catherine of Braganza (1638-1705)**

Mary of Orange (1631-1660) === William II of Orange (d. 1650)

(1) Anne Hyde (1638-1671) === James II, king of England (r. 1685-1688) === **(2) Mary of Modena (1658-1718)**

Elizabeth Stuart (1635-1650)

Henry (d. 1660)

Henrietta Anne (1644-1670) === Philip duke of Orleans (d. 1701)

William III king of England (r. 1689-1702) === **Mary II (1662-1694) queen of England & the Scots (r. 1689-1694)**

Anne (1665-1714) queen of England & Scotland (r. 1702-1707) queen of Britain (r. 1702-1714) m. George of Denmark (d. 1708)

James Francis Edward (The Old Pretender) (d. 1766) === **Clementina Sobieski (1702-1735)**

Louise of Stolberg-Gedern (1752-1824) === Charles Edward (The Young Pretender) (d. 1788)

Henry cardinal of York (d. 1807)

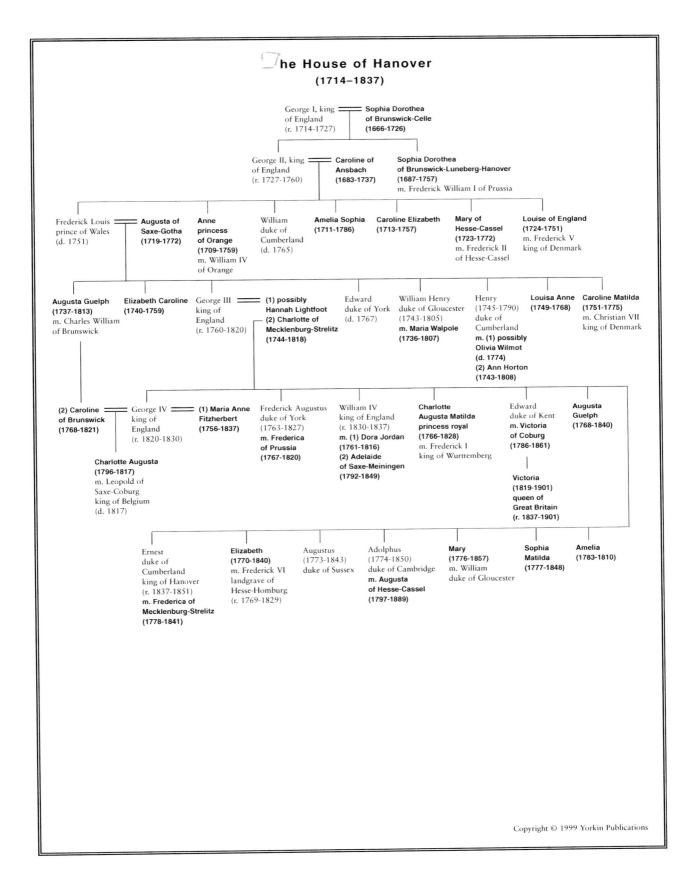

The House of Hanover
(1714–1837)

George I, king of England (r. 1714-1727) ═══ **Sophia Dorothea of Brunswick-Celle (1666-1726)**

George II, king of England (r. 1727-1760) ═══ **Caroline of Ansbach (1683-1737)**

Sophia Dorothea of Brunswick-Luneberg-Hanover (1687-1757) m. Frederick William I of Prussia

Frederick Louis prince of Wales (d. 1751) ═══ **Augusta of Saxe-Gotha (1719-1772)**

Anne princess of Orange (1709-1759) m. William IV of Orange

William duke of Cumberland (d. 1765)

Amelia Sophia (1711-1786)

Caroline Elizabeth (1713-1757)

Mary of Hesse-Cassel (1723-1772) m. Frederick II of Hesse-Cassel

Louise of England (1724-1751) m. Frederick V king of Denmark

Augusta Guelph (1737-1813) m. Charles William of Brunswick

Elizabeth Caroline (1740-1759)

George III king of England (r. 1760-1820) ═══ (1) possibly **Hannah Lightfoot** / (2) **Charlotte of Mecklenburg-Strelitz (1744-1818)**

Edward duke of York (d. 1767)

William Henry duke of Gloucester (1743-1805) m. **Maria Walpole (1736-1807)**

Henry (1745-1790) duke of Cumberland m. (1) possibly **Olivia Wilmot (d. 1774)** (2) **Ann Horton (1743-1808)**

Louisa Anne (1749-1768)

Caroline Matilda (1751-1775) m. Christian VII king of Denmark

(2) **Caroline of Brunswick (1768-1821)** ═══ George IV king of England (r. 1820-1830) ═══ (1) **Maria Anne Fitzherbert (1756-1837)**

Frederick Augustus duke of York (1763-1827) m. **Frederica of Prussia (1767-1820)**

William IV king of England (r. 1830-1837) m. (1) **Dora Jordan (1761-1816)** (2) **Adelaide of Saxe-Meiningen (1792-1849)**

Charlotte Augusta Matilda princess royal (1766-1828) m. Frederick I king of Wurttemberg

Edward duke of Kent m. **Victoria of Coburg (1786-1861)**

Augusta Guelph (1768-1840)

Charlotte Augusta (1796-1817) m. Leopold of Saxe-Coburg king of Belgium (d. 1817)

Victoria (1819-1901) queen of Great Britain (r. 1837-1901)

Ernest duke of Cumberland king of Hanover (r. 1837-1851) m. **Frederica of Mecklenburg-Strelitz (1778-1841)**

Elizabeth (1770-1840) m. Frederick VI landgrave of Hesse-Homburg (r. 1769-1829)

Augustus (1773-1843) duke of Sussex

Adolphus (1774-1850) duke of Cambridge m. **Augusta of Hesse-Cassel (1797-1889)**

Mary (1776-1857) m. William duke of Gloucester

Sophia Matilda (1777-1848)

Amelia (1783-1810)

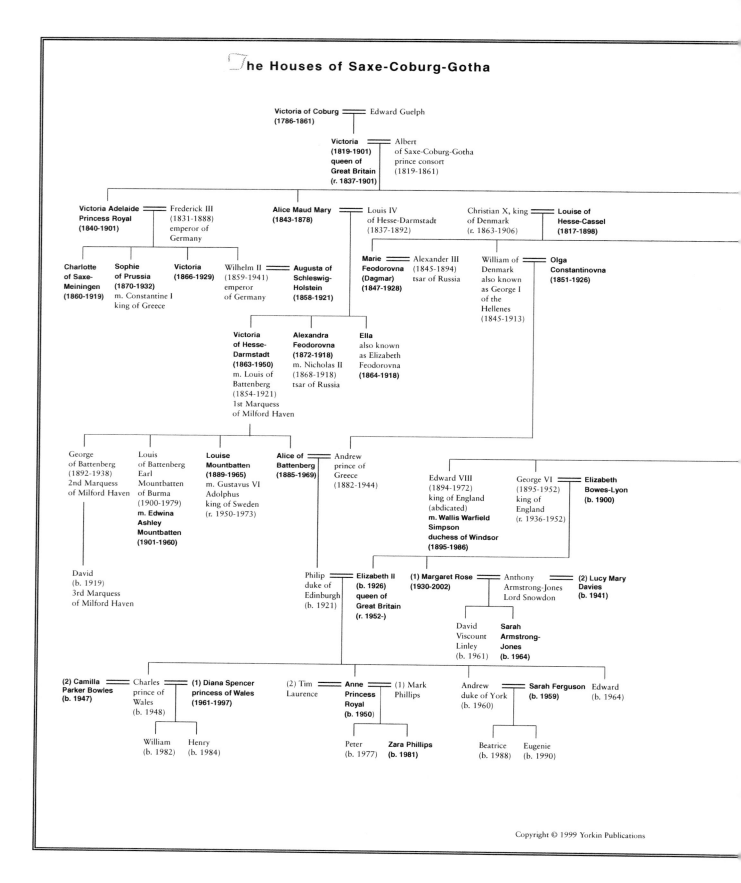

The Houses of Saxe-Coburg-Gotha

Victoria of Coburg (1786-1861) ═══ Edward Guelph

Victoria (1819-1901) queen of Great Britain (r. 1837-1901) ═══ Albert of Saxe-Coburg-Gotha prince consort (1819-1861)

Victoria Adelaide Princess Royal (1840-1901) ═══ Frederick III (1831-1888) emperor of Germany

Alice Maud Mary (1843-1878) ═══ Louis IV of Hesse-Darmstadt (1837-1892)

Christian X, king of Denmark (r. 1863-1906) ═══ Louise of Hesse-Cassel (1817-1898)

Charlotte of Saxe-Meiningen (1860-1919)

Sophie of Prussia (1870-1932) m. Constantine I king of Greece

Victoria (1866-1929)

Wilhelm II (1859-1941) emperor of Germany ═══ Augusta of Schleswig-Holstein (1858-1921)

Marie Feodorovna (Dagmar) (1847-1928) ═══ Alexander III (1845-1894) tsar of Russia

William of Denmark also known as George I of the Hellenes (1845-1913) ═══ Olga Constantinovna (1851-1926)

Victoria of Hesse-Darmstadt (1863-1950) m. Louis of Battenberg (1854-1921) 1st Marquess of Milford Haven

Alexandra Feodorovna (1872-1918) m. Nicholas II (1868-1918) tsar of Russia

Ella also known as Elizabeth Feodorovna (1864-1918)

George of Battenberg (1892-1938) 2nd Marquess of Milford Haven

Louis of Battenberg Earl Mountbatten of Burma (1900-1979) m. Edwina Ashley Mountbatten (1901-1960)

Louise Mountbatten (1889-1965) m. Gustavus VI Adolphus king of Sweden (r. 1950-1973)

Alice of Battenberg (1885-1969) ═══ Andrew prince of Greece (1882-1944)

Edward VIII (1894-1972) king of England (abdicated) m. Wallis Warfield Simpson duchess of Windsor (1895-1986)

George VI (1895-1952) king of England (r. 1936-1952) ═══ Elizabeth Bowes-Lyon (b. 1900)

David (b. 1919) 3rd Marquess of Milford Haven

Philip duke of Edinburgh (b. 1921) ═══ Elizabeth II (b. 1926) queen of Great Britain (r. 1952-)

(1) Margaret Rose (1930-2002) ═══ Anthony Armstrong-Jones Lord Snowdon ═══ (2) Lucy Mary Davies (b. 1941)

David Viscount Linley (b. 1961)

Sarah Armstrong-Jones (b. 1964)

(2) Camilla Parker Bowles (b. 1947) ═══ Charles prince of Wales (b. 1948) ═══ (1) Diana Spencer princess of Wales (1961-1997)

(2) Tim Laurence ═══ Anne Princess Royal (b. 1950) ═══ (1) Mark Phillips

Andrew duke of York (b. 1960) ═══ Sarah Ferguson (b. 1959)

Edward (b. 1964)

William (b. 1982)

Henry (b. 1984)

Peter (b. 1977)

Zara Phillips (b. 1981)

Beatrice (b. 1988)

Eugenie (b. 1990)

Copyright © 1999 Yorkin Publications

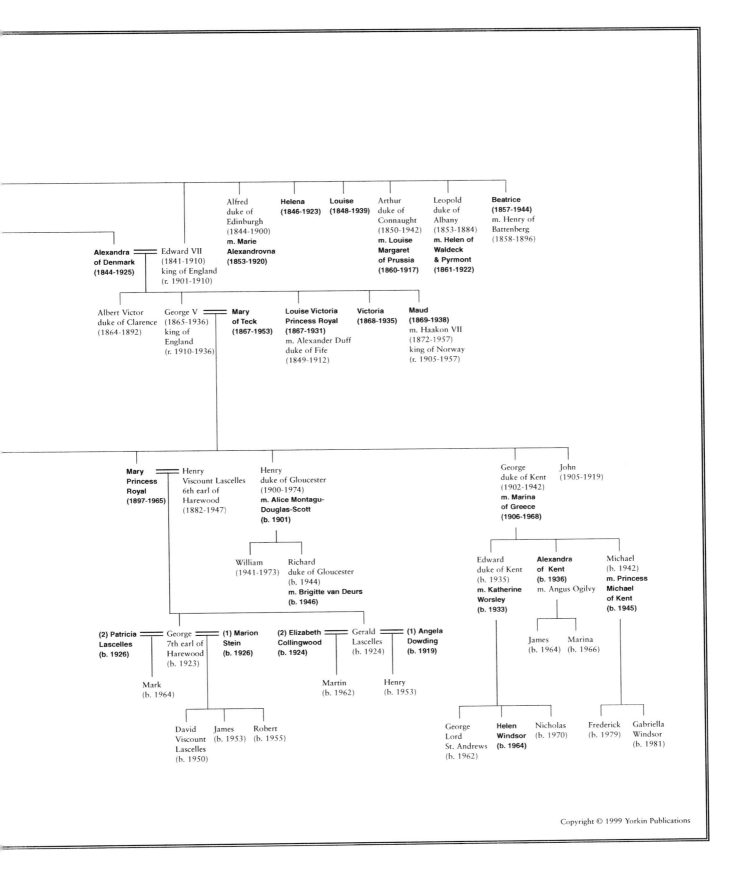

Alfred
duke of
Edinburgh
(1844-1900)
**m. Marie
Alexandrovna
(1853-1920)**

**Helena
(1846-1923)**

**Louise
(1848-1939)**

Arthur
duke of
Connaught
(1850-1942)
**m. Louise
Margaret
of Prussia
(1860-1917)**

Leopold
duke of
Albany
(1853-1884)
**m. Helen of
Waldeck
& Pyrmont
(1861-1922)**

**Beatrice
(1857-1944)**
m. Henry of
Battenberg
(1858-1896)

**Alexandra
of Denmark
(1844-1925)**

Edward VII
(1841-1910)
king of England
(r. 1901-1910)

Albert Victor
duke of Clarence
(1864-1892)

George V
(1865-1936)
king of
England
(r. 1910-1936)

**Mary
of Teck
(1867-1953)**

**Louise Victoria
Princess Royal
(1867-1931)**
m. Alexander Duff
duke of Fife
(1849-1912)

**Victoria
(1868-1935)**

**Maud
(1869-1938)**
m. Haakon VII
(1872-1957)
king of Norway
(r. 1905-1957)

**Mary
Princess
Royal
(1897-1965)**

Henry
Viscount Lascelles
6th earl of
Harewood
(1882-1947)

Henry
duke of Gloucester
(1900-1974)
**m. Alice Montagu-
Douglas-Scott
(b. 1901)**

George
duke of Kent
(1902-1942)
**m. Marina
of Greece
(1906-1968)**

John
(1905-1919)

William
(1941-1973)

Richard
duke of Gloucester
(b. 1944)
**m. Brigitte van Deurs
(b. 1946)**

Edward
duke of Kent
(b. 1935)
**m. Katherine
Worsley
(b. 1933)**

**Alexandra
of Kent
(b. 1936)**
m. Angus Ogilvy

Michael
(b. 1942)
**m. Princess
Michael
of Kent
(b. 1945)**

**(2) Patricia
Lascelles
(b. 1926)**

George
7th earl of
Harewood
(b. 1923)

**(1) Marion
Stein
(b. 1926)**

**(2) Elizabeth
Collingwood
(b. 1924)**

Gerald
Lascelles
(b. 1924)

**(1) Angela
Dowding
(b. 1919)**

James
(b. 1964)

Marina
(b. 1966)

Mark
(b. 1964)

Martin
(b. 1962)

Henry
(b. 1953)

David
Viscount
Lascelles
(b. 1950)

James
(b. 1953)

Robert
(b. 1955)

George
Lord
St. Andrews
(b. 1962)

**Helen
Windsor
(b. 1964)**

Nicholas
(b. 1970)

Frederick
(b. 1979)

Gabriella
Windsor
(b. 1981)

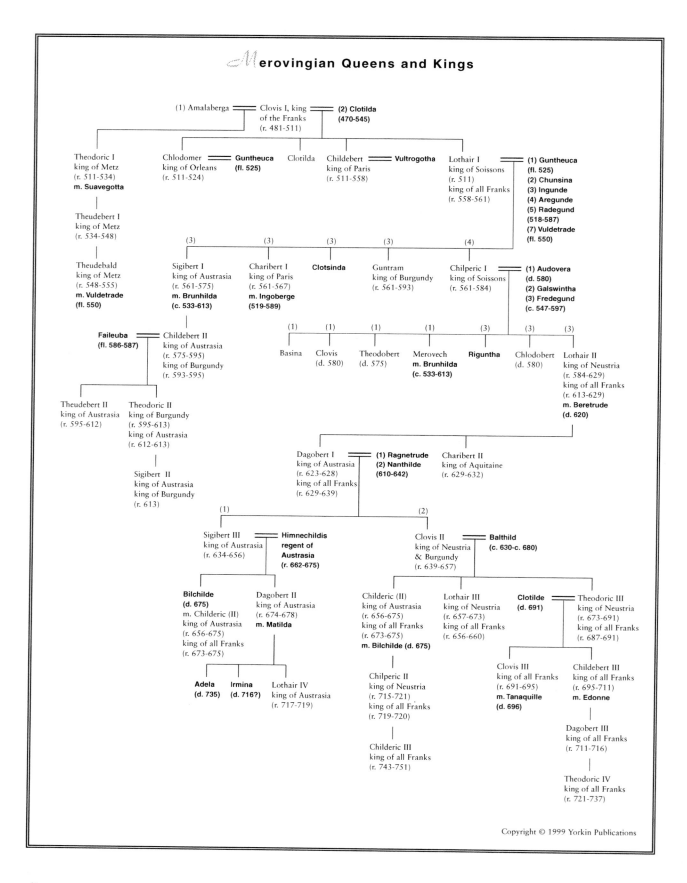

𝓜erovingian Queens and Kings

(1) Amalaberga ══ Clovis I, king ══ **(2) Clotilda**
of the Franks **(470-545)**
(r. 481-511)

Theodoric I
king of Metz
(r. 511-534)
m. Suavegotta

Chlodomer ══ **Guntheuca**
king of Orleans **(fl. 525)**
(r. 511-524)

Clotilda

Childebert ══ **Vultrogotha**
king of Paris
(r. 511-558)

Lothair I ══ **(1) Guntheuca**
king of Soissons **(fl. 525)**
(r. 511) **(2) Chunsina**
king of all Franks **(3) Ingunde**
(r. 558-561) **(4) Aregunde**
(5) Radegund
(518-587)
(7) Vuldetrade
(fl. 550)

Theudebert I
king of Metz
(r. 534-548)

Theudebald
king of Metz
(r. 548-555)
m. Vuldetrade
(fl. 550)

(3)
Sigibert I
king of Austrasia
(r. 561-575)
m. Brunhilda
(c. 533-613)

(3)
Charibert I
king of Paris
(r. 561-567)
m. Ingoberge
(519-589)

(3)
Clotsinda

(3)
Guntram
king of Burgundy
(r. 561-593)

(4)
Chilperic I ══ **(1) Audovera**
king of Soissons **(d. 580)**
(r. 561-584) **(2) Galswintha**
(3) Fredegund
(c. 547-597)

Faileuba ══ Childebert II
(fl. 586-587) king of Austrasia
(r. 575-595)
king of Burgundy
(r. 593-595)

(1)
Basina

(1)
Clovis
(d. 580)

(1)
Theodobert
(d. 575)

(1)
Merovech
m. Brunhilda
(c. 533-613)

(3)
Riguntha

(3)
Chlodobert
(d. 580)

(3)
Lothair II
king of Neustria
(r. 584-629)
king of all Franks
(r. 613-629)
m. Beretrude
(d. 620)

Theudebert II
king of Austrasia
(r. 595-612)

Theodoric II
king of Burgundy
(r. 595-613)
king of Austrasia
(r. 612-613)

Sigibert II
king of Austrasia
king of Burgundy
(r. 613)

Dagobert I ══ **(1) Ragnetrude**
king of Austrasia **(2) Nanthilde**
(r. 623-628) **(610-642)**
king of all Franks
(r. 629-639)

Charibert II
king of Aquitaine
(r. 629-632)

(1)
Sigibert III ══ **Himnechildis**
king of Austrasia **regent of**
(r. 634-656) **Austrasia**
(r. 662-675)

(2)
Clovis II ══ **Balthild**
king of Neustria **(c. 630-c. 680)**
& Burgundy
(r. 639-657)

Bilchilde
(d. 675)
m. Childeric (II)
king of Austrasia
(r. 656-675)
king of all Franks
(r. 673-675)

Dagobert II
king of Austrasia
(r. 674-678)
m. Matilda

Childeric (II)
king of Austrasia
(r. 656-675)
king of all Franks
(r. 673-675)
m. Bilchilde (d. 675)

Lothair III
king of Neustria
(r. 657-673)
king of all Franks
(r. 656-660)

Clotilde ══ Theodoric III
(d. 691) king of Neustria
(r. 673-691)
king of all Franks
(r. 687-691)

Adela
(d. 735)

Irmina
(d. 716?)

Lothair IV
king of Austrasia
(r. 717-719)

Chilperic II
king of Neustria
(r. 715-721)
king of all Franks
(r. 719-720)

Clovis III
king of all Franks
(r. 691-695)
m. Tanaquille
(d. 696)

Childebert III
king of all Franks
(r. 695-711)
m. Edonne

Childeric III
king of all Franks
(r. 743-751)

Dagobert III
king of all Franks
(r. 711-716)

Theodoric IV
king of all Franks
(r. 721-737)

The House of Pepin
(640–814)

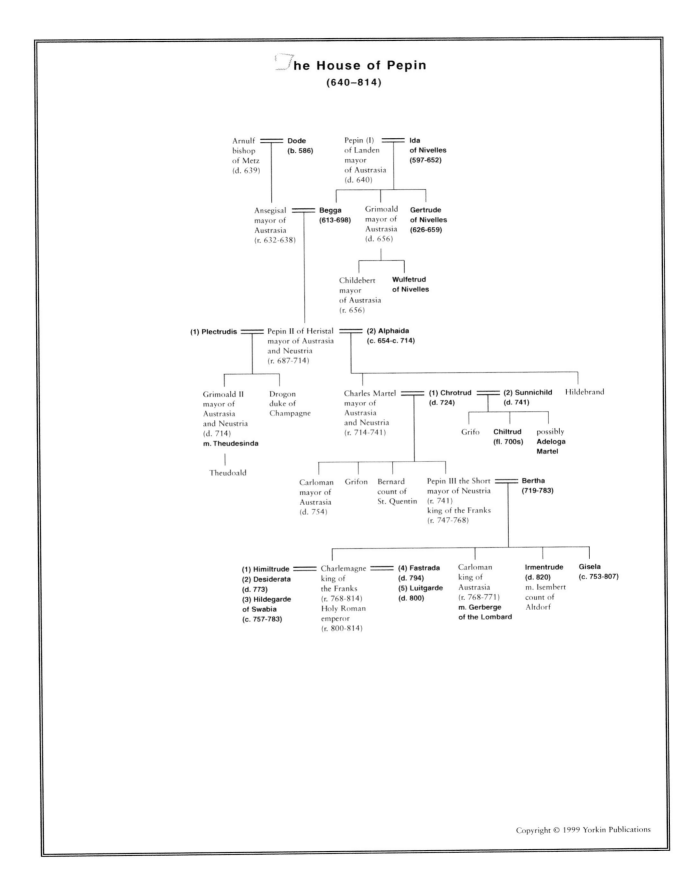

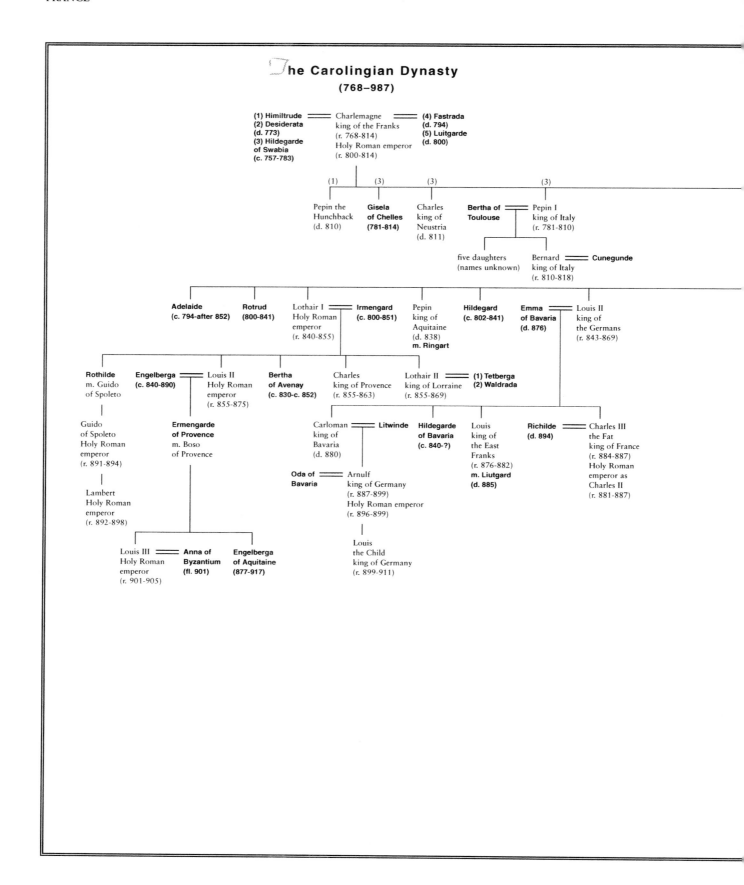

The Carolingian Dynasty
(768–987)

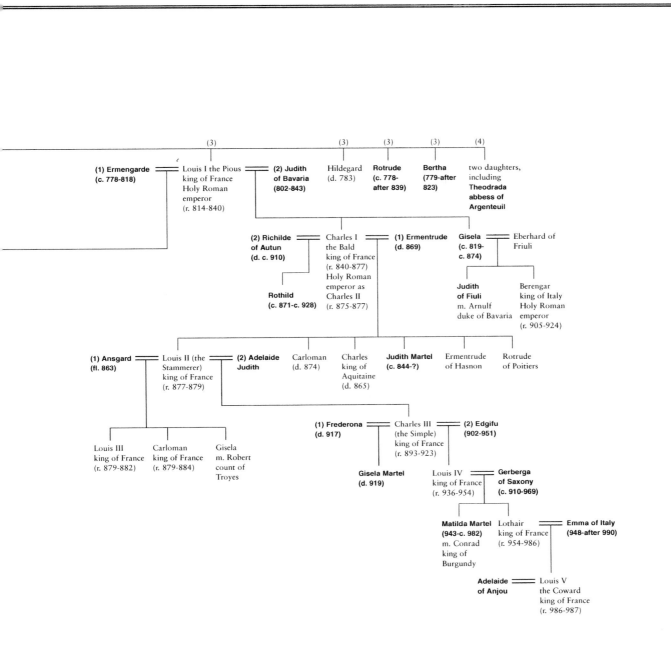

The House of Capet
(987–1328)

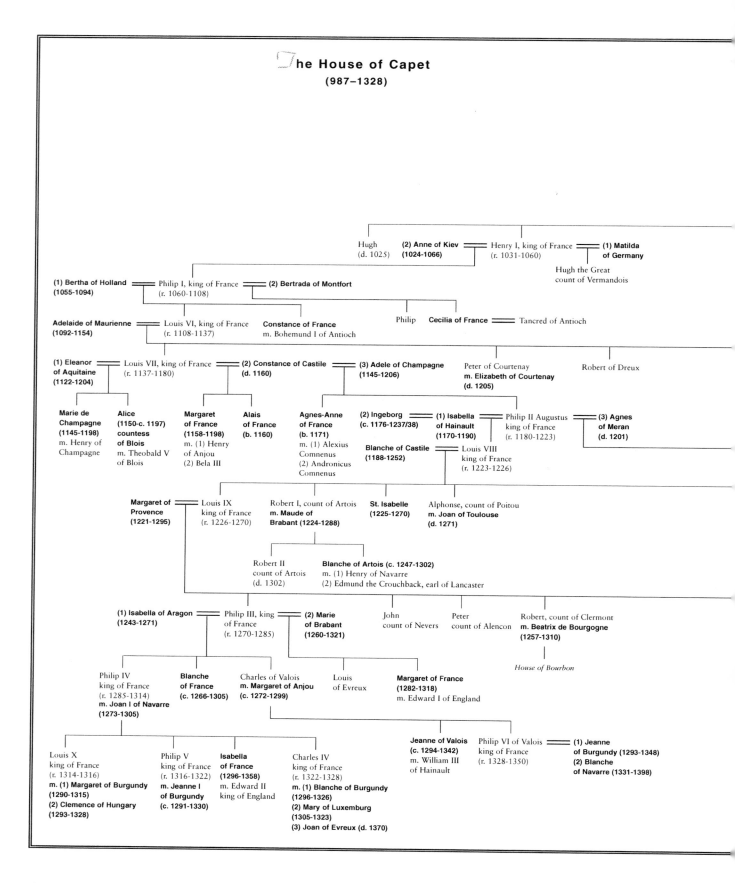

Hugh (d. 1025) — (2) Anne of Kiev (1024-1066) ═══ Henry I, king of France (r. 1031-1060) ═══ (1) Matilda of Germany

Hugh the Great count of Vermandois

(1) Bertha of Holland (1055-1094) ═══ Philip I, king of France (r. 1060-1108) ═══ (2) Bertrada of Montfort

Adelaide of Maurienne (1092-1154) ═══ Louis VI, king of France (r. 1108-1137)   Constance of France m. Bohemund I of Antioch

Philip   Cecilia of France ═══ Tancred of Antioch

(1) Eleanor of Aquitaine (1122-1204) ═══ Louis VII, king of France (r. 1137-1180) ═══ (2) Constance of Castile (d. 1160) ═══ (3) Adele of Champagne (1145-1206)   Peter of Courtenay m. Elizabeth of Courtenay (d. 1205)   Robert of Dreux

Marie de Champagne (1145-1198) m. Henry of Champagne

Alice (1150-c. 1197) countess of Blois m. Theobald V of Blois

Margaret of France (1158-1198) m. (1) Henry of Anjou (2) Bela III

Alais of France (b. 1160)

Agnes-Anne of France (b. 1171) m. (1) Alexius Comnenus (2) Andronicus Comnenus

(2) Ingeborg (c. 1176-1237/38) ═══ (1) Isabella of Hainault (1170-1190) ═══ Philip II Augustus king of France (r. 1180-1223) ═══ (3) Agnes of Meran (d. 1201)

Blanche of Castile (1188-1252) ═══ Louis VIII king of France (r. 1223-1226)

Margaret of Provence (1221-1295) ═══ Louis IX king of France (r. 1226-1270)   Robert I, count of Artois m. Maude of Brabant (1224-1288)   St. Isabelle (1225-1270)   Alphonse, count of Poitou m. Joan of Toulouse (d. 1271)

Robert II count of Artois (d. 1302)   Blanche of Artois (c. 1247-1302) m. (1) Henry of Navarre (2) Edmund the Crouchback, earl of Lancaster

(1) Isabella of Aragon (1243-1271) ═══ Philip III, king of France (r. 1270-1285) ═══ (2) Marie of Brabant (1260-1321)   John count of Nevers   Peter count of Alencon   Robert, count of Clermont m. Beatrix de Bourgogne (1257-1310)

House of Bourbon

Philip IV king of France (r. 1285-1314) m. Joan I of Navarre (1273-1305)

Blanche of France (c. 1266-1305)

Charles of Valois m. Margaret of Anjou (c. 1272-1299)

Louis of Evreux

Margaret of France (1282-1318) m. Edward I of England

Louis X king of France (r. 1314-1316) m. (1) Margaret of Burgundy (1290-1315) (2) Clemence of Hungary (1293-1328)

Philip V king of France (r. 1316-1322) m. Jeanne I of Burgundy (c. 1291-1330)

Isabella of France (1296-1358) m. Edward II king of England

Charles IV king of France (r. 1322-1328) m. (1) Blanche of Burgundy (1296-1326) (2) Mary of Luxemburg (1305-1323) (3) Joan of Evreux (d. 1370)

Jeanne of Valois (c. 1294-1342) m. William III of Hainault

Philip VI of Valois king of France (r. 1328-1350) ═══ (1) Jeanne of Burgundy (1293-1348) (2) Blanche of Navarre (1331-1398)

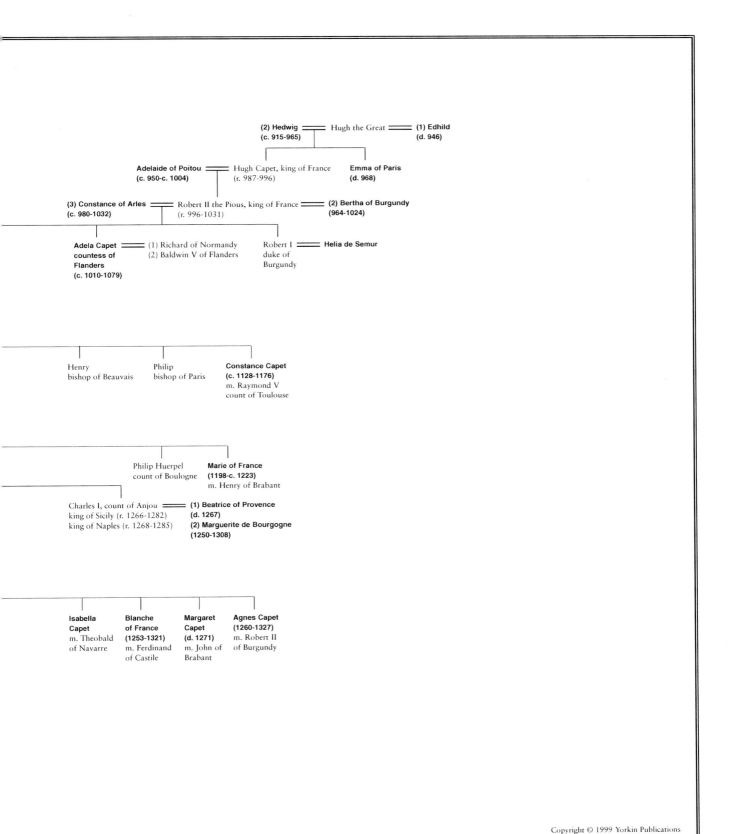

The House of Anjou
(1266–1435)

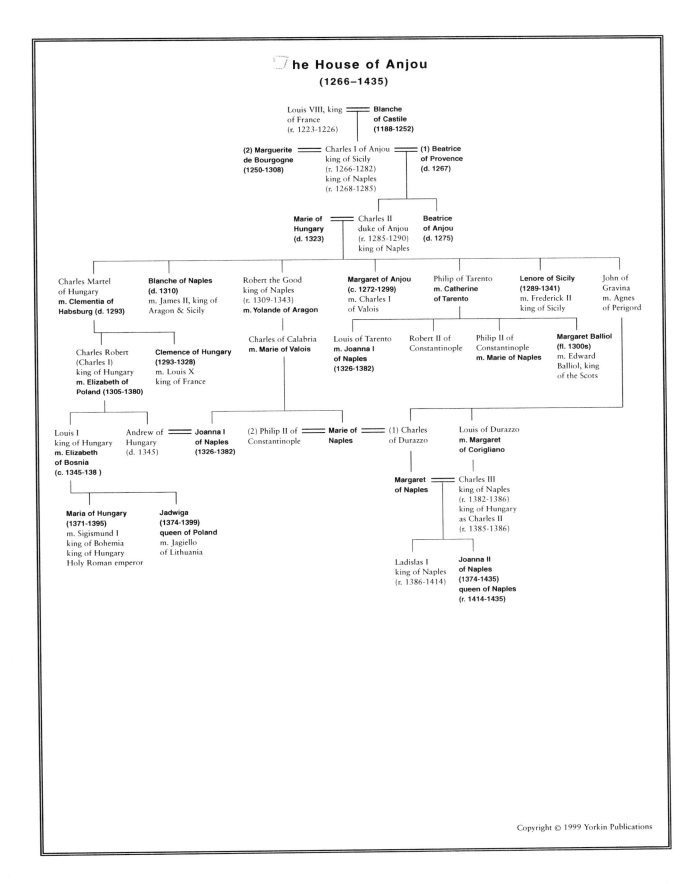

Louis VIII, king of France (r. 1223-1226) ═══ Blanche of Castile (1188-1252)

(2) Marguerite de Bourgogne (1250-1308) ═══ Charles I of Anjou king of Sicily (r. 1266-1282) king of Naples (r. 1268-1285) ═══ (1) Beatrice of Provence (d. 1267)

Marie of Hungary (d. 1323) ═══ Charles II duke of Anjou (r. 1285-1290) king of Naples   Beatrice of Anjou (d. 1275)

Charles Martel of Hungary m. Clementia of Habsburg (d. 1293)

Blanche of Naples (d. 1310) m. James II, king of Aragon & Sicily

Robert the Good king of Naples (r. 1309-1343) m. Yolande of Aragon

Margaret of Anjou (c. 1272-1299) m. Charles I of Valois

Philip of Tarento m. Catherine of Tarento

Lenore of Sicily (1289-1341) m. Frederick II king of Sicily

John of Gravina m. Agnes of Perigord

Charles Robert (Charles I) king of Hungary m. Elizabeth of Poland (1305-1380)

Clemence of Hungary (1293-1328) m. Louis X king of France

Charles of Calabria m. Marie of Valois

Louis of Tarento m. Joanna I of Naples (1326-1382)

Robert II of Constantinople

Philip II of Constantinople m. Marie of Naples

Margaret Balliol (fl. 1300s) m. Edward Balliol, king of the Scots

Louis I king of Hungary m. Elizabeth of Bosnia (c. 1345-138)

Andrew of Hungary (d. 1345) ═══ Joanna I of Naples (1326-1382)

(2) Philip II of Constantinople ═══ Marie of Naples ═══ (1) Charles of Durazzo

Louis of Durazzo m. Margaret of Corigliano

Maria of Hungary (1371-1395) m. Sigismund I king of Bohemia king of Hungary Holy Roman emperor

Jadwiga (1374-1399) queen of Poland m. Jagiello of Lithuania

Margaret of Naples ═══ Charles III king of Naples (r. 1382-1386) king of Hungary as Charles II (r. 1385-1386)

Ladislas I king of Naples (r. 1386-1414)

Joanna II of Naples (1374-1435) queen of Naples (r. 1414-1435)

The House of Burgundy
(1312–1477)

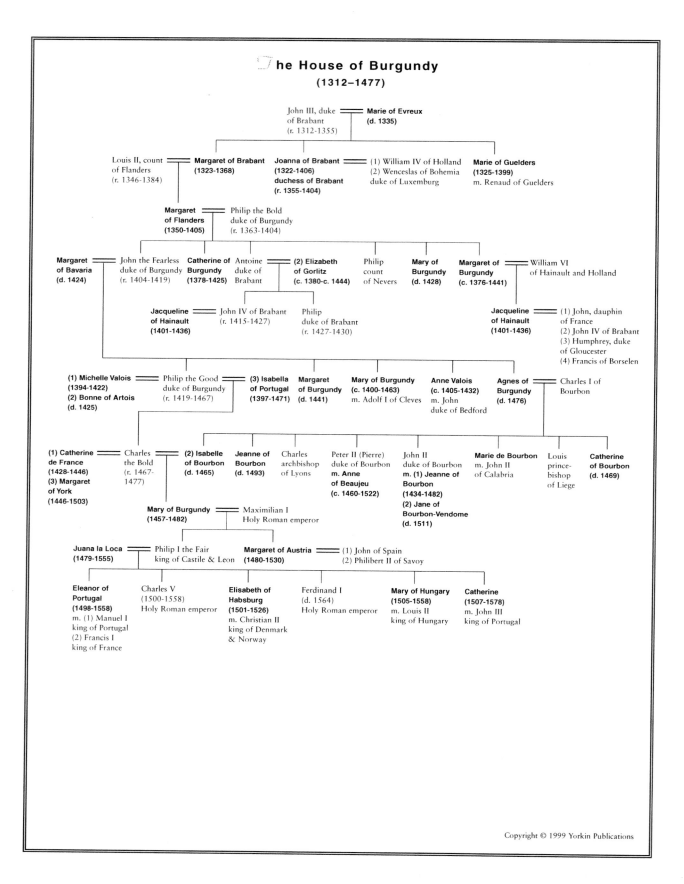

John III, duke of Brabant (r. 1312-1355) ═══ **Marie of Evreux** (d. 1335)

Louis II, count of Flanders (r. 1346-1384) ═══ **Margaret of Brabant (1323-1368)**

Joanna of Brabant (1322-1406) duchess of Brabant (r. 1355-1404) ═══ (1) William IV of Holland (2) Wenceslas of Bohemia duke of Luxemburg

Marie of Guelders (1325-1399) m. Renaud of Guelders

Margaret of Flanders (1350-1405) ═══ Philip the Bold duke of Burgundy (r. 1363-1404)

Margaret of Bavaria (d. 1424) ═══ John the Fearless duke of Burgundy (r. 1404-1419)

Catherine of Burgundy (1378-1425)

Antoine duke of Brabant ═══ (2) **Elizabeth of Gorlitz (c. 1380-c. 1444)**

Philip count of Nevers

Mary of Burgundy (d. 1428)

Margaret of Burgundy (c. 1376-1441) ═══ William VI of Hainault and Holland

Jacqueline of Hainault (1401-1436) ═══ John IV of Brabant (r. 1415-1427)

Philip duke of Brabant (r. 1427-1430)

Jacqueline of Hainault (1401-1436) ═══ (1) John, dauphin of France (2) John IV of Brabant (3) Humphrey, duke of Gloucester (4) Francis of Borselen

(1) **Michelle Valois (1394-1422)** (2) **Bonne of Artois (d. 1425)** ═══ Philip the Good duke of Burgundy (r. 1419-1467) ═══ (3) **Isabella of Portugal (1397-1471)**

Margaret of Burgundy (d. 1441)

Mary of Burgundy (c. 1400-1463) m. Adolf I of Cleves

Anne Valois (c. 1405-1432) m. John duke of Bedford

Agnes of Burgundy (d. 1476) ═══ Charles I of Bourbon

(1) **Catherine de France (1428-1446)** (3) **Margaret of York (1446-1503)** ═══ Charles the Bold (r. 1467-1477) ═══ (2) **Isabelle of Bourbon (d. 1465)**

Jeanne of Bourbon (d. 1493)

Charles archbishop of Lyons

Peter II (Pierre) duke of Bourbon m. **Anne of Beaujeu (c. 1460-1522)**

John II duke of Bourbon m. (1) **Jeanne of Bourbon (1434-1482)** (2) **Jane of Bourbon-Vendome (d. 1511)**

Marie de Bourbon m. John II of Calabria

Louis prince-bishop of Liege

Catherine of Bourbon (d. 1469)

Mary of Burgundy (1457-1482) ═══ Maximilian I Holy Roman emperor

Juana la Loca (1479-1555) ═══ Philip I the Fair king of Castile & Leon ═══ **Margaret of Austria (1480-1530)** ═══ (1) John of Spain (2) Philibert II of Savoy

Eleanor of Portugal (1498-1558) m. (1) Manuel I king of Portugal (2) Francis I king of France

Charles V (1500-1558) Holy Roman emperor

Elisabeth of Habsburg (1501-1526) m. Christian II king of Denmark & Norway

Ferdinand I (d. 1564) Holy Roman emperor

Mary of Hungary (1505-1558) m. Louis II king of Hungary

Catherine (1507-1578) m. John III king of Portugal

The House of Valois
(1328–1515)

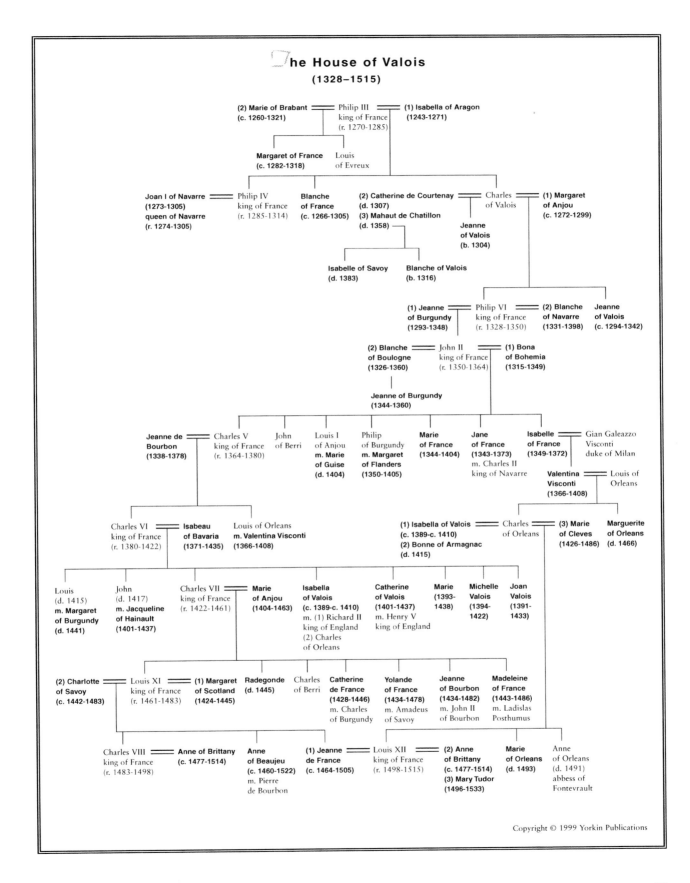

(2) Marie of Brabant (c. 1260-1321) ═══ **Philip III** king of France (r. 1270-1285) ═══ **(1) Isabella of Aragon** (1243-1271)

Margaret of France (c. 1282-1318) — Louis of Evreux

Joan I of Navarre (1273-1305) queen of Navarre (r. 1274-1305) ═══ **Philip IV** king of France (r. 1285-1314) — **Blanche of France** (c. 1266-1305) — **(2) Catherine de Courtenay** (d. 1307) **(3) Mahaut de Chatillon** (d. 1358) ═══ **Charles of Valois** ═══ **(1) Margaret of Anjou** (c. 1272-1299)

Jeanne of Valois (b. 1304)

Isabelle of Savoy (d. 1383) — **Blanche of Valois** (b. 1316)

(1) Jeanne of Burgundy (1293-1348) ═══ **Philip VI** king of France (r. 1328-1350) ═══ **(2) Blanche of Navarre** (1331-1398) — **Jeanne of Valois** (c. 1294-1342)

(2) Blanche of Boulogne (1326-1360) ═══ **John II** king of France (r. 1350-1364) ═══ **(1) Bona of Bohemia** (1315-1349)

Jeanne of Burgundy (1344-1360)

Jeanne de Bourbon (1338-1378) ═══ **Charles V** king of France (r. 1364-1380) — John of Berri — Louis I of Anjou m. Marie of Guise (d. 1404) — Philip of Burgundy m. Margaret of Flanders (1350-1405) — **Marie of France** (1344-1404) — **Jane of France** (1343-1373) m. Charles II king of Navarre — **Isabelle of France** (1349-1372) ═══ Gian Galeazzo Visconti duke of Milan

Valentina Visconti (1366-1408) ═══ Louis of Orleans

Charles VI king of France (r. 1380-1422) ═══ **Isabeau of Bavaria** (1371-1435) — Louis of Orleans m. Valentina Visconti (1366-1408)

(1) Isabella of Valois (c. 1389-c. 1410) **(2) Bonne of Armagnac** (d. 1415) ═══ Charles of Orleans ═══ **(3) Marie of Cleves** (1426-1486) — **Marguerite of Orleans** (d. 1466)

Louis (d. 1415) **m. Margaret of Burgundy** (d. 1441) — John (d. 1417) **m. Jacqueline of Hainault** (1401-1437) — Charles VII king of France (r. 1422-1461) ═══ **Marie of Anjou** (1404-1463) — **Isabella of Valois** (c. 1389-c. 1410) m. (1) Richard II king of England (2) Charles of Orleans — **Catherine of Valois** (1401-1437) m. Henry V king of England — **Marie** (1393-1438) — **Michelle Valois** (1394-1422) — **Joan Valois** (1391-1433)

(2) Charlotte of Savoy (c. 1442-1483) ═══ Louis XI king of France (r. 1461-1483) ═══ **(1) Margaret of Scotland** (1424-1445) — Radegonde (d. 1445) — Charles of Berri — **Catherine de France** (1428-1446) m. Charles of Burgundy — **Yolande of France** (1434-1478) m. Amadeus of Savoy — **Jeanne of Bourbon** (1434-1482) m. John II of Bourbon — **Madeleine of France** (1443-1486) m. Ladislas Posthumus

Charles VIII king of France (r. 1483-1498) ═══ **Anne of Brittany** (c. 1477-1514) — **Anne of Beaujeu** (c. 1460-1522) m. Pierre de Bourbon — **(1) Jeanne de France** (c. 1464-1505) ═══ Louis XII king of France (r. 1498-1515) ═══ **(2) Anne of Brittany** (c. 1477-1514) **(3) Mary Tudor** (1496-1533) — **Marie of Orleans** (d. 1493) — Anne of Orleans (d. 1491) abbess of Fontevrault

Copyright © 1999 Yorkin Publications

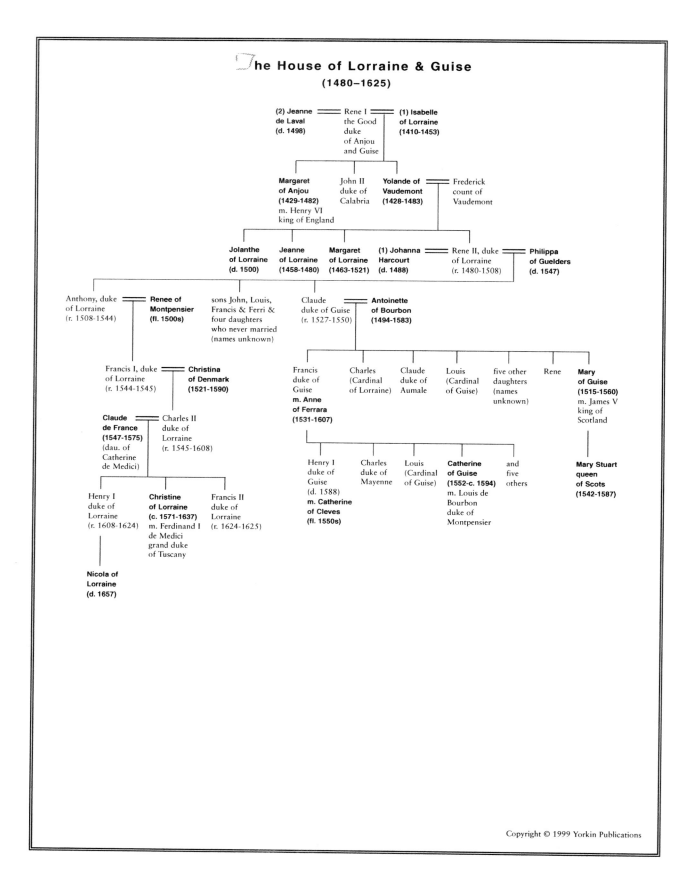

The House of Lorraine & Guise
(1480–1625)

Copyright © 1999 Yorkin Publications

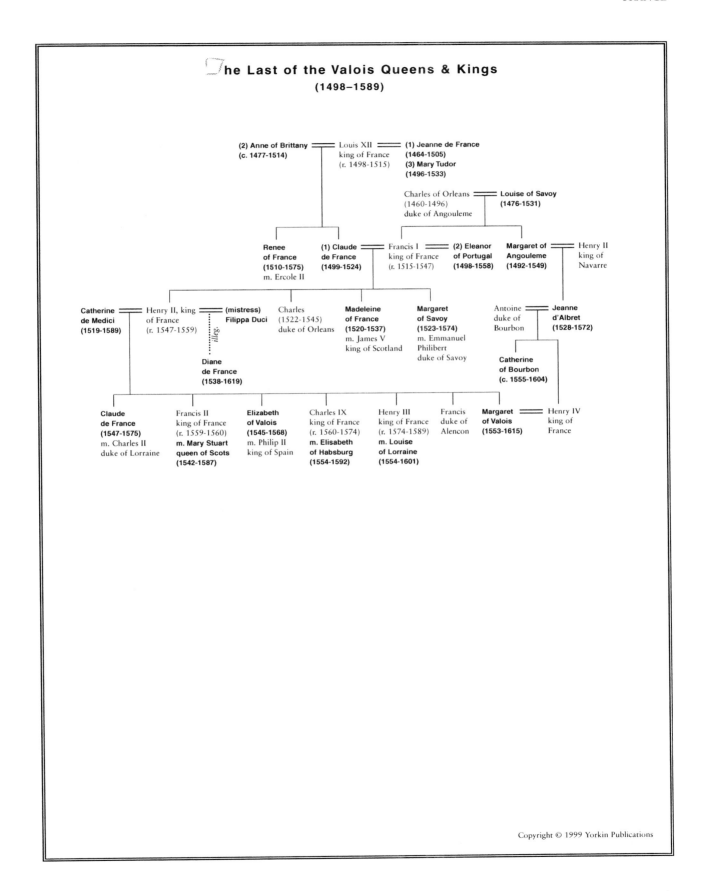

The Last of the Valois Queens & Kings
(1498–1589)

The French Bourbons
(1589–1883)

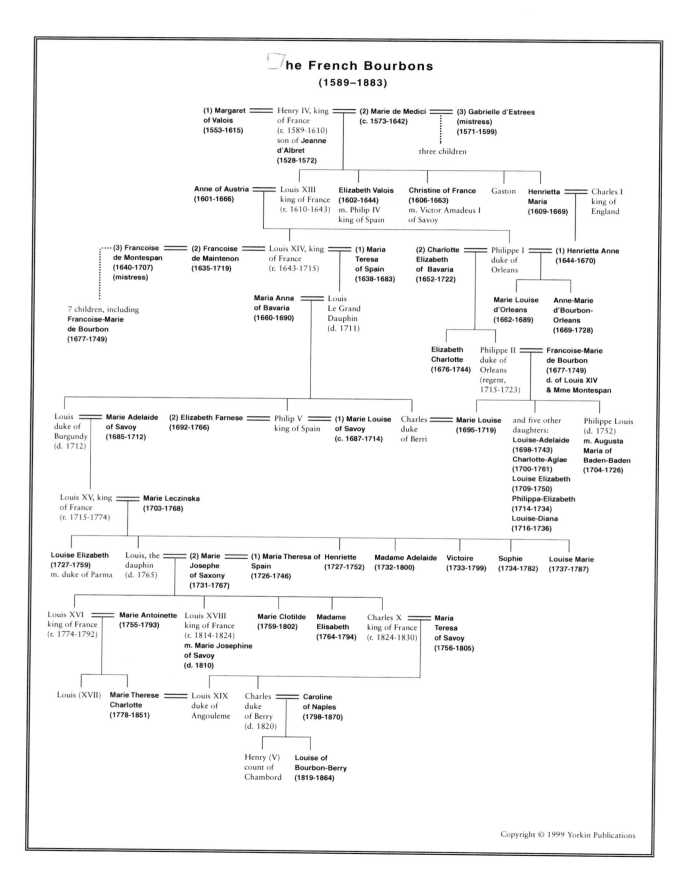

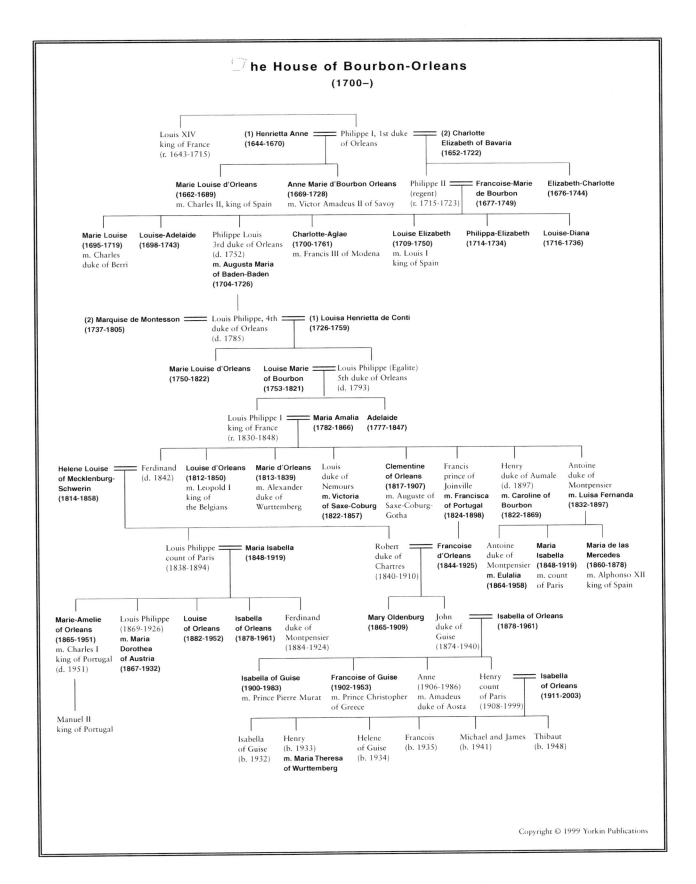

The House of Bourbon-Orleans
(1700–)

Louis XIV
king of France
(r. 1643-1715)

**(1) Henrietta Anne
(1644-1670)** ═══ Philippe I, 1st duke
of Orleans ═══ **(2) Charlotte
Elizabeth of Bavaria
(1652-1722)**

**Marie Louise d'Orleans
(1662-1689)**
m. Charles II, king of Spain

**Anne Marie d'Bourbon Orleans
(1669-1728)**
m. Victor Amadeus II of Savoy

Philippe II ═══ **Francoise-Marie
de Bourbon
(1677-1749)**
(regent)
(r. 1715-1723)

**Elizabeth-Charlotte
(1676-1744)**

**Marie Louise
(1695-1719)**
m. Charles
duke of Berri

**Louise-Adelaide
(1698-1743)**

Philippe Louis
3rd duke of Orleans
(d. 1752)
**m. Augusta Maria
of Baden-Baden
(1704-1726)**

**Charlotte-Aglae
(1700-1761)**
m. Francis III of Modena

**Louise Elizabeth
(1709-1750)**
m. Louis I
king of Spain

**Philippa-Elizabeth
(1714-1734)**

**Louise-Diana
(1716-1736)**

**(2) Marquise de Montesson
(1737-1805)** ═══ Louis Philippe, 4th
duke of Orleans
(d. 1785) ═══ **(1) Louisa Henrietta de Conti
(1726-1759)**

**Marie Louise d'Orleans
(1750-1822)**

**Louise Marie
of Bourbon
(1753-1821)** ═══ Louis Philippe (Egalite)
5th duke of Orleans
(d. 1793)

Louis Philippe I
king of France
(r. 1830-1848) ═══ **Maria Amalia
(1782-1866)**

**Adelaide
(1777-1847)**

**Helene Louise
of Mecklenburg-
Schwerin
(1814-1858)** ═══ Ferdinand
(d. 1842)

**Louise d'Orleans
(1812-1850)**
m. Leopold I
king of
the Belgians

**Marie d'Orleans
(1813-1839)**
m. Alexander
duke of
Wurttemberg

Louis
duke of
Nemours
**m. Victoria
of Saxe-Coburg
(1822-1857)**

**Clementine
of Orleans
(1817-1907)**
m. Auguste of
Saxe-Coburg-
Gotha

Francis
prince of
Joinville
**m. Francisca
of Portugal
(1824-1898)**

Henry
duke of Aumale
(d. 1897)
**m. Caroline of
Bourbon
(1822-1869)**

Antoine
duke of
Montpensier
**m. Luisa Fernanda
(1832-1897)**

Louis Philippe
count of Paris
(1838-1894) ═══ **Maria Isabella
(1848-1919)**

Robert
duke of
Chartres
(1840-1910) ═══ **Francoise
d'Orleans
(1844-1925)**

Antoine
duke of
Montpensier
**m. Eulalia
(1864-1958)**

**Maria
Isabella
(1848-1919)**
m. count
of Paris

**Maria de las
Mercedes
(1860-1878)**
m. Alphonso XII
king of Spain

**Marie-Amelie
of Orleans
(1865-1951)**
m. Charles I
king of Portugal
(d. 1951)

Louis Philippe
(1869-1926)
**m. Maria
Dorothea
of Austria
(1867-1932)**

**Louise
of Orleans
(1882-1952)**

**Isabella
of Orleans
(1878-1961)**

Ferdinand
duke of
Montpensier
(1884-1924)

**Mary Oldenburg
(1865-1909)** ═══ John
duke of
Guise
(1874-1940) ═══ **Isabella of Orleans
(1878-1961)**

Manuel II
king of Portugal

**Isabella of Guise
(1900-1983)**
m. Prince Pierre Murat

**Francoise of Guise
(1902-1953)**
m. Prince Christopher
of Greece

Anne
(1906-1986)
m. Amadeus
duke of Aosta

Henry
count
of Paris
(1908-1999) ═══ **Isabella
of Orleans
(1911-2003)**

Isabella
of Guise
(b. 1932)

Henry
(b. 1933)
**m. Maria Theresa
of Wurttemberg**

Helene
of Guise
(b. 1934)

Francois
(b. 1935)

Michael and James
(b. 1941)

Thibaut
(b. 1948)

The House of Bonaparte

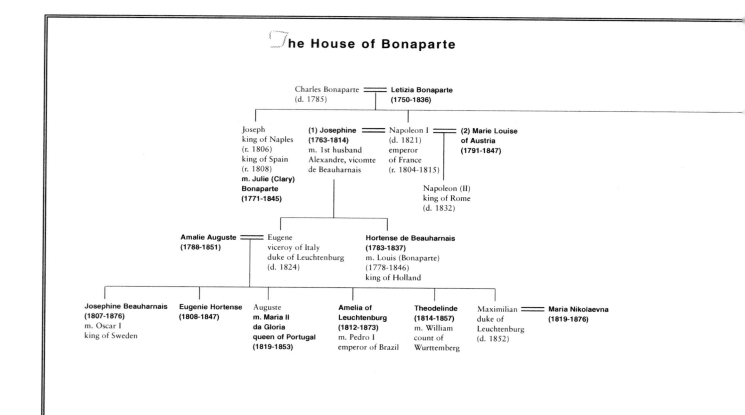

Charles Bonaparte ═══ **Letizia Bonaparte**
(d. 1785)   **(1750-1836)**

Joseph
king of Naples
(r. 1806)
king of Spain
(r. 1808)
**m. Julie (Clary)
Bonaparte
(1771-1845)**

**(1) Josephine
(1763-1814)**
m. 1st husband
Alexandre, vicomte
de Beauharnais

Napoleon I
(d. 1821)
emperor
of France
(r. 1804-1815)

**(2) Marie Louise
of Austria
(1791-1847)**

Napoleon (II)
king of Rome
(d. 1832)

**Amalie Auguste
(1788-1851)** ═══ Eugene
viceroy of Italy
duke of Leuchtenburg
(d. 1824)

**Hortense de Beauharnais
(1783-1837)**
m. Louis (Bonaparte)
(1778-1846)
king of Holland

**Josephine Beauharnais
(1807-1876)**
m. Oscar I
king of Sweden

**Eugenie Hortense
(1808-1847)**

Auguste
**m. Maria II
da Gloria
queen of Portugal
(1819-1853)**

**Amelia of
Leuchtenburg
(1812-1873)**
m. Pedro I
emperor of Brazil

**Theodelinde
(1814-1857)**
m. William
count of
Wurttemberg

Maximilian ═══ **Maria Nikolaevna
(1819-1876)**
duke of
Leuchtenburg
(d. 1852)

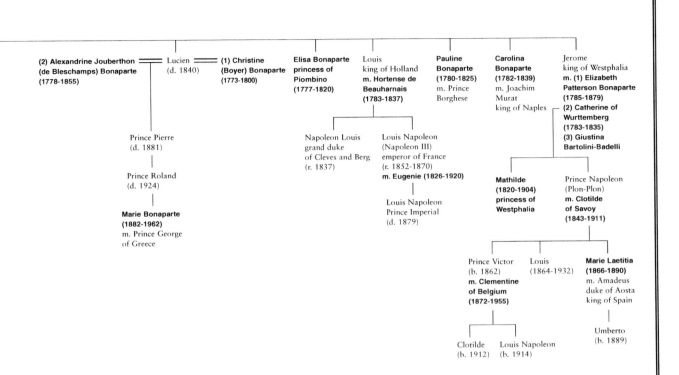

(2) Alexandrine Jouberthon (de Bleschamps) Bonaparte (1778-1855) ══ Lucien (d. 1840) ══ (1) Christine (Boyer) Bonaparte (1773-1800)

Elisa Bonaparte princess of Piombino (1777-1820)

Louis king of Holland m. Hortense de Beauharnais (1783-1837)

Pauline Bonaparte (1780-1825) m. Prince Borghese

Carolina Bonaparte (1782-1839) m. Joachim Murat king of Naples

Jerome king of Westphalia m. (1) Elizabeth Patterson Bonaparte (1785-1879) (2) Catherine of Wurttemberg (1783-1835) (3) Giustina Bartolini-Badelli

Prince Pierre (d. 1881)

Prince Roland (d. 1924)

Marie Bonaparte (1882-1962) m. Prince George of Greece

Napoleon Louis grand duke of Cleves and Berg (r. 1837)

Louis Napoleon (Napoleon III) emperor of France (r. 1852-1870) **m. Eugenie (1826-1920)**

Louis Napoleon Prince Imperial (d. 1879)

Mathilde (1820-1904) princess of Westphalia

Prince Napoleon (Plon-Plon) m. Clotilde of Savoy (1843-1911)

Prince Victor (b. 1862) **m. Clementine of Belgium (1872-1955)**

Louis (1864-1932)

Marie Laetitia (1866-1890) m. Amadeus duke of Aosta king of Spain

Clotilde (b. 1912)

Louis Napoleon (b. 1914)

Umberto (b. 1889)

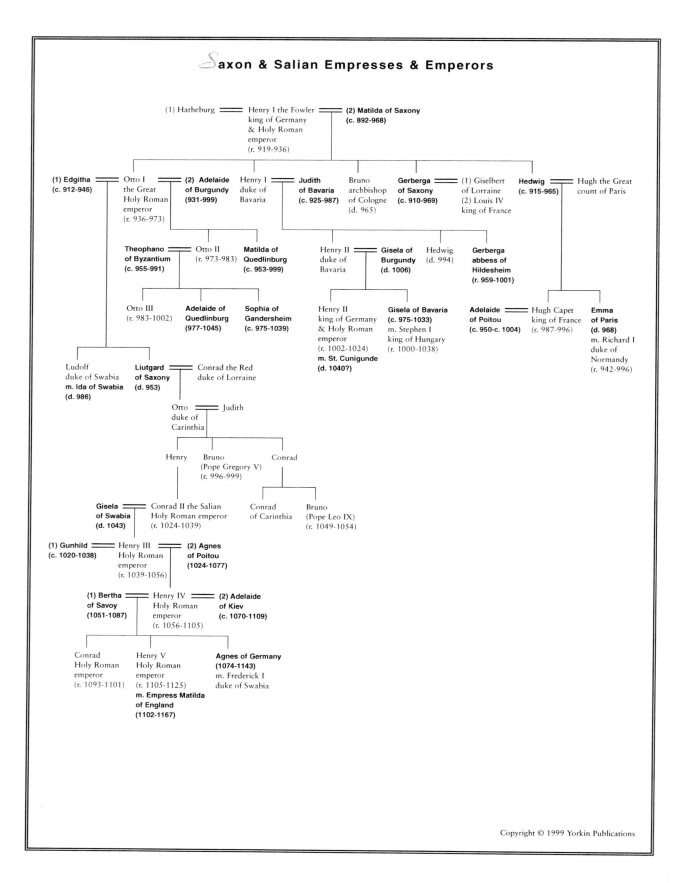

$\mathcal{S}$axon & Salian Empresses & Emperors

(1) Hatheburg ══ Henry I the Fowler ══ **(2) Matilda of Saxony**
king of Germany **(c. 892-968)**
& Holy Roman
emperor
(r. 919-936)

(1) Edgitha ══ Otto I ══ **(2) Adelaide** Henry I ══ **Judith** Bruno **Gerberga** ══ **(1) Giselbert** **Hedwig** ══ Hugh the Great
(c. 912-946) the Great **of Burgundy** duke of **of Bavaria** archbishop **of Saxony** **of Lorraine** **(c. 915-965)** count of Paris
Holy Roman **(931-999)** Bavaria **(c. 925-987)** of Cologne **(c. 910-969)** **(2) Louis IV**
emperor (d. 965) king of France
(r. 936-973)

Theophano ══ Otto II **Matilda of** Henry II ══ **Gisela of** Hedwig **Gerberga**
of Byzantium (r. 973-983) **Quedlinburg** duke of **Burgundy** (d. 994) **abbess of**
(c. 955-991) **(c. 953-999)** Bavaria **(d. 1006)** **Hildesheim**
(r. 959-1001)

Otto III **Adelaide of** **Sophia of** Henry II **Gisela of Bavaria** **Adelaide** ══ Hugh Capet **Emma**
(r. 983-1002) **Quedlinburg** **Gandersheim** king of Germany **(c. 975-1033)** **of Poitou** king of France **of Paris**
(977-1045) **(c. 975-1039)** & Holy Roman m. Stephen I **(c. 950-c. 1004)** (r. 987-996) **(d. 968)**
emperor king of Hungary m. Richard I
(r. 1002-1024) (r. 1000-1038) duke of
m. St. Cunigunde Normandy
(d. 1040?) (r. 942-996)

Ludolf **Liutgard** ══ Conrad the Red
duke of Swabia **of Saxony** duke of Lorraine
m. Ida of Swabia **(d. 953)**
(d. 986)

Otto ══ Judith
duke of
Carinthia

Henry Bruno Conrad
(Pope Gregory V)
(r. 996-999)

Gisela ══ Conrad II the Salian Conrad Bruno
of Swabia Holy Roman emperor of Carinthia (Pope Leo IX)
(d. 1043) (r. 1024-1039) (r. 1049-1054)

(1) Gunhild ══ Henry III ══ **(2) Agnes**
(c. 1020-1038) Holy Roman **of Poitou**
emperor **(1024-1077)**
(r. 1039-1056)

(1) Bertha ══ Henry IV ══ **(2) Adelaide**
of Savoy Holy Roman **of Kiev**
(1051-1087) emperor **(c. 1070-1109)**
(r. 1056-1105)

Conrad Henry V **Agnes of Germany**
Holy Roman Holy Roman **(1074-1143)**
emperor emperor m. Frederick I
(r. 1093-1101) (r. 1105-1125) duke of Swabia
m. Empress Matilda
of England
(1102-1167)

Welf & Hohenstaufen Families

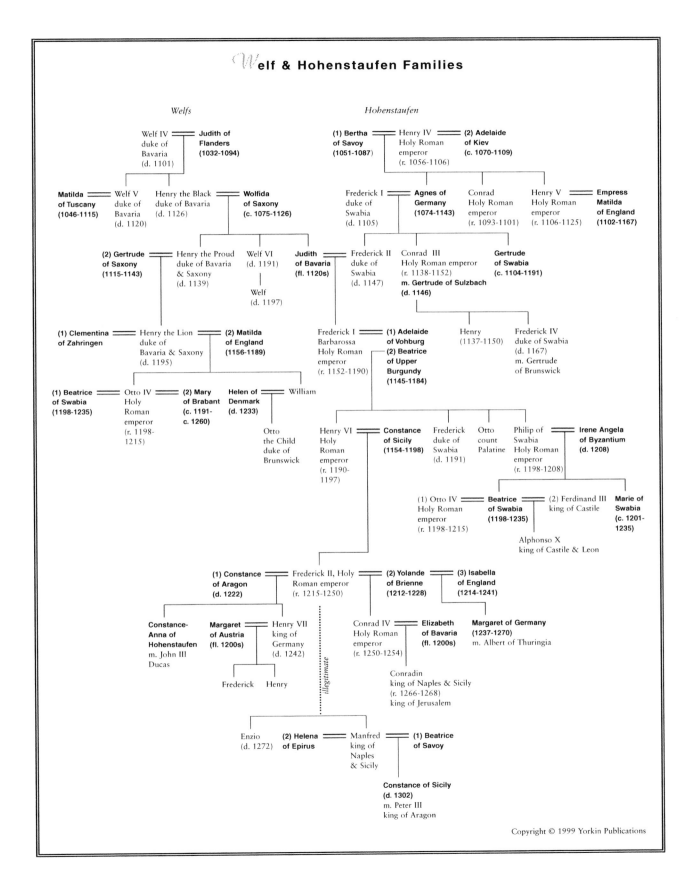

Welfs

Welf IV duke of Bavaria (d. 1101) ═══ **Judith of Flanders (1032-1094)**

Matilda of Tuscany (1046-1115) ═══ **Welf V** duke of Bavaria (d. 1120)

Henry the Black duke of Bavaria (d. 1126) ═══ **Wolfida of Saxony (c. 1075-1126)**

(2) Gertrude of Saxony (1115-1143) ═══ **Henry the Proud** duke of Bavaria & Saxony (d. 1139)

Welf VI (d. 1191)

Welf (d. 1197)

Judith of Bavaria (fl. 1120s) ═══

(1) Clementina of Zahringen ═══ **Henry the Lion** duke of Bavaria & Saxony (d. 1195) ═══ **(2) Matilda of England (1156-1189)**

(1) Beatrice of Swabia (1198-1235) ═══ **Otto IV** Holy Roman emperor (r. 1198-1215) ═══ **(2) Mary of Brabant (c. 1191-c. 1260)**

Helen of Denmark (d. 1233) ═══ **William**

Otto the Child duke of Brunswick

Hohenstaufen

(1) Bertha of Savoy (1051-1087) ═══ **Henry IV** Holy Roman emperor (r. 1056-1106) ═══ **(2) Adelaide of Kiev (c. 1070-1109)**

Frederick I duke of Swabia (d. 1105) ═══ **Agnes of Germany (1074-1143)**

Conrad Holy Roman emperor (r. 1093-1101)

Henry V Holy Roman emperor (r. 1106-1125) ═══ **Empress Matilda of England (1102-1167)**

Frederick II duke of Swabia (d. 1147)

Conrad III Holy Roman emperor (r. 1138-1152) **m. Gertrude of Sulzbach (d. 1146)**

Gertrude of Swabia (c. 1104-1191)

Henry (1137-1150)

Frederick IV duke of Swabia (d. 1167) m. Gertrude of Brunswick

Frederick I Barbarossa Holy Roman emperor (r. 1152-1190) ═══ **(1) Adelaide of Vohburg** / **(2) Beatrice of Upper Burgundy (1145-1184)**

Henry VI Holy Roman emperor (r. 1190-1197) ═══ **Constance of Sicily (1154-1198)**

Frederick duke of Swabia (d. 1191)

Otto count Palatine

Philip of Swabia Holy Roman emperor (r. 1198-1208) ═══ **Irene Angela of Byzantium (d. 1208)**

(1) Otto IV Holy Roman emperor (r. 1198-1215) ═══ **Beatrice of Swabia (1198-1235)** ═══ **(2) Ferdinand III** king of Castile

Marie of Swabia (c. 1201-1235)

Alphonso X king of Castile & Leon

(1) Constance of Aragon (d. 1222) ═══ **Frederick II, Holy Roman emperor (r. 1215-1250)** ═══ **(2) Yolande of Brienne (1212-1228)** ═══ **(3) Isabella of England (1214-1241)**

Constance-Anna of Hohenstaufen m. John III Ducas

Margaret of Austria (fl. 1200s) ═══ **Henry VII** king of Germany (d. 1242)

Frederick   Henry

Conrad IV Holy Roman emperor (r. 1250-1254) ═══ **Elizabeth of Bavaria (fl. 1200s)**

Conradin king of Naples & Sicily (r. 1266-1268) king of Jerusalem

Margaret of Germany (1237-1270) m. Albert of Thuringia

illegitimate

Enzio (d. 1272)

(2) Helena of Epirus ═══ **Manfred** king of Naples & Sicily ═══ **(1) Beatrice of Savoy**

Constance of Sicily (d. 1302) m. Peter III king of Aragon

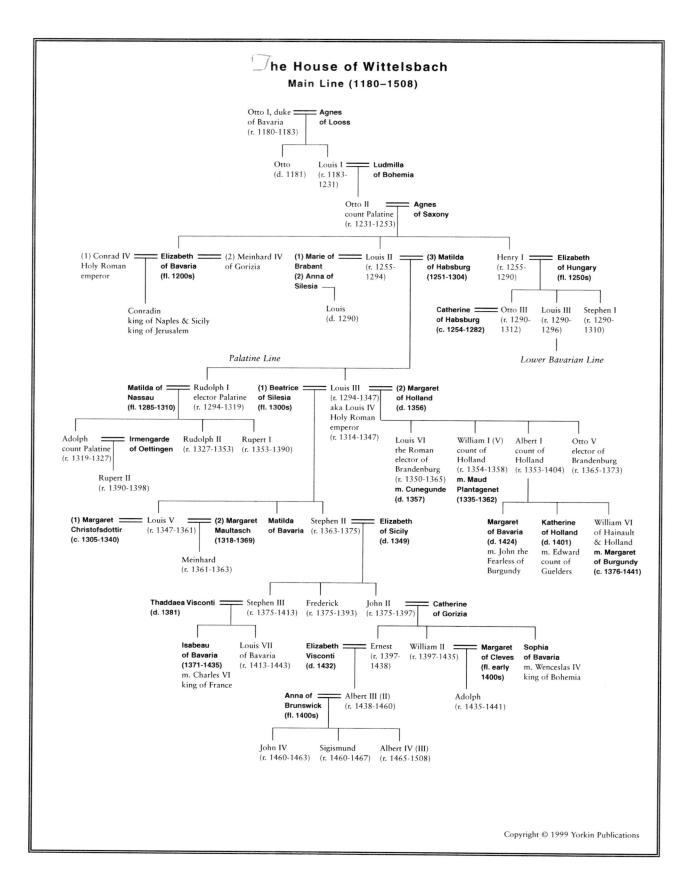

The House of Wittelsbach
Main Line (1180–1508)

Otto I, duke of Bavaria (r. 1180-1183) ══ Agnes of Looss

Otto (d. 1181)

Louis I (r. 1183-1231) ══ Ludmilla of Bohemia

Otto II count Palatine (r. 1231-1253) ══ Agnes of Saxony

(1) Conrad IV Holy Roman emperor ══ Elizabeth of Bavaria (fl. 1200s) ══ (2) Meinhard IV of Gorizia

(1) Marie of Brabant (2) Anna of Silesia ══ Louis II (r. 1255-1294) ══ (3) Matilda of Habsburg (1251-1304)

Henry I (r. 1255-1290) ══ Elizabeth of Hungary (fl. 1250s)

Conradin king of Naples & Sicily king of Jerusalem

Louis (d. 1290)

Catherine of Habsburg (c. 1254-1282) ══ Otto III (r. 1290-1312)

Louis III (r. 1290-1296)

Stephen I (r. 1290-1310)

Palatine Line

Lower Bavarian Line

Matilda of Nassau (fl. 1285-1310) ══ Rudolph I elector Palatine (r. 1294-1319)

(1) Beatrice of Silesia (fl. 1300s) ══ Louis III (r. 1294-1347) aka Louis IV Holy Roman emperor (r. 1314-1347) ══ (2) Margaret of Holland (d. 1356)

Adolph count Palatine (r. 1319-1327) ══ Irmengarde of Oettingen

Rudolph II (r. 1327-1353)

Rupert I (r. 1353-1390)

Louis VI the Roman elector of Brandenburg (r. 1350-1365) m. Cunegunde (d. 1357)

William I (V) count of Holland (r. 1354-1358) m. Maud Plantagenet (1335-1362)

Albert I count of Holland (r. 1353-1404)

Otto V elector of Brandenburg (r. 1365-1373)

Rupert II (r. 1390-1398)

(1) Margaret Christofsdottir (c. 1305-1340) ══ Louis V (r. 1347-1361) ══ (2) Margaret Maultasch (1318-1369)

Matilda of Bavaria

Stephen II (r. 1363-1375) ══ Elizabeth of Sicily (d. 1349)

Margaret of Bavaria (d. 1424) m. John the Fearless of Burgundy

Katherine of Holland (d. 1401) m. Edward count of Guelders

William VI of Hainault & Holland m. Margaret of Burgundy (c. 1376-1441)

Meinhard (r. 1361-1363)

Thaddaea Visconti (d. 1381) ══ Stephen III (r. 1375-1413)

Frederick (r. 1375-1393)

John II (r. 1375-1397) ══ Catherine of Gorizia

Isabeau of Bavaria (1371-1435) m. Charles VI king of France

Louis VII of Bavaria (r. 1413-1443)

Elizabeth Visconti (d. 1432) ══ Ernest (r. 1397-1438)

William II (r. 1397-1435)

Margaret of Cleves (fl. early 1400s)

Sophia of Bavaria m. Wenceslas IV king of Bohemia

Anna of Brunswick (fl. 1400s) ══ Albert III (II) (r. 1438-1460)

Adolph (r. 1435-1441)

John IV (r. 1460-1463)

Sigismund (r. 1460-1467)

Albert IV (III) (r. 1465-1508)

The House of Habsburg
(1273–1519)

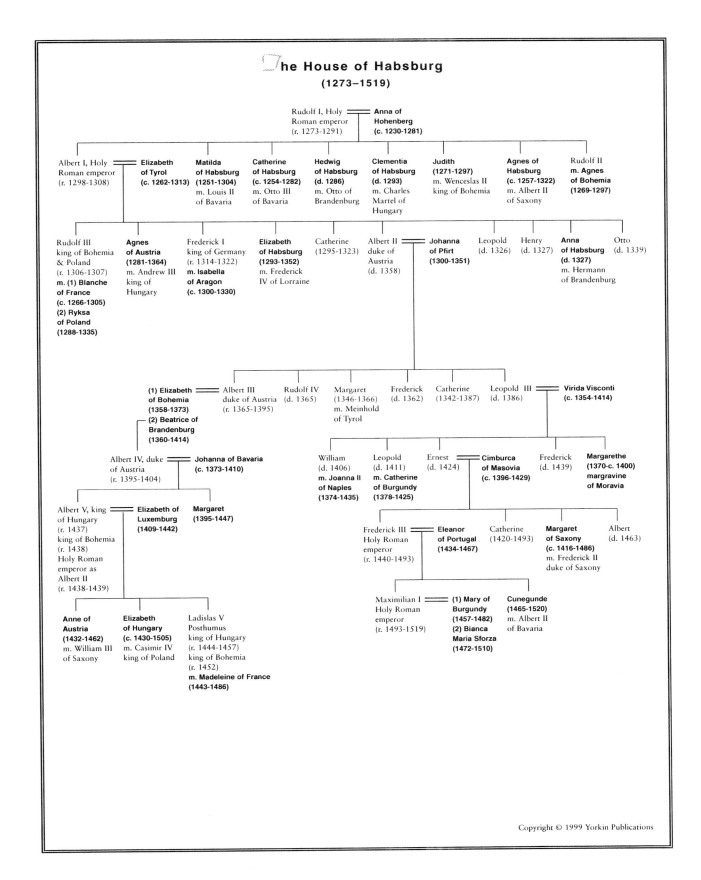

The House of Habsburg
(1493–1780)

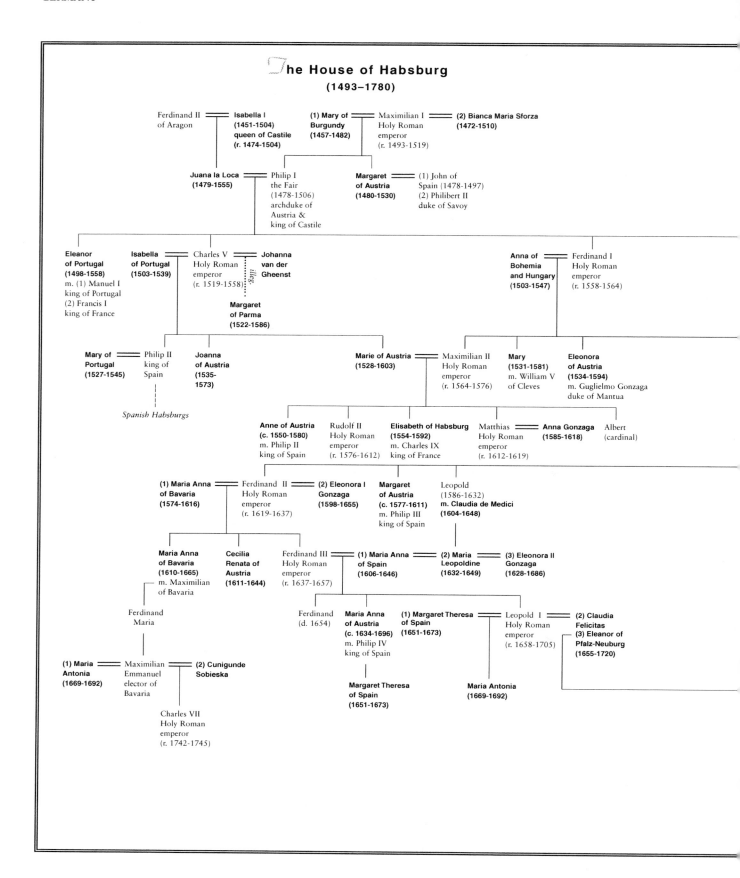

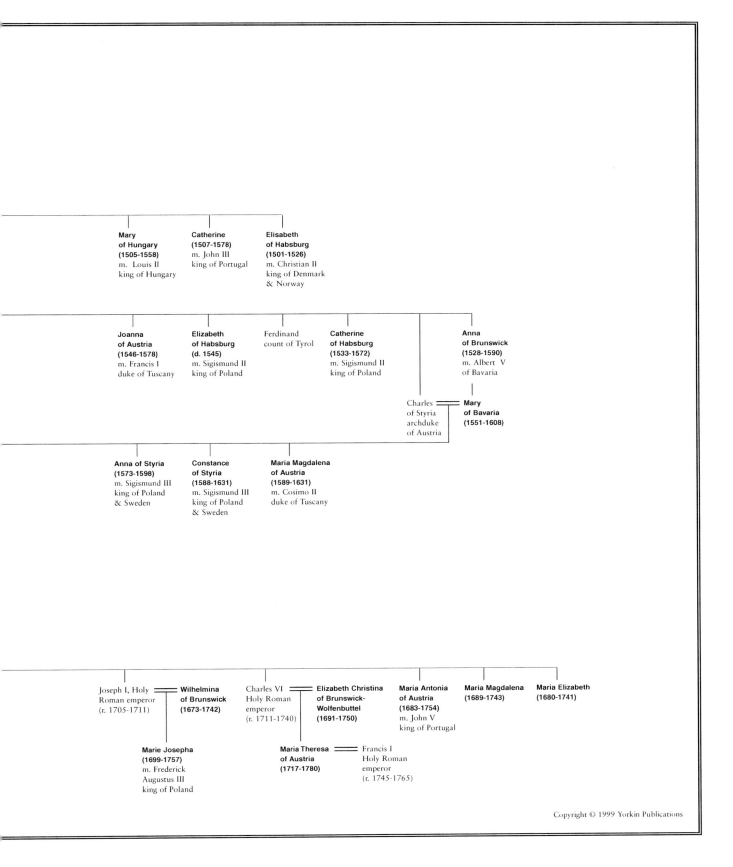

Mary
of Hungary
(1505-1558)
m. Louis II
king of Hungary

Catherine
(1507-1578)
m. John III
king of Portugal

Elisabeth
of Habsburg
(1501-1526)
m. Christian II
king of Denmark
& Norway

Joanna
of Austria
(1546-1578)
m. Francis I
duke of Tuscany

Elizabeth
of Habsburg
(d. 1545)
m. Sigismund II
king of Poland

Ferdinand
count of Tyrol

Catherine
of Habsburg
(1533-1572)
m. Sigismund II
king of Poland

Anna
of Brunswick
(1528-1590)
m. Albert V
of Bavaria

Charles ===== Mary
of Styria   of Bavaria
archduke   (1551-1608)
of Austria

Anna of Styria
(1573-1598)
m. Sigismund III
king of Poland
& Sweden

Constance
of Styria
(1588-1631)
m. Sigismund III
king of Poland
& Sweden

Maria Magdalena
of Austria
(1589-1631)
m. Cosimo II
duke of Tuscany

Joseph I, Holy ===== Wilhelmina
Roman emperor   of Brunswick
(r. 1705-1711)   (1673-1742)

Charles VI ===== Elizabeth Christina
Holy Roman   of Brunswick-
emperor   Wolfenbuttel
(r. 1711-1740)   (1691-1750)

Maria Antonia
of Austria
(1683-1754)
m. John V
king of Portugal

Maria Magdalena
(1689-1743)

Maria Elizabeth
(1680-1741)

Marie Josepha
(1699-1757)
m. Frederick
Augustus III
king of Poland

Maria Theresa ===== Francis I
of Austria   Holy Roman
(1717-1780)   emperor
                     (r. 1745-1765)

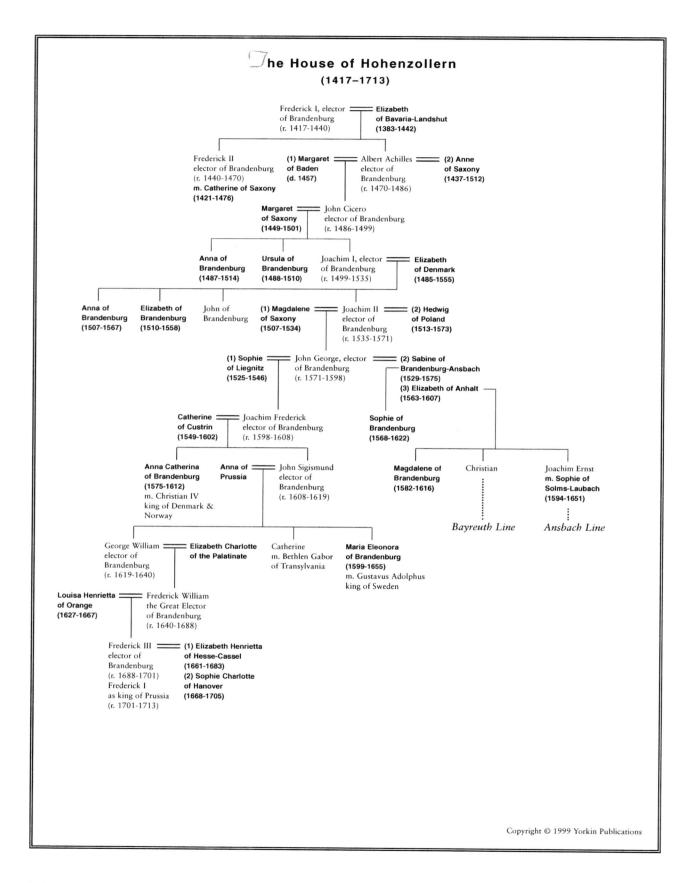

The House of Hohenzollern
(1417–1713)

Frederick I, elector of Brandenburg (r. 1417-1440) ═══ **Elizabeth of Bavaria-Landshut (1383-1442)**

Frederick II elector of Brandenburg (r. 1440-1470) **m. Catherine of Saxony (1421-1476)**

(1) Margaret of Baden (d. 1457) ═══ Albert Achilles elector of Brandenburg (r. 1470-1486) ═══ **(2) Anne of Saxony (1437-1512)**

Margaret of Saxony (1449-1501) ═══ John Cicero elector of Brandenburg (r. 1486-1499)

Anna of Brandenburg (1487-1514)   **Ursula of Brandenburg (1488-1510)**   Joachim I, elector of Brandenburg (r. 1499-1535) ═══ **Elizabeth of Denmark (1485-1555)**

Anna of Brandenburg (1507-1567)   **Elizabeth of Brandenburg (1510-1558)**   John of Brandenburg   **(1) Magdalene of Saxony (1507-1534)** ═══ Joachim II ═══ **(2) Hedwig of Poland (1513-1573)** elector of Brandenburg (r. 1535-1571)

(1) Sophie of Liegnitz (1525-1546) ═══ John George, elector of Brandenburg (r. 1571-1598) ═══ **(2) Sabine of Brandenburg-Ansbach (1529-1575)**
(3) Elizabeth of Anhalt (1563-1607)

Catherine of Custrin (1549-1602) ═══ Joachim Frederick elector of Brandenburg (r. 1598-1608)

Sophie of Brandenburg (1568-1622)

Anna Catherina of Brandenburg (1575-1612) m. Christian IV king of Denmark & Norway   **Anna of Prussia** ═══ John Sigismund elector of Brandenburg (r. 1608-1619)

Magdalene of Brandenburg (1582-1616)   Christian ⋮ *Bayreuth Line*   Joachim Ernst m. **Sophie of Solms-Laubach (1594-1651)** ⋮ *Ansbach Line*

George William elector of Brandenburg (r. 1619-1640) ═══ **Elizabeth Charlotte of the Palatinate**   Catherine m. Bethlen Gabor of Transylvania   **Maria Eleonora of Brandenburg (1599-1655) m. Gustavus Adolphus king of Sweden**

Louisa Henrietta of Orange (1627-1667) ═══ Frederick William the Great Elector of Brandenburg (r. 1640-1688)

Frederick III elector of Brandenburg (r. 1688-1701) Frederick I as king of Prussia (r. 1701-1713) ═══ **(1) Elizabeth Henrietta of Hesse-Cassel (1661-1683)**
(2) Sophie Charlotte of Hanover (1668-1705)

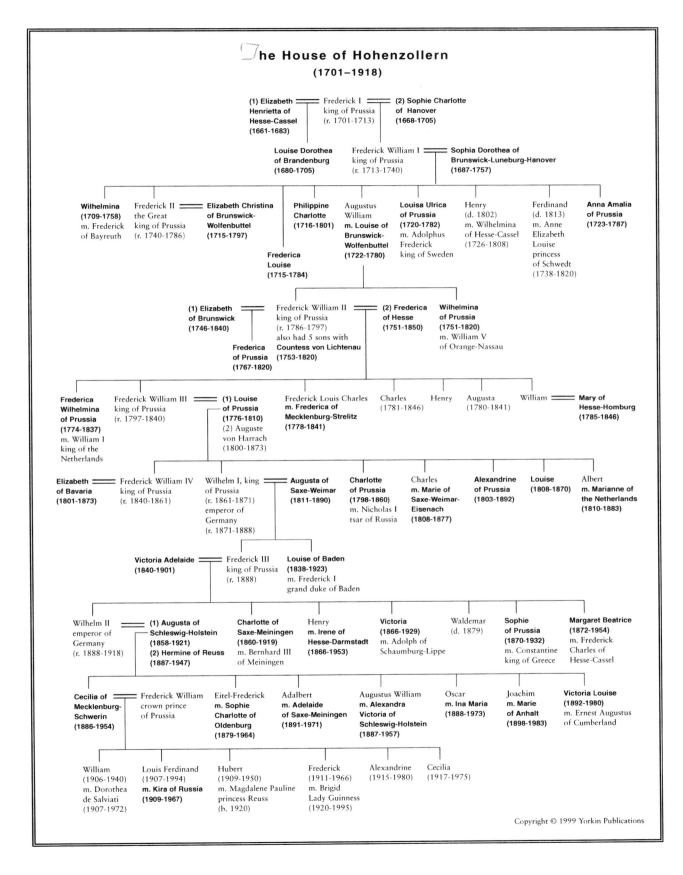

The House of Hohenzollern
(1701–1918)

(1) Elizabeth Henrietta of Hesse-Cassel (1661-1683) ══ Frederick I king of Prussia (r. 1701-1713) ══ (2) Sophie Charlotte of Hanover (1668-1705)

Louise Dorothea of Brandenburg (1680-1705) ══ Frederick William I king of Prussia (r. 1713-1740) ══ Sophia Dorothea of Brunswick-Luneburg-Hanover (1687-1757)

Wilhelmina (1709-1758) m. Frederick of Bayreuth — Frederick II the Great king of Prussia (r. 1740-1786) ══ Elizabeth Christina of Brunswick-Wolfenbuttel (1715-1797) — Philippine Charlotte (1716-1801) — Augustus William m. Louise of Brunswick-Wolfenbuttel (1722-1780) — Louisa Ulrica of Prussia (1720-1782) m. Adolphus Frederick king of Sweden — Henry (d. 1802) m. Wilhelmina of Hesse-Cassel (1726-1808) — Ferdinand (d. 1813) m. Anne Elizabeth Louise princess of Schwedt (1738-1820) — Anna Amalia of Prussia (1723-1787)

Frederica Louise (1715-1784)

(1) Elizabeth of Brunswick (1746-1840) ══ Frederick William II king of Prussia (r. 1786-1797) also had 5 sons with Countess von Lichtenau (1753-1820) ══ (2) Frederica of Hesse (1751-1850) — Wilhelmina of Prussia (1751-1820) m. William V of Orange-Nassau

Frederica of Prussia (1767-1820)

Frederica Wilhelmina of Prussia (1774-1837) m. William I king of the Netherlands — Frederick William III king of Prussia (r. 1797-1840) ══ (1) Louise of Prussia (1776-1810) (2) Auguste von Harrach (1800-1873) — Frederick Louis Charles m. Frederica of Mecklenburg-Strelitz (1778-1841) — Charles (1781-1846) — Henry — Augusta (1780-1841) — William ══ Mary of Hesse-Homburg (1785-1846)

Elizabeth of Bavaria (1801-1873) ══ Frederick William IV king of Prussia (r. 1840-1861) — Wilhelm I, king of Prussia (r. 1861-1871) emperor of Germany (r. 1871-1888) ══ Augusta of Saxe-Weimar (1811-1890) — Charlotte of Prussia (1798-1860) m. Nicholas I tsar of Russia — Charles m. Marie of Saxe-Weimar-Eisenach (1808-1877) — Alexandrine of Prussia (1803-1892) — Louise (1808-1870) — Albert m. Marianne of the Netherlands (1810-1883)

Victoria Adelaide (1840-1901) ══ Frederick III king of Prussia (r. 1888) — Louise of Baden (1838-1923) m. Frederick I grand duke of Baden

Wilhelm II emperor of Germany (r. 1888-1918) ══ (1) Augusta of Schleswig-Holstein (1858-1921) (2) Hermine of Reuss (1887-1947) — Charlotte of Saxe-Meiningen (1860-1919) m. Bernhard III of Meiningen — Henry m. Irene of Hesse-Darmstadt (1866-1953) — Victoria (1866-1929) m. Adolph of Schaumburg-Lippe — Waldemar (d. 1879) — Sophie of Prussia (1870-1932) m. Constantine king of Greece — Margaret Beatrice (1872-1954) m. Frederick Charles of Hesse-Cassel

Cecilia of Mecklenburg-Schwerin (1886-1954) ══ Frederick William crown prince of Prussia — Eitel-Frederick m. Sophie Charlotte of Oldenburg (1879-1964) — Adalbert m. Adelaide of Saxe-Meiningen (1891-1971) — Augustus William m. Alexandra Victoria of Schleswig-Holstein (1887-1957) — Oscar m. Ina Maria (1888-1973) — Joachim m. Marie of Anhalt (1898-1983) — Victoria Louise (1892-1980) m. Ernest Augustus of Cumberland

William (1906-1940) m. Dorothea de Salviati (1907-1972) — Louis Ferdinand (1907-1994) m. Kira of Russia (1909-1967) — Hubert (1909-1950) m. Magdalene Pauline princess Reuss (b. 1920) — Frederick (1911-1966) m. Brigid Lady Guinness (1920-1995) — Alexandrine (1915-1980) — Cecilia (1917-1975)

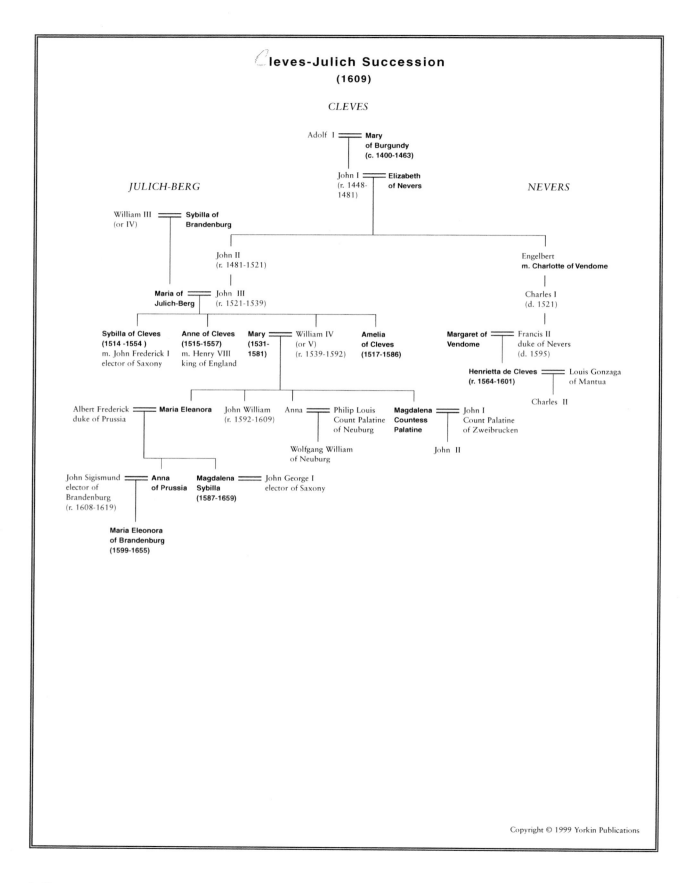

Cleves-Julich Succession
(1609)

CLEVES

Adolf I ══ **Mary**
of Burgundy
(c. 1400-1463)

JULICH-BERG

John I ══ **Elizabeth**
(r. 1448-   **of Nevers**
1481)

NEVERS

William III ══ **Sybilla of**
(or IV)   **Brandenburg**

John II
(r. 1481-1521)

Engelbert
m. Charlotte of Vendome

Maria of ══ John III
Julich-Berg   (r. 1521-1539)

Charles I
(d. 1521)

Sybilla of Cleves
(1514 -1554)
m. John Frederick I
elector of Saxony

Anne of Cleves
(1515-1557)
m. Henry VIII
king of England

Mary ══ William IV
(1531-   (or V)
1581)   (r. 1539-1592)

Amelia
of Cleves
(1517-1586)

Margaret of ══ Francis II
Vendome   duke of Nevers
(d. 1595)

Henrietta de Cleves ══ Louis Gonzaga
(r. 1564-1601)   of Mantua

Charles II

Albert Frederick ══ **Maria Eleanora**
duke of Prussia

John William
(r. 1592-1609)

Anna ══ Philip Louis
Count Palatine
of Neuburg

Magdalena ══ John I
Countess   Count Palatine
Palatine   of Zweibrucken

Wolfgang William
of Neuburg

John II

John Sigismund ══ **Anna**
elector of   **of Prussia**
Brandenburg
(r. 1608-1619)

Magdalena ══ John George I
Sybilla   elector of Saxony
(1587-1659)

Maria Eleonora
of Brandenburg
(1599-1655)

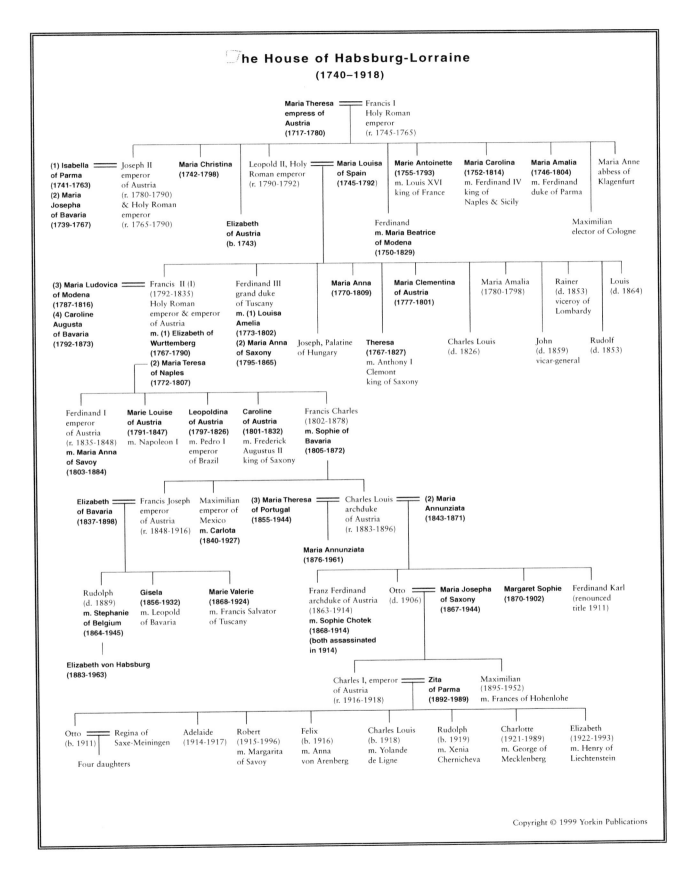

The House of Habsburg-Lorraine
(1740–1918)

Maria Theresa empress of Austria **(1717-1780)** ═══ Francis I Holy Roman emperor (r. 1745-1765)

(1) Isabella of Parma (1741-1763) **(2) Maria Josepha of Bavaria (1739-1767)** ═══ Joseph II emperor of Austria (r. 1780-1790) & Holy Roman emperor (r. 1765-1790)

Maria Christina (1742-1798)

Leopold II, Holy Roman emperor (r. 1790-1792) ═══ **Maria Louisa of Spain (1745-1792)**

Marie Antoinette (1755-1793) m. Louis XVI king of France

Maria Carolina (1752-1814) m. Ferdinand IV king of Naples & Sicily

Maria Amalia (1746-1804) m. Ferdinand duke of Parma

Maria Anne abbess of Klagenfurt

Elizabeth of Austria (b. 1743)

Ferdinand m. Maria Beatrice of Modena (1750-1829)

Maximilian elector of Cologne

(3) Maria Ludovica of Modena (1787-1816) **(4) Caroline Augusta of Bavaria (1792-1873)** ═══ Francis II (I) (1792-1835) Holy Roman emperor & emperor of Austria m. (1) Elizabeth of Wurttemberg (1767-1790) (2) Maria Teresa of Naples (1772-1807)

Ferdinand III grand duke of Tuscany m. (1) Louisa Amelia (1773-1802) (2) Maria Anna of Saxony (1795-1865)

Maria Anna (1770-1809)

Maria Clementina of Austria (1777-1801)

Maria Amalia (1780-1798)

Rainer (d. 1853) viceroy of Lombardy

Louis (d. 1864)

Joseph, Palatine of Hungary

Theresa (1767-1827) m. Anthony I Clemont king of Saxony

Charles Louis (d. 1826)

John (d. 1859) vicar-general

Rudolf (d. 1853)

Ferdinand I emperor of Austria (r. 1835-1848) **m. Maria Anna of Savoy (1803-1884)**

Marie Louise of Austria (1791-1847) m. Napoleon I

Leopoldina of Austria (1797-1826) m. Pedro I emperor of Brazil

Caroline of Austria (1801-1832) m. Frederick Augustus II king of Saxony

Francis Charles (1802-1878) m. Sophie of Bavaria (1805-1872)

Elizabeth of Bavaria (1837-1898) ═══ Francis Joseph emperor of Austria (r. 1848-1916)

Maximilian emperor of Mexico **m. Carlota (1840-1927)**

(3) Maria Theresa of Portugal (1855-1944) ═══ Charles Louis archduke of Austria (r. 1883-1896) ═══ **(2) Maria Annunziata (1843-1871)**

Maria Annunziata (1876-1961)

Rudolph (d. 1889) **m. Stephanie of Belgium (1864-1945)**

Gisela (1856-1932) m. Leopold of Bavaria

Marie Valerie (1868-1924) m. Francis Salvator of Tuscany

Franz Ferdinand archduke of Austria (1863-1914) **m. Sophie Chotek (1868-1914) (both assassinated in 1914)**

Otto (d. 1906) ═══ **Maria Josepha of Saxony (1867-1944)**

Margaret Sophie (1870-1902)

Ferdinand Karl (renounced title 1911)

Elizabeth von Habsburg (1883-1963)

Charles I, emperor of Austria (r. 1916-1918) ═══ **Zita of Parma (1892-1989)**

Maximilian (1895-1952) m. Frances of Hohenlohe

Otto (b. 1911) ═══ Regina of Saxe-Meiningen

Four daughters

Adelaide (1914-1917)

Robert (1915-1996) m. Margarita of Savoy

Felix (b. 1916) m. Anna von Arenberg

Charles Louis (b. 1918) m. Yolande de Ligne

Rudolph (b. 1919) m. Xenia Chernicheva

Charlotte (1921-1989) m. George of Mecklenberg

Elizabeth (1922-1993) m. Henry of Liechtenstein

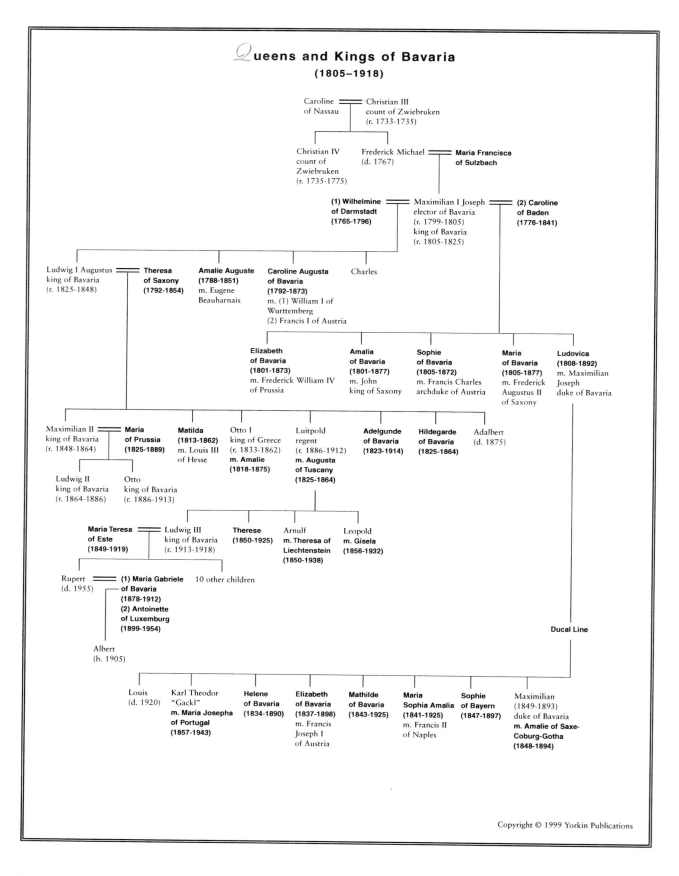

Queens and Kings of Bavaria
(1805–1918)

Caroline of Nassau === Christian III count of Zwiebruken (r. 1733-1735)

Christian IV count of Zwiebruken (r. 1735-1775)

Frederick Michael (d. 1767) === Maria Francisca of Sulzbach

(1) Wilhelmine of Darmstadt (1765-1796) === Maximilian I Joseph elector of Bavaria (r. 1799-1805) king of Bavaria (r. 1805-1825) === (2) Caroline of Baden (1776-1841)

Ludwig I Augustus king of Bavaria (r. 1825-1848) === Theresa of Saxony (1792-1854)

Amalie Auguste (1788-1851) m. Eugene Beauharnais

Caroline Augusta of Bavaria (1792-1873) m. (1) William I of Wurttemberg (2) Francis I of Austria

Charles

Elizabeth of Bavaria (1801-1873) m. Frederick William IV of Prussia

Amalia of Bavaria (1801-1877) m. John king of Saxony

Sophie of Bavaria (1805-1872) m. Francis Charles archduke of Austria

Maria of Bavaria (1805-1877) m. Frederick Augustus II of Saxony

Ludovica (1808-1892) m. Maximilian Joseph duke of Bavaria

Maximilian II king of Bavaria (r. 1848-1864) === Maria of Prussia (1825-1889)

Matilda (1813-1862) m. Louis III of Hesse

Otto I king of Greece (r. 1833-1862) m. Amalie (1818-1875)

Luitpold regent (r. 1886-1912) m. Augusta of Tuscany (1825-1864)

Adelgunde of Bavaria (1823-1914)

Hildegarde of Bavaria (1825-1864)

Adalbert (d. 1875)

Ludwig II king of Bavaria (r. 1864-1886)

Otto king of Bavaria (r. 1886-1913)

Maria Teresa of Este (1849-1919) === Ludwig III king of Bavaria (r. 1913-1918)

Therese (1850-1925)

Arnulf m. Theresa of Liechtenstein (1850-1938)

Leopold m. Gisela (1856-1932)

Rupert (d. 1955) === (1) Maria Gabriele of Bavaria (1878-1912) (2) Antoinette of Luxemburg (1899-1954)

10 other children

Albert (b. 1905)

Ducal Line

Louis (d. 1920)

Karl Theodor "Gackl" m. Maria Josepha of Portugal (1857-1943)

Helene of Bavaria (1834-1890)

Elizabeth of Bavaria (1837-1898) m. Francis Joseph I of Austria

Mathilde of Bavaria (1843-1925)

Maria Sophia Amalia (1841-1925) m. Francis II of Naples

Sophie of Bayern (1847-1897)

Maximilian (1849-1893) duke of Bavaria m. Amalie of Saxe-Coburg-Gotha (1848-1894)

Queens & Kings of Saxony
(1806–1918)

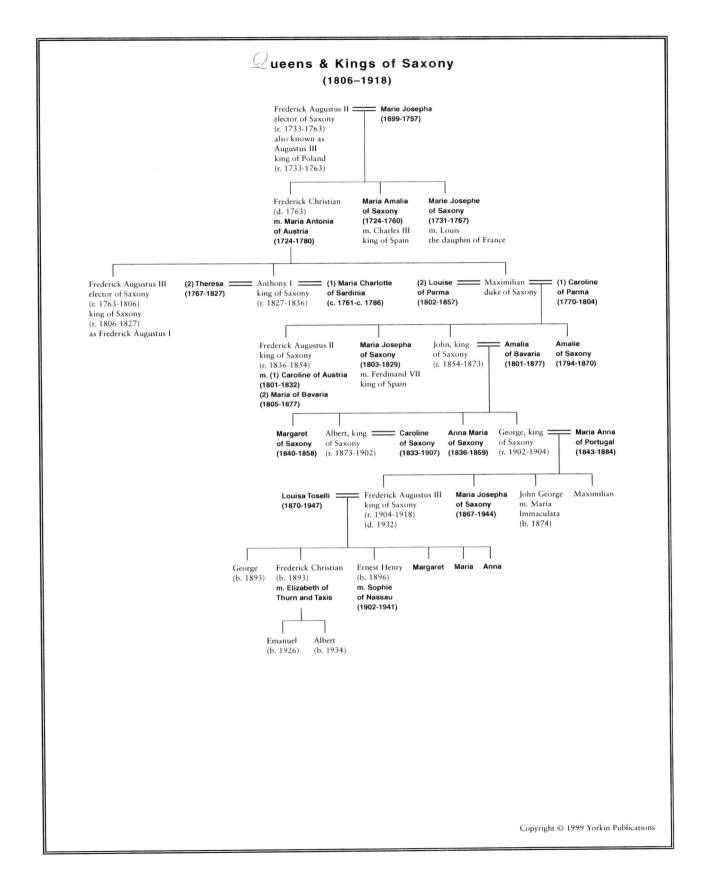

Frederick Augustus II elector of Saxony (r. 1733-1763) also known as Augustus III king of Poland (r. 1733-1763) ═══ **Marie Josepha (1699-1757)**

Frederick Christian (d. 1763) **m. Maria Antonia of Austria (1724-1780)**

Maria Amalia of Saxony (1724-1760) m. Charles III king of Spain

Marie Josephe of Saxony (1731-1767) m. Louis the dauphin of France

Frederick Augustus III elector of Saxony (r. 1763-1806) king of Saxony (r. 1806-1827) as Frederick Augustus I

(2) Theresa (1767-1827) ═══ Anthony I king of Saxony (r. 1827-1836) ═══ **(1) Maria Charlotte of Sardinia (c. 1761-c. 1786)**

(2) Louise of Parma (1802-1857) ═══ Maximilian duke of Saxony ═══ **(1) Caroline of Parma (1770-1804)**

Frederick Augustus II king of Saxony (r. 1836-1854) **m. (1) Caroline of Austria (1801-1832) (2) Maria of Bavaria (1805-1877)**

Maria Josepha of Saxony (1803-1829) m. Ferdinand VII king of Spain

John, king of Saxony (r. 1854-1873) ═══ **Amalia of Bavaria (1801-1877)**

Amalie of Saxony (1794-1870)

Margaret of Saxony (1840-1858)

Albert, king of Saxony (r. 1873-1902) ═══ **Caroline of Saxony (1833-1907)**

Anna Maria of Saxony (1836-1859)

George, king of Saxony (r. 1902-1904) ═══ **Maria Anna of Portugal (1843-1884)**

Louisa Toselli (1870-1947) ═══ Frederick Augustus III king of Saxony (r. 1904-1918) (d. 1932)

Maria Josepha of Saxony (1867-1944)

John George m. Maria Immaculata (b. 1874)

Maximilian

George (b. 1893)

Frederick Christian (b. 1893) **m. Elizabeth of Thurn and Taxis**

Ernest Henry (b. 1896) **m. Sophie of Nassau (1902-1941)**

Margaret

Maria

Anna

Emanuel (b. 1926)

Albert (b. 1934)

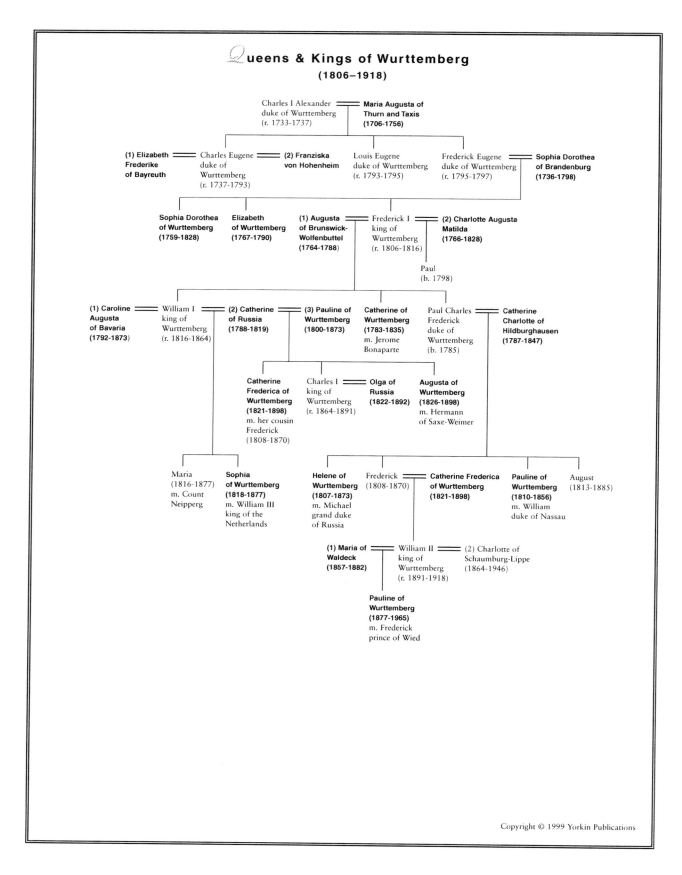

Queens & Kings of Wurttemberg
(1806–1918)

Charles I Alexander duke of Wurttemberg (r. 1733-1737) ═══ **Maria Augusta of Thurn and Taxis (1706-1756)**

(1) Elizabeth Frederike of Bayreuth ═══ Charles Eugene duke of Wurttemberg (r. 1737-1793) ═══ **(2) Franziska von Hohenheim**

Louis Eugene duke of Wurttemberg (r. 1793-1795)

Frederick Eugene duke of Wurttemberg (r. 1795-1797) ═══ **Sophia Dorothea of Brandenburg (1736-1798)**

Sophia Dorothea of Wurttemberg (1759-1828)

Elizabeth of Wurttemberg (1767-1790)

(1) Augusta of Brunswick-Wolfenbuttel (1764-1788) ═══ Frederick I king of Wurttemberg (r. 1806-1816) ═══ **(2) Charlotte Augusta Matilda (1766-1828)**

Paul (b. 1798)

(1) Caroline Augusta of Bavaria (1792-1873) ═══ William I king of Wurttemberg (r. 1816-1864) ═══ **(2) Catherine of Russia (1788-1819)** ═══ **(3) Pauline of Wurttemberg (1800-1873)**

Catherine of Wurttemberg (1783-1835) m. Jerome Bonaparte

Paul Charles Frederick duke of Wurttemberg (b. 1785) ═══ **Catherine Charlotte of Hildburghausen (1787-1847)**

Catherine Frederica of Wurttemberg (1821-1898) m. her cousin Frederick (1808-1870)

Charles I king of Wurttemberg (r. 1864-1891) ═══ **Olga of Russia (1822-1892)**

Augusta of Wurttemberg (1826-1898) m. Hermann of Saxe-Weimer

Maria (1816-1877) m. Count Neipperg

Sophia of Wurttemberg (1818-1877) m. William III king of the Netherlands

Helene of Wurttemberg (1807-1873) m. Michael grand duke of Russia

Frederick (1808-1870) ═══ **Catherine Frederica of Wurttemberg (1821-1898)**

Pauline of Wurttemberg (1810-1856) m. William duke of Nassau

August (1813-1885)

(1) Maria of Waldeck (1857-1882) ═══ William II king of Wurttemberg (r. 1891-1918) ═══ **(2) Charlotte of Schaumburg-Lippe (1864-1946)**

Pauline of Wurttemberg (1877-1965) m. Frederick prince of Wied

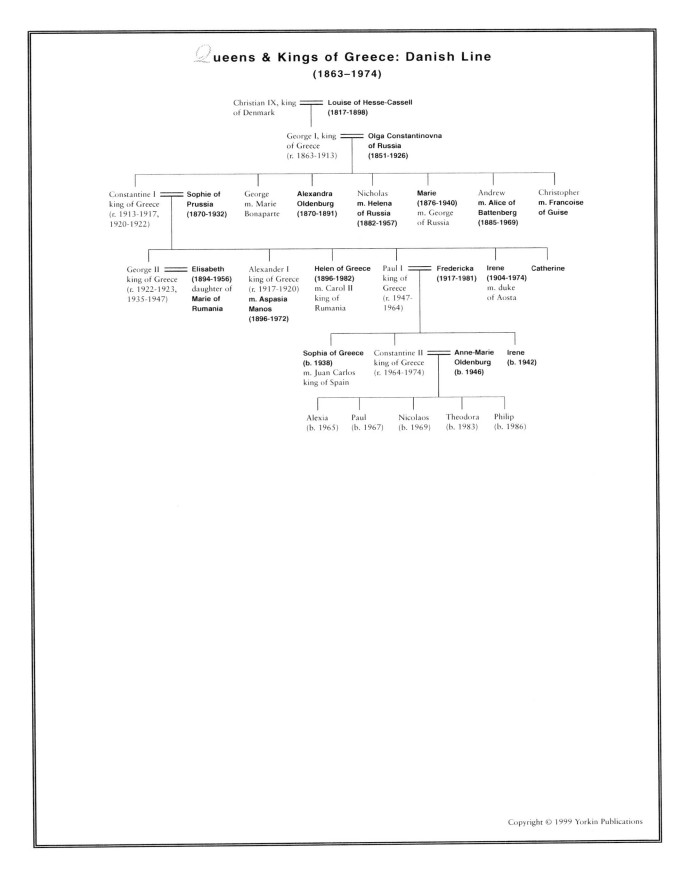

Queens & Kings of Greece: Danish Line
(1863–1974)

Christian IX, king of Denmark ═══ **Louise of Hesse-Cassell (1817-1898)**

George I, king of Greece (r. 1863-1913) ═══ **Olga Constantinovna of Russia (1851-1926)**

- Constantine I king of Greece (r. 1913-1917, 1920-1922) ═══ **Sophie of Prussia (1870-1932)**
- George m. Marie Bonaparte
- **Alexandra Oldenburg (1870-1891)**
- Nicholas **m. Helena of Russia (1882-1957)**
- **Marie (1876-1940)** m. George of Russia
- Andrew **m. Alice of Battenberg (1885-1969)**
- Christopher **m. Francoise of Guise**

- George II king of Greece (r. 1922-1923, 1935-1947) ═══ **Elisabeth (1894-1956) daughter of Marie of Rumania**
- Alexander I king of Greece (r. 1917-1920) **m. Aspasia Manos (1896-1972)**
- **Helen of Greece (1896-1982)** m. Carol II king of Rumania
- Paul I king of Greece (r. 1947-1964) ═══ **Fredericka (1917-1981)**
- **Irene (1904-1974)** m. duke of Aosta
- Catherine

- **Sophia of Greece (b. 1938)** m. Juan Carlos king of Spain
- Constantine II king of Greece (r. 1964-1974) ═══ **Anne-Marie Oldenburg (b. 1946)**
- **Irene (b. 1942)**

- Alexia (b. 1965)
- Paul (b. 1967)
- Nicolaos (b. 1969)
- Theodora (b. 1983)
- Philip (b. 1986)

The Arpad Dynasty
(907–1301)

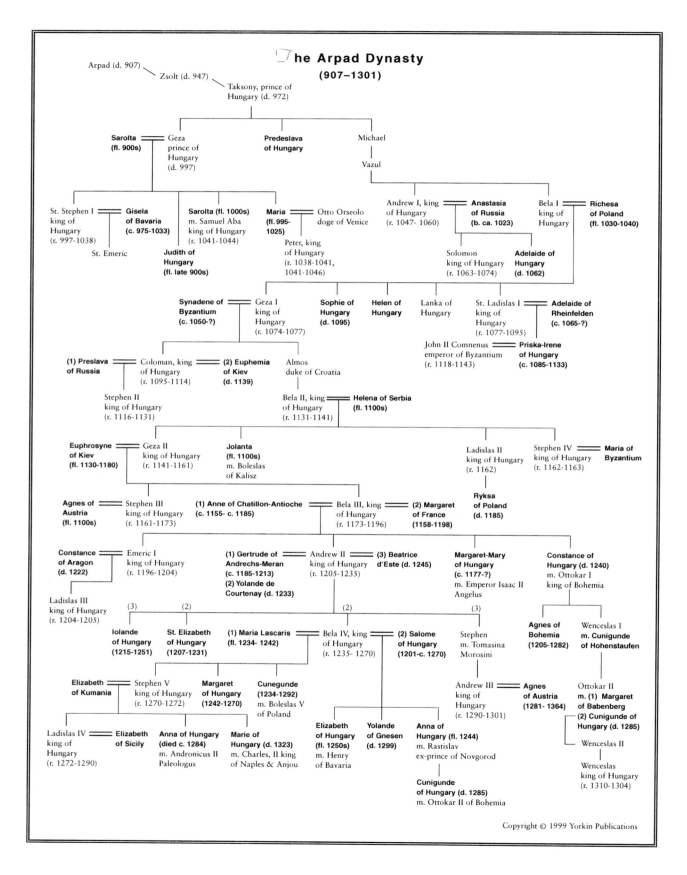

Arpad (d. 907)

Zsolt (d. 947)

Taksony, prince of Hungary (d. 972)

Sarolta (fl. 900s) ═══ Geza prince of Hungary (d. 997)

Predeslava of Hungary

Michael

Vazul

St. Stephen I king of Hungary (r. 997-1038) ═══ Gisela of Bavaria (c. 975-1033)

Sarolta (fl. 1000s) m. Samuel Aba king of Hungary (r. 1041-1044)

Maria (fl. 995-1025) ═══ Otto Orseolo doge of Venice

Andrew I, king of Hungary (r. 1047- 1060) ═══ Anastasia of Russia (b. ca. 1023)

Bela I ═══ Richesa king of Hungary of Poland (fl. 1030-1040)

St. Emeric

Judith of Hungary (fl. late 900s)

Peter, king of Hungary (r. 1038-1041, 1041-1046)

Solomon king of Hungary (r. 1063-1074) ═══ Adelaide of Hungary (d. 1062)

Synadene of Byzantium (c. 1050-?) ═══ Geza I king of Hungary (r. 1074-1077)

Sophie of Hungary (d. 1095)

Helen of Hungary

Lanka of Hungary

St. Ladislas I king of Hungary (r. 1077-1095) ═══ Adelaide of Rheinfelden (c. 1065-?)

John II Comnenus emperor of Byzantium (r. 1118-1143) ═══ Priska-Irene of Hungary (c. 1085-1133)

(1) Preslava of Russia ═══ Coloman, king of Hungary (r. 1095-1114) ═══ (2) Euphemia of Kiev (d. 1139)

Almos duke of Croatia

Stephen II king of Hungary (r. 1116-1131)

Bela II, king of Hungary (r. 1131-1141) ═══ Helena of Serbia (fl. 1100s)

Euphrosyne of Kiev (fl. 1130-1180) ═══ Geza II king of Hungary (r. 1141-1161)

Jolanta (fl. 1100s) m. Boleslas of Kalisz

Ladislas II king of Hungary (r. 1162)

Stephen IV king of Hungary (r. 1162-1163) ═══ Maria of Byzantium

Ryksa of Poland (d. 1185)

Agnes of Austria (fl. 1100s) ═══ Stephen III king of Hungary (r. 1161-1173)

(1) Anne of Chatillon-Antioche (c. 1155- c. 1185) ═══ Bela III, king of Hungary (r. 1173-1196) ═══ (2) Margaret of France (1158-1198)

Constance of Aragon (d. 1222) ═══ Emeric I king of Hungary (r. 1196-1204)

(1) Gertrude of Andrechs-Meran (c. 1185-1213) ═══ Andrew II king of Hungary (r. 1205-1235) ═══ (3) Beatrice d'Este (d. 1245)
(2) Yolande de Courtenay (d. 1233)

Margaret-Mary of Hungary (c. 1177-?) m. Emperor Isaac II Angelus

Constance of Hungary (d. 1240) m. Ottokar I king of Bohemia

Ladislas III king of Hungary (r. 1204-1205)

(3) Iolande of Hungary (1215-1251)

(2) St. Elizabeth of Hungary (1207-1231)

(1) Maria Lascaris (fl. 1234- 1242) ═══ Bela IV, king of Hungary (r. 1235- 1270) ═══ (2) Salome of Hungary (1201-c. 1270)

(3) Stephen m. Tomasina Morosini

Agnes of Bohemia (1205-1282)

Wenceslas I m. Cunigunde of Hohenstaufen

Elizabeth of Kumania ═══ Stephen V king of Hungary (r. 1270-1272)

Margaret of Hungary (1242-1270)

Cunegunde (1234-1292) m. Boleslas V of Poland

Andrew III king of Hungary (r. 1290-1301) ═══ Agnes of Austria (1281- 1364)

Ottokar II m. (1) Margaret of Babenberg
(2) Cunigunde of Hungary (d. 1285)

Ladislas IV king of Hungary (r. 1272-1290) ═══ Elizabeth of Sicily

Anna of Hungary (died c. 1284) m. Andronicus II Paleologus

Marie of Hungary (d. 1323) m. Charles, II king of Naples & Anjou

Elizabeth of Hungary (fl. 1250s) m. Henry of Bavaria

Yolande of Gnesen (d. 1299)

Anna of Hungary (fl. 1244) m. Rastislav ex-prince of Novgorod

Wenceslas II

Wenceslas king of Hungary (r. 1310-1304)

Cunigunde of Hungary (d. 1285) m. Ottokar II of Bohemia

The Ladies & Lords of Milan
(the Visconti & Sforza families, 1310–1535)

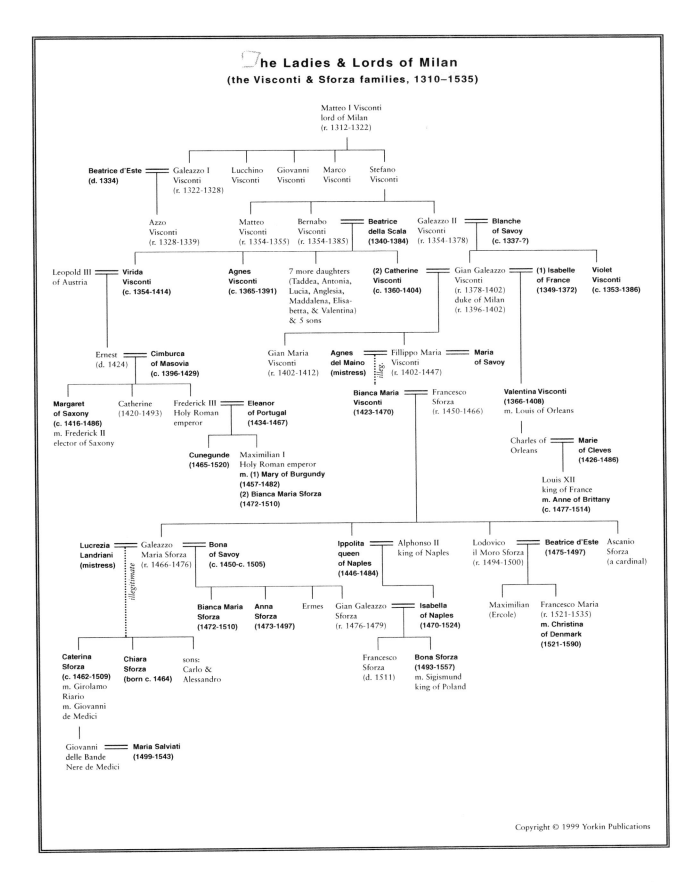

Matteo I Visconti
lord of Milan
(r. 1312-1322)

Beatrice d'Este ══ Galeazzo I   Lucchino   Giovanni   Marco   Stefano
(d. 1334)   Visconti   Visconti   Visconti   Visconti   Visconti
                     (r. 1322-1328)

Azzo   Matteo   Bernabo ══ Beatrice   Galeazzo II ══ Blanche
Visconti   Visconti   Visconti   della Scala   Visconti   of Savoy
(r. 1328-1339)   (r. 1354-1355) (r. 1354-1385) (1340-1384) (r. 1354-1378) (c. 1337-?)

Leopold III ══ Virida   Agnes   7 more daughters   (2) Catherine ══ Gian Galeazzo ══ (1) Isabelle   Violet
of Austria   Visconti Visconti   (Taddea, Antonia,   Visconti   Visconti   of France   Visconti
               (c. 1354-1414) (c. 1365-1391) Lucia, Anglesia, (c. 1360-1404)   (r. 1378-1402)   (1349-1372)   (c. 1353-1386)
                                        Maddalena, Elisa-   duke of Milan
                                        betta, & Valentina)   (r. 1396-1402)
                                        & 5 sons

Ernest ══ Cimburca   Gian Maria   Agnes   Fillippo Maria ══ Maria   Valentina Visconti
(d. 1424)   of Masovia   Visconti   del Maino ┊illeg.┊ Visconti   of Savoy   (1366-1408)
            (c. 1396-1429)   (r. 1402-1412) (mistress)   (r. 1402-1447)   m. Louis of Orleans

Margaret   Catherine   Frederick III ══ Eleanor   Bianca Maria ══ Francesco   Charles of ══ Marie
of Saxony   (1420-1493) Holy Roman   of Portugal Visconti   Sforza   Orleans   of Cleves
(c. 1416-1486)   emperor   (1434-1467) (1423-1470)   (r. 1450-1466)   (1426-1486)
m. Frederick II
elector of Saxony   Cunegunde   Maximilian I   Louis XII
                             (1465-1520) Holy Roman emperor   king of France
                                          m. (1) Mary of Burgundy   m. Anne of Brittany
                                          (1457-1482)   (c. 1477-1514)
                                          (2) Bianca Maria Sforza
                                          (1472-1510)

Lucrezia ══ Galeazzo ══ Bona   Ippolita ══ Alphonso II   Lodovico ══ Beatrice d'Este   Ascanio
Landriani   Maria Sforza   of Savoy   queen   king of Naples il Moro Sforza (1475-1497)   Sforza
(mistress) (r. 1466-1476) (c. 1450-c. 1505) of Naples   (r. 1494-1500)   (a cardinal)
                                          (1446-1484)

            Bianca Maria Anna   Ermes   Gian Galeazzo ══ Isabella   Maximilian   Francesco Maria
            Sforza   Sforza   Sforza   of Naples   (Ercole)   (r. 1521-1535)
            (1472-1510)   (1473-1497)   (r. 1476-1479)   (1470-1524)   m. Christina
                                                                                          of Denmark
                                            Francesco   Bona Sforza   (1521-1590)
                                            Sforza   (1493-1557)
Caterina   Chiara   sons: (d. 1511)   m. Sigismund
Sforza   Sforza   Carlo &   king of Poland
(c. 1462-1509) (born c. 1464) Alessandro
m. Girolamo
Riario
m. Giovanni
de Medici

Giovanni ══ Maria Salviati
delle Bande   (1499-1543)
Nere de Medici

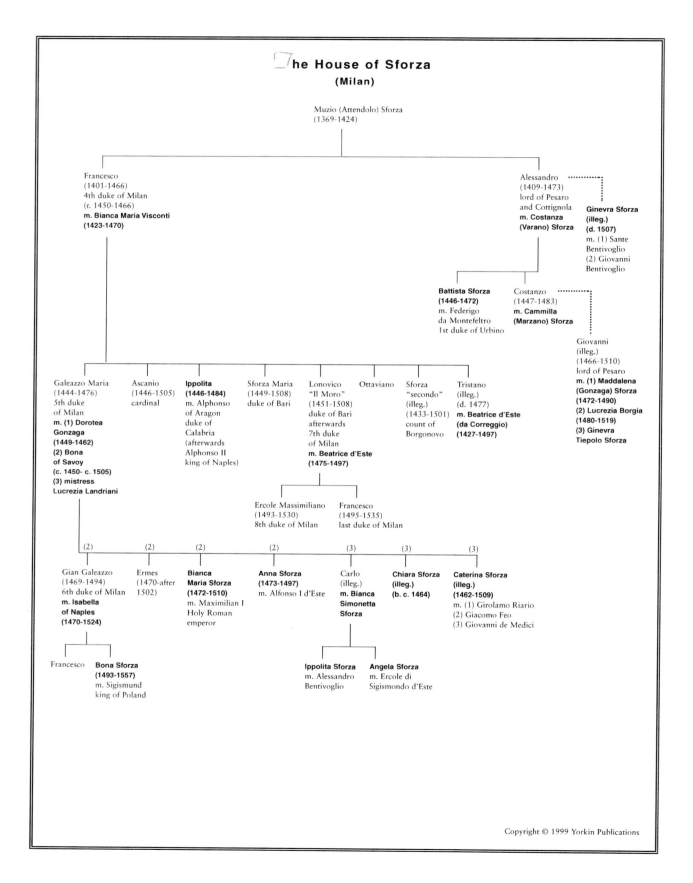

The House of Sforza
(Milan)

Muzio (Attendolo) Sforza
(1369-1424)

Francesco
(1401-1466)
4th duke of Milan
(r. 1450-1466)
m. Bianca Maria Visconti
(1423-1470)

Alessandro
(1409-1473)
lord of Pesaro
and Cottignola
m. Costanza
(Varano) Sforza

Ginevra Sforza
(illeg.)
(d. 1507)
m. (1) Sante
Bentivoglio
(2) Giovanni
Bentivoglio

Battista Sforza
(1446-1472)
m. Federigo
da Montefeltro
1st duke of Urbino

Costanzo
(1447-1483)
m. Cammilla
(Marzano) Sforza

Giovanni
(illeg.)
(1466-1510)
lord of Pesaro
m. (1) Maddalena
(Gonzaga) Sforza
(1472-1490)
(2) Lucrezia Borgia
(1480-1519)
(3) Ginevra
Tiepolo Sforza

Galeazzo Maria
(1444-1476)
5th duke
of Milan
m. (1) Dorotea
Gonzaga
(1449-1462)
(2) Bona
of Savoy
(c. 1450- c. 1505)
(3) mistress
Lucrezia Landriani

Ascanio
(1446-1505)
cardinal

Ippolita
(1446-1484)
m. Alphonso
of Aragon
duke of
Calabria
(afterwards
Alphonso II
king of Naples)

Sforza Maria
(1449-1508)
duke of Bari

Lonovico
"Il Moro"
(1451-1508)
duke of Bari
afterwards
7th duke
of Milan
m. Beatrice d'Este
(1475-1497)

Ottaviano

Sforza
"secondo"
(illeg.)
(1433-1501)
count of
Borgonovo

Tristano
(illeg.)
(d. 1477)
m. Beatrice d'Este
(da Correggio)
(1427-1497)

Ercole Massimiliano
(1493-1530)
8th duke of Milan

Francesco
(1495-1535)
last duke of Milan

(2)
Gian Galeazzo
(1469-1494)
6th duke of Milan
m. Isabella
of Naples
(1470-1524)

(2)
Ermes
(1470-after
1502)

(2)
Bianca
Maria Sforza
(1472-1510)
m. Maximilian I
Holy Roman
emperor

(2)
Anna Sforza
(1473-1497)
m. Alfonso I d'Este

(3)
Carlo
(illeg.)
m. Bianca
Simonetta
Sforza

(3)
Chiara Sforza
(illeg.)
(b. c. 1464)

(3)
Caterina Sforza
(illeg.)
(1462-1509)
m. (1) Girolamo Riario
(2) Giacomo Feo
(3) Giovanni de Medici

Francesco

Bona Sforza
(1493-1557)
m. Sigismund
king of Poland

Ippolita Sforza
m. Alessandro
Bentivoglio

Angela Sforza
m. Ercole di
Sigismondo d'Este

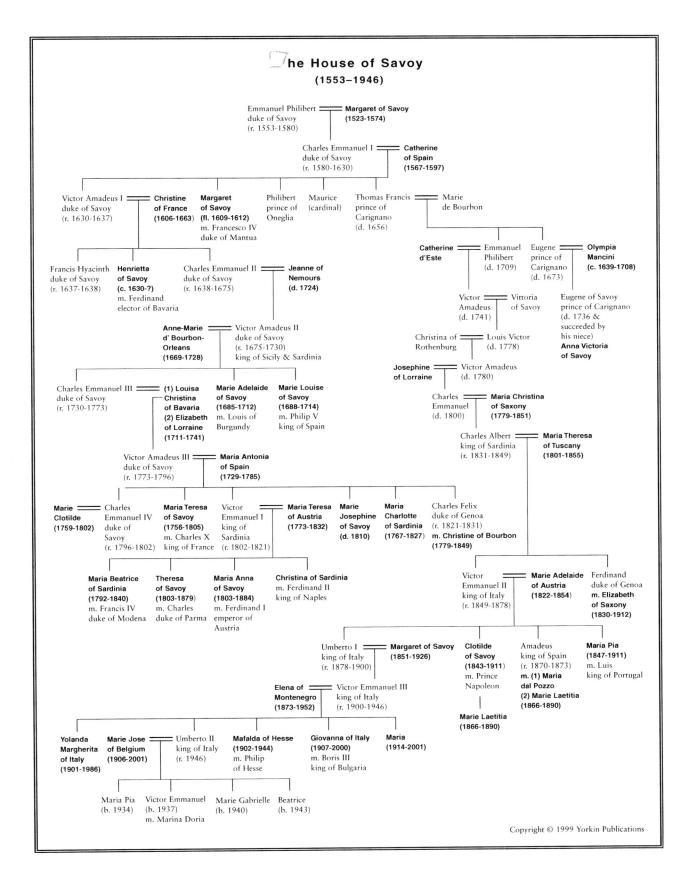

The House of Savoy
(1553–1946)

Emmanuel Philibert duke of Savoy (r. 1553-1580) ═══ **Margaret of Savoy (1523-1574)**

Charles Emmanuel I duke of Savoy (r. 1580-1630) ═══ **Catherine of Spain (1567-1597)**

Victor Amadeus I duke of Savoy (r. 1630-1637) ═══ **Christine of France (1606-1663)**

Margaret of Savoy (fl. 1609-1612) m. Francesco IV duke of Mantua

Philibert prince of Oneglia

Maurice (cardinal)

Thomas Francis prince of Carignano (d. 1656) ═══ Marie de Bourbon

Francis Hyacinth duke of Savoy (r. 1637-1638)

Henrietta of Savoy (c. 1630-?) m. Ferdinand elector of Bavaria

Charles Emmanuel II duke of Savoy (r. 1638-1675) ═══ **Jeanne of Nemours (d. 1724)**

Catherine d'Este ═══ Emmanuel Philibert (d. 1709)

Eugene prince of Carignano (d. 1673) ═══ **Olympia Mancini (c. 1639-1708)**

Victor Amadeus (d. 1741) ═══ Vittoria of Savoy

Eugene of Savoy prince of Carignano (d. 1736 & succeeded by his niece) **Anna Victoria of Savoy**

Anne-Marie d' Bourbon-Orleans (1669-1728) ═══ Victor Amadeus II duke of Savoy (r. 1675-1730) king of Sicily & Sardinia

Christina of Rothenburg ═══ Louis Victor (d. 1778)

Josephine of Lorraine ═══ Victor Amadeus (d. 1780)

Charles Emmanuel III duke of Savoy (r. 1730-1773) ═══ **(1) Louisa Christina of Bavaria (2) Elizabeth of Lorraine (1711-1741)**

Marie Adelaide of Savoy (1685-1712) m. Louis of Burgundy

Marie Louise of Savoy (1688-1714) m. Philip V king of Spain

Charles Emmanuel (d. 1800) ═══ **Maria Christina of Saxony (1779-1851)**

Charles Albert king of Sardinia (r. 1831-1849) ═══ **Maria Theresa of Tuscany (1801-1855)**

Victor Amadeus III duke of Savoy (r. 1773-1796) ═══ **Maria Antonia of Spain (1729-1785)**

Marie Clotilde (1759-1802) ═══ Charles Emmanuel IV duke of Savoy (r. 1796-1802)

Maria Teresa of Savoy (1756-1805) m. Charles X king of France

Victor Emmanuel I king of Sardinia (r. 1802-1821) ═══ **Maria Teresa of Austria (1773-1832)**

Marie Josephine of Savoy (d. 1810)

Maria Charlotte of Sardinia (1767-1827)

Charles Felix duke of Genoa (r. 1821-1831) m. Christine of Bourbon (1779-1849)

Maria Beatrice of Sardinia (1792-1840) m. Francis IV duke of Modena

Theresa of Savoy (1803-1879) m. Charles duke of Parma

Maria Anna of Savoy (1803-1884) m. Ferdinand I emperor of Austria

Christina of Sardinia m. Ferdinand II king of Naples

Victor Emmanuel II king of Italy (r. 1849-1878) ═══ **Marie Adelaide of Austria (1822-1854)**

Ferdinand duke of Genoa m. Elizabeth of Saxony (1830-1912)

Umberto I king of Italy (r. 1878-1900) ═══ **Margaret of Savoy (1851-1926)**

Clotilde of Savoy (1843-1911) m. Prince Napoleon

Amadeus king of Spain (r. 1870-1873) m. (1) Maria dal Pozzo (2) Marie Laetitia (1866-1890)

Maria Pia (1847-1911) m. Luis king of Portugal

Elena of Montenegro (1873-1952) ═══ Victor Emmanuel III king of Italy (r. 1900-1946)

Marie Laetitia (1866-1890)

Yolanda Margherita of Italy (1901-1986)

Marie Jose of Belgium (1906-2001) ═══ Umberto II king of Italy (r. 1946)

Mafalda of Hesse (1902-1944) m. Philip of Hesse

Giovanna of Italy (1907-2000) m. Boris III king of Bulgaria

Maria (1914-2001)

Maria Pia (b. 1934)

Victor Emmanuel (b. 1937) m. Marina Doria

Marie Gabrielle (b. 1940)

Beatrice (b. 1943)

Copyright © 1999 Yorkin Publications

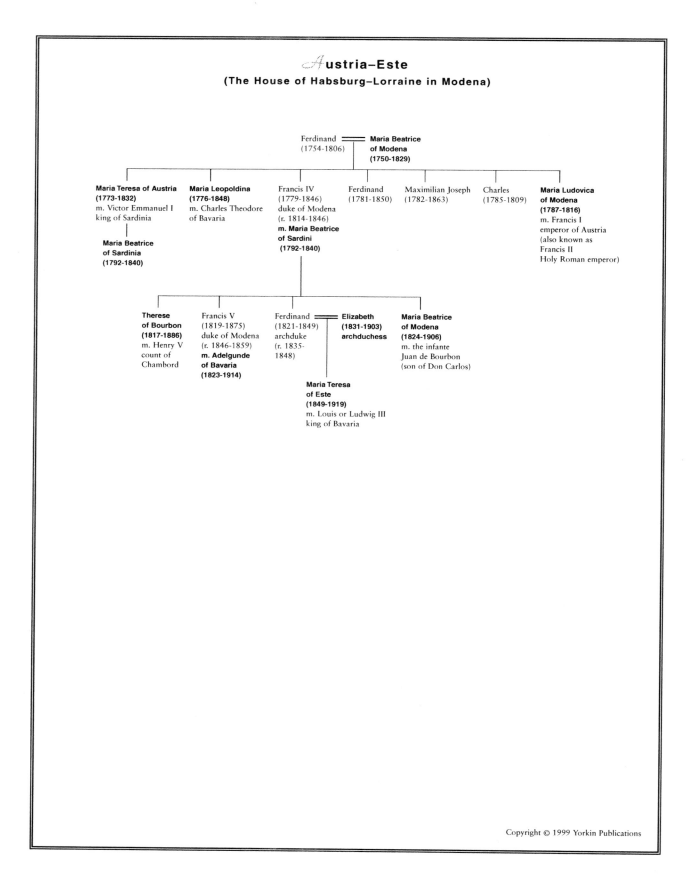

✐ustria–Este
(The House of Habsburg–Lorraine in Modena)

Ferdinand (1754-1806) ═══ **Maria Beatrice of Modena (1750-1829)**

Maria Teresa of Austria (1773-1832) m. Victor Emmanuel I king of Sardinia

Maria Beatrice of Sardinia (1792-1840)

Maria Leopoldina (1776-1848) m. Charles Theodore of Bavaria

Francis IV (1779-1846) duke of Modena (r. 1814-1846) **m. Maria Beatrice of Sardini (1792-1840)**

Ferdinand (1781-1850)

Maximilian Joseph (1782-1863)

Charles (1785-1809)

Maria Ludovica of Modena (1787-1816) m. Francis I emperor of Austria (also known as Francis II Holy Roman emperor)

Therese of Bourbon (1817-1886) m. Henry V count of Chambord

Francis V (1819-1875) duke of Modena (r. 1846-1859) **m. Adelgunde of Bavaria (1823-1914)**

Ferdinand (1821-1849) archduke (r. 1835-1848) ═══ **Elizabeth (1831-1903) archduchess**

Maria Teresa of Este (1849-1919) m. Louis or Ludwig III king of Bavaria

Maria Beatrice of Modena (1824-1906) m. the infante Juan de Bourbon (son of Don Carlos)

The House of Este I

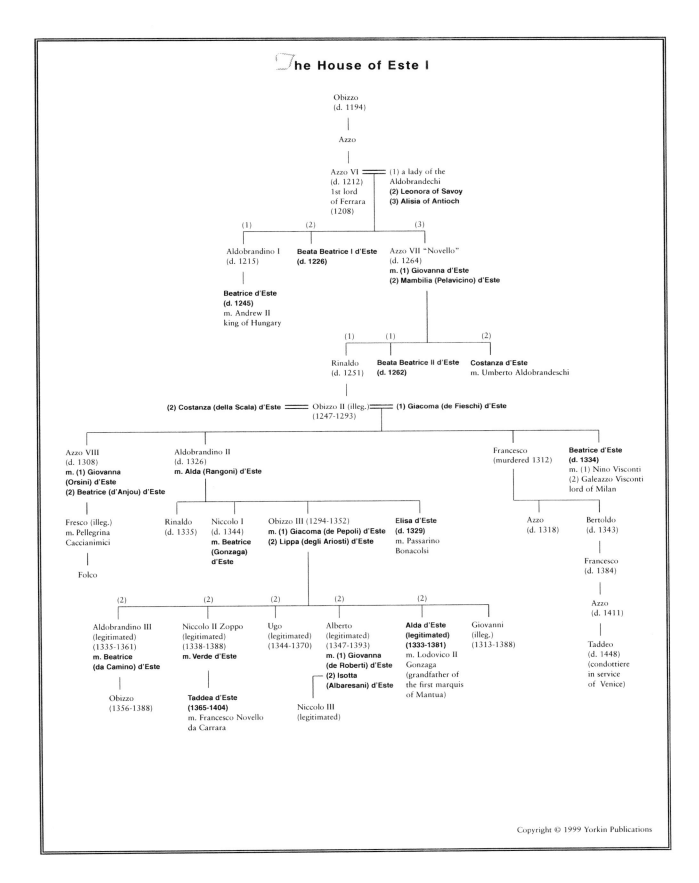

Obizzo
(d. 1194)

Azzo

Azzo VI ══ (1) a lady of the
(d. 1212)   Aldobrandechi
1st lord   (2) **Leonora** of Savoy
of Ferrara (3) **Alisia** of Antioch
(1208)

(1)   (2)   (3)

Aldobrandino I   **Beata Beatrice I d'Este**   Azzo VII "Novello"
(d. 1215)   **(d. 1226)**   (d. 1264)
                                                    m. (1) **Giovanna** d'Este
                                                    (2) **Mambilia (Pelavicino) d'Este**

Beatrice d'Este
(d. 1245)
m. Andrew II
king of Hungary

(1)   (1)   (2)

Rinaldo   **Beata Beatrice II d'Este**   **Costanza d'Este**
(d. 1251)   **(d. 1262)**   m. Umberto Aldobrandeschi

(2) Costanza (della Scala) d'Este ══ Obizzo II (illeg.) ══ **(1) Giacoma (de Fieschi) d'Este**
                                         (1247-1293)

Azzo VIII   Aldobrandino II   Francesco   **Beatrice d'Este**
(d. 1308)   (d. 1326)   (murdered 1312)   **(d. 1334)**
m. (1) Giovanna   **m. Alda (Rangoni) d'Este**   m. (1) Nino Visconti
(Orsini) d'Este   (2) Galeazzo Visconti
(2) Beatrice (d'Anjou) d'Este   lord of Milan

Fresco (illeg.)   Rinaldo   Niccolo I   Obizzo III (1294-1352)   **Elisa d'Este**   Azzo   Bertoldo
m. Pellegrina   (d. 1335)   (d. 1344)   **m. (1) Giacoma (de Pepoli) d'Este**   **(d. 1329)**   (d. 1318)   (d. 1343)
Caccianimici   **m. Beatrice** **(2) Lippa (degli Ariosti) d'Este**   m. Passarino
                                (Gonzaga)   Bonacolsi
                                d'Este
Folco   Francesco
                                                                                                                   (d. 1384)

(2)   (2)   (2)   (2)   (2)   Azzo
                                                                                                                   (d. 1411)
Aldobrandino III   Niccolo II Zoppo   Ugo   Alberto   **Alda d'Este**   Giovanni
(legitimated)   (legitimated)   (legitimated) (legitimated)   **(legitimated)**   (illeg.)
(1335-1361)   (1338-1388)   (1344-1370)   (1347-1393)   **(1333-1381)**   (1313-1388)   Taddeo
m. Beatrice   **m. Verde d'Este**   **m. (1) Giovanna**   m. Lodovico II   (d. 1448)
(da Camino) d'Este   **(de Roberti) d'Este** Gonzaga   (condottiere
                                                  (2) Isotta   (grandfather of   in service
Obizzo   **Taddea d'Este**   **(Albaresani) d'Este** the first marquis   of Venice)
(1356-1388)   **(1365-1404)**   of Mantua)
                   m. Francesco Novello   Niccolo III
                   da Carrara   (legitimated)

The House of Este II

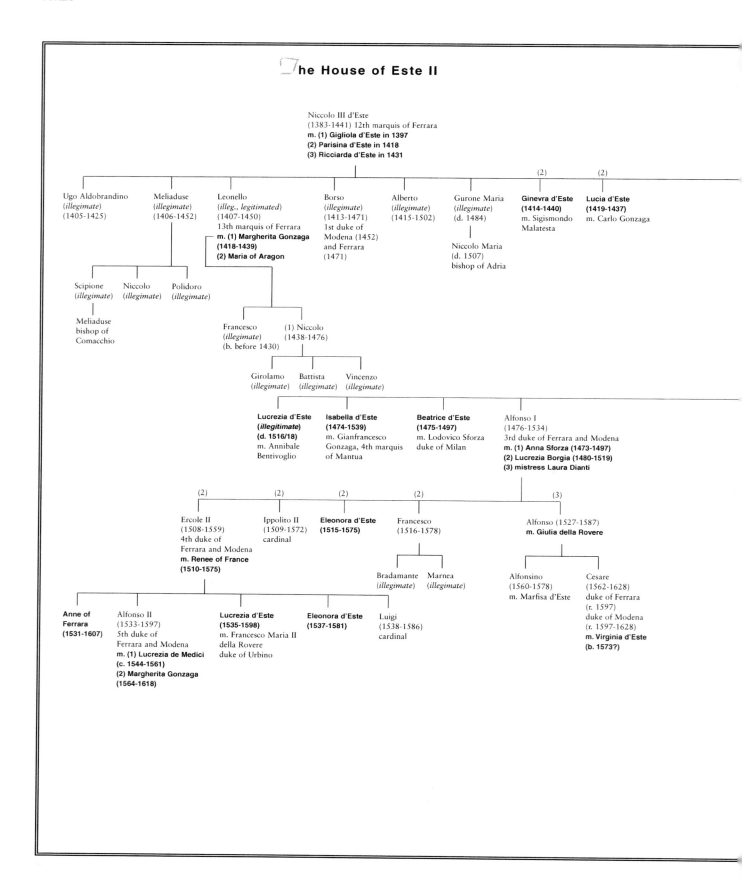

Niccolo III d'Este
(1383-1441) 12th marquis of Ferrara
**m. (1) Gigliola d'Este in 1397
(2) Parisina d'Este in 1418
(3) Ricciarda d'Este in 1431**

Ugo Aldobrandino
(*illegimate*)
(1405-1425)

Meliaduse
(*illegimate*)
(1406-1452)

Leonello
(*illeg., legitimated*)
(1407-1450)
13th marquis of Ferrara
**m. (1) Margherita Gonzaga
(1418-1439)
(2) Maria of Aragon**

Borso
(*illegimate*)
(1413-1471)
1st duke of
Modena (1452)
and Ferrara
(1471)

Alberto
(*illegimate*)
(1415-1502)

Gurone Maria
(*illegimate*)
(d. 1484)

(2) Ginevra d'Este
(1414-1440)
m. Sigismondo
Malatesta

(2) Lucia d'Este
(1419-1437)
m. Carlo Gonzaga

Scipione
(*illegimate*)

Niccolo
(*illegimate*)

Polidoro
(*illegimate*)

Niccolo Maria
(d. 1507)
bishop of Adria

Meliaduse
bishop of
Comacchio

Francesco
(*illegimate*)
(b. before 1430)

(1) Niccolo
(1438-1476)

Girolamo
(*illegimate*)

Battista
(*illegimate*)

Vincenzo
(*illegimate*)

**Lucrezia d'Este
(*illegitimate*)
(d. 1516/18)
m. Annibale
Bentivoglio**

**Isabella d'Este
(1474-1539)**
m. Gianfrancesco
Gonzaga, 4th marquis
of Mantua

**Beatrice d'Este
(1475-1497)**
m. Lodovico Sforza
duke of Milan

Alfonso I
(1476-1534)
3rd duke of Ferrara and Modena
**m. (1) Anna Sforza (1473-1497)
(2) Lucrezia Borgia (1480-1519)
(3) mistress Laura Dianti**

(2) Ercole II
(1508-1559)
4th duke of
Ferrara and Modena
**m. Renee of France
(1510-1575)**

(2) Ippolito II
(1509-1572)
cardinal

**(2) Eleonora d'Este
(1515-1575)**

(2) Francesco
(1516-1578)

(3) Alfonso (1527-1587)
m. Giulia della Rovere

Bradamante
(*illegimate*)

Marnea
(*illegimate*)

Alfonsino
(1560-1578)
m. Marfisa d'Este

Cesare
(1562-1628)
duke of Ferrara
(r. 1597)
duke of Modena
(r. 1597-1628)
**m. Virginia d'Este
(b. 1573?)**

**Anne of
Ferrara
(1531-1607)**

Alfonso II
(1533-1597)
5th duke of
Ferrara and Modena
**m. (1) Lucrezia de Medici
(c. 1544-1561)
(2) Margherita Gonzaga
(1564-1618)**

**Lucrezia d'Este
(1535-1598)**
m. Francesco Maria II
della Rovere
duke of Urbino

**Eleonora d'Este
(1537-1581)**

Luigi
(1538-1586)
cardinal

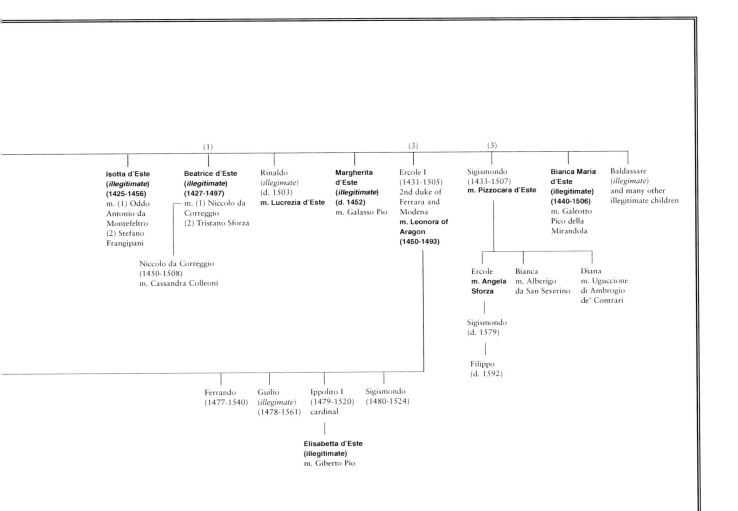

(1)   (3)   (3)

Isotta d'Este **Beatrice d'Este** Rinaldo **Margherita** Ercole I Sigismondo **Bianca Maria** Baldassare
(illegimate) **(illegimate)** (illegimate) **d'Este** (1431-1505) (1433-1507) **d'Este** (illegimate)
(1425-1456) **(1427-1497)** (d. 1503) **(illegimate)** 2nd duke of **m. Pizzocara d'Este** **(illegimate)** and many other
m. (1) Oddo ├ m. (1) Niccolo da **m. Lucrezia d'Este** **(d. 1452)** Ferrara and **(1440-1506)** illegitimate children
Antonio da Correggio m. Galasso Pio Modena m. Galeotto
Montefeltro (2) Tristano Sforza **m. Leonora of** Pico della
(2) Stefano **Aragon** Mirandola
Frangipani **(1450-1493)**

Niccolo da Correggio   Ercole   Bianca   Diana
(1450-1508)   **m. Angela** m. Alberigo   m. Uguccione
m. Cassandra Colleoni   **Sforza**   da San Severino di Ambrogio
                                                                                                                de' Contrari

                                                                                    Sigismondo
                                                                                    (d. 1579)

                                                                                    Filippo
                                                                                    (d. 1592)

                              Ferrando   Guilio   Ippolito I   Sigismondo
                              (1477-1540) (illegimate) (1479-1520)   (1480-1524)
                                          (1478-1561)   cardinal

                              Elisabetta d'Este
                              (illegitimate)
                              m. Giberto Pio

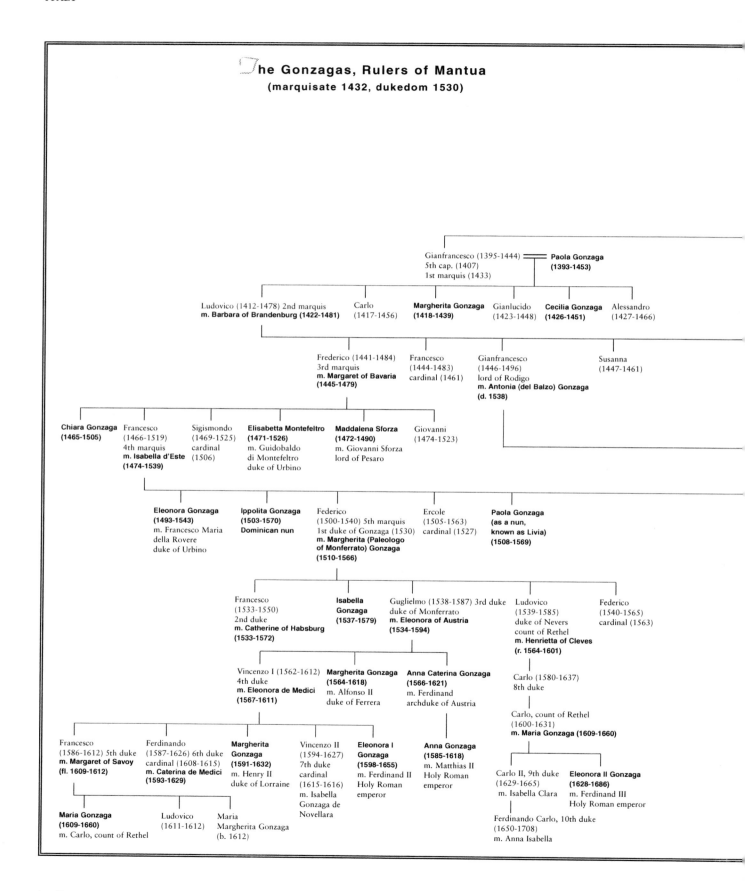

The Gonzagas, Rulers of Mantua
(marquisate 1432, dukedom 1530)

Gianfrancesco (1395-1444) === **Paola Gonzaga**
5th cap. (1407)   **(1393-1453)**
1st marquis (1433)

Ludovico (1412-1478) 2nd marquis · Carlo (1417-1456) · **Margherita Gonzaga (1418-1439)** · Gianlucido (1423-1448) · **Cecilia Gonzaga (1426-1451)** · Alessandro (1427-1466)
m. Barbara of Brandenburg (1422-1481)

Frederico (1441-1484) 3rd marquis **m. Margaret of Bavaria (1445-1479)** · Francesco (1444-1483) cardinal (1461) · Gianfrancesco (1446-1496) lord of Rodigo **m. Antonia (del Balzo) Gonzaga (d. 1538)** · Susanna (1447-1461)

Chiara Gonzaga (1465-1505) · Francesco (1466-1519) 4th marquis **m. Isabella d'Este (1474-1539)** · Sigismondo (1469-1525) cardinal (1506) · **Elisabetta Montefeltro (1471-1526)** m. Guidobaldo di Montefeltro duke of Urbino · **Maddalena Sforza (1472-1490)** m. Giovanni Sforza lord of Pesaro · Giovanni (1474-1523)

Eleonora Gonzaga (1493-1543) m. Francesco Maria della Rovere duke of Urbino · **Ippolita Gonzaga (1503-1570)** Dominican nun · Federico (1500-1540) 5th marquis 1st duke of Gonzaga (1530) **m. Margherita (Paleologo of Monferrato) Gonzaga (1510-1566)** · Ercole (1505-1563) cardinal (1527) · **Paola Gonzaga (as a nun, known as Livia) (1508-1569)**

Francesco (1533-1550) 2nd duke **m. Catherine of Habsburg (1533-1572)** · **Isabella Gonzaga (1537-1579)** · Guglielmo (1538-1587) 3rd duke duke of Monferrato **m. Eleonora of Austria (1534-1594)** · Ludovico (1539-1585) duke of Nevers count of Rethel **m. Henrietta of Cleves (r. 1564-1601)** · Federico (1540-1565) cardinal (1563)

Vincenzo I (1562-1612) 4th duke **m. Eleonora de Medici (1567-1611)** · **Margherita Gonzaga (1564-1618)** m. Alfonso II duke of Ferrera · **Anna Caterina Gonzaga (1566-1621)** m. Ferdinand archduke of Austria · Carlo (1580-1637) 8th duke

Carlo, count of Rethel (1600-1631) **m. Maria Gonzaga (1609-1660)**

Francesco (1586-1612) 5th duke **m. Margaret of Savoy (fl. 1609-1612)** · Ferdinando (1587-1626) 6th duke cardinal (1608-1615) **m. Caterina de Medici (1593-1629)** · **Margherita Gonzaga (1591-1632)** m. Henry II duke of Lorraine · Vincenzo II (1594-1627) 7th duke cardinal (1615-1616) m. Isabella Gonzaga de Novellara · **Eleonora I Gonzaga (1598-1655)** m. Ferdinand II Holy Roman emperor · **Anna Gonzaga (1585-1618)** m. Matthias II Holy Roman emperor

Carlo II, 9th duke (1629-1665) m. Isabella Clara · **Eleonora II Gonzaga (1628-1686)** m. Ferdinand III Holy Roman emperor

Maria Gonzaga (1609-1660) m. Carlo, count of Rethel · Ludovico (1611-1612) · Maria Margherita Gonzaga (b. 1612)

Ferdinando Carlo, 10th duke (1650-1708) m. Anna Isabella

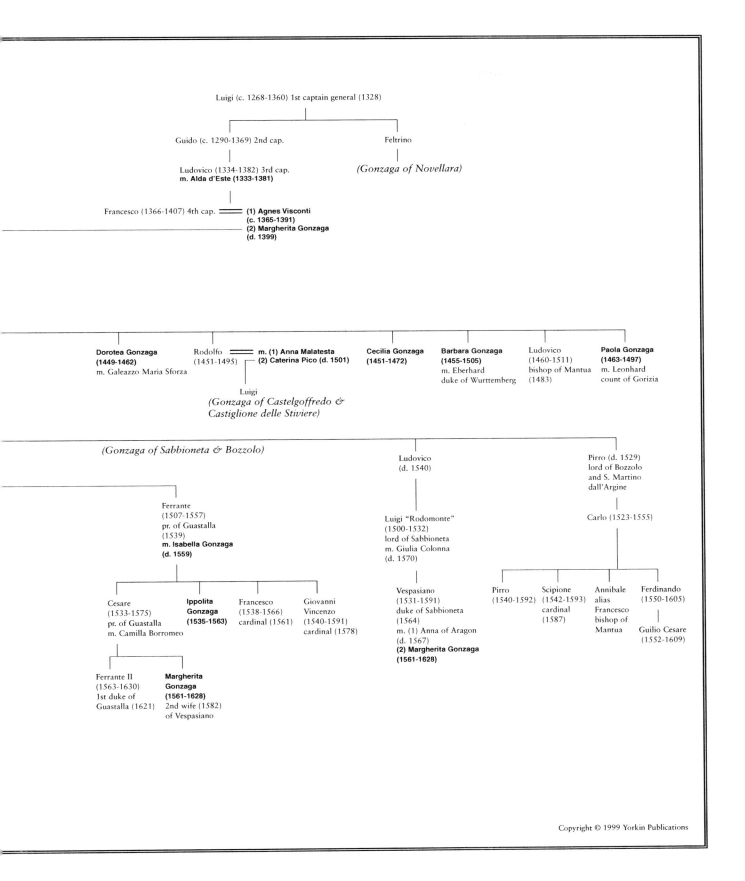

Luigi (c. 1268-1360) 1st captain general (1328)

Guido (c. 1290-1369) 2nd cap.

Feltrino

(Gonzaga of Novellara)

Ludovico (1334-1382) 3rd cap.
m. Alda d'Este (1333-1381)

Francesco (1366-1407) 4th cap. === **(1) Agnes Visconti**
(c. 1365-1391)
(2) Margherita Gonzaga
(d. 1399)

Dorotea Gonzaga
(1449-1462)
m. Galeazzo Maria Sforza

Rodolfo === **m. (1) Anna Malatesta**
(1451-1495) **(2) Caterina Pico (d. 1501)**

Luigi
(Gonzaga of Castelgoffredo &
Castiglione delle Stiviere)

Cecilia Gonzaga
(1451-1472)

Barbara Gonzaga
(1455-1505)
m. Eberhard
duke of Wurttemberg

Ludovico
(1460-1511)
bishop of Mantua
(1483)

Paola Gonzaga
(1463-1497)
m. Leonhard
count of Gorizia

(Gonzaga of Sabbioneta & Bozzolo)

Ludovico
(d. 1540)

Pirro (d. 1529)
lord of Bozzolo
and S. Martino
dall'Argine

Ferrante
(1507-1557)
pr. of Guastalla
(1539)
m. Isabella Gonzaga
(d. 1559)

Luigi "Rodomonte"
(1500-1532)
lord of Sabbioneta
m. Giulia Colonna
(d. 1570)

Carlo (1523-1555)

Cesare
(1533-1575)
pr. of Guastalla
m. Camilla Borromeo

Ippolita
Gonzaga
(1535-1563)

Francesco
(1538-1566)
cardinal (1561)

Giovanni
Vincenzo
(1540-1591)
cardinal (1578)

Vespasiano
(1531-1591)
duke of Sabbioneta
(1564)
m. (1) Anna of Aragon
(d. 1567)
(2) Margherita Gonzaga
(1561-1628)

Pirro
(1540-1592)

Scipione
(1542-1593)
cardinal
(1587)

Annibale
alias
Francesco
bishop of
Mantua

Ferdinando
(1550-1605)

Guilio Cesare
(1552-1609)

Ferrante II
(1563-1630)
1st duke of
Guastalla (1621)

Margherita
Gonzaga
(1561-1628)
2nd wife (1582)
of Vespasiano

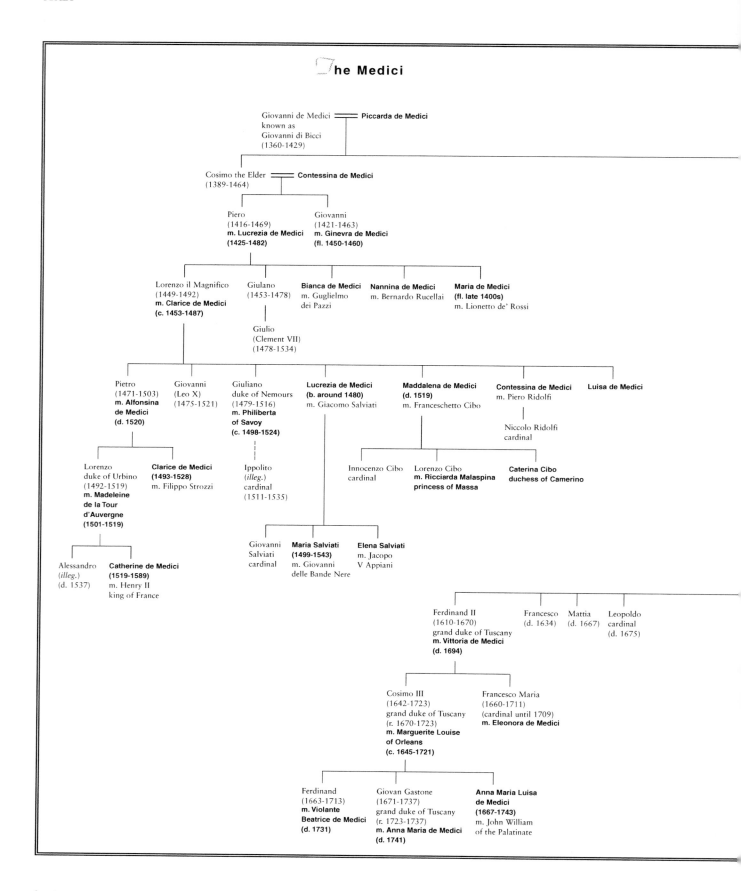

The Medici

Giovanni de Medici known as Giovanni di Bicci (1360-1429) === **Piccarda de Medici**

Cosimo the Elder (1389-1464) === **Contessina de Medici**

Piero (1416-1469) **m. Lucrezia de Medici (1425-1482)**

Giovanni (1421-1463) **m. Ginevra de Medici (fl. 1450-1460)**

Lorenzo il Magnifico (1449-1492) **m. Clarice de Medici (c. 1453-1487)**

Giulano (1453-1478)

Bianca de Medici m. Guglielmo dei Pazzi

Nannina de Medici m. Bernardo Rucellai

Maria de Medici (fl. late 1400s) m. Lionetto de' Rossi

Giulio (Clement VII) (1478-1534)

Pietro (1471-1503) **m. Alfonsina de Medici (d. 1520)**

Giovanni (Leo X) (1475-1521)

Giuliano duke of Nemours (1479-1516) **m. Philiberta of Savoy (c. 1498-1524)**

Lucrezia de Medici (b. around 1480) m. Giacomo Salviati

Maddalena de Medici (d. 1519) m. Franceschetto Cibo

Contessina de Medici m. Piero Ridolfi

Luisa de Medici

Niccolo Ridolfi cardinal

Lorenzo duke of Urbino (1492-1519) **m. Madeleine de la Tour d'Auvergne (1501-1519)**

Clarice de Medici (1493-1528) m. Filippo Strozzi

Ippolito (*illeg.*) cardinal (1511-1535)

Innocenzo Cibo cardinal

Lorenzo Cibo **m. Ricciarda Malaspina princess of Massa**

Caterina Cibo duchess of Camerino

Giovanni Salviati cardinal

Maria Salviati (1499-1543) m. Giovanni delle Bande Nere

Elena Salviati m. Jacopo V Appiani

Alessandro (*illeg.*) (d. 1537)

Catherine de Medici (1519-1589) m. Henry II king of France

Ferdinand II (1610-1670) grand duke of Tuscany **m. Vittoria de Medici (d. 1694)**

Francesco (d. 1634)

Mattia (d. 1667)

Leopoldo cardinal (d. 1675)

Cosimo III (1642-1723) grand duke of Tuscany (r. 1670-1723) **m. Marguerite Louise of Orleans (c. 1645-1721)**

Francesco Maria (1660-1711) (cardinal until 1709) **m. Eleonora de Medici**

Ferdinand (1663-1713) **m. Violante Beatrice de Medici (d. 1731)**

Giovan Gastone (1671-1737) grand duke of Tuscany (r. 1723-1737) **m. Anna Maria de Medici (d. 1741)**

Anna Maria Luisa de Medici (1667-1743) m. John William of the Palatinate

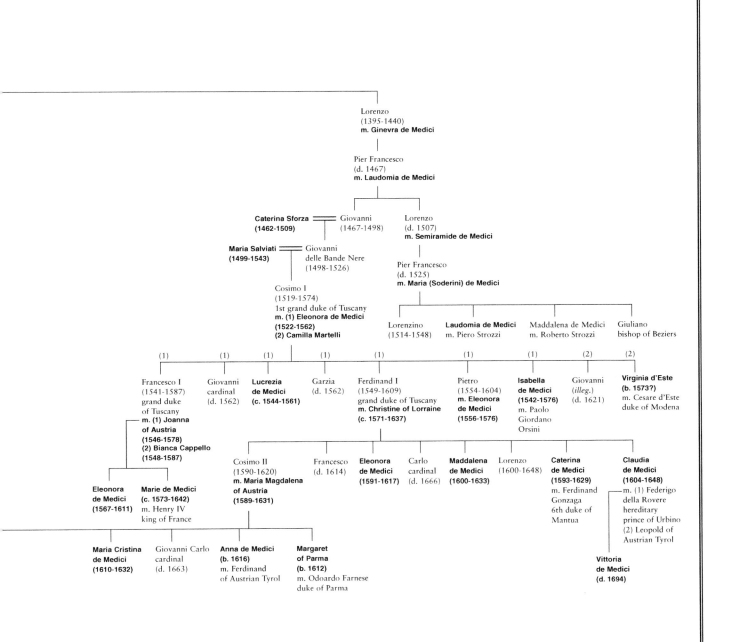

Lorenzo
(1395-1440)
m. Ginevra de Medici

Pier Francesco
(d. 1467)
m. Laudomia de Medici

Caterina Sforza ═══ Giovanni   Lorenzo
(1462-1509)   (1467-1498)   (d. 1507)
                                      m. Semiramide de Medici

Maria Salviati ═══ Giovanni
(1499-1543)   delle Bande Nere
                     (1498-1526)

                                      Pier Francesco
                                      (d. 1525)
                                      m. Maria (Soderini) de Medici

Cosimo I
(1519-1574)
1st grand duke of Tuscany
m. (1) Eleonora de Medici
(1522-1562)
(2) Camilla Martelli

Lorenzino   **Laudomia de Medici**   Maddalena de Medici   Giuliano
(1514-1548)   m. Piero Strozzi   m. Roberto Strozzi   bishop of Beziers

(1)   (1)   (1)   (1)   (1)   (1)   (1)   (2)   (2)

Francesco I   Giovanni   **Lucrezia   Garzia   Ferdinand I   Pietro   **Isabella   Giovanni   **Virginia d'Este**
(1541-1587)   cardinal   de Medici   (d. 1562)   (1549-1609)   (1554-1604)   de Medici   (illeg.)   **(b. 1573?)**
grand duke   (d. 1562)   (c. 1544-1561)**   grand duke   **m. Eleonora   (1542-1576)**   (d. 1621)   m. Cesare d'Este
of Tuscany   of Tuscany   de Medici   m. Paolo   duke of Modena
m. (1) Joanna   **m. Christine of Lorraine** **(1556-1576)** Giordano
of Austria   **(c. 1571-1637)**   Orsini
(1546-1578)
(2) Bianca Cappello
(1548-1587)

                                      Cosimo II   Francesco   **Eleonora   Carlo   **Maddalena   Lorenzo   **Caterina   **Claudia
                                      (1590-1620)   (d. 1614)   de Medici   cardinal   de Medici   (1600-1648)   de Medici   de Medici
                                      m. Maria Magdalena   (1591-1617)** (d. 1666)   (1600-1633)**   (1593-1629)**   (1604-1648)**
                                      of Austria   m. Ferdinand   m. (1) Federigo
Eleonora   **Marie de Medici **(1589-1631)**   Gonzaga   della Rovere
de Medici   **(c. 1573-1642)**   6th duke of   hereditary
(1567-1611)**   m. Henry IV   Mantua   prince of Urbino
                 king of France   (2) Leopold of
                                                                                                                                          Austrian Tyrol

**Maria Cristina Giovanni Carlo   **Anna de Medici   **Margaret   **Vittoria
de Medici   cardinal   (b. 1616)**   of Parma   de Medici
(1610-1632)**   (d. 1663)   m. Ferdinand   (b. 1612)**   (d. 1694)**
                                  of Austrian Tyrol m. Odoardo Farnese
                                                     duke of Parma

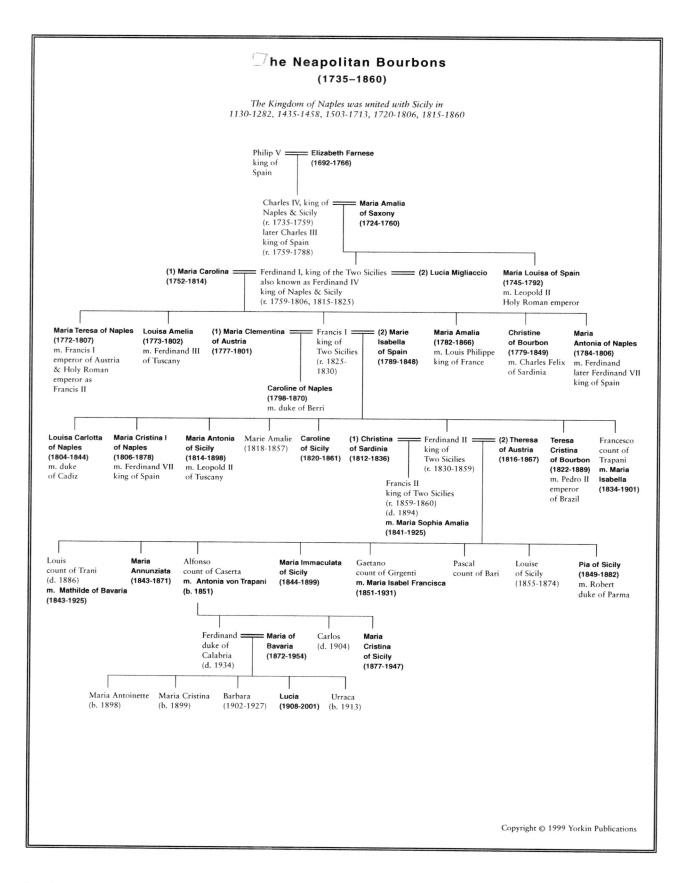

The Neapolitan Bourbons

(1735–1860)

The Kingdom of Naples was united with Sicily in
1130-1282, 1435-1458, 1503-1713, 1720-1806, 1815-1860

Philip V king of Spain ═══ **Elizabeth Farnese (1692-1766)**

Charles IV, king of Naples & Sicily (r. 1735-1759) later Charles III king of Spain (r. 1759-1788) ═══ **Maria Amalia of Saxony (1724-1760)**

(1) Maria Carolina (1752-1814) ═══ Ferdinand I, king of the Two Sicilies also known as Ferdinand IV king of Naples & Sicily (r. 1759-1806, 1815-1825) ═══ **(2) Lucia Migliaccio** **Maria Louisa of Spain (1745-1792)** m. Leopold II Holy Roman emperor

Maria Teresa of Naples (1772-1807) m. Francis I emperor of Austria & Holy Roman emperor as Francis II

Louisa Amelia (1773-1802) m. Ferdinand III of Tuscany

(1) Maria Clementina of Austria (1777-1801) ═══ Francis I king of Two Sicilies (r. 1825-1830) ═══ **(2) Marie Isabella of Spain (1789-1848)**

Maria Amalia (1782-1866) m. Louis Philippe king of France

Christine of Bourbon (1779-1849) m. Charles Felix of Sardinia

Maria Antonia of Naples (1784-1806) m. Ferdinand later Ferdinand VII king of Spain

Caroline of Naples (1798-1870) m. duke of Berri

Louisa Carlotta of Naples (1804-1844) m. duke of Cadiz

Maria Cristina I of Naples (1806-1878) m. Ferdinand VII king of Spain

Maria Antonia of Sicily (1814-1898) m. Leopold II of Tuscany

Marie Amalie (1818-1857)

Caroline of Sicily (1820-1861)

(1) Christina of Sardinia (1812-1836) ═══ Ferdinand II king of Two Sicilies (r. 1830-1859) ═══ **(2) Theresa of Austria (1816-1867)**

Teresa Cristina of Bourbon (1822-1889) m. Pedro II emperor of Brazil

Francesco count of Trapani **m. Maria Isabella (1834-1901)**

Francis II king of Two Sicilies (r. 1859-1860) (d. 1894) **m. Maria Sophia Amalia (1841-1925)**

Louis count of Trani (d. 1886) **m. Mathilde of Bavaria (1843-1925)**

Maria Annunziata (1843-1871)

Alfonso count of Caserta **m. Antonia von Trapani (b. 1851)**

Maria Immaculata of Sicily (1844-1899)

Gaetano count of Girgenti **m. Maria Isabel Francisca (1851-1931)**

Pascal count of Bari

Louise of Sicily (1855-1874)

Pia of Sicily (1849-1882) m. Robert duke of Parma

Ferdinand duke of Calabria (d. 1934) ═══ **Maria of Bavaria (1872-1954)**

Carlos (d. 1904)

Maria Cristina of Sicily (1877-1947)

Maria Antoinette (b. 1898)

Maria Cristina (b. 1899)

Barbara (1902-1927)

Lucia (1908-2001)

Urraca (b. 1913)

Copyright © 1999 Yorkin Publications

The Tuscan Branch of Habsburg-Lorraine

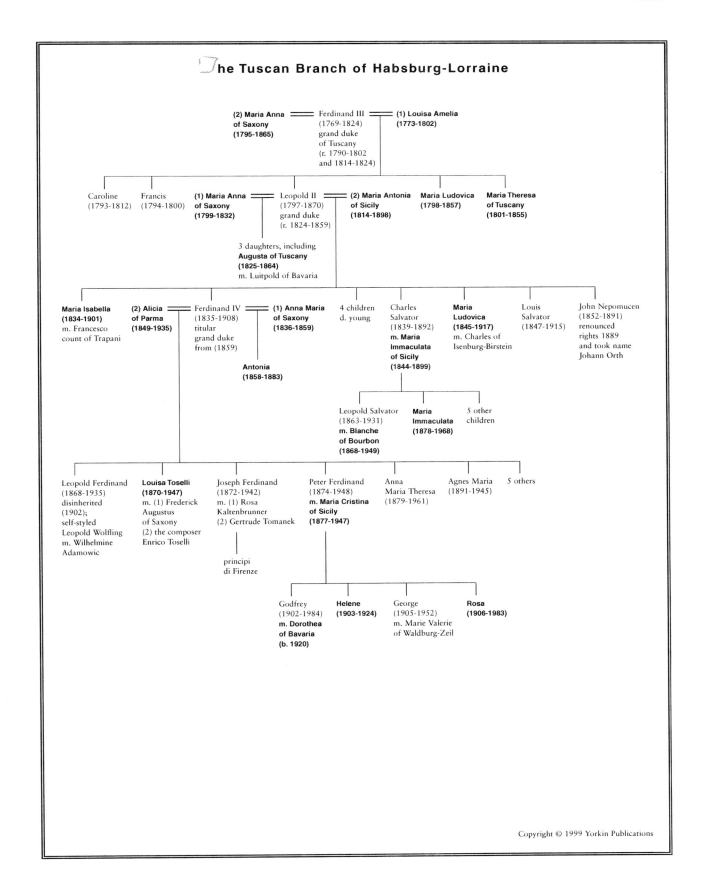

(2) Maria Anna of Saxony (1795-1865) ══ Ferdinand III (1769-1824) grand duke of Tuscany (r. 1790-1802 and 1814-1824) ══ **(1) Louisa Amelia (1773-1802)**

Caroline (1793-1812)

Francis (1794-1800)

(1) Maria Anna of Saxony (1799-1832) ══ Leopold II (1797-1870) grand duke (r. 1824-1859) ══ **(2) Maria Antonia of Sicily (1814-1898)**

Maria Ludovica (1798-1857)

Maria Theresa of Tuscany (1801-1855)

3 daughters, including **Augusta of Tuscany (1825-1864)** m. Luitpold of Bavaria

Maria Isabella (1834-1901) m. Francesco count of Trapani

(2) Alicia of Parma (1849-1935) ══ Ferdinand IV (1835-1908) titular grand duke from (1859) ══ **(1) Anna Maria of Saxony (1836-1859)**

Antonia (1858-1883)

4 children d. young

Charles Salvator (1839-1892) **m. Maria Immaculata of Sicily (1844-1899)**

Maria Ludovica (1845-1917) m. Charles of Isenburg-Birstein

Louis Salvator (1847-1915)

John Nepomucen (1852-1891) renounced rights 1889 and took name Johann Orth

Leopold Salvator (1863-1931) **m. Blanche of Bourbon (1868-1949)**

Maria Immaculata (1878-1968)

5 other children

Leopold Ferdinand (1868-1935) disinherited (1902); self-styled Leopold Wolfling m. Wilhelmine Adamowic

Louisa Toselli (1870-1947) m. (1) Frederick Augustus of Saxony (2) the composer Enrico Toselli

Joseph Ferdinand (1872-1942) m. (1) Rosa Kaltenbrunner (2) Gertrude Tomanek

Peter Ferdinand (1874-1948) **m. Maria Cristina of Sicily (1877-1947)**

Anna Maria Theresa (1879-1961)

Agnes Maria (1891-1945)

5 others

principi di Firenze

Godfrey (1902-1984) **m. Dorothea of Bavaria (b. 1920)**

Helene (1903-1924)

George (1905-1952) m. Marie Valerie of Waldburg-Zeil

Rosa (1906-1983)

*E*mpresses & Emperors of the Imperial House of Japan

According to Japanese tradition, the imperial house of Japan has ruled without interruption from Jimmu to Akihito. Legend depicts Jimmu as a descendant of the sun goddess Amaterasu, and each succeeding empress or emperor has been given the title of tenno *(heavenly ruler). Modern historians generally agree that the forced abdication of Empress Kogyoku in 645 is a trustworthy starting point for more reliable sources of Japanese history.*

		BIRTH AND DEATH DATES	REIGN DATES
1	Jimmu		
2	Suizei		
3	Annei		
4	Itoku		
5	Kosho		
6	Koan		
7	Korei	*legendary emperors*	
8	Kogen		
9	Kaika		
10	Sujin		
11	Suinin		
12	Keiko		
13	Seimu		
14	Chuai		
15	Ojin	*late 4th to early 5th century*	
16	Nintoku		
17	Richu	*first half of the 5th century*	
18	Hanzei		
19	Ingyo		
20	Anko	*mid-5th century*	
21	Yuryaku		
22	Seinei		
23	Kenzo	*latter half of the 5th century*	
24	Ninken		
25	Buretsu		
26	Keitai		
27	Ankan	*first half of the 6th century*	
28	Senka		
29	Kimmei	509-571	531 or 539-571
30	Bidatsu	538-585	572-585
31	Yomei	?-587	585-587
32	Sushun	?-592	587-592
33	**Suiko**	**554-628**	**593-628**
34	Jomei	593-641	629-641
35	**Kogyoku[1]**	**594-661**	**642-645**

Taika Reforms

36	Kotoku	597-654	645-654
37	**Saimei**	**594-661**	**655-661**
38	Tenji	626-672	661-672
39	Kobun	648-672	672
40	Temmu	?-686	672-686
41	**Jito**	**645-703**	**686-697**
42	Mommu	683-707	697-707

Nara Period

43	**Gemmei**	**661-721**	**707-715**
44	**Gensho**	**680-748**	**715-724**
45	Shomu	701-756	724-749
46	**Koken[2]**	**718-770**	**749-758**
47	Junnin	733-765	758-764
48	**Shotoku**	**718-770**	**764-770**
49	Konin	709-782	770-781

Heian Period

50	Kammu	737-806	781-806
51	Heizei	774-824	806-809
52	Saga	786-842	809-823
53	Junna	786-840	823-833
54	Nimmyo	810-850	833-850
55	Montoku	827-858	850-858
56	Seiwa	850-881	858-876
57	Yozei	869-949	876-884
58	Koko	830-887	884-887
59	Uda	867-931	887-897
60	Daigo	885-930	897-930
61	Suzaku	923-952	930-946
62	Murakami	926-967	946-967
63	Reizei	950-1011	967-969
64	En'yu	959-991	969-984
65	Kazan	968-1008	984-986
66	Ichijo	980-1011	986-1011
67	Sanjo	976-1017	1011-1016

		BIRTH AND DEATH DATES	REIGN DATES
68	Go-Ichijo	1008-1036	1016-1036
69	Go-Suzaku	1009-1045	1036-1045
70	Go-Reizei	1025-1068	1045-1068
71	Go-Sanjo	1034-1073	1068-1073
72	Shirakawa	1053-1129	1073-1087
73	Horikawa	1079-1107	1087-1107
74	Toba	1103-1156	1107-1123
75	Sutoku	1119-1164	1123-1142
76	Konoe	1139-1155	1142-1155
77	Go-Shirakawa	1127-1192	1155-1158
78	Nijo	1143-1165	1158-1165
79	Rokujo	1164-1176	1165-1168
80	Takakura	1161-1181	1168-1180
81	Antoku	1178-1185	1180-1185

Kamakura Period

82	Go-Toba	1180-1239	1183-1198
83	Tsuchimikado	1195-1231	1198-1210
84	Juntoku	1197-1242	1210-1221
85	Chukyo	1218-1234	1221
86	Go-Horikawa	1212-1234	1221-1232
87	Shijo	1231-1242	1232-1242
88	Go-Saga	1220-1272	1242-1246
89	Go-Fukakusa	1243-1304	1246-1260
90	Kameyama	1249-1305	1260-1274
91	Go-Uda	1267-1324	1274-1287
92	Fushimi	1265-1317	1287-1298
93	Go-Fushimi	1288-1336	1298-1301
94	Go-Nijo	1285-1308	1301-1308
95	Hanazono	1297-1348	1308-1318

Ashikaga Period

96	Go-Daigo	1288-1339	1318-1339
97	Go-Murakami	1328-1368	1339-1368
98	Chokei	1343-1394	1368-1383
99	Go-Kameyama	?-1424	1383-1392
N1	Kogon	1313-1364	1331-1333
N2	Komyo	1322-1380	1336-1348
N3	Suko	1334-1398	1348-1351
N4	Go-Kogon	1338-1374	1351-1371
N5	Go-En'yu	1359-1393	1371-1382
100	Go-Komatsu	1377-1433	1382-1412
101	Shoko	1401-1428	1412-1428
102	Go-Hanazono	1419-1471	1428-1464
103	Go-Tsuchimikado	1442-1500	1464-1500
104	Go-Kashiwabara	1464-1526	1500-1526
105	Go-Nara	1497-1557	1526-1557

Period of Military Dictatorships

106	Ogimachi	1517-1593	1557-1586
107	Go-Yozei	1572-1617	1586-1611

Tokugawa Period

108	Go-Mizunoo	1596-1680	1611-1629
109	**Meisho**	**1624-1696**	**1629-1643**
110	Go-Komyo	1633-1654	1643-1654
111	Gosai	1637-1685	1655-1663
112	Reigen	1654-1732	1663-1687
113	Higashiyama	1675-1709	1687-1709
114	Nakamikado	1702-1737	1709-1735
115	Sakuramachi	1720-1750	1735-1747
116	Momozono	1741-1762	1747-1762
117	**Go-Sakuramachi**	**1740-1813**	**1762-1771**
118	Go-Momozono	1758-1779	1771-1779
119	Kokaku	1771-1840	1780-1817
120	Ninko	1800-1846	1817-1846
121	Komei	1831-1867	1846-1867

Modern Period

122	Meiji	1852-1912	1867-1912
	Meiji empress (Haruko)	1850-1914	
123	Taisho	1879-1926	1912-1926
	Taisho empress (Sadako)		
124	Hirohito	1901-1989	1926-1989
	& Empress Nagako	b. 1903	
125	Akihito	b. 1989	1989-
	& Empress Michiko	**b. 1934**	

Note: The numbers on the left designate the place of rulers in the order of succession. The names of all the empresses and emperors, except for Hirohito and Akihito, were given posthumously.

[1]Kogyoku (35) later reigned as Saimei (37).
[2]Koken (46) later reigned as Shotoku (48).

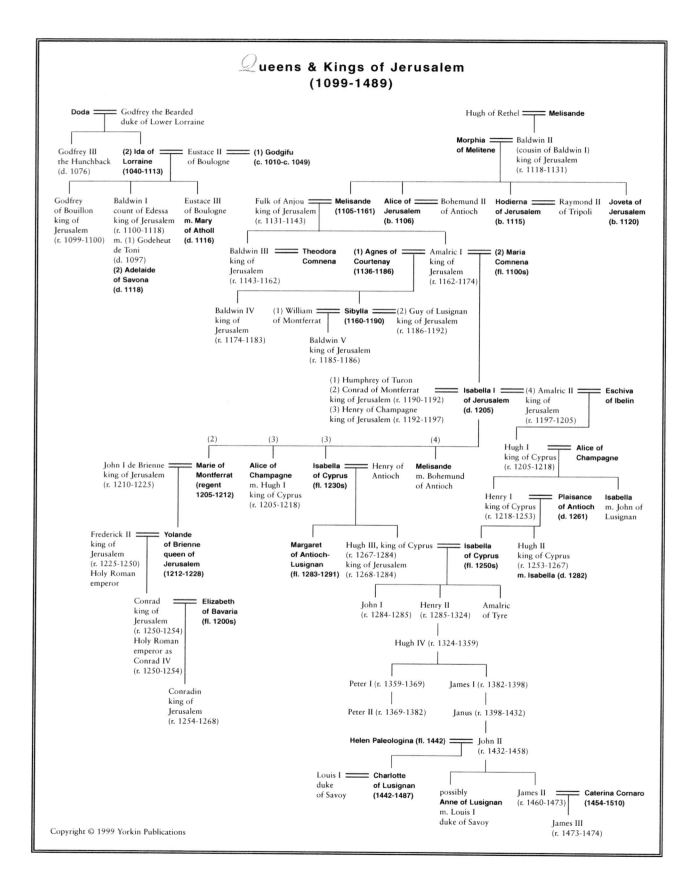

Queens & Kings of Jerusalem
(1099-1489)

Copyright © 1999 Yorkin Publications

Luxemburg Rulers
(1308–1437)

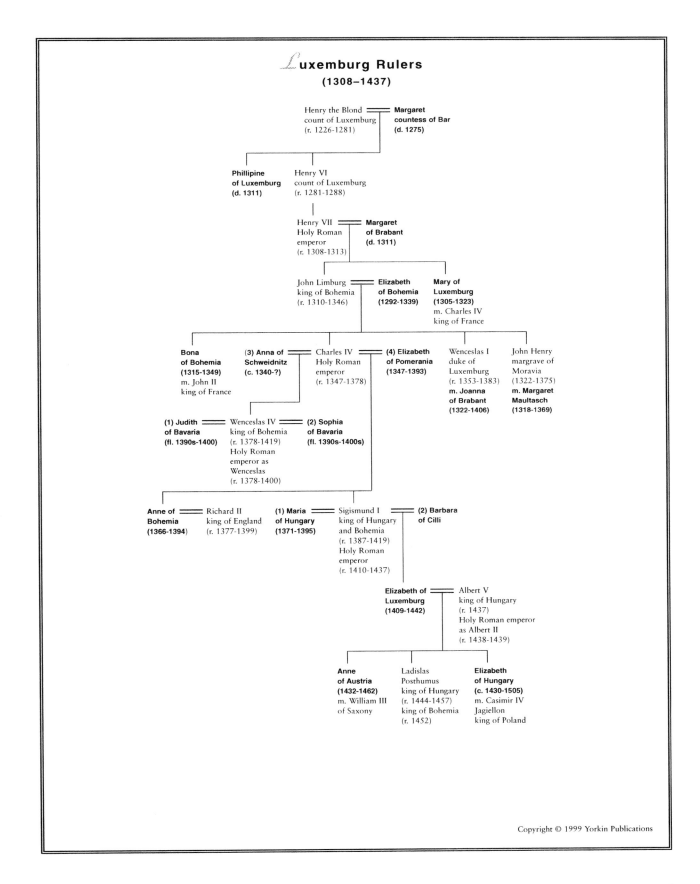

Henry the Blond === Margaret
count of Luxemburg   countess of Bar
(r. 1226-1281)   (d. 1275)

Phillipine   Henry VI
of Luxemburg   count of Luxemburg
(d. 1311)   (r. 1281-1288)

Henry VII === Margaret
Holy Roman   of Brabant
emperor   (d. 1311)
(r. 1308-1313)

John Limburg === Elizabeth   Mary of
king of Bohemia of Bohemia   Luxemburg
(r. 1310-1346)   (1292-1339)   (1305-1323)
                                  m. Charles IV
                                  king of France

Bona   (3) Anna of === Charles IV === (4) Elizabeth   Wenceslas I   John Henry
of Bohemia   Schweidnitz   Holy Roman   of Pomerania   duke of   margrave of
(1315-1349)   (c. 1340-?)   emperor   (1347-1393)   Luxemburg   Moravia
m. John II   (r. 1347-1378)   (r. 1353-1383)   (1322-1375)
king of France   m. Joanna   m. Margaret
                                                                  of Brabant   Maultasch
                                                                  (1322-1406)   (1318-1369)

(1) Judith === Wenceslas IV === (2) Sophia
of Bavaria   king of Bohemia   of Bavaria
(fl. 1390s-1400) (r. 1378-1419) (fl. 1390s-1400s)
               Holy Roman
               emperor as
               Wenceslas
               (r. 1378-1400)

Anne of === Richard II   (1) Maria === Sigismund I === (2) Barbara
Bohemia   king of England   of Hungary   king of Hungary   of Cilli
(1366-1394) (r. 1377-1399)   (1371-1395)   and Bohemia
                                            (r. 1387-1419)
                                            Holy Roman
                                            emperor
                                            (r. 1410-1437)

Elizabeth of === Albert V
Luxemburg   king of Hungary
(1409-1442)   (r. 1437)
                Holy Roman emperor
                as Albert II
                (r. 1438-1439)

Anne   Ladislas   Elizabeth
of Austria   Posthumus   of Hungary
(1432-1462)   king of Hungary   (c. 1430-1505)
m. William III   (r. 1444-1457)   m. Casimir IV
of Saxony   king of Bohemia   Jagiellon
                  (r. 1452)   king of Poland

The House of Orange-Nassau
(1558–)

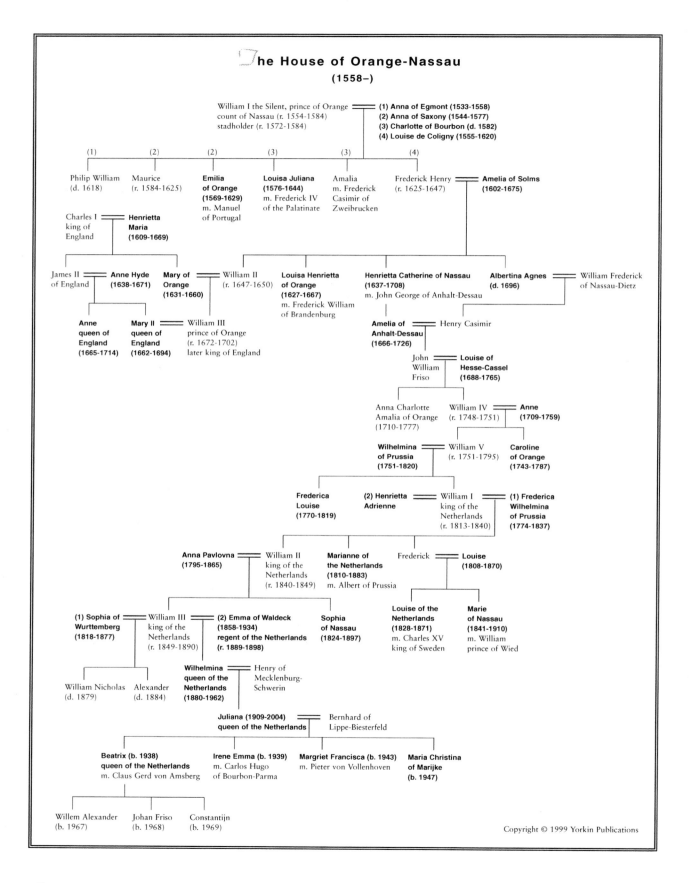

William I the Silent, prince of Orange
count of Nassau (r. 1554-1584)
stadholder (r. 1572-1584)

(1) Anna of Egmont (1533-1558)
(2) Anna of Saxony (1544-1577)
(3) Charlotte of Bourbon (d. 1582)
(4) Louise de Coligny (1555-1620)

(1) Philip William (d. 1618)

(2) Maurice (r. 1584-1625)

(2) **Emilia of Orange (1569-1629)** m. Manuel of Portugal

(3) **Louisa Juliana (1576-1644)** m. Frederick IV of the Palatinate

(3) Amalia m. Frederick Casimir of Zweibrucken

(4) Frederick Henry (r. 1625-1647) — **Amelia of Solms (1602-1675)**

Charles I king of England — **Henrietta Maria (1609-1669)**

James II of England — **Anne Hyde (1638-1671)**

Mary of Orange (1631-1660) — William II (r. 1647-1650)

Louisa Henrietta of Orange (1627-1667) m. Frederick William of Brandenburg

Henrietta Catherine of Nassau (1637-1708) m. John George of Anhalt-Dessau

Albertina Agnes (d. 1696) — William Frederick of Nassau-Dietz

Anne queen of England (1665-1714)

Mary II queen of England (1662-1694) — William III prince of Orange (r. 1672-1702) later king of England

Amelia of Anhalt-Dessau (1666-1726) — Henry Casimir

John William Friso — **Louise of Hesse-Cassel (1688-1765)**

Anna Charlotte Amalia of Orange (1710-1777)

William IV (r. 1748-1751) — **Anne (1709-1759)**

Wilhelmina of Prussia (1751-1820) — William V (r. 1751-1795) — **Caroline of Orange (1743-1787)**

Frederica Louise (1770-1819)

(2) **Henrietta Adrienne** — William I king of the Netherlands (r. 1813-1840) — (1) **Frederica Wilhelmina of Prussia (1774-1837)**

Anna Pavlovna (1795-1865) — William II king of the Netherlands (r. 1840-1849)

Marianne of the Netherlands (1810-1883) m. Albert of Prussia

Frederick — **Louise (1808-1870)**

(1) **Sophia of Wurttemberg (1818-1877)** — William III king of the Netherlands (r. 1849-1890) — (2) **Emma of Waldeck (1858-1934) regent of the Netherlands (r. 1889-1898)**

Sophia of Nassau (1824-1897)

Louise of the Netherlands (1828-1871) m. Charles XV king of Sweden

Marie of Nassau (1841-1910) m. William prince of Wied

William Nicholas (d. 1879)

Alexander (d. 1884)

Wilhelmina queen of the Netherlands (1880-1962) — Henry of Mecklenburg-Schwerin

Juliana (1909-2004) queen of the Netherlands — Bernhard of Lippe-Biesterfeld

Beatrix (b. 1938) queen of the Netherlands m. Claus Gerd von Amsberg

Irene Emma (b. 1939) m. Carlos Hugo of Bourbon-Parma

Margriet Francisca (b. 1943) m. Pieter von Vollenhoven

Maria Christina of Marijke (b. 1947)

Willem Alexander (b. 1967)

Johan Friso (b. 1968)

Constantijn (b. 1969)

Copyright © 1999 Yorkin Publications

Queens & Kings of Norway
(1905–)

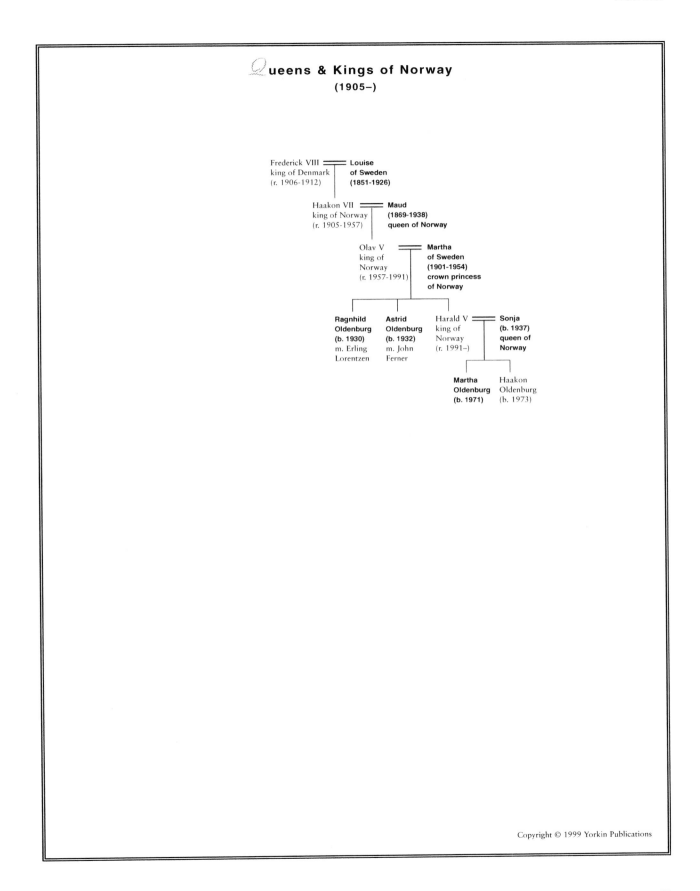

Frederick VIII ═══ **Louise**
king of Denmark　　**of Sweden**
(r. 1906-1912)　　**(1851-1926)**

Haakon VII ═══ **Maud**
king of Norway　**(1869-1938)**
(r. 1905-1957)　**queen of Norway**

Olav V ═══ **Martha**
king of　　**of Sweden**
Norway　　**(1901-1954)**
(r. 1957-1991)　**crown princess**
　　　　　　of Norway

Ragnhild　　**Astrid**　　Harald V ═══ **Sonja**
Oldenburg　　**Oldenburg**　king of　　**(b. 1937)**
(b. 1930)　　**(b. 1932)**　Norway　　**queen of**
m. Erling　　m. John　　(r. 1991–)　**Norway**
Lorentzen　　Ferner

Martha　　Haakon
Oldenburg　Oldenburg
(b. 1971)　(b. 1973)

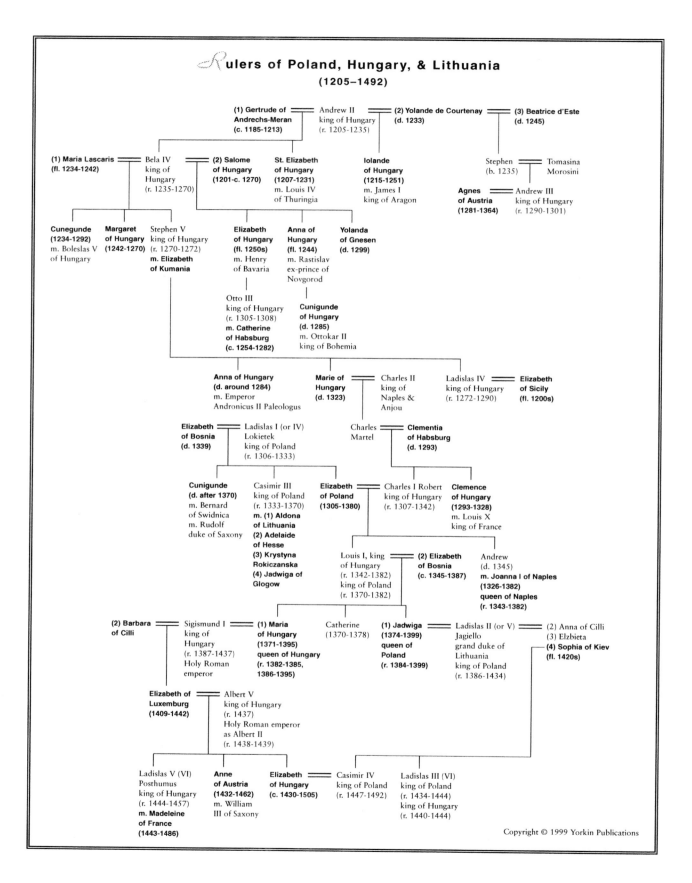

Rulers of Poland, Hungary, & Lithuania
(1205–1492)

(1) Gertrude of Andrechs-Meran (c. 1185-1213) ═ Andrew II king of Hungary (r. 1205-1235) ═ (2) Yolande de Courtenay (d. 1233) ═ (3) Beatrice d'Este (d. 1245)

(1) Maria Lascaris (fl. 1234-1242) ═ Bela IV king of Hungary (r. 1235-1270) ═ (2) Salome of Hungary (1201-c. 1270)

St. Elizabeth of Hungary (1207-1231) m. Louis IV of Thuringia

Iolande of Hungary (1215-1251) m. James I king of Aragon

Stephen (b. 1235) ═ Tomasina Morosini

Agnes of Austria (1281-1364) ═ Andrew III king of Hungary (r. 1290-1301)

Cunegunde (1234-1292) m. Boleslas V of Hungary

Margaret of Hungary (1242-1270)

Stephen V king of Hungary (r. 1270-1272) m. Elizabeth of Kumania

Elizabeth of Hungary (fl. 1250s) m. Henry of Bavaria

Anna of Hungary (fl. 1244) m. Rastislav ex-prince of Novgorod

Yolanda of Gnesen (d. 1299)

Otto III king of Hungary (r. 1305-1308) m. Catherine of Habsburg (c. 1254-1282)

Cunigunde of Hungary (d. 1285) m. Ottokar II king of Bohemia

Anna of Hungary (d. around 1284) m. Emperor Andronicus II Paleologus

Marie of Hungary (d. 1323) ═ Charles II king of Naples & Anjou

Ladislas IV king of Hungary (r. 1272-1290) ═ Elizabeth of Sicily (fl. 1200s)

Elizabeth of Bosnia (d. 1339) ═ Ladislas I (or IV) Lokietek king of Poland (r. 1306-1333)

Charles Martel ═ Clementia of Habsburg (d. 1293)

Cunigunde (d. after 1370) m. Bernard of Swidnica m. Rudolf duke of Saxony

Casimir III king of Poland (r. 1333-1370) m. (1) Aldona of Lithuania (2) Adelaide of Hesse (3) Krystyna Rokiczanska (4) Jadwiga of Glogow

Elizabeth of Poland (1305-1380) ═ Charles I Robert king of Hungary (r. 1307-1342)

Clemence of Hungary (1293-1328) m. Louis X king of France

Louis I, king of Hungary (r. 1342-1382) king of Poland (r. 1370-1382) ═ (2) Elizabeth of Bosnia (c. 1345-1387)

Andrew (d. 1345) m. Joanna I of Naples (1326-1382) queen of Naples (r. 1343-1382)

(2) Barbara of Cilli ═ Sigismund I king of Hungary (r. 1387-1437) Holy Roman emperor ═ (1) Maria of Hungary (1371-1395) queen of Hungary (r. 1382-1385, 1386-1395)

Catherine (1370-1378)

(1) Jadwiga (1374-1399) queen of Poland (r. 1384-1399) ═ Ladislas II (or V) Jagiello grand duke of Lithuania king of Poland (r. 1386-1434) ═ (2) Anna of Cilli (3) Elzbieta (4) Sophia of Kiev (fl. 1420s)

Elizabeth of Luxemburg (1409-1442) ═ Albert V king of Hungary (r. 1437) Holy Roman emperor as Albert II (r. 1438-1439)

Ladislas V (VI) Posthumus king of Hungary (r. 1444-1457) m. Madeleine of France (1443-1486)

Anne of Austria (1432-1462) m. William III of Saxony

Elizabeth of Hungary (c. 1430-1505) ═ Casimir IV king of Poland (r. 1447-1492)

Ladislas III (VI) king of Poland (r. 1434-1444) king of Hungary (r. 1440-1444)

Copyright © 1999 Yorkin Publications

Rulers of Poland & Hungary, House of Jagellon & Vasa
(1447–1668)

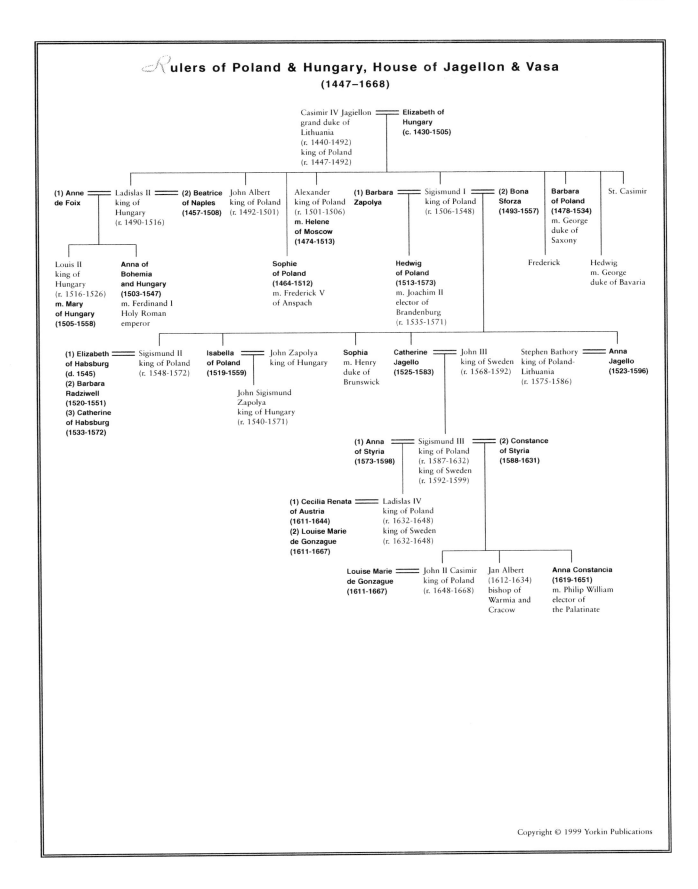

Casimir IV Jagiellon
grand duke of
Lithuania
(r. 1440-1492)
king of Poland
(r. 1447-1492)

**Elizabeth of
Hungary
(c. 1430-1505)**

**(1) Anne
de Foix**

Ladislas II
king of
Hungary
(r. 1490-1516)

**(2) Beatrice
of Naples
(1457-1508)**

John Albert
king of Poland
(r. 1492-1501)

Alexander
king of Poland
(r. 1501-1506)
**m. Helene
of Moscow
(1474-1513)**

**(1) Barbara
Zapolya**

Sigismund I
king of Poland
(r. 1506-1548)

**(2) Bona
Sforza
(1493-1557)**

**Barbara
of Poland
(1478-1534)**
m. George
duke of
Saxony

St. Casimir

Louis II
king of
Hungary
(r. 1516-1526)
**m. Mary
of Hungary
(1505-1558)**

**Anna of
Bohemia
and Hungary
(1503-1547)**
m. Ferdinand I
Holy Roman
emperor

**Sophie
of Poland
(1464-1512)**
m. Frederick V
of Anspach

**Hedwig
of Poland
(1513-1573)**
m. Joachim II
elector of
Brandenburg
(r. 1535-1571)

Frederick

Hedwig
m. George
duke of Bavaria

**(1) Elizabeth
of Habsburg
(d. 1545)
(2) Barbara
Radziwell
(1520-1551)
(3) Catherine
of Habsburg
(1533-1572)**

Sigismund II
king of Poland
(r. 1548-1572)

**Isabella
of Poland
(1519-1559)**

John Zapolya
king of Hungary

Sophia
m. Henry
duke of
Brunswick

**Catherine
Jagello
(1525-1583)**

John III
king of Sweden
(r. 1568-1592)

Stephen Bathory
king of Poland-
Lithuania
(r. 1575-1586)

**Anna
Jagello
(1523-1596)**

John Sigismund
Zapolya
king of Hungary
(r. 1540-1571)

**(1) Anna
of Styria
(1573-1598)**

Sigismund III
king of Poland
(r. 1587-1632)
king of Sweden
(r. 1592-1599)

**(2) Constance
of Styria
(1588-1631)**

**(1) Cecilia Renata
of Austria
(1611-1644)
(2) Louise Marie
de Gonzague
(1611-1667)**

Ladislas IV
king of Poland
(r. 1632-1648)
king of Sweden
(r. 1632-1648)

**Louise Marie
de Gonzague
(1611-1667)**

John II Casimir
king of Poland
(r. 1648-1668)

Jan Albert
(1612-1634)
bishop of
Warmia and
Cracow

**Anna Constancia
(1619-1651)**
m. Philip William
elector of
the Palatinate

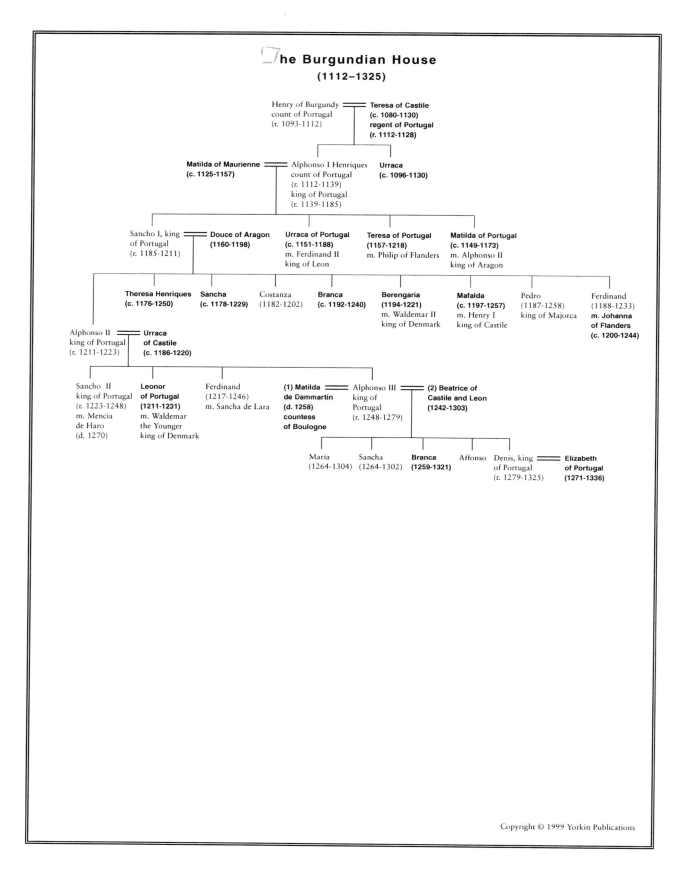

The Burgundian House
(1112–1325)

Henry of Burgundy, count of Portugal (r. 1093-1112) ═══ **Teresa of Castile (c. 1080-1130) regent of Portugal (r. 1112-1128)**

Matilda of Maurienne (c. 1125-1157) ═══ Alphonso I Henriques, count of Portugal (r. 1112-1139) king of Portugal (r. 1139-1185) | **Urraca (c. 1096-1130)**

Sancho I, king of Portugal (r. 1185-1211) ═══ **Douce of Aragon (1160-1198)** | **Urraca of Portugal (c. 1151-1188)** m. Ferdinand II king of Leon | **Teresa of Portugal (1157-1218)** m. Philip of Flanders | **Matilda of Portugal (c. 1149-1173)** m. Alphonso II king of Aragon

Theresa Henriques (c. 1176-1250) | **Sancha (c. 1178-1229)** | Costanza (1182-1202) | **Branca (c. 1192-1240)** | **Berengaria (1194-1221)** m. Waldemar II king of Denmark | **Mafalda (c. 1197-1257)** m. Henry I king of Castile | Pedro (1187-1258) king of Majorca | Ferdinand (1188-1233) m. **Johanna of Flanders (c. 1200-1244)**

Alphonso II, king of Portugal (r. 1211-1223) ═══ **Urraca of Castile (c. 1186-1220)**

Sancho II, king of Portugal (r. 1223-1248) m. Mencia de Haro (d. 1270) | **Leonor of Portugal (1211-1231)** m. Waldemar the Younger king of Denmark | Ferdinand (1217-1246) m. Sancha de Lara | **(1) Matilda de Dammartin (d. 1258) countess of Boulogne** ═══ Alphonso III, king of Portugal (r. 1248-1279) ═══ **(2) Beatrice of Castile and Leon (1242-1303)**

Maria (1264-1304) | Sancha (1264-1302) | **Branca (1259-1321)** | Affonso | Denis, king of Portugal (r. 1279-1325) ═══ **Elizabeth of Portugal (1271-1336)**

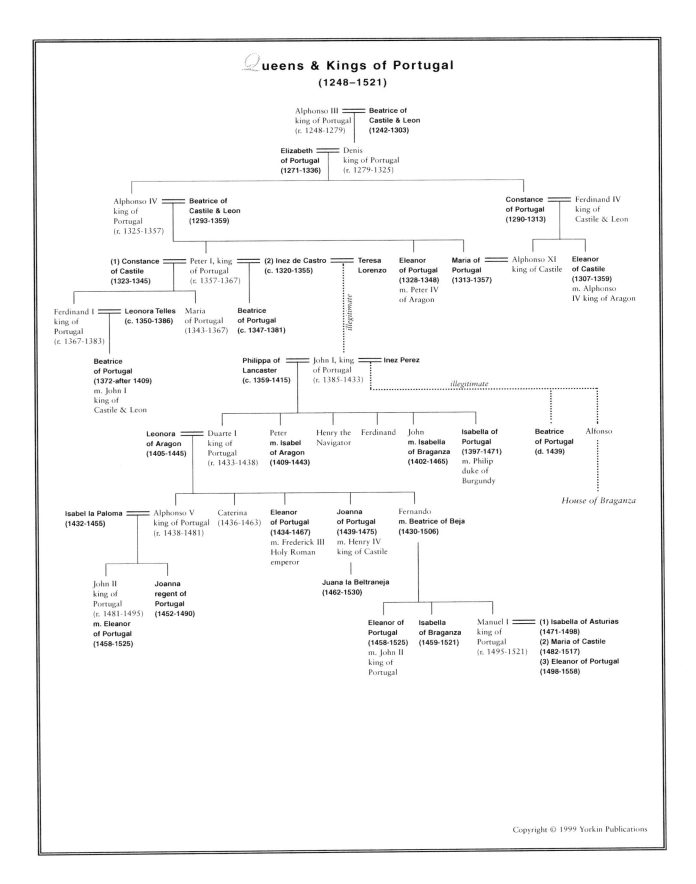

Queens & Kings of Portugal
(1248–1521)

Alphonso III
king of Portugal
(r. 1248-1279)
=== **Beatrice of
Castile & Leon
(1242-1303)**

**Elizabeth
of Portugal
(1271-1336)** === Denis
king of Portugal
(r. 1279-1325)

Alphonso IV
king of
Portugal
(r. 1325-1357)
=== **Beatrice of
Castile & Leon
(1293-1359)**

**Constance
of Portugal
(1290-1313)** === Ferdinand IV
king of
Castile & Leon

**(1) Constance
of Castile
(1323-1345)** === Peter I, king
of Portugal
(r. 1357-1367) === **(2) Inez de Castro
(c. 1320-1355)** === Teresa
Lorenzo

**Eleanor
of Portugal
(1328-1348)**
m. Peter IV
of Aragon

**Maria of
Portugal
(1313-1357)**

Alphonso XI
king of Castile

**Eleanor
of Castile
(1307-1359)**
m. Alphonso
IV king of Aragon

Ferdinand I
king of
Portugal
(r. 1367-1383)
=== **Leonora Telles
(c. 1350-1386)**

Maria
of Portugal
(1343-1367)

**Beatrice
of Portugal
(c. 1347-1381)**

illegitimate

**Beatrice
of Portugal
(1372-after 1409)**
m. John I
king of
Castile & Leon

**Philippa of
Lancaster
(c. 1359-1415)** === John I, king
of Portugal
(r. 1385-1433) === **Inez Perez**

illegitimate

**Leonora
of Aragon
(1405-1445)** === Duarte I
king of
Portugal
(r. 1433-1438)

Peter
m. **Isabel
of Aragon
(1409-1443)**

Henry the
Navigator

Ferdinand

John
m. **Isabella
of Braganza
(1402-1465)**

**Isabella of
Portugal
(1397-1471)**
m. Philip
duke of
Burgundy

**Beatrice
of Portugal
(d. 1439)**

Alfonso

House of Braganza

**Isabel la Paloma
(1432-1455)** === Alphonso V
king of Portugal
(r. 1438-1481)

Caterina
(1436-1463)

**Eleanor
of Portugal
(1434-1467)**
m. Frederick III
Holy Roman
emperor

**Joanna
of Portugal
(1439-1475)**
m. Henry IV
king of Castile

Fernando
m. **Beatrice of Beja
(1430-1506)**

John II
king of
Portugal
(r. 1481-1495)
m. **Eleanor
of Portugal
(1458-1525)**

**Joanna
regent of
Portugal
(1452-1490)**

**Juana la Beltraneja
(1462-1530)**

**Eleanor of
Portugal
(1458-1525)**
m. John II
king of
Portugal

**Isabella
of Braganza
(1459-1521)**

Manuel I
king of
Portugal
(r. 1495-1521)
=== **(1) Isabella of Asturias
(1471-1498)
(2) Maria of Castile
(1482-1517)
(3) Eleanor of Portugal
(1498-1558)**

Copyright © 1999 Yorkin Publications

Queens & Kings of Portugal
(1495–1640)

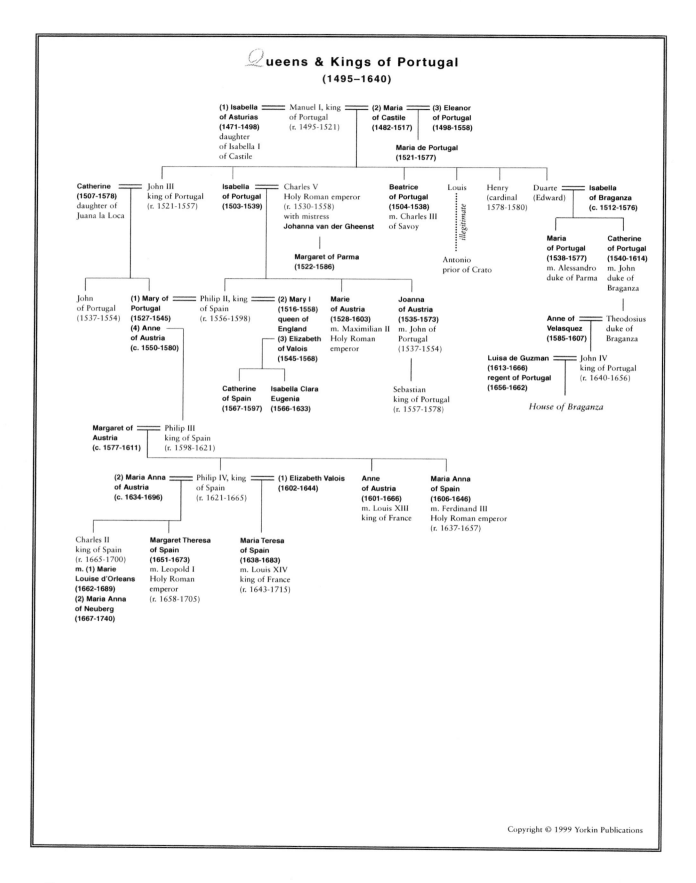

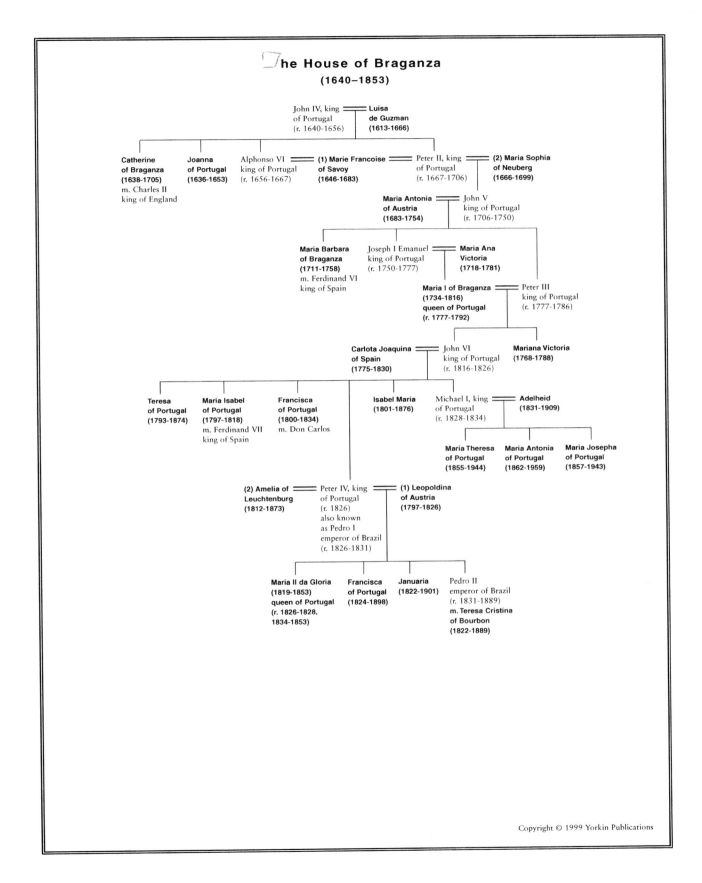

The House of Braganza
(1640–1853)

John IV, king of Portugal (r. 1640-1656) ==== Luisa de Guzman (1613-1666)

Catherine of Braganza (1638-1705) m. Charles II king of England

Joanna of Portugal (1636-1653)

Alphonso VI king of Portugal (r. 1656-1667) ==== (1) Marie Francoise of Savoy (1646-1683) ==== Peter II, king of Portugal (r. 1667-1706) ==== (2) Maria Sophia of Neuberg (1666-1699)

Maria Antonia of Austria (1683-1754) ==== John V king of Portugal (r. 1706-1750)

Maria Barbara of Braganza (1711-1758) m. Ferdinand VI king of Spain

Joseph I Emanuel king of Portugal (r. 1750-1777) ==== Maria Ana Victoria (1718-1781)

Maria I of Braganza (1734-1816) queen of Portugal (r. 1777-1792) ==== Peter III king of Portugal (r. 1777-1786)

Carlota Joaquina of Spain (1775-1830) ==== John VI king of Portugal (r. 1816-1826)

Mariana Victoria (1768-1788)

Teresa of Portugal (1793-1874)

Maria Isabel of Portugal (1797-1818) m. Ferdinand VII king of Spain

Francisca of Portugal (1800-1834) m. Don Carlos

Isabel Maria (1801-1876)

Michael I, king of Portugal (r. 1828-1834) ==== Adelheid (1831-1909)

Maria Theresa of Portugal (1855-1944)

Maria Antonia of Portugal (1862-1959)

Maria Josepha of Portugal (1857-1943)

(2) Amelia of Leuchtenburg (1812-1873) ==== Peter IV, king of Portugal (r. 1826) also known as Pedro I emperor of Brazil (r. 1826-1831) ==== (1) Leopoldina of Austria (1797-1826)

Maria II da Gloria (1819-1853) queen of Portugal (r. 1826-1828, 1834-1853)

Francisca of Portugal (1824-1898)

Januaria (1822-1901)

Pedro II emperor of Brazil (r. 1831-1889) m. Teresa Cristina of Bourbon (1822-1889)

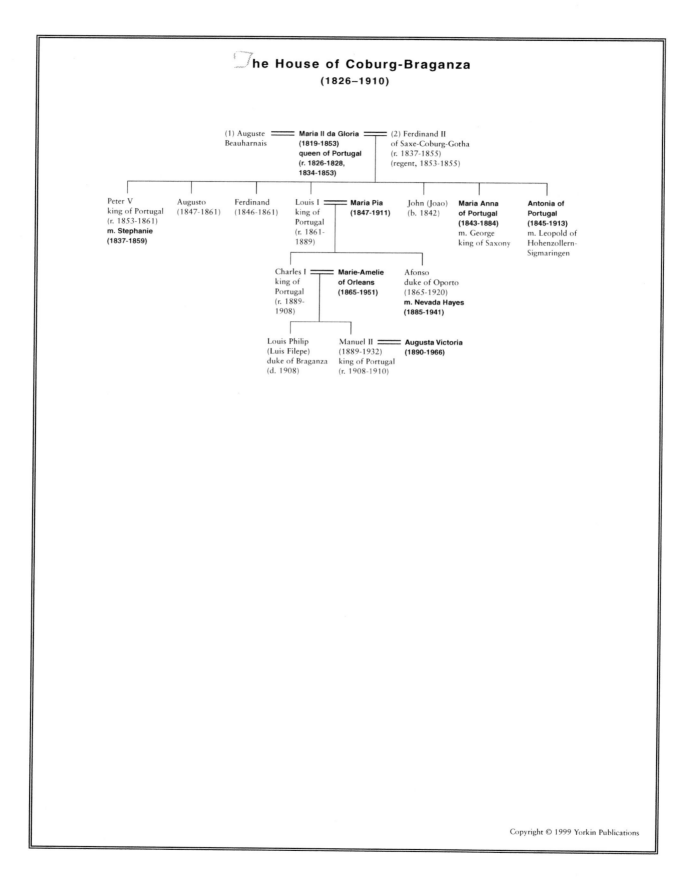

The House of Coburg-Braganza
(1826–1910)

(1) Auguste Beauharnais ══ **Maria II da Gloria (1819-1853) queen of Portugal (r. 1826-1828, 1834-1853)** ══ (2) Ferdinand II of Saxe-Coburg-Gotha (r. 1837-1855) (regent, 1853-1855)

Peter V king of Portugal (r. 1853-1861) **m. Stephanie (1837-1859)**

Augusto (1847-1861)

Ferdinand (1846-1861)

Louis I king of Portugal (r. 1861-1889) ══ **Maria Pia (1847-1911)**

John (Joao) (b. 1842)

Maria Anna of Portugal (1843-1884) m. George king of Saxony

Antonia of Portugal (1845-1913) m. Leopold of Hohenzollern-Sigmaringen

Charles I king of Portugal (r. 1889-1908) ══ **Marie-Amelie of Orleans (1865-1951)**

Afonso duke of Oporto (1865-1920) **m. Nevada Hayes (1885-1941)**

Louis Philip (Luis Filepe) duke of Braganza (d. 1908)

Manuel II (1889-1932) king of Portugal (r. 1908-1910) ══ **Augusta Victoria (1890-1966)**

Copyright © 1999 Yorkin Publications

The Julian Line

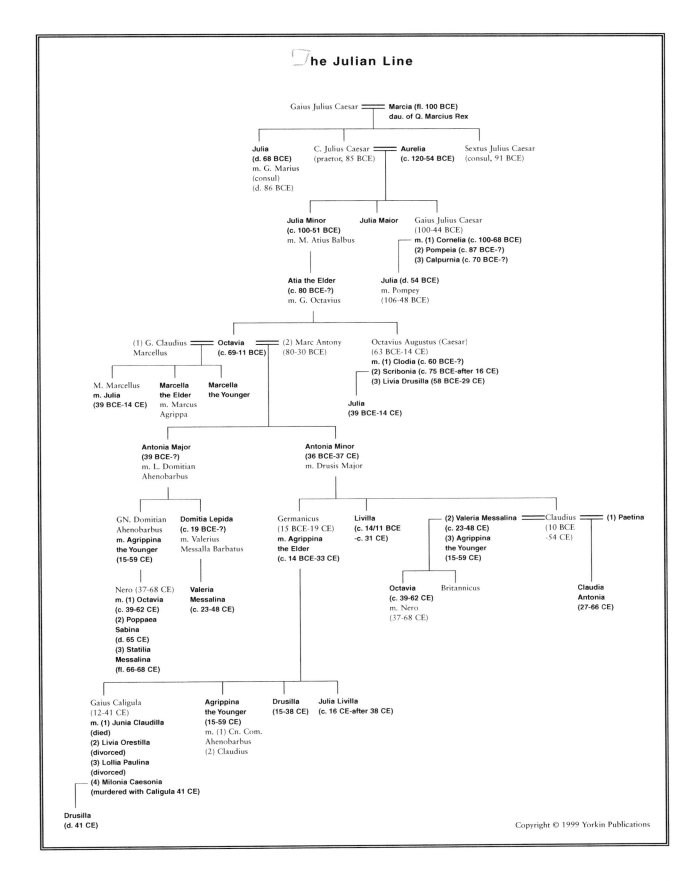

Gaius Julius Caesar ══ **Marcia (fl. 100 BCE)**
dau. of Q. Marcius Rex

Julia
(d. 68 BCE)
m. G. Marius
(consul)
(d. 86 BCE)

C. Julius Caesar ══ **Aurelia**
(praetor, 85 BCE) **(c. 120-54 BCE)**

Sextus Julius Caesar
(consul, 91 BCE)

Julia Minor
(c. 100-51 BCE)
m. M. Atius Balbus

Julia Maior

Gaius Julius Caesar
(100-44 BCE)
m. (1) Cornelia (c. 100-68 BCE)
(2) Pompeia (c. 87 BCE-?)
(3) Calpurnia (c. 70 BCE-?)

Atia the Elder
(c. 80 BCE-?)
m. G. Octavius

Julia (d. 54 BCE)
m. Pompey
(106-48 BCE)

(1) G. Claudius ══ **Octavia** ══ (2) Marc Antony
Marcellus **(c. 69-11 BCE)** (80-30 BCE)

Octavius Augustus (Caesar)
(63 BCE-14 CE)
m. (1) Clodia (c. 60 BCE-?)
(2) Scribonia (c. 75 BCE-after 16 CE)
(3) Livia Drusilla (58 BCE-29 CE)

M. Marcellus
m. Julia
(39 BCE-14 CE)

Marcella
the Elder
m. Marcus
Agrippa

Marcella
the Younger

Julia
(39 BCE-14 CE)

Antonia Major
(39 BCE-?)
m. L. Domitian
Ahenobarbus

Antonia Minor
(36 BCE-37 CE)
m. Drusis Major

GN. Domitian
Ahenobarbus
m. Agrippina
the Younger
(15-59 CE)

Domitia Lepida
(c. 19 BCE-?)
m. Valerius
Messalla Barbatus

Germanicus
(15 BCE-19 CE)
m. Agrippina
the Elder
(c. 14 BCE-33 CE)

Livilla
(c. 14/11 BCE
-c. 31 CE)

(2) Valeria Messalina
(c. 23-48 CE)
(3) Agrippina
the Younger
(15-59 CE)

Claudius
(10 BCE
-54 CE)

(1) Paetina

Nero (37-68 CE)
m. (1) Octavia
(c. 39-62 CE)
(2) Poppaea
Sabina
(d. 65 CE)
(3) Statilia
Messalina
(fl. 66-68 CE)

Valeria
Messalina
(c. 23-48 CE)

Octavia
(c. 39-62 CE)
m. Nero
(37-68 CE)

Britannicus

Claudia
Antonia
(27-66 CE)

Gaius Caligula
(12-41 CE)
m. (1) Junia Claudilla
(died)
(2) Livia Orestilla
(divorced)
(3) Lollia Paulina
(divorced)
(4) Milonia Caesonia
(murdered with Caligula 41 CE)

Agrippina
the Younger
(15-59 CE)
m. (1) Cn. Com.
Ahenobarbus
(2) Claudius

Drusilla
(15-38 CE)

Julia Livilla
(c. 16 CE-after 38 CE)

Drusilla
(d. 41 CE)

Copyright © 1999 Yorkin Publications

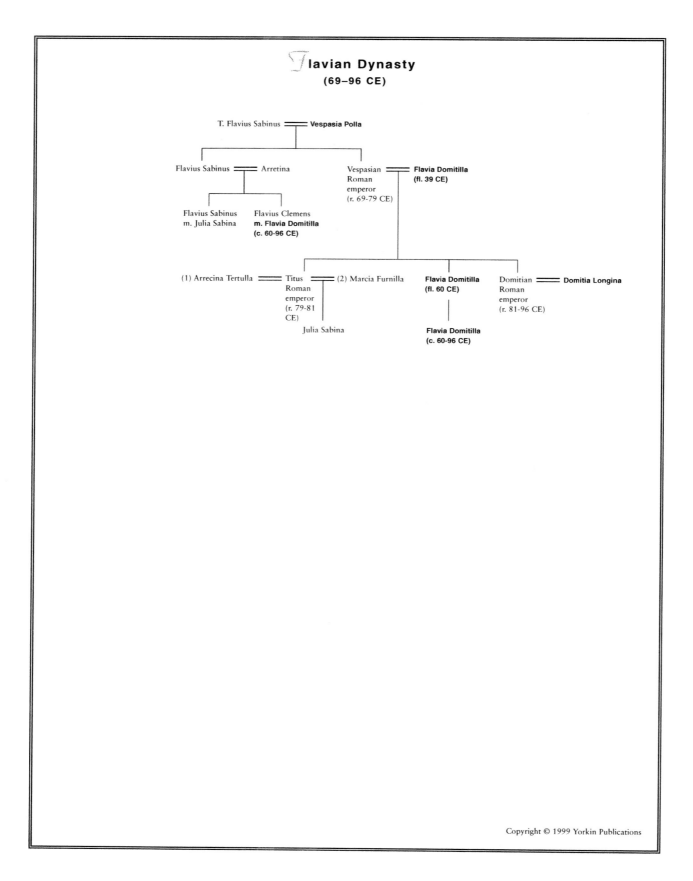

Flavian Dynasty
(69–96 CE)

T. Flavius Sabinus ══ **Vespasia Polla**

Flavius Sabinus ══ Arretina

Vespasian
Roman
emperor
(r. 69-79 CE) ══ **Flavia Domitilla
(fl. 39 CE)**

Flavius Sabinus
m. Julia Sabina

Flavius Clemens
**m. Flavia Domitilla
(c. 60-96 CE)**

(1) Arrecina Tertulla ══ Titus
Roman
emperor
(r. 79-81
CE) ══ (2) Marcia Furnilla

Julia Sabina

**Flavia Domitilla
(fl. 60 CE)**

**Flavia Domitilla
(c. 60-96 CE)**

Domitian
Roman
emperor
(r. 81-96 CE) ══ **Domitia Longina**

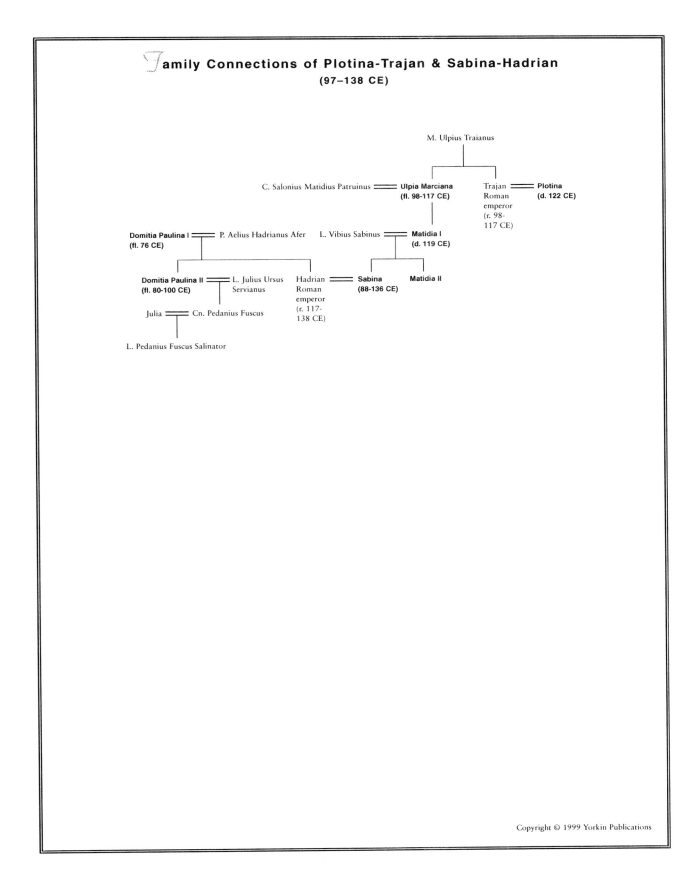

Family Connections of Plotina-Trajan & Sabina-Hadrian
(97–138 CE)

M. Ulpius Traianus

C. Salonius Matidius Patruinus ═══ Ulpia Marciana (fl. 98-117 CE)

Trajan Roman emperor (r. 98-117 CE) ═══ Plotina (d. 122 CE)

Domitia Paulina I (fl. 76 CE) ═══ P. Aelius Hadrianus Afer

L. Vibius Sabinus ═══ Matidia I (d. 119 CE)

Domitia Paulina II (fl. 80-100 CE) ═══ L. Julius Ursus Servianus

Hadrian Roman emperor (r. 117-138 CE) ═══ Sabina (88-136 CE)

Matidia II

Julia ═══ Cn. Pedanius Fuscus

L. Pedanius Fuscus Salinator

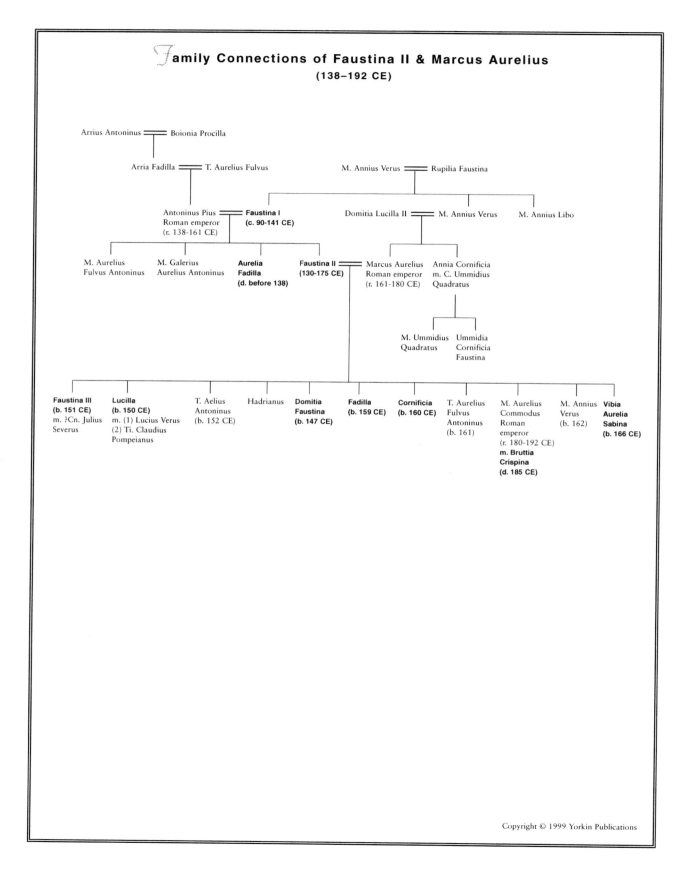

Family Connections of Faustina II & Marcus Aurelius
(138–192 CE)

Arrius Antoninus ══ Boionia Procilla

Arria Fadilla ══ T. Aurelius Fulvus

M. Annius Verus ══ Rupilia Faustina

Antoninus Pius
Roman emperor
(r. 138-161 CE) ══ **Faustina I
(c. 90-141 CE)**

Domitia Lucilla II ══ M. Annius Verus

M. Annius Libo

M. Aurelius
Fulvus Antoninus

M. Galerius
Aurelius Antoninus

**Aurelia
Fadilla
(d. before 138)**

**Faustina II
(130-175 CE)** ══ Marcus Aurelius
Roman emperor
(r. 161-180 CE)

Annia Cornificia
m. C. Ummidius
Quadratus

M. Ummidius
Quadratus

Ummidia
Cornificia
Faustina

**Faustina III
(b. 151 CE)**
m. ?Cn. Julius
Severus

**Lucilla
(b. 150 CE)**
m. (1) Lucius Verus
(2) Ti. Claudius
Pompeianus

T. Aelius
Antoninus
(b. 152 CE)

Hadrianus

**Domitia
Faustina
(b. 147 CE)**

**Fadilla
(b. 159 CE)**

**Cornificia
(b. 160 CE)**

T. Aurelius
Fulvus
Antoninus
(b. 161)

M. Aurelius
Commodus
Roman
emperor
(r. 180-192 CE)
**m. Bruttia
Crispina
(d. 185 CE)**

M. Annius
Verus
(b. 162)

**Vibia
Aurelia
Sabina
(b. 166 CE)**

The House of Constantine
(293–363 CE)

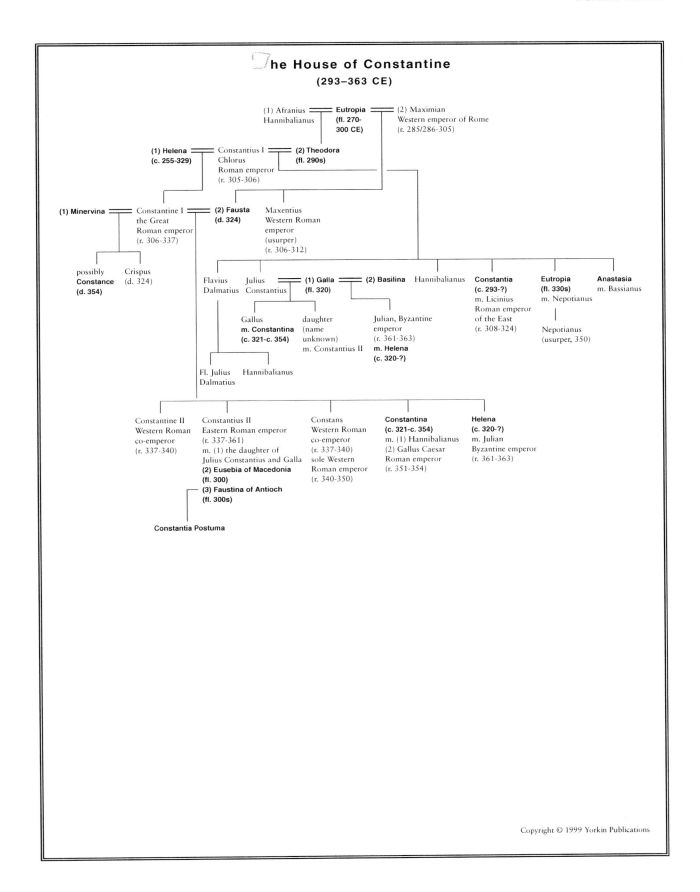

(1) Afranius Hannibalianus ══ **Eutropia (fl. 270-300 CE)** ══ (2) Maximian Western emperor of Rome (r. 285/286-305)

(1) Helena (c. 255-329) ══ Constantius I Chlorus Roman emperor (r. 305-306) ══ **(2) Theodora (fl. 290s)**

(1) Minervina ══ Constantine I the Great Roman emperor (r. 306-337) ══ **(2) Fausta (d. 324)**

Maxentius Western Roman emperor (usurper) (r. 306-312)

possibly **Constance (d. 354)**

Crispus (d. 324)

Flavius Dalmatius

Julius Constantius ══ **(1) Galla (fl. 320)** ══ **(2) Basilina**

Hannibalianus

Constantia (c. 293-?) m. Licinius Roman emperor of the East (r. 308-324)

Eutropia (fl. 330s) m. Nepotianus

Anastasia m. Bassianus

Gallus **m. Constantina (c. 321-c. 354)**

daughter (name unknown) m. Constantius II

Julian, Byzantine emperor (r. 361-363) **m. Helena (c. 320-?)**

Nepotianus (usurper, 350)

Fl. Julius Dalmatius

Hannibalianus

Constantine II Western Roman co-emperor (r. 337-340)

Constantius II Eastern Roman emperor (r. 337-361) m. (1) the daughter of Julius Constantius and Galla **(2) Eusebia of Macedonia (fl. 300)** **(3) Faustina of Antioch (fl. 300s)**

Constans Western Roman co-emperor (r. 337-340) sole Western Roman emperor (r. 340-350)

Constantina (c. 321-c. 354) m. (1) Hannibalianus (2) Gallus Caesar Roman emperor (r. 351-354)

Helena (c. 320-?) m. Julian Byzantine emperor (r. 361-363)

Constantia Postuma

Copyright © 1999 Yorkin Publications

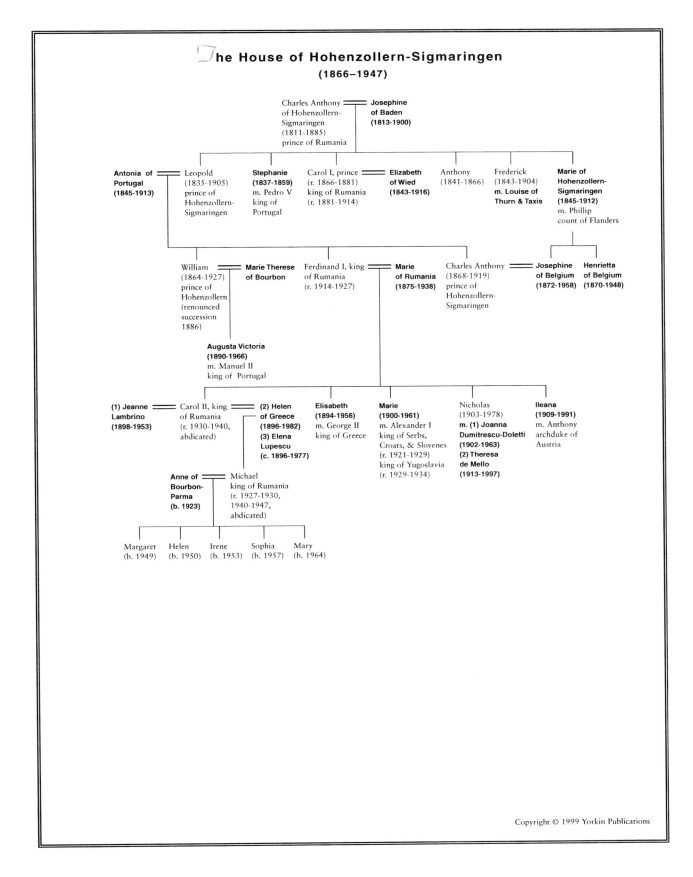

The House of Hohenzollern-Sigmaringen
(1866–1947)

Charles Anthony of Hohenzollern-Sigmaringen (1811-1885) prince of Rumania ══ **Josephine of Baden (1813-1900)**

Antonia of Portugal (1845-1913) ══ Leopold (1835-1905) prince of Hohenzollern-Sigmaringen

Stephanie (1837-1859) m. Pedro V king of Portugal

Carol I, prince (r. 1866-1881) king of Rumania (r. 1881-1914) ══ **Elizabeth of Wied (1843-1916)**

Anthony (1841-1866)

Frederick (1843-1904) **m. Louise of Thurn & Taxis**

Marie of Hohenzollern-Sigmaringen (1845-1912) m. Phillip count of Flanders

William (1864-1927) prince of Hohenzollern (renounced succession 1886) ══ **Marie Therese of Bourbon**

Ferdinand I, king of Rumania (r. 1914-1927) ══ **Marie of Rumania (1875-1938)**

Charles Anthony (1868-1919) prince of Hohenzollern-Sigmaringen ══ **Josephine of Belgium (1872-1958)**

Henrietta of Belgium (1870-1948)

Augusta Victoria (1890-1966) m. Manuel II king of Portugal

(1) Jeanne Lambrino (1898-1953) ══ Carol II, king of Rumania (r. 1930-1940, abdicated) ══ **(2) Helen of Greece (1896-1982)** **(3) Elena Lupescu (c. 1896-1977)**

Elisabeth (1894-1956) m. George II king of Greece

Marie (1900-1961) m. Alexander I king of Serbs, Croats, & Slovenes (r. 1921-1929) king of Yugoslavia (r. 1929-1934)

Nicholas (1903-1978) **m. (1) Joanna Dumitrescu-Doletti (1902-1963)** **(2) Theresa de Mello (1913-1997)**

Ileana (1909-1991) m. Anthony archduke of Austria

Anne of Bourbon-Parma (b. 1923) ══ Michael king of Rumania (r. 1927-1930, 1940-1947, abdicated)

Margaret (b. 1949)

Helen (b. 1950)

Irene (b. 1953)

Sophia (b. 1957)

Mary (b. 1964)

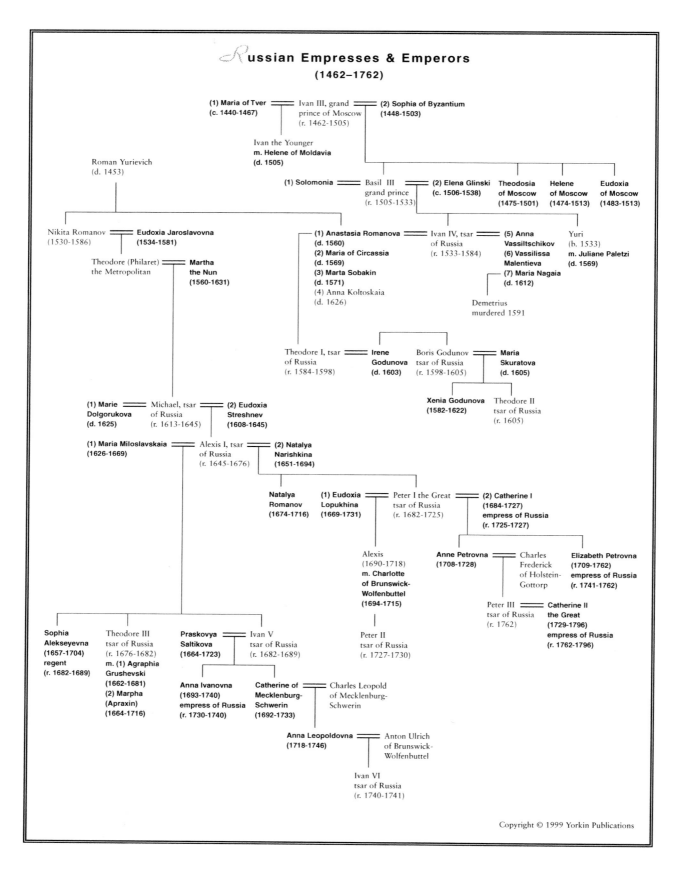

Russian Empresses & Emperors
(1462–1762)

(1) Maria of Tver (c. 1440-1467) ══ Ivan III, grand prince of Moscow (r. 1462-1505) ══ **(2) Sophia of Byzantium** (1448-1503)

Ivan the Younger **m. Helene of Moldavia** (d. 1505)

Roman Yurievich (d. 1453)

(1) Solomonia ══ Basil III grand prince (r. 1505-1533) ══ **(2) Elena Glinski** (c. 1506-1538) | **Theodosia of Moscow** (1475-1501) | **Helene of Moscow** (1474-1513) | **Eudoxia of Moscow** (1483-1513)

Nikita Romanov (1530-1586) ══ **Eudoxia Jaroslavovna** (1534-1581)

(1) Anastasia Romanova (d. 1560) **(2) Maria of Circassia** (d. 1569) **(3) Marta Sobakin** (d. 1571) (4) Anna Koltoskaia (d. 1626) ══ Ivan IV, tsar of Russia (r. 1533-1584) ══ **(5) Anna Vassiltschikov (6) Vassilissa Malentieva (7) Maria Nagaia** (d. 1612) | Yuri (b. 1533) m. Juliane Paletzi (d. 1569)

Theodore (Philaret) the Metropolitan ══ **Martha the Nun** (1560-1631)

Demetrius murdered 1591

Theodore I, tsar of Russia (r. 1584-1598) ══ **Irene Godunova** (d. 1603) | Boris Godunov tsar of Russia (r. 1598-1605) ══ **Maria Skuratova** (d. 1605)

Xenia Godunova (1582-1622) | Theodore II tsar of Russia (r. 1605)

(1) Marie Dolgorukova (d. 1625) ══ Michael, tsar of Russia (r. 1613-1645) ══ **(2) Eudoxia Streshnev** (1608-1645)

(1) Maria Miloslavskaia (1626-1669) ══ Alexis I, tsar of Russia (r. 1645-1676) ══ **(2) Natalya Narishkina** (1651-1694)

Natalya Romanov (1674-1716) | **(1) Eudoxia Lopukhina** (1669-1731) ══ Peter I the Great tsar of Russia (r. 1682-1725) ══ **(2) Catherine I** (1684-1727) empress of Russia (r. 1725-1727)

Alexis (1690-1718) **m. Charlotte of Brunswick-Wolfenbuttel** (1694-1715) | **Anne Petrovna** (1708-1728) ══ Charles Frederick of Holstein-Gottorp | **Elizabeth Petrovna** (1709-1762) empress of Russia (r. 1741-1762)

Peter III tsar of Russia (r. 1762) ══ **Catherine II the Great** (1729-1796) empress of Russia (r. 1762-1796)

Sophia Alekseyevna (1657-1704) regent (r. 1682-1689) | Theodore III tsar of Russia (r. 1676-1682) m. **(1) Agraphia Grushevski** (1662-1681) **(2) Marpha (Apraxin)** (1664-1716) | **Praskovya Saltikova** (1664-1723) ══ Ivan V tsar of Russia (r. 1682-1689) | Peter II tsar of Russia (r. 1727-1730)

Anna Ivanovna (1693-1740) empress of Russia (r. 1730-1740) | **Catherine of Mecklenburg-Schwerin** (1692-1733) ══ Charles Leopold of Mecklenburg-Schwerin

Anna Leopoldovna (1718-1746) ══ Anton Ulrich of Brunswick-Wolfenbuttel

Ivan VI tsar of Russia (r. 1740-1741)

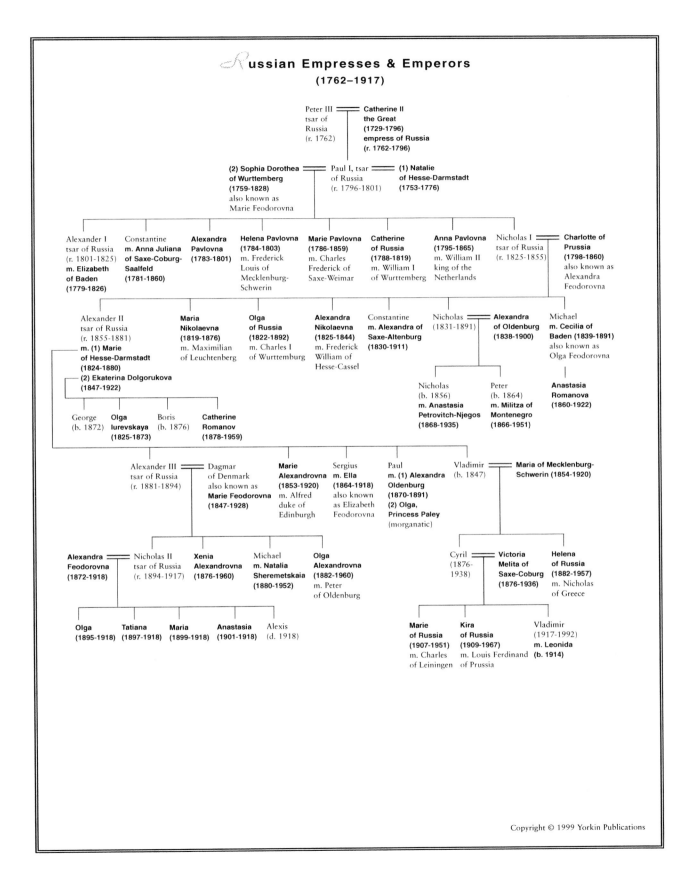

Russian Empresses & Emperors
(1762–1917)

Peter III
tsar of
Russia
(r. 1762)
════
**Catherine II
the Great
(1729-1796)
empress of Russia
(r. 1762-1796)**

**(2) Sophia Dorothea
of Wurttemberg
(1759-1828)
also known as
Marie Feodorovna**
════
Paul I, tsar
of Russia
(r. 1796-1801)
════
**(1) Natalie
of Hesse-Darmstadt
(1753-1776)**

Alexander I
tsar of Russia
(r. 1801-1825)
**m. Elizabeth
of Baden
(1779-1826)**

Constantine
**m. Anna Juliana
of Saxe-Coburg-
Saalfeld
(1781-1860)**

**Alexandra
Pavlovna
(1783-1801)**

**Helena Pavlovna
(1784-1803)**
m. Frederick
Louis of
Mecklenburg-
Schwerin

**Marie Pavlovna
(1786-1859)**
m. Charles
Frederick of
Saxe-Weimar

**Catherine
of Russia
(1788-1819)**
m. William I
of Wurttemberg

**Anna Pavlovna
(1795-1865)**
m. William II
king of the
Netherlands

Nicholas I
tsar of Russia
(r. 1825-1855)
════
**Charlotte of
Prussia
(1798-1860)
also known as
Alexandra
Feodorovna**

Alexander II
tsar of Russia
(r. 1855-1881)
**m. (1) Marie
of Hesse-Darmstadt
(1824-1880)**
**(2) Ekaterina Dolgorukova
(1847-1922)**

**Maria
Nikolaevna
(1819-1876)**
m. Maximilian
of Leuchtenberg

**Olga
of Russia
(1822-1892)**
m. Charles I
of Wurttemburg

**Alexandra
Nikolaevna
(1825-1844)**
m. Frederick
William of
Hesse-Cassel

Constantine
**m. Alexandra of
Saxe-Altenburg
(1830-1911)**

Nicholas
(1831-1891)
════
**Alexandra
of Oldenburg
(1838-1900)**

Michael
**m. Cecilia of
Baden (1839-1891)
also known as
Olga Feodorovna**

George
(b. 1872)

**Olga
Iurevskaya
(1825-1873)**

Boris
(b. 1876)

**Catherine
Romanov
(1878-1959)**

Nicholas
(b. 1856)
**m. Anastasia
Petrovitch-Njegos
(1868-1935)**

Peter
(b. 1864)
**m. Militza of
Montenegro
(1866-1951)**

**Anastasia
Romanova
(1860-1922)**

Alexander III
tsar of Russia
(r. 1881-1894)
════
Dagmar
of Denmark
also known as
**Marie Feodorovna
(1847-1928)**

**Marie
Alexandrovna
(1853-1920)**
m. Alfred
duke of
Edinburgh

Sergius
**m. Ella
(1864-1918)
also known
as Elizabeth
Feodorovna**

Paul
**m. (1) Alexandra
Oldenburg
(1870-1891)
(2) Olga,
Princess Paley**
(morganatic)

Vladimir
(b. 1847)
════
**Maria of Mecklenburg-
Schwerin (1854-1920)**

**Alexandra
Feodorovna
(1872-1918)**
════
Nicholas II
tsar of Russia
(r. 1894-1917)

**Xenia
Alexandrovna
(1876-1960)**

Michael
**m. Natalia
Sheremetskaia
(1880-1952)**

**Olga
Alexandrovna
(1882-1960)**
m. Peter
of Oldenburg

Cyril
(1876-
1938)
════
**Victoria
Melita of
Saxe-Coburg
(1876-1936)**

**Helena
of Russia
(1882-1957)**
m. Nicholas
of Greece

Olga
(1895-1918)

Tatiana
(1897-1918)

**Maria
(1899-1918)**

**Anastasia
(1901-1918)**

Alexis
(d. 1918)

**Marie
of Russia
(1907-1951)**
m. Charles
of Leiningen

**Kira
of Russia
(1909-1967)**
m. Louis Ferdinand
of Prussia

Vladimir
(1917-1992)
**m. Leonida
(b. 1914)**

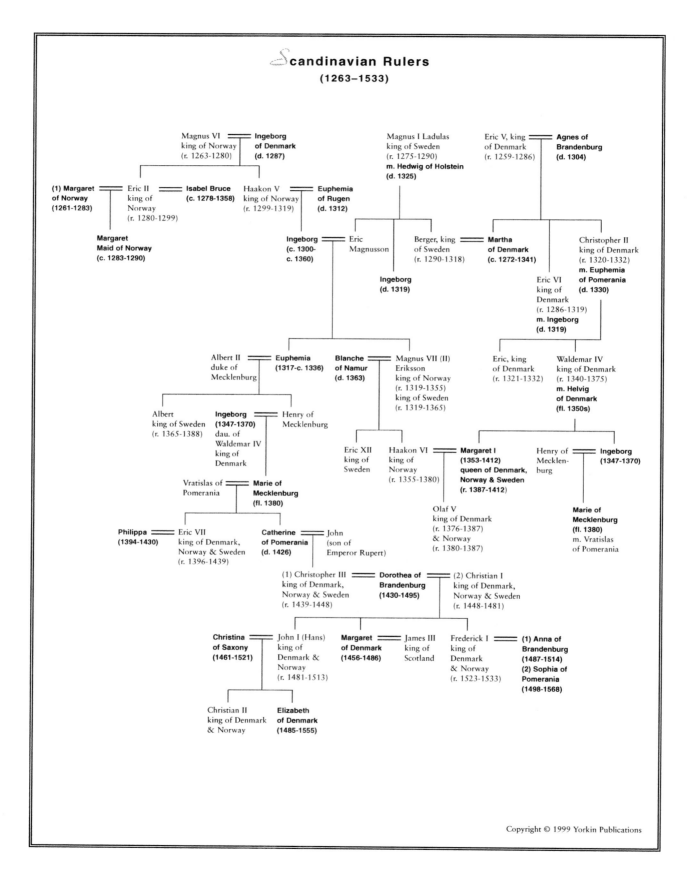

Scandinavian Rulers
(1263–1533)

Magnus VI king of Norway (r. 1263-1280) ═══ **Ingeborg of Denmark (d. 1287)**

Magnus I Ladulas king of Sweden (r. 1275-1290) **m. Hedwig of Holstein (d. 1325)**

Eric V, king of Denmark (r. 1259-1286) ═══ **Agnes of Brandenburg (d. 1304)**

(1) Margaret of Norway (1261-1283) ═══ Eric II king of Norway (r. 1280-1299) ═══ **Isabel Bruce (c. 1278-1358)** ─── Haakon V king of Norway (r. 1299-1319) ═══ **Euphemia of Rugen (d. 1312)**

Margaret Maid of Norway (c. 1283-1290)

Ingeborg (c. 1300- c. 1360) ═══ Eric Magnusson

Berger, king of Sweden (r. 1290-1318) ═══ **Martha of Denmark (c. 1272-1341)**

Christopher II king of Denmark (r. 1320-1332) **m. Euphemia of Pomerania (d. 1330)**

Ingeborg (d. 1319)

Eric VI king of Denmark (r. 1286-1319) **m. Ingeborg (d. 1319)**

Albert II duke of Mecklenburg ═══ **Euphemia (1317-c. 1336)**

Blanche of Namur (d. 1363) ═══ Magnus VII (II) Eriksson king of Norway (r. 1319-1355) king of Sweden (r. 1319-1365)

Eric, king of Denmark (r. 1321-1332)

Waldemar IV king of Denmark (r. 1340-1375) **m. Helvig of Denmark (fl. 1350s)**

Albert king of Sweden (r. 1365-1388) ─── **Ingeborg (1347-1370) dau. of Waldemar IV king of Denmark** ═══ Henry of Mecklenburg

Eric XII king of Sweden

Haakon VI king of Norway (r. 1355-1380) ═══ **Margaret I (1353-1412) queen of Denmark, Norway & Sweden (r. 1387-1412)**

Henry of Mecklenburg ═══ **Ingeborg (1347-1370)**

Vratislas of Pomerania ═══ **Marie of Mecklenburg (fl. 1380)**

Olaf V king of Denmark (r. 1376-1387) & Norway (r. 1380-1387)

Marie of Mecklenburg (fl. 1380) m. Vratislas of Pomerania

Philippa (1394-1430) ═══ Eric VII king of Denmark, Norway & Sweden (r. 1396-1439)

Catherine of Pomerania (d. 1426) ═══ John (son of Emperor Rupert)

(1) Christopher III king of Denmark, Norway & Sweden (r. 1439-1448) ═══ **Dorothea of Brandenburg (1430-1495)** ═══ **(2) Christian I** king of Denmark, Norway & Sweden (r. 1448-1481)

Christina of Saxony (1461-1521) ═══ John I (Hans) king of Denmark & Norway (r. 1481-1513)

Margaret of Denmark (1456-1486) ═══ James III king of Scotland

Frederick I king of Denmark & Norway (r. 1523-1533) ═══ **(1) Anna of Brandenburg (1487-1514) (2) Sophia of Pomerania (1498-1568)**

Christian II king of Denmark & Norway ─── **Elizabeth of Denmark (1485-1555)**

Copyright © 1999 Yorkin Publications

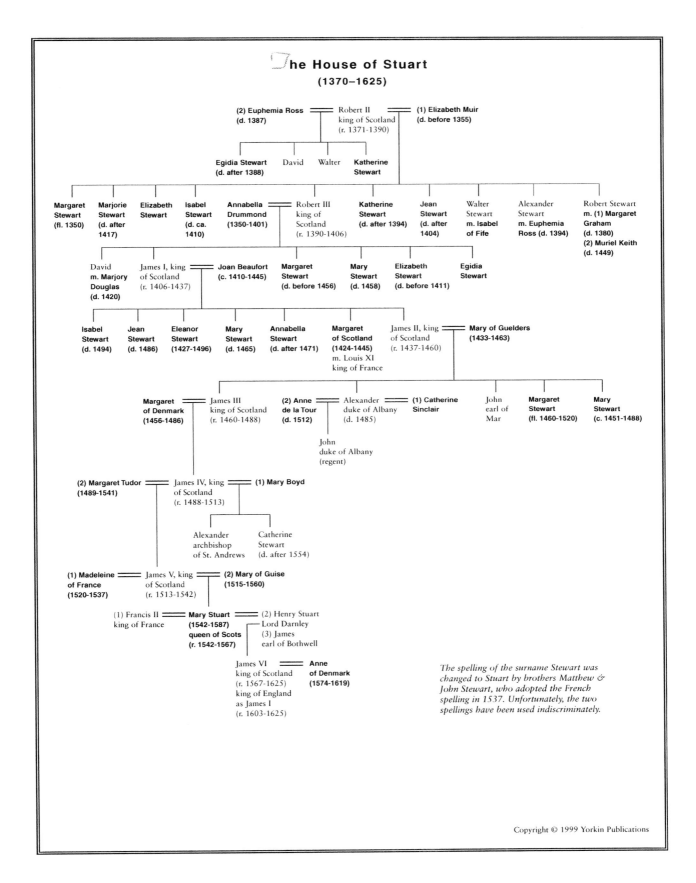

The House of Stuart
(1370–1625)

(2) Euphemia Ross (d. 1387) ═══ Robert II king of Scotland (r. 1371-1390) ═══ **(1) Elizabeth Muir** (d. before 1355)

Egidia Stewart (d. after 1388) — David — Walter — Katherine Stewart

Margaret Stewart (fl. 1350) — **Marjorie Stewart** (d. after 1417) — **Elizabeth Stewart** — **Isabel Stewart** (d. ca. 1410) — **Annabella Drummond** (1350-1401) ═══ Robert III king of Scotland (r. 1390-1406) — **Katherine Stewart** (d. after 1394) — **Jean Stewart** (d. after 1404) — Walter Stewart m. Isabel of Fife — Alexander Stewart m. Euphemia Ross (d. 1394) — Robert Stewart m. (1) Margaret Graham (d. 1380) (2) Muriel Keith (d. 1449)

David m. Marjory Douglas (d. 1420) — James I, king of Scotland (r. 1406-1437) ═══ **Joan Beaufort** (c. 1410-1445) — **Margaret Stewart** (d. before 1456) — **Mary Stewart** (d. 1458) — **Elizabeth Stewart** (d. before 1411) — **Egidia Stewart**

Isabel Stewart (d. 1494) — **Jean Stewart** (d. 1486) — **Eleanor Stewart** (1427-1496) — **Mary Stewart** (d. 1465) — **Annabella Stewart** (d. after 1471) — **Margaret of Scotland** (1424-1445) m. Louis XI king of France — James II, king of Scotland (r. 1437-1460) ═══ **Mary of Guelders** (1433-1463)

Margaret of Denmark (1456-1486) ═══ James III king of Scotland (r. 1460-1488) — **(2) Anne de la Tour** (d. 1512) ═══ Alexander duke of Albany (d. 1485) ═══ **(1) Catherine Sinclair** — John earl of Mar — **Margaret Stewart** (fl. 1460-1520) — **Mary Stewart** (c. 1451-1488)

John duke of Albany (regent)

(2) Margaret Tudor (1489-1541) ═══ James IV, king of Scotland (r. 1488-1513) ═══ **(1) Mary Boyd**

Alexander archbishop of St. Andrews — Catherine Stewart (d. after 1554)

(1) Madeleine of France (1520-1537) ═══ James V, king of Scotland (r. 1513-1542) ═══ **(2) Mary of Guise** (1515-1560)

(1) Francis II king of France ═══ **Mary Stuart** (1542-1587) queen of Scots (r. 1542-1567) ═══ (2) Henry Stuart Lord Darnley (3) James earl of Bothwell

James VI king of Scotland (r. 1567-1625) king of England as James I (r. 1603-1625) ═══ **Anne of Denmark** (1574-1619)

The spelling of the surname Stewart was changed to Stuart by brothers Matthew & John Stewart, who adopted the French spelling in 1537. Unfortunately, the two spellings have been used indiscriminately.

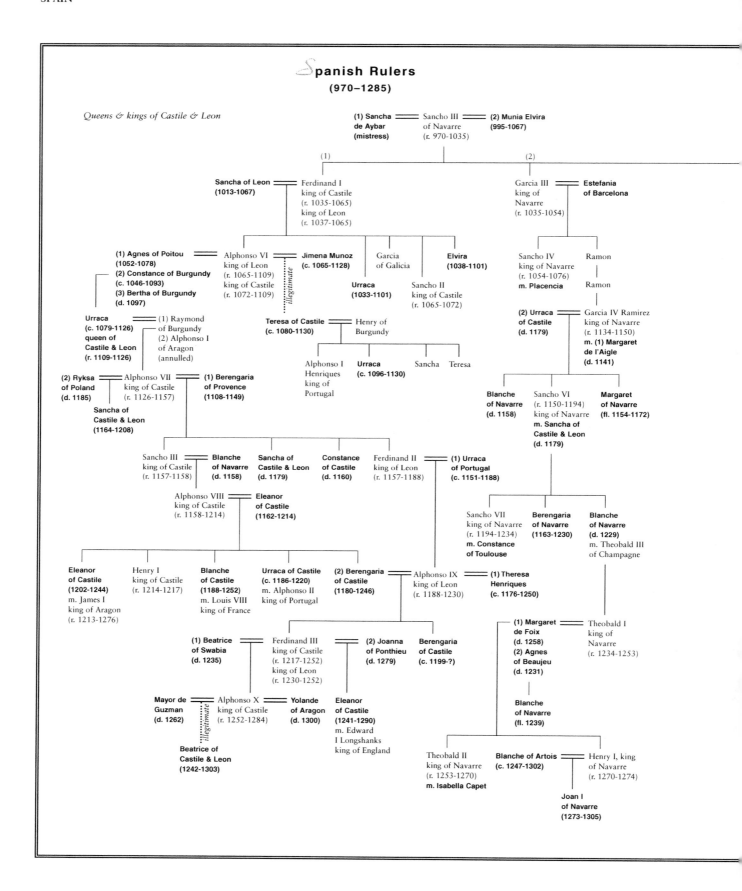

$\mathcal{S}$panish Rulers
(970–1285)

Queens & kings of Castile & Leon

Queens & kings of Aragon

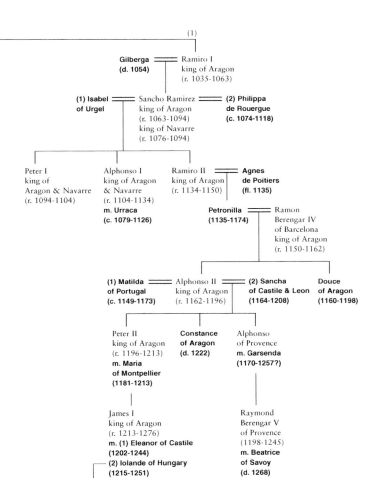

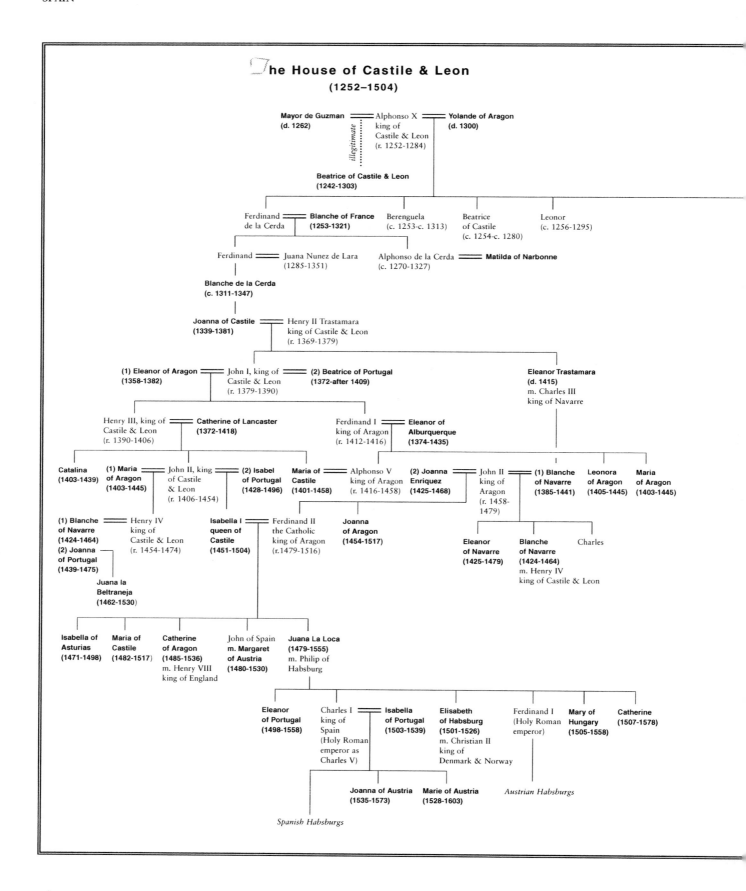

The House of Castile & Leon

(1252–1504)

Mayor de Guzman (d. 1262) ══ *illegitimate* ══ Alphonso X king of Castile & Leon (r. 1252-1284) ══ Yolande of Aragon (d. 1300)

Beatrice of Castile & Leon (1242-1303)

Ferdinand de la Cerda ══ Blanche of France (1253-1321) — Berenguela (c. 1253-c. 1313) — Beatrice of Castile (c. 1254-c. 1280) — Leonor (c. 1256-1295)

Ferdinand ══ Juana Nunez de Lara (1285-1351) — Alphonso de la Cerda (c. 1270-1327) ══ Matilda of Narbonne

Blanche de la Cerda (c. 1311-1347)

Joanna of Castile (1339-1381) ══ Henry II Trastamara king of Castile & Leon (r. 1369-1379)

(1) Eleanor of Aragon (1358-1382) ══ John I, king of Castile & Leon (r. 1379-1390) ══ (2) Beatrice of Portugal (1372-after 1409) — Eleanor Trastamara (d. 1415) m. Charles III king of Navarre

Henry III, king of Castile & Leon (r. 1390-1406) ══ Catherine of Lancaster (1372-1418) — Ferdinand I king of Aragon (r. 1412-1416) ══ Eleanor of Alburquerque (1374-1435)

Catalina (1403-1439) — (1) Maria of Aragon (1403-1445) ══ John II, king of Castile & Leon (r. 1406-1454) ══ (2) Isabel of Portugal (1428-1496) — Maria of Castile (1401-1458) ══ Alphonso V king of Aragon (r. 1416-1458) — (2) Joanna Enriquez (1425-1468) ══ John II king of Aragon (r. 1458-1479) ══ (1) Blanche of Navarre (1385-1441) — Leonora of Aragon (1405-1445) — Maria of Aragon (1403-1445)

(1) Blanche of Navarre (1424-1464) (2) Joanna of Portugal (1439-1475) ══ Henry IV king of Castile & Leon (r. 1454-1474) — Isabella I queen of Castile (1451-1504) ══ Ferdinand II the Catholic king of Aragon (r.1479-1516) — Joanna of Aragon (1454-1517) — Eleanor of Navarre (1425-1479) — Blanche of Navarre (1424-1464) m. Henry IV king of Castile & Leon — Charles

Juana la Beltraneja (1462-1530)

Isabella of Asturias (1471-1498) — Maria of Castile (1482-1517) — Catherine of Aragon (1485-1536) m. Henry VIII king of England — John of Spain m. Margaret of Austria (1480-1530) — Juana La Loca (1479-1555) m. Philip of Habsburg

Eleanor of Portugal (1498-1558) — Charles I king of Spain (Holy Roman emperor as Charles V) ══ Isabella of Portugal (1503-1539) — Elisabeth of Habsburg (1501-1526) m. Christian II king of Denmark & Norway — Ferdinand I (Holy Roman emperor) — Mary of Hungary (1505-1558) — Catherine (1507-1578)

Joanna of Austria (1535-1573) — Marie of Austria (1528-1603)

Austrian Habsburgs

Spanish Habsburgs

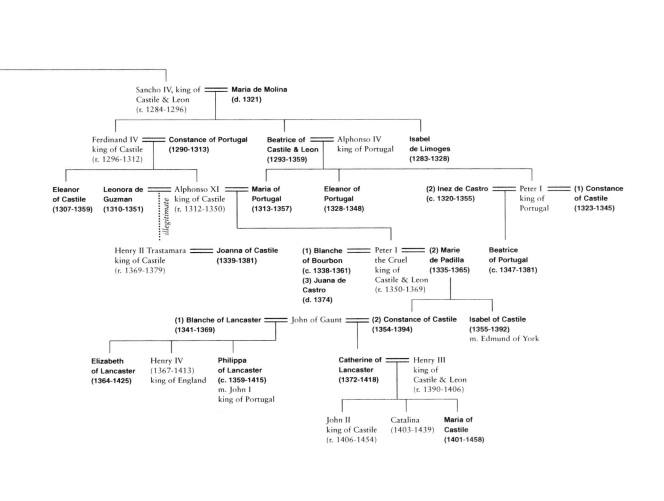

Sancho IV, king of ===== **Maria de Molina**
Castile & Leon   **(d. 1321)**
(r. 1284-1296)

Ferdinand IV ===== **Constance of Portugal**   **Beatrice of** ===== Alphonso IV   **Isabel**
king of Castile   **(1290-1313)**   **Castile & Leon**   king of Portugal   **de Limoges**
(r. 1296-1312)   **(1293-1359)**   **(1283-1328)**

Eleanor   **Leonora de**   Alphonso XI   **Maria of**   **Eleanor of**   **(2) Inez de Castro**   Peter I   **(1) Constance**
of Castile **Guzman**   king of Castile **Portugal**   **Portugal**   **(c. 1320-1355)**   king of   **of Castile**
(1307-1359) **(1310-1351)**   (r. 1312-1350) **(1313-1357)** **(1328-1348)**   Portugal   **(1323-1345)**
                          illegitimate

Henry II Trastamara ===== **Joanna of Castile**   **(1) Blanche** ===== Peter I ===== **(2) Marie**   **Beatrice**
king of Castile   **(1339-1381)**   **of Bourbon**   the Cruel   **de Padilla**   **of Portugal**
(r. 1369-1379)   **(c. 1338-1361)**   king of   **(1335-1365)**   **(c. 1347-1381)**
                                                     (3) Juana de   Castile & Leon
                                                     Castro   (r. 1350-1369)
                                                     (d. 1374)

(1) Blanche of Lancaster ===== John of Gaunt ===== **(2) Constance of Castile**   **Isabel of Castile**
(1341-1369)   **(1354-1394)**   **(1355-1392)**
                                                                                         m. Edmund of York

Elizabeth   Henry IV   **Philippa**   **Catherine of** ===== Henry III
of Lancaster (1367-1413)   **of Lancaster**   **Lancaster**   king of
(1364-1425)   king of England   **(c. 1359-1415)**   **(1372-1418)**   Castile & Leon
                                    m. John I   (r. 1390-1406)
                                    king of Portugal

                                    John II   Catalina   **Maria of**
                                    king of Castile   **(1403-1439)**   **Castile**
                                    (r. 1406-1454)   **(1401-1458)**

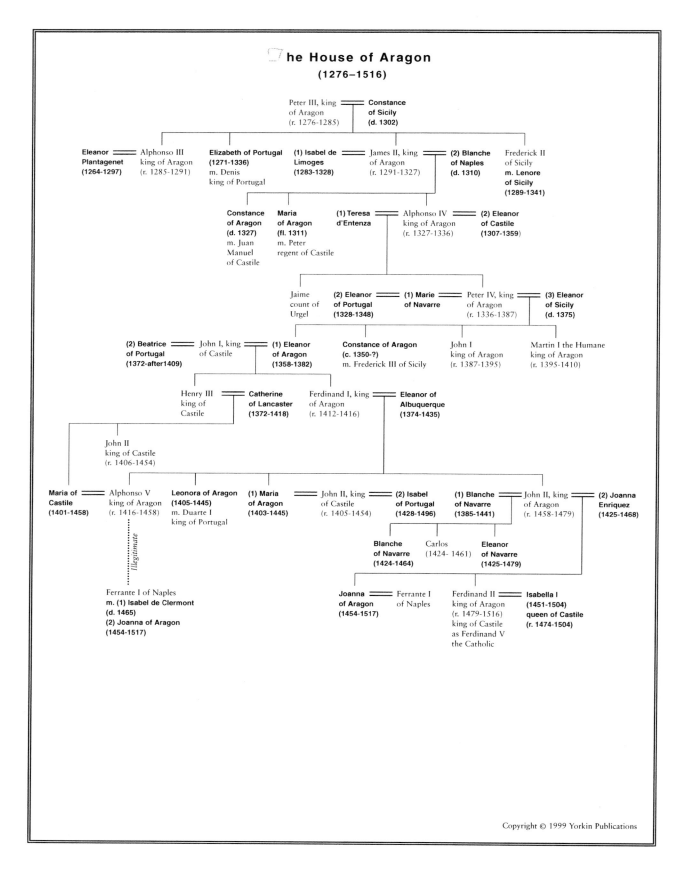

The House of Aragon
(1276–1516)

The Spanish Succession
(1700)

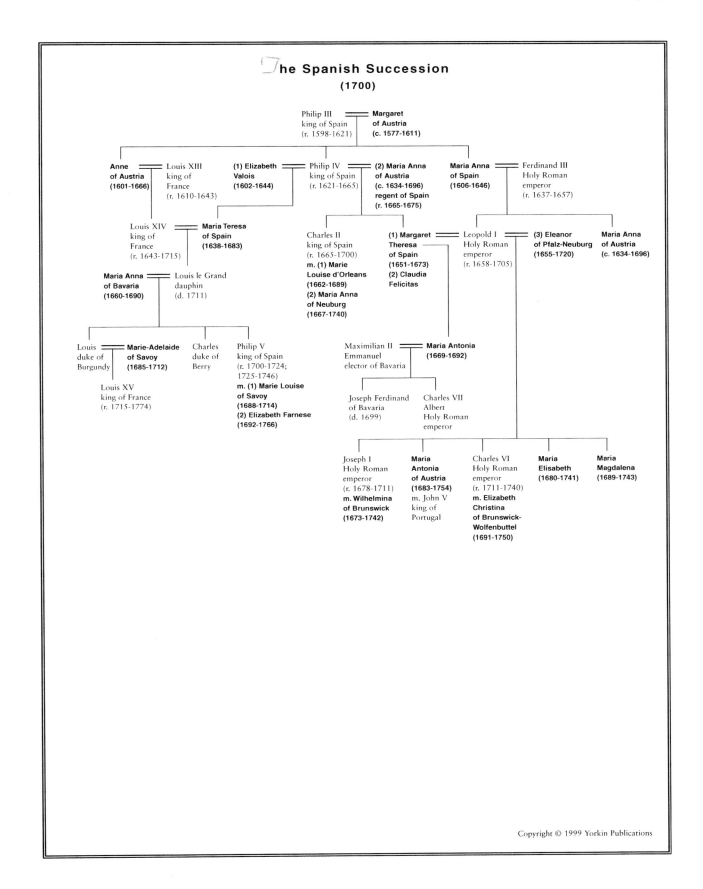

Philip III
king of Spain
(r. 1598-1621)
═══ Margaret
of Austria
(c. 1577-1611)

Anne
of Austria
(1601-1666)
═══ Louis XIII
king of
France
(r. 1610-1643)

(1) Elizabeth
Valois
(1602-1644)
═══ Philip IV
king of Spain
(r. 1621-1665)
═══ (2) Maria Anna
of Austria
(c. 1634-1696)
regent of Spain
(r. 1665-1675)

Maria Anna
of Spain
(1606-1646)
═══ Ferdinand III
Holy Roman
emperor
(r. 1637-1657)

Louis XIV
king of
France
(r. 1643-1715)
═══ Maria Teresa
of Spain
(1638-1683)

Charles II
king of Spain
(r. 1665-1700)
m. (1) Marie
Louise d'Orleans
(1662-1689)
(2) Maria Anna
of Neuburg
(1667-1740)

(1) Margaret
Theresa
of Spain
(1651-1673)
(2) Claudia
Felicitas
═══ Leopold I
Holy Roman
emperor
(r. 1658-1705)
═══ (3) Eleanor
of Pfalz-Neuburg
(1655-1720)

Maria Anna
of Austria
(c. 1634-1696)

Maria Anna
of Bavaria
(1660-1690)
═══ Louis le Grand
dauphin
(d. 1711)

Louis
duke of
Burgundy
═══ Marie-Adelaide
of Savoy
(1685-1712)

Charles
duke of
Berry

Philip V
king of Spain
(r. 1700-1724;
1725-1746)
m. (1) Marie Louise
of Savoy
(1688-1714)
(2) Elizabeth Farnese
(1692-1766)

Maximilian II
Emmanuel
elector of Bavaria
═══ Maria Antonia
(1669-1692)

Louis XV
king of France
(r. 1715-1774)

Joseph Ferdinand
of Bavaria
(d. 1699)

Charles VII
Albert
Holy Roman
emperor

Joseph I
Holy Roman
emperor
(r. 1678-1711)
m. Wilhelmina
of Brunswick
(1673-1742)

Maria
Antonia
of Austria
(1683-1754)
m. John V
king of
Portugal

Charles VI
Holy Roman
emperor
(r. 1711-1740)
m. Elizabeth
Christina
of Brunswick-
Wolfenbuttel
(1691-1750)

Maria
Elisabeth
(1680-1741)

Maria
Magdalena
(1689-1743)

Copyright © 1999 Yorkin Publications

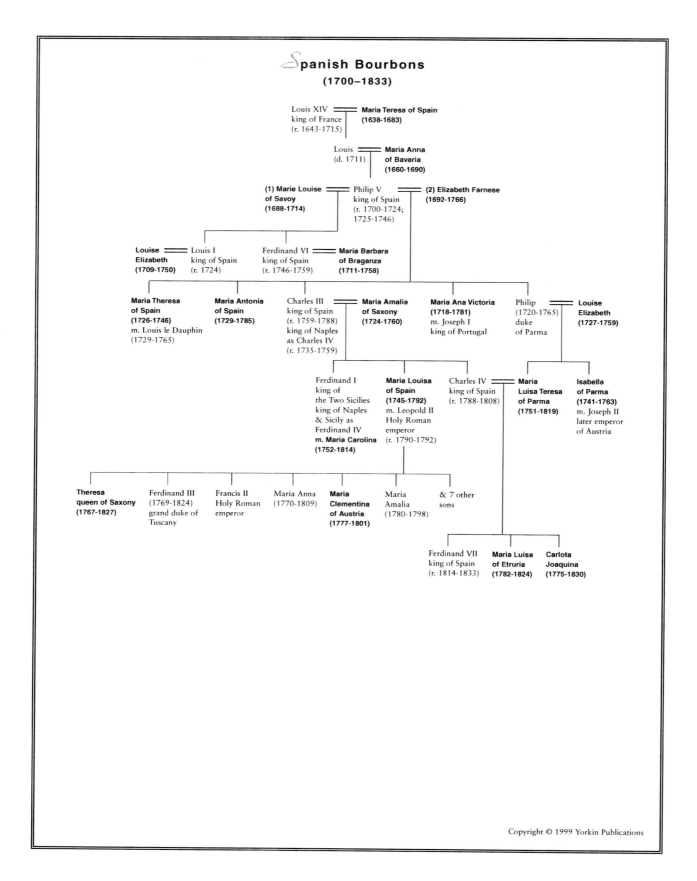

Spanish Bourbons
(1700–1833)

Louis XIV
king of France
(r. 1643-1715) ═══ **Maria Teresa of Spain
(1638-1683)**

Louis
(d. 1711) ═══ **Maria Anna
of Bavaria
(1660-1690)**

**(1) Marie Louise
of Savoy
(1688-1714)** ═══ Philip V
king of Spain
(r. 1700-1724;
1725-1746) ═══ **(2) Elizabeth Farnese
(1692-1766)**

**Louise
Elizabeth
(1709-1750)** ═══ Louis I
king of Spain
(r. 1724)

Ferdinand VI
king of Spain
(r. 1746-1759) ═══ **Maria Barbara
of Braganza
(1711-1758)**

**Maria Theresa
of Spain
(1726-1746)
m. Louis le Dauphin
(1729-1765)**

**Maria Antonia
of Spain
(1729-1785)**

Charles III
king of Spain
(r. 1759-1788)
king of Naples
as Charles IV
(r. 1735-1759) ═══ **Maria Amalia
of Saxony
(1724-1760)**

**Maria Ana Victoria
(1718-1781)**
m. Joseph I
king of Portugal

Philip
(1720-1765)
duke
of Parma ═══ **Louise
Elizabeth
(1727-1759)**

Ferdinand I
king of
the Two Sicilies
king of Naples
& Sicily as
Ferdinand IV
**m. Maria Carolina
(1752-1814)**

**Maria Louisa
of Spain
(1745-1792)
m. Leopold II
Holy Roman
emperor
(r. 1790-1792)**

Charles IV
king of Spain
(r. 1788-1808) ═══ **Maria
Luisa Teresa
of Parma
(1751-1819)**

**Isabella
of Parma
(1741-1763)
m. Joseph II
later emperor
of Austria**

**Theresa
queen of Saxony
(1767-1827)**

Ferdinand III
(1769-1824)
grand duke of
Tuscany

Francis II
Holy Roman
emperor

Maria Anna
(1770-1809)

**Maria
Clementina
of Austria
(1777-1801)**

Maria
Amalia
(1780-1798)

& 7 other
sons

Ferdinand VII
king of Spain
(r. 1814-1833)

**Maria Luisa
of Etruria
(1782-1824)**

**Carlota
Joaquina
(1775-1830)**

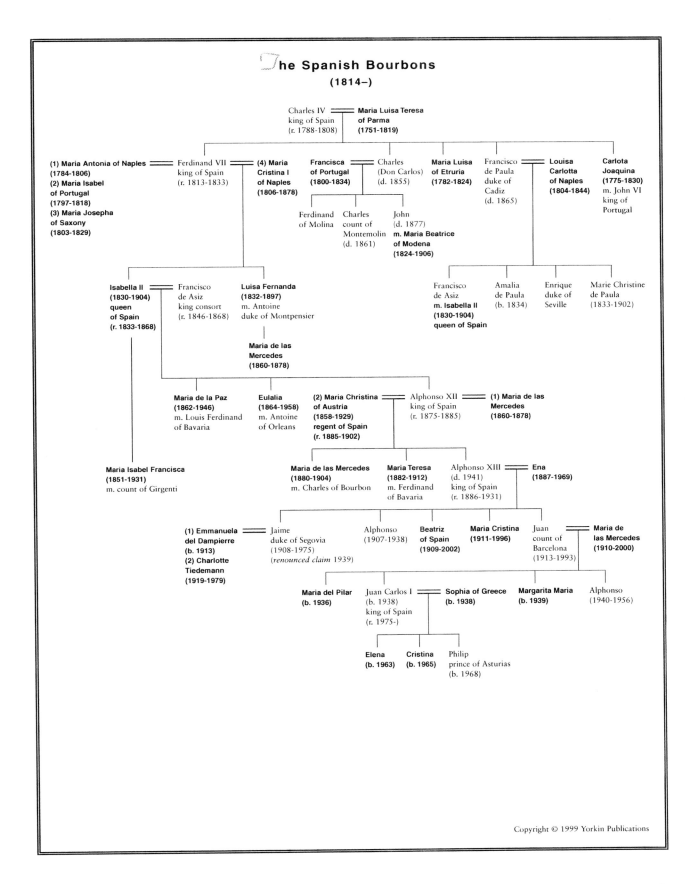

The Spanish Bourbons
(1814—)

Charles IV
king of Spain
(r. 1788-1808)
═══ **Maria Luisa Teresa
of Parma
(1751-1819)**

**(1) Maria Antonia of Naples
(1784-1806)
(2) Maria Isabel
of Portugal
(1797-1818)
(3) Maria Josepha
of Saxony
(1803-1829)** ═══ Ferdinand VII
king of Spain
(r. 1813-1833) ═══ **(4) Maria
Cristina I
of Naples
(1806-1878)**

**Francisca
of Portugal
(1800-1834)** ═══ Charles
(Don Carlos)
(d. 1855)

Maria Luisa
of Etruria
(1782-1824)

Francisco
de Paula
duke of
Cadiz
(d. 1865) ═══ **Louisa
Carlotta
of Naples
(1804-1844)**

**Carlota
Joaquina
(1775-1830)**
m. John VI
king of
Portugal

Ferdinand
of Molina

Charles
count of
Montemolin
(d. 1861)

John
(d. 1877)
**m. Maria Beatrice
of Modena
(1824-1906)**

Francisco
de Asiz
**m. Isabella II
(1830-1904)
queen of Spain**

Amalia
de Paula
(b. 1834)

Enrique
duke of
Seville

Marie Christine
de Paula
(1833-1902)

**Isabella II
(1830-1904)
queen
of Spain
(r. 1833-1868)** ═══ Francisco
de Asiz
king consort
(r. 1846-1868) ═══ **Luisa
Fernanda
(1832-1897)**
m. Antoine
duke of Montpensier

**Maria de las
Mercedes
(1860-1878)**

**Maria de la Paz
(1862-1946)**
m. Louis Ferdinand
of Bavaria

**Eulalia
(1864-1958)**
m. Antoine
of Orleans

**(2) Maria Christina
of Austria
(1858-1929)
regent of Spain
(r. 1885-1902)** ═══ Alphonso XII
king of Spain
(r. 1875-1885) ═══ **(1) Maria de las
Mercedes
(1860-1878)**

**Maria Isabel Francisca
(1851-1931)**
m. count of Girgenti

**Maria de las Mercedes
(1880-1904)**
m. Charles of Bourbon

**Maria Teresa
(1882-1912)**
m. Ferdinand
of Bavaria

Alphonso XIII
(d. 1941)
king of Spain
(r. 1886-1931) ═══ **Ena
(1887-1969)**

**(1) Emmanuela
del Dampierre
(b. 1913)
(2) Charlotte
Tiedemann
(1919-1979)** ═══ Jaime
duke of Segovia
(1908-1975)
(*renounced claim* 1939)

Alphonso
(1907-1938)

**Beatriz
of Spain
(1909-2002)**

**Maria Cristina
(1911-1996)**

Juan
count of
Barcelona
(1913-1993) ═══ **Maria de
las Mercedes
(1910-2000)**

**Maria del Pilar
(b. 1936)**

Juan Carlos I
(b. 1938)
king of Spain
(r. 1975-) ═══ **Sophia of Greece
(b. 1938)**

**Margarita Maria
(b. 1939)**

Alphonso
(1940-1956)

**Elena
(b. 1963)**

**Cristina
(b. 1965)**

Philip
prince of Asturias
(b. 1968)

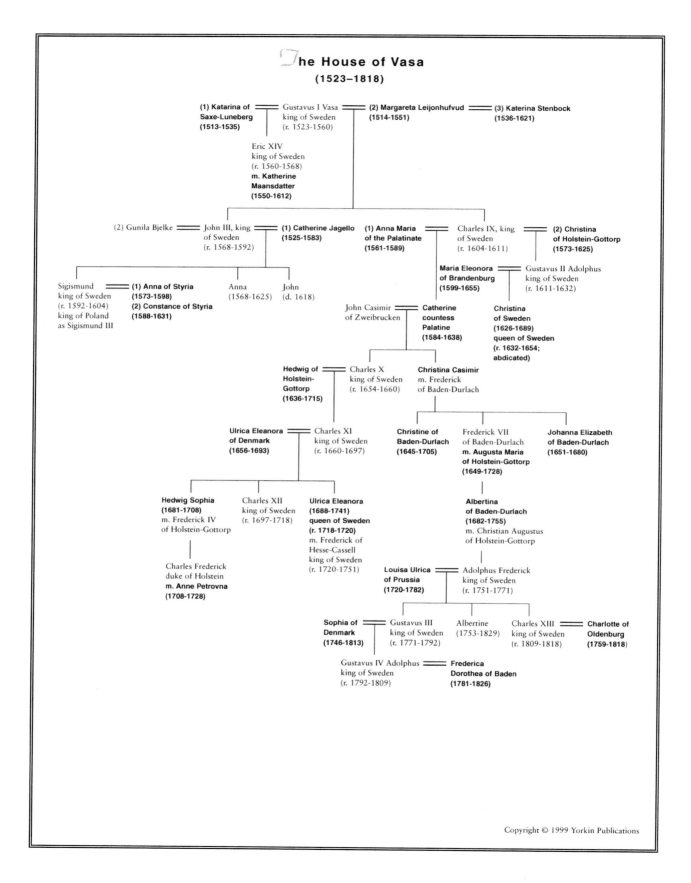

The House of Vasa
(1523–1818)

(1) Katarina of Saxe-Luneberg (1513-1535) ══ Gustavus I Vasa king of Sweden (r. 1523-1560) ══ **(2) Margareta Leijonhufvud (1514-1551)** ══ **(3) Katerina Stenbock (1536-1621)**

Eric XIV king of Sweden (r. 1560-1568) **m. Katherine Maansdatter (1550-1612)**

(2) Gunila Bjelke ══ John III, king of Sweden (r. 1568-1592) ══ **(1) Catherine Jagello (1525-1583)**   **(1) Anna Maria of the Palatinate (1561-1589)**   Charles IX, king of Sweden (r. 1604-1611) ══ **(2) Christina of Holstein-Gottorp (1573-1625)**

Sigismund king of Sweden (r. 1592-1604) king of Poland as Sigismund III ══ **(1) Anna of Styria (1573-1598)** **(2) Constance of Styria (1588-1631)**

Anna (1568-1625)

John (d. 1618)

Maria Eleonora of Brandenburg (1599-1655) ══ Gustavus II Adolphus king of Sweden (r. 1611-1632)

John Casimir of Zweibrucken ══ **Catherine countess Palatine (1584-1638)**

Christina of Sweden (1626-1689) queen of Sweden (r. 1632-1654; abdicated)

Hedwig of Holstein-Gottorp (1636-1715) ══ Charles X king of Sweden (r. 1654-1660)   Christina Casimir m. Frederick of Baden-Durlach

Christine of Baden-Durlach (1645-1705)   Frederick VII of Baden-Durlach **m. Augusta Maria of Holstein-Gottorp (1649-1728)**   **Johanna Elizabeth of Baden-Durlach (1651-1680)**

Ulrica Eleanora of Denmark (1656-1693) ══ Charles XI king of Sweden (r. 1660-1697)

Albertina of Baden-Durlach (1682-1755) m. Christian Augustus of Holstein-Gottorp

Hedwig Sophia (1681-1708) m. Frederick IV of Holstein-Gottorp

Charles XII king of Sweden (r. 1697-1718)

Ulrica Eleanora (1688-1741) queen of Sweden (r. 1718-1720) m. Frederick of Hesse-Cassell king of Sweden (r. 1720-1751)

Charles Frederick duke of Holstein **m. Anne Petrovna (1708-1728)**

Louisa Ulrica of Prussia (1720-1782) ══ Adolphus Frederick king of Sweden (r. 1751-1771)

Sophia of Denmark (1746-1813) ══ Gustavus III king of Sweden (r. 1771-1792)   Albertine (1753-1829)   Charles XIII king of Sweden (r. 1809-1818) ══ **Charlotte of Oldenburg (1759-1818)**

Gustavus IV Adolphus king of Sweden (r. 1792-1809) ══ **Frederica Dorothea of Baden (1781-1826)**

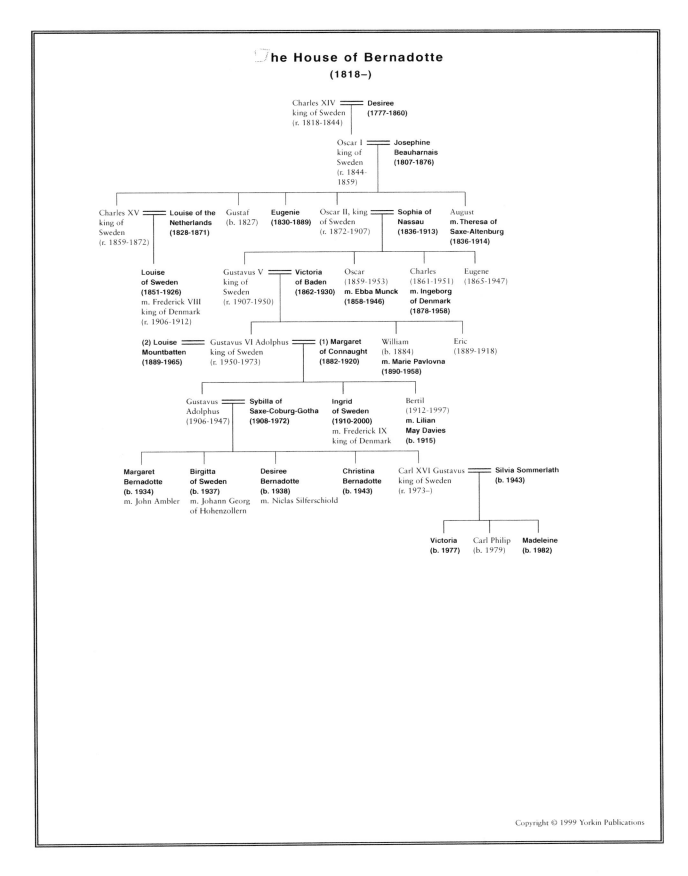

The House of Bernadotte
(1818–)

Charles XIV
king of Sweden
(r. 1818-1844) ═══ **Desiree
(1777-1860)**

Oscar I
king of
Sweden
(r. 1844-
1859) ═══ **Josephine
Beauharnais
(1807-1876)**

Charles XV
king of
Sweden
(r. 1859-1872) ═══ **Louise of the
Netherlands
(1828-1871)** — Gustaf
(b. 1827) — **Eugenie
(1830-1889)** — Oscar II, king
of Sweden
(r. 1872-1907) ═══ **Sophia of
Nassau
(1836-1913)** — August
m. **Theresa of
Saxe-Altenburg
(1836-1914)**

**Louise
of Sweden
(1851-1926)**
m. Frederick VIII
king of Denmark
(r. 1906-1912)

Gustavus V
king of
Sweden
(r. 1907-1950) ═══ **Victoria
of Baden
(1862-1930)** — Oscar
(1859-1953)
m. **Ebba Munck
(1858-1946)** — Charles
(1861-1951)
m. **Ingeborg
of Denmark
(1878-1958)** — Eugene
(1865-1947)

**(2) Louise
Mountbatten
(1889-1965)** ═══ Gustavus VI Adolphus
king of Sweden
(r. 1950-1973) ═══ **(1) Margaret
of Connaught
(1882-1920)** — William
(b. 1884)
m. **Marie Pavlovna
(1890-1958)** — Eric
(1889-1918)

Gustavus
Adolphus
(1906-1947) ═══ **Sybilla of
Saxe-Coburg-Gotha
(1908-1972)** — **Ingrid
of Sweden
(1910-2000)**
m. Frederick IX
king of Denmark — Bertil
(1912-1997)
m. **Lilian
May Davies
(b. 1915)**

**Margaret
Bernadotte
(b. 1934)**
m. John Ambler — **Birgitta
of Sweden
(b. 1937)**
m. Johann Georg
of Hohenzollern — **Desiree
Bernadotte
(b. 1938)**
m. Niclas Silferschiold — **Christina
Bernadotte
(b. 1943)** — Carl XVI Gustavus
king of Sweden
(r. 1973–) ═══ **Silvia Sommerlath
(b. 1943)**

**Victoria
(b. 1977)** — Carl Philip
(b. 1979) — **Madeleine
(b. 1982)**

Copyright © 1999 Yorkin Publications

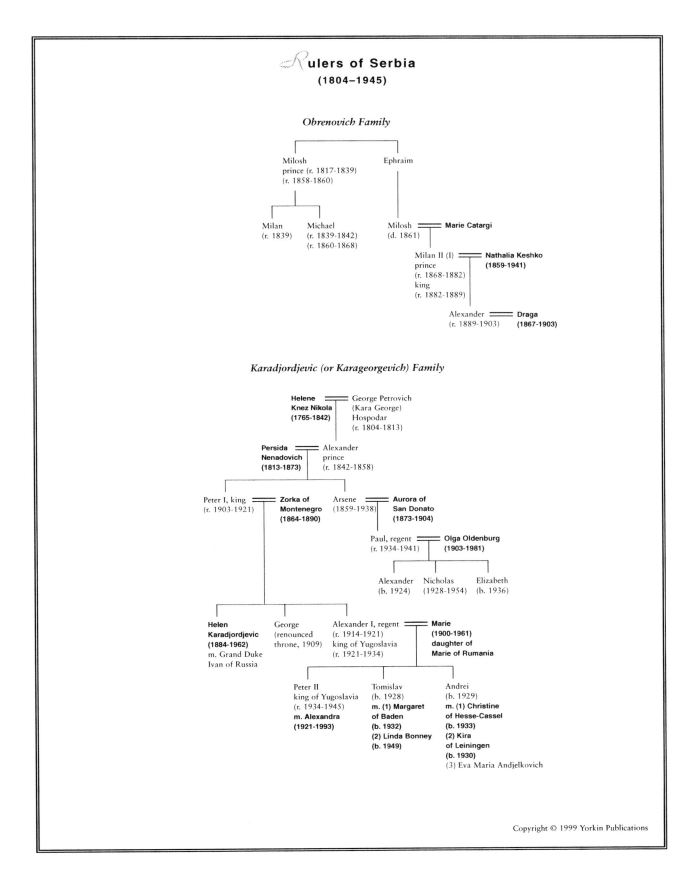

Rulers of Serbia
(1804–1945)

Obrenovich Family

Milosh
prince (r. 1817-1839)
(r. 1858-1860)

Ephraim

Milan
(r. 1839)

Michael
(r. 1839-1842)
(r. 1860-1868)

Milosh
(d. 1861) ══ **Marie Catargi**

Milan II (I)
prince
(r. 1868-1882)
king
(r. 1882-1889) ══ **Nathalia Keshko (1859-1941)**

Alexander
(r. 1889-1903) ══ **Draga (1867-1903)**

Karadjordjevic (or Karageorgevich) Family

Helene Knez Nikola (1765-1842) ══ George Petrovich
(Kara George)
Hospodar
(r. 1804-1813)

Persida Nenadovich (1813-1873) ══ Alexander
prince
(r. 1842-1858)

Peter I, king
(r. 1903-1921) ══ **Zorka of Montenegro (1864-1890)**

Arsene
(1859-1938) ══ **Aurora of San Donato (1873-1904)**

Paul, regent
(r. 1934-1941) ══ **Olga Oldenburg (1903-1981)**

Alexander
(b. 1924)

Nicholas
(1928-1954)

Elizabeth
(b. 1936)

**Helen Karadjordjevic (1884-1962)
m. Grand Duke Ivan of Russia**

George
(renounced throne, 1909)

Alexander I, regent
(r. 1914-1921)
king of Yugoslavia
(r. 1921-1934) ══ **Marie (1900-1961) daughter of Marie of Rumania**

Peter II
king of Yugoslavia
(r. 1934-1945)
m. Alexandra (1921-1993)

Tomislav
(b. 1928)
**m. (1) Margaret of Baden (b. 1932)
(2) Linda Bonney (b. 1949)**

Andrei
(b. 1929)
**m. (1) Christine of Hesse-Cassel (b. 1933)
(2) Kira of Leiningen (b. 1930)**
(3) Eva Maria Andjelkovich

A

AADLAND, Beverly (1943—). American actress. Name variations: Beverly Adland. Born Sept 17, 1943, in Hollywood, California; m. Maurice Jose de Leon, 1961. ❖ At 16, began a relationship with Errol Flynn which was highly publicized; had small parts in such films as *South Pacific* (1958) and *Cuban Rebel Girls* (1959).

AAKESSON, Birgit (1908–2001). Swedish dancer and choreographer. Name variations: Birgit Akesson; called "Picasso of Dance." Born in Malmo, Sweden, Mar 24, 1908; died in Stockholm, Mar 24, 2001; studied with Mary Wigman, 1929–31; children: Mona Moeller-Nielsen. ❖ Debuted in Paris at Vieux Colombier (1934); gave recitals in Sweden and European countries; appeared in Jacob's Pillow Dance Festival in US (1955); staged *Sisyphus* for Royal Swedish Ballet, her 1st production with a professional troupe (1957); staged *The Minotaur* (1958), *Rites* (1960), and *Play for Eight* (1962), and choreographed *Icaros* (1963); while a member of artistic council responsible for policy for Royal Swedish Ballet (1963 on), conceived many ballets in collaboration with Norwegian pianist Kaare Gundersen; considered founding mother of Swedish modern dance along with Birgit Cullberg; awarded the gold medal of the Swedish Academy (1998). ❖ See also *Women in World History.*

AALIYAH (1979–2001). American R&B singer and actress. Name variations: Aaliyah Haughton. Born Aaliyah Dana Haughton, Jan 16, 1979, in Brooklyn, Michigan; grew up in Detroit; killed Aug 25, 2001, in plane crash in Bahamas, near Abaco Island; niece of Gladys Knight (singer). ❖ Made NY stage debut as an orphan in *Annie*; performed in Las Vegas at 11 with Gladys Knight; debut album *Age Ain't Nothing But a Number* went platinum (1994) and included 2 top-10 singles, "Back and Forth" and "At Your Best (You Are Love)"; single "If Your Girl Only Knew" went double platinum (1996); nominated for a Grammy (2001) for Best Female R&B Vocalist for song "Try Again"; made film debut in *Romeo Must Die* (2000); played title role in Anne Rice's *Queen of the Damned* (2000); album *Aaliyah* also went platinum. Sang on soundtrack albums for *Anastasia, Next Friday, Music of the Heart, Sunset Park* and *Dr. Doolittle.*

AALTONEN, Paivi (1952—). See Meriluoto, Paivi.

AARONES, Ann Kristin (1973—). Norwegian soccer player. Name variations: Aarønes. Born Jan 19, 1973, in Norway. ❖ Forward; at World Cup, won a team gold medal (1995) and a team bronze (1999); won a team bronze medal at Atlanta Olympics (1996); played 111 games for the national team, scoring 60 goals; played for New York Power; retired (2001).

AARONS, Ruth Hughes (1918–1980). American table-tennis player. Born Ruth Hughes Aarons, June 11, 1918, in Stamford, Connecticut; died June 1980 in Beverly Hills, California; dau. of Alfred E. (theatrical producer) and Leila (Hughes) Aarons (singer and actress); sister of Alex A. Aarons (theatrical producer). ❖ Won US National singles and mixed-doubles championships (1934–37) and women's doubles (1936); won World title in Prague, Czechoslovakia (1936), becoming 1st American to reach the final rounds in world competition; held title by default the following year; remained the only world singles champion—man or woman—the US ever produced during the 20th century. ❖ See also *Women in World History.*

AARONSOHN, Sarah (1890–1917). Zionist pioneer, spy, and patriot. Name variations: Aaronson or Aharonson. Born in Zikhron Ya'akov, Turkish Palestine, 1890; killed herself during torture by Turks, Oct 1917; dau. of Efrayim Fishel Aaronsohn (1849–1939) and Malkah Aaronsohn (Jewish pioneer settlers); sister of Aaron (1876–1919) and Alexander (1888–1948) Aaronsohn; m. Bulgarian-born Hayyim Abraham, 1914. ❖ Shocked by the Turks' systematic extermination of Armenians in the Ottoman Empire (1915), readily joined brother Aaron's spy ring, Nili, which provided military intelligence to the

British in hopes of overthrowing Turkish rule in Palestine; dispersed the money sent by the British, especially to aid the Jews who were expelled from the cities of Jaffa and Tel Aviv by Ottoman authorities; secretly went to British-occupied Egypt with brother for consultations with British intelligence officials (1917); arrested by Turks (Oct 1, 1917), was tortured for 4 days but refused to reveal information; when Turkish captors decided to take her to Nazareth, where "expert" interrogators could force her to talk, killed herself. Was honored by an Israeli commemorative postage stamp (1991). ❖ See also Ida Cowen and Irene Gunther, *A Spy for Freedom: The Story of Sarah Aaronson* (Lodestar, 1984); and *Women in World History.*

ABADY, Josephine (c. 1950–2002). American director. Born Josephine Abady, c. 1950, in Richmond, Virginia; died of breast cancer, May 24, 2002, in New York, NY; mother was a civil-rights activist in the South; sister of Caroline Aaron (actress); graduate of Syracuse University; Florida State University, MA; married Michael Krawitz (writer). ❖ A leader in the nonprofit theater movement, taught theater at Bennington; was artistic director of the Berkshire Theater Festival in Stockbridge, the Cleveland Playhouse, and (with Theodore Mann) Circle in the Square; plays include *Bus Stop* (with Mary-Louise Parker), *The Rose Tatoo* (with Mercedes Ruehl), *The Boys Next Door* (with Josh Mostel), and David Storey's NY premiere of *March on Russia*; with a grant from AFI, made the short film "To Catch a Tiger" (1994).

ABAIJAH, Josephine (1942—). Papua New Guinea health educator, political leader, and entrepreneur. Name variations: Josephine Abayah; Dame Josephine Abaijah. Born in Wamira Village, Milne Bay, Papua New Guinea, 1942; one of 1st women to be educated in New Guinea. ❖ With Dr. Eric Wright, founded Papua Besena ("Hands off Papua") movement to gain independence from Australian governance (1972); became a health-education administrator and was 1st female member of House of Parliament, the 100-seat House of Assembly of Papua New Guinea (1972–82); an entrepreneur with several retail businesses, returned to politics to serve as chair of Interim Commission (governing body) of National Capital District; co-wrote with Eric Wright, *A Thousand Coloured Dreams*, based on her life, the 1st novel ever published by a woman of Papua New Guinea (Dellasta Pacific, 1991). One of Papua's leading feminists and a leader of the Papua Besena Party, created Dame of the British Empire (1991). ❖ See also *Women in World History.*

ABAKANOWICZ, Magdalena (1930—). Polish sculptor. Name variations: Marta Abakanowicz-Kosmowska. Born in Falenty, Poland, June 20, 1930; Academy of Fine Arts, Warsaw, MA, 1955; m. Jan Kosmowski (civil engineer), 1956. ❖ At 14, during German occupation of Poland, served as a nurse's aide in an improvised hospital; entered work in First International Biennial of Tapestry in Lausanne, Switzerland (1956); turned to organic materials like burlap, rope, and thread, developing an individualistic, rebellious vision of human freedom (1960s); works often represent fragmented human forms, such as *Heads* (1975), *Seated Figures* (1974–79) and *Katharsis* (1985); was an instructor at State College of Arts in Poznan (1965–74), then became an associate professor (1974). Granted 1st prize from Polish Ministry of Culture (1965); gold medals from Polish Artists' Union (1965) and the VIII Sao Paulo Bienal, Brazil (1965); grand prize of Polish Minister for Foreign Affairs (1970); state prize of Polish Folk Republic (1972); golden cross of merit from Polish Folk Republic (1974). ❖ See also Barbara Rose, *Magdalena Abakanowicz* (Abrams, 1994); and *Women in World History.*

ABARBANELL, Lina (1879–1963). German actress and singer. Born Feb 3, 1879, in Berlin, Germany; died Jan 6, 1963, in New York, NY. ❖ Made stage debut at Deutsches Theater, Berlin (1895); sang Hansel in the premiere of *Hansel and Gretel* at the Metropolitan Opera (1905); made 1st appearance on English-speaking stage in NY (1906) as Ilsa in *The Student King*; played Sonia in *The Merry Widow*, Nellie Vaughan in

The Love Cure, Yvonne (her most famous role) in *Madame Sherry* and Princess von Auen in *The Silver Swan.*

ABARCA, Lydia (1951—). American dancer. Born Jan 8, 1951, in New York, NY. ❖ Became an original member of Arthur Mitchell's Dance Theater of Harlem (c. 1968), where she gained fame performing works by Balanchine, including *Concerto Barocco, Agon, Serenade, Allegro Brillante* and *Bugaku;* appeared in Jerome Robbins' *Afternoon of a Faun* and William Dollar's *The Combat,* 2 duets from New York City Ballet repertory; performed in Billy Wilson's *Bubbling Brown Sugar* on Broadway; danced in such films as *A Piece of the Action* (1977) and *The Cotton Club* (1984).

ABARCA, Maria Francisca de (fl. 1640–1656). Spanish painter. Fl. between 1640 and 1656 in Spain. ❖ Working in the 1640s in Madrid, was a portrait painter of such excellence that she was befriended by artists Rubens and Velasquez.

ABASSA (fl. 8th c.). Arabian noblewoman. Name variations: Abbasa. Born c. 765; died c. 803; dau. of al-Mahdi, 3rd Abbasid caliph (or ruler) of Baghdad (now Iraq); half-sister of Musa al-Hadi (4th Abbasid caliph, r. 785–786), Harun al-Rashid (Haroun al-Raschid; 5th Abbasid caliph, r. 786–809), Ulayya (Arabian singer), and Ibrahim ibn al-Mahdi; stepdau. of al-Khaizaran; sister-in-law of singer Dananir al Barmakiyya; m. Jafar (or Jaffar) ibn Yahya al-Barmeki, member of powerful Barmak (Barmek, Barmakis, Barmakids or Barmecide) family; children: twin sons. ❖ Half-sister of Harun al-Rashid, whose 8th-c. court was depicted by Scheherazade in *Arabian Nights;* said to be so beautiful and accomplished that Harun lamented their status as brother and sister; was given to Jafar (Giafar in the *Arabian Nights*), Harun's close companion, in a sham marriage; fell in love with Jafar; had twin sons in secret; deceit discovered (803); saw nearly entire Barmakis family, including Jafar, destroyed. As to her fate: in one version, killed along with two sons; in another, dismissed from court, wandered about, reciting her story in song (some Arabic verses composed by her that commemorate her misfortune are still extant). ❖ See also *Women in World History.*

ABASSOVA, Tamilla (1982—). Russian cyclist. Born Dec 9, 1982, in USSR. ❖ Placed 1st at World Cup in Moscow (2003); won a silver medal for sprint at Athens Olympics (2004).

ABAYAH, Josephine (b. 1942). See *Abaijah, Josephine.*

ABAYOMI, Oyinkansola (1897–1990). Nigerian feminist and nationalist. Name variations: (nickname) Oyinkan; Lady Oyinkansola Abayomi. Born Oyinkansola Ajasa in Lagos, Nigeria, Mar 6, 1897; died in Lagos, Mar 19, 1990; dau. of Sir Kitoyi Ajasa (lawyer, inaugural member of Nigerian Legislative Council, publisher of newspaper *The Standard*) and Lady Cornelia Olayinka (Moore) Ajasa; m. Moronfolu Abayomi (lawyer), May 10, 1923 (died 1923); m. Kofoworola (Kofo) Abayomi, 1930 (died 1979). ❖ Schooled at Anglican Girls' Seminary in Lagos (1903–09); studied in England (1910–17); returned home (1920); became 1st aboriginal supervisor of Nigerian chapter of Girl Guides; 2 months after marriage, 1st husband killed in court; campaigned for Queen's College, secondary school for girls, which was established (1927); escalated work for Girl Guides to obtain recognition equal to Boy Scouts, which was granted (1931); appointed chief commissioner of Girl Guides; joined 2nd husband's cause, the Lagos Youth Movement, later the Nigerian Youth Movement; founded Nigerian Women's Party, uniting several women's organizations (1944). With husband's knighthood, became Lady Oyinkan (1954); given title Life President (1982), and five chief titles, the last being Iya Abiye of Egbaland. ❖ See also Folarin Coker, *A Lady* (Nigeria: Evans, 1987); and *Women in World History.*

ABB (c. 610–c. 683). See *Ebba.*

ABBA. See *Fältskog, Agnetha (1950—).*

ABBA, Marta (1900–1988). Italian actress. Born June 25, 1900, in Milan, Italy; died June 24, 1988, in Milan; sister of Cele Abba (b. 1903, actress); m. Severance A. Millikin. ❖ Appeared throughout major European cities in Italian classics and other plays, including *As You Desire Me, The Enemy, Anna Karenina, A Month in the Country, Hedda Gabler;* made London debut in *Six Characters in Search of an Author* (1925); made English-speaking debut in Bournemouth as the Duchess Tatiana in *Tovarich* (July 1936), and NY debut (Oct 1936) in the same role; was a favorite of Luigi Pirandello and often played the female lead in his plays.

ABBASA (fl. 8th c.). See *Abassa.*

ABBE, Kathryn (1919—). American photographer. Born Sept 22, 1919, New York, NY; dau. of Frank and Katherine (O'Rourke) McLaughlin; twin sister of Frances McLaughlin-Gill; studied photography with Walter Civardi, painting with Yasuo Kuniyoshi at New School for Social Research; m. James Abbe Jr. (photographer); children: 3. ❖ Won *Vogue*'s "Prix de Paris" contest (1941); began working with the magazine's fashion photographer Toni Frissell (1942); contributed photos of actors, musicians, and children to *Good Housekeeping, Better Homes and Gardens* and *Parents;* with sister Frances McLaughlin-Gill, published a book on twins (1980).

ABBÉMA, Louise (1858–1927). French painter. Name variations: Abbema. Born in 1858; died in 1927. ❖ Undertook portrait of Sarah Bernhardt (1876), the beginning of an intense relationship; continued doing portraits of Bernhardt (1876–1922). Awarded Chevalier de la Légion d'Honneur.

ABBING, Justine (1881–1932). See *Bruggen, Carry van.*

ABBOTT, Annie Elizabeth (1877–1946). See *Kelly, Annie Elizabeth.*

ABBOTT, Berenice (1898–1991). American photographer. Born Bernice (changed to Berenice) Abbott, July 17, 1898, in Springfield, Ohio; died in Monson, Maine, Dec 10, 1991; dau. of Charles E. and Alice (Bunn) Abbott. ❖ Proponent of photographic realism and archivist of work of Eugéne Atget, traveled to NYC to study sculpture (1918); continued studies in Europe, under Bourdelle in Paris and at Kunstschule in Berlin (1921); worked as assistant to American photographer Man Ray in Paris (1923–25); established reputation in portraiture of writers, poets, artists, philosophers, philanthropists, and expatriate Americans (1925–29), including James Joyce, Jean Cocteau, André Gide, Janet Flanner, Princess Eugéne Murat, Peggy Guggenheim, Djuna Barnes, Marie Laurencin, Edna St. Vincent Millay, A'Lelia Walker, and Eugéne Atget; returned to NY and started masterwork: a photographic documentation of the city (1929); also taught photography at New School for Social Research (1934–58). Works include: *Changing New York, Greenwich Village Today and Yesterday, Eugéne Atget Portfolio, The World of Atget, A Portrait of Maine, Berenice Abbott Photographs* and *Berenice Abbott: The Red River Photographs.* ❖ See also Hank O'Neal, *Berenice Abbott: American Photographer* (McGraw-Hill, 1982); *Berenice Abbott: A View of the 20th Century* by Kay Weaver and Martha Wheelock (Ishtar Films, 1992); and *Women in World History.*

ABBOTT, Bessie (d. 1937). American soprano. Born Elizabeth Pickens, Riverside, NY; died Feb 1, 1937; granddau. of US Ambassador to St. Petersburg; studied under Bouhy and Mathilde Marchesi. ❖ Made debut at Paris Opera as Juliet in Gounod's *Romeo et Juliette* (1901); appeared at the Élysée and British Embassy, Paris. ❖ See also *Women in World History.*

ABBOTT, Diahnne (1945—). African-American actress. Name variations: Diahnne Eugenia Abbott. Born 1945 in New York, NY; cousin of Gregory Abbott (singer and songwriter); m. Robert De Niro (actor), 1976 (div. 1988); children: Raphael De Niro (actor). ❖ Films include *Taxi Driver* (1976), *Welcome to L.A.* (1976), *New York, New York* (1977), *The King of Comedy* (1983), *Love Streams* (1984) and *Jo Jo Dancer, Your Life is Calling* (1986).

ABBOTT, Diane (1953—). English politician, civil-rights activist, and journalist. Born Diane Julie Abbott, Sept 27, 1953, in Paddington, London, England; dau. of Jamaican parents who had immigrated to London in 1951; attended Newnham College, Cambridge; m. David Thompson, 1991 (div. 1993). ❖ Joined National Council for Civil Liberties; worked as a journalist for Thames Television (1980–82), TV AM (1982–84), and freelance (1984–85); joined Labour Party (1971); appointed press officer for Greater London Council (GLC), then principal press officer for Lambeth Borough Council; served as member of Westminster City Council (1982–86); elected to House of Commons for Hackney North and Stoke Newington (1987), the 1st black woman member of parliament; reelected (1992, 1997, 2001, 2005).

ABBOTT, Edith (1876–1957). American social worker and educator. Born Sept 26, 1876, in Grand Island, Nebraska; died July 28, 1957; dau. of Elizabeth (Griffin) Abbott (noted pioneer in educational work in West); sister of social worker Grace Abbott; graduated from University of Nebraska, 1901. ❖ Advocated using social research to advance social reform; taught economics at Wellesley College (1907–08); was a resident of Hull House (1908–20); served on faculty of University of Chicago (1911–23), before becoming dean of School of Social Service Administration (1924–42) and dean emeritus (1942–53). Author of several books on crime, immigration, and labor, including *Women in Industry* (1910), *The Tenements of Chicago* (1936), and *Public Assistance* (1939).

ABBOTT, Elenore Plaisted (1873–1935). American artist. Born Elenore Plaisted in Lincoln, Maine, 1873 (some sources cite 1875); died in 1935; studied at Pennsylvania Academy of the Fine Arts, Philadelphia School of Design for Women, and in Paris; also attended Drexel Institute where she studied with Howard Pyle, 1899; m. C. Yarnell Abbott. ❖ Exhibited her work at the Académie des Beaux Arts in Paris and at the Pennsylvania Academy of the Fine Arts; illustrated for *Saturday Evening Post, Harper's Magazine* and *Scribner's;* also illustrated such books as *The Minister and the Black Veil,* Defoe's *The Adventures of Robinson Crusoe,* Alcott's *An Old-Fashioned Girl,* Barbour's *That Mainwaring Affair,* Grimm's *Fairy Tales,* Olmsted's *The Land of Never Was,* Stevenson's *Kidnapped* and *Treasure Island* and Wyss' *Swiss Family Robinson.*

ABBOTT, Emma (1850–1891). American soprano. Name variations: Emma Abbott Wetherell. Born in Chicago, Illinois, Dec 9, 1850 (some sources cite 1849); died in Salt Lake City, Utah, Jan 5, 1891; studied in NY with Achille Errani and in Europe with Wartel, Sangiovanni, and Delle Sedie; m. Eugene Wetherell, 1875. ❖ One of the most popular sopranos of her time, debuted at Covent Garden in London as Marie in *La fille du régiment* (1876); debuted in NY in same role (1877); was the 1st woman to establish an opera company, The Emma Abbott English Grand Opera Company (1878), presenting shortened versions of contemporary operas on tour.

ABBOTT, Evelyn (1843–1901). British classical scholar. Born 1843; died 1901; educated at Balliol College, Oxford. ❖ Paralyzed for life because of a spinal cord injury at 23. Author of *History of Greece* (3 vols., 1888–1900) and editor of *Hellenica* (1880).

ABBOTT, Gertrude (1846–1934). *See Abbott, Mother.*

ABBOTT, Grace (1878–1939). American social worker. Born on Grand Island, Nebraska, Nov 17, 1878; died in Chicago, Illinois, June 19, 1939; dau. of Elizabeth (Griffin) Abbott (noted pioneer in educational work in the West); younger sister of Edith Abbott (dean of School of Social Service Administration, University of Chicago); MA in political science from University of Chicago, 1909. ❖ Devoting most of her life to child welfare, became resident of Jane Addams' Hull House (1907); helped organize Immigrants' Protective League with Sophonisba Breckinridge, leading to her studying conditions on Ellis Island, testifying before Congress, and publishing numerous articles along with her book *The Immigrant and the Community* (1917); at invitation of Julia Lathrop, joined staff of US Children's Bureau (1917); succeeded Lathrop as chief of its Child Labor Division (1921) and turned attention to Sheppard-Towner Act, which extended federal aid for maternal and infant health care; oversaw the bureau's opening of 3,000 child-health and prenatal-care clinics throughout US (1921–34); was also president of the National Conference of Social Workers (1924); began serving as professor of public welfare at University of Chicago (1934), where sister Edith Abbott was dean; was editor of *Social Service Review* and a member of President Franklin Delano Roosevelt's Council on Economic Security (1934–35). Authored works on social welfare, including the 2-volume *Child and the State* (1931).

ABBOTT, Lorraine (1937—). Golf coach. Born Dec 9, 1937 in Toledo, Ohio. ❖ Became director of educational services for the National Golf Foundation (1971); as Class A, LPGA teaching-division pro, conducted clinics and workshops (1966–71); achieved LPGA Master Professional status.

ABBOTT, Margaret (1878–1955). American golfer. Name variations: Margaret Abbott Dunne. Born June 15, 1878, in Calcutta, India; died June 10, 1955; dau. of Mary Ives Abbott (novelist); studied art in Paris; m. Finley Peter Dunne (1867–1936, humorist and creator of "Mr. Dooley"), 1902. ❖ Won the 9-hole Olympic golf championship in Paris, France, the 1st year women were allowed to compete in any category and the only year golf was represented in the games (1900). ❖ See also *Women in World History.*

ABBOTT, Mary Martha (1823–1898). Canadian first lady. Born Mary Martha Bethune, 1823; died 1898; m. John Joseph Caldwell Abbott (prime minister of Canada, 1891–92), July 26, 1849 (died Oct 30, 1893); children: 9.

ABBOTT, Maude (1869–1940). Canadian cardiologist. Born 1869 in Montreal, Canada; graduate of McGill University, Montreal; graduate of Bishop's College, Montreal, 1894. ❖ A pioneer in the area of congenital heart disease and "blue babies," worked to break down barriers against women in medicine; awarded an undergraduate degree at McGill University but denied admission to its medical school; accepted at Bishop's College, the 1st institution in Quebec to admit women as medical students; graduated (1894), winning both the chancellor's prize and the senior anatomy medal; appointed assistant curator of medical museum at McGill (1897), then curator (1900), where she developed the *Osler Catalogue of the Circulatory System* and remained for over 30 years; organized and edited *Bulletin of the International Association of Medical Museums* (1907); appointed research fellow in pathology and formally recognized by McGill with honorary MD (1910); served 2-year appointment as visiting professor of pathology and bacteriology at Woman's Medical College of Pennsylvania (1923–24); contributed a section on congenital heart defects for Osler's *System of Medicine;* authored major work, *Atlas of Congenital Cardiac Disease,* a classified bibliography of Osler's writings, which identified 1,000 cases. Received a gold medal—McGill's highest honor—for her presentation on congenital heart disease. ❖ See also H.E. Macdermot, *Maude Abbott* (1941); and *Women in World History.*

ABBOTT, Merriel (c. 1893–1977). American dance director. Born c. 1893, in Chicago, Illinois; died Nov 6, 1977, in Chicago. ❖ Served as teaching assistant to Andreas Pavley and Serge Oukrainsky in Chicago, IL; staged precision acts for Paramount–Publix circuit, based in Chicago; worked as director of entertainment and staff choreographer for The Palmer House in Chicago (starting 1933), later expanding service to entire chain of Hilton hotels; toured internationally with Merriell Abbott Girls (1930s–40s), an acrobatic precision team incorporating somersaults, splits, handstands and more. Merriel Abbott Dancers also appeared in Jack Benny films, *Man About Town* (1939) and *Buck Benny Rides Again* (1940).

ABBOTT, Mother (1846–1934). Australian founder. Name variations: Gertrude Abbott, Mary Jane O'Brien. Born Mary Jane O'Brien in Sydney, Australia, July 11, 1846; died in Sydney, May 12, 1934; dau. of Thomas (schoolmaster) and Rebecca (Matthews) O'Brien. ❖ At 22, entered the order of St. Joseph of the Sacred Heart and assumed the name Sister Ignatius; left convent (1872), returned to Sydney, and became known as Mrs. Gertrude Abbott, or Mother Abbott; eventually founded St. Margaret's Maternity Home (later to become the 3rd largest obstetric hospital in Sydney), which she managed for the next 40 years. ❖ See also *Women in World History.*

ABBOUD, Simonne (c. 1930—). French-American sailor. Born in France, c. 1930. ❖ Immigrated to US (1959); served on the *American Astronaut,* the 1st women to serve on a US cargo ship (1971).

ABDALLAH, Nia (1984—). American taekwondo player. Born Jan 24, 1984, in Houston, Texas. ❖ Won a silver medal for -57kg at Athens Olympics (2004).

ABDEL-AZIZ, Malak (1923—). Egyptian poet and editor. Name variations: Malak 'Abd al-Aziz; Malak 'Abdel 'Aziz; Malak Abdel Aziz. Born 1923 in Egypt; graduated from Department of Arabic at Cairo University. ❖ Influenced by émigré poets, published such poetry collections as *Songs of Youth, The Evening Said, Sea of Silence* and *To Touch the Heart of Things* (1950s–70s).

ABDELLAH, Faye Glenn (1919—). American nursing researcher. Born April 14, 1919, in New York; Ann May School of Nursing, nursing certificate; Columbia University, Teachers College, BS, MA, EdD. ❖ Pioneering nurse researcher credited with saving thousands of lives by developing the nation's 1st tested coronary-care unit; promoted to rear admiral, the 1st nurse to receive the rank of two-star admiral; during career in the Public Health Service, changed the focus of nursing theory from disease-centered to patient-centered; was the 1st nurse and 1st woman to serve as US deputy surgeon general; founded the Graduate School of Nursing at the Uniformed Services University of the Health Sciences and served as its 1st dean; wrote *Better Nursing Care through Nursing Research* and *Patient-Centered Approaches to Nursing.* Inducted into Women's Hall of Fame at Seneca Falls, NY (2000).

ABDEL RAHMAN, Aisha (1913–1998). Egyptian literary critic and educator. Name variations: Aisha Abdel-Rahman, Aisha 'Abd al-Rahman; (pseudonyms) Bint El Shatei, Bint el-Shati or Bint-al-Shah. Born Aisha 'Abd al-Rahman, Nov 6, 1913, in Damietta (Dumyat), Egypt; died Jan 12, 1998; father taught at Dumyat Religious Institute; Cairo University, BA, 1939, MA, 1941, PhD, 1944; m. Amin El-Kholy (professor), 1944 (died 1969). ❖ Became an assistant lecturer in literature at Cairo University (1939); began serving as Inspector of Arabic Language and Literature for Ministry of Education (1942); taught at Ain Shams University (1950–62), becoming assistant professor (1957); was a professor of Arabic literature at University College for Women; best known for her literary criticism, which reflects a strong interest in women of Islam, including *New Values in Arabic Literature* (1961), *Contemporary Arab Women Poets* (1963), and *The Mother of the Prophet* (1966); also wrote 3 books on the wives of Muhammad.

ABDO, Reema (1963—). Canadian swimmer. Born May 19, 1963, in Aden, South Yemen. ❖ Began swimming career in Kingston, Ontario (1975); in Canada, won 14 national championship medals in the backstroke (7 gold, 4 silver, and 3 bronze); at Los Angeles Olympics, won a bronze medal in the 4x100-meter medley relay (1984); became a swimming coach.

ABEGG, Elisabeth (1882–1974). German antiwar activist. Born Mar 3, 1882; grew up in Alsace (now a part of France) when it was a province of the German Reich; died 1974. ❖ Early critic of Hitler's Third Reich who rescued countless Jews in Berlin and has been honored for her work during the Holocaust; moved to Berlin (1918); became involved with relief work of the Quakers; earned a doctorate and became a history teacher at the prestigious *Luisenschule,* an all-girls' school; denied the right to teach because of her refusal to advance the Nazi party line (1940), began to actively rescue Jews, using her apartment to provide temporary shelter; created an extensive rescue network consisting of her Quaker friends as well as former students. ❖ See also *Women in World History.*

ABEL, Annie Heloise (1873–1947). English-American historian. Name variations: Annie Heloise Abel-Henderson. Born Annie Heloise Abel in Fernhurst, Sussex, England, Feb 18, 1873; died in Aberdeen, Washington, Mar 14, 1947; University of Kansas, 1898, MA, 1900; Yale, PhD, 1905; m. George C. Henderson (Australian scholar), 1922 (sep. 1924). ❖ At 12, immigrated to Salina, Kansas; taught at Wells College before teaching at Woman's College of Baltimore (Goucher College), where she became full professor and head of department (1914); also taught English at Johns Hopkins (1910–15) and Smith College (1916–22); published the 3-volume *The Slaveholding Indians* (1915–25); taught at Sweet Briar College (1924–25); became professor of history at University of Kansas (1928) where she researched British colonial and Indian policy while continuing to publish her findings. ❖ See also *Women in World History.*

ABEL, Hazel (1888–1966). American politician. Born Hazel Pearl Hemple in Plattsmouth, Nebraska, July 10, 1888; died in Lincoln, Nebraska, July 30, 1966; graduated from the University of Nebraska, 1908; married George Abel, 1916. ❖ Republican from Nebraska, 83rd Congress (Nov 8, 1954-Dec 1, 1954); was active in the Nebraska State Republican Party and vice chair of the State Republican Central Committee; filled a two-month vacancy in US Senate because of a technicality in Nebraska's election law; during brief tenure, served on the Committee on Finance, and Committee on Interstate and Foreign Commerce; also joined the majority in voting to censure Senator Joseph McCarthy; resigned (Dec 31, 1954); came in second in a run for the Republican primary for nomination as governor (1960).

ABEL, Irene (1953—). East German gymnast. Born Feb 12, 1953, in Berlin, East Germany; children: Katja Abel (b. 1983, champion German gymnast). ❖ At Munich Olympics, won an all-around team silver medal (1972); became a coach in Berlin.

ABEL, Theodora (1899–1998). American clinical psychologist. Name variations: Theodora Mead Abel. Born Theodora Mead, Sept 9, 1899, in Newport, Rhode Island; died Dec 2, 1998, in Forestburgh, NY; dau. of Robert Mead Jr. and Elsie (Cleveland) Mead; Columbia University, PhD (1925); m. Theodore Abel, 1923; children: 3. ❖ Known largely for work in ethnology; worked at Manhattan Trade School for Girls (1923–25); received position at University of Illinois (1925); served on staff at Cornell University (1926–28) and performed research on galvanic skin reflex; served as instructor at Sarah Lawrence College (beginning 1929) and became director of psychoanalysis at Postgraduate Center for Mental Health; with Elaine Kinder, published 1st book *The Subnormal Adolescent Girl* (1942); served as research psychologist at Letchworth Village (1940s); became expert in Rorschach technique; served as instructor at Long Island University and clinical professor at University of New Mexico Medical School; published *Culture and Psychotherapy* (introduction by Margaret Mead, 1975).

ABEL-HENDERSON, Annie Heloise (1873–1947). *See Abel, Annie Heloise.*

ABERCROMBIE, M.L.J. (1909–1984). English zoologist. Name variations: Minnie Louie Johnson Abercrombie; Minnie Louie Johnson. Born Minnie Louie Jane Johnson, Nov 14, 1909, in England; died Nov 25, 1984; University of Birmingham, BS, 1930, PhD, 1932; m. Michael Abercrombie (scientist), 1939. ❖ Authority on teaching medical students, collaborated with husband on the well-known *Penguin Dictionary of Biology* (1971) and *New Biology,* which ran for 31 vols. (1st published, 1945); served as lecturer in zoology department at University of Birmingham (1932–46), and in department of anatomy at University College, London. Writings on education include (with S. Hunt and P. Stringer) *Selection and Academic Performance of Students in a University School of Architecture* (1967) and *Aims and Techniques of Group Teaching* (1970); also published in *Journal of Experimental Biology* and *Proceedings of the Zoological Society of London.*

ABERDEEN, Countess of (1857–1939). *See Aberdeen, Ishbel Maria Gordon, Lady.*

ABERDEEN, Ishbel Maria Gordon, Lady (1857–1939). British women's-rights activist, philanthropist, and social reformer. Name variations: Lady Aberdeen; Countess of Aberdeen; Marchioness of Aberdeen; Ishbel Gordon. Born Ishbel Maria Marjoribanks, Mar 1857, in London, England; died April 18, 1939, in Scotland; youngest dau. of Lord Tweedmouth; m. John Campbell Gordon (governor-general of Canada, 1893–98, and lord lieutenant of Ireland, 1906–15), 7th earl of Aberdeen (later Marquess of Aberdeen and Temair), 1877; children: 5, including Marjorie Lady Pentland. ❖ With husband, founded the Haddo House Association (Onward and Upward Association); founded National Council of Women of Canada (NCWC, 1893); was president of International Council of Women (1893–99, 1904–36); despite strong opposition from medical establishment, founded Victoria Order of Nurses (VON) for Canada (1898), to provide services to Canadians in remote areas; founded the May Court Clubs of Canada (1898); following WWI, convinced League of Nations to open secretarial posts to women as well as men; founded Women's National Health Association in Ireland and was president of its Irish Industries Association; served as chair of the Scottish Council for Women's Trades; was one of the 1st women to become a JP. ❖ See also memoir with husband *We Twa'* (1925); John Saywell, ed. *The Canadian Journal of Lady Aberdeen: 1893–1898* (1960); Marjorie Lady Pentland, *A Bonnie Fechter* (1952).

ABERDEEN, Marchioness of (1857–1939). *See Aberdeen, Ishbel Maria Gordon, Lady.*

ABERNETHY, Moira (1939—). South African swimmer. Born May 29, 1939, in South Africa. ❖ At Melbourne Olympics, won bronze medal for the 4x100-meter freestyle relay (1956).

ABIERTAS, Josepha (1894–1929). Filipino lawyer and feminist. Born in Capiz, Philippines, 1894; died of tuberculosis in 1929. ❖ Was the 1st woman to graduate from the Philippine Law School.

ABIGAIL (fl. 1010 BCE). Biblical woman. Name variations: Abigal. Fl. c. 1010 BCE; dau. of Jesse of Bethlehem; sister of King David (r. 1010–970 BCE); m. Jether (Ishmaelite); children: Amasa. ❖ Was the sister of King David who ruled Judah and Israel (c. 1010–c. 970 BCE); was also the mother of Amasa who commanded the army of Absalom.

ABIGAIL (fl. 1000 BCE). Biblical woman. Name variations: Beautiful Peacemaker. Born in Carmel, a town in hill country of Judah (ruins of which still remain under name Kurmul, about 10 miles south-southeast of Hebron); fl. c. 1000 BCE; m. Nabal (died); m. King David (David appears to have ruled Judah and Israel from approximately 1010 BCE to approximately 970 BCE, capturing Jerusalem in about 1000 BCE); children: Chileab (in Bible called also Daniel). ❖ Warned of the danger to her imperious husband by the army of David, brought offerings of bread, wine, grain, raisins, and figs to David's camp; her diplomacy and bearing softened David's heart, and his small army turned back; following Nabal's death, became David's 2nd wife, sharing the honors of royalty.

ABIGAL. *Variant of Abigail.*

ABIHAIL (fl. 970 BCE). Biblical woman. Fl. c. 970 BCE; 2nd wife of King Rehoboam (r. 975–958 BCE), a descendant of Eliab, David's oldest brother.

ABINGDON, Mrs. W.L. (1877–1961). *See Fernandez, Bijou.*

ABINGTON, Frances (1737–1815). English actress. Name variations: Frances or Fanny Barton. Born Frances Barton, 1737, in London, England; died Mar 4, 1815, in London; dau. of private soldier in King's Guards; m. her music-master, one of royal trumpeters (soon sep.). ❖ Was a domestic servant, flowergirl, and streetsinger in St. James's Park under the name "Nosegay Fan"; made London stage debut as Miranda in *The Busybody* (1755); rose to prominence and enjoyed a successful career for 43 years; originated over 30 characters, including Lady Bab in *High Life Below Stairs,* Betty in *Clandestine Marriage,* Charlotte in *Hypocrite,* Charlotte Rusport in *West Indian,* Roxalana in *Sultan,* Miss Hoyden in *Trip to Scarborough* and, most important, Lady Teazle in *The School for Scandal;* starred at the Drury Lane (1764–82) and at Covent Garden (1782–90); retired (1799). ❖ See also *Women in World History.*

ABISHAG OF SHUNEM (fl. 1000 BCE). Biblical woman. Fl. c. 1000 BCE. ❖ A Shunammite woman, was brought to serve David and keep him warm in bed, though they had no sexual relations; became one of his wives (1 Kings 1:3, 4, 15).

ABITAL (fl. 1000 BCE). Biblical woman. Fifth wife of King David.

ABLA POKOU (c. 1700–c. 1760). *See Pokou.*

ABRABANEL, Benvenida (d. 1560). Jewish noblewoman of Italy. Born in Naples, Italy; died 1560 in Ferrara, Italy; dau. of Joseph Abrabanel; m. 1st cousin Samuel Abrabanel (d. 1547), before 1541 in Naples. ❖ A wealthy Jewish entrepreneur and benefactor, was born into a family that enjoyed prosperity and royal favor in Spain until 1492, the year that Spanish monarchs expelled all practicing Jews from the Iberian peninsula; moved with family to Naples; received an excellent education and was asked to tutor Eleonora de Medici (1522–1562), later duchess of Tuscany; eventually married 1st cousin, the merchant Samuel Abrabanel, with whom she moved to Ferrara (1541) when the government of Naples expelled the Jews from that city; created a sort of salon, opening home to scholars and artists from across Italy; following husband's death (1547), took over his commercial enterprises, which prospered under her management; gained renown for her learning, business acumen, and charity, as she gave freely to aid the less fortunate Jews of Ferrara. ❖ See also *Women in World History.*

ABRAHAM, Caroline Harriet (1809–1877). New Zealand artist. Name variations: Caroline Harriet Hudson, Caroline Harriet Palmer. Born Caroline Harriet Hudson, July 1, 1809, in Leicestershire, England; died at Bournemouth, England, June 17, 1877; dau. of Charles Thomas Hudson (changed name to Palmer, 1813) and Harriet (Pepperell) Hudson; m. Charles John Abraham (Anglican bishop), 1850; children: 1. ❖ Spent early life in England, caring for invalid mother and performing charitable work among poor; accompanied husband to New Zealand (1850); recorded New Zealand through detailed sketches and watercolors; helped prepare privately published book on Maori people, *Extracts of Letters from New Zealand on the War Question* (1861); returned to England (1870); collections of work at Auckland City Art Gallery and Alexander Turnbull Library, Wellington. ❖ See also *Dictionary of New Zealand Biography* (Vol. 1).

ABRAHAM, Constance Palgrave (1864–1942). New Zealand equestrian, tennis player, golfer, and social worker. Name variations: Constance Palgrave Martyn. Born Constance Palgrave Martyn, May 12, 1864, at Palgrave, Suffolk, England; died on Oct 3, 1942, at Te Ranara, New Zealand; dau. of Charles John Martyn (curate) and Catherine Elizabeth (Harrison) Martyn; m. Lionel Augustus Abraham (merchant, d. 1939), 1890; children: 4 daughters and 3 sons. ❖ Active volunteer in community social work; accomplished equestrian, tennis player, and golfer, won many championships; only woman member of Palmerston North Hospital Board (1921–35); elected 1st president of Palmerston North branch of YWCA (1930). Made Member of British Empire (MBE, 1919); received King George V Silver Jubilee Medal (1935). ❖ See also *Dictionary of New Zealand Biography* (Vol. 3).

ABRAHAMOWITSCH, Ruth (1907–1974). German concert dancer. Name variations: Ruth Sorel Abrahamowitsch; Ruth Sorel. Born 1907 in Halle-auf-Saale, Germany; died April 1, 1974, in Warsaw, Poland. ❖ Performed in Mary Wigman's dance troupe (1923–28); danced works by Lizzie Maudrik for Berlin Stadtische Oper (Municipal Opera), including *Legend of Joseph* (1930), for which she won recognition as character dancer; performed with George Groke in various recitals in Berlin and abroad; won award at International Solo Dance Festival in Warsaw (1933); danced concerts throughout US and Canada with Groke (starting

c. 1934), performing own works including *Salome* (1933), *Dance after a Picture by Pisanello* (1934), and *Jeanne d'Arc* (1935). Further works include *Death Lament* (1935), *Conjurer* (1935, co-choreographed with Groke), *Diabolic Figure* (1935), *Sillouettes Exchanges* (1935), *A Pair of Lovers at Evening's Rest* (1935) and *Mea Culpa* (1948).

ABRAHAMS, Doris Cole (1925—). American producing manager. Born Doris Cole in New York, New York, Jan 29, 1925; dau. of Mark Harris Cole and Florence May (Kleinman); attended Goucher College and Ohio University; trained for the stage at the Leland Powers School of Theatre in Boston; married Gerald M. Abrahams. ❖ Originally an actress and literary and theatrical agent, produced 1st play, *Blue Holiday*, at Belasco in NY (May 1945); after moving to London, produced *Enter a Free Man* (1968), *Out of the Question* (1968), *Enemy* (1969), and *Child's Play* (1971); in NY, produced or co-produced *Equus* (1974), *Travesties* (1975), and *Once a Catholic* (1977).

ABRAHAMS, Ottilie Grete (1937—). Namibian political leader and physician. Born Ottilie Grete Schimming in Windhoek, South West Africa (now Namibia), 1937; graduate of University of Cape Town, 1961; m. Kenneth Godfrey Abrahams, 1961. ❖ Founding member of the South West Africa Student Body (SWASB), a predecessor of the major nationalist parties; deeply involved with the newly formed South West Africa People's Organisation (SWAPO); served as secretary-general of the Namibian Independence Party (NIP); her efforts were crucial in the establishment of an independent Namibia. ❖ See also *Women in World History.*

ABRAMOVA, Anastasia (1902—). Russian ballet dancer. Born in Russia, 1902; studied with Yekaterina Geltzer and Yekaterina Vazem; entered Bolshoi School, 1910, graduated, 1917; trained with Liubov Bank, Valentina Kudriavtseva, and Nina Podgoretskaya, under direction of Alexander Gorsky and Vassily Tikhomirov at Bolshoi Theater. ❖ Made debut at the Bolshoi as Lise in *La Fille Mal Gardée* (1922) and was known there for her Swanilda in *Coppélia* and Aurora in *The Sleeping Beauty;* other roles included Jeanne in *Flames of Paris,* Tao-Hoa in *The Red Flower,* and Stepmother and Fairy in *Cinderella;* retired (1948).

ABRAMOVA, Nelli (1940—). Soviet volleyball player. Born Aug 18, 1940, in USSR. ❖ At Tokyo Olympics, won bronze medal in the team competition (1964).

ABRAMS, Harriett (c. 1758–c. 1822). English composer and soprano. Born of Jewish descent c. 1758; died c. 1822; sister of singers Theodosia Abrams (c. 1765–c. 1834) and Eliza Abrams (c. 1772–c. 1830); studied with composer Thomas Arne. ❖ Made debut at Drury Lane in *May Day* (1775); left Drury Lane (1780) to become a singer in fashionable concerts; appeared in Handel Commemoration concerts and in some of the Antient Music concerts (1784); limited appearances to exclusive programs in the homes of the nobility; staged annual benefits where Haydn played the piano (1792, 1794, 1795); a composer as well as a singer, published 2 sets of Italian and English canzonets, a collection of Scottish songs, and a number of ballads, including "Crazy Jane," which was quite popular (1799–1800). ❖ See also *Women in World History.*

ABRANTÈS, Laure d' (1784–1838). French novelist. Name variations: Laurette de St. Martine-Permon, Laure Permon, Duchesse d'Abrantès or Abrantes; (pseudonym) Madame Junot. Born at Montpellier, France, 1784 (some sources cite 1785); died in Paris, June 6(?), 1838; dau. of Corsican mother (friend of Letizia Bonaparte); m. General Junot (one of Napoleon's generals), later duke of Abrantès or duc d'Abrantès; children: Constance Aubert (b. 1803). ❖ Became lady-in-waiting to Letizia Bonaparte, mother of Napoleon; after husband committed suicide, began to write; published her 18-volume *Mémoires de Mme la duchesse d'Abrantès ou Souvenirs historiques sur Napoléon, la Révolution, le Directoire, le Consulat, l'Empire et la Restauration* (1831–35); also wrote *Histoire des salons de Paris* (1836–38). ❖ See also *Women in World History.*

ABRASHITOVA, Elena (1974—). Ukrainian gymnast. Born Mar 21, 1974, in Kherson, Ukraine. ❖ At Australian Grand Prix, won a team gold and a silver for vault (1989); at World Sports Fair, won a silver for vault (1990).

ABROSIMOVA, Svetlana (1980—). Russian basketball player. Born Svetlana Olegovna Abrosimova, July 9, 1980, in St. Petersburg, Russia; graduated from University of Connecticut, 2001. ❖ Forward; placed 5th on the UConn career scoring list with 1,598 points; drafted by Minnesota Lynx of WNBA in 1st round (2001); won a silver medal with Russian National team at World championships (1998); was a member of the Russian National team at Sydney Olympics (2000). Twice named Kodak All-American.

ABUKAWA, Ginko (1938—). *See Chiba, Ginko.*

ABZUG, Bella (1920–1998). US politician, attorney, feminist and peace activist. Born Bella Savitsky, July 24, 1920, in New York, NY; died in New York, NY, Mar 31, 1998; dau. of Emmanuel (Russian immigrant and meat-market owner) and Esther Savitsky; graduate of Hunter College; Columbia Law School, LLB, 1947; m. Martin Abzug (stockbroker), June 1945; children: Eve Gail (Egee) Abzug; Liz Abzug. ❖ Helped found the Women's Strike for Peace (1961) and was active in the peace movement (1960s and 1970s); was an early supporter and founder of the National Organization for Women (NOW) and remained active in feminist issues (late 1960–98); was active in reform politics in NY and elected to Congress, serving in the US House of Representatives (1970–76); gained fame for her outspoken support of the women's liberation movement and supported legislation that promoted federal job programs, public transportation, and individual right to privacy; ran unsuccessfully for the US Senate from NY (1976); served as chair of the National Advisory Council on Women (1977–78); remained active in women's issues and co-founded the National Women's Political Caucus (1971). ❖ See also *Women in World History.*

ACARIE, Barbe (1566–1618). French nun and mystic. Name variations: Jeanne Avrillot; Marie de l'Incarnation. Born Jeanne Avrillot in 1566; died 1618; dau. of Nicolas Avrillot (wealthy aristocrat) and mother from old Parisian family; educated at convent of Longchamps; m. Pierre Acarie (d. 1613), viscount of Villemare, 1584; children: 6. ❖ Though known for her piety and desire to become a nun, was married at 16 at urging of parents (1584); while husband squandered the family fortune, turned her Paris home into a spiritual salon frequented by many, including Vincent de Paul and Francis de Sâles; influenced the court of King Henry IV to introduce the reformed order of the Carmelites to France (1603); was also instrumental in helping Madame de Sainte-Beuve in establishing the French Ursulines; after husband died, became a lay sister at Carmelite convent at Amiens and assumed the religious name of Marie de l'Incarnation; beatified (1794). ❖ See also L.C. Sheppard, *Barbe Acarie, Wife and Mystic* (1953); and *Women in World History.*

ACCAIUOLI, Laudomia. *See Medici, Laudomia de.*

ACCA LARENTIA. *See Larentia, Acca.*

ACCORAMBONI, Vittoria (c. 1557–1585). Duchess of Bracciano. Name variations: Virginia; Vittoria Corombona. Born c. 1557; murdered in Padua, Dec 22, 1585; m. Francesco Peretti, 1573 (murdered 1581); m. Paolo or Paulo Giordano Orsini (d. 1585), duke of Bracciano (or Brachiano). ❖ Known for her great beauty and wit, was involved in a series of intrigues culminating in multiple murders, including her own and those of her two husbands; after 1st husband Francesco Peretti was murdered at instigation of Paolo Orsini, wed Orsini; upon his death (Nov 13, 1585), became involved in litigation with Ludovic Orsini, concerning her inheritance, and was murdered by him. These events were altered and adapted by John Webster for his play *The White Devil or Vittoria Corombona,* 1st presented around 1612; her history was also written by Gnoli (1870) and was made the subject of a novel by L. Tieck, *Vittoria Accoramboni* (1840). ❖ See also *Women in World History.*

ACE, Jane (1905–1974). American radio actress. Born Jane Sherwood, Oct 12, 1905, in Kansas City, Missouri; died Nov 11, 1974; married Goodman Ace (radio actor and writer), 1928. ❖ With husband, starred on the urbane radio show "Easy Aces" (1928–45); portrayed the amiable but ditzy wife while he played the indulgent husband, generally tagging her non-sequiturs with "Isn't that awful," or another line, famously purloined by Ronald Reagan in a campaign debate with Walter Mondale, "There you go again." ❖ See also Goodman Ace, *Ladies and Gentlemen—Easy Aces* (Doubleday, 1970).

ACEDO, Carmen (1975—). Spanish rhythmic gymnast. Name variations: Carmen Acedo Jorge. Born Jan 5, 1975, in Lerida, Spain. ❖ Was the Spanish national rhythmic gymnast champion (1993); won the World championship title on clubs (1993); retired (1993).

ACEDO JORGE, Carmen (1975—). *See Acedo, Carmen.*

ACEVEDO, Angela de (d. 1644). Spanish playwright. Name variations: Doña Ángela de Acevedo. Born in Lisbon, Portugal; died in 1644; dau. of Juan de Acevedo Pereira, a noble, and Isabel de Oliveira. ❖ Was a court favorite of Queen Elizabeth Valois (1602–1644), wife of Philip IV of Spain; plays, all performed, include *El muerto disimilado* (The Hidden Corpse), *La Margarita del Tajo* (The Pearl of the Tiger), *Dicha y desdicha del juego* (The Joys and Sorrows of Gambling), and *Devoción de la Virgen* (Devotion to Our Lady).

ACHATOWA, Albina (1976—). *See Akhatova, Albina.*

ACHESON, Anne Crawford (1882–1962). Irish sculptor. Born 1882 in Portadown, Co. Armagh, Ulster; died in 1962; attended Victoria College, Belfast, Belfast School of Arts, and Royal College of Art, London; studied sculpture under Lanteri. ❖ In early years, worked in wood before turning to metal, stone and concrete; often exhibited at Royal Academy and internationally; was a member of Royal Society of British Sculptors and Society of Artists in Watercolor; during WWI, worked with the Surgical Requisites Association. Awarded CBE (1919) for work with Surgical Requisites; received Feodora Gleichen Memorial Award (1938).

ACHESON, Carrie (1934—). Irish politician. Born Carrie Barlow, Sept 1934, in Tipperary, Ireland; sister of Senator Tras Honan; m. Hugh Acheson. ❖ Served as mayor of Clonmel (1981–82); representing Fianna Fáil, elected to 22nd Dáil for Tipperary South (1981–82).

ACHKINA, Rita (fl. 1968). Russian cross-country skier. Born in USSR. ❖ Won a bronze medal for 3x5km relay at Grenoble Olympics (1968).

ACHMATOWA, Anna (1889–1966). *See Akhmatova, Anna.*

ACHSAH. Biblical woman. Only dau. of Caleb (1 Chr. 2:49). ❖ Was offered in marriage to Othniel, as a reward for his conquest of the city of Debir, or Kirjath-sepher; requested the springs of Upper and Lower Gullath as a wedding gift.

ACHURCH, Janet (1864–1916). English actress. Name variations: Janet Achurch Sharp. Born Jan 17, 1864, in Lancashire, England; died Sept 11, 1916; descended from old acting family; great granddau. of Achurch Ward (manager of Theatre Royal, Manchester); m. Charles Charrington (actor). ❖ The 1st English actress to play Ibsen, won acclaim as Nora in *A Doll's House* (1899); soon after, formed her own company and toured with the play in Australia, India, and America; also appeared in Shaw's *Candida* (title role) and *Captain Brassbound's Conversion* (as Cecily Waynflete); became addicted to morphine and cocaine, effectively leaving the stage (1913). ❖ See also *Women in World History.*

ACKER, Jean (1893–1978). American actress. Name variations: Jean Acker Valentino, Jean Mendoza. Born Oct 23, 1893, in Trenton, New Jersey; died Aug 16, 1978, in Los Angeles, California; m. Rudolph Valentino (actor), 1919 (div. 1921). ❖ Films include *Checkers, Lombardi Ltd., Brewster's Millions, The Ladder of Lies, The Woman in Chains* and *Spellbound.*

ACKER, Kathy (1943–1997). American novelist and performance artist. Born Kathy Lehman, April 18, 1943, in New York, NY; grew up in Manhattan; died of breast cancer, Nov 30, 1997, at an alternative treatment center in Tijuana, Mexico; dau. of Donald Lehman and Clare Lehman; attended Brandeis University and University of California; studied poetry under Jerome Rothenburg; m. Robert Acker; m. Peter Gordon. ❖ Influenced by Black Mountain poets, William Burroughs, and French modernists, wrote *The Childlike Life of the Black Tarantula by the Black Tarantula* (1975), *The Adult Life of Toulouse Lautrec by Henri Toulouse Lautrec* (1975), *Hello, I'm Erica Jong* (1982), *Great Expectations* (1983), *Blood and Guts in High School* (1984), *Empire of the Senseless* (1988), *In Memoriam to Identity* (1990), and *Pussy, King of the Pirates* (1995); also wrote essays and reviews for magazines; lived and worked in London (1980s).

ACKERMAN, Paula (1893–1989). American rabbinical pioneer. Name variations: Paula H. Ackerman. Born Dec 7, 1893; died Jan 12, 1989, in Mississippi; m. William Ackerman, a rabbi (died 1950). ❖ Following death of husband (rabbi at Temple Beth Israel in Meridian, Mississippi), took over his 100-member Reform congregation as an interim spiritual leader (1951–54), the 1st woman to perform the full duties of a rabbi.

ACKERMAN, Val (1959—). American basketball player, lawyer, and business executive. Born Valerie Ackerman, Nov 7, 1959, in Lakewood, New Jersey; graduate of University of Virginia, 1981; graduate of University of California at Los Angeles School of Law, 1985; m. Charles Rappaport (lawyer); children: Emily and Sally Rappaport. ❖ Was a 4-year starter on women's basketball team at University of Virginia and 2-time All-American; played professional basketball in France; joined the NBA (1988) as staff attorney; served as president of the WNBA (1996–2004).

ACKERMAN, Vicki (1972—). *See Goetze, Vicki.*

ACKERMANN, Louise Victorine (1813–1890). French poet. Born Victorine Choquet in Paris, France, Nov 30, 1813; died in Nice, Aug 3, 1890; m. Paul Ackermann (d. 1846, German poet and philologist), 1843. ❖ Widowed after 3 years of marriage, wrote poems of pessimism, passion, and despair; retired near Nice where she wrote *Contes* (1855), *Poésies, Premières poésies* (1863), *Poésies philosophiques* (1871), and *Pensées d'une solitaire* (*Thoughts of a Lonely Woman*, 1882). ❖ See also *Women in World History.*

ACKERMANN, Rosemarie (1952—). East German high jumper. Name variations: Rosi Ackermann. Born April 4, 1952, in Lohsa, East Germany. ❖ Broke the world record with 1.94 meters (1974); won a gold medal at European championships (1974); won a gold medal in Montreal Olympics at 1.93 meters (6′4, 1976); cleared the bar at 2.0 meters in West Berlin (1977). ❖ See also *Women in World History.*

ACKLAND, Valentine (1906–1969). British author. Born Mary Kathleen McCrory Ackland in London, England, 1906; died Nov 9, 1969, in Dorset, England; elder sister of Joan Ackland; m. Richard Turpin; lived with Sylvia Townsend Warner for 30 years. ❖ Works include (with Sylvia Townsend Warner) *Whether a Dove or Seagull* (1934), *Country Conditions* (1936), *The Nature of the Moment* (1973), *Further Poems* (1978), *For Sylvia, An Honest Account* (1985). ❖ See also Wendy Mulford, *This Narrow Place: Sylvia Townsend Warner and Valentine Ackland: Life, Letters and Politics, 1930–1951* (Pandora, 1988); and *Women in World History.*

ACKTÉ, Aino (1876–1944). Finnish soprano. Name variations: Aïno Ackté or Ackte; Aino Ackté-Jalander. Born in Helsinki, Finland, April 23, 1876; died in Nummela, Aug 8, 1944; dau. of Lorenz Nikolai Ackté (baritone and conductor) and Emmy Strömer Ackté (soprano); sister of Irma Tervani (1887–1936, leading mezzo-soprano); attended Paris Conservatoire; studied with Duvernoy. ❖ Made debut at Grand Opera in Paris as Marguerite in Gounod's *Faust* (1897); interpreted many parts with great success, including Elsa in *Lohengrin,* Elizabeth in *Tannhäuser,* Benjamin in Méhul's *Joseph,* and other leading roles; under baton of Sir Thomas Beecham, was triumphant as the 1st British Salome in Strauss' opera; helped found the Finnish National Opera and was its director (1938–39).

ACLAND, Lady Harriet (1750–1815). English memoirist. Born Christian Henrietta Caroline, Jan 3, 1750; died at Tetton, near Taunton, England, July 21, 1815; dau. of Stephen, 1st earl of Ilchester; m. Major John Dyke Acland. ❖ Following marriage, accompanied husband, who was under the command of General John Burgoyne when the British army invaded NY (1777); recorded her adventures in her memoirs, which helped chronicle this facet of the Revolutionary War. ❖ See also *Women in World History.*

ACOSTA, Mercedes de. *See de Acosta, Mercedes*

ACOSTA DE SAMPER, Soledad (1833–1913). Colombian journalist and novelist. Name variations: Soledad Samper; (pseudonyms) Bertilda Aldebarán, Olga Aldebarán, Aldebarán, Bertilda, Renato, and Andina. Born Soledad Acosta in Bogotá, Colombia, May 5, 1833; died in Colombia, Mar 17, 1913; dau. of Joaquín Acosta (Colombian scholar and politician) and Caroline Kemble Acosta; educated in Paris; m. José Maria Samper Agudelo (editor of *El Neo-Granadino* (*The New Granadan*), 1855 (died 1888); children: 4 daughters. ❖ Historian, educator, journalist, novelist and short-story writer, considered one of the most important intellectuals in South America, was sent to Halifax, Nova Scotia, at 12, to live with maternal grandmother; studied in Paris for several years, writing under pseudonyms Aldebarán, Bertilda, Renato, and Andina; began to publish (1858); with husband, moved to Lima, Peru (1862), where they founded a magazine *Revista Americana;* also helped found and edit *La Mujer* (*Woman*), the 1st periodical sustained exclusively by women, which ran from 1878 to 1881; returned to Bogota where husband served in Congress; following his death (1888), returned to Paris; wrote over 45 novels, including *Los piratas en Cartagena* (The Pirates in Cartagena, 1885), *La familia del tio Andrés, El talismán de Enrique, Biografía del general Joaquin Acosta, Dolores, Cuadros de la vida de un mujer, La Monja, Un chistoso de aldea,* and *Historia de dos familias.*

ACQUANETTA (1921–2004). American actress. Name variations: Burnu Acquanetta; Burnu Davenport. Born Mildred Davenport (some sources erroneously cite Burnu Acquanetta), July 17, 1921, of Arapaho descent in Cheyenne, Wyoming; died of Alzheimer's disease, Aug 16, 2004, in Ahwatukee, Arizona; sister of Horace Davenport (Pennsylvania judge);

m. Jack Ross (owner of a car dealership, 1950s) (div. 1980s); children: Jack, Lance, Tom and Rex Ross. ❖ B-movie actress, best known for her role in *Tarzan and the Leopard Woman* (1946), began career as a model; also appeared in *Captive Wild Woman* and *The Sword of Monte Cristo;* founded a theater in Scottsdale.

ACTE (fl. 55–69). Mistress of the Roman emperor Nero. Name variations: Claudia Acte or Akte. Born in Asia Minor; brought to Rome as slave in imperial house of Nero or Claudius; fl. bet. 55 and 69. ❖ Imperial freedwoman, became the mistress of Nero (55), causing a split between Nero and his mother Agrippina the Younger; helped to avert the seduction of Nero by Agrippina (59); assisted at Nero's funeral (69), a testimony of her devotion. ❖ See also *Women in World History.*

ACTON, Eliza (1799–1859). English writer. Name variations: Elizabeth Acton. Born in Battle, England, April 17, 1799; died in Hampstead, Feb 13, 1859. ❖ Wrote poetry during early years, but is best remembered as one of the 1st women to prepare a cookbook; her popular work, *Modern Cookery for Private Families* (1845), went through numerous editions and influenced Isabella Beeton; brought out her last work, *The English Bread Book* (1857).

ACUÑA, Dora (fl. 1940s). Paraguayan poet. Name variations: Dora Gomez Bueno de Acuña; Dora Acuna. Born in Paraguay; fl. in 1940s. ❖ Seen as a master of erotic poetry in the tradition of Uruguayan poet Delmira Agustini, works include *Flor de caña* (Reed Flower, 1940), *Barro celeste* (Heavenly Mud, 1943), and *Luz en el abismo* (Light in the Abyss, 1954); also published in journals and newspapers.

AD, Mrs. (c. 1886–1945). *Topperwein, Elizabeth "Plinky."*

ADA (c. 380–c. 323 BCE). Ruler of Caria. Born c. 380 BCE in Caria (Southwestern Turkey); died c. 323 BCE; dau. of Hecatomnus, satrap of Caria (r. 392–377); sister of Mausolus (r. 377–353), Artemisia (r. 353–351), Idrieus (r. 351–344), and Pixodarus (r. 341–336); m. brother Idrieus; adopted Alexander the Great as royal heir (334). ❖ Ruled Caria jointly with brother-husband Idrieus (351–344), before assuming the throne on his death; saw her rule contested by her younger brother, Pixodarus, who seems to have seized most of Caria by 341; refusing to surrender her claim to the throne, regained control of Caria with the help of Alexander the Great, whom she (being childless) adopted and made her royal heir (334); after her death (c. 323), her family died out and Caria, already absorbed into the Macedonian sphere of influence, came to be ruled by the Macedonian, Philoxenus. ❖ See also *Women in World History.*

ADA-MAY (1898–1978). *See Weeks, Ada May.*

ADAH. Biblical woman. First wife of Lamech; children: Jabal and Jubal.

ADAH. Biblical woman. Name variations: Bashemath. Dau. of Elon the Hittite; was the 1st of Esau's 3 wives.

ADAIR, Bethenia Owens (1840–1926). *See Owens-Adair, Bethenia.*

ADAIR, Jean (1872–1953). Canadian-born stage and screen actress. Name variations: Jennet Adair. Born Violet McNaughton, June 13, 1872, in Hamilton, Ontario, Canada; died May 11, 1953, in New York, NY. ❖ Made NY debut as Mary Grayson in *It's a Boy* (1922); appeared in over 25 plays in such roles as Mertie Ferguson in *That Ferguson Family,* Mrs. Fisher in *The Show Off,* Madame Tanqueray in *Murder at the Vanities,* Demetria Riffle in *On Borrowed Time,* Cora Swanson in *Mornings at Seven,* Miss Holyrod in *Bell Book and Candle,;* also portrayed Martha Brewster in *Arsenic and Old Lace* for three years on stage (1941–43) and on film; made film debut in *Advice to the Lovelorn* (1933).

ADAIR, Virginia Hamilton (1913–2004). American poet. Born Mary Virginia Hamilton, Feb 28, 1913, in the Bronx, NY; raised in Montclair, New Jersey; died Sept 16, 2004, in Claremont, California; dau. of Robert Browning Hamilton; Mount Holyoke College, BS; Radcliffe, MA; m. Douglass Adair (prominent historian), 1936 (committed suicide 1968); children: Katharine Adair Waugh, Robert Adair, and Douglass Adair. ❖ Was an English professor at California Polytechnic University in Pomona for 22 years; wrote poetry for 73 years before publishing 1st collection, *Ants on the Melon,* at age 83, which sold more than 28,000 copies.

ADAM, Jean (1710–1765). Scottish poet. Name variations: Mrs. Jane Adam; Mrs. Jane Adams. Born 1710 in Crawfordsdyke, Renfrewshire, Scotland; died April 3, 1765, in Glasgow. ❖ Orphaned young; employed as governess; began publishing poems by subscription under title *Miscellany Poems, by Mrs. Jane Adams, in Crawfordsdyke* (1734); shortly thereafter, opened a girls' school in Crawford Bridge; when poems didn't sell, had to close school and resort to peddling; died in a poorhouse in Glasgow.

ADAM, Juliette la Messine (1836–1936). French feminist, journalist, political activist, and salonnière. Name variations: Juliette Lamber Adam, Juliette Lamber, Juliette Lambert; (pseudonyms) La Messine or de la Messine, Paul Vasili, La Grande Française. Born Juliette Lambert in Verberie, Picardy, Oct 4, 1836; died in Callian, Aug 25, 1936; m. Alexis de la Messine (government official), div. 1867; m. Edmond Adam (journalist and political activist), 1868–1877; children: (1st m.) daughter. ❖ Ran a successful Parisian salon for 4 decades; made contributions to journals, beginning with a letter to the editor of *Le Siècle* (1856); founded the journal *La Nouvelle Review* (1879); known particularly for fighting for women's suffrage and for her work against the German threat to France; wrote plays, memoirs, and essays, including *Idées anti-proudhoniennes sur l'amour, la femme et le mariage* (1858), and *Blanches de Coucy* (1858); also wrote the biography *Garibaldi, sa vie d'après des documents inédits* (1859), and such novels as *Grecque* (1879), *Païenne* (1883), *Chrétienne* (1913). ❖ See also *Women in World History*.

ADAM, Madge (1912–2001). English solar physicist. Name variations: Madge Gertrude Adam. Born Mar 6, 1912, near Highbury, north London, England; died Aug 25, 2001. ❖ Acclaimed for research on sunspots and interferometry, served as lecturer in department of astrophysics at University of Oxford Observatory (1937–79); served as research fellow and senior research fellow at St. Hugh's College, Oxford (1957–80); worked at Mt. Stromlo Observatory in Australia (1963–64).

ADAM SMITH, Janet (1905–1999). Scottish editor, author and journalist. Born Janet Buchanan Adam Smith, Dec 9, 1905, in Glasgow, Scotland; died 1999; dau. of Sir George (minister and university principal) and Lady Lilian (Buchanan) Adam Smith; attended Cheltenham Ladies' College (scholar), Somerville College, Oxford; Aberdeen University, LLD (1962); m. William Edward Roberts (poet as Michael Roberts), 1935 (died 1948); m. John Dudley Carleton (headmaster of schools), 1965 (died 1974); children: (1st m.) three sons, one daughter. ❖ Worked for BBC (1928–35), *Listener* (assistant editor, 1930–35), *New Statesman & Nation* (assistant literary editor, 1949–52, literary editor, 1952–60); wrote several well-received biographies, including two on author John Buchan; edited a number of books for both children and adults, including *The Faber Book of Children's Verse*, *Henry James and Robert Louis Stevenson: A Record of Friendship and Criticism* (correspondence), and *The Living Stream: An Anthology of Twentieth Century Verse*; translator of several climbing books with Nea Morin, including *Annapurna*; served as president, Royal Literary Fund.

ADAM-SMITH, Patsy (1924–2001). Australian historian. Name variations: Patricia Jean Adam-Smith; Patricia Jean Beckett; Patsy Adam Smith. Born Patricia Jean Smith, May 31, 1924, in Nowingi, Victoria, Australia; died Sept 21, 2001, in Melbourne, Victoria, Australia; grew up throughout remote districts of Victoria; father was a fettler on the railway; mother tended small-town train or post stations. ❖ One of Australia's best-known writers, was educated through correspondence school; during WWII, served with the Australian Medical Women's Service (1943–44); was the 1st woman radio operator on an Australian merchant ship (1954–60); subsequently served as an adult education officer in Hobart (1960–67) and manuscripts field officer for the State Library of Victoria (1970–82); served as president of Australian Writers, Victoria, and federal president of the Fellows Australian Writers, Victoria (1973); published *The Anzacs* (1978), which shared *The Age* Book of the Year Award and was later made into a popular 13-part tv series; roamed the world researching history, folklore, and tradition; wrote 28 books, including the semi-autobiographical *Hear the Train Blow* (1964) and *Good-Bye Girlie* (1995), as well as *Moonbird People* (1965), *Australian Women at War* (1984), and *Prisoners of War* (1992). Awarded OBE (1980) and Officer of the Order of Australia (1994).

ADA MAY (1898–1978). *See Weeks, Ada May.*

ADAMEK, Donna (1957—). American bowler. Born Feb 1, 1957, in Duarte, California. ❖ Won 5 major titles: Women's Open (1978, 1981), WIBC Queens (1979, 1980), and WPBA national championship (1980). Named Woman Bowler of the Year (1978–81); also teamed with Nikki Gianulias to win WIBC doubles title (1980); rolled 3 perfect 300 games (1981–82).

ADAMOVA, Adela (1927—). Italian-born Argentine ballerina, actress and singer. Born in Turin, Italy, 1927; became an Argentine citizen; studied with Michel Borovski. ❖ Left Italy to join the Teatro Colón in Buenos Aires (1942), promoted to soloist (1947), then ballerina (1948); appeared as guest artist at the Paris Opéra, Teatro all Scala, Milan, Maggio Musicale Fiorentino (1953); repertoire included *Sueño de Niña, Evolucion del Movimiento, Hamlet, Les Patineurs, Apollon Musagète, Coppélia, The Sleeping Beauty, The Nutcracker* and works of Margarethe Wallmann: *Offenbachiana, Aubade, Saloman* and *La Boutique Fantasque*; also recorded songs in Spanish, Portuguese, Italian, and English.

ADAMS, Abigail (1744–1818). American first lady. Born Abigail Smith in Weymouth, Massachusetts, Nov 11, 1744; died Oct 28, 1818, in Quincy, Massachusetts; dau. of Reverend William Smith (1706–1783, pastor) and Elizabeth (Quincy) Smith (1721–1775); m. John Adams (1735–1826, US president), Oct 25, 1764; children: Abigail (Nabby, 1765–1813); John Quincy (b. July 11, 1767–1848); Susanna (Suky, b. Dec 28, 1768–1770); Charles (b. May 29, 1770–1800); Thomas Boylston (b. Sept 15, 1772–1832). ❖ An early advocate of gender equality in the American revolutionary and early national eras, married John Adams and took up residence in Braintree (Oct 25, 1764); managed family and farm during husband's absences to the Continental congresses (1774–77) and during his stay in Europe (1778–84); witnessed Battle of Bunker Hill (June 17, 1775); resided in Europe (1784–88); served as wife of the 1st vice president (1789–97); served as first lady (1797–1801); reigned as matriarch of the Adams family (1801–18); spent a lifetime working to overcome the disadvantages suffered by women of her day; through hundreds of letters, advocated a philosophy that refused to accept female inferiority. ❖ See also Charles W. Akers, *Abigail Adams: An American Woman* (Little, Brown, 1980); Phyllis Lee Levin, *Abigail Adams* (St. Martin's, 1987); Lynne Withey, *Dearest Friend: A Life of Abigail Adams* (Free Press, 1981); and *Women in World History*.

ADAMS, Abigail First daughter. Name variations: (nickname) Nabby; Abigail Adams Smith. Born July 14, 1765; died 1813; dau. of Abigail Adams (1744–1818) and John Adams (US president); sister of John Quincy Adams (US president); m. Colonel William Stephens Smith; children: 4. ❖ See also *Women in World History*.

ADAMS, Abigail Brooks (1808–1889). American Brahmin. Name variations: Abby. Born 1808; died 1889; dau. of Peter Chardon Brooks (merchant); m. Charles Francis Adams (1807–1886, lawyer, diplomat); children: Louisa (1831–1870); John Quincy II (1833–1894); Charles Francis Jr. (1835–1915); Henry Brooks Adams (1838–1918, historian who m. Clover Adams); Arthur (1841–1846); Mary (1845–1918); Brooks (1848–1917, a historian). ❖ See also *Women in World History*.

ADAMS, Adrienne (1906–2002). American artist, illustrator, and author of children's books. Born Feb 8, 1906, in Fort Smith, Arkansas; died Dec 3, 2002; dau. of Edwin Hunt (accountant) and Sue (Broaddus) Adams; attended American School of Design, 1926; m. John Lonzo Anderson (writer, under name Lonzo Anderson), Aug 17, 1935. ❖ Taught in a rural school in Oklahoma (1927); designed displays, murals, textiles, greeting cards, in New York City (1929–45); served as art director for Staples-Smith Displays, New York City (1945–52); illustrated more than 30 books for a number of children's authors, including husband, Lonzo Anderson, as well as her own work, such as *A Woggle Of Witches* (1971) and the anthology, *Poetry of Earth* (1972). Received Caldecott honors for *Houses from the Sea* (1960) and *The Day We Saw the Sun Come Up* (1962), as well as a Rutgers Award for contributions to children's literature (1973), and a Medallion from the University of Southern Mississippi (1977).

ADAMS, Alice (1926–1999). American novelist and short-fiction writer. Born Aug 14, 1926, in Fredericksburg, Virginia; grew up near Chapel Hill, North Carolina; died May 27, 1999, in San Francisco, California; dau. of Nicholson Adams (Spanish professor) and Agatha Boyd Adams (writer); graduated from Radcliffe College, 1946; m. Mark Linenthal Jr., 1947 (div. 1958); children: Peter Adams Linenthal (b. 1951). ❖ Known for her wry and witty fiction, worked in publishing in New York City; wrote 11 novels, including *Careless Love* (1966), *Families and Survivors* (1974), *Listening to Billie* (1978), *Rich Rewards* (1980), *Superior Women* (1984), *Caroline's Daughter* (1991), *Almost Perfect* (1993), *A Southern Exposure* (1995), *After the War* (2000) and *Second Chances* (1988), which is considered her best work; short story–collections include *To See You*

Again (1982), *The Last Lovely City* (1999) and *The Stories of Alice Adams* (2002).

ADAMS, Annette (1877–1956). American lawyer and jurist. Born Mar 12, 1877; died in Sacramento, California, 1956; State Normal School, Chico, California, 1897; University of California–Berkeley, 1904, J.D., 1912, the only woman in her class. ❖ Became active in Democratic Party; named federal prosecutor for Northern District of California, the 1st woman to hold the post; named special US attorney in San Francisco (1918), then promoted to assistant attorney general in Washington, DC (1920), where her position involved overseeing prosecution of violators of prohibition's Volstead Act under A. Mitchell Palmer; returned to private practice (1921), until Franklin Roosevelt asked her to serve as assistant special counsel under California Supreme Court Judge John Preston, to handle prosecution in *US v. Standard Oil;* elected to a 12-year term as jurist on the California 3rd District Court of Appeals (1944), the 1st woman in that Western state to hold such a high-ranking judicial position.

ADAMS, Betty (b. 1926). See Adams, Julie.

ADAMS, Carolyn (1943—). African-American dancer. Born Aug 6, 1943, in New York, NY; father was managing editor of the *Amsterdam News;* mother was a writer, pianist and composer; sister of Julie Adams Strandberg (dancer); studied at Martha Graham School and attended Sarah Lawrence College. ❖ Joined Paul Taylor Dance Company as company's only black member (1965) and toured with repertory, creating roles in *Post Meridian* (1966), *Orbs* (1966), *Public Domain* (1968), *Le Sacré du Printemps* (1980), and others; taught dance composition in London and Denmark; founded Harlem Dance Foundation with sister, a school and center for community preservation and restoration that was originally located in family's historic brownstone residence.

ADAMS, Catherine (1893–1959). See Adams, Kathryn.

ADAMS, Charity (1917–2002). African-American military officer. Name variations: Charity Earley. Born Charity E. Adams, Dec 5, 1917, in Kittrell, North Carolina; died Jan 13, 2002, in Dayton, Ohio; graduate of Wilberforce University. ❖ Was the 1st black commissioned officer in the Women's Army Auxiliary Corps and commander of the only battalion of black women to serve overseas during WWII; retired as a lieutenant colonel (1946) and turned to teaching. ❖ See also memoir *One Woman's Army: A Black Officer Remembers the WAC* (1989).

ADAMS, Claire (1898–1978). Canadian-born actress. Name variations: Clara Adams, Clare Adams, Peggy Adams. Born Sept 24, 1898, in Winnipeg, Manitoba, Canada; died Sep 25, 1978, in Melbourne, Australia; sister of Gerald Drayson Adams (screenwriter); m. Benjamin B. Hampton (producer), 1924 (died 1932); m. Donald MacKimmon (sportsman), 1938. ❖ Appeared opposite Lon Chaney in *The Penalty;* other films include *Riders of the Dawn, Black Beauty, Where the North Begins, Fast Set, Devil's Cargo, Souls for Sables, The Big Parade* and *The Sea Wolf.*

ADAMS, Clara (1898–1978). See Adams, Claire.

ADAMS, Clara (born c. 1899). American aviation pioneer. Name variations: Mrs. Clara Adams; The Flying Widow. Born c. 1899; lived in Maspeth, Long Island, NY, and on Riverside Drive in Manhattan. ❖ Was aboard some of the most famous flights of her day, including on the *Graf Zeppelin* from US to Germany (1928), on the *Hawaii Clipper,* which made the 1st passenger flight from US to Hawaii (Oct 1936), and on a record-breaking commercial around-the-world flight on board the *Dixie Clipper* (Jun. 28–Jul 15, 1939); was also the 1st woman passenger on a flight from South America to North America (1931).

ADAMS, Clare (1898–1978). See Adams, Claire.

ADAMS, Clover (1843–1885). American Brahmin, scholar and salonnière. Name variations: Marian Hooper Adams, Marian "Clover" Hooper. Born Marian Hooper in 1843; committed suicide, Dec 6, 1885; dau. of Robert William Hooper and Ellen (Sturgis); sister of Ellen "Nella" Hooper Gurney (1838–1887); attended Elizabeth Agassiz's school for young ladies in Cambridge, the forerunner of Radcliffe; m. Henry Adams (1838–1918, historian and author), June 27, 1872. ❖ Spirited wife of Henry Adams, is completely missing in his famous autobiography, *The Education of Henry Adams,* whose 20th chapter is dated 1871, the year before he married her, and subsequent chapter is entitled "Twenty Years After"; accompanied husband on his trips for historical research, often helping him; was portrayed by Henry James as Mrs. Bonnycastle in *Pandora* and Marcellus Cockerel in *The*

Point of View. A six-foot statue, a memorial to her by Augustus Saint-Gaudens, commissioned by her husband, stands in Rock Creek Cemetery in Washington, DC. ❖ See also Friedrich Otto, *Clover* (Simon & Schuster, 1979); and *Women in World History.*

ADAMS, Constance (1874–1960). American stage and screen actress. Name variations: Mrs. Cecil B. De Mille; Constance De Mille. Born April 27, 1874, in Orange, New Jersey; died July 17, 1960, in Hollywood, California; m. Cecil B. De Mille (director-producer), Aug 16, 1902 (died 1959); children: Cecilia De Mille. ❖ Appeared in the film *Where the Trail Divides* (1914).

ADAMS, Diana (1927–1993). American ballet dancer. Born in Staunton, Virginia, 1927; died in San Andreas, California, Jan 1993; studied with stepmother, Emily Hadley Adams; studied at Ballet Arts School, NY, with Agnes de Mille and Edward Caton. ❖ A leading ballerina with both the New York City Ballet and the American Ballet Theater (ABT), made Broadway debut in the Rodgers and Hammerstein musical *Oklahoma!* (1943); joined ABT (1944), where she was seen in the title role of David Lichine's *Helen of Troy* and as Queen of the Wilis in *Giselle;* created role of the mother in Agnes de Mille's *Fall River Legend* (1948); danced with New York City Ballet (1950–63), performing in many of George Balanchine's major ballets, and is especially remembered for the difficult *pas de deux* danced with Arthur Mitchell in the Balanchine-Stravinsky *Agon* (1957); also appeared in the Danny Kaye film *Knock on Wood* (1954) and Gene Kelly's *Invitation to the Dance* (1956); following retirement (1963), taught at the School of American Ballet in NY.

ADAMS, Donna (1921–1986). See Reed, Donna.

ADAMS, Dorothy (1900–1988). American character actress. Name variations: Dorothy Adams Foulger. Born Jan 8, 1900, in Hannah, North Dakota; died Mar 16, 1988, in Woodland Hills, California. ❖ Appeared in over 40 films, including *Bedtime Story, So Proudly We Hail, Laura, Since You Went Away, Down to the Sea in Ships, Carrie, The Man in the Gray Flannel Suit, The Big Country* and *From the Terrace.*

ADAMS, Edie (1927—). American comedic stage, tv, and screen actress and singer. Name variations: Edie Kovacs. Born Elizabeth Edith Enke, April 16, 1927, in Kingston, Pennsylvania; m. Ernie Kovacs (comedian), 1955 (died 1962). ❖ Appeared on Broadway in *Wonderful Town,* among others; on tv, was a regular on "The Ernie Kovacs Show"; as a spokesperson for Muriel cigars, made famous the phrase "Why don'tcha pick me up and smoke me sometime"; films include *The Apartment, Lover Come Back, It's a Mad Mad Mad Mad World, Under the Yum Yum Tree, Love with the Proper Stranger, The Best Man, The Oscar, Happy Hooker Goes to Hollywood* and *Boxoffice.* Won a Tony award for her performance as Daisy Mae in *Lil' Abner* (1956).

ADAMS, Evangeline Smith (1873–1932). American astrologer. Born in Jersey City, New Jersey, 1873; died 1932; educated at private school, Andover, Massachusetts. ❖ Originated "Adams' Philosophy," a synthesis of the occult theories of the Orient and the West; after building a reputation as a successful astrologer in US, attempted to see astrology legalized in Great Britain, where she became well known as a radio broadcaster and newspaper columnist on the subject and was credited with having correctly forecast the death date of King Edward VII.

ADAMS, Fae Margaret (1918—). American doctor. Born in San Jose, California, 1918. ❖ Served as a 1st lieutenant and reserve medical officer in the Women's Army Corps, becoming the 1st female doctor to receive a regular US Army commission (1953); after the military, practiced gynecology and obstetrics in Albuquerque, New Mexico.

ADAMS, Glenda (1939—). Australian novelist. Born 1939 in Sydney, Australia; dau. of Leonard Henry and Elvira (Wright) Fulton; University of Sydney, BA, 1962, Columbia University, MA, 1965; children: 1 daughter. ❖ Taught Indonesian at University of Sydney; moved to NY to study journalism at Columbia (1964); worked as newswriter at AP, New York, and as press officer at UN; returned to Sydney to teach at University of Technology (1990); has been writer-in-residence at University of Western Australia, Macquarie University, and University of Adelaide; works include *Lies and Stories* (1979), *The Hottest Night of the Century: Short Stories* (1979), *Games of the Strong* (1982), *Longleg* (1990), and *The Tempest of Clemenza* (1996); also published stories in anthologies and magazines, including *The Australian, Bananas, Harper's, Mother Jones,* and *Ms;* wrote articles, essays, and reviews for, among others, *Australian Cultural History, The New York Times Book Review, The Observer* (London), *The Village Voice,* and *Vogue Australia.* Miles

Franklin Award for *Dancing on Coral* (1987); received NBC Banjo Award for *Longleg* (1991).

ADAMS, Hannah (1755–1831). American writer. Born in Medfield, Massachusetts, Oct 2, 1755; died in Brookline, Massachusetts, Nov 15, 1831 (some sources cite 1832); dau. of Eleanor (Clark) Adams and Thomas Adams (bibliophile). ❖ The 1st American woman to make writing a profession, compiled *Views of Religious Opinions* (1784); also wrote *History of New England* (1799), *Evidences of Christianity* (1801), and *History of the Jews* (1812). ❖ See also *Memoir* (1832); and *Women in World History.*

ADAMS, Harriet Chalmers (1875–1937). American explorer and lecturer. Born in Stockton, California, Oct 22, 1875; died in Nice, France, July 17, 1937. ❖ While traveling through Mexico, became a student of Latin American affairs (1900), after which she made a 3-year journey through Central and South America, reaching many points previously unknown to any white woman; lectured in US (1906–08); crossed Haiti on horseback (1910), then traveled through the Philippines, and from Siberia to Sumatra, studying ancient races; was a war correspondent at French front (1916); organized and was 1st president of the Society of Women Geographers (1925); wrote regularly for *National Geographic* and was a fellow and member of various geographical and scientific associations throughout the world.

ADAMS, Harriet Stratemeyer (c. 1893–1982). American writer and publisher. Name variations: (pseudonyms) Victor Appleton II, May Hollis Barton, Franklin W. Dixon, Laura Lee Hope, Carolyn Keene. Born Oct 22, c. 1893, in Newark, New Jersey; died Mar 27, 1982, in Pottersville, New Jersey; dau. of Edward L. Stratemeyer (author) and Magdalene Stratemeyer; sister of Edna Stratemeyer; graduate of Wellesley College, 1914; m. Russell Vroom Adams, 1915; children: Russell Jr. (died WWII), Patricia Adams Harr, Camilla Adams McClave, Edward Stratemeyer Adams. ❖ When her father died (1930), took over the reigns of his Stratemeyer Syndicate; for the next 52 years, like her father before her, created hundreds of chapter-by-chapter book outlines for various series books, which were completed by a stable of writers, most anonymous, many former journalists; also authored an estimated 200 books under various pseudonyms: Carolyn Keene for the Nancy Drew series; Franklin W. Dixon for the Hardy Boys; Victor W. Appleton II for Tom Swift, Jr.; and Laura Lee Hope for The Bobbsey Twins. ❖ See also Carol Billman, *The Secret of the Stratemeyer Syndicate* (Ungar, 1986); and *Women in World History.*

ADAMS, Ida (c. 1888–1960). American actress. Born c. 1888; died Nov 4, 1960. ❖ Made NY debut as Miss Glick in *The Candy Shop* (1909); plays include *Ziegfeld Follies of 1912*, *Houp-La!* and *Inside the Lines.*

ADAMS, Irene (1947—). Scottish politician and member of Parliament. Born Dec 27, 1947; m. Allen Adams, 1968 (MP, 1979–90, died 1990). ❖ Representing Labour, elected to House of Commons for Paisley North (1991, 1997, 2001); named chair of Scottish Affairs (2001); left Parliament (2005).

ADAMS, Jacqueline (1926—). See Adams, Nancy M.

ADAMS, Jane (1710–1765). See Adam, Jean.

ADAMS, Jane (1921—). American screen actress. Name variations: Poni Adams. Born Betty Jane Adams, Aug 7, 1921, in San Antonio, Texas; m. Tom Turnage, 1945. ❖ Began career as a model for Harry Conover Agency; made film debut as Nina in *House of Dracula* (1945); other films include *Lost City of the Jungle* (serial), *The Brute Man*, *Batman and Robin* (serial), and *Masterminds* with the Bowery Boys.

ADAMS, Julie (1926—). American actress. Name variations: Betty Adams. Born Betty May Adams, Oct 17, 1926, in Waterloo, Iowa; m. Ray Danton (actor). ❖ Lead player in B films, including *The Man from Alamo, Creature from the Black Lagoon, Six Bridges to Cross, The Private War of Major Benson, Away All Boats, McQ, Goodbye Franklin High* and *Champions.*

ADAMS, Kathryn (1893–1959). American silent-screen actress. Name variations: Catherine Adams. Born Ethalinda Colson, May 25, 1893, in St. Louis, Missouri; died Feb 17, 1959, in Hollywood, California. ❖ Appeared in early one- and two-reel films for the Thanhouser Company; starred in De Mille's *The Squaw Man* (1914); other films include *Riders of the Purple Sage, Little Brother of the Rich*, and *Brute Breaker.*

ADAMS, Léonie Fuller (1899–1988). American poet and educator. Name variations: Leonie. Born in Brooklyn, NY, Dec 9, 1899; died

in New Milford, Connecticut, June 27, 1988; m. William Troy, 1933. ❖ Best known for her lyric poetry, penned collections that include *Those Not Elect* (1925), *High Falcon* (1929), and *This Measure* (1933); won several awards, including the Harriet Monroe Poetry Award, Shelley Memorial Award, and Bollingen Prize; taught and lectured at various colleges, including Sarah Lawrence, Bennington, and Columbia University, and was poetry consultant to Library of Congress (1948–49).

ADAMS, Lily Moresby (c. 1862–1931). See Beck, Elizabeth Louisa.

ADAMS, Louisa Catherine (1775–1852). American first lady. Born Louisa or Catherine. Born Louisa Catherine Johnson in London, England, Feb 12, 1775; died in Washington, DC, May 15, 1852; dau. of Joshua Johnson (American merchant) and Catherine (Nuth or Young; Englishwoman) Johnson; m. John Quincy Adams, July 26, 1797 (US president, died 1848); children: George Washington (1801–1828), John II (1803–1833); Charles Francis (b. 1807); Louisa Catherine Adams II (1811–1812). ❖ Wife and political partner of John Quincy Adams who wrote about crucial national and diplomatic events of early republican America, everyday life in the late 18th and early 19th centuries, and her 50-year alliance with America's preeminent ruling family; moved with family to France (1778); moved back to England (1782); met John Quincy Adams (1795); joined him on diplomatic mission in Prussia (1797–1801); sailed with family to America (1801); became a senator's wife (1803–08); joined husband in diplomatic mission to Russia (1808–15); journeyed alone from St. Petersburg to Paris (1815); went on diplomatic mission to England (1815–17); returned to America as wife to secretary of state and to campaign for husband's presidency (1817–24); organized the Jackson Ball (1824); served as 1st lady (1824–28), then retired to Quincy, MA; returned to Washington as US representative's wife (1830). ❖ See also Paul C. Nagel, *The Adams Women: Abigail and Louisa Adams, their Sisters and Daughters* (Oxford U. Press, 1987); Jack Shepherd, *Cannibals of the Heart: A Personal Biography of Louisa Catherine and John Quincy Adams* (McGraw-Hill, 1980); and *Women in World History.*

ADAMS, Lucinda (1937—). See Williams, Lucinda.

ADAMS, Lynn (c. 1958—). American racquetball player. Born c. 1958, lives in Libertyville, Illinois; attended Orange Coast College; m. Jim Carson (her coach, div.); m. Richard Clay, 1990; children: Kristen (b. 1994); (adopted) Jasmine. ❖ Joined the Women's Professional Racquetball Association (WPRA) at its inception (1979); was 4-time defending WPRA national champion; won 6 national titles (1982–83, 1985–88); won 7 overall championships (1982–83, 1985–88 and 1990), and 6 pro-tour season titles (1982–83, 1985–88); diagnosed with MS (1987); retired (1991). Inducted into Racquetball Hall of Fame (1997); 5-time Player of the Year.

ADAMS, Marion Hooper (1843–1885). See Adams, Clover.

ADAMS, Mary (d. 1702). English thief. Born at Reading in Berkshire, England; hanged at Tyburn, June 16, 1702. ❖ After giving birth to an illegitimate child, left Reading for London; worked in Drury Lane as prostitute, picking the pockets of her clients; arrested while attempting to cash stolen bank note, was tried and sentenced to death.

ADAMS, Mary Grace (1898–1984). English broadcasting pioneer. Born Mary Grace Campin, 1898, in England; died 1984; dau. of Edward Bloxham Campin; University College, Cardiff, 1st class, botany (1921); m. Samuel Vyvyan Adams, 1925. ❖ Served as the 1st woman tv producer for the BBC (1936–39); employed as director of Home Intelligence at the Ministry of Information (1939–41); worked for the North American Service Broadcasting (1942–45); was head of tv talk shows, BBC (1948–54); wrote for *Punch.* Awarded an Order of the British Empire (OBE, 1953). ❖ See also *Women in World History.*

ADAMS, Mary Manning (1906–1999). See Manning, Mary.

ADAMS, Maude (1872–1953). American actress, lighting designer, and professor of drama. Born Maude Ewing Adams Kiskadden, Nov 11, 1872, in Salt Lake City, Utah; died July 17, 1953, in Tannersville, NY; dau. of Asenath Ann Adams Kiskadden (Annie Adams, actress) and James Henry Kiskadden (businessman); lived with Louise Boynton. ❖ At 9 months, carried on stage by mother in the play *The Lost Child;* appeared frequently with her and eventually took her maiden name; left school after father's death (1883); after appearing in many roles in San Francisco and other theaters in Southwest, appeared as the maid in *The Paymaster* in NY (1888); played Nell in *Last Paradise*, staged by Charles Frohman (1891), then began to appear opposite John Drew (Oct 1892); appeared in *Little Minister,* written for her by British playwright James Barrie (1897); formed her own company and continued to star in Barrie's plays, including *Quality Street* (1901), *Peter Pan* (1905), *What Every Woman Knows* (1908), *The Legend of Leonora* (1914), and *A Kiss for Cinderella* (1916); performed *Peter Pan* more than 1,500 times; fell dangerously ill during flu epidemic (1918) and retired from the stage for 13 years; began another career as a lighting designer for General Electric, developing an incandescent bulb widely used in color film (both 1921); returned to theater playing Portia to Otis Skinner's Shylock in national tour of *The Merchant of Venice* (1934); was a professor of drama at Stephens College in Columbia, Missouri (1937–46). ❖ See also Acton Davies' *Maude Adams* (Stopes, 1901), Ada Patterson's *Maude Adams* (B. Blom, 1971), Phyllis Robbins' *Maude Adams* (Putnam, 1956); and *Women in World History.*

ADAMS, Millicent (1942—). American convicted of manslaughter. Born in 1942; wealthy Philadelphia socialite; attended Bryn Mawr; children: Lisa (born out of wedlock). ❖ Fell in love with Axel Schmidt, post-graduate student, who broke off relationship in favor of another woman; after testing a .22 caliber Smith & Wesson on a St. Bernard, murdered Schmidt, the father of the child she was carrying (1962); successfully pleaded temporary insanity; served 3 years in mental-health facility and released.

ADAMS, Miriam (1907—). English actress. Born Oct 29, 1907, in Heworth, York, England; attended RADA; m. Douglas Muir. ❖ Made stage debut as Mary in *Br'er Rabbit* (1922); performed with the Stratford-on-Avon Company (1927–30); other portrayals include Miss Hoyden in *A Trip to Scarborough,* Joan Saunders in *Strange Barrier,* Phebe in *As You Like It* at the Old Vic, and Anne Brontë in *The Brontës of Haworth Parsonage.*

ADAMS, Nancy M. (1926—). New Zealander scientist and botanical illustrator. Name variations: Jacqueline Nancy Mary Adams. Born Jacqueline Nancy Mary Whittaker, May 19, 1926, in New Zealand. ❖ Botanical illustrator and seaweeds expert, served as assistant to Dr. Lucy B. Moore at Plant Research Bureau in Department of Scientific and Industrial Research (beginning 1942); served as assistant curator and artist in Botany department at National Museum in Wellington (1956–87); received Loder Cup for work on publications about national parks in New Zealand (1964); received Queen's Service Order (1989) and Commemoration Medal (1990). Writings include *Mountain Flowers in New Zealand* (1980) and *Wild Flowers in New Zealand* (1980).

ADAMS, Peggy (1898–1978). *See Adams, Claire.*

ADAMS, Poni (1921—). *See Adams, Jane.*

ADAMS, Sarah Flower (1805–1848). English poet and hymn writer. Name variations: Sally; signed articles S.Y. Born Sarah Flower at Great Harlow, Essex, England, Feb 22, 1805; died from consumption, Aug 1848; dau. of Benjamin Flower (publisher of the *Cambridge Intelligencer,* died 1829) and Eliza (Gould) Flower; sister of Eliza Flower (1803–1846); m. William Bridges Adams (noted inventor), 1834. ❖ Wrote articles, stories, and essays for the *Monthly Repository;* produced her longest work, *Vivia Perpetua* (1840), a dramatic poem about the early life of the Christians; her hymns include "He sendeth sun, He sendeth shower," and "Nearer, my God, to Thee" which was played to comfort passengers on the sinking *Titanic.* ❖ See also *Women in World History.*

ADAMS, Sharon Sites (c. 1930—). American sailor. Born c. 1930; grew up in the high desert of central Oregon. ❖ Took 1st sailing lesson at Marina Del Ray, California (1964); sailed solo from Marina Del Ray to Hawaii in a 25′ Folkboat *Sea Sharp* (1965); soloed from Yokohama, Japan, to San Diego, CA, in a 31′ ketch, *Sea Sharp II* (May 12–Jul 25, 1969), the 1st successful solo sail across the Pacific Ocean by a woman.

ADAMS, Susan Boylston (d. 1797). Mother of John Adams. Born Suzanne or Susan Boylston; died April 21, 1797; m. Deacon John Adams (farmer and cordwainer); remarried, 1766; children: John Adams (1735–1826, 2nd president of US); Peter (b. 1737); Elihu (b. 1741). ❖ See also *Women in World History.*

ADAMS, Susanna Boylston (1769–1828). Member of prestigious Adams family. Eldest dau. of Charles Adams and Sarah Smith Adams (1769–1828). ❖ See also *Women in World History.*

ADAMS, Truda (1890–1958). English ceramist. Name variations: Truda Sharp; Truda Carter; Gertrude Adams. Born Gertrude Sharp in 1890; died in 1958; studied at Royal Academy Schools, London; m. John Adams (artist, div.); m. Cyril Carter (1931). ❖ Married and moved to Durban, South Africa (1914); with Harold Stabler and Cyril Carter, set up the Poole Pottery in Dorset, England (1921), where she became resident designer and continued floral designs until 1950; entered work at Royal Academy Ceramic Exhibition (1935) and International Exhibition in Paris (1937).

ADAMS, Victoria (1974—). *See Beckham, Victoria.*

ADAMS, Violet (1913—). *See Marsh, Marian.*

ADAMSON, Catherine (1868–1925). New Zealand diarist. Name variations: Catherine Mary Ann Friend. Born Catherine Mary Ann Friend, Oct 13, 1868, in Fitzroy, Victoria, Australia; died on Aug 9, 1925, in Hokitika, New Zealand; dau. of Samuel Friend (laborer) and Ann Elizabeth (Langham) Friend; m. Robert Adamson (farmer), 1888; children: 5. ❖ Traveled with family to New Zealand as infant (1866); went to Volis station with husband to farm heavily forested land; kept diary that recorded daily routine of pioneers (1895–1906). ❖ See also *Dictionary of New Zealand Biography* (Vol. 3).

ADAMSON, Joy (1910–1980). Austrian-born writer and naturalist. Born Friederike Victoria Gessner in Troppau, Silesia, in Austro-Hungary, Jan 20, 1910; murdered in Nairobi, Kenya, Jan 3, 1980; dau. of Victor (architect and town planner) and Trauta Gessner; m. Victor von Klarwill (Austrian), 1935; m. Peter Bally (Swiss), 1938; m. George Adamson (senior warden in Kenya game department), 1944. ❖ Writer in Kenya whose bestselling book *Born Free* was pivotal in changing attitudes worldwide toward the value of preserving wildlife and habitat; after growing up on an estate near Vienna, was educated in Vienna, earning a music degree before studying sculpting and medicine; went to Kenya on vacation (1937); painted flowers in Kenya for botanical books for 15 years, spending time camped out in the wild; became interested in African customs, ornaments, and costumes, which she began painting as well; adopted three lion cubs; kept Elsa, the smallest, and wrote *Born Free,* followed by *Living Free* and *Forever Free,* which told of experiences living with the lion and returning her to the wild; proved that captive wild animals could be reeducated to live in their natural habitat, a practice widely used today; alerted the world to the loss of species and habitat, a topic on which she became an early crusader. ❖ See also *The Searching Spirit: Joy Adamson's Autobiography* (Harcourt, 1979); Caroline Cass, *Joy Adamson: Behind the Mask* (Weidenfeld & Nicolson, 1993); and *Women in World History.*

ADASSE (fl. 1348). German moneylender. Jewish resident of Gorlitz, Germany; granted citizen's rights c. 1348. ❖ Became wealthy lending money to the Christian residents of the town, and attained a high social standing in her community; was given the privileges of citizenship, a rare event for a medieval townswoman and extremely rare for a Jew. ❖ See also *Women in World History.*

ADATO, Perry Miller. American film director. Born in Yonkers, NY; studied at Marshalov School of Drama and New School for Social Research, both NY. ❖ The 1st woman to win an award from the Directors Guild of America (DGA), with her documentary on Georgia O'Keeffe (1977), also did documentaries on Carl Sandburg (1982) and Eugene O'Neill (1986), as well as Gertrude Stein, Mary Cassatt, Louise Nevelson, Pablo Picasso, and Dylan Thomas; began career working as director of Film Advertising Center in NY; was then a film consultant and researcher for CBS (NY) before becoming an associate producer, then producer, of cultural documentary films for WNET, the Public Broadcasting System.

ADAWIYYA or ADAWIYYAH, Rabi'a al- (c. 714–801). *See Rabi'a.*

ADCOCK, Fleur (1934—). New Zealand poet. Name variations: Karen Fleur Adcock. Born Karen Fleur Adcock, Feb 10, 1934, in Papakura, near Auckland, New Zealand; dau. of Cyril John Adcock and Irene Robinson Adcock; attended Wellington Girls' College; Victoria University, MA with 1st class honors, 1955; m. Alistair Campbell (poet), 1952 (div. 1958); m. Barry Crump, 1962; children: Andrew. ❖ Immigrated to England (1963); worked as librarian until becoming full-time writer (1979); works include *The Eye of the Hurricane* (1964), *The Scenic Route* (1974), *The Inner Harbour* (1979), *Selected Poems* (1983), *Meeting the Comet* (1988), *Time Zones* (1991), and *Looking Back* (1997); also edited volumes of poetry and published translations of Latin and Romanian poetry, including *The Virgin and the Nightingale: Medieval Latin Poems* (1983) and *Orient Express: Poems by Grete Tartler* (1989).

ADDAMS, Dawn (1930–1985). English actress. Born Dawn Addams in Felixstowe, Suffolk, England, Sep 21, 1930; died of cancer May 7, 1985, in London; dau. of Ethel Mary (Hickie) and James Ramage Addams; educated in India, England, and California; trained for stage at RADA; married Prince Vittorio Massimo, 1954 (div. 1971); married James White (businessman), 1974; children: (1st m.) Prince Stefano. ❖ Made professional debut in London as Amy Spettigue in *Charley's Aunt* (1949); best remembered for role opposite Charlie Chaplin in *A King in New York* (1957); abandoned Hollywood career for marriage to Italy's Prince Vittorio Massimo, though she continued to appear in European films as well as on London stage and tv; films include *Night into Morning* (1951), *Plymouth Adventure* (1952), *Young Bess* (1953), *The Moon is Blue* (1953), *The Robe* (1953), *The Silent Enemy* (1958), *Come Fly with Me* (1963), and *The Thousand Eyes of Dr. Mabuse*.

ADDAMS, Jane (1860–1935). American settlement-house founder. Born Sep 6, 1860, in Cedarville, Illinois; died in Chicago, May 21, 1935; dau. of John (Illinois entrepreneur and legislator) and Sarah (Weber) Addams; graduate of Rockford Female Seminary, 1881 (granted degree when it became Rockford College, 1882); attended Woman's Medical College of Pennsylvania for one year. ❖ One of the heroes and legends of American liberalism who, in an age dominated by *laissez-faire* conservatism, worked to restore a fractured sense of American community and to bring the full benefits of national life to the poorest and most recent immigrants; enrolled at Rockford Seminary (1877); advocated progressive reforms, pacifism, and cultural diversity; made 1st visit to Europe (1883) and 2nd visit with Ellen Gates Starr (1887); with Starr, founded Hull House, a Chicago settlement house, which became the influential center of a national movement aimed at bringing education, sanitation, recreation, and political representation to the most disadvantaged citizens of the new urban civilization (1889); elected chair of Women's Peace Party and the Women's International League for Peace and Freedom (1916); awarded the Nobel Peace Prize (1931). Writings include *Democracy and Social Ethics* (1902), *Newer Ideals of Peace* (1907), *The Spirit of Youth and the City Streets* (1912), *Peace and Bread in Time of War* (1922), *The Excellent Becomes the Permanent* (1932), and *My Friend, Julia Lathrop* (1935). ❖ See also memoirs *Twenty Years at Hull House* (1910) and *The Second Twenty Years at Hull House* (1930); Allen Freeman Davis, *American Heroine: The Life and Legend of Jane Addams* (Oxford U. Press, 1973); John C. Farrell, *Beloved Lady* (Johns Hopkins, 1967); and *Women in World History*.

ADDIE, Pauline Betz (b. 1919). *See Betz, Pauline.*

ADDISON, Agnes (c. 1841–1903). New Zealand draper. Name variations: Agnes Broomfield. Born Agnes Broomfield, c. 1841 or 1842, in Edinburgh, Scotland; died Jan 28, 1903, at Hokitika, New Zealand; dau. of Joseph Broomfield and Margaret (Fairbairn) Broomfield; m. Robert Addison (carpenter), 1874 (died 1885); children: 4 daughters. ❖ Immigrated with husband to New Zealand (1875); established drapery shop, becoming one of Hokitika's leading businesswomen in the 1890s. ❖ See also *Dictionary of New Zealand Biography* (Vol. 2).

ADDISON, Carlotta (1849–1914). English actress. Name variations: Mrs. C.A. LaTrobe or La Trobe. Born July 9, 1849, in Liverpool, Eng.; died June 14, 1914; dau. of E.P. Addison (former proprietor of the Theatre Royal, Doncaster); m. C.A. LaTrobe (died July 1909). ❖ Made stage debut as a child in *Nine Points of the Law*; made London debut as Lady Dolly Touchwood in *The Belle's Stratagem* (1866); other portrayals include Bella in *School*, Nerissa in *The Merchant of Venice*, Ethel Grainger in *Married in Haste*, Grace Harkaway in *London Assurance*, and Mabel Ransom in *Mabel*.

ADDISON, Laura (d. 1852). English actress. Born in England; died in 1852. ❖ Made debut at Worcester, England (1843), playing Desdemona to George Macready's Othello; also performed at Sadler's Wells and at the Haymarket; roles included Juliet, Portia, Isabella, Imogen, Miranda, and Lady Macbeth.

ADDOR, Ady (c. 1935—). Brazilian ballet dancer. Born c. 1935, in Rio de Janeiro, Brazil. ❖ Made debut as ballerina in corps of Teatro Municipal, Rio de Janeiro, and continued to perform there throughout most of career, including ballets of Leonid Massine such as *Gaité Parisienne*, *Les Présages* and *Le Beau Danube*; performed in Aurel Milloss' company, Sao Paulo (1953); went to New York with Igor Schwekoff, where she danced with the American Ballet Theater (1957–61); continued to dance in works by Massine; added to personal repertory with parts in David Lichine's *Graduation Ball*, Agnes de Mille's *Rodeo*, Antony Tudor's *Pillar of Fire*, and others; toured with Alicia Alonso; danced as prima ballerina in National Ballet of Cuba, Ballet of Venezuela, and IV Centenario de Sao Paulo; taught classes in Sao Paulo, Brazil.

ADEA EURYDICE (c. 337–317 BCE). *See Eurydice.*

ADEHEID (931–999). *See Adelaide of Burgundy.*

ADELA. *Variant of Adele.*

ADELA (d. 735). Frankish saint. Died Dec 24, 735; dau. of St. Dagobert II, Merovingian king of Austrasia (r. 674–678), and Matilda (Anglo-Saxon princess); sister of Saint Irmina (d. 716); m. Alberic (noble); children: one son. ❖ Followed her sister into religious life; founded convent of Palatiolum (c. 690), not far from Trier (on site of town of Pfalzel) and became its 1st abbess; canonized as saint. ❖ See also *Women in World History*.

ADELA (fl. 900s). French noblewoman. Born in Brittany, France; d. of Hubert I, Count of Senlis; m. William I, duke of Normandy (r. 932–942); children: Richard I the Fearless, duke of Normandy (r. 942–996); grandmother of Emma of Normandy (c. 985–1052).

ADELA CAPET (c. 1010–1079). Countess of Flanders. Name variations: Adela of France. Born c. 1010; died Jan 8, 1079, at Messinesmonastre, France; dau. of Robert II the Pious (972–1031, son of Hugh Capet), aka Robert I, king of France (r. 996–1031), and Constance of Arles (c. 980–1032); sister of Henry I (1008–1060), king of France (r. 1031–1060), and Robert, duke of Burgundy (r. 1031–1076); m. Richard III, 5th duke of Normandy, Jan 1026 or 1027; became 2nd wife of Baldwin V (c. 1012–1067), count of Flanders (r. 1035–1067), 1028; children: (2nd m.) possibly Baldwin VI, count of Flanders (d. 1070); Matilda of Flanders (c. 1031–1083); Judith of Flanders (1032–1094). ❖ Following death of 2nd husband, Baldwin V, count of Flanders, entered a convent. ❖ See also *Women in World History*.

ADELA H. (1936–1985). *See Kirkwood, Julieta.*

ADELA OF BLOIS (1062–c. 1137). Countess of Blois and Chartres. Name variations: Adele; Adela of Normandy; Adela of England. Born 1062 in Normandy, France; died Mar 8, c. 1137 or 1138, at convent of Marcigny, France; 4th dau. of Matilda of Flanders (1031–1083) and William the Conqueror, duke of Normandy (r. 1035–1087), king of England (r. 1066–1087); sister of Henry I, king of England; m. Stephen Henry, aka Etienne (d. 1102), count of Blois, Tours, Chartres, and Champagne; children: 7, though some authorities claim 9, including William de Blois; Stephen, king of England (r. 1135–1154); Thibaut, aka Theobald II, count of Champagne (whose daughter was Adele of Champagne, 1145–1206); Henry (bishop of Winchester); Philip (held the See of Chalone); Matilda de Blois (drowned in 1120); Lucy de Blois (drowned in 1120). ❖ Known by historians as "heroine of the 1st Crusade," was deeply religious, extremely well-educated, and could read and write in several languages, including Latin; married Stephen Henry of Blois, one of her father's supporters, and became his trusted companion; was named regent of their lands when Stephen left to participate in the 1st Crusade; setting aside needlework on famous Bayeux tapestry, which her mother Matilda of Flanders had left her to complete, ruled ably (1096–1109); also became known as a generous patron of poets and writers; on husband's death (1102), continued to rule and saw son Stephen claim the throne of England; retired to convent of Marcigny (1130s), and died there, age 75; was buried, along with mother and sister Cecilia (c. 1059–1126), in Abbey of the Holy Trinity at Caen, France. ❖ See also *Women in World History*.

ADELA OF ENGLAND (1062–c. 1137). *See Adela of Blois.*

ADELA OF LOUVAIN (c. 1102–1151). *See Adelicia of Louvain.*

ADELA OF MEISSEN (fl. 1100s). German royal. Born in Meissen, Germany; fl. 1100s; dau. of Otto II, margrave of Meissen; was 1st wife of Ottokar I (d. 1230), king of Bohemia (r. 1198–1230); children: Dagmar of Bohemia (d. 1212). Ottokar's 2nd wife was Constance of Hungary.

ADELA OF NORMANDY (1062–c. 1137). *See Adela of Blois.*

ADELAIDE. *Variant of Adelicia.*

ADELAIDE (c. 794–after 852). French princess. Name variations: Alpaid. Born c. 794; died after 852; dau. of Ermengarde (d. 818) and Louis I the Pious (778–840), king of Aquitaine (r. 781–814), king of France (r. 814–840), and Holy Roman emperor (r. 814–840); sister of Lothair I, Holy Roman emperor (r. 840–855); m. Count Bego; children: Susannah (b. around 805).

ADELAIDE (fl. 860s). Countess of Anjou and Blois. Name variations: Fl. c. 860; dau. of Eberhard III, count of Alsace; m. Robert the Strong

(c. 825–866), count of Anjou and Blois, marquis of Neustria; children: Eudes or Odo (c. 860–898), count of Paris and king of France (r. 888–898); Robert I (c. 865–923), king of France (r. 922–923).

ADELAIDE (1777–1847). Princess of Orléans. Name variations: Adélaïde; Adelaide d'Orleans; Adelaide of Orleans; Mademoiselle d'Orléans or Orleans. Born Adelaide Eugenie Louise in Paris, France, Aug 23 or 25, 1777; died Dec 31, 1847; dau. of Louis Philippe Joseph (Philippe-Égalité), duke of Orléans (1785–1793), Montpensier (1747–1752), and Chartres (1752–1785), and Louise Marie of Bourbon (1753–1821); sister of Louis Philippe, king of France (r. 1830–1848); m. Baron Athelin. ❖ Was influential in persuading her brother Louis Philippe, the Citizen King, to accept the crown of France. ❖ See also *Women in World History.*

ADELAIDE (1821–1899). Duchess of Schleswig-Holstein-Sonderburg-Glucksburg. Born Adelaide Christine Juliana Charlotte, Mar 9, 1821; died on July 30, 1899; m. Frederick, duke of Schleswig-Holstein-Sonderburg-Glucksburg; children: 4, including Frederick Ferdinand, duke of Schleswig-Holstein-Sonderburg-Glucksburg.

ADELAIDE (c. 1884–1959). American vaudeville and ballet dancer. Name variations: Mary Adelaide Dickey; La Petite Adelaide. Born Mary Adelaide Dickey, 1884, in New York, NY; died 1959 (some sources cite 1960). ❖ As a child, performed as La Petite Adelaide in acrobatic dances; danced ballet specialty act starting at 7; performed variations of signature dance, the Doll Dance (c. 1887–1910), including an act on point on horseback; known for her uses of toe techniques in theatrical dance, danced in musicals, including *Lady Slavey* (1900), *The Orchid* (1907), *Up and Down Broadway* (1910); formed dancing team with J.J. Hughes (1911), with whom she performed in Europe, later in New York on Broadway and on Keith circuit in vaudeville as Adelaide and Hughes; on Broadway, appeared with Hughes in *Passing Show of 1912*, *Monte Christo Jr.* (1914) and *Town Topics* (1915); co-choreographed dances with Hughes for vaudeville, including *Chantecleer* (1911), *Pierrot and Pierrette* (1914), *The Dancing Divinities* (1917), *Classics of an Age* (1917) and *The Garden of the World* (1917).

ADÉLAÏDE, Madame (1732–1800). French princess. Name variations: Adélaïde; Marie Adelaide de France. Born Marie Adelaide at Versailles, France, May 3, 1732; died at Trieste, Feb 18, 1800; dau. of Louis XV (1710–1774), king of France (r. 1715–1774) and Marie Leczinska (1703–1768); sister of Louise Elizabeth (1727–1759), Victoire (1733–1799), Louise Marie (1737–1787), and Louis le dauphin (father of Louis XVI). ❖ The best-loved dau. of Louis XV, grew into a haughty royal who loathed her niece-in-law Marie Antoinette; with sister Victoire, given the castle of Bellevue to live out her years; with the Revolution brewing, sought permission to leave France to "spend Easter in Rome," but request was met with suspicion by the Assembly (1791); made a hasty and discreet departure to seek refuge abroad; migrated to Rome, then settled in Caserta (1796); moved to Trieste (1799). ❖ See also *Women in World History.*

ADELAIDE, Queen of Lombardy (931–999). *See Adelaide of Burgundy.*

ADELAIDE, Saint (931–999). *See Adelaide of Burgundy.*

ADELAIDE AND HUGHES. *See Hughes, Adelaide.*

ADELAIDE DE CONDET (fl. 12th c.). English patron. Name variations: Alice de Condet. Lived outside Lincoln, England; m. Robert de Condet; children: Roger. ❖ Commissioned a translation of the *Proverbs of Solomon,* a moral treatise, into Anglo-Saxon (c. 1150). ❖ See also *Women in World History.*

ADELAIDE JUDITH (fl. 879). Queen of France. Fl. c. 879; dau. of Adelard, count of the Palace; 2nd wife of Louis II the Stammerer (846–879), king of France (r. 877–879), children: Charles III the Simple (879–929), king of France (r. 898–923). ❖ Louis II's 1st wife was Ansgard (fl. 863).

ADELAIDE OF ANJOU (fl. 10th c.). Queen of France. Married Stephen, count of Gevaudun; m. Louis V the Coward (c. 967–987), king of France (r. 986–987). Louis V's 2nd wife was Blanca, dau. of William II, count of Auvergne, and Gerletta.

ADELAIDE OF AUSTRIA (d. 1854). *See Marie Adelaide of Austria.*

ADELAIDE OF BURGUNDY (931–999). Empress of the Holy Roman Empire. Name variations: Adeheid, Adelheid, Adelheide, Adelaide, Queen of Lombardy; Saint Adelaide. Born Adelaide in Burgundy, 931; died at Seltz in Alsace, Dec 16, 999; dau. of Rudolf aka Rudolph II of Burgundy and Bertha of Swabia; m. Lothar aka Lothair (d. 950), king of Italy, 947; became 2nd wife of Otto I the Great (912–973), king of Germany (r. 936–973), Holy Roman emperor (r. 962–973), 951; children: (1st m.) Emma of Italy (b. 948); (2nd m.) Matilda of Quedlinburg (c. 953–999) and Otto II (955–983), Holy Roman emperor (r. 973–983); grandmother of Adelaide of Quedlinburg (977–1045), German abbess and founder. ❖ Empress of the Holy Roman Empire at the time of its reorganization under husband Otto I, who was not only active in imperial governments, but also endowed many churches and monasteries so as to earn the title of saint; married Lothair, king of Italy (947), who was poisoned 3 years later by Berengar II (Berenguer), a rival for the Italian throne; imprisoned for refusing to marry Adalbert, Berengar II's son (951); escaped and married Otto I later the same year; crowned empress by Pope John XII (962); following husband's death (973), devoted much of her energy and wealth to the church and was an active benefactor of many religious foundations, particularly supportive of the monastic reform movement centered at Cluny; was also personally active in the care of the poor, especially at her daughter's monastery at Quedlinburg; because of tension with son Otto II, left the imperial court and lived with brother Conrad in Burgundy (978–80); when Otto II appealed to her for aid in calming political unrest in Italy, used her influence to calm the crisis and agreed to return to a more active political life; when Otto II died (983), acted in concert with daughter Matilda and daughter-in-law Theophano to counter political challenges and firmly establish Theophano as regent for her grandson Otto III; when Theophano died (991), served as regent to her grandson (991–95); in last months, undertook a pilgrimage to the various religious shrines of Northern Italy, Burgundy, and Germany. ❖ See also Gertrude Baumer, *Adelheid, Mutter der Königreiche* (Stuttgart: R. Wunderlich, 1949); and *Women in World History.*

ADELAIDE OF BURGUNDY (d. 1273). Duchess of Brabant. Name variations: Adelaide de Bourgogne; Alix of Burgundy. Died Oct 23, 1273; dau. of Yolande de Dreux (1212–1248) and Hugh IV (1213–1272), duke of Burgundy (r. 1218–1272); m. Henry III (d. 1261), duke of Brabant (r. 1248–1261), 1251; children: Henry IV (c. 1251–1272), duke of Brabant; John I (c. 1252–1294), duke of Brabant; Marie of Brabant (c. 1260–1321), queen of France.

ADELAIDE OF FRANCE (1092–1154). *See Adelaide of Maurienne.*

ADELAIDE OF HOHENLOHE-LANGENBURG (1835–1900). Duchess of Schleswig-Holstein-Sonderburg-Augustenberg. Name variations: Adelaide von Hohenlohe-Langenburg. Born July 20, 1835; died Jan 25, 1900; dau. of Ernest, 4th prince of Hohenlohe-Langenburg, and Feodore of Leiningen (half-sister of Queen Victoria); m. Frederick, duke of Schleswig-Holstein-Sonderburg-Augustenberg, Sept 11, 1856; children: 5, including Augusta of Schleswig-Holstein (1858–1921, 1st wife of Kaiser Wilhelm II); Caroline Matilda of Schleswig-Holstein-Sonderburg-Augustenberg (1860–1932).

ADELAIDE OF HUNGARY (d. 1062). Queen of Bohemia. Died Jan 27, 1062; dau. of Anastasia of Russia (c. 1023–after 1074) and Andrew I (c. 1001–1060), king of Hungary (r. 1047–1060); became 2nd wife of Vratislav II (c. 1035–1092), king of Bohemia (r. 1061–1092), c. 1058.

ADELAIDE OF KIEV (c. 1070–1109). Holy Roman empress. Name variations: Eupraxia of Kiev. Born c. 1070; died July 10, 1109; dau. of Vsevolod I, prince of Kiev, and Anna of Cumin (d. 1111); m. Henry, count of Stade; became 2nd wife of Henry IV (1050–1106), king of Germany and Holy Roman emperor (r. 1056–1106), Aug 17, 1089 (div. 1093).

ADELAIDE OF LOUVAIN (c. 1102–1151). *See Adelicia of Louvain.*

ADELAIDE OF MAURIENNE (1092–1154). Queen of France and religious founder. Name variations: Adelaide of France; Adelaide of Savoy; Agnes of Maurienne; Alix. Born 1092 (some sources cite 1110); died Nov 18, 1154 at Montmartre, France; dau. of Humbert II of Maurienne aka Umberto II, count of Savoy, and Gisela of Burgundy (dau. of William I, count of Burgundy); m. Louis VI the Fat (1081–1137), king of France (r. 1108–1137), 1115; children: Philip (d. 1131); Louis VII (c. 1121–1180), king of France (r. 1137–1180); Robert, count of Dreux; Peter of Courtenay; Henry, bishop of Beauvais and Rouen; Philip, bishop of Paris; Constance Capet (c. 1128–1176, who m. Raymond V, count of Toulouse). ❖ One of the most dominant queens in French history, married Louis VI (1115) while in her teens; clever and insightful, revealed a nature well-suited to politics and state affairs; quickly became a trusted advisor to her husband as well as an important ruler in her own right; because queen-consorts were then allowed to exercise royal authority under their own names, performed many royal functions, including signing charters, making judicial decisions, and appointing church and lay officials; when Louis died (1137), refused to retire from handling state matters; instead, remained at center of government in Paris with her 15-year-old son Louis (now Louis VII); in later years, however, was virtually forced to retire due to advancing age and growing influence of daughter-in-law, Eleanor of Aquitaine. A deeply religious woman, founded the Abbey of Montmartre with her own money. ❖ See also *Women in World History*.

ADELAIDE OF MONTSERRAT (fl. 1100). Regent of Normandy. Mother of Count Roger II of Normandy. ❖ One of many medieval noblewomen who, though not in theory allowed to rule, actually governed large domains in practice; when son Roger left Normandy to participate in the 1st Crusade (c. 1096), was named to act as his regent during his years of absence. ❖ See also *Women in World History*.

ADELAIDE OF POITOU (c. 950–c. 1004). Queen of France. Name variations: Adelaide of Guyenne; Adelaide of Aquitaine. Born c. 950 (some sources cite 945); died c. 1004; dau. of Guillaume aka William I (or III) Towhead, count of Poitou, duke of Aquitaine, and Adele of Normandy (c. 917–c. 962); m. Hugh Capet, duke of France (r. 956–996), king of France (r. 987–996), 1st of the Capetian kings, 970; children: Robert II (b. 972), king of France (r. 996–1031).

ADELAIDE OF QUEDLINBURG (977–1045). German abbess of Quedlinburg. Name variations: Adelheid of Germany; Adelheid of Quedlinburg. Born in 977 in Holy Roman Empire; died at abbey of Quedlinburg, Germany, 1045; dau. of Holy Roman emperor Otto II (r. 973–983) and Empress Theophano of Byzantium (c. 955–991); sister of Otto III, Holy Roman emperor (r. 983–1002) and Sophia of Gandersheim; granddau. of Adelaide of Burgundy (931–999), Italian queen and empress. ❖ Born into the ruling family of Germany, received an excellent education as a child; at age 7, was kidnapped to be used as a political pawn by the supporters of her parents' rebellious enemy, Henry the Quarrelsome of Bavaria; was eventually returned safely to family, and a defeated Henry was required to give her the abbey of Vreden as compensation; entered the religious life as a young woman, taking nun's vows and continuing her studies; eventually served as abbess of several convents, including the wealthy establishment of Quedlinburg, famous for the great learning of its nuns; became known for her excellent learning and true piety. ❖ See also *Women in World History*.

ADELAIDE OF RHEINFELDEN (c. 1065–?). Queen of Hungary. Born c. 1065; m. St. Ladislas I (1040–1095), king of Hungary (r. 1077–1095); children: Priska-Irene of Hungary (c. 1085–1133, who m. Emperor John II Comnenus).

ADELAIDE OF SAVONA (d. 1118). Countess and regent of Sicily who later became queen of Jerusalem. Name variations: Adelaide of Salona; Adelaide of Sicily. Reigned 1101–1112; died 1118 in Sicily; dau. of Marquis Manfred of Savona; niece of Boniface of Savona; m. Count Roger I of Sicily (1031–1101, brother of Robert Guiscard), 1089; m. Baldwin I of Boulogne, king of Jerusalem (r. 1100–1118), 1113; children: Simon of Sicily (r. 1101–1103); Roger II of Sicily (1095–1154). Baldwin I was also m. to Godeheut de Toni (d. 1097), dau. of Ralf III, seigneur de Conches. ❖ The dau. of the reigning marquis of Savona, became the 3rd wife of Roger I, count of Sicily, and moved to Sicily (1089) as marquessa; after husband died (1101), acted as regent in the name of their small son; was an able ruler and, when son came of age (1113), left him with a fairly prosperous and peaceful island-state; became 3rd wife of Baldwin I of Boulogne, king of Jerusalem; moving to Jerusalem, began a new life as queen-consort, but when Baldwin fell ill (1117), he repented his sins and had the marriage annulled; stripped of her wealth, returned to Sicily; known as a religious founder, provided the seed money for the monastery of S. Marie del Patirion. ❖ See also *Women in World History*.

ADELAIDE OF SAVOY (1092–1154). See *Adelaide of Maurienne*.

ADELAIDE OF SAXE-COBURG (1792–1849). See *Adelaide of Saxe-Meiningen*.

ADELAIDE OF SAXE-MEININGEN (1792–1849). Queen of England. Name variations: Adelaide Louisa Theresa; Adelaide of Saxe-Coburg. Born in Meiningen, Thuringia, Germany, Aug 13, 1792; died Dec 2, 1849, in Stanmore, London, England; buried at St. George's Chapel, Windsor, Berkshire, England; dau. of George I, duke of Saxe-Coburg-Meiningen, and Louise of Hohenlohe-Langenburg (1763–1837);

m. William, duke of Clarence, July 18, 1818; became queen of England (1830) on his accession as William IV until his death (1837); children: Charlotte Guelph (1819–1819, died day of birth); Elizabeth Guelph (1820–1821, died age three months), and four other unnamed babies who died in childbirth, including twins. ❖ At 26, considered plain and religious by contemporaries, was married to the 53-year-old William, duke of Clarence (later William IV), specifically to bear legitimate children (he had already fathered 10 with his mistress, actress Dora Jordan); though she gave birth to 6 children who did not survive infancy, proved to be an extremely tolerant wife, accepting without quibble William's other children and the arrival of another mistress, Mrs. Fitzherbert; took an interest in the model cottages under construction at Windsor and the children who lived in them, and showed kindness to her young niece (and future queen) Victoria, whose mother, Victoria of Coburg, was on bad terms with the court; despite her virtues, was an unpopular queen, since the public found it easier to vindicate the King and blame her influence when he did something to offend. ❖ See also *Women in World History*.

ADELAIDE OF SAXE-MEININGEN (1891–1971). Duchess of Saxony. Name variations: Adelheid; Countess Lingen. Born Adelaide Erna Caroline in Cassel, Sept 16, 1891; died in La Tour de Peilz, Switzerland, April 25, 1971; dau. of Frederick Johann (b. 1861), duke of Saxony, and Adelaide Caroline Matilde, Princess Lippe (1870–1889); m. Adalbert Ferdinand Berengar, count Lingen, Aug 3, 1914; children: Victoria Marina (1917–1981), countess Lingen (who m. Kirby Patterson); William Victor (b. 1919), count Lingen.

ADELAIDE OF SCHAERBECK (d. 1250). Flemish saint. Born Alix of Schärbeck. Birth date unknown; died June 11, 1250. ❖ A nun at the Cistercian abbey of Cambre in Brussels, became a leper and went blind. ❖ See also *Women in World History*.

ADELAIDE OF SCHAUMBURG (1875–1971). German royal. Born Fredericka Adelaide Mary Louise Hilda Eugenie on Sept 22, 1875; died on Jan 27, 1971; 3rd dau. of Prince William of Schaumburg-Lippe and Princess Bathildis of Anhalt; m. Ernest II, duke of Saxe-Altenburg, c. 1898 (div. 1920); children: 4, including Charlotte of Saxe-Altenburg.

ADELAIDE OF SICILY (d. 1118). See *Adelaide of Savona*.

ADELAIDE OF VOHBURG (fl. 1140s). Duchess of Swabia. Name variations: Adelheid von Vohburg. Fl. around 1140s; dau. of Diepold III, margrave of Vohburg, and Adelaide (dau. of Ladislas I Herman, king of Poland); became 1st wife of Frederick I Barbarossa (1123–1190), duke of Swabia (r. 1147), Holy Roman emperor (r. 1152–1190), 1147 (div. 1153). Frederick Barbarossa's 2nd wife was Beatrice of Upper Burgundy (1145–1184).

ADELE. *Variant of Adela.*

ADELE (r. 1017–1031). Co-ruler of Vendôme. Birth and death dates unknown; m. Bouchard I, count of Vendôme, Paril, and Corbeil (ruler of Vendôme from 958–1012); children: 3 sons, Renaud (bishop of Paril); Bouchard II; Foulques d'Oison. ❖ Sometime after 1016, co-ruled Vendôme with 2nd son Bouchard II, but he died soon after; then co-ruled with 3rd son Foulques d'Oison until 1031, when she sold the duchy to Foulques' uncle Geoffrey Martel, count of Anjou. ❖ See also *Women in World History*.

ADELE OF BLOIS (1062–c. 1137). See *Adela of Blois*.

ADELE OF BLOIS (1145–1206). See *Adele of Champagne*.

ADELE OF CHAMPAGNE (1145–1206). Queen of France. Name variations: Adela or Adele of Blois; Alix or Alice of Champagne. Born 1145 in Champagne; died in Paris, 1206; dau. of Count Theobald II of Champagne aka Thibaut of Blois (who was the son of Adela of Blois) and Maud Carinthia (c. 1105–1160); became 3rd wife of Louis VII (1120–1180), king of France (r. 1137–1180), 1160; children: Philip "Dieu-donne" (b. Aug 21, 1165–1223), later Philip II Augustus, king of France (r. 1180–1123); Agnes-Anne of France (b. 1171). ❖ At 15, became the 3rd wife of King Louis VII of France (1160), a marriage that represented a sort of peace treaty between her father and the crown; gave birth to the long-awaited male heir, Philip II Augustus (1165), who would be one of the most important kings in the development of the French monarchy; did not share in the administration of government during Louis' reign, but after he died (1180) retained her title as queen and acted as ruler during Philip's minority; proved to be a capable and energetic regent, handling the myriad royal responsibilities with political shrewdness, developed over her years as a member of two eminent feudal houses; remained at court after Philip came of age, though her direct participation in government lessened; appointed to act as regent of the kingdom when Philip left France to join Richard I of England on the 3rd Crusade (1190–91); after Philip's return, retired from politics. ❖ See also *Women in World History.*

ADELE OF NORMANDY (c. 917–c. 962). Countess of Poitou. Born c. 917 in Normandy, France; died in France after Oct 14, 962; dau. of Rollo aka Robert (b. 870), duke of Normandy, and Gisela Martel (d. 919); m. William I (III) Towhead (c. 915–963), count of Poitou (r. 934–963), duke of Aquitaine, 935; children: Adelaide of Poitou (c. 950–c. 1004); William II (IV) Ironarm (b. around 937), count of Poitou.

ADELGUNDE OF BAVARIA (1823–1914). Duchess of Modena. Born Adelgund. Born Mar 19, 1823, in Wurzburg; dau. of Theresa of Saxony (1792–1854) and Ludwig I (b. 1786), king of Bavaria (r. 1825–1848); died in Wurzburg, Oct 28, 1914; m. Franz or Francis V (1819–1875), duke of Modena (r. 1846–1859), Mar 30, 1842; children: Anna Beatrice (1848–1849).

ADELHEID. *Variant of Adelaide.*

ADELHEID (1831–1909). Queen of Portugal. Name variations: Adelheid Rosenberg. Born Adelheid Rosenberg on April 3, 1831, in Kleinheubach; died Dec 16, 1909, at St. Cecilia's Convent, Ryde, Isle of Wight; dau. of Prince Constantine Rosenberg and Marie Agnes, princess of Hohenlohe-Langenburg; m. Miguel aka Michael I (1802–1866), king of Portugal (r. 1828–1834), Sept 24, 1851; children: Maria da Neves (1852–1941, who m. Alphonse Carlos, duke of San Jaime); Miguel (b. 1853); Maria Theresa of Portugal (1855–1944); Maria Josepha of Portugal (1857–1943); Adelgunde of Portugal (1858–1946), duchess of Guimaraes (who m. Henry, count of Bardi); Marie-Anne of Braganza (1861–1942); Maria Antonia of Portugal (1862–1959, who m. Robert, duke of Bourbon-Parma). ❖ See also *Women in World History.*

ADELHEID OF HOLSTEIN (fl. 1314). Danish royal. Name variations: Adelheid von Holstein. Born c. 1297; dau. of Henry I (b. 1258), count of Holstein, and Heilwig or Helwig of Bronkhorst; m. Eric Waldemarsson, 1313; children: Valdemar or Waldemar III (b. 1314), king of Denmark; Helvig of Denmark.

ADELHEID VON HOLSTEIN (fl. 314). *See Adelheid of Holstein.*

ADELHEIDE. *Variant of Adelaide.*

ADELICIA (1029–1090). Countess of Ponthieu, Lenz, and Champagne. Name variations: Adelaide; Adeliza of Normandy. Born in 1029; died 1090; dau. of Robert I, duke of Normandy (r. 1027–1035) and Arlette (fl. 1010); sister of William I the Conqueror, king of England (r. 1066–1087); m. Enguerrand III, count of Ponthieu; m. Lambert, count of Lenz; m. Odo III, count of Champagne; children: (2nd m.) Judith of Normandy (c. 1054–after 1086).

ADELICIA DE WARRENNE (d. 1178). Countess of Huntingdon. Birth date unknown; died 1178; dau. of William de Warrenne, 2nd earl of Warrenne and Surrey, and Isabel of Vermandois; m. Henry Dunkeld, 1st earl of Huntingdon, 1139; children: Margaret of Huntingdon (c. 1140–1201); Malcolm IV (1142–1165), king of Scots (r. 1153–1165); William I the Lion, king of Scots (r. 1165–1214); David Dunkeld (c. 1144–1219), 1st earl of Huntingdon; Ada Dunkeld (c. 1145–1206); Matilda (c. 1152–1152); Isabella (who m. Robert, baron Ros of Wark).

ADELICIA OF LOUVAIN (c. 1102–1151). Queen of England and patron of literature. Name variations: Adeliza; Adelaide; Adela, Fair Maid of Brabant. Born in 1102 or 1103 in Louvain, France; died in Afflighem, Flanders, Belgium, Mar 23, 1151; dau. of Count Godfrey (Barbatus) of Louvain, duke of Brabant or Lower Lorraine aka Lotharingia (r. 1106–1139), and Ida of Namur; became 2nd wife of Henry I (c. 1068 or 1069–1135), king of England (r. 1100–1135), Jan 24, 1121; m. William d'Aubigny aka William de Albini, later earl of Arundel, 1138; children: (2nd m.) seven who survived, including Reyner d'Aubigny, Henry d'Aubigny, Godfrey d'Aubigny, Alice d'Aubigny, Olivia d'Aubigny, and Agatha d'Aubigny. ❖ Born into a ruling noble family of the Low Countries (modern Belgium and Flanders), received an excellent education and showed a great interest in language and literature; after death of Queen Matilda of Scotland, married the bereaved Henry I as part of a political and economic agreement; as queen, commissioned literary works and rewarded writers amply; became known as a generous patron, especially of the French troubadours; on Henry's death (1135), lost authority when Stephen, son of her sister-in-law Adela of Blois,

claimed the throne of England, though Stephen would have to fight a civil war for many years against Adelicia's stepdaughter Empress Matilda of England (1102–1167); married England's William d'Aubigny, who was later named earl of Arundel (1138); after 11 years of a reputedly happy marriage, withdrew to a convent in Flanders. ❖ See also *Women in World History.*

ADELIZA. *Variant of Adelicia.*

ADELIZA (d. 1066?). Anglo-Saxon princess. Name variations: Adelaide, Adelicia, Alice. Died around 1065 or 1066; dau. of William I the Conqueror, duke of Normandy (r. 1035–1087), king of England (r. 1066–1087), and Matilda of Flanders (c. 1031–1083); possibly betrothed to Harold II Godwineson, 1062. ❖ Became a nun. ❖ See also *Women in World History.*

ADELSTEIN, Angelica (1921—). *See Rozeanu, Angelica.*

ADELWIP (fl. 13th c.). *See Hadewijch.*

ADIE, Kate (1945—). English tv reporter. Born in Sunderland, 1945; attended Newcastle University. ❖ Major BBC journalist, became a technician at BBC radio (1969), then producer; worked for BBC-TV South (1977–79); began reporting on BBC network news (1979); became chief news correspondent (1989). Won Monte Carlo International TV News award (1981, 1990); received BAFTA Richard Dimbleby Award (1989); named OBE (1993).

ADIVAR, Halide Edib (c. 1884–1964). Turkish author, warrior, and political activist. Name variations: Halide Salih, Halidé Edip or Edib; Mrs. H.E. Adivar. Born in 1883 or 1884 in Istanbul (then Constantinople); died in Istanbul, Turkey, Jan 9, 1964; dau. of Mehmet Edib or Edip; 1st Muslim Turkish girl to graduate from the American Girls' College; m. Salih Zeki (noted mathematician; div.); m. Dr. Abdülhak Adnan Adivar (1881–1955), 1917; children: 2 sons. ❖ An ardent nationalist, was also outspoken in her attacks against the Allied forces occupying Istanbul and risked her life to defy them; joined the nationalist movement of national rebirth led by Mustafa Kemal Pasha (later Kemal Atatürk); commissioned a sergeant major by Atatürk himself, served on the General Staff and then participated directly at the front lines when the Greeks made their ill-fated attack on the infant Turkish Republic (1922); with husband, banished from Turkey because of outspoken notions of individual liberty, and moved abroad (1920s); returned to Turkey (1938) and continued to write novels and plays in which she attacked the traditional concept of a woman's role. Writings include *Doktor Abdulhak Adnan Adivar* (1956), *Shirt of Flame* (1924), *The Clown and His Daughter* (1935), *The Daughter of Smyrna: A Story of the Rise of Modern Turkey* (1940), *Masks or Souls?* (1953), *Turkey Faces West* (1973), *The Conflict of East and West in Turkey* (1963); many motion pictures and novels are based on her life. ❖ See also *Memoirs of Halidé Edib* (1972) and *The Turkish Ordeal: Being the Further Memoirs of Halide Edib* (1928); and *Women in World History.*

ADLAND, Beverly (1943—). *See Aadland, Beverly.*

ADLER, Alexandra (1901–2001). American neurologist and psychiatrist. Born Sept 24, 1901, in Vienna, Austria; died Jan 4, 2001, in New York, NY; dau. of Alfred Adler (pioneer psychoanalyst) and Raissa Timofeyevna Epstein Adler (radical socialist); sister of Valentine Adler (editor); received medical degree at University of Vienna; m. Dr. Halfdan Gregersen (erstwhile dean and professor of Romance languages at Williams College), 1959 (died 1980). ❖ Among the earliest women to practice as a neurologist in Vienna, fled the fascist regime of Dollfuss and came to US (1935); taught and practiced at Harvard Medical School and Massachusetts General Hospital; joined the faculty of New York University (1946), becoming a full professor of psychiatry at its medical school (1969); an expert on schizophrenia, worked at the New York City Department of Correction for 20 years; was medical director of the Alfred Adler Mental Hygiene Clinic in Manhattan; best known for her work on brain damage and alexia, was also among the first to bring attention to post-traumatic stress syndrome; writings include *Guiding Human Misfits.*

ADLER, C.S. (1932—). American children's writer. Name variations: Carole Schwerdtfeger Adler. Born Carole Schwerdtfeger, Feb 23, 1932, in Long Island, NY; dau. of Oscar Edward and Clarice (Landsberg) Schwerdtfeger; Hunter College (now Hunter College of the City University of New York), BA (cum laude), 1953; Russell Sage College, MS, 1967; m. Arnold R. Adler (engineer), June 1952; children: Steven and Clifford (twins), Kenneth. ❖ Began career as a middle-school English teacher in upstate NY; author of *Down by the River, The Shell*

Lady's Daughter, The Silver Coach, Footsteps on the Stairs, One Sister Too Many, With Westie and the Tin Man, Always and Forever Friends, Eddie's Blue Winged Dragon, Ghost Brother, among others. Received the William Allen White Award and the Golden Kite Award, both for *Magic of the Glits* (1979).

ADLER, Celia (1890–1979). American actress. Born 1890; died after a stroke, Jan 31, 1979, in New York, NY; dau. of Jacob Adler (actor) and his 1st wife Dinah Feinman (actress); half-sister of actors Luther and Stella Adler (1902–1993); m. 3 times; children: 1 son. ❖ The 1st lady of the Yiddish theater, began acting career in the arms of her mother at 6 months; helped launch the Yiddish company of Maurice Schwartz at Irving Place Theater (1918); starred in many productions, including Sholom Aleichem's *Stempenya* (1929); also appeared with Paul Muni and Marlon Brando in *A Flag is Born* (1946). ❖ See also *Women in World History.*

ADLER, Emma (1858–1935). Austrian socialist and women's-rights activist. Born Emma Braun in Debrecen, Hungary, May 20, 1858; died in exile in Zurich, Switzerland, Feb 23, 1935; m. Victor Adler (leader of the Austrian socialist movement), 1878; children: 3, including Friedrich (Fritz) Adler, who assassinated the Austrian Prime Minister, Count Carl Stürgkh. ❖ Leader of the women's movement in the Habsburg Empire, edited anthologies aimed at youth, particularly the influential *Buch der Jugend;* published a number of works, including a history of the role of women in the French Revolution and a biography of Jane Welsh Carlyle; when Democratic Socialism was suppressed in a bloodbath in the Austrian Republic (Feb 1934), was forced to flee Vienna; died in exile. ❖ See also *Women in World History.*

ADLER, Frances (d. 1964). American actress. Died Dec 13, 1964, age 73, in New York, NY; eldest dau. of Maurice Heine and Sara Adler (1858–1953, actress); half-sister of actors Luther Adler, Stella Adler (1902–1993), and Julia Adler (1897–1995). ❖ Appeared with her mother and stepfather Jacob Adler, star of the Yiddish theater, in repertory; also performed in *The Flies* (1947) and *Electra* (1959); taught acting.

ADLER, Francie (1879–1952). *See Alda, Frances.*

ADLER, Henrietta J. (1906–1988). *See Jacobson, Henrietta.*

ADLER, Julia (1897–1995). American actress. Name variations: Julia Adler Foshko. Born Philadelphia, Pennsylvania, July 4, 1897; died June 3, 1995, Englewood, New Jersey; dau. of Jacob P. and Sara (Lewis) Adler (actors and producing managers in Yiddish theater); sister of Frances Adler, Stella Adler, Luther, and Jay; half-sister of Abe, Charles, and Celia Adler; m. Joseph Foshko (artist). ❖ Generally overshadowed by her legendary theatrical family, portrayed Jessica in David Warfield Broadway production of *The Merchant of Venice* and title role in David Belasco's *Rosa Machree* (1920s); appeared in revival of Clifford Odets' *Awake and Sing,* in a role originated by sister Stella (1939); toured with brother Luther in *Tovarich* (1952). ❖ See also *Women in World History.*

ADLER, Lola (1902–1993). *See Adler, Stella.*

ADLER, Lydia (1704–?). English woman convicted of manslaughter. Born 1704 in England; death date unknown; m. John Adler; children: at least 1 daughter, Hannah. ❖ Known to fight often with husband, apparently threw him to the ground and kicked him in the groin (June 11, 1744); after he died 2 weeks later (June 23), blaming her for his impending demise, was tried at Old Bailey, convicted of manslaughter (thanks to testimony of doctor who claimed husband had been suffering from a hernia when she kicked him), and sentenced to burning on the hand with a branding iron.

ADLER, Margarete (1896–?). Austrian-Jewish swimmer. Born Feb 13, 1896, in Austria; death date unknown. ❖ At Stockholm Olympics, won bronze medal in the 4x100-meter freestyle relay (1912); was Austrian national champion in the 100-meter freestyle (1915, 1921–24), 300-meter freestyle (1915–16, 1918, 1921), and 400-meter freestyle (1922–24); was Austrian diving champion (1915).

ADLER, Polly (1899–1962). American bordello operator. Name variations: (aliases) Ann Bean, Pearl Davis, Joan Martin. Born Pearl Adler in Yanow, a White Russian village near Polish border, April 16, 1899; died June 10, 1962; eldest of nine children of Isidore (Jewish tailor) and Sarah Adler; became naturalized citizen (May 20, 1929). ❖ Successful American madam who ran an opulent bordello in the heart of Manhattan (1920–45). ❖ See also autobiography *A House Is Not a Home* (Rinehart, 1953); and *Women in World History.*

ADLER, Renata (1938—). American novelist and journalist. Born in Milan, Italy, 1938, of German parents who were fleeing the Nazis; grew up in Danbury, Connecticut; attended Bryn Mawr, Harvard, and the Sorbonne. ❖ Began working for *The New Yorker* (1962); served as film critic for *New York Times* (1968–69); books include *A Year in the Dark* (1969), *Toward a Radical Middle* (1970), *Speedboat* (1976) and *Pitch Dark* (1983); also wrote *Reckless Disregard* (1986) which tracks William Westmoreland's libel suit against CBS.

ADLER, Sara (1858–1953). Russian-American actress. Born Sara Levitzky (changed to Lewis) in Odessa, Russia; died April 28, 1953, in New York, NY; studied singing at Odessa Conservatory; m. Maurice Heine (div. 1890); m. Jacob Adler (1885–1926, Yiddish actor), 1890; children: (1st m.) Frances Adler; Stella Adler (1902–1993, actress, director, teacher of acting); Julia Adler (1897–1995, actress); Luther Adler; Jay Adler. ❖ Foremost tragedian of the Yiddish stage, whose place in American theater history is often overshadowed by husband Jacob Adler, played a major part in establishing the Yiddish theater in NYC, and was an impressive actor in her own right, with over 300 leading roles to her credit; also introduced "realism" in acting before it became a leading theater movement in US; best known for her performance as Katusha Maslova in Gordin's dramatization of Tolstoy's *Resurrection;* also won acclaim for her portrayal of the abandoned and unbalanced wife in Gordin's *Homeless.* ❖ See also *Women in World History.*

ADLER, Stella (1902–1993). American actress, director, acting teacher, and studio founder. Name variations: Lola Adler (stage name), Stella Ardler (film name). Born Stella Adler Feb 10, 1902, in New York, NY; died Dec 21, 1992, in Los Angeles, California; dau. of Jacob P. and Sara (Lewis) Adler (foremost tragedians of the Yiddish stage); sister of Frances, Julia Adler (1897–1995), Luther, and Jay; half-sister of Abe, Charles, and Celia Adler (1890–1979); attended NYU; studied acting with Maria Ouspenskaya; m. Horace Eleascheff (div.); m. Harold Clurman, 1943 (div. 1960); m. Mitchell Wilson; children: (1st m.) Ellen Oppenheim. ❖ Grand dame of the stage and influential teacher, performed in over 200 productions, from the classics to the new realism; made her theatrical debut at father's theater, The Grand, NY, in *Broken Hearts* (1906); performed in repertory with parents (1906–18); made London debut (1919); 1st appeared on Broadway in *The World We Live In* by Karel Capek (1922); with brother Luther, joined the Group Theater (1931), a repertory founded by Harold Clurman, Lee Strasberg, and Cheryl Crawford, modeled after the Moscow Art Theater; appeared as Geraldine Connelly in The Group's 1st production, Paul Green's *The House of Connelly* (1931); played Bessie Berger in Clifford Odets' *Awake and Sing!* (1935); also appeared in plays by Maxwell Anderson, Robert Lewis, and Sidney Kingsley; worked with Stanislavski (1934); had a falling out with Lee Strasberg over interpretation of Stanislavski's methods and made final stage appearance with the Group as Clara in *Paradise Lost* (1935); made film debut in *Love on Toast* under name Stella Ardler; also appeared in *Shadow of the Thin Man* (1941) and *My Girl Tisa* (1948); was associate producer on *Du Barry Was a Lady* and *Madame Curie,* and involved with several Judy Garland films, including *For Me and My Gal;* opened Stella Adler Acting Studio (1949), later named Stella Adler Conservatory of Acting, promoting the acting methods of Stanislavski (graduates include Marlon Brando, Robert De Niro, and Warren Beatty); served as adjunct professor of acting at Yale University's School of Drama; opened a 2nd conservatory in Los Angeles (1986); wrote *The Technique of Acting* (Bantam, 1988). ❖ See also *Women in World History.*

ADLER, Valentine (1898–1942). Austrian communist and editor. Name variations: Vali, Valentine Sas-Adler. Born in Vienna, Austria, May 5, 1898; died in a labor camp, July 6, 1942; dau. of Alfred Adler (1870–1937, the psychologist who would later gain fame for breaking with the teachings of his mentor Sigmund Freud) and Raissa Timofejewna or Timofeyevna Epstein Adler; sister of Alexandra Adler (research fellow in neurology at Harvard); m. Gyula Sas ("Giulio Aquila"). ❖ Was a member of the Austrian Communist Party (1919–21); soon after arriving in Berlin, transferred to the German Communist Party (1921); worked in Berlin until 1933 as an editor and translator; moved to Moscow to be with husband (1933); arrested during the Great Purge (1937); found guilty of "Trotskyite activities" and sentenced to 10 years imprisonment; died in a labor camp (1942); was posthumously rehabilitated by a decree of the Military Collegium of the Supreme Court of the USSR (1956). ❖ See also *Women in World History.*

ADLERSTRAHLE, Maertha (1868–1956). Swedish tennis player. Name variations: Martha or Märtha Adlerstrahle. Born June 16, 1868, in

Sweden; died Jan 1956. ❖ At London Olympics, won bronze medal in the singles–indoor courts (1908).

ADNAN, Etel (1925—). Lebanese poet and painter. Name variations: Etel 'Adnan. Born 1925 in Beirut, Lebanon; father was a Muslim; mother was a Christian Greek; studied philosophy at Sorbonne, University of California at Berkeley, and Harvard; moved to US, 1955. ❖ Taught French literature at the Ahliga School for Girls for 3 years; moved to Paris to study philosophy (1950); taught philosophy at Dominican College of San Rafael, CA (1959–72); while protesting Vietnam War, wrote political poetry in both French and English; returned to Beirut for a brief editorial stint at French Lebanese paper *L'Orient-le Jour* (1972); left Beirut after outbreak of war and lived in US and France; works include *Moonshots* (1966), *Five Senses for One Death* (1971), *Jebu et l'Express Beyrouth-Enfer* (1973), *Pablo Neruda is a Banana Tree* (1982), *The Indian Never Had a Horse and Other Poems* (1985), *The Arab Apocalypse* (1989), *Paris When It's Naked* (1993), *Of Cities and Women: Letters to Fawwaz* (1993), *To Write in a Foreign Language* (1996), and *Sitt Marie Rose: A Novel* (1997).

ADOFF, Virginia Hamilton (1936–2002). See *Hamilton, Virginia.*

ADOLF, Helen (1895–1998). Austrian-born educator. Born in Vienna, Austria, Dec 31, 1895; died Dec 13, 1998, in State College, Pennsylvania; dau. of Jakob Adolf (attorney) and Hedwig (Spitzer) Adolf (artist); sister of Anna Adolf Spiegel (b. 1893, a medical doctor). ❖ Professor of German language and literature who made major contributions to several areas of scholarship; after earning a PhD in literature, went to Leipzig, Germany, to work in a publishing house; with Nazi Anschluss, fled to US (1939); joined the staff of Pennsylvania State University (1943), becoming a full professor (1953); wrote *Visio Pacis* (1960). Awarded the Republic of Austria's Cross of Honor, 1st Class, in Arts and Letters (1972).

ADORÉE, Renée (1898–1933). French actress. Name variations: Renee Adoree. Born Jeanne de la Fonte in Lille, Nord, Nord-Pas de Calais, France, Sept 30, 1898; died age 35 of tuberculosis, Oct 5, 1933, in Tujunga, California; m. Tom Moore (actor), 1921 (div. 1924); m. Sherman Gill, 1925. ❖ Began career as a toe dancer, horseback dancer, and acrobat in parents' touring circus; danced with Folies-Bergère; fled Europe during WWI; appeared in Australia in 1st film *1500 Reward* (1918); on Broadway, introduced "The Rocker," a popular fox trot, in *Oh, Uncle!, Oh, What a Girl*; attained stardom as Melisande in King Vidor's *The Big Parade* (1925); other films include *Parisian Nights* (1925), *La Bohème* (1926), *The Cossacks* (1928), *The Michigan Kid* (1928), *The Pagan* (1929), *Tide of Empire* (1929), and *Redemption* (1930). ❖ See also *Women in World History.*

ADORNO, Catherine (1447–1510). See *Catherine of Genoa.*

ADRET, Françoise (1920—). French ballet dancer. Name variations: Francoise Adret. Born Aug 7, 1920, in Versailles, France. ❖ Became ballet master of, and toured with, Petit Ballets de Paris (1948); choreographed for European companies including Netherlands Opera (c. 1951–58), Warsaw Opera, Nice Opera (1960–64), for which she staged opera divertissements and modern ballets; formed Ballet-Théâtre Contemporain in Paris and Angiers, France; works include *La Conjuration* (1948); *Quatre Mouvements* (1952); *Le Sanctuaire* (1956); *Otello* (1958); *Barbaresques* (1960); *Le Manteau Rouge* (1963); *Le Mandarin Merveilleux* (1965); *Incendio* (1967); *La Follia de Orlando* (1972).

ADRIAN, Iris (1912–1994). American actress. Born Iris Adrian Hostetter, May 29, 1912, in Los Angeles, California; died Sept 17, 1994, in Hollywood, California; m. Charles Over, 1935 (div., 1936); m. George Jay; m. "Fido" Murphy (well-known football player and consultant to the Chicago Bears). ❖ Debuted as a dancer in the Ziegfeld Follies (1929); as one of Hollywood's popular wise-cracking actresses (1930s), appeared in over 150 films, including *Gold Diggers of 1937, Road to Zanzibar, Roxie Hart, To the Shores of Tripoli, Orchestra Wives, Ladies of Burlesque, Bluebeard, The Paleface, Blue Hawaii* and *That Darn Cat.*

ADRIAN, Jane (1921–2004). See *Sterling, Jan.*

ADRIENNE, Jean (b. 1905). India-born actress, dancer and singer. Born Oct 23, 1905, in Mussoorie, India; attended George Watson College, Edinburgh; studied dance in London; m. Andrea Meazza. ❖ Made stage debut at Duke of York in a season of Russian dances (1920); toured with Tamara Karsavina and Anna Pavlova; toured the provinces and made many appearances in Glasgow.

ADU, Helen Folasade (1959—). See *Sade.*

ADU, Sade (1959—). See *Sade.*

ADY, Mrs. Henry (1851–1924). See *Cartwright, Julia.*

AE. See also, *E for names beginning AE.* (Originally the Teutonic [Germanic] Æ was used, such as Aethelflaed or Aethelfleda, before the 11th century, but in some citations was later dropped from common usage, becoming Ethelflaed or Ethelfleda).

AEBBA (c. 610–c. 683). See *Ebba.*

AEBBE (c. 610–c. 683). See *Ebba.*

AEBI, Tania (1966—). American yachtswoman. Born in 1966; lived in New York City. ❖ Completed a 30-month circumnavigation of the world in 26-foot sloop *Varuna* (Nov 6, 1987), but was not considered the 1st American woman to sail solo around the world, since a friend had joined her for 80 miles of the trip while she was in the South Pacific. ❖ See also memoir (with Bernadette Brennan) *Maiden Voyage.*

AEDELERS or AELDERS, Etta Palm d' (1743–1799). See *Palm, Etta.*

AELFFLAED. See *Elflaed.*

AELFGIFU (c. 985–1052). See *Emma of Normandy.*

AELFGIFU (d. 1002). See *Elfgifu.*

AELFLED. See *Elflaed.*

AELFTHRYTH (c. 945–c. 1000). See *Elfthrith.*

AELFWYN. See *Elfwyn.*

AELGIFU (c. 1000–c. 1040). See *Elfgifu.*

AELIA ARIADNE (fl. 457–515). See *Ariadne.*

AELIA FLAVIA FLACCILLA (c. 355–386). See *Flaccilla.*

AELIA GALLA PLACIDIA (c. 390–450). See *Placidia, Galla.*

AELIA PULCHERIA (c. 398–453). See *Pulcheria.*

AELITH DE POITIERS (c. 1123–?). French noblewoman. Name variations: Petronilla. Born c. 1123; death date unknown; dau. of William X, duke of Aquitaine, and Aénor of Châtellerault (d. 1130); sister of Eleanor of Aquitaine (1122–1204). ❖ See also *Women in World History.*

AEMILIA (fl. 195 BCE). Roman patrician. Fl. in 195 BCE; dau. of Lucius Aemilius Paullus (consul in 219 and 216 BCE); sister of Lucius Aemilius Paullus (consul in 182 and 168 BCE); m. Publius Cornelius Scipio Africanus (the Roman victor over Hannibal in the 2nd Punic War); children: two sons and two daughters who lived to adulthood, including Publius (who adopted Scipio Aemilianus); Lucius (praetor in 174); and Cornelia (c. 195–c. 115 BCE). ❖ See also *Women in World History.*

AEMILIA HILARIA (fl. 350 CE). Gallo-Roman doctor. Name variations: Aemilia; Aemilia Hilaria (Aemilia the Jolly); (nickname) Hilarus. Born c. 300 CE in the small city of Aquae Tarbellicae (modern Dax), Roman Gaul (modern France); died at age 63 at an unspecified date; dau. of Caecilius Agricius Arborius and Aemilia Corinthia Maura, apparently both impoverished nobles from Gaul; had one brother, Aemilius Magnus Arborius, who became a tutor to a son of Emperor Constantius, and 2 sisters: Aemilia Dryadia, who died in infancy, and Aemilia Aeonia, mother of Ausonius. ❖ One of the few female doctors in the Roman Empire of whom a record has come down from antiquity—a single line of a long Latin poem, the *Parentalia,* written by her nephew, Decimus Magnus Ausonius, the Gallo-Roman senator and tutor to Emperor Gratian. ❖ See also *Women in World History.*

AÉNOR OF CHÂTELLERAULT (d. 1130). Duchess of Aquitaine. Name variations: Aenor of Chatellerault; Anor; Aenor Aimery; Eleanor of Châtellerault. Born after 1107 (some sources cite 1103); died in Talmont, France, 1130; dau. of Aimery, viscount of Châtellerault, and Dangereuse (mistress of William IX, duke of Aquitaine); m. William X (1099–1137), duke of Aquitaine, 1121; children: Eleanor of Aquitaine (1122–1204); Aelith de Poitiers (born c. 1123 and sometimes referred to as Petronilla); William de Poitiers (died in infancy, 1130). ❖ Was the dau. of Dangereuse (La Maubergeonne), who had been abducted by William IX, duke of Aquitaine, and kept in a tower; died when her children were quite young. ❖ See also *Women in World History.*

AESARA OF LUCANIA (fl. 400s–300s BCE). Pythagorean philosopher. Born in Lucania, Italy. ❖ Her work earned her such esteem that she was praised in Roman poetry and Greek lectures; wrote *Book on Human Nature.* ❖ See also *Women in World History.*

AETHEL-. *See Ethel-.*

AETHELBURG. *See Ethelberga.*

AETHELFLEDA. *See Ethelflaed.*

AETHELFRYTH (c. 945–c. 1000). *See Elfthrith.*

AETHELTHRITH. *See Elthelthrith.*

AETHERIA (fl. 4th c.). *See Egeria.*

AFIFI, Hidaya (1898–1969). *See Barakat, Hidaya Afifi.*

AFLATUN, Inge. *See Efflatoun, Inji.*

AFOLABI, Bisi. Nigerian runner. Born Olabisi Afolabi in Nigeria. ❖ Won a silver medal for the 4x400-meter relay at Atlanta Olympics (1996).

AFRA (fl. c. 304). German saint. Possibly dau. of St. Hilaria who was martyred at the tomb of Afra in the 4th century. ❖ The local saint of Augsburg, suffered martyrdom under Diocletian; said to have originally been a prostitute. Feast day is Aug 5. ❖ See also *Women in World History.*

AFRASILOAIA, Felicia (1954—). Romanian rower. Born Jan 16, 1954, in Romania. ❖ At Montreal Olympics, won bronze medal in the Quadruple sculls with coxswain (1976).

AFUA KOBA (fl. 1834–1884). Asantehemaa of the Ashanti Empire. Name variations: Afua Kobi; Efua Kobiri. Married Kwasi Gyambibi (tribal chief); children: Kofi Kakari (or Kofi Karikari, asantehene, 1867–1874) and Mensa Bonsu (asantehene, 1874–1883). ❖ Enstooled as queenmother, or asantehemaa (1834), and held the position, naming several sons as asantehene, until the family was deposed (1884) for cooperating with British colonialists (including an 1881 intervention in hopes of preventing a bloody, deadly battle). ❖ See also *Women in World History.*

AGACHE, Lavinia (1966—). Romanian gymnast. Born Feb 11, 1966, in Caiute, Romania; trained under Bela and Marta Karolyi; m. Tom Carney, 1995. ❖ At World championships, won a silver medal for vault, silver for uneven bars, and bronze for beam (1983); at European championship, placed 2nd all-around and 1st in balance beam (1983); at Los Angeles Olympics, won a bronze medal in vault and a gold medal in all-around team (1984); broke kneecap (1985); turned to coaching.

AGANOOR POMPILJ, Vittoria (1855–1910). *See Pompilj, Vittoria Aganoor.*

AGAOGLU, Adalet (1929—). Turkish dramatist, novelist and short-story writer. Name variations: 'Adalet Agoglu. Born 1929 in Ankara Province, Turkey; graduated from French Department at University of Ankara. ❖ During her tenure as director of the Ankara Radio Theatre, wrote her best-known play, *Yasamak,* which was broadcast originally in Turkey (1955), and subsequently in France and Germany; writings include *To Lie Down* (1973), *The Delicate Rose of My Mind* (1976), *The Wedding Night* (1979), *The End of Summer* (1980), *A Few People* (1984), *No...* (1987), *The High Voltage* (1974), *The First Sound of Silence* (1978), *Come On Let's Go* (1982), *A Chill in the Soul* (1991), and *A Romantic Viennese Summer* (1993); also published plays, essays, and translations of Sartre, Brecht, and Anouilh. Won Turkish Language Society drama award (1974), Sedat Simawi prize (1979), Sait Faik Short Story award (1975), and Is Bankasi Grand Award for theater (1992).

AGAPE OF THESSALONICA (d. 304). Saint. Name variations: Agape. Born in Roman Empire; died 304; sister of Irene and Chionia (saints). ❖ With sisters, accused of being in possession of the Holy Scriptures, a crime punishable by death, and burned alive. Feast day is April 3. ❖ See also *Women in World History.*

AGAR, Eileen (1899–1991). Argentine-born British surrealist artist. Born Eileen Agar in Buenos Aires, Argentina, Dec 1, 1899; died in London, Nov 17, 1991; dau. of James and Mamie Agar; educated at Heathfield, Ascot; studied art under sculptor Leon Underwood (1924), at Slade School of Art under Henry Tonks (1925–26), and in Paris (1928–30); m. Robin Bartlett (painter), 1925 (sep. 1926); m. Joseph Bard (Hungarian-born writer), 1940. ❖ Artist, known as a surrealist, whose artistic works such as *Quadriga* were enormously popular; with family, settled permanently in London (1911); separated from husband and began lifelong relationship with Hungarian-born author Joseph Bard

(1926) who was then married; broke away from conventional art and began developing her own style; set up a studio in the Rue Schoelcher in Paris (1929); became attracted to the formations in natural history, especially fossils, which culminated in her large work *Autobiography of an Embryo* (1934); continuing her fascination with nature, began gathering odd shapes from the Dorset beaches, such as cork, wood, shells, and stone; exhibited her work *Angel of Anarchy* in the London Gallery as part of the Exhibition of Surrealist Poems and Objects (1937) and became a major celebrity in the London gallery scene; was one of the few women, and the main British woman, who came to be recognized as part of the predominantly male surrealist movement; after WWII, work began to take on the characteristics of Abstract Expressionism, or the "New York School"; continued artistic work well into old age, remaining influential in London art circles. Paintings include *Self-Portrait* (1927), *Movement in Space* (1931), *The Modern Muse* (1931), *Autobiography of an Embryo* (1933–34), *Ceremonial Hat for Eating Bouillabaisse* (1936), *Battle Cry/ Bullet Proof Painting* (1938) and *Marine Object* (1939). ❖ See also autobiography *A Look at My Life* (1988); and *Women in World History.*

AGARISTE (fl. 515 BCE–490 BCE). Greek noblewoman, mother of Pericles. Fl. around 515 BCE–490 BCE; m. Xanthippus; children: Pericles (c. 495 BCE–429 BCE), Greek general, politician, and diplomat. ❖ Was an Alcemeonid, an old and influential aristocratic family (her uncle Clisthenes inaugurated his democratic reforms in 507 BCE and her husband Xanthippus was one of the most important public figures of his generation). ❖ See also *Women in World History.*

AGASSIZ, Elizabeth Cary (1822–1907). American naturalist, college founder, and educator. Name variations: Elizabeth Cabot Agassiz. Born Elizabeth Cabot Cary in Boston, Massachusetts, Dec 5, 1822; died in Arlington Heights, Massachusetts, June 27, 1907; dau. of Thomas Graves Cary (lawyer and businessman) and Mary Ann Cushing Perkins (homemaker); m. (Jean) Louis Agassiz (Swiss scientist), 1850; stepchildren: Alexander Agassiz (eminent marine zoologist), Pauline Agassiz Shaw (1841–1917); Ida Agassiz, who m. historian Francis Parkman. Louis Agassiz's 1st wife was Cécile Braun. ❖ An important figure in the history of women's higher education in America, was the co-founder and 1st president of Radcliffe College; in her early years, as a self-taught naturalist and educator, operated a select school for girls out of her home (1856–64); published *A First Lesson in Natural History* (1859), followed by *Seaside Studies in Natural History,* co-written with stepson Alexander Agassiz (1865); was a member of a scientific expedition to Brazil (1865); published *A Journey in Brazil,* co-written with husband Louis Agassiz (1867); embarked on a deep-sea dredging expedition through the straits of Magellan and the Galapagos (1871); co-founded and operated the Anderson School of Natural History (1872); published 2-vol. biography, *Louis Agassiz: His Life and Correspondence* (1885); helped found the Society for the Collegiate Instruction of Women, known as the "Harvard Annex" (1879); elected president of the Society (1882); continued in her capacity as president of the newly incorporated Radcliffe College (1894); resigned from active duty and became honorary president of Radcliffe College (1899); honored when a student's hall, the Elizabeth Cary Agassiz House, was established at Radcliffe (1902); resigned as honorary president (1903). ❖ See also *Women in World History.*

AGASSIZ, Pauline (1841–1917). *See Shaw, Pauline Agassiz.*

AGATE, May (1892–1960). English actress and writer. Born Dec 29, 1892, in Manchester, England; died 1960; sister of James Agate, drama critic and author; m. Wilfrid Grantham. ❖ Studied and made stage debut with Sarah Bernhardt at her theater in Paris in *La Samaritaine* (1912); made London debut as Lady Howard in the Bernhardt starrer *La Reine Elizabeth* (1912); also appeared in Bernhardt's *Phèdre* (1913) and *Les Cathédrales* (1913); other portrayals include Mrs. 'Enderson in *The Beetle,* Mrs. Harold in *Craig's Wife,* Mrs. Vanderpool in *Hocus-Pocus,* and Duchess Ludoviska in *Elizabeth of Austria.* Wrote a biography of Bernhardt, *Madame Sarah* (1945); with husband, under pseudonym Grant Yates, adapted *Night's Candles* (1933); adapted "The Woman of Samaria" for radio (1945).

AGATHA (d. 251). Sicilian saint. Born at Palermo, though date of birth is unknown; died Feb 5, 251. ❖ Patron saint of Malta and of the cities Catania and Palermo in Sicily, was a 3rd-century Sicilian noblewoman of great beauty, who repeatedly rejected the illicit advances of the Roman prefect Quintianus, governor of Sicily; was whipped, burnt with hot irons, torn with hooks, and then placed on a bed of live coals and glass during the persecutions of the Christians by the emperor Decius (251 CE). Feast day is Feb 5. ❖ See also *Women in World History.*

AGATHA (fl. 1060). English princess. Fl. around 1060; buried in Bayeux, Normandy, France; dau. of William I the Conqueror (c. 1027–1087), duke of Normandy (r. 1035–1087), king of England (r. 1066–1087), and Matilda of Flanders (c. 1031–1083); betrothed to Harald or Harold II Godwineson (c. 1022–1066), king of the English (r. 1066); betrothed to Alphonso VI, king of Castile and Leon. ❖ See also *Women in World History.*

AGATHA OF HUNGARY (c. 1025–?). Saxon noblewoman. Born c. 1025; died after 1067 in Scotland; some sources erroneously claim that she was the dau. of Stephen I, king of Hungary, and Gisela of Bavaria (d. 1033); other sources claim that she was the dau. of St. Cunigunde and Henry II, Holy Roman emperor; more than likely she was the dau. of Bruno, bishop of Augsburg (brother of Henry II, Holy Roman emperor); m. Edward the Exile also known as Edward the Atheling (son of King Edmund II), before 1045; children: Edgar the Atheling (b. around 1050); St. Margaret (c. 1046–1093); Christina (fl. 1086). ❖ See also *Women in World History.*

AGATHA OF LORRAINE (fl. 1100s). Countess of Burgundy. Name variations: Agathe de Lorraine. Dau. of Simon I, duke of Lorraine; m. Rainald also known as Renaud III, count of Burgundy and Macon; children: Beatrice of Upper Burgundy (1145–1184). ❖ See also *Women in World History.*

AGHDASHLOO, Shohreh (1952—). Iranian actress. Born May 11, 1952, in Tehran, Iran; m. Houshang Touzie (actor). ❖ Nominated for an Academy Award for Best Supporting Actress for film *The House of Sand and Fog* (2003), was the 1st Iranian and Middle Eastern actress to be nominated for an Oscar; other films include *Shatranje bad* (1976), *Gozaresh* (1977), *Sooteh-Delan* (1978), *Guests of Hotel Astoria* (1989), *Maryam* (2000), *Surviving Paradise* (2000), *America So Beautiful* (2001), and *The Exorcism of Emily Rose* (2005).

AGNELLI, Susanna (1922—). Italian politician and writer. Name variations: Susanna Rattazzi, Countess Rattazzi. Born in Turin, Italy, April 24, 1922; dau. of Edoardo Agnelli and Princess Virginia Bourbon del Monte Agnelli; sister of industrialists Giovanni and Umberto Agnelli; m. Count Urbano Rattazzi, a lawyer (div. 1971); children: 6. ❖ The 1st Italian woman to hold the post of foreign minister, grew up in a family of immense wealth and influence (her paternal grandfather was the industrialist Giovanni Agnelli, founder of FIAT automobile company); entered the public arena relatively late in life, serving as town councillor and mayor of Monte Argentario (1974–84); elected for 2 terms to Italian Parliament on Republican Party ticket (1976, 1979); was a member of the European Parliament (1979–81); elected to Italian Senate (1983); appointed to post of undersecretary of state for foreign affairs with responsibility for South and North American Affairs (1983); member of the World Commission on Environment and Development, Geneva (1984–87); became Italy's 1st woman minister of foreign affairs (Jan 1995). ❖ See also autobiography *We Always Wore Sailor Suits* (Viking, 1975); and *Women in World History.*

AGNES (d. possibly c. 304). Saint and Christian martyr. Name variations: Formerly Annes, Annis, Annice; (French) Agnūs. Born in Rome, though date of birth unknown; some historians place her death around 254 (under emperor Decius), some about 304 (under Diocletian); dau. of a noble Roman family; foster sister of St. Emerentiana (d. around 305). ❖ At 12, was sought after by wealthy suitors for marriage; when she refused, saying she wanted to devote her life to Christ, was denounced as a Christian to the Roman governor; unmoved by threats of torture, was sent to the public brothel (there, only one man dared touch her, and he was stricken blind until his sight was restored in answer to her prayers); though scholars disagree as to the date of her death, it is thought that she was beheaded in Rome by order of the emperor Diocletian. Through the centuries, young girls observed St. Agnes' Eve (Jan 20–21) with rites that supposedly divined the form of their future husbands; John Keats used this superstition as *mise en scène* for his poem "The Eve of St. Agnes" (1819); another poem, "Saint Agnes' Eve," was written by Alfred Lord Tennyson. ❖ See also *Women in World History.*

AGNES, Lore (1876–1953). German politician. Born Lore Benning in Bochum, Germany, June 4, 1876; died in Cologne, June 9, 1953; m. Peter Agnes. ❖ A lifelong Social Democrat, represented the Düsseldorf electoral district as a deputy to the German Reichstag (1919–33); after the Nazi takeover (1933), continued to work in the underground Social

Democratic movement and was consequently persecuted and imprisoned by the Nazi authorities on many occasions. ❖ See also *Women in World History.*

AGNES, Mere (1593–1671). *See Arnauld, Jeanne Catherine*

AGNES, Saint (1274–1317). *See Agnes of Monte Pulciano, Saint.*

AGNES CAPET (1260–1327). Duchess of Burgundy. Name variations: Agnes of Burgundy; Agnes of France. Born 1260; died Dec 19, 1327, in Chateau de Lanthenay, France; dau. of Louis IX, king of France, and Margaret of Provence (1221–1295); m. Robert II, duke of Burgundy, 1279; children: John of Burgundy (1279–1283); Blanche of Burgundy (1288–1348); Margaret of Burgundy (1290–1315, 1st wife of Louis X of France); Jeanne of Burgundy (1293–1348, who m. Philip VI of France); Hugh V, duke of Burgundy; Eudes IV, duke of Burgundy; Louis (1297–1316), king of Thessalonica; Marie of Burgundy (1298–c. 1310), who m. Edward I, count of Bar); Robert (1302–1334), count of Tonnerre. ❖ See also *Women in World History.*

AGNES DE CASTRO (c. 1320–1355). *See Castro, Inez de.*

AGNES DE DAMPIERRE (1237–1288). Ruler of Bourbon. Name variations: Agness. Born in 1237; died Sept 7, 1288, in Bourbon; dau. of Count of Guy (or Gui) II de Dampierre and Mahaut I (r. 1215–1242); sister of Mahaut II (ruler of Bourbon, 1249–1262, ruler of Nevers, 1257–1266); granddau. of Mahaut de Courtenay (ruler of Nevers, 1182–1257); m. Jean de Bourgogne, also known as John of Burgundy, in Feb 1247; children: Beatrix de Bourgogne (1257–1310), ruler of Bourbon (r. 1287–1310). ❖ On death of sister Mahaut II (1262), inherited the barony of Bourbon and held it until her death. ❖ See also *Women in World History.*

AGNES DE NEVERS (r. 1181–1192). Countess and ruler of Nevers. Reigned (1181–92); m. Pierre de Courtenay; children: Mahaut de Courtenay, ruler of Nevers (r. 1192–1257). ❖ Succeeding Count Guillaume V, also known as William V, became the ruler of Nevers, located in central France (1181). ❖ See also *Women in World History.*

AGNES DE POITIERS (fl. 1135). Queen of Aragon. Name variations: Agnes of Aquitaine. Fl. around 1135; dau. of William IX, duke of Aquitaine, and Philippa de Rouergue (dau. of William IV of Toulouse); m. Ramiro II (c. 1075–1157), king of Aragon (r. 1134–1157), 1135; children: Petronilla (1135–1174), queen of Aragon. ❖ See also *Women in World History.*

AGNES OF ANJOU (c. 1005–1068). *See Agnes of Aquitaine.*

AGNES OF AQUITAINE (c. 995–1068). Duchess of Aquitaine. Name variations: Agnes of Anjou; Agnes of Burgundy; Agnes, countess of Burgundy. Born c. 995 in Burgundy; died Nov 10, 1068, at convent of Notre Dame des Saintes, France; dau. of Otto William, duke of Burgundy, and Ermentrude de Roucy; m. William V the Grand or the Pious (d. 1030), duke of Aquitaine, 1019; m. Geoffrey Martel, count of Anjou, c. 1032 or 1040 (m. dissolved, 1050); children: (1st m.) William VII, duke of Aquitaine; another son; Agnes of Poitou (1024–1077), Holy Roman empress. ❖ Born into the Burgundian ruling house, was extremely well-educated, even in the web of loyalties and enmities between the ruling feudal families of France; showed an ambitious nature and was pleased with her arranged marriage to the powerful Duke William V the Grand of Aquitaine (1019); upon William's death (1030), struggled to gain control of the duchy for her children, because her husband's eldest son (William VI) from a previous marriage had inherited title of duke; when her eldest son, also William, inherited the duchy upon William VI's death (1038), retained her title as duchess and became regent of Aquitaine in his name; even after he came of age, played a principal role in the administration of the large duchy; married Geoffrey Martel, count of Anjou (c. 1040); when marriage dissolved and Geoffrey remarried (1050), refused to give up her dower lands that he had bestowed on his new wife (in the ensuing war, her son William VII died in battle); more or less withdrew from politics and turned to more spiritual endeavors, using her wealth to found the abbey of Notre Dame des Saintes and Abbey of the Trinity. ❖ See also *Women in World History.*

AGNES OF ASSISI (1207–1232). Italian abbess. Name variations: (Italian) Agnese. Born in Assisi, Umbria, in Central Italy, 1207; died 1232; dau. of Favorone (or Favarone) Offreduccio (noble and Crusader) and Ortolana; sister of Clare of Assisi. ❖ Born into a wealthy Italian family, was about 13 years younger than sister Clare of Assisi; when Clare founded Poor Clares (Franciscan order for women) and established a convent at San Damiano, joined the convent as a nun and helped sister in role of spiritual advisor; though sometimes overshadowed by Clare, drew admiration from the people of Italy for her own selfless devotion to serving the poor and sick; founded a convent in Monticelli (near Florence) and became its abbess (1219); died young from an undiagnosed illness, about age 25. ❖ See also *Women in World History.*

AGNES OF AUSTRIA (fl. 1100s). Hungarian queen and German princess. Married Stephen III, king of Hungary (r. 1161–1173).

AGNES OF AUSTRIA (1281–1364). Hungarian queen and German princess. Born 1281 (some sources cite 1280); died June 11, 1364, in Königsfelden; dau. of German king Albert I of Habsburg (1255–1308), Holy Roman emperor (r. 1298–1308), and Elizabeth of Tyrol (c. 1262–1313); sister of Frederick the Handsome, king of Germany, Anna of Habsburg (d. 1327), Rudolf III, king of Bohemia and Poland, and Elizabeth of Habsburg (1293–1352); m. Andrew III, king of Hungary (r. 1290–1301), 1296. ❖ When her father was murdered by a nephew (May 1, 1308), pursued all connected with his murder; also backed her brother Frederick the Handsome in his long war with Ludwig of Bavaria for the imperial crown; as a widow, lived with mother Elizabeth of Tyrol in Vienna, acting as secretary, adviser and deputy; after Elizabeth's death, continued her mother's charities from the convent Elizabeth had founded at Königsfelden; resided at the convent for the last 50 years of her life; one of the richest German princesses of her day, lived simply while heaping gifts on the church and the poor; also directed a successful peace campaign, bringing an end to the war over Laupen (1340) and concluding alliances for the house of Austria with Berne (1341) and Strassburg, Basel, and Freiburg (1350). Meister Eckhart, the European mystic, wrote one of his best known tracts, *Book of Divine Consolation* (1308–11), for her. ❖ See also *Women in World History.*

AGNES OF BARBY (1540–1569). Princess of Anhalt. Name variations: Agnes von Barby. Born Jun 23, 1540; died Nov 27, 1569; dau. of Wolgang, count of Barby; married Joachim Ernst, prince of Anhalt, Mar 3, 1560; children: Elizabeth of Anhalt (1563–1607); Sibylle of Anhalt (1564–1614); John George I (b. 1567), prince of Anhalt.

AGNES OF BAVARIA (1024–1077). *See Agnes of Poitou.*

AGNES OF BEAUJEU (d. 1231). French noblewoman. Died July 11, 1231; dau. of Richard IV of Beaujeu; became 2nd wife of Teobaldo or Theobald I also known as Theobald IV of Champagne (1201–1253), king of Navarre (r. 1234–1253), 1222 (div. 1227); children: probably Blanche of Navarre (fl. 1239), duchess of Brittany.

AGNES OF BOHEMIA (1205–1282). Hungarian princess. Born in Prague; died 1282; dau. of Otakar or Ottokar I, king of Bohemia and Hungary (r. 1198–1230), and Constance of Hungary (d. 1240); sister of Wenceslas I (1205–1253), king of Bohemia (r. 1230–1253). ❖ Revered as a saint but never canonized, was renowned for her piety; saw 2 betrothals broken off when young and began to show a great interest in charitable work; had 2 more offers of marriage (from Henry III of England and Emperor Frederick II), but successfully petitioned the pope for permission to pursue a religious life (1233); joined Franciscan order of the Poor Clares (1234); though the pope commanded that she be abbess, maintained that she was not superior to other nuns and insisted on performing all menial tasks; heightened her growing fame when she reconciled her brother Wenceslas with his rebellious son Ottokar II, king of Bohemia; because of her popularity, the Franciscan order was spread throughout Bohemia; also founded several convents as well as a monastery and a hospital at Prague; was so revered that after her death at age 77, many of the sick wore her relics and prayed to Blessed Agnes in the belief that her spirit could effect miracles of healing. ❖ See also *Women in World History.*

AGNES OF BOHEMIA (1269–1297). Princess of Bohemia and duchess of Austria. Name variations: Anezka. Born Sept 1269; died May 17, 1297, in Prague (some sources cite 1290 or 1296); dau. of Otakar or Ottokar II (b. 1230?), king of Bohemia (r. 1253–1278), duke of Austria and Styria (r. 1252), and Cunigunde of Hungary (d. 1285); m. Rudolf II (1270–1290, son of Rudolf I, Holy Roman emperor, and Anna of Hohenberg), duke of Austria (r. 1282–1290); children: John the Parricide (1291–1313). ❖ See also *Women in World History.*

AGNES OF BOURBON (d. 1287). Countess of Artois. Died Sept 7, 1287; dau. of Archimbaud or Archambaud VII, ruler of Bourbon, and Alix of Burgundy (1146–1192); became 2nd wife of Robert II (1250–1302), count of Artois (r. 1250–1302), in 1277; stepmother of Mahaut (c. 1270–1329).

AGNES OF BRANDENBURG (d. 1304). Queen of Denmark. Died Oct 1, 1304; dau. of Jutta of Saxony (d. 1267) and John I, margrave of Brandenburg; m. Erik V Klipping or Clipping (1249–1286), king of Denmark (r. 1259–1286), Nov 11, 1273; children: daughter Regitze also known as Richeza Eriksdottir (who m. Nicholas II von Werle); Erik VI, king of Denmark (r. 1286–1319); Christopher I, king of Denmark (r. 1319–26, 1330–32); Martha of Denmark (c. 1272–1341); Valdemar; Katherina (1283–1283); Elizabeth (1283–1283).

AGNES OF BURGUNDY (c. 995–1068). *See Agnes of Aquitaine.*

AGNES OF BURGUNDY (1260–1327). *See Agnes Capet.*

AGNES OF BURGUNDY (d. 1476). Duchess of Bourbon. Died 1476; dau. of Margaret of Bavaria (d. 1424) and John the Fearless, duke of Burgundy (r. 1404–1419); sister of Philip the Good (1396–1467), duke of Burgundy (r. 1419–1467); m. Charles I, duke of Bourbon (r. 1434–1456); children: Isabelle of Bourbon (d. 1465); Charles (c. 1434–1488), archbishop of Lyons; Peter II also known as Pierre de Beaujeu (who m. Anne of Beaujeu); Louis, prince-bishop of Liege; Marie de Bourbon (who m. John II of Calabria); John II (1426–1488), duke of Bourbon (r. 1456–1488, who m. Jeanne of Bourbon [1434–1482]); Catherine of Bourbon (d. 1469); Jeanne of Bourbon (d. 1493).

AGNES OF COURTENAY (1136–1186). Queen of Jerusalem. Born 1136; died 1186; dau. of Joscelin II and Beatrice; sister of Joscelin III and Sibylla; 1st wife of Amalric I, king of Jerusalem (r. 1162–1174); m. Hugh of Ramleh also known as Hugh of Ibelin (died 1169); m. Reginald also known as Reynald of Sidon, lord of Sidon; children: (1st m.) Baldwin IV, king of Jerusalem (r. 1174–1183) and Sibylla (1160–1190). Amalric's 2nd wife was Maria Comnena. ❖ A dynamic politician who greatly influenced events in the Frankish principality of Jerusalem, was born a princess in Edessa when the Holy Land was controlled by Christian knights; moved to Jerusalem (1149) at age 13; married Amalric I, king of Jerusalem (1157), but marriage was annulled on grounds of consanguinity soon after Amalric assumed the throne, despite 2 children (1163); married and widowed twice more, began to regain power as mother of Baldwin IV, who had succeeded to his father's throne despite the annulment; became a major participant in the politics of the royal court, arranging, among other accomplishments, her daughter's marriages and securing the loyalty of Jerusalem's nobles and churchmen to her son; when Baldwin's leprosy incapacitated him, became ruler of Jerusalem in practice if not in name; arranged the coronation of her grandson as Baldwin V before her son's death (1185), thus ensuring a peaceful succession. ❖ See also *Women in World History.*

AGNES OF FRANCE (c. 1170–?). *See Agnes-Anne of France.*

AGNES OF GERMANY (1024–1077). *See Agnes of Poitou.*

AGNES OF GERMANY (1074–1143). German princess. Born 1074; died Sept 24, 1143; dau. of Holy Roman emperor Henry IV (r. 1056–1106) and Bertha of Savoy (1051–1087); sister of Henry V and Conrad, both Holy Roman emperors; granddau. of Agnes of Poitou (1024–1077); m. Frederick I, duke of Swabia, 1089; m. Leopold III, margrave of Austria of the Babenberg line; children: (1st m.) Frederick (d. 1147), duke of Swabia (who m. Judith of Bavaria [fl. 1120s]); Conrad III (1st emperor of the Hohenstaufen line); Gertrude of Swabia (c. 1104–1191, who m. Hermann, pfalzgraf of Lotharingen); (2nd m.) Leopold IV, margrave of Austria; Henry Jasomirgott, 1st duke of Austria; the historian Otto, bishop of Freising. ❖ With husband Frederick, was responsible for the beginnings of a German dynasty, the House of Hohenstaufen (their son Conrad III ruled Germany [r. 1138–52], their grandson Frederick I Barbarossa [r. 1152–90] unified Germany). ❖ See also *Women in World History.*

AGNES OF GUIENNE (1024–1077). *See Agnes of Poitou.*

AGNES OF HABSBURG (c. 1257–1322). Electress of Saxony. Name variations: Gertrud. Born c. 1257; died Oct 11, 1322, in Wittenberg; dau. of Anna of Hohenberg (c. 1230–1281) and Rudolph or Rudolf I of Habsburg (1218–1291), king of Germany (r. 1273), Holy Roman emperor (r. 1273–1291); m. Albert II, elector of Saxony.

AGNES OF HESSE (1527–1555). Electress of Saxony. Born May 31, 1527; died Nov 4, 1555; dau. of Christine of Saxony (1505–1549) and Philip I the Magnanimous, landgrave of Hesse; m. Maurice, elector of Saxony, Jan 9, 1541; m. John Frederick II, elector of Saxony, May 26, 1555; children: (1st m.) Anna of Saxony (1544–1577).

AGNES OF HUNTINGDONSHIRE (fl. 13th c.). English doctor. Fl. in 13th century. ❖ One of numerous medieval women doctors, was well-respected for her healing abilities in Huntingdonshire, though she practiced medicine without university training—a privilege denied most medieval women. ❖ See also *Women in World History.*

AGNES OF JOUARRE (fl. early 13th c.). French abbess. Fl. early 13th c. ❖ A learned, pious woman, entered religious life as a young girl and eventually became abbess at convent of Jouarre, France; not content with the decreasing power of abbesses in the increasingly centralized church hierarchy, petitioned Pope Innocent III for independent status for Jouarre, which meant that the abbey was no longer responsible to local bishops and other church officials, but had to answer only to the pope himself. ❖ See also *Women in World History.*

AGNES OF LOOSS (fl. 1150–1175). Duchess of Bavaria. Fl. between 1150 and 1175; m. Otto I (b. around 1120), duke of Bavaria (r. 1180–1183); children: Otto (d. 1181); Ludwig also known as Louis I (b. 1174), duke of Bavaria (r. 1183–1231), who m. Ludmilla of Bohemia and was assassinated in 1231).

AGNES OF MARCH (1312–1369). *See Dunbar, Agnes.*

AGNES OF MAURIENNE (1092–1154). *See Adelaide of Maurienne.*

AGNES OF MEISSEN (1184–1203). *See Agnes of Quedlinburg.*

AGNES OF MERAN (d. 1201). Queen of France. Name variations: The White Lady; Agnes of Neran; Agnes de Méranie or Meranie. Died July 20, 1201, in Paris, France; dau. of Berthold III of Andrechs, marquis of Meran, count of Tirol, and duke of Carinthia and Istria, and Agnes of Dedo; sister of Gertrude of Andrechs-Meran, queen of Hungary, and Saint Hedwig of Silesia (1174–1243); m. Philip II Augustus (1165–1223), king of France (r. 1180–1223), 1196; children: Philip Hurepel (1200–1234), count of Boulogne; Marie of France (1198–c. 1223). ❖ Born into a German noble family, became mistress of French king Philip II Augustus; was made his queen in all but title, since neither the church nor the Danish or French people accepted his divorce from Ingeborg of Denmark as legitimate; married (1196), though the marriage was invalid; acted as queen and presided over the French court, much to the scandal of the rest of Europe; gave birth to a son, Philip Hurepel, and daughter, Marie of France (after Agnes' death, Philip reinstated Ingeborg, but managed to have Agnes' son Philip legitimized as heir to the throne). ❖ See also *Women in World History.*

AGNES OF MONTE PULCIANO (1274–1317). Italian abbess and saint. Name variations: Agnese, Agnes of Montepulciano, Agnes of Procena. Born c. 1274 in Monte Pulciano, Italy; died 1317 at convent of Monte Pulciano. ❖ At 9, entered a Franciscan convent known as the Sackins; well-respected for her devotion to the poor and sick, earned the position of abbess at convent of Procena, probably around age 20; remained there for some years but later answered a call to establish her own religious foundation; returning to Monte Pulciano, started a Dominican double monastery, again acting as abbess; was soon known throughout Italy for having the gifts of prophecy and healing; was canonized after her death. Feast day is April 20. ❖ See also *Women in World History.*

AGNES OF POITOU (1024–1077). Holy Roman Empress and regent. Name variations: Agnes of Aquitaine; Agnes of Bavaria; Agnes of Germany; Agnes of Guienne. Born 1024 in Poitou, France; died Dec 14, 1077, in an Italian convent; dau. of William V the Pious, duke of Aquitaine, and Agnes of Aquitaine (c. 995–1068); became 2nd wife of Henry of Germany (1017–1056) also known as Henry III, Holy Roman emperor (r. 1039–1056), Nov 1, 1043; children: Henry IV (b. 1050), Holy Roman emperor (r. 1056–1106). ❖ Over her decade as empress, presided over a brilliant court and became known as a generous patron of writers, painters, and poets, attracting Europe's most creative minds to Germany; when husband Henry III died and 6-year-old son succeeded as Henry IV, became regent of the empire but suffered from the lasting enmity towards Henry III and her own ignorance of the mood of the German people; unskilled in negotiating and ill-advised by her councillors, soon saw the empire threatened by foreign armies and internal religious strife; when her son the emperor was kidnapped by supporters of Anno, archbishop of Cologne (May 1062), abandoned the regency to the archbishop and left politics altogether; retired to an Italian convent. ❖ See also *Women in World History.*

AGNES OF POITOU (1052–1078). Queen of Castile and Leon. Name variations: Ines of Poitou or Pointou. Born 1052; died June 6, 1078; dau.

of Guillaume also known as William VIII (or VI), duke of Aquitaine; became 1st wife of Alphonso VI (c. 1030–1109), king of Leon (r. 1065–1070, 1072–1109) and Castile (r. 1072–1109), in 1069 (div. 1077). Some sources claim that Agnes was the mother of Teresa of Castile, though most historians believe Teresa was the illeg. dau. of Jimena Muñoz.

AGNES OF POLAND (1137–after 1181). Princess of Kiev. Born 1137; died after 1181; dau. of Salomea (d. 1144) and Boleslaw III Krzywousty also known as Boleslaus III the Wrymouthed (1085–1138), king of Poland (r. 1102–1138); m. Mstislav II, prince of Kiev, 1151.

AGNES OF PROCENA (1274–1317). *See Agnes of Monte Pulciano.*

AGNES OF QUEDLINBURG (1184–1203). German abbess and artist. Name variations: Agnes of Meissen. Born 1184 in Meissen, Germany; died 1203 at abbey of Quedlinburg. ❖ Entered the large, wealthy convent of Quedlinburg at a young age, where she received an exceptional education which included calligraphy, miniature painting, and other aspects of manuscript production; gained attention for her artistic abilities; was a talented writer familiar with works of the ancient pagan philosophers as well as those of contemporary writers and painted both miniatures and scenes from Greek mythology for the abbey, as well as contributing to the abbey's tapestry production; was chosen abbess of Quedlinburg before age 20, a rare occurrence, though she died a short time later. ❖ See also *Women in World History.*

AGNES OF SAARBRUCKEN (fl. 1130). Duchess of Swabia. Agnes von Saarbrücken. Fl. around 1130; dau. of Frederick, count of Saarbrucken; became 2nd wife of Frederick II (c. 1090–1147), duke of Swabia (r. 1105–1147), around 1130 or 1135. Frederick's 1st wife was Judith of Bavaria, mother of Frederick I Barbarossa.

AGNES OF SAXONY (fl. 1200s). Countess Palatine and duchess of Bavaria. Fl. in the 1200s. Married Otto II, count Palatine and duke of Bavaria (r. 1231–1253); children: Elizabeth of Bavaria; Ludwig also known as Louis II the Stern (b. 1229), duke of Bavaria (r. 1255–1294); Henry I, duke of Lower Bavaria (r. 1255–1290).

AGNES SOREL (1422–1450). *See Sorel, Agnes.*

AGNES-ANNE OF FRANCE (b. 1171). Byzantine empress. Name variations: Agnes of France. Born 1171; died after 1240; dau. of Louis VII (1120–1180), king of France (r. 1137–1180), and Adele of Champagne (1145–1206); sister of Philip II Augustus, king of France (r. 1180–1223); became childbride of Alexius II Comnenus (1167–1183), Byzantine emperor (r. 1180–1183), on Easter 1179 (Alexius was killed in 1183); m. Andronicus I Comnenus, Byzantine emperor (r. 1183–1185), 1183; m. Theodor Branas in 1204; children: (2nd m.) possibly Manuel. ❖ Though she grew up with intended husband Alexius II, was forced to marry Andronicus I Comnenus after he had killed Alexius (1182); when Andronicus was killed by a mob during a revolt (1185), mourned his loss deeply. ❖ See also *Women in World History.*

AGNESE. *Variant of Agnes.*

AGNESI, Maria Gaetana (1718–1799). Italian mathematician. Name variations: Agnese. Born Maria Gaetana Agnesi, May 16, 1718, in Milan, Italy; died Jan 9, 1799, in Milan; dau. of Pietro Agnesi (wealthy merchant with ties to the University of Bologna) and Anna Fortunata (Brivio) Agnesi; sister of Italian composer Maria Teresa Agnesi (1720–1795); tutored privately; no formal education; never married; no children. ❖ The 1st woman in Europe to distinguish herself in the field of mathematics, is credited with calculating the bell-shaped curve known as the "Witch of Agnesi"; participated in debates at her father's house with learned guests, from the age of 9 until 1739, when she withdrew from public life to concentrate on the study of mathematics; was a member of Academia della Scienze (Bologna); published *Instituzioni Analitiche* (Foundations of Analysis), a systematic compilation of developments in algebra, calculus, differential equations and analytic geometry (1748); appointed by Pope Benedict XIV as honorary chair of Mathematics and Natural Philosophy at the University of Bologna (1750–52); devoted herself to the study of theology and to charity work (after 1752); made director of women at Pio Instituto Trivulzio (1771), where she took up residence (1783) and lived until her death (1799). ❖ See also *Women in World History.*

AGNESI, Maria Teresa (1720–1795). Italian musician. Name variations: Maria Theresa. Born in Milan, Italy, Oct 17, 1720; died in Milan on Jan 19, 1795; dau. of Pietro Agnesi (wealthy merchant with ties to the University of Bologna) and Anna Fortunata Brivio; sister of Maria

Gaetana Agnesi (1718–1799, a mathematician); m. Pier Antonio Pinottini on June 13, 1752. ❖ One of the 1st female composers, considered a forerunner of great Italian opera composers, was also a harpsichordist, singer, and librettist, whose collections of arias were widely known in Italy and German-speaking Europe; had 1st theatrical work, *Il ristoro d'Arcadia*, successfully presented in Milan's ducal theater (1747); used her own libretto for next opera, *Ciro in Armenia* (1753); wrote *Insubria consolata* (1766) to honor engagement of Beatrice d'Este and the Archduke Ferdinand. Her portrait hangs in the theater museum of La Scala. ❖ See also Anzoletti, *L. Maria Gaetana Agnese* (1900); and *Women in World History*.

AGNESS. *Variant of Agnes.*

AGNODICE (fl. 4th c. BCE). Athenian midwife. Fl. 4th c. BCE. ❖ The 1st woman of her city to be trained in midwifery and to practice as a professional, successfully fought before the court of Areopagus for the right to continue to practice. ❖ See also *Women in World History*.

AGOGLIA, Esmeralda (1926—). Argentine ballerina. Born in Buenos Aires, Argentina, 1926; studied with Mercedes Quintana, Michel Borovski, and Esmée Bulnes. ❖ Joined the Teatro Colón (1941), and became a ballerina (1949); directed ballet appearances on tv (1951, 1958–59); appeared on tv with Nathalie Krassovska and Igor Youskevitch (1961); danced Odile in the full-length *Swan Lake* (1963); repertoire includes *Prodigal Son, Capriccio Espagnol, Apollon Musagète, Firebird, Rouge et Noir, Swan Lake, Les Sylphides, Giselle, Interplay* and *Concierto Goreografico.*

AGOGLU, 'Adalet (1929—). *See Agaoglu, Adalet.*

AGOSTINA (1788–1857). Spanish heroine. Name variations: The Maid of Saragossa or Zaragoza; Augustina. Born in 1788; died 1857. ❖ During the French siege of Saragossa (1808), moved through the streets and urged resistance; when Napoleon's army broke through a hole in the city walls and the Spaniards were ready to desert, seized a flaming torch from a dying artillery soldier and took his place at the cannon; rallied the men and saved the city; immortalized as "The Maid of Saragossa," in the 1st canto of Lord Byron's *Childe Harold.* ❖ See also *Women in World History.*

AGOSTON, Judit (1937—). *See Mendelenyine-Agoston, Judit.*

AGOULT, Marie d' (1805–1876). French author and salonnière. Name variations: Marie de Flavigny, comtesse d'Agoult; (pseudonym) Daniel Stern. Born Marie Catherine Sophie de Flavigny in Frankfurt am Main, Germany, Dec 31, 1805; died in Paris, France, Mar 5, 1876; m. the Comte d'Agoult, 1827, but left him and formed a liaison with Hungarian composer Franz Liszt; children: (with Liszt) 3 daughters, including Cosima Wagner (1837–1930). ❖ Wrote the semi-autobiographic romance *Nélida* (1845), *Lettres Républicaines* (1848), *Histoire de la Révolution de 1848* (1851), *Mes Souvenirs, 1806–33* (1877), *Florence et Turin* and *Dante et Goethe.* Her *Esquisses Morales et Politiques* (1849) is considered her best work. ❖ See also *Women in World History.*

AGREDA, Sor María de (1602–1665). Spanish writer of religious books. Name variations: Marie of Agreda; Mary of Agreda; Coronel de Jesús. Born María Coronel y Arana at Agreda, Spain, 1602; died at Agreda, May 24, 1665; never married; no children. ❖ A 17th-century religious woman, who claimed that she was directed in part by a personal revelation from Mary the Virgin, became a nun at 17; experienced trances in which she traveled to areas of New Mexico, Arizona, and Texas to preach to Native Americans; convinced that the Virgin Mary had imparted her life story in a revelation, wrote the biography *Mystical City of God*, which was published in 1670, 5 years after her death; was one of King Philip IV's most influential political and spiritual advisors. ❖ See also *Women in World History.*

AGRIPPINA I (14 BCE–33 CE). *See Agrippina the Elder.*

AGRIPPINA II (15–59 CE). *See Agrippina the Younger.*

AGRIPPINA MAJOR (14 BCE–33 CE). *See Agrippina the Elder.*

AGRIPPINA MINOR (15–59 CE). *See Agrippina the Younger.*

AGRIPPINA THE ELDER (c. 14 BCE–33 CE). Roman woman. Name variations: Agrippina I; Agrippina Major; Vipsania Agrippina. Born c. 14 BCE; died in exile in 33 CE in Pandateria; dau. of Julia (39 BCE–14 CE) and Marcus Agrippa; granddau. of Caesar Augustus; sister of Gaius (b. 20 BCE), Lucius (b. 17 BCE), Julia (b. 15? BCE); m. Germanicus in 5 CE (died 19 CE); children: nine, including Nero Julius Caesar (d. 31

CE); Drusus III Julius Caesar (d. 33 CE); Gaius (12–41 CE, the future emperor Caligula); Drusilla (15–38 CE); Agrippina the Younger (15–59 CE, mother of the future emperor Nero); Julia Livilla (b. 16? CE). ❖ Popular Roman whose independence and ambition for her children annoyed Tiberius and led to her exile and subsequent suicide by starvation; was the granddaughter of Augustus and the daughter of Marcus Agrippa, Augustus' closest political associate; had 2 brothers named as Augustus' heirs to the Roman Empire before their premature deaths; was married to Germanicus, an heir of Augustus' successor, Tiberius; had a loving marriage, producing 9 children, before Germanicus died of a sudden illness (19 CE); since Germanicus' relationship with Tiberius had been deteriorating for some time before Germanicus' death, accused Tiberius of having her husband poisoned; remained Tiberius' implacable foe, even after the aging emperor named her 2 oldest sons as his political heirs (23 CE), though neither son lived long enough to inherit the empire, for Sejanus (the commander of Rome's Praetorian Guard) conspired against them and convinced Tiberius to punish their "treason" with exile and execution; died in exile before she saw the ultimate accession of her youngest son Caligula. ❖ See also *Women in World History.*

AGRIPPINA THE YOUNGER (15–59 CE). Roman wife of Claudius. Name variations: Julia Agrippina (often designated "Agrippina Minor"); Agrippina II. Born at Ara Ubiorum (modern-day Cologne) on Nov 6, 15 CE; slain at Baiae by order of her son, Emperor Nero, 59 CE; eldest dau. of Germanicus (the great Roman general) and Agrippina the Elder ("Major," granddau. of the great Augustus); sister of Drusilla (15–38), Caligula (12–41), and Julia Livilla; m. Gnaeus Domitius Ahenobarbus (died 40 CE), in 28; m. C. Sallustius Passienus Crispus (died 47 CE); m. Claudius (died 54 CE), Roman emperor, in 49; children: (with Gnaeus Domitius Ahenobarbus) Emperor Nero. ❖ Prominent Roman intimately involved in power politics in the Roman Empire, who was often designated by her relationship to three emperors: sister of Caligula, wife of Claudius, and mother of Nero; received various formal honors along with her sisters (37 CE); accused of treachery by Caligula and exiled (39); recalled by the succeeding Emperor Claudius (41); married Claudius (49); succeeded in having Nero adopted by Claudius and received the prestigious title "Augusta" (50); poisoned Claudius and succeeded in having Nero made emperor (54); published an autobiography, no longer extant, which was used by other classical historians as a source for Roman imperial history. ❖ See also *Women in World History.*

AGSTERIBBE, Estella (1909–1943). Dutch-Jewish gymnast. Name variations: Stella Blits-Agsteribbe. Born April 6, 1909, in the Netherlands; killed at Auschwitz concentration camp, Sept 17, 1943, with her 2-year-old son Alfred and 6-year-old daughter Nanny. ❖ At Amsterdam, won a gold medal for all-around team (1928), the 1st time women's gymnastics was on the Olympic program (no indiv. medals were awarded).

AGUERO, Taimaris (1977—). Cuban volleyball player. Name variations: Taimarys Aguero Leyva; Taimaris Agüero. Born Mar 5, 1977, in Cuba. ❖ Setter, won World Cup (1999); won team gold medals at Atlanta Olympics (1996) and Sydney Olympics (2000).

AGUILAR, Grace (1816–1847). English writer. Pronunciation: ah-gee-lär. Born at Hackney, London, England, June 2, 1816; died in Frankfort-on-Main, Germany, Sept 16, 1847; eldest child of Emanuel Aguilar (merchant); mother's name unknown; both parents were Jews of Spanish origin; educated at home; family moved to Devon in 1828; never married, no children. ❖ Writer who educated the general public about Judaism; a semi-invalid, was educated at home; by 14, had published a volume of poems; at 24, accomplished her chief work on the Jewish religion, *The Spirit of Judaism* (1842), a controversial attack on the formalities of institutionalized theology; published *The Jewish Faith: Its Spiritual Consolation, Moral Guidance, and Immortal Hope* (1846), followed by *The Women of Israel*, a series of essays on Biblical history, and *Essays and Miscellanies.* ❖ See also *Women in World History.*

AGUIRRE, Lilia Izquierdo (1967—). *See Izquierdo, Lilia.*

AGUIRRE, Mirta (1912—). Cuban poet and essayist. Born Oct 18, 1912, in Havana, Cuba. ❖ Wrote largely political and revolutionary verse, as well as essays; publications include *Juegos y otros poemas* (Games and Other Poems, 1974) and *Ayer de hoy* (Yesterday Today, 1980). ❖ See also *Women in World History.*

AGUSTINI, Delmira (1886–1914). Uruguayan poet. Born 1886 in Montevideo, Uruguay; murdered by husband, from whom she had separated, who then committed suicide, 1914. ❖ Explored themes of sex, love, and death in such works as *El libro blanco* (1907), *Cantos de* *mañana* (1910), and *Los Calizes vacíos* (1913); letters published posthumously as *Correspondencia intima* (1969).

AHARONSON, Sarah (1890–1917). *See Aaronsohn, Sarah.*

AHAT-MILKI or AHATMILKU (fl. 1265 BCE). *See Akhat-milki.*

AHEARN, Theresa (1951–2000). Irish politician. Born May 1951 in Golden, Tipperary, Ireland; died Sept 20, 2000; m. Liam Ahearn. ❖ Representing Fine Gael, elected to the 26th Dáil (1989–92) for Tipperary South; returned to 27th–28th Dáil (1992–2000); died while in office; championed Equal Status and Employment Equality legislation.

AHERN, Catherine Ita (1915—). Irish politician. Name variations: Kit Ahern. Born Catherine Ita Liston, Jan 13, 1915, in Athea, Co. Limerick, Ireland; m. Dan Ahern, 1941. ❖ Began career as a secondary schoolteacher; unsuccessfully contested the general elections (1965, 1969, 1973) as a Fianna Fáil candidate; elected to 21st Dáil for Kerry North (1977–81); was Taoiseach Sean Lemass's nominee for Seanad (1964–65), casual vacancy (1965–77).

AHERN, Kathy (1949–1996). American golfer. Name variations: Kathleen Ahern. Born Kathleen Ahern, May 7, 1949, in Pittsburgh, Pennsylvania; died of breast cancer, July 6, 1996, in Fountain Hills, Arizona. ❖ Won the Texas Public Links title at age 15 (1964); won Texas state amateur and junior titles (1965); medalist and runner-up USGA Junior (1966); turned pro (1967); won Southgate Open (1970); won the George Washington and Eve-LPGA (1972).

AHERN, Kit (1915—). *See Ahern, Catherin Ita.*

AHERN, Lizzie (1877–1969). Australian socialist. Born Elizabeth Ahern in Ballarret, Victoria, Australia, 1877; died 1969; dau. of an Irish goldminer and a radical; m. Arthur Wallace (radical, later a Member of Parliament), 1905; children: a son. ❖ Became a member of the Social Questions Committee (forerunner of the Victorian Socialist Party, 1905); an eloquent orator, was a conspicuous member of the Free Speech Campaign in Prahra, Melbourne, and was imprisoned for defending the right to speak in public places (1906); founded the Women's Socialist League (1909); with husband, led the anti-draft campaign during WWI; in later life, worked for the Australian Labour Party; also became a justice of the peace and a children's court magistrate. ❖ See also *Women in World History.*

AHERN, Mary Eileen (1860–1938). American librarian. Born Oct 1, 1860, in Marion County, Indiana; died May 22, 1931, near Atlanta, Georgia. ❖ Served as Indiana's state librarian (1893–95); became editor of periodical *Public Libraries* (1896), which became *Libraries* (1926); particular interests included the school librarian, standards for library training, library administration, and cooperation among international libraries; organized the Indiana Library Association and served as secretary (1889–96); ceased publication of *Libraries* at time of retirement (1931).

AHERN, Nuala (1949—). Irish politician. Born Nuala McDowell, Feb 5, 1949, in Belfast, Northern Ireland; dau. of Vincent McDowell (founder member and vice-chair of civil rights movement in Northern Ireland). ❖ Began career as a counseling psychologist; campaigned for the closure of the Sellafield nuclear reprocessing plant near Dunkalk; founder member of the Irish Women's Environmental Network; representing the Green Party, elected member of the European Parliament for Leinster (MEP, 1994–99, 1999–2004).

AHHOTEP (r. 1570–1546 BCE). Queen-regent of Egypt. Name variations: Ahotep. Ruled c. 1570–1546 BCE (there is some debate concerning the chronology of this period of Egyptian history as dates are dependent upon data derived from lunar observations; 3 separate chronologies have been put forth); children: Egyptian rulers King Kamose (d. 1570); Ahmose I (Ahmosi or Amasis), who is generally credited with founding the 18th Dynasty in Egypt; and daughter Ahmose-Nefertari (reigned c. 1570–1546 BCE). ❖ While son Ahmose I drove the Hyksos kings (rulers of ancient Egypt between 13th and 18th dynasties) out of Egypt, ruled Thebes in Upper Egypt (modern-day Luxor), together with daughter Ahmose-Nefertari. ❖ See also *Women in World History.*

AHINOAM (fl. 1020 BCE). Biblical woman. Fl. around 1020 BCE; dau. of Ahimaaz; wife of Saul (1st king of the Jewish nation); children: Jonathan and others; including 2 daughters, one of whom was Michal. ❖ Was the wife of King Saul and the mother of Michal, 1st wife of David, the greatest Israelite king in the Old Testament. ❖ See also *Women in World History.*

AHINOAM OF JEZREEL (fl. 1000 BCE). Biblical woman. Second wife of King David (Israelite king who unified Israel and Judah; r. 1010–970 BCE); children: Amnon.

AHLANDER, Thecla (1855–1925). Norwegian-born actress. Name variations: Thecla Ottilia Åhlander. Born June 3, 1855, in Norway; died 1925. ❖ Made stage debut (1877); achieved renown as Belise in *Lärt folk in stubb*, Madam Rask in *Ensam*, Ane in *Geografi and Kärlek*, Fru Bonivard in *Duval's skilsmässa*, Fru Heinecke in *Åra*, Mormor in *Familjelycka*, Nille in *Erasmus Montanus*, Fru Perichon in *Herr Perichon's resa*, Fru Stockmann, in *En folkfiende* (*The Enemy of the People*), Hedda in *Dardanell och hans upptag*, Ankefru Lüderts in *Guldkarossen*, and Madam Olsen in *Lynggard.*

AHLBERG, Janet (1944–1994). English writer and illustrator. Born and grew up in Huddersfield, England; died at home in Leicestershire, England, Nov 15, 1994, of cancer; Sunderland College of Education, teaching diploma, 1966; married Allan Ahlberg (author), 1969; children: one daughter. ❖ Worked as a magazine layout artist and freelance designer; launched career as an author-illustrator (1972); often collaborated with husband on such books as "The Brick Street Boys" series, *Burglar Bill* (Greenwillow), *The Jolly Postman* (Little, Brown) and *The Jolly Christmas Postman.* Won Kate Greenaway Medal for Illustration (1978) for *Each Peach Pear Plum.*

AHLEFELD, Charlotte von (1781–1849). German novelist. Name variations: (pseudonyms) Elisa or Elise Selbig, Ernestine, Natalie. Born Charlotte Elisabeth Sophie Louise Wilhelmine von Seebach at Stedten, near Erfurt, Germany, Dec 6, 1781; died at Teplitz, Bohemia, July 27, 1849; dau. of Alexander Christoph August von Seebach and Albertine Wilhelmine (Ingersleben) von Seebach; m. Count Johann Rudolph von Ahlefeld, 1798 (div. 1807); children: 2. ❖ Grew up in Weimar and published her 1st novel, *Liebe und Trennung*, at 16; author of over 50 popular novels, travel narratives, and poetry collections; works include *Louise und Meiland* (1803), *Therese* (1805), *Melanie, das Findelkind* (1805), *Die Kokette* (1810), *Der Mohrenknabe* (1821), *Die Frau von 40 Jahren* (1829), and *Der Stab der Pflicht* (1832).

AHLERS, Anny (1906–1933). German actress and opera singer. Name variations: Anni Ahlers. Born Dec 21, 1906, in Hamburg, Germany; died Mar 14, 1933, a suicide, in London, England. ❖ At 7, made stage debut at Hamburg Opera House (1913); was première child danseuse at Vienna Opera (1920) and Berlin State Opera (1922); made operatic singing debut as Venus in *Orpheus in the Underground* at Volks Operahous in Hamburg (1924); gained renown in title roles of *Lady Hamilton* (Breslau) and *Madame Pompadour* (Berlin); created the role of Viktoria in *Viktoria and Her Hussar;* made London debut as Jeanne in *The Dubarry* (1932).

AHLGREN, Ernst (1850–1888). *See Benedictsson, Victoria.*

AHMAD, Fathiyya (c. 1898–1975). Egyptian singer. Born c. 1898; died 1975; daughter of a Qur'an reciter; married a wealthy landowner; children: 2. ❖ Popular singer and manager of the Sala Badi'a, began theatrical career (c. 1910); was also a widely recorded vocalist; retired (1950).

AHMANN, Crissy (1970—). *See Ahmann-Leighton, Crissy.*

AHMANN-LEIGHTON, Crissy (1970—). American swimmer. Name variations: Cristine Ahmann-Leighton; Crissy Ahmann; Crissy Leighton. Born Cristine Leighton, May 20, 1970; attended University of Arizona. ❖ At Barcelona Olympics, won a silver medal in the 100-meter butterfly, a gold medal in the 4x100-meter medley relay, and a gold medal in the 4x100-meter freestyle relay (1992); won a Pacific 10 conference championship and national championship (1992).

AHMANSON, Caroline (1918–2005). American bank executive, charm-school founder, and philanthropist. Name variations: Caroline Leonetti or Caroline Leonetti Ahmanson; Mrs. Howard Ahmanson. Born Caroline Leonetti in San Francisco, California, 1918; died June 21, 2005; attended University of California, Berkeley; 2nd wife of Howard F. Ahmanson (died 1968). ❖ Served as chair and executive officer of Caroline Leonetti, Ltd., the charm school she founded in 1957; served as chair of the Los Angeles branch of the Federal Reserve Bank of San Francisco (1978–1979) and chair of the Federal Reserve Bank of San Francisco, 12th District (1981); began serving on President's Committee on the Arts and Humanities (1984).

AHMANSON, Mrs. Howard (1918–2005). *See Ahmanson, Caroline.*

AHMOSE-NEFERTARI (c. 1570–1535 BCE). Queen of Egypt. Name variations: Ahmose-Nofretari; Ahmes-Nefertary. Ruled with her mother Ahhotep around 1570 to 1546 BCE; dau. of Ahhotep; m. her brother Ahmose I; children: Ahmose (the mother of Hatshepsut), and Amenhotep I. ❖ Queen of Egypt at the start of the New Kingdom (her husband being the 1st king of the illustrious 18th Dynasty), who, upon widowhood, ruled the land as regent for her under-aged son; bore the title Female Chieftain of Upper and Lower Egypt; is credited with restoring temples and official cults throughout the land after decades of neglect by the Hyksos dynasty; also founded a college of Divine Votaresses at the Karnak temple where she was herself a high priestess, holding the title of God's Wife of Amun; when she died, was placed in a coffin 12 feet long and fitted with a lofty plumed crown; was deified after death, and her cult was popular among the common people, particularly in Upper Egypt, for at least 4 centuries. ❖ See also *Women in World History.*

AHOLIBAMAH. *See Judith.*

AHOTEP (r. 1570–1546 BCE). *See Ahhotep.*

AHRENHOLZ, Brigitte (1952—). East German rower. Born Aug 8, 1952, in Potsdam, Germany. ❖ At Montreal Olympics, won a gold medal in the coxed eights (1976); won European championships for coxed eights (1974); became a doctor.

AHRENS, Marlene (1933—). Chilean javelin thrower. Born July 27, 1933, in Chile. ❖ At Melbourne Olympics, won a silver medal in the javelin throw (1956).

AHRWEILER, Hélène (1916—). French historian and educator. Name variations: Helene Ahrweiler; Helene Ahrweiler-Glycatsi; Helene Ahrweiler-Glykatzi. Born Hélène Glykatzi (also seen as Glycatsi), 1916, in Athens, Greece. ❖ Studied medieval history and archeology in Greece; moved to France (1950) and became an expert in Byzantine history; became 1st female head of department of history at Sorbonne (1967) and 1st female president of the Sorbonne (1976), serving until 1981; at the Sorbonne, divided the schools of humanities and social science into separate entities; served as chancellor of the Universities of Paris (1982–89), vice president of the Council of National Education (1983), and president of the Centre Nationale d'Art et de Culture Georges Pompidou (1989–91); president of the University of Europe; writings include *Studies on the Internal Diaspora of the Byzantine Empire.*

AICEGA, Magdalena (1973—). Argentinean field-hockey player. Born Maria Magdalena Aicega, Nov 1, 1973, in Argentina. ❖ Won a team silver medal at Sydney Olympics (2000); while captaining the Argentina team, won a bronze medal at Athens Olympics (2004); won Champions Trophy (2001), World Cup (2002), and Pan American Games (2003).

AICHER-SCHOLL, Inge (d. 1998). *See Scholl, Inge.*

AICHINGER, Ilse (1921—). Austrian short-story and fiction writer. Born in Vienna, Austria, 1921; studied medicine for 2 years; m. Günter Eich (poet), 1953 (died); lives in Bayrisch Gmain, Upper Bavaria. ❖ Wrote novella *Speech Beneath the Gallows,* which won the Gruppe 47 prize (1952); also wrote *The Greater Hope* (1948), *Der Gefesselte* (The Bound Man, 1953), *Knöpfe* (Buttons, 1953), *Zu keiner Stunde* (At No Hour, 1957), *Besuch im Pfarrhaus* (Visit at the Parsonage, 1961), *Wo ich wohne* (Where I Live, 1963), *Eliza, Eliza* (1965), *My Language and I* (1968), *Auckland* (1969), *Nachricht vom Tag* (News of the Day, 1970), *Dialoge, Erzählungen, Gedichte* (Dialogues, Stories, Poems, 1970), and *Advice Freely Given* (1978). ❖ See also J.C. Aldridge, *Ilse Aichinger* (Dufour, 1969).

AIDOO, Ama Ata (1942—). Ghanaian playwright, poet, novelist, and short-story writer and political activist. Name variations: Christina Ama Ata Aidoo. Born Christina Ama Aidoo, Mar 23, 1942, in Abeadzi Kyiakor, near Dominase, Gold Coast (now Ghana); dau. of a chief of Abeadzi Kyiakor; grew up in a royal household; educated at Wesley Girls' High School in Cape Coast; graduated from University of Ghana at Legon, 1964; also studied creative writing at Stanford University; children: daughter Kinna. ❖ Important activist-writer whose work explores the tension between African and Western values and the impact of post-colonialism on women; worked with Efua Sutherland (1960s); gained 1st notice with her play *The Dilemma of a Ghost* (1965); was a junior research fellow at Institute of African Studies at University of Ghana (1964–66); served as consulting professor to Washington bureau of Phelps-Stokes Fund's Ethnic Studies Program (1975–75); served as Ghanaian Secretary for Education under Jerry Rawlings (1981–83); moved to Harare,

Zimbabwe, to work for the curriculum development unit of the Zimbabwe Ministry of Education (1983) and served as chair of Zimbabwe Women Writers Group; was a professor of English at University of Ghana and distinguished visiting professor of English at Oberlin College; published *Changes: A Love Story* (1991), which was awarded the Commonwealth Writers Prize, Africa Division (1993); plays include *Anowa* (1970); also published short story collection *No Sweetness Here* (1970), novels including the semi-autobiographical *Our Sister Killjoy: Or, reflections From a Black-Eyed Squint* (1977), the poetry collection *Someone Talking to Sometime* (1986), and the children's book *The Eagle and the Chickens* (1987).

A'IEN (1856–1926). *See Baker, Louisa Alice.*

AIHARA, Toshiko (1939—). Japanese gymnast. Name variations: Toshiko Shirasu. Born June 3, 1939, in Japan; m. Nobuyuki Aihara (gymnast); children: Makoto Aihara and Yutaka Aihara (both gymnasts). ❖ At Tokyo Olympics, won a bronze medal in the all-around team (1964).

AIHERIA (fl. 4th c.). *See Egeria.*

AIKATERINI. *Variant of Catherine.*

AIKATERINI OF BULGARIA (fl. 1050). *See Catherine of Bulgaria.*

AIKEN, Anna L. (1743–1825). *See Barbauld, Anna.*

AIKEN, Joan (1924–2004). English writer. Born Joan Delano Aiken, Sept 4, 1924, in Rye, Sussex, England; died Jan 4, 2004, at home in Petworth, West Sussex, England; dau. of Jessie (McDonald) Aiken and Conrad (Potter) Aiken (the poet); stepdau. of writer Martin Armstrong; m. Ronald George Brown (journalist), July 7, 1945 (died 1955); m. Julius Goldstein (painter and teacher), Sept 2, 1976; children: (1st m.) John Sebastian Brown, Elizabeth Delano Brown. ❖ At 17, adapted children's stories for stepfather's BBC radio show; published 1st novel *The Wolves of Willoughby Chase* (1962), then wrote 4 more books featuring Dido Twite; other books include *Black Hearts in Battersea, Night Birds on Nantucket, The Whispering Mountain, The Cuckoo Tree, Kingdom under the Sea, Tales of Arabel's Raven* and *Mortimer and the Sword Excalibur;* adult novels include *The Silence of Herondale, The Embroidered Sunset, Died on a Rainy Sunday, The Smile of the Stranger* and *Mansfield Revisited* (1984), sequel to Jane Austen's *Mansfield Park;* with daughter, wrote a series of tv adaptations of her work for BBC, as well as the play *Winterthing* (music by son John Sebastian Brown), which was 1st produced at the Young Vic (1970); wrote "Midnight Is a Place" (13-part serial) for Southern Television (1977). Received, among others, the *Guardian* Award for Children's Fiction and Carnegie Award runner-up for *The Whispering Mountain* (1969), Edgar Allan Poe Award for Best Juvenile Mystery for *Night Fall* (1972), and the *New York Times* Outstanding Book citation for *Midnight Is a Place* (1974).

AIKEN, Kimberly (c. 1975—). Miss America. Name variations: Kimberly Aiken Cockerham. Born Kimberly Clarice Aiken c. 1975; graduate of New York University; m. Haven Cockerham; children: one. ❖ Named Miss America (1994), representing South Carolina; motivational speaker on homelessness; worked in public accounting for Ernst & Young.

AIKENHEAD, Mary (1787–1858). Founder of the Irish Sisters of Charity. Born Mary Stackpole Aikenhead on Jan 19, 1787, in Cork, Ireland; died July 22, 1858, in Dublin, Ireland; dau. of David (physician and chemist) and Mary (Stackpole) Aikenhead. ❖ After a 3-year noviate at the Bar Convent of the Institute of the Blessed Virgin Mary, in York, England, returned to Dublin with one associate to establish the Sisters of Charity in the William Street Orphanage (1815); resided at the motherhouse, which was established at Mount St. Anne's, Milltown, Dublin; opened St. Vincent's Hospital in Dublin (1834), the 1st Catholic hospital in Ireland and a pioneering effort in the staffing and management of hospitals by religious women trained in nursing. ❖ See also *The Life and Work of Mary Aikenhead: Foundress of the Congregation of Irish Sisters of Charity 1787–1858* (Longmans, 1924); and *Women in World History.*

AIKENS, Charlotte (c. 1868–1949). American nurse and editor. Name variations: Charlotte Albina Aikens. Born c. 1868 in Mitchell, Ontario, Canada; died Oct 20, 1949, in Detroit, Michigan. ❖ Worked as volunteer nurse during Spanish-American War; served as director of Sibley Memorial Hospital (Washington, DC), and as superintendent of nurses at Methodist Hospital (Des Moines, IA) and Columbia Hospital (Pittsburgh, PA); named associate editor of *National Hospital Record* (1902); became associate editor (1911), then editor (c. 1915), of *Trained*

Nurse and Hospital Review; authored several nursing texts including *Studies in Ethics for Nurses* (1916).

AIKENS, Diane (c. 1963–2003). *See Geppi-Aikens, Diane.*

AIKIN, Anna Letitia (1743–1825). *See Barbauld, Anna Letitia.*

AIKIN, Lucy (1781–1864). English historian and biographer. Name variations: edited under pseudonym Mary Godolphin. Born at Warrington, Lancashire, England, Nov 6, 1781; died at Hampstead, England, Jan 29, 1864; dau. of John Aikin (physician and author [1747–1822]) and Martha (Jennings) Aikin; niece of Anna Letita Barbauld. ❖ One of the most accomplished literary women of her time, received a classical education from her father, who taught in a nonconformist academy; after assisting him and her aunt, Anna Letitia Barbauld, in their literary work, published a volume of poetry *Epistles to Women* (1810); a staunch Unitarian and feminist, protested the view of women's roles in 19th-century England; edited many children's books under the name Mary Godolphin, but is best remembered for her memoirs of the courts of Elizabeth I (1818), James I (1822), and Charles I (1833), and her *Life of Addison* (1843).

AILIAN DAI (b. 1916). *See Dai Ailian.*

AILING SOONG (1890–1973). *See Song Ailing.*

AIMÉE, Anouk (1932—). French actress. Name variations: Anouk Aimee; Anouk. Born Françoise Sorya Dreyfus in Paris, France, April 27, 1932; dau. of Henry Murray (actor) and Geneviève Sorya (actress); studied acting and dancing in France and England; m. Edouard Zimmerman, 1949 (div. 1950); m. Nico Papatakis (director), 1951 (div. 1954); m. Pierre Barouh, 1966 (div. 1969); m. Albert Finney (actor), 1970 (div. 1978). ❖ Best known for her work in *A Man and a Woman*, made film debut at 14 in *La Maison Sous La Mer* (1947); came to prominence in France in Cayette's *Les Amants de Vérone* (*The Lovers of Verona*, 1949); had international breakthrough as the nymphomaniac in Fellini's *La Dolce Vita* (1960), and followed that with the flighty Lola in Demy's new-wave film *Lola*; was also seen in Fellini's *8½* (*Otté e Mezzo*, 1963); starred with Jean-Louis Trintignant in Claude Lelouch's *Un Homme et une Femme* (*A Man and a Woman*, 1966), for which she won Britain's highest award for Best Foreign Actress; reprised role in *Un Homme et une Femme: 20 Ans déjà* (*A Man and a Woman: 20 Years Later*, 1986); other films include *L'Imprevisto* (1961), *Il Giudizio Universale* (1961), *Sodoma e Gomorra* (1961), *Les Grands Chemins* (*Of Flesh and Blood*, 1963), *Justine* (1969), *The Appointment* (1969), *Mon Premier Amour* (*My 1st Love*, 1978), *Arrivederci e Grazie* (1988), and *Il y a des jours ... et des lunes* (1990). Named Best Actress at Cannes for her role in *Salto nel Vuoto* (*Leap Into Void*), 1980. ❖ See also *Women in World History.*

AIMERY, Aenor (d. 1130). *See Aénor of Châtellerault.*

AINARDI, Sylviane H. (1947—). French politician. Born Dec 19, 1947, in Ugines, Savoie, France. ❖ Member of Toulouse Municipal Council (1989–94) and the PCF (French Communist Party) national council (2000—); representing the Confederal Group of the European United Left/Nordic Green Left (GUE/NGL), elected to 4th and 5th European Parliament (1994–99, 1999–2004); named chair of the French delegation Bouge l'Europe of the GUE/NGL Group (1999).

AINDILI, Eirini (1983—). Greek rhythmic gymnast. Name variations: Irini Aindili. Born Mar 11, 1983, in Greece. ❖ Won a bronze medal for team all-around at Sydney Olympics (2000).

AINIANOS, Aganice (1838–1892). Greek poet. Born 1838 in Athens, Greece; died 1892; studied Classics, French, and painting. ❖ Fled to countryside after involvement in uprising against King Otto; poetry was influenced by contact with country people and reflects sympathy for rural poor, especially women; work was not published until after death.

AINSWORTH, Ruth (1908–1984). English children's writer. Name variations: Ruth Gallard Ainsworth Gilbert. Born Oct 16, 1908, in Manchester, England; died in 1984; dau. of Percy Clough (Methodist minister) and Gertrude (Fisk) Ainsworth; attended Froebel Training Centre, Leicester, England; m. Frank Lathe Gilbert (managing director of chemical works), Mar 29, 1935; children: Oliver Lathe, Christopher Gallard, Richard Frank. ❖ Best known for her "Listen With Mother Tales," based on the BBC radio show of the same name, and for her 8 "Rufty Tufty the Golliwog" books; began full-time writing career (1947) when Heinemann published her collection of children's verse, *All Different;* collaborated with Ronald Ridout on a number of educational books, and wrote several plays and stories for television.

AIOE, Marie (c. 1790–1850). *See Dorion, Marie.*

AIRY, Anna (1882–1964). British painter and etcher. Born in London, England, June 1882; died in Playford, England, Oct 23, 1964; dau. of Wilfrid Airy; granddau. of Sir George Biddell Airy (1801–1892), Astronomer Royal of Great Britain; studied at Slade School; exhibited as a young artist at Royal Academy (1905); m. Geoffrey Buckingham Pocock (painter and etcher). ❖ Began to exhibit at Royal Academy (1905); over the years, became proficient in figure subjects, portraits, and flowers in oils, watercolors and pastels, and etchings; commissioned by the British Ministry of Munitions, produced a series of 5 paintings (1918), including *Women Working in a Gas Retort House, A Shell Forge,* and *The "L" Press,* which were placed in the Imperial War Museum. ❖ See also *Women in World History.*

AISENBERG-SELOVE, Fay (b. 1926). *See Ajzenberg-Selove, Fay.*

A'ISHAH BINT ABI BAKR (c. 613–678). Wife of Muhammad. Name variations: Aisha or Ayesha; also known as Umm al-Mu'minin ("Mother of Believers"). Born A'ishah bint Abu Bakr (dau. of Abu Bakr) at Mecca (Makka) c. 613 or 614 CE; died at Madinah on July 8, 678; dau. of a prominent family of the city; m. Muhammad, in 623 or 624. ❖ Third and favorite wife of Muhammad, Prophet of Islam, whose prominence in early Islamic history is testimony to the high position held by women in Arabian society, before the suffocating atmosphere that began to prevail in the Middle East led to their seclusion from public life; an extraordinary woman of remarkable intelligence, was betrothed to her relative, Jubair ibn Mutimi; taken by her father on the flight of Muhammad and his followers to Madinah (622); married to Muhammad (623 or 624); suspected of unfaithfulness and accused by Muhammad's son-in-law, 'Ali, but exonerated (627); following Muhammad's death (632), father reigned as caliph "successor" (632–634); became increasingly drawn into the politics of the nascent Muslim state; protested assassination of Caliph 'Uthman and moved from Madinah to Mecca (June 656); joined forces against the new caliph, 'Ali; left Mecca for Basrah, Iraq, with a force of 1,000 men of the Kuraysh clan seeking revenge; clashed with 'Ali in the Battle of the Camel (Dec 656); though captured, was treated with respect due her position as the Prophets' widow and allowed to return to Mecca; retired to Madinah; in her last years, became an increasingly revered figure in the Islamic world, one of the last links with the Prophet and a font of knowledge concerning his views and practices. ❖ See also Nadia Abbot, *Aishah the Beloved of Mohammed* (University of Chicago Press, 1942); and *Women in World History.*

A'ISHAH BINT TALHAH (fl. 7th c.). Niece of A'ishah bint Abi Bakr. Dau. of Umm Kulthum (half-sister of A'ishah bint Abi Bakr) and Talhah; sister of Zakariya; m. 'Abd Allah.

AISSA KOLI (1497–1504). Queen of Kanem-Bornu. Born 1497; died 1504; dau. of Ali Gaji Zanani, ruler of Kanem-Bornu, located in West Africa; her mother was a Bulala. ❖ Succeeding her father, ruled Kanem-Bornu for 7 years—the fixed term of rule in many African nations; when a brother who had been put in protective exile was discovered and became king (1504), continued as his advisor. ❖ See also *Women in World History.*

AISSE (c. 1694–1733). Circassian slave. Name variations: Mlle äisse or Aïsse (originally Haïdé). Pronunciation: Ah-EE-say. Born in the Caucasus, Russia, 1694; died in Paris, France, 1733; dau. of a Circassian chief; given the name Charlotte-Elisabeth Aïcha. ❖ At 5, was carried off from her Russian home by Turkish rovers and sold at Constantinople to the French ambassador, Baron de Ferriol, who took her to Paris and educated her; raised at court by his sister-in-law, Madame de Ferriol, sister of Madame de Tencin; gained celebrity for her beauty and accomplishments; her *Letters* to her friend Madame Calandrini in Geneva was published (1787) with notes by Voltaire. ❖ See also *Women in World History.*

AITCHISON, Helen (1881–?). British tennis player. Name variations: F. Helen Aitchinson. Born 1881 in Great Britain; death date unknown. ❖ At Stockholm Olympics, won a silver medal in the mixed doubles–indoor courts (1912).

AITKEN, Jane (1764–1832). Scottish-American bookbinder. Born in Paisley, Scotland, 1764; died in Philadelphia, Pennsylvania, 1832; dau. of Robert Aitken (bookbinder who published the 1st English Bible in America, 1782). ❖ Followed in the footsteps of her father, taking over the business after his death (1802); published more than 60 books before going out of business (1813), including the Thomson Bible.

AITKEN, Janet Gladys (1908–1988). British aristocrat. Born July 9, 1908; dau. of William Maxwell Aitken, Baron Beaverbrook, and Gladys Henderson Drury; married Ian Douglas Campbell (1903–1973), 11th duke of Argyll, Dec 12, 1927 (div. 1934).

AITKEN, Jessie (1867–1934). New Zealand political activist, labor activist, and social worker. Name variations: Jessie Fraser. Born Jessie Fraser, April 14, 1867, at Ecclesmachan, Linlithgow, Scotland; died on Jan 18, 1934, in Wellington, New Zealand; dau. of Walter Fraser (plowman) and Janet (Hearne) Fraser; m. John Barr Aitken (coal miner, d. 1907), 1884; children: 7 daughters and 4 sons. ❖ Immigrated with family to New Zealand (1874); after husband's death, became active in several women's organizations and advocated for political roles for women and enhancement of welfare programs for women and children; joined Wellington Housewives' Union and was elected to executive and social committees of Social Democratic Party (SDP) (1916); member of Women's Anti-Conscription League during WWI; elected president of Wellington branch of Women's International League (1916–18); elected to Wellington Hospital and Charitable Aid Board as Labour candidate (1917); 1st woman to stand for election to Wellington City Council (1919). ❖ See also *Dictionary of New Zealand Biography* (Vol. 3).

AITKIN, Yvonne (1911—). Australian agriculturalist. Name variations: (nickname) Miss Peabody. Born 1911 in Horsham, Victoria, Australia. ❖ Served as demonstrator (1936–45), lecturer (1945–56), senior lecturer (1957–74), and reader (1975–76) in Agricultural Science at University of Melbourne; became the 1st woman doctor of agricultural science at University of Melbourne (1970); received Medal of the Order of Australia for work in agricultural science (1989); discovered methods to increase germination rate of *Trifolium subterraneum* and worked extensively in field of peas. Writings include *Flowering Time, Climate, and Genotype* (1974), *Agricultural Science—An Introduction for Australian Students and Farmers* (co-author, 1962), and more than 40 research papers.

AIU, Thelma Kalama (1931–1999). *See Kalama, Thelma.*

AJAKAIYE, Deborah Enilo (c. 1940—). Nigerian geologist and geophysicist. Born c. 1940 in Nigeria; Adhadu Bello University, Nigeria, PhD (1970). ❖ The 1st woman physics professor in West Africa, 1st woman dean of science in Nigeria, and the 1st woman fellow of Nigerian Academy of Science, studied Nigeria's geophysics to assist in identifying the country's natural resources; conducted survey for geophysical map of northern Nigeria; served as professor at Adhadu Bello University and as professor of physics and dean of natural science faculty at Nigeria's University of Jos.

AJUNWA, Chioma (1970—). Nigerian runner and long jumper. Born Dec 25, 1970, in Umuihiokwu, Nigeria. ❖ Won a bronze medal for the 4x100-meter relay at Commonwealth Games (1990); won a gold medal for the long jump at Atlanta Olympics (1996).

A.J.V. (1781–1852). *See Vardill, Anna Jane.*

AJZENBERG-SELOVE, Fay (1926—). German-born American nuclear physicist. Name variations: Aisenberg. Born in Berlin, Germany, 1926; dau. of Moisei Abramovich Aisenberg and Olga (Naiditch) Aisenberg; m. Walter Selove (physicist), 1955; awarded doctorate from University of Wisconsin, Madison (1952). ❖ Of Russian-Jewish descent, fled Europe (1940); enrolled as an engineering student at the University of Michigan, the only woman in her class, but later focused on physics; taught at Smith College, worked at the Van de Graaff Laboratory of the Massachusetts Institute of Technology, and began to collaborate with Thomas Lauritsen of the California Institute of Technology; with Lauritsen, produced the annual compilation, *Energy Levels of Light Nuclei*, for several decades; took a tenured position at Haverford College while husband became an associate professor at University of Pennsylvania, then accepted an untenured position at the University of Pennsylvania (1970); was the 1st woman elected to a leadership position in the American Physical Society; successfully sued to obtain a full professorship at the University of Pennsylvania, becoming the 2nd female professor its School of Arts and Sciences; author of many scientific articles. ❖ See also autobiography, *A Matter of Choices: Memoirs of a Female Physicist* (Rutgers University Press, 1994); and *Women in World History.*

AKAZOME EMON (d. 1027). Japanese poet. Birth date unknown; died in 1027; dau. of Taira no Kanemori (poet and lady-in-waiting at court) and Oe no Masahira. ❖ Belonged to a famous group of women poets and was a contemporary of Lady Murasaki Shikibu.

AKED, Muriel (1887–1955). English character actress. Born Nov 9, 1887, in Bingley, Yorkshire, England; died Mar 21, 1955, in Settle, Yorkshire. ❖ Made London stage debut in *The Rose and the Ring* (1923); other appearances include 1st witch in *Macbeth* at the Court (1928), Janet Cannot in *The Great Adventure*, Miss Snell in *Murder on the Second Floor*, Mrs. Melville in *After All*, Mother Vicar in *Cradle Song*, and Queen Charlotte in *The Gay Pavilion*; films include *Rome Express, The Wicked Lady, The Happiest Days of Your Life* and *The Story of Gilbert and Sullivan.*

AKELEY, Delia J. (1875–1970). American explorer, hunter, and author. Born Delia Julia Denning in Beaver Dam, Wisconsin, Dec 5, 1875; died in Daytona Beach, Florida, May 22, 1970; dau. of Margaret (Hanbury) Denning and Patrick Denning; m. Arthur J. Reiss, Oct 17, 1889 (div. 1902); m. Carl Ethan Akeley (hunter, naturalist and taxidermist), Dec 2, 1902 (div. 1923); m. Dr. Warren D. Howe (died 1951), 1939; children: none. ❖ Married 2nd husband (1902) and helped him revolutionize taxidermy; with husband, went on 1st expedition to Africa to collect examples of the African elephant (1905–07); brought back 84 crates to US, causing a sensation at Chicago Field Museum; commissioned by American Museum of Natural History in NY to collect elephants for its African Hall, made 2nd expedition to Africa (1909–11); began observing the behavior of monkeys, and was soon attempting to communicate with them; traveled to France to assist with the war effort (1918); divorced (1923); made 3rd expedition to Africa for the Brooklyn Museum (Oct 1924), studying the Pygmies of the Belgian Congo for several months, then reached the west coast of Africa (Sept 3, 1925), the 1st Western woman to cross equatorial Africa; learned of husband's death in Belgian Congo from fever (1926); made 4th expedition to Africa (Nov 1929), shooting 5,000 feet of film, as well as 1,500 stills; though not a scientist, helped to pioneer the study of primates and indigenous peoples of the African continent; became a popular speaker on lecture circuit. Writings include *J.T., Jr.: The Biography of an African Monkey* (1929) and *Jungle Portraits* (1930). ❖ See also *Women in World History.*

AKELEY, Mary Jobe (1878–1966). American explorer, author, and photographer. Name variations: Mary Lee Jobe. Born Mary Leonore Jobe in Tappan, Ohio, Jan 29, 1878; died in Stonington, Connecticut, July 19, 1966; dau. of Sarah Jane Pittis and Richard Watson Jobe; Scio College, PhB, 1897; Columbia University, AM, 1909; m. Carl Ethan Akeley (hunter and naturalist), Oct 18, 1924 (died Nov 17, 1926); children: none. ❖ A writer and photographer, undertook 1st journey of exploration to Canada (1909); operated Camp Mystic in Mystic, CT (1916–30); with husband, went on African expedition (1924), but forced to return to US after his death from fever in Belgian Congo (1926); was a popular staple on the lecture circuit. Canadian government named Mount Jobe in her honor (1925); awarded Belgium Cross of the Knight (1929); made trustee of the American Museum of Natural Science (1938). ❖ See also *Women in World History.*

AKENEHI HEI. *See Hei, Akenehi.*

AKERMAN, Chantal (1950—). Belgian film director, screenwriter, actress and feminist. Born June 6, 1950, in Brussels, Belgium; studied film in Brussels and Paris. ❖ Credited with evolving "feminist aesthetic" in film and praised for formal innovation, frank exploration of female sexuality, and recognition of extraordinary in everyday life; made 1st feature film in NY, *Hotel Monterey* (1972); made 1st English language film, *Histoires d'Amerique (American Stories,* 1989); other works include *Saute ma ville* (1968), *Je, tu, il, elle* (1974), *Jeanne Dielman* (1975), *23 quai du Commerce* (1975), *1080 Bruxelles* (1975), *Toute une nuit* (1982), *Man with a Suitcase* (1984), *D'Est* (1993), and *A Couch in New York* (1996). Won Best Director awards for *Les rendezvous d'Anna (Rendezvous with Anna)* at the Paris and Chicago film festivals (1980).

AKERS, Dolly Smith (1901–1986). Assiniboine tribal leader and politician. Born Mar 23, 1901, in Wolf Point, Montana; died June 1986, in Wolf Point; educated in southern California at Sherman Institute. ❖ The 1st Native woman elected to Montana state legislature, served with distinction as chair of the Federal Relations Committee; was also the 1st woman in the history of the Assiniboines to be elected chair of the tribal council. ❖ See also *Women in World History.*

AKERS, Elizabeth Chase (1832–1911). *See Allen, Elizabeth Chase.*

AKERS, Iris Carpenter (b. 1906). *See Carpenter, Iris.*

AKERS, Michelle (1966—). American soccer player. Name variations: Michelle Akers-Stahl. Born Feb 1, 1966, in Santa Clara, California; attended University of South Florida, Orlando. ❖ Midfielder, recognized as one of the world's most powerful strikers during 15-year career; joined national team (1985), scoring its 1st official goal; at World Cups, won team gold medals (1991, 1999) and bronze medal (1995); won a gold medal at Atlanta Olympics (1996); was a founding player of Women's United Soccer Association (WUSA); scored over 100 career goals in international play; was the 1st female footballer to sign an endorsement contract (1991); retired (2000). Won (indiv.) Hermann Trophy (1988); named Female Soccer Athlete of the Year (1990, 1991); was the 1st woman to receive FIFA's Order of Merit (1998); named FIFA Player of the Century (2000). ❖ See also autobiography (with Gregg Lewis) *The Game and the Glory: An Autobiography* (Zondervan, 2000) and *Standing Fast,* chronicling her battle with chronic fatigue syndrome, and Jere Longman *The Girls of Summer* (HarperCollins, 2000).

AKESON, Sonja (1926–1977). *See Akesson, Sonja.*

AKESSON, Birgit (1908–2001). *See Aakesson, Birgit.*

AKESSON, Sonja (1926–1977). Swedish poet. Name variations: Akeson or Åkeson; (full name) Sonja Berta Maria Hammarberg Akesson. Born in Buttle, Gotland, Sweden, 1926; died in 1977; grew up on the island of Gotland; married. ❖ Upon moving to Stockholm (1951), began writing of her childhood and everyday domestic conditions; published 1st collection of poems *Situationer* (*Situations,* 1957), followed by *Leva livet* (*Living Life,* 1961), *Husfrid* (*Peace in the House,* 1963), "Be White Man's Slave" (1963), *Pris* (*Prize,* 1968), and *Sagan om Siv* (*The Saga of Siv,* 1974); wrote "Autobiography (reply to Ferlinghetti)" (1963).

AKHAMINOVA, Yelena (1961—). Soviet volleyball player. Born Oct 1961 in USSR. ❖ At Moscow Olympics, won a gold medal in the team competition (1980).

AKHAT-MILKI (fl. 1265 BCE). Syrian dowager queen. Name variations: Ahat-milki, Ahatmilku, Sharelli. Born probably in mid-late 1200s BCE in Amorite Amurru; date of death in Ugarit (present-day Ras Shamra in Northern Syria) unknown; dau. of King DU-Teshub of Amurru; m. Niqmepa of Ugarit, king of Canaanite Ugarit, at an unknown date; children: Khishmi-Sharruma, *ARAD-* Sharruma, Ammishtamru II. ❖ Managed affairs of state as dowager queen for a short time after husband's death. ❖ See also *Women in World History.*

AKHATOVA, Albina (1976—). Russian biathlete. Name variations: Albina Achatowa. Born Nov 13, 1976, in Vologda Region, Russia. ❖ Won a silver medal for 4 x 7.5km relay at Nagano Olympics (1998); won a bronze medal for 4 x 7.5km relay at Salt Lake City Olympics (2002); won a silver medal for 7.5km sprint at World championships (2003); won bronze medals for 15km Individual and 10km Pursuit and a gold medal for 4 x 6km relay at Torino Olympics (2006).

AKHMADULINA, Bella (1937—). Russian poet, translator, and essayist. Born Izabella Akhatovna Akhmadulina, April 10, 1937, in Moscow, USSR; only child of a Tartar father and Russian-Italian mother; raised primarily by maternal grandmother; m. Yevgeny Yevtushenko (poet), 1954; m. Yuri Nagibin (short-story writer), 1960; m. Gennadi Mamlin (children's writer); m. Boris Messerer (artist and stage designer), 1974; children: Elizaveta and Anna. ❖ Though her poetry appeared then abruptly disappeared due to censorship, emerged as one of the most lauded 20th-century poets of her nation, often compared with Anna Akhmatova and Marina Tsvetaeva; with the exception of a brief evacuation during WWII to the Urals, was educated in Moscow schools; graduated from high school (1954); worked for the newspaper *Metrostroevets;* career was launched during the Soviet censorship thaw, with the help of writer Pavel Antokolskii; had 1st poem published (1955); attended Gorky Literary Institute but was soon expelled for writing apolitical verse; aided by Antokolskii, was reinstated and completed her studies at Gorky (1960); came to prominence (1962) with the publication of her 1st book, *Struna* (*The String*); was expelled from the Writers' Union (1960s) and silenced for her participation in the journal *Metropol* (1979), which assisted young writers not published by the official press; was not permitted to publish again until 1983; efforts on behalf of lesser-known writers extended to translations of poets in smaller, former Soviet republics, including Georgia; noted for her lyricism and use of traditional Russian forms, writings include *Oznob* (*Fever,* 1968), *Uroki Muzyki* (*Music Lesson,* 1969), *Metell* (1977), *Sad* (1987), *Poberezhye* (1991), *Gryada Kamnei* (1995), and *Odnazhdy v Dekabre* (1996). ❖ See also Sonia I. Ketchian, *The Poetic Craft of Bella Akhmadulina* (Pennsylvania State University Press, 1993).

AKHMATOVA, Anna (1889–1966). Russian poet, translator, and literary scholar. Name variations: Axmatova, Achmatowa, Akhmátova, Anna Andreevna Akhmatova, Anna Gorenko. Pronunciation: AHN-na An-DRAY-ev-na Akh-MAH-toh-va (Gah-RYEN-kuh). Born Anna Andreevna Gorenko, June 11, 1889, in Bol'shoi Fontan, Russia; died in Domodedovo, a sanatorium outside Moscow, Mar 5, 1966; dau. of Andrei Gorenko and Inna Stogova; m. Nikolai Gumilyov (poet and critic), 1910 (sep. 1916; div. 1918); m. Vladimir Shileyko, 1918 (sep. 1921); lived 15 years with Nikolai Punin; children: (1st m.) son Lev Nikolaevich Gumilyov (b. 1912). ❖ Perhaps the most famous 20th-century Russian poet, published 1st poem (1907), in a small journal edited by 1st husband; because father disapproved of her writing, chose great-grandmother's maiden name as a pseudonym; published 1st book of poems, *Evening* (1912), followed by *Rosary* (1914), a huge success, making her the 1st Russian woman poet to gain widespread fame; early poems are simple but psychologically nuanced, based on the psychological realism of the great 19th-century Russian novel; following WWI and the Russian Revolution, published 3 more books to continuing acclaim, but the growing Soviet literary bureaucracy moved to put an end to her publishing career, because her great popularity and increasing moral authority made her a threat; condemned as a petty-bourgeois writer, made a living by working in the library of the Institute of Agronomy, and more and more by literary translating; poems from this period survived only because they had been memorized; son was arrested during a Stalinist purge (1938); completed the long poem "Requiem," in which she takes on the role of mourning mother, the feminine voice of Russia itself, and powerfully condemns the crimes of Stalinism (it would not be printed in Russia until 1987, 2 decades after her death); during WWII, her poetry was suddenly hot property again because of its resonant patriotism; following war, was once more denounced, expelled from the Writers' Union, and son was rearrested; became desperate enough to write and publish a cycle of 15 poems praising the dictator Stalin in a futile attempt to free her son (1949); outlived Stalin and was acknowledged as the grand old lady of Russian literature; renowned throughout the world, was the 3rd Russian ever to be invited to Oxford University in England to receive an honorary doctorate in literature (1965). ❖ See also Amanda Haight, *Akhmatova: A Poetic Pilgrimage* (Oxford University Press, 1976); Lydia Chukovskaya, *The Akhmatova Journals, Vol. I, 1938–41* (trans. by Milena Michalski and Sylva Rubashova, Farrar, Straus, 1994); and *Women in World History.*

AKHMEROVA, Leylya (1957—). Soviet field-hockey player. Name variations: Lyailya Akhmerova. Born May 1957 in USSR. ❖ At Moscow Olympics, won a bronze medal in the team competition (1980).

AKHURST, Daphne (1903–1933). Australian tennis player. Born in 1903 at Ashfield, Sydney, Australia; died in 1933; married Roy Cozens, Feb 1930. ❖ Won the 1st of her 5 Australian women's singles titles (1925, also won in 1926, 1928, 1930); with Jim Willard, won the Australasian mixed doubles title (1924, 1925); with Sylvia Harper, won Australian women's doubles title (1924, 1925); reached semifinals at Wimbledon; with Esna Boyd, won Australian women's doubles title (1928); with Jean Borotra, won Australian mixed doubles title (1928); won Australian doubles title (1930).

AKHYALIYYA, Layla al- (fl. 650–660). *See Layla al-Akhyaliyya.*

AKIMOTO, Matsuyo (1911—). Japanese dramatist. Born Matsuyo Akimoto in 1911 in Yokohama, Japan; younger sister of Fujio Akimoto (antiwar Haiku poet). ❖ Wrote the play *Suicide for Love,* among others; writings appear in *The Collected Works of Akimoto Matsuyo* (1976).

AKIN, Gülten (1933—). Turkish poet. Name variations: Gulten Akin or Guelten Akin. Born 1933 in Turkey; grew up in Ankara; graduate of Ankara Law School, 1955; married a district governor. ❖ One of Turkey's most distinguished women poets, worked as barrister in Anatolia and as a teacher in various districts in Turkey; writings include *The Hour of the Wind* (1956), *My Black Hair I Cut* (1960), *On the Shoals* (1964), *Red Carnation* (1971), *The Legend of Marash and Okkesh* (1972), *Dirges and Ballads* (1976), *Hymns* (1983), *Love Endures* (1991), *And Then I Aged* (1995), and *Silent Back Yards* (1998). Won the Turkish Language Association Award for Poetry (1961, 1971) and Sedat Simavi Literature Award (1992).

AKIN, Susan (c. 1964—). Miss America. Name variations: Susan Akin Lynch. Born Susan Diane Akin c. 1964 in Meridian, Mississippi. ❖ Named Miss America (1986), representing Mississippi; nearly killed in an auto accident (1987); speaker for the National Down's Syndrome Association.

AKINS, Zoe (1886–1958). American playwright and screenwriter. Born Zoe Akins on Oct 30, 1886, in Humansville, Missouri; died of cancer, Oct 29, 1958, in Los Angeles, California; dau. of Thomas J. Akins and

Elizabeth (Green) Akins; attended Monticello Seminary in Godfrey, IL, and Hosmer Hall in St. Louis, MO; m. Hugo C. Rumbold, 1932 (died a few months later); children: none. ❖ Winner of the Pulitzer Prize for her stage adaptation of Edith Wharton's novella *The Old Maid*, began career as an actress, before turning to writing; often wrote about unorthodox or rebellious women who struggled with society's conventions; had 1st play produced in NY, *The Magical City* (1916); became a solid presence in NY theater with such plays as *Declasse* (1919), *Daddy's Gone a-Hunting* (1921), *The Furies* (1928), and *The Greeks Had a Word For It* (1929); launched a 2nd career as a screenwriter (1928), writing or co-writing such classics as *Camille*, starring Greta Garbo, *Zaza*, starring Claudette Colbert, as well as *Christopher Strong* and *Morning Glory*, both starring Katharine Hepburn. ❖ See also *Women in World History*.

AKIYOSHI, Toshiko (1929—). Japanese-American jazz pianist, composer, and bandleader. Born in Darien, Manchuria (province of China then controlled by the Japanese), Dec 12, 1929; dau. of a Japanese owner of a textile company and steel mill; m. Stan Kenton (bandleader and saxophonist; div. in mid-1960s); m. Lew Tabackin (sax player), 1969. ❖ At 16, played for a dance band; played piano with 3 symphony orchestras and 10 Tokyo jazz groups before forming own jazz combo (1952); became highest paid studio musician in Japan; received scholarship to Berklee, Boston's jazz college; known for unique style which has cross-pollination of cultures; composed works including *Kogun* (which combined pretaped percussion sounds with vocal cries from Japanese Noh drama) and *Children in the Temple Ground* (which begins with long, vocal wails in Japanese blended with a flute and orchestra accompanied by piano); known for work which reflects social themes, such as *Tales of a Courtesan* and *Minamata* (considered by some her crowning achievement); credited with establishing the international nature of jazz. Nominated for Grammy awards for her albums (1976 and 1977). ❖ See also *Women in World History*.

AKOBIA, Marina (1975—). Russian water-polo player. Born Jan 12, 1975, in USSR. ❖ Goalkeeper, won a team bronze medal at Sydney Olympics (2000).

AKSELROD, Liubo (1868–1946). Russian Marxist philosopher and literary critic. Name variations: Lyubov Axel'rod, Axelrod; (pseudonyms) Ortodox, Orthodox; Born Liubo Isaakovna Akselrod in Russia, where she lived until her exile to France in 1887; PhD, University of Berne, Switzerland; returned to Russia, 1906. ❖ A Marxist activist, was exiled from Russia (1887); went to France and then Switzerland; granted amnesty, returned to Russia (1906); was a member of the Social Democratic Party (1906–18) but is better known for her academic Marxism; taught at the Institute of Red Professors (1906–21); was a professor at University of Sverdlov (1921–46); writings include *Against Idealism, Marx as a Philosopher, Critique of the Foundations of Bourgeois Sociology and Historical Materialism, In Defense of Dialectical Materialism, Against Scholasticism* and *The Idealist Dialectic of Hegel and the Materialist Dialectic of Marx*. ❖ See also *Women in World History*.

AKSYONOVA-SHAPOVALOVA, Lyudmila (1947—). Soviet runner. Name variations: Lyudmila Shapovalova. Born April 23, 1947, in USSR. ❖ At Montreal Olympics, won a bronze medal in the 4 x 400-meter relay (1976).

AKTE, Claudia (fl. 55–69 CE). *See Acte.*

AL-. *For Arabic names that begin with al-, see the 2nd component (e.g., al-Khaizaran. See Khaizaran).*

A.L. (c. 1530–c. 1590). *See Locke, Anne Vaughan.*

ALABASTER, Ann O'Connor (1842–1915). New Zealand educator. Name variations: Ann O'Connor Warner, Ann O'Connor Knowles. Born Ann O'Connor Warner, Feb 15, 1842, in Oxford, England; died at Christchurch, New Zealand, Feb 25, 1915; dau. of Sarah (Lyne) Warner and Robert Warner (shoemaker); m. Charles Alabaster (cleric and educator), 1858 (died 1865); m. Francis Knowles (cleric), 1915; children: 2. ❖ Taught at parish school at St Ebbe, Oxford, England; immigrated with husband to New Zealand (1859); cofounded and administered prominent Lincoln Cottage Preparatory School (1862); retired (1880). ❖ See also *Dictionary of New Zealand Biography* (Vol. 1).

ALACOQUE, Marguerite Marie (1647–1690). French nun. Name variations: Margaret Mary Alacoque. Pronunciation: ah-lah-COKE. Born in Lauthecour, Saône-et-Loire, in central France, July 22, 1647; died at Paray-le-Monial, France, Oct 17, 1690. ❖ Attributed a recovery from paralysis to the intercession of the Virgin Mary and entered the convent at Paray; her visions of Christ provided the origin of the Catholic practice of worshipping the Sacred Heart of Jesus; was beatified (1864), and canonized by Benedict XV (1920). Feast day is Oct 17.

ALACSEAL, Virgili (1869–1966). *See Albert, Caterina.*

AL-ADAWIYYA or ADAWIYYAH, Rabi'a (c. 714–801). *See Rabi'a.*

ALAGULOVA, Julia. *See Allagulova, Yulia.*

ALAIN, Marie-Claire (1926—). French organist. Born in St. Germain-en-Laye, France, Aug 10, 1926; dau. of Albert Alain (organist); sister of Jehan Alain (1911–1940), composer and organist; studied with Durfulé, DuPré, and Plé-Caussade. ❖ Won an organ prize at Geneva International Competition (1950) and gave 1st recital at St. Merri in Paris (1950); won Bach Prize of the Amis de l'Orgue in Paris (1951); studied for 2 years with Litaize; performed complete works of her brother Jehan Alain, who was killed in WWII; wrote many articles about the organ; especially interested in 17th- and 18th-century music and in reproducing its sound, sought out organs from the era of the composer when recording or playing: Schnitger or Marcussen organs, when she performed Bach, Clicquot, Gonzalez or Haerpfer, and Erman organs for Couperin and De Grigny.

ALAIS. *Variant of Alice.*

ALAIS (fl. 12th c.). French troubadour. Fl. 12th century. ❖ One of the few female troubadours of southern France, composed a poem with two other women (Iselda and Carenza), which opposed the idea of marriage and referred to the anguish of being someone's wife. ❖ See also *Women in World History*.

ALAIS OF FRANCE (1160–?). Princess of France. Name variations: Alix or Alice. Born Oct 4, 1160; death date unknown; dau. of Constance of Castile (d. 1160) and Louis VII, king of France (r. 1137–1180); half-sister of Philip II Augustus (1165–1223), king of France; betrothed to Richard the Lionheart; possibly m. William II of Ponthieu, count of Ponthieu, c. 1195; children: possibly Joanna of Ponthieu, countess of Aumale (d. 1251). ❖ In an arrangement made to secure peace between her family and the family of Eleanor of Aquitaine, was betrothed to Eleanor's son Richard the Lionheart and sent to England for her upbringing; unfortunately for Alais, marriage was kept from occurring as planned because of conflicts between the English princes and their father, King Henry II; after Henry's death, though Richard would not marry her, became the virtual prisoner of Eleanor and Richard, as the new king and his mother did not want to lose her dower lands by returning her to the French king; installed at the fortress of Rouen under guard; at age 33, was released as part of a truce in the war that had erupted between Richard and Philip II Augustus, Alais' younger half-brother and now king of France; after a 24-year absence, returned to Paris. ❖ See also *Women in World History*.

ALAKIJA, Aduke (1921—). Nigerian lawyer. Born 1921 in Lagos, Nigeria. ❖ Began studying medicine at Glasgow University but switched to social science at London School of Economics; later studied law in UK and called to Bar (1953); was member of Nigerian delegation to UN (1961–65), trustee of Federal Nigeria Society for the Blind, advisor to International Academy of Trial Lawyers, 1st African woman director of Mobil Oil, and president of International Federation of Women Lawyers.

ALAMANDA OF FRANCE (fl. late 12th c.). French troubadour. Was probably from the town of Estang, in Gascony, and, like all the women troubadours, must have been of noble birth because she was well educated. ❖ Only existing poem is a *tenson* composed with the important troubadour Guiraut de Bornelh.

ALARIE, Pierrette (1921—). French-Canadian soprano. Born Marguerite Alarie in Montreal, Canada, Nov 9, 1921; dau. of Sylva (choirmaster) and Amanda Alarie (soprano and actress); studied with Jeanne Maubourg, Salvator Issaurel, Albert Roberval; also studied with Elisabeth Schumann (1943–46); m. Léopold Simoneau, 1946. ❖ Won Metropolitan Opera Auditions of the Air (1945); made Metropolitan debut (1945); with husband, engaged by Paris Opera and the Opéra Comique for 3 years (beginning 1949); appeared in opera houses throughout Europe and concertized widely in North America; won the Grand Prix du disque of the Académie Charles-Cros for recording of Mozart arias made with husband (1961); appeared in a number of opera productions made for tv; began teaching at École Vincent d'Indy (1960s). With husband, awarded the Prix de musique Calixa-Lavallée (1959); made Officer of the Order of Canada (1967). ❖ See also *Women in World History*.

ALASTOR (1836–1874). *See Clare, Ada.*

ALBA, duchess of.
See Cayetana, Maria del Pilar Teresa (d. 1802).
See Cayetana Fitz-James Stuart y Silva, Maria del Rosario (b. 1926).

ALBA, Nanina (1915–1968). African-American poet, short-story writer and educator. Born Nannie Williemenia Champey, 1915, in Montgomery, Alabama; died of cancer in 1968; dau. of Rev. I.C. Champey; attended Haines Institute; Knoxville College, AB, 1935; attended Indiana University; Alabama State College, MA in Education (1955); m. Reuben Andres Alba, Nov 27, 1937; children: daughters, Andrea and Pan(chita) Adams (illustrator). ❖ Taught music, French, and English in public schools of Alabama; became professor of English at Tuskegee Institute; used jazz rhythms and black vernacular in poetry collections *Parchments* (1963) and *Parchments II* (1967); poems also appeared in journals, including *Crisis, Phylon* and *Negro Digest.*

ALBANESE, Licia (1913–). Italian soprano. Born July 22, 1913, in Bari, Italy; m. Joseph Gimma (Italian-American businessman), 1945; studied with Emanuel De Rosa in Bari and Giuseppina Baldassare-Tedeschi in Milan. ❖ At 22, won 1st Italian government-sponsored vocal competition in a field of 300 entrants; in 1st five years of career, sang at Teatro alla Scala, Covent Garden, and the Rome Opera; when Benito Mussolini would no longer let distinguished Italian artists leave the country, escaped to Portugal (1939) and boarded ship bound for US; debuted at Metropolitan Opera (Feb 9, 1940) as Cio-Cio-San; was perhaps the most famous *La Boheme* Mimi of the 1940s; made final Metropolitan Opera performance (1966); received the Lady Grand Cross of the Equestrian Order of the Holy Sepulchre from Pope Pius XII; after retirement, worked for Puccini Foundation, founded by husband, to further survival of opera as art form; awarded President's Medal by Bill Clinton for work in the arts (1995). ❖ See also *Women in World History.*

ALBANESI, Meggie (1899–1923). English actress. Born in Kent, England, Oct 8, 1899; died Dec 9, 1923; dau. of an Italian violin teacher at the Royal Academy of Music and Maria Albanesi (novelist); studied piano, attended Royal Academy of Dramatic Art (RADA), and trained under Helen Hayes; won the Bancroft Medal. ❖ Made stage debut as an understudy in *Dear Brutus;* was then given the lead role of Jill in *The Skin Game,* followed by a triumphant opening night in Clemence Dane's *A Bill of Divorcement* (1921); while in rehearsal for *A Magdalen's Husband,* collapsed; died of a severe hemorrhage a few days later, age 25. ❖ See also *Women in World History.*

ALBANI, Emma (c. 1847–1930). French-Canadian soprano. Born Marie Louise Cécile Lajeunesse in Chambly near Montreal, Canada, Sept 27 or Nov 1, probably in 1847; died in London, England, April 3, 1930; eldest dau. of Joseph Lajeunesse and Mélinda Mignault; m. Ernest Gye, 1878; children: Frederick Ernest (b. 1879). ❖ The 1st Canadian artist to achieve international fame, studied with Gilbert-Louis Duprez and François Benoist; sang for the Prince of Wales (1860); debuted in Milan (1870), Covent Garden (1872), and at the New York Academy of Music (1876); sang Elisabeth at the London premiere of *Tannhäuser;* sang the leading role in Franz Liszt's oratorio *The Legend of Saint Elisabeth* in his presence (1886); debuted at the Metropolitan Opera (1891); retired from the opera (1894); received the Royal Philharmonic Society's gold medal known as the Beethoven Medal (1897); continued concertizing in North America, Europe, India, South Africa, Australia, and New Zealand; sang at a private family funeral service for Queen Victoria (1901) at Windsor Castle; made last public appearance at Royal Albert Hall (1911); made Dame Commander of the British Empire (1925). A street was named for her in Montreal and a plaque marks her birthplace in Chambly; a postage stamp was issued in Canada (1980) to commemorate the 50th anniversary of her death. ❖ See also Cheryl MacDonald, *Emma Albani: Victorian Diva* (Dundurn, 1984); and *Women in World History.*

ALBANIA, queen of (1915–2002). *See Apponyi, Geraldine.*

ALBANY, countess of. *See Louise of Stolberg-Gedern (1752–1824).*

ALBANY, duchess of.
See Keith, Muriel (d. 1449).
See Isabel, Countess of Lennox (d. 1457?).
See Anne de la Tour (d. 1512).
See Anne de la Tour (c. 1496–1524).
See Frederica of Prussia (1767–1820).
See Paca (1825–1860).

See Helen of Waldeck & Pyrmont (1861–1922).
See Victoria Adelaide of Schleswig-Holstein (1885–1970).

ALBERDINGK-THIJN, Mercedes (1962—). *See Coghen Alberdingk, Mercedes.*

ALBERGA, Marcenia Lyle (1921–1996). *See Stone, Toni.*

ALBERGHETTI, Anna Maria (1936—). Italian singer and actress. Born May 15, 1936, in Pesaro, Italy; eldest of three children of Daniele (cellist) and Vittoria Alberghetti (pianist); m. Claudio Guzman (producer-director; now div.); children: Alexander and Pilar. ❖ At 12, made 1st European concert tour; made US debut at Carnegie Hall (1950); made film debut as Monica in Gian-Carlo Menotti's opera *The Medium* (1950); groomed by Paramount to replace Deanna Durbin, gave "standout" rendition of the "Caro Nome" aria from *Rigoletto* in *Here Comes the Groom* (1951), which featured Bing Crosby; won Tony Award for starring role in Broadway musical *Carnival;* retired (1961). Other films include *The Stars Are Singing* (with Rosemary Clooney, 1953), *The Last Command* (1955), *10,000 Bedrooms* (1957), *Duel at Apache Wells* (1957), and *Cinderfella* (1960).

ALBERS, Anni (1899–1994). German-born textile and graphic artist. Born Anni Farman, June 12, 1899, in Berlin-Charlottenburg, Germany; died in 1994 (some sources cite 1993); dau. of S. and T. (Ullstein) Farman; studied under Paul Klee at Bauhaus in Weimar; m. Josef Albers (artist and teacher), 1925. ❖ Made her artistic reputation as a weaver during Bauhaus days at the famous design school in Weimar Germany (1922–30); became a leader in abstract textile design, concentrating on "a weaver's concern with threads as an artistic vehicle"; with rise of Nazism, moved to US with husband and others from Bauhaus (1933); served as assistant professor of art, Black Mountain College, NC (1933–49); became a naturalized US citizen (1937); moved to New Haven, CT (1950), where husband was appointed chair of department of design at Yale, and she freelanced; published an edition of her 1st lithographs under auspices of Tamarind Lithography Workshop in Los Angeles (1964). Awarded Medal of American Institute of Architects in the Field of Craftsmanship (1961); awarded citation by the Philadelphia Museum College of Art (1962). ❖ See also *Women in World History.*

ALBERT, Caterina (1869–1966). Catalonian author. Name variations: Catarina; Víctor Català; Virgili Alacseal. Born Caterina Albert i Paradís, Sept 11, 1869, in L'Escala, Spain, on the Costa Brava; died in L'Escala in 1966; dau. of Lluis Albert i Paradeda and Dolors Paradís i Farrés. ❖ Considered the greatest Catalonian woman writer, adopted pseudonym Virgili Alacseal and won the Jocs Florals Prize for her 1st monologue, "La Infanticida" (The Infanticide, 1898); as Víctor Català, published 3 more dramatic pieces and a collection of poetry, *El cant dels messos* (*Song of the Months*), and was praised as one of the leading male writers of Catalan (1901); revealed her true gender following publication of 2nd volume of poetry (1902); published 1st novel, *Solitud* (*Solitude*), which was serialized in 46 segments by the journal *Joventut* (1905). ❖ See also *Women in World History.*

ALBERT, Marie-Madeleine d' (fl. 18th c.). *See d'Albert, Marie-Madeleine Bonafous.*

ALBERT, Octavia V.R. (1853–c. 1899). African-American historian. Born Octavia Victoria Rogers in Oglethorpe, Georgia, Dec 24, 1853; died c. 1899, in Houma, Louisiana; studied at Atlanta University; m. Reverend A.E.P. Albert, 1874; children: Laura T.F. Albert. ❖ Though born into slavery, was emancipated at end of Civil War; married and moved to Houma, LA, where husband was a minister of the Methodist Episcopal church; when their home became a gathering place for former slaves, recorded their oral histories; published *The House of Bondage: or Charlotte Brooks and Other Slaves* (1891).

ALBERTA, Baronesa (1913–1995). *See Ballesteros, Mercedes.*

ALBERTA FIVE. *See individual entries on Henrietta Muir Edwards, Nellie McClung, Louise McKinney, Emily Murphy, and Irene Parlby.*

ALBERTAZZI, Emma (1813–1847). English singer. Born Emma Howson, 1813, possibly in London, England; died of consumption in 1847; dau. of Francis Howson; studied under Sir Michael Costa, 1827, and in Italy under Professor Celli. ❖ Made successful appearances in Milan, Madrid, Paris, and London.

ALBERTI, Sophie (1826–1892). German writer. Name variations: (pseudonym) Sophie Verena. Born in Potsdam, Germany, Aug 5, 1826; died in Potsdam, Aug 15, 1892. ❖ Wrote the popular novel *A Son of the South* (1859) and a collection of tales entitled *Old and New* (1879).

ALBERTINA, Sister (1840–1930). *See Polyblank, Ellen Albertina.*

ALBERTINA AGNES (d. 1696). Princess of Orange. Name variations: Albertina Orange-Nassau. Born Albertina Agnes; died 1696; dau. of Frederick Henry, prince of Orange (r. 1625–1647), and Amelia of Solms (1602–1675); m. William Frederick of Nassau-Dietz (died 1664); children: Henry Casimir (1657–1696), cousin of King William III.)

ALBERTINA OF BADEN-DURLACH (1682–1755). Duchess of Holstein-Gottorp. Born July 3, 1682; died Dec 22, 1755; dau. of Augusta Maria of Holstein-Gottorp (1649–1728) and Frederick VII, margrave of Baden-Durlach; m. Christian Augustus, duke of Holstein-Gottorp, Sept 3, 1704; children: 12, including Sofie, abbess of Herford (1705–1764); Karl (b. 1706); Anna (1709–1758, who m. Wilhelm of Saxe-Gotha); Adolphus Frederick (1710–1771), king of Sweden; Johanna Elizabeth of Holstein-Gottorp (1712–1760, mother of Catherine II the Great); Friederike (1713–1713); Wilhelm Christian (b. 1716); Friedrich Konrad (b. 1718); George (b. 1719).

ALBERTINE (1753–1829). Swedish princess. Born 1753; died 1829; dau. of Louisa Ulrica of Prussia (1720–1782) and Adolphus Frederick, king of Sweden.

ALBERTINE (1797–1838). Duchess of Broglie. Name variations: Albertine de Staël. Born Albertine Ida Gustavine de Staël in Paris, France, June 8, 1797; died Sept 22, 1838; illeg. dau. of Germaine de Staël and Benjamin Constant; m. (Achille Charles Léonce) Victor, duc de Broglie (1785–1870, French minister of the interior, 1830, and foreign affairs, 1832–34 and 1835–36), Feb 1816; children: Jacques Victor Albert, duc de Broglie (b. 1821, French politician, publicist, and historian who was ambassador to London, 1871, and premier, 1873–74 and 1877). ❖ Cherishing the causes of her grandmother Suzanne Necker rather than those of her mother, wrote moral and religious essays which were collected after her death under the title *Fragments sur divers sujets de religion et de morale* (1840). ❖ See also *Women in World History.*

ALBERTINE, Viv (1955—). French-English musician. Name variations: The Slits. Born 1955 in France. ❖ Guitarist for British punk-rock band, the Slits (formed 1976 in London), began career playing with backing band, Flowers of Romance; replaced Kate Korus as guitarist for the Slits (1977); with group, released debut album, *Cut* (1978), which included song "Typical Girls" (group disbanded in 1981). Other Slits releases include *Return of the Giant Slits* (1981), *The Peel Sessions* (1989) and *In the Beginning* (1997).

ALBERTSON, Lillian (1881–1962). American actress and producer. Born Aug 6, 1881, in Noblesville, Indiana; died Aug 24, 1962, in Los Angeles, California. ❖ On Broadway, appeared in *Paid in Full, The Talker* and *The Six-Fifty*; on West Coast, produced operettas, including *White Collars, The Desert Song* and *New Moon.*

ALBERTSON, Mabel (1901–1982). American stage, screen and tv actress. Born July 24, 1901, in Lynn, Massachusetts; died Sept 28, 1982, in Santa Monica, California; sister of Jack Albertson (1907–1981, actor). ❖ On Broadway, appeared in *The Return of Ulysses, The Egg* and *Xmas in Las Vegas,* among others; films include *So This is Love, Forever, Darling, The Long Hot Summer, Home Before Dark, Don't Give Up the Ship, Period of Adjustment, Barefoot in the Park, Ma and Pa Kettle at Waikiki, On a Clear Day You Can See Forever*; on tv, had recurring roles in "Those Whiting Girls," "Tom Ewell Show" and "Bewitched."

ALBIA DOMNICA (fl. 4th c.). Byzantine empress. Married Valens, Byzantine and Roman emperor (r. 364–378).

ALBIN-GUILLOT, Laure (c. 1880–1962). French photographer. Born c. 1880, presumably in France; died in Nogent-sur-Marne, France, 1962; m. Albin Guillot (scientific researcher), 1901. ❖ Specializing in portraits, nudes, and photomicrography, was at the center of Parisian photographic circles during the 1920s and '30s, with her photos frequently appearing in magazines; served as head of Photography, Archives Service Beaux-Arts, Paris (1932) and as president of French Société Artistes Photographes (1935); with husband, spent 30 years amassing a collection of micrographic specimens, including crystallizations, plant cells, and animal organisms. ❖ See also *Women in World History.*

ALBONI, Marietta (1823–1894). Italian contralto. Name variations: Contessa Pepoli. Born Maria Anna Marzia on Mar 6, 1823, in Città di Castello, Italy; died June 23, 1894, in Ville d'Avray, France; m. Count Pepoli (died 1867), 1853; m. Charles Ziéger, 1877. ❖ One of the 19th century's outstanding contralto voices, studied with Mombelli in Bologna and with Rossini (1841); regarded as a protégé by Rossini, who helped arrange her debut at Teatro Communale in Bologna (1842), as well as her 1st appearance at Teatro alla Scala, where she appeared in his *Siege of Corinth;* performed in Russia, Germany, Great Britain, France, and US; sang in 10 of 17 operas performed in Covent Garden's 1st season; appeared widely in Italy until her performance in Turin (1851), which proved to be her last in Italy. ❖ See also A. Pougin, *Marietta Alboni* (1912); and *Women in World History.*

ALBRECHT, Angele (1942—). German ballet dancer. Born Dec 13, 1942, in Freiburg, Germany. ❖ Performed at Hamburg Opera Ballet, Germany (1960s), and won acclaim for performances in classics such as *Swan Lake, Les Sylphides,* Balanchine's *Apollo* and *Palais de Cristal;* became member of Maurice Béjart's company (1969), where she created roles in *Actus Tragicus* (1969), *Beaudelaire* (1972), *I Trionfi* (1973), *Pli selon pli* (1975), and others; created individualized system of notation for Béjart's works, which has been showcased as art in New York and Europe.

ALBRECHT, Bertie (?–1943). French partisan. Born of Swiss parents in Marseille; died at Fresnes prison on May 29, 1943. ❖ Sought out Henri Frenay in Vichy (1940), whose group would eventually be known as Combat; typed and distributed their underground newspaper, "Petites Ailes"; moving to Lyon, took a cover job as regional director for unemployed women at the Ministry of Labor; arrested, was transferred to a concentration camp by Vichy government (1942); feigned insanity and was taken to an asylum at Bron, where fellow Combat regulars helped her escape; plunged once more into underground work, even replacing Frenay when he was away; arrested by the Gestapo, hung herself in the cell she was occupying at Fresnes prison. ❖ See also *Women in World History.*

ALBRECHT, Brigitte (1970—). *See Albrecht-Loretan, Brigitte.*

ALBRECHT, Sophie (1757–1840). German actress and author. Born Sophie Bäumer in Erfurt, Germany, 1757; died in 1840; dau. of a professor of medicine who died when she was 15; m. J.F.E. Albrecht (doctor). ❖ Acting career flourished when husband turned to writing and managing theater productions; on tour with him, became a successful figure on the German stage; during late 20s, also produced 3 volumes of fiction, drama and verse.

ALBRECHT, Sylvia (1962—). East German speedskater. Name variations: Sylvia Heckendorf-Albrecht. Born Oct 28, 1962, in East Berlin, Germany. ❖ Won a bronze medal for 1,000 meters at Lake Placid Olympics (1980).

ALBRECHT-LORETAN, Brigitte (1970—). Swiss cross-country skier. Name variations: Brigitte Loretan; Brigitte Albrecht. Born Nov 6, 1970, in Lax, Switzerland. ❖ Won a bronze medal for the 4x5km relay at Salt Lake City Olympics (2002).

ALBRET, Jeanne III d' (1528–1572). *See Jeanne d'Albret.*

ALBRIER, Albertine (c. 1810–1846). *See Coquillard-Albrier, Albertine.*

ALBRIGHT, Lola (1925—). American actress. Born in Akron, Ohio, July 20, 1925; married for 4 years in her teens; m. Jack Carson (actor), 1952 (div. 1958); m. Bill Chadney (musician-restaurateur), 1961 (div. 1975); no children. ❖ Made film debut in *The Pirate* (1948) and followed that with *Champion* a year later; was lauded for performance in film *A Cold Wind in August* (1961); other films include *Easter Parade* (1948), *The Good Humor Man* (1950), *Sierra Passage* (1951), *The Silver Whip* (1953), *Magnificent Matador* (1955), *The Tender Trap* (1955), *The Monolith Monsters* (1957), *Kid Galahad* (1962), *Lord Love a Duck* (1966), *The Way West* (1967), *Where Were You When the Lights Went Out?* (1968), *The Impossible Years* (1968), and *The Money Jungle* (1968); was also a regular on "Peter Gunn" tv series (late 1950s).

ALBRIGHT, Madeleine (1937—). American diplomat, Cabinet official, and UN ambassador. Born Madeleine Korbel, May 15, 1937, in Prague, Czechoslovakia; Wellesley College, BA with honors; Columbia University, MA and PhD; m. Joseph Albright, 1961 (div. 1981); children: 3 daughters. ❖ Immigrated to US (1950); became US citizen (1957); served on staff of National Security Council in Carter Administration (1978–81); co-founded Center for National Policy (1981); earned professorship at Georgetown University's School of Foreign Service (1982); became US representative to UN (1992); named US secretary of state (1996), the 1st female secretary of state and highest-ranking woman in the history of US government. ❖ See also memoir, *Madame Secretary* (Miramax, 2003); Thomas Blood, *Madame Secretary: The Biography of Madeleine Albright* (1999); Michael Dobbs, *Madeleine Albright: A Twentieth-Century Odyssey* (1999); Thomas W. Lippman, *Madeleine Albright and the New American Democracy* (2000).

ALBRIGHT, Tenley (1935—). American figure skater. Born Tenley Emma Albright, July 18, 1935, in Newton Center, Massachusetts; graduated from Radcliffe College, 1957, and Harvard Medical School, MD, 1961; m. Tudor Gardiner, 1962 (divorced); m. Gerald W. Blakeley. ❖ Earned regional championship title for age 12 and under (1947); won US Novice championship at 13; won US Jr. title at 14; won US National championships 5 times (1952–56); won a silver medal at Oslo Olympics (1952); was 1st American woman to win a World title (1953) and 1st American to capture an Olympic gold medal in figure skating, at Cortina (1956); was 1st woman to be named to US Olympic Committee (1976). Was 1st woman admitted to Harvard University Hall of Fame (1974); inducted into US Figure Skating Hall of Fame (1976) and Olympic Hall of Fame (1988). ❖ See also *Women in World History.*

ALBRIZZI, Isabella Teotochi, Contessa d' (1770–1836). Italian writer and salonnière. Name variations: Isabella Teotochi-Albrizzi. Pronunciation: ahl-BREET-tsee. Born on the Greek island of Corfu in 1770; died in Venice, Italy, Sept 27, 1836; dau. of a Greek father and Venetian mother; m. a Venetian at 16 (annulled); m. a noble of Venice. ❖ Wrote a study of the works of Canova (*Descrizione delle opere di Canova,* 1821–25), wrote essays on celebrated contemporaries, which were published as *Ritratti* (*Portraits*), and completed a biography of Vittoria Colonna (1836); her home was a gathering place for the literati, including the dramatist Vittorio Alfieri, the writer Ugo Foscolo, and the poet Lord Byron, who dubbed her "the Madame de Staël of Venice."

ALCANTARA, Dolores Jimenez (1909–1999). Spanish Flamenco singer. Name variations: La Niña de Puebla. Born Dolores Jimenez Alcantara in La Puebla de Cazalla, near Seville, Spain, 1909; died June 14, 1999, in Malaga, Spain. ❖ Blinded during childhood, took the name "La Niña de Puebla" ("Girl of the Town") and made her singing debut (1931); specialized in fandangos and zambras.

ALCAYA, Lucila Godoy (1889–1957). *See Mistral, Gabriela.*

ALCAYAGA, Lucila Godoy (1889–1957). *See Mistral, Gabriela.*

ALCIPE (1750–c. 1839). *See Alorna, Marquesa de.*

ALCOCK, Mary (1742–1798). British poet. Born 1742 in Northamptonshire, England; died May 28, 1798, in Northamptonshire; youngest dau. of Denison Cumberland (vicar, later bishop of Clonfert in Ireland, then of Kilmore) and Joanna Bentley (dau. of Richard Bentley, master of Trinity College, Cambridge); sister of Richard Cumberland, playwright; m. John Alcock (archdeacon). ❖ Active in literary circles (1780s–90s), was often compared to Romantic poets like William Blake; poems allude to political events and such figures as Thomas Paine and Mary Wollstonecraft; wrote *The Air Balloon; or The Flying Mortal* (1784) and posthumous collection *Poetical Writer* (1799).

ALCOCK, Nora (1874–1972). Scottish plant pathologist. Name variations: Nora Lilian Scott Alcock. Born Nora Lilian Scott in 1874; died Mar 31, 1972; m. a professor of medicine, 1905 (died 1913); children: 4. ❖ Performed laboratory work in Department of Physiology at University of London; worked in Plant Pathology Laboratory at Ministry of Agriculture in Kew Gardens and later Harpenden (1913–24); served as plant pathologist in Department of Agriculture for Scotland at Royal Botanic Garden in Edinburgh (1924–37); was the 1st government plant pathologist appointed in Scotland; researched disease-resistant strawberries and supervised breeding program; pioneered study of seed pathology; made MBE (1935).

ALCOCK, Vivien (1924–2003). English children's writer. Name variations: Vivien Garfield. Born Sept 23, 1924, in Worthing, Sussex, England; died Oct 11, 2003; attended Oxford School of Art; m. Leon Garfield (children's writer); children: Jane Garfield. ❖ Began career as a commercial artist; at age 56, published 1st book, *The Haunting of Cassie Palmer* (1980); wrote more than 20 books in 20 years, including *The Stonewalkers* (1981), *The Cuckoo Sister* (1985), *The Trial of Anna Cotman* (1989), *The Dancing Bush* (1991), and *The Boy Who Swallowed a Ghost* (2001). ❖ See also *Women in World History.*

ALCOFORADO, Mariana (1640–1723). Portuguese nun. Name variations: Mariana Alcoforada. Baptized in the Portuguese city of Beja, April

22, 1640; died July 28, 1723; dau. of Francisco da Costa Alcoforado and Leonor Mendes. ❖ Nun whose love for Noël Bouton, the Marquis of Chamilly, reportedly led her to write 5 love letters, which gained fame as the Lettres portugaises (1669), celebrated examples of amorous correspondence; placed in Our Lady of the Conception convent in Beja (1652); met Noël Bouton de Chamilly when his detachment quartered in and around Beja (mid-1666); after he departed for France (late 1667), allegedly wrote 5 letters to him (Dec 1667–June 1668) which were published as *Lettres portugaises* in Paris (Jan 4, 1669) and went through 5 editions in 7 months; lost election to serve as abbess of convent (July 30, 1709). French scholar Jean François Boissonade claimed she authored the letters (1810). ❖ See also *Women in World History.*

ALCORTA, Gloria (1915—). Argentinean author and sculptor. Born in 1915 in Argentina; dau. of a French diplomat; granddau. of author Eduarda Mansilla de García. ❖ In Paris, studied dramatic arts (1932–38); launched career as a sculptor, winning prizes in both Buenos Aires and Paris; at 20, published 1st volume of verse in French, *La prison de l'enfant* (*The Child's Prison*); wrote 2 plays in French, which were produced in Paris; wrote novel *El hotel de la luna* (*The Moon Hotel,* 1958) in Spanish, which was her most recognized work.

ALCOTT, Amy (1956—). American golfer. Born Feb 22, 1956, in Kansas City, Missouri; lives in Santa Monica, California. ❖ Won US Junior Girls' title (1973); placed 2nd at the Canadian Amateur (1974); joined Ladies' Professional Golf Association (LPGA) Tour (1975); won Orange Blossom Classic and named Rookie of the Year (1976); won LPGA Classic and Colgate Far East Open (1977) and Peter Jackson Classic (1979); won US Women's Open and Vare Trophy (1980); took the Nabisco-Dinah Shore title (1983, 1988, 1991) and the Lady Keystone Open (1984); won a tournament in each of her 1st 12 years on the Tour, a record shared with Louise Suggs and Betsy Rawls.

ALCOTT, Anna Bronson (1831–1893). American preservationist. Name variations: Anna Alcott Pratt. Born Anna Bronson Alcott, Mar 16, 1831; died July 1893; dau. of Bronson (writer, educator, and Transcendentalist) and Abigail (May) Alcott; sister of Louisa May Alcott and May Alcott; m. John Pratt (insurance firm employee), 1860; children: 2 sons. ❖ Sister of Louisa May Alcott, was caretaker of Orchard House. ❖ See also *Women in World History.*

ALCOTT, Louisa May (1832–1888). American author. Name variations: (pseudonyms) Flora Fairfield; A.M. Barnard. Born in Germantown, Pennsylvania, Nov 29, 1832; died in Dunreath Place, Roxbury, Massachusetts, Mar 6, 1888; 2nd child of Bronson Alcott (writer, educator, and Transcendentalist) and Abigail (May) Alcott; never married; no children. ❖ Author whose best-known work, the classic *Little Women,* is often said to have its basis in her life; like Jo, took refuge in books when young, frequently withdrawing to her room to read and think; unlike Jo, was dominated by her father and bore the financial weight of her sisters and mother; sequestering herself at home, journeyed out only as required to make a living for the Alcotts; writings include *Flower Fables* (1855), *Hospital Sketches* (1863), *Moods* (1865), *Little Men* (1871), *Jo's Boys* (1886), and over 30 others. ❖ See also Ednah D. Cheney, ed., *Louisa May Alcott: Her Life, Letters, and Journals* (Roberts, 1889); Myerson and Shealy, *The Journals of Louisa May Alcott* (Little, Brown, 1989); Martha Saxton, *Louisa May Alcott* (Houghton Mifflin, 1977); Madeleine Stern, ed., *Behind a Mask: The Unknown Thrillers of Louisa May Alcott* (Morrow, 1975); and *Women in World History.*

ALCOTT, May (1840–1879). American artist. Born Abby May Alcott, July 26, 1840; died Dec 1879, about a month after giving birth; dau. of Bronson (writer, educator, and Transcendentalist) and Abigail (May) Alcott; sister of Louisa May Alcott and Anna Bronson Alcott; studied art in Paris; m. Ernest Nieriker (Swiss businessman), Mar 22, 1878, and settled in a Parisian suburb; children: Louisa May Nieriker (b. Nov 8, 1879). ❖ See also Caroline Ticknor, *May Alcott: A Memoir* (Little, Brown, 1927); and *Women in World History.*

ALDA, Frances (1879–1952). New Zealand soprano. Name variations: Fanny Jane Davis, Francie Adler. Born Frances Jeanne Davis on May 31, 1879, in Christchurch, New Zealand; died Sept 18, 1952, in Venice, Italy; dau. of David Davis (merchant) and Leonore (Simonsen) Davis; granddau. of famous opera impresarios, Fanny and Martin Simonsen; m. Giulio Gatti-Casazza (general manager of Metropolitan Opera), April 3, 1910 (div. 1928); m. Ray Vir Den (advertising executive), 1941. ❖ Began career in light opera, performing as Francie Adler for theatrical organizations of J.C. Williamson and Harry Rickards (1897–1901); studied with Mathilde Marchesi in Paris; made debut as Manon at the Opéra-Comique in Paris (1904); appeared in Brussels (1905–08), Covent Garden (1906), and Teatro alla Scala (1908); debuted at the Metropolitan Opera as Gilda in *Rigoletto* (1908), then performed there 250 times until 1930; premiered Damrosch's *Cyrano* as Roxanne (1913), Herbert's *Madeleine* (1914), and Hadley's *Cleopatra's Night* (1920); early recording star, made 130 gramophone recordings for the Victor Company (1909–23); performed with leading tenors of the time, including Beniamino Gigli and Enrico Caruso. ❖ See also memoir *Men, Women, and Tenors* (1937).

ALDEBARÁN (1833–1913). *See Acosta de Samper, Soledad.*

ALDEBARÁN, Bertilda or Olga (1833–1903). *See Acosta de Samper, Soledad.*

ALDECOA, Josefina R. (1926—). Spanish educator and author. Born Josefina Rodriquez in La Roba (León), Spain, 1926; earned doctorate in philosophy from University of Madrid; m. Ignacio Aldecoa (writer), 1952 (died 1969); children: Susanna (b. 1954). ❖ With husband, made over 100 trips to less privileged regions of Spain to spread education and culture (1951–53); moved to Blasco de Garay (1956), then to America (1958), when she received a grant to study education in the States; returning to Spain (1959), founded Estilo, a private school for children from 2 to 17; wrote articles and stories for the reviews *Espadaña* and *Revista española,* and published a volume of short stories (1960s); following husband's death, published her memoirs and her 1st novel; writings include *El arte del niño* (The Art of the Child, 1960), *A ninguine parte* (Going Nowhere, 1961), *Los niños de la gueraa* (Children of Wartime, 1983), *La enredadera* (The Clinging Vine, 1984), *Porque éramos jóvenes* (Because We Were Young, 1986), and *El vergel* (The Orchard, 1988).

ALDEGUND (c. 630–684). Frankish abbess. Name variations: Aldegundis. Born c. 630; died of cancer in 684; dau. of St. Walbert and St. Bertilia; sister of St. Wandru; aunt of Madelberte and St. Aldetrude, abbess of Maubeuge. ❖ Born into a wealthy noble family of Hainault, dedicated herself to a religious life as a young woman; used her fortune to build a double monastery-abbey at Hautmount, where she took vows of poverty, chastity, and obedience; was soon elected abbess; influenced many of her fellow nobles to use their wealth for charitable purposes. ❖ See also *Women in World History.*

ALDEN, Cynthia Westover (1862–1931). American social worker and journalist. Born Cynthia May Westover, May 31, 1862, in Afton, Iowa; died Jan 8, 1931, in Brooklyn, NY; m. John Alden, 1896. ❖ Worked for *New York Recorder, Brooklyn Eagle, Tribune* (NY), and *Ladies Home Journal;* with fellow journalists, organized the Sunshine Society, which sent Christmas cards and gifts to shut-ins (1896); after society was incorporated as International Sunshine Society (1900), served as president for rest of life, while society worked to provide care, services, and legislation for blind infants and children. Works include *Manhattan, Historic and Artistic* (1892), *Women's Ways of Earning Money* (1904), and *The Baby Blind* (1915).

ALDEN, Hortense (1903–1999). American actress. Name variations: Hortense Farrell; Mrs. James T. Farrell. Born Jan 13, 1903; died June 22, 1999, in Jacksonville, Florida; married James T. Farrell (writer), 1941 (div. 1955); children: 2. ❖ Made stage debut in Washington, DC, and NY debut (both 1919) as Hortense in *Tumble Inn;* other appearances include Marie in *Liliom* (1921), Audrey in *As You Like It,* Emelia in *The Firebrand,* Laila in *Arabesque,* Regina in *Ghosts,* Dina in *Right You Are If You Think You Are* and Myrrhina in *Lysistrata;* also appeared off-Broadway in *Garden District.*

ALDEN, Isabella (1841–1930). American religious author. Name variations: (pseudonym) Pansy. Born Isabella Macdonald in Rochester, NY, Nov 3, 1841; died in Palo Alto, California, 1930; dau. of Myra (Spafford) and Isaac Macdonald; aunt of novelist Grace Livingston Hill; Gustavus R. Alden (Presbyterian minister). ❖ Published 1st book, *Helen Lester,* which won the Christian Tract Society prize (1866); primarily a religious writer, wrote and edited over 120 books; also founded and edited the Sunday School magazine *Pansy* as well as the *Presbyterian Primary Quarterly;* her novels about the Chautauqua region helped found the Chautauqua movement and Christian summer camps (1870s). ❖ See also autobiography, *Memories of Yesterday* (1931).

ALDEN, Mary (1883–1946). American silent-film actress. Born Mary Maguire Alden, June 18, 1883, in New York, NY; died July 2, 1946, in Woodland Hills, California. ❖ Silent-film actress, portrayed the mulatto housekeeper Lydia Brown in D.W. Griffith's *Birth of a Nation*

(1915); other films include *The Second Mrs. Roebuck, Home Sweet Home* (1914), *The Unpardonable Sin* (1919), *The Witching Hour* (1921), *Babbitt* (1924), *Brown of Harvard* (1926), and *The Potter* (1927).

ALDEN, Priscilla (c. 1602–c. 1685). American colonist. Name variations: Mollins or Mollines. Born Priscilla Mullens or Mullins in Dorking, Surrey, England, c. 1602; died c. 1685; dau. of William Mullens (shopkeeper); m. John Alden (1599–1687, American colonist and barrel-maker), probably in 1622; children: at least 11. ❖ Came to America on the *Mayflower;* wed John Alden and lived in Plymouth until around 1631; moved north to settle the town of Duxbury. The site of the Alden home in Duxbury, Massachusetts, has been preserved. ❖ See also *Women in World History.*

ALDERSON, Georgiana (1827–1899). *See Cecil, Georgiana.*

ALDERSON, Joan. *See Rosazza, Joan.*

ALDETRUDE (fl. 7th c). Abbess of Maubeuge. Name variations: Saint Aldetrude; fl. in the 7th century; dau. of St. Wandru and St. Vincent Madelgaire; sister of Madelberte. ❖ Feast day is Feb 25.

ALDGYTH. *Variant of Edith.*

ALDIS, Dorothy (1896–1966). American children's author. Born Dorothy Keeley, Mar 13, 1896, in Chicago, Illinois; died July 4, 1966; dau. of James Keeley (Chicago *Tribune* journalist) and Gertrude Keeley; attended Miss Porter's School in Connecticut and Smith College; m. Graham Aldis (real-estate executive), June 15, 1922; children: Mary (b. 1923), Owen (b. 1925), Peggy and Ruth (b. 1927). ❖ Became a columnist for Chicago *Tribune;* published 1st volume of children's verse (1927), beginning 4 decades of constant publication of works primarily for children and adolescents; also wrote adult novels and contributed to *The New Yorker, Harper's* and *Ladies Home Journal.*

ALDIS, Mary (1872–1949). American watercolor artist and writer. Born Mary Reynolds in 1872; died in 1949; married Arthur Taylor Aldis, 1892. ❖ Wrote *Plays for Small Stages* (1915), *The Princess Jack* (1915), *Drift* (1918), and *No Curtain* (1935).

ALDONA OF LITHUANIA (d. 1339). Polish royal. Name variations: Anna of Lithuania; Anna Aldona. Died 1339; dau. of Gediminas, duke of Lithuania; became 1st wife of Kazimierz also known as Casimir III the Great, king of Poland (r. 1333–1370), 1325; children: possibly Elizabeth of Poland (d. 1361); possibly Cunegunde (d. 1357, who m. Louis VI the Roman, duke of Bavaria); possibly Anna.

ALDOUS, Lucette (1938—). New Zealand-born ballet dancer. Born Sept 26, 1938, in Auckland, New Zealand; m. Alan Alder (Australian dancer). ❖ As a member of Ballet Rambert in London (1957–63), danced in revivals of Tudor's *Gala Performance* and *Dark Elegies,* Cranko's *Variations* and *La Reja,* and others; danced with London Festival Ballet (1963–66), performing in such classics as *Giselle, Les Sylphides* and *The Nutcracker;* toured with Royal Ballet (1966–70); joined Australian Ballet, Sydney (early 1970s), appeared in soubrette roles in *The Merry Widow* and *Don Quixote* and toured in US and Europe; performed opposite Rudolf Nureyev in film version of *Don Quixote* (1973).

ALDREDGE, Theoni V. (1932—). Greek-born costume designer. Born Theoni Athanasiou Vachlioti, Aug 22, 1932, in Salonika, Greece; m. Thomas Aldredge (actor). ❖ Began designing costumes for the Goodman Theater in Chicago (1950); NY credits include *Sweet Bird of Youth, The Best Man, Under Milk Wood, I Can Get It for You Wholesale, Who's Afraid of Virginia Woolf, Any Wednesday, Ilya Darling, That Championship Season, A Chorus Line* and *42nd Street;* designed such films as *You're a Big Boy Now, No Way to Treat a Lady, I Never Sang for My Father, Rich and Famous, Ghostbusters, Moonstruck, Addams Family Values* and *First Wives Club.* Won an Academy Award for *The Great Gatsby* (1974) and Tony Awards for *Annie* (1977) and *Barnum* (1980).

ALDRICH, Ann (1927—). *See Meaker, Marijane.*

ALDRICH, Anne Reeve (1866–1892). American poet and novelist. Born April 25, 1866, in New York, NY; died June 22, 1892, in New York, NY. ❖ Wrote *The Rose of Flame* (1889), *The Feet of Love* (1890), and *Songs about Life, Love, and Death* (1892).

ALDRICH, Bess Streeter (1881–1954). American author. Name variations: (pseudonym) Margaret Dean Stevens. Born in Cedar Falls, Iowa, Feb 17, 1881; died in Lincoln, Nebraska, Aug 3, 1954; dau. of James and Mary Anderson Streeter; m. Charles S. Aldrich (lawyer), 1907 (died 1925); children: 1 daughter, 3 sons. ❖ Following husband's death, turned to writing to support children, publishing *The Rim of the Prairie* (1925); had a bestseller with *A Lantern in Her Hand* (1928); produced 10 novels and more than 150 stories. ❖ See also *Women in World History.*

ALDRICH-BLAKE, Louisa (1865–1925). English surgeon. Name variations: Dame Louisa Aldrich Blake. Born Louisa Brandreth Aldrich in Essex, England, 1865; died 1925; London University, 1892, Maryland, 1894, master in surgery, 1895. ❖ The 1st woman to be qualified as an English surgeon, was named dean of the London School of Medicine for Women (1914).

ALDRUDE (fl. 1172). Italian countess. Fl. in 1172. ❖ As the countess of Bertinoro in Italy, was an efficient military leader; commanded the army that successfully lifted an imperial siege of the town of Aucona (1172). ❖ See also *Women in World History.*

ALEANDRO, Norma (1936—). Argentinean actress, screenwriter, and director. Born Norma Aleandro Robledo, May 2, 1936, in Buenos Aires, Argentina; dau. of actress María Luisa Robledo and actor Pedro Aleandro; sister of María Vaner (actress); m. Oscar Ferrigno (actor, div.); children: Oscar Ferrigno Jr. ❖ Made stage debut as a child, eventually becoming one of Argentina's leading actresses of stage, tv and film; spent many years in exile in Uruguay and Spain because of outspoken liberal views (1970s); returned to Buenos Aires (1982); films include *Cousins, Cién Veces No Debo, Vital Signs, One Man's War, The Tomb, Autumn Sun* and *Son of the Bride*; wrote short stories, poems, and collaborated on screenplay of *Los Herederos.* Named Best Actress at Cannes for *La Historia Oficial* (*The Official Story,* 1985) and nominated for Oscar for *Gaby—A True Story* (1987).

ALEGRÍA, Claribel (1924—). Nicaraguan writer. Name variations: Alegria. Pronunciation: Clar-ee-BEL Al-eh-GREE-uh. Born May 12, 1924, in Estelí, Nicaragua; dau. of Dr. Daniel Alegría and Ana Maria Vides; George Washington University, BA, 1948; m. Darwin B. Flakoll (journalist), Dec 1947, in Wendte, South Dakota; children: daughters Maya, Patricia, and Karen; son Erik. ❖ Writer of poetry, narrative, and testimony about political upheaval in Central America from the perspective of popular resistance; with family, forced into political exile in El Salvador because of father's opposition to US Marine occupation of Nicaragua (1925); published 1st poems in *Reportorio Americano* (1941); admitted to George Washington University (1944); published 1st book of poetry, *Anillo de silencio* (*Ring of Silence*), in Mexico (1948); moved with husband and children to Mexico; moved with family to Santiago, Chile, to work with husband on anthology of Latin American writers and poets (1953); returned to US (1956); moved to foreign service post in Uruguay (1958); posted to Argentina (1960); moved with family to Paris and began collaboration on a novel (1962); moved to Majorca (1966); co-wrote with journalist husband the novel *Cenizas de Izalco* (*Ashes of Izalco*), widely recognized as a seminal work in Central American literature; published poetry collection *Aprendizaje* (*Apprenticeship,* 1970), which would be burned by army (1972); won the Casa de las Américas Prize (1978); after the Sandinista rebels gained power in Nicaragua, began research with husband for history of Sandinista movement (1979); delivered eulogy at Sorbonne for assassinated Monsignor Arnulfo Romero, archbishop of San Salvador, resulting in exile (1980); co-authored history of the Sandinista revolution. Writings include *Suite* (1951), *Vigilias* (*Vigils,* 1953), *Acuario* (*Aquarium,* 1953), *Huésped de mi tiempo* (*Guest of My Time,* 1961), *Vía Unica* (*One-Way Traffic,* 1965), *Luisa in Realityland* (1987), *Pagaré a cobrar* (*Installment Payments,* 1973), *El detén* (*The Talisman,* 1977), *Sobrevivo* (*I Survive,* 1978), *Suma y sique* (*Add and Carry,* 1981), (edited with Flakoll) *Nuevas Voces de Norteamerica* (*New Voices of North America,* 1981), *Flowers from the Volcano* (poetry collection translated by Carolyn Forché, 1982), (edited with Flakoll) *Nicaragua: La Revolucíon sandinista: Un crónica política 1955–1979* (*Nicaragua: The Sandinista Revolution, a Political chronicle,* 1982), *Despierta mi bien despierta* (*Awake, My Love, Awake,* 1986), *Woman of the River* (poetry trans. by Flakoll, 1989), *Y este poema-rio* (*And This River Poem,* 1989), and *Fugas* (*Fugues,* 1993). ❖ See also Sandra M. Boschetto-Sandoval and Marcia Phillips McGowan, eds., *Claribel Alegría and Central American Literature* (Ohio University); and *Women in World History.*

ALEKSANDRA. *Variant of Alexandra.*

ALEKSANDROVNA, Vera (1895–1966). Russian émigré literary critic, historian, and editor. Born Vera Aleksandrovna Mordvinova in Russia, 1895; died in New York, NY, in 1966; studied in Odessa and Moscow; m. S.M. Shvarts (Menshevik activist), who introduced her to Marxist theories, in 1919. ❖ Opposed to Lenin's concept of a proletarian dictatorship, became a Menshevik with beliefs similar to that of the Social Democratic movements of Western Europe; with husband, went into exile in Germany (1921), where she contributed to the émigré Menshevik magazine *Sotsialisticheski vestnik* (*Socialist Herald*); with the advent of Nazism, fled to France (1933); with invasion of France, fled to US (1940) where she contributed to émigré journals *Novoe russkoe slovo* and *Novyi zhurnal* and wrote for a number of English-language periodicals; worked with anthropologist Margaret Mead; served as editor-in-chief of Chekhov Publishing House (1951–56), one of the leading voices of Russian émigré intelligentsia; worked on English-language editions of histories of Soviet literature, which gained wide critical acclaim. ❖ See also *Women in World History.*

ALEKSEEVA, Galina (1946—). *See Alekseyeva, Galina.*

ALEKSEEVA, Lidiya (1909—). Russian émigré poet. Name variations: Lidiia Alekseevna Alekseeva. Born Lidiya Alekseeva Devel in Dvinsk, Russia, 1909. ❖ At 7, began to write poetry; with the advent of Bolshevism, left Russia for Yugoslavia (1920), where she spent the next 2 decades, then immigrated to US (1949); was a significant poet of the Russian literary emigration; also published a number of delicately tinted, lyrical prose miniatures. ❖ See also *Women in World History.*

ALEKSEYEVA, Galina (1946—). Soviet diver. Name variations: Galina Alekseeva. Born Nov 27, 1946, in USSR. ❖ At Tokyo Olympics, won a bronze medal in platform (1964).

ALEKSEYEVA, Galina (1950—). *See Alekseyeva-Kreft, Galina.*

ALEKSEYEVA-KREFT, Galina (1950—). Soviet kayaker. Name variations: Galina Alekseeva Kreft; Galina Alexeyeva. Born Mar 14, 1950, in USSR. ❖ At Olympics, won a gold medal in K2 500 meters in Montreal (1976) and a silver medal in Moscow (1980).

ALEKSEYEVNA, Sophia (1657–1704). *See Sophia Alekseyevna.*

ALEKSIU, Elli (1894–1988). *See Alexiou, Elli.*

ALENÇON, Emilienne d' (fl. late 1800s). French courtesan. Name variations: Emilienne d'Alencon. Fl. in the late 1800s. ❖ Famed courtesan, ran away from home at 15 with a Gypsy (Roma) violinist; appeared at the Cirque d'Eté; had the "protection" of Leopold II, king of the Belgians, and Jacques, Duc d'Uzès, until his mortified family shipped him off to a regiment in Africa where he died of dysentery. ❖ See also *Women in World History.*

ALENIKOFF, Frances (1920—). American dancer. Born Aug 20, 1920, in New York, NY. ❖ Worked in composition workshops with Doris Humphrey, Anna Sokolow, Lester Horton and others; founded own Aviv Theater of Dance and Song (1959); began integrating film, slides, and musical scores in multimedia works (1968); participated in Kei Takei's *Light,* part VIII (c. 1974); collaborated as choreographer with numerous visual artists, poets and composers and created photomontages for exhibits; also worked for theater in *Zaide* (1957), *Josephine Baker Show on Broadway* (1964), *Joan and the Devil* (1978); worked on films including *Alenka* (1969) and *Shaping Things—A Choreographic Journal* (1977); works of choreography include *Incantation* (1956); *And the Desert Shall Rejoice* (1959); *Shango* (1963); *Interior Journey* (1967); *Territories and Refractions* (1968); *The One of No Way* (1970); *Pomegranate* (1973); *Moon of the Break Up of Ice* (1974); *Fresh Water-Earth* (1976); *Line Drawings* (1978).

ALEOTTI, Raffaella (c. 1570–c. 1646). Italian composer. Probably born in 1570; probably died in 1646; dau. of Giovanni Battista (architect to Alphonso II d'Este, duke of Ferrara); elder sister of Vittoria Aleotti; studied harpsichord and composition with Alessandro Milleville and Ercole Pasquini; entered the Augustinian convent of San Vito, Ferrara; wrote some of the earliest Italian music in the concertante style. ❖ After entering the Augustinian convent at a young age, took her vows (1590); took over the direction of the *concerto grande,* the convent's main ensemble (1593), which consisted of 23 singers and instrumentalists who played the harpsichord, lute, bass viol, flute, cornet, and trombone; performed with ensemble in the presence of Pope Clement VIII and the queen of Spain, Margaret of Austria (1598); probably composed a great deal of music but only her *Sacrae cantiones... liber primus* for 5, 7, 8 and 10 voices has survived.

ALEOTTI, Vittoria (c. 1573–c. 1620). Italian composer. Probably born in 1573; probably died 1620; dau. of Giovanni Battista (architect to Alphonso II d'Este, duke of Ferrara); younger sister of Raffaella Aleotti; studied harpsichord and composition with Alessandro Milleville and

Ercole Pasquini. ❖ After entering the San Vito convent at Ferrara, assisted sister Raffaella with the musical ensemble, writing many pieces for the group; saw one of her madrigals for 5 voices included alongside leading Ferrarese madrigalists in the famous anthology *Il giardino de musici ferrarsei* (1591); also wrote 4-part madrigals which were included in *Ghirlanda de madrigali*, compiled by her father.

ALERAMO, Sibilla (1876–1960). *See Pierangeli, Rina Faccio.*

ALEXANDER, Annie Montague (1867–1949). American naturalist. Born in Honolulu, Hawaii, 1867; died in 1949; lived with Louise Kellogg. ❖ Devoting her life to the fields of paleontology, botany, ornithology, and mammology, went on a series of expeditions to Alaska, where she collected a large number of skulls of different mammal species and discovered a new subspecies of grizzly bear, *Ursus alexandrae*, which was named after her; founded the Museum of Vertebrate Zoology and the Museum of Paleontology at the University of California, Berkeley; with Louise Kellogg, collected over 17,851 botanical specimens for University of California Herbarium, including a new and rare species of grass, named *Swallennia alexandrae*. ❖ See also *Women in World History.*

ALEXANDER, Buffy (c. 1977—). Canadian rower. Born c. 1977 in North York, Ontario, Canada. ❖ Won a bronze medal for coxed eights at Sydney Olympics (2000).

ALEXANDER, Caroline (1859–1932). *See Wittpenn, Caroline.*

ALEXANDER, Cecil Frances (1818–1895). Irish children's hymn writer and poet. Name variations: C.F. Alexander; Mrs. Cecil Frances Alexander. Born Cecil Frances Humphreys in Co. Wicklow in 1818; died in Londonderry, Oct 12, 1895; dau. of Major John Humphreys; m. William Alexander, Protestant bishop of Derry (afterwards archbishop of Armagh and primate of all Ireland), 1850; children: 2 girls and 2 boys, including Robert, who was awarded the Newdigate Prize for English Verse while at Oxford. ❖ With Lady Harriet Howard, wrote tracts for the Oxford Movement; wrote 400 hymns, while her poetry, celebrating the rugged beauty of rural Ireland, was the impetus for many others, including "Once in Royal David's City," "Roseate Hue of Early Dawn," "There is a Green Hill Far Away," and "All Things Bright and Beautiful"; most famous poems were "The Siege of Derry" and "The Burial of Moses." ❖ See also *Women in World History.*

ALEXANDER, Claire (1898–1927). American film dancer. Born 1898 in New York, NY; died of double pneumonia, Nov 16, 1927, in Alhambra, California. ❖ Appeared on screen as one of Mack Sennett's Bathing Beauties and frequently in crowd scenes dancing the Charleston or Black Bottom; appeared in Vitaphone "Jerry" serials (1914–17), including *Jerry's Big Mystery, Jerry's Brilliant Scheme, Jerry's Romance, Jerry's Best Friend;* other films include *A Girl of Yesterday* (1915) and *Charlie the Hero* (1919).

ALEXANDER, Dorothy (1904–1986). American ballet dancer and choreographer. Name variations: Dorothea Sydney Moses. Born Dorothea Sydney Moses, April 22, 1904, in Atlanta, Georgia; died Nov 17, 1986, in Atlanta; graduated from Atlanta Normal Training School, 1925; studied at University of Georgia and Emory University; Oglethorpe College, BA in Education, 1930; studied dance during summers with Michel Fokine, Irma Duncan, Yeichi Nimura, Tatiana Chamié, Bronislava Nijinska, Ted Shawn, Hanya Holm, and at Sadler's Wells (now Royal) Ballet School in London. ❖ Major contributor to regional ballet movement in US and founder of the Atlanta Ballet, studied dance in New York and London before opening her own studio in Atlanta, La Petite École de Dance (1921), now the Atlanta School of Ballet; introduced dance classes in Atlanta public schools (starting 1927) where she recruited dancers to join Dorothy Alexander Concert Group (1929), 1st regional ballet company, later becoming Atlanta Civic Ballet (1944) and Atlanta Ballet; worked as artistic director and principal choreographer for Atlanta Ballet, the country's oldest civic ballet, until retirement (mid-1960s); hosted 1st regional ballet festival (1956) bringing together companies from all over southeastern US, a festival which helped lead to the establishment of National Association for Regional Ballet (1963); choreographed such works as *A Benefit Bridge Party, Gypsy Interlude, Kasperle; The Little Fairy Who Couldn't Dance, Pierrot's Song, Woman in War* (late 1940s), *Fireworks Suite* (1956), *Green Altars* (1958), (with Hilda Gumm) *Twelve Dancing Princesses* (late 1950s), and *Soliloquy* (1963).

ALEXANDER, Ella (1858–1952). *See Boole, Ella.*

ALEXANDER, Florence (1904–1993). American artist's agent. Born in 1904; died of pneumonia at New York University Hospital on Nov 30, 1993. ❖ After a publishing career in Philadelphia, moved to Manhattan to work in advertising; later founded her own agency, representing such artist-illustrators as Tomie dePaola, Gail Gibbons, Janet Stevens and Marilyn Hirsh.

ALEXANDER, Francesca (1837–1917). Author, artist, folklorist and charitable worker. Name variations: Esther Frances Alexander; Francesca or Fanny Alexander. Born Francesca Alexander, Feb 27, 1837, in Boston, Massachusetts; died in Florence, Italy, Jan 21, 1917; dau. of Lucia Gray (Swett) and Francis Alexander. ❖ Settled in Florence and attended the Christian Evangelical Church; dedicated life, as well as money earned from portraits and drawings, to assisting poor and sick; collected folklore of the Italian peasants, which she recorded in art and writing; made 1st contact with John Ruskin (1882), who promoted her works, including the illus. "Roadside Songs of Tuscany" (pub. by Ruskin as *Roadside Songs* in 1884–85), earning her international renown. Other writings include *The Story of Ida* (1883), *Christ's Folk in the Apennines* (1887–89), *Tuscan Songs* (1897) and *The Hidden Servants and Other Very Old Stories Told Over* (1900). ❖ See also Constance Grosvenor Alexander, *Francesca Alexander: A "Hidden Servant"* (1927); Lucia Gray Swett, *John Ruskin's Letters to Francesca and Memoirs of the Alexanders* (1931).

ALEXANDER, Gwen (1951—). *See Cheeseman, Gwen.*

ALEXANDER, Hattie (1901–1968). American microbiologist, pediatrician, and researcher. Born Hattie Elizabeth Alexander in Baltimore, Maryland, April 5, 1901; died June 24, 1968, in New York, NY; dau. of William B. and Elsie M. (Townsend) Alexander; Goucher College, AB, 1923; Johns Hopkins, Maryland, 1930; never married; no children; lived with Elizabeth Ufford. ❖ An early pioneer in DNA research, was the 1st woman to serve as president of the American Pediatric Society; discovered the 1st cure for pediatric influenza meningitis; was one of the 1st researchers to note bacterial resistance to antibiotics; collaborated with Grace Leidy, noting changes in DNA, which was very early research in this field. Received the E. Mead Johnson Award for Research in Pediatrics (1942), the prestigious Stevens Triennial Prize (1954), and the Oscar B. Hunter Memorial Award of the American Therapeutic Society (1961). ❖ See also *Women in World History.*

ALEXANDER, Jane (1939—). American actress. Born Jane Quigley, Oct 28, 1939, in Boston, Massachusetts; m. Edwin Sherrin (director); children: Jace Alexander (actor). ❖ Made stage debut in Boston as a child; appeared at the Arena Stage in Washington, DC (1966–69, 1970); made Broadway debut in *The Great White Hope* (1961), followed by *6 Rms Riv Vu, Find Your Way Home, Hamlet* (Gertrude), *The Heiress* and *First Monday in October;* films include *The New Centurions, All the President's Men* and *The Betsy;* on tv, appeared in "Eleanor and Franklin" (1976); appointed chair of the National Endowment for the Arts (1993). Received Tony (1961) and an Oscar nomination (1970) for performance in *The Great White Hope*; won an Emmy for Best Supporting Actress in "Playing for Time" (1981); nominated for Oscars for *Kramer vs. Kramer* (1979) and *Testament* (1983).

ALEXANDER, Janet (d. 1961). English actress. Name variations: Mrs. Lauderdale Maitland. Born in Ewell, Surrey, England; died June 28, 1961; m. Lauderdale Maitland. ❖ Made West End debut as Kate Meredith in *A Man of His Word* (1901); other appearances include Lady Eileen in *Love in a Cottage*, Mary Brooke in *Brooke of Brazenose*, Hortense in *The Great Conspiracy*, and Lady Amberley in *Nell Gwynne*; made film debut (1916).

ALEXANDER, Janet (1907–1994). *See McNeill, Janet.*

ALEXANDER, Jessie (1876–1962). New Zealand deaconess and missionary. Born on June 2, 1876, in Brantford, Ontario, Canada; died on Mar 27, 1962, in Auckland, New Zealand; dau. of William Alexander (carpenter) and Mary (Munro) Alexander. ❖ Immigrated to New Zealand with family as child; trained at Presbyterian Women's Training Institute in Dunedin, then was ordained deaconess (1913); assigned to Nuhaka, a remote village east of Wairoa; studied Maori language and carried out medical work in community; instrumental in establishment of hospital in Nuhaka; opened missionary work in Waikaremoana, where she was regarded as a healer; after retirement (mid-1930s), established hostels in Auckland for young Maori seeking jobs; was a founding member of United Maori Mission and taught Maori at New Zealand Bible Training Institute. MBE, 1947.

ALEXANDER, Julie (1938–2003). English model and actress. Born May 9, 1938, in Fulham, West London, England; died of Alzheimer's disease, Jan 31, 2003, in Battersea; m. Robert Breckman, 1979. ❖ Successful model (1960s); as an actress appeared as Rosalie Dawn in the comedy film classic *The Pure Hell of St. Trinian's* (1960); was also featured in *Dentist in the Chair* (1960), *The Terror of Tongs* (1961) and *A Matter of Who;* collected Staffordshire ceramics that were eventually donated to Victoria and Albert Museum; diagnosed with Alzheimer's (1993), entered a nursing center (1996).

ALEXANDER, Katherine (1898–1981). American actress. Name variations: Katharine Alexander. Born Sept 22, 1898, in Fort Smith, Arkansas; died Jan 10, 1981, in Tryon, North Carolina; m. William A. Brady Jr. ❖ Made stage debut in Washington, DC, and NY debut (both 1917) as Julie Partington in *A Successful Calamity;* other appearances include Peggy O'Neal Eaton in *That Awful Mrs. Eaton,* Sally in *Gentle Grafters,* Princess Anne in *The Queen's Husband,* and alternating the part of Raina in *Arms and the Man* with Lynn Fontanne; made film debut (1933) in *Should Ladies Behave?;* other films include *The Barretts of Wimpole Street, The Painted Veil, The Hunchback of Notre Dame* and *Kiss and Tell.*

ALEXANDER, Leni (1924—). German-born Chilean composer. Born June 8, 1924, in Breslau, Germany (today Wroclaw, Poland). ❖ Lived in Hamburg, Germany, until 1939 when forced by Nazi persecution to flee with family to Chile; continued musical studies in Santiago, concentrating on piano and cello; began to study composition (1949); became Chilean citizen (1952); studied in France and Italy (1954–55) with such composers as René Leibowitz, Olivier Messiaen, Luigi Nono, and Bruno Maderna; as a modernist, did not expect her compositions to become popular, but many of them gained her respect from fellow composers and small but growing circles of listeners. ❖ See also *Women in World History.*

ALEXANDER, Lisa (1968—). Canadian synchronized swimmer. Born Sept 22, 1968, in Toronto, Ontario, Canada. ❖ Won gold medals for solo and duet at Commonwealth Games (1994); won a team silver medal at Atlanta Olympics (1996). Won Helen Vanderburg Trophy (1991, 1993–95).

ALEXANDER, Lucy Maclay (fl. 1950s). American chef. Born Lucy Maclay Alexander in Maryland; dau. of Margaret Elizabeth Maclay and Robert Alexander. ❖ Employed by the US Bureau of Home Nutrition and Home Economics, where she developed recipes using the lesser cuts of meat available in America during WWII rationing; received the Distinguished Service Medal of the US Department of Agriculture (1950), the 1st woman to be so honored.

ALEXANDER, Mary (1693–1760). American businesswoman. Name variations: Mary Provoost. Born Mary Spratt, April 17, 1693, in New York, NY; died April 18, 1760, in New York, NY; m. Samuel Provoost, Oct 15, 1711 (died c. 1720); m. James Alexander, Jan 5, 1721; children: (1st m.) 3; (2nd m.) 7, including William (6th earl of Stirling).i ❖ Invested nheritance in trading enterprises of 1st husband, then continued after his death; promoted career of 2nd husband, a leading NY and NJ political figure, and maintained a strong interest in NY politics in her own right; operated a successful store which sold colony products as well as a large quantity of imported goods.

ALEXANDER, Mrs. (1825–1902). *See Hector, Annie French.*

ALEXANDER, Muriel (1898–1975). Irish actress. Born Sept 12, 1898, in Dublin, Ireland (some sources cite Cape Town, South Africa); died Mar 1975, in Johannesburg, South Africa; attended RADA; m. Dr. J. Reid-Banks. ❖ Made stage debut in Belfast in *My America* (1916), London debut as Dot Carrington in *Over Sunday* (1920); other appearances include Fanny Willoughby in *Quality Street,* Paula Towers in *The Torchbearers,* Peg in *Peg o' My Heart* and Lisbeth Rysing in *If Four Walls Told.*

ALEXANDER, Sadie (1898–1989). African-American lawyer and civil-rights activist. Born Sadie Tanner Mosell, Jan 2, 1898, in Philadelphia, Pennsylvania; died Nov 1, 1989, in Philadelphia; dau. of Aaron Albert Mossell and Mary Louise Tanner; University of Pennsylvania, BS, 1918, MA, 1919; graduate of University of Pennsylvania School of Law, 1927; m. Raymond Pace Alexander (lawyer), Nov 29, 1923; children: Mary Alexander Brown and Rae Alexander Minter. ❖ Was the 1st African-American woman to practice law in Pennsylvania; served as secretary of the National Bar Association; was an activist for civil rights; appointed by Jimmy Carter to chair White House Conference on Aging.

ALEXANDER, Sheila (b. 1928). *See Lerwill, Sheila.*

ALEXANDER, Wendy. Scottish politician. Born in Glasgow, Scotland. ❖ Served as special advisor to Donald Dewar (1997) and was involved in drafting the White Paper that led to the establishment of the Scottish Parliament; elected as a Labour candidate to represent for Paisley North in the Scottish Parliament (1999) and appointed minister of Communities; appointed minister for Enterprise (2000), then transport minister (2001); resigned (2002).

ALEXANDRA (r. 76–67 BCE). Queen of Judea. Name variations: Salome Alexandra; Alexandra Salome. Birth date unknown; died 67 BCE; m. King Alexander Jannaeus (or Jannæus) of the Asmonean, also known as the Hasmonean or Hasmonian, dynasty (Syria), who ruled from 103–76 BCE; children: John Hyrcanus II (d. 30 BCE); Aristobulus II. ❖ Succeeding her husband, was the ruler of the Maccabees in Judea (76–67 BCE, some sources cite 78–69) during the continued conflict between the Sadducees and Pharisees; in a reversal of husband's policies, supported the Pharisees. ❖ See also *Women in World History.*

ALEXANDRA (d. 27 BCE). Hasmonian royal. Died in 27 BCE; dau. of John Hyrcanus II (d. 30 BCE); granddau. of Alexandra (r. 76–67 BCE); m. her cousin Alexander (d. 49 BCE, son of Aristobulus II); children: Mariamne the Hasmonian (d. 29 BCE); Aristobulus III (d. 36 BCE).

ALEXANDRA (1921–1993). Queen of Yugoslavia. Name variations: Alexandra Oldenburg; Alexandra of Greece. Born in Athens, Greece, Mar 25, 1921; died at home outside London, Sept 30, 1993; dau. of Alexander I, King of the Hellenes, and Aspasia Manos (dau. of a royal equerry); great-grandchild of Queen Victoria; m. Peter II, the last king of Yugoslavia, Mar 20, 1944, at Yugoslav Legation in London (died 1970); children: Alexander Karadjordjevic (b. July 17, 1945). ❖ Born into Greek royalty (1921), 5 months after her father died of blood poisoning from the bite of a pet monkey; by age 3, was exiled in England because of shifting Greek politics; did not reappear in Greece until 13 years later, when her uncle King George II returned to rule (1935); when the Germans overran Greece during WWII, fled with mother to London; while there, met Peter II, king of Yugoslavia, who was in exile and studying at Cambridge; married Peter (1944) but was formally deposed when Marshal Tito established a communist regime in Yugoslavia; was left virtually penniless when the royal property was confiscated. ❖ See also *Women in World History.*

ALEXANDRA, Queen of England (1844–1925). *See Alexandra of Denmark.*

ALEXANDRA FEODOROVNA (1798–1860). *See Charlotte of Prussia.*

ALEXANDRA FEODOROVNA (1872–1918). Empress of Russia. Name variations: Alix or Alexandra of Hesse-Darmstadt; christened Princess Alix Victoria Helena Louise Beatrice, Princess of Hesse-Darmstadt, changed name to Russian form and took a Russian title of nobility, becoming Grand Duchess Alexandra Feodorovna at the time of marriage. Born June 6, 1872, in city of Darmstadt, in German principality of Hesse-Darmstadt; murdered along with family by Communist authorities, July 16–17, 1918, at Ekaterinburg in western Siberia; dau. of Prince Louis of Hesse-Darmstadt and Princess Alice Maud Mary (1843–1878) of Great Britain; granddau. of Queen Victoria; m. Nicholas II, tsar of Russia, 1894; children: Olga (1895–1918); Tatiana (1897–1918); Marie (1899–1918); Anastasia (1901–1918); Alexis (1904–1918). ❖ Played a major role in undermining the stability of the Russian monarchy during the 1st part of the 20th century; married Nicholas, who had just become Tsar Nicholas II on death of Alexander III (1894); gave birth to 4 girls (1895–1901); during Russo-Japanese War, gave birth to Alexis (1904), who suffered from hemophilia, for which she felt responsible (hemophilia is passed down to a child by its mother); searched desperately for people outside regular medical community who could help her son, and began to rely heavily on Rasputin, who saved Alexis from a critical attack (1905); dismissed popular unrest in Russia and urged Nicholas to resist any moves to change the top-heavy political system; with husband, isolated herself at Tsarskoe Seloe palace outside St. Petersburg, as hundreds were shot in front of the Winter Palace on "Bloody Sunday" (1905); with outbreak of revolution, exerted an important influence on Nicholas, strengthening his own conservative inclinations; objected when Rasputin was expelled from St. Petersburg (1911); her dependency on Rasputin grew along with his influence; during WWI, persuaded husband to leave St. Petersburg to command Russian army (1915); with Rasputin at her side, took over role of ruling monarch; was devastated when conservative plotters murdered Rasputin (1916); with husband, dethroned during March Revolution, then arrested and exiled to Siberia in November Revolution (1917); executed with Nicholas and their children (1918). ❖ See also Robert K. Massie, *Nicholas and Alexandra* (Atheneum, 1967); G. King, *The Last Empress* (Birch Lane, 1995); and film "Nicholas and Alexandra," starring Janet Suzman (Columbia, 1971); and *Women in World History.*

ALEXANDRA GUELPH (1882–1963). Grand Duchess of Mecklenburg-Schwerin. Born Alexandra Louise Marie Olga in Gmunden, Austria, Sept 29, 1882; died in Glucksburg, Schleswig-Holstein, Germany, Aug 30, 1963; dau. of Ernest Augustus, 3rd duke of Cumberland and Teviotdale, and Thyra Oldenburg (sister of Alexandra of Denmark and Empress Marie Feodorovna of Russia); m. Frederick Francis IV, grand duke of Mecklenburg-Schwerin, June 7, 1904; children: Frederick Francis (b. 1910), Christian Louis (b. 1912, duke of Mecklenburg-Schwerin), Thyra Anastasia (b. 1919), and Anastasia Alexandrine (b. 1922).

ALEXANDRA NIKOLAEVNA (1825–1844). Landgravine of Hesse-Cassel. Name variations: Alexandra Nicholaievna; Alexandra Romanov. Born June 12, 1825; died Aug 10, 1844; dau. of Charlotte of Prussia (1798–1860) and Nicholas I (1796–1855), tsar of Russia (r. 1825–1855); m. Frederick William, landgrave of Hesse-Cassel, Jan 28, 1844. Frederick William was also m. to Anne Frederica (1836–1918).

ALEXANDRA OF DENMARK (1844–1925). Queen-consort of England. Name variations: Princess Alexandra of Schleswig-Holstein-Sönderborg-Glücksborg; Alexandra Oldenburg; Queen Alexandra; Alix, Princess of Wales. Born Alexandra Caroline Marie Charlotte Louise Julia, Dec 1, 1844, at Gule Palace in Copenhagen, Denmark; died at Sandringham, Norfolk, England, Nov 20, 1925; eldest dau. of Prince Christian of Schleswig-Holstein-Sönderborg-Glücksborg (future Christian IX) and Louise of Hesse-Cassel (dau. of the Landgrave William of Hesse-Cassel); sister of Thyra Oldenburg and Marie Feodorovna (1847–1928, Russian empress and wife of Tsar Alexander III of Russia); m. Albert Edward, prince of Wales (heir to the British throne as Edward VII), Mar 10, 1863; children: (2 sons) Albert Victor (duke of Clarence, who predeceased his father) and George (duke of York, prince of Wales, and King George V); (3 daughters) Louise Victoria (1867–1931, princess royal and duchess of Fife), Victoria (1868–1935), and Maud (1869–1938, queen of Norway). ❖ Remembered for her classical beauty and interest in charities and social relief programs, met the Prince of Wales (1861); betrothed (1862), then married (1863); a breathtakingly handsome woman with a graceful demeanor, became an immediate and lasting favorite of the British public; made official trips with husband to several countries (1864–81); became queen-consort to King Edward VII on his accession to the throne (1902); tolerated husband's many liaisons and stood by his side in scandals; established Queen Alexandra Imperial Military Nursing Service (1902); raised large amounts of revenue to help unemployed workmen during economic crisis (1906); invited Edward's current mistress, Alice Keppel, to visit him during his fatal illness; became dowager queen following Edward VII's death (1910). Granted Order of the Garter (1902); "Alexandra Day" established in her honor (1913). ❖ See also Georgina Battiscombe, *Queen Alexandra* (Houghton Mifflin, 1969); Graham and Heather Fisher *Bertie and Alix: Anatomy of a Marriage* (R. Hale, 1974); George C.A. Arthur, *Queen Alexandra* (Chapman & Hall, 1934); and *Women in World History.*

ALEXANDRA OF HESSE-DARMSTADT (1872–1918). *See Alexandra Feodorovna.*

ALEXANDRA OF KENT (1936—). Princess. Name variations: Princess Alexandra Windsor; The Hon. Mrs. Angus Ogilvy. Born Alexandra Helen Elizabeth Olga Christabel, Dec 25, 1936, in London, England; dau. of George Windsor, 1st duke of Kent, and Marina of Greece (1906–1968); studied at Heathfield School, 1947, 1st British princess to attend a public school; m. Angus Ogilvy, April 24, 1963; children: James Ogilvy (b. 1964), Marina Ogilvy (b. 1966). ❖ Patron of many charities, including Princess Mary's RAF Nursing Service.

ALEXANDRA OF OLDENBURG (1838–1900). Russian royal. Born Alexandra Fredericka Wilhelmina, June 2, 1838; died April 25, 1900; dau. of Peter (b. 1812), duke of Oldenburg, and Therese of Nassau (b. 1815); granddau. of Duke William of Nassau and Louise of Saxe-Altenburg; m. Nicholas Nicholaevitch (son of Nicholas I of Russia and Charlotte of Prussia), Feb 6, 1856; children: Nicholas Nicholaevitch (b. 1856, who m. Anastasia Petrovitch-Njegos); Peter Nicholaevitch (b. 1864, who m. Militza of Montenegro).

ALEXANDRA OF SAXE-ALTENBURG (1830–1911). Russian royal. Name variations: Elizabeth Alexandra of Saxe-Altenburg. Born Alexandra Fredericka Henrietta Pauline Marianne Elizabeth, July 8, 1830; died July 6, 1911; dau. of Joseph, duke of Saxe-Altenburg, and Amelia of Wurttemberg (1799–1848); m. Constantine Nicholaevitch (son of Nicholas I of Russia and Charlotte of Prussia), Sept 11, 1848; children: Nicholas (b. 1850); Olga Constantinovna (1851–1926, who m. George I, king of the Hellenes); Vera Constantinovna (1854–1912); Constantine Constantinovitch (b. 1858); Dmitri (b. 1860); Vladislav (b. 1862).

ALEXANDRA OLDENBURG (1844–1925). *See Alexandra of Denmark.*

ALEXANDRA OLDENBURG (1870–1891). Greek princess. Name variations: Alexandra of Greece. Born Aug 18, 1870; died at age 21, 6 days after birth of son, Sept 12, 1891; dau. of George I, king of Hellenes, and Olga Constantinovna; m. Paul Alexandrovitch (son of Alexander II of Russia and Marie of Hesse-Darmstadt, grand duke, June 5, 1889; children: Marie Pavlovna (1890–1958); Dmitri Pavlovitch (b. 1891).

ALEXANDRA PAVLOVNA (1783–1801). Archduchess of Austria. Born Aug 9, 1783; died Mar 16, 1801; dau. of Sophia Dorothea of Wurttemberg (1759–1828) and Paul I (1754–1801), tsar of Russia (r. 1796–1801); m. Joseph, archduke of Austria, Oct 30, 1799; children: Alexandrine (1801–1801).

ALEXANDRA SAXE-COBURG (1878–1942). Princess of Hohenlohe-Langenburg. Name variations: Alexandra of Saxe-Coburg. Born Alexandra Louise Olga Victoria, Sept 1, 1878, in Coburg, Bavaria, Germany; died April 16, 1942, at Schwabisch Hall, Baden-Wurttemberg, Germany; dau. of Alfred Saxe-Coburg, duke of Edinburgh (son of Queen Victoria) and Marie Alexandrovna (1853–1920); sister of Marie of Rumania; m. Ernest, 7th prince of Hohenlohe-Langenburg, April 20, 1896; children: Godfrey (b. 1897), 8th prince of Hohenlohe-Langenburg; Marie-Melita of Hohenlohe-Langenburg (b. 1899); Alexandra of Hohenlohe-Langenburg (b. 1901); Irma of Hohenlohe-Langenburg (1902–1986); Alfred (b. 1911).

ALEXANDRA VICTORIA (1891–1959). Princess Arthur of Connaught, duchess of Fife. Name variations: Alexandra Duff and Countess of Macduff. Born Alexandra Victoria Alberta Edwina Louise Duff, May 17, 1891, in Richmond-upon-Thames, Surrey, England; died Feb 26, 1959, in London; elder dau. of Alexander Duff, 1st duke of Fife, and of Louise Victoria (1867–1931, dau. of Edward VII); m. Arthur Windsor, Prince Arthur of Connaught, 1913; children: Alastair Windsor, 2nd duke of Connaught and Strathearn. ❖ Succeeded father, becoming duchess of Fife (1912); took up nursing and practiced at St. Mary's Hospital in Paddington (1915–19), while with husband in South Africa (1920–23), and at University College and Charing Cross hospitals; also ran the Fife Nursing Home in London (1939–49).

ALEXANDRA VICTORIA OF SCHLESWIG-HOLSTEIN (1887–1957). German royal. Name variations: Alexandra of Schleswig; Alexandra Victoria of Schleswig-Holstein-Sonderburg-Glucksburg. Born Alexandra Victoria Augusta Leopoldine Charlotte Amelia Wilhelmina, April 21, 1887, in Grunholz, Germany; died April 15, 1957, in Lyon, France; dau. of Frederick Ferdinand, duke of Schleswig-Holstein-Sonderburg-Glucksburg, and Caroline Matilda of Schleswig-Holstein (1860–1932); m. Augustus William (son of Kaiser Wilhelm II and Augusta of Schleswig-Holstein), Oct 22, 1908 (div. 1920); m. Arnold Rumann, Jan 7, 1922 (div. 1933); children: (1st m.) Alexander Ferdinand (b. 1912), prince of Prussia.

ALEXANDRINA OF BADEN (1820–1904). Duchess of Saxe-Coburg and Gotha. Name variations: Alexandrine. Born Alexandrina Louise Amelia Fredericka Elizabeth Sophia Zahringen on Dec 6, 1820; died Dec 20, 1904; dau. of Leopold, grand duke of Baden, and Sophia of Sweden (1801–1865, dau. of Gustavus IV Adolphus of Sweden); m. Ernest II, duke of Saxe-Coburg and Gotha, May 3, 1842.

ALEXANDRINA OF MECKLENBURG-SCHWERIN (1879–1952). Queen of Denmark. Name variations: Alexandrine Augustine, Duchess of Mecklenburg-Schwerin. Born Alexandrina Augusta von Mecklenburg-Schwerin, Dec 24, 1879; died Dec 28, 1952; dau. of Frederick Francis III, grand duke of Mecklenburg-Schwerin, and Anastasia Romanova (1860–1922, granddau. of Nicholas I of Russia and Charlotte of Prussia); m. Christian X, king of Denmark (r. 1912–1947), April 26, 1898; children: Frederick IX, king of Denmark (r. 1947–1972), who m. Ingrid of Sweden); Knud also known as Canute (b. 1900).

ALEXANDRINE OF PRUSSIA (1803–1892). Grand Duchess of Mecklenburg-Schwerin. Born Feb 23, 1803; died April 21, 1892; dau. of Louise of Prussia (1776–1810) and Frederick William III (1770–1840), king of Prussia (r. 1797–1840); m. Paul Frederick (b. 1800), grand duke of Mecklenburg-Schwerin; children: Frederick Francis II (b. 1823), grand duke of Mecklenburg; William, duke of Mecklenburg-Schwerin (b. 1827).

ALEXEEVNA, Sophia (1657–1704). *See Sophia Alekseyevna.*

ALEXEYEVA, Galina (1950—). *See Alekseyeva-Kreft, Galina.*

ALEXIOU, Elli (1894–1988). Greek novelist, playwright, and teacher. Name variations: Elli Aleksiu or Alexiu; Elli Alexioy. Born in 1894 in Herakleion, Crete; died 1988 in Athens, Greece; dau. of a prominent journalist; sister of Galateia Kazantzaki (writer and wife of writer Nikos Kazantzakis); studied at Sorbonne in Paris, France; m. Vasso Daskalakios (Greek writer). ❖ Joined the Greek Communist Party (1928) and remained involved with various left-wing causes throughout her life; during WWII, worked with a Communist resistance group; deprived of her Greek citizenship, lived in Eastern Europe (1950s); returned to Greece (1962); writings include *Hard Struggles for a Short Life* (1931), *The Third Christian School for Girls* (1934), *Louben* (1940), *Tributaries* (1956), *Spondi* (1963), *And So On* (1965), *That He May Be Great* (1966), *The Reigning One* (1972), and *Demolished Mansions* (1977). ❖ See also Deborah Tannen, "Elli Alexiou: An Informal Portrait" in *The Charioteer* issue on Nikos Kazantzakis (22 and 23: 1980–81).

ALEXIOY, Elli (1894–1988). *See Alexiou, Elli.*

ALEXSANDRA. *Variant of Alexandra.*

ALEXSEYEVNA, Yekaterina or Catherine (1684–1727). *See Catherine I.*

ALEY, Ellen Elizabeth (1869–1930). *See Ferner, Ellen Elizabeth.*

ALF, Fé (c. 1910—). German dancer. Name variations: Fe Alf. Born c. 1910 in Germany. ❖ Joined Mary Wigman school and danced in *Totemal* (1929); moved to New York to assist Hanya Holm, who was then director of Wigman school in US (1931); opened own studio (1933) and performed as concert dancer primarily in own works, including *Rhapsodic Dance* (1933), *Cycle of the City* (1933–37), and *Duet for Clarinet and Dancer* (1937); formed Theater Dance Company, a cooperative dance group, with George Bockman, William Bales, Sybil Shearer, and others (1938), but soon merged with Jack Cole's nightclub act due to lack of concerts; ceased performing (c. 1939) and taught dance classes in and around NYC. Further works of choreography include *Summer Witchery* (1933); *Dance Song* (1933); *Promenade* (1935); *Upon the Death of the Loved Ones* (1935); *Birds and Man* (1935); *Triadic Progression* (1937); *Sola* (1937).

ALFEYEVA, Lidiya (1946—). Soviet long jumper. Name variations: Lidia Alfeyeva. Born Jan 17, 1946, in USSR. ❖ At Montreal Olympics, won a bronze medal in the long jump (1976).

ALFIFA (c. 1000–1044). *See Elfgifu of Northampton.*

ALFON, Estrella (1917–1982). Filipino fiction writer. Born in Cebu City, Philippines, 1917; died in 1982. ❖ Published short-story collection *Magnificence and Other Stories* (1960).

ALFORD, Marianne Margaret (1817–1888). English artist. Name variations: Lady Marian Alford, Viscountess Alford. Born 1817; died 1888; dau. of Spencer Compton, 2nd marquis of Northampton; m. John Hume Cust, Viscount Alford (son of Earl Brownlow), 1841. ❖ Friend to leading artists of her day, helped found the Royal School of Art Needlework in Kensington and published *Needlework as Art* (1886).

ALGERANOVA, Claudie (1924—). English ballet dancer. Name variations: Claudie Leonard. Born April 24, 1924, in Paris, France; m. Harcourt Algeranoff, 1945 (div. 1959). ❖ As Claudie Leonard, performed with Mona Inglesby's International Ballet in *Gaité Parisienne, Coppélia* and *For Love or Money*; immigrated to Australia with husband to dance with the Borovansky Ballet (1953) and soon began work with Australian Children's Theater; returned to Europe (late 1950s), where she performed and taught in opera ballets of Lucerne, Switzerland and Graz, Austria; worked as master of Bavarian state opera in Munich, Germany.

AL-HASHEMI, Akila (1953–2003). *See Hashemi, Akila al-.*

AL-HASHEMI, Aqila (1953–2003). *See Hashemi, Akila al-.*

ALI, Aruna Asaf (c. 1909–1996). Indian resistance leader. Name variations: Aruna Ganguly, Ganguli, or Gangulee. Born Aruna Ganguly, July 16, c. 1909, in Kalka, India; died July 29, 1996, in New Delhi, India; m. Asaf Ali (lawyer and politician), 1928 (d. 1953). ❖ Indian revolutionary who believed in secularism and advocated social reform through education and improvement of primary health care; helped found All India Women's Education Fund Association; was imprisoned for participation in civil disobedience movement against British government (1932, 1941); became prominent by hoisting Indian flag at Gwalia Tank Maidan in Mumbai (Bombay), despite crackdown by British authorities against nationalist leaders during "Quit India" movement (Aug 9, 1942); with reward posted for capture, went underground, and traveled country trying to rally nationalist forces (1942–46); was elected 1st mayor of Delhi (1958); founded newspaper, *The Patriot,* and magazine, *Link* (1958); was associated with the Socialist Party, Left Socialist Party, and Communist Party of India; was involved with Indo-Soviet Cultural Society, All-India Peace Council, and National Federation of Indian Women. Received numerous honors, including Lenin Prize for Peace (1975), Nehru Award for International Understanding (1992), and Bharat Ratna (1998).

ALI-ZADEH, Franghiz (1947—). Azerbaijani composer. Born May 28, 1947, in Baku, Azerbaijan; lives in Berlin, Germany; studied piano under U. Khalilov at Music School of Baku, 1954–65; studied under Kara Karayev at Azerbaijani State Conservatory, 1974–76; m. Dzhangir Gasanga Zeinalov (filmmaker), 1982. ❖ Published a piano sonata in memory of Alban Berg, then followed with a tribute to Gustav Mahler; wrote First Symphony (1976) and *Songs about Motherland* (1978), *Three Water-Colours* (1987), and *From Japanese Poetry* (1990); wrote the rock opera *Legend about White Rider* (1985); major influences are Western music and trans-Caucasian folk music; became a professor at State Conservatory (1989).

ALIANORA. *Variant of Eleanor.*

ALIANORE. *Variant of Eleanor.*

ALIBERTY, Soteria (1847–1929). Greek feminist and educator. Born 1847 in Greece; died 1929; educated in Greece and Italy. ❖ Important figure in Greek feminism, became schoolteacher at Zappeion school for girls in Constantinople; moved to Romania and, with other Greek women, founded girls' school; returned to Athens (1893) where she founded women's association Ergani Athena, edited literary journal *Pleiades,* wrote for *Women's Newspaper,* and wrote biographical studies of women.

ALICE. *Variant of Alix.*

ALICE (1201–1221). Duchess of Brittany and Richmond. Name variations: Alice de Thouars; Alice of Brittany. Born 1201; died Oct 21, 1221; dau. of Guy, viscount of Thouars, and Constance of Brittany (1161–1201); m. Pierre also known as Peter I, duke of Brittany, around 1211 or 1213; children: John I, duke of Brittany. ❖ See also *Women in World History.*

ALICE (1150–c. 1197). Countess of Blois. Name variations: Alisa; Alix; Alice Capet. Born 1150; died c. 1197; dau. of Louis VII, king of France (r. 1137–1180), and Eleanor of Aquitaine (1122–1204); sister of Marie de Champagne (1145–1198); m. Thibaut or Theobald V, count of Blois, around 1164; children: Louis Blois; Isabel de Blois; and possibly Marguerite, countess of Blois (r. 1218–1230).

ALICE (1280–1291). English princess. Name variations: Alice Plantagenet. Born Mar 12, 1280, in Woodstock, Oxfordshire, England; died 1291, age 11; dau. of Edward I Longshanks, king of England (r. 1272–1307), and Eleanor of Castile (1241–1290).

ALICE (1856–1926). *See Dawson, Louisa Alice.*

ALICE, Princess (1883–1981). *See Alice of Athlone.*

ALICE, Princess (1901–2004). *See Montagu-Douglas-Scott, Alice.*

ALICE, princess of Greece and Denmark (1885–1969). *See Alice of Battenberg.*

ALICE DE BRYENE (d. 1435). English noble. Married a petty noble as a young girl; widowed (1386). ❖ Left correspondence and household accounts which provide a look into the day-to-day life of a woman; led active widowed life, moving to be near family in Suffolk; managed estates carefully, overseeing all aspects of financial affairs herself; negotiated marriages for 2 daughters and was also in correspondence with Richard

II over marriage plans of 2 young noblewomen being raised in her home. ❖ See also *Women in World History.*

ALICE DE CONDET (fl. 12th c.). See *Adelaide de Condet.*

ALICE DE COURTENAY (d. 1211). Countess of Angoulême. Name variations: Alice de Courteney. Died c. Sept 14, 1211; dau. of Peter I de Courtenay (c. 1126–1180) and Elizabeth of Courtenay (d. 1205); m. Aymer Taillefer, count of Angoulême; children: Isabella of Angoulême (2nd wife of King John I Lackland).

ALICE DE JOINVILLE (fl. 14th c.). Countess of Lancaster. Second wife of Henry (1281–1345), 3rd earl of Lancaster. Henry's 1st wife was Maud Chaworth.

ALICE DE LUSIGNAN. See *Alice le Brun.*

ALICE DE WARRENNE (d. around 1338). See *Fitzalan, Alice.*

ALICE LE BRUN (d. 1255). Countess of Warrenne and Surrey. Name variations: Alice de Lusignan. Died Feb 9, 1255; dau. of Isabella of Angoulême and her 2nd husband Hugh de Lusignan (Isabella's 1st husband was King John I Lackland); half-sister of Henry III, king of England; m. John de Warrenne (1231–1304), 7th earl of Warrenne and Surrey (r. 1240–1304), Aug 1247; children: Isabel de Warrenne (b. 1253, m. John Balliol, king of Scots); Eleanor de Warrenne (who m. Henry Percy, the 7th baron Percy); William de Warrenne (d. 1286).

ALICE MAUD MARY (1843–1878). Princess of Great Britain and Ireland, duchess of Saxony, and grand duchess of Hesse-Darmstadt. Name variations: Alice Saxe-Coburg. Born April 25, 1843, at Buckingham Palace, London, England; died of diphtheria, Dec 14, 1878, in Darmstadt, Hesse, Germany; 2nd dau. of Queen Victoria and Prince Albert; m. Prince Louis of Hesse-Darmstadt (1837–1892), also known as Grand Duke Louis IV, in 1862; children: 7, including Victoria of Hesse-Darmstadt (1863–1950, who m. Louis Alexander of Battenberg, marquis of Milford Haven, and was the mother of Lord Mountbatten); Ella (1864–1918, who m. Grand Duke Serge of Russia and became Elizabeth Feodorovna); Irene (1866–1953, who m. Prince Henry of Prussia); Ernest (who m. Victoria Melita of Edinburgh); Alix (1872–1918, who became empress Alexandra Feodorovna of Russia and m. Nicholas II); Mary Victoria (b. May 1874–1878, who died of diphtheria in infancy, the same year as her mother). ❖ Founded the Women's Union for Nursing Sick and Wounded in War.

ALICE OF ATHLONE (1883–1981). Princess of Great Britain and Northern Ireland, countess of Athlone. Name variations: Princess Alice; Alice Saxe-Coburg. Born Alice Mary Victoria Augusta Pauline, princess of Great Britain and Ireland and the countess of Athlone, at Windsor Castle, Berkshire, England, Feb 25, 1883; died at Kensington Palace, London, Jan 3, 1981; dau. of Prince Leopold Albert, duke of Albany (Queen Victoria's 4th and youngest son) and Princess Helen of Waldeck-Pyrmont; last surviving grandchild of Queen Victoria; great-aunt of Queen Elizabeth II; m. Prince Alexander of Teck, earl of Athlone (younger brother of Mary of Teck), Feb 1904; children: 4, including May Helen Emma (1906–1994, who m. Henry Abel Smith); Rupert Alexander George Augustus, Viscount Trematon (1907–1928); Maurice (1910–1910). ❖ One of the monarchy's most popular royals, was outspoken, independent and public-spirited, particularly in role of highly successful fund raiser as chancellor of University of the West Indies; active in public life until her final months. ❖ See also Theo Aronson, *Princess Alice, Countess of Athlone* (Cassell, 1981); and *Women in World History.*

ALICE OF BATTENBERG (1885–1969). Princess of Greece and Denmark. Name variations: Princess Andrew, Princess Alice. Born Victoria Alice Elizabeth Julia Mary at Windsor Castle, Berkshire, England, Feb 25, 1885; died in Buckingham Palace, Dec 5, 1969; dau. of Prince Louis Alexander Battenberg, 1st marquess of Milford Haven, and Princess Victoria of Hesse-Darmstadt (1863–1950); sister of Louise Mountbatten (1889–1965) and Earl Mountbatten of Burma; m. Prince Andrew of Greece (1882–1944), Oct 7, 1903; children: Margaret Oldenburg (1905–1981, who m. Godfrey, 8th prince of Hohenlohe-Langenburg); Theodora Oldenburg (1906–1969, who m. Berthod, margrave of Baden); Cecily Oldenburg (1911–1937, who m. George Donatus of Hesse); Sophia of Greece (b. 1914, who m. Christopher of Hesse-Cassell and George Guelph); Prince Philip (b. 1921, also known as Philip Mountbatten, duke of Edinburgh, husband of Queen Elizabeth II of England). ❖ After husband's family's expulsion from Greece (1923), lived in exile; during WWII, returned to Greece and hid Jewish refugees

in her home at the risk of her own life, protecting them from certain death in Nazi-occupied Greece; named a "Righteous Gentile" by Yad Vashem, Israel's Holocaust memorial museum and research center (1994). ❖ See also *Women in World History.*

ALICE OF CHAMPAGNE (1145–1206). See *Adele of Champagne.*

ALICE OF CHAMPAGNE (fl. 1200s). Queen of Cyprus. Name variations: Fl. in 1200s; dau. of Isabella I of Jerusalem (d. 1205) and Henry II of Champagne, king of Jerusalem (r. 1192–1197); m. her stepbrother Hugh I, king of Cyprus (r. 1205–1218); children: Henry I, king of Cyprus (r. 1218–1253); Isabella (who m. John of Lusignan).

ALICE OF FRANCE (c. 1160–?). See *Alais of France.*

ALICE OF JERUSALEM (c. 1106–?). Princess and regent of Antioch. Name variations: Alais or Alix. Reigned (1135–36); born c. 1106 in the Frankish principality of Jerusalem; died after 1162 in Antioch; 2nd dau. of Baldwin II, count of Edessa, later king of Jerusalem (r. 1118–1131), and Morphia of Melitene (fl. 1085–1120); sister of Hodierna of Jerusalem (c. 1115–after 1162), Melisande (1105–1161), and Joveta of Jerusalem; m. Bohemond or Bohemund II, prince of Antioch (r. 1126–1130), in 1126; children: Constance of Antioch (1128–1164), co-ruler of Antioch (r. 1130–1163). ❖ Intelligent and well-educated, married Bohemund II, newly crowned prince of Antioch (1126); when Bohemund was killed in battle (1130), assumed the regency for daughter Constance rather than wait for her father Baldwin II, overlord of Antioch, to appoint one; lost support of the Antiochenes, who wanted a strong, adult male warrior-prince to protect Antioch from its enemies; in a move to retain her authority, sent a messenger to Muslim *atabeg* (prince) Zengi, offering to pay him homage if he would help her retain Antioch, but her father's troops captured the messenger and had him hanged for treason; though forgiven by father for her rebellion, was removed from the regency and banished to Lattakieh, her dower lands; on Baldwin II's death, when her sister Melisande's husband Fulk V of Anjou succeeded to throne of Jerusalem, unsuccessfully challenged his right to rule as overlord of Antioch, resulting in her loss of power to the city's Patriarch Bernard; when Bernard died (1135) and the populace of Antioch elected Radulph of Domfront to succeed him, appealed to her sister Melisande to help regain power; was allowed to return to Antioch, where she shared the rule with Radulph, until he fell from power a short time later; ruling alone but without a solid base of support, sought a means of securing her position and that of her daughter; offered Constance's hand to the son of the Byzantine emperor Manuel Comnenus, causing even more turmoil and loss of support, though many Antiochenes recognized, too late, the wisdom of her pro-Byzantine policies; retired to her estates once again, where she spent the remainder of her life. ❖ See also *Women in World History.*

ALICE OF NORMANDY (fl. 1017–1037). Countess of Burgundy. Name variations: Adelaide, Adeliza, and Judith. Born before 1017; died after 1037; dau. of Richard II the Good (d. 1027), duke of Normandy, and Judith of Rennes (c. 982–1018, dau. of Conan I, duke of Brittany); m. Renaud I, count of Burgundy.

ALICE OF SALUZZO (fl. 1285). See *Fitzalan, Alice.*

ALICE OF VERGY. See *Alix of Vergy.*

ALICIA OF PARMA (1849–1935). Grand duchess of Tuscany. Name variations: Alice of Bourbon-Parma; Alice of Parma; Alix of Parma. Born Alice Maria, Dec 27, 1849, in Parma; died Jan 16, 1935, in Schwertberg, Upper Austria; dau. of Louise of Bourbon-Berry (1819–1864) and Charles III, duke of Parma; became 2nd wife of Ferdinand IV (1835–1908), titular grand duke of Tuscany (r. 1859–1908), Jan 11, 1868; children: Leopold Ferdinand (1868–1935, who m. Wilhelmine Adamowic); Louisa Toselli (1870–1947); Joseph Ferdinand (1872–1942); Peter Ferdinand (1874–1948, who m. Maria Cristina of Sicily); Anna Maria Theresa (1879–1961); Agnes Maria (1891–1945); and 5 others.

AL-IDLIBI, 'Ulfah. See *Idlibi, 'Ulfah al-.*

ALIEN (1856–1926). See *Dawson, Louisa Alice.*

ALIENOR or ALIÉNOR. Variant of *Eleanor.*

ALIGER, Margarita Iosifovna (1915–1992). Soviet journalist and lyrical poet. Born into a poor Jewish family in Odessa, Russia, Oct 7, 1915; died in 1992; m. Konstantin Makarov-Rakitin, 1936; children: 2 daughters and a son who did not survive infancy. ❖ At 16, went to Moscow; published 1st poems (1933); published 1st book-length collection, *God* *rozhdeniya* (*Year of Birth,* 1938), which praised the triumphs of Stalinist industrialization; was awarded a Soviet decoration (1939), the 1st of many she would receive in her long literary career; after husband died in combat (1941), became increasingly active in Soviet organizations, including the internationally known Jewish Antifascist Committee; wrote a number of patriotic works, including *To the Memory of the Brave* and *Zoya,* a long narrative poem honoring Zoya Kosmodemyanskaya (both published in 1942); earned a State Prize of the USSR and the Stalin Prize; joined the Soviet Communist Party (1942); after the war, when the latent anti-Semitism of Joseph Stalin and his inner circle began to reassert itself, published *Your Victory* (1946), which took on anti-Semitic slanders, but some lines were banned by Stalin's censors (though not printed, they were circulated widely in manuscript form); with Stalin's death, began writing with a renewed spirit and won a number of medals and awards, including the Order of the Red Banner of Labor (1965) and the Order of Friendship of the Peoples (1975); became a venerable figure of Russian literature. ❖ See also *Women in World History.*

ALI KHAN, Begum Liaquat (d. 1991). *See Khan, Begum Liaquat Ali.*

ALINE (1982—). *See Pellegrino, Aline.*

ALINE SITOE (c. 1920–1944). Queen of Diola Tribe, Casamance. Born c. 1920 in Kabrousse, West Africa (section of modern-day Senegal); died of scurvy, May 22, 1944; reigned (c. 1936–43). ❖ Incited rebellion against French occupation (1942), fomenting a boycott of French goods, discouraging use of French language, and encouraging her people to revive their own culture (1942); when Diola warriors killed 3 French soldiers and the French held Kabrousse under siege for 16 days (1943), surrendered to avoid watching the town destroyed by fire; taken into custody, was condemned to a 10-year exile in Timbuktu; died of scurvy the following year and was buried in Timbuktu's Sidi el Wafi Cemetery. Plans were made to return her remains to Senegal (1983). ❖ See also *Women in World History.*

ALISIA OF ANTIOCH (fl. 1100s). Ferrarese noblewoman. Third wife of Azo also known as Azzo VI d'Este (1170–1212), 1st lord of Ferrara (r. 1208–1212); children: Azzo VII Novello (d. 1264).

ALIX. *Variant of Alice.*

ALIX, countess of Blois (1150–c. 1197). *See Alice.*

ALIX, princess of Wales (1844–1925). *See Alexandra of Denmark.*

ALIX DE VERGY. *See Alix of Vergy.*

ALIX OF BURGUNDY. *See Alix of Vergy.*

ALIX OF FRANCE (c. 1160–?). *See Alais of France.*

ALIX OF HESSE-DARMSTADT (1872–1918). *See Alexandra Feodorovna, empress of Russia.*

ALIX OF VERGY (d. after 1218). Duchess of Burgundy. Name variations: Alice de Vergy; Alix of Burgundy. Died after 1218 in Burgundy, France; dau. of Count Hugues de Vergy; m. Eudes III (d. 1218), duke of Burgundy, in 1199; children: one son. ❖ Upon death of husband (1218), became regent of Burgundy for young son; took an active role in bettering the lives of her people; passed laws to strengthen the Burgundian economy, aided the growth of towns by confirming charters protecting their right to some self-rule, and preserved peace by forming an alliance with the powerful overlord of Champagne, Count Theobald; remained an important part of Burgundian government even after her son came of age. ❖ See also *Women in World History.*

ALIX OF VERGY (r. 1248–c. 1290). Countess, ruler of Burgundy. Name variations: Alix de Vergy. Died sometime before 1290; dau. of Count Otto II, count of Burgundy, and Countess Beatrix (dau. of Count Otto I); sister of Otto III, count of Burgundy; m. Hugh of Chalon; children: son Otto IV (d. 1302). ❖ Inherited Burgundy (present-day Eastern France, 1248) upon death of brother Otto III; ruled for over 40 years.

ALIYA, Fatima (1862–1936). *See Aliye, Fatima.*

ALIYE, Fatima (1862–1936). Turkish author and translator. Name variations: Fatma Aliye, Fatima Aliya. Born in 1862 in Turkey; died in 1936 in Turkey; dau. of Ahmad Cevdet (or Gaudat) Pasha (statesman and historian); educated at home; m. a Turkish army officer. ❖ After marrying an army officer, traveled with him to his various postings; translated French texts from the sciences and arts and spoke out for women's education; wrote a biography of her father and a *History of Women of Islam* (1892).

AL-KAHINA (fl. 695–703). *See Kahina.*

AL-KHAIZURAN (d. 790). *See Khaizuran.*

AL-KHANSA (c. 575–c. 645). *See Khansa, al-.*

AL-KHIRNIQ (fl. late 6th c.). *See Khirniq.*

ALKHATEEB, Sharifa (1946–2004). Muslim-American feminist, scholar, and journalist. Born Sharifa Ahmad, June 6, 1946, in Philadelphia, Pennsylvania; died Oct 12, 2004, in Ashburn, Virginia; dau. of a Yemini father and Czech mother; sister of Nafeesa Ahmad; attended University of Pennyvania; Norwich University, MA in comparative religion; m. Mejdi Alkhateeb (Iraqi-born US citizen), 1969; children: daughters Layla, Maha, and Nasreen Alkhateeb. ❖ Advocate for Muslim culture in US, lived in Saudi Arabia (1978–87); helped place courses in Middle Eastern cultures and Arabic in US public schools; founded the North American Council for Muslim Women (1992); created the Peaceful Families Project (2000), to raise awareness of domestic violence in Muslim communities; co-authored *The Arab World Notebook,* wrote for the English-language *Saudi Gazette,* and edited an English translation of the Koran.

ALLAGULOVA, Yulia. Russian short-track speedskater. Name variations: Yuliya or Julia Alagulova; Ioulia Allagoulova. Born in USSR. ❖ Won a bronze medal for 3,000-meter relay at Albertville Olympics (1992).

ALLAN, Elizabeth (1908–1990). English actress. Born April 9, 1908, in Skegness, Lincolnshire, England; died July 27, 1990, in England; m. W.J. O'Bryen (d. 1977, a theatrical agent and her manager), 1932. ❖ Made stage debut with the Old Vic (1927); appeared in several British movies, then played the lead in more than a dozen US films; sued MGM for replacing her in the lead of *The Citadel* with Rosalind Russell, effectively cutting short her career in Hollywood; is best remembered as the mother of Freddie Bartholomew in *David Copperfield* (1934); returned to England (1937) and continued her career in movies, theater, and tv; had a popular tv show "Swap Shop" (1955–60); retired (1977). Films include *The Lodger* (1933), *The Shadow* (1933), *Men in White* (1934), *Mark of the Vampire* (1934), *A Tale of Two Cities* (1936), *A Woman Rebels* (1936), *Camille* (1937), *Slave Ship* (1937), *No Highway* (*No Highway in the Sky,* 1951), and *The Heart of the Matter* (1954).

ALLAN, Liz (1947—). *See Allan-Shetter, Liz.*

ALLAN, Maude (1883–1956). Canadian-born interpretive dancer and choreographer. Born 1883 in Toronto, Ontario, Canada; raised in San Francisco; died Oct 7, 1956, in Los Angeles, California; educated in San Francisco, Vienna, and Berlin. ❖ Trained as a musician, set out to revive the Greek classic dance; made successful debut in Vienna in *The Vision of Salomé* (1903) which brought her fame as an erotic dancer; interpretive dancer, often compared to Isadora Duncan, toured London, Moscow, St. Petersburg (1909), US (1910), as well as South Africa, India, Malaya, China, Australia, New Zealand, South America, Egypt, Gibraltar, and Malta; danced Tchaikovsky's Sixth Symphony at Hollywood Bowl (1925); following retirement (1928), taught in England. Wrote several articles for magazines. ❖ See also autobiography *My Life and Dancing* (1908).

ALLAN, Stella May (1871–1962). *See Henderson, Stella May.*

ALLAN-SHETTER, Liz (1947—). American waterskier. Name variations: Liz Allan; Liz Shetter; Liz Allan Reid. Born Elizabeth Allan in 1947 in West Germany, where father was stationed; moved to Winter Park, Florida, at age 5; dau. of Colonel William D. Allan (with Army Corps of Engineers); m. William B. (George) Shetter. ❖ Won 42 US national titles and 8 individual World titles (1 tricks, 3 slalom, and 4 jumps); won overall World championship (1965, 1969, 1973); won all 4 titles for a Grand Slam (1969); won a gold medal at Munich Olympics (1972), when waterskiing was a demonstration sport; retired from competition (1975).

ALLARD, Julia (1844–1940). *See Daudet, Julia.*

ALLARD, Marie (1742–1802). French ballerina. Born Marie Allard in 1742; died in 1802; children: (with balletmaster Gaëtan Vestris) Marie-Jean-Augustin Vestris (Mar 27, 1760–1842), a major ballet dancer known as Auguste Vestris. ❖ Born to poor parents, was offered to the Comédie de Marseille and a certain Monsieur V; with mother, went to the Lyon opera and was engaged among the *premieres danseuses*; by 14, was settled in a small apartment in Paris with a job at the Comédie-Française (1756); capitalized on the attentions of her lovers; at 18, made her Paris Opera debut in *Zaïs* by Cahusac and Rameau (1761); danced

35 roles in her 1st 10 years at the Opera, and was lauded for her *pas de deux* with Dauberval in *Sylvie* (1766–67); also helped train son, Auguste, who would become the dance marvel of the age. ❖ See also *Women in World History.*

ALLART, Hortense (1801–1879). French feminist, novelist, and essayist. Name variations: Allart de Meritens. Born in 1801; died 1879. ❖ Was deeply involved in the women's movement of 19th-century France; as an established novelist and essayist, was an integral part of the *Gazette des Femmes*—a "Journal of Legislation, Jurisprudence, Literature, Theater, Art, Commerce, Law, Music, and Fashion" for women—especially aimed at analyzing French law as it pertained to the rights of women; published *La Femme et la Démocratie de Notre Temps* (Women and Democracy Today, 1836); notorious for her many love affairs, including one with the writer Chateaubriand, also published the novel *Les Enchantements de Prudence* (The Delights of Prudence), which was largely autobiographical and detailed the life of a woman who flouts the social conventions of the time; was also noted for *Novum Organum, ou Saintete Philosophique* (1857), a 300-page philosophical work in which she argued for a common foundation for religion and science. ❖ See also *Women in World History.*

ALLBRITTON, Louise (1920–1979). American actress. Name variations: Louise Collingwood; Mrs. Charles Collingwood. Born July 3, 1920, Oklahoma City, Oklahoma; died Feb 16, 1979, in Puerto Vallarta, Mexico; m. Charles Collingwood (CBS news correspondent), 1946. ❖ Films include *Parachute Nurse, Danger in the Pacific, Not a Ladies' Man, It Comes Up Love, Good Morning, Judge, Son of Dracula, Follow the Boys, This Is the Life, Her Primitive Man, San Diego, I Love You, Bowery to Broadway, The Men in Her Diary, That Night With You, Tangier, The Egg and I, Sitting Pretty, Walk a Crooked Mile, Don't Trust Your Husband* and *The Doolins of Oklahoma.*

ALLBUT, Barbara (1940—). American vocalist. Name variations: The Angels (originally known as the Starlets). Born Sept 24, 1940, in Orange, New Jersey; sister of Phyllis "Jiggs" Allbut Meister (vocalist, b. 1942). ❖ With sister Phyllis "Jiggs" Allbut and Linda Jansen, formed The Angels (Orange, NJ, 1961), one of most successful girl groups (early 1960s); released million-selling hit "My Boyfriend's Back" (1963), which reached #1 pop and #2 R&B. Other Angels' singles include "I Adore Him" (1963), "Thank You and Goodnight" (1963), "Wow Wow Wee (He's the Boy for Me)" (1964), and (last single for a major-label) "Papa's Side of the Bed" (1974).

ALLBUT, Jiggs (1942—). See Allbut, Phyllis.

ALLBUT, Phyllis (1942—). American vocalist. Name variations: Phyllis Allbut Meister; Jiggs Allbut; The Angels (originally known as the Starlets). Born Sept 24, 1942, in Orange, New Jersey; sister of Barbara Allbut (vocalist, b. 1940). ❖ With sister Barbara and Linda Jansen, formed The Angels (Orange, NJ, 1961), one of most successful girl groups (early 1960s); with Angels, released million-selling hit "My Boyfriend's Back" (1963) which reached #1 pop and #2 R&B. Other Angels' singles include "I Adore Him" (1963), "Thank You and Goodnight" (1963), "Wow Wow Wee (He's the Boy for Me)" (1964), and (last single for a major-label) "Papa's Side of the Bed" (1974).

ALLEGRO (1867–1924). See Salov'eva, Poliksena.

ALLEINE, Theodosia (fl. 17th c.). British writer. Born probably after 1632 in Ditcheat, Somerset, England; died before 1685; dau. of Reverend Richard Alleine; m. Joseph Alleine (dissenting cleric), 1655 (died 1668). ❖ Set up boarding school in Taunton and was a successful teacher and businesswoman; supported herself during husband's two imprisonments; wrote a sizeable portion of the hagiography of her husband, *The Life and Death of that Excellent Minister of Christ, Mr. Joseph Alleine, Late Teacher of the Church at Taunton, in Somersetshire, Assistant to Mr. Newton* (1672). ❖ See also C. Stanford, *Joseph Alleine: His Companions and Times* (1861).

ALLEN, Adrianne (1907–1993). English actress. Born Feb 7, 1907, in Manchester, England; died Sept 14, 1993, in Montreux, Switzerland; m. Raymond Massey (actor), 1929 (div. 1939); m. William Dwight Whitney, 1939 (died 1973); children: (1st m.) Daniel Massey (actor, b. 1933) and Anna Massey (actress, b. 1937). ❖ Made screen debut with *Loose Ends* (1930); also appeared in *The Night of June 13th, Merrily We Go to Hell, The Morals of Marcus, The October Man, Vote for Huggett, The Final Test* and *Meet Mr. Malcolm;* made her final stage appearance in London in *Five Finger Exercise* (1958).

ALLEN, Annie Jane (1835–1905). See Schnackenberg, Annie Jane.

ALLEN, Barbara Jo (1906–1974). See Vague, Vera.

ALLEN, Betty (1936—). Scottish chef and entrepreneur. Born 1936 in Bathgate, West Lothian, Scotland; m. Eric Allen; children: Graeme Allen (b. 1966). ❖ With husband, Eric, ran a hotel in Largo (1973–78), then opened the Airds Hotel in Port Appin, Argyll (1978); has won worldwide acclaim as a chef. Along with Hilary Brown, received a Michelin star (1990), the 1st women in Scotland to be so honored.

ALLEN, Betty Molesworth (1913–2002). New Zealand botanist. Born Betty Eleanor Gosset Molesworth in 1913 in New Zealand; died Oct 11, 2002, in Marbella, Spain; attended University of New Zealand; m. Geoffrey Allen (fighter pilot and amateur ornithologist), 1947 (died 1985); no children. ❖ Discoverer of the living fossil *Psilotum nudum* in Spain, a plant thought only to be found in the tropics, began career mounting specimens collected by Joseph Banks and Daniel Solander during the voyage of *HMS Endeavour* at Auckland Museum, under the tutelage of Lucy Cranwell; came under the influence of J. Holloway at University of New Zealand; succeeded Cranwell at Auckland Museum (1946); went on a series of expeditions in Borneo and Thailand; also worked in the herbarium of the Singapore Botanic Gardens; with husband, retired and moved to Los Barrios in southern Spain (1963); writings include Appendix 2 of Holttum's *Ferns of Malaya* and *A Selection of Flowers of Andalucia* (1993), among others. Named OBE (1998).

ALLEN, Bill (1906–1949). See Allen, Margaret.

ALLEN, Charlotte Vale (1941—). Canadian novelist. Name variations: (pseudonym) Katharine Marlowe. Born Jan 19, 1941, in Toronto, Ontario, Canada; m. Walter Allen, 1970; children: 1 daughter. ❖ One of Canada's most successful novelists, lived in England (1961–64), where she worked as a tv actress and singer; immigrated to US (1966); published 1st novel, *Love Life* (1976); wrote over 30 novels, including *Meet Me in Time* (1978), *Acts of Kindness* (1979), *Intimate Friends* (1983), *Dream Train* (1988), *Painted Lives* (1990), *Mood Indigo* (1997), *Grace Notes* (2002), *Fresh Air* (2003), and *Sudden Moves* (2004). ❖ See also autobiography *Daddy's Girl* (1980).

ALLEN, Debbie (1950—). African-American dancer and director. Name variations: Deborah Allen; Debra Allen. Born Deborah Kaye Allen, Jan 16, 1950, in Houston, Texas; dau. of Andrew Allen (dentist) and Vivian Ayers-Allen (poet); sister of Phylicia Rashad (actress); graduate of Howard University; m. Win Wilford, 1975 (div. 1983); m. Norman Nixon (former NBA player), 1984; children: (2nd m.) Vivian Nixon (b. 1984), Norm Jr. (b. 1987). ❖ Joined Houston Foundation for Ballet on full scholarship and as company's 1st black dancer (1964); danced with George Faison's Universal Dance Experience in NY (early 1970s); appeared on Broadway in such shows as *Purlie* (1971), *Raisin* (1973), *Truckload* (1975) and *Ain't Misbehavin'* (1980); nominated for Tony award and won Drama Desk Award for portrayal of Anita in Broadway revival of *West Side Story* (1980); nominated for a Tony for *Sweet Charity* (1986); made film debut in *Ragtime* (1981), then appeared as Lydia Grant in the film version of *Fame* and the tv series of the same name, which brought her international recognition; began directing "A Different World" (1988); hosted tv special "The Debbie Allen Show" and tv musical "Polly" (both 1989); directed episodes of tv's "Fresh Prince of Bel Air" and "Quantum Leap" (1990–91); produced Steven Spielberg's *Amistad* (1997); directed musical *Brothers of the Knight* at Kennedy Center, Washington DC (1998); founded the Debbie Allen Dance Institute. Won Essence awards (1992, 1995).

ALLEN, Deborah (1950—). See Allen, Debbie.

ALLEN, Dede (1923—). American film editor. Born Dorothea Carothers Allen in 1923 in Cleveland, Ohio; attended Scripps College; m. Steve Fleischman (tv writer and producer); children: 2. ❖ One of the few film editors to win a solo credit board on screen, moved to New York (1950) and began editing film; got 1st major break with *Odds Against Tomorrow* (1959); edited 6 pictures for Arthur Penn, 3 for Sidney Lumet, 2 for George Roy Hill, 2 for Paul Newman, and one each for Robert Wise, Elia Kazan, and Robert Rossen; growing confident in her craft, began to experiment with such things as pre-lapping sound and startling transitions, most notably in *Bonnie and Clyde* with its unmatched cuts, fade-outs and cut-ins; films include *America, America* (1963), *Rachel, Rachel* (1968), *Little Big Man* (1970), *Slaughterhouse Five* (1972), *Serpico* (1974), *Slapshot* (1977), *The Wiz* (1978), *The Breakfast Club* (1985), *The Milagro Beanfield War* (1988), and *The Addams Family* (1991). Won

British Academy Award for *Dog Day Afternoon* (1975); nominated for American Academy Awards for *Dog Day Afternoon* (1975) and *Reds* (1981); nominated for Ace Eddie awards for *The Hustler* (1961), *Dog Day Afternoon* (1975), and *Reds* (1981); received Crystal Award from Women in Film (1982) and Ace Lifetime Achievement Award (1994). ❖ See also *Women in World History.*

ALLEN, Elizabeth Chase (1832–1911). American poet. Name variations: Elizabeth Akers Allen and Elizabeth Chase Akers; (pseudonym) Florence Percy. Born Elizabeth Anne Chase in Strong, Maine, Oct 9, 1832; died in Tuckahoe, New York, Aug 7, 1911; attended Farmington Academy (later Maine State Teachers College); m. Marshall S.M. Taylor, 1851 (div.); m. Benjamin Paul Akers (Maine sculptor), 1860 (died 1861); m. Elijah M. Allen, 1865. ❖ Under pseudonym Florence Percy, published 1st book of poems, *Forest Buds from the Woods of Maine* (1856); as Elizabeth Akers, published *Poems* (1866), containing the once-popular ballad "Rock Me to Sleep" which opened with the familiar lines: "Backward, turn backward, O time, in your flight,/ And make me a child again, just for to-night"; other works include *The Silver Bridge* (1866), *Queen Catherine's Rose* (1885), *Two Saints: A Tribute to the Memory of Henry Bergh* (founder of the ASPCA, 1888), *The High-Top Sweeting* (1891), *The Ballad of the Bronx* (1901), and *The Sunset Song* (1902); a correspondent for Maine's *Portland Transcript* and the *Boston Evening Gazette*, was also a frequent contributor to the *Atlantic Monthly.*

ALLEN, Florence Ellinwood (1884–1966). American pacifist and champion of women's rights. Born Florence Ellinwood Allen, Mar 23, 1884, in Salt Lake City, Utah; died of a stroke, Sept 12, 1966, in Cleveland, Ohio; dau. of Clarence Emir (classical scholar, congressional delegate, and mining company executive) and Corinne Marie (Tuckerman) Allen (one of the 1st women to attend Smith College); attended New Lyme Institute in Ashtabula County, Ohio, 1895–97, and Salt Lake College, 1897–99; graduate of Western Reserve University (Phi Beta Kappa), 1904; studied music in Berlin, Germany, 1904–06; Western Reserve, AM in political science, 1908; New York University Law School, LLB, 1913; never married; no children. ❖ The 1st woman assistant county prosecutor in Ohio, the 1st woman to preside over a 1st-degree murder trial and to pronounce the death sentence, the 1st woman to sit in a court of general jurisdiction (the Ohio Court of Common Pleas), the 1st woman to preside as a judge in a court of last resort (the Ohio Supreme Court), the 1st woman appointed to a Federal Court of Appeals, and the 1st woman to serve as chief judge of such a court, was admitted to Ohio bar (1914); campaigned for municipal suffrage for women; appointed assistant county prosecutor of Cuyahoga County, OH (1919); elected to common pleas court (1920); elected to Ohio Supreme Court (1922), re-elected (1928); served on the 6th Circuit Court of Appeals (1934–59) and was chief judge (1958); was a member of various professional associations, serving on several committees and attending numerous international conferences. Was the 1st woman to receive the Albert Gallatin Award from New York University (1960); granted 25 honorary degrees. ❖ See also memoirs, *To Do Justly* (1965); and *Women in World History.*

ALLEN, Frances S. (1854–1941). American photographer. Born in Wapping, Massachusetts, 1854; died Feb 14, 1941, in Deerfield, Massachusetts; sister of Mary E. Allen. ❖ With sister, attended State Normal School in Westfield and obtained a job as a teacher; like sister, began going deaf, probably as the result of a childhood illness; with teaching future in jeopardy, turned to photography in order to make a living, specializing in portraits, genre, and scenic views; enjoyed considerable success selling souvenir views of "Old Deerfield" and typical scenes of New England life. ❖ See also *Women in World History.*

ALLEN, Gracie (1902–1964). American comedian. Born Grace Ethel Cecile Rosalie Allen, July 26, 1902, in San Francisco, California; died Aug 27, 1964; one of five children of George and Margaret (Darragh) Allen (both vaudevillians); m. George Burns (comedian), Jan 7, 1926; children: (adopted) Sandra Jean and Ronald Jon. ❖ Smart enough to play the dumbest woman in show-business history, left school at 14 to join her sisters—Hazel, Bessie, and Pearl—in a vaudeville act; after sisters left the company one by one, became a headliner; teamed with George Burns (1923) and remained together for 40 years: on radio, film, tv, and in an offstage marriage that endured the rigors of show business and a probing public; began as the "straightman," but soon delivered the punch lines; began hosting radio show with Burns (1932), which would continue for close to 20 years, attract an audience of 45 million, and make famous the signature line, "Say goodnight, Gracie"; ran for president of US on a new 3rd party ticket, the Surprise Party (1940); starred on "The

Burns & Allen Show" on tv (Oct 12, 1950–June 4, 1958); films include *The Big Broadcast* (1932), *College Humor* (1933), *International House* (1933), *Six of a Kind* (1934), *We're Not Dressing* (1934), *Love in Bloom* (1935), *Big Broadcast of 1936* (1935), *Big Broadcast of 1937* (1936), *A Damsel in Distress* (1937), *College Swing* (1938), *The Gracie Allen Murder Case* (1939), *Honolulu* (1939), *Mr. and Mrs. North* (1942), and *Two Gentleman and a Sailor* (1944). ❖ See also George Burns, *Gracie: A Love Story* (Putnam, 1989); and *Women in World History.*

ALLEN, Hannah Archer (fl. 1680s). British autobiographer. Born Hannah Archer in England in 1600s; dau. of John Archer of Snelston, Derbyshire; m. Hannibal Allen; m. Charles Hatt. ❖ When merchant husband was lost at sea, became suicidal; published autobiography, *Satan's Methods and Malice Baffled* (1683), which described her depression.

ALLEN, Jay Presson (1922–2006). American playwright, screenwriter and producer. Born Jay Presson, Mar 3, 1922, in Fort Worth, Texas; died May 1, 2006, in New York, NY; m. Lewis M. Allen (producer). ❖ On Broadway, plays include *Forty Carats, Tru*, and the adaptation of Muriel Sparks' *The Prime of Miss Jean Brodie* (1966); films include *Wives and Lovers, Marnie, Cabaret, Travels with My Aunt, Funny Lady, Just Tell Me What You Want* (from her novel), *Prince of the City, Deathtrap* and *Lord of the Flies;* created the long-running tv series "Family." Received Oscar nomination for screenplay of *The Prime of Miss Jean Brodie* (1969).

ALLEN, Kate (1974—). Australian field-hockey player. Name variations: Katie Allen. Born Feb 28, 1974, in Adelaide, SA, Australia. ❖ Fullback; won a team gold medal at Sydney Olympics (2000).

ALLEN, Katherine (1970—). Australian triathlete. Born April 25, 1970, in Geelong, Australia. ❖ Won gold medal at Athens Olympics (2004).

ALLEN, Margaret (1906–1949). English murderer. Name variations: Bill Allen. Born 1906 at Rawtenstall, England; hanged Jan 12, 1949, at Strangeways Prison. ❖ Cross-dressed as man from early age and became known as Bill Allen; confessed to murder of 68-year-old widow Nancy Ellen Chadwick, whom she beat to death with coal hammer (1948).

ALLEN, Mary E. (1858–1941). American photographer. Born in Wapping, Massachusetts, 1858; died Feb 18, 1941, in Deerfield, Massachusetts; sister of Frances S. Allen. ❖ With sister, attended State Normal School in Westfield and obtained a job as a teacher; like sister, began going deaf; turned to photography in order to make a living, specializing in portraits, genre, and scenic views; enjoyed considerable success selling souvenir views of "Old Deerfield" and other scenes of New England life. ❖ See also *Women in World History.*

ALLEN, Mary Sophia (1878–1964). British police administrator. Born Mary Sophia Allen, Mar 12, 1878, in England; died in Croydon, England, Dec 16, 1964; educated at Princess Helena College, Ealing, London. ❖ As a militant suffragist, served 3 terms of imprisonment for her activities; co-founded the women's police service in London and was appointed to rank of sub-commandant (1914); was promoted to commandant of the service (1919); argued persuasively for women's expanded role in police work, publishing 3 books on the subject; also founded and served as editor of *The Policewoman's Review* (1927–37); because she was favorably impressed by the "restoration of order" in Nazi Germany and a supporter of the fascist Franco, created heated controversy regarding her suitability as a leading police executive in a democratic society threatened by dictatorial regimes; retired under a cloud of controversy and criticism (1938). ❖ See also *Women in World History.*

ALLEN, Maryon (1925—). American politician and journalist. Born Maryon Pittman in Meridian, Mississippi, Nov 30, 1925; attended University of Alabama; m. James B. Allen (Alabama's lieutenant governor and US senator), Aug 1964. ❖ Democrat of Alabama, served in 95th Congress (June 8, 1978–Nov 7, 1978); wrote a syndicated Washington-based column called "The Reflections of a News Hen"; later was a columnist for the *Washington Post.*

ALLEN, Monique (1971—). Australian gymnast. Born in 1971 in Australia. ❖ Won Australian Nationals (1988, 1989, 1990); placed 3rd at Konica Grand Prix (1988) and 2nd at Commonwealth Games (1990), winning a gold medal in uneven bars; won gold medals in uneven bars and balance beam at Seiko Grand Prix (1991).

ALLEN, Pamela Kay (1934—). New Zealand children's writer and illustrator. Born April 3, 1934, in Auckland, New Zealand; m. Jim Allen, 1964; children: 2. ❖ Works include *Mr Archimedes' Bath* (1980), *Bertie and the Bear* (1983), *Mr McGee* (1987), *My Cat Maisie*

(1990), *Waddle Giggle Gargle* (1996), *The Pear in the Pear Tree* (1999), and *The Potato People* (2002). Received Children's Book Council of Australia Picture Book of the Year Award (1983, 1984) and New Zealand Library Association's Russell Clark Award (1986).

ALLEN, Paula Gunn (1939—). American scholar, literary critic, poet, novelist and educator. Name variations: Paula Marie Francis. Born Paula Marie Francis, Oct 24, 1939, in Albuquerque, New Mexico, of Laguna Pueblo, Sioux, and Lebanese descent; grew up in the Laguna and Acoma Pueblo Indian communities in Cubero, NM; dau. of E. Lee Francis (Lt. Gov. of New Mexico, 1967–70) and Ethel Francis; sister of Carol Lee Sanchez (writer); cousin of Leslie Marmon Silko (writer); attended St. Vincent's Academy in Albuquerque, then Colorado Women's College; University of Oregon, BA, 1966, MFA, 1968; received doctorate in American studies from University of New Mexico; twice married, twice divorced; children: (1st m.) 1 son, 1 daughter; (2nd m.) twin sons. ❖ Taught at several universities, including DeAnza Community College, San Francisco State University, University of New Mexico, Fort Lewis College, University of California at Berkeley, where she was professor of Native American/Ethnic Studies, and University of California at Los Angeles from which post (professor of English, Creative Writing and American Indian Studies) she retired (1999); was a feminist and antiwar activist; poetry includes *The Blind Lion* (1974), *A Cannon between My Knees* (1981), *Shadow Country* (1982), *The Woman Who Owned the Shadows* (1983), and *Life is a Fatal Disease* (1996); scholarly works include *The Sacred Hoop* (1986), *Grandmothers of the Light* (1991), *Studies in American Indian Literature: Critical Essays and Course Designs* (ed., 1983), *Voice of the Turtle: American Indian Literature, 1900–1970* (ed., 1994), and *Song of the Turtle: American Indian Literature, 1974–1995* (ed., 1996). Won Susan Koppelman Award (1990) and Native American Prize for Literature (1990).

ALLEN, Phylicia (1948—). *See Rashad, Phylicia.*

ALLEN, Rita (d. 1968). American theatrical producer. Died July 2, 1968, age 56, in New York, NY; m. 2nd husband Milton Cassel (stockbroker). ❖ On Broadway, co-produced *The Grass Harp, My Three Angels* and *The Cut of the Axe*; off-Broadway, produced *The Wise Have Not Spoken, The Making of Moo,* and 5 plays at the Rita Allen Theatre.

ALLEN, Rosalie (1924–2003). American singer and radio show host. Name variations: Julia Marlene Bedra; Julia Gilbert. Born Julia Marlene Bedra on June 27, 1924, in Old Forge, Pennsylvania; died Sept 23, 2003, in Palmdale, California; married; children: at least 1 daughter. ❖ Won national yodeling contest and earned name, "Queen of the Yodelers" (1939); joined radio show "Swing Billies" in NYC (1943); was host on radio program "Prairie Stars" on WOV (1944–56); became partner in Rosalie Allen's Hillbilly Music Center in NYC (mid-1940s); performed in 1st country-music program at Carnegie Hall, NYC (1947); became country-show host on NBC-TV (late 1940s); hit songs included "Guitar Polka," "Never Trust a Man," and "Yodel Boogie," and duets, with Elton Britt, "Beyond the Sunset (Should You Go First)" and "Quicksilver"; wrote articles and columns on country music for several publications, including *Hoedown* and *National Jamboree*. Was the 1st woman inducted into Country Radio Broadcaster DJ Hall of Fame.

ALLEN, Sadie (c. 1868–?). American daredevil. Born c. 1868; death date unknown. ❖ Along with partner George Hazlett and 500 pounds of sand, had a successful and memorable ride over Niagara Falls in a barrel (Nov 28, 1886).

ALLEN, Samantha (1836–1926). *See Holley, Marietta.*

ALLEN, Sandra (1978—). Australian softball player. Born Oct 11, 1978, in Blacktown, NSW, Australia. ❖ Outfielder; won a team bronze medal at Sydney Olympics (2000) and a team silver medal at Athens Olympics (2004).

ALLEN, Sarita (1954—). American dancer. Born Nov 2, 1954, in Seattle, Washington. ❖ Became member of Alvin Ailey Repertory Workshop (early 1970s) and joined senior company soon after; was principal dancer and danced feature parts in Ailey's *Hidden Rites* (1973), *The Mooche* (1975), *Night Creature* (1975), *Three Black Kings* (1976), and more; created major roles in Jennifer Muller's *Crossword* (1977) and Rael Lamb's *Butterfly* (1978); joined faculty of the Harbor Conservatory for the Performing Arts in NY (2003).

ALLEN, Susan Westford (c. 1865–1944). American musical-comedy actress. Born Susan Leonard, c. 1865, in Chicago, Illinois; died June 13, 1944, at Bayshore, Long Island, NY; sister of Lillian Russell (actress); m. Robert Westover (actor, died 1916). ❖ Appeared with her sister in many Broadway successes, including *The Grand Duchess, Goddess of Truth, Queen of Diamonds, Widow's Might* and *Wildfire*; retired (1922).

ALLEN, Tori (1988—). American climber. Born Victoria Ann Allen, July 30, 1988, in Indianapolis, Indiana. ❖ Set world record as youngest person to on-site a 5.13a "Harvest" (Red River Gorge, KY, 2000); was undefeated in 2001 JCCA Season Events; set world record as youngest woman to summit—The Nose, El Capitan, Yosemite, CA (2001); won USCCA Junior Nationals four years in a row (1999–2002); won gold in climbing at Gorge Games (2001); won gold in Women's Speed at X Games (Summer 2002); other 1st-place finishes include: ABS National Championship, Boulder, CO (2002); Canadian National Championships, Toronto, Canada (2002); TEVA Mountain Dyno Competition (2002); and Telluride 360 (2002).

ALLEN, Vera (1897–1987). American stage, radio, tv, and screen actress. Born Vera Klopman, Nov 27, 1897, in New York, NY; died Aug 10, 1987, in Croton-on-Hudson, NY; m. John Malcolm Schloss. ❖ Made stage debut at the Neighborhood Playhouse in *The Grand Street Follies of 1925*, followed by *The Dybbuk* and *The Critic*; appeared on Broadway in *I Was Waiting for You, The Silver Cord, Susan and God, The Philadelphia Story, The Two Mrs. Carrolls, Strange Fruit* and *Ladies of the Corridor*; on tv, appeared as Ida Weston on "Search for Tomorrow" (1969–72) and as Grandma Matthews on "Another World" (1964–65); co-founded and was president of the American Theatre Wing.

ALLEN, Viola (1867–1948). American actress. Born Oct 27, 1867, in Huntsville, Alabama; died May 9, 1948, at her home in New York, NY; dau. of actors Charles Leslie Allen and Sara Jane (Lyon) Allen; m. Peter Cornell Duryea (Kentucky horse breeder), 1905 (died 1944); children: none. ❖ Performed on stage for 35 years, appearing in over 80 different roles, including her debut in the title role of *Esmeralda* (1882); often appeared as one of Shakespeare's heroines; donated her large collection of theater memorabilia to the Museum of the City of New York.

ALLENBY, G. (1889–1974). *See O'Malley, Mary Dolling.*

ALLENBY, Kate (1974—). English pentathlete. Born Mar 16, 1974, in Devon, England; spent early years in Australia. ❖ Won 2 World Jr. championship titles; won European title (1997) and World Cup final (1998); won a bronze medal for modern pentathlon at Sydney Olympics (2000).

ALLENBY, Peggy (1905–1967). American actress. Born Eleanor Byrne Fox, Feb 14, 1905, in New York, NY; died Mar 23, 1966; m. John McGovern. ❖ Made NY debut as Louise Huldane in *Two Strangers from Nowhere* (1924); other appearances include Kate Camden in *The Sap*, Patrick Longworth in *The Little Spitfire*, Aggie Lynch in *Within the Law*, Ruth Winship in *Conflict*, and Louise in *A Widow in the Green*.

ALLENDE, Isabel (1942—). Chilean author. Born Aug 2, 1942, in Lima, Peru; dau. of Tomás Allende (diplomat) and Francisca (Llona Barros) Allende; 2nd cousin of Salvador Allende Gossens (ex-president of Chile); m. Miguel Frías, 1962; children: 1 daughter, 1 son. ❖ Worked as journalist for women's magazine *Paula* and children's magazine *Mampato* and as interviewer for television and documentary films (1964–75); exiled to Venezuela (1975) due to coup d'etat which ousted 2nd cousin Salvador Allende (1st democratically elected Marxist-socialist president of Chile); worked as writer for *El Nacional* in Venezuela (1975–84); achieved international acclaim as fiction writer with *Casa de los espíritus* (*The House of the Spirits*); has enjoyed wide popular success with many works of fiction, including *Eva Luna* (*Eva Luna*), *El plan infinito* (*The Infinite Plan*), *Paula* (1994), *La hija de fortuna* (*Fortune's Daughter*), *Mi país inventado* (*My Invented Country*); taught creative writing at several American universities (1985–89), including Barnard College and University of California at Berkeley; has also written works for young adults, including *La ciudad de las bestias* (*City of the Beasts*, 2002); employs elements of magic realism; used novels to expose and denounce atrocities committed after 1973 coup d'etat in Chile, as well as to explore more personal themes, such as death of daughter, Paula. Received many prestigious awards including Grand Roman d'Evasion Prize (1984), Brandeis University Major Book Collection Award (1993), Gabriela Mistral Award (1994), and Dorothy and Lillian Gish Prize (1998), as well as 6 honorary doctoral degrees. ❖ See also John Rodden, *Conversations with Isabel Allende* (University of Texas Press, 1999).

ALLEYNE, Ellen (1830–1894). *See Rossetti, Christina.*

ALLFREY, Phyllis Shand (1915–1986). Dominican author and politician. Born Phyllis Byam Shand in Dominica, West Indies, Oct 24, 1915; died in Dominica in 1986; dau. of Francis Byam Berkeley Shand and Elfreda (Nicholls) Shand; m. Robert Allfrey; children: 5, including Philip and Josephine Allfrey (d. 1977); 3 of her children were adopted. ❖ In England, worked as a secretary for novelist Naomi Mitchison; subsequently worked for the Parliamentary Committee for West Indian Affairs and joined the Labour Party and Fabian Society; produced 2 volumes of poetry; published 1st novel, *The Orchid House* (1953), based on her childhood in Dominica; returned to Dominica (1954), where she helped found the Labour Party to help tropical fruit workers command fair pay; was elected minister for labour and social affairs (1958); with husband, edited the *Dominican Star* (1965–82). ❖ See also *Women in World History.*

ALLGOOD, Mary (1885–1952). *See O'Neill, Máire.*

ALLGOOD, Molly (1885–1952). *See O'Neill, Máire.*

ALLGOOD, Sara (1883–1950). Irish actress. Born in Dublin, Ireland, Oct 31, 1883; died in Hollywood, California, Sept 13, 1950; sister of actress Molly Allgood, whose stagename was Máire O'Neill (1885–1952); apprenticed to an upholsterer; joined Inghinidehe na héireann, founded by Maude Gonne; m. Gerald Henson (actor), Sept 1916 (died 1918); children: daughter who died at birth (Jan 1918); became an American citizen (1945). ❖ Legendary actress, was a founding member of Dublin's Abbey Theatre, then known as the Irish National Theatre Society, making debut as Cathleen in Synge's *Riders to the Sea* (1904); appeared at Irish National for next decade, originating such roles as Mrs. Fallon in Lady Gregory's *Spreading the News* (1904), Widow Quin in Synge's *The Playboy of the Western World* (1907), Lavarcham in *Deirdre of the Sorrows* (1910), and title role in *Cathleen ni Houlihan* (1913); was also involved with the inception of Liverpool Rep and Annie Horniman's company at Manchester; in London, created role of Nannie Webster in Barrie's *The Little Minister,* Juno Boyle in O'Casey's *Juno and the Paycock* and Bessie Burgess in *The Plough and the Stars*; made film debut in Hitchcock's *Blackmail* (1929), followed by *Juno and the Paycock* (1930); arriving in Hollywood (1940), began to be typecast as a loveable Irish mother or grandmother; was nominated for Best Supporting Actress for her role in *How Green Was my Valley* (1941); made over 40 films. ❖ See also *Women in World History.*

ALLILUYEVA, Svetlana (1926—). Soviet writer. Name variations: Svetlana Stalin, but for most of her life used mother's maiden name Alliluyeva (also spelled Allilluyeva). Born Svetlana Iosifovna Stalina, Feb 28, 1926, in Moscow, USSR; youngest child and only dau. of Joseph Stalin and Nadezhda Alliluyeva-Stalin; graduated Moscow University, 1949; graduate study, Academy of Social Sciences, Moscow; m. Grigory Morozov, 1943 (div. 1947); m. Yury Zhdanov, 1949 (div.); reportedly m. Mikhail L. Kaganovich, 1951; married, in common law, Brijesh Singh, c. 1963 (died 1966); m. James Wesley Peters, 1970 (sep. 1971); children: (1st m.) Joseph Alliluyev (b. 1945); (2nd m.) Ekaterina (Katya, b. 1950); (4th m.) Olga Peters. ❖ Mother shot herself (1932); remained close to father until he learned of her affair with Jewish filmmaker Alexei Kapler and banished him to Lubianka Prison in Siberia for 10 years; father died (1953); defected to US (1967); wrote *Twenty Letters to a Friend,* the story of her mother's family; returned to Russia (1984), in a well-publicized visit with her 14-year-old daughter, Olga. ❖ See also *Women in World History.*

ALLILUYEVA-STALIN, Nadezhda (1901–1932). Soviet writer. Name variations: Nadya or Nadejda Alliluieva, Alliluleva, or Allileyevna. Born in the Caucasus, Russia, 1901; committed suicide in Moscow, USSR, Nov 8, 1932; dau. of Sergei Alliluyev and Olga Fedorenko (Georgian); younger sister of Anna Alliluyeva Redens; m. Joseph V. Stalin, 1918 (his 1st wife was Ekaterina [Keke] Svanidze, who died in 1907 and gave birth to his son Yakov); children: Vassily and Svetlana Alliluyeva (1926—). ❖ Second wife of Joseph Stalin, was the daughter of a political colleague; worked as a secretary in the Commissariat of Nationalities and worked briefly for the journal *Revolution and Culture*; began to turn from Stalin's ideas and policies; after a public argument with him, was found dead the next morning, apparently of a self-inflicted gunshot wound; left a suicide note that was both personally and politically critical of Stalin. ❖ See also *Women in World History.*

ALLINGER, Cathy. *See Priestner, Cathy.*

ALLINGHAM, Helen Patterson (1848–1926). English watercolorist and illustrator. Born Helen Patterson, Sept 26, 1848; died at Haslemere in 1926; dau. of A.H. Patterson (doctor); attended Birmingham School of Design and the Royal Academy Schools; m. William Allingham (Irish poet), 1874. ❖ Influenced by the work of Fred Walker, devoted her illustrations to domestic and rural life; achieved 1st success illustrating the serialization of Thomas Hardy's *Far from the Madding Crowd* for *The Cornhill Magazine* (1874); was frequently given one-woman shows by the Fine Art Society (1880s–1890s); also illustrated books of Juliana Horatia Ewing, including *A Flat Iron for a Farthing* (1872) and *Jan of the Windmill* (1876). ❖ See also *Women in World History.*

ALLINGHAM, Margery (1904–1966). British mystery novelist. Born Margery Louise Allingham in Ealing, London, England, 1904; died of cancer, June 30, 1966; dau. of Herbert J. Allingham (wrote a popular weekly serial) and Emily Jane (Hughes) Allingham; educated at Perse High School, Cambridge; m. Philip Youngman Carter (artist), 1927. ❖ Best known for her Albert Campion mystery-thrillers, wrote fiction for Britain's *Sexton Blake* and *Girls' Cinema* at 15; published 1st novel (1922); introduced her meek, bespectacled detective Albert Campion in *The Crime at Black Dudley* (1929); created Campion's manservant Lugg in her next novel, *Mystery Mile* (1930); also wrote a small number of plays, nearly 150 articles and book reviews, 60 short stories, and four novellas—*Flowers for the Judge* (1936), *The Tiger in the Smoke* (1952), *The Beckoning Lady* (1955), and *Cargo of Eagles.* ❖ See also *Women in World History.*

ALLISON, Fran (1907–1989). American tv host. Born Nov 20, 1907, in La Porte City, Iowa; died June 13, 1989, in Sherman Oaks, California; graduate of Coe College; m. Archie Levington, 1941 (died 1978). ❖ Television pioneer and popular host, who counseled puppets Kukla and Ollie on tv series "Kukla, Fran and Ollie" (1947–57); also hosted "The Quiz Kids" and appeared as Aunt Fanny on the "Don McNeill TV Club" (1950).

ALLISON, May (1890–1989). American actress. Born on a farm in Rising Fawn, Georgia, June 14, 1890; died Mar 27, 1989, in Bratenahl, Ohio; dau. of John S. Allison and Nannie Wise Allison; educated in Birmingham, Alabama; m. Robert Ellis, 1920 (div. 1923); m. James R. Quirk (*Photoplay* editor) 1926 (died 1932); m. Carl N. Osborne (businessman, died 1982). ❖ One of MGM's stars of the silent screen, started out with a successful career on stage, featured in *Everyman* and *The Quaker Girl* on Broadway; made 1st film, *A Fool There Was* (1915), then starred opposite Will Rogers in *David Harum;* shot 8 movies opposite Harold Lockwood (1915–17); also co-starred with 1st husband Robert Ellis in *Peggy Does Her Darndest* and *In for Thirty Days*; other films include *The Great Question* (1915), *The End of the Road* (1915), *One Increasing Purpose, The Testing of Mildred Vane* (1918), *Fair and Warmer* (1919), *The Woman Who Fooled Herself* (1922), *Flapper Wives* (1924), *I Want My Man* (1925), *Wreckage* (1925), *The Greater Glory* (1926), *Men of Steel* (1926), and *The City* (1926); retired from the screen (1927). ❖ See also *Women in World History.*

ALLITT, Beverley Gail (1969—). English nurse and murderer. Born 1969 in Grantham, Lincolnshire, England. ❖ Allegedly suffering from Munchausen Syndrome by Proxy, murdered 4 children while working on children's ward at Grandtham and Kesteven District Hospital (1991); sentenced to life in prison (1993).

ALLRED, Gloria (1941—). American lawyer, feminist, and social activist. Born Gloria Rachel Bloom, July 3, 1941, in Philadelphia, Pennsylvania; University of Pennsylvania, BA with honors; New York University, MA; Loyola University School of Law, JD, cum laude, 1974; married and div.; children: Lisa (attorney who anchored a daily show on Court TV). ❖ Taught at an African-American boys' school in Philadelphia; after Los Angeles riots (1965), moved to Watts to teach; specializing in family law, started law firm of Allred, Maroko, Goldberg and Ribakoff; turned to cases involving employment discrimination, sexual harassment and civil rights and civil litigation; founded and served as president of the Women's Equal Rights Legal Defense and Education Fund; was a talk-show host on KABC TalkRadio in Los Angeles for 14 years; became a columnist for legal newspaper, *The Daily Journal.* Voted Best Lawyer in America (1987, 1991).

ALLUCCI, Carmela (1970—). Italian water-polo player. Born Jan 22, 1970, in Italy. ❖ At World championships, won team gold medals (1998, 2001); was captain of Italy's World Cup squad (2003); driver, won a team gold medal at Athens Olympics (2004).

ALLWYN, Astrid (1905–1978). American actress and singer. Born Nov 27, 1905, in South Manchester, Connecticut; died Mar 31, 1978, in Los

Angeles, California; m. Robert Kent (actor, div.); m. L.J. Fee (insurance exec); children: three, including Vicki Fee and Melinda O. Fee (both actresses). ❖ Began career as a singer and Broadway actress; films include *Lady with a Past, Beggars in Ermine, White Parade, One More Spring, Way Down East, Charlie Chan's Secret, Follow the Fleet, Dimples, Mr. Smith Goes to Washington* and *Hit Parade of 1943.*

ALLYN, Ellen (1830–1894). *See Rossetti, Christina.*

ALLYSON, June (1917—). American actress. Born Kathryn Ann Eleanor "Ella" van Geisman, Oct 7, 1917, in the Bronx, NY; dau. of Arthur van Geisman (building superintendent) and Clare van Geisman; m. Dick Powell (actor-director), Aug 19, 1945 (died 1963); m. Alfred Glenn Maxwell (Dick Powell's barber), 1963 (div. 1965, rem. 1966, div.); m. David Ashrow (dental surgeon), Oct 30, 1976; children: (1st m.) Pamela (adopted Aug 10, 1948); Richard Jr. (b. Dec 24, 1950); (stepchildren) Ellen Powell and Norman Powell. ❖ Popular star of the 1940s and 1950s, with her husky-voice, tiny lisp, and Peter Pan collars, 1st appeared in the chorus line in Broadway's *Sing Out the News* (1938); shared a showstopper "The Three B's" with Nancy Walker and Erlene Schools in hit musical *Best Foot Forward;* arrived in wartime Hollywood (1943), having been signed for *Best Foot Forward,* then landed a part in *Girl Crazy,* followed by *Thousands Cheer* and *Meet the People*; made 1st appearance in trademark bangs for *Two Girls and a Sailor*; typecast as the girl-next-door, made movie after movie in rapid succession: *Music for Millions, Her Highness and the Bellboy, The Sailor Takes a Wife, Two Sisters from Boston* and *Look for the Silver Lining;* also appeared as Jo in the remake of Louisa May Alcott's *Little Women* (1949); left MGM and signed on for the highly successful *Glenn Miller Story* opposite Jimmy Stewart at Universal; teamed with Stewart for 2 more pictures: *The Stratton Story* and *Strategic Air Command;* against type, played the insanely possessive wife in *The Shrike* (1955). ❖ See also autobiography (with Frances Spatz Leighton), *June Allyson* (Putnam, 1982); and *Women in World History.*

ALMADA, Filipa de (fl. 15th c.). Portuguese poet and noblewoman. Lived and wrote under the rule of Portuguese kings Alphonso V (1438–1481) and John II (1481–1495). ❖ Because of her nobility and stature in the Avis dynasty, had the luxury of being an educated woman in 15th-century Portugal; poetry appeared in Garcia de Resende's *Cancioneiro Geral (General Songbook,* 1516), an anthology of Spanish and Portuguese poetry, which is called "palace poetry" because its audience and authors were largely royalty.

AL-MALAIKA, Nazik (1923–1992). *See Malaika, Nazik al-.*

ALMANIA, Jacqueline Felicie de (fl. 1322). *See de Almania, Jacqueline Felicia.*

ALMEDINGEN, E.M. (1898–1971). Russian-born author. Name variations: Edith Martha Almedingen. Born Martha Edith von Almedingen in 1898 in St. Petersburg, Russia; died in 1971 in England; educated at Xenia Nobility College and University of Petrograd. ❖ Specializing in medieval history and philosophy, lectured at Petrograd in English medieval history and literature (1920–23); moved to England (1923); wrote poetry, plays, novels, and biographies for both children and adults, using St. Petersburg and the Russian landscape as her setting; began teaching at Oxford University as a lecturer on Russian history and literature (1951); lived in England for nearly two-thirds of her life; had more than 10 books to her credit, including *Out of Seir* (1943), *Storm at Westminster* (1952), *The Empress Alexandra, 1872–1918* (1961), and *Anna* (1972).

ALMEIDA, Brites de (fl. 1385). Portuguese heroine. Lived in Aljubarotta, a small town in Portugal, about 63 miles north of Lisbon. ❖ Known as the Portuguese Joan of Arc, gained national prominence during the Battle of Aljubarotta when she led her townspeople against the Castilians, seven of whom she killed with her own hand. A decisive event in the history of Portugal: the battle established the country's independence. ❖ See also *Women in World History.*

ALMEIDA, Filinto de (1862–1934). *See Almeida, Julia Lopes de.*

ALMEIDA, Julia Lopes de (1862–1934). Brazilian novelist. Name variations: (pseudonyms) A. Jalinto, Filinto de Almeida, Eila Worns. Born Julia Lopes in 1862 in Brazil; died in 1934; m. Filinto de Almeida (Portuguese author); children: 3 sons. ❖ Considered one of Brazil's most important novelists in the period before modernism, produced more than 40 books, the majority of which are highly romantic and present a woman's view of Brazilian life. Works include *A viuva Simões* (The Widow Simões, 1987), *Ansia eterna* (Eternal Desire, 1903), *A*

intrusa (The Intruder, 1908), and *A família Medeiros* (The Medeiros Family, 1919). ❖ See also *Women in World History.*

ALMEIDA GARRETT, Teresa (1953—). Portuguese lawyer and politician. Born Aug 28, 1953, in Porto, Portugal. ❖ Lecturer at the Catholic University in the Faculties of Law and of Economics and Business; as a member of the European People's Party (Christian Democrats) and European Democrats (EPP), elected to 5th European Parliament (1999–2004).

ALMERIA (1758–1816). *See Hamilton, Elizabeth.*

ALMOG, Ruth (1936—). Israeli novelist and journalist. Born into an Orthodox family of German descent in 1936 in Petah Tikva, Israel; studied at Tel-Aviv University. ❖ Worked as teacher; has served as a journalist and on the editorial staff of the leading Israeli newspaper *Ha'aretz* since 1967; writings include (short stories) *Hasdei Ha'Laila Shel Margerita* (Marguereta's Night Grace, 1969), (for children) *Naphy Nasich Ha'Karnafim* (Naphy, 1979), (novel) *Mavet Ba'Geshem* (Death in the Rain, 1982), (novel) *Shorshey Avir* (Roots of Light, 1987), (stories) *Nashim* (Women, 1987), (for children) *Hasibor* (The Wonderbird, 1991), (novel) *Meahev Mushlam* (A Perfect Lover, 1995), (for children) *Hamasa Sheli im Alex* (My Journey with Alex, 1999) and (for children) *Od Chibuk Echad* (Just One More Hug, 2003). Received the Brenner Prize (1989) and Agnon Prize (2001).

ALMON, Baylee (1994–1995). American child. Born in Oklahoma City, Oklahoma, April 18, 1994; killed in Oklahoma City, April 19, 1995; dau. of Aren Almon (who married Stan Kok in 1997 and gave birth to a daughter, Bella Almon Kok, 1998). ❖ One day after the celebration of her 1st birthday, became a painful symbol of the 17 children and 165 adults killed in the bombing of the Alfred P. Murrah Federal Building in Oklahoma City (April 19, 1995). The photo of a firefighter cradling her body, his right elbow uplifted as he gazed down at her, became an unforgettable image. ❖ See also *Women in World History.*

ALMOND, Linda (1881–1987). American children's author. Born Linda Stevens in 1881 in Seaford, Delaware; died Jan 10, 1987, in Plymouth Meeting, Pennsylvania. ❖ Carried on the Beatrix Potter series and wrote the "Buddy Bear" and "Penny Hill" series.

ALMUCS DE CASTELNAU (fl. 12th c.). French noblewoman. Probably born in Provence, France, c. 1140; m. Guiraut de Simiane, lord of Castelnau; children: 4 sons, including Raimbaut. ❖ A noblewoman of Provence, composed poetry and was a patron of troubadours; as a young teenager, became 2nd wife of Guiraut de Simiane; had 4 sons, one of whom, Raimbaut, became a troubadour and patron of troubadours. ❖ See also *Women in World History.*

ALMY, Mary Gould (1735–1808). American diarist. Born Mary Gould in Newport, Rhode Island, 1735; died in Newport, Mar 1808; dau. of James and Mary (Rathbone) Gould; m. Benjamin Almy, 1762; children: 6. ❖ On marriage, though a Loyalist at heart, supported husband's revolutionary ways; when the British invaded the American colonies and husband enlisted as a Patriot, took in boarders to help pay the expenses; her diaries, later published as *Mrs. Almy's Journal,* detail the hardships of the Revolution. ❖ See also *Women in World History.*

ALMY, Millie (1915–2001). American psychologist. Born Millie Corinne Almy, June 19, 1915, on a farm in Clymer, NY; died Aug 16, 2001, in San Leandro, California; graduate of Vassar College, 1936; Columbia Teachers College, MA, 1945, PhD, 1948; never married; no children. ❖ Among the 1st to advocate special training for teachers in early childhood education, began teaching career at University of Cincinnati; was a professor of psychology and education at Columbia (1952–71), then joined the faculty at University of California, Berkeley (1971); retired (1980); writings include *Young Children's Thinking* and *Ways of Studying Children.*

A.L.O.E. (1821–1893). *See Tucker, Charlotte Maria.*

ALONI, Shulamit (1931—). Israeli government official. Born in Tel-Aviv in 1931; dau. of Russian parents; educated at the Ben Shemers school; received a law degree, 1956; m. a civil administrator; children: 3. ❖ Fought with the Haganah, the underground Jewish defense force (1948); was a member of parliament for the Labour Party (1965–69), chaired the Israeli Consumer Council (1966), founded the Civil Rights Party (1973), was appointed Minister without Portfolio (1974), and became Civil Rights MP in the Knesset (1977); books include *The Citizen and His Country, The Rights of the Child in Israel* and *Woman as a Human Being.*

ALONSO, Alicia (1921—). Cuban ballet dancer. Born Alicia Martinez in Havana, Cuba, Dec 21, 1921; dau. of Antonio Martinez (army officer) and Ernestina (Hoyo) Martinez; studied ballet with Alexandra Fedorova, Leon Fokine, Anatole Vilzak, and Vera Volkova; m. Fernando Alonso, 1937; children: Laura Alonso (ballerina). ❖ At 10, gave 1st public performance, dancing a waltz in an abridged version of Tchaikovsky's *The Sleeping Beauty*; married and moved to NYC (1937); made American professional dancing debut in chorus line of Broadway musical *Great Lady* (1938), followed by *Stars in Your Eyes* (1939), choreographed by George Balanchine; was chosen by the newly formed Ballet Theater for its corps de ballet (1941); diagnosed with a detached retina (1941), lost peripheral vision; replacing an indisposed Alicia Markova in *Giselle,* had a huge success; promoted to principal dancer of Ballet Theater (1946) and danced the Accused in *Fall River Legend;* returned to Havana in order to found her own company, the Ballet Alicia Alonso (1948), then commuted between Havana and NY; opened her own dance school in Havana, the Alicia Alonso Academy of Ballet (1950); because of the machinations of Batista, had to disband both her dance company and ballet school (1956); danced with the famed Ballet Russe de Monte Carlo (1956–59); was the 1st ballerina from the West to be invited to perform in the Soviet Union; danced *Giselle* in Moscow and Leningrad (1957) and starred in the Leningrad Opera Ballet's 3-act *Path of Thunder,* a denunciation of South Africa's apartheid system; with Castro's overthrow of Batista, returned to Cuba and received funds from the revolutionary government to form a new ballet company, Ballet Nacional de Cuba, and reopen her dance school (1959); within a few years, her company began taking top honors in numerous international dance competitions; with her ensemble, appeared in Western and Eastern Europe (1960–90); performed occasionally in Canada (1967, 1971) and US (1975, 1976). Received *Dance Magazine* Award (1958). ❖ See also *Women in World History.*

ALONSO, Carmen de (1909—). *See de Alonso, Carmen.*

ALONSO, Dora (1910–2001). Cuban author. Name variations: (pseudonyms) Nora Lin, D. Polimita. Born Dora Alonso on Dec 22, 1910, in Máximo Gómez, Cuba; died Mar 21, 2001, in Cuba. ❖ Published story "Humildad," which won a top prize from the journal *Bohemia* (1931); moved to Havana (1935), where she contributed to a number of Latin American journals; published 1st novel, *Tierro adentro* (1944); a dedicated member of the Communist Party, traveled throughout Mexico, Europe, and the former Soviet Union; works include *Cain* (1955) and *Once caballos* (Eleven Horses, 1970). ❖ See also *Women in World History.*

ALORNA, Marquesa de (1750–c. 1839). Portuguese poet and salonnière. Name variations: (pseudonym) Alcipe. Born Leonor de Almeida Portugal de Lorena e Lencastre in Portugal in 1750; died c. 1839; married the count of Oeynhausen, 1779. ❖ At 8, was confined, along with mother and sister, at convent of Chellas (1758), while father was imprisoned for conspiring against King Joseph I Emanuel; released from the convent, age 27, upon death of the king; married a diplomat and moved to Vienna (1779), where he would later become minister of Vienna; after husband died (1793), moved with 2 children to England, then Lisbon; though she wrote and published poetry, is best remembered for her salon and her influence on young writers, such as Manuel Bocage and Alexandre Herculano; returned to Portugal (1814) and reclaimed the titles and properties that had been stripped from the family by the king.

ALÓS, Concha (1922—). Spanish novelist. Name variations: Alos. Born María Concepción "Concha" Alós Domingo in Valencia, Spain, 1922; dau. of Francisco Alós Tárrega and Pilar Domingo Pardo; m. Eliseo Feijóo, 1943. ❖ Though she had been writing for some time, received recognition when she entered her novel *Los enamos* (*The Dwarfs*) for the prestigious Planeta Prize and won (1962); published *Os habla Electra* (*Electra Speaking,* 1975), perhaps her best-known work. ❖ See also *Women in World History.*

ALOYSIA, Sister (1809–1886). *See Hardey, Mary Aloysia.*

ALOZIE, Glory (1977—). Spanish-Nigerian hurdler. Name variations: Gloria Alozie. Born Dec 30, 1977, in Nigeria. ❖ At World championships, won a silver medal for 100-meter hurdles (1999); won a silver medal for the 100-meter hurdles at Sydney Olympics (2000), soon after her fiance Hyginus Anugo, an Olympic competitor, was hit and killed by a car outside the Olympic village; at European championships, running for Spain, won a gold medal for 100-meter hurdles (2002).

ALPAIDA (c. 654–c. 714). *See Alphaida.*

ALPAR, Gitta (1900–1991). Hungarian soprano. Name variations: Gitta Alpár. Born in Budapest, Hungary, Feb 5, 1900; died Feb 17, 1991, in Los Angeles, California; married twice, the 2nd time to Gustav Frölich (German actor who would later marry Lida Baarova). ❖ Studied with Laura Hilgermann before launching singing career in Budapest (1923); sang in Munich, Berlin, and Vienna; though she sang Gilda, Rosina, and the Queen of the Night, greatest success was in operetta; was particularly remembered for appearances in Millöcker's *Der Bettelstudent* at the Meropolteater in Berlin and for premiering in Lehár's *Schön ist die Welt* (1930); sang title role in Millöcker's *Gräfin Dubarry* (1931); forced to flee Europe because of Nazi menace (1936), reestablished operetta career in US and appeared in several films. ❖ See also *Women in World History.*

ALPENNY, Caroline Cadette (1821–?). *See Howard, Caroline Cadette.*

ALPERS, Mary Rose (1906–2002). *See Coulton, Mary Rose.*

ALPHAIDA (c. 654–c. 714). Noblewoman of the House of Pepin. Name variations: Alpaida; Alpoide or Alpoïde; Chalpaida; Elphide. Born c. 654; died c. 714; 2nd wife of Pepin II of Herstol or Heristal, mayor of Austrasia and Neustria (r. 687–714); children: Charles Martel (c. 690–741), mayor of Austrasia and Neustria (r. 714–741); Hildebrand (Chilebrand).

ALPHONSA, Mother (1851–1926). *See Lathrop, Rose Hawthorne.*

ALPOIDE (c. 654–c. 714). *See Alphaida.*

AL-RADI, Nuha (1941–2004). *See Radi, Nuha al-*

AL-RAHMAN, Aisha 'Abd (1913–1998). *See Abdel Rahman, Aisha.*

AL-SAMMAN, Ghada (1942—). *See Samman, Ghada al-.*

ALSHAMMAR, Therese (1977—). Swedish swimmer. Born Aug 26, 1977, in Stockholm, Sweden. ❖ At SC European championships, won gold medals for 50-meter freestyle (1998, 2000), 100-meter freestyle (1998, 2000), and 50-meter butterfly (2001); won silver medals for 50- and 100-meter freestyle and a bronze for 4x100-meter freestyle relay at Sydney Olympics (2000); at LC European championships, won gold medals for 50-meter freestyle (2000), 100-meter freestyle (2000), and 50-meter butterfly (2002); at SC World championships, won gold medals for 50-meter freestyle (2000, 2002), 100-meter freestyle (2000, 2002).

AL-SHAYKH, Hanan (1945—). *See Shaykh, Hanan al-.*

ALSOP, Mary O'Hara (1885–1980). *See O'Hara, Mary.*

ALSOP, Susan Mary (d. 2004). American political hostess and writer. Name variations: Susan Mary Patten. Born Susan Mary Jay, c. 1918, in Rome; grew up in South America and Europe; died Aug 18, 2004, at her home in Georgetown, Washington, DC; dau. of a diplomat; descendant of John Jay (1st chief justice of US); attended Foxcroft boarding school in Middleburg, VA, and Barnard College; m. William S. "Bill" Patten (member of the Foreign Service), Oct 1939 (died Mar 1960); m. Joseph Alsop (newspaper columnist), 1961 (div. 1973, died 1989); children: (1st m.) Bill Patten and Anne Milliken. ❖ Grand dame of Washington society, dined with presidents and prime ministers, including Winston Churchill, Franklin Roosevelt and John F. Kennedy, and the world's elite; began career giving well-known parties in Paris while 1st husband was an embassy official stationed there (1945–60); wrote *Lady Sackville: A Biography* (1978), *Yankees at the Court: The First Americans in Paris* (1982) and *The Congress Dances: Vienna 1814–1815* (1984); was a contributing editor to *Architectural Digest.* ❖ See also her collection of letters to her friend Marietta Tree, *To Marietta from Paris: 1945–1960* (1975).

ALSTON, Barbara (1945—). American singer. Name variations: The Crystals. Born 1945 in Brooklyn, NY. ❖ Began singing with girl-group the Crystals (1961), the 1st act signed to Phil Spector's Phillies Label; with group, had hit singles, including "There's No Other (Like My Baby)" (1961), "Uptown" (1962), "Da Doo Ron Ron" (1963), and "Then He Kissed Me" (1964), though their #1 hit, "He's a Rebel," was recorded by session singers the Blossoms, not the Crystals. Crystals albums include *He's a Rebel* (1963) and *The Best of the Crystals* (1992).

ALSTON, Shirley (1941—). *See Owens, Shirley.*

ALSTON, Theodosia (1783–1813). *See Burr, Theodosia.*

AL-TAYMURIYYA, 'Aisha 'Esmat (1840–1902). *See Taymuriyya, 'A'isha 'Ismat al-.*

ALTHENHEIM, Gabrielle Beauvain d' (1814–1886). *See Beauvain d'Althenheim, Gabrielle.*

ALTWEGG, Jeanette (1930—). English figure skater. Born Sept 8, 1930, in Great Britain. ❖ Won British Nationals (1947–50); won the World Championship (1951) and the European championship (1951, 1952); won a bronze medal at St. Moritz Olympics (1948) and a gold medal at Oslo Olympics (1952), the only indiv. medal won by Great Britain in either of those games; retired (1952) to work at the Pestalozzi Children's Village in Trogen, Switzerland.

ALULI, Irmgard (c. 1912–2001). Hawaiian songwriter and performer. Name variations: Auntie Irmgard. Born Irmgard Keali'iwahinealohanohokahaopuamana Farden. c. 1912, in Lahaina, Maui; died Oct 4, 2001, in Honolulu, Hawaii; sister of Diana Farden; m. Nane Aluli (died 1968). ❖ Began singing and playing guitar with the Annie Kerr Trio, comprised of sister Diana and steel guitarist Annie Kerr (1926), then performed with the Farden Sisters, a family quintet; led her own group, Puamana (1960s–90s); wrote and recorded Hawaiian music (1930s–40s); for over 70 years, composed over 120 songs, including "Puamana," "Laupahoehoe Hula," and "E Maliu Mai."

ALUPEI, Angela (1972—). Romanian rower. Name variations: Angela Tamas or Alupei-Tamas. Born May 1, 1972, in Bacau, Romania. ❖ Won a gold medal for lightweight double sculls at Sydney Olympics (2000) and at Athens Olympics (2004).

ALVAR (1838–1892). *See Mansilla de Garcia, Eduarda.*

ALVARADO, Elvia (1938—). Honduran social and political activist. Born Jan 25, 1938, in Honduras; children: 6. ❖ Under auspices of Catholic Church, served as organizer of mother's clubs in Honduran villages; was among founders of Federation of Campesina Women (FEHMUC); as member of National Campesina Union (UNC) and a founder (1985) of National Congress of Rural Workers (CNTC), worked on behalf of land recovery for peasants and was targeted for persecution by government; jailed at least 6 times in 1980s; collaborated with Medea Benjamin on testimonial autobiography *Don't Be Afraid Gringo* (1987), which was written for US audience; conducted speaking tours in US to educate international community about situation facing Honduran peasants and impact of US military presence in Honduras.

ALVARES, Ana (1965—). Brazilian volleyball player. Name variations: Ana Margarida Álvares Viera; Ana Margarita Alvares; Ida Alvares. Born Jan 22, 1965, in Brazil. ❖ Middle hitter; won team World Grand Prix (1994, 1996, 1998); won South American championship (1991, 1995, 1997); won a team bronze medal at Atlanta Olympics (1996).

ALVAREZ, Anita (1920—). American dancer. Born Oct 13, 1920, in Tyrone, Pennsylvania. ❖ Joined Martha Graham's company (1934–41) where she danced in *Celebration* (1934), *Horizons* (1936), and *American Lyric* (1937); appeared as solo and specialty dancer in numerous Broadway shows, including *Something for the Boys* (1942), *A Connecticut Yankee in King Arthur's Court* (1943), as Susan Mahoney in *Finnian's Rainbow* (1947), and in *Gentlemen Prefer Blondes* (1950); on film, was featured dancer in *Tars and Spars* (1945).

ALVAREZ, Carmen (c. 1936—). American theatrical dancer. Name variations: Carmen Álvarez. Born July 2, c. 1936, in Hollywood, California. ❖ Danced in corps de ballet of Radio City Music Hall; made debut performance on Broadway in Bob Fosse's *The Pajama Game* (1954) and went on to dance major parts in numerous shows, including *Li'l Abner* (1956), *West Side Story* (1957), *Bye Bye Birdie* (1960), and *Zorba* (1968); danced in variety shows on tv such as *Arthur Murrays' Dance Party* (1961), *American Bandstand* (1961), and *The Ernie Kovacs Show* (1962); appeared as Moonbeam McSwine in film version of *Li'l Abner* (1959).

ALVAREZ, Lili de (1905—). Spanish tennis player. Name variations: Lili d'Alvarez; comtess de la Valdene. Born 1905 in Rome, Italy, of Spanish descent; lived in Spain. ❖ Termed brilliant but erratic, played in the finals at Wimbledon (1926, 1927, 1928) and introduced the 1st culottes to be seen there (1931); won French Open doubles with Kea Bouman (1929); won 1st ever Italian championship (1930); was one of Europe's most popular tennis stars. ❖ See also *Women in World History.*

ALVAREZ DE TOLEDO, Luisa Isabel (1936—). Spanish duchess, novelist, historian and activist. Name variations: Luisa-Isabel Alvarez de Toledo; Luisa Alvarez de Toledo; Duchess of Medina Sidonia; Red Duchess. Born Luisa Isabel Alvarez de Toledo y Maura, Aug 13, 1936, in Nace, Spain; dau. of Joaquin Alvarez de Toledo y Caro, 20th duke of Medina Sidonia, and Maria Carmen Maura y Herrara. ❖ The 21st duchess of Medina Sidonia and Spanish grandee, a controversial figure, was jailed for political activism (1969); had other radical episodes which were often reported in the press; works include *La huelga* (1967), *La base* (1971), and *La cacería* (1977) which are anti-capitalist and reflect sympathy for workers; has become a respected historian.

ALVAREZ RIOS, Maria (1919—). Cuban poet, playwright and educator. Born 1919 in Cuba. ❖ Professor of music; works include *Cosecha* (Harvest, 1948), *Poemario* (Book of Poems, 1948), *Martí 9* (Tuesday 9th, 1952), *Según el color* (According to Color, 1955), *Funeral* (1958), and *La Victima* (The Victim, 1959).

ALVES LIMA, Daniela (1984—). Brazilian soccer player. Name variations: Daniela. Born Jan 12, 1984, in Brazil. ❖ Midfielder, won a team silver medal at Athens Olympics (2004).

AL-ZAYYAT, Latifa (b. 1923). *See Zayyat, Latifa al-.*

AMACHREE, Mactabene (1978—). Nigerian basketball player. Born Jan 30, 1978, in Port Harcourt, Nigeria. ❖ Signed as free agent with New York Liberty of the WNBA (2001); signed with Seattle Storm (2003).

AMADIO, Florence (1894–1968). *See Austral, Florence.*

AMALABERGA (fl. 400s). Visigothic princess. Fl. in the 5th century; 1st wife of Chlodovechs or Clodovic also known as Clovis I (465–511), king of the Franks (r. 481–511); children: possibly Theodoric I, king of Metz (r. 511–534).

AMALASUNTHA (c. 498–535). Regent of Ostrogothic Italy. Name variations: Amalswinthe, Amalaswintha, Amalasontha, Amalasuentha. Born c. 498 in Italy; killed in 535 (or 534) in Italy; dau. of Theodoric the Great, king of Italy, and Audofleda (sister of King Clovis); m. Eutharic (d. 522), in 515; m. her cousin Theodat also known as Theodahad or Theodatus; children: (1st m.) son Athalaric or Athalric; daughter Matasuntha. ❖ Daughter of Theodoric the Great, who had conquered Italy with his Ostrogothic armies and declared himself king; when he died without a male heir (526), inherited the kingdom as guardian of her son; intelligent and cultured, reigned for 9 years and earned the enmity of her Ostrogothic nobles for conciliatory foreign policies to Justinian and Theodora of the later Roman capital at Byzantium (Istanbul); aware of her risky position, promised Justinian that if her throne were lost, she and the Ostrogothic treasury would move to Constantinople; after successfully thwarting a rebellion of her nobles (533), put to death 3 of its instigators; when her 17-year-old son died (534), married and became co-ruler with cousin Theodat to gain support against her rebellious subjects; overthrown by husband (534) and banished to an island in the lake of Bolsena (Tuscany, Italy); while in her bath, was strangled to death by relatives of the 3 nobles she had put to death (535). ❖ See also *Women in World History.*

AMALASWINTHA or AMALSWINTHE (c. 498–535). *See Amalasuntha.*

AMALIA. *Variant of Amalie.*

AMALIA (d. 690). Flemish saint. Name variations: Amaliaburga or Amelia. Born in Brabant; died in Flanders in 690; related to Pepin I of Landin. ❖ Married before becoming a Benedictine nun, is the patron saint of arm pain and bruises, and is usually depicted standing on a large fish, thought to be a sturgeon; her relics have been kept in St. Peter's Abbey in Ghent since 1073. Feast day is July 10.

AMALIA, Anna, duchess of Saxe-Weimar (1739–1807). *See Anna Amalia of Saxe-Weimar.*

AMÁLIA, Narcisa (1852–1924). Brazilian poet and feminist. Name variations: Narcisa Amalia. Born Narcisa Amália de Oliveria Campos in São João de Barra, Brazil, 1852; died 1924; dau. of Joaquim Jácome de Oliveria Campos Filho (writer); m. twice. ❖ At 11, moved to Resende; in her 20s, wrote and published 2 volumes of poetry, *Nebulosas* (Starry Skies, 1872) and *Flores do Campo* (Flowers of the Field, 1874), and edited the literary magazine *A Gazetinha de Resende* (The Resende Gazette); moved to Rio (1888) where she worked as a teacher; an outspoken advocate for change in the status of women, is viewed as a foremother in her country's feminist movement.

AMALIABURGA (d. 690). *See Amalia.*

AMALIA OF BAVARIA (1801–1877). Queen of Saxony. Born 1801; died 1877; dau. of Maximilian I Joseph, elector of Bavaria (r. 1799–1805), king of Bavaria (r. 1805–1825), and Caroline of Baden (1776–1841);

twin sister of Elizabeth of Bavaria (1801–1873); m. Johann also known as John (1801–1873), king of Saxony (r. 1854–1873); children: Albert (1828–1902), king of Saxony (r. 1873–1902); George (1832–1904), king of Saxony (r. 1902–1904); Anna Maria of Saxony (1836–1859); Margaret of Saxony (1840–1858).

AMALIA OF OLDENBURG (1818–1875). *See Amalie.*

AMALIE (1818–1875). Queen of Greece and princess of Oldenburg. Name variations: Amalia. Born Marie Friederike Amalie, Dec 21, 1818; died May 20, 1875; eldest dau. of Grand Duke Augustus of Oldenburg and Adelheid of Anhalt-Bernburg-Schaumburg (b. 1800); m. Otho, also known as Otto I (1815–1867), king of Greece (r. 1833–1862, deposed), Nov 22, 1836. ❖ Was unpopular during reign with husband Otto I, because of his taxation, his attempt to establish a central bureaucratic system, his use of German advisors, and her interference (Otto had been imposed as King of the Hellenes by the London Conference in 1832, when the Greeks were given their independence); deposed by a revolutionary government (Oct 1862).

AMALIE AUGUSTE (1788–1851). Duchess of Leuchtenburg. Name variations: Princess Amalie Auguste of Bavaria; Augusta of Bavaria; Auguste, princess of Bavaria. Born June 21, 1788; died May 13, 1851; dau. of Maximilian I Joseph, king of Bavaria (r. 1805–1825), and Wilhelmine of Darmstadt (1765–1796); m. Eugène de Beauharnais, duke of Leuchtenburg, Jan 4, 1806; children: August or Auguste (1810–1835, m. Queen Maria II da Gloria); Maximilian (1817–1852), duke of Leuchtenburg (m. Maria Nikolaevna [1819–1876]); Josephine Beauharnais (1807–1876, m. Oscar I, king of Sweden); Eugénie Hortense (1808–1847); Amelia of Leuchtenburg (1812–1873, m. Pedro I, emperor of Brazil); Theodelinde (1814–1857, m. Count William of Württemberg). ❖ With husband, founded the landgraviate of Leuchtenburg in Bavaria, and their children formed connections with several royal families. ❖ See also *Women in World History.*

AMALIE OF HESSE-DARMSTADT (1754–1832). Princess of Padua and Baden. Born June 20, 1754; died July 21, 1832; dau. of Louis IX, landgrave of Hesse-Darmstadt, and Caroline of Zweibrucken-Birkenfeld (1721–1774); m. Charles Louis of Padua (b. 1755), prince of Padua and Baden, July 15, 1774; children: Caroline of Baden (1776–1841); Elizabeth of Baden (1779–1826), empress of Russia; Frederica Dorothea of Baden (1781–1826), queen of Sweden; Mary-Elizabeth of Padua (1782–1808); Karl Friedrich (b. 1784); Karl Ludwig, also known as Charles Louis (b. 1786); Wilhelmine of Baden (1788–1836).

AMALIE OF SAXE-COBURG-GOTHA (1848–1894). Duchess of Bavaria. Born Oct 23, 1848, in Coburg, Germany; died May 6, 1894, in Schloss Biederstein, Munich; dau. of Clementine of Orleans (1817–1907) and Augustus, prince of Saxe-Coburg-Gotha; m. Maximilian (1849–1893), duke of Bavaria, Sept 20, 1875; children: Sigfrid August of Bavaria; Christopher Joseph of Bavaria; Leopold of Bavaria.

AMALIE OF SAXONY (1794–1870). German composer, harpsichordist, singer, author, and duchess of Saxony. Name variations: (pseudonyms) Amalie Heiter and Amalie Serena. Born Amalie Marie Friederike Auguste, Aug 10, 1794, in Dresden, Saxony; died in Dresden, Sept 18, 1870; dau. of Maximilian, duke of Saxony, and Caroline of Parma (1770–1804); sister of kings Frederick Augustus II and John of Saxony; studied with private tutors and lived her entire life in Pillnitz Castle in Dresden. ❖ Composed mostly operas and liturgical works; highly educated and intellectually curious, also composed an operetta to a French-language libretto and wrote comedies under the pseudonyms Amalie Heiter and Amalie Serena. ❖ See also *Women in World History.*

AMANAR, Simona (1979—). Romanian gymnast. Born Oct 7, 1979, in Constanta, Romania. ❖ At Atlanta Olympics, won a gold medal for vault, silver for floor exercises, and bronze for team all-around and indiv. all-around (1996); at European championships, won gold medals for vault, uneven bars and team (1996), team (1998), and vault (2000); at World championships, won a gold medal for team all-around (1994), team and vault (1995), team and vault (1997), and team (1999); won Hungarian International (1996), International Championships of Romania (1996, 1998, 1999), Romanian Nationals (1997), and World Cup (1998); at Sydney Olympics, won gold medals for indiv. all-around and team all-around and a bronze for floor exercises (2000).

AMANISHAKHETE (r. c. 41–12 BCE). Queen of Meroe. Name variations: Candace. Born in Meroe, an extensive kingdom ranging from just south of Aswan and the 1st Cataract of the Nile in the north to well into modern Ethiopia in the south. ❖ Influential queen of the kingdom of Meroe, negotiated peace with the Roman Empire after an ill-conceived raid into Egypt brought a Roman punitive expedition upon Meroe. ❖ See also *Women in World History.*

AMANPOUR, Christiane (1958—). Iranian-American news reporter. Born Jan 12, 1958, in London, England; spent early years in Tehran, Iran; eldest of 4 daughters of Mohamed Amanpour (Iranian airline executive) and Patricia Amanpour (British); attended Holy Cross Convent School in Buckinghamshire, England, then New Hall School; University of Rhode Island, BA in journalism; m. Jamie Rubin (spokesman for the State Department), 1998; children: Darius John Rubin (b. 2000). ❖ During the Islamic revolution (1979), parents were forced to flee Iran; moved to US to major in journalism at University of Rhode Island; joined CNN as an assistant for the international news desk (1983); became producer-correspondent at its NY bureau (1986), then Frankfurt (1989), where she was CNN's main reporter during the pro-democracy movement in Eastern Europe; came to prominence reporting from Kuwait during the 1st Gulf War; also reported on the violence in Bosnia and Herzegovina.

AMANTOVA, Ingrida. Russian luge athlete. Born in USSR. ❖ Won a bronze medal for singles at Lake Placid Olympics (1980).

AMARILIS (fl. 17th c.). Peruvian poet. Fl. in 17th century in Huanuco, Peru; may have been Doña Maria de Alvarado, a descendant of the explorer Alvarado. ❖ Sent her verses to Spanish poet Lope de Vega and he responded with his *Epístola a Belardo,* published in his *Filomena* (1621); some attribute her poems to de Vega himself.

AMATHILA, Libertine Appolus (1940—). Namibian political leader and health expert. Born Libertine Appolus in 1940 in Fransfontein, South West Africa (today Namibia); m. Ben Amathila (Namibian political activist). ❖ Joined the growing Namibian independence movement; went into exile (1962) and lived for some time in Tanzania, where she applied for, and received, a scholarship to study in Poland; while becoming a leading SWAPO activist in Europe, completed a medical education in Poland, Sweden, and London; served as director of the Women's Council of SWAPO (late 1960s–1970s); a universally recognized figure by the time Namibian independence was achieved (1990), was easily elected to the Assembly of a newly independent Namibia and named minister of Local Government and Housing. ❖ See also *Women in World History.*

AMATI, Olga (1924—). Italian ballet dancer. Born Jan 19, 1924, in Milan, Italy. ❖ Studied at school of Teatro alla Scala, Milan, and became a member of La Scala Ballet (1942–56) where she danced leading roles in Aurel Milloss' *Le Creature de Prometo, Folli e Viennesi* and *Evocazioni,* among others; performed in company productions of Balanchine's *Ballet Imperial,* Massine's *Gaité Parisienne,* as well as in *Giselle* and *Swan Lake;* retired as a performer and taught dance classes in Rome.

AMATO, Serena (1974—). Argentinean sailor. Name variations: Serena Babiana Amato. Born Sept 10, 1974, in Buenos Aires, Argentina; sister of Augusto Amata (athlete). ❖ Won South African championship (1999); won a bronze medal for single-handed (Europe) at Sydney Olympics (2000).

AMAYA, Carmen (1913–1963). Spanish flamenco dancer. Born 1913 in Barcelona, Spain; died in Bagur, Spain, Nov 19, 1963; dau. and granddau. of dancers; m. Juan Antonio Aguero (guitarist). ❖ One of Spain's greatest flamenco dancers, made 1st public appearance at 7; made US debut (1941), where she appeared in night clubs and toured with her group, comprised of her father and two sisters; appeared in the movie *Los Tarantos,* which was released in US (1964). Granted the Medal of Isabela la Catolica by the Spanish government (1963). ❖ See also *Women in World History.*

AMAZON ARMY OF DAHOMEY (1818–1892). Army of women in West Africa who fought a war against French expansionism. Fl. 1818–92. ❖ In early 18th century, King Agadja formed an army against encroachments of neighboring tribes and European colonizers that included women; women became a permanent part of the Dahoman force (1818), when the usurping King Gezo enlisted his many wives to form a permanent phalanx to defend him in civil war; these women helped secure the independence for the people of Dahomey, called the Fon (1818–22); there were about 2,500 Amazons, most of whom were official wives of the king; their weapons were muskets, blunderbusses, bows and arrows, duck-guns, and short swords that were used in close fighting, and they were especially fond of the military tactic of ambush, though they killed only in self-defense; they were involved in the war with the Egba (1840s), attacks on Yoruba towns (1851, 1864, 1883, and 1885), and took on the French in a major conflict (1890); though they fought bravely and with ferocity, the Amazon army was effectively wiped out. ❖ See also *Women in World History.*

AMBAPALI (fl. c. 540 BCE). Indian courtesan and holy woman. Born in Vaisali, India, in 6th century BCE; lived during the time of Siddhartha Gautama, the Buddha (c. 563–483 BCE). ❖ Said to be one of the greatest courtesans of her time, owned a large home with mango groves when Siddhartha passed through Vaisali; deeply impressed by him, retired from her lucrative profession, began to study his teachings, and offered him her groves; became an *arhat* (holy one), a state so high that it is achieved by few, which was a major accomplishment, since it was believed at the time that only men could attain such a place of nirvana; seems to have been the basis for Kamala the courtesan in Hermann Hesse's *Siddhartha.*

AMBLER, Mary Cary (fl. 1700s). American diarist. Fl. in 1700s. ❖ While living in Jamestown, Virginia, discovered that doctors in Baltimore, Maryland, had learned how to inoculate children against smallpox; with her children in tow, headed north, keeping a journal of her 3-month trek which was later published as *The Diary of M. Ambler* (1770).

AMBOISE, Francise d' (1427–1485). French founder and duchess of Brittany. Born 1427; died 1485; dau. of Louis d'Amboise; m. Peter II, duke of Brittany. ❖ Daughter of a powerful lord, longed to pursue a religious calling but was unable to escape a political marriage; became duchess of Brittany when she married Duke Peter II; managed to use her position to accomplish some of her religious goals; founded the 1st Carmelite monastery in Brittany, popularizing that order, which led to its diffusion into other areas of northern France; helped feed and shelter the poor, which gained her a reputation for sincere piety. ❖ See also *Women in World History.*

AMBREE, Mary (fl. 1584). Military leader. Fl. in 1584. ❖ When the Spanish captured Ghent in the Netherlands (1584), joined other Dutch and English volunteers to liberate the city; said to be avenging the death of her lover, a sergeant major slain in the siege; has often been the subject of poems and ballads. ❖ See also *Women in World History.*

AMBROSE, Alice (1906–2001). American philosopher. Name variations: Alice Lazerowitz. Born Nov 25, 1906; died Jan 25, 2001, in Northampton, Massachusetts; Millikin University, BA (1928); University of Wisconsin, MA (1929), PhD (1932); attended Cambridge University, 1932–35; m. Morris Lazerowitz. ❖ Author of the "Blue and Yellow Books" based on Wittgenstein's lectures, was an assistant professor at Smith College (1943–51), professor (1951–64), Sophia and Austin Smith professor of philosophy (1964–72), and professor emeritus (1972—); edited the *Journal of Symbolic Logic* (1953–68).

AMBROSETTI, Bianca (1914–1929). Italian gymnast. Born Mar 1, 1914, in Italy; died 1929. ❖ At Amsterdam Olympics, won a silver medal in all-around team (1928).

AMBROSIE, Christie (1976—). American softball player. Born Dec 21, 1976, in Overland Park, Kansas; m. Regan Earl. ❖ Won a team gold medal at Sydney Olympics (2000).

AMBROSIUS, Johanna (b. 1854). German poet. Born at Lengwethen, a parish village in East Prussia, Aug 3, 1854; death date unknown; dau. of an artisan; m. a peasant's son by the name of Voigt, 1874. ❖ Led the life of a peasant woman until she began writing verse in middle age; submitting poems to a German weekly, caught the attention of Dr. Schrattenthal, who collected her verses and published them in one volume, which went through 26 editions; published other poems and stories that were also extremely popular.

AMELIA (1783–1810). English princess. Name variations: Amelia Guelph. Born Aug 7, 1783, in Buckingham House, London, England; died Nov 2, 1810, in Windsor, Berkshire, England; buried at St. George's Chapel, Windsor, Berkshire; 15th and youngest child of George III, king of England, and Charlotte of Mecklenburg-Strelitz; possibly m. to Charles Fitzroy.

AMELIA (1865–1951). *See Marie-Amelie of Orleans.*

AMELIA OF ANHALT-DESSAU (1666–1726). Princess of Nassau-Dietz. Name variations: Henriette Amalie von Anhalt-Dessau. Born Aug 26, 1666; died April 17, 1726; dau. of John George II, prince of Anhalt-Dessau, and Henrietta Catherine of Nassau (1637–1708); m. Henry Casimir of Orange-Nassau (1657–1696, cousin of King William III), prince of Nassau-Dietz; grandmother of William IV, prince of Orange; children: John William Firso of Orange-Nassau (1686–1711, who m. Louise of Hesse-Cassel.

AMELIA OF CLEVES (1517–1586). English noblewoman. Born 1517; died 1586; dau. of John III, duke of Cleves, and Maria of Julich-Berg; sister of Anne of Cleves (1515–1557).

AMELIA OF DENMARK (1580–1639). Duchess of Holstein-Gottorp. Name variations: Augusta Oldenburg. Born April 8, 1580; died Feb 5, 1639; dau. of Sophia of Mecklenburg (1557–1631) and Frederick II (1534–1588), king of Denmark and Norway (r. 1559–1588); m. John Adolphus, duke of Holstein-Gottorp, Aug 30, 1596; children: Frederick III (b. 1597), duke of Holstein-Gottorp.

AMELIA OF LEUCHTENBURG (1812–1873). Empress of Brazil. Name variations: Amelie or Amélie; Amalie von Leuchtenberg. Born July 31, 1812, in Milan; died Jan 26, 1873, in Lisbon; dau. of Amalie Auguste (1788–1851) and Eugène de Beauharnais, duchess and duke of Leuchtenburg; became 2nd wife of Dom Pedro I, emperor of Brazil (r. 1822–1831), also known as Peter IV, king of Portugal (r. 1826), Oct 17, 1829; children: Maria Amelia Augusta (1831–1853), princess of Brazil. ❖ See also Maria II da Gloria in *Women in World History.*

AMELIA OF ORLEANS (1865–1951). *See Marie-Amelie of Orleans.*

AMELIA OF SOLMS (1602–1675). Princess of Orange. Name variations: Amalia or Amelia von Solms-Braunfels. Born Aug 31, 1602; died Sept 8, 1675 (some sources cite 1667); m. Frederick Henry, prince of Orange (r. 1625–1647); children: William II (1626–1650), prince of Orange (r. 1647–1650); Louisa Henrietta of Orange (1627–1667); Henrietta Catherine of Nassau (1637–1708); Albertina Agnes (d. 1696).

AMELIA OF WURTTEMBERG (1799–1848). Duchess of Saxe-Altenburg. Name variations: Amalie von Wurttemberg. Born Amelia Theresa Louise Wilhelmina Philippina, June 28, 1799; died Nov 28, 1848; dau. of Louis Frederick, duke of Wurttemberg (brother of King Frederick I) and Henrietta of Nassau-Weilburg (1780–1857); m. Joseph, duke of Saxe-Altenburg, April 24, 1817; children: 6, including Mary of Saxe-Altenburg (1818–1907); Elisabeth of Saxe-Altenburg (1826–1896); Alexandra of Saxe-Altenburg (1830–1911); Therese of Saxe-Altenburg.

AMELIA SOPHIA (1711–1786). English princess. Name variations: Amelia Guelph. Born Amelia Sophia Eleanor, June 10, 1711, in Herrenhausen, Germany; died Oct 31, 1786, in London, England; buried in Westminster Abbey, London; dau. of George II (1683–1760), king of Great Britain and Ireland (r. 1727–1760) and Caroline of Ansbach (1683–1737).

AMELING, Elly (1938—). Dutch soprano. Born Elisabeth Sara in Rotterdam, The Netherlands, Feb 8, 1938; studied with Pierre Bernac. ❖ Debuted in London (1966) and NY (1968); focusing on the concert stage, was particularly known for her French songs as well as for her Schubert *lieder;* performed works of Mozart and Handel and more modern composers like Satie, Mahler, Ravel, Stravinsky, and Britten. Won the Hertogenbosch Prize (1956), Geneva Prize (1957), and Edison Prize (1965, 1970); was made a Knight of the Order of Oranje Nassau (1971). ❖ See also *Women in World History.*

AMERICA³ TEAM (1995—). Yachting team. Pronunciation: America Cubed. ❖ Crew of the 1st all-women America's Cup Team to compete in the 144-year history of the America's Cup race (1995): Jennifer (J.J.) Isler (San Diego, CA); Ann Nelson (San Diego, CA); Elizabeth (Lisa) Charles (Provincetown, RI); Hannah Swett (Jamestown, RI); Joan Lee Touchette (Newport, RI); Shelley Beattie (Malibu, CA); Stephanie Armitage-Johnson (Auburn, WA); Dawn Riley (Detroit, MI); Merritt Carey (Tenants Harbor, ME); Amy Baltzell (Wellesley, MA); Courtenay Becker-Dey (The Dalles, OR); Sarah Bergeron (Middletown, NJ); Sarah Cavanagh (Denver, CO); Leslie Egnot (born in South Carolina but moved to Auckland, New Zealand); Christie Evans (Marblehead, MA); Diana Klybert (Annapolis, MD); Susanne (Suzy) Leech Nairn (Annapolis, MD); Linda Lindquist (Chicago, IL); Stephanie Maxwell-Pierson (Somerville, NJ); Jane Oetking (Rockwell, TX); Merritt Palm (Fort Lauderdale, FL); Katherine (Katie) Pettibone (Coral Gables, FL); Marci Porter (Oarton, VA); Melissa Purdy (Tiburon, CA). ❖ See also *Women in World History.*

AMES, Adrienne (1907–1947). American actress. Born Adrienne Ruth McClure, Aug 3, 1907, in Fort Worth, Texas; died May 31, 1947, in New York, NY; sister of Gladys MacClure (1914–1933, actress); m. Stephen Ames (div.); m. Bruce Cabot (actor), 1933 (div. 1937). ❖ Leading lady, made film debut in *Girls about Town* (1931); other films include *Husband's Holiday, A Bedtime Story, You're Telling Me* and *Panama Patrol;* had her own radio show; appeared on stage only once (1945), in *The Beggars Are Coming to Town.*

AMES, Blanche (1878–1969). Botanical illustrator, inventor, and crusader for women's rights. Born Feb 18, 1878, in Lowell, Massachusetts; died in North Easton, Massachusetts, 1969; dau. of Adelbert Ames (Civil War general, US Senator, and governor of Mississippi during Reconstruction) and Blanche (Butler) Ames; Smith College, BA, 1899; m. Oakes Ames (renowned botanist), May 15, 1900; children: Pauline (Mrs. Francis T.P. Plimpton); Oliver; Amyas; Evelyn (Mrs. John Paschall Davis). ❖ Married a young botany instructor at Harvard University (1900); illustrated the various species of orchids he identified; over a period of 17 years, published a definitive 7-volume series, *Orchidaceae Illustrations and Studies of the Family Orchidaceae,* with husband; also devoted hours to her own oil painting, some of which are displayed at Phillips Exeter Academy, Columbia University, and Dartmouth College; a staunch suffragist, drew a number of political cartoons; a co-founder of the Birth Control League of Massachusetts, wrote and illustrated pamphlets describing methods for homemade diaphragms and spermicidal jelly; invented and patented several devices, including an antipollution toilet, a hexagonal lumber cutter, and a snare for catching low-flying enemy planes during WWII; published *Adelbert Ames, 1835–1933: Broken Oaths and Reconstruction in Mississippi* (1964). ❖ See also *Women in World History.*

AMES, Eleanor Maria (1830–1908). American writer. Name variations: (pseudonym) Eleanor Kirk. Born Eleanor Maria Easterbrook in 1830; died 1908; lived in Brooklyn, NY. ❖ Under pseudonym Eleanor Kirk, wrote *Up Broadway* (1870), *Information for Authors* (1888) and *Perpetual Youth.*

AMES, Fanny Baker (1840–1931). American reformer. Born Julia Frances Baker, June 14, 1840, in Canandaigua, NY; died Aug 21, 1931, in Barnstable, Massachusetts; attended Antioch College; m. Charles Gordon Ames (Unitarian minister); children: Alice Ames Winter (1865–1944, writer and social activist). ❖ With Unitarian minister husband, founded the Relief Society of Germantown, Pennsylvania (1873), the 1st visiting social-worker service in US; on her suggestion, Women's Auxiliary Conference of the Unitarian Church founded (1880); was incorporator (1883) and member of the 1st board of the Children's Aid Society and Bureau of Information; was also active in a number of woman suffrage associations.

AMES, Frances (1920–2002). South African neurologist, psychologist and anti-apartheid activist. Born Frances Rix Ames, 1920, in Pretoria, South Africa; died of leukemia, Nov 11, 2002, in Cape Town, South Africa; dau. of a nurse; was the 1st woman to earn an MD from University of Cape Town; m. David Castle (liberal journalist, died 1967); children: 4 sons. ❖ As head of neurology at University of Cape Town Medical School, forced the South African Medical and Dental Council (SAMDC) to reopen its inquiry into the conduct of two doctors involved in the medical care of Steven Biko following his death while in detention (1977); when the SAMDC refused, successfully took the council to the Supreme Court; retired (1985); wrote of her 30-year relationship with her domestic worker, *Mothering in an Apartheid Society* (2001). Awarded the Star of Africa by Nelson Mandela (1999).

AMES, Jessie Daniel (1883–1972). American reformist. Name variations: Daniel Ames, Jessie. Born Jessie Daniel on Nov 2, 1883, in Palestine, Texas; died Feb 21, 1972, of crippling arthritis in an Austin, TX, nursing home; dau. of Laura Leonard (teacher and nurse) and James Malcolm Daniel (railroad worker); Southwestern College, BA, 1902; m. Roger Post Ames, June 28, 1905 (died 1914); children: Frederick Ames (b. 1907); Mary Ames (b. 1912); Lulu Ames (b. 1915). ❖ Founding president of the Association of Southern Women for the Prevention of Lynching, succeeded in increasing positive race relations and decreasing lynching in the South; entered college at 13; was founding president of the Texas League of Women Voters (1919); served as representative to the Pan-American Congress (1923); acted as a delegate-at-large to the national Democratic Party conventions (1920, 1924); appointed executive director of the Texas Commission on Interracial Cooperation and field representative for the Southwest (1922–25); appointed 1st president

of the Texas Interracial Commission (1922); helped found and was the 1st president of the American Association of University Women (AAUW, 1926); appointed director of the women's program for all Commission on Interracial Cooperation branches, which resulted in a move to Atlanta (1929–37); was founding president of the Association of Southern Women for the Prevention of Lynching (1930–42); served as general field secretary of Commission on Interracial Cooperation for 13 Southern states (1937–44). ❖ See also Jacquelyn Dowd Hall, *Revolt Against Chivalry: Jessie Daniel Ames and the Women's Campaign Against Lynching* (Columbia University Press, 1979); and *Women in World History.*

AMES, Lucy True (1856–1936). *See Mead, Lucia Ames.*

AMES, Mary Clemmer (1831–1884). American writer. Name variations: Mary E. Ames; Mary Clemmer, Mrs. Hudson. Born Mary Clemmer, May 6, 1831, in Utica, NY; died Aug 18, 1884, in Washington, DC; m. Daniel Ames, 1851 (div., 1874); m. Edmund Hudson (journalist), June 19, 1883. ❖ Best known for her regular "Woman's Letter from Washington" in the New York *Independent* (beginning 1866) which addressed contemporary political issues; was reportedly the highest paid woman journalist in the country while writing for the *Brooklyn Daily Union* (1869–72); works include 3 novels (among them *Eirene; or, a Woman's Right* [1871]), a *Memorial of Alice and Phoebe Cary* (1873), and *Poems of Life and Nature* (1882).

AMES, Rosemary (1906–1988). American actress. Born Dec 11, 1906, in Evanston, Illinois; died April 15, 1988, in Truth or Consequences, New Mexico; studied at RADA; m. Ogden Ketting (div.); m. Bertie Meyer (div.); m. Abner J. Stillwell (div.). ❖ Made stage debut in London as Jenny in *Late Night Final* (1931); other appearances include Shirley Holmes in *The Holmeses of Baker Street* and Sylvia Lang in *Virginia Lang;* films include *Mr. Quincy of Monte Carlo* (1933), *I Believed in You, Gigolette* and *Our Little Girl.*

AMICIE DE COURTENAY (d. 1275). Countess of Artois. Name variations: Amicia de Courteney. Dau. of Peter de Courtenay; died in 1275; m. Robert II (1250–1302), count of Artois, 1262; children: Mahaut (c. 1270–1329), countess of Artois.

AMICO, Leah (1974—). American softball player. Name variations: Leah O'Brien; Leah O'Brien-Amico. Born Sept 9, 1974, in Chino, California; attended University of Arizona; m. Thomas Amico. ❖ Led Arizona Wildcats to 3 College World Series titles (1993, 1994, 1997); won team World championship (2002); won team gold medals at Atlanta Olympics (1996), Sydney Olympics (2000), and Athens Olympics (2004).

AMIEL, Josette (1930—). French ballet dancer. Born Nov 29, 1930, in Vanves, France. ❖ Joined Paris Opéra Ballet, France (1949), where she danced in company productions of such classics as *Giselle* and *Swan Lake* and was company étoile (star, or principal dancer, 1958–71); joined faculty of Paris Opéra Ballet after retirement as dancer; further performances include parts in Serge Lifar's *Chemin de Lumière* (1957), Venusberg divertissement for *Tannhauser* (1956), and premieres of Flemming Flindt's *La Leçon* (1963), *Symphonie de Gounod* (1964), and *Le Jeune Homme à Marier* (1965).

AMIN, Adibah (1936—). Malaysian novelist, actress and journalist. Name variations: Khalida Adibah binti Haji Amin; Khalidah Adibah bt Amin; (pseudonym) Sri Delima. Born Feb 19, 1936, in Johor Bahru, Malaysia; elder dau. of Ibu Zain who published women's magazine *Bulan Melayu.* ❖ With Habsah Hassan, published radio plays in the collection *Pulang Gadisku Pulang* (1977); translated Shanon Ahmad's *Ranjau Sepanjang Jalan* as *No Harvest But a Thorn* and John Ong's *Garam Gula Duka Bahagia* (1982) as *Sugar and Salt;* novels include *Puteri Asli* (1949), *Gadis Sipu* (1949), *Seroja Masih di Kolam* (1968), and the autobiographical *Tempat Latuh Lagi Dikenang* (Remembrances, 1983); also contributed short stories to women's magazine *Ibu* and wrote column "As I Was Passing" for English-language paper *New Straits Times;* film appearances include *Adik Manja* (1980), *Hati Bukan Kristal* (1989) and *Mat Som* (1990). Named Malaysian Journalist of the Year (1979); named Best Supporting Actress at 1st Malaysia Film Festival (1980); received South East Asia WRITE Award (1983) and ESSO-GAPENA Promotion Award for spread of literature (1991).

AMINA (died c. 576). Mother of Muhammad. Fl. around 550; lived in Makkah; of the Quraish, then the ruling tribe of Mecca; m. Abd Allah (died c. 569); children: Muhammad (the prophet, b. c. 570). ❖ Died when her son was 6.

AMINA (c. 1533–c. 1598). Queen of Zaria. Born c. 1533 in the region of Zazzau, during the reign of the Sarkin Zazzau Nohir; dau. of Queen Turunku Bakwa; sister of Zaria. ❖ One of the most important leaders of West Africa in the last 3rd of the 16th century, was sovereign ruler of the Hausa Empire in what is today the northern region of Nigeria; at outset of reign, policies were based on warfare and a political strategy of unambiguous expansionism; was soon known in much of West Africa as the fearsome ruler who personally led a well-trained army of 20,000 warriors, eventually expanding the frontiers of the new state of Zaria to the Atlantic coast and to the River Niger; by end of reign, had made Zaria the leading state of the Hausa people, establishing the economic as well as military foundations of a great state, introducing and encouraging the spread of the cola nut as a crop. ❖ See also *Women in World History.*

AMINI-HUDSON, Johari (1935—). American poet. Name variations: Jewel Lattimore; Johari Amini; Johari Amini Hudson. Born Jewel Lattimore in 1935 in Philadelphia, Pennsylvania; married young. ❖ A founding member of the Third World Press and an important figure in the Organization of Black American Culture, served as founder and editor of *Black Books Bulletin;* writings include *Images in Black* (1967), *Black Essence* (1968), and *Let's Go Somewhere* (1970); also contributed to such magazines as *Black World* and *Black Books Bulletin;* published the broadside *A Hip Tale in the Death Style* (1970).

AMLINGYN, Katherine (fl. late-15th c.). Erfurt merchant. Fl. in late-15th century. ❖ With daughter, ran a trading company specializing in woad, a plant of the mustard family from which blue textile dye was made; ran a large operation, dealing with buyers in cities all across southern Europe.

AMMA (1953—). See Amritanandamayi, Mata.

AMMERS-KÜLLER, Johanna van (1884–1966). Dutch novelist and playwright. Born Johanna Küller, Aug 13, 1884, in Delft, Holland, the Netherlands; died in 1966 in Amsterdam, Holland; m. in 1904; children: two sons. ❖ Considered the foremost interpreter of Dutch middle-class life after WWI, won international acclaim with her depiction of Holland's youth in *The Rebel Generation* (1925), which was translated into 10 languages; was also an activist with Holland's PEN. Writings include *The House of Joy* (1929), *Tantalus* (1930), *No Surrender* (1931), *Masquerade* (1932), and *The House of Tavelinck* (1938).

AMOHAU, Merekotia (1898–1978). New Zealand tribal singer, entertainer, and composer. Born April 16, 1898, at Ohinemutu, Rotorua, New Zealand; died Dec 30, 1978, in Rotorua; dau. of Henare Mete Amohau and Tukau Te Hira; m. Rongomaiwhiti Winiata (clerk), 1939 (died 1953); children: (1st m.) 3, and 3 from other unions. ❖ Regarded as authority on Te Arawa historical chants, performed with F.A. Bennett's Maori Opera Company as young girl; toured successfully throughout New Zealand; member of Rotorua Maori Choir; foundation member of Te Ropu o te Ora Maori Women's Health League (1937); composed traditional and contemporary Maori music.

AMOORE, Judith Pollock (1940—). Australian runner. Name variations: Judy Pollock; Judith Amoore-Pollock; Judy Amoore. Born Judith Amoore, June 25, 1940, in Melbourne, Australia. ❖ At Tokyo Olympics, won a bronze medal for Australia in the 400-meters (1964); won a gold medal for the 440 yards at Commonwealth Games (1966); competed in 3 Olympics and set many world records.

AMOR, Guadalupe (1920—). Mexican poet. Born in 1920 in Mexico. ❖ Through her metaphysical poetry, widely read in Mexico, explored the human condition; writings include *Yo soy mi casa* (I Am My House, 1946), *Círculo de anguista* (Circle of Anguish, 1948), *Polvo* (Dust, 1949), *Como reina de barajas* (Queen of Cards, 1966), *A mí me ha dado en escriber sonetos* (I Have Taken to Writing Sonnets, 1981), and *Soy dueña del universo* (I Am the Mistress of the Universe, 1984).

AMOR LIMA, Sisleide (1967—). See Sissi.

AMORY, Katherine (1731–1777). American diarist. Born 1731; lived in Boston; died 1777 in London, England. ❖ To escape consequences of being a British Loyalist in Boston during the American Revolution, sailed for London (1775), where she remained. *The Journal of Mrs. John Amory, 1775–1777,* describes her voyage across the Atlantic.

AMOS, Tori (1963—). American singer, songwriter, and pianist. Born Myra Ellen Amos on Aug 22, 1963, in Newton, North Carolina; m. Mark Hawley (music engineer), 1998. ❖ As child prodigy, began playing classical piano at 5; had band, Y Kant Tori Read, which released one self-titled album (1988); known for songs about the female experience, made solo debut with *Little Earthquakes* (1992), which included the song "Me and a Gun," about her experience of being raped; serves as chair of the Rape, Abuse and Incest National Network (RAINN), which she co-founded (1994). Albums include *Crucify* (EP, 1992), *Under the Pink* (#12, 1994, platinum), *Boys for Pele* (#2, 1996, platinum), *Hey Juniper* (1996), *From the Choirgirl Hotel* (#5, 1998), and *To Venus and Back* (#12, 1999).

AMOSOVA, Zinaida (fl. 1976). Russian cross-country skier. Name variations: Sinaida Amossowo. Born in USSR. ❖ Won a gold medal for 4x5km relay at Innsbruck Olympics (1976).

AMOSSOWO, Sinaida. See Amosova, Zinaida.

AMPARO RUIZ DE BURTON, Maria (1832–1895). American novelist. Born María Amparo Ruiz, 1832, in Baja, California; died in 1895; m. Henry S. de Burton, 1849; children: 2. ❖ Chicana who wrote *The Squatter and the Don* (1885), the 1st novel in English to depict plight of Californios after US annexation of California; also wrote *Don Quixote de la Mancha. A Comedy in five acts taken from Cervantes novel of that name* (n.d.), and *Who Would Have Thought It?* (1872).

AMPHLETT, Christina (c. 1960—). Australian vocalist and songwriter. Name variations: Divinyls; Chrissie Amphlett. Born Oct 25, 1959, in Geelong, Victoria, Australia. ❖ Served as vocalist for Australian band Divinyls (formed 1981 in Sydney); costarred in film *Monkey Grip* and with Divinyls released EP of the same name (1982); after band dissolved, continued working as Divinyls with cowriter and guitarist Mark McEntee with whom she released hit single "I Touch Myself" (#4, 1991). Other albums by Divinyls include *Desperate* (1983), *What a Life!* (1985), *Temperamental* (1988), *Divinyls* (1991), *Essential Divinyls* (1991), and *Underworld* (1996).

AMRANE, Djamila (1939—). French-Algerian political terrorist, educator and novelist. Name variations: Danièle Djamila Amrane-Minne; Danielle or Daniele Minne; (nom de guerre) Djamila. Born Danièle Minne in 1939 in France; grew up in Algeria; dau. of a communist professor and Jacqueline Guerroudj (French communist secondary school teacher and terrorist). ❖ Along with Djamila Bouhired and Zohra Drif, was one of the *poseuses de bombes* (bomb carriers) during battle of Algiers (1956); arrested and jailed (Dec 1956); was sentenced to 16 years in French prison but liberated after the independence (1962); used PhD thesis as the basis for her book *Les Femmes algériennes dans la guerre* (1991), concerning the participation of women in the liberation struggle; taught at University of Toulouse-le-Mirail; was a historian and senior lecturer at University of Algiers.

AMRIT, Princess (1889–1964). See Kaur, Rajkumari Amrit.

AMRITANANDAMAYI, Mata (1953—). Indian spiritual leader. Name variations: Amma or Ammachi which means "Mother"; Amritanandamayi which means "Mother of Absolute Bliss." Born Sept 27, 1953, into a poor, low-caste family in Parayakadavu, in the Quilon district of Kerala, India; named Sudhamani. ❖ Ran away from home when young, took a vow of celibacy, and dedicated her life to the uplifting of human suffering by a loving embrace (darshan); called "The Hugging Saint," has dispensed hugs to millions of followers, including 18,000 in one marathon session in India; a Hindu, began delivering hugs at 21, but does not attempt to convert people of other religions, nor does she call herself a healer; has raised tens of millions for such charities as soup kitchens, shelters for battered women, and an AIDS center in India; has built 25,000 homes for the homeless in India and provides pensions for 50,000 destitute women; founded an 800-bed hospital in Cochin, a medical college, and a university; founded an ashram in Kerala and about 25 ashrams abroad; attracts thousands wherever she speaks; served as president of the Centenary Parliament of World Religions in Chicago; was a speaker at the UN's 50th anniversary commemoration (1995). Received UN's Gandhi-King Award for Nonviolence (2002).

AMROUCHE, Fadhma Mansour (1882–1967). Algerian-born Berber poet and folksinger. Name variations: Fadhma Aith Mansur. Born 1882 in the Kabylia region of Eastern Algeria; died in Brittany, July 9, 1967; an out-of-wedlock child, she was raised by French nuns; m. Belkacem-ou-Amrouche, 1899; children: eight, including Marie-Louise Amrouche (1813–1976) and Jean Amrouche (poet). ❖ Was one of the 1st Berber women to receive a Western-style education in colonial Algeria; uneasily suspended between Berber and French culture, recorded the vicissitudes of her life in autobiography *My Life Story: The Autobiography of a Berber Woman* (1946); was eventually recognized for preserving the Berber culture of her ancestors. ❖ See also *Women in World History.*

AMROUCHE, Marie-Louise (1913–1976). Algerian folklorist and novelist. Name variations: Taos Amrouche; Marguerite Taos Bourdil. Born Marie-Louise Taos Amrouche in 1913 in Tunisia, Algeria; died in 1976 in France; dau. of Fadhma Mansour Amrouche (author) and Belkacem-ou-Amrouche, sister of Jean Amrouche (poet). ❖ The 1st Algerian woman to publish a novel, rose to fame with her translation and performance of traditional Berber (Kabylia) songs in French (c. 1937); moved to France (1945), where she published the novel *Jacinthe noir* (*Black Hyacinth*), followed by *Rue des Tambourins* (1960), and *Le grain magique* (*The Magic Grain*), written in Kabylia and translated to French (1966); published mother's autobiography, *The Story of My Life* (1968), and was instrumental in the creation of a chair of Berber literature and sociology at the University of Algeria.

AMROUCHE, Taos (1913–1976). *See Amrouche, Marie-Louise.*

AMUNDRUD, Gail (1957—). Canadian swimmer. Born April 6, 1957, in British Columbia, Canada; attended Arizona State University, 1978–81. ❖ At Commonwealth Games, won gold medals for 4 x 10-meter freestyle relay and 4 x 100-meter medley relay (1974) and 4 x 100-meter freestyle relay (1978); at Montreal Olympics, won a bronze medal in the 4 x 100-meter freestyle relay (1976); won gold medal for 200-meter freestyle at US Nationals (1977); was the 1st Canadian female to break 1:00.00 in 100-meter freestyle long course and 2:00.00 in 200-meter freestyle short course. Inducted into British Columbia Hall of Fame (1999).

AMY, Sister (1869–1928). *See Archer-Gilligan, Amy.*

AN SANG-MI. South Korean short-track speedskater. Born in South Korea. ❖ Won a gold medal for 3,000-meter relay at Nagano Olympics (1998).

AN ZHONGXIN. Chinese softball player. Fl. 1996. ❖ Catcher and pitcher, won a silver medal at Atlanta Olympics (1996).

ANABLE, Gloria Hollister (1903–1988). American zoologist and explorer. Name variations: Gloria Hollister. Born 1903; died 1988. ❖ While working with William Beebe in exploring the sea in his bathysphere, set the women's record for depth at 1,208 feet (Aug 1931); while flying a light plane in British Guiana (1936), discovered 43 unmapped waterfalls, including Kaieteur Falls, which is 5 times the elevation of Niagara; was a fellow with the New York Zoological Society and the Geographical Society.

ANACÁONA (fl. 1492). Indian princess of Haiti. Name variations: Anacaona; name means "Golden Flower." Fl. around 1492; sister of Behechio; m. Caonabo (cacique of Haiti). ❖ An Indian princess, was the sister of Behechio and wife of Caonabo, both caciques of Haiti when it was discovered by Christopher Columbus (1492); after the capture and death of Caonabo, advocated submission to the Spaniards and received Bartholomew Columbus with great hospitality (1498); succeeded her brother as ruler of his tribe, and friendly relations with the whites continued until 1503, when she entertained Ovando and his Spanish forces, who attacked her village, massacred a great number of her people, and carried her to Santo Domingo where she was hanged. ❖ See also *Women in World History.*

ANAGNOS, Julia (1844–1886). American poet. Born Julia Rowana Howe in Rome, Italy, 1844; died 1886; dau. of Samuel Gridley Howe and Julia Ward Howe (1819–1910); sister of Laura E. Richards and Maud Howe Elliott; m. M. Anagnos (superintendent of the Perkins Institute for the Blind in Boston, MA), 1870. ❖ Wrote *Stray Chords* (1883) and *Philosophiæ Quæstor.* ❖ See also Maud Howe Elliott, *Three Generations* (Little, Brown, 1923); and *Women in World History.*

ANAGNOSTAKI, Loula (1940—). Greek playwright. Born 1940 in Thessaloniki, Greece. ❖ Plays include *Overnight Stay, The City, Parade* (collected as *The City,* 1974), *Victory* (1978), *Nike, The Sound of the Gun, Diamonds and Blues, The Distant Trip* and *The Purple Sky.*

ANAN (fl. 9th c.). Arabic poet. Name variations: 'Anan. Died c. 846. ❖ Lived in Baghdad as slave to al-Natifi, who invited poets and intellectuals to meet her; wrote poems modeled on measures of classical Arabic poems, erotic poems (*mujun*) exchanged with poet Abu Nuwas, and love lyrics to poet Abbas ibn al-Ahnaf.

ANANKO, Tatyana (1984—). Belarusian rhythmic gymnast. Name variations: Tatiana Ananko. Born June 26, 1984, in Belarus. ❖ Won a silver medal for team all-around at Sydney Olympics (2000).

ANASTAISE (fl. 1400). French manuscript illuminator. Fl. in Paris c. 1400. ❖ A professional illuminator of manuscripts specializing in painting borders and flowers, her fame is documented in *Book of the City of Ladies* by Christine de Pizan.

ANASTASI, Anne (1908–2001). American psychologist. Born Dec 19, 1908, in New York, NY; died May 4, 2001, at her home in Manhattan; mother was office manager at *Il Progreso,* an Italian newspaper; attended Rhodes Preparatory School; Barnard College, degree in psychology, 1928; Columbia University, PhD, 1930; m. John Porter Foley Jr. (industrial psychologist), 1933. ❖ Pioneer in the field of testing to measure intelligence, aptitude, personality and creativity, began career as an instructor of psychology at Barnard (1930–39); became chair of psychology department at Queens College of City University of New York (1939); joined the faculty at Fordham University (1947), becoming full professor (1951); wrote *Psychological Testing* (1954), which became required reading in college courses, as well as more than 150 books, monographs and articles; was the 3rd woman elected president of American Psychological Association (APA, 1972). Received gold medal for lifetime achievement from APA (1984) and National Medal of Science (1987).

ANASTASIA (fl. 54–68). Christian martyr. Slain during the reign of Nero (r. 54–68). ❖ With Saint Basilissa, said to have been beheaded for burying the bodies of their teachers, St. Peter and St. Paul. Their martyrdom is commemorated on April 15.

ANASTASIA (d. 304). Christian saint. Name variations: Anastasia of Sirmium. Died 304. ❖ A Roman of noble birth, suffered martyrdom during persecution of Christians in Sirmium (modern-day Yugoslavia) under Roman emperor Diocletian; when Christian mother died, forced to marry a pagan by father; treated cruelly by husband on learning belatedly that she was a Christian; after he died, devoted herself to secret works of charity, using what remained of her fortune to relieve the Christian poor; when her works caused suspicion, was arrested with 3 female servants and all were ordered to sacrifice to idols; on refusal, was banished, and servants were executed; brought back to Rome and burned alive. In the Orthodox Church, her feast is celebrated Dec 22; in Roman Catholic Church, she is the only saint to be celebrated on a major feast day, receiving a special commemoration in the 2nd Mass of Christmas Day. ❖ See also *Women in World History.*

ANASTASIA (fl. 500s). Byzantine courtesan. Born on island of Cyprus, or more likely in Syria, c. 500; dau. of Acacius (guardian of the bears for the Greens at the Hippodrome in Constantinople) and an unnamed actress; sister of Empress Theodora and Comitona. ❖ By late teens, was a favorite both on the stage, where she "undraped the beauty of which she was so proud," and off, where she followed in the footsteps of sister Comitona as a prostitute or courtesan (in the context of the time, actress was synonymous with prostitute). ❖ See also *Women in World History.*

ANASTASIA (fl. 600s). Byzantine empress. Fl. in 600s; m. Constantine IV Pogonatus (r. 668–685); children: Justinian II Rhinotmetos, Byzantine emperor (r. 705–711).

ANASTASIA (fl. 800s). Byzantine princess. Dau. of Theophilus and Empress Theodora (fl. 842–856); sister of Pulcheria, Mary, Thecla, Anna, and Michael III.

ANASTASIA (d. about 860). Christian saint. Name variations: Athanasia. Born and lived on the island of Aegina. ❖ Was forced into an advantageous marriage, even though she had looked forward to the life of a religious from childhood; when husband was killed in defense of Aegina, forced to marry a 2nd time, but new husband was as wealthy and generous as she, and their home became a refuge for the poor; after husband became a monk and left her his possessions, gathered companions to her home and trained them for the religious life; with the help of a priest called Matthias, went with them into the wilderness of Timia where she built her convent, which she directed until her death; reputedly corresponded with the empress Theodora the Blessed (fl. 842–856). Feast day is Aug 14. ❖ See also *Women in World History.*

ANASTASIA (1901–1918). Russian grand duchess. Name variations: Anastasia Romanov (Romanoff or Romanovna), June 18, 1901, in Peterhof, Russia; executed July 17, 1918, at Ekaterinburg, in Central Russia; youngest dau. of Tsar Nicholas II and Alexandra Feodorovna (1872–1918, known also as Alix of Hesse-Darmstadt). ❖ When Civil War broke out (1918), was moved—along with parents, sisters Tatiana, Olga, and Marie, and brother Alexis—to Ekaterinburg, east of the Ural Mountains; executed with family on Lenin's orders. As rumors circulated that 17-year-old Anastasia had survived the death squad, theories abounded as to her whereabouts; the most convincing conjecture was that she reappeared in Germany under the name Anna Anderson, though DNA comparisons finally debunked Anderson's claim; speculation continues around the "missing children" whose remains have not been found—Alexei and either Anastasia or Maria. ❖ See also film *Anastasia,* starring Ingrid Bergman; and *Women in World History.*

ANASTASIA (1902–1984). *See Anderson, Anna.*

ANASTASIA OF MONTENEGRO (1868–1935). *See Anastasia Petrovitch-Njegos.*

ANASTASIA OF RUSSIA (c. 1023–after 1074). Queen of Hungary. Name variations: Anastasia Agmunda of Kiev. Born c. 1023 in Kiev, Ukraine; died after 1074; dau. of Yaroslav I the Wise (b. 978), grand prince of Kiev (r. 1019–1054), and Ingigerd Olafsdottir (c. 1001–1050); m. Andrew I (c. 1001–1060), king of Hungary (r. 1047–1060), around 1046; children: Salamon also known as Solomon, king of Hungary (r. 1063–1074, deposed); Adelaide of Hungary (d. 1062).

ANASTASIA OF SIRMIUM (d. 304). *See Anastasia.*

ANASTASIA PETROVITCH-NJEGOS (1868–1935). Russian royal. Name variations: Anastasia of Montenegro; (nickname) Stana. Born Jan 4, 1868; died Nov 15, 1935; dau. of Nicholas, king of Montenegro, and Milena (1847–1923); m. Nicholas Nicholaevitch (grandson of Nicholas I of Russia and Charlotte of Prussia), May 12, 1907. ❖ Fond of psychics and faith healers, had a hand in introducing Rasputin into the Romanov household of Empress Alexandra Feodorovna.

ANASTASIA ROMANOVA (d. 1560). Russian empress. Name variations: Romanovna. Died Aug 7, 1560; dau. of Roman Yurievich, a non-titled landowner (d. 1543) and Juliane Feodorovna (d. 1550); sister of Nikita Romanov (d. 1586); became 1st wife of Ivan IV (1530–1584), tsar of Russia (r. 1533–1584), Feb 3, 1547; children: Anna (1548–1550); Dmitri (b. 1552, drowned in 1553); Maria (1551–1554); Ivan Ivanovich (b. 1554, killed by his father in 1581); Eudoxia (1556–1558); Fyodor also known as Theodore I (1557–1598), tsar of Russia (r. 1584–1598).

ANASTASIA ROMANOVA (1860–1922). Russian royal and grand duchess of Mecklenburg-Schwerin. Name variations: Grand Duchess Anastasia; Romanov. Born Anastasia Michaelovna Romanov, July 28, 1860; died Mar 11, 1922; dau. of Michael Nicholaevitch (son of Nicholas I of Russia and Charlotte of Prussia) and Cecilia of Baden (1839–1891); m. Frederick Francis III, grand duke of Mecklenburg-Schwerin, Jan 24, 1879; children: Alexandrina of Mecklenburg-Schwerin (1879–1952); Frederick Francis IV, grand duke of Mecklenburg-Schwerin; Cecilia of Mecklenberg-Schwerin (1886–1954).

ANASTASIA THE PATRICIAN (d. 567). Christian saint. Died 567. ❖ Served as lady-in-waiting to Empress Theodora; to escape attentions of Emperor Justinian I, fled from the court of Constantinople and, dressed as a male, lived the life of a hermit in the desert of Scete for 28 years. ❖ See also *Women in World History.*

ANASTASOVSKI, Svetlana (1961—). Yugoslavian handball player. Name variations: Svetlana Obucina. Born April 26, 1961, in USSR. ❖ At Olympics, won a silver medal in Moscow (1980) and a gold medal in Los Angeles in team competition (1984).

ANCELOT, Marguerite (1792–1875). French author and salonnière. Born Marguerite Louise Virginie Chardon in Dijon, France, 1792; died 1875; m. Jacques Arsène Polycarpe Ancelot (1794–1854, French dramatist). ❖ Had one of the most fashionable salons during the period of the July monarchy (1831–1848) and was influential in the works of Prosper Merimée and Stendhal; writings include *Un mariage raisonable* (*A Sensible Marriage,* 1835), *Marie ou les trois époques* (*Marie or the Three Epochs,* 1836), *Renée de Varville* (1853), and *The Banker's Niece* (1853).

ANASTOS, Rosemary Park (1907–2004). *See Park, Rosemary.*

ANCHER, Anna (1859–1935). Danish painter. Name variations: AN-ker. Born Anna Kirstine Bröndum in Skagen, the northernmost village in Denmark, 1859; died 1935; dau. of Erik and Anna (Hedvig) Bröndum; studied under Professor Vilhelm Kyhn, 1875–78, and Pierre Puvis de Chavannes in Paris, 1888–89; m. Michael Ancher (painter), 1880; children: Helga Ancher (painter, b. 1883). ❖ Painter of portraits and interiors, known for her masterful use of color and light, made debut at the Spring Exhibition of Paintings at Charlottenborg in Copenhagen

(1880), but before then she had already painted *Lars Gaihede Whittling a Stick;* developed and refined an outstanding sense of color all her own, thereby becoming a pioneer of modern Danish art; was elected a member of the Copenhagen Academy (1904); lived and died in Skagen, where her house became an important museum (June 23, 1967); paintings include *The Maid in the Kitchen* and *Sunshine in the Blue Room.* ❖ See also *Women in World History.*

ANCHUTINA, Leda (1915–1989). Russian-born ballet dancer. Name variations: Leda Eglevsky. Born Mar 23, 1915, in Irkustk, Siberia; died Dec 15, 1989, in Massapequa, NY; m. André Eglevsky (ballet dancer, died Dec 1977). ❖ Danced as one of George Balanchine's 1st pupils in US at School of American Ballet, NY; created roles as part of Balanchine's American Ballet and at Metropolitan Opera in works including *Serenade* (1934), *Reminiscence* (1935), *Jeu de Cartes* (1937), and *Le Baiser de la Fée* (1937); danced in 1st season of Balanchine students' Ballet Caravan; worked with William Dollar at Radio City Music Hall as première danseuse in *The Three Glass Hearts* (1939), and others; opened dance school with husband in Massapequa, Long Island, NY, where she taught classes; became school's director upon Eglevsky's death (1977).

ANCKARSVARD, Karin (1915–1969). Swedish children's author. Pronunciation: Ank-er-sord. Born Karin Inez Maria Olson, Aug 10, 1915, in Stockholm, Sweden; died Jan 16, 1969; dau. of Oscar Emil (doctor) and Iris (Forssling) Olson; attended Oxford University (1934–35); m. Carl M. Cosswa Anckarsvard, Jan 20, 1940; children: Marie Christine, Marie Cecile, Marie Madeleine, Mikael, Carl Henrik. ❖ Following the births of her children, published *Bonifacius the Green,* which was translated from Swedish to English by husband; wrote 13 more books for children, including the "Aunt Vinnie" series; as a journalist, contributed to Sweden's daily newspaper *Expressea.*

ANCKER-JOHNSON, Betsy (1927—). American physicist. Name variations: Betsy Ancker Johnson. Born Betsy Ancker, April 29, 1927, in St. Louis, Missouri; m. Harold Johnson (mathematician), 1958. ❖ Conducted research in solid state physics for Sylvania (1956–58), then RCA (1958–61); made primary contributions to plasma and solid state physics while at Boeing (1961–73); supervised Boeing's solid state and plasma electronics laboratory and managed the company's advanced energy systems (early 1970s); served as assistant secretary of commerce in charge of science and technology (1973–77), vice president in charge of environmental activities at General Motors (1979–92), and director of World Environment Center; served on board of directors: Society of Automotive Engineers, Varian Associates, Motor Vehicle Manufacturers Association, General Mills; became fellow of the Institute of Electrical and Electronic Engineers and the American Physical Society. Patent holder in solid state physics and semiconductor electronics.

ANDAM, Aba A. Bentil (c. 1960—). Ghanaian physicist. Name variations: A.A. Bentil Andam; Aba Andam. Born c. 1960 in Ghana. ❖ Studied charmed mesons (subatomic particles) at the Deutsches Elektronen-Synchrotron in Hamburg, Germany (1986–87); focused research primarily on radioactive gas radon, surveying levels of the gas in varying locations in Ghana with "closed can technique" to determine amount of radiation from radon people are exposed to and work toward reducing that level; became teacher at Ghana's University of Science and Technology in Kumasi; conducts research at the Nuclear Research Laboratory (Kumasi) in applied nuclear physics; became participant in secondary-school program science clinics (begun in 1987) which introduces girls to women scientists.

ANDERS, Beth (1951—). American field-hockey player and coach. Born Nov 13, 1951, in Norristown, Pennsylvania; graduated Ursinus College, 1973. ❖ Was on the US national team (1969–80) and won a team bronze medal at Los Angeles Olympics (1984); as head coach at Old Dominion, long held one of the most impressive win-loss records of any field hockey program, with teams winning 9 NCAA Division I titles, 3 of them consecutively (1982–84); was the 1st Div. I field hockey coach to capture 400 wins (2001); coached on the international level as well. Voted Amateur Athlete of the Year for Field Hockey by US Olympic Committee (1981, 1984) and Co-Athlete of the Year (with Charlene Morett) by *Olympian* magazine (1982); inducted into Pennsylvania Hall of Fame (1998).

ANDERS, Luana (1938–1996). American actress. Name variations: Lu Anders. Born May 12, 1938; died July 21, 1996, in Mar Vista, California; children: Allison Anders (b. 1954, filmmaker). ❖ Made film debut in *Reform School Girl* (1957), followed by *Life Begins at 17, The Pit and the Pendulum, Night Tide, The Last Detail, Shampoo, The*

Missouri Breaks, and Personal Best, among others; appeared as Lisa in *Easy Rider* and as Rona on tv's "Santa Barbara" (1991–92).

ANDERS, Merry (1932—). American actress. Born Mary Helen Anderson, May 22, 1932, in Chicago, Illinois. ❖ Made close to 50 films, including *Belles on Their Toes, Wait Till the Sun Shines Nellie, Les Miserables, How to Marry a Millionaire, Desk Set, Escape from San Quentin, Young Jesse James, Air Patrol, House of the Damned, Young Fury* and *Airport;* appeared as Joyce Erwin on tv's "The Stu Erwin Show" (1954–55) and made numerous guest appearances on leading tv shows, including "Gunsmoke," "Dragnet," "Maverick," and "Lassie."

ANDERSEN, Anja Jul (1969—). Danish handball player. Born Feb 5, 1969, in Denmark. ❖ Debuted on national team (1989); won a team gold medal at Atlanta Olympics (1996); won team European championships (1994, 1996) and World championships (1997); retired (1999). Named World's Best Handballer by International Handball Federation (1998).

ANDERSEN, Astrid Hjertenaes (1915–1985). Norwegian poet. Born Sept 5, 1915, in Horten, Norway; died April 21, 1985. ❖ One of Norway's foremost postwar poets, published 14 poetry collections in a career that spanned more than 40 years, including *De ville traner* (1945) and *Samlede dikt* (1985).

ANDERSEN, Camilla (1973—). Danish handball player. Born Camilla Røseler Andersen, July 5, 1973, in Bagsvaerd, Denmark. ❖ Won a team gold medal at Atlanta Olympics (1996) and at Sydney Olympics (2000); won team European championships (1994, 1996) and World championships (1997).

ANDERSEN, Catherine Ann (1870–1957). New Zealand teacher and writer. Name variations: Catherine Ann McHaffie. Born Catherine Ann McHaffie, Aug 1, 1870, at Onehunga, Auckland, New Zealand; died on Sept 15, 1957, in Auckland, New Zealand; dau. of James McHaffie and Ellen (Leatherbarrow) McHaffie; m. Johannes Carl Andersen (clerk), 1900. ❖ Trained as teacher at Christchurch Normal School and was certified in 1891; taught at Normal School until 1900; worked to establish free kindergarten in Christchurch (1910); helped found Canterbury Women's Club (1913); active in Wellington After-care Association (1920s); helped found Wellington Lyceum Club, which fostered creative writing and published their work in *Lyceum* (1932). ❖ See also *Dictionary of New Zealand Biography* (Vol. 3).

ANDERSEN, Dorothy Hansine (1901–1963). American pathologist and pediatrician. Born Dorothy Hansine Andersen in Asheville, North Carolina, May 15, 1901; died in New York, NY, Mar 3, 1963; only child of Hans Peter and Mary Louise (Mason) Andersen (descendant of Sir John Wentworth, colonial governor of New Hampshire, and of Benning Wentworth, for whom the town of Bennington, Vermont, was named); graduate of Saint Johnsbury Academy, 1918, Mount Holyoke College, 1922, Johns Hopkins Medical School, 1926; Columbia University, MD, 1935; never married; no children. ❖ While still in medical school, published 2 research papers in *Contributions to Embryology;* after graduation (1926), taught anatomy for a year before beginning an internship in surgery at Strong Memorial Hospital in Rochester, NY; denied both a residency in surgery and an appointment in pathology because she was a woman, took a position in the department of pathology at College of Physicians and Surgeons at Columbia University where she began research on the relationship of the endocrine glands to the female reproductive cycle; was appointed an instructor in pathology (1930); moved to Babies Hospital at Columbia-Presbyterian Medical Center, where as a pathologist she researched congenital heart defects in infants and would later share her expertise with pioneers in open-heart surgery; discovered and named the hereditary disease cystic fibrosis (1935) and eventually developed a simple, definitive test to diagnose the disease; named chief of pathology at Babies Hospital (1952); became a full professor at College of Physicians and Surgeons (1958); left an indelible mark on the field of pediatric medicine. Received Borden Award for research in nutrition and the distinguished service medal of Columbia-Presbyterian Medical Center. ❖ See also *Women in World History.*

ANDERSEN, Greta (1927—). Danish long-distance swimmer. Born May 1, 1927, in Copenhagen, Denmark. ❖ At London Olympics, won a gold medal in the 100-meter freestyle and a silver medal in the 4x100-meter freestyle relay (1948); set a world record for the 100 meters (58.2) that stood for 7 years; held 24 national titles and 4 European championships; repeatedly beat men in long-distance swimming; defeated

27 swimmers in a 26-mile competition along the coast of Guaymas, Mexico (1958); placed 1st in 18-mile Lake St. John swim in Quebec with a time of 8:17; swam from US mainland to Catalina in 11:7, breaking Florence Chadwick's record; swam across Lake Michigan, a distance of 50 miles, further than any long-distance swimmer had gone (1962). Elected to International Swimming Hall of Fame (1969).

ANDERSEN, Kjerstin (1958—). Norwegian handball player. Born Nov 25, 1958, in Norway. ❖ At Seoul Olympics, won a silver medal in the team competition (1988).

ANDERSEN, Kristine (1976—). Danish handball player. Born April 1976, in Aalborg, Denmark. ❖ Pivot, won a team gold medal at Atlanta Olympics (1996) and a team gold medal at Athens Olympics (2004).

ANDERSEN, Lale (1905–1972). German singer. Born Mar 23, 1905, in Lehe-Bremerhaven, Germany; died Aug 29, 1972, of a heart attack at the Vienna Airport, Austria. ❖ Became a moderately successful cabaret performer; traveled the circuit, appearing in small clubs throughout Germany and Central Europe; recorded "Lilli Marlene" in 1939 (though Anderson had a reputation of being openly critical of the Nazi regime, the song became a war-time hit in Germany and around the world and was later performed by Marlene Dietrich); after years in obscurity, recorded the theme from *Never on Sunday,* a smash hit both as a movie and as a song (1960); won the Eurovision Song Contest (1961). ❖ See also *Women in World History.*

ANDERSEN, Linda (1969—). Norwegian yacht racer. Born June 15, 1969, in Norway. ❖ At Barcelona Olympics, won a gold medal in the European class (1992).

ANDERSEN, Lisa (1969—). American surfer. Born Mar 8, 1969, in Ormond Beach, Fl. ❖ Collected 35 trophies in an 8-month stretch; won US Amateur championship (1987); turned pro (1988); won 4 consecutive World Surfing championships (1994–97). Named Rookie of the Year (1988). ❖ See also film "Greats of Women's Surfing" and Andrea Gabbard, *Girl in the Curl* (Seal Press).

ANDERSEN, Nina (1972—). See *Nymark Andersen, Nina.*

ANDERSEN, Roxanne (1912–2002). Canadian hurdler. Name variations: Roxy Atkins; Roxy Andersen. Born Jun 26, 1912, in Montreal, Quebec, Canada; died Sep 6, 2002. ❖ Was a top sprinter-hurdler for Canada (1930s), placing 4th at British Empire Games (1934); won US indoor hurdles title (1934); ran for Canada at Berlin Olympics (1936); after WWII, married, moved to California, and became a US citizen; pioneered women's and age group track-and-field programs that became national models. Received President's Award (1982); inducted into USATF Hall of Fame (1991).

ANDERSEN-SCHEISS, Gabriela (1945—). Swiss marathon runner. Born Mar 20, 1945, in Switzerland. ❖ At Los Angeles Olympics, suffering from heat prostration, crossed the finish line 29 minutes after Joan Benoit, taking 5:44 to finish the final lap.

ANDERSON, Adela Blanche (1846–1910). See *Stewart, Adela Blanche.*

ANDERSON, Anna (1902–1984). Impersonator of Russia's Grand Duchess Anastasia. Name variations: mistakenly, Anastasia; allegedly, Franziska Schanzkowskia; Anna Anderson Manahan. Born 1902; died in Charlottesville, Virginia, 1984; m. John E. "Jack" Manahan (retired university lecturer who backed her case for a decade); identity probably that of Franziska Schanzkowskia, dau. of Polish peasants. ❖ Maintained until her death that she was the Grand Duchess Anastasia, youngest daughter of Russia's Tsar Nicholas II and Empress Alexandra Feodorovna, and had escaped the execution of her family in July 1918. Scientists used DNA tests to compare her remains with those from the family of Anastasia and confirmed that Anderson was an impostor (1994). ❖ See also *Women in World History.*

ANDERSON, Anne (1874–1930). British-Argentinean illustrator of children's books. Born 1874; died 1930; m. Alan Wright (painter), with whom she collaborated. ❖ During height of career, was one of the most popular illustrators for children, following in the tradition and style of Jessie M. King and Charles Robinson; accomplished in both black-and-white line drawing and watercolor, was also successful as a greeting-card designer. ❖ See also *Women in World History.*

ANDERSON, Barbara (1926—). New Zealand novelist and short-story writer. Born 1926 in Hastings, New Zealand; educated in Hawkes Bay; University of Otago, BSc, 1947; Victoria University of Wellington, BA,

1984. ❖ For 30 years, worked as a laboratory technician and teacher in the sciences, before earning an arts degree (1984); was in her 60s before she began her career as a bestselling author; works include *I Think We Should Go Into the Jungle: Short Stories* (1989), *Girls' High* (1990), *Portrait of the Artist's Wife* (1992), *The House Guest* (1995), *Glorious Things, and Other Stories* (1999), *The Swing Around* (2001), and *Change of Heart* (2003).

ANDERSON, Bella (1864–?). American kidnapper. Born 1864 in US; death date unknown. ❖ As a trained nurse working for the Clarke family in NY, abducted their 20-month-old daughter Marion in a much-publicized kidnapping (mid-May 1899); after the child was returned home safely (late May), was arrested with George and Addie Barrow (the 3 had intended to make money by mass kidnapping children from families of average means); cooperated with prosecutors and received a lesser sentence than the Barrows.

ANDERSON, Beth (1950—). American composer and pianist. Born 1950 in Lexington, Kentucky; studied under John Cage, Robert Ashley, and Terry Riley. ❖ Worked as a concert pianist and accompanist; founded and co-edited *EAR* magazine (1973–79); was a performing member of Hysteresis (1973–75), a women composers' group; best known for her opera *Queen Christina* (1973).

ANDERSON, Bette B. (c. 1929—). American undersecretary of the Treasury. Name variations: Bette Anderson Wood. Born in Savannah, Georgia, c. 1929. ❖ Served as president of the National Association of Bank Women (1976); appointed undersecretary to the Treasury by President Jimmy Carter (1977); while in Washington, managed a budget of $5 billion; introduced the Susan B. Anthony dollar coin (1979).

ANDERSON, Betty (1895–1964). *See Anderson, Claire.*

ANDERSON, Blanche (1855–1875). *See Whiteside, Jane.*

ANDERSON, Caroline Still (1848–1919). African-American physician and educator. Name variations: Caroline Still. Born Caroline Virginia Still in Philadelphia, Pennsylvania, Nov 1, 1848; died in Philadelphia, June 1, 1919; dau. of William Still (abolitionist and prominent figure in the Philadelphia Underground Railroad); attended Oberlin College, 1865; attended medical school at Howard University and Woman's Medical College in Pennsylvania, 1875–78; interned at New England Hospital for Women and Children in Boston, 1878–79; m. Edward A. Wiley, 1869 (died 1873); m. Matthew Anderson, 1880; children: (2nd m., 3 of 5 survived) Helen, Maude, and Margaret. ❖ Papers are housed in the Charles L. Blockson Afro-American Collection, Temple University, in Philadelphia. ❖ See also *Women in World History.*

ANDERSON, Catherine (1835–1918). *See Charteris, Catherine.*

ANDERSON, Chantelle (1981—). African-American basketball player. Born Jan 22, 1981, in Vancouver, Washington; graduate of Vanderbilt, 2003. ❖ Center, was Vanderbilt's all-time leading scorer (2,604); selected in 1st round of WNBA draft by Sacramento Monarchs (2003); won a team gold medal at Athens Olympics (2004).

ANDERSON, Claire (1895–1964). American actress and dancer. Name variations: Betty Anderson, Cora Anderson. Born Claire Mathes (or Mathis) Anderson, May 8, 1895, in Detroit, Michigan; died Mar 23, 1964, in Venice, California. ❖ Danced in vaudeville locally; made film debut in Mack Sennett comedy (1919), subsequently appearing in movies with Tom Mix, John Gilbert, Gloria Swanson, and Ben Turpin; films include *The Road Demon, Cinders of Love, The Lion and the Girl, His Baby Doll, The Yellow Stain, The Clean-Up* and *The Hidden Spring.*

ANDERSON, Claire (fl. 1940s). American actress and dancer. Born in Pittsburgh, Pennsylvania. ❖ Appeared on Broadway in *Pal Joey* (1940–41) and *Mexican Hayride* (1944–45).

ANDERSON, Cora (1895–1964). *See Anderson, Claire.*

ANDERSON, Doris (1921—). Canadian journalist, novelist, and editor. Born Doris Hilda McCubbin, Nov 10, 1921, in Calgary, Alberta, Canada; dau. of Thomas and Rebecca (Laycock) McCubbin; educated at University of Alberta; m. David Anderson (lawyer), May 24, 1957 (div. 1972); children: Peter, Stephen, and Mitchell. ❖ Began publishing in magazines at 16; was a journalist for *Star Weekly;* joined the staff of *Chatelaine* (1951) and became the magazine's editor (1958), a position she would hold for 18 years; published 1st novel, *Two Women* (1978), followed by *Rough Layout* (1981); served as president of the Canadian

Advisory Council on the Status of Women and wrote *The Unfinished Revolution.*

ANDERSON, Elda E. (1899–1961). American health physicist and medical researcher. Name variations: Elda Emma Anderson. Born Oct 5, 1899, in Green Lake, Wisconsin; died April 1961, in Oak Ridge, Tennessee. ❖ Served as dean and teacher of physics and mathematics, and chemistry teacher, at Iowa's Estherville Junior College (1924–27); taught high-school science in Wisconsin; assisted in organization of physics department at Milwaukee-Downer College (1929), of which she served as professor and became chair (1934); took sabbatical from teaching to work at Princeton University's office of Scientific Research and Development (1941); joined scientists at Los Alamos Scientific Laboratory in New Mexico (1943), working on Manhattan Project to develop the atomic bomb; performed work with spectroscopy and experimental measurements of neutron cross-sections which was integral to development of atomic bomb and design of nuclear power reactors; witnessed "Trinity event" (1945); left Los Alamos and resumed teaching (1947–49); concerned about dangers of radiation, dedicated rest of life to developing the then-new field of health physics so as to research, and examine preventative measures for, radiation exposure; became 1st chief of education and training at Oak Ridge National Laboratory in Tennessee and established American Board of Health Physics; developed leukemia (1956), possibly as result of her exposure to radiation, then breast cancer (1961); was fellow of American Association for the Advancement of Science; published *Manual of Radiological Protection for Civil Defense* (1950). The Elda E. Anderson Award from the Health Physics Society was established in her memory.

ANDERSON, Elizabeth (c. 1893–1973). *See Anderson-Ivantzova, Elizabeth.*

ANDERSON, Elizabeth Garrett (1836–1917). English doctor. Name variations: Elizabeth Garrett. Born June 9, 1836, in London, England; died Dec 17, 1917, in Aldeburgh, England; 2nd dau. of Newson Garrett (successful merchant) and Louisa Dunnell Garrett; attended Miss Browning's School for Girls, London, 1849–51; studied medicine privately and at various hospitals in Britain, 1860–65; Sorbonne, MD, 1870; m. James Skelton Anderson (ship owner and businessman), Feb 9, 1871; children: Louisa Garrett Anderson; Margaret Skelton Anderson; Alan Garrett Anderson. ❖ The 1st British woman doctor, attended lectures by Elizabeth Blackwell, an American doctor, and resolved to pursue a medical career (1859); passed examinations for London Society of Apothecaries, allowing her to practice medicine in Britain, and became the 2nd woman (after Blackwell) listed on the British Medical Register (1865); helped found the Women's Suffrage Committee and opened a dispensary for women and children in London (1866); after years of struggle and study, marked by rebuffs from the medical establishment and from virtually every British university and medical school, became the 1st woman to receive an MD degree from the Sorbonne and the 1st British female doctor, opening the field for the thousands of women who followed (1870); became one of the 1st two women to be elected to the newly established London School Board (1870); opened the New Hospital for Women, the 1st hospital in Britain staffed entirely by women (1872); elected to the British Medical Association (1874); helped found the London School of Medicine for Women, the 1st medical school for women in Britain, serving as a lecturer and board member for the school (1874) and as its dean (1883–1902); elected mayor of Aldeburgh, becoming the 1st female mayor in Britain (1908); published numerous articles on women in medicine, education for girls, and various medical subjects, in publications such as *The Edinburgh Review, The British Medical Journal* and *The Times of London* (1867–1910). ❖ See also Louisa Garrett Anderson, *Elizabeth Garrett Anderson* (Faber and Faber, n.d.); Jo Manton, *Elizabeth Garrett Anderson* (Methuen, 1964); and *Women in World History.*

ANDERSON, Elizabeth Milbank (1850–1921). American philanthropist. Born Elizabeth Milbank in New York, NY, 1850; died in 1921; m. Abram A. Anderson (portrait painter), 1887. ❖ With brother Joseph Milbank, made liberal contributions to Teachers College and Barnard College ($3 million), to the Children's Aid Society of New York ($500,000), and to many other social-welfare agencies; also established the Milbank Memorial Fund, with interest income to be used to "improve the physical, mental, and moral condition of humanity."

ANDERSON, Ellen Alice (1882–1978). New Zealand district nurse. Born on June 22, 1882, in Eketahuna, New Zealand; died on Feb 4, 1978, in Palmerston North, New Zealand; dau. of Anders Anderson (farmer) and Johanna (Manson) Anderson. ❖ Enrolled at Masterton Hospital (1905); appointed district nurse at Eketahuna by Masterton Board (1919); retired from nursing (1935); papers and possessions formed foundation for Eketahuna museum.

ANDERSON, Erica (1914–1976). Austrian-born American filmmaker. Born Erika Kellner in Vienna, Austria, Aug 8, 1914; died in Great Barrington, Massachusetts, Sept 1976; dau. of Eduard Kellner and Ilona Rosenberg Kellner; m. Dr. Lawrence Collier Anderson (British physician), June 1940 (div. 1942). ❖ Moved to NY (1939); made documentaries of important 20th-century figures such as Henry Moore, Carl Jung and Albert Schweitzer, as well as Grandma Moses, with script and narration by Archibald MacLeish, which was released to rave reviews (1950). ❖ See also *Women in World History.*

ANDERSON, Ernestine (1928—). American jazz singer. Born Nov 11, 1928, in Houston, Texas. ❖ Sang with bands of Russell Jacquet and Johnny Otis (1940s); had 1st hit while singing with Shifty Henry's band (1947); worked with Lionel Hampton (1952–53) and recorded with GiGi Gryce (1955); recorded "Hot Cargo" with Harry Arnold's band in Sweden (1957); sang for soundtrack of Sidney Poitier's movie *The Lost Man;* lived in England in semi-retirement (1965–76); recorded for Concord Records (1976–91); rendition of "Never Make Your Move Too Soon" (1981) considered a classic. Albums include: *Hot Cargo* (1958), *Live from Concord to London* (1976), *Hello Like Before* (1976), *Never Make Your Move Too Soon* (1980), *Be Mine Tonight When the Sun Goes Down* (1984), *Now and Then* (1993), *Blue, Dues Love News* (1996), *I Love Being Here with You* (2002). ❖ See also *Women in World History.*

ANDERSON, Ethel Mason (1883–1958). Australian author. Born 1883 in Leamington, England; died in 1958; grew up in Australia; dau. of Cyrus and Louise (Scroggie) Mason (both Australian); m. A.T. Anderson (British army officer), 1904. ❖ With husband, lived in England and India for 22 years (1904–26), before returning to Australia (1926); though she considered herself a poet, is most respected for her stories and essays of experiences in India; also an artist, helped paint several frescoes in Australian churches; writings include *Squatter's Luck* (1942), *Adventures in Appleshire* (1944), *Timeless Garden* (1945), *Sunday at Yarralumla* (1947), *Indian Tales* (1948), *At Paramatta* (1956), and *The Little Ghosts* (1957).

ANDERSON, Eugenie Moore (1909–1997). American ambassador. Name variations: Helen Eugenie Moore Anderson. Born Helen Eugenie Moore on May 26, 1909, in Adair, Iowa; died in Red Wing, Minnesota, April 14, 1997; dau. of Reverend Ezekiel Arrowsmith Moore (Methodist minister) and Flora Belle (McMillen) Moore (schoolteacher); attended Stephens College (Columbia, MO), Simpson College (Indianola, IA), and Carleton College (Northfield, MN); m. John Pierce Anderson, Sept 9, 1930; children: Johanna and Hans Pierce. ❖ Served as ambassador to Denmark (1949–53), the 1st woman in the history of US to achieve that high diplomatic rank; was chair of Minnesota Commission for Fair Employment Practices (1955–60); under President John F. Kennedy, was named US envoy to Bulgaria (1962–65), the 1st American woman to function as chief of a mission to an Eastern European country; served as US representative on the Trusteeship Council of UN (1965–68), special assistant to the secretary of state (1968–72), and as a member of the Commission on the Future of Minnesota until her retirement. ❖ See also *Women in World History.*

ANDERSON, Evelyn (1907–1994). African-American dancer. Born in 1907; died of pneumonia, Oct 29, 1994, in Philadelphia, Pennsylvania. ❖ The last surviving member of *La Revue Nègre,* returned to America after the group disbanded (1926) but continued to visit Europe often; was detained by the Nazis (1941) and held for 3 years, 1st in a Dutch internment camp, then in a German convent; was eventually released as part of a prisoner-exchange program with US.

ANDERSON, Evelyn N. (1909–1977). German-born British journalist. Name variations: Lore Seligmann. Born Lore Seligmann, May 13, 1909, in Frankfurt am Main, Germany; died in London, England, Jan 8, 1977; dau. of a prosperous family; studied economics and sociology at several German universities and at Sorbonne (1927–32), ending studies with a doctorate in political science; m. Paul Anderson, 1934. ❖ Joined German Communist Party (KPD, 1927), but was quickly disillusioned; joined Social Democratic Party (SPD, 1929), but noted the near-paralysis of the SPD leadership when confronted by a growing Nazi movement; immigrated to Great Britain (1933); worked as an editor and announcer for anti-Nazi radio broadcasting stations in England and was a member of the circle of advisors around British Labour Party leader

Aneurin Bevan; contributed articles to the newspaper *Tribune* (1943–52), and also worked as BBC editor for Eastern European questions (1953–76), as well as making BBC broadcasts from Germany (1946, 1952 and 1963); wrote *Hammer or Anvil* (1945), a history of the German working class. ❖ See also *Women in World History.*

ANDERSON, Helen Eugenie (1909–1997). See *Anderson, Eugenie Moore.*

ANDERSON, Isabel Perkins (1876–1948). American author. Born Isabel Perkins in Boston, Massachusetts, Mar 29, 1876; died in 1948; dau. of George Perkins (commodore in US navy) and Anna (Weld) Perkins; George Washington University, Litt.D., 1918, Boston University, LLD, 1930; married Larz Anderson (US diplomat), June 10, 1897. ❖ A prolific writer, wrote more than 40 books, plays, travel guides and volumes of poetry; also produced her own plays.

ANDERSON, Ivie (1904–1949). African-American jazz singer. Born July 10, 1904, in Gilroy, California; died Dec 28, 1949, in Los Angeles, California; studied with Sara Ritt in Washington, DC. ❖ Elegant stylist, made pro debut at Tait's Club in Los Angeles; worked at the Cotton Club (1925), then toured with the "Shuffle Along" revue; sang for bands led by Earl Hines and Paul Howard, before a highly successful stint with Duke Ellington (1931–42); recorded "It Don't Mean a Thing," "I Got It Bad," "Mood Indigo," and "Solitude" and appeared in the Marx Brothers' movie *A Day at the Races.* ❖ See also *Women in World History.*

ANDERSON, Janet (1949—). English politician and member of Parliament. Born Dec 6, 1949; dau. of Ethel Pearson Anderson and Tom Anderson (Labour Party agent); m. Vincent William Humphreys, 1972 (div.). ❖ Representing Labour, elected to House of Commons for Rossendale and Darwen (1992, 1997, 2001, 2005); member of joint committee on House of Lords reform (2003).

ANDERSON, Janet (1956—). American golfer. Born Mar 10, 1956, in Phoenix, Arizona. ❖ Won US Open (1982).

ANDERSON, Jennie (1855–1875). See *Whiteside, Jane.*

ANDERSON, Jessica (1916—). Australian novelist. Name variations: Jessica Margaret Anderson. Born Sept 25, 1916, in Gayndah, Queensland, Australia; grew up in Brisbane; attended Yeronga State School and Brisbane State High; studied at Brisbane Technical College Art School. ❖ Began career writing for radio; works include novels *An Ordinary Lunacy* (1963), *The Last Man's Head* (1970), *The Commandment* (1975), which was based on Captain Logan and the Moreton Bay penal settlement, *Tirra Lirra By the River* (1978), *The Only Daughter* (1980), *The Impersonators* (1980), *Taking Shelter* (1989), *One of the Wattle Birds* (1994), and short-story collection *Stories from the Warm Zone* (1987). Won Miles Franklin Award for *Tirra Lirra By the River* (1978) and *The Impersonators* (1980).

ANDERSON, Jodi (1957—). American track-and-field athlete. Born Nov 10, 1957, in Chicago, Illinois; attended California State–Northridge. ❖ Won AIAW long jump (1977, 1979) and pentathlon (1979); was US national outdoor long jump champion (1977, 1978, 1980, 1981); appeared in the role of Pooch in the film *Personal Best* (1982).

ANDERSON, Judith (1898–1992). Australian-born actress. Name variations: 1st performed as Frances Anderson and finally as Judith Anderson in 1923; Dame Judith Anderson as of 1960. Born Frances Margaret Anderson-Anderson in Adelaide, Australia, Feb 10, 1898; died in Santa Barbara, CA, Jan 3, 1992; dau. of James Anderson-Anderson and Jessie Margaret Saltmarsh; attended Rose Park School (1908–12) and Norwood School (1913–16); m. Benjamin Harrison Lehman (professor of English at University of California), May 18, 1937 (div., Aug 23, 1939); m. Luther Greene (producer-director), July 11, 1946 (div., June 36, 1951); no children. ❖ One of the greatest actresses of the 20th century, made stage debut in *A Royal Divorce* at Theatre Royal, Sydney (1915); arrived in America (1918); made Broadway debut under name Frances Anderson in *On the Stairs* (1922); came to prominence as Elise Van Zile in *The Cobra* (1924); appeared in several plays, including *The Dove* (1926), which cemented her reputation as a young actress to be watched; starred as Lavinia Mannon in *Mourning Becomes Electra* (1931); made film debut in the unlikely role of a gangster's moll in *Blood Money* (1933); of all her film roles, is best remembered as Mrs. Danvers, the villainous housekeeper in *Rebecca,* directed by Alfred Hitchcock, a performance that earned her a 7-year contract at MGM (1940); other films include *The Strange Love of Martha Ivers* (1946), *The Furies* (1950), *Salome* (1953), and *The Ten Commandments* (1956); played Gertrude to John Gielgud's Hamlet (1938); made London debut playing Lady Macbeth to critical acclaim opposite Laurence Olivier (1939); appeared in NY as Virgin Mary in *Family Portrait* (1939); had greatest triumph in the Robinson Jeffers adaptation of *Medea* (1947); after Sarah Bernhardt, became the 2nd woman to attempt the role of Hamlet (1968); appeared regularly on the tv series "Santa Barbara" (1984). Received Donaldson Award and New York Critics' Award for Medea (1948); received Emmy awards for performances as Lady Macbeth (1954, 1961); made Dame Commander of the British Empire (1960). ❖ See also *Women in World History*.

ANDERSON, Katherine (1944—). African-American pop singer. Name variations: Katherine Schaffner; Marvelettes. Born in 1944 in Inkster, Michigan. ❖ Was a member of the Marvelettes, a popular Motown group whose songs "Don't Mess With Bill," "Please Mr. Postman," "I Keep Holding On," and "Beachwood 4–5789" reached the top of the charts (early 1960s); other members included Gladys Horton, Georgia Dobbins, Juanita Cowart. ❖ See also *Women in World History*.

ANDERSON, Laurie (1947—). American performance artist. Born June 5, 1947, in Chicago, Illinois; MFA in sculpture, Columbia University, 1972. ❖ Innovative performance artist who gained mainstream audience, 1st performed publicly (1973), presenting work at festivals, museums, and concert halls; had British pop hit with recording "O Superman" (1981); followed up debut album *Big Science* (1982) with *Mister Heartbreak* (1983), a collaboration with Peter Gabriel; premiered 7-hour multimedia piece *United States, I-IV* (1983) at Brooklyn Academy of Music; composed musical score for performance artist Spalding Gray's films *Swimming to Cambodia* (1987) and *Monster in a Box* (1991); published many books, including *The Package: A Mystery* (1971), *Transportation* (1974), *Notebook* (1977), *Stories from the Nerve Bible* (1994), and *Laurie Anderson* (2000); incorporates graphics, sculpture, film, slides, lighting, mime, spoken and printed language in work.

ANDERSON, Lea (1959—). British dancer and choreographer. Name variations: Cholmondeley Sisters. Born June 13, 1959, in London, England; attended Middlesex College, 1977, and St. Martin's School of Art, London, 1978–79; studied dance at Laban Centre, London (1981–84). ❖ Co-founded female dance-trio, the Cholmondeley Sisters (1986), later named the Cholmondeleys (pronounced 'chumleez'); co-founded Featherstonehaughs (1988), an all-male company that performed with the Cholmondeleys in several pieces, including *Flag* (1988) and *Birthday* (1992); received commissions from numerous dance and theater companies, and took on large projects such as choreographing part of a parade for the French government (1989); wrote and presented 2 seasons of *Tights, Camera, Action!* for British tv (starting 1992); made an honorary fellow of Laban Centre, London (1997); received numerous honors, including 3 Time Out Awards and 2 London Dance and Performance Awards. Major works include *The Cholmondeley Sisters* (1984), debut dance; *Baby, Baby, Baby* (1986); *Marina* (1986); *Flesh and Blood* (1989, revised 1997); *Cold Sweat* (1990), *Immaculate Conception* (1992); *Car* (1995).

ANDERSON, Lucille (1897–1948). See Bogan, Lucille.

ANDERSON, Lucy (1797–1878). English pianist. Born Lucy Philpot on Dec 12, 1797, in Bath, England; died in London, Dec 24, 1878; m. George Frederick Anderson (1793–1876). ❖ Performing Hummel's B minor Concerto, was the 1st woman pianist to play at a concert of the Royal Philharmonic Society in London; while husband served as Master of the Queen's Musick (1848–70), taught piano to Queen Victoria and her children; had a long and successful career, appearing the last time at the Royal Philharmonic concerts as soloist in Beethoven's Choral Fantasia (1862).

ANDERSON, Margaret (1900–1997). English biochemist and indexer. Name variations: Margaret Dampier Whetham Anderson. Born Margaret Dampier Whetham, April 21, 1900, in England; died 1997; m. Alan Bruce Anderson (clinical pathologist), Sept 12, 1927. ❖ Served as biochemical researcher at Newnham College in Cambridge (1920–27) and worked with Marjory Stephenson on projects, including the washed cell suspensions technique for cell analysis; coauthored 4 papers with Stephenson; served as abstractor for *British Chemical Abstracts* (1948–51) and *Food Science Abstracts* (1950–57); became freelance indexer at age 60 (1960) and compiled indexes for 567 books (both scientific and nonscientific); for Society of Indexers, served as treasurer (1965–72), membership secretary, member of board of assessors, and vice president; received Wheatley Medal in 1975 (for index to *Copy-editing: The Cambridge Handbooks*) and the Carey Award (1983). Works include:

Book Indexing (1971), *Cambridge Readings in the Literature of Science* (with W.C.D. Whetham, 1924), and *Reformers and Rebels* (1946).

ANDERSON, Margaret Carolyn (1886–1973). American founder, editor and magazine publisher. Born Margaret Carolyn Anderson on Nov 24, 1886, in Indianapolis, Indiana; died from emphysema, Oct 15, 1973, at Le Cannet, France; dau. of Arthur Aubrey (electric railway executive) and Jessie (Shortridge) Anderson; attended 2-year junior preparatory classes at Western College in Miami, Ohio; lived with Georgette Leblanc (French singer, 1922–41); never married; no children. ❖ Founder, editor, and publisher of the avant-garde literary magazine the *Little Review*, began career as book critic of the *Chicago Evening Post* (1912); made editor of *The Continent* (1914); founded *Little Review* in Chicago (1914), to subvert literary oppression by filling the magazine "with the best conversation the world has to offer"; moved magazine to NY (1916); over the next 15 years, introduced such artists as Amy Lowell, Djuna Barnes, H.D. (Hilda Doolittle), Dorothy Richardson, Sherwood Anderson, Carl Sandburg, Vachel Lindsay, Gertrude Stein, Ernest Hemingway, Ezra Pound, and William Butler Yeats; began serialization of James Joyce's *Ulysses* in the *Little Review* (1918); convicted, along with editor Jane Heap, on obscenity charges for publishing *Ulysses* (1921); published final issue of the *Little Review* in Paris (1929); considered a member of the group known as the Chicago Renaissance. ❖ See also memoirs *My Thirty Years' War* (1969) and *The Strange Necessity* (1969); and *Women in World History*.

ANDERSON, Marian (1897–1993). African-American concert singer. Born Marian Anderson, Feb 27, 1897, in Philadelphia, Pennsylvania; died April 8, 1993, in Portland, Oregon; m. Orpheus H. Fisher (architect), 1943. ❖ Widely acclaimed as one of the world's greatest contraltos (1925–65), made triumphant NY debut at the amphitheater accompanied by NY Philharmonic Orchestra (1925); signed with impresario Arthur Judson; toured eastern and southern US (1926); performed at Carnegie Hall (Mar 2, 1930), the 1st black female to do so; performed at London's Wigmore Hall (1930); toured Europe and Scandinavia (1933–34), singing before King Gustav of Sweden and King Christian X of Denmark; appeared in Paris and London (1934); signed with impresario Sol Hurok (1935) and gave a homecoming recital at New York's Town Hall; kept from singing at Constitution Hall by its owners, Daughters of the American Revolution (DAR), because of its segregation policy, held a free open-air concert at the Lincoln Memorial with some 75,000 Americans in attendance (Easter Sunday, 1939); asked to give a solo concert at the White House (1939); entertained troops during WWII and Korean War; debuted at NY Metropolitan Opera (1955), the 1st black to sing as a regular member of the company; toured India and Far East as goodwill ambassador, sponsored by US State Department (1957); appointed delegate to UN Human Rights Committee (1958); sang at Eisenhower and Kennedy inaugurations (1957 and 1961); sang at the March on Washington (1963); gave last concert (April 19, 1965), at Carnegie Hall. Given the Spingarn Medal (1939), Probenignitate Humana of Finland (1940), Bok award (1941), American Medal of Freedom (1963), and National Medal of Arts (1986). ❖ See also autobiography *My Lord, What a Morning* (Viking, 1956); Shirlee P. Newman, *Marian Anderson: Lady from Philadelphia* (Westminster, 1966); and *Women in World History*.

ANDERSON, Mary (1859–1940). American actress. Name variations: Mary de Navarro, Madame de Navarro. Born Mary Antoinette Anderson in Sacramento, California, July 28, 1859; died in Worcestershire, England, May 29, 1940; educated at the Ursuline Convent in Louisville, Kentucky; studied elocution with Vandenhoff; m. Antonio F. de Navarro, 1890; children: son. ❖ Made 1st appearance on American stage as Juliet in an amateur production at Macauley's Theater in Louisville, KY (1875), and scored an immediate success; during next 10 years, played in all the principal cities of US and was immensely popular, one of the most famous actress of her day; appeared in England (1885–89), where she repeated her American triumphs, her most notable portrayals being Perdita, Hermione, Galatea, Rosalind, Lady Macbeth, Bianca, Pauline, Meg Merrilees, and Juliet; married and remained in England; during WWI, frequently appeared at special performances for the benefit of wounded soldiers and, later, in support of the poor; co-authored, with Robert Hichens, the long-running play *The Garden of Allah*. ❖ See also autobiography *A Few Memories* (1896); and *Women in World History*.

ANDERSON, Mary (1872–1964). Swedish-born American union leader. Born Mary Anderson, Aug 27, 1872, on her parents' farm outside of Lidköping, Sweden; died of a stroke at her home in Washington, DC, Jan

29, 1964; dau. of Magnus and Matilda (Johnson) Anderson (both farmers); graduated from a Lutheran grammar school at top of her class; never married; no children. ❖ Fought for acceptance of the principles of collective bargaining and arbitration and became the 1st director of the Women's Bureau of the US Department of Labor; immigrated to America (1889); worked as a domestic and briefly in the garment trade before finding work as a stitcher in a shoe factory outside Chicago; joined International Boot and Shoe Workers Union (BSWU, 1899); elected president of women's stitchers Local 94 (Chicago, 1900); was a member, BSWU national executive board (1906–19); joined Women's Trade Union League (WTUL, 1905); appointed full-time WTUL organizer (1911); named assistant director, Women in Industry Service (1918), appointed director (1919); served as director of Women's Bureau of US Department of Labor (1920–44), the 1st director of a federal agency devoted to the issues of women's employment; named WTUL delegate to both the Paris Peace Conference and International Congress of Working Women (1919); organized Bryn Mawr Summer School for Women Workers (1921). Given honorary degree, Smith College (1941), and Award of Merit, US Labor Department (1962). ❖ See also autobiography *Woman at Work* (1951); and *Women in World History*.

ANDERSON, Mary Patricia (1887–1966). New Zealand labor activist. Name variations: Aunt Flora. Born on Mar 17, 1887, at Moonlight in Grey River valley of Westland, New Zealand; died Feb 18, 1966, in Greymouth, New Zealand; dau. of Anton Anderson (miner) and Catherine (Flaherty) Anderson. ❖ Taught in local schools and served as local postmaster (early 1900s); was a founding member of Greymouth branch of New Zealand Labor Party (1917) and served as secretary (1918–56); served on board of local Labor newspaper *Grey River Argus* and edited children's page as Aunt Flora for brief period; active in welfare organizations such as Plunket Society; appointed justice of peace (1943); sat on Magistrate's Court bench (1945); was one of the 1st women members of Labor government to be appointed to sit in Legislative Council (1946–50); became 1st woman to chair New Zealand parliamentary committee (1948); served on Grey Hospital Board (1950–62).

ANDERSON, Mary Reid (1880–1921). *See Macarthur, Mary Reid.*

ANDERSON, Maybanke (1845–1927). Australian feminist reformer. Born Maybanke Susannah Selfe at Kingston-on-Thames, England, Feb 16, 1845; died in Paris, France, April 15, 1927; one of 3 children and only daughter of Bessie (Smith) Selfe and Henry Selfe (plumber); m. Edmund Kay Wolstenholme (timber merchant), 1867 (div. 1893); m. Francis Anderson (philosophy professor at University of Sydney), 1899; children: (1st m.) 7 (4 died of tuberculosis-related diseases in infancy). ❖ At 9, moved with family to Sydney, Australia; deserted by husband, opened Maybanke College for young ladies to support herself and children; served as president of Womanhood Suffrage League (1893–97); founded biweekly feminist journal, *Woman's Voice* (1894); served as the founding president of the Kindergarten Union, which opened its 1st free kindergarten (1896); was also appointed as the 1st registrar of Teachers' Central Registry (1897); under name "Lois," began writing for *Sydney Morning Herald,* covering topics ranging from politics to travel; published *Australian Songs for Australian Children* (1902); as founding president of Playgrounds Association, authored *Play and Playgrounds* (1914), to publicize the cause; published *The Root of the Matter: Social and Economic Aspects of the Sex Problem* (1916), covering the wartime spread of venereal diseases and concerns about proposals for compulsory notification; also wrote *Mother Lore* (1919), which enjoyed wide success and was reprinted several times.

ANDERSON, Mignon (1892–1983). American silent-film actress. Born Mar 31, 1892, in Baltimore, Maryland; died Feb 25, 1983, in Burbank, California; dau. of Frank Anderson and Hallie Howard (stage actors); m. J. Morris Foster, 1920 (died 1966). ❖ One of the pioneering actresses of the cinema, joined the Thanhouser Company (1910); starred in *The Early Life of David Copperfield* (1911), *The Merchant of Venice* (1912), *The Mill on the Floss* (1915), *The City of Illusion* (1916), *Mountain Madness* (1920), and *Kisses* (1922), her last film.

ANDERSON, Regina M. (1900–1993). African-American librarian, playwright, and arts patron. Name variations: Regina Anderson Andrews; (pseudonym) Ursula Trelling. Born in Chicago, Illinois, May 21, 1900; died Feb 6, 1993, in Ossining, NY; dau. of William Grant (attorney) and Margaret (Simons) Anderson; attended Normal Training School and Hyde Park High School in Chicago; studied at Wilberforce University in Ohio, University of Chicago, and City College of New York; received library science degree from Columbia University Library

School; m. William T. Andrews, 1926; children: Regina Andrews. ❖ Instrumental in launching careers of countless black artists who in turn gave rise to the Harlem Renaissance, moved to NY from Chicago; became assistant librarian at Harlem's 135th Street branch of New York Public Library (later named the Schomburg Center for Research in Black Culture); helped plan the famous Civic Club dinner (1924), with guests like Jean Toomer, Countee Cullen, Langston Hughes, W.E.B. Du Bois, and James Weldon Johnson; became involved with the fledgling Krigwa Players, which served as the parent group of the Negro Experimental Theater (also known as the Harlem Experimental Theater); became 2nd vice president of the National Council of Women as well as National Urban League representative to US Commission for UNESCO; also worked with the State Commission for Human Rights. ❖ See also *Women in World History.*

ANDERSON, Roberta Joan (1943—). *See Mitchell, Joni.*

ANDERSON, Robin (1948–2002). Australian filmmaker. Born Robin Snyder, Sept 11, 1948, in Perth, Western Australia, Australia; died of cancer, Mar 8, 2002, age 51, in Sydney, NSW, Australia; Columbia University, MA in sociology; m. Bob Connolly (director of documentaries); children: daughters Katherine and Joanna. ❖ With husband, made 5 full-length films, including *First Contact* (1983), which examined tribal life in Papua New Guinea and was nominated for an Academy Award; *Joe Leahy's Neighbors* (1989), *Black Harvest* (1992), *Rats in the Ranks* (1996), and *Facing the Music* (2001). Received a top prize from the Cinéma du Réel festival.

ANDERSON, Sophie (1823–1903). French-born painter. Born Sophie Gengembre, 1823, in France; died 1903 (some sources cite 1898); dau. of a Parisian architect and English mother; m. Walter Anderson (English painter). ❖ Pre-Raphaelite, known for her sentimental pictures of Victorian children, was largely self taught; during Revolution of 1848, moved to US where she became a successful portrait painter; with husband, moved to Cumberland, England (1854), then Capri, Italy (1871), then Falmouth, England (1894); her depiction of nature was almost photographic; best known work is *No Walk Today, Shepherd Piper* and *Elaine* (also known as *The Lily Maid of Astolat*).

ANDERSON-IVANTZOVA, Elizabeth (c. 1893–1973). Russian ballet dancer. Born c. 1893, in Moscow, Russia; died Nov 10, 1973, in New York, NY. ❖ Studied at Moscow school of Imperial Ballet; danced with Bolshoi Ballet (1910s), most notably as Aurora in *Sleeping Beauty*; joined Chauve-Souris tour and immigrated to NY (1924), remaining there until death; taught dance classes at her own studio, which was considered one of most disciplined within the dance world.

ANDERSON-SCOTT, Carol (1935–2003). American winemaker. Name variations: Carol G. Anderson; Carol Scott. Born Carol Gregson, Jan 15, 1935, in Chicago, Illinois; died June 8, 2003, in Yountville, California; studied dental hygiene at Occidental College and University of Southern California; m. Stanley Anderson (dentist), 1961 (died 1994); m. Tom Scott. ❖ One of the 1st female winemakers in Napa Valley, launched S. Anderson winery with husband (1971).

ANDERSSON, Agneta (1961—). Swedish kayaker. Born April 25, 1961, in Karlskogas, Sweden. ❖ At Los Angeles Olympics, won a silver medal in K4 500 meters and gold medals in the K2 500 meters and K1 500 meters (1984); at Barcelona Olympics, won a bronze medal in the K4 500 meters and a silver medal in the K2 500 meters (1992); won a bronze medal for K4 500 meters and a gold medal for K2 500 meters (with Susanne Gunnarsson) at Atlanta Olympics (1996).

ANDERSSON, Bibi (1935—). Swedish actress. Name variations: Bibbi Andersson. Born Birgitta Andersson, Nov 11, 1935, in Kungsholmen, Stockholm, Sweden; sister of Gerd Andersson (dancer and actress); m. Kjell Grede (director), 1960 (div. 1973); m. Per Ahlmark (chair of Sweden's Liberal Party), 1978. ❖ Made film debut in *Fröken Julie* (1951); appeared on stage in Malmö under direction of Ingmar Bergman before he gave her a small role in *Sommarnattens leende* (*Smiles of a Summer Night,* 1955); has appeared in nearly 100 films, including *The Seventh Seal, Wild Strawberries, Persona, Duel at Diablo, The Passion of Anna, The Kremlin Letter, Scenes from a Marriage, I Never Promised You a Rose Garden, An Enemy of the People, Quintet, Two Women, The Dark Side of the Moon, Babette's Feast* and *Dreamplay.* Received a Best Actress award at Cannes for performance in *Brink of Life* (1958).

ANDERSSON, Gerd (1932—). Swedish ballet dancer. Born June 11, 1932, in Stockholm, Sweden; older sister of Bibi Andersson (actress).

❖ Studied at Royal Swedish Ballet and joined repertory company (1948) for which she danced classics, including *Coppélia*'s Swanilda; known for her collaboration with contemporary choreographers such as Janine Charrat in *Abraxas* (1951), Birgit Cullberg in *Miss Julie*, and Antony Tudor in *Echoes of Trumpets* (1963); appeared in films *Kvinnors väntan* (*Secrets of Women*, 1952), *Flyg-Bom* (1952), *Karneval* (1961), *Fanny and Alexander* (1982) and *The Mozart Brothers*.

ANDERSSON, Harriet (1932—). Swedish actress. Born Feb 14, 1932, in Stockholm, Sweden; m. Jörn Donner (director). ❖ Made film debut in *Hamnstad* (1948); had breakthrough role in *Monika* (1953), written for her by Ingmar Bergman; other films include *Smiles of a Summer Night, Through a Glass Darkly, A Sunday in September, Loving Couples, The Deadly Affair, Anna, Cries and Whispers, Cry of Triumph, Fanny and Alexander, Sabina, Raskenstam, Blankt vapen, Happy End* and *Dogville*; on tv, appeared in the series "Gösta Berlings saga" (1986), "Destination Nordsjön" (1990), and "Majken" (1995), among others. Won Best Actress award in Venice for performance in *Att älska* (*To Love*, 1964).

ANDERTON, Elizabeth (1938—). English ballet dancer. Born May 2, 1938, in London, England. ❖ Received the 1st C.W. Beaumont scholarship with which she trained at Sadler's Wells School in London; joined Sadler's Wells repertory company (1955) where she danced in revivals of classics and was featured in contemporary works; danced in Sadler's Wells offspring the Royal Ballet; collaborated with major choreographers of English ballet such as John Cranko in *Sweeney Todd* (1959), Frederick Ashton in *Les Deux Pigeons* (1961), and Antony Tudor in *Knight Errant* (1968); served Robert Helpmann as assistant with the Australian Ballet as well as additional projects; appeared in Tchaikovsky's *Swan Lake* on film (1988).

ANDICS, Erzsebet (1902–1986). Hungarian Communist militant. Born in Hungary in 1902; died in Hungary in 1986. ❖ Joined the Communist Party of Hungary at its inception (1918); with the collapse of the Soviet regime, narrowly escaped imprisonment or death (1919) and fled to Soviet Russia; sent back to Hungary by the Communist International as an underground operative (early 1920s), was arrested and imprisoned but exchanged for Hungarian captives; returned to Hungary after WWII (1945); one of the few women among the cadre of veteran Communists, quickly joined the inner circle; was a member of the Hungarian Politburo (1948–56); even after the failed revolution of 1956, remained a hard-line Marxist-Leninist up to the time of her death (1986), a scant 3 years before the collapse of Communism in Hungary. ❖ See also *Women in World History*.

ANDILLY, Angelique de Saint-Jean Arnauld d' (1624–1684). *See Arnauld, Angelique."*

ANDINA (1833–1913). *See Acosta de Samper, Soledad.*

ANDING, Carola (1960—). East German cross-country skier. Born Dec 29, 1960, in East Germany. ❖ Won a gold medal for 4x5km relay at Lake Placid Olympics (1980).

ANDJAPARIDZE, Veriko (1900–1987). Georgian actress and theater founder. Name variations: Vera Iulianovna Andzhaparidzi or Andzhaparidze; Veriko Ivlianovna Andzhaparidze; Veriko. Born Veriko Ivlianovna Andzhaparidze, Oct 6, 1900, in Kutaisi, Russia (now Georgia); died Jan 31, 1987; dau. of a notary; sister of Meri Andjaparaidze (film director); aunt of Giorgi Danelia (actor); children: Sofiko Chiaureli (actress, b. 1937). ❖ Queen of the Soviet theater, was also one of the founders of the Georgian theater; studied in Tbilisi and acted for Rusthaveli Theater, Moscow Realistic Theater, and others; was director of Mardzhanishvili Theater; gave epic performance as grandmother in the play *The Trees Die Standing*; also appeared in close to 30 films, including *Otaraant qvrivi* (1958) and *Monanieba* (1987), in which her character asks a victim of the Soviet regime, "Is this the way to the Temple," a line that became a motto of Perestroika. Awarded Stalin Prize (1943, 1936, 1952) and Order of Lenin.

ANDO, Misako (1971—). Japanese softball player. Born Mar 21, 1971, in Japan. ❖ Won a team silver medal at Sydney Olympics (2000).

ANDRA, Fern (1893–1974). American actress and producer. Name variations: Fern Andrée. Born Fern Andrews, Nov 24, 1893, in Watseka, Illinois; died Feb 8, 1974, in Aiken, South Carolina; m. Sam Edge Dockrell (commandant of Putnam Phalanx); m. Ian Keith, 1932 (div. 1934); m. Baron Von Welchs. ❖ Began career as an aerialist with Millman Trio, touring US and Europe; as actress, became a student of Max Reinhardt and made film debut in Vienna in *Crushed*; formed her own company in Berlin during WWI, producing over 80 silent films, appearing in many of them; returned to US after Nazi takeover.

ANDRADE, Leny (1943—). Brazilian jazz singer. Born 1943 in Rio de Janeiro, Brazil; attended Brazilian Conservatory of Music. ❖ At 15, debuted as a professional singer with Permínio Gonçalves Orchestra; performed at nightclubs Bacará (with Sergio Mendes trio) and Bottle's Bar; came to prominence with the show "Genimi V" at the Porao 73, performing with Pery Ribeiro and Bossa Três; lived in Mexico for 5 years; recorded albums *Alvoroço* (1973) and *Leny Andrade* (1975), mixing samba with avant-garde music, and *Registro* (1979), a combination of samba and jazz; considered Brazil's first lady of jazz, also recorded *Embraceable You*, a collection of American standards in a bossa-nova style; other albums include *Luz Néon* (1989), *Eu Quero Ver* (1990), *Maiden Voyage* (1994), *Luz Negra* (1995), and *Leny Andrade Canta Altay Veloso* (2000).

ANDRE, Gwili (1908–1959). Danish actress and model. Born Gurli Andresen, Feb 4, 1908, in Copenhagen, Denmark; died Feb 5, 1959, when fire swept her Venice, California, apartment. ❖ Top NY model; signed with RKO and starred opposite Richard Dix in *Roar of the Dragon*.

ANDRÉ, Valerie (1922—). French military physician. Name variations: Andre. Born Valerie Marie André in Strasbourg, France, April 21, 1922; dau. of Philibert André (professor at Strasbourg Lycée); m. Alexis Santini, 1963. ❖ After receiving a medical doctorate, served in Vietnam; became a helicopter pilot and flew over 150 medical missions; named commanding officer of helicopter pilots at the Gialam air base in Tonkin province; became a lieutenant-colonel in the Medical Corps (1965); achieved rank of colonel (1970), then Médecin général (1976), thus becoming a general officer—the 1st female general in the history of France; received equivalency of the rank and prerogatives of a major general (1976); became a founding member of the French National Air and Space Academy (1983); received many awards. ❖ See also *Women in World History*.

ANDRÉ-DESHAYS, Claudie (1957—). *See Haigneré, Claudie.*

ANDREA, Novella d' (fl. 1360s). *See d'Andrea, Novella.*

ANDREAE, Felicity (1914—). English ballet dancer. Name variations: Felicity Gray. Born 1914 in Southampton, England. ❖ Considered one of the last English freelance ballerinas, performed with Leon Woizikovski at Opéra Comique, Paris, and with the Camargo Society and Vic-Wells Ballets in London (1930s); collaborated with Antony Tudor on one of the 1st works for tv (1937); performed with numerous theatrical companies around England, including the Old Vic; wrote for tv and print, including the series *Ballet for Beginners* (for the BBC), which was later published (1952).

ANDREAS-SALOMÉ, Lou (1861–1937). Russian-born author, biographer, novelist, and essayist. Name variations: Louise von Salomé, Lelia, Lyolya, Frau Lou; (pseudonym) Henri Lou. Pronunciation: Loo Ahn-DRAY-us Saa-low-MAY. Born Louise Salomé, Feb 12, 1861, in St. Petersburg, Russia; died of uremia, Feb 5, 1937, in Göttingen, Germany; dau. of Gustav Ludwig Salomé (Russian noble and general) and Louise (Wilm) Salomé (dau. of a sugar refiner); university study in Zurich; m. Fred Charles (later changed to Friedreich Carl) Andreas, June 1887; children: none. ❖ Celebrated figure in turn-of-the-century Central Europe, whose brief relationship with Nietzsche formed only a small part of a much more complex life; traveled to Zurich with mother for study (1880); with mother, traveled to Italy and welcomed into the salon of Malwida von Meysenburg (1882); had an intense friendship with Friedreich Nietzsche, which was to founder under the hostility of his sister, Elisabeth Förster-Nietzsche; though relationship with Nietzsche was brief and rancorous, left a lasting impression on him as a "presence and catalyst"; published 1st work of sustained scholarship, *Hendrik Ibsens Frauengestalten* (*Ibsen's Heroines*, 1892); attracted by the avant-garde intellectuals of the Naturalist movement, penned numerous articles for *Die Freie Bühne* (*The Free Theater*) and published 2nd scholarly book, *Friedreich Nietzsche in seinen Werken* (*Friedreich Nietzsche in His Works*, 1894); her psychological novels, often patterned on her own experiences, appeared in rapid succession and were mostly well received: *Ruth* (1895), *Aus fremder Seele* (*From a Troubled Soul*, 1896), *Fenitschka* (1898), *Menschenkinder* (*Children of Man*, 1899), *Ma* (Mom, 1901), and *Im Zwischenland* (*The Land Between*, 1902); also wrote a number of influential essays on the experience and psychology of religion, catching the attention of René Maria Rilke; had a profound effect on Rilke during time they were lovers (1897–1903); enjoyed celebrity as an established essayist and novelist; published several new novels, including *Das Haus* (*The House*, 1919) and *Rodinka* (1923), and collected several earlier essays into a book, *Die Erotik* (*Eroticism,* 1910); met Sigmund Freud (1911) and immersed herself in the study of psychology (1912–13); published book on Rilke (1928), followed by *Mein Dank an Freud* (*My Thanks to Freud,* 1931); was the subject of Giuseppe Sinopoli's opera *Lou Salomé* (1981). ❖ See also autobiographical novel, *Im Kampf um Gott* (*A Struggle for God,* 1885) and *Looking Back: Memoirs*; Rudolph Binion, *Frau Lou: Nietzsche's Wayward Disciple* (Princeton University Press, 1968); Angela Livingstone, *Salomé: Her Life and Work* (Moyer Bell, 1984); Biddy Martin, *Woman and Modernity: The (Life) Styles of Lou Andreas-Salomé* (Cornell University Press, 1991); and *Women in World History.*

ANDREASSEN, Gunn Margit (1973—). Norwegian biathlete. Born July 23, 1973, in Kristiansand, Norway. ❖ Won a bronze medal at Nagano Olympics (1998) and a silver medal at Salt Lake City Olympics (2002), both for the 4x7.5km relay.

ANDREE, Elfrida (1841–1929). Swedish composer and organist. Born in Visby, Sweden, Feb 19, 1841; died in Stockholm, Jan 11, 1929; dau. of W. Sohrling; sister of the noted opera singer Fredricka Stenhammar; studied at the Stockholm Conservatory under L. Norman and H. Berens. ❖ Though trained as a singer, hoped to be an organist—a difficult feat since Swedish law forbade women organists; eventually served as organist of the Finnish Reformed Church (1861–67) and of the French Reformed Church in Stockholm (1862–67); elected cathedral organist in Göteborg, was put in charge of its people's concerts, directing 800; was the 1st woman to write an organ symphony; also composed for the orchestra, piano, and chamber groups; was also one of the 1st women elected to the Swedish Academy of Music (1879).

ANDRÉE, Fern (1893–1974). *See Andra, Fern.*

ANDREEVA, Maria Fedorovna (1868–1953). Russian actress, theatrical manager and founder. Name variations: (stage name) Maria Andreeva; also known as Maria Fyodorovna or Feodorovna Andreyeva; (real name) Maria Yurkovskaya. Born Maria Yurkovskaya in 1868; died in Moscow, Dec 8, 1953; studied at Moscow Conservatory; m. A.A. Zhelyabuzhsky (state official who worked for the railroad department). ❖ One of the founders of the Bolshoi Drama Theatre in St. Petersburg, joined the Russian Society of Art and Literature (1894); was an actress at the Moscow Art Theatre (1898–1905) where she worked with Constantin Stanislavski; appeared in premiere of Gorky's *The Lower Depths* (1900); left husband for Gorky (1903); began work with the Marxist Bolshevik Party led by Lenin (1904); during Russian uprising (1905), edited the party paper *Novaia zhin'* (New Life); with Gorky, left Russia in an effort to raise funds for underground groups (1906); lived on island of Capri (1907–13), serving as Gorky's secretary and translator as he continued to write; returned to Russia and resumed acting career in Kiev and elsewhere; did other work for the Bolsheviks and earned nickname "Phenomenon"; after the Feb 1917 Revolution, was made chief of Municipal Theatres under the State Duma, then appointed the commissar of Theatre and Entertainment of the Northern Commune as well as chief of the Commission of Experts of the Commissariat of Foreign Trade (1918); still pursuing acting career, portrayed Lady Macbeth at Alexandrinsky Theatre (1918); co-founded the Bolshoi Theatre of Drama in Petrograd (St. Petersburg) (1919); was made chief of the Petrograd section of the Commissariat of Enlightenment (1920); relationship with Gorky ended (1921); directed the Moscow House of Scholars (1930–48). ❖ See also *Women in World History.*

ANDREEVA-BABAKHAN, Anna Misaakovna (1923—). Soviet actress. Name variations: Anna Andreyeva or Andreva. Born Jan 1, 1923, in Kharkov, USSR; m. Vasily Grigorievich Vitrishchak. ❖ Made stage debut at Russian Drama Theater, Ordzhonikidze (1941); over next 16 years, played 65 lead roles in classical and modern rep in many theaters; joined the Moscow Art Theatre Company (1957); especially remembered for her portrayal of the title role in *Anna Karenina.*

ANDREIA (1977—). *See Suntaque, Andreia.*

ANDREINI, Isabella (1562–1604). Italian poet and actress. Name variations: Isabella Canali. Born Isabella Canali in 1562 in Padua, republic of Venice; died July 10, 1604, in Lyon, France; m. Francesco Andreini (actor-manager), 1578; children: 7. ❖ Celebrated leading lady of the Compagnia dei Gelosi, the most famous of the early commedia dell'arte companies, and one of the 1st great European actresses; married at 16 and joined husband's troupe, Il Gelosi; became famed for beauty and talent; wrote pastoral fable *Mirtilla* (1588) and collection of poems *Rime* (1601, 1603); husband published her *Lettere* (1607) and *Fragmenti di alcune scritture* (1620).

ANDREJANOVA, Yelena Ivanovna (1816–1857). *See Andreyanova, Yelena Ivanovna.*

ANDRESEN, Sophia de Mello Breyner (1919–2004). Portuguese author of poetry, children's books, and short stories. Born Nov 6, 1919, in Oporto, Portugal; died July 2, 2004; educated at University of Lisbon; children: 5. ❖ One of Portugal's most respected poets, published 1st collection, *Poesia,* at 25; over the next 50 years, produced 11 more volumes of verse, as well as short stories and children's books; is also known for her translations, including works of Shakespeare.

ANDRESS, Ursula (1936—). Swiss actress. Born Mar 19, 1936, in Berne, Switzerland; m. John Derek (actor), 1957 (div. 1966). ❖ Came to prominence in James Bond movie *Dr. No* (1962); made over 50 films in many nations, including *Sins of Casanova, 4 for Texas,* title role in *She, What's New Pussycat?, The Blue Max, Casino Royale, Scaramouche, Clash of the Titans, Liberté Egalité Choucroute* and *Class Meeting.*

ANDREU, Blanca (1959—). Spanish poet. Born in 1959 in La Coruña, Spain; educated at Madrid University. ❖ Made literary debut with *De una niña de provincias* (*From a Provincial Girl,* 1980), which won the *Premio Adonais* in Spain; followed that success with *Báculo de Babel* (Babel's Wand, 1982), and *Elphistone* (1988), also critically acclaimed.

ANDREW, Janice (1943—). Australian swimmer. Name variations: Jan Andrew. Born Nov 25, 1943, in Australia. ❖ Won a bronze medal in the 100-meter butterfly and a silver medal in the 4x100-meter medley relay in the Rome Olympics (1960).

ANDREW, Princess (1885–1969). *See Alice of Battenberg.*

ANDREWS, Ann (1890–1986). American actress. Born Oct 13, 1890, in Los Angeles, California; died Jan 23, 1986, in New York, NY. ❖ Made Broadway debut in the title role in *Nju* (1917); other plays include *Josephine, Papa, Up from Nowhere, The Hottentot, The Champion, The Royal Family, Dinner at 8, Dark Victory, Reflected Glory, When We Are Married* and *Four Winds.*

ANDREWS, Barbara (c. 1934–1978). American Lutheran minister. Born Barbara Louise Andrews, c. 1934, in US; died in Detroit, Michigan, Mar 31, 1978. ❖ The 2nd woman to be ordained by the Lutheran Church in America, began her ministry at Edina Community Lutheran in Minneapolis, MN (Dec 10, 1970), serving there until 1974; served as staff chaplain for Lutheran Social Service of Michigan; served as interim pastor of the Resurrection Lutheran Church in Detroit, MI; a paraplegic, was unable to escape when a fire broke out in her Detroit apartment, and she died in 1978.

ANDREWS, Cicily Fairfield (1892–1983). *See West, Rebecca.*

ANDREWS, Corinne (1892–1983). *See West, Rebecca.*

ANDREWS, Doris (1920–2003). American preservationist and watercolorist. Born Doris Bass, Aug 14, 1920, in Louisville, Kentucky; died May 25, 2003, in Danbury, Connecticut; attended Erskine School in Boston and Art Students League in Manhattan; m. Sperry Andrews, 1947; children: Catherine Barrett Andrews, Charles Sperry Andrews IV, and Albert Ballard Andrews. ❖ With husband, pursued the preservation of Weir Farm (now the Weir Farm National Historic Site) in Ridgefield and Wilton, CT, with programs for both artists and the public.

ANDREWS, Eliza Frances (1840–1931). American author and botanist. Name variations: (pseudonym) Elzey Hay. Born in Washington, Georgia, Aug 10, 1840, a member of the Southern landowning class; died in Rome, Georgia, Jan 21, 1931; dau. of Garnett Andrews and Annulet Ball Andrews. ❖ Escaped the devastation of the Civil War (1861–65), but became impoverished after father died (1873); her diary of the Civil War became a classic chronicle of the conflict, compared by some historians to the famous diary of Mary Boykin Chesnut; wrote novels, taught in public schools, and became a noted botanist whose scientific knowledge was self-taught; unafraid of espousing new ideas and indifferent to peer pressure, proclaimed herself a Marxian Socialist in a region hostile to any form of social or political radicalism. ❖ See also *The War-Time Journal of a Georgia Girl, 1864–1865;* and *Women in World History.*

ANDREWS, Elizabeth Bullock (1911–2002). American politician. Born Leslie Elizabeth Bullock in Geneva, Alabama, Feb 12, 1911; died Dec 3, 2002, in Birmingham, Alabama; graduated from Montevallo College, 1932; married George Andrews (US congressional representative). ❖ Following husband's death during his 15th term in Congress, was the Democratic party's nominee for election to the vacant seat; ran without

Republican opposition for 92nd Congress; as a representative for Alabama (April 4, 1972–Jan 3, 1973), served on the Committee on Post Office and Civil Service, and introduced several amendments to protect Social Security and medical benefits; co-sponsored a bill establishing a Tuskegee Institute national historical park; did not run for renomination.

ANDREWS, Elsie Euphemia (1888–1948). New Zealand teacher and pacifist. Born on Dec 23, 1888, at Huitangi, Taranaki, New Zealand; died on Aug 26, 1948, at New Plymouth, New Zealand; dau. of John Andrews and Emily (Young) Andrews. ❖ Was infant mistress at Fitzroy School, New Plymouth (1912–35); founded New Plymouth High School for Old Girls' Association (1907); was a member of New Plymouth branch of New Zealand Educational Institute and New Zealand Women Teachers' Association; helped revive local branch of National Council of Women of New Zealand (NCW, 1930), then resigned as president upon outbreak of WWII; active in Pan-Pacific Women's Association; following Honolulu convention (1930), became a pacifist and frequently addressed meetings of women's groups, including Young Women's Christian Association (YMCA). Awarded British Empire Medal (1938).

ANDREWS, Fannie Fern (1867–1950). American pacifist. Born Fannie Fern Phillips, Sept 25, 1867, in Margaretville, Nova Scotia, Canada; died Jan 23, 1950, in Somerville, Massachusetts; Radcliffe College, AB in education and psychology, 1902, PhD in international law, 1923; m. Edward Gasper Andrews. ❖ President of the Boston Home and School Association (1914–18); founded the American School Peace League (1908), renamed the American School Citizenship League (1918), of which she served as secretary until her death; during WWI, devoted her work to the goal of international organization; was a vigorous campaigner for the League of Nations; assisted in the organization of the Harvard-Radcliffe Research Bureau.

ANDREWS, Mrs. Henry Maxwell (1892–1983). *See West, Rebecca.*

ANDREWS, Jane (1833–1887). American educator and children's writer. Born Dec 1, 1833, in Newburyport, Massachusetts; died July 15, 1887, in Newburyport; graduated valedictorian from State Normal School, 1853. ❖ An invalid due to spinal problems, opened a progressive primary school in her home that continued for 25 years (Alice Stone Blackwell was one of her pupils); wrote 1st book, *Seven Little Sisters Who Live on the Round Ball That Floats in the Air* (1861), as a supplement to her geography lessons; also wrote *Ten Boys Who Lived on the Road from Long Ago to Now* (1886) and *Only a Year and What it Brought* (1887). Six of her works, published by Ginn & Co., were used as elementary-school reading for half a century after her death.

ANDREWS, Julie (1935—). English actress and singer. Name variations: Julie Edwards; Dame Julie Andrews. Born Julia Elizabeth Wells, Oct 1, 1935, in Walton-on-Thames, Surrey, England; m. Tony Walton (set designer), 1959 (div. 1968); m. Blake Edwards (director), 1969; children: (1st m.) Emma Kate Walton; (adopted daughters) Amy and Joanna; (stepchildren) Geoffrey and Jennifer Edwards (actress). ❖ Musical-comedy star, began performing as a child in England; made London stage debut at the Hippodrome (1947), singing operatic arias in *Starlight Roof*; made NY stage debut in *The Boyfriend* (1954), then starred as Eliza Doolittle in *My Fair Lady* (1956) and much later in title role in *Victor/Victoria*; films include *The Americanization of Emily* (1964), *Torn Curtain* (1966), *Hawaii* (1966), *Thoroughly Modern Millie* (1967), *Star* (1968), *Darling Lili* (1970), *The Tamarind Seed* (1974), *10* (1979), *S.O.B.* (1981), *The Man Who Loved Women* (1983), *That's Life!* (1986), *Duet for One* (1986), *The Princess Diaries* (2001) and *Princess Diaries 2* (2004); starred on tv series "Julie" (1992); with Carol Burnett, starred in "Julie and Carol at Carnegie Hall" (1962) and "Julie and Carol at Lincoln Center" (1971); an operation on vocal chords left her singing voice badly damaged (1998); writes children's books under name Julie Edwards, including *Mandy, The Last of the Really Great Whangdoodles* and *Little Bo: The Story of Bonnie Boadicea.* Won Academy Award for Best Actress for *Mary Poppins* (1964) and nominated as well for *The Sound of Music* (1965) and *Victor/Victoria* (1982); named Dame Commander of the Order of the British Empire by Queen Elizabeth II (DBE, 1999); honored by the president in the Kennedy Center Honors (2001).

ANDREWS, LaVerne (1911–1967). American singer. Name variations: Laverne. Born July 6, 1911, in Minneapolis, Minnesota; died of cancer in Hollywood, California, May 8, 1967; sister of Maxene and Patti Andrews; m. Louis Rogers, 1948. ❖ As one of the Andrews Sisters

(1932–1953), toured with vaudeville shows (1930s); released 1st hit record (1937); appeared on national radio shows and in feature films (1940–53); with US entry into WWII and subsequent formation of United Services Organization (USO), began touring military facilities in US and abroad as part of the effort to entertain troops and keep morale high (1941); dissolved act (1953). Selected discography: "Bei Mir Bist du Schön," "The Hut Sut Song," "Three Little Fishies," "Hold Tight-Hold Tight," "Beer Barrel Polka," "Well, All Right," "Oh Johnny," "Ferryboat Serenade," "Boogie Woogie Bugle Boy," "In Apple Blossom Time," "Aurora," "Elmer's Tune," "Chattanooga Choo Choo," "Pennsylvania Polka," "Sonny Boy," "Beat Me Daddy, Eight to the Bar," "Oh! Ma-ma!," "Rum and Coca Cola." ❖ See also *Women in World History.*

ANDREWS, Lois (1924–1968). American stage and screen actress. Born Lorraine Gourley, Mar 24, 1924, in Huntington Park, California; died April 4, 1968, in Encino, California; m. George Jessel (actor and comedian); m. David Street (singer); m. Steve Brodie (actor); m. Leonard Kleckner (army colonel); children: four. ❖ On Broadway, appeared in Earl Carroll's *Vanities*, George White's *Scandals*, and the revue *Starlets*; married George Jessel at age 16, had a daughter, and divorced him two years later; appeared in such films as *Meet Me after the Show, Roger Toughy, Gangster* and *Dixie Dugan.*

ANDREWS, Mary Raymond (1860–1936). American author. Born Mary Raymond Shipman, April 2, 1860, in Mobile, Alabama; died Aug 2, 1936, in Syracuse, NY; dau. of Jacob Shaw Shipman (Episcopalian minister) and Ann Louise Gold (Johns) Shipman; m. William Shankland Andrews (lawyer and later judge), Dec 31, 1884; children: Paul Shipman Andrews (b. 1887, became dean of the College of Law at Syracuse University). ❖ Author of short books, stories, poems and articles who contributed to many periodicals over a long career, primarily *Scribner's Magazine;* known for sentimental plots and romantic characters, published best-known story, *The Perfect Tribute,* about the Gettysburg Address, in *Scribner's* (July 1906); wrote over 20 books, including *A Lost Commander* (1929), a biography of Florence Nightingale.

ANDREWS, Maxene (1916–1995). American singer. Name variations: sometimes mistakenly spelled Maxine. Born Jan 3, 1916, in Minneapolis, Minnesota; died of a heart attack while vacationing in Hyannis, Massachusetts, Oct 21, 1995; sister of Patti and LaVerne Andrews; m. Lou Levy (their manager), July 28, 1941 (div. 1950). ❖ As one of the Andrews Sisters (1932–1953), appeared on national radio shows and in feature films; especially known for appearances at morale-boosting USO shows during WWII. ❖ See also autobiography (with Bill Gilbert) *Over Here, Over There: The Andrews Sisters and the USO Stars in WWII* (Kensington, 1993); and *Women in World History.*

ANDREWS, Michelle (1971—). Australian field-hockey player. Born Nov 19, 1971, in Australia. ❖ Striker, won a team gold medal at Atlanta Olympics (1996).

ANDREWS, Nancy (1924–1989). American actress and singer. Born Dec 16, 1924, in Minneapolis, Minnesota; died July 29, 1989, in Queens, NY; m. Parke N. Bossart (div.). ❖ Began career as a singer and pianist in cabarets; made Broadway debut in revue *Touch and Go* (1949); other musicals include *Plain and Fancy, Pipe Dream, Juno, Madame Aphrodite* and *Little Me;* films include *Summer Wishes Winter Dreams* and *W.W. and the Dixie Dance Kings;* frequently appeared on tv variety programs, including "The Ed Sullivan Show," "The Perry Como Show," and "The Tonight Show."

ANDREWS, Patti (1918—). American singer. Born Feb 16, 1918, in Minneapolis, Minnesota; sister of LaVerne and Maxene Andrews; m. Martin Melcher (agent and future husband of Doris Day), Oct 1947 (div. 1950); m. Walter Wescheler (the group's accompanist), Dec 25, 1951. ❖ Performed as one of the Andrews Sisters (1932–1953), one of the most popular singing trios in America during the WWII era. Filmography: *Argentine Nights* (1940); *Buck Privates* (1941); *In the Navy* (1941); *Hold That Ghost* (1941); *What's Cookin'?* (1942); *Private Buckaroo* (1942); *Give Out Sisters* (1942); *Always a Bridesmaid* (1943); *How's About It?* (1943); *Swingtime Johnny* (1943); *Follow the Boys* (1944); *Moonlight and Cactus* (1944); *Hollywood Canteen* (1944); (dubbed vocals only) *Make Mine Music* (1946); *Road to Rio* (1947); (dubbed vocals only) *Melody Time* (1948); (cameo for Patti) *The Phynx* (1970). ❖ See also *Women in World History.*

ANDREWS, Regina Anderson (1900–1993). *See Anderson, Regina M.*

ANDREWS, Theresa (1962—). American swimmer. Born Aug 25, 1962; trained in Baltimore, Maryland; attended Indiana University. ❖ Won 6 Big Ten titles (1986); at Los Angeles Olympics, won gold medals for 4x100-meter medley relay and 100-meter backstroke (1984).

ANDREWS SISTERS.
See Andrews, Laverne.
See Andrews, Maxene.
See Andrews, Patti.

ANDREYANOVA, Yelena Ivanovna (1816–1857). Russian ballet dancer. Name variations: Elena Ivanovna Andreyanova, Andrejanova or Andrianova. Born July 13, 1816, in St. Petersburg, Russia; died Oct 26, 1857, in Anteuil, France. ❖ Began training at school of Imperial Ballet, St. Petersburg; made debut at Maryinsky Theater, St. Petersburg (1837), where she danced the company's 1st Giselle (1842); performed at Paris Opéra Ballet in France (c. 1845) and at La Scala Ballet in Italy (c. 1846); danced further feature roles in Phillipe Taglioni's *Robert le Diable* and *Salterello*.

ANDREYEVA, Maria Fyodorovna (1868–1953). *See Andreeva, Maria Fedorovna.*

ANDREYUK, Yelena (1958—). Soviet volleyball player. Born Nov 23, 1958, in USSR. ❖ At Moscow Olympics, won a gold medal in team competition (1980).

ANDREZEL, Pierre (1885–1962). *See Dinesen, Isak.*

ANDRIANOVA, Yelena Ivanovna (1816–1857). *See Andreyanova, Yelena Ivanovna.*

ANDRIESSE, Emmy (1914–1953). Dutch photographer. Born at The Hague, the Netherlands, 1914; died in Amsterdam, 1953; attended Koninklijke Academie voor Beeldende Kunsten, The Hague, 1932–37; m. Dilck Elffers, 1941. ❖ Primarily known for her portraits, especially of artists, studied graphic design and photography with Dutch avant-garde teachers Gerrit Kiljan, Paul Schuitema, and Piet Zwart; during German occupation, was a member of a group of photographers using disguised cameras (*Ondergedoken Camera*, 1940–45); was invited by the director of the Stedelijk Museum in Amsterdam to photograph 13 sculptors in Paris and Belgium (1951); also began photography for a book on the artist Vincent Van Gogh, which was published posthumously (1953) as *The World of Van Gogh;* two of her photographs appeared in Edward Steichen's show, *The Family of Man* (1955).

ANDRUNACHE, Georgeta (1976—). *See Damian, Georgeta.*

ANDRUS, Ethel Percy (1884–1967). American reformer and founder. Born Sept 21, 1884, in San Francisco, California; died July 1967 in Long Beach, California; 2nd of 2 daughters of Lucretia Frances (Duke) Andrus and George Wallace Andrus (lawyer); graduate of University of Chicago, 1903; University of Southern California at Los Angeles (UCLA), MA (1926), PhD (1930). ❖ Upon retiring from over 40 years as a teacher and public-school principal (1944), founded the National Retired Teachers Association (NRTA, 1947); founded the American Association of Retired Persons (AARP, 1958); was asked to join the national advisory committee for White House Conference on Aging (1961); was also a founder and editor of *Modern Maturity,* the magazine of the AARP.

ANDUJAR, Claudia (1931—). Swiss-born photographer. Born in Neuchâtel, Switzerland, 1931; moved to São Paulo, Brazil. ❖ Specializing in ethnographic documentation and photojournalism, documented the Carja and Bororo Indians in central Brazil (1955); began an ongoing project with Yanomami Indians along the Catrimani River in northern Brazil (1970s), which included examining their daily life and rituals; chaired the commission that, in 1983, successfully petitioned the Brazilian government to set aside a 19-million-acre reserve as a park for the Yanomami; freelanced for *Time, Life, Look* and *Esquire* magazines and published several books dealing with Indians, including *Yanomami* (1978) and *Amazonia* (1979).

ANDZHAPARIDZI, Vera (1900–1987). *See Andjaparidze, Veriko.*

A NEW CANTERBURY PILGRIM (1895–1982). *See Marsh, Edith Ngaio.*

ANEZKA. *Variant of Agnes.*

ANGEL, Albalucía (1939—). Colombian author. Name variations: Albalú; Albalucia Marulanda Angel. Born Sept 27, 1939, in Pereira, Risaralda, Colombia. ❖ Prominent figure in literature of Colombia and Latin America, had links with members of the Nadaista movement; studied art and art history with Marta Traba; works include: (novels) *Los*

girasoles en invierno (Sunflowers in Winter, 1970), *Dos veces Alicia* (Alice, Twice Over, 1972), *Estaba la pájara pinta sentada en el verde limón* (The Petite Painted Bird Perched on the Green Lemon Limb, 1975), *Misiá señora* (Missus-Lady, 1982), and *Las andariegas* (The Wayfarers, 1984); (short-story collections) *¡Oh Gloria inmarcesible!* (Oh, Boundless Glory, 1979); and (theater works) *Siete lunas y un espejo* (Seven Moons and a Mirror, 1984) and *La Manzana de piedra* (The Stone Apple, 1983).

ANGEL, Heather (1909–1986). English actress. Born Heather Grace Angel, Feb 9, 1909, in Oxford, England; died Dec 13, 1986, in Santa Barbara, California; attended London Polytechnic of Dramatic Arts; m. Ralph Forbes, 1934 (div. 1937); m. Henry Wilcoxon (actor, div.); m. Robert B. Sinclair (director), 1944 (stabbed to death by an intruder, 1970); children: (2nd m.) Barbara and Anthony Robert. ❖ Joined Old Vic (1926); filmed 1st sound version of *Hound of the Baskervilles* (1932); appeared in more than 60 films, including *Night in Montmarte, Berkeley Square, The Informer, The Three Musketeers, The Last of the Mohicans, Pride and Prejudice, That Hamilton Woman, Lifeboat, The Saxon Charm, Premature Burial,* and as Phyllis Clavering in 5 of the "Bulldog Drummond" series.

ANGELA, Mother (1824–1887). *See Gillespie, Mother Angela.*

ANGELA MERICI (1474–1540). *See Angela of Brescia.*

ANGELAKI-ROOKE, Katerina (1939—). *See Anghelaki-Rooke, Katerina.*

ANGELA OF BRESCIA (1474–1540). Founder of the Ursuline nuns. Name variations: Angela Merici. Born Angela Merici, Mar 21, 1474, at Grezze on Lake Garda in Italy, though a local legend persists that she was born in town of Desenzano, a few miles away; died Jan 27, 1540, in Brescia; dau. of John Merici (well-to-do vintner), and Signora Merici (of Biancosi merchant family from Salo); never married, no children. ❖ Founder of the Ursuline nuns, a Roman Catholic order focused on teaching young girls and young women; was orphaned in early teens and moved to Salo; became a member of the 3rd Order of St. Francis, a lay order dedicated to charitable works and teaching; experienced a vision that told her to found an order of women in Brescia (c. 1495). Dedicated to St. Ursula, the order was formally approved as an unenclosed group of women devoted to teaching children, especially young girls (Aug 8, 1536). ❖ See also Philip Caraman, *Saint Angela: The Life of Angela Merici, Foundress of the Ursulines* (Farrar, Straus, 1963); Sister Mary Monica, *Angela Merici and Her Teaching Idea (1474–1540)* (The Ursulines of Brown County, 1945); and *Women in World History*.

ANGELA OF FOLIGNO (1249–1309). Saint and writer. Born in Umbria in 1249; died 1309; married with several children. Beatified in 1693. ❖ Revered as a woman of exceptional piety, dictated a work about her life, which came to be called the *Divine Consolations of the Blessed Angela of Foligno.* ❖ See also *Women in World History.*

ANGELBERGA (c. 840–890). *See Engelberga.*

ANGELES, Victoria de (1923—). *See Los Angeles, Victoria de.*

ANGELICA, Mother (1923—). Catholic nun and tv host. Born Rita Antoinette Rizzo, April 20, 1923, in Canton, Ohio; only child of John and Mae (Gianfrancisco) Rizzo (became a nun). ❖ Joined the Poor Clares (1944); became abbess of Our Lady of the Angeles Franciscan monastery in Irondale, Alabama, a suburb of Birmingham; invited by Episcopalians in Birmingham to lead some seminars (1973), gained fame as a spiritual teacher; began to appear on Pat Robertson's Christian Broadcasting Network; founded Eternal World Television Network (EWTN, 1981), hosting twice-weekly shows from a studio near the Irondale monastery; deeply conservative, preaches total loyalty to the pope and often attacks feminists and Catholic liberals.

ANGELI, Pier (1932–1971). Italian actress. Born Anna Maria Pierangeli in Cagliari, Sardinia, Italy, June 19, 1932; dau. of a construction engineer father and an amateur actress mother; committed suicide, Sept 10, 1971; twin sister of Maria Luisa Pierangeli, who performed under the screen name Marisa Pavan; m. Vic Damone (singer), Nov 24, 1954 (div. 1959); m. Armando Travajoli (Italian bandleader), 1962 (sep. 1963); children: (1st m.) Perry Rocco Damone (b. 1955); (2nd m.) Howard Andrea (called Popino, b. 1963). ❖ While her father opposed a show-business career and her mother fostered it, made her debut opposite Vittorio de Sica in Leonide Moguy's *Domani é troppo Tardi* (Tomorrow is Too Late, 1949), then filmed the sequel, *Domani é un altro Giorno* (1950); appeared in the title role of *Teresa* (1951), an American film made in Italy; moved to Hollywood; starred in many Hollywood films, including *The Light*

Touch (1951), *The Devil Makes Three* (1952), *The Story of Three Loves* (1953), *Sombrero* (1953), *The Silver Chalice* (1955), *Somebody Up There Likes Me* (1956), *Merry Andrew* (1958), and *Battle of the Bulge* (1965); on tv, starred in "Song of Bernadette" (1958) and "The Moon and Sixpence" (1959); returned to Italy following breakup of 1st marriage. ❖ See also *Women in World History.*

ANGELILLI, Roberta (1965—). Italian politician. Born Feb 1, 1965, in Rome, Italy. ❖ Served as secretary-general of the Youth Front (1993–96), president of Youth Action (1996–97), and director of the environmental association, Fare Verde (1985–92); representing Union for Europe of the Nations Group (UEN), elected to 4th and 5th European Parliament (1994–99, 1999–2004). Founded the international voluntary work organization, Movimento Comunità.

ANGELINI, Enif (1886–1976). *See Robert-Angelini, Enif.*

ANGELIQUE, Mere (1591–1661). *See Arnauld, Jacqueline.*

ANGELIQUE DE SAINT-JEAN, Mere (1624–1684). *See Arnauld, Angelique.*

ANGELL, Helen Cordelia (1847–1884). English painter. Name variations: Helen Cordelia Coleman. Born Helen Coleman, 1847, in England; died 1884 in England; sister of William Coleman (pottery painter). ❖ One of the best flower painters of 19th century, was trained as an artist by brother and in return assisted with his decorative work for Minton Pottery; earned reputation as flower painter; married postmaster for southwest London and continued to paint; joined Dudley Gallery because of freedoms granted to women in exhibitions (1865); benefitted from Queen Victoria's support of women artists; appointed "Flower Painter in Ordinary" by Queen Victoria (1879); elected member of Royal Watercolor Society (1879).

ANGELL, Katharine S. (1892–1977). *See White, Katharine S.*

ANGELOPOULOS-DASKALAKI, Gianna (1955—). Greek politician and executive. Name variations: Gianna Daskalaki. Born Gianna Daskalaki, 1955, in Greece; studied law at Aristotelian University of Thessaloniki; m. Theodore Angelopoulos (businessman), 1990; children: 2 sons and 1 daughter. ❖ Elected councilor in the Municipality of Athens (1986); representing the New Democracy Party in the Athens first Region Constituency, elected Member of Parliament (1989, 1990); became involved in shipping business; named vice chair of Harvard University's John F. Kennedy School of Government (1994); served as president of the Athens Organizing Committee for the Olympics Games (2000–04).

ANGELOU, Maya (1928—). African-American author, actress, and dancer. Born Marguerite Annie Johnson, April 4, 1928, in St. Louis, Missouri; dau. of Bailey and Vivian Baxter Johnson (div. 1931); m. Tosh Angelos (ex-sailor), c. 1950 (div. c. 1952); m. Vusumzi Make (South African freedom fighter), c. 1960 (div. 1963); m. Paul Du Feu (builder and writer), 1973 (div. c. 1981); children: Guy Johnson. ❖ Studied dance with Pearl Primus (1952), then Martha Graham and Ann Halprin; joined the touring company of *Porgy and Bess;* was northern coordinator for Martin Luther King's Southern Christian Leadership Council (1960–61); lived in Ghana, serving as a writer and editor for *Ghanian Times* and *African Review,* and as an assistant administrator for School of Music and Drama at University of Ghana in Legon-Accra (1963–66); returned to US (1966), wrote and developed several dramatic projects, including *Black, Blues, Black,* a 10-part tv series on African traditions in America (1968); published autobiography *I Know Why the Caged Bird Sings* (1970), which was nominated for National Book Award; published 1st volume of poetry, *Just Give Me a Cool Drink of Water 'Fore I Diiie* (1971), which was nominated for a Pulitzer Prize; became the 1st black woman to have an original screenplay produced (*Georgia, Georgia,* 1972); made Broadway acting debut in *Look Away,* which brought her a Tony nomination (1973); had teaching posts and residency-fellowships at University of Kansas, Yale, and Wake Forest, among others; used popularity to advocate on behalf of feminist and race issues, and was recognized by several US presidents with posts to committees and organizations; offered the Reynolds Chair at Wake Forest University (1982), a lifetime post; delivered the inaugural poem at Bill Clinton's inauguration (1993); works include 5 autobiographies, 5 collections of poetry, and a book of essays, *Wouldn't Take Nothing for My Journey Now.* ❖ See also *Women in World History.*

ANGELS, The. *See Allbut, Barbara.*

ANGELUS, Muriel (1909–2004). Scottish actress and singer. Born Muriel Angelus Findlay, Mar 10, 1909, in London, England, of Scottish parents; died Aug 22, 2004, in Virginia; m. John Stuart (Scottish actor), 1928 (div. 1938); m. Paul Lavalle (Radio City music hall conductor), 1946 (died 1997); children: (2nd m.) Suzanne Lavalle (reporter for NBC). ❖ Following a long stage career in England, starred on Broadway in *The Boys from Syracuse* (1938), introducing the song "Falling in Love with Love"; made 4 US films: *The Light That Failed* (1939), *The Way of All Flesh* (1940), *Safari* (1940), and Preston Sturges' 1st feature, *The Great McGinty* (1940); films in England include *The Ringer* (1928), *No Exit* (1930), *Hindle Wakes* (1931), *Let's Love and Laugh* (1931), *My Wife's Family* (1932) and *So You Won't Talk* (1935); also starred on London stage in *Balalaika* (1936) and on Broadway in *Early to Bed* (1943–44); retired (1946); with husband, recorded *Tribute to Rodgers and Hammerstein* (1961).

ANGER, Jane (fl. c. 1580). British essayist. Fl. around 1580. ❖ In response to the pamphlet "Boke, his Surfeyt in love," which chided women for their moral corruption, responded with "Jane Anger, Her Protection for Women," claiming that females were the purer sex, corrupted only by men who drew them astray (the writer's identity has never been ascertained).

ANGERER, Nadine (1978—). German soccer player. Born Nov 10, 1978, in Lohr/Main, Germany. ❖ Won team European championship (1997); won FIFA World Cup (2003); goalkeeper, won a team bronze medal at Sydney Olympics (2000) and Athens Olympics (2004).

ANGERS, Félicité (1845–1924). French-Canadian novelist and historian. Name variations: Marie-Louise-Félicité Angers; Felicite Angers; (pseudonym) Laure Conan. Born Marie-Louise-Félicité Angers, 1845, in Murray Bay, Quebec, Canada; died 1924 in Quebec, Canada; dau. of Élie Angers and Marie (Perron) Angers; attended Ursuline Convent in Quebec City; never married; no children. ❖ Quebec's 1st woman novelist, began writing novels (1870s); led a solitary life in Murray Bay, living most of her life at her family home in La Malbaie; made a living from writing; works, which evoke French-Canadian history and resist Quebec's patriarchal culture, include *Un amour vrai* (1878), *À l'oeuvre et á l'épreuve* (1891), *L'obscure souffrance* (1919), *La Vaine Foi* (1919), *La Sève immortelle* (1925), and her best-known the epistolary *Angéline de Montbrun* (1884, trans. 1974); wrote moral and religious articles including *Si les Canadiennes le voulaient* (1886).

ANGES, Jeanne des. *See des Agnes, Jeanne.*

ANGEVILLE, Henriette d' (1795–1871). *See D'Angeville, Henriette.*

ANGHARAD (d. 1162). Queen of Wales. Died 1162; m. Gruffydd ap Cynan, king of Gwynedd, around 1095; children: 8, including Owen Gwynedd, prince of Gwynedd, and Susan of Powys.

ANGHARAD (fl. 13th c.). Princess of Wales. Dau. of Llywelyn II the Great (1173–1240), prince of Gwynedd and ruler of All Wales, and Tangwystl (once his mistress); m. Maelgwn Fychan.

ANGHELAKI-ROOKE, Katerina (1939—). Greek poet. Name variations: Katerina Anghelaki Rooke (also seen wrongly as Katerina Angelaki-Rooke); Katerina Rooke. Born 1939 in Athens, Greece; studied foreign languages and literature at the universities of Athens, Nice, and Geneva. ❖ Poet who uses ancient Greek myths to depict lives of contemporary women; works include *Wolves and Clouds* (1963), *The Body is the Victory and the Defeat of Dreams* (1975), *The Suitors* (1984), *Beings and Things: Poems by Katerina Anghelaki-Rooke* (1986), and *Collected Poems* (1998). Awarded National Prize for Poetry (1985).

ANGIOLINI, Giuseppina (c. 1800–?). Italian ballet dancer. Name variations: Giuseppina Angiolini-Cortesi. Born c. 1800, in Italy, possibly Milan; death date unknown; probably dau. of Pietro Angiolini (choreographer); m. Antonio Cortesi, c. 1824. ❖ Appeared at Teatro alla Scala, Milan, in works by Pietro Angiolini and Domenico Rossi (c. 1813–20); appeared at theaters throughout Italy, including in Cremona, Sinigalia, Teatro Reggio in Turin, and Canobbiano in Milan (1810s–20s); danced as prima ballerina at Teatro Reggio and was director of its ballet school; best known for dancing in early works by Cortesi, including *Il Castello del Diavolo* (1826), *Don Chisciotte* (1827), and *Aladino* (1827).

ANGLADA, Maria Angels (1930–1999). Spanish novelist. Born 1939 in Osona, Spain; died April 23, 1999, in Spain; m. Jordi Geli. ❖ Catalan writer whose works include *Les Closes* (1979), *No em dic Laura* (1981), *Viola d'amore* (1983), *Paisatge amb poetes* (1988), *Paradis amb poetes* (1993), and *El violi d'Auschwitz* (1994). Won Joseph Plà Prize for 1st novel, *Les Closes,* about 19th-century Catalan society.

ANGLIN, Margaret (1876–1958). Canadian-born American actress. Born Margaret Mary Anglin in Ottawa, Canada, 1876; died in 1958; dau. of Honorable Timothy Warren Anglin (speaker of Canadian House of Commons); sister of Francis A. Anglin, Canadian supreme court judge; studied in NY; m. Howard Hull, 1911. ❖ Scored 1st success as Roxane in Richard Mansfield's presentation of *Cyrano de Bergerac;* after appearing in a number of important American productions, including *Camille* (1903–04), *Zira* (1905–06), and *The Great Divide* (1906–07), toured Australia in Shakespearean roles (1908), distinguished herself with her revivals of the Greek tragedies; also played the lead in Margaret Deland's *The Awakening of Helena Richie.*

ANGOULÊME, countess of.
See Alice de Courtenay (d. 1211).
See Isabella of Valois (1389–1410).
See Louise of Savoy (1476–1531).
See Margaret de Rohan (fl. 1449).

ANGOULÊME, duchess of.
See Marie Therese Charlotte (1778–1851).
See Diane de France (1538–1619).

ANGOULÊME, Marguerite d'. See Margaret of Angoulême (1492–1549).

ANGUISSOLA, Anna Maria (c. 1545–?). Italian painter. Name variations: Angussola or Anguisciola. Pronunciation ang-GWEE-sho-la or ang-GOOS-so-la. Born c. 1545 or 1546 in Cremona, Italy; date of death unknown; dau. of Amilcare Anguissola (noble) and Bianca Ponzone; sister of Sofonisba, Elena, Europa, and Lucia Anguissola; m. Giacopo Sommi, c. 1570. ❖ Received formal art training from sister Sofonisba and collaborated with her on a *Madonna with the Christ Child and Saint John.* ❖ See also *Women in World History.*

ANGUISSOLA, Elena (c. 1525–after 1584). Italian painter. Name variations: Angussola or Anguisciola. Pronunciation ang-GWEE-sho-la or ang-GOOS-so-la. Born c. 1525 in Cremona, Italy; died after 1584; 2nd dau. of Amilcare Anguissola (noble) and Bianca Ponzone; sister of Sofonisba, Anna Maria, Europa, and Lucia Anguissola. ❖ Trained with sister Sofonisba and also under the mannerist artist Bernardino Campi (1546–49); joined the Convent of the Holy Virgin at San Vincenzo in Mantua as a Dominican nun. ❖ See also *Women in World History.*

ANGUISSOLA, Europa (c. 1542–?). Italian painter. Name variations: Angussola or Anguisciola. Pronunciation ang-GWEE-sho-la or ang-GOOS-so-la. Born c. 1542 or 1544 in Cremona, Italy; date of death unknown; dau. of Amilcare Anguissola (noble) and Bianca Ponzone; sister of Sofonisba, Elena, Anna Maria, and Lucia Anguissola; m. Carlo Schinchinelli, 1568; children: Antonio Galeazzo. ❖ Though it is known that she painted, no secure attributions have been made and no signed paintings are known to exist. ❖ See also *Women in World History.*

ANGUISSOLA, Lucia (c. 1536–1565). Italian painter. Name variations: Angussola or Anguisciola. Pronunciation ang-GWEE-sho-la or ang-GOOS-so-la. Born c. 1536 or 1538 in Cremona, Italy; died in 1565; dau. of Amilcare Anguissola (noble) and Bianca Ponzone; sister of Sofonisba, Elena, Europa, and Anna Maria Anguissola. ❖ Trained with sister Sofonisba; painted *Self-Portrait* (c. 1557), which portrays her in a seated pose, one hand on the bodice of her dress, the other holding a book. ❖ See also *Women in World History.*

ANGUISSOLA, Sofonisba (1532–1625). Italian artist. Name variations: Sephonisba or Sophonisba Angussola or Anguisciola. Pronunciation: ang-GWEE-sho-la or ang-GOOS-so-la. Born Sofonisba Anguissola, 1532, in Cremona, Italy; died in Palermo, Sicily, 1625; dau. of Amilcare Anguissola (noble) and Bianca Ponzone; sister of Lucia, Elena, Europa, and Anna Maria Anguissola; m. Don Fabrizio de Moncada, c. 1570 (died 1578); m. Orazio Lomellino, 1580; children: none. ❖ Known for her portraits, was court painter to Philip II of Spain and the 1st professional woman artist of the Italian Renaissance; drew *Self-Portrait with Old Woman* (c. 1545), a chalk sketch, which shows the artist in her early teens with a woman who, by dress, appears to be a servant of the household; began training with Bernardino Campi (c. 1546); went to Rome (1554), where she was offered advice and guidance by Michelangelo; began to receive commissions for portraits from the nobility and clergy; went to Milan (1558), where she was commissioned to paint the portrait of the Duke of Alba; became painter at the Spanish court in Madrid (1560) and was a great favorite of the queen, Elizabeth of Valois; painted last known self-portrait (c. 1620); a successful professional painter of widespread fame, paved the way for other women artists. The 50 or so securely attributed paintings and drawings of hers, of which at least 13 are self-portraits,

include *Bernardino Campi Painting Sofonisba Anguissola* (c. 1550), *The Chess Game* (1555), *Boy Pinched by a Crayfish* (1557), *Portrait of a Lady* and *Madonna Nursing her Child* (1588). ❖ See also Ilya Sandra Perlingieri, *Sofonisba Anguissola: The First Great Woman Artist of the Renaissance* (Rizzoli, 1992); and *Women in World History.*

ANGUS, Dorothy (1891–1979). Scottish embroiderer. Born Anna Dorothy Angus, Feb 19, 1891, in Stirling, Scotland; died April 24, 1979, in Scotland; dau. of James Angus (minister of the West United Free Church in Stirling); trained at Edinburgh College of Art. ❖ Important figure in the transformation of British embroidery into a dynamic modern art form and away from its nostalgic referencing of the arts and craft tradition established by William Morris, became head of department of Embroidery and Weaving at Gray's School of Art, Aberdeen (1920), where she taught (1920–55).

ANGUS, Rita (1908–1970). New Zealand artist. Name variations: signed work Rita Cook (1930–46); changed name to Henrietta Catherine McKenzie (father's middle name) by deed poll. Born Henrietta Catherine Angus, Mar 12, 1908, in Hastings, New Zealand; died Jan 25, 1970, in New Zealand; studied painting at Canterbury School of Art, Christchurch, and Elam School of Fine Arts, Auckland; m. Alfred Cook (artist), 1930 (div. 1934). ❖ Helped establish a distinct New Zealand style of painting and landscape (1930s–40s); best known paintings include *Cass* (1936), *Head of a Maori Boy* (1938), *Portrait of Betty Curnow* (1942), *Sun Goddess* (1949), and *Self-portrait* (1966).

ANGWIN, Maria L. (1849–1898). Canadian physician. Born Sept 21, 1849, in Newfoundland; died April 25, 1898. ❖ Moved with family to Nova Scotia (1865); became school teacher to raise money for medical school; because no medical schools were open to women in Canada, graduated from Woman's Medical College of the New York Infirmary (1882); became 1st woman with license to practice medicine in Halifax, Nova Scotia, when she opened medical practice; was active with Woman's Christian Temperance Union.

ANGYAL, Eva (1955—). Hungarian handball player. Born April 18, 1955, in Hungary. ❖ At Montreal Olympics, won a bronze medal in team competition (1976).

ANÍCHKOVA, Anna (1868–1935). Russian author, translator, and salonnière. Born Anna Mitrofanovna in 1868 in Russia; died in 1935 in Russia; m. E.V. Aníchkov (literary critic). ❖ With husband, moved to Paris (late 1890s), where she created a literary salon frequented by such writers as Anatole France and Viacheslav Ivanov; wrote novels in French, the most popular of which, *L'ombre de la maison* (1904), was translated into English as *The Shadow of the House;* also contributed to several French periodicals and penned a collection of essays on Russian intellectuals; returned to Russia (1909); after the revolution, devoted her time exclusively to translation (1917–35).

ANIKEEVA, Ekaterina (1965—). Russian water-polo player. Born Jan 21, 1965, in USSR. ❖ Won a team bronze medal at Sydney Olympics (2000).

ANI PACHEN (c. 1933–2002). See Dolma, Pachen.

ANISIMOVA, Natalya (1960—). Soviet handball player. Born Nov 16, 1960, in USSR. ❖ Won an Olympic bronze medal in team competition at Seoul (1988) and at Barcelona (1992).

ANISIMOVA, Nina (1909—). Soviet dancer and choreographer. Born Jan 27, 1909, in St. Petersburg, Russia; studied under Maria Romanova, Agrippina Vaganova, and Alexander Shiryayev at the Leningrad ballet school, 1919–26. ❖ Created many notable roles in the dramatic ballets of the 1930s, including Therese in Vassily Vainonen's *Flames of Paris;* one of the 1st Soviet women choreographers, worked on *Gayané* for the Leningrad Kirov Theater (1945); for her long association with the Maly Opera Theater in Leningrad, created *The Magic Veil* (1947), *Coppélia* (new version, 1949), *Schéhérazade* (new version, 1950), and *Willow Tree* (1957); retired as a dancer (1957), when she began to focus solely on choreography.

ANISIMOVA, Tatyana (1949—). Soviet hurdler. Name variations: Tatiana Anisimova. Born Oct 19, 1949, in USSR. ❖ At Montreal Olympics, won a silver medal in the 100-meter hurdles (1976).

ANISIMOVA, Vera (1952—). Soviet runner. Born May 25, 1952, in USSR. ❖ At Olympics, won a bronze medal in Montreal (1976) and a silver medal in Moscow (1980), both in the 4x100-meter relay.

ANISSINA, Marina (1975—). Russian-born ice dancer. Born Aug 30, 1975, in Moscow, Russia; dau. of Vyacheslav Anissin (hockey player) and Irina Cherniyeva (figure skater who with partner Vassily Blagov won the Soviet Nationals and finished 6th at Sapporo Olympics, 1972). ❖ With partner Ilya Averbukh, won two World Jr. titles (1990, 1992); with partner Gwendal Peizerat and representing France, won Nations Cup and Trophée de France (1995), NHK Trophy (1996, 1999, 2000, 2001), Trophée Lalique (1997, 1999, 2000, 2001), Skate America (1999) and Skate Canada (2001); with Peizerat, also won silver medals (1998, 1999, 2001) and a gold medal (2000) at World championships, a bronze medal at Nagano Olympics (1998), placed 1st at French Nationals (1996, 1997, 1998, 1999, 2000, 2001) and the European championships (2000, 2002), and won a gold medal at Salt Lake City Olympics (2002).

ANITAS, Herta (1967—). Romanian rower. Born Aug 18, 1967, in Romania. ❖ At Seoul Olympics, won a bronze medal in the coxed fours and a silver medal in the coxed eights (1988).

ANKE, Hannelore (1957—). East German swimmer. Born Dec 8, 1957, in Germany. ❖ Won gold medals for 100 meters, 200-meter breaststroke, and relay at World championships (1973); at Montreal Olympics, won gold medals for the 4x100-meter medley relay and 100-meter breaststroke (1976).

ANKER, Nini Roll (1873–1942). Norwegian novelist. Name variations: (pseudonyms) Jo Nein and Kaare P. Born Nicoline Magdalen Roll in Molde, Norway, 1873; died in 1942; dau. of Ferdinand Roll; m. Peter Anker, 1892 (div. 1907); m. Johan Anker, 1910. ❖ Published 1st novel *I blinde (Blind,* 1898) under pseudonym Jo Nein, followed by *Benedicte Stendal,* a novel in diary form (1909); in all, produced 29 books and many articles and essays.

ANKER-DOEDENS, Alida van der (1922—). Dutch kayaker. Born July 28, 1922, in the Netherlands. ❖ At London Olympics, won a silver medal in K1 500 meters (1948).

ANKERS, Evelyn (1918–1985). English actress. Born in Valparaiso, Chile, Aug 17, 1918; died Aug 29, 1985, in Haiku, Maui, Hawaii; dau. of British parents; m. Richard Denning (actor), Sept 6, 1942; children: daughter Dee. ❖ Known as the screamer or the queen of the horror movies, debuted in England before coming to US; films include *The Villiers Diamond* (UK, 1933), *Rembrandt* (1936), *Fire Over England* (1937), *Hold that Ghost* (1941), *The Wolf Man* (1941), *The Ghost of Frankenstein* (1942), *Eagle Squadron* (1942), *Sherlock Holmes and the Voice of Terror* (1942), *Captive Wild Woman* (1943), *Son of Dracula* (1943), *Pearl of Death* (1944), *Pillow of Death* (1945), *Queen of Burlesque* (1946), *Black Beauty* (1946), *Spoilers of the North* (1947), *Flight to Nowhere* (1946), *The Lone Wolf in London* (1947), and *Tarzan's Magic Fountain* (1949); moved with actor husband Richard Denning to Maui (1968).

ANN-MARGRET (1941—). Swedish-born film actress and dancer. Name variations: Ann-Margret Olsson. Born Anna Olsson, April 28, 1941, in Valsjöbyn, Jämtland, Sweden; raised in Wilmette, Illinois; attended Northwestern University; m. Roger Smith (actor), May 8, 1967. ❖ Performed frequently in Las Vegas night clubs and on tv specials until her screen debut in *State Fair* (1964); has appeared in over 50 productions for film and tv, including *Bye Bye Birdie* (1963), *Viva Las Vegas* (1964), *Stagecoach* (1966), *The Villain* (1979), *Twice in a Lifetime* (1985), *Our Sons* (1991), *Grumpy Old Men* (1993), and *Grumpier Old Men* (1995); received Academy Award nominations for work in *Carnal Knowledge* (1971) and *Tommy* (1975); survived a 22-foot fall from a stage while performing at Lake Tahoe (1972), which derailed her career for some time; appeared at MGM Grand in Las Vegas (2003).

ANNA. *Variant of Anne or Hannah.*

ANNA. Biblical woman. Born into the tribe of Asher; dau. of Phanuel. ❖ After 7 years of marriage, husband died; during long widowhood, attended daily temple services; at age 84, entered the temple at the moment when Simeon uttered his words of praise and thanks to God for sending his Son into the world; thus, Anna recognized the infant Jesus as the Messiah (Luke 2:36, 37). ❖ See also *Women in World History.*

ANNA, Saint (fl. 1st c.). *See Anne, Saint.*

ANNA AMALIA OF PRUSSIA (1723–1787). German composer and princess. Name variations: Princess Anna Amalia. Born Nov 9, 1723, in Berlin, Germany; died Mar 30, 1787, in Berlin (some sources cite 1788); dau. of Sophia Dorothea of Brunswick-Lüneburg-Hanover (1687–1757) and Frederick William I (1688–1740), king of Prussia

(r. 1713–1740); youngest sister of Frederick II the Great; aunt of Anna Amalia of Saxe-Weimar (1739–1807); studied harpsichord and piano under Gottlieb Hayne and counterpoint with Johann Philipp Kirnberger. ❖ Youngest sister of Frederick II the Great, was a product of the Enlightenment, a period when women played an important role in public affairs; was trained by court musicians; began composing in mid-40s, concentrating on marches for military regiments for certain generals, a genre rarely adopted by women; founded a music library collection, which includes autographed scores of Johann Sebastian Bach and other composers (known as the Amalien Bibliothek, it exists today in its entirety); was also a patron of music, and musicians throughout Germany were employed by the court. ❖ See also *Women in World History.*

ANNA AMALIA OF SAXE-WEIMAR (1739–1807). German composer, patron of the arts, and duchess of Saxe-Weimar. Name variations: Amalia, Duchess of Saxe-Weimar. Born at Wolfenbüttel, Oct 24, 1739; died in Weimar, April 10, 1807; dau. of Charles (Karl) I, duke of Brunswick-Wolfenbüttel, and Duchess Philippine Charlotte (1716–1801); niece of Frederick II the Great and Anna Amalia of Prussia (1723–1787); m. Ernst August Konstantin (Ernst Wilhelm Wolff), duke of Saxe-Weimar, 1756 (died 1758); children: 2 sons, including Charles Augustus. ❖ Studied with Friedrich G. Fleischer, organist and composer, and Ernst Wilhelm Wolff; named regent of Saxe-Weimar for infant son Charles Augustus, after husband's death (1758); administered affairs of the duchy with great prudence, strengthening its resources and improving its position despite the troubles of the Seven Years' War; known for her work in the new German opera genre of the Singspiel; composed *Erwin und Elmire,* based on a text by Goethe (1776), and *Das Jahrmarksfest zu Plunderweisen,* also based on Goethe's text (1778); created the Musenhof, or court of muses, known throughout Europe for its rich musical and cultural life. A memorial of the duchess is included in Goethe's works under title *Zum Andenken der Fürstin Anna-Amalia.* ❖ See also *Women in World History.*

ANNA ANACHOUTLOU (r. 1341–1342). Queen of Trebizond. Reigned as queen of Trebizond (in present-day Turkey) from 1341 to 1342; dau. of King Alexius II (r. 1297–1330). ❖ Following the removal of Irene Palaeologina from the throne, was crowned, then deposed in favor of Michael, son of former King John II (1341); was restored to the throne and ruled for one more year. ❖ See also *Women in World History.*

ANNA ANGELINA (d. 1210?). Nicaean empress. Died c. 1210; dau. of Alexius III Angelus, emperor of Byzantium (r. 1195–1203) and Euphrosyne (d. 1203); m. Theodore I Lascaris, emperor of Nicaea (r. 1204–1222); children: Irene Lascaris (who m. John III Ducas, Byzantine emperor); Maria Lascaris (who m. Bela IV, king of Hungary). ❖ See also *Women in World History.*

ANNA CARLOVNA (1718–1746). *See Anna Leopoldovna.*

ANNA CATHERINA OF BRANDENBURG (1575–1612). Queen of Denmark and Norway. Name variations: Anna Catherine of Brandenburg; Anne Catherine Hohenzollern. Born June 26, 1575; died Mar 29, 1612; dau. of Catherine of Custrin (1549–1602) and Joachim Frederick (1546–1608), elector of Brandenburg (r. 1598–1608); m. Christian IV (1577–1648), king of Denmark and Norway (r. 1588–1648), Nov 27, 1597; children: Christian or Christiane (1603–1647); Elizabeth (1606–1608); Frederick III (b. 1609), king of Norway and Denmark (r. 1648–1670); Ulrich (b. 1611). Christian IV's 2nd wife was Kirsten Munk (1598–1658).

ANNA COMNENA (1083–1153/55). Byzantine princess, scholar and historian. Name variations: (Greek) Anna Komnena, called "The Tenth Muse" and the "Pallas of Byzantine Greece." Born Dec 2, 1083; died at age 70–72, sometime between 1153 and 1155; dau. of Alexius I Comnenus, emperor of Byzantium (r. 1081–1118), and Irene Ducas or Ducaena (c. 1066–1133); m. Byzantine noble, Nicephorus Bryennius, 1098 (died 1138); children: Alexius Comnenus (b. 1098); John Ducas (b. 1100); Irene Ducas or Ducaena (b. ca. 1101/1103); and a daughter whose name is unknown. ❖ One of the most remarkable women in history prior to the emergence of the Western World, was the 1st known woman historian, and perhaps the best-educated woman in the entire Mediterranean world between the 5th and the 15th centuries; born and proclaimed heir to Byzantine throne (1083); as the daughter of an emperor, had profound education with the best tutors but much of what she mastered came from a lifelong devotion to classical learning; read Homer, the great writers of Greek tragedy, Aristophanes and the lyric poets, works of the philosophers Plato and Aristotle, those of orators

Isocrates and Demosthenes but, above all, those of the great historians, Thucydides and Polybius; lost the right of succession when brother John was proclaimed heir to the throne (1091); when father died and John was named emperor (1118), worked to secure the throne for her own husband; launched a plot to assassinate her brother but her husband could not go through with it; retired from public life, spending much of her time at convent of Kecharitomene, where she surrounded herself with a circle of philosophers and men of letters, forming a kind of salon of which she was the director and chief inspiration; was particularly drawn to the works of Aristotle and encouraged the writers of commentaries upon them, in particular Michael of Ephesus; found the tranquility to compose the history of her father's reign, *The Alexiad* (1148), one of the most original works of Byzantine historiography (it also began the Byzantine classical renaissance, which lasted for 300 years until the empire's demise). ❖ See also Georgina Buckler, *Anna Comnena: A Study* (Oxford University, 1929); Rose Dalven, *Anna Comnena* (Twayne, 1972); and *Women in World History*.

ANNA CONSTANCIA (1619–1651). Electress of the Palatinate. Name variations: Anna Katherina Constance. Born Aug 7, 1619; died Oct 8, 1651; dau. of Constance of Styria (1588–1631) and Sigismund III, king of Poland (r. 1587–1632), king of Sweden (r. 1592–1599); m. Philip William of Neuburg, elector of the Palatinate, June 8, 1642.

ANNA DALASSENA (c. 1025–1105). Byzantine empress. Birth date unknown, possibly c. 1025; died c. 1105; dau. of Alexius "Charon" Dalassenus (Byzantine governor of Italy); m. John Comnenus or Komnenos (d. 1067, brother of Isaac Comnenus, r. 1057–1059); children: 8, including Manuel; Isaac (d. ca. 1106); Alexius I Comnenus (1048–1118), Byzantine emperor (r. 1081–1118); Adrian (d. 1105); Nicephorus; and 3 daughters (names unknown: one m. Michael Taronite; another m. Nicephorus Melissenus; the youngest m. Constantine Diogenes); grandmother of Anna Comnena. ❖ Mother of the Comneni, helped found the Comnenid Dynasty; born into a powerful family, married into an even more powerful family and spent her life at court, where she learned the art of royal intrigue, acquired a thorough grasp of politics, and became skilled in navigating the corridors of Byzantine power; when husband refused the throne (1059), determined to win it back; exercised enormous influence over sons; was the power behind the coup d'etat (1081), which set the Comnenian dynasty upon the throne for more than a century; when son Alexius had himself crowned, was granted the title empress; for 20 years, ruled jointly with her son and governed well; retired voluntarily from public life to become a nun in the convent of Pantepoptes, which she had founded (1100). ❖ See also *Women in World History*.

ANNA DE MEDICI (b. 1616). *See Medici, Anna de.*

ANNA HOHENZOLLERN (1576–1625). *See Anna of Prussia.*

ANNA IOANNOVNA (1693–1740). *See Anna Ivanovna.*

ANNA IVANOVNA (1693–1740). Russian empress. Name variations: Anny Ioannovny; Ioannovna; Anne of Courland. Born Anna Ivanovna on Jan 28, 1693, in Moscow, Russia; died in St. Petersburg, Russia, Oct 17, 1740; 2nd dau. of Ivan V (Alekseevich) and Praskovya Saltykova (1664–1723); niece of Peter the Great; secular education by Western tutors and religious training from the church; m. Frederick-William Kettler, duke of Courland (nephew of the king of Prussia), 1710 (died 1711); no children. ❖ Russian empress who ruled from 1730 to 1740 in a reign characterized by the continuation of the Westernization of Russia initiated by Tsar Peter I; along with family, became dependent on Peter I when her father Ivan V died (1696); widowed on wedding trip (1710); resided in Mitau, capital of Courland (until 1730); succeeded Peter II as tsar (1730); overthrew the Supreme Privy Council and re-established autocracy; succeeded by Ivan VI at her death (1740). Her reign remains controversial; historians have depicted her absolutist reign as a dark page in Russian history in which German favorites exploited the policies, resources, and interests of Russia, but some now believe that foreign domination has been overemphasized, and that the German advisors were actually capable and loyal servants of Russia who improved many aspects of Russian society. ❖ See also Mina Curtiss, *A Forgotten Empress: Anna Ivanovna and Her Era, 1730–1740* (Frederick Ungar, 1974); Philip Longworth, *The Three Empresses: Catherine I, Anne and Elizabeth of Russia* (Holt, Rinehart and Winston, 1972); and *Women in World History*.

ANNA JAGELLO (1523–1596). Queen of Poland. Name variations: Jagiello, Jagiellonica or Jagiellonka. Born in 1523; died in 1596; dau. of Bona Sforza (1493–1557) and Zygmunt I Stary also known as

Sigismund I the Elder (1467–1548), king of Poland (r. 1506–1548); m. Istvan also known as Stefan Batory or Stephen Bathory (1533–1586), king of Poland-Lithuania (r. 1575–1586).

ANNA JULIANA OF SAXE-COBURG-SAALFELD (1781–1860). Russian royal. Name variations: Anna Juliane. Born Sept 23, 1781; died Aug 15, 1860; dau. of Francis Frederick, duke of Saxe-Coburg-Saalfeld, and Augusta of Reuss-Ebersdorf (1757–1831); m. Constantine Pavlovich Romanov (1779–1831, son of Paul I, tsar of Russia, who renounced his succession), Feb 26, 1796 (div. 1820). Constantine Romanov also entered into a morganatic marriage with Johanna von Grudna-Grudczinski, princess of Lowicz (1799–1831), May 24, 1820.

ANNA KARLOVNA (1718–1746). *See Anna Leopoldovna.*

ANNA LEOPOLDOVNA (1718–1746). Russian regent. Name variations: Anna Carlovna or Karlovna. Born Elisabeth Katharina Christine, Dec 18, 1718; died in exile, Mar 18 or 19, 1746; dau. of Catherine of Mecklenburg-Schwerin (1692–1733) and Charles Leopold, duke of Mecklenburg-Schwerin; m. Anton Ulrich (b. 1714), duke of Brunswick, 1739 (died 1775); children: Ivan VI (b. 1740), emperor of Russia (r. 1740–1741); Catherine of Brunswick-Wolfenbuttel (1741–1807); Elizabeth of Brunswick-Wolfenbuttel (1743–1782); Peter (b. 1745); Alexei (b. 1746). ❖ After Empress Anna Ivanovna died (1740), declared herself regent to her son Ivan who was heir to the throne; knew little of the character of the people with whom she had to deal, was ignorant of the Russian mode of government, and quarrelled with key supporters; when Elizabeth Petrovna, daughter of Peter the Great, incited the guards to revolt and was proclaimed Empress Elizabeth I, was banished to a small island in the river Dvina (son Ivan was thrown into prison where he soon died). ❖ See also *Women in World History*.

ANNA MARIA DE MEDICI (d. 1741). *See Medici, Anna Maria de.*

ANNA MARIA LUDOVICA (1667–1743). *See Medici, Anna Maria Luisa de.*

ANNA MARIA LUISA DE MEDICI (1667–1743). *See Medici, Anna Maria Luisa de.*

ANNA MARIA LUISA OF THE PALATINATE (1667–1743). *See Medici, Anna Maria Luisa de.*

ANNA MARIA OF SAXE-LAUENBURG (d. 1741). *See Medici, Anna Maria de.*

ANNA MARIA OF SAXONY (1836–1859). Grand duchess of Tuscany. Name variations: Anna of Saxony; Maria Anna of Saxony. Born April 1, 1836, in Dresden, Germany; died Feb 10, 1859, in Florence, Italy; dau. of Amalia of Bavaria (1801–1877) and Johann also known as John (1801–1873), king of Saxony (r. 1854–1873); became 1st wife of Ferdinand IV (1835–1908), titular grand duke of Tuscany from 1859 to 1908, Nov 24, 1856; children: Antonia (1858–1883). Ferdinand IV's 2nd wife was Alicia of Parma (1849–1935). ❖ See also *Women in World History*.

ANNA MARIA OF THE PALATINATE (1561–1589). Swedish royal. Name variations: Maria of the Palatinate. Born July 24, 1561; died July 29, 1589; dau. of Louis of the Palatinate; became 1st wife of Charles IX (1550–1611), king of Sweden (r. 1604–1611); children: Catherine, countess Palatine (1584–1638, who m. John Casimir of Zweibrücken, count Palatine); Margaret Elizabeth (1580–1585); Elizabeth Sabine (1582–1585); Ludwig or Louis (b. 1583); Gustav (1587–1587); Marie (1588–1589); Christine (1593–1594).

ANNA MARIA THERESA (1879–1961). Princess of Hohenlohe. Born Oct 17, 1879, in Lindau; died May 30, 1961, in Baden-Baden, Germany; dau. of Alicia of Parma (1849–1935) and Ferdinand IV (1835–1908), titular grand duke of Tuscany from 1859 to 1908.

ANNAN, Alyson (1973—). Australian field-hockey player. Born Alyson Regina Annan, June 21, 1973, in Campbelltown, NSW, Australia. ❖ Forward; won team gold medal at Atlanta Olympics (1996) and Sydney Olympics (2000).

ANNA OF BOHEMIA (fl. 1230s). Duchess of Silesia. Fl. in 1230s; m. Henry II the Pious, duke of Silesia (r. 1238–1241); children: Boleslaw II Lysy of Legnica; Henry III of Breslaw; Conrad I of Glogow; Ladislas, archbishop of Salzburg; Elizabeth of Silesia (fl. 1257).

ANNA OF BOHEMIA (fl. 1318). Bohemian princess. Name variations: Anne. Fl. around 1318; dau. of Wenceslas II, king of Bohemia (r. 1278–1305) and Judith (d. 1297); m. Henry of Carinthia

(d. 1335), king of Bohemia (r. 1306–1310); children: Margaret Maultasch (1318–1369).

ANNA OF BOHEMIA AND HUNGARY (1503–1547). Holy Roman Empress. Name variations: Anna of Hungary. Born 1503 in Prague; died 1547 in Prague; dau. of Vladislav or Wladyslaw also known as Ladislas II of Bohemia, king of Bohemia (r. 1471–1516), and Anne de Foix; sister of Louis II, king of Hungary (r. 1516–1528); m. Ferdinand I, Holy Roman emperor (r. 1556–1564), 1521; children: Elizabeth of Habsburg (d. 1545); Maximilian II (1527–1576), Holy Roman emperor (r. 1564–1576); Anna of Brunswick (1528–1590, who m. Albert V of Bavaria); Mary (1531–1581, who m. William V, duke of Cleves); Magdalena (1532–1590); Catherine of Habsburg (1533–1572); Eleonora of Austria (1534–1594); Margaretha (1536–1566); Charles of Styria (1540–1590); Ferdinand, count of Tyrol; Helen (1543–1574); Joanna of Austria (1546–1578, who m. Francis I de Medici, grand duke of Tuscany).

ANNA OF BRANDENBURG (1487–1514). Danish royal. Name variations: Anna von Brandenburg. Born Aug 27, 1487; died May 3, 1514, in Kiel; dau. of Margaret of Saxony (1449–1501) and John Cicero (1455–1499), elector of Brandenburg (r. 1486–1499); became 1st wife of Frederick I, king of Denmark and Norway (r. 1523–1533), April 10, 1502; children: Christian III (1503–1559), king of Denmark and Norway (r. 1534–1559); Hans; Dorothea Oldenburg (1504–1547, who m. Albert, duke of Prussia).

ANNA OF BRANDENBURG (1507–1567). Duchess of Mecklenburg-Schwerin. Name variations: Anna Hohenzollern. Born 1507; died June 19, 1567; dau. of Elizabeth of Denmark (1485–1555) and Joachim I Nestor, elector of Brandenburg (r. 1499–1535); m. Albert V (1488–1547), duke of Mecklenburg-Schwerin (r. 1519–1547), Jan 17, 1524; children: John Albert (b. 1525), duke of Mecklenburg-Gustrow; Ulrich III (b. 1528), duke of Mecklenburg-Gustrow; Christof (b. 1537).

ANNA OF BRUNSWICK (fl. 1400s). Duchess of Bavaria. Married Albert III the Pious (1401–1460, sometimes referred to as Albert II), duke of Bavaria (r. 1438–1460); children: John IV (b. 1437), duke of Bavaria (r. 1460–1463); Sigismund (b. 1439), duke of Bavaria (r. 1460–1467; abdicated in 1467); Albert IV (1447–1508, sometimes referred to as Albert III), duke of Bavaria (r. 1465–1508).

ANNA OF BRUNSWICK (1528–1590). Duchess of Bavaria. Name variations: Anna Habsburg or Hapsburg. Born July 7, 1528, in Prague; died Oct 17, 1590, in Munich; dau. of Anna of Bohemia and Hungary (1503–1547) and Ferdinand I, Holy Roman emperor (r. 1558–1564); m. Albert V (d. 1579), duke of Bavaria; children: William V the Pious, duke of Bavaria (r. 1579–1597, abdicated); Mary of Bavaria (1551–1608).

ANNA OF BYZANTIUM (fl. 901). Holy Roman empress. Dau. of Leo VI the Wise, Byzantine emperor (r. 886–912) and one of his 4 wives, possibly Zoë Carbopsina (c. 890–920); m. Louis III the Blind of Provence (c. 880–928), Holy Roman emperor (r. 901–905); children: Charles Constantine of Vienne (b. 901), count of Vienne.

ANNA OF BYZANTIUM (963–1011). Grand-duchess of Kiev. Born Mar 13, 963; died 1011; dau. of Theophano (c. 940–?) and Romanus II, Byzantine emperor (r. 959–963); sister of Constantine VIII (r. 1025–1028) and Basil II (r. 976–1025), both Byzantine emperors, and Theophano of Byzantium (c. 955–991); m. Vladimir I, grand-duke of Kiev, around 989; children: St. Gleb; St. Boris; and one daughter.

ANNA OF CUMIN (d. 1111). Princess of Kiev. Died Oct 7, 1111; became 2nd wife of Vsevolod I, prince of Kiev (r. 1078–1093), 1067; children: Anna of Kiev, abbess of Janczyn (b. around 1068); Adelaide of Kiev (c. 1070–1109); Katherine of Kiev (nun). Vsevolod's 1st wife was Irene of Byzantium (d. 1067).

ANNA OF DENMARK (1532–1585). Princess of Denmark and electress of Saxony. Born Nov 22, 1532; died Oct 1, 1585; dau. of Christian III, king of Denmark and Norway (r. 1535–1559), and Dorothea of Saxe-Lauenburg (1511–1571); m. Augustus (1526–1586), elector of Saxony on Oct 7, 1584; children: Christian I (b. 1560), elector of Saxony; Dorothea of Saxony (1563–1587). ❖ See also *Women in World History.*

ANNA OF EGMONT (1533–1558). Countess of Egmont. Name variations: Anne. Born 1533; died Mar 24, 1558; dau. of Max, count of Egmont and Büren; became 1st wife of William I the Silent (1533–1584), prince of Orange, count of Nassau, stadholder of Holland, Zealand, and Utrecht (r. 1572–1584), July 8, 1551; children: Philip William (d. 1618).

ANNA OF HABSBURG (d. 1327). German princess. Born in late 1270s; died Mar 1327; dau. of Elizabeth of Tyrol (c. 1262–1313) and Albrecht, aka Albert I, of Habsburg (1255–1308), king of Germany (r. 1298–1308), Holy Roman emperor (r. 1298–1308, but not crowned); m. Hermann of Brandenburg.

ANNA OF HOHENBERG (c. 1230–1281). Holy Roman empress. Name variations: Gertrud of Hohenberg became Anna of Hohenberg at her crowning at Aachen in 1273. Born Gertrud of Hohenberg between 1230 and 1235; died Jan 16, 1281, in Vienna; m. Rudolph or Rudolf I of Habsburg (1218–1291), king of Germany (r. 1273), Holy Roman emperor (r. 1273–1291); children: Albert I (1250–1308), king of Germany (r. 1298–1308), Holy Roman emperor (r. 1298–1308, but not crowned); Hartmann (c. 1263–1281); Matilda of Habsburg (1251–1304, who m. Louis II of Bavaria); Catherine of Habsburg (c. 1254–1282, who m. Otto III of Bavaria); Hedwig of Habsburg (d. 1286, who m. Otto of Brandenburg); Clementia of Habsburg (d. 1293, who m. Charles Martel of Hungary); Judith (1271–1297, who m. Wenceslas II of Bohemia); Agnes of Habsburg (c. 1257–1322, who m. Albert II of Saxony); Rudolf II (1270–1290, who m. Agnes of Bohemia). ❖ With husband Rudolph, skillfully arranged for the marriage of their offspring to other royal houses, thereby establishing a resourceful Habsburg tactic and solidifying the Habsburg claim to preeminence in European affairs, establishing a political power base in Austria where the family ruled for nearly 7 centuries until 1918. ❖ See also *Women in World History.*

ANNA OF HUNGARY (fl. 1244). Hungarian princess. Fl. around 1244; dau. of Salome of Hungary (1201–c. 1270) and Bela IV, king of Hungary (r. 1235–1270); m. Rastislav of Chernigov (b. around 1225), prince of Novgorod, prince of Kiev, in 1244; children: Cunigunde of Hungary (d. 1285, who m. Ottokar II, king of Bohemia).

ANNA OF HUNGARY (d. around 1284). Byzantine empress. Died young, c. 1284; dau. of Stephen V, king of Hungary (r. 1270–1272), and Elizabeth of Kumania; became 1st wife of Andronicus II Paleologus (1259–1332), emperor of Nicaea (r. 1282–1328), in 1274; children: Michael IX Paleologus (d. 1320), Byzantine co-emperor (r. 1295–1320); Constantine. Andronicus II's 2nd wife was Irene of Montferrat.

ANNA OF MOSCOW (1393–1417). Russian royal. Born 1393; died of the plague in 1417; dau. of Basil I, prince of Moscow, and Sophie of Lithuania (b. 1370); became 1st wife of John VIII Paleologus (1391–1448), emperor of Nicaea (r. 1425–1448), in 1411.

ANNA OF PRUSSIA (1576–1625). Electress of Brandenburg. Name variations: Anna Hohenzollern. Born Jul 3, 1576; died on June 30, 1625; dau. of Maria Eleanora (1550–1608) and Albert Frederick, duke of Prussia; m. John Sigismund (1572–1619), elector of Brandenburg (r. 1608–1619); children: Maria Eleonora of Brandenburg (1599–1655); George William (1595–1640), elector of Brandenburg (r. 1619–1640); Catherine (who m. Bethlen Gabor of Transylvania).

ANNA OF RUSSIA (1795–1865). *See Anna Pavlovna.*

ANNA OF SAVOY (c. 1320–1353). *See Anne of Savoy.*

ANNA OF SAVOY (1455–1480). Noblewoman of Savoy. Born 1455; died 1480; dau. of Yolande of France (1434–1478) and Amedée, also known as Amadeus IX, duke of Savoy (r. 1465–1472); m. Frederick IV (1452–1504), king of Naples (r. 1496–1501, deposed), Sept 11, 1478. Frederick's 2nd wife was Isabella del Balzo (d. 1533).

ANNA OF SAXONY (1420–1462). Landgravine of Hesse. Born June 5, 1420; died Sept 17, 1462; dau. of Fredrick I the Warlike (b. 1370), elector of Saxony; sister of Catherine of Saxony (1421–1476); m. Louis II the Peaceful, landgrave of Hesse, Sept 13, 1436; children: Henry III the Rich (b. 1440), landgrave of Hesse; Louis III the Frank (b. 1438), landgrave of Hesse.

ANNA OF SAXONY (1544–1577). Princess of Orange and countess of Nassau. Name variations: Anne of Saxony. Born Dec 23, 1544; died Dec 18, 1577; dau. of Agnes of Hesse (1527–1555) and Maurice, elector of Saxony; became 2nd wife of William I the Silent (1533–1584), prince of Orange, count of Nassau, stadholder of Holland, Zealand, and Utrecht (r. 1572–1584), Aug 24, 1561 (div. in 1574); children: Maurice, prince of Orange, count of Nassau (r. 1584–1625); Emilia of Orange (1569–1629). ❖ Became the 2nd wife of William I the Silent; caused him endless distress, defying him publicly, denying him access to his children;

eventually had an affair with an older German lawyer; when it was discovered, confessed her part and pleaded that William kill both her and her lover (William quietly divorced her and pardoned the lawyer). ❖ See also *Women in World History.*

ANNA OF SCHWEIDNITZ (c. 1340–?). Holy Roman empress. Born c. 1340; dau. of Henry II, duke of Schweidnitz; 3rd wife of Charles IV, Holy Roman emperor (r. 1347–1378); children: Wenceslas IV (1361–1419), duke of Luxemburg (r. 1383–1419), king of Bohemia (r. 1378–1419), and Holy Roman emperor as Wenceslas (r. 1378–1400).

ANNA OF SILESIA (fl. 1200s). Duchess of Bavaria. Second wife of Louis II the Stern (1229–1294), count Palatine (r. 1253–1294), duke of Bavaria (r. 1255–1294); children: Louis (d. 1290). ❖ See also *Women in World History.*

ANNA OF STYRIA (1573–1598). Queen of Poland and Sweden. Name variations: Anna of Austria. Born Aug 16, 1573; died Feb 10, 1598; dau. of Charles (1540–1590), archduke of Austria, and Mary of Bavaria (1551–1608); sister of Margaret of Austria (c. 1577–1611) and Constance of Styria (1588–1631); became 1st wife of Sigismund III (1566–1632), king of Poland (r. 1587–1632), king of Sweden (r. 1592–1599), May 31, 1592; children: Karol Ferdinand, bishop of Breslau; Alexander Karol; Wladyslaw, also known as Ladislas IV (b. 1595), king of Poland (r. 1632–1648); Anna Marie (1593–1600); Katherina (1596–1597). Following Anne of Styria's death in 1598, Sigismund m. her younger sister Constance of Styria. ❖ See also *Women in World History.*

ANNA OF THE PALATINATE (fl. 1300s). Holy Roman empress. Dau. of Rudolf, elector Palatine; 2nd wife of Charles IV Luxemburg, Holy Roman emperor (r. 1347–1378).

ANNA OF TYROL (1585–1618). *See Gonzaga, Anna.*

ANNA PALEOLOGINA (d. 1340). Regent of Epirus. Name variations: Palaeologina. Birth date unknown; died after 1340 in Thessalonica (Greece); m. John Orsini, despot of Epirus (r. 1323–1335); children: Nicephorus, later Nicephorus II of Epirus. ❖ A princess of the Byzantine ruling family, married the despot of the northwest Greek principality of Epirus; despised husband and arranged to have him murdered by poison (1335); with son Nicephorus, co-ruled Epirus; remained in power for only 5 years, during which time she tried to appease the Byzantine emperor Andronicus III Palaeologus, whose extensive empire and powerful army posed the greatest threat to Epirus; overthrown and forced to flee with Nicephorus (1340); died in exile in Thessalonica. ❖ See also *Women in World History.*

ANNA PALEOLOGINA-CANTACUZENE (fl. 1270–1313). Regent of Epirus. Name variations: Palaeologina-Cantacuzena, Palaiologina. Born before 1270 in Byzantium; died after 1313 in Epirus; dau. of Princess Eulogia Paleologina (fl. 1200s); niece of Emperor Michael VIII Paleologus; m. Nicephorus I of Epirus (died 1296); children: Thomas of Epirus; Tamara (fl. 1300s, who m. Philip of Tarento). ❖ Born into Palaeologi house, the imperial family of Byzantium, which led to marriage to despot Nicephorus I, ruler of Epirus; on his death (1296), took over the government in her infant son's name; as regent, quickly became embroiled in the civil struggles between those favoring stronger ties to the Greek emperor, whom she supported, and those seeking to ally Epirus with neighboring kingdoms against the Byzantine Empire; during 17 years of regency, successfully repelled invasions and threats to her power; turned over government to her son when he came of age (1313). ❖ See also *Women in World History.*

ANNA PAVLOVNA (1795–1865). Grand duchess of Russia and queen of the Netherlands. Name variations: Anna of Russia; Anne Romanov. Born Jan 18, 1795, in St. Petersburg, Russia; died Mar 1, 1865, at The Hague, Netherlands; dau. of Sophia Dorothea of Wurttemberg (1759–1828) and Paul I (1754–1801), tsar of Russia (r. 1796–1801); sister of Marie Pavlovna (1786–1859), Nicholas I, tsar of Russia and Alexander I, tsar of Russia; grandmother of Wilhelmina (1880–1962), queen of the Netherlands; m. William II, king of the Netherlands, Feb 21, 1816; children: William III (b. 1817), king of the Netherlands (r. 1840–1849); Alexander (b. 1818); Henry (b. 1820); Ernest (b. 1822); Sophia of Nassau (1824–1897).

ANNA PETROVNA (1757–1758). Princess of Russia. Born Dec 9, 1757; died Mar 8, 1758; dau. of Catherine II the Great (1729–1796) and Stanislas Poniatowski, later king of Poland.

ANNA SOPHIA OF DENMARK (1647–1717). Electress of Saxony. Name variations: Anne Sophia Oldenburg. Born Sept 11, 1647; died July 1, 1717; dau. of Sophie Amalie of Brunswick-Lüneberg (1628–1685) and Frederick III (1609–1670), king of Denmark and Norway (r. 1648–1670); m. John George III (1647–1691), elector of Saxony (r. 1680–1691), Oct 19, 1666; children: John George IV (1668–1694), elector of Saxony (r. 1691–1694); Frederick Augustus I the Strong (1670–1733), elector of Saxony (r. 1694–1733), king of Poland (r. 1697–1704, 1709–1733).

ANNA SOPHIA OF PRUSSIA (1527–1591). Duchess of Mecklenburg-Gustrow. Born June 11, 1527; died Feb 6, 1591; dau. of Dorothea Oldenburg (1504–1547) and Albert (1490–1568), duke of Prussia (r. 1525–1568); m. John Albert, duke of Mecklenburg-Gustrow, Feb 24, 1555; children: John V (b. 1558), duke of Mecklenburg-Schwerin.

ANNA VICTORIA OF SAVOY (fl. 18th c.). Princess of Savoy-Carignan. Probably dau. of Emmanuel Philibert (d. 1709) and Catherine d'Este. ❖ Succeeded her uncle, Eugene of Savoy.

ANNA VON MUNZINGEN (fl. 1327). German abbess and biographer. Name variations: Anna of Adelshausen. Birth date unknown; died after 1327 at convent of Adelshausen, Germany. ❖ Born into the German nobility, entered Dominican convent of Adelshausen, probably as a young girl; highly educated by convent nuns, became abbess of Adelshausen; gathered stories of nuns who experienced visions and heard prophetic voices in her *Chronicle of the Mystics of Adelshausen.* ❖ See also *Women in World History.*

ANNABELLA (1909–1996). French actress. Born Suzanne Georgette Charpentier in La Varenne-Saint-Hilaire, near Paris, France, July 14, 1909; died Sept 18, 1996, in Neuilly-sur-Seine, France; dau. of a publisher; m. Jean Murat (actor, div.); m. Tyrone Power (actor), 1939 (div. 1948); children: (1st m.) Anna Murat (who was m. to German actor Oskar Werner). ❖ At 16, made film debut with a small role in Abel Gance's *Napoleon;* had 1st break starring in René Clair's *Le Million* (1931); was also featured in his *La Quatorze Juillet* (1933); one of France's most celebrated young performers, was voted Best Actress at Venice Biennale for performance in *Veille d'Armes* (1935); made 3 films in England: *Under the Red Robe, Dinner at the Ritz,* and the 1st color film made there, *Wings of the Morning* (all 1937); worked in Britain, France, Hungary, Germany, and Austria, and interspersed Hollywood sojourns with stage work, appearing in Chicago in *Blithe Spirit* and on Broadway in *Jacobowsky and the Colonel* (1944) and Jean-Paul Sartre's *No Exit* (1946), directed by John Huston; retired to her farm in the French Pyrenees and volunteered for prison welfare work (1949). ❖ See also *Women in World History.*

ANNABELLE (1878–1961). American theatrical dancer. Name variations: Annabelle Whitford; Annabelle Moore; Annabelle Whitford Moore Buchan. Born Annabelle Whitford Moore, July 6, 1878, in Chicago, Illinois; died Dec 1, 1961, in Chicago. ❖ Made debut performance as "The Peerless Annabelle" at Chicago Columbian Exposition (1893) as a skirt dancer on point; made several films for Edison Motion Picture Productions and Biograph (1894–97), which won her great popularity, including *Butterfly, Fire, Serpentine* and *Skirt;* starred in the 1st *Ziegfeld Follies* as the "Gibson Girl" (1907), then as the "Nell Brinkley Girl" in a later edition; made last theatrical appearance in *The Charity Girl* (1912); retired from the stage on marriage.

ANNE (fl. 1st c.). Saint. Name variations: Ann, Anna; (Hebrew) Hanna or Hannah. Born in 1st century into the tribe of Juda; m. Joachim; children: Mary the Virgin. ❖ In the apocryphal gospels, was the mother of Mary the Virgin (names of Mary's parents are not found in the New Testament). Her principal shrines, Ste. Anne d'Auray in Brittany, France, and Ste. Anne de Beaupré in Quebec, Canada, are famous places of pilgrimage; Emperor Justinian built a basilica in her honor in Constantinople (550); Feast Day is July 26. ❖ See also *Women in World History.*

ANNE (1665–1714). Queen of Great Britain and Ireland. Name variations: Mrs. Morley. Born Anne Stuart, Feb 6, 1665, at St. James's Palace in London, England; died at Kensington Palace in London on Aug 1, 1714; dau. of King James II, king of England (r. 1685–1688), and Anne Hyde (1638–1671); sister of Mary II (1662–1694); m. Prince George of Denmark, July 28, 1683; children: 17, including Anne Stuart-Oldenburg (May 12, 1686–Feb 2, 1687), but only William, duke of Gloucester, survived infancy. ❖ The last Stuart monarch, whose devotion to the Church of England and adherence to the Act of Settlement of 1701 undid much of the harm of the earlier Stuart kings; was raised a Protestant, upon acquiescence of her father James and insistence of King Charles II; when Charles II died (1685) and her father James II was crowned king, became heir presumptive behind sister Mary, who now resided in Holland; became a rallying point for militant Anglicans who opposed James' pro-Catholic policies; sought an intimate friend and confidante and found one in Sarah Jennings Churchill; during Glorious Revolution, overthrew father in favor of sister Mary II and her husband William III (1688); succeeded William III (1702); declared war on France when Louis XIV set out to place his grandson Philip of Anjou on the throne of Spain, launching the War of Spanish Succession (1702–13); attended most cabinet meetings, read all petitions, made all necessary religious and political appointments, and performed a myriad of other monarchical duties; was politically astute in never totally trusting either the Whig or Tory political factions; conscientious and pious, effectively coped with the religious tensions and sweeping events that threatened her nation and reign; achieved a beneficial political settlement with Scotland in the Act of Union which created the Kingdom of Great Britain (1707); signed Treaty of Utrecht (1713). ❖ See also Beatrice Curtis Brown, *The Letters and Diplomatic Instructions of Queen Anne* (Cassell, 1935); David Green, *Queen Anne* (Scribner, 1970); Edward Gregg, *Queen Anne* (Routledge & Kegan Paul, 1986); G.M. Trevelyan, *England Under Queen Anne* (3 vols. Longmans, Green, 1930–1934); Gila Curtis, *The Life and Times of Queen Anne* (Weidenfeld & Nicolson, 1972); and *Women in World History*.

ANNE (1709–1759). Princess of Orange. Name variations: Anne Guelph; Anne of England, princess royal. Born Oct 22 (some sources cite Nov 2), 1709, in Hanover, Lower Saxony, Germany; died Jan 12, 1759, in The Hague, Netherlands; dau. of George II (1683–1760), king of Great Britain and Ireland (r. 1727–1760), and Caroline of Ansbach (1683–1737); m. William IV, prince of Orange (r. 1748–1751), Mar 25, 1734; children: son (1735–1735); daughter (1736–1736); daughter (1739–1739); Caroline of Orange (1743–1787); Anne Marie (1746–1746); William V (1748–1806), prince of Orange (r. 1751–1795, deposed).

ANNE, Countess of Winchelsea (1661–1720). See Finch, Anne.

ANNE, Countess of Sunderland (1684–1716). See Churchill, Anne.

ANNE, Princess (1950—). British princess and equestrian champion. Name variations: Anne, Princess of the United Kingdom. Born Anne Elizabeth Alice Louise, Aug 15, 1950, in Clarence House, London, England; 2nd child and only dau. of Queen Elizabeth II (b. 1926), queen of England (r. 1952–) and Prince Phillip (b. 1921); attended Benenden School in Kent; m. Mark Phillips (captain of the Queen's Dragoon Guards and twice a medalist in three-day eventing at Olympic games), 1973 (sep. 1989; div. April 1992); m. Tim Laurence (naval commander), Dec 12, 1992; children: (1st m.) Peter Mark Andrew (b. 1977) and Zara Phillips (b. 1981). ❖ On her horse Doublet, was the 1st royal rider to win the Raleigh Trophy (1971); at European championships, won silver medals for indiv. and team competitions (1975); served as president of the British Olympics Association and Save the Children Fund; declared Princess Royal (1987). ❖ See also John Parker, *The Princess Royal* (Hamish Hamilton, 1989); and *Women in World History*.

ANNE BOLEYN (1507?–1536). See Boleyn, Anne."

ANNE DE BRETAGNE (c. 1477–1514). See Anne of Brittany.

ANNE DE FOIX. See Foix, Anne de.

ANNE DE FRANCE (c. 1460–1522). See Anne of Beaujeu.

ANNE DE GONZAGA (1616–1684). See Simmern, Anne.

ANNE DE LA TOUR (d. 1512). Duchess of Albany. Died Oct 3, 1512, at La Rochette Castle, Savoy; interred at the Carmelite Monastery de la Rochette in Savoy; dau. of Bertrand de la Tour, count of Auvergne, and Louise de la Tremoille; m. Alexander Stewart (c. 1454–1485), 1st duke of Albany, Jan 19, 1480; m. Louis, count de la Chambre, Feb 15, 1487; children: (1st m.) John Stewart (b. 1484), 2nd duke of Albany.

ANNE DE LA TOUR (c. 1496–1524). Duchess of Albany and countess of Auvergne. Born c. 1496; died June 1524 at Castle of St. Saturnin, France; dau. of John de la Tour (b. 1467), count of Auvergne, and Jane Bourbon-Vendome (d. 1511); m. John Stewart, 2nd duke of Albany, July 8, 1505.

ANNE-ELEANOR OF HESSE-DARMSTADT (1601–1659). Duchess of Brunswick. Born July 30, 1601; died May 6, 1659; dau. of Magdalene of Brandenburg (1582–1616) and Louis V, landgrave of Hesse-Darmstadt;

m. George of Brunswick-Luneberg, duke of Brunswick, Dec 14, 1617; children: Christian Louis (b. 1622), duke of Brunswick-Zelle; George William (b. 1624), duke of Brunswick-Zelle; John Frederick (b. 1625), duke of Brunswick; Sophia Amelia of Brunswick-Lüneberg (1628–1685); Ernest August (b. 1629), duke of Brunswick-Lunen.

ANNE HENRIETTE LOUISE (1647–1723). Princess de Condé. Name variations: Princess de Condé. Born July 23, 1647; died Feb 23, 1723; dau. of Anne de Gonzaga (1616–1684) and Edward Simmern (1624–1663), duke of Bavaria and count Palatine of the Rhine; married Henry Julius, prince of Condé, Dec 11, 1663; children: Louis, duke of Bourbon; Marie de Conti; Louise of Maine, duchess of Maine.

ANNE HYDE (1638–1671). See Hyde, Anne.

ANNE-MARIE D'BOURBON-ORLEANS (1669–1728). Queen of Sicily and Sardinia. Name variations: Ana Maria of Orleans. Born May 11, 1669; died Aug 26, 1728; dau. of Henrietta Anne (1644–1670) and Philip Bourbon-Orleans, 1st duke of Orléans; m. Victor Amadeus II (1666–1732), duke of Savoy (r. 1675–1713), king of Sicily (r. 1713–1718) and Sardinia (r. 1718–1730), April 10, 1684; children: Marie Adelaide of Savoy (1685–1712), duchess of Burgundy (mother of Louis XV of France); Marie Louise of Savoy (1688–1714), 1st wife of Philip V of Spain); Charles Emmanuel III (1701–1773), king of Sardinia (r. 1730–1773), and duke of Savoy; Vittorio (d. 1715).

ANNE MARIE LOUISE D'ORLEANS (1627–1693). See Montpensier, Anne Marie Louise d'Orleans.

ANNE MARIE OF BRUNSWICK (1532–1568). Duchess of Prussia. Born 1532; died Mar 20, 1568; dau. of Elizabeth of Brandenburg (1510–1558) and Erik I the Elder, duke of Brunswick; became 2nd wife of Albert, duke of Prussia, Feb 26, 1550; children: Albert Frederick (b. 1553), duke of Prussia.

ANNE-MARIE OLDENBURG (1946—). Queen of Greece. Name variations: Anne Marie of Denmark; Anne Marie of Greece. Born Anne Marie Mary Dagmar Ingrid Oldenburg, Aug 30, 1946, in Copenhagen, Denmark; dau. of Frederick IX, king of Denmark (r. 1947–1972), and Ingrid of Sweden (b. 1910); m. Constantine II, king of the Hellenes (r. 1964–1973, deposed 1973), Sept 18, 1964; children: Alexia (b. 1965); Paul (b. 1967); Nicholas (b. 1969); Theodora (b. 1983); and Philip (b. 1986).

ANNE NEVILLE (1456–1485). See Anne of Warwick.

ANNE OF AUSTRIA (1432–1462). Duchess of Luxemburg. Born 1432; died 1462; dau. of Elizabeth of Luxemburg (1409–1442) and Albert V (1404–1439), duke of Austria, king of Germany, also known as Albert II as Holy Roman emperor (r. 1438–1439), June 20, 1446; m. William III the Brave of Saxony, duke of Luxemburg; children: Margaret of Saxony (1449–1501).

ANNE OF AUSTRIA (c. 1550–1580). Queen of Spain. Name variations: Anne or Anna Habsburg. Born c. 1549 or 1550; died 1580; dau. of Maximilian II, Holy Roman emperor (r. 1564–1576), and Marie of Austria (1528–1603, dau. of Charles V, Holy Roman emperor); sister of Rudolf II (1552–1612), Holy Roman Emperor (r. 1576–1612), Elisabeth of Habsburg (1554–1592), and Matthew (1557–1619), king of Bohemia and Holy Roman emperor as Matthias; became 4th wife of Philip II (1527–1598), king of Spain (r. 1544–1598), in 1570; children: Philip III (1578–1621), king of Spain (r. 1598–1621).

ANNE OF AUSTRIA (1601–1666). Spanish princess and regent. Name variations: Anne d'Autriche; Anne Hapsburg or Habsburg. Born Ana Maria Mauricia, Sept 22, 1601, in Valladolid, Castile and Leon, Spain; died of breast cancer, Jan 20, 1666, in Paris, France; dau. of Philip III, king of Spain (r. 1598–1621), and Margaret of Austria (c. 1577–1611); educated at Spanish royal court; m. Louis XIII, king of France (r. 1610–1643), Nov 24, 1615; children: Louis de Dieudonne (1638–1715), later Louis XIV, king of France (r. 1643–1715); Phillipe I, duke of Orleans (1640–1701). ❖ Spanish princess who ruled France as regent and gave birth to its most famous king, Louis XIV; married Louis XIII and became queen of France at age 14 (1615); acted as regent for Louis XIII (1620); suffered miscarriage (1622) and was estranged from Louis; accused of treason by Richelieu but pardoned (1637); governed France as regent for Louis XIV (1643–52), with Mazarin as a close adviser; during rebellion known as the Fronde (1648–53), the product of grievances that stretched back into reign of Louis XIII and Richelieu, maintained her loyalty to Mazarin even though it damaged her reputation; when son was crowned king of France (1654), kept her position on the king's council and often met with Louis and Mazarin. ❖ See also Meriel Buchanan, *Anne of*

Austria, the Infanta Queen (Hutchinson, 1937); Martha Walker Freer, *The Regency of Anne of Austria* (Tinsley Brothers, 1866); Ruth Kleinman, *Anne of Austria: Queen of France* (Ohio State University Press, 1985); and *Women in World History.*

ANNE OF BEAUJEU (c. 1460–1522). French princess and regent. Name variations: Anne de Beaujeu, Anne de France, Anne of France. Born April 1460 or 1461; died Nov 14, 1522; dau. of Charlotte of Savoy (c. 1442–1483), queen of France, and Louis XI (1423–1483), king of France (r. 1461–1483); sister of Jeanne de France (1464–1505) and Charles VIII, king of France; m. Pierre de Bourbon, also known as Peter II, lord of Beaujeu, Nov 3, 1473; children: only one, Suzanne of Bourbon (1491–1521), survived to adulthood. ❖ Since her brother, the future Charles VIII, was too young to rule at the time of her father's death, named regent of France (1483); ruled France skillfully, strengthening not only the power of the royal family in France, but the position of France itself; to forge new political ties with England, supplied troops to Henry VI; also lowered taxes, ordered troops to the borders of the country to repel foreign invaders, and managed successfully to crush several attempted internal revolts; engaged in several skirmishes with armies of Brittany and Orléans until 1488, when her troops defeated them in a decisive battle; regency ended (1492), when her strong-minded sister-in-law, Anne of Brittany, forced her to take a much lesser role in the governance of the country. ❖ See also *Women in World History.*

ANNE OF BOHEMIA (1366–1394). Queen of England. Name variations: Anne Limburg. Born May 11, 1366, in Prague, Bohemia; died June 7, 1394, in Sheen Palace, Richmond, Surrey, England; dau. of Charles IV, Holy Roman emperor (r. 1347–1378), and Elizabeth of Pomerania (1347–1393); became 1st wife of Richard II (1367–1400), king of England (r. 1377–1400), Jan 22, 1383; no children. ❖ Born into the royal family of Germany, was 13 when an alliance between England and the Holy Roman Empire resulted in a contract for her marriage to King Richard II of England; married and crowned queen a week later (1382); grew close to husband, sharing a love that would last the length of their married lives; became popular with the English people during the 12 years of her reign and was remembered by her subjects as "Good Queen Anne"; was known as a generous patron of writers and poets, including Geoffrey Chaucer. ❖ See also *Women in World History.*

ANNE OF BOURBON-PARMA (1923—). Princess of Bourbon-Parma. Name variations: Anne Antoinette Francoise Charlotte, Sept 18, 1923, in Paris, France; dau. of Rene, prince of Bourbon-Parma, and Margaret Oldenburg (b. 1895, granddau. of Christian IX of Denmark); m. Michael I (b. 1921), king of Romania (r. 1927–1930, 1940–1947), June 10, 1948; children: Margaret (b. 1949); Helen (b. 1950); Irene (b. 1953); Sophia (b. 1957); Mary (b. 1964).

ANNE OF BRITTANY (c. 1477–1514). French queen and patron of the arts. Name variations: Anne de Bretagne; duchess of Brittany. Born in Nantes, France, Jan 26, 1477 (some sources cite 1476); died after childbirth, Jan 9, 1514 (some sources cite 1512); dau. of Marguerite de Foix (fl. 1456–1477) and François, also known as Francis II, duke of Brittany; m. Charles VIII (1470–1498), king of France (r. 1483–1498), in 1491; shortly after his death, m. his successor, Louis XII (1462–1515), king of France (r. 1498–1515), Jan 8, 1499; children: (2nd m.) Charles-Orland (1492–1495); and two daughters who survived infancy, Claude de France (1499–1524), queen of France, and Renée of France (1510–1575), duchess of Ferrara, Italy. ❖ A powerful force in her brief lifetime, was only 14 when her father died; aware she had to marry someone of political importance if she was to retain any kind of control of Brittany at all, married Charles VIII, king of France; stipulated in the marriage contract that if she survived her husband, Brittany would revert to her and that she would marry the next king of France to avoid a repetition of the conflict between the two states; stood her ground against regent Anne of Beaujeu, who was then forced to step down; involved herself in every aspect of court life; was a great patron of the arts, and had many tapestries, paintings, and sculptures made in France and imported from other countries to decorate the royal family's palaces, especially her favorite, the Château of Amboise; when Charles died (1498), started directing Brittany's affairs of state and married Louis, duke of Orléans (now Louis XII), a popular contender for the throne; remained active in politics, even at one time joining her Breton troops with Louis' French soldiers in an unsuccessful campaign against the Turks; amassed one of the most impressive libraries in Europe; also commissioned magnificent religious books, some of which survive today as outstanding examples of late medieval illumination. ❖ See also Helen H. Sanborn, *Anne of*

Brittany; The Story of a Duchess and Twice-Crowned Queen (Lothrop, Lee, and Shepard, 1917); and *Women in World History.*

ANNE OF BYZANTIUM (c. 1320–1353). *See Anne of Savoy.*

ANNE OF CHATILLON-ANTIOCHE (c. 1155–c. 1185). Queen of Hungary. Name variations: Agnes Chatillon. Born c. 1155; died c. 1185; dau. of Constance of Antioch (1128–1164) and Reynald of Chatillon; 1st wife of Bela III (1148–1196), king of Hungary (r. 1173–1196); children: Emeric I, king of Hungary (r. 1196–1204); Andrew II (1175–1235), king of Hungary (r. 1205–1235); Margaret-Mary of Hungary (c. 1177–?, who m. Emperor Isaac II Angelus, Eastern Roman Emperor); Constance of Hungary (d. 1240, who m. Ottokar I, king of Bohemia).

ANNE OF CLEVES (1515–1557). Queen of England. Born Sep 22, 1515, in Cleves, Germany; died of cancer, July 16, 1557, in England; 2nd of four children of John III, duke of Cleves, and Maria of Julich-Berg; m. Henry VIII (1491–1547), king of England (r. 1509–1547), in Jan 1540 (div. July 1540). ❖ German royal, who was briefly married to Henry VIII (Jan 1540–July 1540); due to her strict upbringing, was never told the "facts of life" and, as a result, was unaware that her marriage had not yet been consummated; after Henry fell in love with Catherine Howard and divorced Anne to marry her, lived the rest of her life in England as the king's "good sister."

ANNE OF COURLAND (1693–1740). *See Anna Ivanovna.*

ANNE OF CYPRUS (b. around 1430). *See Anne of Lusignan.*

ANNE OF DENMARK (1574–1619). Danish princess, queen of Scotland, 1st queen consort of Great Britain, and patron of the arts. Name variations: Anna of Denmark. Born Anna at Skanderborg Castle, Jutland, Denmark, Dec 12 (some sources cite Oct 14), 1574; died at Hampton Court, near London, Mar 2 or 4, 1619; interred at Westminster Abbey, London; dau. of Frederick II (b. 1534), king of Denmark and Norway (r. 1559–1588), and Sophia of Mecklenburg (1557–1631); sister of Christian IV, king of Denmark and Norway, Elizabeth of Denmark (1573–1626), and Hedwig of Denmark (1581–1641); m. James VI (1566–1625), king of Scotland (r. 1567–1625), later king of England as James I (r. 1603–1625), Nov 23, 1589; children: Henry Frederick (1594–1612); Elizabeth of Bohemia (1596–1662); Margaret (1598–1600); Charles (Charles I, king of England, 1600–1649); Robert (1601–1602); Mary (1605–1607); Sophia (1606–1606). ❖ At 14, married James VI and was crowned queen of Scotland (1590); opposed James sending their infant son to be raised by others; with James absent in the country (1595), hatched a plot to seize her son through armed force, but a tipped-off king forestalled any action; with James proclaimed King James I of England on death of Elizabeth I (1603), successfully regained possession of son and was crowned queen of England (1603); had to reinvent her role as queen-consort, a position that had been vacant in England for nearly 60 years; found herself more politically circumscribed than in Scotland; indulged her passion for court pageantry and commissioned premier dramatists to compose court masques in which she sometimes acted, including Ben Jonson's *Mask of Blackness* (1604) and *Mask of Queens* (1609), and Samuel Daniel's *Tethys Festival* (1610); also patronized Inigo Jones, England's foremost architect; because of her spending, however, contributed to the nation's growing dissatisfaction with the profligacy of the Stuart Court, which it compared unfavorably with the frugality of the late Queen Elizabeth. ❖ See also E.C. Williams, *Anne of Denmark* (London, 1971); and *Women in World History.*

ANNE OF FERRARA (1531–1607). Duchess of Guise. Name variations: Anne of Este or Anna d'Este; Anne d'Este-Ferrare; Anne of Guise. Born 1531; died 1607; dau. of Renée of France (1510–1575) and Ercole II (1508–1559), 4th duke of Ferrara and Modena; sister of Lucrezia d'Este (1535–1598) and Eleonora d'Este (1537–1581); m. Francis (1519–1563), 2nd duke of Guise; m. Jacques, duke of Geneva; children: (1st m.) Henry (1550–1588), 3rd duke of Guise; Carlo also known as Charles (1554–1611), duke of Mayenne; Louis (1555–1588), 2nd cardinal of Guise; Catherine of Guise (1552–c. 1594, who m. Louis de Bourbon, duke of Montpensier); and 3 others; (2nd m.) Charles Emmanuel (b. 1567), duke of Nemours; Henry, duke of Nemours and Aumale.

ANNE OF FRANCE (c. 1460–1522). *See Anne of Beaujeu.*

ANNE OF KIEV (1024–1066). Queen of France. Name variations: Anne of Russia. Born 1024; died 1066 (some sources cite after 1075); dau. of Jaroslav, also known as Yaroslav the Wise (978–1054), prince of Kiev

(r. 1019–1054), and Ingigerd Olafsdottir (c. 1001–1050); became 2nd wife of Henry I (1008–1060), king of France (r. 1031–1060), 1051 (some sources cite Jan 29, 1044); m. Raoul II de Crépi, 1061 (div. 1067); children: (1st m.) Philip I (1052–1108), king of France (r. 1060–1108).

ANNE OF LUSIGNAN (b. before 1430). Duchess of Savoy. Name variations: Anne de Lusignan; Anne of Cyprus. Born before 1430; possibly dau. of John II, king of Cyprus (r. 1432–1458); possibly half-sister of Charlotte of Lusignan (1442–1487); m. Louis I, duke of Savoy (r. 1440–1465); children: Charlotte of Savoy (c. 1442–1483); Bona of Savoy (c. 1450–c. 1505); Agnes of Savoy (who m. Francis, duc de Longueville); Margaret of Savoy (d. 1483, who m. Pierre II, count of Saint-Pol); Marie of Savoy (who m. Louis, constable of Saint-Pol); Philip II of Bresse, later duke of Savoy (d. 1497, who m. Margaret of Bourbon and was the father of Louise of Savoy [1476–1531]); Amadée also known as Amadeus IX (d. 1472), duke of Savoy (r. 1465–1472); Jacques de Romont (d. 1486); Janus of Geneva (d. 1491), count of Geneva (r. 1441–1491); Louis of Geneva (d. 1482), count of Geneva.

ANNE OF SAVOY (c. 1320–1353). Empress of Byzantium. Name variations: Anna; Anne of Byzantium. Born c. 1320 in Savoy, Italy (modern-day southeastern France); died 1353 in Byzantium; dau. of Amadeus V the Great (c. 1253–1323), count of Savoy (r. 1285–1323); became 2nd wife of Andronikos, aka Andronicus III Paleologus (d. 1341), emperor of Byzantium (r. 1328–1341), in 1326; children: John V Paleologus (b. 1331), Byzantine or Nicaean emperor (r. 1341–1347, 1355–1391); Michael; Maria (who m. Francesco Gattilusio). Andronicus III's 1st wife was Irene of Brunswick. ❖ Born into an important Italian noble family, was betrothed and married to Emperor Andronicus III of Byzantium at age 6; age 16, became empress of Byzantium; when Andronicus died (1341), was named regent for 9-year-old son John, who succeeded his father as John V Paleologus; struggled to keep herself and her son in power, even appealing to Pope Clement VI for aid against enemies; faced opposition from husband's chief minister, John Cantacuzene (John VI), who claimed the regency as well; when he became involved in a foreign war, took advantage of his absence to arrest his supporters and consolidate her own power; because of continued conflict with John Cantacuzene, faced increasing unpopularity with the Byzantine people during her years of rule, due to the civil unrest and her efforts to reunite the Eastern and Western Christian churches; surrendered the regency to John Cantacuzene (1347). ❖ See also *Women in World History.*

ANNE OF SAXONY (1437–1512). Electress of Brandenburg. Born Mar 7, 1437; died Oct 31, 1512; dau. of Margaret of Saxony (c. 1416–1486) and Frederick II the Gentle (1412–1464), elector of Saxony; became 2nd wife of Albert Achilles (1414–1486), elector of Brandenburg as Albert III (r. 1470–1486), Nov 12, 1458; children: Frederick V of Ansbach (b. 1460), margrave of Ansbach.

ANNE OF VELASQUEZ (1585–1607). Duchess of Braganza. Born 1585; died Nov 7, 1607, at Villa Vicosa, Evora; dau. of John de Velasco or Velasquez, duke of Frias; m. Teodosio, also known as Theodosius II (1568–1630), 7th duke of Braganza (son of Catherine of Portugal), June 17, 1603; children: Joao, also known as John IV (1604–1656), king of Portugal (r. 1640–1656, house of Braganza).

ANNE OF WARWICK (1456–1485). Queen of England. Name variations: Anne Neville; duchess of Gloucester. Born June 11, 1456, at Warwick Castle, Warwickshire, England; died of tuberculosis, Mar 16, 1485, at Westminster, London; dau. of Richard Neville, count of Warwick (the Kingmaker), and Anne Beauchamp (1426–1492); m. Edward Plantagenet, prince of Wales (son of Henry VI), July 25, 1470 (killed 1471); m. Richard, duke of Gloucester, later Richard III, king of England, July 12, 1472; children: (2nd m.) Edward of Middleham, prince of Wales (d. 1484). ❖ Was heiress of titles and extensive estates of Warwick during the turbulent years of the English civil war, the War of the Roses; in teens, was married to Edward Plantagenet, prince of Wales, son of the Lancastrian king Henry VI (not long after, both Henry and Edward were killed by partisans of the enemy House of York, 1471); under father's arrangement, entered into a loveless marriage with one of the Yorkist leaders, Duke Richard of Gloucester (future Richard III); crowned queen of England (1483), when Richard seized the crown on the death of his brother, Edward IV; attempted to create a court for royal husband, but the constant intrigues, battles, and unstable conditions made normal royal life impossible; died after a long illness (possibly tuberculosis), though there was a popular belief that Richard had poisoned her. Portrayed by Claire Bloom in film *Richard II* (1955). ❖ See also *Women in World History.*

ANNE OF YORK (fl. 13th c.). English doctor. Fl. 13th century. ❖ Was a respected doctor in England; though she probably had no formal training, served the poor and ailing with distinction at Saint Leonard's hospital in York for many years.

ANNE PARR (d. 1552). *See Parr, Anne.*

ANNE PETROVNA (1708–1728). Princess of Russia and duchess of Holstein. Name variations: Anna Petrovna. Born Mar 9, 1708; died June 1, 1728; dau. of Catherine I (1684–1727), empress of Russia (r. 1725–1727) and Peter I the Great, tsar of Russia (r. 1682–1725); sister of Elizabeth Petrovna (1709–1762); m. Charles Frederick (1700–1739), duke of Holstein-Gottorp (r. 1702–1739), June 1, 1725; children: Peter III (b. 1728), tsar of Russia (1728–1762, who m. Catherine II the Great). ❖ See also *Women in World History.*

ANNE PLANTAGENET (1383–1438). Countess of Stafford. Name variations: Anne Stafford. Born April 1383; died Oct 16, 1438 and buried at Llanthony Priory, Gwent, Wales; dau. of Thomas of Woodstock, 1st duke of Gloucester, and Eleanor de Bohun (1366–1399); m. Thomas Stafford, 3rd earl of Stafford, 1392; m. Edmund Stafford, 5th earl of Stafford, 1398; m. William Bourchier, count of Eu, 1404; children: (2nd m.) Humphrey Stafford, 1st duke of Buckingham; Anne Stafford (d. 1432); Philippa Stafford (died young); (3rd m.) Henry Bourchier, 1st earl of Essex; Thomas Bourchier (cardinal archbishop of Canterbury); John Bourchier (1st Baron Berners); William Bourchier (Lord Fitzwarren); Anne Bourchier (d. 1474).

ANNE PLANTAGENET (1439–1476). Duchess of Exeter. Name variations: Anne Holland. Born Aug 10, 1439, at Fotheringhay, Northamptonshire, England; died Jan 14, 1476; buried at St. George's Chapel, Windsor, Berkshire; dau. of Richard Plantagenet, 3rd duke of York, and Cecily Neville; m. Henry Holland, 2nd duke of Exeter, July 30, 1447 (div., Nov 12, 1472); m. Thomas St. Leger, c. 1473; children: (1st m.) Anne Holland; (2nd m.) one.

ANNE ROMANOV (1795–1865). *See Anna Pavlovna.*

ANNE VALOIS (c. 1405–1432). Duchess of Bedford. Name variations: Anne of Burgundy. Born c. 1405 in Arras, Burgundy, France; died in Paris, France, Nov 14, 1432; interred at Chartreuse de Champnol, Digon, Burgundy; dau. of John the Fearless (1371–1419), duke of Burgundy, and Margaret of Bavaria (d. 1424); m. John Plantagenet, duke of Bedford, April 17, 1423; children: one (b. 1432 and died in infancy).

ANNEKE, Mathilde Franziska (1817–1884). German-born American author and women's rights activist. Name variations: Giesler-Anneke. Born Mathilde Franziska Giesler, April 3, 1817, in Lerchenhausen, Westphalia; died in Milwaukee, Wisconsin, Nov 25, 1884; dau. of Karl and Elisabeth Hülswitt Giesler; m. Alfred von Tabouillot, 1836 (div. and retained maiden name after a long court battle); m. Fritz Anneke, 1847; children: (1st m.) Fanny. ❖ An early advocate of women's political and social rights, fought alongside husband in the German revolution of 1848; fled to US after the revolution failed; began publishing a militant monthly newsletter about women's rights, the *Deutsche Frauenzeitung* (1852); addressed the women's rights convention held in NYC (1853); opened a progressive girls' school, the Milwaukee Töchter Institut; founded a women's suffrage association in Wisconsin (1869). ❖ See also *Women in World History.*

ANNENKOVA, Julia (c. 1898–c. 1938). Soviet activist and journalist. Name variations: Julia Gamarnik. Born Julia Ilyishchna Annenkova in Riga, Latvia, c. 1898; killed herself in a labor camp c. 1938; m. Yan Borisovich Gamarnik (1894–1937), deputy people's commissar of defense. ❖ Joined Communist Party in her teens, at the time of the Bolshevik Revolution; wrote and edited many articles explaining the Revolution; after several promotions, was appointed editor-in-chief of Moscow's *Deutsche Zentral-Zeitung*, the central organ for the Soviet Union's German-speaking minority (1934); gained respect in Moscow's intellectual circles; during Stalin's massive purges of Soviet Communist leaders (1936), was summarily removed from her editorial position and arrested on a trumped-up charge of anti-Soviet activities (husband, having also been charged, committed suicide); was sent to the Magadan labor camp where she learned that her 10-year-old son had denounced her publicly as a traitor. ❖ See also *Women in World History.*

ANNENKOVA-BERNÁR, Nina Pávlovna (1859/64–1933). Russian stage actress and author. Name variations: Nina Annenkova-Bernard. Born ánna Pávlovna Bernárd between 1859 and 1864 in Russia; died in Orenberg, Russia, 1933; m. twice, 1st to Druzhinin, 2nd to Borisov. ❖ As an actress, made debut on Russian stage in a provincial theater (1880); worked in smaller venues (1880–88), until she won a place in a Moscow theater company; performed primarily in Moscow and St. Petersburg (1889–93), before she left the stage to devote herself to writing; under pen name Nina Pávlovna Annenkova-Bernár, published short story "Noose" (1896) in a journal; other stories appeared regularly in journals (1896–1900); wrote and starred in *Daughter of the People*, about Joan of Arc (1903); retired to Orenberg (1917), where she ran a theater studio for children.

ANNES. *Variant of Agnes.*

ANNETTE (1942—). See *Funicello, Annette.*

ANNIA AURELIA GALERIA LUCILLA (b. 150 CE). See *Lucilla.*

ANNIA GALERIA FAUSTINA I (c. 90–141 CE). See *Faustina I.*

ANNIA GALERIA FAUSTINA II (130–175 CE). See *Faustina II.*

ANNICE. *Variant of Agnes.*

ANNING, Mary (1799–1847). English fossil collector. Born at Lyme Regis, England, May 1799; died Mar 9, 1847; dau. of Richard Anning (cabinetmaker and one of the earliest collectors and dealers in fossils). ❖ At 12, discovered the 1st skeleton of an ichthyosaur (1811); found the remains of a new saurian, the plesiosaurus (1821); unearthed the remains of a pterodactyl (Dimorphodon), the 1st time such a discovery had been made in England (1828).

ANNIS, Francesca (1944—). English actress. Born May 14, 1944, in London, England; children: (with Patrick Wiseman) 3. ❖ Made film debut in *The Cat Gang* (1958); starred in *The Eyes of Annie Jones* (1964); other films include *Murder Most Foul* (1964), *The Pleasure Girls* (1965), *Run with the Wind* (1966), *The Walking Stick* (1970), *The Tragedy of Macbeth* (1971), *Krull* (1983), *Dune* (1984), *Under the Cherry Moon* (1986) and *Onegin* (1999); on tv, portrayed Estella in "Great Expectations" (1967), Lillie Langtry in "Edward the King" (1975), Emma Bovary in "Madame Bovary" (1975), Lillie Langtry in "Lillie" (1978), Lily Amberville in "I'll Take Manhattan" (1987), Paula Croxley in "Inside Story" (1988), Angela Berridge in "Between the Lines" (1993), Anna Fairley in "Reckless" (1997) and Margrethe Bohr in "Copenhagen" (2002).

ANNIS. *Variant of Agnes.*

ANNO, Noriko (1976—). Japanese judoka. Born May 23, 1976, in Yamaguchi, Japan; attended Meiji University. ❖ At World championships, placed 1st for 72kg (1997) and 78kg (1999, 2001, 2003); won a gold medal for 78kg at Athens Olympics (2004).

ANNORA DE BRAOSE (d. 1241). See *Braose, Annora de.*

ANNUNCIATA OF SICILY (1843–1871). See *Maria Annunziata.*

ANNY IOANNOVNY (1693–1740). See *Anna Ivanovna.*

ANOIS, Marie (c. 1650–1705). See *Aulnoy, Marie Catherine, Comtesse d.*

A NONG (c. 1005–1055). Zhuang/Nung shaman and warrior. Pronunciation: Ah Nung. Born A Nong c. 1005, in the area now bordering the northernmost region of Vietnam and southern China; executed by Chinese in 1055; dau. of a noted chieftain of the Nong clan of the minority people known today in China as the Zhuang, and in Vietnam as the Nung; m. Nong Quanfu (leader of the Nong clan), c. 1020; children: several, the most famous of whom was her son Nong Zhigao (b. 1025). ❖ Powerful shaman and leader of the Zhuang/Nung minority peoples of the Sino-Vietnamese frontier, who led her people in resisting the encroachment of both the Chinese and Vietnamese states; in concert with father, husband, and son, led her people in attempting to found a Zhuang/Nung kingdom (1035); escaped with son Nong Zhigao at the time of husband's capture and execution (1039); after years of political strategy and warfare, declared a 2nd independent state (1052); captured by the Chinese and executed (1055). ❖ See also *Women in World History.*

ANOR OF CHÂTELLERAULT (d. 1130). See *Aénor of Châtellerault.*

ANOUK (b. 1932). See *Aimée, Anouk.*

ANSBACH, margravine of (1750–1828). See *Craven, Elizabeth.*

ANSCHUTZ, Jody (1962—). See *Rosenthal, Jody.*

ANSCOMBE, G.E.M. (1919–2001). English philosopher. Born Gertrude Elizabeth Margaret Anscombe in 1919; died Jan 5, 2001, in Cambridge, England; dau. of Allen Wells and Gertrude Elizabeth Anscombe; attended St. Hugh's College, Oxford, 1941; m. Peter Geach (Wittgenstein scholar), 1941; children: 3 sons, 4 daughters. ❖ One of the most distinguished woman philosophers in England, obtained research fellowships at Oxford and Newnham College, Cambridge (1941–44); named research fellow, Somerville College, Oxford (1946–64); named fellow, Somerville College (1964–70); became professor of philosophy, Cambridge (1970–86); named fellow, New Hall, Cambridge (1970–86); edited and translated the work of Ludwig Wittgenstein. ❖ See also *Women in World History.*

ANSELL, Jan (1925—). See *Harding, Jan.*

ANSELL, Mary (1877–1899). English murderer. Born 1877 in England; hanged, age 22, July 19, 1899. ❖ Took out an insurance policy worth 22 pounds on her sister Caroline, an inmate in the Leavesden Asylum in Waterford; mailed Caroline a cake laced with phosphorus (Mar 1899); after Caroline died in agony having eaten the gift, was found guilty of murder.

ANSELMI, Tina (1927—). Italian politician. Born in Castelfranco Veneto, Italy, 1927. ❖ At 16, worked with the Cesare Battista Brigade in Resistance movement during WWII, for which she later received the military cross for valor; joined the Christian Democratic Party (1944), was head of the local textile trade union (1945–48), and then local party representative; as party spokeswoman on youth (1960–68) and national women's representative, concentrated efforts on industrial relations, family issues, and status of women; became vice president of European Feminist Union (1966); elected to Italian Parliament (1968); as Italy's 1st woman cabinet minister, served as minister of labor (1976–78) and minister of health (1978–79).

ANSGARD (fl. 863). Queen of France. Name variations: Ansgarde; Ansgarde of Burgundy. Fl. around 863; dau. of Count Harduin; became 1st wife of Louis II the Stammerer (846–879), king of France (r. 877–879), 862; children: Louis III (863–882), king of France (r. 879–882); Carloman (866–884), king of France (r. 879–884); Gisela (who m. Robert, count of Troyes). The name of Louis the Stammerer's 2nd wife was Adelaide Judith, mother of Charles III the Simple (879–929), king of France (r. 898–923).

ANSON, Laura (1892–1968). American silent-film actress. Born Jan 2, 1892, in Omaha, Nebraska; died July 15, 1968, in Woodland Hills, California; m. Phil McCullough (actor). ❖ Appeared in *Our Gang* comedies and starred in a number of movies opposite Fatty Arbuckle; films include *The Easy Road, The Little Clown, Bluebeard Jr., Flames of Passion, The Silent Partner* and *The Call of the Canyon.*

ANSPACH, Caroline of (1683–1737). See *Caroline of Ansbach.*

ANSPACH, Elizabeth, margravine of (1750–1828). See *Craven, Elizabeth.*

ANSPACH, margravine of (1750–1828). See *Craven, Elizabeth.*

ANSTEI, Olga Nikolaevna (1912–1985). Russian-born poet and translator. Name variations: Ol'ga. Born Olga Shteinberg, Mar 1, 1912, in Kiev, Russia; died May 30, 1985, in New York, NY; m. Anglaia Shishova (div.); m. Ivan Elagin, 1937 (div.); m. Boris Filippov (div.). ❖ With 2nd husband, emigrated from Russia (1943), spending time in Prague and Berlin; moved to Munich (1946), living in a barracks for displaced persons (DP) and producing a collection of DP poetry; also began to publish regularly in Russian émigré journals, which led to 1st collection *Door in the Wall* (1949); moved to NY (1950); found a position at UN as secretary and translator; also translated such authors as Housman, Tennyson, Rilke, and Benét. ❖ See also *Women in World History.*

ANSTICE, Sophia (1849–1926). New Zealand draper and dressmaker. Name variations: Sophia Catesby, Sophia King. Born Sophia Catesby, Nov 5, 1849, in Marylebone, London, England; died Aug 1, 1926, in Nelson, New Zealand; dau. of Edward Catesby (carpenter) and Caroline (Bailey) Catesby; m. Edwin George King (salesman), 1873 (died 1880); m. John Snook Anstice (baker), 1886 (died 1917); children: (1st m.) 4, (2nd m.) 2. ❖ Immigrated with 1st husband to New Zealand (1874); established dressmaking business at Karamea settlement (1876); after several harsh years and her husband's ill health, moved to Nelson; following 2nd marriage, opened a large drapery and dressmaking business with several branches. ❖ See also *Dictionary of New Zealand Biography* (Vol. 2).

ANSTRUDE OF LAON (fl. 7th c.). Frankish abbess. Fl. in 7th century; dau. of Blandinus Boson and Salaberga of Laon (Frankish nobles). ❖ One of early medieval Europe's great abbesses, followed mother into the religious life, taking a nun's vows at age 12; highly educated, showed a considerable depth of piety; as abbess of Laon, supervised the spiritual and material well-being of both the convent and the monastery; earned widespread admiration for her faith and great administrative skills; turned Laon into one of France's most important learning centers; also managed a scriptorium where books were copied and illustrated. ❖ See also *Women in World History.*

ANSTRUTHER, Joyce (1901–1953). *See Maxtone Graham, Joyce.*

ANTAL, Dana (1977—). Canadian ice-hockey player. Born 1977 in Canada. ❖ Won a gold medal at World championships (2001) and a gold medal at Salt Lake City Olympics (2002).

ANTAL, Marta (1937—). *See Rudasne-Antal, Marta.*

ANTARE, Eeva (1921–2004). *See Joenpelto, Eeva.*

ANTARJANAM, Lalitambika (1909–1987). Indian author. Name variations: Lalithambika Antharjanam. Born Mar 30, 1909, in Kerala, India; died in 1987; dau. of poets; married Narayanan Namboodri, 1927. ❖ Was active in the Indian effort for independence from Britain, working with both the Indian National Congress and the Marxist Party of Kerala; published only novel, *Agnisaksi* (*Testimony of Fire,* 1976), for which she received the Kerala Sahitya Akademi Award as best literary work of the year; also wrote 9 collections of short fiction, 6 volumes of verse, and several children's books.

ANTHARJANAM, Lalithambika (1909–1987). *See Antarjanam, Lalithambika.*

ANTHON, Marian Graves (1853–1915). *See Fish, Marian.*

ANTHONIOZ, Genevieve (1921–2002). *See de Gaulle, Genevieve.*

ANTHONY, Bessie (1880–1912). American golfer. Born 1880 in Chicago, Illinois; died Nov 22, 1912, in Chicago. ❖ Won the USGA Women's Amateur (1903), defeating J. Anna "Johnnie" Carpenter in the final, 7 and 6, despite a turned ankle; also won the Western Women's Amateur (1901, 1902, 1903).

ANTHONY, Katharine Susan (1877–1965). American writer and feminist. Born Katharine Susan Anthony in Roseville, Arkansas, Nov 27, 1877; died in 1965; dau. of Ernest Augustus Anthony (brother of suffragist Susan B. Anthony) and Susan Jane (Cathey) Anthony; niece of Susan B. Anthony; attended Peabody College for Teachers in Nashville, Tennessee, for 2 years; granted BS from University of Chicago; spent 1 year abroad studying at universities of Frieburg and Heidelberg; never married; no children. ❖ After teaching at Wellesley College, moved to NY to write; also did social research and editorial work for Russell Sage Foundation; influenced by aunt and mother, both pioneers in the woman suffrage movement, continued working in that area with books and articles; wrote *Mothers Who Must Earn* (1914), *Feminism in Germany and Scandinavia* (1915), *Margaret Fuller: A Psychological Biography* (1920), *Catherine the Great* (1925), *Queen Elizabeth I* (1929), *Marie Antoinette* (1923), *Louisa May Alcott* (1937), and *Susan B. Anthony: Her Personal History and Her Era* (1954), among others.

ANTHONY, Mary (c. 1920—). American dancer. Born 1920 in Newport, Kentucky. ❖ Studied with Hanya Holm, Martha Graham and Louis Horst in New York City (early 1940s); appeared in *Orestes and the Furies* with Holm's company (1943), among others; taught composition and began to choreograph (early 1950s); danced in John Butler's *Three Promenades with the Lord* and *Frontier Ballad* (both 1955); formed own company, Mary Anthony Dance Theatre (1956); received Ann Dewey Beinecke Endowed Chair for Distinguished Teaching at American Dance Festival in Durham, NC; choreographed numerous works which have been added to repertoires of companies, including the Pennsylvania Ballet, Bat-Dor Company of Israel, Dublin City Ballet, and National Institute of the Arts of Taiwan. Major choreographies include *Threnody* (1956); *Blood Wedding* (1958); *Antiphon* (1968); *A Ceremony of Carols* (1971); *Lady of the Sea* (1980).

ANTHONY, Saint (1684–1706). *See Beatrice, Dona.*

ANTHONY, Sister (1814–1897). *See O'Connell, Mary.*

ANTHONY, Sophia Lois (1893–1990). *See Suckling, Sophia Lois.*

ANTHONY, Susan B. (1820–1906). American women's rights activist, educator, and reformer. Name variations: "Aunt Susan." Born Susan Brownell Anthony, Feb 15, 1820, at Adams, Massachusetts, a small village in Berkshire Mountains; died Mar 13, 1906, at home in Rochester, NY; dau. of Daniel Anthony (prosperous Quaker mill owner and merchant) and Lucy Read Anthony (Baptist homemaker and mother of 7 children, one of whom died in infancy); attended Deborah Moulson's Female Seminary in Hamilton, PA, 1837–38; never married; no children. ❖ Activist whose lifelong effort on behalf of women culminated in passage of the 19th "Anthony" Amendment, which enfranchised women in the US; taught school (1838–52); organized New York State Woman's Temperance Association (1852); meeting with Elizabeth Cady Stanton began lifelong collaboration (1852); attended 1st women's rights convention (1852), beginning of commitment to woman suffrage; spearheaded petition drive for abolition of slavery during Civil War, resulting in 400,000 signatures; co-founded and edited *The Revolution,* a weekly paper devoted to women's rights (1868–70); founded the Working Woman's Association (1868); co-founded and led National Woman Suffrage Association (1869–90); served as president of National American Woman Suffrage Association (1892–1900); was arrested and tried for voting in presidential election (1872); organized International Council of Women (1888); met repeated disappointments with the resilience that led her to say, "Failure is impossible." ❖ See also Katharine Susan Anthony, *Susan B. Anthony: Her Personal History and Her Era* (Doubleday, 1954); Kathleen Barry, *Susan B. Anthony: A Biography of a Singular Feminist* (New York University Press, 1988); Ida Husted Harper, *Life and Work of Susan B. Anthony* (3 vols., Hollenbeck, 1898); Lynn Sherr, *Failure Is Impossible: Susan B. Anthony in Her Own Words* (Random House, 1995); and *Women in World History.*

ANTHONY, Susan B., II (1916–1991). American writer and feminist. Born in Pennsylvania, 1916; died in Boca Raton, Florida, 1991, a few days before her 75th birthday; great niece of Susan B. Anthony (1820–1906). ❖ A journalist and one of the 1st women to be hired by the *Washington Star,* is best known for book *Out of the Kitchen—Into the War* (1943); in last years, after successfully battling her own alcohol addiction, retired in Florida where she co-founded Wayside House in Delray Beach for women alcoholics and wrote for the *Key West Citizen.*

ANTHUSA (c. 324/334–?). Mother of John Chrysostom, the Father of the Eastern Church. Born 324 or 334; death date unknown; m. Secundus (high-ranking military officer in the Roman army of Syria), around 343; children: John Chrysostom (c. 344/354–407). ❖ Takes her place in history as a young widow whose son John would become the Father of the Eastern Church and patriarch of Constantinople; nurtured his Christian character, provided his classical education, and molded him into the man who would become one of the great reformers and ascetics in the church. ❖ See also *Women in World History.*

ANTIN, Mary (1881–1949). Russian-born writer. Name variations: Mary Antin Grabau. Born June 13, 1881, in Polotzk (Poltzk, Polotsk), Russia; died in Suffern, NY, May 15, 1949; educated at Teachers College and Barnard College of Columbia University; m. Amadeus W. Grabau (professor of paleontology), Oct 1901; children: 1 daughter. ❖ Immigrated to US with family (1894); wrote 1st book *From Plotzk to Boston* in Yiddish (1899); came to prominence with autobiographical book *The Promised Land* (1912), which was 1st serialized in the *Atlantic Monthly* and dealt with the immigrant experience in America; lectured about immigration (1913–18); also spoke on behalf of the Progressive Party and campaigned against bills in Congress that restricted immigration; next book *They Who Knock at Our Gates* (1914) also dealt with the foreign experience. ❖ See also *Women in World History.*

ANTISTIA (fl. 80 BCE). Roman woman. Fl. 80 BCE; dau. of Publius Antistius; became 1st wife of Gnaeus Pompeius Strabo, also known as Gnaeus Pompeius Magnus or Pompey the Great (106–48 BCE, Roman general and consul), in 86 BCE (div. c. 83 BCE). Pompey was also married to Aemilia (d. c. 81 BCE); Mucia; Julia (d. 54 BCE); and Cornelia (c. 75-after 48 BCE).

ANTOINETTE, Marie (1755–1793). *See Marie Antoinette.*

ANTOINETTE OF BOURBON (1494–1583). Duchess of Guise and Lorraine. Born Dec 25, 1494 (some sources cite 1493); died Jan 22, 1583; dau. of Marie of Luxemburg (d. 1546) and François, also known as Francis of Bourbon, count of Vendôme; m. Claude I (1496–1550), duke of Guise-Lorraine, June 9, 1513 (some sources cite 1510); children: Mary of Guise (1515–1560); Francis, 2nd duke of Guise (1519–1563); Charles (b. 1524), cardinal of Lorraine; Claude (1526–1573), marquis of Mayenne and duke of Aumâle; Louis (d. 1578), 1st cardinal of Guise;

René (1536–1566), marquis of Elbeuf; and 5 other daughters (names unknown).

ANTOINETTE OF LUXEMBURG (1899–1954). Princess of Nassau. Born Oct 7, 1899; died July 31, 1954; dau. of Marie-Anne of Braganza (1861–1942) and William IV (1852–1912), grand duke of Luxemburg (of the House of Nassau); became 2nd wife of Crown Prince Rupprecht, also known as Rupert of Bavaria (1869–1955), April 7, 1921; children: Henry (b. 1922); Irmingard (b. 1923); Editha (b. 1924); Hilda (b. 1926); Gabriele (b. 1927); Sophie (b. 1935).

ANTOINETTE SAXE-COBURG (1779–1824). Duchess of Wurttemberg. Born 1779; died 1824; dau. of Francis, duke of Saxe-Coburg-Saalfeld, and Augusta of Reuss-Ebersdorf (grandmother of Queen Victoria); m. Alexander, duke of Wurttemberg (uncle of Queen Victoria); children: Mary of Wurttemberg (1799–1860); Alexander, duke of Wurttemberg; Ernest of Wurttemberg.

ANTOLIN, Jeanette (1981—). American gymnast. Born Oct 5, 1981, in Paradise, California. ❖ Tied for 1st at US Classic (1996); won Como Cup (1998).

ANTONAKAKIS, Suzana (1935—). Greek architect. Name variations: Suzana Maria Antonakakis. Born 1935 in Athens, Greece; studied at National Technical University School of Architecture; m. Dimitris Antonakakis. ❖ With husband, formed partnership, co-founded award-winning Atelier 66, and published work on important settlements in Cyclades (1974); served as president of Department of Architecture, Technical Chamber of Greece (1982–83); received numerous awards.

ANTONELLI, Laura (1941—). Italian actress. Born Laura Antonaz, Nov 28, 1941, in Pola, Italy (now Pula, Croatia). ❖ Appeared in 45 films, including *Le Sedicenni* (1965), *Le Malizie di Venere* (1969), *A Man Called Sledge* (1970), *Incontro d'amore* (1970), *Il Merlo maschio* (1971), *Docteur Popaul* (1972), *Malizia* (1973), *Simona* (1975), *Mogliamante* (1977), *Inside Laura Antonelli* (1979), *Casta e pura* (1981), *Tranches de vie* (1985), *La Gabbia* (1986), *L'Avaro* (1990) and *Malizia 2000* (1992).

ANTONIA (1456–1491). Italian painter. Born 1456; died 1491; dau. of Paolo Ucello (painter). ❖ Taught by her father, eventually became a painter of renown; after she took the vows of a nun and entered a Carmelite convent, however, did most of her paintings for the aesthetic and financial benefit of the Carmelite house.

ANTONIA (1858–1883). Tuscan noblewoman. Name variations: Maria Antonia; Antonette. Born Jan 10, 1858, in Florence, Italy; died April 13, 1883, in Cannes; dau. of Anna Maria of Saxony (1836–1859) and Ferdinand IV (1835–1908), titular grand duke of Tuscany from 1859 to 1908.

ANTONIA AUGUSTA (36 BCE–37 CE). *See Antonia Minor.*

ANTONIA DEL BALZO (d. 1538). *See Gonzaga, Antonia.*

ANTONIA MAIOR (39 BCE–?). *See Antonia Major.*

ANTONIA MAJOR (39 BCE–?). Roman imperial and grandmother of Emperor Nero. Name variations: Antonia Maior, Antonia the Elder. Born 39 BCE; death date unknown; dau. of Marc Antony (80–30 BCE) and Octavia (c. 69 BCE–11 BCE); sister of Antonia Minor; at age 2, was betrothed to L. Domitius Ahenobarbus, 37 BCE (they were married much later); children: Domitia Lepida (c. 19 BCE–?); Gnaeus Domitius Ahenobarbus. ❖ See also *Women in World History.*

ANTONIA MINOR (36 BCE–37 CE). Roman noblewoman. Name variations: Antonia the Younger, Antonia Augusta (given the title Augusta [Revered] by Caligula posthumously in 37 CE). Born Jan 31, 36 BCE, in Rome; died in Rome, either by suicide or was poisoned by grandson Caligula, May 1, 37 CE; dau. of Marc Antony and Octavia (c. 69 BCE–11 BCE, the sister of Octavian, later Caesar Augustus); sister of Antonia Major; m. Drusus the Elder (also known as Nero Drusus, brother of the future emperor Tiberius), in 18 BCE; remained a widow after his death in 9 BCE; children: Germanicus (b. 15 BCE–19 CE); Livilla (c. 14/11 BCE–c. 31 CE); and the emperor Claudius (10 BCE–54 CE); grandchildren: the emperor Gaius (Caligula), Drusilla (15–38), Agrippina the Younger, and Julia Livilla (c. 16 CE–after 38). ❖ Ranking Roman woman at center of imperial power under the 1st Caesars; reared in Augustus' household (32–18 BCE); accompanied Drusus the Elder to Lugdunum (modern Lyons, 10 BCE); became effective head of her family after Drusus' death; as mother of heir-apparent, Germanicus, visited her father's former possessions in the Roman East (17 CE); under Tiberius, wielded great influence in the imperial family; voted thanks by Roman

senate for helping to convict the conspirator Gnaeus Piso (19 CE); informed Tiberius of the conspiracy of Sejanus (31 CE); executed her daughter Livilla by starvation for her ties to Sejanus; granted public honors by Caligula (37 CE); commemorated on scores of surviving inscriptions, coin-issues, portraits and statues throughout the Roman Empire (12 BCE–74 CE). ❖ See also Nikos Kokkinos, *Antonia Augusta: Portrait of a Great Roman Lady* (Routledge, 1992); and *Women in World History.*

ANTONIA OF PORTUGAL (1845–1913). Princess of Hohenzollern-Sigmaringen. Name variations: Antonia Saxe-Coburg. Born Feb 17, 1845, in Lisbon, Portugal; died Dec 27, 1913, in Sigmaringen; dau. of Maria II da Gloria (1819–1853), queen of Portugal, and Ferdinand of Saxe-Coburg Gotha; m. Leopold (1835–1905), prince of Hohenzollern-Sigmaringen, Sept 12, 1861; children: William (1864–1927), prince of Hohenzollern; Ferdinand I (b. 1865), king of Romania (r. 1914–1927); Charles Anthony (1868–1919), prince of Hohenzollern.

ANTONIA THE ELDER (39 BCE–?). *See Antonia Major.*

ANTONIA THE YOUNGER (36 BCE–37 CE). *See Antonia Minor.*

ANTONIETTA OF BOURBON-TWO SICILIES (1814–1898). *See Maria Antonia of Sicily.*

ANTONINI, Theresa (1785–1809). German murderer. Born Theresa Marschall in 1785 in Berlin; beheaded 1809; married a criminal named Antonini. ❖ With husband, enlisted help of her 15-year-old brother Carl in committing the murder of Dorothea Blankenfeld, whom they intended to rob; all 3 apparently participated in the beating that killed Blankenfeld (1809); unlike Carl, who received 10-year prison sentence, was sentenced to death with husband, but she was the only one beheaded (husband starved himself to death in his cell).

ANTONISKA, Mariela (1975—). Argentinean field-hockey player. Born Mariela Andrea Antoniska, May 20, 1975, in Argentina. ❖ Goalkeeper, won a team silver medal at Sydney Olympics (2000) and a bronze medal at Athens Olympics (2004); won Champions Trophy (2001), World Cup (2002), and Pan American Games (2003).

ANTONOVA, Elena (1974–). Russian synchronized swimmer. Born Oct 10, 1974, in USSR. ❖ Won a team gold medal at Sydney Olympics (2000).

ANTONOVA, Yelena (1952—). Soviet rower. Born Aug 21, 1952, in USSR. ❖ At Montreal Olympics, won a bronze medal in the single sculls (1976).

ANTONY, Hilda (1896–?). Chilean-born actress. Born Hilda Antonietti, July 13, 1886, in Santiago, Chili; death date unknown; m. Owen Roughwood. ❖ Made stage debut at the Vaudeville, London, as the Red Knight in *Alice in Wonderland* (1900); other appearances include Elizabeth in *The Education of Elizabeth,* Hilda Bouverie in *Stingaree,* Emma Brooks in *Paid in Full,* Kitty Bailey in *Mrs. Bailey's Debts,* and Katherina Ivanovna in *The Brothers Karamazov;* succeeded Lilian Braithwaite as Donna Lovelace in *Comedienne* (1938).

ANTREMONT, Marie-Henriette-Anne Payan Delestang, Marquise d' (1746–1802). *See Bourdic-Viot, Marie-Henriette Payad d'Estang de.*

ANTRIM, Angela (1911–1984). Irish artist. Name variations: Countess of Antrim. Born Angela Sykes in 1911; died 1984; educated privately; studied in Belgium under sculptor D'Havlosse; attended British School in Rome; m. the 8th earl of Antrim. ❖ Known for her large-scale sculptures, did a number of public commissions in stone, including those at St. Joseph's Church, Ballygally, Co. Antrim, and at parliament buildings, Newfoundland; exhibited with Royal Hibernian Academy and Irish Exhibition of Living Art; after an injury to her hand put an end to sculpting (1962), worked mostly with models cast in bronze.

ANTRIM, countess of (d. 1865). *See Vane-Tempest, Frances Anne Emily.*

ANTTILA, S. Inkeri (1916—). Finnish criminologist and minister of justice. Pronunciation: SIL-Vee EN-ker-EE AN-til-AH. Born Sylvi Inkeri Metsämies, Nov 29, 1916 (some sources cite the 21st or 26th), at Viipuri, Finland; dau. of Veini Ireneus (lawyer) and Sylvi Airio Metsämies; graduated University of Helsinki, Cand. Jur., 1936, LLD in criminal law, 1946, Lic. Sociology, 1954, D. Political Sciences (honorary), 1976; m. Sulo Anttila, Dec 1934; children: Veini, Liisa, and Mirja. ❖ Recognized internationally for her work in professionalizing the study of victimology, raised victimology to the level of a genuine sociological discipline, enhanced her profession, and pioneered judicial reforms with an international reach; qualified for the bar in Finland (1942); made director of the Training School for Prison Service (1949–61); appointed professor of criminal law, University of Helsinki Law School (1961—); made director, Finland's Institute of Criminology in Ministry of Justice (1963–74); appointed director, Research Institute of Legal Policy (1974); appointed minister of justice (1975—); elected president, Fifth United Nations Congress on the Prevention of Crime and Treatment of Offenders (1975); named chair of the board of the International Center of Comparative Criminology (1977); author of many books and articles. ❖ See also *Women in World History.*

ANTYUKH, Natalia (1981—). Russian runner. Born June 26, 1981, in Leningrad (now St. Petersburg), Russia. ❖ Won a gold medal for the 4x400-meter relay at the World Indoor championships (2003); won a silver medal in the 400 at the Super Grand Prix (2004); won a bronze medal for 400 meters and a silver medal for 4x400-meter relay at Athens Olympics (2004).

ANUFRIEVA, Oksana (1976—). See *Rakhmatulina, Oxana.*

ANULA (r. 47–42 BCE). Queen of Ceylon (modern-day Sri Lanka). Birth date unknown; reigned 47–42 BCE; m. King Darubhatika Tissa; children: King Kutakanna Tissa (died 47 BCE); children. ❖ Upon the death of King Kutakanna Tissa (47 BCE), governed for 5 years.

ANYTE OF TEGEA (fl. 3rd c. BCE). Greek poet. Born in Tegea, Peloponnesus, in the 3rd century. ❖ Poet famous for her elegantly crafted dedications, whose emotional sensitivity looked back to the achievement of Sappho, while her romantic portrayal of animals and pastoral settings looked forward to the urbane sophistication of poets such as Theocritus. ❖ See also *Women in World History.*

ANZALDÚA, Gloria E. (1942–2004). Mexican-American poet and fiction writer. Name variations: Gloria E. Anzaldua. Born Glora Evangelina Anzaldúa, Sept 26, 1942, in the Rio Grande Valley of south Texas; died of complications from diabetes, May 16, 2004, in California; dau. of Urbano and Amalia Anzaldúa (both Mexican immigrants); Pan American University, BA; University of Texas at Austin, MA; had nearly completed doctorate at University of California in Santa Cruz, 2004. ❖ Chicana feminist and lesbian, whose work calls attention to conditions of those living on borders of society, especially *mestiza* and gay women; is best known for *Borderlands/La Frontera: The New Mestiza* (1987), a hybrid collection of poetry and prose; other works include *This Bridge Called My Back: Writings by Radical Women of Color* (1981), *Making Face, Making Soul—Haciendo Caras* (1990), and the children's book, *Friends from the Other Side—Amigos del Otro Lado* (1993). Won NEA Fiction Award, Lesbian Rights Award (1991) and Sappho Award of Distinction (1992).

AOKI, Mayumi (1953—). Japanese swimmer. Born May 1, 1953, in Japan. ❖ At Munich Olympics, won a gold medal in the 100-meter butterfly (1972).

AOKI, Tsuru (1892–1961). Japanese actress. Name variations: Mrs. Sessue Hayakawa. Born Sept 9, 1892, in Tokyo, Japan; died Oct 18, 1961, in Tokyo; attended St. Margaret's Hall Boarding School in San Francisco; m. Sessue Hayakawa (actor), 1914. ❖ After costarring with husband in *The Typhoon* (1914), starred in *The Wrath of the Gods* (1914), *The Call of the East* (1917), *Five Days to Life* (1922), and *The Danger Line* (1924); was the 1st Japanese leading lady in American films.

AOKI, Yayoi (1927—). Japanese scholar, literary critic and feminist. Name variations: Yayohi Aoki. Born 1927 in Japan. ❖ Works examine women, gender, and sexuality; published *Woman, Gender and Mythology* and *A Culture of Sexual Difference.*

AOUA KÉITA (1912–1979). See *Kéita, Aoua.*

AOUCHAL, Leila (1937—). French-Algerian novelist. Born 1937 in Caen, France; became Algerian citizen after marriage; m. an Algerian immigrant. ❖ Works include her autobiographical *Une autre vie* (Another Life, 1978).

APAMA (fl. 324 BCE). Bactrian mother of Antiochus I Soter. Name variations: Apame. Fl. around 324 BCE; born in Bactria; 1st wife of Seleucus I Nicator, Seleucid king (r. 301–281 BCE); children: Antiochus I Soter (born c. 324). Seleucus I Nicator was also m. to Stratonice I.

APAMA (c. 290 BCE–?). Seleucid princess. Name variations: Apame. Born c. 290 BCE; dau. of Antiochus I and Stratonice I (c. 319–254 BCE); sister of Antiochus II, Stratonice II (c. 285–228 BCE); m. Magas; children:

Berenice II of Cyrene (c. 273–221 BCE). ❖ See also *Women in World History.*

APAMA (fl. 245 BCE). Queen of Bithynia. Fl. around 245 BCE; dau. of Stratonice II and Demetrius II, king of Macedonia; m. Prusias I, king of Bithynia.

APEL, Katrin (1973—). German biathlete. Born May 4, 1973, in Erfurt, Germany. ❖ Won a gold medal for 4x7.5km relay and bronze medal for 7.5km at Nagano Olympics (1998), a gold medal for 4x7.5km relay at Salt Lake City Olympics (2002), and a silver medal for 4x6km relay at Torino Olympics (2006); at World championships, won gold medals for team (1996) and relay (1996, 1997, 1999).

APGAR, Virginia (1909–1974). American physician, researcher and administrator. Pronunciation: APP-gar. Born Virginia Apgar, June 7, 1909, in Westfield, New Jersey; died Aug 7, 1974, in New York, NY; dau. of Charles Emory (automobile salesman) and Helen May (Clarke) Apgar; Mount Holyoke College, BA in zoology, 1929; Columbia University College of Physicians and Surgeons, MD, 1933; Johns Hopkins University, MPH, 1959; never married; no children. ❖ Known for her contributions in the prevention of birth defects and development of the Apgar Score for Evaluating New-Born Infants, was granted 2-year surgical internship at Presbyterian Hospital after receiving her MD degree (1933); served a residency in anesthesiology at University of Wisconsin and Bellevue Hospital, New York City (1937); was instructor of anesthesiology at Columbia University (1938); was assistant professor and clinical director of the Department of Anesthesiology at Columbia-Presbyterian Medical Center (1938); appointed associate professor, Columbia (1942), then full professor (1949); presented her now classic Apgar Scoring System at an International Anesthesia Research Society meeting (1952), proposing that infants be evaluated in 5 categories within 1 minute of birth and then again within 5 minutes after delivery; headed the Division on Congenital Malformations, The National Foundation (1967); was a lecturer in teratology, Cornell University Medical Center (1965); served as senior vice president for Medical Affairs, the National Foundation (1973); was clinical professor of pediatrics, Cornell University (1971) and lecturer in genetics, Johns Hopkins University (1973). ❖ See also *Women in World History.*

APINÉE, Irena (c. 1930—). Latvian ballet dancer. Name variations: Irena Apinee. Born c. 1930, in Riga, Latvia. ❖ Immigrated to Canada (early 1950s); began dancing with National Ballet of Canada (1954) in such classics as *The Nutcracker* and *Les Sylphides;* joined Ludmilla Chiriaeff and her newly founded company Les Grands Ballets Canadiens (c. 1956), the 1st professional ballet company in Quebec; danced Balanchine pieces, including *Themes and Variations* and *Coppélia*, with Jury Gotchalk for a season at American Ballet Theater in New York City; appeared with Gotchalk at Radio City Music Hall and on numerous occasions thereafter.

APOSTEANU, Angelica (1954—). Romanian rower. Born Aug 21, 1954, in Romania. ❖ At Moscow Olympics, won a bronze medal in coxed eights (1980).

APOSTOL, Chira (1960—). Romanian rower. Born June 1, 1960, in Romania. ❖ At Los Angeles Olympics, won a gold medal in coxed fours (1984).

APOSTOLOY, Electra (1911–1944). Greek resistance leader. Name variations: Ilektra Apostolou. Born 1911 in Iraklion-Attikis, a suburb of Athens; executed, July 26, 1944; sister of Lefteris Apostoloy (1903–1981), Communist leader; received secondary education in a German-language school in Athens; married briefly to a doctor; children: daughter Agni. ❖ A Communist, was arrested by the political police and sentenced to 2 years' imprisonment for disseminating subversive "anti-Greek" literature (1936); founded EPON (1943), a communist youth group; during final months of Nazi occupation of Greece in WWII, was arrested for her resistance activities; after being tortured, was executed. ❖ See also *Women in World History.*

APPEL, Anna (1888–1963). Romanian-born Yiddish stage, screen, and tv actress. Born May 1, 1888, in Bucharest, Romania; died Nov 19, 1963, in New York, NY; m. Isadore Appel (died 1909); m. Sigmund Ben Avi (died 1924). ❖ Appeared on Yiddish stage for 50 years; on Broadway, credits include *Did I Say No, Good Neighbors, All You Need is One Good Break, Highway Robbery, Abie's Irish Rose* and *The Golem;* made film debut in *Broken Hearts* (1926), followed by *The Heart of New York* and *Faithless,* among others.

APPEL, Gabriele (1958—). West German field-hockey player. Born Jan 17, 1958, in Germany. ❖ At Los Angeles Olympics, won a silver medal in team competition (1984).

APPELDOORN, Tessa (1973—). Dutch rower. Born April 29, 1973. ❖ Won a silver medal for coxed eight at Sydney Olympics (2000).

APPHIA. Biblical woman. Possibly wife of Philemon. ❖ A Christian at Colossae mentioned in the address of the letter to Philemon (Philemon 2), supposed by some to have been the wife of Philemon. ❖ See also *Women in World History.*

APPLEBEE, Constance (1873–1981). English-born coach and promoter of field hockey. Name variations: Connie, "The Apple." Born Constance Mary Katherine Applebee in Chigwall, Essex, England, June 4, 1873; died in Burley, Hampshire, England, Jan 26, 1981; graduate of British College of Physical Education in London; never married; no children. ❖ Traveled to US to study at Harvard University (1901); founded the American Field Hockey Association (AFHA, 1901); appointed director of athletics at Bryn Mawr College (1904); founded US Field Hockey Association (USFHA), superseding the AFHA (1922); edited and published *The Sportswoman*, the 1st sports magazine for American women (1922); convinced of the importance of physical education to well being, advanced the development of women's athletics. Inducted into US Field Hockey Association Hall of Fame and the International Women's Sports Hall of Fame; received the Distinguished Service Award of the American Association for Health, Physical Education, and Recreation, and the Award of Merit of the Association of Intercollegiate Athletics for Women. ❖ See also *Women in World History.*

APPLEBY, Dorothy (1906–1990). American actress. Name variations: Doris Appleby. Born Jan 6, 1906, in Portland, Maine; died Aug 9, 1990, in Long Island, NY; m. Morgan Hughes Galloway (div.); m. Paul Drake (musician), c. 1943. ❖ Made stage debut as a child of two in *East Lynne* in Portland; made NY debut (1923); came to prominence in role of Constance Sinclair in *Young Sinners* (1929); films include *North of Nome, Make a Wish, Small Town Boy* and *Making the Headlines;* often appeared in Columbia 2-reel comedies with Buster Keaton, Andy Clyde, Harry Langdon, and the Three Stooges.

APPLETON, Frances (1819–1861). See *Longfellow, Fanny Appleton.*

APPLETON, Honor C. (1879–1951). British illustrator. Born in 1879; died in 1951. ❖ Illustrated *The Bad Mrs Ginger* (1902), *Songs of Innocence* (1910), *Babies Three* (1921), *The Book of Animal Tales* (1932) and the "Josephine" series by Mrs. H.C. Cradock, which includes *Josephine and Her Dolls* (1916), *Josephine is Busy* (1918), and *Josephine Keeps School* (1925); also wrote and illustrated the "Dumpy" books.

APPLETON, Jean (1911–2003). Australian painter. Born Jean Appleton, 1911, in Sydney, NSW, Australia; died Aug 2003 in Australia; dau. of Charles Appleton (died 1935) and Elizabeth Appleton; attended East Sydney Technical College and the Westminster School in London; m. Eric Wilson (painter), 1943 (died 1946); m. Tom Green (painter), 1952 (died 1981); children: (2nd m.) Elisabeth Green von Krusenstiena (Buddhist nun). ❖ While in London, created two of Australia's earliest cubist paintings, *Still Life 1937* and *Painting IX 1937;* returned home and began teaching at Church of England Girls Grammar School in Canberra (1940); had 1st solo exhibit at Macquarie Galleries in Sydney (1940); began teaching at Julian Ashton Art School (1946), then East Sydney Technical College (1947); with husband, moved to Moss Vale in the Southern Highlands (1960s). Won the Rockdale Art Prize (1958), D'Arcy Morris Memorial prize (1960), Bathurst Art prize (1961), and Portia Geach Memorial award (1965).

APPLETON, Martha O'Driscoll (1922–1998). See *O'Driscoll, Martha.*

APPLEYARD, Beatrice (1918–1994). English dancer and choreographer. Born in Maidenhead, Berks, England, 1918; died in 1994; studied with Ninette de Valois, Tamara Karsavina, and Bronislava Nijinska. ❖ One of the 1st English dancers to achieve celebrity in early days of English ballet, performed in 2 early Frederick Ashton theater works, *Pomona* and *High Yellow;* was an original member of the Vic-Wells Ballet, dancing in *The Lord of Burleigh* (1931), *Dances Sacrées et Profanes* and *The Scorpions of Ysit* (1932), *Les Rendezvous* (1933), *The Haunted Ballroom* (1934), and *Casse Noisette;* was also soloist with the Markova-Dolin Ballet and the Windmill Theater, London, and choreographer for several London musicals; moved to Ankara, Turkey (1951), where she taught.

APPLING, A.L. (1934–2004). See *Eastman, Carole.*

APPOLUS, Libertine (b. 1940). See *Amathila, Libertine Appolus.*

APPONYI, Geraldine (1915–2002). Queen of Albania. Name variations: Countess Apponyi or Appony; Geraldine of Albania; Geraldine de Nagy-Appony. Born Geraldine de Nagy-Appony in Budapest, Hungary, Aug 6, 1915; raised in Budapest by her uncle and guardian, Count Charles Apponyi; died Oct 22, 2002, in France; elder dau. of Gladys Stewart (also seen as Steuart, later Girrault) of New York City and Count Gyula (Julius) Nagi-Apponyi (also seen as de Nagy-Appony) of Hungary; m. Ahmed Bey Zogu (1895–1961), also known as Scanderbeg III or Zog I (r. 1928–39), king of Albania, April 27, 1938 (died 1961); children: son Leka (b. April 5, 1939). ❖ Was a clerk in the souvenir shop of the Budapest National Museum; married King Zog of Albania (1938), whose country was in close collaboration with Italy, until Mussolini invaded Albania (1939), two days after she gave birth to the Albanian heir; was put into an ambulance with newborn child and sent down 160 miles of rough road to neighboring Greece; lived in England and Egypt during WWII; at end of WWII, was officially deposed with husband by the Communists (1946); resided with family in France.

APRÉLEVA, Elena Ivanovna (1846–1923). Russian author. Name variations: Apreleva; (pseudonym) E. Ardov. Born 1846 in St. Petersburg, Russia; dau. of a Greek mother and a French geodesist in the Russian army; died 1923 in Belgrade, Yugoslavia; married. ❖ In her early 20s, began writing books for children; under pseudonym E. Ardov, published 1st short story and a novel *Guilty but Guiltless* (both 1877); over the years, wrote a number of short, moralistic stories which were collected in *Quick Sketches* (1893).

APTHEKER, Bettina (1944—). American sociologist and feminist. Born in 1944; dau. of Herbert Aptheker (Marxist historian). ❖ While teaching women's studies at San Jose State University and University of California at Santa Clara, gained recognition in the protest and feminist movements (1960s); was also one of the directors of the American Institute for Marxist Studies; collaborated with father on *Racism and Reaction in the United States* (1971); teamed with Angela Davis for *If They Come in the Morning: Voices of Resistance* (1971), then wrote an account and analysis of the Davis trial, *The Morning Breaks* (1975); also wrote *The Academic Rebellion* (1972) and *Woman's Legacy: Interpretative Essays in US History* (1980).

APULIA, duchess of.
See *Aubrey of Buonalbergo (fl. 1000s).*
See *Sichelgaita of Salerno (1040–1090).*

AQUASH, Anna Mae (1945–1976). Native-rights activist. Name variations: Anna Mae Pictou; Annie Mae. Born on the Micmac reserve in Shubenacadie, Nova Scotia, Canada, Mar 27, 1945; murdered on Feb 24, 1976, on Pine Ridge Indian Reservation, South Dakota; 3rd dau. of Mary Ellen Pictou and Frances Levi; attended Wheelock College; scholarship to Brandeis University (unused); m. Jake Maloney (Micmac), in 1962 (later div.); m. Nogeeshik Aquash (Ojibwa artist), 1973, at Pine Ridge; children: (1st m.) 2 daughters. ❖ Moved to Boston (1960s) where she became active on the Boston Indian Council, a group established to aid Native American alcoholics; was also employed as a social worker in the predominately black area of Boston called Roxbury; organized for the American Indian Movement (AIM, 1970–76) which sought to address problems of Native Americans and to rekindle a sense of tribal identity, a group Richard Nixon had put under FBI surveillance; participated in demonstrations like the Mayflower II Thanksgiving Day protest and the Trail of Broken Treaties; traveled to Oglala Nation's Pine Ridge Reservation at Wounded Knee, SD; when tensions there between AIM and the FBI were at their deadliest, was raped and shot in the head, execution style, with a .38 caliber pistol (1976); though an investigation was ordered and a grand jury convened to look into links between the FBI and the events surrounding the Aquash murder, the results were never released. John Graham and Arlo Looking Cloud were indicted in her murder (Dec 2003): Looking Cloud was convicted (2004); John Graham is fighting extradition from Canada. ❖ See also Johanna Brand, *The Life and Death of Anna Mae Aquash* (James Lorimer, 1978); and *Women in World History.*

AQUINO, Corazon (1933—). Philippine president. Name variations: Cory. Born Maria Corazon Cojuangco, Jan 25, 1933, in Tarlac Province, Philippines; 6th of 8 children of José Cojuangco and Demetria "Metring" Sumulong (dau. of Juan Sumulong, a nationally known Philippine senator; the Sumulongs were among the wealthiest landowners of Rizal Province); educated at an exclusive girls' school in Manila; finished education at 2 Roman Catholic convent schools—Raven Hill Academy in

Philadelphia and Notre Dame School in NY City; graduated from Mount St. Vincent College with a major in French, 1953; m. Benigno Aquino Jr. (1932–1983, governor), Oct 11, 1954; children: 5. ❖ Political leader and president of the Philippines (1986–92), who led a quiet revolution that overthrew the Marcos regime without a single shot; before becoming a major opponent of Ferdinand Marcos, served as political wife while husband Benigno Aquino Jr. served as mayor, senator, and governor; saw husband and thousands of the opposition arrested (1972); became speaker for Benigno, lobbying for his release; when husband was released from prison for reasons of health, family went into exile in US (1980); after husband, returning to the Philippines, was murdered as he stepped off the plane (Aug 21, 1983), became his surrogate, leading a revolution in the streets that ousted the Marcos regime; was sworn in as president (Feb 25, 1986); cleaned up corruption, instituted land reform, and rewrote the constitution; saw opposition to her term of office continue and six coups staged against her administration; despite immense challenges, brought the Philippines through troubled times, leaving a more stable democracy when her term ended (1992). ❖ See also Lucy Komisar, *Corazon Aquino: The Story of a Revolution* (George Braziller, 1987); and *Women in World History*.

AQUINO, Iva d' (b. 1916). *See Toguri, Iva.*

AQUINO, Melchora (1812–1919). Philippine revolutionary and hero. Name variations: known as Matandang Sora or Tandang Sora. Pronunciation: Ah-KEEN-o. Born in barrio Banlat, Caloocan, Rizal (now part of Quezon City), Jan 6, 1812; died in Pasong Tamo, Feb or Mar 1919; dau. of Juan Aquino (farmer) and Valentina de Aquino; m. Fulgencio Ramos; children: Juan, Simon, Epifania (also seen as Estefania), Saturnina, Romualdo, and Juana. ❖ Considered "Mother of the Philippine Revolution," became an insurrectionist when she was well into her 80s; sympathizing with Filipino rebels fighting Spanish domination, let them use her store to hold meetings and to stock supplies and weapons; when her house became a rendezvous to plan the Philippine Revolution (1896), was captured and deported to Guam; set free (1898) when US defeated the Spanish and established an American colonial regime over the Philippines. ❖ See also *Women in World History*.

ARABIA (fl. 570). Byzantine princess. Fl. 570; dau. of Justus II, emperor of Byzantium and Rome, and Sophia (c. 525–after 600); married Baduarius (a military commander); children: daughter, Firmina.

ARABELLA STUART (1575–1615). *See Stuart, Arabella.*

ARAD, Yael (1967—). Israeli judoist. Born May 1, 1967, in Tel Aviv, Israel. ❖ Judo champion, won 1st international title in middleweight competition (1984); won a silver medal for half-middleweight (61 kg) at Barcelona (1992), the 1st Israeli woman to win an Olympic medal.

ARAGON, Jesusita (1908—). American midwife. Name variations: Doña Jesusita. Born 1908 on a ranch in Sapello, known as El Rancho Trujillo, northern New Mexico; granddau. of Dolores "Lola" Gallegos (midwife); children: son and daughter (born out of wedlock). ❖ Among the most respected figures in tradition of Hispanic midwifery in northern NM, delivered 1st baby alone at 13; assisted her midwife grandmother; earned title "la partera" (midwife) at age 14 and delivered an estimated 12,000–15,000 children during an 8-decade career; received Sage Femme Award from Midwives' Alliance of North America (1989). ❖ See also Fran Leeper Buss, *La Partera: Story of a Midwife* (University of Michigan Press, 1980).

ARAGON, Mme. (1896–1970). *See Triolet, Elsa.*

ARAGON, queen of.
See Matilda of Portugal (c. 1149–1173).
See Sancha of Castille and Leon (1164–1208).
See Eleanor Plantagenet (1264–1297).
See Eleanor of Portugal (1328–1348).
See Eleanor of Sicily (d. 1375).
See Maria of Castile (1401–1458).

ARAGONA, Tullia d' (1510–1556). Italian poet. Born in 1510 in Italy; died in Italy in 1556. ❖ Acquainted with the leading artists and politicians of her time, moved through Italian society as a *cortegiana onesta* ("honest courtesan"); published 1st book of poetry, *Rhymes* (1547), then wrote *Dialogue on the Infinity of Love* (1552); a prolific writer, last major book, *Meschino, Otherwise Known as Guerrino*, was published 4 years after her death.

ARAKIDA, Yuko (1954—). Japanese volleyball player. Born Feb 14, 1954, in Japan. ❖ At Montreal Olympics, won a gold medal for team competition (1976); won team World championships (1974, 1977).

ARANGO, Débora (1907—). Colombian artist. Name variations: Debora Arango; Débora Arango Pérez. Born Nov 11, 1907, in Medellín, Colombia. ❖ Studied with Pedro Nel Gómez and Eladio Vélez; preferring watercolor as medium, often focused on the nude; was condemned by government and church because work challenged the status quo; though ignored during 1970s, work was shown again as of 1980s, including exhibitions at the Biblioteca Luis Angel Arango (1984) and the Museo de Arte Moderno de Medellín (1984, 1995, and 1996); painted works include *Bailarinas en reposo* (Dancers at Rest, 1939) and *Actriz retirada* (Veteran Actress, 1944).

ARANYI, Adila d' (1886–1962). *See Fachiri, Adila.*

ARANYI, Jelly d' (1895–1966). Hungarian-born British violin virtuosa. Name variations: Yelly d'Arányi or Arányi. Born as Jelly Eva Aranyi de Hunyadvar in Budapest, Hungary, May 30, 1895; died in Florence, Italy, Mar 30, 1966; sister of Adila Fachiri (1886–1962, violinist); grandniece of Joseph Joachim (Austro-Hungarian violinist, conductor, and composer); studied with Jenö Hubay at Hungarian Royal Academy. ❖ One of the most dynamic musicians of the 1st half of the 20th century, began career (1908) in a series of joint recitals with sister Adila Fachiri in several cities, including Vienna, where they received rave reviews; with sister, settled in Great Britain (1913) on eve of WWI and quickly became known for exquisite performances of such works as Johann Sebastian Bach's Concerto for Two Violins and Orchestra; eventually surpassed the musical reputation of her sister with the warmth and almost improvisational nature of her playing; her style, often described as rhapsodic, worked well for many compositions, including a number of works written for her by contemporary composers, including both of Bela Bartók's Sonatas for Violin and Piano, and Maurice Ravel's *Tzigane*; formed a piano trio with cellist Guilhermina Suggia and pianist Fanny Davies (1914); formed another group with cellist Felix Salmond and pianist Myra Hess (1930s). ❖ See also Joseph Todd Gordon Macleod, *The Sisters d'Aranyi* (Allen & Unwin, 1969); and *Women in World History*.

ARAUJO, Alexandra (1972—). Brazilian-Italian water-polo player. Born July 13, 1972, in Brazil. ❖ At World championships, won team gold medals (1998, 2001); center forward, won a team gold medal at Athens Olympics (2004).

ARAÚZ, Blanca (d. 1933). Nicaraguan rebel. Name variations: Arauz. Died in childbirth, 1933; married Agusto César Sandino (1895–1934, guerrilla leader), 1927. ❖ A trained telegrapher, ran the rebel forces communications units for husband.

ARAZ, Nezihe (1922—). Turkish author of religious poetry and children's books. Born in Konya, Turkey, 1922; educated at Ankara's Girls Lycée; graduate of University of Ankara, 1946, with a degree in philosophy and psychology. ❖ A religious and cultural conservative, was influenced by the teachings of Rumi; published several books of poetry inspired by Islamic history, including the spiritual growth of the Prophet Muhammad and the saints of Anatolia; also took on journalistic assignments for several of Turkey's conservative pro-Islamic newspapers, including *Yeni Sabah* and *Yeni Istanbul;* her writings influenced the resurgence of Islamic fundamentalism in Turkey in the last decades of 20th century. ❖ See also *Women in World History*.

ARBA, Rodica (1962—). *See Arba-Puscatu, Rodica.*

ARBA-PUSCATU, Rodica (1962—). Romanian rower. Name variations: Rodica Arba; Rodica Puscatu. Born Rodica Puscatu, May 1962, in Romania. ❖ At Moscow Olympics, won a bronze medal in coxed eights (1980); at Los Angeles Olympics, won a gold medal in coxless pairs (1984); at Seoul Olympics, won a silver medal in coxed eights and a gold medal in coxless pairs (1988).

ARBATOVA, Mia (c. 1910—). Latvian ballet dancer. Born c. 1910, in Dribin, Mogilev, Belarus; raised in Riga, Latvia. ❖ A major contributor to the development of ballet in Israel, trained at Paris Opera Ballet School, where a company tour led to her 1st trip to Palestine (1934); danced with Ballet Russe de Monte Carlo, London, and Mikhail Mordkin Ballet, New York, before returning to Palestine (1938), where she taught ballet classes at Gertrude Krauss' studio; associated with the Haganah (late 1940s), the Zionist military organization in Palestine that later became Israel Defense Forces; performed political cabaret in Tel Aviv, Israel, and with Habimah Theater; her widespread teaching helped lead to establishment of Israel Classical Ballet (1968).

ARBENINA, Stella (1885–1976). Russian-born actress. Born Sept 27, 1885, in St. Petersburg, Russia; died April 26, 1976, in London, England; great-granddau. of Lord Ellenborough; m. Baron Paul Meyendorff. ❖ Made professional stage debut as Catherine in *The Storm* (1918); arrested and imprisoned by the Bolsheviks (1918), escaped to Estonia; played over 100 parts in Estonia (1919–21); appeared with Max Reinhardt's company in Berlin (1921–22); made London debut as Antoinette de Mauban in *The Prisoner of Zenda* (1923); other parts include title role in *Yvelle*, Elmire in *Tartuffe*, Natasia Philipovna in *The Idiot*, The Mother Superior in *The Painted Veil*, Joanne de Beaudricourt in *The Wandering Jew*; made film debut in *Der Brennende Acker* (1926). ❖ See also autobiography *Through Terror to Freedom* (1929).

ARBER, Agnes (1879–1960). English botanist. Born Agnes Robertson, Feb 23, 1879, in London, England; died Mar 22, 1960; granted B.Sc., London, 1899; attended Newnham College, Cambridge, 1901–02; was Quain student in biology, 1903–08; awarded DSc, London University, 1905; married E.A.N. Arber, 1909 (died 1918). ❖ Hailed as the most distinguished as well as the most erudite British plant morphologist, was a lecturer in botany at University College, London (1908–09), before researching plant anatomy in Balfour Laboratory, Newnham (1909–27); published such books as *Herbals: Their Origins and Evolution* (1912), *Waterplants* (1920), *Monocotyledons* (1935), *Gramineae* (1934), *The Natural Philosophy of Plant Form* (1950), and *The Mind and the Eye* (1954).

ARBLAY, Madame d' (1752–1840). See Burney, Fanny.

ARBUCKLE, Minta (1897–1975). See Durfee, Minta.

ARBUS, Diane (1923–1971). American photographer. Name variations: Diane Nemerov. Pronunciation: surname sometimes pronounced DE-yan. Born Diane Nemerov, Mar 14, 1923, in New York, NY; committed suicide, July 26, 1971, in New York, NY; 2nd child and 1st dau. of David (retailer) and Gertrude (Russek) Nemerov; sister of essayist, novelist, and critic Howard Nemerov (1920–1991); sister of Renée Sparkia, a sculptor whose work is in collections at Palm Beach Institute and Lord Beaverbrook's museum in New Brunswick; m. Allan Arbus (photographer), Mar 10, 1941 (div. 1969); children: Doon Arbus (b. 1945, writer) and Amy Arbus (b. April 16, 1954, photographer). ❖ Artist whose work had a profound influence on American documentary photography; during WWII, became fascinated with the possibilities offered by photography for both documentation and creative expression; established fashion photography studio with husband (1947), shooting for magazines like *Glamour* and *Vogue* and advertising agencies like Young & Rubicam and J. Walter Thompson; dissolved partnership with husband (1957); studied photography with Lisette Model (1958–59); began to seek out circuses and other venues where she found individuals living on the margins of society—transvestites, dwarves, midgets, contortionists, people deformed from birth or by accident; got 1st assignment with *Esquire* when the magazine was devoting an entire issue to Manhattan (1959); also shot celebrities on assignment; had at least 30 of her photographs included in "New Documents" exhibition at Museum of Modern Art (1967); given the Robert Levitt Award from American Society of Magazine Photographers for outstanding achievement (1970); work exhibited at Venice Biennale (1972); retrospective, Museum of Modern Art (1972). ❖ See also Patricia Bosworth, *Diane Arbus* (Norton, 1984); and *Women in World History*.

ARBUTHNOT, May Hill (1884–1969). American children's writer and educator. Name variations: May Hill. Born May Hill, Aug 27, 1884, in Mason City, Iowa; died Oct 2, 1969, in Cleveland, Ohio; dau. of Frank Hill and Mary Elizabeth (Seville) Hill; m. Charles Crisswell Arbuthnot (professor of economics), 1932. ❖ Well-known reviewer of children's books, was kindergarten director at Superior (WI) State Normal School (1912–17); taught summer school courses on children's literature at University of Chicago (1913–22); became principal of Cleveland Kindergarten-Primary Training School (1922); established 1st nursery schools in OH (late 1920s), of which University Nursery School (1929) became most famous; served as national vice president of International Kindergarten Union (later renamed Association for Childhood Education, 1927–29); served on original committee for White House Conference on Children (1930); was associate professor of education at Western Reserve University, later Case Western Reserve University (1927–50); was review editor of children's books at *Childhood Education* (1933–43) and at *Elementary English* (1948–50); won many awards and honors, including Women's National Book Association's

Constance Lindsay Skinner Medal for distinguished contribution to field of books (1959) and Regina Medal from Catholic Library Association for distinguished contributions to field of children's literature (1964). Co-authored, with William S. Gray, *Basic Readers: Curriculum Foundation Series* (1940, 1946); authored *Children and Books* (1947); edited *Time for Poetry* (1951), *Time for Fairy Tales, Old and New* (1952), *Time for True Tales* (1953).

ARBUTHNOT, Patricia (1914–1989). See Cockburn, Patricia.

ARBUTINA, Andjelija (1967—). Yugoslavian basketball player. Born Mar 29, 1967, in Yugoslavia. ❖ At Seoul Olympics, won a silver medal in team competition (1988).

ARC, Jeanne d' or Arc, Joan of (c. 1412–1431). See Joan of Arc.

ARCAIN, Janeth (1969—). Brazilian basketball player. Name variations: Janet dos Santos Arcain. Born April 11, 1969, in Sao Paulo, Brazil. ❖ Guard; drafted by Houston Comets of the WNBA (1997); representing Brazil, won a team silver medal at Atlanta Olympics (1996) and a team bronze medal at Sydney Olympics (2000).

ARCANGELA, Sor (1604–1652). See Tarabotti, Arcangela.

ARCASIA (fl. 1669). See Boothby, Frances.

ARCEO, Liwayway (1924—). Filipino author. Born in 1924 in the Philippines. ❖ In more than 5 decades, wrote more than 50 novels and 900 short stories; in her native Tagalog, the national tongue of the Philippines, is considered a modernist and a feminist, whose frequent subject is the virtue and importance of women; edited the weekly journal *Liwayway* for many years; also wrote a radio serial, *Ilaw ng Tahanan* (*Light of the Home*), which ran for several years.

ARCHAMBAULT, Mademoiselle (c. 1724–?). French feminist essayist. Born c. 1724 in Laval, France; died after 1750. ❖ Defending women, wrote the essay *Dissertation sur la question: lequel de l'homme ou de la femme est plus capable de constance?* ("Essay on the Question: Are Men or Women More Loyal?") (1750); followed this with a piece questioning the equality of women and men in intellectual and physical strength.

ARCHBOLD, Helen Kemp (1899–1987). See Porter, Helen Kemp.

ARCHER, Caroline Lilian (1922–1978). Australian Aboriginal and social reformer. Born at Cherbourg Aboriginal Reserve in 1922; died in Narrabri, Australia, Sept 8, 1978; illeg. dau. of Lilian Brown (later Fogarty) and a white father; married Frederick Archer (photographer), Dec 29, 1951; children: two daughters and a son. ❖ Began a craft center and shop to sell Aboriginal art; started training Aborigine women to become shop assistants and typists, which led to her involvement with OPAL (One People of Australia League), a multiracial organization formulated to promote good will between whites and Aborigines, and to develop a common culture; served as executive officer of OPAL.

ARCHER, Maria (1905–1982). Portuguese author. Name variations: Maria Emília Archer Eyrolles Baltazar Moreira. Born Jan 4, 1905, in Lisbon, Portugal; died 1982. ❖ Popular and prolific writer, was concerned with the subjugation of women in an authoritarian society, an opinion she made clear in nonfiction like *Os Últimos Dias do Fascismo Português* (*The Last Days of Portuguese Fascism*, 1961), and fiction like *Casa Sem Pão* (*House Without Bread*, 1946), which was banned in Portugal.

ARCHER, Robyn (1948—). Australian singer, director and actress. Name variations: Robyn Smith. Born Robyn Smith on June 18, 1948, in Adelaide, Australia; dau. of Lykke "Cliff" Smith (club entertainer and comedian). ❖ Famed worldwide as singer, actress, and director most often associated with cabaret, as well as for role as artistic director and public advocate of arts; came from showbiz family and began singing publicly at age 4; worked in vaudeville, folk, nightclubs, tv, country music, jazz and revue before specializing in Brecht-Weill-Eisler repertoire; studied briefly at Berliner Ensemble (1980) and recorded 2 albums of German cabaret music at Abbey Road with London Sinfonietta; has sung in, written and directed cabaret (writing many original works with political bent) and music theater; known for stage successes such as *A Star is Torn* and *Tonight Iola Blau*; achieved notoriety as well for songwriting, including political songs in shows like *Pack of Women* and *Kold Komfort Kaffee*; published numerous essays and regular newspaper column; curated many notable arts festivals in Australia (National Festival of Australian Theater 1993–95, Adelaide Festival 1998–2000, Melbourne Festival 2002–03) and created and curated ongoing Tasmanian festival, Ten Days on the Island (since 2003). Numerous awards and honors include: Sydney Critics' Circle Award (1980); ARIA Awards (Best Soundtrack—*Pack of Women*, 1986 and Best Children's Album—*Mrs. Bottle*, 1989); Australian Creative Fellowship (1991–93); Australian Women's Network Executive Woman of the Year (1998); SA Great's Arts and Culture Award (1998 and 2000); Officer of the Order of Australia (2000); Chevalier du l'Ordre des Artes et des Lettres (2001); Member, Australian International Cultural Council; Doctor of the University (Flinders University).

ARCHER, Violet Balestreri (1913–2000). Canadian composer, pianist, and teacher. Born Violet Balestreri in Montreal, Canada, April 24, 1913; died in 2000; studied with Douglas Clarke and Claude Champagne at McGill Conservatory, earning her Bachelor of Music in 1936; studied with Bela Bartók, 1942, and with Paul Hindemith, 1949, both of whom strongly influenced her orchestral and choral works. ❖ Preoccupied with Canadian folklore, often used folk music as a source of creative material; taught at McGill (1944–47), at North Texas State University, where she was also composer-in-residence (1950–53), at University of Oklahoma (1953–61), and at University of Alberta, where she became professor and chair of the theory and composition department after 1962. Won the Woods-Chandler composition prize at Yale; was the 1st woman composer to be chosen Composer of the Year by the Canadian Music Council (1984).

ARCHER EYROLLES BALTAZAR MOREIRA, Maria Emilia (1905–1982). *See Archer, Maria.*

ARCHER-GILLIGAN, Amy (1869–1928). American poisoner. Name variations: Amy Archer Gilligan; Sister Amy. Born 1869 in US; died 1928 in an insane asylum; married 5 times, including Michael Gilligan (who died suddenly). ❖ Opened rest home for seniors in Windsor, CT (1907); married, took out insurance, then poisoned to death elderly men in her care; also poisoned women in her facility, whose wills had been changed to make her beneficiary (1907–16); caught by an undercover policewoman and sentenced to life imprisonment; relocated from Weathersfield Prison to an insane asylum.

ARCO, Countess von (1879–1958). *See Lichnowsky, Mechthilde.*

ARCONVILLE, Geneviève d' (1720–1805). *See d'Arconville, Geneviève.*

ARCY, Ella d' (c. 1856–1937). *See D'Arcy, Ella.*

ARDEN, Alice (1516–1551). English murderer. Born in 1516 in England; burned at the stake in Canterbury to cheers of hundreds, Mar 14, 1551; stepdau. of Sir Edward North; m. Thomas Arden (murdered Feb 15, 1551). ❖ Began affair with family servant named Richard Mosby (or Mosbie), which she continued after her marriage to Thomas Arden, a man of high standing who was twice her age; was assisted in her plot to murder husband by one of his enemies, a man named Green, whom she paid to hire 2 assassins, known as Black Will and Shakebag; after assassins killed Thomas with help from Mosby, made sure husband was dead by stabbing him 7 or 8 times (Feb 15, 1551). Once the crime was discovered, the outcry was so enormous that at least 9 people were ultimately executed in connection with the killing, including at least 2 who were innocent of murder; a play about the murder, now known as *Arden of Faversham* (1st published anonymously as *The Lamentable and True Tragedie of M. Arden of Feversham in Kent*, 1592), continues to inspire debate over identity of the author, whom many believe to be Shakespeare.

ARDEN, Daphne (1941—). British runner. Name variations: Daphne Arden Slater. Born Dec 29, 1941, in Great Britain. ❖ At Tokyo Olympics, won a bronze medal in the 4x100-meter relay (1964).

ARDEN, Elizabeth (1878–1966). Canadian-born cosmetics entrepreneur. Name variations: Florence Graham; Elizabeth N. Graham. Born Florence Nightingale Graham, Dec 31, 1878, in Woodbridge, Ontario, Canada; died in New York, NY, Oct 18, 1966; 4th of 5 children, 3rd of 3 daughters of Susan Tadd Graham and William Graham (market gardener); m. Thomas Jenkins Lewis, Nov 29, 1915, and became an American citizen (div. 1934); m. Prince Michael Evlanoff (Russian émigré), Dec 30, 1942 (div. 1944). ❖ Entrepreneur who introduced a scientific program to the manufacture of cosmetics and built a multi-million-dollar empire based on her "total woman" approach; left high school out of necessity to seek employment; joined brother William in NY (1907); was employed at Eleanor Adair's, a beauty specialist, where she began learning the elementary formulas for manufacturing and selling cosmetics; entered into a partnership with Elizabeth Hubbard, establishing a beauty salon at 509 Fifth Avenue (1910); bought out Hubbard; opened a salon at 673 Fifth Avenue and a wholesale department at

665 Fifth Avenue, to supply the growing demand for her preparations in stores throughout the country (1915); saw business empire grow under the name Elizabeth Arden; opened branches in Los Angeles, Palm Springs, and Miami Beach (1929); eventually sold products in 78 countries; was also one of the nation's top owners of thoroughbreds, a venture in which she also made a great deal of money. ❖ See also Alfred Allen Lewis and Constance Woodworth, *Miss Elizabeth Arden* (Coward, McCann, 1972); and *Women in World History.*

ARDEN, Eve (1907–1990). American actress. Born Eunice Quedens in Mill Valley, California, April 30, 1907; died Nov 12, 1990; dau. of Lucille (Frank) and Charles Peter Quedens; attended Mill Valley Grammar School and Tamalpais High School; m. Edward G. Bergen (literary agent), 1938 (div.); m. Brooks West (actor, c. 1916–1984); children: Douglas Brooks West; (adopted) Liza Connie and Duncan Paris West. ❖ Best known as "Our Miss Brooks," joined the Henry Duffy Stock Company in San Francisco; toured with Bandbox Repertory Company (1933), then appeared at Pasadena Playhouse in *Lo and Behold*; made NY debut with *The Ziegfeld Follies of 1934*, then was featured in *Parade* with Jimmy Savo (1935), as well as a 2nd *Follies* (1936), singing "I Can't Get Started with You" with Bob Hope; also appeared on Broadway in the Kern-Hammerstein musical *Very Warm Day*, followed by *Two for the Show* and *Let's Face It* (with Danny Kaye); made 1st film, *Oh, Doctor* (1937); came to screen prominence with *Stage Door* (1937); other films include *A Day at the Circus* (with Marx Brothers), *Comrade X, Ziegfeld Girl, One Touch of Venus, Cover Girl, Tea for Two* and *Anatomy of a Murder*; starred in radio series "Our Miss Brooks" (1948–56), then on tv (1956–60); was also seen on "The Eve Arden Show" and "The Mothers-in-Law." Nominated for an Academy Award for Best Supporting Actress for *Mildred Pierce* (1945). ❖ See also autobiography *Three Phases of Eve* (St. Martin, 1985); and *Women in World History.*

ARDEN, Margaretta (1934—). *See D'Arcy, Margaretta.*

ARDEN, Toni (fl. 1950s). American singer. Fl. 1950s. ❖ Pop vocalist, sang with Al Trace (1945) and Joe Reichman (1946); was an important singing star for Columbia Records and Decca (1950s); known for such songs as "I Can Dream, Can't I?," "Padre," and "Kiss of Fire."

ARDERIU, Clementina (1899–1976). Spanish poet. Born Clementina Arderiu, 1899, in Barcelona, Spain; died 1976; dau. of artisans; studied languages and music in Barcelona; m. Carles Riba (Catalan poet and Loyalist), 1916 (died 1959); children: 1 son. ❖ Catalan writer; when the Nationalists took control of Barcelona (1939), went into exile in France with family and author Antonio Machado; allowed to return to Catalonia (1943); works include *Cançoni i elegies* (Songs and Elegies, 1916), *L'Alta lliberat* (Lofty Liberty, 1920), *Cant i paraules* (Song and Word, 1936), *Sempre i ara* (Always and Now, 1946), *Es a dir* (1958), *Antologia poètica* (Poetic Anthology, 1961), *Obra poètica* (Poetic Work, 1973), *Contraclaror: Antologia Poètica* (View Against the Light: Poetic Anthology, 1985).

ARDLER, Stella (1902–1993). *See Adler, Stella.*

ARDOV, E. (1846–1923). *See Apréleva, Elena Ivanovna.*

ARDZHANNIKOVA, Lyudmila (1958—). Soviet archer. Born Mar 15, 1958, in USSR. ❖ At Barcelona Olympics, won a bronze medal in the team round (1992).

AREGUNDE (fl. 6th c.). Queen of the Franks. Name variations: Aregunda. Sister of Ingunde (d. 517); 4th wife of Chlothar, also known as Clothaire, Clotar, or Lothair I (497–561), king of Soissons (r. 511), king of the Franks (r. 558–561); children: Chilperic I (523–584), king of Soissons (Neustria).

AREMBURG (d. 1126). *See Ermentrude, countess of Maine.*

ARENAL, Concepción (1820–1893). Spanish poet and essayist who worked for prison reform. Name variations: Concepcion. Born Jan 30, 1820, in El Ferrol, Galicia, Spain; died in 1893 in Vigo; m. Fernando Garcia Carrasco (editor of *La Iberia*), 1848; children: daughter (b. around 1848 and died in infancy); sons Fernando (b. 1850) and Ramón (b. 1852). ❖ Lived in Madrid when husband was made editor of the liberal newspaper *La Iberia*; in poor health, took up writing (1852), beginning with a series of poems, "Anales de la virtus" (Annals of Virtue); also wrote several plays, and published *Fábulas en verso* (Fables in Verse, 1854); when husband fell ill, continued his work at *La Iberia*, including writing articles that the paper published under his name; following husband's death (1855), took the post of inspector of the women's prisons in Galicia and moved to La Coruña; founded Las

Magdalenas (1864), an organization to assist women during imprisonment and after their release; established the magazine *La voz de la caridad* (1870), a frequent forum for over 400 of her articles. Her complete works constituted 23 volumes. ❖ See also *Women in World History*.

ARENAL, Julie (1942—). American dancer and choreographer. Born 1942 in New York, NY; m. Barry Primus (actor); children: 1 daughter. ❖ Worked as assistant to Anna Sokolow at Lincoln Repertory Theater (mid-1960s); danced in works by Sophie Maslow, John Butler, José Limón and Kazuko Hirabayashi; choreographed the musical *Hair* for Broadway (1968), then restaged it for major cities, including Los Angeles, San Francisco and London; worked on pieces for Ballet Hispanico de Nueva York, NY, including *Fiesta* (1972) and *A Puerto Rican Soap Opera* (1973); has worked Off-Broadway on numerous pieces including Tom Eyen's *2008½* (1974); has worked on numerous pieces for further Hispanic companies in NY, including *I Took Panama* for Puerto Rican Traveling Theater (1977) and *The Sun Always Shines for the Cool* for The Family (1979); choreographed for such films as *King of Gypsies* (1979), *Soup for One* (1981), *Mistress* (1992), *Great Expectations* (1998) and *Meet the Parents* (2000); taught movement for actors at HB Studio and Puerto Rican Traveling Theater in New York City. Further works of choreography include *Indians* on Broadway (1970), *Isabel's a Jezebel* in London (1970), *Siamese Connection* (1971), *Butterfinger's Angel* (1974), and *Boccacio* on Broadway (1975), and *Funny Girl* in Tokyo (1980).

ARENDSEE, Martha (1885–1953). German Socialist and Communist leader. Born in Berlin, Germany, Mar 29, 1885; died in East Berlin, May 22, 1953; m. Paul Schwenk (1880–1960). ❖ Served as one of the few female Communist deputies to the Prussian provincial assembly (1921–24); elected to the Reichstag (1924); arrested by the Nazis (1933), escaped to the Soviet Union (1934); arrested in Stalin's purges but survived with husband (1930s); worked against the Nazi invasion of the USSR during WWII; became a founding member of the Central Women's Council of the Berlin municipal government (Aug 1945); elected a member of the Central Committee of the Communist Party of Germany (KPD, 1946), and served as a member of the 1st party executive committee of the newly created Socialist Unity Party of Germany (SED, 1946–47). ❖ See also *Women in World History*.

ARENDT, Gisela (1918–1969). German swimmer. Born Nov 5, 1918, in Germany; died Feb 18, 1969. ❖ At Berlin Olympics, won a bronze medal in the 100-meter freestyle and a silver medal in the 4 x 100-meter freestyle relay (1936).

ARENDT, Hannah (1906–1975). German-American political theorist and philosopher. Pronunciation: AIR-ent. Born Oct 14, 1906, in Hannover, Germany; died Dec 4, 1975, in New York, NY; dau. of Paul Arendt (engineer) and Martha Cohn Arendt; attended universities of Marburg, Freiburg, and Heidelberg; University of Heidelberg, PhD, 1928; m. Günther Stern, Sept 1929 (div. 1936); m. Heinrich Blücher, Jan 16, 1940 (died Oct 30, 1970). ❖ Famed for her analyses of totalitarianism and the trial of Nazi war criminal Adolf Eichmann, provided distinctive and iconoclastic explanations for the disasters that overtook Europe in the 1st half of the 20th century; used home as underground railroad for fleeing Jewish refugees before moving to France (1933); visited Palestine (1935); worked to help Jewish refugees arriving in Paris (1938); placed in French internment camp (1941); came to US (1941); worked for the Committee for a Jewish Army (1941–42); co-founded, with Joseph Maier, the Young Jewish Group as a replacement for that committee (1942); served as research director of the Conference on Jewish Relations (1944–46); named chief editor of Schocken Books (1946–48); appointed executive director of Jewish Cultural Reconstruction (1948–52); became a US citizen (1951); won Sigmund Freud Prize (1957), Lessing Prize (1959), and Sonning Prize (1974); taught at University of Chicago, Princeton University, University of California at Berkeley, the Rand school, Columbia University, and New School for Social Research, among others (1950–74); writings include *Eichmann in Jerusalem: A Report on the Banality of Evil* (1976), *The Human Condition* (1958), *The Life of the Mind* (1978), *On Revolution* (1973), and *The Origins of Totalitarianism* (1986). ❖ See also George Kateb, *Hannah Arendt: Politics, Conscience, Evil* (Rowman and Allanheld, 1983); David Watson, *Arendt* (Fontana Press, 1992); Elisabeth Young-Bruehl, *Hannah Arendt: For Love of the World* (Yale University Press, 1982); and *Women in World History*.

ARESTY, Esther B. (1908–2000). American book collector and writer. Born Esther Bradford, Mar 26, 1908, in Syracuse, NY; grew up in Iowa; died Dec 23, 2000, in Princeton, New Jersey; dau. of Lithuanian immigrants;

attended Purdue University; m. Julia Aresty (retail executive, died 1999); children: Robert Aresty and Jane Aresty Silverman. ❖ Collector of rare books on etiquette and culinary arts, was responsible for the Esther B. Aresty Collection on the Culinary Arts at University of Pennsylvania; also wrote 3 books, *The Delectable Past* (1964), *The Best Behavior* (1970) and *The Exquisite Table* (1980). ❖ See also *Women in World History*.

ARETE OF CYRENE (fl. 4th c. BCE). Greek philosopher. Fl. in 4th century BCE; dau. of Aristippus; married; children: Aristippus. ❖ Greek philosopher of the 4th century BCE who followed her father Aristippus as the head of the Cyrenaic school, which came to hold that virtue and pleasure were one. ❖ See also *Women in World History*.

ARETINA (1737–1814). See Moody, Elizabeth.

ARETZ, Isabel (1909—). Argentinean-born composer, ethnomusicologist, and folklorist. Name variations: Isabel Aretz de Ramón y Rivera; Isabel Aretz-Thiele. Born in Buenos Aires, Argentina, April 13, 1913; studied piano with Rafel González and composition with Athos Palma at the Buenos Aires National Conservatory of Music; instrumentation with Heitor Villa-Lobos in Brazil; and anthropology with Carlos Vega; received her doctorate in musicology at the Argentine Catholic University in 1967; m. Luis Felipe Ramón y Rivera. ❖ Universally recognized as a leading authority on South American folk music, was appointed the 1st professor of ethnomusicology at the Escuela Nacional de Danzas de Argentina (1950), where she continued her role as a scholar and composer; traveled extensively throughout Hispanic America, collecting folk music that she analyzed and used as a basis for research papers. ❖ See also *Women in World History*.

ARGENTINA, La (c. 1886–1936). See Mercé, Antonia.

ARGENTINITA (1898–1945). See Lopez, Encarnación.

ARGERICH, Martha (1941—). Argentinean pianist. Born June 5, 1941, in Buenos Aires, Argentina; studied with Vincenzo Scaramuzza, Friedrich Gulda, Arturo Benedetti Michelangeli, Nikita Magaloff, and Madeleine Lipatti. ❖ Considered by many to be one of the most passionate pianists of the late 20th century, made debut in Buenos Aires (1949); won Busoni International Competition in Bolzano (1957) and Chopin International Competition in Warsaw (1965); was a master performer of such disparate composers as Brahms, Schumann, and Prokofiev; lauded for recording of Ravel's *Gaspard de la nuit*.

ARGIRIADOU, Chryssoula (1901–1998). Greek poet, playwright and essayist. Name variations: Hrisoula Pendziki; Hrisoula Aryiriadou; Chryssoula or Chrisoula Argyriadou; (pseudonym) Zoe Karelli or Zoi Karelli. Born Hrisoula Pendziki, 1901, in Thessaloniki, Greece; died July 16, 1998, in Thessaloniki; sister of Nikos-Gavril Pentzikis (writer). ❖ Published 1st work, the short story "Moods" (1935), and 1st collection of poetry, *Pathway* (1940); became a member of the Greek National Academy. Twice awarded Greek national poetry award.

ARGYLE, Pearl (1910–1947). South African-born ballerina and actress. Born Pearl Wellman, Nov 7, 1910, in Johannesburg, South Africa; died Jan 29, 1947, in New York, NY; studied with Marie Rambert; m. Curtis Bernhardt (American film producer), 1938. ❖ Made debut in England with Ballet Club (later Ballet Rambert, 1926); rose quickly to leading roles, creating La Fille in *Bar aux Folies-Bergère*, Hebe in *Descent of Hebe*, the wife in *Les Masques*, and the title roles in Andrée Howard's *Cinderella* and *Mermaid*; joining the Sadler's Wells (1935), danced *Les Syphides*, *Swan Lake*, and created the Queen in *Le Roi Nu*; was also seen in many English films, including *That Night in London* (1935), as well as revues; following marriage (1938), lived in America and danced in several Broadway musicals, including *One Touch of Venus*.

ARGYLL, duchess of.
See Gunning, Elizabeth (1734–1790).
See Louise (1848–1939).
See Mathilda (1925–1997).

ARGYRIADOU, Chrisoula (1901–1998). See Argiriadou, Chryssoula.

ARI, Carina (1897–1970). Swedish ballet dancer. Born April 14, 1897, in Stockholm, Sweden; died Dec 24, 1970, in Buenos Aires, Argentina. ❖ Danced with Ballets Suedois throughout its existence (starting 1920), a company that fused traditional ballet and new expressionism of early 20th-century choreographers; performed in most repertory pieces by company's major star and ballet master Jean Börlin, including *Dangsille*, *Danse pour les Ciseaux* and *Les Maries de la Tour Eiffel*; created own ballets for Opéra Comique, Paris, such as *Sous-Marine* (1925) and *Les Valses de Brahms* (1933); performed in works by Sege Lifar.

ARIADNE (fl. 457–515). Byzantine empress. Name variations: Aelia Ariadne. Born before Feb 7, 457; died in Constantinople, late 515; dau. of the future Leo I, Byzantine emperor (r. 457–474), and Empress Verina; m. the future Emperor Zeno (Tarasicodissa Rousoumbladeotes) in 466 or 467 (died April 9, 491); m. Emperor Anastasius I Dicorus (r. 491–518), May 20, 491; children: (1st m.) Leo II (b. around 467). ❖ Fifth-century Byzantine empress and daughter of Leo I, whose 2 marriages preserved the dynasty until her death; son Leo II became emperor (473), but died the following year, leaving Zeno as ruler (474); styled "Augusta" during reigns of Zeno and Anastasius (474–515); possibly involved in the revolt of Basiliscus (475–76); conspired in unsuccessful plots against the general Illus (477, 478, and 480–81); dominated court after death of husband (491); chose and married his successor, Anastasius I (491). ❖ See also *Women in World History.*

ARIADNE (fl. 1696). British playwright. Flourished around 1696. ❖ Wrote comedy *She Ventures and He Wins* (1696). First woman to publish plays after Aphra Behn.

ARIB (797–890). *See Oraib.*

ARIGNOTE (fl. 6th c. BCE). Pythagorean philosopher. Born in Crotona, Italy, to Pythagoras of Samos (philosopher, mathematician, politician, spiritual leader) and Theano of Crotona (Pythagorean philosopher); sister of Myia, Damo, Telauges and Mnesarchus; educated at the School of Pythagoras. ❖ Was educated in the Pythagorean school and adopted that life, which involved the study of mathematics and the contemplation of mathematic's role in the order of the universe, particularly in regard to physical relationships and astronomy; wrote several of the Pythagorean *Sacred Discourses, Epigrams on the Mysteries of Ceres, Mysteries of Bacchus,* and an unnamed work on Dionysius. ❖ See also *Women in World History.*

ARIMORI, Yuko (1966—). Japanese long-distance runner. Born Dec 17, 1966, in Okayama City, Japan. ❖ At Barcelona Olympics, won a silver medal in the marathon (1992), the 1st Japanese woman to win a marathon medal at Olympics; at Atlanta Olympics, won a bronze medal for marathon (1996); established the Hearts of Gold foundation (1998) to raise funds for victims of land mines in Cambodia; became a Goodwill Ambassador for United Nations Population Fund (UNFPA).

ARISTARETE. Ancient Greek painter. Birth and death dates unknown; born to the painter Nearchus and an unknown mother; taught to paint by her father. ❖ Painted an Asclepius. ❖ See also *Women in World History.*

ARIYOSHI, Sawako (1931–1984). Japanese author. Born Sawako Ariyoshi, Jan 20, 1931, in Wakayama City, Japan; died Aug 30, 1984, in Tokyo, Japan; dau. of Shinji and Akitsu; educated at Tokoyo Christian Women's University; m. Jin Akira (director), Mar 1963 (div. 1964); children: daughter, Tamao (b. Nov 1963). ❖ Began career working for Kabuki theater companies and publications (1952); published 1st short story (1955); earned numerous prizes for short stories and plays; published 1st novel *Kinokawa (The River Ki,* 1959), one of her best known; released most of her novels 1st in serial form in popular Japanese magazines, often running over a 6-month period; published *Kōkotsu no hito (The Twilight Years,* 1972), which sold more than one million copies, followed by a serialization that became the novel *Fukugo osen (Compound Pollution);* works, including more than 35 nonfiction, fiction, and dramatic volumes, have been translated into 12 languages.

ARJEMAND or ARJUMAND, Princess (c. 1592–1631). *See Mumtaz Mahal.*

ARKHIPOVA, Anna (1973—). Russian basketball player. Born July 27, 1973, in Stavropol, USSR. ❖ Guard, won a team bronze medal at Athens Olympics (2004); placed 2nd at World championships (2002) and 1st at European championships (2003); played for European clubs and UMMC Ekaterinburg.

ARLETTE (fl. c. 1010). French noblewoman and mother of William the Conqueror. Name variations: Herleva or Herleve. Born c. 1010; death date unknown; dau. of Fulbert (the tanner) of Falaise; liaison with Robert I, duke of Normandy (d. 1035); m. Herluin, viscount of Conteville; children: (with Robert I) William I the Conqueror, duke of Normandy (r. 1035–1087), king of England (r. 1066–1087); Adelicia (c. 1029–1090); (1st m.) Odo, earl of Kent, and Robert, count of Mortain (d. 1091).

ARLETTY (1898–1992). French actress. Name variations: Arlette. Born Léonie Bathiat in Courbevoie, France, May 15, 1898; died in Paris on July 24, 1992; dau. of a miner and a laundress; never married; no children. ❖ One of the immortals of the golden age of French cinema, known as "the Garbo of France," is famed for her work in *Les Enfants du Paradis* and *Hôtel du Nord,* and for her brief affair with a German flyer; made stage debut in a small part as a courtesan in *L'école des Cocottes* (1920); on film, had supporting parts in *Le Grand Jeu* (1934) and *Pension Mimosas* (1935); teamed with Marcel Carné for a supporting role in his *Hôtel du Nord* (1938), effectively walking away with the film; reunited with Carné for 3 more films: *Le Jour se lève (Daybreak,* 1939), *Les Visiteurs du Soir* (1943), and one of the most celebrated films in French cinema, *Les Enfants du Paradis (Children of Paradise,* 1945); was accused of what was called *collaboration horizontale* (sleeping with the enemy) and placed under house arrest for 18 months (1945–46); waited four years before completing next major film *Portrait d'un Assassin* (1949); returned to the stage as Blanche in *Un tramway nommé désir (A Streetcar Named Desire),* adapted by Cocteau (1951); other plays include *Les Compagnons de la Marjolaine* and *La Descente d'Orphée (Orpheus Descending);* played Inez in the film *Huis Clos* (1945), followed by *Maxime, Drôle de Dimanche, La Loi des Hommes* and *The Longest Day,* among others. ❖ See also memoir *La Défense* (1948) and autobiography *Je Suis comme Je Suis (I Am as I Am,* 1971); and *Women in World History.*

ARLEY, Maryse (1922–1967). *See Carol, Martine.*

ARLINGTON, Lizzie (1876–1917). American baseball player. Name variations: Lizzie Stride; Lizzie Stroud; Arlington was a professional name. Born Elizabeth Stride, 1876 (some sources cite 1877), in Mahonoy City, Pennsylvania; died 1917. ❖ Was the 1st woman to sign a contract in the baseball minor leagues (Atlantic League, 1898). ❖ See also *Women in World History.*

ARLISS, Florence (1871–1950). English actress. Name variations: Florence Montgomery; Mrs. George Arliss. Born Florence Montgomery, 1871, in London, England; died Mar 11, 1950, in London; m. George Arliss (actor), Sept 16, 1899. ❖ Appeared in many of her husband's productions, including both the stage and film version of *Disraeli;* other films include *The Devil, The Millionaire* and *The House of Rothschild.*

ARMAND, Inessa (1874–1920). Russian revolutionary and feminist. Name variations: Comrade Inessa, Elena Blonina. Pronunciation: In-es-a Ar-mand. Born Elizabeth Stéphane, May 8, 1874, in Paris, France; died of cholera in Nal'chik, Russia, Sept 24, 1920; dau. of Théodore Pécheux d'Herbenville (opera singer who performed under the name Théodore Stéphane) and Nathalie Wild (part-time actress and voice teacher); tutoring at home led to teaching certificate, 1891; auditor, University of Moscow, 1906–1907; license, New University of Brussels, 1910; m. Alexander Armand, Oct 3, 1893; children: (with husband) Alexander, Fedor, Inna, and Varvara; (with brother-in-law, Vladimir Armand) Andre. ❖ One of the most important women in the early Soviet state, was an underground propagandist, Bolshevik Party organizer, and champion of women's equality; devoted 5 years to teaching peasant children (1893–98); as a feminist, sought to rehabilitate prostitutes in Moscow; served as Russian vice-president of Women's International Progressive Union (1899) and president of Moscow Society for Improving the Lot of Women (1900–03); joined Russian Social Democratic Labor Party (1904); was an underground propagandist (1904–07); arrested 4 times and exiled to Mezen in northern Russia (1907–08); escaped, went abroad where she assisted V.I. Lenin in organizing Bolshevik Party (1910–17); served as chair, Committee of Foreign Organizations (1911–12); established and edited *Rabotnitsa,* the 1st Bolshevik paper for women workers (1914); represented the Bolsheviks at numerous international socialist conferences (1914–16); was a member, Left Communist opposition (1918); worked for economic reconstruction as chair of the Moscow Provincial Economic Council (1918–19); was a member, All-Russian Central Executive Committee (1918–19); was 1st director, Women's Section (Zhenotdel) of the Central Committee of the Russian Communist Party (1919–20); was editor, *Kommunistka* (Female Communist, 1920), and organizer and chair, 1st International Conference of Communist Women (1920). ❖ See also R.C. Elwood, *Inessa Armand: Revolutionary and Feminist* (Cambridge University Press, 1992); Michael Pearson, *Lenin's Mistress* (Random House, 2002); and *Women in World History.*

ARMASESCU, Mihaela (1963—). Romanian rower. Born Sept 1963 in Romania. ❖ Won a silver medal in coxed eights at Los Angeles Olympics (1984) and Seoul Olympics (1988).

ARMATRADING, Joan (1947—). West Indian-British singer and guitarist. Born 1947 in St. Kitts, West Indies. ❖ Highly regarded in Britain, especially in the women's movement, because of her independence, feminist lyrics, and imaginative guitar playing; moved with family to Birmingham, England (1958); with friend Pam Nestor, began recording with Cube records, releasing debut album *Whatever's for Us* (1972); ended partnership with Nestor and moved to A&M; albums include *Back to the Night* (1975), *Joan Armatrading* (1976), *Stepping Out* (1979), *Me, Myself and I* (1980), *Walk Under Ladders* (1981), and *Secret Secrets* (1985); songs include "Love and Affection," "Down to Zero," and "Drop the Pilot"; asked to write a tribute song for Nelson Mandela (1999), wrote "The Messenger." Made a Member of the British Empire (MBE, 2001).

ARMBRUST, Barbara (1963—). Canadian rower. Born Aug 13, 1963, in Canada. ❖ At Los Angeles Olympics, won a gold medal in coxed fours (1984).

ARMBRUST, Roma (1927–2003). American conservationist. Born Sept 30, 1927, in Los Angeles, California; died Oct 10, 2003, in Ventura, California; m. Bill Armbrust; children: Kurt Armbrust and Vikki McCarter. ❖ With Jean Harris, successfully fought to preserve about 750 acres of Ventura County wetlands (1989–2003).

ARMEN, Kay (1920—). American pop singer and songwriter. Born Armen Manoogian, Nov 2, 1920, in Chicago, Illinois; dau. of a professional wrestler billed as "The Terrible Turk." ❖ Had early career in Chicago clubs and on Nashville radio; appeared on tv's "Stop the Music" (1948–51) and in such films as *Hit the Deck* (1955), *Hey Let's Twist!* (1961) and *Paternity* (1981); recorded "Come On-A My House" before Rosemary Clooney; wrote such songs as "Be Good to Yourself," "My Love and I," and "It's a Sin to Cry Over You."

ARMEN, Margaret (1921–2003). American tv writer. Born Sept 9, 1921, in Washington, DC; died Nov 10, 2003, at her home in Woodland Hills, California; dau. of a naval officer; University of California at Los Angeles, BS; married with children. ❖ One of the 1st successful female tv writers, wrote episodes for "The Rifleman," "The Big Valley," "The Lawman," "Star Trek," "Barnaby Jones," "Flamingo Road" and "Marcus Welby, M.D.," among others; also wrote the novel *The Hanging of Father Miguel* (1984).

ARMENTIÈRES, Péronelle d' (fl. 14th c.). French poet. Name variations: Peronelle d' Armentieres. Born into a gentry family c. 1340 in France; death date unknown; dau. of Gonthier d'Unchair of Champagne. ❖ Taught and wrote poetry; at 18, began a correspondence with poet and musician Guillaume de Machaut. The book *Voir Dit* (*Seeing Said*) documents their relationship, letters and poems.

ARMER, Laura Adams (1874–1963). American artist and author. Born in Sacramento, California, Jan 12, 1874; died 1963; youngest of 3 children; studied under Arthur Mathews at California School of Design in San Francisco, 1893; m. Sidney Armer (artist), 1902; children: one son, Austin, 1903. ❖ At 50, 1st visited the Navajo region that would figure so prominently in writings; set up a wilderness camp at base of Blue Canyon cliffs in the Hopi mesas (1925); lived with only a young Navajo girl to cook and interpret, while she immersed herself in Indian culture, including the religious ritual of sandpainting; published a series of books, many self-illustrated (1931–39), including *Dark Circle of Branches* (1933), *Cactus* (1934), *Southwest* (1935), *The Traders' Children* (1937), *Farthest West* (1939), and *In Navajo Land* (1962). Won the Newbery Medal for *Waterless Mountain* (1932) and the Caldecott Medal for *The Forest Pool* (1939). ❖ See also *Women in World History*.

ARMITAGE, Alan (1875–1960). *See Kenny, Alice Annie.*

ARMITAGE, Ella (1841–1931). English archaeologist. Name variations: Ella Sophia Bulley Armitage. Born Ella Sophia Bulley, Mar 3, 1841, in Liverpool, England; died Mar 20, 1931; m. Rev. Elkanah Armitage (nonconformist minister), 1874 (died 1929). ❖ The 1st research student at Newnham College, Cambridge, taught history in Women's Department of Owen's College in Manchester (1874–84); worked with well-known scholars to prove that the mottes (or mounds) in Anglo-Saxon Britain did not appear until after Norman invasion; published *The Early Norman Castles of the British Isles* (1912); became founder and 1st president of Yorkshire Congregational Women's Guild of Christian Service; served in many voluntary posts in field of education and was 1st woman elected to Rotherham school board (1887).

ARMITAGE, Goody (fl. 1643). American innkeeper. Flourished around 1643. ❖ When she received permission from the General Court of Massachusetts to "keepe the ordinary, but not to drawe wine," apparently became the 1st woman innkeeper in the colonies (1643).

ARMITAGE, Heather (1933—). British runner. Name variations: Heather Armitage Young. Born Mar 17, 1933, in Great Britain. ❖ Won bronze medal in Helsinki Olympics (1952) and silver medal in Melbourne Olympics (1956), both for 4 x 100-meter relay.

ARMITAGE, Karole (1954—). American dancer. Born Mar 3, 1954, in Madison, Wisconsin; attended North Carolina School of the Arts; studied with Bill Evans at University of Utah, 1971–72, and at School of American Ballet and Harkness School of Dance. ❖ Under Patricia Neary, made professional debut with Grand Théâtre de Genève (Geneva Opéra Ballet), Switzerland (1972–75); gained wide recognition while dancing in Merce Cunningham Dance Company (1976–80); made choreographic debut with *Ne* (1978); founded Armitage Dance Company (1980), based in NY, which became the Armitage Ballet (1986); continued choreographic career in Europe (1980s), where she worked in frequent collaboration with Charles Atlas in such works as *Drastic Classicism* (1981) and worked on numerous pieces with painter David Salle, including *Mollino Room* (1985); received Guggenheim fellowship (1986); wrote and directed film *Hall of Mirrors* (1992); works as freelance choreographer for various European countries; appointed artistic director of MaggioDanza, Florence, Italy (1996); has also choreographed for numerous music videos, including those of Madonna and Michael Jackson. Further works include *-p = dH/dq* (1985, renamed *The Watteau Duets*), with Salle, *The Elizabethan Phrasing of the Late Albert Ayler* (1986), *Les Anges ternis* (The Tarnished Angels, 1987), *Duck Dances* (1988), *The Dog is Us* (1994), *Hovering at the Edge of Chaos* (1994), *Weather of Reality* (1997), and Handel's *Apollo e Dafne* (1997).

ARMITAGE, Pauline. Northern Ireland politician. Married with one daughter. ❖ Served as mayor of Coleraine (1995–97); as an Independent Unionist, elected to the Northern Ireland Assembly for Londonderry East (1998).

ARMITAGE, Rachelina Hepburn (1873–1955). New Zealand social-welfare worker. Name variations: Rachelina Hepburn Stewart. Born Rachelina Hepburn Stewart, April 22, 1873, at Dunedin, New Zealand; died May 14, 1955, in Dunedin; dau. of William Downie Stewart (lawyer) and Rachel (Hepburn) Stewart; Somerville College, University of Oxford, BA, 1896; m. George Whitefield Armitage (accountant, died 1943), 1903; children: 2 sons. ❖ First New Zealand woman to complete BA course at University of Oxford (1896); joined Women's University Settlements Scheme to help improve women's position in education and work place (late 1890s); returned to New Zealand (1899); established Temuka branch of New Zealand Federation of Women's Institutes; active in Society of Health of Women and Children (Plunkett Society) (1914–28). ❖ See also *Dictionary of New Zealand Biography* (Vol. 3).

ARMOUR, Mary Nicol Neill (1902–2000). Scottish painter. Name variations: Mary Nicol Neill Steel; Mary Steel; Dr. N.N. Mary Armour. Born Mary Nicol Neill Steel in 1902 in Blantyre, Lanarkshire, Scotland; died 2000 in Kilbarchan, Scotland; studied under David Forrester Wilson and Maurice Greiffenhagen at Glasgow School of Art (1920–25); m. William Armour (artist), 1927. ❖ One of Scotland's most important modern painters, won scholarship to Hamilton Academy at 11, where she studied with Penelope Beaton; executed mural commission for Royal Navy and elected Associate of Royal Scottish Academy (RSA, both 1941); focused primarily on landscape and flower studies; taught at Glasgow School of Art (1951–62), period during which paintings became more free in handling and brighter in color; elected to Royal Scottish Water Colour Society (1956) and to Royal Scottish Academy (1958); showed paintings at Royal Scottish Academy and Glasgow Institute and Fine Art Society; precluded from continuing to paint due to failing eyesight (1988); lived out life in artistic community of Kilbarchan, Scotland.

ARMOUR, Rebecca (1846–1891). Canadian novelist. Name variations: Rebecca Agatha Armour Thompson; Mrs. John G. Thompson. Born Rebecca Agatha Armour, 1846, in Fredericton, New Brunswick, Canada; died 1891; dau. of Joseph A. Armour (grocer) and Margaret (Hazlett) Armour; m. John G. Thompson (carriage maker), 1885. ❖ Daughter of Irish immigrants, had a working-class Canadian upbringing; attended a teachers' college; taught in Fredericton (1864–73), then in southern New

Brunswick and Lancaster; wrote 4 novels depicting Fredericton society, including *Lady Rosamund's Secret* (1878) and *Marguerite Verne; or, Scenes from Canadian Life* (1886).

ARMOUR, Toby (1936—). American postmodern dancer and choreographer. Born Sept 27, 1936, in New York, NY. ❖ Began choreographing for Judson Dance Theater in New York City and solo concerts (early 1960s); created works for Dancing Ladies concert (1972) and The New England Dinosaur, her own Boston company; danced in Living Theater workshops in NY with James Waring; performed solo recitals of Waring's works in Paris, including *Moonlight Sonata* (1974), *Intrada* and *Phrases*; continued in solo concerts, dancing in Aileen Passloff's *Variations on an Original Theme* and in her own works, *Bagatelle* and *Epilogue for an Endless Dance* (1979); also choreographed *Godmother* (1962), *Fragments of a Minor Murder* (1966), *Reveries of a Solitary Walker* (1967), *Ruby Turnpike* (1971), *Walrus and Carpenter* (1975), *Window Nocturne* (1976) and *Oompah* (1980).

ARMSTEAD, Izora (1942–2004). African-American pop singer. Name variations: Izora Rhodes; Izora Rhodes-Armstead; The Weather Girls. Born 1942 in Texas; grew up in San Francisco; died of heart failure, Sept 16, 2004, in San Leandro, California; attended San Francisco Conservatory; children: 11, including singer Dynell Rhodes. ❖ Sang with the gospel group News of the World; was backup vocalist for disco singer, Sylvester (1970s); with Martha Wash, sang as Two Tons o' Fun (1979), then as The Weather Girls, and released a hit disco anthem, "It's Raining Men" (1984); living in Germany, relaunched The Weather Girls with daughter Dynell (1990s). Albums include *Success, Big Girls Don't Cry* and *Weather Girls*.

ARMSTRONG, Anne L. (1927—). American politician. Born Anne Legendre in New Orleans, Louisiana, Dec 27, 1927; dau. of Armant (coffee importer) and Olive (Martindale) Legendre; attended Foxcroft School in Middleburg, VA, valedictorian of 1945 graduating class; graduated Phi Beta Kappa from Vassar College, 1949; m. Tobin Armstrong (rancher), April 12, 1950; children: John, Katharine, Sarita, and twin boys, Tobin Jr. and James. ❖ Served as Republican national committeewoman for Texas (1968–73); was the 1st woman to be national co-chair of the Republican Party (1971–73); became a champion of women in the Republican Party, lending her support to the Equal Rights Amendment; was 1st woman in either party to deliver the keynote speech at a major national convention (1972); because of a growing dismay among women's groups at Nixon's failure to name women to high-ranking posts, was appointed counselor to the president, with full Cabinet status (1972); established the Office of Women's Programs in the White House, which tripled the number of women in government policy-making positions; acted as liaison with Hispanic Americans; was a member of the Council of Wage and Price Stability, Domestic Council, and Commission on the Organization of Government for the Conduct of Foreign Policy; served as a delegate to UN food conference in Rome (1974); named US ambassador to Great Britain (1975); was chair of the Advisory Board Center for Strategic and International Studies and chair of the president's Foreign Intelligence Advisory Board; also served as a member of the board of overseers of the Hoover Institute (1978–90) and co-chaired the Reagan-Bush presidential campaign (1980). Named to the Texas Women's Hall of Fame (1986) and awarded the Presidential Medal of Freedom (1987). ❖ See also *Women in World History*.

ARMSTRONG, Debbie (1963—). American Alpine skier. Born Deborah Armstrong, Dec 6, 1963, in Salem, Oregon. ❖ Won the gold medal in the giant slalom at Sarajevo Olympics (1984); was national giant slalom champion (1987); was also a member of US Olympic ski team (1988). ❖ See also *Women in World History*.

ARMSTRONG, Eileen (1894–1981). English diver. Born Jan 11, 1894, in Great Britain; died Mar 12, 1981. ❖ At Antwerp Olympics, won a silver medal in platform (1920).

ARMSTRONG, Gillian (1950—). Australian film director. Born Gillian May Armstrong, Dec 18, 1950, in Melbourne, Australia; father worked in real estate; mother was a teacher; lives with film editor John Pffefer; children: 2 daughters. ❖ Acclaimed film director, part of the "Australian New Wave," studied theater design and then film, winning a scholarship to Film and Television School at Swinbourne College in Sydney; made documentaries after graduation as well as drama *The Singer and the Dancer* (1976), which won Australian Film Institute award for Best Short; won 11 Australian Film Institute awards, including Best Film and Best Director for *My Brilliant Career* (1979),which was the 1st

feature film directed by an Australian woman since the 1930s and was also selected for Cannes Film Festival; invited to Hollywood after early success, but elected to continue working in Australia until 1984; has mostly directed films that focus on difficulties facing independent women, such as *The Last Soffel* (1984), *High Tide* (1987), and *The Last Days of Chez Nous* (1993); also directed musical comedy *Starstruck* (1982); other films include *Fires Within* (1991), *Little Women* (1994), *Oscar and Lucinda* (1997) and *Charlotte Gray* (2001). Won Dorothy Arzner Directing Award (1995).

ARMSTRONG, Helen Porter (1861–1931). See *Melba, Nellie*.

ARMSTRONG, Hilary (1945—). English politician and member of Parliament. Name variations: Rt. Hon. Hilary Armstrong. Born Nov 30, 1945; dau. of Hannah Armstrong and Ernest Armstrong (MP for Durham North West, 1966–87); attended Monkwearmouth Comprehensive School, West Ham College of Technology, and University of Birmingham, m. Dr. Paul Corrigan, 1992. ❖ As a VSO volunteer, taught at a girl's school in Kenya; served as a councillor on Durham County Council (1985–87); representing Labour, elected to House of Commons for Durham North West (1988, 1992, 1997, 2001, 2005); served as opposition frontbench spokesperson on Education (1988–92), Treasury Affairs (1994–95), and Environment and London (1995); appointed minister of state at Department of Environment, Transport and the Regions (1997); made a member of the Privy Council (1999); promoted to the Cabinet and named government chief whip (2001).

ARMSTRONG, Jenny (1970—). New Zealand-born sailor. Born Mar 3, 1970, in Dunedin, New Zealand; m. Erik Stibbe (Olympic sailing coach). ❖ Competed for New Zealand at Barcelona Olympics, placing 4th in Europe class (1992); crewed the all-female Elle Racing entry for the Whitbread 60 around-the-world race (1996); became an Australian citizen (1998); won a gold medal for double-handed dinghy (470) at Sydney Olympics (2000); won World championships in double-handed dinghy class (2002).

ARMSTRONG, Lil Hardin (1898–1971). African-American jazz pianist, bandleader, composer, and vocalist. Name variations: Lillian Hardin Armstrong, Lil Hardin, Lilian. Born Lillian Hardin, Feb 3, 1898, in Memphis, Tennessee; died of a heart attack, Aug 27, 1971, in Chicago, Illinois; studied classical piano at Fisk University; m. Jimmy Johnson, early 1920s (div. 1924); m. Louis Armstrong (trumpeter and bandleader), Feb 5, 1924 (div. 1938). ❖ Was a member of Joe "King" Oliver's Creole Jazz Band (1921–24); recorded nearly 50 tunes with Louis Armstrong's Hot Fives, Hot Sevens, and Lil's Hot Shot (1925–27); led all-woman bands (1932–36); became house pianist for Decca Records, leading many all-star recording sessions (late 1930s); toured Europe, playing with Sidney Bechet and others (1952); wrote over 150 compositions and led bands that included Louis Armstrong, Kid Ory and Johnny Dodds; played many extended engagements in Chicago until her death. Selected discography: *Lil Hardin Armstrong And Her Swing Orchestra 1936–1940, Forty Years of Women In Jazz, Born to Swing, Safely Locked Up in My Heart, Women in Jazz: Pianists, Satchmo and Me, The Louis Armstrong Story, Young Louis: "The Side Man"* and *Mean Mothers: Independent Women's Blues*. ❖ See also *Women in World History*.

ARMSTRONG, Margaret (1894–1973). See *Du Pont, Patricia*.

ARMSTRONG, Margaret Neilson (1867–1944). American botanist and author. Born Margaret Neilson Armstrong, Sept 24, 1867, in New York, NY; died July 18, 1944, in New York, NY; dau. of David Maitland and Helen Neilson Armstrong; granddau. of Peter Stuyvesant (mayor); sister of Helen Maitland Armstrong (painter and stained-glass artist) and Hamilton Fish Armstrong (author and editor of *Foreign Affairs*). ❖ Spent several years in the American West, working on *Field Book of Western Wild Flowers*, which was published in 1915; completed father's memoirs *Day Before Yesterday* (1920), then wrote a biography of the Armstrong family, *Five Generations* (1930), as well as portraits of actress Fanny Kemble and adventurer Edward Trelawny; also authored two mysteries.

ARMSTRONG, Nellie (1861–1931). See *Melba, Nellie*.

ARMSTRONG, Nettie Florence (1875–1974). See *Keller, Nettie Florence*.

ARMSTRONG, Penny (1946—). American nurse and midwife. Name variations: Penny Bradbury Armstrong. Born Penelope Bradbury, Jan 23, 1946, in Aroostook County, Maine; m. Richard Armstrong. ❖ Directed drug-abuse education council as regional health planner in Portland, ME (early 1970s); received certificate in midwifery from Glasgow College of Midwifery in Scotland (1978); as director of Dry Hill Clinic (Gordonville, PA), attended an estimated 1,400 births primarily in Amish and Mennonite communities of Lancaster County, PA; (with Sheryl Feldman) authored *A Midwife's Story* (1986) and *A Wise Birth: Bringing Together the Best of Natural Childbirth with Modern Medicine* (1990); served as family-planning practitioner (Houlton, ME), staff nurse-midwife in group at Bassett Hospital (Cooperstown, NY), and project director of Behavioral Science and Community Health Curriculum Project at University of New England College of Osteopathic Medicine (Biddeford, ME).

ARMSTRONG-JONES, Margaret (b. 1930). *See Margaret Rose, Princess.*

ARMSTRONG-JONES, Sarah (1964—). English royal. Name variations: Lady Sarah Chatto. Born Sarah Frances Elizabeth, May 1, 1964, in Clarence House, London, England; dau. of Princess Margaret Rose (b. 1930) and Anthony Armstrong-Jones, earl of Snowdon; sister of David, Viscount Linley; m. Daniel Chatto (artist and actor), 1994; children: Samuel and Arthur.

ARMYTAGE, G. (1860–1911). *See Watson, Rosamund.*

ARMYTAGE, R. (1860–1911). *See Watson, Rosamund.*

ARNALDI, Edith von Haynau (1884–1978). *See von Haynau, Edith.*

ARNAUD, H. Pierre (1802–1871). *See Reybaud, Fanny.*

ARNAUD, Henriette (1802–1871). *See Reynaud, Henriette.*

ARNAUD, Yvonne (1892–1958). English actress and pianist. Born Yvonne Germaine Arnaud in Bordeaux, France, Dec 20, 1892; died in Surrey, England, Sept 20, 1958; dau. of Charles Léon Arnaud and Antoinette (de Montegut) Arnaud; educated in Paris; m. Hugh McLellan (theater manager). ❖ At 13, awarded 1st prize for piano at Paris Conservatoire (1905) and subsequently toured Europe and America as a youthful prodigy; made acting debut as Princess Mathilde in *The Quaker Girl* at London's Adelphi Theater (1911); had success as Suzanne in *The Girl in the Taxi* (1912); advanced career in light comedies and musicals throughout WWI, aware that her French accent was a chief asset; added Shaw and Shakespeare to her repertoire, playing the Princess of France in *Henry V* (1934) and Mrs. Frail in *Love for Love* (1943); appeared for 50 years on English stage; with husband, created and managed the Yvonne Arnaud Theatre in Guildford; made movie debut (1924) and appeared in such films as *On Approval* (1931), *A Cuckoo in the Nest* (1933), *The Improper Duchess* (1936), *Stormy Weather* (1936), *Neutral Port* (1940), *Tomorrow We Live* (1942), and *The Ghosts of Berkeley Square* (1947).

ARNAULD, Agnès (1593–1671). *See Arnauld, Jeanne Catherine*

ARNAULD, Angélique (1624–1684). French abbess. Name variations: Angélique de Saint-Jean Arnauld D'Andilly, Mère Angélique de Saint-Jean. Born Angélique Arnauld in 1624; died Jan 29, 1684; niece of Jacqueline Marie Arnauld (Mère Angélique) and Jeanne Catherine Arnauld (Mère Agnès); one of ten children of their eldest brother Robert Arnauld (successful lawyer who later became a hermit at Port Royal) and Catherine de la Boderie (who died when Angélique was only 13). ❖ Known as Mère Angelique de Saint-Jean, spent her life as a nun during a period which saw the height of Port Royal's power and influence and lasted into the days of its persecution and decline, keeping a faithful record of all that she experienced, including the period of her imprisonment for resisting royal authority; was present at the deaths of both her abbess aunts and recorded both in moving descriptions, together with insightful summaries of their characters; is known as the historian of Port Royal for composing the 3-volume account *Memoires pour Servir a l'Histoire de Port Royal* as well as the *Portrait de la Mère Catherine Agnès;* more intellectually gifted than either of her abbess aunts, worked with Agnès to compose the order's Constitutions and, in Port Royal's time of greatest trial, worked with Agnès to produce the *Advice given to the nuns of Port Royal on their conduct (la conduit qu'elles devraient garder)* in case of a change in the government of the house; twice elected abbess of Port Royal. ❖ See also *Women in World History.*

ARNAULD, Jacqueline Marie (1591–1661). French abbess. Name variations: Angélique-Marie de Sainte-Magdeleine Arnauld, Mère Angélique, Mère Marie Angélique. Born Jacqueline Marie Arnauld, Sept 8, 1591; died Aug 6, 1661; 2nd of 6 daughters of Antoine Arnauld (lawyer) and Catherine Marion Arnauld (d. 1641; dau. of Simon Marion, avocat general at Parlement of Paris). ❖ Abbess of Port Royal des Champs, known as Mère Angélique, who believed she was attempting nothing

more than to follow the original monastic rule as strictly as possible, when her convent provoked the suspicions of the king and was subject to intense persecution; appointed abbess of Port Royal des Champs at age 8 (1599) and ordained a nun the following year (1600); intent upon returning the convent to the strict rule of St. Benedict, imposed sharing of all property, frequent prayer, and long periods of complete silence upon the community; her mother and all her sisters, as well as many male relatives, would eventually seek the religious life at Port Royal, which became an influential center of spirituality and education; her convent began to incur the suspicion of royal authorities because of its apparent sympathies with the reformist ideas of Cornelius Jansen (1638). An important place of refuge during the civil wars (1648–49, 1652), Port Royal came under increasing scrutiny, its schools were closed, and many of its supporters were in hiding when she died (1661). ❖ See also *Women in World History.*

ARNAULD, Jeanne Catherine (1593–1671). French abbess. Name variations: Jeanne Catherine de Sainte Agnès Arnauld, Agnès de Saint-Paul Arnauld, Mère Agnès, Mère Catherine Agnès de Saint Paul. Born Jeanne Catherine Arnauld in 1593; died of inflammation of the lungs on Feb 19, 1671; 3rd dau. of Antoine Arnauld (lawyer) and Catherine Marion Arnauld (d. 1641); younger sister of Jacqueline Marie Arnauld (Mère Angélique). ❖ Known as Mère Agnès, joined her elder sister Jacqueline Arnould at Port Royal, serving as prior and abbess there and bravely bearing the full brunt of royal persecution after Jacqueline's death; as a child, appointed abbess of St. Cyr at age 6 but soon joined her sister at Port Royal des Champs and spent most of her life either there or in the Paris convent; often alternated with her sister in holding the office of abbess of Port Royal, though reluctant to assume the highest office; also served as abbess of Tard for 6 years; held out bravely against the persecution which enveloped Port Royal, at 1st signing and then retracting agreement to a formulary which was imposed upon the nuns; more inclined to mystical forms of devotion than her more practical sister, wrote a number of devotional works and also composed the Constitutions or Rule of Port Royal. ❖ See also *Women in World History.*

ARNDT, Eva (1919—). *See Riise-Arndt, Eva.*

ARNDT, Hermina (1885–1926). New Zealand artist. Name variations: Mina Arndt. Born Hermina Arndt, April 18, 1885, near Arrowtown, New Zealand; died on Dec 22, 1926, in Wellington, New Zealand; dau. of Herman Arndt (merchant) and Marie (Beaver) Arndt; m. Lionel Manoy (merchant), 1917; children: 1 son. ❖ Studied art at Wellington Technical College in 1905 and 1906, and attended art school in London, Berlin, Cornwall (early 1900s); briefly interned at outset of WWI, but released in women-prisoner exchange; returned to New Zealand and opened studio (1914); exhibited throughout New Zealand, Australia, and Europe; most notable painting was *The Red Hat*; work held in private collections and galleries in New Zealand, England, Australia, and France. ❖ See also *Dictionary of New Zealand Biography* (Vol. 3).

ARNDT, Judith (1976—). German cyclist. Born July 23, 1976, in Leipzig, Germany. ❖ Won a bronze medal for indiv. pursuit at Atlanta Olympics (1996); won World championship for pursuit (1997); placed 2nd in UCI Points Standing (2001); won a silver medal for road race at Athens Olympics (2004).

ARNDT, Mina (1885–1926). *See Arndt, Hermina.*

ARNE, Sigrid (1894–1973). Swedish-American journalist. Name variations: Sigrid Holmquist; adopted Sigrid Arne as a pen name. Born Sigrid Holmquist in New York City, possibly April 6, 1894; died, possibly in Feb 1973 in Manistique, Michigan; dau. of Magnus Holmquist (manufacturer) and Hulda (Larson) Holmquist; University of Michigan, BA, 1922. ❖ As a journalist, wrote stories about local issues and causes for newspapers in Cleveland, Oklahoma and Detroit; joined the staff of the Washington bureau of the Associated Press (1932); began working as a roving reporter for the AP (1941), which led to her analysis of the UN in her book *The United Nations Primer* (1945); served as president of American News Women's Club (1950–51).

ARNE, Susannah Maria (1714–1766). *See Cibber, Susannah.*

ARNELL, Amy (1919—). American singer. Born May 18, 1919, in Portsmouth, Virginia. ❖ Sang with Tommy Tucker band (1937–43); best known for hit record, "I Don't Want to Set the World on Fire" (1941).

ARNESEN, Liv (1953—). Norwegian skier and explorer. Born in Bærun, outside Oslo, Norway, 1953; studied graduate of University of Oslo, 1979; taught school in Norway; m. Einar Glestad, 1990. ❖ With Julie Maske, traversed the Greenland ice cap in 24 days (1992); became the 1st woman to ski solo from the Antarctic coast to the US research base at the South Pole, a 745-mile trek (1994); was a member of a team climbing Mount Everest's North Face (1996); with American Ann Bancroft, crossed the 1,700-mile Antarctic landmass in 97 days (2001), the 1st two women to cross Antarctica's landmass by sail and ski; as a teacher and coach, has been involved in education for more than two decades; is also known for her work in the rehabilitation of drug addicts. ❖ See also (with Ann Bancroft) *No Horizon Is so Far* (2003); and *Women in World History.*

ARNETT, Charlotte (c. 1795–1855). *See Brown, Charlotte.*

ARNIM, Bettine von (1785–1859). German letter writer. Name variations: Bettina; Bettina Brentano; Bettine. Pronunciation: AR-neem. Born Elizabeth Catharina Brentano, 1785, in Frankfurt am Main; died in Berlin, 1859; dau. of Maximiliane von La Roche Brentano and Peter Anton Brentano (Frankfurt merchant); sister of poet Clemens Brentano; granddau. of Sophie von La Roche; m. (Ludwig) Achim von Arnim (1781–1831, German poet and novelist), 1811; children: Freimund (b. 1812); Sigmund (b. 1813); Friedmund (b. 1815); Kühnemund (b. 1817); Maximiliane (b. 1818); Armgard von Arnim (b. 1821); Gisela von Arnim (b. 1827). ❖ Writer, who is best known for her epistolary works published from correspondence with Johann von Goethe, Clemens Brentano, and Karoline von Günderrode, and social activist, whose writings on behalf of the poor, of political agitators, and of social reform annoyed many, including the Prussian King Friedrich Wilhelm IV and the Berlin Magistrate; published 1st work *Goethes Briefwechsel mit einem Kinde* (Goethe's Correspondence with a Child, 1835), after husband had died (1831); through her later political works and deeds, was held partially responsible for the revolt of the Silesian weavers; was arrested and publication of her work was temporarily stopped; sympathized with the 1848 revolution and wrote on behalf of imprisoned insurgents; sentenced to 3 months in prison for lese-majesty; acquitted after trial. Writings include *Die Günderode* (1840), *Clemens Brentanos Frühlingskranz* (Clemens Brentano's Spring Wreath, 1844), *Dies Buch gehört dem König* (1843), (fairytale co-authored with daughter Gisela von Arnim) *Reichsgräfin Gritta von Rattenzuhausbeiuns* (1843), *Das Armenbuch* (Book of the Poor, 1844), *Ilius Pamphilius und die Ambrosia* (1848), and *Gespräche mit Dämonen* (1852). ❖ See also Elke Frederiksen and Katherine Goodman, eds. *Bettina Brentano-von Arnim: Gender and Politics* (Wayne State University Press, 1995); and *Women in World History.*

ARNIM, Elizabeth von (1866–1941). New Zealand-born novelist. Name variations: Mary Annette Russell, Countess Russell; Elizabeth Mary Russell; (pseudonyms) Elizabeth and Anne Cholmondely. Born Mary Annette Beauchamp in New Zealand, Aug 31, 1866; died in Charleston, South Carolina, Feb 9, 1941; 6th and last child of Henry Beauchamp (English shipping magnate) and Elizabeth "Louey" Lassetter (Australian); cousin of Katherine Mansfield; attended Miss Summerhayes' school in Ealing and Royal College of Music; m. Henning August von Arnim-Schlagenthin (Prussian count), 1891 (died 1910); m. Francis, 2nd Earl Russell, brother of philosopher Bertrand Russell (sep. 1919); children: (1st m.) 5, including daughter Leslie de Charms (writer). ❖ At 3, moved to London with family; at 18, met and married a Prussian count and moved into his depleted estate in Pomerania, the setting of her best-known book, *Elizabeth and her German Garden*, published anonymously (1898); published early books under the name Elizabeth: *The Benefactress* (1901), *Fraulein Schmidt and Mr. Anstruther* (1907), and *The Caravanners* (1909); used pseudonym Anne Cholmondely for *Christine* (1917); after an affair with H.G. Wells and a failed 2nd marriage, set a bleaker tone in such books as *The Pastor's Wife* (1914), *Vera* (1921), and *The Enchanted April* (1923), which was filmed by Miramax (1992). ❖ See also memoir *All the Dogs of My Life* (1936); and *Women in World History.*

ARNIM, Mary Annette, Countess von (1866–1941). *See Arnim, Elizabeth von.*

ARNOLD, Becky (1936—). American postmodern dancer and choreographer. Born Sept 21, 1936, in Blossten, Indiana. ❖ Moved to New York City and danced for Helen Tamiris in *Women's Song, Memoirs* (both 1960), and *Arrows of Desire* (1963), among others; performed in the premiere of Yvonne Rainer's *Continuous Project Altered Daily* (1966), considered crucial in the development of postmodern dance; was

founding member of improvisational troupe The Grand Union, with whom she performed 2 years; continues to choreograph for own company. Further works include *Motor Dance* (1975), *Bonaja Transit* (1976), *Solo Dance and Film* (1977), *Dancing Fats* (1978), and *Encounters* (1980).

ARNOLD, Bené (1953—). American ballet dancer. Name variations: Bene Arnold. Born 1953 in Big Springs, Texas. ❖ Studied at San Francisco Ballet School under Arnold Christensen; joined San Francisco Ballet (1950) and danced in *Coppélia, Swan Lake, The Nutcracker* and most prominently as The Bearded Lady in Lew Christensen's *Jinx;* served as the company's ballet master (1960–63), then as ballet master at Utah Civic Ballet (1963–75), which evolved into Ballet West; joined the dance faculty at University of Utah's ballet department (1975) where she remained until retirement (2001); continued to work with Ballet West throughout, appearing in such character roles as *The Sleeping Beauty*'s Carabosse.

ARNOLD, Dorothy (1917–1984). American actress and singer. Name variations: Dorothy DiMaggio. Born Dorothy Arnoldine Olson, Nov 21, 1917, in Duluth, Minnesota; died Nov 13, 1984, in Palm Springs, California; m. Joe DiMaggio (famed baseball player), 1939 (div. 1944); m. George Schuster, 1946 (div. 1950); m. Gary Peck; children: Joe DiMaggio Jr. (1941–1999). ❖ Began career as a nightclub singer; started appearing in films (1938), including *The Storm, House of Fear, The Phantom Creeps* (serial), *Family Next Door, Hers for a Day* and *Lizzie;* owned and performed in Charcoal Charley's, a supper club in Palm Springs.

ARNOLD, Emily (1939—). *See McCully, Emily Arnold.*

ARNOLD, Emmy (1884–1980). German-born leader of the Bruderhof movement. Born Emmy von Hollander in 1884 in Riga, Latvia; died 1980; m. Eberhard Arnold, Dec 1909; children. ❖ With husband, founded a small Christian pacifist commune in the village of Sannerz-Schlüchtern, near Fulda, called the Bruderhof (1920); husband died (1935); fled to Great Britain after persecution by the Nazis (1939); with group, provided shelter for many Jewish refugees; after the war, immigrated to Paraguay and then to upstate (Rifton) New York with members of the Bruderhof. ❖ See also Gertrud Hüssy, *A Joyful Pilgrimage: Emmy Arnold 1884–1980* (Plough, 1980); Yaacov Oved, *Witness of the Brothers: A History of the Bruderhof* (trans. by Anthony Berris, Transaction, 1995); and *Women in World History.*

ARNOLD, Eve (1913—). American photojournalist. Born in Philadelphia, Pennsylvania, 1913; dau. of Russian immigrant parents (Arnold's maiden name unknown); studied medicine before switching to photography classes at New School for Social Research, 1947; studied under Alexey Brodovitch, art director for *Harper's Bazaar.* ❖ Was the 1st woman to photograph for Magnum Photos (1951), an international cooperative of photographers, becoming an associate member (1955) and a full member (1957); focused on stories about women, including the poor, elderly, and African-Americans; moved to London (1961), working mainly for the *Sunday Times* but also frequently contributing to *Life* magazine and other periodicals in US and abroad; made 1st of 5 trips to Soviet Union (1965); intermittent travels to Afghanistan and Egypt (1967–71) resulted in film *Behind the Veil,* which disclosed daily life in a harem; published several collections, including *The Unretouched Woman* and *Flashback! The '50s* (1978); published *In China* (1980), the culmination of 2 extended trips there (1979), which won the National Book Award; also published *In America, All in a Day's Work* (1989) and *Marilyn Monroe—An Appreciation* (1987). Shared a Lifetime Achievement Award with Louise Dahl-Wolfe from American Association of Magazine Publishers (1979). ❖ See also memoir *In Retrospect* (Knopf, 1995); and *Women in World History.*

ARNOLD, Helen (1943—). *See Quinn, Helen.*

ARNOLD, June (1926–1982). American novelist and publisher. Born June Davis, Oct 27, 1926, in Greenville, South Carolina; died of cancer, Mar 11, 1982, in Houston, Texas; dau. of Robert Cowan and Cad Wortham Davis; attended Vassar College and Rice Institute; m. Gilbert Harrington Arnold, 1953; children: 4. ❖ With partner Parke Bowman, founded the feminist press, Daughters, Inc., which published the work of new and radical women writers, including Rita Mae Brown's *Rubyfruit Jungle;* was a member of National Institute for Women and Texas Institute of Letters; a Southern regional writer of feminist and lesbian fiction, published *Applesauce* (1967), *The Cook and the Carpenter* (1973), *Sister Gin* (1975), and, posthumously, *Baby Houston* (1987); also contributed to magazines and periodicals.

ARNOLD, Margaret (1760–1804). *See Shippen, Peggy.*

ARNOLD, Mary Beth (1981—). American gymnast. Born July 11, 1981, in Reno, Nevada. ❖ Won a bronze medal at World championships and a gold medal at Pan American Games (1995), both for team all-around; won Tournoi International (1994).

ARNOLD, Monica (1980—). *See Monica.*

ARNOLD, Peggy (1760–1804). *See Shippen, Peggy.*

ARNOTHY, Christine (1930—). French novelist and journalist. Born Nov 20, 1930, in Budapest, Hungary. ❖ Left Hungary with parents (1948), moving to Paris; wrote about her experiences during WWII's siege of Budapest in autobiographical novels: *J'ai quinze ans et je ne neux pas mourir* (*I am Fifteen and I Don't Want to Die*, 1956) and *Il n'est pas si facile de vivre* (*It is Not so Easy to Live*, 1958); other works include *La saison des Americains* (1964), *Le Jardin noir* (1971), *Aviva* (1971), *Chiche!* (1974), *J'aime la vie* (1978), *La piste Africaine* (1997), *Malins plaisirs* (1998), and *Complot de femmes* (2000).

ARNOUL, Françoise (1931—). Algerian-born actress. Born Françoise Gautsch, June 3, 1931, in Constantine, Algeria; studied acting in Paris. ❖ Made film debut in *L'Epave* (1950); initially typecast as a sultry sex symbol, moved into a wide variety of lead and supporting roles in such films as *Nous Irons à Paris, Quai De Grenelle* (*The Strollers*), *Le Désir et l'Amour, Le Fruit défendu, Paris Palace-Hôtel, Napoléon, La Chatte, La Morte-Saison des Amours, Compartiment tueurs* (*The Sleeping Car Murder*), *Le Dimanche de la Vie, Le Petit Théâtre de Jean Renoir, Violette et François, Dernière Sortie avant Roissy, Bobo Jacco, Ronde de nuit, Les Années campagne* and *Photo de famille*.

ARNOULD, Sophie (1740–1802). French operatic singer. Born Madeleine-Sophie Arnould, Feb 13, 1740, in Paris; died Oct 22, 1802, in Paris; studied with Marie Fel and Hippolyte Clarion. ❖ Renowned for her beauty and sharp wit, held the diva spotlight for 2 decades in the 18th century; at age 17, made her operatic debut (1757); performed most notably in operas by Raneau and is often associated with Gluck's *Iphigénie en Aulide;* retired from the stage at age 38; made home in Paris a salon for such writers as Rousseau, Diderot and d'Alembert. ❖ See also *Women in World History.*

ARNOULD-PLESSY, Jeanne (1819–1897). French actress. Name variations: Jeanne Plessy. Born Jeanne Sylvanie Plessy in Metz on Sept 7, 1819; died in 1897; dau. of a local actor named Plessy; m. J.F. Arnould (playwright), 1845 (died 1854). ❖ A pupil of Samson at Paris Conservatoire (1829); met instant success with debut as Emma at the Comédie Française (1834), in *La Fille d'honneur;* suddenly left Paris at height of success (1845) and moved to London, marrying the playwright J.F. Arnould; was effectively sued for damages by Comédie Française; accepted an engagement at French theater at St. Petersburg, Russia, where she played for 9 years; following death of husband, returned to Paris (1855) and was readmitted to Comédie Française as *pensionnaire* (resident) with an engagement for 8 years; had triumphs in such new plays as *Le Fils de Giboyer* and *Maître Guerin;* retired (1876). ❖ See also *Women in World History.*

ARNOW, Harriette Simpson (1908–1986). American writer. Name variations: H. Arnow, Harriette Simpson Arnow, Harriette Simpson, H.L. Simpson. Born Harriette Louisa Simpson, July 7, 1908, in Wayne County, Kentucky; died in Ann Arbor, Michigan, Mar 22, 1986; dau. of Elias Thomas Simpson (teacher, farmer, and oil driller) and Millie Jane (Denney) Simpson (teacher and homemaker); attended Berea College, 1924–26; University of Louisville, BS, 1931; m. Harold B. Arnow, Mar 11, 1939; children: Marcella Jane Arnow; Thomas Louis Arnow. ❖ Began career teaching in a remote one-room rural school, experiences that would become the material for 1st novel, *Mountain Path* (1936); after 2 more teaching jobs, in Pulaski County and Louisville, gave up the classroom and took waitress jobs in Michigan and Ohio in order to write; sold 1st short story, "Marigolds and Mules" to *Kosmos* (1934); worked for Federal Writers Project; when husband took a job as a reporter with *Detroit Times,* moved to Detroit and found a rental in one of the wartime housing projects (1944); published novel *Hunter's Horn* (1949); published what is generally considered greatest work, *The Dollmaker* (1954), about a family's eventual disintegration after it journeys from a rural community to the industrialized city (it was the 2nd place selection for National Book Award and adapted into an Emmy award-winning tv film starring Jane Fonda); wrote 2 works of social and cultural history of her native region, *Seedtime on the Cumberland* (1960) and *Flowering of the Cumberland* (1963); published several additional books: 2 novels, *The Weedkiller's Daughter* (1970) and *The Kentucky Trace* (1974), and a work

of nonfiction, *Old Burnside* (1978). ❖ See also Wilton Eckley, *Harriette Arnow* (Twayne, 1974); and *Women in World History.*

ARNST, Bobbe (1903–1980). American theater dancer. Born Oct 11, 1903, in New York, NY; died Nov 25, 1980, in Los Angeles, California. ❖ At 15, made debut on Broadway in *Greenwich Village Follies of 1924;* worked as vocalist and danced in musical comedies (1920s), including on tour with Ted Lewis Band; returned to Broadway in *A la Carte* (1927), followed by *Le Maire's Affairs* (1927), and sang "Isn't She a Pretty Thing" in *Rosalie;* performed as dance satirist in plays by Kaufman and Hart such as *The Fabulous Invalid* (1930) and *You Can't Take It With You;* appeared at New York clubs with satirical acts (1930s–40s), and in the films *Wine, Women and Song* (1933), *Torch Singer* (1933) and *Beloved* (1934), among others.

ARNSTEIN, Fanny von (1758–1818). Austrian-Jewish patron and philanthropist, and salonnière. Name variations: Baroness von Arnstein. Born Franziska Itzig in Berlin, Germany, Nov 29, 1758; died in Dreihaus near Vienna, June 8, 1818; dau. of Daniel Itzig (1723–1799, wealthy banker and court financier) and Marianne (Wulff) Itzig (1725–1788); never converted to Christianity, preferring to keep her Jewish faith; m. Baron Nathan Adam von Arnstein (Viennese banker), 1776; children: daughter Henriette (1780–1879, the Baroness Pereira). ❖ Known throughout Europe for her Viennese salon that attracted many of the leading composers, musicians, writers, artists, political leaders, and thinkers of the day; played a major role in the cultural life of Vienna, supporting Mozart and Beethoven; helped found Society of the Friends of Music; encouraged many talented artists; wielded enormous influence during Congress of Vienna (1814–15), when "the Congress danced" in her ballrooms; as one of Europe's intellectual and social arbiters, played an important role in the Age of Enlightenment and set new styles, including the introduction of Christmas trees to Vienna; an ardent Austrian patriot, organized the nursing of soldiers wounded in Napoleonic wars. ❖ See also Hilde Spiel, *Fanny von Arnstein: A Daughter of the Enlightenment, 1758–1818* (trans. by Christine Shuttleworth, Berg, 1991); and *Women in World History.*

ARNSTEIN, Margaret (1904–1972). American nurse. Born Margaret Gene Arnstein, Oct 27, 1904, in New York, NY; died Oct 8, 1972, in New Haven, Connecticut; dau. of Leo Arnstein (businessman) and Elsie (Nathan) Arnstein (social worker); niece of NY governor Herbert H. Lehman; graduated from Ethical Culture School (1921); Smith College, AB in biological sciences, 1925; New York Presbyterian Hospital School of Nursing, nursing diploma, c. 1928; Teachers College, Columbia University, MA in public health nursing, 1929; Johns Hopkins University, MA in public health, 1934. ❖ Celebrated for leadership in public health nursing, worked at Westchester County Hospital in White Plains, NY, and at New York State Department of Health's communicable disease division (as consultant nurse); taught public health nursing at University of Minnesota (1938–40); took leave from New York Health Department to work with United Nations Relief and Rehabilitation Administration (UNRRA) in Balkan countries (1943–45); began work at US Public Health Service (USPHS) as assistant to chief nurse Lucile Petry (1946), serving as chief of nursing division (1957–64); was then named senior nursing advisor for the International Health Office of the US Surgeon General's office (1964); left USPHS to head University of Michigan's public health nursing program (1966); served as dean of Yale University School of Nursing until retirement (1967–72); directed 1st International Conference on Nursing Studies in Sèvres, France (1956); writings include World Health Organization's *A Guide for National Studies of Nursing Resources* (1953). Was the 1st holder of Annie W. Goodrich Chair of Nursing at Yale University School of Nursing (1958).

AROL, Victoria Yar (1948—). Sudanese politician. Born in 1948 in Sudan; studied economics and political science at University of Khartoum; m. Toby Maduat; children: 3. ❖ Became a member of African Nationalist Front and later helped form the Sudanese Women's Union; represented women at National People's Assembly and won seat on People's Regional Assembly in Bahr el Ghazal Province; served as chair of committee to investigate corruption.

AROLDINGEN, Karin von (1941—). *See von Aroldingen, Karin.*

ARON, Geraldine (1941—). South African playwright and screenwriter. Born 1941 in Galway, Ireland; moved to South Africa, 1965; spent most of her life in Zambia, Zimbabwe, and South Africa, living in Cape Town. ❖ Plays include *Bar and Ger* (1975), *Mr. McConkey's Suitcase* (1977), *Joggers* (1979), *Zombie* (1979), *The Spare Room* (1981), *My Brilliant*

Divorce and *Spider;* plays collected in *Seven Plays and Four Monologues* (1985); wrote screenplay *Toscanini* for Franco Zeffirelli.

AROUET, Louise (c. 1710–1790). *See Denis, Louise.*

AROVA, Sonia (1927–2001). Bulgarian-born ballet dancer. Name variations: Sonia Sutowski. Born Sonia Errio, June 20, 1927, in Sofia, Bulgaria; died Feb 11, 2001, in San Diego, California; trained at the Sofia Opera Ballet; m. Thor Sutowski (dancer and choreographer), 1965; children: Ariane Sutowski. ❖ Performed with, and created roles in, numerous companies throughout Europe, including a role in *Design with Strings* for the Metropolitan Ballet (1948), "Odette" in *Swan Lake* for Ballet Rambert, and more; relocated to US (c. 1955) and performed with Ballet Theater in such pieces as *Design with Strings* and *Pas de Quatre* (both 1955); joined Ruth Page Ballet, later renamed Ruth Page's Chicago Opera Ballet, in Illinois (c. 1955), where she performed throughout most of her career; danced the "Don Quixote" pas de deux with Rudolf Nureyev at Brooklyn Academy of Music for his NY debut (1962); danced with National Ballet in Washington in pieces by her husband, including *Bachianas Brasileiras;* served as director of the Norwegian National Ballet (1966–70) and of the San Diego Ballet and Ballet Alabama; was also an early partner of Erik Bruhn.

ARQUIMBAU, Rosa Maria (1910—). Spanish novelist and journalist. Name variations: (pseudonym) Rosa de Sant Jordi. Born in Barcelona, Spain, 1910. ❖ During Spain's Second Republic, was a journalist for several leftist periodicals; published *Historia d'una noia i vont braçalets* (Story of a Girl and Twenty Bracelets, 1934) and *Home i dona* (Man and Woman, 1936); when Spanish Civil War began, was on the side of the Loyalists who, by 1939, had been defeated; went into exile; reemerged in Spain with *40 anys perduts* (Forty Years Lost, 1971).

ARRIA MAJOR (d. 42 CE). Roman matron. Name variations: Arria Maior; Arria the Elder. Died 42 CE in Rome by a self-inflicted wound; grandmother of Fannia; m. Caecina Paetus (Roman senator); children: Arria Minor. ❖ Impressed Roman writers of the 1st and 2nd centuries primarily because of her resolution during the arrest, trial and punishment of her husband, the senator Caecina Paetus. ❖ See also *Women in World History.*

ARRILA DE PÉREZ, Eulalia (c. 1773–1878). *See Pérez, Eulalia Arrila de.*

ARROM, Madame de (1796–1877). *See Böhl von Faber, Cecilia.*

ARRON, Christine (1973—). French runner. Born Sept 13, 1973, in Les Abymes, Guadaloupe. ❖ Moved to France (1990); placed 1st at World Championships for 4 x 100-meter relay (2003); won a bronze medal for the 4 x 100-meter relay at Athens Olympics (2004); won 6 Grand Prix and Super Grand Prix events in the 100 and 200 meters (2003, 2004). Named European Female Athlete of the Year (1998).

ARRONDO, Ines (1977—). Argentinean field-hockey player. Name variations: Inés Arrondo. Born Nov 28, 1977, in Buenos Aires, Argentina. ❖ Won a team silver medal at Sydney Olympics (2000) and a bronze medal at Athens Olympics (2004); won Champions Trophy (2001) and World Cup (2002).

ARROWSMITH, Mary Anne (c. 1833–1897). *See Swainson, Mary Anne.*

ARROYO, Gloria Macapagal (1947—). President of the Philippines. Born Gloria Macapagal, April 5, 1947, in San Juan, a suburb of Manila, Philippines; dau. of Diosdado P. Macapagal (president of the Philippines, 1961–65); studied economics at Georgetown University in Washington, DC; graduated magna cum laude from Assumption College, Manila, 1968; Ateneo de Manila University, MA in economics, 1978; University of the Philippines, PhD in economics, 1986; m. Mike Arroyo; children: 3. ❖ Was a university professor when appointed undersecretary of trade and industry by Corazon Aquino; won a seat in the Senate (1992); was reelected (1995) and wrote 55 laws on economic and social reform; following election to the vice presidency (1998), was named secretary of social welfare and development; when scandal began to embroil the president, Joseph Estrada, resigned the Cabinet post to oppose him (2000); when Estrada resigned, became the 14th president of the Philippines (2001).

ARROYO, Martina (1935—). African-American soprano. Born Feb 2, 1935, in New York, NY; studied with Marinka Gurevich and at Hunter College with Joseph Turnau. ❖ Was co-winner of Metropolitan Opera Auditions with Grace Bumbry (1958); debuted at Metropolitan Opera (1959) as the Celestial Voice in *Don Carlos;* appeared in Vienna, Frankfurt, Berlin and Zurich (1963–68) and at Covent Garden (1968–80); excelled in Verdi operas that called for a lirico-spinto soprano voice, especially as Aïda, Amelia (in *Un ballo in maschera*), Leonora (in *La forza del destino*), and Donna Anna and Donna Elvira (in *Don Giovanni*). ❖ See also *Women in World History.*

ARSENAULT, Samantha (1981—). American swimmer. Born Oct 11, 1981, in Peabody, Massachusetts; attended University of Michigan. ❖ Won a gold medal for 800-meter freestyle relay at Sydney Olympics (2000).

ARSIENNIEVA, Natalia (1903—). Belarussian poet. Born in Baku, Azerbaijan, Nov 20, 1903; studied at University of Vilna; m. an officer of the Polish Army. ❖ Known for her nationalistic writing, lived in Poland (1922–40), before Soviet occupation authorities deported her as a "bourgeois nationalist intellectual" to Kazakhstan; was released after Belarussian intellectuals protested; landed in a German displaced persons camp (1945); immigrated to US (1950), where she continued to write and publish in émigré journals.

ARSINDE (fl. 934–957). French countess and ruler. Born in Carcassonne (southwestern France); died in 957 in Carcassonne; dau. of Acfred II, count of Carcassonne; m. Arnaud de Comminges; children: at least one surviving son, Roger (later Roger I of Carcassonne). ❖ Born into the ruling feudal house of Carcassonne, in what is now southwestern France; inherited title and lands on death of father (934); held complete control of her homeland as countess for 23 years. ❖ See also *Women in World History.*

ARSINOE (fl. 4th c. BCE). Egyptian princess. Name variations: Arsinoë. Born during 4th century BCE; m. Lagus (Loqus); children: Ptolemy I Soter of Egypt. ❖ The 1st Arsinoe of the Ptolemaic dynasty, was a concubine of Philip II of Macedon; presented by him in marriage to a Macedonian soldier named Lagus shortly before the birth of her son, Ptolemy I Soter. ❖ See also *Women in World History.*

ARSINOE I (d. 247 BCE). Egyptian princess. Birth date unknown; died 247 BCE; dau. of Lysimachus, king of Thrace, and Nicaea (dau. of Macedonian general Antipater); became 1st wife of Ptolemy II Philadelphus (r. 285–247 BCE), c. 285; children: Ptolemy III Euergetes; Berenice Syra (c. 280–246 BCE); and others. ❖ Accused of conspiring against husband Ptolemy II Philadelphus, who may have already been contemplating a 2nd marriage with his sister (Arsinoe II Philadelphus), was banished to Coptos, in Upper Egypt (c. 275 BCE). ❖ See also *Women in World History.*

ARSINOE II PHILADELPHUS (c. 316–270 BCE). Egyptian queen. Name variations: Arsinoë II Philadelphos ("Philadelphus" was added after last marriage). Probably born in 316 BCE; died 270 BCE; oldest child of Ptolemy I Soter and Berenice I (c. 345–275 BCE); m. Lysimachus (the 60-year-old monarch of Macedonia, Thrace, and Anatolia in order to secure an alliance for her father), in 300; m. Ptolemy Ceraunus (her half brother); m. Ptolemy II Philadelphus (her full brother, c. 275 BCE); children: (1st m.) 3 sons, including Ptolemy. ❖ Was daughter of Ptolemy I (founder of the Macedonian dynasty that ruled Egypt for almost 300 years) and 3 times a queen; little is known about her before c. 283 when she became embroiled in the vicious dynastic struggle that threatened Lysimachus' realm and led to his death (281); with her 3 sons, fled Lysimachus' Asian domain for the European city of Cassandrea, in which she fortified herself awaiting the opportunity to foster her children's interests; while there, was offered marriage by Ptolemy Ceraunus, though this was nothing but a ploy, for this Ptolemy only proposed in order to murder Arsinoe's sons and thus fortify his claim to the dead Lysimachus' realm; though her oldest son escaped (fearing treachery, he fled before the carnage), witnessed the slaughter of her 2 other sons (280–279); immediately thereafter, sought refuge in Egypt; eventually married her full brother, Ptolemy II (c. 275), 8 years her junior; had a successful and popular joint reign that ended with her death (270); her memory lived on, especially since she received divine honors while still alive—at that time a novel development in a rapidly changing world. ❖ See also *Women in World History.*

ARSINOE III (fl. c. 250–210/05 BCE). Egyptian princess. Birth date unknown; died between 210 and 205 BCE; dau. of Ptolemy III Euergetes and Berenice II of Cyrene (c. 273–221 BCE); (following a Pharaonic practice) sister and wife of Ptolemy IV Philopator; children: Ptolemy V Epiphanes. ❖ With her presence, greatly encouraged the troops at battle of Raphia in 4th Syrian War (217), in which Antiochus III the Great was defeated; was put to death by brother-husband Ptolemy IV Philopator to please his mistress Agathocleia, a Samian dancer. ❖ See also *Women in World History.*

ARSINOE IV (d. 41 BCE). Queen of Egypt. Birth date unknown; killed at Miletus in 41 BCE; youngest dau. of Ptolemy XI Auletes; sister of Cleopatra VII, Ptolemy XII, and Ptolemy XIII. ❖ During Caesar's siege of Alexandria (48 BCE), was looked on by the Egyptians as sole queen (47 BCE); was captured by Caesar and led triumphantly through Rome; though eventually allowed to return to Alexandria, her years were brief; after battle of Philippi, was put to death at Miletus (or in temple of Artemis at Ephesus) by order of Marc Antony, at request of her sister Cleopatra. ❖ See also *Women in World History.*

ARTAMONOVA, Evguenia (1975—). Soviet volleyball player. Name variations: Yevgeniya Artamonova. Born July 17, 1975, in Ekaterinburg, Russia. ❖ Outside hitter, made debut on national team (1991); won European team championship (1993, 1997, 1999) and World Grand Prix (1997, 1999, 2002); placed 3rd at World championships (1994, 1998, 2002); won a team silver medal at Barcelona Olympics (1992), team silver at Sydney Olympics (2000), and team silver at Athens Olympics (2004). Named Best Player of Europe (1998).

ARTEMISIA I (c. 520–? BCE). Queen of Halicarnassus (present-day Turkey). Born c. 520 BCE; died after 480 BCE; dau. of Lygdamis of Halicarnassus. ❖ Under the umbrella of the Persian Empire, ruled much of southwestern Anatolia; when Xerxes invaded Greece (480), went along with a naval contingent which was the 2nd largest of the many which composed the Persian navy; though she warned Xerxes not to fight a naval battle in the strait between the coast of Attica and the island of Salamis, when the battle occurred, fought bravely; after the battle, returned to Asia with Xerxes and continued to rule over the lands she had inherited. ❖ See also *Women in World History.*

ARTEMISIA II (c. 395–351 BCE). Carian queen. Born c. 395; died in 351 BCE; oldest dau. and perhaps primary heir of Hekatomnus (Hekatomnos), the 1st Carian to rule over his native land as a satrap of the Persian Empire; sister of Ada (c. 380–323 BCE), Idreus, and Pixodarus; m. full-brother, Mausolus, c. 377 BCE. ❖ Carian daughter of Hekatomnus, was a devoted wife, co-ruler, and the primary patron behind the construction of the Mausoleum—one of the Seven Wonders of the ancient world; helped secure her family's claim to a more independent Caria, albeit without breaking away from the Persian Empire; with husband, helped frustrate the renewal of the Athenian imperial vision, which took concrete form in the 2nd Delian Confederacy; after Mausolus' death (353 BCE), devoted the rest of her life to glorifying his memory in the form of the "Mausoleum," a burial compound so large and magnificent that it became one of the most common tourist destinations in the ancient world; died of grief over the loss of her husband (351 BCE), her reign as the lone satrap of Caria lasting but 2 years; after her death, her authority passed without incident to the joint reign of her brother and sister—respectively, Idrieus and Ada, who, like Mausolus and Artemisia, were husband and wife; these were followed on the satrapal throne of Caria by Pixodarus, the youngest of Artemisia's siblings. ❖ See also *Women in World History.*

ARTESHINA, Olga (1982—). Russian basketball player. Born Nov 27, 1982, in Samara, USSR. ❖ Forward, won a team bronze medal at Athens Olympics (2004); placed 2nd at World championships (2002) and 1st at European championships (2003).

ARTHUR, Bea (1923—). American actress. Name variations: Beatrice Arthur. Born Bernice Frankel, May 13, 1923, in New York, NY; raised in Maryland; m. Robert Alan Arthur (div.); m. Gene Saks (director), 1950 (div. 1978); children: (2nd m.) Matthew (b. 1961) and Daniel (b. 1964). ❖ Was a regular on Sid Caesar's show, "Caesar's Hour" (1950s); appeared on stage in *Threepenny Opera;* came to prominence as Yente the Matchmaker in *Fiddler on the Roof* (1964); appeared on the sitcom "All in the Family" as Maude Findlay (1971), which led to her own series, "Maude" (1972–78); appeared on "The Golden Girls" (1985–92). Won a Tony award for performance as Vera Charles in *Mame.*

ARTHUR, Charthel (1946—). American ballet dancer. Born Oct 8, 1946, in Los Angeles, California. ❖ Began apprenticeship at Joffrey Ballet (1965) and became a company member soon thereafter; danced featured roles in company revivals of Fokine's *Petrouchka,* Joos' *The Green Table,* Massine's *Le Beau Danue,* and Robbins' *Interplay,* among others; performed in Joffrey's *Pas des Déesse* and the premiere of *Remembrances;* also appeared in John Cranko's *Pineapple Poll,* Ruthanna Boris' *Cakewalk,* Gerald Arpino's *Trinity, Cello Concerto,* and *Viva Vivaldi!.*

ARTHUR, Daphne (1925—). English stage, tv, and screen actress. Born Mar 6, 1925, in London, England. ❖ Made stage debut with York Rep as Joan in *Lord Babs* (1943); made London debut as Margaret Knox in *Fanny's First Play* (1944); subsequently appeared as Gwen in *Trespass,* Jean Fane in *A Man Must Die,* Lady Caroline Lamb in *Caro William,* and Margaret in *The Holly and the Ivy,* for which she won the Clarence Derwent award (1950); films include *That Dangerous Age.*

ARTHUR, Ellen Herndon (1837–1880). American philanthropist. Born Ellen Lewis Herndon, Aug 30, 1837, in Culpeper, Virginia; died Jan 12, 1880, in New York, NY; only child of Frances Elizabeth (Hansbrough) Herndon and William Lewis Herndon (explorer of the Amazon); m. Chester Alan Arthur (later president of US), Oct 25, 1859; children: William Lewis Herndon (b. 1860, lived only 3 years); Chester Alan Jr. (b. 1864); Ellen Arthur (b. 1871). ❖ A gifted singer, lent her talent to countless charities, and her philanthropic efforts were well known and admired; died one year before husband took office as president. ❖ See also *Women in World History.*

ARTHUR, Jean (1900–1991). American actress. Born Gladys Georgianna Greene, Oct 17, 1900, in Plattsburg, NY; died June 19, 1991, in Carmel, California; dau. of a NY photographer; m. Julian Anker, 1928 (annulled 1928); m. Frank J. Ross Jr., 1932 (div. 1949). ❖ Made film debut in a supporting role in John Ford's silent *Cameo Kirby* (1923), then made one forgettable movie after another, mostly for Paramount; dissatisfied with roles, returned to NY (1931) to hone acting skills; played leads in short-run stage productions: *Foreign Affairs, The Man Who Reclaimed His Head* and *The Curtain Rises* (1931–34); in Hollywood, reunited with Ford for breakthrough part in *The Whole Town's Talking* (1935); starred in 3 Frank Capra classics: *Mr. Deeds Goes to Town* (1936), *Mr. Smith Goes to Washington* (1939), and *You Can't Take It With You* (1938); also appeared in *Public Hero Number One* (1935), *Diamond Jim* (1935), *The Ex-Mrs. Bradford* (1936), *The Devil and Miss Jones* (1941), and *The Talk of the Town* (1942); when contract expired (1944), walked away from Columbia; made only 2 more films: *A Foreign Affair* for Billy Wilder (1948), followed by her masterful swan song in *Shane* (1953); scored a major success on Broadway in *Peter Pan* (1955) and had a short-lived tv series "The Jean Arthur Show" (1966). Won an Academy Award nomination for Best Actress for *The More the Merrier* (1943). ❖ See also *Women in World History.*

ARTHUR, Julia (1869–1950). Canadian-born actress. Born Ida Lewis, May 3, 1869, in Hamilton, Ontario, Canada; died Mar 29, 1950, in Boston, Massachusetts; m. Benjamin Pierce Cheney, Feb 23, 1898. ❖ Had 1st success as Queen Fortunetta in *The Black Masque of the Red Death* at Union Square Theatre, NY (1891); appeared with A.M. Palmer's stock company in a number of works, including the lead opposite Maurice Barrymore in *Lady Windermere's Fan* (1893); appeared on London stage with Sir Henry Irving's Lyceum Theatre company; organized her own company and starred in *A Lady of Quality* (1897); worked for Red Cross during WWI; made film debut as Edith Cavell in *The Woman the Germans Shot* (1918); retired from stage (1924).

ARTIUKHINA, Alexandra (1889–1969). *See Artyukhina, Aleksandra.*

ARTOIS, countess of.
See Amicie de Courtenay (d. 1275).
See Jeanne I of Burgundy (c. 1291–1330).
See Jeanne II of Burgundy (1308–1347).
See Agnes of Bourbon (d. 1287).
See Margaret of Artois (d. 1382).
See Maude of Brabant (1224–1288).
See Maude of Brabant (fl. 1240s).

ARTÔT, Désirée (1835–1907). Belgian soprano and mezzo-soprano. Name variations: Joséphine Désirée Artôt; Desiree Artot. Born Marguerite-Joséphine Désirée Montagney in Paris, France, July 21, 1835; died in Berlin, Germany, April 3, 1907; dau. of Jean Désiré Montagney (1803–1887, a horn player whose professional name was Artôt); studied with Pauline Viardot in London; m. Mariano Padilla y Ramos (singer), 1864; children: daughter, Lola Artôt de Padilla (1876–1933), also a well-known singer. ❖ Appeared throughout continental Europe; promoted by composer Giacomo Meyerbeer, appeared as Fidès (1858); toured France and Belgium as Rosina and Leonora in *Il trovatore;* performed in Italy and at the Victor Theater in Berlin (1859); sang at Her Majesty's Theatre in London (1863) and appeared at Covent Garden (1864); following marriage (1869), performed opera with husband in Germany, Austria, and Russia. ❖ See also *Women in World History.*

ARTYUKHINA, Aleksandra (1889–1969). Soviet politician and champion of women's rights. Name variations: Aleksandra Vasil'evna Artiukina; Alexandra Vasilevna or Vasilyevna Artyukhina; Alexandra Artiukhina. Born in 1889 in Russia; died in 1969 in Soviet Union. ❖ Politician and early champion of women's rights in Soviet Union, worked in textile factory in pre-revolutionary Russia and was active in union movement; was arrested by tsarist government several times for political activities; held various government posts after Russian Revolution (1917); appointed head of *zhenotdel* (Department of Working Women and Peasant Women), women's section of Communist Party of Soviet Union (1927); helped continue work of *zhenotdel* comrades Alexandra Kollantai and others, organizing literacy schools, publishing weekly bulletin and monthly journal *Kommunitska* (The Communist Woman), instructing women of newly-won rights and deepening political awareness (and cooperation); pressed for and won changes to support women's role as worker outside of the home in rapidly industrializing country including state-run childcare and dining facilities; lost position when *zhenotdel* was shut down by Stalinists who did not wish discussion of conditions of life nor change in male dominance of political power; continued to hold government positions but these were more honorific than real. ❖ See also Carmen Scheide, "Born in October: The Life and Thought of Aleksandra Vasil'evna Artyukina 1889–1969" in Melanie Ilic ed., *Women in the Stalin Era* (Macmillan, 2001).

ARUNDALE, Sybil (1882–1965). English actress. Born Sybil Kelly, June 20, 1882, in London, England; died Sept 5, 1965, in London; sister of Grace Arundale. ❖ Performed in music halls with sister Grace as the Sisters Arundale; while continuing to work in music halls, appeared on stage as Oberon in *Midsummer Night's Dream*, Lady Molly Martingale in *My Lady Molly*, Gina Ekdal in *The Wild Duck*, Jennifer in *The Young Idea*; toured Malta with her own company (1931); was a prominent member of the BBC repertory (1939–42); with Herbert Jay, was responsible for building the Embassy Theater (1928).

ARUNDEL, Ann (1557–1630). Countess of Arundel. Name variations: Ann or Anne Arundell; Anne Howard. Born Mar 21, 1557; died April 19, 1630, at Shifmal Manor, Shropshire, England; dau. of Thomas Dacre, 4th Lord Dacre of Gilsland, and Elizabeth Leyburne; m. Philip Howard, 17th earl of Arundel, 1571 (died in the Tower of London, Nov 1595); children: Thomas Howard (1585-1646), earl of Arundel.

ARUNDEL, Anne (d. 1642). English noblewoman. Name variations: Lady Baltimore; Arundell. Born in England; died in England in 1642; dau. of a Roman Catholic peer; m. Cecil Calvert, 2nd Lord Baltimore (1606–1675), 1629. ❖ As the wife of Cecil Calvert, the 1st lord proprietor of Maryland, her name still marks Anne Arundel County, Maryland, though neither she nor her husband ever set foot on American soil. ❖ See also *Women in World History*.

ARUNDEL, Blanche (1583–1649). English noblewoman. Name variations: Lady Blanche Arundell; Blanche Somerset, Baroness Arundell of Wardour. Born 1583 in Worcester, England; died 1649; 6th of 7 daughters of Edward, 4th earl of Worcester, and Elizabeth (3rd and youngest dau. of Francis Hastings, 2nd earl of Huntingdon); m. Thomas, 2nd Lord Arundel of Wardour, in Wiltshire; children: Henry, 3rd Baron Arundel (1606?–1694); Catherine (who m. Francis Corwallis); Anne (who m. Roger Vaughan); and Clara (who m. Humphrey Weld of Lulworth Castle in Dorsetshire). ❖ Was born into the ruling family of Worcestershire and married Thomas, lord of Arundel; was responsible for economic and financial management of husband's extensive lands, as well as the health and well-being of all the officials, peasants, servants, and laborers who lived on those lands; saw husband only rarely, as he was absent from home while serving King Charles I at court or at war; during civil war (1643), had to handle the consequences of husband's political and military machinations, for his enemies were a constant threat to the safety of her household; when Sir Edward Hungerford approached her residence, Wardour Castle, with a few soldiers and demanded admittance (1643), refused; when he returned with a Parliamentary force of 1,300 men, still refused; under bombardment for six days and nights, finally surrendered but on her terms (though the Parliamentary force immediately broke the treaty). ❖ See also *Women in World History*.

ARUNDEL, countess of.
See Fitzalan, Alice (fl. 1285).
See Fitzalan, Alice (d. around 1338).
See Eleanor Plantagenet (c. 1318–1372).
See Fitzalan, Elizabeth (d. 1385).
See Mortimer, Philippa (1375–1401).
See Beatrice of Portugal (d. 1439).
See Woodville, Margaret (fl. 1450s).
See Percy, Anne (fl. 1470s).
See Neville, Joan (fl. 1480s).
See Fitzalan, Katherine (b. around 1520).
See Fitzalan, Mary (d. 1557).
See Arundel, Ann (d. 1630).

ARUSMONT, Frances Wright d' (1795–1852). *See Wright, Frances.*

ARVANITAKI, Angélique (1901–1983). French neurobiologist. Name variations: Angélique Arvanitaki; Angélique or Angelique Arvanitaki-Chalanozitis; Angélique Arvanitaki Chalanozitis; Angélique Chalanozitis. Born 1901 in Cairo, Egypt; died 1983 in France; University of Lyons, PhD (1938); m. Nicolas Chalanozitis (physician and scientist). ❖ Played instrumental role in developing field of cellular neurophysiology; worked for most of career at Oceanographic Museum of Monaco; collaborated at times with husband; worked on giant nerve endings of squid and developed technique for studying nerve cells of sea-slug *Aplysia;* provided major impetus to understanding cellular mechanisms of neural functioning; groundbreaking studies include: "Effects Evoked in an Axon by the Activity of a Contiguous One" (1942) and "Excitatory and Inhibitory Processes Initiated by Light and Infra-red Radiations in Single Identifiable Nerve Cells (Giant Ganglion Cells of Aplysia)" (1961).

ARVELO, Enriqueta (1886–1963). *See Arvelo Larriva, Enriqueta.*

ARVELO LARRIVA, Enriqueta (1886–1963). Venezuelan poet. Name variations: Enriqueta Arvelo. Born Enriqueta Arvelo Larriva in 1886 in Barinitas, Venzuela; died 1962 in Venezuela; sister of Alfredo Arvelo Larriva (poet); self-educated. ❖ As a poet, walked in the shadow of her brother; championed a number of causes, including the opportunity for women to live in liberation and, through the Viernes Group, the right of minorities to own land (Viernes was also concerned with the recovery of native myth, tradition and legend); works include *El cristal nervioso* (The Narrow Mirror, 1931), *Poemas perseverantes* (Persistent Poems, 1963), and *Mandato del canto* (Mandate of the Song, 1957).

ARVIDSON, Linda (1884–1949). American actress. Name variations: Linda A. Griffith. Born Linda Arvidson Johnson, 1884, in San Francisco, California; died July 26, 1949, in New York, NY; m. D.W. Griffith (motion-picture director), 1906 (div. 1936). ❖ As 1st wife of movie director David Wark Griffith, played leads in many of his early silents and contributed a valuable look at his early work with her autobiography *When the Movies Were Young* (1925); also starred in her own screenplay of *Enoch Arden* (1911); other films include *The Adventures of Dollie* (1908), *Balked at the Altar* (1909), *After Many Years* (1909), *An Awful Moment* (1909), *The Test of Friendship* (1909), *The Helping Hand* (1909), *The Cord of Life* (1909), *Edgar Allan Poe* (1909), *The Politician's Love Story* (1909), *A Drunkard's Reformation* (1909), *The Cricket on the Hearth* (1909), *The Mills of the Gods* (1909), *Lines of White on a Sullen Sea* (1909), *Pippa Passes, The Day After* (1909), *The Rocky Road* (1910), *The Converts* (1910), *The Unchanging Sea* (1910), *Fisher Folks* (1911), *The Scarlet Letter* (1913), *A Fair Rebel* (1914), *The Wife* (1914), *The Gambler of the West* (1915), and *Charity* (1916). ❖ See also *Women in World History.*

ARWA (1052–1137). Yemeni queen. Name variations: Sayyidah. Born 1052; died 1137 in Jiblah, Yemen; m. al-Mukarram Ahmad (Sulayhid ruler), 1065 (died 1091); children: 4. ❖ Was a member of the Sulaihid Dynasty in southern Arabia; when husband became sultan, was handed power; ruling wisely, suppressed tribal disputes, strengthened trade and agriculture, lowered prices, and supervised tax-collection; commanded that capital of Yemen be moved to Dhu Jibla (1088); after husband died and her rule was threatened, married his successor and maintained power; her death brought end to Sulaihid power in the region. ❖ See also *Women in World History.*

ARYIRIADOU, Hrisoula (1901–1998). *See Argiriadou, Chryssoula.*

ARZHANNIKOVA, Tatiana (1964—). Russian gymnast. Born Nov 20, 1964, in Vitebsk, Belarus. ❖ At World championships, won gold medals for all-around team (1978, 1981); won Simo Sappinen Memorial (1977).

ARZNER, Dorothy (1897–1979). American director. Born in San Francisco, California, Jan 3, 1897; died in La Quinta, California, Oct 1, 1979; only dau. and one of two children of Louis Arzner (restaurant manager); graduated from the private Westlake girls' school, 1915; studied pre-med at University of Southern California, 1915–1917; lived with Marion Morgan (dancer and choreographer); never married; no children. ❖ The only woman director of the era, who developed a substantial body of work within the Hollywood system; became a cutter and editor at Realart, subsidiary of Paramount, cutting 32 movies in one year and becoming chief editor; edited Rudolph Valentino's *Blood and Sand* (1922); edited and was sometimes scriptwriter for several pictures for James Cruze: *The Covered Wagon, Ruggles of Red Gap, Merton of the Movies* and *Old Ironsides*; made directoral debut with the light comedy *Fashions for Women*, starring Esther Ralston (1927), followed by *Ten Modern Commandments* (1927); signed a long-term contract with Paramount; directed Clara Bow in *Get Your Man* and in Paramount's 1st talkie *The Wild Party;* because Bow was nervous with the new medium of sound, reputedly took a microphone and put it on a fishpole to give the actress freedom of movement (thus, the boom was born); moved to RKO to direct Katharine Hepburn's 2nd film, *Christopher Strong;* signed as an associate producer at Columbia and embarked on her most successful film, *Craig's Wife* (1934); was the 1st woman admitted to the Director's Guild of America and the 1st to insist that directors have control over their films; took over an RKO production of *Dance, Girl, Dance* (1940), starring Lucille Ball and Maureen O'Hara, now recognized as her best-known film; other films include *Sarah and Son, Anybody's Women, Honor among Lovers,* the imaginative *Working Girls, Merrily We Go to Hell, Nana, The Last of Mrs. Cheyney, The Bride Wore Red* and *First Comes Courage.* ❖ See also Judith Mayne, *Directed by Dorothy Arzner* (Indiana University Press, 1994); and *Women in World History.*

ASA (c. 800–c. 850). Norwegian queen and regent. Born c. 800 in Agdir, Norway; died c. 850 in Agdir; dau. of King Harald Redbeard of Agdir; m. King Gudrod of Vestfold; children: one son, Halfdan "the Swarthy," king of Agdir. ❖ Born into royal family of Agdir, was kidnapped and forced to marry Gudrod of Vestfold who was responsible for the death of her father; gave birth to son Halfdan, then supposedly murdered Gudrod to avenge father and took child back to Agdir, where, as heir to his grandfather, the infant was made king; ruled as regent for son until he came of age. ❖ See also *Women in World History.*

ASAKAWA, Hitomi (1948). Japanese ballet dancer. Born Oct 13, 1948, in Kochi, Japan; trained with Nishino Ballet and school. ❖ Joined Ballet du XXième Siècle in Belgium (mid-1960s), later becoming a member of Maurice Béjart's company; danced principal roles such as "Siva" in Béjart's *Bhakti* (1970) and Juliet in *Romeo and Juliet.*

ASAKAWA, Takako (1938—). Japanese dancer and choreographer. Born Feb 23, 1938, in Tokyo, Japan; m. David Hatch Walker (choreographer and dancer). ❖ Came to New York City early in career with the revue, *Holiday in Japan;* was a member of the Graham Company (1962–79), creating roles in Graham works, including *Archaic Hours* (1969), *Adorations* (1975), and *Eagles* (1976), and Yuriko's *Wind Drum* (1965); performed briefly with Alvin Ailey Dance Theater; founded her own company, Asakawalker, with husband (1970). Choreographed works include *Fantasy II* (1972), *Eclipse* (1973), *Ambrosia* (1974), *Reflections of Romance* (1977), and *Opalescence* (1978).

ASANOVA, Dinara (1942–1985). Soviet filmmaker. Born Nov 24, 1942, in Kirghizia, one of the 15 republics of the USSR, located in central Asia (now Bishkek, Kazakhstan); died April 4, 1985, in Murmansk, USSR; attended VGIK (All-union State Institute of Cinematography). ❖ Began film career in her national studio, Kirgizfilm, before becoming one of the few non-Russians to be accepted into the prestigious VGIK, the Soviet Union's premiere film school; one of the most notable Soviet directors of her time, made 9 feature films that were critically and financially successful, including *Tough Kids* (Patsany, 1983). ❖ See also *Women in World History.*

ASANTEWAA, Yaa (c. 1850–1921). See Yaa Asantewaa.

ASCARELLI, Devora (fl. 1601). Jewish poet of Italy. Birth and death dates unknown; m. Joseph Ascarelli, a merchant. ❖ An active participant in Italian Renaissance, devoted much of her time to the religious education of her community by preparing translations of hymns and other religious works from Hebrew into Italian; gained considerable fame for her translations, yet proved herself a talented poet as well, publishing verse on various religious themes in Italian.

ASCHAM, Margaret Howe (c. 1535–1590). English letter writer. Born Margaret Howe c. 1535 in England; died in England in 1590; m. humanist scholar Roger Ascham (1515–1568). ❖ After husband's death (1568), arranged for the publication of his final work, a treatise

on practical education published as *The Scholemaster* (*The Schoolmaster*), which quickly became a seminal text of humanism, and remains one of the most important documents of 16th-century humanist thought. ❖ See also *Women in World History.*

ASCHE, Mrs. Oscar (1876–1953). See Brayton, Lily.

ASCLEPIGNIA (c. 375–?). Greek philosopher and educator. Born in Athens c. 375; dau. of Plutarch the Younger of Athens (philosopher and founder of a school following the pagan philosophy of Plotinus who died in 430); sister of Hierius. ❖ Was a teacher and then director at Plutarch's school; was a contemporary of Hypatia, with whom she expounded different versions of Plotinus' teaching; was also a teacher of Proclus, who revolutionized Plotinian doctrine, bolstering it against the popularity of Christianity. ❖ See also *Women in World History.*

ASCUE, Anne (c. 1521–1546). See Askew, Anne.

ASENATH. Egyptian woman of the Bible. Dau. of Potipherah, priest of On or Heliopolis; m. Joseph (Gen. 41:45); children: Manasseh and Ephraim. ❖ See also *Women in World History.*

ASENSIO, Manola (1946—). Swiss ballet dancer. Born May 7, 1946, in Lausanne, Switzerland. ❖ Made debut at Geneva's Grand Théâtre, Switzerland; danced with Het National Ballet in Amsterdam and the New York City Ballet; was a member of Harkness Youth and later Harkness Ballet Company (1969–72), where she performed in contemporary repertory including Ben Stevenson's *Bartok Concerto* and *Three Preludes,* Brian MacDonald's *Firebird* and Vincente Nebrada's *Sebastien;* returned to classical repertory at London Festival Ballet in company productions of *The Nutcracker, The Sleeping Beauty, Giselle,* and others.

ASH, Caroline (1925—). See Pearce, Caroline.

ASH, Maie (b. 1888). English actress. Born May 31, 1888, in London, England; m. Stanley Brett (div. 1913). ❖ Made stage debut at the Shaftesbury as Lily in *A Little Un-fairy Princess* (1902); plays include *The Cherry Girl, My Darling, The Gay Gordons* and *Goody Two-Shoes.*

ASH, Mary Kay (1918–2001). American entrepreneur. Born Mary Kathlyn Wagner, May 12, 1918, in Hot Wells, Texas; died Nov 22, 2001, in Dallas, Texas; m. Ben Rogers (Houston radio personality, div.); m. Mel Ash (sales representative), 1966 (died 1980); children: 3, including Marilyn Theard (died 1991) and Richard Rogers (co-founder, chair and CEO of Mary Kay Inc.). ❖ Founder & CEO of Mary Kay cosmetics; known as the high priestess of pink; was one of the most famous women in American business; served as national sales director for World Gifts (1949–63); intent on empowering herself and other women, bought a formulation for a skin-care cream and founded Mary Kay Cosmetics (1963), with a sales force of 11 that grew to more than 750,000, mostly women, in 37 countries; retired as its chair (1987); wrote the bestsellers *Mary Kay on People Management* (1984) and *Mary Kay—You Can Have It All* (1995). ❖ See also autobiography *Mary Kay* (1981).

ASHANTI, Queen of the.
See Afua Koba (fl. 1834–1884).
See Pokou (c. 1700–1760).

ASHBRIDGE, Elizabeth (1713–1755). British autobiographer. Born in 1713 in Middlewich, Cheshire, England; died May 16, 1755, in Ireland; dau. of Mary and Thomas Sampson; m. three times, including Aaron Ashbridge in 1746. ❖ *Some Account of the Fore Part of the Life of Elizabeth Ashbridge* was published in 1774. ❖ See also *Women in World History.*

ASHBROOK, Jean (1934—). American politician. Born Emily Jean Spencer in Cincinnati, Ohio, Sept 21, 1934; graduated from Ohio State University, 1956; m. John M. Ashbrook (served 11 terms as US congressional representative, died April 24, 1982). ❖ Republican of Ohio, 97th Congress (June 29, 1982–Jan 3, 1983), won special election to finish husband's term in US House of Representatives; during tenure, introduced a bill that would have denied federal-law enforcement or criminal-justice assistance to any jurisdictions that implemented certain gun-control ordinances, and another to prescribe mandatory minimum sentences for anyone convicted of federal felonies against senior citizens; after 6 months in office, her seat was eliminated through reapportionment and redistricting.

ASHBY, Margery Corbett (1882–1981). See Corbett-Ashby, Margery.

ASHCRAFT, Juanita (1921—2000). Assistant secretary in the US Air Force. Born probably Dec 3, 1921; probably died Sept 5, 2000, in Hanford, California. ❖ Served on the California State Employment Board and as an assistant appointments secretary to Ronald Reagan, then governor of California; appointed as an assistant secretary for manpower and reserve affairs by President Gerald Ford (1976), the highest civilian appointive position which had ever been bestowed on a woman in the US Air Force.

ASHCROFT, Peggy (1907–1991). English actress. Born Edith Margaret Emily Ashcroft in Croydon, Surrey, England, Dec 22, 1907; died in England, June 14, 1991; dau. of William Worsley Ashcroft and Violetta Maud (Bernheim) Ashcroft; attended Central School of Dramatic Art under the tutelage of Elsie Fogerty; m. Rupert Charles Hart-Davis (publisher, div.); m. Theodore Komisarjevsky (Russian director and architect, div.); m. Jeremy Nicholas Hutchinson (lawyer), 1940 (div.); children: (3rd m.) son Nicholas (director) and daughter Eliza. ❖ One of the finest English actresses of her day, made stage debut at Birmingham Rep as Margaret in *Dear Brutus;* 1st appeared in London as Bessie in *One Day More* (1927); dazzled critics as Naomi in *Jew Süss* (1929), then appeared as Desdemona opposite Paul Robeson's Othello; performed regularly at Old Vic (1932–33); played Juliet in *Romeo and Juliet,* Portia in *The Merchant of Venice,* Irina in *The Three Sisters,* Lady Teazle in *The School for Scandal,* and the queen in *Richard II;* also emerged as one of the great interpreters of Chekhov; starred in *Edward, My Son* (1947) and *The Heiress* (1949); appeared at Shakespeare Memorial Theater (1949–56); made NY debut as Lise in *High Tor* (1937); had another triumph in title role in *Hedda Gabler* (1954); played Margaret of Anjou in *The War of the Roses* (1963); also appeared in *Happy Days, The Chalk Garden* and *The Deep Blue Sea;* made film debut in *The Wandering Jew* (1933); other films include *The Thirty-nine Steps* (1939), *The Nun's Story* (1958), *Sunday, Bloody Sunday* (1971), and *Joseph Andrews* (1976); tv appearances included roles in *The Cherry Orchard* (1962), *Rosmersholm* (1965), *Dear Liar* (1966), *Edward and Mrs. Simpson* (1978), *Little Eyolf* (1982), *The Jewel in the Crown* (1984) and *A Perfect Spy* (1987); named director of Royal Shakespeare Company (1968). Won Ellen Terry Award for performance in *Edward My Son* (1947); named Commander of the British Empire (1951), then Dame Commander of the British Empire (1956); received British Academy of Film and Television Arts Award for Frau Messner in *Caught on a Train* and for Jean Wilsher in *Cream in my Coffee* (both 1980) and British Theater Association Special Award for her career in the theater (1983); won British Academy of Film and Theater Arts Award for performance in *The Jewel in the Crown* (1984); won British Academy of Film and Television Arts Award, Academy Award, Golden Globe Award, and NY Film Critics' Circle Award, all for Best Supporting Actress for performance as Mrs. Moore in *A Passage to India* (1984, 1985); given Special Laurence Olivier Award for Lifetime Achievement in the Theater (1991). ❖ See also Robert Tanitch, *Ashcroft* (Hutchinson, 1987); and *Women in World History.*

ASHER, Elise (c. 1912–2004). American poet and painter. Name variations: Elise Kunitz; Mrs. Stanley Kunitz. Born c. 1912 in Chicago, Illinois; died Mar 7, 2004, in New York, NY; attended Art Institute of Chicago; graduate of Simmons School of Social Work; m. Stanley Kunitz (poet laureate of US), 1958. ❖ Had a solo show at Tanager Gallery in NY (1953); published collection of poetry, *The Meandering Absolute* (1955) and *The Visionary Gleam: Texts and Transformations* (1994), which included her paintings.

ASHER, Katherine Te Rongokahira (1873–1939). See *Parata, Katherine Te Rongokahira.*

ASHER, Maata Mahupuku (1890–1952). See *Mahupuku, Maata.*

ASHERSON, Renée (1915—). English actress. Born Renée Ascherson in London, England, May 19, 1915; dau. of Charles Stephen Ascherman and Dorothy Lilian (Wiseman) Ascherman; educated in Maltman's Green, Gerrard's Cross, Switzerland, and Anjou, France; studied for the stage at the Webber-Douglas Dramatic School; m. Robert Donat (actor), 1953 (died 1958). ❖ Made stage debut at age 15, playing a walk-on in John Gielgud's production of *Romeo and Juliet;* mostly known for work on stage and tv, played Katherine in Laurence Olivier's film of *Henry V* (1944); other films include *The Way Ahead* (1944), *The Way to the Stars* (1944), *Caesar and Cleopatra* (1945), *The Small Back Room* (1949), *Pool of London* (1950), *Malta Story* (1953), *The Day the Earth Caught Fire* (1962), *Rasputin, the Mad Monk* (1966), *Theatre of Blood* (1973), and *A Man Called Intrepid* (1979).

ASHFORD, Daisy (1881-1972). British children's author. Born Margaret Mary Julia Ashford, April 7, 1881, in Petersham, Surrey, England; died in Hellesdon, Norwich, England, Jan 15, 1972; dau. of William Henry Roxburghe and Emma Georgina (Walker) Ashford; m. James Devlin, 1920. ❖ At 8, wrote *The Young Visiters* (1889), which appeared years later and achieved enormous success (1919), though her identity was not revealed until after her death. ❖ See also *Women in World History.*

ASHFORD, Evelyn (1957—). African-American runner. Born April 15, 1957, in Shreveport, Louisiana; m. Ray Washington. ❖ Competed at Montreal Olympics (1976); won World Cup sprints (1981, 1983); at Los Angeles, won Olympic gold medals for 4x100-meter relay and 100 meters, the 1st woman to run under 11 seconds in Olympic history (1984); won Olympic gold medal in 4x100-meter relay and silver in the 100 meters at Seoul (1988); won Olympic gold medal in 4x100-meter relay at Barcelona (1992). Received Flo Hyman award, Women's Sports Foundation (1989). ❖ See also *Women in World History.*

ASHFORD, Margaret Mary (1881–1972). See *Ashford, Daisy.*

ASHFORD AND SIMPSON. See *Simpson, Valerie (b. 1948).*

ASHLEY, Edwina (1901–1960). See *Mountbatten, Edwina.*

ASHLEY, Elizabeth (1939—). American stage, tv, and screen actress. Born Elizabeth Ann Cole, Aug 30, 1939, in Ocala, Florida; m. James McCarthy (1976, div. 1981); m. James Farentino (actor), 1962 (div. 1965); m. George Peppard (actor), 1966 (div. 1972); children: Christian Peppard (writer). ❖ Appeared on Broadway as Corie Bratter in *Barefoot in the Park* (1963) and Maggie in *Cat on a Hot Tin Roof* (1974); made screen debut in *The Carpetbaggers* (1964), followed by *Ship of Fools, The Third Day, 92 in the Shade, Coma, Split Image, Dragnet* and *Vampire's Kiss,* among others; appeared as Aunt Frieda on tv's "Evening Shade" (1990–94). Won a Tony award for Best Actress for *Take Her She's Mine* (1962), her Broadway debut. ❖ See also autobiography *Actress—Postcards from the Road.*

ASHLEY, Jean (1939—). See *Crawford, Jean Ashley.*

ASHLEY, Laura (1925–1985). Welsh textile designer and entrepreneur. Born Laura Mountney in Wales, Sept 7, 1925; died in Wales, Sept 17, 1985; eldest of four children of Stan (civil service clerk) and Bessie (Davies) Mountney; m. Bernard Albert Ashley, Feb 1949; children: Laura Jane (b. 1953); David (b. 1954); Nick (b. 1956); Emma Mary Ashley (b. 1965). ❖ Designer who, with husband, built an international fashion and home-decoration business, specializing in prim necklines, muted Victorian prints, and long concealing skirts; unable to find fabrics with small prints, stripes, or flowers in one color, suitable for a patchwork quilt, set out to print her own, pouring over books to learn how to construct a silk screen; launched the fledgling Ashley Mountney Company, providing single-design table mats and scarves; by mid-'60s, had established a profitable factory and shop, Gwalia House, in Machynlleth, Wales, where she began experimenting with new prints and clothing design; moved to larger quarters in Carno, Wales; handled the design aspects of the business while husband took care of operations; formed Ashley Shops Ltd. expressly for retailing (1968), and opened the 1st "Laura Ashley" shop in London's Kensington district; by 1975, owned 40 shops and 3 factories, and employed 1,000 people worldwide; entered into licensing agreements with major US companies to produce "Laura Ashley" designs on sheets, wallpaper, and other home furnishings. ❖ See also Anne Sebba, *Laura Ashley: A Life by Design* (Weidenfeld & Nicolson, 1990); and *Women in World History.*

ASHLEY, Merrill (1950—). American ballet dancer. Name variations: Linda Merrill. Born Linda Michelle Merrill, Dec 2, 1950, in St. Paul, Minnesota; raised in Rutland, Vermont. ❖ Graduated from New York City Ballet school and joined the company (1966); performed in numerous Balanchine repertory works including *Square Dance, Divertimento No. 15, Symphony in C* and *Tchaikovsky Piano Concerto;* created roles in *Requiem Canticles* (1972), *Coppélia* (1974), *Cortège Hongrois* (1973), *Ballade* (1980), and others; also performed roles choreographed for her by Jerome Robbins and Twyla Tharp; retired from performance career (1997) to teach at New York City Ballet. ❖ See also autobiography *Dancing for Balanchine* (1984).

ASHLEY, Pauline (1932–2003). English political campaigner. Name variations: Lady Ashley of Stoke. Born Pauline Crispin, Aug 2, 1932, in Liverpool, England; died July 28, 2003; dau. of an insurance company manager; studied mathematics at Girton College, Cambridge; London

School of Economics, MA in social administration, 1977; m. Jack Ashley (Labour member of Parliament), c. 1952; children: 3 daughters, Jackie, Jane and Caroline Ashley. ❖ Campaigned often to improve the lives of the disadvantaged; served as deaf husband's adviser, researcher and tactician; wrote *The Money Problems of the Poor* (1983); founded Hearing Research Trust (1985) and was its chair for 10 years.

ASHOUR, Radwa (1946—). See Ashur, Radwa.

ASHRAWI, Hanan (1946—). Palestinian political leader. Name variations: Hanan Mikhail-Ashrawi. Born Hanan Mikhail in Ramallah, about 6 miles north of Jerusalem (which became the Israeli-occupied West Bank) in 1946; youngest of 5 daughters of Daoud (doctor) and Wad'ia Mikhail; attended American University in Beirut, Lebanon, MA in literature (1960s); received a doctorate in English literature at University of Virginia (1981); m. Emile Ashrawi (photographer, filmmaker, and artist); children: two daughters, Amal and Zeina. ❖ Was active in the General Union of Palestinian Students (GUPS); was the only woman from Lebanon on the GUPS delegation at an international conference in Amman, Jordan (1969); joined the teaching staff of Bir Zeit University in the West Bank (1973); rejoined the faculty at Bir Zeit as a professor of English, and became dean of the Faculty of Arts; known in some circles as the "Nightline Palestinian," sought self-determination for her people, espousing pragmatic approaches with calm and projecting an apparent willingness to reason, while continuing to appear on Western evening news shows; quit Palestinian Cabinet post as minister of Higher Education in protest over lack of accountability in the Palestinian government (1998). ❖ See also memoir *This Side of Peace: A Personal Account* (Simon & Schuster, 1995); Barbara Victor, *A Voice of Reason: Hanan Ashrawi and Peace in the Middle East* (Harcourt, Brace, 1994); and *Women in World History.*

ASHTON, Helen (1891–1958). British novelist. Born Helen Rosaline Ashton on Oct 18, 1891, in London, England; died in 1958; dau. of Arthur J. (king's counsel) and Emma (Burnie) Ashton; sister of Leigh Ashton (director of the Victoria and Albert Museum); educated at London University; earned a medical degree from London University, but largely applied her medical knowledge to her writing; m. Arthur Edward North Jordan (lawyer), 1927. ❖ Was house physician at Great Ormond Street Children's Hospital in London; at 22, published 1st novel *Pierrot in Town;* continued to write novels and fictionalized biographies, which would total 26 books by the end of her career.

ASHTON, Kiti (1870–1927). See Riwai, Kiti Karaka.

ASHTON, Winifred (1888–1965). See Dane, Clemence.

ASHTON-WARNER, Sylvia (1908–1984). New Zealand writer and teacher. Name variations: Sylvia Henderson, Sylvia. Born Sylvia Constance Warner, Dec 17, 1908, in Stratford, New Zealand; died April 28, 1984, in Tauranga, New Zealand, of abdominal cancer; dau. of Margaret (Maxwell) Warner (teacher) and Francis Ashton Warner (house-husband); attended Wairarapa College in Masterton, 1926–1927; Auckland Teacher's Training College, 1928–1931; m. Keith Dawson Henderson (teacher), Aug 23, 1931; children: Jasmine, Elliot, Ashton. ❖ Achieved international fame as an innovator of child-based educational methods, vivifying her experiences teaching Maori children, and promulgating an educational scheme based on "organic" integration of the inner and outer self; with husband, taught in several country schools in New Zealand with largely Maori populations (1931–55); described her experiences in autobiographical novels and educational treatises that profoundly influenced child-based educational methods throughout world (beginning mid-1950s); taught in alternative elementary school, Aspen Colorado (1970–71); was professor of education, Simon Fraser University, Vancouver, British Columbia (1971–73); writings include *Spinster* (1958), *Incense to Idols* (1960), *Teacher* (1963), *Bell Call* (1964), *Greenstone* (1966), *Myself* (1967), *Three* (1970), *Spearpoint: Teacher in America* (1972), *O Children of the World* (1974), and *Stories from the River* (1986). Received New Zealand Book Award (1980) for *I Passed This Way;* made a Member of the Order of the British Empire (1982). ❖ See also Lynley Hood, *Sylvia!* (Viking, 1988); and *Women in World History.*

ASHUMOVA, Irada (1958—). Azerbaijani shooter. Born Feb 25, 1958, in Baku, Azerbaijan. ❖ Set a world record (1152) in the women's 10m air pistol (1985); won a bronze medal for 25m pistol at Athens Olympics (2004).

ASHUR, Radwa (1946—). Egyptian novelist, critic and educator. Name variations: Radwa Ashour or Radwa 'Ashur. Born 1946 in Manial, Egypt;

m. Murid al-Barghouti (Palestinian poet and writer), 1970. ❖ Graduated from University of Cairo (1967) and began teaching literature; helped found Higher National Committee for Writers and Artists (1973); is a professor of literature at Ain Shams University; probably best known for her *Thulathiyyat granata* (*Granada Trilogy*, published in Arabic, 1994–95), with 1st volume published in English as *Granada: A Novel* (2003); other works include *The Journey* (1983), *Warm Stone* (1985), *Khadija and Sawsan* (1989), *I Saw the Date Palms* (1989), *Siraj* (1992), *Apparitions* (1998) and *A Clean Kill.* Won best novel award for *Granada Trilogy* at International Cairo Book Fair (1994).

ASHWELL, Lena (1872–1957). English actress. Name variations: Lady Simson. Born Lena Pocock in 1872; died in 1957; dau. of C. Ashwell B. Pocock, R.N.; educated in Toronto, Canada; studied singing at Lausanne Conservatoire and Royal Academy of Music; m. Arthur Playfair (actor), 1896 (div. 1908); m. a Dr. Simson, 1908. ❖ One of London's leading actresses at turn of the century, portrayed Elaine in Sir Henry Irving's production of *King Arthur* at the Lyceum (1895) and would again act for him in *Dante* (1903); scored 1st major triumph in *Mrs. Dane's Defence* (1900); starred under her own management at the Kingsway Theatre (1907); during WWI, provided concerts and plays for troops at the front; ran the Lena Ashwell Players (1918–28), which toured the suburbs; also founded the Century Theatre to provide quality plays at quality prices and to give opportunities for beginning actors. Awarded the Order of the British Empire (OBE, 1917).

ASHWORTH, Jeanne (1938—). American speedskater. Born Jeanne Chesley Ashworth, July 1, 1938, in Burlington, Vermont; grew up in Wilmington, Massachusetts. ❖ Won National indoor titles (1957–59); won a bronze medal for the 500 meters at Squaw Valley Olympics (1960); won 9 National titles; became town supervisor of Wilmington (the equivalent of mayor, c. 2000).

ASILIAN, Dimitra (1972—). Greek water-polo player. Born July 10, 1972, in Greece. ❖ Won team silver medal at Athens Olympics (2004).

ASKEW, Anne (c. 1521–1546). English Protestant martyr. Name variations: Askewe, Ascue, Ayscoughe; (m. name) Kime, Kyme, Keme. Pronunciation: ASS-que. Born Anne Askew at Stallingborough, near Grimsby in Yorkshire, England, c. 1521; burned at the stake in London, July 16, 1546; dau. of Sir William Askew (knight); mother unknown; m. Thomas Kyme (sep.); children: 2. ❖ One of England's most famous religious martyrs, whose adherence to Sacramentarian doctrines led to her execution and subsequent renown as one of the heroines of the Reformation; a humanist, earned a reputation for her intellectual abilities; married Thomas Kyme against her will; following separation from husband, moved to London (1545); was arrested for heresy (1545) and examined under the terms of the Six Articles, which attached severe penalties to the denial of certain traditional religious beliefs; had run afoul of the 1st of the Six Articles, the one having to do with the proper interpretation of the Eucharist (radical Protestants like Askew argued that the bread and wine taken in Communion remained bread and wine in substance and thus had a merely symbolic function); throughout examinations for heresy, was protected by her considerable wit and circumspection; was acquitted and set free; under renewed accusations of heresy (1546), was examined for several successive days during which the Privy Councillors urged her to "confess the Sacrament to be flesh, blood, and bone"; refused, even under torture, and was burned at the stake. ❖ See also *Women in World History.*

ASKEW, Sarah B. (c. 1863–1942). American librarian. Name variations: Sarah Byrd Askew. Born Sarah Byrd Askew on Feb 15, c. 1863, in Dayton, Alabama; died Oct 20, 1942, in Trenton, New Jersey; dau. of Samuel Horton Askew and Thyrza (Pickering) Askew; stepdau. of Kittie Reeves. ❖ Worked with Cleveland Public Library (1904–05); worked for New Jersey Public Library Commission as "organizer and missionary," visiting towns without libraries, and gaining support from State Teachers' Association and Federation of Women's Clubs (1905–09); established summer school to train librarians (1906); was reference librarian for State Library at Trenton, NJ (1909–15); served as president of NJ Library Association (1913–14 and 1939–40); worked with Commission, founding county library program and establishing 12 new libraries in NJ (1915–42); created system to provide books to military camps, troopships, and patients in military hospitals (WWI); designed Model-T book truck to supply books to people without library services (1920); was a member of Trenton Board of Education (1923–33); was chair of children's reading for National Congress of Parents and Teachers (1924–29); served as vice president of American Library Association

(1938–39); helped organize Victory Book Campaign (WWII). Granted 1st honorary degree awarded by New Jersey College for Women (later Douglass College) of Rutgers University (1930).

ASLEY OF STOKE, Lady (1932–2003). *See Ashley, Pauline.*

ASMĀ (c. 1028–1084). Yemeni queen. Name variations: Asma. Born c. 1028 in Yemen; died c. 1084; m. Alī al-Sulaihī (founder of Sulaihid Dynasty who established power of Fatimid caliphs); children: Al-Mukarram. ❖ Highly cultured queen, was famed as patron of poetry and music; following husband's murder (1080), was imprisoned for 2 years until rescued by son; ruled until her death.

ASP, Anna (1946—). Swedish production designer. Born in 1946 in Sweden; attended Stockholm's Academy of Fine Arts and Dramatic Institute. ❖ Designed sets for Scandinavia's major directors: Ingmar Bergman, Andrei Tarkovsky, and Bille August; films include *Giliap* (1973), *Ansikte mot ansikte* (*Face to Face*, 1976), *Hostsonaten* (*Autumn Sonata*, 1978), *Min Alskade* (1979), *After the Rehearsal* (1984), *Offret-Sacrificatio* (*The Sacrifice*, 1986), *Pelle Erobreren* (*Pelle the Conqueror*, 1987), and *Katinka* (1988). Won an Academy Award for art direction on *Fanny and Alexander* (1982). ❖ See also *Women in World History.*

ASPASIA MANOS (1896–1972). *See Manos, Aspasia.*

ASPASIA OF MILETUS (c. 464 BCE–c. 420 BCE). Greek philosopher. Pronunciation: As-PAS-ia. Fl. around 430 BCE; dates of birth and death unknown. Born in Miletus (in modern Turkey) around 464 BCE; died, probably, in Athens around 420 BCE; dau. of Axiochus; mother unknown; most likely attended schools of the Sophists in Miletus and Athens; attended and engaged in philosophical disputations with Socrates; mistress of Pericles, c. 442 (died 429); mistress of Lysicles, 429 (died 428); children: (with Pericles) a son, Pericles (original name unknown); (with Lysicles) a son, Poristes (name uncertain). ❖ One of the most famous women of the ancient Greek world, known for her philosophical and rhetorical education, political influence, and charm; may have attended or had contact with the schools of the Sophists in Miletus before she came to Athens (mid-440s); came to the notice of Pericles—the most powerful man in Athens—shortly after her arrival, and then became his mistress, thus ensuring that she could live in the city (an official marriage was recognized only between a man and a woman whose parents had been Athenian); is said to have been part of Socrates' circle and to have taught Socrates rhetoric; is said to have been the author of public funeral speeches, including the famous one delivered by Pericles (431); because of her association with Pericles, was the subject of much abuse, aimed at harming him as well; was prosecuted in court on a charge of sacrilege, which was a common accusation against the Sophists (and against Socrates, 431–430); after Pericles died from the plague, lived with a popular leader named Lysicles; died and was buried in Attica, in the region of Athens, and her grave site was famous in antiquity; is one of the best known, and least typical, women of ancient Greece. ❖ See also *Women in World History.*

ASPASIA THE YOUNGER (fl. 415–370 BCE). Greek concubine. Name variations: real name, according to Plutarch, was Milto; Aspasia the Wise. Flourished around 415–370; dau. of Hermotimus. ❖ Born free and well educated, was the favorite concubine of Cyrus the Younger who named her Aspasia; when Cyrus was murdered by his brother Artaxerxes, became Artaxerxes' favorite as well. ❖ See also *Women in World History.*

ASPIN, Rhoda Alice (1889–1980). *See Bloodworth, Rhoda Alice.*

ASPINALL, Nan Jane (fl. 1911). American messenger on horseback. Fl. 1911. ❖ The 1st woman to cross America on horseback alone, traveled 4,500 miles to deliver a letter from the mayor of San Francisco to the mayor of New York City (Sept 1, 1910–Jul 8, 1911).

ASQUITH, Cynthia (1887–1960). British author. Born Cynthia Mary Evelyn Charteris in Wiltshire, England, 1887; died in 1960; dau. of Hugo (Lord Elcho, 11th earl of Wemyss) and Mary (Wyndham) Charteris; m. Herbert Asquith (2nd son of Prime Minister Herbert Henry Asquith and 1st wife Helen Melland), in 1910; children: John (b. 1911); Michael (b. 1914); Simon (b. 1919). ❖ After WWI put an end to husband's career as a lawyer, supplemented the family income by writing autobiographies, biographies, novels, children's stories, a play, and diaries of the war years; was secretary to playwright James M. Barrie, a position she held for 20 years; writings include *Portrait of J.M. Barrie, Married to Tolstoy*, an account of the tempestuous union between Leo and Sonya Tolstoy, *Her Majesty, the Queen* (1937), *Haply I May Remember* (1950), *Remember and be Glad* (1952), and *Diaries 1915–1918* (1969).

❖ See also Nicola Beauman, *Cynthia Asquith* (Hamish Hamilton, 1988); and *Women in World History.*

ASQUITH, Emma Alice Margaret (1864–1945). *See Asquith, Margot Tennant.*

ASQUITH, Lady (1887–1969). *See Bonham-Carter, Violet.*

ASQUITH, Margot Tennant (1864–1945). British writer and prime-ministerial wife. Born Margaret Emma Alice Tennant in Peebleshire, Scotland, 1864; died July 28, 1945, in London, England; 6th daughter and 1 of 12 children of Sir Charles (industrialist) and Emma (Winsloe) Tennant; m. Herbert Henry Asquith (prime minister, 1908–16, and Liberal leader until 1926), May 10, 1894; children: (5) only 2, Anthony (1902—) and Elizabeth Bibesco (1897–1943), survived infancy; (5 stepchildren) Raymond (1878–1916); Herbert (1881–1947); Arthur (1883–1939); Cyril (1890–1954); Violet Bonham-Carter (1887–1969), also known as Lady Asquith of Yarnbury. ❖ Brilliant and witty hostess, attracted a vast circle of smart and influential friends, including Benjamin Jowett, vice-chancellor of Oxford, and prime minister William Gladstone, as well as writers John Addington, John Symonds, and Virginia Woolf; was a member of The Souls, a group of aesthetes who, in addition to intellectual and literary pursuits, advocated greater freedom for women, particularly in self-expression and dress; a prolific writer, kept diaries from an early age and actively corresponded by letter; published the 1st of her 2-volume autobiography (1920) which was greeted with embarrassment from family and friends, condemned by critics, and sold well because of its indiscretions and revelations about English politics and society; authored several less controversial books: one on travel, *Places and Persons* (1925), essays entitled *Lay Sermons* (1927), a biographical novel, *Octavia* (1928), and 2 additional books of reminiscence. ❖ See also Mark Bonham Carter, ed. *The Autobiography of Margot Asquith* (Riverside, 1962); and *Women in World History.*

ASQUITH, Ruby (c. 1910—). American ballet dancer. Name variations: Ruby Christensen. Born c. 1910, possibly in Portland, Oregon; m. Harold Christensen (dancer). ❖ Performed with the Christensen Brothers' vaudeville act; with the brothers, appeared in the musical *The Great Waltz* (1935), then joined the School of American Ballet, where she performed in numerous Balanchine works; was an original member of the touring troupe Ballet Caravan—which consisted of dancers from American Ballet—where she created roles in such works as *Air and Variations* (1936), *Yankee Clipper* (1937), *Charade* (1939); joined William Christensen's San Francisco Ballet (early 1940s) where she appeared in *Now the Brides* (1941), *Sonata Pathétique* (1943), and *Prince Siegfried* (1944); upon retiring from performance career, became dance faculty member of school of San Francisco Ballet.

ASQUITH OF YARNBURY, Baroness (1887–1969). *See Bonham-Carter, Violet.*

ASSANDRA, Caterina (fl. 1580–1609). Italian composer. Name variations: Catterina Alessandra. Born in Pavia between 1580 and 1609; sometimes confused with another composer of this name who appeared in 1772; studied with Benedetto Re. ❖ Became a nun in the cloister of Sant' Agata in Lomello near Pavia; during 1st half of 17th century, composed many works, including *Siren colestis* and *Promptuarium musicum;* published motets for a few voices and organ continuo in the new concertato style.

ASSELIN, Marie-Claude. Canadian freestyle skier. Lives in St. Hubert, Quebec. ❖ Pioneer female "hotdogger," won FIS World Cup Grand Prix for aerials (1981, 1982, 1983). Won Elaine Tanner Award (1982); inducted into Honor Roll of Canadian Skiing (1991).

ASSIA (1912–1998). *See Noris, Assia.*

ASSING, Ludmilla (1821–1880). German writer and journalist. Born at Hamburg, Germany, Feb 22, 1821; died at Florence, Italy, Mar 25, 1880; David Assur Assing (Jewish physician) and Rosa Maria Varnhagen; sister of Ottilie Assing (writer); niece of Karl Varnhagen von Ense and Rahel Varnhagen (1771–1833). ❖ Moved to Berlin to live with uncle (1842), Karl Varnhagen von Ense; edited several works of her uncle as well as several by Alexander von Humboldt; supported the revolution from 1848; wrote articles and books that were published anonymously; became a political exile in Florence where she wrote for leading German newspapers as an Italian correspondent; was imprisoned for libel by Prussian government (1863–64).

ASSING, Ottilie (1819–1884). German-American journalist and essayist. Born 1819 in Hamburg, Germany; committed suicide in 1884; dau. of

David Assur Assing (Jewish physician) and Rosa Maria Varnhagen; sister of Ludmilla Assing (1821–1880, writer); niece of Karl Varnhagen von Ense and Rahel Varnhagen (1771–1833). ❖ Immigrated to US and worked for German paper *Morgenblatt* in NY; settled in Hoboken, NJ; met ex-slave Frederick Douglass (c. 1855) and they became lovers; exchanged letters with Douglass for 26 years until her suicide upon hearing of his marriage to Helen Pitts; wrote against slavery and for women's suffrage; some essays published in *Was die Deutschen aus Amerika berichten, 1828–1865* (1885); other essays and letters to Frederick Douglass published in *Radical Passion: Ottilie Assing's Reports from America and Letters to Frederick Douglass* (Christoph Lohmann, ed., 1999). ❖ See also Maria Diedrich, *Love Across Color Lines: Ottilie Assing and Frederick Douglas* (Hill and Wang, 1999).

ASSISI, Clara d' (c. 1194–1253). *See Clare of Assisi.*

AST, Pat (1941–2001). American actress and model. Born Oct 21, 1941, in Brooklyn, NY; died Oct 3, 2001, in West Hollywood, California. ❖ Appeared in Andy Warhol films, including *Heat* (1972); met designer Halston and became a model in his Madison Avenue store; other films include *Reform School Girl* and *The Incredible Shrinking Woman.*

ASTAFEI, Galina (1968—). Romanian high jumper. Born June 7, 1968, in Romania. ❖ At Barcelona Olympics, won a silver medal in the high jump (1992).

ASTAFIEVA, Serafima (1876–1934). Russian dancer and teacher. Name variations: Serafina or Serafine. Born in St. Petersburg, Russia, 1876; died Sept 13, 1934, in London, England; graduate of St. Petersburg Imperial School of Ballet in 1895; m. Joseph Kchessinksy-Nechui (older brother of ballerina Matilda Kshesinskaia), 1896 (div. 1905). ❖ One of the most influential teachers of Russian classical ballet technique, began in the corps de ballet of the Maryinsky Theater; following divorce (1905), resigned from the theater; was a member of Diaghilev's Ballets Russes, dancing principal roles in Fokine's *Cléopâtre* and *Khovantchina* (1909–11); opened a ballet school in London and trained, among many others, Alicia Markova, Margot Fonteyn, and Anton Dolin. ❖ See also *Women in World History.*

ASTAIRE, Adele (1898–1981). American dancer and actress. Born Adele Austerlitz in Omaha, Nebraska, Sept 10, 1898; died Jan 25, 1981, in Arizona; dau. of Ann (Geilus) and Frederick E. Austerlitz (traveling salesman); older sister of Fred Astaire; m. Lord Charles Cavendish, 1932 (died 1944); m. Kingman Douglass (Wall Street investment broker); children: (1st m.) 3 (all died shortly after their birth). ❖ One half of the most famous brother-and-sister act in Broadway history, studied at Ned Wayburn School of Dance and at Metropolitan Ballet School; with brother, toured US as a dance team on Orpheum and Keith vaudeville circuits (1906–16), made Broadway debut in Sigmund Romberg's *Over the Top* (1917), and had 1st major success in *The Passing Show of 1918;* appeared as Molly in *Apple Blossoms* (1919) and as Aline Moray in *Love Letter* (1921); with brother, performed in *Lady Be Good,* dancing to the tunes of "Fascinating Rhythm," "So Am I," and "Oh, Lady, Be Good" (1924), and reprising roles in London (1926); followed that with *Funny Face* (1927) and *The Band Wagon* (1931); married and retired (1932); made only one film: Mary Pickford's *Fanchon the Cricket* (1915). ❖ See also *Women in World History.*

ASTAKHOVA, Polina (1936—). Soviet gymnast. Born Oct 30, 1936; grew up in Ukraine. ❖ At Melbourne Olympics, won a bronze medal for team all-around, portable apparatus, and gold medal for team all-around (1956); at Rome Olympics, won a bronze medal for indiv. all-around, silver for floor exercises, and gold medals for team all-around and uneven bars (1960); at Tokyo Olympics, won bronze medal in indiv. all-around, silver for floor, and gold for team all-around and uneven bars (1964); at World championships, won team all-around (1958, 1962); at European championships, won a gold medal in balance beam (1959), then uneven bars and balance beam (1961); won USSR Cup (1965).

ASTELL, Mary (1666–1731). English writer. Name variations: Madonella. Pronunciation: as-TELL. Born Mary Astell, Nov 12, 1666, in Newcastle-upon-Tyne, England; died in London, May 9, 1731, from breast cancer; dau. of Peter (coal merchant) and Mary (Errington) Astell; no formal education, but was tutored for a few years by her father's older brother Ralph; never married; no children. ❖ Writer of feminist, political, and religious works that addressed some of the most controversial issues of her time, including the education of women, the institution of marriage, and the role of God in everyday life; probably had a conventional middle-class

upbringing for girls of that period, though the death of her father when she was 12 left the financial stability of the family threatened; moved to London to live on her own (mid-1680s); came to attention of archbishop of Canterbury (1689); published 1st work, *A Serious Proposal to the Ladies, For the Advancement of Their True and Greatest Interest* (1694); active as a writer until 1709, when she helped to establish a school for girls and became headmistress; some of her works reissued (1722 and 1730); other writings include *Letters Concerning the Love of God* (1695), *A Serious Proposal To The Ladies, Part II, Wherein a Method is Offer'd for the Improvement of Their Minds* (1697), *Some Reflections upon Marriage* (1700), *Moderation Truly Stated* (1704), *A Fair Way with Dissenters and Their Patrons* (1704), *An Impartial Enquiry into the Late Causes of Rebellion and Civil War* (1704), *The Christian Religion as Profess'd by a Daughter of the Church* (1705), and *Bart'lemy Fair: or, An Inquiry after Wit* (1709). ❖ See also Bridget Hill, ed. *The First English Feminist: Reflections upon Marriage and other Writings by Mary Astell* (St. Martin, 1986); Ruth Perry, *The Celebrated Mary Astell: An Early English Feminist* (University of Chicago Press, 1986); and *Women in World History.*

ASTHON SOSI (1877–1945). *See Wetherill, Louisa Wade.*

ASTIN (fl. 5th c. BCE). *See Vashti.*

ASTIN, Patty Duke (1946—). *See Duke, Patty.*

ASTLEY, Thea (1925–2004). Australian novelist. Born Beatrice May Astley, Aug 25, 1925, in Brisbane, Queensland; dau. of Cecil Astley and Eileen (Lindsay) Astley; died Aug 2004, in Byron Bay, Queensland, Australia; dau. of Cecil Astley (journalist); attended All Hallows Convent; University of Queensland, arts degree, 1947; attended Teachers Training College; m. Edmund John (Jack) Gregson, Aug 27, 1948, in Sydney (died Jan 2003); children: one son, Ed Gregson (tv producer). ❖ Traveling with father, a journalist with the newspaper *The Queenslander,* became acquainted with the ruggedness of rural Australia and its amalgam of people, imagery she would later use in her satirical writing; taught in rural schools for 5 years; moved to Sydney (1948) and took a teaching position at a local high school; published *Girl With a Monkey* (1958) and *A Descant for Gossips* (1960); was a senior tutor at Macquarie University in Sydney (1968–80); wrote short stories, novellas, and novels, which emphasized the social intricacies and prejudices of small-town life; selected works include *Girl With a Monkey* (1958); other writings include *A Boatload of Home Folk* (1968), *The Acolyte* (1972), *Hunting the Wild Pineapple* (1979), *Beachmasters* (1985), *Reaching Tin River* (1990), *Vanishing Points* (1992), *Coda* (1994), *The Multiple Effects of Rainshadow* (1997) and *Drylands* (2000). Won 4 Miles Franklin awards, the Patrick White award, the gold medal of the Australian Literature Society, and the inaugural Steele Rudd award.

ASTON, Luise (1814–1871). German author and feminist pioneer. Name variations: Louisa. Born Luise Hoche, Nov 26, 1814, in Gröningen near Halberstadt, into a conservative Lutheran family; died in obscurity, Dec 21, 1871, in Wangen-Allgäu, in southern Germany; dau. of Johann Gottfried Hoche (Lutheran minister and church official); twice married Samuel Aston (English industrialist); m. Eduard Meier (physician from Bremen), 1850. ❖ Became a well-known and controversial spokeswoman for women's rights in her verse and novels (early 1840s); had brief moment of fame during ill-fated revolution (1848), when her writings were much discussed; fleetingly served as editor of a radical journal; like other German revolutionaries, was unable to reach a broadly based audience and quickly faded from the spotlight after the suppression of the revolution (1849); writings include the poetry collection, *Wilde Rosen* (*Wild Roses*), famed for its emotional eroticism. ❖ See also *Women in World History.*

ASTOR, Augusta (fl. 1820s–1890s). American philanthropist. Name variations: Mrs. John Jacob III. Born Charlotte Augusta Gibbes; m. John Jacob Astor III (1822–1890); children: William Waldorf Astor (1848–1919, who m. Mary Dahlgren Paul). ❖ Known as Mrs. John Jacob Astor III, gave balls, held a literary circle, and gave $225,000 for the Astor Pavilion, the 1st building of the Memorial Hospital for the treatment of cancer; also supported Children's Aid Society and helped pay transportation costs for 1,500 NY slum youths who were resettled in foster homes in midwest.

ASTOR, Brooke (b. 1902). American foundation executive and civic worker. Name variations: Mrs. Vincent Astor. Born Brooke Russell in Portsmouth, New Hampshire, Mar 31, 1902; dau. of John Henry (marine commandant) and Mabel (Howard) Russell; Columbia University, LLD, 1971; m. J. Dryden Kuser, 1918 (div., c. 1929); m. Charles "Buddie" Marshall (stockbroker who died in 1952);

m. Vincent Astor, Oct 1953 (died 1959); children: (1st m.) Anthony (who took the name of Marshall). ❖ Known as the Fairy Godmother of New York City, gave away every penny in the family foundation that had been funded by John Jacob Astor's fur trade and real estate fortune; over a span of 38 years, handed out $193,317,406 to charitable causes around the city—Carnegie Hall, The Bronx Zoo, the South Street Seaport, industrial projects in the Bronx, rebuilding Bedford-Stuyvesant in Brooklyn—then closed the foundation (Mar 1998); was a consulting and feature editor for *House and Garden*. Received hundreds of awards, including the Governor's Arts Award (May 1985), Presidential Citizen's Medal and National Medal of Arts Award from Ronald Reagan (both 1988), and Presidential Medal of Freedom from Bill Clinton (1998). ❖ See also autobiographies, *Patchwork Child* (1962) and *Footprints* (1980).

ASTOR, Caroline Schermerhorn (1830–1908). American arbiter of New York Society. Born Caroline Webster Schermerhorn in New York, NY, Sept 22, 1830; died in her Fifth Avenue mansion, Oct 30, 1908, in New York, NY; dau. of a wealthy Dutch merchant; m. William Backhouse Astor Jr. (1830–1892, grandson of John Jacob and Sarah Todd Astor), 1853; children: Emily Astor Van Alen (who m. James J. Van Alen and died in childbirth); Helen Astor Roosevelt (who m. James Roosevelt); Charlotte Augusta Astor Drayton (who m. James Coleman Drayton); Caroline Astor Wilson (who m. Orme Wilson); and John Jacob Astor IV (who m. Ava Lowle Willing and Madeleine Talmadge Force). ❖ The Grande Dame of American society from the 1860s to the turn of the century, made sure that those who belonged to the powerful elite were separated from those who did not. ❖ See also *Women in World History.*

ASTOR, Gertrude (1887–1977). American actress. Born in Lakewood, Ohio, Nov 9, 1887; died on 90th birthday, Nov 9, 1977, in Woodland Hills, California. ❖ Though usually cast as a vamp or the other woman, is also remembered for her brilliant comedic timing in silent film *The Strong Man* (1926); at 13, began career as a stage actress, before joining Universal 14 years later, where she became one of the most popular leading ladies in that studio's silents; worked with many directors, including George Cukor, Allan Dwan, Henry Hathaway, and John Ford; made over 300 movies, including *The Devil's Pay Day* (1917), *The Impossible Mrs. Bellew* (1922), *Flaming Youth* (1923), *Alice Adams* (1923), *The Torrent* (1924), *Stage Struck* (1925), *The Boy Friend* (1926), *The Old Soak* (1926), *Kiki* (1926), *Uncle Tom's Cabin* (1927), *The Taxi Dancer* (1927), *The Cat and the Canary* (1927), *Rose-Marie* (1928), *Hold Back the Dawn* (1941), *Father Makes Good* (1950), *Around the World in 80 Days* (1956), *All in a Night's Work* (1961), and *The Man Who Shot Liberty Valance* (1962). ❖ See also *Women in World History.*

ASTOR, Mrs. John Jacob (1761–1832). See Astor, Sarah Todd.

ASTOR, Mrs. John Jacob III (fl. 1820s–1890s). See Astor, Augusta.

ASTOR, Lady (1879–1964). See Astor, Nancy Witcher.

ASTOR, Madeleine Talmadge (c. 1893–1940). American socialite. Name variations: Madeleine Force Astor; Madeline. Born c. 1893; died 1940; m. John Jacob Astor IV, 1911 (who died April 15, 1912, on the *Titanic*); m. twice more; children: John Jacob Astor V (b. Aug 14, 1912). John Jacob Astor's 1st wife was Ava Willing Astor, the mother of Vincent Astor (b. 1891). ❖ Had been married to John Jacob Astor IV for only a few months when she boarded the *Titanic* at Cherbourg; though husband went down with the ship, she and her dog survived. ❖ See also *Women in World History.*

ASTOR, Mary (1906–1987). American actress. Born Lucile Vasconcellos Langhanke in Quincy, Illinois, May 3, 1906; died of complications from emphysema, Sept 25, 1987, in Los Angeles, California; dau. of Otto Ludwig Langhanke and Helen (Vasconcells); m. Kenneth Hawks (producer; brother of Howard Hawks), Feb 24, 1928 (died in a plane crash, Jan 2, 1930, while on film assignment); m. Franklyn Thorpe (gynecologist), June 29, 1931 (div. 1935); m. Manuel del Campo, 1937 (div. 1941); m. Thomas Gordon Wheelock (stockbroker), Dec 24, 1945 (sep. 1951, div. 1955); children: (2nd m.) Marylyn Hauoli (b. June 15, 1932); (3rd m.) Anthony Paul (b. June 5, 1939). ❖ Urbane actress, best known for her courtroom battle for child custody and her role as Brigid O'Shaughnessy in *The Maltese Falcon*, was pushed by parents to embark on film career; moved with them to NY (1919); made 1st feature, a small part in *John Smith*; signed with Famous Players and was sent to the West Coast (1923); came to prominence appearing opposite John Barrymore in the silents *Beau Brummel* and *Don Juan*; appeared in over 35 other silent films; following 1st marriage, was sued by father for maintenance

of the family house, though she was living elsewhere; endured a highly visible battle for custody of daughter when portions of her diary landed in the *Los Angeles Examiner* (1930s); appeared in about 80 sound films, including *Red Dust, Dodsworth, Prisoner of Zenda, The Hurricane, Across the Pacific* and *The Palm Beach Story*; starting at 38, began getting type-cast in a series of mother roles: *Thousands Cheer, Cynthia, Meet Me in St. Louis, Desert Fury* and *Little Women;* wrote several novels, including *The Incredible Charlie Carewe* and *A Place Called Saturday.* Won an Oscar for Best Supporting Actress for *The Great Lie.* ❖ See also autobiographies *My Story* (1959) and *A Life on Film* (1967); and *Women in World History.*

ASTOR, Minnie (1906–1978). See Fosburgh, Minnie Astor.

ASTOR, Nancy Witcher (1879–1964). British politician. Name variations: Lady Astor; Nancy Viscountess Astor; Viscountess Astor of Hever Castle; Nancy Langhorne Shaw. Born Nancy Witcher Langhorne, May 19, 1879, at Danville, Virginia; died May 2, 1964, at Grimsthorpe, Lincolnshire; 5th child of Chiswell Dabney Langhorne (railroad developer) and Nancy Witcher Keene; sister of Irene Gibson (the Gibson girl); aunt of actress Joyce Grenfell; m. Robert Gould Shaw, Oct 1897 (div., Feb 1903); m. Waldorf Astor (parliamentary secretary to Prime Minister David Lloyd George, then viscount), May 3, 1906; children: (1st m.) Robert (Bobbie) Shaw; (2nd m.) William (Bill) Waldorf, Nancy Phyllis Louise (Wissie), Francis David Langhorne, Michael Langhorne, John Jacob (Jakie). ❖ First woman member of the House of Commons, who was known for her iconoclastic wit and the many controversies into which she entered; when husband was elevated to House of Lords (1918), agreed to stand for Parliament in his place in the by-election, running as a Conservative supporter of Lloyd George coalition; became the 1st woman to sit in the British Parliament (1919), remaining in the Commons for 26 outspoken years; in Parliament, continually pressed issues concerning women and children, which included votes for females at 21, equal rights in the civil service, better conditions in women's prisons, the preservation of the women's police forces, milk for the needy, allowances for widows, birth control, the suppression of prostitution, and the elimination of venereal disease; was equally active on behalf of children, fighting child labor in unregulated trades and calling for the protection of the young from indecent assault, the raising of the school age, and the introduction of juvenile courts. ❖ See also Maurice Collis, *Nancy Astor* (Dutton, 1960); John Grigg, *Nancy Astor: A Lady Unashamed* (Little, Brown, 1980); Elizabeth Langhorne, *Nancy Astor and Her Friends* (Praeger, 1974); Christopher Sykes, *Nancy: The Life of Nancy Astor* (Harper & Row, 1972); and *Women in World History.*

ASTOR, Sarah Todd (1761–1832). German-born American entrepreneur. Born Sarah Todd in New York, NY, 1761; died in 1832; only dau. and youngest child of Adam and Sarah (Cox) Todd; m. John Jacob Astor, Sept 19, 1785; children: 8, 5 of whom lived to adulthood, including William Backhouse Astor (1792–1875, who m. Margaret Rebecca Armstrong) and Magdalen Astor (who m. Danish major-general Adrien Benjamin de Bentzon, grandfather of Marie Thérèse Blanc). ❖ Fur trader who worked with, and consulted for, husband in their successful business and philanthropic ventures. ❖ See also Lucy Kavaler, *The Astors: A Family Chronicle of Pomp and Power* (Dodd, Mead, 1966); and *Women in World History.*

ASTOR, Mrs. Vincent (b. 1902). See Astor, Brooke.

ASTOR, Mrs. William Backhouse, Jr. (1830–1908). See Astor, Caroline Schermerhorn.

ASTOR OF HEVER CASTLE, Nancy Witcher Astor, Viscountess (1879–1964). See Astor, Nancy Witcher.

ASTORGA, Nora (1949–1988). Nicaraguan diplomat and revolutionary. Born Nora Astorga Gadea in 1949; died of cancer in Managua on Feb 14, 1988; studied at Catholic University in Washington, DC; studied for a law degree at Managua's Universidad Centroamericana; m. Jorge Jenkins; children: five, including one adopted son. ❖ Became an attorney; a social radical, joined the Sandinista National Liberation Front (FSLN); in a controversial move, assisted in the assassination of General Reynaldo Perez Vega, security chief for the Somozas (1978); for Sandinista loyalists, became an instant heroine; was a founding member of the Association of Women Confronting the National Problem (AMPRONAC), the Sandinista organization of women supporters of the FSLN; was appointed chief special prosecutor for the trials of some 7,500 members of Somoza's National Guard, many of whom drew long prison terms (1980); served as deputy minister of foreign affairs; was appointed chief Nicaraguan delegate to UN (1986). ❖ See also *Women in World History.*

ASTRID. *Variant of Estrith.*

ASTRID (fl. 1100s). Norwegian royal. Fl. 1100s; married Sverre (c. 1152–1202), king of Norway (r. 1177–1202); children: Haakon III, king of Norway (r. 1202–1204); Sigurd Laward; Ingeborg Sverresdottir (who m. Charles, prince of Sweden); Cecilie Sveresdottir (who m. Einar Kongesvoger). ❖ Sverre was also married to Margaret (d. 1209) (dau. of St. Eric, king of Sweden).

ASTRID BERNADOTTE or ASTRID OF BELGIUM (1905–1935). *See Astrid of Sweden.*

ASTRID OF SWEDEN (1905–1935). Queen of the Belgians. Name variations: Astrid Bernadotte; Astrid of Belgium. Born Astrid Sofia Lovisa Thyra Bernadotte, princess of Sweden, Nov 17, 1905, in Sweden; died in automobile accident, Aug 29, 1935, near Küssnacht, Switzerland; buried in Laeken, Brussels, Belgium; dau. of Charles of Sweden and Ingeborg of Denmark (1878–1958); m. Leopold III (b. 1901), king of the Belgians, Nov 4, 1926; children: Baudoin (1930–1993), king of the Belgians; Albert II (b. 1934), king of the Belgians; Josephine-Charlotte of Belgium (b. 1927). ❖ Popular in Belgium, assumed the title of queen when her husband ascended the throne (1934), but their royal glow was short-lived; did not survive an auto accident in Switzerland (1935). ❖ See also *Women in World History.*

ASTRID OF THE OBOTRITES (c. 979–?). Queen of Sweden. Born c. 979; m. Olof or Olaf Sköttkonung or Skötkonung, king of Sweden (r. 994–1022); children: Ingigerd Olafsdottir (c. 1001–1050); Anund Jakob, king of Sweden (r. 1022–1050). Olaf also had children with Edla. ❖ See also *Women in World History.*

ASTRITH. *Variant of Estrith.*

ASTROLOGES, Maria (1951—). American golfer. Name variations: Maria Astrologes Combs. Born Aug 10, 1951, in Valparaiso, Indiana; attended San Fernando Valley State College and University of New Mexico. ❖ In 2nd year on pro tour, won more than $21,000, was 21st on money list, and 20th in scoring average; won the LPGA Birmingham Classic (May 1975), in a playoff against Judy Rankin and JoAnne Carner.

ASTRUP, Heidi (1972—). Danish handball player. Born 1972 in Denmark. ❖ Debuted on national team (1990); played for Viborg; won a team gold medal at Atlanta Olympics (1996); won team European championships (1994, 1996); retired (1996).

ASTURIAS, princess of (1972—). *See Ortiz, Letizia.*

ASZKIELOWICZOWNA, Halina (1947—). Polish volleyball player. Born Feb 1947 in Poland. ❖ At Mexico City Olympics, won a bronze medal in team competition (1968).

ATENCIA, Maria Victoria (1931—). Spanish poet. Born Nov 28, 1931, in Malaga, Spain; m. Rafael Leon; children: 4. ❖ Studied music and painting but abandoned studies to pursue poetry writing; works include *Tierra mojada* (1953), *Arte y parte* (1961), *Cañada de los ingleses* (1961), *Marta y Maria* (1976), *Los sueños* (1976), *Paulina. El libro de las aguas* (1984), *De la llama en que arde* (1988), *La señal* (1990), *El puente* (1992), and *A orillas del Ems* (1997). Won Premio Andalucia de la Critica (1998) and Premio Nacional de la Critica (1998).

ATHALIAH (r. 842–836 BCE). Biblical woman. Name variations: Athalia. Fl. between 860 and 836 BCE; assassinated in 836 BCE; dau. of Ahab and Jezebel of Israel; m. Jehoram (or Joram), king of Judah; children: son Ahaziah (or Azariah). ❖ Daughter of Ahab and Jezebel of Israel, was married to Jehoram of Judah thereby allying the two kingdoms; after her husband's death and assassination of her son Ahaziah, seized control of Judah (842 BCE), which she ruled until a coup, led by those who objected to Athaliah's foreignness and to her religious toleration; was murdered and replaced with her grandson, Joash. The story of Athaliah forms the subject of one of Racine's best tragedies; it has also been musically adapted by Handel and Mendelssohn. ❖ See also *Women in World History.*

ATHANASIA (d. about 860). *See Anastasia.*

ATHENAIS, empress (c. 400–460). *See Eudocia.*

ATHERTON, Candy (1955—). English politician and member of Parliament. Born Sept 21, 1955; dau. of Pamela Osborne Atherton (former mayor of Falmouth) and Denis Gordon Atherton (journalist); m. Broderick Ross, 2002. ❖ Launched magazine *Everywoman* (1985); representing Labour, elected to House of Commons for Falmouth and Camborne (1997, 2001); lost general election (2005).

ATHERTON, Gertrude (1857–1948). American author of novels and short stories. Born Gertrude Franklin Horn, Oct 30, 1857, in San Francisco, California; died in San Francisco, June 14, 1948; dau. of Thomas L. (businessman) and Gertrude (Franklin) Horn (homemaker); attended Clark Institute, St. Mary's Hall, and Sayre Institute; m. George Henry Bowen Atherton, Feb 15, 1876 (died 1887); children: George (d. 1882), Muriel. ❖ Moved to NY (1888); published 1st novel, *What Dreams May Come* (1888), followed by *Hermia Suydam*, which engendered a storm of criticism from the guardians of Victorian morality; began a peripatetic pattern that would take her back and forth to Europe, to Cuba, to West Indies, to Egypt, and to San Francisco for her last decade; published the controversial *Black Oxen*, the bestseller of 1923, which was made into a film the following year; wrote of loveless marriages, of women who defied convention, of young girls instructed by wise older men, of disillusionment in over 50 books, including *The Doomswoman* (1892), *Patience Sparrowhawk and Her Times* (1897), *The Californians* (1898), *Senator North* (1900), *The Conqueror: Being the True and Romantic Story of Alexander Hamilton* (1902), *The Living Present* (1917), *The White Morning* (1918), *The Immortal Marriage* (1927), *The Jealous Gods* (1928), *Dido, Queen of Hearts* (1929), *The Sophisticates* (1931) and *The Horn of Life* (1942). Elected to National Institute of Arts and Letters (1938); chosen 1st recipient of California's Most Distinguished Woman award (1940). ❖ See also autobiography, *Adventures of a Novelist* (1932); Emily Wortis Leider, *California's Daughter: Gertrude Atherton and Her Times* (Stanford, 1991); and *Women in World History.*

ATHOLL, duchess of (1874–1960). *See Stewart-Murray, Katharine Marjory.*

ATIA THE ELDER (c. 80 BCE–?). Roman noblewoman. Name variations: Atia Maior or Major; Atia the Elder. Born c. 80 BCE; dau. of Julia Minor (c. 100–51 BCE, sister of Julius Caesar) and M. Atius Balbus; m. G. Octavius (native of Velitrae to the north of Rome who died in 59 BCE); m. L. Marcius Philippus; children: (1st m.) Gaius Julius Caesar Octavianus, also known as Octavian (63 BCE–14 CE, later Augustus Caesar); and Octavia (c. 69–11 BCE). ❖ See also *Women in World History.*

ATKINS, Anna (1797–1871). English botanist and photographer. Born Anna Children, Mar 16, 1797 (some sources cite 1799), in Tonbridge, Kent, England; died June 9, 1871, in Halstead Place, England; dau. of John George Children (zoologist and fellow and secretary of the Royal Society); m. John Pelly Atkins (railway promoter and owner of Jamaican coffee plantations), in 1825. ❖ The 1st person to publish a book illustrated with photographs, worked closely with her father, a respected scientist and longtime associate of the British Museum; began career by producing drawings for his translation of Jean-Baptiste-Pierre-Antoine de Monet de Lamarck's *Genera of Shells* (1823); produced a study of algae titled *British Algae: Cyanotype Impressions* (1843), containing her own original cyanotypes; produced *Cyanotypes of British and Foreign Flowering Plants and Ferns* (1864). ❖ See also *Women in World History.*

ATKINS, Babs (1917–2004). English educator and conservationist. Born June 3, 1917, in England; died Mar 30, 2004, on St. George's Island, Cornwall, England; dau. of a merchant seaman; sister of Evelyn Atkins (potter, died 1997). ❖ With sister, bought St. George's Island (also known as Looe Island) off the coast at West Looe in southeast Cornwall and lived there for 35 years; leased the island to the Cornwall Wildlife Trust (2000), for the annual rent of one peppercorn and a bottle of whisky; was previously deputy head of a 1,500-pupil school at Surrey. ❖ See also Evelyn Atkins, *We Bought an Island* (1976).

ATKINS, Charlotte (1950—). English politician and member of Parliament. Born Charlotte Atkins, Sept 24, 1950; m. Gus Brain, 1990. ❖ Representing Labour, elected to House of Commons for Staffordshire Moorlands (1997, 2001, 2005); named assistant government whip.

ATKINS, Eileen (1934—). English actress. Name variations: Dame Eileen Atkins. Born Eileen June Atkins on June 16, 1934, in Clapton, London, England; m. Julian Glover (actor), 1957 (div. 1966); m. Bill Shepherd (filmographer), 1978. ❖ Versatile English actress who has played a wide range of roles on stage and screen, made London debut at Open Air

Theater (1953); was a member of Shakespeare Memorial Theater in Stratford-upon-Avon (1957–59); joined Bristol Old Vic (1959) and enjoyed numerous substantial successes with company, notably as Childie in *The Killing of Sister George* (1965); with Jean Marsh, created the classic British drama series "Upstairs, Downstairs" (1971); served as both producer and leading actress in Marguerite Duras's *Suzanna Andler* (1973); won widespread acclaim for one-woman show *A Room of One's Own* (1989), which earned her a New York Critics Citation; wrote and performed in successful play *Vita and Virginia* (1994), based on letters of Vita Sackville-West and Virginia Woolf; frequent tv appearances include "The Three Sisters" (1970), "The Duchess of Malfi" (1972), "Sons and Lovers" (1981), "The Maitlands" (1993), "Cold Comfort Farm" (1995), "A Dance to the Music of Time" (1997), and "Wit" (2001); films include *Inadmissible Evidence* (1968), *Equus* (1977), *The Dresser* (1983), *Gosford Park* (2001), *The Hours* (2002), *Cold Mountain* (2003), and *Vanity Fair* (2004). Nominated for 3 Tony awards, including Best Actress for *The Retreat from Moscow* (2004); received London Critics Circle Theatre Award for Best Actress for *The Night of the Iguana* (1992) and London Evening Standard Theatre Award for Best Actress for *A Delicate Balance* (1997); inducted into Theatre Hall of Fame in New York; received 4 Laurence Olivier Theatre Awards: Best Performance in Supporting Role for *Cymbeline* and *Mountain Language* (1989), Best Actress for *The Unexpected Man* (1999) and *Honour* (2004); made CBE (1990) and DBE (2001).

ATKINS, Evelyn (c. 1910–1997). English writer. Born c. 1910; died 1997 in Cornwall, England; dau. of a merchant seaman; sister of Babs Atkins. ❖ Was head of personnel at ICI, then took up pottery; with sister, lived and owned St. George's Island (also known as Looe Island) off the coast at West Looe in southeast Cornwall for 35 years; wrote *We Bought an Island* (1976) and *Tales from our Cornish Island* (1986).

ATKINS, Gillian (1963—). British field-hockey player. Born 1963 in Great Britain. ❖ At Barcelona Olympics, won a bronze medal in team competition (1992).

ATKINS, Mary (1819–1882). American educator. Born July 7, 1819, in Jefferson, Ohio; died Sept 14, 1882, in Benicia, California. ❖ Became principal and proprietor of the Young Ladies' Seminary at Benicia, California (1855), which prospered under her leadership; sold seminary to Susan and Cyrus Mills (c. Jan 1866) and observed school systems in Europe; reacquired seminary and her post as principal (1879); was highly respected on the West Coast as an educator of young women. Mills College regards the Benicia Seminary as its founding institution.

ATKINS, Roxy (1912–2002). *See Andersen, Roxanne.*

ATKINS, Susan (1948—). American murderer (accused). Name variations: Sadie Atkins. Born May 7, 1948, in San Gabriel, California; m. Donald Lee Laisure, 1980; m. James Whitehouse, 1987. ❖ Met Charles Manson in San Francisco and moved to commune in Los Angeles; with other Manson gang members, committed murders of Gary Hinman, Sharon Tate, Jay Sebring, Abigail Folger, Voytek Frykowski, and Leno and Rosemary La Bianca; arrested for auto theft with other gang members (1969) and then cooperated in prosecution of Charles Manson and others; charged with murders and sentenced to death (1971); sentence commuted to life.

ATKINS, Vera (c. 1908–2000). British officer. Name variations: Adkins. Born in Romania c. 1908; died in Hastings, England, July 2000. ❖ Officer for the SOE during WWII who recruited and trained nearly 500 secret agents and also made sure that murderers of agents were eventually brought to trial for war crimes; a conducting officer at Orchard Court, was 2nd in command to Colonel Maurice Buckmaster, head of the British SOE (Special Operations Executive).

ATKINSON, Carolina Louisa Waring (1834–1872). *See Atkinson, Louisa.*

ATKINSON, Eleanor (1863–1942). American author. Name variations: (pseudonym) Nora Marks. Born Eleanor Stackhouse, Jan 7, 1863, in Renselaer, Indiana; died Nov 4, 1942, in Orangeburg, NY; dau. of Isaac M. and Margaret (Smith) Stackhouse; educated at Indianapolis Normal Training School; m. Francis Blake Atkinson (journalist), 1891; children: 2 daughters (who write under the pseudonyms Dorothy and Eleanor Blake). ❖ Wrote 11 books, primarily for children, including *Johnny Appleseed* (1915); wrote for the Chicago *Tribune* under pseudonym Nora Marks; with husband, produced *The Little Chronicle*, a weekly paper for grammar and high-school students. ❖ See also *Women in World History.*

ATKINSON, Eudora Clark (1831–?). American state-reformatory superintendent. Born Dec 20, 1831, in Andover, Massachusetts. ❖ Served as the 1st superintendent of the Massachusetts Reformatory for Women in Sherborn (the 1st reformatory in the country solely for women prisoners) which opened in 1877; after contending with overcrowding and understaffing, resigned amid public disappointment in her performance (1880). Now located in Framingham, the facility was renamed the Reformatory for Women (1911).

ATKINSON, Jane Maria (1824–1914). New Zealand letter writer and diarist. Name variations: Jane Maria Richmond. Born Jane Maria Richmond, Sept 15, 1824, in London, England; died at Nelson, New Zealand, Sept 29, 1914; dau. of Christopher Richmond (barrister) and Maria (Wilson) Richmond; attended school for young women at Highgate; m. Arthur Samuel Atkinson, 1854; children: 4. ❖ Immigrated to Taranaki, New Zealand, and settled with family (1853); through letters and diary entries, recorded communal life in colonial region, British mismanagement, and the abandonment of the settlement (early 1860s); relocated to Nelson (1867), where she started a school for family's children; involved in women's suffrage and temperance movements; purported to have been the 1st white woman to climb Mt Egmont. ❖ See also *Dictionary of New Zealand Biography* (Vol. 1); Frances Porter, *Born to New Zealand: A Biography of Jane Maria Atkinson* (Bridget Williams Books, 1985).

ATKINSON, Juliette P. (1873–1944). American tennis player. Born April 15, 1873, in Rahway, New Jersey; died Jan 12, 1944; sister of Kathleen Atkinson (tennis player). ❖ Won US national women's doubles with Helen Hellwig and mixed doubles with Edwin P. Fischer (1894); won singles national title (1895) and both doubles titles (1895, 1896); with sister, won women's national doubles (1897, 1898), then won again with Myrtle McAteer (1901) and Marion Jones (1902).

ATKINSON, Lily May (1866–1921). New Zealand feminist and reformer. Name variations: Lily Kirk. Born Lily May Kirk, Mar 29, 1866, in Auckland, New Zealand; died July 19, 1921, in Wadestown, NZ; dau. of Sarah Jane Mattocks and Thomas Kirk (lecturer); m. Arthur Richmond Atkinson (barrister), 1900; children: Janet Atkinson (b. 1904). ❖ Joined the Women's Christian Temperance Union (WCTU, 1885), serving as dominion recording secretary (1887–1901), president of Wellington branch (1896), and dominion president (1901–06); became a popular speaker on women's suffrage, welfare of children, rights of illegitimate children, and evils of alcohol; named to executive committee of the New Zealand Alliance (1894), and served as its vice president (1895–1921).

ATKINSON, Louisa (1834–1872). Australian novelist and botanist. Name variations: Carolina Louisa Waring Atkinson; Carolina L.W. Calvert. Born Carolina Louisa Waring Atkinson, Feb 25, 1834, in Berrima, New South Wales, Australia; died April 28, 1872, 3 weeks after the birth of her daughter; dau. of James Atkinson; m. James Snowdon Calvert. ❖ Self-taught student of natural history, wrote articles on botany and did botanical illustrations; had several plants named after her; as the 1st published Australian-born female novelist, wrote *Gertrude the Emigrant: A Tale of Colonial Life* (1857), *Cowanda, the Veteran's Grant* (1959), and *Tom Hellicar's Children* (1983).

ATKINSON, Ti-Grace (1939—). American feminist. Born 1939 in US; University of Pennsylvania, BA (1964); attended Columbia University. ❖ Second-Wave feminist who abandoned liberal politics of National Organization for Women (NOW) in favor of more radical feminist agenda as laid out in her collection of essays *Amazon Odyssey* (1974); an early member of NOW, became president of NY chapter, but resigned (1968); co-founded leaderless group The Feminists, dedicated to the elimination of marriage and patriarchy; fought for rights of gays and lesbians and end to all social constructions oppressive to women; was a professor at Tufts University.

ATLAS, Consuelo (1944–1979). American dancer. Name variations: Consuelo Baraka. Born Consuelo Baraka, 1944, in West Medford, Massachusetts; died Nov 23, 1979, age 35, in Boston; m. Henry Atlas (dancer and teacher). ❖ Performed with the Alvin Ailey Dance Theater in New York City (1966–72) where she created roles in Ailey's *Quintet* (1968) and *Myth* (1971), Miguel Godreau's *Circle of the Sunconscious* (1969), and Kelvin Rotardier's *Child of the Earth* (1971); retired from performance (early 1970s) to teach classes in and around Boston; taught and directed at Impulse Dance Company with husband.

ATLER, Marilyn (c. 1937—). *See Van Derbur, Marilyn.*

ATLER, Vanessa (1982—). American gymnast. Born Feb 17, 1982, in Valencia, California. ❖ Won Canberra Cup (1997) and Australia Cup (1998); won US Nationals (1997) and US Classic (2000); won gold medals for vault and floor exercises at Goodwill Games (1998).

ATOSSA (c. 545–c. 470s BCE). Persian queen. Born c. 545 BCE; probably died in 470s BCE; dau. of Cyrus II the Great (c. 590–529 BCE), 1st Persian king, and possibly Cassandane; m. Cambyses II (died 522 BCE); m. Smerdis, 522 BCE; m. Darius I the Great, 521 BCE; children: (3rd m.) Xerxes I, king of Persia (c. 518–465 BCE). ❖ Subsequent to father's death, was married to (probably) half-brother, Cambyses, to the pseudo-Smerdis, and finally to Darius, all of whom attempted to consolidate their control of the Persian Empire by marrying her; a figure much respected within the royal harem, greatest influence seems to have been felt when her support for the accession of her son Xerxes secured for him the Persian throne after the death of Darius (486). ❖ See also *Women in World History.*

ATTAR, Samar (1940—). Syrian poet, novelist and educator. Name variations: Samar 'Attar. Born 1940 in Damascus, Syria; University of Damascus, Licences en Lettres in English and Arabic; Dalhousie University, Halifax, Canada, BA; State University of New York, Binghamton, PhD. ❖ Taught Arabic and English at several universities in Algeria, Germany, US, and Australia; moved to Australia (c. 1978); works include *Lena, Portrait of a Girl of Damascus* (1982) and *The House on Arnus Square* (1988); translated *Journey at Night*, poems by Abd Al-Sabur.

ATTENBOROUGH, Sheila (1922—). *See Sim, Sheila.*

ATTWELL, Mabel Lucie (1879–1964). English artist, illustrator, and author of children's stories and verse. Born June 4, 1879, in Mile End, London; died Nov 5, 1964, in Fowey in Cornwall; attended Heatherley's and St. Martin's School of Art; m. Harold Earnshaw (illustrator), 1908; children: Peggy (b. 1909), Peter (b. 1911), and Brian (1914–1936). ❖ Gained worldwide recognition with her trademark wide-eyed, chubby-kneed tots; illustrated books by May Baldwin, Mrs. Molesworth, Mabel Quiller-Couch, and others, usually providing between four and eight color plates for each volume; also illustrated *Grimm's Fairy Tales and Stories* and *Legends* (both 1910), *Alice in Wonderland* (1911), *Grimm's Fairy Stories* (1912), *Hans Andersen's Fairy Tales* (1914), *The Water Babies* (1915), *Children's Stories from French Fairy Tales* (1917), *Peter Pan and Wendy* (1921), and *The Lucie Attwell Annual* (1922). ❖ See also Chris Beetles, *Mabel Lucie Attwell* (Pavilion); and *Women in World History.*

ATTWOOD, Julie Maree (1957—). Australian politician. Born May 31, 1957, in Bundaberg, Queensland, Australia. ❖ As a member of the Australian Labor Party, elected to the Queensland Parliament for Mount Ommaney (1998); named chair of the Members' Ethics and Parliamentary Privileges Committee (2001).

ATTWOOLL, Elspeth (1943—). Scottish politician. Born Feb 1, 1943, in Chislehurst, Kent, England. ❖ Lectured in jurisprudence and comparative law, University of Glasgow (1966–98); was a member of the executive committee, Scottish Liberal Democrats (1996—), and president of Scottish Women Liberal Democrats (1998—); as a member of the European Liberal, Democrat and Reform Party, elected to 5th European Parliament (1999–2004) from UK.

ATWATER, Edith (1911–1986). American actress. Born April 22, 1911, in Chicago, Illinois; died Mar 14, 1986, in Los Angeles, California; m. Hugh Marlowe (actor, div.); m. Joseph Allen Jr. (div.); m. Kent Smith (actor, died 1985). ❖ Made NY debut as Miss Jones in *Springtime for Henry* (1931), followed by *The Country Wife, Susan and God, R.U.R., State of the Union, The Best Man* and *The Child Buyer*, among others; originated the role of Maggie Cutler in *The Man Who Came to Dinner* (1940); made film debut in *We Went to College* (1936); other films include *The Body Snatcher, Sweet Smell of Success, Sweet Bird of Youth, True Grit* and *Zabriskie Point.*

ATWATER, Helen (1876–1947). American home economist. Born in Somerville, Massachusetts, May 29, 1876; died in Washington, DC, June 26, 1947; graduated from Smith College, Northampton, 1897. ❖ Joined the staff of the Office of Home Economics in US Department of Agriculture; as a frequent contributor to *Journal of Home Economics*, a publication of American Home Economics Association, went to work for them in 1923, becoming their 1st

woman editor that year, and stayed until her retirement in 1941; participated in White House Conference on Child Health and Protection (1930), and served as chair of Committee on Hygiene in Housing of the American Public Health Association (1942). ❖ See also *Women in World History.*

ATWELL, Winifred (1914–1983). Trinidad-born British pianist and entertainer. Name variations: Winnie Atwell; also seen incorrectly as Winnifred Atwell. Born Feb 27, 1914, in Tunapuna, Trinidad; died Feb 28, 1983, in Sydney, Australia; trained as a classical pianist; m. Lew Levisohn (comedian). ❖ Dominated the pop charts in the 1950s; moved to London (1946); playing medleys in a honky-tonk style, had 1st hit with George Botsford's "Black and White Rag" (1952); recorded "Flirtation Waltz," "Britannia Rag" and "Coronation Rag" for the coronation of Queen Elizabeth II (1953); hit the top of the charts with sing-along album "Let's Have a Party"; had a string of hits in the Top 20, including "Poor People of Paris" (1956); was 1st artist from United Kingdom to be awarded 2 gold records at same time.

ATWOOD, Donna (c. 1923—). American figure skater. Born in Newton, Kansas, Feb 14, c. 1923; m. John H. Harris, 1949 (div. 1956); children: twin sons and a daughter. ❖ Won jr. women's figure-skating title and national senior pairs title, skating with Eugene Turner; was the star of the Ice Capades (1949–56).

ATWOOD, Margaret (1939—). Canadian novelist, poet and literary critic. Born Margaret Eleanor "Peggy" Atwood, Nov 18, 1939, in Ottawa, Ontario, Canada; grew up in northern Quebec and Toronto; dau. of a forest entomologist; attended Victoria College; University of Toronto, BA, 1961; Radcliffe College, MA, 1962; also studied at Harvard University, 1962–63, 1965–67. ❖ Canada's most eminent novelist, worked in Canada, Italy, England, and US; taught at University of British Columbia and Sir George William University; her works often focus on environment, women's issues, and Canadian culture; collections of poetry include *The Circle Game* (1964), *Power Politics* (1971), *You are Happy* (1974), *True Stories* (1981), *Margaret Atwood Poems 1965–1975* (1991), and *Eating Fire: Selected Poems, 1965–1995* (1998); novels include *The Edible Woman* (1969), *Surfacing* (1972), *Lady Oracle* (1977), *Life Before Man* (1980), *Bodily Harm* (1981), *The Handmaid's Tale* (1985), *Cat's Eye* (1989), *The Robber Bride* (1993), *Alias Grace* (1996), *The Blind Assassin* (2000), and *Oryx and Crake* (2003); also published nonfiction, short stories, and children's books; was president of Writers Union of Canada (1981–82) and PEN, Canada (1984–86). Recipient of several awards, including Governor General's Award, Norwegian Order of Literary Merit, and French Chevalier dans l'Ordre des Arts et des Lettres; won the Booker Prize for *The Blind Assassin* (2000).

ATWOOD, Susan (1953—). American swimmer. Name variations: Susie Atwood. Born June 1953 in Long Beach, California. ❖ Won 5 silver medals and a bronze at Pan American Games (1971); at Munich Olympics, won a bronze medal for the 100-meter backstroke and a silver medal for the 200-meter backstroke (1972); a 4-time World record holder in the 200-meter backstroke, captured 23 national titles during career; became a swimming coach at Ohio State University. Received World Swimmer of the Year award 6 times.

AUBERT, Constance (1803–?). French journalist and novelist. Born 1803 in France; dau. of Laure d'Abrantès (1784–1838, novelist and biographer) and General Junot. ❖ Collaborated with mother on several novels; worked as a fashion columnist for *Le Temps*, as a contributor for *Journal des Dames* (*Ladies Journal*) and *Journal des Femmes* (*The Women's Journal*) and as an editor for several fashion and style publications, including *Les Abeilles parisiennes* (*The Bees of Paris*); published *Manuel d'économie élégante* (*Handbook of Economy and Style*, 1859).

AUBERT, Marie Henriette Suzanne (1835–1926). *See Aubert, Mary Joseph.*

AUBERT, Mary Joseph (1835–1926). New Zealand nun, nurse, herbalist, teacher, social worker, writer, and religious order founder. Name variations: Marie Henriette Suzanne Aubert, Suzanne Aubert. Born Marie Henriette Suzanne Aubert, June 19, 1835, in Saint-Symphorien-de-Lay, Loire, France; died Oct 1, 1926, in Wellington, New Zealand; dau. of Louis Aubert (bailiff) and Henriette Catherine Clarice (Périer) Aubert. ❖ Immigrated to New Zealand (1860); became novice of Sisters of Mary (1861); taught Maori girls in Auckland (1860–69); performed teaching and nursing missionary work among the Maori (1870s); published Maori language catechism in 1879, and Maori grammar (1885); became interested in native herbal remedies and marketed them (1890s); performed social work among urban poor throughout early 1900s, establishing various institutions, including soup kitchen, day nursery, and home for incurables; founded Sisters of Compassion to respond to numerous local needs (1917); became national figure for more than six decades of work. ❖ See also *Dictionary of New Zealand Biography* (Vol. 2).

AUBERT, Suzanne (1835–1926). *See Aubert, Mary Joseph.*

AUBESPINE, Madeleine de l' (1546–1596). French poet and salonnière. Name variations: Madame de Laubespine; Dame de Villeroy. Born in 1546 in France; died in 1596 in France; dau. of Jean de Brabant; m. Nicolas de Neufville. ❖ Became lady-in-waiting to Catherine de Medici; after marriage to the king's secretary, Nicolas de Neufville, turned to writing poetry; also provided an impetus for other French poets by creating one of the earliest salons, opening her home for writers and poets to share their works; her writings, mostly sonnets, earned her the admiration and respect of many of Europe's finest poets, including Pierre de Ronsard.

AUBIGNY, Agatha d' (fl. 1100s). English noblewoman. Dau. of William d'Aubigny, earl of Arundel, and Adelicia of Louvain (2nd wife of King Henry I of England); sister of Alice and Olivia d'Aubigny.

AUBIN, Penelope (c. 1685–1731). British author and translator. Born c. 1685 in London, England; died in England c. 1731; m. a government employee, name unknown. ❖ Foremother of the fictional novel, reportedly required no fee for her work which bore a strict moral message; published 3 poetic pamphlets (1707); published 6 novels, which sold well and were widely enjoyed, including *The Strange Adventures of the Count de Vinevil* (1721), *The Life of Madame de Beaumont* (1721), *The Life of Charlotta DuPont* (1723), and *The Life and Adventures of the Lady Lucy* (1726); also published 4 translations (from French and Asian works), a drama, and a moral treatise.

AUBRAC, Lucie (1912—). French Resistance leader. Name variations: Lucie Bernard, Lucie Samuel. Born Lucie Bernard in the Mâcon area of Burgundy, France, June 29, 1912; dau. of winegrowers; graduated from Sorbonne with an *agrégée d'histoire* (one of France's highest academic degrees), 1938; m. Raymond Samuel (Raymond Aubrac), Dec 14, 1939; children: Jean-Pierre (b. May 3, 1941), Catherine (b. Feb 19, 1944), Elisabeth (b. 1946). ❖ One of the most active members of the Resistance during WWII, participated in raids, arranged contacts, delivered patriots from the Gestapo, and specialized in organizing prison escapes, 3 of which included her Jewish *résistant* husband; helped found the powerful Libération Sud ("Liberation South") and its underground press, to incite popular revolt and a general strike and to alert the French to the treacherous machinations of Pétain's Vichy government (1940); dealt directly with Klaus Barbie and other Nazis to help husband and others escape (1943); in danger, was flown with family to England where the underground made her a representative of United Resistance Movement with a seat at the conservative assembly of the French Committee of National Liberation in Algiers in 1944 (thus, she became the 1st French woman parliamentarian); testified against Barbie in Lyon (1983); wrote *La Résistance* (*Naissance et Organisation,* 1945). ❖ See also memoir, *Ils partiront dans l'ivresse* (*Outwitting the Gestapo*) (1984); film *Lucie Aubrac;* and *Women in World History.*

AUBRAY, Marie-Madeleine Marguerite d' (1630–1676). *See Brinvilliers, Marie de.*

AUBREY, Madge (1902–1970). English actress. Born Marjorie Alexandra Witham, Feb 2, 1902, in Liverpool, England; died Oct 21, 1970. ❖ Made 1st professional stage appearance in *The Fatal Wedding* (1912); made London debut in *The Best People* (1926), followed by *The Gold Diggers, This Year of Grace* and *Lucky Break,* among others.

AUBREY OF BUONALBERGO (fl. 1000s). Duchess of Apulia. Fl. in 1000s; 1st wife of Robert Guiscard (d. 1085), Frankish noble, duke of Apulia and Calabria, count of Sicily (r. 1057–1085); children: Bohemund I of Antioch (r. 1098–1111, who m. Constance of France). ❖ Robert Guiscard's 2nd wife was Sichelgaita of Salerno.

AUBRY, Cécile (1928—). French actress. Name variations: Cecile Aubry. Born Anne-Marie-José Bénard in Paris, France, Aug 3, 1928; m. a Moroccan prince (later div.); children: Mehdi El Glaoui (actor). ❖ Discovered by Henri-Georges Clouzot, starred in his highly popular film *Manon,* based on a modernization of Abbé Prévost's novel *Manon Lescaut* (1949); other films include *The Black Rose* (US, 1950), *Barbe-Bleu* (Bluebeard, 1951), *Bonjour la*

Chance (1954), and *The Reluctant Thief* (Italian, 1955); went on to write and illustrate children's books and produce for children's tv.

AUCH, Susan (1966—). Canadian speedskater. Born Jan 3, 1966, in Winnipeg, Manitoba, Canada; sister of Andrea Auch. ❖ Won a gold medal for the 3,000-meter relay at the World Short Track championships (1986); won a bronze medal in the 3,000-meter relay at the Calgary Olympics (1988); won a silver medal for the 500 meters at Lillehammer Olympics (1994); won a silver medal for the 500 meters at Nagano Olympics (1998).

AUCLERT, Hubertine (1848–1914). French feminist. Name variations: "Liberta," Jeanne Voitout. Pronunciation: o-CLAIR. Born Marie-Anne-Hubertine Auclert, April 10, 1848, in the village of Tilly, in the department of Allier, France; died in her apartment in Paris, France, April 8, 1914; 5th of 7 children of Jean-Baptiste (well-to-do peasant landowner) and Marie (Chanudet) Auclert (dau. of neighboring landowners); residential pupil at the Catholic Convent of the Dames de l'enfant Jésus in Montmirail (Allier, France) from 9 to 16 (1857–64); m. Antonin Lévrier (judge in the French colonial service) in Algiers, July 1888 (died Feb 1892); no children. ❖ Founder of the women's suffrage movement in France who struggled for 30 years to win the vote through her suffrage league, her militant newspaper, and dramatic tactics including a tax boycott and violent demonstrations; father died (1861); rejected in effort to join Sisters of Charity of St. Vincent de Paul at end of her studies (1864); sent back to convent as a pensioner by her oldest brother on the death of their mother (1866); inherited independent fortune at age 21 (1869); claimed inheritance and moved to Paris (1873), joining pioneering feminist league of Léon Richer and Maria Deraismes (1876); split from Richer and Deraismes during feminist congress of 1878, to seek women's suffrage; participated in socialist congress of 1879 to seek feminist-socialist alliance; organized voter registration campaign and feminist tax boycott in Paris (1880–81); founded feminist society, Women's Suffrage, and suffragist newspaper, *La Citoyenne* (The Citizeness, 1881); led numerous petition campaigns and demonstrations (1881–85); ran as illegal candidate for French parliament (1885); left Paris to marry her longtime feminist collaborator (1888–92); returned to Parisian feminism as newspaper columnist (1893); resumed suffragist petition campaigns (1898); took active role in feminist congress and revived Women's Suffrage (1900); led militant demonstration to burn French Civil Code (1904); led violent election-day demonstrations and convicted of misdemeanor (1908); ran as illegal candidate for French parliament (1910); remained leading voice of militant suffragism as moderate suffragist movement grew in France (1910–14). ❖ See also Steven C. Hause, *Hubertine Auclert: The French Suffragette* (Yale University Press, 1987); and *Women in World History.*

AUDATA (fl. 358 BCE). Illyrian princess. Fl. 358 BCE; dau. of Bardylis (Illyrian chieftain); was the 1st of Philip II of Macedonia's 7 wives; children: Cynnane (c. 357–322 BCE). ❖ Philip's other wives included Olympias, Meda, Nicesipolis, Philinna, Roxane.

AUDELEY, Eleanor (1590–1652). *See Davies, Eleanor.*

AUDINA, Mia (1979—). Indonesian badminton player. Name variations: Mia Audina Tjiptawan. Born Aug 22, 1979, in Jakarta, Indonesia; moved to Rotterdam, Netherlands; m. Tylio Lobman (Dutch gospel singer). ❖ Won a silver medal for singles at Atlanta Olympics (1996); won Indonesia Open (1998) and Dutch Open (2001); became a Dutch national (2000); representing the Netherlands, won a silver medal for singles at Athens Olympics (2004).

AUDLEY, Alice (d. 1374). Baroness Neville of Raby. Name variations: Alice Neville; Baroness Neville of Raby. Died in 1374; m. Ralph Neville, 2nd baron Neville of Raby; children: John Neville, 3rd baron Neville of Raby; Margaret Neville (d. 1372).

AUDLEY, Margaret (fl. 1340s). Countess of Stafford. Fl. 1340; dau. of Hugh Audley, earl of Gloucester, and Margaret de Clare (c. 1293–1342); m. Ralph Stafford, 1st earl of Stafford; children: Ralph (d. 1348), 1st earl of Stafford; Hugh (c. 1344–1386), 2nd earl of Stafford; Beatrice Stafford (who m. Thomas Roos, 5th baron Ros).

AUDLEY, Margaret (d. 1564). Duchess of Norfolk. Name variations: Margaret Howard. Died Jan 9, 1564; dau. of Thomas Audley and Elizabeth Grey; m. Henry Dudley; m. Thomas Howard, 3rd duke of Norfolk, after 1557; children: Thomas Howard (1561–1626), earl of Suffolk; William Howard (1563–1640). ❖ When sister Mary Audley died unmarried, inherited her father's property.

AUDLEY, Maxine (1923–1992). English actress. Born in London, England, April 29, 1923; died July 23, 1992, in London; dau. of Henry Julius Hecht and Katharine (Arkandy) Hecht; educated at Westonbirt School; trained for the stage at the Tamara Daykharhanova School in New York and at the London Mask Theatre School; m. Leonard Cassini (div.); m. Andrew Broughton (div.); m. Frederick Granville (div.). ❖ Made 1st stage appearance as a walk-on in *Midsummer Night's Dream* at the Open Air Theatre (July 1940); following years of stage work, also appeared in such films as *Anna Karenina* (1947), *The Sleeping Tiger* (1954), *The Barretts of Wimpole Street* (1957), *The Prince and the Showgirl* (1957), *King in New York* (1957), *The Dunkirk Story* (1958), *The Vikings* (1958), *Our Man in Havana* (1959), *The Trials of Oscar Wilde* (1960), *The Agony and the Ecstasy* (1965), *House of Cards* (1969), and *The Looking-Glass War* (1970); appeared on tv as Queen Elizabeth I in *Kenilworth,* Celia in *The Cocktail Party,* Tanis in *Portrait in Black,* Mrs. Wilton in *John Gabriel Borkman;* also appeared in tv serials "The Voodoo Factor" and "Danger Man," and as Mrs. Marlow on "Prime Suspect."

AUDOFLEDA (c. 470–?). Queen of Italy. Born c. 470; dau. of Childeric; sister of King Clovis I (c. 466–511); m. Theodoric the Great, king of the Ostrogoths; children: Amalasuntha (c. 498–535). ❖ See also *Women in World History.*

AUDOUARD, Olympe (1830–1890). French novelist, travel writer, and journalist. Pronunciation: OH-dö-är. Born in 1830; died in 1890; m. and div. ❖ Founded various journals in Paris (including literary review *Le Papillon*), and made a successful lecture tour in US (1868–69); interested in the occult, was also an ardent advocate of women's rights; novels and books of travel include *How Men Love* (1861), *The Mysteries of the Seraglio and of the Turkish Harems* (1863), *War on Man* (1866), *Across America* (1869–71), and *Parisian Silhouettes* (1883).

AUDOUX, Marguerite (1863–1937). French novelist. Born in 1863 in France, orphaned; died in 1937. ❖ Worked as a servant and wrote in her spare time; published the autobiographical *Marie-Claire* (1910), which received critical acclaim and international recognition for its realistic depiction of working-class life in France.

AUDOVERA (d. 580). Merovingian queen. Name variations: Audovere or Audovère. Fl. in 560s; put to death by orders of Fredegund (c. 547–597) around 580; 1st wife of Chilperic I, king of Soissons (Neustria, r. 561–584); children: daughter Basina (who became a nun at Poitiers) and 3 sons, Chlodovech, also known as Clovis (d. 580); Theudebert, also known as Theodobert (d. 575); Merovech (d. 577 or 578, who m. his aunt, Brunhilda). ❖ Because of machinations of Fredegund, was ordered to a convent with her daughter Basina sometime before 567, then put to death (c. 580).

AUDRAN, Monique (1924—). See Tcherina, Ludmilla.

AUDRAN, Stéphane (1932—). French actress. Born Colette Suzanne Jeannine Dacheville in Versailles, France, Nov 2, 1932; m. Jean-Louis Trintignant (div.); m. Claude Chabrol (director), 1964 (div. in late 1980s). ❖ An enormously popular star in France, is known for her ability to play the vapid sophisticate or elegant mannequin, while hinting at far more intensity below the surface; 1st starred in *L'Oeil du Matin* (*The Third Lover,* 1962); appeared in nearly 50 films, 21 of them directed by her ex-husband Claude Chabrol, including *Paris Vu Par* (*Six in Paris,* 1965) and *Les Biches* (1968); was also lauded for her performance in the title role of *Babette's Feast* (1987); other films include *Le Signe de Lion* (*The Sign of Leo,* 1962), *Landru* (*Bluebeard,* 1963), *La Ligne de Démarcation* (1966), *Le Scandale* (*The Champagne Murders,* 1967), *La Femme Infidèle* (1969), *La Rupture* (*The Break Up,* 1970), *Le Boucher* (1970), *La Dame dans l'Auto avec des Lunettes et us Fusil* (*The Lady in the Car with Glasses and a Gun,* 1970), *La Peau de Torpedo* (1970), *Folies Bourgeoises* (1976), *And Then There Were None* (1974), *Le Gagnant* (1979), *The Big Red One* (1980), *Brideshead Revisited* (1981), *Le Beau Monde* (1981), *Boulevard de Assassins* (1982), *Thieves After Dark* (1983), *The Sun Also Rises* (1984), *La Cage aux Folles III* (1985), *Les Saisons du Plaisir* (1987), *Poor Little Rich Girl* (1987), *Sons* (1989), *Jours tranquilles à Clichy* (*Quiet Days in Clichy,* 1990), and *Betty* (1993). Received Britain's Academy Award for *Juste Avant la Nuit* (*Just Before Nightfall,* 1971) and *The Discreet Charm of the Bourgeoisie* (1972); won a César award for performance in *Violette Nozière* (*Violette,* 1978). ❖ See also *Women in World History.*

AUDRY, Jacqueline (1908–1977). French film director. Born Jacqueline Audry in Orange, France, Sept 25, 1908; died in 1977; sister of Colette Audry (1906–1990, novelist, playwright, literary critic, and screenwriter

of *The Battle of the Rails* [*Bataille du Rail*]); m. Pierre Laroche (1902–1962, a scriptwriter). ❖ Began film career in continuity (1933); served as assistant director to such luminaries as G.W. Pabst, Jean Delannoy, and Marcel Ophüls (1933–43); directed 1st film, a short entitled *Les Chevaux du Vercors* (1943), followed by 1st full-length feature *Les Malheurs de Sophie* (1944); subsequently directed a number of films popular in France, many of which were written by husband Pierre Laroche; brought two of Colette's stories to the screen: *Mitsou* and *Gigi* (not the musical); released *Olivia* (1951), script by Colette, a milestone because of its exploration of lesbian themes, a subject then considered taboo; also directed Jean-Paul Sartre's *Huis clos* (*No Exit,* 1954). ❖ See also *Women in World History.*

AUEL, Jean (1936—). American novelist. Name variations: Jean M. Auel. Pronunciation: Auel pronounced owl, like the bird. Born Jean Marie Untinen, Feb 18, 1936, in Chicago, Illinois; dau. of a housepainter; Portland State University, MA in Business, 1976; m. Ray Bernard Auel; children: 5. ❖ Gained international renown with her "Earth's children" series, books that contain detailed descriptions of prehistoric life, including *Clan of the Cave Bear* (1980), *The Valley of Horses* (1982), *The Mammoth Hunters* (1985), *Plains of Passage* (1990), and *The Shelters of Stone* (2002).

AUEN, Signe (1894–1966). See Owen, Seena.

AUER, Johanna (1950—). Austrian politician. Born Oct 8, 1950, in Rust am See, Austria. ❖ Elected to the Bundesrat (Austrian Parliament) in 2000; served as president of the Bundesrat (Dec 28, 2000–Dec 31, 2000).

AUER, Judith (1905–1944). Swiss-born German political activist. Born Judith Vallentin in Zurich, Switzerland, Sept 19, 1905; died by the guillotine at Berlin's Plötzensee Penitentiary, Oct 27, 1944; m. Erich Auer, 1926; children: one daughter (b. 1929). ❖ Fought against the Nazi regime despite constant threats to her life; was active in youth activities in Berlin, joining the German Communist Party (KPD, 1927); centered her work in the Communist-dominated working-class district of Wedding, known as "Red Wedding" during the Weimar Republic; was active in underground resistance activities, including the preparation and distribution of pamphlets and flyers warning the populace of Hitler's plans for war (1930s); was a member of the Saefkow-Jacob-Bästlein resistance group (1940–44); arrested and sentenced to death for high treason (1944). ❖ See also *Women in World History.*

AUERBACH, Beatrice Fox (1887–1968). American business executive. Name variations: Beatrice Fox. Born in Hartford, Connecticut, July 7, 1887; died Nov 29, 1968; eldest dau. of Moses and Theresa Stern Fox; m. George Auerbach (died 1927). ❖ For many years the only female department-store president in the country, came into the family business, G. Fox & Co., when husband died (1927); became company president (1938); introduced the 5-day work week, retirement and medical plans, and a subsidized lunchroom; was one of the 1st to hire African-Americans in jobs that were not dead-end positions; initiated a statewide toll-free telephone service, a free delivery service, and fully automated billing. By 1959, G. Fox & Co. was the largest privately owned department store in US. ❖ See also *Women in World History.*

AUERBACH, Charlotte (1899–1994). German-born Scottish geneticist. Name variations: Lotte Auerbach. Born May 14, 1899, in Krefeld, Germany; died Mar 17, 1994, in Scotland; achieved doctorate in genetics from the University of Edinburgh in 1935; never married; children: adopted a girl and a boy. ❖ Universally recognized for her studies on the effects of radiation on mutation of genes, left Nazi Germany to escape persecution (1933); completed doctorate in genetics from University of Edinburgh (1935); became a laboratory technician despite her qualifications, slowly working up the career ladder; appointed lecturer (1947) and reader (1958); researched the mutagenic action of chemicals, which resulted in many publications, including several books for general audiences, like *Genetics in the Atomic Age* (1956) and *The Science of Genetics* (1962). Awarded the DSc from Edinburgh (1947); elected to a Royal Society of Edinburgh fellowship (1949); became a fellow of Royal Society of London (1957), foreign associate member of Royal Danish Academy of Science (1968), foreign associate member of US National Academy of Sciences (1970); received Darwin Medal of London's Royal Society (1976). ❖ See also *Women in World History.*

AUERBACH, Edith (1903—). German physician. Born on Oct 14, 1903, in Berlin; married Theodor Auerbach (Marxist). ❖ A Marxist, escaped to Belgium with husband (1933), after the Nazis seized power in

Germany, then USSR (1935); arrested with husband on suspicion of anti-Soviet activities during the Stalinist purges (1937); survived WWII and returned to East Germany (1956); joined the dominant Socialist Unity Partya and was appointed to a post in the Buch Clinic and the hospital reserved for high state officials.

AUERBACH, Ellen (1906–2004). German-American photographer. Born Ellen Rosenberg in Karlsruhe, Germany, May 20, 1906; died in New York, age 98, July 31, 2004; studied sculpture at Kunstakademie, Karlsruhe, Germany, 1924–1927; married Walter Auerbach (stage designer), in London, 1936 (div. 1945). ❖ Known for her advertising images, documentation, portraits, experimental photography, and powerful photos of children, began training as a sculptor at Kunstakademie and later in Stuttgart; traveled to Berlin to study photography privately with Bauhaus professor Walter Peterhans (1928); with Grete Stern, set up a studio in Dessau (1932), Ringl + Pit, one of the world's 1st female-run commercial photographic firms, where they photographed leading figures, including Bertolt Brecht; with the rise of Hitler, immigrated to Palestine (1933) and opened a children's portrait studio in Tel Aviv; on marriage, moved to US (1937) and worked with husband at the Lessing Rosenwald Print Collection in Philadelphia, using photography to restore prints; combined photography with work in education at the Menninger Foundation in Kansas (1946–49), where she used film and still photography to study the behavior of young children; photographed extensively in Argentina, Greece, Majorca, Germany, and Austria; chose Mexico for her last photographic journey, in collaboration with Eliot Porter, documenting Mexico's church art and religious celebrations in *Mexican Churches* (1987) and *Mexican Celebrations* (1990); was an educational therapist in New York (1965–80).

AUERSWALD, Ingrid (1957—). East German runner. Born Sept 1957 in East Germany. ❖ At Moscow Olympics, won a bronze medal in the 100 meters and a gold medal for the 4 x 100-meter relay (1980); at Seoul Olympics, won a silver medal for the 4 x 100-meter relay (1988).

AUFLES, Inger. Norwegian cross-country skier. Born in Norway. ❖ Won a bronze medal for 10 km and a gold medal for 3 x 5km relay at Grenoble Olympics (1968); won a bronze medal for 3 x 5km relay at Sapporo Olympics (1972).

AUGARDE, Adrienne (d. 1913). English actress. Born in England; died Mar 17, 1913; niece of Amy Augarde (actress). ❖ Made London debut in *The Toreador* (1903), followed by *The Duchess of Dantzic, The Mystery of Edwin Drood* and *The Sins of Society*, among others; created the title role in *Lady Madcap* (1904) and the Princess in *The New Aladdin* (1905); toured US in title role of *Peggy Machree*. ❖ See also Sandra M.A. Sardeson's *Born to Music: The Story of the Augarde Family in England* (Heritage Lincolnshire, 1999).

AUGARDE, Amy (1868–1959). English actress and singer. Born Amy Florence Augarde, July 7, 1868, in Westminster, Middlesex, England; died April 1, 1959, in Reigate, Surrey; sister of Louise Augarde (actress and singer); aunt of Adrienne Augarde (actress). ❖ Made 1st stage appearance in the chorus of the D'Oyly Carte Opera company (1884); starred in such plays and musicals as *Dorothy, La Fille de Madame Angot, The Wizard of the Nile, Bilberry of Tilbury, The Chocolate Soldier, The Girl in the Taxi, Love and Laughter, Véronique, Cash on Delivery, The Red Mill, The Naughty Princess, The Last Waltz* and *The Damask Rose*; sang the parts of Pitti-Sing and Katisha for a Gilbert and Sullivan Gramophone recording of *The Mikado* (1906), and Hebe and Little Buttercup for *H.M.S. Pinafore* (1908). ❖ See also Sandra M.A. Sardeson's *Born to Music: The Story of the Augarde Family in England* (Heritage Lincolnshire, 1999).

AUGARDE, Louise (1863–1909). English actress and singer. Name variations: Louise Augarde King. Born Louise Adele Augarde, Feb 24, 1863, in Westminster, Middlesex, England; died Aug 1, 1909, in Brixton, Surrey; elder sister of Amy Augarde (actress); aunt of Adrienne Augarde (actress); m. Sebastian King (actor and singer). ❖ Made professional stage debut (1882); joined D'Oyly Carte Rep (1884); with sister Amy, traveled to US with the 1st American *Mikado* company (1885–86). ❖ See also Sandra M.A. Sardeson's *Born to Music: The Story of the Augarde Family in England* (Heritage Lincolnshire, 1999).

AUGSPURG, Anita (1857–1943). Major leader of the German women's movement. Name variations: Augsburg. Pronunciation: OWGS-purk. Born Anita Johanna Theodora Sophie Augspurg, Sept 22, 1857, in Verden an der Aller, Germany; died Dec 20, 1943, in Zurich, Switzerland; dau. of Augustine (Langenbeck) Augspurg (from a ministerial and medical family) and Wilhelm Augspurg (lawyer); attended private schools and universities of Berlin and Zurich; granted law degree from University of Zurich; never married; no children; lived with Lida Heymann. ❖ A major leader of the German women's movement during early 20th century, combined feminism with pacifism, insisting that Europe would be spared future wars only when women had the right to vote; 1st wanted to become a teacher; studied drama at University of Berlin and acted at theaters in Meiningen, Riga, and Altenburg, Germany (1881–85); studied jurisprudence at University of Zurich (1893–97); edited *Journal for Female Suffrage* (1907–12); with Lida Heymann, was among 13 co-founders of the German Union for Women's Suffrage (1902), participated in the German Women's Suffrage League (1907), worked in International Women's Suffrage Alliance (1904–09), attended a women's meeting at The Hague which established the Women's International League for Peace and Freedom (1915), edited the journal *Woman in the State* (1918–33) and moved to Zurich (1933); opened highly successful photographic studio in Munich (1900). ❖ See also *Women in World History*.

AUGUST, Bonnie (1947–2003). American fashion designer. Name variations: Bonnie J. August. Born Jan 2, 1947, in River Edge, New Jersey; died of ovarian cancer, Aug 9, 2003, in New York, NY; attended Syracuse University; married; children: Bryan. ❖ Known for her stretchy materials and bodywear based on leotard and tights, created her most influential designs while working for Danskin (1975–1983), including the disco look: a one-piece bodysuit worn with a wraparound skirt; started Bonnie August Activewear and Bodywear (1984). Won Coty Award (1978). ❖ See also *Women in World History*.

AUGUSTA, Empress of Germany (1811–1890). *See Augusta of Saxe-Weimar.*

AUGUSTA, Mlle (1806–1901). German-born dancer. Name variations: Performed as Comtesse de Saint-James or Augusta, Countess of St. James. Born Caroline Augusta Josephine Thérèsa Fuchs, 1806, in Munich, Germany; died Feb 17, 1901; trained in Munich, then Paris under François Albert. ❖ Was in the corps de ballet of the premiere of *l'Orzie* (1831); had greatest success with her US debut in *Les Naïades* (1836), then toured intermittently for 10 years; was the 1st to dance *Giselle* in NY (Feb 1846), a month after Mary Anne Lee had danced the ballet in Boston; was also known for her versions of *La Bayadère, La Sylphide* and *La Muette de Portici;* retired (c. 1850) and returned to Europe.

AUGUSTA GUELPH (1737–1813). Duchess of Brunswick-Wolfenbuttel. Name variations: Princess royal. Born July 31, 1737, at St. James's Palace, London, England; died Mar 23, 1813, in London; buried at St. George's Chapel, Windsor; dau. of Frederick Guelph, prince of Wales, and Augusta of Saxe-Gotha (1719–1772); sister of George III, king of England; m. Charles Bevern, duke of Brunswick-Wolfenbuttel, Jan 17, 1764; children: seven, including Augusta of Brunswick-Wolfenbuttel (1764–1788), who m. Frederick I, king of Wurttemberg); Caroline of Brunswick (1768–1821), who m. George IV, king of England); Amelia Caroline Dorothea (1772–1773).

AUGUSTA GUELPH (1768–1840). English princess. Name variations: Princess Augusta, Augusta Sophia. Born August Sophia on Nov 8, 1768, at Buckingham House, London, England; died Sept 22, 1840, in London; buried at St. George's Chapel, Windsor; dau. of George III, king of England, and Charlotte of Mecklenburg-Strelitz.

AUGUSTA GUELPH (1822–1916). Duchess of Mecklenburg-Strelitz. Name variations: Augusta Caroline Charlotte Elizabeth Mary Sophia Louise Guelph on July 19, 1822; died Dec 4, 1916, in Neustrelitz, Mecklenburg, Germany; dau. of Adolphus Guelph, 1st duke of Cambridge, and Augusta of Hesse-Cassel (dau. of Landgrave Frederick III); m. Frederick, grand duke of Mecklenburg-Strelitz, June 28, 1843; children: 2, including Adolphus Frederick V, grand duke of Mecklenburg-Strelitz.

AUGUSTA MARIA OF BADEN-BADEN (1704–1726). Duchess of Orleans. Name variations: Augusta-Marie of Baden; Augusta Maria von Baden-Baden. Born Nov 10, 1704; died Aug 8, 1726, shortly after giving birth to a daughter; dau. of Louis William (b. 1655), margrave of Baden-Baden; m. Philippe Louis, also known as Louis Philip or Philippe (1703–1752), 3rd duke of Orleans (r. 1723–1752), July 13, 1724; children: Louis-Philippe (1725–1785), 4th duke of Orleans (1752–1785); Louise Magdalen (1726–1726, lived seven days).

AUGUSTA MARIA OF HOLSTEIN-GOTTORP (1649–1728). Margravine of Baden-Durlach. Name variations: Augusta Marie. Born in 1649; died in 1728; dau. of Marie Elizabeth of Saxony (1610–1684) and Frederick III, duke of Holstein-Gottorp; m. Frederick VII, margrave of Baden-Durlach, May 15, 1670; children: Albertina of Baden-Durlach (1682–1755); Charles III William, margrave of Baden-Durlach (b. 1679).

AUGUSTA OF BAVARIA (1788–1851). *See Amalie Auguste.*

AUGUSTA OF BRUNSWICK-WOLFENBUTTEL (1764–1788). Queen of Wurttemberg. Name variations: Augusta Caroline of Brunswick. Born Augusta Caroline Fredericka Louise Bevern on Dec 3, 1764; died age 24 on Sept 27, 1788; dau. of Augusta Guelph (1737–1813) and Charles II Bevern, duke of Brunswick-Wolfenbuttel; m. Frederick II (1754–1816), duke of Wurttemberg (r. 1797–1802), elector of Wurttemberg (r. 1802–1806), also known as Frederick I, king of Wurttemberg (r. 1806–1816), Oct 11, 1780; children: William I, king of Wurttemberg (r. 1816–1864); Catherine of Wurttemberg (1783–1835); Sophia Dorothea (1783–1784); Paul Charles Frederick (1785–1852), duke of Wurttemberg (b. 1785).

AUGUSTA OF HESSE-CASSEL (1797–1889). Duchess of Cambridge. Born July 25, 1797, at Cassell, Germany; died April 6, 1889, at St. James's Palace, London, England; buried at St. George's Chapel, Windsor; dau. of Frederick III, landgrave of Hesse-Cassel, and Caroline of Nassau-Usingen (1762–1823); m. Adolphus Guelph, 1st duke of Cambridge, May 7, 1818; children: George Guelph, 2nd duke of Cambridge; Augusta Guelph (1822–1916); Mary Adelaide (1833–1897).

AUGUSTA OF REUSS-EBERSDORF (1757–1831). Duchess of Saxe-Coburg-Saalfeld. Born Jan 9, 1757; died Nov 16, 1831; dau. of Henry XXIV, count of Reuss-Ebersdorf, and Caroline Ernestine, countess Erbach-Schonberg (b. 1727); grandmother of Victoria, queen of England; m. Francis Frederick (1750–1806), duke of Saxe-Coburg-Saalfeld; children: Sophie (b. 1778); Antoinette Saxe-Coburg (1779–1824); Anna Juliana of Saxe-Coburg-Saalfeld (1781–1860); Ernest I, duke of Saxe-Coburg and Gotha (b. 1784); Ferdinand Saxe-Coburg (b. 1785); Victoria of Coburg (1786–1861, mother of Queen Victoria); Marianne (b. 1788); Leopold I, king of Belgium (b. 1790); Maximilian (b. 1792).

AUGUSTA OF SAXE-GOTHA (1719–1772). Princess of Wales and mother of George III of England. Name variations: Augusta of Saxe-Coburg, Augusta of Saxe-Gotha-Altenburg; Augusta of Saxe-Coburg Gotha. Born Augusta, princess of Saxe-Gotha-Coburg, Nov 30, 1719, in Gotha, Thuringia, Germany; died Feb 8, 1772, at Carlton House, London, England; buried at Westminster Abbey; dau. of Frederick II, duke of Saxe-Gotha-Altenburg, and Madeleine of Anhalt-Zerbst (1679–1740); m. Frederick Louis, prince of Wales (1706–1751, son of George II and Caroline of Ansbach), April 27, 1736; children: Augusta Guelph (1737–1813), princess royal; George William Frederick (1738–1820), later George III, king of England; Edward Augustus (1739–1767), duke of Albany and York; Elizabeth Caroline (1740–1759); William Henry (1743–1805), duke of Gloucester; Henry Frederick (b. 1745), duke of Cumberland; Louisa Anne (1749–1768); Frederick William (1750–1765); Caroline Matilda (1751–1775). ❖ At 17, married Frederick Louis, prince of Wales; because of Frederick's influence at court, evicted with husband from their palace apartments by King George; gave birth to 9 children in 14 years, before death of husband (1751); was heavily influential in the life of royal son, future George III, and heavily influenced by her close friend, the earl of Bute. ❖ See also *Women in World History.*

AUGUSTA OF SAXE-WEIMAR (1811–1890). Empress of Germany and queen of Prussia. Name variations: Marie Louise Augusta of Saxe-Weimar; Empress Augusta of Germany. Born Marie Luise Katharina Augusta, princess of Grand Duchy of Saxe-Weimar, Sept 30, 1811, in Saxe-Weimar, Germany; died in Berlin, Jan 7, 1890; 2nd dau. of Karl Friedrich, also known as Charles Frederick, grand duke of Saxe-Weimar, and Marie Pavlovna (1786–1859); m. William I (1797–1888), the future Kaiser Wilhelm I, emperor of Germany (r. 1871–1888), June 11, 1829; children: Frederick Wilhelm III, also known as Frederick III (b. 1831), king of Prussia and emperor of Germany (r. 1888); Louise of Baden (1838–1923). ❖ Raised as a scholar; at 18, married the future Wilhelm I (1829), though he was in love with his cousin, Elisa Radziwill; as a learned liberal, freely announced her opinions, often in direct contrast with her husband; was also known for her impassioned displays, passionate friendships and explosions of anger; led a separate existence from husband, sequestered on different floors at home in Berlin; by the time Wilhelm was named king of Prussia (1858), had done away with any pretense of a unified marriage, often spending time away, either with brother in Weimar or with daughter Louise of Baden; as she aged under

layers of make-up and finery, became an object of quiet ridicule in Germany. ❖ See also *Women in World History.*

AUGUSTA OF SCHLESWIG-HOLSTEIN (1858–1921). Empress of Germany. Name variations: Augusta Victoria; (Ger.) Auguste Viktoria. Born Augusta Victoria Fredericka Louise Feodore Jenny, Oct 22, 1858, in Dolzig, Germany; died April 11, 1921, at Doorn, Netherlands; eldest dau. of Frederick, duke of Schleswig-Holstein-Sonderburg-Augustenburg, and Adelaide of Hohenlohe-Langenburg (1835–1900); m. William II (1859–1941), also known as Wilhelm II, kaiser of Germany (r. 1888–1918), Feb 27, 1881; children: Frederick William (1885–1951, crown prince of Prussia, who m. Cecilia of Mecklenburg-Schwerin); Eitel-Frederick (1883–1942, who m. Sophie Charlotte of Oldenburg); Augustus William (1887–1949, who m. Alexandra Victoria of Schleswig-Holstein); Adalbert (who m. Adelaide of Saxe-Meiningen); Oscar; Joachim (who m. Marie of Anhalt); Victoria Louise (1892–1980, who m. Ernest Augustus of Cumberland). Following the death of Augusta in 1921, Wilhelm II m. Hermine of Reuss, Nov 5, 1922.

AUGUSTA OF TUSCANY (1825–1864). Austrian archduchess. Name variations: Auguste Ferdinand; Augusta of Austria. Born Jan 4, 1825, in Florence, Italy; died April 26, 1864, in Munich; dau. of Maria Anna of Saxony (1799–1832) and Leopold II, grand duke of Saxony; m. Luitpold (1821–1912), regent of Bavaria from 1886 to 1912; children: Ludwig III, king of Bavaria (r. 1913–1918); Therese (1850–1925); Leopold (1846–1930); Arnulf (1852–1907).

AUGUSTA OF WURTTEMBERG (1826–1898). Princess of Saxe-Weimar. Born Augusta Wilhelmina Henrietta, Oct 4, 1826; died Dec 3, 1898; dau. of Pauline of Wurttemberg (1800–1873) and William I (1781–1864), king of Wurttemberg (r. 1816–1864); m. Hermann Henry, prince of Saxe-Weimar, June 17, 1851; children: Pauline of Saxe-Weimar (1852–1904); William Charles (b. 1853); Bernard William (b. 1855), count of Crayenberg; Alexander William (b. 1857); Ernest Charles (b. 1859); Olga Marie (1869–1924, who m. Leopold Wolfgang, prince of Ysemburg-Birste).

AUGUSTA VICTORIA (1890–1966). Countess Douglas. Name variations: Auguste Victoria Hohenzollern. Born Aug 19, 1890, in Potsdam, Germany; died Aug 29, 1966, in Münchhof, Kr. Stockach, Baden, Germany; dau. of William (1864–1927), prince of Hohenzollern, and Marie Therese of Bourbon; m. Manuel II (1889–1932), king of Portugal (r. 1908–1910, deposed in 1910), Sept 4, 1913; m. Carl Robert, count Douglas, April 23, 1939; children: (2nd m.) possibly Dagmar Rosita Douglas who m. John George Spencer-Churchill, 11th duke of Marlborough.

AUGUSTAT, Elise (1889–1940). German Reichstag deputy. Born Elise Queck on July 29, 1889, in Waldheim, Germany; died Mar 13, 1940, as a result of injuries sustained while imprisoned at Ravensbrück. ❖ Was 1st elected to German Reichstag (Sept 1930), representing Hamburg on Communist ticket; was arrested on charges of high treason soon after Hitler came to power but was released (1933); at beginning of WWII, was arrested once more and sent to Ravensbrück. ❖ See also *Women in World History.*

AUGUSTESEN, Susanne (1956—). Danish soccer player. Born in Denmark in 1956. ❖ At World championship finals (1971), as a 15-year-old schoolgirl, helped Denmark defeat Mexico 3–0 by scoring all 3 goals.

AUGUSTINE, Rose (1910–2003). American guitar-string maker. Born Rose Lipschitz (later changed by family to Lewis), Feb 10, 1910, in New York, NY; grew up in the Bronx; died April 21, 2003, in New York, NY; attended Hunter College; Columbia University, MA; m. Albert Augustine (Danish-born luthier) 1928 (died 1967). ❖ Began career as a chemistry teacher; founded the journal *Guitar Review* (1946) and was publisher and editor; with husband, developed nylon strings to replace animal gut strings for guitar, and founded guitar string-making company, Augustine Strings, Ltd. (1947), becoming president (1967); was a close friend of Andrés Segovia; underwrote concerts, and commissioned guitar works from composers (beginning 1980); chief sponsor of Augustine Foundation Concert Series, was named "The Matriarch of the Guitar." Received numerous honors, including Guitar Foundation of America's Lifetime Achievement Award (2002), Vahdah Olcott Bickford Award, and honorary degree from Manhattan School of Music.

AULAIRE, Ingri d' (1904–1980). *See d'Aulaire, Ingri.*

AULENTI, Gae (1927—). *Italian architect.* Name variations: Gaetana Aulenti. Born 1927 in Palazzolo dello Stello, Italy. ❖ Best known for her furniture and exhibition design, trained and later taught at the Milan Polytechnic School of Architecture (Milan Politecnico); established private practice in Milan; held visiting professorships in Italy and Spain; came to prominence with designs for Fiat and Olivetti; designed houses, schools, and stage sets; conceived lamps, displays and show-rooms for Knoll International; redesigned the Musée d'Orsay in Paris (1980–86).

AULNOY, Marie Catherine, Countess d' (c. 1650–1705). *French author.* Name variations: Aunoy or Anois; wrote under pseudonyms of Dunnois and Madame D. Born Marie Catherine Jumel de Barneville, c. 1650, at Barneville near Bourgachard (Eure); died in Paris, France, Jan 14, 1705; her mother became the marquise de Gudaigne at the time of her 2nd marriage; niece of Marie Bruneau des Loges (friend of Malherbe and Balzac, called the "tenth Muse"); m. François de la Motte (gentleman in the service of César, duc de Vendôme, who became Baron d'Aulnoy in 1654), Mar 8, 1666; children: 5, not all with her husband. ❖ Married Baron d'Aulnoy then became embroiled in a plot with her mother to have him committed for high treason; when conspiracy was exposed, fled with mother to England, then Spain, but was eventually allowed to return to France; won instant success with 1st novel *Histoire d'Hypolite comte du Duglas* (*Hippolyte, Count of Douglas*), an adventure-romance set in England (1690); a prolific writer, was especially noted for her *Contes nouvelles ou fées à la mode*, 24 fairy tales from the original stories found in the *Pentamerone* (1637) by Giovanni Battista Basile, a collection that included *L'Oiseau blue* (*The Blue Bird*), *La Chatte Blanche* (*The White Cat*), and her best known, *La Belle aux cheveux d'or* (*Goldilocks*). ❖ See also *Women in World History*.

AULT, Marie (1870–1951). *English stage and screen actress.* Born Mary Cragg, Sept 2, 1870, in Wigan, Lancashire, England; died May 9, 1951, in London; m. James Alexander Paterson. ❖ Spent the 1st 20 years of career touring the provinces; made London debut in *Petronella* (1906), followed by *Rutherford and Son, Strife, East of Suez* (to great success), *The Elopement, The Little Minister, Prisoners of War, The Fanatics, Little Eyolf, Love on the Dole, Jane Eyre, Anna Christie* and *Bedtime Story*; films include *Woman to Woman, The Lodger, Hobson's Choice, Major Barbara, Love on the Dole, We Dive at Dawn, I See a Dark Stranger* and *Madness of the Heart.*

AUMA, Alice (1960—). See *Lakwena, Alice.*

AUNG SAN SUU KYI (1945—). *Burmese human-rights activist, scholar, and writer.* Born Suu Kyi in Rangoon, Burma (now Yangon and Myanmar, respectively), June 19, 1945; youngest of three children of Aung San (leader of the Burmese nationalist movement in 1940s, which culminated in 1948 in the nation's attaining its independence from 50 years of British rule and three years of Japanese occupation) and Khin Kyi (Burma's ambassador to India and 1st woman to head a Burmese diplomatic mission); attended Lady Sri Ram College and Delhi University; St. Hugh's College at Oxford University, BA (1967); attended University of Kyoto in Japan (1985) and School of Oriental and African Studies at London University (1987); m. Michael Aris (scholar of Tibetan civilization), 1972; children: sons, Alexander and Kim. ❖ At 15, left the country when mother became Burma's ambassador to India; worked in England as a teacher and at UN; returned to Rangoon to care for dying mother (1988); when armed soldiers killed as many as 3,000 citizens because of uprisings against the dictatorial Burma Socialist Program Party, made her 1st major public appearance in front of 500,000, speaking of human rights, including freedom to choose one's government; attempted to reconcile civil and military authorities; founded National League of Democracy and became its secretary-general (1988); though the government banned political demonstrations of over four persons and reaffirmed the right to arrest and sentence citizens without trial, defied the ban and continued her efforts for "Burma's second struggle for independence"; lived under house arrest at family home in Rangoon (1989–95); freed (2002); detained once more (2003); wrote *Freedom From Fear & Other Writings* (Viking, 1991) and (with Alan Clements) *The Voice of Hope* (Seven Stories, 1997). Received the Nobel Peace Prize in recognition of her nonviolent quest for democracy in her ravaged nation (1991). ❖ See also *Women in World History*.

AUNLI, Berit. *Norwegian cross-country skier.* Name variations: Berit Kvello. Born Berit Kvello in Norway; m. Ove Aunli (skier). ❖ Won a bronze medal for 4 x 5km relay at Lake Placid Olympics (1980); won a gold medal for 4 x 5km relay and a silver for 5 km at Sarajevo Olympics (1984).

AUNOY, Marie (c. 1650–1705). See *Aulnoy, Marie Catherine, Countess d.*

AUNT DAISY (1879–1963). See *Basham, Maud Ruby.*

AUNT FANNY
See *Gage, Frances D. (1808–1884).*
See *Barrow, Frances Elizabeth (1822–1894).*

AUNT HATTY (1815–1893). See *Baker, Harriette Newell.*

AUNT HILDA (1893–1972). See *Burns, Violet Alberta Jessie.*

AUNT JEMIMA (1897–1950). See *Gardella, Tess.*

AUNT KATE (1854/55?–1946). See *Powell, Mary Sadler.*

AUNTIE IRMGARD (c. 1912–2001). See *Aluli, Irmgard.*

AUNTIE MAME (1891–1985). See *Tanner, Marion.*

AURA POKOU (c. 1700–c. 1760). See *Pokou.*

AURELIA (c. 120 BCE–54 BCE). *Roman noblewoman and mother of Julius Caesar.* Born c. 120 BCE; died 54 BCE in Rome; dau. of Aurelius Cotta; m. Gaius Julius Caesar Maior (judge); children: Roman emperor (Gaius) Julius Caesar Minor (c. 100–44 BCE); Julia Minor (c. 100 BCE–51 BCE); Julia Maior. ❖ Was known to have had some education, because she spoke a learned Latin; oversaw the education of her son until he was 7, after which he was turned over to his father and uncles; remained in charge of daughters, one of whom, Julia Minor, would be the grandmother of Rome's 1st emperor, Augustus. ❖ See also *Women in World History.*

AURELIA FADILLA (d. before 138). *Roman noblewoman.* Born before 138; dau. of Faustina I (c. 90–141 CE) and Antoninus Pius (r. 138–161); sister of Faustina II (130–175 CE); married.

AURIOL, Jacqueline (1917–2000). *French aviator.* Born Jacqueline Marie Thérèse Suzanne Douet on Nov 5, 1917, at Challans, France; died in 2000; dau. of Pierre Douet (shipbuilder and importer of Scandinavian wood); attended school in Nantes; studied art at L'école du Louvre, Paris; m. Paul Auriol (son of Vincent Auriol, French diplomat and 1st president of Fourth Republic [1947–1954]), 1938; children: two sons, Jean-Claude and Jean-Paul. ❖ Famed pilot, attended flying school at Villacoublay and received license (1948), then soloed an additional 10 hours to receive a 2nd-degree license; demonstrated skills in an air show outside Paris (1949), the only woman among 20 famous French flyers; was severely injured when a seaplane in which she was a passenger crashed into the Seine (1949); underwent over 20 operations to rebuild her face; qualified for a helicopter pilot's license (1951); won the title of "fastest woman in the world" (1951), then broke her own speed record (Dec 21, 1952); went on to become one of France's top test pilots, the only woman in her country engaged in that profession, and made headlines again as the Concorde's 1st pilot (1971). Awarded the Cross of Chevalier of the French Legion of Honor; won the Harmon International Trophy (1951 and 1952). ❖ See also autobiography *I Live To Fly* (trans. by Pamela Swinglehurst, M. Joseph, 1970); and *Women in World History.*

AUROI, Danielle (1944—). *French politician.* Born Feb 29, 1944, in Clermont-Ferrand, France. ❖ Member of the Auvergne Regional Council (1992–99) and the Greens' Executive Committee (1995–97); representing Group of the Greens/European Free Alliance, elected to 5th European Parliament (1999–2004).

AURORA OF SAN DONATO (1873–1904). *Princess of Yugoslavia.* Name variations: Aurora Demidoff. Born Nov 15, 1873; died June 28, 1904; dau. of Paul Demidoff, prince of San Donato; m. Arsen or Arsene Karadjordjevic (b. 1859), prince of Yugoslavia, May 1, 1892 (div. 1896); children: Paul, prince and regent of Yugoslavia.

AURY, Dominique (1907–1998). *French editor and writer.* Name variations: (pseudonym) Pauline Réage or Reage. Born at Rochefort-sur-Mer, France, 1907; died April 26, 1998, in France. ❖ A well-known translator, worked for Gallimard in Paris, starting 1950; did not claim authorship for *The Story of O,* the sado-masochistic "classy porn classic," until 1994, when she was 86, even though the book was awarded the Deux-Magots, one of France's premiere literary awards, in 1955. ❖ See also *Women in World History.*

AUS DER OHE, Adele (1864–1937). *German pianist.* Born in Hannover, Germany, Dec 11, 1864; died in Berlin on Dec 7, 1937; studied with

Theodor Kullak, then studied for 7 years with Franz Liszt. ❖ Made American debut in NY, performing Liszt's First Piano Concerto (1886), followed by 17 annual US tours; played with Boston Symphony on 51 occasions (1887–1906); performed Tchaikovsky's First Piano Concerto at Carnegie Hall with the composer conducting (1891); appeared again as soloist in the same concerto with the composer conducting in St. Petersburg, Russia (1893), a few days before his sudden death; had to abandon career because of a crippling illness.

AUSLANDER, Mrs. Joseph (1911–1960). *See Wurdemann, Audrey Mary.*

AUSLÄNDER, Rose (1901–1988). Austro-Hungarian poet. Born Rosalie Scherzer in 1901 into a German-speaking Jewish family and raised in Czernowitz (now Chernovtsy), Ukraine; died in 1988; m. Ignaz Ausländer (div. 3 years later). ❖ One of the foremost lyrical poets detailing the war and postwar experience of the Jews, left Europe for US (1921); returned to Czernowitz (1931) and spent the war years hiding in the ghetto cellars of the town; writing in German, published 1st volume of poetry (1965), but did not receive critical acclaim until 1970s; works include *Blindar Summer* (Blind Summer, 1965), *Inventar* (Inventory, 1972), *Doppelspiel* (Double Game, 1977), *Mutterland* (Motherland, 1978), and *Ein Stück weiter* (A Little Further, 1979).

AUSSEM, Cilly (1909–1963). German tennis player. Name variations: Cilly or Cäcilie Aussem. Born Cäcilie Aussem, Jan 4, 1909, in Cologne, Germany; died Mar 1963 in Portofino, Italy; m. Murai della Corte Brae (Italian count), 1935. ❖ Won German mixed-doubles championship in Berlin (1926); won German national singles title (1927); won French mixed-doubles championships with Bill Tilden and women's singles title (1930); won Wimbledon's women's singles title (1931), the only German to hold a Wimbledon title before 1985; ill health forced retirement (1935). ❖ See also *Women in World History.*

AUSTEN, Alice (1866–1952). American photographer. Name variations: Elizabeth Alice Austen. Born Elizabeth Alice Munn in 1866 in New York; died in 1952 on Staten Island, NY; dau. of Edward Stopford Munn and Alice (Austen) Munn; attended Miss Errington's School for Young Ladies. ❖ By 18, was a serious photographer with professional standards, though she never tried to sell any of her thousands of glass-plate negatives; did much of her work in Manhattan, documenting working people and immigrants of various ethnic backgrounds; also spent many summers abroad; lived in the poorhouse (1945–50), until historian Oliver Jensen interested magazines in her exceptional work. ❖ See also *Women in World History.*

AUSTEN, Elizabeth Alice (1866–1952). *See Austen, Alice.*

AUSTEN, Jane (1775–1817). British novelist. Name variations: Jennie. Born Jane Austen on Dec 16, 1775, in the village of Steventon, England; died July 18, 1817, in Winchester, England, probably of Addison's disease; dau. of George Austen (cleric) and Cassandra (Leigh) Austen; sister and lifelong companion of Cassandra; attended boarding school for girls in Oxford, then Southampton, run by Ann Cooper Cawley, 1783, and the Abbey School in Reading, 1784–86; never married; no children. ❖ Novelist, whose domestic satires of 19th-century British gentry, with their witty and astute depictions of human nature, continue to enthrall modern readers, lived with family in Steventon (1775–1801), Bath (1801–06), Southampton (1801–09), and Chawton (1809–1817), and moved to Winchester for medical care shortly before her death; read widely; wrote short stories and comedies for the family's amusement; published 1st novel, *Sense and Sensibility,* anonymously at her own expense (1811) to immediate success; continued to publish anonymously because the customs of the time, to which she firmly adhered, prescribed that ladies of good breeding shun the limelight; other writings, impervious to changes in taste and literary fashion, include *Pride and Prejudice* (1813), *Mansfield Park* (1814), *Emma* (1815), *Northanger Abbey* and *Persuasion* (1818). ❖ See also John Halperin, *The Life of Jane Austen* (Johns Hopkins University Press, 1984); Marghanita Laski, *Jane Austen and her World* (Viking, 1969); Penelope Hughes-Hallett, ed. *My Dear Cassandra: The Letters of Jane Austen* (Clarkson Potter, 1991); David Nokes, *Jane Austen* (Farrar, Straus, 1997); Claire Tomalin, *Jane Austen* (Knopf, 1997); and *Women in World History.*

AUSTEN, Winifred (1876–1964). English wildlife artist. Name variations: Winifred Marie Louise Austen, Winifred M.L. Austen, "Spink." Born in 1899 in Ramsgate, England; died Nov 1, 1964, in Orford, Suffolk, England; dau. of a naval surgeon. ❖ Accomplished wildlife artist, took up painting professionally at an early age; exhibited many paintings and etchings at Royal Academy and was active on the London art scene (1899–1907); moved to village of Orford in Suffolk (1926) after a brief marriage; produced paintings, etchings, drawings and illustrations of wildlife; also painted postcards for Valentine company to make a living, signing some of these "Spink," which is a local name for chaffinch; illustrated numerous books, including *Birds Ashore and Aforeshore* by Patrick Chalmers.

AUSTIN, Debbie (1948—). American golfer. Name variations: Deborah E. Austin. Born Deborah E. Austin, Feb 1, 1948, in Oneida, NY; attended Rollins College. ❖ Was the youngest finalist in the NY State Amateur at age 16; joined the LPGA tour (1968); won Birmingham Classic, Hoosier Classic, Pocono Classic, Long Island Charity Classic, and Wheeling Classic (1977); was Australian Open champion (1978); won American Cancer Society Classic (1978) and Mayflower Classic (1981); coached women's golf squad at Rollins College for one year; now plays on the Women's Senior Golf Tour, resides in Orlando, FL.

AUSTIN, Debra (1955—). American ballet dancer. Born July 25, 1955, in Brooklyn, NY. ❖ Received scholarship to School of American Ballet at age 12; joined New York City Ballet (1971), creating numerous roles in such works as Jacques D'Ambroise's *Sinfonietta* (1975) and Jerome Robbins' *Chansons Madécasse* (1975); joined Geneva Opéra Ballet in Switzerland (1980); danced with Zurich Ballet and toured with company throughout Europe; became a principal of the Pennsylvania Ballet, dancing in *Swan Lake, Coppélia* and *A Midsummer's Nights Dream,* among others; joined artistic staff of Carolina Ballet as ballet master.

AUSTIN, Jane Goodwin (1831–1894). American novelist. Born in Worcester, Massachusetts, Feb 25, 1831; died in Boston on Mar 30, 1894; educated in Boston. ❖ Often wrote of the Pilgrim fathers and early colonists of Massachusetts; writings included *Fairy Dreams* (1860), *Moonfolk* (1874), *Mrs. Beauchamp Brown* (1880), *A Nameless Nobleman* (1881), *The Desmond Hundred* (1882), *Nantucket Scraps* (1882), *Standish of Standish* (1889), *Betty Alden* (1891), and *David Alden's Daughter and Other Stories* (1892).

AUSTIN, Lovie (1887–1972). American pianist, arranger, and leader of Lovie Austin's Blues Serenaders. Born Cora Calhoun, Sept 19, 1887, in Chattanooga, Tennessee; died in Chicago, Illinois, July 10, 1972; studied music at Roger Williams' University in Nashville and at Knoxville College; married a Detroit movie-house owner; married a variety artist (who toured with a partner as "Austin and Delaney"). ❖ Was music director at the Monogram Theater in Chicago for 20 years; later directed at the Gem and Joyland Theaters; name appeared often on blues releases of the Paramount label (1923–26), both as pianist and leader of Lovie Austin's Blues Serenaders, backing such Paramount's stars as Ida Cox, Alberta Hunter, and Ma Rainey, and occasionally contributing some group instrumentals on her own; wrote "Down Hearted Blues" (recorded by Bessie Smith). ❖ See also *Women in World History.*

AUSTIN, Margaret (1933—). New Zealand politician. Born Margaret Leonard, April 1, 1933. ❖ Was a secondary school science teacher and administrator; elected Labour MP for Yaldhurst (1984); re-elected (1990) and promoted to Cabinet as Minister of Science and Technology, Internal Affairs; served as chair of New Zealand National Commission for UNESCO: Membership, and as chancellor of Lincoln University.

AUSTIN, Mary Hunter (1868–1934). American author. Name variations: refers to herself as both I-Mary and Mary-by-Herself; (pseudonym) Gordon Stairs. Born Mary Hunter, Sept 9, 1868, in Carlinville, Illinois; died in Santa Fe, New Mexico, Aug 13, 1934; dau. of Captain George (lawyer) and Susannah Savilla Graham Hunter (nurse); attended State Normal School at Bloomington and graduated from Blackburn College of Carlinville, 1888; m. Stafford Wallace Austin (vineyardist, irrigation manager, schoolteacher), May 18, 1891 (div., Aug 21, 1914); children: Ruth (1892–1918). ❖ Writer primarily of naturalist fiction about the Southwest, who celebrated the environment, preserved Native American and Spanish Colonial culture, and mingled with the cultural icons of her times; moved to California (1888); taught school (1897–99); published 1st book *The Land of Little Rain* (1903); moved to artists colony of Carmel (1906); lived through and reported San Francisco earthquake and fire (1906); commuted between New York City and Carmel (1911–24); was publicist for the Panama-Pacific Exposition (1915); served as advisor for Herbert Hoover's US Food Administration (1917); named associate in Native American Literature at School of American Research (1918); built house in Santa Fe (1925); organized Spanish Colonial Arts Society of Santa Fe (1927); served as delegate to Seven States Conference (1927); bequeathed most of her estate to Indian

Arts Fund (1933); writings include *Isidro* (1905), *Lost Borders* (1909), (as Gordon Stairs) *Outland* (1910), *Woman of Genius* (1912), *The Ford* (1917), *The Man Jesus* (1925), *Starry Adventure* (1931), *One Smoke Stories* (1934) and (with Ansel Adams) *Taos Pueblo* (1930). ❖ See also autobiography *Earth Horizon* (1932); Augusta Fink, *I-Mary: A Biography of Mary Austin* (University of Arizona Press, 1983); and *Women in World History*.

AUSTIN, Sarah (1793–1867). English author. Born Sarah Taylor in Norwich, England, 1793; died at Weybridge, England, Aug 8, 1867; dau. of John Taylor (wool-stapler, who died in 1826) and Susannah Cook Taylor; great-granddau. of Dr. John Taylor (1694–1761), pastor of the Presbyterian church in Norwich; m. John Austin (London barrister), 1820 (died 1859); children: Lucie Duff-Gordon (1821–1869). ❖ Cultivated a large circle of friends, including Jeremy Bentham, James Mill, and historians George and Harriet Grote; attempted few original works, involving herself mainly with translations, of which the most important are the *Characteristics of Goëthe* (3 vols., 1833), Leopold von Ranke's *History of the Reformation in Germany* and *History of the Popes* (1840), and *Report on the State of Public Instruction in Prussia* (1834); from the French, translated V. Cousin and F.W. Carove's *The Story without an End* (1864); following husband's death (1859), edited his *Lectures on Jurisprudence*. ❖ See also Janet Anne Duff-Gordon Ross, *Three Generations of Englishwomen* (1888); and *Women in World History*.

AUSTIN, Tracy (1962—). American tennis player. Born Dec 12, 1962, in Rolling Hills, California; sister of John Austin and Pam Austin (tennis players); m. Scott Holt (mortgage broker). ❖ Won 25 US National Jr. titles; won 2 US Open championships (1979, 1981) and the Italian Open (1979); with brother John, won mixed doubles at Wimbledon (1980); does tennis commentary for tv networks. Was the youngest player ever inducted into the International Tennis Hall of Fame. ❖ See also *Women in World History*.

AUSTRAL, Florence (1894–1968). Australian opera singer. Name variations: Florence Amadio, Florence Fawaz, Florence Wilson. Born Mary Wilson on April 16, 1892, in Richmond, Victoria, Australia; died May 16, 1968, in Newcastle, New South Wales, Australia; attended Newcastle Conservatorium, Melbourne, Australia (1917); m. John Amadio (virtuoso flautist), 1925. ❖ One of world's greatest Wagnerian sopranos, won an entrance exhibition to Newcastle Conservatorium in Melbourne (1917); traveled to New York to study Italian opera (1919); adopted Austral as stage name (1921), prior to debut with British National Opera Company at Convent Garden, London (1922); toured US and Canada (1920s) and appeared in complete cycles of *The Ring* at Convent Garden and at Berlin State Opera; married flautist John Amadio in London (1925) and toured widely with him in US and Australia; joined Berlin State Opera as principal (1930); appeared frequently with Sir Henry Wood and BBC Symphony Orchestra; made many recordings with other contemporary leading singers; toured Australia (1930, 1934–35), North America (1931–33) and Holland (1931, 1933–34); appeared in benefit concerts during WWII; returned to Australia after WWII, almost completely paralyzed by multiple sclerosis; taught with Newcastle branch of New South Wales State Conservatorium of Music despite affliction until retirement (1959).

AUSTREBERTHA (635–704). Medieval abbess. Born 635; died 704; dau. of Count Badefroi of the Palatine and Frametilda (who was canonized). ❖ Much admired as a holy woman, refused to go along with parents' wishes for an arranged marriage, preferring to live as a servant of God; to escape the wedding, secretly took vows of a nun from a local bishop; during long life, served as abbess at 2 establishments, in Port and later Pavilly; charitable works and leadership abilities gained her the admiration of believers across Western Europe. ❖ See also *Women in World History*.

AUSTRIA, archduchess of.
See Visconti, Virida (1350–1414).
See Eleanor Stewart (d. 1496).
See Joanna of Austria (1546–1578).
See Elizabeth of Habsburg (1554–1592).
See Gonzaga, Anna Caterina (1566–1621).
See Isabella Clara Eugenia (1566–1633).
See Maria Antonia of Austria (1683–1754).
See Alexandra Pavlovna (1783–1801).
See Maria of Wurttemberg (1797–1855).
See Sophie of Bavaria (1805–1872).
See Maria Annunziata (1843–1871).

See Augusta of Tuscany (1825–1864).
See Marie Annunziata of Naples (d. 1877).
See Elizabeth (1831–1903).
See Maria Theresa of Portugal (1855–1944).
See Marie Valerie (1868–1924).
See Maria Cristina of Sicily (1877–1947).
See Elizabeth von Habsburg (1883–1963).
See Ileana (1909–1991).

AUSTRIA, duchess of.
See Margaret of Babenberg (fl. 1252).
See Cunigunde of Hungary (d. 1285).
See Agnes of Bohemia (1269–1297).
See Johanna of Pfirt (1300–1351).
See Elizabeth of Bohemia (1358–1373).
See Beatrice of Brandenburg (1360–1414).
See Johanna of Bavaria (c. 1373–1410).
See Catherine of Burgundy (1378–1425).
See Cimburca of Masovia (c. 1396–1429).
See Elizabeth of Luxemburg (1409–1442).
See Mary of Bavaria (1551–1608).

AUSTRIA, empress of.
See Maria Theresa of Austria (1717–1780).
See Maria Josepha of Bavaria (1739–1767).
See Maria Louisa of Spain (1745–1792).
See Maria Teresa of Naples (1772–1807).
See Maria Ludovica of Modena (1787–1816).
See Maria Anna of Savoy (1803–1884).
See Elizabeth of Bavaria (1837–1898).

AUSTRIAN TYROL, archduchess of. See Medici, Claudia de (1604–1648).

AUVERGNE, duchess of (1606–1627). See Marie de Bourbon.

AUZELLO, Blanche (d. 1969). See Rubenstein, Blanche.

AUZOU, Pauline Desmarquets (1775–1835). French painter. Name variations: Mme Auzou; Pauline Desmarquêts Auzou. Born in Paris in 1775; died in 1835; studied under Regnault. ❖ Influenced by Marguérite Gérard, began painting interior scenes (1790s), portraying young women reading or playing musical instruments; won a *médaille de première classe* with this theme (1808); most popular works were French historical paintings and portraits, including *Diana of France and Montmorency*.

AV-PAUL, Annette (1944—). Swedish-born ballet dancer. Name variations: Annette Wiedersheim-Paul; Annette MacDonald. Born 1944, in Stockholm, Sweden; m. Brian MacDonald (choreographer), c. 1964. ❖ Performed with Opera Ballet and Royal Swedish Ballet (1962–72); won recognition when Bolshoi choreographer Yuri Grigorovich cast her as the lead Katerina in *The Stone Flower* (1962); performed in abstract works by Antony Tudor, including *Echoes of Trumpets* (1963) and *Pillar of Fire*; danced with Nureyev, Fonteyn, Bruhn, and Orlando Sagrado; performed in such classics as *Les Sylphides*, *Swan Lake* and *The Sleeping Beauty*; served as artistic director of the Harkness Ballet and Royal Winnipeg Ballet (1960s–70s); danced as reigning ballerina with Les Grands Ballets Canadiens; became founding artistic director of Ballet British Columbia upon retiring (1984); works as artistic director of dance program at Banff Center for the Arts in Canada.

AVA OF MELK (d. 1127). German religious writer. Name variations: Frau Ava. Birth date unknown; died in 1127 in Melk, Austria; married; 2 children. ❖ The earliest female writer known to have written in German, wrote poems and prose with themes from the New Testament, as well as translations of saints' lives; retired to a convent but was not a nun. ❖ See also *Women in World History*.

AVEDON, Barbara Hammer (1930–1994). American tv writer and pacifist. Name variations: Barbara Hammer (ceased using married name in 1990s). Born Barbara Hammer, June 29, 1930, in New York, NY; died in Palm Springs, California, Aug 31, 1994; m. and div.; children: one son, Josh. ❖ With Barbara Corday, created "Cagney and Lacey" and episodes for "The Doctors," "Medical Center," "Maude," "Sons and Daughters," "Fish," "Trapper John, M.D.," "Grandpa Goes To Washington," "Harper Valley PTA," "Turnabout (1969–83); also wrote tv movie: "This Girl For Hire" (1983); a longtime political activist, founded the antiwar organization, Another Mother For Peace, with actress Donna Reed. ❖ See also *Women in World History*.

AVELINA DE FORZ (1259–1274). Countess of Holderness. Born Jan 20, 1259; died Nov 10, 1274, in Stockwell, England; buried at Westminster Abbey; dau. of William de Forz, 2nd count of Aumale, and Isabella de Redvers (1237–1293); m. Edmund the Crouchback (c. 1245–1296), 1st earl of Lancaster, April 9, 1269.

AVELLANEDA, La (1814–1873). *See Gómez de Avellaneda, Gertrudis.*

AVERINA, Tatiana (1950–2001). Russian speedskater. Name variations: Tatyana Averina, Tatyana Barabash-Averina. Born Tatyana Borisovna Averina, June 25, 1950, in Gorki, USSR; died on Aug 22, 2001. ❖ Won gold medals in the 1,000 and 3,000 meters and bronze medals in the 500 and 1,500 meters at Innsbruck Olympics (1976); at World championships, won silver medals (1974, 1975, 1976) and a gold medal (1978).

AVERKOVA, Oksana (1970—). Russian gymnast. Born Aug 12, 1970, in Moscow, USSR. ❖ Won a bronze medal for all-around and a gold medal for uneven bars (1985) and a gold medal in all-around at Moscow News (1986); won gold medals for vault and balance beam at Belgian Gym Masters (1986).

AVERY, Ellen (1840–1910). *See Foster, J. Ellen.*

AVERY, Judith Ellen (1840–1910). *See Foster, J. Ellen.*

AVERY, Martha (1851–1929). American socialist and Catholic missionary. Born Martha Gallison Moore, April 6, 1851, in Steuben, Maine; died Aug 8, 1929, in Medford, Massachusetts; m. Millard Filmore Avery, Mar 18, 1880; children: Katharine (b. 1881). ❖ Active and relatively prominent member of the socialist movement, founded the Karl Marx Class (1896), which became the Boston School of Political Economy (1901), of which her close associate David Goldstein served as secretary; with Goldstein, left the socialist movement (c. 1902) and published *Socialism: The Nation of Fatherless Children* (1903); baptized as a Roman Catholic (1904), pioneered the Catholic social-justice movement; served as president of the Common Cause Society (1922–1929); with Goldstein, launched the Catholic Truth Guild.

AVERY, Mary Ellen (1927—). American pediatrician. Born May 6, 1927, in Camden, New Jersey; father was a Pennsylvania manufacturer and mother was vice-principal of a high school; graduate of Wheaton College, summa cum laude, with a degree in chemistry, 1948; 1 of only 4 women to graduate from Johns Hopkins University medical school in 1952. ❖ Discovered and developed artificial surfactant and glucocorticoid treatment for infant respiratory distress syndrome (RDS); after being diagnosed with tuberculosis (1952), specialized in pulmonary disease; completed residency and internship in pediatrics; studied premature infants with RDS (formerly hyaline membrane disease) on a Harvard Medical School research fellowship; worked with Harvard School of Public Health professor Dr. Jere Mead to study origins of fluid that normally lines lungs on healthy babies; studied the research of Dr. John A. Clements and then correctly hypothesized that surfactant is necessary to retain air in lungs and that its lack causes premature babies' lungs to collapse; established discipline known as "metabolism of the lung"; served as physician-in-chief of Boston's Children's Hospital (1974–85) and as president of the American Association for the Advancement of Science (AAAS); elected to the National Academy of Sciences (1994) and became its president (2003). Received National Medal of Science (1991) and Harvard University's Thomas Morgan Rotch Distinguished Professor of Pediatrics.

AVERY, Rachel G. (1858–1919). American suffragist. Born Rachel Foster, Dec 30, 1858, in Pittsburgh, Pennsylvania; died Oct 26, 1919, in Philadelphia, PA; m. Cyrus Miller Avery, Nov 8, 1888; children: 3 daughters. ❖ Met Susan B. Anthony (1879); served as corresponding secretary of the National Woman Suffrage Association (1880–1901), where she worked closely with Anthony; helped organize and finance several state suffrage campaigns; served as corresponding secretary of the International Council of Women (1891–94), secretary of the International Woman Suffrage Alliance (1904–1909), and vice-president of the National American Woman Suffrage Association (1907–1910).

AVES, Isabel Annie (1887–1938). New Zealand abortion provider. Name variations: Isabel Annie Michaelsen, Isabel Annie Craike. Born on Mar 18, 1887, in Waipawa, Hawke's Bay, New Zealand; died on Oct 3, 1938, in Napier, New Zealand; dau. of Harald Michaelsen (clerk) and Kate Layton (Fraser) Michaelsen; m. John Oliver Craike (grape-grower), 1907 (died 1931); m. Charles James Aves (music teacher), 1932 (died 1937); children: (1st m.) 3. ❖ Orphaned as young child, entered domestic service and later worked as institutional cook to support children after separation from 1st husband; following 2nd marriage, began to provide abortions at her home and to hold men financially responsible for fees; successfully evaded numerous attempts at prosecution; was shot and killed by an angry fiancé, after a client of hers became ill and was hospitalized.

AVICE OF GLOUCESTER (c. 1167–1217). *See Avisa of Gloucester.*

AVILÉS PEREA, María Antonia. Spanish politician. Fl. 1980s. ❖ Member of the Zaragoza City Council (1979–83) and the National Executive Committee of the People's Party; as a member of the European People's Party (Christian Democrats) and European Democrats, elected to 5th European Parliament (1999–2004).

AVILOVA, Lidya (c. 1864–1943). Russian memoirist and short-story writer. Name variations: Lidiia Alekseevna Avilova or Lidiia Alekseevna Avílova; Lydia Avilova; L.A. Avilova. Born Lidiia Alekseevna, c. 1864, in Russia; died 1943; married; children: daughter. ❖ Tutored by Anton Chekhov, published 1st collection of stories (1896); stories received praise from Leo Tolstoy and Ivan Bunin but judged uneven by many critics; lived with daughter in Czechoslovakia (1922–24); published other story collections, 1906, 1913, and 1914; best-known work, *Chekhov in My Life*, published posthumously (1947).

AVISA OF GLOUCESTER (c. 1167–1217). Queen of England. Name variations: Avice of Gloucester; Hadwisa; Isabella or Isabelle of Gloucester; Isabelle de Clare. Born c. 1167; died in 1217; dau. of William Fitzrobert (d. 1183), 2nd earl of Gloucester, and Hawise Beaumont (d. 1197); sister of Amicia Fitzrobert (d. 1225); m. Prince John (1166–1216), later John I Lackland, king of England (r. 1199–1216), 1189 (div. 1200); m. Geoffrey de Mandville, earl of Essex; children: none. ❖ See also *Women in World History*.

AVISON, Margaret (1918—). Canadian poet. Born April 23, 1918, in Galt, Ontario, Canada; grew up in Regina and Calgary; attended universities of Indiana and Chicago; University of Toronto, 1936–40, MA, 1963–65. ❖ Taught at Scarborough College, University of Toronto (1967–68); was writer-in-residence at University of Western Ontario; was secretary at Mustard Seed Mission (1978–86); poetry collections include *Winter Sun* (1960), *The Dumbfounding* (1966), *Sunblue* (1978), *Collected Poems* (1990), and *Concrete and Wild Carrot* (2003); also wrote *History of Ontario* (1951), as well as book reviews for *Canadian Forum, Poetry, Contemporary Verse* and *Origin;* delivered 1993 Pascal Lectures at Waterloo University, published as *A Kind of Perseverance.* Awarded Governor General's Award, three honorary doctorates, and Order of Canada; won Griffin Poetry Prize for *Concrete and Wild Carrot* (2003).

AVOIE (c. 915–965). *See Hedwig.*

AVON, Lady (b. 1920). *See Eden, Clarissa.*

AVRIL, Jane (1868–1943). French dancer. Name variations: Jeanne Richepin. Born Jeanne Richepin, June 1868, in Montmartre, France; died Jan 16, 1943, in Paris, France. ❖ Though she received little professional dance training, was considered one of the major popular dancers of La Belle Epoque; won recognition throughout Europe as a specialty dancer at the Moulin Rouge in Paris where she performed "La Mélanite," an improvised waltz act; performed the same act at numerous venues in major European cities, including the Théâtre de Champs Elysees (1894), Folies-Bergère (1897) and Paris Exposition of 1900; performed in the theatrical production of Lugne-Poé's *Peer Gynt* at his Nouvelle Theatre; gained lasting fame through the paintings of Henri de Toulouse-Lautrec.

AVRIL, Suzanne (fl. 1920s). French actress. Name variations: Suzanne Delaroche. Born in France; fl. 1920s. ❖ Associated with Réjane's theater for many years; plays include *La Course du Flambeau, La Souris, Paris—New York, Zaza, Raffles, La Passerelle, La Plus heureuse des trois, La Fille Sauvage, Nono* and *Je t'aime.*

A.W., Mrs. (fl. 1650s). *See Weamys, Anna.*

AWASHONKS (fl. mid-late 17th c.). Sunksquaw of the Sakonnet tribe. Name variations: The Queen. Born Awashonks in the middle to late 1600s in the vicinity of present-day Little Compton, Rhode Island; death date unknown; married Tolony. ❖ Though *sunksquaw* is the title given the hereditary female head of state of the Wampanoag Confederacy tribes, was one of the numerous women warriors misidentified as a queen by early British colonists; along with Wetamoo and Magnus, participated as a tribal chieftain during Metacom's (King Philip's) War

(1675–76); unlike her counterparts, when forced to surrender, convinced her warriors to fight with the British, in order to save her people from being sold into slavery in the West Indies.

AWIAKTA (1936—). Cherokee-Appalachian poet and essayist. Name variations: Marilou Awiakta; Marilou Bonham Thompson; Marilou Awiakta Bonham. Born Marilou Awiakta Bonham, Jan 24, 1936, in Knoxville, Tennessee; grew up in Oak Ridge, TN; dau. of Bill and Wilma Bonham; University of Tennessee, BA, 1958; m. Paul Thompson; children: 3. ❖ Conducted poetry workshops in women's prison in Tennessee; was co-founder of Far-Away Cherokee Association (now Native American Intertribal Association); draws on Cherokee–Appalachian heritage for her writings, which include *Abiding Appalachia: Where Mountain and Atom Meet* (1978), *Rising Fawn and the Fire Mystery: A Story of Heritage, Family, and Courage 1833* (1983), and *Selu: Seeking the Corn-Mother's Wisdom* (1993); also published short stories in anthologies.

AWOLOWO, Hannah (1915—). Nigerian businesswoman and philanthropist. Name variations: Chief (Mrs) H.I.D. Awolowo, Mama H.I.D. Born Hannah Idowu Dideolu Adelana, Nov 25, 1915, at Ikenne Remo, Nigeria; dau. of Chief Moses Odugbemi Adelana (prince) and Elizabeth Oyesile-Adelana (businesswoman and member of Nigerian royalty); attended Saint Saviour's Anglican School, Saint Peter's School, and Methodist Girls' High School in Lagos; m. Obafemi Awolowo (journalist), Dec 26, 1937; children: Segun, Olusegun, Omotola, Oluwole, and Ayo. ❖ Entrepreneur whose early ventures in trade grew into a business empire that generated a fortune, allowing husband to devote himself to politics as a nationalist leader; entered business after departure of husband to study in England (1944); founded Didelou Stores Ltd., Ligu Distribution Services Ltd. (after 1946); backed the founding of *The Nigerian Tribune*, later expanded to include the African Newspapers of Nigeria Ltd., and African Press Ltd. (1949); husband became prime minister of the western region of Nigeria (1951), lost bid for national leadership (1959), imprisoned for treason (1962), and released after government coup (1966); campaigned for him in 2 unsuccessful bids for the national presidency (1979 and 1983); continued her philanthropic activities after husband's death (1987); awarded the 1,000-year-old chieftaincy title of Yeye-Oba for life (1980). ❖ See also Tola Adeniyi, *The Jewel: The Biography of Chief (Mrs) H.I.D. Awolowo* (Ibandan, Nigeria: Gemini Press, 1993); and *Women in World History*.

AWURA POKOU (c. 1700–c. 1760). *See Pokou.*

AXELROD, Luibo (1868–1946). *See Akselrod, Luibo.*

AXIOTHEA OF PHLIUS (fl. 4th c. BCE). Greek student of philosophy. Born into a wealthy Peloponnesian family in Phlius, near Corinth, in 4th century BCE. ❖ Donned masculine clothes and travelled to Athens to study philosophy under Plato. ❖ See also *Women in World History*.

AXIOTI, Melpo (1906–1973). Greek novelist and poet. Name variations: Melpo Axiote. Born 1906 in Athens, Greece; died 1973 in Greece; attended school at a Roman Catholic convent on the island of Tinos (1918–22). ❖ Joined Communist Party (1936) and fought in Greek resistance during WWII; went to France to escape possible imprisonment for political activities (1947) and met important intellectuals, including Paul Eluard and Louis Aragon; expelled from France (1950), went to East Germany, where she taught Modern Greek at the Classics Institute of Humboldt University; returned to Greece (1964); works include poetry collection *Coincidence* (1939) and novels *Difficult Nights* (1938), *Shall We Dance, Maria?* (1940), *Twentieth Century* (1946), and *Kadmo* (1972).

AXIS SALLY (1900–1988). *See Gillars, Mildred E.*

AXMATOVA, Anna (1889–1966). *See Akhmatova, Anna.*

AXTON, Estelle (1918–2004). American music entrepreneur. Born Estelle Stewart, Sept 11, 1918, in Middleton, Tennessee; died Feb 25, 2004, in Memphis, Tennessee; m. Everett Axton, 1941; children: Doris Axton Fredrick and Charles "Packy" Axton (saxophonist). ❖ Founded Satellite Records with brother Jim Stewart (1958) and had hit songs "Cause I Love You," with Rufus Thomas and his daughter Carla, and "Last Night," with son Charles Axton and the Mark-Keys (1960); forced to change the name of their company, co-founded the legendary Memphis label Stax Records, featuring such artists as Otis Redding, Sam and Dave, Wilson Pickett, Booker T and the MGs, Isaac Hayes, the Staple Singers, Eddie Floyd, and Johnnie Taylor; sold her share of the company (1970), set up Fretone Records and scored a hit with "Disco Duck" by Rick Dees (1976). ❖ See also *Women in World History*.

AXTON, Mae Boren (1914–1997). American songwriter. Born Mae Boren, Sept 14, 1914, in Bardwell, Texas; died April 9, 1997, in Nashville, Tennessee; sister of David Boren (US senator from Oklahoma); m. John T. Axton, high-school football coach; children: Hoyt Axton (1938–1999, singer and songwriter); grandmother of Mark Axton (singer and songwriter). ❖ Wrote several hit songs (1950s); co-wrote "Heartbreak Hotel," Elvis Presley's 1st single on RCA (1956); had about 200 numbers recorded in all, including "Honey Bop" (Wanda Jackson) and "I Won't Be Rockin' Tonight."

AXUM, Donna (c. 1924—). Miss America. Name variations: Donna Axum Whitworth. Born c. 1924 in El Dorado, Arkansas; University of Arkansas, MA; m. Gus Mutscher (Speaker of the House of Representatives in Texas); m. J. Bryan Whitworth; children: 2. ❖ Named Miss America (1964), representing Arkansas; served on the President's Advisory Committee on the Arts for the John F. Kennedy Center in Washington, DC. ❖ See also Frank Deford, *There She Is* (Viking, 1971).

AY, Evelyn (c. 1934—). Miss America. Name variations: Evelyn Sempier. Born Evelyn Margaret Ay c. 1934 in Ephrata, Pennsylvania; attended University of Pennsylvania; m. Carl Sempier; children: two daughters. ❖ Named Miss America (1954), representing Pennsylvania; motivational speaker. ❖ See also Frank Deford, *There She Is* (Viking, 1971).

AYALA, Josefa de (1630–1684). *See de Ayala, Josefa.*

AYDY, Catherine (1937—). *See Tennant, Emma.*

AYER, Harriet Hubbard (1849–1903). American cosmetics entrepreneur and journalist. Born Harriet Hubbard in Chicago, Illinois, 1849; died 1903; graduated from Convent of the Sacred Heart, Chicago; m. Herbert C. Ayer (div.); children: two daughters. ❖ One of the 1st cosmetic notables, went to work as a saleswoman in a fashionable NY furniture store after husband lost his fortune; while in Paris on a buying junket, purchased the formula for a cream supposedly made for Mme Récamier from a chemist in Paris; put the Hubbard coat of arms, as well as her name, on the jars and obtained backing (1886); crafted imaginative pamphlets about Récamier's beauty secrets, and used the endorsements of society friends and actress Lillie Langtry; resurfaced on staff of New York *World* (1896), writing a beauty column; published the bestseller, *Harriet Hubbard Ayer's Book: A Complete and Authentic Treatise on the Laws of Health and Beauty* (1899). ❖ See also *Women in World History*.

AYESHA (c. 613–678). *See A'ishah bint Abi Bakr.*

AYLING, Jean (1894–1976). *See Wrinch, Dorothy.*

AYLING, Sue (1945–2003). English tv producer. Born Susan May Ayling, May 31, 1945, in Brighton, England; died of cancer, Mar 20, 2003, in England; attended New Hall, Cambridge; m. David Dickinson (div.); children: Patrick and Ellie. ❖ Highly regarded talk-show producer, began career as 1st woman editor of *Granta* magazine; joined BBC news (1970); was with "Nationwide" (1972–75), then Robin Day's "Newsday" program (1977–78), before following him to "Panorama" (1977); produced "Question Time" (1994–98).

AYLWARD, Gladys (1902–1970). English missionary. Name variations: Ai-weh-deh, Ai Weh Teh, Hsiao Fu-jeh. Pronunciation: AIL-wood. Born Gladys May Aylward, Feb 24, 1902, in Edmonton, north of London, England; died of influenza, Jan 2, 1970, in Taipei, Taiwan; dau. of a postman and a postal worker; left school at 28, studied for 3 months at the China Inland Mission in London; never married; children: adopted 5 officially, many unofficially. ❖ Missionary in China and Taiwan who worked to end the traditional Chinese practice of binding women's feet, led a large group of orphans out of occupied China, and set up orphanages in Hong Kong and Taiwan; left school to work as a shop assistant; later went into domestic service; became an evangelical Christian at 18 (1920); began training at China Inland Mission but was not recommended for further training (1928); went back into domestic service in London; finally departed for China on her own (1930); settled in Yangcheng in Shensi (or Shansi) province; helped set up an inn and appointed Inspector of Feet; adopted Chinese nationality (1936); led about 100 orphans out of war-torn China to safety in Sian (1940); worked in Tsingsui, near Lanchow in northwest China (1944); moved to Chengtu, Szechwan, where she continued her missionary work and was appointed Biblewoman at the Chinese Seminary (1945); returned to England (1949); went to Hong Kong and then Taiwan, settling in Taipei where she set up an orphanage (1957). ❖ See also *Gladys Aylward: One of the Undefeated* (Edinburgh House, 1950); Alan Burgess, *The Small Woman* (Evans, 1957); C. Hunter, *Gladys Aylward*

(Coverdale, 1970); Phyllis Thompson, *A London Sparrow: The Story of Gladys Aylward* (Word, 1971); film *The Inn of the Sixth Happiness* (1958); and *Women in World History*.

AYMAR, Luciana (1977—). Argentinean field-hockey player. Born Luciana Paula Aymar, Aug 10, 1977, in Rosario, Argentina. ❖ Won a team silver medal at Sydney Olympics (2000) and a bronze medal at Athens Olympics (2004); won Champions Trophy (2001), World Cup (2002), and Pan American Games (2003). Named International Hockey Federation's Women's Player of the Year (2001).

AYRES, Agnes (1896–1940). American actress. Name variations: Agnes Eyre. Born Agnes Eyre Hinkle, Sept 4, 1896, in Carbondale, Illinois; died Dec 25, 1940; m. Frank P. Schuker, 1921; m. Manuel Reachi (div. 1927); children: 1. ❖ American leading lady of the silent screen, began working in Essanay shorts (c. 1915); was at height of career when she played opposite Rudolph Valentino in *The Sheik* (1921) and also starred opposite Wallace Reid; retiring with the advent of sound, returned to the screen only once, for a bit in movie *Souls at Sea* (1937).

AYRES, Anne (1816–1896). Protestant religious. Name variations: Sister Anne. Born in London, England, Jan 3, 1816; died at St. Luke's Hospital in New York, NY, Feb 9, 1896; came to the US in 1836. ❖ As Sister Anne, became the 1st member of an American sisterhood in the Protestant Episcopal Church (1845), then founded the Sisterhood of the Holy Communion (1852), which was affiliated with the Church of the Holy Communion in NY City; became head of housekeeping and nursing at newly constructed St. Luke's Hospital in NY (1858); with William Augustus Muhlenberg, also opened St. Johnland, a refuge for orphans, the homeless, and the handicapped, on Long Island (1865); wrote *Evangelical Sisterhood* (1867) and *Life of William Augustus Muhlenberg* (1880).

AYRES, Mary Andrews (fl. 1970s). American advertising executive. Fl. 1960s–70s. ❖ At Sullivan, Stauffer, Colwell & Bayles, served as senior vice president (1967), then executive vice president (1968); was the 1st woman to be elected director of the American Association of Advertising Agencies (1971). Won Matrix Award (1972).

AYRES, Ruby Mildred (1883–1955). English novelist. Born in 1883 in Watford, Hertshire, England; died Nov 14, 1955, in Weybridge, England; m. Reginald William Pocock (insurance broker), 1909. ❖ Published 1st novel, *Castles in Spain* (1912); wrote approximately 150 books over the next 41 years, with sales totaling more than 8 million; published last book *Dark Gentleman* (1953); also authored the play, *Silver Wedding*, produced in 1932. ❖ See also *Women in World History*.

AYRTON, Hertha Marks (1854–1923). British physicist. Name variations: adopted the name Hertha while at Girton College; Phoebe Sarah Ayrton. Born Phoebe Sarah Marks in Portsmouth, England, April 28, 1854; died Aug 26, 1923; 3rd of 5 children of Alice and Levi Marks (clockmaker and jeweler); attended boarding school, London; Girton College, Cambridge (1876–1880); Finsbury Technical College (1884–1885); m. William Edward Ayrton (prof of applied physics), 1885 (died 1908); one daughter, Barbara Bodichon (Barbie) Ayrton, 1892. ❖ Bolstered by her success in obtaining a patent for an instrument for dividing lines into any number of equal parts (a boon to architects, engineers, and artists), entered Finsbury Technical College with the help of Barbara Bodichon (1884); began experiments with electricity (1893), presenting papers on her work while making plans to publish a book; became the 1st woman member of the Institution of Electrical Engineers (1898); began investigating ripple marks in sand and finished book *The Electric Arc* (1901), which became the accepted textbook on the subject and cemented her reputation; became 1st woman to present a paper ("The Origin and Growth of Ripple Marks") to the Royal Society (1904); worked for War Office and Admiralty on electric searchlights (a project inherited from husband for which she produced several reports that were ultimately credited to him, 1905–10); invented the Ayrton fan, a device to ward off poisonous gases in the trenches of WWI; was an outspoken suffragist. Awarded the Hughes Medal for original research by Royal Society (1906). ❖ See also *Women in World History*.

AYSCOUGH, Anne (c. 1521–1546). *See Askew, Anne.*

AYSCOUGH, Florence (1875/78–1942). American poet and translator. Born Florence Wheelock between 1875 and 1878 in Shanghai, China; died April 26, 1942, in Chicago, Illinois; dau. of Thomas Reed and Edith Haswell (Clarke) Wheelock; educated at Mrs. Quincy Shaw's School in Brookline, Massachusetts; m. Francis Ayscough (British importer),

c. 1895 in Shanghai (died 1933); m. Harley Farnsworth MacNair, 1935. ❖ Taught Chinese art and literature at the college level and wrote 8 books encompassing Chinese history, literary criticism and translation, including *Chinese Women Yesterday and Today* (1939); took a lecturing post at University of Chicago (1935). ❖ See also *Florence Ayscough and Amy Lowell: Correspondence of a Friendship* (1945); and *Women in World History*.

AYTON, Sarah (1980—). English sailor. Born April 9, 1980, in Ashford, Kent, England. ❖ Won a gold medal for Yngling class at Athens Olympics (2004), a debut event.

AYUSO GONZÁLEZ, María del Pilar (1942—). Spanish agricultural engineer and politician. Name variations: Maria del Pilar Ayuso Gonzalez. Born June 16, 1942, in Badajoz, Spain. ❖ As a member of the Castile-La Mancha Parliament, served as assistant spokesperson for the PP Group (1991–94), vice-chair of the Committee on Agriculture (1994–96), and director-general responsible for Food, Ministry of Agriculture, Fisheries and Food (1996–99); as a member of the European People's Party (Christian Democrats) and European Democrats, elected to 5th European Parliament (1999–2004).

AYVERDI, Samiha (1906–1993). Turkish writer. Born in 1906 in Istanbul, Turkey; died in 1993. ❖ Wrote essays on politics and religion, including explications of Islamic Jihad; published several novels, including *So This Is Love* (1939), *A Night in the Temple* (1940), *The Fire Tree* (1941), *Living Dead* (1942), and *The Chaplain* (1948).

AYVOISE, Marie (c. 1790–1850). *See Dorion, Marie.*

AZAROVA, Elena (1973—). Russian synchronized swimmer. Born June 5, 1973, in Moscow, Russia. ❖ Won a team World championship (1998); won a team gold medal at Sydney Olympics (2000) and a team gold medal at Athens Olympics (2004).

AZEVEDO, Maria (1871–1920). *See Júlia, Francisca.*

AZIZ, Malak 'Abd al- (1923—). *See Abdel-Aziz, Malak.*

AZNAVORYAN, Karina (1974—). *See Aznavourian, Karina.*

AZNAVOURIAN, Karina (1974—). Russian fencer. Name variations: Karina Aznavuryan or Aznavoryan. Born Sept 20, 1974, in Baku, Armenia. ❖ Won a bronze medal at Atlanta Olympics (1996), a gold medal at Sydney Olympics (2000), and a gold medal at Athens Olympics (2004), all for team épée.

AZON, Sandra (1973—). Spanish yacht racer. Born Nov 12, 1973, in Barcelona, Spain. ❖ Won World championship for Yngling class (2002); won a silver medal for double-handed dinghy (470) at Athens Olympics (2004).

AZUBAH. Biblical woman. Wife of Caleb (1 Chr. 2:18, 19).

AZUBAH (fl. 860 BCE). Biblical woman. In 1 Kings 22:42; dau. of Shilhi; children: Jehoshaphat, king of Judah (r. 873–849 BCE).

AZURDUY DE PADILLA, Juana (1781–1862). Argentine heroine. Name variations: Juana Azurduy. Born in Chuquisaca (now Sucre, Bolivia) in 1781; died in 1862; m. Manuel Asencio Padilla, 1805 (died 1816); children: one daughter. ❖ Heroine in the Argentine struggle for independence, whose military exploits have long been celebrated throughout Latin America; became a nun; after a few years, left the cloister to marry a soldier (1805); when the independence struggle against Spain in the Viceroyalty of La Plata began (1810), fought side by side with husband; after he died in battle at Viloma (1816), withdrew with rebel forces to Salta, where General Manuel Belgrano won a significant victory; admired for her courage and élan, received an officer's appointment from the national executive of the provisional rebel government, Juan Martín Pueyrredón (1816). ❖ See also *Women in World History*.

AZZA AL-MAILA (fl. c. 707). Arabian composer and singer. Name variations: (nickname) Maila. Died around 707. ❖ Was taught music of the older days by Ra'iqa and learned Persian airs from Nashit and Sa'ib Kathir. A Christian freed woman of Medina and one of the most important professional musicians of her era, composed many songs in the Persian idiom. ❖ See also *Women in World History*.

AZZI, Jennifer (1968—). American basketball player. Born Aug 31, 1968, in Oak Ridge, Tennessee; graduated from Stanford University, 1990. ❖ Point guard; won a team gold medal at World championships (1990) and Goodwill Games (1994); played for Arvika Basket in

Sweden (1995–96); also played in Viterbo, Italy, and Orchies, France; won a team gold medal at Atlanta Olympics (1996); joined the San Jose Lasers of the American Basketball League; drafted by the Detroit Shock of the WNBA (1999); traded to Utah Starzz (2000). Named Kodak All-American (1989, 1990); received Wade Trophy (1990); named Naismith Player of the Year and NCAA Final Four MVP (1990).

B

BÂ, Mariama (1929–1981). Senegalese novelist. Name variations: Ba or Baâ. Born to Muslim parents in Dakar, Senegal, 1929; died after a long illness in Dakar in 1981; dau. of a civil servant; attended École Normal for girls in Rufisque; married a Senegalese politician (div.); children: 9. ❖ Worked as secretary before becoming a grade-school teacher (1947); joined various Senegalese women's organizations and wrote essays on such topics as polygamy and clitoridectomy; published epistolary 1st novel *Une Si longue lettre* (*So Long a Letter*) (1979), which won 1st Noma Award for Publishing in Africa; works include the posthumously published *Le Chant écarlate* (*Scarlet Song*). ❖ See also *Women in World History*.

BA TRIEU (225–248). Vietnamese resistance fighter. Name variations: Trieu Thi Chinh, Trieu Thi Trinh, Trieu Tring Nuong, Lady Trieu; Trieu Au (used by Chinese, though considered disrespectful by Vietnamese). Pronunciation: Bah Tcheel. Born c. 225; lived in Nui Nua, Thanh Hoa province, Vietnam; committed suicide on Tung Mountain, age 23, in 248; sister of Trieu Quoc Dat, a headman in Quang An, Thanh Hoa (northern Vietnam). ❖ Denounced crimes of Chinese Wu Dynasty and appealed to Vietnamese citizens to take up arms to save the country; at 19, rallied 1,000 fighters and trained them for battle on Nua Mountain; was so admired by her brother's soldiers that she took over as leader after his death and led her troops in 30 battles; killed herself on Tung Mountain, rather than give in to the enemy; commended for loyalty and bravery during early Ly Dynasty in 6th century by King Nam De who ordered construction of temple in her honor; serves as inspiration for national defiance against foreign domination; called the Vietnamese Joan of Arc by Western scholars. ❖ See also *Women in World History*.

BA YAN (1962—). Chinese basketball player. Born Dec 18, 1962, in China. ❖ At Los Angeles Olympics, won a bronze medal in team competition (1984).

BAADER, Amalie (b. 1763). Bavarian engraver. Born 1763 in Erding, Bavaria. ❖ An amateur engraver, studied under J. Dorner; her mark—an A & B interlaced—is found on copies of Rembrandt, Schmidt, and some Italian masters.

BAARD, Francina (1901–1997). South African activist. Name variations: Frances "MaBaard" Baard. Born in Port Elizabeth, South Africa, 1901; died 1997; husband died, 1953; children. ❖ Worked as a domestic servant, then as a teacher; joined ANC (1948) and was involved in organizing ANC's Women's League; was secretary of Women's League in Port Elizabeth by 1952; served as a leading member of Food and Canning Workers' Union and South African Congress of Trade Unions (SACTU) Local and Management Committees; was among ANC's 156 members and allies caught up in government sweep (1956); tried for treason, was eventually released but charged again under the Suppression of Communism Act (1963) and held in jail in solitary confinement for 1 year before trial; was imprisoned for 5 more years; released (1969) and "endorsed out" to Mabopane, near Pretoria.

BAAROVA, Lida (1914–2000). German actress. Name variations: Lída Baarová. Born in Prague, Czechoslovakia, Sept 7, 1914 (one source cites May 12, 1910); died Oct 28, 2000, in Salzburg, Austria; dau. of a civil servant; attended State Conservatory of Prague; m. Gustav Fröhlich (actor and star of *Metropolis*, who had been married earlier to Gitta Alpar); m. Jan Kopecky (theatrical agent), 1947 (div. 1956). ❖ Worked with National Theater in Prague before turning to film; found stardom in Germany with *Barbarole, Ein Teufelskerl, Einer zuviel an Bord* and *Die Stunde der Versuchung*; after husband had a conflict with Nazi Joseph Goebbels over Goebbels' apparent interest in her, was banished from German films and sent back to Prague; made 4 films in Italy (1942) before Mussolini fell from power; accused of collaboration with the Axis (1945), was interned in Pankrac Prison in Prague until Dec 1946; moved to Argentina, then Spain; made additional films in Italy, including

Fellini's *I vitelloni*, for which she earned a Silver Ribbon at Venice Film Festival (1953); moved to Salzburg and returned to the stage. ❖ See also autobiography *Escapes* (1983); and *Women in World History*.

BAAS, Christina (1938—). See Baas-Kaiser, Christina.

BAAS-KAISER, Christina (1938—). Dutch speedskater. Name variations: Stien Kaiser; Christina Kaiser; Christina Baas. Born Christina Wilhelmina Kaiser, May 20, 1938, in Delft, Netherlands. ❖ At World championships, won bronze medals for small allround (1965–66), gold medals (1967–68) and silver medals (1969–72); won bronze medals for 3,000 meters and 1,500 meters at Grenoble Olympics (1968); won a silver medal for 1,500 meters and a gold medal for 3,000 meters at Sapporo Olympics (1972), the oldest woman to win a gold medal in an indiv. event (33 years, 268 days).

BABAKHAN, Anna (1923—). See Andreeva-Babakhan, Anna Misaakovna.

BABAKOVA, Inga (1967—). Ukrainian high jumper. Born June 27, 1967, in Ashkabad, Turkmenistan. ❖ Won a bronze medal at Atlanta Olympics (1996); at World championships, won a gold medal (1999) and silver medals (1997, 2001).

BABANINA, Svetlana (1943—). Soviet swimmer. Born Feb 1943 in USSR. ❖ At Tokyo Olympics, won a bronze medal in the 4 x 100-meter medley relay and a bronze medal in the 200-meter breaststroke (1964).

BABANOVA, Maria (b. 1900). Russian actress. Name variations: Maria or Mariya Ivanovna Babanova. Born 1900 in Russia. ❖ Worked under Theodore Komisarjevsky; began to play leading roles for Meyerhold in Theatre Workshop (1920); later worked with A. Dikie at Moscow Art Theatre where she became leading actress; notable performances include Pauline in Ostrovsky's *Place of Profit* (1922), Juliet in Popov's *Romeo and Juliet*, and the heroine in Arbuzov's *Tanya*, for which she received Stalin Prize (1941); films include *Starets Vasili Gryaznov* (1924) and *Odna* (1931).

BABASHOFF, Shirley (1957—). American swimmer. Born Shirley Frances Babashoff, Jan 31, 1957, in Whittier, California. ❖ Won silver medals for the 200-meter and 100-meter freestyle and a gold medal for the 4 x 100-meter freestyle relay at Munich Olympics (1972); won silver medals for the 200-meter, 400-meter, and 800-meter freestyle and 4 x 100-meter relay and a gold medal for the 4 x 100-meter relay at Montreal Olympics (1976); won 27 national championships; won World championships for 200- and 400-meter freestyle (1975). Inducted into International Swimming Hall of Fame and US Olympic Hall of Fame. ❖ See also *Women in World History*.

BABB-SPRAGUE, Kristen (1968—). American synchronized swimmer. Name variations: Kristin Babb Sprague. Born July 29, 1968. ❖ At Barcelona Olympics, won a gold medal in solo competition (1992).

BABBIGE, Dora (c. 1872–1950). See Dean, Dora.

BABBIN, Jacqueline (1921–2001). American producer. Born Jacqueline T. Babbin, July 26, 1921, in New York, NY; died Oct 6, 2001, in Kent, Connecticut; graduate of Smith College, 1941; m. Alan Shayne (president of Warner Bros. Television, div.); no children. ❖ Theater, film and tv producer, was one of the 1st women head producers, presenting several tv network series, including "Armstrong Circle Theater," "DuPont Show of the Week," and "Beacon Hill"; established her own company, Clovis; won Peabody Award for "J.T." (1969) and Emmy for "Sybil" (1976); became vice president of novels and mini-series at ABC (1976); produced "All My Children" (1982–86) and "Loving" (1990–91); wrote 2 mystery novels.

BABCOCK, Maud May (1867–1954). American educator. Born Maud May Babcock in East Worcester, Otsego Co., New York, May 2, 1867;

died Dec 31, 1954, in Salt Lake City, Utah; dau. of William Wayne Babcock (doctor) and Sarah Jane (Butler) Babcock; Welles College, BA, 1884; Philadelphia National School of Oratory, BE in elocution, 1886; attended Harvard University, 1890–92; granted diploma, American Academy of Dramatic Art, 1890; pupil of Albert Ayres, 1891; studied in London and Paris 1 year, and University of Chicago, 1901; never married; no children. ❖ Taught in NYC public schools(1888–89); was visiting professor of oratory and speech, Rutgers College; taught at School of Physical Education of Harvard University (1890–92); became the 1st woman professor at University of Utah in Salt Lake City, Utah Territory (1892), where her classes in oratory, speech, and physical education became basis for the earliest university theater in US; with brother, Dr. William Wayne Babcock, provided equipment for 1st women's gymnasium in Utah (1893); directed 1st public performance (1893); served as guest director for Washington Square and Provincetown Players (1916); conducted 1st university Little Theatre west of Mississippi (1917); served as manager of Utah Theatre (now Playhouse) and other theatrical companies performing in the intermountain region; served on board of trustees of State School for Deaf and Blind (1897–1917) and was board president for 12 years, the 1st woman to preside over the trustees of a state institution. ❖ See also *Women in World History.*

BABCOCK, Winnifred (1875–1954). Canadian-American novelist. Name variations: Onoto Watanna; Winnifred Eaton. Born Winnifred Eaton in 1875 in Montreal, Canada; died 1954; dau. of a Chinese mother and English father; sister of Edith Eaton, also known as Sui Sin Far (writer); educated in Canadian public schools; married B.W. Babcock, 1901. ❖ Adopted Japanese persona and published 17 bestselling novels, all under pen name Onoto Watanna, including *The Old Jinriksha* (1895), *Miss Nume of Japan* (1899), *A Japanese Nightingale* (1901), *The Wooing of Wisteria* (1902), *The Heart of Hyacinth* (1903), *Daughters of Nijo* (1904), *The Diary of Delia* (1911), *Honorable Miss Moonlight* (1912) and *His Royal Nibs* (1924); lived in US. ❖ See also *Me: A Book of Remembrance* (Century, 1915).

BABER, Esther Mary (1871–1956). New Zealand headmistress. Born Mar 21, 1871, at Christchurch, New Zealand; died Nov 19, 1956, in Karori, New Zealand; dau. of Thomas Primrose Baber (corn merchant) and Jane (Wood) Baber; University of New Zealand, MA, 1898. ❖ Appointed to teaching staff at Fitzherbert Terrace School (1897); helped establish Pipitea Private School (1899–1906); purchased and administered Fitzherbert Terrace School (1907–31); remained on school's board of governors until 1956. ❖ See also *Dictionary of New Zealand Biography* (Vol. 3).

BABER, Liz (1938—). See *Calder, Liz.*

BABILENSKA, Gertruda (1902–1997). Polish-born Holocaust rescuer. Name variations: Name variations: Babilinska. Born near Danzig (Gdansk), Poland, 1902; died 1997; children: (adopted) Michael Stolowitzky. ❖ Worked for 15 years as an untutored Polish domestic for wealthy Jewish family named Stolowitzky; raised the son as her own after deaths of his parents and worked to conceal his Jewish identity during WWII; after the war, took him to Palestine on legendary ship *Exodus.* Her story, "Mamusha," appeared on "Rescuers: Stories of Courage," on "Showtime" cable network (1997). ❖ See also *Women in World History.*

BABILONIA, Tai (1959—). American pair skater. Born Tai Raina Babilonia, Sept 22, 1959; children: Scout. ❖ With partner Randy Gardner (1968–96), won the World championship (1979) and US nationals (1980), and was the 1st to complete the throw triple salchow in competition; had to withdraw from Lake Placid Olympics after Gardner pulled a groin muscle (1980).

BABIN, Vitya Vronsky (1909–1992). See *Vronsky, Vitya.*

BABOIS, Marguerite-Victoire (1760–1839). French poet. Name variations: Marguerite Victoire Babois. Born 1760 in Versailles, France; died 1839; dau. of a shopkeeper; married 1780 (sep. 1788); children: daughter (died 1792). ❖ Published *Elégie sur la mort de ma fille,* about death of her daughter (1792); other elegies published in *Elégies et poésies diverses* (1810).

BABY MARIE (1911—). See *Osborne, Marie.*

BABY PEGGY (b. 1917). See *Montgomery, Peggy.*

BABY RUTH (1892–1937). See *Roland, Ruth.*

BABY SPICE (1976—). See *Bunton, Emma.*

BACALL, Lauren (1924—). American actress. Born Betty Joan Perske, Sept 16, 1924, in Bronx, NY; m. Humphrey Bogart (actor), 1945 (died 1957); m. Jason Robards Jr. (actor), 1961 (div. 1969); children: (1st m.) Stephen and Leslie Bogart; (2nd m.) Sam Robards (actor). ❖ Began career as a model; made film debut opposite Humphrey Bogart in *To Have and Have Not* (1945); other films include *The Big Sleep, Dark Passage, Key Largo, Young Man with a Horn, How to Marry a Millionaire, Blood Alley, Designing Woman, Written on the Wind, Murder on the Orient Express, The Shootist, The Fan* and *The Venice Project;* appeared on Broadway in *Goodbye Charlie* and *Cactus Flower,* among others. Won Tony Award for *Applause* (1970).

BACCELLI, Giovanna (c. 1753–1801). Italian ballerina. Born Giovanna Zanerini in Venice in 1753; died in London, England, May 7, 1801. ❖ At 21, made London debut at King's Theatre, Haymarket, as Rose in Jean Lany's *Le Ballet des Fleurs* (1774); remaining at King's Theatre (1772–83), was featured in *La Polonaise favorite* (1772), *Les Amans surpris* (1780), *Médée et Jason* (1781), *Les Amans réunis* (1782) and *Les Petites Reins* (1781); made Paris Opéra debut (1782); was the mistress of the 3rd duke of Dorset for 15 years, then of the earl of Pembroke; during career, danced with Gaetan Vestris and Charles Le Picq; had portrait rendered by Sir Joshua Reynolds and Thomas Gainsborough. ❖ See also *Women in World History.*

BACCIOCCHI, Elisa (1777–1820). See *Bonaparte, Elisa.*

BACEWICZ, Grazyna (1909–1969). Polish violinist and composer. Born in Lodz, Poland, Feb 5, 1909; died in Warsaw, Jan 17, 1969; studied at Lodz Conservatory, Warsaw Conservatory, and Warsaw University as well as with Nadia Boulanger; m. Andrzej Biernacki (physician, professor of medicine, and secretary of Polish Academy of Science). ❖ Widely considered the most gifted composer of her time, began performing at 7; won 1st prize at Young Composers' Competition for a wind quintet in Paris (1933); won 2nd prize for *Trio* at Publishing Polish Music Society in Warsaw (1936); recorded *Overture* (1946); premiered *Concerto for String Orchestra* in US (1952); published *Music for Strings, Trumpets, and Percussion* (1958), which was played throughout the world. Received gold medal from Belgian government at International Composers' Competition (1965); had 2 streets in Poland named for her, one in Warsaw and one in Gdansk. ❖ See also *Women in World History.*

BACH, Anna Magdalena (1701–1760). German musician. Born Anna Magdalena Wilcken (or Wilcke), Sept 22, 1701, in Zeitz, Germany; died Feb 1760; dau. of Johann Caspar Wilcken (court trumpeter) and Margaretha Elisabeth Liebe, part of a musically gifted family; became 2nd wife of Johann Sebastian Bach (1685–1750), Dec 3, 1721; children: 13, including Johann Christoph Friedrich, Johann Christian (the "London" Bach), and 7 who died in infancy. ❖ As a soprano, held a position as a "princely singer" at court of Anhalt-Zerbst; retained singing post on marriage, drawing a salary equal to half of her husband's; often sang church cantatas written for her by husband; assisted him in copying his scores; eventually died in an almshouse, left penniless after his death. ❖ See also *Women in World History.*

BACH, Maria (1896–1978). Austrian composer, pianist, and violinist. Born in Vienna, Austria, Mar 11, 1896; died in Vienna, Feb 26, 1978; related to Johann Sebastian Bach; 1 of 4 daughters of Lenore von Bach (well-known soprano and concert singer) and Robert Freiherr von Bach (violinist and government official); studied with Josef Marx and Ivan Boutnikoff. ❖ Began musical career at 6; gave 1st concert at 10; studied violin under Arnold Rose but returned to piano and studied under Paul de Conne; at 19, wrote *Flohtanz,* a piece for piano which attracted attention; studied composition with Josef Marx and instrumentation under conductor Ivan Boutnikoff; composed *Narrenlied* (1924), which established her reputation in Vienna; won Premio Internationale para Compositores Buenos Aires prize (1962); as an orchestral, chamber, and piano composer, set the works of Hesse, Rilke, Rimbaud, Nietzsche and others to music. ❖ See also *Women in World History.*

BACH, Maria Barbara (d. 1720). First wife of JS Bach. Died July 1720, while husband was away on a tour in Karlsbad; married her cousin Johann Sebastian Bach (1685–1750, composer), Oct 17, 1707; children: 7, 4 of whom lived to maturity, including Carl Philipp Emanuel Bach and Wilhelm Friedemann Bach (both distinguished composers).

BACHAUER, Gina (1913–1976). Greek pianist. Born in Athens, Greece, May 21, 1913; died in Athens, Aug 22, 1976; dau. of Austrian father and Italian mother; married 2nd husband Alec Sherman (conductor). ❖ Began serious piano instruction at age 5, studying in Athens and then Paris with Alfred Cortot; won Medal of Honor at Vienna international competition (1933); made concerto debut in Athens with Dmitri Mitropoulos conducting (1935); repeated that triumph in Paris under baton of Pierre Monteux (1937); during WWII, lived in Alexandria, Egypt, and gave 100s of performances for Allied soldiers throughout Middle East; made London debut with conductor Alec Sherman (1946); had a large repertoire, which included Liszt, Tchaikovsky, and Rachmaninoff, the major works of Mozart, and such modernists as Igor Stravinsky. Gina Bachauer International Competition, held in Salt Lake City, UT, is dedicated to her memory. ❖ See also *Women in World History.*

BACHE, Sarah (1743–1808). American patriot. Name variations: Sarah Franklin Bache; Sarah Franklin. Born Sept 11, 1743; died 1808; only dau. of Benjamin Franklin and Deborah Read Rogers (his common-law wife); m. Richard Bache (Philadelphia merchant); children: 8. ❖ During Revolutionary War, led an effort whereby over 300,000 Continental dollars were collected by Philadelphia women for soldiers' relief and allocated for dry goods; established her home as gathering place for women who sewed while discussing financial strategy; employed more than 2,000 women in sewing uniforms for the army; also served in the hospitals; was host to prominent government leaders at home on Market Street in Philadelphia, where Franklin lived his last years. ❖ See also *Women in World History.*

BACHERACHT, Therese von (1804–1852). German novelist and travel writer. Born 1804; died 1852; dau. of a diplomat; married a Russian consul. ❖ Lauded by contemporaries especially for novels *Falkenberg* (1843), *Lydia* (1844) and *Heinrich Burkart* (1846); at urging of her lover, writer Karl Gutzkow, published diaries and letters concerning her travels to Russia and the Far East: *Briefe aus dem Süden* (Letters from the South, 1841) and *Menschen und Gegenden* (People and Places, 1845); credited for publishing Wilhelm von Humboldt's *Letters to a Friend* (1847).

BACHMAN, Maria Martin (1796–1863). See *Martin, Maria.*

BACHMANN, Ingeborg (1926–1973). Austrian-born author. Pronunciation: BOCK-mun. Born Ingeborg Bachmann, June 25, 1926, in Klagenfurt in Carinthia, southern Austria; died Oct 17, 1973, in Rome from burns suffered in a house fire and complications resulting from drug withdrawal; dau. of Mathias Bachmann (teacher) and Olga (Haas) Bachmann; studied philosophy and law in Innsbruck and Graz, 1945–46; continued studies in Vienna, 1946–50; wrote PhD dissertation on the reception of Martin Heidegger's existential philosophy and was awarded doctorate, 1950; never married but had long-term relationships with composer Hans Werner Henze and writer Max Frisch; no children. ❖ Considered one of 20th century's most significant German-language authors, published 1st story, "Die Fähre" (The Ferry, 1946), and 1st poems 3 years later; traveled to Paris and London (1950); after returning to Vienna, worked as a scriptwriter and editor for radio station Red-White-Red until 1953; worked as a dramaturg for Bavarian tv (1957–58); wrote several opera libretti; published novel *Malina* (1971) and a volume of stories *Simultan* (1972); awarded numerous prizes, including the Gruppe 47 prize for her poetry volume *Die gestundete Zeit* (Borrowed Time, 1953), the Georg Büchner prize (1964) and the Austrian State Prize (1968); made member of German Academy of Language and Literature (1957). Other writings include "Ein Geschäft mit Träumen" (A Business with Dreams, radio play, 1952), "Die Zikaden" (The Cicadas, radio play, 1955), *Anrufung des Grossen Bären* (Invocation of the Great Bear, poetry, 1957), "Der gute Gott von Manhattan" (The Good God of Manhattan, radio play, 1958), *Der Prinz von Homburg* (The Prince of Homburg, opera libretto, 1960), *Das dreissigste Jahr* (The Thirtieth Year, stories, 1961), "Der junge Lord" (The Young Lord, opera libretto, 1965) and "Der Fall Franza" (The Case of Franza, novel fragment, 1966). ❖ See also Karen R. Achberger, *Understanding Ingeborg Bachmann* (South Carolina U. Press, 1995); Peter Beicken, *Ingeborg Bachmann* (Beck, 1988); Kurt Bartsch, *Ingeborg Bachmann* (Metzler, 1988); and *Women in World History.*

BACHMANN, Tina (1978—). German field-hockey player. Born Aug 1, 1978, in Germany. ❖ Won a team gold medal at Athens Olympics (2004).

BACHOR, Isabell (1983—). German soccer player. Born July 10, 1983, in Trier, Germany. ❖ Won a team bronze medal at Athens Olympics (2004).

BACHRACH, Elise Wald (1899–1940). American artist. Born Elise Wald in New York, NY, June 20, 1899; died Mar 8, 1940; attended Horace Mann School; studied painting abroad; married a man named Bachrach. ❖ Had a brief but successful painting career; though she started painting late and died young at age 41, her landscapes and still-lifes were widely exhibited throughout US; lived in Great Neck, Long Island, and maintained a studio in Woodstock, NY.

BACINETTI-FLORENZI, Marianna (1802–1870). Italian philosopher and translator. Name variations: Marchesa Marianna Bacinetti-Florenzi Waddington. Born into a wealthy family in Ravenna, Italy, 1802; died April 1870; educated privately in Faenza by Torrigiani; m. Marquis Lodovico e Carlotta (died); m. Evelino Waddington; children: (1st m.) 2. ❖ Known far and wide for her philosophical writing and her deft interpretations of philosophers, was instrumental in introducing the philosophy of Friedrich Schelling to Italy; translated much of his work into Italian, including some of his unpublished writings; received some opposition from Catholic Church for her own philosophy; also trans. Gottfried Wilhelm Leibniz; writings include *Taluui Pensieri* (1843), *Letters filesofiche* (1848), *Alcune Riflessioni sopra il Socialismo ed il Comunismo* (1860), *Filosofemini di Cosmologia e di Antologia* (1863), *Saggi di Psicologia e di Logica* (1864), *Saggio sulla Natura* (Dante, il poeta del pensiero, 1866), *Saggio sulla filosofia dello spirito* (1867), *Della Immortalita dell'Anima Umana* (1868), *La Facolta di Sentire* (1868) and *Corrispondenza inedita di Vittorio Cousin con la marchesa Florenzi* (1870).

BACINSKAITE-BUCIENE, S. (1904–1945). See *Neris, Salomeja.*

BACKANDER, Helge (1891–1958). Swedish gymnast. Born Oct 13, 1891; died Nov 11, 1958. ❖ At Antwerp Olympics, won a gold medal in all-around, Swedish system, teams (1920).

BACKER, Harriet (1845–1932). Norwegian painter. Born Jan 21, 1845, in Holmestrand, on the Oslofjord, Norway; died Feb 1932; dau. of Consul Nils Backer (shipowner) and Sophie (Petersen) Backer; sister of Agathe Backer-Grondahl; studied in Germany and Italy, as well as Paris with Bonnat. ❖ Known for paintings of interiors from all levels of society—Paris salons, Breton and Norwegian farmhouses, her own background, and in particular the interiors of Norwegian churches—all of them with figures, mainly of women; moved to Paris (1878) and made debut in Paris Salon (1880); divided time in following decade between France and Norway; was in circle of leading Norwegian painters and foremost Norwegian writers of the day; returned to Norway for good (1888), painting during the summer in the valleys north of Christiania with another Norwegian artist Kitty Kielland, and spending the rest of the year teaching young artists at her own painting school which she ran until 1912; paintings include *By Lamplight* (1890), *Blue Interior* (1892) and *Baptism at Tanum Church* (1892); decorated with the Order of St. Olav. Many of Backer's paintings are in the collections of the National Gallery, Oslo, and the Rasmus Meyer Gallery, Bergen, Norway. ❖ See also Else Christie Kielland, *Harriet Backer* (Aschehoug, 1958); Marit Lange, *Harriet Backer* (Gyldendal, 1995); *Store Norske Leksikon* (Kunnskapsforlaget, 1991); and *Women in World History.*

BACKER-GRONDAHL, Agathe (1847–1907). Norwegian pianist and composer. Born in Holmestrand, on the Oslofjord, Norway, Dec 1, 1847; died in Ormoen near Christiana, Norway, June 16, 1907; dau. of Consul Nils Backer (shipowner) and Sophie (Petersen) Backer; sister of Harriet Backer; studied with Theodor Kullak and Hans von Bülow; married; children: Fridtjof (pianist and composer) and Nils (professor of medicine at University of Bergen). ❖ Well regarded in her lifetime, had a large repertoire; also wrote piano compositions, effectively in the style of Mendelssohn and Schumann. ❖ See also Inga Hoegsbro Christensen, *Biography of the Late Agathe Backer-Grondahl* (Roy, 1913); and *Women in World History.*

BACKHOUSE, Elizabeth (b. 1917). Australian author. Born Elizabeth Backhouse, May 21, 1917, in Northam, Western Australia; dau. of Hilda (Booth) Backhouse and William Backhouse; never married; no children. ❖ Wrote 1st novels while serving with Women's Auxiliary Australian Air Force (WWII), including *In Our Hands* (1940) and *The Sky Has Its Clouds* (1943); lived in England after the war, working for Korda Films; returned to Australia (1951); published novels *Death Came Uninvited* (1957), *Death Climbs a Hill* (1963) and *The Web of Shadows* (1966); turned to writing for stage and tv; published *Against Time and Place* (1990), which provides an anecdotal history of her parents' families, several of whose members emigrated from England; also wrote *The Thin Line* (1968) and *The Fourth Picture* (1974).

BACLANOVA, Olga (1899–1974). Russian actress and dancer. Pronunciation: Bah-CLAHN-ova. Born in Moscow, Russia, Aug 19,

1899; died Sept 6, 1974, in Vevey, Switzerland; studied at Cherniavsky Institute and Moscow Art Theater; married a man named Zoppi (div.); m. Nicholas Soussanin; m. Richard Davis (film exhibitor and distributor); children: (2nd m.) Nicholas Soussanin Jr. (also known as Nicholas Saunders). ❖ At 16, made stage debut at Moscow Art Theater and soon appeared in leading roles as one of company's top draws; while on tour in America (1923), decided to remain; played parts in 2 Josef von Sternberg films: *The Docks of New York* (as Lou) and *Street of Sin,* both opposite Emil Jannings; had most prominent leading role in Tod Browning's cult classic *Freaks;* appeared on Broadway with Bela Lugosi in *Murder at the Vanities* (1930s); hosted her own radio program; returned to Broadway as Madame Daruscha in *Claudia* and repeated the role in film version; lived in Switzerland following retirement; films include *He Who Gets Slapped* (1916), *The Man Who Laughs* (1928), *The Wolf of Wall Street* (1929), *Cheer Up and Smile* (1930), *The Great Lover* (1931), *The Monster Show* (1932), and *Billion Dollar Scandal* (1933). ❖ See also *Women in World History.*

BACON, Albion Fellows (1865–1933). American housing reformer. Born April 8, 1865, in Evansville, Indiana; grew up in McCutchanville; died in Evansville, Dec 10, 1933; dau. of Albion (Methodist minister) and Mary (Erskine) Fellows; younger sister of Annie Fellows Johnston (1863–1931); m. Hilary E. Bacon (banker and merchant), Oct 1888; children: 4. ❖ Became aware of river-front slums of Evansville, Indiana, and worked with Evansville Civic Improvement Society; organized the Men's Circle of Friendly Visitors, the Flower Mission for poor working girls, a Working Girls' Association, an Anti-Tuberculosis League, and the Monday Night Club; after years of effort, managed to have a tenement-house law included in cities' building codes for Evanston and Indianapolis (1909); helped organize Indiana Housing Association (1913); responsible for law involving the condemnation of unsafe or unsanitary buildings (1917). ❖ See also autobiography *Beauty for Ashes* (1914); and *Women in World History.*

BACON, Alice Mabel (1858–1918). American writer and educator. Born Alice Mabel Bacon, Feb 26, 1858, in New Haven, Connecticut; died May 1, 1918, in New Haven; dau. of Leonard Bacon and Catherine E. (Terry) Bacon. ❖ Taught at Hampton Normal and Agricultural Institute, Hampton, VA (1883–88, 1889–99); taught English at Peeresses' School in Tokyo, Japan, for daughters of nobility (1888–89); founded Dixie Hospital for nursing education and to care for local community (1891); raised funds to establish nurse's training for blacks; with Umé Tsuda, wrote *Japanese Girls and Women* (1891), *A Japanese Interior* (1893), and Japanese folk tales, *In the Land of the Gods* (1905); with Tsuda, founded Girls' English Institute (later Tsuda College), the 1st non-mission school for advanced training for women in Japan (1900), becoming chief assistant; taught at Tokyo Women's Higher Normal School; returned to New Haven (1902); taught at Miss Capen's School, Northampton, MA (1908–10); established, and during summer managed, Deep Haven Camp on Squam Lake, Holderness, New Hampshire.

BACON, Anne Cooke (1528–1610). English writer. Name variations: Ann Bacon, Lady Anne Bacon; (pseudonym) A.C. Born 1528 in Gidea Hall, Essex, England; died Aug 1610 in Gorhambury, Hertfordshire, England; dau. of Anthony Cooke (scholar and tutor) and Anne Fitzwilliam Cooke; sister of Mildred Cooke Cecil and Elizabeth Russell; m. Nicholas Bacon, 1556; children: 2 sons, Anthony and Francis Bacon (1561–1626, theologian). ❖ With sisters, educated by father who was tutor of King Henry VIII's only son, Edward (later King Edward VI); learned to speak and write several languages, including Latin and possibly Greek; was devoted follower of new Protestant faith and produced many English translations of Protestant works, thus contributing to spread of Protestantism in England; at 22, published her translations from Italian of works by Barnadine Ochine; published English edition of the Latin "Apology in Defense of the Church of England" by John Jewett, one of her more important translations (1564); lived long enough to see her younger son, Sir Francis Bacon, gain international renown for his theological writings on the new faith. ❖ See also *Women in World History.*

BACON, Delia Salter (1811–1859). American author. Born Delia Salter Bacon, Feb 2, 1811, in Tallmadge, Ohio; died Sept 2, 1859, in Hartford, Connecticut; dau. of Alice (Parks) Bacon and Reverend David Bacon (congregationalist missionary); educated at Harriet Parson's School and Catharine Beecher's School; never married; no children. ❖ The 1st person to theorize publicly that Francis Bacon was the true author of Shakespeare's plays, began career publishing the sentimental *Tales of the Puritans* anonymously (1831), and received attention for the work once

her identity was discovered; taught literature, philosophy, sciences, and history to women in CT; became subject of controversy when a young minister, Alexander MacWhorter, asserted that she had proposed to him; received ruling from hearing that MacWhorter had behaved questionably, but incident damaged her reputation; with help from Elizabeth Palmer Peabody, became an established lecturer in Boston; obsessed with her Baconian theory, received support from Ralph Waldo Emerson and Nathaniel Hawthorne; after years of effort, published her theory in *Philosophy of the Plays of Shakespeare Unfolded* (1857) and was fiercely denounced; died in an institution for the mentally ill 2 years later; while her theory has been taken up by others, it has never been proven; was basis for character of Miss Ophelia in *Uncle Tom's Cabin.* ❖ See also Theodore Bacon, *Delia Bacon: A Biographical Sketch* (Houghton, 1888); and *Women in World History.*

BACON, Faith (1909–1956). American dancer and performer. Born 1909 in Los Angeles, California; committed suicide, Sept 26, 1956, in Chicago, Illinois; trained with Albertina Rasch. ❖ Debuted on Broadway as a model in *Artists and Models* (1925); appeared as a showgirl in *Earl Carroll's Vanities* (1925–30) and in the last edition of the *Ziegfeld Follies* (1931); performed as an interpretive dancer (1932–35) and became a strip-tease artist in burlesque (1935); created numerous works, including *Bird of Paradise, The Afternoon of a Faun* (unrelated to Fokine's) and *Dance of the Living Orchids* (1935–39) with which she headlined the World's Fair Congress of Beauty in NY and later performed versions on Paramount/Publix Circuit; appeared in film *Prison Train* (1938).

BACON, Georgeanna (1833–1906). *See Woolsey, Georgeanna.*

BACON, Gertrude (1874–1949). British aeronaut, writer, and lecturer. Born Gertrude Bacon, April 19, 1874, in England; died Dec 22, 1949; dau. of Rev. John Mackenzie Bacon (balloonist and scientist); m. Thomas J. Foggitt (chemist and botanist), 1929 (died 1934). ❖ During 1st flight of Stanley Spencer's 84-foot-long craft, became 1st woman to fly in an airship (1904); on a Farman plane, was the 1st Englishwoman to fly in an airplane (1909); was the 1st passenger in a hydroplane (1912) and 1st woman in a hydromonoplane; lectured in England, wrote books on flying, and was active in botany; codiscovered *Carex microglochin,* a species of rush new to Britain (1923); writings include: *Memories of Land and Sky* (1928) and *The Record of an Aeronaut: Being the Life of John M. Bacon* (1907).

BACON, Josephine Dodge (1876–1961). American writer. Name variations: Josephine Dodge Daskam. Born Josephine Dodge Daskam, Feb 17, 1876, in Stamford, Connecticut; died July 29, 1961, in Tannersville, New York; dau. of Anne (Loring) and Horace Sawyer Daskam; graduate of Smith College, 1898; m. Selden Bacon (lawyer), July 25, 1903; children: Anne, Deborah and Selden Jr. ❖ Author of juvenile and adult satires, had 1st major success with the *Smith College Stories* (1900); published most popular book *The Memoirs of a Baby* (1904), a satire on child rearing, which became bestseller; served on executive committee of Girl Scouts (1915–25), and as editor of official handbook and *Girl Scout Magazine;* published more than 35 books in 60 years, including *Sister's Vacation and Other Girls' Stories* (1900), *The Imp and the Angel* (1901), *Fables for the Fair* (1901), *The Madness of Philip* (1902), *The Inheritance* (1912), *Square Peggy* (1919), *Counterpoint* (1927), *Kathy* (1933), *Cassie-on-the-Job* (1937) and *The House By the Road* (1937).

BACON, Mabel (fl. 1910). American yacht racer. Flourished 1910. ❖ With husband, raced their 46½-foot cabin cruiser *Yo Ho* to Hamilton, Bermuda (June 25–29, 1910), taking 2nd place in the contest (1910), as members of Maine's Kennebec Yacht Club; took her regular turn at the wheel as part of the 3-person crew, becoming the 1st woman in US history to participate in a power-boat race.

BACON, Mary (1948–1991). American jockey. Born 1948 in Chicago, Illinois, to a carnival family; committed suicide in Fort Worth, Texas, June 8, 1991; m. Johnny Bacon (jockey), 1968. ❖ After attending Porelock Vale Riding School in Somerset, England, awarded a certificate as a British Horse Society Assistant; began professional career racing thoroughbreds the 1st year women were licensed as jockeys in US (1969); in 2 decades of thoroughbred racing, won 286 races. Named Most Courageous Athlete of the Year by Philadelphia Sports Writer Association (1973). ❖ See also Lynn Haney, *The Lady is a Jock* (Dodd, Mead, 1973); and *Women in World History.*

BACON, Peggy (1895–1987). American artist and illustrator. Name variations: Peggy B. Brook (legally since 1920). Born Margaret Frances

Bacon, May 2, 1895, in Ridgefield, Connecticut; died Jan 4, 1987, in Kennebunk, Maine; dau. of Elizabeth (Chase) Bacon and Charles Roswell Bacon (both artists); attended School of Applied Arts for Women, NY, 1913–14, and New York School of Fine and Applied Arts, 1914–15; studied painting at Art Students League, NY, 1915–20; m. Alexander Brook, 1920 (div. 1940); children: Belinda Bacon (b. 1920), Alexander "Sandy" Brook (b. 1922). ❖ Admired for her drypoint caricatures and satirical glimpses of New Yorkers, taught at Art Students League (1935, 1949–51), School of the Corcoran Gallery of Art, Washington, DC (1942–44), Fieldston Ethical Cultural School, Bronx (1933–38), Moore College of Art, Philadelphia (1963–64), and other schools; illustrated more than 60 books (1919–66), 17 of which she wrote herself, including *The True Philosopher and Other Cat Tales,Funerealities,The Terrible Nuisance and Other Tales, Animosities, Cat-Calls, The Mystery at East Hatchett,The Ghost of Opalina* and *The Magic Touch;* established reputation as America's leading caricaturist with *Off With Their Heads* (1934), satirical portraits in black-and-white pastel of notables; began to do genre pictures in pastel (after 1937), which are regarded as her most important contribution to history of US art; had major retrospective, *Pens and Needles* (1942); limited herself to painting (after 1955); received gold medal of American Academy and Institute of Arts and Letters (1960); published mystery novel *The Inward Eye,* which received Edgar Allan Poe Award (1953); recognized with year-long retrospective exhibit, *Peggy Bacon: Personalities and Places,* at Smithsonian (1975); works are in collections of Metropolitan Museum of Art, Whitney Museum, MoMA, Brooklyn Museum, Art Institute of Chicago, among others; illustrated such books as T. Robinson's *Buttons* (1938), T.S. Eliot's *The Hollow Men* (1925) and Carl Sandberg's *Rootabaga Country* (1929), and for such magazines as *The New Yorker,Vanity Fair* and *Town and Country.* ❖ See also William Murrell, ed., *Peggy Bacon* (Fisher, 1922); Roberta K. Tarbell, *Peggy Bacon: Personalities and Places* (Smithsonian, 1975); and *Women in World History.*

BADARZEWSKI-BARANOWSKA, Tekla (1834–1861). Polish composer. Born in Warsaw, Poland, 1834; died in Warsaw, Sept 24, 1861. ❖ Known chiefly for her piece *The Maiden's Prayer,* one of the 1st musical pieces to sell on the international music market (1856); by 1859, over 80 publishers had printed versions. ❖ See also *Women in World History.*

BADDELEY, Angela (1904–1976). English actress. Born Madeleine Angela Clinton-Baddeley, July 4, 1904, in London, England; died 1976; dau. of W.H. Clinton-Baddeley and Louise (Bourdin) Clinton-Baddeley; sister of actress Hermione Baddeley (1906–1986); m. Stephen Kerr Thomas (div.); m. Glen Byam Shaw. ❖ Made stage debut at Old Vic as the little Duke of York in *Richard III* (1915); frequently appeared as Jenny Diver in *The Beggar's Opera* (1920–23); played other roles including Anne Boleyn in Sybil Thorndike's revival of *Henry VIII* (1925), title role in *Marigold* (1927), title role in *Sadie Dupont* (1928), Lady Teazle in *The School for Scandal* (1929), Sylvette in *The Fantasticks* (1933), Olivia Grayne in *Night Must Fall* (1935), Lady Anne in *Richard III* at the Old Vic (1937), Natasha in *Three Sisters* (1938), Constance in *The Mad Woman of Chaillot* (1951) and Madame Ranevsky in *The Cherry Orchard* (1965); made US stage debut in *Night Must Fall* (1936); appeared as Mrs. Bridges, the cook, in "Upstairs, Downstairs" for British tv; films include *Arms and the Man* (1932), *The Ghost Train* (1932), *The Citadel* (1938) and *Tom Jones* (1963. ❖ See also *Women in World History.*

BADDELEY, Hermione (1906–1986). English actress. Born Hermione Clinton-Baddeley, Nov 13, 1906, in Broseley, Shropshire, England; died 1986; dau. of W.H. Clinton-Baddeley and Louise (Bourdin) Clinton-Baddeley; sister of actress Angela Baddeley (1904–1976); m. David Tennant (div.); m. Captain J.H. Willis. ❖ At 12, made London debut as Le Nègre in *La Boîte à Joujoux* at Court Theatre (1918); had 1st notable success as Florrie Small in *The Likes of Her* (1923); made NY debut as Helen in Delaney's *A Taste of Honey* (1959); nominated for Oscar (1959) for Best Supporting Actress for *Room at the Top;* appeared in tv series "The Good Life" (1971) and as Mrs. Naugatuck in "Maude" (1974–77); films include *A Daughter in Revolt* (1926), *The Guns of Loos* (1928), *No Room at the Inn* (1948), *The Pickwick Papers* (1952), *The Unsinkable Molly Brown* (1964), *Mary Poppins* (1964) and *There Goes the Bride* (1980). ❖ See also *Women in World History.*

BADDELEY, Sophia (1745–1786). English actress. Name variations: Sophia Snow. Born Sophia Snow, 1745, in London, England; died 1786 in Edinburgh, Scotland; dau. of Valentine Snow (sergeant-trumpeter); m. Robert Baddeley (1733–1794, actor). ❖ Celebrated Shakespearian

actress and singer of great beauty, who was renowned for her vanity and notorious conduct; eloped with actor Robert Baddeley at 18 (1763); made stage debut at Drury Lane as Ophelia in *Hamlet* (1765); appeared as a singer at Ranelagh and Vauxhall; excelled as Shakespearian heroine; had stormy relationship with husband who fought a bloodless duel over her with the brother of David Garrick; though separated from husband, continued to act with him at Drury Lane; suffering from addiction to laudanum, took refuge from creditors in Edinburgh, the site of her last appearance on stage (1784). ❖ See also Elizabeth Steele, *Memoirs of Mistress Sophia Baddeley* (1781).

BADEA, Ioana (1964—). Romanian rower. Born Mar 22, 1964. ❖ At Los Angeles Olympics, won a gold medal in quadruple sculls with coxswain (1984).

BADEA, Laura (1970—). Romanian fencer. Name variations: Laura Gabriela Badea; Laura Badea Carlescu; Laura Carlescu Badea. Born Laurei or Laura Gabriela Badea, Mar 26 (also seen as Mar 20 and 28), 1970, in Bucharest, Romania; m. Adrian Carlescu. ❖ At Barcelona Olympics, won a bronze medal in team foil (1992); won World championship for foil (1995); at Atlanta Olympics, won a gold medal for indiv. foil and a silver medal for team foil (1996); won European championships (1996–97).

BADEN, grand duchess of.
See Stephanie de Beauharnais (1789–1860).
See Sophia of Sweden (1801–1865).
See Louise of Baden (1838–1923).
See Margaret of Baden (b. 1932).

BADEN, margravine of.
See Marie Louise (1879–1948).
See Theodora Oldenburg (1906–1969).

BADEN, princess of.
See Amalie of Hesse-Darmstadt (1754–1832).
See Elizabeth of Wurttemberg (1802–1864).
See Louise of Baden (1811–1854).

BADEN-DURLACH, margravine of.
See Christina Casimir.
See Augusta Maria of Holstein-Gottorp (1649–1728).

BADEN-POWELL, Agnes (1858–1945). English founder. Born 1858; died June 1945; dau. of Rev. B. Baden Powell (1796–1860, Savilian professor of geometry, known for his research on optics and radiation); sister of George Smyth Baden-Powell (1847–1898, Conservative MP), and Robert Stephenson Smyth, 1st baron Baden-Powell (1857–1941), who founded the Boy Scouts. ❖ Co-founded the Girl Guides (1910), serving as its president until 1917 and issuing *Handbook of the Girl Guides;* remained vice president of the organization until her death.

BADEN-POWELL, Olave (1889–1977). English leader of international Girl Scout movement. Born Olave St. Clair Soames in Chesterfield, Derbyshire, England, Feb 22, 1889; died 1977; youngest dau. of Harold Soames; m. Sir Robert Stephenson Smyth Baden-Powell (founder of the Boy Scout movement and chief scout, who was made a baronet, and, 1929, elevated to the peerage as the 1st Baron Baden-Powell of Gilwell), 1912; children: Peter (b. 1913); Heather Baden-Powell (b. 1915); Betty Baden-Powell (b. 1917). ❖ Met future husband on trip to West Indies (1912); ran YMCA canteen in Calais (WWI); became guide commissioner of Sussex for Girl Guide Association (1916); organized, publicized, and solicited leadership for Girl Guide movement; became chief commissioner (1917) and extended network of Girl Guide organizations to every county in Great Britain, as well as overseas; published *Training Girls as Guides* (1917); elected permanent chief guide (1918); made chief guide of the world at World Conference (1930); documented worldwide travels in 2 books, *Travelogues* and *Guide Links;* lent expertise to World Bureau, headquartered in London. Made Dame of the Grand Cross of Order of the British Empire (1932); received numerous additional honors, including Order of the White Rose from Finland and Order of the Sun from Peru. ❖ See also autobiography, *Window on My Heart* (1973); and *Women in World History.*

BADGER, Charlotte (fl. 1806–1808). New Zealand convict. Born Charlotte Badger, c. 1778 (baptized July 31, 1778), in Bromsgrove, Worcestershire, England; died after 1816, perhaps on Island of Tonga in South Pacific; dau. of Thomas and Ann Badger; children: 1. ❖ Convicted of felony housebreaking and sentenced to 7 years deportation, arrived in

Port Jackson, Sydney, Australia, aboard convict ship (1801); served 5 years at Parramatta Female Factory, where she gave birth to a daughter; assigned as servant to settler in Hobart to complete sentence, boarded *Venus* with other convicts for Tasmania (1806); was among those who seized the ship in Port Dalrymple and were put ashore at Rangihoua in Bay of Islands, where she lived among the Maori and became one of 1st white women to settle in New Zealand; may have later accepted passage to Tonga in South Pacific. ❖ See also *Dictionary of New Zealand Biography* (Vol. 1); Angela Badger, *Charlotte Badger, Buccaneer* (historical fiction; Indra, 2002).

BADGLEY, Helen (1908–1977). American silent-film actress. Born Dec 1, 1908, in Saratoga Springs, NY; died Oct 25, 1977, in Phoenix, Arizona. ❖ As a child, was a member of the Thanhouser Co. of New Rochelle (1911–17), billed as the Thanhouser Kidlet (as was Marie Eline).

BADHAM, Mary (1952—). American actress. Name variations: Mary Badham Wilt. Born Oct 7, 1952, in Birmingham, Alabama; dau. of a retired army officer who became president of Bethlehem Steel; sister of John Badham (director); m. Dick Wilt (computer science teacher); children: 2. ❖ Appeared as Scout in film version of *To Kill a Mockingbird* (1962) and was nominated for a Best Supporting Actress award; also appeared as Sport Sharewood in "The Bewitchin' Pool" episode of "Twilight Zone" (1964).

BADIA, Baahissat el (1886–1918). *See Nassif, Malak Hifni.*

BADIYA, Bahithat al- (1886–1918). *See Nassif, Malak Hifni.*

BADLESMERE, Elizabeth (fl. 1315–1342). Countess of Northampton. Dau. of Bartholomew Badlesmere (d. 1322), Lord Badlesmere, and Margaret de Clare (fl. 1280–1322); m. Edmund Mortimer (d. around 1331), 3rd baron of Wigmore; m. William Bohun (c. 1312–1360), 1st earl of Northampton; children: (1st m.) Roger Mortimer (1328–1359), 2nd earl of March; (2nd m.) Elizabeth Fitzalan (d. 1385); Humphrey Bohun (1342–1372), earl of Hereford, Essex, and Northampton.

BADLESMERE, Lady (fl. 1280–1322). *See Clare, Margaret de.*

BADLESMERE, Maud (d. 1366). Countess of Oxford. Name variations: Maud de Vere. Born c. 1312; died May 24, 1366, in Earls Colne; dau. of Bartholomew Badlesmere (d. 1322), Lord Badlesmere, and Margaret de Clare (fl. 1280–1322); m. John de Vere, 7th earl of Oxford, before Mar 27, 1336; children: John de Vere (b. around 1335); Margaret de Vere; Thomas de Vere (c. 1337–1371), 8th earl of Oxford; Aubrey (c. 1340–1400), 10th earl of Oxford; Robert de Vere; Maud de Vere; Elizabeth de Vere.

BADOREK, Gabriele (1952—). East German handball player. Born 1952 in East Germany. ❖ At Montreal Olympics, won a silver medal in team competition (1976).

BADULINA, Svetlana (1960—). Soviet volleyball player. Born Oct 26, 1960, in USSR. ❖ At Moscow Olympics, won a gold medal in team competition (1980).

BAELS, Liliane (1916–2002). Queen of the Belgians. Name variations: Mary Liliane Baels; Princess Lilian of Belgium; princess of Rethy. Born Nov 28, 1916, in Highbury, London, England; died June 7, 2002; became 2nd wife of Leopold III, king of the Belgians (r. 1934–1951), Sept 11, 1941; children: Alexandre (b. 1942); Marie Christine (b. 1951, who m. Paul Druker); Marie Esmeralda (b. 1956).

BAESINGER, Barbara (d. 1497). *See Fugger, Barbara Baesinger.*

BAEZ, Joan (1941—). American folksinger and civil-rights activist. Born Joan Chandos Baez, Jan 9, 1941, in Staten Island, NY; dau. of Albert Vinicio Baez (taught at Massachusetts Institute of Technology) and Joan Bridge Baez; sister of Mimi Farina (1945–2001, guitarist); briefly attended Boston University; m. David Harris (draft resister and activist), 1968 (div.); children: Gabriel Earl Harris (b. 1969). ❖ Began singing in coffeehouses in Cambridge, MA, and then appeared at Newport Folk Festival (1959); drew on ballads, southern, country, and protest music, and earned praise from fans and critics; released 1st album, *Joan Baez* (1960), which was a huge success, followed by *Joan Baez, Volume Two* (1961) and *Joan Baez in Concert* (1962); appeared at Monterey Folk Festival with Bob Dylan (1963); toured US, Europe, and Japan, and became involved in civil-rights activism and anti-war protests; founded institute for study of non-violence (1965); had hit single with "There But For Fortune" (1965); was a headliner at Woodstock (1969); earned several Grammy nominations. Other albums include *Farewell Angelina* (1965), *Noel* (1966), *Baptism* (1968), *Any Day Now* (1969), *David's*

Album (1969), *Blessed Are. . .* (1971), *Come from the Shadows* (1972), *Gracias a la Vida* (1974), *Diamonds and Rust* (1975), *Gulf Winds* (1976), *Blowin' Away* (1977), *Play Me Backwards* (1992), and *Gone from Danger* (1997). ❖ See also autobiographies *Daybreak* (1968) and *And a Voice to Sing With* (1987).

BAEZ, Mimi (1945–2001). *See Farina, Mimi.*

BAFFA, Sultana (d. 1603). *See Safiye.*

BAFFO, Cecelia Venier (1525–1583). *See Nurbanu.*

BAGE, Freda (1883–1970). Australian biologist and educator. Born Anna Frederica Bage, in St. Kilda, Melbourne, Australia, April 11, 1883; died in Brisbane, Oct 27, 1970; dau. of Edward (junior partner in a chemists and manufacturing firm) and Mary Charlotte (Lange) Bage; University of Melbourne, BS, 1905, MS, 1907. ❖ Champion of education and vocational guidance for women, became a lecturer in biology at the newly established University of Queensland (1913), then appointed the 1st principal of the Women's College within the university (1914); had a long association with Queensland National Council of Women; organized the Queensland Women Graduates' Association (which later became Queensland Association of University Women), and served as president of Australian Federation of Women Graduates (1928–29); was the 1st woman member on the Senate of the University of Queensland (1923–50); was also president of Queensland Women's Hockey Association (1925–31).

BAGENAL, Mabel (c. 1571–1595). Irish noblewoman. Born c. 1571; died at Dungannon, Dec 1595; dau. of Marshal Bagenal, leader of the army in Ireland; sister of Henry Bagenal (c. 1556–1598); m. Hugh O'Neill (1550–1616), 3rd Baron Dungannon and 2nd earl of Tyrone, Aug 1591. ❖ When her brother Henry Bagenal, marshal of the army in Ireland, refused to allow her to marry the twice-married Hugh O'Neill, defied him and eloped (1591); saw her dowry held back by brother for 2 years. Early historians often made her the cause of ill will between O'Neill and Henry Bagenal, calling her the "Helen" of the Elizabethan Bagenal wars, though this theory has been discredited.

BAGER, Louise (1982—). *See Noergaard, Louise Bager.*

BAGLEY, Amelia (1870–1956). New Zealand hospital matron, midwife, and nursing administrator. Born Oct 2, 1870, at Dunedin, New Zealand; died Jan 30, 1956, in Auckland; dau. of Benjamin Bagley and Amelia (Prictor) Bagley. ❖ Trained at Dunedin Hospital (1892–95); after working at Auckland Hospital (1895–1902), became matron of Masterton Hospital (1903–05); following passage of Midwives Act (1904), trained and became one of 1st registered midwives in New Zealand (1905); appointed assistant inspector in Department of Hospitals and Charitable Aid (1908); after setting up nursing stations at Te Karaka and Te Araroa, and dealing with outbreaks of typhoid and smallpox, was appointed supervisor of native health nurses (1913); served as matron of hospital ships (1917–18); and assisted with influenza pandemic of 1918; established basis for specialist branch of nursing and its own postgraduate training course (1928). ❖ See also *Dictionary of New Zealand Biography* (Vol. 3).

BAGLEY, Sarah (b. 1806). American labor leader. Born Sarah George Bagley in Meredith, New Hampshire, April 29, 1806; died after 1847; dau. of Nathan (farmer and entrepreneur) and Rhoda (Witham) Bagley. ❖ Entered Hamilton Manufacturing Corporation as operative (1837); was founder and president, the Lowell Female Reform League (1844–47); left mill job and became full-time organizer; active in Ten-Hour Day movement (1844–45); was founder and member of the Lowell Union of Associationists (1844–47), serving as vice-president (1846); organized Lowell Industrial Reform Lyceum (1845); edited *Voice of Industry* (1846); was a delegate to National Industrial Congress in Boston and National Reform Convention in Worcester (both 1846); served as superintendent of Lowell telegraph office and became 1st woman telegraph operator in US (1846). ❖ See also *Women in World History.*

BAGNOLD, Enid (1889–1981). English author. Name variations: Lady Jones; (pseudonym) "A Lady of Quality." Born Enid Algerine Bagnold, Oct 27, 1889, in Rochester, Kent, England; died in St. John's Wood, London, Mar 31, 1981; dau. of Arthur Henry (colonel in Royal Engineers) and Ethel (Alger) Bagnold; attended Prior's Field, as well as finishing schools in Germany, Switzerland and France; studied painting and drawing in London with British impressionist artist Walter Sickert; m. Sir George Roderick Jones, July 8, 1920; children: Laurian (b. 1921); Timothy Angus (b. 1924); Richard Bagnold (b. 1926); Dominick

(b. 1930). ❖ Known particularly for popular children's novel *National Velvet* and immensely successful play *The Chalk Garden*, published 1st book *The Sailing Ship and Other Poems* (1917); joined Red Cross and served as nurse's aide in Royal Herbert Hospital; wrote about experience in *A Diary Without Dates* (1918), which resulted in her dismissal from hospital; joined a corps of ambulance drivers in France, the experience of which influenced *The Happy Foreigner*, her 1st novel (1920); published children's book *Alice and Thomas and Jane* (1930), followed by highly acclaimed *National Velvet* (1935); worked for the Babies Club, 1st private welfare clinic in London; devoted postwar career mostly to theater, writing plays including *Dottie Dundass*, an English murder mystery (1941), *Poor Judas* (1946), and her greatest theatrical success, *The Chalk Garden*, which was 1st produced in NY (1955), then opened to great acclaim in London (1956); had hit play *The Chinese Prime Minister* in NY (1964); worked wtih Katharine Hepburn on *A Matter of Gravity*, produced in NY (1976); received Arts Theatre Prize, Commander of the British Empire, and American Academy of Arts and Letters silver medal. Other writings include *Serena Blandish* (1924), (trans.) *Alexander of Asia* (1935), *The Squire* (1938), *Letters to Frank Harris and Others* (1980) and *Poems* (1978). ❖ See also *Enid Bagnold's Autobiography* (Little, Brown, 1969); Lenemaja Friedman, *Enid Bagnold* (Twayne, 1986); Anne Sebba, *Enid Bagnold* (Taplinger, 1986); and *Women in World History*.

BAGNOLD, Lisbeth (1947—). American dancer. Born Oct 10, 1947, in Bronxville, NY; attended University of California at Los Angeles. ❖ Performed under Valerie Bettis in *On Ship* (1971) while at University of California, and also worked with Gus Solomons, José Limón and Alwin Nikolais; joined Nikolais' company in New York City (1971); performed in company's repertory and Nikolais group works (1972–78), including *Grotto* (1973); began teaching at Nikolais studio in NY and a Nikolais sponsored school in Paris; choreographed *Quiescence* (1980), among others.

BAGRYANA, Elisaveta (1893–1991). Bulgarian poet. Name variations: Yelisaveta Bagryana, Elizaveta Bagriana; (real name) Elisaveta Lyubomirova Belcheva Likov; Elisaveta Belcheva. Born Elisaveta Lyubomirova Belcheva, April 16, 1893, in Sofia, Bulgaria; died Mar 23, 1991; dau. of Maria and Lyubomir Belchev; educated at University of Sofia; m. Ivan Shapkarev, 1919 (div. 1925); m. Aleksandur Likov, 1944 (died 1954); children: (1st m.) son Lyubomir (b. 1919). ❖ Published 2 early poems (1915); began publishing under pseudonym Elisaveta Bagryana (1922); started earning national and European attention (1922), writing for literary magazine *Zlatorog*; released 1st volume of poetry *Vechnata i svyatata* (*The Eternal and the Sacred*), one of the most celebrated collections in Bulgarian poetry (1927); made lifetime arrangement with publisher Khemus (c. 1929); lost most of her personal papers when house was destroyed by bomb (WWII); traveled widely and was known for many love affairs. Considered among Bulgaria's greatest poets for her visions of her homeland, its traditions and peasant life. Other works include *Zvezda ne moryaka* (*The Mariner's Star*) (1932), *Pet zvezdi* (*Five Stars*) (1953), *Ot bryag do bryag* (*From Shore to Shore*) (1963) and *Counterpoint* (1970). ❖ See also *Women in World History*.

BAGRYANTSEVA, Irina (1957—). See *Nazarova-Bagryantseva, Irina*.

BAGRYANTSEVA, Yelizaveta (1920—). Soviet discus thrower. Born Nov 12, 1920. ❖ Won a silver medal in the discus throw in Helsinki Olympics (1952).

BAGSHAW, Elizabeth (1881–1982). Canadian physician. Born Oct 19, 1881, in Ontario, Canada; died Jan 5, 1982; dau. of John and Eliza (Beatty) Bagshaw; attended Ontario Medical College for Women and University of Toronto; never married; children: (adopted) John and Voureen. ❖ Served in private practice under Emma Leila Skinner; opened own practice in Hamilton, Ontario (1906); studied birth-control methods at Margaret Sanger's NY clinic; served as medical director of Birth Control Society of Hamilton (later part of Planned Parenthood Society), which was the 1st birth control clinic in Canada (1932–66). Named Hamilton's Citizen of the Year (1970); received Order of Canada Medal (1973).

BAHISSAT EL BADIA, or Bahithat al-Badiya (1886–1918). See *Nassiv, Malak Hifni*.

BAHMANN, Angelika (1952—). East German kayaker. Born April 1, 1952. ❖ At Munich Olympics, won a gold medal in the K1 slalom (1972).

BAHR-MILDENBURG, Anna (1872–1947). Austrian soprano. Born Anna Mildenburg, Nov 29, 1872, in Vienna, Austria; died Jan 27,

1947, in Vienna; studied with Rosa Papier-Paumgartner; m. Hermann Bahr (writer), 1909. ❖ Debuted in Hamburg as Brünnhilde in a performance conducted by Gustav Mahler (1895); began a relationship with Mahler; appeared with Mahler at Vienna Hofopera (1898–1916) and at Bayreuth (1897–1914); also appeared in 1st London performance of Richard Strauss' *Elektra* (1910). ❖ See also *Women in World History*.

BAHRKE, Shannon (1980—). American freestyle skier. Born Nov 7 (some sources cite Nov 11), 1980, in Reno, Nevada. ❖ Won a silver medal for moguls at Salt Lake City (2002); won a bronze medal at World championships and a gold medal at US Freestyle championships (2003), both for dual moguls.

BAI FENGXI (1934—). Chinese actress and playwright. Born 1934 in China. ❖ One of the most important women playwrights in contemporary China, began career as an actress (1950s); writings include the "Women Trilogy" (*First Bathed in Moonlight, Once Loved and in a Storm Returning* and *Say, Who Like Me Is Prey to Fond Regret*) which was staged and televised, achieving popular success; often writes about women's issues.

BAI, Lakshmi (c. 1835–1858). See *Lakshmibai*.

BAI, Putli (1929–1958). See *Putli Bai*.

BAI WEI (1894–1987). Chinese playwright. Born 1894 in China; died 1987. ❖ Playwright, recognized in her day as one who defied traditions, wrote and starred in own plays, which include *Tragic Life, Lin Li* (1925), and *Patricide*; her love letters to Yang Sao (1924–32) were compiled as short pieces of prose and entitled *Zuoye* (*Last Night*, 1995).

BAÏDAR-POLIAKOFF, Olga. See *Poliakoff, Olga*.

BAIDYCHEVA, Nina. See *Baldycheva, Nina*.

BAIER, Anke (1972—). East German speedskater. Name variations: Anke Baier-Loef or Baier-Löf. Born May 22, 1972, in Eisenach, Thüringen, East Germany. ❖ Was World Jr. champion (1991); won a silver medal for 1,000 meters at Lillehammer Olympics (1994).

BAIER, Maxi (1920—). See *Herber, Maxi*.

BAIK MYUNG-SUN (1956—). Korean volleyball player. Born Feb 12, 1956. ❖ At Montreal Olympics, won a bronze medal in team competition (1976).

BAIKAUSKAITE, Laimute (1956—). Soviet runner. Born June 10, 1956. ❖ At Seoul Olympics, won a silver medal in the 1,500 meters (1988).

BAILES, Margaret Johnson (1951—). African-American runner. Born Jan 23, 1951, in The Bronx, NY. ❖ Won the Amateur Athletic Union (AAU) national titles in the 100 and 200 meters (1968); won an Olympic gold medal in the 4 x 100-meter relay in Mexico City (1968).

BAILEY, Abigail Abbott (1746–1815). American memoirist. Born Abigail Abbott, Feb 2, 1746, in Rumford, Connecticut; died Feb 11, 1815, in Bath, New Hampshire; dau. of Deacon James Abbott; m. Major Asa Bailey, 1767; children: 17, including Samuel, Asa, Abigail, Caleb and Anna (twins), Chloe, Amos, Olive, Phinehas, Judith, and Patience. ❖ Began writing *Memoirs of Mrs. Abigail Bailey* (sometime after 1789) when she discovered that husband was sexually abusing one of their elder daughters; upon proof of his assaults, kicked husband out (1790); memoirs were published (1815), one of the few accounts written by a woman about domestic violence in early America. ❖ See also *Women in World History*.

BAILEY, Aleen (1980—). Jamaican runner. Born Nov 25, 1980, in St. Mary, Jamaica; attended University of South Carolina. ❖ Won a gold medal for the 4 x 100-meter relay at Athens Olympics.

BAILEY, Angela (1962—). Canadian runner. Born in Coventry, England, of Jamaican parentage, Feb 28, 1962. ❖ At Commonwealth Games, won a silver medal (1978); won a silver medal in 4 x 400-meter relay at Los Angeles Olympics (1984); was a finalist in the 100- and 200-meter races in World championships (1983). ❖ See also *Women in World History*.

BAILEY, Ann (1742–1825). Legendary frontier scout. Name variations: "White Squaw of the Kanawha" and Mad Ann. Born Ann Hennis in Liverpool, England, 1742; died in Gallia Co., Ohio, Nov 22, 1825; came to America, probably as an indentured servant, 1761; m. Richard Trotter (died 1774); m. John Bailey; children: 1 son. ❖ Arrived in America from England (1761); after husband's death, donned male attire, armed herself with tomahawk and rifle, and forged new life as frontier scout, "Indian fighter," messenger, and spy; in less than 3 days, rode 200 miles through forest and enemy territory, to and from Fort Union (now Lewisburg), to replace supply of gun powder (1791). ❖ See also *Women in World History.*

BAILEY, Anna Warner (1758–1851). American patriot. Name variations: Mother Bailey. Born Anna Warner, Oct 11, 1758, in Groton, Connecticut; died Jan 10, 1850, in Groton; an orphan, was raised by her uncle Edward Mills; m. Captain Elijah Bailey (postmaster of Groton). ❖ When British soldiers under command of Benedict Arnold stormed Fort Griswold near Groton (Sept 6, 1781), walked to the battle site where she found her uncle mortally wounded; at his bidding, hurried home, saddled a horse for her aunt, and carried her infant cousin back in her arms for a final reunion of the family; also assisted soldiers in defense of New London against a blockading British fleet by providing her flannel petticoat for use as cartridge wadding (1813).

BAILEY, Barbara Vernon (1910–2003). English nun and artist. Name variations: Sister Mary Barbara; Barbara Vernon. Born Barbara Vernon, 1910, at Bulkeley Hall, in Woore, Shropshire, England; died at her convent, May 4, 2003, in Haywards Heath, West Sussex, England; dau. of Cuthbert Bailey (general manager of Royal Doulton's factory at Burslem, in Stoke-on-Trent). ❖ Nun whose whimsical watercolors inspired Royal Doulton's line of Bunnykins nursery dishes and were the model for Bunnykins figurines (now all collectors' items); trained as a nurse and teacher; at 19, went into the religious life in Sussex, an enclosed Roman Catholic order known as the Augustinian Canonesses of the Lateran (1929); at request of her father, began her rabbit drawings for use on cups, plates and other children's tableware (1934); working late at night, eventually rendered around 1,000 pictures.

BAILEY, Carolyn Sherwin (1875–1961). Author and editor of children's books. Born Oct 25, 1875, in Hoosick Falls, New York; died Dec 24, 1961, in Concord, Massachusetts; dau. of Charles Henry (scientist and traveler) and Emma Frances (Blanchard) Bailey (teacher and writer); attended Lansingburgh Academy, near Albany, NY; graduate of Columbia University Teachers College, 1896; attended Montessori School (Rome) and New York School of Social Work; m. Eben Clayton Hill, 1936. ❖ Worked as public-school teacher and kindergarten principal; did resident social work at Warren Goddard House in NY; wrote collection *For the Children's Hour* (1906), which remained in print for over 40 years; served as editor of children's department of *Delineator* and *American Childhood;* wrote 4-vol. series about pioneer arts and crafts (*Children of the Handcrafts* [1935], *Tops and Whistles* [1937], *Homespun Playdays* [1940], and *Pioneer Art in America* [1944]), which are considered by some critics as her finest achievements; won Newbery award (1947) for *Miss Hickory;* also wrote *Montessori Children* (1915), *Letting in the Gang* (1916), *Old Man Rabbit's Dinner Party* (1949), *The Little Red Schoolhouse* (1957) and *Flickertail* (1962), among others. ❖ See also *Women in World History.*

BAILEY, Chris (1972—). American ice hockey player. Born Feb 5, 1972, in Marietta, NY; graduate of Providence College, 1994. ❖ Won a team gold medal at Nagano (1998), the 1st Olympics to feature women's ice hockey; won a team silver medal at World championships (1997, 1999, 2000, 2001) and a team silver at Salt Lake City Olympics (2002). ❖ See also Mary Turco, *Crashing the Net: The U.S. Women's Olympic Ice Hockey Team and the Road to Gold* (HarperCollins, 1999); and *Women in World History.*

BAILEY, Elizabeth (1938—). American economist. Born Nov 26, 1938, in New York, NY; Radcliffe College, BA (magna cum laude), 1960; Stevens Institute of Technology, MS, 1966; Princeton University, PhD, 1972. ❖ Was an associate professor of economics at New York University (1973–77); was the 1st woman on Civil Aeronautics Board, filling an unexpired term, then served a full term (1977–83); was named dean of Graduate School of Industrial Administration at Carnegie Mellon University, the 1st woman to hold such a position at a major graduate business school; served as head of economics research department at Bell Labs and was on board of Honeywell, Philip Morris, CSX Corporation and Natwest Bancorp; was a founding member of Harbor School for Learning Disabilities.

BAILEY, Florence (1863–1948). American ornithologist and nature writer. Name variations: Florence Merriam. Born Florence Augusta Merriam in Locust Grove, NY, Aug 8, 1863; died in Washington, DC, Sept 22, 1948; dau. of Clinton (banker) and Caroline (Hart) Merriam; sister of Clinton Hart, 1st chief of the US Biological Survey; Smith College, BA, 1921; m. Vernon Bailey (naturalist), Dec 16, 1899.

❖ Published 1st book *Birds Through an Opera Glass* (1889), based on early articles she had written for *Audubon Magazine;* often accompanied husband on arduous field expeditions in Texas, California, Arizona, Pacific Northwest and Dakotas; published *Handbook of Birds of the Western United States* (1902), which became a standard; became 1st woman to receive Brewster Medal of American Ornithologists' Union, for *Birds of New Mexico;* at 75, published last work of note, *Among the Birds in the Grand Canyon National Park* (1939); was founding member of Audubon Society of District of Columbia; taught classes in basic ornithology; became 1st woman associate member (1885) and 1st woman fellow (1929) of American Ornithologists' Union; writings include *My Summer in a Mormon Village* (1894), *A-Birding on a Bronco* (1896), *Birds of New Mexico* (1928), and *Among the Birds in the Grand Canyon National Park* (1939). In her honor, a variety of chickadee from the mountains of southern California named *Parus gambeli baileyae* (1908). ❖ See also *Women in World History.*

BAILEY, Frankie (1859–1953). American dancer. Name variations: Francesca or Frankie Walters; The Girl with the Million Dollar Legs. Born Francesca Walters, May 29, 1859, in New Orleans, Louisiana; died July 8, 1953, in Los Angeles, California; m. Frank Robinson. ❖ One of the best-known chorus dancers of her era, performed as lead chorus dancer in Weber and Fields' Music Hall in New York (c. 1896–1912), where she appeared in *Whirl-i-gig* (1899), *Fiddle-Dee-Dee* (1900), *The Ginger Bread* (1905) and *Hokey-Pokey* (1912), among others; retired from stage work (1916); appeared on film in numerous roles—as mother, maid, or commoner—including in *The Famous Mrs. Fair* (1923), *Flower of Night* (1925), *Thank You* (1925) and *The Crown of Lies* (1926).

BAILEY, Hannah Johnston (1839–1923). American suffragist, philanthropist, and activist for peace. Born Hannah Clark Johnston, July 5, 1839, in Cornwall-on-the-Hudson, New York; died in Portland, Maine, Oct 23, 1923; dau. of David Johnston (tanner, farmer, and Quaker minister) and Letitia (Clark) Johnston; attended Friends boarding school; m. Moses Bailey, Oct 13, 1868 (died 1882); children: Moses Melvin. ❖ One of most effective publicists in US dedicated to the cause of peace and internationalism, began career as a schoolteacher (1858–67); undertook religious mission to New England (1867); served as 1st superintendent of National Woman's Christian Temperance Union's department of peace and arbitration (1887–1916); transformed department into most active separate women's peace agency in US; founded peace department of World WCTU and became superintendent (1889); used private wealth to advance cause of peace; was long active in Quaker Meeting; began publishing peace journals, *The Acorn* and *Pacific Banner* (1889); served as president of Maine Equal Suffrage Association (1891–97); joined Woman's Peace Party (1915) and Woman's International League for Peace and Freedom (1918). ❖ See also *Women in World History.*

BAILEY, Marion Sheahan (1892–1994). See Sheahan, Marion.

BAILEY, Mary (1890–1960). British pilot. Name variations: Lady Mary Bailey; Dame Mary Bailey. Born in England, 1890; died 1960; dau. of 5th Lord Rossmore; m. Sir Abe Bailey, 1911. ❖ Obtained pilot's license (1927); made solo flight from Croydon, England, to Cape Town, South Africa (Mar 1928–Jan 1929); awarded Britannia Trophy and Dame of the British Empire (1930).

BAILEY, Mildred (1903–1951). American jazz singer. Born Mildred Rinker, Feb 27, 1903, in Tekoa, near Seattle, Washington; died Dec 12, 1951, in Poughkeepsie, NY; sister of Al Rinker, who sang with Paul Whiteman's Rhythm Boys; m. 2nd husband Red Norvo (bandleader and xylophonist), 1933 (div. 1945). ❖ Sang with Paul Whiteman's Band (1929–33), Ben Berney's Orchestra (1934), Red Norvo and his Orchestra (1936–39), the Dorsey Brothers' and Benny Goodman's orchestras (from 1939 on); as the 1st white female to be completely accepted in jazz circles, helped move the genre into US mainstream; made many recordings which are considered classics, and was especially known for her recording of Hoagy Carmichael's "Ol' Rockin' Chair." ❖ See also *Women in World History.*

BAILEY, Mother (1758–1851). See Bailey, Anna Warner.

BAILEY, Pearl (1918–1990). African-American jazz singer, actress, writer and activist. Born Mar 29, 1918, in Newport News, Virginia; died Aug 17, 1990; dau. of Joseph James Bailey (evangelical preacher) and Ella Mae Bailey; graduate of Georgetown University, with a degree in theology and a Dean's Award (1985); married a drummer (lasted only 18 months), then a soldier just returned from overseas during WWII (div.); m. John Randolph Pinkett Jr., Aug 31, 1948 (div. Mar 1952); m. Louis Bellson Jr. (drummer and bandleader), 1952. ❖ After winning an amateur contest (1933), began touring with several bands, singing and dancing; signed 1st recording contract, with Columbia (1945), and recorded 1st hit, "Tired," (its opening line—"Honey, aren't you tired?"—became her trademark); debuted on Broadway in *St. Louis Woman* (1946) and named most promising newcomer; dispatched on 1st of a long series of overseas tours as part of US's growing cultural presence in the postwar world, rubbing elbows easily with heads of state (1952); won Tony Award (1968) for performance in all-black version of *Hello, Dolly!*; appeared in such films as *Isn't It Romantic?* (1948), *Carmen Jones* (1955), *St. Louis Blues* (1958), *Porgy and Bess* (1959), *All The Fine Young Cannibals* (1960), *The Landlord* (1970) and *Norman . . . Is That You?* (1976); had her own tv show (1970s); appointed by Gerald Ford to US Mission to the UN (1975), then reappointed to 3 more terms. Awarded Medal of Freedom by President Ronald Reagan (1988). ❖ See also autobiographies *The Raw Pearl* (Harcourt, 1968) and *Between You and Me* (Doubleday, 1989); and *Women in World History.*

BAILEY, Temple (c. 1869–1953). American author. Born Irene Temple Bailey in Petersburg, Virginia, c. 1869; died July 6, 1953, in Washington, DC; dau. of Emma (Sprague) and Milo Varnum Bailey; never married; no children. ❖ Romance novelist who sold an estimated 3 million books, was a favorite author of department-store magnate John Wannamaker (he bought and distributed her works); earned $60,000 from *McCall's* for a single serial and $325,000 from *Cosmopolitan* for the right to 3 serials and several short stories; writings include *Judy* (1907), *Glory of Youth* (1913), *Adventures in Girlhood* (1917), *The Blue Window* (1926), *Little Girl Lost* (1932), *Fair as the Moon* (1935), *I've Been to London* (1937), *The Pink Camellia* (1942) and *Red Fruit* (1945).

BAILEY, Tonja (1970—). See Buford-Bailey, Tonja.

BAILIN, Gladys (1930—). American dancer and choreographer. Born Feb 11, 1930, in New York, NY; trained at Henry Street Settlement House. ❖ Joined Nikolais' company (1948) where she appeared in nearly all his tv works; performed on stage for Nikolais' in *Totem* (1959), *Imago* (1963) and *Galaxy* (1965), among others; created roles with Murray Louis troupe as a charter member, including in *Family Albums* (1954), *Signal* (1960), and *Chorus I*; performed in notable duets with Don Redlich such as *Alice and Henry* and *Couplet* (both 1967); choreographed works for numerous concerts with other Nikolais dancers; taught at Nikolais/Louis Dance Theater Lab and New York University School of the Arts. Works of choreography include *Quiet Vision* (1954), *Five Ladies* (1954), *Harlequinade* (c. 1956), *Prelude and Courante* (1957) and *Koto* (1957).

BAILLIE, Grisell (1822–1921). Scottish philanthropist and deaconess in Church of Scotland. Name variations: Grisell, Grizelda, Lady Grizel Baillie or Lady Grisell Baillie. Born Grisell Baillie, 1822, in Scotland; died 1921 in Scotland; dau. of George Baillie of Mellerstain; great-great-granddau. of Grizel Baillie (1665–1746); also a descendent of Robert Baillie, the martyr, and John Knox; sister of Katherine Charlotte Baillie (memoirist-biographer). ❖ Lauded as Church of Scotland's 1st deaconess, supported the local church in Dryburgh, both financially and through good works, such as teaching Sunday school for 50 years, visiting sick parishioners and organizing charity events; ordained as 1st deaconess of Church of Scotland in Bowden Kirk, Roxburgh (1888); also supported such causes as YWCA, Scotland Women's Guild, and temperance movement. ❖ See also Countess of Ashburnham, *Lady Grisell Baillie. A Sketch of Her Life by the Countess of Ashburnham* (R&R Clark, 1893).

BAILLIE, Grizel (1665–1746). Scottish songwriter. Name variations: Grisell, Grizelda, Lady Grizel Baillie, Lady Grizel Hume. Born Grizel Hume at Redbraes Castle, Berwickshire, Dec 25, 1665; died Dec 6, 1746; eldest dau. of Sir Patrick Hume (or Home) of Polwarth, afterwards earl of Marchmont, and Grisell Ker; m. George Baillie, 1692; children: Grizel (who m. Sir Alexander Murray of Stanhope and was known as Lady Murray of Stanhope) and Rachel, Lady Binning. ❖ At 12, carried letters from her father to imprisoned Scottish patriot Robert Baillie of Jerviswood (1677); also supplied father with food as he hid from the troops of England's King Charles II; married George Baillie (1692), son of the executed patriot. Some of her songs were printed in Allan Ramsay's *Tea-Table Miscellany*, while another, "And werena my heart light I wad dee," the most famous, originally appeared in *Orpheus Caledonius* (1725); "The Legend of Lady Grizelda Baillie" forms one of Joanna Baillie's *Metrical Legends of Exalted Character.* ❖ See also *Memoirs of the Lives and Characters of the Right Hon. George Baillie of Jerviswood and Lady Grisell*

Baillie, by their daughter, Lady Murray of Stanhope (1822); George Baillie's *Correspondence (1702–1708),* edited by Lord Minto (1842); and *Women in World History.*

BAILLIE, Isobel (1895–1983). Scottish soprano. Name variations: Dame Isobel Baillie. Born Isabella Baillie, Mar 9, 1895, in Hawick, Roxburghshire, Scotland; died Sept 24, 1983, in Manchester, England; youngest child of a master baker; studied with Guglielmo Somma in Milan, 1925–26. ❖ Following inaugural London season (1923), became one of England's most sought after singers for the works of Handel, Haydn, Brahms and Elgar; was especially noted for her singing in Handel's *Messiah,* Gluck's *Orphée,* and her recording of "I Know That My Redeemer Liveth"; was also one of the 1st British opera stars to sing in Hollywood Bowl (1933); gave many performances of Gounod's *Faust* in New Zealand, made frequent appearances with Royal Choral Society, and sang for 26 years with Hallé orchestra; went on to teach at Royal College of Music (1955–57, 1961–64), Cornell University (1960–61), and Manchester College of Music. Named Commander of the British Empire (CBE, 1951) and Dame of the British Empire (DBE, 1978). ❖ See also autobiography *Never Sing Louder than Lovely* (1982); and *Women in World History.*

BAILLIE, Jackie (1964—). Scottish politician. Born 1964 in Hong Kong. ❖ Became chair of the Scottish Labour Party (1997); elected to Scottish Parliament for Dumbarton (1999); was deputy minister for Communities (1999–2000) and minister for Social Justice (2000–01).

BAILLIE, Jane Welsh (1801–1866). See Carlyle, Jane Welsh.

BAILLIE, Joanna (1762–1851). English dramatist and poet. Born Sept 11, 1762, in Bothwell, Lanarkshire, Scotland; died Feb 23, 1851, at Hampstead Heath; dau. of Reverend Dr. Baillie (descendant of Scottish patriot William Wallace) and Dorothea Hunter; never married; no children. ❖ Well-known poet and dramatist of early 19th century, published 28 plays and 2 vols. of poetry, *Fugitive Verses* and *Metrical Legends,* which were highly praised by contemporaries; was famous for *Plays on the Passions,* which, with several other of her plays, were produced in leading theaters in England, Scotland, Ireland and US; was educated in Glasgow until father's death (1778), then lived in London, where she published 1st book of poems and began wrote to plays (1779–91); moved to Hampstead and published 3 vols. of *Plays on the Passions,* as well as several poems (1791); enjoyed close friendship with Sir Walter Scott (1808–51); published religious pamphlet defending the human nature of Christ (1831); published complete works in London (1851); remained active in literary community into her 80s; compared favorably with William Shakespeare and Sir Walter Scott; considered pioneer in development of new style of drama which examined "motives and personality." ❖ See also Margaret S. Carhart, *The Life and Work of Joanna Baillie* (Yale U. Press, 1923); and *Women in World History.*

BAIN, May (1887–1964). *Dreaver, Mary.*

BAIN, Wilhelmina Sherriff (1848–1944). New Zealand teacher, librarian, feminist, pacifist, and writer. Name variations: Wilhelmina Elliot, William Sherif. Born Wilhelmina Sherriff Bain (registered as William Sherif), Sept 5, 1848, in Edinburgh, Scotland; died Jan 26, 1944, in Auckland, New Zealand; dau. of John Bain (merchant) and Elizabeth (Middlemass) Bain; m. Robert Archibald Elliot (merchant), 1914 (died 1920). ❖ Taught school in Invercargill area (c. 1893–96), before becoming librarian at Christchurch; served as president of Canterbury Women's Institute and frequently promoted antiwar views; continued to teach until 1904; worked as journalist (1910–13); contributed to *Southland Times* (1911); established Aparima Peace Union (1912); traveled to London and published book of poetry, *From Zealandia,* and novel *Service: A New Zealand Story* (c. 1920s). ❖ See also *Dictionary of New Zealand Biography* (Vol. 3).

BAINBRIDGE, Beryl (1933—). British novelist. Born Beryl Margaret Bainbridge, Nov 21, 1933, in Liverpool, England; dau. of Richard Bainbridge (salesman) and Winifred Baines Bainbridge; m. Austin Davies (painter), 1954 (div. 1959). ❖ Focused on working-class life in post-WWII Liverpool where she grew up; writings include *A Weekend with Claud* (1967), *Another Part of the Wood* (1968), *Harriet Said* (1972), *The Secret Glass* (1973), *Sweet William* (1975), the autobiographical *A Quiet Life* (1976), *Injury Time* (1977), *Winter Garden* (1980), *English Journey, or, The Road to Milton Keynes* (1984), *Watson's Apology* (1984), (short stories) *Mum and Mr. Armitage* (1985), *Filthy Lucre, or, The Tragedy of Ernest Ledwhistle and Richard Soleway* (1986), *Forever England* (1987), *The Birthday Boys* (1995), *Every Man for Himself*

(1996), and *According to Queenie* (2001). *The Dressmaker* (1973), *The Bottle Factory Outing* (1974), and *An Awfully Big Adventure* (1989) were all shortlisted for the Booker Prize. ❖ See also Elizabeth Wenno, *Ironic Formula in the Novels of Beryl Bainbridge* (Acta Universitatis Gothoburgensis, 1993).

BAINES, Eveline Willert (1849–1916). *See Cunnington, Eveline Willert.*

BAINS, Ethel Betts (b. 1878). *See Betts, Ethel Franklin.*

BAINTER, Fay (1891–1968). American stage and screen actress. Born Dec 7, 1891, in Los Angeles, California; died April 16, 1968, in Beverly Hills, California; aunt of Dorothy Burgess (actress); m. Reginald Venable (lieutenant commander), 1922 (died 1964); children: Richard Venable. ❖ Had a successful career on stage, 1st appearing in stock at age 4 in *The Jewess;* made Broadway debut in musical *The Rose of Panama* (1912), followed by *The Willow Tree, East is West, Fallen Angels, She Stoops to Conquer, The Admirable Crichton* and *Dodsworth,* among others; came to Hollywood at age 41 and appeared in 39 films, including *Bill of Divorcement, Quality Street, Mrs. Wiggs of the Cabbage Patch, Young Tom Edison, Our Town, The Children's Hour, State Fair, Woman of the Year, Journey for Margaret* and *The Human Comedy.* Nominated for Academy Award for Best Actress for *White Banners* and won for Best Supporting Actress for *Jezebel* (both 1938).

BAIRD, Cora (c. 1912–1967). American actress and puppeteer. Name variations: Cora Burlar. Born c. 1912; died Dec 7, 1967, in New York, NY; m. Bil Baird (puppeteer), 1937 (died 1987); children: Peter Baird (1952–2004, actor who did voice overs). ❖ As actress under name Cora Burlar, appeared on stage in *Valley Forge, Winterset* and *Dr. Faustus;* with husband, formed the Bil and Cora Baird Marionettes, performing on stage in *Ziegfeld Follies, Ali Baba and the Forty Thieves* and *Man in the Moon,* and on film in *The Sound of Music;* appeared on many tv variety shows, including "Snarky Parker" (1950–50), "The Bil Baird Show" (1953), and CBS's "The Morning Show" (1954). Received Outer Circle award (1967) for having founded a permanent puppet theater off-Broadway.

BAIRD, Dorothea (1875–1933). English actress. Name variations: Dorothea Irving; Lady Irving. Born May 20, 1875, in Teddington, England; died Sept 24, 1933, in Broadstairs, England; m. H.B. Irving (actor-manager, author, and son of Sir Henry Irving), 1896; children: Laurence Henry Forster Irving (artist and author, b. 1897); Elizabeth Irving (actress, b. 1904). ❖ Made London debut as Hippolyta in *A Midsummer Night's Dream* (1895); scored a triumph in the title role of *Trilby* (1895); other plays include *As You Like It, The Happy Life, The Medicine Man* (with Henry Irving), *A Court Scandal, The Wedding Guest, Nero, Caesar Borgia, The Lyons Mail, Charles I, The Merchant of Venice* and title role in *Mauricette.*

BAIRD, Helen Stephen (1875–1956). *See Cowie, Helen Stephen.*

BAIRD, Frances (d. 1708). Duchess of Cumberland. Died 1708; m. Rupert (1619–1682), duke of Cumberland and commander of the Royalist Army (r. 1644–1682), contrary to the Royal Marriages Act.

BAIRD, Irene (1901–1981). Canadian novelist. Name variations: Irene Todd. Born Irene Todd, April 9, 1901, in Carlisle, Cumberland Co., England; died April 19, 1981, in Victoria; m. Robert Baird; children: Robert and Jane. ❖ At 18, immigrated with family to Canada (1919); moved to Victoria (1937); worked for National Film Board, Canadian civil service, and as reporter for Vancouver *Sun;* served as information chief for Department of Indian Affairs and Northern Development; works include *John* (1937), *Waste Heritage* (1939), considered a classic novel of the depression in Canada, *He Who Rides the Sky* (1941) and *The Climate of Power* (1971).

BAIRD, Leah (1883–1971). American actress and screenwriter. Born June 20, 1883, in Chicago, Illinois; died Oct 3, 1971, in Hollywood, California; m. Arthur Beck (producer), 1914. ❖ As actress, starred on Broadway opposite Douglas Fairbanks in *Gentleman from Mississippi* and appeared in numerous films, including *Chumps, Adam and Eve, Ivanhoe* (as Rebecca), *The Anarchist, Neptune's Daughter, The Lights of New York, The Volcano, The Radio Flyer* and *The Unnamed Woman;* also starred in and wrote screenplays for *A Soul in Bondage, Don't Doubt Your Wife* and *The Destroying Angel;* as screenwriter, credits include *Barriers Burned Away, Devil's Island, Stolen Pleasures, The Return of Boston Blackie, Lady Gangster, King's Row, Mildred Pierce, My Reputation* and *Shadow of a Woman;* had her own production company (1920s).

BAIRD, Vera (1951—). English politician and member of Parliament. Born Vera Thomas, Feb 13, 1951; m. David John Taylor-Gooby, 1972 (div. 1978); m. Robert Brian Baird, 1978 (died 1979). ❖ Called to the bar (1975), specializing in criminal law; contested Berwick (1983); representing Labour, elected to House of Commons at Westminster (2001, 2005) for Redcar.

BAISSAC, Lise de (1905–2004). *See Villameur, Lise.*

BAITOVA, Svetlana (1972—). Belarus gymnast. Born Sept 3, 1972, in Belarus, Soviet Union. ❖ Won USSR nationals (1986); at American Cup, finished 1st in vault, uneven bars, and floor exercises and 2nd in team all-around (1988); at Seoul Olympics, won a gold medal in team all-around (1988); at World championships, won a gold medal in team all-around (1989).

BAIUL, Oksana (1977—). Ukrainian figure skater. Born Oksana Sergeevna Baiul, Nov 16, 1977, in Dnepropetrovsk, Ukraine. ❖ Lost her father (by abandonment) at 2 and her mother (by death) at 13; at 15, won World championship (1993); won a gold medal at Lillehammer Olympics (1994); moved to US. ❖ See also autobiography *Oksana: My Own Story* and "A Promise Kept: The Oksana Baiul Story" (CBS-TV).

BAJANOVA, Svetlana (1972—). *See Bazhanova, Svetlana.*

BAJER, Matilde (1840–1934). Danish feminist. Name variations: Mathilde. Born 1840 in Denmark; died 1934; m. Frederik Bajer (influential Member of Parliament). ❖ Leading feminist in late 19th century who with husband founded Society of Danish Women to "improve the intellectual, moral and economic status of women, and make them an active and independent member of the family and the nation"; made increasing economic opportunities for women primary goal; with husband, opened women's trade school in Copenhagen (1872); founded Danish Women's Progress Association (1886), harbinger of suffrage movement. ❖ See also *Women in World History.*

BAJKUSA, Vesna (1970—). Yugoslavian basketball player. Born May 21, 1970. ❖ At Seoul Olympics, won a silver medal in team competition (1988).

BAJZA, Helene (1840–1905). *See Beniczky-Bajza, Helene.*

BAJZA, Ilona (1840–1905). *See Beniczky-Bajza, Helene.*

BAKANIC, Ladislava (1924—). American gymnast. Born May 1924. ❖ At London Olympics, won a bronze medal in all-around team (1948).

BAKER, Anita (1958—). American vocalist. Born Jan 26, 1958, in Toledo, Ohio; grew up in Detroit; m. Walter Bridgforth, 1988; children: Walter Baker Bridgforth (b. 1993) and Edward Carlton (b. 1994). ❖ Known for a return to traditional vocalizing in her own style of jazz-influenced R&B, began professional career in Detroit with Chapter 8 band; released 1st solo album *The Songstress* (1983), which earned her the 1st of 7 Grammy Awards (for "Angel"); served as executive producer and helped write some songs for the album *Rapture* (1988), which sold more than 6 million copies; released *Giving You the Best That I've Got* (1990), which went to #1. Other albums include *Compositions* (1994) and *Rhythm of Love* (1994).

BAKER, Augusta (1911–1998). African-American storyteller and librarian. Born Augusta Braxton in Baltimore, Maryland, April 1, 1911; died Feb 22, 1998; dau. of Winfort J. and Mabel (Gough) Braxton (both teachers); attended University of Pittsburgh, 1927–29; New York State College, AB, 1933, BS in Library Science, 1934; m. James Baker (div.); m. Gordon Alexander, Nov 23, 1944; children: (1st m.) James Baker III. ❖ Pioneer in efforts to bring an honest portrayal of ethnic groups to children's literature, became assistant to children's librarian at New York Public Library's 135th Street branch, which served Harlem's black community (1937); distressed by lack of material about black history and culture, as well as by often deplorable depictions of blacks in literature, founded the James Weldon Johnson Memorial Collection (1939); became assistant coordinator (1953), and later coordinator, of Children's Services; became visiting lecturer in school of library service at Columbia University; produced several reference guides for storytellers; published bibliography *The Black Experience in Children's Books* (revised every 5 years since 1974); began series of weekly broadcasts, "The World of Children's Literature," on WNYC-Radio (1974); received Constance Lindsay Skinner Award (1971) and Regina Medal (1981), and was 1st recipient of Zora Neale Hurston Award (1989); retired (1974) after 37-year career as children's librarian and storyteller with New York Public Library. ❖ See also *Women in World History.*

BAKER, Bea (b. 1929). *See Baker, LaVern.*

BAKER, Belle (1893–1957). American actress, singer, and entertainer. Born Bella Becker in New York, NY, Dec 25, 1893; died in Los Angeles, California, April 29, 1957. ❖ Made Broadway debut in *Vera Violetta* (1911); starred in the short-lived *Betsy* (1926), in which she introduced Irving Berlin's "Blue Skies"; in vaudeville, popularized a number of songs, including "All of Me" and "My Yiddische Mama," which came to be associated with her friend Sophie Tucker; also appeared in the films *The Song of Love* (1929) and *Atlantic City* (1944); played the Palace one last time (1950); was featured on tv show "This is Your Life" (1955) and appeared as herself in the film *Atlantic City* (1944).

BAKER, Bonnie (b. 1917). American pop singer. Name variations: Wee Bonnie Baker. Born Evelyn Nelson in Orange, Texas, April 1, 1917; m. Billy Roger (her accompanist), 1950. ❖ With a baby voice that matched her diminutive size, hired as vocalist by bandleader Orrin Tucker (1936); rose to fame with recording of "Oh Johnny, Oh Johnny," (1939); signed for spots on the popular radio show "Your Hit Parade" and featured in film *You're the One* (1941); after a string of hits, including "Billy," "My Resistance Is Low," and "You'd Be Surprised," left Tucker and went solo, singing with such notables as Stan Kenton and Tony Pastor; toured for USO with all-girl band; retired (1963). ❖ See also *Women in World History.*

BAKER, Carlee (1978—). Singaporean snowboarder. Name variations: Cee Bee Baker. Born Jan 2, 1978, in Singapore. ❖ Won silver medal in Snowboarder X at X Games (Winter 2000).

BAKER, Carroll (1931—). American actress. Born May 28, 1931, in Johnstown, Pennsylvania; m. Louie Ritter (furrier), 1953 (div. 1953); m. Jack Garfein (director), 1955 (div. 1969); m. Donald Burton (actor), 1982; children: Blanche Baker (b. 1956, actress). ❖ Made film debut in *Easy to Love* (1953); appeared in tv dramas and on Broadway in *All Summer Long* (1955), before being cast as Luz Benedict in the film *Giant* (1956); other films include *The Big Country, The Carpetbaggers, The Miracle, How the West Was Won, Cheyenne Autumn, The Greatest Story Ever Told, Harlow, Star 80* and *Ironweed;* moved to Italy, then Spain, making films in many countries; made London stage debut in *Rain* (1977). Nominated for Oscar for performance in *Baby Doll* (1956). ❖ See also autobiography *Baby Doll* (1983).

BAKER, Cee Bee (1978—). *See Baker, Carlee.*

BAKER, Charlotte (b. 1957). *See Bredahl, Charlotte.*

BAKER, Daisy (1889–1965). *See Dumont, Margaret.*

BAKER, Diane (1938—). American actress and producer. Born Feb 25, 1938, in Hollywood, California; dau. of Dorothy Harrington (stage actress). ❖ Made screen debut as Margot Frank in *Diary of Anne Frank* (1959); other films include *The Best of Everything, Journey to the Center of the Earth, Nine Hours to Rama, The Prize, Strait-Jacket, Marnie, Mirage, The Silence of the Lambs, The Joy Luck Club, Courage under Fire, Murder at 1600* and *The Keeper* (also produced); directed the documentary *Ashyana* (also seen as *Ashiana,* 1986) and produced *Portrait of Grandpa Doc* and tv mini-series "A Woman of Substance," among others.

BAKER, Dorothy (1907–1968). American novelist. Born Dorothy Dodds, April 21, 1907, in Missoula, Montana; died of cancer, June 17, 1968, in Terra Bella, California; dau. of Raymond Branson Dodds and Alice (Grady) Dodds; educated at Occidental College and Whittier College; University of California, Los Angeles, BA, 1929, MA, 1933; m. Howard Baker, Sept 2, 1930; children: Ellen (b. 1940) and Joan (b. 1943). ❖ After publication of short story "A Glance Around" in *The Magazine* (1934), began to write full time; earned Houghton Mifflin fellowship (1937) for work loosely based on life of jazz legend Bix Beiderbecke, which was published to rave reviews as *Young Man with a Horn* (1938); struggled for rest of career to equal success of 1st novel; published *Trio* (1943), which received cold reception; collaborated with husband on tv drama *The Ninth Day* (1957); renewed reputation with last novel *Cassandra at the Wedding* (1962). ❖ See also *Women in World History.*

BAKER, Eleanor Southey (1879–1969). *See Baker McLaglan, Eleanor Southey.*

BAKER, Elizabeth (d. 1962). English playwright. Born in London, England; died, age 86, Mar 8, 1962; m. James E. Allaway. ❖ Wrote *Chains,* 1st produced at the Court (1909); also wrote *Miss Tassey, Cupid in Clapham, Edith, The Price of Thomas Scott, Beastly Pride, Over a Garden Wall, Partnership, Miss Robinson, Bert's Girl, Penelope Forgives* and *One of the Spicers,* among others.

BAKER, Ella (1903–1986). African-American activist. Name variations: Ella Jo or Ella Josephine Baker. Born Ella Josephine Baker, Dec 13, 1903, in Norfolk, Virginia; died Dec 13, 1986, in Harlem, New York; dau. of Blake (waiter on steamship ferry) and Georgianna Baker (schoolteacher); earned bachelors degree at Shaw, 1927; m. T.J. Roberts, late 1930s; children: none, but raised a niece. ❖ Moved to NY; did editorial work for *American West Indian News* and *National News* (1929–1930s); with George Schuyler, founded Young Negro Cooperative League, organizing consumer food co-ops during Depression (1932); worked for WPA (Works Progress Administration) consumer education project; began association with National Association for the Advancement of Colored People (NAACP, 1938); named NAACP national field secretary (1941), then national director of branches (1943); ran unsuccessfully for NY City Council on Liberal Party ticket (1951); named president of NY branch of NAACP and began working to end de facto segregation in NYC schools (1954); helped found SCLC (Southern Christian Leadership Conference) with Dr. Martin Luther King Jr. (1957); set up SCLC office in Atlanta and became associate director (1958); worked to register African-American voters during "Crusade for Citizenship" (1958–60); named executive director of SCLC (1959); helped found Student Nonviolent Coordinating Committee (SNCC, 1960); helped focus SNCC on voter registration, culminating in successful "Freedom Summer" (1964), which influenced passage of Voting Rights Act of 1965; presented keynote address at Mississippi Freedom Democratic Party convention in Jackson (1964) and organized an MFDP office in Washington, DC; joined staff of interracial social-justice group, Southern Conference Education Fund (SCEF, 1967); continued activism as vice-chair of Mass Party Organizing Committee (1972), as national board member of Puerto Rican Solidarity Committee, and as public speaker and advisor to human-rights groups. ❖ See also Joanne Grant, *Ella Baker: Freedom Bound* (Wiley, 1998); (film) *"Fundi"—the Story of Ella Baker* (1981), produced by Grant; and *Women in World History.*

BAKER, Ellen Anne (1843–1926). *See Hewitt, Ellen Anne.*

BAKER, Elsie (1909–2003). English priest. Name variations: Rev. Elsie Baker. Born Mar 28, 1909, in south London, England; died June 8, 2003; children: (adopted) Pat (later a headteacher). ❖ One of the 1st English women to be ordained by the Church of England, had to wait until her 80s for the ceremony (1994); became a deaconess at the College of Greyladies, Blackheath (1938); served as a social worker, preacher and evangelist in a series of south London parishes; after WWII, helped revive the heavily bombed Church of All Saints, Walworth; became head of religious education at Sydenham comprehensive school; served the parish of Church of the Ascension (1968–81).

BAKER, Florence von Sass (1841–1916). Hungarian-born explorer of Africa. Name variations: Barbara Maria Szasz; Florence Barbara Maria Szasz Baker; Florence or Florenz Finnian von Sass; Florence von Sass-Baker. Born Florence Barbara Maria Finnian von Sass (some sources claim she was born Barbara Maria Szasz), 1845, in Transylvania, Hungary (now Romania); died 1916 in England; m. Sir Samuel White Baker (explorer, governor-general of Sudan), 1859. ❖ One of the few women to make major contributions to the exploration of Africa, was also an opponent of slavery; lived comfortable existence as child in military family in Transylvania, but was orphaned during 1848 Hungarian Revolution; abducted from refugee camp into harem in Ottoman Empire, was raised to become concubine; was sold at slave market at 14 to the pasha of Viddin but smuggled to Austro-Hungarian Empire by Sir Samuel White Baker who married her (1860); set off with husband to explore uncharted regions of Africa (1861), discovering Murchison Falls (1864), as well as the source of the Nile which they named Lake Albert (Albert Nyanza); fluent in Arabic, often acted as interpreter; returned to England where husband was granted gold medal from Royal Geographical Society and knighthood from the queen; commissioned by viceroy of Egypt, joined husband in nearly fatal quest to end slave trade in Africa; traveled with husband to southern Sudan where he served as governor-general; outlived husband by 23 years. ❖ See also Pat Shipman, *To the Heart of the Nile: Lady Florence Baker and the Exploration of Central Africa* (Harper Collins, 2004).

BAKER, Harriette Newell (1815–1893). American writer for children. Name variations: (pseudonyms) Madeline Leslie and Aunt Hatty. Born

Harriette Woods, 1815; died 1893; dau. of Reverend Leonard Woods; married Reverend S.R. Baker. ❖ Prolific writer with several of her works translated into German and French, wrote *Tim the Scissors-Grinder* (1861, sequel in 1862), *The Two Homes* (1862), *The Organ-Grinder* (1863), *White and Black Lies* (1864), *Worth and Wealth* (1864), *Tim's Sister* (1864), *Wheel of Fortune* (1865), *Paul Barton* (1869), *Fashion and Folly* (1869), *Lost but Found* (1969), *Ingleside* (1886), *This and That* (1887). Her most popular work, *Up the Ladder*, was published in 1862.

BAKER, Irene Bailey (1901–1994). American politican. Born Edith Irene Bailey, in Sevierville, Tennessee, Nov 17, 1901; died in Loudon, Tennessee, April 2, 1994; m. Howard H. Baker (Congressman 1951–1964); stepson Howard H. Baker Jr. served as US senator from Tennessee (1967–1985) and chief of staff to Ronald Reagan (1987–1988). ❖ Served as court clerk in Sevier Co., TN; helped husband's political campaigns and chaired a state Republican committee to recruit new women voters; served as Republican National Committeewoman from TN (1960–1964); after husband's death (1964), won Tennessee's 2nd District Republican endorsement as candidate in special election to determine his successor; defeated Democratic rival and served as US Representative, Republican of Tennessee, 88th Congress (Mar 10, 1964–Jan 3, 1965); served on Committee on Government Operations and supported a Social Security cost of living increase; served as director of public welfare in Knoxville, TN (1965–71). ❖ See also *Women in World History.*

BAKER, Iris (b. 1901). English actress. Born May 23, 1901, in India. ❖ Made 1st stage appearance in Holborn in the chorus of *The Trojan Women* (1922); appeared in many productions under the management of Lena Ashwell, and Lewis Casson and Sybil Thorndike; joined Old Vic (1928), appearing as Ophelia, among others; other plays include *Queer Fish, Two Olivers, An Average Man, As You Like It, While Parents Sleep, Alison's House, These Two, Misalliance, The White Devil, The House of Borgia* and *The Ivory Tower.*

BAKER, Isabel Noeline (1878–1958). New Zealand suffragist and gardener. Born Dec 25, 1878, at Opawa, Christchurch, New Zealand; died Aug 25, 1958, at Stewart Island, New Zealand; dau. of John Holland Baker (surveyor) and Isabel (Strachey) Baker. ❖ Lived in England as child and attended Slade School of Fine Art, London; was a member of National Union of Women's Suffrage Societies, then founding member of Guildford branch (1910); worked on women's farm labor committee and for Women's Land Army during WWI; returned to New Zealand (1930) and created botanically significant garden on 34 acres of land; donated Moturau Moana, which boasted primarily indigenous plants, to government (1948).

BAKER, Janet (1933—). British mezzo-soprano. Name variations: Dame Janet Baker. Born Janet Abbott Baker, Aug 21, 1933, in York, England; studied with Helene Isepp and Meriel St. Clair; studied at Mozarteum in Salzburg; attended master classes with Lotte Lehmann; m. James Keith Shelly, 1956. ❖ Won Kathleen Ferrier Prize (1956); joined Glyndebourne Festival chorus (1956); began operatic career (1957); won Queen's Prize from Royal College of Music (1959); toured British Isles, Sweden, France, and USSR with Benjamin Britten's English Opera Group (early 1960s); made US debut at NY's Town Hall (1966); performed mainly with the English Opera Co., Glyndebourne Opera, and Covent Garden in London (1970s); retired from opera (1982) but continued to concertize; varied operatic roles included the Sorceress in Purcell's *Dido and Aeneas,* Pippo in Rossini's *La Gazza Ladra,* Lucretia in Britten's *The Rape of Lucretia,* and Polly Peachum in Britten's *The Beggar's Opera.* Named Commander of the Order of the British Empire (1970) and Dame Commander (1976). ❖ See also autobiography *Full Circle* (MacRae, 1982); Alan Blyth, *Janet Baker* (Ian Allen, 1973); and *Women in World History.*

BAKER, Josephine (1906–1975). African-American singer, dancer, music-hall entertainer, civil-rights activist. Born June 3, 1906, in St. Louis, Missouri; died in Paris, France, April 14, 1975; illeg. dau. of Carrie McDonald and Eddie Carson; m. Willie Wells, 1919; m. William Howard Baker, 1921; m. Jean Lion, 1937; m. Jo Bouillon, 1947; children: adopted 12 (the "Rainbow Tribe"), 1954–1965. ❖ Joined Jones Family Band, St. Louis (1919); became a member of "Dixie Steppers" (1920); appeared in shows, *Shuffle Along* and *Chocolate Dandies* (1921–25); moved to Paris (1925); appeared in *Revue Nègre* and at Folies-Bergère (1926), becoming a music-hall sensation when she danced the Charleston wearing nothing but a string of bananas; opened club Chez Joséphine in Paris (1926); lived with Giuseppe (Pepito)

Abatino ("Count di Abatino," 1927–36); went on world tour (1928–29); starred at Casino de Paris (1930–33); starred in Offenbach's *La Créole* (1934); starred in Ziegfeld Follies, NY (1936); became French citizen (1937); fled Paris (1940) and worked for French Resistance (1940–44); toured US; determined to smash racial barriers, was the 1st black allowed to register at a first-class hotel in Miami, the 1st to perform for a non-segregated audience in that city, and insisted that blacks be hired as musicians and stagehands for her shows; was soundly criticized for her verbal attacks on America and praise of French racial attitudes; appeared in Carnegie Hall, NY (1973). Awarded Legion of Honor and Medal of the Resistance. ❖ See also autobiography (with Jo Bouillon) *Josephine* (Harper & Row, 1977); Lynn Haney, *Naked at the Feast* (Dodd, 1981); Phyllis Rose, *Jazz Cleopatra* (Doubleday, 1989); Jean-Claude Baker, *Josephine: The Hungry Heart* (Random House, 1993); and *Women in World History.*

BAKER, Kate (1861–1953). Australian teacher and literary benefactor. Born Catherine Baker, April 23, 1861, in Cappoquin, Co. Waterford, Ireland; died 1953 in Australia; never married; no children. ❖ Known to Australians for support of author Joseph Furphy, began to teach for Victoria School Department (1881); sent to head the Wanalta Creek State School (1886); met Furphy (1887) and became his critic, editor and benefactor, providing funds for his early publications; dedicated life to Furphy and, after his death, to perpetuating his work, spending her remaining 40 years editing and publishing his poetry; edited *The Poems of Joseph Furphy* (1916) and wrote (with Miles Franklin) *Joseph Furphy: The Legend of a Man and His Book* (1944); received Office of the Order of the British Empire (OBE, 1937). ❖ See also *Women in World History.*

BAKER, Kathleen M. (1901–1957). *See Drew-Baker, Kathleen M.*

BAKER, Kathy (1961—). American golfer. Name variations: Kathy Baker Guadagnino; Kathy Baker-Guadagnino. Born Mar 20, 1961, in Albany, NY. ❖ Joined LPGA tour (1983); won US Women's Open (1985). Inducted into South Carolina Golf Hall of Fame.

BAKER, Laurie (1976—). American ice-hockey player. Born Nov 6, 1976, in Concord, Massachusetts. ❖ Won a team gold medal at Nagano (1998), the 1st Olympics to feature women's ice hockey; won a team silver medal at World championships (1997 and 2000) and a team silver medal at Salt Lake City Olympics (2002). ❖ See also Mary Turco, *Crashing the Net: The U.S. Women's Olympic Ice Hockey Team and the Road to Gold* (HarperCollins, 1999); and *Women in World History.*

BAKER, LaVern (1929–1997). African-American singer. Name variations: The Countess, Little Miss Sharecropper, Bea Baker. Born Delores Williams in Chicago, Illinois, Nov 11, 1929; died Mar 10, 1997, in New York, NY. ❖ Considered one of rock and roll's finest singers, had 20 pop hits (1955–66); while performing as a teenager in Chicago clubs, was billed as Little Miss Sharecropper (the name she also recorded under for RCA and National Records); recorded for Columbia as Bea Baker; debuted as LaVern Baker (1953) with "Soul on Fire" on Atlantic; had breakthrough recording with novelty song "Tweedle Dee" (1954), and became one of Atlantic's 1st performers to crossover to the pop charts, even though Georgia Gibbs was hired to rerecord the song (a common practice was to have a white cover artist re-record black hits); left Atlantic for Decca's Brunswick label (1965); began touring military bases overseas, becoming the entertainment director at Subic Military Base in Philippines; after a self-imposed exile of 20 years, returned to US (late 1980s) and continued to do live-performance work; inducted into Rock & Roll Hall of Fame (1991). Selected singles: "Bop Ting-a-Ling" (1955), "Play It Fair" (1955), "Jim Dandy" and "Jim Dandy Got Married" (1957), "I Cried a Tear" (1958), "Fee Fi Fo Fum," "I Can't Love You Enough," "I Waited Too Long" and "See See Rider." ❖ See also *Women in World History.*

BAKER, Louisa (fl. 1812). *See Brewer, Lucy.*

BAKER, Louisa Alice (1856–1926). New Zealand journalist and novelist. Name variations: Louisa Alice Dawson; (pen names) Alice, Alien and Dot. Born Louisa Alice Dawson, Jan 13, 1856, in Warwickshire, England; died Mar 22, 1926, in Deal, Kent, England; dau. of Henry Joseph Dawson (carpenter) and Elizabeth (Bratt) Dawson; m. John William Baker (house painter, died 1916); children: 1 son, 1 daughter. ❖ Immigrated to New Zealand with family (1863); wrote successful women's and children's columns under pen names Alice and Dot for *Otago Witness* (1886–early 1890s); returned to England with daughter (1894); referred to as "a colonial George Eliot," wrote 14 novels and volume of short fiction, which dealt with contemporary feminist issues, including *A Daughter of the King* (1894), *The Majesty of Man* (1895), *In Golden Shackles* (1896), *Wheat in the Ear* (1898), *The Devil's Half Acre* (1900), *A Slum Heroine* (1904), *The Perfect Union* (1908), and *A Maid of Mettle* (1913); penned weekly column from England for *Otago Witness* under name Alien (1903). ❖ See also *Dictionary of New Zealand Biography* (Vol. 3).

BAKER, Mary Ann (1834–1905). Australian bush ranger. Born Mary Ann Brigg near Berrico, in upper Gloucester River valley, Australia, 1834; died April 12, 1905; dau. of James (convict shepherd assigned to Australian Agricultural Co.) and Charlotte Brigg; m. Edmond Baker, 1848; met and traveled with Fred Ward, later known as Captain Thunderbolt, with whom she had at least 3 children; possibly m. John Burrows after 1866, and had more children. ❖ Probably aided in prison escape of horse thief Fred Ward (later known as Captain Thunderbolt); with Ward, traveled as outlaw in the bush in northern New South Wales (1860s) and had several children; to feed family, said to have developed own brand of cattle rustling; with children, captured by police (1866); details of later life uncertain. ❖ See also *Women in World History*.

BAKER, Nina Brown (1888–1957). American children's author. Born Nina Brown, Dec 31, 1888, in Galena, Kansas; died Sept 1, 1957, in Brooklyn Heights, NY; dau. of Frank and Belle (Warren) Brown; University of Colorado (teaching certificate, 1911); m. Sidney J. Baker, 1915; children: Berenice and Nina. ❖ Wrote set of biographies for children which focused on historical and world leaders; ran rural school in Alison, Colorado; moved with family to Brooklyn Heights (1938); wrote mystery for girls *The Secret of Hallam House* (1931), followed by 6 more, before she turned to biographies for young people in 1940; earned greatest praise for *He Wouldn't Be King* (1941), about Simón Bolívar; wrote on other famous men, including Benito Juarez, Sun Yat-Sen, Christopher Columbus and Amerigo Vespucci. ❖ See also *Women in World History*.

BAKER, Nora (1914–1944). See Khan, Noor Inayat.

BAKER, S. Josephine (1873–1945). American physician. Name variations: Sara Josephine Baker. Born Nov 15, 1873, in Poughkeepsie, NY; died Feb 22, 1945, in NY, NY; dau. of Orlando D.M. Baker (lawyer) and Jenny Harwood (Brown) Baker; Women's Medical College, New York Infirmary, MD, 1898; Bellevue Medical College (New York University), Doctor of Public Health, 1917; lived with Florence Laighton; never married. ❖ After 1-year internship in Boston, opened private practice (1901) and began medical work in NY slums when babies died at rate of 1,500 a week during hot summer weather; appointed assistant to Commissioner of Health (1907) and gained some notoriety for tracking down and arresting "Typhoid Mary" (Mary Mallon); appointed director of Bureau of Child Hygiene of NY Department of Health (1908) and had 1,200 fewer infant deaths in district than previous year; by time of retirement as director (1923), had influenced all 48 states to set up divisions of Child Hygiene; founded American Child Hygiene Association (1908) and Children's Welfare Federation (1911); lectured on child hygiene at Columbia and New York universities; became consultant to US Public Health Service Children's Bureau; began monthly advice column on baby and child care for *Ladies' Home Journal* (1922); thesis on transmission of respiratory diseases led to adoption of practices to prevent spread of influenza among school children (1918); her ideas on child care and prevention of illness in children became commonplace; was also active in women's suffrage. Writings include *Healthy Children* (1920), *The Growing Child* (1923) and *Child Hygiene* (1925). ❖ See also autobiography, *Fighting for Life* (Macmillan, 1939); and *Women in World History*.

BAKER, Sara Josephine (1873–1945). See Baker, S. Josephine.

BAKER, Sarah (1736–1816). English theater manager. Born 1736 in Kent, England; died 1816 in England; children: 3. ❖ England's 1st woman theatrical manager, was widowed in 1769 with 3 young children; assumed control of mother's theatrical company and established a touring circuit in county of Kent; introduced more ambitious repertoire (1777), including Shakespeare and Sheridan; began building permanent theaters in towns frequented by her company (1789), ultimately founding 10; was a successful theatrical entrepreneur for 50 years.

BAKER McLAGLAN, Eleanor Southey (1879–1969). New Zealand physician and writer. Name variations: Eleanor Southey Baker. Born Eleanor Southey Baker, Sept 13, 1879, in Akaroa, New Zealand; died Sept 20, 1969, in Auckland; dau. of Thomas Southey Baker (stock owner) and Josephine Harriet Anne (Dicken) Baker; University of

Otago Medical School, 1903; m. Sydney Leopold Temple McLaglan (military officer), 1923. ❖ Served in various medical positions throughout New Zealand before returning to Kopuru, Northland, to establish a country practice in 1914; acted as agent of Department of Public Health during smallpox epidemic (1913); appointed to school medical service in Canterbury-Westland by Department of Education, where she brought innovative treatments to children (1914); published in *New Zealand Medical Journal* (1920s); retired from school medicine (1940); helped to administer geriatric hospital near Wellington until early 1950s. ❖ See also autobiography, *Stethoscope and Saddlebags* (1965); *Dictionary of New Zealand Biography* (Vol. 3).

BAKKEN, Jill (1977—). American bobsledder. Born Jan 25, 1977, in Portland, Oregon. ❖ Won 2 World Cup races and finished 2nd in overall standings (1999–2000); with brakeman Vonetta Flowers, won a gold medal for the two-man bobsleigh at Salt Lake City Olympics (2002), the 1st women's bobsleigh competition in Winter Games history.

BAKOGIANNI, Niki (1968—). Greek high jumper. Born June 9, 1968, in Lamia, Greece. ❖ Placed 1st at Balkan Games (1990, 1992, 1994); won a silver medal for high jump at Atlanta Olympics (1996) and a silver medal at European Indoor championships (1996).

BAKOVA, Ani (1957—). Bulgarian rower. Born Feb 22, 1957. ❖ At Moscow Olympics, won a bronze medal in quadruple sculls with coxswain (1980).

BAKWA. See Turunku Bakwa.

BALABANOFF, Angelica (1878–1965). Russian-born socialist. Name variations: (Russian) Angelika Balabanova. Born Anzhelika Balabanova, 1878, in Chernigov, Russia; died in Rome, Italy, Nov 25, 1965; dau. of Isaak Balabanov (wealthy merchant and landowner); attended Princess Obolenskaia Institute in Kharkov, 1889–95, and New University of Brussels, 1897–99; never married; no children. ❖ Renounced family inheritance to engage in university study; met leaders of German Social Democratic Party (SPD); moved to Italy (1901) and joined Italian Socialist Party (1902); served as propagandist among Italian women working in Switzerland (1903–07); served as member of Executive Committee of Italian Socialist Party in Switzerland (1904–07); was co-editor of *Su, Compagne!* (1904–06); in Switzerland, came into frequent contact with exiled Russian Social Democrats and met many leaders of the RSDRP—including Lenin, Julius Martov, and Leon Trotsky—and on occasion translated their Russian speeches into Italian, French, German and English; returned to Italy (1912) and served as member of Executive Committee of Italian Socialist Party (1912–17); was co-editor with Benito Mussolini of *Avanti!* (1912–13) and took the same position more than decade later (1928); denounced Mussolini for his support of WWI and fled to neutral Switzerland, where she became a leader in fight against the war; named Italian representative to International Socialist Bureau (c. 1912–14); co-founded the Zimmerwald Movement (1915–17); served as secretary of International Socialist Commission (1915–19); returned to Russia (June 1917) and shortly thereafter joined Bolshevik Party; was Bolshevik propagandist and agent in Sweden and Switzerland (July 1917–Nov 1918); in recognition of high standing in European socialist movement, served as 1st secretary of Communist International (1919–20); was soon isolated from real work of Comintern and her complaints about its dubious operations were ignored; served as commissar of foreign affairs for Ukraine (1919–20); protested the growing use of Red terror against members of other revolutionary parties; left Russia (Dec 1921); expelled from Russian Communist Party when she expressed disapproval of Soviet actions (1924); involved in various anti-communist and anti-fascist movements in Vienna (1922–26), Paris (1926–36) and NY (1936–46); returned to Italy (1946); participated in formation of Italian Social Democratic Party (1947) and was a member of its Executive Committee; spent rest of life fighting for cause of socialism against threats of Italian fascism and Russian communism. ❖ See also autobiography *My Life as a Rebel* (Harper & Brothers, 1938) and her *Impressions of Lenin* (trans. by Isotta Cesari, U. of Michigan Press, 1964); Ronald Florence, *Marx's Daughters: Eleanor Marx, Rosa Luxemburg, Angelica Balabanoff* (Dial, 1975); and *Women in World History*.

BALABANOVA, Hanna (1969—). Ukrainian kayaker. Born Dec 10, 1969, in Vinnytsya, USSR. ❖ Won a bronze medal for K4 500 at Athens Olympics (2004).

BALACHOVA, Alexandra (1887–1905). Russian ballerina. Name variations: Alexandra Balashova. Born 1887 in Moscow, Russia; died

Jan 5, 1979, in New York, NY; graduate of Bolshoi Ballet School (1905). ❖ One of last prima ballerinas of tsarist Russia, made professional debut as Tsar-Maiden in *Humpbacked Horse* (c. 1906); fled Soviet Union (c. 1928); taught ballet in Paris (until 1972); danced as Aurora in *Sleeping Beauty*, Medora in *Le Corsair*, Kitri in *Don Quixote*, Nikia in *La Bayadere*, Odette-Odile in *Swan Lake* and title role in *La Fille Mal Gardée.*

BALAN, Anisoara (1966—). See Dobre-Balan, Anisoara.

BALAN, Doina (1963—). See Snep-Balan, Doina Liliana.

BALAS, Iolanda (1936—). Romanian high jumper. Born Dec 12, 1936, in Timosoaru, Romania. ❖ One of the greatest high jumpers ever, won gold medals at Rome Olympics (1960) and Tokyo Olympics (1964); won European championship (1958, 1962); claimed the world high-jump record 14 times (1956–61); had 140 consecutive victories (1956–1967). ❖ See also *Women in World History.*

BALATKOVA, Helena (1949—). See Sikolova, Helena.

BALAZS, Erzsebet (1920—). Hungarian gymnast. Born Oct 15, 1920. ❖ At London Olympics, won a silver medal in all-around team (1948).

BALBILLA (fl. 130). Greco-Roman poet. Name variations: Iulia Balbilla; Julia Balbilla. Born c. 100 CE; date of death unknown; dau. of C. Iulius Antiochus Epiphanes and Claudia Balbilla; granddau. of Tiberius Claudius Balbillus, prefect of Egypt under Emperor Nero, and of Antiochus IV, king of Commagene. Visited Egypt as part of the imperial entourage, 130 CE. ❖ A woman of royal Macedonian descent, who is known for 3 or possibly 4 poems of hers that survive as inscriptions on the right foot of Colossus of Memnon in the sacred city of Thebes in Upper Egypt (poems commemorate pilgrimage she made there with Hadrian and Sabina on Nov 20, 130 CE); her poems use a highly literary Greek in which Aeolic dialect—dialect of archaic Greek poet Sappho—predominates. ❖ See also *Women in World History.*

BALCH, Emily Greene (1867–1961). American director of the Women's International League for Peace and Freedom. Born Emily Greene Balch, Jan 8, 1867, in Jamaica Plain, Massachusetts; died Jan 9, 1961, at Cambridge, Massachusetts; dau. of Francis Vergnies Balch (attorney) and Ellen (Nelly) Maria (Noyes) Balch (former schoolteacher); never married; no children. ❖ Published pioneer sociological study *Public Assistance of the Poor in France* (1893); began academic career at Wellesley (1896) and received 5-year appointment as professor and chair of department of economics and sociology (1913); was a founder and president of Boston Women's Trade Union League (1903); after researching Slavic immigration, published the groundbreaking *Our Slavic Fellow Citizens* (1910); during WWI, began work as peace activist and attended International Congress of Women (ICW) at The Hague, then co-edited the Congress proceedings, *Women at the Hague* (1915); as envoy for ICW, visited rulers of Scandinavian countries and Russia to secure backing to end the conflict through mediation by neutral countries; also met with Woodrow Wilson over the Stockholm plan (1916); had professorship terminated at Wellesley (1918); joined editorial staff of *The Nation* (1918); attended 2nd International Congress of Women (1919), which established itself as permanent organization under name Women's International League for Peace and Freedom (WILPF); held influential offices of US and international WILPF, including international secretary, president of US section (1931), and honorary international president (1937); during WWII, called for unity between pacifists and non-pacifists, based on common aims of civil liberties, aid to conscientious objectors, and keeping the nation out of war, but agreed that fighting was only option after Pearl Harbor; attacked policy of unconditional surrender for prolonging the war; awarded Nobel Peace Prize (1946), which she shared with John R. Mott. Writings include *Approaches to the Great Settlement* (1918), *Occupied Haiti* (1927) and *Vignettes in Prose* (1952). ❖ See also Mercedes M. Randall, *Improper Bostonian: Emily Greene Balch* (Twayne, 1964) and Mercedes Randall, ed. *Beyond Nationalism: The Social Thought of Emily Greene Balch* (Twayne, 1972); and *Women in World History.*

BALDECHILD, Baldhild, or Baldhilda (c. 630–c. 680). See Balthild.

BALDINA, Alexandra Maria (1885–1977). Russian ballet dancer and teacher. Name variations: Alexandra Kosloff. Born Sept 27, 1885, in St. Petersburg, Russia; died Sept 6, 1977, in Hollywood, California; m. Theodore Kosloff (dancer and teacher, died 1956). ❖ Graduated from Imperial Ballet in St. Petersburg into the Maryinsky Ballet (1903); joined Bolshoi Ballet in Moscow (1904) where she danced principal parts

in Petipa'a *Esmeralda* and Ivanov's *Nutcracker* and created the "ballerina of the Prelude" role in *Les Sylphides* (1909); joined Diaghilev Ballet Russe, where she toured and performed for next 15 years; moved to US with husband, his brother Alexis, and Alexis' wife Juliette Mendez, where—as a quartet—they performed on Orpheum circuit (1910); danced for Gertrude Hoffmann's Saison des Ballets Russe company in NY (1911); toured with Hoffmann and the Kosloffs in Diaghilev repertory, dancing in *Schézhérezade, Les Sylphides* and *Cléopatre;* toured US with Kosloff quartet in a company which included Anatole Bourman and Natasha Rambova; with husband, appeared on Broadway in *The Passing Show of 1915, The Awakening* and *Maid in America* (c. 1915); began teaching classes in and around Los Angeles (1910s) and in schools founded by husband across the country; had her own private studio (1956–77), then retired.

BALDO, Marta. Spanish rhythmic gymnast. Name variations: Marta Baldo Marin. Born in Spain. ❖ Won a team gold medal at Atlanta Olympics (1996).

BALDUS, Brita Pia (1965—). German diver. Born June 4, 1965. ❖ At Barcelona Olympics, won a bronze medal in springboard (1992).

BALES, Susan Ford (1957—). See Ford, Susan.

BALMER, Fanny (1861–1943). See McHugh, Fanny.

BALDWIN, Charlotte Fowler (1805–1873). Hawaiian missionary and educator. Born Charlotte Fowler in White Hollow, Connecticut, Nov 7, 1805; died in Lahaina, Maui, Hawaii, Oct 2, 1873; dau. of Solomon (deacon) and Olive (Douglas) Fowler; attended boarding school of Rev. Herrick in New Haven, Connecticut; married Dwight Baldwin (physician and preacher), Dec 3, 1830; children: David Dwight, Abigail Charlotte, Mary Clark, Charles Fowler, Douglas Hoapili, Henry Perrine, Emily Sophronia, and Harriet Melinda. ❖ Began missionary work in New Jersey, setting up Sunday schools in the state's black neighborhoods; with husband, set sail for Hawaii (Dec 3, 1830) to begin missionary work in a district covering 60 miles, including Kohala, Waimea, and Hamakua, on the Big Island; opened a school for girls; during a stay in the district of Kohala, established more schools for women, who in turn became teachers of Hawaiian children; moved to last mission site at Lahaina, Maui (1833), and continued a strenuous schedule for next 37 years.

BALDWIN, Ethel Frances (1879–1967). Hawaiian philanthropist. Born Ethel Frances Smith in Honolulu, Hawaii, Nov 17, 1879; died Sept 20, 1967; dau. of William Owen (served in legislature of Hawaiian kingdom and later appointed attorney general) and Mary Abby (Hobron) Smith; attended Punahou School; married Henry "Harry" Alexander Baldwin (US Congressional representative), July 19, 1897; children: Leslie Alexander (1898–1901); Jared Smith (1899–1914); Frances Hobron (b. 1903). ❖ Civic leader and philanthropist and one of Maui's outstanding early leaders, was executive secretary of American Red Cross on Maui during WWI; was instrumental in establishing the Kula Sanitarium for tubercular patients (1916–26); secured passage of a bill establishing a Board of Child Welfare and Old Age Pension in each county (1919) and served as its chair until 1937; was president of the Maui Woman's Suffrage Association (1919–20); took particular interest in beautification projects of the Outdoor Circle, resulting in a public park adorned with shower trees.

BALDWIN, Faith (1893–1978). American novelist. Born in New Rochelle, New York, Oct 1, 1893; died in Norwalk, Connecticut, Mar 18, 1978; dau. of Stephen C. Baldwin (well-known trial lawyer) and Edith Hervey (Finch) Baldwin; educated in Brooklyn, in private schools, and in Dresden, Germany, 1914–16; m. Hugh H. Cuthrell, 1920 (died 1953); children: 2 boys, Hugh and Stephen, and 2 girls, Hervey and Ann. ❖ Popular novelist of light fiction, began literary career as poet; published 1st work (1911); wrote over 60 novels, one book of poetry (*Signposts*, 1924), children's books, and numerous short stories, serials, and articles for popular magazines; also wrote for the screen, including *The Moon's Our Home* (1936), *Men Are Such Fools* (1937), *Apartment for Peggy* (1950) and *Queen for a Day* (1951); novels include *Mavis of Green Hill* (1921), *Alimony* (1928), *Office Wife* (1930), *Week-end Marriage* (1932), *Medical Center* (1940), *Washington, D.C.* (1943), *You Can't Escape* (1943), *Woman on Her Way* (1946), *Golden Shoestring* (1949), *Whole Armor* (1951), *The Juniper Tree* (1952), and *American Family* (1935), which details her family history.

BALDWIN, Maria Louise (1856–1922). African-American educator. Name variations: Mollie. Born in Cambridge, Massachusetts, Sept 13,

1856; died in Boston, Massachusetts, Jan 9, 1922; dau. of Peter L. (letter carrier) and Mary E. Baldwin; graduate of Cambridge training school for teachers. ❖ Leading social and intellectual figure in the progressive community of Cambridge, had 40-year association with Agassiz School; became master of Agassiz School's 12 teachers and 500 students (1916), the 1st black woman to hold the post of master in a school in New England; was perhaps the only black woman in US to lead a primarily white faculty and student body; was also the 1st woman to deliver Washington's Birthday address to Brooklyn Institute (1897). ❖ See also *Women in World History*.

BALDWIN, Ruth Ann (fl. 1915–1921). American screenwriter and director. Fl. from 1915 to 1921. ❖ Among the pioneers of the motion-picture industry, was hired by Universal to write the serial *The Black Box* for Herbert Rawlinson and Anna Little (1915); after co-directing feature film *End of the Rainbow* (1916), became a full-time director; had 1st major success with *Retribution* (1916), starring Cleo Madison; spent much of her career working for Universal but also directed 2 pictures—*Broken Commandments* and *Puppets of Fate*—for rival Metro; career apparently ended abruptly (after 1921).

BALDWIN, Sally (1940–2003). Scottish educator. Born Nov 4, 1940, in Coatbridge, north Lanarkshire, Scotland; died in an accident in Rome, Italy, Oct 28, 2003; University of Glasgow, 1st-class degree in English Language and Literature; diploma in social administration, York University; m. Joe Callan; children: Emma and Julia. ❖ Social sciences academic, spent over 30 years at York University; became director of Social Policy Research Unit (SPRU) at York (1973), researching social security, disablement, and policies for carers; made a professor (1990), then head of York's department of social policy (1994); writings include *The Cost of Caring: Families with Disabled Children* (1985); was a supporter of women's studies departments.

BALDYCHEVA, Nina. Russian cross-country skier. Name variations: Baldytschewa; Baidycheva. ❖ Won a gold medal for 4 x 5 km relay and a bronze for 5 km at Innsbruck Olympics (1976); won a silver medal for 4 x 5 km relay at Lake Placid Olympics (1980).

BALFOUR, Alison (d. 1596). Scottish woman accused of witchcraft. Lived in Ireland, a village in Orkney; burned at Gallow Hill in Kirkwall, Orkney, Dec 16, 1596. ❖ Accused of witchcraft in the reign of James VI (1594), was held for 2 days in "cashielaws," an iron vice for the leg to which fire was applied (June 1596); was required to watch as her son was placed in an iron boot and received 57 blows, her 7-year-old daughter was put in thumbscrews, and her 81-year-old husband was crushed to death; finally confessed, but was burned anyway, protesting her innocence just before she died.

BALFOUR, Betty (1867–1942). English suffragist. Nv: Elizabeth Lytton; Elizabeth Edith Bulwer-Lytton. Born Elizabeth Edith Bulwer-Lytton, June 12, 1867; died Mar 28, 1942; dau. of (Edward) Robert Bulwer Lytton, 1st earl of Lytton (1831–1891), author and viceroy of India) and Lady Edith Villiers Lytton; sister of Constance Lytton (1869–1923) and Emily Lytton (1874–1964); sister-in-law of Frances Balfour; m. Gerald William Balfour, 2nd earl of Balfour; children: Eve Balfour (1898–1990), agriculturalist) and Robert Arthur Lytton Balfour, 3rd earl of Balfour (1902–1968). ❖ With Frances Balfour, attempted to persuade Arthur Balfour to support women's suffrage in House of Commons (though supportive philosophically, he was unwilling to fight for the cause).

BALFOUR, Betty (1903–1979). English actress. Born in London, England, Mar 27, 1903; died Nov 4, 1979, in Weybridge, Surrey, England. ❖ One of Britain's more popular stars of the silent screen, made debut at 17 in *Nothing Else Matters* and came to prominence with title role in *Squibs* (1921); was huge audience draw throughout 1920s, starring mostly in comedies produced by her own company; turned to supporting roles with arrival of sound; films include *Mary Find the Gold* (1921), *Squibs Wins the Calcutta Sweeps* (1922), *Squibs' Honeymoon* (1923), *Squibs MP* (1923), *Love Life and Laughter* (1923), *Reveille* (1924), *Somebody's Darling* (1925), *Monte Carlo* (1925), *La Petite Bonne du Palance* (1926), *The Little People* (1926), *Croquette* (1927), *The Vagabond Queen* (1929), *Bright Eyes* (1929), *Paddy the Next Best Thing* (1933), *Evergreen* (1934), *My Old Dutch* (1934), *Eliza Comes to Stay* (1936) and *29 Acacia Avenue* (1945).

BALFOUR, Clara Lucas (1808–1878). English writer and reformer. Born Clara Liddell in New Forest, Hampshire, Dec 21, 1808; died at Croydon, July 3, 1878. ❖ Beginning in 1841, wrote articles and lectured on topics, including temperance and women's influence; authored numerous works designed chiefly to promote the temperance cause.

BALFOUR, Eve (1898–1990). British agriculturalist. Name variations: Evelyn Barbara Balfour; Lady Eve Balfour. Born Evelyn Barbara Balfour, July 16, 1898, in England; died Jan 16, 1990; dau. of Gerald William Balfour, 2nd earl of Balfour, and Elizabeth Edith Bulwer-Lytton (1867–1942), known as Betty Balfour; sister of Robert Arthur Lytton Balfour, 3rd earl of Balfour (1902–1968); graduate of University of Reading, one of the 1st women to study agriculture at a British university. ❖ Responsible for launching organic movement in British farming, 1st trained girls in farm work with the Land Army (1918); purchased New Bells Farm at Haughley (1919) and began Haughley Experiment (1939), to compare organic and inorganic methods of farming; founded Soil Association (1946); made OBE (1990); writings include *The Living Soil* (1943) and 3 detective novels, of which *Paper Chase* (1927) was most successful.

BALFOUR, Frances (1858–1931). English writer and suffragist. Name variations: Lady Frances Balfour. Born 1858; died 1931; 10th of 12 children of duchess of Argyll and 8th duke of Argyll; sister of Blanche Balfour; sister-in-law of Betty Balfour; m. E.J.A. Balfour (brother of philosopher and statesman Arthur J. Balfour), 1879. ❖ Left with chronic pain and a limp from hip-joint disease in childhood; was devout Liberal and loyal supporter of William Gladstone; with Marie Corbett and Eva Maclaren, formed Liberal Women's Suffrage Society (1887); with Betty Balfour, attempted to persuade Arthur Balfour to support women's suffrage in House of Commons; as a fervent supporter of Church of Scotland, organized rebuilding of London's Crown Court Church; wrote several memoirs and reminiscences including autobiography *Me Obliviscaris* (Hodder and Stoughton, 1930). ❖ See also *Women in World History*.

BALFOUR, Jean (1927—). Scottish conservationist and land manager. Born Elizabeth Jean Drew, Nov 4, 1927, in Scotland; University of Edinburgh, BS with honors, 1949; m. John Charles Balfour, 1950. ❖ Served as partner-owner of Balbirnie Home Farms and Balbirnie Dairy Farm, as director of A&J Bowen and Co. (1960–97) and as chair of Countryside Commission for Scotland (1972–83); involved in forestry, land management, and agriculture; made botanical expeditions to Greenland, Ellesmere Island, Franz Joseph Land, Novaya Zemlya, and arctic Siberia, among others; served as governor of East Scotland College of Agriculture for 30 years and as vice president (1982–88); named to Cabinet as deputy chair of Committee on Women in Science, Engineering, and Technology in Office of Science and Technology (1993); at government's request, wrote report of recommendations, *A New Look at the Northern Ireland Countryside* (1984). Made CBE (1981), awarded Order of the Falcon (Iceland, 1994), and received Institute of Chartered Foresters Medal for services to British Forestry (1996).

BALFOUR, Katharine (c. 1921–1990). American stage, tv, and screen actress. Born c. 1921 in New York, NY; died of amyotropic lateral sclerosis, April 3, 1990, in New York, NY. ❖ In Dallas, created the role of Alma in the original production of Tennessee Williams' *Summer and Smoke*; films include *America, America, Love Story* and *Teachers*.

BALFOUR, Nora (1845–1936). *See Sidgwick, Eleonora Mildred.*

BALIN, Ina (1937–1990). American actress. Born Ina Rosenberg, Nov 12, 1937, in Brooklyn, NY; died June 20, 1990, in New Haven, Connecticut; children: (adopted) 3 Vietnamese girls (1976). ❖ Films include *The Black Orchid, From the Terrace, The Young Doctors, The Patsy, The Greatest Story Ever Told* and *The Projectionist*; helped evacuate hundreds of Vietnamese orphans following war in Vietnam.

BALIN, Mireille (1911–1968). French actress. Born in Monte Carlo, July 20, 1911; died Nov 8, 1968, in Paris, France. ❖ International star of French films throughout 1930s, appeared opposite Fyodor Chaliapin, played Dulcinea in G.W. Pabst's *Don Quixote* and originated role of the femme fatale, opposite Jean Gabin, in *Pépé le Moko* (1937); during Nazi occupation of France, fell in love with an officer of the Wehrmacht; at war's end, was imprisoned in Fresnes until her release (Jan 1945); retired (1947). Other films include *Vive la Classe* (1932), *Le Sexe faible* (1933), *Marie des Angoisses* (1935), *Jeunes Filles de Paris* (1936), *Naples au Baiser de Feu* (*The Kiss of Fire*, 1937), *Le Vénus de l'Or* (1938), *Menaces* (1940), *Macao l'Enfer du Jeu* (1940), *Dernier Atout* (1942), *Malaria* (1943) and *La Dernière Chevauchée* (1947). ❖ See also *Women in World History*.

BALKAMA (fl. 10 c. BCE). *See Sheba, queen of.*

BALKANSKA, Mimi (b. 1902). Bulgarian soprano. Born in Ruse, Bulgaria, June 23, 1902. ❖ As Bulgaria's most popular operetta star, appeared throughout Europe as well as in Turkey, Israel, and the former Yugoslavia; founded and worked at the Cooperative Theater in Sofia (1922–38); moved to the Odeon Operetta Theater (1938); became director of the Khudojestven Operetta Theater (1942), appearing in all her productions; retired (1968). ❖ See also *Women in World History.*

BALKIS (fl. 10 c. BCE). *See Sheba, queen of.*

BALL, Anne Elizabeth (1808–1872). Irish naturalist. Born 1808; lived in Youghal, Ireland; died 1872. ❖ Collected seaweeds, flowering plants, and butterflies along Irish coast; gathered seaweed specimens for Dr. W.H. Garvey who named *Ballia callitricha* and *Cladophora balliana* after her. The herbarium at University College, Cork, houses seaweeds she collected (1834–36); 96 of her drawings (probably copied from already published plates) are located at herbarium of National Museum, Dublin.

BALL, Catherine (1951—). American swimmer. Born Sept 30, 1951. ❖ At Mexico City Olympics, won a gold medal in 4 x 100-meter medley relay (1968).

BALL, Frances (1794–1861). Irish founder of the Loreto Institute. Name variations: Mother Teresa, Mother Teresa Ball, Mother Frances Mary Theresa, Mother Ball, Mrs. Ball. Born Frances Ball, early Jan 1794, in Dublin, Ireland; died in Dalkey, near Dublin, May 19, 1861; dau. of John (merchant) and Mabel (Bennett) Ball; educated at Convent of the Institute of the Blessed Virgin Mary, York; never married. ❖ Entered the Bar convent at York as novice (1814) and became Sister Mary Teresa; took final vows as nun (1816); left York and returned to Dublin (1821); encouraged by Dr. John Murray (later archbishop of Dublin) to establish and lead a sisterhood which would have as its mission the creation of a system of middle-class female education, established 1st house of Irish Institute of the Blessed Virgin Mary, known as the Loreto Institute, at Rathfarnham (1821); set up new fee-paying day school at Harcourt Street in Dublin (moved to St. Stephen's Green, 1841), which became one of leading Catholic girls' schools in country; established network of schools throughout Ireland for education of Catholic middle-class girls; sent sisters to run convent school in Calcutta (1841), followed by other overseas projects in Mauritius and Gibraltar (1845), Canada (1847), and Manchester and Cadiz (1851); appealed to the pope to end dispute at Stephen's Green, whose members apparently resented her authority; by time of her death (1861), had established 37 houses of her Order throughout the world. ❖ See also Henry James Coleridge, *The Life of Mother Frances Mary Teresa Ball* (Gill, 1881); Desmond Forristal, *The First Loreto Sister* (Dominican, 1994); William Hutch, *Mrs. Ball: A Biography* (Duffy, 1879); Mother Evangeline MacDonald, *Joyful Mother of Children* (1961); and *Women in World History.*

BALL, Lucille (1911–1989). American actress. Name variations: Lucy. Born Lucille Ball, Aug 6, 1911, in Jamestown in western New York State; died in Los Angeles, California, April 26, 1989; dau. of Henry Ball (electrician) and Desirée ("DeDe") Hunt (saleswoman); m. Desi Arnaz, Nov 30, 1940 (div. 1961); m. Gary Morton, Nov 19, 1961; children: (1st m.) Lucie Arnaz (actress) and Desi Arnaz Jr. ❖ Star of tv show "I Love Lucy" and co-founder and president of Desilu Productions, which revolutionized tv production in America and world, 1st modeled for Bergdorf Goodman and Hattie Carnegie (1926–28); went to Hollywood for 6-week stint as Goldwyn Girl, appearing in *Roman Scandal* (1933); made more than 60 films, including *Stage Door, The Big Street, DuBarry Was a Lady* and *The Fuller Brush Girl* (1933–50), and starred in CBS-radio show "My Favorite Husband" (1948–50); starred as the wacky, star-struck housewife Lucy Ricardo in the groundbreaking and wildly successful "I Love Lucy" and its spin-off "The Lucy-Desi Comedy Hour" (1951–60) with then-husband Desi Arnaz, with whom she founded Desilu Productions; starred in Broadway Musical *Wildcat* (1960–61); starred in 3 "Lucy" tv-series (1962–74); served as president of Desilu Productions (1962–67); starred in film *Mame* (1974), tv-movie "Stone Pillow" (1985), and short-lived series "Life with Lucy" (1986); received countless honors, including Emmys for best comedienne (1952 and 1967), induction into Television Academy Hall of Fame (1984), and Kennedy Center Honors for Lifetime Achievement (1986). ❖ See also Bart Andrews, *The "I Love Lucy" Book* (Doubleday, 1985); Jim Bochu, *Lucy in the Afternoon* (Morrow, 1990); Kathleen Brady, *Lucille: The Life of Lucille Ball* (Hyperion, 1994); Eleanor Harris, *The Real Story of Lucille Ball*

(Farrar, Straus, 1954); Stefan Kanfer, *Ball of Fire* (2004); and *Women in World History.*

BALL, Suzan (1933–1950). American actress and singer. Born Susan Ball, Mar 3, 1933, in Jamestown, NY; died Aug 5, 1955, in Hollywood, California; 2nd cousin of Lucille Ball; m. Richard Long (actor), 1954. ❖ Sang with Mel Baker Orchestra (1948–53); made film debut in *Untamed Frontier* (1952), followed by *East of Sumatra, Yankee Buccaneer, City Beneath the Sea, War Arrow* and *Chief Crazy Horse,* among others; developed tumors in right leg that had to be amputated (1954); died of cancer at age 22.

BALL, Mother Teresa (1794–1861). *See Ball, Frances.*

BALLANGER, Felicia (1971—). French cyclist. Name variations: Félicia Ballanger. Born June 12, 1971, in La Roche-sur-Yon, France. ❖ Won a gold medal for sprint at Atlanta Olympics (1996); won gold medals for sprint and 500-meter time trial at Sydney Olympics (2000); won 5 consecutive World sprint titles (1995–1999).

BALLANTYNE, Sara (c. 1964—). American mountain-bike racer. Name variations: Sara Haaland. Born in Indiana, Pennsylvania, c. 1964; graduate of University of Colorado, 1982. ❖ Pioneer in US mountain biking, was the 1st American woman to race full-time in Europe (1990); won 1st overall at European championships (1988–89) and 1st overall at World championships (1987–89); won team National and World championships; began adventure racing with Team Vail, winning the Eco-Challenge twice (1998, 2001). Inducted into Mountain Bike Hall of Fame (1992).

BALLARD, Florence (1943–1976). African-American singer. Name variations: The Supremes. Born June 30, 1943, in Detroit, Michigan; died in 1976; dau. of Lurlee Ballard; m. Tommy Chapman (sep. 1973). ❖ With Mary Wilson, organized a singing group called "The Primettes" (1959); joined by Diana Ross, recorded 1st song for Motown (1964), under name "The Supremes"; with group, saw recording of "Where Did Our Love Go" reach *Billboard*'s Top 100, had 7 #1 hits, and was rarely out of the Top 10 (1965–69) with such songs as "Your Heart Belongs to Me" (1964), "Baby Love" (1964), "Come See about Me" (1964), "Stop! In the Name of Love" (1965), "Back in My Arms Again" (1965), "Nothing But Heartaches" (1965), "I Hear a Symphony" (1965), "My World Is Empty Without You" (1966), "You Can't Hurry Love" (1966), "You Keep Me Hangin' On" (1966), "Love Is Here and Now You're Gone" (1967), "Love Child" (1968) and "Someday We'll Be Together" (1969); left the group when its name was changed to "Diana Ross and The Supremes" (1967). Inducted into Rock and Roll Hall of Fame (1988). ❖ See also (play) *Dreamgirls,* loosely based on The Supremes (1981); and *Women in World History.*

BALLARD, Kaye (1926—). American comedian. Born Catherine Gloria Ballotta, Nov 20, 1926, in Cleveland, Ohio. ❖ Began career in vaudeville as an impressionist and singer; was a frequent guest star on tv, a regular on "The Perry Como Show" (1961–63) and "Hollywood Squares" (1968), and starred in series "The Mothers-in-Law" (1967) and "The Doris Day Show" (1970–71); films include *The Girl Most Likely* (1957), *Freaky Friday* (1976), *The Ritz* (1976), *Falling in Love Again* (1980), *Fate* (1990) and *The Million Dollar Kid* (2000).

BALLARD, Lucinda (1906–1993). American costume designer. Born Lucinda Davis Goldsborough, April 3, 1906, in New Orleans, Louisiana; died June 19, 1993, in Los Angeles, California; m. Howard Dietz. ❖ Made design debut with *As You Like It* (1937); won Tony Awards for Costumes for 5 plays: *Happy Birthday, Another Part of the Forest, Street Scene, John Loves Mary* and *Chocolate Soldier* (1947); also won a Tony for *The Gay Life* (1962); other plays include *I Remember Mama, Streetcar Named Desire* and *Night of the Iguana;* retired (1986).

BALLARD, Martha Moore (1735–1812). American midwife and diarist. Name variations: Martha Moore in Oxford, Massachusetts, 1735; died in Augusta, Maine, June 1812; dau. of Dorothy and Elijah Moore; great-aunt of Clara Barton; m. Ephraim Ballard, 1754 (died 1821); children: Lucy (b. 1756), Triphene, Jonathan, Dorothy (d. 1769), Martha, Cyrus, Hannah (b. 1769), Dorothy "Dolly" (b. 1773), and Ephraim (b. 1779). ❖ Received sufficient education from an uncle and brother to maintain diary and keep track of family finances; could make poultices, emulsions, treatments for cold, cough, dysentery and frostbite, as well as other general remedies; lost 3 of her children to diphtheria outbreak in 10 days (1769); moved to Hallowell, Maine (1777), and delivered 1st baby (1778); made 1st diary entry (1785) and maintained diary as combination of daybook which detailed daily events and finances, and almanac, which helped plot weather patterns and crops for farmers; captured drama of life in new settlement by recounting her work; performed 816 deliveries (1785–1812) and tended to general health needs of the community. Following her death (1812), the diary was passed down through the family until it was donated more than 100 years later to Maine State Library. ❖ See also Laurel Thatcher Ulrich, *A Midwife's Tale: The Life of Martha Moore Ballard, Based on Her Diary, 1785–1812* (Knopf, 1990); "A Midwife's Tale" on "American Experience" (1998); and *Women in World History*.

BALLESTEROS, Mercedes (1913–1995). Spanish journalist and novelist. Name variations: (pseudonyms) Baronesa Alberta; Rocq Morris; Sylvia Visconti. Born Mercedes Gaibrois de Ballesteros in 1913 in Madrid, Spain; died 1995; dau. of Mercedes Gaibrois y Riaño de Ballesteros (1891–1960, historian), and Antonio Ballesteros Beretta (count of Beretta and university professor); m. Claudio de la Torre (writer). ❖ Humorist whose works include *Así es la vida* (1953), *Eclipse de tierra* (1954), *Este mundo* (1955), *La cometa y el eco* (1956), *Mi hermano y yo por esos mundos* (1962), *La sed* (1965), *El chico* (1967) and *Los amores de cinco minutes* (with José Ortega, 1995); also wrote *Las mariposas cantan*.

BALLESTREM, Eufemia von (1859–1941). German novelist and poet. Name variations: Countess von Ballestrem. Born in Ratibor, Germany, Aug 18, 1859; died April 21, 1941; married Major von Adlersfeld, 1884; lived at Karlsruhe. ❖ Wrote *Lady Melusine* (1878) and *The Falconers of Falcon Court* (1890); poetry was published as *Drops in the Ocean* (1878) and *Raoul the Page* (1881).

BALLIN, Mabel (1887–1958). American silent-screen actress. Name variations: Mabel Croft. Born Mabel Croft, Jan 1, 1887, in Philadelphia, Pennsylvania; died July 24, 1958, in Santa Monica, California; m. Hugo Ballin (producer-director, died 1956). ❖ Had stage career as Mabel Croft; appeared opposite Tom Mix in *Riders of the Purple Sage;* starred in husband's productions *Jane Eyre, Vanity Fair* and *Married People,* among others; other films include *East Lynne;* retired (1925).

BALLINGER, Margaret (1894–1980). South African politician. Born Violet Margaret Livingstone Hodgson in Scotland in 1894; died 1980; educated in Port Elizabeth, Wellington; University College of Rhodes, BA; attended Somerville College, Oxford, 1914; m. William Ballinger. ❖ Immigrated to South Africa with parents at 10; served as history lecturer at Witwatersrand University in Johannesburg; with husband, collaborated on major study of the protectorates: Bechuanaland (now Botswana), Basutoland (now Lesotho), and Swaziland; drafted (1937) to run for 1 of 4 seats designated for nonwhite voters under 1936 Representation of the Natives Act; won Eastern Cape seat and was reelected 5 times before her seat was eventually abolished by the Bantu Self-Government Act, which ended representation of Africans in House and Senate; within the Congress, was a founding member of Liberal Party (1953) and was its 1st national chair; attacked racial discrimination and crusaded against apartheid; founded home for crippled African children (eventually closed by Group Areas Act of 1950); was instrumental in establishing scholarships for African students; lectured briefly at Australian Institute of International Affairs, then began work on major historical analysis, *From Union to Apartheid: a Trek to Isolation* (1968). ❖ See also *Women in World History*.

BALLIOL, Ada (fl. 1256). Scottish royal. Name variations: Baliol; Ada de Baliol. Born before 1256; dau. of John Balliol (d. 1269) and Devorgilla (d. 1290); sister of John Balliol (1249–1315), king of Scots (r. 1292–1296); m. William Lindsay of Lambarton; children: Christina de Lindsay.

BALLIOL, Cecily (d. before 1273). Scottish royal. Name variations: Cecilia Balliol or Baliol; Cecily de Burgh. Died before 1273; dau. of John Balliol (d. 1269) and Devorgilla (d. 1290); sister of Ada Balliol (fl. 1256), Margaret Balliol (c. 1255–?), and John Balliol (1249–1315), king of Scots (r. 1292–1296); m. John de Burgh; children: Devorgilla de Burgh (1255–1284, who m. Robert, 1st baron FitzWalter); Hawise de Burgh (who m. Robert de Grelley); Marjorie de Burgh (nun at Chicksands Priory).

BALLIOL, Devorgilla (d. 1290). *See Devorgilla.*

BALLIOL, Eleanor (fl. 1230). Scottish royal. Name variations: Eleanor Percy. Fl. around 1230; dau. of Ingelram Balliol; m. William Percy (d. 1245); children: Henry Percy (d. 1272, who m. Eleanor de Warenne).

BALLIOL, Eleanor (c. 1255–?). *See Balliol, Margaret.*

BALLIOL, Isabel (fl. 1281). *See Isabel de Warenne.*

BALLIOL, Margaret (c. 1255–?). Scottish royal. Name variations: Alianora or Eleanor; Mary. Born c. 1255; death date unknown; dau. of Devorgilla (d. 1290) and John Balliol; sister of John Balliol (c. 1250–1313), king of the Scots (r. 1292–1296); m. John Comnyn; children: John "Red" Comyn.

BALLIOL, Margaret (fl. 1300s). Scottish royal. Name variations: Margherita of Taranto or Tarento. Flourished in the 1300s; dau. of Philipp or Philip of Tarento (d. 1332), prince of Tarent and Catherine of Tarento; m. Edward Balliol (c. 1283–1364), king of the Scots (r. 1332–1338); m. Francisco II del Balzo, duke of Andria. ❖ See also *Women in World History*.

BALLISER, Helen (fl. 1914). American ambulance doctor. Graduate of Cornell Medical School. ❖ With Ana Tjohnlands, became the 1st women ambulance doctors, taking positions at Bellevue Hospital (1914); also served in the European theater during WWI.

BALLON, Ellen (1898–1969). Canadian pianist. Born 1898 in Montreal, Canada, of Russian immigrants; died in Montreal, Dec 21, 1969. ❖ Child prodigy, won the director's prize at McGill Conservatory at age 6; made NY concerto debut (1910); went on a major European tour (1927) to great acclaim; lived and performed in Great Britain and Europe (1930s); returned to Canada and settled in Montreal (1939); gave world premiere of Heitor Villa-Lobos' First Piano Concerto under his baton in Rio de Janeiro (1946) and made a number of pioneering recordings of Villa-Lobos' piano compositions; appeared on CBC French-language tv series "Heure du concert." Was invited to perform at the White House (1912, 1934, 1954). ❖ See also *Women in World History*.

BALLOU, Esther Williamson (1915–1973). American composer, teacher, and pianist. Born July 17, 1915, in Elmira, New York; died Mar 12, 1973; studied with Luening, Wagenaar, and Riegger. ❖ Had career on hold while crippled by arthritis (1943–53); joined faculty of American University, where she composed and orchestrated *Beguine for two pianos* (1958), performed by National Symphony Orchestra; also composed *A Babe is Born* (1959), and for orchestra and band: *In memoriam* (1952), *Prelude and allegro for string orchestra and piano* (1952), *Oboe concertino* (1953), *Adagio for bassoon and string orchestra* (1962), *Early American Portrait* (1962), *Concerto for piano and orchestra* (1965), *Concerto for solo guitar and chamber orchestra* (1966), *Konzertstück* (1970) and *Intermezzo for orchestra.* ❖ See also *Women in World History*.

BALLOU, Germaine (b. 1899). American ballet dancer and teacher. Name variations: Germaine Douglas. Born Germaine Douglas, Dec 14, 1899, in Seattle, Washington; sister of Ann Douglas (dancer). ❖ With younger sister, trained at Douglas Dancing School in Seattle, then at Denishawn School in Los Angeles (1920–27); appeared in numerous films as an extra or exotic dancer in denishawnesque numbers, including in *The Persian Market* (1924), *Wild Orchids* (1929) and *Lives of the Bengal Dancers* (1935); with sister, taught at and directed numerous studios in Los Angeles, Hollywood, and Manhattan Beach (starting 1921); switched from teaching Denishawn style to Cecchetti ballet technique (1960s).

BALOGH, Beatrix (1974—). Hungarian handball player. Name variations: Beatrix Balogh Csatane. Born Dec 12, 1974, in Hungary. ❖ Won a team silver medal at Sydney Olympics (2000).

BALOGH, Suzanne (1973—). Australian trapshooter. Born May 8, 1973, in Queanbeyan, Australia; dau. of Steven Balogh (trapshooter). ❖ Won World Cup in double trap at Seoul (2001); won a gold medal for trap at Athens Olympics (2004).

BALTECHILDIS (c. 630–c. 680). *See Balthild.*

BALTEIRA, La. *See Perez, Maria.*

BALTHASAR, Ramona (1964—). East German rower. Born Jan 9, 1964. ❖ At Seoul Olympics, won a gold medal in coxed eights (1988).

BALTHILD (c. 630–c. 680). Queen of the Franks. Name variations: Balthildis, Bathildis, Bathilde, Baltechildis, Baldechild, Baldhilda, Baldhild. Born c. 630 CE in England; died c. 680 at convent of Chelles, France; m. Clovis II (634–657), king of Neustria and Burgundy (r. 639–657), king of the Franks (r. 639–657), in 649; children: Childeric II (650–675), king of Austrasia (r. 656–675), king of the Franks (r. 673–675); Chlothaire or Lothair III (654–673), king of Neustria and Burgundy (r. 657–673); Thierry or Theoderic III (d. 691), king of Neustria and Burgundy (r. 673/75–691), king of the Franks (r. 687–691). ❖ Influential queen of the Franks, helped enact laws to improve the conditions of slaves' and prevent Christians from being sold into slavery; as a young woman, was kidnapped and sold as a slave in Gaul (c. 641); was purchased by the mayor (ruler) of Neustria (northeastern France); managed to deter his ardor by dressing in rags and hiding until he forgot about her; married Frankish king Clovis II (648); unlike many early medieval queens, was not a passive queen-consort and had the considerable duties of managing the royal court and controlling all charitable funds; gave birth to 3 sons, all of whom were to become rulers; helped the poor by decreasing their heavy tax burden; when Clovis died (657), became regent for the minority of her son Lothair; during these years, attempted to realize the ambitious goal of unifying the kingdom of the Franks; when Lothair came of age (c. 665), retired to the convent at Chelles which she had founded with her own wealth, along with the monastery of Saint Peter at Corbie, an important center of learning. ❖ See also *Women in World History.*

BALTHILDIS (c. 630–c. 680). *See Balthild.*

BALTIMORE, Lady (d. 1630). *See Arundel, Anne.*

BALY, Monica E. (1914–1998). English nurse historian. Born May 24, 1914, in England; died Nov 12, 1998; Open University, BA, 1979; London University, PhD, 1983. ❖ Qualified as nurse (1938); worked for Princess Mary's Royal Air Force Nursing Service in Middle East and Italy (WWII); became chief nursing officer at Royal College of Nursing (RCN, 1949); represented nurses as area officer for RCN for 24 years (1952–76); worked successfully for nurses' pay raise (1972); lectured in history of nursing and social policy; founded RCN History of Nursing Society and became known as a leading nurse historian; after retirement (1974), published *Florence Nightingale and the Nursing Legacy* (1986); also wrote *Nursing and Social Change* (1973).

BALZAC, Madame (1801–1882). *See Hanska, Eveline, Countess.*

BALZER, Karin (1938—). East German hurdler. Born June 1938. ❖ At Tokyo Olympics, won a gold medal in the 80-meter hurdles (1964); at Munich Olympics, won a bronze medal in 100-meter hurdles (1972).

BAMBACE, Angela (1898–1975). American union organizer and leader. Name variations: Angela Camponeschi. Born Angela Bambace, Feb 14, 1898, in Santos, Brazil; died April 3, 1975, in Baltimore, Maryland; dau. of Antonio and Giuseppina (Calabrese) Bambace; m. Romolo Camponeschi, June 1919 (div. 1927); children: 2 sons (b. 1920, 1923). ❖ Labor leader, organized strike for International Ladies' Garment Workers' Union (ILGWU, 1919); left work after marriage but rejoined ILGWU (1925); moved to Baltimore and organized women garment workers, who were denied entry to male-dominated union, into a local (1934); served as assistant manager of ILGWU Maryland Department and worked to increase union's influence in state (1930s–40s); appointed manager of MD-VA District (1942); became head of Upper South Department (formerly MD-VA District) (1947); established outpatient clinic (1956) and pension fund (1957) for union members; became 1st non-Jewish woman to be elected a vice president of ILGWU's general executive board (resigned 1972); appointed to Commission on Status of Women by John F. Kennedy (1962); fought anti-Semitism and racism against black union members in Upper South Department; participated in war-relief programs; worked with Histadrut (Zionist labor movement), Americans for Democratic Action, Italian American Labor Council, and American Civil Liberties Union.

BAMBARA, Toni Cade (1939–1995). African-American novelist, short-story writer and filmmaker. Born Miltona Mirkin Cade, Mar 25, 1939, in Harlem, NY; died from colon cancer, Dec 9, 1995, in Philadelphia, Pennsylvania; dau. of Helen Cade; Queens College, BA, 1959; City College (CCNY), MA, 1964. ❖ Taught at City College New York, Livingstone College, and Spelman College; traveled extensively (1970s); came to prominence as a short-story writer with *Gorilla, My Love* (1972); won American Book Award for 1st novel, *The Salt Eaters* (1980); other books include 2 edited works, *The Black Woman* (1970) and *Tales and Stories for Black Folks* (1971), as well as the short-story collection, *The Sea Birds Are Still Alive* (1977); also made 2 documentary films: *The Bombing of Osage Avenue* (1986), for which she won an Academy Award for Best Documentary, and *W.E.B. Du Bois: A Biography in Four Voices* (1995). *Deep Sightings and Rescue Missions*

(1996) and *Those Bones Are Not My Child* (1999) were published posthumously.

BAMPTON, Rose (1907—). American soprano and mezzo-soprano. Name variations: Rose Bampton Pelletier. Born Nov 28, 1908, in Lakewood, Ohio; dau. of English father and German pianist mother; m. Wilfrid Pelletier (conductor), 1937; trained at Curtis Institute of Music, where she studied with Horatio Connell and Queena Mario; also studied with Martha Graham, Elena Gerhardt and Lotte Lehmann. ❖ Well known for radio work and recordings, made debut as Siebel in *Faust* at Chautauqua (1929); made Metropolitan opera debut as Laura in *La Gioconda* (1932); sang with New York City Opera; retired (1950), then taught at Manhattan School, North Carolina School of the Arts, Drake University, and Juilliard School. ❖ See also *Women in World History.*

BAN HUI-JI (c. 45–c. 120 CE). *See Ban Zhao.*

BAN JIEYU (c. 48–c. 6 BCE). Chinese poet and royal concubine. Born c. 48 BCE; died c. 6 BCE; great-aunt of Ban Zhao. ❖ A royal concubine to Emperor Cheng of Han dynasty, lost favor and was relegated to serving dowager empress. Her indignation informed her poetry, including "Resentful Song," which was inscribed on a round fan. ❖ See also *Women in World History.*

BAN, Oana (1986—). Romanian gymnast. Born Jan 11, 1986, in Cluj-Napoca, Romania. ❖ Won a team all-around gold medal at Athens Olympics (2004).

BAN ZHAO (c. 45–c. 120). Chinese poet, historian and writer. Name variations: Pan Chao; also known in the Chinese literary world by the alternate name Ban Hui-ji and by the title Cao Dagu. Born sometime between 45 and 51; died sometime between 114 and 120; dau. of Ban Biao (3–54, noted scholar and administrator of the powerful Chinese Ban family which included a number of famous literary figures, and a highly educated mother (name unknown); both her great-aunt and her mother were also literary figures; received a broad education with noted tutors and established a reputation as a poet and woman of letters; sister of Ban Gu and Ban Chao (Pan Ch'ao, 32–102, famous Chinese traveler and military official in northern frontiers); m. Cao Shishu; children: several sons. ❖ After brother Ban Gu died, finished his dynastic history, *Han Shu* (History of the Han), which is said to be the 2nd most noted of many dynastic histories of China (while her exact contributions to the work have been obscured by time and by later Confucian disregard for women, some scholars have given her credit as primary author); served as tutor to Empress Deng (fl. 105–121) and as noted court memorialist; is most famous for classic work *Lessons for Women,* which became a standard treatise prescribing rules for behavior of women within Chinese family for almost 2,000 years and made her the most noted Chinese woman of letters prior to 20th century; also wrote many volumes of poetry and a wide range of literary miscellany, such as epitaphs and memorials; was a model for subsequent generations of Chinese female intellectuals well into the modern era. ❖ See also Nancy Lee Swann, *Pan Chao: Foremost Woman Scholar of China* (Russell & Russell, 1932); and *Women in World History.*

BANAHAN, Frances (1855/56?–1932). *See Banahan, Mary Gertrude.*

BANAHAN, Mary Gertrude (1855/56?–1932). New Zealand nun and teacher. Name variations: Frances Banahan. Born Frances Banahan, c. 1855 or 1856, in Mountrath, Co. Laois, Ireland; died Mar 17, 1932, in Pahiatua, New Zealand; dau. of Cornelius (grazier) and Margaret (McManus) Banahan. ❖ Joined Brigidine sisterhood (1876); immigrated to Australia (1883); helped to expand Brigidine congregation in New South Wales and in Wairarapa, New Zealand (1880s–1920s). ❖ See also *Dictionary of New Zealand Biography* (Vol. 3).

BANCROFT, Ann (1955—). American explorer. Born 1955 in Mendota Heights, Minnesota. ❖ Became the 1st known woman to cross the ice to the North Pole, as a member of the Steger International Polar Expedition which used dogsleds to travel 1,000 miles in 55 days (1986); led the 1st east to west crossing of Greenland by American women (1992); led a 4-woman American Women's Expedition to South Pole, becoming the 1st woman to cross the ice to both Poles (1993); with Norwegian explorer Liv Arnesen, became the 1st to cross Antarctica's landmass by sail and ski (2001); is an instructor at Wilderness Inquiry and founder of the Ann Bancroft Foundation which celebrates the achievements of women and girls. ❖ See also memoir (with Arnesen) *No Horizon is so Far* (2003).

BANCROFT, Anne (1931–2005). American actress. Name variations: Anne Marno. Born Anna Maria Louise Italiano, Sept 17, 1931, in the Bronx, NY; died June 6, 2005, in New York, NY; m. Martin A. May, 1953 (div. 1957); m. Mel Brooks (actor, producer), 1964; children: Max Brooks. ❖ Began career on tv (1950), appearing under name Anna Marno in numerous productions, including "The Goldbergs"; made Broadway debut as Gittel Mosca in *Two for the Seesaw* (1958), for which she received a Tony award; other plays include *Mother Courage and Her Children, The Devils, The Little Foxes* and *A Cry of Players;* made film debut in *Don't Bother to Knock* (1952), followed by *7 Women, Silent Movie, To Be or Not to Be, The Elephant Man, Garbo Talks, 84 Charing Cross Road* and *Point of No Return.* Won a Tony award (1959) and Oscar (1962) for performance in *The Miracle Worker;* nominated for Oscars for *The Pumpkin Eater* (1964), *The Graduate* (1967), *The Turning Point* (1977) and *Agnes of God* (1985).

BANCROFT, F. (1892–1947). *See Slater, Frances Charlotte.*

BANCROFT, Jane (1847–1932). *See Robinson, Jane Bancroft.*

BANCROFT, Jessie (1867–1952). American physical-education expert. Name variations: Jessie Hubbell Bancroft or Jessie H. Bancroft. Born Jessie Hubbell Bancroft, Dec 20, 1867, in Winona, Minnesota; died Nov 13, 1952, in Pittsfield, Massachusetts; dau. of Edward Hall Bancroft and Susan Maria (Hubbell) Bancroft. ❖ Pioneer of NY gymnastics, helped create 1st public school gymnasium and used anthropometric measurements of children to provide them with appropriately sized school furniture; influenced fields as varied as shoemaking, manufacture of furniture, and design of subway-train seats; began traveling through Iowa and Illinois conducting classes in, and giving demonstrations of, physical exercise (1889–91); taught physical education at schools and colleges in NYC (1891–93); served as director of physical training at Brooklyn Public Schools (1893–1903) and as assistant director of NYC Schools (1904–28); was founder and president of American Posture League; was 1st woman to earn Gulick Award for distinguished service in physical education (1924); authored *School Gymnastics with Light Apparatus* (1897) and *The Posture of School Children* (1913); was 1st woman to be a member of American Academy of Physical Education.

BANCROFT, Lady (1839–1921). English stage star and theater manager. Name variations: Marie Wilton; Marie Bancroft. Born Marie Effie Wilton, Jan 12, 1839, in Doncaster, England; died May 22, 1921, in London; dau. of Robert Pleydell Wilton (actor) and Georgiana Jane (Faulkner) Wilton; m. Squire Bancroft (actor-manager), 1867 (died 1926). ❖ With father, appeared on stage as a child (1845); made London debut with Charles Dillon in *Belphegor* (1856), followed by Perdita in William Brough's musical version of *A Winter's Tale;* with playwright H.J. Byron and later her husband, managed the Prince of Wales (1865–80), appearing there in *La Sonnambula, Society, Ours, Caste, Play, School, MP, Man and Wife, Sweethearts, The Vicarage, Diplomacy* and *London Assurance,* among others, making it the leading house for comedy in England; with husband, managed the Haymarket (1880–85), appearing there in *Odette, Fédora* and *Lords and Commons.* Wrote 3 plays, the novel *Shadow of Neeme,* and collaborated with husband on *Mr. and Mrs. Bancroft: On and Off the Stage.*

BANCROFT, Marie (1839–1921). *See Bancroft, Lady.*

BANDA (1898–1919). *See MacLeod, Juana-Luisa.*

BANDARANAIKE, Sirimavo (1916–2000). Sri Lankan politician. Name variations: Sirimavo Ratwatte Dias Bandaranaike. Born Sirimavo Ratwatte (or Ratevatte) in Ratnapura, Balangoda, in southern Ceylon (now Sri Lanka), April 17, 1916; died Oct 10, 2000; dau. of Barnes Ratwatte and Rosemund (Mahawalatenne) Ratwatte; educated at St. Bridget's Convent, Colombo; m. Solomon West Ridgeway Dias Bandaranaike, Oct 1940; children: son, Anura (b. 1949); 2 daughters, Sunethra Rupasinghe and Chandrika Kumaratunga (elected president of Sri Lanka in 1994). ❖ Served as treasurer of Social Service League (until early 1940); married (1940) and moved to capital at Colombo; joined Lanka Mahila Samiti (1941), the primary women's movement organization in Ceylon; after husband's assassination (1959), succeeded him as leader of Sri Lanka Freedom Party (SLFP), then as prime minister (1960–65, 1970–77), becoming 1st woman prime minister in world; dedicated to democratic, socialist, and non-aligned policies, led country through stressful period of national growth and raised Sri Lanka to respectable position in community of Asian nations; served as external affairs minister (1960–65) and remained member of Senate (until 1965); a dedicated Buddhist, pressed hard to satisfy Buddhists' demands, and her

government took over country's Christian-run schools (1960), which effectively weakened role of Christian churches; tried to restore Sinhalese over English, a move strongly opposed by Tamil-speaking minority; established country's position of positive neutralism, which enabled her to initiate peace moves over the Sino-Indian border dispute (1962); after losing elections to UNP (1965), remained leader of the opposition and was reelected prime minister (1970); led "United Front" coalition government in promulgating new constitution to remove various British elements (1972); failed to enlist support of Tamil minority, who comprised about 11% of Ceylonese population and who were being forced into positions of 2nd-class citizenship; criticized for allowing too much power to pass into hands of her family members, suffered humiliating defeat at polls (1977); found guilty of abuse of power in office by Presidential Commission under President J.R. Jayewardene (1980) and was denounced and stripped of civic rights for 7 years. ❖ See also Maureen Seneviratne, *Sirimavo Bandaranaike: The World's First Woman Prime Minister* (Hansa, 1975); and *Women in World History.*

BANDETTINI, Teresa (1763–1837). Italian poet. Born at Lucca, Aug 12, 1763; died 1837; married Pietro Landucci, 1789. ❖ Works include *La Morte di Adonide, Il Polidoro* and *La Rosmunda.*

BANDLER, Faith (1918—). Australian author and Aboriginal activist. Born Ida Lessing Faith Mussing, Sept 27, 1918, in Tumbulgum, Murwillumbah, New South Wales; dau. of Ida and Wacvie Mussingkon (Pacific Islander whose name was anglicized to Peter Mussing); educated at Murwillumbah public schools and Cleveland Street Night School; m. Hans Bandler, 1952; children: 1 daughter. ❖ A primary force in Aboriginal rights, 1st became involved in politics after she was accused of having Communist sympathies and had her passport seized when she returned to Australia from Bulgaria; became activist for Aboriginal rights and helped found Aboriginal-Australian Fellowship (AAF) with Pearl Gibbs; active in The Federal Council for Advancement of Aborigines; refused offer of Medal of the Order of the British Empire (1976) for her activism, denying English claim to her country; received Medal of Order of Australia (1984); published *Wacvie* (1977), the life story of her father; with Len Fox, wrote several histories of Aboriginal culture and history, including *Marani in Australia* (1980), *The Time Was Right* (1984) and *Turning the Tide* (1988); also wrote *Welon, My Brother* (1984). ❖ See also *Women in World History.*

BANFALVI, Klara (1931—). *See Friedne-Banfalvi, Klara.*

BANG, Nina (1866–1928). Danish historian and minister of education. Born Nina Henriette Wendeline Ellinger in Copenhagen, Denmark, 1866; died 1928; dau. of Heinrich August David Ellinger and Charlotte Ida Friedericke Preuss; University of Copenhagen, PhD, 1895; m. Gustav Bang (historian), 1895. ❖ Focused studies on history of trade in 1500s, becoming especially knowledgeable about accounts of Sound Tariffs collected from ships trading in Baltic; as Marxist historian, used tariff accounts to illuminate material and spiritual social conditions; published findings in 2-vol. work which offered new insights into history of English, Dutch, and Scandinavian trade; with husband, became 1st academicians to join Social Democratic Party (1895); worked as writer for *Social-Demokraten* (1898); served as member of party's executive board (1903–28); was council member for city of Copenhagen (1913–18); became member of Parliament (1918) and was reelected (1920 and 1924); at formation of Denmark's 1st social-democratic government (1924), appointed minister of education, the 1st woman Cabinet member in the world; her chief concern as minister of education was promotion of stronger local rule with greater responsibility for schools and improved education for teachers. ❖ See also *Women in World History.*

BANG, Soo-Hyun (1972—). South Korean bandminton player. Born Sept 13, 1972, in South Korea. ❖ Won a silver medal at Barcelona Olympics (1992) and a gold medal at Atlanta Olympics (1996), both for singles.

BANGLES, The. *See Steele, Micki.*

BANISTER, Zilpah Polly Grant (1794–1874). *See Grant, Zilpah.*

BANISZEWSKI, Gertrude Wright (1929–1990). American murderer. Name variations: Nadine Van Fossan. Born Gertrude Van Fossan, 1929, in Indianapolis, Indiana; died of lung cancer, 1990; m. John Baniszewski (div.); m. Edward Guthrie (div.); remarried John Baniszewski (div.); lived with Dennis Lee Wright; children: 7, including Stephanie, Paula, John, Dennis. ❖ Hired to care for the Likens sisters, Sylvia (16) and Jenny (15), while their parents traveled (July 1965);

abused the sisters, particularly Sylvia who was beaten and burned, and encouraged her children and others to participate; in one of the most infamous crimes of the century, branded the words "I am a prostitute and proud of it" onto Sylvia's stomach and the girl eventually died of her injuries (Oct 26, 1965); received life sentence, while her children Paula and John were convicted of lesser charges, and charges were dropped against daughter Stephanie; was released on parole (1985) and relocated to Iowa. ❖ See also John Dean, *The Indiana Torture Slaying* (Borf, 1999); Kate Millet, *The Basement: Meditations on Human Sacrifice* (Simon & Schuster, 1991).

BANKES, Mary (1598–1661). British royalist. Name variations: Lady Mary Bankes or Banks; Brave Dame Mary. Born Mary Hawtrey, 1598, in Ruislip, England; died April 11, 1661, in Damory Court, Blanford, Dorset, England; dau. of Ralph Hawtrey of Ruislip and Mary Althan (aristocrats); m. Sir John Bankes (prosecutor and later chief justice of Court of Common Pleas), 1618; children: 8 daughters, 6 sons. ❖ During English Civil Wars, was a Royalist who held Dorset's Corfe Castle while husband stayed with King Charles I in London; eventually turned over 4 remaining guns of castle to local Parliamentary Committee on their demands (1643); when a force of some 600, led by Sir Walter Earle, attacked with 2 siege engines (1643), personally defended the upper ward of the castle with only 5 soldiers, her daughters, and her women attendants, and prevented a breach in the castle's defenses; was besieged again after husband's death (1645), but a traitor apparently gave the enemy entry to the castle; permitted to depart without injury to herself and children. ❖ See also *Women in World History.*

BANKHEAD, Tallulah (1902–1968). American actress. Born Tallulah Brockman Bankhead, Jan 31, 1902, in Huntsville, Alabama; died New York, NY, Dec 12, 1968; dau. of William "Will" Brockman (US congressional delegate and speaker of the house) and Adelaide "Ada" Eugenia (Sledge) Bankhead; m. John Emery (actor), Aug 31, 1937 (div., June 13, 1941); no children. ❖ Actress who eventually eclipsed her own career with the force of her public personality, went to New York (1917); moved into Algonquin Hotel (1918); on stage, played a flapper in Crother's *Nice People* (1921) and patterned her personality after the character; appeared in *The Dancers* in England (1923); signed with Paramount (1931); on Broadway, appeared as Regina Giddens in *The Little Foxes* (1939); other stage roles include Penelope Penn in *39 East* (1919), Sadie Thompson in *Rain* (1935), Cleopatra in *Antony and Cleopatra* (1937), Lily Sabina in *The Skin of our Teeth* (1942), Amanda Prynne in *Private Lives* (1944, 1948), Blanche DuBois in *A Streetcar Named Desire* (1956) and title role in *Midgie Purvis* (1961); purchased "Windows" (1943); appeared as Constance Porter in film *Lifeboat* (1944); other films include *Tarnished Lady* (1931), *The Devil and the Deep* (1932), *Faithless* (1932) and *A Royal Scandal* (1945); on radio, was Mistress of Ceremonies of "The Big Show" (NBC, 1950–52); hosted ABC's "All-Star Revue" (1952); appeared for last time on Broadway as Mrs. Goforth in *The Milk Train Doesn't Stop Here Anymore* (1964); filmed *Die! Die! Darling!* in England (1964); appeared on *Batman* (1967). ❖ See also *Tallulah: My Autobiography* (Harper, 1952); Denis Brian, *Tallulah, Darling: A Biography of Tallulah Bankhead* (Macmillan, 1972); Lee Israel, *Miss Tallulah Bankhead* (Putnam, 1972); and *Women in World History.*

BANKS, Mrs. G. Linnaeus (1821–1887). See Banks, Isabella.

BANKS, Isabella (1821–1897). British author. Name variations: (pseudonyms) Isabella Varley; Mrs. G. Linnaeus Banks. Born Isabella Varley, Mar 25, 1821, in Manchester, England; died May 5, 1897, in Dalston, England; dau. of James and Amelia (Daniels) Varley; educated at Miss Hannah Spray's Ladies' Day School and Rev. John Wheeldon's academy; m. George Linnaeus Banks (poet and journalist), 1846; children: Agnes, Esther, George, and 5 who died in infancy. ❖ At 17, established School for Young Ladies in Manchester suburb of Cheetham; published poetry in local publications before release of collection *Ivy Leaves* (1844); faced with husband's alcoholism, turned to writing to support family and published 1st novel *God's Providence House* (1865), which was followed by more than 50 others in next 25 years; wrote most famous work *The Manchester Man*, which remains a widely read depiction of industrial revolution in Manchester; published *Caleb Booth's Clerk* (1878) and *Wooers and Winners* (1880), sealing her reputation as the "Lancashire novelist"; also wrote (with G. Linnaeus Banks) *Daisies in the Grass* (1865), *Geoffrey Oliphant's Folly* (1886) and *The Bridge of Beauty* (1894). ❖ See also E. L. Burney, *Mrs. G. Linnaeus Banks* (Morten, 1969); and *Women in World History.*

BANKS, Lynne Reid (1929—). British novelist and children's writer. Name variations: Lynne Reid-Banks. Born July 31, 1929, in London, England; dau. of James Reid-Banks (physician) and Muriel (Marsh) Reid-Banks (actress); m. Chaim Stephenson (Israeli sculptor), 1965; children: 3. ❖ Evacuated to Canada during WWII; worked as actress, secretary, journalist, and a scriptwriter for England's ITV News (1960s–70s); spent time in Israel (1960–72), which influenced several works; returned to England with family (1972); published *The L-Shaped Room* (1961), which was filmed with Leslie Caron (1962), followed by its sequels: *The Backward Shadow* (1971) and *Two is Lonely* (1974); other adult novels include *An End to Running* (1962) and *Children at the Gate* (1969); achieved greatest recognition for children and young adult novels, including *Dark Quartet: The Story of the Brontës* (1976), *Melusine: A Mystery* (1988) and *The Indian in the Cupboard* (1980), which was also filmed (1995), and its sequels. Received many awards for children's fiction.

BANKS, Margaret (1924—). Canadian ballet dancer. Born 1924 in Vancouver, British Columbia, Canada. ❖ Danced with Ballet Theater in New York for 6 seasons, in revivals of Fokine's *Les Sylphides, Carnaval* and *Petrouchka,* and created roles in Balanchine's *Waltz Academy* (1944), Lichine's *Fair at Sorochinsk* (1943), and Nijinska's *Harvest Time* (1945); performed in Jerome Robbins' *Look Ma, I'm Dancing* on Broadway (1948); began dancing for tv in "54th Street Revue" (1949–50), one of the earliest hour-long variety shows; worked as dance director for numerous tv shows, including "Dinah Shore Show" (1956–63); directed dance and variety specials for competitions and award ceremonies, including Academy Awards; worked on film as camera dance assistant or assistant choreographer with Jack Cole, Hermes Pan, Charles O'Curran, Jerome Robbins (*West Side Story*), and others; works for film include *The Children's Hour* (1962) and *Two for the Seesaw* (1962).

BANKS, Sarah Sophia (1744–1818). British naturalist. Born 1744, probably at Revesby Abbey, Lincolnshire; died 1818 in London, England; dau. of Sarah (Bate) Banks and William Banks; sister of botanist Joseph Banks (1743–1820). ❖ Earned reputation by assisting her brother, botanist Joseph Banks; transcribed much of his work; copied entire manuscript of his Newfoundland voyage journal (published 1766). ❖ See also *Women in World History.*

BANKY, Vilma (1898–1991). Austro-Hungarian actress. Born Vilma Lonchit in Nagyrodog, near Budapest, Hungary, Jan 9, 1898; died Mar 18, 1991, in Los Angeles, California; dau. of a prominent politician; m. Rod La Rocque (1898–1969, film star), 1927 (died 1969). ❖ Popular silent-screen star of 1930s, made stage debut in Vienna, then appeared in films in Austria and Hungary (from 1920); brought to Hollywood by Samuel Goldwyn, was promoted as "The Hungarian Rhapsody"; starred opposite Rudolph Valentino in *The Eagle* (1925) and *Son of the Sheik* (1926); teamed with Ronald Colman for *The Dark Angel;* made last film *The Rebel* in Germany (1932); spoke little English and ostensibly retired with advent of sound; was women's golf champion at Wilshire Country Club (throughout 1940s); other films include *Im letzten Augenblick* (1920), *Hotel Potemkin* (1924), *The Winning of Barbara Worth* (1926), *The Awakening* (1928), *Two Lovers* (1928) and *Innocent;* also made talkies: *This is Heaven* (1929) and *A Lady to Love* (1930). ❖ See also *Women in World History.*

BANNERJEE, Karuna (1919–2001). Indian actress. Name variations: Karuna Bannerji. Born 1919 in India; died Nov 13, 2001, in Kolkata, India. ❖ Starred as Sarbojaya Ray in *Pather Panchali* (1955) and *Aparajito* (1957), 2 films in Satyajit Ray's trilogy; other films include *Manmoyee Girls' School* (1958), *Kato Ajanare* (1959), *Devi* (1960) and *Calcutta 71* (1971).

BANNERMAN, Helen (1862–1946). Scottish children's writer. Born Helen Brodie Cowan Watson, Feb 25, 1862, in Edinburgh, Scotland; died Oct 13, 1946, in Edinburgh; dau. of Robert Boog Watson (army chaplain) and Helen Cowan Watson; married William Burney Bannerman (surgeon), 1889 (died 1924); children: 2 daughters, 2 sons. ❖ Spent childhood moving from army post to army post throughout British Empire; received LLA through correspondence courses, St. Andrew's University, London (1887); married an army doctor (1889) and spent next 30 years in India, where husband worked to eliminate the plague in Madras and Bombay; wrote and illustrated her most-famous book, *The Story of Little Black Sambo* (1899), which became a classic in England and US until it was banned for racism from many children's libraries, not so much because of the story, but because of the character's names and her illustrations, which exaggerated and caricatured the facial features of her protagonist (African-American writer Julius Lester introduced a new version with illustrator Jerry Pinkney retitled *Sam and the Tigers* [1996]); also wrote and illustrated *The Story of Little Black Mingo* (1901), *The Story of Little Black Quibba* (1903), *Little Dechie-Head: An Awful Warning to Bad Babas* (1903), *Pat and the Spider: The Bitter Bit* (1904), *The Story of the Teasing Monkey* (1907) and *Sambo and the Twins: A New Adventure of Little Black Sambo* (1936).

BANNERMAN, Jane (c. 1835–1923). New Zealand religious leader and philanthropist. Name variations: Jane Burns. Born Jane Burns, c. 1835 (baptized Feb 24, 1835), in Ayr, Scotland; died Oct 9, 1923, in Dunedin, Otago, New Zealand; dau. of Thomas (cleric) and Clementina (Grant) Burns; m. William Bannerman (minister), 1856 (died 1902); children: 6. ❖ Immigrated with family to New Zealand (1848); after marriage and birth of children, settled in South Otago and assisted in husband's ministry; relocated to Puerua (1866); raised funds to assist Presbyterian missions in New Hebrides, and became involved in other philanthropic activities (1880s); became 1st president and international secretary of Presbyterian Women's Missionary Union (1905). ❖ See also *Dictionary of New Zealand Biography* (Vol. 1).

BANNERMAN, Kay (1919–1991). English actress and screenwriter. Born in Hove, Sussex, England, Oct 11, 1919; died Mar 31, 1991; dau. of Robert George and Chicot (Mowat) Bannerman; attended Royal Academy of Dramatic Art; m. Harold Brooke (writer). ❖ On stage, appeared as Emmanuele in *Asmodée* (1939), Suzanne in *Prison Without Bars* (1939), Sarah in *Major Barbara* (1939), Ann Sheldon in *Other People's Houses* (1942), Mary Jefferson in *One Flight Up* (1942), Raina in *Arms and the Man* (1943), Polina in *The Gambler* (1945) and Diana Temple in *High Horse* (1946); with Harold Brooke, wrote *Fit for Heroes* (1945), *The Nest Egg* (1952), *All For Mary* (1954), *The Call of the Dodo* (1955), *Handful of Tansy* (1959), *Don't Tell Father* (1962), *The Snowman* (1965), *She Was Only an Admiral's Daughter* (1972) and *Take Zero* (1974).

BANNERMAN, Margaret (1896–1976). Canadian-born stage and screen actress. Born Dec 15, 1896, in Toronto, Ontario, Canada; died April 25, 1976, in Englewood, New Jersey; m. Pat Somerset (div.); m. Anthony Prinsep (div.). ❖ Won 1st acclaim on London stage as Lady George Grayston in *Our Betters* (1923); made Broadway debut in *By Jupiter* (1942), followed by, among others, *One Touch of Venus*, *Rebecca*, *John Loves Mary* and *My Fair Lady;* films include *The Love of Madame duBarry*, *Cluny Brown* and *The Homestretch.*

BANNING, Margaret Culkin (1891–1982). American author. Born Margaret Culkin in Buffalo, Minnesota, Mar 18, 1891; died Jan 4, 1982, in Tryon, North Carolina; dau. of William Edgar Culkin and Hannah Alice (Young) Culkin; Vassar College, BA, 1912; research fellow of the Russell Sage Foundation; m. Archibald Tanner Banning, 1914; children: 2 daughters, 2 sons. ❖ Widely read author of chiefly light fiction, wrote over 40 books and 400 short stories; novels include *Too Young to Marry* (1938), *Clever Sister* (1947), *Give Us Our Years* (1949), *Fallen Away* (1951) and *The Vine and the Olive;* nonfiction includes *Women for Defense* (1942), *Letters from England* (1943), (with Mabel Louise Culkin) *Conduct Yourself Accordingly* (1944) and *Salud: A South American Journal.* ❖ See also *Women in World History.*

BANNON, Ann (1932—). American novelist. Name variations: Ann Weldy; (married name) Ann Thayer. Born Ann Weldy, 1932 in Midwest; raised in Joliet, Illinois; dau. of Jane and Paul Weldy; Stanford University, PhD in linguistics; married immediately after college (div.); children: 2 daughters. ❖ Writer, who published under pseudonym Ann Bannon because husband would not allow her to use real name, was a dean at California State University at Sacramento; challenged gender identities and offered portrayals of lesbian life in such writings as *Odd Girl Out* (1957), *I Am a Woman* (1959), *Women in the Shadows* (1959), *Journey to a Woman* (1960) and *Beebo Brinker* (1962). Appeared in the documentary film *Before Stonewall.*

BANOTTI, Mary (1939—). Irish politician. Born Mary O'Mahony, May 29, 1939, in Dublin, Ireland; grandniece of Michael Collins (1890–1922, Irish nationalist) and Margaret Collins-O'Driscoll (1878–1945, TD); sister of Nora Owen (TD, Dublin North); m. Giovanni Banotti (sep.). ❖ Began career as a registered nurse; was a social worker with Irish Distillers (1972–84); hosted an RTE tv program on social welfare; elected member of the European Parliament for Dublin (MEP, 1984–1999, 1999—); representing Fine Gael, ran unsuccessfully for the Irish presidency (1997); appointed UN Population Fund Goodwill Ambassador for Ireland (1999), to campaign for reproductive

health care and education. Named by the European Environmental Bureau, Brussels, as one of the best legislators in the EP on environmental issues; won Ireland's European of the Year award (1997).

BANOVICI, Sofia (1956—). *See Corban-Banovici, Sofia.*

BANTI, Anna (1895–1985). *See Longhi, Lucia Lopresti.*

BANTI, Brigitta (c. 1756–1806). Italian operatic singer. Name variations: Brigitta Banti-Giorgi; Brigitta Giorgi. Born Brigitta Giorgi in c. 1756 in Monticelli D'Ongina, Italy; died Feb 18, 1806; studied with Abel, Piozzi, and Antonio Sacchini; m. Zaccaria Banti (dancer). ❖ Discovered as street singer and taken to Paris Opéra; made debut (1776); moved to London (1778) and became principal soloist for Pantheon concerts but, unable to read music, was eventually dismissed; performed widely and became more popular in Europe, appearing as principal in King's Theatre until retirement (1802); sang in premiere of *Eraldo ed Emma* and created title role for Mount Edgcumbe's *Zenobia.*

BAÑUELOS, Romana Acosta (1925—). Hispanic business executive and politician. Name variations: Romana Acosta Banuelos. Born Mar 20, 1925, in Miami, Arizona; grew up in Mexico in the states of Sonora and Chihuahua; returned to US (1947); div.; children: 2. ❖ The 1st Mexican-American woman in US history to hold a Cabinet office, began career investing in a small tortilla factory in Los Angeles, a business that grew into a $5 million enterprise; founded Pan American National Bank of East Los Angeles (1964); served as treasurer of US (1971–74), under the Nixon administration.

BANUS, Maria (1914–1999). Romanian poet. Born in Bucharest, Romania, 1914; died July 14, 1999, in Bucharest; studied law and philology. ❖ Known as grande dame of Romanian poetry, had 1st work published at 14; active in anti-fascist movements (1930s), worked for the Resistance in Romania during WWII; though named an official "Stalinist poet" following the war and the occupation of Romania, was soon disenchanted with Soviet regime and returned to her own voice; translated poetry from German, Russian, Spanish, Turkish and French, including poems of Goethe, Pushkin, Neruda, Hikmet and Rimbaud; works include *The Girl's Country* (1937), *Joy* (1947), *I Am Speaking to You, America!* (1955), *Metamorphosis* (1963) and *Anyone and Something* (1972). *Demon in Brackets* was trans. into English by Dan Dutescu and published by Dufour (1994).

BAR, countess of.
See Philippa de Dreux (d. 1240).
See Margaret (d. 1275).
See Eleanor Plantagenet (1264–1297).
See Marie of France (1344–1404).

BAR, duchess of.
See Isabelle of Lorraine (1410–1453).
See Jeanne de Laval (d. 1498).
See Catherine of Bourbon (c. 1555–1604).
See Elizabeth-Charlotte (1676–1744).

BARA, Theda (1885–1955). American silent-film star. Name variations: Theodosia Goodman, Theodosia de Coppet. Born Theodosia de Coppet Goodman, July 20, 1885, in Cincinnati, Ohio; died April 7, 1955, in Los Angeles, California; dau. of Bernard (tailor) and Pauline Louise (de Coppet) Goodman; attended University of Cincinnati, 1903–05; moved to New York City with family about 1905; m. Charles J. Brabin (film director), 1921. ❖ As Theodosia de Coppet, appeared on Broadway in *The Devil* (1908); appeared in film *The Stain* (1908); signed with Fox studios (1914) and was given new personal background and name, Theda Bara (was 1st star whose off-screen character was created entirely by a publicity campaign); starred in *A Fool There Was* (1915) as a seductive woman who schemes to trap and ruin a prosperous married man, and the character became prototype for other films in which she played "the vamp," a term her performances introduced into English language; appeared in 39 other Fox "vamp" films (through 1919); also appeared in *The Two Orphans* (1915) and *Romeo and Juliet* (1916); appeared in play *The Blue Flame* (1920); attempted film comeback in *The Unchastened Woman* (1925) and *Madame Mystery* (1926); retired (1926). ❖ See also *Women in World History.*

BARAKA, Consuelo (1944–1979). *See Atlas, Consuelo.*

BARAKAT, Hidiya Afifi (1898–1969). Egyptian feminist. Name variations: Hidiya Hanim Barakat, Hidiya Afifi. Born in Cairo, Egypt, 1898; died in Cairo, 1969; dau. of Ahmad Pasha Afifi (magistrate connected with the royal palace); educated at French convent of Notre

Dame de la Mère; m. Bahieddine Barakat (professor of law at Cairo University), May 1918. ❖ Leading Egyptian feminist was known as the "little soldier" during Revolution of 1919; organized The Société de la Femme Nouvelle, which concentrated on education for girls, and the Mabarra, which was concerned with clinics and women's health care.

BARAKSANOVA, Irina (1969—). Uzbekistan gymnast. Born July 4, 1969, in Tashkent, Uzbekistan. ❖ Won Jr. European championships (1984); at World championships, won a gold medal for team all-around (1985).

BARANDAS, Ana Eurídice Eufrosina de (1806–1856). Brazilian poet and novelist. Name variations: Ana Euridice de Barandas; Ana Eurydica Eufrozina de Barandas. Born 1806 in Brazil; died 1856. ❖ Regarded as the 1st Brazilian woman novelist, wrote O ramalhete ou flores escolhidas no jardim da imaginação (1845) and A filosofia do amor (1845).

BARANET, Nancy (1933—). See Nieman, Nancy.

BARANOVA, Elena (1972—). Russian basketball player. Name variations: Yelena Baranova. Born Jan 28, 1972, in Frunze, USSR. ❖ Forward, began professional career at 16 with the Dynamo Moscow (1988); won a team gold medal at Barcelona Olympics (1992) and a team bronze medal at Athens Olympics (2004); placed 2nd at World championships (1998, 2002); in WNBA, played for Utah Starzz (1997–99), Miami Sol (2001), then signed with New York Liberty (2003); played in 4 official games for the Mytischi Biso (Moscow men's team, 1999).

BARANOVA, Lyubov. Russian cross-country skier. Name variations: Ljubow Baranowa; Lyubov Kozyreva, Kosyryeva, Kosyrjeva, Kosyrewa, Kosytiyeva. Born Lyubov Kozyreva in USSR. ❖ Won a gold medal for 10 km and a silver for 3 x 5 km relay at Cortina Olympics (1956); won a silver medal for 10 km and a silver medal for 3 x 5 km at Squaw Valley Olympics (1960).

BARANOVA, Yelena (1972—). See Baranova, Elena.

BARANOVSKAYA, Vera (c. 1870–1935). Russian actress. Name variations: Baranovskaia or Baranowskaia. Born in Russia c. 1870 (some sources cite 1885); died Dec 7, 1935, in Paris, France; studied with Constantin Stanislavski. ❖ A favorite of Stanislavski, was a leading lady of the Moscow Art Theater; achieved international recognition with lead in Vsevolod Pudovkin's classic film The Mother (1926) and a role in Pudovkin's The End of St. Petersburg (1927); left Russia to further career in Czechoslovakia, Germany and France, and retired 4 years later; films include The Thief (1916), The Burden of Fate (1917), The Wolves (1925), Ruts (1928), Such is Life (1929), Poison Gas (1929), Monsieur Albert (1932) and Les Aventures du Roi Pausole (1933).

BARANOWSKA, Tekla Badarzewski (1834–1861). See Badarzewski-Baranowska, Tekla.

BARANSKAYA, Natalia (b. 1908). Russian short-story writer and feminist. Name variations: Natalya or Natál'ia Baránskaia or Baranskaia. Born Natalia Vladmírovna Baranskaya, Dec 31, 1908, in St. Petersburg, Russia; dau. of revolutionaries who never married; graduated from Moscow State University, 1930; married 1928 (div. 1932); married a cousin (soldier), mid-1930s (killed in battle, 1943); children: (2nd m.) 2. ❖ Spent infancy in hiding from tsarist police; parents imprisoned (1910); on their release, fled with them to Switzerland, then Germany, where she lived until the outbreak of WWI; returned to Russia with mother; worked as curator at Pushkin museum in Moscow (1958–66); at 61, published Nedelia kak nedelia (1969), detailing the day-to-day experiences of a mother, wife, homemaker and professional, which has been translated into 6 languages, including English (A Week Like Any Other); also wrote Den' pominoveniia (Memorial Day, 1989) and short stories, some of which appear in Images of Women in Contemporary Fiction (1976) and Soviet Women Writing (1981).

BARAQUIO, Angela Perez (1976—). Miss America. Born Angela Perez Baraquio, June 1, 1976, in Mililani, Hawaii; dau. of Claudio and Rigolette Baraquio; graduate of University of Hawaii at Manoa, 1999. ❖ Representing Hawaii, named Miss America (2001), the 1st teacher and 1st Asian-American to be crowned; teaches phys. ed. at Holy Family Catholic Academy.

BARASCU, Aurica (1974—). Romanian rower. Born Sept 21, 1974, in Romania. ❖ At World championships, placed 2nd for coxed eight (2003); won a gold medal for coxed eight at Athens Olympics (2004).

BARAT, Madeleine Sophie (1779–1865). French saint. Born in Joigny, France, Dec 12, 1779; died in Paris, France, May 25, 1865; dau. of

Jacques (vinegrower) and Marie-Madeleine (Fouffé) Barat; educated at home by her brother Louis, a priest; accompanied him to Paris in 1880 to continue her education. ❖ With 4 other women, established 1st Society of the Sacred Heart in Amiens (1802), where she became superior general and head of school for girls; devoted herself to expanding schools of "Madames of the Sacred Heart," a religious congregation known in Europe and US primarily for education of young ladies of wealth and position, which numbered 86 at time of her death (1865); after death, body 1st taken to Conflans, but when her nuns were driven out of France it was removed to Jette, Belgium, where it was enshrined; beatified (1908) and canonized (1925). ❖ See also Mother C.E. Maguire, Saint Madeleine Sophie Barat (Sheed & Ward, 1960); and Women in World History.

BARATOTTI, Galerana (1604–1652). See Tarabotti, Arcangela.

BARBARA (fl. 3rd c.). Christian martyr and saint. Lived and suffered martyrdom in the city of Nicomedia in Bithynia, Asia Minor, c. 235; the place of her martyrdom is variously given as Heliopolis, as a town of Tuscany, and as Nicomedia, Bithynia; dau. of Dioscorus. ❖ Spent youth receiving philosophers, orators, and poets dispatched by father to instruct her in meaning of all things; without his knowledge, became converted to Christianity by a follower of Origen and secretly baptized; threw out statues of the "false gods" and resolved to remain a virgin, dedicated to God; when father threatened to kill her, fled to the mountains but was captured and handed over to Martianus, Roman governor of Bithynia, to be dealt with by law; when Martianus failed in his attempts to make her repudiate Christianity, her head was cut off by father in punishment (he was then struck by lightning); became patron saint of storms and artillery. Feast day is Dec 4. ❖ See also Women in World History.

BARBARA, Agatha (1923–2002). Maltese president. Born Mar 11, 1923, in Zabbar, Malta; died Feb 4, 2002; honored by a state funeral; eldest dau. and 2nd of 9 children of Joseph and Antonia Barbara. ❖ Educated in Valletta and became a schoolteacher; contested General Elections (1947) for Malta Labour Party and became 1st woman elected to House of Representatives; sentenced to 43 days hard labor for picketing in the national strike (1958); served as minister of Education (1958–58, 1971–74), introducing compulsory and full-time education up to age 14; also served as minister of Labour, Culture, and Welfare, and acting prime minister several times; became 1st female president of Malta (1982), serving until 1987; was the 1st woman to successfully contest every election from 1947 until her retirement; served on many delegations to international conferences.

BARBARA OF BRAGANZA (1711–1758). See Maria Barbara of Braganza.

BARBARA OF BRANDENBURG (1422–1481). Marquesa of Mantua. Name variations: Barbara Gonzaga. Born 1422; died 1481; dau. of John III the Alchemist, margrave of Brandenburg, and Barbara of Saxe-Wittenberg (c. 1405–1465); sister of Dorothea of Brandenburg (1430–1495), queen of Norway, Denmark, and Sweden; m. Louis also known as Ludovico Gonzaga (1412–1478), 2nd marquis of Mantua (r. 1444–1478); children: Federico (1441–1484), 3rd marquis of Mantua (r. 1478–1484); Francesco (1444–1483, a cardinal); Gianfrancesco (1446–1496), lord of Rodigo; Susanna Gonzaga (1447–1461); Dorotea Gonzaga (1449–1462); Rodolfo (1451–1495); Cecilia Gonzaga (1451–1472); Barbara Gonzaga (1455–1505); Louis also known as Ludovico (1460–1511, bishop of Mantua); Paola Gonzaga (1463–1497).

BARBARA OF BYZANTIUM (d. 1125). Grand princess of Kiev. Name variations: Barbara Comnena. Died Feb 28, 1125; m. Svyatopolk also known as Sviatopolk II, prince of Kiev (r. 1093–1113), around 1103; children: possibly Zbyslawa (d. 1110).

BARBARA OF CILLI (fl. 1390–1410). Queen of Hungary and Bohemia. Name variations: Borbala Cillei; Barbara Cilli. Flourished from 1390 to 1410; dau. of Count William of Cilli; 2nd wife of Zygmunt also known as Sigismund I of Luxemburg, king of Hungary and Bohemia (r. 1387–1437), Holy Roman emperor (r. 1410–1437); children: Elizabeth of Luxemburg (1409–1442), who m. Albert II, king of Hungary). Sigismund I's 1st wife was Maria of Hungary (1371–1395). ❖ See also Women in World History.

BARBARA OF POLAND (1478–1534). Duchess of Saxony. Born July 15, 1478; died Feb 15, 1534; dau. of Casimir IV Jagiellon (or Kazimierz), grand duke of Lithuania (r. 1440–1492), king of Poland (r. 1446–1492), and Elizabeth of Hungary (c. 1430–1505); m. George the Bearded (1471–1539), duke of Saxony (r. 1500–1539),

Nov 21, 1496; children: Christine of Saxony (1505–1549); Magdalene of Saxony (1507–1534).

BARBARA OF SAXE-WITTENBERG (c. 1405–1465). Margravine of Brandenburg. Born c. 1405; died Oct 10, 1465; dau. of Rudolf III, duke of Saxe-Wittenberg; m. John III the Alchemist (b. 1406), margrave of Brandenburg, 1412; children: Dorothea of Brandenburg (1430–1495); Barbara of Brandenburg (1422–1481).

BARBARA RADZIWELL (1520–1551). Queen of Poland. Name variations: Radziwill. Born 1520; died 1551; dau. of a Lithuanian *Hetman* (general); sister of Nicholas the Black Radziwell and cousin of Nicholas the Red Radziwell, both princes of Lithuania; married the last of the Gasztolds (died); became 2nd wife of Zygmunt August also known as Sigismund II Augustus, king of Poland (r. 1548–1572). ❖ Secretly eloped with Sigismund, shocking her mother-in-law Bona Sforza, as well as the Polish Sejm (Parliament). ❖ See also *Women in World History.*

BARBARA ZAPOLYA (fl. 1500). Queen of Poland. Name variations: Barbara Zápolya of Hungary; Szapolyai. Sister of John or Jan Zapolya, king of Hungary (r. 1526–1540); 1st wife of Sigismund I the Elder, king of Poland (r. 1506–1548); children: Hedwig of Poland (1513–1573, who m. Joachim II, elector of Brandenburg). Sigismund's 2nd wife was Bona Sforza (1493–1557).

BARBARINA, La (1721–1799). *See Campanini, Barbara.*

BARBAULD, Anna Letitia (1743–1825). English author. Born Anna Laetitia Aikin in Kibworth-Harcourt, Leicestershire, England, June 20, 1743; died Mar 9, 1825, in Stoke-Newington, London; dau. of John Aikin (Unitarian minister and schoolmaster, who taught her Latin and Greek); sister of English physician John Aikin; aunt of Lucy Aikin; m. Reverend Rochemont Barbauld, 1774 (died 1808). ❖ Published 1st volume, *Poems* (1773), which ran through 4 editions in a year; co-authored (with brother) volume of *Miscellaneous Pieces in Prose* and, later, series of prose sketches, *Evenings at Home* (1792–95); with husband, founded a boys' boarding school in Suffolk (1774) and wrote *Hymns in Prose and Early Lessons* for the pupils; wrote devotional works *Early Lessons for Children* and *Devotional Pieces;* became well known in London literary circles; wrote life of Samuel Richardson; edited Mark Akenside's *Pleasures of the Imagination,* William Collins' *Odes,* and a collection of *British Novelists* with memoirs and criticisms; produced works distinguished by pure moral tone, simplicity, and sincerity; authored books for children which were considered among best of their class; wrote last work, "Eighteen Hundred and Eleven," an ode which gave a pessimistic view of Britain and its future. A collected edition of her works, with memoir, was published by her niece, Lucy Aikin, in 2 vols. (1825). ❖ See also A.L. le Breton, *Memoir of Mrs Barbauld* (1874); G.A. Ellis, *Life and Letters of Mrs. A.L. Barbauld* (1874); Lady Thackeray Ritchie, *A Book of Sibyls* (1883); and *Women in World History.*

BARBER, Alice (1858–1932). *See Stephens, Alice Barber.*

BARBER, Fanny (c. 1864–1952). Irish murderer. Name variations: Fanny Malone. Born c. 1864 in Ireland; died 1952 in prison; m. William Barber, 1912. ❖ Shot husband to death in home in Cultra, Ireland (1933); arrested (1934), was charged with murder; tried and sentenced to death by hanging (1935), had sentence commuted to life in prison; maintained her innocence until she died (1952).

BARBER, Margaret Fairless (1869–1901). British mystic and nature writer. Name variations: (pseudonym) Michael Fairless. Born Margaret Fairless Barber, May 7, 1869, in Castle Hill, Rastrick, Yorkshire, England; died Aug 24, 1901, in Mock Bridge, Henfield, England; youngest of 3 daughters of Fairless (lawyer) and Maria (Musgrave) Barber; sister of A.M. Haggard, writer; educated at Torquay and London, and a children's hospital near London; never married; no children. ❖ As a nurse, was the "Fighting Sister" in the London slum of Jago, known for breaking up street fights and fending off violent patients (1886–91); during a philanthropic venture to London (1899), grew suddenly ill, was taken in by the Dowson family, and never left; turned to art, of which her greatest success was a crucifix for a London church; took up writing, publishing *Brother Hilarius* in a magazine under the name Michael Fairless (1901), then dictated the last chapter of *The Roadmender* as she lay dying. The publication of *The Roadmender* (1902), a meditative exploration of the road to heaven, created an instant clamor for information about its mystical author; already admired for a tract about the Black Death, she remained unidentified, until her sister, A.M. Haggard, revealed her true identity (1913); later works published

include *The Child King* (1902), *Grey Brethren* (1905) and *The Complete Works of Michael Fairless* (1931). ❖ See also Palmer, William Scott (M.E. Dowson) and A.M. Haggard, *Michael Fairless: Her Life and Writing* (1913).

BARBER, Mary (c. 1690–1757). Irish poet. Name variations: (pseudonym) Sapphira. Born c. 1690 in Ireland; died 1757 in Dublin; m. Jonathan Barber; children: 4, including Constantine Barber (president of Irish College of Physicians). ❖ Encouraged in 1730s by Jonathan Swift to publish poetry, wrote *Poems on Several Occasions* (1734); poems also appeared in collections *Poems by Eminent Ladies* (1755), *Brookiana* (1804) and *Eighteenth-Century Women Poets* (1989).

BARBER, Mary (1911–1965). English pathologist. Born April 3, 1911, in England; killed in a road accident, Sept 1965; London School of Medicine for Women, MB and BS, 1936, MD, 1940. ❖ Published 1st paper on *Listeria* meningitis (1937); issued results showing increase of penicillin resistance in staphylococci (1947); served as assistant pathologist and lecturer in bacteriology (1940–48), reader in clinical bacteriology (1958–63), and professor (1963–65) at British Postgraduate Medical School (BPMS), Hammersmith; studied cross-infection by staphylococci and developed policy at Hammersmith Hospital restricting use of antibiotics and recommending use of antibacterial drugs in combination; served at other hospitals, including Hill End and the City Hospitals, St. Albans (1939–40), and St. Thomas's Hospital (1948–58); published in many journals and coauthored (with L.P. Garrod) *Antibiotic and Chemotherapy* (1963); was among the 1st pathologists to show development of bacteria that was resistant to penicillin.

BARBER, Mary (1919–2004). *See Henderson, Mary.*

BARBERI, Maria (1880–?). Italian-American murderer. Born 1880. ❖ At 15, promised marriage by her lover Domenico Cataldo who apparently had no intention of marrying her; after he refused her pleas to make her an honest woman, sliced his throat in NY saloon (1895); convicted of 1st-degree murder, was sentenced to death by electrocution; her cause became national issue as progressives and conservatives alike opposed execution of the 15-year-old; won a new trial at which defense successfully argued "physical epilepsy" (term now replaced with "insanity"); though found to be insane, was released.

BARBERINA, La (1721–1799). *See Campanini, Barbara.*

BARBI, Alice (1862–1948). Italian mezzo-soprano and lieder singer. Born June 1, 1862, in Modena, Italy; died in Rome, Italy, Sept 4, 1948; m. 2nd husband Pietro della Torretta (Italian ambassador to Great Britain). ❖ Debuted as a concert singer in Milan (1882), which was soon followed by a highly successful appearance in Rome; enjoyed star status as a concert performer throughout Italy, specializing in lieder; appeared in Great Britain (1884), drawing large crowds at London's Popular Concerts series, then performed in Russia, Germany and Austria; upon marriage, gave farewell recital in Vienna (Dec 21, 1893); also composed some small-scale works and edited a collection of ancient Italian airs; for many decades a major celebrity in the highest strata of European diplomacy and the arts, having chosen as her 2nd husband the Italian ambassador to Great Britain; largely remembered for having been "the last love of Johannes Brahms"—a platonic friendship that brightened his final years. ❖ See also *Women in World History.*

BARBIER, Adèle Euphrasie (1829–1893). New Zealand nun, teacher, religious founder. Name variations: Marie du Coeur de Jésus. Born Adèle Euphrasie Barbier, Jan 4, 1829, at Caen, Normandy, France; died Jan 18, 1893, at Westbere, Kent, England; dau. of Louis-Désiré Barbier (shoemaker) and Jeanne Adèle (Le Cler) Barbier. ❖ Joined Sisters of Calvary and trained as teacher (1848); founded Congregation of Our Lady of the Missions (1860s); recruited sisters for new order, founding 8 houses and establishing school for Maori girls. ❖ See also *Dictionary of New Zealand Biography* (Vol. 2).

BARBIER, Marie-Anne (c. 1670–1742). French dramatist. Born c. 1670 in Orléans, France; lived in Paris; died 1742 in France; married; children: 1 daughter. ❖ One of the most successful dramatists of her day, had 4 of her tragedies staged at Comédie-Française (1702–10); despite her achievements, and those of a small number of other female dramatists, no further tragedies by women were produced (1717–49), so she moved on to other works, including editing the journal *Saisons littéraires* (1714), which documented many of her feminist ideals; writings include *Brutus, tragédie* (1691), *Arrie et Pétrus* (1702), *Cornélie, mère des Graques* (Cornelia, Mother of the Gracchi, 1703), *Tomyris* (adapted from Madelaine de Scudéry's *Le Grand Cyrus,* 1707), *La mort de César*

(The Death of Caesar, 1710), *Le Théâtre de l'amour et de la fortune* (The Theater of Love and Fortune, 1713); *Les fêtes de l'été, ballet* (Summer Festivities, a Ballet, 1716); *Le jugement de Paris, pastorale héroique* (The Judgment of Paris, a Historic Pastoral, 1718), *La Faucon, comédie* (The Falcon, a Comedy, 1719), *Les plaisirs de la campagne, ballet* (Country Delights, a Ballet, 1719).

BARBIERI, Fedora (1919–2003). Italian mezzo-soprano. Born June 4, 1919, in Trieste, Italy; died Mar 4, 2003, in Florence, Italy; studied with Luigi Toffolo and Giulia Tess; m. Luigi Barlozzetti (music director), 1943 (died 1993); children: 2 sons. ❖ Debuted in Florence as Fidalma in *Matrimonio segreto* (1940); made debut as Meg Page in *Falstaff* at Teatro alla Scala (1942); after 1946, was a regular performer at Teatro alla Scala; made Metropolitan Opera debut as Eboli in Verdi's *Don Carlos* (1950); appeared often at the Met (1950–68), singing 95 performances of 11 roles; also debuted at Covent Garden (1950); other roles included Azucena, Amneris, and Mistress Quickly in "Falstaff." ❖ See also *Women in World History.*

BARBIERI, Margaret (1947—). South African ballet dancer. Born Mar 2, 1947, in Durban, South Africa; great-great niece of Enrico Cecchetti. ❖ Trained in South Africa before moving to London to study at school of Royal Ballet; joined Royal Ballet (1965) and appeared in such works as John Cranko's *Pineapple Poll*, Peter Wright's *El Amor Brujo*, and as "Swanilda" in *Coppélia*; created roles in numerous works, including Antony Tudor's *Knight Errant* (1968), Joe Layton's *O.W.* (1972), Ronald Hynd's *Charlotte Brontë* (1974) and David Drew's *Sacred Circles* (1974).

BARBIROLLI, Evelyn (b. 1911). *See Rothwell, Evelyn.*

BARBOSA, Pilar (1898–1997). Puerto Rican historian. Born Pilar Barbosa de Rosario, July 4, 1897, in San Juan, Puerto Rico; died in San Juan, Jan 22, 1997; dau. of José Celso Barbosa (founder of Puerto Rican statehood movement); her mother died when she was quite young; University of Puerto Rico, BEd, 1924; Clark University, MA, 1925; m. José Ezequiel Rosario (economics professor), 1927 (died 1963); no children. ❖ Widely regarded as the conscience of the ruling New Progressive Party, taught at University of Puerto Rico (1926–67); established and headed history and social sciences department at university, the 1st woman to head a department there (1927); collaborated with Dr. Antonio S. Pedreira on series of articles on history of Puerto Rico (1937); was president and founder of La Obra de José Celso Barbosa y Alcalá, Inc.; received 1st of four 1st prizes from Puerto Rican Institute of Literature for book on Puerto Rican autonomism (1887); with others, founded Historical Society of Puerto Rico (1967); retired from university (1967); received Golden Book Award for 50 years service to Puerto Rican education (1967); recognized by University of Puerto Rico as professor emeritus (1975); given US Outstanding Leadership Award by President Ronald Reagan and National Institute of Education (1984); appointed Official Historian of Puerto Rico (1993); at 99, honored with plaque for lifetime achievement by House of Representatives of Puerto Rico (1997). ❖ See also *Women in World History.*

BARBOUR, Joyce (1901–1977). English stage actress. Born Mar 27, 1901, in Birmingham, England; died Mar 14, 1977. ❖ Made London debut in the chorus of *Tonight's the Night* (1915), followed by *Yes Uncle, Irene, London Calling, The Punch Bowl, Shake Your Feet, Ever Green, Fanfare, Words and Music, Hay Fever, The Greeks Had a Word For It, George and Margaret, Blithe Spirit* and *Cry Liberty*, among others; made Broadway debut in *Havoc* (1924), followed by *Present Arms, Spring is Here* and *Jonica*; also appeared in films.

BARBULOVA-KELBECHEVA, Siyka (1951—). Bulgarian rower. Born Dec 1, 1951. ❖ Won a gold medal at Montreal Olympics (1976) and a bronze medal at Moscow Olympics (1980), both in coxless pairs.

BARCA, Frances Calderón de la (1804–1882). *See Calderón de la Barca, Frances.*

BARCA-THEODOSIA (fl. 800s). Byzantine empress. Married Leo V Gnuni, the Armenian, Byzantine emperor (r. 813–820).

BARCELO, Gertrudis (c. 1820–1852). Entrepreneur and monte dealer. Name variations: La Tules (diminutive of Gertrudis); Doña Gertrudis; Señora Doña Gertrudis Barcelo. Born c. 1820, possibly in Valencia Co., New Mexico; death date unknown; buried in Santa Fe, New Mexico, Jan 17, 1852; dau. of Juan Ignacio and Dolores Herrero (Barcelo); m. Manuel Antonio Sisneros, June 20, 1823; children: Jose Pedro (b. 1823) and Miguel Antonio (b. 1825). ❖ Settled in Santa Fe, New

Mexico, and learned to play Spanish-American card game of monte well enough to become expert at dealing; saved enough from winnings to establish her own gambling house and saloon of repute, or disrepute, depending on the account (though accusations of prostitution surfaced, there seems to be no solid proof of impropriety); amassed a relative fortune and lived well; said by some to have provided assistance to poor and church, but did not seem to be known for her philanthropy; at time of death, was reportedly worth about $10,000, a great sum for the day. ❖ See also *Women in World History.*

BARCELONA, countess of. *See Maria de las Mercedes (b. 1910).*

BARCITOTTI, Galerana (1604–1652). *See Tarabotti, Arcangela.*

BARCLAY, Florence Louisa (1862–1921). English romance author. Name variations: (pseudonym) Brandon Roy. Born Florence Louisa Charlesworth, Dec 2, 1862, in Limpsfield, Surrey, England; died Mar 10, 1921; dau. of Reverend Samuel Charlesworth; niece of Maria Charlesworth (children's author); sister of Maud Ballington Booth (1865–1948); m. Reverend Charles W. Barclay, 1881; children: 6 daughters, 2 sons. ❖ Published romance novels, including *The Rosary* (1910), which sold more than 1 million copies by 1921; other writings include *The Wheels of Time* (1908), *The Following of the Star* (1911) and *The White Ladies of Worcester* (1917). ❖ See also *The Life of Florence L. Barclay: By One of Her Daughters* (1921); and *Women in World History.*

BARCLAY-SMITH, Phyllis (1903–1980). British ornithologist. Name variations: Phyllis Ida Smith. Born 1903 in England; died Jan 2, 1980; dau. of a professor of anatomy at Cambridge University. ❖ Served as assistant secretary at Royal Society for the Protection of Birds (1924–35); served as assistant secretary (1935–46), secretary (1946–74), and secretary general (beginning 1974) at International Council for Bird Preservation and is credited with building up the organization to its current status; served as editor of *Avicultural Magazine* (1939–73); trans. ornithology books from French and German, including *Birds of the World* (1954) and *The Bird* (1951); writings about birds (under name Phyllis Smith) include *British and American Game Birds* (1939), *Birds of Lake, River, and Stream* (1939), *Garden Birds* (1945), *A Book of Ducks* (1951) and *Woodland Birds* (1955). Was the 1st woman named Member of the British Empire (MBE) for work in conservation (1958); made CBE (1971).

BARD, Mary (1904–1970). American writer. Name variations: Mary Ten Eyck Bard; Mary TenEyck Bard; Mary TenEyck Bard Jensen. Born Nov 21, 1904, in Butte, Montana; died 1970; dau. of Darsie Campbell Bard (mining engineer) and Elsie Tholimar (Sanderson) Bard; sister of Betty MacDonald (writer, 1908–1958); University of Washington, 1924–26; m. Clyde Reynolds Jensen (pathologist), 1934; children: Mary, Sally, Heidi. ❖ Wrote several books that detailed events in her personal life with humorous slant, including *The Doctor Wears Three Faces* (1949), *Forty Odd* (1952) and *Just Be Yourself* (1956); also wrote several books for young girls, including *Best Friends* (1955), *Best Friends in Summer* (1960), and *Best Friends at School*. ❖ See also *Women in World History.*

BARDACH, Georgina (1983—). Argentinean swimmer. Born Aug 18, 1983, in Argentina. ❖ Won a bronze medal for 400-meter indiv. medley at Athens Olympics (2004).

BARDET, Anne-Lise (1974—). French kayaker. Name variations: Anne Lise Bardet. Born Nov 1974 in Oyannax, France. ❖ Won a bronze medal for K1 slalom at Sydney Olympics (2000).

BARDI, Contessina de. *See Medici, Contessina de.*

BARDIN, Madeleine (c. 1920—). French ballet dancer. Born c. 1920 in Paris, France. ❖ Joined ballet company of Paris Opéra and danced there for most of her career; gave most notable performances in works by Serge Lifar, including *Les Mirages, La Péri* and *Le Chevalier et la demoiselle*; moved to New York City to perform in Cyril Richard's *La Péricole* (c. 1956) and remained in US.

BARDOTTE, Brigitte (1934—). French actress. Name variations: BB. Born Sept 28, 1934, in Paris, France; m. Roger Vadim (director), 1952 (div. 1957); m. Jacques Charrier, 1959 (div, 1962); m. Gunther Sachs, 1966 (div. 1969); m. Bernard d'Ormale, 1992; children: Nicholas Charrier (actor). ❖ Made film debut in *Le Trou normand* (Crazy for Love, 1952); came to prominence in *Et Dieu créa la Femme* (And God Created Woman, 1956); other films include *Dear Brigitte, Contempt, Viva Maria!, Babette Goes to War, Helen of Troy, Don Juan, Spirits of the Dead, Come Dance with Me!, La Vérité, Vie privée, Love on a Pillow, Shalako* and

Les Femmes; retired from acting (1973); established Foundation for the Protection of Distressed Animals (1976). ❖ See also Simone de Beauvoir's *Brigitte Bardot and the Lolita Syndrome* (1960).

BARDWAY, Mohini (1978—). *See Bhardwaj, Mohini.*

BARDWELL, Leland (1928—). Irish novelist, playwright and poet. Born Leland Hone, 1928, in India, of Irish parents; brought to Ireland at age 2, grew up in Leixlip, Co. Kildare; attended Alexandra College, Dublin, and London University; m. Michael Bardwell (sep.); children: 6. ❖ Poetry includes *The Mad Cyclist* (1970), *Dostoevsky's Grave: New and Selected Poems* (1991), and *The White Beach: New and Selected Poems 1960–1998* (1998); novels include *Girl on a Bicycle* (1978), *That London Winter* (1981), *The House* (1984), *There We Have Been* (1989) and *Mother to a Stranger* (2002); also published short stories and stage and radio plays.

BAREA, Ilse (1902–1973). *See Kulcsar, Ilse.*

BAREA COBOS, Maria (1966—). Spanish field-hockey player. Born Oct 1966. ❖ At Barcelona Olympics, won a gold medal in team competition (1992).

BAREL, Olesya (1960—). Soviet basketball player. Born Feb 9, 1960. ❖ At Seoul Olympics, won a bronze medal in team competition (1988).

BARET, Jeanne (1740–after 1795). French adventurer. Name variations: Jeanne Barret, Jeanne Mercadier. Born into modest circumstances in Bourgogne, France, 1740; died after 1795; married a soldier named Antoine Barnier (or Antoine Du Bernat). ❖ Worked in Paris as servant for botanist Philibert Commerson; posing as a male valet named Bonnefoy, became the 1st woman to circumnavigate the globe by participating in an expedition led by Louis-Antoine de Bougainville (1764); while on the expedition, assisted Commerson in his botanical field trips, on which they discovered a sizeable body of new botanical data, including the South American climbing plant *Bougainvillea,* named for the captain; returned to France after Commerson's death (1773); achieved status of celebrity and was granted an annual pension by Louis XV; had reputation further enhanced by Bougainville's favorable description of her participation, published in his account of voyage (1771). The genera *Baretia* and a species of plant, *Bonna fidia,* were named in her honor. ❖ See also *Women in World History.*

BARFOOT, Joan (1946—). Canadian novelist. Born May 17, 1946 in Owen Sound, Ontario, Canada; University of Western Ontario, BA in English (1969). ❖ One of Canada's most prominent contemporary writers, worked as a journalist for *London Free Press, The Owen Sound Sun-Times, The Windsor Star* and *The Toronto Sun;* published 1st novel *Abra* (1978), followed by *Dancing in the Dark* (1982) which was made into an award-winning film; other novels include *Duet for Three* (1985), *Family News* (1989), *Plain Jane* (1992), *Charlotte and Claudia Keeping in Touch* (1994), *Some Things About Flying* (1997) and *Getting Over Edgar* (1999). Received YM-YWCA Women of Distinction award (1986) and Marian Angel award (1992); was short-listed for Trillium Award for *Critical Injuries* (2001).

BARI, Judi (1949–1997). American environmentalist. Born Judith Beatrice Bari, Nov 7, 1949, in Baltimore, Maryland; died of breast cancer, Mar 2, 1997, near Willits, California; dau. of Arthur and Ruth Bari; sister of Gina Kolata (science reporter for *New York Times*); attended University of Maryland; m. Mike Sweeney, 1979 (div.); children: Lisa and Jessica. ❖ Principal leader of the non-violent Earth First! movement in northern California, who was crippled by a car bomb while fighting to save California's redwood forests (May 24, 1990).

BARI, Lynn (1913–1989). American stage, tv, and screen actress and dancer. Born Marjorie Schuyler Fisher, Dec 18, 1913, in Roanoke, Virginia; died Nov 20, 1989, in Santa Barbara, California; m. 2nd husband Sid Luft (producer). ❖ Made film debut as a member of the chorus in *Dancing Lady* (1933); appeared in musical films, including *Search for Beauty* (1934), *George White Scandals* (1935), *Sing and Be Happy* (1937) and *Pigskin Parade* (1936); hung up tap shoes and played leads and second leads in such films as *Thanks a Million, Sun Valley Serenade, The Magnificent Dope, Orchestra Wives, The Bridge of San Luis Rey, Margie* and *The Women of Pitcairn Island;* also appeared in several Charlie Chan and Mr. Moto mysteries; joined the touring cast of *Follies* (1973).

BARI, Nina K. (1901–1961). Russian mathematician. Born Nina Karlovna Bari, Nov 19, 1901, in Moscow, Russia; died by falling in front of train on Moscow Metro, July 15, 1961; dau. of a physician; m. V.V. Nemytski. ❖ Studied under Luzin at Moscow School of Mathematics; taught (from 1921) and performed research (from 1926) at Research Institute of Mathematics and Mechanics, Moscow State University; received doctorate for work on trigonometric series (1926); became professor at Moscow State University and published 1st textbook, *Higher Algebra* (1932); published 2nd textbook, *The Theory of Series* (1936); edited complete works of Luzin and trans. into Russian *Lebesgue's* book on integration; wrote more than 50 articles and edited 2 mathematical journals.

BARI, Tania (1936—). Dutch dancer. Born July 5, 1936, in Rotterdam, the Netherlands. ❖ Joined Maurice Béjart troupe Ballet de l'Etoile (1955), before becoming a charter member of Béjart's Ballet du XXième Siècle in Brussels, Belgium (1960); created roles in numerous Béjart works throughout career, including *Sonate à Trois* (1957); *Sacre du Printemps* (1959), *Ninth Symphony* (1964) and *Bhakti* (1968); retired from stage (1973).

BARIATINSKY, Princess (1869–1921). *See Yavorska, Lydia.*

BARINE, Arvède (1840–1908). French biographer and historian. Name variations: Arvede Barine or Arvede-Baraine; Mme Charles Vincens. Born 1840 in France; died 1908; m. Charles Vincens. ❖ Works include *Portraits de femmes* (1887), *Princesses et grandes dames* (1890) and *Poètes et névrosés* (1898); also wrote literary essays, philosophical articles, and socio-political commentary for major journals.

BARKENTIN, Marjorie (c. 1891–1974). American publicist and writer. Born c. 1891; died Feb 24, 1974, age 83, in New York, NY. ❖ Was a founder member of the Association of Theatrical Press Agents and Managers; under the supervision of Padraic Colum, dramatized *Ulysses in Nighttown* (1970–71).

BARKER, A.L. (1918–2002). British novelist and short-story writer. Name variations: Audrey Lillian Barker. Born Audrey Lillian Barker, April 13, 1918, in Kent, England; died Feb 21, 2002; dau. of Harry Barker and Elsie A. Dutton Barker. ❖ Best known for short stories which were often described as ghostly, surreal, or Kafkaesque, also wrote novels; works include *Innocents: Variations on a Theme* (1947), *Apology for a Hero* (1950), *A Case Examined* (1965), *The Middling* (1967), *John Brown's Body* (1969), *A Source of Embarrassment* (1974), *No Word of Love* (1985), *The Gooseboy* (1987) and *Seduction* (1994). Was 1st recipient of Somerset Maugham award (1947); elected fellow of Royal Society of Literature (1970).

BARKER, Audrey Lillian (1918–2002). *See Barker, A.L.*

BARKER, Mrs. C.F. (1902–1995). *See Cooper, Susie.*

BARKER, Cicely Mary (1895–1973). British children's-book author and illustrator. Born in Waddon, Croydon, Surrey, England, June 28, 1895; died in Worthing, Sussex, England, Feb 16, 1973; dau. of Walter (seed merchant and woodcarver) and Mary Eleanor Oswald Barker; sister of Dorothy Barker (b. 1893); attended Croyden School of Art. ❖ Began commercial career at 15, with sale of painted postcards to printer-publisher Raphael Tuck; became youngest member of Croydon Art Society and served as vice-president (1961–72); best known for "Flower Fairies" series of self-illustrated children's books; also produced portraits and church murals, and a painting, "The Darling of the World is Come," which was purchased by Queen Mary of Teck. ❖ See also *Women in World History.*

BARKER, Florence (b. 1908). English swimmer. Born 1908 in Great Britain. ❖ At Paris Olympics, won a silver medal in 4 x 100-meter freestyle relay (1924).

BARKER, Francine (1947—). American singer. Name variations: Francine Hurd, Francine Hurd Barker; Peaches and Herb. Born Francine Hurd in 1947 in Washington, DC. ❖ Was lead singer of group, Sweet Things; with Herb Fame, formed duo Peaches and Herb (1965) and had hit with 1st single, "Let's Fall in Love" (1967), on pop and rhythm-and-blues charts; other hits include "Close Your Eyes" (1967), "United" (1968) and "When He Touches Me" (1969); left Peaches and Herb (1968–69); with Fame, signed with Columbia Records, but was unsuccessful, then released singles on duo's own label, BS (mid-1970s); was replaced by Linda Green (1977).

BARKER, Helen Granville (d. 1950). *See Granville-Barker, Helen.*

BARKER, Jane (1652–1732). British novelist and poet. Name variations: (pseudonyms) Galesia, Fidelia, A Young Lady. Born May 17, 1652, in Blatherwicke, Northamptonshire, England; died Mar 29, 1732, in Saint Germain-en-Laye, France; dau. of Thomas Barker (tenant farmer) and

Anne (Connock) Barker; sister of Edward Barker; never married; no children. ❖ Early feminist and one of the 1st female British novelists, grew up in rural Lincolnshire and was assured education through Royalist brother's encouragement and tutoring, becoming one of the rare, educated women of the 17th century; moved to London with mother after death of brother and father, who had gone to battle on behalf of Charles I against the usurpation of William III of Orange; because of Catholic sympathies, fled to France with exiled court of James II; returned to England (1713) and began publishing; works include *Poetical Recreations: Consisting of Original Poetry Songs, Odes & c. With Several New Translations* (1688), *Love Intrigues; or, the history of the amours of Bosvil and Galesia* (1713), *Exilius, or, The Banish'd Roman* (1715), *The Christian Pilgrimage* (1718), *The Entertaining Novels of Mrs. Jane Barker* (1719), *A Patch-Work Screen for the Ladies* (1723); *Lining of the Patch-Work Screen* (1726) and *The Galesia Trilogy and Selected Manuscript Poems of Jane Barker* (1997).

BARKER, Kate "Ma" (1872–1935). *See Barker, Ma.*

BARKER, Kylene (c. 1956—). Miss America. Name variations: Kylene Hibbard. Born c. 1956; graduate of Virginia Polytechnic Institute and State University; m. Ralph Hibbard (Canadian businessman and dept. store owner), 1992. ❖ Named Miss America (1979), representing Virginia; made frequent tv appearances; author of *Southern Beauty*; co-owner with husband of Great American Sportswear in Toronto (1992–2000).

BARKER, M.C. (1879–1963). American educator and union leader. Name variations: Mary Barker; Mary Cornelia Barker; Mary C. Barker. Born Mary Cornelia Barker, Jan 20, 1879, in Atlanta, Georgia; died Sept 15, 1963, in Atlanta; dau. of Thomas Nathaniel Barker and Dora Elizabeth (Lovejoy) Barker. ❖ Educator who combined creative teaching methods with discipline and worked for higher salaries and continuing education for teachers; taught at Ivy Street School (1904–21), then was principal (1922–23); served as principal at John B. Gordon School (1923–44), in Atlanta, GA; was a founder (1905) and board member of Atlanta Public School Teachers' Association; served as president of Local 89 (1921–23); supported adoption of constitutional amendment to ban child labor (1924); served as 3rd president of American Federation of Teachers (1925–31); joined organizing committee of Southern Summer School for Women Workers in Industry (1926) and chaired the school's central committee (1927–44).

BARKER, Ma (1872–1935). American outlaw. Name variations: Arizona Donnie Clark; Kate "Ma" Barker. Born Arizona Donnie Clark, near Springfield, Missouri, 1872; died in Oklawaha, Florida, Jan 16, 1935; m. George Barker, c. 1892; children: Herman, Lloyd, Dock and Fred. ❖ Middle-aged woman with a motherly face who had an outlaw mentality rivaling that of Jesse James, lived as a model Presbyterian wife and mother of 4 boys before setting up "cooling off" service for convicts or crooks on the run; masterminded robberies, kidnappings, and murders for Barker Gang (also known as the Holden-Keating Gang) in the Missouri-Oklahoma area for 12 years (1920s), terrorizing businessmen and bankers; died in fierce shootout with FBI agents (1935). ❖ See also *Women in World History.*

BARKER, Mary Anne (1831–1911). British Commonwealth writer. Name variations: Lady Mary Anne Barker; Lady Broome. Born Mary Anne Stewart, 1831, in Spanish Town, Jamaica; died Mar 6, 1911, in London, England; dau. of W.G. Stewart (Jamaican Island secretary); educated in England; m. Captain George Barker (officer in Royal Artillery), c. 1852 (died 1861); m. Frederick Napier Broome, June 21, 1865 (died 1896); children: (1st m.) John Stewart (b. 1853) and Walter George (b. 1857); (2nd m.) Hopton Napier (1866–1866), Guy Saville (b. 1870), and Louis Egerton (b. 1875). ❖ A literary legend and trailblazer in New Zealand, who is best known for her early histories of colonial life there, arrived in New Zealand with 2nd husband (1865); returned to England (1868) and took up journalism to help support family; published letters she had penned to family while in New Zealand as *Station Life in New Zealand* (1870); earned appointment as superintendent for National Training School for Cookery (London) for *First Lessons in the Principles of Cookery* (1874); joined husband on assignments in a number of British-held territories and documented colonial life; after 2nd husband was knighted (1884), became Lady Broome; also wrote *Travelling About Over Old and New Ground* (1871), *A Christmas Cake in Four Quarters* (1872), *Station Amusements in New Zealand* (1873), *A Year's Housekeeping in South Africa* (1877), *Letters to Guy* (1885) and *Colonial Memories* (1904).

BARKER, Mary Cornelia (1879–1963). *See Barker, M.C.*

BARKING, abbess of.
See Ethelburga (d. 676?).
See Segrave, Anne (fl. 1300s).
See Katherine of Sutton (d. 1376).

BARKLEY, Jane Hadley (1911–1964). American memoirist. Name variations: Elizabeth Rucker; Jane Hadley. Born Elizabeth Jane Rucker, 1911, in Keytesville, Ohio; died Sept 6, 1964, in Washington, DC; m. (2nd m.) Alben W. Barkley (35th vice president of US who had been married to Dorothy Brower), Nov 1949; children: (stepchildren) David Murrel Barkley, Marion Frances Barkley, and Laura Louis Barkley. ❖ Widowed at 34, later married the 78-year-old widowed Vice President Alben W. Barkley, then serving under President Harry S. Truman (1949), becoming the 1st woman to marry a vice president who was already in office; wrote *I Married the Veep* (1958), two years after his death.

BARKMAN, Jane (1951—). American swimmer. Born Sept 20, 1951. ❖ At Mexico City Olympics, won a bronze medal in the 200-meter freestyle and a gold medal in the 4 x 100-meter freestyle relay (1968); at Munich Olympics, won a gold medal in the 4 x 100-meter freestyle relay (1972).

BARKOVA, Anna Aleksandrovna (1901–1976). Russian writer. Name variations: Ánna Aleksándrovna Barkóva; (pseudonym) Kalika Perekhozhaia (Wandering Cripple or Wandering Beggar-Bard). Born Anna Aleksandrovna Barkova, July 16, 1901, in Ivanovo-Voznesensk, Russia; died April 29, 1976, in Moscow; never married; no children. ❖ Joined "Circle of Genuine Proletarian Poets" and published 1st poems in their newspaper *Workers' Land*; was invited to Moscow by Lenin's commissioner of education, Anatoli Lunarcharski, who promised to advance her poetry and offered her work as his secretary (1922); published 1st vol. of collected poems, *Woman* (1922); received help from Marie Ulyanova, Lenin's sister, who assisted in securing work at *Pravda*; left in peril after Lenin's death and Stalin's assumption of power; arrested for writings (1934); released (1939) and exiled to Kaluga for duration of WWII; imprisoned again (1947) and not released until Khrushchev's general amnesty (1956); convicted a year later of mailing manuscripts with content "dangerous to society" and returned to prison for another 8 years; released for last time (1965) and forbidden to publish; lived in Moscow, "rehabilitated" (from 1967); work rediscovered after *glasnost* (1989). ❖ See also *Women in World History.*

BARLOIS, Valerie (1969—). French fencer. Name variations: Valerie Barlois-Mevel, then Valerie Barlois-Leroux. Born May 28, 1969, in France. ❖ Won a silver medal for indiv. épée and a gold medal for team épée at Atlanta Olympics (1996).

BARLOW, Billie (1862–1937). English actress and singer. Name variations: Minnie Barlow. Born Minnie Barlow, July 18, 1862, in London, England; died Feb 11, 1937; m. E.M. Stuart. ❖ As Minnie Barlow, made stage debut in *H.M.S. Pinafore* (1878) and NY debut as Isabel in *The Pirates of Penzance* (1879); other plays include *Patience* and *Adonis*; made 1st variety show appearance at the Metropolitan (1888), followed by the Alhambra, London Pavilion, Tivoli, and Paragon; popularized such songs as "It's English, Quite English, You Know," "See Me Dance the Polka," "Do Buy Me that, Mama Dear," "I Want to Look as Well as You," "Mashing the Band," "Save a Nice One for Me" and "Bubbles."

BARLOW, Hannah (1851–1916). English ceramic decorator. Born Hannah Bolton Barlow, 1851, in Little Hadham, Hertfordshire, England; died 1916 in England; dau. of Benjamin Iram Barlow (bank manager) and Hannah Barlow; attended Lambeth School of Art and Design, 1868–70. ❖ The 1st woman artist to work for Henry Doulton's pottery firm, excelled in wildlife decorations; along with brother Arthur, sister Florence, and other local artists, helped secure the success of the firm through innovative decorating, turning utilitarian stoneware and earthenware into artistic creations; exhibited terracotta reliefs and sculptures at Royal Academy (1881–90); also exhibited at Dudley Gallery, Society of British Artists and Walker Art Gallery, Liverpool.

BARLOW, Jane (c. 1857–1917). Irish poet and critic. Born Jane Barlow in Clontarf, Co. Dublin, Ireland, c. 1857; died April 17, 1917, in Bray, Ireland; dau. of Reverend James William Barlow (vice provost of Trinity College, Dublin) and Mary Louisa Barlow; educated at home; never married; no children. ❖ Received honorary degree from Trinity College (1904), though institution did not formally accept women;

published 1st book *Bogland Studies* (1892); wrote some dozen or so volumes during 20-year career; writings, which often concerned peasant-life in Ireland, include *Irish Idylls* (1892), *Kerrigan's Quality* (1893), *Maureen's Fairing* (1895), *Strangers at Lisconnel* (1895), *Ghost-Bereft* (1901), *By Beach and Bogland* (1905), *Flaws* (1911) and *In Mio's Path* (1917).

BARLOW, Lucy (c. 1630–1658). See *Walter, Lucy.*

BARLOW, Minnie (1862–1937). See *Barlow, Billie.*

BARNACLE, Nora Joseph (1884–1951). See *Joyce, Nora.*

BARNARD, A.M. (1832–1888). See *Alcott, Louisa May.*

BARNARD, Lady Anne (1750–1825). See *Lindsay, Lady Anne.*

BARNARD, Hannah Jenkins (d. 1825). American Quaker minister. Born c. 1754, most likely in Nantucket, Massachusetts; died 1825; m. Peter Barnard, before 1780. ❖ In Hudson (NY) Quaker colony, served as highly respected minister of the Hudson Monthly Meeting (beginning 1793); conducted a religious visit to Friends in England, Scotland and Ireland with Elizabeth Hosier Coggeshall (beginning July 1798); charged with heresy at the London Yearly Meeting, was eventually censured and ordered home; silenced as a minister in America (1802) and disowned by the local meeting.

BARNARD, Kate (1875–1930). American political reformer. Born Catherine Ann Barnard in Geneva, Nebraska, May 23, 1875; died in Oklahoma City, Oklahoma, Feb 23, 1930; dau. of John Barnard (lawyer and surveyor) and Rachel (Shiell) Barnard (died 1877); attended Oklahoma City Business College; never married; no children. ❖ Ran for commissioner of Oklahoma's newly formed charities and corrections department (c. 1907) and defeated Republican opponent by over 35,000 votes, making her, at 32, the 1st woman ever elected to statewide post by an all-male electorate; served 2 terms; worked on behalf of child-labor laws, compulsory education, progressive labor legislation, homeless children, improving care of mental patients, providing juvenile offenders a better chance for reform, securing pension benefits for laborers' widows, and prison reform; also worked for safety laws and inspections in mines and factories; battled Indian guardianship fraud. ❖ See also *Women in World History.*

BARNARD, Marjorie (1897–1987). Australian author. Name variations: (joint pseudonym with Flora Eldershaw) M. Barnard Eldershaw. Born Marjorie Faith Barnard, Aug 16, 1897, in Sydney, Australia; died 1987 in Sydney; dau. of Ethel Frances (Ashford) and Oswald Holmes Barnard; educated at University of Sydney; never married; no children. ❖ With Flora Eldershaw, wrote more than 20 books under joint pseudonym M. Barnard Eldershaw; contributed the majority of the books' text, while Eldershaw cultivated publishers and readers; though a fiction writer, had a greater passion for the history of Australia, particularly Sydney; under her name alone, published *Macquarie's World* (1941), begun as Barnard-Eldershaw project, initiating some independent work on each writer's behalf; served for 12 years as librarian at Sydney Technical College (beginning 1920); writings—as M. Barnard Eldershaw—include *A House is Built* (1929), *Green Memory* (1931), *The Glasshouse* (1936), *Plaque with Laurel* (1937) and *Tomorrow and Tomorrow* (1947); writings as Marjorie Barnard include *The Ivory Gate* (1920), *The Persimmon Tree and Other Stories* (1943), *Sydney: The Story of a City* (1956), *Australia's First Architect: Francis Greenway* (1961), *A History of Australia* (1962) and *Miles Franklin* (1967). ❖ See also Louise E. Rorabacher, *Marjorie Barnard and M. Barnard Eldershaw* (Twayne, 1973); and *Women in World History.*

BARNES, Binnie (1903–1998). English-born actress. Born Gittel Enoyce Barnes, Mar 25, 1903, in London, England; died July 27, 1998, in Beverly Hills, California; m. Samuel Joseph, 1931 (div. 1937); m. Mike Frankovich (producer), 1940 (died 1992); children: Peter and Michael Frankovich Jr. and Michelle Frankovich De Motte (b. 1944). ❖ Made London stage debut in *Charlot 1928*, followed by *The Silver Tassie, Little Tommy Tucker* and *Cavalcade*; made film debut in England (1929), then appeared in 26 two-reel comedies for Stanley Lupino; portrayed Catherine Howard in *The Private Life of Henry VIII* (1933), then left for Hollywood (1934); other films include *Diamond Jim* (as Lillian Russell), *The Last of the Mohicans, Broadway Melody of 1938, Holiday, The Three Musketeers* and *The Trouble with Angels.*

BARNES, Catharine (1851–1913). See *Ward, Catharine Barnes.*

BARNES, Charlotte Mary Sanford (1818–1863). American poet, playwright, novelist and actress. Name variations: Charlotte Mary Sanford Barnes Connor. Born Charlotte Mary Sanford Barnes, 1818; died April 14, 1863, in New York, NY; dau. of Mary Barnes (actress); m. Edmund Sheppard Connor (actor), 1847. ❖ Made stage debut at the Tremont in Boston (1933), playing Juliet to her mother's Romeo; writings include retelling of story of Pocahontas, *The Forest Princess* (1848), and of a 19th-century murder, *Octavia Bradaldi* (1837).

BARNES, Debra Dene (c. 1947—). Miss America. Name variations: Debra Miles. Born Debra Dene Barnes, c. 1947, in Moran, Kansas; majored in music at Kansas State College of Pittsburgh; m. Mitchell Miles (minister); children: 2 daughters. ❖ Named Miss America (1968), representing Kansas; serves as music director at husband's church; teaches piano at Missouri Southern State College. ❖ See also Frank Deford, *There She Is* (Viking, 1971).

BARNES, Djuna (1892–1982). American writer. Name variations: (pseudonym) Lydia Steptoe. Born Djalma Barnes Chappell, Jan 12, 1892, in Cornwall-on-Hudson, New York; died in New York, NY, June 18, 1982; dau. of Elizabeth Chappell and Henry Budington (later Wald Barnes); studied painting at Pratt Institute and at Art Students League in NY, 1915–16; m. Courtenay Lemon, 1917 (div. 1919); lived with Thelma Wood, 1920–31. ❖ Left home for Greenwich Village (1912); started publishing short stories (1913); published 1st book *The Book of Repulsive Women* (1915); established herself as writer of the avant-garde (1915–20); moved to Paris (1920); published *Ladies Almanack* (1928), which centers on lesbian circles she frequented (especially that surrounding Natalie Clifford Barney) and *Ryder* (1928), which uses mock-Elizabethan style to chronicle her family history; contributed to *Vanity Fair, New Republic, The New Yorker* and other publications, sometimes under name Lydia Steptoe; published *Nightwood* (1936), which became cult classic and earned her needed financial support; returned to NY (1939); published play about her family, *The Antiphon* (1958), which earned positive reviews after premiere at Royal Theatre, Stockholm (1961), but was never produced in English; served as trustee, Dag Hammarskjöld Foundation (beginning 1961); offered membership by National Institute of Arts and Letters; with radical departure from realism and conventional narrative structures, embraced dense symbolism and earned reputation as leader of modernist movement along with James Joyce, T.S. Eliot, and Ezra Pound; also known for focus on women's sexuality, on social circles dominated by women, and on same-sex attraction between women. ❖ See also Andrew Field, *Djuna: The Life and Times of Djuna Barnes* (Putnam, 1983); Phillip Herring, *The Life and Work of Djuna Barnes* (Viking, 1995); and *Women in World History.*

BARNES, Jhane (1954—). American designer. Born Mar 4, 1954, in Baltimore, Maryland. ❖ Won the coveted Coty Award, the 1st year it was offered for menswear (1980); served as president of the New York based Jhane Barnes, Inc.

BARNES, Josephine (1912–1999). English obstetrician and gynecologist. Name variations: Dame Josephine Barnes; Josephine Warren. Born Alice Josephine Mary Taylor Barnes, Aug 18, 1912, in Shorlingham, Norfolk, England; died Dec 28, 1999; dau. of a Methodist minister and a pianist; Lady Margaret Hall, Oxford, BA with honors in physiology, 1934, MA, BM, BCh, 1937; University College Hospital Medical School, MD, 1941; m. Sir Brian Warren (lieutenant in Royal Army Medical Corps), 1942; children: 3. ❖ During WWII, delivered babies during bombing in London; held various positions at University College Hospital, including deputy academic head of the Obstetric Unit (1947–52); headed steering committee for 2 government maternity surveys (1948–70); held positions at Radcliffe Infirmary, Oxford (1939–45), Elizabeth Garrett Anderson Hospital (1945–77), and Marie Curie Hospital (surgeon 1947–67), among others; was the 1st woman to be appointed consultant gynecologist at Charing Cross Hospital (1954); served as 1st woman president of British Medical Association (1979–80); writings include *Gynaecological Histology* (1948) and *Essentials of Family Planning* (1976). Made DBE (1974).

BARNES, Juliana (c. 1388–?). See *Berners, Juliana.*

BARNES, Kirsten (1968—). Canadian rower. Born Mar 26, 1968. ❖ At Barcelona Olympics, won a gold medal in coxed eights and a gold medal in coxed fours (1992).

BARNES, Lucy. See *Brown, Lucy.*

BARNES, Margaret Ayer (1886–1967). American novelist and playwright. Born Margaret Ayer, April 8, 1886, in Chicago, Illinois; died Oct 25, 1967, in Cambridge, Massachusetts; dau. of Janet and Benjamin F. Ayer (general counsel to Illinois Central Railroad); sister of Janet Ayer Fairbank (novelist); attended University School for Girls, Chicago; graduate of Bryn Mawr College, 1907; m. Cecil Barnes (lawyer), May 21, 1910; children: Cecil Jr. (b. 1912), Edward Larrabee (b. 1915) and Benjamin Ayer (b. 1919). ❖ Began writing while bedridden after car accident, publishing in *Pictorial Review;* published novel *Years of Grace* (1930), which won the Pulitzer Prize (1931); subjects included the social history of upper-class Midwest and the need, regardless of financial or social status, for women to have a vocation to broaden the scope of their daily lives; following death (1967), her manuscripts were donated to Harvard and New York Public libraries; writings include (play) *The Age of Innocence* (1928), (play) *Jenny* (1929), (play) *Dishonored Lady* (1930), *Westward Passage* (1931), *Within This Present* (1933) and *Wisdom's Gate* (1938). ❖ See also Lloyd C. Taylor Jr., *Margaret Ayer Barnes* (Twayne, 1974); and *Women in World History.*

BARNES, Mary Ann (1836–1885). See Colclough, Mary Ann.

BARNES, Mary Downing (1850–1898). American educator. Born Mary Downing Sheldon in Oswego, NY, Sept 15, 1850; died 1898; dau. of educator Edward Austin Sheldon (1823–1892), who founded the Oswego State Normal School; studied at Oswego State Normal School, University of Michigan, and in Cambridge and Zurich; m. Earl Barnes, 1885. ❖ The 1st teacher in US to use the Pestalozzian method in teaching history, joined staff of Wellesley College (1876) and began experimenting with what she called the "source" method, which emphasized use of various source materials and promoted critical thought; returned to Oswego Normal School to teach history, Latin, Greek, and botany (1882); moved to CA (1891) and joined history department at Stanford; published *Studies in American History: Teachers' Manual* (1892). ❖ See also *Women in World History.*

BARNES, Monica (1936—). Irish politician. Born Monica McDermott, Feb 1936, in Carrickmacross, Co. Monaghan, Ireland; m. Bob Barnes, 1962. ❖ Served as secretary, Council of the London Stock Exchange; served as administrator, Council for the Status of Women (1978–81); representing Fine Gael, elected to the 24th Dáil (1982–87) for Dún Laoghaire; returned to 25th–26th Dáil (1987–1992) and 28th Dáil (1997–2002); elected to Seanad from Labour Panel (1982).

BARNES, Pancho (1901–1975). American stunt pilot. Born Florence Lowe in Pasadena, California, 1901; died in Boron, California, 1975; dau. of a wealthy Pasadena family that suffered reverses in the 1929 Depression. ❖ Appeared in Howard Hughes' movie *Hell's Angels* (1929), the 1st woman stunt pilot in motion pictures; flew in 1st Women's Air Derby, taking 1st place in the 2nd stage of the race before damaging plane and withdrawing; set new women's speed record of 196.19 miles per hour; became 1st woman to fly from Los Angeles to Mexico City; helped launch a transcontinental race for women (1931); was part of flying group that supplied emergency disaster assistance; purchased 80-acre ranch abutting Edwards Air Force Base in the Mojave desert (1933), which she later turned into a resort facility.

BARNES, Ryllis (1906–1978). See Hasoutra.

BARNES, Winifred (1894–1935). English actress and singer. Born Dec 18, 1894, in England; died April 5, 1935; m. Roy Faulkner. ❖ Made stage debut in *Our Miss Gibbs* (1909), followed by *A Country Girl, The Happy Day, Anthony in Wonderland, Soldier Boy, Maggie, Angel Face, The Three Graces* and title role in *Arlette.*

BARNES, Zadel (1841–1917). Feminist writer. Name variations: Zadel Budington (also seen as Buddington); Zadel Barnes Gustafson. Born Zadel Barnes in 1841; died 1917; married Henry Budington (div. c. 1879); married once more; children: Henry Budington Jr. (known as Ward Barnes); grandmother of Djuna Barnes (writer). ❖ Published stories and poems under maiden name in major magazines, including *Harper's* (1870s–80s); wrote novels with feminist themes. ❖ See also *Women in World History.*

BARNETT, Etta Moten (1902–2004). See Moten, Etta.

BARNETT, Henrietta (1851–1936). English philanthropist and social-welfare activist. Name variations: Dame Henrietta Octavia Weston Barnett. Born Henrietta Octavia Weston Rowland, 1851, in Clapham, London, England; died 1936 in England; m. Samuel Augustus Barnett (Anglican curate of St Mary's, Bryanston Square; canon of St Jude's Whitechapel; co-founder of Toynbee Hall), 1873. ❖ Worked with social-activist Octavia Hill at St. Mary's, Bryanston Square; moved with husband to parish of St. Jude's Whitechapel, supporting him in an arduous 33-year ministry; participated in founding and running Toynbee Hall, part of the settlement-house movement which called for university-educated young people to settle in areas of poverty to promote social welfare; helped open evening schools for adults, Saturday schools for children, vocational training and construction model dwellings for poor, and Henrietta Barnett School for girls (1911); advocated Christian Socialism, as expounded in husband's *Practicable Socialism* (1885); developed independent interests which included welfare of servants and children, Children's Country Holiday Fund, London Pupil Teachers' Association, and preservation of Hampstead Heath. Named Dame Commander of British Empire (DBE, 1924).

BARNETT, Ida B. or Ida Wells (1862–1931). See Wells-Barnett, Ida.

BARNETT, Pamela (1944—). American golfer. Born Mar 2, 1944, in Charlotte, North Carolina; graduate of Winthrop College. ❖ Dominated Carolina golf for several years as an amateur; joined LPGA tour (1966); won Southgate Open (1971); tied for 2nd in USGA Women's Open (1972).

BARNEY, Alice Pike (1857–1931). American portrait artist. Born Alice Pike in 1857; died in Hollywood, California, 1931; dau. of Samuel Pike (Dutch-Jewish entrepreneur who built an opera house for Cincinnati); m. Albert Clifford Barney (industrialist, president of Barney Railroad Car Foundry); studied in Paris with James McNeill Whistler; married, at age 52, 22-year-old Christian Dominick Hemmick, c. 1909; children: (1st m.) Natalie Clifford Barney (1876–1972, writer) and Laura Barney (b. 1879). ❖ Heiress and bohemian activist, known for her portraiture, who arrived in Washington DC with 1st husband and set out to change the city (1889); built Studio House in Sheridan Circle and hosted diverse endeavors, including her theatrical productions. Following her death (1931), her daughters donated the house to Smithsonian Institution, which sponsored the exhibit *Alice Pike Barney: Pastel Portraits from Studio House* (1985). ❖ See also *Women in World History.*

BARNEY, Elvira Dolores (c. 1905–c. 1936). English woman charged with murder. Born c. 1905 in England; died c. 1936; married (sep.). ❖ After her 24-year-old lover Michael Scott Stephen was found shot to death at her Knightsbridge home (May 31, 1932), claimed shooting was accidental; tried for murder at Old Bailey, was defended by Patrick Hastings and found not guilty; moved to France; found dead 4 years later in a Paris hotel bedroom.

BARNEY, Maginel Wright (1881–1966). See Wright, Maginel.

BARNEY, Natalie Clifford (1876–1972). American-born expatriate author. Born Natalie Clifford in Dayton, Ohio, Oct 31, 1876; died in Paris, France, Feb 3, 1972; dau. of Alice Pike Barney (painter and arts patron) and Albert Clifford Barney (industrialist, president of Barney Railroad Car Foundry); sister of Laura Barney (b. 1879); never married; had a 50-year relationship with Romaine Brooks. ❖ Author, translator, and foremother of feminist literature, lived in Paris with sister and mother (1887–1901); began affair with famous courtesan Liane de Pougy (c. 1899), the 1st of many; engaged briefly to Lord Alfred-Douglas, Oscar Wilde's former lover (1900); met and began affair with Anglo-American writer and poet, Renée Vivien (1900); after father's death (1902), became independently wealthy and moved permanently to Paris; wrote 6 of her 14 books during liaison with Vivien; met painter Romaine Brooks sometime before WWI and started long-term liaison; moved to 20 rue Jacob in Faubourg St. Germain and launched salon for leading writers and intellectuals of the day (1909); met influential but reclusive writer and critic Remy de Gourmont (1910), who published Brooks-Barney correspondence with Barney's approval in *Mercure de France* (1912–13), establishing Barney as a literary figure; remained in Paris and ran salon during WWI; launched Académie des Femmes (Academy of Women) to celebrate and support women writers (1927); moved to Florence with Brooks during WWII (1939); after the war, revived salon in Paris and ran it until 1968; writings include *Quelques portraits-sonnets de femmes* (1900), *Cinq petits dialogues grecs* (1901), *The Woman Who Lives with Me* (1904), *Eparpillements* (1910), *Je me souviens* (1910), *Pensées d'une Amazone* (1920), *Aventures de l'esprit* (1929), *The One Who Is Legion, A.D.'s After-Life* (1930), *Souvenirs indiscrets* (1960) and *Traits et portraits* (1963). ❖ See also Natalie Clifford Barney, *Adventures of the Mind* (trans. by John Gatton, New York U. Press, 1992); Jean Chalon, *Portrait of a Seductress* (Crown, 1979); George

Wickes, *The Amazon of Letters: The Life and Loves of Natalie Barney* (Putnam, 1976); and *Women in World History.*

BARNEY, Nora (1883–1971). American civil engineer and architect. Name variations: Nora Blatch or Nora Stanton Blatch; Nora de Forest; Nora Stanton Barney or Nora Stanton Blatch Barney. Born Nora Stanton Blatch, Sept 30, 1883, in Basingstoke, England; died Jan 18, 1971, in Greenwich, Connecticut; dau. of William Henry Blatch and Harriot Stanton Blatch (1856–1940, feminist); granddau. of Elizabeth Cady Stanton; Cornell University, graduated cum laude, 1905, the 1st woman at Cornell to receive a degree in civil engineering; m. Lee de Forest (inventor of the radio vacuum tube), Feb 1908 (div. May 1912); m. Morgan Barney (naval architect), 1919; children: (1st m.) Harriet de Forest (b. 1909); (2nd m.) Rhoda Barney (b. 1920), John Barney (b. 1922). ❖ The 1st woman member of the American Society of Civil Engineers, began career as an assistant engineer and chief draftsman for Radley Steel Construction Co., then as assistant engineer for New York Public Service Commission; as an active member of Women's Political Union (WPU), campaigned to gain voting rights for women in NY (1909–17); edited WPU publication, *Women's Political World,* and served as union's executive secretary, becoming union president (1915); designed and built homes in CT (1923–71); was appointed engineering inspector for Public Works Administration in CT and RI (1934); wrote pamphlet, *World Peace Through a Peoples Parliament* (1944); investigated by House Committee on Un-American Activities for being a member of Congress of American Women (1950), but never testified; was a strong supporter of Equal Rights Amendment.

BARNICOAT, Constance Alice (1872–1922). New Zealand secretary, interpreter, mountaineer, and journalist. Name variations: Constance Alice Grande. Born Constance Alice Barnicoat, Nov 27, 1872, in Richmond, Nelson, New Zealand; died Sept 16, 1922, in Geneva, Switzerland; dau. of John Wallis Barnicoat (politician) and Rebecca Lee (Hodgson) Barnicoat; Canterbury College, BA, 1895; m. Israel Julian Grande (journalist and lecturer), 1911. ❖ Versed in several languages, became New Zealand's 1st official woman shorthand reporter (1896); worked as translator for *Review of Reviews* (1898) and joined reviewing staff (early 1900s); served as secretary and interpreter at Hague Peace Conference (1899); actively pursued mountaineering, participating in expeditions throughout Europe (1905–11); with husband, edited multilingual monthly journal to counter German propaganda during WWI. Mt. Barnicoat in Southern Alps named in her honor. ❖ See also *Dictionary of New Zealand Biography* (Vol. 3).

BARNS, Cornelia Baxter (1888–1941). American illustrator and political activist. Name variations: Cornelia Barns Garbett. Born Cornelia Baxter Barns in Philadelphia, Pennsylvania, 1888; died 1941; dau. of Charles Barns (impresario); studied art at Philadelphia Academy of Fine Arts; m. Arthur Selwyn Garbett (music critic); children: Charles (b. 1915). ❖ One of the few women illustrators to appear in the Socialist press, contributed drawings to radical magazine *The Masses* (1914–17) until its suppression by government; stricken with tuberculosis, moved to California (1917); continued to draw and also worked as a journalist; contributed to such journals as *Liberator, New Masses, Suffragist* and *Woman Voter;* served briefly as associate editor and art director of *Birth Control Review* (1921); for many years, published daily editorial vignette, "My City Oakland," which appeared in *Oakland Post Enquirer.* ❖ See also *Women in World History.*

BARNS-GRAHAM, Wilhelmina (1912–2004). Scottish painter. Name variations: Willie Barnes-Graham. Born June 8, 1912, in St. Andrews, Fife, Scotland; died Jan 26, 2004; attended Edinburgh College of Art, 1932–37; m. David Lewis (writer), 1949 (div. 1960s). ❖ Widely-regarded as one of most popular abstract painters in Scotland, moved to Cornwall upon graduation from college and became a founding member of the Penwith Society of Arts, working with Ben Nicholson and Barbara Hepworth; traveled widely throughout Europe; joined St. Ives Group, a younger group of artists which included Roger Hilton and writer David Lewis, who would become husband (1949); taught at Leeds School of Art (1956–57) and in London (1960–63); worked initially in figurative tradition but embraced abstraction (1960s–70s), with square becoming dominant motif; returned to live and work in St. Andrews (1973); revitalized career with survey exhibition *St. Ives 1939–64* at Tate Gallery in London (1985); returned later to direct painting, particularly large watercolors and gouaches in brilliant color; had many highly acclaimed shows, including retrospective (1989–90) and *W Barns-Graham at 80* (1992–93) as well as 3 exhibitions with Art First (1995, 1997, 1999); included in public collections throughout UK, including Scottish National Galley of Modern Art, Arts Council of Great Britain, British Museum, Tate Gallery and Victoria and Albert Museum; painted well into late 80s, living in St. Ives. Named Commander of British Empire (CBE, 2001).

BARNUM, Gertrude (1866–1948). American labor reformer. Born Sept 29, 1866, in Chester, Illinois; died June 17, 1948, in Los Angeles, California. ❖ Served in Chicago at Jane Addams' Hull House (1890s) and as head worker of Henry Booth House (1902–03); was national organizer for National Women's Trade Union League (early 1900s), special agent of International Ladies' Garment Workers' Union (1911–16), special agent for President Wilson's US Commission on Industrial Relations (1914), assistant director of investigation service at Department of Labor (1918–19), and officer of Harriot Stanton Blatch's Equality League of Self-Supporting Women.

BARNWELL, Barbara Olive (c. 1919–c. 1977). American staff sergeant. Possibly born Aug 14, 1919; lived in Pittsburgh, Pennsylvania; possibly died April 1977 in Santa Barbara, California. ❖ Staff sergeant and reservist in the US Marines, saved a drowning soldier (1952); was awarded the US Navy-Marine Corps medal for heroism (Aug 7, 1953), the 1st woman to receive this distinction.

BARON, Devorah (1887–1956). Israeli novelist. Name variations: Deborah Baron. Born 1887 in Uzda, Russia; died 1956 in Israel; dau. of a Russian rabbi; m. Joseph Aharonovitz (magazine editor). ❖ Emigrated from Russia to Palestine (1911); began publishing stories of shtetl life in journal *Ha-Po'el ha Za'ir* (The Young Worker), edited by soon-to-be-husband Joseph Aharonovitz; managed literary supplement for *Ha-Po'el;* writings include (stories) *Sipurim* (1927), (episodes) *Parshiyot* (1968), and *The Thorny Patch* (1969); also trans. Flaubert's *Madame Bovary.* ❖ See also *Women in World History.*

BARON, Emilie (c. 1834–1852). French ballet dancer. Name variations: Marie Pescaline Dreville. Born Marie Pescaline Dreville, c. 1834, possibly in Paris; died Nov 19, 1852, in St. Louis, Missouri. ❖ Debuted at Thomas Placide's Théâtre des Variétés, Paris (1849); performed for Placide for 3 consecutive years including in his *La Fête de Terpsichore, La Statue vivante, Le Carnaval de Venise* and *Giselle;* helped differentiate between ballet dancer and specialty dancer when she sued Placide for demanding she dance polka comedy "as an artiste in ballets and fairy scenes" (1851); died in fire caused by gas lighting during performance in St. Louis.

BARON, Mietje (1908–1948). Dutch swimmer. Born Marie Baron, Feb 5, 1908, in Rotterdam, Netherlands; died July 23, 1948, in Rotterdam. ❖ At Amsterdam Olympics, won a silver medal in the 200-meter breaststroke (1928).

BARON, Ria. See Falk, Ria.

BARONE, Marian E. (1924–1996). American gymnast. Name variations: Marian Twining. Born Marian Twining, Mar 18, 1924, in Philadelphia, Pennsylvania; died May 1996 in Philadelphia. ❖ At London Olympics, won a bronze medal in all-around team (1948); won US gymnastic championships for uneven bars (1945, 1951) and vault (1950).

BARONESS ALBERTA (1913–1995). See Ballesteros, Mercedes.

BARONESS OF STOKE NEWINGTON (1942—). See Blackstone, Tessa.

BARONI, Adriana Basile (c. 1590–c. 1640). See Basile, Adriana.

BARONI, Leonora (1611–1670). Italian opera singer. Born 1611; died 1670; dau. of Adriana Basile (Italian singer) and Mutio Baroni; sister of Caterina Baroni (1620–?). ❖ Famed as a singer in Italy and France, was often accompanied by her mother on the theorbo, while her sister Caterina Baroni played the harp.

BARONOVA, Irina (1919—). Russian ballerina. Born Mar 13, 1919, in Petrograd (now St. Petersburg), Russia; studied at College Victor-Hugo, Paris; studied ballet with Olga Preobrazhenska in Paris; m. German Sevastianov, 1940 (div.); m. Cecil G. Tennant, 1949 (died 1967); children: (2nd m.) 3. ❖ Discovered by George Balanchine while attending Preobrazhenska School in Paris; at 13, with Tatiana Riabouchinska and Tamara Toumanova, was one of the "baby ballerinas" of Ballet Russe de Monte Carlo (1932); created roles of princess in *The Hundred Kisses,* Passion in *Les Présages,* Josephina in *Choreartium, Scuola di Ballo,* Boulotte in *Bluebeard,* Helen in *Helen of Troy* and First Hand in *Le Beau Danube;* also danced *Aurora's Wedding, Swan Lake, Les Sylphides, Coq d'Or, Coppélia, La Fille Mal Gardée, Petrouchka, Le Spectre de la Rose* and *Jeux d'Enfants;* danced in films *Florian* (MGM, 1939) and

Yolanda (Mexico, 1942), in musical *Follow the Girls* (1944), with Léonide Massine's *Ballet Russe Highlights* (1945), and in musical *Bullet in the Ballet* and comedy *Black Eyes* (both England, 1946); retired from stage (1946). ❖ See also *Women in World History*.

BAROT, Madeleine (1909–1995). **French anti-Nazi resistance leader.** Born July 4, 1909, in Chateauroux, France; died Dec 29, 1995, in Paris. ❖ Human-rights activist, Protestant leader in ecumenical movement, and celebrated hero of the French Resistance, joined the French Reformed Church and was leader at First World Conference of Christian Youth (1939); appointed general secretary of refugee relief organization, Comité Inter-Mouvement Auprés des Evacués (CIMADE); joined resistance and risked life to assist Jews escaping Spain and Switzerland; worked for social reconstruction and ecumenical cooperation after WWII; served on board of Young Women's Christian Association (1945–50); worked for World Council of Churches (1953–73) and was appointed director of Department on the Co-operation of Men and Women in Church and Society (1953–66); staunch defender of women's rights, worked to promote greater role for women in Protestant church; joined Christian Action for the Abolition of Torture (ACAT) and worked through Protestant relief agency CIMADE on industrial, rural and social education in developing countries. Named Righteous Gentile by Israel's Yad Vashem; received French Legion of Honor.

BARR, Amelia Huddleston (1831–1919). **British-American author.** Name variations: Amelia Edith Barr. Born Amelia Faith Huddleston, Mar 29, 1831, in Ulverston, Lancashire, England; died Mar 10, 1919, in New York; dau. of Mary Singleton and William Henry Huddleston (Methodist minister); educated at home and in private schools; m. Robert Barr (1826–1867), July 11, 1850, in Kendal, England; children: 13, including 4 who died at birth, and Mary (b. 1851), Eliza (called Lilly, b. 1853), Edith (b. 1854), Calvin (b. 1857), Alice (b. 1859), Ethel (b. 1861), Alexander (b. 1863), Archibald (b. 1864), and Andrew (b. 1867). ❖ Left England for New York (1853); began writing career; was a regular contributor to Henry Ward Beecher's *Christian Union;* won critical acclaim with publication of *Jan Vedder's Wife* (1885); known for her historical tales that dealt with religious persecution and for her scenes of Scotland, the north of England, and Dutch New York; produced more than 80 books in 40 years of writing. ❖ See also autobiography, *All the Days of My Life* (1913).

BARR, Beth (1971—). **American swimmer.** Name variations: Cynthia Barr. Born Dec 17, 1971, in US. ❖ At Seoul Olympics, won a silver medal in the 4 x 100-meter medley relay (1988).

BARR, Cynthia (1971—). See Barr, Beth.

BARR, Margaret Scolari (1901–1987). **Italian-born American art historian.** Born Margaret Scolari, 1901, in Rome; died in New York, NY, Dec 30, 1987; dau. of Virgilio Scolari (antiques dealer) and Mary Fitzmaurice Scolari; studied at University of Rome, 1919–22; m. Alfred Barr (founding director of Museum of Modern Art), 1930; children: daughter Victoria (painter). ❖ Came to US (1925); taught at Vassar College (1925–29); helped husband accrue MoMA exhibits (1930–81); during WWII in France, was active with the Emergency Rescue Committee (1940–41), which brought to US artists whose lives were threatened in Nazi-occupied Europe, including Max Ernst, Piet Mondrian, Jacques Lipchitz, Yves Tanguy and André Masson; taught art history at Spence School (1943–80). ❖ See also *Women in World History*.

BARR, Roseanne (b. 1952). See Roseanne.

BARRA (c. 590–640/41). See Zaynab bint Jahsh.

BARRA, Emma de la (1861–1947). **Argentinean novelist, singer and painter.** Name variations: Ema de la Barra; Emma de la Barra de Llanos; (pseudonym) César Duayen or Cesar Duayen. Born 1861 in Rosario, Argentina; died 1947 in Buenos Aires; dau. of Federico de la Barra and Emilia Gonzalez Funes; married her uncle Juan de la Barra (died 1904); m. Julio Llanos. ❖ After death of husband, began writing and painting; wrote articles and short stories for magazines and newspapers; novels include *Stella* (1905), *Mecha Iturbe* (1906) and *Eleanora*.

BARRAINE, Elsa (1910–1999). **French composer.** Born Jacqueline Elsa Barraine, Feb 13, 1910, in Paris, France; died Mar 20, 1999, in Strasbourg; studied at Paris Conservatory with Paul Dukas for composition and Jean Gallon for harmony. ❖ Considered one of the most gifted composers since Lili Boulanger, won the Prix de Rome for *La vierge guerriere* (1929); was Chef du Chant for RTF (Radio Télevision Français, 1936–39); during WWII, was with Front National des Musiciens; appointed professor of musical analysis at the Paris Conservatory (1953); composed 3 symphonies, a comic opera, and several pieces for chorus.

BARRAUD, Sarah Maria (c. 1823–1895). **New Zealand letter writer.** Name variations: Sarah Maria Style. Born Sarah Maria Style, c. 1823 (baptized, Aug 10, 1823), at Wraysbury, near Windsor, England; died Mar 8, 1895, at Wellington, New Zealand; dau. of Robert Style (farmer) and Elizabeth (Haines) Style; m. Charles Decimus Barraud (pharmacist and artist), 1849; children: 9. ❖ Immigrated with husband to Wellington (1849); wrote numerous letters to relatives describing domestic life in New Zealand. ❖ See also *Dictionary of New Zealand Biography* (Vol. 1).

BARRAULT, Marie-Christine (1944—). **French actress.** Born Mar 21, 1944, in Paris, France; niece of Madeleine Renaud (1903–1944, actress) and Jean-Louis Barrault (actor); m. Daniel Toscan du Plantier (div.); m. Roger Vadim (director), 1990 (died 2000); children: (1st m.) 2. ❖ Made film debut in *Ma nuit chez Maud* (My Night at Maude's, 1969); came to prominence in *Cousin, cousine* (1975); other films include *Le Distrait* (1970), *Les Intrus* (1972), *Du côté des tennis* (1976), *The Medusa Touch* (1978), *Ma chérie* (1980), *Stardust Memories* (1980), *Table for Five* (1983), *Pianoforte* (1984), *Paradigma* (1985), *Vaudeville* (1986), *Sanguine* (1988), *Bonsoir* (1994), *La Dilettante* (1999), *Azzurro* (2000) and *L'Empreinte de l'ange* (2004); frequently appeared on French tv, including in such miniseries as "Que ferait donc Faber?" (1969), "Le Miroir 2000" (1971), "Le Village sur la colline" (1982), "L'Ami Maupassant" (1986), "Marie Curie, une femme honorable" (1990), "La Nouvelle tribu" (1996) and "Garonne" (2002).

BARRE, Alexandra (1958—). **Canadian kayaker.** Born Jan 29, 1958. ❖ At Los Angeles Olympics, won a bronze medal in the K4 500 meters and silver medal in the K2 500 meters (1984).

BARRE, Margot de la (d. 1390). **French woman.** Name variations: Du Coignet. ❖ Accused of sorcery, was tried and burned at the stake (1390).

BARRENO, Maria Isabel (1939—). **Portuguese writer and feminist.** Name variations: The Three Marias. Born in Lisbon, Portugal, July 10, 1939; granted degree in historic and philosophical sciences from Lisbon Arts Faculty; married with children. ❖ Employed in the National Institute of Industrial Research; participated in the writing of *A Condicão da Mulher Portuguesa* (1968); published 1st novel, *De Noite as Arvores São Negras* (1968); with Maria Velho da Costa and Maria Teresa Horta, wrote and published *Novas Cartas Portuguesas* (*The New Portuguese Letters,* 1972), which led the modern feminist literary movement in Portugal and achieved notoriety because of the government's attempt to suppress the work; arrested on charges of pornography and offenses against public morality, went on trial as one of the "The Three Marias" (1971–74); following the ousting of the Portuguese dictatorship, was declared innocent, with all charges dismissed (1974); published a series of novels and short stories, including *Morte da Mãe* (1977), *Inventário de Ana* (1982), *Célia e Celina* (1985), *O Enviado* (1991), *O Senhor das Ilhas* (1994) and *Os Outros Legitimos Superiores*; also studied the Portuguese media's portrayal of women in *A Imagem da Mulher na Imprensa* (1976) and sexual discrimination in education in *Falso Neutro: Um Estudo sobre a Discriminação no Ensino* (1985). ❖ See also *The Three Marias: New Portuguese Letters* (trans. by Helen R. Lane, 1975); and *Women in World History*.

BARRER, Nina Agatha Rosamond (1879–1965). **New Zealand teacher and eugenicist.** Name variations: Nina Agatha Rosamond Greensill. Born Aug 9, 1879, in Picton, New Zealand; died Sept 17, 1965, in Masterton, New Zealand; dau. of John Abraham Roberts Greensill and Selina Rebecca (Downes) Greensill; Canterbury College, MA, 1902; m. Thomas Robert Barrer (engineer), 1904 (died 1951); children: 3 sons, 1 daughter. ❖ Was scholastic head mistress for Queen Victoria School for Maori Girls at Parnell (1903); helped to establish Wairarapa High School (1923); served as president of Masterton branch of Women's Division of New Zealand Farmers' Union (1927–30) and edited division's magazine, *New Zealand Country-woman* (1933–35); promoted eugenicist arguments and published pamphlet, *The Problem of Mental Deficiency in New Zealand* (1933). Awarded British Empire Medal (1959).

BARRET, Dorothy (1917–1987). American dancer and choreographer. Born, possibly Sept 7, 1917, near Berkeley, California; died, possibly Jan 1987 in Nesconset, NY. ❖ Presented 1st known choreography at University of Berkeley, CA, in pageant Parthneia while studying there under Louise La Gai; moved to New York City and trained with teachers of diverse dance styles, including Albertina Rasch, Pierre Vladimiroff, George Balanchine, Martha Graham, Hanya Holm, and at the Humphrey-Weidman studio; performed with company of Felicia Sorel and Senia Gluck-Sandor's Dance Center in *El Amor Brujo* and *Petrouchka;* choreographed numerous works, including *Little Attitudes* (1938), *The Evolution of the Modern Dance* (1940), *Spring Fever* (1941), *In a World I Never Made* (1942), *Ariadne Leads the Way* (1944), *Epitaph* (1944), *Flirtation Waltz* (1944) and *Saturday Afternoon* (1944).

BARRET, Jeanne (1740–after 1795). *See Baret, Jeanne.*

BARRET, Shirley (c. 1953—). *See Cothran, Shirley.*

BARRETT, Angela Mortimer (1932—). *See Mortimer, Angela.*

BARRETT, Edith (1906–1977). American stage and screen actress. Born Jan 19, 1906, in Roxbury, Massachusetts; died Feb 22, 1977, in Albuquerque, New Mexico; m. Vincent Price (actor, div.). ❖ Made stage debut with Walter Hampden in *Cyrano de Bergerac* (1923); other plays include *Trelawny of the Wells, Merchant of Venice, Hamlet, Becky Sharp, Symphony, Parnell, Wuthering Heights* and *Mrs. Moonlight,* her greatest success; also appeared in films, including *Ladies in Retirement, Jane Eyre, Keys of the Kingdom, Song of Bernadette* and *The Swan.*

BARRETT, Elizabeth (1806–1861). *See Browning, Elizabeth Barrett.*

BARRETT, Grace (1907–1955). *See Hartman, Grace.*

BARRETT, Hiria (1870–1943). *See Kokoro-Barrett, Hiria.*

BARRETT, Janie Porter (1865–1948). African-American welfare worker. Born Janie Porter, Aug 9, 1865, in Athens, Georgia; died in Hampton, Virginia, Aug 27, 1948; graduated from Hampton Institute, 1884; m. Harris Barrett, Oct 1889; children: 4. ❖ Worked as teacher; opened small day-care school in her home in Hampton, VA, which was later formally organized as Locust Street Social Settlement (1890), the nation's 1st such settlement for blacks; received support from Hampton Institute, at which she had taught; founded and became president of Virginia State Federation of Colored Women's Clubs (1908), through which she worked to raise money to begin residential industrial school for black female juvenile delinquents; founded Virginia Industrial School for Colored Girls (1915) on 147-acre farm called Peaks Turnout; became school's superintendent (1915); received William E. Harmon Award for Distinguished Achievement among Negroes (1929) and was participant in White House Conference on Child Health and Protection (1930). The Virginia Industrial School was later renamed Janie Porter Barrett School for Girls (1950). ❖ See also *Women in World History.*

BARRETT, Kate Waller (1857–1925). American social worker. Born Kate Harwood Waller in Falmouth, Virginia, Jan 24, 1857; died in Alexandria, Virginia, Feb 23, 1925; attended Arlington Institute for Girls, Florence Nightingale Training School and St. Thomas' Hospital, London; Women's Medical College of Georgia, MD, 1892; m. Rev. Robert S. Barrett, July 1876; children: 7. ❖ Known for work on behalf of prostitutes and unwed mothers, opened a Florence Crittenton home for unwed mothers in Atlanta (1893); moved to Washington, DC (c. 1894), and aided in the foundation of the National Florence Crittenton Mission; served as vice president and general superintendent of nationwide chain, then president upon death of Charles Crittenton (1909); published *Some Practical Suggestions on the Conduct of a Rescue Home* (1903); was special representative of Labor Department on commission investigating treatment of women deported from country on moral grounds (1914). ❖ See also *Women in World History.*

BARRETT, Kay B. (1903–1995). *See Brown, Kay.*

BARRETT, Minnette (1880–1964). American vaudevillian and actress. Born Mar 25, 1880, in Gainesville, Georgia; died June 20, 1964, in Whitestone, Queens, NY. ❖ Was a headliner in vaudeville; appeared in the original production of *The Bat,* as well as a revival (1937); other credits include *The Show-Off, Lovely Lady, Mrs. McThing* (with Helen Hayes), and *Desire under the Elms;* active with the American Theatre Wing.

BARRETT, Rona (1934—). American tv columnist. Born Oct 8, 1934, in New York, NY; m. Bill Trowbridge, 1973 (died 2001). ❖ Hollywood gossip columnist, became a columnist for Bell-McClure–NANA newspaper syndicate (1957); began broadcasting over KABC-TV in Los Angeles; was a correspondent for tv shows "Dateline: Hollywood" (1967), "Good Morning America" (1975) and "Entertainment Tonight" (1985–86), and a regular on "Television: Inside and Out" (1981); retired (1991). ❖ See also autobiography *Miss Rona.*

BARRETT, Rose Tyler (b. 1889). American city manager. Born 1889 at XYZ Ranch, Spink Co., South Dakota. ❖ Receiving only a 5th-grade education, married at 19 and was a widow by 24; studied commercial law at night school and opened a real-estate business; came to wealth as a result of land investments in Warrenton, Oregon; became the 1st woman city manager when she took the post in Warrenton (c. 1920), heading a corporate entity with a capital worth of $3 million.

BARRIE, Elaine (1915–2003). American actress. Name variations: Elaine Barrie Barrymore. Born Elaine Jacobs, July 16, 1915; changed name to Barrie for the stage; died Mar 1, 2003, in New York, NY; attended Hunter College; m. John Barrymore, 1936 (div. Nov 27, 1940); no children. ❖ Better known for her tumultuous marriage as the 4th wife of actor John Barrymore than for acting career, appeared with him in the play *My Dear Children;* films include the short, *How to Undress in Front of Your Husband* (1937), and the feature, *Midnight* (1939). ❖ See also autobiography *All My Sins Remembered* (1964).

BARRIE, Mona (1909–1964). English-born stage and screen actress. Born Mona Smith, Dec 18, 1909, in London, England; died June 27, 1964, in Los Angeles, California. ❖ Was active on English and Australian stage; made film debut in *Sleepers East* (1933), followed by *One Night to Love, Charlie Chan in London, A Message to Garcia, Love on the Run, When Ladies Meet, Never Give a Sucker an Even Break, Skylark, Storm over Lisbon, Cass Timberlane* and *Plunder of the Sun.*

BARRIE, Wendy (1912–1978). English-born actress. Born Marguerite Wendy Jenkins, April 18, 1912, in Hong Kong; died Feb 2, 1978, in Englewood, New Jersey; goddau. of J.M. Barrie; m. David Meyer (div.). ❖ Made London stage debut (1930); appeared as Jane Seymour in *The Private Life of Henry VIII* (1933); came to Hollywood (1934) and subsequently appeared in numerous films, including *The Big Broadcast of 1936, Wings over Honolulu, Dead End, The Saint Strikes Back, Hound of the Baskervilles, The Saint Takes Over* and *It Should Happen to You;* retired from the screen; hosted a radio program and an early tv talk show "The Wendy Barrie Show" (1948–50); was once engaged to Bugsy Siegel.

BARRIENTOS, Maria (1884–1946). Spanish soprano. Born in Barcelona, Spain, Mar 10, 1884; died in Ciboure, Basses Pyrénées, Aug 8, 1946. ❖ At 12, wrote a symphony at the Barcelona Conservatory and conducted it when she graduated that same year; took singing lessons and debuted at Teatro de Novidades in Barcelona; sang in Covent Garden (1903) and at La Scala (1904); appeared in many of the world's opera houses before finally debuting at the Metropolitan Opera (1916); recorded frequently. ❖ See also *Women in World History.*

BARRINGER, Emily Dunning (1876–1961). American surgeon and gynecologist. Born Emily Dunning in Scarsdale, New York, Sept 27, 1876; died in New Milford, Connecticut, April 8, 1961; Cornell University, BS, 1896; Cornell Medical School, MD, 1901; m. Benjamin Stockwell Barringer, 1904; children: Benjamin Lang, Emily Velona. ❖ Graduated 2nd in class from Cornell Medical School and won 1st place in competitions for positions at both Mount Sinai and Gouverneur Hospital in NYC, but was denied both appointments due to gender (1901); came to attention of reform mayor Seth Low who vowed that if a woman qualified for place at Gouverneur Hospital he would ratify her placement; took examination again, won 4th place, and began 2-year internship and residency at Gouverneur as 1st woman ambulance surgeon in NYC; became member of Gouverneur staff (c. 1905), the 1st woman to serve in such position in a NY hospital; during distinguished 50-year career, was president of Women's Medical Association of NY and fellow of College of Surgeons and the New York Academy of Medicine; worked for passage of progressive medical legislation, including right for women medical doctors to receive commissions in military. ❖ See also *Women in World History.*

BARRINGTON, E. (c. 1862–1931). *See Beck, Elizabeth Louisa.*

BARRINGTON, Margaret (1896–1982). Irish short-story writer. Born in Malin, Co. Donegal, Ireland, 1896; died in West Cork, Ireland, 1982; attended Trinity College, Dublin; m. 2nd husband, Liam O'Flaherty. ❖ Worked in England (1930s), writing woman's page for *Tribune;* helped refugees from Nazi Germany and supported Republicans in Spanish Civil War; returned to Ireland (1940s); wrote numerous short stories and the novel *My Cousin Justin* (1939). ❖ See also *Women in World History*.

BARRIO GUTIERREZ, Sonia (1969—). Spanish field-hockey player. Born Dec 13, 1969. ❖ At Barcelona Olympics, won a gold medal in team competition (1992).

BARRIOS DE CHAMORRO, Violeta (b. 1929). See *Chamorro, Violeta*.

BARRIOS DE CHÚNGARA, Domitila (1937—). Bolivian political activist and writer. Name variations: Domitila Chungara. Born May 7, 1937, in Bolivia; married 1958; children: 11. ❖ Elected general secretary of Comité de Amas de Casa de Siglo XX (Housewives Committee of the Twentieth Century, 1963 and 1977) which pressured the government to improve conditions for miners; imprisoned and tortured for voicing opposition to the "Massacre of San Juan" (1967); published testimonial book *"Si me permiten hablar . . ." Testimonio de Domitila, una mujer de las minas de Bolivia* (1977, trans. as *Let Me Speak! Testimony of Domitila, a Woman of the Bolivian Mines*, 1978); with 4 other women, organized historic hunger strike (1977–78), which included 4,000 strikers and created sufficient pressure to overthrow Hugo Banzer's military regime; organized women's march in Copenhagen, Denmark, to protest atrocities against miners by the military; opened Escuela Móvil Domitila (Domitila Mobile School) in Bolivia (1990). Other writings include *!Aquí también Domitila!* (Here Domitila Also!, with David Acebey, 1985) and *La mujer y la organización* (Women and Organization, 1980).

BARRISCALE, Bessie (1884–1965). American actress. Born Elizabeth Barry Scale in Hoboken, New Jersey, Sept 30, 1884; died June 30, 1965, in Kentfield, California; cousin of actresses Edith and Mabel Taliaferro; m. Howard Hickman (director and actor). ❖ Began career on stage; was brought to Hollywood by Jesse Lasky with his Famous Players Co.; starred in De Mille films and films directed by Thomas Ince, typically romantic melodramas, during her prominent years (1914–20); established own film company; films include *Eileen of Erin* (1913), *Rose of the Rancho* (1914), *The Golden Claw* (1915), *The Painted Soul* (1915), *Plain Jane* (1916), *Wooden Shoes* (*Dutch Shoes*, 1917), *Madam Who* (1918), *Blindfolded* (1918), *Patriotism* (1918), *The White Lie* (1918), *The Notorious Mrs. Sands* (1920), *The Broken Gate* (1920), *The Breaking Point* (1921), *Show Folks* (1928), *Beloved* (1934) and *The Man Who Reclaimed His Head* (1935).

BARRON, Dorothy (1897–1953). See *Shepherd-Barron, Dorothy*.

BARRON, Gayle (c. 1947—). American marathon runner. Born c. 1947 in Atlanta, Georgia; attended University of Georgia. ❖ Won the 1st Peachtree 10k Road Race (1970), then won 4 more; won the Boston Marathon (1978). Inducted into Georgia Sports Hall of Fame (2003).

BARRON, Hannah Ward (1829–1898). New Zealand shopkeeper and innkeeper. Name variations: Hannah Dorney, Joanna Dorney, Hannah Ward. Born Joanna Dorney, probably July 14, 1829, in Cork, Ireland; died Nov 10, 1898, in Bluff (Campbelltown), New Zealand; dau. of Thomas (shopkeeper) and Elizabeth (Lynch) Dorney; m. William Ward, 1850 (died 1860); m. John Barron (butcher), 1862; children: 8. ❖ Followed 1st husband to Australia (1853); established a small shop and boarding house for miners; left 2nd husband and moved to New Zealand (1863); established boarding house for sailors, which prospered into the Club Hotel in Bluff. ❖ See also *Dictionary of New Zealand Biography* (Vol. 2).

BARRON, Jennie Loitman (1891–1969). American judge. Name variations: Jennie Loitman. Born Jennie Loitman, Oct 12, 1891, in Boston, Massachusetts; died Mar 28, 1969, in Boston, MA; dau. of Morris Loitman (founder of the Hebrew Progressive Lodge) and Fannie (Castleman) Loitman; m. distant cousin Samuel Barron Jr. (lawyer), June 23, 1918; children: Erma (b. 1919); Deborah (1923–1956); Joy (b. 1931). ❖ In 30-year career as judge, promoted rehabilitation over imprisonment; organized Boston University's equal suffrage league; as president of Massachusetts Association of Women Lawyers, successfully campaigned to permit women notaries (1918); wrote League of Women Voters' statement, which supported jury duty for women; was delegate to federal commission on uniform marriage and divorce laws; with husband, practiced law at Boston firm, Barron and Barron (1918–37); served as only woman member of Boston School Committee (1926–29); was 1st president of Women's Auxiliary of Beth Israel Hospital (1926–29) and New England Women's Division of American Jewish Congress; was director of Home Owners Federal Savings and Loan Association

(1933–37); served as Massachusetts' assistant attorney general (1934–35) and special justice of Western Norfolk District Court (1934–37); was associate justice of Boston Municipal Court (1938–59), becoming 1st woman in Commonwealth to be full-time judge and only woman to serve on court; was 1st woman to serve as associate justice of MA Superior Court (1959–69); named American Mother of the Year (1959).

BARROS, Leila (1971—). Brazilian volleyball player. Name variations: Leila Gomes Barros. Born Sept 30, 1971, in Brasilia, Brazil. ❖ Wing spiker, won team World Grand Prix (1994, 1996, 1998); won South American championship (1991, 1995, 1997); won team bronze medals at Atlanta Olympics (1996) and Sydney Olympics (2000). Named MVP at World Grand Prix (1996, 1998).

BARROS, Lorena (d. 1976). Filipino hero. Born in Philippines; killed Mar 1976. ❖ While in college, founded Makibaka (which means "led struggle" in Tagalog), the 1st underground organization dedicated to women's rights; made it a force to be reckoned with during the years of oppression; when martial law was declared by Marcos during an anti-insurgency campaign, was arrested but escaped from her prison cell in Bicutan; organized the 1st women's unit of the New People's Army which was fighting for liberation; was killed in action by the military.

BARROS, Zoila (1976—). Cuban volleyball player. Name variations: Zoila Barros Fernandez. Born Aug 6, 1976, in Cuba. ❖ Won a team gold medal at Sydney Olympics (2000) and a team bronze medal at Athens Olympics (2004).

BARROSO, Maria Alice (1926—). Brazilian novelist and short-story writer. Born 1926 in Miracema, Rio de Janeiro, Brazil. ❖ Works include *Os Posseiros* (1955), *Un nome para matar* (1967), *Quem matou Pacífico?* (1969), *Globo da morte* and *Cavalo indomado*.

BARROW, Frances Elizabeth (1822–1894). American author. Name variations: (pseudonym) Aunt Fanny. Born in Charleston, South Carolina, Feb 22, 1822; died in New York, NY, May 7, 1894; educated in New York; married James Barrow. ❖ Wrote numerous books for children under the name Aunt Fanny, including *Six Nightcaps*, which was translated into French, German and Swedish, and *The Letter G* (1864); also wrote the novel *The Wife's Stratagem*.

BARROW, Nita (1916–1995). First female governor-general of Barbados. Name variations: Dame Nita Barrow. Born Ruth Nita Barrow, Nov 15, 1916, in Barbados; died Dec 19, 1995, in Barbados; dau. of Bishop Reginald Barrow (Anglican priest and political martyr); sister of Errol Barrow (who led Barbados to political independence); attended Columbia University (NY), University of Toronto, and Edinburgh University. ❖ Respected internationally for her community service, work in women's movement, and involvement in the struggle against apartheid; held nursing and public health posts in Barbados and Jamaica (1940–56); was matron of University Hospital in Jamaica (1954); served as principal nursing officer, Jamaica (1956–62); was nursing adviser, Pan American Health Organization (1967–71); worked as associate director, Christian Medical Commission of World Council of Churches, Geneva (1971–75); was president of World YWCA (1973–83); served as director, Christian Medical Commission of World Council of Churches, Geneva (1975–80); served as health consultant, World Health Organization (1981–86); was president of International Council for Adult Education (1982), was 1st black female president of World Council of Churches (1983), and member of Commonwealth Group of Eminent Persons on South Africa (1986); was permanent representative of Barbados to UN (1986–90); served as governor-general of Barbados (1990–95). ❖ See also *Women in World History*.

BARROWS, Bella S. (1845–1913). See *Barrows, Isabel Hayes*.

BARROWS, Isabel Hayes (1845–1913). American editor, surgeon, and penologist. Name variations: Katharine I. Barrows; Bella S. Barrows. Born Katharine Isabel Hayes in Iras, Vermont, April 16, 1845; died in Croton-on-Hudson, New York, 1913; attended Woman's Medical College of the New York Infirmary for Women and Children, 1868; studied ophthalmology in Vienna, Austria, 1869; m. Samuel June Barrows (author and eventually Unitarian minister), 1865. ❖ Replaced husband as stenographic secretary to Secretary of State William H. Seward (1868), becoming 1st women employed by US Department of State in Washington, DC; studied medicine in NYC and Vienna; opened private medical practice in US while teaching at Howard University in Washington; served as editor of *Proceedings of the National Conference of*

Charities and Correction for 20 years; honored for notable service as secretary to National Prison Association.

BARROWS, Katherine I. (1845–1913). *See Barrows, Isabel Hayes.*

BARRY, Ann Street (1734–1801). Irish actress. Name variations: Mrs. Spranger Barry, Mrs. Barry, Ann, Anne or Annie Crawford, Ann Dancer. Born in Bath, England, 1734; died Nov 29, 1801; married an actor named Dancer; m. Spranger Barry (Irish actor), 1768 (died 1777); m. a Mr. Crawford, 1778. ❖ Considered the equal of Peg Woffington and Susannah Cibber in tragedy and to have surpassed both in comedy, 1st appeared on stage (c. 1756) under name Ann Dancer; not to be confused with actress Elizabeth Barry (who was known as "the great Mrs. Barry"). Lyrics to "Kathleen Mavourneen" have been attributed to her by John Bartlett, though Louise Macartney Crawford is generally considered the author.

BARRY, Bonny (1960—). Australian politician. Name variations: Veronica Lesley Barry. Born Jan 30, 1960, in Blackall, Australia. ❖ Began career as a nurse; as a member of the Australian Labor Party, elected to the Queensland Parliament for Aspley (2001).

BARRY, Deidre (1972—). American cyclist. Born Oct 8, 1972, in Milwaukee, Wisconsin. ❖ Won a silver medal for indiv. time trial at Athens Olympics (2004).

BARRY, Elaine (d. 1948). American dancer. Name variations: The Barrys. Died Jan 30, 1948, in auto accident near Etowah, Tennessee; studied with Chester Hale; m. Fred Barry (dancer). ❖ Was a member of the Capitol Theater Ballet; for 13 years, danced with husband in nightclubs and on stage in *Show Time, Priorities of '42, Mexican Hayride* and *Up in Central Park,* specializing in whirlwind turns. Following her death, Fred Barry performed with Susan Graves for 3 years.

BARRY, Elizabeth (1658–1713). English actress. Name variations: Mrs. Barry. Born 1658; died Nov 7, 1713; buried at Acton; children: a child with Lord Rochester and a 2nd with Sir George Etheredge. ❖ One of the most famous tragic actresses of her time, also created over 100 roles in comedy, including Lady Brute in *The Provoked Wife;* said to have so delighted Charles II and the duke and duchess of York (James II and Anne Hyde) with performance of Isabella, queen of Hungary, in earl of Orrery's *Mustapha* (1673), that the duchess took lessons in English from her; when the duchess became queen was loaned her coronation robes in which Barry appeared as Elizabeth II in *Earl of Essex;* was particularly successful in plays of Thomas Otway; retired from stage (1709); known as "the great Mrs. Barry" (not to be confused with Ann Street Barry). ❖ See also *Women in World History.*

BARRY, Iris (1895–1969). English-American author and museum official. Born in Birmingham, England, 1895; died 1969; educated in England and at Ursuline Convent, Verviers, Belgium. ❖ Authoritative film critic and historian, worked as movie critic for *The Spectator* and movie editor for London's *Daily Mail* (1925–30); settled in US; served as librarian of Museum of Modern Art, NY (1932–35), and as curator, then director, of its motion-picture collection (1935–50); was a founding member of London Film Society (1925); elected president of International Federation of Film Archives (1946); awarded Chevalier of the French Legion of Honor (1949) before retiring (1950). Writings include *Let's Go to the Pictures* (1926), *D.W. Griffith: American Film Master* (1940), and a widely distributed series of pamphlets comprised of program notes for exhibitions of motion pictures arranged by Museum of Modern Art (1935–50).

BARRY, James (c. 1795–1865). *See Stuart, Miranda.*

BARRY, Jeanne Bécu, Comtesse du (1743–1793). *See du Barry, Jeanne Bécu, Comtesse.*

BARRY, Leonora M. (1849–1930). American labor organizer and temperance leader. Name variations: Mrs. Barry-Lake, Mother Lake, Leonora Marie Lake. Born Leonora Marie Kearney in Kearney, Co. Cork, Ireland, Aug 13, 1849; died in Minooka, Illinois, July 15, 1930; only child of John and Honor Granger (Brown) Kearney; m. William E. Barry, Nov 30, 1871 (died 1881); m. Obadiah Read Lake, April 17, 1890 (died 1923); children: (1st m.) Marion Frances (b. 1873), William Standish (b. 1875), Charles Joseph (b. 1880). ❖ Immigrated to US with parents (1852); after death of husband and daughter (both 1881), took job in knitwear factory in Amsterdam, NY, to support sons; turned to trade-union movement to alleviate some hardships of working conditions; joined local assembly of Knights of Labor (1884), where she moved into positions of leadership, 1st on local level as

president of her local, the Victory assembly (made up of 1,500 female knitwear workers); became president of District Assembly 65 (1885) and a national organizer (by 1886); retired from organizing (1889); worked on behalf of temperance and women's suffrage; spoke before World's Representative Congress of Women at Chicago's Columbian Exposition on "The Dignity of Labor" (1893); was active in both Woman's Christian Temperance League and Catholic Total Abstinence Union of America; sometimes referred to as "Mother Lake," was in demand as a speaker for Redpath and Slayton agencies and on the Chautauqua circuit until shortly before death. ❖ See also *Women in World History.*

BARRY, Madame du (1743–1793). *See du Barry, Jeanne Bécu, Comtesse.*

BARRY, Mary Ann (1855–1874). English murderer. Born 1855 in England; hanged 1874; married Edwin Bailey (common law). ❖ Petty thief and alcoholic, was arrested with common-law husband for murder of their 1-year-old child; in uncustomary triple execution, was hanged with husband and a man who had murdered his girlfriend (1874).

BARRY, Mrs.
See Barry, Elizabeth (1658–1713).
See Barry, Ann Street (1734–1801).

BARRY, Myra (1957—). Irish politician. Born June 1957 in Fermoy, Co. Cork, Ireland; dau. of Dick Barry (TD, Cork North East, 1953–81, parliamentary secretary to minister for health, 1973–77). ❖ Won a by-election representing Fine Gael to the 21st Dáil for Cork North East (1979); returned to 22nd–24th Dáil (1981–87); was a member of the joint committee on women's rights and joint committee on marriage breakdown (both 1983).

BARRY, Mrs. Spranger (1734–1801). *See Barry, Ann Street.*

BARRY, Veronica Lesley (1960—). *See Barry, Bonny.*

BARRY-LAKE, Mrs. (1849–1930). *See Barry, Leonora M.*

BARRYMORE, Diana (1921–1960). American actress. Born Diana Strange Blythe (actual name of Barrymore family), Mar 3, 1921; died in New York, NY, Jan 25, 1960; dau. of Blanche Oelrichs Thomas Barrymore Tweed (who, as poet and playwright, used the pseudonym Michael Strange) and John Barrymore; m. Bramwell Fletcher (div.); m. John Howard (tennis player); m. Bob Wilcox. ❖ At 16, began studying at American Academy of Dramatic Arts, NY; signed for season of summer stock at Ogunquit Playhouse and appeared on cover of *Life* magazine (1939); made Broadway debut as Caroline Bronson in *Romantic Mr. Dickens;* made 1st film *Eagle Squadron;* with 1st husband, opened in Theatre Guild production of *Rebecca* (1944); suffering from alcoholism, was replaced by Faye Emerson after arriving drunk to telecast of "The Diana Barrymore Show" on CBS; had numerous fresh starts, many affairs, and more than one suicide attempt; with help of Gerold Frank, wrote her autobiography *Too Much, Too Soon* which became bestseller (1957); at 38, committed suicide. ❖ See also Hollis Alpert, *The Barrymores* (Dial, 1964); and *Women in World History.*

BARRYMORE, Elaine (1915–2003). *See Barrie, Elaine.*

BARRYMORE, Ethel (1879–1959). American actress. Born Ethel Mae Blyth in Philadelphia, Pennsylvania, Aug 15, 1879; died June 18, 1959; dau. of actors Georgiana Drew (1854–1893) and Maurice Barrymore (whose actual name was Herbert Blyth); sister of actors John and Lionel Barrymore; granddau. of Louisa Lane Drew; aunt of actress Diana Barrymore; grandaunt of actress Drew Barrymore; m. Russell Griswold Colt, Mar 24, 1909 (div. 1923); children: Samuel (b. 1910), Ethel Barrymore Colt (b. 1912, actress), and John (b. 1913). ❖ First Lady of the American Theater and the last of "fabulous" Barrymores, made acting debut at 11 in *The Lady of the Camellias,* with brothers in supporting cast; at 15, made professional debut in NY in *A School for Scandal* (1894); received 1st leading role, in *Captain Jinks of the Horse Marines* (1901); starred in *A Doll's House* (1905) and *Alice-Sit-by-the-Fire* (1906), becoming one of the foremost actresses in US; appeared in 1st film *The Nightingale* (1914), then signed 2-year contract with Metro Pictures, for which she shot 5 well-received films (1915–17); preferring stage to film, opened the Ethel Barrymore Theater in NY (1928), appearing in *The Kingdom of God;* legendary among fellow actors for professionalism and sang-froid on stage; appeared with brothers in MGM's *Rasputin and the Empress* (1933); won Oscar for Best Supporting Actress (1945) for *None But The Lonely Heart;* continued working until heart disease forced slow down; retired (1958). Films include *The Awakening of Helen Ritchie* (1917), *Our Mrs. McChesney* (1918), *The Spiral Staircase* (1946), *The Farmer's Daughter* (1947), *The Paradine Case* (1948), *Portrait of Jennie*

(1949), *Pinky* (1949), *The Story of Three Loves* (1953), *Main Street to Broadway* (1953) and *Young at Heart* (1955). ❖ See also Ethel Barrymore, *Memories: An Autobiography* (Harper, 1955); Hollis Alpert, *The Barrymores* (Dial, 1964); James Kotsilibas-Davis, *The Barrymores: The Royal Family in Hollywood* (Crown, 1981); Margot Peters, *The House of Barrymore* (Knopf, 1990); and *Women in World History*.

BARRYMORE, Georgiana Drew (1854–1893). *See Drew, Georgiana.*

BARRYMORE, Irene (1887–1936). *See Fenwick, Irene.*

BARRYS, The. *See Barry, Elaine.*

BARSKAYA, Margarita A. (1903–1938). Soviet actress, scenarist, and filmmaker. Name variations: Margarita Barskaia; Margarita Chardinina-Barskaya or Chardynina-Barskaya. Born June 19, 1903, in Baku, Russia; died 1938 (some sources cite 1939) in a Soviet gulag; m. Petr Chardynin (director). ❖ Gained reputation as actress in pre-revolutionary Russia; with husband, had successful career during and after Bolshevik takeover; made major contribution as pioneer in children's films; opened Laboratory for Children's Cinema (1930) and eventually directed enormously successful *Torn Boots*, a landmark in Soviet film history which was the 1st realistic movie geared toward young audience; directed *Father and Son* (1937), which outraged authorities; arrested and sent to concentration camp where she died (1938).

BARSLUKOVA, Julia (1978—). *See Barsukova, Yulia.*

BARSTOW, Edith (1907–1960). American dancer and choreographer. Born 1907 in Ashtabula, Ohio; raised in Tacoma, Washington; died Jan 6, 1960, in Sarasota, Florida. ❖ Began appearing on Pantages vaudeville circuit with family (c. 1917); performed toe tapping and exhibition ballroom act with brother Richard in cabarets and theaters; worked in midwest with Merriell Abbott on Balaban and Katz circuit, before staging shows with Abbott at Palmer House in Chicago; continued to tour worldwide with brother, performing *Funny Face* as far as Australia; worked at Ringling Brothers and Barnum and Bailey Circus with brother (1949–60); served as choreographer on such tv shows as "Colgate Comedy Hour" (1950–54), "Garroway at Large" (1949–54), "Milton Berle's Texaco Star Theater" (1948–55) and "The Frankie Laine Show" (1955–56).

BARSTOW, Mrs. Montagu (1865–1947). *See Orczy, Baroness.*

BARSUKOVA, Yulia (1978—). Russian rhythmic gymnast. Name variations: Youlia Barsoukova; Julia Barsoukova or Barslukova. Born Dec 31, 1978, in Moscow, Russia. ❖ Won a gold medal for indiv. all-around at Sydney Olympics (2000).

BARTEL, Jean (c. 1924—). Miss America. Born c. 1924 in Los Angeles, California. ❖ Named Miss America (1943); instituted scholarship program and was the 1st to refuse to pose in a swimsuit following the competition; appeared on Broadway and in film; headed an international communications consulting firm. ❖ See also Frank Deford, *There She Is* (Viking, 1971).

BARTELME, Mary (1866–1954). American judge and juvenile reformer. Name variations: Mary Margaret Bartelme; (nickname) "Suitcase Mary." Born Mary Margaret Bartelme, July 24, 1866, in Chicago, Illinois; died July 25, 1954, in Carmel, California; dau. of Balthazar Bartelme and Jeannette (Hoff) Bartelme; attended Cook Co. Normal School; graduated as only woman in class at Northwestern University Law School. ❖ Lawyer who proposed reduction of female delinquency by providing sex education and extending women's minimum working age to 16, was admitted to Illinois bar (1894), then US bar, and began private practice in Chicago (1896); served as Cook Co. public guardian (1897–1913); with other members of Chicago Woman's Club, established Chicago juvenile court (1899); served as assistant to juvenile court judge (1913–23); created several halfway houses for dependent girls (1914) and for semi-delinquent girls (1916); served as Cook Co. Circuit Court associate justice (1923–27) and as presiding judge of juvenile court (1927–33).

BARTELS, Tineke (1951—). Dutch equestrian. Name variations: Maria Anna Bartels de Vries; Tineke Bartels-de Vries. Born Feb 6, 1951, in the Netherlands; m. Joep Bartels (equestrian); children: Imke Schellekens-Bartels (equestrian) and Gijs Bartels. ❖ Won Dutch national championship (1974), on Irene; was a member of the Dutch national team (1984–97); won team silver medals in dressage at Barcelona

Olympics (1992) and Atlanta Olympics (1996), on Barbria. ❖ See also *Big Pony Book* and *Riding with Tineke Bartels*.

BARTET, Jeanne Julia (1854–1941). French actress. Born Jeanne Julia Regnault, Oct 8, 1854, in Paris, France; died 1941; trained at the Conservatoire. ❖ Began successful career at the Vaudeville (1872); engaged at Comédie Française (c. 1879), of which she became a *sociétaire*, or shareholder (1880); played leading parts, both in tragedy and comedy, and was known for elegance and grand style, which made her supreme among younger actresses on French stage; played season in London (1908). ❖ See also *Women in World History*.

BARTH, Beatrice Mary (1877–1966). New Zealand music teacher. Born May 11, 1877, in London, England; died Jan 14, 1966, in Dunedin, New Zealand; dau. of Arthur James Barth (professor of music) and Ellen (Thompson) Barth. ❖ Immigrated to New Zealand with family (1881); after father's death (1905), began to teach music, founding Barth Pianoforte Music School (later Barth School of Music, 1921); was a founding member of Society of Women Musicians of Otago (1925) and served as president (1928); helped to administer Dunedin Center of Trinity College of Music, London. ❖ See also *Dictionary of New Zealand Biography* (Vol. 3).

BARTHOLOMEW, Ann Sheppard (1811–1891). English composer, pianist, organist, and teacher. Born Ann Mounsey, April 17, 1811, in London, England; died in London, June 24, 1891; studied under Logier (1817), then with Louis Spohr, Samuel Wesley and Thomas Attwood. ❖ Became an organist (1828); appointed to same position at St. Vedast's (1837), remaining there for 50 years; wrote many pieces for organ and piano as well as over 100 songs, an oratorio, and a cantata; gave regular concerts of sacred classical music and introduced a number of Felix Mendelssohn's organ compositions to public; became an associate of Philharmonic Society (1834) and a member of Royal Society of Musicians (1839). ❖ See also *Women in World History*.

BARTHOLOMEW, Susan (1969—). American triathlete. Name variations: Susan Bartholomew-Williams or Susan Bartholomew Williams. Born June 17, 1969, in Long Beach, California; attended University of Alabama; children: daughter Sydney. ❖ Won a bronze medal at Athens Olympics (2004).

BARTKOWICZ, Peaches (1949—). American tennis player. Name variations: Jane Bartkowicz. Born Jane Bartkowicz, April 16, 1949, in Hamtramck, Michigan; trained by Jean Hoxie. ❖ Won 17 age-group titles before turning professional; at 15, was the youngest player to win the Jr. Wimbledon tournament; won a silver medal for women's singles at Mexico City Olympics (1968) and bronze medals for doubles and mixed doubles; during pro career, won 14 tournaments. Inducted into Michigan Sports Hall of Fame (2002).

BARTLESON, Nathalie (1968—). *See Schneyder, Nathalie.*

BARTLETT, Adelaide (c. 1856–?). English woman accused of murder. Born c. 1856 in England; m. Edwin Bartlett, c. 1875. ❖ Began liaison with Wesleyan minister Rev. George Dyson (1885), which was sanctioned by husband; after husband died suddenly (Jan 1, 1886), was charged with murder along with Dyson, when a post-mortem revealed liquid chloroform in husband's stomach, but not on his mouth or throat; though the case was dropped against Dyson, admitted at sensational murder trial at Old Bailey to sprinkling chloroform on husband's handkerchief only to aid him in sleep (April 1886); was acquitted by jury due to lack of evidence as to the manner in which the large amounts had been administered.

BARTLETT, Caroline (1858–1935). *See Crane, Caroline Bartlett.*

BARTLETT, Ethel (1896–1978). English pianist. Born in Epping Forest, England, June 6, 1896; died in Los Angeles, California, April 17, 1978; studied with Tobias Matthay and Artur Schnabel; married Rae Robertson (1893–1956, pianist). ❖ With husband, founded a duo-piano team that was famed in United Kingdom (1930s); made annual tours in Europe and US and gave 1st performance of Sir Arthur Bax's duo-piano sonata (1931).

BARTLETT, Mary (d. 1789). American letter writer. Born in Newton, New Hampshire; died July 14, 1789; dau. of Joseph Bartlett and Sarah Hoyt; m. Josiah Bartlett, 1754; children: 12. ❖ "The Letters of Josiah and Mary Bartlett" describe difficulties of agrarian life and give details about illnesses, domestic trials, and farming; also provide insight into Josiah Bartlett, signer of the Declaration of Independence.

BARTLOW, Jericho. *See Poppler, Jericho.*

BARTOK, Ditta Pasztory (1902–1982). Hungarian pianist. Born Ditta Pasztory in 1902; died in Budapest, Nov 21, 1982; became 2nd wife of Béla Bartok (composer), 1923. ❖ Performed with husband in Europe and US, where they arrived as exiles from the Nazis (1940); with husband, made several recordings of his compositions, including the *Sonata for Two Pianos and Percussion* and selections from *Mikrokosmos*, and gave world premiere of his *Concerto for Two Pianos* with NY Philharmonic (1943); also performed works other than those of her husband, including Mozart concertos. ❖ See also *Women in World History.*

BARTOK, Eva (1926–1998). Hungarian actress. Born Eva Martha Szöke, June 18, 1926, in Kecskemet, Hungary; died Aug 1, 1998, in London, England; m. Geza Kovacs, 1941 (annulled, 1942); m. Alexander Paal (film producer), 1948 (div. 1951); m. William Wordsworth (publicist), 1951 (div. 1952); m. Curt Jurgens (actor), 1955 (div. 1957). ❖ Spent several years in a German concentration camp, eventually marrying a Nazi officer, but marriage was annulled on grounds of coercion of a minor; made film debut in Hungary in *The Prophet of the Fields* (1947); left Communist Hungary (1949); had an international career in such films as *A Tale of Five Cities, The Crimson Pirate, The Venetian Bird, The Last Waltz, The Gamma People, Madeleine, Beyond the Curtain* and *Savina.* ❖ See also autobiography, *Worth Living For* (1959).

BARTOLINI-BADELLI, Giustina (fl. 1840). Third wife of Jérôme Bonaparte. Name variations: Giustina Pecori. Born Giustina Pecori-Suárez Grimaldi; m. Jérôme Bonaparte (1784–1860), brother of Napoleon I, in a religious ceremony, 1840, and later in a civil ceremony, 1853. ❖ Widow of an Italian noble, married Jérôme Bonaparte after bailing him out of debt; in return, Jérôme was unfaithful and squandered her money.

BARTOLOMEI or BARTOLOMMEI, Angelica (1798–1875). *See Palli, Angelica.*

BARTON, Clara (1821–1912). Founder of American Red Cross. Born Clarissa Harlowe Barton in North Oxford, Massachusetts, Dec 25, 1821; died in Glen Echo, Maryland, April 12, 1912; dau. of Captain Stephen (farmer) and Sarah (Stone) Barton; never married; no children. ❖ The 1st woman diplomat in US history and a pioneer in development of first aid and attentive care to war and disaster victims, began career teaching school (1839); started work at US Patent Office (1854); began volunteer Civil War relief work (1861), providing direct assistance to wounded; as news of her work spread, dubbed "Angel of the Battlefield" by press; after fighting ended, went with War Department expedition to Andersonville, GA (scene of Confederate prison camp in which more than 10,000 Union prisoners had died), and helped to mark graves (1865); began touring country on lecture circuit (1866), describing adventures at battlefronts; recuperated in Corsica after nervous collapse (1869); worked in Franco-Prussian War; campaigned in Washington, DC, for American involvement in Red Cross (1878); received support from President Chester Arthur, and, with his encouragement, the Senate confirmed American participation in the Convention (1882); led American Red Cross for next 23 years; went on innumerable relief expeditions, including visits to 2 more theaters of war (Turkey in 1896 and Cuba during Spanish-American War of 1898); represented US government at 4 international conferences: in Geneva (1884), Carlsruhe (1887), Vienna (1897), and St. Petersburg (1902); ousted from Red Cross leadership (1904). ❖ See also William E. Barton, *The Life of Clara Barton: Founder of the American Red Cross* (2 vols., Houghton, 1922); Elizabeth Brown Pryor, *Clara Barton: Professional Angel* (U. of Pennsylvania Press, 1987); Ishbel Ross, *Angel of the Battlefield: The Life of Clara Barton* (Harper, 1956); and *Women in World History.*

BARTON, Donna (c. 1967—). American jockey. Name variations: Donna Brothers. Born c. 1967 in Edgewood, Kentucky; dau. of Patti Barton (jockey who rode 1,202 winners, 1969–84); sister of Jerry Barton (trainer); m. Frankie Brothers (trainer). ❖ The 2nd-winningest female rider in total earnings after Julie Krone, began riding (1993) and spent over 11 years competing; had over 1,000 wins; retired from racing (Sept 1998).

BARTON, Dora (1884–1966). English stage actress. Name variations: Mrs. Antony Caton Woodville. Born Dora Brockbank in 1884, in London, England; died Sept 13, 1966, in London; m. Anthony Caton Woodville, 1908 (div.). ❖ Made stage debut in Liverpool in *A Man's Shadow* (1892); London credits include *The Black Cat, Editha's Burglar, The Puritan, The Girl I Left Behind Me, Hearts are Trumps, Arizona, The*

Rich Mrs. Repton, Monsieur Beaucaire, Strife, The Heart of a Child, Three's a Crowd, Thunder on the Left, The Lady with a Lamp, Many Mansions and *Muted Strings;* toured US with Lillie Langtry.

BARTON, Elizabeth (c. 1506–1534). English zealot. Name variations: The maid of Kent, Nun of Kent, or Holy Maid of Kent. Born, according to her statement, 1506 at Aldington, Kent; executed at Tyburn, April 20, 1534. ❖ Was a servant in the house of Thomas Cobb, caretaker of estate near Aldington owned by William Warham, archbishop of Caterbury; at 19, came to attention of Warham after an illness resulted in "religious hysteria"; with ravings of "marvellous holiness in rebuke of sin and vice," was believed to be divinely inspired; pronounced sincere by monk Edward Bocking and gained admission as Benedictine nun to St. Sepulchre's convent, Canterbury; attracted many followers who believed her to be in direct communication with the Virgin Mary; objected to Henry VIII's divorce from Catherine of Aragon; brought before Archbishop Thomas Cranmer and confessed to feigning trances; condemned to death and executed. ❖ See also *Women in World History.*

BARTON, Emma (1872–1938). British photographer. Name variations: Mrs. G.A. Barton. Born Emma Rayson in Birmingham, England, 1872; died at Isle of Wight, England, 1938; dau. of a railway porter; m. George Albert Barton; children: 3 daughters, 2 sons. ❖ Highly regarded for portraits and allegorical studies, began exhibiting (c. 1901) and was represented in competitions and exhibitions in Britain, Europe, and US; had work published in number of magazines; received medal at Royal Photographic Society exhibition for her well-known photograph *The Awakening* (1903), which appeared in British section of Louisiana Purchase Exposition in St. Louis, Missouri (1904); established residence on Isle of Wight (1929).

BARTON, Fanny or Frances (1737–1815). *See Abington, Frances.*

BARTON, Mrs. G.A. (1872–1938). *See Barton, Emma.*

BARTON, Gertrude (d. 1972). *See Bonfils, Helen.*

BARTON, Glenys (1944—). English sculptor. Born 1944 in Stoke-on-Trent, England; attended Royal College of Art in London, 1968–71. ❖ Accomplished sculptor, had 1st exhibit at Museum of Decorative Art, Copenhagen (1973); was artist-in-residence at Wedgewood factory (1976–77), where she experimented with clay and techniques of ceramic figure design; displayed work from Wedgewood period in landmark exhibition "Glenys Barton at Wedgewood" at Crafts Council Gallery, London (1977–78); began to focus on human head (1980s), in such exhibitions as "Heads—Sculpture and Drawings" (London, 1986), "The Face" (Little Rock, Arkansas, 1988), and "The Portrait Now" (National Portrait Gallery, 1993–94); work is included in Scottish National Gallery, National Portrait Gallery and Victoria and Albert Museum, as well as National Museum of Victoria, Melbourne, and Pennsylvania State University of Modern Art.

BARTON, Jane (1851–1938). Australian prime-ministerial wife. Name variations: Jeanie Barton; Lady Barton. Born Jane Mason Ross, June 11, 1851, in London, England; died Mar 23, 1938, in Sydney, Australia; m. Edmund Barton (1st prime minister of Australia, 1901–03), 1877; children: 6. ❖ Charming and well-educated, furthered the cause of Federation through social networks as vice-president of the 2nd Sydney Women's Federal League; participated in the inauguration of the Commonwealth and in the opening ceremony of the 1st parliament in Melbourne (Jan and May 1901); was founding president of the Queen's Club in Sydney (1912–14).

BARTON, Jeanie (1851–1938). *See Barton, Jane.*

BARTON, Lady (1851–1938). *See Barton, Jane.*

BARTON, Mary (d. 1970). English actress. Born in Warwickshire, England; died Mar 8, 1970; m. Tristan Rawson. ❖ Made London stage debut in *The Philanderer* (1907), followed by *Joy, Waste* and *The Treasure;* joined Charles Frohman's repertory group (1909), appearing in *Strife, Arsène Lupin* and *The Twelve-Pound Look,* among others; later appeared with Lena Ashwell's company; made NY debut in *Fanny's First Play* (1912), followed by *A Midsummer Night's Dream* and *Nan;* other London plays include *The Winter's Tale, The Crossing, A Family Man, Quality Street, Twelfth Night, Richard III, The Madras House, Marigold, A Doll's House* and *On the Frontier.*

BARTON, Pam (1917–1943). English golfer. Born Pamela Barton, Mar 4, 1917, in London, England; died in plane crash in England, Nov 14, 1943. ❖ Placed 2nd (1934, 1935), then 1st (1936, 1939) at the British

Women's championship; won USGA Women's Championship (1936), the 1st English woman to hold English and American titles in the same year; enlisted in the Women's Auxiliary Air Force during WWII and was killed while on duty. ❖ See also *Women in World History.*

BARTOSIK, Alison (1983—). American synchronized swimmer. Born April 20, 1983, in Flagstaff, Arizona. ❖ With Anna Kozlova, won a bronze medal for duet at Athens Olympics (2004), as well as a bronze medal for team.

BARTOSOVA, Marie (1882–1967). *See Majerová, Marie.*

BARWIRTH, Anita (1918—). German gymnast. Born Aug 30, 1918. ❖ At Berlin Olympics, won a gold medal in all-around team (1936).

BARYARD, Malin (1975—). Swedish equestrian. Born April 10, 1975, in Norrk, Sweden. ❖ Placed 2nd in team jumping at World Equestrian games (2002); on Butterfly Flip, won bronze medal for team jumping at Athens Olympics (2004).

BARYKOVA, Anna Pavlovna (1839–1893). Russian poet. Name variations: Barýkova. Born Anna Pavlovna Kamenskaia in St. Petersburg, Russia, Dec 22, 1839; died at Rostov on Don, Russia, May 31, 1893; dau. of Maria Kamenskaia (writer); granddau. of Fyodor Tolstoi (artist); educated at Ekaterininskii Institute; married twice; children: 4. ❖ Began writing poetry as teenager; employed as translator for Lev Tolstoy's publishing company, Intermediary; released 1st vol. of poetry *My Muse* (1878), which was followed by satiric portrait of Alexander III, *Tale of How Tsar Akhreian Went to Complain to God* (1883), published anonymously; because writings represented populist, revolutionary spirit of 1870s and 1880s, was imprisoned briefly for political beliefs; also wrote *A Votary of Aesthetics* (1884).

BARYSHEVA, Olga (1954—). Soviet basketball player. Born Aug 24, 1954. ❖ Won a gold medal at Montreal Olympics (1976) and a gold medal at Moscow Olympics (1980), both in team competition.

BAŞAR, Sukufe Nihal (1896–1973). Turkish poet and novelist. Name variations: Süküfe Nihal Basar. Born 1896 in Istanbul, Turkey; died Sept 24, 1973, in Istanbul. ❖ After graduation from University of Istanbul, taught literature and geography; worked for women's rights and movement for National Defense; published 7 vols. of poetry (1919–60), 6 novels (1928–51), and a travel book on Finland (1935).

BASCH, Anamarija (1893–after 1945). Yugoslav-Jewish activist. Born in Felz Sentivan, Yugoslavia, 1893; died after 1945; m. Andreas Basch (engineer); children: son, Jan (b. 1921). ❖ Active in radical politics, fled Yugoslavia with husband after it became increasingly repressive (early 1930s); settled in Belgium, then went to Spain (1936) to lend support to embattled Republican government; returned to Belgium after defeat of Spanish Republic (1939); during WWII, was active in Belgian resistance; though husband was captured by Gestapo and killed, survived and moved with son to Hungary after the war. ❖ See also *Women in World History.*

BASCOM, Florence (1862–1945). American geologist. Born Florence Bascom, July 14, 1862, in Williamstown, Massachusetts; died in Northampton, Massachusetts, June 18, 1945; dau. of John (president of University of Wisconsin) and Emma Curtiss (schoolteacher); University of Wisconsin, BA, BL, 1882, BS, 1884, MS, 1887; became 1st woman in US to earn a PhD in geology and 1st woman awarded PhD in any discipline by Johns Hopkins University (1893). ❖ Studied geology with some of best scholars in country; while at John Hopkins, revealed that Precambrian rocks of South Mountain were actually formed from ancient lava flows not sediments, and introduced term aporhyolite into geological jargon to explain how volcanics undergo extreme metamorphosis; served as instructor and associate professor at Ohio State University (1893–95); at Bryn Mawr College, was reader (1895–1903), associate professor (1903–06), professor (1906–28), professor emeritus (1928–45), and created graduate program that gained prominence internationally (hers was the 1st geology department at a women's college); introduced optical crystallography methods to US scientists and showed them how to use a 2-circle contact goniometer that she had developed to teach crystallography; studied paleontology and stratigraphy to complement work in petrography and structural geology; trained the most important female geologists in world (1930s); served as geologist, US Geological Survey, publishing major folios (1896–1938); with US Geological Survey, surveyed territory from NJ to VA, and her reports are considered her most important geological contribution; work led to preparation of survey maps which indicate areas feasible for

economic development and provide scientific insight to North American continent's physical history; was associate editor for *American Geologist* (1896–1905); was 2nd woman appointed fellow (1894) and 1st woman elected an officer (1924) of Geological Society of America; published approximately 40 articles on petrology, geomorphology, and history of geology. ❖ See also Isabel Fothergill Smith, *The Stone Lady: A Memoir of Florence Bascom* (Bryn Mawr College, 1981); and *Women in World History.*

BASFORD, Kathleen (1916–1998). English botanist. Born Sept 6, 1916, in Grantham, Lincolnshire, England; died Dec 20, 1998; University of Manchester, MS; m. Dr. Freddie Basford, 1936; children: 3. ❖ Developed interest in cultivation of fuchsias (late 1940s); published paper in *Journal of the Fuchsia Society* (1952) about a cross between a Mexican and New Zealand fuchsia which had existed 20–30 million years ago; received post in botany department at University of Manchester as a result; researched maize breeding in Peru with S.C. Harland; worked in department of diagnostic cytology at Christie Cancer Hospital, Manchester; in retirement, researched significance of mythical Green Man, resulting in *The Green Man* (1978).

BASHAM, Maud Ruby (1879–1963). New Zealand singer, radio broadcaster, and writer. Name variations: Maud Ruby Taylor, Aunt Daisy. Born Aug 30, 1879, in London, England; died July 14, 1963, in Wellington, New Zealand; dau. of Robert (carpenter) and Eliza Taylor; m. Frederick Basham, 1904 (died 1950); children: 3. ❖ Immigrated to New Zealand with family (1891); was a music and choral teacher and soloist (1918–24); following radio performance as Aunt Daisy, broadcast half-hour daily program for women (1930s); also wrote cookbooks and helpful hints books. Awarded British Empire Medal (1956).

BASHEMATH. Biblical woman. Name variations: Mahalath. Dau. of Ishamel; m. Esau, the last of his 3 wives; children: son Reuel, founder of the 4 tribes of Edomites.

BASHEMATH (fl. 900 BCE). Biblical women. Dau. of Solomon; m. Ahimaaz (one of his officers).

BASHIR, Marie (1930—). Australian psychiatrist and politician. Born Marie Roslyn Bashir, 1930, in Narrandera, NSW, Australia, of Lebanese-born parents; graduate of Women's College of University of Sydney, 1956; m. Sir Nicholas Shehadie (Lord Mayor of Sydney, 1971–73); children: 3. ❖ Often focusing on the underprivileged, helped Cambodian child refugees integrate into Australian society (1970s); served as clinical professor of psychiatry at University of Sydney (1993–2001), area director of Mental Health Services for Central Sydney (1994–2001) and senior consultant to the Aboriginal Medical Service, Redfern (1996–2001); helped found Women for Wik (1997), to support the Aboriginal Wik group gain land rights; became governor of New South Wales (2001), its 1st female governor. Appointed Officer of the Order of Australia (1988) and Companion of the Order of Australia (2001).

BASHKIRTSEFF, Marie (1859–1884). Russian-born painter and diarist. Name variations: (Russian form) Maria Konstantinovna Bashkirtseva; (pseudonym) Miss Hastings. Pronunciation: Bash-KEERT-sev, Bash-KEERT-seva. Born Marie Bashkirtseff, probably Jan 24, 1859 (some authorities place her birth as early as Nov 1858), outside Kiev, Ukraine; died in Paris, France, Oct 31, 1884; dau. of Konstantin Bashkirtseff (Russian noble and landowner) and Marie (Babanina) Bashkirtseff; trained in art at Academy Julian (or Julien) in Paris, 1877–84; never married; no children. ❖ Rising young painter and daughter of wealthy Russian expatriates in Paris who, before her early death, produced one of the most notable diaries of 19th century; left Russia, along with mother and members of her mother's family (1870); began diary and had love affair at a distance with Lord Hamilton (1873); began to paint (1875); settled in Paris (1877); had 1st painting accepted at Paris Salon (1880); was diagnosed with TB and met Bastien-Lepage (1882); corresponded with Guy de Maupassant; produced painting *The Meeting,* which was hailed in Parisian press and led to sale of several other works; most frequently defined by critics as "genre painter," best known works are portraits and street scenes; paintings include *The Académie Julian* (1880) and *Jean and Jacques* (1883). After death (1884), her diary covering the last 10 years of her life was published by her mother (1887); a remarkable psychological portrait of girl passing to young womanhood, it appealed to readers on both sides of Atlantic, and was used by Simone de Beauvoir as a major source for *The Second Sex.* ❖ See also D.J. Baynes, *The Life of Marie Bashkirtseff* (1943); *The Journal of Marie Bashkirtseff* (trans. by Mathilde Blind, Virago,

1985); Doris Langley Moore, *Marie & the Duke of H.: The Daydream Love Affair of Marie Bashkirtseff* (Lippincott, 1966); and *Women in World History*.

BASHKIRTSEVA, Maria Konstantinovna (1859–1884). *See Bashkirtseff, Marie.*

BASICH, Tina (1969—). American snowboarder. Born June 29, 1969, in Sacramento, California. ❖ Won gold (Winter 1998), silver (Summer 1998), and bronze (Winter 1997) in Big Air at X Games; competes in Big Air and Slopestyle; became founding member of Boarding for Breast Cancer (B4BC); active in clothing and board design. Other 1st-places finishes include ESPN Freeride, Aspen, Colorado, in big air (1997); MTV Big Air, Snow Summit, CA (1999); and Boarding for Breast Cancer, Sierra-at-Tahoe, CA, in Big Air (1999).

BASILE, Adriana (c. 1590–c. 1640). Italian opera singer. Name variations: Adreana, Adriana Basile Baroni. Born Adriana Basile in Posillip, near Naples, c. 1590 (some sources cite 1580); died in Rome, c. 1640; sister of Giovanni Battista (poet) and singers Vittoria and Margherita Basile (d. 1636?); m. Mutio Baroni; children: 3, including daughters Leonora (1611–1670) and Caterina Baroni (1620–?) who were also singers and performed with their mother at their salon in Rome. ❖ Began singing in the Mantuan court (c. 1610); performed in Mantua, Naples and Rome; awarded a barony.

BASILISSA (fl. 54–68). Christian martyr and saint. Name variations: Basilissa of Rome. Slain during the reign of Nero (r. 54–68). ❖ With Saint Anastasia, said to have been beheaded for burying the bodies of St. Peter and St. Paul. Martyrdom is commemorated on April 15.

BASILISSA (d. 780). Benedictine abbess. Name variations: Saint Basilissa of Horren. Died in 780. ❖ Was abbess of Horren near Trier. Feast day is Dec 5th.

BASILISSA OF HORREN (d. 780). *See Basilissa, Saint.*

BASILISSA OF ROME (fl. 54–68). *See Basilissa.*

BASINE (fl. 428). Frankish queen. Married Clodion, chief of the Franks (r. 428–447).

BASINE (fl. 465). Merovingian queen of the Salian Franks. Married Childeric I (436–481), king of the Salian Franks (r. 457–481), in 463; children: Clovis I (465–511), king of the Salian Franks (r. 481–511), who m. St. Clotilda (470–545).

BASINGER, Barbara (d. 1497). *See Fugger, Barbara Baesinger.*

BASQUETTE, Lina (1907–1995). American actress. Born Lena Baskette, April 19, 1907, in San Mateo, California; died in Wheeling, West Virginia, Sept 30, 1995; dau. of Gladys Basquette Belcher and stepdau. of Ernest Belcher (dance instructor); half-sister of actress-dancer Marge Champion; m. Sam Warner (movie producer), 1925 (died 1927); m. J. Peverell Marley (cinematographer); also married to Jack Dempsey's trainer as well as Nelson Eddy (the actor), and 3 others; children: (1st m.) Lita; 1 son from another marriage. ❖ Began performing at 1915 San Francisco World Fair, where she was featured as "Baby Ballerina" for Victor Talking Machine Co. exhibition; signed contract with Universal at age 9; endured demands of legendary stage mother, 6 marriages, vicious custody battle, and 2 suicide attempts, before settling into 2nd career as owner of Honey Hollow Kennels, one of finest Great Dane kennels in US; films include "Lena Baskette Featurettes," *Penrod* (1922), *Serenade* (1927), *The Younger Generation* (1929), *Goldie* (1931), *Hello Trouble* (1932), *The Midnight Lady* (1932), *Phantom Express* (1932), *Ebb Tide* (1937), *The Buccaneer* (1938), *Four Men and a Prayer* (1938), *A Night for Crime* (1943) and *Paradise Park* (1991).

BASS, Charlotta Spears (1880–1969). African-American editor and civil-rights advocate. Name variations: Charlotta A. Bass; Charlotta Spears. Born Charlotta Spears, Oct 1880, in Sumter, South Carolina; died April 12, 1969, in Los Angeles, California; dau. of Hiram Spears and Kate Spears; m. Joseph Bass (newspaper founder and editor), mid-1910s (died 1934). ❖ Sold subscriptions for newspaper *The Eagle* (later *The California Eagle*) in Los Angeles (1910–12); managed and edited *The California Eagle*, focusing on social activism (1912–50s); won libel suit brought by Ku Klux Klan against newspaper (1925); worked for Wendell Wilkie's presidential campaign (1940); was the 1st black grand-jury member at Los Angeles Co. Court (1943); ran unsuccessfully for Los Angeles City Council (1945) and for Congress (1950); testified before Tenney Committee on suspicion of being "un-American" (1946); helped found Progressive Party (late 1940s); visited Paris and Prague for Peace

Committee of the World Congress (1950); was 1st black candidate for vice presidency, representing Progressive Party (1952); helped establish several organizations to assist minorities, including Progressive Educational Association (1917), Industrial Business Council (1930), and Home Protective Association; argued for creation of permanent fair-employment practices committee and equal rights for minorities; supported banning of atomic bomb (1950) and end to Cold War and Korean War. ❖ See also autobiography, *Forty Years: Memoirs from the Pages of a Newspaper* (1960).

BASS, Mary Elizabeth (1876–1956). American physician. Name variations: Elizabeth Bass. Born in Carley, Mississippi, 1876; died 1956; dau. of Issac Esau and Mary Eliza (Wilkes) Bass; graduate of Woman's Medical College of Pennsylvania, MD, 1904. ❖ With sister, joined 5 other woman physicians to found New Orleans Hospital for Women and Children (1908), which was later named the Sara Mayo Hospital; became one of 1st 2 women appointed to unpaid faculty position at Tulane University's School of Medicine (c. 1911); was later promoted to rank of instructor of clinical medicine, and became full professor (1920); wrote column "These Were the First" for *Journal of the American Women's Medical Association* (1946–56), which chronicled careers of early women physicians. Received Elizabeth Blackwell Centennial Medal Award (1953). ❖ See also *Women in World History*.

BASSEPORTE, Magdalene (?–c. 1780). French artist. Name variations: Madeleine Basseporte. Born Frances Magdalene Basseporte; died c. 1780. ❖ Painted subjects from natural history in watercolors, executing 3 books of flowers which were engraved by Avril; also engraved some plates for Crozat College and others, including *The Martyrdom of S. Fidelio de Sigmaringa* (after the work of P.A. Robert) and *Diana and Endymion* (after a design by Sebastiano Conca).

BASSET, Florence Knoll (b. 1917). *See Knoll, Florence.*

BASSET, Mary Roper (fl. 1544–1572). English writer and translator. Born before 1544 in England; died in England in 1572; dau. of Margaret More Roper (1505–1544) and William Roper (both Protestant scholars); m. Stephen Clarke (died); m. James Basset. ❖ As granddaughter of humanist scholar Sir Thomas More and daughter of Margaret More Roper, arguably one of the best-educated women in 16th-century Europe, grew up surrounded by humanist writers and philosophers and received classical education; contributed to growth of English humanism through her translations into English of significant humanist works. Among her translations were *Treatise on the Passion* (1557), written in Latin by Thomas More, and translation into English from mother's Latin edition of Eusebius' history of the church.

BASSETT, Angela (1958—). African-American actress. Born Aug 16, 1958, in New York, NY; raised in St. Petersburg, Florida; dau. of single mother, Betty Bassett (social worker); Yale University, BA, in African-American studies, 1980; Yale Drama School, MA, 1983; m. Courtney B. Vance (actor), 1997. ❖ On tv, appeared on "F/X" (1986), portrayed the mother of the Jacksons in "The Jacksons: An American Dream" (1992) and starred in "The Rosa Parks Story" (2002); was also a regular on the soap, "Guiding Light"; nominated for Academy Award and won Golden Globe for her performance as Tina Turner in *What's Love Got to Do with It?*; other films include *Boyz n the Hood* (1991), *Passion Fish* (1992), *Malcolm X* (1992), *Vampire in Brooklyn* (1995), *Waiting to Exhale* (1995), *How Stella Got Her Groove Back* (1998), *Supernova* (2000), *Boesman and Lena* (2000), *Sunshine State* (2002), *The Lazarus Child* (2004) and *Mr. and Mrs. Smith* (2005).

BASSETT, Ann (1878–1956). American outlaw. Name variations: Queen Ann, Ann Bassett Willis. Born in Brown's Park, Colorado, 1878; died in Leeds, Utah, May 9, 1956; dau. of Herbert (rancher and horse exporter) and May Elizabeth (Chamberlain) Bass; married H.H. "Hi" Bernard, 1904 (div. 1911); m. Frank Willis, 1920. ❖ Raised in western settlement of Brown's Hole, Colorado, may have been 1st cowgirl in US to wear divided skirt so she could ride in a man's saddle; attended Boston finishing school; when large cattle companies threatened to buy out town and "squeeze out the settlers," took steps to rally residents and defend town; was said to have headed band of outlaws, but this fact is questionable; remained controversial figure, denying that she was a rustler; involved in a court case when her foreman was accused of stealing and butchering a heifer (1911), but received favorable verdict. ❖ See also *Women in World History*.

BASSETT, Mary (1842–1935). *See Mumford, Mary.*

BASSEY, Shirley (1937—). Welsh singer. Name variations: Dame Shirley Bassey. Born Shirley Veronica Bassey, Jan 8, 1937, in Cardiff, Wales; raised in Tiger Bay, a working-class area; dau. of a West Indian seaman who died when she was 2; m. Sergio Novak; m. Kenneth Hume; children: daughter who drowned (1985). ❖ Made professional debut at 16 in the touring revue "Memories of Al Jolson"; had 1st major hit with "The Banana Boat Song"; had mega-hit with "Goldfinger" from the James Bond film of the same name (1964); also sang title songs for films *Diamonds Are Forever* (1971), *Moonraker* (1979) and *La Passione* (1996), among others; after 24 years, was back in the Top-40 charts with hit single "History Repeating" (1997), while singing with the Propellerheads. Awarded CBE (1993) and DBE (1999).

BASSI, Laura (1711–1778). Italian anatomist and natural philosopher. Born Laura Maria Caterina Bassi in Bologna, Italy, 1711; died 1778; awarded PhD from University of Bologna, 1731 or 1732; m. Dr. Giuseppe Veratti (physician and professor), 1738; children: 12. ❖ Renowned scholar, held public disputation on philosophy at 21; received, among many honors, doctor's degree from University of Bologna, where she was eventually appointed to chair of physics; published 2 Latin dissertations but was noted more for teaching than research; corresponded with many eminent European intellectuals, including Voltaire, for whom she secured membership in the Accademia; known as deeply religious woman of "good character," gave generously to poor. A medal in her honor was coined by Senate of Bologna. ❖ See also *Women in World History.*

BASTANCHURY-BOOTH, Jane (1948—). *See Booth, Jane Bastanchury.*

BASTEN, Alice (1876–1955). New Zealand accountant and politician. Born Alice Henrietta Gertrude Basten, Jan 24, 1876, in Auckland, New Zealand; died Mar 6, 1955, in Auckland; dau. of George John Basten (coachbuilder) and Rachel (Lang) Basten. ❖ Ran a secretarial and accounting business with sister in Auckland (1904–40s); also trained hundreds of young women in clerical practice until 1922; elected to Auckland City Council (1927); was a member of delegation to Pan-Pacific Women's Association conference (1934).

BASTIDAS, Micaela (1745–1781). Peruvian revolutionary leader. Born Micaela Bastidas Puyucahua (also seen as Puyurawa), a pure-blooded Spaniard, in Pampamarca, Cuzco, Peru, 1745; died May 18, 1781; m. José Gabriel Condorcanqui, Túpac Amarú II (revolutionary leader and great-great-grandson of Tupac Amaru [c. 1544–1572]), 1760; children: 3 sons, Hipólito, Fernando, Mariano. ❖ One of the most prominent women in the great Inca revolt (1780–83), worked as commandant of secretariat located in rebel stronghold of San Felipe de Tungasuca; with status as wife of rebel chieftain, had level of control which solicitor general of Cuzco described as allowing her to command "with more authority and rigor than her husband"; warned local governors of penalties for desertion and issued numerous directives forbidding banditry; captured by Spanish colonial authorities, was found guilty of complicity in the rebellion and executed in Cuzco's *Plaza Mayor.* ❖ See also *Women in World History.*

BASTOS, Regina (1960—). Portuguese lawyer and politician. Born Nov 4, 1960, in Veiros-Estarreja, Portugal. ❖ Voting member of the Estarreja Municipal Assembly (1989–93, 1997—); Estarreja municipal councillor (1993–97) and assistant to the Aveiro Civil Governor (1994–95); as a member of the European People's Party (Christian Democrats) and European Democrats (EPP), elected to 5th European Parliament (1999–2004).

BAT (r. 267–272). *See Zenobia.*

BAT-MIRIAM, Yocheved (1901–1980). Israeli poet. Name variations: Yocheved Zhelezniak. Born Yocheved Zhelezniak, 1901, in Keplits, Belorussia (now Belarus); died 1980; studied at universities of Odessa and Moscow; children: son Zuzik (killed in War of Independence, 1948). ❖ Immigrated to Palestine (1928); published 1st book of verse (1929); following death of son (1948), never wrote again; collections include *Merahok* (1932), *Eretz Israel* (1937), *Shirim La'ghetto* (1946) and *Shirim* (1963). Awarded the Bialik Prize (1964) and Israel Prize (1972).

BATCHELOR, Joy (1914–1991). English film animator. Born May 12, 1914, in London, England; m. John Halas (b. April 16, 1912), in Budapest. ❖ One of the most prolific and successful animators in British history, teamed with husband to form an animation studio (1940); made films for war effort (1941–45), including *Digging for Victory*, with composer Matyas Seiber; after war, made instructional and public-relations films; won international fame for adaptation of Orwell's *Animal Farm* (1954), the 1st full-length animated feature to come out of UK; animated US tv series, including "Popeye" (c. 1958), which ran for at least 2 decades in syndication; worked on several cartoon series for children produced by Hanna-Barbera (1970s), most notably "The Addams Family," "The Jackson Five" and "The Osmonds. ❖ See also Roger Manvell, *The Story of Halas and Batchelor: Animation Studio 1940–1980* (1980); and *Women in World History.*

BATCHELOR, Mary (1927—). New Zealand politician. Born Mary Foley, Jan 7, 1927, in Christchurch, NZ; m. Arthur Batchelor, 1945; children: 2. ❖ Was a trade union organizer; served as Labour MP for Avon (1972–87); served on the Select Committee on Women's Rights. Worked toward better legislation concerning domestic violence and rape.

BATE, Dorothea (1879–1951). Welsh geologist. Born Dorothea Minola Alice Bate, Nov 8, 1879, in Carmarthenshire, Wales; died Jan 13, 1951. ❖ Authority on birds of Mediterranean islands and Pleistocene mammals, educated herself in anatomy while working in bird room at National History Museum, London, in her teens; published 1st paper (1901); found fossils, including *Elephas cypriotes* and *Hippopotamus minutus* (both Cyprus), *E. creticus* (Crete), and *Myotragus* (Balaeric Islands); worked under Dorothy Garrod on animal remains found in Wady el-Mughara Caves, Mount Carmel, and published *The Fossil Fauna of the Wady el Mughara Caves* (1937); at 68, worked with Louis S.B. Leakey at Rusinga Island, Lake Victoria; served as officer in charge of National History Museum in Tring, Hertfordshire (1947–51).

BATEHAM, Josephine (1829–1901). American temperance reformer. Born Josephine Abiah Penfield, Nov 1, 1829, in Alden, NY; died Mar 15, 1901, in Oberlin, Ohio; m. Rev. Richard Cushman, July 20, 1848 (died c. 1949); m. Michael Boyd Bateham (horticulturist and editor), Sept 27, 1850; children: 7. ❖ Performed missionary work with 1st husband in Haiti (c. 1849); was editor of the ladies' department of the *Ohio Cultivator* (published by 2nd husband); served as president of the State Temperance Society of the Women of Ohio (1853) and was active in the state and national Women's Christian Temperance Union (WCTU); was superintendent of the national WCTU's Department for the Suppression of Sabbath Desecration (1884–96).

BATEMAN, Hester (1709–1794). English silversmith. Born Hester Needham in 1709; died 1794; m. John Bateman; children: 5. ❖ One of 18th century's greatest silversmiths, probably learned the craft from husband who worked in silver and gold; following his death (1761), took over family business and registered her own hallmark, "H.B."; with 2 sons and an apprentice, worked for other silversmiths, but shop eventually won acclaim for its own beautiful domestic silver, especially tea and coffee pots, spoons, and other tableware; also produced some church and presentation pieces, known for their refined—almost austere—lines and decoration; retired (1790).

BATEMAN, Jessie (1877–1940). English actress. Born Aug 2, 1877, in England; died Nov 14, 1940; m. Captain G.A. Ashfordby Trenchard (died 1902); m. Wilfred G. Chancellor; m. Captain Kenneth Duncan Bond. ❖ At 10, made stage debut in London as a dancer; appeared as Cobweb in *A Midsummer Night's Dream* (1889), followed by *The Rose and the Ring, Ivanhoe, The Guinea Stamp, Mr. Martin, A Little Ray of Sunshine, A Message from Mars, The Man from Blankley's, Beauty and the Barge, The Cabinet Minister, Raffles, Dear Brutus, Dulcy* and *The Painted Veil*; made NY debut in *A Brace of Partridges* (1898); appeared in the film *Account Rendered.*

BATEMAN, Kate (1842–1917). American actress. Name variations: Mrs. George Crowe. Born Kate Josephine Bateman in Baltimore, Maryland, Oct 7, 1842; died in 1917; 2nd child of H.L. Bateman (theatrical manager) and Frances Bateman (actress and playwright); sister of Ellen Bateman (also a child actor who retired from the stage in 1856 and later m. Claude Greppo); m. George Crowe, Oct 1866. ❖ Born into theatrical family and hailed as child prodigy, toured England with sister Ellen; played title role in *Evangeline* (1860), written by mother, based on Longfellow poem; achieved star status as Julie in *The Hunchback;* had success as Lady Gay Spanker in *London Assurance* and Lady Teazel in *The School for Scandal;* played signature role "Jewess" Leah, who was deserted by her Christian lover, in *Leah, the Forsaken* in England (1860); appeared with Henry Irving in *Macbeth* and played title role in Tennyson's *Queen Mary;* established acting school in London (1882), where she taught for many years. ❖ See also *Women in World History.*

BATEMAN, Mary (1768–1809). British murderer. Name variations: Yorkshire Witch. Born Mary Harker in Aisenby, Yorkshire, England,

1768; executed Mar 20, 1809; dau. of James Harker (farmer); m. John Bateman, c. 1792; children: 1. ❖ Known as the Yorkshire Witch, found victims among uneducated villagers of 18th-century England, who were awed and terrified by her reported supernatural powers; employed phony witchcraft schemes to extort large sums of money from her victims; after a plot involving poison resulted in death of a young woman (1806), was found guilty of murder and sentenced to hang.

BATEMAN, Virginia Frances (1853–1940). *See Compton, Virginia.*

BATES, Barbara (1925–1969). American actress. Born Aug 6, 1925, in Denver, Colorado; committed suicide by carbon monoxide poisoning, Mar 18, 1969, in Denver; m. Cecil Coen, 1945 (died 1967); m. William Reed, 1968. ❖ Made film debut in *Salome Where She Danced* (1945); other films include *Johnny Belinda, Adventures of Don Juan, The House Across the Street, Cheaper by the Dozen, All About Eve, I'd Climb the Highest Mountain, Belles on Their Toes, The Outcasts of Poker Flat, The Caddy, Rhapsody* and *Apache Territory.*

BATES, Blanche (1873–1941). American actress. Name variations: The Girl of the Golden West; Blanche Lyon Bates. Born Aug 25, 1873, in Portland, Oregon; died Dec 25, 1941, in San Francisco, California; m. Milton F. Davis; m. George Creel (police commissioner, Denver, Colorado), Nov 28, 1912. ❖ Made stage debut in San Francisco in *The Picture* (1894) and NY debut as Bianca in Augustin Daly's production of *The Taming of the Shrew* (1897); had great success as Miladi in *The Musketeers* (1899); began work with David Belasco in *Naughty Anthony* (1900); achieved national fame as Cho-Cho-San, the original *Madame Butterfly*, and was critically acclaimed as Yo-San in *The Darling of the Gods* and Minnie Smith in *The Girl of the Golden West* (1905); other NY appearances include *Under Two Flags, Nobody's Widow, Diplomacy, Getting Together,* and the title roles in *Medea* and *The Famous Mrs. Fair,* among others; after ending her relationship with Belasco (1912), had continued success in a variety of works, including *Witness for the Defense* (1913), *Molière* (1919) and *Mrs. Partridge Presents* (1925); following retirement (1926), performed in 2 supporting roles (1933).

BATES, Carrie (1968—). *See Steinseifer, Carrie.*

BATES, Charlotte Fiske (1838–1916). American poet. Name variations: Mme Adolphe Rogé or Roge; Charlotte Fiske Rogé. Born in New York, NY, Nov 30, 1838; died 1916; dau. of Harvey Bates; educated in Cambridge, Massachusetts. ❖ Assisted Henry Wadsworth Longfellow in compiling *Poems of Places;* also edited the *Cambridge Book of Poetry and Song* (Boston, 1882), contributed to magazines, and published *Risk and Other Poems* (1879).

BATES, Clara Doty (1838–1895). American author. Born Clara Doty in Ann Arbor, Michigan, Dec 22, 1838; died in Chicago, Oct 14, 1895; m. Morgan Bates (Chicago publisher). ❖ Lived in Chicago and published many juvenile books in the 19th century; also wrote *From Heart's Content* (1892).

BATES, Daisy Lee (1914–1999). American civil-rights activist. Name variations: Daisy Gatson Bates, Mrs. L.C. Bates. Born Daisy Lee Gatson, Nov 11, 1914, in Huttig, Arkansas; died Nov 4, 1999, in Little Rock, Arkansas; adopted by Orlee and Susan Smith as an infant; attended Shorter College and Philander Smith College, both in Little Rock; m. L(ucius) C(hristopher) Bates, 1941 (died Aug 1980). ❖ As teenager, moved to Memphis and graduated from high school there (1934); married, moved to Little Rock and, with husband, founded *Arkansas State Press* (1941); elected Arkansas state president of NAACP branches (1952); led in effort to integrate all grades of Little Rock public schools (1956); served as spokeswoman, counselor, "surrogate mother" for the "Little Rock Nine" students chosen to pioneer the integration of Central High (1957); worked successfully with NAACP lawyers to reverse Governor Faubus' segregation orders (Sept 1957); became target for segregationists (1957–59); arrested and fined for resisting city ordinance requiring disclosure of names of NAACP members and contributors to city council (US Supreme Court reversed conviction in *Bates v. Little Rock,* 1960); saw *State Press* bankrupted by advertisers boycott (Oct 30, 1959); moved to NY to write memoirs and continue civil-rights activism (1960); enlisted by Kennedy Administration to work in voter registration project, Democratic National Committee; named director of Mitchelville, Arkansas, Office of Economic Opportunity during Johnson Administration (1964); worked with O.E.O. officials and others in community revitalization project in Mitchelville; made headlines during Nixon administration, protesting Nixon's cancellation

of O.E.O. programs; received more than 210 different awards. Author of *The Long Shadow of Little Rock* (McKay, 1962). ❖ See also *Women in World History.*

BATES, Daisy May (1859–1951). Irish-born anthropologist in Australia. Born Daisy May O'Dwyer, Oct 16, 1859, at Ballychrine, Co. Tipperary, Ireland; died April 18, 1951, at Prospect, near Adelaide, South Australia; only dau. of Marguarette (Hunt) and James Edward O'Dwyer; m. Edwin Henry Murrant (said to have been "Breaker" Morant), Mar 13, 1884, at Charters Towers (no record of a divorce exists); m. Jack Bates (cattle rancher), Feb 17, 1885; children: Arnold (b. 1886). ❖ Arrived in Australia (1883), seeking warm climate due to pulmonary tuberculosis; developed interest in Aborigines due to influence of Reverend George Stanton, 1st Anglican bishop of North Queensland; worked as apprentice journalist in England and approached London *Times* offering to investigate rumors about living conditions among Aborigines; in Australia, traveled over 800 miles to remote mission run by Trappist monks at Beagle Bay and spent months carrying out extensive investigations into status of Aborigines in surrounding area which were subsequently documented in a series of articles in the *Times;* at a time when great majority of white Australians had no interest in native culture, embarked on 1st systematic study of Aboriginal kinship affiliations and customs; with funds granted by government of Western Australia (1904), studied Bibbulmun tribe who resided on the Maamba reserve in southwest corner of the state; contributed important paper to *Victoria Geographical Journal* (1905), the 1st comparative study of the marriage customs between the Aborigines in Western Australia and those in other parts of the country; appointed "traveling protector" of Aborigines in Western Australia (1910); made principal concern the condition of elderly and sick natives; received name of *Kabbarli* (grandmother) from Aborigines; submitted perhaps her most important report to Western Australian government (1912) which recommended establishment of reservations in remote parts of the country, and these recommendations were subsequently accepted in part by state government which established a series of "Aboriginal Protection Boards"; established new residence at Eucla, near the border with Southern Australia, among Mirning tribe; established residence at Ooldea and worked to alleviate distress of Aborigines there (1919); created a Commander of the British Empire (1934); writings include *The Passing of the Aborigines* (1938) and numerous articles in Australian and British newspapers. ❖ See also Ernestine Hill, *Kabbarli: A Personal Memoir of Daisy Bates* (University Press, 1973); and *Women in World History.*

BATES, Elizabeth (1947–2003). American researcher and psychologist. Born Elizabeth Ann Bates, July 26, 1947, in Wichita, Kansas; died Dec 13, 2003, in San Diego, California; graduate of St. Louis University; University of Chicago, PhD in human development; m. George Carnevale (physicist); children: Julia Carnevale. ❖ An expert on how the brain processes language, was also a professor of cognitive science at University of California at San Diego; served as director of the department's Center for Research in Language; was also a visiting scholar at National Research Council Institute of Psychology in Rome; writings include *Rethinking Innateness* (1996).

BATES, Florence (1888–1954). American actress and lawyer. Born Florence Rabe, April 15, 1888, in San Antonio, Texas; died Jan 31, 1954, in Burbank, California; m. Will Jacoby, 1929 (died 1951). ❖ Became the 1st woman lawyer in Texas (1914); at 47, moved to CA and joined the Pasadena Playhouse; made film debut in Hitchcock's *Rebecca,* followed by *Kitty Foyle, The Devil and Miss Jones, The Chocolate Soldier, We Were Dancing, The Moon and Sixpence, Heaven Can Wait, Since You Went Away, Kismet, Tonight and Every Night, Saratoga Trunk, Cluny Brown, The Diary of a Chambermaid, Claudia and David, The Secret Life of Walter Mitty, I Remember Mama, A Letter to Three Wives, Portrait of Jennie, On the Town, Lullaby of Broadway* and *Les Miserables.*

BATES, Harriet Leonora (1856–1886). American poet and novelist. Name variations: Harriet L. Vose; (pseudonym) Eleanor Putnam. Born Harriet Leonora Vose in 1856; died 1886; married Arlo Bates (1850–1918, novelist, Boston newspaper editor, and professor of English at Massachusetts Institute of Technology). ❖ Was the author of *A Woodland Wooing* and *Old Salem;* with husband, co-wrote the novel *Prince Vance* (1888); was also the subject of his elegy *Sonnets in Shadow* published in 1887, one year after her death.

BATES, Katherine Lee (1859–1929). American author and educator. Born Aug 12, 1859, at Falmouth, Massachusetts; died Mar 28, 1929, at Wellesley, Massachusetts; dau. of William Bates (Congregational minister) and Cornelia Frances (Lee) Bates; attended Wellesley College and Oxford University; lived with Katharine Coman (Wellesley professor of economics); never married; no children. ❖ Appointed professor and permanent head of Wellesley English department (1891); joined a prairie wagon ascent of Pike's Peak and at top of the mountain heard the words in her mind which would become lyrics for "America the Beautiful": "O Beautiful for Spacious Skies, for Amber waves of grain. For Purple Mountains Majesties. . . ."; reworked her poem for some time, finally publishing it on Fourth of July (1895) in *The Congregationalist;* also published children's stories, other poetry, and scholarly work; named director of International Institute for Girls in Spain; gathered outstanding group of women scholars in Wellesley English department; designated professor emeritus (1925); edited numerous English and American classics. Other writings include *Yellow Clover, a Book of Remembrance* (1922), *English Religious Drama* (1893), *Sigurd our Golden Collie and Other Comrades of the Road* (1919), *Rose and Thorn* (1889), and *Spanish Highways and Byways* (1900). ❖ See also Dorothy Burgess, *Dream and Deed: The Story of Katherine Lee Bates* (U. of Oklahoma Press, 1952); and *Women in World History.*

BATES, Kathy (1948—). American actress. Born Kathleen Doyle Bates, June 28, 1948, in Memphis, Tennessee; dau. of Langdon Doyle Bates (mechanical engineer); Southern Methodist University, BFA in Theater, 1969; m. Tony Campisi, 1991 (div. 1997). ❖ Appeared on NY stage; as Bobo Bates, made film debut in *Taking Off* (1971); appeared as Stella Mae in *Come Back to the Five and Dime, Jimmy Dean, Jimmy Dean* (1982); came to prominence and won an Oscar for performance as Annie Wilkes in *Misery* (1990), followed by *Fried Green Tomatoes* (1991); on tv, appeared in "Johnny Bull" (1986), "Roe vs. Wade" (1989), "Hostages" (1993), "The Late Shift" (1996) and "Annie" (1999); other films include *Arthur 2* (1988), *Dick Tracy* (1990), *At Play in the Fields of the Lord* (1991), *Used People* (1992), *The Road to Mecca* (1992), *Curse of the Starving Class* (1994), *Dolores Claiborne* (1995), *Diabolique* (1996), *The War at Home* (1996), *Titanic* (1997), *Primary Colors* (1998), *About Schmidt* (2002) and *The Bridge of San Luis Rey* (2004).

BATES, Mrs. L.C. (b. 1914). See Bates, Daisy Lee.

BATES, Lynda (1942—). See Chalker, Lynda.

BATES, Mary (1861–1954). American physician. Name variations: Mary Elizabeth Bates. Born Feb 25, 1861, in Manitowoc, Wisconsin; died 1954; dau. of William Wallace Bates and Marie (Cole) Bates (graduate of New York Hydropathic Medical College); earned medical degree from Woman's Medical School in Chicago (now part of Northwestern University, 1881). ❖ Became 1st woman intern at Cook Co. Hospital in Chicago, Illinois (1881); served as lecturer in minor surgery, demonstrator in anatomy, and professor at alma mater Woman's Medical School (Chicago); served on staff of Chicago Hospital for Women and Children; settled in Denver, Colorado (1891), and had large private practice which focused on diseases of women and children; served as surgical editor of *Medical Woman's Journal;* founded Denver School for Practical Nurses; was a suffragist and lobbyist for laws protecting children.

BATES, Ruby (1913–1976). Key American participant in Scottsboro case. Name variations: Ruby Schut. Born in Huntsville, Alabama, 1913; died in Yakima, Washington, Oct 27, 1976; m. Elmer Schut. ❖ Was key participant in notorious Scottsboro case of Alabama, which made clear to the American public the full extent of racial injustice in those Southern states whose legal and social systems were based on de jure segregation; was 1 of 2 white women (with Victoria Price) who accused 9 "black boys" ranging in age from 13 to 21 of raping them; after the 9 were tried without adequate legal counsel and all but 1 received death sentences, changed her testimony; served briefly as speaker for International Labor Defense and then vanished into obscurity. Attorneys for the Scottsboro boys agreed to an unusual plea bargain (1937) whereby 4 of them were released while the other 5 remained in prison; the last of them was not released until 1950. ❖ See also *Women in World History.*

BATES, Sophia Ann (1817–1899). New Zealand teacher and postmaster. Born Sophia Ann Bates, Mar 6, 1817, at Westminster, London, England; died Nov 28, 1899, at Onehunga, New Zealand; dau. of John (tinsmith) and Elizabeth Hix (Brown) Bates. ❖ Immigrated with parents to New Zealand (1847); lived in Fencible settlement at Onehunga, Auckland; became schoolmistress soon after settlement; served as sub-deputy postmaster supervising delivery of mail to Onehunga beginning 1849,

then appointed as 1st woman postmaster (1855); continued to teach until retirement (1860). ❖ See also *Dictionary of New Zealand Biography* (Vol. 1).

BATES, Vietta M. (1922–1972). American soldier. Born June 11, 1922; died July 1972; lived in New Jersey. ❖ Enlisted in the Women's Auxiliary Army Corps (WAAC, Mar 1945); when WAAC became part of the regular army (June 1949), was the 1st woman sworn into the Women's Army Corps (WAC, July 8, 1949); assigned to duty with the Military District of Washington, DC.

BATESON, Mary (1865–1906). British specialist in medieval sociology. Born Sept 12, 1865, in Ings House, Robin Hood's Bay, near Whitby, England; died Nov 30, 1906, in Cambridge, England; dau. of William Henry Bateson (1812–1881) and Anna Aikin; sister of biologist William Bateson (1861–1926, pioneer in study of genetics); attended Newnham College, Cambridge (1887); became a member of the Council at Newnham College. ❖ Was a lecturer at Newnham College (1888–1906); influenced by Mandell Creighton, focused on monastic history; published *The Register of Crabhouse Nunnery* (1889); turned to municipal history, editing *Records of the Borough of Leicester* (3 vols., 1899–1905), *The Charters of the Borough of Cambridge* (1901), *The Cambridge Gild Records* (1903), and *Grace Book B* (2 vols. 1903–05); edited many works for antiquarian societies; was a Warburton lecturer at Manchester University and an ardent suffragist. ❖ See also *Women in World History.*

BATH, marchioness of (1735–1825). See Cavendish-Bentinck, Elizabeth.

BATHIAT, Arlette-Léonie (1898–1992). See Arletty.

BATHILDE (c. 630–c. 680). See Balthild.

BATHILDIS (c. 630–c. 680). See Balthild.

BATHILDIS OF SCHAUMBURG-LIPPE (1873–1962). Princess of Waldeck and Pyrmont. Born Bathildis Mary Leopoldine Anne Augusta, May 21, 1873; died April 6, 1962; m. Frederick, prince of Waldeck and Pyrmont; children: Helen of Waldeck and Pyrmont (1899–1948).

BATHORY, Countess Erzsébet (1560–1614). See Bathory, Elizabeth.

BATHORY, Elizabeth (1560–1614). Hungarian countess, influential landowner, and mass murderer. Name variations: Countess Erzsébet Báthory or Bathori; "The Blood Countess," "Tigress of Csejthe." Born 1560 into a Hungarian noble family at Castle Ecsed, Transylvania; convicted for murder and imprisoned in Cachtice Castle where she died in 1614; dau. of George and Anna Bathory; m. Count Ferencz Nadasdy; children: 1 out-of-wedlock (name unknown) and 4 by marriage, Anna, Ursula, Katherina, and Paul. ❖ Tortured and killed perhaps 650 women, thereby becoming one of the horrific legends of Europe. ❖ See also *Women in World History.*

BATHSHEBA (fl. 1010–975 BCE). Biblical woman. Name variations: Bethsabee. Married Uriah, the Hittite (killed); 4th (some sources say 2nd) wife of King David (r. 1010–970 BCE); children: 4 sons, including Solomon (born c. 985 BCE c. 925 BCE). ❖ As the wife of Uriah the Hittite, a soldier in King David's army, was seen bathing by David who became infatuated with her beauty, sent for her and slept with her; became pregnant; married David after he appointed her husband to an exposed position in his armies to secure his death; gave birth to a son who died; gave birth to 4 more sons, the 1st of whom was Solomon, who ultimately succeeded David on throne of Israel; is generally described as a woman who possessed a highly cultivated mind and vast knowledge (her son Solomon owed much of his wisdom and reputation to her, as well as a great part of the practical philosophy embodied in his Proverbs).

BATH ZABBAI (r. 267–272). See Zenobia.

BATIRSHINA, Jana (1979—). See Batyrchina, Jana.

BATKOVIC, Suzy (1980—). Australian basketball player. Born Dec 17, 1980, in Lambton, Australia. ❖ Forward and center, placed 1st at Oceania championships (2001, 2003); won a team silver medal at Athens Olympics (2004).

BATOUKHTINA, Elena (1971—). See Tiourina, Elena.

BATSCHAUER, Lina (1903–1983). See Radke, Lina.

BATSIUSHKA, Hanna (1981—). Belarusian weightlifter. Born Oct 24, 1981, in USSR. ❖ Placed 1st for 63kg snatch at World championships (2003); won a silver medal for 63kg at Athens Olympics (2004).

BATSON, Flora (1864–1906). African-American concert singer. Born April 16, 1864, in Washington, DC; died Dec 1, 1906, in Philadelphia, Pennsylvania; educated and studied music in Providence, Rhode Island; m. James G. Bergen (her manager), Dec 13, 1887 (died c. 1896); m. Gerard Millar. ❖ Known as the "Double-Voiced Queen of Song" because of her range from baritone to high soprano, joined Bergen Star Concert Co. (1885) and won international fame; her numerous world-wide tours were highlighted by appearances before England's Queen Victoria, Pope Leo XIII, and Queen Liliuokalani of Hawaii; also gave concerts in Fiji, India, China and Japan. ❖ See also Gerard Millar, *Life, Travels, and Works of Miss Flora Batson, Deceased Queen of Song;* and *Women in World History.*

BATSON, H.M. (1859–1943). See Batson, Henrietta M.

BATSON, Henrietta M. (1859–1943). British novelist. Name variations: H.M. Batson; Mrs. Stephen Batson. Born May 30, 1859, in Hamilton, Ontario, Canada; died Nov 30, 1943, in Dorset, England; dau. of Thomas John Mark Willoughby Blackman and Anne Gunn; m. Alfred Stephen Batson, 1879. ❖ Spent childhood in Canada and moved to Foxfield, Wilshire, England (1869); like Thomas Hardy, set novels in fictional English counties; works include *Dark: A Tale of the Down County* (1892), *Such a Lord is Love: A Woman's Heart Tragedy* (1893), *Adam the Gardener* (1894), *The Earth Children* (1897) and *A Splendid Heritage* (1910); also wrote books on gardening including *The Book of the Country and the Garden* (1903) and *A Concise Handbook of Garden Flowers* (1903).

BATSON, Mrs. Stephen (1859–1943). See Batson, Henrietta M.

BATTAGLIA, Letizia (1935—). Italian photojournalist. Born 1935 in Palermo, Sicily; dau. of a navy officer; married and sep.; children: 3 daughters. ❖ As photography director of Palermo's left-wing daily, *L'Ora,* began to document atrocities committed by the Sicilian Mafia; despite continuous threats, photographed hundreds of crime scenes during a bloody period in Palermo (1974–90); her photos had an enormous influence on the anti-Mafia campaign and some were put in evidence against Giulio Andreotti, the corrupt prime minister of Italy; also known for her photos of street life; founded the publishing house, Edizioni della Battaglia; books include *Passion, Justice, Freedom: Photographs of Sicily* (1999). Received Lifetime Achievement Award (1999).

BATTELLE, Ann (1968—). American freestyle skier. Born Jan 18, 1968, in Yonkers, NY. ❖ Won World Cup (1999, 2000); was World moguls champion (1999); competed in 3 Olympics.

BATTEN, Edith Mary (1905–1985). See Batten, Mollie.

BATTEN, Guin (1967—). English rower. Born Sept 27, 1967, in Cuckfield, Sussex, England; younger sister of Miriam Batten (rower); attended Southampton University. ❖ Won a silver medal for quadruple sculls at Sydney Olympics (2000), the 1st woman's rowing medal ever won by Britain; retired (2003).

BATTEN, Jean Gardner (1909–1982). New Zealand aviator. Born Jean Gardner Batten, Sept 15, 1909, in Rotorua, New Zealand Nov 22, 1982, in Majorca, Spain; dau. of Ellen Blackmore Batten (artist) and Frederick Harold Batten (dental surgeon). ❖ Became world famous for her aviation exploits; earned a private pilot's license (1930) and a commercial license (1932) in London; undertook a series of solo flights, setting world records (1930s); set women's record on solo flight from England to India (1933); became 1st woman to fly from England to Australia (1934) and from Australia to England (1935); became 1st woman to fly across the South Atlantic Ocean from Africa to South America (1935); made the 1st direct flight to Auckland, New Zealand, from England, setting world record (1936), and from Australia to England with a record solo time (1937); won US Challenge Trophy (1934, 1935, 1936), US Harmon Trophy (1935, 1936, 1937), Johnston Memorial Air Navigation Trophy (1935) and Segrave Trophy (1936); awarded officer of the Brazilian Order of the Southern Cross (1935); named Commander of the British Empire (1936); given the chevalier of the French Legion of Honor (1936). Jean Batten archive was established at the Royal Air Force Museum (1972), and British Airways christened an airliner the "Jean Batten" (1981). ❖ See also autobiographies *My Life* (G.G. Harrap, 1938 [republished as *Alone in the Sky,* Airlife, 1979]) and *Solo Flight* (1934); and *Women in World History.*

BATTEN, Kim (1969—). African-American runner. Born Mar 29, 1969, in McRae, Georgia. ❖ Won a silver medal for 400-meter hurdles at Atlanta Olympics (1996); at World championships, won a gold medal for 400-meter hurdles (1995), bronze for 400-meter hurdles and silver for 4 x 400 meters (1997).

BATTEN, Miriam (1964—). English rower. Born Nov 4, 1964, in Dartford, Kent, England; elder sister of Guin Batten (rower). ❖ Won World championship for double sculls (1998) and a silver medal for quadruple sculls at Sydney Olympics (2000).

BATTEN, Mollie (1905–1985). English social-work pioneer. Name variations: Edith Mary Batten. Born 1905 in London, England; died 1985 in England; graduated from Southport Girls' High School; attended Liverpool University and London School of Economics; studied theology at St. Anne's, Oxford, 1947–49. ❖ Became warden of Birmingham University Settlement (1933) and developed training for both youth and social workers; worked for Ministry of Labor during WWII but declined permanent civil service appointment, choosing instead to read theology at St. Anne's; served as principal of William Temple College, bringing together people from industry, civil service, social work and education (1950–66); supported Labour Party as well as ordination of women into priesthood. Awarded Order of the British Empire (OBE, 1948).

BATTENBERG, Princess of (1857–1944). See Beatrice.

BATTERHAM, Mary Rose (c. 1870–1927). American nurse. Born c. 1870 in England; died April 4, 1927, in North Carolina; dau. of William and Mary Rose Batterham; came to NY at age 20; graduate of Brooklyn City Hospital nurse program, 1893, and Brooklyn City Hospital. ❖ In North Carolina, served as head nurse at Oakland Heights Sanitarium and as a Metropolitan Life nurse; was charter member and 1st vice president of North Carolina State Nurses' Association; registered as nurse in Buncombe Co., NC (June 5, 1903), when North Carolina became 1st state to require nurses' registration; was the 2nd registered nurse in the US (1st was Josephine Burton of Craven Co., NC, who registered the day before).

BATTERSEA, Lady (1843–1931). See Rothschild, Constance de.

BATTLE, Kathleen (1948—). African-American soprano. Born Aug 13, 1948, in Portsmouth, Ohio; dau. of a steelworker; earned Bachelor's and Master's degrees from College Conservatory of Music, University of Cincinnati. ❖ Made professional debut at the Spoleto Festival (1972) and Metropolitan debut 5 years later as the Shepherd in *Tannhauser* (1977); has appeared at the world's leading opera houses and often sang under the baton of James Levine; 5-time Grammy winner, became renowned for her interpretations of the light lyric repertoire, especially the soubrette roles of Mozart and Richard Strauss, as well as for recitals of German Lieder and Negro spirituals; presented André Previn's song cycle *Honey and Rue* (text by Toni Morrison) at Carnegie Hall (1992).

BATTLE, Tara (1968—). See Cross-Battle, Tara.

BATUKHTINA, Elena (1971—). See Tiourina, Elena.

BATYRCHINA, Jana (1979—). Russian rhythmic gymnast. Name variations: Ianina or Yanina Batyrchina, Batyrshina or Batirshina. Born Oct 7, 1979, in Tashkent, Uzbekistan. ❖ At World championships, won a bronze medal for all-around (1995) and team gold medals (1996–99); at European championships, won silver medals in all-around and ball (1996); at Atlanta Olympics, won a silver medal in indiv. all-around (1996); won Grand Prix Final (1996). Holder of the Honored Master of Sports title.

BAU, Sabine (1969—). West German fencer. Name variations: Sabine Christiane Bau. Born July 19, 1969, in Würzburg, Germany. ❖ At Seoul Olympics, won a silver medal in indiv. foil and a gold medal in team foil (1988); won a silver medal at Barcelona Olympics (1992), a bronze medal at Atlanta Olympics (1996), and a bronze medal at Sydney Olympics (2000), all for team foil; won the World championship (1989, 1993, 1998, 1999); spent 17 years on the national team, winning 23 medals.

BAUCHENS, Anne (1881–1967). American motion-picture editor. Born in Saint Louis, Missouri, Feb 2, 1881; died May 7, 1967, in Woodland Hills, California, at the Motion Picture Country Hospital; never married; no children. ❖ Served as assistant editor on Cecil B. DeMille's film *We Can't Have Everything* (1919), then continued to edit every DeMille film; nominated for Academy Awards for Best Editing for *Cleopatra* (1934), *The Greatest Show On Earth* (1952), and *The Ten Commandments* (1956); received the Oscar for *Northwest Mounted Police* (1940); other films include *The Squaw Man* (1918), *Till I Come*

Back to You (1918), *For Better or Worse* (1919), *The Affairs of Anatol* (1921), *Fool's Paradise* (1921), *Adam's Rib* (1923), *The King of Kings* (1927), *Chicago* (1928), *Craig's Wife* (1928), *Dynamite* (1929), *Ned McCobb's Daughter* (1929), *Lord Byron of Broadway* (1930), *Madam Satan* (1930), *The Squaw Man* (1931), *The Sign of the Cross* (1932), *Cradle Song* (1933), *Cleopatra* (1934), *The Crusades* (1935), *The Plainsman* (1937), *The Buccaneer* (1938), *Bulldog Drummond in Africa* (1938), *Union Pacific* (1939), *Commandos Strike at Dawn* (1942), *Mrs. Wiggs of the Cabbage Patch* (1942), *Reap the Wild Wind* (1942), *The Story of Dr. Wassell* (1944), *Love Letters* (1945), *Unconquered* (1947), and *Samson and Delilah* (1952). Received the Life Achievement Award given by the American Cinema Editors (ACE).

BAUDISCH-WITTKE, Gudrun (1907–1982). Austrian ceramist. Name variations: Gudrun Baudisch; Gudrun Baudisch-Teltscher. Born Gudrun Baudisch, Mar 17, 1907, in Pöls, Styria, Austria; died Oct 16, 1982, in Salzburg, Austria; attended University of Graz, Austria, and Vienna School of the Arts and Crafts; married a man named Teltscher (div.); m. Karl Wittke. ❖ An accomplished ceramist and member of the 20th-century crafts collective Wiener Werkstätte, studied ceramics and sculpture at Graz, then moved to Grünbach and became the youngest member in the Kunstlerwerkstätte at 19; established herself as one of the top designers in Weiner Werkstätte (Vienna), specializing in heads and figurines (1926–30); was included in International Exhibition of Ceramic Art at Metropolitan Museum in NY (1928); opened own studio in Vienna (1930s); moved to Berlin following the Anschluss (1938); worked with architect Clemens Holzmeister, designing architectural faience for churches in Turkey, Austria and Germany; with 2nd husband Karl Wittke, settled in Hallstatt in Austria (1946) and set up the pottery workshop, Keramic Hallstatt; retired (1977) and turned pottery studio over to group of ceramists she had organized, Gruppe H. Created sculptures and decorations for many public and private buildings including Stadttheater in Gmunden (1949), Salzburg Festival Building (1959–60), and Bruckner Conservatory in Linz (1970).

BAUER, Alice (1927–2002). American golfer. Born Oct 6, 1927, in Eureka, South Dakota; died Mar 6, 2002 in Palm Desert, California; sister of Marlene Bauer Hagge (golfer); children: Heidi Gussa and David Hovey. ❖ Turned pro (1950); was one of the founders of the LPGA.

BAUER, Catherine Krouse (1905–1964). American housing expert. Name variations: Catherine Bauer Wurster. Born Catherine Krouse Bauer, May 11, 1905, in Elizabeth, New Jersey; died Nov 22, 1964, in Berkeley, California; dau. of Jacob Louise Bauer and Alberta Louise (Krouse) Bauer; m. William Wilson Wurster (architect), Aug 13, 1940; children: Sarah Louise Wurster, known as Sadie (b. 1945). ❖ Authored articles on European architecture while living in Paris (late 1920s); met and was influenced by Lewis Mumford (late 1920s); appointed executive secretary of Regional Planning Association in NYC (1931); wrote *Modern Housing* (1934); as executive secretary of Labor Housing Conference, helped create around 75 labor housing committees, leading to passage of Wagner-Steagall Housing Act (1937); served as director of research and information at US Housing Authority (1937–40); was Rosenberg Professor of Public Social Services at University of California at Berkeley (1940–43); worked at University of California at Berkeley (1950–64), as professor of city and regional planning and associate dean of College of Environmental Design; authored what became foundation for the President's Commission on National Goals, "Framework for an Urban Society" (*Goals for Americans*, 1960); co-founded National Association of Housing Officials; was vice president of National Public Housing Conference and honorary member of American Institute of Planners; urged better public housing and coordination of housing, transportation and land control policies.

BAUER, Charita (1922–1985). American stage, radio, tv, and screen actress. Born Dec 20, 1922, in Newark, New Jersey; died Feb 28, 1985, in NYC. ❖ Appeared on Broadway in *Thunder on the Left, The Women, Life of Riley,* and *Good Morning Corporal;* for over 35 years, appeared as Bert Bauer on the soap opera "The Guiding Light" on radio and tv. Received the Lifetime Achievement Award from the Academy of Television Arts and Sciences.

BAUER, Helene (1871–1942). Austrian journalist and educator. Born Helene Gumplowicz in Cracow, Russian Poland, Mar 13, 1871; died in Berkeley, California, Nov 20, 1942; dau. of Ludwig Gumplowicz; studied in Vienna and Zurich; received doctorate in 1905; m. Max Landau, 1895; m. Otto Bauer (1881–1938), 1914; children: (1st m.) Wanda Lanzer, Zbigniew Landau. ❖ Wife and collaborator of Social Democratic leader Otto Bauer, was also a significant Marxist personality in her own right, with an impressive career in both the Polish and Austrian working-class movements; was active in the Polish Social Democratic movement in early years; worked as an editor and journalist in Vienna for Social Democratic Party; was editor-in-chief of *Der Kampf;* played key role in founding an important Marxist student organization, the Socialist Working Group for Economics and Politics (Sozialistische Arbeitsgemeinschaft für Wirtschaft und Politik); taught evening courses at the Workers' University; fled Austria (1934) for Czechoslovakia; moved to Paris (1938), remaining active in SPÖ affairs; relocated to Stockholm (1939) and then to US (1941). ❖ See also *Women in World History.*

BAUER, Karoline (1807–1877). German actress. Name variations: Countess Montgomery. Born in Heidelberg, Mar 29, 1807; died in Zurich, Switzerland, Oct 18, 1877; morganatic wife of Prince Leopold of Coburg (later king Leopold I of Belgium), 1829, under name Countess Montgomery; m. Count Ladislas de Broel-Plater of Poland, 1844. ❖ Noted German actress, was famous for talents in both comedy and tragedy; after early retirement, returned to the stage when her husband Prince Leopold of Coburg became King Leopold I of the Belgians in 1831; retired again (1844) when she married a Polish count. ❖ See also *Posthumous Memoirs.*

BAUER, Klara (1836–1876). German novelist. Name variations: (pseudonym) Karl Detlef. Born in Swinemünde, June 23, 1836; died in Breslau, June 29, 1876. ❖ Known primarily for her engrossing character studies, wrote *Indissoluble Bonds* (1877) and *Must It Be?* (1872) under the pseudonym Karl Detlef.

BAUER, Margaret (1927—). Austrian ballet dancer. Born May 24, 1927, in Vienna, Austria. ❖ Equally successful as a dancer in classical as well as contemporary ballets throughout career, danced intermittently for Vienna State Opera Ballet (1945–71) until her retirement; received recognition for roles in contemporary ballets by Erika Hanka, including *Homeric Symphony* and *Classical Symphony.*

BAUER, Marion (1887–1955). American composer and teacher. Born Marion Eugenie in Walla Walla, Washington, Aug 15, 1887; died in South Hadley, Massachusetts, Aug 9, 1955; studied with Nadia Boulanger. ❖ Co-founded American Music Guild (1921); taught at New York University, becoming an associate professor (1930); served on faculty of Juilliard School (1940–44); composed throughout career, writing over 30 impressionist pieces; also wrote regularly for music journals. ❖ See also *Women in World History.*

BAUER, Marlene (b. 1934). *See Hagge, Marlene Bauer.*

BAUER, Sybil (1903–1927). American swimmer. Born Sept 18, 1903, in Chicago, Illinois; died Jan 31, 1927; attended Northwestern University. ❖ At Paris Olympics, won a gold medal in the 100-meter backstroke (1924); won 11 US national championships and held world records in every backstroke distance. Was engaged to marry Ed Sullivan, then a Chicago sportswriter who late became a tv host, but died of cancer at 23.

BAUER, Veronika (1979—). Canadian freestyle skier. Born Oct 17, 1979, in North York, Ontario, Canada. ❖ Began career competing on trampoline; won Canadian nationals for aerials (2000, 2001); won a gold medal for aerials at FIS Freestyle World championships (2001), the 1st Canadian woman to win a freestyle world title.

BAUER, Viola (1976—). German cross-country skier. Born Dec 13, 1976, in Neudorf, Germany. ❖ Won a gold medal for the 4 x 5 km relay at Salt Lake City Olympics (2002) and a silver medal for 4 x 5 km relay at Torino Olympics (2006).

BAUERNSCHMIDT, Nola (1895–1994). *See Luxford, Nola.*

BAUERSCHMIDT, Maritta (1950—). East German gymnast. Born Mar 23, 1950. ❖ At Mexico City Olympics, won a bronze medal in team all-around (1968).

BAUERSMITH, Paula (1909–1987). American stage, radio, and tv actress. Born July 26, 1909, in Oakmont, Pennsylvania; died Aug 6, 1987, in NYC; m. Dr. B.M. Warren (died); children: Jennifer Warren (actress). ❖ Made Broadway debut as Carmen Bracegirdle in *Lean Harvest* (1931), followed by *East of Broadway, The Warrior's Husband, Bury the Dead, 200 Were Chosen, The Anatomist, Let Freedom Ring, 20th Century* and *Sail Away,* among others; toured with the National Repertory Company.

BAUGH, Emma (b. 1912). *See Kitchell, Iva.*

BAUGH, Laura (1955—). American golfer. Name variations: Laura Baugh Cole. Born May 31, 1955, in Gainesville, Florida; m. 2nd husband Bobby Cole (PGA Tour pro golfer), 1980 (div. 1985, remarried 1988, sep. 1998); attended California State–Long Beach. ❖ At age 16 (1971), became the youngest US Women's Amateur golf champion in history (13 days younger than Beatrix Hoyt when she won in 1896); won Southern Amateur championships (1970, 1971); turned pro (1973); though she never won an LPGA tournament, reaped a harvest of commercial endorsements for her California blonde good looks. Named Rookie of the Year (1973). ❖ See also autobiography *Out of the Rough* (Routledge).

BAUGHAN, Blanche Edith (1870–1958). New Zealand poet, writer, penal reformer. Born Jan 16, 1870, in Surrey, England; died Aug 20, 1958, at Akaroa, New Zealand; dau. of John Baughan (scrivener) and Ruth (Catterns) Baughan; Royal Holloway College, University of London, BA, 1891, with 1st-class honors. ❖ One of the 1st women to attend Royal Holloway College, performed social work in East London slums following graduation (1893–98); traveled to New Zealand (1900); wrote stylistic and modernist poetry (1893–1910), until illness affected her creativity; was active in prison reform and became official visitor at Addington Reformatory for Women in Christchurch (1920s); an outspoken opponent of capital punishment, published controversial study of prisoners, *People in Prison* (1930s); published poetry includes: *Reuben and Other Poems* (1903), *Shingleshort and Other Verses* (1908), and *Poems from the Port Hills* (1923); prose sketches include: *Brown Bread from a Colonial Oven* (1912), and *Studies in New Zealand Scenery* (1916); also contributed to London *Spectator* from 1902. Received King George V Jubilee Medal for work in social reform (1935). ❖ See also *Dictionary of New Zealand Biography* (Vol. 3).

BAULD, Alison (1944—). Australian composer, singer and actress. Born 1944 in Sydney, Australia; studied piano with Alexander Sverjensky at New South Wales Conservatorium of Music; studied drama at National Institute of Dramatic Art; University of York, PhD in composition; married with 2 children. ❖ Worked as actress in theater, tv, and radio; traveled to UK to study with Elisabeth Lutyens and Hans Keller; also wrote music for Royal Ballet, Scottish Workshop, and London Contemporary Dance Company; became music director of Laban Centre for Dance at London University, worked briefly in Sydney, and returned to London; received several commissions from BBC; works include *On the Afternoon of the Pigsty* (1971), *Pumpkin 2* (1973), *Exiles* (1974), *The Baker's Story* (1978), and *Once Upon a Time* (1986); noted for dramatic structure and effective combination of musical forms in compositions.

BAUM, Marianne (1912–1942). German-Jewish anti-Nazi activist. Born Marianne Cohn in Saarburg, Saar Province, Dec 9, 1912; executed Aug 18, 1942; m. Herbert Baum (1912–1942, resistance leader). ❖ Leading member of the Herbert Baum resistance circle, joined the Communist Youth League of Germany (1931); along with husband, helped organize resistance cells that undertook many acts of defiance and sabotage against Nazi rule in Berlin (starting 1933); with husband, began building an illegal resistance organization (1936–37), primarily with young Jewish women and men who had been members of the Bund Deutsch-Jüdischer Jugend (Union of German-Jewish Youth), a strongly anti-Nazi Jewish youth group; supported husband's decision to establish ties between their organization and another Communist group in Berlin, the cells led by Robert Uhrig (1939); worked as a slave laborer (1940–42); was involved in the fire-bombing of Propaganda Minister Joseph Goebbels' anti-Soviet propaganda display (May 18, 1942); with husband and 3 others, arrested by Gestapo (May 22); sentenced to death by a special Nazi tribunal (July 16, 1942), and executed at Berlin's Plötzensee prison. ❖ See also *Women in World History*.

BAUM, Marie (1874–1964). German-Jewish social worker. Born in Germany, Mar 23, 1874; died in Heidelberg, Germany, Aug 8, 1964; was a descendent of Felix Mendelssohn through mother's family. ❖ Entered politics when the regime of Imperial Germany collapsed (Nov 1918); elected as a Reichstag deputy on the German Democratic party ticket (1919) and represented Schleswig-Holstein and Lübeck (1919–21); an innovative thinker in the field of social work, achieved a national reputation by 1920s; appointed to a lectureship at University of Heidelberg (1928), but lost position after Nazi takeover (Jan–Mar 1933); interrogated by Gestapo, who also maintained surveillance over her daily doings, but refused to be cowed; had a private printing of her autobiography, *Rückblick auf mein Leben* (*Looking Back at My Life*, 1939); remained in Germany and was one of a handful of Germans of Jewish origin to survive the war without deportation to a concentration or extermination camp; lived almost 2 decades following the defeat of the Third Reich and enjoyed the resumption of her teaching duties at the University of Heidelberg (1947); saw the publication of her autobiography in a commercial edition (1950). ❖ See also *Women in World History*.

BAUM, Vicki (1888–1960). German-born writer. Born Victoria Baum, Jan 24, 1888, in Vienna, Austria; died in Hollywood, California, Aug 29, 1960; dau. of Mathilde Donat and Hermann Baum; m. Max Prels, 1906 (div., c. 1912); m. Richard Lert (conductor), July 17, 1916; children: (2nd m.) Wolfgang and Peter. ❖ After publishing numerous short stories, wrote *Der Weg* (*The Way*, 1925); signed a contract with Ullstein Publishers and began writing for the mass market (1926); published novel *stud. chem. Helene Willfüer* (*Chemistry Student Helene Willfüer*) to great success (1928); published most famous book *Menschen im Hotel* (*Grand Hotel*, 1930); fled to US with family because of growing anti-Semitism in Nazi Germany (1931); published *Liebe und Tod auf Bali* (*Tale of Bali*, 1937), followed by *Hotel Shanghai* (1939); switched to writing exclusively in English with novel *The Ship and the Shore* (1941); published *Marion Alive* (1942); published *The Weeping Wood* about a Brazilian rubber plantation (1943); *Hotel Berlin '43* (1944), *Mortgage on Life* (1946), and *Headless Angel* (1948); attempted to write more complex plots, producing *The Mustard Seed* (1953), followed by *Written on Water* (1956), and *Theme for Ballet* (1958), her last novel; successfully wrote about women's liberation, abortion, drug use, and isolation in terms millions could understand. Other writings include *Der Eingang zur Bühne* (1920, published in English as *Once in Vienna*, 1943), *Die Tänze der Ina Raffay* (1921), *Bubenreise* (1923), *Die Welt ohne Sünde* (1923), *Ulle, der Zwerg* (1923), *Feme* (1927, published in America as *Secret Sentence*, 1932), *Hell in Frauensee* (1927, published in English as *Martin's Summer*, 1931), *Das Leben ohne Geheimnis* (1932, published in English as *Falling Star*, 1934), *Das grosse Einmaleins* (1935, published in America as *Men Never Know*, 1935), *Die Karriere der Doris Hart* (1936, published in English as *Sing, Sister, Sing*, 1936), *Der grosse Ausverkauf* (1937, published in London as *Central Stories*, 1940), *Die grosse Pause* (1941, published in London as *Grand Opera*, 1940), *The Christmas Carp* (1941), and *Danger from Deer* (1951). ❖ See also *It Was All Quite Different: The Memoirs of Vicki Baum* (1964); and *Women in World History*.

BAUMA, Herma (1915–2003). Austrian javelin thrower. Born Jan 23, 1915; died Feb 2003. ❖ At London Olympics, won a gold medal in the javelin throw (1948).

BAUMANN, Edith (1909–1973). German political activist. Name variations: Edith Honecker. Born Aug 1, 1909, in Berlin, Germany; died April 7, 1973; dau. of a bricklayer; received secondary education; became 1st wife of Erich Honecker, 1947; children: Erika Honecker (lawyer). ❖ One of the few women to reach a high position in the political life of the German Democratic Republic (GDR), came from working-class origins; worked as activist in Social Democratic youth movement (1925–31), then for Socialist Workers Party (1931–33); arrested and sentenced to 3 years' imprisonment (1933); joined Social Democratic Party (1945) and the Socialist Unity Party (1946); was one of the few women to occupy a significant political post in the Soviet Occupation Zone of Germany in years after 1946; served as professional youth movement administrator and deputy chair of Free German Youth (1946–49); was a member of Central Committee of Socialist Unity Party (1946–73); was a delegate to the Volkskammer ("People's Chamber"), the legislature of the GDR, from 1949 until her death; represented women's interests in the Socialist Unity Party (SED) Central Committee and held high posts in the municipal administration of East Berlin for the last 2 decades of her life. ❖ See also *Women in World History*.

BAUMANN, Edith (1949—). *See Eckbauer-Baumann, Edith.*

BAUME, Madame de la (fl. 17th c.). French transcriber. Fl. in the 17th century in Paris, France. ❖ Transcribed and circulated manuscript of Roger de Bussy-Rabutin's *Histoires amoureuses des Gaules* (1665); later accused by Bussy-Rabutin of adding scurrilous passages to the novel.

BAUME, Rosetta Lulah (1871–1934). New Zealand teacher, feminist, and social reformer. Name variations: Rosetta Lulah Leavy, Rosetta Lulah Kane. Born Rosetta Lulah Leavy, July 1871, at San Francisco, California; died Feb 22, 1934, at Wellington, New Zealand; dau. of Charles Maurice Leavy (civil service commissioner) and Francesca (Simon) Leavy; University of California, BA, 1891; m. Frederick

Ehrenfried Baume (lawyer), 1899 (died 1910); m. Edward William Kane (clerk of House of Representatives), 1921; children: (1st m.) 4 sons. ❖ Was 1st woman high-school teacher in California (1891); immigrated to New Zealand with 1st husband (1898); became active in educational and community work following husband's death and was 1st woman to serve on Auckland Education Board and Auckland Grammar School Board (1911–13); involved in numerous women's groups and supported numerous social-welfare reform initiatives from 1913; stood for election to Parliament (1919); appointed to board of governors of Wellington College and Wellington Girls' College; became member of Wellington branch of League of Nations Union of New Zealand; became justice of peace (1931). ❖ See also *Dictionary of New Zealand Biography* (Vol. 3).

BAUMER, Daniela. Swiss kayaker. Lived in Switzerland. ❖ Won a silver medal for K4 500 meters at Atlanta Olympics (1996).

BÄUMER, Gertrud (1873–1954). German feminist, politician, and writer. Name variations: Baumer. Pronunciation: BOY-mer. Born Sept 12, 1873, in Hohenlimburg in the German state of Westphalia; died Mar 24, 1954, in Bethel, Germany; dau. of a teacher-theologian; University of Berlin, PhD, 1904; lived with Helen Lange. ❖ The most politically active of all leaders of the German women's movement, expressed views on marriage and motherhood which contributed to the rightward direction of German feminism (1910–30s), declaring that the natural and honorable role for women in German society was as housewives and mothers; taught schools in Magdeburg and other German cities (1892–97); went to Berlin to study at University of Berlin (1898); became full-time secretary to Helene Lange (1899); elected to steering committee for League of German Women's Associations (1900); became an editor for journal *Die Hilfe* (1912); served as president of the League of German Women's Associations (1910–19); during WWI, co-sponsored Women's National Service, finding common ground in this area with women's leaders whom she regarded as "radicals"; served as member of the National Assembly of Germany (1919) and member of the German Reichstag (1919–33); worked as a high official in the German Ministry of the Interior (1920–33); edited the journal *Die Frau* (1921–44); was deprived of Reichstag and Ministry of Interior positions by new Nazi government (1933), though permitted to retain her editorship of *Die Frau;* after war, was regarded with suspicion by American and British military in occupied Germany; viewed as a possible Nazi sympathizer, was denied permission to resume publication of *Die Frau.* Writings include *Die Frau im neueren Lebensraum* (1931), *Die Frau in Volkswirtschaft und Staatsleben der Gegenwart* (1914), (with Helene Lange), *Handbuch der Friedensbewegung* (1901–06), and *Lebensweg durch eine Zeitenwende* (1933). ❖ See also *Women in World History.*

BAUMGARTNER, Ann (c. 1923—). American aviator. Born c. 1923; formerly a journalist. ❖ At 21, flew a YP-59A, America's 1st experimental jet, reaching 350 miles per hour and an altitude of 35,000 feet (at Wright Field in Dayton, Ohio, Oct 1944).

BAUR, Clara (1835–1912). German-born music teacher and founder. Born in 1835 in Germany; died in 1912; aunt of Bertha Baur (d. 1940). ❖ Founded the Cincinnati Conservatory of Music (1867); traveled to Europe to recruit a 1st-rate faculty; her niece Bertha Baur took over the reins of the Conservatory after her death. The Conservatory merged with the College of Music to become the Cincinnati College–Conservatory of Music (1955), then became the 14th college at the University of Cincinnati (1962).

BAUR, Margrit (1937—). Swiss novelist. Born Oct 9, 1937, in Adliswil, Switzerland. ❖ German-speaking novelist whose writings include *Von Straßen, Plätzen und ferneren Umständen* (1971), *Zum Beispiel irgendwie* (1977), *Überleben, eine unsystematische Ermittlung gegen die Not aller Tage* (1981), *Geschichtenflucht* (1988), and *Alle Herlichkeit* (1993).

BAUSCH, Pina (1940—). German choreographer. Born July 27, 1940 in Solingen, Germany. ❖ Credited with reviving modern dance in postwar Germany, began dance studies at Folkwang School in Essen where she came under influence of Kurt Jooss; continued studies at Juilliard School in New York and performed there with New American Ballet and Metropolitan Opera Ballet; returned to Germany and became soloist in Folkwang Ballet; served as director of Uppertal Opera Ballet, later called Tanztheater Wuppertal Pina Bausch; works, which are noted for their episodic structure, repetition, haunting quality of dances, and absence of sustainable plot, include *Ich bring dich um di Ecke, Spring Sacrifice, Legend of Chastity* (1979), *1980* and *Arias.*

BAVARIA, duchess of.
See Judith of Fiuli (*fl. 910–925*).
See Judith of Bavaria (*c. 925–987*).
See Gisela of Burgundy (*d. 1006*).
See Agnes of Poitou (*1024–1077*).
See Judith of Flanders (*1032–1094*).
See Wolfida of Saxony (*c. 1075–1126*).
See Ludmilla of Bohemia (*fl. 1100s*).
See Gertrude of Saxony (*1115–1143*).
See Agnes of Looss (*fl. 1150–1175*).
See Matilda of England (*1156–1189*).
See Agnes of Saxony (*fl. 1200s*).
See Matilda of Habsburg (*1251–1304*).
See Beatrice of Silesia (*fl. 1300s*).
See Visconti, Thaddaea (*d. 1381*).
See Elizabeth of Sicily (*d. 1349*).
See Catherine of Gorizia (*fl. late 1300s*).
See Visconti, Elizabeth (*fl. late 1300s*).
See Blanche (*c. 1392–1409*).
See Margaret (*1395–1447*).
See Margaret of Cleves (*fl. early 1400s*).
See Anna of Brunswick (*fl. 1400s*).
See Cunegunde (*1465–1520*).
See Anna of Brunswick (*1528–1590*).
See Maria Sophia Amalia (*1841–1925*).
See Amalie of Saxe-Coburg-Gotha (*1848–1894*).

BAVARIA, electress of.
See Maria Anna of Bavaria (*1610–1665*).
See Henrietta of Savoy (*c. 1630–?*).
See Maria Antonia (*1669–1692*).
See Cunigunde Sobieska (*fl. 1690s*).
See Caroline of Baden (*1776–1841*).
See Maria Leopoldina (*1776–1848*).
See Ludovica (*1808–1892*).

BAVARIA, queen of.
See Caroline of Baden (*1776–1841*).
See Theresa of Saxony (*1792–1854*).
See Ludovica (*1808–1892*).
See Maria of Prussia (*1825–1889*).
See Maria Teresa of Este (*1849–1919*).

BAVENT, Madeleine (fl. 1642). French prisoner. Accused of witchcraft at Louviers (1642), sentenced to life in prison by the bishop of Evreux. ❖ See also *Women in World History.*

BAVEREL, Myriam (1981—). French taekwondo player. Born Jan 14, 1981, in Chambéry, France. ❖ At World championships, placed 2nd for 67–72kg (2003); won a silver medal for 67kg at Athens Olympics (2004).

BAVIER, Frances (1902–1989). American stage, tv, and screen actress. Born Dec 14, 1902, in NYC; died Dec 6, 1989, in Siler City, North Carolina. ❖ On Broadway, appeared in *The Black Pit, The Mother, Native Son, Kiss and Tell, Jenny Kissed Me* and *Point of No Return;* probably best remembered as Aunt Bea on tv series "Andy Griffith Show," for which she received an Emmy; films include *The Day the Earth Stood Still, Bend of the River* and *It Started with a Kiss.*

BAWDEN, Nina (1925—). British novelist and children's writer. Name variations: Nina Bawden Kark. Born Nina Cushing, Jan 19, 1925, in London, England; dau. of Charles Mabey Cushing and Ellalaine Ursula (May) Cushing; Somerville College, BA, 1946, MA, 1951; m. H.W. Bawden, 1946; m. Austen Steven Kark, 1954 (died 2002); children: 4. ❖ Worked as a lay-magistrate; wrote mysteries, horror stories, domestic comedies, including *Anna Apparent* (1972), *George Between a Paper Moon* (1974), *Afternoon of a Good Woman* (1976), *Walking Naked* (1981), *The Ice House* (1983), *Circles of Deceit* (1987), *Family Money* (1991), *A Nice Change* (1997), and *Ruffian on the Stair* (2001); also wrote children's books, including *The Secret Passage* (1963), *The Witch's Daughter* (1966), *Squib* (1971), *Carrie's War* (1973), *The Outside Child* (1989), and *The Real Plato Jones* (1993); made a fellow of the Royal Literary Society; served as president of the Society of Women Writers and Journalists; several works made into films and tv serials. *Circles of Deceit* shortlisted for Booker Prize.

BAWR, Alexandrine de (1773–1860). French playwright and novelist. Name variations: Alexandrine Sophie Goury de Champgrand, Baronne de Bawr; Baroness de Bawr; Alexandrine Sophie, countess de Saint Simon; S. de Bawr. Born Alexandrine Sophie Goury de Champgrand, 1773 (some sources cite 1776) in Stuttgart, Germany, of French parents; died 1860 (some sources cite 1861) in Paris, France; dau. of an aristocratic father and an actress; m. Comte de Saint-Simon (div.); married a Russian officer named de Bawr (crushed by a cart years later). ❖ Fiction includes *Le Rival obligeant* (1811), *Le Double stratagème* (1811) *Auguste et Frédéric* (1817), and *Cecilia* (1852); also wrote two guides *Cours de littérature* (1821) and *Histoire de la musique* (1823).

BAXLEY, Barbara (1923–1990). American actress. Born Barbara Angie Rose Baxley, Jan 1, 1923, in Porterville, California; died June 7, 1990, in NYC. ❖ Made NY debut in *Private Lives* with Tallulah Bankhead; appeared in such films as *East of Eden, All Fall Down, No Way to Treat a Lady, Nashville,* and as Sally Field's mother in *Norma Rae;* shared an apartment with Bankhead for years. Nominated for a Tony award for *Period of Adjustment* (1960).

BAXTER, Anne (1923–1985). American film actress. Born in Michigan City, Indiana, May 7, 1923; suffered a stroke in New York City on Dec 4 and died Dec 12, 1985; dau. of Kenneth Stuart and Catherine Wright Baxter (dau. of architect Frank Lloyd Wright); attended private schools in New York City; studied acting with Maria Ouspenskaya; m. John Hodiak, 1946 (div. 1953); m. Randolph Galt, 1960 (div. 1968); children: (1st m.) Katrina (b. 1951); (2nd m.) Melissa (b. 1961), Maginal (b. 1963). ❖ Made auspicious Broadway debut at 13 in *Seen but Not Heard;* reached high point of career at 23, with portrayal of Sophie MacDonald in film *The Razor's Edge* (1946) for which she won an Academy Award for Best Supporting Actress; had 2nd outstanding role as Eve in *All About Eve* (1950), which earned her an Oscar nomination; on tv, appeared in "Batman" and "Marcus Welby, M.D.," and was nominated for an Emmy Award for "The Bobbie Currier Story," an episode from the series "The Name of the Game" (1969); replaced Lauren Bacall as Margo Channing on Broadway in *Applause* (1971). Films include *The Great Profile* (1940), *Charley's Aunt* (1941), *The Magnificent Ambersons* (1942), *The Pied Piper* (1942), *Crash Dive* (1943), *Five Graves to Cairo* (1943), *The North Star (Armored Attack,* 1943), *The Sullivans* (1944), *The Eve of St. Mark* (1944), *A Royal Scandal* (1945), *Homecoming* (1948), *Yellow Sky* (1949), *You're My Everything* (1949), *A Ticket to Tomahawk* (1950), *The Outcasts of Poker Flat* (1952), *O. Henry's Full House* (1952), *I Confess* (1952), *The Blue Gardenia* (1953), *Carnival Story* (1954), *Bedevilled* (1955), *One Desire* (1955), *The Spoilers* (1956), *The Ten Commandments* (1956), *Chase a Crooked Shadow* (1958), *Summer of the Seventeenth Doll* (1959), *Cimarron* (1960), and *Walk on the Wild Side* (1962). ❖ See also autobiography *Intermission: A True Story* (Putnam, 1976); and *Women in World History.*

BAXTER, Annie Maria (1816–1905). *See Dawbin, Annie Maria.*

BAXTER, Jane (1909–1996). English actress. Born Feodora Forde, Sept 9, 1909, in Bremen, Germany; died Sept 13, 1996, in London, England; dau. of an English father Henry Bligh Forde and German mother Hedwig (von) Dieskau; studied acting under Italia Conti; m. Clive Dunfee; m. Arthur Montgomery. ❖ Made London stage debut in *Love's Prisoner* (1925); made 1st NY appearance as Cecily Cardew in *The Importance of Being Earnest* (1947); appeared on stage for 5 decades, most notably as Sheila Wendice in *Dial M For Murder* (1952); went on to play gentle-mannered leads in American and British films, including *Bed and Breakfast, Down River, The Constant Nymph, Blossom Time, Enchanted April, Royal Cavalcade, The Man Behind the Mask, Murder Will Out* and *Death of an Angel;* began work in British tv (1951).

BAXTER, Millicent Amiel (1888–1984). New Zealand pacifist. Name variations: Millicent Amiel Macmillan Brown. Born Millicent Amiel Macmillan Brown, Jan 8, 1888, in Christchurch, New Zealand; died July 3, 1984, near Dunedin, New Zealand; dau. of John Macmillan Brown (founding professor of Canterbury College) and Helen (Connon) Brown (school principal); University of Sydney, BA, 1908; Newnham College, University of Cambridge (degrees not then conferred to women), 1912; m. Archie Baxter (farmer), 1921 (died 1970); children: 2 sons. ❖ Studied languages in New Zealand and in Germany, returning to New Zealand before outbreak of WWI; worked with Red Cross and other support groups during war and became pacifist (1918); actively involved in peace campaigns and groups throughout her life. ❖ See also *Dictionary of New Zealand Biography* (Vol. 3).

BAY, Mrs. Charles Ulrick (1900–1962). *See Bay, Josephine.*

BAY, Josephine Perfect (1900–1962). American financier. Name variations: Mrs. Charles Ulrick Bay; Josephine Bay Paul. Born Josephine Holt Perfect in Anamosa, Iowa, Aug 10, 1900; died in New York, NY, Aug 6, 1962; dau. of Otis Lincoln and Tirzah (Holt) Perfect; sister of Tirzah Perfect (Mrs. Frederick W. Dunn); graduated from Brooklyn Heights Seminary, 1916; attended Colorado College at Colorado Springs, Colorado, 1918–19; m. Charles Ulrick Bay (Wall Street financier), 1942 (died 1955); m. C. Michael Paul, in Jan 1959; children: (adopted) Christopher Bay, Synnova Bay, Frederick Bay. ❖ The 1st woman to head a member firm of the New York Stock Exchange (A.M. Kidder, 1956), was mentored in business by husband Charles Ulrick Bay; accompanied him to Norway (1946), where he served as ambassador until 1953; became president of the Charles Ulrick and Josephine Bay Foundation (1950), through which the pair made numerous charitable gifts and grants, including scholarships to Norwegian students for study in America and a medical fund for research and prevention of cerebral palsy among Norwegian children; honored for humanitarian efforts with Norway's Commander's Cross of the St. Olav's order (1957); when husband took ill (1955), succeeded him as director of the American Export Lines (passenger and shipping firm) and was elected chair of the executive committee (1956); boosted profits and won reputation as savvy businesswoman in her own right; following husband's death, became a limited partner in A.M. Kidder; after being elected unanimously, served as president and chair of board of A.M. Kidder (1956–62); served as chair of the board of American Export Lines (1959–60). ❖ See also *Women in World History.*

BAYARD, Sylviane (1957—). French ballet dancer. Born Oct 8, 1957, in Bergerac, France. ❖ Trained early on with Fokine student Desha Delteil; had feature role in the film *L'Age en Fleurs* (1972); joined the Stuttgart Ballet in Germany (1974), where she performed repertory works by John Cranko to great acclaim; appeared in such contemporary works as William Forsythe's *Flore Subsimplici* and Rosemary Halliwell's *Mirage;* danced principal roles for Metropolitan Opera House in New York, Royal Swedish Ballet, Théâtre du Châtelet Paris, Béjart's Ballet du XXième Siècle, Teatro Massimo Palermo, Australian Ballet, among others; served as ballet master at Leipzig Opera (1995–97) and Berlin Opera thereafter; became ballet director at Berlin Opera (1999–2000).

BAYER, Adèle (1814–1892). American Catholic welfare worker. Name variations: Adele Bayer. Born Adèle Parmentier, July 1, 1814, in Enghien, Belgium; died Jan 22, 1892, with a requiem mass celebrated in her honor on the *Vermont* in the Navy Yard; m. Edward Bayer, Sept 8, 1841. ❖ Known chiefly for her Catholic ministering and welfare work among naval seamen during Civil War, drew a sizable following with her visits to the Brooklyn Navy Yard and other points of embarkment; established a private allotment system to oversee the accounts of sailors; was instrumental in securing an appointment for the 1st Roman Catholic chaplain by the US Navy (1888).

BAYER, Johanna (1915–2000). Austrian politician. Name variations: Dr. Johanna Bayer. Born Jan 23, 1915, in Berlin, Germany; died Feb 5, 2000, in Graz; received a doctorate in dairy farming, 1937. ❖ Was a member of the Upper House of Parliament (1953–57); was presiding officer of the Austrian Parliament (July 1, 1952–Dec 31, 1953).

BAYES, Nora (1880–1928). American singer and actress. Born Dora (also cited as Leonora or Eleanor) Goldberg in Milwaukee, Wisconsin (various sources also cite Los Angeles and Chicago as birth places), 1880; died in New York, NY, Mar 19, 1928; m. Jack Norwood, 1908 (one of 5 husbands). ❖ Made vaudeville debut in Chicago (1899) and Broadway debut in *The Rogers Brothers in Washington* (1901); gained recognition performing "Down Where the Wurzburger Flows," (1902) at Orpheum Theatre in Brooklyn; toured in variety shows and musicals in Europe (1904–07); appeared in 1st edition of *Ziegfeld Follies* (1907); married and teamed with Jack Norworth (1908); introduced and popularized many songs, including "Has Anyone Here Seen Kelly?," "Take Me Out to the Ball Game," "Japanese Sandman," George M. Cohan's "Over There," and her theme song, "Shine on Harvest Moon," written by Norwood and introduced in *Ziegfeld Follies of 1908;* inaugurated Nora Bayes Roof at 44th Street Theatre, with a performance in the musical *Ladies First* (1919); later appeared in *Her Family Tree* (1920), *Snapshots of 1921* and *Queen o'Hearts* (1922). ❖ See also *Women in World History.*

BAYLEY, Mrs. John Oliver (1919–1999). *See Murdoch, Iris.*

BAYLIS, Lilian (1874–1937). British theater manager. Name variations: The Lady. Pronunciation: BAY-lis. Born Lilian Mary Baylis, May 9, 1874, in Marylebone, London, England; died in Stockwell, London, Nov 25, 1937; dau. of Edward William (Newton) Baylis and Elizabeth (Liebe) Cons Baylis; attended private school and St. Augustine's, Kilburn; never married; no children. ❖ Performed as a child with parents' concert group; went to South Africa and toured with family (1890); taught music in Johannesburg (1892–97); returned to England (1897) and became assistant to Emma Cons, manager of the Old Vic Theater; succeeded Cons as manager (1912); extended the work of theater during and after WWI to include seasons of Shakespeare and opera; acquired Sadler's Wells Theater (1926), which became the home of permanent opera and ballet companies (1930s); helped found the companies which became Britain's Royal National Theatre, English National Opera, and the Royal Ballet; contributed regularly to *Old Vic* (later *Old Vic and Sadler's Wells*) *Magazine* [1919–37]); with Cicely Hamilton, wrote *The Old Vic* (1926). ❖ See also Harcourt Williams *Vic-Wells: The Work of Lilian Baylis* (Cobden-Sanderson, 1938); Richard Findlater, *Lilian Baylis* (Allen Lane, 1975); and *Women in World History.*

BAYLIS, Meredith (1929–2002). American dancer and teacher. Born Meredith J. Baylis, April 4, 1929, in Burbank, California; died July 26, 2002, in Los Angeles, California; great-niece of Lilian Baylis (founder of the Old Vic). ❖ Prominent teacher at the Joffrey Ballet School in Manhattan for 15 years, toured with the national company of *Carousel;* danced with the Ballet Russe de Monte Carlo (1951–62); was on the faculty of the Joffrey School (1969–84); directed her own ballet school in Los Angeles (1990–2000).

BAYLIS, Nadine (1940—). English theatrical designer. Born June 15, 1940, in London, England. ❖ Collaborated with choreographer Glen Tetley on numerous occasions, designing for his *Embrace Tiger and Return to Mountain* (1968), *Field Figures* (1970), *Rag Dances* (1971), among others; worked with Norman Morrice mostly at Ballet Rambert; worked with Norman Morrice on such ballets as *That Is the Snow* (1971) and *Blind-Sight;* designed *There Was a Time* (1973), *Ancient Voices of Children* (1975), *Black Angels,* and others for Christopher Bruce and Ballet Rambert; has designed for Netherlands Dance Theater, Munich Ballet, American Ballet Theater, Australian Ballet, Tanz Forum in Cologne, and others; has taught stage design at Croyden School of Design and Central School of Arts and Design in London; also designed Tetley's *Ziggurat* (1967), *Circles, Imaginary Films* and *Small Parades;* Graham Lustig's *The Edge of Silence* (1988) and *Paramour* (1990), both for Sadler's Wells (now Birmingham) Royal Ballet; Lustig's *Peter Pan* (1996), for Hong Kong Ballet; and Ben Stevenson's *Alice in Wonderland* (1992).

BAYLISS, Blanche (fl. 1894). American actress. Birth and death date unknown. ❖ Starred in *Miss Jerry* (1894), produced at New York City's Carbon Studio, which was the 1st magic lantern show to feature a plot, characters, and titles.

BAYLISS, Lisa (1966—). English field-hockey player. Born Nov 27, 1966. ❖ At Barcelona Olympics, won a bronze medal in team competition (1992).

BAYLY, Ada Ellen (1857–1903). British novelist. Name variations: Edna Lyall. Born Mar 25, 1857, in Brighton, Sussex, England; died Feb 8, 1903, in Eastbourne, England; dau. of Mary (Winter) Bayly and Robert Bayly (lawyer); educated at home and at boarding school in Brighton; never married; no children. ❖ Popular novelist who wrote 17 books, all with a religious theme; published 1st book, *Won by Waiting,* under pseudonym Edna Lyall at 22; came to prominence with another Lyall tome, *Donovan* (1882), about an agnostic who returns to his faith; after the rumor spread that the author of these popular books was insane and institutionalized, publicly announced her identity; defended herself in *Autobiography of a Slander* (1887); with notoriety continuing to promote sales, amazed literary community by selling 9,000 copies on the 1st day of the publication of *Hope the Hermit* (1898); published final works, the autobiographical *The Burges Letters* and *The Hinderers* (both 1902). ❖ See also J.M. Escreet, *The Life of Edna Lyall* (1904); Reverend George A. Payne, *Edna Lyall* (John Heywood, 1903); and *Women in World History.*

BAYLY, Mary (c. 1623–1698). *See Fisher, Mary.*

BAYNE, Beverly (1894–1982). American silent-screen star. Born Beverly Pearl Bain in Minneapolis, Minnesota, 1894; died Aug 12, 1982, in Scottsdale, Arizona; m. Francis X. Bushman (actor), 1918 (div. 1924); m. Charles T. Hvass, 1937 (died 1953); children: (1st m.) son Richard.

❖ Best known for films with Francis X. Bushman, made film debut at Essanay Studios in *The Loan Shark;* made 500 movies before retirement, many of which were 1- and 2-reelers, but by far the most successful were those with Bushman, beginning with *Under Royal Patronage* (1914); with Bushman, catapulted to stardom with 1st film version of *Romeo and Juliet* (1916), then orchestrated $15,000 deal to co-star in the serial *The Great Secret* for Metro Pictures (1917); after divorce from Bushman (1924), never again achieved star status, though she had some success on vaudeville circuit (1920s); performed in some plays (1920s–30s), including *The Road to Rome, Once in a Lifetime* (1931), and *The Shining Hour* (1934); made last movie, *Seven Keys to Baldpate* (1935), with Gene Raymond; returned to Broadway in *Loco* (1946). ❖ See also *Women in World History.*

BAYNE, Margaret (1798–1835). Scottish missionary. Name variations: Margaret Wilson. Born Margaret Bayne, Nov 5, 1795, in Greencock, Scotland; died April 19, 1835, in India; sister of Anna and Hay Bayne who continued her educational work in India after her death; m. John Wilson (missionary). ❖ A pioneer in female missionary work in India, was a gifted linguist and administrator; following marriage to Bombay missionary John Wilson, went with him to India; established schools for girls in India and trained teachers for them (beginning 1829); learned many Indian languages; preached of need for female education as means of achieving moral and intellectual progress for India.

BAYNES, Deserie (1960—). Australian shooter. Name variations: Deserie Wakefield or Wakefield-Baynes; Deserie Huddleston. Born Deserie Joy Wakefield, 1960, in South Australia; m. 2nd husband Stephen Baynes (her coach). ❖ Won a bronze medal for double trap at Atlanta Olympics (1996).

BAYNES, Pauline (1922—). English illustrator. Born Sept 9, 1922, in Brighton, England; dau. of Frederick William Wilberforce (commissioner in the Indian Civil Service) and Jessie Harriet Maude (Cunningham) Baynes; attended Farnham School of art, 1937; Slade School of Art, 1939–40; m. Fritz Otto Gasch (garden contractor), Mar 25, 1961. ❖ Made her reputation on illustrations for C.S. Lewis, for such books as *The Lion, the Witch, and the Wardrobe* (1950), *Prince Caspian* (1951), *The Voyage of the "Dawn Treader"* (1952), and *The Silver Chair* (1953); began to draw at an early age; entered Farnham Art School (1937); did volunteer work during WWII; hired by printer Perry Powell to illustrate books for popular Puffin collection; received commission to illustrate Victoria Stevenson's *Clover Magic;* illustrated 1st work for J.R.R. Tolkien, *Farmer Giles of Ham,* and later illustrated other Tolkien works, including *Smith of Wootton Major* (1967), *Bilbo's Last Song,* and the cover for *The Lord of the Rings;* writings (all self-illustrated) include *Victoria and the Golden Bird* (1947), *How Dog Began* (1986) and *Good King Wenceslas* (1987). Also illustrated Edmund Spenser, *Saint George and the Dragon* (1961), Alison Uttley, *The Little Knife That Did All the Work* (1962), Rumer Godden, *The Dragon of Oq* (1981), Mary Norton, *The Borrowers Avenged* (1982), R. Godden, *Four Dolls* (1983), Peter Dickinson, *The Iron Lion* (1983), Rudyard Kipling, *How the Whale Got His Throat* (1983), Anna Sewell, *Black Beauty* (1984), Cecil Frances Alexander, *All Things Bright and Beautiful* (1986), George Macbeth, *Daniel* (1986), and Beatrix Potter, *Country Tales* (1987). ❖ See also *Women in World History.*

BAYNTON, Barbara (1857–1929). Australian short-story writer. Name variations: Lady Headley. Born Barbara Janet Ainsleigh Lawrence, 1857, in Scone, NSW, Australia; died May 28, 1929, in Melbourne, Australia; 5th daughter and 8th of 9 children of Elizabeth and John Lawrence (aka Robert Kilpatrick, a carpenter); educated in public schools; married Alexander Frater Jr., June 24, 1880 (div. Mar 4, 1890); married Dr. Thomas Baynton (then a 70-year-old retired surgeon), Mar 5, 1890 (died June 1904); married George Allanson-Winn, 5th Lord Headley, Feb 21, 1921 (sep. 1922); children: (1st m.) Alexander III (b. 1881), Robert (b. 1883) and Elizabeth Penelope (b. 1885); great-grandmother of Penne Hackforth-Jones. ❖ Author who primarily depicted women of the Australian bush, was a well known literary hostess and collector of antiques in London; created a persona for herself equal to any character in her stories, reworking her past in order to escape from her blue-collar roots in New South Wales, Australia, into blue-blood society in England; works, which depict harshness of life for women in Australian bush, include *Bush Studies* (1902) and *Human Toll* (1907). ❖ See also Penne Hackforth-Jones, *Barbara Baynton: Between Two Worlds* (Penguin, 1989); Thea Astley, *Three Australian Writers* (Townsville Foundation for Australian Literary Studies, 1979).

BAZÁN, Emilia Pardo (1851–1921). *See Pardo Bazan, Emilia.*

BAZANOVA, Marina (1962—). Soviet handball player. Born Dec 25, 1962. ❖ Won bronze medals in team competition at Seoul Olympics (1988) and Barcelona Olympics (1992).

BAZHANOVA, Svetlana (1972—). Russian speedskater. Name variations: Svetlana Bajanova. Born Dec 1, 1972, in Chelyabinsk, Russia. ❖ At European championships, won bronze medals (1993, 1998) and a silver medal (1994), all for all-around; won a gold medal for the 3,000 meters at Lillehammer Olympics (1994).

BAZIN, Janine (1923–2003). French film and tv producer. Born Janine Kirsch, Jan 29, 1923, in Paris, France; died May 31, 2003; m. Andre Bazin (film critic and theorist who co-founded *Cahiers du Cinema*), 1949 (died 1958); children: Florent Bazin (cinematographer). ❖ Champion and producer of the French new wave, who carried on husband's flame after his death by co-producing the tv series "Cineastes De Notre Temps"; created the international film festival in Belfort; also played a major role in the life of François Truffaut.

BAZINCOURT, Mlle Thomas de (fl. 18th c.). French poet. Fl. in the 18th century in France. ❖ Wrote *Abrégé historique et chronologique des figures de la Bible* (1768), as an educational text for young women.

BAZON-CHELARIU, Adriana (1963—). Romania rower. Name variations: Adriana Chelariu. Born July 5, 1963. ❖ Won Olympic silver medals in coxed eights at Los Angeles (1984), Seoul (1988), and Barcelona (1992).

BAZUS, Florence de or Leslie de (1836–1914). *See Leslie, Miriam Folline Squier.*

BB. *See Nairne, Carolina.*

BEACH, Amy Cheney (1867–1944). American composer and pianist. Name variations: Mrs. H.H.A. Beach, Amy Marcy Cheney. Born Amy Marcy Cheney, Sept 5, 1867, in Henniker, New Hampshire; died of heart failure in NY, Dec 27, 1944; only child of Charles Abbott Cheney (paper manufacturer and importer) and Clara Imogene (Marcy) Cheney (singer and pianist); at 6, began studying piano with mother; studied piano with Ernst Perabo, 1876–82, and Carl Baermann, starting 1880; studied harmony with Junius W. Hill, 1881–82; taught herself orchestration and fugue, translating treatises by Berlioz and François-Auguste Gevaert; m. Dr. Henry Harris Aubrey Beach (Boston physician and lecturer), 1885 (died 1910). ❖ The 1st American woman to overcome gender bias in music, attained an international reputation as a composer of large-scale classical music; moved with family to Chelsea, a suburb of Boston (1871), then Boston (1875); made Boston debut as pianist (1883); debuted with Boston Symphony (1885); began publishing compositions (1885); wrote Mass in E-Flat, op. 5, the 1st mass composed by an American woman, which was performed by Boston's Handel and Haydn Society (1892); premiered *Eilende Wolken,* op. 18, with NY Symphony Society (1892); premiered *Festival Jubilate,* op. 17, for the dedication of Woman's Building at Chicago's Columbian Exposition (1893); performed 1st piano recital devoted to her own compositions, at Wellesley College (1894); composed *Gaelic Symphony,* op. 32, the 1st symphony by an American woman, which was presented by Boston Symphony Orchestra (1896); premiered Piano Concerto in C-Sharp minor, op. 45 (1900); premiered Piano Quintet in F-Sharp minor, op. 67 (1908); lived in Europe (1911–14); began composing at MacDowell Colony, Peterborough, NH (1921); named 1st president of Society of American Women Composers (1924); finished only opera, *Cabildo,* op. 149 (1932); elected 1st vice president of Edward MacDowell Association (1934); performed at White House (1934 and 1936); premiered Piano Trio, op. 150, in NY (1939); recognized on her 75th birthday by Phillips Memorial Gallery of Washington, DC, which presented 2 concerts of her music (1942). ❖ See also Walter S. Jenkins, *The Remarkable Mrs. Beach* (Harmonie Park Press, 1994); Jeanell Wise Brown, *Amy Beach and her Chamber Music* (Scarecrow, 1994); and *Women in World History.*

BEACH, Cyprian (1893–1951). American actress. Born April 23, 1893, in New Jersey; died of cancer, July 26, 1951; dau. of Sylvester Woodbridge Beach (American Presbyterian minister) and Eleanor (Orbison) Beach (born in a missionary family in India); younger sister of Sylvia Beach; studied music with Jean Alexis Perier; lived with Helen Eddy. ❖ While living in Paris at the Palais Royale with her sister Sylvia, studied opera and, unbeknownst to her parents, secretly pursued a film career; knew

early success when she portrayed Belle-Mirette in the French serial *Judex.* ❖ See also *Women in World History.*

BEACH, Mrs. H.H.A. (1867–1944). *See Beach, Amy Cheney.*

BEACH, Holly (b. 1884). American philanthropist. Name variations: Holly Beach Dennis. Born Mary Hollingsworth Morris Beach, June 17, 1884, in New Jersey; eldest dau. of Sylvester Woodbridge Beach (American Presbyterian minister) and Eleanor (Orbison) Beach; sister of Sylvia Beach; m. Frederic James Dennis, Jan 21, 1929 (died 1945). ❖ Joined a Red Cross mission to Serbia during WWI; helped fund sister's bookstore. ❖ See also *Women in World History.*

BEACH, Sylvia (1887–1962). American bookseller. Name variations: changed 1st name to Sylvia, 1901. Born Nancy Woodbridge Beach in Baltimore, Maryland, Mar 14, 1887; died in Paris, France, Oct 5, 1962; 2nd dau. of Sylvester Woodbridge Beach (American Presbyterian minister) and Eleanor (Orbison) Beach (who was born in a missionary family in India); educated mainly at home; never married; companion of Adrienne Monnier (bookseller, died 1955); no children. ❖ Owned and ran Shakespeare and Company, a Paris bookshop (1920s–30s), which became the community center for lost-generation intellectuals from Britain and America, including Djuna Barnes, Kay Boyle, Natalie Barney, Mina Loy, Margaret Anderson, Gertrude Stein, Ezra Pound, Ernest Hemingway, John Dos Passos, and Stephen Spender, as well as prominent French writers like Paul Valéry, André Gide, and Paul Claudel; was responsible for the publication of James Joyce's *Ulysses* and supported Joyce for many years; befriended Man Ray, who made portraits of many of her regular customers, in addition to photographing life at Shakespeare and Company; also helped promote the many little magazines which her friends started in 1920s; her bookstore was a famous stop for all American visitors to Paris by 1935; interned by Germans during WWII; published her memories of Joyce (1956). ❖ See also memoirs, *Shakespeare and Company* (Harcourt Brace, 1959); Noel Riley Fitch, *Sylvia Beach and the Lost Generation* (Norton, 1983); and *Women in World History.*

BEACHLEY, Layne (1972—). Australian surfer. Born May 24, 1972, in Sydney, NSW, Australia. ❖ Won 5 of 11 World Champion Tour events to clinch the World title (1998), then went on to win 4 more World titles (1999–2002).

BEALE, Dorothea (1831–1906). English educator. Born Dorothea Beale, Mar 21, 1831, in London, England; died in Cheltenham in 1906; dau. of Dorothea Margaret (Complin) Beale and Miles Beale (physician); taught at home by governesses; attended boarding school in Essex and a finishing school on the Champs Élysées in Paris; enrolled at Queens College, London, 1849; never married; no children. ❖ Reforming head teacher who helped revolutionize education for middle-class girls in England, was a student and tutor at Queens College (1849–57), the 1st teaching post held by a woman at Queens; named head teacher at the Clergy Daughters' School at Casterton (1857), but was dismissed for criticizing the conservative-minded establishment; served as head teacher at Cheltenham Girls School (1858–1906), transforming it into one of the most prestigious in England; also helped found St. Hilda's College at Cheltenham to train secondary teachers (1885), St. Hilda's College at Oxford (1893) and St. Hilda's in Shoreditch to educate working-class women; gave evidence to the Taunton Commission and edited the 20-volume assistant commissioner's reports which presented a pessimistic picture of education for girls (1865); was joint founder of Association for Headmistresses (1874); sat on Bryce Commission (1894), the 1st women to be appointed to such a body, whose recommendations were embodied in the 1902 Education Act, which transformed secondary education in England; elected president of Association for Headmistresses (1895). Named Officier d'Academie (1889); was a corresponding member of the National Education Association of US (1898); served on advisory board of the University of London (1901); granted Freedom of the borough of Cheltenham (1901). ❖ See also Josephine Kamm, *How Different From Us: A Biography of Miss Buss and Miss Beale* (1958); Elizabeth Raikes, *Dorothea Beale of Cheltenham* (Constable, 1909); F. Cecily Steadman, *In the Days of Miss Beale* (1931); and *Women in World History.*

BEALE, Mary (1632–1699). English artist. Born Mary Cradock in Suffolk, England, 1632; died in 1699 (some sources cite 1697); dau. of a minister and amateur artist; studied with Robert Walker and Thomas Flatman; m. Charles Beale (cloth manufacturer); children: two sons, including Charles Beale (artist). ❖ Portrait painter and miniaturist whose works have often been confused with those of Sir Peter Lely and other noted painters;

established herself as an independent artist, working out of a studio in Covent Garden; her portraits in pastels, watercolor, and oils were much in demand, and many of the city's most prominent people sat for her; also gained popularity for her portraits of children; did numerous copies of Lely's work, as well as her own, which may have ultimately caused the confusion surrounding her original paintings. ❖ See also *Women in World History.*

BEALS, Jessie Tarbox (1870–1942). Canadian-American photographer. Born Jessie Richmond Tarbox, in Hamilton, Ontario, Canada, Dec 23, 1870; died in New York, NY, May 31, 1942; daughter and youngest of 4 children of John Nathaniel (machinist and inventor) and Marie Antoinette (Bassett) Tarbox; attended Collegiate Institute of Ontario; m. Alfred T. Beals, 1897 (div.); children: Nanette Tarbox Beals (b. 1911). ❖ America's 1st female press photographer, known also for her portraits, architectural documentation, landscapes, and gardens, took a teaching position in a remote country school near Williamsburg, Massachusetts (1886), where she had settled with her mother; began work in photography; became the 1st woman in America to have news photos published and credited in the press (1900); landed a job as a staff newspaper photographer in Buffalo (1902); became a fully accredited press photographer when a St. Louis newspaper claimed she carried "the 1st permit to be issued to a woman authorizing the taking of photographs on the World's Fair Grounds" (1904); settled in NY's Greenwich Village (1905); shot a number of documentation projects around NY, including a haunting series on children of the slums; also traveled a great deal, taking assignments from Maine to Minnesota; in later years, photographed gardens of the wealthy for major gardening magazines; won four Grand Awards in the yard-and-garden photographic competition run by *New York Herald Tribune* (1936); received more exposure than any other female photographer of her era. ❖ See also Alexander Alland, Sr. *Jessie Tarbox Beals: First Woman News Photographer* (Camera-Graphic Press, 1978); and *Women in World History.*

BEAMAN, Hana (1982—). American snowboarder. Born Aug 25, 1982, in Santa Barbara, California. ❖ 1st-place finishes include USASA nationals, Mammoth, CA, in Slopestyle (2001), World championships, Vail, Colorado, in both Slopestyle and Big Air (2002), and Yahoo! Big Air & Style, Breckenridge, Colorado, in HIP—TIE (2003). Won silver in Slopestyle at X Games (Winter 2003).

BEAMES, Adrienne. Australian runner. Born in Australia. ❖ Was Victorian squash champion (1966–68); was the 1st woman to break the 3-hour barrier for women's marathon at 2:46:24 in Werribee, Victoria (Aug 31, 1971).

BEAN, Ann (1899–1962). See *Adler, Polly.*

BEAN, Janet Beveridge (1964—). American musician. Name variations: Eleventh Day Dream; Freakwater. Born Feb 10, 1964, in Louisville, Kentucky; m. Rick Rizzo (musician). ❖ Became founding member of alternative Midwest band, Eleventh Day Dream, serving as vocalist and drummer; sang and played guitar as a member of 1990s alternative country group Freakwater. Albums include (with Eleventh Day Dream) *Eleventh Day Dream* (1987), *Lived to Tell* (1991), *El Moodio* (1993), *Ursa Major* (1994), *The Stalled Parade* (2000); (with Freakwater) *Freakwater* (1989), *Dancing Underwater* (1991), *Feels Like the Third Time* (1993), *Old Paint* (1995), and *Endtime* (1995).

BEAR-CRAWFORD, Annette (1853–1899). Australian feminist. Born Annette Ellen Bear in East Melbourne, Australia, 1853; died in London, England, June 7, 1899; eldest of 8 children of Annette Eliza (Williams) Bear and John Pinney Bear (stock and station agent); attended Cheltenham Ladies' College, Gloucestershire, England; m. William Crawford, 1894. ❖ Trained in social work in England, where she became acquainted with the women's movement and was active in the National Vigilance Committee; following death of father (1890), rejoined mother in Melbourne, becoming a leader in Melbourne's women's movement; with the support of the Woman's Christian Temperance Union, formed the Victorian Women's Suffrage League; was instrumental in the founding of the United Council for Women's Suffrance (1894), serving as its 1st president; organized the successful Queen's Willing Shilling fund to found Queen Victoria Hospital for Women (1897). ❖ See also *Women in World History.*

BEARD, Amanda (1981—). American swimmer. Born Oct 29, 1981, in Irvine, California; attended University of Arizona. ❖ At age 14, won a silver medal for 100-meter breaststroke, setting an American record of 1:08.09, a silver medal for 200-meter breaststroke, and a gold medal for

4 x 100-meter relay at Atlanta Olympics (1996); won a bronze medal for 200-meter breaststroke at Sydney Olympics (2000); won 100-meter and 200-meter breaststroke at Pan Pacific championships (2002); at World championships, placed 1st in 200-meter breaststroke (2003); won silver medals for 200-meter indiv. medley and 4 x 100-meter medley relay and a gold medal for 200-meter breaststroke at Athens Olympics (2004); won 5 US National titles.

BEARD, Betsy (1961—). American rower. Name variations: Betsy Beard Stillings. Born Sept 16, 1961, in Seattle, Washington; attended University of Washington. ❖ At Los Angeles Olympics, won a gold medal in coxed eights (1984).

BEARD, Mary (1876–1946). American nurse. Born Nov 14, 1876, in Dover, New Hampshire; died Dec 4, 1946, in New York, NY; dau. of Ithamar Warren Beard and Marcy (Foster) Beard; graduate of New York Hospital School of Nursing (1903). ❖ Known largely for increasing standards of public-health nursing education, became director of Boston Instructive District Nursing Association (BIDNA, 1912), which provided nursing to low-income patients and would become the largest visiting nurse association in US under her direction; at Rockefeller Foundation in NY, served as special assistant to director of division of studies (1925–27), assistant to director of division of medical education (1927–30), and associate director of international health division (1930–38); became director of nursing for American Red Cross (1938).

BEARD, Mary Ritter (1876–1958). American historian and feminist. Born Mary Ritter in Indianapolis, Indiana, Aug 5, 1876; died in Phoenix, Arizona, Aug 14, 1958; dau. of Narcissa (Lockwood) Ritter (teacher) and Eli Foster Ritter (banker); DePauw University, 1897; postgraduate work, Columbia University, 1902–04; m. Charles Austin Beard (historian), Mar 8, 1900; children: William and Miriam Beard (both historians). ❖ Foremost historian of her generation, wrote extensively on the worldwide history of women and on American culture; joined staff of National Women's Trade Union League; served as editor of *The Woman Voter* (1910–12); joined staff of Wage Earners' Suffrage League; was on staff of Congressional Union (later National Woman's Party, 1913–17); with husband, wrote high-school textbook *American Citizenship* (1914), which consciously sought to bring women into the study of the body politic; published with husband, *The Rise of American Civilization* (1927), followed by its sequels: *The Making of American Civilization* (1937), *America in Midpassage* (1939) and *The American Spirit* (1942); published *On Understanding Women* (1931), an advanced intellectual and social history of the entire Western tradition; conducted a worldwide crusade for women's studies as an autonomous discipline, drafting a 50-page syllabus for a women's studies program, published by the American Association of University Women (1934); published *Woman as Force in History* (1946); other writings include *Woman's Work in Municipalities* (1915), *A Short History of the American Labor Movement* (1920), (with C.A. Beard) *A History of the United States* (1921), (ed.) *America Through Women's Eyes* (1933), (ed. with Martha B. Bruère) *Laughing Their Way: Women's Humor in America* (1934), (with C.A. Beard) *The Force of Women in Japanese History* (1953) and *The Making of Charles A. Beard* (1955). ❖ See also Nancy F. Cott, ed. *A Woman Making History: Mary Ritter Beard through Her Letters* (Yale U Press, 1991); Ann J. Lane, *Mary Ritter Beard: A Sourcebook* (Schocken, 1977); and *Women in World History.*

BEARDEN, Bessye (1888–1943). African-American political and civic worker. Born Bessye Jeanne Banks in Goldsboro, North Carolina, Oct 1888; died Sept 16, 1943, in New York, NY; dau. of George T. and Clara (Carrie Ocott) Banks; attended Hartshorn Memorial College; graduate of Virginia Normal Industrial Institute; post-graduate work at University of Western Pennsylvania; studied journalism at Columbia University; m. Richard Howard Bearden; children: Romare Bearden (b. 1914, artist). ❖ Appointed to New York City Board of Education (1922), where she was elected chair of the 12th District, the 1st black woman member of the board; wrote a society column for *Chicago Defender*, weekly African-American newspaper; named deputy collector in internal revenue for 3rd New York Collection District (1935), the 1st African-American appointed to that position; became active in Democratic Party politics as founder and president of the Colored Women's Democratic League in NY (1930s); elected delegate to 1st Judicial District Convention (1937), where she was involved in congressional campaigns and rallies to reelect President Franklin Roosevelt. ❖ See also *Women in World History.*

BEARNISH, Geraldine (1885–1972). English tennis player. Born June 23, 1885; died May 10, 1972. ❖ At Antwerp Olympics, won a silver medal in doubles (1920).

BEAT, Janet Eveline (1937—). English composer. Name variations: Janet Beat. Born 1937 in Streetly, Staffordshire, England; University of Manchester, bachelor's degree; attended Birmingham University; studied with Alexander Goehr. ❖ Worked as freelance horn player (1960–65) and as teacher and musicological researcher; published 1st compositions (1972) and was appointed lecturer at Royal Scottish Academy of Music and Drama in Glasgow; became pioneer of electronic music with Alexander Goehr; joined Scottish Society of Composers (1980) and Scottish Electro-Acoustic Music Society (1987); founded Soundstrata (1989), a group that performs music for acoustic instruments (including voice) with taped and electronically produced sound; works include *A Vision of the Unseen* (1988), *Mandala* (1990) and *Vincent* (1979–80).

BEATH, Betty (1932—). Australian composer. Name variations: Elizabeth Margaret Beath Cox. Born Elizabeth Margaret Eardley, Nov 19, 1932, in Gooburrum district near Bundaberg, Queensland; studied at Sydney Conservatorium of Music (1950); m. John Beath (patrol officer), 1953; m. David Cox (writer and artist), 1970. ❖ Writer of chamber, choral, and instrumental music as well as music for theater, collaborated with 2nd husband on a 40-minute opera for children, *The Strange Adventures of Marco Polo* (1972), and another opera, *The Raja Who Married an Angel;* based her next work, *Songs from the Beasts' Choir,* on poems by Carmen Bernos de Gasztold, which premiered at Carnegie Hall; developed a program about women composers which came to be a regular feature on Australian radio (1984). ❖ See also *Women in World History.*

BEATRICE (1242–1275). English princess and duchess of Brittany. Name variations: Beatrice Plantagenet. Born June 25, 1242, in Bordeaux, Aquitaine, France; died Mar 24, 1275, in London, England; dau. of Henry III (1206–1272), king of England (r. 1216–1272) and Eleanor of Provence (c. 1222–1291); sister of Edward I Longshanks, king of England (r. 1272–1307); m. John II (1239–1305), duke of Brittany (r. 1286–1305), 1260; children: Arthur II (d. 1312), duke of Brittany (r. 1305–1312), and 6 others.

BEATRICE (fl. c. 1100s). Countess of Edessa. Married Joscelin II, count of Edessa; children: Joscelin III; Sibylla; Agnes of Courtenay (1136–1186).

BEATRICE (1857–1944). Princess of England. Name variations: Beatrice of Battenberg; Princess of Battenberg; Princess Henry of Battenberg; Beatrice Saxe-Coburg; Beatrice of Saxe-Coburg. Born Beatrice Mary Victoria Feodora (or Feodore), April 14, 1857, at Buckingham Palace, London, England; died Oct 26, 1944, in Balcombe, West Sussex, England; 5th and youngest dau. of Queen Victoria (1819–1901) and Prince Albert Saxe-Coburg; sister of King Edward VII of England; m. Prince Henry Maurice of Battenberg, July 23, 1885 (died 1896); children: Alexander Mountbatten, marquess of Carisbrooke (1886–1960); Victoria Eugenie of Battenberg (1887–1969), who m. Alphonso XIII, king of Spain, and was known as Queen Ena); Leopold Mountbatten; Maurice Mountbatten. ❖ Of all Queen Victoria's children, was the closest to her mother; became her confidante, secretary, factotum and nurse—until the day that she fell in love with a Prussian, Prince Henry of Battenberg, causing her mother's fury; agreed to live in the royal household after marriage; after Henry joined the British Expeditionary Force sent to quell the angry Ashanti and died of malaria (1896), returned to mother's side and remained there; also took on husband's duties as governor of the Isle of Wight; following mother's death (1901), spent next 30 years editing her mother's letters and journals, sometimes rewriting total passages and striking out anything that might put Victoria in a bad light, then burned the originals. ❖ See also *Women in World History.*

BEATRICE, Dona (c. 1684–1706). Congolese religious leader. Name variations: Kimpa Vita, Saint Anthony. Born Kimpa Vita, c. 1684, in Belgian Congo (now Republic of Congo); burned at the stake, 1706; children: 1 son. ❖ Rose to power in the Belgian Congo, during a period when the area, reduced to a Portuguese conquest, was ravaged by clan rivalry and famine; established herself as a religious leader and savior of her people; built a church and formed her own sect, called Antonianism, a synthesis of European and African culture, and preached national unity; for 2 years, preached throughout the country, attracting many followers and threatening the power of the Portuguese missionaries and the Catholic Church; fell in love, became pregnant, fled with lover; found with her lover and infant by the king's men, was brought to trial and sentenced to death. ❖ See also *Women in World History.*

BEATRICE, Sister (1829–1921). *See Rogers, Elizabeth Ann.*

BEATRICE D'ESTE. *See Este, Beatrice d'.*

BEATRICE OF ANJOU (d. 1275). Titular empress of Constantinople. Beatrix. Died 1275; dau. of Beatrice of Provence (d. 1267) and Charles I of Anjou (brother of Louis IX, king of France), king of Sicily (r. 1266–1282) and Naples (r. 1268–1285); m. Philipp de Courtenay, titular emperor of Constantinople, Oct 15, 1273; children: Catherine de Courtenay (d. 1307).

BEATRICE OF ARAGON (1457–1508). *See Beatrice of Naples.*

BEATRICE OF BATTENBERG (1857–1944). *See Beatrice.*

BEATRICE OF BEJA (1430–1506). Duchess of Beja and Viseu. Name variations: Beatriz. Born 1430; died Sept 30, 1506, in Beja; dau. of Isabella of Braganza (1402–1465) and Joao or John of Portugal, grand master of Santiago; m. Fernando also known as Ferdinand, duke of Beja and Viseu, Mar 16, 1452; children: Joao, duke of Beja and Viseu (1456–1483); Eleanor of Portugal (1458–1525); Isabella of Braganza (1459–1521); Diego (1460–1484), duke of Beja and Viseu; Duarte (b. 1462, died young); Diniz or Denis (b. 1464, died young); Simiao (b. 1467, died young); Caterina (1467, died young); Alfonso (b. 1468, died young); Emmanuel or Emanuel also known as Manuel I the Fortunate (1469–1521), king of Portugal (r. 1495–1521). ❖ Son Manuel ascended the throne of Portugal (1495); her descendants reigned in that country until Manuel II abdicated (1910).

BEATRICE OF BRANDENBURG (1360–1414). Duchess of Austria. Name variations: Beatrix of Zollern. Born 1360 in Nurnberg; died June 10, 1414, in Perchtoldsdorf, Lower Austria; 2nd wife of Albrecht also known as Albert III (c. 1349–1395), duke of Austria (r. 1365–1395); children: Albert IV (1377–1404), duke of Austria.

BEATRICE OF BURGUNDY (d. 1310). *See Beatrix de Bourgogne.*

BEATRICE OF CANOSSA (c. 1020–1076). *See Beatrice of Lorraine.*

BEATRICE OF CASTILE (d. 1179). *See Sancha of Castile and Leon.*

BEATRICE OF CASTILE AND LEON (1242–1303). Queen of Portugal. Name variations: Beatriz; Beatriz de Guillén. Born in 1242; died Oct 27, 1303; illeg. dau. of Alphonso X, king of Castile and Leon (r. 1252–1284), and Mayor Guillen de Guzman (d. 1262); m. Alphonso III (1215–1279), king of Portugal (r. 1248–1279), 1253 or 1254; children: Branca (1259–1321); Fernando (1260–1262); Affonso (1263–1321); Sancha (b. Feb 2, 1264–1302); Maria (b. Nov 21, 1264–1304); Vicente (1268–1271); Diniz or Denis the Farmer (1261–1325), king of Portugal (r. 1279–1325); Costanza (b. before Nov 23, 1271). Alphonso's 1st wife was Matilda de Dammartin (d. 1258).

BEATRICE OF CASTILE AND LEON (1293–1359). Queen of Portugal. Name variations: Beatriz. Born in Toro, Spain, 1293; died Oct 25, 1359, in Lisbon, Portugal; dau. of Maria de Molina (d. 1321) and Sancho IV, king of Castile (r. 1284–1296); m. Alphonso IV, king of Portugal (r. 1325–1357), Sept 12, 1309; children: Maria of Portugal (1313–1357), who m. Alphonso XI of Castile); Alfonso or Alphonso (1315–1315); Diniz or Denis (1317–1318); Pedro also known as Peter I (1320–1367), king of Portugal (r. 1357–1367); Isabel (1324–1326); Joao (1326–1327); Eleanor of Portugal (1328–1348, who m. Peter or Pedro IV of Aragon).

BEATRICE OF CENCI (1577–1599). Noblewoman of Rome. Name variations: Beatrice Cenci; "the Beautiful Parricide." Born 1577 (some sources cite 1583); executed Sept 11, 1599; dau. of Francesco Cenci (1549–1598) and his 1st wife whose name is unknown. ❖ The youngest of 12 children, was treated reprehensibly by father Francesco, then sexually abused; her friend Olimpio Calvetti and a hired assassin drove a large nail into Francesco's brain while he lay sleeping (Sept 9, 1598); when the crime was discovered, was tortured along with brother Giacomo; though Giacomo confessed, continued to declare her innocence; was beheaded. The tragedy inspired a number of literary works, including *The Cenci* by Percy Bysshe Shelley and a novel by Francesco Guerrazzi. ❖ See also *Women in World History.*

BEATRICE OF FALKENBURG (c. 1253–1277). *See Falkenstein, Beatrice von.*

BEATRICE OF KENT (d. after 1280). English abbess and author. Died after 1280 at Lacock Abbey, Wiltshire, England; never married. ❖ Entered convent at Lacock Abbey in Wiltshire sometime after its founding in 1239; elected abbess (1257); composed a biography of predecessor Countess Ela, though no copies are extant; also wrote poetry; retired from position (c. 1269). ❖ See also *Women in World History*.

BEATRICE OF LORRAINE (c. 1020–1076). Marchioness and regent of Tuscany. Name variations: Beatrice of Tuscany; Beatrice of Canossa. Born in Upper Lorraine c. 1020; died 1076 in Tuscany, Italy; dau. of Frederick, duke of Upper Lorraine; niece of Conrad II; became 2nd wife of Count Boniface II of Canossa, Marquess of Tuscany, around 1040 (died 1052); m. Godfrey the Bearded, duke of Upper Lorraine, 1054 (died 1069); children: 3 from 1st marriage, including Matilda of Tuscany. ❖ With 1st husband, supported Pope Gregory's authority over Henry III; when husband Boniface was assassinated (1052) and her only surviving child, 6-year-old Matilda, inherited father's titles and estates, became regent of Tuscany, ruling by herself for 2 years; married Godfrey the Bearded (1054), another supporter of the papacy; arrested along with daughter by Holy Roman emperor (1055), remained a prisoner in Germany for about a year, until Godfrey and Henry reached a settlement; took up reins of government again in Matilda's name, arranging a marriage for Matilda with Godfrey's son, Godfrey III the Hunchback; after Godfrey the Bearded died (1069), co-ruled Tuscany (with Matilda) for the remaining 6 years of her life. ❖ See also *Women in World History*.

BEATRICE OF MODENA (1750–1829). *See Maria Beatrice of Modena.*

BEATRICE OF NAPLES (1457–1508). Queen of Hungary. Name variations: Beatrice of Aragon. Born 1457; died Sept 23, 1508, in Ischia; dau. of Isabel de Clermont (d. 1465) and Ferdinand also known as Ferrante I (1423–1494), king of Naples (r. 1458–1494); m. Matthias Corvinus, king of Hungary (r. 1458–1490), 1476; m. Vladislas also known as Ladislas II of Bohemia, king of Bohemia (r. 1471–1516) and Hungary (r. 1490–1516), 1490 (div., 1500). ❖ Ladislas' 1st wife was Anne de Foix.

BEATRICE OF NAZARETH (c. 1200–1268). Belgian nun, mystic, philosopher, and prioress at Notre-Dame-de-Nazareth. Name variations: Beatrijs; Beatrice of Tirlemont. Born between 1200 and 1205; died 1268 at Nazareth priory in Brabant; dau. of Bartholoméus (also mentioned as Bartholomaeus, Bartholomew, Barthélémy) de Vleeschouwer of Tirlemont (merchant and lay brother) and Gertrudis; had one brother and two sisters, Christina (Christine) and Sybilla (Sibylle); educated at the school of the Beguines at Léau, at Bloemendaal (Florival) Convent, and at Rameia (La Ramée); never married; no children. ❖ Experienced visions of God and described the nature of mystical experience in such works as: *The Seven Modes of Sacred Love, On the Intensive Use of Time, On the Threefold Exercise of Spiritual Affections, On the Two Cells Which She Constructed in Her Heart, On the Fruitful Garden of Her Own Heart, On Her Aspirations to Achieve Self-Knowledge, On a Certain Rule of Spiritual Life Which She Kept for Some Time*; also wrote 2 prayers, *Oh, Righteous Lord* and *Oh, Most Righteous and Almighty God*. ❖ See also *Women in World History*.

BEATRICE OF PORTUGAL (c. 1347–1381). Countess of Albuquerque. Born c. 1347; died July 5, 1381, in Ledesma; probably the dau. of Inez de Castro (c. 1320–1355) and Pedro also known as Peter I, king of Portugal (r. 1357–1367); m. Sancho (b. 1373), count of Albuquerque, 1373; children: Fernando or Ferdinand, count of Albuquerque (b. 1373); Eleanor of Albuquerque (1374–1435).

BEATRICE OF PORTUGAL (1372–after 1409). Queen of Castile and Leon. Name variations: Beatrix, Beatriz, Brites. Born in Feb 1372 (some sources cite 1373) at Coimbra, Portugal; died after 1409 in Madrigal, Portugal; dau. of Fernando also known as Ferdinand I the Handsome, king of Portugal (r. 1367–1383), and Leonora Telles (c. 1350–1386); m. Edward, duke of York, in July 1381 (annulled 1382); became 2nd wife of Juan also known as John I, king of Castile and Leon (r. 1379–1390), April 30, 1383; children: none. John of Castile's 1st wife was Eleanor of Aragon (1358–1382). ❖ Was illeg. daughter Ferdinand I, king of Portugal, and Leonora Telles, his mistress; when it became clear that Ferdinand would have no sons, was officially legitimized and named heir; at 12, married John I of Castile (1383), the same year her father died; was refused support by the Portuguese as their queen because accepting her rule meant accepting the rule of her Castilian husband (instead, they supported the weaker claims of an illeg. half-brother of King Ferdinand, who was crowned as King John I of Portugal); saw marriage annulled (1387); returned to Portugal. ❖ See also *Women in World History*.

BEATRICE OF PORTUGAL (d. 1439). Countess of Arundel. Died Oct 23, 1439, in Bordeaux, France; interred at Collegiate Church, Arundel; illeg. dau. of Inez Perez and João I also known as John I (1385–1433), king of Portugal (r. 1385–1433); m. Thomas Fitzalan, 12th earl of Arundel, Nov 26, 1405; m. John Holland, duke of Huntington, Jan 20, 1432.

BEATRICE OF PORTUGAL (1504–1538). Duchess of Savoy. Name variations: Beatriz; Maria Beatrix, countess d'Asti. Born Dec 31, 1504, in Lisbon; died Jan 8, 1538, in Nice; dau. of Manuel I the Fortunate (1469–1521), king of Portugal (r. 1495–1521), and Maria of Castile (1482–1517); m. Carlo also known as Charles III (d. 1552), duke of Savoy (r. 1504–1553), Sept 29, 1520; children: Emmanuel Philibert (1528–1580), 10th duke of Savoy (r. 1553–1580).

BEATRICE OF PROVENCE (d. 1267). Queen of Sicily. Name variations: Countess of Provence. Died in 1267; dau. of Beatrice of Savoy (d. 1268) and Raymond Berengar or Berenger IV (some sources cite V), count of Provence and Forcalquier; sister of Eleanor of Provence (c. 1222–1291), Sancha of Provence (c. 1225–1261), and Margaret of Provence (1221–1295); m. Charles I of Anjou (brother of Louis IX, king of France), king of Sicily (r. 1266–1282) and Naples (r. 1268–1285), 1246; children: Charles II, duke of Anjou (r. 1285–1290), king of Naples (r. 1285–1309); Beatrice of Anjou (d. 1275).

BEATRICE OF RETHEL (fl. 1150s). Queen of Sicily. Married Roger II, king of Sicily (r. 1103–1154), duke of Apulia (r. 1128–1154); children: Roger of Apulia; William I the Bad, king of Sicily (r. 1154–1166); Constance of Sicily (1154–1198).

BEATRICE OF SARDINIA (1792–1840). *See Maria Beatrice of Sardinia.*

BEATRICE OF SAVOY (d. 1268). Countess of Provence. Name variations: Beatrice de Savoie. Died in 1268 (some sources cite 1266); 1 of 10 children of Thomas I, count of Savoy, and Margaret of Geneva; m. Raymond Berengar V (1198–1245), count of Provence, Dec 1220; children: Margaret of Provence (1221–1295), queen of France; Eleanor of Provence (c. 1222–1291); Sancha of Provence (c. 1225–1261, who m. Richard, 1st earl of Cornwall and king of the Romans); Beatrice of Provence (d. 1267, who m. Charles of Anjou, brother of Louis IX). ❖ Beatrice of Savoy and her husband Raymond Berengar were renowned for their learning and influence on the arts.

BEATRICE OF SAVOY (fl. 1240s). Queen of Naples and Sicily. Name variations: Beatrix of Savoy. Married Manfred, king of Naples and Sicily (r. 1258–1266), illeg. son of Frederick II, Holy Roman emperor); children: Constance of Sicily (d. 1302).

BEATRICE OF SAXE-COBURG (1857–1944). *See Beatrice.*

BEATRICE OF SAXE-COBURG (1884–1966). Duchess of Galliera. Born Beatrice Leopoldine Victoria, April 20, 1884, in Eastwell Park, Kent, England; died July 13, 1966, in Sanlucar de Barrameda, Andalusia, Spain; dau. of Alfred Saxe-Coburg, duke of Edinburgh, and Marie Alexandrovna (1853–1920); sister of Marie of Rumania (1875–1928); m. Alphonso Bourbon, 5th duke of Galliera, July 15, 1909; children: Alvaro (b. 1910); Alonso (b. 1912); Ataulfo (b. 1913).

BEATRICE OF SILESIA (fl. 1300s). Holy Roman empress. Name variations: Beatrix of Glogau. Was 1st wife of Louis III, duke of Bavaria (r. 1294–1347), also known as Ludwig IV of Bavaria or Louis IV, Holy Roman emperor (r. 1314–1347); children: Matilda of Bavaria; Louis V (1315–1361), margrave of Brandenburg (r. 1347–1361, who m. Margaret Maultasch); Stephen II, duke of Bavaria (r. 1363–1375). Louis IV's 2nd wife was Margaret of Holland (d. 1356).

BEATRICE OF SWABIA (1198–1235). Queen of Castile and Leon. Name variations: Beatrice Hohenstaufen; Beatrice von Hohenstaufen. Born 1198; died in Toro, Castile and Leon, Spain, Aug 11, 1235; dau. of Philip of Swabia (1176–1208), Holy Roman emperor (r. 1198–1208), and Irene Angela of Byzantium (d. 1208); sister of Marie of Swabia (c. 1201–1235); granddau. of Beatrice of Upper Burgundy (1145–1184); became 1st wife of Otto IV of Brunswick (c. 1175–1218), earl of York, count of Ponthieu, duke of Bavaria, king of the Romans (r. 1198–1209), and Holy Roman emperor (r. 1209–1215), July 2, 1212; became 1st wife of Fernando also known as Saint Ferdinand or Ferdinand III (1199–1252), king of Castile (r. 1217–1252) and Leon (r. 1230–1252), Nov 30, 1219; children: Alphonso X (c. 1226–1284), king of Castile and Leon (r. 1252–1284); Fadrique (d. 1277); Enrique also known as Henry (d. 1304); Felipe, archbishop of Seville; Leonor (died young); Berenguela (nun); Sancho (1233–1261), archbishop of Toledo and Seville; Manuel of Castile (1234–1283); Maria (1235–1235). Otto's 2nd wife was Mary of Brabant (c. 1191–c. 1260). ❖ Ferdinand's 2nd wife was Joanna of Ponthieu (d. 1279).

BEATRICE OF TIRLEMONT (c. 1200–1268). *See Beatrice of Nazareth.*

BEATRICE OF TUSCANY (c. 1020–1076). *See Beatrice of Lorraine.*

BEATRICE OF UPPER BURGUNDY (1145–1184). Holy Roman empress and queen of Germany and Italy. Name variations: Beatrice of Burgundy; Beatrix of Burgundy. Born 1145; died Nov 15, 1184; dau. of Rainald also known as Renaud III, count of Burgundy and Macon, and Agatha of Lorraine; m. Frederick I Barbarossa (1123–1190), Holy Roman emperor (r. 1152–1190), June 10, 1156; children: Henry VI (c. 1165–1197), Holy Roman emperor (r. 1190–1197); Frederick (d. 1191), duke of Swabia; Otto, count Palatine; Philip of Swabia (c. 1176–1208), Holy Roman emperor (r. 1198–1208). ❖ Frederick Barbarossa's 1st wife was Adelaide of Vohburg.

BEATRICE OF VERMANDOIS (880–931). Queen of France. Name variations: Beatrice de Vermandois. Born 880; died 931; dau. of Hubert I, count of Senlis; m. Robert I (c. 865–923), king of France (r. 922–923), around 893 or 895; children: Emma of Burgundy (d. 939); Hugh the Great also known as Hugh the White (c. 895–956), count of Paris and duke of Burgundy; Adela (who m. Herbert II, count of Vermandois).

BEATRICE OF WITTELSBACH (1344–1359). Swedish royal. Name variations: Beatrix Wittelsbach. Born 1344; died Dec 25, 1359; dau. of Louis IV the Bavarian, Holy Roman emperor, and possibly Margaret of Holland (d. 1356); m. Erik XII (c. 1339–1359), co-regent of Sweden (r. 1356–1359), in Dec 1355; children: 2 sons.

BEATRICE PLANTAGENET (1242–1275). *See Beatrice.*

BEATRICE PORTINARI (c. 1265–1290). Florentine woman. Born c. 1265 or 1266; died June 9, 1290; dau. of Folco Portinari (Florentine noble); m. Simone di Geri de Bardi (or Pardi). ❖ Some say Beatrice Portinari was the heroine and inspiration of Dante's *La Vita Nuova* (The New Life), of his *Divine Comedy,* and of his life; her identity and allegorical significance in the *Divine Comedy* (*Divina Commedia*) has been the subject of extensive literature. ❖ See also *Women in World History.*

BEATRIJS. *Variant of Beatrice.*

BEATRIX. *Variant of Beatrice.*

BEATRIX (b. 1938). Queen of the Netherlands. Name variations: Beatrix Wilhelmina; Beatrix Wilhelmina Armgard van Orange-Nassau; Beatrice. Born Beatrix Wilhelmina Armgard van Orange-Nassau, Jan 31, 1938, in Soestdijk, Netherlands; dau. of Juliana (b. 1909), queen of the Netherlands (r. 1948–1980), and Prince Bernard of Lippe-Biesterfeld; received doctorate in law, University of Leiden, 1961; m. Claus Gerd von Amsberg (German diplomat), Mar 10, 1966; children: Willem or William Alexander, crown prince of the Netherlands (b. 1967, who m. Maxima Zorreguieta of Argentina); Johan Friso (b. 1968); and Constantijn or Constantine (b. 1969). ❖ The granddau. of Queen Wilhelmina, began her reign with the abdication of her mother Queen Juliana (1980); at 2, escaped from Holland to Ottawa, Canada, with rest of family when the German army invaded the Netherlands (May 1940); attended primary school in Ottawa until family returned to Holland at end of war (1945); recognized as heir to the throne when it became clear that Juliana would not have sons to succeed her (1947); turned 18 and officially joined Dutch Reformed Church (1956); as crown princess, also became a member of her mother's council of state; made 1st state visit, to US (1959); helped launch a European version of the Peace Corps (1961); announced engagement to 38-year-old German diplomat Claus von Amsberg to great hue and cry (1966), when it was learned that he served in Nazi army during WWII; has concerned herself with international problems such as underdevelopment in Third World and other social welfare issues, especially involving the former Dutch colonies in Asia. ❖ See also *Women in World History.*

BEATRIX DA SILVA (1424–1490). Spanish saint. Born 1424; died 1490. ❖ Was said to be so beautiful that she had to escape the Spanish court to ward off admirers; founded the order of the Conceptionists, in honor of the Virgin Mary (1484), which followed the Cistercian rule, before adopting that of St. Francis of Assisi in 1511.

BEATRIX DE BOURGOGNE (1257–1310). Duchess of Bourbon. Name variations: Beatrice of Burgundy, Beatrice of Bourbon; Béatrix.

Born 1257; died Oct 1, 1310, at Château-Murat; dau. of Jean de Bourgogne also known as John of Burgundy and Agnes de Dampierre (1237–1287); m. Robert of France (1256–1317), count of Clermont, 1271 or 1278; children: Louis I le Grand (1270–1342), count of Clermont. ❖ Born into noble houses of Burgundy and Bourbon, received an excellent education; was betrothed early and married Robert of France, son of count of Clermont; as her parents had no surviving sons, was named heir; when mother died (1287), inherited the duchy of Bourbon (located in modern-day central France); ruled as duchess for 23 years, until death. ❖ See also *Women in World History.*

BEATRIX OF BURGUNDY (1145–1184). *See Beatrice of Upper Burgundy.*

BEATRIX OF FALKENBURG (c. 1253–1277). *See Falkenstein, Beatrice von.*

BEATRIX OF GLOGAU (fl. 1300s). *See Beatrice of Silesia.*

BEATRIX OF LENS (d. around 1216). French saint. Died around 1216; dau. of a noble of Lens. ❖ Founded a Cistercian monastery in the neighborhood of Mons.

BEATRIX OF MODENA-ESTE (1750–1829). *See Maria Beatrice of Modena.*

BEATRIZ. *Variant of Beatrice.*

BEATRIZ OF SPAIN (1909–2002). Spanish princess. Name variations: Beatriz; the Infanta; Beatriz Torlonia; Countess Torlonia. Born Beatriz Isabel Frederica Alfonsa, June 22, 1909, in La Granja, San Ildefonso, Segovia; died in Rome, Italy, Nov 2002; dau. of Ena (1887–1969) and Alphonso XIII (1886–1941), king of Spain (r. 1886–1931); m. Alessandro Torlonia, prince of Civitella-Cesi, Jan 14, 1935; children: Sandra Vittoria Torlonia (b. 1936, who m. Clemente, count Lequio di Assaba); Marco Alfonso (b. 1937), prince Civitella-Cesi; Marino Riccardo (b. 1939); Olimpia Emanuela Torlonia (b. 1943, who m. Paul-Annik Weiller).

BEATTIE, Ann (1947—). American writer. Born 1947 in Washington, DC; American University, BA, 1969; University of Connecticut, MA, 1970; m. Lincoln Perry (painter), 1988. ❖ Prolific novelist and short-story writer who focuses on disaffected upper-middle-class Americans, 1st gained attention with short stories in *The New Yorker* (early 1970s); came to prominence with novel *Chilly Scenes of Winter* and short-story collection *Distortions* (both 1976); worked as visiting lecturer at University of Virginia and Harvard University; other novels include *Falling in Place* (1981), *Picturing Will* (1990), *Another You* (1995) and *The Doctor's House* (2002); short-story collections include *The Burning House* (1983), *What Was Mine* (1991), *Park City* (1998) and *Perfect Recall* (2000). Received award for literature from American Academy of Arts and Letters.

BEATTIE, Mollie (1947–1996). American environmentalist. Name variations: Mollie H. Beattie. Born April 27, 1947; died of a brain tumor, June 27, 1996, in Townshend, Vermont; dau. of Pat Beattie; earned degree in forestry from University of Vermont; Harvard University, MA in public administration; m. Rich Schwolsky. ❖ Was commissioner of Vermont Department of Forests, Parks, and Recreation; was the 1st woman director of the Fish and Wildlife Service (1993–96); during her tenure, added 15 wildlife refuges, saw 100 conservation habitat plans agreed on between landowners and the government, and introduced the gray wolf into the Northern Rockies.

BEATTY, Bessie (1886–1947). American journalist, author, and radio commentator. Born Jan 27, 1886, in Los Angeles, California; died April 6, 1947; dau. of Thomas Edward and Jane Mary (Boxwell) Beatty; attended Occidental College in Los Angeles; m. William Sauter (actor), Aug 15, 1926. ❖ While still in college, began writing for Los Angeles *Herald* (1904); within 3 years, was *Herald's* drama editor and chief editor of women's page; published 1st book, *Who's Who in Nevada* (1907); as a reporter for San Francisco *Bulletin* (1907–17), wrote on a range of topics: from the Progressive movement in Washington to life in Alaska; initiated a series called "Around the World in Wartime" (1917), which took her to Japan, China, and finally Russia, where she spent 8 months observing the Revolution firsthand; published *The Red Heart of Russia* (1918); edited *McCall's* magazine (1918–21), before returning to Russia as a correspondent for *Good Housekeeping* and Hearst's *International* magazine; interviewed Lenin and Trotsky, then visited Turkey to study women under the new regime; with Jack Black, wrote the play *Salt-chunk Mary;* started her own public-relations bureau; launched a 45-minute chat-radio program on NY's WOR (1940), which received the highest ratings of any program of its kind (1942). ❖ See also *Women in World History.*

BEATTY, Josephine (1895–1984). *See Hunter, Alberta.*

BEATTY, May (1880–1945). New Zealand singer and actress. Name variations: May Lauri. Born May Beatty, June 4, 1880, in Christchurch, New Zealand; died April 1, 1945, near Los Angeles, California; dau. of George Beatty (innkeeper and theater manager) and Emma (Furby) Beatty; m. Edward Lauri (comedian), 1908 (died 1919); children: 1 daughter. ❖ Began professional career at age 11 with Pollard's Lilliputian Opera Co.; excelled at musical comedy (late 1890s); toured Australia, New Zealand, England and Ireland with husband; after husband's death, settled outside Los Angeles, California. ❖ See also *Dictionary of New Zealand Biography* (Vol. 2).

BEATTY, Patricia (1936—). Canadian dancer, teacher and choreographer. Born May 15, 1936, in Toronto, Canada; attended Bennington College; studied ballet as well as modern dance with Gladys Forrester, Gwynneth Lloyd, Pearl Lang, and at Martha Graham School. ❖ One of Canada's most influential teachers of modern dance, founded New Dance Group (1966), which soon merged with the concert group of David Earle and Peter Randazzo to become Toronto Dance Theater (1967); served as artistic director and teacher at Dance Theater, where she also choreographed works, most notably *Hot and Cold Heroes* (1970) and *Harold Morgan's Delicate Equilibrium* (1974); choreographed *Momentum* (1967), *First Music* (1969), *Study for a Song in the Distance* (1970), *Los Sencillos* (1972), *The Reprieve* (1975) and *Seastill* (1979).

BEAUCHAMP, Anne (1426–1492). Countess of Warwick. Name variations: Lady Anne de Beauchamp. Born Sept 1426 in Caversham; died Sept 20, 1492; dau. of Richard Beauchamp (1381–1439), 5th earl of Warwick, and Isabel Despenser (1400–1439); m. Richard Neville the Kingmaker (1428–1471), 16th earl of Warwick (r. 1449–1471), 1434; children: Isabel Neville (1451–1476); Anne of Warwick (1456–1485, m. King Richard III).

BEAUCHAMP, Catherine (c. 1313–1369). *See Mortimer, Catherine.*

BEAUCHAMP, Eleanor (1408–1468). Duchess of Somerset. Born 1408; died Mar 6, 1468, in London, England; dau. of Richard Beauchamp, 5th earl of Warwick, and Elizabeth Berkeley; m. Thomas Roos, 9th baron Ros; m. Edmund Beaufort, 1st duke of Somerset, before 1436; children: (2nd m.) Henry Beaufort (1436–1464), 2nd duke of Somerset; Edmund Beaufort (1438–1471), 3rd duke of Somerset; John Beaufort (d. 1471); Margaret Beaufort (d. 1474); Eleanor Beaufort (d. 1501); Elizabeth Beaufort (d. before 1492, who m. Henry Lewes); Anne Beaufort (who m. William Paston); Joan Beaufort (d. after 1492, who m. Robert Howth, Lord of Howth, and Richard Fry); and 2 others.

BEAUCHAMP, Elizabeth (fl. 1420). Countess of Ormonde. Name variations: Elizabeth Butler. Fl. around 1420; dau. of William Beauchamp, Lord Abergavenny; m. James Butler (known as The White Earl), 4th earl of Ormonde; children: James Butler (c. 1390–1452), 5th earl of Ormonde; John Butler, 6th earl of Ormonde; Thomas Butler (c. 1424–1515), 7th earl of Ormonde.

BEAUCHAMP, Elizabeth (d. around 1480). English baroness. Died c. 1480; dau. of Richard Beauchamp, 5th earl of Warwick, and Elizabeth Berkeley (dau. of Thomas, Viscount L'Isle); m. George Neville (d. 1469), 1st baron Latimer; children: Henry Neville.

BEAUCHAMP, Elizabeth (fl. 1400s). Baroness Abergavenny. Dau. of Isabel Despenser (1400–1439) and Richard Beauchamp, earl of Worcester; stepdau. of Richard Beauchamp, the 5th earl of Warwick; m. Edward Neville, 1st baron Abergavenny (r. 1438–1476); children: Richard Neville; George Neville (d. 1492), 4th lord Abergavenny. ❖ Edward Neville's 2nd wife was Catherine Howard (d. after 1478).

BEAUCHAMP, Isabel (fl. 1285). Countess of Winchester. Name variations: Isabel Despenser; Isabel Chaworth. Fl. around 1285; dau. of William Beauchamp, 1st earl of Warwick, and Maud Fitzjohn; m. Patrick Chaworth; m. Hugh Despenser, Sr. (c. 1262–1326), earl of Winchester (executed, Oct 1326); children: (1st m.) Maud Chaworth (1282–c. 1322); (2nd m.) Hugh Despenser Jr. (c. 1285–1326); Isabel Despenser (who m. John Hastings, 2nd baron Hastings).

BEAUCHAMP, Isabel (1400–1439). *See Despenser, Isabel.*

BEAUCHAMP, Kathleen (1888–1923). *See Mansfield, Katherine.*

BEAUCHAMP, Margaret (d. 1482). Countess of Somerset. Died Aug 8, 1482; dau. of John Beauchamp, 3rd baron Beauchamp of Bletso, and Edith Stourton; m. Oliver St. John; m. John Beaufort, earl of Somerset, 1439; m. Lionel Welles, 6th baron Welles; children: (1st m.) Edith St. John (who m. Geoffrey Pole, grandfather of the archbishop of Canterbury); Oliver St. John (Lord St. John); John St. John; (2nd m.) Margaret Beaufort (1443–1509); (3rd m.) John Welles, 1st viscount Welles (d. 1499).

BEAUCHAMP, Mary Annette (1866–1941). *See Arnim, Elizabeth von.*

BEAUCHAMP, Philippa (fl. 1368–1378). *See Stafford, Philippa.*

BEAUCLERK, Diana (d. 1742). *See Vere, Diana de.*

BEAUDET, Louise (1861–1947). Canadian-born stage actress and singer. Born 1861 in St. Emilie, Quebec, Canada; died Jan 1, 1948, in New York, NY. ❖ Appeared on stage for over 50 years and was last seen in *White Lilacs* and *Hay Fever;* made film debut in *My Lady of Idleness* (1913), followed by over 20 films.

BEAUFORT, Anne (1673–1763). *See Coventry, Anne.*

BEAUFORT, duchess of. *See Estrées, Gabrielle d' (1573–1599).*

BEAUFORT, Eleanor (d. 1501). Countess of Ormonde. Died Aug 16, 1501; dau. of Edmund Beaufort, 1st duke of Somerset, and Eleanor Beauchamp (1408–1468); m. James Butler, 5th earl of Ormonde, April 1458; m. Robert Spencer; children: (2nd m.) Margaret Spencer (b. 1471).

BEAUFORT, Jane (c. 1410–1445). *See Beaufort, Joan.*

BEAUFORT, Joan (c. 1379–1440). Countess of Westmoreland. Name variations: Joanna Neville. Born illeg. at Beaufort Castle, Anjou, France, c. 1379; died at Howden, Humberside, England, Nov 13, 1440; dau. of John of Gaunt (1340–1399), duke of Lancaster, and Catherine Swynford (c. 1350–1403); half-sister of Henry IV, king of England (r. 1399–1413); grandmother of kings Edward IV and Richard III; m. Sir Robert Ferrers, 2nd baron Ferrers of Wemme, 1392 (died); m. Sir Ralph Neville of Raby (created 1st earl of Westmoreland by Richard II, 1397), 1396 (died 1425); children: (1st m.) Elizabeth Ferrers (1392–1434); Mary Ferrers (d. 1457); (2nd m.) Catherine Neville (c. 1397–1483); Richard (1400–1460), earl of Salisbury; William (d. 1463), lord of Fauconberg and earl of Kent; George (d. 1469), lord of Latimer (who m. Elizabeth Beauchamp); Edward (d. 1476), lord of Abergavenny; Robert (d. 1457), bishop of Durham; Cuthbert; Henry; Thomas; Eleanor Neville (c. 1413–1472), countess of Northumberland; Anne Neville (d. 1480), duchess of Buckingham; Jane also known as Joan Neville (who became a nun); Cecily Neville (1415–1495), duchess of York. ❖ Was instrumental in the creation of the Beaufort political faction in 15th-century England; betrothed to Sir Robert Ferrers (1386); legitimated, along with other Beaufort children, by Papal Bull (1396), and by royal writ and act of parliament (1397); father died (1399); legitimation confirmed by Henry IV (1407); became patron of poet Thomas Hoccleve (1421); awarded custody of Richard, duke of York (1423); her 2nd husband died (1425) and inheritance contested (1429); daughter Cecily married Richard, duke of York (1429); founded Chantry in the name of mother Catherine Swynford at Lincoln Cathedral (1437). ❖ See also *Women in World History.*

BEAUFORT, Joan (c. 1410–1445). Queen of Scotland. Name variations: Jane Beaufort; Queen Joan; Jane or Johanna. Born in England, c. 1410; died in Dunbar Castle, Lothian, Scotland, July 15, 1445, and buried in church of the Carthusian Monastery in Perth; dau. of Margaret Holland (1385–1429) and John Beaufort, earl of Somerset; m. James I (1394–1437), king of Scotland (r. 1406–1437), Feb 1424; m. Sir James Stewart of Lorne, July 1439; children: (1st m.) Margaret of Scotland (1424–1445); Isabel Stewart (d. 1494); Jean Stewart (d. 1486); Eleanor Stewart (d. 1496); (twins) Alexander (1430–1430) and James II (1430–1460), king of Scotland (r. 1437–1460); Mary Stewart (d. 1465), countess of Buchan; Annabella Stewart (d. after 1471); (2nd m.) James; John Stewart, 1st earl of Atholl (c. 1440–1512); Andrew. ❖ Crowned queen of Scotland (May 21, 1424) and nobility swore fealty (1428); gave birth to twin sons (Oct 16, 1430) and nobility swore fealty (1435); daughter Margaret married French dauphin (June 1436); attempted unsuccessfully to shield husband from assassination (Feb 20–21, 1437); remarried; tried to strengthen position by assuming the powers of regent but was arrested and imprisoned (Aug 3, 1439); release was negotiated by Parliament, but conditions of release, set out in the Appoyntement Agreement, were extremely favorable to her imprisoner who was awarded custody of James II (Sept 4, 1439); negotiated successful marriages of her daughters: Isabel married Francis I, duke of Brittany, and Mary married Wolfaert, count of Grandpre (1444); when she negotiated the marriage of daughter Jean to earl of Angus, resisted governmental opposition; continued to defy wishes of government and died while her castle was under siege (1444). ❖ See also *Women in World History.*

BEAUFORT, Margaret (c. 1407–?). Countess of Devon. Name variations: Margaret Courtenay. Born c. 1407; dau. of John Beaufort, marquess of Somerset (son of John of Gaunt and Catherine Swynford) and Margaret Holland (1385–1429); sister of Joan Beaufort (c. 1410–1445); m. Thomas Courtenay (1414–1458), 5th earl of Devon; children: Thomas (b. 1432), 6th earl of Devon (executed in 1461); John (c. 1435–1471), 7th earl of Devon; Henry Courtenay (executed in 1466); Joan Courtenay (who m. Sir Roger Clifford); Elizabeth Courtenay (who m. Sir Hugh Conway).

BEAUFORT, Margaret (d. 1474). English noblewoman. Died 1474; dau. of Edmund Beaufort, 1st duke of Somerset, and Eleanor Beauchamp (1408–1468); cousin and sister-in-law of Margaret Beaufort (1443–1509); m. Humphrey Stafford (d. 1455), 7th earl of Stafford, before 1454; m. Richard Darell; children: (1st m.) Henry Stafford, 2nd duke of Buckingham, and one other; (2nd m.) one.

BEAUFORT, Margaret (1443–1509). Countess of Richmond and Derby. Name variations: Lady Margaret; Margaret of Lancaster. Born Margaret Beaufort, May 31, 1443 (some sources cite 1441, but 1443 is documented), at Bletso in Bedfordshire; died at Westminster, June 29, 1509; dau. of John Beaufort (c. 1404–1444), 1st duke of Somerset, and Margaret Beauchamp (d. 1482); betrothed to John de la Pole, 1st duke of Suffolk, 1450 (dissolved, 1453); m. Edmund Tudor (d. 1456), earl of Richmond, 1455; m. Henry Stafford (d. 1471), 1458; m. Thomas Stanley (d. 1504), earl of Derby, 1472; children: (1st m.) Henry (b. Jan 28, 1457), later Henry VII, king of England (r. 1485–1509). ❖ One of the great women of her century, who might have tried to claim the throne of England but instead secured that position for her son, Henry VII, and all the Tudor line; involved in political conflicts of Wars of Roses (1459–71 and 1483–87); declared *femme sole* (1485); took vow of chastity (1499), though last husband was still living; founded divinity professorships at Oxford and Cambridge (1502), Cambridge preachership (1503), Christ's College (1505), and licensed St. John's College (1508) which was founded in her memory (1511); translated *De Imitatione Christi* from French to English (1504) and *Mirror of Gold for the Sinful Soul* (1506). ❖ See also Jones and Underwood, *The King's Mother: Lady Margaret Beaufort, Countess of Richmond and Derby* (Cambridge U. Press, 1992); E.M.G. Routh, *Lady Margaret: A Memoir* (Oxford U. Press, 1924); Linda Simon, *Of Virtue Rare: Margaret Beaufort, Matriarch of the House of Tudor* (Houghton, 1982); and *Women in World History.*

BEAUGRAND, Léontine (1842–1925). French ballet dancer. Name variations: Leontine Beaugrand. Born April 26, 1842, in Paris, France; died May 25, 1925, in Paris. ❖ Made debut performance at Paris Opéra in Marie Taglioni's *Le Papillon* (1860) and performed there for the next 20 years; danced in *Giselle* and *Coppélia* and held principal parts in Saint-Léon's *Diavolina* (1864) and Louis Mérante's *Gretna Green.*

BEAUHARNAIS, Eugénie Hortense de or Hortense de (1783–1837). See *Hortense de Beauharnais.*

BEAUHARNAIS, Fanny de (1737–1813). French novelist, poet and salonnière. Name variations: Marie-Anne-Françoise Mouchard, Comtesse de Beauharnais; Countess of Beauharnais. Born Marie Anne Françoise Mouchard in 1738 in Paris, France; died 1813; m. Claude de Beauharnais (uncle of Empress Josephine). ❖ Held literary salon in Paris and was a friend of Napoleon; contributed to *Journal des Dames* and wrote tales and poetry; probably collaborated with her lover, Dorat, on the novel *Sacrifices de l'amour* (1771); also wrote *Lettres de Stéphanie* (1778) and *La Fausse Inconstance* (1787). Beauharnais and Marie Anne Fiquet du Bocage were the only women admitted to the academy at Lyon.

BEAUHARNAIS, Josephine de.
See *Josephine, Empress (1763–1814).*
See *Josephine Beauharnais (1807–1876).*

BEAUHARNAIS, Marie-Anne-Françoise Mouchard, Comtesse de (1737–1813). See *Beauharnais, Fanny de.*

BEAUHARNAIS, Stephanie de (1789–1860). See *Stephanie de Beauharnais.*

BEAUJEU, Anne de (c. 1460–1622). See *Anne de Beaujeu.*

BEAUMER, Madame de (d. 1766). French journalist and novelist. Born in France; possibly a Huguenot; died 1766 in Holland. ❖ One of the 1st women to use feminine words for editor (*éditrice*) and author (*autrice*), served as editor of *Journal des Dames* (1760–65), which was censored for radical and feminist views; her various writings were collected as *Ouevres mêlées* (1760); also wrote *Lettres de Magdelon Friquet* and *Dialogue entre Charles XII roi de Suède et Mandarin* (1760). *Lettres de Magdelon Friquet* was deemed unpublishable by censors and is no longer extant.

BEAUMONT, Agnes (1652–1720). English religious autobiographer. Born 1652 in Edworth, Bedfordshire, England; died 1720 in England; was 7th and youngest child of yeoman farmer. ❖ Joined one of John Bunyan's congregations at Gamblingay (1672); was locked out of her parental home by father for 2 days, for continuing to attend the meetings in defiance of his wishes (1674); when the strain of the incident killed him, was accused of conspiring with Bunyan to poison father (1674); was eventually cleared of charges, which stemmed from the persecution of Nonconformist religious movements in England; wrote of experiences in *Narrative of the Persecution of Agnes Beaumont*, which survives in manuscript form and was published in the collection *An Abstract of the Gracious Dealings of God with Several Eminent Christians* (1760). ❖ See also Vera J. Camden, ed., *The Narrative of the Persecutions of Agnes Beaumont* (Michigan State U. Press, 1992).

BEAUMONT, Alice (fl. 1318). See *Comyn, Alice.*

BEAUMONT, Amicia (fl. 1208). See *Montfort, Amicia.*

BEAUMONT, Anne Louise Elie de (1730–1783). See *Elie de Beaumont, Anne Louise.*

BEAUMONT, countess of.
See *Jeanne of Valois (c. 1304–?).*
See *Blanche of France (1328–1392).*

BEAUMONT, Diana (1909–1964). English stage, tv, and screen actress. Born May 8, 1909, in Thames Ditton, England; died June 21, 1964, in London; m. John Barter (div.); m. Gabriel Toyne. ❖ Made stage debut in London in *Peter Pan,* followed by *Easy Virtue* (1926); other plays include *Baa Baa Black Sheep, While Parents Sleep, Admirals All, After October, Three Blind Mice, Life with Father, Fortune Came Smiling* and *Room with a View;* made film debut in *Adam's Apple* (1928), followed by *Alibi, When London Sleeps, Mannequin, Birds of a Feather, Black Limelight* and *North Sea Patrol.*

BEAUMONT, Eleanor (c. 1318–1372). See *Eleanor Plantagenet.*

BEAUMONT, Elizabeth (c. 1104–d. after 1172). See *Beaumont, Isabel.*

BEAUMONT, Ermengarde (d. 1234). See *Ermengarde of Beaumont.*

BEAUMONT, Florence (c. 1912–1967). American antiwar protester. Born c. 1912 in La Puente, California; died Oct 15, 1967, in Los Angeles, California; children: 2. ❖ One of 8 Americans known to have set themselves on fire to protest US involvement in the Vietnam War, soaked herself in gasoline and set herself alight in front of the Federal Building in Los Angeles, CA (Oct 15, 1967).

BEAUMONT, Hawise (d. 1197). Countess of Gloucester. Died 1197; dau. of Robert Beaumont (1104–1167), 2nd earl of Leicester, and Amicia de Waer; m. William Fitzrobert (d. 1183), 2nd earl of Gloucester, 1119; children: Amicia Fitzrobert (d. 1225); Mabel Fitzrobert; Avisa of Gloucester (c. 1167–1217).

BEAUMONT, Isabel (c. 1104–d. after 1172). English countess. Name variations: Elizabeth Beaumont; Isabel de Beaumont; born c. 1104; died after 1172; dau. of Isabel of Vermandois (d. before 1147) and Robert of Meulan, 1st earl of Leicester; had liaison with Henry I, king of England; married Gilbert de Clare, 1st earl of Pembroke; married Hervey de Montmorency, constable of England; children: (with Henry I) Isabel (b. c. 1120); Maud of Montivilliers, abbess of Montivilliers (1st m.) Richard de Clare (b. 1130), 2nd earl of Pembroke; Basilea de Clare.

BEAUMONT, Isabel (d. 1368). Duchess of Lancaster. Name variations: Isabel de Beaumont; Isabel of Lancaster. Died 1368; dau. of Henry Beaumont, 1st baron Beaumont, and Alice Comyn; m. Henry of

Grosmont (c. 1299–1361), 1st duke of Lancaster, around 1334; children: Maud Plantagenet (1335–1362); Blanche of Lancaster (1341–1369).

BEAUMONT, Lyne (1978—). Canadian synchronized swimmer. Born Jan 23, 1978, in Quebec City, Quebec, Canada. ❖ Won a team bronze medal at Sydney Olympics (2000).

BEAUMONT, Marie Le Prince de (1711–1780). *See Le Prince de Beaumont, Marie.*

BEAUMONT, Mary (d. 1632). Countess of Buckingham. Acceded on July 1, 1618; died April 19, 1632; dau. of Anthony Beaumont; m. Sir George Villiers; m. Sir William Rayner, June 19, 1606; m. Sir Thomas Compton; children: (1st m.) John Villiers, 1st viscount Purbeck; George Villiers, 1st duke of Buckingham; Christopher Villiers, 1st earl of Anglesey; Susan Villiers.

BEAUMONT, Muriel (1881–1957). English stage actress. Name variations: Muriel du Maurier; Lady du Maurier. Born April 14, 1881, in England; died Nov 27, 1957, in England; m. Sir Gerald du Maurier (actor-manager); children: Daphne du Maurier (novelist, 1907–1989). ❖ Made stage debut in non-speaking part at the Haymarket in *The Little Minister* (1898); had 1st substantial role as Lady Agatha Lazenby in *The Admirable Crichton* (1903); other plays include *The Walls of Jericho, The Merchant of Venice, The Fascinating Mr. Vanderveldt, The Barrier, Dear Old Charlie, Making a Gentleman* and *Glass Houses;* retired (1911).

BEAUPREY, Jeanne (1961—). American volleyball player. Born June 21, 1961. ❖ At Los Angeles Olympics, won a silver medal in team competition (1984).

BEAUREGARD, Robin (1979—). American water-polo player. Born Feb 23, 1979, in Huntington Beach, California; attended University of California, Los Angeles. ❖ Central defender, won a team silver medal at Sydney Olympics (2000) and a team bronze at Athens Olympics (2004); won World championship (2003).

BEAUVAIN D'ALTHENHEIM, Gabrielle (1814–1886). French poet and novelist. Name variations: Gabrielle Soumet, Mme Gabrielle Soumet, or Gabrielle Soumet Altenheim; Mme B. Daltenheym; Dame Beuvain d'Altenheim. Born Gabrielle Soumet, 1814, in France; died 1886; dau. of Alexandre Soumet (playwright, 1786–1845). ❖ Through father, met leading Romantic writers and composed epic by age 9; her fiction and poetry, which achieved great popular success, includes *Les Filiales* (1836), *Nouvelles Filiales* (1838), *Berthe Bertha* (1843), *Les Deux Frères* (1858) and *La Croix et la lyre;* also wrote 2 plays with father, *Le Gladiateur* (1841) and *Jane Grey* (1844).

BEAUVAU, Marie Charlotte (1729–1807). French memoirist. Name variations: Marie Charlotte de Rohan-Chabot, princesse de Beauvau; Princess of Beauvau; Princesse de Beauvau. Born Marie Charlotte de Rohan-Chabot in 1729; died 1807; widowed, 1749; m. Maréchal de Beauvau (of the Académie Française), 1764. ❖ Wrote *Souvenirs de la Maréchale Princesse De Beauvau,* detailing the loss of her 2nd husband, which was later published by her granddaughter, Sabine de Standish (nee Noailles), 1872.

BEAUVOIR, Simone de (1908–1986). French writer. Name variations: (nickname) le Castor (the Beaver). Born Simone Lucie Ernestine Marie Bertrand de Beauvoir in Paris, France, Jan 9, 1908; died in Paris, April 14, 1986; dau. of Georges Bertrand de Beauvoir and Françoise Brasseur; received *baccalauréat* degree from Cours Désir at 17; attended Institut Catholique and Institut Sainte-Marie; at 21, earned degree from Sorbonne (*license-ès-lettres*) and the prestigious *agrégation* in philosophy from École Normale Supérieure, the youngest *agrégée de philosophie* in France, 1929; never married; no children. ❖ Novelist, memoir writer, essayist, pioneer of modern feminism, and intellectual companion of French philosopher Jean-Paul Sartre for 51 years; at 10, developed a deep friendship with classmate Elizabeth Le Coin ("Zaza"); long after Le Coin died (1929), would try unsuccessfully to immortalize her in her fiction; met Sartre, the future founder of Existentialism (1929); taught in lycées (1931–43); published *L'Invitée* (*She Came to Stay*, 1943), which brought fame; wrote *Pyrrhus and Cineas,* a series of essays on human relationships, personal responsibility, and the nonexistence of God (1944); gained further recognition with publication of *The Blood of Others* (1945) and *All Men are Mortal* (1946); with Sartre, established and edited influential journal, *Les Temps Modernes* (*Modern Times*), a vehicle for disseminating existentialist and eventually feminist thought (1944); published Vol. I of her noted study of women, *The Second Sex*

(Oct 1949), beginning a lifelong involvement with feminist issues (over 200,000 copies of the book sold in a week, despite being banned by Catholic Church); undeterred, published 2nd volume which caused an even greater sensation; was openly antipathetic to the government of Charles de Gaulle and in favor of Algerian independence, unpopular sentiments in France (1950s); wrote 4 vols. of memoirs, the 1st published in 1958, the last in 1972; met Sylvie Le Bon (later her adopted daughter, Nov 1960); served as president of "Choisir" (To Choose, June 1972), promoting contraception; served as president of League of Women's Rights (Jan 1974), working to end sex discrimination in France; mourned death of Sartre (April 15, 1980) and published *Adieux—Farewell to Sartre* (1981); accepted the post of honorary chair of the Commission on Women and Culture offered by François Mitterand (1981); inspired other women in the quest for their humanity. Received Goncourt Prize for *The Mandarins* (1954). ❖ See also Deirdre Bair, *Simone de Beauvoir: A Biography* (Summit, 1990); Margaret Crosland, *Simone de Beauvoir: The Woman and Her Work* (Heinemann, 1992); Renée Winegarten, *Simone de Beauvoir: A Critical View* (Berg, 1988); Carole Asher, *Simone de Beauvoir: A Life of Freedom* (Beacon Press, 1981); Mary Evans, *Simone de Beauvoir: A Feminist Mandarin* (Tavistock, 1985); Francis and Gontier *Simone de Beauvoir* (St. Martin, 1987); and *Women in World History.*

BEAUX, Cecilia (1855–1942). American artist. Name variations: (nicknames) Leilie and Bo. Pronunciation: Boe. Born Eliza Cecilia Beaux, May 1, 1855, in Philadelphia, Pennsylvania; died at Gloucester, Massachusetts, Sept 17, 1942; dau. of Jean Adolphe Beaux (silk manufacturer) and Cecilia Kent (Leavitt) Beaux (grandmother of historian Catherine Drinker Bowen); trained as a painter in Catherine Ann Drinker's studio, at Adolf Van der Whelan's art school and privately with William Sartain; later on, studied in Paris at Académie Julien, 1888–89; never married; no children. ❖ In a career devoted entirely to portraiture, was acclaimed during America's Gilded Age as the greatest living "woman artist"; brought up by grandmother and 2 aunts in Philadelphia; awarded Mary Smith Prize from Pennsylvania Academy of Fine Arts for painting *Les Derniers Jours d'Enfance,* which was exhibited in Paris Salon (1885); won 3 more annual Mary Smith awards for the best painting by a resident woman artist (1887–89); went abroad for further study, to Paris, Italy and England (1888–89); reaped numerous honors over next few years; taught at Pennsylvania Academy of the Fine Arts (1895–1915); moved studio to New York City (1900); built Green Alley, her famous summer home in Gloucester (1905); was commissioned to do 3 portraits of Allied WWI leaders at Paris Peace Conference (1919); invited to paint self-portrait for Uffizi Gallery at Florence (1924); broke hip in France (1924), which thereafter curtailed her mobility and painting career; was one of the 12 most influential women in America (1920s–30s). Paintings include *Les Derniers Jours d'Enfance* (1883), *Little Girl* (1887), *William R. Darwin* (1889), *Cynthia Sherwood* (1892), *Mrs. Stetson* (1893), *Sita and Sarita* (1893–94), *Ernesta Drinker with Nurse* (1894), *The Dreamer* (1894), *Mrs. Alexander Biddle* (1897), *Mr. and Mrs. Anson Phelps Stokes* (1898), *The Dancing Lesson* (1899–1900), *Mrs. Theodore Roosevelt with her daughter Ethel* (1901), *Man with the Cat* (1902), *A Girl in White: Ernesta* (1914), *Georges Clemenceau* (1920) and *Self-Portrait No. 4* (1925). ❖ See also autobiography, *Background With Figures* (1930); Catherine Drinker Bowen, *Family Portrait* (Little, Brown, 1970); Henry S. Drinker, *The Paintings and Drawings of Cecilia Beaux* (Pennsylvania Academy of Fine Arts, 1955); Tara Leigh Tappert, *Cecilia Beaux and the Art of Portraiture* (Smithsonian, 1995); and *Women in World History.*

BEAVERS, Louise (1902–1962). African-American actress. Born in Cincinnati, Ohio, Mar 8, 1902; died in Los Angeles, California, Oct 26, 1962; graduate of Pasadena High School, June 1920; m. LeRoy Moore. ❖ After performing the song "Pal of My Cradle Days" in an amateur contest at the Philharmonic Auditorium, received a call from Central Casting in Hollywood; made film debut in silent version of *Uncle Tom's Cabin* for Universal (1927); was only occasionally provided the opportunity to avoid the part of maid or white-child's "mammy" in her 125 films; was allowed to display the range of her talent in *Imitation of Life* (1934) and *The Jackie Robinson Story* (1950); replaced Hattie McDaniel on radio and tv series "Beulah" with great success (early 1950s); was a member of the board of Screen Actors Guild; other films include *Golddiggers of Broadway* (1929), *She Couldn't Say No* (1930), *Freaks* (1932), *Old Man Minick* (1932), *She Done Him Wrong* (1933), *Rainbow on the River* (1936), *Made for Each Other* (1939), *No Time for Comedy* (1940), *Belle Starr* (1941), *Shadow of the Thin Man* (1941), *Holiday Inn* (1942), *DuBarry Was a Lady* (1943), *Dixie Jamboree*

(1944), *Follow the Boys* (1944), *Mr. Blandings Builds His Dream House* (1948), *My Blue Heaven* (1949), *Never Wave at a Wac* (1953), *Tammy and the Bachelor* (1957), *The Goddess* (1958), *All the Fine Young Cannibals* (1960) and *The Facts of Life* (1961). Inducted into the Black Filmmakers Hall of Fame (1957). ❖ See also *Women in World History.*

BEAVIS, Sandra (1942—). *See Morgan, Sandra.*

BÉBEL-GISLER, Dany (1935–2003). Gaudeloupean sociolinguist and ethnologist. Name variations: Dany Bebel Gisler. Born April 7, 1935, in Pointe-à-Pitre, Guadeloupe; died Sept 28, 2003, in Lamentin, Guadeloupe; dau. of landowner father and agricultural worker. ❖ Focused on the tension between the French and Creole language and culture and called for recognition of Creole; worked with Bwadoubout Centre Project to promote teaching in Creole; writings include *La langue créole, force jugulée* (1976), *Le défi culturel Gaudeloupéen* (1989) and (novel) *Léonora* (1985).

BECCARY, Madame (fl. 18th c.). French novelist. Flourished between 1761 and 1778. ❖ Wrote 4 novels as supposed translations from the English: *Lettres de Milady Bedfort* (1769), *Mémoires de Lucie d'Olbery* (1770), *Mémoires de Fanny Spingler* (1781) and *Milord d'Ambi* (1778).

BECHARD, Kelly (1978—). Canadian ice-hockey player. Born 1978 in Canada. ❖ Won a gold medal at World championships (2001) and a gold medal at Salt Lake City Olympics (2002).

BECHER, Eliza (1791–1872). *See O'Neill, Eliza.*

BECHER, Hilla (1934—). German photographer. Born Hilla Wobeser in Potsdam, Germany, 1934; married Bernhard (Bernd) Becher (photographer), 1961; children: Max (b. 1964). ❖ With family, fled Russian troops during WWII and later returned to Potsdam; began a 4-year apprenticeship with a commercial photographer (1951); worked as an aerial photographer with a commercial studio in Hamburg; moved to Düsseldorf and found work at advertising agency (late 1950s); with husband, enrolled at Staatliche Kunstakademie, then traveled and photographed in Germany, Netherlands and Belgium, documenting structures for the concrete company that he worked for, and photographing other structures—especially water towers—for own interest; also did freelance work for industrial fairs and exhibitions, as well as some teaching; work has been exhibited internationally in solo and group shows.

BECHER, Lilly (1901–1976). East German writer and publicist. Name variations: Lilly Korpus. Born Lilly Korpus in Nuremberg, Germany, Jan 27, 1901; died in East Berlin in 1976; dau. of a naval officer (one of the few officers of Jewish origin to serve in German Navy) and a mother who was the stepdau. of Albert Ballin, the Jewish director of the Hamburg-America Line and an advisor of Kaiser Wilhelm II; m. Johannes R. Becher. ❖ Joined Communist Party of Germany (KPD, 1919); did editorial work on Communist newspapers and journals in Berlin; appointed to high leadership positions within KPD (1924–25); fled to France (1933); worked with Willi Münzenberg in Paris to produce the 1st documentation of Nazi anti-Semitism, *Der gelbe Fleck;* fled France for Soviet Union (1935), where she broadcast for Radio Moscow; returned to Germany (1945); served as editor-in-chief of *Neue Berliner Illustrierte;* was founding member of Democratic Women's League and chair of German-Soviet Friendship Society. Awarded Silver Medal for Service of the GDR. ❖ See also *Women in World History.*

BECHKE, Elena (1966—). Russian pairs skater. Born Elena Yurievna Bechke, Jan 7, 1966, in St. Petersburg (then Leningrad), Russia; m. Denis Petrov, 1990 (div. 1995). ❖ With Valeri Kornienko, won Skate Canada (1984) and placed 3rd at European championships (1986); with Denis Petrov, won NHK Trophy (1990, 1991), Soviet nationals (1992), placed 3rd at World championships (1989) and 2nd at European championships (1991, 1992), and won a silver medal at Albertville Olympics (1992); turned pro (1992).

BECHTEL, Louise Seaman (1894–1985). American editor, author and lecturer on children's literature. Born Louise Seaman, June 29, 1894, in Brooklyn, NY; died 1985; dau. of Charles Francis Seaman (railroad accountant) and Anna (Van Brunt) Seaman; attended Packer Collegiate Institute, 1909–11; Vassar College, AB, 1915; graduate study at Yale University, 1915–18; m. Edwin De Turck Bechtel, 1929 (died 1957). ❖ Served as editor and head of Juvenile Book Department of Macmillan in NY (1919–34); worked as freelance writer and lecturer; was the editor of children's section of *New York Herald Tribune Book Review* (1948–56) and associate editor of *The Horn Book Magazine* (1939–57).

BECHTEREVA, Natalia (1924—). Russian physician specializing in brain research. Name variations: Natalia Petrovna Bechtereva. Born July 7, 1924, in Russia. ❖ Conducted majority of research at Institute of Experimental Medicine (part of Leningrad's Academy of Medical Sciences), of which she served as head of department of human neurophysiology; performed work on brain function which assisted in treatment of disorders including severe epilepsy (1950s–60s); was 1st to use electrodes to study normal brain function; with coworkers, discovered type of signal that reflected emotions; extended research to examine thinking (1960s); received Century Award from International Organization of Psychophysiology (1998). Was a member of Russian Academy of Sciences, Institute of the Human Brain, and Finnish Academy of Science and Letters.

BECIRSPAHIC, Mirsada (1957—). Yugoslavian basketball player. Born Dec 1957. ❖ At Moscow Olympics, won a bronze medal in team competition (1980).

BECK, Audrey P. (1931–1983). American economist and politician. Name variations: Audrey Phillips Beck. Born Audrey Phillips, Aug 6, 1931, in Brooklyn, NY; died Mar 11, 1983, in Willington, Connecticut; University of Connecticut, BA, MA; m. Curt Frederick Beck (political science professor at University of Connecticut); children: Meredith Wayne Beck (b. 1951); Ronald Person Beck (b. 1953). ❖ Joined faculty of economics department at University of Connecticut (1961); served on state board of directors of League of Women Voters (1962–65); served in Connecticut House of Representatives (1967–1975), where she was assistant minority leader for Democrats (1973); was the 1st woman president of American Society of Planning Officials; elected to Connecticut State Senate (1975), where she served as assistant majority leader (1977–83); during 4th senate term, apparently committed suicide.

BECK, Beatrix (1914—). Belgian novelist. Name variations: Béatrix. Born Beatrix Beck in Villars-sur-Ollon, Switzerland, July 30, 1914; dau. of Christian Beck (Belgian novelist) and an Irish mother; educated at University of Grenoble; married Naum Szapiro, Sept 26, 1936. ❖ Her father, a respected novelist, died in WWI, when she was 2; husband was killed during WWII; published *Barny* (1948); began supporting herself as secretary to André Gide (1950); other novels, which were heavily based on her life, include *Léon Morin, Prête* (*The Priest,* 1952), which won the Goncourt Prize, *Noli* (1978), *La Décharge* (The Discharge, 1979), and *La Petite Italie.*

BECK, Elizabeth Louisa (c. 1862–1931). Canadian romance-fiction writer. Name variations: Eliza Louisa Moresby Beck; (pseudonyms) Lily Adams Beck or L. Adams Beck or Lily Moresby Adams, E. Barrington and Louis Moresby. Born Elizabeth Louisa Moresby in England, c. 1862; died in Kyoto, Japan, Jan 3, 1931; dau. of Jane Willis (Scott) Moresby and John Moresby (navy admiral); married. ❖ As an admiral's daughter, lived in India, China, Burma, Tibet and Japan, leading to a love of Oriental culture and history, which informed her novels; wrote under 3 pseudonyms (oriental historical romance under Louis Moresby, historical under E. Barrington, and books about oriental culture as Lily Adams Beck or L. Adams Beck); settled in Canada (1922); published 1st book (1922); produced more than 25 books in next 9 years; also assisted father with his memoirs; returned to Japan near the end of her life; works include *The Ninth Vibration and Eight Other Stories* (1922), *Dreams and Delights* (1922), *The Key of Dreams* (1922), *The Chaste Diana* (1923), *The Divine Lady* (1924); *Glorious Apollo* (1925), *The Treasure of Ho* (1925), *The Thunderers* (1927), *The Garden of Vision* (1929), *The Irish Beauties* (1931) and *The Great Romantic* (1933).

BECK, Emily Morison (1915–2004). American book editor. Born Emily Marshall Morison, Oct 15, 1915, in Boston, Massachusetts; died at home, Mar 28, 2004, in Canton, MA; dau. of Samuel Eliot Morison (Harvard historian) and Elizabeth Greene Shaw; attended Dragon School in Oxford, England, Concord Academy in Massachusetts, and Radcliffe; m. Brooks Beck (lawyer), 1946 (died 1969); children: Cameron, Gordon and Emily M. Beck. ❖ Began career as an editor for Harper & Brothers, then Knopf; moved to Boston and became an editor at Atlantic Monthly Press; at same time, joined editorial staff of *Bartlett's Familiar Quotations* at Little, Brown (1952), serving as editor for 13th, 14th, and 15th editions (1955, 1968, 1980); continued working for Atlantic Monthly press until 1975.

BECK, L. Adams (c. 1862–1931). *See Beck, Elizabeth Louisa.*

BECK, Lily Adams (c. 1862–1931). *See Beck, Elizabeth Louisa.*

BECK, Maria (1959—). See Epple, Maria.

BECK, Martha (c. 1921–1951). American swindler and murderer. Born c. 1921; electrocuted at Sing Sing Prison, Mar 8, 1951. ❖ Answered advertisement from Raymond Fernandez, a confidence man, in lonely hearts magazine; after meeting (Dec 1947) and falling in love, began tricking vulnerable women out of their savings with his help, a life of crime which soon turned into a killing spree; with Fernandez, was thought responsible for more than 20 murders (they were known as the Lonely Hearts Killers); tried in NY for murder of Janet Fay, widow in her 60s, and found guilty.

BECK, Sophie (1858–?). American swindler. Born 1858; death date unknown. ❖ After operating as a minor confidence artist, relocated from New York to Philadelphia where she sold stock in a phony Story Cotton Co.; accepted cash-only investments and made away with over $2 million before escaping to Europe (1903).

BECKER, Britta (1973—). German field-hockey player. Born May 11, 1973. ❖ At Barcelona Olympics, won a silver medal in team competition (1992).

BECKER, Carolyn (1958—). American volleyball player. Born Nov 8, 1958. ❖ At Los Angeles Olympics, won a silver medal in team competition (1984).

BECKER, Christiane (1778–1797). German actress. Born Christiane Luise Amalie Neumann at Krossen in Neumark, Germany, Dec 15, 1778; died at Weimar, Sept 17, 1797; dau. of Johann Christian Neumann (well-known German actor); m. Heinrich Becker (German actor). ❖ Famed actress, performed in both comedy and tragedy; was admired by Goethe who, after her death at a young age, wrote of her in the elegy "Euphrosine."

BECKER, Elizabeth (1903–1989). See Becker-Pinkston, Elizabeth.

BECKER, Ellen (1960—). West German rower. Born Aug 3, 1960, in Germany. ❖ At Los Angeles Olympics, won a bronze medal in coxless pairs (1984).

BECKER, Ingrid (1942—). See Mickler, Ingrid.

BECKER, Jillian (1932—). South African novelist and historian. Born 1932 in Johannesburg, South Africa; m. Gerry Becker. ❖ Moved to England (1961), but early novels focus on interracial tension and life in South Africa; works of fiction include *The Keep* (1967), *The Union* (1971) and *The Virgins* (1976); nonfiction includes *Hitler's Children: The Story of the Baader-Meinhof Terrorist Gang* (1978), *The P.L.O.: The Rise and Fall of the Palestinian Liberation Organization* (1984) and *Giving Up: The Last Days of Sylvia Plath* (2003); also edited *The Soviet Union and Terrorism* (1984).

BECKER, Lucy (1916–2004). See Freeman, Lucy.

BECKER, Lydia (1827–1890). English botanist and women's-rights advocate. Born Lydia Ernestine Becker, Feb 24, 1827, in Manchester, England; died at health resort of Aix-les-Bains, July 18, 1890; dau. of Hannibal Becker (owner of chemical works in Manchester) and Mary (Duncuft) Becker; never married; no children. ❖ In a lifetime devoted to women's rights, established the Manchester Ladies Literary Society (1865), as a forum for the study of scientific subjects among women; co-founded and became secretary of Manchester Women's Suffrage Committee (1867), which became National Society for Women's Suffrage later that year; edited *Women's Suffrage Journal* (1870–90), as well as other pamphlets on women's suffrage.

BECKER, Marie Alexander (1877–194?). Belgian housewife and mass poisoner. Born Marie Alexander, 1877, in Belgium; date of death went unreported during WWII German occupation of Belgium; married to a cabinet maker. ❖ Embarked on an affair with Lambert Beyer that led her to poison her cabinetmaker husband with digitalis; soon bored with Beyer, dispatched him in the same manner; to obtain money for subsequent romances with a series of gigolos, began poisoning elderly women patrons of her new dressmaking shop, stealing what she could; murdered 10 in all. ❖ See also *Women in World History*.

BECKER, May Lamberton (1873–1958). American writer. Born May Lamberton in New York, NY, Aug 26, 1873; died April 27, 1958; dau. of Emma (Packard) Lamberton (teacher) and Ellis Tinkham Lamberton; m. Gustav Louis Becker (pianist and composer), 1894 (div. 1911); children: Beatrice Becker Warde. ❖ Critic and journalist who edited a column titled "Reader's Guide" for 40 years; launched "Reader's Guide"

at New York *Evening Post* (1915); moved column to the *Saturday Review of Literature* (1924), then to *Herald Tribune* (1933), where it ran until she retired (May 1, 1955). ❖ See also *Women in World History*.

BECKER, Paula (1876–1907). See Modersohn-Becker, Paula.

BECKER, Sabine (1959—). East German speedskater. Born Aug 13, 1959, in Karl-Mark-Stadt (present-day Chemnitz), East Germany. ❖ Won a bronze medal for 1,500 meters and a silver for the 3,000 meters at Lake Placid Olympics (1980); fled East Germany to West Berlin (1986); won national titles over single distances in West Germany; became a professional singer.

BECKER-DEY, Courtenay (1965—). American sailor. Name variations: Courtenay Becker; Courtenay Becker Dey. Born Courtenay Becker, April 27, 1965, in Greenwich, Connecticut; grew up in Rye, NY; Eckerd College, BA, 1987; m. Jim Dey (pro windsurfer). ❖ Ranked #1 on US Sailing Team (1989–94); won a gold medal at USYRU Singlehanded championships (1988); won a bronze medal for single-handed dinghy (Europe) at Atlanta Olympics (1996); was navigator on America³, the 1st all-woman America's Cup Team (1995). Named Rolex Yachtswoman of the Year (1990).

BECKER-MODERSOHN, Paula (1876–1907). See Modersohn-Becker, Paula.

BECKER-PINKSTON, Elizabeth (1903–1989). American swimmer. Name variations: Elizabeth Becker; Elizabeth Pinkston; Elizabeth Pinkston-Becker; Betty Becker Pinkston Campbell; Elizabeth P. Campbell. Born Elizabeth Becker, Mar 6, 1903, in Philadelphia, PA; died in Detroit, Michigan, April 6, 1989; lived in West Palm Beach, Florida; m. Clarence Pinkston (1900–1961, American diver), 1925 (died Nov 18, 1961); m. once more; children: (1st m.) twins (b. 1926). ❖ The 1st woman to win 2 Olympic diving titles, won gold medals for springboard at Paris as Elizabeth Becker (1924) and for platform at Amsterdam as Elizabeth Pinkston (1928); also won a silver medal for platform in Paris; was US indoor 3-meter champion (1922, 1923, 1926). ❖ See also *Women in World History*.

BECKER-STEINER, Marion (1950—). West German javelin thrower. Born Jan 21, 1950. ❖ At Montreal Olympics, won a silver medal in the javelin throw (1976).

BECKETT, Margaret (1943—). English politician and member of Parliament. Name variations: Rt. Hon. Margaret Beckett. Born Margaret Jackson, Jan 15, 1943, in Ashton-under-Lyne, Lancashire, England; dau. of a carpenter and teacher; trained as an engineer at Manchester College of Science and Technology; m. Lionel Arthur Beckett, 1979. ❖ Served as industrial policy researcher, Labour Party (1970–74), and principal researcher, Granada Television (1979–83); was political adviser, Ministry of Overseas Development (1974); representing Labour, elected MP for Lincoln (1974) and served as under-secretary of state for the Department of Education and Science (1976–79); elected to House of Commons for Derby South (1983); served as Opposition front bench spokesperson on health and social security (1984–89), shadow chief secretary to the Treasury (1989–92), shadow leader of the House and campaigns coordinator (1992–94), deputy leader (1992–94), chair of committee for Modernization of House of Commons (1998–2001); named secretary of state for Environment, Food, and Rural Affairs; reelected (2005).

BECKETT, Mary (1926—). Irish novelist. Born 1926 in Belfast, Ireland; children: 5. ❖ Writings, which often focus on women living through social conflict, include *A Belfast Woman* (1980), *Give Them Stones* (1989) and *A Literary Woman* (1990); also wrote books for children, including *Orla at School* (1991), *A Family Tree* (1992) and *Hannah or Pink Balloons* (1992). Won Bisto Merit Award (1995).

BECKETT, Patricia Jean (1924–2001). See Adam-Smith, Patsy.

BECKHAM, Victoria (1974—). English singer. Name variations: Victoria Adams, Victoria Caroline Beckham, Posh Spice, The Spice Girls. Born Victoria Caroline Adams, April 17, 1974, in Essex, England; m. David Beckham (football player), July 4, 1999; children: Brooklyn Joseph (b. Mar 5, 1999), Romeo James (b. Sept 1, 2002). ❖ Singer who shot to fame as part of pop-quintet, The Spice Girls, and cemented star status with marriage to football star, 1st performed with pop group Touch; with other members of Touch band, formed Spice Girls in London (1994); with group, released "Wannabe," the 1st debut single by an all-girl band to enter international charts at #1 (1997), then album, *Spice*, which went to #1 in UK charts and was the 1st debut album by UK performers to enter US charts at #1 (1997); had other Top-10 singles, including "Say You'll be There" and "2 Become 1"; released smash-hit album *Spiceworld* and film of same name (1997); like other members of the group, took on solo projects after unsuccessful Spice album, *Forever* (2000); had mixed solo career, releasing album *Victoria Beckham* (2001) and several singles, including "Not Such an Innocent Girl" (2001) and "A Mind of Its Own" (2002); signed with Telstar Records (2001) and Rocc-A-Fella Records (2003). ❖ See also Victoria Beckham, *Learning to Fly* (Michael Joseph, 2001).

BECKMAN-SHCHERBINA, Elena (1881–1951). Russian pianist. Born 1881; died 1951; studied under Konstantin Igumnov. ❖ Trained in Russian School of virtuoso pianism; was a highly respected artist who left behind an impressive recorded legacy of music by Anton Rubinstein, Sergei Rachmaninoff, and Alexander Scriabin; knew Scriabin personally and frequently played his music for him. ❖ See also *Women in World History.*

BECKMANN, Gudrun (1955—). West German swimmer. Born Aug 17, 1955. ❖ At Munich Olympics, won a bronze medal in the 4 x 100-meter medley relay and the 4 x 100-meter freestyle relay (1972).

BECKWITH, Martha Warren (1871–1959). American folklorist, ethnographer, teacher and author. Born in Wellesley Heights, Massachusetts, Jan 19, 1871; died in Berkeley, California, Jan 28, 1959, and buried in Makawao cemetery, Maui; youngest child of George Ely and Harriet Winslowe (Goodale) Beckwith (both school-teachers); grandniece of Lucy Goodale Thurston; graduate of Mt. Holyoke College, 1893; Columbia University, MA in anthropology, 1906. ❖ Close childhood friend of naturalist Annie Alexander, grew up on Maui; taught at Punahou School for 2 years, then at Mt. Holyoke, Smith, and Vassar for next 10 years, before studying anthropology under Frank Boaz at Columbia; returned to teaching at Vassar (1920), retiring (1938); wrote firsthand accounts of the folklore and ethnography of Hawaiians, Jamaicans, Native Americans, and the Portuguese residents of Goa in such books as *The Hawaiian Romance of Laieikawai* (1919), *Folklore in America* (1931), *Hawaiian Mythology* (1940) and *The Kumulipo* (1951).

BECLEA-SZEKELY, Violeta (1965—). Romanian runner. Name variations: Violeta Beclea; Violeta Beclea Szekely. Born Violeta Beclea, Mar 26, 1965, in Dolhestii Mari, Romania. ❖ Won a silver medal for the 1,500 meters at Sydney Olympics (2000); won a silver medal at World championships and a gold medal at European championships (2001), both for 1,500 meters; at European won IAAF Grand Prix (2001).

BÉCU, Marie Jeanne (1743–1793). *See Du Barry, Jeanne Bécu.*

BEDACIER, Catherine (d. 1736). *See Durand, Catherine.*

BEDARD, Myriam (1969—). Canadian biathlete. Name variations: Myriam Bédard. Born Dec 22, 1969, in Ancienne-Lorette, Quebec, Canada; m. Jean Pacquet (biathlete). ❖ Won Canadian Jr. championship (1987); was 1st Canadian to win a World Cup biathlon event (1991); won a bronze medal for 15 km at Albertville (1992), the 1st North American to win an Olympic medal in biathlon; won a World championship (1993); won gold medals for 15 km and 7.5 km at Lillehammer (1994), the 1st Canadian woman to win 2 Olympic gold medals; competed at Nagano Olympics but did not medal (1998); retired (1999); became co-host of Radio-Canada's tv series "Parents d'aujourd'hui." Inducted into Canada's Sports Hall of Fame (1998).

BEDDINGFIELD, Ann (1742–1763). English murderer. Born in England, 1742; burned alive at the stake, April 8, 1763, in Rushmore, England; m. John Beddingfield. ❖ Convinced her 19-year-old servant-lover (Richard Ringe) to kill husband (Mar 1763); caught and placed on trial (April 1763). Though Ringe was hanged, she was burned alive at the stake, a form of punishment then reserved for unfaithful, murderous wives. ❖ See also *Women in World History.*

BEDDINGTON, Rosa (1956–2001). English embryologist. Name variations: Dr. Rosa Susan Penelope Beddington. Born Mar 23, 1956 in Hurstbourne Tarrant, Hampshire, England; died May 18, 2001, in Tew, Oxfordshire, England; m. Rev. Robin A. Denniston. ❖ An experimental biologist, produced insights into the way an embryo becomes a fetus in mammals; was among the 1st women to be admitted to Brasenose College at Oxford to study medicine; though a skilled microsurgeon, made embryology her career; headed the mammalian development section of National Institute for Medical Research in London.

BEDE, Shelda (1973—). Brazilian beach volleyball player. Name variations: Shelda Kelly Bruno Bede. Born Jan 1, 1973, in Fortaleza, Brazil; sister of Shaylyn Bede (b. 1981, beach volleyball player). ❖ With Adriana Behar, was FIVB Tour champion (1997–2001), won World championships (1999 and 2001), won a silver medal at Sydney Olympics (2000) and a silver medal at Athens Olympics (2004).

BEDELL, Catherine Dean (1914–2004). *See May, Catherine Dean.*

BEDELL, Harriet M. (1875–1969). American missionary and religious leader. Born in Grand Island, New York, Mar 19, 1875; died in Davenport, Florida, 1969; dau. of Horace Ira and Louisa Sophia (Oberist) Bedell; graduate of State Normal School, Buffalo, 1894. ❖ Deacon, known as the "white sister" of the Florida Seminole Indians, left her teaching position in Buffalo, NY, to train as a mission teacher through the Protestant Episcopal Church; spent remainder of life as a missionary in service of the Cheyenne Indians of northwestern Oklahoma, the Alaskan Indians in the remote Alaskan Arctic Circle, and the Mikasuki Seminole Indians of Florida; lost her world-renowned Glade Cross Mission House and most of her personal possessions to Hurricane Donna (1960). ❖ See also William and Ellen Hartley *A Woman Set Apart: The Remarkable Life of Harriet Bedell* (Dodd, 1963).

BEDELLS, Phyllis (1893–1985). English dancer. Born Aug 9, 1893, in Bristol, England; died May 2, 1985, in London; trained with Theodore Gilmer in Nottingham, then with Malvina Cavallazzi at the Empire Theatre; also studied with Alexander Genée, Nicholas Legat, Enrico Cecchetti and Adolf Bolm; m. Ian Gordon Macbean. ❖ Made stage debut as First Oyster in *Alice in Wonderland* (1906); appeared at the Empire (1907–15), in such productions as *The Debutante, The Bell of the Ball, Ship Ahoy!* and *Watch Your Step*, before succeeding Adeline Genée as *première danseuse* (1914); other appearances include *Pastoral, The Dancing Master, Razzle-Dazzle, Zig-Zag, Smile* and *Johnny Jones and His Sister Sue*; often appeared in variety theaters with Anton Dolin, as well as at the Palladium with her own company; retired from stage (1935) and turned to teaching; was one of the founders of Royal Academy of Dancing. ❖ See also autobiography *My Dancing Days* (1954).

BEDERKHAN, Leila (b. around 1903). Persian interpretive dancer. Born c. 1903 in Kurdistan. ❖ Raised in Egypt after Turkish invasion of Kurdistan, and later exiled during the conflict between Egypt and Turkey (1917), studied both music and medicine for some time in Switzerland; made professional debut in Vienna (1926), performing native and interpretive dances; won acclaim throughout Austria, US and Italy; appeared as exotic dancer in production of *Belkis, Reine de Saba* at Teatro alla Scala in Milan (1934), but otherwise performed mainly own works; solo choreographies include *Snake, Heirogliphe, Bridal Song, Profane, On the Island* and *Kurdistani Dances*.

BEDFORD, B.J. (1972—). American swimmer. Name variations: Barbara Bedford. Born Barbara Bedford, Nov 9, 1972, in Hanover, New Hampshire; University of Texas, BFA, 1994. ❖ Won a gold medal for 4 x 100-meter medley relay at Sydney Olympics (2000); won 7 national titles in the 50-, 100-, and 200-meter backstroke.

BEDFORD, Barbara (1903–1981). American silent-film actress. Born July 19, 1903, in Eastman, Wisconsin; died Oct 25, 1981, in Jacksonville, Florida. ❖ Noted for her performance in Maurice Tourneur's *The Last of the Mohicans* (1920), made 170 films, including *Tumbleweeds* (opposite William S. Hart), *Souls for Sale, The Mad Whirl, Mockery* and *The Port of Missing Girls*.

BEDFORD, Barbara (1972—). *See Bedford, B.J.*

BEDFORD, countess of.
See Isabella (1332–1382).
See Russell, Lucy (c. 1581–1627).

BEDFORD, duchess of.
See Anne Valois (c. 1405–1432).
See Jacquetta of Luxemburg (c. 1416–1472).
See Woodville, Katherine (c. 1442–1512).
See Russell, Mary du Caurroy (1865–1937).

BEDFORD, Lillian (1881–1956). *See Leonard, Marion.*

BEDFORD, Marie (1907—). South African swimmer. Born Mar 27, 1907. ❖ At Amsterdam Olympics, won a bronze medal in the 4 x 100-meter freestyle relay (1928).

BEDFORD, Sybille (1911–2006). Anglo-German journalist, novelist and biographer. Born Sybille Von Schoenebeck in Charlottenburg, Germany, Mar 16, 1911; died Feb 17, 2006, in London, England; dau. of Elizabeth Bernard and Maximilian Von Schoenebeck; educated at village and private schools in Germany, Italy, England and France; m. Walter Bedford, 1935, but the marriage was brief. ❖ At 19, living alone in England while her mother was in drug rehabilitation in Italy, wrote 1st novel *A Legacy* (1930), which would be published more than 2 decades later (1956); worked as a law reporter; over 20 years, produced 6 books, including 2-vol. set on Aldous Huxley, commissioned by his family; spent more than a decade working on her autobiographical *Jigsaw: An Unsentimental Education* (1989); other writings include *Faces of Justice* (1961), *Favourite of the Gods* (1963) and *A Compass Error* (1968).

BEDLINGTON, Viva (1893–1970). *See Donaldson, Viva.*

BEDOTT, Widow (1811–1852). *See Whitcher, Frances Miriam Berry.*

BEDRA, Julia (1924–2003). *See Allen, Rosalie.*

BEDREGAL, Yolanda (1916–1999). Bolivian poet and essayist. Name variations: Yolanda de Bolivia. Born Sept 21, 1916, in La Paz, Bolivia; died May 22, 1999, in La Paz; attended Barnard College in NY. ❖ Professor of aesthetics, whose poems and essays have been published in many Bolivian journals, has been dubbed Yolanda de Bolivia by compatriots; writings include *Naufragio* (1936), *Poemar* (1937), *Ecos* (1940), *Almadía* (1942), *Nadir* (1950), *Del mar y la ceniza* (1957) and *Bajo el oscuro sol* (1970). Won National Poetry Prize.

BEEBE, Candace (1946—). *See Pert, Candace B.*

BEEBE, Elswyth (1900–1984). *See Thane, Elswyth.*

BEEBE, Mrs. William (1900–1984). *See Thane, Elswyth.*

BEEBY, Doris (1894–1948). Australian union organizer. Born Doris Isabel Beeby, July 30, 1894, in Australia; died Oct 17, 1948 in Australia; dau. of Helena Maria (West) Beeby and Sir George Stephenson Beeby (labor politician and judge); attended University of Sydney as an unmatriculated arts student. ❖ Began career as an associate to her father (1920) following his appointment as a judge of the New South Wales Industrial Court of Arbitration and president of the Board of Trade; continued with father after his appointment to the Commonwealth Arbitration Court (1926); while in London (1939), joined the Spanish Relief Movement which offered aid to refugees from Spain's Civil War, as well as to those from Great Britain's Communist Party; returning to Sydney, joined the Australian Communist Party and worked as an organizer for the Sheetmetal Workers' Union; through the United Associations of Women, supported the Women for Canberra Movement and the Australian Women's Charter; also wrote for the *Tribune* and the *Australian Women's Digest,* the monthly publication of the United Associations of Women. ❖ See also *Women in World History.*

BEECH, Olive Ann (1903–1993). American entrepreneur. Name variations: O.A. Beech. Born Olive Anne Mellor in Waverly, Kansas, Sept 25, 1903; died July 6, 1993, in Wichita, Kansas; dau. of Frank B. (carpenter and building contractor) and Suzannah (Miller) Mellor; attended American Secretarial and Business College, Wichita; m. Walter H. Beech, Feb 24, 1930; children: Suzanne Mellor Beech and Mary Lynn Beech. ❖ Aviation pioneer and co-founder and chief executive officer of Beech Aircraft Corporation, began work in aviation as secretary-bookkeeper (1920s); became knowledgeable in various aspects of aviation (1930s); co-founded Beech Aircraft Co. (1932); because of husband's poor health during WWII, ran Beech Aircraft during a time of rapid expansion; became president and chair of the company after his death (1950); elected Woman of the Year by Women's National Aeronautical Association of the US (1951); retired from presidency (1968); sold company (1980). Under her leadership, Beech Aircraft became a leading manufacturer of private aircraft, also winning major missile and space contracts. ❖ See also *Women in World History.*

BEECHER, Catharine (1800–1878). American writer and educator. Born Catharine Esther Beecher, Sept 6, 1800, in East Hampton, Long Island; died May 12, 1878, in Elmira, NY; dau. of Reverend Lyman Beecher and Roxana (Foote) Beecher; sister of Harriet Beecher Stowe (author); attended private school in Litchfield; never married; no children. ❖ Activist who campaigned for women to assume the role of redeemers of their society through values learned in their domestic duties as mothers and wives; moved with Beecher family to Litchfield, Connecticut (1810); became woman of the house after death of mother (1816); taught school in New London (1820); fiancé Alexander Metcalf

Fisher died (1822); opened Hartford Female Seminary (1823); moved to Cincinnati, where she established the Western Female Institute (1831); conservative in outlook, was often isolated from the major developments in the history of American reform, believing that good manners were essential even in social agitation and debate; held that all Christian women were abolitionists by definition but urged gradual rather than immediate emancipation; took part in a published exchange with Angelina Grimké over abolitionism and the duties of American women (1837); toured the West, establishing female teaching academies (1837–47); founded the National Popular Education Association, later known as the American Woman's Educational Association (1847); taught briefly in Massachusetts and Connecticut; wrote on domestic science and critiqued the direction of American feminism up to the time of her death; writings include *The Elements of Mental and Moral Philosophy, Founded on Experience, Reason, and the Bible* (1831), *Letters on the Difficulties of Religion* (1836), *A Treatise on Domestic Economy* (1841), *The Domestic Receipt Book* (1846) and *The American Woman's Home* (1869). ❖ See also Milton Rugoff, *The Beechers, An American Family in the Nineteenth Century* (Harper & Row, 1981); Kathryn K. Sklar, *Catharine Beecher: A Study in American Domesticity* (Yale U. Press, 1973); Jeanne Boyston, *The Limits of Sisterhood: The Beecher Sisters on Women's Rights and Woman's Sphere* (U. of North Carolina Press, 1988); Marie Caskey, *Chariot of Fire: Religion and the Beecher Family* (Yale U. Press, 1977); Barbara A. White, *The Beecher Sisters* (Yale U. Press, 2004); and *Women in World History.*

BEECHER, Isabella (1822–1907). *See Hooker, Isabella Beecher.*

BEECHER, Janet (1884–1955). American stage and tv actress. Born Janet Meysenburg, Oct 21, 1884, in Jefferson City, Missouri; died Aug 6, 1955, in Washington, Connecticut, at the home of her sister, Olive Wyndham (actress); m. Harry R. Guggenheimer (div. 1919); m. Richard H. Hoffman (div. 1935). ❖ On stage, created role of Helen Arany in *The Concert* and Catherine Apley in *The Late George Apley;* films include *Gallant Lady, Dark Angel, So Red the Rose, The 13th Chair, Big City, Lady Eve, Love Before Breakfast* and *Judge Hardy's Children.*

BEECHMAN, Laurie (c. 1955–1998). American actress and singer. Born c. 1955 in Philadelphia, Pennsylvania; died of complications from ovarian cancer, Mar 8, 1998, in White Plains, NY; attended New York University. ❖ Made Broadway debut in *Annie* (1977); nominated for Tony Award for performance in *Joseph and the Amazing Technicolor Dreamcoat;* appeared as Grizabella in *Cats;* sang at President Clinton's inaugural gala (1997).

BEEK, Carin ter. *See ter Beek, Carin.*

BEEMAN, Ruth Coates (1925—). American nurse-midwife. Born Jan 10, 1925, in Harriston, Virginia. ❖ Served as nurse-midwife for Maternity Center Association (MCA) home birth service in NY (1950–52); was key participant in formation of American College of Nurse-Midwifery and instrumental in development of early accreditation standards for nurse-midwifery programs; trained midwives in West Africa (mid-1950s); became professor and chair of department of nursing and nurse-midwifery at Graduate School of Nursing of New York Medical College (1962); served as family-planning nurse consultant for NY Bureau of Family Planning (1970–76); served as director of Frontier School of Midwifery and Family Nursing in Kentucky (1983–88); led formation of Community-Based Nurse-Midwifery Education Program (CNEP).

BEEMER, Hilda (1911–1992). *See Kuper, Hilda B.*

BEER, Patricia (1919–1999). British poet and literary critic. Born Nov 4, 1919, in Exmouth, Devon, England; died 1999. ❖ Early poetry often explored the landscape and history of Devon; later work, which was more experimental, includes *The Loss of the Magyar* (1959), *The Survivors* (1963), *Driving West* (1975), *Selected Poems* (1979) and *The Lie of the Land* (1983); also wrote critical works, *An Introduction to the Metaphysical Poets* (1972) and *Reader, I Married Him* (1974), and the essay collection *As I Was Saying Yesterday* (2002). ❖ See also autobiographical works, *Just Like the Resurrection* (1967) and *Mrs Beer's House* (1968).

BEERBOHM, Lady.
See Kahn, Florence(1878–1951).
See Jungmann, Elisabeth (d. 1959).

BEERBOHM, Mrs. Max.
See Kahn, Florence(1878–1951).
See Jungmann, Elisabeth (d. 1959).

BEERBOHM TREE, Mrs. (1858–1937). See *Tree, Maud Holt.*

BEERE, Estelle Girda (1875–1959). New Zealand dance teacher. Born July 23, 1875, in Wanganui, New Zealand; died Sept 20, 1959, in Wellington; dau. of Edward Holroyd Beere (surveyor) and Mary (Brewer) Beere. ❖ After studying dance at Wellington School of Design, studied ballet in England (1895); returned to Wellington and established successful dance studio, where she taught for more than 60 years; also taught dance at Solway College in Masterton, Scots College, Fitzherbert Terrace School, and Queen Margaret College in Wellington; was the 1st dance teacher in Australasia to be named Officer of British Empire (1958). ❖ See also *Dictionary of New Zealand Biography* (Vol. 3).

BEERE, Thekla (1901–1991). Irish civil servant. Name variations: T.J. Beere. Born Thekla June Beere, June 20, 1901, in Streete, Co. Westmeath, Ireland; died Feb 19, 1991, in Dublin; dau. of Rev. Francis John Armstrong Beere (Church of Ireland cleric) and Lucie M. (Potterton) Beere; attended Alexandra School and College, 1916–19, and Trinity College, University of Dublin, 1919–23; prizes in political economy, criminal and constitutional law, jurisprudence and international law; graduated 1923 with senior moderatorship in legal and political science and degree of Bachelor of Laws (LLB); never married; no children. ❖ The 1st female head of an Irish government department and the 1st chair of Commission on the Status of Women, supervised the publication of the Commission's report on the Status of Women, a landmark for women's rights in Ireland, which provided a blueprint for effective action over the next decade and beyond (1972); began career by joining Irish civil service (1924); had Rockefeller fellowship for study in US (1925–27); returned to Irish civil service, department of Industry of Commerce (1927); served as senior staff officer, Statistics Branch (1927–41); co-founded (1931) and later became president of An Óige (Irish Youth Hostel Association); served as superintending officer and principal officer, transport and marine division, Department of Industry and Commerce (1941–53); worked as secretary (1949–55) and president (1971–74) of Statistical and Social Inquiry Society of Ireland; served as assistant secretary, Department of Industry and Commerce (1953–59); served as secretary, Department of Transport and Power (1959–66); awarded LLD, University of Dublin (1960); served as member of Council of Alexandra College (1962–86); named member of Public Service Organisation Review Group (Devlin Committee, 1966–69); served as 1st chair of Government Commission on Status of Women (1970–75); appointed governor of Irish Times Trust (1974); named Irish delegate to World Population Conference, Bucharest (1974); was governor of the Rotunda Hospital and president of the Irish Film Society. ❖ See also *Women in World History.*

BEERS, Ethel Lynn (1827–1879). American poet. Name variations: (pen name) Ethel Lynn. Born Ethelinda Eliot, Jan 13, 1827, in Goshen, NY; died Oct 11, 1879, in Orange, New Jersey; descendent of John Eliot (Indian missionary); m. William H. Beers, Mar 1846. ❖ Published poem "The Picket Guard" in *Harper's Magazine* (1861), which was the basis for Civil War lyric, "All Quiet Along the Potomac," a rallying point during the war; published other popular poems, including "Weighing the Baby" and "Which Shall It Be?"; other works include *General Frankie: A Story for Little Folks* (1863).

BEESE, Lotte (1903–1988). German architect, city planner, and experimental photographer. Name variations: Charlotte Stam-Beese. Born in Reisicht, Germany (now in Poland), 1903; died in Krimpen, the Netherlands, 1988; studied art, weaving, and architecture at Bauhaus; received Dutch diploma in architecture, 1944; married Mart Stam (Dutch architect), 1935. ❖ Primarily an architect and city planner, also experimented with photography; began career with architect Bohuslav Fuchs (1929), then traveled to Soviet Union (1930), as an architect and town planner; married and established an office in Amsterdam (1940); worked as an architect for city of Rotterdam (1946–68).

BEETHAM, Thyra Talvase (1882–1972). See *Bethell, Thyra Talvase.*

BEETON, Isabella Mary (1836–1865). English home economist. Name variations: Mrs. Beeton. Born Isabella Mary Mayson, Mar 14, 1836, in Cheapside, London, England; died of puerperal fever, Feb 6, 1865, in Grandhithe, Kent, England; eldest dau. of Benjamin (soft-goods merchant) and Elizabeth Mayson; m. Sam Beeton (publisher), 1856; children: 4 sons, 2 of whom died in childhood. ❖ Authority on cooking and domestic science, best known for her popular book *Household Management,* began writing articles for husband's *The Englishwoman's*

Domestic Magazine, which was aimed at the young, middle-class Victorian woman; tried out recipes sent to the magazine and experimented with her own; traveled to Paris for fashion plates and illustrations and consulted experts for advice on financial and health matters; spent 4 years preparing her lavishly illustrated *Household Management* which became a reference "Bible" for homemakers, containing recipes, as well as information on nutrition and budgeting; extracted *Dictionary of Cookery* from the main volume, which also became a bestseller. ❖ See also *Women in World History.*

BEETON, Mrs. (1836–1865). See *Beeton, Isabella Mary.*

BEGARD, Isabelle (1960—). French fencer. Born July 1960. ❖ At Moscow Olympics, won a bronze medal in team foil (1980).

BEGG, Anne (1955—). Scottish politician and member of Parliament. Born Dec 6, 1955; dau. of Margaret Begg and David Begg (MBE). ❖ Began career as a teacher; representing Labour, elected to House of Commons for Aberdeen South (1997, 2001, 2005).

BEGGA (613–698). Belgian saint. Name variations: Beggha; Beggue of Austrasia. Born 613; died 698 (some sources cite 693 or 694) at Ardenne; dau. of Ida of Nivelles (597–652) and Pepin I of Landen (d. 640), mayor of Austrasia; sister of Gertrude of Nivelles (626–659); m. Ansegisel, also known as Auseghisel, Anchises, and Ansegisal, mayor of Austrasia (r. 632–638, son of St. Arnulf of Metz and Dode); children: Pepin II of Heristal (c. 640–714), mayor of Austrasia and Neustria (r. 687–714). ❖ Upon death of husband who was killed while hunting (c. 638), made a pilgrimage to Rome; returning home, retired to the abbey that she had founded at Ardenne in present-day Belgium; also founded 6 other churches at Ardenne of the Meuse. Feast day is Dec 17.

BEGGA OF EGREMONT (fl. 7th c.). Irish saint. Name variations: Beggha. Born in Ireland in 7th century. ❖ Daughter of a king of Ireland, was betrothed to the king of Norway; determined to remain a virgin, fled on eve of wedding; received the veil from St. Aidan and founded a convent at Copeland. Feast day is Oct 31. ❖ See also *Women in World History.*

BEGGHA. Variant of *Begga.*

BEGGUE OF AUSTRASIA (613–698). See *Begga.*

BEGLIN, Elizabeth (1957—). American field-hockey player. Born April 1957. ❖ At Los Angeles Olympics, won a bronze medal in team competition (1984).

BEGLYAKOVA, Irina (1933—). Soviet discus thrower. Born Feb 1933. ❖ At Melbourne Olympics, won a silver medal in the discus throw (1956).

BEGTRUP, Bodil (1903–1987). Danish diplomat. Born Bodil Gertrud Andreasen in Nyborg, Denmark, Nov 12, 1903; died Dec 12, 1987, in Denmark; dau. of Judge Christian A. Andreasen (1867–1941) and Carla Sigrid (Locher) Andreasen (1876–1938); University of Copenhagen, MA in economics, 1929; m. Erik Begtrup, Feb 21, 1929 (div. 1936); m. L.B. Bolt-Jorgensen, 1948 (died); children: (1st m.) Marianne Begtrup (b. 1931). ❖ Delegate to United Nations and crusader for women's rights, who was Denmark's 1st female ambassador; was a member of the Executive Committee of the National Council of Women (1929), vice-chair (1931), chair (1946–49); was a member of the joint Council of the Maternity Welfare Service (1939–59); was a member of the Danish delegation to 19th Assembly of League of Nations (1938); was a member of the Danish delegation to General Assembly of UN (1946–52); served as chair of UN Commission on the Improvement of the Social Status of Women (1947, 1948–49); served as Envoy Extraordinary and Minister Plenipotentiary, Reykjavik (1949); served as ambassador (1955); was head of department, Ministry for Foreign Affairs (1956); was a member of the Council of the "Norden" Association (1956); served as Permanent Representative of Denmark to the Council of Europe, Strasbourg (1956); served as ambassador to Berne (1959–68); served as ambassador to Lisbon (1968–Dec 1973); was head of Danish delegation to World Population Conference, Bucharest (1974); shunned the honors frequently bestowed upon her throughout her long, distinguished career. Granted Order of the Falcon of Ireland, 1st Class. ❖ See also *Women in World History.*

BEGUE, Laetitia (1980—). French gymnast. Born Sept 30, 1980, in Monaco. ❖ Won a silver medal at Jr. European team championships (1992); tied with Elodie Lussac for French National championship

(1994); won City of Popes (1994) and French National championship (1996).

BEGUM SHAH JAHAN (c. 1592–1631). *See Mumtaz Mahal.*

BEHAR, Adriana (1969—). Brazilian beach volleyball player. Name variations: Adriana Brandão Behar. Born Feb 14, 1969, in Rio de Janeiro, Brazil; attended Rio de Janeiro University. ❖ With Shelda Bede, was FIVB Tour champion (1997–2001), won World championships (1999 and 2001), won a silver medal at Sydney Olympics (2000) and a silver medal at Athens Olympics (2004).

BEHLE, Petra (1969—). German biathlete. Name variations: Petra Schaaf. Born May 5, 1969, in Offenbach, Germany. ❖ As Petra Schaaf, won a silver medal for 3 x 7.5 km relay at Albertville Olympics (1992) and a silver medal for 4 x 7.5 km relay at Lillehammer Olympics (1994); as Petra Behle, won a gold medal for 4 x 7.5 km relay at Nagano Olympics (1998); won 9 World champion titles; co-hosted (with Christa Haas) a German tv show.

BEHMER-VATER, Anke (1961—). East German heptathlete. Born June 5, 1961. ❖ At Seoul Olympics, won a bronze medal in the heptathlon (1988).

BEHN, Aphra (1640?–1689). English playwright and novelist. Name variations: Afra, Aphara, Ayfara; (pseudonym) Astrea. Possibly born in Wye, Surrey, or Canterbury, Kent, c. 1640; died 1689 and is buried in Westminster Abbey; dau. of Amy and John Johnson, or Amis; m. a city merchant of Dutch background named Behn, c. 1658 (widowed by 1666); no known children. ❖ Restoration dramatist and novelist, usually acclaimed as the 1st English woman to make her living as a writer, wrote during the English Restoration, the period immediately following the return of the Stuart monarchy to the throne in 1660; had lived an exotic adolescence in British West Indies when father was appointed to the post of lieutenant-general of Surinam; father died at sea; at about 18, returned to London; married, was widowed, then sent to Antwerp as a spy during 2nd Dutch War (1666); returned to London to earn her living writing for the newly restored theater, amusing Charles II and his court with her wit; 1st recorded performance was the play *The Forced Marriage; or, the Jealous Bridegroom* (1670), which ran for 6 nights, a good run for a 1st play; her play *The Rover; or, The Banish't Cavaliers* was her most popular, both in her lifetime and subsequently, and she wrote a sequel to it late in her career; her most popular novel, *Oroonoko*, the 1st treatment of black slavery in English literature, depends on those early years in Surinam and has remained in print to the present day. ❖ See also William J. Cameron, *New Light on Aphra Behn* (U. of Auckland Press, 1961); Angeline Goreau, *Reconstructing Aphra* (Dial, 1980); Heidi Hutner, ed. *Rereading Aphra Behn* (U. Press of Virginia, 1993); Maureen Duffy, *The Passionate Shepherdess: Aphra Behn* (Cape, 1977); Janet Todd, *The Secret Life of Aphra Behn* (Rutgers U. Press, 1998); and *Women in World History.*

BEHRENDT, Kerstin (1967—). East German runner. Born Sept 2, 1967. ❖ At Seoul Olympics, won a silver medal in the 4 x 100-meter relay (1988).

BEHRENDT-HAMPE, Jutta (1960—). East German rower. Name variations: Jutta Hampe. Born 1960. ❖ At Seoul Olympics, won a gold medal in single sculls (1988).

BEHRENS, Hildegard (1937—). German soprano. Born in Oldenburg, Germany, Feb 9, 1937; law degree from University of Freiburg; studied voice with Ines Leuwen at Freiburg Music Academy. ❖ Debuted in Freiburg as the Countess in *Le nozze di Figaro* (1971); appeared at Deutsche Oper am Rhein in Düsseldorf; performed several roles in Berg's *Wozzeck;* debuted at Covent Garden and Metropolitan Opera (1976); known as a Wagnerian soprano, appeared as Salome in Salzburg (1977) and sang Brünnhilde at Bayreuth (1983); also appeared in such non-Wagnerian roles as Elektra in Mozart's *Idomeneo,* Elena in Janácek's *The Makropoulous Case,* and the Empress in Richard Strauss' *Die Frau ohne Schatten.* ❖ See also *Women in World History.*

BEIER, Roswitha (1956—). East German swimmer. Born Dec 22, 1956. ❖ At Munich Olympics, won a silver medal in the 4 x 100-meter medley relay and a silver medal in the 100-meter butterfly (1972).

BEIG, Maria (1920—). West German novelist and poet. Born Oct 8, 1920, in Tettnang, West Germany. ❖ Was a 62-year-old retired knitting teacher when she published 1st novel *Rabenkrächzen* (Raven's Croak, 1982), an unsparing portrait of country life; also published *Hochzeitslose* (trans. as *Lost Weddings,* 1983), *Urgroßelternzeit* (1985), *Töchter und Söhne* (1995) and *Buntspechte* (2002). Won Allemannischen Literature Prize (1983) and Literature Prize of the City of Stuttgart (1997).

BEIMLER-HERKER, Centa (1909—). German anti-Nazi activist. Born Centa Dengler in Munich, Mar 12, 1909; dau. of a construction worker and a washerwoman; sister of Maxi Dengler; married Hans Beimler (founding member of Bavarian Communist Party, member of German Reichstag, and anti-Nazi hero), 1930 (died 1936); married Hans Herker (artist), 1945 (died 1964); children: (2nd m.) Christa (b. 1948). ❖ Worked in a law office and became a Communist activist (mid-1920s); helped husband in his illegal political work after Nazi takeover (1933); arrested and imprisoned along with mother and sister (1933); husband escaped from Dachau (1933), but was killed in Spanish Civil War (1936); with sister, was transferred to Moringen concentration camp (1936); released from Moringen (1937), returned to anti-Nazi work; rearrested (1939 and 1942).

BEINHORN, Elly (1907—). German aviator and author. Name variations: Elly Beinhorn-Rosemeyer. Born Elly Beinhorn, May 30, 1907, in Hanover, Germany; m. Bernd Rosemeyer (racing driver), 1936 (died in racing accident, 1938). ❖ Known as "Germany's Amelia Earhart," was one of the few women in Nazi Germany to have a widely reported career; made a number of dramatic flights, including one to Africa from Berlin to Timbuktoo (1931), a Round-the-World Flight (1931–32), for which she was awarded the Hindenburg Cup, a Round-Africa Flight (1933), and a Western Hemisphere Flight (1934–35); as a prolific author, published a number of articles and books, including *180 Studen über Afrika* (1933), *Flying Girl* (trans. by Winifred Ray, Holt, 1935), *Grünspecht wird ein Flieger: Werdegang eines Flugschülers* (1935), *Mein Mann, der Rennfahrer: Der Lebensweg Bernd Rosemeyers* (1938), *180 Studen über Afrika: Mein Flug zu den Deutschen in unseren ehemaligen Kolonien* (1937), *Berlin—Kapstadt—Berlin: Meine 28,000-km-Flug nach Afrika* (1939), *Ich fliege um die Welt* (1952) and *So waren diese Flieger* (1966). ❖ See also *Women in World History.*

BEISER, Trude (1927—). Austrian Alpine skier. Name variations: Trude Jochum-Beiser; Trude Beiser-Jochum; Trude Jochum. Born Trude Beiser, Sept 2, 1927, in Lech am Arlberg, Austria. ❖ Won a silver medal for downhill and a gold medal for combined at St. Moritz (1948), the 1st woman skier to win 2 Olympic medals; won a gold medal downhill at Oslo Olympics (1952); at World championships, won a gold medal and silver medal (1950).

BEJARANO, Esther (1924—). German-Jewish singer. Born Esther Loewy (or Löwy) in Saarlouis, Saar Territory (then French-controlled Germany), Dec 15, 1924; sister of Ruth Loewy, who was killed by German security forces after being expelled from Switzerland; m. Nissim Bejarano. ❖ Holocaust survivor who built a successful career as a singer of folk and political songs; parents deported to Kaiserwald concentration camp near Riga, where they were killed (1941); sent to Auschwitz (April 20, 1943) and assigned to play the accordion in women's camp orchestra conducted by Alma Rosé; liberated (1945); immigrated to Israel; 20 years later, returned to Germany and became an acclaimed performer at music festivals dedicated to German-Jewish reconciliation; remained active on Auschwitz Committee which she helped found. ❖ See also *Women in World History.*

BEJART, Geneviève (c. 1622–1675). French actress. Name variations: Geneviève Hervé. Born c. 1622; died 1675; dau. of Joseph (official in the Chief Bureau of Forests and Waterways) and Marie (Hervé) Bejart. ❖ Performed under mother's maiden name of Hervé. ❖ See also *Women in World History.*

BEJART, Madeleine (1618–1672). French actress. Name variations: Béjart. Born Madeleine Bejart in 1618; died Feb 17, 1672; dau. of Joseph (official in the Chief Bureau of Forests and Waterways) and Marie (Hervé) Bejart. ❖ Headed a traveling company, which included her siblings Geneviève, Joseph, and Louis, before meeting Molière and forming the Illustre Théâtre (June 1643); acted in the troupe and also managed its finances until her death; her most famous roles, some of which were created especially for her by Molière, were Marotte in *The Affected Young Ladies* (1659), Lisette in *The School for Husbands* (1661) and Dorine in *Tartuffe* (1664). ❖ See also *Women in World History.*

BEJART, Armande (c. 1642–1700). French actress. Name variations: Mlle Menou, "Miss Puss." Born Armande Grésinde Claire Elizabeth Bejart in 1642 or 1643; died 1700; possibly dau. of Madeleine Bejart and the Count of Modène; m. Molière (the dramatist), 1662 (died 1673); m. Isaac-François Guérin d'Estriché (actor), 1677; children: (with Molière) daughter Ésprit-Madeleine (b. 1666), and 2 sons (both of whom died in infancy). ❖ Actress, belonging to a 17th-century theatrical family, who originated roles in the plays of Molière; said to be a charming actress and the best interpreter of his plays, was at her finest as Celimène in *Le Misanthrope* and was deemed outstanding as Angélique in *The Imaginary Invalid;* after Molière's death, merged the troupe with the failing Theatre du Marais, to form the Troupe du Roi, which would merge once more to become the renowned Comédie Française. ❖ See also *Women in World History.*

BEKATOROU, Sofia (1977—). Greek yacht racer. Born Dec 26, 1977, in Athens, Greece; attended Metsovio University. ❖ Won World championships for 470 class (2001, 2002, 2003); won a gold medal for double-handed dinghy (470) at Athens Olympics (2004). With Emilia Tsoulfa, named ISAF Female World Sailor of the Year (2002).

BEKESI, Ilona (1953—). Hungarian gymnast. Born Dec 11, 1953. ❖ At Munich Olympics, won a bronze medal in the team all-around (1972).

BEKKER, Elizabeth (1738–1804). Dutch novelist. Name variations: Elisabeth Bekker; Elizabeth Betjen Wolff; Elizabeth Wolff-Bekker; Betje Wolff. Born at Vlissingen, northern Netherlands, July 24, 1738; died in The Hague, Nov 5, 1804; m. Adriaan Wolff (Reformed cleric at Beemster), 1759 (died 1777). ❖ Daughter of Calvinist merchants, entered into a theoretical marriage with Adriaan Wolff, a vicar 31 years her senior; writing debut (1763) consisted of poetry of moral contemplation, though her later poetry became satirical; after husband's death (1777), began to write with her close companion Aagje Deken; while living in Burgundy with Deken, was exposed to some of the dangers of the Revolution, and is said to have escaped the guillotine only by her presence of mind; lived with Deken for nearly 30 years before her death (Deken died 9 days later).

BEKKEVOLD, Kristin (1977—). Norwegian soccer player. Born April 19, 1977. ❖ Won a team gold medal at Sydney Olympics (2000).

BELAN, Tatyana (1982—). Belarusian rhythmic gymnast. Name variations: Tatiana Belan. Born Nov 10, 1982, in Belarus. ❖ Won a silver medal for team all-around at Sydney Olympics (2000).

BELAND, Lucy (1871–1941). American drug peddler. Name variations: Mrs. Lucy Beland; Ma Beland. Born in Texas, 1871; died in Texas, 1941; m. J.H. Beland (deceased); children: 6. ❖ With a *modus operandi* paralleling Ma Barker, used her children to commit crimes, turning them into drug addicts and prostitutes in an illegal drug wholesaling operation that peaked in late 1930s; as the major wholesaler of illegal drugs in the Southwest, grew rich and powerful, especially after the passage of Harrison Narcotics Act of 1914, when drugs became scarce; trapped while making a drug deal with an undercover agent (1937). ❖ See also *Women in World History.*

BELBIN, Tracey (1967—). Australian field-hockey player. Born June 24, 1967. ❖ At Seoul Olympics, won a gold medal in team competition (1988).

BELCHEVA, Elisaveta (1893–1991). *See Bagryana, Elisaveta.*

BELEN (1931—). *See Kaplan, Nelly.*

BELESTICHE or BELISTICHE (fl. 268–264 BCE). *See Bilistiche.*

BELFIORE, Liliana (1952—). Argentinean ballet dancer. Born Oct 12, 1952, in Buenos Aires, Argentina. ❖ Danced with Ballet Festio Argentino and Ballet Contemporena; joined Ballet de Teatro Colón in Buenos Aires where she performed in numerous classics, including *Daphnis et Chloe, Firebird, Cinderella, Giselle* and *Swan Lake;* danced principal roles in further classics upon joining London Festival Ballet (1976), including in *Etudes, Conservatoire* and *Les Sylphides;* partnered with Rudolf Nureyev on a regular basis; danced for Vienna State Opera, National Ballet of Cuba, Opera Ballet of Bordeaux, Opera Ballet of Venezuela and performed in major theaters throughout Europe, Asia, Australia, South and Central America; directed tv series "Con el Arte en el Alma" (1994–99); began serving as teacher, choreographer and director at Centro de Danzas Liliana Belfiore (c. 1994).

BELFRAGE, Sally (1936–1994). American journalist. Born Sally Mary Caroline Belfrage in Hollywood, California, Oct 4, 1936; died in London, Mar 14, 1994; dau. of Cedric Belfrage and Molly Castle (both British journalists); studied in New York City and at London School of Economics; m. Bernard Pomerance (writer), 1965; children: Eve and Moby. ❖ Traveled to Moscow as a member of the US delegation to the World Youth Festival (1957); defied a Washington ban and traveled to People's Republic of China; on return to Moscow, worked at Foreign Languages Publishing House and met British spy Donald Maclean; wrote about experiences in *A Room in Moscow,* a worldwide bestseller (1958); spent a year in Egypt, Israel, Jordan and Syria and contracted a sham marriage with Sari Nashashibi, son of a distinguished Palestinian family, in order to help him acquire US citizenship; was active in the civil-rights movement and wrote *Freedom Summer;* investigated violence in Northern Ireland, resulting in *Living With War: A Belfast Year* (1987); other writings include *Flowers of Emptiness: Reflections on an Ashram* (1981) and the autobiographical *Un-American Activities: A Memoir of the Fifties* (1994). ❖ See also *Women in World History.*

BEL GEDDES, Barbara (1922–2005). American actress. Born in New York, NY, Oct 31, 1922; died Aug 8, 2005, at her home in Northeast Harbor, Maine; dau. of Norman Bel Geddes (stage designer, producer, and theater architect) and Helen Belle (Sneider) Bel Geddes; m. Carl Schreuer (engineer), Jan 1944 (div. 1951); m. Windsor Lewis (producer and director); children: (1st m.) daughter; (2nd m.) daughter. ❖ Made acting debut as a walk-on in *School for Scandal* at Clinton Playhouse in Connecticut (1940); made NY debut in *Out of the Frying Pan* (1941); won New York Drama Critics Award for performance as Genevra Langdon in *Deep Are the Roots* (1945); made film debut in *The Long Night* (1947); nominated for Best Supporting Actress for film *I Remember Mama* (1948); career stalled when she was made to appear before the House Un-American Activities Committee hearings (1950s); turned to live tv, appearing in dramas for "Studio One," "Schlitz Playhouse" and "Alfred Hitchcock Presents"; had Broadway success as Patty O'Neill in *The Moon is Blue* (1951), created role of Maggie the Cat in *Cat on a Hot Tin Roof* (1955) and triumphed in Jean Kerr's *Mary, Mary* (1961); sidelined with cancer (1971–73), returned to the stage in *Finishing Touches* (1973); appeared as Miss Ellie Ewing on tv series "Dallas" (1978–90); other films include *Panic in the Streets* (1950), *Vertigo* (1958), *The Five Pennies* (1959), *Five Branded Women* (1959), *By Love Possessed* (1961) and *Summertree* (1971). ❖ See also *Women in World History.*

BELGIANS, queen of the.
See Louise d'Orleans (1812–1850).
See Maria Henrietta of Austria (1836–1902).
See Astrid of Sweden (1905–1935).
See Baels, Liliane (b. 1916).
See Paola (b. 1937).

BELGIOSO, Cristina (1808–1871). Italian revolutionary and author. Name variations: Countess of Belgioso; Principess di Belgioso, Belgioioso, or Belgiojoso; Cristina Trivulzio. Born in Milan, Italy, June 28, 1808; died 1871; dau. of Gerolamo Trivulzio (d. 1812, distinguished figure at the court of Napoleon's viceroy) and Vittoria Trivulzio; m. Prince Emilio Barbiano di Belgioso d'Este, Sept 24, 1824; children: Marie Barbiano, countess of Belgioso (b. 1838, who m. Marchese Ludovico Trotti). ❖ Before the Italian Revolution of 1848, worked in Paris writing articles advocating political justice and constitutional democracy for Italy; founded *Gazzetta Italiana* (1843) and also contributed articles for *Constitutionnel* and *Revue des deux mondes;* held a famous salon in France (1835–43), befriending Honoré de Balzac, Heinrich Heine, Franz Liszt and Alfred de Musset; also produced 4-vol. study, *Essai sur la formation du dogme Catholique;* returning to Naples (1840s), organized a legion of volunteers and led them into Milan to participate in the attempt to drive Austrian troops from northern Italy; when the revolution was defeated, spent years in exile, but was allowed to return to Milan (1855); later works include *Souvenirs d'Exil* (1850), *Histoire de la Maison de Savoie* (1860) and *Réflexions sur l'État Actuel de l'Italie et sur son Avenir* (1869). ❖ See also Beth Archer Brombert, *Cristina: Portraits of a Princess* (Knopf, 1977); and *Women in World History.*

BELGIUM, countess of.
See Johanna of Flanders (c. 1200–1244).
See Margaret of Flanders (1202–1280).

BELGIUM, queen of. *See Belgians, queen of the.*

BELIKOVA, Anastasia (1979—). Russian volleyball player. Name variations: Anastassia Belikova. Born July 22, 1979, in Tchelyabinsk, Russia. ❖ Made national team debut (1997); won European team championship (1997, 1999) and World Grand Prix (1997, 1999, 2002); won a team silver medal at Sydney Olympics (2000).

BELISHOVA, Liri (1923—). Albanian politician and partisan leader. Born in the village of Belishova. 1923; graduate of Tirana Girls Pedagogical Institute; m. Nako Spiru (member of Communist Politburo). ❖ While fighting against German and Italian occupying forces (1941–44), was wounded and lost an eye; served as president of People's Youth (1946–47); because of suicide of husband (1947), was purged and exiled, then politically rehabilitated and elected to Central Committee of Albanian Communist Party (ACP, 1948); elected to Central Committee and Politburo of ACP; elevated to important post of secretary of the party secretariat (1954), among the few women in Albania's leadership elite. ❖ See also *Women in World History.*

BELITA (1923–2005). English ice-skater and dancer. Name variations: Maria Belita. Born Gladys Lyne Jepson-Turner, Oct 25, 1923, in Garlogs, Hampshire, England; died Dec 18, 2005; trained for ballet under Anton Dolin; m. James Kenney (died 1982). ❖ Professional skater from age 4, was featured in an ice ballet at 11; starred in London's *Opera on Ice,* then toured US and starred for 4 years with *Ice Capades* (1939–43); skated in films *Ice Capades* (1941) and *Silver Skates* (1943); turned to jazz dancing for such films as *Lady Let's Dance, Suspense, The Gangster, The Man on the Eiffel Tower, Never Let Me Go, Invitation to the Dance, Silk Stockings* and *The Terrace.*

BELL, Acton (1820–1849). *See Brontë, Anne.*

BELL, Mrs. Alexander Graham (1857–1923). *See Bell, Mabel Hubbard.*

BELL, Currer (1816–1855). *See Brontë, Charlotte.*

BELL, Eileen (1943—). Northern Ireland politician. Born Aug 15, 1943, in Dromara, Co. Down, Northern Ireland. ❖ Was active in the peace movement; as a member of the Alliance Party, elected to Northern Ireland Assembly for North Down (1998); became deputy leader of the Alliance Party (2001).

BELL, Elizabeth Viola (1897–1990). New Zealand teacher and sports administrator. Born June 4, 1897, in San Francisco, California; died Dec 25, 1990, in Auckland, New Zealand; dau. of John William Bell (boilermaker) and Elizabeth (Brown) Bell; Auckland University, BA, 1922. ❖ Immigrated with family to New Zealand via Canada, Australia and Figi (1902); taught at Taumarunui District High School (1923–24); served as senior assistant mistress at Matamata Junior High School (Matamata College after 1946, 1925–50s); helped form Matamata Basketball Association (1932) and served as president for 36 years; also elected vice president of New Zealand Basketball Referees' Association (early 1940s). Received British Empire Medal (1976).

BELL, Ellis (1818–1848). *See Brontë, Emily.*

BELL, Florence (1909—). Canadian runner. Born 1909. ❖ At Amsterdam Olympics, won a gold medal in the 4 x 100-meter relay (1928).

BELL, Gertrude (1868–1926). British archaeologist, writer and traveler. Born Gertrude Margaret Lowthian Bell, July 14, 1868, at Washington Hall in Co. Durham, England; died July 12, 1926, in Baghdad, Iraq; dau. of Sir Hugh Bell (iron and steel industrialist) and Mary Bell; granddau. of Sir Isaac Lowthian Bell; at Oxford University received a "First" Honors in Modern History, 1888; studied at Bibliothèque Nationale in Paris; never married; no children. ❖ Distinguished scholar, poet, author, historian, archaeologist, linguist, explorer, and mountaineer, one of the most remarkable figures of her time, is best known for her role in the Middle East as an intelligence advisor for the British government; went to the Middle East (1892); studied Arabic and Persian (Farsi) and published 1st two books, *Safah Nameh—Persian Pictures* (1894) and *Poems from the Divan of Hafiz* (1897), which she had translated from Farsi into English; began 1st excursions into the desert from Jerusalem, excursions which included Petra, Palmyra, Beirut, Damascus, and other locations in Syria and Palestine which were at that time under the banner of the Ottoman Empire (1899–1900); published *The Desert and the Sown* which made the bestseller list in US (1907); from Syria, crossed the desert to Mesopotamia and had her 1st meeting with T.E. Lawrence (1911); traveled into interior of Arabia (1913); appointed to military intelligence staff, then as political secretary at Baghdad (1917); helped mold postwar administration of Mesopotamia, siding with forces bringing Faisal to throne of Iraq (1921); other writings include (with Sir William Ramsay) *The Thousand and One Churches* (1909), *The Monasteries of Tur Abdin* (1910), *Amurath to Amurath* (1911), and (archaeological work) *The Palace and Mosque of Ukhaidir* (1914). ❖ See also Lady Bell *The Letters of Gertrude Bell* (2 vols., Boni & Liveright, 1927);

Elizabeth Burgoyne, *Gertrude Bell: From Her Personal Papers, 1889–1914 and 1914–1926* (2 vols., Benn, 1958); H.V.F. Winstone, ed. *Gertrude Bell* (Cape, 1978); Josephine Kamm, *Gertrude Bell: Daughter of the Desert* (Vanguard, 1956); Janet Wallach, *Desert Queen: The Extraordinary Life of Gertrude Bell* (Doubleday, 1996); and *Women in World History.*

BELL, Jane (1873–1959). Scottish-Australian nurse. Born Mar 16, 1873, at Middlebie, Dumfriesshire, Scotland; died Aug 6, 1959, in Melbourne, Australia; dau. of Helen (Johnstone) Bell and William Bell (farmer); nurses training at Royal Prince Alfred Hospital, Sydney, Australia; midwifery training at Queen Charlotte's Hospital, London. ❖ Hospital matron and advocate of nurses education and reform, lost parents and 4 siblings to TB before she was 13; served as senior assistant lady superintendent of nursing at Edinburgh Royal Infirmary; was superintendent at Melbourne Hospital (1910–34); during WWI, paved the way for a reorganization of the Australian Army Medical and Nursing Services; devoted years to restructuring nurses organizations and updating qualifications, working through Australian Trained Nurses' Association (of which she was a foundation member), Victorian Trained Nurses' Association (later Royal Victorian College of Nursing), and Nurses' Board; served as president of College of Nursing (1931–34, 1935–46). Named OBE (1944).

BELL, Jocelyn (b. 1943). *See Burnell, Jocelyn Bell.*

BELL, Laura (1829–1894). Irish missionary and courtesan. Born 1829 in Antrim, Ireland; died 1894 in England; dau. of the bailiff to Marquis of Hertford; m. Augustus Frederick Thistlethwayte, 1852. ❖ Well-known courtesan, gained respectability as an evangelical preacher, who, through her work with Prime Minister William Gladstone, aided London prostitutes. ❖ See also *Women in World History.*

BELL, Lilian (1867–1929). American fiction writer. Name variations: Mrs. Arthur Hoyt Bogue. Born in Kentucky, 1867; died 1929; married Arthur Hoyt Bogue. ❖ Wrote *The Love Affairs of an Old Maid* (1893), *Why Men Remain Bachelors, and Other Luxuries* (1906), *Angela's Quest* (1910), *The Land of Don't-Want-To* (1916) and *A Little Sister to the Wilderness.*

BELL, Lynette (1947—). Australian swimmer. Born Jan 24, 1947. ❖ At Tokyo Olympics, won a silver medal in the 4 x 100-meter freestyle relay (1964).

BELL, Lynn Colella (1950—). *See Colella, Lynn.*

BELL, Mabel Hubbard (1857–1923). American philanthropist. Name variations: Mabel Hubbard; Mrs. Alexander Graham Bell. Born Mabel Gardiner Hubbard, Nov 25, 1857, in Cambridge, Massachusetts; died of pancreatic cancer, Jan 3, 1923, in Canada; dau. of Gertrude McCurdy Hubbard and Gardiner Greene Hubbard (lawyer, businessman, and member of Massachusetts State Board of Education, died 1897); m. Alexander Graham Bell (inventor), July 11, 1877 (died 1922); children: Elsie May Bell (b. May 8, 1878, who m. Gilbert Grosvenor), Maian (Daisy) Bell (b, Feb 15, 1880, who m. David Fairchild), Edward (1881–1881), Robert (1883–1883). ❖ After a bout with scarlet fever at age 5, was left totally deaf; had an excellent education, then began studying under Alexander Bell who would eventually become a partner of her father's; engaged to Bell at 18, urged him to continue his work with telephone; with father, was instrumental in establishing schools for deaf children; moved to Washington DC, where she became a popular host; served as president of Montessori Educational Association and was a patron of aviation; had a summer home in Canada, where she founded the Canadian Home and School Association. ❖ See also Ann J. Bishundayal, *Mabel Hubbard Bell.*

BELL, Maggie (1945—). Scottish singer. Name variations: Stone the Crows. Born Jan 12, 1945, in Scotland. ❖ Scottish vocalist, fronted soul band Stone the Crows, formed in Glasgow (1969), before going solo; began career with Les Harvey, heading the group Power, which performed in clubs and at US Army bases in Europe, before being discovered by Led Zeppelin manager Peter Grant, who renamed band Stone the Crows; with group, released such albums as *Ode to John Law* (1970), *Teenage Licks* (1971) and *'Ontinuous Performance* (1972); worked with Rod Stewart on *Every Picture Tells a Story* (1971); won 1st of several Top Girl Singer awards in Britain (1972); pursued solo career after group disbanded with such albums as *Queen of the Night* (1973), *Suicide Sal* (1975) and *Great Rock Sensation* (1977); appeared in tv series, "Your Cheatin' Heart" (1990) and in tv film, "Down Among the Big Boys" (1993).

BELL, Margaret Anne (b. 1921). *See Bell, Peggy Kirk.*

BELL, Margaret Brenda (1891–1979). New Zealand radio pioneer. Born Oct 18, 1891, in Otago, New Zealand; died Aug 10, 1979, in Dunedin; dau. of Alfred Dillon Bell and Gertrude Eliza (Robinson) Bell; sister of Francis Wirgman Dillon Bell. ❧ Shared father's and brother's early interest in wireless communication; worked as military hospital cook in England during World Wars I and II; assumed duties of wireless station and became New Zealand's 1st woman amateur radio operator (1920s); became 1st New Zealander to contact South Africa (1927); broadcast talk show on Dunedin radio station 4YA (late 1940s). Received Queen's Service Medal (1979).

BELL, Marie (1900–1985). French actress. Born Marie-Jeanne Bellon-Downey, Dec 23, 1900, in Bègles, Gironde, Aquitaine, France; died May 16, 1985, in Neuilly-sur-Seine, France; studied drama at Paris Conservatory. ❧ At 13, made debut as a dancer in England; turned to acting and began a string of supporting roles in French silent films (1924); became a member of Comédie Française (1928); with advent of sound, moved to film leads; in her 2 most successful films, played a dual role in Feyder's *Le Grand Jeu* (1934) and a rich widow in Duvivier's *Un Carnet de Bal* (*Life Dances On,* 1937); other films include *Paris* (1924), *Madame Récamier* (1928), *Figaro* (1929), *La Nuit est à nous* (*The Night is Ours,* 1930), *La Fédora* (1934), *Polichè* (1934), *Pantins d'Amour* (1937), *Légion d'Honneur* (1938), *Ceux du Ciel* (1940), *Vie privée* (1942), *Le Colonel Chabert* (1943), *Hotel Paradiso* (1966) and *Les Volets clos* (1973). Awarded Legion of Honor by General de Gaulle for her activity in the French resistance during WWII. ❧ See also *Women in World History.*

BELL, Marilyn (1937—). Canadian marathon swimmer. Name variations: Marilyn Bell Di Lascio. Born Oct 19, 1937, in Toronto, Ontario, Canada; m. Joe Di Lascio. ❧ Was the 1st woman to complete the 20-mile Atlantic City Marathon (1954); was the 1st person to swim Lake Ontario (Sept 9, 1954); was the youngest person (age 17) to swim the English Channel (1955); swam the straits of Juan de Fuca (1956); moved to Willingboro, NJ, with husband. Won Lou Marsh Trophy (1953); named "Woman of the Year" by women editors of Canadian Press (1954, 1955). ❧ See also tv-movie "Heart: The Marilyn Bell Story" (2001), starring Caroline Dhavernas; and *Women in World History.*

BELL, Marion (1919–1997). American actress and singer. Name variations: Marion Lerner. Born Nov 16, 1919, in St. Louis, Missouri; died Dec 14, 1977, in Culver City, California; m. Thomas Charlesworth (div.); m. Jack Holliman (div.); m. Alan J. Lerner (lyricist, author) 1947 (div. 1949, was the 2nd of his 6 wives). ❧ In Broadway debut, created role of Fiona MacLaren in *Brigadoon* (1947); appeared in film *Ziegfeld Follies* (1946).

BELL, Marjorie (1919—). *See Champion, Marge.*

BELL, Mary (c. 1957—). Convicted murderer at age 11. Name variations: Mary Flora Bell. Born c. 1957. ❧ At age 11, was among the 1,200 children questioned after 4-year-old Martin Brown and 3-year-old Brian Howe were found dead in Newcastle (1968); during questioning, accused 13-year-old Norma Joyce Bell (no relation) of strangling Brian Howe, while Norma accused her in return; arrested with Norma (Aug 5, 1968), was charged with Howe's murder; at trial, found guilty of manslaughter and sentenced to life detention (Dec 1968), while Norma was acquitted; at 20, made 3-day getaway from Moor Court open prison (Sept 1977); released from prison (1980). ❧ See also Gitta Sereny, *Cries Unheard: The Story of Mary Bell* (Macmillan, 1998).

BELL, Mary Hayley (1911–2005). English actress, playwright and novelist. Name variations: Mary Hayley Mills. Born Jan 22, 1911, in Shanghai, China; died Dec 1, 2005, in England; m. John Mills (actor), 1941; children: Juliet Mills (b. 1941) and Hayley Mills (b. 1946), both actresses, and Jonathan Mills (b. 1949). ❧ Made stage debut in Shanghai in *The Barretts of Wimpole Street* (1932); made London debut in *Vintage Wine* (1934), followed by *Summer's Lease, The Composite Man* and *The Peaceful Inn,* among others; wrote plays *Men in Shadow, Duet for Two Hands, Angel, Dear Enemy, The Uninvited Guest, Foreign Field, Feather on the Water* and *Treble Key;* wrote novels *Arolena, Whistle Down the Wind* and *Far Morning,* and the film *Bats with Baby Faces.*

BELL, Muriel Emma (1898–1974). New Zealand nutritionist, medical researcher, and professor. Name variations: Muriel Emma Saunders, Muriel Emma Hefford. Born Jan 4, 1898, at Murchison, New Zealand; died May 2, 1974, in Dunedin; dau. of Thomas Bell (farmer) and Eliza (Sheat) Bell; Victoria University College, c. 1917; University of Otago Medical School, MB, ChB, 1922, MD, 1926; m. James Saunders (laborer), 1928 (died 1940); m. Alfred Ernest Hefford (fisheries inspector), 1942 (died c. 1957). ❧ The 1st woman awarded an MD by University of Otago (1926), worked there as an assistant in physiology (1922) and lecturer in physiology (1923–27); was house surgeon at Dunedin Hospital (1920s); performed research on vitamins at University College, London (1930–32); worked as pathologist at Elizabeth Garrett Anderson Hospital (c. 1932); became a lecturer in physiology and experimental pharmacology at Otago Medical School (1935); was a founding member of Medical Research Council (1937), which conducted surveys into diets of workers in tramway and boot and shoe industry, and into Maori diets; served as director of nutrition research at Otago Medical School and state nutritionist (1964); contributed more than 100 articles to *Listener* from 1941; fought for fluoridation in New Zealand and conducted research into cholesterol and heart disease; made a fellow of New Zealand Institute of Chemistry (1941), Royal Society of Medicine and Royal Australasian College of Physicians (1959). Made CBE (1959).

BELL, Nora Kizer (1941–2004). American educator. Born Nora Kizer, July 25, 1941, in Charleston, West Virginia; died Jan 24, 2004, in Roanoke, Virginia; attended Randolph-Macon Woman's College; University of South Carolina, MA; University of North Carolina, PhD; m. Dr. David A. Bell (president of Macon State College); children: 3. ❧ Taught at University of South Carolina for 16 years; served as dean of College of Arts and Sciences at University of North Texas for 5 years; was president of Wesleyan College; was president of Hollins University (2002–04).

BELL, Peggy Kirk (1921—). American golfer. Name variations: Margaret Anne Kirk. Born Margaret Anne Kirk, Oct 28, 1921, in Findlay, Ohio; attended Sargent Physical Education School in Boston, MA; graduate of Rollins College in Florida; m. Warren E. ("Bullet") Bell (pro basketball player, 1953). ❧ As an amateur, won the North, South, and Eastern Women's titles; went on to win the Titleholders in Augusta, the 1st to break 300 in that tournament; teaming up with Babe Zaharias, won the International Four-Ball (1947); joined Curtis Cup team; turned pro (1950) and became a charter member of Ladies' Professional Golf Association (LPGA); turned to teaching and was voted Teacher of the Year by the LPGA (1961); with husband, bought (1953) and built Pine Needles Lodge and Country Club in North Carolina. Published *A Woman's Way to Better Golf* (1966); received Ellen Griffin Rolex Award (1989).

BELL, Regla (1971—). Cuban volleyball player. Name variations: Regla Maritza Bell McKenzie (also seen as Mackenzie). Born July 6, 1971, in Havana, Cuba. ❧ Outside hitter, won a team gold medal at Barcelona Olympics (1992); won a team World championship (1994); won a team gold medal at Atlanta Olympics (1996) and at Sydney Olympics (2000).

BELL, Sandy Neilson- (1956—). *See Neilson, Sandy.*

BELL, Teresa Z. (1966—). American rower. Name variations: Teresa Zarceny. Born Teresa Zarczeny, Aug 28, 1966, in Washington Crossing, New Jersey. ❧ Won a silver medal for lightweight double sculls at Atlanta Olympics (1996).

BELL, Vanessa (1879–1961). English painter. Name variations: Vanessa Stephen, 1879–1906; Vanessa Bell 1906–1961. Born Vanessa Stephen in London, England, May 30, 1879; died April 7, 1961; dau. of Sir Leslie Stephen (author and editor) and Julia (Jackson) Stephen (widow at age 24 of Herbert Duckworth); sister of Virginia Woolf; studied at Royal Academy and Slade School of Art, London; m. Clive Bell (art critic), 1906; children: (with Bell) sons, Julian (1908–1937) and Quentin (b. 1910); (with Duncan Grant) daughter, Angelica Garnett (b. 1918, writer). ❧ One of the Bloomsbury group, was the center of an influential circle of friends, of whom the most famous was her younger sister, novelist Virginia Woolf; studied drawing from a fellow of Royal Academy, Arthur Cope, took lessons from John Singer Sargent, and then won a competitive exam to enter Royal Academy schools to study painting technique; during marriage, had a liaison with art critic Roger Fry (1911–13); began to live with artist Duncan Grant (1914); became a well-known feature of English intellectual and artistic life; had 1st solo exhibition of paintings (1922); a popular post-Impressionist, her work is valued as much because it illustrates the characters and settings of Bloomsbury Group as for its intrinsic merits; paintings include *Lady Robert Cecil* (1905), *Iceland Poppies* (1909), *Lytton Strachey* (1911), *The Bathers in a Landscape* (1911), *Studland Beach* (1912), *Landscape* with *Haystack, Asheham* (1912), *Nursery Tea* (1912), *A Conversation* (1913–16), *Mrs. Mary Hutchinson* (1914), *Iris Tree* (1915), *The Madonna Lily* (1915), *The Tub* (1918), *Quentin Bell* (1919), *Interior with a Table, San Tropez* (1921), *The Open Door, Charleston* (1926), *Portrait of Aldous Huxley* (c. 1929–30), *Roger Fry* (1933), *Interior with Housemaid* (1939), *Poppies and Hollyhocks* (c. 1941), *Self-Portrait* (1958) and *Henrietta Garnett* (1959). ❖ See also Regina Marler, ed. *Selected Letters of Vanessa Bell* (Pantheon, 1993); Frances Spalding, *Vanessa Bell* (Harcourt, 1985); and *Women in World History*.

BELL, Vera (1906—). Jamaican poet. Born 1906 in Jamaica; educated in Jamaica; attended Columbia University School of Library Service and London University. ❖ Worked for Jamaica's Welfare Commission; was editor of *Jamaican Writer;* contributed to *Jamaican Short Stories* (1950), *New Ships: An Anthology of West Indian Poems* (1972) and *You Better Believe It: Black Verse in English from Africa, the West Indies and the United States* (1973); wrote the well-known poem, "Ancestor on the Auction Block" (1962).

BELL BURNELL, Jocelyn (b. 1943). *See Burnell, Jocelyn Bell.*

BELL MARTIN, Mrs. (1815–1850). *See Martin, Mary Letitia.*

BELLA, Antoinetta (b. 1863). Italian ballet dancer. Born Jan 17, 1863, in Italy. ❖ Trained with Vautier in Turin and later at Teatro alla Scala in Milan; performed in premieres of Luigi Manzotti's *Sieba* in Turin (1878) and *Escelçior* in Milan (1881); toured East Coast of US (1884), winning popularity for her Italian ballet spectacles.

BELLAMY, Elizabeth (1845–1940). New Zealand missionary and teacher. Born Mar 19, 1845, in Birmingham, England; died Aug 18, 1940, in Dunedin, New Zealand; dau. of Robert Bellamy (cordwainer) and Ann (White) Bellamy. ❖ Worked for 22 years in British Syrian Mission in Beirut, Lebanon, which she helped found in 1871; became Arabic scholar; briefly relocated to Australia due to ill health, before settling in New Zealand (1893); ran non-denominational school for children in Dunedin's Lebanese community. ❖ See also *Dictionary of New Zealand Biography* (Vol. 3).

BELLAMY, Elizabeth Whitfield (1839–1900). American author and teacher. Name variations: (pseudonym) Kamba Thorpe. Born Elizabeth Croom near Quincy, Florida, 1837; died in Mobile, Alabama, 1900. ❖ Teacher who also wrote romantic novels of life in the South, including *Four Oaks* (1867), *Little Joanna* (1876), *Old Man Gilbert* (1888) and *The Luck of the Pendennings.*

BELLAMY, George Anne (1727–1788). Irish actress. Name variations: Mrs. Bellamy. Born George Anne Bellamy at Co. Fingal, Dublin, Ireland, by her own account, on St. George's Day, April 23, 1733, but more probably in 1727; died in London, England, Feb 16 (some sources cite Feb 10), 1788; illeg. dau. of James O'Hara, 2nd Baron Tyrawley (British ambassador) and a Quaker named Miss Seal; educated at a convent in Boulogne, France; married twice, once bigamously (West Digges, 1763). ❖ Celebrated actress, 1st appeared at Covent Garden in *Love for Love* (1742); considered the better of the Juliets, played Juliet to David Garrick's Romeo at Drury Lane; published 5-vol. *Apology,* containing her "amours, adventures, and vicissitudes" (1785), the year of her retirement, to great success. ❖ See also *Women in World History.*

BELLAMY, Madge (1899–1990). American actress. Born Margaret Philpott in 1899 (some sources cite 1902) in Hillsboro, Texas; died Jan 24, 1990, in Upland, California; dau. of William Bledsoe (English professor and football coach at Texas A&M) and Anne "Annie" Margaret (Derden) Philpott; attended St. Mary's Hall, a junior college affiliated with Vassar; m. Logan Metcalf, 1928 (div. 1928). ❖ One of the few silent stars who arrived in Hollywood by way of Broadway, was among the most highly regarded and highest paid actresses of that era; made stage debut at 9 in a touring company of *Aida* and Broadway debut in the chorus of *The Love Mill;* had stage roles in *Dear Brutus* and *Peg O' My Heart* and played Geraldine Farrar's daughter in the film *The Riddle: Woman,* before winning a screen test for Thomas Ince Studio and moving to Hollywood with her mother; won title role in *Lorna Doone* (1922), directed by Maurice Tourneur; made 1st talkie, *Mother Knows Best,* based on life of Elsie Janis (1928) and received raves from critics; walked out of Fox contract (1928), virtually putting an end to starring roles; jilted by lumber tycoon Stan Murphy, fired three shots at him as he was leaving the Commonwealth Club in San Francisco (1941). Other films include *Passing Thru* (1921), *The Iron Horse* (1924), *The Dancer* (1925), *Lightnin'* (1925), *Havoc* (1925), *Lazybones* (1925), *Bertha, The Sewing Machine Girl* (1926), *Colleen* (1927), *Riot Squad* (1933), *Gordon of Ghost*

City (serial in 12 chapters, 1933), *Charlie Chan in London* (1934), *The Great Hotel Murder* (1935) and *Northwest Trail* (1945). ❖ See also autobiography *A Darling of the Twenties* (Vestal, 1989); and *Women in World History.*

BELLANCA, Dorothy (1894–1946). Latvian-American labor leader and political activist. Born Dorothy Jacobs, Aug 10, 1894, in Zemel, Latvia; died in New York, NY, Aug 16, 1946; dau. of Harry (tailor) and Bernice Edith (Levinson) Jacobs; m. August Bellanca (Amalgamated Clothing Workers of America [ACWA] organizer), Aug 1918; no children. ❖ Immigrated to US with family (1900); by 13, was working 10 hours a day in a Baltimore mens' overcoat factory, making buttonholes for $3 a week; by 1909, had helped form Local 170 of United Garment Workers of America (UGWA); led her local into the recently organized Amalgamated Clothing Workers of America (ACWA, 1914); elected to ACWA executive board (1916) and became the union's 1st full-time woman organizer (1917); was head of ACWA Women's Bureau (1924–26) and participated in several strikes; named to a maternal and child-welfare national advisory committee by US Secretary of Labor Frances Perkins (1938); founded American Labor Party (ALP, 1936) and was twice elected its state vice-chair (1940, 1944). ❖ See also *Women in World History.*

BELLE, Anne (1935–2003). American filmmaker. Born June 10, 1935, in Chile; died June 18, 2003, in Los Angeles, California; studied ballet in London; New York University Graduate Institute of Film and Television, MA, 1968; m. John Belle (architect); children: David and Antonia Belle. ❖ Documentary filmmaker who specialized in portraits of New York City Ballet dancers, began career with "Baymen—Our Waters Are Dying" and "Henry," both for PBS; produced "Reflections of a Dancer: Alexandra Danilova" (1987), followed by "Dancing for Mr. B: Six Balanchine Ballerinas," which she co-directed with Deborah Dickson (1989); with Dickson, was nominated for Academy Award for "Suzanne Farrell: Elusive Muse" (1996).

BELLE, Regina (1963—). American vocalist. Born Regina Edna Belle, July 15, 1963, in Englewood, New Jersey. ❖ Gospel- and jazz-influenced contemporary soul singer, released debut album *All by Myself* (1987), which included the #2 R&B hit, "Show Me the Way"; sang pop duet with Peabo Bryson, "A Whole New World (Aladdin's Theme)," for Disney's *Aladdin,* which reached #1 on pop charts (1992) and received 3 Grammy awards and an Oscar; released #1 R&B album *Stay With Me* (1993). Other albums include *Passion* (1995), *Reachin' Back* (1997) and *Baby Come to Me: The Best of Regina Belle* (1998).

BELLEVILLE, Jeanne de (fl. 1343). *See Jeanne de Belleville.*

BELLEVILLE-OURY, Anna Caroline de (1808–1880). French-German pianist. Born Anna Caroline de Belleville in Landshut, Germany, June 24, 1808, of French descent; died in Munich, Germany, July 22, 1880; dau. of the director of Bavarian Court Opera; m. Antonio James Oury (violinist), 1831. ❖ Though parents were French, spent most of her life in Germany; studied with Czerny in Vienna for 4 years, making her debut in that city; toured Europe, settled in London; on marriage (1831), toured Europe and Russia with husband as a highly successful chamber-music team; composed many piano works, over 180 of which were published. ❖ See also *Women in World History.*

BELLEW, Kyrle (1887–1948). English actress and theater manager. Born Mar 23, 1887, in Hampstead, England; died Jan 25, 1948; dau. of Louis Hance Faulk and Charlotte (Harcourt-Bellew) Faulk; m. Arthur Burchier; m. John Beckett. ❖ Prior to stage career, appeared in films; made stage debut as Lady Gwendolen in *Raffles* (1914), followed by *Peter Ibbetson, The Green Flag, The Arm of the Law, Stand and Deliver, Cheating Cheaters, The Knife, Scandal, The Crimson Alibi, The Storm* and *Tilly of Bloomsbury;* was proprietor of the Strand Theatre (1927–35).

BELLIL, Samira (1972–2004). Algerian-born writer and activist. Born Nov 27, 1972, to Algerian parents in Algiers; grew up in Parisian suburb of Seine-Sainte-Denis; died from stomach cancer, age 31, Sept 4, 2004. ❖ Shocked France with her autobiographical book, *Dans l'Enfer des tournantes* (In the Hell of Gang Rapes, 2002), forcing the nation to look at life in its deprived ghettos (the banlieue), especially the predilection for gang rapes (she had been gang raped at 14); organized Ni Putes, Ni Soumises (Neither Whores Nor Submissive), to publicly address the issue of violence against French Muslim women.

BELLINCIONI, Gemma (1864–1950). Italian soprano. Born Aug 18, 1864, in Monza, Italy; died in Naples, April 23–24, 1950; dau. of Cesare Bellincioni (buffo bass) and Carlotta Savoldini (contralto); studied with father and husband, as well as Luigia Ponti dell'Armi and Giovanni Corsi; m. Roberto Stagno (tenor). ❧ Made debut in Dell'Orefice's *Il segreto della duchessa* (1879); sang in Spain and Portugal and appeared in Rome (1885); sang at Teatro alla Scala (1886); appeared as 1st Italian Salome under Strauss' baton in Turin (1906); continued to appear occasionally in The Netherlands in 1920s; idolized in Italy, won acclaim in opera houses throughout Europe; made several early recordings: 4 titles for the Gramophone and Typewriter Company (1903) and 10 for Pathé (1905); her interpretation of the aria from *Cavalleria rusticana* is considered a model for subsequent interpreters of the role of Santuzza. ❧ See also autobiography *Io e il palcoscenico* (Milan, 1920).

BELLOC, Louise (1796–1881). French children's writer and translator. Born Louise Swanton in 1796; died 1881; dau. of an Irish army officer; m. Jean-Hilaire Belloc (French painter). ❧ Published the educational journal *La Ruche;* wrote books for children, including *Histories et Contes de la grand-mère* (1871) and *Le Fond du sac de la grand-mère* (1873).

BELLOC-LOWNDES, Marie (1868–1947). British writer. Name variations: Mrs. Belloc Lowndes, Marie Belloc, Philip Curtin, Elizabeth Rayner. Born Marie Adelaide Belloc in London, England, Aug 5, 1868; died in Eversley Cross, Hampshire, England, Nov 14, 1947; dau. of Elizabeth (Bessie) Rayner (Parkes) (writer and feminist known as Bessie Parkes) and Louis S. Belloc (lawyer); sister of Hilaire Belloc (writer); m. Frederick S.A. Lowndes (journalist and editor for the *Times*), Jan 9, 1896; children: Charles (b. 1898), Susan and Elizabeth. ❧ Author of novels, short stories, plays and memoirs, 69 volumes in all, began career as a journalist in England and France for *Pall Mall Gazette;* became a bestselling author in England and abroad with such books as *The Heart of Penelope* (1904), *Barbara Rebell* (1905), *The Pulse of Life* (1907), *The Lodger* (1913), *The End of Her Honeymoon* (1914), *I, Too, Have Lived in Arcadia* (1941), *Where Love and Friendship Dwelt* (1943) and *Merry Wives of Westminster* (1946). ❧ See also Susan Lowndes, ed. *Diaries and Letters of Marie Belloc Lowndes* (Chatto & Windus, 1971).

BELLON, Denise (1902–1999). French photographer. Born Denise Hulmann in Paris, France, 1902; died in 1999; studied psychology at the Sorbonne; m. Jacques Bellon (div. early 1930s); m. Armand Labin (deceased); children: (1st m.) Yannick (film director) and Loleh (actress and writer); (2nd m.) Jérôme. ❧ Following divorce (c. 1930), took up photography, establishing herself through the group agencies Studio Zuber and Alliance-Photo; was widely published in art magazines; became interested in the surrealistic art movement and photographed the group's exhibitions in Paris, while making portraits of notable artists of the movement, including Marcel Duchamp, Joan Miró and Salvador Dalí; commissioned by Paris-Match, also went to French Africa.

BELLONCI, Maria (1902–1986). Italian journalist and novelist. Born 1902 in Rome, Italy; died 1986; m. Goffredo Bellonci. ❧ Organized the literary group Amici della domenica which awards the Strega Prize; writings include *Lucrezi Borgia, la sua vita e i suoi tempi* (1939), *I segreti dei Gonzaga* (1947), *Pubblici segreti* (1965), *Tu vipera gentile* (1972), *Diletto di Stato* (1982), *Marco Polo* (1984), *Rinascimento privato* (1986), *Io el il premio Strega* (1987) and *Segni sul muro* (1988). Won Strega Prize (1986).

BELLUTTI, Antonella (1968—). Italian cyclist. Born Nov 7, 1968, in Bolzano, Italy. ❧ Won a gold medal for indiv. pursuit at Atlanta Olympics (1996) and points race at Sydney Olympics (2000); won 7 Italian titles and 3 European World Cups.

BELMEGA, Viorica (1939—). See Viscopoleanu, Viorica.

BELMONDO, Stefania (1969—). Italian cross-country skier. Born Jan 13, 1969, in Vinadio, Italy. ❧ Won a gold medal for the 30 km, silver medal for the Combined 5 km + 10 km pursuit, and bronze medal for the 4 x 5 km relay at Albertville Olympics (1992), the 1st Italian woman to win an Olympic cross-country skiing medal; won bronze medals in the Combined 5 km + 10 km pursuit and 4 x 5 km relay at Lillehammer Olympics (1994); won a silver medal for the 30 km and bronze medal for the 4 x 5 km relay at Nagano (1998); won a gold medal in the 15 km mass and silver medal in the 30 km at Salt Lake City (2002); retired from competition (2002); also won 4 indiv. world titles (2 in 1993, 2 in 1999); finished in the top 10 in World Cup standings 11 consecutive times and lit the flame at the Torino Olympics (2006).

BELMONT, Alva Smith (1853–1933). American socialite and social reformer. Name variations: Mrs. O.H.P. Belmont; Mrs. Oliver Belmont; Mrs. William K. Vanderbilt; Alva E. Belmont; Alva Murray Smith. Born Alva Erskine (or Ertskin) Smith, Jan 17, 1853, in Mobile,

Alabama; died Jan 26, 1933, in Paris, France; educated in France; m. William Kissam Vanderbilt I (1849–1920), 1875 (div. 1895); m. Oliver Hazard Perry Belmont (d. 1908), in Jan 1896; children: (1st m.) Consuelo Vanderbilt (1877–1964), duchess of Marlborough; William Kissam Vanderbilt II (1878–1944); Harold Stirling Vanderbilt (1884–1970). ❧ Focusing on the cause of women's rights, lent support to the striking garment workers (1909), organizing meetings and encouraging wealthy friends to boycott non-union dress manufacturers; financed a speaking tour by English suffragist Christabel Pankhurst; co-authored a feminist operetta, *Melinda and Her Sisters* (1916); authored the slogan "Pray to God; she will help you"; was elected president of the National Woman's Party (1921), a post she held to the end of her life; became a noted architectural designer, restoring a 15th-century castle, among other projects; was one of the 1st women elected to American Institute of Architects. ❧ See also *Women in World History*.

BELMONT, Mrs. August (1879–1979). *See Belmont, Eleanor Robson.*

BELMONT, Eleanor Robson (1879–1979). English-American actress and philanthropist. Name variations: Mrs. August Belmont. Born Eleanor Elise Robson, Dec 13, 1879, in Wigan, Lancashire, England; died Oct 26, 1979, in New York, NY; dau. of Charles Robson (musician and conductor) and Madge Carr-Cook (actress); attended St. Peter's Academy on Staten Island, NY; m. August Belmont Jr., Feb 26, 1910 (died 1924). ❧ Known as "the woman who single-handedly saved the Metropolitan Opera," made Broadway debut playing the lead in Augustus Thomas' *Arizona;* appeared in *Merely Mary Ann* (1904); had a successful London tour; gave up successful acting career to marry wealthy widower August Belmont Jr.; throughout a 2nd career as a philanthropist, her extraordinary efforts on behalf of numerous organizations, most notably the American Red Cross and the Metropolitan Opera, were unparalleled; during the Depression, chaired Women's Division of the Emergency Unemployment Relief Commission for NY; also collaborated with Harriet Ford, adapting Ford's novel *In the Next Room* into a successful play (1924). ❧ See also *Women in World History*.

BELMONT, Mrs. O.H.P. (1853–1933). *See Belmont, Alva Smith.*

BELMORE, Bertha (1882–1953). English actress. Born Bertha Cousins, Dec 22, 1882, in Manchester, England; died Dec 14, 1953, in Barcelona, Spain; m. Herbert Belmore. ❧ Made stage debut as a child in the pantomime *Robinson Crusoe* (1890) and also appeared at leading English variety houses as one of the Belmore Sisters for 7 years; made NY debut as Portia in *Julius Caesar* (1912), followed by *Ziegfeld Follies;* made London debut in *Irene* (1920); played both sides of the Atlantic for many years in such plays as *Give Me A Ring, Reunion in Vienna, Bobby Get Your Gun, Peace Comes to Peckham, Show Boat, Johnny Belinda, By Jupiter, Rhapsody, Harlequinade* and *Caesar and Cleopatra;* also appeared in films, including *Keep It Quiet, Blossom Time* and *Royal Cavalcade.*

BELO, Jane (1904–1968). *See Tannenbaum, Jane Belo.*

BELOFF, Nora (1919–1997). English author and journalist. Born in London, England, Jan 24, 1919; died Feb 12, 1997; 3rd of 5 children of Simon and Marie (Spivak) Beloff; sister of Anne Beloff-Chain (1921–1991) and Max Beloff; Lady Margaret Hall, Oxford, BA, 1940; m. Clifford Makins (sports editor for *Observer*), Mar 7, 1977 (died 1990); no children. ❧ The 1st woman correspondent in Britain, began career in British Foreign Office, then joined Reuters News Agency (1946), and wrote for *The Economist* in Paris; became an editorial leader writer for British *Observer* (1948), living on assignment in Washington and Moscow (1950s); by 1964, was a political correspondent in most of the major capital cities of the world, holding that position until 1976; left the *Observer* (1978) and began to freelance, exploring Soviet Union and former Yugoslavia; was eventually arrested in Russia and expelled from Yugoslavia; writings include *The General Says No* (1963), *Transit of Britain* (1973), *Freedom under Foot: The Battle over the Closed Shop in British Journalism* (1976), *No Travel Like Russian Travel* (1979, published as *Inside the Soviet Empire: The Myth, the Reality,* 1980), and *Tito's Flawed Legacy.* ❧ See also *Women in World History*.

BELOFF-CHAIN, Anne (1921–1991). British biochemist. Name variations: Anne Beloff Chain. Born in London, England, June 26, 1921; died in London, Dec 2, 1991; dau. of Simon and Marie (Spivak) Beloff; sister of Nora Beloff (1919–1997) and Max Beloff; earned DPhil. at Oxford University, then quickly picked up 1st-class honors degree from University College London; m. Ernst Boris Chain (1906–1979, Nobel Prize winner for his work on penicillin), 1948; children: 2 sons (both scientists). ❖ Biochemist internationally recognized for her work on the metabolism of carbohydrates and hormonal aspects of diabetes, worked on a number of joint projects at the Department of Biochemistry of the Instituto Superiore di Sanita with husband (1948–64); taught at Imperial College, London (1964–86), receiving a personal chair (1983); taught at University of Buckingham (1986–91); discovered a new insulin secretagogue hormone beta-cell tropin present at abnormal levels in the blood of the obese which enabled researchers to establish a key link between diabetes and obesity. ❖ See also *Women in World History.*

BELOGLAZOVA, Galina (1967—). Russian rhythmic gymnast. Born June 10, 1967, in Astrakhan, Russia; m. Heino Endo (basketball player). ❖ Won Jr. Intervision Cup (1980); at World championship, won gold medals for ball and ribbon, a silver for hoop, and tied for silver for clubs (1983); won European championship (1984) and placed 3rd (1986); placed 3rd at Goodwill Games (1986). Inducted into FIG Hall of Fame (1999).

BELOT, Madame (1719–1804). French essayist and translator. Born 1719 in France; died 1804; m. Parisian parliamentary lawyer (died); m. President Durey de Meinières (parliamentary president and antiquary), also seen as President du Rey de Meynières. ❖ Published 2 essays, *Réflexions d'une provinciale sur le discours de J.J. Rousseau* (1756) and *Observations sur la novelese et le tiers état* (1758); translations include Samuel Johnson's novels *The Prince of Abyssinia* and *The History of Ophelia* and Hume's history of the Plantagenets.

BELOTE, Melissa (1956—). American swimmer. Name variations: Melissa Belote Ripley. Born Oct 10, 1956, in Springfield, Virginia; attended Arizona State University. ❖ Won gold medals for 100-meter backstroke, 400-meter medley relay, and 200-meter backstroke at Munich Olympics (1972); won AAU outdoor 100-meter backstroke (1973), outdoor 200-meter backstroke (1973, 1975), and indoor 200-yard backstroke (1972); won 4 AIAW championships. ❖ See also *Women in World History.*

BELOUSOVA, Ludmila (1935—). See *Protopopov, Ludmila.*

BELOVA, Elena (1965—). Russian biathlete. Name variations: Yelena Belova. Born July 25, 1965, in USSR. ❖ Won bronze medals for 7.5 km and 3 x 7.5 km relay at Albertville Olympics (1992).

BELOVA, Irina (1968—). Russian heptathlon champion. Born Irina Ilyichova, Mar 27, 1968, in Irkutsk, Russia. ❖ Won a silver medal for the heptathlon at Barcelona Olympics (1992); won non-championship pentathlon at World championships (1993), but was disqualified after failing drug tests, resulting in a 4-year suspension; won Götzis heptathlon (1998); placed 2nd at European Cup (1999).

BELOVA, Irina (1980—). Russian rhythmic gymnast. Born 1980 in Nizhny Novgorod, Russia. ❖ Won a team World championship (1989, 1999) and a team gold medal at Sydney Olympics (2000); won 2 team European championships.

BELOVA-NOVIKOVA, Yelena (1947—). Soviet fencer. Born July 28, 1947. ❖ Six-time Olympic medal winner, won gold medals in team foil and individual foil in Mexico City (1968), a gold medal in team foil in Munich (1972), a bronze medal in individual foil and a gold medal in team foil in Montreal (1976), and a silver medal in team foil in Moscow (1980).

BELOVSOVA, Ludmila (1935—). See *Protopopov, Ludmila.*

BELTRAN, Daima (1972—). Cuban judoka. Name variations: Daima Mayelis Beltran; Dayma Beltran Guisado. Born Sept 10, 1972, in Cuba. ❖ Won World open weight championships (1997, 1999); won a silver medal for +78kg heavyweight at Sydney Olympics (2000); won a silver medal for +78kg at Athens Olympics (2004).

BELTRAN, Lola (1932–1996). Mexican singer. Name variations: Lola Béltran; Lola la Grande (Lola the Great). Born Lucila Beltran Ruiz, Mar 7, 1932, in El Rosario, Sinaloa, Mexico; died of a stroke in Mexico City, Mar 24, 1996; m. Alfredo Leal (bullfighter); children: Maria Elena Leal and (adopted) Jose Quintin Entriquez. ❖ La Reina de La Musica Ranchera (Queen of Ranchera Music), whose emotional Spanish renditions of mariachi ballads entertained Latin Americans for 50 years, 1st signed with the Peerless Label; recorded many records that went gold that included such songs as "Huapango Torero, La Cigarra" and "Paloma Negra"; appeared in 38 films, including *El Cantor del circo*

(1940), *La Bandida* (1963), *Cucurucucú Paloma* (1965), *Me caiste del cielo* (1975), as well as the tv series "Aun hay mas" (1972) and "Mi rival" (1973). Received Medalla del Artistica del Extranjero (1982).

BÉLTRAN, Manuela (fl. 18th c.). Colombian hero. Born in El Socorro, Colombia; beheaded in 1781. ❖ Opposing the Spanish government of Charles III, organized a peasant revolt over excess taxes in the cities of the northeast (1780), which resulted in a revolution throughout New Granada; the 1st person to publicly challenge Spanish exploitation, is a well-known hero in Colombia.

BELTRAN GUISADO, Dayma (1972—). See *Beltran, Daima.*

BELTRANO, Aniella (1613–1649). See *Rosa, Anella de.*

BELUGUINA, Olesia (1984—). Russian rhythmic gymnast. Born Jan 2, 1984, in USSR. ❖ Won 3 group competition events at World championships (2003); won team all-around gold medal at Athens Olympics (2004).

BEMBERG, Maria Luisa (1922–1995). Argentine director and screenwriter. Born in Argentina, April 14, 1922; died in Buenos Aires, Argentina, May 7, 1995; dau. of influential German immigrants in Argentina; married, 1942 (div. 1952); children: 4. ❖ One of Latin America's foremost female film directors, began career financing and making 2 documentaries, *El mundo del mujeres* and *Juguetes,* the latter a groundbreaking film which argued that traditional toys reinforce stereotypes; wrote 1st feature-length screenplay, the highly successful *Crònica de una señora* (1972), which was autobiographical; her next film, *Triangulo de cuatro,* was also a great success; wrote, produced and directed *Momentos* (1981), a film about a love affair gone sour which explored role reversals; also filmed *Senora de nadie;* earned Oscar nomination for Best Foreign Film for *Camila* (1984), based on story of Camila O'Gorman; cast Julie Christie in title role of *Miss Mary;* filmed *Yo, la peor de todas,* which portrays life of poet Juana Inés de la Cruz; completed final and perhaps most controversial film, *De eso no se habla,* with Marcello Mastroianni (1993). ❖ See also *Women in World History.*

BEMBO, Antonia (1643–1715). Italian composer. Name variations: V. Antonia Bembo. Born 1643 in Venice, Italy; died 1715; received musical training in Venice. ❖ For unknown reasons, fled Venice for Paris (c. 1675), where she lived in a religious community and produced music for court circles; vocal compositions were collected into the manuscript vols. *Produzioni armoniche* (1697–1707).

BEMIS, Polly (1853–1933). See *Nathoy, Lalu.*

BEN, Myriam (1928–2001). See *Ben-Haim, Marylise.*

BEN, Helena van der (1964—). See *van der Ben, Helena.*

BEN-HAIM, Marylise (1928–2001). Algerian novelist and painter. Name variations: Myriam Ben; Myriam Ben Haim or Haïm. Born Marylise Ben Haim in 1928 in Algiers, Algeria; died 2001. ❖ Sentenced to 20 years hard labor for participation in Algerian war; writings include *Ainsi naquit un homme* (1982), *Sur le chemin de nos pas* (1984) and *Sabrina, ils t'ont volé ta vie* (1986).

BEN-YEHUDA, Hemda (1873–1951). Israeli short-story writer. Born 1873 in Glubokoye, Vilna, Lithuania (maiden name was Jonas); died 1951; dau. of Samuel Naphtali Herz Jonas; sister of Deborah Jonas Ben-Yehuda (1st wife of Eliezer Ben-Yehuda, died 1891); m. Eliezer Ben-Yehuda (1858–1922, Hebrew writer and lexicographer who was born Eliezer Yitzhak Perelman), c. 1892; children: Ehud; Dola Wittman. ❖ Wrote sentimental stories about life in Palestine; helped husband with Hebrew dictionary and published biography about him, *Yehuda, hayav umif'alo* (1940).

BEN-YUSUF, Zaida (fl. 1897–1907). British photographer. Born in England; died presumably in United States. ❖ Highly regarded for her portraits, flowers, and photographs of Japan, came to US from Britain (c. 1890); probably began photographing in 1895; with encouragement from George Davidson, a leading British pictorialist, opened a portrait studio in NY (1897) and received 1st commission from *Century* magazine; traveled extensively in Europe and Japan, contributing articles and photographs for various publications, including *Architectural Record* ("Period of Daikan") and *Century* ("Flowers of Japan"); in addition to individual portraits of notable personalities, including one of Theodore Roosevelt, produced a series of photographs of artists for *American Art News;* gained great recognition, then disappeared from the art world (1907).

BENADERET, Bea (1906–1968). American radio and television actress. Born April 4, 1906, in New York, NY; died Oct 13, 1968, in Los Angeles, California; m. Jim Bannon (actor), 1938; m. Gene Twombley (sound technician), 1957; children: 2, including Jack Bannon (b. 1940, actor). ❖ Character actress, appeared as a regular on such tv shows as "Burns and Allen," "The Beverly Hillbillies," and "Petticoat Junction."

BENARIO, Olga (1908–1942). German-Jewish revolutionary. Name variations: Olga Benario Prestes, Olga Benario-Prestes. Born Olga Benario in Munich, Germany, Feb 12, 1908; gassed in Feb 1942; dau. of Leo Benario (wealthy Social Democratic attorney) and Eugenie Guttmann Benario (socialite); received extensive leadership training ranging from Marxist theory to skydiving in USSR; m. Luis Carlos Prestes (unofficially); children: Anita Leocádia Prestes (b. Nov 1936). ❖ Joined the underground Young Communist League in Munich in order to counter the growing danger of fascism; became one of the most promising young women in the German Communist movement (1923); after engineering the rescue of political radical Otto Braun from Moabit Prison in Berlin, fled with him to Soviet Union (1928); traveled to France, Belgium and England on Communist Youth International mission (1931); assigned by Comintern to go to Brazil with Brazilian revolutionary leader Luis Carlos Prestes to lead a revolutionary upheaval which failed (Nov 1935); captured with Prestes by the fascist regime of Getulio Vargas, was held until shipped, 7 months pregnant, to Nazi Germany, where she gave birth to her daughter in prison (1936); transported to Ravensbrück concentration camp. Honored with streets named after her in 7 cities of the former German Democratic Republic, as well as 91 schools, factories and workers' brigades. ❖ See also Fernando Morais, *Olga* (trans. by Ellen Watson, 1990); and *Women in World History*.

BENATAR, Pat (1953—). American singer. Born Patricia Andrzejewski, Jan 10, 1953, in Brooklyn, NY; m. Dennis Benatar (div.); m. Neil Giraldo (guitarist); children: daughters, Haley (who has a pop trio, Glo) and Hana. ❖ One of the most successful women hard-rock singers during 1980s, had 6 platinum albums: *In the Heat of the Night* (1979), *Crimes of Passion* (1980), *Precious Time* (1981, multiplatinum), *Get Nervous* (1982), *Live From Earth* (1983) and *Tropico* (1984); co-wrote most songs with husband Neil Giraldo; was 4-time Grammy winner as Best Rock Vocal Performance, Female (1981, 1982, 1983, and 1984); performed at 1st Lilith Fair. Hit singles include "Heartbreaker" (1980), "Hit Me With Your Best Shot" (1980), "Fire and Ice" (1981), "Love Is a Battlefield" (1983) and "We Belong" (1984).

BENCHLEY, Belle (1882–1973). American zoo director. Born Belle Jennings, Aug 28, 1882, near Larned, Kansas; died Dec 17, 1973; dau. of Fred Merrick Jennings and Ida Belle (Orrell) Jennings; graduate of San Diego Teachers College, 1902; m. William L. Benchley, June 25, 1906 (div. 1924); children: Edward Jennings. ❖ Director of San Diego Zoo (1927–53), became a temporary bookkeeper in Zoological Garden of San Diego (1925); was appointed head of San Diego Zoo, with the title executive secretary (1926); acquired 2 gorillas, Mbongo and Ngagi, the largest in captivity, and fell in love with her charges, resulting in her book *My Friends, the Apes*; championed the trend toward the natural habitat, where animals could be displayed without undo confinement; gained renown through speaking engagements, radio broadcasts, appearances in newsreels, and articles she contributed to *Nature Magazine, Westways, Recreation* and *Zoonooz*; retired (1953). ❖ See also memoir *My Life in a Man-Made Jungle* (1940); Emily Hahn, *Eve and the Apes* (Weidenfeld & Nicolson, 1988); and *Women in World History*.

BENCI, Ginevra de' (b. 1457). Florentine intellectual. Name variations: Ginevra d'Benci. Born 1457 in Florence, Italy; dau. of a wealth Florentine banker; m. Luigi Niccolini, Jan 15, 1474. ❖ Considered one of the most gifted intellectuals of her day, was the subject of a painting by Leonardo da Vinci, probably at the time of her marriage; had a platonic affair with Bernardo Bembo, Venetian ambassador to Florence; in later years, went into self-imposed exile in hopes of recovering from a serious illness. ❖ See also "Ginevra's Story," narrated by Meryl Streep, PBS-TV.

BENDA, Pauline (1877–1985). See Simone, Madame.

BENDER, Kate (1849—). American murderer. Name variations: Professor Kate Webster. Born 1849 in US. ❖ Moved with mother, father, and brother to rural Kansas where they established a roadside inn 9 miles from Cherryvale (1872); calling herself Professor Kate Webster, gave séances and healing lectures in several small towns, attracting men who then visited the inn; with family, murdered them and stole their belongings (11 graves were found near the inn, and they were suspected in at least 2

dozen additional killings); in fear of being caught (May 5, 1873), fled premises with family. Accounts of their subsequent whereabouts (one which included their deaths at the hands of a posse) have never been substantiated. ❖ See also Fern M. Wood, *The Benders: Keepers of the Devils Inn* (1992).

BENDISH, Bridget (c. 1650–1726). English celebrity. Born Bridget Ireton c. 1650; died 1726; dau. of General Henry Ireton (1611–1651) and Bridget Cromwell (dau. of Oliver Cromwell); granddau. of Oliver Cromwell. ❖ Was mostly famed for her physical resemblance to her grandfather, Oliver Cromwell.

BENE, Adriana Gabrieli del (c. 1755–1799). Italian soprano. Born Adriana Gabrieli La Ferraresi, c. 1755, in Ferrara, Italy; died 1799 in Venice; studied with Antonio Sacchini at Conservatorio dei Mendicanti in Venice; m. Luigi del Bene, 1783. ❖ Sang in London (1785–86), at the Teatro alla Scala (1787), and as prima donna at Burgtheater in Vienna (1788–91); as Susanna in *Le nozze di Figaro* (*Marriage of Figaro*), sang 2 new arias Mozart composed for her (1789); premiered as Fiordiligi in Mozart's *Cosi fan tutte* (1790); sang in Warsaw (1792–93). ❖ See also *Women in World History*.

BENEDETTA (1897–1977). See Marinetti, Benedetta Cappa.

BENEDICT, Crystal Eastman (1881–1928). See Eastman, Crystal.

BENEDICT, Ruth (1887–1948). American anthropologist. Name variations: (pseudonym) Anne Singleton. Born Ruth Fulton in Shenango Valley, New York, June 5, 1887; died in New York, NY, Sept 17, 1948; dau. of Beatrice (Shattuck) Fulton and Frederick Fulton (died 1889); sister of Margery Fulton (b. 1889); Vassar College, AB 1909; New School for Social Research, MA, 1921; Columbia University, PhD, 1923; m. Stanley Rossiter Benedict (biochemist), June 18, 1914 (sep. 1931, died 1936); no children. ❖ Social scientist whose research on Native Americans, as well as contemporary Europeans and Asians, made her a leading member of the culture and personality school of anthropology; traveled to Europe (1909); worked for the Charity Organization Society, Buffalo, NY (1911); taught at Westlake School for Girls, Los Angeles (1911–12) and Orton School for Girls, Pasadena (1912–14); completed biography of Mary Wollstonecraft (1917); enrolled at New School for Social Research, NY (1919), then Columbia University (1921), studying under Franz Boas and befriending Margaret Mead; wrote dissertation challenging Durkheim's assertion that the source of religious values are imbedded in social structures (1923); undertook field work on Serrano Indians (1922); lectured at Columbia University (1923–26); undertook field research on Zuni Pueblo Indians (1924) and Pima Indians (1927), recording their ceremonies and myths; served as editor of *Journal of American Folklore* (1924–39); named assistant professor in department of anthropology at Columbia University (1931), then associate professor (1937); served as a member of National Research Council (1941–43); employed by Office of War Information (1943–46); served as leader of Columbia University Contemporary Cultures Project (1946–48); elected president of American Anthropological Association (1947); appointed full professor at Columbia University (1948); her legacy is the continued emphasis on the comparative approach to culture, and values and themes which give cultures their distinct personalities; writings include the pioneering study *Patterns of Culture* (1934), *Zuni Mythology* (1935), and the bestsellers *Race: Science and Politics* (1940), in which she coined the term "racism," and *The Chrysanthemum and the Sword: Patterns of Japanese Culture* (1946). ❖ See also Margaret Mead, *An Anthropologist At Work: Writings of Ruth Benedict* (Atherton, 1966) and *Ruth Benedict* (Columbia U. Press, 1974); Judith Modell *Ruth Benedict: Patterns of a Life* (U. of Pennsylvania, 1983); and *Women in World History*.

BENEDICTA, Mother (1825–1862). See Riepp, Mother Benedicta.

BENEDICTA, Sister (1891–1942). See Stein, Edith.

BENEDICTA OF ASSISI (d. 1260). Italian saint and abbess. Name variations: Benedetta. Died 1260. ❖ Succeeded Clare of Assisi as abbess of St. Damian at Assisi.

BENEDICTSSON, Victoria (1850–1888). Swedish novelist. Name variations: Victoria Benedictson; (pseudonym) Ernst Ahlgren. Born Victoria Maria Bruzelius in Skåne, Sweden, Mar 6, 1850; committed suicide in Copenhagen, Denmark, July 22, 1888; dau. of Helena Sophia Finérus and Thure Bruzelius; m. Christian Benedictsson (postmaster), 1871; children: 2. ❖ Under pseudonym Ernst Ahlgren, wrote gothic thrillers for a daily newspaper and began writing novels (1880s); kept a personal journal, published in 1978 as *Stora Boken* (The Big Book), which documents her friendship and romantic liaison with Danish critic Georg Brandes; writings include *Från Skåne* (From Skåne, 1884), *Pengar* (Money, 1885) and *Fru Marianne* (Mrs. Marianne, 1887).

BENEDIKTE (1944—). Danish princess. Name variations: Benedikte Oldenburg. Born Benedikte Astrid Ingeborg Ingrid, April 29, 1944, in Amalienborg Palace, Copenhagen, Denmark; dau. of Ingrid of Sweden (1910—) and Frederick IX, king of Denmark (r. 1947–1972); sister of Margrethe II, queen of Denmark (b. 1940), and Anne-Marie Oldenburg (b. 1946); m. Richard, 6th prince of Sayn-Wittgenstein-Berleburg, Feb 3, 1968; children: Gustav (b. 1969); Alexandra of Sayn-Wittgenstein (b. 1970); Nathalie of Sayn-Wittgenstein (b. 1975).

BENERITO, Ruth (1916—). American inventor and chemist. Name variations: Ruth Rogan Benerito. Born 1916; grew up in New Orleans, Louisiana; Sophie Newcomb College, BS in Chemistry, 1935; Tulane University, MS in Physics, 1938; attended Bryn Mawr College, 1935–36; University of Chicago, PhD in Physical Chemistry, 1948. ❖ While working at US Department of Agriculture laboratories in New Orleans (1950s), invented cotton wash-and-wear, wrinkle-free clothes, effectively putting an end to hours of ironing for women; spent 33 years with the Department, producing 55 patents; also taught chemistry at Randolph-Macon Women's College, Tulane University, and University of New Orleans. Received Garvan Medal of American Chemical Society, as well as Lemelson–MIT Lifetime Achievement Award for her patented processes in textiles (2002), among others.

BENESH, Joan (1920—). English dancer and notator. Born Joan Dorothy Rothwell, Mar 24, 1920, in Liverpool, England; m. Rudolf (accountant, painter, and musician, 1916–1975). ❖ Danced with Sadler's Wells Ballet (late 1940s); with husband, developed a dance notation system to record and decipher dance steps, now known as the Benesh Movement Notation (BMN, 1955), then wrote *An Introduction to Benesh Dance Notation* (1956); notated 1st score written in Benesh Movement Notation, Royal Ballet's version of *Petrouchka* (1957); founded Benesh Institute of Choreology with husband (1962), where she served as principal (1965–75); with husband, received Royal Academy of Dancing's Queen Elizabeth II Coronation Award. The Benesh notation system is now used to document all dance in England and as a teaching medium at Royal Academy of Dancing and Rambert School.

BENET, Laura (1884–1979). American poet, biographer, and novelist. Name variations: Laura Bénet. Born June 1, 1884, in Fort Hamilton, NY; died Feb 17, 1979, in New York, NY; dau. of Colonel James Walker and Frances Neill Rose Benet; graduate of Emma Willard School; Vassar College, BA, 1907; Moravian College, LittD. ❖ Was a worker at Spring Street Settlement in NY (1915–17), placement worker at Children's Aid Society (1917), sanitary inspector, American Red Cross in Augusta, GA (1917–19), worker at St. Bartholomew's House (1924–25), secretary and assistant book page editor, *New York Evening Post* (1927–28), assistant editor at *New York Sun* (1928–29); began freelance writing (1930); poetry includes *Fair Bred* (1921), *Noah's Dove* (1929), *A Basket for a Fair* (1934), *Is Morning Sure* (1947), *In Love with Time* (1959); fiction includes *Goods and Chattels*, *The Hidden Valley* (1938), *Roxana Ramphant* (1940), *Come Slowly, Eden: A Novel about Emily Dickinson* (1942); biographies include *The Boy Shelley* (1937), *Enchanting Jenny Lind* (1939), *Young Edgar Allan Poe* (1941), *Famous American Poets* (1950), *Famous American Humorists* (1959) and *Famous Storytellers* (1968).

BENETT, Etheldred (1776–1845). English geologist. Born in 1776; died Jan 11, 1845; 2nd dau. of Thomas Benett, of Pyt House near Tisbury. ❖ One of the earliest of English women geologists, devoted herself to collecting and studying the fossils of her native county for more than 25 years; contributed "A Catalogue of the Organic Remains of the County of Wilts" to Sir R.C. Hoare's *County History*.

BENETTON, Guiliana (1935—). Italian designer. Born May 13, 1935, in Treviso, Italy; sister of Luciano, Gilberto and Carlo Benetton; married with 4 children. ❖ As a child, worked in knitting atelier in Treviso and later began selling hand-knitted sweaters; with brothers, started business and opened store in Bellino (1965), and the company expanded rapidly to over 7,000 outlets worldwide by 2004 (Benetton is now the world's largest manufacturer of knitwear and largest consumer of virgin wool); serves on board of directors of Edizione Holding (the family-owned financial holding company) and Benetton Group.

BENGELSDORF, Rosalind (1916–1979). *See Browne, Rosalind Bengelsdorf.*

BENGER, Elizabeth (1778–1827). British biographer and poet. Born Elizabeth Ogilvy Benger, Feb 1778, in Wells, Somerset, England; died Jan 9, 1827, in London, England; dau. of John Benger (purser in the navy, died 1796) and Mary (Long) Benger; niece of Sir David Ogilvy. ❖ Writer, whose historical work often focused on women of intellect, befriended Laetitia Barbauld, Lucy Aikin, Elizabeth Hamilton, Joanna Baillie and Madame de Staël; wrote novels *Marian* (1812) and *The Heart and the Fancy, or, Valsinore* (1813), as well as poetry; biographies, which were frequently reprinted, include *Memoirs of the late Mrs. Elizabeth Hamilton* (1818), *Memoirs of the Life of Anne Boleyn* (1821) and *Memoirs of the Life of Mary, Queen of Scots* (1823).

BENGERD OF PORTUGAL (1194–1221). *See Berengaria.*

BENGTSSON, Birgitta (1965—). Swedish yacht racer. Born May 16, 1965, in Sweden. ❖ At Seoul Olympics, won a silver medal in 470 class (1988).

BEN HADDOU, Halima (fl. 1980s). Moroccan novelist. Name variations: Halima Benhaddou. Born in Nador, Morocco. ❖ Paralyzed by polio at age 9; wrote *Aicha la rebelle* (1982), which became an immediate bestseller.

BENHAM, Dorothy (c. 1956—). Miss America and opera singer. Born c. 1956 in Edina, Minnesota; m. Paul Shoemaker; children: 6. ❖ Named Miss America (1977), representing Minnesota; appeared in *Jerome Robbins' Broadway* (1989); continued career as lyric-coloratura soprano; made two CD recordings (2000).

BENHAM, Gertrude (1867–1938). British mountain climber. Born 1867 in England; died at sea in 1938, while returning from Africa. ❖ Spent more than 30 years walking the world, including 17 visits to Switzerland, a walk across South America from Valparaiso to Buenos Aires (1908), and a walk across Africa from west to east (1913); climbed more than 300 peaks of 10,000 feet or over; was the 1st woman to conquer the 19,700-foot Kilimanjaro (1909).

BENHASSI, Hasna (1978—). Moroccan runner. Born June 1, 1978, in Morocco. ❖ Won the 800 meters at the Mediterranean Games (1997); set 4 Moroccan records (1998); placed 8th in 800 meters at Sydney Olympics (2000); at World Indoor championship, placed 1st for 1,500 meters (2001); won a silver medal for 800 meters at Athens Olympics (2004).

BENICZKY-BAJZA, Helene (1840–1905). Hungarian novelist. Name variations: Helene von Beniczky-Bajza; Helene Bajza; Illona or Ilona Beniczky-Bajza; Ilona Bajza. Pronunciation: Ben-IS-skee By-tsa. Born in Budapest, June 1840; dau. of József Bajza (critic and theater manager, 1804–1858). ❖ One of the most prolific writers in Hungary in 19th century, is best-known for *Prejudice and Enlightenment* (1872), *It Is She* (1888), *Martha* (1890) and *The Mountain Fairy* (1890).

BENIDA, Nouria (1970—). Algerian runner. Name variations: Nouria Merah-Benida. Born Oct 19, 1970, in Algeria. ❖ Won a gold medal for the 1,500 meters at Sydney Olympics (2000).

BENINCASA, Caterina or Catherine di (1347–1380). *See Catherine of Siena.*

BENINCASA, Ursula (1547–1618). Italian religious. Born 1547; died 1618. ❖ Founded the Oblate Sisters of the Immaculate Conception of the Blessed Virgin Mary (1583), whose members were known as Theatines, or Theatine nuns.

BENISLAWSKA, Konstancja (1747–1806). Polish religious poet. Name variations: Konstancia Benislawska of Ryki. Born 1747 in Livonia, Poland; died 1806; dau. of impoverished nobles; married into the wealthy and well-educated Benislawski family; children: 22. ❖ Ranked as one of the better mystical poets, wrote *Piesni sobie spiewanr od Konstancji z Rykow Benislawskie...*(Songs Sung to Herself, at the Instigation of Friends, Brought by Konstancja of Ryki Benislawska from Rural Shade to the Daylight of Publication, 1776), a cycle of notable religious poetry.

BENITEZ, Lucienne (1905–1968). *See Benitez-Rexach, Lucienne.*

BENITEZ-REXACH, Lucienne (1905–1968). French cabaret singer. Name variations: Mome Moineau or Môme Moineau; Lucienne Benitez Rexach; Lucienne Benitez; Lucienne d'Hotelle de Benitez Rexach. Born Lucienne d'Hotelle in a caravan in France in 1905 (one source cites 1909); died Jan 18, 1968; dau. of traveling marketsellers; m. Felix Benitez Rexach (wealthy Puerto Rican engineer and friend of Trujillo), in San Juan, Puerto Rico, 1928 (died 1975). ❖ Well known as a child flowerseller at Fouquet's on the Champs Elysées, began career as a cabaret singer with the help of the couturier Paul Poiret, acquiring the name La Môme Moineau (kid sparrow); worked in theater until 1930; married well and led an extravagant life; while living in San Pedro de Marcoris, Cuidada Trujillo, Dominican Republic, bought a PC-461 Class submarine chaser with galley facilities to serve 100 guests (June 1947), then challenged Onassis to a yacht race; also lived in France (1946–52); became cultural attaché at San Domingo.

BENIZELOS, Philothey (fl. 1650). Greek abbess. Fl. 1650 in Greece; never married; no children. ❖ Founded a convent school (c. 1650) which became a popular refuge for local women; seems to have come into conflict with local authorities over her management of the abbey's lands, and was forced to take arms against the rebellious peasants who were tenants on her properties; eventually sentenced to prison, was apparently murdered soon after.

BENJAMIN, Ethel Rebecca (1875–1943). New Zealand lawyer and restaurateur. Name variations: Ethel Rebecca De Costa. Born Jan 19, 1875, in Dunedin, New Zealand; died Oct 14, 1943, at Northwood, Middlesex, England; dau. of Henry Benjamin and Lizzie (Mark) Benjamin; University of Otago, LLB, 1897; m. Alfred Mark Ralph De Costa, 1907 (died c. 1940/41). ❖ The 1st woman lawyer in New Zealand (1897), established a successful practice in Dunedin; also represented New Zealand Society for the Protection of Women and Children (1899); took over large restaurant in New Zealand International Exhibition (1906); moved to England (c. 1910). ❖ See also *Dictionary of New Zealand Biography* (Vol. 2).

BENJAMIN, Hilde (1902–1989). German lawyer and judge. Born Hilde Lange in Bernburg an der Saale, Germany, Feb 5, 1902; died in East Berlin, April 18, 1989; dau. of a sales director of a department store; m. Georg Benjamin (1895–1942, a physician); children: Michael (b. 1932). ❖ Communist lawyer and much-feared judge, known as "Red Hilde" in German Democratic Republic (GDR) where she served as a hard-line minister of justice, joined German Communist Party (1926); became a lawyer (1928); was forbidden to practice law by the Nazis (1933); joined German Central Judicial Authority (1946); served as vice-president of GDR Supreme Tribunal (1949–53), then minister of justice (1953–67); was notorious for presiding over 1950s political show trials; was a member of Socialist Unity Party central committee (1954–81); writings include *Vorschläge zum neuen deutschen Familienrecht* (1949), (with others) *Grundriss des Strafrechtsverfahrens der Deutschen Demokratischen Republik* (1953), *Die Hauptaufgaben der Justiz bei der Durchführung des neuen Kurses* (1953), *Karl Liebknecht, zum Wesen und zu Erscheinungen der Klassenjustiz* (1976), *Zur Geschichte der Rechtspflege der DDR 1945–1949* (1976), *Georg Benjamin: Eine Biographie* (1977) and *Zur Geschichte der Rechtspflege der DDR 1949–1961* (1980). ❖ See also *Women in World History*.

BENJAMIN, Lois (1932–2002). *See Gould, Lois.*

BENKO, Lindsay (1976—). American swimmer. Born Nov 29, 1976, in Elkhart, Indiana; attended University of Southern California, Los Angeles. ❖ Won a gold medal for 800-meter freestyle relay at Sydney Olympics (2000); at SC World championships, won gold medals for 400-meter freestyle (2000) and 200-meter freestyle and 200-meter backstroke (2002); won a gold medal for 4 x 200-meter freestyle relay at Athens Olympics (2004).

BENNEDSEN, Dorte (1938—). Danish politician. Name variations: Marianne Bennedsen. Born Dorte Koch, July 2, 1938, in Frederiksberg, Denmark; dau. of Hans Harald Koch (1904–1963, Doctor of Divinity and former Minister for Ecclesiastical Affairs) and Bodil Thastrum Koch (1903–1972, minister); Copenhagen University, degree in divinity, 1964; m. Jorgen Bennedsen, Sept 29, 1961; children: Mette (b. 1962), Mads (b. 1964) and Morten (b. 1966). ❖ Served as curate of Holmen Church (1965–68) and general secretary of Danish Youth Council (1968–71); was a member of the management committee for Social Democratic Party's 2nd constituency, Frederiksberg (1968–71) and member of the management committee for Danish Association for International Cooperation (1969–71); member of UNESCO national commission (1968–71) and of Ulandsrået (1968–71); chair of the Consumer Council (1974–79); vice-chair of the Parliamentary Social Democratic Party (1977–79); became chair of Danish Association for Nordic Collaboration (1984), serving as president (1987–91);

became a member of Nordic Council (1984); chair of Folketing's Municipal Affairs committee (1987–88) and of Folketing's Naturalization committee (1998).

BENNETT, Agnes (c. 1750–1808). *See Bennett, Anna Maria.*

BENNETT, Agnes Elizabeth Lloyd (1872–1960). New Zealand physician. Born June 24, 1872, in Sydney, Australia; died Nov 27, 1960, in Wellington, New Zealand; dau. of William Christopher Bennett (engineer) and Agnes Amelia (Hays) Bennett; University of Sydney, BSc, 1894; Medical College for Women, University of Edinburgh, Scotland, MB, ChM, 1899, MD, 1911. ❖ Assumed practice of Dr Isabella Watson, Wellington (1905–30); appointed medical officer to St. Helens Hospital, Wellington (1908); named honorary physician to children's ward, Wellington Hospital (1910); during WWI, served in New Zealand Medical Corps, working in military hospitals in Cairo, Egypt, until 1916; appointed commanding officer, 7th Medical Unit, Scottish Women's Hospitals for Foreign Service (1916); served as medical officer on troop and cargo ships (1917–18); during retirement, became part of flying doctor service in Queensland (1939); helped to establish Women's War Service Auxiliary (early 1940s); returned to New Zealand and lectured to servicewomen primarily on sex education (1942); worked briefly in Chatham Islands (1947). Received Order of St. Sava, 3rd class, of Serbia (1917), Cross of Honour of Serbian Red Cross (1917), and Order of British Empire (1948). ❖ See also *Dictionary of New Zealand Biography* (Vol. 3).

BENNETT, Alice (1851–1925). American physician. Born Jan 31, 1851, in Wrentham, Massachusetts; died May 31, 1925, in NY; Woman's Medical College of Pennsylvania, MD, 1876, PhD in anatomy (1880). ❖ The 1st woman to receive a PhD from University of Pennsylvania, was also one of the 1st women administrators at an American mental hospital, serving as superintendent of women's section at Pennsylvania State Hospital for the Insane in Norristown, PA (1880–86); advocated eliminating restraints, instituted a program of occupational therapy and had only women physicians treat women patients; after leaving Pennsylvania State Hospital, worked on volunteer basis at New York Infirmary for Women and Children (1910–25).

BENNETT, Alma (1889–1958). American silent-film actress. Born April 9, 1889, in Seattle, Washington; died Sept 16, 1958, in Los Angeles, California. ❖ Lead player in 1920s, films include *The Face on the Barroom Floor, Lilies of the Field, Don Juan's Three Nights* and *Long Pants*.

BENNETT, Anna Maria (c. 1750–1808). British novelist. Name variations: Agnes Bennett. Born Anna Maria Evans, c. 1750, in Merthyr Tydfil, Glamorgan, Wales (or Bristol); died Feb 12, 1808, in Brighton, Sussex, England; dau. of David Evans (Bristol grocer); married a tanner. ❖ Championed women intellectuals and members of the underclass in such works as *Anna, or, Memoirs of a Welch Heiress, Interspersed with Anecdotes of a Nabob* (1785), *Juvenile Indiscretions, a Novel* (1786) and *The Beggar Girl and Her Benefactors* (1797).

BENNETT, Barbara (1906–1958). American actress. Name variations: Mrs. Morton Downey. Born Aug 13, 1906; died in Montreal, Canada, Aug 9, 1958; dau. of actor Richard Bennett and actress Adrienne Morrison; sister of actresses Constance Bennett (1904–1965) and Joan Bennett (1910–1990); m. Morton Downey (singer), Jan 28, 1929 (div. 1941); m. Addison Randall, 1941 (died 1945); m. Laurent Surprenant (Canadian journalist), 1954; children: (1st m.) Michael (adopted), Sean, Lorelle Ann, Anthony, Kevin. ❖ Began her brief theatrical career as a dancer, touring with renowned exhibition dancer Maurice Mouve; went on to dance in a few Broadway musicals and an occasional movie, including *Syncopation* (1929), *Mother's Boy* (1929) and *Love among the Millionaires* (1930). ❖ See also *Women in World History.*

BENNETT, Belle (1891–1932). American stage, vaudeville, and screen actress. Born April 22, 1891, in Milcoon Rapids, Iowa; died Nov 4, 1932, in Los Angeles, California; m. Jack Oaker; m. William Macy (div.); m. Fred Windemere (film director), 1924. ❖ Best remembered for her performance in the title role in the original *Stella Dallas* (1925); appeared in over 65 films, including *East Lynne, His Supreme Moment, The Fourth Commandment, The Battle of the Sexes, The Iron Mask* and John Ford's *Mother Machree;* on Broadway, earned accolades for performance in *The Wandering Jew* (1921).

BENNETT, Belle Harris (1852–1922). American church worker. Born Isabel Harris Bennett, Dec 3, 1852, in Whitehall, near Richmond, Kentucky; died July 20, 1922, in Richmond; educated privately in Kentucky and Ohio. ❖ The 1st woman elected a delegate to the

Southern Methodist Church's General Conference (1919), began long career as a Sunday-school teacher; undertook a plan to establish the Scarritt Bible and Training School (1889), which was dedicated in Kansas City (1892) and later moved to Nashville, Tennessee, and renamed Scarritt College for Christian Workers; opened the Sue Bennett Memorial School in London, Kentucky, in honor of her older sister (1897); as president of the newly organized Woman's Board of Home Missions (1898), helped establish more than 40 "Wesley Community Houses" for whites and "Bethlehem Houses" for blacks throughout the segregated South; became president of the unified Woman's Mission Council (1910), a post she held until her death. ❖ See also *Women in World History.*

BENNETT, Brooke (1980—). American swimmer. Born May 6, 1980, in Tampa, Florida. ❖ Won a gold medal for 800-meter freestyle at Atlanta Olympics (1996) and a gold medal for 800-meter freestyle at World championships (1998); won gold medals for 400-meter freestyle and 800-meter freestyle at Sydney Olympics (2000); holds 13 US national titles.

BENNETT, Constance (1904–1965). American actress. Born in New York, NY, Oct 22, 1904; died in Fort Dix, New Jersey, July 24, 1965; dau. of actor Richard Bennett and actress Adrienne Morrison; sister of actresses Barbara Bennett (1902–1958) and Joan Bennett (1910–1990); m. Chester Moorehead, 1921 (annulled); m. Philip Plant, 1925 (div. 1929); m. Henri Falaise (Marquis de la Coudraye), 1931 (div. 1940); m. Gilbert Roland, 1941 (div. 1944?); m. John Coulter, 1946; children: (2nd m.) Peter Bennett; (4th m.) Lorinda and Christina Consuelo ("Gyl"). ❖ Had 1st major screen role in *Cytherea* (1924), which led to a number of roles in the silents; established herself as a leading lady in her 1st talkie, the fast-moving comedy *This Thing Called Love* (1929); lending her husky voice to both sophisticated comedies and melodramatic tear-jerkers, is especially remembered for her role as the heroine of *Topper* (1937) and *Topper Takes a Trip* (1939); made stage debut touring in *Easy Virtue* (1940); other films include *Three Faces East* (1930), *Rockabye* (1932), *Our Betters* (1933), *Bed of Roses* (1933), *After Tonight* (1933), *Moulin Rouge* (1934), *The Affairs of Cellini* (1934), *Tail Spin* (1939), *Law of the Tropics* (1941), *Two-Faced Woman* (1941), *Wild Bill Hickock Rides* (1942), *Madame Spy* (1942), *Paris Underground* (1945), *Centennial Summer* (1946), *As Young As You Feel* (1951), *It Should Happen to You* (1954) and *Madame X* (1966). ❖ See also *Women in World History.*

BENNETT, Eileen (1920—). English actress. Born July 8, 1920, in London, England; m. Thomas W. Hammond (American army officer), 1945 (died 1970); children: David Hammond and Nicholas Hammond (actor who played the eldest von Trapp child in *Sound of Music*). ❖ On London stage, played the ingenue lead in *Arsenic and Old Lace* (1942–45); films include *Thursday's Child* and *Much Too Shy;* on marriage, moved to US.

BENNETT, Enid (1893–1969). Australian actress. Born July 15, 1893, in York, Western Australia, Australia; died May 14, 1969, in Malibu, California; sister of actresses Marjorie Bennett (c. 1896–1982) and Catherine Bennett; m. Sidney Franklin (director); m. Fred Niblo (director), 1918; children: (with Niblo) Louis, Peter, and Judith. ❖ Was touring with an Australian stage troupe when she arrived in US during WWI; discovered by Thomas Ince, starred as Maid Marion opposite Douglas Fairbanks Sr. in *Robin Hood* (1922); also appeared in *The Sea Hawk* (1924); other films include *The Battle of Gettysburg* (1914), *Princess of the Dark* (1917), *The Biggest Show on Earth* (1918), *The Vamp* (1918), *Stepping Out* (1919), *Keeping Up with Lizzie* (1921), *The Bootlegger's Daughter* (1922), *The Courtship of Miles Standish* (1923), *The Red Lily* (1924), *Waterloo Bridge* (1931), *Intermezzo* (1939) and *Strike Up the Band* (1940); retired from the screen soon after marriage to Fred Niblo; accompanied him to Italy (1926), assisting him on the filming of *Ben-Hur.* ❖ See also *Women in World History.*

BENNETT, Estelle (1944—). American singer. Born July 22, 1944, in New York, NY; sister of Ronnie Spector (singer); m. Teddy Vann (producer). ❖ With sister Ronnie and cousin Nedra Talley, sang and danced as the Darling Sisters at Peppermint Lounge in NYC (1961), then recorded for Colpix as Ronnie and the Relatives, then as the Ronettes (1962); with Ronettes, signed with producer Phil Spector's Phillies label (1963), and sang background vocals for label's other performers, including Darlene Love and Bob B. Soxx and the Blue Jeans; with group, released song, "Be My Baby" (1963), which hit #2. Other successful Ronettes songs include "Baby I Love You" (1963), "Walking in the Rain" (1964) and "Is This What I Get For Lovin' You?" (1965).

BENNETT, Evelyn (b. 1905). American theater dancer. Born 1905 in New York, NY. ❖ Toured in Gus Edwards' Kiddie Cabaret, partnered in one number with Eddie Cantor, George Jessel and Walter Winchell; performed tap number on Pacific circuit at age 13; headlined a dance act in Pantages theaters (c. 1918–20); starred as a specialty dancer on NY stage in *The Clinging Vine* (1922), *Lollipop* (1924), *Suzanna* (1924) and *Merry-Go-Round* (1927); was the highest paid vaudevillian for over a decade, winning greatest acclaim for 2 solo numbers in *Americana*: "Tabloid Papers" and "Why D'ya Roll Those Eyes" (1928).

BENNETT, Gwendolyn B. (1902–1981). African-American writer. Born July 8, 1902, in Giddings, Texas; died in Reading, Pennsylvania, May 30, 1981; dau. of Joshua Robin Bennett (lawyer) and Mayme F. (Abernathy) Bennett (beautician); studied fine arts at Columbia University Teachers College for 2 years; transferred to Pratt Institute in Brooklyn; m. Alfred Joseph Jackson (physician), 1927 (died); m. Richard Crosscup (died Jan 9, 1980). ❖ Artist, poet, writer, and educator whose work as a columnist for *Opportunity* encouraged the growth of cultural life in Harlem, and whose poetry, incorporating themes of her African heritage and her training as a painter, placed her among the finest of the writers of the Harlem Renaissance; shortly after her birth, moved with family to Nevada, where parents taught on an Indian reservation, and later to Washington, DC; while still young, parents divorced, leaving her in mother's custody; at 7, was kidnapped by father and would not see mother again until she was an adult; graduated from Brooklyn Girls High School (1921), where she became the 1st black student elected to the literary and dramatic societies; became an instructor of watercolor and design at Howard University; received Delta Sigma Theta's foreign scholarship (1924), which allowed her to travel to Paris to study at the Julian and Colarossi academies, as well as at the École de Pantheon; in Paris, became acquainted with the modern French painter Frans Masereel; resumed teaching at Howard (1926) and became assistant editor of the magazine *Opportunity,* where she wrote the column "The Ebony Flute" (1926–28); was 1 of 2 African-American artists selected to study the modern and primitive art collections of the Barnes Foundation (1927); poetry appeared in numerous magazines, including *Fire!, Crisis* and the *American Mercury* (1922–34); continued teaching at Howard University and also served as director of the Harlem Community Arts Center (1937–40). Little is known of her life after the 1940s. ❖ See also *Women in World History.*

BENNETT, Helen (1896–1963). *See Black, Helen McKenzie.*

BENNETT, Isadora (d. 1980). American theatrical publicity agent. Born in Missouri; died Feb 8, 1980, age 79, in New York, NY; m. Daniel Reed (actor, died); children: Susan Reed (folk singer). ❖ Began career as reporter for *Chicago Daily News;* worked as a publicist for the Martha Graham Dance Co. for many years, starting 1939, and was among the 1st to champion American dance.

BENNETT, Isobel (b. 1909). Australian marine biologist. Born July 9, 1909, in Brisbane, Australia. ❖ Worked in variety of capacities, including research assistant for zoology professor William J. Dakin at University of Sydney (1933–48); was crew member on the university's research ship *Thistle;* did field work on Victorian and Tasmanian coasts (1950s); became expert in marine biology, specializing in ecology of intertidal area; was 1 of the 1st 4 women scientists from Australia to visit Antarctica, where she studied intertidal shore life (1957); made 1st visit to Macquarie Island with ANARE relief ship (1959), followed by 3 additional visits (1960, 1965, 1968); served as dean of women on the *Te Vega,* Stanford University research ship (1963); was delegate to 11th Pacific Congress (Tokyo, 1966); retired from university (1971); surveyed coastal rock platforms at Jervis Bay and Ulladulla (1973, 1974, 1977); performed fieldwork on Lord Howe Island (1974), Norfolk Island (1980) and Flinders Island (1981); continued visits to Heron Island until 1995; wrote 9 books, some of which became popular textbooks. Received Mueller Medal from Australia and New Zealand Association for the Advancement of Science (1982), Order of Australia (1984), and Ruth Readford Award for Lifetime Achievement (2000).

BENNETT, Jill (1931–1990). British actress. Born Dec 24, 1931, in Penang, Federated Malay States (now Malaysia); committed suicide, Oct 4, 1990, in London, England; dau. of James Randle and Nora Adeline (Beckett) Bennett; attended Priors Field, Godalming; attended Royal Academy of Dramatic Art; m. Willis Hall (div.); m. John Osborne (1929–1994, playwright), 1968 (div. 1977). ❖ Actress who often played in the works of playwright husband, made stage debut at Shakespeare

Memorial Theatre, Stratford-on-Avon (1949), followed by London debut in *Captain Carvallo* (1950); had 1st success as Isabelle in *Dinner with the Family* (1957); won *Evening Standard* and Variety Club Awards for Best Actress for performance as Pamela in *Time Present* (1968); also appeared as Helen Eliot in *The Night of the Ball* (1955), Masha in *The Seagull* (1956), Mrs. Marin in *The Bald Prima Donna* (1956), Susan Roper in *Breakfast for One* (1961), Feemy Evans in *The Showing-Up of Blanco Posnet*, Ophelia in *Castle in Sweden* (1962), Isabelle in *The Love Game* (1964), Countess Sophia Delyanoff in *A Patriot for Me* (1965), Frederica in *West of Suez* (1971), Hedda in *Hedda Gabler* (1972), Fay in *Loot* (1975), Sally in *Watch It Come Down* (1976), and Mrs. Shankland and Miss Railton-Bell in *Separate Tables* (1977), among others; made a number of films, including *The Charge of the Light Brigade, Inadmissible Evidence, Julius Caesar* and *I Want What I Want*; also appeared on British tv. ❖ See also memoir *Godfrey: A Special Time Remembered,* concerning her relationship with Sir Godfrey Tearle.

BENNETT, Joan (1910–1990). American actress. Born in Palisades, New Jersey, Feb 27, 1910; died in Scarsdale, New York, Dec 7, 1990; dau. of actor Richard Bennett and actress (Mabel) Adrienne Morrison; sister of actresses Constance Bennett (1904–1965) and Barbara Bennett (1906–1958); m. John Fox, Sept 15, 1926 (div., Aug 1928); m. Gene Markey, 1932 (div. 1937); m. Walter Wanger, 1940 (div. 1965); m. David Wilde, 1978; children: (1st m.) Adrienne Ralston (b. 1928); (2nd m.) Melinda (b. 1934); (3rd m.) Stephanie (b. 1943) and Shelley (b. 1948). ❖ One of the most popular leading ladies of 1930s and 1940s, made stage debut as an ingenue opposite her father in *Jarnegan* (1928); had 1st major screen role in *Bulldog Drummond,* then appeared in *Disraeli* (both 1929); acclaimed for her portrayal of Amy in *Little Women* and her performances in 2 films directed by Fritz Lang: *The Woman in the Window* (1944) and *Scarlet Street* (1945); also worked for Jean Renoir in *The Woman on the Beach* (1947); changed from blonde to brunette for the film *Trade Winds* (1938), which furthered her career to such a degree that she stayed brunette; other films include *The Mississippi Gambler* (1929), *Puttin' on the Ritz* (1930), *Moby Dick* (1930), *Scotland Yard* (1930), *Doctor's Wives* (1931), *Me and My Gal* (1932), *Mississippi* (1935), *Two for Tonight* (1935), *The Man Who Broke the Bank at Monte Carlo* (1935), *Artists and Models Abroad* (1938), (as Queen Maria Theresa) *The Man in the Iron Mask* (1939), *The House Across the Bay* (1940), *The Son of Monte Cristo* (1940), *Nob Hill* (1945), *The Macomber Affair* (1947), *Father of the Bride* (1950), *Father's Little Dividend* (1951), *We're No Angels* (1955) and *Navy Wife* (1956); after husband Walter Wanger shot and wounded her agent Jennings Lang in a jealous rage (1951), her career was effectively destroyed; appeared in several stage productions (1950s–60s), including *Janus, The Pleasure of His Company* and *Never Too Late;* appeared in the Gothic tv soap opera "Dark Shadows" (1966–71). ❖ See also autobiography, *The Bennett Playbill* (1970); and *Women in World History.*

BENNETT, Louie (1870–1956). Irish trade unionist. Born Louie Guillemine Bennett in Dublin, Ireland, 1870; died in Dublin, 1956; dau. of James Cavendish Bennett (auctioneer); never married; no children. ❖ Founded the Irish Women's Suffrage Federation and the Irish Women's Reform League (1910); founded the Irish Women's International League (1914); an ardent pacifist, reorganized the Irish Women Workers' Union with a less nationalistic sentiment (IWWU, 1916); served as IWWU vice-president (1917) and general secretary (1919–55); went to US to help publicize British brutalities against the Irish, specifically the use of British police forces known as the Black and Tans (1920); elected president of Irish Trades Union Congress (1932), the 1st woman to hold that office; struggled to improve labor conditions for the working women of Ireland for much of her life; also wrote 2 romantic novels. ❖ See also *Women in World History.*

BENNETT, Louise Simone (1919—). Jamaican poet, actress, folklorist, singer and radio personality. Name variations: Miss Lou; Miss Lulu; Louise Bennett-Coverly. Born in Kingston, Jamaica, Sept 7, 1919; educated at St. Simon's College, Friends College and Royal Academy of Dramatic Art; m. Eric "Chalk Talk" Coverly, 1954. ❖ Often working in the Jamaican Creole dialect, wrote stories of Jamaica and its people, finding humor in even the most serious subjects; performed her poetry at outdoor theaters and was occasionally published, but Jamaican literary community was difficult to penetrate; studied acting in London and eventually appeared on a radio show there; moved to NY to work in theater (1953); with Eric Coverly, coproduced folk musical *Day in Jamaica;* with husband, returned to Jamaica (1955), where respect for Jamaican dialect was increasing; as an artistic envoy for Jamaican Social Welfare Commission, traveled the country performing and teaching; began to draw crowds of 60,000. Works include *M's Lulu Sez:*

A Collection of Dialect Poems (1949), *Laugh With Louise* (1961) and *Jamaica Labrish* (1966). ❖ See also *Women in World History.*

BENNETT, Marjorie (1896–1982). Australian stage, screen, and tv actress. Name variations: Margery Bennett; Marjorie E. Bennett. Born Jan 15, 1896, in York, Australia; died June 14, 1982, in Hollywood, California; sister of Enid Bennett (1893–1969, silent star) and Catherine Bennett. ❖ Films include *Monsieur Verdoux, Perfect Strangers, Limelight, Young at Heart, Autumn Leaves, Sabrina, Rat Race, Whatever Happened to Baby Jane?, Mary Poppins, Coogan's Bluff* and *Charley Varrick;* appeared regularly on such tv series as "Dobie Gillis," "December Bride," "Eve Arden Show," "Bob Cummings Show" and "Chips."

BENNETT, Mary Jane (c. 1816–1885). New Zealand lighthouse keeper. Name variations: Mary Jane Hebden. Born Mary Jane Hebden, c. 1816 (baptized Dec 11, 1816), at Pateley Bridge, Yorkshire, England; died July 6, 1885, at Dacre Banks, Yorkshire, England; dau. of William and Mary Hebden; m. George White Bennett (seed merchant and lighthouse keeper), 1840 (died 1855); children: 5. ❖ Immigrated to Wellington, New Zealand (Feb 1840); assumed lighthouse duties after husband drowned; became 1st keeper of permanent lighthouse in New Zealand and only woman to hold that position (1859); returned to England with children (c. 1865). ❖ See also *Dictionary of New Zealand Biography* (Vol. 1).

BENNETT, Mary Katharine (1864–1950). American churchwoman. Born Mary Katharine Jones, Nov 28, 1864, in Englewood, New Jersey; died April 11, 1950, in Englewood; m. Fred Smith Bennett, July 20, 1898. ❖ Served as president of the Woman's Board of Home Missions (1909–23) and vice president of the Presbyterian Board of National Missions (1923–41); traveled nationally and abroad to promote home missions; was president of the interdenominational Council of Women for Home Missions (1916–24) and president of the interchurch Board for Christian Work in Santo Domingo (1920–36); in later years, focused largely on work with migrants and American Indians.

BENNETT, Mary Montgomerie (1881–1961). English-born writer, reformer and educator. Born Mary Montgomerie Christison in London, England, July 8, 1881; died at Kalgoorlie, Australia, Oct 6, 1961; eldest of 3 children of Robert (pastoralist and meatworks owner) and Mary (Goodsall) Christison; attended Royal Academy of the Arts, 1903–08; matriculated at University of London, 1944; married Charles Douglas Bennett (ship's captain), Aug 18, 1914. ❖ Crusader for Aboriginal rights, was 29 before making 1st trip to Australia, accompanying father to Queensland; returned to England, where she married and took up residence in London; widowed (1927), set out to teach the Aborigines, using crafts as a medium; learned spinning and weaving before embarking for Australia (1930), where, after extensive travel through Aboriginal territories, she applied her teaching theories with some success at the Mt. Margaret Mission, near Laverton; publicized the exploitation of Aboriginal pastoral workers, who suffered with no wage laws and were required to ask permission to leave their place of employment; also opposed the policy of removing Aboriginal children from their mothers; writings include *The Australian Aboriginal as a Human Being* (1930), *Teaching the Aborigines: Data from Mount Margaret Mission, W.A.* (1935), *Hunt or Die* (1950) and *Human Rights for Australian Aborigines* (1957).

BENNETT, Mavis (1900–1990). English coloratura soprano. Born Mar 28, 1900, in Redditch, Worcestershire, England; died Jan 28, 1990, in Stalbridge, Dorset, England. ❖ Known as the "Nightingale of the Wireless," joined the D'Oyly Carte Repertory Co. chorus (1921); appeared on the concert stage and in several London shows; became an overnight sensation when she sang with Dutch violinist De Groot for BBC radio (1925); was soon appearing on radio in England and on the Continent; frequently recorded for HMV; performing career ended when an operation damaged her throat (1939); became a vocal teacher.

BENNETT, Olga (1947—). Irish politician. Born Oct 1947 in Dublin, Ireland; m. Eamon Bennett. ❖ Representing Fianna Fáil, nominated to the Seanad by Taoiseach Charles J. Haughey (1989), serving until 1993.

BENNETT, Patricia (1947—). American vocalist. Name variations: The Chiffons. Born April 7, 1947, in Bronx, NY. ❖ With Barbara Lee, Judy Craig, and Sylvia Peterson, sang as a member of the Chiffons; released such hits as "He's So Fine" (1963), "One Fine Day" (with Carole King on Piano, 1963), "Nobody Knows What's Going On" (1965), and "Sweet Talkin' Guy" (1966). Chiffons albums include *He's So Fine* (1963) and *Sweet Talkin' Guy* (1966).

BENNETT, Ronnie (1943—). See Spector, Ronnie.

BENNETT, Wilda (1894–1967). American musical star. Born Dec 19, 1894, in Asbury Park, New Jersey; died Dec 20, 1967, in Winnemucca, Nevada; m. Pepe D'Albreu (div.); m. Anthony J. Wettach (div.); married twice more. ❖ Made stage debut as Conscience in *Everyman* (1911); also appeared as Queen Mab in *The Good Little Devil*, Sylva Veraska in *Riviera Girl*, Mariana in *Lady in Ermine*, Nancy in *Apple Blossoms*, the title role in *Mme. Pompadour* and in *The Music Box Revue*.

BENNINGA, Carina (1962—). Dutch field-hockey player. Born Aug 18, 1962. ❖ Won a gold medal at Los Angeles Olympics (1984) and a bronze medal at Seoul Olympics (1988), both in team competition.

BENNION, Lianne (1972—). American rower. Name variations: Lianne Nelson; Lianne Nelson-Bennion. Born Lianne Bennion, June 15, 1972, in Houston, Texas; attended Princeton University. ❖ Won a silver medal for coxed eights at Athens Olympics (2004); won 2 World Cups in coxed eights (2004).

BENOIS, Nadia (1896–1975). Russian painter and set designer. Name variations: Nadezhda Leontievna Benois; Nadia Ustinov. Born Nadezhda Leontievna Benois, May 17, 1896, near St. Petersburg, Russia; died 1975 in England; dau. of Louis Benois (architect in tsarist court and professor of architecture); studied under Alexandre Benois (uncle who designed sets for Diaghilev) and Jacovleff Choukhaieff; attended private academy in St. Petersburg; m. Iona (Jonah) Ustinov (officer in tsarist army), 1920; children: Peter Ustinov (actor, playwright). ❖ Moved with husband to England following marriage (1921); had 1st solo exhibition at Little Gallery, the Adelphi (1924); traveled to Scotland, France, Wales and Ireland which inspired impressionist landscape paintings; exhibited work in London and Paris and in Canada; began exhibiting with New English Art Club (1929) and was a member (1937–41); began designing sets (1932) and collaborated with son Peter on the play *House of Regrets* (1942); worked as set designer for several ballet companies, including Ballet Rambert; also worked closely with French avante-garde theater company, Compagnie Quinze.

BENOIST, Françoise-Albine (1724–1809). French novelist and playwright. Name variations: Francoise Albine Benoist; Françoise-Albine Puzin de la Martinière Benoist. Born 1724 in Lyon, France; died 1809. ❖ Novels include *Journal en forme de lettres* (1757), *Célianne* (1766), *Elisabeth* (1766), *Lettres du colonel Talbert* (1767), *Les aveux d'une jolie femme* (1782), *Les Erreurs d'une jolie femme ou la nouvelle Aspasie* (1781) and *Lettres sur le désir de plaire* (1786); published 2 plays: *La Supercherie réciproque* (1768) and *Le Triomphe de la probité* (1768).

BENOIST, Marie (1768–1826). French painter. Name variations: Comtesse Benoist. Born Marie Guillemine (or Guilhelmine) Lerouix de la Ville in 1768 in Paris, France; died 1826 in Paris; dau. of an administrative official; student of Elisabeth Vigée-Lebrun, Adelaide Labille-Guiard and Jacques Louis David; m. Pierre Vincent Benoist (royalist), 1793. ❖ Encouraged by father, was about 13 when she began studying painting with Vigée-Lebrun, who influenced her early pastel portraits; was then placed under tutelage of Jacques Louis David who moved her into the more linear and brilliant history paintings and formal portraits, exhibited at the Salon of 1791, that would dominate the rest of her career; painted best-known work *Portrait of a Negress* (1800); was officially commissioned to paint Napoleon's portrait for the Palais de Justice at Ghent (c. 1804), for which she received a gold medal. ❖ See also *Women in World History*.

BENOIT, Joan (b. 1957). See Samuelson, Joan Benoit.

BENSON, Gertrude (1886–1964). New Zealand professor. Name variations: Gertrude Helen Rawson. Born Jan 25, 1886, in Bradford, Yorkshire, England; died Feb 20, 1964, in Dunedin, New Zealand; dau. of Joseph Cordingley Rawson and Agnes Annie (Cragg) Rawson; Newnham College, University of Cambridge, BSc, 1919; m. William Noel Benson (geologist), 1923 (died 1957). ❖ Became professor of home science and dean of faculty at School of Home Science, University of Otago (1920); was founder of New Zealand branch of Federation of University Women (1920); was a member of Senate of University of New Zealand (1939–48).

BENSON, Linda (c. 1944—). American surfer. Born c. 1944 in Encinitas, California. ❖ At 15, was the youngest contestant to enter the International Championship at Makaha, then won (1959); was the 1st woman to ride Waimea; was Pacific Coast women's champion (1959, 1960, 1961); won the 1st women's US championship (1959), then defended the title (1960, 1961, 1964, 1968); was Annette Funicello's double in the "Beach Party" films and doubled for Deborah Walley in

surfing action sequences for film *Gidget Goes Hawaiian;* was one of the best-known female surfers of her day.

BENSON, Mary (1919–2000). South African novelist, biographer, historian and anti-apartheid activist. Born Dorothy Mary Benson, Dec 8, 1919, in Pretoria, South Africa; died June 20, 2000, in London, England; never married. ❖ Joined South African women's army (1941–45), becoming captain and serving as personal assistant to British generals in Egypt and Italy; became personal assistant to David Lean and secretary to Michael Scott (1950); was involved in anti-apartheid activities and founded, with Michael Scott and David Astor, the Africa Bureau in London; served as secretary to Treason Trials Defence Fund (1957) and helped to smuggle Nelson Mandela out of South Africa (1962); was served with a banning order and subjected to house arrest; left South Africa (1966) and continued to work in London against apartheid; writings include *Tshekedi Khama* (1960), *The African Patriots* (1963), *Chief Albert Luthuli* (1963), *At the Still Point* (1969), *Nelson Mandela* (1986) and *A Far Cry: The Making of a South African* (1989); edited Athol Fugard's *The Sun Will Rise: Statements from the Dock by South African Political Prisoners* (1974) and *Notebooks: 1960–1977* (1983); also wrote radio plays on Nelson Mandela and Rivonia trial and scripted Winnie Mandela's *Part of My Soul* (1985).

BENSON, Mildred (1905–2002). American writer, journalist and pilot. Name variations: Mildred Augustine; Mildred Wirt Benson; Mildred A. Wirt; Ann Wirt; (pseudonyms) Frank Bell, Joan Clark, Don Palmer, Dorothy West; (collective pseudonyms) Julia K. Duncan, Alice B. Emerson, Frances K. Judd, Carolyn Keene, Helen Louise Thorndyke. Born Mildred Augustine in Ladora, Iowa, July 10, 1905; died May 28, 2002, in Toledo, Ohio; dau. of J.L. (doctor) and Lillian (Mattison) Augustine; University of Iowa, BA, 1925, MA, 1927, the 1st woman to receive an MA from the University's journalism school; m. Asa Alvin Wirt (affiliated with the Associated Press, died 1947); m. George A. Benson (editor of *Toledo* [Ohio] *Times*), 1950 (died 1959); children: (1st m.) Margaret Wirt. ❖ Effectively the creator of the character of "Nancy Drew," wrote over 100 series books for the Stratemeyer Syndicate using her own name and a variety of pseudonyms (1927–59); after receiving a brief plot and character outline for the 1st Nancy Drew book, *The Secret of the Old Clock*, crafted a smart, adventurous heroine, one she hoped would break the stereotypical mold; for years, as Carolyn Keene, produced a 200-page Nancy Drew story every 6 weeks or so, writing 22 of the next 29 books in the series, and frequently drawing on her own experiences for inspiration; also worked on several other Stratemeyer projects, including the "Doris Force," "Kay Tracy" and "Dana Girls" series; published volumes under her own name, or variations of her own name, including the "Ruth Darrow Flying Stories"; well into her 80s, piloted her own plane; in her 90s, continued writing the weekly column, "On the Go," for *The Blade* in Toledo, Ohio. ❖ See also *Women in World History*.

BENSON, Rita Romilly (1900–1980). American actress and acting teacher. Born Rita Romilly, Sept 7, 1900; died April 4, 1980, age 79, in New York, NY; m. Martin Benson (1971). ❖ Began career as an actress; became director of the American Academy of Dramatic Arts.

BENSON, Sally (1900–1972). American writer. Name variations: (pseudonym) Esther Evarts. Born Sara Mahala Redway Smith, Sept 3, 1900, in St. Louis, Missouri; died July 19, 1972, in Woodland Hills, California; dau. of Alonzo Redway (cotton broker) and Anna (Prophater) Smith; attended Mary Institute, St. Louis, Missouri; Horace Mann High School, New York, NY; m. Reynolds Benson, Jan 25, 1919 (div.); children: Barbara. ❖ Best remembered as the creator of Judy Graves, the heroine of her "Junior Miss" stories that began in *The New Yorker*, started writing as an interviewer for the New York *Morning Telegraph;* sold her 1st short story to *The New Yorker;* published *People are Fascinating* (1936), a collection of her *New Yorker* stories which contains "The Overcoat" and "Suite 2049," two O. Henry prize stories; was astonished by the success of the "Junior Miss" collection, which included a stage play (1941), 2 radio shows, films and a tv movie; published the highly successful novel *Meet Me in St. Louis* (1942), based on her childhood memories; adapted the musical *Seventeen* from the novel by Booth Tarkington; wrote numerous film scripts, including *Shadow of a Doubt* (1943), *Experiment Perilous* (1944), *National Velvet* (1944), *Come to the Stable* (1949), *No Man of Her Own* (1950), *The Belle of New York* (1952), *The Farmer Takes a Wife* (1953), *The Adventures of Huckleberry Finn* (1960), *Bus Stop* (1961), *Summer Magic* (1962), *Viva Las Vegas* (1963), *Signpost to Murder* (1963) and *The Singing Nun* (1966). Nominated for Academy Award for screenplay for *Anna and the King of Siam* (1946). ❖ See also *Women in World History*.

BENSON, Stella (1892–1933). English novelist, poet, and travel writer. Name variations: Stella Benson O'Gorman Anderson. Born Stella Benson, Jan 6, 1892, in Shropshire, England; died Dec 6, 1933, in Hongay in Chinese province of Tongking (now Vietnam); dau. of Caroline Essex (Cholmondeley) and Ralph Beaumont Benson, both landed gentry; m. Shaemus (James) O'Gorman Anderson (Chinese government customs official), Sept 29, 1921; children: none. ❖ Writer who actively campaigned for women's rights before and during WWI and in Hong Kong during early 1930s; began lifelong practice of writing diary (1901); at 21, left home in Shropshire for an independent life in London, where she took up a series of jobs to support herself, producing novels which eventually brought her fame as a modernist writer and launching her own "private Stellarian Suffrage Campaign" of argument and persuasion; wrote *I Pose* (1915), a feminist satire about the suffrage movement; wrote novels, poems, and short stories, mixing fantasy and satire; traveled alone, often ill but self-supporting, to Berkeley, California (1918–19), to China and India (1920–21); traveled to US with husband; moved to China with husband, settling in Mengtsz (1922–25), then Shanghai, followed by Lung Ching Tsun (1925–27), Nanjing (1929–30), Hong Kong (1930–31) and Pakhoi (1931–33); writings include *This Is the End* (1917), (poems) *Twenty* (1918), *Living Alone* (1919), *Kwan-Yin* (1922), *The Poor Man* (1922), *Pipers and a Dancer* (1924), (self-illustrated essays) *The Little World* (1925), *The Awakening: A Fantasy* (1925), *Goodbye, Stranger* (1926), (self-illustrated essays) *Worlds within Worlds* (1928), *The Man Who Missed the Bus: A Story* (1928), *The Far-Away Bride* (1930, republished as *Tobit Transplanted*, 1931), *Hope Against Hope and Other Stories* (1932), *Christmas Formula and Other Stories* (1931) and *Mundos: An Unfinished Novel* (1935). Received French Vie Heureuse Prize (1932) for *Tobit Transplanted* (published in US as *The Far-Away Bride*) and A.C. Benson silver medal for service to literature (1932). ❖ See also Joy Grant, *Stella Benson: A Biography* (Macmillan, 1987); Richard Ellis Roberts, *Portrait of Stella Benson* (Macmillan, 1939); and *Women in World History*.

BENT, Buena (c. 1890–1957). English actress. Born c. 1890 in London, England; died Dec 17, 1957, in England; m. T.C. Maxwell. ❖ Made stage debut in *La Poupée*, followed by numerous appearances in musical halls and vaudeville; plays include *Bought and Paid For, Within the Law, The Wild Widow, Bran Pie, The Risk, A House of Cards, Third Time Lucky, After All, Major Barbara, The Merry Wives of Windsor* and *Vanity Fair*; also appeared as Mrs. Malaprop in *The Rivals*; films include *Amazing Quest* with Cary Grant (1937, released in US as *Amazing Adventure*).

BENTHAM, Ethel (1861–1931). British doctor. Born Jan 5, 1861; died Jan 19, 1931, in England; attended Alexandra School and College, Dublin, London School of Medicine for Women, 1890–94, and Rotunda Hospital in Dublin; University of Brussels, MD, 1895. ❖ Served as general practitioner at Newcastle upon Tyne, Gateshead, and North Kensington; a pioneer in efforts to provide for needs of preschool children and mothers' health, served as organizer and consultant medical officer at Margaret O. MacDonald Memorial Clinic for Children under School Age and as a member of Metropolitan Asylums Board; representing East Islington, became successful Labour Party candidate for House of Commons (1929).

BENTINCK, Margaret (1714–1785). Duchess of Portland. Name variations: Margaret Cavendish; Margaret Cavendish Harley; Peggy Bentinck. Born Margaret Cavendish Harley in 1714 (some sources cite 1715); died July 17, 1785; dau. of Edward Harley, 2nd earl of Oxford; m. William Bentinck, 2nd duke of Portland, 1734; children: Elizabeth Cavendish-Bentinck (1735–1825, who m. Sir Thomas Thynne, 1st marquess of Bath); Henrietta Cavendish-Bentinck (1737–1827); William Henry Cavendish-Bentinck, 3rd duke of Portland (1738–1809); Edward Charles Cavendish-Bentinck (1744–1819). ❖ One of the foremost private collectors of her day, acquired a number of shells from Captain Cook's expeditions; friend of Bluestockings, Mary Granville Delany and Elizabeth Montagu.

BENTIVOGLIO, Ippolita. See Sforza, Ippolita.

BENTIVOGLIO, Lucrezia (d. 1516/18). See Este, Lucrezia d'.

BENTLEY, Catherine (fl. 1635). English-Flemish nun. Name variations: Sister Magdalene Augustine. Dau. of English parents; never married; no children. ❖ Entered the order of Poor Clares in Douai (Flanders) and took the name Sister Magdalene Augustine; well educated by nuns of her order, showed an aptitude for languages which led her to complete several translations of devotional works, among these the life of St. Clare of Assisi, founder of the Poor Clares (1635).

BENTLEY, Elizabeth Turrill (1908–1963). American anti-Communist. Born in New Milford, Connecticut, 1908; died in New Haven, Connecticut, Dec 3, 1963; graduate of Vassar College, 1930; Columbia University, MA, 1933. ❖ Anti-Communist witness during McCarthy era in US, joined Communist Party while a student at Columbia (1935); served as secretary to Jacob Golos, head of a Soviet espionage network; later claimed that as a Soviet spy courier she had uncovered a vast network of treason in Washington, DC (1930s–45); played an important role in anti-Communist investigations and prosecutions during early years of the Cold War; described by media as the "Red Spy Queen," her testimony was significant in bringing about the convictions of Ethel and Julius Rosenberg, though she had never met either of them, and William Remington, who had dared to sue her for libel. ❖ See also autobiography *Out of Bondage: The Story of Elizabeth Bentley* (Devin-Adair, 1951); and *Women in World History*.

BENTLEY, Gladys (1907–1960). African-American pianist and blues singer. Born Aug 12, 1907, in Philadelphia, Pennsylvania; died of influenza during a flu epidemic, 1960; dau. of Mary Mote Bentley (Trinidadian) and George L. Bentley (American); left home at 16; m. Charles Roberts, 1952 (div.). ❖ One of the most notorious and successful lesbian entertainers of the 1920s and '30s, performed in top hat and white tuxedo at swank NY nightclubs, inventing scandalous lyrics to the tunes of the day; recorded 5 discs for Excelsior Label (1945).

BENTLEY, Helen Delich (1923—). American politician. Born in Ruth, Nevada, Nov 28, 1923; dau. of Michael (miner) and Mary (Kovich) Ivanesvich; attended University of Nevada and George Washington University; University of Missouri School of Journalism, BA, 1944; m. William Roy Bentley (schoolteacher), June 7, 1959. ❖ US Congressional Representative (Jan 3, 1985—Jan 3, 1995), began a long association with the Baltimore *Sun* (1945), as a reporter specializing in labor matters; became the 1st woman to cover an American Federation of Labor convention (1947); began writing and producing a weekly tv show, *The Port that Built a City and State*, for a Baltimore station (1950); after serving as maritime editor at the *Sun* (1952–68), with her "Around the Waterfront" column syndicated in 15 newspapers, was appointed chair of the Federal Maritime Commission by President Richard Nixon (1969); as a Republican from Maryland, elected to US House of Representatives (1984); served 4 consecutive terms, during which she was a member of the Committee on Merchant Marine and Fisheries, the Committee on Public Works and Transportation, the Budget Committee and the Select Committee on Aging; continued her efforts as an advocate of a more powerful American merchant marine. ❖ See also *Women in World History*.

BENTLEY, Irene (d. 1940). American actress and singer. Died in Baltimore, Maryland, June 3, 1940, age 70; aunt of actress Irene Bentley (1904–1965); m. J.T. Sothoron; m. Henry B. Smith (librettist). ❖ Made stage debut in *Little Christopher* (1895); became a popular actress on both sides of the Atlantic, starring or featured in *The Merry World, The Belle of New York, The Rounders, The Strollers, The Wild Rose, The Girl from Dixie* and *The Belle of Mayfair*.

BENTLEY, Irene (1904–1965). American actress. Born Nov 12, 1904, in New York, NY; died Nov 1965, in Palm Beach, Florida; niece of Harry B. Smith (composer) and Irene Bentley (actress); m. Kenneth Niemann (div.); m. Richard Hemingway, 1935; m. George S. Kent (div.). ❖ Appeared in such films as *My Weakness, Smoky* and *Frontier Marshal*.

BENTLEY, Muriel (1917–1999). American ballet dancer. Name variations: Muriel S. Bentley. Born June 26, 1917, in New York, NY; died Mar 8, 1999, in Los Angeles, California. ❖ Performed with José Greco touring company; joined Metropolitan Opera Ballet in NY (1938); performed in Fokine Ballet's concerts at Lewisohn Stadium; danced with Ballet Theater in New York for 15 years, creating roles in Antony Tudor's *Pillar of Fire* (1942) and Agnes de Mille's *Tally-Ho* (1944) and *Fall River Legend* (1948); performed in Jerome Robbins' *Fancy Free* (1944) and *Interplay* (1945); on Broadway, was a principal dancer in *Call Me Madam* (1950–52) and Anita in *West Side Story* (1957–59).

BENTLEY, Phyllis (1894–1977). English novelist. Born Phyllis Eleanor Bentley in Halifax, Yorkshire, England, Nov 19, 1894; died in Halifax,

June 27, 1977; dau. of Eleanor (Kettlewell) Bentley and Joseph Edwin Bentley (cloth manufacturer and mill owner); educated at Cheltenham Ladies' College, BA, 1914; never married; no children. ❖ Writer of regional novels of life in West Riding, published *Environment* and *The Infamous Bertha* to modest sales (1922); began to lecture effectively on the regional novel, an area in which she was considered a new talent; when her greatest success, *Inheritance,* was published (1932), her reputation as a West Riding novelist was secure; also wrote *The Spinner of the Years* (1928), *The Partnership* (1928), *Trio* (1930), *A Modern Tragedy* (1934), *Sleep in Peace* (1938), *Take Courage* (1940), *Manhold* (1941), *Rise of Henry Morcar* (1947), *Some Observations on the Art of Narrative* (1947), *Life Story* (1948), *Quorum* (1951) and *Tales of West Riding* (1974). ❖ See also *"O Dreams, O Destinations": An Autobiography* (Gollancz, 1963); and *Women in World History.*

BENTLEY, Ursula (1945–2004). English novelist. Born Ursula Mary Bentley, Sept 18, 1945, in England; died of cancer, age 58, April 7, 2004, in Suffolk, England; sister of Paul Bentley (actor, librettist); attended Manchester University; m. Alan Bruce Thompson (geologist, div.); children: Alexis and Ishbel Verena Thompson. ❖ Became a publishing sensation with 1st novel, *The Natural Order* (1983); also wrote *Private Accounts* (1986), *The Angel of Twickenham* (1996) and *The Sloping Experience* (1999).

BENTOS, Annita (c. 1821–1849). *See Garibaldi, Anita.*

BENTUM, Cornelia van (1965—). Dutch swimmer. Born Aug 12, 1965. ❖ Won an Olympic bronze medal in Moscow (1980), a silver medal at Los Angeles (1984), and a silver medal at Seoul (1988), all in the 4 x 100-meter freestyle relay.

BENTZEN, Th. (1840–1907). *See Blanc, Marie Thérèse.*

BENZELL, Mimi (1922–1970). American actress and operatic singer. Born 1922; died Dec 23, 1970, in Manhasset, NY; m. Walter Gould. ❖ As a member of the Metropolitan Opera (1944–50), sang 60 roles; became a nightclub performer and appeared on Broadway in *Milk and Honey;* hosted a daily radio show.

BENZONI, Juliette (1920—). French romance-fiction writer. Born Oct 30, 1920, in France; grew up in Saint-Germain-des-Prés; m. Maurice Gallois (Dijon doctor); children: 2. ❖ Published over 60 historical romance novels, many of which have been translated; writings include *Catherine, ma vie* (1967) and *Marianne et l'inconnu de Toscane* (1971).

BEN ZVI, Rachel Yanait (1886–1979). First lady of Israel. Born Rachel Yanait in Russia in 1886; died 1979; m. Itzhak Ben Zvi (2nd president of Israel). ❖ Co-founded the Poalei Zion movement in Russia (1906); came to Eretz Israel (1908), where she established a Hebrew high school and the country's 1st socialist journal, *Ahdut;* was often a delegate to World Zionist Congresses; was first lady of Israel (1952–63); with husband, founded the Shomer, Israel's 1st defense force; after WWII, became known as an educator of both female agricultural workers and youth; wrote *Before Golda,* the biography of Manya Shochat (1976). ❖ See also autobiography *Anu Olim* (1959) (trans. into English as *Coming Home,* 1964); and *Women in World History.*

BERANGER, Clara (1886–1956). American screenwriter and director. Name variations: Clara De Mille. Born Clara Strouse, Jan 14, 1886, in Baltimore, Maryland; died Sept 10, 1956, in Hollywood, California; attended Goucher College; m. Albert Berwanger (div.); m. William C. De Mille (1878–1955, film director), 1928; children: (1st m.) Frances Beranger (actress). ❖ Screenwriter for 3 decades, arrived in Hollywood after having worked as a successful New York City journalist; wrote scenarios for silent-film companies like Vitagraph and Edison; for "talkies," wrote primarily for MGM and Pathé; films include *Tale of Two Cities* (1917), *Miss Lulu Bett* (1921), *Sheltered Daughters* (1921), *Clarence* (1922), *The Fast Set* (1924), *Icebound* (1924), *Men and Women* (1925), *Don Juan's Three Nights* (1926), *Craig's Wife* (1928), *His Double Life* (1933) and *Social Register* (1934); also authored *Writing for the Screen* (1950), long considered a classic on the subject. ❖ See also *Women in World History.*

BERBER, Anita (1899–1928). German dancer. Born into a middle-class family in Leipzig in 1899 (some sources cite 1898); died of TB and drug addiction in 1928; dau. of Felix Berber (concertmaster of the Leipzig Gewandhaus Orchestra). ❖ Dancer who epitomized the decadent spirit of the Berlin cabaret scene of the Weimar Republic, moved to Berlin (1918); quickly became a celebrity, 1st appearing in a Rudolf Nelson revue, dancing the Shimmy dressed in a dinner jacket; gravitated toward *Nacktballet,* instantly becoming a superstar; in chalk-white makeup and generally in the nude, danced uninhibitedly at such night spots as the White Mouse; became known as "Queen of the Bohemians." ❖ See also (in German) Lothar Fischer, *Tanz zwischen Rausch und Tod: Anita Berber 1918–1929 in Berlin;* (West German film) *Anita—Tänze des Lasters,* directed by Rosa von Praunheim (1988); and *Women in World History.*

BERBERIAN, Cathy (1925–1983). American singer and composer. Born Catherine Berberian, July 4, 1925, in Attleboro, Massachusetts, of Armenian parentage; died Mar 6, 1983, in Rome, Italy; attended Columbia University and New York University (1942–43); m. Luciano Berio (composer and teacher of music), 1950 (div. 1966). ❖ Known for her agile soprano voice and striking stage presence, was married to composer Luciano Berio, who wrote many works for her, including *Circles* (1960), *Sequenza III* (1963) and *Recital* (1971); inspired other composers to write pieces for her, including John Cage, Stravinsky and Henri Pousseur; performed works from a variety of musical styles, from Monteverdi to Lennon-McCartney; also composed music, including *Stripsody* (1966) and *Morsicat(h)y* (1971) for piano.

BERBEROVA, Lalka (1965—). Bulgarian rower. Born June 11, 1965. ❖ At Seoul Olympics, won a silver medal in coxless pairs (1988).

BERBEROVA, Nina (1901–1993). Russian-born writer. Name variations: Berbérova. Born Nina Nikolaevna Berberova in St. Petersburg, Russia, Aug 8, 1901; died in Philadelphia, Pennsylvania, Sept 26, 1993; dau. of Nikolai and Natalia (Karaulova) Berberova; lived with the poet Vladislav Khodasevich for over a decade, starting 1922; m. Nikolai Makeyev (div.); m. George Kochevitsky, 1954 (div. 1983). ❖ Writer whose life as an exile was vividly portrayed in her autobiography, *The Italics Are Mine,* grew up in the last years of pre-Bolshevik Russian literary and artistic culture; left Russia (1922) after Communist takeover, living mostly in Paris (1920s–30s); existed in near-poverty, at the same time writing novels that remained unpublished in France; survived WWII, hiding in French countryside; immigrated to US (1950); had successful academic career at Yale and Princeton universities (1958–71); visited Russia (1989); became famous in English-speaking countries in later years; wrote several books, including her bestselling autobiography, collection of poetry, biography of Moura Budberg, and history of Russian Freemasonry in 20th century; also wrote *The Tattered Cloak and Other Novels* (trans. by Marian Schwartz, 1991) and *The Ladies from St. Petersburg* (trans. by Schwartz, 1998). Made a Chevalier dans l'Ordre des Arts et des Lettres in France (1989). ❖ See also *Women in World History.*

BERBIE, Jane (1931—). French mezzo-soprano. Born May 6, 1931, in Villefranche-de-Lauragais, France; studied at Conservatory in Toulouse. ❖ One of the most popular mezzo-sopranos in mid-20th century, was a natural for ingenue parts and "trouser" roles in comic operas; made operatic debut in Ravel's *L'Enfant et les sortilèges* at La Scala (1958); came to prominence as the young wife in Ravel's *L'heure espagnole ;* joined the Paris Opera (1959), debuting as Mercedes in *Carmen;* was a stand-out in soubrette roles of Zerlina in *Don Giovanni,* Despina in *Cosi fan tutte* and Marcellina in *Nozze di Figaro,* and excelled as Rosina in *The Barber of Seville.*

BERENDT, Rachel (d. 1957). French stage star. Name variations: Rachel Bérendt. Born Monique Arkell in Paris, France; died Jan 19, 1957, in Paris; dau. of Henry V. Arkell and Rosy (Robertson) Arkell; granddau. of T.W. Robertson (playwright); m. Pierre Fresnay (actor) 1917 (div. 1919). ❖ Made stage debut in Paris at the Odéon in the role in *Pamela Giraud* (1918); made NY debut as Celie in *L'Aventurière* (1922), followed by *Le Duel;* played leads at the Odéon (1924–29); made London debut in *Phèdre* (1925), followed by an engagement at the Old Vic in her grandfather's play *Caste;* back in France, appeared in *Chaud et froid, Le Témoin, Le Cid, Le Mainson Monestier* and the title role in *Judith;* toured in classical plays in Brazil and Argentina (1936–38); also appeared in films.

BERENGARE. *Variant of Berengaria.*

BERENGARIA (1194–1221). Queen of Denmark. Name variations: Berengaria Henriques, Enriques or Enriquez; Berengaria of Portugal; Bengerd of Portugal; (Span.) Berenguela. Born 1194; died Mar 27, 1221, in Ringsted, Denmark; dau. of Sancho I, king of Portugal (r. 1185–1211 or 1212), and Douce of Aragon (1160–1198), queen of

Portugal; became 2nd wife of Valdemar also known as Waldemar II the Victorious, king of Denmark (r. 1202–1241), 1213; children: Sophia of Denmark (1217–1248); and 3 kings of Denmark—Eric IV Ploughpenny (1216–1250), king of Denmark (r. 1241–1250); Abel (r. 1250–1252); and Christopher I (r. 1252–1259). Waldemar II's 1st wife was Dagmar of Bohemia (d. 1212).

BERENGARIA OF CASTILE (1180–1246). Queen of Leon. Name variations: Berengeria, Berengare; (Spanish) Berenguela. Born in 1180 in Castile; died Nov 8, 1246, in Castile; dau. of Alphonso VIII, king of Castile and Leòn (d. 1214), and Eleanor of Castile (1162–1214, dau. of Eleanor of Aquitaine); sister of Blanche of Castile (1188–1252) and Urraca of Castile (1186–1220); m. Conrad II, duke of Swabia, 1188 (annulled); became 2nd wife of Alphonso IX (1171–1230), king of Leòn, 1197 (annulled in 1204); children: (2nd m.) Ferdinand III (St. Ferdinand, 1199–1252), king of Castile (r. 1217–1252) and Leon (r. 1230–1252); Berengaria of Castile (b. around 1199, who m. John I de Brienne); Constanza of Castile (1200–1242); Leonor (1202–1202); Alfonse de Castilla (c. 1204–1272). ❖ Acted as regent of Castile for younger brother Henry (1214–17); inherited kingdom but abdicated in favor of son, Ferdinand III; when former husband Alphonso XI, king of Leòn, died (1230), aided her son in inheriting his throne; continued to advise son on matters of state until her death. ❖ See also *Women in World History.*

BERENGARIA OF CASTILE (b. around 1199). Empress of Constantinople. Name variations: Infanta of Castile; Queen of Jerusalem. Born c. 1199; death date unknown; dau. of Berengaria of Castile (1180–1246) and Alphonso IX, king of Leòn; m. John I de Brienne, king of Jerusalem (r. 1210–1225), emperor of Constantinople (r. 1228–1237), in 1224; children: Alfons d'Acre, count of Eu; Jean de Brienne (d. 1296); Louis de Brienne; possibly Marie de Brienne.

BERENGARIA OF NAVARRE (c. 1163–c. 1230). Queen of England. Name variations: Berengare, Berengeria. Born in Pamplona, in the kingdom of Navarre, c. 1163 (some sources cite 1165); died after 1230 in l'Epau Abbey, near Le Mans, France; dau. of Sancho VI the Wise, king of Navarre (r. 1150–1194), and Sancha of Castile and Leon (d. 1179); daughter-in-law of Eleanor of Aquitaine; m. Richard I the Lionheart, king of England (r. 1189–1199), May 12, 1191, in Cyprus; no children. ❖ Spanish princess who reigned as queen of England with Richard the Lionheart, though she never set foot on English soil. ❖ See also *Women in World History.*

BERENGARIA OF PROVENCE (1108–1149). Queen of Castile. Name variations: Berengeria, Berengare; (Spanish) Berenguela of Barcelona. Born 1108; died Feb 3, 1149, in Valencia; dau. of Raymond Berengar I, count of Provence, also known as Ramòn Berenguer IV, conde de Barcelona (r. 1131–1162), and Douce I, countess of Provence; m. 2nd husband Alphonso VII (1105–1157), king of Leòn and Castile (r. 1126–1157), 1128; children: Sancho III (b. 1134), king of Castile (r. 1157–1158); Constance of Castile (d. 1160, who m. Louis VII, king of France); Garcia (died young); Sancha of Castile and Leon (d. 1179, who m. Sancho VI, king of Navarre); Ferdinand II (1137–1188), king of Leon. Following Berengaria's death, Alphonso married Ryksa of Poland (d. 1185); he also had a daughter, Urraca of Castile (d. 1179), with Gontrada Perez.

BERENGERIA. *Variant of Berengaria.*

BERENGUELA. *Spanish variant of Berengaria.*

BERENGUER, Amanda (1924—). Uruguayan poet. Born 1924 in Montevideo, Uruguay. ❖ Writings include *El través de los tiempos que llevan a la gran calma* (1940), *Elegía por la muerte de Paul Valéry* (1945), *El río* (1952), *La invitación* (1957), *Contracanto* (1961), *Quehaceres e invenciones* (1962), *Declaración conjunta* (1964), *Materia prima* (1966) and *Composición de lugar* (1976). Won prize from Universidad de la República for *Los signos sobre la mesa* (1986).

BERENICE (c. 35 BCE–?). Jewish princess who was the mother of Herod Agrippa I. Name variations: Bernice. Pronunciation: Ber-e-NEE-kay. Born into Herodian family c. 35 BCE; death date unknown; dau. of Salome (sister of Herod the Great) and Costobar (executed about 25 BCE after he was probably found guilty of plotting with Parthians against Herod's life); m. Aristobulus (son of Herod the Great) c. 15 BCE; m. Theudion (brother of Herod's wife Doris, who was also the mother of Antipater); children: (1st m.) 3 sons, Aristobulus (who m. Jotape, dau. of the king of Emesa), Herod (became king of Chalcis), and Agrippa (born c. 10 BCE and became Herod Agrippa I, king of Judea); and 2 daughters,

Herodias (who would take as her 2nd husband, Herod Antipas, son of Herod the Great by Malthace, another of his 10 wives), and Mariamne II. ❖ Born into a court filled with intrigue and rivalries, married Aristobulus (c. 15 BCE), a son of Herod the Great; with Aristobulus, had 5 children, one of whom, Herod Agrippa, was sent to Rome to be educated and make political connections, and subsequently became king of Judea; after intense court machinations (7 BCE), her husband and his full-brother (Alexander) were executed by Herod the Great for treason, then Herod married her off to Theudion, the brother of Herod's wife. ❖ See also *Women in World History.*

BERENICE (fl. 1st c. CE?). See Veronica.

BERENICE (28 CE–after 80 CE). Jewish princess. Name variations: Julia Berenice; Bernice. Pronunciation: Ber-e-NEE-kay. Born in 28 CE; died after 80 CE; eldest dau. of Herod Agrippa I and Cypros (both grand-children of Herod the Great); m. Marcus Julius Alexander (scion of one of Alexandria's [in Egypt] most prominent Jewish families), in 41; m. her uncle King Herod of Chalcis, in 46 (died 48); lived with brother Agrippa II, who was Herod's successor, until 53; m. Polemon, priest-king of Olba in Anatolian Cilicia; became intimate with Titus (Roman general and future emperor) during period of his Jewish conquests (67–70). ❖ Was 1st married to Marcus Julius Alexander, and subsequently to King Herod of Chalcis (her uncle) until his death; thereafter, lived incestuously with brother Herod Agrippa, and for a time was married to Polemon, the Priest/King of Olba in Cilicia; soon returned to the embrace of her brother and remained active in the affairs of Judea; a supporter of Rome against Judea during the period of the Jewish revolt, met and bedazzled the future Roman emperor Titus, son of Vespasian; lived with Titus in Rome as his mistress, until popular opinion forced him to reject her before his accession to the Roman throne. ❖ See also *Women in World History.*

BERENICE I (c. 345 BCE–c. 275 BCE). Macedonian-born queen of Egypt. Born in Macedonia c. 345 BCE; died c. 275 BCE; probably dau. of Lagus (Macedonian aristocrat) and Antigone (niece of Antipater, who was well-connected in Macedonian circles); m. a Macedonian named Philip (widowed); m. half-brother Ptolemy I Soter (d. 283); children: (1st m.) Magas (eventually king of Cyrene) and several daughters, including Antigone (who m. Pyrrhus, king of Epirus) and Theoxena (who m. Agathocles, tyrant of Syracuse); (2nd m.) Arsinoe II Philadelphus (c. 316–270 BCE); Ptolemy II Philadelphus (r. 285–247 BCE). ❖ Widowed after 1st marriage, attached herself to entourage of 2nd cousin, Eurydice (fl. 321 BCE) when that heiress married Ptolemy I (c. 322); not long after, was favored by Ptolemy, so much so that he took her as a 2nd wife and began to favor her children over those he fathered with Eurydice; her children from both marriages would rule as kings, queens and the consorts of tyrants for various lengths of time in Cyrene, Epirus, Macedonia, Thrace, Anatolia, Sicily and Egypt; her son Ptolemy II eventually succeeded his father to the throne of Egypt over the claims of the older Ptolemy Ceraunus, Ptolemy I's son by Eurydice; loved and greatly honored by her husband in life, her stature was in no way diminished in death, for Ptolemy II instituted a cult which worshipped both her and Ptolemy I as "savior gods"; associated with the persona of the goddess Aphrodite, her divine status thereafter religiously helped to legitimize the Ptolemaic dynasty in the eyes its subjects. ❖ See also *Women in World History.*

BERENICE II OF CYRENE (c. 273–221 BCE). Queen of Egypt. Name variations: Berenice of Cyrene. Pronunciation: Ber-e-NEE-kay. Born c. 273 BCE; died c. 221 BCE; dau. of Magas, ruler of Cyrene (and stepson of Ptolemy I of Egypt) and Apama (dau. of the Seleucid king Antiochus I); betrothed to Ptolemy III, Euergetes, of Egypt; m. Demetrius (half-brother of Macedonian king Antigonus I); m. Ptolemy III (died 222 BCE); children: (2nd m.) 5, including Ptolemy IV, Magas, Alexander, an unnamed son, and a daughter, Arsinoe III (who m. her brother Ptolemy IV and shared his throne). ❖ Betrothed to Ptolemy III of Egypt as part of a compromise which allowed her father to claim royal status while remaining under umbrella of Egyptian power; in actuality, was married at mother's insistence to a Demetrius, the half-brother of the Macedonian king, who himself was an ally of the Seleucids; caught mother in bed with Demetrius and had him executed; arranged her own marriage to Ptolemy III and thus aligned Cyrene with Egypt; had a happy marriage and was co-ruler of Egypt, providing with Ptolemy more or less competent leadership for both Egypt and Cyrene until he died (222); shared the throne briefly with oldest son Ptolemy IV; when Ptolemy IV started exhibiting hedonistic tenancies, began to favor another son, Magas, as Egypt's king; was executed by command of Ptolemy IV. ❖ See also *Women in World History.*

BERENICE III (c. 115–80 BCE). *See Cleopatra Berenice III.*

BERENICE IV (fl. 79–55 BCE). **Egyptian queen.** Born after 79 BCE; died in 55 BCE; reigned between 58 and 55; eldest child of Ptolemy XII Theos (or Auletes) and Cleopatra V Tryphaena; older sister of the famous Cleopatra VII; briefly m. to a man nicknamed Cybiosactes (fishmonger) by the Alexandrians; briefly m. to Archelaus; no children. ❖ Grew up at a dissolute court, which decreased in popularity among its subjects as time went on; when father Ptolemy XII angered his subjects who expelled him in favor of her (58), was thrust into a dynastic struggle which only ended after Ptolemy's bribery spurred Rome to restore him to his throne; was quickly put to death at her father's command. ❖ See also *Women in World History.*

BERENICE SYRA (c. 280–246 BCE). **Queen of the Seleucid Empire.** Born c. 280 BCE; murdered in 246 BCE; dau. of Ptolemy II Philadelphus and Arsinoe I of Egypt (fl. 280 BCE); m. Antiochus II, king of the Seleucid Empire, 252 BCE; children: 1 son. ❖ Grew up at a court dominated by father and his 2nd wife Arsinoë II Philadelphus; doted on by a loving father, was married to Antiochus II, king of the Seleucid Empire, after Egypt had fought the Seleucids twice for control of the harbors of the eastern Mediterranean (Antiochus had to reject his 1st wife Laodice and two sons, whom he loved, so as to establish Berenice as his one and only legitimate queen); after giving birth to a son, was left by Antiochus who returned to his 1st wife; when diplomatic pressure was applied for Antiochus to return to Berenice and Laodice had Antiochus poisoned and Berenice's child kidnapped, sought to protect her son in vain; was executed under Laodice's orders; her murder sparked an aggressive reaction in Ptolemy III (her brother), who for vengeance, began to ravage Seleucid possessions, thus beginning a 3rd war between Egypt and Syria. ❖ See also *Women in World History.*

BERENIKE. *Variant of Berenice.*

BERENS-TOTENOHL, Josefa (1891–1969). **German poet and novelist.** Name variations: Josefa Berens Totenohl. Born Mar 30, 1891, in Grevenstein, Germany; died June 6, 1969, in Meschede, Germany. ❖ Novels, which draw from German folk tradition, include *Der Femhof* (1934), *Frau Magdlene* (1935), *Der Fels* (1943) and *Im Moor* (1944).

BERENSON, Alys (1866–1951). *See Russell, Alys Smith.*

BERENSON, Berry (1948–2001). **American fashion photographer and actress.** Born Berenthia Berenson, 1948, in New York, NY; died Sept 11, 2001, on American Airlines flight 11 that crashed into the World Trade Center; dau. of Marquesa Gogo Berenson di Cacciopooti (also seen as Marchesa Cicciapouti di Guilliano); grandniece of Bernard Berenson; granddau. of Elsa Schiaparelli; sister of Marisa Berenson (actress); m. Tony Perkins (actor), 1973 (died 1992); children: 2 sons. ❖ Began career at *Vogue* and *Harper's Bazaar;* photographed many Hollywood stars, including Tuesday Weld, Ray Brock, Pilar Crespi and Candice Bergen, and did covers for *Life;* films include *Remember My Name, Winter Kills* and *Cat People;* appeared on tv in "Scruples" (1980).

BERENSON, Marisa (1946—). **American model and actress.** Born Feb 15, 1946, in NYC; dau. of Marquesa Gogo Berenson di Cacciopooti (also seen as Marchesa Cicciapouti di Guilliano); grandniece of Bernard Berenson; granddau. of Elsa Schiaparelli; sister of Berry Berenson. ❖ Films include *Death in Venice, Cabaret* and *Barry Lyndon;* wrote a fashion book *Dressing Up,* with photos by sister Berry Berenson.

BERENSON, Mary (1864–1944). **American art historian.** Name variations: Mary Pearsall Smith; (pseudonym) Mary Logan. Born Mary Smith, 1864, in Philadelphia, Pennsylvania; died in Italy, 1944; dau. of Hannah (Whitall) Smith (1832–1911) and Robert Smith (Quaker preacher); sister of Alys Smith Russell (1st wife of Bertrand Russell); attended Smith College and Harvard Annex (later Radcliffe College); m. Frank Costelloe (London barrister) Sept 3, 1885 (died 1899); m. Bernard Berenson (art scholar), Dec 29, 1900; children: (1st m.) 2 daughters, Ray Costelloe (Ray Strachey, 1887–1940) and Karin Costelloe (who m. Adrian Stephen, brother of Virginia Woolf). ❖ Art expert whose 50-year union with Bernard Berenson was a tumultuous one, and whose villa, I Tatti, northeast of Florence, was visited by some of the most celebrated personalities of the period, including Edith Wharton, Gertrude Stein, Gabriele D'Annunzio, John Maynard Keynes and

Isabella Gardner; an invaluable partner to her husband, both in his business ventures and as the editor of almost all his writings, established her own reputation as an art critic with publication of her *Guide to the Italian Pictures at Hampton Court* (1894) and various other magazine articles and reviews; also wrote *A Modern Pilgrimage* (1933), chronicling her travels in Palestine and Syria. ❖ See also Barbara Strachey and Jayne Samuels, eds. *Mary Berenson: A Self-Portrait from Her Diaries and Letters* (Norton, 1983); and *Women in World History.*

BERENSON, Senda (1868–1954). **Jewish-American basketball innovator and physical educator.** Born Senda Valvrojenski in Biturmansk (or Butrimonys), Lithuania, Mar 19, 1868; died 1954; sister of Bernard Berenson (noted art collector); attended Boston Normal School of Gymnastics (1890–92); m. Hebert Vaughn Abbott (English professor at Smith College), June 15, 1911. ❖ Began teaching physical education at Smith College (1892), where she was to lead that department of the all-female university for 19 years; modified and wrote the rules for women's basketball which remained in use until 1960s, which included a court divided into 3 zones which kept players from crossing the dividing lines; chaired American Association for the Advancement of Physical Education (AAAPE) Committee on Basketball for Girls for 12 years; became director of physical education at Mary A. Burnham School in Northampton, Massachusetts, where she would remain until her retirement in 1921. Inducted into Naismith Memorial Hall of Fame and International Women's Sports Hall of Fame (1984). ❖ See also *Women in World History.*

BERÈS, Pervenche (1957—). **French politician.** Name variations: Pervenche Beres. Born Mar 10, 1957, in Paris, France. ❖ Served as adviser to Lauren Fabius, president of the National Assembly (1988–92) and Socialist Party national secretary responsible for development cooperation (1993–95); as a European Socialist, elected to 4th and 5th European Parliament (EP, 1994–99, 1999–2004); named chair of the French Socialist delegation in the EP (1997).

BERESFORD, Anne (1919—). **British poet.** Born Anne Beresford, Sept 10, 1919, in Redhill, Surrey, England; dau. of Richard Beresford and Margaret Kent Beresford; m. Michael Hamburger (poet), 1951, remarried him, 1974. ❖ Worked as BBC broadcaster, teacher, musician, and actress; collections of poetry include *Walking Without Moving* (1967), *The Lair* (1968), *The Courtship* (1972) and *The Sele of the Morning* (1988); collections with husband include *Struck by Apollo* (1965) and *Words* (1977).

BERESFORD, Monica Massy- (1894–1945). *See Massy-Beresford, Monica.*

BERESFORD-HOWE, Constance (1922—). **Canadian novelist.** Name variations: Constance Beresford Howe. Born Nov 10, 1922, in Montreal, Canada; educated at McGill and Brown universities. ❖ Taught literature at McGill and Ryerson Polytechnical Institute; writings include *The Unreasoning Heart* (1946), *Of This Day's Journey* (1947), *My Lady Greensleeves* (1955), *The Book of Eve* (1973), *A Population of One* (1977), *The Marriage Bed* (1981), *Night Studies* (1985), *Prospero's Daughter* (1988) and *A Serious Widow* (1993).

BERETRUDE (d. 620). **Queen of Neustria and the Franks.** Name variations: Bérétrude; Berthetrude; Bertrude. Died in 620 (some sources cite 610); m. Chlothar also known as Clotaire or Lothair II (584–629), king of Neustria (r. 584–629), king of the Franks (r. 613–629); children: Dagobert I (c. 606–639), king of Austrasia (r. 623–628), king of the Franks (r. 629–639); Caribert or Charibert II (606–632), king of Aquitaine (r. 629–632).

BERETTA, Caterina (1839–1911). **Italian ballet dancer and teacher.** Name variations: also seen erroneously as Catarina Beretta. Born 1839 in Milan, Italy; died Jan 1911 in Milan. ❖ Studied at Teatro alla Scala school of dance in Milan and performed with the company throughout her career; danced in numerous works by Pasquale Borri, including *Rodolfo* (1858) and *Fiamella* (1866); performed in premiere productions of Lucien Petipa's *Rilla, ossia la Fête de Provence* (1855), Paul Taglioni's *Léonilda* (1869), and Hyppolyte Monplaisir's *Brahma* (1870); served a directorship at Maryinsky Theater in St. Petersburg for short period (1877); taught classes at school of Teatro alla Scala for many years, for such students as Ria Teresa Legnani and Marie Giuri, who later danced Swanilda in US premiere of *Coppélia* at Metropolitan Opera.

BEREZHNAYA, Elena (1977—). **Russian pairs skater.** Name variations: Yelena Berezhnaya or Berezhnaia. Born Oct 11, 1977, in Stavropol, Russia. ❖ With partner Oleg Shliyachov, represented Latvia at the Lillehammer Games, placing 8th (1994); with partner Anton

Sikharulidze, placed 1st at World championships (1998, 1999) and 2nd (2001); won European championships (1998, 2001) and Russian nationals (1999–2001); won a silver medal at Nagano Olympics (1998); at Salt Lake City Olympics, won a gold medal but had to share the podium with Canadian pairs partners Jamie Sale and Davie Pelletier (2002), after a judging scandal brought about the IOC decision for a 2nd gold-medal award.

BEREZHNAYA, Lyubov (1955—). See *Odinokova-Berezhnaya, Lyubov.*

BERG, Aina (b. 1902). Swedish swimmer. Born Jan 7, 1902, in Sweden. ❖ Won Olympic bronze medals in the 4 x 100-meter freestyle relay in Antwerp (1920) and Paris (1924).

BERG, Edith (d. 1931). American early airplane passenger. Name variations: Lena Berg; Mrs. Hart Berg. Born in Aledo, Illinois; died Mar 1, 1931; m. Hart O. Berg (European business manager for Wright brothers). ❖ During a promotional exhibit in Le Mans, France, flew with Wilbur Wright over a racetrack to show the Wright plane's dependability for licensing in that country (Oct 7, 1908). During the 2 min. and 3 sec. flight, a wire was used to tether the plane to a rock while she and Wright flew at an altitude of 50 feet.

BERG, Gertrude (1899–1966). American actress, producer, and author. Born Gertrude Edelstein, Oct 3, 1899, in New York, NY; died Sept 14, 1966, in New York, NY; dau. of Jacob and Diana Netta (Goldstein) Edelstein; m. Lewis Berg, Dec 1, 1918; children: Harriet and Cherney Robert. ❖ Famed for her creation "The Goldbergs," made a career playing the loquacious, lovable Jewish housewife Molly Goldberg; premiered the radio broadcast of "The Rise of the Goldbergs" (1929), which was shortened to "The Goldbergs" (1931); wrote, acted in, and produced over 5,000 radio scripts featuring her fictitious family from the Bronx; starred in her own stage play *Me and Molly* (1948); launched tv version of "The Goldbergs" (1949); appeared in film *Molly* (1950); won Tony for her performance in long-running play, *A Majority of One* (1959), then starred in *Dear Me, the Sky is Falling* (1963). ❖ See also memoirs, *Molly and Me* (1961); and *Women in World History.*

BERG, Mrs. Hart (d. 1931). See *Berg, Edith.*

BERG, Helene (b. 1906). German political activist. Name variations: Lene Berg; Lene Ring. Born in Mannheim, Germany, April 4, 1906; attended Lenin School in Moscow, 1931–32. ❖ One of the very few women to play a significant role in the leadership of the German Democratic Republic (GDR), trained to be a dressmaker; joined the Socialist Worker's Youth League (1921); joined the Communist Party of Germany (KPD, 1927); was involved in underground activities against the Nazis (1933–35); immigrated to Soviet Union (1935), but barely escaped the gulag; returned to Germany (1946); was active in propaganda and ideological work for Socialist Unity Party (SED); served as director of Institute for Social Sciences, Berlin (1951–58); was a candidate and member of Central Committee of SED (1958–89); was active in political life of GDR until collapse of Communist rule (1989). ❖ See also *Women in World History.*

BERG, Jacomina van den (1909—). Dutch gymnast. Born Dec 28, 1909. ❖ At Amsterdam Olympics, won a gold medal in team all-around (1928).

BERG, Laura (1975—). American softball player. Born Jan 6, 1975, Santa Fe Springs, California; attended Fresno State University. ❖ Outfielder, won team World championship (2002); won team gold medals at Atlanta Olympics (1996), Sydney Olympics (2000) and Athens Olympics (2004).

BERG, Leila (1917—). English children's writer and editor. Born 1917 in Salford, Lancashire, England; children: son and daughter. ❖ Writer and editor of books for and about children which highlight urban and working-class environments, was raised in a Jewish immigrant neighborhood; started career as a journalist for *The Daily Worker*; began writing for children after birth of 2nd child; influenced by psychologist Susan Isaacs and by her own children, became interested in children's rights, alternative education and informal teaching methods; wrote many well-loved children's books, such as *A Box for Benny* (1958) and the "Nippers" series for primary-school readers; wrote the influential *Look at Kids* (1972), illustrated with black-and-white photographs of urban life, and *Rising Hill: Death of a Comprehensive School* (1968); worked as children's book editor at Metheun, then Macmillan. Received Eleanor Farjeon Medal (1973) for services to children's literature. ❖ See also autobiographical *Flickerbook* (Granta, 1997).

BERG, Lena (d. 1931). See *Berg, Edith.*

BERG, Lisbeth (1948—). See *Korsmo, Lisbeth.*

BERG, Patty (1918—). American golfer. Born Patricia Jane Berg, Feb 13, 1918, in Minneapolis, Minnesota; never married. ❖ Foremost American golfer and 1st president of the LPGA, won 29 amateur events (1934–41) and over 60 professional golf tournaments (1941–62), including 15 majors; played in the Curtis Cup (1936, 1938); served as a lieutenant in the Marine Corps during WWII; won 3 Vare Trophies for the lowest average score (1953, 1955, and 1956). Named Associated Press Woman Athlete of the Year (1938, 1943, 1955); received Bob Jones Award (1963); given Ben Hogan Award for playing despite a handicap (1975); received Herb Graffis Award for contributions to golf as recreation (1981). ❖ See also *Women in World History.*

BERGAGLI, Luisa (1703–1779). See *Bergalli, Luisa.*

BERGALLI, Luisa (1703–1779). Italian poet and playwright. Name variations: Luisa Bergalli Gozzi; Luisa Bergagli; Contessa Luisa Bergagli Gozzi; Irminda Partenide. Born Irminda Partenide, April 15, 1703, in Venice, Italy, into a respectable Piemontese family; died July 18, 1779; m. Gasparo Gozzi, 1738; children: 5. ❖ With husband, unsuccessfully managed Teatro Sant'Angelo (1747); writings include *Agide* (1725), *L'Elensà* (1730), *Le avventure del poeta* (1730) and *Teba* (1738).

BERGANZA, Teresa (1934—). Spanish mezzo-soprano. Born Mar 16, 1934, in Madrid, Spain; studied with Lola Rodriguez Aragon; m. Felix Lavilla (composer). ❖ Won a singing prize in Madrid (1954); debuted at Aix-en-Provence Festival as Dorabella in *Cosi fan tutte* (1957); debuted at Piccola Scala and Glyndebourne (1958); made American debut in Dallas (1958); debuted at Covent Garden (1960) and Metropolitan Opera (1967); specialized in early Italian opera, singing roles by Monteverdi, Purcell, and Handel although later became known for roles by Mozart and Rossini; frequently performed as Rosina in *Il barbiere di Siviglia* (*Barber of Seville*) and as Cinderella. ❖ See also *Women in World History.*

BERGEN, Candice (1946—). American actress. Born Candice Patricia Bergen, May 9, 1946, in Beverly Hills, California; dau. of Edgar Bergen (ventriloquist and radio host) and Frances Bergen (model and actress); sister of Kris Bergen (film and tv editor); attended University of Pennsylvania; m. Louis Malle (film director), 1980 (died 1995); m. Marshall Rose (NY real-estate magnate), 2000; children: Chloe Malle (b. 1985). ❖ Began career as a photographer and model; was a spokesperson for Revlon; came to prominence in screen debut in *The Group* (1966); was the 1st female host of "Saturday Night Live" (1975); starred on tv series "Murphy Brown" (1988–98) and joined cast of "Boston Legal" (2004); other films include *The Sand Pebbles* (1966), *The Day the Fish Came Out* (1967), *Vivre pour vivre* (1967), *The Magus* (1968), *Getting Straight* (1970), *Soldier Blue* (1970), *Carnal Knowledge* (1971), *T.R. Baskin* (1971), *The Wind and the Lion* (1975), *The Domino Principle* (1977), *A Night Full of Rain* (1978), *Oliver's Story* (1978), *Starting Over* (1979), *Rich and Famous* (1981), *Gandhi* (1982), *Stick* (1985), *Miss Congeniality* (2000) and *The In-Laws* (2003).

BERGEN, Larisa (1949—). Soviet volleyball player. Born July 22, 1949, in USSR. ❖ At Montreal Olympics, won a silver medal in team competition (1976).

BERGEN, Nella (1873–1919). American actress and singer. Name variations: Mrs. DeWolf Hopper. Born Dec 2, 1873, in Brooklyn, NY; died 1919; sister of Edith Shayne (actress); m. DeWolf Hopper (div. 1913). ❖ Made earliest appearances as a singer with bandmaster P.S. Gilmore; made NY stage debut in *The Bride Elect* (1898), followed by *The Charlatan, Wang, The Baroness Fiddlesticks, The Free Lance, The Talk of New York* and *He Came from Milwaukee,* among others.

BERGEN, Polly (1929—). American actress, singer, writer and producer. Name variations: Polly Burgin. Born Nellie Paulina Burgin, July 14, 1930, in Knoxville, Tennessee; m. Jerome Courtland (actor), 1954 (div. 1955); m. Freddie Fields, 1956 (div. 1975); m. Jeffrey Endervelt, 1982 (div.) 1990; children: 3 (2 adopted). ❖ At 14, as Polly Burgin, began singing professionally on radio; made film debut as Polly Bergen in *At War with the Army* (1950), followed by *Escape from Fort Bravo, Cape Fear, Move Over Darling* and *A Guide for the Married Man,* among others; on tv, hosted "The Polly Bergen Show" (1957–58) and was a panelist on "To Tell the Truth" (1956–61); appeared as Rhoda Henry on tv miniseries: "The Winds of War" (1983) and "War and Remembrance" (1988); wrote and produced "Leave of Absence" (1994); launched her own cosmetics company (late 1960s) and was co-chair of the National Business Council for the

Equal Rights Amendment. Won Emmy for performance in "The Helen Morgan Story" (1957); nominated as Best Featured Actress for Broadway revival of *Follies* (2001). ❖ See also *Polly's Principles* (1974).

BERGEN, Veritas Leo (1847–1912). *See Troll-Borostyani, Irma von.*

BERGER, Erna (1900–1990). German soprano. Born Oct 19, 1900, in Cossebaude, near Dresden; died June 14, 1990, in Essen; studied with Hertha Boeckel and Melitza Hirzel in Dresden. ❖ Debuted in Dresden as the First Boy in Mozart's *Die Zauberflöte* (*The Magic Flute*) (1925) and was a member of the Dresden Opera (1926–34); sang the role of the Shepherd in *Tannhäuser* at Bayreuth (1929); sang with the Berlin Städtische Oper and the Berlin Staatsoper (1930–53); debuted at Covent Garden (1935); after WWII, was one of the 1st German singers to perform in London and NY, debuting at Metropolitan Opera (1949); retired from opera (1955); continued to concertize until 1964; taught at Hamburg Musikhochschule (1959 on). Awarded German Service Cross (1953, 1976); made honorary member of Berlin Academy of Arts (1980). ❖ See also *Women in World History.*

BERGER, Maria (1956—). Austrian politician. Name variations: Maria Margarethe Berger. Born Aug 19, 1956, in Perg, Austria. ❖ Served as federal chair of Young Socialists (1984–87) and vice-president of the University of Krems (1995–96); member of Perg municipal council (1997—); as a European Socialist, elected to 4th and 5th European Parliament (1994–99, 1999–2004).

BERGER, Nicole (1934–1967). French actress. Born Nicole Gaspey, June 12, 1934, in Paris, France; died in a road accident, April 13, 1967, in Rouen, Seine-Maritime, France. ❖ Leading lady of the French cinema, whose career was cut short by her death at 33, starred with Edwige Feuillère in an adaptation of Colette's novella *Le blé en herbe* (*Game of Love* or *The Ripening Seed*, 1954); other films include *Juliette* (1952), *Le Premier Mai* (1957), *Love is My Profession* (1958), *Les Dragueurs* (also known as *The Young Have No Morals* or *The Chasers*, 1959), and *Tirez sur le pianiste* (*Shoot the Piano Player*, 1962). ❖ See also *Women in World History.*

BERGER, Senta (1941—). Austrian actress. Born May 13, 1941, in Vienna, Austria; m. Michael Verhoeven, 1966; children: Simon Verhoeven (actor, b. 1972). ❖ Made film debut in *Die Unentschuldigte Stunde* (1957); made over 100 films, including *Ramona* (1961), *Frauenarzt Dr. Sibelius* (1962), *Das Testament des Dr. Mabuse* (*The Terror of Dr. Mabuse*, 1962), *The Victors* (1962), *Major Dundee* (1965), *Cast a Giant Shadow* (1966), *The Quiller Memorandum* (1966), *Poppies Are Also Flowers* (1966), *Diabolically Yours* (1967), *The Ambushers* (1967), *Vienna* (1968), *Cuori solitari* (1969), *Roma bene* (1971), *Die Moral der Ruth Halbfass* (1972), *Reigen* (1973), *Cross of Iron* (1977) and *Killing Cars* (1985); often appeared on tv and was an active environmentalist and pacifist. ❖ See also *Women in World History.*

BERGERE, Ouida (1885–1974). American screenwriter and playwright. Name variations: Ouida Fitzmaurice, Ouida Bergère, Ouida Rathbone, Mrs. Basil Rathbone. Born Dec 14, 1885 (some sources cite 1886), in Spain; died Nov 29, 1974, in New York, NY; sister of B.C. Branch; m. Louis Weadock (div.); m. George Fitzmaurice (film director; div.); m. Basil Rathbone (actor), April 18, 1926 (died July 1967); children: Cynthia (adopted, Oct 1939). ❖ Began career as child actor with Shubert Stock Co. in Brooklyn, then played in vaudeville; made Broadway debut in *The Stranger* (1911); appeared as actress in films and collaborated on screenplays with 1st husband, among them *On With the Dance* and *The Cheat* (1920s); wrote screenplays for Paramount, including *Idols of Clay, Bella Donna, Garden of Allah* and *Peter Ibbetson;* during WWI, started a talent agency, with such clients as Alla Nazimova and Richard Barthelmess; following war, wrote screenplays for MGM, Pathe and Paramount, as well as several plays, including *The Vicious Circle, That Woman* and *Sherlock Holmes* (1953).

BERGERE, Valerie (1872–1938). French-born actress and vaudevillian. Born Mar 11 (some sources cite Feb 2), 1872, in Metz, Alsace-Lorraine, France; died Sept 16, 1938, in Hollywood, California; m. Napoleon E. Daignault; m. Herbert Warren. ❖ Made 1st stage appearance in the chorus of the Heinrich Conried Opera company; played 1st English-speaking part in San Francisco in *The Harbor Lights* (1892), followed by *The Journalist;* toured US with many stock companies, then appeared in vaudeville, heading the bill for many years; plays include *Congai, Inspector Kennedy, Penny Arcade, Melody* and *Moon over Mulberry Street.*

BERGERON, Marian (1918–2002). Miss America and singer. Name variations: Marian Bergeron Setzer, Marian Leeds. Born Marian Bergeron in 1918 in West Haven, Connecticut; died Oct 22, 2002, in West Haven, Connecticut; m. Donald Ruhlman (research representative); m. once more. ❖ Named Miss America (1933), representing Connecticut; performed as a band singer with Rudy Vallee, Tommy Dorsey, and Guy Lombardo under stage name Marian Leeds. ❖ See also Frank Deford, *There She Is* (Viking, 1971).

BERGGOLTS, Olga (1910–1975). Russian poet and playwright. Name variations: Ol'ga Fëdorovna Berggól'ts; Olga Fyodorovna Berggolts; Olga Bergholz. Born 1910 in Leningrad, USSR; died 1975; dau. of a Leningrad doctor; briefly married to poet Boris Kornilov (victim of the Stalinist purges in 1939); married once more (died 1942). ❖ First husband shot in purge and second died of starvation during Nazi blockade of Leningrad; imprisoned for 2 years; worked on radio during blockade and helped Anna Akhmátova deliver appeal to citizens; works include fictionalized autobiography *Diurnal Stars* (1959), lyric poetry, children's stories, and plays; published *Collected Works* (1972–73).

BERGGREN, Evy (1934—). Swedish gymnast. Born June 16, 1934. ❖ Won an Olympic gold medal at Helsinki (1952) and a silver medal at Melbourne (1956), both in the teams all-around, portable apparatus.

BERGHAUS, Ruth (1927–1996). German theater and opera director. Born in Dresden, Germany, July 2, 1927; died of cancer at her home in Berlin, Jan 25, 1996; m. Paul Dessau (composer), 1954 (died 1979). ❖ One of postwar Germany's most innovative stage directors, known throughout Europe for her often controversial productions, began career as a dancer, studying at the Palucca School in Dresden (1947–50); became a member of Socialist Unity Party and remained in the German Democratic Republic (GDR) at a time when many artists fled to West Germany; became a choreographer for Berliner Ensemble (1964), then director (*intendantin*, 1971), a post she held until 1977; began directing husband's operas (1960s) and staged operas for East Berlin's Deutsche Staatsoper, including Rossini's *Barber of Seville,* which remained in the repertory for more than 2 decades; other notable productions include *The Abduction from the Seraglio* (1981) and Wagner's *Ring* (1985–87). ❖ See also *Women in World History.*

BERGHMANS, Ingrid (1961—). Belgian judoka. Name variations: Ingrid Vallot. Born Aug 24, 1961, in Koersel, Belgium; m. Marc Vallot (Belgian judoka), 1990. ❖ One of the most successful judokas in the history of the sport, won 4 World titles in open class (1980, 1982, 1984, 1986) and 2 in 72kg (1984 and 1989); also won 4 silver medals and a bronze; won a gold medal at Seoul Olympics (1988), when judo was still a demonstration sport; was European champion at 72kg (1985, 1988, 1989) and open (1983, 1987, 1988); won British Open numerous times, along with Japan's Fukuoka title and Canadian Open title.

BERGHOLZ, Olga (1910–1975). *See Berggolts, Olga.*

BERGMAN, Ingrid (1915–1982). Swedish actress. Born Ingrid Bergman, Aug 29, 1915, in Stockholm, Sweden; died Aug 29, 1982, in London, England; dau. of Justus Samuel Bergman and German-born Friedel (Adler) Bergman; m. Petter Lindstrom (dentist), July 10, 1937; m. Roberto Rossellini (Italian director); m. Lars Schmidt, 1958: children: (1st m.) Pia Lindstrom (b. 1938); (2nd m.) Robertino (b. Feb 2, 1950), and (twin girls) Isabella Rossellini and Isotta Rossellini (b. June 18, 1952). ❖ One of the most beloved, condemned, and beloved-again stars in the history of the silver screen, snagged her 1st film role in the comedy *The Count of the Monk's Bridge* (1934), followed by *Ocean Breakers*—considered one of Sweden's best films of 1935; made 6 films in Sweden in quick succession before coming to prominence in *Intermezzo* (1936); came to Hollywood to do an English remake of *Intermezzo,* then opened on Broadway in *Liliom* (1940); filmed *Adam Had Four Sons* (1941), *Rage in Heaven* (1941) and *Dr. Jekyll and Mr. Hyde* (1941); starred as Maria in *For Whom the Bell Tolls,* for which she was nominated for an Academy Award, followed by the classic, *Casablanca* (both 1943); won Academy Award for Best Actress for *Gaslight* (1944); had one triumph after another with such films as *Spellbound* (1945), *Saratoga Trunk* (1945), *The Bells of St. Mary's* (1945) and *Notorious* (1946); opened on Broadway in Anderson's *Joan of Lorraine* (1946), a sizeable hit; starred in film *Joan of Arc* to mixed reviews (1948); left for Italy to film *Stromboli* (1949); with husband and child back home in CA, fell in love with her director Roberto Rossellini and became pregnant, unleashing a tidal wave of negative publicity; condemned on floor of US Senate; married Rossellini 2 months later; had American career rebirth with *Anastasia* (1956), for which she won an Academy Award for Best Actress, followed by *Indiscreet* (1958) and *The*

Inn of the Sixth Happiness (1958); other films include *Goodbye Again* (*Aimez-vous Brahms?*, 1961), *Der Besuch* (*The Visit*, 1964), *The Yellow Rolls-Royce* (1964), *Cactus Flower* (1969), *A Walk in the Spring Rain* (1970), *From the Mixed-Up Files of Mrs. Basil E. Frankweiler* (1973), *Murder on the Orient Express* (1974), *A Matter of Time* (1976) and *Herbstsonate* (*Autumn Sonata*, 1978); on stage, starred in *Tea and Sympathy* (1956), *A Month in the Country* (1965), *More Stately Mansions* (1967), *Captain Brassbound's Conversion* (1971–72), *The Constant Wife* (1975), and *Waters of the Moon* (1979); on tv, appeared in "The Turn of the Screw" (1959), winning an Emmy for Best Dramatic Performance, "Hedda Gabler" (1960), "The Human Voice" (1966), and the 4-hour miniseries "A Woman Called Golda" (1982), for which her daughter Pia accepted a posthumous Emmy. ❖ See also autobiography (with Alan Burgess) *Ingrid Bergman: My Story* (Delacorte, 1980); Laurence Leamer, *As Time Goes By: The Life of Ingrid Bergman* (Harper & Row, 1986); Donald Spoto, *Notorious: The Life of Ingrid Bergman* (HarperCollins, 1997); and *Women in World History.*

BERGMAN, Marilyn (1929—). American lyricist and songwriter. Born Marilyn Keith, Nov 10, 1929, in New York, NY; dau. of Albert A. Katz (in the clothing business); graduate of New York University; m. Alan Bergman (lyricist), Feb 9, 1958; children: Julie (b. 1960). ❖ One half of one the most important wife-husband lyric-writing teams in the history of American popular music, co-wrote lyrics for such films as *The Way We Were* and *Tootsie ;* had 1st success with lyrics for "Yellow Bird," a West Indian folk tune (1957); co-wrote the lyrics for "Nice and Easy" for Frank Sinatra (1960); co-wrote theme song "The Windmills of Your Mind," for *The Thomas Crown Affair* (1968), which won an Oscar and a Golden Globe; also won Oscars for overall score of *Yentl*, as well as its 2 lead songs, "The Way He Makes Me Feel" and "Papa Can You Hear Me?" (1984); captured another Oscar, two Grammys, and a Golden Globe for title song of *The Way We Were* (1973), which became Barbra Streisand's 1st gold single; co-wrote theme songs for several hit tv shows, including "Maude," "Good Times" and "The Sandy Duncan Show,"; won 2 Emmys for the score of *Queen of the Stardust Ballroom* (1974); elected president of American Society of Composers, Authors and Publishers (ASCAP, 1994, 1996); other films include *Any Wednesday* (lyr., 1966), *The Happy Ending* (song, 1969), *Sometimes a Great Notion* (lyr., 1970), *Forty Carats* (lyr., 1973), *Ode to Billy Joe* (lyr., 1975), *A Star Is Born* (lyr., 1976), *Same Time Next Year* (lyr., 1978), *Starting Over* (lyr., 1979), *Big* (song, 1988) and *Shirley Valentine* (lyr., 1989). ❖ See also *Women in World History.*

BERGMANN, Gretel (b. 1914). *See Lambert, Margaret Bergmann.*

BERGMANN-POHL, Sabine (1946—). East German politician and head of state. Born Sabine Schulz, April 20, 1946, in Eisenach, Thuringia; m. twice (surname is a result of 2 marriages). ❖ The last head of state of the German Democratic Republic (GDR), began career as a physician, specializing in respiratory diseases; joined Christian Democratic Union (CDU, 1981), a satellite controlled by the ruling Socialist Unity Party; earned a reputation for competence in her medical area as well as in the field of social welfare; following the collapse of the Communist dictatorship (1989), made a strong showing in Mar 1990 elections to *Volkskammer* ("People's Chamber"), coming in 2nd to the new prime minister, Lothar de Maziere; a month later, was elected president of the *Volkskammer*, in effect, becoming head of state of the German Democratic Republic, the only democratically elected one in its 40-year history; after unification of the 2 German states, entered the Bundestag, joining Chancellor Helmut Kohl's cabinet as minister without portfolio (1990). ❖ See also memoirs, *Abschied ohne Tränen: Rückblick auf das Jahr der Einheit* (*Departure without Tears: A Look Back at the Year of Unity*, 1991); and *Women in World History.*

BERGNER, Elisabeth (1897–1986). Austrian-born actress. Born Elisabeth (Ella) Ettel, Aug 22, 1897, in Drohobycz, Austrian Galicia (now Drogobych, Ukraine); died in London, England, May 12, 1986; grew up in Vienna; dau. of a Jewish merchant; m. Paul Czinner (1890–1972), producer-director), 1933. ❖ Stage and screen actress who fascinated audiences in Europe for over 50 years with her androgynous persona, made stage debut in Innsbruck (1915); performed in Zurich (1916–18); in Vienna, performed in several Wedekind plays, including *Earth Spirit* and *Pandora's Box* (1919), and appeared in role of *Miss Julie* at Vienna's Burgtheater (1920); moved to Berlin (1922), where she starred in *Vatermord* and performed at Max Reinhardt's Deutsches Theater; came to prominence as Rosalinde in *As You Like It*, breaking all German records with her 560-consecutive performances; made 1st motion picture, the silent film *Der Evangelimann*; ruled the German stage

and screen (1923–33); began collaboration with future husband (1924), appearing in his film, *Nju, A Tragicomedy of Daily Life ;* starred in her most successful silent film, *Miss Else* (1929); wrote screenplay for her film *The Dreaming Lips* (1932); with rise of Nazism, fled to London (1932), where she was a sensation as Gemma Jones in *Escape Me Never* (1933); took *Escape Me Never* to NY (1935), where it was highly acclaimed; starred with Laurence Olivier in film version of *As You Like It* (1936); with husband, came to US (1940); had a major Broadway hit in *The Two Mrs. Carrolls* (1943–44), but had much less success in America than Britain, collaborating with Bertolt Brecht and involved in exile politics (Council for a Democratic Germany); toured Germany and Israel (1949–50); because of Cold War tensions and McCarthyism, returned to England (1950); appeared in a German production of Rattigan's *The Deep Blue Sea* in West Berlin (1954), reestablishing herself as one of the leading actresses in German theater; elected member of Arts Academy of Berlin (1956); performed on stage and tv in Germany and UK (1950s–70s); performed last stage role but continued to make tv films (1973); other films include *Der Geiger von Florenz* (*The Violinist of Florence*, 1926), *Köulein Luise* (Queen Louise, 1927), *Ariane* (*The Loves of Ariane*, 1931), *Catherine the Great* (1934), *Paris Calling* (1942), *Cry of the Banshee* (1970) and *Feine Gesellschaft* (1982). ❖ See also memoirs (in German) *Bewundert viel und viel gescholten . . . Elisabeth Bergners unordentliche Erinnerungen* (1978); and *Women in World History.*

BERGQVIST, Kajsa (1976—). Swedish high jumper. Born Oct 12, 1976, in Sollentuna, Sweden. ❖ Tied with Oana Pantelimon for a bronze medal at Sydney Olympics (2000); at European championship, won a gold medal (2002).

BERGROTH, Kersti (1886–1975). Finnish dramatist, novelist, and critic. Name variations: Kersti Solveig Bergroth. Born Jan 24, 1886, in Karelia, Finland; died Jan 24, 1975, in Helsingissä, Finland. ❖ Best known for her rustic comedies portraying life in Karelia, also wrote 5 novels, including *Kiirashni* (1922) and *Balaisuntemme* (1955), and a series of books for young girls; during 1920s and 1930s, was editor of 2 Finnish avant-garde literary magazines which had a great influence on cultural life; though she lived in Rome for a prolonged period, continued to contribute anecdotes and stories to Finnish papers.

BERGSMA, Deanne (1941—). South African ballet dancer. Born Deanne Harrismith, 1941, in Pretoria, South Africa; trained with Marjorie Sturman in Johannesburg. ❖ Joined Royal Ballet in London (1959), where she created roles in Ray Powell's *One in Five* and Frederick Ashton's *Enigma Variations* (both 1968), among others; danced in England and on tour in numerous works to great acclaim, such as Tetley's *Field Figures*, and Ashton's *Daphnis and Chloe, Swan Lake* and *The Sleeping Beauty ;* best known for her mime portrayal of the Polish mother in Britten's opera *Death in Venice* (1973); appeared in "Field Figures" segment of the film *I Am a Dancer* (1973).

BERI, Beth (c. 1904—). American theater dancer. Born c. 1904, near Los Angeles, California. ❖ Had interpretive dance act on Keith and Orpheum circuits (1918–21); billed as the "most beautiful dancer of the world," danced numerous pieces, often to Chopin; performed interpretive dances on Broadway in *Kid Boots* (1923), *Jack and Jill* (1923) and *Rufus LeMaire's Affairs* (1927).

BERINGER, Aimée Daniell (1856–1936). American-born playwright and novelist. Name variations: Aimee Beringer, Mrs. Oscar Beringer. Born Aimée Daniell, 1856, in Philadelphia; died Feb 17, 1936; m. Oscar Beringer (musician and composer); children: Esmé Beringer and Vera Beringer (actresses). ❖ Wrote plays *Tares, Katherine Kavanagh, Holly Tree Inn, The Prince and the Pauper, That Girl, Salve, Bess, A Bit of Old Chelsea, The Plot of His Story, The Agitator*, and novels *Beloved of the Gods, A Left-Handed Marriage* and *The New Virtue.*

BERINGER, Esmé (1875–1972). English actress. Born Sept 5, 1875, in London, England; died Mar 31, 1972; dau. of Oscar Beringer (composer) and Aimée Daniell Beringer (playwright and novelist); sister of Vera Beringer (actress, 1879–1964). ❖ Made stage debut as Dick Tipton in *The Real Little Lord Fauntleroy* (1888), followed by *The Prince and the Pauper, The Three Wayfarers, The Benefit of the Doubt, The Pilgrim's Progess, The White Knight, In Days of Old, Captain Kettle, The Maid's Tragedy, Hamlet, The Winter's Tale, The Cradle, Julius Caesar, The Cat and the Canary, Gruach* and *Richard III*, among numerous others; caused a sensation appearing as Romeo opposite her sister's Juliet at a matinee performance at Prince of Wales' Theatre (1896); in US, appeared at the Palace to great success.

BERINGER, Mrs. Oscar (1856–1936). *See Beringer, Aimée Daniell.*

BERINGER, Vera (1879–1964). English actress and playwright. Born Mar 2, 1879, in London, England; died 1964; dau. of Oscar Beringer (composer) and Aimée Daniell Beringer (playwright and novelist); sister of Esmé Beringer (actress). ❧ Made stage debut as Jack in her mother's play *Tares* (1888); was the original Little Lord Fauntleroy; appeared as Juliet opposite her sister's Romeo at a matinee at Prince of Wales's Theatre (1896); other plays include *The Broken Melody, The Odd Woman, Lucky Jim, The Blue Stockings, The Man from Blankley's, Lover's Meeting* and *Hamlet*; as playwright, wrote *A Penny Bunch, The Absent-Minded Husband,* (adaptation) *The Blue Stockings, Lucky Jim, Darling, Beltane Night, The Painted Lady, South East and South West, What Happened to George, It Might Happen To You, Nanny* and *Happy Birthday.*

BERIOSOVA, Svetlana (1932–1998). Lithuanian-born British ballerina. Born 1932 in Kaunas, Lithuania; died Nov 1998 in London, England; dau. of Nicholas Berisov-Berżaitis. ❧ Beloved British ballerina during the great days of the Royal ballet, was noted for her acting ability and superior technique; 1st trained as dancer by father; moved with family to US (1940) and studied ballet at Vilzak Scholler School; danced with Grand Ballet de Monte Carlo, Metropolitan Ballet in London, and as soloist for Sadler's Wells; toured widely and appeared in many roles, including The Hostess in *Les Biches,* the Bride in *Les Noces,* title role in *Persephone,* Fairy in *The Fairy's Kiss,* and Lady Elgar in *Enigma Variations;* also known for her Swan Lake and Sleeping Beauty; appeared in film *The Soldier's Tale* (1963); retired (1975) in order to teach. ❧ See also A.H. Franks, *Svetlana Beriosova: A Biography* (1978).

BERK, Lotte (1913–2003). German-born dancer and entrepreneur. Born Liselotte Heymansohn, Jan 17, 1913, in Cologne, Germany; died Nov 4, 2003, in Hungerford, Berkshire, England; dau. of a Russian father and German mother (both Jews); studied modern dance with Mary Wigman in Cologne; m. Ernest Berk (British dancer), 1933 (div. c. 1963); m. once more (for about 3 weeks); children: Esther Berk Fairfax. ❧ With husband, danced at Cologne's National Theatre to great acclaim; fled the Reich (1938), settling in Britain where she worked with Marie Rambert, among others; opened her own exercise center in a basement in the West End; came to prominence with her set of exercises to help slim waists and trim thighs, called the Lotte Berk method, which became a phenomenon in London, NY, and California (1960s), shaping the abdomens of the likes of Joan Collins, Brit Ekland and Shirley Conran.

BERKE, Dorothea (c. 1900—). American theatrical and choreographer. Name variations: Dorothea Schlesinger. Born Dorothea Schlesinger, c. 1900, near Chicago, Illinois. ❧ Performed vaudeville dance acts in her teens and worked in Prologs; helped introduce ballet style as a theatrical technique through her early work at The Capitol Theater (1920s); served as dance director for Balaban and Katz Theater chains in Chicago (as of 1925); began working with performers on tour once theaters were absorbed into Paramount-Publix conglomerate, for which she staged acts suitable for a range of theaters, including the Capitol, Palace, Roxy and Paramount; collaborated with soprano Grace Moore for many years for whom she staged operetta revivals including the widely acclaimed production of *The Dubarry* on Broadway (1932); retired (late 1930s).

BERKELEY, Elizabeth (fl. 1390–1410). English royal. Name variations: Elizabeth Beauchamp. Dau. of Thomas Berkeley, viscount L'Isle, and Margaret Warren; m. Richard Beauchamp, 5th earl of Warwick; children: Margaret Beauchamp (who m. John Talbot, earl of Shrewsbury); Eleanor Beauchamp (1408–1468); Elizabeth Beauchamp.

BERKELEY, Elizabeth (fl. 1408–1417). *See Fitzalan, Elizabeth.*

BERKELEY, Elizabeth (1576–1635). *See Carey, Elizabeth.*

BERKELEY, Elizabeth (1661–1709). *See Burnet, Elizabeth.*

BERKELEY, Frances (1634–after 1695). American supporter of the Green Spring faction. Name variations: Lady Frances Berkeley; Frances Culpeper. Born Frances Culpeper, baptized May 27, 1634, in Kent, England; died at Green Spring, Virginia, after 1695; buried at Jamestown; dau. of Thomas and Katherine (St. Leger) Culpeper; cousin of Thomas, Lord Culpeper (colonial governor); m. Samuel Stephens (governor of Albemarle settlement in North Carolina and owner of Roanoke Island), 1652 (died Dec 1669); m. Sir William Berkeley (governor of Virginia), 1670 (died 1677); m. Philip Ludwell, c. 1680; no children. ❧ Wife of 3 colonial governors, was a considerable political force in Virginia; immigrated with family to Virginia colony (1650);

when her cousin Nathaniel Bacon headed a revolt against her husband (1676), returned to England with husband to lobby on his behalf at the court; on her return, discovered that husband's plantation at Green Spring near Jamestown had been reduced to shambles by Bacon's Rebellion (1677); led the "Greenspring faction" to violently retaliate against the followers of Bacon; following husband's death, married Colonel Philip Ludwell of Rich Neck plantation, her late husband's chief supporter, and thwarted royal representatives from imposing arbitrary measures on the Virginia colony.

BERKSOY, Semiha (1910–2004). Turkish soprano. Born 1910 in Istanbul, Turkey; died Aug 15, 2004, in Istanbul; attended Istanbul conservatory to study music and visual arts; attended Berlin Music Academy; children: Zeliha Berksoy. ❧ The first lady of Turkish opera, made stage debut at 19; starred in the 1st Turkish sound movie, *Istanbul Sokaklari* (The Streets of Istanbul); appeared in the 1st Turkish opera, *Ozsoy;* in Germany, sang the lead in *Ariadne Auf Naxos* (1939), the 1st Turkish opera singer to star in Europe; helped establish the 1st opera house in Ankara.

BERLEPSCH, Emilie von (1755–1830). German essayist and travel writer. Name variations: Emilie von Berlepsch Harms. Born Emile von Oppel in 1755; died 1830; married a noble named von Berlepsch of the Hanover court. ❧ Wrote *Caledonia* (1802–04), about travels through Scotland; also published essays on marriage and repression of women.

BERLIN, Elaine (1932—). *See May, Elaine.*

BERLIN NIGHTINGALE, The (1900–1980). *See Korjus, Miliza.*

BERLIOZ, Madame (1800–1854). *See Smithson, Harriet Constance.*

BERMAN, Sara Mae (1936—). American marathon runner. Born Sara Mae Sidore, May 14, 1936, in the Bronx, NY; lived in Cambridge, Massachusetts; m. Larry Berman (runner). ❧ "Unofficially" won the Boston Marathon (1969, 1970, 1971).

BERNADETTE OF LOURDES (1844–1879). French nun and saint. Name variations: Bernadette Soubirous. Born Bernadette Soubirous in Lourdes, French Pyrenees, Jan 7, 1844; died 1879; dau. of François and Louise (Casterot) Soubirous. ❧ Born into a poor family, was placed in domestic service from 12 to 14, until she returned home to prepare for 1st Communion; at 14, claimed that the Virgin Mary appeared in the crevasse of a rock on the bank of the Gave as she was collecting firewood with her sister and a friend (Feb 11, 1858), and that the Virgin reappeared 18 times from then until July 16 (the visions were declared authentic by Roman Catholic Church, and the Lourdes grotto became a shrine for pilgrims); joined Sisters of Charity at Nevers, France (1866); nursed the wounded in Franco-Prussian war (1870–71); became a nun (1877); was beatified (1925) and canonized (1933). *The Song of Bernadette,* a film based on the novel of the same name by Franz Werfel, starred Jennifer Jones (1943); feast day is April 16. ❧ See also *Women in World History.*

BERNADINA, Mother. *See Mathews, Ann Theresa.*

BERNADOTTE, Astrid (1905–1935). *See Astrid of Sweden.*

BERNADOTTE, Bridget (b. 1937). *See Birgitta of Sweden.*

BERNADOTTE, Christina (b. 1943). *See Christina Bernadotte.*

BERNADOTTE, Desiree (b. 1938). *See Desiree Bernadotte.*

BERNADOTTE, Ingeborg (1878–1958). *See Ingeborg of Denmark.*

BERNADOTTE, Louise (1851–1926). *See Louise of Sweden.*

BERNADOTTE, Madeleine (b. 1982). *See Madeleine Bernadotte.*

BERNADOTTE, Margaret (b. 1934). *See Margaret Bernadotte.*

BERNADOTTE, Margaretha (1899–1977). *See Margaretha of Sweden.*

BERNADOTTE, Martha (1901–1954). *See Martha of Sweden.*

BERNADOTTE, Victoria (b. 1977). *See Victoria Bernadotte.*

BERNAL, Emilia (1884–1964). Cuban poet. Born 1884 in Camagüey, Cuba; grew up in Nuevitas; died 1964 in Washington DC; dau. of a primary schoolteacher. ❧ Lived most of life outside Cuba; published poems in newspapers; works include *Alma errante* (1916), *Poesías inéditas* (1922), *Los nuevos motivos* (1925), *Vida* (1928), *América* (1937) and *Mallorca* (1938).

BERNÁR, Nina Annenkova (1859/64–1933). *See Annenkova-Bernár, Nina.*

BERNARD, Catherine (1662–1712). French novelist. Born 1662 in Rouen, France; died 1712 in Paris; never married; no children. ❖ Well-educated, probably wealthy woman, moved to Paris at 17; made her way into the elite of Parisian society, where her imaginative stories found a receptive, intellectual audience; supported herself through her writing, probably from commissions; dedicated herself to producing plays, novels, short stories, and fairy tales; works, which centered on the theme of love, both happy and tragic, include *The Misfortunes of Love* (1687) and *Ines of Cordoba* (1696).

BERNARD, Dorothy (1890–1955). South African-born stage and screen actress. Born July 25, 1890, in Port Elizabeth, South Africa; died Dec 14, 1955, in Hollywood, California; m. A.H. Van Buren (actor); children: Marjorie "Midge" van Buren (1910–1997), worked at Screen Actors Guild, 1933–75). ❖ Joined Biograph (1909), appearing in such D.W. Griffith films as *The Cricket on the Hearth, The Girl and Her Trust, The Goddess of Sagebrush Gulch* and the "Jonesy" series; appeared opposite William Farnum in numerous films, including *Les Miserables ;* other films include *The Wild Goose, The Contrast, Princess Romanoff* and *Little Women;* played Margaret in the 7-year run of *Life with Father* on Broadway, as well as on tv.

BERNARD, Jessie (1903–1996). American sociologist. Born Jessie Ravitch in Minneapolis, Minnesota, 1903; died in Washington, Oct 6, 1996; dau. of Romanian-Jewish parents who were immigrant shop-keepers; attended the University of Minnesota; Washington University, PhD, 1935; m. Luther Lee Bernard (died 1951); children: 3. ❖ At the advent of the feminist movement (1963), was a 60-year-old widowed professor at Penn State, 1 year away from retirement; over next 16 years, published a list of books that earned her a reputation as the foremost scholar of the women's movement, including *Academic Women* (1964), *The Sex Game* (1968), *The Future of Marriage* (1972), *The Future of Motherhood* (1974), *Women, Wives, Mothers* (1975) and *The Female World* (1980). ❖ See also autobiographical *Self Portrait of a Family* (1978); and *Women in World History*.

BERNARD, Karen (1948—). American dancer. Born Sept 14, 1948, in Boston, Massachusetts; studied dance with her father and art at Boston Museum School; trained at School of Contemporary Dance in London (1969–72), and at the Merce Cunningham and Erick Hawkins studios in NY; also studied contact improvisation with David Woodberry. ❖ Worked in kinesiology and ideokinesiology in New York; worked with David Tremlette on a conceptual project in London (1972); taught and performed with the Art Bus in New York City, a mobile workshop; began choreographing (1974), frequently in collaboration.

BERNARDINA, Sister (1732–1800). *See Mathews, Ann.*

BERNARDINO, Minerva (1907–1998). Dominican Republic feminist. Born in Seibo, Dominican Republic, 1907; died Aug 29, 1998, in Dominican Republic; dau. of Alvaro and Altagracia Bernardino. ❖ Pioneer among Latin American feminists, was the predominant force in founding the UN Commission on the Status of Women; pursued a career in the civil service, eventually becoming head of the file office of Dominican Republic's Department of Development and Communications (1926), chief of a section of the Department of Agriculture (1928), and chief of the statistics section of the Department of Education (1931); by 1929, was also a leader in Acción Feminista Dominica, a women's-rights organization credited for successfully leading the battle to insert suffrage and civil rights for Dominican women into the amended Constitution of 1942; was appointed Dominican delegate to the Inter-American Commission of Women to be held in Montevideo (1933), becoming its rapporteur (1938), vice chair (1939), and chair (1943); attended founding conference for the UN in San Francisco (1945) and was one of only four women to sign the UN Charter; with others, demanded the document contain the phrase "to ensure respect for human rights and fundamental freedoms without discrimination against race, sex, condition, or creed"; was appointed her country's Minister Plenipotentiary to United Nations (1950). Awarded Pan American Union's Bolivar and San Martin medal (1948); granted Hispanic Heritage Award for excellence in education. ❖ See also *Women in World History*.

BERNAUER, Agnes (d. 1435). Bavarian who was condemned for witchcraft. Drowned 1435; dau. of an Augsburg baker; m. Albert (1401–1460), c. 1432. ❖ Secretly married Albert, son of Ernest, the duke of Bavaria-Munich (c. 1432); while Albert was away, was seized by order of her father-in-law and condemned to death for witchcraft; was

drowned in the Danube near Straubing. Her story afforded material for several German dramas: Adolf Böttger, Friedrich Hebbel and Otto Ludwig have each written works entitled *Agnes Bernauer.* ❖ See also *Women in World History*.

BERNAYS, Marie (1883–1939). German-Jewish social worker. Born in Munich, Germany, 1883; died in a monastery in 1939; father taught the history of literature at University of Munich. ❖ Was an active member of the Deutsche Volkspartei (DVP), the German People's Party; with Elisabeth Altmann-Gottheimer, founded the School of Women's Social Work in Mannheim, serving as its director (1919–32); won a seat in the *Landtag* (Provincial Assembly, 1921), serving until 1925; distressed both by the rightward drift of the DVP and the rise of Nazism, entered a convent (1933) and converted to the Roman Catholic faith. ❖ See also *Women in World History*.

BERNDT, Catherine Webb (1918–1994). Australian anthropologist. Name variations: Catherine H. Berndt. Born Catherine Helen Webb, May 8, 1918, in Auckland, New Zealand; died May 12, 1994, in Perth, Western Australia; Victoria University of Wellington, BA; studied anthropology with H.D. Skinner and A.P. Elkin in Sydney; Sydney University, MA with 1st class honors; also attended London School of Economics; m. Ronald M. Berndt, 1941. ❖ Known largely for studies in Aboriginal Australia and Papua New Guinea, often focused on status of Aboriginal women; performed fieldwork with husband in various locations, including Ooldea, South Australia (1941), North Australia (1946–51), and Papua New Guinea (1951–52); in US, surveyed relations between anthropology and sociology; at University of Western Australia, lectured in anthropology (1963–84), then began serving as honorary research fellow in Anthropology from 1984; with Aboriginal illustrator Djoki Yunupingu, received New South Wales Premier's Special Children's Book Award for *Land of the Rainbow Snake* (1980); published numerous works, including "Women's Changing Ceremonies in Northern Australia" (1950).

BERNERS, Juliana (c. 1388–?). English writer. Name variations: Julyans or Julians Barnes or Bernes. Born c. 1388; either the dau. of Sir James Berners, who was beheaded in 1388, or the wife of the holder of the manor of Julians Barnes near St. Albans. ❖ Considered one of earliest published women writing in Britain, wrote on hawking and hunting; her treatise, "Explicit Dam Julyans Barnes in her boke of huntyng" is contained in the *Boke of St. Albans.* The theory that she had been prioress of Sopwell nunnery, Hertfordshire, near St. Albans, is thought to be false, though there is a gap in the records of the priory of Sopwell between 1430 and 1480. ❖ See also *Women in World History*.

BERNHARD, Ruth (1905—). German-born photographer. Born Ruth-Maria Bernhard in Berlin, Germany, Oct 14, 1905; dau. of Lucien Bernhard (graphic and typeface designer); parents divorced when she was an infant; raised by schoolteachers Helene and Katarina Lotz; attended Academy of Fine Arts, Berlin, 1927; became US citizen, 1935. ❖ Photographer of nudes, still lifes and portraits, as well as advertising and fashion work, immigrated to US (1927); did freelance work for *The New York Times* and *Advertising Art,* as well Macy's and Sloane's department stores; became photographer for *Machine Age,* a publication of the Museum of Modern Art (1934); moved to Santa Monica, California, resuming her freelance career in Los Angeles; had a fascination with shells that led to a collaboration with conchologist Jean Schwengel (1940s); moved to San Francisco (1953); published 2 portfolios of prints, *The Gift of the Common place* and *The Eternal Body,* as well as a monograph of her work *Collecting Light ;* considered one of the preeminent 20th-century photographers of the female nude. Received Dorothea Lange award at Oakland Museum (1971). ❖ See also *Women in World History*.

BERNHARDI, Sophie (1775–1833). German novelist and short-story writer. Name variations: Sophie Tieck; Sophie Tieck-Bernhardi or Bernhardi-Tieck; Sophie Tieck-Bernhardi. Born Anna Sophie Tieck, 1775, in Germany; died 1833; dau. of Johann Ludwig Tieck and Anna Sophie Tieck; sister of Christian Friedrich Tieck (1776–1851) and Ludwig Tieck (1773–1853, romantic poet and writer); m. August Bernhardi. ❖ Wrote collection of short stories *Straußfedern* (1795), as well as plays, fairytales, and 2 novels; well-known for her *Flore und Blancheflur* (1822), a rework of a medieval poem.

BERNHARDT, Sarah (1844–1923). French actress. Name variations: The, or, La Divine Sarah. Born (Sarah-Marie-?) Henriette-Rosine Bernard, or Bernardt, or Bernhardt, probably on Oct 22 or 23, 1844 (born between 1841 and 1845, with 1844 the preferred choice) in Paris;

adopted the name Sarah Bernhardt in early teens; died in Paris, Mar 26, 1923; dau. of Judith ("Youle") Van Hard (aka Julie Bernard, or Bernardt, or Bernhardt, a Dutch-Jewish courtesan) and an unknown French father; educated at Paris Conservatoire (1860–62); m. Ambroise-Aristide (aka Jacques) Damala, 1882–89; children: (with Prince Henri de Ligne) son, Maurice Bernhardt (b. 1864). ❖ Actress, generally considered her country's greatest, whose ego, extravagance, eccentricities, numerous affairs, immense talent, magnetism, energy, will, and courage made her one of the most famous women of her time; appeared at Comédie-Française (1862–63), but contract was canceled for misbehavior; became well-known at the Odéon (1866–72), where she ran a hospital during Franco-Prussian War (1870–71); returned and starred at the Comédie (1872–80); left the Comédie to strike out on her own after sensational appearances in London (1879); initiated the 1st of 9 tours in North America (1880–81), followed by numerous European tours and nearly annual seasons in London, and established an immense international reputation; leased and produced and acted at Porte Saint-Martin theater (1883–93), Théâtre de la Renaissance (1893–98), and Théâtre de la Nation, renamed the Théâtre Sarah-Bernhardt (1899–1923); made gigantic world tour to Europe, Americas, Hawaii, Australia, New Zealand, and Dakar, Africa (1891–93); made last grand tour of Europe (1908–09); awarded the Legion of Honor (1914); right leg amputated (1915); made last American tour (1916–18); returned to the Paris stage after a 6-year absence (1920); gave last performance, in Turin, Italy (1922). Most notable roles include Zacherie in *Athalie*, Anna Damby in *Kean*, Zanetto in *Le Passant*, Queen Maria in *Ruy Blas*, title roles in *Zaïre* and *Phèdre*, Doña Sol in *Hernani*, title role in *Adrienne Lecouvreur*, Gilberte in *Froufrou*, Marguerite Gautier in *La Dame aux Camélias*, title role in *Fédora*, Floria Tosca in *La Tosca*, title role in *Jeanne d'Arc*, title roles in *Cléopâtre* and *Gismonda*, Melissinde in *La Princesse lointaine*, Photine in *La Samaritaine*, title role in *Hamlet*, Duc de Reichstadt in *L'Aiglon*, Zoraya in *La Sorcière*, Pelléas in *Pelléas et Mélisande*, and Strasbourg in *Les Cathédrales*; also appeared in silent films *La Reine Elisabeth* and *La Dame aux Camélias* (1911). ❖ See also *My Double Life: Memoirs of Sarah Bernhardt* (Heinemann, 1907); Elaine Aston, *Sarah Bernhardt* (Berg, 1989); Gold and Fizdale, *The Divine Sarah* (Knopf, 1991); Joanna Richardson, *Sarah Bernhardt and Her World* (Putnam, 1977); Cornelia Otis Skinner, *Madame Sarah* (Houghton, 1966); Lysiane Bernhardt, *Sarah Bernhardt: My Grandmother* (trans. Hurst & Blackett, 1945); and *Women in World History*.

BERNICE. *Variant of Berenice.*

BERNIER, Sylvie (1964—). Canadian diver. Born Jan 31, 1964. ❖ At Los Angeles Olympics, won a gold medal in springboard (1984).

BERNING, Susie Maxwell (1941—). American golfer. Name variations: Susie Maxwell. Born Susan Maxwell, July 22, 1941, in Pasadena, California; married (1968); children: Robin Berning (member of Ohio State women's golf team). ❖ Was the 1st female to attend Oklahoma City University (OCU) on a golf scholarship, playing on the men's team; turned pro (1964) and was LPGA Rookie of the Year; won two LPGA titles (1965); won USGA Women's Open (1968, 1972, 1973). Inducted into OCU Sports Hall of Fame (1973) and National Golf Coaches Association Hall of Fame (1986).

BERNSON, Kathryn (1950—). American dancer. Born Sept 9, 1950, in Los Angeles, California; trained with Carmelita Maracchi and David Lichine; attended Bennington College. ❖ Created a large repertory with Stormy Mullis; taught numerous technique classes at universities and in interdisciplinary programs at art schools, including Pratt Institute in Brooklyn, NY; choreographed concert works include *House Dances* (1972), *Real Costumes* (1974), (with Mullis) *Prospect Park* (1975), *True Stories* (1977), (with Mullis) *Ladder/Mother of Three* (1977), *Otterduck Pond* (1977), and (with Mullis) *Bugs* (1980).

BERNSTEIN, Aline (1882–1955). American scenic designer and writer. Born Hazel Frankau, Dec 22, 1882, in New York, NY; died Sept 7, 1955, in New York, NY; dau. of Joseph Frankau (actor) and Rebecca (Goldsmith) Frankau; sister of Ethel Frankau; attended New York School for Applied Design and studied with Robert Henri; m. Theodore Bernstein, Nov 1902; children: Theo (1904–1949) and Edla (b. 1906). ❖ Possibly remembered as much for her love affair with author Thomas Wolfe as for her work as a theatrical designer and writer, perhaps because of the enormous impact she had on Wolfe's short writing career; her relationship with him is documented through the character of Esther Jack in his *The Web and the Rock* (1939) and *You Can't Go Home Again* (1940), and in her own short stories and novels; began designing

scenery, costumes and props for Neighborhood Playhouse (1913); invited to work with designer Lee Simonson on Shaw's *Back to Methuselah* (1922), then collaborated with him often on Theatre Guild productions; remained with Neighborhood Playhouse through its dissolution in 1927, achieving notice with *The Little Clay Cart* and *The Grand Street Follies* (both 1924); executed her most famous designs for the Guild's *The Dybbuk* (1925) and *Ned McCobb's Daughter* (1926); became the 1st woman member of Local 829, the Brotherhood of Painters, Decorators and Paperhangers (1926); worked as resident designer for Eva Le Gallienne's Civic Repertory; designed for 5 Lillian Hellman plays, including *The Children's Hour* (1934) and *The Little Foxes* (1939); also designed the costumes for 1st movie, *She*, followed by *The Last Days of Pompeii*; writings include (short stories) *Three Blue Suits*, (novel) *The Journey Down*, and (play) *Harriet*, based on Harriet Beecher Stowe, which starred Helen Hayes; designed the ballet *The Spellbound Child*; taught costume design at Vassar. Won Tony Award for designs for *Regina* (1949). ❖ See also Carole Klein, *Aline* (Harper & Row, 1979); and *Women in World History*.

BERNSTEIN, Felicia (d. 1978). *See Montealegre, Felicia.*

BERNSTEIN, Hilda (1915—). South African painter, memoirist and novelist. Born Hilda Watts, 1915, in London, England; moved to South Africa, 1933; dau. of Simeon Watts (Russian ambassador to UK) and Dora Watts; m. Rusty Bernstein (anti-apartheid activist). ❖ Joined South African Communist Party (1940); served as a member of Johannesburg City Council and co-founded Transvaal Peace Council and Federation of South African Women; arrested (1946), placed under banning orders (1950s–60s), detained without trial (1960); after arrest of husband during Rivonia trial, fled with him on foot to Botswana and then moved to London; continued anti-apartheid work in London and on behalf of African National Congress's Women's League; began working as painter and graphic artist; writings include *South Africa: The Terrorism of Torture* (1972), *For Their Triumphs and For Their Tears: Women in Apartheid South Africa* (1978), *No. 46—Steve Biko* (1978), *Death is Part of the Process* (1983) and *A Life of One's Own* (2002). Received Lituli Silver Award for services assisting the foundation of a non-racial South Africa (2004). ❖ See also political autobiography, *The World That Was Ours* (1967).

BERNSTEIN, Sylvia (1915–2003). American civil-rights activist. Born Nov 6, 1915, in Washington, DC; died Nov 23, 2003, in Washington, DC; dau. of Russian immigrants; m. Albert Bernstein (union activist, died Feb 2003); children: Carl Bernstein (Watergate reporter for *Washington Post*). ❖ With husband, was a member of the Communist Party (1940s) and a target of government scrutiny; fought to desegregate Washington, DC (1950s); also advocated home rule for the city, and protested the Vietnam war and the development of nuclear weapons. ❖ See also Carl Bernstein *Loyalties* (1989).

BERNSTEIN, Theresa Ferber (1890–2002). American painter. Name variations: Theresa F. Meyerowitz. Born Theresa Ferber Bernstein, Mar 1, 1890, in Philadelphia, Pennsylvania; died Feb 1, 2002, in New York, NY; attended Philadelphia School of Design for Women (now Moore College); studied under William Merritt Chase at Art Students League; m. William Meyerowitz (painter). ❖ At Milch Galleries, NY, had 1st solo exhibition (1914); paintings, often portraits, include *Portrait of a Young Girl* (1923), *Miss Hadded* (1923), as well as *The Fair* and *Jerusalem*; summered for 70 years at her home in East Gloucester, MA.

BERNYE, Elizabeth (d. 1603). *See Grymeston, Elizabeth Bernye.*

BERONIKE. *Variant of Berenice.*

BERRY, Agnes (c. 1405–1479). *See Paston, Agnes.*

BERRY, duchess of.
See Margaret of Angoulême (1492–1549).
See Margaret of Savoy (1523–1574).
See Marie Louise (1695–1719).
See Caroline of Naples (1798–1870).

BERRY, Halle (1966—). African-American actress and model. Born Halle Maria Berry, Aug 14, 1966, in Cleveland, Ohio; dau. of Jerome Berry (African-American) and Judith Berry (Caucasian psychiatric nurse); sister of Heidi Berry; m. David Justice, Dec 31, 1992 (div. 1996); m. Eric Benét, Jan 24, 2001 (sep. 2004). ❖ Representing Ohio, won Miss Teen All-American Pageant (1985) and was 1st runner-up in Miss USA Pageant (1986); became a model; appeared in tv series "Living Dolls" (1989); came to prominence as a crack addict in

Spike Lee's film *Jungle Fever* (1991); acclaimed for performances in cable tv's "Introducing Dorothy Dandridge," for which she won a Golden Globe for Best Actress (1999), and *Monster's Ball,* for which she became the 1st African-American woman to win an Academy Award for Best Actress (2002); other films include *Boomerang* (1992), *The Flintstones* (1994), *Losing Isaiah* (1995), *Bulworth* (1998), *X-Men* (2000), *Swordfish* (2001), *Die Another Day* (2002), *X2* (2003) and *Catwoman* (2004).

BERRY, Harriet Morehead (1877–1940). American civic worker. Born July 22, 1877, in Hillsborough, North Carolina; died Mar 24, 1940, at Chapel Hill, NC. ❖ Served in various capacities at North Carolina State Geological and Economic Survey, of which she acted as director during WWI; while serving as secretary of North Carolina Good Roads Association (1902–17), developed a statewide road system and secured legislation which provided $50 million for the venture (1921); employed by State Department of Agriculture (1925); was responsible for the organization of credit unions across NC; was also superintendent and organizer of savings and loan associations (1927–37); served as vice-president of the state Equal Suffrage League.

BERRY, Martha McChesney (1866–1942). American educator. Born Martha McChesney Berry, Oct 7, 1866, near Rome, Georgia; died Feb 27, 1942, in Atlanta, Georgia; dau. of Thomas (cotton dealer) and Frances (Rhea) Berry; attended Edgewood Finishing School, Baltimore, 1882. ❖ One of the most outstanding women in Georgia's history, devoted her life to educating poor Southern mountain children; used the land she had inherited to build a small day school, followed by 3 others; opened the 1st Boys' Industrial School (1902), a crude log building outfitted with castoffs, and hired Elizabeth Brewster, graduate of Leland Stanford University; opened a school for girls (1909); offered high school-age students scholastic as well as vocational, agricultural, and domestic training, in a religious but nondenominational setting (by 1912, the state of Georgia had opened 11 schools using her model; other states soon followed); established Berry College (1926); at time of her death (1942), her schools, known as Berry's Schools, were housed in 125 buildings on 35,000 acres of land in the mountains of northwestern Georgia (of the 1,300 students enrolled, most did not pay tuition but earned their education instead by working for the institution). Awarded Theodore Roosevelt Memorial Medal for Distinguished Service (1925) and gold medal from National Institute of Social Sciences (1939). ❖ See also Harnett T. Kane with Henry Inez, *Miracle in the Mountains* (Doubleday, 1956); and *Women in World History.*

BERRY, Mary (1763–1852). English writer. Born in Kirkbridge, Yorkshire, England, Mar 16, 1763; died Nov 20, 1852, in London; dau. of Robert Berry and Elizabeth Seaton Berry (died 1763); sister of Agnes Berry. ❖ Began writing a journal while on a European tour with her father (1783); became a friend of Horace Walpole (1788) and edited 9 vols. of his works (1798–1825), as well as the *Letters of Mme Deffand* to Walpole and Voltaire; wrote *Social Life of England and France, from Charles II to 1830,* the play *Fashionable Friends,* and a biography of Lady Rachel Russell (1636–1723); her *Journals,* published after her death (1865), span 70 years. ❖ See also *Women in World History.*

BERRY, Miriam (1811–1852). See Whitcher, Frances Miriam Berry.

BERSIANIK, Louky (1930—). See Durand, Lucile.

BERTA. *Spanish variant of Bertha.*

BERTAUD, Marie Rosalie (c. 1700–?). French engraver. Born in Paris, c. 1700; studied with S. Aubin and Choffard. ❖ Best known for replicating the pictures of Vernet.

BERTHA (719–783). Queen of the Franks. Name variations: Bertrada, Berthrada; Berthe au grand pied; Bertrada II of Laon. Born 719; died at Choisy, July 12, 783; dau. of Heribert also known as Caribert, count of Laon; m. Pepin III the Short (715–768), mayor of Neustria (r. 741), king of the Franks (r. 747–768), in 741; children: Charles also known as Charlemagne (c. 742–814), who ruled as king of the Franks for 46 years and as Holy Roman emperor for 13 years); Irmentrude (d. 820); Carloman also known as Karlman (c. 751–771); Gisela (c. 753–807). ❖ The mother of Charlemagne, was called *Berthe au grand pied* (Bertha with the large foot), because one foot was greater than the other; has been celebrated with poems and legends for many centuries. Some romances have made Bertha the dau. of an emperor of Constantinople; others trace her descent from Flore, king of Hungary, and queen Blanche-Fleur. ❖ See also *Women in World History.*

BERTHA (779–after 823). Frankish princess. Born 779; died after 823; dau. of Hildegarde of Swabia (c. 757–783) and Charles I also known as Charlemagne (742–814), king of the Franks (r. 768–814), Holy Roman emperor (r. 800–814); associated with Angilbert, the abbott of St. Riquier; children: (with Angilbert) Nithard (b. around 800, the historian); Hartnid.

BERTHA-EUDOCIA THE FRANK (fl. 900s). Byzantine empress. Fl. in 900s young; 1st wife of Romanos or Romanus II, Byzantine emperor (r. 959–963); no children. Romanus II's 2nd wife was Theophano (c. 940–?).

BERTHA-IRENE OF SULZBACH (d. 1161). Byzantine empress. Name variations: Bertha of Sulzbach; Irene of Sulzbach. Born Bertha of Sulzbach; died 1161; dau. of Berengar II, count of Sulzbach; sister of Gertrude of Sulzbach (d. 1146); sister-in-law of Conrad III (1093–1152), Holy Roman emperor (r. 1138–1152); became 1st wife of Manuel I Comnenus, emperor of Byzantium (r. 1143–1180), 1146; children: 2 daughters. ❖ Was sister-in-law of Holy Roman emperor Conrad III, who arranged her betrothal to Manuel Comnenus, emperor of Byzantium; married at Constantinople (1146); as new empress, changed christened name of Bertha to Irene, a name more familiar to the Greeks; became a devoted wife and, by the simplicity of her manner, contrasted favorably with most Byzantine queens of the age; her husband, however, had numerous affairs. ❖ See also *Women in World History.*

BERTHA OF AVENAY (fl. 6th c.). Frankish saint. Died at end of 6th century; m. Gumbert (also canonized as a saint). ❖ After husband was martyred in Ireland where he had gone as a missionary, founded a convent near Avenay in Champagne and became its abbess; was killed there by her nephews who objected to the generous gifts she had bestowed on the church. Feast day is May 1.

BERTHA OF AVENAY (c. 830–c. 852). Abbess of Avenay. Born c. 830; died after 852; dau. of Irmengard (c. 800–851) and Lothair also known as Lothar I (795–855), Holy Roman emperor (r. 840–855).

BERTHA OF BIBURG (d. 1151). German saint. Died in 1151; buried at her abbey. ❖ Founded the abbey of Biburg. Feast Day is Aug 6.

BERTHA OF BLANGY (d. 725). French saint. Possibly born in Artois; died c. 725; m. a noble; children: several (one of her daughters succeeded her as abbess). ❖ Following death of husband, a noble of the Merovingian court, founded the abbey of Blangy, where she went into seclusion with her 2 daughters; eventually resigned as abbess and spent the rest of her life in enclosure, living in a cell beside the abbey church. Feast day is July 4. ❖ See also *Women in World History.*

BERTHA OF BRITTANY (d. 1163). Duchess of Brittany. Name variations: Bertha Fergaunt. Birth date unknown; died 1163; dau. of Conan III, duke of Brittany, and Matilda (illeg. dau. of King Henry I of England); m. Odo of Porhoet, duke of Brittany; m. Alan III, 1st earl of Richmond; children: Conan IV, duke of Brittany.

BERTHA OF BURGUNDY (964–1024). Queen of France. Born c. 964; died 1024; dau. of Matilda Martel (943–c. 982) and Conrad, king of Burgundy (r. 937–993); became 2nd wife of her cousin Robert II the Pious (972–1031, son of Hugh Capet) sometimes known as Robert I, king of France (r. 996–1031), in 996 (marriage annulled in 998); children: Almaric Montfort. ❖ See also *Women in World History.*

BERTHA OF BURGUNDY (d. 1097). Queen of Castile and Leon. Died in 1097; dau. of William I, count of Burgundy, and Etienette de Longwy; became 3rd wife of Alphonso VI (c. 1030–1109), king of Leon (r. 1065–1070, 1072–1109) and Castile (r. 1072–1109), in 1093.

BERTHA OF CHARTRES (d. 1084). Countess of Brittany. Died 1084; dau. of Odo II, count of Blois, and possibly Emelia; m. Alan III, count of Brittany; m. Hugo IV, count of Maine, in 1046; children: (1st m.) Conan II, duke of Brittany; Hawise of Brittany (d. 1072).

BERTHA OF HOLLAND (1055–1094). Queen of France. Name variations: Bertrada. Born 1055; died 1094 (some sources cite 1093); dau. of Florent I, count of Holland; stepdau. of Robert the Frisian; became 1st wife of Philip I the Fair (1052–1108), king of France (r. 1060–1108), in 1072 (div. 1092); children: Louis VI (c. 1081–1137), king of France (r. 1108–1137); Constance of France (fl. 1100s, who m. Bohemund of Taranto, prince of Antioch).

BERTHA OF KENT (c. 565–c. 616). Queen of Kent and religious founder. Born c. 565 in Paris; died c. 616 in Kent, England; dau. of Cherebert also known as Caribert or Charibert I, king of Paris (r. 561–567), and possibly Ingoberge (519–589); great-granddau. of Clotilda (470–545); m. St. Ethelbert (Aethelbert), king of Kent (r. c. 560–616), before 589; children: Aethelbald also known as Eadbald, king of Kent (r. 616–640); Ethelberga of Northumbria (d. 647), later queen of Northumbria; great-grandmother of Elflaed, abbess of Whitby (fl. 640–713). ❖ Born into Merovingian house of France, was brought up as a Christian and married King Ethelbert of Kent; as queen of Kent, brought Merovingian Christian culture to southeast England; since marriage treaty stipulated she have free exercise in her religion, was active in promoting Christianity, and her husband was the 1st English king to convert to the new faith; convinced him to receive Augustine, legate of Pope Gregory the Great, along with 40 monks, an event which led to the conversion of all of Kent (597); with husband, founded Canterbury Church, still one of England's most important religious establishments. ❖ See also *Women in World History.*

BERTHA OF MARBAIS (d. 1247). Saint. Name variations: Bertha de Marbais. Died 1247; related to Johanna of Flanders (d. 1244). ❖ Was a nun at the abbey of Aywières, then abbess of the abbey of Marquette. Feast day is July 18. ❖ See also *Women in World History.*

BERTHA OF SAVOY (1051–1087). Holy Roman empress. Born Sept 21, 1051; died Dec 27, 1087, in Mainz, Germany; dau. of Otto, count of Savoy, and Adelaide of Turin; m. Henry IV (1050–1106), king of Germany and Holy Roman emperor (r. 1056–1106), in 1066; children: Conrad (d. 1101), king of Germany (r. 1087) and Holy Roman emperor (r. 1093–1101); Henry V (1081–1125), king of Germany and Holy Roman emperor (r. 1106–1125); Agnes of Germany (1074–1143). ❖ Was with husband (1076), when, threatened with excommunication, he made his famous midwinter dash across the Alps to meet with Matilda of Tuscany and Pope Gregory VII at Canossa. Following Bertha's death, Henry married Adelaide of Kiev. ❖ See also *Women in World History.*

BERTHA OF SULZBACH (d. 1161). *See Bertha-Irene of Sulzbach.*

BERTHA OF SWABIA (fl. 900s). Queen of Burgundy. Born in German province of Swabia; m. Rudolf II of Burgundy also known as Rudolf of Lorraine (died 937); m. Hugh of Provence, king of Italy; children: (1st m.) Adelaide of Burgundy (931–999); Conrad of Burgundy.

BERTHA OF TOULOUSE (fl. late 700s). Queen of Italy. Married Pippin also known as Pepin I (773–810), king of Italy (r. 781–810), 795; children: Bernard (c. 799–818), king of Italy (r. 810–818); and 5 daughters (names unknown).

BERTHE. *Variant of Bertha.*

BERTHEROY, Jean (1868–1927). *See Roy de Clotte le Barillier, Berthe.*

BERTHGYTH (fl. 8th c.). English nun and letter writer. Born in England in 8th century in Thuringia (modern Germany); dau. of Cynehild (scholar and teacher); never married; no children. ❖ Traveled to Thuringia with mother who had been asked by St. Boniface to teach and help convert the native population to Christianity; remained in Thuringia for the rest of her life, deeply involved in Boniface's missionary work even after his death (754) and mother's death some years later. Her life has been preserved through 3 letters she wrote to her brother Balthard in England. ❖ See also *Women in World History.*

BERTHOD, Madeleine (1931—). Swiss Alpine skier. Name variations: Madeleine Chamot. Born Feb 1, 1931, in Switzerland. ❖ Placed 6th in downhill and slalom at Oslo Olympics (1952); won a gold medal for downhill at Cortina Olympics (1956), with a margin of victory 4 times larger than any other woman in the event's history; at World championships, won 2 silver medals (1954); also competed at Squaw Valley Olympics but did not medal.

BERTHOD, Sylviane (1977—). Swiss Alpine skier. Born July (some sources cite Apr) 25, 1977, in Sion, Switzerland. ❖ Won World Jr. championship in downhill (1995) and super-G (1996); at World championships, placed 7th in super-G and 13th in downhill (1999); placed 7th in downhill at Salt Lake City Olympics (2002).

BERTHOLD, Ernst (1797–1870). *See Robinson, Therese Albertine Louise von Jakob.*

BERTHRADA (d. 783). *See Bertha.*

BERTIE, Catharine (1519–1580). Duchess of Suffolk. Name variations: Katherine or Catherine Willoughby; Dowager of Suffolk. Born Mar 22, 1519, in Parham, Suffolk; died Sept 19, 1580; only child of William

Willoughby, 8th baron Willoughby of Eresby, and Mary de Salinas; m. Charles Brandon (1484–1545), duke of Suffolk (r. 1514–1545), Sept 7, 1534 or 1536; m. Richard Bertie (1516–1582), MP, 1553; children: (1st m.) Henry Brandon (b. 1535), 2nd duke of Suffolk; Charles Brandon (b. 1537), 3rd duke of Suffolk; (2nd m.) Peregrine Bertie (b. 1555), Lord Willoughby of Eresby. ❖ Was a fervent advocate for the Reformation. Husband Charles Brandon was also married to Anne Browne (d. 1511), Margaret Neville (b. 1466), and Mary Tudor (1496–1533). ❖ See also *Women in World History.*

BERTILDA (1833–1913). *See Acosta de Samper, Soledad.*

BERTILLE (d. 705/713). French saint. Born into a landowning family near Soissons, France; died between 705 and 713. ❖ Became a nun at abbey of Jouarre, which followed the strict rule of St. Columbanus; became director of abbey of Chelles (658), remaining in that position for next 46 years. Feast day is Nov 5. ❖ See also *Women in World History.*

BERTIN, Louise Angélique (1805–1877). French poet and composer. Born Feb 15, 1805, in Roches, near Bièvre, France; died April 26, 1877, in Paris, France. ❖ Wrote the operas *Guy Mannering* (Opera Comique, 1827), *Fausto* (Italiens, 1831), *La Esméralda*, text by Victor Hugo (Grand Opera, 1836), and *Le Loup-garou.* Her volume of poems, *Les Glanes* (1842), was honored by the French Academy.

BERTINI, Francesca (1888–1985). Italian actress. Born Elena Seracini Vitiello in Florence, Italy, April 11, 1888; died Oct 13, 1985, in Rome; dau. of a stage actress; m. Paul Cartier (Swiss count), 1921. ❖ Italy's 1st screen diva, made film debut in *La Dea del Mare* (1907); had 1st Italian success in *Il Trovatore* (1910) and 1st international success in *Assunta Spina* (1915), directed by Gustavo Serena; prominent in the early period of Italian cinema, influenced fashion the world over; retired on marriage (1921), but returned sporadically, most notably in Bertolucci's *1900* (1976); other films include *Ernani* (1911), *Giulietta e Romeo* (1911), *Tristano e Isota* (1911), *Francesca da Rimini* (1911), *Re Lear* (1911), *Lorenzo il Magnifico* (1911), *Il Mercante di Venezia* (1912), *La Rosa di Tebe* (1912), *Idillio tragico* (1912), *La Gloria* (1913), *La Madre* (1913), *Salome* (1913), *La Signora dalle Camelie* (*Camille,* 1915), *Fedora* (1916), *Odette* (1916), *La Tosca* (1918), *Frou-Frou* (1918), *Anima allegra* (1918), *La Donna nuda* (1918), *La Contesa Sarah* (1919), *Beatrice* (1919), *Marion* (1921), *La Giovinezza del Diavolo* (1921), *Conseulita* (1922), *Monte Carlo* (1928), *Odette* (1928), *Possession* (1929), *Dora* (1943) and *A Sud Niente di Nuovo* (1956). ❖ See also autobiography (in Italian) *Il Resto non conta* (1969) and film *The Last Diva* (1983).

BERTKEN, Sister (c. 1427–1514). Dutch nun and writer. Born c. 1427; died 1514. ❖ Spent 57 years of her life in a convent in Utrecht; her poems are allegorical and frequently laced with Biblical allusions.

BERTOLACCINI, Silvia (1959—). Argentinean golfer. Born Jan 30, 1950, in Rafaela, Argentina; attended National College of Argentina. ❖ Won the Argentinean Amateur (1972) and Colombian Amateur (1974); turned pro (1975); won Colgate-Far East Open (1977, 1979); Cavitan Open (1978); Mazda Classic of Deer Creek (1984).

BERTOLINI, Livia (fl. 1920s–1930s). Italian mountaineer. Fl. in 1920s and 1930s. ❖ With Tina Bozzino and Nina Pietrosanta, climbed the Italian side of Mont Blanc: the Brenva and Puterey ridges.

BERTRADA. *See Bertha (d. 783).*

BERTRADA OF EVREUX (fl. 1170s). Countess of Chester. Name variations: Bertrade d'Evreux. Dau. of Simon, count of Evreux, and Amice de Beaumont; m. Hugh de Kevilioc, 3rd earl of Chester; children: Ranulf de Blondville, 4th earl of Chester (c. 1172–1232, who was 2nd husband of Constance of Brittany [1161–1201]); Maude of Chester (1171–1233); Hawise, countess of Lincoln; Adeliz de Keveliock; Agnes, Lady of Chartley.

BERTRADA OF MONTFORT (d. after 1117). Queen of France. Name variations: Bertrada de Montfort; Bertha; countess of Anjou. Died after 1117; m. Fulk IV the Rude, count of Anjou, in 1089 (annulled before 1093); became 2nd wife of Philip I the Fair (1052–1108), king of France (r. 1060–1108), in 1092 or 1095; children: (1st m.) Fulk V the Younger, count of Anjou and king of Jerusalem; (2nd m.) Philip; Cecilia of France (who m. Tancred, prince of Antioch). Philip I was also married to Bertha of Holland (1055–1094). ❖ Following death of her 2nd husband Philip I (1108), entered the convent and became a nun.

BERTRAM, Elsie (1912–2003). English entrepreneur. Born Elsie Hacking, June 6, 1912, in Co. Durham, England; died Oct 26, 2003, in England; m. Edward Bertram (salesman), 1935 (died 1987); children: Christopher "Kip" Bertram and Nigel Bertram. ❖ Though never a reader, revolutionized book distribution in the UK; because of the inefficient distribution service from publishers to booksellers in 1960s, established the highly successful Bertram Books to take on wholesale distribution throughout the nation. Awarded MBE (1987).

BERTRANA, Aurora (1899–1974). Spanish novelist. Name variations: Aurora Bertrana Salazar. Born Aurora Bertrana i Salazar in 1899 in Gerona, Spain; died 1974; dau. of Prudenci Bertrana (Catalan writer, 1867–1941) and Neus Salazar. ❖ Wrote novels *Tres presoners* (Three Prisoners, 1957) and *Entre dos silencis* (Between Two Silences, 1958), which focus on the Spanish Civil War; also wrote the novels *La nimfa d'argili* (1959), *Fracàs* (1966) and *Vent de grop* (1967), among others.

BERTSCH, Marguerite (1889–1967). American scenarist and director. Born Dec 14, 1889, in New York, NY; died in 1967. ❖ For many years, was head of the Scenario department for Vitagraph, a leading producer of silent films; wrote many of the scenarios for the company; with William P.S. Earle, directed the film *The Law Decides;* had 1st solo directing job with *The Devil's Prize* (1916); wrote *How To Write for Moving Pictures* (1917).

BERURIAH (fl. 2nd c.). Woman of the Talmud. Lived in 2nd century, during the revolt of Bar Kochba (132–135 CE); dau. of Rabbi Hanina ben Teradion; m. Rabbi Meir. ❖ Known as the only woman of Talmudic literature whose views were seriously considered by scholars, was a teacher in the academy, a highly unusual position for a woman; expressed her own view as to the rabbinic attitude toward her gender by subtly confronting the prejudice against women. ❖ See also *Women in World History.*

BERVOETS, Marguerite (1914–1944). Belgian resistance leader, teacher, and poet. Born in La Louviere, Belgium, in 1914; executed in Aug 1944; studied literature and philosophy in Brussels and taught at the École Normale in Tournai. ❖ Active in underground activities from the start of the Nazi occupation of her country, produced an illegal newspaper in her home, *La Délivrance,* and also was involved in procuring weapons and recruiting new members for the underground in Northern France; captured (1942); deported to Germany (1943); after captivity in many prisons and concentration camps, sentenced to death (Mar 1944), a sentence that was carried out in August of that year. ❖ See also *Women in World History.*

BERWICK, duchess of (1926—). See *Cayetana Fitz-James Stuart y Silva, Maria del Rosario.*

BERWICK, Mary (1825–1864). See *Procter, Adelaide.*

BERZINA, Valentina (1956—). See *Lutayeva-Berzina, Valentina.*

BESANT, Annie (1847–1933). British journalist, social reformer, Theosophist, and political leader. Name variations: Annie Wood; (pseudonym) Ajax. Born Annie Wood, Oct 1, 1847, in London, England; died Sept 20, 1933, in Madras, India; dau. of William Burton Persse (insurance underwriter) and Emily (Morris) Wood; London University, BSc, 1880; m. Frank Besant, Dec 21, 1867; children: Arthur Digby (b. 1869) and Mabel Emily (b. 1870); (wards) Krishnamurti and Nityananda Naryaniah. ❖ In a career spanning over 60 years, used her role as an influential journalist, political activist, and social reformer to challenge and reform existing attitudes about birth control, religion, the plight of industrial laborers and the growth of Indian nationalism; her many controversial and contradictory campaigns had a dramatic and lasting impact on British and Indian political and social development in late 19th and early 20th centuries; lived in and was educated by Ellen Marryat (1855–63); published short stories in *Family Herald* (beginning 1870); joined National Secular Society and began writing regular columns and articles under pseudonym Ajax for *National Reformer;* convicted under obscenity laws for disseminating birth-control information (1877); founded and edited *Our Corner* and *Link;* joined Fabian Society (1885); participated in Bloody Sunday riot and began to organize trade unions; elected to London School Board (1889); joined Theosophical Society and repudiated atheism and earlier stance on birth control (1890); assumed leadership of main Theosophical Society faction and moved to India (1893); established schools and lectured on need for social reform and Indian self-autonomy; founded and edited *Commonweal* and *New India;* elected president of Indian National Congress in 1917. Writings include *Auguste Comte* (1875), *The Gospel of Atheism* (1877), *Autobiographical Sketches* (1885), *Why I Became a Theosophist* (1889), *Reincarnation* (1892), *An Autobiography*

(1893), *Death and After* (1893), *Four Great Religions* (1897), *Dharma* (1899), *The Story of the Great War* (1899), *Pedigree of Man* (1903), *A Study in Consciousness* (1904), *Theosophy and the New Psychology* (1904), *Hints on the Bhagavad Gita* (1905), *Wisdom of the Upanishats* (1906), *H.P. Blavatsky and the Masters of Wisdom* (1907) and *India a Nation* (1930). ❖ See also Rosemary Dinnage, *Annie Besant* (Penguin, 1986); Elizabeth Longford, *Eminent Victorian Women* (Knopf, 1981); Anne Taylor, *Annie Besant* (Oxford U. Press, 1992); and *Women in World History.*

BESELIENE, Vida (1956—). Soviet basketball player. Born Aug 17, 1956. ❖ At Moscow Olympics, won a gold medal in team competition (1980).

BESFAMILNAYA, Nadezhda (1950—). Soviet runner. Born Dec 17, 1950. ❖ At Montreal Olympics, won a bronze medal in the 4 x 100-meter relay (1976).

BESKOW, Elsa (1874–1953). Swedish author and illustrator of children's books. Born Elsa Maartman, Feb 11, 1874, in Stockholm, Sweden; died 1953; dau. of Bernt (businessman) and Augusta (Fahlstedt) Maartman; attended Stockholm Technical School (now National College of Art, Craft, and Design); m. Fredrik Natanael Beskow (minister and headmaster), in 1892 or 1897; children: 6 sons. ❖ Wrote and illustrated 33 books and 8 collections of fairy tales (1897–52), which were praised for their insight into a child's perspective and for the accuracy and fine detail of their illustrations; writings include *Tant Grroen, Tant Brun, och Tant Gredelin* (1924, published in America as *Aunt Green, Aunt Brown, and Aunt Lavender,* 1928), *Pelle's New Suit* (1929), *The Tale of the Wee Little Old Woman* (1930) and *The Adventures of Peter and Lotta* (1931). Won a number of awards, including the Swedish Library Association, Nils Holgersson Plaque (1952); the Elsa Beskow Award for best Swedish picture book illustrator was established in her honor. ❖ See also *Women in World History.*

BESNYÖ, Eva (1910–2003). Hungarian-Dutch photographer. Name variations: Besnyo. Born in Budapest, Hungary, in 1910; died Dec 12 2003, in Laren, Netherlands; children: (with Wim Brusse) 2. ❖ After training with Budapest photographer Jozsef Pécsi, began career in Berlin, shooting for magazines and industry; during liaison with Dutch photographer John Fernhout, moved to Amsterdam, where she joined the Dutch Photographers' Society and worked commercially in architecture, portraits, and fashion, while also doing large mural work; helped organize the exhibition *Foto 37* at Stedelijk Museum (1937); was associated with the activist feminist group Dolle Mina (1970–76). A retrospective of her work was exhibited at Historisch Museum in Amsterdam (1982).

BESSA-LUÍS, Agustina (1922—). Portuguese novelist and playwright. Name variations: Agustina Bessa Luis; also seen as Augustina Bessa-Luis. Born María Agustina Bessa Luís, Oct 15, 1922, in Vila Mea, Amarante, Portugal; married; grandmother of Leonor Baldaque (actress). ❖ Known as the grand dame of contemporary Portuguese literature, came to prominence with *A Sibila* (The Sibyl, 1953); wrote over 30 books, often set in her hometown and often based on historical figures, including *Adivinhas de Pedro e Ines* (Riddles of Pedro and Ines, 1983), which concerns the romance between Peter I and Inez de Castro; also wrote *A Muralha* (1957), *O Inseparável* (1958), *As Relações Humanas* (1964), *A Brusca* (1971), *O Mosteiro* (1980), *Sebastião José* (1982), *Os Meninos de Ouro* (1983) and *Memórias laurentinas* (1996), among others. Won Camoes Award (2004).

BESSARABO, Hera (b. 1868). See *Myrtel, Hera.*

BESSBOROUGH, countess of (1761–1821). See *Spencer, Henrietta Frances.*

BESSERER, Eugénie (1868–1934). American character actress. Name variations: Eugenie Besserer. Born Dec 25, 1868, in Watertown, NY (some sources cite Marseille, France); died May 30, 1934, in Los Angeles, California; educated in a Canadian Convent. ❖ Following stage career, made film debut in the silent version of *The Wizard of Oz* (1910), followed by *The Profligate, The Count of Monte Cristo, The Rosary, The Crisis, The Garden of Allah, The Curse of Eve, A Hoosier Romance, Little Orphan Annie, Forty-Five Minutes from Broadway, Penrod, Anna Christie* (as Marthy, 1923), *Flesh and the Devil, Lilac Time, Illusion, Madame X* and *The Bridge of San Luis Rey,* among many others; best remembered as Al Jolson's mother in Hollywood's 1st talker *The Jazz Singer* (1927); also appeared in D.W. Griffith's *Scarlet Days, The Greatest Question* and *Drums of Love.*

BESSMERTNOVA, Natalia (1941—). Russian ballet dancer. Name variations: Natalya Igorevna Bessmertnova. Born July 19, 1941, in Moscow, Russia; m. Yuri Grigorovich (choreographer and Bolshoi master). ❖ Trained at the Bolshoi Ballet in Moscow where she continued to perform professionally throughout career; created female title role in Kasyan Goleizovsky's *Leili and Medsjhnun* (1964) and principal parts in 2 ballets by husband, *Ivan the Terrible* (1975) and *Angara* (1976); appeared as Odette/Odile, Swanilda, Giselle and Juliet at Bolshoi Ballet; starred in film versions of numerous Bolshoi productions, including *Ivan the Terrible* (1977), *Romeo and Juliet* (1976) and *Spartacus* (1977).

BESS OF HARDWICK (1518–1608). *See Talbot, Elizabeth.*

BESSON, Colette (1946—). French runner. Born April 7, 1946, in Royan, France. ❖ At Mexico City Olympics, won a gold medal in the 400 meters (1968).

BESSONOVA, Anna (1984—). Ukrainian rhythmic gymnast. Born July 29, 1984, in Kiev, Ukraine. ❖ Won World championship in clubs and hoop (2003) and team all-around (2001); won an indiv. all-around bronze medal at Athens Olympics (2004).

BEST, Edna (1900–1974). English stage and screen actress. Born Mar 3, 1900, in Hove, East Sussex, England; died Sept 18, 1974, in Geneva, Switzerland; m. Seymour Beard (actor, div.); m. Herbert Marshall (actor), 1928 (div. 1940); m. Nat Wolff, 1940 (died); children: (1st m.) twin sons; (2nd m.) Sarah Marshall (b. 1933, actress). ❖ Debuted on London stage in *Charley's Aunt* (1917) and had a great stage success in *The Constant Nymph* (1926); made British film debut in *Tilly of Bloomsbury* (1921); made Broadway debut in *These Charming People* (1925); other plays include *The Browning Version, Harlequinade, Captain Brassbound's Conversion* and *Ladies of the Corridor;* moved to Hollywood (1939) where she appeared in many films, including *Intermezzo, Escape, The Key, The Man Who Knew Too Much, The Late George Apley, The Ghost and Mrs. Muir* and *Iron Curtain*. Became US citizen (1950).

BEST, Mary Ellen (1809–1891). English artist. Born 1809 in York, England; died in Darmstadt, 1891. ❖ Primarily a watercolorist, whose subjects were mainly women; gave a unique glimpse into many aspects of English provincial life (1828–40). ❖ See also Caroline Davidson, *Women's Worlds: The Art & Life of Mary Ellen Best 1809–1891* (Crown, 1985).

BESTEMIANOVA, Natalia (1960—). Russian ice dancer. Born Jan 6, 1960, in Moscow, Russia. ❖ With Andrei Bukin, won a silver medal at Sarajevo Olympics (1984) and a gold medal at Calgary Olympics (1988); won Russian nationals (1982–83, 1987), European championships (1983, 1985–88), and World championships (1985–88).

BESTON, Elizabeth (1893–1986). *See Coatesworth, Elizabeth.*

BETANCOURT, Ingrid (1961—). Colombian politician. Born 1961 in Bogota, Colombia; grew up in France and Colombia; dau. of Yolanda Pulecio (ex-senator) and the ambassador to UNESCO; attended Institute of Political Studies in France; married and divorced; m. Juan Carlos Lecompte; children: Melanie and Lorenzo. ❖ Worked for the Ministry of Finance; was 1st elected to House of Representatives (1994), then to the Senate (1998), garnering the most votes in that election; published *Si sabia* and *La rabia en el corazón* (Rage in My Heart); created the New Colombia/Green Oxygen Party; as a candidate for president of Colombia (2002), was campaigning against corruption when she was kidnapped, along with her campaign manager Clara Rojas, by the Revolutionary Armed Forces of Colombia (FARC) guerrillas (Feb 23, 2002); as of Nov 4, 2004, had been held hostage for 1,000 days, while FARC continued to demand a prisoner exchange.

BETBEZE, Yolande (1930—). Miss America. Name variations: Yolande Fox. Born 1930; attended University of Alabama; m. Matthew Fox (film tycoon); children: 1 daughter. ❖ Named Miss America (1951), representing Alabama; refused to pose in a swimsuit, causing a stir with pageant sponsor Catalina (Catalina withdrew sponsorship and started the Miss Universe pageant); was active in the feminist movement. ❖ See also Frank Deford, *There She Is* (Viking, 1971).

BETHAM-EDWARDS, Matilda (1836–1919). British novelist and travel writer. Born Matilda Barbara Betham-Edwards at Westerfield, Suffolk, England, Mar 4, 1836; died at Hastings, Sussex, England, Jan 4, 1919; dau. of Edward Edwards (East Anglian farmer) and Barbara Betham; niece of Matilda Betham (1776–1852, poet and diarist); cousin of Amelia Blanford Edwards (author and Egyptologist); never married. ❖ As a teenager, wrote *The White House by the Sea,* which was published when she was 21 and reprinted for 40 years; left home to make her living as an author and journalist, covering French topics for the *Daily News;* with longtime friend Barbara Bodichon, traveled through Europe and wrote guides of the experience; other friends included Frederic Harrison and Henry James, whose correspondences and anecdotes she shared in her *Mid-Victorian Memories* (1919); also wrote *A Winter with the Swallows* (1866), *Through Spain to the Sahara* (1867), *Forestalled* (1880) and *Love and Marriage* (1884). ❖ See also autobiography, *Reminiscences* (1898); and *Women in World History.*

BETHÂNIA, Maria (1946—). Brazilian singer. Name variations: Maria Bethania. Born 1946 in Santo Amaro da Pruificaçao, Bahia, Brazil; sister of Caetano Veloso. ❖ One of the titans of modern Brazilian pop, was the 1st Brazilian singer to sell 1 million CDs, with *Álibi* (1978); made stage debut in Salvador (1963), singing a samba in the play *Boca de Ouro;* came to prominence singing "Carcará" and recorded her 1st CD (1965); released more than 30 CDs, including *Maricotinha Ao Vivo* (2002).

BETHELL, Mary Ursula (1874–1945). New Zealand social worker and poet. Name variations: Ursula Bethell; (pseudonyms) Evelyn Hayes or E.H. Born Oct 6, 1874, at Horsell, Surrey, England; died Jan 15, 1945, at Christchurch, New Zealand; dau. of Richard Bethell (barrister) and Isabella Anne (Lillie) Bethell; educated at Christchurch Girls High School, a Swiss finishing school, and Oxford; longtime companion of Effie Pollen. ❖ After studying in Germany and Switzerland, worked with Lady Margaret Hall Settlement in London (c. 1895); joined Women Workers for God in London (1899) and also assisted with Dundee Social Union in Scotland; performed social work for Church of England Central Society for Providing Homes for Waifs and Strays (1904); returned to Christchurch following WWI; donated family home to Anglican church to house St. Faith's House of Sacred Learning (1935); conceived most of her poetry in her garden, which overlooked a valley in Christchurch, and the view was often reflected in her lines; originally, only shared her work with correspondents, then permitted publication under the pseudonym Evelyn Hayes or under a reference to a former publication ("by the author of *Time and Place*"); remained anonymous during lifetime; poetry includes *From a Garden in the Antipodes* (1929), *Time and Place* (1936) and *Day and Night: Poems 1924–1934* (1939); contributed poems to Christchurch *Press* and *North Canterbury Gazette* under initials E.H.

BETHELL, Thyra Talvase (1882–1972). New Zealand society leader. Name variations: Thyra Talvase Beetham. Born Dec 5, 1882, in Wairarapa, New Zealand; died Nov 16, 1972, at Culverden, New Zealand; dau. of Hugh Horsley Beetham and Ruth (Bidwill) Beetham; m. Marmaduke Bethell (politician), 1904 (died 1955); children: 2 sons. ❖ Organized Red Cross nursing during WWI and supervised emergency measures during influenza pandemic of 1918; helped establish Amuri Hospital (1922); founded Culverden branch of Women's Division of New Zealand Farmers' Union (1929).

BETHELL, Ursula (1874–1945). *See Bethell, Mary Ursula.*

BETHOC (fl. 1000). Heiress of Scone. Name variations: Beatrice or Beatrix, heiress of Scone. Dau. of Malcolm II, king of Scots; m. Grimus also known as Crinan (d. 1045), mormaer of Atholl and abbot of Dunkeld, c. 1000; children: Duncan I (c. 1001–1040), king of Scots (r. 1034–1040); Maldred Dunkeld (d. after 1045), and a daughter (name unknown, who had a son Moddan).

BETHOC (fl. 11th c.). Scottish princess. Dau. of Donalbane or Donelbane also known as Donald III (c. 1033–1099), king of the Scots (r. 1093–1098) and Margaret, queen of Scots; married Hadria of Tynedale.

BETHSABEE (fl. 1010–975 BCE). *See Bathsheba.*

BETHUNE, Elizabeth (fl. 16th c.). Scottish royal mistress. Mistress of James V (1512–1542), king of Scotland (r. 1513–1542); children: (with James V) Jean Stuart.

BETHUNE, Jennie Louise (1856–1913). *See Bethune, Louise Blanchard.*

BETHUNE, Joanne (1770–1860). Canadian-American school founder. Born Feb 1, 1770, in Fort Niagara, Canada; died July 28, 1860, in New York, NY; dau. of John and Isabella Marshall Graham (1742–1814, educator). ❖ Taught in New York City at the school opened by her mother; organized the Orphan Asylum Society in NY (1806); founded the Female Union Society for the Promotion of Sabbath-Schools (1816); inspired by Swiss educator Pestalozzi, established the Infant School

Society, the 1st free school for infants in NY (1827); added 8 additional schools designed to assist working-class parents, with facilities to serve children between 18 months and 5 years of age.

BETHUNE, Louise Blanchard (1856–1913). American architect. Name variations: Jennie Louise Bethune. Born Jennie Louise Blanchard, July 21, 1856, in Waterloo, New York; died Dec 18, 1913, in Buffalo, NY; m. Robert Bethune (architect), Dec 1881. ❖ The 1st woman elected to the American Institute of Architects (1888) and their 1st woman fellow (1889), began career as a draftsperson in the architectural office of Richard A. Waite; at 25, opened her own architectural office in partnership with Robert Bethune (1881), whom she later married; worked on a broad range of structures, including stores, factories, chapels, banks, schools, houses and apartment buildings; designed 18 schools, including the Lockport Union High School in western NY; completed Buffalo's 225-room Hotel Lafayette (1904); became the best-known woman practicing architecture in the country. ❖ See also *Women in World History*.

BETHUNE, Mary McLeod (1875–1955). African-American educator and civil-rights activist. Pronunciation: Beth-OON. Born Mary McLeod, July 10, 1875, near Mayesville, South Carolina; died May 18, 1955, in Daytona Beach, Florida; dau. of Samuel McLeod (farmer) and Patsy McIntosh; educated at Scotia Seminary and Moody Bible Institute; m. Albertus Bethune, 1898; children: Albert (b. 1899). ❖ One of America's most outstanding educators, as well as a major advocate of racial equality and civil rights, began career as a teacher at Lucy Laney's Haines Institute; founded what was to become one of the most important educational establishments in the South, the Daytona Normal and Industrial Institute for Girls (1904); embarked on a program of fund raising, organizing her pupils into a choir which raised money by giving concerts throughout Florida, launching a series of lecture tours; purchased land and built new facilities (1906), while enrollment at the school expanded to some 250 pupils (which now included boys); was one of the prime movers in organizing what became known as the McLeod Hospital (1911); merged her school with the Cookman Institute, a co-educational college located in Jacksonville, Florida (1923), which, as Bethune-Cookman College, become one of the leading junior colleges in US; served 2 terms as president of National Association of Colored Women (NACW, 1924 and 1928); founded National Council of Negro Women (NCNW, 1935), serving as president for 14 years; during Roosevelt's presidency, began serving as director of Minority Affairs in the New Deal's National Youth Administration (1936); became director of Division of Negro Affairs (1939), at that time the most important appointment an African-American woman had held in US government service; during WWII, was a special assistant to the secretary of war and responsible for the selection of the 1st females for officer-training schools, insisting on a fixed portion of available places for African-American women; represented National Association for the Advancement of Colored People's (NAACP) at the conference in San Francisco to write the inaugural charter for the UN (1945). Was the 2nd African-American woman to receive Spingarn Medal (1935); a monument was dedicated to her in Washington DC's Lincoln Park, the 1st statue in the capital to honor either an African-American or a woman (1974). ❖ See also Rackham Holt, *Mary McLeod Bethune* (Doubleday, 1964); Emma Gelders Sterne, *Mary McLeod Bethune* (Knopf, 1957); and *Women in World History*.

BETKER, Jan (c. 1960—). Canadian curler. Born c. 1960 in Regina, Saskatchewan, Canada. ❖ Won a gold medal for curling at Nagano Olympics (1998); with Team Schmirler, won the World championship (1993, 1994, 1997), the only 3-time winner in the history of the sport. ❖ See also *Gold on Ice* (Coteau Books, 1989).

BETKIN, Elisabeth (fl. 1476). *See Scepens, Elizabeth.*

BETTERTON, Mrs. (d. 1712). *See Saunderson, Mary.*

BETTIGNIES, Louise de (d. 1918). *See de Bettignies, Louise.*

BETTINA (1785–1859). *See Arnim, Bettine von.*

BETTIS, Valerie (1919–1982). American dancer and choreographer. Born Valerie Elizabeth Bettis in Houston, Texas, Dec 20, 1919; died Sept. 26, 1982, in New York, NY; dau. of Royal Holt and Valerie Elizabeth (McCarthy) Bettis; attended University of Texas; studied dance with Rowena Smith and Tina Flade in Houston; m. Bernardo Segall (Brazilian concert pianist and composer), 1943 (div.); m. Arthur A. Schmidt. ❖ Studied under Hanya Holm in whose *Trend* she made her professional debut (1937); was a member of the Hanya Holm company (1938–40); had 1st major solo in *The Desperate Heart* (1943); founded

her own group (1944), presenting, among others, *As I Lay Dying* and *Domino Furioso;* choreographed *Virginia Sampler* for Ballet Russe de Monte Carlo (1947); enjoyed a huge success on Broadway as Tiger Lily in the musical *Inside USA* (1948); choreographed for tv (1940s); in Hollywood, worked on 2 Rita Hayworth films: *Affair in Trinidad* and *Salomé* (1951); also choreographed and appeared in off-Broadway and London productions of *Ulysses in Nighttown* (1958); founded her own dance studio in NY (1963) and also taught at Perry-Mansfield School at Connecticut College.

BETTJEMAN, Agnes Muir (1885–1964). New Zealand nurse and midwife. Name variations: Nancy Muir Bettjeman, Agnes Muir McNab, Nancy Muir McNab. Born July 4, 1885, at Port Glasgow, Renfrewshire, Scotland; died 1964; dau. of James McNab (ship carpenter) and Mary (Mirk) McNab; m. Frederick Charles Bettjeman (engineer), 1916; children: 5. ❖ Immigrated to New Zealand (1919); became involved in nursing during influenza pandemic of 1918; provided unofficial nursing and midwifery services in Whanganui River valley, with supplies provided by Red Cross.

BETTJEMAN, Nancy Muir (1885–1964). *See Bettjeman, Agnes Muir.*

BETTS, Anna Whelan (1873–1959). American illustrator. Born 1873 in Philadelphia, Pennsylvania; died 1959; sister of Ethel Franklin Betts (children's book illustrator); attended Pennsylvania Academy of the Fine Arts and Drexel Institute, both Philadelphia; studied with Robert Vannoh and Howard Pyle. ❖ Rendered delicate color illustrations for such popular magazines as *St. Nicholas, Harper's Monthly, The Ladies' Home Journal* and *The Century Magazine;* at height of career, developed eye trouble and had to stop illustrating; became a director and art teacher at Solebury School in New Hope, Pennsylvania, a post she held for 20 years; was also a member of the Philadelphia Watercolor Society.

BETTS, Doris (1932—). American novelist and short-story writer. Born June 4, 1932, in Statesville, North Carolina; only child of William Elmore Waugh (cotton mill worker) and Mary Ellen (Freeze) Waugh; attended Woman's College of University of North Carolina at Greensboro and University of North Carolina; m. Lowry Betts (lawyer), 1952; children: 3. ❖ Began teaching creative writing at University of North Carolina at Chapel Hill (1966), becoming Alumni Distinguished Professor of English there and serving 2 terms as chair of the faculty, the 1st woman to achieve that distinction; published 1st short-story collection, *The Gentle Insurrection* (1954), which won the Putnam prize; followed that with *The Astronomer and Other Stories* (1966), which is considered her masterpiece, and *Beasts of the Southern Wild* (1973); novels include *Tall Houses in Winter* (1957), *The Scarlet Thread* (1964), *The River to Pickle Beach* (1972), *Heading West* (1981) and *Souls Raised from the Dead* (1994). Won Southern Book Award; her short story "Violet" was filmed and won an Academy Award (1982).

BETTS, Ethel Franklin (1878—). American illustrator. Name variations: Ethel Betts Bains. Born 1878; death date unknown; sister of Anna Whelan Betts; studied with Howard Pyle at Drexel Institute in Philadelphia. ❖ Popular illustrator of children's books during the "Golden Age of Illustration," moved with sister to Wilmington, Delaware, to continue studying with Pyle when he established a school there; books include *The Raggedy Man* (1907), *Fairy Tales from Grimm* (1917), *The Complete Mother Goose* and *The Six Swans,* which won a bronze medal at Panama-Pacific International Exposition (1915).

BETZ, Pauline (1919—). American tennis player. Name variations: Bobbie Betz, Pauline Betz Addie. Born Pauline May Betz, Aug 6, 1919, Dayton, Ohio; grew up in Los Angeles; graduated Rollins College, 1943; m. Bob Addie (sportswriter for *Washington Post*). ❖ A baseline player, won US singles title (1942–44, 1946), but international career was mostly dormant because of WWII; won Wimbledon championship (1946). Inducted into International Tennis Hall of Fame (1965).

BEUMER, Catharina (1947—). Dutch swimmer. Born July 1947. ❖ At Tokyo Olympics, won a bronze medal in the 4 x 100-meter freestyle relay (1964).

BEURTON, Ruth (1907–2000). *See Kuczinski, Ruth.*

BEUS, Bernadette de (1958—). *See de Beus, Bernadette de.*

BEUTLER, Maja (1936—). Swiss novelist. Born Dec 8, 1936, in Berne, Switzerland. ❖ German-speaking writer, came to prominence with her semi-autobiographical *Fuß fassen (Gaining a Foothold,* 1980), about a mother confronted by cancer; other writings include *Flissingen fehlt auf der Karte* (1976), *Die Wortfalle* (1983), *Das Marmelspiel* (1985), *Das*

Bildnis der Doña Quichotte (1989) and *Die Stunde, da wir fliegen lernen* (1994).

BEUTLER, Margarete (1876–1949). German poet and playwright. Name variations: Margarethe or Margaretha Beutler. Born 1876 in Pomerania, Germany; died 1949. ❖ Worked as an editor in Munich; studied medicine and became a gynecologist; poetry, which focuses on woman's position in society, includes *Gedichte* (1902); also wrote the play *Das Lied des Todes* (1911) and translated plays by Molière.

BEVAN, Mrs. Aneurin (1904–1988). *See Lee, Jennie.*

BEVANS, Philippa (1913–1968). English actress. Born Feb 10, 1913, in London, England; died May 10, 1968, in New York, NY; dau. of Viola Roache (actress, 1885–1961). ❖ Began career on the London stage as a child; made Broadway debut in *The Stepdaughters of the War* (1930); other plays include *Ah Wilderness, Dream Girl, The Long Voyage Home, Mr. Pickwick, My Fair Lady* and *What Did We Do Wrong?*; appeared in such films as *The Notorious Landlady, The World of Henry Orient* and *The Group.*

BEVEL, Diane Nash (1938—). *See Nash, Diane.*

BEVIER, Isabel (1860–1942). American educator and reformer. Born near Plymouth, Ohio, Nov 14, 1860; died in Urbana, Illinois, Mar 17, 1942; graduate of Wooster College, 1885, MA, 1888; attended Case School of Applied Science, 1888–89, Harvard, 1891, Wesleyan, 1894, Western Reserve, and Massachusetts Institute of Technology. ❖ Vital force in educational reform, brought the subject of home economics into the realm of scientific study on the university level; for 9 years, taught science courses at Pennsylvania College for Women in Pittsburgh; was appointed head of the new home-economics department at University of Illinois (Urbana), which she quickly renamed the department of "household science" (1900) and established one of the 1st home-economics laboratories; served as the 2nd president of American Home Economics Association (1910–15); during WWI, served briefly in Washington, DC, as an advisor on food conservation; also chaired the home-economics department of University of California, Los Angeles (1921–23), and is credited with the idea of using a thermometer in the cooking of meat. ❖ See also *Women in World History.*

BEVILACQUA, Alma (1910–1988). Italian novelist. Name variations: (pseudonym) Giovanna Zangrandi. Born 1910 in Galliera, Bologna, Italy; died 1988. ❖ Worked as science teacher; was active in Resistance during WWII; wrote about countryside and of partisans after war in such works as *Leggende delle Dolomiti* (1950), *I Brusaz* (1954), *Il campo rosso* (1959), *I giorni veri, 1943–45* (1963), *Anni con Attila* (1966), and *Il diario di Chiara* (1972).

BEVINGTON, L.S. (1845–1895). British poet and essayist. Name variations: Louisa Sarah Bevington; Louisa S. Guggenberger; (pseudonym) Arbor Leigh. Born Louisa Sarah Bevington, 1845, in London, England; died 1895 in London; dau. of Alexander Bevington and Louisa (De Hermes) Bevington; m. Ignatz Guggenberger, 1883. ❖ Acquired strong sense of social justice from Quaker parents, but became an agnostic and anarchist; spent time in Germany with husband, then returned to England and associated with international atheists and anarchists; works of poetry include *Key Notes* (1876), *Poems, Lyrics, and Sonnets* (1882) and *Liberty Lyrics* (1895); published articles on anarchism and socialism, including "Atheism and Morality" (1879), "Why I am an Expropriationist" (1894) and "Anarchism and Violence" (1896).

BEWLEY, Lois (c. 1936—). American ballet dancer and designer. Born c. 1936 in Louisville, Kentucky. ❖ Performed with numerous companies at start of career, including Ballet Russe de Monte Carlo (c. 1955–57), Ballet Theater (c. 1957–58), Alicia Markova's touring group (1958), and Jerome Robbins' Ballets: U.S.A.; joined New York City Ballet (1960), where she appeared in works of Balanchine and Robbins; was acclaimed for performances in 2 comic ballets by Todd Bolender, *Souvenirs* and *Creation of the World;* formed trio dance group with Charles Bennett and William Carter, performing at Pablo Casals Festival in Puerto Rico (1960) and in her own piece *Pi-r²* to enthusiastic NY audiences (1961); returned to stage in solo recitals in NY (as of 1976), performing 10 ballets she created and designed; retired from performing (1980) to design fashion and streetwear.

BEWS, Mary Ellen (1856–1945). New Zealand school principal and founder. Born Aug 20, 1856, in Glasgow, Scotland; died Mar 29, 1945, in Auckland, New Zealand; dau. of David Bews and Ann (Anderson) Bews. ❖ Studied in Europe and became accomplished linguist; immigrated to New Zealand with family (1885); co-founded secondary school for girls in Auckland, Mount Eden College (1895) and served as principal. ❖ See also *Dictionary of New Zealand Biography* (Vol. 2).

BEY, Hannelore (1941—). German ballet dancer. Born Nov 6, 1941, in Leipzig, Germany. ❖ Performed with Gret Palucca's Dresden State Opera Ballet in East Germany; joined Berlin Comic Opera where she was featured in 19th-century classics as well as neo-romantic ballets by Tom Schilling, including his *La Mer, Cinderella* (1968), *Ondine* (1970) and *Romeo and Juliet* (1973).

BEYER, Helga (1920–1942). German-Jewish member of the anti-Nazi resistance. Born in Breslau (now Wroclaw, Poland), May 4, 1920; murdered near Dessau, Feb 1942; dau. of Adolf Beyer (Jewish businessman) and Else Beyer (who was not Jewish); sister of Ursel Beyer (b. 1918). ❖ Joined an anti-Nazi resistance cell (1933); became a member of German-Jewish youth group Kameraden, resisting Fascism under the sign of the Weisse Möwe (White Gull); for more than 3 years, worked as a courier in a resistance cell organized by a group of Communist Oppositionists in Breslau; arrested (Jan 28, 1938), convicted of "preparation for high treason," and sentenced to 3 years imprisonment; though sentence was scheduled to end Aug 1941, was moved to the women's concentration camp, Ravensbrück; taken to Bernburg near Dessau and killed as part of a group of other female "undesirables." ❖ See also *Women in World History.*

BEYERMANN, Ina (1967—). West German swimmer. Born April 11, 1967. ❖ At Los Angeles Olympics, won a bronze medal in the 200-meter butterfly and a silver medal in the 4 x 100-meter medley relay (1984).

BEYNON, Francis Marion (1884–1951). Canadian novelist, journalist and women's-rights activist. Name variations: F.M. Beynon. Born Francis Marion Beynon, 1884, in Ontario, Canada; grew up on a homestead near Hartney, Manitoba; died 1951; dau. of Ontario immigrant farmers; sister of activist Lillian Beynon Thomas (1874–1961). ❖ Trained as a teacher but worked as a catalogue writer for T. Eaton Co.; with sister, formed the Quill Club (1908), a group of intellectuals and journalists; worked for women's suffrage and opposed conscription; became editor of the Women's Page for *Grain Grower's Guide* (1912), and was soon a prominent voice for the rights of rural women; with sister, friend Nellie McClung and others, helped form Political Equality League (1912); wrote *Aleta Dey* (1919), expressing opposition to militarism in Canadian life. ❖ See also Wendy Lill (play) *The Fighting Days* (2004), which focuses on Beynon and Nellie McClung.

BEYNON, Lillian (1874–1961). *See Thomas, Lillian Beynon.*

BEYONCÉ (1981—). *See Knowles, Beyoncé.*

BHANDARI, Mannu (1931—). Indian novelist and short-story writer. Born 1931 in India; dau. of a scholar who compiled the 1st Hindi dictionary. ❖ Taught Hindi at University of Delhi; writings in Hindi include *Apala Banti* (1974), *Mahabhoj* (1979, adapted for the stage, then for the BBC as *The Great Feast* 1981), *Apane se Pare* (1981), *Svami* (1982), and *Bunty* (1983), and the short-story collections *Meri Priya Kahaniyan* and *Trishanku.*

BHANUREKHA or BHANUREKHA, Baby (1954—). *See Rekha.*

BHARDWAJ, Mohini (1978—). American gymnast. Name variations: Mohini Bardway. Born Sept 29, 1978, in Philadelphia, Pennsylvania. ❖ Won a bronze medal for team all-around at World championships (2001); won a silver medal for team all-around at Athens Olympics (2004). Won Honda Award (2000).

BHATIA, June (1919—). Canadian novelist. Name variations: (pseudonym) Helen Forrester. Born 1919 in Hoylake, Cheshire, England; grew up in Liverpool; m. Avadh Behari Bhatia (physics professor at University of Alberta), 1950 (died 1985); children: 1 son. ❖ Married and lived in India; immigrated to Canada (1953), settling in Alberta (1953); autobiographical works portraying childhood of poverty in England are *Twopence to Corss the Mersey* (1974), *Minerva's Stepchild* (1979), *By the Waters of Liverpool* (1981) and *Lime Street at Two* (1985); novels include *Most Precious Employee* (1976), *Liverpool Daisy* (1979), *The Latchkey Kid* (1985), *Thursday's Child* (1985) and *Yes, Mama* (1988).

BHREATHNACH, Naimh (1945—). Irish politician. Born June 1945 in Dublin, Ireland; m. Tom Ferris. ❖ Began career as a remedial teacher;

representing Labour, elected to the 27th Dáil (1992–97) for Dún Laoghaire; served as minister for Education (1993–97).

BHUTTO, Benazir (1953—). Pakistani political leader and prime minister. Born in Karachi, West Pakistan, June 21, 1953; dau. of Zulfikar Ali Bhutto (president of Parkistan, 1971–77) and Nusrat Bhutto (b. 1929); attended Radcliffe College, Harvard University; graduated with honors from Lady Margaret Hall, Oxford University, 1976; m. Asif Ali Zardari; children: 3, including son Bilawal (b. 1988) and daughter Asifa. ❖ Came to prominence when she spoke out over her father's arrest and subsequent hanging as the result of a coup; was placed under house arrest (1977–84); along with mother, became leader in exile of Pakistan People's Party; returned to Pakistan (1986) to lead the Movement for the Restoration of Democracy; was appointed prime minister (1988), becoming the 1st woman to head a modern Muslim state; removed from office on charges of corruption (1990); served 2nd term as prime minister (1993–96); in college days, was also elected to a 3-month term as president of the Oxford Union, the 1st foreign woman to be accorded this honor (1976); writings include *Pakistan: The Gathering Storm* (1983) and *The Way Out: Interviews, Impressions, Statements, and Messages* (1988). ❖ See also *Daughter of Destiny: An Autobiography* (Simon and Schuster, 1989); and *Women in World History*.

BHUTTO, Nusrat (1929—). First lady of Pakistan and politician. Name variations: Begum Nusrat Bhutto. Born Nusrat Isphahani in Bombay, India, Mar 23, 1929; dau. of Mirza Mohamed Isphahani and Fatima Sultana Isphahani; m. Zulfikar Ali Bhutto (president and prime minister of Pakistan, 1971–77), in 1951; children: 2 daughters, including Benazir Bhutto (b. 1953, politician), and 2 sons, including Shahwanaz (d. 1985). ❖ Began career as a university lecturer; was captain in the Women's National Guard (1947–48); was first lady of Pakistan (1971–77); served as chair of Pakistan Red Crescent Society (1974–77); elected to National Assembly (1977); following coup against husband, was imprisoned (1977–80); became head of Pakistan People's Party (PPP), the leading member of the Movement for the Restoration of Democracy; with daughter Benazir, became co-chair of the party (1986); began to serve on National Assembly (1988); when Benazir Bhutto became prime minister of Pakistan (1988), was appointed senior minister; saw fortunes rise and fall with those of her daughter. ❖ See also *Women in World History*.

BI WENJING (1981—). Chinese gymnast. Name variations: Bi Wenjiing. Born July 28, 1981, in China. ❖ At Atlanta Olympics, won a silver medal in uneven bars (1996).

BIANCA. *Variant of Blanche.*

BIANCA DE MEDICI (1548–1587). *See Cappello, Bianca.*

BIANCA MARIA SFORZA (1472–1510). *See Sforza, Bianca Maria.*

BIANCA MARIA VISCONTI (1423–1470). *See Visconti, Bianca Maria.*

BIANCA OF NAVARRE. *See Blanche of Navarre.*

BIANCA OF SICILY (1385–1441). *See Blanche of Navarre.*

BIANCHEDI, Diana (1969—). Italian fencer. Born Nov 4, 1969, in Milan, Italy. ❖ Won a gold medal at Barcelona Olympics (1992) and a gold medal at Sydney Olympics (2000), both for team foil; at World championships, won team gold medals (1991, 1995).

BIANCHINI, Angela (1921—). Italian essayist, novelist and literary critic. Born 1921, of Jewish parents in Italy. ❖ With family, fled Mussolini's racist Italy before WWII; studied French semantics at Johns Hopkins; returned to Italy and became director of Sarah Lawrence College there, in charge of American studies; contributed to magazines, radio, and tv; writings include *Romanzi d'amore e d'avventura* (1957), *Lungo equinoxio* (1962), *Spiriti costretti* (1963), *Le nostre distanze* (1965), *Il romanzo di appendice* (1969), *Cent'anni di romanzo spagnolo* (1971) and *Voce Donna* (1979).

BIANCO, Margery Williams (1881–1944). English novelist, translator, and children's writer. Name variations: wrote under Margery Williams, Margery Williams Bianco, and Margery Bianco. Born Margery Williams, July 22, 1881, in London, England; died Sept 4, 1944, in New York, NY; dau. of Robert (barrister, distinguished classical scholar, and journalist) and Florence (Harper) Williams; m. Francesco Bianco (dealer in rare books and manuscripts), 1904; children: Cecco Bianco; Pamela Bianco (artist and illustrator of children's books). ❖ Best remembered for her children's classic *The Velveteen Rabbit* (1922), published 1st book, *The Late Returning*, in England (1902), but wrote most of stories after her

children were nearly grown; following *The Velveteen Rabbit,* produced *The Little Wooden Doll* (1925), illustrated with daughter Pamela's early drawings; other writings include *Poor Cecco* (1925), *The Apple Tree* (1926), *The Adventures of Andy* (1927), *The Skin Horse* (1927), *The House That Grew Smaller* (1931), *The Hurdy-Gurdy Man* (1933), *The Good Friends* (1934), (with J.C. Bowman) *Green Grows the Garden* (1936), *Tales from a Finnish Tupa* (1936), *Winterbound* (1936), *Rufus the Fox* (1937), (with G. Loeffler) *Franzi and Gizi* (1941), *Bright Morning* (1942), *The Five-and-a-half Club* (1942), *Penny and the White Horse* (1942) and *Herbert's Zoo* (1949). ❖ See also autobiographical *Bright Morning* (1942); and *Women in World History.*

BIANCO, Pamela (1906–1994). English-born artist and writer for children. Name variations: Pamela B. Hartmann. Born Dec 31, 1906, in London, England; died Dec 1994, in New York, NY; dau. of Francesco Giuseppe (bibliographer and poet) and Margery (Williams) Bianco (writer); m. Robert Schlick, 1930 (div. 1955); m. Georg Theodor Hartmann (artist), July 25, 1955 (died 1976); children: (1st m.) Lorenzo Bianco. ❖ At 11, drawings were exhibited at Circolo degli Artisti in Turin; received an invitation to exhibit at Anderson Galleries in New York (1922); wrote and illustrated *The Starlit Journey* (1933), *Joy and the Christmas Angel* (1949), *Paradise Square* (1950), *Little Houses Far Away* (1951), *The Look-Inside Easter Egg* (1952), *The Doll in the Window* (1953), *The Valentine Party* (1954) and *Toy Rose* (1957); illustrated books for her mother and others. ❖ See also *Women in World History.*

BIANCO, Suzannah (1973—). American synchronized swimmer. Born Suzanne Dyroen, May 5, 1973, in San Jose, California; sister of Becky Dyroen-Lancer (synchronized swimmer); attended West Valley College; m. Brad Bianco (cyclist). ❖ Won a team gold medal at Atlanta Olympics (1996).

BIAS, Fanny (1789–1825). French ballet dancer. Name variations: Fanny la Désossée or la Desossee. Born 1789 in Paris, France; died Sept 6, 1825, in Paris. ❖ Premiere danseuse at the Paris Opéra, trained and performed there throughout most of professional career; danced in Milon's *Clari* (1820), and in revivals of Jean Aumer's *Les Pages du Duc de Vendôme* and François Décombe Albert's *Cendrillon* (Cinderella); performed under ballet master André Jean-Jacques Deshayes at King's Theatre in London (1821).

BIBBY, Mary Ann (c. 1832–1910). New Zealand shopkeeper. Name variations: Mary Ann Woodhouse. Born Mary Ann Woodhouse, c. 1832 (baptized, June 10, 1832), in Heaton, Lancashire, England; died Jan 13, 1910, at Waipawa, New Zealand; dau. of Thomas Woodhouse (fisherman and miller) and Ann Woodhouse; m. Edward Bibby (carpenter), 1861 (died 1901); children: 4 sons, 4 daughters. ❖ Immigrated with husband to New Zealand (1861); opened store with him in Abbottsford (Waipawa, 1862); imported goods through brother in Liverpool and developed a successful mail-order business. ❖ See also *Dictionary of New Zealand Biography* (Vol. 2).

BIBESCO, Elizabeth (1897–1943). English writer. Name variations: Princess Bibesco. Born Elizabeth Asquith in 1897; died 1943; dau. of Herbert Henry Asquith (1852–1928, later earl of Oxford and Asquith) and Margot (Tennant) Asquith; stepsister of Violet Bonham-Carter (1887–1969); m. Prince Antoine Bibesco, 1919. ❖ Wrote *I Have Only Myself to Blame* (1921), *Balloons* (1923), *There is No Return* (1927) and *Portrait of Caroline* (1931). ❖ See also *Women in World History.*

BIBESCO, Marthe Lucie (1887–1973). Romanian novelist and essayist. Name variations: Princess Bibesco; (pseudonym) Lucile Decaux. Born Marthe Lucile Lohovary, Jan 28, 1887, in Romania; died in Paris, Nov 29, 1973; dau. of Jean Lohovary (minister for foreign affairs and president of the Senate) and Princess Smaranda "Emma" (Mavrocordato) Lohovary (collateral descendant of the Prince Mavrocordato); m. Prince George Bibesco (grandson of the Prince of Wallachia, now Romania), in 1902. ❖ At 18, produced her 1st travel book; during career, wrote numerous books under her own name and 6 historical novels under pseudonym Lucile Decaux (only one of which, *Katia,* was translated into English); wrote in French, though her books were translated into various European languages; best known for her reminiscences of titled and diplomatic circles; novels include *Catherine-Paris* (1928), *The Green Parrot* (1929), *Balloons* (1929) and *Worlds Apart* (1935); nonfiction includes (travel memoir) *The Eight Paradises* (1923), *Isvor: The Country of Willows* (1924), *Royal Portraits* (1928), *Lord Thomson of Cardington* (1932), *Alexander of Asia* (1935), *A Daughter of Napoleon* (1937) and *Flowers: Tulips, Hyacinths, Narcissi* (1940). ❖ See also Christine Sutherland, *Enchantress: Marthe Bibesco and Her World* (Farrar, 1996); and *Women in World History*.

BIBESCO, Princess (1887–1973). *See Bibesco, Marthe Lucie.*

BIBESCO, Princess (1897–1945). *See Bibesco, Elizabeth.*

BIBIANA (d. 363). Roman martyr. Name variations: Vivian. Died in Rome in 363; dau. of Flavian (formerly prefect of Rome) and Dafrosa. ❖ During the Christian-baiting reign of Roman emperor Julian the Apostate (355–363), was tied to a pillar by Apronianus and beaten with leaded cords until she died. Feast day is Dec 2. ❖ See also *Women in World History*.

BIBLE, Frances L. (1919–2001). American mezzo-soprano. Born 1919 in Sackets Harbor, NY; died Jan 29, 2001, in New York, NY; studied voice at Juilliard School. ❖ Starred at New York City Opera for nearly 30 years, making debut as the Shepherd in *Tosca* (1948); created roles in several contemporary works, including Augusta Tabor in Douglas Moore's *Ballad of Baby Doe* (1956) and Elizabeth Proctor in Robert Ward's *Crucible* (1961); also sang in the premiere of *Dybbuk*.

BICHEROVA, Olga (1966—). Soviet gymnast. Born Oct 26, 1966, in Moscow, Russia; m. Valentin Mogilny (gymnastic champion), 1986 (sep). ❖ At World championships, won gold medals in team all-round and all-around (1981) and team all-around (1983); at Chunichi Cup, placed 1st in all-around, vault, and balance beam (1981); at World Cup, won gold medals in all-around, vault, and floor exercise, a silver medal in uneven bars, and a bronze medal in balance beam (1982); at European championship, won gold medals in all-around, vault, and floor exercise (1983); moved to France and provides tv commentary for French Eurosport.

BICHOVSKY, Elisheva (1888–1949). Russian poet. Name variations: Élishéva Bichovsky; Elisaveta Ivanovna Zirkowa; (pseudonym) Elisheva. Born Elisaveta Ivanovna Zirkowa in 1888 in Russia; died 1949; dau. of the village schoolteacher and an English mother; m. Shimon Bichovsky, 1920. ❖ Born into a Christian family but began to live in Jewish community and study Hebrew and Jewish culture (1907); immigrated with husband to Eretz Israel (1925); writings, written in Hebrew, include *Kos Ketana* (1926), *Harouzim* (1928), *Mikreh Tafel* (1929), *Shirim* (1946) and *Yalkout Shirim* (1970); also translated English and Hebrew poetry into Russian.

BICHYK, Yuliya (1983—). Belarusian rower. Born April 1, 1983, in Minsk, USSR. ❖ At World championships, placed 2nd for coxless pair and quadruple sculls (2003); won a bronze medal for coxless pair at Athens Olympics (2004).

BICKERDYKE, Mary Ann (1817–1901). American nurse. Name variations: Mary Anne Ball Bickerdyke or Byckerdyke; Mother Bickerdyke. Born Mary Ann Ball, July 19, 1817, in Knox Co., Ohio; died in Bunker Hill, Kansas, Nov 8, 1901; dau. of Hiram Ball (farmer and businessman) and Anne (Cassady) Ball; m. Robert Bickerdyke (widower, housepainter, and musician), April 27, 1847 (died 1859); children: John Ball (b. 1849), James Rodgers (1850–1904), Hiram Ball (1854–1909), and Martha M. (1858–1860). ❖ Nurse and Sanitary Commission agent in the Civil War, whose strength, tireless devotion, and care for the wounded "boys in blue" earned her the respect and friendship of generals; moved with family to Galesburg, Illinois (1858); volunteered as a "nurse" in the Civil War (1861–65); worked with the Chicago Home for the Friendless (1866–67); operated a boarding house for veterans in Salina, Kansas (1867–69); worked for the Protestant Board of City Missions in NY (1870–74); helped Kansas locust plague victims (1874); worked at US Mint in San Francisco (1876–87); granted a pension from Congress (1886); returned to Kansas (1887). A monument was erected to her memory in Galesburg, Illinois (1903). ❖ See also Julia A. Houghton Chase, *Mary A. Bickerdyke, "Mother"* (1896); Martin Litvin, *The Young Mary, 1817–1861* (Log City, 1977); and *Women in World History*.

BICKERDYKE, Mother (1817–1901). *See Bickerdyke, Mary Ann.*

BICKNELL, Jessie (1871–1956). New Zealand nurse and hospital matron. Born Mar 27, 1871, in Oamaru, New Zealand; died Oct 13, 1956, in Auckland, New Zealand; dau. of Frederick Bicknell (postmaster) and Elizabeth (Armstrong) Bicknell. ❖ Trained as nurse at Nelson Hospital, qualifying in 1903; named assistant inspector in Department of Hospital and Charitable Aid (1907); appointed deputy matron in chief of New Zealand Army Nursing Service (1915); made associate of Royal Red Cross and was active in New Zealand Overseas Women War Workers' Association during WWI; became 1st New Zealand-born director of nursing in Department of Health (1923); helped establish post-graduate course in nursing at University of New Zealand (1928); active in New Zealand Trained Nurses' Association. ❖ See also *Dictionary of New Zealand Biography* (Vol. 3).

BID'A (856–915). Arab composer and singer. Born 856; died 915; studied under Oraib. ❖ Sang for Caliph al-Mutamid (r. 870–892) and became enormously wealthy. ❖ See also *Women in World History*.

BIDAUD, Laurence (1968—). Swiss curler. Born Mar 22, 1968, in Switzerland. ❖ Won a silver medal for curling at Salt Lake City Olympics (2002).

BIDDER, Anna McClean (1903–2001). British marine biologist. Born Anna McClean Bidder, May 4, 1903, in Cambridge, England; died Oct 1, 2001; dau. of George Parker Bidder III (zoologist) and Marion Greenwood Bidder (1862–1932, physiologist); Newnham College, Cambridge, PhD, 1934. ❖ Specializing in squids, cuttlefish, and pearly nautilus, worked at Marine Laboratory, Plymouth (1927, 1929, and 1930); occupied Cambridge table at Stazione Zoologica, Naples (1928 and 1930); performed marine fieldwork at Banyuls-sur-Mer (1929); taught in zoology department (1929–65) and served as curator of mollusks (1963–70) at Cambridge University; taught physiology and botany at Newnham and Girton Colleges; researched cephalopods; cofounded Lucy Cavendish College, Cambridge, and served as president (1965–70); joined Society of Friends and served on several Quaker committees.

BIDDER, Marion Greenwood (1862–1932). British physiologist. Born Marion Greenwood, Aug 24, 1862, at Myton, Hull, England; died Sept 25, 1932; attended Girton College, Cambridge, 1879–83, 1883–84; m. George Parker Bidder III (zoologist), June 8, 1899; children: Caroline Bidder (b. 1900) and Anna McClean Bidder (zoologist, 1903–2001). ❖ Served as lecturer in physiology (1885–87) and head of laboratory (1890–99) at Balfour Laboratory, University of Cambridge; served as lecturer and director of biology studies at Newnham and Girton colleges, Cambridge (1888–89); became one of 1st women at Cambridge to conduct independent research; became 1st woman to present her own paper at meeting of Royal Society; gave up professional scientific work upon marriage (1899). With Florence Baddeley, wrote *Domestic Economy in Theory and Practice* (1901).

BIDDLE, Esther (1629–1696). *See Biddle, Hester.*

BIDDLE, Hester (1629–1696). British religious writer. Name variations: Esther Biddle. Born 1629 in England; grew up in Oxford; died 1696; m. Thomas Biddle; children: 3. ❖ Brought up as Anglican in Oxford but became a Quaker (1640s); published such tracts as *Wo to thee city of Oxford* (1655) and *The Trumpet of the Lord God* (1662), which denounced sins of the flesh and called for social justice and reform; as public speaker, was arrested several times for preaching in the streets.

BIDDY OF THE BULLER (c. 1802/27–1899). *See Goodwin, Bridget.*

BIDIOUANE, Nouzha (1969—). Moroccan hurdler. Born 1969 in Morocco. ❖ Won a gold medal at World championships (1997) and a bronze medal at Sydney Olympics (2000), both for 400-meter hurdles.

BIDSTRUP, Jane (c. 1956—). Danish curler. Born c. 1956; sister of Lene Bidstrup (curler). ❖ Skipped for the Danish team at the World Curling championships (1983–84); won a silver medal for curling at Nagano Olympics (1998), the 1st-ever Danish medal in any sport at Winter Olympics.

BIDSTRUP, Lene (1966—). Danish curler. Born Aug 10, 1966, in Denmark; sister of Jane Bidstrup (curler). ❖ As skip, placed 3rd at World championships (1999, 2001).

BIEBL, Heidi (1941—). West German Alpine skier. Born Feb 17, 1941, in Oberstaufen, West Germany. ❖ Won a gold medal for the downhill at Squaw Valley Olympics (1960).

BIECHI, Anni (1940—). West German runner. Born Mar 17, 1940. ❖ Won a silver medal in the 4 x 100-meter relay in the Rome Olympics (1960).

BIEDA, Jaroslawa (1937—). *See Jozwiakowska, Jaroslawa.*

BIEHL, Amy (1967–1993). American activist. Born 1967 in Newport Beach, California; murdered, Aug 25, 1993, in Cape Town, South Africa; dau. of Peter Biehl (died 2002) and Linda Biehl (both philanthropists and activists); graduated from Stanford University with honors. ❖ As a Fulbright Scholar, went to South Africa (1992); based at the University of the Western Cape in Cape Town, was working in underprivileged communities and helping with black voter registration in advance of the elections; while driving black co-workers to their homes in Gugulethu township outside Cape Town, was dragged from her car and beaten and stabbed to death by 4 black youths (Aug 25, 1993), a killing that drew international attention to racial violence in South Africa. Her parents, who eventually reconciled with her killers, formed the Amy Biehl Foundation.

BIEHL, Charlotta Dorothea (1731–1788). Danish novelist and playwright. Name variations: Charlotte Biehl. Born 1731 in Copenhagen, Denmark; died 1788; dau. of the inspector of Charlottenborg Castle (died 1777); never married. ❖ One of the best-known authors in 18th-century Norway and Denmark, learned German, French, Italian and Spanish despite father's refusal to allow schooling; her sentimental comedies had a strong influence on Danish theater; writings include *Den kierlige Mand* (1764), *Moralske Fortællinger* (1781–82), *Brevveksling mellem fortrolige Venner* (1783) and *Mit ubetydelige Levnetsløb* (1787).

BIELENBERG, Christabel (1909–2003). English writer. Born Christabel Burton, June 18, 1909, in Totteridge, England; died at home, Nov 2, 2003, in rural Ireland; dau. of P.C. Burton (lieutenant colonel) and Christabel Rose (Harmsworth) Burton (both of Irish stock); m. Peter Bielenberg (German lawyer), Sept 29, 1934 (died 2001); children: John (b. 1935), Nicky (b. 1936), Christopher (b. 1942). ❖ While studying to become an opera singer in Hamburg (1934), met and married a German law student and traded in her British passport; enjoyed the friendship of liberals and intellectuals, including Adam and Clarita von Trott zu Solz, and Helmut Moltke; moved to Berlin (1939); over next 12 years, witnessed the cruelties of the Reich and desperately tried to enlist Allied support to start a revolution from within; became tangentially involved in the failed plot to assassinate Hitler (July 20, 1944); chronicled her story in *The Past Is Myself* (1968), reprinted as *Christabel* (1984), which was adapted for "Masterpiece Theatre" (1989); wrote the sequel *The Road Ahead* (1992).

BIERMANN, Aenne (1898–1933). German photographer. Name variations: changed name to Aenne or Anne when she began to take photographs. Born Anna Sibilla Sternefeld in Goch am Niederrhein, Germany, 1898; died in Gera, Germany, 1933; m. Herbert Biermann, 1920; children: Helga and Gershon (Gerd). ❖ Collaborated with geologist Rudolf Hundt (1927), photographing minerals, and then expanded her work to include close-up plant studies; produced approximately 3,000 negatives (1929–32), from which 400 prints have survived; had solo exhibitions at Kunstkabinett, Munich (1928) and Kunstverein, Gera (1930); was also represented in several important group exhibitions, including *Film und Foto* (Stuttgart, 1929) and *Die neue Fotografie* (Basel, 1930); photographs were published by the German art historian and photographer Franz Roh in *60 Fotos*.

BIESENTHAL, Laryssa (1971—). Canadian rower. Name variations: Larissa. Born June 22, 1971, in Walkerton, Ontario, Canada. ❖ Won bronze medals for coxed eights and quadruple sculls at Sydney Olympics (2000).

BIGELOW, Kathryn (1951—). American director and screenwriter. Born Nov 27, 1951, in San Carlos, California; attended San Francisco Art Institute; graduate of Columbia Film School; m. James Cameron (film director), 1989 (div. 1991). ❖ As director, films include *The Set-Up* (1978), *The Loveless* (1982, also wrote screenplay), *Near Dark* (1987, also wrote screenplay), *Blue Steel* (1990, also wrote screenplay), *Point Break* (1991), *Strange Days* (1995), *The Weight of Water* (2000) and *K-19: The Widowmaker* (2002); also directed 4-part miniseries, "Wild Palms" (1993).

BIGGS, Rosemary (1912–2001). English hematologist. Born 1912 in London, England; died June 29, 2001, in England; University of London, BS in Botany; University of Toronto, PhD in Mycology; London School of Medicine for Women, MD, 1943; children: (adopted) daughter. ❖ One of the foremost hematologists of her generation, was internationally acclaimed for pioneering work on diagnosis and treatment of hemophilia and related bleeding disorders; served as graduate assistant in department of pathology at Radcliffe Infirmary in Oxford, studying blood coagulation (1944–59); helped develop preparations of anti-hemophilic factor, which proved invaluable in treatment; took over running of Medical Research Council's Blood Coagulation Research Laboratory (1967) and served as director of newly established Oxford Haemophilia Centre until retirement in 1977; served as editor of *British Journal of Haemotology and of Thrombosis and Haemostasis*; was founding member of British Society for Haemotology and International Society on Thrombosis and Haemostasis; credited with describing clotting disorder "Christmas disease"; co-authored several influential textbooks.

BIG MAYBELLE (1924–1972). *See Smith, Mabel.*

BIGOT DE MOROGUES, Marie (1786–1820). Alsatian pianist. Born in Colmar, Alsace, Mar 3, 1786; died in Paris, France, Sept 16, 1820. ❖ Admired by both Haydn and Beethoven, reputedly played Beethoven's *Appassionata* Sonata at sight from manuscript (1814). An 1807 letter to her from Beethoven strongly suggests that he was in love with her, though she was married. ❖ See also *Women in World History.*

BIGOTTINI, Emilie (1784–1858). French ballet dancer and actress. Born April 16, 1784, in Toulouse, France; died April 28, 1858, in Paris; dau. of an Italian actor who toured the provinces as a well-known harlequin; sister of Louise Bigottini, who became Mme Milon, wife of the dancer Louis-Jacques Milon; studied with Louis-Jacques Milon; children: 4. ❖ *Premiere danseuse*, known for her acting, made 1st public appearance in *Pygmalion*, staged by Milon (1799); debuted in Gardel's *Psyché* (1800); danced title roll in *Nina, ou la folle par amour* (Nov 23, 1813), title role in *Clari, ou la Promesse de Mariage* (1820), and Suzanne in *Le Page inconstant*; also appeared in Aumer's *Alfred le Grand, Cendrillon* and *Aline, Reine de Golconde.* ❖ See also *Women in World History.*

BIG TWANG. *See Macy, Robin Lynn.*

BIHERON, Marie-Catherine (1719–1786). French anatomist. Born 1719 in France; died 1786; dau. of an apothecary. ❖ Studied illustration under Madeleine Basseport; became known for her skill at wax modeling (which was then used for medical instruction, especially in gynecology); received invitation to present work to academics at French court (1759); demonstrated working model of pregnant women in varying stages of labor to Académie Royale des Sciences (1770), which continue to consider her models as the best in their field as late as 1830; was regarded as a rival by Parisian doctors (though she was outside the official medical community). Some of her works were acquired by Catherine the Great for the St. Petersburg Academy of Sciences.

BIJESSE, Diane. *See Dunbar, Diane.*

BIJNS, Anna (1493/94–1575). Flemish religious poet. Name variations: Byns; Sappho of Brabant. Born in 1493 or 1494 in Antwerp (Netherlands); died April 10, 1575, probably in Antwerp; never married; no children. ❖ Known as the Brabantine Sappho, was one of many women whose religious writings found a receptive audience in the 16th century, though she was one of the few to achieve success who was not a nun; along with teaching, wrote poetry, often lamenting the attacks made on Catholicism and making her own attacks on the leaders and ideas of the Protestant movement; also composed some poetry on secular themes; founded her own school (1530s); published 3 collections of her verses on religious themes.

BIKCIN, Hamide (1978—). Turkish taekwondo player. Name variations: Hamide Bikcin Tosun. Born 1978 in Turkey. ❖ Won a bronze medal for 49–57kg at Sydney Olympics (2000).

BILANSKY, Ann (1820–1860). American accused of murder. Born Mary Ann Evards Wright, 1820; hanged 1860 in Minnesota; m. Stanislaus Bilansky. ❖ Only woman to be legally executed in Minnesota (Mar 23, 1860), poisoned husband's soup with arsenic after finding nephew more desirable; though nephew was released, found guilty and hanged. It has since been suggested that her conviction may have been based on questionable testimony and circumstantial evidence; Jeffrey Hatcher's play *A Piece of the Rope* is a retelling of the story.

BILCHILDE (d. 675). Queen of Austrasia and the Franks. Name variations: Bilichild; Blitilde. Died 675; dau. of Hymnegilde also known as Himnechildis, regent of Austrasia (r. 662–675), and Sigebert or Sigibert III (630–656), king of Austrasia (r. 634–656); m. Childeric II (656–675), king of Austrasia (r. 656–675), king of the Franks (r. 673–675), in 668; sister of St. Dagobert; children: Chilperic II (670–721), king of Neustria (r. 715–721).

BILECK, Pamela (1968—). American gymnast. Name variations: Pammy Bileck, Palm Bileck-Flat. Born Dec 1, 1968, in California. ❖ Placed 1st in balance beam at US nationals (1984); at Los Angeles Olympics, won a silver medal in team all-around (1984).

BILHAH. Biblical woman. Name variations: Bala. Handmaid of Rachel who was Jacob's wife; children: sons Dan and Naphtali.

BILISTICHE (fl. 268–264 BCE). **Chariot racer.** Name variations: Belestiche, Belistiche, Blistiche. Pronunciation: Bee-lee-STEE-kay. Various sources list her birthplace as Argos, the coast of Macedonia, or in an unspecified "barbarian" region before 246 BCE in Canopus (modern-day Maadie); dau. of an otherwise unknown Philo; one of the mistresses of Ptolemy II, king of Egypt. ❖ Owner of winning 4-colt chariot at the Olympic games (268 BCE) and of the victorious 2-colt chariot in the games (264 BCE); was processional basket-bearer in Alexandria (251–250 BCE); deified after her death, was worshipped as "Aphrodite Bilistiche." ❖ See also *Women in World History.*

BILKAS or BILKIS (fl. 10th c. BCE). *See Sheba, Queen of.*

BILLANY, Zillah Smith (1859–1937). *See Gill, Zillah Smith.*

BILLINGTON, Adeline (1825–1917). **English actress.** Name variations: Mrs. John Billington; Adeline Mortimer. Born Adeline Mortimer, Jan 4, 1825, in England; died 1917; m. John Billington (actor). ❖ Made London debut in *Cupid and Psyche* at the Adelphi, where she remained for 16 years, often appearing with husband; appeared in several theatrical adaptations of Dickens' works, including *Dot*, a dramatization of *Cricket on the Hearth.*

BILLINGTON, Elizabeth (c. 1765/68–1818). **English soprano.** Born Elizabeth Weichsell or Weichsel in London, England, between 1765 and 1768; died in Venice, Aug 25, 1818; dau. of Carl Weichsell (German-born oboist and clarinet player); mother was a well-known singer and pupil of Johann Christian Bach; m. James Billington, 1783 (died c. 1795); m. Fellissent or Felican. ❖ Before age 12, composed 2 sets of piano sonatas; at 14, sang at a concert in Oxford; gained international renown in Naples appearing in the title role of a new opera, *Inez di Castro*, written for her by F. Bianchi (1794); was in such demand in England that she sang at Covent Garden and Drury Lane, on alternate nights, and Haydn wrote "Arianna abbandonata" for her. The term "a Billington" became synonymous with "a great singer." ❖ See also *Women in World History.*

BILLINGTON, Francelia (1895–1934). **American silent-film actress and camerawoman.** Born Feb 1, 1895, in Dallas, Texas; died Nov 24, 1934, in Glendale, California. ❖ Worked as a camerawoman at Reliance and Majestic studios (1914); as an actress, films include *Blind Husbands, The Terror, Hearts Are Trumps* and *What a Wife Learned.*

BILLINGTON, Mrs. John (1825–1917). *See Billington, Adeline.*

BILLINGTON-GREIG, Teresa (1877–1964). **English suffragist.** Born Teresa Billington, 1877, in Lancashire, England; died 1964; dau. of an English shipping clerk; attended Blackburn Convent and Manchester University extension classes; m. F.L. Greig, 1907, with both partners taking their combined surnames. ❖ Employed as a teacher when she began working for the equal-pay movement (1904); was a national organizer for, and member of, the Women's Social and Political Union (1903–07), when she left to found the Women's Freedom League with Charlotte Despard and Edith How-Martyn; wrote for *The Vote;* endured 2 imprisonments for her political activities, but after 1911 was critical of extremist tactics; writings include *Towards Women's Liberty* (1906), *The Militant Suffrage Movement* (1911) and *Women and the Machine* (1913).

BILLOUT, Marguerite (1893–1983). *See Broquedis, Marguerite.*

BILSTON, Catherine Julia (1864–1944). *See Mackay, Catherine Julia.*

BILTAUERE, Astra (1944—). **Soviet volleyball player.** Born Oct 1944 in USSR. ❖ At Tokyo Olympics, won a silver medal in team competition (1964).

BIMOLT, Klena (1945—). **Dutch swimmer.** Born June 1945. ❖ At Tokyo Olympics, won a silver medal in the 4 x 100-meter medley relay (1964).

BIN, Queen (d. 1895). *See Min, Queen.*

BINCHY, Maeve (1940—). **Irish novelist and journalist.** Born Maeve Binchy, Mar 28, 1940, in Dublin, Ireland; grew up in Dalkey; eldest of 4 children of Maureen (Blackmore) Binchy (nurse) and William T. Binchy (lawyer); graduate of University College, Dublin, c. 1961; m. Gordon Snell (children's author and BBC correspondent), 1975; no children. ❖ Though she grew up Catholic, was a teacher at the Zion Schools in Dublin and worked on a kibbutz in Israel; became a columnist for *Irish Times* (1968), then its London correspondent (1970); saw production in Dublin of her one-act play, "End of Term," and a release of a collection of *Times* articles, *My First Book* (1976), followed by

Maeve's Diary (1979); published a book of short fiction, *The Central Line* (1977); other short-story collections include *Victoria Line* (1980) and *The Lilac Bus* (1984); published 1st novel, *Light a Penny Candle* (1982), an instant commercial success; other novels include *Echoes* (1984), *Silver Wedding* (1988), *Circle of Friends* (1990), which was the basis for the film of the same name, *The Glass Lake* (1994) and *Quentins* (2002). Her tv play, *Deeply Regretted By,* won 2 Irish Jacob's Awards and Best Script Award at Prague Film Festival.

BINDER, Aranka (1966—). **Yugoslavian shooter.** Born June 19, 1966. ❖ At Barcelona Olympics, won a bronze medal in air rifle (1992).

BING, Ilse (1899–1998). **German photojournalist.** Born in Frankfurt, Germany, 1899; died in New York City, Mar 17, 1998; pursued a degree in history of art at University of Frankfurt; m. Konrad Wolff (pianist and musicologist), 1937. ❖ Began photographing architecture to illustrate her doctoral thesis on German architect Friedrich Gilly (1928); moved to Paris to photograph full time (1930); primarily a photojournalist, also worked in advertising; was included in *Modern European Photography: Twenty Photographers* exhibition (1932); on marriage (1937), relocated to New York; continued to work until 1959, after which she was virtually forgotten until 1976, when her photographs appeared in 2 NY exhibitions: one at Museum of Modern Art and another at Witkin Gallery.

BINGAY, Roberta Gibb. *See Gibb, Roberta.*

BINGHAM, Amelia (1869–1927). **American actress-manager.** Born Amelia Smiley, Mar 20, 1869, in Hicksville, Ohio; died Sept 1, 1927, in New York, NY; attended Ohio Wesleyan College; m. Lloyd Bingham (manager of a traveling professional theater company). ❖ The 1st American actress to succeed at both producing and performing, began career touring the West Coast with the McKee Rankin Co.; headed to NY (1892) to appear in a series of melodramas, including *The Struggle for Life, The Power of Gold* and *A Man Among Men;* won 1st important role in *The Mummy*, opposite Robert Hilliard (1896); now extremely popular, played leading roles under management of Charles Frohman (1897–1901); as an actress-manager (1900), leased the Bijou Theatre, assembled a company, and successfully produced Clyde Fitch's *The Climbers,* in which she played Mrs. Sterling; went on to appear in different stock companies, then toured UK in *Big Moments from Great Plays* (1909); performed in *The New Henrietta* with Douglas Fairbanks (1913–16); following husband's death (1915), retired from the stage but returned in *Trelawney of the Wells* (1925); gave final performance in *The Pearl of Great Price* (1926). ❖ See also *Women in World History.*

BINGHAM, Anne Willing (1764–1801). **American socialite and salonnière.** Born Anne Willing, Aug 1, 1764, in Philadelphia, Pennsylvania; died May 11, 1801, in St. George's, Bermuda; m. William Bingham (merchant, banker, member of Continental congress, and also US senator, 1795–1801), in 1780. ❖ Known for her 18th-century Philadelphia salon, attracted the city's literary and political personalities, as well as distinguished foreign guests; with the new federal government centered in Philadelphia, her salon became the acknowledged "Republican Court," attracting Federalist leaders, including George Washington.

BINGHAM, Henrietta (1901–1968). **American socialite.** Born Henrietta Worth Bingham in 1901; died 1968; dau. of Judge Robert Worth Bingham (American ambassador to Court of St. James), and Eleanor E. Miller Bingham (killed, c. 1911); aunt of Sallie Bingham; lover of Dora Carrington. ❖ At 10, was in an automobile accident in which her mother was killed; her father married twice more, but both marriages were unsuccessful (he was all but accused of murdering his 2nd wife, Mary Lily Flagler Bingham, one of the richest women in America, a scandal that made the front page of newspapers throughout the nation in 1917). ❖ See also Marie Brenner, *House of Dreams: The Bingham Family of Louisville* (Random House, 1988); and *Women in World History.*

BINGHAM, Millicent Todd (1880–1968). **American geographer, conservationist, author, and educator.** Born Millicent Todd, Feb 5, 1880, in Washington, DC; died Dec 1, 1968; dau. of David Peck (astronomer specializing in the study of eclipses) and Mabel Loomis Todd (writer and lecturer); Vassar College, BA, 1902; Radcliffe College, MA in geography, 1917; Harvard University, PhD in geography, 1923; m. Walter Van Dyke Bingham (psychologist), Dec 4, 1920 (died 1952). ❖ As the 1st woman to receive a doctorate in geology and geography from Harvard and a leading expert on Emily Dickinson, distinguished herself in the fields of both geography and literature; devoted several decades to editing many of Dickinson's unpublished letters and poems; as a legacy of her lifelong concern with conservation, presented the Todd Wildlife Sanctuary on Hog Island, Maine, to the National Audubon Society as a perpetual preserve (1960); writings include (biography) *Life of Mary E. Stearns* (1909), (biography of maternal grandfather) *Elben Jenks Loomis* (1913), *La Floride du sud-est et la ville de Miami* (1932), (ed.) *Letters of Emily Dickinson* (1931), *Mabel Loomis Todd: Her Contribution to the Town of Amherst* (1935), (ed. with Mabel Loomis Todd) *Bolts of Melody* (1945), *Beyond Psychology* (1953), (ed.) *Emily Dickinson: A Revelation* (1954) and *Emily Dickinson's Home: Letters of Edward Dickinson and his Family, with Documentation and Comment* (1955). ❖ See also *Women in World History.*

BINGHAM, Sybil Moseley (1792–1848). American missionary. Born in Westfield, Massachusetts, Sept 14, 1792; died in Easthampton, Massachusetts, Feb 27, 1848; dau. of Pliny and Sophia (Pomeroy) Moseley; m. Hiram Bingham (missionary), Oct 11, 1819; children: Sophia Bingham (1820–1887, who m. William Augustus Moseley); Levi Parsons (1822–1823); Jeremiah Evarts (1824–1825); Lucy Whiting Bingham (1826–1890, who m. Charles Olmstead Reynolds); Elizabeth Kaahumanu Bingham (1829–1899); Hiram II (1831–1908); Lydia Bingham (1834–1915). ❖ With new husband, set sail from Boston for Hawaii to lead a mission (1820); helped found the 1st Christian mission established in Hawaiian Islands by New England Congregationalists; during her 21 years of service, used her talent as a teacher to establish the 1st school on the islands; planned, supervised, and participated with students in the construction of an adobe brick schoolhouse, which was completed in 1835; often made the treacherous journey to missionary posts on neighboring islands to assist with childbirth or other medical emergencies; worked with the other missionaries to turn the islanders' vocal sounds into written words through the formation of an alphabet. ❖ See also *Women in World History.*

BINGLEY, Blanche (b. 1864). See Hillyard, Blanche Bingley.

BING XIN (1900–1999). See Xie Wanying.

BINH, Nguyen Thi (1920–1992). See Nguyen Thi Dinh.

BINKIENE, Sofija (1902–1984). Holocaust rescuer. Born 1902; died 1984; m. Kazys Binkiene (writer); children: 4, including Lilianne. ❖ Starting with the Nazi occupation of Lithuania (summer 1941), harbored Jews in the family home; even after husband died of a heart ailment (1942), continued to assist Jews; after 1945, worked for the children's service of the Lithuanian Radio and wrote a book about Lithuanians who had saved Jewish lives during the 3 years of Nazi occupation; honored as one of the Righteous by Yad Vashem, Jerusalem. ❖ See also autobiography *Ir be ginklo kariai* (Vilnius: Mintis, 1967); and *Women in World History.*

BINNEY, Constance (1896–1989). American silent-film actress. Born June 28, 1896, in New York, NY; died Nov 15, 1989, in Whitestone, LI, NY; sister of Faire Binney (actress); m. Henry Wharton Jr.; m. Charles E. Cotting, 1926 (div. 1932); m. Geoffrey Cheshire, 1947. ❖ Made NY stage debut as Lucy Delaney in *Saturday to Monday* (1917), followed by *Oh Lady Lady!* and *39 East;* as a Paramount starlet, was in such films as *Sporting Life, Erstwhile Susan, 39 East, A Bill of Divorcement, Erstwhile Susan, The Case of Becky* and *Midnight.*

BINNS, Hilda May (1945—). Canadian wheelchair athlete. Born Hilda May Torok, Oct 20, 1945, in Hamilton, Ontario, Canada; m. David Binns (paraplegic athlete, div.). ❖ A paraplegic, contracted polio (1955); won 2 gold and 1 silver medal at International Stoke Mandeville Games for the Paralyzed (1968), followed by 1 gold and 2 silver medals (1972); won 5 gold, 1 silver, and 4 bronze medals at the Wheelchair Pan American Games (1969), then 5 gold, 2 silver and 1 bronze medal (1971).

BINNUNA, Khanatta (1940—). Moroccan novelist and short-story writer. Born 1940 in Morocco. ❖ Active in politics and women's rights campaigns; short stories often deal with silencing of women in Arab culture, but also focus on plight of Arabs in general; works include *Down With Silence* (1967), *Fire and Choice* (1971), *The Storm* (1979), *Anger and Tomorrow* (1981) and *Articulate Silence* (1987).

BINO (1908–1987). See Ward, Polly.

BINOCHE, Juliette (1964—). French actress. Born Mar 9, 1964, in Paris, France; dau. of an actress and a sculptor; sister of actress-photographer Marion Stalens; m. Andre Halle (professional scuba diver), 1993; lived with French actor Benoit Magimel, 1999–2003; children: (with Halle) Raphaël (b. 1993); (with French actor Benoit Magimel) Hannah

(b. 2000). ❖ Came to prominence in *The Unbearable Lightness of Being* (1988); starred in *Les Amants du Pont-Neuf* (1991), *Wuthering Heights* (1992), *Damage* (1992), *Trois couleurs: Bleu* (1993), *Trois couleurs: Rouge* (1994), *Le Hussard sur le toit* (1995), *Alice et Martin* (1998), *Les Enfants du siècle* (1999), *La Veuve de Saint-Pierre* (2000), *Chocolat* (2000), *Country of My Skull* (2004); won an Oscar for Best Supporting Actress for performance in *The English Patient* (1996).

BINS, Patrícia (1930—). Brazilian novelist, artist, journalist and translator. Name variations: Patricia Doreen Bins. Born 1930 in Brazil. ❖ Worked as teacher, plastic artist, and journalist in southern Brazil; works include *Jogo de fiar* (1983) and *Antes que o amor acabe* (1984). ❖ See also H.R. Franco (PhD thesis) "Organization and Analysis of the Archives of the Contemporary Brazilian Author Patricia Bins" (U. of New Mexico, 1999).

BINT-AL-SHAH (1913–1998). See Abdel Rahman, Aisha.

BINT EL SHATEI (1913–1998). See Abdel Rahman, Aisha.

BINT EL-SHATI (1913–1998). See Abdel Rahman, Aisha.

BINT JAHSH, Zaynab (c. 590–640). See Zaynab bint Jahsh.

BIRACREE, Thelma (1904–1997). American ballet dancer. Name variations: Thelma Biracree Schnepel. Born Feb 4, 1904, in Buffalo, NY; died May 12, 1997, in Fort Wayne, Indiana. ❖ Studied with Martha Graham, among others, and at Eastman School of Music in Rochester, NY; became a member of Graham's 1st performance group and danced in premieres of Graham works, including *Dance Languide* (1926); studied with Theodore Kosloff and Mary Wigman on West Coast and Europe for many years; served as director of the ballet program at Eastman School in Rochester; collaborated with Howard Hanson and Walter Piston, among others, on development of new American scores.

BIRCH, Gina (1956—). English musician. Name variations: The Raincoats. Born 1956 in England. ❖ Played bass and sang for English punk group, the Raincoats, an all-girl band formed in London (1977) with singer-guitarist Ana Da Silva, violinist Vicky Aspinall, and former Slits drummer Palmolive; with group, opened for punk group Chelsea (1978) and recorded 1st single, "Fairytale in the Supermarket" (1979); also released *Odyshape* (1981), toured US, recorded *Kitchen Tapes* (1983) and *Moving,* then disbanded (1984); after Nirvana frontman Kurt Cobain released all 3 Raincoat albums on band label DGC, reunited with Da Silva for US East Coast tour (1994), then released *Extended Play* (1995) and *Looking in the Shadows* (1996).

BIRCH, Patricia (c. 1930—). American theatrical choreographer and dancer. Name variations: Pat Birch. Born c. 1930 in Scarsdale, NY. ❖ Joined Martha Graham Company (1950) and was featured in *Letter to the World* (1954) and *Seraphic Dialogues* (1954); served as rehearsal director for the company for many years; danced in Choreographers' Workshop recital in Eleanor King's *Brandenburg No. 2 (1950),* and continued to work in the theater thereafter; earned 1st choreographic credit for *Carefree Tree,* at Phoenix Theater (1956); on Broadway, choreographed acclaimed musical numbers for *Grease* (1972), *Pacific Overtures* (1976), *Zoot Suit* (1979), *Anna Karenina* (1992) and *Band in Berlin* (1999), and was nominated for 5 Tony awards for Best Choreography, including for *Grease, Over Here!* and *Parade;* also choreographed *You're a Good Man Charlie Brown* (1967), *Up Eden* (1968), the tango sequence in *The Prime of Miss Jean Brodie* (1969), *Bread and Circus* (1980), and *Gilda Radner—Live from New York* (1980); for film, choreographed for *Roseland* (1977), *A Little Night Music* (1977), *Grease* (1978), *Sgt. Pepper's Lonely Heart's Club Band* (1979), *Big* (1988), *Stella* (1990), *Billy Bathgate* (1991), *The First Wives Club* (1996) and *The Human Stain* (2003).

BIRCH, Pearl (1907–1983). See Choate, Pearl.

BIRCH-PFEIFFER, Charlotte (1800–1868). German playwright and actress. Born Charlotte Karoline Pfeiffer in Stuttgart, Germany, June 23, 1800; died in Berlin, Aug 24, 1868; dau. of an estate agent named Pfeiffer; m. Christian A. Birch (historian), 1825; children: Wilhelmine von Hillern (writer). ❖ At 18, made stage debut in Munich; toured Europe as the lead in tragic roles; managed the Zurich theater (1837–43); accepted an engagement at the royal theatre in Berlin (1844), where she remained until her death; her popular novels and tales, *Gesammelte Novellen und Erzählungen,* were collected in 3 vols. (1863–65); her 70 plays, adapted and original, fill 23 vols., *Gesammelte dramatische Werke* (1863–80). ❖ See also *Women in World History.*

BIRCHFIELD, Constance Alice (1898–1994). New Zealand trade unionist, political activist, and bookseller. Name variations: Constance Alice Rawcliffe. Born July 27, 1898, at Haydock, Lancaster, England; died May 9, 1994, in Wellington, New Zealand; dau. of John Rawcliffe (police constable) and Catherine (Williamson) Rawcliffe; m. Albert James Birchfield (linesman), 1936 (died 1984); children: 2 daughters. ❖ Immigrated to New Zealand (1923); joined New Zealand Labour Party and served as executive member of Wellington Hotel, Club and Restaurant Workers' Union (1920s); belonged to New Zealand section of Friends of the Soviet Union and stood 4 times for Wellington City Council, twice for Wellington Hospital Board, and 5 times for House of Representatives; expelled from Communist Party for factionalism.

BIRD, Billie (1908–2002). American comedic actress on tv and screen. Name variations: Billie Bird Sellen. Born Feb 28, 1908, in Pocatello, Idaho; died Nov 27, 2002, in Granada Hills, California; m. Edwin Sellen (died 1966); children: 3. ❖ Orphaned as a child; at 8, hired to tour circuits with a vaudeville troupe; films include *The Odd Couple, Ernest Saves Christmas, Jury Duty, Dennis the Menace* and *Home Alone;* had recurring role on "Dear John" (1988–92); often entertained troops in Vietnam with USO.

BIRD, Bonnie (1914–1995). American dancer and choreographer. Born 1914 in Portland, Oregon; died 1995 in England; studied with Martha Graham; m. Ralph Gundlach, 1938. ❖ Influential modern dancer, choreographer and teacher who introduced new elements to dance and dance education in US and England, was one of the original members of Martha Graham Dance Co. and one of the 1st official teachers of the Graham technique; served as head of dance at Cornish School of Fine Arts in Seattle, Washington (1937–40), where students included Merce Cunningham and Jane Dudley; founded Merry-Go Rounders dance company after WWII; chaired American Dance Guild (1965–67) and was partly responsible for founding of Congress on Research in Dance; moved to England and with Marion North reshaped the Laban Centre for Movement and Dance (1974), introducing professional training for dancers and Britain's 1st degree course in dance studies (1977); formed Transitions Dance Co. (1983), to provide student dancers with experience in new choreography; founded Bonnie Bird Choreography Fund (1984); provided inspiration for *Dance Theatre Journal* (1983) and acted as editorial advisor until her death.

BIRD, Dorothy (c. 1913—). Canadian dancer. Born c. 1913 on Vancouver Island, British Columbia, Canada. ❖ Made professional debut with Martha Graham Co. in *Primitive Mysteries* (1931); remained with company until 1937, performing in such works as *Tragic patterns* (1933), *American Provincials* (1934) and *Horizons* (1936); choreographed for recitals with Miriam Blecher, Si-Lan Chen, José Limón, and others (1938–47); performed regularly on Broadway, where credits include Agnes de Mille's *Hooray for What?* (1937), Albertina Rasch's *Around the World* (1946) and *Sleepy Hollow* (1948); also choreographed *Opening Dance* (1938), *Nostalgic Portrait* (1938), *Songs of the Hill Country* (1945), *Woman by the Sea* (1947) and *Incantations* (1947).

BIRD, Grace (1864–1943). *See Hewlett, Hilda.*

BIRD, Isabella (1831–1904). *See Bishop, Isabella Bird.*

BIRD, Lorraine. Australian politician. ❖ As a member of the Australian Labor Party, served in the Queensland Parliament for Whitsunday (1989–98); was shadow minister for Public Works and Administrative Services (1996–97).

BIRD, Nancy (1915—). Australian aviator. Name variations: Nancy Bird-Walton. Born 1915 in Sydney, NSW, Australia; m. Charles Walton (Englishman), 1939; children: Anne Marie and John. ❖ One of Australia's aviation pioneers, was the 1st female poilot in the Commonwealth to carry passengers; began flight training under Sir Charles Kingsford Smith (1933); was hired to operate an air ambulance service in outback New South Wales (1935); founded the Australian Women's Pilots Association (1950), remaining its president until 1990. Named OBE (1966). ❖ See also autobiographies, *Born to Fly* and *My God! It's a Woman.*

BIRD, Rata Alice (1894–1969). *See Lovell-Smith, Rata Alice.*

BIRD, Sue (1980—). American basketball player. Born Suzanne Brigit Bird, Oct 16, 1980, in Syosset, NY; attended Christ the King High School; graduated from University of Connecticut, 2002. ❖ Point guard; while at UConn, won NCAA championships (2000, 2002); selected by Seattle Storm of the WNBA in 1st round (1st pick overall), 2002; won a team gold medal at Athens Olympics (2004). Was 3-time Nancy Lieberman Cline Point Guard of the Year winner; received Honda Award and Wade Trophy (2002); named AP and Naismith Player of the Year (2002).

BIRDSONG, Cindy (1939—). African-American singer. Name variations: The Supremes. Born Dec 15, 1939, in Camden, New Jersey; dau. of Lloyd and Annie Birdsong. ❖ Appeared with Motown's Patti LaBelle and the Bluebelles; replaced Florence Ballard when she left the Supremes (1967). Inducted into Rock and Roll Hall of Fame (1988). ❖ See also *Women in World History.*

BIRELL, Tala (1907–1958). German-Romanian actress. Born Natalie Bierl, Sept 10, 1907, in Bucharest, Romania (some sources cite Vienna, Austria); died Feb 17, 1958, in Landstuhl i.d. Pfalz, Rhineland–Palatinate, Germany. ❖ Starred on the European stage; brought to Hollywood as "another Garbo," made US film debut in *Nagana* (1933), followed by such films as *Let's Fall in Love, The Captain Hates the Sea, Air Hawks, Crime and Punishment* and *Bringing Up Baby;* with film career a disappointment, returned to Europe (1951), eventually settling in Eastern Europe, behind the Iron Curtain.

BIRET, Idil (1941—). Turkish pianist. Born in Ankara, Turkey, 1941; studied in Paris with Alfred Cortot and in Germany with Wilhelm Kempff. ❖ Made debut in Paris to great success (1952); revived many neglected piano works which came to be included in the classical repertoire, recording Ravel's *Gaspard de la nuit*, Alban Berg's Piano Sonata, and Liszt's transcription of the Berlioz *Symphonie fantastique.* ❖ See also *Women in World History.*

BIRGITTA. *Variant of Bridget.*

BIRGITTA AV VADSTENA. (1303–1373). *Bridget of Sweden.*

BIRGITTA OF SWEDEN (1937—). Swedish royal and princess of Hohenzollern. Name variations: Bridget Bernadotte. Born Birgitta Ingeborg, Jan 19, 1937, at Haga Palace, Stockholm, Sweden; dau. of Gustavus Adolphus (1906–1947), duke of Westerbotten, and Sybilla of Saxe-Coburg-Gotha (1908–1972); sister of Carl XVI Gustavus, king of Sweden; m. Johann Georg, prince of Hohenzollern, May 25 or 30, 1961; children: Carl Christian (b. 1962); Desiree Margaretha (b. 1963); Hubertus Gustaf (b. 1966).

BIRGITTA OF VADSTENA (1303–1373). *See Bridget of Sweden.*

BIRIUKOVA, Alexandra (1929—). *See Biryukova, Alexandra.*

BIRKETT, Viva (1887–1934). English actress. Name variations: Viva Merivale. Born Feb 14, 1887, in Exeter, Devon, England; died June 26, 1934, in London; m. Philip Merivale (actor). ❖ Made London stage debut in *Monsieur Beaucaire* (1906) and NY debut in *The Hypocrites* (1906); other plays include *The Brass Bottle, David Garrick, Peter Pan, Loaves and Fishes, Twelfth Night, The Jew of Prague, Officer 666* and *Trust the People;* toured with George Arliss.

BIRMINGHAM FOUR.
See Collins, Addie Mae.
See McNair, Denise.
See Robertson, Carol.
See Wesley, Cynthia.

BIRNEY, Alice McLellan (1858–1907). American founder. Born Alice McLellan Birney in Marietta, Georgia, Oct 19, 1858; died in Chevy Chase, Maryland, Dec 20, 1907; attended Mt. Holyoke Seminary, 1875. ❖ Was a founding member and the 1st president of the National Congress of Mothers (1897), which convened in Washington, DC; the year after her death (1908), her organization was renamed the Parent-Teacher Association. ❖ See also *Women in World History.*

BIRTLES, Mary (1859–1943). Canadian nurse. Born Mary Ellen Birtles, 1859, in Hepworth, near Yorkshire, England; died June 22, 1943. ❖ One of the 1st trained nurses in the Canadian west, immigrated with family to Brandon, Manitoba (1883); became assistant nurse at Medicine Hat General Hospital in Alberta (1890), then head nurse at a hospital in Brandon; appointed matron of Calgary General Hospital (1894), where she created Calgary General Hospital Training School; returned to Brandon (1898) and served as matron of the General Hospital until 1919.

BIRYUKOVA, Alexandra (1929—). Soviet politician. Name variations: Alexandra Pavolvna Biryukova; Alexandra Biriukova. Born 1929 in

USSR. ❖ Trained as textile engineer; took minor official jobs while still working in factory but had to leave upon accepting position of secretary of Trade Union Presidium (1968), later serving as the Presidium's deputy chair (1985); wrote *The Working Woman in the USSR* (1973); selected for secretariat of Central Committee of Communist Party, as consumer affairs specialist (1986); appointed deputy prime minister responsible for Social Development (1988); was made non-voting candidate member of Politburo (1988), the 1st woman to achieve this distinction since Ekaterina Fursteva in 1957; was pushed aside in political turmoil of 1990–91.

BISCHOFF, Ilse (1903–1976). American illustrator and engraver. Name variations: Ilse Marthe Bischoff. Born Nov 21, 1903, in New York, NY; died 1976; attended Art Students League, NY; studied in Paris and Munich. ❖ Beginning in 1938, spent her summers at 150-year-old pink brick house in Vermont, where she painted, created wood engravings, and wrote; her illustrated books were twice selected to appear in the Fifty Books of the Year Exhibition; her wood prints were purchased by the Metropolitan Museum of New York and the Fine Arts Museums of Boston and Baltimore.

BISCHOF, Martina (1957—). East German kayaker. Born Nov 23, 1957, in East Germany. ❖ At Moscow Olympics, won a gold medal in K2 500 meters (1980).

BISCHOFF, Sabine (1958—). West German fencer. Born May 21, 1958. ❖ At Los Angeles Olympics, won a gold medal in team foil (1984).

BISHOP, Ann (1899–1990). British scientist. Born Dec 19, 1899, in Manchester, England; died May 7, 1990; dau. of a furniture maker; Manchester University, BS, 1921, MS, 1922, DSc, 1932; Cambridge University, PhD, 1926, DSc, 1941. ❖ Leading protozoologist and parasitologist, best known for researching the development of drug resistance in malaria-causing parasites, served as part-time lecturer in zoology department at University of Cambridge and as scientific assistant to protozoologist Clifford Dobell at Medical Research Council, Mount Vernon, Hampstead; held Beit Memorial fellowship at Molteno Institute, Cambridge (beginning 1929), then served as staff member (1942–48) and director (1948–64); led parasitology group at Institute of Biology (1950s); became chair of British Society for Parasitology upon its founding (1960).

BISHOP, Ann Rivière (1810–1884). English singer. Name variations: Madame Anna Bishop, Ann Reviere Bishop. Born 1810 in London, England; died in New York, Mar 18, 1884; m. Sir Henry Rowley Bishop (English musician, composer), 1831 (died April 30, 1855); m. a Mr. Schultz, 1858. ❖ A singer of oratorio and opera known as Madame Anna Bishop, made her debut on the concert stage (1837); retired (1883). ❖ See also *Women in World History*.

BISHOP, Bernice Pauahi (1831–1884). Hawaiian high chiefess and philanthropist. Born Bernice Paki, Dec 19, 1831, in Honolulu, Hawaii; died in Honolulu, Oct 16, 1884; only dau. of Abner (adviser to King Kamehameha III, judge of Supreme Court, and acting governor of Oahu) and Konia Paki; by tradition, was taken as an infant to live with high chiefess and co-ruler Kinau from 1832–1839; after Kinau gave birth to a daughter, was returned to her parents at their request; m. Charles Reed Bishop (1822–1915, customs collector), June 4, 1850. ❖ Active in church and charitable organizations, became a social leader in Honolulu; by hosting visiting international dignitaries, served as a link between Hawaiian and American communities; through her will, established the Kamehameha Schools. In 1889, Charles Bishop established the Bernice Pauahi Bishop Museum in Honolulu, which is dedicated to Hawaiian and Polynesian ethnology. ❖ See also *Women in World History*.

BISHOP, Cath (1971—). English rower. Born Nov 22, 1971, in Southend-on-Sea, England. ❖ At World championships, won a gold medal for coxless pair (2003); won a silver medal for coxless pair at Athens Olympics (2004).

BISHOP, Claire Huchet (1898–1993). French-American author and political activist. Born Claire Huchet, Dec 30, 1898, in Brittany, France, or Geneva, Switzerland; became a US citizen; died Mar 11, 1993, in Paris; attended the Sorbonne; married Frank Bishop (pianist). ❖ Was instrumental in opening the 1st French children's library, L'Heure Joyeuse, following WWI; married and came to US; joined staff of New York Public Library, where she became a popular storyteller; wrote *The Five Chinese Brothers*, a modern classic; also wrote *The Man Who Lost His Head*, *Pancakes-Paris* (runner-up for Newbery Medal, 1948), *Twenty and Ten*, *All Alone*, *A Present from Petros* and *Yeshu*,

Called Jesus; was actively involved as a lecturer and writer for various social movements in France; served as president of Jewish Christian Fellowship of France (1968–81) and International Council of Christians and Jews (1975–77).

BISHOP, Elizabeth (1911–1979). American poet. Born Feb 8, 1911, in Worcester, Massachusetts; died in Boston, Oct 6, 1979; dau. of William Thomas (executive with J.W. Bishop Co.) and Gertrude Bulmer Bishop; Vassar College, AB in English Literature, 1934; lived with Lota de Macedo Soares for 15 years; never married; no children. ❖ Generally regarded as one of the finest and most influential poets in the 20th century, spent a short time in early childhood with maternal grandparents in Nova Scotia, after her father's untimely death and her mother's subsequent breakdown; lived with paternal grandparents (Worcester) and then an aunt (Boston) from age 6 until she went away to school; began writing, mostly short fiction, while at Vassar; made 1st trip abroad, to Paris (1935); moved to Florida (late 1930s); lived in Key West until after end of WWII; lived in Mexico for 9 months (1943); published *North & South* (1946); served as Consultant in Poetry, Library of Congress (1949–50); set off on a trip around South America and the Straits of Magellan (1951); while visiting Rio de Janeiro, suffered a violent allergic reaction to cashew fruit and was forced to curtail her journey; remained in Brazil for next 15 years, sharing a house near Petropolis with a Brazilian friend, Lota de Macedo Soares; returned to US (1966); became a life member of National Institute of Arts and Letters (1954); published *Poems: North & South—A Cold Spring* (1955) and won Pulitzer Prize for Poetry (1956); published *The Diary of "Helena Morley"* (1957), followed by *Brazil* (1962) and *Questions of Travel* (1965); published *Selected Poems* (1967) and *The Ballad of the Burglar of Babylon* (1968); won National Book Award for *The Complete Poems* (1970); published *An Anthology of Twentieth-Century Brazilian Poetry* (1972); wrote *Geography III* and became a member of American Academy of Arts and Letters (1976); taught for 2 terms at University of Washington in Seattle; lived intermittently in Brazil and US for a number of years; taught at Harvard University as poet in residence until mandatory retirement (1977); continued to write poetry until her death. Received American Academy of Arts and Letters Award (1951), Shelley Memorial Award (1952), Merrill Foundation Award (1969), Order of Rio Branco, Brazil (1970), Harriet Monroe Award (1974) and National Book Critics Circle Poetry Award (1976). ❖ See also Anne Stevenson, *Elizabeth Bishop* (Twayne, 1966); Robert Giroux, ed. *One Art: Letters of Elizabeth Bishop* (Farrar, 1994); Lorrie Goldensohn, *Elizabeth Bishop* (Columbia U. Press, 1992); Brett C. Millier, *Elizabeth Bishop: Life and the Memory of It* (U. of California Press, 1993); and *Women in World History*.

BISHOP, Georgianna M. (1878–1971). American golfer. Born Oct 15, 1878, in Bridgeport, Connecticut; died Sept 1, 1971, in Fairfield, Connecticut. ❖ Won USGA Women's championship (1904), defeating E.F. Sanford, 5 and 3, in the final; won the Metropolitan Women's Championship (1907, 1908), and was runner-up 5 times; took the Connecticut Women's title (1921, 1922, 1927).

BISHOP, Harriet E. (1817–1883). American missionary. Born Jan 1, 1817, in Panton, Addison Co., Vermont; died Aug 8, 1883, in St. Paul, Minnesota; m. John McConkey, Sept 12, 1858 (marriage dissolved, Mar 13, 1867). ❖ Became a Baptist early in life; arrived in St. Paul (then a Sioux Indian trading post of no more than 20 families), to open the 1st permanent citizen day school in the area (1847); introduced Sunday schools from which St. Paul's early Baptist, Presbyterian, and Methodist churches developed; elected vice-president of American Equal Rights Association (1869); also championed the temperance movement; wrote 3 books dealing with Minnesota.

BISHOP, Hazel (1906–1998). American chemist and cosmetics manufacturer. Born Hazel Gladys Bishop, Aug 17, 1906, in Hoboken, New Jersey; died Dec 5, 1998; dau. of Henry (entrepreneur and pioneer motion-picture exhibitor) and Mabel (Billington) Bishop; Barnard College, BA, 1929; graduate study at Columbia University. ❖ Became research assistant to a leading dermatologist (1935); during WWII, was a senior organic chemist for Standard Oil; continued petroleum research with Socony Vacuum Oil Co. (1945); spent evenings developing and testing a formula for a "no-smear" lipstick; formed Hazel Bishop, Inc., to manufacture the lipstick and launch the product (1950); over a dispute with majority stockholders, resigned as president, sold remaining stock and severed all connection with the firm (Nov 1951); founded H.B. Laboratories to conduct research into consumer-oriented chemical products; elected to New York Academy of Sciences and named a fellow of American Institute of Chemists and a member of Society of Cosmetic

Chemists; appointed head of cosmetics and marketing program at Fashion Institute of Technology (1978) and was the 1st to occupy the Revlon chair at that institution. ❖ See also *Women in World History.*

BISHOP, Isabel (1902–1988). American artist. Born Isabel Bishop, Mar 3, 1902, in Cincinnati, Ohio; died Feb 1988 in Riverdale, New York; dau. of Dr. J. Remsen Bishop (educator) and Anna Bartram (Newbold) Bishop; attended John Wicker's Art School, Detroit, 1917; New York School of Applied Design for Women, 1918; Art Students League of New York, 1922–24; m. Harold George Wolff (physician), Aug 9, 1934 (died Feb 21, 1962); children: son, Remsen Wolff (b. April 6, 1940, photographer). ❖ Artist of genre scenes, best known for paintings of working women and men of New York City's Union Square, rented her 1st studio in Union Square (1926); produced *Self-Portrait* (1927), the 1st of a series of self-portraits and female nudes that are considered by some as unique among American women painters, reminiscent more of Europeans like Käthe Kollwitz and Paula Modersohn-Becker; rendered *Dante and Virgil in Union Square,* a precursor of her "Walking Pictures"; had 1st solo show with Midtown Galleries where she would exhibit throughout career; sold her oil, *Two Girls,* to Metropolitan Museum of Art (1935), bringing her national attention; became an instructor at Art Students League (1935); commissioned by US Treasury to execute a mural for a post office in New Lexington, Ohio, one of her few large-scale works (1938); elected an associate of National Academy of Design in NY; was the 1st woman to be elected an officer of National Institute of Arts and Letters (1946); had a retrospective at Whitney Museum (1974); received Gold Medal for Painting of the American Academy and Institute of Arts and Letters (1987); illustrated *Pride and Prejudice* (1976). ❖ See also Karl Lunde, *Isabel Bishop* (Abrams, 1975); Helen Yglesias, *Isabel Bishop* (Rizzoli, 1989); and *Women in World History.*

BISHOP, Isabella (1831–1904). English travel writer and explorer. Name variations: Isabella Bird, Isabella Bird Bishop, Isabella Lucy Bishop, Isa, IB. Born Isabella Lucy Bird, Oct 15, 1831, in Boroughbridge, Yorkshire, England; died Oct 7, 1904, in Edinburgh, Scotland; dau. of Reverend Edward (barrister turned cleric) and Dora (Lawson) Bird; m. John Bishop (physician), Mar 8, 1881; no children. ❖ After many years of illness, including a spinal tumor, traveled to Canada and North America on advice of doctor (1854); as a result, traveled throughout life and published many authoritative works on what she observed; major trips include Australia and New Zealand (1872), returning via the Sandwich Isles (now Hawaii) and US (1873), Japan (1878), Malaya (1879), Kashmir and Ladakh in northern India, and Tibet (1889), Persia (now Iran, 1890), Kurdistan (area of Middle East inhabited by Kurds which today includes parts of Turkey, Iran and Iraq, 1891), Japan, Korea, and China (1894–96) and Morocco (1901); was one of the 1st women to be made a fellow of Royal Geographical Society, London; though always a sharp and critical observer of religion in all its forms, her deep interest in everything she saw was stronger than her Victorian sensibilities, and she took everything in her stride, from nakedness to opium smoking; was also a gifted writer and her books are particularly important because it was the cultures of native peoples that she sought out on her travels, not Western-style comforts. Writings include *The Englishwoman in America* (1856), *Six Months in the Sandwich Islands* (1875), *A Lady's Life in the Rocky Mountains* (1879), *Unbeaten Tracks in Japan* (1880), *Journeys in Persia and Kurdistan* (1891), *Among the Tibetans* (1894), *Korea and Her Neighbours* (1898) and *The Yangtze Valley and Beyond* (1899). ❖ See also Pat Barr, *A Curious Life for a Lady: The Story of Isabella Bird* (Murray, 1970); Cicely Palser Havely, *This Grand Beyond: The Travels of Isabella Bird Bishop* (Century, 1984); Anna Stoddart, *The Life of Isabella Bird (Mrs Bishop)* (Murray, 1906); and *Women in World History.*

BISHOP, Julie (1914–2001). American actress. Name variations: Jacqueline Wells, Diane Duval. Born Jacqueline Brown, Aug 30, 1914, in Denver, Colorado; died Aug 30, 2001, in Mendocino, California; m. Walter Booth Brooks, 1936 (div. 1939); m. Clarence A. Shoop (vice-president of Hughes aircraft), 1944 (died 1968); m. William F. Bergin (surgeon), 1968; children: Steve Shoop (physician); Pamela Shoop (actress). ❖ Began film career as a child star under name Jacqueline Wells; as an adult, returned to the screen in Hal Roach comedies, then played leads in many films; signed with Warner's and changed name to Julie Bishop (1941); made over 50 films as Wells, including *Maytime, Dorothy Vernon of Haddon Hall, Tillie and Gus, Highway Patrol, Spring Madness* and *Flight into Nowhere;* made over 30 films as Bishop, including *Northern Pursuit, Action in the North Atlantic, Sands of Iwo Jima, Rhapsody in Blue, The High and the Mighty* and *The Big Land.*

BISHOP, Kate (b. 1847). English actress. Name variations: Kate Bishop Löhr; Kate Lohr or Loehr. Born Oct 1, 1847, in England; sister of Alfred Bishop; m. Lewis J. Löhr (treasurer of Melbourne Opera House in Australia); children: Marie Löhr (1890–1975, actress). ❖ Made stage debut in a juvenile play in Bristol (1863); made London debut as Venus in *Ixion* (1866), followed by a string of appearances; was the original Violet Melrose in Byron's *Our Boys,* sustaining the part for over 4 years; appeared in Australia for many years and on tour with the Kendals.

BISHOP, Kelly (1944—). American theatrical dancer. Born Carole Bishop, Feb 28, 1944, in Colorado Springs, Colorado; m. Lee Leonard (tv host in New Jersey), 1981. ❖ Failing an audition at American Ballet Theatre, joined the corps de ballet at Radio City Music Hall; appeared at World's Fair in Michael Kidd's *Wonderland* (1964); performed in numerous cabaret shows in Las Vegas; appeared on Broadway in *Golden Rainbow* (1968), *Promises, Promises* (1968), *On the Town* (1971–72), *Precious Sons* (1986), *Six Degrees of Separation* (1990–92), *Bus Stop* (1996), *The Last Night of Ballyhoo* (1997–98) and *Proposals* (1997–98); won Tony Award for Best Featured Actress as Sheila in *A Chorus Line* (1976); films include *An Unmarried Woman* (1978), *O'Hara's Wife* (1982), *Miami Rhapsody* (1995) and *Private Parts* (1997); on tv, appeared as Emily Gilmore on "The Gilmore Girls" (2000).

BISLAND, Elizabeth (1863–1929). American writer. Name variations: Bessie Bisland; Elisabeth Bisland Wetmore. Born in St. Mary Parish, Louisiana, 1863; died 1929; grew up in Natchez; married a man named Wetmore. ❖ An associate editor of *Cosmopolitan* magazine, published *A Flying Trip around the World,* an account of her 1889 trip performed in 76 days (1891); also wrote *A Widower Indeed,* with Rhoda Broughton (1892). ❖ See also Jason Marks, *Around the World in 72 Days: The Race between* Pulitzer's *Nellie Bly and* Cosmopolitan's *Elizabeth Bisland* (Gemittarius Press).

BISMARCK, Johanna von (1824–1894). German wife of Bismarck. Name variations: Johanna von Puttkamer Bismarck. Born Johanna von Puttkamer, April 11, 1824, in Viartlum, Pommern; died Nov 27, 1894, in Varzin, Pommern; m. Otto von Bismarck (1815–1898), 1st German Chancellor, 1847; children: Maria (b. 1848), Herbert (b. 1849), and Wilhelm (b. 1851). ❖ Had little interest in politics and was not ambitious, but provided husband with an emotionally secure household for over 40 years.

BISSELL, Emily (1861–1948). American welfare worker and founder. Born Emily Perkins Bissell, May 31, 1861, in Wilmington, Delaware; died Mar 8, 1948, in Wilmington; dau. of Champion Aristarcus Bissell (banker and real-estate investor) and Josephine (Wales) Bissell; educated at Miss Charlier's in New York City. ❖ Founder of Christmas Seals, was active in a number of charities her entire life; organized the 1st chapter of the American Red Cross for Delaware and created the 1st public playground and the 1st free kindergarten in Wilmington; persuaded American Red Cross to mount a nationwide strategy to sell Christmas stamps (1907); was the 1st lay person to be awarded the Trudeau Medal of National Tuberculosis Association (1942); honored on US stamp (1980).

BITTENBENDER, Ada Matilda (1848–1925). American suffragist, temperance reformer, and attorney. Born Ada Matilda Cole, Aug 3, 1848, in Bradford Co., Pennsylvania; died Dec 15, 1925, in Lincoln, Nebraska; m. Henry Clay Bittenbender, Aug 9, 1878. ❖ Helped organize the Nebraska Woman Suffrage Association (1881), of which she served as president (1882); became Nebraska's 1st female lawyer (May 1882); was superintendent of temperance legislation for Nebraska Woman's Christian Temperance Union (1883–89); focused on federal laws as superintendent of legislation and petitions for National WCTU (beginning 1887), and attorney for the organization (1888–89); credited with drawing up the bill which raised the statutory age of consent to 16 for women (enacted 1889); in Nebraska, was a candidate for supreme court judge on the Prohibition ticket (1891). Writings include *The National Prohibitory Amendment Guide* (1889) and *Tedos and Tisod: A Temperance Story* (1911).

BJARKLIND, Unnur Benediktsdóttir (1881–1946). Icelandic poet and short-story writer. Name variations: (pseudonym) Hulda. Born 1881 in Iceland; died 1946. ❖ Neo-romantic lyric poet, was extremely popular during her lifetime; wrote 7 poetry collections, including *Kvæði* (1909); also wrote novels.

BJEDOV, Djurdica (1947—). Yugoslavian swimmer. Born April 1947. ❖ At Mexico City Olympics, won a gold medal in the 100-meter breaststroke and a silver medal in the 200-meter breaststroke (1968).

BJEDOV, Mira (1955—). Yugoslavian basketball player. Born Sept 7, 1955. ❖ At Moscow Olympics, won a bronze medal in team competition (1980).

BJELKE-PETERSEN, Marie (1874–1969). Danish-Australian novelist. Born Marie Bjelke-Petersen at Jagtvejen, near Copenhagen, Denmark, Dec 23, 1874; died at Lindisfarne, Hobart, Tasmania, Oct 11, 1969; only dau. of Georg Peter and Caroline Vilhellmine (Hansen) Bjelke-Petersen; attended schools in Denmark, Germany and London. ❖ Immigrated with family to Tasmania (1891); contributed a number of romantic religious stories to Sydney papers, three of which were published as *The Mysterious Stranger* (1913); at 42, published 1st novel *The Captive Singer*, which enjoyed immense popularity, followed by 8 more sentimental novels, each containing an evangelical theme; gained greater popularity in US and England than Australia; helped establish the Tasmanian Fellowship of Australian Writers. Received King's Jubilee Medal for literature (1935).

BJERKRHEIM, Susan Goksoer (1970—). See Goksoer, Susann.

BJERREGAARD, Ritt (1941—). Danish politician. Born May 19, 1941, in Copenhagen, Denmark; dau. of Gudmund (cabinetmaker) and Rita Bjerregaard; attended Odense University, 1968–70. ❖ Social Democrat, was a member of the Folketing for Funen Co. constituency (1971–1995) and for Roskilde Co. constituency (2001); served as minister for Education (1973–75, 1975–78), minister of Social Affairs (1981), and minister of Food, Agriculture and Fisheries (2000–2001); was commissioner of the European commission (1995–99); writings include *Strid* (Struggle, 1979), *Til venner og fjender* (To Friends and Enemies, 1982), *Heltindehistorier* (Stories of Heroines, 1983), and *I opposition* (In Opposition, 1987).

BJOERGEN, Marit (1980—). Norwegian cross-country skier. Name variations: Marit Björgen. Born Mar 21, 1980, in Norway. ❖ Won a silver medal for the 4 x 5 km relay at Salt Lake City Olympics (2002) and a silver medal for 10 km Classical at Torino Olympics (2006).

BJÖRGEN, Marit (1980—). See Bjoergen, Marit.

BJORK (1965—). Icelandic singer. Name variations: Bjork Gudmundsdottir. Born Bjork Gudmundsdottir, Nov 21, 1965, in Reykjavik, Iceland; children: 1 son, 1 daughter. ❖ Eccentric vocalist known for distinctive voice, recorded 1st album at age 11; joined Icelandic hard-rock band, Theyr, while still in teens; co-founded KUKL (1984), theatrical rock band, which became The Sugarcubes; sang lead vocals on Sugarcubes' debut *Life's Too Good* (1986); sang vocals and co-wrote songs on *Here Today, Tomorrow, Next Week!* (1989) and *Stick Around for Joy* (1992); collaborated with Soul II Soul's Nellee Hooper on 1st US solo album *Debut* (1993); released solo albums *Post* (1995), *Telegram* (1997) and *Selmasongs* (2000); drew acclaim playing lead in Lars von Trier's *Dancer in the Dark* (2000).

BJÖRK, Anita (1923—). Swedish actress. Name variations: Anita Bjork. Born April 25, 1923, in Tällberg, Sweden; attended Royal Dramatic Theatre School, Stockholm. ❖ One of Sweden's leading actors of stage and screen, made film debut at 19 in Alf Sjöberg's *The Road to Heaven*; came to prominence in title role of another Sjöberg film, an adaptation of Strindberg's *Miss Julie*; subsequently appeared in several Ingmar Bergman films, including *Secrets of Women* (1952), and in Nunnally Johnson's *Night People* (1954), an American film shot in Germany; in later years, appeared at Royal Dramatic Theatre in Stockholm and on Swedish tv. ❖ See also *Women in World History.*

BJORKLAND, Penny (1941—). American murderer. Born Rosemarie Diane Bjorkland in 1941 in US. ❖ As teenager, stole .38-caliber pistol from friend's home (Jan 1959); left her house in Daly City, California, intending to commit a murder (Feb 1959); offered a ride by gardener August Norry, shot him 18 times; confessed and received life sentence at trial; when asked about her motive, reportedly said that for a year or more she'd had an urge to kill.

BJØRN, Dinna (1947—). Danish ballet dancer. Name variations: Dinna Bjørn or Bjoern. Born Dinna Bjørn Larsen, Feb 14, 1947, in Copenhagen, Denmark; dau. of Niels Bjørn Larsen (dance teacher). ❖ Trained at Royal Danish Ballet school, where her father was on the faculty; joined Royal Danish Ballet (1964), then won acclaim in Jerome Robbins' *Afternoon of a Faun ;* was later recognized for performances in revived works by Bournonville, especially *Kermesse in Bruges, La Sylphide, La Ventana, Far from Denmark* and *A Folk Tale;* taught classes in Bournonville technique; accompanied father on tour, giving lectures and demonstrations of his dance and mime work.

BJORNSON, Maria (1949–2002). English set and costume designer. Name variations: Maria Bjørnson. Born Feb 16, 1949, in Paris, France; grew up in London; died Dec 13, 2002, in London, England; dau. of Mia Prodan (Romanian who worked in the BBC Romanian service at Bush House) and Bjorn Bjornson (Norwegian businessman); granddau. of Bjornstjerne Bjornson (who won Nobel Prize for Literature in 1903); studied at Glen Byam Shaw School and Central School of Art and Design; never married. ❖ Began designing career at Glasgow Citizens Theater; won Tony Awards for set and costumes for *Phantom of the Opera* (1988); designed for Francesca Zambello's production of *Don Giovanni* at Royal Opera House (2001) and *Troyens* at Metropolitan Opera (2002); also designed for Royal Shakespeare Company's *The Tempest,* Welsh National Opera's Janacek cycle, *From the House of the Dead,* Royal Ballet's *Sleeping Beauty,* among many others.

BJURSTEDT, Anna "Molla" (1884–1959). See Mallory, Molla.

BLACHÉ, Alice Guy (1875–1968). See Guy-Blaché, Alice.

BLACH, Helena. See Lavrsen, Helena.

BLACHFORD, Theodosia (1745–1817). Irish reformer. Born Theodosia Tighe in 1745; died 1817; m. Reverend William Blachford, 1770 (died 1773). ❖ Prominent in the Methodist movement in Ireland, was present at the inaugural meeting of the Friends of the Female Orphan House (1790); founded House of Refuge on Baggot Street (1802); also authored a number of tracts.

BLACK, Ana (1907–1953). See Hato, Ana Matawhaura.

BLACK, C.C. (1862–1946). See Garnett, Constance.

BLACK, Cilla (1943—). English pop singer and television host. Born Priscilla Maria Veronica White, May 27, 1943, in Liverpool, England; dau. of John Patrick White (dock worker) and Priscilla White (market-stall owner); attended Anfield Community College (typing course); m. Bobby Willis (her manager), 1969 (died 1999); children: 3 sons. ❖ Became mini-celebrity in Liverpool, performing alongside legendary acts that established the Mersey Sound, such as the Beatles, Gerry and the Pacemakers, and the Hurricanes; debuted on British singles charts with Lennon-McCartney song, "Love of the Loved"; hit #1 with Burt Bacharach's "Anyone Who Had a Heart" (1964), then the biggest selling single of all time by a British female recording artist; hit #1 again with "You're My World"; was at the forefront of the British pop scene with 20 consecutive Top-40 hits on singles and albums; appeared at sell-out concerts throughout Europe and Australia (1963–78); fading as a pop icon (late 1960s), had last hit, "Surround Yourself with Sorrow" (1969); starred in her own popular variety show for BBC and went on to host "Blind Date" (1985–2003) and "Surprise! Surprise!" (1998–2001); released album "Beginnings" (2003). ❖ See also autobiography, *What's It all About?* (Ebury, 2004).

BLACK, Clementina (1854–1922). English trade unionist and writer. Born in Brighton, England, in 1854; died at her home in Brighton, 1922; dau. of David Black (solicitor) and Maria (Patten) Black (successful portrait painter); never married; no children. ❖ Concerned with issues of work and wages for women, became secretary of Women's Protective and Provident League (1886); created a Consumers' League, supported the London Match Girls' Strike, and initiated the Equal Pay resolution at the Trade Union Congress (1888); joined the new Women's Trade Union Association and took up the cause against sweatshop labor; became a founding member of Women's Industrial Council (1894), of which she would later serve as president; was also vice-president of National Anti-Sweating League; was a member of National Union of Women's Suffrage Society and editor of *Common Cause;* initiated the suffrage petition (1906); writings include *A Sussex Idyll* (1877), (novel) *An Agitator* (1895), (novel) *The Princess Desirée* (1896), (novel) *The Pursuit of Camilla* (1899), *Sweated Industry and the Minimum Wage* (1907), (novel) *Caroline* (1908), *Makers of Our Clothes: a Case for Trade Boards* (1909), (novel) *The Linleys of Bath* (1911) and *Married Women's Work* (1915).

BLACK, Dora (1894–1986). See Russell, Dora.

BLACK, Elinor F.E. (1905–1982). Canadian physician. Born Elinor Frances Elizabeth Black, Sept 9, 1905, in Nelson, British Columbia; died 1982; dau. of Francis Mollison Black and Margaret Elizabeth (McIntosh) Black; graduated cum laude from University of Manitoba Medical School, 1930. ❖ Studied childbirth techniques at Annie McCall Maternity Hospital, London; opened private practice in obstetrics and gynecology in Winnipeg, Canada (1930s); became 1st woman Canadian member (1938) and 1st woman fellow (1949) of Royal College of Obstetricians and Gynaecologists in England; as 1st woman Canadian physician to lead a major medical department, served as head of obstetrics and gynecology at University of Manitoba and at Winnipeg General Hospital (1951–64); served temporary professorship of obstetrics and gynecology at University of the West Indies (beginning 1969). ❖ See also Julie Vandervoort, *Tell the Driver: A Biography of Elinor F.E. Black, M.D.*

BLACK, Helen McKenzie (1896–1963). New Zealand political host and politician. Name variations: Helen McKenzie Murray, Helen McKenzie Bennett. Born Aug 16, 1896, in Aberdeen Scotland; died Oct 17, 1963, in Christchurch, New Zealand; dau. of Alexander Innes Murray (shipmaster) and Helen (McKenzie) Murray; m. Leslie Douglas Stuart Murray (military officer), 1921 (div. c. 1924); m. Robert Sheriff Black (fur merchant), 1924 (died 1939); m. Stanley George Bennett (tea planter), 1960; children: 2 daughters, 2 sons. ❖ Served as political host for 2nd husband, who was mayor of Dunedin (1929–33); stood unsuccessfully for Parliament (1935, 1954); active in Women's War Service Auxiliary, National Council of Women of New Zealand and Navy League; published autobiography (1947). Awarded British Empire Medal (1952).

BLACK, Julie (1970—). *See Richards, Julie Burns.*

BLACK, Marilyn (1944—). Australian runner. Born May 20, 1944. ❖ At Tokyo Olympics, won a bronze medal in the 200 meters (1964).

BLACK, Martha Louise (1866–1957). Canadian politician and writer. Born Martha Louise Munger in 1866 in Chicago, Illinois; died 1957; attended St. Mary's College, Notre Dame; m. William Purdy, 1887 (died); m. George Black (commissioner of the Yukon and member of Parliament [1921–35 and 1940–49]), in 1904; children: (1st m.) 3. ❖ Separated from husband (1898) and took her children to the Yukon, where she joined the Klondike Gold Rush, working a claim and managing a sawmill; was elected to represent the Yukon (1935–40), only the 2nd woman after Agnes Macphail to serve as an MP; wrote well-known autobiography *My Seventy Years,* which documents her transformation from ordinary wife and mother to mining pioneer and politician.

BLACK, Shirley Temple (1928—). American actress and diplomat. Born Shirley Temple, April 23, 1928, in Santa Monica, California; dau. of George Francis and Gertrude Amelia (Krieger) Temple; m. John Agar (actor), Sept 19, 1945 (div. 1950); m. Charles Alden Black, Dec 16, 1950; children: (1st m.) Linda Susan; (2nd m.) Charles Alden Jr. and Lori Alden. ❖ Child movie star whose famous dimples saved 20th Century-Fox from bankruptcy, began work for Educational Films Corp. (1932); appeared in short films, followed by 1st full-length film *Red-Haired Alibi* for Tower Productions (1932); signed contract with Fox Films (1934); appeared and starred in over 30 features (1934–49), including *Stand Up and Cheer* (1934), *Little Miss Marker* (1934), *Baby Take a Bow* (1934), *Bright Eyes* (1934), *The Little Colonel* (1935), *Curly Top* (1935), *The Littlest Rebel* (1935), *Captain January* (1936), *Poor Little Rich Girl* (1936), *Dimples* (1936), *Wee Willie Winkie* (1937), *Heidi* (1937), *Rebecca of Sunnybrook Farm* (1938), *Little Miss Broadway* (1938), *Just Around the Corner* (1938), *The Little Princess* (1939), *Susannah of the Mounties* (1939), *The Blue Bird* (1940), *Since You Went Away* (1944), *I'll Be Seeing You* (1945), *The Bachelor and the Bobby-Soxer* (1947), *The Story of Seabiscuit* (1949) and *A Kiss for Corliss* (1949); named #1 box-office attraction in US (1935–38); narrated and appeared in tv series "Shirley Temple's Storybook" (1958–61); entered Republican politics, campaigning for Richard Nixon (1960); ran for Congress (1967); appointed representative to 24th General Assembly of United Nations (1969–70); served as ambassador to Ghana (1974–76); served as US chief of protocol (1976–77); was officer and founding member of American Academy of Diplomacy (1981); appointed 1st Honorary Foreign Service Officer of the US (1981); served as ambassador to Czechoslovakia (1989). ❖ See also *Child Star: An Autobiography* (McGraw-Hill, 1988); Anne Edwards, *Shirley Temple: American Princess* (Morrow, 1988); and *Women in World History.*

BLACK, Winifred Sweet (1863–1936). American journalist. Name variations: Winifred Black Bonfils; (pseudonym) Annie Laurie. Born Winifred Sweet, Oct 14, 1863, in Chilton, Wisconsin; died May 25, 1936, in San Francisco, California; dau. of Benjamin Jeffrey (attorney) and Lovisa Loveland (Denslow) Sweet; m. Orlow Black, June 1892 (div. 1897); m. Charles A. Bonfils (sep. 1909); children: (1st m.) 1 son (died in childhood drowning accident); (2nd m.) 1 daughter; 1 son (died in childhood). ❖ Writing under pen name "Annie Laurie," began career with *San Francisco Examiner;* soon made the undercover story a Hearst trademark, covering the lepers on Hawaiian island of Molokai, polygamy among the Mormons in Utah, and an investigation of juvenile court system in Chicago; became the 1st woman to report a prize fight and the 2nd to interview a president; as colorful as her exposés, made her mark in the daredevil style of Nellie Bly (Elizabeth Seaman), often risking her life, or engaging in elaborate stunts, to get a scoop; in a career that spanned 50 years, helped build a newspaper empire for William Randolph Hearst and proved to be one of the most versatile journalists of her time. ❖ See also *Women in World History.*

BLACKADDER, Elizabeth (1931—). Scottish artist. Born Sept 24, 1931, in Falkirk, Stirlingshire, Scotland; attended Edinburgh University and Edinburgh College of Art, 1949–54; m. John Houston (painter), 1956. ❖ Landscape and still life painter, held 1st solo exhibition at 57 Gallery, Edinburgh (1959); lectured in drawing and painting at Edinburgh College of Art (1962–86); though early work was mostly landscapes, began to concentrate on still life (1970s), combining recognizable objects with apparently random associations (cats, fans, ribbons, etc.) depicted on an empty abstract background; had solo exhibitions of work, both nationally and internationally, and participated extensively in group exhibitions from 1961, notably in Canada, Germany, US, Japan, Brazil, Australia, Russia and UK; began to include flowers and plants in later works which increasingly came to dominate compositions; elected to Royal Scottish Academy (1972) and Royal Academy (1976), the 1st woman to be a full member of both; also elected member of The Royal Glasgow Institute of Fine Arts (1983). Received Guthrie Award from Royal Scottish Academy (1962), Pimms Award from Royal Academy (1983); appointed Her Majesty's Painter and Limner in Scotland (2001).

BLACK AGNES (1312–1369). *See Dunbar, Agnes.*

BLACKBURN, Doris Amelia (1889–1970). Australian civil-rights activist, peace campaigner, and politician. Born Doris Amelia Hordern, Sept 18, 1889, in Auburn, Victoria; died Dec 12, 1970; dau. of Louisa Dewson (Smith) and Lebbeus Hordern; attended Hessle School; m. Maurice Blackburn (lawyer and Labor Party politician), Dec 1914; children: 2 sons, 2 daughters (1 died in infancy). ❖ Joined husband's efforts against conscription and war (1914); served as president of Women's International League for Peace and Freedom (1928–30); was a member of the Free Kindergarten Movement and retained a lifelong interest in pre-school education; wrote for newspapers and journals; as an independent Labor candidate, elected to Parliament (1944), where she focused on women's rights, social and family welfare, and opposition to the testing and use of guided missiles; was defeated for re-election (1949); helped establish Aboriginal Advancement League, which evolved into Federal Council for Advancement of Aborigines and Torres Strait Islanders.

BLACKBURN, Helen (1842–1903). Irish suffragist. Born in Knightstown, Valentia Island, Co. Kerry, Ireland, May 25, 1842; died in London, England, Jan 11, 1903; buried in Brompton cemetery; dau. of a civil engineer who was manager of the Knight of Kerry's slate quarries on the island. ❖ Moved from Ireland to London (1859); began work on behalf of women's suffrage (1874), serving as secretary for National Society of Women's Suffrage until 1895; served as editor of *Englishwoman's Review* (1881–90) and secretary of West of England Suffrage Society; writings include a classic history, *Women's Suffrage: A Record of the Movement in the British Isles* (1902), as well as several books on women in industry.

BLACKBURN, Mrs. Hugh (1823–1909). *See Blackburn, Jemima.*

BLACKBURN, Jemima (1823–1909). Scottish Painter. Name variations: Jemima Wedderburn; Mrs. Hugh Blackburn. Born 1823 in Edinburgh, Scotland; died 1909 in Lochailort, Inverness Co., Scotland; dau. of James Wedderburn (solicitor-general for Scotland) and Isabella Clerk of Penicuik; studied with John Ruskin and Sir Edwin Landseer, and with a professor of anatomy at Royal College of Surgeons; m. Hugh Blackburn (professor of mathematics at Glasgow University), 1848; children: 3 sons, 1 daughter. ❖ One of the foremost illustrators of the Victorian Age, is best remembered for her visual diaries depicting life in the Scottish Highlands; sent to London to complete education (1840), promised to send mother a drawing a day, initiating a visual diary that she maintained for next 60 years; with husband, traveled throughout Europe, sketchbook in hand, then bought Roshven Estate (1854), on the shores of Loch Ailort; hosted some of the most celebrated figures of 19th century, including John Ruskin, Sir John Everett Millais, Anthony Trollope, Benjamin Disraeli, Lord Lister, and her 1st cousin, James Clerk-Maxwell; painted wildlife of countryside as well; a watercolorist of outstanding techniques and keen observations, also showed talent with lithographic crayon; was also a leading birder and skilled ornithological illustrator; asked to contribute to 1st exhibition of contemporary British art in America (1857), exhibited as well in Edinburgh, Glasgow and London. Work resides in British Museum, British Library, Natural History Museum, The Royal Collection, National Portrait Gallery and Scottish National Portrait Gallery.

BLACKBURN, Jessy (1894–1995). English aviator. Name variations: Jessica Blackburn, Jessica Thompson. Born Jessica Thompson, 1894, in Cradley, Worcestershire, England; died 1995 in England; orphaned at early age; m. Robert Blackburn (aircraft engineer), 1914 (div. 1936); remarried twice, briefly; children: 2 sons. ❖ An early aviation enthusiast, married Robert Blackburn (1914) and used her inheritance to help him establish Blackburn Aircraft, Ltd., which supplied military planes to British government during WWI and WWII; undertook 1st flight in Roundhay Park, Leeds, one of the 1st women to fly a monoplane before WWI; competed twice in King's Cup Air Races (1922, 1928); following divorce (1936), ended direct involvement with Blackburn Aircraft.

BLACKBURN, Kathleen (1892–1968). British botanist. Name variations: Kathleen Bever Blackburn. Born Feb 23, 1892, in UK; died Aug 20, 1968; Bedford College, BS, 1913, MS, 1916, DSc, 1924. ❖ Served as lecturer in botany at Southlands Training College, Battersea (1914–18); was lecturer (1918–47) and reader in cytology (from 1947) at Armstrong College, Newcastle-upon-Tyne (later Newcastle University); was an early teacher of practical plant cytology; performed most important research with Heslop Harrison in cytotaxonomy of Salicaceae (willows) and genus *Rosa;* with Harrison, became 1st to document sex chromosomes in flowering plants; served as president of Northern Naturalist Union (1935).

BLACKBURN, Molly (c. 1931–1985). South African civil-rights activist. Born c. 1931; died in automobile accident, Dec 28, 1985, near Port Elizabeth, South Africa. ❖ One of South Africa's leading white anti-apartheid advocates, joined the Black Sash (1960); as a member of South Africa's official opposition party, the Progressive Federals, joined the Cape Provincial Council (1975); was instrumental in arranging medical and legal assistance for victims of South Africa's violent unrest; through the years, was arrested on a number of occasions for attending illegal gatherings or entering black townships without the necessary permit; was one of the 1st whites arrested after Botha's crackdown on dissidents (July 1985), which gave the country's security forces unlimited powers to search, seize and arrest. ❖ See also *Women in World History.*

BLACKBURNE, Anna (1726–1793). British naturalist. Born 1726 at Orford Hall, near Warrington, Manchester, England; died Dec 30, 1793; dau. of a wealthy landowner. ❖ Began collection of natural specimens and was in contact with scientists, including taxonomist Linnaeus; collected some North American specimens which were used by Thomas Pennant for descriptions in his *Arctic Zoology;* had several species named after her, including the beetle *Scarabaeus blackburnii* (now *Geotrupes blackburnii*) and the Blackburnian warbler *Dendroica fusca.*

BLACK DAHLIA, The (1925–1947). See *Short, Elizabeth.*

BLACKETT, Annie Maude (1889–1956). New Zealand librarian. Born July 30, 1889, at Newcastle upon Tyne, England; died June 12, 1956, in Wanganui, New Zealand; dau. of Thomas Robert Blackett and Annie (Pile) Blackett. ❖ Immigrated to New Zealand (1907); one of 1st chief librarians to have trained in New Zealand, served as chief librarian of Wanganui Public Library (1918–50); planned and administered Alexander Library in Queens Park (1933); was president of New Zealand Library Association (1944–45).

BLACKHAM, Dorothy Isabel (1896–1975). Irish artist. Born 1896, in Dublin, Ireland; died 1975; attended Royal Hibernian Academy, Metropolitan School of Art and Goldsmith's College, London. ❖ Working in oils, watercolor, and tempera, designed posters and Christmas cards, as well as creating drawings for various magazines, including the *Bell;* received medals at Tailteann Festivals (1928 and 1932) and was widely exhibited throughout Ireland, including the Ulster Women Artists'

Group, the Watercolour Society of Ireland, and the Arts and Crafts Society of Ireland; works are held by Hugh Lane Municipal Gallery, in Dublin.

BLACKIE, Jeannetta Margaret (1864–1955). New Zealand teacher and church administrator. Name variations: Jeannetta Margaret Walker. Born June 19, 1864, in London, England; died May 4, 1955, in Dunedin, New Zealand; dau. of Alexander Walker (printer) and Anne Jane (Randall) Walker; m. James Blackie (minister), 1893 (died 1897); children: 2 daughters. ❖ Opened small private school in Queenstown, New Zealand (1900); appointed superintendent of Presbyterian Women's Training Institute in Dunedin and presided over training of deaconesses (1903–18). ❖ See also *Dictionary of New Zealand Biography* (Vol. 3).

BLACKLER, Betty (1929—). English actress. Born Elizabeth Anne Felicity Blackler, Nov 19, 1929, in London, England. ❖ Came to prominence withh stage debut as Elizabeth Bullett in *Panama Hattie.*

BLACKMAN, Elizabeth (1836–1900). See *Pulman, Elizabeth.*

BLACKMAN, Honor (1926—). English stage and screen actress. Born Dec 12, 1926, London, England; m. Bill Sankey, 1946 (div. 1956); m. Maurice Kaufmann, 1963 (div. 1975); children: (2nd m.) 2. ❖ Made London stage debut as Monica Cartwright in *The Gleam* (1946); other plays include *The Blind Goddess, The Fifth Season, Wait Until Dark, Mr. and Mrs., Who Killed Santa Claus?* and *The Deep Blue Sea;* on tv, appeared as Cathy Gale on "The Avengers" (1962–64) and as Laura West in "The Upper Hand," among others; appeared in such films as *Fame Is the Spur, Quartet, So Long at the Fair, Diplomatic Passport, A Night to Remember, Serena, Jason and the Golden Fleece, Life at the Top, Moment to Moment, A Twist of Sand, Shalako, The Virgin and the Gypsy, Something Big, Fright, Lola, The Cat and the Canary, To Walk with Lions, Bridget Jones's Diary,* and as Pussy Galore in James Bond's *Goldfinger* (1964).

BLACKMAN, Liz (1949—). English politician and member of Parliament. Born Sept 26, 1949; m. Derek Blackman (div. 1999). ❖ Representing Labour, elected to House of Commons for Erewash (1997, 2001, 2005).

BLACK MARY (c. 1832–1914). See *Fields, Mary.*

BLACK MEG (1202–1280). See *Margaret of Flanders.*

BLACKSTONE, Tessa (1942—). English sociologist, educator and politician. Name variations: Tessa Blackstone; Baroness Tessa Ann Vosper Evans Blackstone; Baroness of Stoke Newington. Born Tessa Ann Vosper Blackstone, 1942, in Bures, Suffolk, England; attended London School of Economics; m. Thomas Evans, 1963 (div., died 1985). ❖ Known as the "Red Baroness" while in academia, lectured in sociology at Enfield College of Technology (1965–66) and in social administration at London School of Economics for 9 years; served as advisor to Central Policy Review Staff in Cabinet Office (1975–78) and as professor of Educational Administration at University of London Institute of Education (1978–83); became director of education at Inner London Education Authority, before being appointed master of London University's Birkbeck College (1987); awarded Labour life peerage (1987) and served in House of Lords as opposition bench speaker on education and science (1988–92) and on foreign affairs; served on board of Royal Opera House for 10 years, 6 of them as chair of Royal Ballet; wrote several books on education and social issues, including *Prisons and Penal Reform* (1990); was Labour's education spokesperson (1997–2001); appointed minister for the arts (2001); became vice-chancellor of University of Greenwich (2004).

BLACKWELL, Alice Stone (1857–1950). American feminist and reformer. Born Sept 14, 1857, in Orange, New Jersey; died in Cambridge, Massachusetts, Mar 15, 1950; dau. of Lucy Stone (1818–1893) and Henry Browne Blackwell (both reformers); niece of medical pioneers Elizabeth Blackwell, Emily Blackwell and Antoinette Brown Blackwell; graduated Phi Beta Kappa from Boston University, 1881; never married; no children. ❖ Joined editorial staff of her mother's *Woman's Journal,* an organ of American Woman Suffrage Association, and soon became its primary force, a tenure that lasted for more than 3 decades; also wrote a syndicated column that was printed in mainstream newspapers throughout the country; published a biography of her mother, *Lucy Stone* (1930), which she had worked on for 40 years. ❖ See also *Women in World History.*

BLACKWELL, Antoinette Brown (1825–1921). See *Brown Blackwell, Antoinette.*

BLACKWELL, Elizabeth (1821–1910). English-born physician. Born Feb 3, 1821, in Counterslip, England, near Bristol; died May 31, 1910, in Hastings, England; dau. of Samuel (sugar refiner and reform activist) and Hannah Lane Blackwell; sister of Emily Blackwell; sister-in-law of Lucy Stone (who m. Henry Browne Blackwell) and Antoinette Brown Blackwell (who m. Samuel Blackwell); aunt of Alice Stone Blackwell; Geneva College, MD, 1849; additional medical study at La Maternité, Paris, and St. Bartholomew's Hospital, London; children: Katharine Barry (b. 1847, adopted 1854). ❧ The 1st woman doctor of modern times, who worked to expand professional medical opportunities for women and to provide quality medical care for poor women and children, emigrated from England to New York with family (1832); moved to Cincinnati, Ohio (1838); after stints as a teacher in Ohio, Kentucky and North Carolina, entered medical school at Geneva College in NY (1847), graduating at top of her class; because of prejudices against women doctors in US, continued her medical training in Paris and London; contracted ophthalmia, resulting in the loss of an eye; opened dispensary for poor women and children in New York City (1853); during Civil War, provided nurses for Union army; founded Women's Medical College of New York Infirmary (1868); moved to England and worked for repeal of the Contagious Diseases Acts and for dissemination of sanitary knowledge (1869); was a renowned figure in US and Europe, and an inspiration to the many female doctors who followed in her pioneering path. Writings include *Counsel to Parents on the Moral Education of Their Children* (1880), *Wrong and Right Methods of Dealing with Social Evil* (1883), *The Human Element in Sex* (1884) and *Essays in Medical Sociology* (1899). ❧ See also autobiography, *Pioneer Work in Opening the Medical Profession to Women* (1895); Ishbel Ross, *Child of Destiny* (Harper, 1949); Elinor Rice Hays, *Those Extraordinary Blackwells* (Harcourt, 1967); and *Women in World History.*

BLACKWELL, Ellen Wright (1864–1952). New Zealand writer and botanist. Name variations: Ellen Wright Maidment; (pseudonym) Grace Winter. Born Oct 7, 1864, in Northamptonshire, England; died Feb 24, 1952, in Portsmouth, England; dau. of John Blackwell (master hosier) and Annie Maria (Bumpus) Blackwell; m. Thomas Maidment, 1910. ❧ Under pseudonym Grace Winter, wrote religious books for children, beginning 1900; traveled to New Zealand (1903); co-authored *Plants of New Zealand* (1906), which became botanical classic for several decades; returned to England (c. 1906). ❧ See also *Dictionary of New Zealand Biography* (Vol. 3).

BLACKWELL, Emily (1826–1910). English-born physician. Born Oct 8, 1826, in Bristol, England; died Sept 1910 in York Cliffs, Maine; dau. of Samuel Blackwell (sugar refiner and reform activist) and Hannah Lane Blackwell; sister of Elizabeth Blackwell; sister-in-law of Lucy Stone (who m. Henry Browne Blackwell) and Antoinette Brown Blackwell (who m. Samuel Blackwell); aunt of Alice Stone Blackwell; attended Rush Medical College, 1852; Western Reserve University, MD, 1854; studied in Edinburgh with Sir James Simpson, and in Paris, London, Berlin and Dresden; children: Anna (b. 1871, adopted). ❧ Pioneer in opening the medical profession to women, who served as physician to generations of poor women and children and facilitated other women's entry into medicine through her work as dean and professor at the Women's Medical College in New York; immigrated with family to US (1832); following medical training, joined sister Elizabeth in her dispensary practice (1856), which was chartered as the New York Infirmary for Women and Children (1858); devoted all her time to the infirmary practice, serving as administrator as well as physician, and never developed a private practice of her own; took over administration of the Women's Medical College (1869), as well, serving as dean and professor of obstetrics and gynecology; elected to New York County Medical Society (1871). ❧ See also *Women in World History.*

BLACKWELL, Lucy Stone (1818–1893). *See Stone, Lucy.*

BLACKWOOD, Beatrice (1889–1975). British social anthropologist. Born Beatrice Mary Blackwood, May 3, 1889, in London, England; died 1975; dau. of James Blackwood (publisher); sister of Mary French; graduated from Somerville College at Oxford, 1912, but did not receive BA and MA until 1920, when Oxford granted women their degrees; Oxford University, BSc in embryology, 1923; never married. ❧ Became assistant to Arthur Thomson at anatomy department of Oxford University (c. 1920); performed archaeological research in France and England; served as demonstrator and lecturer in ethnology at Oxford (1923–59); in US, performed psychological tests to research intelligence (1920s); as one of 1st women to perform field research in Melanesia, studied 2 communities in Solomon Islands (the Petats and Kurtatchi,

1929–30), and published the results in *Both Sides of Buka Passage* (1935); served as assistant curator at Pitt Rivers Museum and as founding editor of museum publication series.

BLACKWOOD, Hariot (c. 1845–1891). Irish reformer and author. Name variations: Lady Dufferin; Marchioness of Dufferin and Ava, Hariot Hamilton. Born Hariot Rowan Hamilton, c. 1845; died after 1891; dau. of Captain A. Rowan Hamilton, of Killyleagh Castle, Down; m. Frederick Temple Hamilton-Temple-Blackwood, 1st marquis of Dufferin and Ava (1826–1902, British diplomat); children: 3 daughters, 4 sons, including Terence (b. 1866). ❧ When husband was appointed governor-general, accompanied him to Canada (1872–79), and other posts; after he was appointed viceroy of India (1884), started the Countess of Dufferin's Fund in Support of the National Association for Supplying Female Medical Aid to the Women of India, which provided better medical treatment for native women; recorded her experiences in *Our Viceregal Life in India* (1889) and *My Canadian Journal* (1891). ❧ See also *Women in World History.*

BLACKWOOD, Helen Selina (1807–1867). British-Irish poet. Name variations: Lady Dufferin, Countess of Dufferin, Countess of Gifford; Helen Selina Dufferin, Helen Selina Sheridan; (pseudonym) Impulsia Gushington. Born Helen Selina Sheridan, 1807; died June 13, 1867, at Dufferin Lodge, Highgate, Middlesex, England; dau. of Thomas Sheridan (colonial treasurer) and Caroline Henrietta (Callander) Sheridan (novelist); granddau. of Richard Brinsley Sheridan and Elizabeth Linley (1754–1792); sister of Caroline Norton (1808–1877) and Georgiana Seymour, duchess of Somerset (d. 1884); m. Price Blackwood (naval officer), 4th baron Dufferin, 1825 (died 1841); married on his deathbed, George Hay, earl of Gifford, Oct 13, 1862; children: (1st m.) Frederick Temple Hamilton-Temple-Blackwood, 1st marquis of Dufferin and Ava (1826–1902, British diplomat who m. Hariot Blackwood). ❧ Journeyed down the Nile with son (1863), which she recorded in her *Lispings from Low Latitudes, or Extracts from the Journal of the Honorable Impulsia Gushington,* a satire on high life in the 19th century; is commemorated by the "Helen's Tower" put up by her son in her honor at Clandeboye (the Irish seat of the Blackwoods); her songs and lyrics, collected into 1 vol. (1895), include "The Bay of Dublin," "Katey's Letter," "Terence's Farewell" and "Irish Emigrant's Lament." ❧ See also *Women in World History.*

BLACKWOOD, Margaret (1909–1986). Australian botanist and geneticist. Born Margaret Blackwood, April 26, 1909; died of cancer in 1986; youngest dau. of Robert Leslie (sub-Warden of Trinity College, Melbourne University) and Muriel Pearl Blackwood; attended Melbourne Church of England Girls Grammar School, University of Melbourne; Cambridge University, PhD, 1951. ❧ Pioneer in cytogenetics in Australia, taught herself techniques of cytogenetics and began developing reputation as scientist; was the Caroline Kay Research Scholar at University of Melbourne (1939–41); left scientific community to serve in Women's Australian Auxiliary Airforce (1941); after discharge, did doctoral work on B chromosomes of maize at Cambridge; served as dean of Women at Mildura campus of Melbourne University (1947); at University of Melbourne (1952–74), worked as lecturer, senior lecturer, and reader in botany department and grew her research collection of 1,000 maize plants; was appointed 1st female deputy chancellor at University of Melbourne (1980); elected fellow of Trinity College and fellow of Australian and New Zealand Association for the Advancement of Science. Named MBE; named DBE (1981).

BLAGG, Mary Adela (1858–1944). British astronomer. Born in Cheadle, North Staffordshire, England, May 17, 1858; died in Cheadle, April 14, 1944; dau. of Charles Blagg (lawyer); educated at private boarding school, London. ❧ Self-taught astronomer, became involved in the process of standardizing lunar nomenclature, which 1st necessitated clarifying some of the inconsistencies in the use of names to describe lunar formations; as part of a committee formed in 1907, was appointed to collate the names given to lunar formations on existing maps of the moon; after her preliminary list was published (*Collected List of Lunar Formations Named or Lettered in the Maps of Nelson, Schmidt, and Madler,* 1913), was appointed to the Lunar Commission of the newly founded International Astronomical Union, and served on the subcommittee that prepared the definitive list of lunar names that subsequently became the standard authority (*Named Lunar Formations*); also became involved in the study of variable stars with astronomer H.H. Turner; elected to Royal Astronomical Society (1915). ❧ See also *Women in World History.*

BLAGOEVA, Stella Dimitrova (1887–1954). Bulgarian Communist revolutionary and diplomat. Name variations: Stela. Born 1887 in Bulgaria; died in Moscow, Feb 16, 1954; dau. of Dimitur Blagoev (near-legendary revolutionary leader) and Vela Blagoeva (teacher and novelist); studied music, history and philology and became a high school teacher. ❖ Joined Socialist Party (1915) and Communist Party (1919); removed from teaching post after failure of Communist uprising (Sept 1923); fled to Soviet Union (1926); worked in Communist International (Comintern) until its dissolution (1943), advancing to the post of director of the cadre section of the Latin-language countries, which included France, Spain, Italy, and all of Latin America; returning to Bulgaria after the defeat of Nazi Germany, became the most visible woman political leader in the newly created People's Republic of Bulgaria; served as vice-president of Bulgarian Pan-Slav Committee (1946–49) and as Bulgarian ambassador to the Soviet Union (1949–54). ❖ See also *Women in World History.*

BLAGOEVA, Yordanka (1947—). Bulgarian high jumper. Born Jan 19, 1947, in Bulgaria. ❖ Won an Olympic silver medal at Munich (1972) and a bronze medal at Montreal (1976), both in the high jump.

BLAHETKA, Marie Leopoldine (1811–1887). Austrian pianist. Born in Guntramsdorf, Austria, Nov 15, 1811; died in Boulogne, France, Jan 12, 1887; studied with Moscheles and Friedrich Kalkbrenner. ❖ A child prodigy, was the darling of the Viennese concert stage (1820s); was also a prolific composer, with *Konzertstück* for Piano and Orchestra, Op. 25 her best-known composition.

BLAHOSKI, Alana (1974—). American ice-hockey player. Born April 29, 1974, in St. Paul, Minnesota. ❖ Won a team gold medal at Nagano (1998), the 1st Olympics to feature women's ice hockey; won the team silver medal at World championships (1997, 1999, 2000, 2001). ❖ See also Mary Turco, *Crashing the Net: The U.S. Women's Olympic Ice Hockey Team and the Road to Gold* (HarperCollins, 1999); and *Women in World History.*

BLAINE, Anita McCormick (1866–1954). American philanthropist. Name variations: Anita McCormick or Anita Eugénie McCormick; Anita Eugénie McCormick Blaine. Born Anita Eugénie McCormick, July 4, 1866, in Manchester, Vermont; died Feb 12, 1954, in Chicago, Illinois; dau. of Cyrus Hall McCormick (inventor & industrialist) and Nettie Fowler McCormick (1835–1923, philanthropist); sister of Cyrus Hall McCormick II, Mary Virginia McCormick, Harold Fowler McCormick (who m. Edith Rockefeller McCormick), and Stanley Robert McCormick (who m. Katharine McCormick); m. Emmons Blaine (lawyer and businessman and son of James G. Blaine, presidential candidate), Sept 26, 1889 (died 1892); children: Emmons Jr. (1890–1918). ❖ Benefactor who believed strongly in world cooperation and ardently backed the United Nations, founded the Chicago Institute (1899), which was then joined with the University of Chicago School of Education (1901); also founded the Francis W. Parker School (1901); co-founded City Homes Association (1900) and served as chair of tenement committee; was a member of the Chicago Board of Education (1905–07) and the Juvenile Court and Truancy committees; was a board member of Bureau of Charities and served on National Child Labor Committee; after WWI, argued for US to join League of Nations and gave financial support to League of Nations Association until late 1930s; gave $1 million to help form Foundation for World Government (1948); served as vice chair of World Citizens Association; after undergoing surgery, did not regain health (1949).

BLAINE, Jan (1911–1983). *See Mantle, Winifred Langford.*

BLAINE, Vivian (1921–1995). American actress and singer. Born Vivian Stapleton, Nov 21, 1921, in Newark, New Jersey; died Dec 9, 1995, in New York, NY; dau. of Lionel P. and Wilhelmina (Tepley) Stapleton; attended American Academy of Dramatic Arts; m. Manuel George Frank (div.); m. Milton Rackmil, 1959 (div. 1961); m. Stuart Clark. ❖ Best remembered for her portrayal of Miss Adelaide, the long-suffering chorus girl in the musical *Guys and Dolls,* for which she introduced the songs "A Bushel and a Peck," "Take Back Your Mink" and "Adelaide's Lament," began performing in vaudeville at 3; made film debut in *Through Different Eyes* (1942), and appeared in a number of musicals and light films during 1940s, most notably as Emily Edwards in the 1st version of *State Fair* (1945); later starred on Broadway in *Say Darling* (1958) and *Enter Laughing* (1963), and made numerous tv appearances; other films include *Something for the Boys* (1944), *Nob Hill* (1945), *Doll Face* (1945), *Three Little Girls in Blue* (1946) and *Skirts Ahoy!* (1952). ❖ See also *Women in World History.*

BLAIR, Betsy (1923—). American actress. Born Betsy Boger, Dec 11, 1923, in New York, NY; m. Gene Kelly (dancer and actor), 1947 (div. 1957); m. Karel Reisz (director), 1963 (div. 1969); married a 3rd time to a physician. ❖ Following a stage career, made film debut in *The Guilt of Janet Ames* (1947); though usually a supporting player, starred in film *Marty* (1955), winning an Oscar and Cannes Festival Award, both for Best Actress; later worked in Europe, notably in Bardem's *The Lovemaker* and Antonioni's *The Outcry*; other films include *A Double Life* (1948), *Another Part of the Forest* (1948), *The Snake Pit* (1948), *Kind Lady* (1951) and *A Delicate Balance* (1973). ❖ See also *Women in World History.*

BLAIR, Bonnie (1964—). American speedskater. Born Bonnie Blair, Mar 18, 1964, in Cornwall, NY; m. Dave Cruikshank (speedskater), 1996. ❖ Won a gold medal in the 500 meters and a bronze in 1,000 meters at Calgary Olympics (1988); won gold medals in the 500 and 1,000 meters at Albertville Olympics (1992); won overall gold medal at World Sprint championships (1994); won gold medals in the 500 and 1,000 at Lillehammer Olympics (1994), becoming the 1st American woman in any sport to win gold medals in consecutive Winter Olympics, and 1st American speedskater to win gold medals in more than one Olympics; was the most decorated American Winter Olympian of all time. Named Associated Press Female Athlete of the Year (1994); received Babe Zaharias Female Amateur Athlete Award (1994). ❖ See also *Women in World History.*

BLAIR, Catherine (1872–1946). Scottish pottery painter and suffragist. Born 1872 in Bathgate, Midlothian, Scotland; died 1946 in Scotland. ❖ Became active in women's suffrage movement in her late 30s; lived at Hoprig Mains Farm near Gladsmuir; was founding member of Scottish Women's Rural Institute, one of early feminist organizations and guilds designed to develop employment for women; founded Mak' Merry Pottery in Macmerry, East Lothian (1920); sold pieces at exhibitions and roadside markets, as well as organizing thriving export trade; moved studio eventually to North Berwick, East Lothian, continuing to produce high-quality pottery; took both 1st and 2nd places at Rural Industries Exhibition (late 1930s); received order for crockery set from Queen Mother; remained outspoken champion of cottage industry.

BLAIR, Cherie (1954—). English lawyer and judge. Name variations: Cherie Booth. Born Cherie Booth, Sept 23, 1954, in Bury, Lancashire, England; dau. of Tony Booth (actor and Labour activist) and actress Gale Smith; m. Tony Blair (prime minister of England), 1980; children: Euan, Nicholas, Kathryn and Leo. ❖ Achieved considerable success as lawyer and judge, but came to prominence as wife of British Prime Minister Tony Blair; was brought up in a working-class, Roman Catholic family in Bury, Lancashire, which became single-parent household when father left (1956); earned law degree at London School of Economics with highest mark of the year in bar exams; met husband while both were training to be barristers (1976); as an active supporter of Labour Party, is thought to have inspired husband's increased involvement; unsuccessfully campaigned for no-hope seat of Thanet North, Kent, in general election (1983), the same year husband won a safe seat in Sedgefield, Co. Durham; worked in well-paid job as barrister (1980s), helping family through lean years while husband was a backbencher MP; struggled to find acceptable image when husband became leader of Labor Party (1994); opinionated, was frequently compared to former US first lady, Hillary Clinton; continued to practice employment and discrimination law; lectured widely on human rights and advised on implications of Human Rights Act; appeared in European Court of Justice and in Commonwealth jurisdictions, and sat as an international arbitrator; accredited as mediator under ADR Chambers/Harvard Law Project scheme.

BLAIR, Rev. David (1766–1840). *See Fenwick, Eliza.*

BLAIR, Emily Newell (1877–1951). American feminist and politician. Name variations: Emily Blair or Emily Jane Newell Blair; Emily Newell or Emily Jane. Born Emily Jane Newell, Jan 9, 1877, in Joplin, Missouri; died Aug 3, 1951, in Alexandria, Virginia; dau. of James Patton Newell (mortgage broker) and Anna Cynthia (Gray) Newell; m. Harry Wallace Blair (lawyer), Dec 24, 1900; children: Harriet and Newell Blair. ❖ Democratic party official, joined Missouri Equal Suffrage Association (1910); became press and publicity chair and 1st editor of *Missouri Woman* (monthly suffrage publication) (1914); during WWI, became vice chair of Missouri Woman's Committee of Council of National Defense, and then head of news and publicity for council's national Woman's Committee; helped found League of Women Voters (1920); elected woman representative from Missouri to Democratic National Committee (1921) and appointed national vice chair; helped found Woman's National Democratic Club, serving as secretary (1922–26) and becoming president (1928); was reelected to DNC and, as the only national woman official, served as 1st vice president (1924–28); was associate editor of *Good Housekeeping* magazine (1925–33); became Consumers' Advisory Board member (1933) and served as chair (1935); wrote novel *A Woman of Courage* (1931); was appointed chief of women's interests section in War Department's bureau of public relations (1942); suffered debilitating stroke (1944).

BLAIR, Janet (1921—). American actress and singer. Born Martha Janet Lafferty, April 23, 1921, in Altoona, Pennsylvania. ❖ Began career as band vocalist; made film debut in *Three Girls About Town* (1941), followed by 2 of her best roles in *Broadway* and *My Sister Eileen* (both 1942); other films include *Two Yanks in Trinidad, Something to Shout About, Once Upon a Time, Tonight and Every Night, Tars and Spars, The Fabulous Dorseys, The Fuller Brush Man, Boys' Night Out* and *The One and Only Genuine Original Family Band* (1968); launched a successful 2-year tour in the stage musical *South Pacific* (1950); worked as a nightclub performer, made occasional tv appearances, and co-starred with Henry Fonda in tv series "The Smith Family" (1971–72).

BLAIR, Lottie May (c. 1858–1937). See *Parker, Lottie Blair.*

BLAIR, Mary (c. 1895–1947). American stage actress. Born c. 1895; died Sept 17, 1947, in Pittsburgh, Pennsylvania. ❖ Appeared in several plays by Eugene O'Neill; retired from stage (1930).

BLAIR, Pamela (1949—). American theatrical dancer. Name variations: Pam Blair. Born Dec 5, 1949, in Arlington, Virginia. ❖ Debuted on Broadway in *Promises, Promises* (1968), followed by *Wild and Wonderful* (1971), *Sugar* (1972), *Seesaw* (1973), *Of Mice and Men* (1974), as Val in the original cast of *A Chorus Line* (1975), *The Best Little Whorehouse in Texas* (1978), *King of Hearts* (1978), *The Nerd* (1987) and *A Few Good Men* (1989).

BLAIS, Marie-Claire (1939—). Canadian novelist and playwright. Born Oct 5, 1939, in Quebec City, Canada; attended Laval University. ❖ Dominant figure in Canadian letters, was praised by Edmund Wilson and others; works, which were noted for their lyrical intensity, depictions of violence, and surreal effects, address homosexual issues and often present characters in conflict with society; novels, which have all been written in French and translated into English, include *La Belle Bête* (1959, *Mad Shadows*), *Tête blanche* (1960, *White Head*), *Une Saison dans la vie d'Emmanuel* (1965, *A Season in the Life of Emmanuel*), *L'Insoumise* (1966, *The Fugitive*), *David Sterne* (1967), *Les Manuscrits de Pauline Archange* (1968, *The Manuscripts of Pauline Archange*), *Le Loup* (1972, *The Wolf*); *Le Sourd dans la ville* (1979, *Deaf to the City*), *Visions d'Anna* (1982, *Anna's World*), *L'Ange de la solitude* (1989), *Un Jardin dans la tempête* (1990) and *Soifs* (1995, *These Festive Nights*); also published poetry and plays. Received Governor-General's Literary Award (1969, 1979, 1996), Prix Medicis (1965), Prix d l'Académie française (1983) and Prix Athanase-David (1982); elected to Belgian Académie française.

BLAKE, Amanda (1929–1989). American actress. Born Beverly Louise Neill, Feb 20, 1929, in Buffalo, NY; died of AIDS-related complications, Aug 16, 1989, in Sacramento, California; m. William Henry Dixon (div.); m. Jason Day, 1964 (div.); m. Frank Gilbert, 1967 (div. 1982); m. Mark Spaeth, 1984 (div.). ❖ Best known for long-running role of Miss Kitty on tv's "Gunsmoke" (1955–75); films include *Duchess of Idaho, Stars in My Crown, Lili, Sabre Jet, A Star is Born, About Mrs. Leslie, High Society* and *The Glass Slipper;* helped form the Arizona Animal Welfare League (1971).

BLAKE, Lillie Devereux (1833–1913). American suffragist, reformer, and writer. Born Elizabeth Johnson Devereux in Raleigh, North Carolina, Aug 12, 1833; died in Englewood, New Jersey, Dec 30, 1913; dau. of George P. (wealthy southerner of Irish descent) and Sarah Elizabeth (Johnson) Devereux; m. Frank G. Quay Umsted (Philadelphia lawyer), June 1855 (died May 1859); m. Grenfill Blake (NY merchant), 1866 (died 1896); children: (1st m.) 2. ❖ Delivered addresses on women's suffrage throughout the country; also spoke on education and was an active promoter in the founding of Barnard College; as president of New York State Woman's Suffrage Association (1879–90), was instrumental in securing laws permitting woman's suffrage in school elections, providing for matrons in police stations (1891), and requiring storekeepers to provide seats for saleswomen; delivered a series of lectures in reply to the Lenten discourses on "the calling of a

Christian Woman" by Reverend Morgan Dix (1883), which attracted much attention and were published as *Woman's Place Today;* also wrote *Southwold* (1859), *Rockford* (1863), *Fettered for Life, or Lord and Master* (1874) and *A Daring Experiment* (1892), among others.

BLAKE, Louisa Aldrich (1865–1925). See *Aldrich-Blake, Louisa.*

BLAKE, Marie (1895–1978). See *MacDonald, Blossom.*

BLAKE, Mary Jane (1834–1891). See *Safford, Mary Jane.*

BLAKE, Mrs. (c. 1842–1893). See *Lord, Lucy Takiora.*

BLAKE, Sophia Jex (1840–1912). See *Jex-Blake, Sophia.*

BLAKER, Eliza Ann (1854–1926). American kindergarten founder. Born Eliza Ann Cooper, Mar 5, 1854, in Philadelphia, Pennsylvania; died Dec 4, 1926, in Indianapolis, Indiana; m. Louis J. Blaker, Sept 15, 1880. ❖ Known largely for her kindergarten-teacher training program, which began in her home (1882) and became the Teachers College of Indianapolis, served as president until her death (approximately 20,000 girls were educated under her leadership); also opened the 1st free kindergarten in Indianapolis (c. 1882), which she also supervised (60 kindergartens were opened by the Society over next several decades).

BLALOCK, Jane (1945—). American golfer. Born Sept 19, 1945, in Portsmouth, New Hampshire; graduate of Rollins College. ❖ Joined LPGA tour (1969) and was Rookie of the Year; won 5 LPGA tourneys, including the Colgate-Dinah Shore Classic (1972); won 3 major tournaments (1974) and was 2nd in the Vare Trophy for low-scoring average with 73.11 strokes per round; won Colgate Triple Crown (1975); following a win at McDonald's championship, was the 7th player in LPGA history to cross the $1 million mark in career earnings (1983); won the Women's Kemper Open and the Mazda Japan Classic (1985); won 29 LPGA tournaments during 15-year professional career; founded The Jane Blalock Co., a Boston-based sports management agency (1987); created LPGA Golf Clinics for Women; was instrumental in the formation of the LPGA Senior Women's Golf Association (2000).

BLAMAN, Anna (1905–1960). See *Vrugt, Johanna Petronella.*

BLAMIRE, Susanna (1747–1794). English writer. Born Susanna Blamire at Cardew Hall, near Dalston, in Cumberland, England, Jan 12, 1747; died in Carlisle, England, April 5, 1794; dau. of Isabella (Simpson) Blamire (died 1754) and William Blamire (yeoman); educated at village schools; never married; no children. ❖ Known as the Muse of Cumberland for her regional poetry and songs, the most popular of which are "The Nabob," "And ye shall walk in silk attire" and "What ails this heart o' mine." Her poems, which were not collected during her lifetime, were 1st published by Henry Lonsdale as *The Poetical Works of Miss Susanna Blamire*, with a memoir by Patrick Maxwell (1842).

BLAMIRES, Jane Annie (1869–1955). See *Collier, Jane Annie.*

BLANC, Isabelle (1975—). French snowboarder. Born July 1975 in Nimes, France. ❖ Was Jr. World Champion (1994); at World Cup, won for slalom (1996) and giant parallel slalom (2000, 2002); won the World championship for giant parallel slalom (1999); won a gold medal for giant parallel slalom at Salt Lake City (2002).

BLANC, Marie-Thérèse (1840–1907). French novelist and literary critic. Name variations: Blanc usually appears under her pseudonym (derived from her mother's maiden name), variously given as Th. Bentzon, Th. Bentzen, or Thérèse or Théodore Bentzon; yet she is sometimes referred to by contemporaries as Thérèse de Solms or, simply, as Mme Blanc. Born Marie-Thérèse de Solms, Sept 21, 1840, in Seine-Port, France; died in Paris, 1907; dau. of the German count of Solms and Olympe de Bentzon (Danish dau. of Major-General Adrien Benjamin de Bentzon, one-time governor of the Danish Antilles); m. M. Blanc (French banker), 1856 (div. 1859). ❖ Prolific novelist and literary critic, primarily of American and English authors, who devoted much of her work to popularizing the history and attainments of the American women's movement for French readers; literary output spanned the years 1868–1907, during which she published 51 books and 116 articles—mostly literary criticism for the *Revue des Deux Mondes*, a prestigious French literary journal—and translated or wrote prefaces to 16 American or English literary works; writings include *Un divorce* (1871), *Un remords* (acclaimed by the French Academy, 1878), *Tony* (acclaimed by French Academy, 1884), *The Condition of Woman in the United States: A Traveller's Notes* (English trans. of *Notes de Voyages: Les Américaines chez elles* by Abby Langdon Alger, 1895, also acclaimed by French Academy), *Choses et Gens d'Amérique* (1898), *Notes de Voyages: Nouvelle France et*

Nouvelle-Angleterre (1899), *Femmes d'Amérique* (1900), *Questions américaines* (1901) and *En France et en Amérique* (1909, posthumously). ❖ See also *Women in World History.*

BLANCA. *Variant of Blanche.*

BLANCA, Nida (1936–2001). Filipino actress. Born Dorothy Acueza Jones, Jan 6, 1936, in Gapan, Nueva Ecija, Philippines; murdered Nov 7, 2001, in San Juan, Metro Manila, Philippines; out-of-wedlock dau. of John William Jones Jr. (half-American) and Inocencia Guinto; m. 2nd husband Roger Lawrence Strunk (American actor, known as Rod Lauren), 1981; children: (1st m.) Kay. ❖ During a 50-year film career, starred in over 160 films, usually as a spunky, strong-willed woman; often appeared on tv; was repeatedly stabbed and left to die in the back seat of her car in a parking garage in Greenhills, San Juan; her death caused an outpouring of grief in the Philippines, and the killer surrendered to police 2 weeks later, saying he had been hired by her husband (he later claimed he'd been tortured to confess and point the finger at Strunk); husband is fighting extradition from US.

BLANCA DE NAVARRE. *See Blanche of Navarre.*

BLANCA MARIA (1423–1470). *See Visconti, Bianca Maria.*

BLANCARD, Jacqueline (1909—). French-born pianist. Born in Paris, France, 1909; studied at Paris Conservatory. ❖ Studied with Isidor Philipp, then continued training with Alfred Cortot, mastering both standard German repertoire and modern French school; highly regarded as a Schumann specialist, also made the 1st recording of Debussy's *etudes* and was the 1st pianist to record Maurice Ravel's Concerto for the Left Hand (1938); performed 3 Mozart concertos in triumphant NY debut (1948). ❖ See also *Women in World History.*

BLANCHARD, Caroline Cadette (1821–?). *See Howard, Caroline Cadette.*

BLANCHARD, Dorothy (1899–1987). *See Hammerstein, Dorothy.*

BLANCHARD, Madeleine Sophie (1778–1819). French balloonist. Born Marie-Madeleine-Sophie Armand, Mar 25, 1778, in Trois-Canons, France; died in a balloon accident in Paris, July 6, 1819, the 1st woman to die in an aviation accident; dau. of Madame Armand; m. Jean-Pierre Blanchard (1753–1809), 1796. ❖ Married pioneer balloonist Jean-Pierre Blanchard (1796) and became his partner in adventures; with husband, developed an act that included acrobatics on a net that hung from their balloon gondola and became a sensation throughout Europe, appearing at fairs and other public events in France, England and Germany; following husband's death (1809), was the 1st woman to fly alone under a variety of circumstances; appointed to honorary post of chief of Air Services by Napoleon, toured Europe and France as an ambassador and flew in balloons at State festivals; on her 67th ascent, died when her balloon exploded in a fireball. ❖ See also *Women in World History.*

BLANCHARD, Mari (1927–1970). American actress. Born Mary Blanchard, April 13, 1927, in Long Beach, California; died May 10, 1970, in Woodland Hills, California; m. Vincent Conti (photographer). ❖ Began career as a model; films include *On the Riviera, Ten Tall Men, Assignment Paris, Veils of Bagdad, Destry, Son of Sinbad, Return of Jack Slade* and *McClintock!*; starred in tv series "Klondike" (1960–61).

BLANCHARD, Theresa Weld (1893–1978). American skater. Name variations: Theresa Weld; Theresa Weld-Blanchard or Blanchard-Weld. Born Theresa Weld, Aug 21, 1893, in Brookline, Massachusetts; died Mar 12, 1978; m. Charles Blanchard, 1920. ❖ Under Theresa Weld, won US nationals (1914–20); while skating with Nathaniel W. Niles, won 9 gold medals in US pairs competition; won a bronze medal in singles at Winter Olympics (1920), the 1st US medal in winter Olympics history; was influential in US Figure Skating Association for many years. ❖ See also *Women in World History.*

BLANCHE (c. 1392–1409). Duchess of Bavaria. Name variations: Blanche Plantagenet. Born c. April 1392 in Peterborough Castle, Cambridgeshire, England; died May 22, 1409; dau. of Henry IV, king of England, and Mary de Bohun (1369–1394); m. Louis, duke of Bavaria, July 6, 1402; children: 1.

BLANCHE, Ada (1862–1953). English actress and music-hall star. Born July 16, 1862, in London, England; died Jan 1, 1953. ❖ Made London stage debut as Dandini in *Cinderella* (1878); other plays include *The Vicar of Wakefield, Miss Esmeralda, Little Bo-Peep, A Royal Star, The Medal and the Maid, The Arcadians* and *The Rebel Maid*; toured with *The Telephone Girl* (1897–1900), and with Robert Courtneidge (1903–05).

BLANCHE, Marie (1893—). English actress and singer. Born Nov 5, 1893, in Scarborough, England; dau. of William Peacock and Addie Blanche (actress as Mrs. Adelaide Emily Peacock); niece of Ada Blanche and Robert Courtneidge; m. Edmund Lewis Waller (son of Lewis Waller). ❖ Musical-comedy star, made stage debut in Worthing in title role of *Priscilla Runs Away* (1911); made London debut in *Princess Caprice* (1912), followed by *The Joy-Ride Lady, The Chorus Girl, All Scotch, Samples, High Jinks, Carminetta, Babes in the Wood* and title role in *Cherry*, among others; often toured with George Robey and was romantically linked; retired (1932) to become director of White Rose Players at Harrogate Grand Opera House and of the Empire, York.

BLANCHE CAPET (c. 1247–1302). *See Blanche of Artois.*

BLANCHECOTTE, Augustine-Malvina (1830–1895). French poet. Name variations: Auguste Malvina Blanchecotte; d'Augustine-Malvina Blanchecotte; Augustine-Malvina Souville-Blanchecotte; Mme Blanchecotte. Born 1830 in Paris, France, of humble beginnings; died 1895. ❖ A seamstress, whose works were recognized by the Académie Française, attempted to give an alternate view of women's position in society; writings include *Rêves et Réalités* (1855), *Impressions d'une femme, pensées, sentiments et portraits* (1868), *Tablettes d'une femme pendant la Commune* (1972) and *Les Militants* (1875).

BLANCHE OF ARTOIS (c. 1247–1302). Queen of Navarre and countess of Lancaster. Name variations: Blanche Capet; duchess of Lancaster. Born c. 1247; died May 2, 1302, in Paris, France; dau. of Robert I (1216–1250), count of Artois, and Maude of Brabant (1224–1288); m. Henry I the Fat, king of Navarre (r. 1270–1274), also known as Henry III of Champagne, in 1269; m. Edmund the Crouchback (1245–1296), 1st earl of Lancaster (r. 1267–1296), before Feb 3, 1276; children: (1st m.) Joan I of Navarre (1273–1305), queen of Navarre; (2nd m.) Thomas (1276–1322), 2nd earl of Lancaster; Henry (1281–1345), 3rd earl of Lancaster; John (c. 1286–c. 1327 or 1337), lord of Beaufort; Mary Plantagenet (died young).

BLANCHE OF BOULOGNE (1326–1360). Countess of Auvergne. Name variations: sometimes referred to as Jeanne of Boulogne or Joan of Boulogne. Born May 8, 1326; died Sept 29, 1360, at Château d'Argilly; dau. of Robert of Auvergne; m. Philip Capet (d. 1346, son of Eudes IV of Burgundy), Sept 26, 1338; became 2nd wife of John II (1319–1364), king of France (r. 1350–1364), Feb 19, 1350; children: (1st m.) Jeanne of Burgundy (1344–1360); Marguerite (b. 1345, died young); Philip of Rouvres (b. 1346), count of Artois. King John II's 1st wife was Bona of Bohemia (1315–1349).

BLANCHE OF BOURBON (c. 1338–1361). Queen of Castile and León. Name variations: Bianca; Blanche of Castile. Born in France c. 1338 or 1339; died at Medina Sidonia, Spain, in 1361; dau. of Pierre also known as Peter I, duke of Bourbon, and Isabelle of Savoy (d. 1383); m. Pedro el Cruel also known as Peter I the Cruel (1334–1369), king of Castile and Leon (r. 1350–1369), June 3, 1353. ❖ During marriage to Peter the Cruel, was unjustly accused of infidelity and imprisoned; her death has been ascribed to poisoning. Her tragic fate has frequently been documented in verse. ❖ See also *Women in World History.*

BLANCHE OF BOURBON (1868–1949). Grand duchess of Tuscany. Name variations: Blanka of Bourbon-Castile. Born Sept 7, 1868; died Oct 25, 1949, in Viareggio; dau. of Margaret of Parma (1847–1893) and Charles, duke of Madrid; m. Leopold Salvator, grand duke of Tuscany (1863–1931), Oct 24, 1889; children: 5 daughters and 5 sons, including Margaretha (1881–1986, known as Meg); Maria Dolores (1891–1974); Maria Immaculata (1892–1971); Rainer Karl (1895–1930); Leopold (1897–1958); Maria Antonia (1899–1977); Franz Joseph (1905–1975); Charles Pius Salvator (1909–1953).

BLANCHE OF BURGUNDY (1288–1348). Countess of Savoy. Name variations: Blanche de Bourgogne. Born in 1288; died July 28, 1348, in Dijon; dau. of Agnes Capet (1260–1327) and Robert II (b. 1248), duke of Burgundy; m. Edward the Liberal, count of Savoy, Oct 18, 1307.

BLANCHE OF BURGUNDY (1296–1326). Princess of Burgundy. Name variations: Blanche Capet. Born 1296; died 1326; dau. of Otto IV, count of Burgundy, and Mahaut (c. 1270–1329); sister of Jeanne I of Burgundy (c. 1291–1330); m. Charles IV the Fair (c. 1294–1328), king of France (r. 1322–1328), in 1307 (annulled, Sept 1322). Charles IV was also married to Mary of Luxemburg (1305–1323) and Joan of Evreux (d. 1370).

BLANCHE OF CASTILE (1188–1252). Queen of France. Name variations: Blanca of Castille. Born Mar 4, 1188, in Valencia, Castile (some sources cite 1187); died Nov 27, 1252, in an abbey near Melun, France; 3rd dau. of Alphonso VIII (b. 1155), king of Castile (r. 1158–1214), and Eleanor of Castile (1162–1214); sister of Urraca of Castile, queen of Portugal (1186–1220), Berengaria of Castile (1180–1246), and Eleanor of Castile (1202–1244); m. Louis VIII (1187–1226), king of France (r. 1223–1226), May 23, 1200, in Normandy; children: (12, 5 of whom lived to adulthood) Louis IX (1214–1270), king of France (r. 1226–1270); Robert I (1216–1250), count of Artois; Alphonse (1220–1271), count of Poitiers and Toulouse; Blessed Isabelle (1225–1270); Charles of Anjou (1226–1285), king of Sicily (r. 1266–1282), king of Naples (r. 1268–1285), who m. Beatrice of Provence. ❖ One of the most important women of the 13th century, married future king Louis VIII in Normandy (1200); had an extremely happy marriage and 12 children; when Louis invaded England and needed more support, rode about France gathering troops and raising additional money to assemble a fleet which she personally organized; became queen of France (1223); when Louis VIII died (1226), was named regent for son Louis IX and would be actual ruler for 14 years of his reign (1226–34); because of rebellion of French nobles, had to deal with constant outbreaks and conspiracies (1226–30); broke the back of the nobles' rebellion (1230); when Louis came of age, continued at his side as a virtual co-ruler; through her example, her son became a champion of the poor, lowly, and oppressed; remained as a member of Louis' council and sometimes represented the crown as a secret negotiator; when Louis went on Crusade, made regent again (1248–52); under her administration, son Louis IX, king in Paris, could truly be called "king of France." ❖ See also Regine Pernoud, *Blanche of Castille* (trans. by Henry Noel, Collins, 1975); and *Women in World History*.

BLANCHE OF DREUX (c. 1396–c. 1418). Countess of Armagnac. Name variations: Blanche de Dreux. Born c. 1396; died c. 1418; dau. of John IV de Montfort, 5th duke of Brittany (r. 1364–1399) and #Joanna of Navarre (c. 1370–1437); married John (Lomagne), count of Armagnac.

BLANCHE OF FRANCE (1253–1321). French princess. Name variations: Blanche Capet. Born 1253 in Jaffa; died 1321 in Paris, France; dau. of Margaret of Provence (1221–1295) and Saint Louis also known as Louis IX (1214–1270), king of France (r. 1226–1270); sister of Philip III the Bold (1245–1285), king of France (r. 1270–1285); m. Ferdinand de la Cerda of Castile and Leon (son of Alphonso X), Oct 30, 1268; children: Alphonso de la Cerda (c. 1270–1327); Ferdinand de la Cerda (b. 1272).

BLANCHE OF FRANCE (c. 1266–1305). French princess. Name variations: Blanca. Born c. 1266 (some sources cite a much later date); died Mar 19, 1305, in Vienna; dau. of Isabella of Aragon (1243–1271) and Philip III the Bold (1245–1285), king of France (r. 1270–1285); 1st wife of Rudolph or Rudolf III (1281–1307), king of Bohemia and Poland (r. 1306–1307).

BLANCHE OF FRANCE (1328–1392). Duchess of Orléans and countess of Beaumont. Name variations: Duchess of Orleans. Born 1328; died 1392; dau. of Joan of Evreux (d. 1370) and Charles IV the Fair (1294–1328), king of France (r. 1322–1328); m. Philippe also known as Philip (1336–1375), count of Beaumont and Valois, duke of Orléans (brother of John II, king of France).

BLANCHE OF LANCASTER (1341–1369). Duchess of Lancaster. Born 1341; died of the Black Death, Sept 12, 1369, at Bolingbroke Castle, Lincolnshire, England (while John of Gaunt was away in Spain fighting Henry II Trastamara of Castile and his French allies); dau. of Henry of Lancaster (c. 1299–1361), 1st duke of Lancaster, and Isabel Beaumont (d. 1368); m. John of Gaunt, duke of Lancaster (1340–1399), in 1359; children: Philippa of Lancaster (c. 1359–1415, who m. John I, king of Portugal); John (1362–1365); Elizabeth of Lancaster (1364–1425, who m. John Holland, duke of Exeter); Edward (1365–1368); John (1366, died young); Henry Bolingbroke (1367–1413), later Henry IV, king of England (r. 1399–1413); Isabel (c. 1368, died young).

BLANCHE OF NAMUR (d. 1363). Queen of Sweden and Norway. Name variations: Blanca of Namur; Blanka of Namur. Died 1363; dau. of John, count of Namur; m. Magnus II Eriksson or Erikson (1316–1374), king of Sweden (r. 1319–1356, 1359–1365), king of Norway as

Magnus VII (r. 1319–1350), in 1335; children: Erik XII (c. 1339–1359), king of Sweden (r. 1356–1359); Haakon VI (c. 1339–1380), king of Norway (r. 1355–1380); and 3 daughters (names unknown).

BLANCHE OF NAPLES (d. 1310). Queen of Sicily and Aragon. Died 1310; dau. of Charles II, duke of Anjou (r. 1285–1290), king of Naples (r. 1285–1309), and Marie of Hungary (d. 1323); sister of Lenore of Sicily (1289–1341); m. Jaime also known as James II, king of Sicily and Aragon (r. 1291–1327); children: Alphonso IV the Benign (1299–1336), king of Aragon (r. 1327–1336); Constance of Aragon (d. 1327, who m. Juan Manuel "el Scritor" of Castile); Maria of Aragon (who m. Peter, regent of Castile).

BLANCHE OF NAVARRE (d. 1158). Queen of Castile. Name variations: Blanche Jimeno. Born after 1133; died Aug 11 or 12, 1158; dau. of Garcia IV, king of Navarre (r. 1134–1150), and Marguerite de l'Aigle (d. 1141); m. Sancho III (1134–1158), king of Castile (r. 1157–1158), Jan 30, 1151; children: Alphonso VIII (b. 1155), king of Castile (r. 1158–1214).

BLANCHE OF NAVARRE (d. 1229). Countess of Champagne. Born after 1177; died in childbirth, 1229; dau. of Sancho VI the Wise, king of Navarre (r. 1194–1234), and Sancha of Castile and Leon (d. 1179); only sister of Berengaria of Navarre (c. 1163–c. 1230); m. Thibaut also known as Theobald, count of Champagne, July 1, 1199; children: Teobaldo or Theobald I (1201–1253), king of Navarre (r. 1234–1253, also known as Theobald IV of Champagne).

BLANCHE OF NAVARRE (fl. 1239). Duchess of Brittany. Fl. around 1239; dau. of Theobald I, king of Navarre (r. 1234–1253), and probably Agnes of Beaujeu (d. 1231); m. John I the Red, duke of Brittany; children: John II (1239–1305), duke of Brittany (r. 1286–1305).

BLANCHE OF NAVARRE (1331–1398). Queen of France. Born (Spanish) Blanca de Navarra. Born 1331 (some sources cite 1330); died 1398; dau. of Philip III, king of Navarre (r. 1328–1349), and Joan II of Navarre (1309–1349), queen of Navarre (r. 1328–1349); m. Philip VI of Valois (1293–1350), king of France (r. 1328–1350), in 1349; children: Jeanne (who m. John of Aragon, duke of Gironda). ❖ See also *Women in World History*.

BLANCHE OF NAVARRE (1385–1441). Queen of Navarre and Sicily. Name variations: Bianca of Navarre, Bianca of Sicily, Blanche of Sicily; (Spanish) Blanca de Navarre, Doña Blanca. Born in 1385 (some sources cite 1386 or 1391) in Navarre; died April 3, 1441, in Santa Maria de Nieva, Aragon; dau. of Charles III, king of Navarre, and Eleanor Trastamara (d. 1415); m. Martin I the Younger (d. 1410), king of Sicily (r. 1390–1409), in 1404; m. John II (1398–1479), king of Sicily and Aragon (r. 1458–1479), Jan 18, 1419, or 1420; children: (2nd m.) Carlos also known as Charles (1421–1461), prince of Viana; Juana of Aragon (1423–1425); Eleanor of Navarre (1425–1479); Blanche of Navarre (1424–1464), queen of Castile, who m. Henry also known as Enrique IV). King Martin's 1st wife was Maria of Sicily (d. 1402). ❖ At 19, married Martin I, king of Sicily; when he died without heirs (1410), inherited throne of Sicily; after landholders reasserted ancient rights to land and income, which were supposedly the king's property, and refused to support the crown, was forced to borrow money from private sources and power quickly slipped away; assembled a committee of nobles to choose new king, Ferdinand I of Castile, then returned to homeland of Navarre (1412); married John II of Aragon (1419); succeeded her father Charles III of Navarre as queen (1425). ❖ See also *Women in World History*.

BLANCHE OF NAVARRE (1424–1464). Queen of Castile and Leon. Name variations: (Spanish) Blanca de Navarra; Bianca. Born June 9, 1424, in Olite; died Dec 2, 1464, in Orthez; dau. of Juan also known as John II, king of Aragon (r. 1458–1479), and Blanche of Navarre (1385–1441); sister of Charles (Carlos), prince of Viana, and Eleanor of Navarre (1425–1479); became 1st wife of Enrique also known as Henry IV (b. 1425), king of Castile and Leon (r. 1454–1474), Sept 15, 1440 (div. 1453); children: none.

BLANCHE OF ROSSI (d. 1237). Italian noblewoman and soldier. Born in Rossi, Italy; died 1237 in Ezzelino, Italy; m. Battista of Padua. ❖ Was a participant in the Italian war between 2 powerful political factions, the Ghibellines and the Guelfs; fought alongside husband to protect town of Ezzelino (1237). ❖ See also *Women in World History*.

BLANCHE OF SAVOY (c. 1337–?). Milanese noblewoman. Name variations: Bianca of Savoy. Born Blanche Mary in Savoy c. 1337; dau. of

Aymon, count of Savoy; sister of Amadeus VI, count of Savoy; m. Galeazzo II Visconti, lord of Milan (r. 1354–1378), in Aug of 1350; children: Gian Galeazzo Visconti, lord of Milan (r. 1378–1402), duke of Milan (r. 1396–1402); Violet Visconti (c. 1353–1386).

BLANCHE OF SICILY (1385–1441). *See Blanche of Navarre.*

BLANCHE OF VALOIS (c. 1316–?). Holy Roman empress. Born c. 1316; dau. of Mahaut de Chatillon (d. 1358) and Charles I, count of Valois (1270–1325, son of Philip III, king of France); half-sister of Philip VI of Valois (1293–1350), king of France (r. 1328–1350), and Jeanne of Valois (c. 1294–1342); 1st wife of Charles IV Luxemburg (1316–1378), Holy Roman emperor (r. 1347–1378).

BLANCHETTE, Marcia Frederick (1963—). *See Frederick, Marcia.*

BLANCHFIELD, Florence (1884–1971). American nurse. Born Florence Aby Blanchfield, April 1, 1884, in Sheperdstown, West Virginia; died May 12, 1971, in Washington, DC; dau. of Joseph Plunkett (stone mason) and Mary Louvenia (Anderson) Blanchfield (nurse); attended University of California and Columbia University; graduate of South Side Training School for Nurses, Pittsburgh, 1906; additional training at Johns Hopkins Hospital. ❖ The 1st woman to receive a regular commission in US Army, held a succession of civilian nursing positions before enlisting in Army Nurse Corps (1917); spent WWI on battlefields of France; after war, rejoined the Corps and served over next 15 years in various posts in US, China and Philippines; was on surgeon general's staff in Washington (1935); when WWII broke out, was assistant to Colonel Julia Flikke, superintendent of Army Nurse Corps (1942); succeeded Flikke (1943), supervising some 60,000 nurses on fronts from Australia to Alaska; finally achieved full rank (1947) after the Army-Navy Nurse Act was passed, granting nurses full status; awarded the 1st regular commission ever given to a woman in US Army; writings include *The Army Nurse Corps in World War II* (1948) and *Organized Nursing and the Army in Three Wars* (1950). Awarded Distinguished Service Medal (1945). ❖ See also *Women in World History.*

BLANCHI, Elisa (1987—). Italian rhythmic gymnast. Born Oct 13, 1987, in Velletri, Italy. ❖ Won team all-around silver medal at Athens Olympics (2004).

BLANCO, Kathleen (1942—). American politician. Name variations: Kathleen Babineaux Blanco. Born Kathleen Babineaux, Dec 15, 1942, in New Iberia, Louisiana; attended University of Louisiana at Lafayette; m. Raymond Blanco, 1964; children: 6. ❖ As a Democrat, elected to Louisiana House (1984); worked for Louisiana Public Service Commission (1989–95); served 2 terms as lieutenant governor starting 1996; became Louisiana's 1st female governor (2003), and was criticized for her response to Hurricane Katrina.

BLAND, Alexander (1908–2004). *See Lloyd, Maude.*

BLAND, Dorothea (1761–1816). *See Jordan, Dora.*

BLAND, Edith (1858–1924). *See Nesbit, Edith.*

BLAND, Harriet (1915–1991). American runner. Born Feb 13, 1915; died Nov 6, 1991. ❖ At Berlin Olympics, won a gold medal in the 4 x 100-meter relay (1936).

BLAND, Lilian (1878–1971). British aviator. Name variations: Lillian Bland. Born in Kent, England, 1878; lived in Carnmoney, Co. Antrim, Ireland; died 1971; granddau. of a dean of Belfast. ❖ The 1st woman in the British Isles, possibly in the world, to design, build, and fly her own plane, first established a reputation as a press photographer and sportswriter before undertaking the construction of a bi-plane glider; successfully flew her plane, the *Mayfly* (1910), after modifying it with the addition of an engine; was also a successful press photographer and sports journalist. ❖ See also *Women in World History.*

BLAND, Maria Theresa (1769–1838). English soprano. Name variations: Maria Romanzini. Born Maria Romanzini, 1769, in London, England; died Jan 15, 1838, in London; studied with Dibdin; m. George Bland (actor), 1790; children: Charles (tenor) and James (1798–1861, a buffo bass). ❖ Made London debut at the Hughes' Riding School (1773), then Drury Lane debut (1786); was a member of Drury Lane Co. (1789–1824), excelling in operas of Storace and Arnold; also sang at the Haymarket and Vauxhall; suffering from depression, abandoned career (1824).

BLANDIANA, Ana (1942—). *See Coman, Otilia.*

BLANDICK, Clara (1880–1962). American actress. Born June 4, 1880, on American ship anchored in Hong Kong; committed suicide, April 15,

1962, in Hollywood, California. ❖ Character actress, played Aunt Polly in *Tom Sawyer* (1930) and *Huckleberry Finn* (1931), but best remembered for role of Auntie Em in *The Wizard of Oz* (1939); other films include *Anthony Adverse* (1936), *A Star Is Born* (1937), *Drums Along the Mohawk* (1939), *Northwest Mounted Police* (1940), *Heaven Can Wait* (1943) and *Life With Father* (1947).

BLANDINA (d. 177). Christian martyr and saint. Tortured in the amphitheater at Lyons in 177. ❖ A female slave during the persecution of Christians, who was brought into the amphitheater at Lyons to be put to death (177); along with Biblis, Pothinus, Maturus, Sanctus, Ponticus, Attalus, and other martyrs, was hung by her arms to a post, then animals were let into the arena; amazingly, along with Ponticus, went untouched by animals; was subjected to even more horrors on last day of spectacle, but pagans swore they had never seen a woman suffer with such courage. Feast day is June 2. ❖ See also *Women in World History.*

BLANDY, Mary (1719–1752). English murderer. Born at Henley-on-Thames, England, in 1719; convicted of murder and hanged at Oxford, England, 1752; only dau. of Francis Blandy (lawyer). ❖ Was engaged to Captain William Henry Cranstoun (titled son of a Scottish peer), when her father discovered that Cranstoun was already married and the father of 2; with the help of Cranstoun, poisoned her father; was tried, convicted and hanged (Cranstoun successfully fled to France). ❖ See also *Women in World History.*

BLANE, Sally (1910–1997). American actress. Born Elizabeth Jane Young in Salt Lake City in 1910; died in Palm Springs, California, Aug 27, 1997; sister of Loretta Young (actress), Polly Ann Young, and Georgiana Young; m. Norman Foster (actor-director), in 1934 (died 1976). ❖ Made film debut during silent era, appearing in *Casey at the Bat* (1927); other films include *Outlawed* (1929), *Annabelle's Affairs* (1931), *The Spirit of Notre Dame* (1931), *Ten Cents a Dance* (1931), *I Am a Fugitive from a Chain Gang* (1932), *The Phantom Express* (1932), *Pride of the Legion* (1932), *Advice to the Lovelorn* (1933), *The Story of Alexander Graham Bell* (1939) and *Way Down South* (1939).

BLANGY, Hermine (c. 1820–c. 1865). French ballet dancer. Born c. 1820; died c. 1865 in New York. ❖ As a member of the Paris Opéra ballet (1835–42), danced in Philippe Taglioni's *La Sylphide* (after 1838), Joseph Mazillier's *Le Diable Amoureux,* and as "Myrthe" in *Giselle;* spent one season at Theater Royal in Munich, Germany; toured US 3 times, appearing on East Coast and Mississippi Circuit, performing in *The Vengeance of Diana, Giselle* (as "Giselle"), *La Vivandière, l'Illusion d'un Peintre* and *La Fille de Marbre,* introducing the repertory of the Romantic era.

BLANK, Arapera (1932—). *See Hineira, Arapera.*

BLANK, Carla (c. 1940—). American choreographer and dancer. Name variations: Carla Reed. Born c. 1940 in Pittsburgh, Pennsylvania; trained with Anna Sokolow, Richard Thomas, Ann Halprin, and at Martha Graham and Merce Cunningham studios; m. Ishmael Reed (writer), 1970; children: daughter, Tennessee Reed. ❖ Studied composition with James Waring at Living Theater in New York City, which soon led to involvement with Judson Dance Theater (1965); choreographed and collaborated extensively with Suzushi Hanayagi in NY, Japan, and the Bay area of San Francisco; choreographed *Turnover* (1963), *Untitled Chase* (1965), *Everybody's Independent & Grand Nation Spirit Show* (1976) and *Kore at Eleusis* (1979); with Hanayagi, choreographed *Spaced* (1965), *Sidelights* (1966), *Ghost Dance* (1973) and *Trickster Today* (1977).

BLANKENBURG, Lucretia L. (1845–1937). American suffragist and municipal reformer. Name variations: Lucretia Longshore. Born Lucretia Longshore near New Lisbon, Ohio, May 8, 1845; died in Philadelphia, Pennsylvania, Mar 29, 1937; dau. of Thomas Ellwood Longshore (schoolteacher) and Hannah E. Longshore (1819–1901, physician); m. Rudolph Blankenburg (mayor of Philadelphia), April 18, 1967 (died 1918); children: 3, all died young. ❖ Named for Lucretia Mott who was a frequent visitor to her parents' home; active with Philadelphia's Society for Organizing Charitable Relief (1878) and the New Century Club; enlisted by Susan B. Anthony in the cause of woman suffrage (1884) and served as president of Pennsylvania Woman Suffrage Association (1892–1908); became auditor (1908) and served as 1st vice-president (1912–14) of General Federation of Women's Clubs, working to secure the woman's club movement on the side of suffrage; as an independent Republican, supported municipal reform, prohibition and world peace.

BLANKERS-KOEN, Fanny (1918–2004). Dutch track-and-field athlete. Name variations: Fanny Koen. Born Francina Elsje Koen, April 26, 1918, Baarn, Soestdyk, Netherlands; died Jan 5, 2004, in Amsterdam, Netherlands; m. Jan Blankers (athlete and coach), Aug 1940; children: Jantje (b. 1941); Fanneke (b. 1946). ❖ Greatest woman track-and-field star of her generation, who won 4 Olympic gold medals, set 13 world records, and won 58 Dutch titles; won every sprinting event in Holland, as well as 2 competitions in Germany; tied for 6th place in the high jump at Berlin Olympics (1936); took 3rd at the European championships (1938); won 80-meter hurdles at European championships (1946); won 4 gold medals at London Olympics—the 100 meters in 11.9 seconds, 200 meters in 24.4, 80-meter hurdles in 11.2 and 4 x 100-meter relay while anchoring the Dutch women's team (1948); competed at Berne, Switzerland, sweeping all 5 1st places in pentathlon and collecting 4,185 points (1951); made a final, unsuccessful appearance at Helsinki Olympics (1952). Voted Female Athlete of the Century by the International Association of Athletic Federations (1999).

BLASBERG, Claudia (1975—). German rower. Born Feb 14, 1975, in Dresden, Germany; dau. of rowers. ❖ For lightweight double sculls, won a silver medal at Sydney Olympics (2000) and a silver at Athens Olympics (2004); also won World championships for lightweight double sculls (2001 and 2003).

BLASCO SOTO, Miriam (1963—). Spanish judo champion. Born Dec 12, 1963. ❖ At Barcelona Olympics, won a gold medal in lightweight—56 kg (1992).

BLATCH, Harriot Stanton (1856–1940). American reformer. Born Harriot Eaton Stanton in Seneca Falls, New York, Jan 20, 1856; died in Greenwich, Connecticut, Nov 20, 1940; dau. of Elizabeth Cady Stanton (1815–1902, the suffragist) and Henry B. Stanton (abolitionist, politician, and journalist); Vassar College, BA, 1878, MA, 1894; m. William Henry Blatch (English businessman), 1882 (died 1915); children: 2 daughters (one died in infancy). ❖ Assisted her mother and Susan B. Anthony on *History of Woman Suffrage;* after marriage, lived in England for 20 years (1882–1902), during which she was prominent in the reform work of the Fabian Society and also collaborated with British sociologist Charles Booth on a statistical study of English villages; on return to US, became involved with Women's Trade Union League and National American Woman Suffrage Association; founded Equality League of Self Supporting Women (1907), which became Women's Political Union (1910), until it merged in 1916 with Congressional Union (later National Woman's Party) under Alice Paul; during WWI, was head of the speakers bureau of the wartime Food Administration and a director of Woman's Land Army; writings include *Mobilizing Woman-Power* (1918), and *A Woman's Point of View* and *Roads to Peace* (both 1920); co-edited *Elizabeth Cady Stanton, as Revealed in Her Letters, Diary and Reminiscences* (1922). ❖ See also autobiography (with Alma Lutz), *Challenging Years* (1940); and *Women in World History.*

BLATCH, Nora (1883–1971). See Barney, Nora.

BLATTER, Barbara (1970—). Swiss mountain biker. Born Dec 22, 1970, in Switzerland. ❖ Won a silver medal for cross-country at Sydney Olympics (2000); won World Cup overall (2000, 2001).

BLAUGDONE, Barbara (c. 1609–1705). English Quaker and author. Born c. 1609 in England; died 1705 in England; never married; no children. ❖ Became active in the early period of the Quaker movement in England, traveling extensively around England and Ireland to promote the new ideas of Society of Friends; writings reveal the freedoms she enjoyed, as well as the hardships and dangers a lone female minister faced, especially as Quaker ideas grew in popularity and English authorities began to crack down on its heretical leaders. ❖ See also autobiography *An Account of the Travels, Sufferings, and Persecutions of Barbara Blaugdone* (1691).

BLAVATSKY, Helena (1831–1891). Russian spiritual leader, author, mystic, and a founder of the Theosophical Society. Name variations: Madame Blavatsky or simply HPB. Born Helena (Elena or Helen) Petrovna Gan, July 31, 1831, in Ekaterinoslav, Russia; died May 8, 1891, in London, England; dau. of Captain (later Colonel) Peter Alekseevich Gan (1798–1873, career military officer) and Elena Andreevna (Fadeeva) Gan (1814–1842, author who wrote novels as "Zinaida R-va"); sister of writer Vera Zhelikhovskaya (1835–1896); m. Nikifor Vasileevich Blavatsky, 1849; children: Nikolai, who died a few years after his birth. ❖ Termed both a charlatan and a great thinker, occasionally at the same time, established an international organization that preached a Universal brotherhood of all peoples, and introduced, albeit in a slightly altered form, Eastern philosophies to Western audiences; at the same time, much of her fame was and is based on the numerous psychic illusions and tricks that she and her followers experienced—phenomena she almost certainly staged herself; spent most of the 1850s traveling extensively throughout Europe, as well as Turkey and Egypt; immigrated to US (1873), where she settled in New York City; met Henry Steel Olcott (1832–1907) and began a collaboration, writing and translating articles on Spiritualism and related subjects, that was to continue for most of the rest of her life; turned away from orthodox Spiritualism when she revealed that she was communicating telepathically with an organization of learned men living in Egypt, the Brotherhood of Luxor, who were serving as her spiritual mentors; with Olcott and William Judge, established the Theosophical Society, which was based on the teaching she was receiving from the Brotherhood (1875). Theosophy, a blend of Buddhism, Hinduism, and the occult, was open to those of any nationality, race, or religious faith; its aims were no less than the discovery and teaching of the truths that govern the Universe. Theosophists believe that all religions have the same goal, the pursuit of truth, and the Society's motto is "there is no religion higher than truth." ❖ See also *H.P. Blavatsky Collected Writings* (14 vols., compiled by Boris de Zirkoff, 1950–91); Sylvia Cranston, *HPB: The Extraordinary Life and Influence of Helena Blavatsky* (Putnam, 1993); Marion Meade, *Madame Blavatsky: The Woman Behind the Myth* (Putnam, 1980); and *Women in World History.*

BLAYNEY, May (1875–1953). English stage actress. Born July 6, 1875, in England; died Feb 10, 1953, in Johannesburg, South Africa; m. A.E. Matthews. ❖ Made London debut as Kate Cunliffe in *Lady Fortune* (1892); spent many years under the managements of Charles Frohman, George Edwardes, Cyril Maude, Sir Charles Wyndham and Sir Herbert Tree, with greatest successes as Julie Alardy in *The Little Damozel* (1909) and Ann Whitefield in *Man and Superman* (1912); appeared on Broadway in *The Walls of Jericho, Love Among the Lions, The Importance of Being Earnest* and *Chantecler.*

BLAZE DE BURY, Rose (?–1894). French-English journalist and novelist. Name variations: Baroness Blaze de Bury; Baronne Blaze de Bury or Mme la Baronne Blaze de Bury. Born Marie Pauline Rose Stewart; died 1894; thought to be the illeg. dau. of an English lord; married possibly (Ange) Henri Blaze de Bury (1813–1888, librettist). ❖ Wrote in French and English; published articles on French life in English papers, including *Daily News;* wrote travel account *Voyage en Autriche, en Hongrie et en Allemagne pendant les événements de 1848 et de 1849* (1851).

BLAZEJOWSKI, Blaze (b. 1957). See Blazejowski, Carol.

BLAZEJOWSKI, Carol (1957—). American basketball player. Name variations: Blaze Blazejowski. Born Carol Blazejowski, Sept 29, 1956, in Cranford, New Jersey; attended Montclair State University. ❖ During college career, was 3-time All-American, amassing 3,199 points, setting a record of 52 points in a single game (1977); won a team silver medal at World University Games (1977); missed out on Moscow Olympics (1980), because of President Jimmy Carter's Russian boycott; signed with New Jersey Jems (1981); joined NY Club of Women's American Basketball Association (1984); became director of Women's Basketball Development for National Basketball Association (NBA); named vice president and general manager for newly formed New York Liberty of the WNBA (1997). Was the 1st woman to be awarded the Margaret Wade Trophy (1978); inducted into Basketball Hall of Fame (1994).

BLAZKOVA, Milada (1958—). Czech field-hockey player. Born May 30, 1958. ❖ At Moscow Olympics, won a silver medal in team competition (1980).

BLEARS, Hazel Anne (1956—). English politician and member of Parliament. Born Hazel Anne Blears, May 14, 1956; m. Michael Halsall, 1989. ❖ Solicitor; representing Labour, elected to House of Commons for Salford (1997, 2001, 2005); named parliamentary undersecretary of state, Department of Health; named minister of State, Crime Reduction, Policing & Community Safety (2003).

BLEARS, Laura (c. 1951—). See Ching, Laura Blears.

BLECHER, Miriam (1912–1979). American dancer and choreographer. Name variations: Miriam Sklar. Born Feb 23, 1912, in New York, NY; died Sept 19, 1979, in Los Angeles, California; m. George Sklar (playwright). ❖ First trained at Henry Street Settlement House in New York City in a program run by Martha Graham and Louis Horst; an active member of the American Dance Association and New Dance League, created anti-Fascist works during the buildup to WWII, including *Van de Lubbe's Head;* also created numerous solo works, performed in concert recitals with fellow members of the Dance League, including Si-Lan Chen, Lily Mehlman, and Anna Sokolow; moved to Los Angeles, CA, with husband (c. 1940), where she worked in dance therapy; best remembered works include *Three Dances to Poems* (1934), *East Side Sketches: The Bum* (1937), *Me and Robert Taylor* (1937), *Negro Poems* (1938), and the series of *Masks* (of Wealth, War, and Hatred, 1938).

BLEECKER, Ann Eliza (1752–1783). American author. Name variations: (incorrectly) Ann Eliza Bleeker. Born Ann Eliza Schuyler, Oct 1752, in New York, NY; died at Tomhanick, NY, 1783; dau. of Brandt Schuyler (died 1752) and Margaret Van Wyck Schuyler; m. John James Bleecker, Mar 29, 1769; children: 2, including Margaretta V. Faugeres (writer). ❖ Known for her writing on the rural life of the American frontier, died at 31 (1752), having endured hardships during the Revolutionary War; her writings, including poetry and prose narrative, appeared posthumously in the *New York Magazine. The Posthumous Works of Ann Eliza Bleecker, in Prose and Verse* was supplemented with work by her daughter, Margaretta V. Faugeres (Oct 1793).

BLEECKER, Margaretta Van Wyck (1771–1801). *See Faugeres, Margaretta V.*

BLEEKER, Ann Eliza (1752–1783). *See Bleecker, Ann Eliza.*

BLEEKER, Caroline Emilie (1897–1985). Dutch physicist. Name variations: Lili Bleeker. Born Jan 17, 1897, in Netherlands; died Nov 12, 1985; University of Utrecht, PhD, 1928; m. Adrian W.P. Keg. ❖ Became assistant (1919) and head assistant (1926) in physics laboratory at Utrecht University; opened successful factory to produce scientific apparatus and later optical equipment; participated in Dutch resistance during WWII, which resulted in closing of her factory; awarded royal distinction for wartime activities; from its opening (1949), served as director of NED-OPTIFA factory in Zeist, the 1st factory to produce phase contrast microscope invented by Frits Zernike.

BLEEKER, Lili (1897–1985). *See Bleeker, Caroline Emilie.*

BLEIBTREU, Hedwig (1868–1958). Austrian actress. Born in Linz, Austria, Dec 23, 1868; died in Pötzleinsdorf, a suburb of Vienna, Jan 25, 1958; dau. of Sigmund Bleibtreu (1819–1894, actor) and Amalie (Hirsch) Bleibtreu (1835–1917, actress); sister of actress Maximiliane Bleibtreu (1870–1923); graduate of Vienna Conservatory, 1884; m. Alexander Rompler, 1900; m. Max Paulsen, 1911. ❖ Actress who had a long and distinguished career as one of the greatest tragediennes in German-speaking Central Europe, made stage debut in Augsburg, Germany; returned to Austria (1887), starring at the theater in Brunn, Moravia; became a member of Vienna's Burgtheater (1893), an association that would last almost half a century, as she excelled in the roles of mothers and mature women in drawing-room comedies; began acting in motion pictures (1923); acted in Salzburg Festivals (1920s–30s); received countless awards including the Burgtheater Ring (1930); appeared in the film *The Third Man.* ❖ See also *Women in World History.*

BLEIBTREY, Ethelda M. (1902–1978). American swimmer. Born Feb 27, 1902, in Waterford, NY; died May 6, 1978; children: daughter who was also a swimmer. ❖ Won gold medals in the 100-meter freestyle, 300-meter freestyle, and 4 x 100 freestyle relay at Antwerp Olympics (1920); won US Outdoor nationals in the 100 yards (1920–21), 440-yard freestyle (1919, 1921), 880-yard freestyle (1919–21), 1-mile freestyle (1920), and 3-mile freestyle (1921); won US Indoor nationals in the 100-yard freestyle (1930, 1922) and 100-yard backstroke (1920).

BLEICH, Lela (1908—). *See Brooks, Lela.*

BLEILER, Gretchen (1981—). American snowboarder. Born April 10, 1981, in Toledo, Ohio. ❖ Wins include 1st Overall at Vans Triple Crown, Season End 2002; US championships, Northstar-at-Tahoe, CA, in Halfpipe (2002); and gold medal at X Games in Superpipe (Winter 2003); won a silver medal for Halfpipe at Torino Olympics (2006).

BLESCHAMPS, Madame de (1778–1855). *See Bonaparte, Alexandrine.*

BLESCHKE, Johanna (1894–1936). German writer. Name variations: (stage name) Rahel Sanzara. Born Feb 9, 1894 in Jena, Germany; died Feb 8, 1936, in Berlin. ❖ Under stage name Rahel Sanzara, began appearing on the stages of Prague, Darmstadt, and Berlin as a dancer (1918); as an actress, made film debut (1917); wrote the novel, *Das verlorene Kind* (The Lost Child, 1926), about the rape and murder of a

4-year-old girl, which went through several editions (because of her Jewish-sounding name, her book was banned in Nazi Germany).

BLESSINGTON, countess of (1789–1849). *See Blessington, Marguerite.*

BLESSINGTON, Marguerite, Countess of (1789–1849). Irish writer. Name variations: Marguerite Gardiner; Marguerite Power; Lady Blessington; Margaret, Sally. Born Marguerite Power, Sept 1, 1789, at Knockbrit, near Clonmel, Co. Tipperary, Ireland; died in Paris, France, June 4, 1849; dau. of Edward (or Edmund) Power (magistrate and newspaper editor) and Ellen (Sheehy) Power; m. Captain Maurice St. Leger Farmer, 1804 (died 1817); m. Charles John Gardiner, 1st earl of Blessington, 1817 (died 1829); no children. ❖ Author who published a number of popular novels of fashionable life and for many years presided over the most brilliant salon in London, published 1st book (1822); embarked with husband on a lengthy European tour (1822), visiting Italy and France; following husband's death (1829), returned to London in reduced financial circumstances; for many years, supported herself and her partner, Count d'Orsay, by her writing, while entertaining the leading figures in the arts and politics at her home, Gore House, in Kensington; endured acute financial difficulties (mid-1840s); fled to Paris to escape debtors (1849), dying there shortly afterwards. Writings include *The Magic Lantern, or Sketches of Scenes in the Metropolis* (1822), *Grace Cassidy, or the Repealers* (1833), *Conversations with Lord Byron* (1834), *The Two Friends* (1835), *Confessions of an Elderly Gentleman* (1836), *The Victims of Society* (1837), *Confessions of an Elderly Lady* (1838), *The Governess, Desultory Thoughts and Reflections* and *The Idler in Italy,* Vols I and II (1839), *The Idler in Italy,* vol III, and *The Belle of a Season* (1840), *The Idler in France* (1841), *Lottery of Life and Other Tales* (1842), *Strathern* (1843), *The Memoirs of a Femme de Chambre* (1846) and *Marmaduke Herbert* (1847). ❖ See also J. Fitzgerald Molloy, *The Most Gorgeous Lady Blessington* (1896); R.R. Madden, *The Literary Life and Correspondence of the Countess of Blessington* (1855); and *Women in World History.*

BLEY, Carla (1938—). American composer. Born Carla Borg, May 11, 1938, in Oakland, California; m. Paul Bley (pianist); m. Michael Mantler (trumpeter, sep.); children: (2nd m.) Karen Mantler (musician). ❖ Composer and band conductor who has experimented in numerous arenas, including free jazz, punk rock, and big band orchestras; formed Jazz Composers Orchestra with 1st husband (1964); with 2nd husband, founded JCOA (Jazz Composers Orchestra Association) Records (1966) and formed New Music Distribution Service, which handled independent labels, including their own Watt Records; received Grammy nomination for Best Jazz Big Band Album for *Big Band Theory* (1995). Other works include *Escalator over the Hill* (1972), *Dinner Music* (1978), *European Tour 1977* (1977), *Duets* (1988), *The Very Big Carla Bley Band* (1991), *Songs with Legs* (1995), *Are We There Yet?* (1999) and *Carla Bley 4 x 4* (2000).

BLIER, Henriette (c. 1864–1961). *See Pelletier, Henriette.*

BLIGE, Mary J. (1971—). American R&B and pop singer. Born Jan 11, 1971, in Bronx, NY. ❖ Released debut album *What's the 411?* (1992) which reached #1; consistently topped R&B charts with singles, including "You Remind Me" (1992), "Real Love" (1992), "I'll Be There for You/You're All I Need to Get By" (Grammy winner with Method Man, 1995), and "Not Gon' Cry" (1996). Other albums include *My Life* (1994, #1 R&B), *Share My World* (1997, #1 R&B), *Mary* (1999), *No More Drama* (2001) and *Love and Life* (2003).

BLIGH, Anna Maria. Australian politician. Name variations: Hon. Anna Maria Bligh. ❖ As a member of Australian Labor Party, elected to the Queensland Parliament for South Brisbane (1995); named minister for Education (2001), the 1st woman in Queensland to become Education Minister.

BLIND, Mathilde (1841–1896). German-English poet. Name variations: (pseudonym) Claude Lake. Born Mathilde Cohen in Mannheim, Germany, Mar 21, 1841; died in London, England, Nov 26, 1896, bequeathing her property to Newnham College, Cambridge; dau. of Friederike Ettlinger and Cohen Ettlinger (banker) but assumed the name Blind from her adoptive stepfather Karl Blind (1826–1907, political writer). ❖ Under pseudonym Claude Lake, published 1st vol. of poems (1867), dedicated to her friend, Italian nationalist Giuseppe Mazzini; wrote a critical essay on poetical works of Shelley for *Westminster Review* under her own name (1870) and an account of the life and writings of Shelley, to serve as an introduction to a selection of his poems in the Tauchnitz edition (1872); won fame with her own writings, which included the longer poems: "The Heather on Fire" (1886), "The Ascent of Man," and "The Prophecy of St. Oran" (1881); wrote biographies of George Eliot (Mary Anne Evans, 1883) and Madame Roland (1886), and trans. *The Memoirs of Marie Bashkirtseff* (1890); wrote 1st novel, *Tarantella* (1885); was an ardent advocate of the betterment of the position of woman in society and the state. ❖ See also *Women in World History*.

BLINKS, Susan (1957—). American equestrian. Name variations: Sue Blinks. Born Oct 5, 1957, in Mount Kisco, NY. ❖ Won a team bronze medal for dressage at Sydney Olympics (2000), on Flim Flam. Named USOC Female Equestrian of the Year (1998).

BLISS, Anna (1843–1925). American educator. Name variations: Anna Elvira Bliss. Born Anna Elvira Bliss, Jan 14, 1843, in Jericho, Vermont; died July 25, 1925, in Wellington, South Africa; dau. of Genas Bliss and Elvira (Chamberlain) Bliss. ❖ Closely linked with Abbie Ferguson, left for South Africa with Ferguson (1873); opened Huguenot Seminary, a school for girls (1874); took charge of lower department of Huguenot Seminary (1875); with Ferguson, founded Women's Missionary Society (later Vrouwen Zending Bond) at Huguenot; became principal when Huguenot Seminary developed into Huguenot Girls High School (1898); after Ferguson retired, served as president of Huguenot College (1910–20), which was renamed Huguenot University College, then incorporated by Parliament into University of South Africa (1916). Received honorary degree from Mount Holyoke College (1910).

BLISS, Catherine (1908–1989). English religious-education leader. Name variations: Dr. Kathleen Bliss. Born 1908 in London, England; died 1989 in England; studied theology at Cambridge University; m. Rev. Rupert Bliss. ❖ Leader in religious education who worked extensively with ecumenical World Council of Churches and pushed for an expanded role for women in the church, served on British Council of Churches (1942–67); chaired committee on Laity for World Council of Churches (WCC, 1948) and took keen interest in lay and educational concerns of organization; helped form commission on Life and Work of Women in Churchs (1949); published *The Service and Status of Women in the Churches* (1952) and *The Future of Religion* (1969); served as secretary of Church of England board of education (1957–66); lecturer in religious studies at University of Sussex (1966–73).

BLISS, Eleanora (1883–1974). See Knopf, Eleanora Bliss.

BLISS, Kathleen (1908–1989). See Bliss, Catherine.

BLISS, Lillie (1864–1931). American philanthropist. Name variations: Lizzie Plummer Bliss. Born Lizzie Plummer Bliss in Boston, Massachusetts, April 11, 1864; died in New York City, Mar 13, 1931; dau. of Cornelius Newton Bliss (textile commission merchant and secretary of the interior under President McKinley) and Elizabeth Mary (Plummer) Bliss; never married; no children. ❖ Co-founder of New York Museum of Modern Art, purchased 2 Renoirs, 1 Degas, and 2 Redons at the Armory Show (1913), initiating a collection of modern French art that would become one of the finest in US; in subsequent years, acquired paintings by Gauguin, Cézanne, Seurat, Matisse, Modigliani and Picasso, as well as by Arthur B. Davies, whose work she continued to collect until her death; with Abby Aldrich Rockefeller and Mary Sullivan, launched Museum of Modern Art (1929); encouraged and supported freedom of expression in the art world, and through her efforts established the modern-art movement in US and guaranteed its continuance. ❖ See also *Women in World History*.

BLISS, Mary Elizabeth (1824–1909). American first daughter and White House hostess. Name variations: Betty Taylor; Betty Bliss. Born Mary Elizabeth Taylor in 1824; died 1909; dau. of Margaret Smith Taylor (1788–1852) and Zachary Taylor (1784–1850, president of the US); sister of Knox Taylor; m. William Wallace Smith Bliss (1815–1853, Zachary Taylor's adjutant and confidential secretary); m. Philip Pendleton Dandridge; no children. ❖ Often called the "Wild Rose of the White House," functioned as social hostess for her mother Margaret Smith Taylor. ❖ See also *Women in World History*.

BLISS, Mildred Barnes (1879–1969). American art collector and philanthropist. Name variations: Mrs. Robert Woods Bliss. Born Mildred Barnes in New York City in 1879; died in Washington, DC, Jan 17, 1969; dau. of Demas Barnes and Anna Dorinda Blaksley; m. Robert Woods Bliss (1875–1962, diplomat). ❖ Patron of the arts who, with husband, commissioned and collected works of art for their home, Dumbarton Oaks; with landscape gardener Beatrix Jones Farrand, worked for 25 years to bring the most appropriate shrubs and trees to the garden of Dumbarton Oaks (1922–47); with husband, amassed a collection of pre-Columbian artifacts, then gave Dumbarton Oaks to Harvard University so that the academic world could benefit from the history they had collected (1940). ❖ See also *Women in World History*.

BLISS, Mrs. Robert Woods (1879–1969). See Bliss, Mildred.

BLISTICHE (fl. 268–264 BCE). See Bilistiche.

BLITCH, Iris Faircloth (1912–1993). American politician. Born near Vidalia, Georgia, April 25, 1912; died in San Diego, California, Aug 19, 1993; m. Brooks E. Blitch Jr., Oct 1929. ❖ Won election to the Georgia Senate (1946) and to the state House of Representatives (1948), but was defeated for reelection (1950); elected to the state Senate (1952), at which time she also served the Democratic Party as secretary of the state executive committee and as a state representative on the National Committee; as a Democrat from Georgia, elected to US House of Representatives (1954), serving 4 terms (84th–87th Congresses, Jan 3, 1955–Jan 3, 1963); along with 95 other senators and representatives from 11 southern states, signed the "Southern Manifesto," a pledge to work to reverse the 1954 Supreme Court decision outlawing racial segregation in public schools (1956); left the Democratic Party to support Republican presidential candidate Senator Barry M. Goldwater (1964). ❖ See also *Women in World History*.

BLITS-AGSTERIBBE, Stella (1909–1943). See Agsteribbe, Estella.

BLIXEN, Karen (1885–1962). See Dinesen, Isak.

BLOCH, Suzanne (1907–2002). Swiss-born musician and teacher. Born 1907 in Geneva, Switzerland; died Jan 29, 2002, in New York, NY; dau. of Ernest Bloch (musician and teacher); studied with Nadia Boulanger in Paris. ❖ The 1st famous lutenist of modern times, spurred interest in the lute, an 18th-century instrument that had become obscure; moved to NY with family (1916); taught at Juilliard School (1942–85); also played the recorder and the virginal, a small version of the harpsichord.

BLODGETT, Katharine Burr (1898–1979). American physicist. Born Katharine Burr Blodgett, Jan 10, 1898, in Schenectady, New York; died Oct 12, 1979, in Schenectady; dau. of George Bedington (patent attorney) and Katharine Buchanan (Burr) Blodgett; Bryn Mawr, AB, 1917, University of Chicago, MS, 1918; was the 1st woman to earn a PhD in physics from Cambridge University, 1926; never married; no children. ❖ Best known for her invention of non-reflecting glass, became the 1st woman research scientist hired by General Electric laboratories, Schenectady, NY (1918); developed color gauge to measure extremely thin films (1933); invented non-reflecting glass (1938), which would ultimately find widespread application, benefitting not only high-tech users of optical devices like astronomers and photographers, but every driver of an automobile; devised smokescreen for Allied military use in WWII; received American Association of University Women's Annual Achievement Award (1945); won Francis P. Garvan Medal for women in chemistry presented by American Chemical Society (1951); starred in 7th edition of American Men of Science; retired from General Electric (1963). ❖ See also *Women in World History*.

BLOEDE, Gertrude (1845–1905). American poet and novelist. Name variations: (pseudonym) Stuart Sterne. Born in Dresden, Germany, 1845; died in Baldwin, New York, 1905. ❖ Came to America as a child; under the pseudonym Stuart Sterne, wrote *Angelo* (1879) and *Giorgio and Other Poems* (1881); also wrote the novel *The Story of Two Lives*.

BLOIS, countess of.
See Adelaide (fl. 860s).
See Maud of Normandy (d. 1107).
See Adela of Blois (1062–c. 1137).
See Maud Carinthia (c. 1105–1160).
See Alice (1150–c. 1197).
See Marguerite (r. 1218–1230).
See Marie de Chatillon (r. 1230–1241).
See Jeanne de Chatillon (d. 1292).
See Jeanne de Penthièvre (c. 1320–1384).
See Françoise-Marie de Bourbon (1677–1749).

BLOIS, Natalie de (1921—). See de Blois, Natalie.

BLOM, Gertrude Duby (1901–1993). See Duby-Blom, Gertrude.

BLOMBERG, Vanja (1929—). Swedish gymnast. Born Jan 28, 1929, in Sweden. ❖ At Helsinki Olympics, won a gold medal in the teams all-around, portable apparatus (1952).

BLOMFIELD, Dorothy (1858–1932). British poet and hymn writer. Born Dorothy Frances Blomfield in London, England, Oct 1858; died in London, England, 1932; dau. of Frederick G. Blomfield (Anglican minister); sister of Katherine, Isabella, and Daisy Blomfield; granddau. of Rt. Rev. C.J. Blomfield (distinguished bishop of London); m. Gerald Gurney (Anglican minister), 1897. ❖ Best known for her oft-sung wedding hymn, "O Perfect Love," which she wrote for her sister's wedding (1883); also produced several volumes of quotable verse, including the popular poem "God's Garden." ❖ See also *Women in World History.*

BLOND, Elizabeth Le (1861–1934). *See Le Blond, Elizabeth.*

BLONDAL, Patricia (1926–1959). Canadian novelist. Born Patricia Jenkins, 1926, in Souris, Manitoba, Canada; died 1959 in Montreal, Canada; dau. of Nathanial Jenkins (railroad engineer); attended United College, 1944–47; m. Harold Blondal, 1946; children: 2. ❖ Moved to Winnipeg with family (1930s); began to write seriously (1955); published novel *From Heaven With a Shout,* which was 1st serialized in *Chatelaine* (1963); died of cancer before her book *A Candle to Light the Sun* was released to considerable acclaim (1960).

BLONDEAU, Barbara (1938–1974). American experimental photographer. Born in Detroit, Michigan, 1938; died in Philadelphia, Pennsylvania, 1974; School of the Art Institute of Chicago, BFA in painting, 1961; Institute of Design, Illinois Institute of Technology, MS, 1968. ❖ Widely known for her experimentation, taught in various colleges around the country, including Saint Mary's College, Notre Dame, Indiana, and Moore College of Art and Design in Philadelphia; was also chair of the Department of Photography and Film at Philadelphia College of Art.

BLONDELL, Joan (1906–1979). American actress. Born Aug 30, 1906, in New York, NY; died Dec 25, 1979, in Santa Monica, California; dau. of Eddie (stage comedian, one of the original Katzenjammer Kids) and Kathryn (Cain) Blondell (vaudeville performer); sister of Gloria Blondell, who also appeared in film and tv; m. George Scott Barnes, 1933 (div. 1935); m. Dick Powell, 1936 (div. 1945); m. Mike Todd, 1947 (div. 1950): children: (1st m.) Norman Scott Barnes (b. 1934); (2nd m.) Ellen Powell (b. 1938). ❖ At 3, joined parents' vaudeville act, "Ed Blondell and Company," and debuted in Sydney, Australia; toured with the act for 15 years; landed a small part in a Broadway production of *Tarnished,* which was followed by roles in *The Trial of Mary Dugan* and the *Ziegfeld Follies;* with James Cagney, appeared in the plays *Maggie the Magnificent* (1929) and *Penny Arcade;* signed with Warner Bros. and began playing the cynical, wisecracking blonde with a heart of gold, making some 20 films (1931–33), including *Public Enemy* and *Gold Diggers of 1933;* appeared in more than 80 movies, most memorably as Aunt Sissy in *A Tree Grows in Brooklyn* (1945); received Academy Award nomination as Best Supporting Actress for *The Blue Veil* (1951); on tv, appeared in "Here Comes the Bride," for which she was nominated for 2 Emmys; wrote the novel *Center Door Fancy* (1972). Other films include *Footlight Parade* (1933), *Dames* (1934), *Stage Struck* (1936), *Three Men on a Horse* (1936), *Topper Returns* (1941), *Nightmare Alley* (1947), *Desk Set* (1957), *The Cincinnati Kid* (1964), *Support Your Local Gunfighter* (1971), *Won Ton Ton, The Dog Who Saved Hollywood* (1976), *Grease* (1978) and *The Champ* (1979). ❖ See also *Women in World History.*

BLONDIE. *See Harry, Deborah.*

BLOODWORTH, Rhoda Alice (1889–1980). New Zealand labor activist and feminist. Name variations: Rhoda Alice Aspin. Born June 22, 1889, in Skipton, Yorkshire, England; died Dec 23, 1980, at Remuera, Auckland, New Zealand; dau. of James Aspin (loomer) and Maria Jane Aspin; m. Thomas Bloodworth (carpenter), 1912 (died 1974); children: 1. ❖ Immigrated with parents to New Zealand (1901); was a founding member of Women's Progressive Society (1913); helped establish Workers' Educational Association (1915); member of Auckland Women's International and Political League, served as president in 1918; also belonged to Women's Christian Temperance Union of New Zealand, and New Zealand Society for the Protection of Women and Children; elected to Auckland Electric Power Board (1955).

BLOODY MARY.
See Mary I (1516–1558).
See Lord, Lucy Takiora (c. 1842–1893).

BLOOM, Claire (1931—). English actress. Born Patricia Claire Blume, Feb 15, 1931, in North Finchley, London, England; sister of John Blume (film editor); niece of British actress Mary Crew; m. Rod Steiger (actor), Sept 19, 1959 (div. 1969); m. Hillard Elkins (producer, director), Aug

14, 1969 (div. 1979); m. Philip Roth (novelist), 1990 (div. 1995); children: (1st m.) Anna Steiger. ❖ Made stage debut as Jessie Killigrew in *It Depends What You Mean* at Oxford Rep (1946), followed by a triumphant Ophelia at Stratford-upon-Avon in *Hamlet* (1948); came to international prominence as Juliet in the Old Vic production of *Romeo and Juliet* and her star turn in Charlie Chaplin's *Limelight* (1953); other plays include *The Damask Cheek, The Lady's Not for Burning, Ring 'Round the Moon,* Helena in *All's Well That Ends Well,* Viola in *Twelfth Night,* Virgilia in *Coriolanus,* Miranda in *The Tempest,* Cordelia in *King Lear,* Nora in *A Doll's House,* Hedda in *Hedda Gabler,* and Mary Queen of Scots in *Vivat! Vivat Regina!;* films include *Richard III, Alexander the Great, The Brothers Karamazov, The Buccaneer, Look Back in Anger, The Chapman Report, The Haunting, The Outrage, The Spy Who Came in from the Cold, Charley, The Illustrated Man, Three into Two Won't Go, A Severed Head, Red Sky at Morning, A Doll's House, Clash of the Titans, Crimes and Misdemeanors* and *Mighty Aphrodite.* Won Plays and Players Award for portrayal of Blanche du Bois in *A Streetcar Named Desire* (1974). ❖ See also memoirs, *Limelight and After: The Education of an Actress* (Harper & Row, 1987) and *Leaving a Doll's House* (Little, Brown, 1997).

BLOOM, Ursula (1893–1984). British writer. Name variations: (pseudonyms) Deborah Mann, Sheila Burns, Mary Essex, Rachel Harvey, Sara Sloane, Lozania Prole (joint). Born Ursula Bloom in Chelmsford, England, Dec 1893; died in Nether Wallop, Hampshire, England, Oct 29, 1984; dau. of Mary and J. Harvey Bloom; m. Arthur Denham-Cooke, Nov 1916 (died 1918); m. Charles Gower Robinson (naval officer), Nov 1925; children: (1st m.) Pip Denham-Cooke (b. Nov 1917). ❖ Author of historical and romance novels totaling 564 volumes, became a crime reporter for the *Empire News* in Harlow; published 1st novel (1924), producing an average of 10 books a year until 1976. ❖ See also autobiography, *Life Is No Fairy Tale* (1976); and *Women in World History.*

BLOOM, Verna (1939—). American actress. Born Aug 7, 1939, in Lynn, Massachusetts; m. Jay Cocks (screenwriter and music critic). ❖ Made Broadway debut as Charlotte Corday in *Marat/Sade;* made film debut in *Medium Cool* (1969); other films include *The Hired Hand, High Plains Drifter, Animal House* and *The Last Temptation of Christ;* on tv, appeared in "Playing for Time," among others.

BLOOMER, Amelia Jenks (1818–1894). American reformer. Born Amelia Jenks, May 27, 1818, in Homer, Cortland Co., New York; died Dec 30, 1894, in Council Bluffs, Iowa; dau. of Augustus Jenks (clothier) and Lucy Jenks; m. Dexter C. Bloomer, 1840; children: none. ❖ Feminist and temperance crusader, best known for her advocacy of dress reform, became a founding member of the nationally based Ladies Temperance Society and was elected to the governing council; in Seneca Falls, was appointed assistant postmaster (1849), the 1st woman to hold such a position in US; wrote numerous articles for feminist and temperance journals; was editor and publisher of *The Lily* (1849–55), a monthly publication and the 1st of its kind produced by a woman in North America; adopted a militant stance on questions of women's rights and social reform, which accurately reflected the increasingly combative attitude assumed by the nation's leading feminists; also began to advocate a revolution in women's style of dress; fought against "fashionable" clothes comprised of tightly laced stays and at least half a dozen cumbersome skirts that, because of their length, frequently became coated in dust and mud; advocated a style (not of her invention) that would later be called "Bloomers," consisting of a three-quarter length tunic, belted at the waist, over a knee-length skirt which was completed by a pair of ankle-length baggy pantaloons (or trousers); by 1853, was a popular lecturer and enjoyed worldwide fame. ❖ See also Dexter C. Bloomer, *The Life and Writings of Amelia Bloomer* (1895); and *Women in World History.*

BLOOMFIELD-MOORE, Clara (1824–1899). *See Moore, Clara Sophia.*

BLOOMFIELD-ZEISLER, Fannie (1863–1927). *See Zeisler, Fanny Bloomfield.*

BLOOR, Ella Reeve (1862–1951). American reformer. Name variations: Ella Reeve Ware, Ella Reeve Cohen, Mother Bloor. Pronunciation: Bloor rhymes with more. Born Ella Reeve, July 8, 1862, on Staten Island, NY; died in Richlandtown, Pennsylvania, Aug 10, 1951; dau. of Harriet Amanda (Disbrow) Reeve and Charles Reeve (owner of a drug store); attended University of Pennsylvania; m. Lucien Ware, 1881 (div. 1896); m. Louis Cohen, 1897 (div. 1902); m. Andrew Omholt, 1930; assumed the surname of her companion Richard Bloor while on a trip to Chicago and was thereafter known by that name; children: (1st m.) Pauline (1882–1886), Charles (1883–1886), Grace (b. 1885), Helen (b. 1887), Harold (1889–1935), Hamilton (b. 1892); (2nd m.) Richard (b. 1898) and Carl (b. 1900). ❖ Labor organizer, suffragist, journalist, and Communist Party leader, known the world over by the affectionate name of Mother Bloor, who was a living symbol of the American Communist movement for 3 decades, and a rabble-rouser who stirred up many audiences with her fiery oratory; while giving birth to 6 children in 10 years, became active in the suffrage and temperance movements and joined the Knights of Labor and the Ethical Culture Society (1880s); joined Social Democracy of America (1897); joined Socialist Labor Party (1900), then the Socialist Party (SP, 1902); ran for secretary of state in Connecticut on the SP ticket (1908); elected SP state organizer for Ohio (1910); worked with Elizabeth Gurley Flynn for Workers Defense Union (WDU, 1917–19); joined the newly formed Communist Labor Party and appointed national organizer for the Eastern Division (1919); was organizer for International Labor Defense Council (ILD, 1920s); appointed organizer for United Farmers League (1931); elected to US Communist Party (CPUSA) Central Executive Committee (1932–48); named delegate to the Women's International Congress Against War and Fascism, held in Paris (1934); appointed chair of the Pennsylvania CP and ran for Congress on the CP ticket (1940); made 80th Birthday Tour, part of the CPUSA "Win the War Against Fascism" campaign (1942); arrested 36 times; writings include *Three Little Lovers of Nature* (1895), *Talks About Authors and Their Works* (1899) and *We Are Many* (1940); devoted over 50 years seeking justice for the working class. ❖ See also Anne Barton, *Mother Bloor: The Spirit of '76* (1937); Elizabeth Gurley Flynn, *Daughters of America: Ella Reeve Bloor and Anita Whitney* (1942); and *Women in World History*.

BLOOR, Maria Sophia (1818–1909). See *Pope, Maria Sophia*.

BLOSSOMS, The. See *Love, Darlene*.

BLOUNT, Anne (1837–1917). See *Blunt, Anne*.

BLOUNT, Elizabeth (c. 1502–c. 1540). Mistress of Henry VIII. Name variations: Bessie Blount; Lady Talboys. Born c. 1502; died c. 1540; dau. of John Blount; m. Gilbert Talboys, Lord Talboys of Kyme; children: (with Henry VIII) Henry Fitzroy, duke of Richmond.

BLOUNT, Gertrude (c. 1504–1558). See *Courtenay, Gertrude*.

BLOUNT, Martha (1690–1762). English literary executor. Born near Reading, England, June 15, 1690; died in Berkeley Row, Hanover Square, London, 1762; educated at Hammersmith and in Paris. ❖ Was an intimate friend of Alexander Pope, who dedicated his *Epistle on Women* to her (1735).

BLOW, Susan Elizabeth (1843–1916). American educator. Born Susan Elizabeth Blow, June 7, 1843, in Carondelet (now St. Louis), Missouri; died Mar 26, 1916, in New York, NY; dau. of a congressional representative. ❖ Studied teaching methods of Friedrich Froebel while in Germany and later studied with Maria Kraus-Boelté in NY; opened the 1st public kindergarten in America at the Des Peres School (1873); established a training school for kindergarten teachers (1874); was a lecturer at Columbia University Teachers College (1905–09). ❖ See also *Women in World History*.

BLOWER, Elizabeth (1763–after 1816). British novelist and actress. Born 1763 in Worcester, England; died after 1816. ❖ At 17, published *The Parsonage House* (1780), followed by *George Bateman* (1782), *Maria* (1785), and *Features from Life, or, A Summer Visit* (1788); published some poetry and worked as an actress in England and Ireland (1782–88).

BLUE, Rita Hassan (c. 1905–1973). American actress, producer, and drama critic. Born c. 1905; died Oct 13, 1973, age 68, in Westport, Connecticut. ❖ Produced such Broadway shows as *Skydrift, Under the Roof, Alice in Wonderland, Sing out the News* and *Mamba's Daughter*; wrote drama criticism for *Show Business*.

BLUEBELL, Miss (1910–2004). See *Kelly, Margaret*.

BLUE DOVE (1921–1997). See *De Luce, Virginia*.

BLUFFSTEIN, Sophie (1854–1891). Russian swindler. Name variations: The Golden Hand. Born 1854 in Russia; died 1891 in Russia. ❖ Known to criminal colleagues as the "Golden Hand," often posed as a well-to-do woman and ordered rare jewels; after valuables arrived, made off with the goods before payment could be collected; wanted by authorities throughout Europe, was apprehended in Smolensk, Russia, where she was set free by the

governor, whom she seduced; caught again by police, served in the Alexandrovsk Prison in Siberia; after release, opened an inn in Vladivostok.

BLUM, Arlene (1945—). American mountaineer, author, and chemist. Born 1945; raised in Chicago, Illinois; dau. of a physician and a violinist; graduate of Reed College and University of California, Berkeley; children: 1 daughter. ❖ Organized and led the 1st all-women's expedition to the summit of Mount Denali, Alaska (1970); organized and led the 1st all-female expedition to the summit of Annapurna I in the Himalayas (1978); hiked entire length of the Great Himalaya Range; did scientific research that led to the ban of a carcinogenic chemical from use in American clothing; taught at Stanford University, Wellesley College, and University of California, Berkeley. Awarded Gold Medal from Society of Women Geographers. ❖ See also memoir, *Annapurna: A Woman's Place* (Sierra Club, 1980); and *Women in World History*.

BLUM, Klara (1904–1971). German-Jewish poet and short-story writer. Name variations: Zhu Bailan. Born Nov 27, 1904, in Czernowitz/Bukowina, Romania (now part of the Ukraine); died May 4, 1971, in Canton, China; m. Zhu Xiangcheng (director and journalist, died 1943). ❖ Moved from Romania to Vienna with mother (1913); worked as a journalist and joined the SPO; after winning Communist prize for anti-fascist poetry, lived in Moscow (1934–47) where she published several books of poetry in German and had a romantic relationship with Zhu Xiangcheng; when he mysteriously disappeared, having been carted off to one of Stalin's Siberian camps, set out for China to find him (1947); became a professor of German language and literature at University of Nanking (1952), then University of Canton (1957); took the name Zhu Bailan; novellas and later poems were collected in *Das Lied von Hongkong* (The Song of Hong Kong, 1960); also wrote *Der Hirte und die Weberin* (1951).

BLUME, Judy (1938—). American novelist and children's writer. Born Judith Sussman, Feb 12, 1938, in Elizabeth, New Jersey; dau. of Rudolf Sussman and Esther Sussman; New York University, BS in education, 1961; m. John L. Blume, Aug 15, 1959 (div. 1975); m. Thomas A. Kitchens, 1976 (div. 1978); m. George Cooper (writer), 1987; children: Randy Lee Blume (b. 1961, airplane pilot) and Lawrence Andrew Blume (b. 1963, filmmaker). ❖ Popular author, whose books for children have often been banned because of their language and frank approach to sexuality, has been an active spokesperson for the National Coalition Against Censorship; writings include *The One in the Middle is the Green Kangaroo* (1969), *Are You There God? It's Me, Margaret* (1970), *Iggie's House* (1970), *Then Again, Maybe I Won't* (1971), *Tales of a Fourth Grade Nothing* (1972), *Otherwise Known as Sheila the Great* (1972), *Deenie* (1973), *Forever* (1975), *Blubber* (1974), *Starring Sally J. Freedman as Herself* (1977), *Superfudge* (1980), *The Judy Blume Memory Book* (1988), *Here's to You, Rachel Robinson* (1993) and *Places I Never Meant to Be* (1999); adult novels include *Wifey* (1978), *Smart Women* (1984) and *Summer Sisters*. Received over 90 literary awards, including Margaret A. Edwards Award from ALA for Lifetime Achievement (1996).

BLUMENTAL, Felicja (1908–1991). Polish pianist. Born Dec 28, 1908, in Warsaw, Poland; died in Israel, 1991; studied composition at Warsaw Conservatory with Karol Szymanowski. ❖ Made debut (1938); escaped Nazi-occupied Poland (1942), launching successful career in Brazil (1940s); gave world premiere of Heitor Villa-Lobos' *Fifth Piano Concerto* (1956), with London Philharmonic Orchestra; made well-received recordings of a number of neglected concertos by Ries, Clementi and others, and championed the music of Polish composer Karol Szymanowski, recording his *Symphonie* concertante, Op. 60; also performed *Partita* for Harpsichord and Orchestra which was composed for her by Krysztof Penderecki.

BLUNDELL, Heather (b. 1941). See *McKay, Heather*.

BLUNT, Anne (1837–1917). British explorer. Name variations: Baroness Wentworth; Anne Blount. Born Anne Isabella King, Sept 22, 1837; died in Cairo, Egypt, 1917; dau. of Ada Byron, countess of Lovelace (1815–1852), and Lord William Noel King, 1st earl of Lovelace; m. Wilfrid Scawen Blunt (1840–1922, poet, traveler, and diplomat), 1869; children: 1 daughter. ❖ Arabic scholar, equestrian, musician, traveler and writer, was the 1st Englishwoman to explore the Arabian peninsula; with husband, traveled in Turkey, Algiers, Egypt, and visited India (1878 and 1883–84); described the desert journey from Aleppo to Baghdad in *The Bedouin Tribes of the Euphrates* (1878); other desert excursions, including penetration of the unknown territory of Nedj, is described in *Pilgrimage* *to Nedj* (1881); settled in Egypt (1906), trading and breeding Arabian horses.

BLUNT, Katharine (1876–1954). American educator. Born in Philadelphia, Pennsylvania, May 28, 1876; died July 29, 1954; dau. of Stanhope English (army officer and author of technical articles) and Fanny (Smyth) Blunt; Vassar College, BA; University of Chicago, PhD in organic chemistry. ❖ The 1st woman president of Connecticut College, began her teaching career at Pratt Institute in Brooklyn (1913); was then appointed to the home-economics faculty at University of Chicago, where she remained until 1925, becoming chair of the department and raising the study of home economics to the graduate level; during WWI, worked for the Federal government as an expert on nutrition; collaborated with Florence Powdermaker on a series of lesson plans for colleges called *Food and the War* (1918); became active in American Home Economics Association, serving as national president (1924–26); appointed the 3rd president of Connecticut College (1929), the only college in the state offering a 4-year course for women; oversaw the construction of 18 buildings (1929–42). ❖ See also *Women in World History*.

BLUWSTEIN, Rachel (1890–1931). Israeli poet. Name variations: (pseudonym) Rachel. Born 1890 in Vyatka, Russia; died 1931 in Tel Aviv, Israel. ❖ At 19, moved to Eretz-Israel; went to France to study agriculture (1913), then to Russia where she contacted tuberculosis; returned to Eretz-Israel (1919); wrote about pioneering life in Jordan valley; works include *Saphiach* (1927), *Mineged* (1930), *Nevo* (1932) and *Shirat Rachel* (1961).

BLY, Nellie (1864–1922). *See Seaman, Elizabeth Cochrane.*

BLYTH, Ann (1928—). American actress and singer. Born Ann Marie Blyth in Mt. Kisco, NY, Aug 16, 1928; studied voice and spent 3 years as a soprano with the San Carlo Opera Co.; m. James McNulty (doctor, and brother of singer-comedian Dennis Day), June 27, 1953; children: 5. ❖ Often remembered for her dazzling smile and soprano voice in musicals *The Student Prince* and *Kismet,* was also a fine dramatic actress, nominated for an Oscar for Best Supporting Actress for *Mildred Pierce* (1945); other films include *Another Part of the Forest* (1948), *Mr. Peabody and the Mermaid* (1948), *Our Very Own* (1950), *The Great Caruso* (1951), *Sally and Saint Anne* (1952), *All the Brothers Were Valiant* (1953), *Rose Marie* (1954), *The Student Prince* (1954), *The Buster Keaton Story* (1957) and *The Helen Morgan Story* (1957). ❖ See also *Women in World History*.

BLYTHE, Betty (1893–1972). American actress. Born Elizabeth Blythe Slaughter in Los Angeles, California, Sept 1, 1893; died April 7, 1972, in Woodland Hills, California; niece of writer Samuel G. Blythe; attended University of Southern California; m. Paul Scardon, 1924 (died 1954). ❖ Leading lady of the silent era, best remembered for her title role in the hit *The Queen of Sheba* (1921), landed a role on Broadway in *High Jinks* (1915), and the following year went on the road with *So Long Letty;* hired by Vitagraph in Brooklyn, appeared in *She* (1917), *The Silver Horde* (1920), *Nomads of the North* (1920), *Chu Chin Chow* (1923), *Snowbound* (1927), *The Girl from Gay Paree* (1927), *Tom Brown of Culver* (1932), *Only Yesterday* (1933), *The Scarlet Letter* (1934), *Conquest* (1937), *Honky Tonk* (1941) and *Docks of New York* (1945). ❖ See also *Women in World History*.

BLYTHE, Coralie (1880–1928). English actress. Name variations: Mrs. Lawrence Grossmith. Born 1880 in Norwich, England; died July 24, 1928; dau. of W. Blythe Jr. and Jennie Blythe (actress); sister of Vernon Castle (dancer); sister-in-law of Irene Castle; m. Lawrence Grossmith (1877–1944, actor). ❖ Made stage debut in the pantomime *Santa Claus* (1894) and subsequently appeared in music halls for many years; plays include *A Greek Slave, The Toreador, The Gold Diggers, Two Naughty Boys, The Girl Behind the Counter* and *Dorothy.*

BLYTON, Enid (1897–1968). English writer. Name variations: Mary Pollock. Born Enid Mary Blyton, Aug 11, 1897, in East Dulwich, London; died Nov 28, 1968 in Hampstead, London; dau. of Thomas Carey Blyton Jr. (worker in a wholesale clothing business) and Theresa Mary (Harrison) Blyton; m. Major Hugh Alexander Pollock, Aug 28, 1924 (div. 1943); m. Kenneth Darrell Waters, Oct 20, 1943 (died Sept 15, 1967); children: (1st m.) Gillian Mary (b. July 15, 1931); Imogen Mary (b. Oct 27, 1935). ❖ Prolific writer of children's stories who has been consistently popular with young readers for over 50 years, but whose writing has been frequently condemned by librarians, teachers, and literary critics; had 3 poems accepted by *Nash's Magazine* (1916–18);

taught at Bickley Park School (1919); worked as nursery governess (1920–24); wrote *Child Whispers* (1922), followed by *Teachers' World* (1923–45); began to edit *Sunny Stories* (1926), then turned it into a weekly (1937); withdrew from editing *Sunny Stories* and edited fortnightly *Enid Blyton Magazine* (1953–59); had 1st performance of *Noddy in Toyland* (1954). Wrote well over 400 publications, not counting numerous articles and stories in periodicals, including (fantasy) *Adventures of the Wishing Chair* (1937); (holiday adventure) *The Secret Island* (1938), *Five on a Treasure Island* (1942), *The Island of Adventure* (1944), *The Rockingdown Mystery* (1949); (detective fiction) *The Mystery of the Burnt Cottage* (1943), *The Secret Seven* (1949); (circus stories) *Mr. Galliano's Circus* (1938); (family stories) *The Children of Cherry Tree Farm* (1940); (school stories) *Naughtiest Girl in the School* (1940), *The Twins at St. Clare's* (1941), *1st Term at Mallory Towers* (1946); and (nursery stories) *Mary Muse and the Dolls' House* (1942), *Little Noddy Goes to Toyland* (1949); has been translated into more than 126 languages and dialects. ❖ See also autobiography, *The Story of My Life* (Pitkins, 1952); Bob Mullan, *The Enid Blyton Story* (Boxtree, 1987); Sheila Ray, *The Blyton Phenomenon* (Deutsch, 1982); Imogen Smallwood, *A Childhood at Green Hedges* (Methuen, 1989); and *Women in World History*.

BOADICEA (26/30–60 CE). *See Boudica.*

BOARD, Lillian (1948–1970). English runner. Born Dec 13, 1948, in Durban, South Africa; died of cancer, Dec 26, 1970, in England. ❖ At Mexico City Olympics, won a silver medal in the 400 meters (1968); won gold medals at European championships for 800 meters and 4 x 400-meter relay (1969). Awarded MBE (1970).

BOARDMAN, Diane (c. 1950—). American dancer and choreographer. Born c. 1950 in Brooklyn, NY. ❖ Began dance training at age 5 at Henry Street Settlement in New York City, with Murray Louis, Phyllis Lamhut and Gladys Bailin; danced with the Lamhut company where she appeared in *Hearts of Palm, Extended Voices, Brainwaves* and *Country Mozart* (1971–77), among others; performed in concerts by Murray Louis and Alwin Nikolais; formed own dance troupe (1971), performing in theaters in NY and in residencies throughout US; works are known for their imagination and wit, characteristic of Lamhut pieces; choreography includes *Love Story* (1971), *Player Piano Piece* (1972), *Oolite* (1974), *Baguette* (1974), *Set Up* (1977), *Dynamis* (1978) and *Man Made* (1979).

BOARDMAN, Eleanor (1898–1991). American actress. Born in Philadelphia, Pennsylvania, Aug 19, 1898; died in Santa Barbara, California, Dec 12, 1991; attended Academy of Fine Arts, Philadelphia; m. King Vidor (film director), 1926 (div. 1931); m. Harry d'Abbadie d'Arrast (film director), 1940 (died 1968); children: (1st m.) 2 daughters. ❖ At 16, gained national attention as the Kodak girl on publicity posters for Eastman Kodak; appeared in films of MGM (1922–32), playing in comedies as well as romantic dramas, including *Vanity Fair* (1923), *Three Wise Fools* (1923), *The Circle* (1925), *Memory Lane* (1926), *Bardelys the Magnificent* (1926), *Tell It to the Marines* (1926), *She Goes to War* (1929), *Mamba* (1930), *Redemption* (1930), *The Flood* (1931) and *The Squaw Man* (1931); best remembered for her leading role in *The Crowd* (1928), a realistic study of life in an American city, directed by King Vidor; after divorce and bitter custody battle over daughters, left for Europe (1933), where she made her last screen appearance in *The Three-Cornered Hat*. ❖ See also *Women in World History*.

BOARDMAN, Mabel (1860–1946). American Red Cross leader. Born Mabel Thorp Boardman in Cleveland, Ohio, Oct 12, 1860; died in Washington, DC, Mar 17, 1946; dau. of William Jarvis and Florence (Sheffield) Boardman. ❖ Called "the administrative genius" of the American Red Cross, is credited with transforming the turn-of-the-century, 300-member society into a thriving institution, with 29 million junior and senior members; marked by an early struggle to break from the authoritarian leadership of Clara Barton, spent 44 years, primarily behind the scenes, as head of the Volunteer Special Services; appointed 1st woman member of the Board of Commissioners of the District of Columbia (1920); retired as director of Volunteer Services (1940); wrote *Under the Red Cross Flag at Home and Abroad* (1915). Decorated by the king of Sweden and the Italian government (1909); received French Medal of Merit, 1st Class, and the Légion d'Honneur, as well as recognition from Japan, Belgium, Portugal, Serbia and Chile; received the 1st Distinguished Service Medal ever awarded by the Red Cross (1944). ❖ See also *Women in World History*.

BOARDMAN, Virginia (1889–1971). *See Eames, Virginia.*

BOARDMAN, Sarah Hall (1803–1845). *See Judson, Sarah Boardman.*

BOBATH, Berta (1907–1991). German-born physiotherapist. Name variations: Berta Othilie Bobath. Born Dec 5, 1907, in Germany; moved to England (1938); died Jan 20, 1991, in England; m. Karel Bobath (pediatric neurologist), 1941. ❖ Pioneer of treatment of cerebral palsy and adult hemiplegics, served as a therapist at Princess Louise Hospital (1944–51); received diploma in physiotherapy (1950); established private clinic, Western Cerebral Centre (1951), where her husband served as honorary consultant physician (the clinic, which moved to Hampstead and became known as the Bobath Centre in 1957, became the world leader in treatment for children with cerebral palsy); with husband, received Harding Award for outstanding work for the disabled. Made MBE (1978).

BOBBETTES, The.
See Dixon, Reather.
See Gathers, Helen.
See Pought, Emma.
See Pought, Jannie.
See Webb, Laura.

BOBEICA, Iulia (1967—). Romanian rower. Born July 1967 in Romania. ❖ At Barcelona Olympics, won a silver medal in coxed eights (1992).

BOBER, Phyllis (1920–2002). American scholar. Born Phyllis Pray, Dec 2, 1920; died May 30, 2002, in Ardmore, Pennsylvania; attended Institute of Fine Arts at New York University; m. Harry Bober (art historian, div. 1973); children: Jonathan and David Bober. ❖ A scholar of Renaissance art and pioneering scholar in culinary history, spent 40 years working on the monumental project, "The Census of Classical Works Known to the Renaissance"; founded the department of fine arts of New York University in the Bronx, and served as its chair (1967–73); became the dean of Bryn Mawr College Graduate School of Arts and Sciences (1973); often lectured on historical cooking; writings include *Art, Culture and Cuisine* (1999).

BOBIS, Ildiko (1945—). Hungarian fencer. Name variations: Ildiko Bobis-Ferkasinszky. Born Sept 1945 in Hungary. ❖ Won an Olympic silver medal in team foil at Mexico City (1968), silver medals in individual foil and team foil at Munich (1972), and a bronze medal in team foil in Montreal (1976).

BOBKOVA, Hana (1929—). Czech gymnast. Born Feb 19, 1929. ❖ At Helsinki Olympics, won a bronze medal in the team all-around (1952).

BOBOC, Loredana (1984—). Romanian gymnast. Born May 12, 1984, in Bucharest, Romania. ❖ At Sydney Olympics, won a gold medal for team all-around (2000).

BOBOLINA (1771–1825). *See Bouboulina, Laskarina.*

BOBROVA, Natalia (1978—). Soviet gymnast. Born Aug 24, 1978, in Siberia, Russia. ❖ Won a bronze medal in floor exercises at the World championships (1993); came in 3rd overall at the Moscow News/Stars competition (1993) and the Russian Cup (1995).

BOCAGE, Marie-Anne Le Page du (1710–1802). French playwright, poet, and salonnière. Name variations: Marie-Anne Le Page du Boccage; Marie Anne Fiquet du Bocage. Born Marie Anne Le Page in 1710 in Rouen, France; died 1802. ❖ Held literary salon in Paris; wrote *Les Amazones*, which was performed at Comédie Française (1749) but not well received; nicknamed "Le Milton français," wrote the long poem *Le Paradis Terrestre* in imitation of John Milton (1748); also wrote *La Colombiade* and visited Voltaire at his home in Ferney, near Geneva.

BOCANEGRA, Gertrudis (1765–1817). Mexican freedom fighter. Born in Pátzcuaro, Mexico, in 1765; died by execution in Pátzcuaro in 1817; m. Lazo de la Vega (soldier for the Spanish royalists turned revolutionary); children: a son and daughters. ❖ Founded schools for Indian children in Mexico; during War of Independence (1810), along with husband and son, aligned with the insurgents against the Spanish government; carried important messages between the rebel groups, and organized an underground army of women, which eventually included her daughters, to join in the fighting, considerably aiding the attack on the city of Valladolid; after husband and son were killed in battle, was captured in Pátzcuaro; tried and executed (1817).

BOCCHI, Dorotea (fl. 1390–1430). Italian teacher of medicine. Name variations: Dorotea Bucca; dau. of a professor of medicine. ❖ Was appointed professor of medicine at University of Bologna (1390), succeeding her father, who was an educator and physician; continued in that capacity for 40 years.

BOCHAROVA, Nina (1924—). Soviet gymnast. Born Sept 24, 1924, in USSR. ❖ At Helsinki Olympics, won a silver medal in the teams all-around, portable apparatus, a silver medal in the individual all-around, a gold medal in team all-around, and a gold medal in balance beam (1952).

BOCHATAY, Fernande (1946—). Swiss Alpine skier. Born Jan 23, 1946, in Marecottes, Switzerland. ❖ Won a bronze medal for giant slalom at Grenoble Olympics (1968).

BOCHER, Joan (d. 1550). Anabaptist martyr. Name variations: Boucher or Butcher; Joan of Kent. Executed in 1550. ❖ A friend of Anne Askew's, maintained that Christ did not "take flesh of the virgin"; after being interrogated by Thomas Cranmer, archbishop of Canterbury, was imprisoned and later burned at Smithfield. ❖ See also *Women in World History.*

BOCHINA, Natalya (1962—). Soviet runner. Born Jan 1962 in USSR. ❖ At Moscow Olympics, won a silver medal in the 200 meters and a silver medal in the 4 x 100-meter relay (1980).

BOCHKAREVA, Maria (b. 1889). *See Botchkareva, Maria.*

BOCK, Amy Maud (1859–1943). New Zealand confidence artist. Name variations: Amy Maud Christofferson, Molly Shannon, Agnes Vallance. Born May 18, 1859, at Hobart, Tasmania, Australia; died Aug 29, 1943, at Bombay, New Zealand; dau. of Alfred Bock and Mary Ann Parkinson; m. Charles Edward Christofferson (farmer), 1914. ❖ Arrived in New Zealand (late 1880s); established pattern of securing domestic work and then defrauding employers; used several names and served frequent prison sentences for fraud, including posing as wealthy sheepfarmer Percival Leonard Carol Redwood and marrying Agnes Ottaway in April 1909 (marriage annulled 2 months later). ❖ See also *Dictionary of New Zealand Biography* (Vol. 2).

BODARD, Mag (1916—). Italian-French film producer. Name variations: Margherita Perato. Born Margherita Perato, Jan 3, 1916, in Turin, Italy; dau. of winegrowers; attended Institution Mainterion in Paris, France; m. Lucian Bodard (journalist, div. after 25 years). ❖ While husband was posted in Vietnam (1948–55), wrote articles about everyday life in Saigon for *France-Soir* and *Elle,* which were later published as *C'est Aussi Comme Ca (It's Also Like That)* to great success; co-produced Jonathan Demy's *Les Parapluies de Cherbourg* (*The Umbrellas of Cherbourg,* 1962), which won the top prize at Cannes Film Festival (1964) and was nominated for Academy Award for Best Foreign Film; her next movie, *Le Bonheur* (*Happiness*), directed by Agnes Varda, won a special jury prize at Berlin Film Festival (1965); working with several top French directors, produced films like Jean-Luc Godard's *La Chinoise* (*The Chinese Girl*), Robert Bresson's *Mouchette,* and Jacques Doniol-Valcroze's *Le Viol* (*A Question of Rape*); also produced for tv; was one of the few independent women producers of her day, as well as one of the most prolific. ❖ See also *Women in World History.*

BODDIE, Barbara White (1940—). American golfer. Name variations: Barbara Fay White. Born Barbara Fay White, April 14, 1940, in Shreveport, Louisiana. ❖ Was twice a member of the Curtis Cup (1964, 1966) and World Cup teams (1964, 1966), with a remarkable record in each; also won the Western Women's (1964, 1965), the Broadmoor (1964), the Southern (1967), and the Louisiana State 3 times.

BÖDDING-ECKHOFF, Inge (1947—). *See Boedding-Eckhoff, Inge.*

BODEN, Margaret (1936—). British psychologist. Born Nov 26, 1936; married c. 1967 (div. 1981); children: 2. ❖ Served as lecturer in philosophy at University of Birmingham (1959–62); began doctoral work at Harvard University (1962); published 1st book, *Purposive Explanation in Psychology* (1972); began teaching at Sussex University (1965) and was among founders of university's Cognitive Studies program (early 1970s); at Sussex, became professor (1980), dean of School of Social Sciences (1985), and dean of the new School of Cognitive and Computing Sciences (c. 1987); through her work, popularized concept that aspects of the human mind can be understood in terms of the computer programming involved in artificial intelligence (AI); has lectured around world and had work translated into 16 languages; awarded OBE (2002); served as vice president of British Academy; served as vice president and chair of council of Royal Institution of Great Britain. Additional works include: *Artificial Intelligence and Natural Man*

(1977, 1987), *Piaget* (1979, 1984), *Minds and Mechanisms* (1981), *Computer Models of Mind* (1988), *Artificial Intelligence in Psychology* (1989), (ed.) *The Philosophy of Artificial Intelligence* (1989, 1990), *The Creative Mind* (1990) and (ed.) *The Philosophy of Artificial Life* (1996).

BODENDORF, Carla (1953—). East German runner. Born Aug 13, 1953. ❖ At Montreal Olympics, won a gold medal in the 4 x 100-meter relay (1976).

BODENWIESER, Gertrud (1886–1959). Austrian dancer and choreographer. Born 1886 in Vienna, Austria; died 1959 in Sydney, Australia. ❖ Taught at State Academy of Music and Drama in Vienna (c. 1921–38); founded a dance troupe to perform her constructivist works in Austria-Hungary and Germany (mid-1920s); won more widespread recognition on tours to London (1927) and Italy (1932) with such pieces as *The Daemon Machine, or Dance of Work* (1932); immigrated to Australia (1938) and continued to teach and perform with a new dance troupe formed in Sydney; works include *An Exotic Orchestra* (1972), *Le Ore Solenne* (1932), *Waltzes of Delirium* (1933), *Narcissus* (c. 1936), *Visions from Painters* (c. 1944) and *Cinderella of Old Vienna* (c. 1945).

BODET, Stéphanie (1976—). French climber. Name variations: Stephanie Bodet. Born 1976 in France. ❖ Became Championne de France Junior (1994), University Championne de France (1995 and 1996), and Championne de France (1997); other 1st-place finishes include Signal Rock 'n' roll Challenge in Crans Montana, Switzerland, and Cortina d' Ampezzo, Italy (both 1998), as well as World Cup (Block) Bardonecchia, Italy, and Chamonix, France (both 1999), X Games (1999), and World Cup (Difficulty) in Chamonix (2000).

BODICHON, Barbara (1827–1891). English feminist and educator. Name variations: Barbara Leigh-Smith or Barbara Leigh Smith. Born Barbara Leigh-Smith at Watlington, Norfolk, England, April 8, 1827; died at Robertsbridge, Sussex, June 11, 1891; illeg. dau. of Benjamin Leigh Smith (1783–1860, long an M.P. for Norwich) and Anne Longden (milliner's apprentice); sister of Anne Leigh Smith; 1st cousin of Florence Nightingale; enrolled at Bedford College for Women, 1849; m. Dr. Eugéne Bodichon (French physician), 1857. ❖ With Elizabeth Whitehead, opened Portman Hall School in Paddington (1852); published a *Brief Summary in Plain Language of the Laws of England Concerning Women* (1869), which helped advance the passage of the Married Women's Property Act; with Emily Davies, promoted the extension of university education to women, with the 1st small experiment at Benslow House, Hitchen (1866), which developed into Girton College; exhibited watercolors at the Salon and elsewhere, and hosted a London salon that included many of the literary and artistic celebrities of her day, including Mary Anne Evans (George Eliot); also helped finance the *Englishwomen's Journal* and wrote *Women and Work* (1857), *Reasons for the Enfranchisement of Women* (1866) and *Objections to the Enfranchisement of Women Considered* (1866).

BODIL OF NORWAY (fl. 1090s). Queen of Denmark. Married Erik Ejegod or Erik Egode, king of Denmark (r. 1095–1103); children: Knud or Canute Lavard (who m. Ingeborg of Russia).

BODIN DE BOISMORTIER, Suzanne (c. 1722–?). French novelist. Born Suzanne Bodin de Boismortier c. 1722, in Perpignan, France; dau. of Joseph Bodin de Boismortier (1689–1755, composer) and Marie Valette. ❖ Wrote *Mémoires historiques de la comtesse de Marienberg* (1751), *Histoire de Jacques Féru et de la valeureuse demoiselle Agathe Mignard* (1766) and short-story collection *Histoires morales* (1768).

BODKIN, A.M. (1875–1967). *See Bodkin, Maud.*

BODKIN, Maud (1875–1967). British literary critic and educator. Name variations: Amy Maud Bodkin; A.M. Bodkin. Born Amy Maud Bodkin, Mar 30, 1875, in Chelmsford, Essex, England; died May 18, 1967; dau. of William Bodkin; attended University College of Wales, Aberystwyth. ❖ Became lecturer in pedagogy at training college in Cambridge; studied Carl Jung (1920s), a central influence on her highly regarded 1st work, *Archetypal Patterns in Poetry: Psychological Studies of Imagination* (1934); also wrote *The Quest for Salvation in an Ancient and a Modern Play* (1941) and *Studies of Type-Images in Poetry, Religion, and Philosophy* (1951), among others.

BODLEY, Rachel (1831–1888). American chemist and botanist. Born in Cincinnati, Ohio, Dec 7, 1831; died of a heart attack in Philadelphia, Pennsylvania, 1888; dau. of Anthony (carpenter) and Rebecca (Talbott) Bodley (educator); attended private school in Cincinnati; graduate of Wesleyan Female College, 1849, and Polytechnic College, Philadelphia, 1860. ❖ Credited with helping to raise the profile of women in science, attended a private school run by her mother before enrolling at Wesleyan Female College; embarked on her teaching career at the Cincinnati Female Seminary (1862); was named 1st chair of chemistry at Female Medical College (later Woman's Medical College, 1865); became dean of the school and was elected school director in Philadelphia's 29th School District; was one of the 1st women appointed to the State Board of Public Charities (1883); classified and mounted an extensive collection of plants.

BODZIAK, Ericleia (1969—). Brazilian volleyball player. Name variations: Ericléia Bodziak; (nickname) Filo or Filó Bodziak. Born Sept 26, 1969, in Curitiba, Brazil. ❖ Outside hitter, won a team bronze medal at Atlanta Olympics (1996).

BOE, Anette. Norwegian cross-country skier. Born in Norway. ❖ Won a bronze medal for 4 x 5 km relay at Lake Placid Olympics (1980); won World championship in the 5 and 10 km events (1985).

BOEDDING-ECKHOFF, Inge (1947—). West German runner. Name variations: Bödding-Eckhoff; Inge Boedding Eckhoff. Born Mar 29, 1947. ❖ At Munich Olympics, won a bronze medal in the 4 x 100-meter relay (1972).

BOEGLI, Lina (1858–1941). *See Bögli, Lina.*

BOEHM, Annett (1980—). German judoka. Name variations: Annett Böhm or Bohm. Born Jan 8, 1980, in Meerane, Germany; attended University of Leipzig. ❖ Won a bronze medal for 70kg at Athens Olympics (2004).

BOEHM, Helen F. (b. early 1920s). American porcelain studio owner. Born Helen Francesca Franzolin in early 1920s in Brooklyn, NY; dau. of working-class Italian immigrants; m. Edward Marshall Boehm (1913–1969, porcelain artist), 1944. ❖ With husband, moved to Trenton, New Jersey (1950), where they opened a small studio in a basement; became chair of the Boehm porcelain studios after his death (1969); heavily involved with the National Center for Missing and Exploited Children for which the Helen F. Boehm Museum in Alexandria, VA, was dedicated (2002). Boehm porcelain, which is shown in more than 130 leading museums and institutions around the world, has been requested by 9 US presidents as gifts for heads of state; the Gregorian Etruscan Museum at the Vatican Museum was dedicated to Edward Boehm (June 19, 1992), the 1st time in half a century that a museum at the Vatican had been dedicated to someone other than a pope, nobility or royalty.

BOEHM, Mary Louise (1924–2002). American pianist and painter. Born 1924 in US; died Nov 29, 2002, in Spain; studied with her mother, then with Robert Casadesus in Paris and Walter Gieseking in Saarbrücken. ❖ Well-known as a recitalist, 1st specialized in the compositions of lesser Romantic composers like Moscheles and Hummel, then diligently worked to champion the works of American composers, including Amy Beach; her discography includes works by C.P.E. Bach, Abel, Schroeder, Field, Kalkbrenner, and Spohr; began painting (1960s), working in oils, watercolors, and inks.

BOEKHORST, Josephine (1957—). Dutch field-hockey player. Born Dec 18, 1957. ❖ At Los Angeles Olympics, won a gold medal in team competition (1984).

BOELTE, Amely (1811–1891). *See Bolte, Amely.*

BOELTÉ, Maria (1836–1918). *See Kraus-Boelté, Maria.*

BOENISCH, Yvonne (1980—). German judoka. Name variations: Yvonne Bonisch or Bönisch. Born Dec 29, 1980, in Ludwigsfelde, Germany. ❖ At A Tournament, placed 1st for 57kg (2003, 2004); placed 2nd at World championships for 57kg (2003); won a gold medal for 57kg at Athens Olympics (2004).

BOERNER, Jacqueline (1965—). *See Börner, Jacqueline.*

BOESLER, Martina (1957—). East German rower. Born June 18, 1957. ❖ At Moscow Olympics, won a gold medal in coxed eights (1980).

BOESLER, Petra (1955—). East German rower. Born Sept 19, 1955. ❖ At Montreal Olympics, won a silver medal in double sculls (1976).

BOFILL, Angela (1954—). American singer. Born 1954 in New York, NY; dau. of a Cuban father (singer) and Puerto Rican mother. ❖ Was singing on Latin club circuit with the Group while in high school; served as singer, dancer, composer, and arranger for Dance Theater of Harlem;

released debut album *Angie* (1979), which became best-selling jazz album. Other albums include *Angel of the Night* (1979), *Something About You* (1981), *Too Tough; Teaser* (1983), *Intuition* (1988), *I Wanna Love Somebody* (1993) and *Love in Slow Motion* (1996).

BOG, Harriet (b. 1922). *See* Holter, Harriet.

BOGAN, Louise (1897–1970). American poet and literary critic. Born Aug 11, 1897, in Livermore Falls, Maine; died in Washington Heights, New York, Feb 4, 1970; dau. of Daniel Joseph Bogan (superintendent of a paper mill) and Mary "May" Helen Murphy (Shields) Bogan; m. Curt Alexander (German-born captain in the army), Sept 4, 1916 (died 1920); m. Raymond Holden (writer), July 10, 1925 (legally sep., 1934); children: Maidie Alexander (b. Oct 19, 1917). ❖ Poet and *New Yorker* critic, one of America's most influential women of letters, began contributing to *Poetry, The New Republic, Vanity Fair, Voices* and *The Liberator,* among others (1921); published 1st book of poems, *Body of this Death* (1923); started writing criticism (1924); published next book of poems, *Dark Summer* (1929); began reviewing poetry for *The New Yorker* (1931), a job she would continue for the next 38 years; wrote the reverie "Journey Around My Room" (1932); published *The Sleeping Fury* (1937), her last important work, followed by 1st collected edition *Poems and New Poems* (1941), which was well received; became a fellow in American Letters of Library of Congress (1944) and a consultant in poetry (1945–46); taught poetry at many colleges and universities, including New York University, University of Arkansas, University of Washington, Brandeis University, as well as at 92nd Street YMHA in Manhattan (1949–60); published last book of poetry, *The Blue Estuaries: Poems, 1923–1968* (1968); elected to membership in Academy of American Poets (1969); during lifetime, endured frequent bouts of depression and frequent hospital stays. ❖ *See also* Elizabeth Frank, *Louise Bogan: A Portrait* (Knopf, 1985); Ruth Limmer, ed. *What the Woman Lived: Selected Letters of Louise Bogan, 1920–1970* (1973) and *Journey Around My Room* (1980); and *Women in World History.*

BOGAN, Lucille (1897–1948). African-American blues singer. Name variations: recorded under the name Bessie Jackson. Born Lucille Anderson, April 1, 1897, in Amory, Mississippi; died in Los Angeles, California, Aug 10, 1948; m. Nazareth Bogan; reportedly m. James Spencer. ❖ One of the greatest blueswomen of all time, sang down-and-gritty songs dealing with sex, violence, dope and the underworld; moved to Chicago (1927); recorded for Paramount and Brunswick (1928–30), particularly "Alley Boogie," with pianist Charles Avery, and "They Ain't Walking No More" (later remade with its uncensored title "Tricks Ain't Walking No More"). ❖ *See also Women in World History.*

BOGDANOVA, Krasimira (1949—). Bulgarian basketball player. Born June 5, 1949. ❖ Won a bronze medal in team competition at Montreal Olympics (1976) and a silver in Moscow (1980).

BOGDANOVA, Svetlana (1964—). Soviet handball player. Born June 12, 1964, in USSR. ❖ At Barcelona Olympics, won a bronze medal in team competition (1992).

BOGDANOVA, Yuliya (1964—). Soviet swimmer. Born April 27, 1964, in USSR. ❖ At Moscow Olympics, won a bronze medal in 200-meter breaststroke (1980).

BOGEN, Erna (1906—). Hungarian fencer. Born Dec 31, 1906; m. Aladár Gerevich (fencer). ❖ Won the Olympic bronze medal in Los Angeles in individual foil (1932).

BOGGS, Lindy (1916—). American politician. Born Corinne Morrison Claiborne at Brunswick Plantation, Louisiana, Mar 13, 1916; dau. of Roland and Corinne (Morrison) Claiborne; graduate of Sophie Newcomb College of Tulane University, 1935; m. Thomas Hale Boggs (US Congressional representative and majority leader), Jan 22, 1938 (died Mar 1973); children: Barbara Boggs Sigmund (mayor of Princeton, NJ, from 1984 until her death in 1990); Thomas Hale Boggs (Washington lawyer and lobbyist); Corinne "Cokie" Roberts (b. 1944, TV correspondent). ❖ Beginning in 1948, ran husband's campaigns, managed his Capitol Hill office, and headed a number of other organizations, including the Women's National Democratic Club, Democratic Wives' Forum, and Congressional Club; succeeded husband (Mar 1973), 5 months after his small plane vanished over Alaska during a campaign trip; had a 17-year legislative career as US Representative, Democrat of Louisiana, in 93rd–101st Congresses (1973–1991), earning a reputation for tenacity and Southern charm; had wide-ranging legislative interests, including equal opportunity for women and minorities, housing-policy issues, technological development, and Mississippi River

transportation; became the 1st woman to preside over a national political convention when she served as chair of the Democratic National Convention (1976); chaired the Commission on the Bicentenary of US House of Representatives for 3 terms and was a member of the Commission on the Bicentennial of US Constitution; was appointed US ambassador to the Vatican (1997). ❖ *See also* (with Katherine Hatch) *Washington Through a Purple Veil: Memoirs of a Southern Woman* (Harcourt, 1994); Cokie Roberts, *We Are Our Mothers' Daughters* (Morrow, 1998); and *Women in World History.*

BOGINSKAYA, Svetlana (1973—). Belarusian gymnast. Name variations: Svetlana Boguinskaia. Born Feb 9, 1973, in Minsk, Belarus, Soviet Union; m. William Yee. ❖ Won Hungarian International (1985), Riga (1987), European championship (1989, 1990), Moscow News (1989), World championship (1989), World Sports Fair (1989), Blume Memorial (1990, 1991), French International and Chunichi Cup (1990), DTB Cup and Gander Memorial (1992); while competing for Russia at Seoul Olympics, won a bronze medal in the all-around indiv., silver medal in floor exercises, team gold in all-around, and gold medal in vault (1988); competing for Unified Team in Barcelona Olympics (1992), won team gold in all-around; competing at Atlanta Olympics representing Belarus, placed a team 6th (1996).

BOGLE, Helen McDermott (1871–?). American kidnapper. Name variations: also seen as Helen Boyle. Born Helen McDermott in 1871 in US; death date unknown; m. James H. Bogle. ❖ With husband, was responsible for the kidnapping of Willie Whitla (Mar 18, 1909), 8-year-old son of wealthy attorney James P. Whitla of Sharon, PA (relation of steel tycoon Frank Buhl); after receiving $10,000 in ransom, released Willie (Mar 22) and was caught only hours later; along with husband, received a life sentence; was apparently the mastermind behind the plot.

BOGLE, Sarah C.N. (1870–1932). American librarian. Born Sarah Comly Norris Bogle in Milton, Pennsylvania, Nov 17, 1870; died in White Plains, NY, Jan 11, 1932; dau. of John Armstrong Bogle (chemical engineer) and Emma Ridgway (Norris) Bogle; attended University of Chicago; graduate of Drexel Institute, 1904. ❖ Leader in children's library work, library education, and international library service, became head of children's department at Carnegie Library of Pittsburgh (1911) and principal of the training school for children's librarians (which became Carnegie Library School); served as president of Association of American Library Schools (1917–18), assistant secretary of American Library Association (ALA, 1920–32), secretary to the ALA's Board of Education for Librarianship (1924–32), and director and primary fund raiser for Paris Library School (1923–29); active on many international library committees; elected to Library Hall of Fame (1951). The Sarah C.N. Bogle Memorial Fund of the ALA became the Bogle International Library Travel Fund (1982).

BÖGLI, Lina (1858–1941). Swiss travel writer. Name variations: Lina Bogli or Boegli. Born 1858 in Switzerland; died 1941. ❖ German-speaking Swiss writer, worked as maid in Italy and Poland and as teacher in England; wrote accounts of 2 round-the-world trips: *Forward* (in English, 1905) and *Immer Vörwarts* (in German, 1913); her 1st world voyage lasted 10 years.

BOGLIOLI, Wendy (1955—). American swimmer. Born Mar 1955. ❖ At Montreal Olympics, won a bronze medal in the 100-meter butterfly and a gold medal in the 4 x 100-meter freestyle relay (1976).

BOGOMOLOVA, Ludmilla (1932—). Russian ballet dancer. Name variations: Lyudmila or Ludmila Bogomolova. Born Mar 25, 1932, in Moscow, Russia. ❖ Trained at school of Bolshoi Ballet in Moscow, where she performed throughout her career and created numerous roles, including in Mikhail Lavrosky's *Pages of Life* (1961) and Alexander Lapauri's *Lieutenant Kijé* (1963); danced as Kitri in *Don Quixote,* title role in *Fadetta* and was featured in Asaf Messerer's *Spring Waters.*

BOGOMILOVA, Tanya (1964—). *See* Dangalakova-Bogomilova, Tanya.

BOGORAZ, Larisa (c. 1930–2004). Russian dissident. Born c. 1930 in USSR; died April 6, 2004, in Moscow, Russia; received doctorate in linguistics, 1965; m. Yuli Daniel (satirist and poet); m. Anatoly Marchenko (dissident, arrested 1980 and died in exile); children: (1st m.) Aleksandr Daniel (historian). ❖ Became active in human-rights issues after 1st husband was arrested for anti-Soviet essays (1965); stood in Red Square with 6 others to protest the Soviet invasion of Czechoslovakia (1968), the 1st public demonstration of the dissident era; sentenced to 4 years in Siberia; co-wrote the underground book *Memory,* chronicling Stalin's reign of terror; was a leading contributor to the underground publication, "Chronicle of Current Events," and campaigned to free all political prisoners.

BOGOSLOVSKAYA, Olga (1964—). Soviet runner. Born May 20, 1964, in USSR. ❖ At Barcelona Olympics, won a silver medal in the 4 x 100-meter relay (1992).

BOGUE, Mrs. Arthur Hoyt (1867–1929). See Bell, Lilian.

BOGUINSKAIA, Svetlana (1973—). See Boginskaya, Svetlana.

BOHEMIA, duchess of. See Hemma of Bohemia (c. 930–c. 1005).

BOHEMIA, queen of.
See Libussa (c. 680–738).
See Drahomira of Bohemia (d. after 932).
See Adelaide of Hungary (d. 1062).
See Cunigunde of Hohenstaufen (fl. 1215–1230).
See Constance of Hungary (d. 1240).
See Margaret of Babenberg (fl. 1252).
See Cunigunde of Hungary (d. 1285).
See Judith (1271–1297).
See Ryksa of Poland (1288–1335).
See Elizabeth of Poland (fl. 1298–1305).
See Elizabeth of Bohemia (1292–1339).
See Maria of Hungary (1371–1395).
See Sophia of Bavaria (fl. 1390s–1400s).
See Barbara of Cilli (fl. 1390–1410).
See Foix, Anne de (fl. 1400s).
See Madeleine (c. 1425–1486).
See Maria Anna of Bavaria (1574–1616).
See Elizabeth of Bohemia (1596–1662).
See Gonzaga, Eleonora I (1598–1655).
See Maria Anna of Spain (1606–1646).
See Gonzaga, Eleonora II (1628–1686).
See Maria Leopoldine (1632–1649).

BOHEMIA, regent of. See Ludmila (859–921).

BÖHL VON FABER, Cecilia (1796–1877). Spanish novelist. Name variations: Cecilia Böhl de Faber or Bohl de Faber, Madame de Arrom; Bohl; (pseudonym) Fernán Caballero. Born Cecilia Francisca Josefa Böhl von Faber in Morgues, Switzerland, Dec 25, 1796 (some sources cite 1797); died in Seville, Spain, April 7, 1877; educated in Germany. ❖ Considered the creator of the modern novel in Spanish literature, was 52 years old when her 1st novel *Mouette* (*The Sea-Gull*) was published under the pseudonym Fernán Caballero; was Spain's most renowned novelist of the 19th century until the Revolution of 1868 and the advent of realism; also wrote *A Summer Season at Bornos, Elia, Sola* (written in German and published anonymously in 1840), *Lágrimas* (*Tears*, 1850), *Clemencia* (1852), *Poor Dolores, Lucas Garcia, Un servilón y un liberalito* (*A Groveller and a Little Liberal*, 1855), and *La Familia Albareda* (*The Family of Alvareda*, 1880); short stories are collected under the titles *Cuadros de Costumbres* (*Tales of Customs*, 1862) and *Relaciones* (1857).

BÖHLAU, Helene (1859–1940). German author. Name variations: Bohlau or Boehlau. Born Helene Böhlau in Weimar, Germany, Nov 22, 1859; died in Widdersberg, Germany, Mar 28, 1940; dau. of Therese and Hermann Böhlau (publisher); educated privately; m. Friedrich Helwig Arnd, 1886 (died 1911); children: 1 son. ❖ Launched 1st book, a collection of novellas, at father's publishing house (1882); met with early success, though her popularity would wane with time; writings include *Rathsmädelgeschichten* (Stories of Councilors' Daughters, 1888), *Der Rangierbahnhof* (The Railway Junction, 1896), *Das Recht der Mutter* (The Right of the Mother, 1896) and *Halbtier!* (Half-animal!, 1899).

BOHLEY, Bärbel (1945—). German political activist. Born in Berlin, Germany, May 24, 1945. ❖ Known as the "Mother of the Revolution," was arrested and imprisoned on several occasions as a leading member of the East German opposition (1980s); was also appraised by the Stasi (secret police) in her file as the "mother of the underground"; was instrumental in the founding of the New Forum organization which focused the grievances of the population against the Communist regime of Erich Honecker (Sept 1989); believing that a radically reformed GDR could survive as an independent state, opposed German unification (though her organization New Forum played a major role in transforming East Germany [1989], it virtually disappeared in the 1st free elections [Mar 1990]); withdrew from politics with the achievement of German unity. ❖ See also *Women in World History*.

BOHM, Annett (1980—). See Boehm, Annett.

BOHM-SCHUCH, Clara (1879–1936). German political activist. Born Dec 5, 1879, in Stechow, Westhavelland; died as a result of mistreatment, May 6, 1936. ❖ Was active as a member of the Social Democratic Party of Germany and in humanitarian educational work; represented a Berlin district in the German Reichstag, serving with considerable distinction (Jan 1919–early 1933), until the Nazis seized power; having protested Nazi atrocities (1933), was arrested and harshly interrogated, which destroyed her health; writings include *Die Kinder im Weltkriege* (1916), *Willst Du mich hören? Weckruf an unsere Mädel* (1928) and (ed.) *Die Vorgeschichte des Weltkrieges* (vols. X–XI, 1930). ❖ See also *Women in World History*.

BOHMER, Caroline (1763–1809). See Schlegel-Schelling, Caroline.

BOHR, Margrethe (1890–1984). Danish wife of Niels Bohr. Born Margrethe Norlund in 1890 in Slagelse, Denmark; died 1984; dau. of a pharmacist; m. Niels Bohr (major force in the field of quantum physics), 1912 (died 1962); children: 6 sons, including Aage Bohr. ❖ Was studying French for a teacher's certificate, when she met Niels Bohr; acted for years as his assistant; was also his sounding board for many of his scientific ideas; after the Danish goverment moved family into a palatial mansion, officiated over the many receptions held for visiting scientists and dignitaries; during WWII, was concerned when the German physicist Werner Heisenberg came to Copenhagen to talk with her part-Jewish husband (1941); escaped to Sweden (1943). Portrayed in Michael Frayn's play, *Copenhagen.*

BOHRA, Katharina von (1499–1550). See Bora, Katharina von.

BOHUN, Alianore (d. 1313). Countess of Hereford and Essex. Died Feb 20, 1313; interred at Walden Abbey; dau. of Eleanor de Braose (fl. 1250s) and Humphrey Bohun (d. 1265), 6th earl of Hereford and Essex; m. Robert de Ferrers, earl of Derby, June 26, 1269; children: John (b. 1271), baron Ferrers of Chartley; Alianore de Ferrers (who m. Robert, 1st baron FitzWalter).

BOHUN, Eleanor (fl. 1327–1340). Countess of Ormonde. Name variations: Eleanor Butler; Eleanor Dagworth. Fl. between 1327 and 1340; dau. of Humphrey Bohun, 4th earl of Hereford, 3rd of Essex, and Elizabeth Plantagenet (1282–1316); m. James Butler (c. 1305–1338), 1st earl of Ormonde, in 1327; m. Thomas Dagworth, Lord Dagworth; children: (1st m.) James Butler (1330–1382), 2nd earl of Ormonde.

BOHUN, Eleanor (1366–1399). Duchess of Gloucester. Name variations: Eleanor de Bohun. Born 1366; died Oct 2, 1399; buried in Westminster Abbey, London; dau. of Humphrey Bohun, 7th earl of Hereford, Essex, and Northampton, and Joan Fitzalan (d. 1419); m. Thomas of Woodstock, 1st duke of Gloucester (r. 1356–1397), in 1374; children: Humphrey (c. 1382–1399); Anne Plantagenet (1383–1438); Joan (1384–1400); Isabel (1386–1402); Philippa (c. 1389–1399). ❖ Following murder of husband Thomas of Woodstock, entered a convent; appears in Shakespeare's *Richard II.*

BOHUN, Elizabeth (1282–1316). See Elizabeth Plantagenet.

BOHUN, Elizabeth (d. 1385). See Fitzalan, Elizabeth.

BOHUN, Joan (fl. 1325). See Fitzalan, Joan.

BOHUN, Joan (d. 1419). See Fitzalan, Joan.

BOHUN, Margaret (fl. 1330). See Courtenay, Margaret.

BOHUN, Mary (1369–1394). See Mary de Bohun.

BOHUN, Maud (fl. 1240s). Countess of Pembroke. Name variations: Maud de Bohun. Dau. of Maud of Lusignan (d. 1241) and Humphrey Bohun (1200–1275), 2nd earl of Hereford, 1st of Essex (r. 1220–1275), and constable of England (some sources cite him as 6th earl of Hereford and Essex); m. Anselme Marshall (d. 1245), 6th earl of Pembroke (some sources cite 9th earl of Pembroke); m. Roger de Quincy, 2nd earl of Winchester, after 1245.

BOHUN, Maud (fl. 1275). Countess of Hereford and Essex. Name variations: Maud de Fiennes; Maud de Bohun. Flourished in 1275 before 1298; interred at Walden; dau. of Enguerrand II de Fiennes (d. 1270) and a dau. of Jacques de Condé; m. Humphrey Bohun, 3rd earl of Hereford, 2nd of Essex (some sources cite 7th earl of Hereford and Essex), in 1275; children: Humphrey Bohun (1276–1321), 4th earl of Hereford, 3rd of Essex.

BOHUSZ, Cicely (b. 1918). See Saunders, Cicely.

BOHUSZEWICZOWNA, Maria (1865–1887). Polish revolutionary. Born into a family of impoverished nobles, Jan 4, 1865, in Cepercach near Slutsk, Poland; died in Russia en route to her designated place of exile in Siberia in 1887; grandniece of Tadeusz Kosciuszko; trained to be a teacher. ❖ Key member of the generation of "Socialist martyrs," whose organization was destroyed by the tsarist-occupation authorities; was among the founding members, at 17, of a group of Marxists who formed the 1st modern revolutionary party in Warsaw (1882); became director of the organization's welfare section, named "Red Cross" to render assistance to the families of imprisoned members; took over the leadership of the organization (Aug 1884); was arrested (Sept 30, 1885) and endured more than a year of interrogations by Russian police officials; sentenced to banishment in Siberia, left Warsaw in police custody (May 12, 1887), but died several weeks later en route to Siberia. ❖ See also *Women in World History.*

BOIARDI, Helen (1905–1995). Italian-American businesswoman. Born 1905 in Italy; died in Shaker Heights, Ohio, July 1995; m. Hector Boiardi (1898–1985); children: Mario. ❖ With husband, arrived in US as an immigrant, then ran a successful Italian restaurant in the financial district of Cleveland, Ohio; went into the packaged-food business (1928), calling the new company Chef Boiardi, then changed the name to the phonetic "Chef Boyardee." ❖ See also *Women in World History.*

BOISMORTIER, Suzanne Bodin de (c. 1722–?). *See Bodin de Boismortier, Suzanne.*

BOISSEVAIN, Inez M. (1886–1916). American suffrage leader and lawyer. Born Inez Milholland, Aug 6, 1886; died in Los Angeles, California, Nov 25, 1916; graduate of Vassar College, 1909; attended law school at New York University; m. Eugene Boissevain (Dutch electrical engineer), 1913. ❖ As a speaker and organizer, was invaluable to the Woman's Party (1912–15); overtaken by illness during a speaking tour, died at age 30.

BOISSEVAIN, Mia (1878–1959). Dutch feminist. Name variations: Maria. Pronunciation: Bwha-se-VAY. Born Maria Boissevain, April 8, 1878, in Amsterdam, the Netherlands; died Mar 8, 1959, in London, England; dau. of Jan Boissevain (director of a shipping company) and Petronella Brugmans; University of Amsterdam, MA in biology; University of Zurich, PhD, 1903; never married; children: 2 (adopted). ❖ With Rosa Manus, organized a major exhibition on the status of women (1913), was an advocate of women's suffrage, women's rights and the worldwide peace movement, and worked to aid war refugees; active in the International Woman Suffrage Alliance from 1908, organized an exhibition on the position of women, entitled "Woman 1813–1913"; was a member of the women's committee (and the general committee) to help mobilized families during WWI. Writings include *The Women's Movement in the Netherlands* (1915), and *Een Amsterdamsche familie* (1967). ❖ See also *Women in World History.*

BOIT, Elizabeth Eaton (1849–1932). American manufacturer. Born July 9, 1849, in Newton, Massachusetts; died Nov 14, 1932; dau. of James Henry Boit (stationary engineer) and Amanda Church (Berry) Boit. ❖ Established partnership with Charles N. Winship (1888) and founded the Harvard Knitting Mill, the 5th largest knitting mill in Massachusetts (1909–10); turned her interest in the Mill over to Winship (late 1920s); was known for generosity to charities in Wakefield.

BOIVIN, Marie Anne (1773–1847). French midwife. Born Marie Anne Victoire Gillain in Montreuil, France, 1773; died 1847 (some sources cite 1841); educated by nuns; married in 1797. ❖ Spent 3 years in study of anatomy; widowed with a baby daughter, undertook the study of midwifery at La Maternité Hospital, as an assistant to Marie Lachapelle; appointed chief superintendent of the institution (1801); received an order of civil merit and degree of MD; published *Mémorial de l'art des accouchements* (1824), which went through many editions. ❖ See also *Women in World History.*

BOIZOT, Marie (1748–?). French painter. Born Marie Louise Adelaide Boizot in Paris, France, in 1748; death date unknown. ❖ Studied with J.J. Flipart and "engraved with neatness" both portraits and other subjects.

BOK, Mary Louise Curtis (1876–1970). *See Zimbalist, Mary Louise Curtis.*

BOKEL, Claudia (1973—). German fencer. Born Aug 30, 1973, in Ter Apel, Netherlands. ❖ Won a silver medal for épée team at Athens Olympics (2004); at World championships, placed 1st for indiv. épée (2001) and 2nd for team épée (1993, 1997, 2003).

BOLAND, Bridget (1904–1988). British playwright and screenwriter. Born Mar 13, 1913, in London, England; died Jan 19, 1988. ❖ Wrote the screenplay for *Gaslight* (1940) and screen adaptations for *The Prisoner* (1955), *War and Peace* (1956) and *Anne of the Thousand Days* (1969), for which she won a Golden Globe and was nominated for an Academy Award; wrote the play *Cockpit,* which was filmed as *The Lost People* (1949).

BOLAND, Eavan (1944—). Irish poet and essayist. Born Eavan Aisling Boland, Sept 24, 1944, in Dublin, Ireland; dau. of Frederick Boland and Frances Kelly Boland; graduate of Trinity College; m. Kevin Casey, 1969. ❖ Taught at Trinity College, Bowdoin College, University College, and Stanford University; was a reviewer for *Irish Times;* collections of poetry include *The War Horse* (1975), *In Her Own Image* (1980), *Night Feed* (1982), *The Journey* (1987), *Outside History* (1990), *The Lost Land* (1998) and *Against Love Poems* (2001); also published essays on Irish literature and *A Kind of Star: The Woman Poet in a National Tradition* (1989).

BOLAND, Mary (1880–1965). American actress. Born in Philadelphia, Pennsylvania, Jan 28, 1880; died June 1965; dau. of W.A. Boland (actor from Detroit); attended Sacred Heart Convent school in Detroit. ❖ Made debut in Detroit (1901), as Eleanor Burnham in *A Social Highwayman,* and played in various stock companies while still a teen; made Broadway debut (1905), as Dorothy Nelson in *Strongheart;* though she began as a tragedian, was at her best portraying madcap wives and mothers on stage (1920s) and in films (1930s); on stage, portrayed the stepmother in *Clarence* (1919), the flighty matron in *The Vinegar Tree* (1930) and the domineering mother in *Lullaby* (1954); on film, appeared opposite Charlie Ruggles in *Ruggles of Red Gap* (1935), as well as in *Trouble in Paradise* (1932), *If I had a Million* (1932), *Here Comes the Groom* (1934), *People Will Talk* (1935), *The Big Broadcast of 1936* (1935), *The Women* (1939), *Pride and Prejudice* (1940), *In Our Time* (1944), *Julia Misbehaves* (1948) and *Guilty Bystander* (1950). ❖ See also *Women in World History.*

BOLAND, Veronica Grace (1899–1982). American politician. Born in Scranton, Pennsylvania, Mar 18, 1899; died in Scranton, June 19, 1982; m. Patrick J. Boland (Congressman 1931–1942). ❖ Running as the unopposed Democratic candidate in a special election (Nov 3, 1942), completed the term of her late husband Patrick J. Boland who had been majority whip of the House of Representatives.

BOLANOS, Raisa O'Farrill (1972—). *See O'Farrill, Raisa.*

BOLDEN, Jeanette (1960—). African-American runner. Born Jan 26, 1960, in Los Angeles, California. ❖ Held 5 indoor American records and 7 indoor records at various distances; won Olympic gold medal for the 4 x 100-meter relay in Los Angeles (1984).

BOLDUC, Marie (1894–1941). French-Canadian singer and musician. Name variations: La Bolduc; Mary Travers. Born Marie or Mary-Rose-Anne Travers in Newport, Gaspésie, Quebec, Canada, June 4, 1894; died in Montreal, Quebec, Feb 20, 1941; m. Édouard Bolduc (plumber), 1914. ❖ Considered Canada's 1st great *chansonnière,* left home at 13 to earn a living in Montreal (1907); an excellent musician, equally adept at playing an accordion, harmonica, violin and the Jew's harp, began to perform professionally (1927); composed more than 80 songs to address the concerns of working people and made many recordings (1930s), including "La Cuisinière," "La Servante," "Le Commerçant des rues," "L'Enfant volé," "Les Cinq Jumelles," "Les Colons canadiens," "La Grocerie du coin," "Les Agents d'assurance" and "Les Conducteurs de chars." Canadian postage stamp issued to commemorate the centenary of her birth (1994). ❖ See also (in French) Réal Benoit, *La Bolduc* (Les Éditions de l'Homme, 1959); Pierre Day, *Une histoire de la Bolduc* (VLB éditeur, 1991); David Lonergan, *La Bolduc: La vie de Mary Travers* (Isaac-Dion éditeur, 1992); and *Women in World History.*

BOLEN, Lin (1941—). American television executive. Born 1941 in Benton, Illinois; attended City College of New York. ❖ After producing tv commercials, was hired by NBC's prime-time programming department in Los Angeles (1972); became head of the network's daytime programming in NY, the highest-ranking position then held by a woman at any network (during her tenure, NBC reached number one in daytime programming ratings for 1st time); left NBC and formed Lin Bolen Productions (1976); joined Fred Silverman's InterMedia Entertainment (1982), as head of creative affairs. Faye Dunaway's character of Diana Christensen in film *Network* is thought to have been modeled on Bolen.

BOLENA, Anna (1507–1536). *See Boleyn, Anne.*

BOLEY, May (1881–1963). American actress. Born May 29, 1881, in Washington, DC; died Jan 7, 1963, in Hollywood, California. ❖ Made stage debut in Victor Herbert's *The Singing Girl* (1900); other credits include *Ziegfeld Follies of 1913, Why Worry?* and *Jubilee;* best remembered for her performance in *Hit the Deck* (1926).

BOLEYN, Anne (c. 1507–1536). Queen of England. Name variations: Nan Bullen; Anne of the Thousand Days. Born 1507 (some sources cite 1501) in England; executed May 19, 1536, in London; dau. of Thomas Boleyn, earl of Wiltshire (diplomat and courtier) and Elizabeth Howard (dau. of earl of Surrey); m. Henry VIII, king of England, Jan 25, 1533; children: Elizabeth (1533–1603, later Elizabeth I, queen of England); Henry Tudor, duke of Cornwall (1534–1534), and an unnamed baby (1536–1536). ❖ Precipitated the English Reformation and gave birth to England's most famous queen, Elizabeth I; appointed lady-in-waiting to Catherine of Aragon (1526); beloved by Henry VIII (1527); became Henry's mistress (1532); crowned queen of England (1533); miscarried male child (Jan 1536); accused of adultery and treason (May 1536). ❖ See also E.W. Ives, *Anne Boleyn* (Basil Blackwell, 1986); Retha Warnicke, *The Rise and Fall of Anne Boleyn* (Cambridge U. Press, 1989); film *Anne of the Thousand Days,* starring Genevieve Bujold (1969); and *Women in World History.*

BOLEYN, Mary (d. 1543). Sister of Anne Boleyn. Name variations: Mary Carey; Mary Stafford. Died July 19, 1543; dau. of Thomas Boleyn, earl of Wiltshire, and Elizabeth Howard; m. William Carey (gentleman of the privvy), Jan 31, 1521; m. William Stafford; children: (1st m.) Henry Carey (c. 1524–1596), 1st baron Hunsdon; Catherine Carey (1529–1569, who was chief lady of the bedchamber).

BOLGER, Deirdre (1938—). Irish politician. Born July 27, 1938, in Dublin, Ireland; m. David F. Bolger; children: 5 sons. ❖ Representing Fine Gael, elected to the Seanad from the Industrial and Commercial Panel: Nominating Bodies Sub-Panel (1981–82) and from the Oireachtas Sub-Panel (1982–83).

BOLHUIS-EYSVOGEL, Marjolein (1961—). Dutch field-hockey player. Name variations: Marjolein Eysvogel. Born June 16, 1961. ❖ Won an Olympic gold medal in team competition at Los Angeles (1984) and a bronze medal in Seoul (1988).

BOLKAN, Florinda (1941—). Brazilian-Italian actress. Born Florinda Soares Bulcao, Feb 15, 1941, in Ceara, Brazil; dau. of José Pedro Bulcao (poet and congressional representative) and Maria Hosana Bulcao (part Indian). ❖ Made screen debut in *Candy e il suo pazzo mondo* (1968); other films include *Investigation of a Citizen Above Suspicion, The Last Valley, Hearts and Minds, Love at the Top, The Devil's Bed, Terrore, Royal Flash, Assassination in Sarajevo, Manaos, Some Girls, Prisoner of Rio, La Gabbia, L'Enigma di un Giorno, Sisters* and *Bella Donna;* appeared as the prostitute in Luchino Visconti's *The Damned* (1969) and the working wife in Vittorio de Sica's *Une breve vacanza (A Brief Vacation)* (1973); directed *Eu nao conhecia Tururu (I Didn't Know Tururu)* (2000); made stage debut in *Metti una sera a cena* (1984), followed by *Uncle Vania;* starred in the Italian tv series "La piovra." Won Donatello awards (Italian oscar) for *Metti una sera a cena (One Night at Dinner), Anonimo Veneziano (The Anonymous Venetian),* and *Dear Parents;* received Best Actress award from Los Angeles Film Critics for *A Brief Vacation.*

BOLLAND, Adrienne (1895–1975). French aviator. Born Nov 25, 1895 in Arcueil, France; died 1975. ❖ Pioneer aviator, was a test pilot for Caudron, the French aircraft maker; became the 1st woman to fly over the Andes in Argentina (1921), having to avoid mountain peaks that were higher than her plane could fly.

BOLLIN, Caroline Cadette (1821–?). *See Howard, Caroline Cadette.*

BOLLINGER, Anne (c. 1923–1962). American soprano. Born c. 1923 in Lewiston, Iowa; died July 11, 1962, age 39, in Zurich, Switzerland; m. Jack T. Nielsen. ❖ Made debut at the Metropolitan Opera in *Carmen* (1949) and remained there until 1935; made many guest appearances in Europe.

BOLLMANN, Minna (1876–1935). German politician. Born Minna Zacharias, Jan 31, 1876, in Halberstadt, Saxony, Germany; committed suicide in Halberstadt, Dec 9, 1935; married; children: Otto Bollmann (anti-Nazi activist, died 1951). ❖ Social Democratic Reichstag and Landtag deputy who represented her working-class constituents throughout the troubled history of the Weimar Republic; representing the Magdeburg-Anhalt electoral district, won a seat in the Reichstag (Jan 1919), serving until June 1920; ran successfully on Social Democratic ticket for a seat in the Prussian Landtag (Provincial Assembly), serving from 1921 until 1933; with the onset of the Nazi dictatorship and the outlawing of the Social Democratic movement in Germany (1933), lost legislative seat and was interrogated on several occasions by Gestapo agents. ❖ See also *Women in World History.*

BOL POEL, Martha (1877–1956). Belgian feminist. Name variations: Baroness Bol Poel. Born Martha De Kerchove de Deuterghem in Ghent, Belgium, in 1877; died 1956; dau. of a distinguished Ghent family; attended Kerchove Institute, founded by her grandfather; studied painting at Académie Julien, Paris, 1895; m. Bol Poel (industrialist and politician), 1898. ❖ Established a maternity center at husband's metal works at La Louvrière, the 1st of its kind; during German occupation of Belgium in WWI, organized a secret correspondence service which led to her imprisonment; while incarcerated, became seriously ill and was exchanged for another prisoner (1917), whereupon she went into exile in Switzerland; resurfaced (1920s) as a leading figure in the Belgian women's movement, serving as president of the National Council of Women (1934) and of the International Council of Women (1935–40); after German invasion of Belgium (1940), again became active in underground; following WWII, resumed activities with the International Council of Women.

BOLT, Carol (1941–2000). Canadian playwright. Born Carol Johnson, Aug 25, 1941, in Winnipeg, Canada; grew up in Vancouver; died Nov 28, 2000, in Toronto, Ontario; University of British Columbia, BA, 1961; m. David Bolt; children: 1. ❖ Created plays in Toronto for Theatre Passe Muraille and Toronto Workshop Productions; was a founding member of Playwrights Co-op; also wrote for film, radio and tv; works include *Buffalo Jump* (1972), *Gabe* (1973), *Red Emma: Queen of the Anarchists* (1973), *Shelter* (1975), *One Night Stand* (1977) and *Escape Entertainment* (1981); children's plays include *My Best Friend is Twelve Feet High* (1972), *Cyclone Jack* (1972), *Tangleflags* (1973), *Maurice* (1974) and *Finding Bumble* (1975).

BOLTE, Amely (1811–1891). German novelist. Name variations: Amely Bölte or Boelte; Amely Charlotte Elise Marianne Bölte. Born Oct 6, 1811, in Rhena, Mecklenburg, Germany; died Nov 15, 1891, in Wiesbaden; niece of Fanny Tarnow. ❖ Worked as governess in Germany and then as translator in England, where she wrote novels in the vein of Charlotte Brontë; returned to Germany and wrote biographies and historical novels; worked on behalf of unemployed women.

BOLTON, Frances Payne (1885–1977). American politician. Born Frances Payne Bingham in Cleveland, Ohio, Mar 29, 1885; died in Lyndhurst, Ohio, Mar 9, 1977; dau. of Charles William and Mary Perry (Payne) Bingham; m. Chester Castle Bolton (US congressional representative, 1929–1937, and 1939), Sept 14, 1907; children: Charles Bingham, Kenyon Castle, and Oliver Payne Bolton (US congressional representative). ❖ Because of her lifelong interest in nursing and public health, established the Payne Fund, through which she made philanthropic donations; endowed a nursing school at Cleveland's Western Reserve University (1923); served as vice chair of Republican national program committee and as a member of the Republican Central Committee of Ohio; running for the seat left vacant by the death of her husband (1939), became the 1st congresswoman to be elected from Ohio; entered Congress as an isolationist and a critic of Roosevelt's New Deal; voted against the Lend-Lease program; gained national attention by opposing the conscription policies of the selective service bill (1941); once the US entered the war, strongly supported the military effort; during 2nd term, sat on the Committee on Foreign Affairs, a post she would hold throughout congressional career; voted for creation of the Women's Auxiliary Army Corps (1942) and authored the Bolton Act of 1943, which created the US Cadet Nurse Corps; headed up a tour of the Middle East, Soviet Union and Poland (1947), the 1st woman to lead a congressional mission; appointed to the advisory committee of Foreign Service Institute (1949); appointed US delegate to UN General Assembly (1950s); by 1960, was the longest-serving woman sitting in US House of Representatives (76th–90th Congresses, Feb 27, 1940–Jan 3, 1969) and a ranking Republican on Foreign Affairs. ❖ See also David Loth, *A Long Way Forward: The Biography of Congresswoman Frances P. Bolton* (Longmans, 1957); and *Women in World History.*

BOLTON, Mildred Mary (1886–1943). American murderer. Born 1886; died Aug 29, 1943, in women's penitentiary in Dwight, Illinois; m. Charles Bolton (businessman), 1922. ❖ Fired revolver at husband in his office and he died of his injuries within hours (June 15, 1936); received death sentence which was converted to 199 years without parole; served less than 10, committing suicide at women's penitentiary at Dwight by cutting her wrists.

BOLTON, Ruthie (1967—). African-American basketball player. Name variations: Ruthie Bolton-Holifield. Born Alice Ruth Bolton, May 25, 1967, in Lucedale, Mississippi; one of 20 children of Reverend Linwood and Leola Bolton; graduate of Auburn University with a degree in Exercise Physiology, 1989; m. Mark Holifield, 1991. ❖ Guard; selected to Southeastern Conference (SEC) All-Academic Teams (1988–89); won 3 SEC championships; named to NCAA Mideast Region All-Tournament Teams (1988–89) and NCAA Final Four All-Tournament Team (1988); made 4 NCAA Tournament appearances and advanced to NCAA championship game twice (1989, 1990); won a gold medal with World University team (1991), a bronze with the World Championship team (1994) and a gold with the Goodwill team (1994); played professionally with Visby in Sweden (1989–90), Tungstrum in Hungary (1991–92), Erreti Faenz in Italy (1992–95), and Galatsaray in Turkey (1996–97); won a team gold medal at Atlanta Olympics (1996) and at Sydney Olympics (2000); signed with WNBA to play for the Sacramento Monarchs (1997). Named USA Basketball Female Player of the Year (1991); 2-time WNBA All-Star.

BOLTON, Sarah Knowles (1841–1916). American writer. Born Sept 15, 1841, in Farmington, Connecticut; died Feb 21, 1916, in Cleveland, Ohio; dau. of John S. Knowles; graduate of Hartford Female Seminary, 1860; m. Charles E. Bolton, 1866; children: Charles Knowles Bloton (b. 1872). ❖ Active in temperance and reform movements, taught school in Natchez, Mississippi, until outbreak of Civil War; was associate editor of *Congregationalist* (1878–81); wrote numerous poems, children's books and biographical sketches (1864–1902).

BOLTON, Sarah T. (1814–1893). American poet. Name variations: Sarah Tittle Barrett Bolton; Sarah Reese. Born Sarah Tittle Barrett, Dec 18, 1814, in Newport, Kentucky; died Aug 4, 1893; dau. of Esther (Pendleton) Barrett and Jonathan Belcher Barrett; m. Nathaniel Bolton (editor), Oct 15, 1831; m. Addison Reese (judge), Sept. 15, 1863; children: 2. ❖ At 13, published 1st verse in Indiana's *Madison Banner;* considered for many years the unofficial Hoosier laureate, published poetry primarily in newspapers and magazines; an early leader for the legal rights of women, also wrote many articles on the subject; collected works include *Poems* (1865), *The Life and Poems of Sarah T. Bolton* (1880) and *Songs of a Life-Time* (1892).

BOMBAL, María Luisa (1910–1980). Chilean writer. Born María Luisa Bombal in Viña del Mar, Chile, June 8, 1910; died in Chile, May 6, 1980; educated at French boarding schools; graduate of Sorbonne, 1931; m. Count Raphael de Saint-Phalle (French financier), c. 1945 (died 1970); no children. ❖ Author of early Latin American feminist fiction in the style of magical realism, went to France at 12; returning briefly to Chile, received an invitation to Buenos Aires, where she wrote *La ultima niebla* (*The Final Mist*) at Pablo Neruda's kitchen table; moved to Argentina to work on scripts for Sonofilm and sold movie rights to her 2nd novel, *La amortajada* (*The Shrouded Woman*); during a domestic dispute (1940), shot and severely wounded her lover, political activist Eulogio Sánchez Errazuriz; banished from Chile, settled in New York; published *El Canciller* (*The Foreign Minister*, 1946), but grew progressively more dependent on alcohol. ❖ See also *Women in World History.*

BOMBECK, Erma (1927–1996). American humor columnist and author. Born Erma Louise Fiste, Feb 21, 1927, in Dayton, Ohio; died April 22, 1996, in San Francisco, California; dau. of Cassius and Erma (Haines) Fiste; University of Dayton, BA, 1949; m. William L. Bombeck, Aug 13, 1949; children: Betsy, Matthew and Andrew. ❖ With her syndicated column "At Wit's End," a string of best-selling books, and 11 years as a correspondent on ABC's "Good Morning America," was known for almost 30 years as a wisecracking champion of the suburban housewife; writings include *The Grass Is Always Greener over the Septic Tank* (1976), *If Life Is a Bowl of Cherries, What Am I Doing in the Pits?* (1978), *Aunt Erma's Cope Book* (1979), *Motherhood: The Second Oldest Profession* (1984), *I Want to Grow Hair, I Want to Grow Up, I Want to Go to Boise* (1989), *A Marriage Made in Heaven—or, Too Tired for an Affair* (1993) and *All I Know About Animal Behavior I Learned in*

Loehmann's Dressing Room (1995). ❖ See also *Women in World History.*

BOMPARD, Gabrielle (1869–?). French murderer. Born 1869 in France. ❖ With lover Michel Eyraud, murdered a court bailiff named Toussaint-Augustin Gouffé (1889); traveled through Marseilles, London, NY, Canada and San Francisco, was arrested on her return to Paris; tried for murder with Eyraud and found guilty; sentenced to 20 years' hard labor (Feb 1891), while Eyraud was guillotined.

BONA. *Variant of Bonna.*

BONACCI BRUNAMONTI, Maria Alinda (1841–1903). Italian poet and watercolorist. Name variations: Alinda Bonacci-Brunamonti. Born Aug 21, 1841, in Perugia, Italy; died Feb 3, 1903, in Perugia; dau. of Gratiliano Bonacci; m. Pietro Brunamonti. ❖ Encouraged by father to write; befriended and corresponded with important writers and artists; started herbarium and made watercolor paintings of flowers and herbs found in Umbria; paintings collected as *Flora Umbra* (c. 1888); works include *Canti* (1856), *Canti nazionali* (1860), *Versi* (1875), *L'ultimo sonno—la seconda vita* (1876), *Nuovi canti* (1887) and *Ricordi di viaggio* (1907); also published work of art criticism *Discorsi d'arte* (1898).

BONAFINI, Hebe de (1928—). Argentinean political activist. Name variations: Hebe María Pastor, Kika Pastor. Born Hebe María Pastor, Dec 4, 1928, in La Plata, Buenos Aires, Argentina; m. Humberto Bonafini (or Toto), Nov 9, 1949 (died 1982); children: several. ❖ After disappearance of politically active son Raúl (1977), began making trips to army regiment in Palermo to try to locate him; met other mothers searching for answers from government about their lost children and with them formed the Mothers of the Plaza de Mayo (1977), which conducted marches and other activities to bring international attention to the disappeared; served as president of Mothers of the Plaza de Mayo, traveled internationally to meet with government officials, and received many awards from numerous countries for her human-rights work.

BONALY, Surya (1973—). French figure skater. Born Dec 15, 1973, in Nice, France; adopted dau. of Suzanne and George Bonaly. ❖ Made the French team at 12; placed 1st in French nationals (1989–97), at Trophee Lalique (1989, 1990, 1992, 1993), at European championships (1991, 1992, 1993, 1994, 1995), at Skate Canada (1991) and Skate America International (1994); placed 2nd at World championships (1993, 1994); turned pro and began appearing with Champions on Ice (1993).

BONANNI, Laudomia (1907–2002). Italian novelist and short-story writer. Born 1907 in L'Aquila, Abruzzes, Italy; died in 2002 in Rome, Italy. ❖ Wrote for Italian newspapers and magazines, often about children's issues and cases in juvenile courts; writings include *Il fosso* (1949), *Palma e sorelle* (1955), *L'adultera* (1964), *Vietato ai minori* (1974), *Il bambino di pietra: Una nevrosi femminile* (1979) and *Le droghe* (1982). Won the Prix Viareggio for her novel *L'imputata* (1960).

BONANNI, Pearl (1967—). *See Sinn, Pearl.*

BONA OF BOHEMIA (1315–1349). Bohemian princess. Name variations: Bonne de Luxemburg; Judith de Luxembourg or Judith of Luxemburg. Born 1315; died of the plague in 1349; dau. of Elizabeth of Bohemia (1292–1339) and John I of Luxemburg also known as John of Bohemia, king of Bohemia (r. 1310–1346); sister of Charles IV Luxemburg, Holy Roman emperor (r. 1347–1378), and John Henry, margrave of Moravia (d. 1375); became 1st wife of John II the Good (1319–1364), king of France (r. 1350–1364), July 28, 1332; children: Charles V the Wise (1338–1380), king of France (r. 1364–1380, who m. Jeanne de Bourbon); Jane of France (1343–1373); Marie of France (1344–1404); Agnes (1345–1349); Margaret (1347–1352); Isabelle of France (1349–1372); Philip the Bold (1342–1404), duke of Burgundy (who m. Margaret of Flanders [1350–1405]); John of Berri; Louis I (1339–1384), duke of Anjou. King John II's 2nd wife was Blanche of Boulogne (1326–1360).

BONA OF PISA (c. 1156–1207). Italian saint. Name variations: Bonna of Pisa. Born in Pisa about 1156; died May 29, 1207; buried in the church of San Martino in Pisa. ❖ Reportedly, throughout childhood was blessed with visions; returning from a pilgrimage to Jerusalem, met a hermit who encouraged her to undertake the task of converting the Saracens, but the Saracens had her imprisoned; upon her release, continued her pilgrimages to sacred places, including Santiago de Compostela and tomb of St. Peter in Rome; declared patron saint of flight attendants because of her frequent travels. Feast day is May 29. ❖ See also *Women in World History*.

BONA OF SAVOY (c. 1450–c. 1505). Duchess of Milan. Name variations: Bona di Savoia; Bona Sforza. Born c. 1450 in Savoy; died c. 1505 in Italy; dau. of Louis, duke of Savoy, and Anne of Lusignan; sister of Charlotte of Savoy (c. 1442–1483), queen of France; m. Galeazzo Maria Sforza (1444–1476), 5th duke of Milan (r. 1466–1476); children: Gian Galeazzo Sforza (1469–1494), 6th duke of Milan (r. 1476–1479); Ermes (1470–after 1502); Bianca Maria Sforza (1472–1510), Holy Roman empress; and Anna Sforza (1473–1497); (stepchildren) Carlo (b. 1461); Caterina Sforza (c. 1462–1509); Chiara Sforza (b. around 1464); and Alessandro. ❖ Born into ducal house of Savoy, married Galeazzo Maria Sforza and moved to Milanese court (1468); known to be a loving mother to son Gian Galeazzo and daughters Bianca Maria and Anna, was said to have loved her stepchildren as well; had been married for 8 years when Galeazzo was murdered by political foes (1476); named regent of Milan for young son Gian Galeazzo; had moderately successful years of governing, given the chaotic and warlike condition of Italian politics at the time; fell in love with Antonio Tassino (1480), who was beneath her socially, and the Milanese people disapproved of their relationship; eventually lost the support of the Milanese by maintaining the connection; usurped by the Italian noble Ludovic Sforza, "Il Moro" (1480); forced to retire to France. ❖ See also *Women in World History*.

BONAPARTE, Alexandrine Jouberthon (1778–1855). Second wife of Lucien Bonaparte. Name variations: Madame de Bleschamps. Born Alexandrine Bleschamps in 1778; died 1855; dau. of a lawyer; daughter-in-law of Letizia Bonaparte (1750–1836); sister-in-law of Napoleon I, emperor of France (r. 1804–1815); m. Jean-François-Hippolyte Jouberthon, around 1797 (died); became 2nd wife of Lucien Bonaparte, in May 1803 (he was 1st m. to Christine (Boyer) Bonaparte [1773–1800]); children: (1st m.) 2; (2nd m.) Charles or Carlo, prince of Canino; Laetitia; Jeanne; Paul; Lucien; Pierre; Antoine; Marie; Constance; and one who died in infancy. ❖ See also *Women in World History*.

BONAPARTE, Carlotta (1780–1825). See Bonaparte, Pauline.

BONAPARTE, Carolina (1782–1839). Queen of Naples. Name variations: Caroline Murat; Countess Lipona, Countess of Lipona. Born Maria Annunciata or Maria-Nunziata Caroline at Ajaccio, Corsica, Mar 25, 1782; died of stomach cancer in Florence, Italy, May 18, 1839; dau. of Letizia Bonaparte (1750–1836) and Carlo Bonaparte (Corsican lawyer); youngest sister of Napoleon I, emperor of France (r. 1804–1815); m. Joachim Murat, king of Naples, in 1800 (died); m. Francesco Macdonald; children: (1st m.) Napoléon Murat; Laetitia Murat; Lucien Murat; Louise Murat. ❖ As ambitious as brother Napoleon, became queen of Naples (1808); encouraged husband to betray Napoleon (1814), which led ultimately to husband's defeat and execution (1815); renamed herself Countess of Lipona and took refuge with children in Trieste; secretly married Francesco Macdonald, a soldier formerly in Napoleon's service (1816). ❖ See also *Women in World History*.

BONAPARTE, Christine (1773–1800). First wife of Lucien Bonaparte. Name variations: Christine-Eléonore; Catherine Boyer. Born Christine Boyer in 1773; died in childbirth in 1800; dau. of Pierre-André and Rosalie (Fabre) Boyer; became 1st wife of Lucien Bonaparte (1775–1840), May 4, 1794; daughter-in-law of Letizia Bonaparte (1750–1836); sister-in-law of Napoleon I, emperor of France (r. 1804–1815); children: Charlotte Bonaparte; Christine Bonaparte; and two who died in infancy. ❖ Was the illiterate sister of an innkeeper with whom Lucien Bonaparte had lodged. ❖ See also *Women in World History*.

BONAPARTE, Elisa (1777–1820). Grand duchess of Tuscany and princess of Piombino. Name variations: changed name from Marie Anna to Elisa after marriage; Elisa Lucca; Elisa Bacciochi, Marie Anna Bonaparte; Contessa di Compignano. Born Marie Anna at Ajaccio, Corsica, Jan 3, 1777; died near Trieste, Aug 7, 1820; dau. of Letizia Bonaparte (1750–1836) and Carlo Bonaparte (Corsican lawyer); eldest sister of Napoleon I, emperor of France (r. 1804–1815); m. Felice Pasquale Bacciochi, May 1, 1797; children: Jérôme; Frederic; Napoléon; Elisa Baccioci. ❖ Disliked by brother Napoleon, was made princess of Lucca where she became a successful and respected sovereign; became princess of Piombino (1806) and grand duchess of Tuscany (1809); intellectual and ambitious, was known to surround herself with interesting, intelligent people; had a number of affairs, including one

with violinist Paganini, whom she appointed court musician. ❖ See also *Women in World History*.

BONAPARTE, Elizabeth Patterson (1785–1879). American socialite who married into the family Bonaparte. Name variations: Betsy Patterson; Elizabeth Patterson; Elizabeth Bonaparte-Patterson; Madame Patterson. Born Elizabeth Patterson in Baltimore, Maryland, Feb 6, 1785; died in Baltimore, April 4, 1879; dau. of William Patterson (president of Baltimore's largest bank); daughter-in-law of Letizia Bonaparte (1750–1836); sister-in-law of Napoleon I, emperor of France (r. 1804–1815); m. Jérôme Bonaparte (1784–1860), king of Westphalia, in Baltimore, Dec 24, 1803 (div. 1813); children: Jerome ("Bo," b. July 7, 1805), from whom the American Bonapartes descended. ❖ The belle of Baltimore, met 19-year-old Jérôme Bonaparte, younger brother of Napoleon, on his visit to US (1803); though he was underage and forbidden to marry without consent, married him within a month of the meeting; with husband, set sail for Lisbon but was not permitted to land; traveling on to England, gave birth to son (July 7, 1805); granted annual pension of $12,000 by Napoleon who arranged for a nullification of the marriage (Oct 1806), despite protests from the pope; eventually returned to Baltimore and was granted a divorce by Maryland legislature (1813), but refused to drop name Bonaparte; returned to Europe (1815), where she was admired for her wit and beauty, and courted by many important men of the day, including Arthur Wellesley, Duke of Wellington; though reunited with the Bonaparte family and her son was finally declared legitimate, saw Jérôme only once more; returned to Baltimore (1861), where she lived in obscurity until her death. ❖ See also *Women in World History*.

BONAPARTE, Hortense de Beauharnais (1783–1837). *See Hortense de Beauharnais.*

BONAPARTE, Josephine (1763–1814). *See Josephine.*

BONAPARTE, Julie Clary (1771–1845). Queen of Spain and wife of Joseph Bonaparte. Name variations: Marie Julie; Julie Clary. Born Julie Clary in 1771; died in 1845; dau. of François Clary (prosperous merchant of Marseille); older sister of Désirée (1777–1860), later queen of Sweden, who became a love interest of Napoleon I); daughter-in-law of Letizia Bonaparte (1750–1836); sister-in-law of Napoleon I, emperor of France (r. 1804–1815); m. Joseph Bonaparte, Aug 1, 1794, in Cuges, France; children: Zénaide Bonaparte; Charlotte Bonaparte. ❖ Short and plain in appearance, was known as sweet natured, loving, and exceedingly rich; with marriage to Joseph Bonaparte, helped established the Bonaparte fortune which made her a favorite with mother-in-law Letizia; lived apart from husband more often than not, and some have speculated that this was the reason the union endured; was left in Italy by husband (1815) and reunited (1844). ❖ See also *Women in World History*.

BONAPARTE, Letizia (1750–1836). Corsican mother of Napoleon I. Name variations: Marie-Letizia Bonaparte or Buonaparte; Letitia or Lætitia; Letizia Ramolino; known as Madame Mère. Born Maria Lætitia or Letizia Ramolino at Ajaccio, Corsica, Aug 24, 1750; died in Rome, Feb 2, 1836; dau. of Jean-Jérôme (town official) and Angèle-Maria Ramolino; m. Carlo Bonaparte, June 2, 1764; children: 12, of whom 8 survived, including Joseph (Giuseppe, 1768–1844); Napoleon (Napoleone, 1769–1821), emperor of France (r. 1804–1815); Lucien (Lucciano, 1775–1840); Elisa (Maria-Anna, 1777–1820); Louis (Luigi, 1778–1846); Pauline (Maria-Paola, 1780–1825); Carolina (Maria-Annunziata, 1782–1839); Jérôme (Girolamo, 1784–1860). ❖ The mother of three kings, a queen, two princesses, and Napoleon I, was born into obscurity, married at 13, and widowed at 34 with 8 children; became the center of her eccentric family, binding them to their Corsican roots and struggling to maintain peace and unity among their ranks. ❖ See also Alain Decaux, *Napoleon's Mother* (Cresset, 1961); Monica Stirling, *Madame Letizia: A Portrait of Napoleon's Mother* (Harper & Brothers, 1961); and *Women in World History*.

BONAPARTE, Marie (1882–1962). Princess of Greece. Born July 2, 1882; died 1962; dau. of Prince Roland Bonaparte (1858–1924) and Marie Blanc (1859–1882); m. Prince George of Greece (son of George I of Greece and Olga Constantinovna), Dec 12, 1907; children: Peter Oldenburg (b. 1908, anthropologist); Eugénie Oldenburg (b. 1910, who m. Dominique Rainer, Prince Radziwill, and Raymond, duke of Castel).

BONAPARTE, Maria-Letizia (1750–1836). *See Bonaparte, Letizia.*

BONAPARTE, Maria-Nunziata Caroline (1782–1839). *See Bonaparte, Carolina.*

BONAPARTE, Maria-Paoletta or Marie Pauline (1780–1825). *See Bonaparte, Pauline.*

BONAPARTE, Marie Julie (1771–1845). *See Bonaparte, Julie Clary.*

BONAPARTE, Pauline (1780–1825). Princess Borghese and duchess of Guastalla. Born Marie Pauline; Maria-Paoletta. Born Carlotta Bonaparte in Ajaccio, Corsica, Oct 20, 1780; died in Florence, Italy, June 9, 1825; dau. of Letizia Bonaparte (1750–1836) and Carlo Bonaparte (Corsican lawyer); younger sister of Napoleon I, emperor of France (r. 1804–1815); m. Charles Victor-Emmanuel Leclerc, in 1797 (died); m. Prince Camillo Borghese, Aug 28, 1803; children: (1st m.) one son, Napoléon Dermide. ❖ Napoleon's youngest and favorite sister, was known for her beauty and promiscuity; married C.V.E. Leclerc, a staff officer of Napoleon (1797); following his death, married Prince Camillo Borghese, only to tire of him and return to Paris; received title of duchess of Guastalla (1806), but her shabby treatment of Napoleon's 2nd wife, Marie Louise of Austria, led to her removal from court (1810); retired to Elba with mother (1814) and was legally separated from 2nd husband (1816); died of stomach cancer, as did many of the Bonapartes (1825), after being reconciled with husband for last few months of her life. ❖ See also *Women in World History.*

BONAPARTE-PATTERSON, Elizabeth (1785–1879). *See Bonaparte, Elizabeth Patterson.*

BONA SFORZA. *See Sforza, Bona (b. 1493).*

BONAVENTURI, Bianca (1548–1587). *See Cappello, Bianca.*

BONCHEVA, Rumeliana (1957—). Bulgarian rower. Born April 25, 1957. ❖ At Moscow Olympics, won a bronze medal in quadruple sculls with coxswain (1980).

BOND, Carrie Jacobs (1862–1946). American composer. Name variations: Jacobs-Bond. Born Carrie Jacobs in Janesville, Wisconsin, Aug 11, 1862; died in Hollywood, California, Dec 28, 1946; m. E.J. Smith, 1880 (div. 1888); m. Dr. Frank L. Bond, 1889 (died 1895). ❖ Had been writing songs for years, seeing publication of "Is My Dolly Dead?" and "Mother's Cradle Song" (1894); on death of 2nd husband, moved to Chicago (1895), where she ran a boarding house and gave recitals and concerts in private homes to supplement income; published *Seven Songs as Unpretentious as the Wild Rose* (1901), which included 2 favorites "I Love You Truly" and "Just a-Wearyin' for You"; opened a shop to sell sheet music, which she designed and printed; by 1910, had played at White House for Theodore Roosevelt and performed at recitals in NY and England, where she appeared with Enrico Caruso; published "The End of a Perfect Day," which became her most popular song, selling over 5 million print copies; moved to Hollywood and continued to write some 400 songs (170 of which were published), all in the sentimental style that characterized much of 19th-century music. ❖ See also memoir, *The Roads of Melody* (1927); and *Women in World History.*

BOND, Elizabeth Powell (1841–1926). American educator and author. Born in Dutchess Country, New York, 1841; died 1926. ❖ Was dean of Swarthmore College (1890–1906).

BOND, Jessie (1853–1942). English actress and singer. Born Jan 11, 1853, in London, England; died June 17, 1942; m. Lewis Ransome. ❖ Made stage debut as Hebe in the 1st production of *H.M.S. Pinafore* (1878); was a member of Gilbert & Sullivan's Savoy company (1881–91), appearing as Edith in *Pirates of Penzance,* Lady Angela in *Patience,* Constance in *The Sorcerer,* Phoebe Merryll in *The Yeoman of the Guard,* Tessa in *The Gondoliers,* title role in *Iolanthe,* Melissa in *Princess Ida,* Mad Margaret in *Ruddigore,* and Pitti-Sing in *The Mikado.* Portrayed by Dorothy Atkinson in the film *Topsy Turvy* (1999). ❖ See also *The Life and Reminiscences of Jessie Bond the Old Savoyard as Told by Herself to E. Macgeorge* (1935).

BOND, Lilian (1908–1991). English stage and screen actress. Name variations: Lillian Bond. Born Jan 18, 1908, in London, England; died Jan 25, 1991, in Reseda, California; m. Henry Shulman (div.); m. Sydney A. Smith. ❖ Made stage debut in pantomime *Dick Whittington* (1924); arrived in US (1926); films include *The Squaw Man, The Old Dark House, Affairs of a Gentleman, China Seas, The Westerner* (as Lillie Langtry), *The Picture of Dorian Gray* and *Pirates of Tripoli.*

BOND, Mary (1939—). Scottish painter. Name variations: Marj Bond, Marj McKechnie. Born Mary McKechnie, 1939, in Paisley, Renfrewshire, Scotland; studied under David Donaldson, Mary Armour, and Alex Dick at Glasgow School of Art, 1955–60. ❖ Abstract oil and watercolor painter, taught in Outer Hebrides, Inverness and Perth; traveled to India, Mexico, Ireland and Italy and drew on travels as source of imagery and symbolism; combined ancient traditions and folklore of diverse Western and Eastern cultures in expressionistic paintings; exhibited widely in many venues in Britain, France, Sweden and US, including Torrance Gallery (Edinburgh, 1975), Scottish Art Molle (Sweden, 1984), Four Printmakers (Lyons), Virginia Lynch Gallery (Rhode Island, 1994) and Adam Gallery (London, 2002); elected member of Royal Scottish Society of Painters in Watercolour (1989). Received Hiram Walker Award (1981), Ann Redpath Award (1984), Paper Prize from First Open Printmakers (1989) and Thyne Scholarship from English Speaking Union (1994).

BOND, Sheila (1928—). American actress, dancer and singer. Born Sheila Phyllis Berman, Mar 16, 1928, in New York, NY; trained at Professional Children's School in NY; m. B.L. Goldberg. ❖ Made NY debut in chorus of *Let Freedom Sing* (1942), followed by *Artists and Models;* gained fame in *Street Scene* (1947), dancing the "Moon-Faced, Starry-Eyed" duet with Danny Daniels; also appeared in *Make Mine Manhattan* and *Damn Yankees;* frequently appeared on tv variety shows (1950s), especially "The Ed Sullivan Show," and in such dramatic showcases as "Schlitz Playhouse" and "Playhouse 90." Won Tony Award for Supporting Actress in a Musical for performance as Fay Fromkin in *Wish You Were Here* (1953).

BOND, Sudie (1928–1984). American stage, tv, and screen actress, singer and dancer. Born July 13, 1928, in Louisville, Kentucky; died Nov 10, 1984, in New York, NY; m. Massen Cornelius Noland (div.). ❖ Made NY debut at Circle in the Square as Mrs. Winemiller in *Summer and Smoke;* won acclaim for her portrayal of Grandma in *The American Dream;* films include *A Thousand Clowns, Silkwood, Swingshift, Love Story, Come Back to the Five & Dime, Jimmy Dean and Johnny Dangerously;* made frequent tv appearances on "Maude," "Mary Hartman," "The Guiding Light," "Flo" and "Benson"; co-founded The Paper Bag Players, a children's touring group. Won 3 Obies.

BOND, Victoria (1950—). American conductor and composer. Born 1950 in Los Angeles, California; studied composition with Ingolf Dahl at University of Southern California; studied with Roger Sessions at Juilliard School and was the 1st woman to earn a doctorate degree in orchestral conducting, 1977. ❖ As a composer, has written for every medium, including opera, orchestra, ballet and chamber music; conducted many orchestras, including Houston, Pittsburgh and Buffalo symphonies; recorded with Ray Charles, Billy Taylor and Marian McPartland; 1st opera *Travels* was performed by Opera Roanoke in Virginia; 2nd opera, *Mrs. Satan,* was performed by New York City Opera; also wrote the children's opera, *Everyone is Good for Something;* assisted Paul Glass in composing film scores for Universal and Metromedia studios; served as artistic director at Opera Roanoke (1989–95) and artistic adviser to The Wuhan Symphony in China.

BONDAR, Elena (1958—). Romanian rower. Born Nov 6, 1958. ❖ At Moscow Olympics, won a bronze medal in coxed eights (1980).

BONDAR, Roberta (1945—). Canadian astronaut. Born Roberta Lynn Bondar, Dec 4, 1945, at Sault Ste. Marie, Ontario, Canada; dau. of Edward and Mildred Bondar; University of Guelph, BS, 1968; University of Western Ontario, MS, 1971; University of Toronto, PhD, 1974; McMaster University, MD, 1977. ❖ The 1st Canadian woman astronaut, trained as a neurologist, serving as director of the Multiple Sclerosis Clinic at McMaster University and researching aspects of aerospace medicine; began training with the Canadian Space Agency (1984) and was named chair of Canada's life sciences subcommittee for the space station; as a payload specialist on the Internal Microgravity Laboratory (IML-1) Spacelab mission (Dec 1990), studied microgravity's effects on material processing and living organisms; was the mission's principal investigator for 55 experiments, including studies of taste in space and cerebral blood flow velocity during weightlessness; resigned from astronaut corps (1984) and returned to University of Ottawa to teach. ❖ See also memoir, *On the Shuttle: Eight Days in Space* (1993); and *Women in World History.*

BONDARENKO, Olga (1960—). Soviet runner. Born June 1960 in USSR. ❖ At Seoul Olympics, won a gold medal in 10,000 meters (1988).

BONDFIELD, Margaret (1873–1953). British social reformer. Name variations: Maggie Bondfield; (pseudonym) Grace Dare. Born Margaret Grace Bondfield, Mar 17, 1873, in Furnham, Somerset, England; died in Sanderstead, Surrey, June 16, 1953; dau. of William (foreman of a lace-making factory) and Ann (Taylor) Bondfield; never married; no children. ❖ Trade union organizer, advocate of child welfare improvement, lecturer, and 1st woman member of a British Cabinet, began career apprenticed to a drapery store; joined the National Union of Shop Assistants, Warehousemen and Clerks and became one of its full-time officials (1898), a post she held until 1908; also acted on behalf of the Women's Trade Union League, the National Federation of Women Workers, and the Women's Co-operative Guild; became chief woman officer of National Union of General and Municipal Workers (1920), a post occupied until 1938 but with secondments when she was a Member of Parliament; served as MP for Northampton (1923–24); served as junior minister in the Labour Government (1924); elected MP for Wallsend (1926–31); served as minister of labour in the Labour government (1929–31); was British Information Services lecturer in US (1941–42); writings include *Why Labour Fights* (British Information Services, 1941). ❖ See also memoirs *A Life's Work* (Hutchinson, 1949); Mary Agnes Hamilton, *Margaret Bondfield* (Leonard Parsons, 1924); and *Women in World History.*

BONDI, Beulah (1892–1981). American actress. Born Beulah Bondy, May 3, 1892, in Chicago, Illinois; died in Woodland Hills, California, Jan 12, 1981; dau. of A.O. (realtor) and Eva Bondy; graduate of Valparaiso University, 1913; studied at Chicago Little Theater during WWII. ❖ At 7, made stage debut in *Little Lord Fauntleroy*, then spent 24 years in stock and repertory before Broadway debut in *One of the Family* (1925); after playing the landlady in *Street Scene* (1929), repeated the role in film version (1931); returned to the stage only 4 more times, in *The Late Christopher Bean* (1932), *Mother Lode* (1934), *Hilda Crane* (1950), and *On Borrowed Time* (1953); appeared in over 60 feature films, mostly in supporting character roles, and was nominated for Oscars for *Gorgeous Hussy* (1936) and *Of Human Hearts* (1938); films include *Arrowsmith* (1931), *Rain* (1932), *The Trail of the Lonesome Pine* (1936), *On Borrowed Time* (1939), *Mr. Smith Goes to Washington* (1939), *Remember the Night* (1940), *Our Town* (1940), *Penny Serenade* (1941), *Watch on the Rhine* (1943), *Our Hearts Were Young and Gay* (1944), *And Now Tomorrow* (1944), *Back to Bataan* (1945), *Sister Kenny* (1946), *It's a Wonderful Life* (1946), *The Snake Pit* (1948), *So Dear to My Heart* (1949), *Back From Eternity* (1956) and *Tammy and the Doctor* (1963). ❖ See also *Women in World History.*

BONDS, Margaret (1913–1972). African-American composer, pianist, historian, singer and lecturer. Born Margaret Allison Richardson in Chicago, Illinois, Mar 3, 1913; died in Los Angeles, California, April 26, 1972; dau. of Estella C. Bonds (organist); studied composition and piano with Florence B. Price and William Dawson at Northwestern University and with Robert Starer, Henry Levine, Roy Harris and Emerson Harper at Juilliard. ❖ Known for her sacred and vocal compositions, composed 1st song at 5; received a Rosenwald fellowship, a National Association of Negro Musicians award, and a Rodman Wanamaker award; opened Allied Arts Academy in Chicago (1930s), a school for ballet and music; known for her arrangements of spirituals, was commissioned by Leontyne Price for several to record; composed art songs, popular songs, theatrical and orchestral music, as well as piano pieces which featured jazz harmonies, spiritual materials, and social themes; also appeared on radio in NY and Hollywood; served as musical director for several music theaters in NY; worked with inner-city Cultural Center in Los Angeles (1968–72). A singer as well as a composer, became the 1st black guest soloist to appear with Chicago Symphony, at Chicago World's Fair (1933). ❖ See also *Women in World History.*

BONDS, Rosie (1944—). African-American runner. Born c. 1944; grew up in Riverside, California; attended the Junior College of University of California at Riverside; aunt of Barry Bonds (baseball player). ❖ Won US National Outdoor hurdles championship (1963, 1964), setting an American record in the 80-meter hurdles of 10.8; competed at Tokyo Olympics (1964). ❖ See also *Women in World History.*

BONETA, Prous (d. 1323). French visionary. Burned at the stake, 1325. ❖ A beguine of southern France, began receiving visions of Jesus; believing that God had chosen her to be the incarnation of the Holy Ghost, attacked Pope John XXII, accusing him of being the Antichrist; was tried and burned at the stake at Carcassonne.

BONFANTI, Marietta (1845–1921). Italian ballerina. Name variations: Maria and Marie. Born Feb 16, 1845, in Milan, Italy; died in New York, NY, Jan 25, 1921; studied with Carlo Blasis, and at the ballet school of Teatro all Scala, Milan; m. George Hoffmann (American businessman). ❖ Made debut in *Roberto, il Diavolo*, then danced at Teatro alla Scala for 2 seasons; made US debut in *The Black Crook*, often called the 1st musical comedy, at Niblo's Garden, NY (1866); went on tour throughout US (1869–71); was prima ballerina of Milan Italian Grand Opera (1884) and Metropolitan Opera in NY (1885–86); following several US-European tours (1888–94), opened a ballet school in NY, where she taught until 1916 (Ruth St. Denis was one of her pupils).

BONFILS, Helen (c. 1890–1972). American theatrical producer and actress. Name variations: Gertrude Barton. Born c. 1890, in New York, NY; died June 6, 1972, age 82, in Denver, Colorado; dau. of Frederick G. Bonfils (co-founder and owner of *The Denver Post*); m. George Somnes (died). ❖ Began running *Denver Post* after death of her father (1933); with husband, began producing in NY with *Sun Kissed* (1937); under name Gertrude Barton (mother's maiden name), co-produced and acted in *The Greatest Show on Earth* (1938); produced or co-produced many plays, including *Pastoral, Come Play with Me, A Thurber Carnival, Sail Away, The Beast in Me, Chips with Everything, Slow Dance on a Killing Ground, Beekman Place, The Promise, Enter Laughing, King Lear, Comedy of Errors, The Killing of Sister George* and *Sleuth*; for 10 years, produced and acted at the Elitch Gardens, Denver; built the Bonfils Theatre in Denver (1953).

BONFILS, Winifred Black (1863–1936). See Black, Winifred Sweet.

BONHAM, Marilou (1936—). See Awiakta.

BONHAM-CARTER, Violet (1887–1969). British peer and activist. Name variations: Lady or Baroness Asquith of Yarnbury. Born Helen Violet Asquith, April 15, 1887, in London, England; died Feb 19, 1969; only dau. of Herbert Henry Asquith (1852–1928, later earl of Oxford and Asquith) and Helen Kelsall (Melland) Asquith (died 1891); stepdau. of Margot Asquith; sister of Herbert Asquith (1881–1947) and Raymond Asquith (killed in action in WWI, 1916); stepsister of Elizabeth, Princess Bibesco (1897–1945); grandmother of actress Helena Bonham-Carter (1966—); m. Sir Maurice Bonham Carter, 1915 (died 1960); children: Helen Cressida (who m. Jasper Ridley); Laura Miranda (who m. Joseph Grimond); Mark Raymond; Raymond Henry. ❖ Politically supported father and his Liberal causes (1905–18), including old-age pensions, limiting the House of Lords veto, and the passage of Home Rule for Ireland; was president of the Women's Liberal Federation (1923–25, 1939–45) and of the Liberal Party (1945–47); was vice-chair of the United Europe Movement (1947) and president of the Royal Institute of International Affairs (1964–69); was also governor of the BBC (1940–46) and Old Vic (1945), and the 1st woman to give the Romanes lecture at Oxford (1963); published *Winston Churchill as I Knew Him* (1965). Created a Dame of the British Empire (DBE, 1953) and baroness (1964).

BONHEUR, Juliette (1830–1891). French painter. Name variations: Madame Peyrol. Born 1830; died 1891; dau. of Raimond Oscar-Marie Bonheur (artist and teacher), and Sophie Marquis Bonheur. ❖ Younger sister of Rosa Bonheur by 8 years, painted sentimental studies of pets that sold commercially.

BONHEUR, Rosa (1822–1899). French painter. Pronunciation: Bau-NUR. Born Marie Rosalie Bonheur, Mar 16, 1822, in Bordeaux, France; died in By, France, May 25, 1899; dau. of Raimond Oscar-Marie Bonheur (artist and teacher) and Sophie (Marquis) Bonheur; sister of Juliette Bonheur (1830–1891); trained by father; lived with artist Nathalie Micas (died 1889); lived with American artist Anna Klumpke. ❖ One of the most successful women artists of the 19th century, was famous for her naturalistic depictions of animals; had 1st exhibit at the Paris Salon (1840), *Rabbits Nibbling Carrots*, a simple work, naturalistically depicted; achieved critical recognition for the 1st time when 5 of her works were accepted for exhibition at Paris Salon and she was awarded a Third Class Medal (1845); her painting *Red Oxen of Cantal* sold to a British buyer for the (then) huge sum of £ 600 (1846); received a government commission of 3,000 francs to produce a work on the subject of ploughing, resulting in *Ploughing in the Nivernais* (or *Labourages Nivernais*), which established her reputation as an animal painter and laid the foundation for lifelong financial security; became director of School of Drawing for Young Girls in Paris (1850); exhibited her masterpiece, *The Horse Fair*, at the Salon (1853), the most universally recognized painting in North America in the mid-19th century; was the 1st woman awarded the Cross of the Legion of Honor (1865); befriended, and painted a portrait of, "Buffalo Bill" Cody (1889), which became a familiar image to most Americans. ❖ See also Ashton and Hare, *Rosa Bonheur—A Life and A Legend* (Viking, 1981); Anna Klumpke, *Rosa Bonheur: The Artist's (Auto)biography* (trans. by Gretchen van Slyke, U. of Michigan Press, 1997); Theodore Stanton, *Reminiscences of Rosa Bonheur* (Appleton, 1910); and *Women in World History.*

BONHEYDEN, Louis (1836–1923). See Loveling, Virginie.

BONHOEFFER, Emmi (1905–1991). German anti-Nazi. Born Emmi Delbrück in Berlin, Germany, in 1905; died in Düsseldorf, Mar 12, 1991; dau. of Hans Delbrück (historian and political publicist) and Lina (Thiersch) Delbrück; m. Klaus Bonhoeffer (chief counsel of the German Lufthansa Airline Company, leading civilian member of the military resistance to the Hitler regime, and brother of Dietrich Bonhoeffer), in 1930 (murdered, April 23, 1945); children: 3. ❖ Though occupied raising her children, strongly supported husband's decision to work in the anti-Nazi resistance, assisting him on countless occasions both morally and practically; after the failure of the attempt to assassinate Adolf Hitler (July 20, 1944), husband arrested (Oct 1944), sentenced to death (Feb 1945), murdered by the SS (April 1945); barely escaped being killed when her house was destroyed in the last days of the war; moved with children to Schleswig-Holstein to rebuild their lives (June 1945); was active in activities aiding war refugees, as well as anti-Nazi educational work and various humanitarian efforts. ❖ See also Eberhard Bethge and Renate Bethge, eds. *Last Letters of Resistance: Farewells from the Bonhoeffer Family* (Fortress, 1986); and *Women in World History.*

BONHOTE, Elizabeth (1744–1818). British novelist and essayist. Born 1744 in Bungay, Suffolk, England; died July 1818 in Bungay; m. Daniel Bonhote (died 1804). ❖ Wrote *The Rambles of Mr. Friendly* (1772), *The Fashionable Friend* (1773), *Olivia* (1786), *Darnley Vale* (1789), *Ellen Woodley* (1790) and *Bungay Castle* (1796); also published a collection of essays on education, *The Parental Monitor* (1788), and a book of verse, *Feeling* (1810).

BONINO, Emma (1948—). Italian politician. Born Mar 9, 1948, in Bra, Cuneo province, Italy. ❖ Served as secretary-general of the Transnational Radical Party, European Commissioner (1995–99); as an Independent or Non-attached (NI), elected to 5th European Parliament (1999–2004).

BONINSEGNA, Celestina (1877–1947). Italian soprano. Born Feb 26, 1877, in Reggio Emilia, Italy; died Feb 14, 1947, in Milan; studied with Mattieli in Reggio Emilia and Virginia Boccabadati in Pesaro. ❖ Debuted as Norina (1892) at the Teatro Municipale in Reggio Emilia and at the Teatro Piccinini in Bari (1897); made debut at Covent Garden (1904), Teatro alla Scala (1904–05), Metropolitan Opera as Aïda (1906–07), Boston (1909–10), Barcelona (1912) and St. Petersburg (1913); retired (1923); known more for her recordings (1904–19) than for stage appearances. ❖ See also *Women in World History.*

BONISCH, Yvonne (1980—). See Boenisch, Yvonne.

BONITA, Maria (c. 1908–1938). Brazilian revolutionary. Name variations: Pretty Mary, Dona Maria, Maria Déia, Maria Déia de Nenem. Pronunciation: Boo-NEE-tuh. Born Maria Déia in interior of Brazilian state of Bahia, 1908 or 1909; gunned down in a military ambush at Angicos ranch in the state of Sergipe, July 28, 1938; dau. of José Felipe and Maria de Oliveira Déia; illiterate; m. in her teens to José Nenem (cobbler); children: 1 girl (3 other children, all boys, died in infancy). ❖ Backwoods consort of the famous Brazilian bandit and folk hero Lampião who accompanied her lover on a series of campaigns against government forces in 1930s Brazil and, in so doing, became a legend in her own right; born into primitive circumstances in the most impoverished region of Brazil (c. 1908); spent early years with family just scraping by; married in her teens to a cobbler, José Nenem, but as the match was loveless, spent more and more time with her parents; made acquaintance of Lampião, whose fame as a bandit in the Brazilian backlands had by that time grown to legendary proportions (early 1931); ran away with Lampião; entered a life of adventure and crime that only ended with both of their deaths in an engagement against the army (1938). ❖ See also *Women in World History.*

BONMARTINI, Linda (1873–?). Italian murderer. Name variations: Linda Murri; Countess Bonmartini; Linda Bonmartini-Murri. Born Linda Murri in 1873; m. Count Bonmartini (murdered Sept 2, 1902). ❖ An upperclass woman married to philandering Count Bonmartini, took up with Carlo Secchi (or Secci); expressed unhappiness about her

marriage to her brother Tullio, who apparently harbored his own dislike for the count; after the count was found stabbed to death in his home on the Via Mazzini in Bologna (1902), was tried for the murder, along with Carlo, Tullio, and Tullio's lover Rosina Bonetti, in a case that caused a national furor; with others, was found guilty and received a long prison sentence. ❖ See also *La Grande Bourgeoisie* (film), starring Giancarlo Giannini and Catherine Deneuve as Linda Murri (1974).

BONNA OF PISA (c. 1156–1207). See Bona of Pisa.

BONNE OF ARMAGNAC (d. 1415). Duchess of Orléans. Name variations: Bonne d'Armagnac; duchess of Orleans. Died in 1415 (some sources cite 1435); dau. of Bernard VII d'Armagnac and Bonne of Berry; became 2nd wife of Charles Valois (1391–1465), duke of Orléans, in 1410. Charles Valois' 1st wife was Isabella of Valois (c. 1389–c. 1410); his 3rd was Marie of Cleves (1426–1486).

BONNE OF ARTOIS (d. 1425). Duchess of Burgundy. Name variations: Bona or Bonne d'Artois. Died in 1425; 2nd wife of Philip the Good (1396–1467), duke of Burgundy (r. 1419–1467). Philip the Good's 1st wife was Michelle Valois (1394–1422); his 3rd was Isabella of Portugal (1397–1471).

BONNE OF LUXEMBURG (1315–1349). See Bona of Bohemia.

BONNEAU, Marie (1629–1696). See Miramion, Madame de.

BONNER, Antoinette (1892–1920). Romanian-born jewel thief. Born in Romania in 1892; immigrated to US; died in New York, NY, age 28, 1920. ❖ Known as the "Queen of Diamonds," set up an office, drummed up wealthy clients in search of the perfect diamond, and had jewelers turn their diamonds over to her to sell; disappeared with stones estimated to be worth $1 million (1914); tracked down in Paris, avoided prosecution; caught again in NY (1928), downed strychnine in front of stunned police and fell dead. ❖ See also *Women in World History.*

BONNER, Beth (1952–1998). American marathon runner. Born 1952 in New Orleans, Louisiana; died of injuries in Texas, Oct 1998, when hit by a truck while riding her bike. ❖ Was the 1st woman to win the NYC Marathon (1971) with a time of 2:55:22, becoming arguably the 1st woman to break 3:00 (Adrienne Beames of Australia broke 3:00 earlier but the conditions were suspect); won US National championships in the 3,000 meters (1970).

BONNER, Catherine Sherwood (1849–1883). See Bonner, Sherwood.

BONNER, Elena (1923—). Russian physician and civil-rights activist. Name variations: Luisa (childhood name still used by her family); Yelena or Jelena Bonner. Born Feb 15, 1923, in Merv in Soviet Turkestan; dau. of Levon Sarkisovich Kocharov and Ruth Grigorievna Bonner (subsequently Communist Party official); stepdau. of Gevork Sarkisovich Alikhanov (Communist Party official); attended Herzen Teachers Institute, 1940–41, and 1st Leningrad Medical Institute, 1947–53; m. Ivan Vasilyevich Semyonov, 1950 (sep. 1965); m. Andrei Sakharov, 1971 (died 1989); children (1st m.): Tatyana (b. 1950), Alexei (b. 1956). ❖ Daughter of high-ranking Soviet officials, victims of Stalin's purges, who became a physician, a civil-rights activist in the Soviet Union, and a spokeswoman and representative for husband Andrei Sakharov; parents arrested during a Stalin purge (1937); served as nurse in WWII (1941–45); was wounded in action which destroyed her sight in one eye, leading to a progressive weakening of vision in the other (1941); mother rearrested (1950); attended medical school (1947–53); mother released from imprisonment (1954); separated from 1st husband, joined Communist Party (1965); became a leading member in the Soviet dissident community (1970); met Sakharov at a protest demonstration (1970), then married him (1971); was now linked personally to one of the nation's greatest scientists and by then an internationally renowned critic of Soviet political life; left Communist Party (1972); when Sakharov could not leave the Soviet Union to receive the Nobel Prize awarded him, received it in his place, then received medical treatment in Italy (1975); with Sakharov exiled in Gorky, became his chief spokesperson and link to the outside world (1980); also arrested and sentenced to exile in Gorky (1984); had medical treatment in Italy and the US (1985–86); husband released from exile (1986), then died (1989); following collapse of the Soviet Union (1991), established Sakharov memorial library in Moscow (1994); as a witness to the purges of the 1930s, as a member of the armed forces during WWII, and as a leading dissident in the era following the death of dictator Joseph Stalin, observed and helped to shape the course of her country's history. ❖ See also memoirs *Alone*

Together (1986) and *Mothers and Daughters* (1992); (film) *Sakharov*, starring Jason Robards Jr. and Glenda Jackson (1984); and *Women in World History*.

BONNER, Isabel (1907–1955). American actress. Born June 12, 1907, in Pittsburgh, Pennsylvania; died July 1, 1955, in Los Angeles, CA, on Cathay Circle Stage during a performance of her husband's play *The Shrike*; m. Joseph Kramm (playwright). ❖ Broadway appearances include *Let Freedom Ring, Processional, Uncle Harry* and *Trojan Women*; also appeared as Dr. Barrow in the film version of *The Shrike*.

BONNER, Katherine Sherwood (1849–1883). *See Bonner, Sherwood.*

BONNER, Marita (1899–1971). African-American playwright and short-story writer. Name variations: Marita Bonner Occomy. Born 1899 in Boston, Massachusetts; died 1971 in Chicago, Illinois; dau. of Joseph Andrew Bonner and Mary Anne Bonner; graduate of Radcliffe College; m. William Almy Occomy, 1931; children: 3. ❖ A member of Georgia Douglas Johnson's S Street Salon in Washington DC during the Harlem Renaissance, published short stories in *Crisis* and *Opportunity: A Journal of Negro Life*; plays include *The Pot-Maker: A Play to Be Read* (1927) and *The Purple Flower* (1928), for which she is best known; ceased publishing (1941).

BONNER, Margerie (1905–1988). American actress and writer. Name variations: Margerie Bonner Lowry; Marjorie Bonner. Born Margerie Bonner, 1905, in Washington DC; died Sept 28, 1988, in Los Angeles, California; sister of Priscilla Bonner (actress); m. Jerome Chaffee Jr., 1924; m. Malcolm Lowry (novelist, died 1957). ❖ Made film debut in *Reno* (1923); other films include *Rapid Fire Romance, The Trail of Courage* and *Paying the Price* (with sister Priscilla Bonner, 1927); wrote 2 novels, *The Shapes that Creep* and *The Last Twist of the Night*; with husband Malcolm Lowry, published their unfilmed screenplay of *Tender is the Night*.

BONNER, Mary (1885–1935). American artist. Born in Bastrop, Louisiana, 1885; died in San Antonio, Texas, June 26, 1935; studied etching with Edouard Leon in Paris. ❖ Noted for her etchings of the American West, had 1st exhibition in Europe (1925), which was enthusiastically received and won her the Palmes Academique from the French government; friezes are displayed at New York Public Library and Luxembourg Museum.

BONNER, Priscilla (1899–1996). American actress. Born 1899 in Washington DC; died Feb 21, 1996, in Los Angeles, California; sister of Margerie Bonner (actress and writer); m. Allen Wynes Alexander, 1922 (div. 1926); m. Dr. E. Bertrand Woolfan, 1928 (died 1988). ❖ Ingenue in silent films, starred opposite Charles Ray and Will Rogers, and in Frank Capra's 1st feature *The Strong Man* (1926); other films include *Homer Comes Home, Shadows, Drusilla with a Million, The Red Kimono, Long Pants, It* and *Paying the Price* (with sister Margerie Bonner, 1927).

BONNER, Sherwood (1849–1883). American writer. Name variations: Catherine or Katherine Bonner McDowell; (pen names) Clayton Vaughn, Katharine McDowell, Kate McDowell, Anonymous, A Citizen of Holly Springs, and Bohemian. Born Catherine Sherwood Bonner in Holly Springs, Mississippi, Feb 26, 1849; died in Holly Springs, July 22, 1883; dau. of Charles (planter and physician) and Mary (Wilson) Bonner; sister of Ruth Maring Bonner (b. 1851), Samuel Wilson (b. 1854), and Anne Lea Bonner (b. 1858); m. Edward McDowell, Feb 14, 1871 (div., c. 1881); children: Lilian McDowell (b. 1871). ❖ Writer of the "local color" school whose promising literary career, which spanned 2 decades following the Civil War, was cut short by her death at age 34; is remembered mainly for her short stories and especially for her realistic use of regional dialects and humor; writings include *Like unto Like* (1878), *Dialect Tales* (1883), *Suwanee River Tales* (1884), *Gran'mammy: Little Classics of the South, Mississippi* (1927) and *The Valcours* (novella, 1881). ❖ See also Hubert Horton McAlexander, *The Prodigal Daughter: A Biography of Sherwood Bonner* (Louisiana State U. Press, 1981); and *Women in World History*.

BONNER, Terry Nelson (1942—). *See Yarbro, Chelsea Quinn.*

BONNEVIE, Kristine (1872–1948). Norwegian zoologist. Born Kristine Elisabeth Heuch Bonnevie in Trondheim, Norway, Oct 8, 1872; died Aug 30, 1948; sister-in-law of feminist Margarete Bonnevie; awarded doctorate at University of Oslo, 1906; professor of zoology, University of Oslo (1912); director, Institute of Genetics (1916); pursued studies in Zürich, Würzburg, Naples and New York. ❖ The 1st woman professor

in Norway, whose comparative research into animal and human malformations led to the adoption of the designation "Bonnevie-Ullrich syndrome" for a certain disease in humans, played a role in local and national politics as a Freethinking liberal. Awarded the Order of St. Olav (1945). ❖ See also *Women in World History*.

BONNEVIE, Margarete Ottilie (1884–1970). Norwegian feminist, humanist, and reforming author. Born Margarete Ottilie Skattebøl in Hallingdal, East Norway, 1884; died Mar 28, 1970; dau. of a member of the Storting (Norwegian parliament); m. Thomas Bonnevie (1879–1960), a judge and brother of Kristine Bonnevie. ❖ Wrote half-a-dozen books on family policies, nursery schools, part-time work, and equal pay for women, which included *Patriarkatets siste skanse* (The Last Bastion of Patriarchy, 1948) and *Fra mannssamfunn til menneskesamfunn* (From a Society for Men to a Society for People, 1955); chaired Norsk Kvinnesaksforening (The Norwegian Association for Women's Rights, 1936–46). ❖ See also *Women in World History*.

BONNEY, Anne (1700–?). Irish-born pirate. Name variations: Ann Bonny. Born in 1700 in Co. Cork, Ireland; date of death unknown; illeg. dau. of William Cormac (Irish attorney) and an unknown servant; m. James Bonney, in 1718; children: unknown. ❖ When young, immigrated with family to Charleston, South Carolina; began to frequent the waterfront, disguised as a man; eloped with a young sailor named James Bonney, whom she had met in a dockside tavern; with husband, set sail for the Bahamas, determined to seek fortune on the island of New Providence (1719); fell in love with pirate Calico Jack Rackham, plotted with him to seize a sloop riding at anchor in the harbor, and made for the open sea (1719); captured Dutch merchantship (1719); met Mary Read (1719); captured by Royal Navy and "Calico Jack" Rackham hung (1720); sentenced to death but was pregnant (1720); delivered child, then disappeared (1721). ❖ See also *Women in World History*.

BONNEY, Mrs. Harry (1897–1994). *See Bonney, Lores.*

BONNEY, Linda (1949—). Princess of Yugoslavia. Born Linda Mary Bonney, June 22, 1949, in London, England; dau. of Holbrook Van Dyke Bonney and Joan Evans; became 2nd wife of Tomislav Karadjordjevic (1928–2000), also known as Prince Tomislav (brother of Peter II, king of Yugoslavia), Oct 16, 1982; children: Princess George (b. 1984); Prince Michael (b. 1985).

BONNEY, Lores (1897–1994). Australian aviator. Name variations: Maude Rose Bonney; Mrs. Harry Bonney. Born 1897; died Feb 24, 1994; m. Harry B. Bonney. ❖ Began flying (1931); was the 1st female pilot to fly from Australia to England in a Gypsy Moth (April 15–June 21, 1933); was the 1st pilot to fly between Brisbane and Capetown, South Africa (1937). Awarded MBE. ❖ See also Terry Gwynn-Jones, *Pioneer Airwoman: The Story of Mrs. Bonney* (1979).

BONNEY, Mary Lucinda (1816–1900). American educator and reformer. Name variations: Mary Lucinda Bonney Rambaut. Born in Hamilton, New York, June 8, 1816; died in Hamilton, July 24, 1900; graduate of Emma Willard's Troy Female Seminary, 1835; m. Thomas Rambaut (minister), 1888 (died 1890). ❖ A teacher by profession, opened the Chestnut Street Female Seminary in Philadelphia, of which she served as principal for 38 years (the school was moved to Ogontz, Pennsylvania, and renamed the Ogontz School for Young Ladies, 1883); was also active in the missions of her Baptist church, as well as the interdenominational Woman's Union Missionary Society of America for Heathen Lands; when Congress proposed to abolish the treaties reserving lands in Indian Territory for certain tribes (1879), mounted a petition campaign calling for the treaties to be honored; founded an organization that devoted itself to missionary work among the Native Americans, offering training in English, religion, and domestic skills. ❖ See also *Women in World History*.

BONNEY, Maude Rose (1897–1994). *See Bonney, Lores.*

BONNEY, Thérèse (1894–1978). American photographer and war correspondent. Born Mabel Thérèse Bonney in Syracuse, New York, 1894; died in Neuilly-sur-Seine, France, 1978; dau. of Anthony and Addie Bonney; attended University of California; MS in romance languages from Harvard University; prepared for PhD at Columbia University, but completed studies at Sorbonne, with honors. ❖ After living in Paris and writing for newspapers and periodicals in England, France and US, founded the Bonney Service, the 1st American illustrated-press service in Europe; published her behind-the-scenes series of photographs on the Vatican in *Life* magazine (1938), and later published *The Vatican*; documented the outbreak of the Russo-Finnish War

(1939) and traveled with the 9th Army to photograph the Battle of the Meuse and the Battle of Bordeaux in France (1940). ❖ *See also Women in World History.*

BONNIN, Gertrude Simmons (1876–1938). Yankton Sioux activist and writer. Name variations: Gertrude Simmons; "Zitkala Sa," "Zitkala-Sa," and "Red Bird." Born Feb 22, 1876, at the Yankton Agency in Dakota Territory; died Jan 26, 1938, in Washington, DC; dau. of Ellen Simmons (Yankton Sioux woman) and a white man named Simmons; attended White's Manual Labor Institute in Wabash, Indiana; attended Earlham, a Quaker-affiliated college, in Richmond, Indiana, and New England Conservatory of Music in Boston; m. Raymond T. Bonnin (Yankton man), 1902; children: Raymond O. Bonnin. ❖ Though she was a product of the Euroamerican schooling system, resisted much of the assimilationist viewpoint and championed the worth and resiliency of tribal culture; known often by her Yankton Sioux name "Zitkala Sa," was instrumental in the development of early 20th-century Pan-Indianism through the Society of American Indians and later the National Council of American Indians; helped lay the groundwork for the burst of rejuvenated tribalism and militancy after World War II; writer of fiction and nonfiction, was the 1st indigenous woman to receive a PhD; published her 1st article, "Impressions of an Indian Childhood," in *The Atlantic Monthly* (1900); edited the *American Indian Magazine;* published the collections *Old Indian Legends* (1901) and *American Indian Stories* (1921). ❖ *See also Women in World History.*

BONO, Cher (1946—). *See Cher.*

BONO, Mary (1961—). American politician. Born Mary Whitaker, Oct 24, 1961, in Cleveland, Ohio; grew up in Pasadena, California; dau. of Clay (physician) and Karen Whitaker (chemist); University of Southern California, BA, 1984; m. Sonny Bono (singer and US congressional representative), Feb 1986 (died 1998); m. Glenn Baxley (businessman), Nov 24, 2001; children: Chesare Elan Bono and Chianna Maria Bono. ❖ Republican, elected to Congress from California's 44th District (April 7, 1998) in a special election to fill the seat previously held by late husband; relected (2000, 2002, 2004); served on the Energy and Commerce Committee; founded and co-chaired the Recording Arts and Sciences Caucus and the Intellectual Property Promotion and Piracy Prevention Caucus.

BONOFF, Karla (1952—). American singer and composer. Born Dec 27, 1952, in Los Angeles, California. ❖ In addition to recording her own songs, wrote songs for other artists, including Linda Ronstadt ("Someone to Lay Down Beside Me," "Lose Again" and "If He's Ever Near"), Bonnie Raitt, Nicolette Larson and Wynonna Judd; wrote "All My Life" for Ronstadt's *Cry Like a Rainstorm, Howl Like the Wind* album (1990), which earned Ronstadt and Aaron Neville a Grammy for Best Pop Vocal Duo; contributed tracks for films, including *About Last Night, Footloose* and *8 Seconds;* performs on her own and with the group Bryndle. Albums include *Karla Bonoff* (1977), *Restless Nights* (1981), *Wild Heart of the Young* (1981), *New World* (1988) and *All My Life: The Best of Karla Bonoff* (1999).

BONSTELLE, Jessie (1871–1932). American actress and theater manager. Born Laura Justine Bonesteele near Greece, New York, Nov 18, 1871; died in Detroit, Michigan, Oct 14, 1932; m. Alexander H. Stuart (actor), April 1893. ❖ One of the 1st women theater managers in the country and the driving force behind one of the earliest community-based repertory theaters, organized a stock company for a theater in Rochester (1900); managed stock companies in Buffalo and Detroit; directed the Municipal Theater in Northampton, Massachusetts (1912–17) and the Opera House in Providence, Rhode Island (1922–24); laid the groundwork for the development of a community-supported professional theater by taking over Detroit's Playhouse (1925), which emerged as the Detroit Civic Theater (1928), was in operation until 1933, and served as a model for dozens of civic repertory theaters around the country; is credited with discovering Jessie Royce Landis, Melvyn Douglas, Ann Harding, William Powell, Ben Lyon and Frank Morgan; also employed stage designer Jo Mielziner and director Guthrie McClintic early in their careers. ❖ *See also Women in World History.*

BONTAS, Cristina (1973—). Romanian gymnast. Born Dec 5, 1973, in Bacau, Romania; coached by Nadia Comaneci; m. Gabi Tataru. ❖ At World championships, placed 2nd in team all-around, 2nd (tie) for vault, and 3rd for floor exercise (1989) and 1st in floor exercise and 3rd in all-around (1991); at Romanian nationals, placed 1st all-around (1990); at Chunichi Cup, placed 3rd all-around (1989) and 2nd all-around (1992);

at Barcelona Olympics, won a bronze medal (tie) in floor exercises and a silver medal in team all-around (1992); immigrated to Canada to coach.

BONTECOU, Lee (1931—). American sculptor. Born 1931 in Providence, Rhode Island; raised in Westchester Co., NY; attended Art Students League, 1952–55; studied in Rome; m. Bill Giles (artist); children: daughter. ❖ Began by sculpting animal and bird forms; in NY, started using lightweight frames filled with wire mesh, canvas and muslin to impart a sense of depth and illusion; often added circular openings to her work (1959); the only woman then in the stable of the NY Leo Castelli Gallery, set the art scene alight with what one critic called "belligerent art" (1960s), then seemed to vanish, walking away from Castelli's in 1972; retreated with husband to their Pennsylvania farmhouse (1967), commuting to teach at Brooklyn College in NYC (1971–91); went 30 years without a solo show, but continued to work in a studio on the farm; saw a major retrospective co-organized by the UCLA Hammer Museum and the Museum of Contemporary Art, Chicago, which then traveled to MoMA in NY (2004).

BONTJE, Ellen (1958—). Dutch equestrian. Born June 11, 1958, in Hilversum, Netherlands. ❖ At Barcelona Olympics, won a silver medal in team dressage (1992); won a team silver medal at Sydney Olympics (2000), on Silvano.

BONVILLE, Cecily (1460–1530). English baroness. Name variations: Baroness Harrington. Born 1460; died May 12, 1529, at Shacklewell, Hackney, Middlesex; interred at Astley, Warwick; dau. of William Bonville, Lord Harrington, and Catherine Neville (fl. 1460, sister of the Kingmaker), m. Thomas Grey, 1st marquess of Dorset; m. Henry Stafford, earl of Wiltshire, c. 1540.

BOOGERD-QUAAK, Johanna L.A. (1944—). Dutch politician. Born Mar 1, 1944, in Axel, Netherlands. ❖ Member of Provincial States (Provinciale Staten) of Zeeland (1978–90); as a member of the European Liberal, Democrat and Reform Party, elected to 4th and 5th European Parliament (1994–99, 1999–2004); served as vice-chair of European Economic Area Joint Parliamentary Committee (1994–99); named vice-chair of Committee on Citizens' Freedoms and Rights, Justice and Home Affairs (2003). Named Knight of the Order or Orange Nassau (1999).

BOOGERT, Kristie (1973—). Dutch tennis player. Born Dec 16, 1973, in Rotterdam, Netherlands. ❖ Turned pro (1991); won a silver medal for singles at Sydney Olympics (2000).

BOOIJ, Minke (1977—). Dutch field-hockey player. Born Jan 24, 1977, in Zaanstad, Netherlands. ❖ Won a team bronze medal at Sydney Olympics (2000) and a team silver at Athens Olympics (2004); won Champions Trophy (2000) and European championship (2003).

BOOKER, Cedella Marley (b. 1967). *See Marley, Cedella.*

BOOLE, Ella (1858–1952). American temperance reformer. Name variations: Ella Alexander; Ella A. Boole or Ella Alexander Boole. Born Ella Alexander, July 26, 1858, in Van Wert, Ohio; died Mar 13, 1952, in Brooklyn, NY; dau. of Isaac Newton Alexander (prominent lawyer) and Rebecca (Alban) Alexander; m. William Hilliker Boole (Methodist minister), July 3, 1883 (died 1896); children: Florence Alexander (b. 1887). ❖ Taught high school and Sunday School and spoke at teachers' institutes (1878–83); after marriage, moved to Brooklyn, NY; joined New York branch of Woman's Christian Temperance Union (WCTU, 1883), serving as vice president (1891), then president (1898–1903, 1909–25); served as National WCTU president (1925–33) and International WCTU president (1931–47); was corresponding secretary of Woman's Board of Home Missions of Presbyterian Church (1903–09); participated in successful drive to ban liquor from government buildings, military installations, and Indian reservations; gave speech supporting national prohibition amendment in Washington, DC (1913); worked to ratify 18th amendment in NY; ran unsuccessfully for Senate (1920, 1922, 1926); after WWII, was key in achieving recognition for World WCTU from United Nations. Was ordained deaconess in Presbyterian Church; supported women's suffrage and women's rights; worked for disarmament, world peace, and eradication of international drug trade.

BOOM, Christel (1927–2004). East German spy. Born Oct 6, 1927; died of heart failure, Mar 20, 2004; m. Günter Guillaume (spy, div.); children: 1. ❖ One of East Germany's elite spies, played a major role in penetrating the inner circle of Willy Brandt, chancellor of Germany (1969–74); with husband Günter Guillaume, pretended to be a refugee to infiltrate the Social Democratic Party (SPD); opened a coffee shop in Frankfurt (1956) and was soon relaying NATO documents and SPD policy papers to the Stasi, East Germany's secret police (Günter became policy aide to Brandt in 1969); arrested wtih Guillaume (April 24, 1974), was tried and sentenced; released (1981). Their work caused the resignation of Brandt (May 6, 1974).

BOOMGAARDT, Ageeth (1972—). *Dutch field-hockey player.* Born Nov 16, 1972, in Tilburg, Netherlands. ❖ Won a team bronze medal at Sydney Olympics (2000) and a team silver at Athens Olympics (2004); won Champions Trophy (2000) and European championship (2003).

BOOMSTRA, Johanna (1929–2001). *See Termeulen, Johanna.*

BOONE, Debby (1956—). *American singer and actress.* Born Deborah Boone, Sept 22, 1956, in Hackensack, New Jersey; dau. of Shirley (Foley) Boone (dau. of Red Foley) and Pat Boone (singer); m. Gabriel Ferrer, 1979; children: 4. ❖ Began performing with sisters as Boone Girls (1969); recorded "You Light Up My Life" for a film of the same name, one of longest-running #1 hit singles (10 weeks), which garnered an Oscar for Best Song and earned her 3 Grammy Awards (1977); starred in musicals, including *Seven Brides for Seven Brothers* (1982) and *The Sound of Music* (revival, 1990); works in contemporary Christian and children's music. Albums include *You Light Up My Life* (1977), *Midstream* (1978), *The Promise* (1979) and *Love Has No Reason* (1980). ❖ See also autobiography *Debby Boone . . . So Far* (1981).

BOONLUA (1911–1982). *See Debyasuvan, Boonlua Kunjara.*

BOOP, Betty (1904–1966). *See Kane, Helen.*

BOORAPOLCHAI, Yaowapa (1984—). *Thai taekwondo player.* Born Sept 6, 1984, in Thailand. ❖ Won a bronze medal in -49kg at Athens Olympics (2004).

BOOTH, Adrian (1918—). *American actress and singer.* Name variations: Ginger Pound; Lorna Gray. Born Virginia Mae Pound, July 26, 1918, in Grand Rapids, Michigan; m. David Brian (actor, died 1998). ❖ Began career singing with Roger Pryor's band as Ginger Pound; signed with Columbia Pictures and changed name to Lorna Gray for film debut in *Adventure in Sahara* (1938); appeared in over 50 films during career, including *The Man They Could Not Hang, Red River Range, Deadwood Dick, Mr. Smith Goes to Washington, Under Colorado Skies, So Proudly We Hail, Captain America* (serial), and 2-reel comedies starring Buster Keaton and The Three Stooges; changed name to Adrian Booth (1946), appearing in *Oh! Susanna, The Gallant Legion* and *The Sea Hornet,* among others; retired (1954).

BOOTH, Agnes (1843–1910). *Australian-American actress.* Name variations: Agnes Perry. Born Marian Agnes Land Rookes in Sydney, Australia, Oct 4, 1843; died 1910; m. Harry Perry, 1861 (died 1863); m. Junius Brutus Booth, the younger (actor and elder brother of Edwin and John Wilkes Booth), in 1867 (died 1883); m. John B. Schoeffel (her manager), 1885. ❖ Joined a dance troupe at 14 and arrived in San Francisco the following year; would remain in America for rest of her life; as a member of Edwin Booth's theater company in NY, played supporting roles to Edwin, as well as Edwin Forrest, E.A. Sothern and Lawrence Barrett; while with Palmer's Company (1890), played leads at Madison Square Theater in New York.

BOOTH, Angela Elizabeth (1869–1954). *English-born Australian feminist and advocate of reproductive rights.* Born Angela Elizabeth Josephine Plover in Liverpool, England, in 1869; died 1954; dau. of Thomas Plover (laborer); married James Booth (medical practitioner), Jan 7, 1897. ❖ Immigrated to Queensland, Australia (1896); joined the campaign to eradicate venereal disease, focusing on the double standard and the economic dependency that often led women into prostitution; during WWI, spoke out against condom distribution to soldiers, arguing instead for a change in men's attitudes; as a member of the Racial Hygiene Association, advocated family planning and established the 1st family-planning clinic in New South Wales, but also advocated the sterilizing of the mentally impaired; was one of the 1st women to be appointed as a justice of the peace in Victoria (1927); unsuccessfully sought election as an independent Nationalist for the state seat of Brighton (1929); wrote *Voluntary Sterilisation for Human Betterment* (1938).

BOOTH, Catherine (1829–1890). *English social reformer.* Born Catherine (Kate) Mumford, Jan 17, 1829, in Ashbourne, Derbyshire, England; died Oct 4, 1890, in Clacton-on-Sea, Essex; only dau. of John (coachbuilder) and Sarah (Milward) Mumford; m. William Booth, June 16, 1855; children: William Bramwell (b. Mar 8, 1856); Ballington

(b. July 28, 1857); Catherine (b. Sept 18, 1858); Emma Moss Booth-Tucker (b. Jan 8, 1860); Herbert Henry (Aug 26, 1862); Marian Billups (May 4, 1864); Evangeline Booth (1865–1950, social reformer); Lucy Milward (April 28, 1867); grandmother of Catherine Bramwell-Booth. ❖ Victorian preacher and campaigner against social injustice who, with husband William Booth, founded the Salvation Army; experienced conversion (June 15, 1846); sympathetic to the Reform Movment, was expelled from Wesleyan Church and became a Sunday school teacher in Methodist Reform Church (c. 1850); met William Booth (1851); published 1st pamphlet, *Female Ministry,* urging the rights of women to preach, which is still used as the basis for Salvation Army teaching on the subject and shows a highly enlightened attitude towards the abilities of women (Jan 1860); 1st spoke from pulpit on Whit Sunday and became a sought after preacher (1860), conducting revivalist meetings jointly with husband; began to conduct meetings independently (June 1864); settled in London and came in contact with the Midnight Movement (1865), a Christian organization working with prostitutes; joint ministry with husband began to be called "The Christian Mission or The Salvation Army" (1877); affectionately called the "Mother of the Army," helped form its precepts; was influential in the passing of the Criminal Law Amendment Act (1884), raising the age of consent to 16 and giving greater protection to women generally. ❖ See also Catherine Bramwell-Booth, *Catherine Booth: The Story of her Loves* (Hodder & Stoughton, 1970); and *Women in World History.*

BOOTH, Catherine (1883–1987). *See Bramwell-Booth, Catherine.*

BOOTH, Cherie (1954—). *See Blair, Cherie.*

BOOTH, Edwina (1904–1991). *American actress.* Born Josephine Constance Woodruff, Sept 13, 1904, in Provo, Utah; died May 18, 1991, in Los Angeles, California; m. Rienold Fehlberg (died 1983). ❖ Had small parts in early films, including *Manhattan Cocktail* and *Our Modern Maidens;* came to prominence as the white goddess in *Trader Horn* (1931) and made 2 more serials (1932); came down with an infection from shooting *Trader Horn* in Africa and was bedridden for nearly 5 years, causing rampant speculation that she had died of the illness, rumored to be jungle fever.

BOOTH, Ellen Scripps (1863–1948). *American philanthropist.* Born Ellen Warren Scripps, July 10, 1863, in Detroit, Michigan; died Jan 24, 1948, at Cranbrook, Michigan; dau. of James Edmund Scripps (founder of *Detroit Evening News*) and Harriet Josephine (Messenger) Scripps; niece of Ellen Browning Scripps; m. George Gough Booth (later president of *Detroit Evening News,* then head of Booth Newspapers), June 1, 1887; children: James Scripps Booth (b. 1888), Grace Ellen Scripps Booth (b. 1880), Warren Scripps Booth (b. 1894), Henry Scripps Booth (b. 1897) and Florence Louise Booth (b. 1902). ❖ An heiress, co-founded with husband the educational and cultural center known as the Cranbrook Foundation in Bloomfield Hills, MI (1927), which came to include both a boys' and girls' school, a science institute, and the internationally known Cranbrook Academy of Art.

BOOTH, Eva Gore (1870–1926). *See Gore-Booth, Eva.*

BOOTH, Evangeline (1865–1950). *English social reformer.* Name variations: known as Eva (1865–1904), then Evangeline (1904–50). Born Eveline Cory Booth, Dec 25, 1865, in the East End borough of Hackney, England; died in Westchester Co., New York, July 17, 1950; dau. of William and Catherine Booth (founders of the Salvation Army); never married, no children. ❖ Fourth general of the Salvation Army, daughter of its founder, who was noted for her eloquence and directed the religious and social work of the American Salvation Army for the 1st three decades of the 20th century; was suspected at 1st of being an intrusive agent of British dominance, but soon quieted American Salvationists' fears and became the embodiment of the organization, rising at age 69 to world leadership; preached from age of 15; served as field commissioner of Salvation Army (1885–94); made envoy to US (1896); served as head of Salvation Army in Canada (1896–1904); was head of Salvation Army in US (1904–34); served as general of Salvation Army (1934–39); became an internationally famous figure, and on her return to US from the High Council of 1934 was given an official welcome by mayor of New York and a ticker-tape parade; retired (1939); with Grace Livingston Hill, wrote *The War Romance of the Salvation Army* (1919). ❖ See also Margaret Troutt, *The General Was a Lady: The Story of Evangeline Booth* (Holman, 1980); Wilson P. Whitwell, *General Evangeline Booth* (Revell, 1935); Charles Ludwig, *The Lady General* (Baker, 1962); and *Women in World History.*

BOOTH, Evelyn Mary (1897–1988). Irish botanist. Born Oct 30, 1897, in Ireland; died Dec 13, 1988. ❖ During WWII, worked as nurse in Essex; compiled *Flora of County Carlow* (1979).

BOOTH, Jane Bastanchury (1948—). American golfer. Name variations: Jane Bastanchury-Booth. Born Jane Bastanchury, Mar 31, 1948, in Los Angeles, California; graduate of Arizona State University; m. Michael Booth; children: Kellee Booth (b. 1976, LPGA Rookie of the Year, 2000). ❖ Was on the World Cup Team (1968, 1970, 1972); made the Curtis Cup team (1970, 1972, 1974); won the Women's Western Amateur (1969, 1970) and the Trans-Mississippi (1967, 1969, 1971); won the North and South (1972); won the International Four-Ball, with Martha Wilkinson (1968, 1969, 1970), with Cindy Hill (1974).

BOOTH, Karin (1919–1992). American actress. Name variations: Karen Booth, Katharine Booth. Born Katharine Hoffman, June 20, 1919, in Minneapolis, Minnesota; died 1992. ❖ Began career as a photographer's model; as a contract player for Paramount, was billed as Katharine Booth; signed with MGM and changed name to Karin Booth; films include *Louisiana Purchase, The Fleet's In, This Gun for Hire, Holiday Inn, Swing Shift Maisie, Abbott and Costello in Hollywood, Big City, My Foolish Heart, Seminole Uprising* and *Beloved Infidel*.

BOOTH, Katharine (1919–1992). *See Booth, Karin.*

BOOTH, Margaret (1898–2002). American film editor. Name variations: (nickname) Maggie. Born Jan 14 (some sources cite 16th), 1898, in Los Angeles, California; died Oct 28, 2002, in Los Angeles; sister of actor Elmer Booth; graduate of Los Angeles High School. ❖ Supervising editor at MGM (1937–68), led a pioneering career that spanned 70 years; started as a cutter for D.W. Griffith; edited such classics as *The Bridge of San Luis Rey, The Barretts of Wimpole Street, Romeo and Juliet* and *Camille;* nominated for Academy Award for *Mutiny on the Bounty* (1935); other films include *Bringing Up Father* (1927), *In Old Kentucky* (1927), *Susan Lenox, Her Fall and Rise* (1931), *Smilin' Through* (1932), *Strange Interlude* (1932), *A Yank at Oxford* (1937), *The Owl and the Pussycat* (1970), *The Way We Were* (1973), *Funny Lady* (1975), *Sunshine Boys* (1975), *Murder by Death* (1976), *The Goodbye Girl* (1977), *California Suite* (1978), *Chapter Two* (1979) and *Annie* (1982). Received honorary Academy Award (1977) and granted Lifetime Achievement Award by American Cinema Editors (1990). ❖ See also *Women in World History*.

BOOTH, Mary Louise (1831–1889). American journalist, translator and editor. Born in Millville (now Yaphank), Suffolk Co., Long Island, NY, April 19, 1831; died in New York, NY, Mar 5, 1889; father was a school principal at Williamsburg, Long Island; educated at home, the district school, and Long Island academies. ❖ Translated some 40 important French works, including the writings of Pascal, as well as Victor Cousin's *Secret History of the French Court; or Life and Times of Madame de Chevreuse;* published *History of the City of New York* (1859); also trans. Edouard Laboulaye's *Paris in America* (1863), Count Agénor de Gasparin's *Uprising of a Great People: The United States in 1861,* Augustin Cochin's *The Results of Slavery* and *The Results of Emancipation* (both 1863), and Henri Martin's abridgment of his *History of France* (6 vols., 1880); was the 1st editor of *Harper's Bazaar,* from its inception until her death.

BOOTH, Maud Ballington (1865–1948). American social reformer. Name variations: Mrs. Ballington Booth (upon her marriage to Ballington Booth, adopted both his names); Maud Charlesworth Booth. Born Maud Elizabeth Charlesworth at Limpsfield, Surrey, England, Sept 13, 1865; died in Great Neck, Long Island, Aug 26, 1948; dau. of Reverend Samuel Charlesworth and a welfare-worker mother; niece of Maria Charlesworth (1819–1880, children's author); sister of Florence Louisa Barclay (1862–1921); m. Ballington Booth (son of William and Catherine Booth and leader of Salvation Army in US and Australia), Sept 1886 (died 1940); sister-in-law of Evangeline Booth; became a naturalized US citizen, 1895. ❖ At 17, organized a branch of the Salvation Army in Paris; accompanied Salvationists to Switzerland where, after experiencing setbacks and even imprisonment, succeeded in establishing a Salvation Army corps; with husband, withdrew from Salvation Army (1896) and founded Volunteers of America, of which she became president in 1940; was also one of the founders of the Parent-Teachers Association; writings include *Branded* (1897), *After Prison, What?* (1903) and *Relentless Current* (1912), as well as *Twilight Fairy Tales* (1906) and other books for children. ❖ See also *Women in World History*.

BOOTH, Sarah (1793–1867). English actress. Born 1793; died 1867. ❖ Appeared at the Surrey Theatre (1810); also performed at Covent Garden, where she played Cordelia to Junius Brutus Booth's King Lear (1820).

BOOTH, Shirley (1907–1992). American actress. Born Thelma Booth Ford in New York, NY, Aug 30, 1907; died Oct 16, 1992, in North Chatham, Massachusetts; dau. of Albert J. (IBM district manager) and Shirley (Wright) Ford; m. Edward Gardner (writer and radio producer), Nov 23, 1929 (div. 1942); m. William H. Baker (investment counselor), 1943 (died 1951). ❖ One of the finest character actresses of her time, appeared on stage, screen, radio, and tv for over 5 decades; made stage debut in *Mother Carey's Chickens* at 12; had 1st Broadway role opposite Humphrey Bogart in *Hell's Bells* (1925); for next 10 years, alternated stock engagements with parts in short-lived Broadway plays, appearing in nearly 600 stock productions; came to prominence as a gangster's moll in hit comedy *Three Men on a Horse* which ran for 2 years (1935–37), followed by the hits, *The Philadelphia Story* (1939) and *My Sister Eileen;* performed comedic turn as Miss Duffy in popular radio program "Duffy's Tavern," which was written and produced by husband Ed Gardner; on tv, starred on NBC's "Hazel" (1961–66), for which she received an Emmy; other films include *Main Street to Broadway* (1953), *About Mrs. Leslie* (1954), *The Matchmaker* (1958) and *Hot Spell* (1958). Received Tony Award for Best Supporting Actress for *Goodbye, My Fancy* (1948); won Tony Award (1950) and Academy Award (1952) for Best Actress for her *Come Back, Little Sheba;* received 3rd Tony for *The Time of the Cuckoo* (1952). ❖ See also *Women in World History*.

BOOTH-TUCKER, Emma Moss (1860–1903). American missionary. Born Emma Moss Booth in Gateshead, England, Jan 8, 1860; died near Dean Lake, Missouri, in 1903; dau. of William and Catherine Booth (1829–1890); m. Frederick Booth-Tucker (who also worked for Salvation Army). ❖ As consul for the Salvation Army, worked in India before working in America from 1896 to 1903.

BOOTHBY, Dora (1881–1970). English tennis player. Name variations: Penelope Boothby, Penelope Dora Harvey Boothby. Born Aug 1881 in UK; died July 22, 1970. ❖ As Penelope Boothby, won a silver medal in singles at London Olympics (1908).

BOOTHBY, Frances (fl. 1669). British playwright. Name variations: (pseudonyms) Arcasia; F. Boothby. ❖ Forerunner to Aphra Behn, her only known play is *Marcelia: or the Treacherous Friend* (1669).

BOOTHBY, Penelope (1881–1970). *See Boothby, Dora.*

BOOTHE or BOOTHE-LUCE, Clare (1903–1987). *See Luce, Clare Boothe.*

BOOTHROYD, Betty (1929—). British politician. Born Betty Boothroyd in 1929; dau. of union activists; never married. ❖ The 1st female speaker of the House of Commons, spent 1940s on tour with a dancing troupe called the Tiller Girls; entered politics (1950) as an assistant to several members of Parliament; made a few unsuccessful runs for MP within the Labour Party, before winning (1973); became deputy speaker (1987); was elected speaker in a landslide victory (1992). ❖ See also *Women in World History*.

BORA, Katharina von (1499–1550). German reformer. Name variations: Catherine de Bora or Bohra; Katherine von Bora Luther. Born Katharina von Bora, Jan 1499; died in Wittenburg, Dec 20, 1550; m. Martin Luther, June 13, 1525; children: Hans (b. 1526); Elizabeth (b. 1527, and died young); Magdalene Luther (b. 1529); Martin (b. 1531); Paul (b. 1533); and Margareta Luther (known as Lenchen, 1534–1548). ❖ Wife of German theologian Martin Luther who, in presiding over the 1st Protestant parsonage, did much to determine the tone of German Protestant domestic life; became responsible for the many who flocked to Wittenburg as the new followers; in a building known as the Black Cloister, established a hostel for the many hundreds, perhaps even thousands, of visitors and religious refugees requiring food and rest and sometimes medical care; through her own sense of religious conviction, broke the traditional medieval concept of Christian ministry as the work of men only; with husband, was responsible for shaping the family-centered aspect in Christian ministry, which has dominated Protestant Christianity throughout the world. ❖ See also *Women in World History*.

BORBALA. *Variant of Barbara.*

BORBONI, Paola (1900–1995). Italian actress. Born 1900; died April 9, 1995, in Varese, Italy; m. Bruno Vilar (actor), 1972. ❖ Dubbed "Paola of the Scandals," fomented controversy throughout extraordinary 77-year career; appeared in hundreds of theatrical productions of distinguished playwrights, including those of Pirandello and Shaw. ❖ See also *Women in World History.*

BORCHARDT, Selma Munter (1895–1968). American educator and labor lobbyist. Born Selma Munter Borchardt, Dec 1, 1895, in Washington, DC; died Jan 30, 1968, in Washington, DC; dau. of Newman and Sara (Munter) Borchardt; Syracuse University, AM, 1922, BS in education, 1923. ❖ Activist who worked for legislation to raise teachers' salaries, promote adult literacy, and provide health care for children and financial aid for students; joined public schools' faculty in Washington, DC (1922) and local of American Federation of Teachers (AFT); served as vice president of AFT (1924–35, 1942–62); served as director of World Federation of Education Associations (1927–46), until it disbanded; served as secretary of Education Committee of American Federation of Labor (1929–55); was a delegate to White House Conferences on Children and Youth (1930, 1940, 1950) and to White House Conference on Education (1955); was consultant on education for American Association of University Women (1931–60); retired from teaching (1960); appointed to National Advisory board of National Youth Administration by Franklin Roosevelt (1935); served on Wartime Education Commission (1941–45); served as legislative representative of AFT (1942–62); was a member and director of Educational Planning Committee of Institute of World Studies (1946–48); named to US Commission on UN Educational, Scientific and Cultural Organization and served on committee drafting UNESCO charter (1946–51).

BORCHERS, Christl (b. 1914). *See Cranz, Christl.*

BORCHERS, Cornell (1925—). Lithuanian-born actress. Born Cornelia Bruch, Mar 16, 1925, in Heydekrug, Lithuania. ❖ Made debut in the German film *Anonyme briefe* (1949); made US debut in *The Big Lift,* opposite Montgomery Clift (1950); other films include *Abenteuer in Wien, Haus des Lebens, The Divided Heart, Maxie, Never Say Goodbye, Rot ist die Liebe, Istanbul, Flood Time* and *Arzt ohne Gewissen.*

BORCHERT, Katrin (1969—). German kayaker. Born April 11, 1969, in Waren, Germany. ❖ At Barcelona Olympics, won a silver medal in K4 500 meters (1992); won a bronze medal for K4 500 meters at Atlanta Olympics (1996); at World championships, won gold medals for K2 1,000 (1998, 1999), K2 500 meters (1998); won a bronze medal for K1 500 meters at Sydney Olympics (2000); placed 1st at World Cup for K2 1,000 meters (2000).

BORCHMANN, Anke (1954—). East German rower. Born June 23, 1954. ❖ At Montreal Olympics, won a gold medal in quadruple sculls with coxswain (1976).

BORCKINK, Annie (1951—). Dutch speedskater. Born Oct 17, 1951, in the Netherlands. ❖ Won a gold medal for the 1,500 meters at Lake Placid Olympics (1980).

BORDA, Deborah (1949—). American symphony orchestra director. Born July 15, 1949, in New York, NY; dau. of William and Helene (Malloy) Borda; Bennington College, BA, 1971; attended Royal College of Music in London, 1972–73. ❖ As a violinist, spent 8 years with the San Francisco Symphony Orchestra (1979–86), of which she became general manager; served as director of St. Paul Chamber Orchestra (1986–88), executive director of Detroit Symphony (1988–90) and president of Minnesota Orchestra (1990–91); became managing director of New York Philharmonic (1991) and vice-president and managing director, Los Angeles Philharmonic Association (2000).

BORDEN, Amanda (1977—). American gymnast. Born May 10, 1977, in Cincinnati, Ohio. ❖ Won US Classic (1994); at Pan American Games, won gold medals for team all-around and balance beam and silver medals for all-around and floor exercises (1995); at Atlanta Olympics, won a gold medal for team all-around (1996).

BORDEN, Laura (1862–1940). Canadian first lady. Born Laura Bond, 1862, in Halifax, Nova Scotia; died Sept 7, 1940; m. Robert Laird Borden (prime minister of Canada, 1911–17, 1917–20), Sept 25, 1889 (died 1937); children: none.

BORDEN, Lizzie (1860–1927). American accused of murder. Born Lizbeth Andrew Borden, July 19, 1860, in Fall River, Massachusetts; died June 1, 1927, in Fall River; dau. of Andrew (owner of a yarn mill) and Sarah (Morse) Borden; sister of Emma Lenora Borden (b. 1849); never married; no children. ❖ In a gruesome case that riveted late 19th-century America, was accused of murdering her father and stepmother

with an axe on Aug 4, 1892; though there were many circumstances that led to her guilt, was acquitted with the help of a sympathetic press, sure that the real perpetrator would be from the lower classes (June 1893); became somewhat of a recluse, seen only occasionally around Fall River in her handsome carriage driven by a devoted chauffeur; was the subject of the popular poem, "Lizzie Borden took an axe, And gave her mother forty whacks/ And when she saw what she had done, She gave her father forty-one." Legal scholars and amateur criminologists have been arguing the case and the identity of the "real" murderer ever since. ❖ See also *Women in World History.*

BORDEN, Olive (1906–1947). American silent-screen star. Born Sybil Trinkle, July 14, 1906, in Richmond, Virginia; died Oct 1, 1947, in a hotel for destitute women in Los Angeles, California; cousin of actress Natalie Joyce; m. John Moeller; m. Theodore Spector. ❖ Began screen career in Hal Roach comedies; starred opposite Tom Mix, Lew Cody, and George O'Brien; appeared in early talkies, but career took a dive with talking pictures and the advent of alcoholism; films include *The Overland Limited, Yellow Fingers, The Country Beyond, Sinners in Love* and *Hotel Variety.*

BORDERS, Ila (1975—). American baseball player. Born Feb 18, 1975, in La Mirada, California. ❖ With a fastball clocked at 80 mph, was the 1st woman to earn a baseball scholarship (1993); as a lefthander, made pitching debut with the men's Southern California College Vanguards (1994); transferred to Whittier College (1997); pitched for men's pro-hardball baseball teams, including St. Paul Saints (1997), Duluth-Superior Dukes (1997–98), Madison Black Wolf, posting a 1.67 ERA (1999), all in the Northern League, and the Zion Pioneerzz in Western Baseball League; retired from competition (2000); was the 1st woman to start a pro baseball game and the 1st on record to win.

BORDES, Armonia (1945—). French politician. Born May 3, 1945, in Toulouse, France. ❖ Representing the Confederal Group of the European United Left/Nordic Green Left (GUE/NGL), elected to 5th European Parliament (1999–2004).

BORDES, Marguerite (1893–1983). *See Broquedis, Marguerite.*

BORDONI, Faustina (c. 1700–1781). Italian mezzo-soprano. Name variations: Faustina Hasse. Born c. 1700 in Venice, Italy; died Nov 4, 1781, in Venice; m. Johann Adolf Hasse (composer), 1730; studied with Michelangelo Gasparini. ❖ A superstar in her era, debuted in Venice (1716), Naples (1721), Rome (1722) and Munich (1723); was brought to London by Handel, where she was a huge success as Rossane in his opera *Allessandro* (1726); created many roles for Handel, including Alcestis in *Admeto,* Pulcheria in *Riccardo Primo,* Emira in *Siroe,* and Elisa in *Tolomeo;* appeared on stages throughout Europe until 1751; appeared in concerts in Dresden until 1763. Her portrait by Rosalba Carriera hangs in the Ca'Rezzonico, Venice; was also the subject of an opera by Louis Schubert, *Faustina Hasse* (1879). ❖ See also *Women in World History.*

BORDONI, Irene (1895–1953). Corsican-American musical-comedy star. Born Jan 16, 1895, in Ajaccio, Corsica, France; died Mar 19, 1953, in New York, NY; m. E. Ray Goetz; m. Edgar Becman. ❖ Known for slightly risqué performances, made NY debut in *Broadway to Paris* (1912); introduced such well-known songs as "Do It Again" in *The French Doll* (1922) and "Let's Do It" in *Paris* (1928); also sang Irving Berlin's "It's a Lovely Day Tomorrow" in film *Louisiana Purchase* (1940); performed in vaudeville and straight plays; last major appearance was as Bloody Mary in a touring production of *South Pacific* (1951). ❖ See also *Women in World History.*

BORELLA, Francesca Bortolozzi (1968—). *See Bortolozzi, Francesca.*

BORELLI, LaVerne (1909—). American murderer. Born 1909 in US; death date unknown; m. Gene Borelli. ❖ After discovering husband's infidelity, shot him to death in his sleep (May 9, 1946); made failed suicide attempt after the murder; was represented by Jake Erlich who managed to get charge reduced to manslaughter despite her lack of cooperation at trial; was paroled (Mar 10, 1953), following time in women's prison at Tehachapi.

BOREMAN, Linda (1952–2002). *See Lovelace, Linda.*

BORG, Anita (1949–2003). American computer scientist. Born Anita Borg Naffz, 1949, in Chicago, Illinois; died April 27, 2003, in Sonoma, California; dau. of Beverly Naffz; New York University, PhD in computer science, 1981; m. Winfried Wilcke (physicist). ❖ Devoted much of her career to the advancement of women in computer science;

launched Systers (1987), an electronic mailing list on technical subjects, for women highly trained in engineering; founded the Institute for Women and Technology (IWT) in Palo Alto (1998).

BORG, Dorothy (1901–1993). American historian. Born in Elberon, New Jersey, Sept 4, 1901; died in New York, NY, Oct 1993; dau. of Sidney C. and Madeleine (Beer) Borg; graduate of Wellesley College; Columbia University, AM, PhD. ❖ Scholar on modern East Asia and defender of academic freedom during McCarthy era, studied in China (1940s); when Joseph McCarthy hurled unsubstantiated charges of treason against many distinguished professors and State Department experts on Chinese and East Asian affairs, helped defend Owen Lattimore and other scholars whose reputations were being assassinated; taught at Harvard and Columbia universities; writings include *The United States and the Far Eastern Crisis, 1933–1938* (1965); edited with Waldo Heinrichs, *Uncertain Years: Chinese-American Relations, 1947–1950* (1980). ❖ See also *Women in World History.*

BORG, Veda Ann (1915–1973). American actress. Born Jan 11, 1915, in Boston, Massachusetts; died Aug 16, 1973, in Hollywood, California; m. Paul Herrick, 1942 (div.); m. Andrew McLaglen (director), 1946 (div. 1957); children: Mary McLaglen (production manager) and Andrew McLaglen Jr. ❖ Began career as a New York model; debuted in film in *Three Cheers for Love* (1936); following auto accident (1939), had to have face reconstructed by plastic surgery; other films include *Alcatraz Island, Mildred Pierce, Big Town, Big Jim McLain, Three Sailors and a Girl, Guys and Dolls* and *The Alamo.*

BORGESE, Elisabeth Mann (d. 2002). *See Mann, Elisabeth.*

BORGESE FRESCHI, Maria (1881–1947). Italian poet and novelist. Name variations: Maria Borghese Freschi; (pseudonym) Erinni. Born Maria Freschi, 1881, in Italy; died 1947; m. Giuseppe Antonia Borgese (1882–1952, writer, div.); children: Leonardo and Giovanna. ❖ Wrote reviews for periodicals; under pseudonym Erinni, published collection of poetry, *I canti dell'alba e della sera* (Songs of the Dawn and the Evening, 1909); also wrote narrative and historical fiction; writings include *Aurora la amata* (1930), *Dodici donne e due cane* (1935), *Anime scompagnate* (1937), *Quelli che vennero prima* (1942), *Benvenuto* (1945), *La pelle della volpe* (1946) and *L'appassionata di Byron* (1949).

BORGIA, Lucrezia (1480–1519). Duchess of Ferrara. Name variations: Madonna Lucrezia; Lucrece Borgia. Pronunciation: BOR-jha. Born in Rome, April 18, 1480; died in childbirth in Ferrara, Italy, June 24, 1519; dau. of Rodrigo Borgia (later named Pope Alexander VI) and Vannozza Cattanei; m. Giovanni Sforza, June 1493 (div. 1497); m. Alfonso di Biselli (Alphonso of Aragon), 1498 (killed 1500); m. Alfonso I d'Este (1476–1534), 3rd duke of Ferrara and Modena, Nov 1501; children: (2nd m.) Rodrigo di Biselli (1499–1512); (3rd m.) Ercole II (1508–1559), 4th duke of Ferrara and Modena (who m. Renée of France); Cardinal Ippolito II (1509–1572); Alessandro (1514–1516); Eleonora d'Este (1515–1575); Francesco d'Este (1516–1578). ❖ Known alternately as a monster, a pawn, a beauty, a loving mother, and a great patron of the arts, was born into a powerful and dangerous family and survived many scandals and intrigues before she finally made a place for herself at the court of Ferrara. Rumors begun by rivals and gossips of her era survived well into the 19th century, providing a basis for Victor Hugo's play, *Lucrece Borgia*, and Gaetano Donizetti's opera by the same name; in those fictional accounts, she's represented as a murderer and sexual fiend; early in the 20th century, however, historians began working out the complicated details of her life, and biographies written in the 1930s and 1940s offer a far more sympathetic representation of her. ❖ See also *Women in World History.*

BORGSTRÖM, Hilda (1871–1953). Swedish actress. Name variations: Borgstrom. Born Oct 13, 1871, in Stockholm, Sweden; died 1953; studied drama and ballet at Stockholm's Royal Dramatic Theater. ❖ One of Sweden's most admired silent-screen actresses, trained for the ballet as a child; appeared in the films of Victor Sjöström and other great directors of the silent era; went on to play supporting roles in countless talkies throughout 1940s, including an early film directed by Ingmar Bergman. ❖ See also *Women in World History.*

BORI, Lucrezia (1887–1960). Spanish soprano. Born Lucrecia Borja y Gonzales de Riancho, Dec 4, 1887, in Valencia, Spain; died May 14, 1960, in New York, NY; studied with Melchiorre Vidal in Milan and at Valencia Conservatory. ❖ Debuted as Micaela in *Carmen* in Rome (1908), at Teatro alla Scala (1909) and in Paris (1910); debuted at Metropolitan Opera in *Manon Lescaut* (1912), continuing to appear

there until 1936; was the 1st woman elected to the Metropolitan Opera board of directors and served in that position (1935–60). ❖ See also *Women in World History.*

BORING, Alice Middleton (1883–1955). American scientist. Born in Philadelphia, Pennsylvania, 1883; died in Cambridge, Massachusetts, 1955; dau. of Edwin (pharmacist) and Elizabeth (Truman) Boring; Bryn Mawr College, BA, 1904, MA, 1905, PhD, 1910; fellow at University of Pennsylvania, 1905–06. ❖ Cytologist, geneticist, and zoologist who bridged scientific understanding between East and West, taught for years in the University of Maine's zoology department (1910–18); accepted 2-year teaching post as assistant professor of biology at China's Peking Union Medical College (1918); taught briefly at Wellesley College (1920), only to return to China as soon as a position opened at Peking University (later called Yenching University); began the study of China's lizards and amphibians, making contributions to literature in the field; spent WWII in a Japanese concentration camp; co-authored some 36 works with Thomas Hunt Morgan. ❖ See also *Women in World History.*

BORIS, Ruthanna (1918—). American ballet dancer and choreographer. Born Mar 17, 1918, in Brooklyn, NY. ❖ Trained as a child at ballet school of Metropolitan Opera in NY with Giuseppe Bonfiglio, Margaret Curtis, and others; was among Balanchine's 1st students in US and a founding student at Balanchine's School of Ballet in NY (1934); toured with Ballet Caravan, including in title role in Lew Christensen's *Pocahontas* (1936); appeared on Broadway in Agnes de Mille's *Hooray for What?* and returned to Metropolitan Opera for several seasons (1937–42); danced with Ballet Russe de Monte Carlo in *Spectre de la Rose, Serenade, Paquita* and *Bluebird,* among others; with Frank Hobi, created numerous pieces for Boris-Hobi Concert Co. and Royal Winnipeg Ballet, where she also performed (1956–57); began teaching at University of Washington in Seattle (1965).

BORISOVA, Verka (1955—). Bulgarian volleyball player. Born Feb 26, 1955. ❖ At Moscow Olympics, won a bronze medal in team competition (1980).

BORJA, Ana de (c. 1640–1706). Vice-queen of Peru. Name variations: Countess of Lemos. Pronunciation: BOR-ha. Born in Spain, c. 1640; died Sept 23, 1706; dau. of duke of Bejar; 3rd wife of Pedro Fernandez de Castro, Andrade y Portugal, Count of Lemos (1634–1672). ❖ Accompanied husband to Peru when he was appointed viceroy of Peru (1667); during his absence in Charcas, was left in charge of the government (1668–69), a singular event for a woman in Spanish America.

BORKH, Inge (1917—). Swiss soprano. Born Ingeborg Simon, May 26, 1917, in Mannheim, Germany, of Swiss and Austrian parents; studied acting at Max Reinhardt seminar in Vienna and singing at Salzburg Mozarteum in Milan; m. Alexander Welitsch (singer). ❖ Performed comfortably in both Italian and German; debuted in Lucerne as Czipra in *Der Ziguenerbaron* (1940–41) and remained in Switzerland until 1951; came to prominence in Basel as Magda in the 1st German-language performance of *The Consul* (1951); debuted in San Francisco as Verdi's Lady MacBeth (1955); debuted at Metropolitan Opera as Salome (1958); gave 1st Covent Garden performance (1967); crowning achievement was probably as Elektra in Richard Strauss' opera; retired (1973).

BORMANN, Gerda (1909–1946). German Nazi. Name variations: Mrs. Martin Bormann. Born Gerda Buch in 1909; died of cancer in Merano, Italy, Mar 22, 1946; dau. of Walter Buch (chair of Nazi Party Court); married Martin Bormann (1900–1945, member of Hitler's inner circle), 1929; children: 10. ❖ Personable and committed to the ideals of National Socialism, supported husband both personally and ideologically as a model Nazi wife, even giving her blessing to his choosing a mistress; was particularly militant on the "Jewish Question"; began career as a kindergarten teacher.

BORMANN, Maria Benedita Câmara de (1853–1895). Brazilian novelist. Name variations: Maria Benedita Camara de Bormann; (pseudonym) Délia or Delia. Born 1853 in Brazil; died 1895; married to a marshal of the Paraguay war. ❖ Wrote *Aurélia* (1883), *Una vítima* (1884), *Duas irmãs* (1884), *Lésbia* (1890) *Madalena* (1891), *Celeste* (1893) and *Angelina* (1894).

BORNE, Bonita (1952—). American ballet dancer. Born 1952 in Los Angeles, California. ❖ Joined New York City Ballet (1971) and appeared in most of its repertory works over next 10 years; created roles in Richard Tanner's *Concerto for Two Solo Pianos* (1971), Lorca Massine's

Four Last Songs (1971), and others; danced in many works by George Balanchine, Jerome Robbins, and John Taras, including *Apollo, Concerto Barocco, Chaconne* and *Divertimento No. 15;* danced in film, *Balanchine: Dance in America* (1977).

BÖRNER, Jacqueline (1965—). East German speedskater. Name variations: Boerner or Borner. Born Mar 30, 1965, in Wismar, East Germany. ❖ Placed 3rd in all-around at European championships (1987, 1989) and 2nd (1990); won World championship for all-around (1990); sidelined when hit by a car while on a training bike (Aug 1990–92); won a gold medal for the 1,500 meters at Albertville Olympics (1992).

BORON, Kathrin (1969—). German rower. Born Nov 4, 1969, in Eisenhüttenstadt, Brandenburg, Germany. ❖ Won a gold medal in double sculls at Barcelona Olympics (1992) and Sydney Olympics (2000); won a gold medal for quadruple sculls at Atlanta Olympics (1996) and Athens Olympics (2004); at World championships, won gold medals for quadruple sculls (1989, 1997, 1998) and double sculls (1990, 1991, 1997, 1999, 2001).

BORONAT, Olimpia (1867–1934). Italian soprano. Born 1867 in Genoa, Italy; died 1934; studied at Milan Conservatory under Pietro Leoni; married a Polish count, Count Rzewuski, 1893. ❖ Made debut in Naples (c. 1885), then sang in Central and South America; guest starred at the Maryinsky Theatre in St. Petersburg (1891), followed by engagements in Moscow, Kiev and Warsaw; became a favorite singer of the tsar; retired (1914); after WWI, opened a school for singing in Warsaw.

BOROS, Ferike (1880–1951). Hungarian-American actress. Born Aug 2, 1880, in Nagvarad, Hungary; died Jan 16, 1951, in Hollywood, California. ❖ Character actress of 1930s–40s, appeared in over 40 films, including *No Living Witness* (1932), *Eight Girls in a Boat* (1934), *Love Affair* (1939), *Bachelor Mother* (1939), *The Light That Failed* (1939), *Lillian Russell* (1940) and *Christmas in July* (1940).

BOROSTYANI, Irma von Troll- (1847–1912). *See Troll-Borostyani, Irma von.*

BOROZNA, Lyudmila (1954—). Soviet volleyball player. Born Jan 1954 in USSR. ❖ At Munich Olympics, won a gold medal in team competition (1972).

BORREGAARD OTZEN, Christina (1975—). Danish sailor. Born Oct 4, 1975, in Denmark. ❖ Won a bronze medal for Yngling class at Athens Olympics (2004), a debut event.

BORREL, Andrée (1919–1944). French spy. Name variations: Andree Borrel; SOE code name, Denise. Born Nov 18, 1919, near Paris, France; killed July 6, 1944, at Natzwiller, Bas-Rhin, France. ❖ At start of WWII, trained as a nurse's aid with Association des Dames de France; worked in Beaucaire, treating wounded soldiers; with fall of France, joined the French resistance, helping British airmen who had been shot down over France to escape; with Nazis closing in, fled to Lisbon (Dec 1941), then London (April 1942); joined the French section of the Special Operations Executive (SOE); with Lise de Baissac, parachuted into France (Sept 24, 1942), the 1st female agents to do so; became 2nd in command of Paris network; captured and held at Fresne (June 1943); shipped to the Natzwiller-Struthof concentration camp in Alsace (May 1944). Awarded the Croix de Guerre.

BORRERO, Dulce María (1883–1945). Cuban poet and artist. Name variations: Dulce Maria Borrero; Maria Borrero. Born 1883 in Cuba; died 1945; dau. of Esteban Borrero Echeverría; sister of Juana Borrero (poet). ❖ Active feminist who also published essays and lectures on education and art; writings include *Horas de me vida* (1912); also published poetry in *Revista de Cayo Hueso.*

BORRERO, Juana (1877–1896). Cuban poet and artist. Born 1877 in Cuba; died 1896; dau. of Esteban Borrero Echeverría; sister of Dulce María Borrero (poet). ❖ Educated in Cuba and US; studied painting in Washington, DC; writings include *La Habama Elegante, El Fígaro* and *Gris y Azul.*

BORRERO, Maria (1883–1945). *See Borrero, Dulce María.*

BORROWMAN, Agnes (1881–1955). Scottish-born pharmaceutical chemist. Name variations: Agnes Thompson or Thomson Borrowman. Born 1881 near Melrose, Scotland; died Aug 20, 1955. ❖ Served as researcher at Pharmaceutical Society School of Pharmacy in London (beginning 1909); took over pharmacy in Clapham, London, with 3 other women, including Margaret Buchanan, where women

pharmaceutical students could further skills; became sole proprietor of business after WWI; was the 1st woman appointed to Pharmaceutical Society's board of examiners (1924); served as president of South-West London Chemists' Association (1929–31) and helped establish National Association of Women Pharmacists. Assisted with compiling *Pharmocopedia* and provided work for 2 editions of *British Pharmaceutical Codex* (1911 and 1923).

BORST-EILERS, Els (1932—). Dutch doctor and politician. Name variations: Els Borst; Dr. E. Borst-Eilers. Born Mar 22, 1932, in Amsterdam, Netherlands; graduate in medicine from University of Amsterdam, 1958; studied pediatrics, 1958–60, and immunohematology, 1960–65; took doctoral degree in medicine, 1972; m. Johan Borst (physician, died 1988); children: 3. ❖ Worked as scientific employee in immunohematology at University of Utrecht (1965–69); became head of the blood bank at Academic Hospital Utrecht (1969), then medical director (1976); served as vice-chair of the Health Council (1986–94); was appointed fellow of Royal College of Physicians in Edinburgh (1977); appointed minister of Health, Welfare and Sports (1994), then deputy prime minister and minister of Health, Welfare and Sports (1998); was the 1st female politician in the Netherlands charged with advising the crown on the Cabinet formation.

BORTOLOZZI, Francesca (1968—). Italian fencer. Name variations: Francesca Bortolozzi Borella. Born May 4, 1968, in Padua, Italy. ❖ At Seoul Olympics, won a silver medal in team foil (1988); at Barcelona Olympics, won a gold medal in team foil (1992); won a gold medal for team foil at Atlanta Olympics (1996); at World championships, won gold medals for team foil (1990, 1991, 1995) and indiv. foil (1993).

BORYSENKO, Nataliya (1975—). Ukrainian handball player. Born Dec 3, 1975, in Ukraine. ❖ Won a team bronze medal at Athens Olympics (2004).

BORZENKOVA, Galina (1964—). Soviet handball player. Born Feb 2, 1964, in USSR. ❖ At Barcelona Olympics, won a bronze medal in team competition (1992).

BOS, Alida van den (1902—). Dutch gymnast. Born Jan 18, 1902. ❖ At Amsterdam Olympics, won a gold medal in team all-around (1928).

BOSAKOVA-VECHTOVA, Eva (1931–1991). Czech gymnast. Name variations: Eva Vechtova. Born Dec 18, 1931; died Jan 10, 1991. ❖ At Helsinki Olympics, won a bronze medal in team all-around (1952); at Melbourne Olympics, won a silver medal in balance beam (1956); at Rome Olympics, won a silver medal in team all-around and a gold medal for balance beam (1960).

BOSBOOM-TOUSSAINT, Anna (1812–1886). Dutch novelist. Name variations: Anna Louisa Toussaint. Born Anna Louisa Geertruida Toussaint at Alkmaar in north Holland, Sept 16, 1812; died at The Hague, April 13, 1886; dau. of a local chemist named Toussaint; m. Johannes Bosboom (1817–1891, Dutch painter), 1851. ❖ Wrote historical romance novels, including *Almagro* (1837), *Graaf van Devonshire* (*The Earl of Devonshire,* 1838), *Engelschen te Rome* (*The English at Rome,* 1840) and *Het Huis Lauernesse* (*The House of Lauernesse,* 1841), an episode of the Reformation which was translated into many European languages; fascinated with Dutch history, published *Leycester in Nederland* (3 vols.), *Vrouwen uit het Leycestersche Tydperk* (*Women of Leicester's Epoch,* 3 vols.), and *Gideon Florensz* (3 vols.), a series dealing with Robert Dudley's adventures in the Low Countries; her novels were published in a 25-volume collected edition (1885–88).

BOSCAWEN, Fanny (1719–1805). British writer and salonnière. Name variations: Frances Boscawen. Born Frances Evelyn Glanville, July 23, 1719, in St. Clere, Kent, England; died Feb 26, 1805, in London, England; dau. of Frances and William Evelyn Glanville (politician and sheriff); m. Edward Boscawen (naval officer), Dec 11, 1742 (died 1761); children: Edward Hugh (1744–1774); Frances (b. 1746, who m. John Leveson-Gower); Elizabeth (b. 1747); William (1751–1769); Benjamin (b. 1758). ❖ Diarist, correspondent, and member of the Bluestocking group, described political, social and familial scenes in letters to her husband and friends, which would later detail England's military and colonial decline during the 18th century; after a period of seclusion following husband's death (1761), emerged to enliven the Bluestocking group, a roundtable of intellectual women whom she and Elizabeth Montagu gathered. ❖ See also Cecil Aspinall-Oglander, *Admiral's Widow* (Hogarth, 1942) and *Admiral's Wife* (Longman, 1940); and *Women in World History.*

BOSCH, Aurora (c. 1940—). Cuban ballet dancer. Born c. 1940 in Havana, Cuba. ❖ Studied with Alicia Alonso and José Parés in Cuba; performed with Ballet Nacional de Cuba in *Coppélia, Antigona,* and *Tarde en la siesta,* among others; remained associated with the company throughout performing career and also danced with Ballet Clássico de México; won 2 Varna competition prizes; taught and served as ballet master at Ballet Nacional de Cuba; also taught at Instituto Superior de Arte, an acclaimed art institute, in Cuba.

BOSCH, Edith (1980—). Dutch judoka. Born May 31, 1980, in the Netherlands. ❖ Won a silver medal for 70kg at Athens Olympics (2004).

BOSCHEK, Anna (1874–1957). Austrian labor leader. Born in Vienna, Austria, May 14, 1874; died in Vienna, Nov 19, 1957; dau. of a locksmith and a former agricultural laborer; never married; no children. ❖ Socialist pioneer who organized strikes, gave countless speeches, and played a major role in building up a strong women's section within the Austrian Social Democratic movement; worked at various unskilled factory jobs; attended night school and joined Social Democratic movement (early 1890s); involved in strikes and political agitation; became secretary of the Social Democratic Party (SDP) trade union commission (1894); was an advocate of the political organization of Austrian working-class women; was a member of Austrian delegation to International Socialist Women's Conference (1907); was the 1st woman to serve in SDP Executive Committee (1909); served in various capacities in Austrian Parliament (1919–34); was responsible for several major pieces of social legislation; unable to resume political career after 1945 due to declining health, remained active within Social Democratic circles. ❖ See also *Women in World History.*

BOSCHETTI, Amina (1836–1881). Italian ballet dancer and choreographer. Born 1836 in Milan, Italy; died 1881 in Naples, Italy. ❖ At 12, debuted at Teatro alla Scala in Milan and continued to perform there for next 16 years; danced featured roles at La Scala in works by Paul Taglioni, Pasquale Borri, Salvatore Taglioni, and Giuseppe Rota; created roles in numerous works by Rota, including in his *La Maschera* (1865); choreographed many solos and a full-length ballet *Il Vello d'Ore,* which is said to have premiered the day she died.

BOSCO, María Angélica (1917—). Argentinean novelist, translator and essayist. Name variations: Maria Angelica Bosco. Born 1917. ❖ Works include *La muerte baja en el ascensor* (1954), *La Trampa* (1960), *Historia privada* (1972), *Cartas de mujeres* (1975), *En la estela de un secuestro* (1977), *En la piel de otro* (1981) and *La muerte vino de afuero* (1983); also translated Kierkegaard, Flaubert, Zola and Rimbaud.

BOSCO, Monique (1927—). Austrian-Canadian novelist. Born June 8, 1927, in Vienna, Austria. ❖ Immigrated to Canada (1948) and worked as journalist and professor of French at University of Montreal; novels include *Un Amour Maladroit* (1961), *Les Infusoires* (1965), *La femme de Loth* (1970), *New Medea* (1974) and *Charles Lévy M.D.* (1977); poetry includes *Jéricho* (1971), *Schabbat 70–77* (1978) and *Amen* (2002).

BOSE, Abala (1865–1951). Indian educator and reformer. Born Abala Das in 1865; died 1951; dau. of Durgahohan Das (founder of the Sadharan Brahma Samaj and Brahmamoijee); attended Bethune Collegiate School for Girls (est. by father) and Calcutta University; studied medicine in Madras; m. Jagadish Chandra Bose (physicist), in 1887. ❖ With sister Sarla, was one of the 1st women to attend Calcutta University; studied medicine in Madras; as secretary of the Brahmo Balika Shikshalaya (School for Girls), became an educational innovator, broadening the curriculum to include self-defense and introducing new methods such as the Maria Montessori system; launched the Nari Shiksha Samiti to help spread education to women throughout the country (1919), then established the Sister Nivedita Adult Education Fund; established a home for widows (1925); opened the Women's Industrial Co-operative Home in Calcutta (1935), which later became a relief and rehabilitation center for women from Bangladesh; established the Sadhuna Ashram in Calcutta.

BOSÉ, Lucia (1931—). Italian actress. Name variations: Lucia Bose. Born Lucia Borlani, Jan 28, 1931, in Milan, Italy; m. Luis-Miguel Dominguín (bullfighter and actor), 1955 (div. 1967); children: Miguel Bosé (b. 1956, singer and composer) and Paola Dominguín (actress). ❖ Named Miss Italy (1947); made film debut in De Santis's *Non c'è pace tra gli ulivi* (*Under the Olive Tree,* 1950); other films include Antonioni's *Cronaca di un Amore* and *La Signora senza camelie,* Bardem's *Death of a Cyclist,* and Buñuel's *Cela s'appelle l'aurore,* as well as *Satyricon, Jurtzenka, Ciao*

Gulliver, La Controfigura, La Casa de las palomas, Ceremonia sangrienta, Vera un cuento cruel, Lumière and *Ehrengard;* directed *El Niño de la luna* (1989).

BOSERUP, Esther (1910–1999). Danish economist. Name variations: Esther Talke Boserup. Born Esther Talke Börgesen, May 18, 1910, in Frederiksberg, Denmark; died Sept 24, 1999, in Ascona, Switzerland; studied at Copenhagen University; m. Mogens Boserup, 1931; children: 3. ❖ Influential specialist in economic development, worked for Danish government (1936–47), then at Research Division of UN Economic Committee for Europe (1947–57); also did freelance work worldwide, including in India (1957–59) and Senegal (1964–65); served on UN committee of Development Planning, Scandinavian Institute of Asian Studies, and UN International Research and Training Institute for Advancement of Women; was the 1st to bring world attention to the role of women in economic development. Writings include *Conditions of Agricultural Growth* (1965), *Women's Role in Economic Development* (1970) and *Population and Technological Change* (1981).

BOŠKOVIĆ, Anica (1714–1804). Croatian poet. Name variations: Anica Boskovic. Born 1714 in Dubrovnik, Croatia; died 1804; sister of Rudjer Boskovic (philosopher and scientist, 1711–1787); never married. ❖ Translated poetry from Latin and Italian; anonymously published *Razgovor pastirski vrhu porodjenja Gospodinova jedne djevočice Dubrovkinje* in Venice (1758).

BOSOMWORTH, Mary (c. 1690–c. 1763). *See Musgrove, Mary.*

BOSONE, Reva Beck (1895–1983). American politician. Born Reva Zilpha Beck in American Fork, Utah, April 2, 1895; died in Vienna, Virginia, July 21, 1983; dau. of Christian M. and Zilpha (Chipman) Beck; graduate of Westminster Junior College in Salt Lake City, 1917; University of California, Berkeley, BA, 1920; University of Utah, Doctor of Laws, 1930; m. Joe P. Bosone (lawyer), Oct 8, 1929 (div.); children: Zilpha Theresa Bosone. ❖ With husband, opened a private law practice, Bosone and Bosone; elected to State legislature (1932 and 1934) and served as Democratic floor leader; elected a police and traffic court judge of Salt Lake City Municipal Court (1936), becoming Utah's 1st woman judge; was an official observer at United Nations' founding conference in San Francisco (1945); served as the 1st director of Utah State Board for Education on Alcoholism (1937–48); became the 1st woman from Utah to be elected to US House of Representatives (1948) and won a 2nd term (1950); served on the Committee on Public Lands, the Committee on House Administration and the Committee on Interior and Insular Affairs, 81st–82nd Congresses (Jan 3, 1949–Jan 3, 1953). ❖ See also Beverly B. Clopton, *Her Honor, the Judge: The Story of Reva Beck Bosone* (Iowa State U. Press, 1980); and *Women in World History.*

BOSSE, Harriet (1878–1961). Norwegian-born Swedish actress. Name variations: Mrs. August Strindberg; Harriet Bosse-Vingård or Bosse-Wingard. Born Harriet Sofie Bosse, Feb 19, 1878, in Christiania (now Oslo), Norway; died Nov 2, 1961, in Oslo; dau. of Johann Heinrich Wilhelm Bosse (1836–1896, publisher and bookseller) and Anne Marie Lehman Bosse (1836–1893); sister of Dagmar Bosse (opera singer) and Alma Bosse (actress); attended Royal Conservatory of Music in Stockholm, 1894–97; became 3rd wife of August Strindberg (1849–1912, playwright), May 6, 1901 (div. 1904); m. Gunnar Wingard, 1908 (div. 1911); m. Edvin Adolphson, 1927 (div. 1932); children: (1st m.) Anne Marie Strindberg (b. 1902); (2nd m.) 1 son (b. 1909). ❖ One of the greatest Scandinavian actresses of modern times, began acting career in 1896; had starring role in Strindberg's *To Damascus I* in Stockholm (1900); besides performing starring roles in Strindberg's plays, became a leading actress in plays by Maeterlinck, Sudermann, von Hofmannsthal and other major playwrights of early years of 20th century; her enduring influence is to be found in the late work of Strindberg, whom she inspired, and in the modern style of acting she pioneered in Sweden; also appeared in several Swedish motion pictures. ❖ See also Carla Waal, *Harriet Bosse: Strindberg's Muse and Interpreter* (Southern Illinois U. Press, 1990); *Letters of Strindberg to Harriet Bosse: Love Letters from a Tormented Genius* (ed. and trans. by Arvid Paulson, Grosset, 1959); and *Women in World History.*

BOSSHARDT, Alida M. (1913—). Dutch social reformer. Born Alida Margaretha Bosshardt in the Netherlands, June 8, 1913. ❖ Lieutenant colonel in the Salvation Army, spent the greater part of her career living and working in the section of the Old City of Amsterdam called the *Zeedijk,* home of the notorious Red Light district; joined the Salvation Army (June 19, 1932); commissioned (1934), was stationed at the Children's Home, "Zonnehoek," in Amsterdam, where she stayed until after WWII; was given an administrative post at the Territorial Headquarters across from the Central station and bordering the city's Red Light district, staying there for 10 years; well known in the Netherlands, was one of three honored guests received by Queen Juliana (1960); was promoted to lieutenant-colonel and received a knighthood in the Order of Oranje Nassau (1966); retired (1978). ❖ See also Denis Duncan, *Here Is My Hand: The Story of Lieutenant Colonel Alida Bosshardt of the Red Light Area, Amsterdam* (Hodder & Stoughton, 1977); and *Women in World History*.

BOSSHART, Dominique (1977—). Swiss-Canadian taekwondo player. Born Oct 7, 1977, in Morges, Switzerland; immigrated to Landmark, Manitoba, Canada (1981). ❖ Won a bronze medal for +67kg at Sydney Olympics (2000); won 7 national titles (1993–2000); won gold medal at Pan American Games (2000).

BOSTON, Lucy Maria (1892–1990). British author of children's books. Born Lucy Maria Wood in Southport, Lancashire, England, Dec 10, 1892; died in Hemingford Grey, Huntingdonshire, England, May 25, 1990; dau. of James (engineer) and Mary (Garrett) Wood; attended Somerville College, Oxford; married an officer in the Royal Flying Corps, 1917 (div., 1935); children: Peter. ❖ Started writing at 62 and, within a short time, had distinguished herself in juvenile fiction; her books (many of which were illustrated by son Peter) were often inspired by and set in her 12th-century manor house in Hemingford Grey, which, through extensive renovations, became her work of art. Most notable among her writings is the "Green Knowe" series, which includes *A Stranger at Green Knowe,* winner of Carnegie Medal (1961), and *The Children of Green Knowe,* winner of Lewis Carroll Shelf Award (1969). ❖ See also autobiography, *Perverse and Foolish: A Memoir of Childhood and Youth* (1979); Jasper Rose, *Lucy Boston* (Bodley Head, 1965); and *Women in World History*.

BOSURGI, Silvia (1979—). Italian water-polo player. Born April 17, 1979, in Italy. ❖ At World championships, won team gold medal (2001); driver, won a team gold medal at Athens Olympics (2004).

BOSWELL, Annabella (1826–1916). Australian memoirist. Name variations: Annabella Innes. Born Annabella Innes, 1826, in Australia; died 1916; dau. of George Innes (died 1839); niece of Archibald Clunes Innes (1800–1857, commandant at the prison at Port Macquarie) and Margaret Macleay (1802–1858, dau. of the colonial secretary, Alexander Macleay); lived at their Lake Innes Cottage in Port Macquarie, 1839, 1843–48; attended school in Sydney. ❖ Published journal about her Australian girlhood (illus. with her own watercolors) as *Early Recollections and Gleanings from an Old Journal* (1908) and *Further Recollections of my Early Days in Australia* (1911). It was reprinted as *Annabella Boswell's Journal* (1965).

BOSWELL, Cathy (1962—). African-American basketball player. Born Nov 10, 1962, in Joliet, Illinois. ❖ Was all-time women's scoring leader at Illinois State University; won a team gold medal for basketball at Los Angeles Olympics (1984). Won the Willye White Award (1979). ❖ See also *Women in World History*.

BOSWELL, Connee (1907–1976). American jazz singer. Name variations: changed spelling of name to Connee when she went solo. Born Connie Boswell in New Orleans, Louisiana, Dec 3, 1907; died in New York, NY, Oct 11, 1976; sister of Helvetia Boswell ("Vet") and Martha Boswell (singers); m. Harold Leedy (her manager), 1935; crippled at age 3, performed in a wheelchair. ❖ With sisters, formed a trio called the Boswell Sisters (Connee played cello, piano, alto sax, and trombone, Martha the piano, and Vet the violin); signed with the Dorsey Brothers' Band; secured recording contracts (Brunswick) and headlined radio shows; when sisters retired following their marriages (1935), embarked on a solo career; was a frequent radio guest on "Bing Crosby & Kraft Music Hall," and entertained the troops during WWII; also appeared in several movies, including *Moulin Rouge, Artists and Models, Transatlantic Merry-Go-Round, The Big Broadcast of 1932* and *Kiss the Boys Goodbye;* gave last performance (1975), with Benny Goodman at Carnegie Hall. ❖ See also *Women in World History*.

BOTA, Kinga (1977—). Hungarian kayaker. Born Aug 22, 1977, in Hungary. ❖ At World championships, placed 1st for K4 500 and 1000 and K2 500 (2001), K4 200 and 500 and K2 500 and 1000 (2002) and K4 200 and 500 and K2 500 (2003); won a silver medal for K4 500 at Athens Olympics (2004).

BOTCHKAREVA, Evguenia. Russian rhythmic gymnast. Name variations: Eugenia or Evgenia. Born in USSR. ❖ Won a team bronze medal at Atlanta Olympics (1996).

BOTCHKAREVA, Maria (1889–?). Russian military leader. Name variations: Leona Botchkarova, Mariya Bochkareva; nicknamed Yashka. Pronunciation: BOK-car-AVA. Born Maria Leontievna Frolkova, July 1889, in Nikolsko, Russia; date of death unknown; dau. of Leonti Semenovitch Frolkov (Novgorod peasant) and Olga Nazarev Frolkova; m. Afanasi Botchkarev, in 1905; children: none. ❖ Commander who rose from the peasantry during WWI and organized the most successful women's battalion for the Provisional Government in 1917; ran away from husband (1908); spent time in Yakutsk Prison with her lover, Yakov Buk (1912–14); ran away from Yakutsk and joined Russian army (1914); while fighting on Russian-German front, was wounded and won several medals for heroism (1915–17); organized Russian Women's Battalion of Death in an effort to inspire the Russian military and bolster the Provisional Revolutionary Government that replaced the tsar (1917); disbanded Battalion and imprisoned by the Bolsheviks (1917); left Russia for US, where she met with President Woodrow Wilson (1918); returned to Russia, removed from active service and faded into obscurity (1918). ❖ See also autobiography *Yashka: My Life As Peasant, Officer and Exile* (Stokes, 1919); and *Women in World History*.

BOTCHKAROVA, Leona (b. 1889). See Botchkareva, Maria.

BOTELHO, Adélaïde-Marie-Émilie-Filleul, Souza (1761–1836). See Souza-Botelho, Adélaïde-Marie-Émilie-Filleul, Marquise of.

BOTELHO, Fernanda (1926—). Portuguese poet and novelist. Name variations: Maria Fernanda Botelho. Born 1926 in Oporto, Portugal. ❖ Contributed to experimental, anti neo-realist literary journals and magazines; was one of the founders of the magazine *Távola Redonda;* postwar novels include *O enigma de Sete Alíneas* (1956), *O Angula Raso* (1957), *Xerazade e os Outros* (1964), *Terra sem Música* (1969), *Lourenço é un Nome de Jogral* (1971), *Esta Noite Sonhei com Brueghel* (1987) and *Dramaticamente Vestida de negro* (1994); poetic work includes *Coordenadas Líricas* (1951). Won Camilo Castelo Branco prize for best novel for *A Gata e a Fábula* (The Cat and the Fable, 1960).

BOTHA, Wendy (1965—). South African surfer. Born Aug 22, 1965, in East London, South Africa; m. Brent Todd (New Zealand football player). ❖ Won 1st of 4 World titles (1987); moved to Australia (1989), eventually becoming a naturalized citizen and Australia's 1st female professional champion; won 7 events (1989); won 24 events during career; moved to New Zealand (1993) and co-hosted a sports tv show.

BOTKIN, Cordelia (c. 1854–1910). American murderer. Born c. 1854 in US; died Mar 7, 1910, at San Quentin; m. Welcome A. Botkin (sep. sometime before 1898); children: son, Beverly. ❖ While living in San Francisco, took up with journalist John Presley Dunning, who left his wife Elizabeth and child for her; when Dunning was assigned to cover Spanish-American War (1898), feared war would make him return to his wife; seeded a box of candy with arsenic and mailed it to Elizabeth Dunning, killing her and her relative Leila Deane; in highly publicized trial, found guilty of first-degree murder (Dec 31, 1898) and received a life sentence.

BOTSFORD, Anna (1854–1930). See Comstock, Anna Botsford.

BOTSFORD, Beth (1981—). American swimmer. Born Beth Anne Botsford, May 21, 1981, in Baltimore, Maryland; sister of Stacie Botsford (swimmer). ❖ Won a gold medal for 100-meter backstroke and a gold medal for 4 x 100-meter relay at Atlanta Olympics (1996).

BOTSFORD, Susan (c. 1954—). See Perkins, Susan.

BOTTA, Anne C.L. (1815–1891). American poet and essayist. Name variations: Anne Lynch Botta; Anne Lynch. Born Anne Charlotte Lynch in Bennington, Vermont, Nov 11, 1815; died in New York, NY, Mar 23, 1891; graduated with honors from Albany Female Academy; m. Vincenzo Botta (New York University professor), in 1855. ❖ A sculptor of merit, started literary career in Providence and moved to New York (1842); her residence became a center for literary and artistic friends, including Edgar Allan Poe and Margaret Fuller, and is known as the 1st important salon in the history of American letters. ❖ See also *Memoirs of Anne C.L. Botta* (compiled by "Her Friends," 1894); and *Women in World History*.

BOTTERILL, Jennifer (1979—). Canadian ice-hockey player. Born May 1, 1979, in Winnipeg, Manitoba, Canada. ❖ Played for Harvard University; at age 18, as Team Canada's youngest player, won a team silver medal at Nagano for Canada (1998), the 1st Olympics to feature women's ice hockey; won a team gold medal at World championships (2001); won a team gold medal at Salt Lake City Olympics (2002) and at Torino Olympics (2006).

BOTTING, Eirene Adeline (1899–1980). *See White, Antonia.*

BOTTOME, Margaret McDonald (1827–1906). American author and religious organizer. Born Mary McDonald, Dec 29, 1827, in New York, NY; died Nov 14, 1906, in New York, NY; m. Rev. Frank Bottome, in 1850. ❖ With 9 other women, formed a Christian study group called King's Daughters (1886), an outgrowth of her long-standing practice of giving informal talks on the Bible; as president, saw membership increase over next 20 years to approximately 500,000 in US and Canada; also contributed to the Order's magazine, *Silver Cross*, and wrote a column in the *Ladies' Home Journal* for members; other published works include *Crumbs from the King's Table, A Sunshine Trip: Glimpses of the Orient, Death and Life, Seven Questions, After Easter* and *The Guest Chamber.*

BOTTOME, Phyllis (1884–1963). British novelist and lecturer. Born in Rochester, Kent, England, May 31, 1884; died in Hampstead, England, Aug 22, 1963; dau. of William Macdonald Bottome (cleric) and Margaret Leatham; m. A.E. Forbes Dennis, in 1917. ❖ Writer and lecturer whose work concentrated on life in post-Imperial Austria and on the psychological theories of Alfred Adler; grew up in England and US; traveled extensively and published 1st novel, *Raw Material* (1905); showed strong interest in psychology throughout writing career; published almost 50 novels and 2 collections of short stories, including *Old Wine* (1920), *The Advances of Harriet* (1933), *Innocence and Experience* (1935), *Level Crossing* (1936), *The Mortal Storm* (1937), *The Heart of a Child* (1940), *Masks and Faces* (1940), *The Mansion House of Liberty* (1941), *Man and Beast* (1953), *Against Whom?* (1954), *Eldorado Jane* (1956) and *Walls of Glass* (1958). ❖ See also autobiographies, *Search for a Soul* (1947) and *The Goal* (1963); and *Women in World History.*

BOTTOMLEY, Virginia (1948—). Scottish social worker, politician and member of Parliament. Born Virginia Hilda Brunette Maxwell Garnett, Mar 12, 1948, in Dunoon, Scotland; dau. of W. John Garnett (CBE); attended Putney High School, Essex University, and London School of Economics; m. Peter Bottomley (MP), 1967. ❖ Behavioral scientist (1971–84); as a Conservative, unsuccessfully contested 1st seat, Isle of Wight (1983); elected to House of Commons for Surrey South West (1984–2001); worked as parliamentary private secretary under Chris Patten, then Geoffrey Howe; served as junior minister of the Department of the Environment (1988–89); named a health minister (1989); became secretary of state for health (1992) and began reforming the National Health Service, closing several hospitals; became secretary of state for National Heritage (1995); left Parliament (2005).

BOTTZAU, Tina (1971—). Danish handball player. Name variations: Tina Nielsen-Bottzau or Bøttzau. Born Aug 29, 1971, in Denmark. ❖ Won a team gold medal at Atlanta Olympics (1996) and at Sydney Olympics (2000); won team European championships (1996) and World championships (1997).

BOTWINSKA, Adela (b. 1904). Polish-Jewish political activist and nurse. Born Adela Weinraub in Podwoloczyska near Tarnopol, Russian Poland, in 1904. ❖ Experienced the destruction of her hometown and a bloody pogrom (1915); joined Zionist youth movement and immigrated to Palestine (1926); became a nurse and was active in trade union activities (1927–37); traveled to Spain to join nursing staff of the International Brigades during Spanish Civil War (1937); returned to Palestine (1940); worked as a nurse for British forces in Cairo (1941–46); returned to Poland (1947); an ardent Communist, wished to participate in the creation of a "People's Poland," but experienced anti-Semitism and returned to Israel disillusioned (1969).

BOUBOULINA, Laskarina (1771–1825). Greek military leader. Name variations: Lascarina Bobolina or Boubalina; (nickname) Capitanissa. Born on the island of Spétsai (Spetses), 1771 (some sources cite 1783); killed 1825; dau. of a sea captain; twice married, twice widowed; children: 6. ❖ Freedom fighter and naval commander whose heroic exploits became the subject of countless folk songs, ballads and plays; widowed for the 2nd time soon after the outbreak of the Greek War of Independence (1821), supported the struggle against the Ottoman occupiers of her homeland; paid for the outfitting of 4 ships as well as an army unit,

and personally participated in the naval blockades of Monemvasia and Nauplia (1825); killed because of involvement in a family feud. ❖ See also *Women in World History.*

BOUCHER, Denise (1935—). Canadian playwright. Born Dec 12, 1935, in Victoriaville, Quebec, Canada. ❖ Wrote the play *Les Fées ont Soif* (1978, trans. as *The Fairies are Thirsty,* 1982), which was banned from a Montreal theater for its allegedly blasphemous representation of the Virgin Mary (Boucher was attacking the idealization of women); also wrote *Cyprine: Essaicollage Pour Etre Une Femme* (1978) and (with Madeleine Gagnon) *Retailles* (1978).

BOUCHER, Joan (d. 1550). *See Bocher, Joan.*

BOUCHERETT, Jessie (1825–1905). English feminist. Born in Wellingham, Lincolnshire, England, in 1825; died 1905; dau. of a land-owner and High Sheriff; educated at Stratford. ❖ Joined Barbara Bodichon and Adelaide Ann Procter to found the Society for Promoting the Employment of Women (1860), which advocated jobs for women in farming, engraving, nursing, and clerical work, as well as special training courses in arithmetic and bookkeeping; was the editor of *The Englishwoman's Review* (1866–71) and served on the committee to present a petition for women's suffrage to Parliament (1866); writings include a collaboration with Helen Blackburn, *The Condition of Working Women* (1896). ❖ See also *Women in World History.*

BOUCICAULT, Mrs. Dion (1833–1916). *See Robertson, Agnes.*

BOUCICAULT, Irene (1872–1949). *See Vanbrugh, Irene.*

BOUCICAULT, Nina (1867–1950). English actress. Born in Marylebone, England, Feb 27, 1867; died Aug 2, 1950; dau. of Dion Boucicault the Elder (1822–1890, actor and dramatist) and Agnes Robertson (actress); sister of Dion Boucicault the Younger (1859–1929) and Aubrey Boucicault; m. E.H. Kelly; m. Donald Innes Smith. ❖ Made stage debut as Eily O'Connor in *The Colleen Bawn* with father's company in Kentucky; made London debut as Flossie Trivett in *The New Wing* at the Strand (1892), and then played Kitty Verdun in *Charley's Aunt* for 2 years; starred in the original production of *Peter Pan* at the Duke of York Theatre, London, England (1904); best known roles included that of Suzanne de Villiers in *Le Monde ou L'On S'Ennuie* (repeated her performance in an English adaptation) and Susan Throssel in *Quality Street* (1914); also had great success as Bessie Broke in *The Light that Failed* at the Lyric and as Moira Loiney in *Little Mary* at Wyndham's, both 1903.

BOUCOT, Katharine (1903–1987). *See Sturgis, Katharine Boucot.*

BOUDBERG, Moura (1892–1974). *See Budberg, Moura.*

BOUDICA (26/30–60 CE). Queen of the Iceni. Name variations: Boudicca or Boudicaa; the popular spelling, Boadicea, was derived from an error in an influential Renaissance manuscript. Pronunciation: (roughly) Boodika. Born as a member of the Royal House of the Iceni tribe probably between the years 26 CE to 30 in the modern shires of Norfolk and northern Suffolk, England; died c. 62; m. King Prasutagus of the Iceni prior to 49 CE; children: 2 daughters (names unknown). ❖ Fought to drive the Romans from British soil; made regent on behalf of her daughters upon the death of Prasutagus (59 or 60 CE); became queen and led revolt against the Roman occupation of Britain (60); won victories at the modern sites of Colchester, London, and St. Albans and ambushed a Roman force in the field before succumbing to the Romans (60), the same year in which she is believed to have taken her own life. ❖ See also Antonia Fraser, *The Warrior Queens* (Knopf, 1989); Graham Webster, *Boudica: the British Revolt against Rome AD 60* (Batsford, 1978, rev. ed., 1993); and *Women in World History.*

BOUDICAA or BOUDICCA (26/30–60 CE). *See Boudica.*

BOUDIN, Kathy (1943—). American radical. Born May 19, 1943, in New York, NY; dau. of Leonard Boudin (civil-rights attorney, died 1989) and Jean Boudin (died 1994); Bryn Mawr, BA (magna cum laude), 1965; niece of radical journalist I.F. Stone; children: son Chesa. ❖ Was a member of the Weather Underground, which claimed responsibility for 20 bombings (1969–75); served 22 years in prison at Bedford Hills Correctional Facility for participating as a decoy in armored-car robbery (1981) that caused the death of 2 Nyack police officers and a security guard. ❖ See also Susan Braudy, *Family Circle: The Boudins and the Aristocracy of the Left* (Knopf, 2003).

BOUDJENAH, Yasmine (1970—). French politician. Born Dec 21, 1970, in Paris, France. ❖ Member of the French Young Communists'

Movement national bureau (1990–98), 1st national secretary of the Communist students' union (1994–97), and member of the National Council of the French Communist Party (2000—); representing the Confederal Group of the European United Left/Nordic Green Left (GUE/NGL), elected to 5th European Parliament (1999–2004).

BOUDRIAS, Christine (1972—). Canadian short-track speedskater. Born Sept 5, 1972, in Montreal, Quebec, Canada. ❖ Won a silver medal at Lillehammer Olympics (1994) and a bronze medal at Nagano Olympics (1992), both for the 3,000-meter relay.

BOUFFLERS, Madeleine-Angelique, Duchesse de (1707–1787). French Salonnière. Name variations: Madeleine-Angelique de Neufville-Villeroi, duchesse de Luxemburg or Luxemburg; Maréchale de Luxembourg. Born 1707; died 1787; m. Duc de Boufflers; m. Maréchal (Marshal) of Luxembourg. ❖ Held a salon that was a popular meeting place for the cream of society; was a patron of Rousseau.

BOUFFLERS, Marie (1706–1747). Marquise de Boufflers. Born Marie Françoise Catherine de Beauvais-Craon in 1706; died in 1747; sister of the Maréchale de Mirepoix (friend of Mme de Pompadour); children: Stanislas-Jean Boufflers, chevalier de (1737–1815, a cavalry officer and writer of light verse). ❖ A beautiful, witty woman, was one of the charmers of her age; lived in Lorraine, was a friend of Voltaire, and mistress of King Stanislas Leczszinski, ex-king of Poland.

BOUFFLERS-ROUVREL, Marie Charlotte Hippolyte, Countess de (1724–c. 1800). French salonnière. Name variations: Comtesse or Countess Boufflers-Rouvrel; Rouveret. Born in Paris, France, 1724; died c. 1800; m. Comte de Boufflers-Rouvrel (d. 1764). ❖ Following death of husband (1764), became the reputed mistress of the Prince de Conti and hosted his receptions; a leader in Parisian literary circles, was a friend of J.J. Rousseau, Hume, and Grimm; is often confused with Marie Boufflers, mother of author Stanislas-Jean Boufflers and friend of Voltaire. ❖ See also *Women in World History.*

BOUGHTON, Alice (1866–1943). American photographer. Born in Brooklyn, New York, 1866; died in Bay Shore, New York, 1943. ❖ Studied painting in Paris and Rome before becoming an assistant in the studio of Gertrude Käsebier; became an associate of the Photo-Secession (later elected a fellow) and was represented in Alfred Stieglitz's initial exhibition of 1905; specialized in portraits and theatrical work. ❖ See also *Women in World History.*

BOUHIRED, Djamila (1937—). Algerian patriot. Name variations: Djamilah or Jamila. Born 1937 to a middle-class Muslim family in Algiers (some sources cite 1935); m. Jacques Vergès (her French attorney); children: Nadyah (adopted), Maryam, Ilyas. ❖ Algerian heroine of the War of National Liberation from France (1954–62), known throughout the Middle East as "the Arab Joan of Arc"; at 16, convinced that her activities would hasten the day of Algerian independence, was taught to plant bombs by an activist; while under arrest, was fired at by the leader of her organization in order to prevent her from revealing information about him (1957); as soon as she had recovered from her wounds, was interrogated and tortured by French captors for 17 days, but would not reveal any information; was tried before a military court in Algeria (mid-July 1957), which was regarded by many observers as a travesty of justice; was found guilty and sentenced to die on the guillotine, but public opinion—both in France and internationally—had begun to turn against the war; with her cause taken up by French intellectuals, was granted a reprieve from the guillotine; because of international pressure, sentence commuted to life imprisonment (1958); with Algerian independence (1962), was released and returned to Algiers. ❖ See also *The Battle of Algiers* (1966); and *Women in World History.*

BOUILLON, Duchess de (1649–1714). See Mancini, Marie-Anne.

BOULANGER, Lili (1893–1918). French composer. Born Juliette Marie Olga Boulanger, Aug 21, 1893, in Paris, France; died of TB, Mar 15, 1918, in Paris; dau. of Ernest Boulanger (composer) and Raissa or Raïssa (Princess Michetsky or Mychetsky) Boulanger (vocalist from St. Petersburg); sister of Nadia Boulanger (1887–1979). ❖ A child prodigy, entered Paris Conservatoire (1909), where she studied composition with Georges Gaussade and Paul Vidal; found her musical voice almost at once, proving to be a gifted composer despite precarious health; won Prix Lepaulle (1910); was 1st woman to win Premier Grand Prix de Rome for music (1913); wrote *Nocturne* for flute or violin and piano (1911), *Pour les funérailles d'un soldat* for orchestra (1912), *Three psalms* for orchestra (1916–17), an unfinished opera (1917), and a work for

soprano, strings, harp, and organ (1918), the year of her death at age 24. ❖ See also *Women in World History.*

BOULANGER, Nadia (1887–1979). French composer, performer, and teacher. Born Juliette Nadia Boulanger in Paris, France, Sept 16, 1887; died in Paris, Oct 22, 1979; dau. of Ernest (composer and professor of voice at Paris Conservatoire de Musique) and Raissa or Raïssa (Princess Michetsky or Mychetsky) Boulanger (vocalist from St. Petersburg); sister of Lili Boulanger (1893–1918); attended Paris Conservatoire de Musique; never married. ❖ Teacher of music who included among her students Leonard Bernstein, Virgil Thomson, and Aaron Copland, making her one of the most influential musicians of the 20th century; at 11, won the 1st of many 1st place competitions at Paris Conservatoire de Musique (1898); began performing career (1903); began studies with Italian pianist and composer Raoul Pugno (1904); collaborated with Pugno on music for Gabriele d'Annunzio's drama, *La Ville morte,* and began lifelong friendship with Igor Stravinsky (1910); abandoned performing in favor of teaching (1920); made concert tour of US and was offered teaching chair at Curtis Institute in Philadelphia (1924); accepted position at École Normale du Musique in Paris, teaching organ, harmony, counterpoint, and the history of music, an unprecedented appointment for a woman; became 1st woman to conduct the Royal Philharmonic Orchestra in London (1936); repeated the honor with Boston Symphony Orchestra (1938), and NY Philharmonic and Philadelphia orchestras (1939); appointed judge of the prestigious Tchaikovsky Competition in Moscow (1966). Inducted as a Grand Officer of the Legion of Honor (1977). ❖ See also Alan Kendall, *The Tender Tyrant, Nadia Boulanger: A Life Devoted to Music* (1976); Bruno Monsaingeon, *Conversations with Nadia Boulanger* (trans. by Robyn Marsack, Northeastern U. Press, 1988); Léonie Rosenstiel, *Nadia Boulanger: A Life in Music* (Norton, 1982); Jérôme Spycket, *Nadia Boulanger* (trans. by M.M. Shriver, Pendragon, 1987); and *Women in World History.*

BOULAZ, Loulou (1912—). Swiss skier and mountain climber. Born 1912 in Avenches, Switzerland. ❖ As a skier: was a member of the Swiss national team (1936–41) and came in 3rd at World Slalom championships in Chamonix (1937); as a climber: made 1st ascent of one of the classic routes on the big cliff, Les Paturages in the Salève; made 1st ascent by women (with Lulu Durand) of the Southwest Face of the Dent du Géant (1933) and the Dent du Requin (1932); made 1st all-female traverse of the Southwest Face and the Northwest Ridge of the Grands Charmoz (1935), and the Droites (1935); made 1st female ascent (and 2nd ascent by anyone) of the North Face of the Petit Dru with Raymond Lambert (1935); made 1st ascent of the North Face of the Velan and the north shoulder of the Rothorn in the Valais (1941); made 1st female ascents of the North Faces of the Schreckhorn, the Studerhorn, and the Jungfrau in the Bernese Oberland; Montagnes de 'Air, including 1st ascent of Tour Loulou (1977). ❖ See also Birkett and Peascod, *Women Climbing* (A&C Black, 1989); and *Women in World History.*

BOULIAR, Marie Geneviève (1762–1825). French portraitist. Name variations: Bouliard. Born in Paris, France, in 1762; died at Château d'Arcy (Saône-et-Lire) in 1825; only dau. of a tailor, though she may have been related to artists with similar names; studied with Joseph Siffred Duplessis, 1725–1802. ❖ First recorded work, signed and dated 1785, was a portrait of a young woman; initially exhibited at the Salon of 1791 and sent work there until 1817; most famous painting, *Aspasia,* won a Prix d'Encouragement (1795). Though over 40 paintings and drawings are attributed to her through various records, only 10 paintings and 1 drawing have survived.

BOULMERKA, Hassiba (1968—). Algerian runner. Born July 10, 1968, in Constantin, Algeria. ❖ Won the 800-meter and 1,500 meter races at the African Games (1988); won World championship in the 1,500 meters (1991 and 1995), the 1st World title won by an African woman; won a gold medal for 1,500 meters at Barcelona Olympics (1992), the 1st Algerian to win an Olympic gold medal; promoted the cause of women athletes. Awarded Algerian Medal of Merit. ❖ See also *Women in World History.*

BOULOGNE, countess of.
See Ida of Lorraine (1040–1113).
See Mary of Atholl (d. 1116).
See Sybilla of Anjou (1112–1165).
See Constance Capet (c. 1128–1176).
See Marie of Boulogne (d. 1182).

See Ide d'Alsace (r. 1173–1216).
See Matilda de Dammartin (d. 1258).

BOULTER, Rosalyn (1916–1997). English stage and screen actress. Born Feb 1, 1916, in Burton-on-Trent, Staffordshire, England; died Mar 6, 1997, in Santa Barbara, California; m. Stanley Haynes (div.); m. William Sistrom (British film producer), Aug 8, 1952 (died 1972); children: Carol Haynes Johnson. ❖ Made stage debut as Lady Clive in *Clive of India* (1935), followed by *Our Own Lives, Children to Bless You, Number Six* and *Dear Murderer*, among others; starred with Barry Morse in *The Assassin* (1945); made Broadway debut as the ingenue lead Frankie in *George and Martha*; films include *Love at Sea, Holiday's End, The First of the Few* (aka *Spitfire*), *The Gentle Sex, Rhythm Serenade* (with Vera Lynn) and *The Day They Gave Babies Away;* was the foil for George Formby in film *George in Civvy Street* (1946); at time of 2nd marriage, moved to Arizona and worked with the Phoenix Little Theater.

BOULTON, Agnes (1893–1968). English-born writer. Name variations: Agnes Boulton O'Neill. Born in London, England, Sept 19, 1893; died in Point Pleasant, New Jersey, Nov 25, 1968; dau. of Edward W. Boulton (painter); sister of Margery Boulton; married a man named Burton; became 2nd wife of Eugene O'Neill (playwright), April 12, 1918 (div. 1929); m. Morris Kaufman (freelance writer); children: (1st m.) Barbara Burton; (2nd m.) Shane Rudraighe O'Neill (b. Oct 30, 1919); Oona O'Neill Chaplin (b. May 14, 1925). ❖ From age 17, sold stories to better magazines and pulps, including *Black Cat, Cavalier* and the *Evening World;* wrote of her early years in *Part of a Long Story* (1958); also wrote the highly praised *The Road Is Before Us.* ❖ See also *Women in World History.*

BOULTON, Mary Anne (1829–1912). *See Robb, Mary Anne.*

BOUMAN, Kea (1903–1998). Dutch tennis player. Name variations: Cornelia Tiedemann Bouman. Born Nov 23, 1903, in the Netherlands; died Nov 1998. ❖ At Paris Olympics, won a bronze medal in mixed doubles–outdoors (1924); won the French Open doubles with Lili de Alvarez (1930).

BOUMEDIENE-THIERY, Alima (1956—). French politician. Born July 24, 1956, in Argenteuil, France; MA in law and economics (1982) and Doctorate in socio-economic studies (1987). ❖ Representing Group of the Greens/European Free Alliance, elected to 5th European Parliament (1999–2004); named vice-chair to delegation for relations with the Palestinian Legislative Council.

BOUNESS, Elisabeth (1862–1911). *See Bré, Ruth.*

BOUPACHA, Djamila (1942—). Algerian nationalist heroine. Name variations: Djamilah or Jamila. Born in Algeria in 1942; married. ❖ During Algerian war of independence, joined the National Liberation Front (FLN, 1954); arrested, was accused of having bombed the Brasserie des Facultés, a café near the University of Algiers (1961); because she refused to confess to the charges, was beaten, subjected to electric shocks, and raped with an empty bottle; incensed by the nature of the atrocities committed against her, received the support of many of the luminaries of French intellectual life; at trial, was defended by attorney Gisèle Halimi, who took her case through a series of courts in Algeria; transferred to France, won release from prison at the time of Algerian independence (1962); later spoke and wrote on the subject of women's emancipation in a Muslim society. ❖ See also Simone de Beauvoir and Gisèle Halimi. *Djamila Boupacha: The Story of the Torture of a Young Algerian Girl which Shocked Liberal French Opinion* (trans. by Peter Green, Macmillan, 1962); and *Women in World History.*

BOUQUARD, Marilyn Lloyd (b. 1929). *See Lloyd, Marilyn.*

BOURASSA, Jocelyn (1947—). Canadian golfer. Born May 30, 1947, in Shawinigan South, Quebec, Canada; attended University of Montreal. ❖ Considered the "godmother" of Canadian women's golf, won the Canadian Open (1965, 1971), and the New Zealand Amateur (1971); was the 1st woman to be named French-Canadian athlete of the year (1972); turned pro and was Rookie of the Year (1972); won La Canadienne Open, later known as the du Maurier Classic, in its inaugural year (1973), and received Canada's highest honor, a medal presented by the queen; coached at Arizona State University (1979–80); served as director of the du Maurier Classic and the Bank of Montreal Canadian Women's Open. Inducted into Canadian Golf Hall of Fame (1996).

BOURBON, Anne Geneviève de, Duchesse de Longueville (1619–1679). *See Longueville, Anne Geneviève de.*

BOURBON, duchess of.
See Isabelle of Savoy (d. 1383).
See Agnes of Burgundy (d. 1476).
See Jeanne of Bourbon (1434–1482).
See Marie Louise d'Orleans (1750–1822).

BOURBON, ruler of.
See Agnes de Dampierre (1237–1288).
See Beatrix de Bourgogne (d. 1310).
See Mahaut I (r. 1215–1242).

BOURBON-PARMA, duchess of. *See Pia of Sicily (1849–1882).*

BOURBON-PARMA, princess of.
See Zita of Parma (1892–1989).
See Oldenburg, Margaret (1895–1992).
See Charlotte (1896–1985).
See Anne of Bourbon-Parma (1923—).

BOURCHIER, Anne (c. 1417–1474). Duchess of Norfolk. Name variations: Eleanor Bourchier; Anne Mowbray. Born c. 1417; died in 1474; dau. of William Bourchier, count of Eu, and Anne Plantagenet (1383–1438); m. John Mowbray (1415–1461), 3rd duke of Norfolk; children: John Mowbray (b. 1444), 4th duke of Norfolk. Following Anne Bourchier's death in 1474, John Mowbray m. Catherine Neville (c. 1397–1483).

BOURCHIER, Anne (1512–1571). Countess of Essex. Name variations: Baroness Bourchier. Born 1512; died Jan 28, 1571 (some sources cite 1570); dau. of Henry Bourchier, 2nd earl of Essex, and Mary Say; m. William Parr, marquess of Northampton, Feb 9, 1526 (annulled April 1543).

BOURCHIER, Eleanor (c. 1417–1474). *See Bourchier, Anne.*

BOURCHIER, Elizabeth (b. 1598). *See Cromwell, Elizabeth.*

BOURCHIER, Joan (fl. 1468). *See Neville, Joan.*

BOURDIC-VIOT, Marie-Henriette Payad d'Estang de (1746–1802). French poet and essayist. Name variations: Madame d'Antremont; Marquise d'Antremont or d'Entremont; Marie-Henriette-Anne Payan Delestang, Marquise d'Antremont. Born 1746 in Dresden, Germany; died 1802; related to Anne Dacier. ❖ Knew Latin, German, English, and Italian; admitted to Académie de Nîme (1782); contributed to *Journal des Dames*, and her poetry was later collected in *Poésies de Mme la marquise d'Antremont* (1770); collaborated on periodical *L'Almanach de Muses*, which published her poem "Ode au silence"; other works include *Éloge de Montaigne* (1800) and *La Forêt de Brama.*

BOURDIL, Marguerite Taos (1913–1976). *See Amrouche, Marie-Louise.*

BOURETTE, Charlotte Rouyer (1714–1784). French poet. Name variations: Charlotte Bourette; La Muse Limonadière. Born 1714 in France; died 1784. ❖ Father and 2 husbands were *limonadiers,* makers of non-alcoholic beverages; ran Café Allemand in the rue Croix-des-Petits-Champs, Paris, where dissertations and plays were read; published selection of verse *La Muse limonadière* (1755) and play *La Coquette punie.*

BOURGEOIS, Louise (1563–1636). French midwife and medical writer. Born 1563 near Paris (France); died 1636 in France; m. Martin Boursier (barber-surgeon); children: 3. ❖ Talented midwife, gained a widespread reputation for her skill and learning; became the royal midwife to the queen, Marie de Medici (1601), while maintaining her own private practice; supervised close to 2,000 births (1593–1609), while acquiring experience and practical training unsurpassed in Europe; writings include *Various Observations on Sterility, Miscarriage, Fertility, Confinements, and Illnesses of Women and Newborn Infants,Instructions to My Daughter* and *A Collection of the Secrets of Louise Bourgeois.* Her works were used as the leading texts on gynecology and obstetrics for many years. ❖ See also *Women in World History.*

BOURGEOIS, Louise (b. 1911). French-born American sculptor and painter. Born in Paris, France, Dec 25, 1911; dau. of Louis Bourgeois and Josephine (Fauriaux) Bourgeois; sister of Henriette Bourgeois and Pierre Bourgeois; studied mathematics at Lycée Fénelon and the Sorbonne, 1932–35; m. Robert Goldwater, 1938; children: Michel, Jean-Louis, Alain. ❖ A strong voice in 20th-century art, began career working in the atelier of Fernand Léger, mostly in painting and drawing; 1st became aware of surrealism (mid-1930s); married and moved to US (1938); concentrated on printmaking, painting and drawing, but also began work in sculpture, developing a highly subjective style of expression; presented 1st solo show, in NY (1945); remained relatively undiscovered as a major artist until 1970s; saw a retrospective exhibition of her work at NY's Museum of Modern Art, an honor rarely accorded a living artist, which signaled her acceptance into the highest echelons of American art celebrities (1982); presented with National Medal of Arts by President Bill Clinton (1997). ❖ See also Donald Kuspit, *Bourgeois: An Interview with Louise Bourgeois by Donald Kuspit* (Random House, 1988); and *Women in World History.*

BOURGEOIS, Marguerite (1620–1700). *See Bourgeoys, Marguerite.*

BOURGEOIS, Marguerite Taos (1875–1956). *See Mistinguett.*

BOURGEOYS, Marguerite (1620–1700). French founder, social reformer and saint. Name variations: Marguerite Bourgeois; Soeur du Saint-Sacrement. Born April 17, 1620, at Troyes, Champagne, France; died Jan 12, 1700, at Montreal, Canada; dau. of Abraham Bourgeoys and Guillemette (Garnier) Bourgeoys; beatified by Roman Catholic Church, 1950; canonized, 1982. ❖ French Catholic founder of the Congrégation de Notre Dame de Montreal who dedicated most of her long life to educating the poor and underprivileged in the pioneer settlement of Ville-Marie, New France, later to become Montreal, Canada; born into a large and affectionate family in the prosperous French town of Troyes; though not particularly religious, underwent a spiritual experience at age 20 which transformed her life; became dedicated to the service of God and had a particular devotion to the Virgin Mary; well trained in Troyes as an external member of the Congrégation de Notre Dame; refused entry into several established religious orders; was 33 when she accepted the invitation of the governor of Ville-Marie (Montreal) to accompany him to New France (Canada) as a teacher; established the Congrégation de Notre Dame de Montreal, an order of teaching women who were not cloistered nuns but women who served the community by living and working in it. As the settlement grew, so did the number of her pupils, the size of the community of women which she established and the number of her schools; her ideas about pedagogy, based on those of Pierre Fourier, stressed kindness and encouragement rather than punishment; by 1961, there were over 6,000 members of her order in 262 communities in Canada, US and Japan, teaching some 100,000 pupils. ❖ See also Elizabeth Butler, *The Life of Venerable Marguerite Bourgeoys, Foundress of the Congregation of Notre Dame of Montreal* (Kennedy, 1932); Patricia Simpson, *Marguerite Bourgeoys and Montreal, 1640–1665* (McGill-Queen's U. Press, 1997); and *Women in World History.*

BOURGOGNE, countess or duchess of. *See Burgundy, countess or duchess of.*

BOURIGNON, Antoinette (1616–1680). Flemish mystic. Born at Lille, Flanders (now a city in northern France), Jan 13, 1616; died at Franeker, Friesland, Oct 30, 1680. ❖ Convinced that she was the direct recipient of supernatural revelations, entered a convent at 20 before taking charge of a hospital in Lille, followed by one in East Friesland; believing that she had been appointed by God to restore the spirit of early Christianity, disregarded all sects and maintained that her religion could not be found in the canons or practice of any church; her doctrine, known as Bourignianism, became widespread among Roman Catholics and Protestants; after her death, her following dwindled, though in early 18th century, her influence was so prevalent in Scotland that it prompted the condemnation of her doctrines at the Presbyterian general assemblies of 1701, 1709 and 1710. Her writings, an account of her life and of her visions and opinions, were collected by her disciple, Calvinist minister Pierre Poiret (19 vols., Amsterdam, 1679–1686), who also published her life (2 vols., 1679). ❖ See also *Women in World History.*

BOURIN, Jeanne (1922–2004). French historian and novelist. Born 1922 in Paris, France; died Mar 18, 2004, in Paris; attended Victor-Duruy lycée. ❖ Wrote historical novels set in the Middle Ages, including her greatest success, *La Chambre des dames* (The Ladies Room, 1979), and its sequel, *Le Jeu de la tentation* (The Temptation Game, 1981); also wrote *Le Grand Feu* (The Great Fire, 1985) and *La dame de beauté*, a biography of Agnes Sorel.

BOURKE, Mary (1944—). *See Robinson, Mary.*

BOURKE-WHITE, Margaret (1904–1971). American photojournalist. Born June 14, 1904, at Harrison Avenue in the Bronx, New York; died Aug 27, 1971, in Stamford, Connecticut; dau. of Joseph and Minnie (Bourke) White; graduate of Cornell University, 1927; m. Everett Chapman, 1925; m. Erskine Caldwell (writer), 1939; no children. ❖ Pioneer industrial photographer, photojournalist, war-photographer and writer, who became an American celebrity in her own right and was one of the preeminent photographers of 20th-century America, 1st established a studio in Cleveland and began industrial photography (1927); was hired by *Fortune* magazine (1929); undertook 1st visit to Soviet Union (1930); had cover photograph on 1st issue of *Life* (1936); photographed the siege of Moscow (1941); was torpedoed on troop ship in the Mediterranean (1942); photographed Battle of Monte Cassino (1944); was with troops liberating Buchenwald and other camps (1945); visited India and had meetings with Gandhi (1946–48); photographed in Korean War and denied red-baiters' accusations (1952); brave, resourceful, artful in unsnarling bureaucratic obstacles, pioneered in several ways: was the 1st photographer to capture many industrial operations on film, the 1st photographer featured by *Fortune* and *Life* magazines, the 1st to present "photo-essays," and one of the 1st to show the possibilities of aerial photography; like many artists of the interwar years, loved machinery, and one of her best-remembered styles is the romanticized dam, factory and airplane; writings include *Dear Fatherland, Rest Quietly* (1946) and *Eyes on Russia* (1931). ❖ See also autobiography, *Portrait of Myself* (Simon & Schuster, 1963); Sean Callahan and Theodore Brown, *The Photographs of Margaret Bourke-White* (Graphic Society Press, 1972); Vicki Goldberg, *Margaret Bourke-White* (Harper & Row, 1986); and *Women in World History.*

BOUTET, Anne Françoise Hippolyte (1779–1847). *See Mars, Ann Françoise.*

BOUTHIAUX, Anne (1968—). *See Briand, Anne.*

BOUTILIER, Joy (1939—). American dancer and choreographer. Born Sept 30, 1939, in Chicago, Illinois. ❖ Performed in Alwin Nikolais and Murray Louis' concert groups in New York City (mid-1960s); appeared in concert recitals with Louis and other company members, including Phyllis Lamhut and Bill Frank; received great acclaim in NY for 1st solo concert piece *Homunculus* (1968); also choreographed *In Grandma's House* (c. 1967), *Sortilegy* (c. 1968), *Lines of Lewis Carroll* (1968), *Bazooka* (1968) and *Colony* (1971).

BOUVET, Marguerite (1865–1915). American linguist and writer for children. Name variations: Marie Marguerite Bouvet. Born in New Orleans, Louisiana, 1865; died in Reading, Pennsylvania, 1915. ❖ Wrote *Sweet William, Prince Tip-Top, Little Marjorie's Love Story* and *Pierrette.*

BOUVIER, Jacqueline (1929–1994). *See Kennedy, Jacqueline.*

BOUVIER, Jeanne (1865–1964). French feminist and trade unionist. Born Feb 11, 1865, in Salaize-sur-Sanne, Isère, France; died 1964. ❖ At 11, began work in a silk factory; worked as a domestic, then dressmaker; attended meetings of dressmakers' trade union (1902) and became an active trade unionist; published her memoirs, *Mes mémoires* (1936).

BOUVIER, Léone (c. 1929—). French murderer. Name variations: Leone Bouvier. Born into a poor family c. 1929 in the village of Saint-Macaire-en-Mauges, France. ❖ An illiterate, worked in a factory; began a steady relationship with auto-mechanic Emile Clenet (1951); became pregnant, lost her child and her job; when Emile ended relationship, shot him in neck with .22 automatic and killed him (Feb 17, 1952); arrested while at a convent; found guilty at trial at the Assizes of Maine-sur-Loire at Angers (Dec 1953) but premeditation was not proved; sentenced to life imprisonment.

BOVASSO, Julie (1930–1991). American playwright, actress, director and producer. Born Aug 1, 1930, in Brooklyn, NY; died Sept 14, 1991, in New York, NY; m. George Ortman (div.); m. Leonard Wayland (div.). ❖ Made NY stage debut in title role in *Faustina* (1952); founded Tempo Playhouse in NY, producing and directing avant-garde plays, including *The Maids;* wrote and directed *The Moondreamers* (1969), *Gloria and Esperanza* (1970), *The Nothing Kid* and *Standard Safety* (both 1975); films include *Saturday Night Fever* (as Travolta's mother), *Willie and Phil, The Verdict, Staying Alive, Moonstruck* and *Betsy's Wedding.* Received 5 Obie awards.

BOVE, Joan (1901–2001). American entrepreneur. Name variations: Joan Gelb. Born Oct 24, 1901; died July 21, 2001, in Stamford, Connecticut; m. Lawrence M. Gelb (manufacturer, div., died 1980); m. twice more; 3rd husband was Emilio Bove (executive with Alitalia); children: Richard L. Gelb (once chair of Bristol-Myers Squibb and former director of The New York Times Co.); Bruce Gelb (American ambassador to Belgium). ❖ With husband, discovered a hair dye in Paris (1931) and co-founded the Clairol company; while serving as its president (1931–40), traveled the nation giving demonstrations, successfully taking the onus off dyed hair which was then considered vulgar.

BOVERI, Margret (1900–1975). German writer. Born Aug 14, 1900, in Würzburg, Germany; died in West Berlin, July 6, 1975; dau. of Theodor Boveri (1862–1915, professor at University of Würzburg) and Marcella (O'Grady) Boveri (1864–1950, US-born biologist). ❖ One of West Germany's best-known journalists, studied literature and history into her 30s, starting a career as a journalist (mid-1930s); regarding herself a "German patriot," remained in Nazi Germany, working for non-Nazi newspapers and journals; traveled in Asia, the Middle East and US (1936–42) and detailed her impressions in the *Berliner Tageblatt* as well as in the book, *Das Weltgeschehen am Mittelmeer;* worked as a journalist in Portugal and Spain (1942–44); survived the bombing and battle of Berlin (1944–45); began publishing essays on the political and cultural scene in the journal *Der Merkur* (1947), and her highly praised multivolume study of treason in the 20th century (1956); published historical study of the *Berliner Tageblatt,* under title *Wir lügen alle* (*We All Lied* 1965), in which she admitted to having been a collaborator with the Nazi regime to the extent that she, and her colleagues, had consciously decided to remain in Germany and had offered their talents to provide the regime with a more decent, humane image. Writings include *Amerika-Fibel für erwachsene Deutsche: Ein Versuch Unverstandenes zu erklären* (1946), *Minaret and Pipe-Line: Yesterday and Today in the Near East* (1939), *Tage des Überlebens: Berlin 1945* (1968), *Treason in the Twentieth Century* (trans. by Jonathan Steinberg, Putnam, 1963), and *Verzweigungen: Eine Autobiographie* (1977). ❖ See also *Women in World History.*

BOVT, Violette (1927—). American ballet dancer. Born May 1927 in Los Angeles, California. ❖ Began studying at school of Bolshoi Ballet in Moscow (1935); appeared at Stanislavsky and Nemirovich-Danchenko Theater in Moscow (1950s–60s), where she created roles in Chichinadze's *The Wood Fairy* (1960) and *Don Juan* (1962); performed principal roles in numerous classics, including the theater's production of *Carnaval* and in Bourmeister's *Swan Lake;* with Nina Grishina, choreographed *Star Fantasy* (1963).

BOVY, Berthe (1887–1977). Belgian-born actress. Name variations: Betty Bovy. Born Jan 6, 1887, in Liège, Belgium; died Feb 26, 1977; m. Pierre Fresnay (actor), 1923. ❖ Made stage debut at the Comédie Française as Adrienne in *M. Alphonse* (1907), where she continued to appear in classical roles including Lucinde in *Le Médecin Malgré Lui*, Marianne in *L'Avare*, Angélique in *Le Malade Imaginaire*, Henriette in *Les Femmes Savantes*, Psyche in *L'Amour*, Isabelle in *Les Plaideurs*, Chérubin in *Le Mariage de Figaro*, and Rosine in *Le Barbier de Seville;* other plays include *Les Romanesques*, *La Visite de Noces*, *La Robe Rouge*, *L'anglais tel qu'on le parie*, *La Princesse Georges*, *Le Monde où l'on s'ennuie*, *Connais-toi*, and *Poil de Carotte;* created the lead roles in *Polyphème*, *Cher Maître*, *Primerose*, *L'Embuscade*, *La Nouvell Idole*, *L'Envoûtée*, *La Course du Flambeau*, *Les Deux Ecoles*, *Circé* and *La voix humaine* (1932), among others; films include *La Terre*, *Le Déserteur*, *La belle aventure* and *La Maison Bonnadieu*.

BOW, Clara (1904–1965). American actress. Name variations: The 'It' Girl. Born Clara Gordon Bow in Bay Ridge, Brooklyn, New York, July 29, 1904; died in Los Angeles, California, Sept 27, 1965; dau. of Robert and Sarah Gordon Bow; m. Rex Bell (né Beldam, actor), in Dec 1931; children: Rex Lardlow Beldam (b. 1934); George Francis Robert Beldam (b. 1938). ❖ Popular international star of the silent screen and early talkies who was the idol of the "flappers" and, with her spit curls, bee-stung lips, and Kewpie-doll eyes, came to epitomize the devil-may-care, flaming youth of 1920s; won a beauty contest conducted by *Shadowland* magazine, received a screen test, and was cast in *Beyond the Rainbow* (1922), though her part was later cut; signed with Preferred Pictures (1923), appearing in *Down to the Sea in Ships* (1922), *Maytime* (1923), *Daughters of Pleasure* (1924), *Wine* (1924), *This Woman* (1924) and *The Plastic Age* (1925), which brought her stardom; moved to Paramount Studios (1926), where she starred in such silent films as *Dancing Mothers* (1926), *The Runaway* (1926), *Kid Boots* (1926), *It* (1927), *Children of Divorce* (1927), *Rough House Rosie* (1927), *Wings* (1927), *Hula* (1927), *Ladies of the Mob* (1928), *The Fleet's In* (1928), and *Three Weekends* (1928); talking films include *The Wild Party* (1929), *Dangerous Curves* (1929), *Saturday Night Kid* (1929), *Paramount on Parade* (1930), *Her Wedding Night* (1930), *Call Her Savage* (1932) and *Hoopla* (1933); for 7 years, was the queen of the movies, the embodiment of everything that the flapper supposedly was or wanted to be. ❖ See also David Stenn, *Clara Bow: Runnin' Wild* (Doubleday, 1988); Joe Morella and Edward Epstein, *The "It" Girl: The Incredible Story of Clara Bow* (1976); and *Women in World History.*

BOWDEN, Pamela (1925–2003). English mezzo-soprano. Born April 17, 1925, in Rochdale, Lancashire, England; died April 8, 2003; dau. of the town mayor; attended Royal Manchester (now Northern) College of Music; studied with Roy Henderson; m. Derrick Edwards (racing driver, died 2000); children: son and daughter. ❖ Won the Geneva international competition (1954); appeared mainly in recital and oratorio, giving more than 750 performances (1954–79), under such conductors as Josef Krips, Paul Sacher, Solti, Sargent, Boult, Mackerras and Boulez.

BOWDEN, Sally (c. 1948—). American dancer and choreographer. Born c. 1948 in Dallas, Texas. ❖ Studied with Martha Graham, Merce Cunningham and Paul Sanasardo, among others; danced with the Sanasardo company; began choreographing and soon started focusing on improvisation; performed a series of solo works entitled *Sally Bowden dances at . . .;* appeared in improvisational pieces in NY (mid-1970s), including *Five Wednesdays at Nine* and *Wonderful World of Modern Dance: or the Amazing Story of Plié*; continued to work mainly in improvisational format for rest of performance career; works include *Woodfall* (1966), *Opening Dance* (1971), *Rondo* (1971), *Sally Bowden Dances at the Village View Community Center* (1971), *Sally Bowden and David Schiller Dance* (1973), *The Ice Palace* (1973), *The Spiral Thicket* (1975), *Kite* (1978) and *The Potato Piece* (1978).

BOWELL, Harriet (1829–1884). Canadian wife of future prime minister. Born Harriet Louisa Moore, 1829, in Belleville, Ontario, Canada; died April 2, 1884; m. Mackenzie Bowell (prime minister of Canada, 1894–96), Dec 23, 1847; children: 9. ❖ Died while husband was minister of customs, long before he took office as prime minister.

BOWEN, Betty (1775–1865). *See Jumel, Eliza Bowen.*

BOWEN, Catherine Drinker (1897–1973). American writer. Born Catherine Shober Drinker, Jan 1, 1897, in Haverford, Pennsylvania; died Nov 1, 1973, in Haverford; dau. of Henry Sturgis (president of Lehigh University) and Aimee Ernesta (Beaux) Drinker; attended Peabody Conservatory of Music, Baltimore, and Institute of Musical Art, NY; m. Ezra Bowen (economist), 1919 (div. 1936); m. Thomas McKean Downs (surgeon); children: (1st m.) Ezra (b. 1921) and Catherine Drinker (b. 1924). ❖ Acclaimed biographer, wrote 1st book, *The Story of an Oak Tree* (1924); published *Beloved Friends: The Story of Tchaikowsky and Nadejda von Meck* (1937), which was highly praised, especially by music critics, followed by *Free Artist: The Story of Anton and Nicholas Rubinstein*, which was also well-received; had an immediate critical and popular success with *Yankee from Olympus: Justice Holmes and His Family* (1944); won National Book Award with *The Lion and the Throne: The Life and Times of Sir Edward Coke, 1552–1634* (1959); other writings include *John Adams and the American Revolution* (1950), *Adventures of a Biographer* (1959), *Francis Bacon: The Temper of a Man* (1963), *Miracle at Philadelphia: The Story of the Constitutional Convention, May to September, 1787* (1966), *Family Portrait* (1970), and *The Most Dangerous Man in America: Scenes from the Life of Benjamin Franklin* (1974). ❖ See also *Women in World History.*

BOWEN, Elizabeth (1899–1973). Irish novelist and short-story writer. Name variations: Mrs. Alan Cameron. Born Elizabeth Dorothea Cole Bowen in Dublin, Ireland, June 7, 1899; died Feb 22, 1973; dau. of Henry (barrister) and Florence (Colley) Bowen; m. Alan Cameron (secretary to the Central Council of School Broadcasting at BBC), Aug 4, 1923 (died 1952); no children. ❖ Author of the acclaimed *House in Paris, Death of the Heart* and *In the Heat of the Day*, whose work focused on the world of the middle and upper classes and the cracks in their veneer, began writing at age 20; published 1st collection of short stories, *Encounters* (1923); within next 2 years, wrote 2 books, a collection of stories titled *Ann Lee's* and 1st novel *The Hotel* (published in 1926); produced at least 1 book a year, including her 2nd novel *The Last September*, based on the world of Bowen's Court; began to review for *The New Statesman* and *The Tatler* (1931); published 2 novels in quick succession: *Friends and Relations* (1931) and *To the North* (1932); wrote *A House in Paris* (1937); made a member of the Irish Academy of Letters (1937); published one of her most popular books, *The Death of the Heart* (1938); following WWII, published *In the Heat of the Day* (1949), a classic novel of London during the war years; now recognized as a major novelist, was named Commander of the British Empire (1948); made lecture tours outside the country for the British Council; published *The Shelbourne,* her popular history of the Dublin hotel (1951); was writer-in-residence at Vassar as well as the American Academy in Rome and had a fellowship at Bryn Mawr; also wrote *Joining Charles* (short stories, 1929), *Seven Winters* (childhood memoirs, 1942), *The Demon Lover* (short stories, 1945), *A World of Love* (1955), *A Time in Rome* (1960), *After thought* (essays and short stories, 1962), *The Little Girls* (1963), *A Day in the Dark* (collection, 1965) and *Eva Trout* (1968). ❖ See also *Bowen's Court* (1942); autobiography *Pictures and Conversations* (1969); Victoria Glendinning, *Elizabeth Bowen: A Biography* (Knopf, 1978); Edwin J. Kenney, *Elizabeth Bowen* (Bucknell U. Press, 1975); and *Women in World History.*

BOWEN, Gretta (1880–1981). Irish artist. Born in Dublin, Ireland, Jan 1, 1880; died April 8, 1981; m. Matthew Campbell; children: 3 sons, including George and Arthur Campbell, both painters. ❖ Started painting in her 70s, after she worked with some paint left behind by her painter sons; under maiden name, exhibited 3 times in Belfast under the Arts Council of Northern Ireland, and her work was sold to patrons in England, America, France and Morocco; at 100, was invited to contribute to the 1st international exhibition of naïve art (1979). ❖ See also *Women in World History.*

BOWEN, Louise (1859–1953). American philanthropist. Name variations: Louise deKoven Bowen. Born Louise deKoven, Feb 26, 1859, in Chicago, Illinois; died Nov 9, 1953, in Chicago; dau. of John deKoven and Helen (Hadduck) deKoven; attended Dearborn Seminary; m. Joseph Tilton Bowen (businessman), June 1, 1886 (died 1911); children: John (b. 1887), Joseph Tilton Jr. (b. 1889), Helen Hadduck (b. 1891) and Louise deKoven (b. 1893). ❖ Taught Sunday school classes for "bad boys" at St. James Episcopal Cathedral, Chicago (c. 1875–86), and established one of city's 1st boys' clubhouses, Huron Street Club; began work with Hull House (1893), becoming trustee (1903); served on Juvenile Court Committee of Chicago (late 1890s), and became president; served as 1st president when Court Committee became Juvenile Protective Association (1907); while Hull House treasurer (beginning 1907), personally financed construction of Boys' Club and Woman's Club buildings; was instrumental in making the Pullman Co. upgrade its medical facilities for workers and in establishing minimum wage for women at International Harvester (1911); served as president of Woman's City Club and vice president of United Charities (1911–15); served as president of Hull House board (1935–44). Wrote *The Colored People of Chicago* (1913). ❖ See also autobiographies, *Growing Up with a City* (1926), *Baymeath* (1944) and *Open Windows: Stories of People and Places* (1946).

BOWER, Mrs. Albert Bunker (1922—). See *Bower, Alberta.*

BOWER, Alberta (1922—). American golfer. Name variations: Mrs. Albert Bunker Bower; Alberta Freeman Little. Born Alberta Freeman Little, Oct 4, 1922, in Owensboro, Kentucky; m. Albert Bower. ❖ Won state titles in Kentucky (1939), Maryland (1945), Massachusetts (1957), and New York (1964); won the Metropolitan championship (1966 and 1974); won the USGA Women's Senior championship (1975), and continued to compete, appearing in USGA Senior Women's Amateur championship (2002).

BOWER, Beverly (d. 2002). American opera singer. Born in Olean, NY; died Mar 24, 2002, in Washington Township, New Jersey; married; children: Mark. ❖ Began career in radio and tv; joined New York City Opera (1956), appearing there as Donna Anna in *Don Giovanni*, Micaela in *Carmen* and title role in *Amelia Goes to the Ball*; debuted at the Met as Ortlinde in *Walküre* (1965); also sang Musetta in *La Bohème*, Senta in *Der Fliegende Holländer*, and Micaela; sang lead at the 1st performance in the new Metropolitan Opera House at Lincoln Center (April 1, 1966); also appeared with Vienna State Opera (1963).

BOWER, Carol (1956—). American rower. Born June 9, 1956; attended University of Pennsylvania. ❖ At Los Angeles Olympics, won a gold medal in coxed eights (1984).

BOWER, Catherine Olivia Orme Spencer (1905–1982). See *Spencer Bower, Olivia.*

BOWER, Olivia Spencer (1905–1982). See *Spencer Bower, Olivia.*

BOWERS, Bathsheba (c. 1672–1718). American religious writer. Born c. 1672 in Charlestown, Massachusetts; died 1718; 3rd of 12 children of Benanuel Bowers and Elizabeth Dunster; never married. ❖ With sisters, was sent by parents to live in Philadelphia to avoid the persecution of Quakers by the Puritans of Massachusetts; became a Quaker preacher;

wrote *An Alarm Sounded* (1709), which argues for religious rights of women.

BOWERS, Elizabeth Crocker (1830–1895). American actress and manager. Born Elizabeth Crocker in Ridgefield, Connecticut, Mar 12, 1830; died in Washington, DC, in 1895. ❖ Played leading roles in America and England (1846–94); also took on supporting roles in productions with Edwin Booth, Lawrence Barrett, and many others.

BOWERS, Jess (1900–1973). See *Buffington, Adele.*

BOWERS, Lally (1917–1984). English actress. Born Kathleen Bowers, Jan 21, 1917, in Oldham, Lancashire, England; died July 18, 1984, in London, England; dau. of Albert Ernest and Kate (Richardson) Bowers; attended Hulme Grammar School, Oldham; studied with James Bernard. ❖ Joined the Shakespeare Memorial Theater, Stratford-on-Avon, working as an understudy and taking small walk-on roles; after additional experience at Manchester Repertory (1936–38) and Sheffield (1938–43), joined the Old Vic, appearing as Nora in *A Doll's House* and Viola in *Twelfth Night* (1943); made West End debut as Norrie in *The Last of Summer* (1944); appeared in repertory and London productions for 3 decades, winning the Clarence Derwent Award (1958) for her performance as Madame de Montrachet in *Dinner With the Family*; made NY debut as Mrs. Mercy Croft in *The Killing of Sister George* (1966); other roles include Candida, Lady Cicely Wayneflete in *Captain Brassbound's Conversion*, Mrs. Millamant in *The Way of the World*, and Maggie Hobson in *Hobson's Choice.*

BOWES, Alice (c. 1890–1969). English actress. Born in London, England, c. 1890; died Jan 3, 1969, age 79; m. D. A. Clark-Smith. ❖ Made stage debut as Willie Carlyle in *East Lynne* (1904); made London debut in *The Apple of Eden* (1912), followed by *The Queen's Champion, Boy of My Heart, The Moon Rides High, Dandy Dick,* and the title role in *Skittles,* among others; was the original Sal Gratton in *My Old Dutch.*

BOWES-LYON, Elizabeth (b. 1900). See *Elizabeth Bowes-Lyon.*

BOWLES, Camilla Parker (b. 1949). See *Parker-Bowles, Camilla.*

BOWLES, Caroline (1786–1854). See *Southey, Caroline Anne Bowles.*

BOWLES, Eva del Vakia (1875–1943). African-American leader of the YWCA. Born Eva del Vakia Bowles, Jan 24, 1875, in Albany, Athens Co., Ohio; died June 14, 1943, in Richmond, Virginia; dau. of John Hawkes Bowles (postal clerk) and Mary Jane (Porter) Bowles. ❖ Worked as teacher in Kentucky, Florida, North Carolina, and Virginia; on recommendation of Addie Hunton, was appointed secretary, Harlem branch of YWCA (1905); served as caseworker for Associated Charities of Columbus, OH (1908–12); became secretary of subcommittee on colored work for National Board of YWCA (1913); put in charge of Negro work of War Work Council, YWCA (1917); served as general coordinator of Council on Colored Work, YWCA; opposed separatist movement among younger black leaders in organization (1920s); served as secretary to board of directors, New York Urban League; retired from YWCA (1932).

BOWLES, Jane (1917–1973). American novelist and short-story writer. Born Jane Auer, Feb 22, 1917, in New York, NY; grew up in Woodmere, LI, NY; died May 4, 1973, in Malaga, Spain; dau. of Sidney Auer (died 1930) and Claire (Stajer) Auer; m. Paul Bowles (writer), 1938 (though both were homosexual and lived separate sexual lives, remained married). ❖ A writer's writer with a strong following, developed tuberculosis of the knee in adolescence and spent months in traction in a sanatorium in Leysin, Switzerland; traveled widely with husband Paul Bowles; enjoyed friendships with several important literary figures, including Tennessee Williams and William Burroughs; published *Two Serious Ladies* (1943); published several short stories, including the highly regarded "Camp Cataract"; wrote the play *In the Summer House* (1954), which was performed on Broadway to mixed reviews but also had a revival; suffered a serious stroke which affected her sight (1957); published *Plain Pleasures* (1966); lived in Tangier. ❖ See also Millicent Dillon, *A Little Original Sin: The Life and Works of Jane Bowles* (Holt, 1981).

BOWMAN, Deborah (1963—). Australian field-hockey player. Born July 4, 1963. ❖ At Seoul Olympics, won a gold medal in team competition (1988).

BOWMAN, Nellie (b. 1878). English actress. Born Helen Bowman, 1878, in Woolwich, Kent, England; sister of Isa, Maggie and Empsie Bowman (entertainers). ❖ Made stage debut at Theatre Royal in Stratford (1884);

appeared in vaudeville and on stage in *Water Babies, The Little Minister, The Belle of New York, A Midsummer Night's Dream, Oliver Twist, Peter Pan,* and title roles in *The Lady Slavey, La Poupée* and *The Casino Girl,* among others.

BOWMAN, Marjorie (1922–1992). See Gestring, Marjorie.

BOWMAN, Patricia (1904–1999). American dancer. Born Dec 12, 1904, in Washington, DC; died Mar 18, 1999. ❧ Began to study ballet with Mikhail Fokine in New York City at 14; made Broadway debut in George White's *Scandals* (1919) and only returned to Broadway many years later for the 1st of the *Ziegfeld Follies* (1934); danced as prima ballerina at Roxy Theater in New York where she partnered with Leonid Massine (c. 1928–31); performed at Radio City Music Hall in Prolog ballets for 16 years (starting 1932) and was frequently partnered with Paul Haakon; performed at numerous other Prolog theaters, including Boston Metropolitan (1935–38) and Boston Capitol (1938); made debut in classical ballet with Toronto Symphony Orchestra (1936); performed with Fokine Ballet and Mordkin Ballet (1939–40), where she created roles in Mordkin's *Giselle, Voices of Spring* and *The Goldfish* ; was charter member of the Ballet Theater company (1940); choreographed several works, including *Beat Me, Daddy, Eight to the Bar* (1942), *Brilliant* (1950) and *The Penguin* (1950); directed and taught at dance studio in NY (1941–77); also performed on radio with *Roxy's Gang* (mid-1930s) and hosted 13-week tv series, "The Patricia Bowman Show."

BOWNE, Eliza Southgate (1783–1809). American letter writer. Born 1783 in Maine; died Feb 20, 1809, from lingering complications from childbirth; dau. of Robert Southgate and Mary King; attended Susanna Rowson's boarding school; m. Walter Bowne, 1803; children: 2. ❧ Letters, which were collected in *A Girl's Life Eighty Years Ago* (1888), detail the daily life of an upper-class woman and frequently address the topic of marriage.

BOWRING, Eva Kelly (1892–1985). American politician. Born in Nevada, Missouri, Jan 9, 1892; died in Gordon, Nebraska, Jan 8, 1985; married, 1924 (widowed); m. Arthur Bowring, 1928. ❧ Active in local Republican politics and in the Nebraska Stockgrowers Association, was appointed to fill the vacancy in US Senate caused by the death of Dwight Griswold (April 16, 1954–Nov 7, 1954); following her brief tenure in the Senate, served on the national advisory council of the National Institutes of Health and on the board of parole of the Department of Justice. ❧ See also *Women in World History.*

BOW WOW WOW. See Lwin, Annabella.

BOX, Betty E. (1915–1999). British film producer. Name variations: Betty Rogers. Born Betty Evelyn Box, Sept 25, 1915, in Beckenham, Kent, England; died Jan 15, 1999, in London, England; sister of producer Sydney Box; sister-in-law of writer-director Muriel Box; m. Peter Rogers (director, writer, producer), 1949. ❧ Dubbed "Miss Box Office" by the British press, was one of the most prolific and commercially successful producers in the history of British cinema; began working with her brother's documentary production company; during WWII, produced close to 200 British propaganda films; launched 1st feature film, *The Seventh Veil* (1945), followed by *Dear Murderer* (1947), *When the Bough Breaks* (1947), *Miranda* (1948), *The Blind Goddess* (1948), *Vote for Huggett* (1948), *Here Come the Huggetts* (1948), *Don't Ever Leave Me* (1949), and *The Huggetts Abroad* (1949); beginning 1950, her work with the British director Ralph Thomas yielded more than 20 years of lightweight, skillfully executed, and commercially successful movies, including *So Long at the Fair* (1950), *Doctor in the House* (1954), *Doctor at Sea* (1955), *Checkpoint* (1956), *Iron Petticoat* (1956), *Doctor at Large* (1957), *Campbell's Kingdom* (1958), *A Tale of Two Cities* (1958), *Carve Her Name With Pride* (1958), *The 39 Steps* (1959), *Conspiracy of Hearts* (1960), *No, My Darling Daughter* (1961), *A Pair of Briefs* (1961), *Doctor in Distress* (1963), *Deadlier Than the Male* (1966), *Doctor in Clover* (1966), *Doctor in Trouble* (1970), *Percy* (1970) and *Percy's Progress* (1973). Made Officer of the British Empire (OBE, 1958). ❧ See also *Women in World History.*

BOX, Muriel (1905–1991). English writer, director, and producer. Name variations: Violette Muriel Baker, Lady Gardiner. Born Violette Muriel Baker in Surrey, England, in 1905; died 1991; attended Pitman's College; m. Sydney Box, May 23, 1935 (div. 1969); m. Sir Gerald Gardiner, a Lord Chancellor, Aug 28, 1970; children: (1st m.) Leonora (b. 1936). ❧ For 40 years, wrote, co-wrote, produced, or directed some 70 plays, numerous documentaries, and over 3 dozen feature films, making her one of the most prolific talents of the British stage and screen;

with husband, wrote 1st screenplay, *Alibi Inn,* which was well received (1935), along with 50 one-act plays, several full-length plays, and the librettos for a number of musicals (1935–39); during WWII, directed documentary films for the British war effort; with husband, made a long line of financially successful films, including *Street Corner* (1952), *Both Sides of the Law* (1954), *The Truth About Women* (1958) and *Rattle of a Simple Man* (1964); published 1st novel, *The Big Switch* (1964), to glowing reviews; co-founded a publishing company, Femina Books, and wrote the 1st book published by the company, a biography of feminist pioneer Marie Stopes. ❧ See also autobiography, *Odd Woman Out* (1974); and *Women in World History.*

BOXER, Barbara (1940—). American politician. Born Barbara Levy, Nov 11, 1940, in Brooklyn, NY; Brooklyn College, BA in economics, 1962; m. Stewart Boxer; children: Doug Nicole Boxer (who m. Tony Rodham). ❧ Worked as a stockbroker on Wall Street (1962–65), as a journalist and associate editor, Pacific Sun Newspaper (1972–74) and as a congressional aide (1974–76); served for 6 years on the Marin County (CA) board of supervisors (1977–83) and was the 1st woman president of the board; as a Democrat representing California, was elected to US House of Representatives (1983), serving for 10 years; elected to US Senate (1992), won reelection (1998, 2004); focuses on families, children, consumers, human rights, military procurement reform, the environment, and a woman's right to choose; introduced the 401(k) Pension Protection Act (1996) and led the Senate effort to end the suffering of Afghan women under the Taliban; served on the Senate Environment and Public Worlds Committee, on the Commerce Committee, and on the Foreign Relations Committee.

BOXX, Gillian (1973—). American softball player. Born Sept 1, 1973, in Torrance, California; sister of Shannon Boxx (soccer player). ❧ Won a team gold medal at Atlanta Olympics (1996).

BOXX, Shannon (1977—). American soccer player. Born June 29, 1977, in Fontana, California; sister of Gillian Boxx (softball player); attended Notre Dame University. ❧ Midfielder, won a team gold medal at Athens Olympics (2004).

BOY-ED, Ida (1852–1928). German novelist and biographer. Name variations: Ida Boy Ed. Born Ida Ed in 1852 in Bergedorf, Germany; died 1928 in Travemünde; married a Hanseatic businessman. ❧ Wrote short stories, family sagas, and biographies of famous women, including Germaine de Staël and Charlotte von Stein.

BOYACK, Sarah (1961—). Scottish politician. Born May 1961 in Glasgow, Scotland. ❧ As a Labour candidate, elected to the Scottish Parliament for Edinburgh Central (1999); served as minister for Transport and the Environment (1999–2000), then minister for Transport and Planning (2000–01).

BOYARKINA, Svetlana (1972—). See Zhurova, Svetlana.

BOYARSKIKH, Claudia (1939—). Russian cross-country skier. Name variations: Klaudia or Klavdia, or Klavdiya Boyarskikh. Born Nov 11, 1939, in USSR. ❧ Won gold medals for 10 km, 5 km, and 3 x 5 km relay at Innsbruck Olympics (1964).

BOYCE, Ann (c. 1827–1914). New Zealand herbalist. Name variations: Ann Cave. Born Ann Cave, c. 1827 (baptized Nov 20, 1827), in Sydney, NSW, Australia; died Feb 28, 1914, at Motueka, New Zealand; dau. of Charles Samuel Cave (farmer) and Susannah (Dockrell); m. William Boyce (sea captain), 1842 (died 1895); children: at least 12. ❧ Sent to Australia with parents, who were convicts; relocated to New Zealand (1830s); gained vast understanding of medicinal value of plants, becoming respected herbalist, especially among Motueka's large population of Maori people. ❧ See also *Dictionary of New Zealand Biography* (Vol. 1).

BOYCE, Johanna (1954—). American dancer and choreographer. Born May 10, 1954, in Hanover, New Hampshire. ❧ Choreographed many works, often for untrained dancers, in and around New York City (as of 1978), most of which are characterized by her incorporation of ordinary, pedestrian movement; experimented with film and in collaboration with composers; works of choreography include *New Dances (Pas, Styles, Tracings, Forms, Ghost Dance* and *Its How You Play the Game,* 1980), and *New Choreography: Untitled Work in Progress* (1980).

BOYCE, Neith (1872–1951). American writer. Name variations: Neith Boyce Hapgood; Mrs. Hutchins Hapgood. Born Neith Boyce in Mt. Vernon, New York, 1872; died 1951; m. Hutchins Hapgood (1869–1944, writer), June 1899; children: Boyce Hapgood; Charles Hutchins Hapgood; Miriam Hapgood DeWitt (1908–1990, writer); Beatrix

Hapgood. ❖ At one time the only woman reporter for the *New York Globe*, was a founding member of the Provincetown Players, along with husband and others; works, which explore marriage and the conflicts between men and women, include *The Forerunner* (1903), *Eternal Spring* (1906), (with her husband) *Enemies* (1916), *Two Sons* (1917), *Proud Lady* (1923), *Winter's Night* (1927) and an autobiographical novel, *The Bond* (1908). ❖ See also Ellen Kay Trimberger, *Intimate Warriors: Portraits of a Modern Marriage, 1899–1941: Selected Works by Neith Boyce and Hutchins Hapgood* (Feminist Press at the City University of New York, 1991); and *Women in World History*.

BOYD, Ann Carr (b. 1938). *See Carr-Boyd, Ann.*

BOYD, Anne (1946——). Australian composer and flutist. Name variations: Anne Elizabeth Boyd. Born April 10, 1946, in Sydney, NSW, Australia; University of Sydney, BA; University of York, PhD; studied composition in Sydney with Peter Sculthorpe and Richard Meale (from 1963). ❖ Acclaimed composer and flutist whose interest in Asian and indigenous Australian music influences her work, served as founding managing editor for *Music Now*, the 1st contemporary music journal in Australia (1968–69); lectured in music at University of Sussex (1972–77); returned to Australia to work as freelance composer (1977); served as reader and founding head of department of music at University of Hong Kong (1981–90) and as vice-chair of Hong Kong music festival, Fringe (1982–84); founded Hong Kong Society of Music Education and helped organize 1st Contemporary Chinese Composers Festival (1986); created and recorded compositions which reflect interest in ethno-musicology, in Australian Aboriginal music as well as music of Japan and Java; appointed professor and head of department of music at University of Sydney (1990); featured in documentary *Facing the Music*; became president of Federation of Australian Music Clubs (1993). Selected works include: (oratorio) *The Death of Captain Cook*; (chamber works) *My Name Is Tian* and *Cycle of Love*; (choral works) *Coal River* and *The Last of His Tribe*; (pieces for flute an piano) *Red Sun Chill Wind, Cloudy Mountain* and *Revelations of Divine Love*; (orchestral work) *Grathawai*; and children's opera *The Little Mermaid*.

BOYD, Belle (1844–1900). Confederate patriot and spy. Born May 9, 1844, in Martinsburg, Virginia; died June 11, 1900, in Kilbourn (now Wisconsin Dells), Wisconsin; dau. of Benjamin Reed Boyd (business owner) and Mary Rebecca (Glenn) Boyd; m. Samuel Wylde Hardinge, Aug 25, 1864 (later missing, presumed dead); m. John Swainston Hammond, Mar 17, 1869 (div., Nov 1, 1884); m. Nathaniel Rue High Jr., Jan 9, 1885; children: (1st m.) Grace; (2nd m.) Arthur, Byrd, Marie, John. ❖ Celebrated spy and Southern patriot who engaged in courier and espionage activities throughout the Civil War, became revered as a symbol of Southern independence and pride, and later wrote her memoirs and gave dramatic readings of her war exploits; grew up in the Virginia town of Martinsburg, commonly referred to as the "Northern Gateway to the Shenandoah," which was to become the center of activity during the Civil War; when drunken Federal troops attempted to attach a Union flag to her house and a foul-mouthed soldier insulted her mother, shot him; acquitted of the killing, began to relay tidbits of useful military information to the Confederates; caught and released, traveled to Manassas to visit her father who had enlisted in the Confederate army; during her stay, worked as a military courier and assisted, among others, General Stonewall Jackson and General Pierre Beauregard with their communications; endured musket and cannon fire to reach Jackson to tell him to strike at Front Royal, that the Union army had been caught off guard (May 1862); caught giving messages to two "Confederate" soldiers who were Union spies, was brought to the Old Capital Prison in Washington (July 1862); after a month of confinement, was released in a prisoner exchange and sent south to Richmond; arrested and again sent to Washington (1863), was sentenced to "banishment to the South"; intent on becoming a courier of Confederate dispatches to the capitals of Europe, arrived in London; wrote and published her memoirs and began an acting career. ❖ See also *Belle Boyd in Camp and Prison* (Yoseloff, 1968); Ruth Scarborough, *Belle Boyd; Siren of the South* (Mercer U. Press, 1983); Louis A. Sigaud, *Belle Boyd; Confederate Spy* (Dietz, 1944); and *Women in World History*.

BOYD, Carla (1975——). Australian basketball player. Name variations: Carla Porter. Born Carla Porter, Oct 31, 1975, in Australia. ❖ Won a team bronze medal at Atlanta Olympics (1996) and a silver medal at Sydney Olympics (2000); played with Detroit Shock of the WNBA (1998–2001).

BOYD, Elizabeth (fl. 1727–1745). British poet. Name variations: (pseudonyms) Eloisa; Louisa. Fl. between 1727 and 1745. ❖ Suffered from ill health and poverty throughout life; wrote the long poem *Variety: A Poem* (1727) and the collection *Verses on the King's Birthday* (1730); also wrote (novels) *The Happy Unfortunate, of the Female Page* (1732) and *The Humorous Miscellany* (1733).

BOYD, Eva (1945–2003). American singer. Name variations: Little Eva. Born Eva Narcissus Boyd, June 29, 1945, in Belhaven, North Carolina; died April 10, 2003, in Kinston, NC; 10th of 13 children of Laura Boyd; sister of Idalia Boyd (singer who had one minor hit, "Hoola Hooping"); children: 2 daughters, 1 son. ❖ As a teenager, was a baby sitter in NY for songwriters Carole King and Gerry Goffin when they asked her to record "Loco-Motion" (1962); followed that chartbuster with 2 other lesser hits, "Keep Your Hands Off My Baby" (1962) and "Old Smokey Loco-Motion" (1963); was a backup singer for the Drifters, Ben E. King, and others.

BOYD, Liona (1950——). English-Canadian guitarist and composer. Born in London, England, July 11, 1950; moved to Canada as a child and became a citizen in 1975; studied with Alexandre Lagoya, Julian Bream, Alirio Diaz and Narcisco Yepes. ❖ One of the few female classical guitarists, concertized worldwide and was especially popular in Japan and Central and South America; made New York debut in Carnegie Hall (Mar 22, 1975); recording New Age as well as classical music, also performed with Chet Atkins, André Gagnon, and Zamfir; as a composer, wrote pieces as well as incidental film music; often included *Cantarelle* and *Llanto de Gaviota* on programs, as well as her transcriptions of Bach, Beethoven, Cimarosa, Debussy, and Satie. Won the Vanier Award (1979), 4 Juno Awards (1979, 1982–84), and was named classical guitarist of the year by *Guitar Player* magazine (1985–89).

BOYD, Louise Arner (1887–1972). American explorer and geographer. Born Sept 16, 1887, in San Rafael, California; died Sept 14, 1972; dau. of John Franklin (mining operator) and Louise Cook (Arner) Boyd. ❖ Made 1st cruise to Iceland, Greenland, and Lapland (1924), which became the impetus for the 7 expeditions to the Arctic that were to follow; led several friends on what was primarily a hunting expedition to Franz Josef Land (northernmost land in the Eastern Hemisphere), but which included the beginning of the extensive photography of the Arctic that would ultimately become her legacy (1926); learning of the disappearance of polar explorer Roald Amundsen (1928), undertook her own 3-month, 10,000-mile search, making extensive photographic records of her journey, including 20,000 feet of motion-picture film and thousands of still photographs; made 4 additional expeditions from Norway aboard the *Veslekari* (1931, 1933, 1937, 1938), which included the regions in and around Franz Josef Land, Spitsbergen, Greenland, Jan Mayen Island, and eastern arctic Canada; was the 1st to sail to the inner ends of Ice Fjord, Greenland; traveled further north along the Greenland coast than any other American had traveled by sea (1938); made a successful flight over and around the North Pole (1955), taking photographs of the area; writings include *The Fiord Region of East Greenland* (1935) and *Coast of Northeast Greenland* (1949). ❖ See also *Women in World History*.

BOYD, Mary (fl. 1487). Scottish royal. Name variations: Marion Boyd. Dau. of Archibald Boyd of Bonshaw; 1st wife or paramour of James IV (1473–1513), king of the Scots (r. 1488–1513); children: Alexander Stewart, archbishop of St. Andrews (c. 1487–1513); Catherine Stewart (d. after 1554, who m. James Douglas, 3rd earl of Morton).

BOYD, Megan (1915–2001). Scottish maker of fish flies. Born Rosina Megan Boyd, Jan 29, 1915, in England; grew up in the Scottish Highlands; died Nov 15, 2001, in Golspie, Scotland; dau. of a riverkeeper on an estate in Sutherland Co.; never married. ❖ Famed for her expertise in tying delicate fishing flies, which are now in museums and sought after by collectors, moved into a small cottage on a hillside in the village of Kintradwell, at age 20, where she lived for 53 years, spending 14–16 hours a day at her workbench; never charged more than a dollar for her flies, which she preferred selling to fishermen she knew; retired (1985). Awarded the British Empire Medal.

BOYD, Nancy. *See Millay, Edna St. Vincent.*

BOYD, Susan (1949–2004). Scottish tv writer. Born Feb 7, 1949, in Glasgow, Scotland; died June 18, 2004; dau. of Eddie Boyd (screenwriter and journalist) and Katy Gardiner (illustrator); attended Glasgow School of Art; children: Janet. ❖ Wrote episodes for tv-series "EastEnders" for 20 years; also wrote for the series "Casualty" (1986).

BOYD-CARPENTER, Sarah (1946—). *See Hogg, Sarah.*

BOYE, Karin (1900–1941). Swedish poet. Born in Göteborg, Oct 26, 1900; walked into the woods, April 23, 1941, and was found dead, apparently a suicide, a few days later; dau. of Carl Fredrik "Fritz" Boye (manager of insurance business) and Signe (Liljestrand) Boye; m. Leif Björk (div.); no children. ❖ Widely regarded as Sweden's greatest woman poet, lived a short life marked by the conflict between her religious callings and her growing awareness of her sexual preference for women; following the warm reception of her prose masterpiece *Kallocain,* committed suicide at age 40, yet the honesty of her poetry and prose secured for Boye a reputation which informed future generations about her most private, as well as life's most public, dilemmas; writings include *Moln* (Clouds, 1922), *Gömda land* (Hidden Lands, 1924), *Härdarna* (The Hearths, 1927), *Astarte* (1931), *Merit vaknar* (Merit Awakes, 1933), *Kris* (Crisis, 1934), *För trädets skull* (For the Tree's Sake, 1935), *För lite* (Too Little, 1936), *Kallocain* (1941) and (published posthumously) *De sju dödssynderna* (The Seven Deadly Sins, 1941). ❖ See also *Women in World History.*

BOYER, Catherine (1773–1800). *See Bonaparte, Christine.*

BOYER, Pat (1911–1978). *See Paterson, Pat.*

BOYLAN, Mary (1913–1984). American actress and playwright. Born Feb 23, 1913, in Plattsburg, NY; died Feb 18, 1984, in New York, NY. ❖ Made Broadway debut in *Dance Night* (1938); other plays include *Susannah and the Elders, The Walrus and the Carpenter, Our Town, Middle of the Night, Biography of a Woman* and *Women behind Bars*; co-authored and appeared in *Curly McDimple.*

BOYLE, Alice (1869–1957). *See Boyle, Helen.*

BOYLE, Darian (c. 1968—). American skier. Born c. 1968 in Olympic Valley, California. ❖ Won silver in Skier X at X Games (Winter 1999); was NEA winner as Best Female Freeskier (2000); also worked as tv commentator and fashion model.

BOYLE, Desley (1948—). Australian politician. Born Mar 29, 1948, in Newcastle, NSW, Australia. ❖ Psychologist; as a member of the Australian Labor Party, elected to the Queensland Parliament for Cairns (1998).

BOYLE, Eleanor Vere (1825–1916). Scottish writer, illustrator and painter. Name variations: E.V.B. Born Eleanor Vere Gordon, 1825, in Scotland; died 1916; m. Richard Boyle (Somerset rector). ❖ One of the great Victorian children's book illustrators, was also a writer, watercolorist and avid gardener; works include *Child's Play* (1859), *Beauty and the Beast* (1872) and *Days and Hours in a Garden* (1884), which was about her garden at Huntercombe Manor; also illustrated Sarah Austin's *The Story without End.*

BOYLE, Helen (1869–1957). Irish-born psychiatrist. Name variations: Alice Helen Anne Boyle. Born 1869 in Dublin, Ireland; died Nov 20, 1957; London School of Medicine for Women, MD, 1893. ❖ Strong proponent of diagnosis and early treatment of mental disorders, ran a private clinic with Mabel Jones for women and children in Brighton; with Jones, established Lady Chichester Hospital for the Treatment of Early Nervous Disorders (1905) and was in charge of Chichester Hospital for 50 years; with Sir Maurice Craig, founded National Council for Mental Hygiene (1923, now National Council for Mental Health); became the 1st woman president of Royal Medico-Psychological Association (1939, now Royal College of Psychiatrists).

BOYLE, Kay (1902–1992). American writer and poet. Born Katherine Evans Boyle, Feb 19, 1902, in St. Paul, Minnesota; died Dec 27, 1992, in Mill Valley, California; dau. of Katherine Evans and Henry Peterson Boyle; m. Richard Brault, June 24, 1923; m. Laurence Vail (scholar and poet), April 2, 1931; m. Joseph von Franckenstein, Feb 20, 1943; children: (with Ernest Walsh) Sharon Walsh; (2nd m.) Apple-Johan, Kathe, Clover, Faith Carson, Ian Savin. ❖ Expatriate writer and poet, member of the Lost Generation in 1920s and 1930s, who battled fascism, Nazism, McCarthyism, and the Vietnam War, grew up in France and Switzerland, returning to Cincinnati when WWI broke out; studied violin and then architecture at Ohio and Columbia universities; at 18, married and went to France; published *Short Stories* in Paris (1929); won the O. Henry Memorial Award for short stories "The White Horses of Vienna" (1936) and "Defeat" (1941); returned to US as a celebrity to

escape Hitler's armies (1941); published novel *Avalanche,* which became a bestseller (1944), and wrote extensively for magazines like *The New Yorker, Vanity Fair* and *Harper's Bazaar;* was blacklisted for being too leftist during McCarthy reign of terror (1950s); husband, who worked with the State Department, also lost his job, though he was later reinstated; became a professor of English and creative writing at San Francisco State University (1963–79); was a passionate opponent of the Vietnam War, and antiwar experiences are recounted in *The Underground Woman* (1975). Novels include *Plagued by the Nightingale* (1931), *Year before Last* (1932), *Death of a Man* (1936), *Monday Night* (1938), *The Crazy Hunter: Three Short Novels* (1940), *A Frenchman Must Die* (1946), *1939* (1948), *The Seagull on the Step* (1955) and *Generation without Farewell* (1960); nonfiction includes *The Long Walk at San Francisco State and Other Essays* (1972), and *Words that Must Somehow Be Said* (1985); poetry includes *A Statement* (1932), *A Glad Day* (1938), *American Citizen: Naturalized in Leadville, Colorado* (1944), *The Lost Dogs of Phnom Penh* (1968) and *Testament for My Students and Other Poems* (1970); also published numerous collections of short stories. ❖ See also Joan Mellen, *Kay Boyle: Author of Herself* (Farrar, 1994); Sandra Whipple Spanier, *Kay Boyle: Artist and Activist* (Southern Illinois U. Press, 1986); and *Women in World History.*

BOYLE, Mary (1625–1678). *See Rich, Mary.*

BOYLE, Raelene (1951—). Australian runner. Born June 24, 1951. ❖ Won an Olympic silver medal in 200 meters at Mexico City (1968) and silver medals in 200 meters and 100 meters at Munich (1972).

BOYLEN, Christilot (1947—). Canadian equestrian. Name variations: Christilot Hanson. Born Christilot Hanson, April 2, 1947, in Batavia, Indonesia; dau. of of an Australian father and Indonesia mother of Dutch descent; m. James Boylen (horse breeder); children: daughters Billie Jeanne and Christa-Dora Boylen. ❖ Moved to Toronto when young; starred as Princess Summerfall Winterspring on the CBC version of "Howdy Doody" (1956–60); at the Pan American Games, won gold medals for indiv. dressage and team dressage (1971) and a gold medal for indiv. dressage (1975). Wrote *Basic Dressage for North America.* ❖ See also autobiography, *Canadian Entry.*

BOYNE, Eva Leonard (1886–1960). English actress. Born 1886 in London, England; died April 12, 1960, in New York, NY. ❖ Made NY debut as Dora Delaney in *Fanny's First Play* (1912); was also seen in *Little Miss Bluebeard, The Shanghai Gesture, The Letter, The Apple Cart, Victoria Regina, The Corn is Green, O Mistress Mine* and *The Chalk Garden* (1957).

BOYNTON, Katharine (1937—). *See Payne, Katy.*

BOYS, Beverly (1951—). Canadian diver. Born April 7, 1951, in Toronto, Ontario, Canada. ❖ At the Commonwealth Games, won gold medals for 3-meter springboard and 10-meter tower (1970) and a silver medal for 3-meter springboard and a gold medal for 10-meter tower (1974); won a silver medal for 10-meter tower and a bronze medal for 3-meter springboard at the Pan American Games (1971); won 34 Canadian championships on the 1- and 3-meter springboards and 10-meter tower, including 5 sweeps of all 3 events at a single championship (1966–78); retired (1978).

BOYS-SMITH, Winifred Lily (1865–1939). New Zealand science artist and lecturer, professor, and school principal. Born Nov 7, 1865, in Wiltshire, England; died Jan 1, 1939, in Hampshire, England; dau. of John Boys Smith (cleric) and Rosamond Georgiana (Cox) Boys Smith. ❖ Educated in England and published numerous illustrations in contemporary botanical texts (1890s); traveled to US on scholarship to study various education programs, including domestic science (1906–07); was the 1st professor of home science and domestic arts at University of Otago (1911–20); established private school, Amberley Girls' Collegiate School, in Christchurch (1920); returned to England (1921). ❖ See also *Dictionary of New Zealand Biography* (Vol. 3).

BOYSEN, Liberta Schulze (1913–1942). *See Schulze-Boysen, Libertas.*

BOZHURINA, Tsvetana (1952—). Bulgarian volleyball player. Born June 13, 1952, in Bulgaria. ❖ At Moscow Olympics, won a bronze medal in team competition (1980).

BOZYK, Reizl (1914–1993). Yiddish actress. Name variations: Reizel. Born in Poland, 1914; died in New York, NY, Sept 30, 1993; m. Max Bozyk (Yiddish actor 1970). ❖ At 6, began acting in Poland, performing with parents, then with future husband Max Bozyk; with husband, fled the Nazis (1939), traveling to New York City (1941); received top billing for more than 60 years on New York's Yiddish stage, appearing in hundreds of productions as a comedian, and later as the stereotypical mother-in-law who often stole the show; undertook 1st English-language role, the matchmaking grandmother in the film *Crossing Delancey* (1988). ❖ See also *Women in World History.*

BOZZACCHI, Giuseppina (1853–1870). Italian ballerina. Born in Milan, Italy, Nov 23, 1853; died Nov 23, 1870, in Paris, France; studied with Mme Dominique-Venettoza under the sponsorship of Emile Perrin. ❖ Immigrated to Paris with family (1862); at age 16, created the role of Swanilda in *Coppélia* at Paris Opéra (May 1870); died 6 months later, on 17th birthday, a victim of virulent fever (smallpox), made worse by deprivations from the German siege of Paris.

BOZZINO, Tina (fl. 1920s–30s). Italian mountaineer. Born in Italy. ❖ With Nina Pietrosanta and Livia Bertolini, climbed the Italian side of Mont Blanc: the Brenva and Puterey ridges.

BRABANT, countess of.
See Mary of Brabant (c. 1191–c. 1260).
See Maude of Alsace (1163–c. 1210).

BRABANT, duchess of.
See Lutgardis (fl. 1139).
See Marie of France (1198–c. 1223).
See Sophia of Thuringia (1224–1284).
See Margaret (1275–1318).
See Adelaide of Burgundy (d. 1273).
See Margaret of Flanders (d. 1285).
See Marie of Evreux (d. 1335).
See Joanna of Brabant (1322–1406).
See Mathilde of Belgium (1973–).

BRABANT, Marie de (c. 1530–c. 1600). *See Marie de Brabant.*

BRABANTS, Jeanne (1920–). Belgian ballet dancer and choreographer. Born Jan 25, 1920, in Antwerp, Belgium. ❖ A major player in the development of modern ballet in Belgium and the Lowlands, studied modern dance choreography and technique with a variety of teachers, including Kurt Jooss and Sigurd Leeder, and classical ballet under Olga Preobrazhenska; performed intermittently (1939–50s); choreographed works for numerous companies, including Dance Ensembles Brabants, Royal Netherlands Theater, Royal Flemish Opera, and her own company, Ballet Van Vaalanderen of Flanders, which she founded in 1969; has taught at schools including Royal Flemish Opera; choreographed works include *De Reiskameraad* (1961), *Arabesque* (1964), *Rhapsody* (1968), *Presto, Viva Lento* (c. 1971), *Poèma* (c. 1975), *Ulenspiegel de geus* (1977) and *Nostalgie* (1979).

BRACCIANO, duchess of (c. 1642–1722). *See Marie-Anne de la Trémouille, Princess of the Ursins.*

BRACE, Julia (1806–1884). American pioneer. Born in Newington, Connecticut, June 13, 1806; died in Bloomington, Connecticut, Aug 12, 1884; admitted to Hartford Asylum when she was 18. ❖ Famed as the nation's 1st known case of concurrent deafness and blindness, became completely deaf and blind at age five and a half, having learned to read and spell words of two syllables; at 18, entered the asylum for the "deaf and dumb" at Hartford, but never had the attention and thought-out course of instruction that was given to Laura Bridgman. ❖ See also *Women in World History.*

BRACEGIRDLE, Anne (1671–1748). English actress. Name variations: Mrs. Bracegirdle. Born 1671; died in London, England, 1748; buried in the cloisters of Westminster Abbey; mistress and possibly wife of William Congreve. ❖ As a child, was possibly placed under care of actor-playwright Thomas Betterton and his wife, actress Mary Saunderson; is thought to have 1st appeared on stage as the page in premiere of *The Orphan* (1680); played Lucia in Shadwell's *Squire of Alsatia* (1688); also played Araminta in *The Old Bachelor* (1693); made 1st appearance in a comedy as Angelica in Congreve's *Love for Love* (1695); created the parts of Belinda in *Provoked Wife* (1697), Almeria in *Mourning Bride* (1697), and Millamant in *The Way of the World* (1700); also played the heroines in some of Nicholas Rowe's tragedies, as well as acting in contemporary versions of Shakespeare's plays; was the innocent cause of the killing of actor William Mountfort, who was stabbed to death by one of her jealous suitors (1692). ❖ See also *Women in World History.*

BRACETTI, Mariana (1840–c. 1904). Puerto Rican revolutionary. Name variations: Braceti; Brazo de Oro (Golden Arm). Born in Añasco, Puerto Rico, in 1840; died c. 1904 from aphasia; m. 2nd husband Manuel Rojas; m. Santiago Labiosa. ❖ With 2nd husband Manuel Rojas, played an important role in the Puerto Rican insurrection against Spanish rule, known as the "Grito de Lares"; with Rojas, belonged to the Lares Revolutionary Board which was founded on Feb 24, 1868; embroidered the Banner of Lares, a symbol of the 1st Republic of Puerto Rico; briefly imprisoned, was released when the Spanish granted amnesty to political prisoners.

BRACHMANN, Karoline (1777–1822). *See Brachmann, Louise.*

BRACHMANN, Louise (1777–1822). German poet. Name variations: Karoline Louise Brachmann; Luise Brachmann. Born Karoline Luise Brachmann, Feb 9, 1777, in Rochlitz-Sachsen, Germany; died by drowning herself in the Saale, Sept 17, 1822, in Halle-Saale, Germany; dau. of Christian Paul Brachmann and Friederike Louise (Vollhard) Brachmann. ❖ Friend of poet Novalis and dramatist Friedrich Schiller, whose work explored mythological themes, published such poetry collections as "Das Hirtenmädchen," "Columbus," "Meine Wahl," "Treue Lieve," "Der Führer," "Versöhnung," "Terzinen," "Klosterstille," "Roccafrieda," and "Der Befreite."

BRACHVOGEL, Carry (1864–1942). German-Jewish novelist and author. Born in Munich, Germany, June 16, 1864; died in Theresienstadt-Terezin concentration camp, Nov 20, 1942; dau. of Heinrich Hellmann and Zerlina (Karl) Hellmann; m. Wolfgang Josef Emil Brachvogel (author and editor, died 1892); children: son, Heinz (b. 1889). ❖ Enjoyed a solid reputation in the "golden era" of pre-1914 middle-class prosperity, having created a series of highly regarded novels, novellas, and essays; published 1st novel, *Alltagsmenschen* ("Everyday People," 1895); also wrote *Der Erntetag* ("Harvest Day"); completely assimilated into German culture, made no attempt to leave Germany during Nazi years; deported from Munich to the Theresienstadt-Terezin concentration camp (July 1942). In the 1980s, scholars began to discover her as a writer of distinction who had articulated in the years before World War I a clear vision of modern women fully exercising their civil and personal rights. ❖ See also *Women in World History.*

BRACKEEN, JoAnne (1938–). American jazz pianist and composer. Name variations: Joanne Brackeen, Joanne or JoAnne Grogan. Born JoAnne Grogan, 1938 in Ventura, California; attended Los Angeles Conservatory; m. Charles Brackeen (saxophonist), early 1960s; children: 4. ❖ Innovative jazz pianist and prolific composer consistently ranked among world's best, who broke the glass ceiling and became an icon for women in jazz; began playing piano at 9; met and played with many jazz greats in Los Angeles while still in teens, such as Dexter Gordon and Art Farmer; moved to New York (1965), where she enjoyed great success, playing and recording with Paul Chambers, Lee Konitz, George Benson, Pharoah Sanders and Dave Holland; gained distinction as 1st and only female in Art Blakey's Jazz Messengers (1969–72) and went on to perform extensively with Joe Henderson (1972–75) and Stan Getz (1975–77); became successful solo artist and leader, forming own groups with such sidemen as Eddie Gomez, Cecil McBee, Sam Jones, Billy Hart and Freddie Waits; recorded over 2 dozen albums as leader and over 30 as side person; toured extensively worldwide, performing at every major European jazz festival; gave concerts at Carnegie Hall, Kennedy Center, Town Hall, Avery Fisher Hall, Smithsonian Institution and Seattle's Experience Music Project; created a library of more than 300 original compositions ranging in style from bop to Latin to avant-garde, over 100 of which have been recorded; worked as professor at New School and at Berklee College of Music; albums include *Snooze* (1975), *Special Identity* (1981); *Ancient Dynasty* (1988), *Live at Maybeck* (1989), *Where Legends Dwell* (1991) and *Popsicle Illusion* (2000). Was included in Ken Burns' documentary "Jazz"; nominated for Grammy award for album, *Pink Elephant Magic* (1999).

BRACKEN, Grace (1805–1901). *See Hirst, Grace.*

BRACKETT, Anna Callender (1836–1911). American educator. Born May 21, 1836, in Boston, Massachusetts; died Mar 18, 1911, in Summit, New Jersey; graduate of State Normal School, Framingham, Massachusetts, 1856. ❖ After working as a teacher and assistant principal in several schools, served as principal of the St. Louis Normal School in Missouri (1863–72); founded a private girls' school based on progressive educational methods; was editor of a symposium published as *The Education of American Girls* (1874); also edited *Women and the Higher Education.*

BRACKETT, Leigh (1915–1978). American author and screenwriter. Name variations: George Sanders, a pseudonym used for the mystery novel *Stranger at Home*. Born Leigh Douglass Brackett, Dec 7, 1915, in Los Angeles, California; died Mar 18, 1978; dau. of Margaret (Douglass) Brackett and William Franklin Brackett (certified public accountant); m. Edmond Hamilton (science-fiction writer), Jan 1, 1947 (died 1977); no children. ❖ Dubbed the "Queen of Space Opera" for her contribution to the science-fiction genre, began writing and submitting novels to editors (1928); sold 1st story to *Astounding* (1939); published 1st full-length novel, the mystery *No Good from a Corpse* (1944); collaborated with William Faulkner on screenplay of *The Big Sleep* (1944); won 1963 Silver Spur Award for *Follow the Free Wind*, the only western she wrote; was working on the screenplay for George Lucas' *Star Wars: The Empire Strikes Back* when she died (1978); writings include *The Sword of Rhiannon* (1953), *The Galactic Breed* (1955), *The Long Tomorrow* (1955), *The Tiger among Us* (1957), *Rio Bravo* (1959), *The Nemesis From Terra* (1961), *The Secret of Sinharat* (1964), *The Coming of the Terrans* (1967), *The Ginger Star* (1974), *The Best of Planet Stories No. 1* (1975) and (trilogy) *The Book of Skaith* (1976). ❖ See also *Women in World History*.

BRACQUEMOND, Marie (1840–1916). French impressionist painter. Born Marie Quivoron, 1840, at Argenton, Brittany; died 1916; studied painting with M. Wassor; m. Felix Bracquemond (engraver), 1869. ❖ Made 1st submission to the Paris Salon and was accepted (1857); by 1877, was beginning to follow the same pattern as many of the other Impressionists, working outdoors and intensifying the colors in her palette; took part in 1879 and 1880 Impressionist exhibitions with such works as *The Woman in White*; also exhibited at 1886 Impressionist exhibition, perhaps her last concerted effort to advance her career in the face of husband's growing disapproval. In 1919, a retrospective exhibition at the Galerie Bernheim Jeune displayed 156 of her works, most of which are no longer on public display anywhere. ❖ See also *Women in World History*.

BRADDOCK, Bessie (1899–1970). English politician. Name variations: E.M. Braddock. Born Elizabeth Margaret Bamber in Liverpool, England, Sept 24, 1899; died Nov 13, 1970; dau. of Hugh (Socialist) and Mary Bamber (labor organizer); m. John Braddock, in 1972. ❖ Known among her working-class constituents as "Battling Bessie," was a Labour member of Parliament for 35 years (1945–70), during which time she negotiated an end to a 5-week national dock strike, championed a bill nationalizing the trucking industry, uncovered an illegal arms shipment to the Liverpool docks which resulted in a halt on surplus arms shipments, and exposed mistreatment of prisoners in a Liverpool jail which sparked an inquiry by the secretary of state for the Home Department. ❖ See also *Women in World History*.

BRADDOCK, E.M. (1899–1970). *See Braddock, Bessie.*

BRADDON, Mary Elizabeth (1835–1915). English novelist and editor. Name variations: Mrs. M.E. Maxwell or Mrs. John Maxwell; (as an actress) Mary Seyton. Born Mary Elizabeth Braddon, Oct 4, 1835, in London, England (some sources cite 1837); died Feb 4, 1915, in Richmond, Surrey, England; dau. of Henry (lawyer and writer) and Fanny (White) Braddon; sister of Sir Edward Braddon, prime minister of Tasmania; m. John Maxwell (London publisher), 1874; children: 7, including 2 sons, William B. Maxwell and Gerald Maxwell, who became novelists. ❖ Produced 1st novel, *The Trail of the Serpent; or Three Times Dead;* published her most famous novel, *Lady Audley's Secret* (1862), which established her reputation as a novelist; followed that with *Aurora Floyd* (novel with a strong affinity to *Madame Bovary*) and *Eleanor's Victory*, in which murder was a central theme; is credited with introducing an innovation into popular fiction whereby wickedness, traditionally portrayed as ugly, is imbued with grace and beauty; is also known for inventing a crime mystery surrounded by everyday circumstances, yet devoid of the formulaic "detective novel" mechanism; turned out novels in rapid succession, all in the same vein, all achieving instant popularity. ❖ See also *Women in World History*.

BRADEN, Anne (1924–2006). American journalist and civil-rights activist. Born Anne Gamrell McCarty in Louisville, Kentucky, July 28, 1924; died March 6, 2006, in Louisville; attended Stratford and Randolph-Macon colleges; m. Carl Braden (1914–1975, journalist), 1948. ❖ Grew up in Mississippi and Alabama; returned to Louisville (1947); with husband, became involved in labor struggles for the CIO and the Progressive Party; arrested in Mississippi (1951) for protesting execution of a black man; arrested and blacklisted (1954); worked for the Southern Conference Educational Fund (SCEF); opposed witch-hunting tactics of House Un-American Activities Committee (HUAC, 1958);

served prison term and helped launch National Committee to Abolish HUAC; made effective use of media to dramatize struggle for civil rights and racial justice; arrested for "sedition" in Kentucky (1967); retired from SCEF (1972); edited *The Southern Patriot;* continued political activism after husband's death (1975), creating the Southern Organizing Committee for Economic and Social Justice; writings include *The Wall Between* (1958). ❖ See also *Women in World History*.

BRADFORD, Barbara Taylor (1933—). British novelist. Born May 5, 1933, in Upper Armley, Leeds, Yorkshire, England; dau. of Winston Taylor and Freda Taylor (nurse); m. Robert Bradford (American film producer), 1963. ❖ Worked as journalist in Yorkshire and London; became fashion editor for *Woman's Own* in London; worked as a crime and beat reporter for the *London Evening News;* on marriage, moved to New York (1963), where she wrote a syndicated column for *Designing Woman* for 12 years; came to prominence with the novel *A Woman of Substance* (1979); other novels, which usually center on powerful, autonomous females, include *Hold the Dream* (1985), *The Women in His Life* (1990), *Angel* (1993), *Her Own Rules* (1996), *Where You Belong* (2000) and *Emma's Secret* (2003); served on various charities and established Barbara Taylor Bradford Research Fellowship in Pediatric Leukemia. Awards include Matrix Award from New York Women in Communications (1985) and Special Jury Prize for Body of Literature from Deauville Festival of American Film (1994); several of her novels have been serialized for tv.

BRADFORD, Cornelia Foster (1847–1935). American social worker. Born Cornelia Foster Bradford, Dec 4, 1847, probably in Granby, NY; died Jan 15, 1935, in Montclair, New Jersey; dau. of Mary Amory (Howe) Bradford and Benjamin Franklin Bradford; sister of Amory Howe Bradford (Congregational minister). ❖ Visited Toynbee Hall (England) and developed interest in settlement work; lived in Mansfield House (East London settlement house) and worked with Jane Addams' Hull House (Chicago); with help from brother, established Whittier House in Jersey City, the 1st social settlement in NJ (1894); served as 1st and only head of Whittier House (1894–1920s), which established many services for Jersey City, including city's 1st kindergarten (by 1900); became leader in battle for child-labor legislation; appointed to Jersey City Board of Education (1912).

BRADFORD, Cornelia Smith (d. 1755). American printer and editor. Born Cornelia Smith in New York, NY; died 1755 in Philadelphia, Pennsylvania; m. Andrew Bradford (c. 1686–1742), probably 1740. ❖ After death of husband, took over his printing business and store, becoming one of 1st women printers in America; served as sole editor and printer of the *American Weekly Mercury* (1744–46); engaged in bookbinding and other printing, including almanacs, until at least 1751.

BRADLEY, Amber (1980—). Australian rower. Born May 19, 1980, in Wickham, Australia. ❖ Won World championship for quadruple sculls (2003); won a bronze medal for quadruple sculls at Athens Olympics (2004).

BRADLEY, Amy Morris (1823–1904). American educator, Civil War nurse, and administrator. Born Sept 12, 1823, in Vassalboro, Maine; died Jan 15, 1904, in Wilmington, North Carolina; dau. of Abired (shoemaker) and Jane (Baxter) Bradley. ❖ At 21, was named principal of a grammar school in Gardiner, Maine; moved to higher paying positions in Charlestown and Cambridge, Massachusetts, until severe bronchitis forced her to accept a position in the restorative climate of San José, Costa Rica, where she opened an English School for children of various nationalities; shortly after outbreak of Civil War, served the Union effort as a nurse with the Maine volunteers; named superintendent in the regimental hospital tents of the 5th Maine Regiment at Alexandria, Virginia; volunteered for the Sanitary Commission and was appointed superintendent of the floating hospital *Ocean Queen;* assigned as matron and administrator of a Soldiers' Home in Washington, DC (1862); transferred to a neglected convalescent camp dubbed "Camp Misery," where she oversaw the needs of some 5,000 soldiers (1862); after the war, opened a school in Wilmington, North Carolina, for poor white children; three years later, expanded her original classroom of 3 to a school for 75; was named superintendent of the newly restored school system (1869); opened Tileston Normal School in Wilmington, to train local women for teaching positions (1872); retired (1891). ❖ See also *Women in World History*.

BRADLEY, Grace (1913—). American theater and film dancer. Name variations: Grace Boyd; Mrs. William Boyd. Born Sept 21, 1913, in Brooklyn, NY; m. William Boyd (actor), 1937 (died 1972). ❖ A red-haired beauty, was a graceful dancer in *The Third Little Show* (1931) and *Strike me Pink* (1933); received film contract for Harold Lloyd comedies, whereupon she danced in a series of musicals and melodramas, including *Come on Marines* (1934), *She Made Her Bed* (1934) and *The Gilded Lily* (1935); returned to dancing in straight musical comedies after marriage to cowboy star William Boyd (Hopalong Cassidy); other films include *Wharf Angel* (1934), *Old Man Rhythm* (1935), *Thirteen Hours by Air* (1936), *Wake Up and Live* (1937), *The Big Broadcast of 1938* (1938), *Romance on the Run* (1938), *Brooklyn Orchid* (1942), *Taxi, Mister* (1943) and *Two Knights from Brooklyn* (1949).

BRADLEY, Jenny. French literary agent. Name variations: Mrs. William Aspenwall Bradley; Mme Jenny Serruys. Born Jenny Serruys in France; m. William Aspenwall Bradley (b. 1878), 1921. ❖ Was a partner in the literary agency set up in Paris by her husband, to serve such American expatriates as Hemingway and Fitzerald; also introduced the finest French writers, such as Camus and Gide, to the Knopfs for American publication.

BRADLEY, Katharine Harris (1846–1914). British poet and playwright. Name variations: (pseudonyms) Michael Field, Arran Leigh. Born Oct 27, 1846, in Birmingham, England; died Sept 26, 1914, in Richmond, Surrey, England; dau. of Charles Bradley and Emma (Harris) Bradley. ❖ Educated at Newnham College, Cambridge, and College de France, Paris; assumed care of niece, Edith Emma Cooper (1865), with whom she remained until death; under joint pseudonym Michael Field, published plays and poetry with niece, including *The New Minnesinger and Other Poems* (1875), *Bellerophon and Other Poems* (1881), *Long Ago* (1889), *Sight and Song* (1892), *The Race of Leaves* (1901), *Borgia: A Period Play* (1905), *Queen Marianne: A Play* (1908), *Mystic Trees* (1913) and *Dedicated: An Early Work of Michael Field* (1914); was a suffragist and anti-vivisectionist.

BRADLEY, Lillian Trimble (1875–?). American playwright and director. Name variations: Mrs. Trimble Bradley. Born 1875 in Milton, Kentucky; death date unknown; m. George H. Broadhurst (1866–1952, producer, writer, lyricist, director). ❖ Wrote *Mr. Myd's Mystery* (1915) and *The Wonderful Thing* (1920); with husband, wrote *The Red Falcon, Izzy* and *The Woman on the Index;* produced and sometimes staged several plays written by husband and others, including *Wild Oats Lane, The Elton Case, Tarzan of the Apes, The Crimson Alibi* and *Keep It to Yourself.*

BRADLEY, Lisa (1941—). American ballet dancer. Born 1941 in Elizabeth, New Jersey. ❖ Began professional career performing with Garden State Ballet in NJ; joined Joffrey Ballet (1960s), where she created roles in Gerald Arpino's *Incubus* (1962), *Viva Vivaldi!* (1965), *Nightwings* (1966) and *Secret Places* (1968); also danced featured roles in Balanchine's *Square Dance* and *Pas de Dix,* Arpino's *Partita for Four,* and Jerome Robbins' *Moves;* began performing with First Chamber Dance Company (1967); was guest artist at Hartford Ballet (1972–76), under director Michael Uthoff, where she created roles in his *Quartet* (1968), *Aves Mirabiles* (1973), and *Primavera* (1975); made guest appearance with Royal Winnipeg Ballet, in José Limón's *The Moor's Pavane* and Balanchine's *Apollo.*

BRADLEY, Lydia Moss (1816–1908). American philanthropist. Born July 31, 1816, in Vevay, Indiana; died Jan 16, 1908, in Peoria, Illinois; m. Tobias S. Bradley, May 1837; children: 6 (all died young). ❖ Following husband's death (1867), began philanthropic activities with gifts to her church and the establishment of a home for elderly women; obtained a charter for Bradley Polytechnic Institute (1876), later endowing the 28-acre campus with $2 million (it became Bradley University in 1946). ❖ See also *Women in World History.*

BRADLEY, Marion Zimmer (1930–1999). American science-fiction writer. Name variations: (pseudonyms) Lee Chapman; John Dexter; Miriam Gardner; Valerie Graves; Morgan Ives; John J. Wells. Born Marion Zimmer, June 3, 1930, in Albany, NY; died Sept 25, 1999, in Berkeley, CA; attended New York State College for Teachers, 1946–48; Hardin-Simmons University, BA, 1964; attended University of California at Berkeley; m. Robert A. Bradley, 1949 (div. 1963); m. Walter Henry Breen, 1964; children: (1st m.) 1 son; (2nd m.) 1 son, 1 daughter. ❖ Well-known sci-fi writer, wrote the "Darkover" series of novels, including *The Door Through Space* (1961), *Falcons of Narabedla* (1964), *Darkover Landfall* (1972), *The Shattered Chain* (1976), *The House Between the Worlds* (1980), *Web of Light* (1982), *Mists of Avalon* (1983), *Heirs of Hammerfell* (1989) and *Zandru's Forge* (2003); other novels include *I am a Lesbian* (1962), *Knives of Desire* (1966) and *The*

Catch Trap (1979); also published short-story collections, including *The Dark Intruder and Other Stories* (1964) and *Swords of Chaos* (1982).

BRADLEY, Pat (1951—). American golfer. Name variations: Patty Bradley; Patricia E. Bradley. Born Mar 24, 1951, in Westford, Massachusetts; attended Florida International University. ❖ Won the New Hampshire Amateur (1967, 1969) and the New England Amateur (1972–73); named to All-America Women's Intercollegiate Team (1970); joined LPGA tour (1974); won Colgate-Far East in Melbourne, Australia (1975); recorded 1st of 8 multiple-win seasons by winning the Lady Keystone Classic, Hoosier Classic, and Rail Charity Classic; won Greater Baltimore Classic and Peter Jackson Classic (1980); won Women's Kemper Open and US Women's Open (1981); won du Maurier Classic (1985); won 5 LPGA titles, including Nabisco-Dinah Shore, LPGA championship, and du Maurier Classic, the only player to capture 3 of the 4 modern-day majors in a single season (1986); following a bout with Graves Disease, won the Ai Start/Centinela Hospital Classic (1989); won 3 LPGA events, including the Oldsmobile Classic (1990); became the 1st player in LPGA history to surpass the $2, $3, and $4 million mark in earnings; won 4 LPGA titles (1991); won 31st career title, became the 2nd player to cross $5 million in earnings; served as captain of the US Solheim Cup Team (2000). Inducted into the LPGA Hall of Fame (1991); received the Patty Berg Award (2000).

BRADLEY, Mrs. Trimble (b. 1875). *See Bradley, Lillian Trimble.*

BRADLEY, Mrs. William Aspenwall. *See Bradley, Jenny.*

BRADNA, Olympe (1920—). French-born film star. Born Aug 12, 1920, backstage at the famous Olympia Theatre in Paris, France, where her parents were performing a dog act. ❖ Became part of the family circus act at 18 months, later performing solo as a bareback rider and acrobatic dancer; came to US with the Folies-Bergère (1934) and went to Hollywood; films include *Three Cheers for Love, The Last Train From Madrid, Souls at Sea, Say It in French, The Night of Nights, South of Pago Pago* and *International Squadron;* retired following marriage (1941).

BRADSHAW, Elizabeth Rose Rebecca (1827/31–1881). *See Watts Russell, Elizabeth Rose Rebecca.*

BRADSHAW, Maria (1801–1862). English singer and actress. Name variations: Mrs. Bradshaw. Born Ann Maria Bradshaw in 1801; died 1862; sister of Ellen Kean (1805–1880). ❖ Often appeared in roles of Shakespeare's women: Ophelia, Rosalind, Viola and Imogen, as well as Julia in *Two Gentleman of Verona;* retired (1825). ❖ See also *Women in World History.*

BRADSTREET, Anne (1612–1672). American writer. Born Anne Dudley in 1612 in Northamptonshire, England; died Sept 16, 1672, in Andover, Massachusetts; dau. of Thomas Dudley (governor of Massachusetts) and Dorothy Yorke; m. Simon Bradstreet (governor), in 1628; children: Samuel, Dorothy, Sarah, Hannah, Simon, Mercy, Dudley, and John. ❖ America's 1st woman poet, broke into a male-dominated avocation by writing epic and lyric poems, excelling in expression of feeling for life, nature, and love of family; came to New England with family and parents (1630); wrote 1st poem (1632); moved to Agawam (Ipswich), Massachusetts (1635); resided in Andover, Massachusetts (1640s–72); collected poems published in London by brother-in-law, Rev. John Woodbridge (1650); wrote last extant poem, "A Weary Pilgrim, now at Rest" (1669). Six years after her death, a 2nd edition of her work, with poems added to those of the 1st edition, was published in Boston (1678); though she and her family arrived in America at the beginning of settlement in the wilderness and she lived in a strict Puritan society, which denied women identity beyond their domestic duties, led the way in proving that women could achieve fulfillment in marriage and family and still pursue their creative intellectual talents; sounded the message for equality between men and women and even implied criticism of church and political authority. ❖ See also Pattie Cowell and Ann Stanford, eds. *Critical Essays on Anne Bradstreet* (Hall, 1983); Ann Stanford, *Anne Bradstreet, The Worldly Puritan: An Introduction to Her Poetry* (Franklin, 1974); Elizabeth Wade White, *Anne Bradstreet: "The Tenth Muse"* (Oxford U. Press, 1971); John Berryman, *Homage to Mistress Bradstreet* (Farrar, 1956); Josephine K. Piercy, *Anne Bradstreet* (College & U. Press, 1965); and *Women in World History.*

BRADTKE, Nicole (1969—). *See Provis, Nicole.*

BRADWELL, Myra (1831–1894). American publisher. Born Myra Colby, Feb 12, 1831, in Manchester, Vermont; died in Chicago, Illinois, Feb 14, 1894; dau. of Eben (farmer) and Abigail Hurd

(Willey) Colby; attended Ladies Seminary, Elgin, Illinois; m. James Bolesworth Bradwell, May 18, 1852; children: Myra (1854–1861); Thomas (b. 1856); Bessie Bradwell Helmer (b. 1858 who continued her mother's work); James (b. 1862). ❖ Founder, publisher, and editor of *Chicago Legal News* who, denied the right to practice law because of her gender, reformed the legal profession, especially laws discriminating against women; moved with family from Vermont to NY to Illinois; following graduation, taught in schools near Elgin; following marriage, taught in public schools and in a private school run in partnership with husband in Memphis, Tennessee (1853–55); back in Chicago, worked during Civil War with Northwestern Sanitary Commission, with leading role in Sanitary Fairs of 1863, 1865, 1867; read law under husband's tutelage, passed examination, but denied admission to bar on grounds of gender (1869); as founder, manager, and editor of *Chicago Legal News* (1868–94), proposed many reforms for women's rights, the legal profession, and Chicago, which were eventually adopted; appointed representative for Illinois to Centennial Exhibition, Philadelphia (1876); admitted to bar by Illinois Supreme Court on court's own motion (1890); named to Board of Lady Managers, Chicago Columbian Exposition. ❖ See also Jane M. Friedman, *America's First Woman Lawyer: The Biography of Myra Bradwell* (Prometheus, 1993); and *Women in World History.*

BRADY, Alice (1892–1939). American actress. Born in New York City, Nov 2, 1892; died 1939; dau. of William A. Brady (stage and film producer). ❖ Made stage debut at 14; starting screen career (1914), played romantic leads throughout WWI but reappeared on the New York stage (1918) and became a Broadway star; returned to Hollywood (early 1930s), abandoning straight roles for light comedy; nominated for Academy Award for Best Supporting Actress in *My Man Godfrey* (1936) and won Best Supporting Actress for *In Old Chicago* (1938); other films include *When Ladies Meet* (1933), *Beauty for Sale* (1933), *The Gay Divorcée* (1934), *Gold Diggers of 1935* (1935), *Metropolitan* (1935), *Go West Young Man* (1936), *Three Smart Girls* (1937), *Mama Steps Out* (1937), *Goodbye Broadway* (1938), *Zenobia* (1939) and *Young Mr. Lincoln* (1939). ❖ See also *Women in World History.*

BRADY, Julia Trotman (1968—). *See Trotman, Julia.*

BRADY, Mary (1821–1864). Irish-born Civil War nurse. Born in Ireland, 1821; died 1864 in Philadelphia, Pennsylvania; married a lawyer, 1846; children: 5. ❖ Immigrated to America with husband (1846); during Civil War, endured the hardships of the front lines and field hospitals, tending to the sick and wounded; helped found the Soldiers' Aid Society (1862), with the purpose of visiting hospitals, evaluating needs, and distributing supplies from a central-supply depot; personally distributed supplies to some 40 military hospitals in and around Washington, bringing her in contact with 30,000 sick and wounded; over a 2-year period, alternated trips to the front lines with respite at home in Philadelphia, where she became well known for her charitable work. ❖ See also *Women in World History.*

BRADY, Mildred Edie (1906–1965). American journalist. Name variations: Mildred Edie. Born Mildred Edie, June 3, 1906, in Little Rock, Arkansas; died July 27, 1965; dau. of Stewart Carson Edie (pharmacist) and Maude (White) Edie; m. Gerald Fling, 1929 (div. 1931); m. Robert Brady (economist), 1956 (died 1963); children: (with Robert Brady) 2 daughters. ❖ Active in the consumer movement, wrote investigative articles on marketing practices and advocated legislation for consumer rights and information; was an associate editor of *Theatre Arts Monthly* in NY (late 1920s) and a reporter for *Tide* magazine (1930–36); began living with Robert Brady (1936) and took his last name; joined newly formed Consumers Union (CU) and became manager of western branch in Berkeley, CA (1936); became managing editor of reform publication, *Friday*, and helped introduce CU's new weekly, *Bread & Butter*, in NY (1940); edited consumer newsletter for *McCall's* in Washington, DC (1940s); published famous article on Wilhelm Reich in *Harper's Magazine* (April 1947); worked for CU's *Consumer Reports*, becoming feature writer in California (1950) and editorial director and senior editor in Mt. Vernon, NY (1958); participated in International Organization of Consumers Unions.

BRADY, Veronica (1890–1964). Irish-born actress. Born 1890 in Dublin, Ireland; died Jan 19, 1964, in Twickenham, Middlesex, England; m. Hugh Nolan. ❖ Made stage debut in London as a fairy dancer in *A Midsummer Night's Dream* (1900); toured the provinces for many years before appearing at the Prince of Wales in *Are You There?*; other plays include *Samples, Flora, Very Good Eddie, The Last Waltz, Boodle,*

Casanova, Sunshine Sisters, Indoor Fireworks, Henry V and *The Dancing Years;* also appeared in many films and major London music halls.

BRAE, June (1917–2000). English ballerina. Born June Baer, May 18, 1917, in Ringwood, Hants., England; died in 2000; studied with George Goncharov in China; trained at Sadler's Wells Ballet School in London and with Nicholas Legat in Paris; m. David Lucas Breeden. ❖ Made stage debut in Shanghai in *The Blue Bird;* joined the Sadler's Wells Ballet (1936) and remained there for years, scoring 1st success as Josephine in *The Wedding Bouquet,* followed by *Nocturne, Giselle, Les Patineurs, Harlequin in the Street, Checkmate, Dante Sonata, The Sleeping Princess* and *Les Sylphides,* among others; was the 1st to appear as the Lilac Fairy in *The Sleeping Beauty* (1939).

BRAGA, Maria Ondina (1932–2003). Portuguese novelist and short-story writer. Born Jan 13, 1932, in Braga, Portugal; died 2003; educated in Paris and London. ❖ Taught in Goa, Macao, and Beijing, and often based early stories on experiences in the Far East; works include *Eu Vim para Ver a Terra* (1965), *Amor e Morte* (1970), *A Revolta das Palavras* (1975), *Estação Morta* (1980), *A Casa Suspensa* (1983), *Nocturno em Macao* (1991), *A Filha do Juramento* (1995) and *Vidas Vencidas* (1998); also wrote biographies of women in *Mulheres Escritoras* (1980). Won Grand Prize in Literature of ITF (2000).

BRAGA, Sonia (1950—). Brazilian actress. Name variations: Sônia Braga. Born June 8, 1950, in Maringá Paraná, Brazil. ❖ Made film debut in *O Bandido da Luz Vermelha* (1969); appeared as Lidia on tv series "Irmãos Coragem" (1970), as Flavia on "Selva de Pedra" (1972), as Gabriela on "Gabriela" (1975) and Gelly on "Chega Mais" (1980); starred in the film *Dona Flor e Seus Dois Maridos* (*Doña Flor and Her Two Husbands,* 1976); made English-language film debut in *Kiss of the Spider Woman* (1985), followed by *The Milagro Beanfield War* (1988), *Moon over Parador* (1988), *The Rookie* (1990), *Roosters* (1993), *Perfume* (2001), *Angel Eyes* (2001), *Empire* (2002) and *Sea of Dreams* (2004).

BRAGANZA, duchess of.
See Isabella of Braganza (1459–1521).
See Catherine of Portugal (1540–1614).
See Anne of Velasquez (1585–1607).
See Luisa de Guzmán (1613–1666).
See Elizabeth Maria of Thurn and Taxis (1860–1881).

BRAGGIOTTI, Berthe (c. 1900–c. 1925). Italian-American interpretive dancer. Born c. 1900 in Florence, Italy; died c. 1925 in Boston, Massachusetts; sister of Francesca and Gloria Braggiotti. ❖ Studied with Mlle La Roche while growing up in Florence; with sisters, trained at Denishawn's summer encampment in Peterborough, New Hampshire (early 1920s); with sister Francesca, directed school in Boston, MA, while performing in Prologs there.

BRAGGIOTTI, Francesca (1902–1998). Italian-American interpretive dancer and actress. Name variations: Francesca Lodge; Mrs. John Davis Lodge. Born Oct 17, 1902, in Florence, Italy; died Feb 25, 1998, in Marbella, Italy; sister of Berthe and Gloria Braggiotti; m. John Davis Lodge (governor of CT), 1938 (died 1985); children: Lily (b. 1930) and Beatrice (b. 1938). ❖ Studied with Mlle La Roche while growing up in Florence; trained at Denishawn's summer encampment in Peterborough, NH; with sister Gloria, performed in St. Denis' *Cupid and Psyche* (1923); performed solo concerts (1920s) and as part of Denishawn Lewisohn Stadium program, appearing in St. Denis' *The Lamp* (1928); retired from dance (mid-1930s) and returned to Italy to star in film epics; was one of Greta Garbo's Italian dubbers.

BRAGGIOTTI, Gloria (c. 1905—). Italian-American dancer and photographer. Name variations: Gloria Braggiotti Etting; Mrs. Emlen Etting. Born c. 1905 in Florence, Italy; sister of Berthe and Francesca Braggiotti (dancers); m. Emlen Etting (painter, 1905–1993). ❖ Studied with Mlle La Roche while growing up in Florence; with sisters, trained at Denishawn's summer encampment in Peterborough, NH (early 1920s); with sister Francesca, performed in St. Denis' *Cupid and Psyche* (1923); is thought to have continued to appear in Denishawn productions until mid-1930s, when she retired from dancing; worked as a fashion editor at *New York Evening Post,* then turned to photography.

BRAGINA, Lyudmila (1943—). Soviet runner. Name variations: Lyudmila Ivanovna Bragina. Born July 24, 1943, in Sverdlovslt, USSR. ❖ At Munich Olympics, won a gold medal in 1,500 meters with a time of 4:1.4, beating Albert Hill's 1920 gold medal performance by 1.4 seconds (1972); won a silver medal at European championships for 3,000 meters (1974); topped her own world record in the 3,000 meters by 18 seconds (1976), setting a new record of 8:27.1.

BRAHAM, Leonora (1853–1931). English actress and singer. Born Leonora Lucy Abraham, Feb 3, 1853, in Bloomsbury, London, England; died Nov 23, 1931, in London; m. 2nd husband Carter J. Duncan Young (actor, singer), 1886. ❖ Made stage debut in *Ages Ago* (1870) and NY debut in title role of *Princess Toto* (1879); in London, joined the D'Oyly Carte (1881–87, 1896), creating the title role in *Patience* (1881); at the Savoy, created the role of Phyllis in *Iolanthe*, Princess Ida in *Princess Ida*, Yum-Yum in *The Mikado*, and Rose Maybud in *Ruddigore*; other plays include *Gretna Green, Nanon, Paola, The Dove Cot* and *An Artist's Model*; toured US.

BRAHE, Sophia (1556–1643). Danish student of astronomy and chemistry. Born in Denmark in 1556; died 1643; 1 of 10 children of Otto and Beate (Bille) Brahe; sister of astronomer Tycho Brahe (1546–1601); m. Otto Thott (died 1588); m. Erik Lange; children: (1st m.) 1. ❖ Highly educated in classical literature, astrology, and alchemy, assisted her brother with the observations that led to his computation of the lunar eclipse of Dec 8, 1573. ❖ See also *Women in World History*.

BRAHMS, Helma Sanders-. See Sanders-Brahms, Helma.

BRAIN, Marilyn (1959—). Canadian rower. Born April 14, 1959, in Canada. ❖ At Los Angeles Olympics, won a gold medal in coxed fours (1984).

BRAITHWAITE, Lilian (1873–1948). British actress. Name variations: Dame Lilian Braithwaite. Born Lilian Florence Braithwaite in 1873 in Ramsgate, England; died 1948; dau. of a minister; m. Gerald Lawrence (actor); children: daughter, Joyce Carey (b. 1892, actress). ❖ One of the grande dames of the British stage, gained popularity early in career playing a succession of suffering heroines, but in later years expanded her repertoire to become a well-respected actress; joined William Haviland and Gerald Lawrence Shakespearean company (1897), making 1st professional appearances in minor roles in South Africa; made London debut as Celia in *As You Like It;* came to prominence as Lady Olivia Vernon in original Haymarket production of *Sweet Nell of Old Drury* (1900); signing with George Alexander company, was seen in *The Wilderness, Liberty Hall, Paolo and Francesca, The Importance of Being Earnest, Lady Windermere's Fan, Old Heidelberg*, and *Mr. Wu*, a 1913 hit which ran for a year; after considerable success as Margaret Fairfield in *A Bill of Divorcement* (1921), played opposite Noel Coward in *The Vortex* (1924), then appeared as Mrs. Phelps in *The Silver Cord;* subsequently played in a series of Novello comedies, including *The Truth Game, Symphony in Two Flats, Party, Fresh Fields, Full House* and *Comedienne*; during WWII, appeared as Abby Brewster in *Arsenic and Old Lace* for 1,337 performances. ❖ See also *Women in World History*.

BRAKEWELL, Jeanette (1974—). British equestrian. Born Feb 4, 1974, in Yorkshire, England. ❖ On Over To You, won a silver medal at Sydney Olympics (2000) and a silver medal at Athens Olympics (2004), both for team eventing.

BRAMLETT, Bonnie (1944—). American singer. Name variations: Delaney and Bonnie; Bonnie Lynn; Bonnie Sheridan. Born Bonnie Lynn O'Farrell, Nov 8, 1944, in Acton, Illinois; m. Delaney Bramlett (musician), 1967 (div. 1972); children: Bekka Bramlett (b. 1968, singer). ❖ Worked as Ikette with Ike and Tina Turner (mid-1960s); with Delaney Bramlett (as Delaney and Bonnie), had such hits as "Never Ending Song of Love" (1971) and "Only You Know and I Know" (1971). Albums include (as Delaney and Bonnie) *Accept No Substitute: The Original Delaney and Bonnie* (1969), *On Tour With Eric Clapton* (1970), *Motel Shot* (1971) and *Together* (1972); solo albums include *Sweet Bonnie Bramlett* (1973), *It's Time* (1975), *Lady's Choice* (1976) and *Memories* (1978).

BRAMLEY, Jenny Rosenthal (1910–1997). American engineer. Born 1910 in Russia, of Lithuanian parents; died 1997; left Russia with family as part of a hostage exchange between Lithuania and Soviet Union; attended high school in Berlin; University of Paris, ScB, 1926; New York University, MSc, 1927, PhD in physics, 1929; m. Arthur Bramley (engineer), 1943; children: Alan, Timothy, Eleanor. ❖ Cited for achievement in spectroscopy, optics, and mathematical techniques and their applications, was a physicist at US Army Signal Corps Laboratories in Ft. Monmouth, NJ (1942–44, 1948–50, 1950–53), where she and husband did pioneering work applying electroluminescence to solid state display and storage devices; her basic research for the invention of the microwave-pumped, high-efficiency lamp was applied to subsequent

development of high efficiency lasers; also invented techniques of coding and decoding pictorial information, which were later used in classified studies.

BRAMWELL-BOOTH, Catherine (1883–1987). English Salvation Army leader. Name variations: Catherine Booth. Born Catherine Booth (added father's name to her surname, 1929), July 20, 1883, in London, England; died Oct 3, 1987, in England; dau. of William Bramwell Booth and Florence Booth (both administrators in Salvation Army); granddau. of Catherine Booth (1829–1890, social reformer); attended Clapton Salvation Army Training College, 1903. ❖ Involved in Salvation Army, began service by playing and singing in band with sisters at open-air meetings; was sworn in as Salvation Army soldier on 15th birthday and later given responsibility for newly formed "Band of Love"; trained as Salvation Army officer at Clapton (1903) and commissioned (1904); appointed to Bath and Walthamstow and served as home officer for women and later chief side officer at Salvation Army Training College; provided relief to residents of Silvertown, East London, after massive explosion devastated area (1917); became leader of Women's Social Services (1926) and then International Headquarters secretary for Europe, providing relief for women and children after WWII; suffered nervous breakdown and bouts of depression and illness; wrote biography of father; retired from Salvation Army (1948) and lived with sisters in Finchampstead, England, writing biography of grandmother *Catherine Booth: The Story of Her Loves* (1970); emerged from seclusion to conduct memorial and funeral services for mother (1957); continued efforts to evangelize through radio and tv interviews (1970s). Awarded Commander of British Empire (CBE, 1971); received Humanitarian Award of Variety Clubs International (1981); admitted to Salvation Army's Order of the Founder (1983). ❖ See also autobiography, *Commissioner Catherine*; Mary Batchelor, *Catherine Bramwell-Booth: The Story of Her Life* (Lion, 1986).

BRANCA (c. 1192–1240). Portuguese princess. Born c. 1192; died Nov 17, 1240, at Guadalajara; dau. of Douce of Aragon (1160–1198) and Sancho I (1154–1211 or 1212), king of Portugal (r. 1185–1211 or 1212).

BRANCA (1259–1321). Abbess of Lorvano. Born Feb 25, 1259, in Guimaraes; died April 17, 1321, in Burgos; dau. of Beatrice of Castile and Leon (1242–1303) and Alphonso III, king of Portugal (r. 1248–1279).

BRANCH, Anna Hempstead (1875–1937). American poet and social worker. Born Mar 18, 1875, in New London, Connecticut; died Sept 8, 1937, in New London; dau. of John Locke Branch and Mary Lydia (Bolles) Branch (1840–1822, writer). ❖ Served as editor-in-chief of literary monthly at Smith College and worked on poem "The Road 'Twixt Heaven and Hell" (winner, competition by *Century Magazine*); began relationship with the Christodora House social settlement on Lower East Side, NY (c. 1900), where she read her poetry, organized youth club, and served on board of directors; coordinated programs and classes at the Poet's Guild which was established at Christodora House; engaged in writings, including plays, prayers, and poems, for house activities; known for a broad mysticism; authored *Sonnets from a Lock Box* (1929). Best-known poem is "Nimrod."

BRANCH, Elizabeth (1673–1740). English murderer. Born in Philips-Norton, Somersetshire, England, 1673; hanged, May 3, 1740, in Ovelchester, England; m. a farmer named Branch; children: Mary Branch (1716–1740). ❖ Showed cruelty throughout life, particularly to servants whom she physically abused and denied basic necessities; following husband's death, with help of daughter Mary, attacked young servant Jane Buttersworth and killed her; arrested with Mary, was brought to Taunton for trial (Mar 1740); found guilty, was hanged with daughter in the middle of the night with no crowd present, for fear that the two would otherwise be torn apart by public (May 3, 1740).

BRANCH, Mary Lydia Bolles (1840–1922). American children's writer. Born Mary Lydia Bolles, June 1840, in New London, Connecticut; died 1922; m. John Locke Branch; children: Anna Hempstead Branch (poet and social worker). ❖ Known primarily for stories and poems for children, served as assistant editor of *Saturday Evening Post* in Philadelphia, PA (1865); best-known poem is "The Petrified Fern."

BRANCOURT, Karen (1962—). Australian rower. Name variations: Karen Brancourt-Pollock; Karen Pollock. Born Mar 15, 1962, in Australia. ❖ At Los Angeles Olympics, won a bronze medal in coxed fours (1984).

BRANCOVAN, Princess de (1876–1933). *See Noailles, Anna de.*

BRAND, Barbarina (1768–1854). *See Dacre, Barbarina.*

BRAND, Colette. Swiss freestyle aerial skier. ❖ Won a gold medal at Albertville Olympics when aerials was a demonstration sport (1992); though a favorite at Lillehammer Olympics, failed to qualify for final (1994); won a bronze medal in aerials at Nagano Olympics (1998); retired (1998).

BRAND, Esther (1924—). South African high jumper. Born Sept 29, 1924, in South Africa. ❖ At Helsinki Olympics, won a gold medal in the high jump (1952), using the scissors technique, the 1st South African woman to win a gold medal in track and field; won the national high-jump title 9 times (1938–52); set a world record (1941).

BRAND, Mona (1915—). Australian poet and playwright. Name variations: Mona Alexis Fox Brand. Born Oct 22, 1915, in Sydney, NSW, Australia; m. Len Fox (socialist). ❖ Socialist playwright, was an industrial social welfare worker during WWII; lived in Hanoi (1956–57); was a member of the Communist Party until 1970; wrote over 25 plays, which were often produced by the left-wing New Theatre as well as overseas, including the anti-racist *Here Under Heaven* (1947), *Flood Tide* (1955), *Pavement Oasis* (1958), *On Stage Vietnam* (1967) and *Here Comes Kisch!* (1984); poetry includes *Wheel and Bobbin* (1938), *Silver Singing* (1940), *Lass in Love* (1946) and *Daughters of Vietnam, Hanoi* (1958). Awards include New South Wales Arts Council Drama Festival 1st prize for *Our 'Dear' Relation* (1968). ❖ See also *Enough Blue Sky: The autobiography of Mona Brand, an unknown well-known playwright.*

BRAND, Phoebe (1907–2004). American actress and theater founder. Name variations: Phoebe Brand Carnovsky. Born 1907 in Syracuse, NY; grew up in nearby Ilion; died July 3, 2004, in New York, NY; dau. of chief mechanical engineer for Remington typewriters; m. Morris Carnovsky (actor), 1941 (died 1992); children: Stephen Carnovsky. ❖ Began career appearing in Gilbert and Sullivan revivals; with others, formed the prestigious Group Theater (1931), a radical company dealing with social issues; originated several parts with the Group, including Hennie Berger in *Awake and Sing!* and Anna in *Golden Boy;* blacklisted during the McCarthy era along with husband, began to teach acting; helped found Theater in the Street (1960s); made film debut at age 86 in Louis Malle's *Vanya on 42nd Street* (1994).

BRAND, Rebecca (1939—). *See Charnas, Suzy McKee.*

BRAND, Sybil (c. 1899–2004). American philanthropist. Born Sybil Morris, c. 1899, in Chicago, Illinois; grew up in Los Angeles, California; died Feb 17, 2004, in Beverly Hills, California; dau. of Arthur W. Morris (wealthy stockbroker); m. Harry Brand (head of publicity at 20th Century-Fox), 1933 (died 1989); children: George. ❖ Devoted to improving conditions for imprisoned women, was appointed to the Vocational Training Commission (1945), which oversaw jails and other facilities; chaired the commission, which evolved into the Institutional Inspections Commission, then the Sybil Brand Commission, for the rest of her life; helped found the Sybil Brand Institute (1963).

BRANDÃO, Fiama Hasse Pais (1938—). Portuguese poet and playwright. Name variations: Fiama Hasse Pais Brandao. Born 1938 in Lisbon, Portugal; attended St. Julian's School; studied German philology at University of Lisbon. ❖ One of Portugal's major poets, was member of Poesia 61 movement opposed to neo-realism (1960s); her volume of plays, *A Campanho, O Golpe de Estado, Diálogo dos Pastores, Auto de Família* (1969), which were often political in nature, were banned by the Salazar government; published 14 vols. of poetry, including *Em Cada Pedra um Vôo Imóvel* (1957) and *Epistles and Memoranda;* also translated Updike, Novalis, Artaud, Brecht, and Chekhov into Portuguese.

BRANDAO BEHAR, Adriana (1969—). *See Behar, Adriana.*

BRANDEBUSEMEYER, Nicole (1974—). German soccer player. Born Oct 9, 1974, in Georgsmarienhütte, Germany. ❖ Defender and midfielder; won a team bronze medal at Sydney Olympics (2000).

BRANDEGEE, Mary Katharine (1844–1920). American botanist. Name variations: Mary Curran; Katherine Layne. Born Mary Katharine Layne in 1844 in Tennessee; died 1920 in Berkeley, California; dau. of Marshall and Mary (Morris) Layne; University of California at Berkeley, MD, 1878; m. Hugh Curran, 1866 (died 1874); m. Townshend Brandegee (civil engineer), 1889. ❖ Took up the study of plants, concentrating on their medicinal value before expanding to a more general approach; began working at California Academy of Sciences, where she was curator of botany (1883–93); with 2nd husband, Townshend Brandegee, also an avid plant collector, established and edited a series of *Bulletins* of the California Academy of Science and founded *Zoe,* a journal of botanical observations from the western US, in which she published most of her works. ❖ See also *Women in World History.*

BRANDEIS, Friedl Dicker- (1898–1944). *See Dicker-Brandeis, Friedl.*

BRANDENBURG, electress of.
See Cunegunde (d. 1357).
See Elizabeth of Bavaria-Landshut (1383–1442).
See Margaret of Baden (d. 1457).
See Catherine of Saxony (1421–1476).
See Anne of Saxony (1437–1512).
See Margaret of Saxony (1449–1501).
See Elizabeth of Denmark (1485–1555).
See Magdalene of Saxony (1507–1534).
See Hedwig of Poland (1513–1573).
See Sabine of Brandenburg-Ansbach (1529–1575).
See Catherine of Custrin (1549–1602).
See Elizabeth of Anhalt (1563–1607).
See Elenore Hohenzollern (1583–1607).
See Anna of Prussia (fl. 1599).
See Louisa Henrietta of Orange (1627–1667).
See Sophie Charlotte of Hanover (1668–1705).

BRANDENBURG, margravine of.
See Jutta of Saxony (d. around 1267).
See Hedwig of Habsburg (d. 1286).
See Barbara of Saxe-Wittenberg (c. 1405–1465).

BRANDÉS, Marthe (1862–1930). French actress. Name variations: Martha Brandes. Born Marthe Brunschwig, 1862; died in Paris, France, 1930. ❖ Made stage debut in Paris in *Diane de Lys* (1884); at Vaudeville Theatre, Paris, appeared as the 1st French Hedda Gabler (Dec 17, 1891); with the Comédie Française, featured in *Ruy Blas, L'Aventurière, Patrie, Le Mariage de Figaro, Hernani, Les Tenailles, Cabotins, Grosse fortune, Catharine* and *L'Enigme.* Created a Chevalier of the Legion of Honor (1920).

BRANDES-BRILLESLIJPER, Janny (c. 1918–2003). Dutch resistance leader. Name variations: Jannie. Born c. 1918; died Aug 13, 2004, in Amsterdam, Netherlands; children: 2. ❖ The last person known to have seen Anne Frank alive, was a member of the Jewish resistance in occupied Netherlands; with Anne, was deported to Westerbork, then Auschwitz; while working as a nurse in Nazi camps, saw Anne in Bergen-Belsen concentration camp a few days before she died of typhus (spring 1945).

BRANDON, Anne (d. 1557). English baroness. Died Jan 1557; dau. of Charles Brandon (1484–1545), 1st duke of Suffolk (r. 1514–1545), and his 2nd wife Anne Browne (his 1st wife was Mary Tudor [1496–1533]); m. Edward Grey (d. 1552), 3rd baron Grey of Powys; m. Randle Hansworth.

BRANDON, Eleanor (c. 1520–1547). Duchess of Cumberland. Born c. 1520; died Nov 1547 at Brougham Castle, Cumbria, England; buried at Skipton, North Yorkshire, England; dau. of Charles Brandon (1484–1545), 1st duke of Suffolk, and Mary Tudor (1496–1533); m. Henry Clifford, 2nd earl of Cumberland, in June 1527; children: Margaret Clifford.

BRANDON, Frances (1517–1559). Duchess of Suffolk. Name variations: Frances Grey. Born July 16, 1517, in Hatfield, Hertfordshire, England; died Nov 21, 1559, in London, England; dau. of Charles Brandon (1484–1545), duke of Suffolk, and Mary Tudor (1496–1533, younger sister of Henry VIII); m. Henry Grey, marquis of Dorset (later duke of Suffolk), in 1535 (d. 1554); m. Adrian Stokes, Mar 9, 1554; children: (1st m.) Jane Grey (1537–1554); Catherine Grey (c. 1540–1568, later Catherine Seymour); Mary Grey (1545–1578, who m. Thomas Keyes); (2nd m.) Elizabeth Stokes (1554–1554, died at birth).

BRANDSTROM, Elsa (1888–1948). Swedish-born heroine and nurse. Name variations: Elsa Brändström; Elsa Uhlig. Born Mar 26, 1888, in St. Petersburg, Russia; died Mar 4, 1948, in Cambridge, Massachusetts; dau. of General Edvard Brandstrom, Swedish ambassador to Tsar Nicholas II during WWI; m. Robert Uhlig (taught at Harvard University). ❖ Known as the "Angel of Siberia," assisted German POWs in Siberia during WWI, in part privately, in part as a delegate of the Swedish Red Cross; later married and moved to Germany, where she worked among the destitute; with rise of Hitler, fled with husband to US, where they cared for European refugees during WWII.

BRANDT, Julie (1979—). See Glass, Julie.

BRANDT, Marianne (1842–1921). Austrian soprano. Born Marie Bischoff in Vienna, Austria, Sept 12, 1842; died in Vienna, July 9, 1921. ❖ Performed in Berlin (1868–82); studied in Vienna with Janda and Zeller and in Baden-Baden with Pauline Viardot; made Covent Garden debut in *Fidelio* (1872); sang Amneris in the 1st Berlin performance of *Aïda* (1874); appeared as Waltraute in *Götterdämmerung* at the 1st Bayreuth Festival (1876) and Kundry at 2nd performance of *Parsifal* at Bayreuth (1882); though she disliked Wagner, performed his work in Berlin, London and NY; appeared at Metropolitan Opera (1884–88) and gave the 1st American performance of Weber's *Euryanthe* (1887); retired (1890). ❖ See also *Women in World History.*

BRANDT, Marianne (1893–1983). German designer. Born in Germany, Oct 1, 1893; died June 18, 1983; studied painting at Weimar. ❖ Best known for her metal teapot (1924) and various lamps and lighting fixtures, all personifying the Bauhaus tradition of functional design, was an instructor in the Bauhaus metalworking shop; later went on to teach industrial design in Dresden (1949–51) and Berlin (1951–54).

BRANDT, Muriel (1909–1981). Irish painter. Born in Belfast in 1909; died in Our Lady's Hospice, Dublin, June 10, 1981; won a scholarship to the Royal College of Art, London; m. Frank Brandt (artistic adviser); children: 1 son, 2 daughters, including Ruth Brandt (artist). ❖ Gained 1st major commission, a set of panels of Adam and Eve for the Franciscan Church on Merchants' Quay in Dublin; portraits include Sir Alfred Chester Beatty, George O'Brien, as well as a group seating of Michael Mac Liammoir, Christine Longford, and Hilton Edwards, which hangs in the foyer of the Gate Theater.

BRANDY (1979—). American singer and actress. Name variations: Rayana Norwood. Born Rayana Norwood, Feb 11, 1979, in McComb, Mississippi; m. Robert Smith (producer and songwriter), 2001 (sep.); children: 1 daughter. ❖ At 12, became backup singer for R&B group Immature; released debut album *Brandy* which sold more than 4 million copies and featured hit singles "I Wanna Be Down" (1994) and "Baby" (1995); other hits include "Sittin' Up in My Room" (from film *Waiting to Exhale,* 1995), "Missing You" (with Tamia, Gladys Knight, and Chaka Khan, from film *Set It Off,* 1996), and "The Boy Is Mine" (duet with Monica, 1998); with Monica, received Grammy for Best Rhythm & Blues Performance by a Duo with Vocal for "The Boy Is Mine"; made film debut starring in *Moesha* (1996). Other albums include *Never S-a-y Never* (1998) and *Full Moon* (2002).

BRANHAM, Sara Elizabeth (1888–1962). American bacteriologist. Born 1888 in Oxford, Georgia; died 1962; studied biology at Wesleyan College; University of Colorado, PhD, 1923, MD, 1934. ❖ Researcher in the field of public health, who conducted pioneering work on meningitis, demonstrated that sulfa drugs inhibit the activity of meningococcal bacteria helping to pave the way to successful control of the often fatal disease; for 30 years, was a bacteriologist with US Public Health Service (now National Institute of Health, NIH). Named Women of the Year by American Medical Women's Association (1959). ❖ See also *Women in World History.*

BRANIGAN, Laura (1957–2004). American singer. Born July 3, 1957, in Brewster, NY; died of a brain aneurysm, age 47, Aug 26, 2004, in East Quogue, NY; attended Academy of Dramatic Arts; m. Lawrence Kruteck (lawyer, died 1996). ❖ Powerful singer with a 5-octave range, toured Europe as a backup vocalist for Leonard Cohen; signed with Atlantic Records (1982); released debut album *Branigan* (1982), which featured the pop hit "Gloria" and earned her a Grammy nomination for Best Female Pop Vocalist; had other hit singles with "Solitaire" (1983), "How Am I Supposed to Live Without You" (1983), "Self Control" (1984) and "The Power of Love" (1988); starred as Janis Joplin in off-Broadway musical, *Love, Janis* (2002). Other albums include *Branigan 2* (1983), *Self Control* (1984), *Hold Me* (1985), *Touch* (1987), *Laura Branigan* (1990), *Over My Heart* (1993) and *The Best of Branigan* (1995).

BRANITZKA, Nathalie (1905–1977). Russian ballet dancer. Name variations: Nathalie Branitzka von Hoyer. Born July 18, 1905, in St. Petersburg, Russia; died Mar 8, 1977, in New York, NY; m. Jan von Hoyer. ❖ Studied in St. Petersburg and Paris; appeared with Vera Trefilova and Pierre Vladimioff in Berlin (c. 1925); performed with Boris Kniaseff's ballet company in Paris (c. 1930); danced with De Basil's Ballet Russe de Monte Carlo (1932–40); appeared in many works by Leonid Massine, including *Choreartium, Jeux d'Enfants, Beach* and *Scuola di Ballo,* and in Mikhail Fokine's *Carnaval* and *Les Sylphides;* moved to US to teach (1940).

BRANKIN, Rhona. Scottish politician. Born in Glasgow; graduate of Aberdeen University; children: Anna and Ruth. ❖ Taught in the Highlands (1975–94); chair of the Labour Party (1995–96) and a member of the Scottish Constitutional Convention; elected to the Scottish Parliament for Midlothian (1999 and 2003).

BRANNON, Carmen (1899–1974). See Lars, Claudia.

BRANNON, Hazel (1914–1994). See Smith, Hazel Brannon.

BRANSCOMBE, Gena (1881–1977). Canadian-born American composer, conductor, teacher, and pianist. Born Gena Branscombe in Picton near Kingston, Ontario, Canada, Nov 4, 1881; died in New York, NY, July 26, 1977; graduate of Chicago Musical College; studied with Rudolph Ganz, Felix Borowski, and Engelbert Humperdinck; m. John Ferguson Tenney, 1910. ❖ Especially known for choral compositions, began composing at 5 and was still composing at 92; moved to NY (1910); premiered *Quebec Suite* (1910); saw *Coventry's Choir* (1944), a large choral work with piano accompaniment, performed throughout US, Canada, and Great Britain; founded Branscombe Chorale of NY (1933), which performed for over 20 years; was president of Society of American Women Composers and director of National Association of American Composers and Conductors. ❖ See also *Women in World History.*

BRANT, Beth (1941—). Native American essayist and short-story writer. Name variations: Degonwadonti. Born 1941 in Detroit, Michigan, a Bay of Quinte Mohawk from Theyindenaga Mohawk Territory in Michigan; married at 17; children: 3 daughters. ❖ Edited *A Gathering of Spirit: A Collection by North American Indian Women* (1988); wrote *Mohawk Trail* (1985) and *Food and Spirits* (1991); with partner Denise Dorsz, founded Turtle Grandmother archive on Native American women; worked with AIDS survivors in Native American community and as an activist for Native American lesbians. Won Creative Writing Award from Michigan Council for the Arts (1984, 1986), National Endowment for the Arts award (1991), and Canada Council Award in Creative Writing (1992).

BRANT, Mary (c. 1736–1796). See Brant, Molly.

BRANT, Molly (c. 1736–1796). Mohawk tribal leader. Name variations: Mary Brant; (in Mohawk) Koñwatsi'tsiaiéñni. Born c. 1736 in the Mohawk village at Canajoharie, Little Falls, New York; died April 16, 1796, at Kingston, Ontario, Canada; dau. of Margaret and Peter (Christianized Mohawks of the Six Nations Confederacy); granddau. of Sagayeeanquarashtow, Iroquois representative to the English court; sister of Joseph Brant (c. 1742–1807); became 2nd wife of Sir William Johnson (superintendent of Indian Affairs for His Majesty's Northern Colonies), c. 1759; children: Peter (b. 1759); Elizabeth (b. 1761); Magdalene (b. 1763); Margaret (b. 1765); George (b. 1767); Mary (b. 1769); Susanna (b. 1771); Anna (b. 1773) and one child who died shortly after birth. ❖ Mohawk clan mother whose diplomacy and intelligence-gathering during the American Revolution made her a power broker among both the Iroquois nations and British government officials in Canada; accompanied Mohawk delegation to Philadelphia to protest fraudulent sales of tribal lands (1754–55); because of marriage to Superintendent of Indian Affairs for the Northern Colonies, was placed in charge of the Johnson household and estate, and, from time to time, the Indian Department itself (1759–74); as Johnson's widow and a powerful clan mother, persuaded her nation to ally with the Crown during the American Revolution (1775–83); credited with saving St. Leger's Loyalist forces besieging Fort Stanwix from surprise attack by an American relief militia (1777); forced from her Mohawk Valley home by invading rebel colonists, spent most of the war at Fort Niagara and on Carleton Island, New York, negotiating the Crown's interests with other displaced Iroquois; at war's end, resettled her family at Cataraqui (Kingston) Canada; a controversial figure because she was both pro-British and pro-Iroquois, strode with authority in both worlds, asserting her will with Indian chiefs and Anglo officials alike. ❖ See also *Women in World History.*

BRANTENBERG, Gerd (1941—). Norwegian novelist and feminist. Born Oct 27, 1941, in Oslo, Norway; grew up in Fredrikstad in southeastern Norway; graduate of University of Oslo, 1970. ❖ Taught history and English; a feminist, who writes about lesbian life and awakening, made literary debut with the coming-out story, *Opp alle jordens homofile* (1973), published in English as *What Comes Naturally* (1986); depicts lesbian love in *Embraces* (1983); published internationally successful feminist science-fiction novel *Egalias døtre* (*Egalia's Daughters*, 1977), exposing absurdities of patriarchal society by inverting norms; focused on class and sex differences in realist trilogy *The Song of St. Croix* (1979), *At the Ferry Crossing* (1985), and *To The Winds* (1989); tackles prejudices with imagination and humor; was instrumental in the founding of the lesbian movement in Denmark (1974) and Norway (1975).

BRANZELL, Karin (1891–1974). Swedish opera singer. Born Karin Maria Branzell in Stockholm, Sweden, Sept 24, 1891; died in Altadena, California, Dec 15, 1974; studied under Thekla Hofer in Stockholm and with Louis Bachner, Enrico Rosati, and Anna Schoen-René; m. Fedya Reinshagen (opera stage director), 1946. ❖ Singer whose powerful contralto and large frame made her a perfect Wagnerian figure, performed with the Stockholm Royal Opera (1912–18), then Berlin Staatsoper (1918–23), appearing as the Nurse in the Berlin premiere of Strauss' *Die Frau ohne Schatten;* went to Vienna to sing Kundry and debuted in America as Fricka in *Die Walküre* at the Metropolitan (1924); continued singing major contralto roles at Met, including Amneris and Delilah, until 1942; performed at Bayreuth (1930, 1931); appeared at Covent Garden under Sir Thomas Beecham (1935, 1937, 1938); taught singing in NY and California after retirement from the stage. ❖ See also *Women in World History.*

BRAOSE, Annora de (d. 1241). English noblewoman and recluse. Died 1241; dau. of William and Maud de Braose (d. 1211); m. Hugh de Mortimer (wealthy baron). ❖ Was imprisoned by King John for possibly conspiring against him with her family, though the facts of the case remain obscure; after some time, was released through intervention of the papal legate; gained permission to be a recluse and enclosed herself at Iffley (c. 1231); received annual payments from King Henry III, a great supporter of recluses, until her death 10 years later. ❖ See also *Women in World History.*

BRAOSE, Beatrice de (d. 1383). *See Mortimer, Beatrice.*

BRAOSE, Eleanor de (fl. 1250s). English noblewoman. Name variations: Eleanor Bohun; Eleanor de Bohun. Interred at Llanthony, Gloucester; dau. of Eve de Braose (fl. 1220s) and William de Braose, lord of Abergavenny; m. Humphrey Bohun (d. 1265, son of the 6th earl of Hereford and Essex); children: Humphrey Bohun (c. 1248–1298), 3rd earl of Hereford, 2nd of Essex (some sources cite 7th earl of Hereford and Essex); Gilbert Bohun; Alianore Bohun (d. 1313). ❖ Humphrey Bohun's 2nd wife was Joan de Quinci.

BRAOSE, Eve de (fl. 1220s). Lady of Abergavenny. Name variations: Eva Marshal; Eve Marshall. Dau. of William Marshall (b. 1146), 1st earl of Pembroke, and Isabel de Clare (c. 1174–1220); m. William de Braose, lord of Abergavenny; children: Isabel de Braose (d. 1248?); Maud Mortimer (c. 1229–1301); Eleanor de Braose (fl. 1250s).

BRAOSE, Gladys de (d. 1251). *See Gladys the Black.*

BRAOSE, Isabel de (d. 1248?). Welsh queen and princess of Gwynedd. Died before Feb 1248; dau. of William de Braose and Eve de Braose; m. David ap Llywelyn of Wales (David II), prince of Gwynedd (1240–1246), Ruler of All Wales (r. 1240–1246), in 1230.

BRAOSE, Loretta de (d. 1266). English religious activist. Name variations: Loretta de Briouze; Loretta of Leicester. Born before 1186; died 1266 in Hackington, England; dau. of William de Braose and Maud de Braose (d. 1211); sister of Annora de Braose (d. 1241); m. Robert Beaumont, earl of Leicester, around 1196 (died 1204); children: none. ❖ Along with parents and siblings, caught up in King John's political persecutions (1204), though reportedly had been a strong supporter of the king; had lands seized and fled to France; returned to England 10 years later and was granted her properties again; received permission to become a recluse and entered a cell in village of Hackington (1221); became an activist, helping establish the Franciscan order in England and writing to the king asking for favors for her ecclesiastical friends. ❖ See also *Women in World History.*

BRAOSE, Maud de (d. 1211). Baroness. Name variations: Maud de St. Walerie; Maud of St. Valery; Lady Bramber. Died of starvation while in prison, c. 1211, in Windsor, Berkshire, England; m. William de Braose, Lord of Bramber (d. around 1212); children: William de Braose (d. 1211, sheriff of Herefordshire who raised a rebellion in Wales against King John); Reginald de Braose, baron de Braose (d. 1221, who m. Groecia de Bruere); Annora de Braose (d. 1241); Loretta de Braose (d. 1266). ❖ See also *Women in World History.*

BRAOSE, Maud de (c. 1229–1301). *See Mortimer, Maud.*

BRASILEIRA, Uma (1825–1917). *See Reis, Maria Firmina dos.*

BRASLAU, Sophie (1888–1935). American contralto. Born Aug 16, 1888, in New York, NY; died Dec 22, 1935, in NY, NY; dau. of Abel Braslau and Lascha (Goodelman) Braslau (both Russian-Jewish immigrants); attended Institute of Musical Art in NY; never married; no children. ❖ Particularly noted for her 3-octave range as well as volume and quality of voice, studied voice with Arturo Buzzi-Peccia; received contract with Metropolitan Opera (1913), debuting as A Voice in *Parsifal;* performed many roles at Met, including title role in *Shanewis* and parts in *Tosca, Hänsel und Gretel, L'Amore dei Tre Re, Madame Sans-Gêne, L'Oracolo,* and *Carmen;* made 1st concert appearances in Cleveland and Baltimore (1914); gave 1st NY recital at Aeolian Hall (1916) and last performance at Metropolitan (1920), in favor of concert work in US and abroad; toured England, Netherlands, and Scandinavian countries (1931); made last public appearance (1934) in NY at Lewisohn Stadium.

BRASOVA, Natalia or Nathalie (1880–1952). *See Sheremetskaia, Natalia.*

BRASSEUR, Isabelle (1970—). Canadian pairs skater. Born July 28, 1970, in Quebec, Canada; m. Rocky Marval (two-time American pair champion), 1996. ❖ With partner Lloyd Eisler, won 5 Canadian National titles (1989, 1991–94), the World championship (1993), a bronze medal at Albertville Olympics (1992) and a bronze medal at Lillehammer Olympics (1994); turned professional (1994); produced "Dreams on Ice." Inducted into Canadian Figure Skating Hall of Fame (2000). ❖ See also joint autobiographies, *To Catch a Dream* (1996) and *Brasseur and Eisler: The Professional Years* (1999).

BRASSEY, Anna (1839–1887). British travel writer. Name variations: Lady Anna or Annie Brassey, Annie B., Baroness Brassey. Born Anna Allnutt in London, Oct 7, 1839; died at sea in the South Pacific, Sept 14, 1887; dau. of Elizabeth (Burnett) and John Allnutt; educated at home; m. Baron (later Lord) Thomas Brassey (politician and MP), Oct 9, 1860; children: Thomas Allnutt, Mabelle Annie, Muriel Agnes, and Marie Adelaide. ❖ With husband, began sea journeys on the sailing yacht *Eöthen* (1872), commissioned by Parliament to research the culture, economy, and labor of other nations; wrote journal-like letters to father, which were published as *A Cruise in the Eöthen* (1872) to great success; wrote further travel novels for public readership, based on circumnavigation of the globe, including *A Voyage in the "Sunbeam" Our Home on the Ocean for Eleven Months* (1878), which had 19 editions in 10 years, including translations in 5 languages; with family, took at least 8 sailing trips, lasting a minimum of 4, but more commonly 6-to-8 months at sea. ❖ See also *Women in World History.*

BRATHWAITE, Yvonne (b. 1932). *See Burke, Yvonne Brathwaite.*

BRATSBERG, Stine Lise. *See Hattestad, Stine Lise.*

BRATSCH, Jacqueline (b. 1936). *See Means, Jacqueline.*

BRAUMUELLER, Ellen (1910—). German javelin thrower. Name variations: Ellen Braumüller. Born Dec 24, 1910, in Germany. ❖ At Los Angeles Olympics, won a silver medal in javelin throw (1932).

BRAUMÜLLER, Ellen (b. 1910). *See Braumueller, Ellen.*

BRAUN, Carol Mosely (1947—). African-American politician. Name variations: Carol Mosely-Braun. Born Carol Mosely, Aug 16, 1947, in Chicago, Illinois; dau. of a policeman and a medical technician; University of Illinois–Chicago, BA, 1968; law degree from University of Chicago, 1972; married and divorced; children: Matthew (computer engineer). ❖ Worked in the US Attorney's office in Chicago (1973–77), focusing primarily in the civil and appellate law areas; served in the Illinois state legislature (1978–87), becoming assistant majority leader; as a Democrat representing Illinois, became the 4th African-American and 1st African-American woman to be elected to the US Senate (1992); served on the Finance, Banking and Judiciary committees; ran unsuccessfully for reelection (1998); served as US ambassador to New Zealand (1999–2001); taught law and political science at Morris Brown College and DePaul University; ran for nomination for president of US in Democratic primaries (2004).

BRAUN, E. Lucy (1889–1971). American botanist and conservationist. Name variations: Emma Lucy Braun. Born April 19, 1889, in Cincinnati, Ohio; died Mar 5, 1971, in Mt. Washington, Ohio; dau. of George Frederick (school principal) and Emma Moriah (Wright) Braun (amateur botanist); sister of Annette Braun (1884–1978), entomologist and international authority on moths; University of Cincinnati,

AB, 1910, AM in geology, 1912, PhD in botany, 1924. ❖ Pioneering ecologist of the early 20th century, became associate professor of botany at University of Cincinnati (1927) and full professor (1946); early studies and publications centered on the plant life of the Cincinnati region and culminated in the classic book, *Deciduous Forests of Eastern North America* (1950), the most respected of her scholarly works; became the 1st woman president of Ohio Academy of Science (1935); under the auspices of the Academy, later established Ohio Flora Committee (1951) and became its chair; championed conservation of wildlife habitats, contributing numerous articles on the subject; also wrote *The Woody Plants of Ohio: Trees, Shrubs, and Weedy Climbers, Native, Naturalized, and Escaped; A Contribution Toward the Vascular Flora of Ohio* (1961) and *The Monocotyledoneae: Cat-tails to Orchids* (1967). ❖ See also *Women in World History.*

BRAUN, Eva (1912–1945). German mistress. Born Eva Anna Paula Braun in Munich, Germany, Feb 6, 1912; committed suicide with Hitler, April 30, 1945; dau. of Franziska Katharina (Kranburger) Braun and Fritz Braun; sister of Ilse Braun (b. 1909) and Gretl Braun Fegelein (b. 1915); m. Adolf Hitler, April 29, 1945. ❖ Unknown to the world until the final days of the battle of Berlin in April 1945, became Hitler's mistress in 1932; during next 12 years, throughout the span of the Nazi dictatorship, had relationship with Adolf Hitler that was a state secret; often bored by her cocooned isolation, attempted suicide (May 1935); became the woman of the house at Hitler's "Berghof" in Obersalzberg (1936); followed him into his Berlin bunker and married him (April 29, 1945), then committed suicide with him the following day. ❖ See also Nerin E. Gun, *Eva Braun: Hitler's Mistress* (Meredith, 1968); Glenn B. Infield, *Eva and Adolf* (Grosset, 1974); Ib Melchior, *Eva* (Dodd, 1984); and *Women in World History.*

BRAUN, Johanna (1929—). East German science-fiction writer. Born 1929 in Magdeburg, Germany; m. Günter Braun (writer). ❖ With husband, wrote *The Great Magician's Error* (1972), *Uncanny Phenomena on Omega 11* (1974), *The Mistake Factor* (1975), *Conviva Ludibundus* (1978), *The Utofant: A Periodical from the Third Millennium Found in the Future* (1981), *The Spherico-Transcendental Design* (1983), *The Inaudible Sounds* (1984) and "Pantamann" trilogy (1988–91), among others.

BRAUN, Julie (1883–1971). See Braun-Vogelstein, Julie.

BRAUN, Lily (1865–1916). German feminist. Pronunciation: Brawn. Born July 1, 1865, in Halberstadt, Germany; died Aug 9, 1916, at Zehlendorf; 1st child of Hans von Kretschman (captain in Prussian military) and Jenny von (Gustedt) Kretschman; m. Georg von Gizycki, 1893 (died 1895); m. Heinrich Braun, 1896; children: (1st m.) Otto. ❖ Feminist who repudiated her origins in the German aristocracy to assert in her 1901 book *Die Frauenfrage* that capitalism laid a basis for the economic oppression of women; father forced to retire from Prussian military (1889); moved with family to an apartment in Berlin, where she became acquainted with a wide variety of social and cultural reformers (1890); published correspondence of maternal grandmother Jenny von Gustedt with the German poet Goethe (1891 and 1893); began publishing, with Minna Cauer, the twice-monthly journal *Die Frauenbewegung* (1894); joined Social Democratic Party (1895); published her major work *Die Frauenfrage* (1901); worked in Helene Stoecker's League for the Protection of Motherhood and Sexual Reform (1906–10); in several books and more than 100 articles, many translated from her native German and published in up to 4 other European languages, argued that feminists and Marxists battled a common enemy: capitalism; working in the repressive atmosphere of late 19th-century Germany, anticipated many issues still debated in feminist circles; also wrote *Memoiren einer Sozialistin* (1908–09); after her death, her husband Heinrich married Julie Braun-Vogelstein. ❖ See also Alfred G. Meyer, *The Feminism and Socialism of Lily Braun* (Indiana U. Press, 1985); and *Women in World History.*

BRAUN, Maria-Johanna (1911–1982). Dutch swimmer. Born June 22, 1911, in Netherlands; died June 23, 1982; dau. of "Ma" Braun, her swimming coach. ❖ At Amsterdam Olympics, won a gold medal in 100-meter backstroke and a silver medal in 400-meter freestyle (1928).

BRAUN, Sabine (1965—). German heptathlete. Born June 19, 1965, in Essen, Germany. ❖ Won European championships (1990, 1994); won gold medal at World championships (1991, 1997); won a bronze medal at Barcelona Olympics (1992).

BRAUN-VOGELSTEIN, Julie (1883–1971). German-Jewish art historian and author. Name variations: Julie Vogelstein Braun. Born Julie

Vogelstein in Stettin (now Szczecin, Poland), Jan 26, 1883; died in New York City, Feb 6, 1971; dau. of Heinemann Vogelstein (rabbi) and Rosa (Kobrak) Vogelstein; sister of Hermann Vogelstein (1870–1942, rabbi), Theodore Max Vogelstein (1880–1957), and Ludwig Vogelstein (1871–1934); studied art history and Egyptology in Munich and Berlin; University of Heidelberg, PhD, 1919; m. Heinrich Braun (Social Democratic leader), 1920 (died 1927). ❖ Edited and published the posthumous writings of stepson Otto Braun, including his diary (1920), which became a literary sensation; with Nazis in power, emigrated from Germany (1935), 1st settling in France; came to US (1936); was active in German exile circles; published a sweeping interpretation of the artistic heritage of Western civilization, *Art, the Image of the West* (1952); also wrote *Die ionische Säule* (1921), *Lily Braun: Ein Lebensbild* (1922), *Was niemals stirbt: Gestalten und Erinnerungen* (1966) and *Heinrich Braun: Ein Leben für den Sozialismus.* ❖ See also *Women in World History.*

BRAUND, Mary (b. 1765). See Bryant, Mary.

BRAUNSCHWEIG, countess or duchess of. See Brunswick, countess or duchess of.

BRAUNSCHWEIG-LÜNEBURG, Elisabeth von (1519–1558). German ruler and writer. Name variations: Elisabeth of Brunswick-Luneburg. Born in 1519 in Brandenburg (Germany); died in 1558 in Braunschweig-Lüneburg (Germany); dau. of Joachim I, Prince of Brandenburg; m. Erich I, duke of Braunschweig-Lüneburg, in 1534 (died 1540); children: 1 daughter, 1 son. ❖ Following husband's death, took over the governing of the duchy (1540); drawn to the ideas of the new Protestantism, composed a treatise on the new religion, called *The Christian Epistle*, which she published and distributed to her subjects; completed a book of instruction for her daughter and a treatise on government for her son, as well as a book of consolation for other widows; when her Catholic son took over power, was exiled with daughter to Hanover because of religious beliefs. ❖ See also *Women in World History.*

BRAUNSCHWEIG-LÜNEBURG, Sibylle Ursula von (1629–1671). German writer and translator. Name variations: Sibylle von Braunschweig-Luneburg; Sibylle of Brunswick-Luneburg. Born 1629 in Braunschweig-Lüneburg (Germany); died in childbirth in 1671; dau. of August the Younger, duke of Braunschweig-Lüneburg; stepdau. of Sophie Elisabeth von Braunschweig-Lüneburg (1613–1676); married, 1663; children: 4. ❖ Devoted the years prior to her marriage to composing poetry, translating foreign works into German, and writing plays; her more significant work was a novel, *Aramena*, which was completed after her death by her siblings; also composed tracts on her Protestant religious beliefs and was recognized for her excellent translations of French literary works. ❖ See also *Women in World History.*

BRAUNSCHWEIG-LÜNEBURG, Sophie Elisabeth von (1613–1676). German duchess, novelist, composer and playwright. Name variations: Sophie von Braunschweig-Luneburg; Sophie Elisabeth, Duchess of Brunswick-Luneburg. Born 1613; died 1676 in Braunschweig-Lüneburg (Germany); m. August the Younger, duke of Braunschweig-Lüneburg, 1635; children: many stepchildren, including Sibylle Ursula von Braunschweig-Lüneburg (1629–1671). ❖ Highly educated, promoted a lively, intellectual court and patronized baroque artists, for which she became known as the "Juno" of Braunschweig-Lüneburg; also wrote songs, plays, and librettos which were performed at court, completed the novel *The Story of Dorinde,* based on French courtly literature (1652), and composed prayers and various spiritual tracts. ❖ See also *Women in World History.*

BRAVO, Florence (1845–1878). British murderer (accused). Born Florence Campbell, 1845, in London, England; died 1878; dau. of Robert Campbell and Ann Campbell; m. Alexander Ricardo, 1864 (died 1871); m. Charles Delauny Turner Bravo (barrister), 1875 (died April 21, 1876). ❖ Born into wealthy London family, was married to 1st husband at 19; acquired a considerable fortune after husband's death; remarried at 30; after Charles Bravo's death by poisoning, became the subject of an inquest which was a Victorian *cause célèbre*, but was not charged with murder.

BRAXTON, Toni (1967—). American rhythm-and-blues singer. Name variations: Toni Michelle Braxton. Born Toni Michelle Braxton, Oct 7, 1967, in Severn, Maryland. ❖ Husky-voiced R&B vocalist, grew up studying piano and performing with sisters in church choir; shot to success with Grammy-winning debut, *Toni Braxton* (1993); toured with saxophonist Kenny G (1994); sold more than 16 million copies of 1996 album *Secrets;* released many top-10 singles, including "Another Sad Love Song" (1993), "Breathe Again" (1993), "You're Making Me High" (1996), "Unbreak My Heart" (1996) and "He Wasn't Man Enough" (2000); filed for bankruptcy (1998); took over leads in Broadway hits *Beauty and the Beast* (1994) and *Aida* (2000).

BRAY, Anna Eliza (1790–1883). English novelist. Name variations: Mrs. Bray; Anna Eliza Stothard. Born Anna Eliza Kempe at Newington, Surrey, Dec 25, 1790; died in London, England, Jan 21, 1883; dau. of Ann Arrow and John Kempe; m. Charles A. Stothard (artist and son of artist R.A. Stothard), 1818 (died 1821); m. Reverend Edward Atkyns Bray, vicar of Tavistock, 1823 (died 1857). ❖ Wrote about a dozen novels, chiefly historical, including *The Borders of the Tamar and the Tavy* (3 vols., 1836), an account of the traditions and superstitions of the neighborhood of Tavistock in the form of letters to Robert Southey, of whom she was a close friend; following 1st husband's accidental death (1821), completed his work *The Monumental Effigies of Great Britain.* ❖ See also *Women in World History.*

BRAY, Yvonne de (1889–1954). See de Bray, Yvonne.

BRAYLEY, Sally (1937—). English ballet dancer. Name variations: Sally Brayley Bliss. Born 1937 in London, England. ❖ Trained with numerous teachers in Toronto and New York, including Margaret Craske, Antony Tudor, Lillian Moore and William Griffith; apprenticed with National Ballet of Canada, then joined ballet company of Metropolitan Opera in NY, where she appeared in such operas as *La Perichole* and *La Gioconda,* and in numerous works by Antony Tudor, including *Echoing of Trumpets* (1966) and *Concerning Oracles;* danced with City Center Joffrey Ballet for 2 years, performing in Gerald Arpino's *Viva Vivaldi!,* *Elegy,* and others; performed *Prince Igor* and *Manon* at New York City Opera; served as associate director of Joffrey II Company (1970–74), then became director (1975).

BRAYTON, Lily (1876–1953). English stage star. Name variations: Mrs. Oscar Asche. Born June 23, 1876, in Hindley, Lancs., England; died April 30, 1953; m. Oscar Asche (actor, writer, 1871–1936); m. Douglas Chalmers Watson (physician). ❖ Made stage debut with Frank Benson's company as a walk-on in *Richard III* (1896), then appeared for several seasons at the Stratford Shakespeare Festival; through the years, appeared to great acclaim as Rosalind, Katherine, Ophelia, Isabella, Mistress Ford, Helena, Desdemona, Queen Isabella and Viola; as actor and manager, often collaborated with husband Oscar Asche, and appeared opposite him as Zahrat-al-Kulub in his huge hit, *Chu Chin Chow,* for almost 2,000 performances (1916–21).

BRAZIL, Angela (1868–1947). English writer. Born Nov 30, 1868, in Preston, Lancashire, England; died Mar 14, 1947, in Coventry, England; dau. of Clarence (manager of a cotton mill) and Angelica (McKinnell) Brazil; sister of Amy Brazil; studied art at Heatherley's Art College, London; never married; no children. ❖ Known as the English schoolgirl's favorite author, did not begin writing professionally until she was 36; produced at least 1 book a year, over 50 titles in all (1906–47); published 1st work, *A Terrible Tom Boy* (1904), largely autobiographical, followed by *The Fortunes of Philippa* (1906), which was based on her mother's school experiences; other writings include *The Third Class at Miss Kaye's* (1908), *The Nicest Girl in the School* (1910), *A Fourth Form Friendship* (1912), *The Jolliest Term on Record* (1915), *The Madcap of the School* (1917), *Monitress Merle* (1922), *Captain Peggie* (1924), *My Own Schooldays* (1925) and *The School on the Loch* (1946). ❖ See also *Women in World History.*

BRAZIL, empress of.
See Leopoldina of Austria (1797–1826).
See Amelia of Leuchtenburg (1812–1873).

BRÉ, Ruth (1862–1911). German feminist poet and author. Name variations: Ruth Bre; Elisabeth Bouness. Born Elisabeth Bouness in 1862; died Dec 1911; dau. of unmarried parents. ❖ Was an elementary schoolteacher and unsuccessful poet; enjoyed a fleeting period of fame in Germany as a result of having founded the Liga für Mutterschutz (League for the Protection of Mothers, LPM) in 1904, helping the German feminist movement focus its ideas and influencing the development of feminist ideology throughout the Western world. ❖ See also *Women in World History.*

BREAMER, Sylvia (1897–1943). Australian-born silent-film actress. Born June 9, 1897, in Sydney, Australia; died June 7, 1943, in New York, NY; m. Harry W. Martin. ❖ Films include *The Cold Deck, The*

Narrow Trail, My Lady's Garter, Doubling for Romeo, The Girl of the Golden West and *Up in Mabel's Room.*

BRECHOVÁ, Hana. See Brejchová, Hana.

BRECHOVÁ, Jana (1940—). See Brejchová, Jana.

BRECHT, Helene Weigel (1900–1971). See Weigel, Helene.

BRECHT, Marianne (1893–1984). See Zoff, Marianne.

BRECKINRIDGE, Madeline McDowell (1872–1920). American social reformer and suffragist. Born Magdalen McDowell, May 20, 1872, at Woodlake, Kentucky; died Nov 25, 1920, in Kentucky; dau. of Henry Clay McDowell and Anne (Clay) McDowell; attended State College of Kentucky (now University of Kentucky); m. Desha Breckinridge (lawyer brother of Sophonisba Breckinridge), Nov 17, 1898. ❖ Became a founding member of, and principal participant in, Lexington Civic League; raised funds for construction, planned design, and supervised staffing of the Abraham Lincoln School and Social Center; with Civic League, worked to secure state legislation restricting child labor and establishing juvenile court system (1906); served as director of Lexington Associated Charities (1907–20); served in many Kentucky anti-Tuberculosis organizations and helped win legislative and public support for state sanatorium; served as president of Kentucky Equal Rights Association (1912–15 and 1919–20) and vice president of National American Woman Suffrage Association (1913–15); conducted speaking tour in support of Democratic Party and League of Nations (1920). ❖ See also Sophonisba P. Breckinridge, *Madeline McDowell Breckinridge* (U. of Chicago Press, 1921).

BRECKINRIDGE, Margaret E. (d. 1864). American nurse. Date and place of birth unknown, possibly Princeton, New Jersey; died July 27, 1864; dau. of John Breckinridge (minister); granddau. of John Breckinridge of Kentucky (US attorney general, 1806). ❖ Orphaned at 9 and frail of health, was raised and educated by grandparents in Princeton; at onset of Civil War, determined to become a hospital nurse; went to Baltimore, Maryland (1862), where she contracted measles during 1st week of visiting hospital wards; recuperating in Lexington, Kentucky, resumed hospital work there; in St. Louis, worked aboard the transport boats and in the hospitals at Young's Point and Helena; volunteer efforts were cut short by ongoing health problems, forcing her off the transports; died in summer of 1864.

BRECKINRIDGE, Mary (1881–1965). American nurse and midwife. Born Feb 17, 1881, in Memphis, Tennessee; died May 16, 1965, in Hyden, Kentucky; dau. of Clifton Rodes (US congressional representative and US minister to Russia, 1890s) and Katherine (Carson) Breckinridge; granddau. of John Cabell Breckinridge (vice president under James Buchanan); earned nursing degree, Saint Luke's Hospital School of Nursing, NY, 1910; m. Henry Ruffner Morrison, 1904 (died 1906); m. Richard Ryan Thompson, 1912 (div. 1920); children: (2nd m.) Breckinridge (1914–1918); Mary (died in infancy). ❖ Volunteered for wartime duty with American Red Cross (1918), where she was eventually assigned to American Committee for Devastated France during WWI; went to work in Vic-Sur-Aisne, caring for the infant victims of war, as well as pregnant and nursing women; through her work in France and several trips to England, formulated a plan by which nurse-midwives could serve the needs of women and young children in rural America; founded the Kentucky Committee for Mothers and Babies (1925), which in 1928 became the Frontier Nursing Service (FNS); established the Frontier Graduate School of Midwifery (1939), a training program for nurse-midwives; wrote *Wide Neighborhoods: The Story of the Frontier Nursing Service* (1952). ❖ See also *Women in World History.*

BRECKINRIDGE, Mary Marvin (1905–2002). American journalist and photojournalist. Name variations: Mary Marvin Breckinridge Patterson; Mrs. Jefferson Patterson; Marvin Patterson. Born 1905 in New York City; died Dec 11, 2002, at her home in Washington, DC; dau. of John C. Breckinridge of Kentucky and Isabella Goodrich Breckinridge (dau. of B.F. Goodrich); granddau. of John C. Breckinridge (vice president of US under Buchanan); cousin of nurse Mary Breckinridge (1881–1965); graduate of Vassar College, 1927; studied at New School for Social Research, NY; married Jefferson Patterson, member of US State Department, 1940 (died 1977); children: Patricia Marvin Patterson and Mark Julian Patterson. ❖ Pioneering reporter who broke through the gender barrier in radio to become one of the 1st women to report the news during World War II, began career in Washington as a secretary for the Democratic National Committee; went abroad to work as a freelance photographer (1930); was in London

(1939), when Edward R. Murrow put her on the air to report events from a woman's point of view and she became a regular; broadcast from the Netherlands, then temporarily replaced William L. Shirer in Berlin; donated 23-acre family estate in York, Maine, to Bowdoin College (1973); donated her 550-acre farm to State of Maryland (1983), which became Jefferson Patterson Park and Museum.

BRECKINRIDGE, Sophonisba Preston (1866–1948). American social worker and educator. Born in Lexington, Kentucky, April 1, 1866; died in Chicago, Illinois, July 30, 1948; dau. of William Campbell Preston Breckinridge (lawyer who served in Congress) and Issas (Desha) Breckinridge; sister of Desha Breckinridge (editor of *Lexington Herald*); sister-in-law of Madeline McDowell Breckinridge (1872–1920); Wellesley College, SB, 1888; University of Chicago, PhD in political science, 1901, JD, 1904; Oberlin, LLD, 1919. ❖ Pioneer in legislative social work and an early advocate for economic parity for women, became the 1st woman in Kentucky admitted to the state bar (1895); entered University of Chicago (1898), where she was the 1st woman to receive a law degree in the college's history; began instructing there (1903); founded the Chicago School of Civics and Philanthropy with Julia Lathrop (1907), subsequently renamed the University of Chicago School of Social Service Administration (1920); also founded the Immigrants' Protective League (1908), became vice-president of National Woman's Suffrage Association (1911), and was named delegate to the Women's Peace Conference at The Hague (1915); at University of Chicago School of Social Service Administration, was dean and professor of public welfare administration (1925–29), dean of College of Arts, Literature, and Science (1929–33), and professor emeritus of public welfare (1933–42); wrote many books. ❖ See also *Women in World History*.

BRÉCOURT, Jeanne (b. 1837). French courtesan and blackmailer. Name variations: Jeanne de la Cour; Brecourt. Born Jeanne Amenaide Brécourt in 1837 in Paris, France; death date unknown; m. a grocer named Gras, who deserted her. ❖ One of France's most infamous courtesans, destroyed a number of her paramours through blackmail and deceit, while feigning an aristocratic background; after plotting to have a wealthy lover blinded to guarantee his dependence, was brought to trial (1877) and defended by Charles Lachaud, who had also been the attorney for Marie Lafarge. The trial, one of the more spectacular of its day, reportedly attracted the elite of Paris, including journalists, playwrights, and even members of the popular Comédie-Française. ❖ See also *Women in World History*.

BREDAEL, Annelies (1965—). Belgian rower. Born June 15, 1965, in Belgium. ❖ At Barcelona Olympics, won a silver medal in single sculls (1992).

BREDAHL, Charlotte (1957—). American equestrian. Name variations: Charlotte Bredahl Baker or Bredahl-Baker. Born April 21, 1957, in Denmark; m. Joel Baker (financial advisor and polo player); children: Zachary. ❖ Moved to US (1979); at Barcelona Olympics, won a bronze medal in team dressage on Monsieur (1992); on Lugano, won a silver team medal at North American championship (1997).

BREDEN, Christiane von (1839–1901). Austrian poet. Name variations: Christine von Breden; Christiane Breden; (pseudonym) Ada Christen. Born Christine Rosalia Frideriks, Mar 6, 1839, in Vienna, Austria; died May 23, 1901, in Vienna; married, 1864; m. Adalmar von Breden (writer), 1873. ❖ Wrote poetry to support herself after death of 1st husband and child; writings, noted for their eroticism, social radicalism, and depictions of life in Vienna, include *Lieder einer Verlorenen* (1868) and *Aus der Tiefe* (1878).

BREEN, Nellie (c. 1898–1986). American dancer and comedian. Born c. 1898; died April 26, 1986, age 88, in San José, California. ❖ Made Broadway debut at the Hippodrome (1919); also appeared in George White's *Scandals of 1921, The Perfect Fool, The Passing Show of 1922, Take a Chance* and *The Desert Song*, among others; performed the 1st tap dance on radio.

BREER, Murle MacKenzie (1939—). American golfer. Name variations: Murle Lindstrom. Born Murle Lindstrom, Jan 20, 1939, in St. Petersburg, Florida. ❖ Under name Murle Lindstrom, won US Open (1962); won 3 other major tournaments, including San Antonio Civitan (1973); now a golf instructor.

BREESE, Zona (1874–1938). *See Gale, Zona.*

BREGENDAHL, Marie (1867–1940). Danish novelist and poet. Born Nov 6, 1867, in Fly, Denmark; died July 22, 1940, in Copenhagen; dau. of a farmer in Viborg district; m. Jeppe Aakjaer (folk poet), 1893 (div.). ❖ Regional writer who used the Viborg district for her setting, published 1st stories (1902); best known for her novel *En doedsnat* (A Night of Death, 1912) and for her 8-volume series *Billeder af Soedalsfolkenes liv* (Pictures from the Life of the People of Sodal, 1914–23).

BREHM, Marie Caroline (1859–1926). American temperance leader. Born in Ohio, 1859; died in Long Beach, California, 1926. ❖ Ardent prohibitionist, devoted most of her life to lecturing on behalf of the Women's Christian Temperance Union (WCTU); held offices in temperance organizations in Illinois, Nebraska and California; also spoke at international conferences and represented US at World's Congress on Alcoholism in London (1911); ran as the Prohibitionist Party's vice-presidential nominee (1924), the 1st woman nominated by a recognized political party.

BREHMER, Christina (1958—). *See Lathan-Brehmer, Christina.*

BREIKEN, Dagmar (1963—). West German field-hockey player. Born Sept 13, 1963, in Germany. ❖ At Los Angeles Olympics, won a silver medal in team competition (1984).

BREJCHOVÁ, Hana (c. 1943—). Czech actress. Name variations: Hana Brejchova; Hana Brechová; Hana Brejchovou. Born c. 1943 in Prague, Czechoslovakia; younger sister of Jana Brejchová (actress). ❖ Starred as Andula in the film, *The Loves of a Blonde* (1965); also appeared in *Zirafa v okne* (1968), *Amadeus* (1984), *Zastihla me noc* (1986) and *Mandragora* (1997), among others.

BREJCHOVÁ, Jana (1940—). Czech actress and writer. Name variations: Jana Brejchova; Jana Brechová. Born Jan 20, 1940, in Prague, Czechoslovakia; older sister of Hana Brejchová (actress); m. Milos Forman (director), 1951 (div. 1956); m. Ulrich Thein (div.); m. Vlastimil Brodsky (actor, div.); m. Jirí Zahajsky, 1997; children: Tereza Brodská (b. 1968, actress). ❖ One of the Czech Republic's most popular screen stars, made film debut at age 14 in *Oloveny chléb* (1953); came to prominence in *Vyssi princip*, for which she received the Golden Screen at Locarno film festival (1960); other films include *Kdyby tisic klarinetu, Bloudeni, Kazdy den odvahu, Návrat ztraceného syna* and *Faráruv Konec*; won the Golden Film Band for her work in the German film, *Das Haus in der Karpfengasse* (1965).

BREMA, Marie (1856–1925). English mezzo-soprano. Born Minny Fehrmann, Feb 28, 1856, in England; died Mar 22, 1925; children: Francis Braun (baritone) and Tita Brand (actress who m. Emile Cammaerts, Belgian poet). ❖ Appeared as Lola in the English premiere of *Cavalleria Rusticana;* sang at Bayreuth (1894–97); created the role of Beatrice in Stanford's *Much Ado about Nothing* in London (1901); sang the role of Angel in the disastrous 1st performance of Elgar's *The Dream of Gerontius* in Birmingham, walking off with the only good reviews.

BREMER, Edith (1885–1964). American immigrant-welfare worker. Name variations: Edith Terry Bremer. Born Edith Terry, Oct 9, 1885, in Hamilton, NY; died Sept 12, 1964, in Port Washington, NY; dau. of Benjamin Stites Terry (Baptist minister) and Mary (Baldwin) Terry; m. Harry M. Bremer (social welfare leader), Sept 4, 1912. ❖ Pioneer in social-service work who rejected forced Americanization of immigrants, encouraging them to retain their own culture while adapting to US; was a field investigator for Chicago Juvenile Court (1908), special agent for US Immigration Commission, and resident at University of Chicago Settlement and Union Settlement in NYC; became national field secretary for National Board of YWCA (1910); in NY, founded 1st International Institute, helping immigrants learn English and deal with housing, employment, and naturalization problems (1910); served as head of YWCA's Department of Immigration and Foreign Communities and as expert witness on immigrant policy at congressional hearings (1920s–30s); established National Institute of Immigrant Welfare (1944, later named American Federation of International Institutes), serving as executive director (1933–54); also served as acting director of NY International Institute (1955–58). Received Order of the White Lion from Czechoslovakia for immigrant welfare work (1927).

BREMER, Fredrika (1801–1865). Swedish writer. Born Fredrika Bremer near Aabo, Finland, Aug 17, 1801; died Dec 31, 1865; dau. of Carl Fredric Bremer (wealthy iron master and merchant, died 1830) and Brigitta Charlotta (Hollstrom) Bremer; sister of Charlotte Bremer, who edited her letters and works; never married; no children. ❖ Founder of the Swedish novel, who also wrote well-received travel books dealing with social and political conditions of other countries, and became an emblem for women's emancipation in Sweden; anonymously published *Teckningar utur hvardagslivet* (*Sketches of Everyday Life*, 1828), followed by *Familjen H.* (*The H. Family*, 1830–31), a continuation of *Sketches*, which brought her international fame; revealed her identity shortly thereafter; in following years, wrote 4 full-length novels; traveled in US (1849), then published 3 vols. of her observations shortly after her return to Sweden which had been recorded in a series of letters to her younger sister, including *Hemmen i den nya verlden* (*Homes of the New World*, 1853–54); published most famous novel *Hertha* (1856), as well as *Fader och dotter* (*Father and Daughter*, 1858); spent 5 years on the Continent and in Palestine (1856–61); worked for the emancipation of Swedish women and their deliverance from the traditional social restrictions which, in her opinion, violated their natural rights; also wrote *Grannarne* (trans. *The Neighbors*, 1837), *Hemmet* (trans. *The Home or Family Cares and Family Joys*, 1839), *En Dagbok* (trans. *A Diary*, 1843), *Syskonlif* (*Brothers and Sisters*, 1849), *England in 1851 or Sketches of a Tour in England* (1853) and *Lifvet i gamla verlden* (trans. *Life in the old World*, 1850–62). Received the gold medal from the Swedish Academy. ❖ See also Charlotte Bremer, ed. *Life, Letters, and Posthumous Works of Fredrika Bremer* (trans. by F. Milow, Hurd & Houghton, 1868); and *Women in World History*.

BREMER, Lucille (1923–1996). American dancer and actress. Born Feb 21, 1923, in Amsterdam, NY; died April 16, 1996, in La Jolla, California; m. Abelardo Louis Rodriguez (son of a Mexican president), 1948 (div. 1963). ❖ Began career as a Rockette and Broadway chorine; partnered Fred Astaire in *Yolanda and the Thief* and *Ziegfeld Follies;* other films include *Till the Clouds Roll By, Adventures of Casanova* and *Behind Locked Doors;* best remembered for her debut role as eldest daughter Rose in *Meet Me in St. Louis* (1944); retired from screen (1948) and ran a children's dress shop.

BREMNER, Janice (1974—). Canadian synchronized swimmer. Born July 15, 1974, in Burlington, Ontario, Canada. ❖ Won a team silver medal at Atlanta Olympics (1996).

BREMONT, Anna de (1864–1922). See De Brémont, Anna.

BRENCHLEY, Winifred (1883–1953). English botanist. Name variations: Winifred Elsie Brenchley. Born Aug 10, 1883; died Oct 27, 1953; University College London, BS, 1905, DSc, 1911. ❖ Went deaf from measles; named to the staff of Rothamsted Experimental Station in Harpenden, Herfordshire, the 1st woman appointed to an agricultural station (1906); served as head of Botanical Department at Rothamsted (1907–48); research fields included weeds, ecology, plant physiology and nutrition; writings include *Inorganic Plant Poisons and Stimulants* (1914), *The Weeds of Farmland* (1920) and *Manuring of Grass Land for Hay* (1924). Made OBE (1948).

BRENDEL, Daniela (1973—). German swimmer. Born Sept 29, 1973. ❖ At Barcelona Olympics, won a silver medal in 4 x 100-meter medley relay (1992).

BRENNAN, Anna Teresa (1879–1962). Australian lawyer and activist. Born Sept 2, 1879, in Emu Creek, Victoria; died Oct 11, 1962; daughter and 13th child of Michael (farmer) and Mary (Maher) Brennan; attended St. Andrew's College, Bendigo; awarded law degree from University of Melbourne, 1909. ❖ Advocate for women's rights, was a senior partner in her brother's firm, specializing in general and matrimonial law; lobbied for the reform of divorce laws; helped establish the Catholic Women's Social Guild (1916), whose goal was an expanded role for Catholic women in social and political reform; was a founding member of a Melbourne branch of St. Joan's Alliance (1936), an association of Catholic lay women, serving as president (1938–45, 1948–62).

BRENNAN, Eileen (1935—). American stage and screen actress. Born Sept 3, 1935, in Los Angeles, California; dau. of Jean Manahan (silent-screen actress); m. David Lampson (div. 1975). ❖ On NY stage, appeared as Mrs. Molly with Carol Channing in the original *Hello Dolly* and created the title role in long-running off-Broadway musical *Little Mary Sunshine*; made film debut in *Divorce American Style* (1967), followed by *The Last Picture Show, Scarecrow, The Sting, Daisy Miller, Murder by Death, FM, The Cheap Detective, At Long Last Love, Clue, Stella, Texasville, White Palace* and *Changing Habits*, among others; on tv, was a regular on "Laugh-In" (1968) and "Private Benjamin" (1981); hit by a car and seriously injured (1983). Nominated for an Oscar for Best Supporting Actress for the film *Private Benjamin* and won an Emmy for same role on tv; won Obie award for *Little Mary Sunshine*.

BRENNAN, Fanny (1921–2001). French-born artist. Born Fanny Myers, 1921, in France; died July 22, 2001, in New York, NY; dau. of expatriates Richard and Alice Lee Myers; studied at Atelier Art et Jeunesse in Paris; m. Francis "Hank" Brennan (design consultant); children: Richard Lee Brennan and Christopher Herrick Brennan. ❖ Painter of small, surrealist still lifes, fled France on eve of WWII and took a job as Alexey Brodovitch's assistant at *Harper's Bazaar;* was included in 2 shows in Manhattan run by Betty Parsons; published a collection of her works in *Skyshades* (1990).

BRENNAN, Maire (1952—). Irish singer. Name variations: Maire Ni Bhraonain; Moya Brennan. Born Maire Ni Bhraonain, Aug 4, 1952, in Gaoth Dobhair, Co. Donegal, Ireland; sister of Enya (singer); m. Tim Jarvis, 1991; children: 2. ❖ As lead singer for the Irish Celtic pioneering group Clannad, released over 20 albums; as a solo artist, released 5 albums, including *Maire* (1992), *Perfect Time* (1998), *Whisper to the Wild* (1999), which was nominated for a Grammy, and *Two Horizons* (2004).

BRENNAN, Mary (1938—). See Merrell, Mary.

BRENNAN, Moya (1952—). See Brennan, Maire.

BRENNER, Dori (1946–2000). American screen and tv actress. Born Dec 16, 1946, in New York, NY; died Sept 16, 2000, in Los Angeles, California. ❖ Made film debut in *Summer Wishes, Winter Dreams* (1973); other films include *The Other Side of the Mountain, Next Stop Greenwich Village, Altered States, For the Boys* and *Infinity;* appeared in tv series "The Charmings."

BRENNER, Veronica (1974—). Canadian freestyle skier. Born Oct 18, 1974, in Scarborough, Ontario, Canada. ❖ Was World aerials champion (1996–97); won a bronze medal at World championships (1997); won a gold medal at Goodwill Games (2000); won a silver medal for aerials at Salt Lake City (2002).

BRENT, Evelyn (1899–1975). American actress. Name variations: appeared in several early films as Betty Riggs. Born Mary Elizabeth Riggs, Oct 20, 1899, in Tampa, Florida; died 1975; m. Bernie Fineman, 1922 (div., 1927); m. Harry Edwards; m. Harry Fox (died 1959). ❖ Leading lady of the silent era, began career as an extra (c. 1915); appeared opposite John Barrymore in *Raffles, the Amateur Crackman* (1917); following WWI, sailed to England where she was in the chorus of West End production of *The Ruined Lady* (1920); made a number of films while abroad; filmed *The Spanish Jade* in Spain (1922), her 1st success; in US, came to prominence in von Sternberg's masterpiece *Underworld* (1927), followed by *The Last Command* (1928), a small movie that enjoyed enormous success; career suffered with advent of talkies, though her voice was pleasant enough; other films include *The Dragnet* (1928), *Broadway* (1929), *Slightly Scarlet* (1930), *The Silver Horde* (1930), *Madonna of the Streets* (1930), *Hopalong Cassidy Returns* (1936), (serial) *Jungle Jim* (1937), *The Last Train from Madrid* (1937), *Mr. Wong—Detective* (1938), *The Mad Empress* (1940), (serial) *Holt of the Secret Service* (1941), *Westward Ho!* (1942) and *The Golden Eye* (1948); worked as an actor's representative for Thelma White Agency (1950s). ❖ See also *Women in World History*.

BRENT, Linda (1813–1897). See Jacobs, Harriet A.

BRENT, Margaret (c. 1601–1671). American colonist. Born c. 1601; died prior to May 1671; one of 13 children. ❖ Though descended from royalty, inherited little on the death of parents because of English inheritance laws; as a result of that and religious intolerance in then Protestant England (Brent was Catholic), immigrated to the newly founded Maryland colony with a sister and 2 brothers (1638); starting with a land grant from Lord Baltimore, began to acquire more and more land; as far as is known, was the 1st woman to demand representation based on property (1647).

BRENT-DYER, Elinor M. (1894–1969). English children's book writer. Name variations: Elinor Mary Brent-Dyer. Born Gladys Eleanor May Dyer, April 6, 1894, in South Shields, England; died Sept 20, 1969, in Redhill, England; dau. of Charles Morris Brent Dyer and Eleanor "Nelly" Watson Rutherford; attended City of Leeds Training College. ❖ Prolific writer of 98 books for young people, most notably the "Chalet School" and "La Rochelle" series, was schoolmistress at St. Helen's Northwood in Middlesex, at Moreton House School in Dunstable and at Fareham near Portsmouth; adopted name Elinor Mary Brent-Dyer (1920s); wrote 1st book *Gerry Goes to School* (1922) for child actress Hazel Bainbridge; spent holiday in Austrian Tyrol at

Pertisau-am-Achensee (early 1920s), then successfully used the location for her famous "Chalet School" series, beginning with *The School at the Chalet* (1925); sought to use "Chalet" books to discourage parochialism and xenophobia through main character Jo Bettany; became a Roman Catholic (1930); moved to Hereford with mother and stepfather (1933), traveling daily to Peterchurch to work as governess; started Margaret Roper Girl's School in Hereford, serving as headmistress until school's closing in 1948; began writing full-time (1948); later books set in Channel Islands in Wales and in Bernese Oberland; moved to Redhill (1964).

BRENTANO, Bettina or Elizabeth (1785–1859). *See Arnim, Bettine von.*

BRENTANO, Sophie (1770–1806). *See Mereau-Brentano, Sophie.*

BRENT OF BIN-BIN (1879–1954). *See Franklin, Miles.*

BRERETON, Mrs. (1756–1845). *See Kemble, Priscilla.*

BRESHKO-BRESHKOVSKAYA, Ekaterina (1844–1934). *See Breshkovsky, Catherine.*

BRESHKOVSKAIA, Breshkovskaya, or Breshkovskoi, Katerina. *See Breshkovsky, Catherine.*

BRESHKOVSKY, Catherine (1844–1934). Russian revolutionary. Name variations: Ekaterina Breshko-Breshkovskaya, Katerina Breshkovskaia, Breshkovskaya, or Breshkovskoi. Pronunciation: BRESH-kawf-skee. Born Ekaterina Konstantinova Verigo, Jan 13, 1844, in Ivanovo village, Vitebsk, Russia; died in Prague, Czechoslovakia, Sept 12, 1934; dau. of Konstantin Mikhailovich Verigo (lieutenant in Russian Imperial Guards who descended from Polish nobility) and Olga Ivanovna Verigo (née Goremykina); m. Nikolai Breshko-Breshkovsky, 1869; children: Nikolai (b. 1874). ❖ Educator, political leader, and a vocal opponent of the Bolshevik government, who spent decades in a tsarist prison and exile for her political views, devoted her life to bringing social and political change to turn-of-the-century Russia; began political career as a liberal, though she later discarded the path of reform for a brand of revolutionary activism known as populism; following years in tsarist exile (1874–96), helped found the Socialist Revolutionary Party (SRs), a one-time opponent of the Marxist Bolsheviks who eventually came to power; fled to Romania (1903); went to US to raise funds for the party (1905); jailed in St. Petersburg's Peter and Paul Fortress (1907–10); tried as a revolutionary (1910), was sentenced to a lifetime of Siberian exile in town of Kerensk; released with all political prisoners (1917), was made an honorary member of the SR Central Committee; was a fervent supporter of Alexander Kerensky and very active during the period of the Provisional Government; when Kerensky became prime minister, briefly served as his advisor and moved into the Winter Palace, the seat of government; ended political career as an avid anti-Bolshevik, then turned to her other great love, teaching, in effective exile in the new Republic of Czechoslovakia (1919); her years of service to the revolutionary cause earned her the sobriquet "little grandmother of the revolution"; writings include *Hidden Springs of the Russian Revolution* (1931). ❖ See also Good and Jones, *Babushka: The Life of the Russian Revolutionary Ekaterina K. Breshko-Breshkovskaia* (1991); Alice Stone Blackwell, ed. *The Little Grandmother of the Russian Revolution: Reminiscences and Letters of Catherine Breshkovskaya* (Little, Brown, 1918); and *Women in World History.*

BRÉSIL, Marguerite (1880–1923). French stage actress. Name variations: Marguerite Bresil. Born Aug 20, 1880, in Sermaises, Loiret, France; died Nov 9, 1923. ❖ Made stage debut in Paris in *Petit Chagrin* (1899); appeared at all the major Parisian theatres in such plays as *Le Médecin de Coeur, La Meilleure des Femmes,* and the title role in *Zaza.*

BRESLAU, Louise (1857–1927). Swiss artist. Born in 1857 (some sources cite 1856); died in 1927. ❖ Enjoyed early success in the salons of Paris; won many medals for her work; paintings were included in the retrospective section of "Les Femmes Artistes de l'Europe" exhibition (1937), which was held at Musée du Jeu de Paume and Metropolitan Museum of New York. Awarded Chevalier de la Légion. ❖ See also *Women in World History.*

BRESLAUER, Marianne (1909–2001). German photographer. Name variations: (pseudonym) Ipp. Born in Berlin, Germany, 1909; died in Zurich, Switzerland, 2001; m. Dr. Walter Feilchenfeldt (art dealer), 1936. ❖ Trained in Berlin, then went to Paris where she was a student of Man Ray; photographed extensively, specializing in urban documentation and portraits; returning to Berlin (1930), entered the Ullstein studio under Elsbeth Heddenhausen; was soon back in Paris, however, where she continued portrait work, photographing artists Pablo Picasso and

Ambrois Vollard, among others; also traveled to Spain and Zurich to photograph for the Mauritius and Academia agencies; with work restricted under Hitler's Germany, photographed with the Kind agency (1934), under pseudonym "Ipp"; during 1930s, was widely published in German periodicals, including *Frankfurter Illustrierten, Funkstunde, Weltkreir* and *Weltspiegel;* immigrated to Switzerland (1936) and became an art dealer.

BRETAGNE, Anne de (c. 1477–1514). *See Anne of Brittany.*

BRETAGNE, countess or duchess of. *See Brittany, countess or duchess of.*

BRETIN, Flora (c. 1807–c. 1857). *See Fabbri, Flora.*

BREUER, Grit (1972—). East German runner. Born Feb 16, 1972, in Robel, Germany. ❖ At Seoul Olympics, won a bronze medal for 4 x 100-meter relay (1988); at European championships, won gold medals for the 400 meters (1990, 1998) and 4 x 400-meter relay (1990, 1998, 2002); at World championships, won a silver medal for 400 meters (1991) and gold for the 4 x 100-meter relay (1997).

BREUER-DUKAT, Renate (1939—). West German kayaker. Born Renate Breuer, Dec 1, 1939, in Germany. ❖ At Mexico City Olympics, won a silver medal in K1 500 meters (1968).

BREWER, Lucy (fl. 1812). Possibly the first American woman marine. Name variations: George Baker; Louisa Baker. Fl. in 1812. ❖ Published *The Female Marine* (c. 1815), which detailed her adventures from life in a Boston brothel to her service in the Marine Corps during War of 1812; according to her account, dressed as a man, took the name George Baker, and gave 3 years of service aboard the USS *Constitution,* where she participated in 3 sea battles without her gender being discovered. The US Marine Corps, which maintained that it would have been impossible for a woman to serve in the manner claimed by Brewer without being detected, regards her in their Historical Division as "the legendary first woman Marine."

BREWER, Margaret A. (1930—). American brigadier general. Born 1930 in Durand, Michigan. ❖ Commissioned a Marine second lieutenant (Mar 1952); after positions in CA, NY, VA, NC, and KY, promoted to major (Sept 1961); served as executive officer (1963) and later commanding officer of the Woman Officer School at Quantico, VA; promoted to lieutenant colonel (Dec 1966) while in the post of public affairs officer for the 6th Marine Corps District in Atlanta, GA; while serving as director of information at US Marine Corps headquarters in Washington, DC, was named brigadier general (1978), the 1st woman in history to achieve this rank in US Marine Corps; retired (July 1, 1980), after serving as director of public affairs at Marine headquarters in Washington.

BREWER, Teresa (1931—). American pop singer. Born May 7, 1931, in Toledo, Ohio; m. Bob Thiele, 1972. ❖ Began career on radio at age 2; toured with Major Bowes talent show for 7 years; resumed career at age 16; had 1st hit with recording of "Music! Music! Music!" (1950), followed by "'Til I Waltz Again with You," "Ricochet Romance" and "Let Me Go Lover"; made frequent tv and club appearances and appeared in film *Those Red Heads from Seattle* (1953); later albums include those with jazz greats Count Basie, Duke Ellington, and Bobby Hackett. ❖ See also *Women in World History.*

BREWSTER, Anne Hampton (1818–1892). American writer. Name variations: (pseudonym) Enna Duval. Born Anne Hampton Brewster in Philadelphia, Pennsylvania, Oct 29, 1818; died in Siena, Italy, April 1, 1892; dau. of Francis Enoch Brewster (attorney) and Maria Hampton Brewster; never married; no children. ❖ Fiction writer, poet, essayist, and early female foreign correspondent, who published primarily in Philadelphia, New York, and Boston newspapers, struggled daily to maintain her independence; converted to Catholicism (1848); published 1st poem and 1st novel *Spirit Sculpture* (1849); served as an editor at *Graham's American Monthly Magazine* (1850); sued older brother for a portion of their parents' estate (1856); moved to Bridgeton, New Jersey (1858); published 2nd novel *Compensation; or, Always a Future* (1860), followed by *Saint Martin's Summer* (1866); moved to Rome, Italy (1868); became foreign correspondent (1869), contributing to such newspapers as *Boston Daily Advertiser* (1870–83), *Boston Sunday Herald* (1887–88), *Chicago Daily News* (1885–88), *New York World* (1876–78), *Parisian* (1879–80), *Philadelphia Evening Bulletin* (1869–78) and *San Francisco Chronicle* (1885); became member of Arcadia (1873); moved to Siena, Italy (1889); published at least 52 short stories, 11 pieces of nonfiction, and 4 poems in such periodicals as *Atlantic Monthly, Blackwood's Edinburgh Magazine, Godey's Lady's Book, Harper's Magazine* and *Lippincott's*

Magazine. ❖ See also Denise M. Larrabee, *Anne Hampton Brewster: 19th-Century Author and "Social Outlaw"* (1992); and *Women in World History.*

BREWSTER, Barbara (1918–2005). American dancer. Name variations: Naomi Stevenson Brewster; Brewster Twins; Barbara Brewster LeMond. Born Naomi Stevenson, Feb 19, 1918, in Tucson, Arizona; died June 21, 2005, in Oceanside, California; twin sister of Gloria Brewster (dancer); m. Bob LeMond (radio and tv announcer). ❖ With sister, appeared in numerous film musicals as the Brewster Twins, including *Little Miss Broadway* (1938) and *Hold That Co-ed* (1938); was also featured in numerous Broadway shows, including *Josette,* with Simone Simone; as a solo, was a notable specialty dancer in *High Kickers* (1941–42).

BREWSTER, Elizabeth (1922—). Canadian poet, novelist, and short-story writer. Born Aug 26, 1922, in Chipman, New Brunswick, Canada; University of New Brunswick, BA: Radcliffe College, MA; University of Toronto Library School, BLS; Indiana University, PhD; also attended King's College, London. ❖ Worked as a librarian until 1972, then taught at University of Saskatchewan; published 1st book of poetry, *East Coast* (1951), followed by more than 20 collections of poetry, including *Roads, and Other Poems* (1957), *Passage of Summer* (1969), *Sunrise North* (1974), *Digging In* (1982), *Entertaining Angels* (1988), *Wheel of Change* (1993), *Footnotes to the Book of Job* (1995) and *Burning Bush* (2000); was a founding member of *The Fiddlehead* magazine; short-story collections include *It's Easy to Fall on the Ice* (1977), *A House Full of Women* (1983) and *Visitations* (1987); novels include *The Sisters* (1974) and *Junctions* (1983). Received Lifetime Award for Excellence in the Arts (1995).

BREWSTER, Gloria (1918–1996). American dancer. Name variations: Ruth Stevenson Brewster; Ruth Stroud; Brewster Twins; Gloria Brewster Stroud. Born Ruth Stevenson, Feb 19, 1918, in Tucson, Arizona; died Oct 25, 1996, in Denver, Colorado; twin sister of Barbara Brewster (dancer); m. Claude Stroud (1907–1985, actor and one of the Stroud Twins). ❖ With sister, appeared in film musicals as the Brewster Twins, including *Little Miss Broadway* (1938) and *Hold That Co-ed* (1938); also appeared on Broadway; worked with husband on radio.

BREWSTER, Martha Wadsworth (fl. 1725–1757). American colonial poet. Married Oliver Brewster, 1732. ❖ One of only four women to publish a volume of poetry before the American Revolution, lived in Lebanon, Connecticut; her *Poems on Diverse Subjects* was 1st published in New London, CT (1757).

BREXNER, Edeltraud (1927—). Austrian ballet dancer. Born June 12, 1927, in Vienna, Austria. ❖ Joined Vienna State Opera Ballet (1944), where she remained throughout career; danced in numerous works by Erika Hanka, including *Titus Feuerfuchs* (1950), *Abraxas* (1953), *Giselle, Joan von Zarissa, Turandot* and *Romeo and Juliet;* served on faculty of Vienna State Opera Ballet; continued to perform at Austrian heritage celebrations in New York after retirement.

BREYER, Hiltrud (1957—). German politician. Born Aug 22, 1957, in Saarbrücken, Germany. ❖ Representing Group of the Greens/European Free Alliance, elected to 4th and 5th European Parliament (1994–99, 1999–2004).

BRÉZÉ, Charlotte de (c. 1444/49–?). French princess. Name variations: Charlotte de France; Charlotte de Breze. Born between 1444 and 1449; murdered by husband; dau. of Charles VII, king of France, and Agnes Sorel; m. Jacques de Brézé; children: Louis de Brézé (who m. Diane de Poitiers).

BRÉZÉ, Claire-Clémence de Maillé de (1628–1694). French aristocrat. Name variations: Claire-Clemence de Maille de Breze; Claire-Clémence de Maillé-Brézé; Mlle de Breze; Duchesse de Fronsac; Princesse de Condé. Born Feb 25, 1628, in Breze, France; died April 16, 1694, in Chateau de Chateauroux; niece of Cardinal Richelieu; m. Louis II de Bourbon, prince de Condé and duc d'Enghien (1621–1686, known as The Great Condé, who was the leader of the last aristocratic uprising in France, the Fronde), Feb 1641; children: Henri Jules de Bourbon, prince of Condé (1643–1709). ❖ Was married to husband against her will (he would have preferred marriage to his longtime mistress Marthe de Vigean).

BREZHNEVA, Viktoriya (1908–1995). Russian first lady. Name variations: Viktoria Brezhnev. Born Viktoriya Petrovna Denisova in Kursk, 1908; died in Moscow, July 5, 1995; dau. of Pyotr Nikanorovich Denisov (train engineer); m. Leonid Brezhnev (1906–1982, head of Soviet Communist Party), in 1928; children: Galina Brezhneva (b. 1929); Yuri Brezhnev (b. 1933). ❖ First lady of the Soviet Union, who lived in near-total obscurity while husband was a leading Soviet political figure (1964–82), though her family would later become a symbol of the favoritism and corruption of an "Era of Stagnation"; uninterested in politics, enjoyed the perquisites that accrued to her and her family as husband's career in the Communist bureaucracy flourished. ❖ See also *Women in World History.*

BREZHNEVA, Galina (1929—). Soviet first daughter. Born 1929 in USSR; dau. of Viktoriya Brezhneva (1908–1995) and Leonid Brezhnev (1906–1982, head of Soviet Communist Party); m. Evgenii Milaev, 1951 (div. 1959); m. Igor Kio; m. Iruii Churbanov. ❖ Known for her high living and problems with alcohol, made headlines when her circus-performer lover, Boris the Gypsy, was arrested for smuggling; entered a mental asylum (1998).

BRIAN, Mary (1906–2002). American actress. Born Louise Byrdie Dantzler, Feb 17, 1906, in Corsicana, Texas; died Dec 30, 2002, in Del Mar, California; m. briefly to artist Jon Whitcomb, May 4, 1941–Aug 8, 1941; m. film editor George Tomasini, 1947 (died Nov 22, 1967). ❖ One of the most amiable actresses in pictures, was an unfamiliar face when she played Wendy in Paramount's *Peter Pan* (1924); attended high school on Paramount lot while making as many as 7 feature films a year, including the silents *Beau Geste* (1926), *Harold Teen* (1928) and *The Virginian* (1929); appeared in such notable talkies as *Royal Family of Broadway* (1930) and *The Front Page* (1931); also co-starred with James Cagney in *Hard to Handle* (1933) and W.C. Fields in *The Man on the Flying Trapeze* (1935); had a brief stint on tv (1955), as the mother of Janet Waldo in "Meet Corliss Archer" series; turned hobby of painting celebrities into a profitable sideline. ❖ See also *Women in World History.*

BRIAND, Anne (1968—). French biathlete. Name variations: Anne Briand Bouthiaux or Anne Briand-Bouthiaux. Born June 2, 1968, in Mulhouse, France. ❖ Won a gold medal for 3 x 7.5 km relay at Albertville Olympics (1992); won a silver medal for 15 km and a bronze medal for 4 x 7.5 km relay at Lillehammer Olympics (1994); at World championships, won gold medals for team (1993) and sprint (1995).

BRIANZA, Carlotta (1862–1930). Italian ballerina. Born in Milan, Italy, 1862; died 1930 in Paris, France, possibly a suicide; studied with Carlo Blasis; godmother of Sonia Woizikowska (dancer and teacher). ❖ Known as the 1st Aurora, made debut at Arcadia Theater, St. Petersburg (1887), and was subsequently engaged as a guest artist at Maryinsky Theater (later known as the Kirov), where she 1st appeared in Lev Ivanov's *Haarlem Tulip;* performed frequently at Teatro alla Scala, notably in *La Maladetta* (1875); at the Maryinsky, created role of Princess Aurora in the Petipa-Tchaikovsky *Sleeping Beauty* (1890); after leaving Russia (1891), danced and taught in Italy and Paris; made final appearance, as the wicked fairy in Diaghilev's London production of *Sleeping Beauty,* then called *The Sleeping Princess* (1921). ❖ See also *Women in World History.*

BRICKDALE, Eleanor Fortesque (1872–1945). See Fortesque-Brickdale, Eleanor.

BRICE, Carol (1918–1985). African-American contralto. Born in Sedalia, North Carolina, April 16, 1918; died in Norman, Oklahoma, Feb 15, 1985; dau. of John Brice (Presbyterian minister and schoolteacher); sister of Eugene Brice and Jonathan Brice (both singers); niece of Charlotte Hawkins Brown, founder of the Palmer Memorial Institute; attended Talladega College in Alabama and Juilliard School of Music; m. Thomas Carey (vocalist), 1942. ❖ The 1st black American to win the Walter W. Naumberg Award, performed with the Pittsburgh, Boston, and San Francisco symphonies; sang the role of the Voodoo Princess in *Ouanga* at Metropolitan Opera (1956); went on to play Addie in *Regina,* Kakou in *Saratoga,* Maude in *Finian's Rainbow,* Queenie in *Show Boat,* Maria in *Porgy and Bess,* and Harriet Tubman in *Gentlemen, Be Seated;* with husband, joined music faculty at University of Oklahoma and founded the Cimarron Circuit Opera Company. Won a Grammy for *Porgy and Bess.* ❖ See also *Women in World History.*

BRICE, Elizabeth (c. 1885–1965). American musical-comedy singer and dancer. Born Bessie Shaler, c. 1885, in Findlay, Ohio; died Jan 25, 1965, in Forest Hills, NY. ❖ Made Broadway debut in the chorus of *The Chinese Honeymoon* (1906); other appearances include *Ziegfeld Follies, The Belle of New York, Lady Teazle, The Motor Girl, The Winsome Widow* and *Buzzin' Around;* formed a partnership with Charles King, appearing with him in vaudeville, on Broadway, and on the exhibition ballroom circuit (1910); retired (1920).

BRICE, Fanny (1891–1951). American actress, singer, and comedian. Born Fania Borach, Oct 29, 1891, in NY, NY; died May 29, 1951, in California; m. Frank White (businessman), Feb 14, 1909 (div. 1912); m. Nick Arnold (real name, Jules Wilford Arnt Stein), June 11, 1919 (div. 1927); m. Billy Rose (songwriter and producer), Feb 2, 1929 (div. 1938); children: (2nd m.) Frances Arnold Stark (b. 1919); William (b. 1921). ❖ Began performing in amateur shows in early teens, later appearing in burlesque shows on Broadway as a chorus girl, singer, and dancer; discovered by Florenz Ziegfeld and appeared nearly continuously in his long-running *Ziegfeld Follies* (1910–23); through touring, gained a national reputation as a comedian, bolstered by later film appearances and her most famous role as "Baby Snooks" on radio; appeared in such films as *My Man* (1928), *The Man from Blankley's* (1930), *The Great Ziegfeld* (1936), *Everybody Sing* (1938) and *Ziegfeld Follies* (1946); her life served as the basis for the musical and film *Funny Girl* and film *Funny Lady*, all starring Barbra Streisand. ❖ See also Herbert G. Goldman, *Fanny Brice: The Original Funny Girl* (Oxford U. Press, 1992); Barbara Grossman, *Funny Woman: The Life and Times of Fanny Brice* (Indiana U. Press, 1991); Norman Katkov, *The Fabulous Fanny* (Knopf, 1953); and *Women in World History*.

BRICHE, Adelaide de la (1755–1844). French memoirist, travel writer and salonnière. Name variations: Madame de La Briche; Adélaïde-Edmée Prévost de la Briche. Born Adélaïde-Edmée Prévost, Sept 12, 1755, in Nancy, France; died Jan 29, 1844, in Paris; dau. of Bon Prévost, receveur general of the farms of Lorraine; m. Alexis Janvier de La Live de La Briche (secretair honoraire des commandements of Marie Antoinette and brother of Sophie, comtesse d'Houdetot), 1780 (died 1785). ❖ Settled in Paris (1765); traveled in Switzerland, Italy, England, and Scotland and wrote memoir *Les Voyages en Suisse de Mme de la Briche 1785–1832* (1935); held popular salon for 50 years and was the subject of a painting by Elisabeth Vigée-Le Brun.

BRICKELL, Edie (1966—). American pop singer. Born Mar 10, 1966, in Oak Cliff, Texas; attended Southern Methodist University; m. Paul Simon (singer, songwriter), 1992; children: son Adrian; daughter Lulu. ❖ Shy singer known for jazz-inflected vocals, joined touring band New Bohemians; sang lead on band's successful debut album *Shooting Rubber Bands at the Stars* (1988) and follow up *Ghost of a Dog* (1990); released hit singles "What I Am" (1988) and "Circle" (1989); went solo with *Picture Perfect Morning* (1994), produced by husband Paul Simon; shunned spotlight during much of her career.

BRICO, Antonia (1902–1989). Dutch-born American conductor, pianist, and musical pioneer. Born June 26, 1902, in Rotterdam, Netherlands; died in Denver, Colorado, Aug 3, 1989; attended University of California, at Berkeley; studied with Karl Muck and Sigismund Stojowski. ❖ Pioneer in music, came to US at age 6; coached at the Bayreuth Wagner Festival (1928); was the 1st woman to conduct Berlin Philharmonic (1930), a guest appearance that received rave reviews; conducted Hamburg Philharmonic (1931); was the 1st woman to conduct Metropolitan Opera orchestra (Jan 1933); conducted New York Philharmonic (1938); founded New York Women's Symphony Orchestra, which made its 1st appearance in Town Hall (Feb 18, 1935); while WWII stalled the momentum of the feminist movement, went to Denver to teach and conduct a semi-professional orchestra (1942); for next 27 years, led the Denver Businessman's Orchestra, which was later renamed the Brico Symphony in her honor. ❖ See also documentary by Judy Collins, *Antonia: Portrait of the Woman;* and *Women in World History*.

BRIDA, Maud (1881–1944). See Nelson, Maud.

BRIDE. Variant of Bridget.

BRIDE (c. 453–c. 524). See Bridget.

BRIDGE, Ann (1889–1974). See O'Malley, Mary Dolling.

BRIDGER, Bub (1924—). New Zealand poet and short-story writer. Name variations: Ngati Kahungunu. Born 1924 in Napier, New Zealand—part Maori, part English, and part Irish; children: 3 daughters, 1 son. ❖ Published stories and poems in magazines and anthologies; also wrote for tv and acted on stage; works include the poetry collection, *Up Here on the Hill* (1990).

BRIDGES, Alice (1916—). American swimmer. Born July 19, 1916, in US. ❖ At Berlin Olympics, won a bronze medal in the 100-meter backstroke (1936).

BRIDGES, Elizabeth (1887–1977). See Daryush, Elizabeth.

BRIDGES, Fidelia (1834–1923). American artist. Born in Salem, Massachusetts, 1834; died in Canaan, Connecticut, 1923; dau. of a shipmaster in the China trade; studied painting with William Trost Richards. ❖ Set up her own studio in Philadelphia (1862); exhibited many of her early works at Pennsylvania Academy; began to gain recognition for her close-up, fragmented studies of grasses, birds, and flowers, rendered in delicate yet vibrant watercolors; elected an associate of National Academy of Design (1874) and a member of Water Color Society (1875); had a number of commissions for chromolithographic prints from Louis Prang and Co.; paintings include *Milkweeds* (1861), *Daisies and Clover* (1871) and *Thrush in Wild Flowers* (1974). ❖ See also *Women in World History*.

BRIDGES, Ruby (c. 1954—). African-American civil-rights activist. Name variations: Ruby Bridges Hall. Born Ruby Bridges in Tylerton, Mississippi, c. 1954; dau. of Abon (gas station attendant) and Lucile Bridges; m. Malcolm Hall (building contractor); children: 4 sons. ❖ One of 4 black children chosen to integrate the New Orleans public-school system, was accompanied by US federal marshals to the William Frantz Elementary School for her 1st day of 1st grade (Nov 1960); her ordeal was documented by Norman Rockwell in his famous painting, *The Problem We All Live With;* established the Ruby Bridges Educational Foundation (1994) to encourage parental involvement in schools. ❖ See also (juvenile) Robert Coles, *The Story of Ruby Bridges* (1995); tv movie, "Ruby Bridges" (1998); and *Women in World History*.

BRIDGET (c. 453–c. 524). Patron saint of Ireland. Name variations: Brigantia, Brigid, Brigid of Kildare, Brigida, Briget, Brigte; also called Bride. Born at Faugher or Faughart (then Fochart), near Dundalk, Ireland, c. 453; died at Kildare, now in Co. Louth, Feb 1, c. 524; dau. of Dubhthach (pagan chieftain) and Broicsech (also spelled Brotsech or Broseach, his bondwoman and concubine); became a nun, reputedly in 467. ❖ Ranks with Patrick and Columba as one of the 3 patron saints of Ireland; founded the 1st Irish nunnery at Kildare and ruled there as abbess until her death; habitually made gifts to the poor of the money and goods bequeathed to the monastery, much to the consternation of fellow sisters and brothers of Kildare; was known both for her hospitality and love of entertainment as well as for her occasional vehemence when confronted by those of which she disapproved; reputedly traveled widely throughout Ireland, chiefly through the provinces of Leinster, Connacht and Munster. ❖ See also D. O hAodha, ed. and trans, *Bethu Brigte* (Dublin, 1978); and *Women in World History*.

BRIDGET OF SWEDEN (1303–1373). Patron saint of Sweden. Name variations: Birgitta, Birgitta of Vadstena, Brigit, or Brigitta. Born 1303; died 1373; dau. of Sir Birger Persson of Finsta and Lady Ingeborg; m. Ulf Gudmarsson, prince of Nericia, 1317 (died 1342); children: 8 (most of her children either predeceased her or else lived a celibate life, including Catherine, who is known as Saint Catherine of Sweden, c. 1330–1381). ❖ The founder of the Catholic order of Brigettines, became one of the richest people in Sweden upon father's death; growing up on the family estates at Finsta Gaard, was well-educated by governesses and priests, becoming literate 1st in Swedish, later in Latin and Italian; was married at age 14 to a powerful noble, Ulf Gudmarsson, himself 18; became lady-in-waiting and governess to Queen Blanche of Namur (1335); with husband, made pilgrimage to Santiago de Compostella in Spain (1341); adopted penitential life (1342); departed for Rome just before the Black Death plagued Sweden (1349); made pilgrimage to Holy Land (1372). ❖ See also Johannes Jorgensen, *Bridget of Sweden* (2 vols., trans. by Ingeborg Lund, Longmans, Green, 1954, the only book on Saint Bridget in English); and *Women in World History*.

BRIDGMAN, Eliza Jane (1805–1871). American missionary educator. Born Eliza Jane Gillet, May 6, 1805, in Derby, Connecticut; died Nov 10, 1871, in Shanghai, China; dau. of Canfield and Hannah Gillet; m. Elijah Coleman Bridgman (1st American missionary in China), June 28, 1845. ❖ Served 17 years as principal at girls' boarding school (beginning c. 1827); as teacher for China mission (1843), began missionary work in Canton; opened 1st Protestant day school for girls in Shanghai (1850); reached the American Board's North China Mission at Peking (1864); opened school in Peking, the Bridgman Academy (later Woman's College of Yenching University), providing personal funding; participated in development of newly opened girls' school in Shanghai. Writings include *Daughters of China* (1853) and *The Life and Labors of Elijah Coleman Bridgman* (1864).

BRIDGMAN, Laura (1829–1889). American pioneer. Born Laura Dewey Bridgman, Dec 21, 1829, in Hanover, New Hampshire; died May 24,

1889, in South Boston, Massachusetts; dau. of Daniel and Harmony Bridgman (both farmers); had 2 brothers and 3 sisters, two of whom died from the scarlet fever that destroyed her senses of sight, hearing, and smell; educated by Dr. Samuel Gridley Howe at Perkins Institution for the Blind; never married; no children. ❖ First deaf and blind person successfully educated, who paved the way for other disadvantaged people and whose fame spread across America and Europe; at 7, was brought to Perkins, America's 1st school for the blind (1837); aided by intelligence and curiosity, demonstrated that deaf-blind children could learn language and be educated; met Charles Dickens, who wrote an account of their meeting in *American Notes;* lived most of her life at the Perkins Institution; in later years, helped with the education of blind children. ❖ See also Maude Howe Elliott and Florence Howe Hall. *Laura Bridgman: Dr. Howe's Famous Pupil and What He Taught Her* (Little, Brown, 1904); Mary Swift Lamson, *Life and Education of Laura Dewey Bridgman, The Deaf, Dumb, and Blind Girl* (1881); and *Women in World History.*

BRIENESE, Karin (1969—). Dutch swimmer. Born July 17, 1969, in Netherlands. ❖ At Seoul Olympics, won a silver medal in 4 x 100-meter freestyle relay (1988).

BRIERCLIFFE, Nellie (1889–1966). English actress and singer. Born 1889 in England; died Dec 12, 1966; m. George Thirlwater Phillipson (div.). ❖ Made London debut in *A Dear Little Wife* (1913); was a popular member of D'Oyly Carte Co. (1914–18, 1919–20, 1929–30); appeared at the Adelphi in the musical *Our Boys* (1918–19), followed by *The Wild Geese, Kate, A Most Immoral Lady* and *Escape;* appears on all 7 full-length D'Oyly Carte recordings made for H.M.V. (1929–32), as Phoebe, Edith, Iolanthe, Hebe, Angela, Margaret and Melissa.

BRIERLEY, Susan (1885–1948). See Isaacs, Susan.

BRIEST, Karoline von (1774–1831). See Fouqué, Karoline Freifrau de la Motte.

BRIET, Marguerite de (c. 1510–c. 1550). French novelist and translator. Name variations: (pseudonym) Hélisenne de Crenne or Helisenne de Crenne. Born c. 1510 (some sources cite 1500) in Picardy, France; died c. 1550 (some sources cite 1560). ❖ Wrote *Les Angoisses douloureuses qui procedent d'amours* (1538), which was seen by some critics as the 1st feminine journal in French due to its autobiographical elements and factual details; published *Les Epistres familieres et invectives* (1539), possibly the 1st epistolary novel in French; though her view of love follows the chivalric tradition, writings often address female readers and defend women's right of access to intellectual activity; also wrote the 1st French prose translation of Books I–IV of *Aeneid* (1541).

BRIGANTIA (c. 453–c. 524). See Bridget.

BRIGGS, Emily Edson (1830–1910). American journalist. Name variations: (pseudonym) Olivia. Born Emily Pamona Briggs, Sept 14, 1830, in Burton, Ohio; died in Washington, DC, July 3, 1910; m. John R. Briggs (part owner of newspaper, *Daily Whig* in Keokuk, Iowa, and assistant clerk of US House of Representatives), in 1854. ❖ Under pseudonym Olivia, began writing a daily column for *Washington Chronicle,* and its sister paper the *Philadelphia Press* (1861); during Lincoln's administration, became the 1st woman to report from the White House; was also the 1st woman admitted to the congressional press gallery; acquiring a national reputation, became the 1st president of Women's National Press Association (1882); was also a celebrated Washington host; published columns in book form, *The Olivia Letters* (1906). ❖ See also *Women in World History.*

BRIGGS, Karen (1963—). English judoka. Born April 11, 1963, in Hull, England. ❖ Was World judo champion under 48kg (1982, 1984, 1986, 1989) and European judo champion (1982–84, 1986–87); was 5-time winner of Japanese Open championships; won Commonwealth Games (1990); served as Japanese Women's National team coach (1993) and established her own judo club in Hull. Named MBE. ❖ See also autobiography *Judo Champion* (1988).

BRIGGS, Margaret Jane (1892–1961). New Zealand equestrian. Born April 17, 1892, near Manaia in South Taranaki, New Zealand; died Nov 5, 1961, in Palmerston, New Zealand; dau. of Robert Ephraim Briggs (laborer) and Lydia Elsie (Stevens) Briggs. ❖ Began successful show-jumping career at 10; moved to Australia (1922), where she won numerous exhibition prizes and became skilled in wire jumping, bareback jumping, and high jumping; invited to Los Angeles, California (1925), where she gained prominence in rodeo riding and exhibition jumping;

returned to New Zealand (1948). ❖ See also *Dictionary of New Zealand Biography* (Vol. 3).

BRIGHAM, Emma Frances (1855–1881). American sculptor. Born 1855; died 1881; married Eugene Winslow Durkee, 1878. ❖ Carved the bust of Maria Mitchell for Vassar College (a replica was placed in the American Hall of Fame).

BRIGHAM, Mary Ann (1829–1889). American educator. Born in Westboro, Massachusetts, 1829; died 1889. ❖ An associate principal at Brooklyn Heights Seminary (1863–89), was chosen to be the 1st president of Mount Holyoke College, but died before taking office.

BRIGHT, Clarita Heath (c. 1916–2003). See Heath, Clarita.

BRIGHT, Dora Estella (1863–1951). English composer, organist, pianist. Name variations: Mrs. Knatchbull. Born in Sheffield, England, Aug 16, 1863; died in London, Nov 16, 1951; studied at Royal Academy of Music under Walter Macfarren and Ebenezer Prout; m. a Captain Knatchbull of Bath, 1892. ❖ The 1st woman to be awarded the prestigious Lucas Medal for composition (1888), was also the 1st woman to hear her music performed by the London Philharmonic Orchestra (1892), the 1st person to give a recital of purely English music, which she called *From Byrd to Cowen* (1892), and the 1st Englishwoman to play her own concerto in Leipzig, Dresden, and Cologne (played Piano Concerto in A-Minor with Carl Reinecke conducting, 1880); wrote 8 orchestral pieces as well as compositions for chamber orchestra and piano, and music for a ballet scena which was danced by Adeline Genée (1907). ❖ See also *Women in World History.*

BRIGHT, Mary (1954–2002). Scottish curtain designer. Born Jan 11, 1954, in Edinburgh, Scotland; died of lung cancer, Nov 29, 2002, in New York, NY; studied fine arts in London and fashion and millinery in Leeds; m. David Paskin. ❖ Innovative curtain maker whose work became an art form, moved to NY and worked as a milliner (1979); began experimenting with unorthodox materials for curtain making; formed Mary Bright Inc. with husband, working with such clients as Ellen Barkin, Calvin Klein, Bette Midler, Lauren Bacall, and Museum of Modern Art.

BRIGHT, Mary Golding (1857–1945). British short-story writer. Name variations: (pseudonyms) Mary Chavelita Dunne, George Egerton. Born Dec 14, 1857, in Melbourne, Australia; died Aug 12, 1956, in Sussex, England; dau. of Captain John J. Dunne and Isabel George Bynon; m. H.H.W. Melville (bigamist), 1888; m. Egerton Clairmonte (writer), 1891 (div. 1901); m. Reginald Golding Bright (theater critic), 1901. ❖ Known for her short stories which shocked Victorian sensibilities, spent some time in Norway where she had an affair with novelist Knut Hamsun; published *Keynotes* (1893), which created a stir; other collections include *Discords* (1894), *Symphonies* (1897), *Fantasias* (1898) and *Flies in Amber* (1905); also translated several works, including Hamsun's *Hunger* (1926).

BRIGHT EYES (1854–1902). See La Flesche, Susette.

BRIGHTMAN, Sarah (1960—). English singer and actress. Born Aug 14, 1960, in Berkhamsted, Hertfordshire, England; m. Andrew Graham-Stewart (manager of Tangerine Dreams, a German rock band), 1978 (div. Sept 1983); m. Andrew Lloyd Webber (composer), Mar 22, 1984 (div. 1990). ❖ At 12, made West End debut in *I and Albert;* with Pan's People, appeared on tv's "Top of the Pops"; had disco hit single "I Lost My Heart to a Starship Trooper" (1978); originated roles in Lloyd Webber productions, as Jemima in *Cats* and Christine in *The Phantom of the Opera* (1986); also had a huge hit with "Pie Jesu" and starred with Placido Domingo in *Requiem* in NY; albums include *Dive* (1993), *Fly* (1995), *Timeless/Time to Say Goodbye* (1997), *Eden* (1998), *La Luna* (2000) and *Harem* (2003); frequently appears in specials on tv.

BRIGHTWELL, Ann (b. 1942). See Packer, Ann.

BRIGHTWEN, Eliza (1830–1906). British naturalist. Born Eliza Elder at Banff, Scotland, Oct 30, 1830; died at Stanmore, England, May 5, 1906; dau. of Margaret and George Elder; m. George Brightwen, June 5, 1855 (died 1883); no children. ❖ Observed nature from the grounds of her English home, The Grove, in Stanmore; wrote about her findings and experiences in such books as *My Practical Thoughts on Bible Study* (1871), *Wild Nature Won by Kindness* and *More about Wild Nature* (1892). ❖ See also W.H. Chesson, ed. *Eliza Brightwen: The Life and Thoughts of a Naturalist* (1909); and *Women in World History.*

BRIGID. *Variant of Bridget.*

BRIGID OF KILDARE (c. 453–c. 524). *See Bridget.*

BRIGIDA (c. 453–c. 524). *See Bridget.*

BRIGIT.

See Bridget (c. 453–c. 524).
See Bridget of Sweden (1303–1373).

BRIGITHA, Enith Salle (1955—). Dutch swimmer. Born April 15, 1955, in Curaçao, Netherlands Antilles. ❖ The 1st black female swimmer, moved to Holland (1971); won the bronze medal at the inaugural world championships (1973); won bronze medals in the 200-meter freestyle and the 100-meter freestyle at Montreal Olympics (1976).

BRIGITTA (1303–1373). *See Bridget of Sweden.*

BRIGMAN, Anne W. (1869–1950). American photographer. Name variations: Annie Wardrope. Born Anne Wardrope Knott or Nott in Honolulu, Hawaii, 1869 (some sources cite 1868); died in Eagle Rock, California, 1950; descendant of missionaries; sister of Elizabeth Nott, photographer; attended Punahou School, 1882–1883; m. Martin Brigman, c. 1894 (sep. 1910). ❖ Moved to Los Gatos, California, and took up photography (c. 1886); worked on allegorical portraits, nudes, and draped figures in landscapes; elected a fellow of the Photo-Secessionists (1906), forming a close friendship with Alfred Stieglitz who promoted her work; had 1st important exhibitions at Corcoran Gallery of Art in Washington, DC (1904) and Carnegie Institute in Pittsburgh; represented in opening show of the Photo-Secessionists in New York (1905); won a gold medal at Alaska-Yukon-Pacific Exhibition in Seattle (1909); work 1st published in *Camera Work* (1909); also published *Songs of a Pagan* (1949).

BRIGUE, Jehenne de (d. 1391). French soothsayer. Name variations: Jehenna; La Cordière. Born Jehenne Brion in 1882 Le Cordier. ❖ Accused of witchcraft. ❖ See also *Women in World History.*

BRILL, Debbie (1953—). Canadian high jumper. Born Mar 10, 1953, in Mission, British Columbia, Canada. ❖ Was the 1st North American to jump 6 feet (1970); at Commonwealth Games, won a gold medal (1970) and a silver medal (1978); at Pan American Games, won a gold medal (1971) and a bronze medal (1979); won a gold medal at the World Cup (1979); set world indoor record (1982); competed in 3 Olympics (Munich 1972, Montreal 1976, and Los Angeles 1984). Made Officer of the Order of Canada (1983); inducted into Canadian Sports Hall of Fame (1984).

BRILL, Patti (1923–1963). American dancer and actress. Name variations: Patsy Paige. Born Patricia Brilhante, Mar 8, 1923, in San Francisco, California; died Jan 16, 1963, in North Hollywood, California. ❖ As a young child, danced in such films as *Lilies of the Field* (1929) and *The Vagabond Lover* (1929), among others; signed with Universal as an adolescent and danced a specialty lead in *Mad About Music* (1938) and in Deanna Durbin's *1000 Men and a Girl* (1939); other films include *Best Foot Forward* (1940), *Star Spangled Rhythm* (1942) and *Music in Manhattan* (1944); on West Coast, hosted Special Services and USO shows during WWII; was a regular in Paramount comedy films "Henry Aldrich" (1941–47) and RKO thrillers of "The Falcon" (1943–47); hosted early tv show, "Let There Be Stars" (1949).

BRIND, Tessa (1928–1999). *See Brown, Vanessa.*

BRINK, Carol Ryrie (1895–1981). American children's writer and novelist. Born Carol Ryrie, Dec 28, 1895, in Moscow, Idaho; died Aug 15, 1981, in La Jolla, California; dau. of Alexander (1st mayor of Moscow, Idaho) and Henrietta (Watkins) Ryrie; attended University of Idaho, 1914–17; University of California at Berkeley, BA, 1918; married Raymond Woodward Brink (mathematics professor), July 12, 1918 (died); children: David Ryrie, Nora Caroline Brink Hunter. ❖ Won the Newbery Medal (1936) and Lewis Carroll Shelf Award (1959) for *Caddie Woodlawn;* other books include *Anything Can Happen on the River* (1934), *Lad with a Whistle* (1941), *The Headland* (1956), *The Pink Motel* (1959) *Snow in the River* (1966), *The Bad Times of Irma Baumlein* (1972) and *Four Girls on a Homestead* (1978).

BRINKER, Nancy G. (1946—). American leader in fight against breast cancer. Born Nancy Goodman, 1946, in Peoria, Illinois; lives in Florida; sister of Susan G. Komen (1944–1980); University of Illinois at Urbana-Champaign, BA in sociology, 1968; m. 2nd husband, Norman Brinker (restaurateur), 1981; children: son Eric from a previous marriage. ❖ Founded Susan G. Komen Breast Cancer Foundation (1982), the world's leading catalyst in fight against breast cancer, in memory of sister

Susan; appointed to National Cancer Advisory Board by President Reagan (1986); appointed to run President's Cancer Panel and monitor progress of National Cancer Program by President George H.W. Bush (1990); founded In Your Corner, a business for health and wellness products (1994); appointed US ambassador to Hungary by President George W. Bush (2001); wrote *The Race Is Run One Step at a Time* and *1,000 Questions About Women's Health.*

BRINKLEY, Christie (1953—). American model. Born Christie Lee Hudson, Feb 2, 1954, in Detroit, Michigan; raised in Malibu, California; dau. of Don Brinkley, producer-director; m. Jean-François Allaux, 1973 (div. 1981); m. Billy Joel (singer), Mar 23, 1985 (div. 1994); m. Richard Taubman, 1994 (div. 1995); m. Peter Cook, 1996; children: (2nd m.) Alexa Rae Joel (b. 1986); (3nd m.) Jack Paris Taubman (b. 1995); (4th m.) Sailor Lee Cook (b. 1998). ❖ Popular fashion model, began working for Eileen Ford; appeared on over 500 magazine covers, including the *Sports Illustrated* swimsuit issues (1979, 1980, 1981), the 1st model to appear on 3 consecutive covers; was spokesperson for Breck, Prell, MasterCard, Chanel No. 19, and Diet Coke, and had a long-running contract with Cover Girl; had tv series "Living in the 90's with Christie Brinkley" (1992); appeared in the films *National Lampoon's Vacation* and *Vegas Vacation.*

BRINSMEAD, Hesba Fay (1922–2003). Australian novelist. Name variations: Pixie Brinsmead. Born Hesba Fay Hungerford, 1922, in the Blue Mountains settlement of Berambing, Australia; died Nov 2003, in Murwillumbah, NSW, Australia; m. Reg Brinsmead (div.); children: Ken and Bernie. ❖ One of Australia's most important writers for children and young adults, wrote on a wide variety of subjects; came to prominence with 1st book, *Pastures of the Blue Crane* (1964), which won the Children's Book of the Year award; followed this with her landmark *Longtime Passing* (1971), the 1st of her semi-autobiographical trilogy; an environmentalist whose works often reflect fascination with Australian wilderness, also published the 1st of her "Tasmanian" books with the novel *Season of the Briar* (1965), followed by *Echo in the Wilderness* (1972) and *I Will Not Say the Day is Done* (1983); her *The Ballad of Benny Perhaps* (1977) is "increasingly recognized," wrote the *Sydney Morning Herald,*"as one of the lost masterpieces of Australian literature." Received Mary Gilmore Award (1965) and *Pastures of the Blue Crane* was made into tv miniseries. ❖ See also Michael Pollak and Margaret MacNabb, *Days Never Done: The Life and Work of Hesba Fay Brinsmead* (2002).

BRINVILLIERS, Marie de (1630–1676). French poisoner. Name variations: Marie-Madeleine Marguerite d'Aubray, marquise de Brinvilliers. Born Marie-Madeleine Marguerite d'Aubray in Paris, France, 1630; beheaded and body burned, July 16, 1676; dau. of Dreux d'Aubray (civil lieutenant of Paris); m. Antoine Gobelin, marquis de Brinvilliers (French army officer), in 1651. ❖ After husband introduced her to his friend Gaudin de Sainte-Croix, a handsome young cavalry officer, became his lover, causing a public scandal; her outraged father obtained the arrest of Sainte-Croix via a *lettre de cachet*; plotted with Sainte-Croix to poison her father (1666) and her brothers (1670) in order to inherit the family fortune; eventually poisoned over 50 victims. ❖ See also G. La. Roullier, *Marquise de Brinvilliers* (1883); and *Women in World History.*

BRION, Friederike Elisabeth (1752–1813). German paramour. Born April 19, 1752, in Niederrödern, Germany; died April 3, 1813, in Meissenheim bei Lahr, Germany; dau. of a pastor at Sesenheim, near Strasbourg; never married. ❖ Was loved by, and a lover of, Goethe (1770).

BRION, Hélène (1882–1962). French educator and activist. Name variations: Helene Brion. Pronunciation: BREE-on. Born Hélène Brion in 1882 (probably Jan 12) in Clermont-Ferrand, France; died 1962; orphaned at young age and raised by grandmother in the Ardennes; attended the école primaire supérieure Sophie-Germain in Paris; never married; had 2 children by a Russian immigrant around 1905–1907. ❖ Schoolteacher, union activist, pacifist and feminist who—due to her pacifist stance during World War I—was the 1st French woman to be tried before a military tribunal, and who, after the war, researched and wrote her own feminist encyclopedia; taught at a nursery school (*école maternelle*) in Pantin until her revocation in 1917; participated in numerous feminist organizations, including the Feminist University Federation, the League for the Rights of Women, and the French Union for Female Suffrage; belonged to the Socialist Party and to the Confederal Committee of the General Confederation of Work (CGT); during World War I, opened a soup kitchen in Pantin, served as secretary-general of the National Federation of Teachers' Unions

(1915–18), helped oversee an orphanage for poor children in Épône, and belonged to the Committee for the Renewal of International Relations; joined with other pacifist members of the Teachers' Federation in calling for an immediate negotiated peace (1916); arrested for "defeatism" (1917); saw to it that her trial would serve as a soapbox not only for the pacifism for which she was arrested but also for the feminism that defined all of her political and social action; found guilty (Mar 1918) by a military tribunal and given a 3-year suspended sentence; returned to teaching after the war (1925) and maintained contact with militant colleagues but retreated from public life; devoted many of her later years to the research and writing of a feminist encyclopedia. ❖ See also *Women in World History*.

BRIOUZE, Annora de (d. 1241). See Braose, Annora de.

BRIOUZE, Loretta de (d. 1266). See Braose, Loretta de.

BRISCO-HOOKS, Valerie (1960—). African-American runner. Born July 6, 1960, in Greenwood, Mississippi; m. Alvin Hooks (wide receiver for Philadelphia Eagles), 1981 (div., 1984). ❖ At Los Angeles Olympics, won a gold medal in the 4 x 400-meter relay and back-to-back gold medals for the 200 and 400 meters (1984), the 1st Olympian to win both events and the 1st American track-and-field woman to have won 3 Olympic gold medals since Wilma Rudolph in 1960; won a silver medal in the 4 x 400-meter relay at the Seoul Olympics (1988). ❖ See also *Women in World History*.

BRISCOE, Amy Maria (1864–1955). See Hellaby, Amy Maria.

BRISCOE, Lottie (1870–1950). American stage and silent-screen actress. Born April 19, 1870, in St. Louis, Missouri; died Mar 19, 1950, in New York, NY. ❖ Debuted as a child in a play with Ada Rohan, then appeared with Richard Mansfield in *The Devil's Disciple;* starred in films with the Lubin Company, including *The Beloved Adventurer, House of Mirth, The Blinded Heart* and *A Little Family Affair.*

BRISSAC, Virginia (1883–1979). American actress. Born June 11, 1883, in California; died July 26, 1979, in Hollywood, California. ❖ Character actress appeared in over 125 films, including *Honeymoon Limited, Three Godfathers, Artists and Models, Jesse James, Dark Victory, Little Old New York, Black Friday, The Little Foxes, Phantom Lady, A Tree Grows in Brooklyn, Monsieur Verdoux, The Snake Pit, Harriet Craig, Executive Suite* and *Rebel Without a Cause.*

BRISCOE, Vanessa (1955—). See Hay, Vanessa Briscoe.

BRISSON, Therese (1966—). Canadian ice-hockey player. Born Oct 5, 1966 in Fredericton, New Brunswick, Canada. ❖ Played for Mississauga Ice Bears; won a team silver medal at Nagano (1998), the 1st Olympics to feature women's ice hockey; won a team gold medal at World championships (2001); won a team gold medal at Salt Lake City Olympics (2002). Inducted into Concordia University Hall of Fame.

BRISTOL, countess of (1720–1788). See Chudleigh, Elizabeth.

BRISTOW, Lily (fl. 1890s). British mountaineer. Fl. 1890s. ❖ Traversed the Aiguille des Charmoz (1892); climbed the Grépon (1893), the second traverse (guideless), the Petit Dru, and later the Zinal Rothorn and the Matterhorn (14,690 ft.); shared many climbs with Mary Petherick.

BRITAGNE, countess or duchess of. See Brittany, countess or duchess of.

BRITAIN, Radie (1897–1994). American composer. Born Mar 17, 1897, in Silverton, near Amarillo, Texas; died May 23, 1994, in Los Angeles, California; studied at Clarendon College Conservatory of Music, American Conservatory, as well as in Berlin and Munich; m. Edgardo Simone, sculptor (died); m. Ted Morton. ❖ Pioneer for American women composers in 20th century, often mistaken for a man because of her name, made debut as a composer in Munich, when baritone Erich Wildhagen sang several of her songs; won International Award for composition (1930) and was the 1st woman to receive the Juilliard National Prize (1945), for her composition *Heroic Poem*, dedicated to Charles Lindbergh's flight to Paris; joined faculty of American Conservatory of Music in Chicago (1938); wrote over 150 compositions for orchestra, chamber ensembles, stage works, choral, piano, violin, harp and voice, many of which were performed by women's orchestras.

BRITES. *Variant of Beatrice.*

BRITT, May (1933—). Swedish actress. Born Maybritt Wilkens, Mar 22, 1933, in Lidingo, Stockholm, Sweden; m. Ed Gregson, 1958 (div.); m. Sammy Davis Jr. (dancer, singer, actor), 1960 (div. 1968). ❖ Made film debut in Carlo Ponti's *Le Infideli* (1952); other films include

Cavalleria Rusticana, Vergine moderna, War and Peace, The Young Lions, The Hunters, The Tempest, The Blue Angel, Murder Inc. and *The Veil.*

BRITTAIN, Vera (1893–1970). British writer, feminist, and pacifist. Born Vera Mary Brittain, Dec 29, 1893, in Newcastle-under-Lyme, Staffordshire, England; died Mar 29, 1970, in London; dau. of Thomas Arthur (paper manufacturer) and Edith Mary (Bervon) Brittain; attended Somerville College, Oxford, 1914–15, 1919–21, MA, 1925; m. George Edward Gordon Catlin (professor of politics at Oxford and prominent member of Labour Party), June 27, 1925; children: John Catlin; Shirley Williams (b. 1930, politician). ❖ During WWI, fiancé Roland Leighton killed (1915), then brother (1918), then 2 other close friends; as a member of Voluntary Aid Detachments (VAD), served in Malta and France; with Winifred Holtby, became a speaker for League of Nations Union (LNU), a strongly antiwar organization (1920s); contributed to *Time and Tide,* a weekly with strong feminist leanings; with Holtby, became a Socialist (1924); published the novels *The Dark Tide* (1923) and *Not Without Honour* (1924); came to prominence as a writer with *Testament of Youth* (1933), which offered the 1st account of the agonies of WWI as seen through the eyes of a woman; following death of Holtby (1935), saw Holtby's most-admired novel, *South Riding,* to press and commemorated her in her own book, *Testament of Friendship* (1940); also published 2 books of poems: *Verses of a V.A.D.* (1918) and *Poems of the War and After* (1934); was president of Peace Pledge Union (PPU), the leading British pacifist organization (1949–51); the leading pacifist chronicler of her times, also wrote *Honourable Estate: A Novel of Transition* (1936), *War-time Letters to Peace Lovers* (1940), *Account Rendered* (1944), *On Becoming a Writer* (1947), *In the Steps of John Bunyan* (1950), *Lady into Woman: A History of Women from Victoria to Elizabeth II* (1953), *The Women at Oxford* (1960), *Pethick-Lawrence* (1963), *The Rebel Passion* (1964), *Envoy Extraordinary: A Study of Vijaya Lakshmi Pandit* (1965) and *Radclyffe Hall* (1968), among others. ❖ See also *Thrice a Stranger: New Chapters of Autobiography* (1938); *Testament of Experience: An Autobiographical Story of the Years 1925–1950* (1957); *Selected Letters of Winifred Holtby and Vera Brittain, 1920–1935* (1960); Hilary Bailey, *Vera Brittain* (Penguin, 1987); Berry and Bostridge, *Vera Brittain: A Life* (1995); *Chronicle of Youth: War Diary, 1913–1917* (1981); *Testament of a Generation: The Journalism of Vera Brittain and Winifred Holtby* (1985); *Chronicle of Friendship: Diary of the Thirties, 1932–1939* (1986); *Testament of a Peace Lover: Letters from Vera Brittain* (1988); *Wartime Chronicle: Vera Brittain's Diary, 1939–1945* (1989); and *Women in World History.*

BRITTAN, Elizabeth Mary Brittan (1845–1940). See Rolleston, Elizabeth Mary.

BRITTAN, Emily Sophia (1842–1897). See Foster, Emily Sophia.

BRITTAN, Mary Brittan (1845–1940). See Rolleston, Elizabeth Mary.

BRITTANY, countess of. See Constance (c. 1066–1090).

BRITTANY, duchess of.
See Matilda (fl. 1000s).
See Hawise of Normandy (d. 1034).
See Hawise of Brittany (d. 1072).
See Margaret of Huntingdon (c. 1140–1201).
See Constance of Brittany (1161–1201).
See Alice (d. 1221).
See Beatrice (1242–1275).
See Isabel de Limoges (1283–1328).
See Jeanne de Montfort (c. 1310–c. 1376).
See Mary (1344–1362).
See Joan Holland (c. 1356–1384).
See Joan Valois (1391–1433).
See Amboise, Francise d' (1427–1485).
See Marguerite de Foix (fl. 1456–1477).
See Anne of Brittany (c. 1477–1514).

BRITTON, Alison (1948—). English potter. Born 1948 in Harrow, Middlesex, England; attended Leeds College of Art, 1966–67; trained in ceramics at Central School of Art and Design, 1967–70; studied photography at Royal College of Art, 1970–73, before turning to tile work under tutelage of Hans Coper. ❖ Major ceramic artist, curator and writer, who employed strong graphic element in early work, but since 1980s has worked in more sculptural manner; uses slab construction technique, drawing on influences as diverse as prehistoric artifacts, medieval Far East and 20th-century painting and architecture; was joint curator for groundbreaking exhibition "The Raw and the Cooked" (1993); taught at Royal College of Art and lectured at many institutions; exhibitions include "Work of Alison Britton" at Crafts Council, London (1979), Retrospective at Aberystwyth Arts Centre (1990), "Form and Function" at Marianne Heller Gallery, Sandhausen, Germany (1995), and Barrett Marsden Gallery (solo show every 2–3 years since 1998). Awarded Order of the British Empire (OBE, 1990); shortlisted for Jerwood prize for Applied Arts: Ceramics (2001). ❖ See also Peter Dormer and David Cripps, *Alison Britton in Studio* (Bellew, 1985).

BRITTON, Barbara (1919–1980). American tv and screen actress. Born Barbara Brantingham, Sept 26, 1919, in Long Beach, California; died Jan 17, 1980, in New York, NY; m. Dr. Eugene J. Czukor, 1945; children: daughter and son. ❖ Lead player whose films include *Secrets of the Wastelands, Louisiana Purchase, Wake Island, Reap the Wild Wind, So Proudly We Hail, Till We Meet Again, The Story of Dr. Wassell, Captain Kidd, The Virginian, I Shot Jesse James, Bandit Queen, Bwana Devil* and *The Spoilers;* retired from film (1955); appeared occasionally on Broadway; later had recurring roles in tv series "Mr. and Mrs. North" and soap "One Life to Live," and was spokesperson for Revlon cosmetics.

BRITTON, Elizabeth Knight (1858–1934). American botanist. Born Elizabeth Gertrude Knight in New York, NY, Jan 9, 1858; died in New York, NY, Feb 25, 1934; dau. of James Knight and Sophie (Compton) Knight; grew up in Cuba; graduate of Normal College (later Hunter College), NY, 1875; m. Nathaniel Britton (director of New York Botanical Garden), 1885. ❖ Author of close to 350 scientific papers, helped establish and manage the New York Botanical Gardens and was a driving force in conservation efforts; became the unofficial curator of the moss collection at Columbia, which she expanded with the acquisition of the collection of August Jaeger of Switzerland; made honorary curator (1912); was a principal founder of the Sullivan Moss Society (later know as American Bryological Society), serving as president (1916–19); also co-founded the Wild Flower Preservation Society of America (1902). Fifteen species of plants and a moss genus (*Bryobrittonia*) have been named in her honor. ❖ See also *Women in World History.*

BRITTON, Hutin (1876–1965). English actress. Name variations: Nellie Britton, Nellie Hutin Britton. Born April 24, 1876, in Reading, England; died Sept 3, 1965; m. Matheson Lang (1879–1948, actor and manager). ❖ Made stage debut with Frank Benson's Rep company at Brighton in *Henry V* (1901); came to prominence as Dagny in *The Vikings* (1903); with a career that stretched over 4 decades, appeared in such parts as Portia, Ophelia, Lady Macbeth, Volumnia in *Coriolanus,* Hero in *Much Ado about Nothing,* and Lady Elizabeth in *Richard III;* with husband, assisted Lilian Baylis in producing the 1st Shakespeare season at Old Vic (1914); in later years, was on the governing board of the Old Vic. ❖ See also Matheson Lang's *Mr. Wu Looks Back* (1940).

BRITTON, Nan (1896–1991). American paramour. Born Nov 9, 1896, in Claridon, Ohio; died in Oregon, 1991; children: (with Warren Harding) Elizabeth Ann Britton. ❖ Long-time mistress of President Warren G. Harding (1917–23), was smuggled in and out of the White House during his presidency, aided by the Secret Service; after Harding's sudden and mysterious death (Aug 1923), no longer received child support; desperate for money, wrote the infamous tell-all *The President's Daughter* (1927). ❖ See also *Women in World History.*

BRITTON, Nellie Hutin (1876–1965). See Britton, Hutin.

BRITTON, Pamela (1923–1974). American stage, tv and screen actress. Born Mar 19, 1923, in Milwaukee, Wisconsin; died June 17, 1974, in Arlington Heights, Illinois; m. Arthur Steel (hotel executive); children: daughter. ❖ Starred on Broadway in *Brigadoon;* films include *Anchors Aweigh, A Letter from Evie, Key to the City* and *Dead on Arrival;* had recurring roles on tv series, "My Favorite Martian" and "Blondie."

BRITTON, Rosa María (1936—). Panamanian writer and physician. Name variations: Rosa Maria Britton. Born July 28, 1936, in Panama; dau. of a Panamanian mother and Cuban father; married an American engineer; children: at least 2. ❖ Served as only US-trained cancer specialist in Panama; was director of National Oncological Institute of Panama for 18 years and president of Latin American Federation of Cancerology Societies (FLACSA, 1993–96); published 1st novel *El ataúd de uso* (Used Coffin, 1983), which became part of national school curriculum in Panama; received 5 Miró awards and the Golden Pen Award (Panama, 1998) for the sale of more books than any other Panamanian author; themes include love, racism, religion and politics.

Also wrote *El señor de las lluvias y el viento* (The Master of the Rain and the Wind, 1984), *Esa esquina del paraíso* (drama, That Corner of Paradise), *No pertenezco a este siglo* (I Don't Belong to this Country, 1989) and *Todas íbamos a ser reinas* (We Were All Going to Be Queens, 1997), among others.

BRITZ, Jerilyn (1943—). American golfer. Born Jan 11, 1943, in Minneapolis, Minnesota; attended Mankato State College. ❖ Turned pro (1973); won US Open (1979); won Mary Kay Classic (1980); named Golf Digest Most Improved Player (1979); spent 25 years on LPGA tour; coached at New Mexico State.

BRIXEY, Loretta (1960—). See Sanchez, Loretta.

BRLIČ-MAŽURANIĆ, Ivana (1874–1938). Croatian children's writer. Name variations: Ivana Brlic Mazuranic. Born April 18, 1874, in Ogulin, Croatia; died Sept 21, 1938, in Zagreb, Croatia; dau. of Vladimir Mažuranić; m. Vatroslav Brlič. ❖ Called the "Croatian Andersen," was the 1st woman member of the Yugoslav Academy of Science and Arts; works, which remain classics in children's literature, include *The Good and the Mischievous* (1902), *School and Holidays* (1905), *Pictures* (1912), *The Marvellous and Misadventures of Hlapic the Apprentice* (1913), *Tales of Long Ago* (1916), *A Book for Youth* (1923), *Jaš a Dalmatin Viceroy of the Gujarati* (1937) and *Gingerbread Heart* (1939).

BROAD, Helen Hay (1873–1918). See Smith, Helen Hay.

BROAD, Mary (1765–?). See Bryant, Mary.

BROAD, Molly Corbett (c. 1941—). American educator. Born Molly Corbett, c. 1941, in Wilkes-Barre, PA; Syracuse University, BA in economics, 1962; Ohio State University, MA in economics, 1964; m. Robert W. Broad; children: 2 sons. ❖ Served as CEO of Arizona university system (1985–92); served as senior vice chancellor for administration and finance for California State University system (1992–93), then executive vice chancellor (1993–97); was president of University of North Carolina (1997–2006).

BROADFOOT, Eleanor (1878–1934). See Cisneros, Eleanor de.

BROADINGHAM, Elizabeth (d. 1776). English criminal. Died Mar 20, 1776, in England; m. John Broadingham (British smuggler). ❖ Convinced lover Thomas Aikney to murder husband John (Feb 1776); confessed to plotting husband's murder and was executed. Scandal was so sensational that witnesses picked up her ashes for souvenirs.

BROADWICK, Tiny (1893–1978). American parachutist. Name variations: Georgia Broadwick; Georgia Ann Thompson; Georgia Ann Thompson Brown. Born Georgia Ann Thompson, April 8, 1893, near Oxford, Granville Co., North Carolina; died Aug 1978 in Long Beach, California; adopted by Charles Broadwick. ❖ Known as Tiny for her diminutive build (4 feet tall, weighing 85 pounds), suffered broken bones, made landings in swamps and was dragged by her parachute as she made more than 1,100 jumps during her career (many while wearing a silk dress and bloomers with ruffles); at 15, joined Charles Broadwick who had a parachuting act with the James J. Jones Carnival; jumped primarily in aerial barnstorming shows where she was billed as The Doll Girl; was the 1st woman to jump from an aircraft (June 21, 1913), 1st woman to jump from a hydro aeroplane, and 1st woman to make a water jump from an airplane; was also the 1st person to make a premeditated freefall jump (1914), which took place while she was presenting the 1st parachute-jump demonstration to US government; made jumps at San Diego World's Fair (1915, 1916 and 1922); inducted into Curtis Hall of Fame. A parachute and pack used by Broadwick were given to the Smithsonian Institute. ❖ See also Elizabeth Whitley Roberson, *Tiny Broadwick: The First Lady of Parachuting* (Pelican, 2001).

BROCCADELLI, Lucia (1476–1544). See Lucia of Narni.

BROCCOLI, Dana (1922–2004). American actress, novelist and film producer. Name variations: Dana Wilson. Born Dana Natol, Jan 3, 1922, in New York, NY; died Feb 29, 2004, in Los Angeles, California; m. Lewis Wilson (actor, div.); m. Albert R. "Cubby" Broccoli (film producer), 1959 (died 1996); children: (1st m.) Michael Wilson (film producer); (2nd m.) Barbara Broccoli (film producer) and 2 stepchildren, Tony and Tina Broccoli (known as Tina Banta). ❖ As an actress, career peaked with role of Queen Bonga Bonga in *Wild Women* (1951); with husband, helped produce *Chitty Chitty Bang Bang* (1967) and was involved in the production of its musical adaptation for the stage (2002); following husband's death (1996), became president of Danjaq, the company that owned the film rights to Ian Fleming's James Bond novels, and released 3 Bond films starring Pierce Brosnan during her tenure; adapted the stage musical *La Cava* from her own novel *Florinda* for London's West End (2000).

BROCK, Karena (1942—). American ballet dancer. Name variations: Karena Brock-Carlyle or Brock Carlyle. Born Sept 21, 1942; m. John Carlyle (dancer). ❖ During adolescence, danced with Ballet Celeste in San Francisco and Dutch National Ballet in the Netherlands; joined American Ballet Theater upon returning to US where she created roles in Eliot Feld's *Eccentrique* (1971) and Dennis Nahat's *Momentum* (1969), *Mendelssohn Symphony* (1971) and *Some Times* (1972); named principal dancer of Ballet Theater (1973); appeared in Ballet Theater Workshop's staging of Richard Wagner's *Beatrice* (1964), Enrique Martinez' *Balladen der Liebe* (1965), Robert Goldstein's *Way Out* (1970), Tomm Rudd's *Polyandrion* (1973), and numerous others; danced throughout Europe, Asia, and Latin America, as well as US and Canada; performed at White House for 2 presidents; served as artistic director of Savannah Ballet; founded Hilton Head Dance School in SC with husband (1993) and has co-directed the school ever since.

BROCKMAN, Henrietta (1901–1968). *See Drake-Brockman, Henrietta.*

BROCKOVICH, Erin (1960—). American environmental activist. Name variations: Erin Brockovich-Ellis. Born Erin L.E. Pattee, June 1960, in Lawrence, Kansas; dau. of Frank (industrial engineer) and Betty Jo Pattee (journalist); attended Kansas State University; earned Associate in Applied Arts degree at a business college in Dallas, Texas; m. Shawn Brown (restaurant manager), 1982 (div. 1987); m. Steen Brockovich (stockbroker), 1989 (div. 1990); m. Eric Ellis (actor), 1999; children: (1st m.) Matthew and Katie Brown; (2nd m.) Elizabeth Brockovich. ❖ Hired to work as a clerk at the law firm of Masry & Vititoe (1991); on her own, set out to investigate the mysterious illnesses around Hinkley, CA; established that it was caused by exposure to Chromium 6, leaked into the groundwater by the nearby Pacific Gas & Electric Co.; sued Pacific Gas which had to pay $333 million in damages to more than 600 Hinkley residents, the largest toxic tort injury settlement in US history (1996); has spearheaded many other cases; hosted her own Lifetime tv show, "Final Justice." ❖ See also film, *Erin Brockovich,* starring Julia Roberts (2000).

BROCKWELL, Gladys (1894–1929). American actress. Born Gladys Lindeman, Mar 21 (some sources cite Sept 26), 1894, in Brooklyn, NY; died July 4 (some sources cite July 2), 1929, of peritonitis following an auto accident; m. Robert Broadwell; m. Harry Edwards. ❖ At 3, made stage debut; became a popular stage star; made film debut in *The Typhoon* (1914); specialized in fallen woman roles; films include *The End of the Trail* (1916), *Oliver Twist* (1922), *Penrod and Sam* (1923), *The Hunchback of Notre Dame* (1923), *So Big* (1924), *Stella Maris* (1925), *Lights of New York* (1928) and *The Drake Case* (1929); also appeared opposite Janet Gaynor and Charles Farrell in *Seventh Heaven.*

BRODBECK, May (1917–1983). American philosopher and professor. Born in Newark, New Jersey, July 26, 1917; died Aug 2, 1983; New York University, BA, 1941; University of Iowa, MA, 1947, PhD, 1947. ❖ Was an instructor at University of Minnesota (1947–74), then professor of philosophy (1959–74), chair of the department of philosophy (1967–70), dean of graduate school (1972–74), and Carver Professor of Philosophy (1974–83); became University of Iowa Professor Emeritus (1983); achieved outstanding success as an academic philosopher at a time when there were few prominent women in philosophy; writings include *Philosophy in America: 1900–1950* (1952); (ed. with Herbert Fiegel) *Readings in the Philosophy of Science* (1953), and (ed.) *Readings in the Philosophy of the Social Sciences* (1968).

BRODBER, Erna (1936—). Jamaican novelist and poet. Born April 20, 1936, in Woodside, St. Mary, Jamaica; sister of Velma Pollard (b. 1937, writer); University College of the West Indies, London, BA with honors, 1963, MS in Sociology; University of West Indies, Mona, Jamaica, PhD in History. ❖ Won Ford Foundation scholarship for study in US (1967); embraced Rastafarianism and worked as freelance journalist; won critical acclaim for 1st novel, *Jane and Louisa Will Soon Come Home* (1980); won Commonwealth Regional Prize for 2nd novel, *Myal* (1988); named Whichard Distinguished Professorship in Women's Studies at University of West Indies in Kingston, Jamaica (2003); nonfiction works include *Abandonment of Children in Jamaica* (1974), *A Study of Yards in the City of Kingston* (1975), *Perceptions of Caribbean Women: Towards a Documentation of Stereotypes* (1982) and *Oral Sources and the Creation of a Social History in the Caribbean* (1983). Awarded Musgrave Gold award for Literature and Orature from government of Jamaica.

BRODEL, Joan (1925—). *See Leslie, Joan.*

BRODER, Jane (d. 1977). American talent agent. Died June 16, 1977, in New York, NY. ❖ Was a talent agent for 60 years.

BRODERICK, Helen (1890–1959). American comedic actress and singer. Born Aug 11, 1890, in Philadelphia, Pennsylvania; died Sept 25, 1959, in Hollywood, California; m. Lester Crawford; children: Broderick Crawford (actor). ❖ Made stage debut in the chorus of *Ziegfeld Follies* (1907); appeared in vaudeville for several years with husband; other Broadway plays include *Jumping Jupiter, The Band Wagon, Earl Carroll Vanities of 1932* and *As Thousands Cheer;* made film debut in *Fifty Million Frenchmen* (1931), followed by *Top Hat, Swing Time, No No Nanette* and *Stage Door Canteen,* among others.

BRODSGAARD, Karen (1978—). Danish handball player. Name variations: Brødsgaard or Broedsgaard. Born Mar 10, 1978, in Denmark. ❖ Pivot, won a team gold medal at Sydney Olympics (2000) and Athens Olympics (2004).

BROEDSGAARD, Karen (1978—). *See Brodsgaard, Karen.*

BROGAN, Michelle (1973—). Australian basketball player. Name variations: Michelle Griffiths. Born Michelle Brogan, Feb 8, 1973, in Australia. ❖ Forward; won a team bronze medal at Atlanta Olympics (1996) and a silver medal at Sydney Olympics (2000); played for Phoenix Mercury (1998, 2000).

BROGDEN, Cindy (1957—). American basketball player. Born Feb 25, 1957, in US. ❖ At Montreal Olympics, won a silver medal in team competition (1976).

BROGDEN, Gwendoline (1891–?). English actress and singer. Born Sept 28, 1891, in Hull, England; m. Basil Foster (div.). ❖ As a child, made stage debut in London in *Bluebell in Fairyland* (1901), followed by *Miss Hook of Holland, The Merry Widow, Pinkie and the Fairies, Peter Pan, The Marionettes, The Sunshine Girl, A Pantomime Rehearsal, After the Girl, The Passing Show, Vanity Fair* and *Bubbly.*

BRØGGER, Suzanne (1944—). Danish novelist and essayist. Name variations: Suzanne Brogger. Born Nov 18, 1944, in Copenhagen, Denmark; children: daughter (b. 1984). ❖ Radical Marxist and feminist, influenced by Taoism and postmodern philosophy, published such books as *Fri os fra kærligheden* (Deliver Us from Love, 1973), *Crème Fraiche* (1978) and *Kvœlstof* (Nitrogen, 1990).

BROGLIE, Duchesse de (1797–1838). *See Albertine.*

BROHAN, Augustine Suzanne (1807–1887). French actress. Name variations: Suzanne or Susanne Brohan. Born in Paris, France, Jan 22 (some sources cite 29), 1807; died Aug 16 (some sources cite 17), 1887; children: Josephine Félicité Augustine Brohan (1824–1893); Émilie Madeleine Brohan (1833–1900). ❖ Known on the stage as Suzanne, entered the Paris Conservatoire at 11; took the 2nd prize for comedy (1820) and 1st (1821); served apprenticeship in the provinces, making Paris debut at Odéon (1832) as Dorine in Molière's *Tartuffe;* success earned a berth at the Comédie Française, where she made her debut (Feb 15, 1834), as Madelon in *Les Précieuses ridicules,* and as Suzanne in *Le Mariage de Figaro;* forced to retire due to ill health (1842).

BROHAN, Augustine (1824–1893). *See Brohan, Josephine Félicité Augustine.*

BROHAN, Émilie Madeleine (1833–1900). French actress. Name variations: Madeleine Brohan. Born in France, Oct 22, 1833; died 1900; dau. of Augustine Suzanne Brohan (actress); m. Mario Uchard, 1853 (soon sep., div. 1884). ❖ Known on stage as Madeleine Brohan, took 1st prize for comedy at the Conservatoire (1850); debuted at Comédie Française in a play by Scribe and Legouvé, titled *Les Contes de la reine de Navarre,* in which she created the part of Margaret of Angoulême (1850); a polished soubrette, earned immediate success for her talent and beauty; elected *sociétaire* (1852); following marriage (1853), returned to the Comédie Française (1858), playing leading parts until her retirement (1886); her name is associated with a great number of plays, besides those in the classical *répertoire,* notably *Par droit di conquête, Les Deux Veuves,* and *Le Lion amoureux,* the last of which brought one of her greatest successes in the role of the marquise de Maupas.

BROHAN, Josephine Félicité Augustine (1824–1893). French actress. Name variations: Augustine Brohan. Born in France, Dec 2, 1824; died Feb 16, 1893; dau. of Augustine Suzanne Brohan (actress); m. Edmond David de Gheest (secretary to the Belgian legation in Paris), 1866 (died

1885). ❖ Known on stage as Augustine Brohan, was admitted to the Conservatoire when very young; as a soubrette, debuted at Comédie Française (1841), as Dorine in *Tartuffe* and Lise in *Rivaux d'eux-mêmes*; after 18 months, was unanimously elected *sociétaire* (member of the company); a remarkably versatile and brilliant actress, succeeded Rachel at the Conservatoire and soon became a great favorite in the plays of Molière, Jean de Regnard, and Pierre de Marivaux; also wrote plays; retired (1866).

BROHAN, Madeleine (1833–1900). See Brohan, Émilie Madeleine.

BROHAN, Suzanne (1807–1887). See Brohan, Augustine Suzanne.

BROHON, Jacqueline-Aimée (1731–1778). French novelist and essayist. Born 1731 in France; died 1778. ❖ Writings, which reflect influence of Jean-Jacques Rousseau and promote anti-clerical mysticism, include *Les Amants philosophes* (1755), *Instructions édifiants* (1791) and *Réflexions édifiants* (1791).

BROMHALL, Margaret Ann (1890–1967). English radiotherapist. Born Nov 7, 1890, in England; died Jan 5, 1967; Manchester University, MB, ChB, 1924; earned diploma in medical radiology and electrotherapy (DMRE, 1932). ❖ Served as radium officer at North of England Radium Institute, Newcastle-upon-Tyne, and as resident radiotherapist in Perth, Australia; at North Middlesex Hospital, London (1934–54), was 1st radiotherapist to be appointed to a British radiotherapy department.

BROMLEY, Dorothy Dunbar (1896–1986). American editor and writer. Born Dorothy Ewing Dunbar, Dec 25, 1896, near Ottawa, Illinois; died Jan 3, 1986, in Pennsylvania; dau. of Helen Elizabeth (Ewing) and Charles E. Dunbar; Northwestern University, BA, 1917; m. Donald C. Bromley, Aug 1920 (div. early 1920s). ❖ Longtime editor at New York *Herald Tribune*, began career as secretary to the editor at Detroit *Free Press* and was given an opportunity to write reviews; following marriage, moved to NY where she worked as an editor with Henry Holt (1921–25); published 1st book, *Birth Control: Its Use and Misuse* (1934), which contributed to her stint as columnist on the women's page of New York *World-Telegram* (1935–38); with Florence Haxton Britten, wrote *Youth and Sex* (1938); served as columnist with New York *Post* (1940–42); invited to edit the Women's Page of the Sunday edition of New York *Herald Tribune* (1942), replaced club news with national issues. ❖ See also *Women in World History*.

BRON, Eleanor (1934—). English stage, tv, and screen actress and writer. Born Mar 14, 1934, in Stanmore, Middlesex, England. ❖ Began career with The Establishment revue in London (1962); made film debut in *Help!* (1965), followed by *Alfie, Two for the Road, Bedazzled, Women in Love, The National Health, Monty Python Meets beyond the Fringe, Little Dorrit, Black Beauty, A Little Princess, The House of Mirth* and *Iris*; appeared on the miniseries *Vanity Fair* (1998), and co-wrote, with John Fortune, such tv series as "Beyond a Joke," "Where was Spring?" and "Romance: Emily."

BRONDELLO, Sandy (1968—). Australian basketball player. Name variations: Alexandra Brondello. Born Aug 20, 1968, in Mackay, Australia; attended University of Western Sydney. ❖ Won a team bronze medal at Atlanta Olympics (1996), a team silver medal at Sydney Olympics (2000) and a team silver at Athens Olympics (2004); was a member of the European Cup All-Star teams (1994, 1996, 1997); in WNBA, drafted by Detroit Shock (1998), selected by Indiana Fever in expansion draft (1999), traded to Miamo Sol (2000), and signed as free agent with Seattle Storm (2003). Named Australian International Player of the Year (1992).

BRONER, E.M. (1930—). American novelist and essayist. Name variations: Esther Broner; Esther Masserman Broner. Born Esther Masserman, July 8, 1930, in Detroit, Michigan; dau. of Paul Masserman (journalist and Jewish historian) and Beatrice Weckstein Masserman (once an actress in Yiddish theater in Poland); Wayne State University, BA and MFA; Union Graduate School, PhD; m. Robert Broner (artist); children: 4. ❖ Pioneer Jewish feminist whose work addresses themes of motherhood, Jewish heritage, and religion, was a professor at Wayne State University; published 1st book, *Summer is a Foreign Land* (1966); lived in Israel (1970s); for 20 years, was one of the Seder Sisters, a group that consisted of Gloria Steinem, Bella Abzug, and Phyllis Chesler, among others; also wrote *Journal/Nocturnal and Seven Stories* (1968), *Her Mothers* (1975), *A Weave of Women* (1978) and *The Telling* (1993); with Cathy N. Davidson, edited *The Lost Tradition: Mothers and Daughters in Literature* (1980). Her story "New Nobility" was included in O. Henry Prize stories collection (1968).

❖ See also E.M. Broner Collection (1969–1997) at Brandeis University Libraries.

BRONHILL, June (1929–2005). Autralian opera singer. Born June Gough, June 26, 1929, in Broken Hill, NSW, Australia; died Jan 25, 2005; m. Richard Finney; children: daughter. ❖ Opera soprano and musical-comedy performer, adapted stage name from hometown; moved to London, became immediate success at Sadler's Wells in such musicals as *Robert and Elizabeth* and *The Sound of Music* (1954), as well as operettas including *The Merry Widow*; remained regular lead for Sadler's Wells until 1961; starred in *Lucia di Lamermoor* at Convent Garden, London (1959); returned to Australia (1970s) and sang with Australian Opera and Victorian State Opera; back in London (1981), appeared as Mother Abbess in revival of *The Sound of Music*; suffered health problems (1980s), surviving breast cancer, but was forced to retire because of acute deafness (1993); recorded some 30 records. Awarded Order of the British Empire (OBE, 1977).

BRONIEWSKA, Janina (1904–1981). Polish Communist writer and activist. Born in Kalisz, Russian Poland, Aug 5, 1904; died 1981; m. Wladyslaw Broniewski (1897–1962, revolutionary poet). ❖ Contributed articles for children to journals, including *Plomyczek* (*Little Flame*); a political militant, led the teacher's union in a number of strikes (1930s); with the Nazi invasion of Poland (1939), fled with husband to Soviet-occupied eastern Poland; joined a Moscow-sponsored political organization, the Union of Polish Patriots; also served on editorial board of journal *Nowe Widnokregi* (*New Horizons*); though she knew little about military affairs, became chief editor of journal *Polska Zbrojna* (*Armed Poland*, 1944); returning to Poland (1945), published books based on her wartime experiences, including *Marching with the First Army* (1946) and *From the Notebooks of a War Correspondent* (1953); as secretary of the Union of Polish Writers, a position that entailed supervising the political loyalty of the organization's members, earned the animosity of many of Poland's independent-minded writers. Awarded City of Warsaw Literary Prize (1949). ❖ See also *Women in World History*.

BRONNER, Augusta Fox (1881–1966). American clinical psychologist. Born in Louisville, Kentucky, 1881; died in Clearwater, Florida, 1966; Columbia University Teachers College, PhD, 1914; m. William Healy (neurologist), 1932. ❖ Pioneer in the study of delinquent and mentally challenged girls, taught for 5 years before returning to Columbia for PhD, where her groundbreaking thesis proved that, given equal determinates, girls with mental disabilities were no more likely to behave destructively than girls without disabilities (1914); became a research psychologist at Chicago Juvenile Psychopathic Institute; with neurologist William Healy, opened the Judge Baker Foundation (1971), later known as Judge Baker Children's Center.

BRONSART, Ingeborg von (1840–1913). German composer and pianist. Born Ingeborg Starck in St. Petersburg, Russia, Aug 24, 1840, of Swedish parents; died in Munich, Germany, June 17, 1913; m. Hans Bronsart von Schellendorff (known as Hans von Bronsart), 1862. ❖ A child prodigy, mentored by Franz Liszt, undertook a triumphal concert tour in Germany (1860s), including Leipzig, then went on to Paris and St. Petersburg; on marriage, because of husband's position as intendant of the Court Theater in Hanover, was forbidden to perform in public; turning to composing, scored greatest success with opera based on a Goethe text, *Jery und Baetely* (1873), which was performed in Berlin, Weimar, Wiesbaden, Königsberg and Vienna; also wrote choral works, including a patriotic work for mixed choir, *Hurrah Germania*. ❖ See also *Women in World History*.

BRONSKAYA, Eugenia (1882–1953). Russian soprano. Born Feb 1, 1882, in St. Petersburg, Russia; died in Leningrad (St. Petersburg), Dec 12, 1953. ❖ Debuted in Tbilisi and then went to Kiev for 3 years; performed in Moscow (1905–07), then Italy; was a member of the Boston Opera Co. (1909); returned to Russia (1911) and was engaged at Maryinsky and Bolshoi theaters; taught at Leningrad Conservatory (1923–50); was a well-known recording artist in early 20th century. ❖ See also *Women in World History*.

BRONSON, Betty (1906–1971). American film actress. Born Elizabeth Ada Bronson in Trenton, New Jersey, Nov 17, 1906; died 1971; m. Ludwig Lauerhaus (bond specialist), 1932; children: 1 son. ❖ After a few bit parts, became an overnight star when James M. Barrie cast her in the title role of the 1st film version of *Peter Pan* (1924); was never able to sustain her initial popularity; other films include *Are Parents People?* (1925), *A Kiss for Cinderella* (1926), *Ritzy* (1927), *The Singing Fool* (1928) and *The Medicine Man* (1930); following marriage (1932), settled in Asheville, North Carolina; attempted a comeback in *Yodelin' Kid from Pine Ridge* with Gene Autry (1937); on tv, appeared in *Dr. Kildare, My Three Sons* and *Marcus Welby, M.D.* ❖ See also *Women in World History*.

BRONSON, Lillian (1902–1995). American actress. Born Oct 21, 1902, in Lockport, NY; died Aug 2, 1995, in San Clemente, California. ❖ Films include *Family Honeymoon, The Hucksters* and *Spencer's Mountain*.

BRONTË, Anne (1820–1849). English author. Name variations: (pseudonym) Acton Bell. Born Anne Brontë at Thornton, near Bradford, Yorkshire, Jan 1820; died of consumption in Scarborough, May 28, 1849; dau. of Maria Branwell Brontë and Reverend Patrick Brontë (cleric-author). ❖ Victorian author of *Agnes Grey* and *The Tenant of Wildfell Hall*, was the youngest of the Brontë sisters; mother died within months of her birth; with elder sister Emily, developed a world called Gondal; served for 4 years as governess to Robinson family at Thorp Green (1835–39), where she witnessed brother Branwell's attempts to seduce Mrs. Robinson; with sisters Charlotte and Emily, published *Poems by Currer, Ellis and Acton Bell* (1846); published *Agnes Grey* based on a brief experience as governess to the Ingham family (1847); wrote *The Tenant of Wildfell Hall* as a warning against the type of existence that claimed her brother's life; contracted consumption after the deaths of her brother and sister Emily; journeyed to the seaside with Charlotte in hopes of a cure, but damp air hastened her demise; was buried in Scarborough within 6 months of Emily's death; embraced a staunchly religious view in her life and work. ❖ See also Ernest Dimnet, *The Brontë Sisters* (trans. by Louise Morgan Sill, Harcourt, 1928); Rebecca Fraser, *The Brontës* (Fawcett, 1988); Janet Barker, *The Brontës* (St. Martin, 1995); and *Women in World History*.

BRONTË, Charlotte (1816–1855). English author. Name variations: Charlotte Bronte; Charlotte Brontë Nichols; Mrs. Arthur Nichols; (pseudonym) Currer Bell. Born Charlotte Brontë at Thornton in Yorkshire, April 21, 1816; died at Haworth in Yorkshire, Mar 31, 1855; dau. of Maria Branwell Brontë and Reverend Patrick Brontë (Methodist cleric-author); m. Arthur B. Nichols (curate), June 29, 1854, at age 38. ❖ Author of *Jane Eyre* and elder sister to writers Emily and Anne Brontë, whose creative and passionate nature remained locked in perpetual combat with the moral strictures that governed the famous Victorian "cult of womanhood"; lost her mother and 2 older sisters to childbirth complications and consumption by age 8; moved to Haworth (1821); briefly attended Cowan Bridge School, which formed the basis for the austere and unhealthy Lowood of *Jane Eyre*; at 15, began a year of study at Roe Head, which provided governess training for young women (1831); taught 3 years at Roe Head, followed by a period of physical and mental recovery at Haworth before she assumed the duties of a nursery governess (1839); with Emily, enrolled at the Pensionnat de Demoiselles, run by the Heger family in Brussels; saw publication of *Poems by Currer, Ellis and Acton Bell* (1846); following publication of *Jane Eyre* (1847), was transformed into a *cause celèbre*, even though her identity remained ambiguous and her unconventional novel and heroine had inspired considerable controversy; by age 33, saw 2 younger sisters and only brother die within months of each other; married late in life and died within 9 months, from illness associated with pregnancy and, most likely, consumption; other writings include *Shirley, A Tale* (1849), *Villette* (1853), *The Professor, A Tale* (1857), in which she critiqued social hypocrisy and the limitations faced by women and the working class, *Legends of Angria* (1933), *The Twelve Adventurers and Other Stories* (1925) and *Five Novelettes* (1971); a literary giant, her reputation has eclipsed that of her younger sisters, owing to her prodigious literary production. ❖ See also Margaret Howard Blom, *Charlotte Brontë* (Twayne, 1977); Penny Boumelha, *Charlotte Brontë* (Indiana U. Press, 1990); Elizabeth Gaskell, *The Life of Charlotte Brontë* (Penguin, 1975); Ernest Dimnet, *The Brontë Sisters* (trans. by Louise Morgan Sill, Harcourt, 1928); Rebecca Fraser, *The Brontës* (Fawcett, 1988); Janet Barker, *The Brontës* (St. Martin, 1995); and *Women in World History*.

BRONTË, Emily (1818–1848). English author. Name variations: (pseudonym) Ellis Bell. Born Emily Jane Brontë at Thornton, near Bradford, Yorkshire, July 30, 1818; died of consumption at Haworth, Dec 19, 1848; dau. of Maria Branwell Brontë and Reverend Patrick Brontë (Methodist cleric-author). ❖ Victorian author of *Wuthering Heights* and middle sister to writers Charlotte and Anne Brontë, who withdrew into a private imaginative world; following death of mother, moved to Haworth (1821); was reared by an austere and intellectual cleric-father amid the bleak and secluded Yorkshire moors; with younger sister Anne, developed a rich imaginative world called Gondal, that formed the basis for early poems, which were discovered by elder sister Charlotte and published in *Poems by Currer, Ellis and Acton Bell* (1846); published

Wuthering Heights (1847), which received strong, condemnatory reviews and sparked great controversy and speculation about author's identity, which she resolutely guarded until her death; contracted consumption (1848), one month after her brother Branwell died of the same disease and less than 6 months before Anne succumbed as well; holds a place of primacy in the annals of British literature. ❖ See also Richard Benvenuto, *Emily Brontë* (Twayne, 1982); Edward Chitham, *A Life of Emily Brontë* (Blackwell, 1987); Winifred Gérin, *Emily Brontë* (Oxford U. Press, 1971); Muriel Spark and Derek Stanford. *Emily Brontë: Her Life and Work* (Coward-McCann, 1966); Ernest Dimnet, *The Brontë Sisters* (trans. by Louise Morgan Sill, Harcourt, 1928); Rebecca Fraser, *The Brontës* (Fawcett, 1988); Janet Barker, *The Brontës* (St. Martin, 1995); and *Women in World History*.

BROOK, Helen (1907–1997). English family-planning proponent. Name variations: Lady Helen Brook. Born Helen Grace Mary Knewstub, Oct 12, 1907, in England; died Oct 3, 1997; m. George Whittaker, 1925 (div.); m. Sir Robin Brook, 1937. ❖ Served as director of Marie Stopes Memorial Clinic, London (1959–64), and went against rules so as to provide unmarried women with family-planning advice; founded Brook Advisory Centre for Young People, London (1964), and angered public for providing advice to unmarried women under 16. Made freeman of City of London (1993) and CBE (1995).

BROOKE, Annette (1947—). English politician and member of Parliament. Born Annette Kelly, June 7, 1947. ❖ Served as mayor of Poole (1997–98); representing Liberal Democrats, elected to House of Commons at Westminster (2001, 2005) for Mid Dorset and Poole North; named Liberal Democratic whip (2001).

BROOKE, Charlotte (1740–1793). Irish writer. Born Charlotte Brooke in Rantavan, Co. Cavan, Ireland, 1740; died in Kildare, Ireland, 1793; one of 21 children of Lettice (Digby) Brooke (died 1772) and Henry Brooke (dramatist, died 1783); educated at home, learned Gaelic in addition to traditional lessons; never married; no children. ❖ Author and translator of poetry from ancient Irish to English, became her father's primary companion following mother's death; translated a collection of poetry from the ancient Irish, *Reliques of Irish Poetry*, which was published to good reviews (1788); contributed anonymously to other anthologies; her only novel, *Emma, or the Foundling in the Wood*, was released posthumously (1803).

BROOKE, Cynthia (1875–1949). Australian-born actress. Born Dec 15, 1875, in Australia; died Sept 11, 1949; m. F.G. Latham. ❖ Made stage debut in London in *The Green Bushes* (1890); had 1st success as Paula in *The Second Mrs. Tanqueray* on tour (1894–95); other plays include *The Girl I Left Behind Me, The Liars, The Price of Peace, The Lady from Texas, Dr. Jekyll and Mr. Hyde* and *Joseph and His Brethren*; appeared in Australia and New York.

BROOKE, Evelyn Gertrude (1879–1962). New Zealand nurse and hospital matron. Name variations: Evelyn Gertrude Brown. Born Sept 13, 1879, in New Plymouth, New Zealand; died Feb 11, 1962, in Wellington, New Zealand; dau. of Thomas William Brooke (carpenter) and Kate Theresa (Coad) Brooke; m. William John Brown, 1925. ❖ Worked as private nurse before accepting position as ward sister at Wellington Hospital (1910); sailed with New Zealand Expeditionary Force to German Samoa (1914), then served on hospital ships (1915–16); returned to New Zealand as matron of military hospital at Trentham before becoming matron on hospital ship bound for England (1916); served as matron of New Zealand Hospital for Officers at Brighton until end of 1917; transferred to New Zealand Stationary Hospital at Wisques, France (c. 1918); returned to New Zealand to accept post as matron at military hospital at Featherston (1919); served as matron of hospital for disabled veterans in Christchurch (1921). ❖ See also *Dictionary of New Zealand Biography* (Vol. 3).

BROOKE, Frances (1724–1789). English novelist, poet and dramatist. Name variations: Mary Singleton, Spinster. Born Frances Moore in Claypole, Lincolnshire, England, Jan 4, 1724; died in Sleaford, Lincolnshire, England, Jan 23, 1789; dau. of Mary (Knowles) Moore (died 1737) and William Moore (Anglican minister, died 1727); grew up in Lincolnshire and Peterborough; m. Reverend John Brooke, DD (rector of Colney, Norfolk), in 1756 (died 1789); children: John Moore (b. 1757, minister). ❖ Launched periodical, *The Old Maid*, writing under the name Mary Singleton, Spinster, producing 37 issues before ceasing publication in July 1756; undertook translations, most notably Marie-Jeanne Riccoboni's French epistolary novel, which in English became *Letters from Juliet, Lady Catesby* (1760); also wrote the successful and sentimental *History of Lady Julia Mandeville* (1763), which had 10 editions; sailed for Canada to join husband (1763); began *The History of Emily Montague*, a 4-vol. narrative depicting life in Canada (1767), which was the 1st Canadian novel and well-received; with actress Mary Ann Yates, managed Haymarket Opera House (1773–78), where her play *The Siege of Sinope* and musicals *Rosina* and *Marian* were produced (1780s) and remained popular for many years. ❧ See also Lorraine McMullen, *Frances Brooke and Her Work* (ECW, 1983); and *Women in World History*.

BROOKE, Hillary (1914–1999). American actress. Born Beatrice Peterson, Sept 8, 1914, in Astoria, LI, NY; died May 25, 1999, in Fallbrook, California; m. Jack Voglin; m. Raymond A. Klune, 1960 (died 1988). ❧ Made film debut in *New Faces of 1937*; other films include *The Philadelphia Story, Dr. Jekyll and Mr. Hyde, Mr. and Mrs. North, Lady in the Dark, Jane Eyre, Ministry of Fear, The Fuller Brush Man* and *The Man Who Knew Too Much*; appeared regularly on "My Little Margie" (1952–54) and "The Abbott and Costello Show" (1952).

BROOKE, Lady (1861–1938). *See Greville, Frances Evelyn.*

BROOKE-ROSE, Christine (1923—). British novelist, poet and literary critic. Name variations: Christine Brooke Rose. Born Christine Frances Evelyn Rose, Jan 16, 1923, in Geneva, Switzerland; dau. of Alfred Northbrook Rose (died 1934) and Evelyn Blanche (Brooke) Rose (became a Bendictine nun, Mother Anselm); Somerville College, BA, 1949, MA, 1953; University College, London, PhD, 1954; m. Rodney Ian Shirley Bax, 1944 (div. 1948); m. Jerzy Peterkiewicz (Polish poet and novelist), 1948 (sep. 1968); m. Claude Brooke, 1981 (div. 1982). ❧ During WWII, worked at Bletchley Park in British Women's Auxiliary Air Force; moved to Paris (1968) and became teacher of Anglo-American literature at University of Paris VIII; early novels, which are mostly satirical, include *The Languages of Love* (1957) and *The Middlemen: A Satire* (1961); influenced by French postmodern novels (1960s), wrote *Out* (1964), *Such* (1966) and *Between* (1968), as well as her science-fiction novels, *Amalgamemnon* (1984), *Xorandor* (1986), *Verbivore* (1990) and *Textermination* (1991), which form a loose quartet; also wrote literary criticism, including *A Grammar of Metaphor* (1958), *A ZBC of Ezra Pound* (1971), *A Structural Analysis of Pound's Usura Canto* (1976) and *Stories, Theories, and Things* (1991). ❧ See also Sarah Birch, *Christine Brooke-Rose and Contemporary Fiction* (Oxford U. Press, 1994).

BROOKNER, Anita (1928—). British novelist and art historian. Born July 16, 1928, in London, England; dau. of Newson Brookner and Maude Brookner; attended King's College, University of London. ❧ Renowned art historian, was a visiting lecturer at University of Reading (1959–64), then the 1st woman to serve as Slade Professor of Fine Arts at Cambridge (1967–68); a fellow of New Hall, Cambridge, was a reader at Courtauld Institute of Art (1968–88); published works in 18th- and 19th-century art history, including *Watteau* (1968), *The Genius of the Future: Studies in French Art Criticism* (1971) and *Jacques-Louis David* (1980); highly regarded as a practitioner of neo-realist fiction and compared to Woolf, James and Proust, published 22 novels, including *A Start in Life* (1981), *Providence* (1982), *Look at Me* (1983), *Hotel du Lac* (1984), *Family and Friends* (1985), *A Misalliance* (1986), *A Friend from England* (1987), *Latecomers* (1988), *Brief Lives* (1990), *Fraud* (1992), *A Private View* (1994), *Altered States* (1996), *The Bay of Angels* (2001) and *The Next Big Thing* (2001). ❧ See also George Soule, *Four British Women Novelists: Anita Brookner, Margaret Drabble, Iris Murdoch, Barbara Pym* (Scarecrow, 1998).

BROOKS, Angie (1928—). Liberian diplomat and lawyer. Name variations: Angie Brooks-Randolph. Born Angie Elizabeth Brooks in Virginia, Montserrado Co., Liberia, Aug 24, 1928; dau. of a back-country minister of the African Methodist Episcopal Zion Church; Shaw University, Raleigh, North Carolina, BA in social science, 1949; University of Wisconsin, Madison, LLB and MSc in social science and international relations, 1952; University College law school of London University, 1952–53; m. at 14 (div.); m. Isaac Randolph, April 27, 1970; children: (1st m.) Wynston and Richard. ❧ Admitted as a counselor-at-law to the Supreme Court in Liberia (1953); taught at Liberia University (1954–58), where she helped establish a department of law; began long association with United Nations by filling a vacancy on the Liberian delegation (1954); was appointed assistant secretary of state by President Tubman (1958); after serving as the Liberian delegate to UN for 15 years, was elected overwhelmingly to the post of president of the 24th session of the General Assembly (1969), the 1st African woman to serve as such; was also the 1st woman and the 1st African to serve as president of the

Trusteeship Council, the UN's watchdog over its trust territories; championed the advancement of women, particularly Africans. ❧ See also *Women in World History*.

BROOKS, Charlotte (1918—). American photographer. Born in New York, NY, 1918; Brooklyn College, BA, 1940; graduate work in psychology, University of Minnesota, 1941. ❧ Apprenticed with dance photographer Barbara Morgan (c. 1944); was staff photographer for a chain of newspapers and worked on a 1,000-picture project for Standard Oil; became the 1st woman staff photographer for *Look* magazine (1951), a position she held until the magazine folded (1971); at International Center of Photography in New York, participated in the group exhibition *Roy Stryker: USA* (1943–50), which later toured; had solo exhibition at New Britain Museum of American Art (CT), entitled *A Poem of Portraits* (1994).

BROOKS, Dolores (1946—). American singer. Name variations: Dolores "La La" Brooks; The Crystals. Born 1946 in Brooklyn, NY. ❧ As an original member of girl-group The Crystals, the 1st act signed to Phil Spector's Phillies label (1961), had such hit singles as "There's No Other (Like My Baby)" (1961), "Uptown" (1962), "Da Doo Ron Ron" (1963) and "Then He Kissed Me" (1964); also had #1 hit with "He's a Rebel" but it was recorded by session singers The Blossoms, not The Crystals. Crystals albums include *He's a Rebel* (1963) and *The Best of the Crystals* (1992).

BROOKS, Geraldine (1925–1977). American actress. Born Geraldine Stroock in New York, NY, Oct 29, 1925; died in Riverhead, New York, June 19, 1977; dau. of a costume manufacturer and designer; attended American Academy of Dramatic Arts; m. 2nd husband, novelist-screenwriter Budd Schulberg, 1964. ❧ Made film debut in *Possessed* (1947); after playing ingénue roles in a number of films, including *Cry Wolf* (1947), *The Reckless Moment* (1949) and *Challenge for Lassie* (1950), grew disillusioned with the quality of her pictures and went to Italy to play Anna Magnani's younger sister in *Volcano*; stayed in Europe to make a few more films before returning to US, where she concentrated mostly on stage and tv work; in later years, was an accomplished nature photographer, publishing a book of bird photographs, *Swan Watch* (1975); other films include *The Green Glove* (1952), *Street of Sinners* (1956) and *Johnny Tiger* (1966).

BROOKS, Gwendolyn (1917–2000). African-American writer. Born Gwendolyn Brooks, June 7, 1917, in Topeka, Kansas; grew up in Chicago; died Dec 3, 2000, in Chicago, Illinois; dau. of David Anderson Brooks (mechanic and janitor) and Keziah Corine (Wims) Brooks (teacher and homemaker); graduate of Wilson Junior College, 1936; m. Henry Blakely (writer), 1938; children: Henry Jr. (b. 1940), Nora (b. 1951). ❧ Pulitzer Prize-winning poet, novelist, and teacher, published the poem "Eventide" in *American Childhood* magazine at 13; while in high school, contributed to weekly poetry column in *Chicago Defender*, where she would ultimately publish nearly 80 poems; became active in National Association for the Advancement of Colored People (NAACP); received Midwestern Writers' Conference poetry award (1943); published *A Street in Bronzeville,* delineating the indignities of racial injustice and the particular concerns of women (1945); made a fellow of American Academy of Arts and Letters; won Pulitzer Prize for Poetry for *Annie Allen* (1950), the 1st African-American to do so; wrote reviews for a number of Chicago newspapers and published a book of poetry for children, *Bronzeville Boys and Girls;* next major volume of verse, *The Bean Eaters,* appeared during civil-rights movement (1960), followed by *Selected Poems* (1964); published only novel, *In the Mecca* (1968); later works, including *Riot* (1969), *Family Pictures* (1971) and *Beckonings* (1975), deal more with the black experience while early work seemed to focus more on individuals; taught creative writing at Elmhurst College, Northeastern Illinois State, and University of Wisconsin, and took a position at City University of New York as Distinguished Professor of the Arts (1969); named poet laureate of Illinois (1968); appointed poetry consultant to Library of Congress (1985); published *Gottschalk and the Grande Tarantelle* (1988); became professor of English at Chicago State University (1990); was the recipient of more public honors than any other African-American poet, yet her work was not widely included in American literature courses until late in her career. Received National Medal of Arts from President Bill Clinton (1995). ❧ See also autobiography *Report from Part One* (Broadside, 1972); Maria K. Mootry and Gary Smith, eds., *A Life Distilled: Gwendolyn Brooks, Her Poetry and Fiction* (U. of Illinois, 1987); Harry B. Shaw, *Gwendolyn Brooks* (Twayne, 1980); and *Women in World History*.

BROOKS, Hadda (1916–2002). African-American singer and pianist. Born Hadda Hapgood, Oct 29, 1916, in Boyle Heights, Los Angeles, California; died Nov 21, 2002, in Los Angeles; m. Earl Morrison (played for Harlem Globetrotters), 1941 (died 1942). ❖ Torch singer, known as Queen of the Boogie, trained as a classical pianist; began recording boogie-woogie instrumentals for Modern Records (1945), including her 1st hit, "Swingin' the Boogie"; had a number of hits, including "That's My Desire," "Don't Take Your Love from Me," "Trust in Me" and "Dream" (1940s–50s); on Channel 13 in Los Angeles, became the 1st black woman in the nation to host her own tv variety show, "The Hadda Brooks Show" (1951); also sang in several films; retired (1971); was rediscovered (1990s) and played in Johnny Depp's Viper Room, among others. Received Pioneer Award from Rhythm and Blues Foundation (1993).

BROOKS, Harriet (1876–1933). Canadian scientist. Born Harriet Brooks, July 2, 1876, in Exeter, Ontario, Canada; died in Montreal, April 17, 1933; dau. of George Brooks and Elizabeth Agnes (Worden) Brooks; McGill University, BA, 1898, MA, 1901; m. Frank Pitcher (physics instructor at McGill), 1907; children: 3, of which 2 died while in their teens. ❖ Pioneer nuclear scientist, who made significant contributions to the field of radiation, became Sir Ernest Rutherford's 1st graduate student and a key member of what would become his research team; received appointment as nonresident tutor in mathematics at Royal Victoria College (1899), the women's college of McGill University; worked with J.J. Thomson in the Cavendish Laboratory at Cambridge University; began teaching physics at Barnard College in NY (1905); worked on research staff of Marie Curie; was the 1st scientist to show that the radioactive substance emitted from thorium was a gas with a molecular weight of 40 to 100, a discovery crucial to the determination that the elements undergo some transmutation in radioactive decay. ❖ See also Marelene Rayner-Canham and Geoffrey Rayner-Canham, *Harriet Brooks: Pioneer Nuclear Physicist* (McGill-Queen's U. Press, 1992); and *Women in World History*.

BROOKS, Lela (b. 1908). Canadian speedskater. Name variations: Lela Brooks Potter, Lela Brooks Bleich. Born Feb 17 (some sources cite Feb 7), 1908, in Toronto, Ontario, Canada; m. 2nd husband Russ Campbell (died 1967); m. Clifford Bleich, 1972. ❖ Set 6 world records (1925); came in 1st all-around, World championships (1926) and North American Indoor championships (1935); retired (1936). Inducted into Canadian Sports Hall of Fame.

BROOKS, Louise (1906–1985). American actress. Born Nov 14, 1906, in Cherryvale, Kansas; died Aug 8, 1985, in Rochester, New York; dau. of Leonard Porter Brooks (lawyer and assistant attorney general for the state of Kansas) and Myra Rude Brooks; m. Edward Sutherland, 1926 (div., 1928); m. Deering Davis, 1934 (div. 6 months later); no children. ❖ Unique actress, whose highly memorable performance in *Pandora's Box* helped make that film a landmark in the history of international cinema, left home at 15 to pursue a career as a dancer in New York City; studied with Ruth St. Denis and Ted Shawn, before going on tour with their company (1922); danced in George White's *Scandals* (1924) and Ziegfeld *Follies* (1925); signed 5-year contract with Paramount at 19 (1925); with her signature bangs, appeared in 14 films (1925–29), including *The American Venus* (1926), *The Canary Murder Case* (1928) and *A Girl in Every Port* (1928); cast by filmmaker G.W. Pabst to star as Lulu in *Pandora's Box* (1928), became the dominant presence in the silent German film; made only 2 more films in Europe: *Diary of a Lost Girl*, also directed by Pabst (1929), and *Prix de Beauté* (1930), based on a script by René Clair; in Hollywood, made 7 more pictures after returning from Europe, the last in 1938; went into retirement at 34, spending the rest of her life painting, translating books, and writing penetrating character sketches of Hollywood stars. ❖ See also memoir *Lulu in Hollywood* (Knopf, 1982); *Louise Brooks: Portrait of an Anti-Star* (ed. by Roland Jaccard, New York Zoetrope, 1980); Barry Paris, *Louise Brooks* (Anchor, 1990); and *Women in World History*.

BROOKS, Maria Gowen (c. 1794–1845). American poet. Name variations: Maria Gowan Brooks; (pseudonym) Maria del Occidente. Born Abigail Gowen (also seen as Gowan), c. 1794, in Medford, Massachusetts; baptized as Mary Abigail Brooks; died Nov 11, 1845, in Matanzas, Cuba; dau. of Eleanor (Cutter) Gowen and William Gowen (goldsmith); m. John Brooks (Boston merchant), Aug 26, 1810 (died 1823); children: 2 sons, Edgar and Horace, and 2 stepsons. ❖ Referred to by Robert Southey as "the most empassioned and most imaginative of all poetesses," published small verse collection *Judith, Esther, and Other Poems* (1820); known primarily for her romance *Zóphïel; or the Bride of

Seven, published under the pseudonym Maria del Occidente (1833), also wrote romantic autobiography *Idomen: or the Vale of Yumuri* which was serialized in the Boston *Saturday Evening Gazette* (1838); financed a limited edition of *Idomen* (1843).

BROOKS, Mary (1914–1995). *See Brooks, Phyllis.*

BROOKS, Matilda M. (1888–1981). American scientist. Name variations: Matilda Moldenhauer Brooks. Born Matilda Moldenhauer in Pittsburgh, Pennsylvania, possibly Oct 16, 1888; died possibly 1981 in San Francisco, California; dau. of Rudolph and Selma (Neuffer) Moldenhauer; University of Pittsburgh, BA and MA; Harvard University, PhD, 1920; m. Sumner Cushing Brooks (zoologist), 1917 (died 1948). ❖ Biologist who discovered an antidote for cyanide and carbon monoxide poisoning, worked as a biologist for US Public Health Service before her appointment as a research biologist at the University of California, where her husband was also employed. ❖ See also *Women in World History*.

BROOKS, Pauline (1912–1967). American actress. Born Oct 1, 1912, in NYC; died June 7, 1967, in Glendale, California; m. Carl B. Bruck (major). ❖ Films include *Alibi Joe, Make a Million, Age of Indiscretion* and *Beauty for Sale*.

BROOKS, Phyllis (1914–1995). American stage and screen actress. Name variations: Mary Brooks. Born Phyllis Steiller (also seen as Weiler), July 18, 1914, in Boise, Idaho; died Aug 1, 1995, in Cape Neddick, Maine; m. Torbert H. MacDonald (then a Harvard gridiron hero who had roomed with John F. Kennedy, later MA congressional representative), 1945 (died 1976). ❖ Briefly known as Mary Brooks, appeared on Broadway in *Stage Door, Panama Hattie* and *Road Trip*; films include *Rebecca of Sunnybrook Farm, In Old Chicago, Slightly Honorable, Lady in the Dark, Charlie Chan in Honolulu* and *Dangerous Passage*.

BROOKS, Romaine (1874–1970). American artist. Name variations: Beatrice Romaine Goddard. Born Beatrice Romaine Goddard, May 1, 1874, in Rome, Italy; died Dec 7, 1970, in Nice, France; dau. of Major Henry Goddard and Ella Mary Waterman (heiress); studied art at La Scuola Nazionale, Rome, 1896–97; attended Académie Colarossi in Paris, 1899; m. John Ellingham Brooks, June 13, 1903 (sep. 1904); no children. ❖ Portrait artist, whose main theme was "the essential loneliness of the human predicament," went to Capri (1899), where she rented a small studio and mingled with the expatriate community of writers and artists; received her 1st commission for a portrait of R. Barra, an American writer living on Capri; inherited an apartment in Paris, 8 additional apartments around France, and the Château Grimaldi (1902); relying on an extremely limited range of tones (black, white, and grey), produced masterful character studies of women; had 1st exhibit of 13 paintings in the Galeries Durand-Ruel, which established her reputation as a mature, first-rate artist (1910); met and fell in love with Natalie Clifford Barney (1915), remaining close to Barney for over 50 years; had solo exhibition of drawings in New York (1935); wrote memoirs (1930s); painted last portrait (1961); paintings include *Portrait of John Rowland Fothergill* (1905), *Azalées Blanches* (1910), *Le Trajet* (c. 1911), *Gabriele d'Annunzio, Le Poète en Exil* (1912), *Jean Cocteau à Epoque de la Grand Roué* (1914), *Ida Rubenstein* (1917), *Renata Borgatti au Piano* (c. 1920), *Miss Natalie Barney, L'Amazone* (1920), *Una, Lady Troubridge* (1924) and *Marchese Uberto Strozzi* (1961). ❖ See also Meryle Secrest, *Between Me and Life: A Biography of Romaine Brooks* (Doubleday, 1974); and *Women in World History*.

BROOKS-RANDOLPH, Angie (1928—). *See Brooks, Angie.*

BROOKSHAW, Dorothy (1912—). Canadian runner. Born Dec 20, 1912. ❖ At Berlin Olympics, won a bronze medal in the 4 x 100-meter relay (1936).

BROOM, Mrs. Albert (1863–1939). *See Broom, Christina.*

BROOM, Christina (1863–1939). British photographer. Name variations: Mrs. Albert Broom. Born Christina Livingston in 1863, probably in London; died 1939, probably in London; m. Albert Broom; children: Winifred; may have been others. ❖ Often called Britain's 1st woman press photographer, launched career with a shot of the prince and princess of Wales (Mary of Teck) opening tramways at Westminster (1903); was soon documenting national and international events, including the effects of World War I on the home front, 30 years of Oxford and Cambridge boatrace crews, and Edith Cavell's funeral; became especially well known for her documentation of woman suffrage marches and exhibitions; also remained the official photographer of the Senior

Regiment of the First Life Guards until her death. ❖ See also *Women in World History.*

BROOMALL, Anna (1847–1931). American obstetrician. Name variations: Anna Elizabeth Broomall. Born Mar 4, 1847, in Upper Chichester Township, Pennsylvania; died April 4, 1931, in Chester, PA; dau. of John Martin Broomall and Elizabeth (Booth) Broomall (died 1848); graduate of Women's Medical College of Pennsylvania, 1871; studied obstetrics in Vienna and Paris. ❖ As one of 1st woman medical students permitted to attend clinics at Pennsylvania Hospital, sparked protests by male students (1869); appointed chief resident physician at Woman's Hospital and instructor of obstetrics at Woman's Medical College (1875), serving as professor of obstetrics (1880–1903); established Out-Practice Maternity Department in an impoverished area of South Philadelphia, where students received clinical experience while providing high-quality care (1888); maintained private practice and served as gynecologist to Friends' Asylum for the Insane, Frankford, PA (beginning 1883); became one of 1st women members of Philadelphia Obstetrical Society (1892) and was 1st woman to publish in their *Transactions;* served as curator of museum and library for Delaware County Historical Society (1923–31).

BROOME, Lady Mary Anne (1831–1911). *See Barker, Mary Anne.*

BROOMFIELD, Agnes (c. 1841–1903). *See Addison, Agnes.*

BROPHY, Brigid (1929–1995). British-born writer. Born Brigid Antonia Brophy in London, England, June 12, 1929; died in Louth, Lincolnshire, Aug 7, 1995; dau. of Irish parents, John Brophy (novelist and chief fiction critic of *Daily Telegraph*) and Charis Grundy Brophy (feminist and teacher); studied classics at St. Hugh's College, Oxford; m. Sir Michael Levey (author and former director of National Gallery, London), 1954; children: Katharine. ❖ Novelist, critic and playwright, who was one of the most acute and witty critics of 1960s and 1970s, published 1st novel, *Hackenfeller's Ape* (1953); published 4 novels (1962–64) of which 2, *Flesh* and *The Finishing Touch,* are considered among her best; published *In Transit* (1969) and *Palace Without Chairs* (1978), speaking out against sexual prejudice, particularly homophobia, at a time when homosexual activity was still illegal in Britain; had a high profile on tv, radio, and in the press (1960s–70s); with Maureen Duffy, formed the Writers' Action Group (1972) and served as vice-chair of the British Copyright Council (1976–80); was diagnosed with multiple sclerosis (1984), an illness that led to increasing physical infirmity; her novels and critical writings reflected a polymathic range of interests: animal rights, atheism, feminism, opera, pacifism, psychoanalysis and vegetarianism; writings include *The Finishing Touch* (1963), *Mozart the Dramatist* (1964), *Don't Never Forget* (Cape, 1966), (with Michael Levey and Charles Osborne) *Fifty Works of Literature We Could Do Without* (1967), *Beardsley and His World* (1976) and *Baroque 'n' Roll* (1987). ❖ See also *Women in World History.*

BROQUEDIS, Marguerite (1893–1983). French tennis player. Name variations: Marguerite Billout; Marguerite Bordes. Born April 17, 1893, in Pau, France; died April 23, 1983, in Orléans, France. ❖ At Stockholm Olympics, won a bronze medal in the mixed doubles–outdoor courts and a gold medal in singles (1912); won World championship (1912); at French Open (open only to French nationals), was runner-up to Jeanne Matthey (1910 and 1911), then singles champion (1913 and 1914, beating Suzanne Lenglen) and doubles champion with Yvonne Bourgeois (1924); won mixed doubles at Roland Garros with Jean Borotra (1927).

BROSNIHAN, Diane (1963–2001). *See Golden, Diana.*

BROSSARD, Nicole (1943—). Canadian poet, novelist and essayist. Born 1943 in Montreal, Canada; University of Montreal, BA, 1965. ❖ Active in avant-garde poetry movement as well as feminist and lesbian circles, described her work as "writing in the feminine"; co-founded and edited *La Barre du jour* (1965–75), *Les Têtes de pioche* (1976–79) and *La Nouvelle Barre du jour* (1977–79); poetry collections include *Aubé a la saison* (1965), *L'echo bouge beau* (1968), *Le Centre blanc* (1970), *Amantes* (1980) and *Mauve* (1985); fiction includes *Un livre* (1970), *French Kiss* (1974), *Le sens apparent* (1980), and *le Désert Mauve* (1987); also published the essay collection, *La lettre aérienne* (1985); most works translated into English, German, and Spanish. Received Governor General's Prize for *Mécanique jongleuse* (1974) and *Double impression* (1984); won Athanas-David Prize (1991).

BROSTEDT, Charlotte (1958—). *See Montgomery, Charlotte.*

BROTHERS, Donna. *See Barton, Donna.*

BROTHERS, Joyce (1928—). American psychologist. Name variations: Dr. Joyce Brothers. Born Joyce Diane Bauer, Sept 20, 1928, in New York,

NY; graduate of Cornell University; Columbia University, PhD; m. Milton Brothers (internist), 1949 (died); children: Lisa Brothers. ❖ Came to national attention as a winning contestant on tv's "The $64,000 Question"; was a member of the faculty of Hunter College and Columbia University; known as the dean of American psychologists, had her own show on NBC Radio Network; often appeared on tv and in film, usually as herself; wrote a regular column for *Good Housekeeping* magazine and a daily syndicated column for over 350 newspapers.

BROTHERTON, Alice Williams (1848–1930). American poet and magazine writer. Born Alice Williams in Cambridge, Indiana, 1848; died 1930; dau. of Ruth Dodge (Johnson) Williams and Alfred Baldwin Williams; educated in various private schools, as well as St. Louis Eliot Grammar School and Woodward High School of Cincinnati; m. William Ernest Brotherton, 1890; children: 2 sons, 1 daughter (eldest son died 1890). ❖ Contributed prose and verse to periodicals such as *The Century, The Atlantic* and *The Independent;* books include *Beyond the Veil* (1886), *What the Wind Told the Tree-Tops* (prose and verse for children), *The Sailing of King Olaf, and Other Poems* (1887); was in attendance at the Congress of Women in Chicago (1893), contributing the poem "The Feast of Columbia, 1493–1893."

BROUGH, Fanny Whiteside (1854–1914). English actress. Born July 8, 1854, in Paris, France; died Nov 30, 1914; dau. of Robert Brough and Elizabeth (Romer) Brough; niece of William and Lionel Brough; sister of Robert Brough; half-sister of Brenda Gibson (actress); cousin of Mary Brough (actress); m. R.S. Boleyn. ❖ Made stage debut in a pantomime written by her uncle William (1869); made London debut in the title role of *Fernande* (1870); subsequently appeared in *Money, Forced from Home, The World, Harvest, The Lodgers, Civil War, Pleasure, The Wife's Secret, Dear Bill, The Times, A Woman's Revenge, The Man from Blankley's, The Whip* and *The Sins of Society;* came to prominence with portrayal of Mary O'Brien in *The Real Little Lord Fauntleroy* (1888); was president of Theatrical Ladies' Guild.

BROUGH, Louise (1923—). American tennis player. Name variations: A. Louise Brough, Louise Brough Clapp. Pronunciation: Bruff. Born Althea Louise Brough, Mar 11, 1923, in Oklahoma City, Oklahoma; educated at University of Southern California. ❖ Won Wimbledon singles title (1948, 1949, 1950, 1955), doubles title with Margaret Osborne du Pont (1946, 1948, 1949, 1950, 1954) and mixed doubles (1946, 1947, 1948, 1950); won British women's singles (1948, 1949, 1950); won British women's doubles (1946), French doubles (1946, 1947, 1949), and US doubles 12 times (1942–50, 1955–57); won US mixed doubles (1942, 1947, 1948, 1949). ❖ See also *Women in World History.*

BROUGH, Mary (1863–1934). English stage actress. Born April 16, 1863, in London, England; died Sept 30, 1934, in London; dau. of Margaret (Simpson) Brough and Lionel Brough; cousin of Fanny Whiteside Brough (actress). ❖ Specializing in comedy, made stage debut in Brighton in *Nine Points of the Law* (1881); made London debut in *She Stoops to Conquer* (1881); subsequent appearances include *What the Public Wants, The Brass Bottle, The Prodigal Son, Mr. Wu, Double Dutch, Summertime, Fantasia, Pollyanna,* and as Peggoty in *David Copperfield;* made film debut in *Beauty and the Barge,* followed by *A Sister to Assist 'Er, Mr. Pickwick, Lily of the Alley, Rookery Nook, On Approval, Plunder* and *A Night Like This.*

BROUGHTON, Phyllis (1862–1926). English actress, dancer, and singer. Born 1862 in England; died July 21, 1926. ❖ Made London stage debut in *The 40 Thieves* (1880), followed by *Indiana, The Old Guard, Follow the Drum, Paul Jones, Marjorie, Joan of Arc, Blue-Eyed Susan, In Town, Hot House Peach, Biarritz, A Night Out, The Earl and the Girl* and *The Vagabond King,* among others.

BROUGHTON, Rhoda (1840–1920). British novelist. Born Rhoda Broughton in Denbighshire, North Wales, Nov 29, 1840; died in Headington Hill, Oxford, England, June 5, 1920; dau. of Jane (Bennett) Broughton (dau. of a Dublin lawyer) and Delves Broughton (cleric); never married; no children. ❖ Published *Not Wisely but Too Well* (1867); followed by *Cometh Up As a Flower* (1867); routinely released a novel every 2 years, all anonymously written until *Goodbye Sweetheart* (1872); wrote more than 25 works of romantic fiction, including *A Fool in Her Folly* (1920). ❖ See also Marilyn Wood, *Rhoda Broughton: Profile of a Novelist* (Watkins, 1993).

BROULETOVA, Lioubov. Russian judoka. Born in USSR. ❖ Won a silver medal for -48kg extra-lightweight at Sydney Olympics (2000); won European championship (2003).

BROUQUIER, Veronique (1957—). French fencer. Born May 28, 1957, in France. ❖ Won an Olympic gold medal at Moscow (1980) and a bronze medal at Los Angeles (1984), both in team foil.

BROUSNIKINA, Olga (1978—). See Brusnikina, Olga.

BROUSSE, Amy (1910–1963). American spy. Name variations: Elizabeth Pack; Betty Pack; Elizabeth Thorpe; (codename) Cynthia; (pen name) Elizabeth Thomas; (nickname) Betty. Born Amy Elizabeth Thorpe in Minneapolis, Minnesota, Nov 22, 1910; died Dec 1, 1963; dau. of Major George Cyrus Thorpe, US Marines, and Cora (Wells) Thorpe; m. Arthur Pack (diplomat with British foreign service), April 29, 1930 (committed suicide after WWII); m. Charles Brousse (French attaché); children: (1st m.) Anthony George Pack (b. 1930, killed in Korean War), Denise Avril Beresford Pack (b. 1934). ❖ Spy, codenamed Cynthia, who managed to acquire Italy's and Vichy France's naval ciphers, a phenomenal boon to the Allies during WWII; made society debut in Washington, DC (1929); as a diplomat's wife, lived in Chile (1931–35), then Spain (1935); with outbreak of Civil War in Spain, evacuated Madrid (1936); while husband was posted in Warsaw (1937–38), became friends with many in the Polish Foreign Office and a secret agent for British Intelligence; returned to Chile (1939), where she wrote a pro-Allies column in Spanish in *La Nación* under pen name Elizabeth Thomas; given the codename Cynthia by British Intelligence (1940), was assigned duty in Washington DC; soon managed to pry the key to Italy's secret cipher from its naval attaché's office; also penetrated the Vichy French Embassy. ❖ See also H. Montgomery Hyde, *Cynthia* (Farrar, 1965); Mary S. Lovell, *The Life of Betty Pack, the American Spy Who Changed the Course of World War II* (Pantheon, 1992); and *Women in World History.*

BROUWENSTIJN, Gré (1915–1999). Dutch soprano. Name variations: Gre Brouwenstijn or Brouwenstein. Born Gerada Damphina, Aug 26, 1915, in Den Helder, Netherlands; died Dec 14, 1999, in Amsterdam; studied with Japp Stroomenbergh, Boris Pelsky, and Ruth Horna in Amsterdam. ❖ Often called a "great singing actress," debuted in Amsterdam (1940); joined the Netherlands Opera (1946); made Covent Garden debut (1951), singing roles there until 1964; made Chicago debut (1959) and Glyndebourne (1959); retired (1971).

BROUWER, Bertha (1930—). Dutch runner. Born Oct 29, 1930, in Netherlands. ❖ At Helsinki Olympics, won a silver medal in the 200 meters (1952).

BROVAR, Anna Iakovlevna (1887–1917). Russian writer. Name variations: (pseudonyms) Anna Iakovlevna Lenshina; Anna Mar; Princess Daydream. Born 1887 in St Petersburg, Russia; committed suicide by poison, 1917. ❖ Explored themes of sexuality, unrequited love, religious devotion, obsession, and longing; collections of short prose fiction include *Miniatures* (1906), *The Impossible* (1912), and *Blood and Rings* (1916); novellas include *Passers-by* and *For You Alone I Sinned* (1914); also wrote play *When Ships are Sinking* (1915), 10 film scripts, and novel *Woman on the Cross* (1916).

BROWN, Abbie Farwell (1871–1927). American poet and children's writer. Name variations: (pseudonym) Jean Neal. Born Aug 21, 1871, in Boston, Massachusetts; died Mar 5, 1927; dau. of Benjamin F. and Clara (Neal) Brown; sister of Ethel Brown who wrote and illustrated under pseudonym Ann Underhill; graduate of Bowdoin School, 1886; attended Boston Girls' Latin School; attended Radcliffe College, 1891–92 and 1893–94. ❖ Known largely for her leadership in the New England literary community, published 1st and possibly most successful volume, *The Book of Saints and Friendly Beasts* (1900); authored other works for children, including *The Lonesomest Doll* (1901), *A Pocket Full of Posies* (poetry, 1901), *In the Days of the Giants* (1902), and *Fresh Posies* (poetry, 1908); with composer Mabel W. Daniels, wrote "On the Trail" which became official song of Girl Scouts; served as editor of 20-vol. Young Folks' Library (1902); wrote poetry for adults, including *Heart of New England* (1920) and *The Silver Stair* (1926); served as president of New England Poetry Club.

BROWN, Ada (1889–1950). African-American jazz singer and pianist. Born Ada Scott, May 1, 1889, in Kansas City, Kansas; died in Kansas City, Mar 31, 1950; cousin of James Scott, noted ragtime composer and pianist. ❖ Billed in heyday as "Queen of Blues," launched career at Bob Mott's Pekin Theater in Chicago (1910); was a regular with Bennie Moten Band and appeared in black revues and musical comedies on Broadway (1920s); featured at London Palladium (late '30s) and appeared with Fats Waller in film *Stormy Weather* (1943); was one of the original incorporators of The Negro Actors Guild of America (1936). ❖ See also *Women in World History.*

BROWN, Alice (1856–1948). American novelist and dramatist. Born in Hampton Falls, New Hampshire, Dec 5, 1856; died in Boston, Massachusetts, June 21, 1948; attended Robinson Seminary in Exeter. ❖ Best known for her analysis of New England characters and morals in her short stories and novels, also authored biographies of Mercy Otis Warren (1896) and Louise Imogen Guiney (1921), some verse, and a book on English travels; won $10,000 for best play for her *Children of Earth* (1914), which opened at Booth Theater in New York (1915).

BROWN, Alice Regina (1960—). African-American runner. Born Sept 20, 1960, in Jackson, Mississippi; attended California State, 1979–80. ❖ Was a member of Bob Kersee's World Class Track Club; won an Olympic gold medal in the 4 x 100-meter relay and a silver medal in the 100 meters at Los Angeles (1984); won a gold medal for the 4 x 100-meter relay in Seoul Olympics (1988).

BROWN, Alice Seymour (1878–1941). See Frame, Alice.

BROWN, Alice Van Vechten (1862–1949). American art educator. Born June 7, 1862, in Hanover, New Hampshire; died Oct 16, 1949, in Middleton, New Jersey; dau. of Samuel Gilman Brown (Congregational minister and later head of Hamilton College) and Sarah Van Vechten Brown; granddau. of Francis Brown (president of Dartmouth); studied at Art Students League, 1881–85, with William M. Chase and Abbott Thayer. ❖ Appointed assistant director (1891), then director (1894), of Norwich Art School, CT, where her method of teaching art history attracted attention; reorganized art-teaching program at Wellesley College, MA (1897), which became the 1st college in the US to offer art history as a major (1900); served as head of art department at Wellesley for 33 years; also served as director of Wellesley's Farnsworth Museum; coauthored (with William Rankin) *A Short History of Italian Painting* (1914); retired (1930).

BROWN, Ann (1803/11–1869). See Lovell, Ann.

BROWN, Anna (1747–1810). Scottish poet and singer. Born Anna Gordon, 1747, in Scotland; died 1810; dau. of Thomas Gordon. ❖ Was a singer, transmitter, and collector of Scottish ballads, some of which were anthologized in Walter Scott's *Minstrelsy of the Scottish Border.*

BROWN, Antoinette (1825–1921). See Brown Blackwell, Antoinette.

BROWN, Audrey (b. 1913). English runner. Born May 24, 1913, in Great Britain. ❖ At Berlin Olympics, won a silver medal in the 4 x 100-meter relay (1936).

BROWN, Audrey Alexandra (1904–1998). Canadian poet. Born Audrey Alexandra Fonds Brown, Oct 29, 1904, in Nanaimo, British Columbia, Canada; died 1998; dau. of Joseph Miller Brown and Rosa Elizabeth Brown. ❖ With only 4 years of formal schooling, worked as a freelance writer for newspapers; influenced by Romantic poetry, her collections include *A Dryad in Nanaimo* (1931), *The Tree of Resurrection and Other Poems* (1937), *Challenge to Time and Death* (1943), *V-E Day* (1946), and *All Fool's Day* (1948); also wrote an address to Canadian Authors' Association, *Poetry and Life* (1944). Received Memorial Gold Medal of Canadian Women's Press Club (1936); named Officer of the Order of Canada (1967). ❖ See also memoir, *The Log of a Lame Duck* (1938).

BROWN, Benita Fitzgerald (1961—). See Fitzgerald, Benita.

BROWN, Beverly (1941–2002). American dancer and choreographer. Born Beverly Brown, 1941, in Effingham, Illinois; died May 17, 2002, in Kansas City, Missouri; graduate of Carlton College. ❖ Trained with a range of teachers in New York City, including Alvin Ailey, Hanya Holm, Merce Cunningham, Erick Hawkins, and the faculty of the American Ballet Center; performed with Hawkins' company (1967–74), where she appeared in his *Eight Clear Pieces, Here and Now with Watchers, Classic Kite Tails* (1972), and others; appeared in concert recitals by Rod Rogers and Anthony La Giglia; formed own dance troupe, Greenhouse Ensemble; founded Body Voice Theater and Beverly Brown Ensemble, where she experimented with natural sounds and body movement; taught at Colorado University and University of California at Santa Cruz; composed music for Siddha Yoga meditation communities in NY and Kansas City; choreographed numerous works.

BROWN, C. Patra (1905–1995). See Brown, Cleo.

BROWN, Carol Page (1953—). American rower. Born Carol Page Brown, April 19, 1953, in US; dau. of Harper Brown; graduate of Princeton University with a degree in economics and politics, 1975; University of Washington, degree in forest management. ❖ With Janet Youngholm, won the national collegiate title for women's pairs without coxswain (1974); was a member of the 1st US crew to row in the World championships, finishing 2nd; at Montreal Olympics, won a bronze medal in coxed eights (1976).

BROWN, Carolyn (1927—). American dancer and choreographer. Born 1927 in Fitchburg, Massachusetts. ❖ Studied classical ballet at Juilliard School with Antony Tudor, performing in his *Excercise Piece* (1953), and modern dance with Merce Cunningham; joined Merce Cunningham Dancers (1952), where she performed for next 20 years; created roles in more than half of Cunningham's works, including *Fragments* (1953), *Gambit for Dancers and Orchestra* (1959), *Winterbranch* (1965), *Scramble* (1967) and *Tread* (1970); choreographed *Balloon* for Barbara Lloyd and Steve Paxton (1965), *Car Lot* for Manhattan Festival Ballet (1968), and *Balloon II* for Ballet Théâtre Contemporain (1975); formed own dance troupe, Among Company; worked on films *House Party* (1974) and *Dune Dance* (1975); also choreographed *West Country* (1970), *Zellerbach Maul* (1971), *As I Remember It* (1972), *Synergy I, or, Don't Fight It, Bertha* (1973), *Synergy II* (1974), *Cicles* (1975) and *Duetude* (1977).

BROWN, Mrs. Charles S. *See Brown, Lucy.*

BROWN, Charlotte (c. 1795–1855). New Zealand missionary and teacher. Name variations: Charlotte Arnett. Born Charlotte Arnett, 1795 or 1796, in England; died Nov 13, 1855, at Auckland, New Zealand; m. Alfred Nesbit Brown (missionary), c. 1829; children: 3. ❖ Administered girls' school before marriage; accompanied husband to Australia (1829); relocated to Matamata, New Zealand (1830s); assisted in husband's missionary work, supervising education of infants and girls, and caring for needs of other missionaries' wives. ❖ See also *Dictionary of New Zealand Biography* (Vol. 1).

BROWN, Charlotte (1846–1904). American physician and surgeon. Name variations: Charlotte Amanda Blake Brown. Born Charlotte Amanda Blake, Dec 22, 1846, in Philadelphia, Pennsylvania; died April 19, 1904, in San Francisco, California; dau. of Charles Morris Blake (teacher and Presbyterian minister) and Charlotte A. (Farrington) Blake; graduate of Elmira College, 1866; m. Henry Adams Brown, 1867; children: Adelaide Brown (b. 1868), Philip King Brown (b. 1869), and Harriet L. Brown. ❖ With other women, formed Pacific Dispensary for Women and Children (1875); with Dr. Martha E. Bucknell, served as one of 1st two attending physicians at Pacific Dispensary, which was reorganized as a hospital (1878), and later incorporated as San Francisco Hospital for Children and Training School for Nurses (1885); became 1st woman to perform an ovariotomy (1878); embraced medical innovations, designed a milk sterilizer, and recommended that children with contagious diseases be treated at public expense; resigned from San Francisco Hospital for Children (1895) and opened private practice with daughter Adelaide and son Philip. Children's Hospital later merged with Pacific Presbyterian Medical Center as California Pacific Medical Center (1991).

BROWN, Charlotte Elizabeth (1790–1846). *See Tonna, Charlotte Elizabeth.*

BROWN, Charlotte Emerson (1838–1895). American clubwoman. Born Charlotte Emerson, April 21, 1838, in Andover, Massachusetts; died Feb 5, 1895, in East Orange, New Jersey; dau. of a cleric and a relative of Ralph Waldo Emerson; m. Rev. William B. Brown, July 1880. ❖ Founded many clubs, including Euterpe (musical club); served as president of local Woman's Club in East Orange, NJ; with Jane Cunningham Croly, founded the General Federation of Women's Clubs in New York City, an alliance of women's literary clubs and civic reform societies which was one of the most influential women's organizations then in US, serving as its 1st president (1889–94); assisted Woman's Board of Missions of the Congregational Church.

BROWN, Charlotte Hawkins (c. 1883–1961). African-American educator. Name variations: Charlotte Hawkins, Charlotte Eugenia Hawkins, or Lottie Hawkins; Charlotte Eugenia Hawkins Brown. Born Lottie Hawkins, June 11, c. 1883, in Henderson, North Carolina; died Jan 11, 1961, in Greensboro, North Carolina; dau. of Edmund H. Hight and Caroline (Carrie) Frances Hawkins; m. Edward S. Brown (teacher), 1911 (div. 1916); children: attended State Normal School at Salem (MA). ❖ School founder who encouraged interracial cooperation, promoting exchange programs for students, worked with local community and advocated voting and home-ownership for blacks; taught at American Missionary Association's Bethany Institute at McLeansville (later Sedalia), NC (1901); after AMA shut it down, took over school and renamed it Palmer Memorial Institute (PMI, 1902), building its reputation over next few decades; served as president of NC State Federation of Negro Women's Clubs (1915–36) and of NC Teachers Association (1935–37); wrote *Mammy: An Appeal to the Heart of the South* (1919) and *The Correct Thing to Do, to Say, and to Wear* (1941); was the 1st black woman to gain membership in Twentieth Century Club of Boston (1928) and to serve on NC Council of Defense (1940); addressed Congrès International des Femmes in Paris (1945); retired from PMI as president (1952) and as vice president of board and director of finances (1955); co-founded National Council of Negro Women. ❖ See also Constance Marteena, *The Lengthening Shadow of a Woman* (1977).

BROWN, Cindy (1965—). African-American basketball player. Name variations: Cynthia Brown. Born Mar 16, 1955, in California; attended Long Beach State College. ❖ Won team gold medals at FIBA World championships and Goodwill Games (1986); at Seoul Olympics, won a gold medal in team competition (1988); played in the WNBA for the Detroit Shock (1998–99), then Utah Starzz.

BROWN, Cleo (1905–1995). American jazz pianist and vocalist. Name variations: C. Patra Brown. Born Cleopatra Brown, Dec 8, 1905, in Meridian, Mississippi; died April 15, 1995; sister of pianist Everett Brown. ❖ Moved to Chicago (1919); started touring with shows; replaced Fats Waller on his NY radio program; had her own series on WABC and led her own group at the Three Deuces in Chicago; retired (1953); took up inspirational music, playing and singing under name C. Patra Brown (1973). ❖ See also *Women in World History.*

BROWN, Cynthia (1965—). *See Brown, Cindy.*

BROWN, Denise Scott (1931—). *See Scott-Brown, Denise.*

BROWN, Doris (1942—). *See Heritage, Doris Brown.*

BROWN, Dorothy L. (1919–2004). African-American physician and politician. Name variations: "D" Brown. Born Dorothy Lavinia Brown, Jan 7, 1919, in Philadelphia, Pennsylvania; died June 13, 2004, in Nashville, Tennessee; dau. of an unmarried mother who left her in a Troy (NY) orphanage as an infant; Bennett College, BA, 1941; Meharry Medical College, MD, 1948; children: (adopted) Lola Cannon Redmon. ❖ First African-American woman surgeon in the American South, spent a year as an intern at Harlem Hospital in New York City, but was denied a surgical residency because of gender; completed residency at Meharry (1954); practiced in Nashville, becoming a fellow of the American College of Surgery; later became attending surgeon at George W. Hubbard Hospital and professor of surgery at Meharry Medical College; at 40, became the 1st single woman in modern times to adopt a child in the state of Tennessee; was the 1st black woman to be elected to the lower house of Tennessee State Legislature (1966). ❖ See also *Women in World History.*

BROWN, Earlene Dennis (1935—). African-American track-and-field athlete. Born July 11, 1935, in Latexo, Texas. ❖ Placed 4th in discus and won a bronze medal for shot put at Rome Olympics (1960), the 1st American to win an Olympic medal in shot put; was Amateur Athletic Union (AAU) champion in shot put (1956–62, 1964); won AAU championships in discus (1958–59, 1961); placed 6th in shot put and 4th in discus at Melbourne Olympics (1956); won AAU championship, baseball throw (1957); won gold medal in shot put, silver medal in discus at USA-USSR dual meet (1958); took silver medal in shot put at USA-USSR dual meet (1959); was shot put and discus champion at Pan American Games (1959); placed 12th in shot put at Tokyo Olympics (1964); became a Roller Derby superstar on several professional teams (1970s). ❖ See also *Women in World History.*

BROWN, Edith Mary (1864–1956). English-born doctor. Born Mar 24, 1864 in Whitehaven, Cumbria, England; died Dec 6, 1956, in Srinagar, Kashmir. ❖ Established North India Medical School for Christian Women in Ludhiana (1894, later Women's Christian Medical College)—1st medical college for women in India—and served as principal until 1942; trained local midwives and was responsible for fall in childbirth mortality rate; wrote handbook for midwives published in Urdu, Hindi, and Punjabi; awarded Gold Kaiser-I-Hund medal (1922); made DBE (1932). Her meditations, prayers, and poems were published by Friends of Ludhiana as *My Work is for a King* (1994).

BROWN, Elaine (1943—). African-American militant, writer and activist. Born in Philadelphia, Pennsylvania, Mar 2, 1943; grew up in North Philadelphia; dau. of a dress-factory worker; attended Thaddeus Stevens School of Practice and Philadelphia High School for Girls; briefly attended Temple University. ❖ Moved to Los Angeles (1965); became interested in radical politics and worked for the newspaper *Harambee*; joined Black Panther Party, turning it into a supporter of women's rights; became the 1st and only woman to lead the Black Panther Party (1974), and encouraged its involvement in conventional politics; began lecturing on the vision of an inclusive and egalitarian society, focusing on resolving problems of race, gender oppression and class disparity in US; served as president of the non-profit educational corporation, Fields of Flowers, and as director of Political Affairs for the National Alliance for Radical Prison Reform; writings include *New Age Racism and the Condemnation of "Little B"* (2002). ❖ See also autobiographical memoir, *A Taste of Power: A Black Woman's Story* (1992).

BROWN, Eliza (d. 1896). Australian letter writer. Born Eliza Bussey in Oxfordshire, England; died in Australia, 1896; dau. of William Bussey; educated at home; married Thomas Brown (land surveyor), Jan 1836 (died 1863); children: Kenneth, Aubrey, Maitland, Vernon, Matilda and Janet; grandmother of Edith Cowan, the 1st woman in Australian Parliament. ❖ Arrived in Australia (1841); documented early Australian colonial life through letters home to her family in Oxfordshire, England; grandson Peter Cowan edited these letters, which were published as *A Faithful Picture: The Letters of Eliza and Thomas Brown at York in the Swan River Colony 1841–1852* (1977).

BROWN, Elizabeth (1753–1812). American letter writer. Born Elizabeth Brown in 1753; lived in Concord, Massachusetts; died 1812; sister of Rebecca Brown French and Anna Brown Spaulding. ❖ Letters of the three Brown sisters, which express their spiritual and sisterly relationships, were collected as *The Brown Family Letters*.

BROWN, Ellie (1940—). See Moore, Ellie Durall.

BROWN, Evelyn Gertrude (1879–1962). See Brooke, Evelyn Gertrude.

BROWN, Fiona (1974—). See MacDonald, Fiona.

BROWN, Fiorella (1930–1976). See Keane, Fiorella.

BROWN, Foxy (1979—). American singer. Name variations: Inga Fung Marchand or I. Marchand; The Firm. Born Inga Fung Marchand (also seen as Marchaud), Sept 6, 1979, in Brooklyn, NY; parents from Trinidad and Tobago; m. Ricardo Brown, 1999 (sep. 2000). ❖ Performed with major hip-hop and rap artists before releasing debut album *Ill Na Na* (1996) with hits "Get Me Home" and "I'll Be"; joined hip-hop group The Firm (with Nas, AZ, and Nature) which released *The Album* (#1 pop, #1 R&B, 1997); released 2nd solo album *Chyna Doll* (1999) which reached #1 on both pop and R&B charts; other albums include *Broken Silence* (2001).

BROWN, Georgia (1933–1992). British singer and actress. Born Lillian Claire Laizer Getel Klot in London, England, Oct 21, 1933; died in London, June 6, 1992; m. Gareth Wigan, Nov 7, 1974. ❖ Gained early experience as a nightclub singer; made London stage debut as Lucy Brown in *The Threepenny Opera* (1956), then replaced Lotte Lenya in same role for NY debut; shuttled between US and England, appearing as Jeannie in *The Lily White Boys*, title role in *Maggie May*, Widow Begbick in *Man is Man* and *Side by Side by Sondheim*; was seen in such films as *A Study in Terror, The Fixer, Nothing but the Night, The Seven Per Cent Solution* and *The Bawdy Adventures of Tom Jones* (1976); appeared on tv in BBC's "Tophat" (1950), "Show Time" (1954), and a production of *Mother Courage* (1960). Nominated for Tony Award and received the *Variety* Critics Poll Award (England) for performance as Nancy in musical *Oliver!* (1961). ❖ See also *Women in World History*.

BROWN, Georgia Ann (1893–1978). See Broadwick, Tiny.

BROWN, Hallie Quinn (c. 1845–1949). African-American educator and activist. Born Mar 10, c. 1845, in Pittsburgh, Pennsylvania; died in Wilberforce, Ohio, Sept 16, 1949; dau. of Frances Jane (Scroggins) Brown and Thomas Arthur Brown; Wilberforce University, BS, 1873; never married; no children. ❖ Pioneer educator, writer and elocutionist, who was a tireless campaigner for the rights of blacks and women; taught in South Carolina and Mississippi (1873); appointed dean of Allen University (1875); taught in Dayton, Ohio, public school system (1887); appointed dean of women at Tuskegee Institute, Alabama (1892), then professor of elocution at Wilberforce University (1893); addressed World Congress of Representative Women, Chicago (May 18,

1893); made 1st trip to Europe (1894); spoke at World's Women's Christian Temperance Union Conference, London (1895); founded the 1st British Chautauqua, Wales (1895); presented to Queen Victoria (1899); served as president of Ohio State Federation of Women's Clubs (1905–12); was a delegate at World Missionary Conference in Edinburgh (1910); appointed president of National Association of Colored Women (1920); met President Harding to promote anti-lynching legislation (1922); retired from Wilberforce University (1923); addressed Republican National Convention (1924); protested segregated seating at All-American Music Festival of International Council of Women in Washington, DC (1925); writings include *Bits and Odds: A Choice Selection of Recitations for School, Lyceum, and Parlour Entertainment* (1884), *Trouble in Turkeytrot Church* (1917), *Tales My Father Told Me* (1925) and *Pen Pictures of Pioneers of Wilberforce* (1937). Hallie Quinn Brown Memorial Library of Central State University and Hallie Q. Brown Community House in St. Paul, Minnesota, named in her honor. ❖ See also *Women in World History*.

BROWN, Helen (c. 1859–1903). See Connon, Helen.

BROWN, Helen Gurley (1922—). American author and editor. Born Helen Gurley in Green Forest, Arkansas, Feb 18, 1922; dau. of Ira M. and Cleo (Sisca) Gurley; attended Texas State College for Women (now Texas Women's University), 1939–42, and Woodbury Business College, 1942; m. David Brown (film producer), Sept 1959. ❖ Began career in advertising, winning 2 Frances Holmes Advertising Copywriters awards; published controversial bestseller *Sex and the Single Girl* (1962), followed by *Sex and the Office* (1964); appointed editor-in-chief of *Cosmopolitan* (1965); turned *Cosmopolitan* into one of the five top-selling magazines in the US and made the "Cosmo Girl" the ideal among her young readers; achieved personal celebrity, espousing her views on tv and in further publications, including the autobiographical *Having It All* (1982); also wrote *Outrageous Opinions* (1966), *Sex and the New Single Girl* (1970) and *The Late Show: A Semiwild But Practical Survival Plan for Women Over 50* (1993); retired (1997). ❖ See also *Women in World History*.

BROWN, Hilary (1952—). Scottish chef and restaurateur. Born 1952 in Glasgow, Scotland; Glasgow College of Domestic Science, BS in food and nutrition (1973); m. David Brown (restaurateur). ❖ Renowned chef, taught home economics for 2 years before starting La Poitinière in Gullane, East Lothian, with husband (1975); earned widespread acclaim for excellently chosen and executed no-choice menus and impressive wine list, resulting in tables being booked several months in advance; served simple Scottish cooking with gourmet flair; sold restaurant (2000) much to chagrin of food critics; has continued career as chef, writing cookbooks and appearing on tv food shows. Was the 1st woman in Scotland to be honored with Michelin Star, along with Betty Allen (1990).

BROWN, Iona (1941–2004). English violinist and conductor. Born Jan 7, 1941, in Salisbury, England; died June 5, 2004, in Salisbury; dau. of musicians; sister of Timothy Brown (horn player), Ian Brown (pianist), Sally Brown Hallam (viola player); studied with Hugh Maguire in London, Remy Principe in Rome, and Henryk Szeryng in Paris; m. 2nd husband Björn Arnils (bassist). ❖ Celebrated violinist, began career with National Youth Orchestra (1955–60); played in the Philharmonia Orchestra, London (1963–66); joined Academy of St. Martin in the Fields in London (1964), working her way up through the ranks to become a soloist, then served as music director (1974–80); performed many times at London Promenade Concerts and recorded David Blake's Violin Concerto; named artistic director of Norwegian Chamber Orchestra (1981); served as music director of Los Angeles Chamber Orchestra (1987–92, 1995–97); was also guest director of City of Birmingham Symphony Orchestra (1985–89); because of severe arthritis in her wrists (1998), turned to full-time conducting; made many recordings. Made an Officer of the British Empire (1986).

BROWN, Jessica (c. 1900–?). American theatrical dancer. Name variations: Countess of Northesk; Lady Northesk; Jessica Ruth Brown; Jessica Ruth Reinhard; Jessica Cornelius. Born Jessica Ruth Brown, c. 1900, in Buffalo, NY; dau. of F.A. Brown; m. Cyril de Witt Brown (naval contractor and electrical engineer), 1918 (div. 1922); m. David Ludovic George Hopetoun Carnegie (1901–1963), 11th earl of Northesk, July 19, 1923 (div. 1928); m. Vivian Cornelius of Windlesham, Surrey, Dec 18, 1928. ❖ Known for her wide-ranging dance abilities, which included social dance, tap, and high kicks, 1st appeared in the chorus of Ned Wayburn's *Ziegfeld Midnight Frolic of 1918*; performed in numerous shows in New York City, including *Gloriana* (1918), *The Cohan Revue of 1918, Come Along* (1919), *A Lonely Romeo* (1919), *Cinderella on*

Broadway (1920), *Midnight Rounders of 1921,* and 2 editions of the *Ziegfeld Follies* (1921–22); retired to marry the earl of Northesk; though the marriage failed, did not resume career.

BROWN, Jessie (1892–1985). American theatrical ballet dancer and actress. Name variations: Jessica Brown; Jessie Brown Kalmar. Born Jessica Brown, Aug 24, 1892; died Jan 1985 in Sherman Oaks, California; m. Bert Kalmar (composer-songwriter, 1884–1947); children: Bert Kalmar Jr. ❖ Debuted as a specialty dancer in the Hanlon Brothers' show *Superba* (c. 1907), then performed as a toe dancer for many years; toured with Carter de Haven, dancing to pizzicato polkas and popular songs; alongside husband Bert Kalmar, danced ballet numbers on a popular Sunday concert to "I'd Rather Two-Step than Waltz"; toured with Kalmar in *Nurseryland* (1916) and in an act which included a ragtime toe dance set to "Moving Man Don't Take My Baby Grand"; retired (late 1910s); portrayed by Vera-Ellen in the film, *Three Little Words.*

BROWN, Joanne (1972—). Australian softball player. Born Joanne Alchin, April 7, 1972, in Canberra, Australia; m. Stephen Brown (softball player and research economist), 1994. ❖ Won bronze medals at Atlanta Olympics (1996) and Sydney Olympics (2000).

BROWN, Josephine (1892–1976). American actress. Born Sept 27, 1892, in Chicago, Illinois; died April 26, 1976, in Ibiza, Spain; children: Wauna Paul (actress and producer, died 1973). ❖ At 11, made stage debut with Lillian Russell; subsequently appeared with William Gillette, John Barrymore and George Fawcett; plays include *Bachelor Born, I Remember Mama, Gigi, Anniversary Waltz* and *Diary of a Scoundrel;* was sculpted by Auguste Rodin, painted by Augustus John, but spurned Enrico Caruso's offer of marriage.

BROWN, Judi (1961—). American runner. Name variations: Judith Brown. Born July 14, 1961, in East Lansing, Michigan. ❖ At Los Angeles Olympics, won a silver medal in the 400-meter hurdles (1984).

BROWN, Judith (1961—). *See Brown, Judi.*

BROWN, Karen (1955—). African-American ballet dancer. Born Oct 6, 1955, in Okmulgee, Oklahoma. ❖ Trained at American Ballet Center and the school of the Dance Theater of Harlem, where, as principal dancer (1973–95), she performed in works by George Balanchine, Geoffrey Holder, John Taras, and Agnes de Mille; taught in company's community outreach program during yearly residencies at Kennedy Center in Washington, DC; became artistic director of Oakland Ballet (c. 2000), one of the few black women to head a major US dance company.

BROWN, Karen (1963—). English field-hockey player. Born Jan 9, 1963, in Great Britain. ❖ At Barcelona Olympics, won a bronze medal in team competition (1992).

BROWN, Katie (1982—). American climber. Born Oct 4, 1982, in Jacksonville, Florida. ❖ Won gold at X Games in Women's Difficulty (1996, 1997, 1998); became 1st woman to achieve on-sight ascent of a 5.13d (Omaha Beach, Red River Gorge, Kentucky); other 1st-place finishes include: UIAA Youth World championship, Laval, France (1995); UIAA Masters, Rock Masters Arco (1996 and 1997); and UIAA Worldcup, Besancon, France (1999).

BROWN, Kay (1903–1995). American film producer and agent. Name variations: Kay Brown Barrett. Born 1903; died in Hightstown, New Jersey, Jan 18, 1995; graduate of Wellesley College, 1924; m. James Barrett; children: 2 daughters. ❖ Powerful Hollywood agent who once ran Selznick International Pictures in New York, was best known for having prodded David O. Selznick into buying the rights to *Gone with the Wind;* was also responsible for importing European talent, including Ingrid Bergman, Alfred Hitchcock, Vivien Leigh and Laurence Olivier, as well as handling some of early Hollywood's brightest stars; counted among her clients Arthur Miller, Isak Dinesen, Lillian Hellman, John Gielgud and Alec Guinness. ❖ See also *Women in World History.*

BROWN, Leah (1975—). American gymnast. Born June 11, 1975, in Atlanta, Georgia. ❖ Won Dynamo Classic (1991), Peachtree Classic (1992, 1993); won a bronze medal for vault at World University Games (1997).

BROWN, Linda (1943—). African-American civil rights activist. Name variations: Linda Brown Thompson. Born 1943 in Topeka, Kansas; dau. of Reverend Oliver Brown. ❖ As a 4th-grade student at a black elementary school in Topeka, weary of the long walk and bus ride from her home

to school each day, applied to attend a nearby public elementary school for white children (1951); was denied access; her father sued the Topeka Board of Education, and the eventual Supreme Court case, *Brown* v. *Board of Education,* destroyed the legal basis for racial segregation in public schools. ❖ See also *Women in World History.*

BROWN, Lucy (fl. 1895). American golfer. Name variations: Lucy Barnes; Lucy Brown; Mrs. Lucy Barnes Brown; Mrs. Charles S. Brown. Born Lucy Barnes in New York; m. Charles S. Brown; children at least one, son A.M. Brown. ❖ Representing the Shinnecock Hills Long Island Golf Club, won the (unofficial) 1st national women's golf tournament which took place at the Meadow Brook Club in Hempstead, NY (1895); also won the 1st US Women's Amateur championship (Nov 9, 1895).

BROWN, Maggie (1867–1932). *See Brown, Molly.*

BROWN, Marcia (1918—). American author and illustrator. Born in Rochester, New York, July 13, 1918; dau. of Clarence Edward (minister) and Adelaide Elizabeth (Zimber) Brown; New York College for Teachers (now State University of New York at Albany), BA, 1940; studied at New School for Social Research, Art Students League, and Columbia University; studied at Zhejiang Academy of Fine Arts, Hangzhou, China, 1985. ❖ Storyteller and illustrator, taught English and dramatics for several years before moving to New York City, where she finished her 1st four books while employed in the children's department of New York Public Library; lived and painted for periods in Europe (1956–62); wrote and illustrated 1st book, *The Little Carousel* (1946), inspired by her neighborhood in Italian district of Greenwich Village; wrote the much-loved *Stone Soup* (1947), the 1st of her books to be chosen a runner-up for Caldecott Medal; won Caldecott medals for *Cinderella* (1955), *Once a Mouse . . .* (1961) and *Shadow* (1983); other works (all self-illustrated) include *Dick Whittington and His Cat* (1950), *The Steadfast Tin Soldier* (1954), *Felice* (1958), *Tamarindo!* (1960), *Backbone of the King* (1966), *The Neighbors* (1967), *The Blue Jackal* (1977) and *Lotus Seeds: Children, Pictures and Books* (1985). Awarded Regina Medal from Catholic Library Association (1977). ❖ See also *Women in World History.*

BROWN, Margaret (1867–1932). *See Brown, Molly.*

BROWN, Margaret A. (1867–?). Canadian novelist and journalist. Born Margaret Porter in 1867 in western Ontario, Canada; attended Toronto Normal School. ❖ Wrote the Ottawa novel, *My Lady of the Snows* (1908).

BROWN, Margaret Elizabeth (1918—). English biologist. Name variations: Mrs. Varley. Born Margaret Elizabeth Brown, Sept 28, 1918, at Mussoorie, Punjab, India, where her father served in the colonial service; Girton College, Cambridge, MA, 1944, PhD, 1945; Oxford, MA, 1959; m. George Copley Varley (professor), 1955. ❖ An expert on fish biology, worked at various educational and research institutions, including Girton College, University of Cambridge, East African Fisheries Research Organisation in Jinja, Uganda, University of Oxford, and Open University; collaborated with Winifred Frost on New Naturalist volume *The Trout* (1967); published *British Freshwater Fishes: Factors Affecting Their Distribution* (1967); served as vice president of Linnean Society (1982). Some of her works—including *A Manuel of Practical Vertebrate Morphology* (coauthor 1949) and *Physiology of Fishes* (ed., 1957)—were widely used as textbooks.

BROWN, Margaret Wise (1910–1952). American writer. Name variations: (pseudonyms) Golden McDonald, Juniper Sage, and Timothy Hay. Born Margaret Wise Brown, May 23, 1910, in New York, NY; died in Nice, France, Nov 13, 1952; dau. of Robert Bruce Brown (executive with American Manufacturing Co.) and Maude Margaret (Johnson) Brown; Hollins College, BA, 1932; never married; no children. ❖ Author of the classic children's book *Goodnight Moon* and innovator in children's literature, joined an experimental writing group led by Lucy Sprague Mitchell, and associated with the Bureau for Educational Experiment, later known as the Bank Street School (1935); studied children's responses to stories read to them, a technique she would use to test her own writings; published 1st book, *When the Wind Blew* (1937), a fantasy based on a story by Chekhov; served on publications staff of Bank Street School; served as editor at W.R. Scott (1937–41); wrote *The Noisy Book* (1939), her 1st big sales success; as Golden McDonald, wrote *Red Light, Green Light* and *Little Lost Lamb* (both 1944); published *The Little Island* (1946), which featured the setting of her summer house at Vinal Haven, Maine; for the Golden Book series, wrote *The Five Little Firemen* and *Color Kittens,* both of which sold millions of copies in US and abroad (1940s); for Harper and Row, wrote *The Runaway Bunny* (1942), *The House of a Hundred Windows* (1945) and *The Little Fur Family* (1946); had greatest success with *Goodnight Moon* (1947); published what was, in the eyes of many critics, one of her best books, *Mr. Dog: The Dog Who Belonged to Himself* (1952); wrote more than 100 books and lyrics for 21 children's recordings, including *Goodnight Moon.* ❖ See also Leonard S. Marcus, *Margaret Wise Brown: Awakened by the Moon* (Beacon, 1992); and *Women in World History*.

BROWN, Marie (1914–2003). *See Marcus, Marie.*

BROWN, Marilyn Cochran (1950—). *See Cochran, Marilyn.*

BROWN, Martha McClellan (1838–1916). American temperance leader. Born Martha McClellan in Baltimore, Maryland, April 16, 1838; died in Dayton, Ohio, Aug 31, 1916; graduate of Pittsburgh Female College, 1862; m. W. Kennedy Brown (Methodist minister), 1858. ❖ Gained recognition in the temperance movement as a lecturer during Civil War years; as a member of the Order of Good Templars, a fraternal temperance society, served the state executive committee of Ohio Templars as grand vice-templar; served as editor of *Alliance Monitor* (1867–76); helped lay the groundwork for the national Prohibition Party (1869); after being elected world supreme vice-templar (1874), was instrumental in founding in Columbus, Ohio, what may have been the 1st women's state temperance society; helped organize the Woman's Christian Temperance Union; withdrew from the Templars when they refused to admit black members; served on executive committee of Prohibition Party (1876–80); was also a force behind the National Prohibition Alliance, a speakers bureau, of which she served as secretary and principal lecturer. ❖ See also *Women in World History.*

BROWN, Mary Jane (1917–1997). American tap dancer and teacher. Born May 13, 1917, in Syracuse, NY; died 1997. ❖ Began performing tap numbers with family vaudeville act (1929), but soon moved on to solos (c. 1932); appeared frequently with brother; toured with bands of Bob Crosby and Wayne King, among others (1930s); appeared on Broadway in George White's *Scandals of 1940;* appeared at NY clubs, such as Greenwich Village Inn, and on early tv variety shows, including Milton Berle's "Texaco Star Theater"; opened own ballet studio in the Bronx and taught for many years at International Dance School.

BROWN, Mary Willcox (1869–1940). *See Glenn, Mary Willcox.*

BROWN, Melanie (1975—). English singer. Name variations: Melanie B, Mel B, Scary Spice, The Spice Girls. Born Melanie Janine Brown, May 29, 1975, in Leeds, England; sister of Danielle Brown (actress); attended Leeds College of Music and Northern School of Contemporary Dance; m. Jimmy Gulzar (dancer), Sept 13, 1998 (div. Jan 2001); children: daughter Phoenix Chi (b. Feb 19, 1999). ❖ Performed with pop group, Touch; with other members of Touch band, formed Spice Girls in London (1994); with group, released "Wannabe," the 1st debut single by an all-girl band to enter international charts at #1 (1997), followed by the album, *Spice,* which went to #1 in UK charts, and was the 1st debut album by UK performers to enter US charts at #1 (1997); had other Top-10 singles, including "Say You'll be There" and "2 Become 1"; released smash-hit album *Spiceworld* and film of same name (1997); like other members of the group, took on solo projects after unsuccessful Spice album, *Forever* (2000); released several solo hit singles, including "I Want You Back," "Tell Me" and "Word Up"; appeared in tv series, "Burn It" (2002); made stage debut in West End in Eve Ensler's *The Vagina Monologues* (2002). ❖ See also *Catch A Fire: The Autobiography* (Headline, 2002).

BROWN, Michele (1939—). *See Mason-Brown, Michele.*

BROWN, Millicent Amiel Macmillan (1888–1984). *See Baxter, Millicent Amiel.*

BROWN, Minnijean (1942—). African-American civil-rights activist. Name variations: Minnie Jean; Jean Brown Trickey. Born Minnie Jean Brown in 1942; dau. of Imogene Brown (nurse) and Bob Brown (landscaper); attended Southern Illinois University; m. Ray Trickey (zoologist), 1967 (div. 1987); children: 6, including Spirit Trickey (b. 1980) and Leila Trickey (b. 1982). ❖ One of the Little Rock Nine, had been attending all-black Horace Mann High School when the school board, in an attempt to integrate Little Rock's public schools, passed out applications to those interested in transferring to Central; entered Central with 9 other African-Americans (Sept 1957) and endured a year of misery. ❖ See also *Women in World History.*

BROWN, Molly (1867–1932). American philanthropist. Name variations: Margaret or Maggie Tobin Brown; Mrs. J.J. Brown; "The Unsinkable Molly Brown." Born Margaret Tobin in Hannibal, Missouri, 1867; died Oct 26, 1932; dau. of a ditch digger; m. James J. Brown (mine foreman known as "Leadville Johnny"), 1886 (sep. 1909, died 1922); children: Lawrence and Helen. ❖ Survivor of the sinking *Titanic,* became known as the Unsinkable Molly Brown; struck with gold fever (1884), followed brother to Colorado, where she met and married James Brown; after his silver mine yielded a vein of gold worth $2.5 million (1894), moved to Denver; continually snubbed by Denver society who regarded her as uncouth and ignorant, set out to educate herself, eventually mastering 7 languages; made frequent trips to Europe, hobnobbing with artists and the occasional royal; established a home in Newport, Rhode Island, where she was welcomed among the Astors, Whitneys and Vanderbilts; was aboard the ill-fated *Titanic* on its maiden voyage (1912); while in a lifeboat, argued fiercely with the quartermaster to return to the wreck site and pick up more survivors; when he dismissed the flare from an approaching ship as a "shooting star," took control of the boat and got the other women to row; devoted her remaining years to charity work. ❖ See also *The Unsinkable Molly Brown* (film), based on the Broadway musical; and *Women in World History.*

BROWN, Muriel (1912–1998). *See Humphrey, Muriel.*

BROWN, Nancy (1869–1948). *See Leslie, Annie.*

BROWN, Natasha (1967—). *See Kaiser, Natasha.*

BROWN, Olympia (1835–1926). American cleric. Name variations: Olympia Brown Willis. Born Olympia Brown, Jan 5, 1835, in Prairie Ronde, near Schoolcraft, Michigan; died Oct 23, 1926, in Baltimore, Maryland; dau. of Asa (farmer) and Lephia (Brown) Brown; attended Mt. Holyoke Seminary (1854–55); graduate of Antioch College, 1860, and St. Lawrence Theological School, 1863; m. John Henry Willis, April 1873; children: Henry Parker Willis (b. 1874); Gwendolen Brown Willis (b. 1876). ❖ Graduated from St. Lawrence Theological School, one of the 1st women to obtain a theology degree, and was ordained by Universalist Association (1863); with her gift for oratory, soon overcame the initial resistance of members who had not wanted to welcome a "woman preacher"; 1st ministry was to a small congregation in Marchfield, Vermont, another small church in East Montpelier was soon added; served as minister for the Universalist Church in Weymouth Landing, Massachusetts (1864–69), Bridgeport, Connecticut (1869–78), then Racine, Wisconsin (1878–87); grew increasingly involved in the women's rights movement; was a founding member of American Equal Rights Association (1866); helped found the New England Woman Suffrage Association (1868) and the Federal Suffrage Association (1892); assisted in the final editing of *The Woman's Bible* (1898); reorganized the Wisconsin Woman Suffrage Association and served as president for 28 years; was a member and activist for the Congressional Union (1913), which became the Woman's Party (1916); served as publisher of *Racine Times-Call* (1893–1900); helped found and wrote regularly for the suffrage newspaper *The Wisconsin Citizen;* wrote the history of Kansas women's suffrage campaign of 1867 for *History of Woman Suffrage* (Vol. II, 1881, 1882), "Democratic Ideals—A Sketch of Clara Bewick Colby" (1917), *Acquaintances, Old and New, Among Reformers* (1911), and an unpublished autobiography. ❖ See also Charlotte Coté, *Olympia Brown: The Battle for Equality* (Mother Courage, 1988); and *Women in World History.*

BROWN, Pamela (1917–1975). English actress. Born Pamela Mary Brown, July 8, 1917, in London, England; died Sept 18, 1975, in London; attended St. Mary's Convent, Ascot, and Royal Academy of Dramatic Art; briefly married to actor Peter Copley (div. 1953). ❖ Known for her husky voice, made stage debut as Juliet (1936) and would continue to distinguish herself in Shakespearean roles throughout career, performing with Oxford Repertory Company and Old Vic; had 1st outstanding London success in the title role of *Claudia* (1942); made New York debut as Gwendolyn in *The Importance of Being Earnest* (1947) to rave reviews; was heralded for performace as Jennet Jourdemayne in *The Lady's Not for Burning* (1949); also appeared in *The Way of the World, The Country Wife, Heartbreak House* and *A Question of Fact;* made last stage appearance in *This Year, Next Year* (1960); was seen in non-speaking role of Jane Shore in Olivier's *Richard III* (1955); also made sporadic tv appearances, including *Victoria Regina* (1961), for which she received an Emmy; other films include *One of Our Aircraft is Missing* (1942), *Tales of Hoffmann* (1951), *The Second Mrs. Tanqueray* (1952), *The Scapegoat* (1959), *Becket* (1964), *Wuthering Heights* (1970),

On a Clear Day You Can See Forever (1970) and *Lady Caroline Lamb* (1972). ❖ See also *Women in World History.*

BROWN, Phyllis George (1949—). *See George, Phyllis.*

BROWN, Rachel Fuller (1898–1980). American scientist. Born Rachel Fuller Brown, Nov 23, 1898, in Springfield, Massachusetts; died Jan 14, 1980, in Albany, New York; dau. of George Hamilton Brown and Annie (Fuller) Brown; Mount Holyoke, AB in chemistry and history, 1920; University of Chicago, MS and PhD; lived with Dorothy Wakerley; never married; no children. ❖ Following work at University of Chicago, became a chemist at Division of Laboratories and Research in Albany, NY; developed simple tests for standardizing antisera used in treatment of pneumonia, vaccines and purification of antigens (1926–48); improved precipitation tests used to diagnose syphilis; paired with mycologist, Elizabeth Lee Hazen, to find antifungal agents (1948); with Hazen, discovered nystatin (1950), the 1st highly active antifungal agent to be found safe and effective for use in humans; assigned rights and royalties of nystatin to establish the Brown-Hazen Fund (1951); with Hazen, discovered the antibacterial agents, phalamycin (1953) and capacidin (1959). Received Squibb Award in Chemotherapy (1955); elected fellow of New York Academy of Science (1957); received Rhoda Benham Award of Medical Mycology Society of the Americas (1972) and Chemical Pioneer Award (1975). ❖ See also Richard S. Baldwin, *The Fungus Fighters* (Cornell U. Press, 1981); and *Women in World History.*

BROWN, Rita Mae (1944—). American poet and novelist. Born Nov 28, 1944, in Hanover, Pennsylvania; as an orphan, was adopted and raised by a poor family in York; attended public school in Fort Lauderdale, Florida, then University of Florida at Gainesville; attended New York University; Institute for Policy Studies, PhD in English and Political Science (1976). ❖ Participated in civil-rights movements (1960s) and helped found chapter of Student Homophile League; was an early member of NOW, but quit because of the discrimination she encountered as a lesbian; as a result, wrote the oft-quoted essay, "The Woman-Identified Woman"; published the semi-autobiographical *Rubyfruit Jungle* (1973), one of the 1st American novels with a liberated lesbian as its protagonist; other writings, which often celebrate the role of women in Southern history, include (poetry) *The Hand That Cradles the Rock* (1971), *In Her Day* (1974), (essays) *A Plain Brown Rapper* (1976), *Six of One* (1978), *Southern Discomfort* (1982), *High Hearts* (1986), *Wish You Were Here* (1990), *Murder at Monticello* (1994), and *Murder, She Meowed* (1996). ❖ See also autobiography *Rita Will: Memoir of a Literary Rabble-Rouser* (1997).

BROWN, Rosel George (1926–1967). American science-fiction writer. Name variations: Rosel George. Born Mar 15, 1926, in New Orleans, Louisiana; died Nov 1967 in New Orleans; Tulane University, BA, 1946; University of Minnesota, MA, 1950; m. W. Burlie Brown, 1946; children: 1 daughter, 1 son. ❖ Wrote the novels *Earthblood* (with Keith Laumer, 1966), *Sybil Sue Blue* (1966), and *The Waters of Centaurus* (1970), considered her best; also published a collection of short stories, *A Handful of Time* (1963).

BROWN, Rosellen (1939—). American novelist and poet. Born 1939 in Philadelphia, Pennsylvania, to Jewish parents; Barnard College, BA, 1960; Brandeis University, MA in literature, 1962; m. Marvin Hoffman (psychologist); children: Adina (b. 1967); Elana (b. 1970). ❖ Taught Creative Writing at Goddard College, University of Houston, and School of the Art Institute of Chicago; writings include *Some Deaths in the Delta* (1970), *Street Games* (1974), *The Autobiography of My Mother* (1976), *Tender Mercies* (1978), *Civil Wars* (1984), *Before and After* (1992) and *Cora Fry's Pillow Book* (1994).

BROWN, Rosemary (1916–2001). British spiritualist. Born Rosemary Dickeson, July 27, 1916, in Stockwell, South London, England; died Nov 16, 2001, in London; m. Charles Brown (government scientist), 1952 (died 1961). ❖ Former cafeteria worker who alleged that spirits of dead composers dictated music to her; composed over 400 works in styles of various musicians, including Liszt, Chopin, Beethoven, Brahms, and Schubert; also wrote autobiography, *Unfinished Symphonies* (1971), as well as *Immortals at My Elbow* (1974), about psychic philosophy, and *Look Beyond Today* (1986).

BROWN, Rosemary (1930—). Canadian politician and activist. Born Rosemary Wedderburn, June 17, 1930, at Kingston, Jamaica; dau. of Ralph Wedderburn (businessman) and Enid James; raised by grandmother, Imogene Wilson-James, one of the founding members of the left-wing People's National Party (PNP) in Jamaica; niece of Leila

James-Tomlinson, judge; McGill University, BA, 1954; University of British Columbia, Master of Social Work, 1964; m. William (Bill) Brown (clinical psychiatrist), 1955; children: Cleta Brown (b. 1957), Gary (b. 1959), and Jonathon (b. 1965). ❖ Feminist activist and 1st black woman to be elected to any parliament in Canada; became a Canadian citizen; elected to the executive committee of British Columbia Association for the Advancement of Coloured People (BCAACP), an activist organization patterned after the NAACP in US; became involved in the growing feminist and peace movements and spent much of her time lobbying politicians, organizing demonstrations, and writing letters to newspapers; joined the Vancouver Status of Women Council (late 1960s); joined provincial wing of left-leaning New Democratic Party (NDP); in British Columbia, elected to provincial legislature for the riding of Vancouver-Burrard, part of the 1st ever NDP government in the history of the province (1972); was able to retain her seat in the next election (1975); focused on the plight of immigrant women, the lack of affordable housing, foreign ownership of natural resources, corporate control of the environment, and the sexism and paternalism that she believed was rampant in her party; was a member of the National Action Committee on the Status of Women and the federal-government-sponsored Advisory Council on the Status of Women; reelected in the new riding of Burnaby-Edmonds in the provincial election (1979); retired from parliament (1986); continued to speak and lecture throughout Canada and remained active in the international campaign to promote peace. Received the Black Award, National Black Coalition of Canada (1974). ❖ See also autobiography *Being Brown* (1989); and *Women in World History.*

BROWN, Ruth (1928—). African-American jazz and rhythm-and-blues singer. Born Ruth Weston, Jan 20, 1928, in Portsmouth, Virginia; grew up in North Carolina; married 3 times. ❖ Hired to sing at Blanche Calloway's club; debuted on Atlantic Records with "So Long," which reached #6 on R&B charts (1949) and led to such a string of hits that Atlantic became known as "The House that Ruth Built": "Teardrops From My Eyes" (1950), "5-10-15 Hours," "(Mama) He Treats Your Daughter Mean," "Mend Your Ways," "Miss Rhythm," "Oh What a Dream" and "Mambo Baby"; crossed over to the pop charts with "Lucky Lips," which reached #25 (1957); shut out of pop charts when her songs were covered by white artists; left Atlantic Records (1960); worked as a domestic and busdriver for many years; started up the Rhythm & Blues Foundation (1976), which established an R&B archive based in the Smithsonian Institution's National Museum of American History; became host of national radio program *Harlem Hit Parade* (later known as *BluesStage*); appeared as Motormouth Mabel in John Waters' film *Hairspray* (1988). Won Tony Award for performance in *Black and Blue* (1989) and Grammy for album *Blues on Broadway;* inducted into Rock and Roll Hall of Fame (1993). ❖ See also autobiography (with Andrew Yule), *Miss Rhythm: The Autobiography of Ruth Brown* (Fine, 1996); and *Women in World History.*

BROWN, Tina (1953—). English writer and editor. Name variations: Christina Hambley Brown. Born Christina Hambley Brown, Nov 21, 1953, in Maidenhead, Berkshire, England; St. Anne's College, Oxford University, MA, 1974; m. Harold Evans (English journalist, editor and author), 1981; children: George and Isabel. ❖ Controversial magazine editor, began career as journalist for *London Sunday Times, The New Statesman* and *The Sunday Telegraph,* winning Catherine Pakenham Award for most Promising Female Journalist (1973); worked as columnist for *Punch* (1978); became editor-in-chief of *Tatler* (1979), revitalizing the magazine and raising circulation by 300%; moved with husband to New York City (1983), becoming editor-in-chief of Condé-Nast's *Vanity Fair* magazine (1984); was extremely successful with *Vanity Fair* as well, winning 4 National Magazine Awards; appointed 4th editor of *The New Yorker* (1992); enlivened *New Yorker* through use of more color and increased focus on current events but changes brought as much censure as praise; was 1st magazine editor to receive the National Press Foundation's Editor of the Year Award (1992); left *New Yorker* (1998) to found Talk Media, launching *Talk* magazine (soon defunct) and Talk Miramax Book company, a publishing venture that produced 11 titles listed on *New York Times* Bestseller List in a few short years; wrote weekly column for *The Washington Post* and hosted CNBC's *Topic A with Tina Brown;* writings include (play) *Under the Bamboo Tree* (1973), *Loose Talk* (1979) and *Life as a Party* (1983). Awarded Commander of British Empire (CBE, 2000).

BROWN, Trisha (1936—). American choreographer and dancer. Born Patricia Brown, Nov 25, 1936, in Aberdeen, Washington; Mills College, BA in dance, 1958; studied with Anna Halprin, José Limón, Merce

Cunningham, Louis Horst, Robert Dunn. ❖ Taught dance at Reed College, Portland, OR (1958–59); moved to NY (1960); was a founding member of Judson Dance Theater (early 1960s), where she presented 1st works, including *Lightfall* (1963), *Rulegame 5* (1965), and *A String* (1966); began using specialized surfaces and equipment in choreography for such works as *Planes* (1968), *Leaning Duets* (1970) and *Roof Piece* (1971); founded Trisha Brown Company (1970); received New York Dance and Performance awards (1984, 1986) and Samuel H. Scripps American Dance Festival award (1993); appointed to US National Council on the Arts (1994). ❖ See also Lise Brunel, *Trisha Brown* (1987).

BROWN, Vanessa (1928–1999). Austrian-born actress and writer. Name variations: Tessa Brind. Born Smylla Brind, Mar 24, 1928, in Vienna, Austria; died May 21, 1999, in Los Angeles, California; m. Mark Sandrich Jr. (tv director). ❖ At 13, as Tessa Brind, appeared on Broadway in *Watch on the Rhine;* at 16, made screen debut; films include *Margie, The Ghost and Mrs. Muir, The Late George Apley, Mother Wore Tights, The Foxes of Harrow, The Heiress, Tarzan and the Slave Girl, The Bad and the Beautiful, Rosie* and *Bless the Beasts and Children;* also published several books.

BROWN, Vera Scantlebury (1889–1946). Australian physician. Born Vera Scantlebury in Australia, Aug 7, 1889; died July 14, 1946 (some sources cite 1945); dau. of G.J. (doctor) and Catherine (Baynes) Scantlebury; University of Melbourne, MD, 1913; m. Edward Brown (professor of engineering at University of Melbourne), Sept 1926; children: 2. ❖ After residency at Children's Hospital, Melbourne, worked in a London military hospital during WWI before returning to Melbourne (1919); assumed position of medical officer of the newly established Victorian Baby Health Centres Association, where she lectured on mother and infant care to nurse trainees; completed specialized training in children's diseases (1924) and made a study tour to New Zealand, Canada and US; with Henrietta Main, worked on a study comparing infant welfare in Victoria with that in New Zealand; as director of Infant Welfare in Victoria, was instrumental in establishing a system of infant welfare clinics. Awarded OBE (1938). ❖ See also *Women in World History.*

BROWN, Vida (1922—). American ballet dancer. Born 1922 in Oak Park, Illinois. ❖ Performed with Chicago Opera Ballet; joined Ballet Russe de Monte Carlo where she danced numerous roles including the Cowgirl in Agnes de Mille's *Rodeo* and the goose girl in *Igrouchki;* joined New York City Ballet (1950), appearing in many works by Balanchine, including *A Life for the Tsar* (1950) and *La Valse* (1951), and the premiere of Antony Tudor's *Lady of the Camilias* (1951); began serving as ballet master of New York City Ballet (1954), then headed the State Ballet of Missouri ballet school.

BROWN, Virginia Mae (1923–1991). American lawyer and government official. Born in Pliny, Virginia, 1923; died in Charleston, West Virginia, Feb 24, 1991; mother was president of a small bank; graduate of University of West Virginia (Morgantown), 1945, and University of West Virginia School of Law, 1947; married; children: 2 daughters. ❖ Was the 1st woman executive secretary to serve on the Judicial Council of West Virginia (1944–52), the 1st woman to serve as an assistant attorney general (1952–61) and the 1st to be appointed state insurance commissioner (1962); served as council to the governor of West Virginia and as a member of the state public-utilities commission; appointed by President Lyndon Johnson to serve on the 11-member Interstate Commerce Commission (1964), was also chair of the commission (1969–70), during which time she fought to maintain public rail transportation. ❖ See also *Women in World History.*

BROWN BLACKWELL, Antoinette (1825–1921). American minister and suffragist. Name variations: Antoinette Brown; Antoinette Brown-Blackwell. Born Antoinette Louisa Brown, May 20, 1825, in Henrietta, New York; died in New Jersey, Nov 5, 1921; dau. of Joseph Brown (farmer) and Abigail Morse Brown; sister-in-law of Elizabeth Blackwell, Emily Blackwell, and Lucy Stone; aunt of Alice Stone Blackwell (1857–1950); Oberlin College, BA, 1847, MA in theology, 1850 (not recognized by Oberlin until 1908); m. Samuel Blackwell, Jan 24, 1856; children: Florence Blackwell (b. 1856); Mabel Blackwell (b. 1858); Edith Blackwell (b. 1860); Grace Blackwell (b. 1863); Agnes Blackwell (b. 1866); Ethel Blackwell (b. 1869). ❖ First ordained female minister in US and well-known public speaker on women's rights, temperance, and abolition, who successfully combined a career with marriage and motherhood, began public-speaking career on the lyceum circuit in the

northeastern US (1847); ordained as minister and installed as pastor of a Congregational Church in South Butler, NY (1853); became the 1st woman in the US to officiate at a marriage ceremony (1853); after her marriage and birth of 1st daughter (1856), curtailed, but did not eliminate, her public speaking, continuing to tour with Susan B. Anthony and to preach in New York City; wrote several volumes and articles on women's rights and religion, as well as a novel; participated in founding of Association for the Advancement of Women (1873); became a Unitarian and was recognized as a Unitarian minister (1878); founded and preached monthly at a Unitarian Church in Elizabeth, New Jersey (1903); was a featured speaker at the International Council of Women (1888) and the World Parliament of Religions (1893); testified before the Senate on behalf of federal suffrage for women (1906); writings include (novel) *The Island Neighbors* (1871), *The Philosophy of Individuality* (1893), *The Making of the Universe* (1914) and *The Social Side of Mind and Action* (1915). ❖ See also Elizabeth Cazden, *Antoinette Brown Blackwell* (Feminist Press, 1983); Carol Lasser and Marlene Deahl Merrill. *Friends and Sisters: Letters between Lucy Stone and Antoinette Brown Blackwell* (U. of Illinois Press, 1987); and *Women in World History.*

BROWN-MILLER, Lisa (1966—). American ice-hockey player. Born Elizabeth Brown, Nov 16, 1966, in Union Lake, Michigan; graduate of Providence College, 1988; m. John Miller (engineer), 1995. ❖ Served as head coach of the Princeton University women's ice hockey team (1991–96); named ECAC Player of the Year and American Women's Hockey Coaches' Association Player of the Year; named MVP of the US Women's National Team (1992); won a team gold medal at Nagano (1998), the 1st Olympics to feature women's ice hockey; won a team silver medal at World championships (1990, 1992, 1994, 1997). ❖ See also Mary Turco, *Crashing the Net: The U.S. Women's Olympic Ice Hockey Team and the Road to Gold* (HarperCollins, 1999); and *Women in World History.*

BROWN-POTTER, Mrs. (1857–1936). *See Potter, Cora.*

BROWNBILL, Kay. Australian politician. Name variations: Kay Catherine Millin Brownbill. ❖ A Liberal, was the 1st woman elected to the Australian House of Representatives (1966), for Kingston; served until 1969; wrote novel *Blow the Wind Southerly* (1962). Awarded OBE (1980).

BROWNE, Alice Seymour (1878–1941). *See Frame, Alice.*

BROWNE, Anne (d. 1511). Duchess of Suffolk. Died 1511; dau. of Sir Anthony Browne and Lucy Neville; m. Charles Brandon (1484–1545), 1st duke of Suffolk (r. 1514–1545), c. 1508; children: Anne Brandon (d. 1557); Mary Brandon (d. around 1542, who m. Thomas Stanley, Lord Monteagle).

BROWNE, Augusta (1820–1882). American composer, organist and journalist. Born Augusta Garrett in Dublin, Ireland, 1820; died in Washington, DC, Jan 11, 1882. ❖ One of the most prolific woman composers in US before 1870, was brought to US (late 1820s); served as organist at First Presbyterian Church in Brooklyn (1840s–50s); began to publish successful parlor songs and salon piano pieces (1840s), including *The Chieftain's Halls* (1844) and *The Warlike Dead in Mexico* (1848); was also a prominent musical journalist, arguing for the right of women to a complete and equal musical education. ❖ See also *Women in World History.*

BROWNE, Charlotte Elizabeth (1790–1846). *See Tonna, Charlotte Elizabeth.*

BROWNE, Coral (1913–1991). Australian-born actress. Born Coral Edith Brown in Melbourne, Australia, July 23, 1913; died May 29, 1991, in Los Angeles, California; dau. of Leslie Clarence and Victoria Elizabeth (Bennett) Brown; attended Claremont Ladies' College, Melbourne; studied painting at Working Men's College, Melbourne; m. Philip Westrope Pearman, June 26, 1950 (died); m. Vincent Price (actor), 1974. ❖ Accomplished tragic actress as well as an acclaimed comedian, was as comfortable in the role of Shakespeare's Lady Macbeth as she was cavorting as Vera Charles in *Auntie Mame;* in a 50-year career, was seen on stages in Australia, England, and US, as well as in a number of films; made professional stage debut in Melbourne (1931), as Margaret Orme in *Loyalties* and had 28 plays to her credit before leaving Australia for England; made London debut as Nora Swinburne in *Lover's Leap* (1934); played in such London hits as *Mated* (1935), *Death Asks a Verdict* (1936), and *The Taming of the Shrew* (1937); also portrayed Maggie Cutler in *The Man Who Came to Dinner* (1941), Ruth Sherwood in *My*

Sister Eileen (1943), Mrs. Cheyney in *The Last of Mrs. Cheyney* (1944) and Lady Frederick Berolles in *Lady Frederick* (1946); began long association with Old Vic (1951), when she debuted as Emilia in *Othello;* went on to play numerous Shakespearean roles; made Broadway debut in *Tamburlaine the Great;* films include *The Roman Spring of Mrs. Stone* (1961), *Dr. Crippen* (1964), *The Night of the Generals* (1967), *The Legend of Lylah Clare* (1968), *The Killing of Sister George* (1968), *The Ruling Class* (1972), *Theater of Blood* (1973), *The Drowning Pool* (1975) and *Dream Child* (1985). ❖ See also *Women in World History.*

BROWNE, Ethel (1885–1965). See *Harvey, Ethel Browne.*

BROWNE, Felicia Dorothea (1793–1835). See *Hemans, Felicia D.*

BROWNE, Frances (1816–1879). Irish author. Name variations: Blind Poetess of Donegal. Born Frances Browne in Stranolar, Co. Donegal, Ireland, Jan 16, 1816; died in London, Aug 25, 1879; educated at home; never married; no children. ❖ At 18 months, lost her sight due to smallpox; as an adult, contributed regularly to journals and periodicals; published most popular work, *Granny's Wonderful Chair and the Stories It Told* (1856); also wrote *The Star of Alteghei* (1844) and *My Share in the World* (1861), among others.

BROWNE, Harriet Louisa (1829–1906). New Zealand political hostess and letter writer. Name variations: Harriet Louisa Campbell. Born Harriet Louisa Campbell, July 1, 1829, in Scotland; died April 9, 1906, at Brooklands, Weybridge, Surrey, England; dau. of James Campbell and Grace Elizabeth (Hay) Campbell; m. Thomas Robert Gore Browne (governor), 1851 (died 1887); children: 6. ❖ Organized and hosted weekly cultural and political events, bolstering husband's popularity and success as governor of New Zealand; when war erupted over the Crown taking land from Maori (1860), supported husband's controversial stance and wrote numerous letters to people in England and New Zealand seeking support; when husband was appointed governor of Tasmania, Australia (1861), became more involved in social issues, including establishing an industrial reform school, where she also taught. ❖ See also *Dictionary of New Zealand Biography* (Vol. 1).

BROWNE, Helen Edith (1911–1987). English nurse-midwife. Born Helen Edith Browne, Feb 3, 1911, in Bury St. Edmonds, England; died Jan 20, 1987, in Milford, Pennsylvania; dau. of Phil and Agnes (Rice-Capon) Browne; attended St. Bartholomew's Hospital School of Nursing in London, 1931–34, and British Hospital for Mothers and Babies in London, 1934–35; never married; no children. ❖ Celebrated educator, nurse-midwife, and administrator, practiced privately as nurse-midwife (1935–38) and as midwifery supervisor for British Hospital for Mothers and Babies (1937); arrived in Leslie Co., Kentucky (July 1938), to work for Mary Breckinridge's Frontier Nursing Service (FNS) as district midwife at Red Bird-Flat Creek Clinic; joined Frontier Graduate School of Midwifery (FNS' training school) as faculty member (1940); was supervisor of FNS' Hyden Hospital, then assistant director (1947), then director (1965) after Mary Breckinridge's death; raised funds for creation of Mary Breckinridge Hospital. Named Officer of the British Empire (1964) and Commander of the British Empire (1976).

BROWNE, Irene (1896–1965). English stage and screen actress. Born June 29, 1896, in London, England; died July 24, 1965, in London. ❖ Made London stage debut as a dancer (1910); appeared as lead or second lead in numerous plays, including as Margaret Harris in *Cavalcade* and Madame Arcati in *Blithe Spirit;* made Broadway debut at age 14 in *The Red Mill;* films include *Cavalcade, The Letter* and *Berkeley Square.*

BROWNE, Kathleen Anne (b. 1878). Irish politician and nationalist. Born Oct 1878 in Bridgetown, Co. Waterford, Ireland; dau. of Michael Browne. ❖ Was a member of Sinn Féin (1912–27), then Cumann na nGaedheal; jailed briefly during the Rising (1916); elected to 3rd Triennial Seanad to fill the vacancy left by the death of Alice Stopford Green (June 20, 1929); elected to 4th Triennial (1931–34) and 5th Triennial (1934–36); played a crucial role in the preservation of Great Saltee Island bird sanctuary (1938).

BROWNE, Leslie (1958—). American ballet dancer. Name variations: Leslie Brown. Born Leslie Brown, 1958, in New York, NY; raised in Phoenix, Arizona; goddau. of Herbert Ross (choreographer and film producer); dau. of Kelly Brown (1928–1981) and Isabel Mirrow (both dancers with American Ballet Theatre); sister of Kevin Kelly Brown (producer), Ethan Brown (dancer) and Elizabeth Laing (dancer); m. Leonide Slepak. ❖ Trained at School of American Ballet after initial schooling from parents; joined corps of New York City Ballet as adolescent; was cast alongside Mikhail Baryshnikov as the young ballerina in

The Turning Point, a film based loosely on the story of her family; danced roles for Ballet Theater in Baryshnikov's *The Nutcracker* and Antony Tudor's *Jardin aux Lilas;* promoted to principal dancer of American Ballet Theater (1976), where she danced until stage retirement (1993); has taught classes at numerous venues, including Brandywine Ballet in West Chester, PA, and Steps studio in New York City.

BROWNE, Maria da Felicidade do Couto (c. 1797–1861). Portuguese poet and salonnière. Born around 1797 in Portugal; died 1861; married a wealthy merchant of Irish descent. ❖ Held famous literary salon; became lover of novelist Camilo Castelo Branco and exchanged love poems with him in local newspapers; published poetry collections: *A Coruja Trovadora, Sóror Dolores* (1849) and *Virações da Madrugada* (1854).

BROWNE, Marjorie (1910–1990). English actress, singer, dancer. Name variations: Lady Reeve; Marjorie Reeve. Born Florence Marjorie Brown, Mar 13, 1910, in Manchester, England; died Oct 21, 1990; m. (Charles) Trevor Reeve (barrister, knighted 1973). ❖ Made London debut in *One Darn Thing After Another* (1927), followed by *This Year of Grace, Wake Up and Dream, Mother Goose, Jack and the Beanstalk, Sporting Love, On Your Toes, Crazy Days, Rose Marie* and the lead in *Chu Chin Chow;* films include *Lassie from Lancashire, Laugh It Off* and *I Didn't Do It.*

BROWNE, Mary K. (1891–1971). American golfer and tennis player. Born June 3, 1891, in Ventura, California; died Aug 19, 1971, in Laguna Beach, California. ❖ The only person to have played in championship rounds in both tennis and golf, held US National Tennis Singles title (1912–14), National Doubles (1913–14), and National Mixed Doubles (1912–14, 1921); reached the final round of the USGA Women's Amateur, (1924), beating Glenna Collett in the semifinal, then losing to Dorothy Campbell Hurd in the final.

BROWNE, Rosalind Bengelsdorf (1916–1979). American artist. Name variations: Rosalind Bengelsdorf. Born Rosalind Bengelsdorf in 1916 in New York, NY; died 1979 in New York; studied art at Art Students League, the Annot School, and with Hans Hofmann at his newly established school on 57th Street, NY; m. Byron Browne (abstract artist), 1940. ❖ A founding member of the American Abstract Artists, devoted a lifetime to advancing the abstract art movement; was one of a handful of abstract artists to win funding from the Federal Art Project, for a mural for the Central Nurses Home (1938). ❖ See also *Women in World History.*

BROWNE, Mrs. Sedley (1861–1944). See *Crosman, Henrietta.*

BROWNE, Sidney Jane (1850–1941). British nurse. Name variations: Dame Sidney Browne. Born Jan 5, 1850; died Aug 13, 1941. ❖ Known as "the modern Florence Nightingale" for her work nursing soldiers, served in 4 campaigns: the Egyptian War, Sudan campaign, Boer War, and World War I; also served as the 1st president of the Royal College of Nursing.

BROWNELL, Kady (b. 1842). American military leader. Name variations: Kate. Born in Caffraria, on the African coast, in 1842; death date unknown; dau. of a soldier in the British army; m. Robert S. Brownell (soldier). ❖ Civil War hero who served with the Rhode Island Volunteers, joined husband's infantry company (1861); an excellent markswoman, was assigned as color-bearer and fought alongside husband in several battles; is credited with saving the day at Newbern when the regiment, traveling through a dense forest, was fired upon by another group of Union soldiers who mistook them for the enemy; rushed forward, waving the regimental flag until the attackers realized their mistake. ❖ See also *Women in World History.*

BROWNELL, Kate (b. 1842). See *Brownell, Kady.*

BROWNER, Carol M. (1956—). American lawyer, politician, and environmentalist. Born Dec 16, 1955, in Miami, Florida; grew up in southern Florida near Everglades; dau. of professors at Miami-Dade Community College; University of Florida, BS, 1977, JD; m. Michael Podhorzer; children: Zachary. ❖ Skilled negotiator, was the longest-serving director of US Environmental Protection Agency in history; served as general counsel for Florida House of Representatives Government Operations Committee (1979–83); worked for Senator Lawton Chiles, helping to negotiate complex land swap expanding Big Cypress National Preserve (1986–89); worked for Senator Al Gore Jr. (1989–90), drafting amendments to the Clean Air Act; returned to employ of state of Florida when Lawton Chiles became governor, serving as secretary of Department of Environmental Regulation, 3rd largest environmental agency in US (1991–93); brokered widely praised agreement between Walt Disney

World and state of Florida in which company would be allowed to develop property in exchange for $40 million to reclaim 8,500 acres of endangered land and create wildlife refuge; lauded for common sense, cost-effective solutions to public health and environmental challenges; served as director of US Environmental Protection Agency under President Bill Clinton (1993–2000); elected to Audubon Society's board of directors (2001).

BROWNING, Angela (1946—). English politician and member of Parliament. Born Angela Pearson, Dec 4, 1946; m. David Browning, 1968. ❖ Served as chair, Women into Business (1988–92); as a Conservative, elected to House of Commons for Tiverton and Honiton (1992, 1997, 2001, 2005).

BROWNING, Elizabeth Barrett (1806–1861). English poet. Name variations: Elizabeth Barrett (1806–1846); Elizabeth Barrett-Browning (1846–1861). Born Elizabeth Barrett Moulton in Co. Durham, England, Mar 6, 1806; died June 30, 1861, in Florence, Italy; dau. of Edward Barrett Moulton (who would change his name to Barrett for reasons of inheritance) and Mary Graham-Clarke; m. Robert Browning (the poet), Sept 12, 1846; children: Robert "Pen" Wiedemann Browning (b. 1849). ❖ Poet who wrote some of the most exquisite love poems in the English language—the 1st cycle of Petrarchan love sonnets to be written from the woman's rather than the man's point of view; published 1st book, *An Essay on Mind with Other Poems* (1826), anonymously, at age 20; followed up initial triumph with a translation of Aeschylus' *Prometheus Bound* (1833), and a further book of poetry, *The Seraphim and Other Poems* (1838), which for the 1st time carried her name on the title page; by early 1840s, was probably the best-known and most admired woman poet in Britain; developed a serious ailment, a form of tuberculosis, and some biographers have speculated that it was a psychosomatic stratagem, brought on by the tensions of her family life; also suffered from a spinal injury incurred in a riding accident; spent virtually all her time in her work room, allowing only a small circle of close friends to visit her; exchanged greetings with poet Robert Browning (Jan 1845) after he wrote her a letter of admiration for her poems; met with him frequently in her room and wrote him a series of sonnets, the most famous of which, "How do I love thee? Let me count the ways," was included in her *Sonnets from the Portuguese;* married him, returned home without mentioning it, then immigrated with him to Italy the following week; after marriage, remained the more famous half of the couple, and, when William Wordsworth died (1850), her name was mentioned among the candidates for poet laureate; health began to improve; published *Aurora Leigh* (1857), a blank verse, book-length poem in the form of an autobiography, full of echoes of her own life; other writings include *A Drama of Exile and Other Poems* (1845), *The Runaway Slave at Pilgrim's Point* (1849), *Casa Guidi Windows* (1851), *Poems before Congress* (1860), *Last Poems* (1862), and numerous volumes containing her letters to her sister, as well as Mary Russell Mitford, R.H. Horne, Robert Browning, and others. ❖ See also Daniel Karlin, *The Courtship of Robert Browning and Elizabeth Barrett* (Oxford U. Press, 1985); Elvan Kintner, ed. *The Letters of Robert Browning and Elizabeth Barrett-Browning* (Harvard U. Press, 1969); R. Mander, *Mrs. Browning: The Story of Elizabeth Barrett* (Widenfeld & Nicolson, 1980); Raymond and Sullivan, eds. *The Letters of Elizabeth Barrett-Browning to Mary Russell Mitford* (3 vols., Wedgestone, 1983); Barbara Dennis, *Elizabeth Barrett Browning: The Hope End Years* (Dufour, 1996); and *Women in World History.*

BROWNING, Peaches (1910–1956). See Heenan, Frances.

BROWNRIGG, Elizabeth (1720–1767). English murderer. Born Elizabeth Harkly (or Hartley) in 1720; hanged at Tyburn, England, Sept 14, 1767; m. James Brownrigg (plumber); children: 16. ❖ Married to a prospering plumber, lost 13 of her 16 children in infancy, and, in light of her subsequent behavior, it is possible that she was at least a contributory factor in their deaths; went on to build a respected midwifery practice, which kept her so busy that she was forced to take in apprentices from the local workhouse; abused 3 successive teenage apprentices, all named Mary, one of whom died of massive injuries; was hanged in front of one of the largest, and angriest, crowds ever assembled for a public execution in England. ❖ See also *Women in World History.*

BROWNSCOMBE, Jennie Augusta (1850–1936). American painter. Born Dec 10, 1850, near Honesdale, Pennsylvania; died Aug 5, 1936, in New York, NY; dau. of William Brownscombe (English farmer) and Elvira (Kennedy) Brownscombe; attended Cooper Institute School of Design, National Academy of Design, and Art Students League; never married; no children. ❖ Specializing in genre and works depicting early

American history, sold 1st painting "Grandmother's Treasures" (1876); contributed illustrations to Scribner and *Harper's Weekly;* studied in Paris with Henry Mosler (beginning 1882); exhibited at Royal Academy in London (1900), Water Color Society in Rome, and in Philadelphia, NY and Chicago; began association with George Henry Hall (1890); had more than 100 prints copyrighted when magazines, calendar firms, and publishers of prints sought out her work; produced works on historical subjects including "The Peace Ball" (1895–97) and "The First American Thanksgiving"; contributed color illustrations to Pauline Bouvé's *Tales of the Mayflower Children* (1927).

BROWNSON, Josephine (1880–1942). American Catholic religious educator. Born Josephine Van Dyke Brownson, Jan 26, 1880, in Detroit, Michigan; died Nov 10, 1942, in Grosse Pointe, Michigan; dau. of Henry Francis Brownson and Josephine (Van Dyke) Brownson; paternal granddau. of Orestes Brownson; maternal granddau. of James A. Van Dyke (mayor of Detroit); attended Detroit Normal Training School; University of Michigan, AB, 1913; never married; no children. ❖ Began catechetical class and social center in basement of a parochial school (c. 1896); with group of women, founded Weinman Settlement (1904), from which League of Catholic Women developed under her sponsorship (1916); began teaching industrial mathematics at Cass Technical High School (1914) and became 2nd assistant to principal at Cass (1919); organized Catholic Instruction League (1916); wrote syllabus for teachers urging new approach to catechism (*Stopping the Leak*, 1925); wrote widely used elementary-school textbook, *Learn of Me* series, to provide essentials of religious instruction and prepare students for 1st Holy Communion.

BROWNSTEIN, Carrie (1974—). American musician. Name variations: Sleater-Kinney. Born Sept 27, 1974, in Seattle, Washington; graduate of Evergreen State College, Olympia. ❖ Lead singer and guitarist, was part of the band Excuse 17 (early 1990s) and performed on albums *Excuse Seventeen* (1995) and *Such Friends Are Dangerous* (1995); with Corin Tucker and drummer Lora McFarlane, formed alternative rock and punk group, Sleater-Kinney, releasing debut album, *Sleater-Kinney* (1995), which addressed sexism and sexual abuse; with group, released *Call the Doctor* (1996), which included the song, "I Wanna be Your Joey Ramone," and was voted best album of the year; also released *All Hands on the Bad One* (2000), which included "The Ballad of a Ladyman"; with group, appeared on Go-Betweens album, *The Friends of Rachel Worth* (2000). Other acclaimed albums include *Dig Me Out* (1997) and *The Hot Rock* (1999).

BROXON, Mildred Downey (1944—). American science-fiction writer. Name variations: (pseudonym) Sigfridur Skaldaspillir. Born Mildred Downey, June 7, 1944, in Atlanta, Georgia; grew up in Brazil; Seattle University, BA in psychology, 1965, BS in nursing, 1970; m. G.D. Torgerson, 1965 (div. 1969); m. William D. Broxon, 1969 (died 1981). ❖ Worked as teacher's aide and psychiatric nurse; served as vice-president of Science Fiction Writers of America (1975–77); wrote novels *Eric Brighteyes No. 2: A Witch's Welcome* (1979), *The Demon of Scattery* (with Poul Anderson, 1979), and *Too Long a Sacrifice* (1983); published short stories in science-fiction magazines; wrote "Singularity," regarded as her best short story, which was anthologized in *Black Holes* (1979).

BROZ, Jovanka (b. 1924). See Tito, Jovanka Broz.

BRUCE, Betty (1920–1974). American dancer and comedian. Born May 2, 1920, in Brooklyn, NY; died July 18, 1974, in New York, NY. ❖ Trained at Metropolitan Opera Ballet's school as a child until she had to leave due to her exceptional height (5′7); toured with Albertina Rasch's concert troupe for tall dancers, performing a mixture of classical ballet and tap; appeared in numerous clubs throughout NY and across Europe as a popular theatrical and tap dancer; was a featured dancer in Balanchine's *Boys from Syracuse* (1938); danced in a number of Broadway shows, including *Keep Off the Grass* (1940), *High Kickers* (1941–42), *Something for the Boys* (1943–44), and *Gypsy* (1959), and appeared as Tessie Tura in the film version (1962); danced on tv and at Radio City Music Hall, Strand Theater Roof, and other NY performance houses.

BRUCE, Catherine Wolfe (1816–1900). American astronomy patron. Born Jan 22, 1816, in New York, NY; died Mar 13, 1900, in New York; dau. of George (printer and type founder, died 1866) and Catherine (Wolfe) Bruce; cousin of Catharine L. Wolfe (1828–1887, philanthropist); educated privately; never married; no children. ❖ Donated $50,000 (1887), for the George Bruce Branch of New York Free-Circulating

Library (later New York Public Library); translated and printed edition of Tommaso da Celano's *Dies Irae;* began career as patron of astronomical and astrophysical research with 1st gift ($50,000), at age 73, to finance construction of photographic telescope for Harvard College Observatory (1889); made contributions which benefited many astronomers at important stages in their careers; endowed a gold medal for distinguished services to astronomy awarded by Astronomical Society of the Pacific (1897).

BRUCE, Christian (d. 1356). Countess of Mar. Name variations: Lady Christian Bruce; Lady Christian Seton; Christian Moray or Murray; Christina Bruce. Died 1356; dau. of Robert Bruce, earl of Carrick, and Marjorie of Carrick (c. 1254–1292); sister of Robert I the Bruce (1274–1329), king of Scotland (r. 1306–1329); m. Garnait also known as Gratney, 7th earl of Mar, around 1292; m. Christopher Seton, 1305; m. Andrew Murray also known as Andrew Moray of Bothwell, after Oct 12, 1325; children: (1st m.) Donald, 8th earl of Mar; Helen of Mar (who m. John Mentieth, lord of Arran, and Sir James Garioch); (3rd m.) John Moray, lord of Bothwell; Sir Thomas Moray. ❖ During Scotland's wars for independence (1296–1328), defended Kildrummy Castle when it came under siege.

BRUCE, Christina (d. 1356). *See Bruce, Christian.*

BRUCE, Ethel (1879–1967). Australian prime-ministerial wife. Born Ethel Dunlop Anderson, May 25, 1879, in Melbourne, Australia; died Mar 1967 in London, England; m. Stanley Melbourne Bruce (prime minister of Australia, 1923–29), July 12, 1913; children: none. ❖ As the 1st ministerial wife to reside in The Lodge when the seat of government moved from Melbourne to Canberra, had to hire staff and establish a household (1927).

BRUCE, Isabel (c. 1278–1358). Queen of Norway. Born c. 1278; died in 1358; dau. of Robert Bruce, earl of Carrick, and Marjorie of Carrick (c. 1254–1292); sister of Robert I Bruce (1274–1329), king of Scotland (r. 1306–1329); became 2nd wife of Eirik the Priest-Hater also known as Eric II Magnusson (1268–1299), king of Norway (r. 1280–1299), in 1293; children: Ingeborg Ericsdottir (b. 1297, who m. Waldemar, duke of Finland). Eric II's 1st wife was Margaret of Norway (1261–1283).

BRUCE, Isabella (d. 1296). *See Isabella of Mar.*

BRUCE, Kate (1858–1946). American silent-film actress. Name variations: Phyllis Forde. Born 1858 in Columbus, Indiana; died April 2, 1946, in New York, NY. ❖ Character actress, appeared in motherly roles for D.W. Griffith films, including *The Country Doctor, Judith of Bethulia, Hearts of the World, Orphans of the Storm* and *A Bowery Cinderella;* best known as Mrs. Bartlett in *Way Down East* (1920).

BRUCE, Mrs. Lyndhurst (1885–1970). *See Clifford, Camille.*

BRUCE, Margaret (c. 1286–?). Scottish royal. Born c. 1286; dau. of Robert Bruce, earl of Carrick, and Marjorie of Carrick (c. 1254–1292); sister of Robert I the Bruce (1274–1329), king of Scotland (r. 1306–1329); m. William de Carlyle; children: William de Carlyle; John de Carlyle.

BRUCE, Margaret (1296–1316). Scottish princess. Name variations: Marjory or Marjorie Bruce. Born 1296 (some sources cite 1297); died in an accident at age 20, Mar 2, 1316, in Paisley, Strathclyde, Scotland; interred at Paisley Abbey; dau. of Robert I the Bruce (1274–1329), king of Scotland (r. 1306–1329), and Isabella of Mar (died in 1296, shortly after giving birth to Margaret); m. Walter Stewart or Stuart (d. 1326), 6th High Steward of Scotland, in 1315; children: Robert II (1316–1390), king of Scotland (r. 1371–1390). ❖ Captured by the English, along with aunt Mary Bruce (fl. 1290–1316) and Isabella of Buchan (fl. 1290–1310), was placed in a nunnery in Yorkshire (1306); exchanged for English prisoners after battle of Bannockburn and returned to Scotland (1314); married Walter Stewart (1315); was killed while pregnant when she fell from her horse (1316), though her baby, successfully delivered from her dead body, succeeded to the throne as the 1st Stewart monarch of Scotland, Robert II (1371). ❖ See also *Women in World History.*

BRUCE, Margaret (d. 1346). Scottish princess. Died in childbirth, 1346 (some sources cite 1347); dau. of Robert I the Bruce (1274–1329), king of Scotland (r. 1306–1329), and Elizabeth de Burgh (d. 1327); m. William Sutherland, 5th earl of Sutherland, 1343 or 1345; children: John (b. around 1346).

BRUCE, Marjorie.
See Marjorie of Carrick (c. 1254–1292).
See Bruce, Margaret (1296–1316).

BRUCE, Mary (fl. 1290–1316). Scottish royal. Fl. around 1290 to 1316; died before 1323; dau. of Robert Bruce, earl of Carrick, and Marjorie of Carrick (c. 1254–1292); sister of Robert the Bruce also known as Robert I, king of Scotland (r. 1306–1329); m. Neil Campbell of Lochow, c. 1312; m. Alexander Fraser, 1316; children: (1st m.) John of Lochow (b. around 1313), earl of Atholl; Dougal; Duncan; (2nd m.) John of Touch (b. around 1317); Sir William Fraser (b. around 1318).

BRUCE, Mary Grant (1878–1958). Australian journalist and children's writer. Name variations: (pseudonym) Cinderella. Born May 24, 1878, in Sale, Victoria, Australia; died July 12, 1958, in Bexhill-on-Sea, England; dau. of Eyre Lewis Bruce and Mary Whittakers Bruce; m. George Evans, 1914 (died 1946); children: 2. ❖ Worked as children's editor for *The Age;* traveled to England and Ireland (1913) and met future husband; wrote stories for BBC Children's Hour (1930s) and contributed to *Blackwood's Magazine;* returned to Australia (1939); published 37 children's novels, including *A Little Bush Maid* (1910), which became the 1st of 15 books in the "Billabong Series" (1910–42), and *Peter and Co.* (1940); wrote book of aboriginal legends, *The Stone Age of Burkamukk* (1922), and collection of radio talks, *The Power Within* (1940).

BRUCE, Matilda (c. 1285–c. 1326). Countess of Ross. Name variations: Matilda Ross; Maud Bruce. Born c. 1285; died c. 1326; interred at Fearn, Scotland; dau. of Robert Bruce, earl of Carrick, and Marjorie of Carrick (c. 1254–1292); sister of Robert I the Bruce (1274–1329), king of Scotland (r. 1306–1329); m. Hugh Ross (d. 1333), 4th earl of Ross, around 1308; children: Euphemia Ross (d. 1387).

BRUCE, Matilda (d. 1353). Scottish princess. Died July 20, 1353, in Aberdeen Grampian, Scotland; buried in Dunfermline Abbey, Fife, Scotland; dau. of Robert I the Bruce (1274–1329), king of Scotland (r. 1306–1329), and Elizabeth de Burgh (d. 1327); m. Thomas Isaac; children: Joan Isaac, Lady of Lorn (fl. 1300s); Katherine Isaac.

BRUCE, Norma (c. 1908–1966). *See Smallwood, Norma.*

BRUCE, Tonie Edgar (1892–1966). English stage-and-screen actress. Name variations: Tonie Edgar-Bruce. Born Sybil Etonia Bruce, June 4, 1892, in London, England; died Mar 28, 1966; dau. of Lucy (Windham-Lukin) Bruce and Edgar Bruce (actor-manager); m. Vivian R. Barron (div.); m. John Redman (div.). ❖ Made stage debut in *Improper Peter* (1912), followed by *The Little Café, Peter Pan, A Dear Little Lady, The Circle, Quarantine, Benediction, Conflict, This Money Business, Elizabeth of Austria, Nine Til Six* and *Pygmalion;* on death of father, became proprietor of the Prince of Wales's Theatre until 1935; made over 30 films, including *Derby Day, Spitfire, The Last Waltz, Lilies of the Field, Mannequin* and *Lucky Girl.*

BRUCE, Virginia (1910–1982). American actress. Born Helen Virginia Briggs, Sept 29, 1910, in Minneapolis, Minnesota; died Feb 24, 1982, in Woodland Hills, California; m. John Gilbert (actor), 1932 (div. 1934); m. J. Walter Ruben (director), Dec 18, 1937 (died 1942); m. Ali Ipar (Turkish writer-producer), 1946; children: (1st m.) Susan Ann Gilbert; (2nd m.) Christopher Ruben. ❖ Made film debut in *The Love Parade* (1928); appeared in lead roles in a number of films, including *The Great Ziegfeld* (1936), *Born to Dance* (1936), *Between Two Women* (1937), *Arsène Lupin Returns* (1938), *Yellow Jack* (1938), *Invisible Woman* (1941), *Pardon My Sarong* (1942), *Night has a Thousand Eyes* (1948), *The Reluctant Bride* (1952), and as Kim Novak's mother in *Strangers When We Meet* (1960).

BRUCE, Wendy (1973—). American gymnast. Born Mar 23, 1973, in Fort Lauderdale, Florida. ❖ At Barcelona Olympics, won a bronze medal in team all-around (1992).

BRÜCK, Anita (b. 1899). *See Brück, Christa-Anita.*

BRÜCK, Christa-Anita (1899–). German novelist. Name variations: Christa Anita Bruck or Brueck; Anita Brück. Born 1899 in Germany. ❖ Wrote *Schicksale hinter Schreibmaschinen* (1930), *Ein Mädchen mit Prokura* (1932), and *Die Lawine* (1941).

BRÜCKNER, Christine (1921–1996). West German novelist. Name variations: Christine Brueckner, Bruckner or Bruchner. Born Dec 10, 1921, in Schmelinghausen, Hesse, Germany; died Dec 22, 1996, in Kassel, Germany. ❖ Published the 1st of her "Poenichen" trilogy, *Jauche und Levkojen* (Muck and Stocks, 1975, published in English as *Gillyflower Kid*), and its sequels, *Nirgendwo ist Poenichen* (1977, published in English as *Flight of Cranes*, 1982), and *Die Quints* (1985); also wrote *Ehe die Spuren verwehen* (Before All Trace Fades Away, 1954), *Der Kokon* (The Cocoon, 1966), and a collection of fictitious speeches by famous women: *Wenn du gerede hätest, Desdemona. Ungehaltene Reden ungehaltener Frauen* (If Only You Had Spoken, Desdemona: Angry Words from Angry Women, 1983).

BRUDDLAND, Gro Harlem (b. 1939). *See Bruntland, Gro Harlem.*

BRUECK, Christa-Anita (b. 1899). *See Brück, Christa-Anita.*

BRUECKNER, Christine (1921—). *See Brückner, Christine.*

BRUELL, Ilse (1925–1942). *See Brüll, Ilse.*

BRUENING, Elfriede (b. 1910). *See Brüning, Elfriede.*

BRUES, Alice (1913—). American physical anthropologist. Name variations: Alice Mossie Brues. Born Alice Mossie Brues, Oct 9, 1913, in Boston, MA; dau. of Beirne Barrett (amateur field botanist) and Charles Thomas Brues (professor of entomology at Harvard University); sister of Austin M. Brues; Bryn Mawr College, BA, 1933; Radcliffe College, MA, PhD in anthropology, 1940. ❖ Influenced by Ernest Hooton at Radcliffe, served as research associate at Peabody Museum of Harvard (1940–41) and as assistant statistician at Wright Field (1942–44); while serving as assistant professor of anatomy at University of Oklahoma School of Medicine, extended work to population genetics of A-B-O blood group system; published 1st paper in population genetics, "Selection and Polymorphism in the A-B-O Blood Groups" (1954), which became a classic in physical anthropology; served as curator of physical anthropology at Stovall Museum in Norman, Oklahoma (1956–65), chair of anthropology department at University of Colorado at Boulder (1968–71), and vice president (1966–68), then president (1971–73), of American Association of Physical Anthropologists; wrote textbook *People and Races* (1977), but probably best known for her essay "The Spearman and the Archer" (1959).

BRUGGEN, Carry van (1881–1932). Dutch novelist. Name variations: Carry de Haan; (pseudonym) Justine Abbing. Born Carolina Lea de Haan, Jan 1, 1881, in Smulde, Netherlands; died Nov 16, 1932, in Laren; dau. of a Jewish cantor; sister of Jacob Israël de Haan; m. Kees van Bruggen, 1904; married A. Pit. ❖ Writings, which draw on experiences of her childhood in a strict Orthodox Jewish home, include *De verlatene* (1910), *Heleen* (1913), *Het huisje aan de sloot* (1921), *Avontuurtjies* (1922), *Hedendaagsch fetischisme* (1925) and *Eva* (1927).

BRUGHA, Caitlin (1879–1959). Irish politician. Born Caitlin Kingston, Dec 1879, in Birr, Co. Offaly, Ireland; died Dec 1, 1959; m. Cathal Brugha, 1912 (IRA chief of staff, 1917–18, acting president of 1st Dáil, 1919, killed while fighting for Republicans, 1922); children: 5 daughters, and son Ruaidhrí Brugha (TD, Dublin Co., South, 1973–77, senator, 1969–73, 1977–81). ❖ Republican, actively supported Volunteers during the Rising (1916) and served as secretary, Sinn Féin executive, for many years; elected to 4th (abstentionist) and 5th Dáil for Co. Waterford (1923–27); established a drapery business, Kingston's Ltd (1924).

BRUGNOLI, Amalia (c. 1808–?). Italian ballet dancer. Born c. 1808 in Milan, Italy; dau. of Giuseppina Brugnoli (ballerina); m. Paolo Samego (dancer). ❖ Trained at ballet school of Teatro alla Scala in Milan; joined company (1817) and made debut appearance in Salvatore Viganò's *Prometheus;* appeared briefly on stages in Vienna (early 1820s); danced mainly in northern Italy at Teatro San Carlo in Naples, where she made 1st appearance on point and is often considered the inventor of "tiptoe" dancing, and Teatro alla Scala in Milan; danced in Pietro Angiolini's *Haroum-al-Rachid* at Teatro Reggio in Turin (1823); created a role in Louis Henry's *Dircea* at La Scala (1826); danced one season with husband at Théâtre des Bouffes in Paris (1832).

BRUHA, Antonia (1915—). Austrian resistance leader. Born in Vienna, Austria, 1915, into a Czech-speaking working-class family; married. ❖ Was in an anti-Nazi resistance cell with husband; arrested and sent to Ravensbrück concentration camp (1941); emerged as an important organizer of a resistance organization that maintained prisoner morale, supplied them with drugs and additional food when they were ill, and warned them of particularly dangerous situations; survived and was liberated (1945); remained active in anti-Fascist educational work in Vienna. ❖ See also memoirs *Ich war keine Heldin* (I Was Not a Heroine, 1984); and *Women in World History.*

BRUHAT, Yvonne (1923—). *See Choquet-Bruhat, Yvonne.*

BRÜHNE, Vera (1910—). German murderer. Name variations: Vera Bruhne or Bruehne. Born 1910 in Germany; married twice; children: at least 1, Sylvia. ❖ At 50, was mistress to Otto Praun who cast her aside and took back expensive property he'd given her (1960); though Praun's

death was initially thought to be a suicide, was implicated in planning his murder by her 14-year-old daughter, who claimed it was carried out by another of Vera's lovers, Johann Ferbach; convicted with Ferbach; received a life sentence.

BRÜLL, Ilse (1925–1942). Austrian-Jewish Holocaust victim. Name variations: Bruell. Born April 28, 1925, in Innsbruck, Austria; murdered at Auschwitz, Sept 3, 1942; dau. of Rudolf Brüll (furniture manufacturer) and Julie Brüll; educated at primary and secondary public schools in Innsbruck. ❖ Schooling ended (Nov 1938) due to Kristallnacht pogrom; left Austria with a group of Jewish children accepted for resettlement by the Netherlands (April 1939); taken to Hertogenbosch camp (Aug 1941); deported to occupied Poland and killed at Niederkirch, one of the outlying camps of Auschwitz (Sept 1942); parents survived imprisonment and returned to Innsbruck (1945); like Anne Frank, became a symbol in Austria of the millions of young girls murdered during the Holocaust. ❖ See also *Women in World History.*

BRÛLON, Angélique (1772–1859). French military leader. Name variations: Angelique Brulon. Born Marie-Angélique Josephine Duchemin around 1772; died 1859. ❖ Known popularly as Liberté the Fusilier, fought in 7 campaigns in male guise in defense of the island region of Corsica (1792–99), displaying particular courage at Calvi and at the attack on Fort Gesco; was so valuable to the French army that she remained in service after being identified as a woman; retired (1822), received the rank of lieutenant as well as the red ribbon of French Legion of Honor from Napoleon III. ❖ See also *Women in World History.*

BRUN, Friederike (1765–1835). German poet. Name variations: Friederike Sophie Christiane Brun; Friederike Münter, Munter, or Muenter. Born Friederike Sophie Christiane Münter, June 3, 1765, in Gräfentonna, Thüringen, Germany; died Mar 25, 1835, in Copenhagen, Denmark; dau. of Balthasar Munter (well-known Evangelical pastor, died 1794) and Friederike von Wangenheim (died 1808); m. Constantin Brun (Danish consulate in St. Petersburg), 1783; children: 5, including Carl (b. 1784) and Charlotte Auguste Adelaide, known as Ida (b. 1792). ❖ Grew up in educated family; met important literary figures such as Friedrich Gottlieb Klopstock, Johann Andreas Cramer, and the Brothers Stolberg; later corresponded with Johann Gottfried Herder and Wilhelm Grimm; following father's death, suffered an emotional breakdown and lost her hearing; wrote of her travels and published lyric poetry collections, including *Gedichte von Friederike Brun* (1795).

BRUN, Marie-Marguerite de Maison-Forte (1713–1794). French poet and salonnière. Born 1713 in Coligny, France; died 1794. ❖ Wrote *Essai d'un dictionnaire comtois-français* (1753), *L'Amour maternal* (1773) and *L'Amour de Français pour leur roi.*

BRUNAMONTI, Maria Bonacci (1841–1903). *See Bonacci Brunamonti, Maria Alinda.*

BRUNAUER, Esther C. (1901–1959). American government official. Name variations: Esther Caukin or Esther Delia Caukin; Esther Delia Caukin Brunauer. Born Esther Delia Caukin, July 7, 1901, near Jackson, California; died June 26, 1959, in Evanston, Illinois; dau. of Ray Oakheart Caukin (electrician) and Grace Elizabeth (Blackwell) Caukin; Mills College, BA, 1924; Stanford University, PhD in history, 1927; m. Stephen Brunauer (commander in US Navy), July 8, 1931; children: Louis (1934–1934), Kathryn (b. 1938) and Elizabeth (b. 1942). ❖ International affairs expert who was highly regarded for work with UNESCO, led international education program for American Association of University Women (c. 1927–44); received Carl Schurz fellowship and studied effects of Nazism in Berlin (1933); among other works, wrote *Germany, the Nationalist Socialist State* (1934) and "Facing the Nazi Menace," in *Vital Issues* (June 1941); co-founded the Committee to Defend America by Aiding the Allies and served as chair of committee which created the Women's Action Committee for Victory and Lasting Peace (1943–44); joined US Department of State as specialist in international organizational affairs (1944); appointed US representative on Preparatory Committee to United Nations Educational, Scientific, and Cultural Organization (UNESCO), becoming 3rd woman in US to hold diplomatic rank of minister (1946); accused of being a communist by Senator Joseph McCarthy (1950); though cleared by State Department's Loyalty Board and by Senate subcommittee, was suspended (1951) and dismissed (1952) by State Department (was generally believed to be innocent of the charge); worked for Library of Congress, as associate director of Film Council of America and as editor for publishing companies (1950–59).

BRUNDAGE, Jennifer (1973—). American softball player. Born June 27, 1973, in Irvine, California. ❖ Won a team gold medal at Sydney Olympics (2000).

BRUNE, Adrienne (b. 1892). Australian-born stage actress and singer. Born Phyllis Caroline Brune, Oct 27, 1892, in Australia; m. Thomas Habgood Hudson (div.); m. Arthur Pusey (div.); children: (1st m.) Gabrielle Brune (b. 1912, actress). ❖ Made London debut as Jenny Diver in *Polly* (1922), followed by *Head Over Heels, Tonight's the Night, The Merry Widow, Dear Little Billie, The Girl from Cook's, The Rose and the Ring, Waltzes from Vienna* and *Cinderella,* among others.

BRUNE, Gabrielle (b. 1912). English stage actress and singer. Born Feb 12, 1912, in Bournemouth, England; dau. of Thomas Habgood Hudson and Adrienne Brune (actress); m. Walter J. Currie (div.); m. Paul Bowman. ❖ Made stage debut in the chorus of *Chelsea Follies* (1930); made NY debut in *The Two Bouquets* (1938); films include *The Case of the Frightened Lady, The Titfield Thunderbolt* and *Mandy;* appeared in numerous cabarets and revues and 20 films.

BRUNECHILDIS. *Variant of Brunhilda.*

BRUNECHILDIS (c. 533–613). *See Brunhilda.*

BRUNEFILLE, G.B. (1857–1911). *See Campbell, Lady Colin.*

BRUNEHAUT OR BRUNEHILDE. *Variant of Brunhilda.*

BRUNET, Andrée (1901–1993). *See Joly, Andrée.*

BRUNET, Caroline (1969—). Canadian kayaker. Born Mar 20, 1969, in Quebec City, Canada. ❖ Won a silver medal at Atlanta Olympics (1996) and a silver medal at Sydney Olympics (2000), both for K1 500 meters; at World championships, won gold medals for K4 200 (1995), K1 200 (1997, 1998, 1999, 2003), K1 1000 (1997, 1999), and K1 500 (1997, 1998, 1999); won a bronze medal for K1 500 at Athens Olympics (2004). Awarded Lou Marsh Trophy (1999).

BRUNET, Marguerite (1730–1820). *See Montansier, Marguerite.*

BRUNET, Marta (1897–1967). Chilean novelist and short-story writer. Name variations: Marta Brunet Cáraves. Born Aug 9, 1897, in Chillán, Chile; died of a cerebral hemorrhage, Oct 27, 1967, while speaking to the Uruguayan Academy of Letters in Montevideo, Uruguay; dau. of wealthy agriculturists, Ambrosio Brunet Molina (Chilean) and María Presentación Cáraves de Cossio (Spanish); educated by tutors. ❖ Major figure in 20th-century Chilean fiction, worked as a journalist; published 1st and most important novel, *Montaña adentro* (Mountain Interior, 1923); appointed to a consular position in the Chilean Embassy in Buenos Aires, served in the diplomatic corps (1940–52); other writings include (novel) *Bestia dañina* (Harmful Beast, 1926), (short stories) *Aguas abajo* (Waters Below, 1930), (novel) *Humo hacia el sur* (Smoke to the South, 1946), (novel) *María Nadie* (Maria Nobody, 1957), and (novel) *Amasijo* (Mixture, 1962). Awards include Atenea Prize from University of Concepción for *Aguas abajo;* received the National Prize for Literature (1961), only the 2nd woman to be so honored (the 1st was Gabriela Mistral).

BRUNET, Roberta (1965—). Italian runner. Born May 20, 1965, in Gressan (Aosta), Italy. ❖ Won a bronze medal for 5,000 meters at Atlanta Olympics (1996).

BRUNHILDA (c. 533–613). Merovingian queen. Name variations: Brunechildis; Brunehilde, Brunhilde, Brunnhilde, or Brunehaut, queen of Austrasia. Born c. 533; died in 613; dau. of Athanagild (Athangild), king of the Visigoths, and Queen Goinswintha of Spain; sister of Galswintha; m. Sigibert I, king of Austrasia (r. 561–575, assassinated, 575); m. Merovech (son of Chilperic I and Audovera); sister-in-law of Fredegund (c. 547–597); children: Childebert II, king of Austrasia (r. 575–595), king of Burgundy (r. 593–595). ❖ Married Sigibert I, king of Austrasia who was reigning at Metz (567); her sister Galswintha soon married Sigibert's younger brother Chilperic I, king of the west Frankish kingdom of Neustria; when Chilperic assassinated Galswintha, following the instructions of his paramour Fredegund, set out to avenge her sister's death. Bloody deeds, provoked by the enmity of Brunhilda and Fredegund, fill the annals of the next half century in Gaul. ❖ See also *Women in World History.*

BRUNHILDE. *Variant of Brunhilda.*

BRÜNING, Elfriede (1910—). East German novelist. Name variations: Elfriede Bruning or Brueing. Born 1910 in Germany. ❖ Imprisoned briefly in 1930s for communist activities; writings include *Un außerdem ist Sommer* (1934), *Junges Herz muß wandern* (1936), and *. . . damit du weiterlebst* (1949).

BRUNNER, Josefine (1909–1943). Austrian resistance leader. Born Josefine Ragnes in Innsbruck, Austria, Feb 26, 1909; executed with husband at Stadelheim prison, Munich, Sept 9, 1943; m. Alois Brunner (1907–1943, Socialist and resistance leader). ❖ Leading member of Waldemar von Knoeringen's resistance network in the anti-Nazi underground, was a member of the Austrian Social Democratic Party (1932–34); with husband, remained committed Socialists and anti-Nazis after 1933; joined von Knoeringen's underground organization (1936) and underwent special training in use of espionage techniques; worked as courier and provided important military, economic and political information to the anti-Nazi underground; arrested on charges of high treason (1942); sentenced to death (May 28, 1943). ❖ See also *Women in World History.*

BRUNNER, Melitta (1907—). Austrian figure skater. Born 1907 in Vienna, Austria. ❖ At World championships, won a singles bronze medal (1929); with Ludwig Wrede, won a bronze medal for pairs at St. Moritz Olympics (1928), then a bronze medal (1928) and silver medal (1930) at World championships; performed professionally (1932–54) and coached (1932–68); moved to Philadelphia, PA (1959).

BRUNNER, Ursula (1941—). West German swimmer. Born Jan 30, 1941, in Germany. ❖ At Rome Olympics, won a bronze medal in the 4 x 100-meter medley relay and a bronze medal in the 4 x 100-meter freestyle relay (1960).

BRUNNHILDE. *Variant of Brunhilda.*

BRUNO, Gioia Carmen (1965—). American singer. Name variations: Gioia Carmen; Exposé. Born June 11, 1965, in Bari, Italy. ❖ As a member of the vocal trio Exposé, had great success with Latin-tinged dance songs; with trio, released multiplatinum debut album *Exposure* (1987), which broke Beatles' record for most Top-10 hits from a debut album; was replaced on group's 3rd album due to throat problems. Exposé hits include "Come Go With Me" (1987), "Point of No Return" (1987), "Seasons Change" (#1 pop, 1987), and "I'll Never Get Over You (Getting Over Me)" (1993). Albums with Exposé include *Exposure* (1987) and *What You Don't Know* (1989).

BRUNSCHVICG, Cécile (1877–1946). French feminist. Name variations: Cecile Brunschwicg. Pronunciation: say-SEEL BROON-shvig. Born Cécile Kahn in 1877; died 1946; dau. of Arthur Kahn (Alsatian industrialist); m. Léon Brunschvicg (philosopher at Lycée Henri IV and Sorbonne), 1889 (died 1944); children: 4, born 1901–19. ❖ Activist at the heart of her country's women's suffrage movements, joined the suffrage section of the National Council of French Women (CNFF), attended the 1908 Amsterdam congress of International Women's Suffrage Alliance (IWSA), and joined the newly founded French Union for Women's Suffrage (UFSF, 1909); was made head of the membership and propaganda committee, resulting in a dramatic surge in membership; was named secretary-general, from which post she thereafter ran the UFSF; during WWI, was awarded Legion of Honor for her work in finding lodgings for 25,000 refugee families; founded a school to train women factory inspectors to deal with problems arising from the huge wartime employment of women (1917); became president of UFSF, as well as director of the monthly *La Française* (1926–34) and joined the Radical-Socialist Party (1924); was a founder of the Estates-General of Feminism, which convened in 1929, 1931, and 1937; reached the peak of her prominence when Léon Blum made her one of three women under-secretaries of state—a historic 1st in France—in his Popular Front government (June 4, 1936); pressed the Ministry of the Interior for the revision (enacted in Feb 1938) of Article 215 of the Code requiring husbands to give consent for wives to enroll in schools, open bank accounts, or obtain passports; intervened with the ministries of Colonies, Labor, and Foreign Affairs to admit women to their competitive examinations; at the end of her life, was internationally known, sitting on United Nations commissions and the executive committee of the International Democratic Federation of Women; was also honorary president of National Council of Radical-Socialist Women; was by most accounts "the *grande dame* of the feminist movement" in France from 1920s until her death. ❖ See also *Women in World History.*

BRUNSWICK, duchess of.
See Catherine of Pomerania (d. 1526).
See Elizabeth of Brandenburg (1510–1558).
See Elizabeth of Denmark (1573–1626).

See Anne-Eleanor of Hesse-Darmstadt (1601–1659).
See Mary-Elizabeth of Padua (1782–1808).

BRUNSWICK, Ruth Mack (1897–1946). American psychoanalyst. Name variations: Ruth Mack. Born Ruth Jane Mack in Chicago, Illinois, Feb 17, 1897; died in New York, NY, Jan 24, 1946; dau. of Judge Julian Mack; graduate of Radcliffe College, 1918, and Tufts Medical School, 1922; married 2nd husband, Mark Brunswick (American composer), 1928. ❖ Refused entrance to Harvard Medical School because of gender, matriculated at Tufts before heading for Vienna to become an analysand of Sigmund Freud; began her own practice in Vienna (1925); became a member of Vienna Psychoanalytic Society, an instructor at Psychoanalytic Institute, and edited the American journal *Psychoanalytic Quarterly;* following annexation of Austria by Nazis (1938), moved to New York with husband, where she went into private practice. ❖ See also *Women in World History.*

BRUNSWICK-LÜNEBURG, duchess of.
See Helen of Denmark (d. 1233).
See Matilda of Brandenburg (d. 1261).
See Braunschweig-Luneburg, Sophie Elisabeth (1613–1676).
See Victoria Louise (1892–1980).

BRUNSWICK-WOLFENBUTTEL, duchess of.
See Philippine Charlotte (1716–1801).
See Augusta Guelph (1737–1813).

BRUNTLAND, Gro Harlem (1939—). Norwegian politician. Name variations: Bruddland, Brundtland. Born in Oslo, Norway, in 1939; attended university in Oslo and Harvard University; m. Arne Olav, 1960; children: 4. ❖ First woman prime minister of Norway and one of her nation's most influential politicians abroad, was a physician with a particular interest in public health; gained reputation while serving in various local health-care organizations, including the Ministry of Health and Social Affairs, the Oslo City Health Department, and the Oslo School Health Services; appointed Minister of Environmental Affairs (1974); became vice chair of Labor Party (1975); after leaving government service (1979), ran for president of Labor Party, winning overwhelming support from local constituencies; upon resignation of Odvar Nordli, took over as head of the minority government (1980); became 1st woman prime minister of Norway (1981) but served for only an 8-month period; upon reelection (1986), appointed a number of women to Cabinet posts and facilitated the election of more women to governmental positions; also worked on a plan to ease Norway's economic decline; as chair of United Nations Commission of the Environment, led discussions on corporate responsibility for environmental health; resigned (1996). ❖ See also *Women in World History.*

BRUNTON, Ann (1769–1808). *See Merry, Ann Brunton.*

BRUNTON, Dorothy (1893–1977). Australian-born actress and singer. Born Oct 14, 1893, in Melbourne, Australia; died June 5, 1977, in Sydney; dau. of Christine (Neilsen) Brunton and John Brunton (scenic artist); m. Benjamin Dawson. ❖ As a child, made stage debut in Adelaide in *The White Heather;* was a great favorite on the Australian musical stage, playing leads in such plays as *The Girl in the Taxi, The Girl on the Film, The Waltz Dream, The Merry Widow, High Jinks* and *So Long Letty* (1914–18); made London debut in *Shanghai* (1918), followed by *Soldier Boy, The Bantam V.C.* and *Baby Bunting,* among others; appeared often on the London and Australian stage, most notably in Sydney as Betsy Burke in *Dearest Enemy* (1932); made film debut in *Seven Keys to Baldpate;* also appeared in *Clara Gibbings* (1934).

BRUNTON, Elizabeth (1799–1860). *See Yates, Elizabeth.*

BRUNTON, Louisa (c. 1785–1860). English actress. Name variations: Countess of Craven. Born Louisa Brunton around 1785; died 1860; m. William, 1st earl of Craven, 1807. ❖ Famed for her remarkable beauty, made debut as Lady Townley in *Provoked Husband* and Beatrice in *Much Ado About Nothing* (1803); became countess of Craven upon marriage (1807), then retired from the stage.

BRUNTON, Mary (1778–1818). Scottish novelist. Born Mary Balfour, Nov 1, 1778, on the island of Barra, Orkney, on west coast of Scotland; died in Edinburgh, Dec 19, 1818; dau. of Captain Thomas Balfour of Elwick; m. Alexander Brunton (minister of Bolton in Haddingtonshire and later professor of oriental languages at Edinburgh), in 1798. ❖ Wrote 2 novels, which were popular in her day: *Self-control,* published anonymously in 1811 and sold out in one month, and *Discipline* (1814); as well,

authored a fragment, *Emmeline* (1819), which, together with a memoir, was published by husband after her death.

BRUSNIKINA, Olga (1978—). Russian synchronized swimmer. Name variations: Olga Brousnikina. Born Nov 9, 1978, in Moscow, Russia. ❖ Won gold medals for duet and team at Sydney Olympics (2000) and for team at Athens Olympics (2004); won World championship for duet and team (1998), solo (2001) and team (2003).

BRUSSELMANS, Anne (c. 1905—). English resistance leader. Name variations: wrongly seen as Brusselsmans. Born c. 1905; lived in Brussels, Belgium; dau. of a British mother and Belgian father; m. Julien Brusselmans; children: Jacques Brusselmans (1935–2002) and Yvonne Daley-Brusselmans. ❖ One of the unsung heroes of World War II, operated an escape line for Allied soldiers as an English housewife living in Brussels; supervised the passage of more than 150 British and American pilots out of Nazi-controlled territory in 4 years. Named MBE; awarded Belgian Croix de Guerre with Palm Leaf. ❖ See also Yvonne Daley-Brusselmans, *Belgium Rendez-Vous 127 Revisited: Anne Brusselmans, M.B.E.—Resistance, World War II* (Sunflower U. Press).

BRUSTEIN, Norma (c. 1929–1979). American stage and tv actress. Born c. 1929; died April 9, 1979, age 50, in New Haven, Connecticut; m. 2nd husband Robert Brustein (director and dean of Yale Drama School). ❖ On NY stage, appeared in *The Iceman Cometh, The Big Knife, The Warm Peninsula, Career, Threepenny Opera* and *Sganarelle;* taught at Yale Drama School.

BRUTSAERT, Elke (1968—). American mountain biker. Name variations: (nicknames) Tellie Ellie and Mountain Ellie. Born Aug 5, 1968, in Fort Collins, Colorado. ❖ Won a World Cup event in 1st year of racing (1993); won gold in Speed (winter 1998), bronze in Downhill (winter 1998) and bronze in Biker X (winter 1999) at X Games; finished 2nd in final series standings of Visa Downhill national championship series, Mammoth Mountain, CA (2000).

BRUTTIA CRISPINA (d. 185). Roman empress. Died c. 185 CE; m. Marcus Aurelius Commodus (161–192), Roman emperor (r. 180–192). ❖ Banished by husband Emperor Commodus (177) and replaced by Marcia.

BRYAN, Anna E. (1858–1901). American kindergarten educator. Born July 1858 in Louisville, Kentucky; died Feb 21, 1901, in Chicago, Illinois; dau. of Parish G. Bryan (piano maker) and Eliza H. Belle (Richard) Bryan. ❖ Taught in Chicago at Marie Chapel Charity Kindergarten; became head of new training school and Free Kindergarten in Louisville, Kentucky (1887) and fostered a permissive, experimental setting; became principal of kindergarten normal department at Armour Institute (1894); served as chair of the child study committee of International Kindergarten Union (1897–1901).

BRYAN, Florence (1896–1951). *See Mario, Queena.*

BRYAN, Jane (1918—). American actress. Born Jane O'Brien, June 11, 1918, in Hollywood, California; m. Justin Dart (president of Rexall Drug Co.), 1939; children: 3. ❖ Made film debut in *The Case of the Black Cat* (1936), followed by *Marked Woman, Kid Galahad, Confession, A Slight Case of Murder, The Sisters, Girls on Probation, Brother Rat, Each Dawn I Die, The Old Maid, These Glamour Girls, We Are Not Alone* and *Brother Rat and a Baby,* among others; retired (1939).

BRYAN, Margaret (1769–1858). *See Marcet, Jane.*

BRYAN, Mary Edwards (1838–1913). American writer. Born Mary Edwards, May 17, 1838, in Lloyd, Florida; died June 15, 1913, in Clarkston, Georgia; dau. of Major John D. Edwards (1800–1883, planter and member of the Florida senate) and Louisa Crutchfield (Houghton) Edwards (1813–1891); attended Fletcher Institute; m. Iredell E. Bryan (1832–1909), Jan 10, 1854; children: 3. ❖ Contributed to *Georgia Literary and Temperance Crusader* (c. 1858) and became its literary editor (c. 1859); contributed full-length novel to *Southern Field and Fireside;* served as co-editor of *Semi-Weekly Natchitoches Times* (1866–67), associate editor of *Sunny South,* and assistant editor of *Fireside Companion* and *Fashion Bazaar* (both published by George Munro); published many novels, including *Manch* (1880) and *Wild Work* (1881); served as editor of *Half Hour* (1897–1900) and as writer for *Uncle Remus's Magazine* and *Golden Age.*

BRYANT, Alice Gertrude (c. 1862–1942). American surgeon and inventor. Born c. 1862 in Boston, Massachusetts; died July 25, 1942, in Boston. ❖ After graduating from Vassar College (1885) and the

Woman's Medical College of the New York Infirmary (1890), became one of the 1st two women, with Florence West Duckering, to be admitted to the American College of Surgeons (1914); worked as an ear, nose, and throat specialist; a one-time engineering student at Massachusetts Institute of Technology, combined medicine and engineering and invented 3 medical devices: the tonsil-separator, tongue depressor, and bone-gripping forceps; was a member of more than 50 scientific and humanitarian organizations.

BRYANT, Bonnie (1943—). American golfer. Born Oct 5, 1943, in Tulare, California; attended College of the Sequoias. ❖ Joined LPGA (1971); won 1st LPGA title (1974); played on the Women's Senior Golf Tour.

BRYANT, Charlotte (c. 1902–1936). English murderer. Born c. 1902 in England; hanged July 15, 1936, at Exeter Prison; m. Frederick Bryant; children: 5. ❖ Illiterate and given to extramarital affairs, became enamored of a Leonard Parsons and wanted to run away with him; after husband died as result of arsenic poisoning (Dec 22, 1935), was found to have arsenic traces in her coat pockets, while a tin with arsenical weedkiller was discovered behind their cottage; arrested and charged with husband's murder (Feb 10, 1936), was tried at Dorchester Assizes (May 1936) and hanged at Exeter Prison (July 15, 1936).

BRYANT, Deborah (c. 1946—). Miss America. Name variations: Debbie Bryant. Born Deborah Irene Bryant c. 1946; University of Kansas, Phi Beta Kappa; married; children: 5. ❖ Named Miss America (1966), representing Kansas. ❖ See also Frank Deford, *There She Is* (Viking, 1971).

BRYANT, Dorothy (1930—). American writer and feminist. Born 1930 in San Francisco, California; dau. of immigrants from Northern Italy. ❖ Taught English and music in high schools and community colleges for 23 years; published *The Comforter* (1971), which was later published by Random House as *The Kin of Ata Are Waiting for You* (1983) and has been called a utopian allegory; also wrote *Miss Giardino* (1978), *Garden of Eros* (1979), *Prisoners* (1980), *Killing Wonder* (1981), *Day in San Francisco* (1983), *Myths to Lie By* (1984), *Confessions of Madame Psyche* (1986), *Test* (1991) and *Ella Price's Journal* (1997); with husband, formed an independent publishing company, Ata Books.

BRYANT, Ethel Maude (1882–1967). *See Field, Ethel Maude.*

BRYANT, Felice (1925–2003). American country songwriter. Name variations: Matilda Genevieve Scaduto. Born Matilda Genevieve Scaduto, Aug 7, 1925, in Milwaukee, Wisconsin; died April 22, 2003, in Gatlinburg, Tennessee; m. 2nd husband Diadorius Boudleaux Bryant (musician), Sept 5, 1945 (died July 25, 1987); children: 2 sons. ❖ Began writing songs (1935); met future husband and song-writing partner while working as hotel elevator operator in Milwaukee, WI (1945); wrote songs for Acuff-Rose Music Publishing Co. (1948–66); had 1st hit, "Country Boy" (1949); moved to Nashville (1950); founded Showcase Music (mid-1950s); established House of Bryant Publications (1967); with husband, recorded only album as performers, *A Touch of Bryant* (1979), and wrote about 800 songs performed by such singers as the Everly Brothers, Dean Martin, Elvis Presley, and the Beatles, including "Bye Bye Love," "Wake Up Little Susie," "We Could," and "Rocky Top," which became Tennessee's state song (1982); with husband, won 59 BMI awards; owned and operated Rocky Top Village Inn in Gatlinburg, TN. With husband, received numerous honors, such as induction to Nashville Songwriters Hall of Fame (1972), National Songwriters Hall of Fame (1986), and Country Music Hall of Fame (1991); received Nashville Arts Foundation's Living Legend Award (1991).

BRYANT, Hazel (1939–1983). African-American producer and singer. Born 1939; died Nov 7, 1983, in New York, NY; dau. of a preacher in the African Methodist Episcopal Church; graduate of Oberlin, 1962; attended Columbia University. ❖ Toured in opera as a major promoter of black theater, produced over 200 musicals and plays, including Langston Hughes' *Black Nativity* and O'Neill's *Long Day's Journey into Night*, with an all-black cast; organized the Black Theatre Alliance and founded the Richard Allen Center for Culture and Arts.

BRYANT, Lane (1879–1951). American clothing designer and entrepreneur. Born Lena Himmelstein in Lithuania in 1879; died 1951. ❖ The 1st American designer to address the fashion needs of larger women, immigrated to US and set up shop as a seamstress specializing in lingerie and maternity clothing; opened 1st retail shop (1910), catering to pregnant and larger women; by 1917, her stores had sold over $1 million in merchandise. ❖ See also *Women in World History*.

BRYANT, Louise (1885–1936). American journalist. Born Anna Louisa Mohan, Dec 5, 1885, in San Francisco, California; died Jan 6, 1936, in Paris, France; dau. of Hugh J. (journalist) and Anna Louisa (Flick) Mohan (dressmaker); attended University of Nevada, University of Oregon; m. Paul Trullinger, Nov 13, 1909 (div. 1917); m. John Reed (poet and journalist), Nov 9, 1916 (died Oct 19, 1920); m. William C. Bullitt, Dec 23, 1923 (div. Mar 1930); children: (3rd m.) Anne Bullitt (b. 1924). ❖ Journalist who witnessed the Soviet revolution in Russia and became one of its outspoken defenders, began career as society editor of the *Portland Spectator* (1913); met John Reed, one of the finest writers of the American left (Dec 1915); leaving 1st husband behind, moved to New York (1916); contributed to *The Masses;* with press credentials from the just-organized Bell Syndicate, traveled with Reed to Russia (Aug 1917); witnessed the Soviet Revolution, filing press reports all the while; returned to New York (Feb 1918) and devoted herself to telling the American public what she had seen in Russia; joined suffrage picket of White House (1919); testified before Senate subcommittee on Russia (Feb 1919); catapulted to renown by her testimony, embarked on a national speaking tour (1919); deciding to rejoin Reed, returned to Soviet Union (Aug 1919); interviewed Lenin, the 1st he had granted to an American newspaper or press association; following Reed's death, traveled to Middle East (1920–21); diagnosed with incurable disease (1928); writings include *Six Red Months in Russia* (1918) and *Mirrors of Moscow* (1923). ❖ See also Virginia Gardner, *"Friend and Lover": The Life of Louise Bryant* (Horizon, 1982); Mary V. Dearborn, *Queen of Bohemia: The Life of Louise Bryant* (Houghton, 1995); (film) *Reds*, with Diane Keaton as Bryant (1981); and *Women in World History*.

BRYANT, Mary (1765–?). English highway robber. Name variations: Mary Bryant of Fowey; Mary Braund or Broad. Born Mary Broad in Cornwall, England, and baptized on May 1, 1765; dau. of William (mariner) and Grace Broad; m. Will Bryant (convict), Feb 10, 1788; children: Charlotte Spence (b. 1787); Emmanuel (b. 1790). ❖ One of only a handful of convicts to escape from the notorious penal colony at Botany Bay, was apprehended for highway robbery at age 20 (1786); tried and given 7-years transport; was newly pregnant when she was put on board the prison ship *Charlotte* (Jan 1787); sailed to Australia (May 1787), arriving (Jan 1788); with husband, children, and others, escaped by sailing 3,254 miles, 1,200 of which in uncharted ocean waters, in an open boat (1791) and her courage sustained them; landed in the Dutch East Indies; arrested, was returned to England, though husband and son died en route; with the help of James Boswell, was granted a full pardon. Two journals would recount the Bryant voyage, one left behind by husband Will and one by James Martin, another escapee. ❖ See also Judith Cook, *To Brave Every Danger* (Macmillan, 1993); and *Women in World History*.

BRYANT, Millicent (1878–1927). Australian aviator. Born 1878 in Australia; lived in Manly; died Nov 3, 1927; widowed with 3 sons, George, John, Bowen. ❖ Was the 1st Australian woman to gain a pilot's license (Mar 28, 1927); died in ferry accident, when the 7,585-ton passenger liner *Tahiti* cut through the 32-ton Sydney ferry *Greycliffe* off Bradleys Head in Sydney Harbor.

BRYANT, Rosalyn (1956—). African-American runner. Born Jan 7, 1956, in Chicago, Illinois. ❖ At Montreal Olympics, won a silver medal in 4 x 400-meter relay (1976).

BRYANT, Sophie (1850–1922). Irish campaigner for women's education. Name variations: Dr. Sophie Bryant. Born Sophie Willock, 1850, in Sandymount, Ireland; died 1922 while hiking near Chamonix; dau. of Rev. W.A. Willock, DD; attended Bedford College; London University, BSc in Mental and Moral Science and Mathematics, 1881, DSc, 1884; m. Dr. William Hicks Bryant (surgeon), 1869 (died 1870). ❖ The 1st woman with a DSc in England, was also a campaigner for women's education and Irish Home Rule; moved to England with family (1863); elected member of London Mathematical Society and wrote the 1st paper by a woman member (1884); taught at North London Collegiate School, before becoming headmistress (1885); served as member of Board of Studies in Pedagogy for 20 years and on Bryce Commission on Secondary Education (1894–95), positions which provided a forum to promote education for women; was one of the 1st three women appointed to the Senate of London University; during tenure, advocated and achieved founding of the Day Training College for teachers (which later became the Institute of Education); became involved in campaign for Home Rule for Ireland (1886); played instrumental role in the founding of Cambridge Training College for Women (which became Hughes Hall); was founding member of Psychological Society; was 1st woman awarded honorary doctorate from Trinity College, Dublin (1904); wrote books on Irish history and ancient Irish law as well as women's suffrage; retired (1918); an ardent sportswoman, climbed the Matterhorn twice and is said to have been one of the 1st women to own a bicycle.

BRYCE, Cornelia (1881–1960). *See Pinchot, Cornelia.*

BRYCELAND, Yvonne (1926–1992). South African stage actress. Born Yvonne Heilbluth, Nov 18, 1926, in Cape Town, South Africa; died Jan 13, 1992, in London, England; dau. of Adolphus Walter and Clara Ethel (Sanderson) Heilbluth; attended St. Mary's Convent, Cape Town; m. Daniel Bryceland (div.); m. Brian Astbury; children: 3 daughters. ❖ Actress who originated many roles for the plays of Athol Fugard, 1st appeared on stage in *Stage Door* (1947); with the Cape Performing Arts Board (1964–71), played a variety of roles, including Mme. Desmortes in *Ring Round the Moon,* Miss Madrigal in *The Chalk Garden* and Mme. Ranevskaya in *The Cherry Orchard;* for Fugard, created Millie in *People Are Living There* (1969) and Lena in *Boesman and Lena,* in which she also made London debut (July 1971); with Fugard and 2nd husband, founded The Space, Cape Town (Mar 1972), where she portrayed such diverse characters as Frieda in Fugard's *Statements after an Arrest under the Immorality Act,* Amanda Wingfield in *The Glass Menagerie,* as well as Mother Courage and Medea; joined National Theatre Company in London (1978), where she appeared as Queen Margaret in *Richard III* and Emilia in *Othello* (1979–80); appeared in Fugard's *Road to Mecca* (1980), traveling with the play to London and New York and winning both the Theater World Award and an Obie; recreated the role of Lena in film version of *Boesman and Lena* (1972) and appeared on tv in *People Are Living There* and Fugard's *Hello and Goodbye.*

BRYHER (1894–1983). *See Ellerman, Winifred.*

BRYK, Rut (1916–1999). Finnish art ceramist. Born 1916 in Stockholm, Sweden; died 1999; graduate of School of Arts and Crafts in Helsinki, 1939; married Tapio Wirkkala (postwar designer). ❖ Worked for Arabia Finland (1942–90), experimenting with raw material for ceramics that would bring her renown; borrowed from Byzantium, early renaissance, folk art and constructivism for her thickly glazed plaques and tiles. Won the Grand Prix in Milan (1951), Diplome d'Honneur in Milan (1954), silver medal in Cannes (1955).

BRYN, Alexia (1889–1983). Norwegian pairs skater. Name variations: Alexia Schoyen or Schøyen; Alexia Bryn-Schoeien or Bryn-Schoyen. Born Alexia Schøyen, Mar 24, 1889, in Norway; died July 19, 1983; m. Yngvar Bryn (1881–1947, skater), c. 1913. ❖ With Yngvar Bryn, won a silver medal at Antwerp Olympics (1920); placed 2nd at World championships (1923).

BRYNER, Vera (d. 1967). American lyric soprano. Name variations: Vera Brynner. Died Dec 13, 1967, age 51, in New York, NY; sister of Yul Brynner (actor); m. Roy Raymond. ❖ Appeared with New York City opera; won critical praise as the alternate in Menotti's *The Counsel* (1950).

BRYNNER, Vera (d. 1967). *See Bryner, Vera.*

BRYSON, Bernarda (1903–2004). American illustrator. Name variations: Bernarda Bryson Shahn. Born Mar 7, 1903, in Athens, Ohio; died Dec 12, 2004, in Roosevelt, Monmouth Co., New Jersey; dau. of the owner of the Athens *Morning Journal;* studied painting, printmaking and philosophy at Ohio University, Ohio State University, and Cleveland School of Art; m. 2nd husband Ben Shahn (artist), 1969 (having lived with him since 1933); children: son Jonathan (sculptor) and daughters Susanna Watts (died 1967) and Abby Shahn (painter). ❖ Wrote and illustrated children's books, including *The Zoo of Zeus* (1964) and *Gilgamesh* (1967); also did portraits; series of lithographs published as *The Vanishing American Frontier* (1995); later in life, became known for her paintings, which were realistic and mysterious in style; work is in the permanent collection of Whitney Museum, among others.

BRYSTYGIEROWA, Julia (1902–1980). Polish activist. Name variations: Julia Preiss. Born Julia Preiss in 1902; died 1980; earned degree in history at University of Lvov; married. ❖ Polish Communist activist, was a member of the Hashomer Scouts, a Zionist youth group (1920s); joined Communist Party of Poland, a small and illegal group (1930), then the Communist Party of the Ukraine (1939); when Lvov was annexed to Ukrainian Soviet Socialist Republic as a result of Nazi-Soviet alliance, was granted membership in Ukrainian Communist Party and served as director of Lvov branch of International Workers' Relief organization (1939–41); was active in Union of Polish Patriots (UPP, 1943–45) and

presidium secretary (1944), one of the few women to occupy a high position in the UPP; as departmental director in the Ministry of Public Security in Poland, was a major figure in the repression of anti-Communists and other dissidents (1945–56); removed from office as a result of the growing anti-Stalinist movement (Sept 1956), spent final decades writing novels under maiden name of Julia Preiss. ❖ See also *Women in World History.*

BRYUNINA, Mira (1951—). Soviet rower. Born Sept 16, 1951, in USSR. ❖ At Montreal Olympics, won a silver medal in quadruple sculls with coxswain (1976).

BRYZGINA, Olga (1963—). Soviet runner. Born June 30, 1963, in USSR. ❖ At Seoul Olympics, won gold medals in 4 x 400-meter relay and 400 meters (1988); at Barcelona Olympics, won a silver medal in 400 meters and a gold medal in 4 x 400-meter relay (1992).

BUBER, Margarete (1901–1989). *See Buber-Neumann, Margarete.*

BUBER-NEUMANN, Margarete (1901–1989). German author and activist. Name variations: Grete Buber, Margarete Buber, Margaret Buber Neumann. Born Margarete Thüring, Oct 21, 1901, in Potsdam, Germany; died in Frankfurt am Main, Germany, Nov 6, 1989; dau. of Heinrich Thüring (brewery manager, 1866–1942) and Else (Merten) Thüring (1871–1960); had 2 sisters, Babette Gross and Gertrud ("Trude") Thüring, and 2 brothers; trained at Pestalozzi-Fröbel-Haus in Berlin-Schöneberg as a kindergarten teacher; common-law marriage to Rafael Buber (son of philosopher Martin Buber), beginning 1921; common-law marriage to Heinz Neumann (linguist and Communist revolutionary), c. 1928; m. Helmuth Faust (div.); children: (with Rafael Buber) Barbara (b. 1921) and Judith (b. 1924). ❖ Communist activist and prisoner in the Soviet Gulag before being deported to Nazi Germany and incarcerated in the infamous Ravensbrück concentration camp, who devoted the remainder of her life to exposing Stalinist tyranny; joined Communist Youth League of Germany (1921); joined Communist Party of Germany (KPD, 1926); worked in Berlin on editorial staff of *Inprekorr,* journal of the Communist International; fled Germany (1933) with Heinz Neumann, her 2nd common-law husband, going to Spain, Switzerland, France, and the Saar territory; immigrated to Soviet Union (1935); arrested and convicted of being a "socially dangerous element" and sentenced to 5 years' loss of freedom (1938); expelled from USSR to Nazi Germany (1940); imprisoned in Ravensbrück concentration camp until 1945; became a noted author after 1945, whose books played a significant role in exposing the Soviet Gulag; after release, spent 5 years in Sweden; published memoir, *Under Two Dictators,* in Germany (1948), which was then translated into many other languages; returned to Frankfurt (1950), becoming editor of the political journal *Die Aktion* (1951); in Munich, wrote and published *Milena—Kafkas freundin* (1977, *Milena: The Story of a Remarkable Friendship*); continued to write and speak out against Stalinist oppression. ❖ See also *Women in World History.*

BUBLEY, Esther (1921–1998). American photographer. Born in Phillips, Wisconsin, Feb 16, 1921; died Mar 16, 1998, in New York, NY; dau. of Louis and Ida Bubley (Russian immigrants); attended Superior State Teachers College, Superior, Wisconsin, 1937–38; studied art and photography at Minneapolis College of Art and Design, 1939; briefly married to Edwin Locke (writer). ❖ One of the nation's top women photographers, known for her use of "picture story" technique, spent some of her early years in Washington, DC, microfilming rare books at the National Archives; got her break in NY, freelancing for Roy Stryker, then director of Standard Oil's photographic activities (1943); worked on photojournalism assignments for *Ladies' Home Journal* series, "How America Lives" (1948–60); also did a number of assignments for *Life, McCall's, Woman's Day, Saturday Evening Post* and *Good Housekeeping;* photographs were featured in an exhibition curated by Edward Steichen at Museum of Modern Art in New York (1948); was represented in 2 other Steichen exhibitions at MoMA: *Diogenes with a Camera* (1952) and *The Family of Man* (1955). ❖ See also *Women in World History.*

BUCCA, Dorotea (fl. 1390–1430). *See Bocchi, Dorotea.*

BUCGE (d. 751). *See Edburga.*

BUCHAN, Anna (1878–1948). Scottish novelist. Name variations: (pseudonym) O. Douglas. Born Anna Buchan, 1878, in Perth, Scotland; lived in Peebles; died 1948 in Peebles; dau. of a minister; sister of John Buchan, Baron Tweedsmuir (1875–1940, writer and politician); attended Hutcheson's Grammar School in Glasgow. ❖ Writings, which often depict Free Church of Scotland communities, include *Olivia in India*

(1912), *The Setons* (1917), *Penny Plain* (1920), *Ann and Her Mother* (1922) and *Pink Sugar* (1924). ❖ See also autobiography *Farewell to Priorsford* (1950), and her biography of Buchan family, *Unforgettable, Unforgotten* (1945).

BUCHAN, Annabelle (1878–1961). *See Annabelle.*

BUCHAN, countess of.
See Isabella of Buchan (fl. 1290–1310).
See Stewart, Mary (d. 1465).

BUCHAN, Elspeth (1738–1791). Scottish religious founder. Name variations: Elspeth Simpson. Born Elspeth Simpson near Banff, Scotland, in 1738; died near Dumfries, Scotland, in 1791; dau. of John Simpson (innkeeper near Banff); m. Robert Buchan (potter of Greenock); children. ❖ Founder of a religious sect known as the Buchanites, settled with children in Glasgow after separating from husband (1781); convinced Hugh White, minister of the Relief Church at Irvine, that she was the woman described in *Revelations xii* in whom the light of God was restored to men, and that God was the son she had brought forth (1783); along with White and her 46 disciples, was expelled by the presbytery (1784); settled with group on a communal farm, known as New Cample, in Closeburn, Dumfriesshire; convinced them that the millennium was near. ❖ See also *Women in World History.*

BUCHANAN, Dorothy (1899–1985). Scottish civil engineer. Name variations: Dorothy Donaldson Buchanan; Dot Buchanan; Mrs. Dorothy Fleming. Born Dorothy Donaldson Buchanan, Apr 8, 1899, in Dumfriesshire, Scotland; died 1985; married a man named Fleming, 1930. ❖ Inspired from a young age to train as civil engineer, graduated from Edinburgh University (1922); hired by Dorman Long consultant, Ralph Freeman, to work in design office and later in drawing office for Sydney Harbour Bridge; worked on gravity dam (Belfast's waterworks) for S. Pearson and Sons in Northern Ireland's Mourne Mountains; returned to design office of Dorman Long in England and worked on Newcastle's George V Bridge and London's Lambeth Bridge; passed admission exam for Institution of Civil Engineers (1927). Became 1st woman corporate member of Institution of Civil Engineers (ICE, 1927).

BUCHANAN, Isobel Wilson (1954—). Scottish soprano. Born Mar 13, 1954, in Glasgow, Scotland; attended Royal Scottish Academy of Music and Drama (1971); m. Jonathan Hyde (actor), 1980; children: 2 daughters. ❖ Became a principal with Australian Opera (1975–78), singing role of Pamina in Mozart's *The Magic Flute* for professional debut (1976); made sensational debuts at both Glyndebourne and Vienna Staatsoper (1978) and appeared the following year at Santa Fé, Chicago, New York and Cologne; also sang with Scottish Opera, English National Opera and Paris Opéra, as well as at Convent Garden and Carnegie Hall; was the subject of a BBC documentary directed by Michael Radford (1981); performed with Placido Domingo, Jose Carreras and Joan Sutherland and worked with world's leading conductors, notably Sir Georg Solti, Richard Bonynge and Colin Davis; made numerous recordings both of operas and of Scottish folk music.

BUCHANAN, Margaret (1864–1940). English pharmaceutical chemist. Name variations: Margaret Elizabeth Buchanan. Born 1864 in England; died 1940. ❖ Trained with father (doctor) and later with a husband-and-wife team named Kerr in London; became a registered chemist and druggist (1886) and a pharmaceutical chemist (1887); became hospital pharmacist (1888); with Agnes Borrowman and 2 others, started a pharmacy business in Clapham; established and served as 1st president of Women Pharmacists' Association (1905); founded School of Pharmacy for Women (1908) and worked as its principal (1908–25); elected 1st woman member of Pharmaceutical Society's Council (1918); taught at London School of Medicine for Women.

BUCHANAN, Vera Daerr (1902–1955). American politician. Born Vera Daerr in Wilson, Pennsylvania, July 20, 1902; died in McKeesport, Pennsylvania, Nov 26, 1955. m. Frank Buchanan (US congressional representative, 1946–51), in 1929. ❖ US Representative, Democrat of Pennsylvania, 82nd–84th Congresses, July 24, 1951–Nov 26, 1955, won a special election to fill a vacancy left by husband's death; was reelected twice by her largely Democratic, pro-labor constituency; served on the Committee on Merchant Marines and Fisheries, the Committee on Banking and Currency, and the Committee on Public Works. ❖ See also *Women in World History.*

BUCHBINDER, Aline (1928–1991). *See Ehrlich, Aline.*

BUCHINSKAIA, Nadezhda Aleksandrovna (1872–1952). *See Teffi, N.A.*

BÜCHNER, Luise (1821–1877). German poet and novelist. Name variations: Luise Buchner. Born in Germany, June 12, 1821; died Nov 28, 1877, in Darmstadt, Germany; sister of Georg Büchner (1813–1837, poet), Friedrich Karl Christian Ludwig Büchner (1824–1899, physician and philosopher), and Alexander Büchner (1827–1904, critic and historian). ❖ A champion of women's rights, published *Die Frauen und ihr Beruf* (Woman and Their Calling, 1855), a popular work that went through 5 editions by 1883; wrote many other books about women, as well as *From Life* (1861) and *Poet-Voices of Home and Foreign Lands.*

BÜCHNER, Annemarie. German Alpine skier. Name variations: Miri Buchner; Annemarie Buchner-Fischer. Born in West Germany. ❖ Won bronze medals for slalom and giant slalom and a silver medal for downhill at Oslo Olympics (1952).

BÜCHNER, Miri. *See Buchner, Annemarie.*

BUCK, Carrie (d. 1983). American icon. Born Carrie Buck in Charlottesville, Virginia; died in 1983 in Waynesboro, Virginia; only dau. of Emma and Frank Buck; m. William Davis Eagle, May 14, 1932 (died); m. Charles Albert Detamore, April 25, 1965; children: Vivian Elaine, born out of wedlock (d. 1932). ❖ First American woman to be sterilized under the Virginia Compulsory Sterilization Law, was operated on at the State Colony for Epileptics and the Feebleminded in Lynchburg, Virginia (Oct 19, 1927), an operation which was performed without her understanding or agreement and sanctioned by the US Supreme Court. The procedure ultimately altered the lives of 60,000 in the States, and, arguably, had worldwide implications, influencing the German policy of eugenics or "Aryan cleansing" under the Nazi regime, causing the sterilization of over 2 million. The State of Virginia issued an apology (2002). ❖ See also David J. Smith and K. Ray Nelson, *The Sterilization of Carrie Buck* (New Horizon, 1989); and *Women in World History.*

BUCK, Heather (1926—). English poet. Born 1926 in England. ❖ Writings, which combine mystical and religious elements with psychoanalytic theory, include *The Opposite Direction* (1972), *At the Window* (1982), *The Sign of the Water Bearer* (1987), and *Elegy for a Nun* (1987).

BUCK, Karen (1958—). English politician and member of Parliament. Born Aug 30, 1958; partner of Barrie Taylor; children: 1 son. ❖ Specialized in employment for the disabled (1979–86); representing Labour, elected to House of Commons for Regent's Park and Kensington North (1997, 2001, 2005); named parliamentary undersecretary, Department of Transport (2005).

BUCK, Kitty (1907–2001). American entrepreneur. Born Gussie Rubin, June 15, 1907, in Hurleyville, NY; died Jan 9, 2001, in Oceanside, NY; m. Otto Buck (baker), 1930 (died 1959); children: Barbara Halio and Joan Buck. ❖ With husband, founded the famous Cake Masters Bakery on the Upper West Side of Manhattan (1937); opened 14 more outlets in NY; retired (1992).

BUCK, Lillie West Brown (1855–1939). *See Leslie, Amy.*

BUCK, Linda B. (1947—). American immunologist. Born Jan 29, 1947, in Seattle, Washington; University of Washington, BS in psychology, 1975; BS in microbiology, 1975; University of Texas, PhD in immunology, 1980. ❖ Was a postdoctoral fellow at Columbia University (1980–84); was an associate at Howard Hughes Medical Institute at Columbia (1984–91), then assistant investigator (1994–97), associate investigator (1997–2000), and finally named full investigator (2001); was assistant professor in department of neurobiology, Harvard Medical School (1991–96), then associate professor (1996–2001), and professor (2001–02); became full member, Division of Basic Sciences, Fred Hutchinson Cancer Research Center, Seattle (2002). With Dr. Richard Axel, received Nobel Prize in Physiology or Medicine (2004), for determining how people can smell and recall about 10,000 different odors, a discovery they made while working together at Columbia in 1991.

BUCK, Pearl S. (1892–1973). American writer. Name variations: (pseudonym) John Sedges. Born Pearl Comfort Sydenstricker, June 26, 1892, in Hillsboro, Pocahontas Co., West Virginia; died Mar 6, 1973, in Danby, Vermont; dau. of Absalom and Caroline Stulting Sydenstricker (Presbyterian missionaries); spent childhood and youth in China; graduate of Randolph-Macon Woman's College; Cornell University, MA in English, 1936; m. John Lossing Buck (agricultural missionary) 1917 (div. 1935); m. Richard J. Walsh (editor of *Asia Magazine* and head of John Day Co.), in 1935; children: (1st m.) Carol (mentally challenged) and Janice; (adopted) many. ❖ First American woman to win the Nobel

Prize in Literature, was the widely read author of over 100 books which have been translated into 69 languages; learned to speak Chinese before she spoke English; taught English literature at University of Nanking (Nanjing); published 1st novel, "East Wind: West Wind" (1930); had immediate and greatest success with 2nd novel *The Good Earth* (1931); published sequels, *Sons* (1932) and *A House Divided* (1935), followed by numerous books of fiction and nonfiction, including *All Men Are Brothers*, an English translation of the monumental Chinese classic *Shui Hu Chuan* (1933), *The Mother* (1934), *The Exile* (1936), *Fighting Angel* (1936), *A Bridge for Passing* (1962) and *Dragon Seed;* received Nobel Prize in Literature (1938); settled with 2nd husband at Green Hills Farm, Perkasie, Pennsylvania, with large family of adopted children; founded East West Association (1941), Welcome House (1949) and Pearl S. Buck Foundation (1964), to aid homeless Amerasian children in the lands of their birth; made countless appearances urging interracial understanding and world peace; as a member of the national committee of American Civil Liberties Union, spoke out against censorship of books; also wrote children's books, *The Big Wave* and *One Bright Day*. Won the Pulitzer Prize. ❖ See also memoir *My Several Worlds* (John Day, 1954); Theodore F. Harris, *Pearl S. Buck: A Biography* (Vols. I and II, John Day, 1969); Peter S. Conn, *Pearl S. Buck: A Cultural Biography* (Cambridge U. Press, 1998); Cornelia Spencer, *The Exile's Daughter: A Biography of Pearl S. Buck* (Coward-McCann, 1944); and *Women in World History*.

BUCKEL, C. Annette (1833–1912). American physician. Name variations: Chloe Annette Buckel. Born Chloe Annette Buckel, Aug 25, 1833, in Warsaw, NY; died Aug 17, 1912, in Piedmont, California; dau. of Thomas Buckel; mother's name was Bartlett; orphaned soon after birth, grew up with aunts; Woman's Medical College of Pennsylvania, MD, 1858. ❖ Early woman physician in US, performed post-graduate work under Marie Zakrzewska at New York Infirmary for Women and Children; began medical career with founding of dispensary in Chicago for women and children (1859); served as chief of female nurses at Jefferson General Hospital in Jeffersonville, Indiana, during Civil War; appointed resident physician (1868) and attending surgeon (1875) at New England Hospital for Women and Children in Boston, MA; opened medical practice in Oakland, CA, and served as consulting physician at San Francisco's Pacific Dispensary for Women and Children; later work centered on child health and welfare. The Buckel Foundation research fellowship at Stanford University was established with a grant from her estate.

BUCKINGHAM, countess of (d. 1632). *See Beaumont, Mary.*

BUCKINGHAM, duchess of.
See Neville, Anne (d. 1480).
See Woodville, Katherine (c. 1442–1512).

BUCKINGHAM, Rosa (c. 1843–1864). *See Buckingham, Rosetta.*

BUCKINGHAM, Rosetta (c. 1843–1864). New Zealand actress and singer. Name variations: Rosa Buckingham, Rosa Hayes. Born Rosetta Buckingham, c. 1843 or 1844; died 1864; dau. of George Buckingham and Anne (Jessop) Buckingham; children: 1. ❖ Performed plays and concerts with parents and brothers as Buckingham Family in Auckland, New Zealand (beginning mid-1850s); became star of entertainment troupe after parents' death and opened successful hotel with brothers; lived with Captain William Henry (Bully) Hayes, the father of her child; drowned with her child when boat capsized (1864). ❖ See also *Dictionary of New Zealand Biography* (Vol. 1).

BUCKLAND, Jessie Lillian (1878–1939). New Zealand photographer. Born May 9, 1878, at Tumai, Otago, New Zealand; died at sea, June 8, 1939; dau. of John Channing Buckland and Caroline (Fairburn) Buckland. ❖ With family, provided photographic services to community and documented rural life in New Zealand at end of 19th century; had several photographs published in *Auckland Weekly News*. Buckland family albums held by the Hocken Library, Dunedin. ❖ See also *Dictionary of New Zealand Biography* (Vol. 2).

BUCKLAND, Mary Morland (d. 1857). English naturalist. Name variations: Mary Morland. Born Mary Morland at Sheepstead House, near Abingdon, Berkshire, England; died 1857; dau. of Benjamin Morland; m. William Buckland (professor), 1825. ❖ Interested in natural history, family life, and social problems, spent much of her childhood living with the physician Sir Christopher Pegge and his wife; assisted husband, an Oxford University geology professor, with writing, illustrations and note taking, and on his *The Bridgewater Treatise* (1836); created drawings for the geologist William Conybeare.

BUCKMAN, Rosina (1881–1948). New Zealand opera singer and teacher. Name variations: Rosina d'Oisly. Born Mar 16, 1881, in Blenheim, New Zealand; died Dec 31, 1948, in London, England; dau. of John Buckman (carpenter) and Henrietta Matilda (Chuck) Buckman (singer and organist); studied at Birmingham and Midland School of Music in England; m. Emile Maurice d'Oisly (opera singer), 1919. ❖ Received early training from mother and church choir director until 1900, when she moved to England to study under George Breedon; illness forced return to New Zealand, where she began performing with American singer, Hamilton Hodges (1904); made operatic début (1905); continued to perform throughout Australia and New Zealand; persuaded by Nellie Melba and John McCormack to return to England, where she auditioned at Royal Opera House Covent Garden (c. 1912); was a flower maiden in the 1st English performance of *Parsifal* at Covent Garden (1914); invited by Thomas Beecham to become principal dramatic soprano in his newly formed opera company during WWI, where she appeared as Isolde, Butterfly, Mimi, and Aïda; performed at Covent Garden and throughout England in numerous operas following WWI; sang in the only performance of Ethyl Smyth's *The Boatswain's Mate* (1923); gave last performance (1925); taught at Royal Academy of Music (1930s). ❖ See also *Dictionary of New Zealand Biography* (Vol. 3).

BUCUR, Florica (1959—). Romanian rower. Born May 18, 1959, in Romania. ❖ At Moscow Olympics, won a bronze medal in coxed eights (1980).

BUCZYNSKA, Nadezhda Alekseyevna (1872–1952). *See Teffi, N.A.*

BUDAPEST, Z. (1940—). American writer and founder of religious movement. Name variations: Zsusanna Mokcsay; Zsuzsanna Emese Budapest. Born Zsusanna Mokcsay, Jan 30, 1940, in Budapest, Hungary; dau. of Masika Szilagyi (medium and sculptor); attended University of Vienna and University of Chicago; children: 2 sons. ❖ Known for founding the woman-centered, nature-based religion, Dianic Wicca, and for many writings on the subject of spirituality and spiritual power; fled to Austria when Hungarian Revolution broke out (1956), finishing high school in Innsbruck and winning scholarship to University of Vienna to study languages; immigrated to US (1959) and became student at University of Chicago; studied improvisational theater with Second City in Chicago; became involved in women's movement in Los Angeles; founded Susan B. Anthony Coven Number 1, 1st feminist witches coven which became a role model for other spiritual groups being formed across US; opened candle shop in Los Angeles; worked to spread Wiccan religion (1960s–70s), basing spiritual ideas on her own family's traditions of spirituality and worship which emphasize centrality of female deity and of nature; published *The Feminist Book of Lights* (1975); arrested for selling Tarot cards to undercover policewoman (1975), was convicted under anti-divination law that would be struck down 9 years later; in San Francisco Bay Area, served as director of nonprofit Women's Spirituality Forum (founded 1986) and had cable tv show, "13th Heaven"; writings include the bestselling *Holy Book of Women's Mysteries* (1989) and *Grandmother Moon: Lunar Magic in Our Lives—Spells, Rituals, Goddesses, Legends and Emotions Under the Moon* (1991).

BUDBERG, Moura (1892–1974). Russian-born linguist. Name variations: Moura von Benckendorff; Baroness Marie Budberg or Boudberg. Born Maria Ignatievna Zakrevsky or Zakrevskaya in Kharkov, Ukraine, in 1892; died in Tuscany, Italy, Oct 31, 1974; dau. of Count Ignaty Platonovich Zakrevsky (died 1905) and Countess Maria Boreisha Zakrevsky; sister of Alla Zakrevskaya and Assia Zakrevskaya; m. Ioann (Djohn) von Benckendorff (diplomat), 1911 (murdered 1919); m. Baron Nicolai Budberg (Baltic German aristocrat); children: Pavel (Paul); Tania Alexander (writer). ❖ Translator and literary personality, moved to Berlin with 1st husband (1912), where he had been assigned to the Russian Embassy; returned to Russia at start of WWI; following Russian Revolution, got a job as a translator with Maxim Gorky's World Literature publishing house (1918); following husband's murder (April 1919), moved in with Gorky, whose large Moscow flat was shared by a motley group of writers, artists and actors; though married once more, became increasingly intimate with Gorky, while at the same time cultivating what was to be a lifelong friendship with his wife Ekaterina Peshkov; assigned as an interpreter to British writer H.G. Wells when he visited Soviet Russia (1920); left Russia with the Gorky entourage (1921), settling 1st in Germany, then Czechoslovakia, then Italy; translated the works of several noted German writers into English, including Thomas

Mann; moved to London (1928), finding work as a literary agent; rekindled relationship with the aging H.G. Wells, whose wife Catherine Wells had recently died; refused to marry Wells, though their relationship remained passionate until his death; became one of the institutions of London's artistic and intellectual life; translated over 2 dozen books and served as a consultant on films for Sir Alexander Korda; during WWII, worked for *La France Libre*, a monthly magazine published by French emigrés. ❖ See also *Women in World History*.

BUDD, Zola (1966—). South African runner. Name variations: Zola Budd Pieterse. Born 1966 in Bloemfontein, Orange Free State, South Africa; m. Michael Pieterse (businessman). ❖ Banned from competing internationally because of apartheid policies of South African government, applied for British citizenship (1983); competed for England at Los Angeles Olympics and was involved in historic tumble with Mary Decker Slaney (1984); won world cross-country titles (1985, 1986); won European 3,000 meters (1985); returned to South Africa (1988).

BUDDINGTON, Zadel Barnes (1841–1917). See Barnes, Zadel.

BUDGE, Elizabeth Ann (1843–1908). See Mackay, Elizabeth Ann Louisa.

BUDINGTON, Zadel Barnes (1841–1917). See Barnes, Zadel.

BUDKE, Mary Anne (1953—). American golfer. Born Nov 16, 1953, in Salem, Oregon; attended Oregon State University. ❖ Won the National Intercollegiate championship (1974); won USGA Women's championship (1972), at age 18; member of the Curtis Cup team (1974); named captain of the Curtis Cup team (2002). Inducted into the Oregon State (1992), Oregon Sports, and National Golf Coaches Association (1996) Halls of Fame.

BUDZYNSKA-TYLICKA, Justyna (1876–1936). Polish physician and activist. Born 1876 in Lomza, Poland; grew up in an area of Poland under Russian occupation; died in Warsaw, June 8, 1936. ❖ Socialist, feminist, and birth-control pioneer, became a militant Marxist, joining the Polish Socialist Party; served on the party's national council (1931–34); advocated birth control, a position that placed her in conflict with both the Roman Catholic Church and a government that did not permit distribution of contraceptive information; was for many years an active member of the Socialist Women's International. ❖ See also *Women in World History*.

BUEHRMANN, Elizabeth (1886–1954). American photographer. Born 1886; died 1954 (some sources cite 1962). ❖ Specializing in home portraiture, elected an associate of Photo-Secession (1904); work shown in Art Crafts Exhibition (1908) and at annual exhibits of the Art Students League, both at Art Institute of Chicago (1910–11); as a member of the Photo-Club of Paris, exhibited at International Salons of Photography (1910, 1912, and 1913); photographs appeared in *Vogue* and *Vanity Fair*; later career included advertising copy for some well-known products, including Corona typewriters, Packard automobiles, and Yuban coffee.

BUELBRING, Edith (1903–1990). See Bülbring, Edith.

BUELL, Marjorie Henderson (1905–1993). American cartoonist. Name variations: Marge Henderson Buell; (pen name) Marge. Born 1905; died in Elyria, Ohio, May 30, 1993. ❖ Using the pen name "Marge," was the creator of "Little Lulu," which 1st appeared as a single-panel cartoon in *Saturday Evening Post* (June 1935); launched the comic-book series and the long-running newspaper strip with Western Publishing for the Chicago Tribune-New York News syndicate; lost the rights to her own creation (1945). ❖ See also *Women in World History*.

BUENO, Maria (1939—). Brazilian tennis player. Name variations: (nicknames) Little Saber and Sao Paulo Swallow. Born Maria Esther Andion Bueno in Sao Paulo, Brazil, Oct 11, 1939; dau. of a veterinarian who was also an amateur tennis player. ❖ Won 62 titles as an amateur; rated No. 1 in the world (1959, 1960, 1964 and 1966); ranked the world's best woman tennis player (1964); won 8 Wimbledon titles, 3 in singles (1959, 1960, 1964) and 5 in doubles (1958, 1960, 1963, 1965, 1966). ❖ See also *Women in World History*.

BUERGER, Erna (1909–1958). German gymnast. Name variations: Erna Bürger or Burger. Born July 26, 1909, in Germany; died June 26, 1958. ❖ At Berlin Olympics, won a gold medal in team all-around (1936).

BUERI, Piccarda. See Medici, Piccarda de.

BUERKI, Gianna (1969—). See Hablützel-Bürki, Gianna.

BUFALINO, Brenda (1937—). American tap dancer. Name variations: Strickland Sisters. Born 1937 in Lynn, Massachusetts. ❖ At 8, began appearing on nightclub stages throughout Massachusetts, tapping in her mother and aunt's show, The Strickland Sisters (c. 1945); toured for the USO, performing in hospitals after WWII; turned to jazz, and danced with Stanley Brown's dance troupe (starting 1952); often seen as leading figure in tap revival, moved to NY and became immersed in the cultural revolution of bebop, dancing in jazz clubs throughout the city (c. 1954); performed in concert with Charles "Honi" Coles, touring US, England and France; founded American Tap Dance Orchestra (ATDO) in NY (1986); with ATDO, created Woodpeckers Tap Dance Center in Soho, NY (1989); received grant from National Endowment for the Arts for production of documentary *Great Feats of Feet: Portraits of the Jazz Tap Dancer*; received Flo-Vert Lifetime Achievement Award.

BUFANU, Valeria (1946—). Romania hurdler. Born Oct 7, 1946, in Romania. ❖ At Munich Olympics, won a silver medal in the 100-meter hurdles (1972).

BUFERD, Marilyn (1925–1990). Miss America and actress. Name variations: Marilyn Buferd Stevens. Born Jan 30, 1925, in Los Angeles, California; died Mar 27, 1990, in Austin, Texas; m. Franco Barbara (former submarine commander under Mussolini), 1951 (div.); m. Milton Stevens (plumbing magnate, died 1988); children: (1st m.) Nick Barbaro (publisher of *Austin Chronicle*). ❖ Named Miss America (1946), representing California; modeled in Paris, then moved to Italy and appeared in numerous films with such directors as Roberto Rossellini and Pietro Germi; moved to LA, appearing in films and tv. ❖ See also Frank Deford, *There She Is* (Viking, 1971).

BUFF, Charlotte (1753–1828). German literary inspiration. Name variations: Lolette, Lolotte or Lotte Buff; Charlotte Kestner. Born 1753; died 1828; m. Georg Christian Kestner (court councilor), 1773. ❖ Friend and companion of the German author Johann Wolfgang von Goethe, was the inspiration for Lotte in his 1st novel *Die Leiden des Jungen Werthers* (*The Sorrows of Young Werther*, 1774); also inspired Thomas Mann's novel *Lotte in Weimar*. ❖ See also *Women in World History*.

BUFF, Lotte (1753–1828). See Buff, Charlotte.

BUFFALO-CALF-ROAD-WOMAN (fl. 1876). Native American. Born into Cheyenne tribe; sister of Chief Comes-in-Sight. ❖ Rescued brother from George Crook's US Cavalry by swooping him onto her horse in the battle of Rosebud Creek in southern Montana (June 17, 1876), an event known to Cheyennes as the Battle Where the Girl Saved Her Brother.

BUFFET, Marguerite (d. 1680). French grammarian. Born in France; died in France, 1680; never married; no children. ❖ An exceptionally well-educated woman of the French aristocracy, produced written works outlining French grammar and other aspects of the language; only surviving work is *New Observations on the French Language* (1668), a book specifically designed to instruct women in the skills of rhetoric and writing. ❖ See also *Women in World History*.

BUFFINGTON, Adele (1900–1973). American screenwriter. Name variations: (pseudonym) Jess Bowers. Born Adele Burgdorfer, Feb 12, 1900, in St. Louis, Missouri; died Nov 23, 1973, in Woodland Hills, California; dau. of Adolph and Elizabeth (Friedrich) Burgdorfer; educated in public schools. ❖ Wrote scenarios for many of the silent screen's cowboy matinee idols, including Tom Mix, Tim McCoy, and Buck Jones; sold 1st script, *La Petite*, to a film company for $300, at age 19; worked for Thomas Ince; by the time she retired, had more than 150 screen credits either under her own name or pseudonym Jess Bowers; films include *Times Square* (1928), *Ghost Valley* (1932), *The Moonstone* (1934), *When Strangers Meet* (1934), *The Texas Kid* (1943), *The Navajo Trail* (1945), *West of Wyoming* (1950), *Jiggs and Maggie Out West* (1950), *Arizona Territory* (1950), *Overland Telegraph* (1951) and *Bullwhip* (1956). ❖ See also *Women in World History*.

BUFORD-BAILEY, Tonja (1970—). American hurdler. Name variations: Tonja Buford. Born Tonja Buford, Dec 13, 1970, in Dayton, Ohio; graduate of University of Illinois, 1994; m. Victor Bailey, 1995. ❖ Was NCAA Outdoor champion (1992); won a bronze medal for 400-meter hurdles at Atlanta Olympics (1996); won a silver medal at World championships (1995).

BUGARINOVIC, Melanija (1905–1986). Serbian mezzo-soprano. Name variations: Melanie, Melka, Milada. Born in Bela Crkva, June 29, 1905; died in Belgrade, Yugoslavia, May 8, 1986. ❖ Performed regularly with Belgrade Opera (1930–37, 1946–61); sang with Vienna Staatsoper (1938–44) and appeared in role of Herodias in *Salome*, conducted by Richard Strauss (1942); also appeared at Bayreuth (1952–53); was well-known for such Wagnerian roles as Fricka, Erda, Brangäne and Ortrud. ❖ See also *Women in World History.*

BUGBEE, Emma (1888–1981). American journalist. Born May 18, 1888, in Shippensburg, Pennsylvania; died Oct 6, 1981, in Warwick, Rhode Island; dau. of Edwin Howard (language teacher) and Emma Bugbee; graduate of Barnard College; never married. ❖ Grand dame of *New York Herald Tribune,* spent 56 years there as a reporter; gained prominence as one of Eleanor Roosevelt's "girls," a group of women reporters who traveled with the first lady; was a generalist, covering everything from the annual flower show and circus, to murders and local politics; also covered the women's movement; was one of the founders of the Newspaper Women's Club of New York (1922) and served as its president for 3 terms; published the 1st in a series of 5 "Peggy" books (1936), based on her experience as a reporter; retired (1966). ❖ See also *Women in World History.*

BUGGA (d. 751). *See Edburga.*

BUGGE (d. 751). *See Edburga.*

BUGGY, Regina (1959—). American field-hockey player. Born Nov 12, 1959; lived in Plymouth, Pennsylvania. ❖ At Los Angeles Olympics, won a bronze medal in team competition (1984); became head coach of Episcopal Academy.

BUGLISI, Jacqulyn (1951—). American modern dancer. Name variations: incorrectly seen as Jacquelyn. Born Feb 19, 1951, in New York, NY. ❖ Made debut with Pearl Lang (c. early 1970s); joined Martha Graham Dance Company (1977) where she performed as principal artist throughout the world, dancing in company revivals of Graham classics as well as later works, such as *Owl and the Pussy Cat* and *Flute of Pan;* joined Graham faculty and that of Juilliard School (1977); founded her own company, Buglisi-Foreman Dance, with former Graham dancers Donlin Foreman, Terese Capucilli, and Christine Dakin (1994); work has been presented by Jacob's Pillow Dance Festival, John F. Kennedy Center of Performing Arts, Joyce Theater in New York City, and 1999 Melbourne International Festival, among others; received Fiorello LaGuardia Award for Excellence in Field of Dance; has more than 25 ballets to her credit, including *Requiem, Frida, Suspended Women* and *Red Hills.*

BUGRIMOVA, Irina (1910–2001). Russian animal tamer. Born Mar 13, 1910, in Kharkov, Ukraine; died Feb 20, 2001, in Moscow, Russia; m. Aleksandr Buslayev (her coach and acrobatic partner); m. Konstantin Parmakyan (dressage rider). ❖ The 1st Russian woman to train lions and tigers, appeared for 45 years with the Moscow State Circus, the Circus Humberto in Czechoslovakia, and the East German State Circus, among others; retired after being attacked by her lion Nero (1971).

BUHAEV, Agafia (1955—). *See Constantin-Buhaev, Agafia.*

BÜHLER, Charlotte (1893–1974). German-born psychologist. Name variations: Buhler or Buehler. Born Charlotte Bertha Malachowski in Berlin, Germany, Dec 20, 1893; died in Stuttgart, Federal Republic of Germany, Feb 3, 1974; dau. of Hermann Malachowski (architect) and Rose (Kristeller) Malachowski; attended Freiburg im Breisgau, 1913, University of Kiel, 1914; studied under Carl Stumpf at University of Berlin; University of Munich, PhD, 1918; m. Karl Bühler (1879–1963, psychologist), April 4, 1916; children: Ingeborg (b. 1917), Rolf (b. 1919). ❖ One of the leading figures of child psychology in 1st half of the 20th century, published 1st book, *Das Märchen und die Phantasie des Kindes,* a study of children's fantasies and fairy tales (1918); became 1st female *privatdozent* at Dresden Institute of Technology (1920), where both she and husband would later teach until they accepted positions at University of Vienna (1922); recipient of one of the 1st Rockefeller exchange fellowships (1923), worked with Edward Thorndike at Columbia University in US; after returning to Vienna, continued to collaborate with husband, now head of the university's psychological institute; also founded her own institute dedicated to innovative investigations of the psychological development of children; books became world-famous, both in their original German-language editions as well as in translations into a number of languages including English; as a "full-blooded Jewess" who had achieved world fame as an educational reformer, was a particular threat to the Nazi occupiers of Vienna (1938); found sanctuary in Norway, then fled to US; taught at several institutions, including College of St. Catherine in St. Paul (MN), Clark University in Worcester (MA), and City College of New York; became US citizen and moved to Los Angeles (1945); was chief clinical psychologist at Los Angeles County General Hospital until 1953; helped

organize Old Saybrook Conference, which resulted in the birth of the humanistic psychology movement (1964); writings include *Kindheit und Jugend* (1928), *The First Year of Life* (trans. by Pearl Greenberg and Rowena Ripin, 1930), *From Birth to Maturity* (1935), *Psychologie im Leben unserer Zeit* (1962), *The Course of Human Life* (1968) and *An Introduction to Humanistic Psychology* (1972). ❖ See also *Women in World History.*

BUHR-WEIGELT, Liane (1956—). East German rower. Name variations: Liane Weigelt; Liana Weigelt-Buhr. Born Mar 11, 1956, in Germany. ❖ Won a gold medal in quadruple sculls with coxswain at Montreal Olympics (1976) and Moscow Olympics (1980).

BUITENWEG, Kathalijne Maria (1970—). Dutch politician. Born Mar 27, 1970, in Rotterdam, Netherlands. ❖ Served as policy advisor, GroenLinks European delegation (1995–98); representing Group of the Greens/European Free Alliance, elected to 5th European Parliament (1999–2004).

BUI THI XUAN (d. 1771). Vietnamese heroine. Executed around 1771; m. Tran Quang Dieu, a Tay Son general; children: daughter. ❖ Famous general in Vietnamese history, was captured for leading 5,000 rebels in a peasant insurgence, known as the Tay Son Rebellion. ❖ See also *Women in World History.*

BUJDOSO, Agota (1943—). Hungarian handball player. Born June 1943 in Hungary. ❖ At Montreal Olympics, won a bronze medal in team competition (1976).

BUJOLD, Geneviève (1942—). French-Canadian actress. Name variations: Genevieve Bujold. Born July 1, 1942, in Montreal, Quebec, Canada; schooled in Hochelaga Convent; attended Conservatoire d'Art Dramatique; m. Paul Almond (director), 1967 (div. 1973); children: (1st m.) Matthew James Almond (actor and director). ❖ Came to prominence in France in *La Guerre est Finie* (1965), followed by *Le Roi de Coeur* (*King of Hearts,* 1966), *Le Voleur* (1967) and title role in *Isabel* (1968); appeared as Shaw's Saint Joan on tv (1967); made Hollywood film debut as Anne Boleyn in *Anne of the Thousand Days* (1969), for which she was nominated for an Academy Award; other films include *The Trojan Women* (1971), *Kamouraska* (1973), *Earthquake* (1974), *Obsession* (1976), *Alex & the Gypsy* (1976), *Coma* (1978), *Murder by Decree* (1979), *Final Assignment* (1980), *Monsignor* (1982), *Tightrope* (1984), *Choose Me* (1984), *Trouble in Mind* (1985), *The Moderns* (1988), *Dead Ringers* (1988), *Rue du Bac* (1991), *Dead Innocent* (1996), *Eye of the Beholder* (1999), *Jericho Mansions* (2003) and *Downtown: A Street Tale* (2004).

BUKHARINA, Galina (1945—). Soviet runner. Born Feb 14, 1945, in USSR. ❖ At Mexico City Olympics, won a bronze medal in 4 x 100-meter relay (1968).

BUKOVEC, Brigita (1970—). Slovenian hurdler. Name variations: Brigitta Bukovec. Born May 21, 1970, in Ljubljana, Slovakia. ❖ Won a silver medal for 100-meter hurdles at Atlanta Olympics (1996); at European championships, won a silver medal for 100-meter hurdles.

BULARDA-HOMEGHI, Olga (1958—). Romanian rower. Name variations: Olga Bularda; Olga Homeghi. Born May 1, 1958, in Romania. ❖ At Moscow Olympics, won a bronze medal in double sculls (1980); at Los Angeles Olympics, won a gold medal in coxed fours (1984); at Seoul Olympics, won a gold medal in coxed pairs and a silver medal in coxed eights (1988).

BÜLBRING, Edith (1903–1990). German pharmacologist and physiologist. Name variations: Edith Bulbring or Buelbring. Born Dec 27, 1903, in Bonn, Germany; died July 5, 1990; dau. of a professor of English at University of Bonn; mother was Dutch; attended University of Bonn (1923–25). ❖ Known for pharmacology research and expertise in smooth muscle physiology, received medical training in Bonn, Freiburg, and Munich (1925–28); collaborated with Ulrich Friedemann as clinical research assistant at Virchow Hospital's Infectious Disease Unit in Berlin (1933); worked as J.H. Burn's research assistant at London's Pharmaceutical Society (1933–37); moved with him to University of Oxford's Department of Pharmacology, where she served as pharmacology department demonstrator (1937–46), lecturer and university demonstrator (1946–60), reader (1960–67) and professor (1967–71); created and collaborated with international team of smooth-muscle researchers (mid-1950s) until retirement, studying electrical activity, drug and transmitters response, ion levels, oxygen consumption, and nerve activity of smooth muscle. Made a fellow of Royal Society (1958); received Wellcome Gold Medal in Pharmacology (1985).

BULBULIA, Katharine (1943—). Irish politician. Born Katharine O'Carroll, July 1943, in Dublin, Ireland; m. Dr. Abdul Bulbulia. ❖ Representing Fine Gael, elected to the Seanad from the Administrative Panel: Oireachtas Sub-Panel (1981–82); representing Progressive Democrats, elected to the Seanad from the Nominating Bodies Sub-Panel (1982–89); appointed program manager for Progressive Democrats (1997).

BULDAKOVA, Lyudmila (1938—). Soviet volleyball player. Born May 25, 1938, in USSR. ❖ Won a silver medal at Tokyo Olympics (1964), a gold medal at Mexico City Olympics (1968) and a gold medal at Munich Olympics (1972), all in team competition.

BULFINCH, Hannah Apthorp (1768–1841). American letter writer and diarist. Born Hannah Apthorp in 1768; died April 8, 1841; orphaned during American Revolution and raised by grandfather, Stephen Greenleaf, a noted Loyalist; m. Charles Bulfinch (architect), 1788. ❖ Her diary of economically difficult early years of marriage was excerpted in *The Life and Letters of Charles Bulfinch, Architect.*

BULGARIA, queen of.
  See Giovanna of Italy (b. 1907).
  See Marie Louisa of Parma (d. 1899).

BULGARIA, tsarina of.
  See Dessilava (fl. 1197–1207).
  See Irene Lascaris (d. around 1270).
  See Maria Paleologina (fl. 1278–1279).
  See Irene Paleologina (fl. 1279–1280).

BULICH, Vera Sergeevna (1898–1954). Russian poet. Name variations: Vera Sergéevna Búlich; Vera Bulich. Born 1898 in Russia; died 1954. ❖ Émigré poet, fled Russia with family (1920); worked as librarian at Helsinki University in Finland and published poetry in émigré journals; published 4 volumes of poems (1934–54), some of which have been compared to the work of Anna Akhmátova.

BULLEN, Nan (1507?–1536). *See Boleyn, Anne.*

BULLER, Annie (1896–1973). Canadian activist. Born Dec 1896 in Russia or Canada; died Jan 19, 1973, in Toronto, Ontario; dau. of Jewish parents (father was a carpenter); attended Rand School of Social Science in NY, 1919; m. Harry Guralnick, mid-1920s; children: Jimmy. ❖ Prominent speaker and organizer for the Communist Party in Canada, who endured imprisonment and political repression to better the lives of Canadian workers, began work in a tobacco factory (1910); joined socialist youth movement (1917); left Montreal to attend Rand School in New York (1919); developed talent for oratory that would make her a popular figure among Canadian workers; was one of the founding members of Communist Party of Canada (CPC, 1922); sent to Winnipeg, Manitoba, to support workers in the needle trades (1929); arrested along with 26 others for her part in organizing the famous Estevan strike (1931); jailed for 1 year (1933), which she served in solitary confinement; during WWII, jailed for 2 years while Russia was aligned with Germany (1940–42); for Labour Progressive Party (LPP), ran unsuccessfully for alderman in city of Toronto (1932) and for federal election from Spadina Riding (Toronto, 1956); traveled to Soviet Union (1955); for 50 years, worked tirelessly for the building of unions, the production of working-class publications, and the raising of the consciousness of workers of Canada in the hope of bringing her country closer to socialism. ❖ See also Louise Watson, *She Never Was Afraid: The Biography of Annie Buller* (Progress, 1976); and *Women in World History.*

BULLETT, Vicky (1967—). African-American basketball player. Name variations: Victoria Bullett. Born Oct 4, 1967, in Martinsburg, West Virginia; sister of Scott Bullett (b. 1968, baseball player with Pittsburgh Pirates, Chicago Cubs and Cincinnati Reds); attended University of Maryland. ❖ Won an Olympic gold medal at Seoul (1988) and a bronze medal in Barcelona (1992), both in team competition; in WNBA, played for Charlotte Sting (1997–99), then signed with Washington Mystics (2000).

BULLETTE, Julia (d. 1867). English-born courtesan. Name variations: Julia Bulette. Born in London, England; died Jan 20, 1867, in Virginia City, Nevada. ❖ Called the "Darling of the Comstock," was one of the most popular courtesans of Virginia City, Nevada, where she settled in order to cash in on the Western mining boom of the 1850s; was robbed

and murdered by the notorious thief John Millian. ❖ See also *Women in World History.*

BULLIN, Katharina (1959—). East German volleyball player. Born Mar 2, 1959, in East Germany. ❖ At Moscow Olympics, won a silver medal in team competition (1980).

BULLINGER, Anna (c. 1504–1564). Swedish reformer. Born Anna Adlischweiler c. 1504 in Sweden; died of the plague in 1564; m. Heinrich Bullinger (church reformer), 1529; children: 11. ❖ While living in a Zurich convent with her failing mother, met Heinrich Bullinger who was to gain recognition in the church-reform movement; moved with husband to Bremgarten, Argau, Switzerland; as Roman Catholic armies were attacking Protestant ministers during the Reformation (1531), made a home for many refugees of the plague, after nursing husband back to health from his own bout with the disease. ❖ See also *Women in World History.*

BULLITT, Kay (b. 1914). *See Stammers, Kay.*

BULLOCK, Emma (1812–1851). *See Martin, Emma.*

BULLOCK, Margaret (1845–1903). New Zealand journalist and social reformer. Name variations: Madge Bullock; (pseudonym) Tua-o-rangi. Born Margaret Carson, Jan 4, 1845, in Auckland, NZ; died June 17, 1903, at Sydney Place, Wanganui, NZ; dau. of Jane Kennedy Carson and James Carson (road maker); m. George Bullock (warehouseman), Feb 10, 1869 (died 1877); children: 5 sons, including William (died 1892). ❖ Reported for *Wanganui Chronicle* (1870s–80s), becoming one of the 1st women parliamentary correspondents; began writing short stories for magazines (1887); under pseudonym Tua-o-rangi, published Maori novel *Utu;* campaigned for women's rights; established the Wanganui Women's Franchise League (1893, later Wanganui Women's Political League) and served as its president (1893–97); was also a major figure in National Council of Women of New Zealand (NCW), and its vice-president (1900).

BULLOWA, Emilie (1869–1942). American reformer. Born 1869 in New York, NY; died in New York, Oct 25, 1942; dau. of Morris Bullowa and Mary Bullowa; graduate of Law College of New York University, 1900; never married. ❖ Lawyer and philanthropist, opened a law office in Lower Manhattan, from which she and brother Ferdinand Bullowa would practice admiralty law for more than 4 decades; fought for the equal treatment of female lawyers and was a founding member and 1st president of National Association of Women Lawyers; served as a member of platform committee of Women's Democratic Union (1924). ❖ See also *Women in World History.*

BULLRICH, Silvina (1915–1990). Argentinean novelist, poet and screenwriter. Name variations: Sandra Bullrich. Born Oct 4, 1915, in Buenos Aires, Argentina; died July 1990 in Geneva, Switzerland. ❖ Taught French and wrote for newspapers and tv; traveled and lectured abroad and wrote of experiences for *La Nación;* writings include *Vibraciónes* (1935), *Bodas de cristal* (Glass Wedding, 1951), *Teléfono ocupado* (Telephone Engaged, 1955), *Los burgueses* (The Bourgeoisie, 1964), *Los salvadores de la patria* (The Saviors of the Fatherland, 1965), *Mañana digo basta* (Tomorrow I Talk Enough, 1968), and *La creciente* (The Crescent Moon, 1970); collaborated with Jorge Luis Borges on *El Compadrito* (1945); wrote screenplay for *Bajo un mismo rostro* (1962) and adaptions for film: *A momento muy largo* (1964), *Los Pasajeros del jardin* (1982), and her novel *Bodas de cristal* (1975). Won French Academic Award (1982).

BULLWINKEL, Vivian (1915–2000). Australian nurse and prisoner of war. Name variations: Vivian Statham. Born in Kapunda, South Australia, Dec 1915; died in Perth, July 3, 2000; dau. of George Bullwinkel (mining company employee); educated in Broken Hill and District Hospital, 1938; m. Colonel Frank W. Statham, 1977 (died 1999). ❖ Completed midwifery training (1939); served as staff nurse at Kiaora Private Hospital, Hamilton, Victoria (1939–40); served as staff nurse at Jessie McPherson Hospital, Melbourne (1940–41); joined the Australian Army Nursing Service (AANS), as part of the fledgling 13th Australian General Hospital (AGH), and sailed to Singapore on a hospital ship (Sept 1941); when Singapore was attacked by the Japanese and evacuated, boarded the *Vyner Brooke,* which was bombed and sunk by the Japanese in the Banka Strait; with other survivors, reached Banka Island, but was the only woman survivor of the massacre on the beach; interned at Japanese prisoner-of-war camp (1941–44); named president of the College of Nursing (later the Royal College of Nursing), Australia (1970s). ❖ See also *Women in World History.*

BULNES, Esmée (1900–1986). English ballet dancer. Name variations: Esmee Bulnes. Born 1900 in Rock Ferry, Cheshire, England; died in Rimini, 1986. ❖ One of the most influential teachers of ballet in Italy and one of the main perpetuators of the Cecchetti technique, trained with Enrico Cecchetti, Bronislava Nijinska, Lyubov Egorova, and others; traveled to Buenos Aires (1931), to assist Mikhail Fokine in his work as ballet master at Teatro Colón; performed, taught and assisted at Teatro Colón after Fokine's departure; joined faculty of Teatro alla Scala in Milan (late 1940s) and later served as director of the school and ballet company.

BÜLOW, Frieda von (1857–1909). German writer. Name variations: Buelow, Bulow; Baroness von Bülow. Born Frieda Freifräulein von Bülow in Berlin, Germany, Oct 12, 1857; died in Dornburg, Mar 12, 1909; dau. of Hugo Freiherr von Bülow (diplomat); sister of novelist Margarete von Bülow (1860–1884) and Albrecht von Bülow (died 1892). ❖ Creator of the German colonial novel, accompanied brother to German East Africa (1885), where he attempted to create a successful career as a plantation owner; became a strong proponent of a German presence in Africa; from early 1890s to her death, urged German colonial expansionism; convinced that Germans were racially superior to Africans, created the German colonial novel with her work, *Im Lande der Verheissung* (1899), which was populated with racist stereotypes; wrote movingly of her sister Margarete in her last novel, *Die Schwestern* (*The Sisters*, 1909). ❖ See also *Women in World History*.

BÜLOW, Margarete von (1860–1884). German writer. Name variations: Buelow or Bulow. Born Margarete Freifräulein von Bülow in Berlin, Germany, Feb 23, 1860; drowned in Berlin, Jan 2, 1884; dau. of Hugo Freiherr von Bülow (diplomat); sister of Frieda von Bülow (1857–1909) and Albrecht von Bülow; grew up in various countries including England. ❖ Novelist, whose early death while attempting to save a drowning child cut short a promising literary career, lived in England (1876–78), finally settling in Berlin (1881); a prolific writer and sharp-eyed observer, had a large number of unpublished manuscripts prepared for publication in the final months of her life, which were all published posthumously to critical acclaim; writings include *Novellen* (1885), *Jonas Briccius: Erzählung* (1886), *Aus der Chronik derer von Riffelshausen: Erzählung* (1887), *Neue Novellen* (1890), and *Novellen einer Frühvollendeten: Ausgewähltes: Mit einer Einleitung von Adolf Bartels* (1920). ❖ See also *Women in World History*.

BULSTRODE, Emily Mary (1867–1959). New Zealand school principal, missionary, and nurse. Born Nov 21, 1867, at Cookham, Berkshire, England; died Dec 24, 1959, in Slough, Buckinghamshire, England; dau. of William Bulstrode (farmer) and Jane (Taylor) Bulstrode; sister of Jane Helena Bulstrode. ❖ Trained as nurse before following sister Jane Bulstrode to New Zealand (1901); served as principal of Hukarere missionary school (1920–27). ❖ See also *Dictionary of New Zealand Biography* (Vol. 3).

BULSTRODE, Jane Helena (1862–1946). New Zealand school principal and missionary. Born April 1, 1862, at Cookham, Berkshire, England; died Mar 6, 1946, at Rotorua, New Zealand; dau. of William Bulstrode (farmer) and Jane (Taylor) Bulstrode; sister of Emily Mary Bulstrode. ❖ Educated at Craufurd House, Maidenhead; immigrated to New Zealand; served as principal of Hukarere missionary school (1900–19). ❖ See also *Dictionary of New Zealand Biography* (Vol. 3).

BULWER-LYTTON, Constance (1869–1923). See Lytton, Constance.

BULWER-LYTTON, Elizabeth (1867–1942). See Balfour, Betty.

BULWER-LYTTON, Emily (1874–1964). See Lutyens, Emily.

BULWER-LYTTON, Rosina, Lady (1802–1882). English novelist. Name variations: Lady Bulwer-Lytton; Rosina Wheeler. Born Rosina Doyle Wheeler in Ballywhire, Co. Limerick, Ireland, Nov 2, 1802; died in Upper Sydenham, in London, England, Mar 12, 1882; youngest dau. of Francis Wheeler and Anna Doyle Wheeler (dau. of an archdeacon); m. Edward George Earle Lytton Bulwer-Lytton, 1st baron Lytton, Aug 1827 (died 1873); children: Emily Bulwer-Lytton (1828–1848); Edward Robert Bulwer Lytton (1831–1891); grandmother of Lady Constance Lytton. ❖ Popular member of the literary circle surrounding Lady Caroline Lamb, married Edward Bulwer-Lytton despite his mother's wishes and the cessation of his yearly allowance (1827); legally separated from husband because of his volatile temper (and possibly domestic violence) and was given custody of their 2 children (1836); children were taken from her (1838); saw her daughter only once more before the young girl died at age 20; attacked husband in print with her

book *Cheveley, or the Man of Honour* (1839), which met with scandalous success; continued to publicly taunt him until his death. ❖ See also Louisa Devey, *Life of Rosina, Lady Lytton* (1887); Michael Sadleir, *Bulwer, a Panorama: Edward and Rosina, 1803–36* (1931).

BUMBRY, Grace (1937—). African-American mezzo-soprano. Born Grace Ann Bumbry, Jan 4, 1937, in St. Louis, Missouri; studied at Boston and Northwestern universities and with Lotte Lehmann. ❖ Was a winner on "The Arthur Godfrey Show" (1954); made concert debut in London (1959); debuted with Paris Opera as Amneris (1960); was featured as Venus in a new production of Tannhauser at Bayreuth (1961), the 1st black to sing there (won the Wagner Medal); gave more than 170 performances at NY's Metropolitan Opera; scored a tour de force singing both Cassandra in Part I and Dido in Part II of Berlioz's *Les Troyens* at Paris's Bastille Opera (1990); recorded on 4 labels and sang in concerts worldwide, including opera houses in Vienna, London, Salzburg and Milan; performed all of the great Verdi and French mezzo-soprano roles, such as Carmen, Delilah, Azucena, Eboli, and Amneris, as well as soprano parts. Was the 1st recipient of the Lawrence Tibbett Award.

BUNATYANTS, Elen (1970—). Soviet basketball player. Born June 2, 1970, in USSR. ❖ At Barcelona Olympics, won a gold medal in team competition (1992).

BUNBURY, Lady (1745–1826). See Lennox, Sarah.

BUNBURY, Selina (1802–1882). Irish novelist and traveler. Born in Kilsaran, Co. Louth, Ireland, in 1802; died in Cheltenham in 1882. ❖ While teaching in a primary school, wrote books about Ireland, including *A Visit to My Birthplace* (1820) and *Tales of My Country* (1833); moved to Liverpool, where she kept house for her twin brother and continued writing, publishing many popular novels; following brother's marriage (1845), took to the road, publishing books on her travels throughout Europe.

BUNDY, May Sutton (1887–1975). See Sutton, May.

BUNGE DE GÁLVEZ, Delfina (1881–1952). Argentinean poet, novelist and travel writer. Name variations: Delfina Bunge de Galvez. Born 1881 in Buenos Aires, Argentina; died 1952 in Buenos Aires. ❖ Deeply religious writer, published her 1st 2 books, *Simplement* (1911) and *La nouvelle moisson* (1918), in French; also wrote *Las imágines del infinito* (1922), *El tesoro del mundo* (1923), *Los malos tiempos de hoy* (1927), and *Tierras del mar azul* (1928); edited the magazine *Ichthys*.

BUNGU, Nonteta (c. 1875–1935). See Nonteta Bungu.

BUNINA, Anna Petrovna (1774–1829). Russian poet. Name variations: Búnina. Born 1774; died 1829; sixth child born into a gentry family. ❖ Russia's 1st major woman poet, moved to St. Petersburg on death of father (1801); used her small inheritance to educate herself and to support her writing; gained prominence with her poetry, *An Inexperienced Muse* (Vol. 1, 1809, Vol. 2, 1812); to seek treatment for breast cancer, journeyed to England (1815), but wrote very little after 1817, because of illness and pain. ❖ See also Barbara Heldt, *Terrible Perfection*.

BUNKE, Tamara (1937–1967). Argentine-born revolutionary. Name variations: (codename) Tania. Born Tamara Haydée Bunke, Nov 19, 1937, in Buenos Aires, Argentina; killed in ambush by Bolivian army patrol, Aug 31, 1967, at Vado del Yeso, Bolivia; dau. of Erich Otto Heinrich Bunke (German Communist and teacher) and Esperanza Bider (Polish Communist and teacher); m. Mario Martínez Álvarez, briefly, to obtain Bolivian citizenship, 1966; children: none. ❖ Communist double agent in Cuba who was instrumental in planning the guerilla operation in Bolivia in which both she and the famed Cuban revolutionary Ché Guevara died; moved with family to the German Democratic Republic (1948); joined GDR defense training program (1952); recruited for intelligence work by the East German Ministry of State Security (1958); shortly thereafter, was approached by the KGB to work as a double agent for Moscow; in an effort to advance the Communist revolution in Latin America, was sent to Cuba as a translator for the Ministry of Education (1961); recruited for Cuban intelligence (Mar 1963), was given the work of organizing a network to invade Latin America countries and subvert their governments, confronting the power and influence of US whenever possible; sent to La Paz to establish an urban guerrilla network in Bolivia (Oct 1964); after deliberately revealing extent of Cuban involvement in Bolivia (possibly because Moscow wanted Bolivian authorities to know what Guevara's troops were doing), joined Ché Guevara's guerrillas in the jungle (Feb 1967); died not as a victim of the West, but because of infighting within her own party, while her actions also led directly to the death of Ché Guevara. ❖ See also Marta Rojas and Mirta Rodríguez Calderón, eds. *Tania: The Unforgettable Guerrilla* (Vintage, 1971); and *Women in World History*.

BUNKER, Carol Laise (1918–1991). American diplomat. Born Carol Laise in 1918; died in Virginia, 1991; m. diplomat Ellsworth Bunker (ambassador to Vietnam), 1967. ❖ Began career with State Department (1948); served as ambassador to Nepal (1966–73); also served at United Nations and as assistant secretary of state. ❖ See also *Women in World History*.

BUNKOWSKY, Barb (1958—). See Scherbak, Barb.

BUNKOWSKY-SCHERBAK, Barb (1958—). *See Scherbak, Barb.*

BUNN, Anna Maria (1808–1899). See Murray, Anna Maria.

BUNTING, Mary Ingraham (1910–1998). American educator. Born in Hartford, Connecticut, July 10, 1910; died Jan 21, 1998; dau. of Mary Shotwell Ingraham (1887–1981, founder of USO) and Henry Andrews Ingraham; Vassar, BA, 1931; University of Wisconsin, MA, 1932, PhD, 1934; m. Henry Bunting, 1937; children: 4. ❖ Was an instructor in biology at Bennington College (1936–37), instructor in physiology and hygiene at Goucher College (1937–38), research assistant in department of bacteriology at Yale (1938–40, 1948–52), lecturer at Yale (1953–55), lecturer in department of botany, Wellesley College (1946–47), dean of Douglass College at Rutgers University (1955–69), president of Radcliffe College in Cambridge, Massachusetts (1960–72), and assistant to the president at Princeton University (1972–75).

BUNTON, Emma (1976—). English pop singer. Name variations: Baby Spice, The Spice Girls. Born Emma Lee Bunton, Jan 21, 1976, in London, England; attended Sylvia Young Drama School, London, England. ❖ As a child, was featured in numerous advertising campaigns; joined Spice Girls as 5th member of band, replacing Michelle Stephenson; with group, released "Wannabe," the 1st debut single by an all-girl band to enter international charts at #1 (1997), followed by the album, *Spice,* which went to #1 in UK charts, and was the 1st debut album by UK performers to enter US charts at #1 (1997); had other Top-10 singles, including "Say You'll be There" and "2 Become 1"; released smash-hit album *Spiceworld* and film of same name (1997); after unsuccessful Spice album *Forever* (2000), released several solo albums, including *A Girl Like Me* (2001) and *Free Me* (2004).

BUNZEL, Ruth (1898–1990). American cultural anthropologist. Name variations: Maiatitsa (blue bird); Tsatitsa. Born Ruth Leah Bunzel, April 18, 1898, in New York, NY; died Jan 14, 1990, in New York; dau. of Jonas Bunzel and Hattie Bernheim Bunzel; sister of Madeleine Bunzel; Barnard College, degree in European history, 1918; Columbia University, PhD, 1927. ❖ Known for her culture-and-personality studies and her work with female Zuni potters and on Pueblo ceremonialism, became secretary to Franz Boas at Columbia University (c. 1924); traveled with Ruth Benedict to Zuni Pueblo, New Mexico (1924), where she studied Pueblo potters; received Zuni names Maiatitsa (blue bird) and Tsatitsa; published *The Pueblo Potter* (1929), which became a classic; was part of a group of women anthropologists at Columbia, including Margaret Mead, Ruth Benedict, and Elsie Clews Parsons; spent 5 summers and several winters at Zuni (1924–29); did field work in Mexico and was among the 1st US anthropologists to work in and write about Guatemala; during WWII, worked for Office of War Information.

BUONOPARTE. See Bonaparte.

BUONAPARTE, Josephine (1763–1814). See Josephine.

BURAKOVA, Tatyana (1952—). See Prorochenko-Burakova, Tatyana.

BURANI, Michelette (1882–1957). French-born stage actress. Born 1882 in Paris, France; died Oct 27, 1957, in Eastchester, NY. ❖ Appeared on Broadway in *Lilac Time, Enter Madame, The Trial of Mary Dugan, Candle in the Wind, The Time of Your Life, The Two Mrs. Carrolls* and *Detective Story.*

BURBIDGE, Margaret (1919—). English astronomer. Born Eleanor Margaret Peachey in Davenport, England, Aug 12, 1919; dau. of Marjorie Stott Peachey and Stanley John Peachey (lecturer in chemistry); University of London, BSc, 1939, PhD, 1943; m. Geoffrey Burbidge (astronomer), 1948; children: Sarah Burbidge (b. 1956). ❖ Distinguished for her research on the creation of galaxies and quasars, became the 1st female director of the Royal Greenwich Observatory; enrolled at University of London (1935); at London Observatory, was assistant director (1943–50) and acting director (1950–51); served as researcher at Yerkes Observatory

(1951–53) and California Institute of Technology (1955–57); was associate professor at University of Chicago (1957–62) and associate research physicist at University of California at San Diego (1962–64); was a professor at University of California (1964–84); served as Mauze Rockefeller professor, Massachusetts Institute of Technology (1968); was director of the Royal Greenwich Observatory (1971–73); was a member of the Anglo-Australian Telescope Board (1972–74); appointed Virginia Gildersleeve professor, Barnard College (1974); served as president of American Astronomical Society (1976) and director of Center for Astrophysics and Space Science, University of California (1979–88); was president of American Academy of the Arts and Sciences (1982); named professor emeritus, University of California (1990); with husband, wrote *Quasi-Stellar Objects* (1967); her research led to the discovery of pulsars and the source of supernovas, and her subsequent observations led to the 1st accurate estimates of galactic masses. Received Helen B. Warner Prize of American Astronomical Society (1959); became a member of Royal Society of London (1964) and American National Academy of the Arts and Sciences (1978); gave Lindsay Memorial Lecture, NASA (1985); received Einstein Medal (1988). ❖ See also *Women in World History.*

BURCHENAL, Elizabeth (1876–1959). American founder and educator. Born Flora Elizabeth Burchenal in Richmond, Indiana, around 1876; died in Brooklyn, NY, Nov 21, 1959; 2nd of 6 children; Earlham College, Richmond, Indiana, AB in English, 1896; received diploma from Dr. Sargent's School of Physical Training (later part of Boston University), 1898. ❖ Began teaching career in Boston, moved on to Chicago, then took a position at Columbia University Teachers College in NY (1903); at Columbia, began to experiment with the theories of dance educator Melvin Gilbert, who advocated incorporating dance into physical-education classes; subsequently worked for the city's public schools; introduced dancing programs for girls and organized folk festivals in Central Park that often attracted as many as 10,000 school children; retiring from New York public-school system (1916), founded the American Folk Dance Society; represented American folk dance at the 1st International Congress of Folk Arts (1928); when the Folk Dance Society became a division of the National Committee of Folk Arts (NCFA), was its 1st director; wrote 15 books on folk dancing.

BURCICA, Constanta (1971—). Romanian rower. Name variations: Constanta Popota. Born Mar 15, 1971, in Sohatu, Romania. ❖ Won a gold medal at Atlanta Olympics (1996), Sydney Olympics (2000), and Athens Olympics (2004), all for lightweight double sculls; won gold medals at World championships for lightweight double and single sculls (1999) and bronze medal for double sculls (2003).

BURDA, Lyubov (1953—). Soviet gymnast. Born April 11, 1953, in Voronezh, Russia; m. Nikolai Andrianov (gymnast, sep.); children: sons Dmitri and Sergei Andrianov (gymnast). ❖ Placed 3rd all-around (1967) and 1st all-around (1971) at the USSR Spartakiade; placed 1st all-around at USSR nationals (1969, 1970); placed 1st for team all-around and 3rd on vault (tie) at World championships (1970); won 1st all-around at Chunichi Cup (1970); won Olympic gold medals in team all-around at Mexico City (1968) and Munich (1972); at the World University Games, placed 2nd for all-around, vault, uneven bars, and balance beam, and 3rd for floor exercises. Inducted into the International Gymnastics Hall of Fame (2001).

BURDEKIN, Katharine (1896–1963). British science-fiction writer. Name variations: Kay Burdekin; (pseudonym) Murray Constantine. Born Katherine Penelope Cade, July 23, 1896, in Derbyshire, England; died Aug 10, 1963, in Suffolk, England; dau. of Charles James Cade and Mary Casterton Cade; m. Beaufort Burdekin, 1915; children: 2. ❖ Went to Sydney with husband (1915) but returned to London (1922) and later set up home with a female companion; though she wrote realist fiction, is best known as a science-fiction writer; published *Swastika Night* (1937), her most widely read novel, which anticipated Orwell's *1984;* other works include *Quiet Ways* (1930), *Proud Man* (1934), *Venus in Scorpio* (1940) and *The End of This Day's Business* (1989).

BURDETT-COUTTS, Angela (1814–1906). English philanthropist. Name variations: Baroness Burdett-Coutts of Highgate and Brookfield; took name Coutts by royal license, 1837; surname sometimes unhyphenated; created baroness in 1871. Pronunciation: Coots. Born Angela Georgina Burdett, April 21, 1814, in London, England; died in London, Dec 30, 1906; interred in Westminster Abbey, Jan 5, 1907; dau. of Sir Francis Burdett (member of Parliament for Westminster) and Sophia (Coutts) Burdett; m. William Ashmead-Bartlett (later MP for Westminster), 1881 (died 1921); no children. ❖ Heiress who spent a large part of her fortune on various charitable causes, especially to help the very poor, inherited fortune from stepgrandmother, Harriot Mellon (Coutts), duchess of St. Albans (1837); adding Coutts to her own name, moved from father's house to the substantial property that Harriot had occupied, where she lived for the remainder of her life; during the 70 years following her inheritance, encouraged scientific investigation; assisted in the building of churches in poor areas; collaborated closely with Charles Dickens, who dedicated *Martin Chuzzlewit* to her and encouraged her to give money to the Ragged Schools, which provided a basic education for London's poorest and most neglected children; also worked with him to establish a home in which prostitutes might be redeemed; funded the building of 4 blocks of tenements, with accommodation for over 1,000 people, in the Bethnal Green area of London, one of the poorest in the city (1862); to some extent, reflected the conventional views of the time, advocating, for example, emigration as a solution to destitution but also as a means of extending the settlement of English stock in Canada, Australia, and South Africa; was prominent in the Royal Society for the Prevention of Cruelty to Animals; raised to the peerage by Queen Victoria (1871). ❖ See also Edna Healey, *Lady Unknown: The Life of Angela Burdett-Coutts* (Sidgwick & Jackson, 1978); Edgar Johnson, ed. *Letters from Charles Dickens to Angela Burdett-Coutts, 1841–1865* (Cape, 1953); Diana Orton, *Made of Gold: A Biography of Angela Burdett-Coutts* (Hamish Hamilton, 1980); Clara Burdett Patterson, *Angela Burdett-Coutts and the Victorians* (John Murray, 1953); and *Women in World History.*

BURDEYNA, Nataliya (1974—). Ukrainian archer. Name variations: Natalia Burdeyna. Born Jan 30, 1974, in Ukraine. ❖ Won a silver medal for teams at Sydney Olympics (2000).

BURDOCK, Mary Ann (1805–1835). English murderer. Born 1805 in England; hanged April 1835. ❖ While operating a rooming house in Bristol, fell in love with one of her roomers, a sailor named Charles Wade, who did not have money to marry her; to solve the problem, poisoned one of her boarders, Clara Smith, and stole her money; was reported to police by a suspicious relative of Smith's and sentenced to death.

BURESOVA, Charlotte (1904–1984). Czech-Jewish artist. Born Nov 4, 1904, in Prague, Czechoslovakia; died in 1984 in Prague; dau. of a tailor; studied at Prague Academy of Art; married to a non-Jewish lawyer (div. 1940, to prevent the Nazi decrees against Jews from affecting her family); children: 1 son (physician). ❖ Artist, whose work documents her imprisonment at the Terezin-Theresienstadt concentration camp, was a leading artist in Prague and part of that vibrant city's intellectual elite (1930s); as a Jew, was deported to Terezin-Theresienstadt (1942); finding ways to procure the materials necessary, was able to produce a significant number of sketches and paintings depicting the life around her; survived Theresienstadt, along with her paintings; returned to Prague and resumed her career (1945). ❖ See also *Women in World History.*

BURFEINDT, Betty (1945—). American golfer. Born Betty Burfeindt, July 20, 1945, in NY, NY. ❖ Joined the LPGA tour (1969); won the Birmingham and Sealy opens (1972); won the Child and Family title (1973); won LPGA championship (1976); currently plays on the Women's Senior Golf tour.

BURFORD, Anne Gorsuch (1942–2004). American Cabinet member. Born Anne Irene McGill, April 21, 1942, in Casper, Wyoming; died July 18, 2004, in Aurora, Colorado; dau. of a surgeon and Dorothy McGill; earned a bachelor's degree from University of Colorado in two years and finished law school there at age 20; m. David Gorsuch, 1964 (div. 1982); m. Robert Burford (rancher and head of Interior Department's Bureau of Land Management), 1983 (div. 1992, died 1993); children: J.J., Neil and Stephanie Gorsuch. ❖ Colorado conservative who believed states should have control over matters like clean air and water, was the youngest woman admitted to the Colorado bar; worked as deputy district attorney for City of Denver; elected to Colorado House of Representatives (1976); appointed to head the Environmental Protection Agency by President Reagan (Feb 1981); set out to limit regulations, cutting the agency's budget by 22%; slashed EPA enforcement action against polluters and slowed payments for Superfund cleanups; resigned under Congressional fire 22 months later (Mar 1983), when she refused to hand over thousands of pages of documents concerning her agency's handling of toxic waste cleanup.

BURFORD, Barbara (1944—). British novelist. Born in 1944 in Great Britain. ❖ Published 4 poems in *A Dangerous Knowing: Four Black Woman Poets* (1985); wrote short-story collection *The Threshing Floor*

(1986) and play *Patterns,* performed by Changing Women's Theatre (1984); edited *Dancing the Tightrope: New Love Poems by Women* (1987).

BURGEN, Olga (1924—). *See Kennard, Olga.*

BÜRGER, Erna (1909–1958). *See Buerger, Erna.*

BURGER, Fritzi. Austrian figure skater. Born in Austria. ❖ Won a silver medal at St. Moritz Olympics (1928) and a silver medal at Lake Placid Olympics (1932); at World championships, placed 2nd (1929, 1932) and 3rd (1931).

BURGER, Hildegard (1905–1943). Austrian resistance leader. Born Hildegard Freihsl in Zeltweg, Austria, Nov 6, 1905; guillotined in Graz, Sept 23, 1943; dau. of a railway worker and Socialist trade unionist; married. ❖ Anti-Nazi activist and leading member of an underground Communist cell in Graz who was sentenced to death by the infamous People's Court; produced and distributed an anti-Nazi newsletter, *Der rote Stosstrupp* (The Red Shock Troops); arrested by the Gestapo (1941). ❖ See also *Women in World History.*

BURGESS, Annie (1969—). Australian basketball player. Name variations: Annie La Fleur or LaFleur. Born Annie Lillian Burgess, April 10, 1969, in Moresby, Papua New Guinea. ❖ Guard; won a team silver medal at Sydney Olympics (2000); played for Sydney Flames in WNBL; signed as a free agent by Minnesota Lynx in the WNBA (1999); traded to Washington Mystics (2001).

BURGESS, Dorothy (1907–1961). American actress. Born Mar 4, 1907, in Los Angeles, California; died Aug 20, 1961, in Woodland Hills, California; niece of Fay Bainter (actress); dau. of Grace Burgess (actress). ❖ Starred in numerous Broadway plays and musicals as an ingenue; made film debut in *In Old Arizona* (1929); other films include *Protection, Pleasure Crazed, A Song of Kentucky, Taxi!, The Stoker, Ladies They Talk About, Strictly Personal, On Your Guard, Fashions of 1934, Orient Express, Affairs of a Gentleman, Lady for a Night, West Side Kid* and *Man of Courage.*

BURGESS, Georgina Jane (c. 1839–1904). New Zealand innkeeper, midwife, postmaster. Name variations: Georgina Jane Gilbert. Born Georgina Jane Gilbert, c. 1836–1841, in Edinburgh, Scotland; died 1904; dau. of James Gilbert (tailor) and Jane (Currie) Gilbert; m. John Burgess, 1858; children: 6. ❖ Immigrated with family to New Zealand (c. 1844); assisted husband with cooking and housekeeping in Burke Pass hotel; served as midwife to community, traveling long distances; assumed husband's part-time duties as postmaster upon his resignation (1885). ❖ See also *Dictionary of New Zealand Biography* (Vol. 1).

BURGESS, Renate (1910–1988). German-born British art and medical historian. Born Renate Ruth Adelheid Bergius in Hanover, Germany, Aug 2, 1910; died in London, Aug 15, 1988; dau. of Friedrich Bergius (1884–1949, chemist who won Nobel Prize, 1931) and Margarethe (Sachs) Bergius; University of Munich, PhD in art history, 1935; m. Hans Burgess, 1950s (div.). ❖ Stripped of German citizenship because of her part-Jewish ancestry (1935), immigrated to Great Britain (1938); worked as a domestic, factory worker and office clerk (1938–44), then as a nurse and midwife (1944–51); was a clerical officer and translator at General Nursing Council (1952–62); served as curator of paintings, prints and photographs at Wellcome Institute for the History of Medicine (1964–80), cataloguing over 12,000 portraits and prints of physicians and other medical personages that had been collected by Sir Henry Wellcome; had a distinguished career in the area of medical bibliography and iconography. ❖ See also *Women in World History.*

BURGESS, Yvonne (1936—). South African novelist. Born 1936 in Pretoria, South Africa. ❖ Wrote reviews and feature articles for *Eastern Province Herald* (1960–72); fiction, which often employs humor to convey difficulties in lives of South African women, includes *A Life to Live* (1973), *The Strike* (1975), and *Say a Little Mantra for Me* (1979).

BURGH, Elizabeth de.
See *Clare, Elizabeth de (1295–1360).*
See *Elizabeth de Burgh (1332–1363).*

BURGHER, Michelle (1977—). Jamaican runner. Born Mar 12, 1977, in Kingston, Jamaica. ❖ Placed 1st for 4 x 400-meter relay at World championships (2001); won a silver medal for 4 x 400-meter relay at Sydney Olympics (2000) and a bronze medal for 4 x 400-meter relay at Athens Olympics (2004).

BURGHERSH, Joan. *See Mohun, Joan.*

BURGHLEY, Lady (1526–1589). *See Cecil, Mildred Cooke.*

BURGIN, Annie Mona (1903–1985). New Zealand scouting leader, teacher, and headmistress. Born Mar 11, 1903, at Kirk Michael, Isle of Man; died June 15, 1985, at Howick, Auckland, New Zealand; dau. of Robert Burgin (cleric) and Henrietta Jane (Woollcombe) Burgin. ❖ Immigrated to New Zealand with family (c. 1909); established St. Andrew's Girl Peace Scout Troop in Epsom (1921); started Rahiri Ranger Company for older girls (1939); worked with young people in displaced-persons camps in Europe for United Nations Relief and Rehabilitation Administration (1945); wrote 1st New Zealand handbooks for guides and rangers; taught at Dilworth School (1929–60); served as headmistress at Hilltop School (1960–68). Awarded British Empire Medal (1959).

BURGIN, Polly (1929—). *See Bergen, Polly.*

BURGOS, Julia de (1914–1953). *See de Burgos, Julia.*

BURGOS SEGUÍ, Carmen de (1867–1932). Spanish novelist. Name variations: Carmen Burgos de Segui; (pseudonym) Colombine, Raquel, Honorine, Marianela, Duchess Laureana, and Gabriel Luisa, Countess of C***. Born Dec 10, 1867 (some sources cite 1879) in Rodalquilar, Almeria, Spain; died Oct 9, 1932, in Madrid, Spain. ❖ Worked as suffragist and newspaper columnist; writings include *Notas del alma* (1901), *La mujer en España* (1906), *Los inadaptados* (1909), *Siempre en la tierra* (1912), *Los inseparables* (1917), *El extranjero* (1923), *La mujer moderna y sus derechos* (1927), and *Los endemoniados de Jaca* (1932).

BURGUNDOFARA, Saint (d. 667). *See Fara.*

BURGUNDY, duchess of.
See Hedwig (c. 915–965).
See Ermengarde of Anjou (1018–1076).
See Helia de Semur (fl. 1020–1046).
See Alix de Vergy (d. after 1218).
See Agnes Capet (1260–1327).
See Margaret of Flanders (1350–1405).
See Margaret of Bavaria (d. 1424).
See Michelle Valois (1394–1422).
See Bonne of Artois (d. 1425).
See Isabella of Portugal (1397–1471).
See Margaret of York (1446–1503).
See Mary of Burgundy (1457–1482).
See Marie-Adélaïde of Savoy (1685–1712).

BURGUNDY, queen of.
See Faileuba (fl. 586–587).
See Matilda Martel (943–c. 982).

BURIAN, Hildegarde. *See Burjan, Hildegarde.*

BURJAN, Hildegard (1883–1933). Austrian social reformer. Name variations: Burian. Born Hildegard Freund in Gorlitz an der Neisse, Silesia, Jan 30, 1883; died in Vienna, Austria, June 11, 1933; dau. of Adolf Freund (Jewish merchant); University of Zurich, PhD, 1908; m. Alexander Burjan (engineer), 1907; children: Elisabeth. ❖ One of the most influential and respected Roman Catholic women in 20th-century Austria, moved to Vienna (1909); converted to Roman Catholic faith and became involved in issues relating to social reform including abuses of child and domestic labor; was active during World War I in alleviating the suffering of working-class families in Austria; founded a charitable organization, "Caritas Socialis," to aid the poor, aged, and ill (1918), which would grow to become a major social agency of Austria's Roman Catholics in the next decades; elected as the only female deputy of the Christian Social Party to Austrian Parliament (1919); was responsible for numerous social reforms during the 1st Austrian Republic (1919–33); founded "Bahnhofsmission" (1922); revived her "Soziale Hilfe" organization (1924); founded "St.-Elisabeth-Tisch" (1930); was close friend of Cardinal Piffl and Ignaz Seipel. ❖ See also *Women in World History.*

BURK, Martha Jane (1852–1903). *See Cannary, Martha Jane (Calamity Jane).*

BURKA, Ellen Petra (1921—). Dutch-Canadian figure skater and coach. Born Aug 11, 1921, in Amsterdam, Netherlands; children: Petra Burka (figure skater). ❖ Won the Dutch figure-skating championship (1945, 1946); as a skating coach, produced 26 Canadian World and Olympic champions and medalists, including Toller Cranston, Christopher Bowman, Elvis Stojko, and her own daughter.

BURKA, Petra (1946—). Canadian figure skater. Born Nov 17, 1946, in Amsterdam, Netherlands; dau. of Ellen Petra Burka (skating coach). ❖ Placing 4th at the World championship, made history as the 1st female to perform a triple Salchow in competition (Feb 24, 1962); won a bronze medal at Innsbruck Olympics (1964); won the Canadian national title (1964–66), and the North American and World championships (1965); went professional. Inducted into Canadian Figure Skating Hall of Fame (1997). ❖ See also *Women in World History.*

BURKA, Sylvia (1954—). Canadian speedskater and cyclist. Born May 4, 1954, in Winnipeg, Manitoba, Canada. ❖ As a speedskater, placed 1st overall at the Junior World championship (1973), World championship (1976) and World Sprint championship (1977); as a cyclist, won several national titles; retired from competition (1980).

BURKART, Claudia (1980—). Argentine field-hockey player. Born Claudia Ines Burkart, Feb 22, 1980, in Buenos Aires, Argentina. ❖ Won a team bronze medal at Athens Olympics (2004); won Champions Trophy (2001), World Cup (2002), and Pan American Games (2003).

BURKART, Erika (1922—). Swiss poet and novelist. Born Feb 8, 1922, in Aarau, Switzerland; m. Ernst Halter. ❖ Works of poetry include *Der dunkle Vogel* (1953), *Ich lebe* (1964), *Augenzeuge* (1978), *Die Freiheit der Nacht* (1982), *Schweigeminute* (1988), *Die Zärtlichkeit der Schatten* (1991), and *Stille fernster Rückruf* (1997); novels include *Moräne* (1970), *Der Weg zu den Schafen* (1979), *Der Spiele der Erkenntnis* (1985), and *Das Schimmern der Flügel* (1994). Received Prix du Lions Club (1956), Prix de Pro Argovia (1964), and Prix Gottfried-Keller de la Fondation Bodmer (1990).

BURKE, Barbara (1917—). English runner. Born May 13, 1917, in UK. ❖ At Berlin Olympics, won a silver medal in 4 x 100-meter relay (1936).

BURKE, Billie (1885–1970). American actress. Born Mary William Ethelbert Appleton Burke in Washington, DC, Aug 7, 1885; died May 14, 1970, in Los Angeles, CA; dau. of William Burker (singing clown with Barnum & Bailey circus) and Blanche (Beatty) Hodkinson Burke; m. Florenz Ziegfeld (theatrical producer), 1914 (died July 22, 1932); children: Patricia Burke (b. 1916). ❖ Best known for her twittery matron roles and her performance as the good witch Glinda in *The Wizard of Oz*, made stage debut at London Pavilion, singing "Mamie, I Have a Little Canoe," in *The School Girl* (1903), which brought her some celebrity and better roles; back in New York co-starred with John Drew in *My Wife* (1907); made film debut in *Peggy* (1915); did a number of silents with Famous Players-Lasky, including *In Pursuit of Polly* and *The Misleading Widow*; on Broadway, appeared in such hits as Booth Tarkington's *Intimate Strangers* and Noel Coward's *The Marquise*, then took on 1st character role in *The Truth Game*, followed by *The Vinegar Tree*, which led to a new image as a scatterbrained comedian; made talkie debut in *Bill of Divorcement* (1932); other films include *Topper*, its sequel *Merrily We Live* (which earned her an Academy Award nomination), *Christopher Strong* (1933), *Dinner at Eight* (1933), *Becky Sharp* (1935), *A Feather in Her Hat* (1935), *Craig's Wife* (1936), *Parnell* (1937), *The Bride Wore Red* (1937), *Topper Takes a Trip* (1939), *Irene* (1940), *Dulcy* (1940), *Hullabaloo* (1940), *Topper Returns* (1941), *One Night in Lisbon* (1941), *The Wild Man of Borneo* (1941), *The Man Who Came to Dinner* (1942), *The Cheaters* (1945), *The Barkleys of Broadway* (1949), *And Baby Makes Three* (1949), *Father of the Bride* (1950), *Father's Little Dividend* (1951), *The Young Philadelphians* (1959), *Sergeant Rutledge* (1960) and *Pepe* (1960). ❖ See also autobiographies *With a Feather on My Nose* (Appleton, 1949) and *With Powder on My Nose* (1959); and *Women in World History.*

BURKE, Caroline (d. 1964). *See Swann, Caroline Burke.*

BURKE, Fielding (1869–1968). *See Dargan, Olive Tilford.*

BURKE, Frances (c. 1921—). Miss America. Born Frances Marie Burke, c. 1921, in Philadelphia, Pennsylvania. ❖ Named Miss America (1940), representing Pennsylvania; became a prominent East Coast fashion model. ❖ See also Frank Deford, *There She Is* (Viking, 1971).

BURKE, Georgia (1880–1986). African-American stage actress. Born Feb 27, 1880, in Atlanta, Georgia; died Nov 28, 1986, in New York, NY. ❖ Made Broadway debut in Lew Leslie's *Blackbirds*; other plays include *Five Star Final, They Shall Not Die, Mamba's Daughters, Cabin in the Sky, No Time for Comedy, Anna Lucasta, The Grass Harp* and *Porgy and Bess*. Won Donaldson Award for performance in *Decision* (1944).

BURKE, Joan T. (1929—). Irish politician. Born Joan T. Crowley, Feb 1929, in Bandon, Co. Cork, Ireland; m. James Burke (TD, Roscommon,

1954–64). ❖ Following husband's death, won a by-election as a Fine Gael candidate to 17th Dáil, the 1st woman to represent Roscommon (1964–65); returned to 18th–21st Dáil (1965–81); as a state-registered nurse, was later a ward sister in Cherry Orchard Fever Hospital, Dublin.

BURKE, Katherine (1917–1992). *See Field, Virginia.*

BURKE, Kathleen (1913–1980). American screen actress. Born Sept 5, 1913, in Hammond, Indiana; died April 9, 1980, in Chicago, Illinois; m. Glen A. Rardin, Feb 1933 (div. 1934); m. José Fernandez (dancer), Mar 1936; m. Forrest Smith; children: Antonia Fernandez (b. June 1938). ❖ Made film debut as "The Panther Woman" in *Island of the Lost Souls* (1932); other films include *Murders in the Zoo, Bulldog Drummond Strikes Back, Lives of a Bengal Lancer, Craig's Wife* and *Rascals.*

BURKE, Lynn (1943—). American swimmer. Born Mar 22, 1943, in New York, NY; children: 3. ❖ At Rome Olympics, won a gold medal in the 4 x 100-meter medley relay and a gold medal in the 100-meter backstroke (1960), the 1st American woman to win that event in 28 years; won 6 national AAU titles; set 6 World records; was also a model.

BURKE, Martha Jane (1852–1903). *See Cannary, Martha Jane.*

BURKE, Patricia (1917–2003). English actress, singer, dancer. Born Mar 23, 1917, in Milan, Italy; died Nov 23, 2003, in England; dau. of Marie Burke (1894–1988, actress and singer) and Tom Burke (opera singer); m. 2nd husband, John Collingwood. ❖ Came to stage prominence in *The Lisbon Story* (1943–44), singing "Pedro the Fisherman"; joined Old Vic company and triumphed as Katharina in *The Taming of the Shrew* to Trevor Howard's Petruchio; over the years, also appeared as Rosalind, as Trilby, as Doll Common in *The Alchemist*, and as Lampito in *Lysistrata*, among others; films include *The Lisbon Story* (1946), *The Trojan Brothers* (1946), *The Dream of Olwen* (1947), *Forbidden* (1948), *The Happiness of Three Women* (1954), *The Day the Fish Came Out* (1967) and *Soft Beds, Hard Battles* (1974).

BURKE, Sarah (1982—). Canadian skier. Born Sept 3, 1982, in Midland, Ontario, Canada. ❖ Pioneer woman freeskier, competed against men and set example for other women freeskiers, which helped create women's categories at major events; 1st place finishes include: in Slopestyle at US Freeskiing Open (2003), World Skiing Invitational Women's Superpipe (2003), Orage Masters of Freeskiing, and in Ski Superpipe at X Games Global championship (2003). Was ESPN Female Skier of the Year (2001); named Best Skier of the Year in *Powder* reader poll (2004).

BURKE, Selma Hortense (1900–1995). African-American sculptor. Born in Mooresville, North Carolina, 1900; died Aug 29, 1995, in Newtown, Pennsylvania; dau. of an African Methodist Episcopal Zion minister and Mary L. Burke; attended Slater Industrial and State Normal School (later Winston-Salem State University); attended Saint Agnes Training School for Nurses, Raleigh, North Carolina; attended Women's Medical College in Philadelphia, Pennsylvania; studied art at Sarah Lawrence College; Columbia College, MFA, 1941; studied architecture with Frank Lloyd Wright and Josef Hoffman; twice married poet Claude McKay (twice div.); m. Herman Kobbe (architect), late 1940s (died 1950s). ❖ Though best remembered as the sculptor who created the profile of Franklin D. Roosevelt that appears on the US dime, created many other critically acclaimed works in her lifetime, including the bust of Duke Ellington at Performing Arts Center in Milwaukee, portraits of Booker T. Washington and Mary McLeod Bethune, the 8-foot bronze statue of Martin Luther King at Marshall Park, Charlotte, NC, and sculptures of John Brown and President Calvin Coolidge; taught at Livingston College, Swarthmore College, and Harvard University, as well as Friends Charter School in Pennsylvania and Hamlen Center in New York; founded the Selma Burke Art Center in Pittsburgh, Selma Burke School of Sculpture in New York, and Selma Burke Gallery at Winston-Salem State University. ❖ See also *Women in World History.*

BURKE, Sophie Lyons (1848–1924). *See Lyons, Sophie.*

BURKE, Yvonne Brathwaite (1932—). African-American politician. Name variations: Yvonne Brathwaite. Born Pearl Yvonne Watson in Los Angeles, California, Oct 5, 1932; dau. of James T. Watson (janitor at MGM film studios) and Lola (Moore) Watson; attended University of California, Berkeley, 1949; University of California, Los Angeles, BA, 1953; University of Southern California School of Law, JD, 1956; m. Louis Brathwaite, 1957 (div. 1964); m. William A. Burke, June 14, 1972; children: (2nd m.) Autumn Roxanne (b. 1973). ❖ Outspoken and articulate advocate of social welfare, was admitted to California state bar (1956); went into private practice; was an attorney for the McCone

Commission (1965), which investigated the causes of the Watts riot; was the 1st African-American woman to be elected to California General Assembly; elected to Assembly for 3 terms, supported prison reform, child care for underprivileged, equal job opportunities for women, and increased federal aid to education; as a Democrat, served as California's 1st black US congresswoman (93rd–95th Congresses, Jan 3, 1973–Jan 3, 1979); was the 1st congressional representative to be granted a maternity leave (1973), and the 1st woman selected to chair the Congressional Black Caucus (1976); served on Committee on Interior and Insular Affairs and later transferred to Committee on Appropriations, where she called for additional federal funding of community nutrition programs; did not seek reelection (1978); served on Los Angeles County Board of Supervisors (1979–80); elected to 4-year term as a Los Angeles County supervisor (1992), then re-elected (1996). ❖ See also *Women in World History.*

BURKE SHERIDAN, Margaret (1889–1958). *See Sheridan, Margaret.*

BURKHOLDER, Mabel (1881–1973). Canadian journalist and historian. Born 1881 in Hamilton, Ontario, Canada; died 1973. ❖ Well-known historian of the Hamilton area of Ontario, wrote a column for *The Hamilton Spectator* for 16 years; published the novel *The Course of Impatience Carningham* (1912).

BÜRKI, Gianna (1969—). *See Hablützel-Bürki, Gianna.*

BURLAR, Cora (c. 1912–1967). *See Baird, Cora.*

BURLEIGH, Celia C. (1826–1875). American Unitarian minister and women's rights activist. Born at Sept 18, 1826, Cazenovia, NY; died July 25, 1875, in Syracuse, NY; m. C.B. Kellum, 1844 (div.); m. Charles Chauncey Burr, 1851 (div.); m. William Henry Burleigh, 1865 (died Mar 1871). ❖ Writer, editor, and activist on behalf of a number of reform movements, was primarily concerned with women's rights, including woman's suffrage, divorce reform, and dress reform; became the 1st woman to be ordained as a minister in the Unitarian Church (Oct 5, 1871), at a ceremony in Brooklyn, CT, which was officiated by Julia Ward Howe, among others; served as minister of the First Ecclesiastical Society of Brooklyn, CT; resigned due to breast cancer (1873).

BURLET, Delphyne (1966—). French biathlete. Born Nov 24, 1966, in Chamonix, France. ❖ Won a bronze medal for 4 x 7.5 km relay at Lillehammer Olympics (1994); at World championships, won a team gold medal (1993).

BURLIN, Natalie Curtis (1875–1921). American musicologist. Name variations: Natalie Curtis. Born Natalie Curtis in New York, NY, April 26, 1875; killed by an automobile while in Paris to address a congress of art historians, Oct 23, 1921; dau. of Edward Curtis (physician) and Augusta Lawler (Stacey) Curtis; studied under Arthur Friedheim at National Conservatory of Music in NY, with Ferruccio Busoni in Berlin; m. Paul Burlin (painter), July 1917; children: 1 son. ❖ Student of Native American and African-American music, became fascinated with customs and lore of Arizona Native Americans (1900); visiting villages and camps of the Zuñi, Hopi, and other tribes, recorded their songs, poetry, and stories; published *The Indians' Book* (1907), which contained music and lore from 18 tribes; joined David Mannes (1911) to organize the Music School Settlement for Colored People in New York City; was also instrumental in arranging the 1st concert of African-American music performed by black performers at Carnegie Hall (1914); produced a number of volumes of African-American music, including the 4-vol. *Hampton Series Negro Folk-Songs* (1918–19) and *Songs and Tales from the Dark Continent* (1920).

BURMYSTROVA, Ganna (1977—). Ukrainian handball player. Born June 16, 1977, in Ukraine. ❖ Won a team bronze medal at Athens Olympics (2004).

BURN, Margaret Gordon (1825–1918). New Zealand school teacher and principal. Name variations: Margaret Gordon Huie. Born Mar 22, 1825, at Edinburgh, Scotland; died Dec 8, 1918, at Dunedin, New Zealand; dau. of Alexander Huie (accountant) and Eliza Gordon (Edgar) Huie; m. Andrew Burn (educator), 1857 (died 1892); children: 2 sons, 1 daughter. ❖ Immigrated with mother and family to Australia and opened private school (1852); opened Geelong Ladies' College (1860s); immigrated to New Zealand and became principal of Girls' Provincial School (1870–84); served as principal of new Waitaki Girls' High School in Oamaru (1884–92). ❖ See also *Dictionary of New Zealand Biography* (Vol. 2).

BURNAND, Lily (1865–?). English musical-hall star. Born Eleanor Elizabeth Day, 1865, Mile End, London, England; death date unknown;

State University), 1937; m. Bernard Goss (artist), 1939 (div.); m. Charles Gordon Burroughs (poet), 1949; children: (1st m.) Gayle Goss Toller; (2nd m.) Paul Burroughs (adopted). ❖ With 2nd husband Charles Gordon Burroughs, founded Dusable Museum of African American Heritage in Chicago (1961); appointed commissioner with Chicago Park District (1986); writings include *Jasper, The Drummin' Boy* (1947), *What Shall I Tell My Children Who Are Black?* (1963) and *Africa, My Africa* (1970); edited *Did You Feed My Cow? Rhymes and Games from City Streets and Country Lanes* (1955) and (with Dudley Randall) *For Malcolm: Poems on the Life and Death of Malcolm X* (1967).

BURROUGHS, Nannie Helen (c. 1878–1961). African-American educator and school founder. Born in Orange, Virginia, May 2, c. 1878; died in Washington, DC, May 1961; dau. of John Burroughs (farmer and preacher) and Jennie (Poindexter) Burroughs (both ex-slaves). ❖ With 7 students, opened the Training School for Women and Girls located on a 6-acre campus in suburban Washington (1909); spent rest of life administering to, and raising money to sustain, the enterprise; believing that black women could become self-sufficient wage earners, offered courses in unconventional occupations such as shoe repair, printing, barbering, and gardening, in addition to domestic arts and secretarial skills; supplemented vocational training with classical academics, with emphasis on grammar and language; changed school name to National Trades and Professional School for Women (1934); was also an active participant in the club movement among black women; was a founding member of National Association of Colored Women (1896); also founded National Association of Wage Earners and served as its president; sought after as a speaker and writer, promoted her belief in self-help and self-reliance for blacks. After her death from a stroke, the school was renamed the Nannie Burroughs School. ❖ See also *Women in World History.*

BURROWS, Eva (1929—). Australian-born religious leader. Born Eva Evelyn Burrows, Sept 15, 1929, in an Australian mining town; dau. of Salvation Army officers; granted degrees in history and English and a graduate degree in education from Queensland University. ❖ Joined the Salvation Army; spent 17 years at Howard Institute in Zimbabwe, as a teacher and administrator; also acted as an advisor to the Zimbabwe government on planning curriculums for African colleges; leaving Africa (1969), was an administrator at International College for Officers in London; served as leader of Women's Social Services in Great Britain and Ireland (1975); was a territorial commander in Sri Lanka, Scotland, and southern Australia (1977–85); appointed 13th general of the Salvation Army (1986), the 1st woman elected to that high office since Evangeline Booth in 1934; was also the youngest worldwide commander of the evangelical Christian group; during tenure, traveled extensively, commanding the Army's social-welfare operations in 86 countries and working to add to the organization's dwindling ranks; retired (1993). ❖ See also *Women in World History.*

BURROWS-FONTAINE, Evan (1898–1984). American dancer. Name variations: Evan Fontaine; Evan Burroughs Fontaine. Born Evan Burroughs Fontaine, Oct 3, 1898, possibly in Virginia, though she claimed Jan 1, 1900, in London, England; died Dec 1984 in Virginia; dau. of Florence Fontaine; children: at least 1 son. ❖ Claimed to have been trained by Emile Jaques-Dalcroze, but little can be verified about her education or background; danced solo performances *Dance Egyptienne* and *Syvillia* on Denishawn tour across US, and performed in numerous Ted Shawn works, including *Ta-Toa, Chinese Minuet, Dance Modern* and *Waltz–Al Fresco* and *Lu-Lu Fado;* appeared in vaudeville for many years and gained popularity dancing on a movable sphinx in Broadway's *Ed Wynn Carnival* (1920); credited as Evan Burroughs Fontaine for films *Madonnas and Men* (1920) and *Women Men Love* (both 1920); sued Cornelius Vanderbilt Whitney for $1 million, alleging breach of promise of marriage and that he fathered her child.

BURSAC, Marija (1921–1943). Yugoslav war heroine. Born 1921 in Yugoslavia; killed 1943. ❖ Joined Federation of Communist youth (1941) and Communist Party of Yugoslavia (1942); joined partisan forces as a nurse; as a fighter-bomber, was mortally wounded in an attack on the Germans, charging 3 times at a German pillbox; was the 1st woman to be proclaimed a national hero in Yugoslavia (Oct 15, 1943).

BURSTYN, Ellen (1932—). American stage, tv and screen actress. Name variations: (stage names) Edna Rae, Keri Flynn, Erica Dean, Ellen McRae. Born Edna Rae Gilhooley, Dec 7, 1932, in Detroit, Michigan; m. William Alexander, 1950 (div. 1955); m. Paul Roberts, 1957 (div. 1959), m. Neil Burstyn, 1960 (div. 1971); children: (3rd m.) 1 son. ❖ Made Broadway debut in *Fair Game* (1957); as Ellen McRae, appeared on tv series "The Doctors" (1963) and made film debut in *Goodbye Charlie* (1964); as Ellen Burstyn, made such films as *The King of Marvin Gardens, Harry and Tonto, Providence, A Dream of Passion, Twice in a Lifetime, Hanna's War, The Cemetery Club, How to Make an American Quilt* and *Divine Secrets of the Ya-Ya Sisterhood;* on tv, appeared in numerous movies, as well as "The Ellen Burstyn Show" (1986); served as the 1st woman president of Actor's Equity (1982–85) and was co-director (with Al Pacino) of the Actor's Studio (1982–87). Nominated for Oscars for performances in *The Last Picture Show* (1971), *The Exorcist* (1973), *Same Time Next Year* (1978) and *Resurrection* (1980); awarded an Oscar for Best Actress for *Alice Doesn't Live Here Anymore* and a Tony for *Same Time, Next Year* (1975).

BURT, Laura (1872–1952). English-born character actress. Born Sept 16, 1872, in Ramsay, Isle of Man, England; died Oct 17, 1952, in New York, NY; studied at American Academy of Dramatic Art; m. Henry Stanford (actor). ❖ Made 1st appearance on stage as a child; made US debut in *Fantasma;* alternated between London and NY in such plays as *Blue Jeans, In Old Kentucky, The Christian, In the Palace of the King, Dante, Dorothy Vernon of Haddon Hall* and *Damaged Goods.*

BURTON, Annie L. (fl. 19th c.). African-American writer. Born on a plantation near Clayton, Alabama; birth and death date unknown; dau. of a slave woman and white plantation owner from Liverpool, England; m. Samuel L. Burton, 1888. ❖ Provided details of her life in her autobiographical *Memories of Childhood's Slavery Days* (1909), a glimpse into the world of the slave woman. ❖ See also Henry Louis Gates Jr., ed., *Six Women's Slave Narratives* (Oxford U. Press, 1988); and *Women in World History.*

BURTON, Beryl (1937–1996). English cyclist. Born Beryl Charnock, May 12, 1937, in Morley, near Leeds, Yorkshire, England; died May 5, 1996, while riding a racing cycle near her home in Harrogate, Yorkshire, possibly of a heart attack; m. Charles Burton (cyclist), 1954; children: Denise Burton (b. 1956, also a cycling champion). ❖ One of the foremost cyclists of the 20th-century, had a 20-year unbroken record as Best British All-Rounder (1958–1978), winning 73 national titles; regularly beat England's top male riders; raced 277.37 miles in 12 hours, beating the men's best distance cyclist by 10 miles (1967); won the World Championship for 3,000-meters pursuit (1959, 1960, 1962, 1963, 1966); won the World Championship road race (1960, 1967). Awarded MBE (1964) and OBE (1968).

BURTON, Denise (1956—). English cyclist. Born Jan 24, 1956, in Yorkshire, England; dau. of Charles and Beryl Burton (champion cyclist). ❖ Won several national championships; won a bronze medal at World championships for pursuit (1975).

BURTON, Isabel (1831–1896). English traveler. Name variations: Lady Burton. Born Isabel Arundell in London, England, 1831; died of cancer in 1896; dau. of Henry Raymond Arundell; m. Sir Richard Francis Burton (1821–1890, English explorer and scholar), in 1861. ❖ Before marriage, performed social work among London prostitutes; married explorer Richard Burton (1861); accompanied him as much as possible, sharing his posts at Santos, Brazil, and Damascus where they pioneered interracial receptions and went on archaeological expeditions; following his death (1890), wrote *The Life of Sir Richard Burton* (1893); also wrote *Inner Life of Syria* (1875) and *Arabia, Egypt, and India* (1879). ❖ See also Mary S. Lovell, *A Rage to Live: A Biography of Richard and Isabel Burton* (Norton, 1998); Jean Burton, *Sir Richard Burton's Wife* (also called *Life of Lady Burton,* 1942).

BURTON, Joan (1949—). Irish politician. Born Feb 1949 in Dublin, Ireland; m. Pat Carroll (member of Dublin Co. Council). ❖ Representing Labour, elected to the 27th Dáil (1992–97) for Dublin West; was minister of State at the dept. of Social Welfare with responsibility for poverty, including EU Poverty Plans (1992); returned to 29th Dáil (2002).

BURTON, Lady (1831–1896). *See Burton, Isabel.*

BURTON, Pearlie (1904–1993). American midwife. Name variations: Pearlie Hunt. Born April 21, 1904, in Hart Co., Georgia; died Mar 12, 1993, in Royston, Georgia; m. Lafayette Burton. ❖ Having apprenticed with husband's mother (midwife), delivered thousands of babies (1920s–40s) and was often paid in goods if paid at all; unable to have children, adopted many delivered babies with husband; became 1st African-American foster parent for Hart County (1940s). Named Hart County Mother of the Year (1991).

BURTON, Sala (1925–1987). Polish-American politician. Born Sala Galante in Bialystok, Poland, April 1, 1925; died in Washington, DC, Feb 1, 1987; attended San Francisco University; m. Philip Burton (US congressional representative, 1964–83), in 1953. ❖ US Representative (98th–100th Congresses, June 21, 1983–Feb 1, 1987), fled Poland with parents before Nazi occupation (1939) and made a new home in California; as a founder of the California Democratic Council, served as its vice president (1951–54); was president of San Francisco Democratic Women's Forum (1957–59) and held memberships in both San Francisco County and California State Democratic Central Committees; served as president of Democratic Wives of House and Senate (1972–74); elected to US House of Representatives to fill the vacancy left by the death of husband (1983) and was appointed to his former seats on the Committee on Education and Labor and the Committee on Interior and Insular Affairs; during 2nd term, was named to the Committee on Rules. ❖ See also *Women in World History.*

BURTON, Virginia Lee (1909–1968). American children's writer and illustrator. Born in Newton Centre, Massachusetts, Aug 30, 1909; died in Boston, Massachusetts, Oct 15, 1968; dau. of Alfred E. Burton (1st dean of Massachusetts Institute of Technology) and Lena Dalkeith (Yates) Burton; half-sister of Harold H. Burton, Justice of the Supreme Court; studied ballet privately in San Francisco, California; studied art at California School of Fine Arts and Boston Museum School; m. George Demetrios (sculptor and teacher), Mar 28, 1931; children: 2 sons. ❖ After a stint as a sketch artist for the *Boston Transcript,* created her 1st self-illustrated children's book, *Choo Choo* (1935), inspired by an engine on the Gloucester Branch of the Boston & Maine line; won the Caldecott Medal for *The Little House* (1943); also wrote and illustrated *Mike Mulligan and His Steam Shovel* (1939), *Calico, the Wonder Horse* (1941), *Katy and the Big Show* (1943), *Maybelle, the Cable Car* (1952) and *Life Story* (1962). ❖ See also *Women in World History.*

BURY, Charlotte (1775–1861). English novelist. Name variations: Charlotte Campbell; Lady Charlotte Bury. Born Charlotte Susan Maria Campbell in London, England, Jan 28, 1775; died in London, Mar 31, 1861; dau. of Elizabeth Gunning (1734–1790, writer) and John Campbell, 5th duke of Argyll; m. Col. John Campbell, June 14, 1796 (died 1809); m. Rev. Edward John Bury (rector of Lichfield), Mar 17, 1818 (died 1832); children: (1st m.) 9; (2nd m.) 2. ❖ Novelist who wrote romantic fiction, including a thinly veiled account of life at court; widowed (1809) and soon destitute, took a post as lady-in-waiting to Caroline of Brunswick, then princess of Wales, who was separated from Prince George (George IV) and the subject of slander; left royal service upon publication of 1st novel (1815); published *Diary Illustrative of the Times of George IV* (1838), an account of her experiences in Caroline of Brunswick's court and had her 1st bestseller; forced into seclusion by public criticism for having violated the queen's privacy; other writings include *Conduct is Fate* (1822), *Alla Giornata* (1826), *Flirtation, A Marriage in High Life* (1828), *The Exclusives* (1830) and *The History of a Flirt* (1840). ❖ See also *Women in World History.*

BURYAKINA, Olga (1958—). Soviet basketball player. Born Mar 17, 1958, in USSR. ❖ At Seoul Olympics, won a bronze medal in team competition (1988).

BUSBY, Amy (c. 1872–1957). American actress and dancer. Born c. 1872; died July 13, 1957, age 85, in East Stroudsburg, Pennsylvania. ❖ Made stage debut with Stuart Robson in *The Henrietta* (1891); appeared in the American premiere of *Arms and the Man* and with William Gillette in *Secret Service;* retired (1897).

BUSCH, Lydia (1898–1970). *See St. Clair, Lydia.*

BUSCH, Mae (1891–1946). Australian-born actress. Born in Melbourne, Australia, June 18, 1891; died April 19, 1946, in San Fernando Valley, CA; father was conductor of the Australian Symphony Orchestra; mother was a grand-opera singer; educated in a New Jersey convent; m. Francis McDonald (actor). ❖ Spent much of her childhood in Tahiti, until family immigrated to US; made stage debut at 17 and became a popular headliner in vaudeville; had film debut in a Mack Sennett Keystone comedy, *The Agitator* (1912), and 1st major movie success while starring in Erich von Stroheim's *Foolish Wives* (1922); throughout 1930s, appeared in Laurel and Hardy two-reel comedies, sometimes playing Hardy's wife, other times as a foil for their routines; became a foil once again when Jackie Gleason began to use her name in a running gag on his tv program with the phrase "and the ever-popular Mae Busch." ❖ See also *Women in World History.*

BUSCH, Sabine (1962—). East German runner. Born Nov 21, 1962, in East Germany. ❖ At Seoul Olympics, won a bronze medal in 4 x 400-meter relay (1988).

BUSCHSCHULTE, Antje (1978—). German swimmer. Born Dec 27, 1978, in West Berlin, Germany. ❖ Won a bronze medal for 4 x 100-meter freestyle relay at Atlanta Olympics (1996); at SC European championships, won gold medals for 100-meter backstroke (1996) and 200-meter backstroke (1998, 1999); at LC European championships, won a gold medal for 100-meter backstroke (1997); won a bronze medal for 800-meter freestyle relay at Sydney Olympics (2000); at SC World championships, won gold medals for 50- and 200-meter backstroke (2000); at World championships, placed 1st for 100-meter backstroke (2003); won bronze medals for 200-meter backstroke, 4 x 100-meter medley relay, and 4 x 200-meter freestyle relay at Athens Olympics (2004).

BUSH, Barbara (1924—). American first lady. Born Barbara Pierce in Rye, New York, June 8, 1924; dau. of Marvin Pierce (magazine publisher of McCalls-Redbook) and Pauline (Robinson) Pierce; attended Smith College (1943–44); m. George Herbert Walker Bush (US president), Jan 6, 1945; children: George Walker Bush (b. 1946, governor of Texas and US president); Robin Bush (1949–1953, died of leukemia); John "Jeb" Ellis Bush (b. 1953, governor of Florida); Neil Mallon Bush (b. 1955); Marvin Pierce Bush (b. 1956); Dorothy Walker Bush (b. 1959). ❖ From husband's early days as a Texas businessman to political posts as a US Congressional representative, ambassador to the United Nations, US Envoy in China, director of the CIA, and vice president, lived in 29 homes in 17 cities and blossomed from a shy housewife into a savvy political advisor and campaigner; as first lady (1989–93), arrived on the scene with a shock of white hair, undisguised wrinkles, and a down-to-earth demeanor; her main focus while in the White House was on behalf of literacy and learning disabilities; set aside proceeds from her 2 books, *C. Fred's Story* and *Millie's Book,* for the literacy foundation; often accompanied husband on visits in US and abroad; maintained strong opinions on many controversial issues but fielded questions of a controversial nature with the stock answer, "Let me tell you how George Bush feels." ❖ See also *Barbara Bush: A Memoir* (Scribner, 1994); and *Women in World History.*

BUSH, Dorothy V. (1916–1991). American Democratic party secretary. Name variations: Dorothy Vredenburgh. Born Dorothy McElroy, Dec 8, 1916, in Baldwyn, Mississippi; died Dec 21, 1991, in Naples, Florida; m. Peter Vredenburgh, 1940 (died); m. John W. Bush, 1962. ❖ At 27, was named national Democratic party secretary (1944), becoming the 1st woman officer for either major US political party; called the roll of States and kept the vote count for Democratic presidential nominees through the administrations of 10 presidents; known as an American institution by the time of her retirement (1989).

BUSH, Frances Cleveland (d. 1967). American musical-comedy singer. Name variations: Cleva Creighton, Cleva Creighton Chaney, Frances Chaney, Mrs. Lon Chaney, Cleva Fletcher. Died Nov 21, 1967, in Sierra Madre, California; m. Lon Chaney (actor), 1905 (div. 1914); children: (Creighton) Lon Chaney Jr. (b. 1906). ❖ Appeared in many musical comedies and Gilbert & Sullivan operettas; portrayed in *Man of a Thousand Faces* by Dorothy Malone.

BUSH, Kate (1958—). British singer and songwriter. Born Katherine Bush (also seen as Catherine Bush), July 30, 1958, in Bexleyheath, England; sister of Paddy Bush; children: Albert (b. 1998). ❖ Popular singer-songwriter whose wide stylistic range has influenced artists, including Sinéad O'Connor, Torie Amos, and Björk; had such hit singles in UK as "Wuthering Heights" (#1), "Running Up That Hill" (1985), and "The Man With the Child in His Eyes" (1987). Albums include *The Kick Inside* (1978), *Lionheart* (1978), *The Dreaming* (1982), *Kate Bush* (1983), *The Hounds of Love* (1985), *The Whole Story* (1983) and *The Red Shoes* (1993).

BUSH, Laura (1946—). American first lady. Born Laura Welch, Nov 4, 1946, in Midland, Texas; only child of Harold Bush (home builder) and Jenna Bush (bookkeeper); Southern Methodist University, BS, 1968; University of Texas at Austin, MA, 1973; m. George W. Bush (president of US), 1977; children: (twins) Jenna and Barbara Bush. ❖ Quiet, reserved and highly respected first lady, whose special interest is education, taught in the public schools of Dallas and Houston; earned MA in library science (1973), then served as a public school librarian in Austin; quit working after marriage; after some difficulty, conceived twins Jenna and Barbara, named after their grandmothers; convinced husband to give up drinking after his habit became problematic for family (mid-1980s); was forced into public eye when husband became governor of Texas (1995); maintained interest in reading and education, kicking off Texas Book Festival to raise money for libraries, and took up literacy and breast cancer awareness as causes; at first was adamant about not getting involved in husband's political campaigns but eventually went on the stump, especially after he entered the White House; played an active role in husband's successful bids for presidency (2000 and 2004), giving 1st major speech at 2000 Republican National Convention in Philadelphia; called attention to the oppression of women and children under the Taliban. ❖ See also Ann Gerhart, *The Perfect Wife: The Life and Choices of Laura Bush* (Simon & Schuster, 2004).

BUSH, Lesley (1947—). American diver. Name variations: Lesley L. Bush. Born Sept 17, 1947, in Orange, New Jersey. ❖ At Tokyo Olympics, won a gold medal in platform (1964); won a gold medal for platform at Pam-American games (1967).

BUSH, Noreen (1905–1977). English ballet dancer and teacher. Born 1905 in Nottingham, England; died Aug 7, 1977, in London, England; dau. of Pauline Bush; trained by mother and Edouard Espinosa; m. Victor Leopold (tap dancer). ❖ Appeared in numerous West End musicals and operettas, such as *The Last Waltz* (1932), *Our Nell* (1924) and *Betty in Mayfair* (1952); named head scholarship teacher at Royal Academy of Dancing (1929), where she served for over 40 years; with husband, founded dance school which soon merged with the Marjorie Davies' school, becoming The Bush-Davies School, a notable London studio of ballet and general dance (1939).

BUSH, Pauline (1886–1969). American actress. Born May 22, 1886, in Lincoln, Nebraska; died Nov 1, 1969, in San Diego, California; m. Allan Dwan (director), 1915. ❖ Lead player with American Film Co. and Universal (1911–15), often shared the screen with J. Warren Kerrigan; films include *The Poisoned Flame* (1911), *Richelieu* (1914), *Her Escape* (1914), *The Struggle* (1915) and *The Enemy Sex* (1924).

BUSHFIELD, Vera Cahalan (1889–1976). American politician. Born in Miller, South Dakota, Aug 9, 1889; died in Fort Collins, Colorado, April 16, 1976; graduate of Stout Institute in Menominee, Wisconsin, 1912; attended Dakota Wesleyan University and University of Minnesota; m. Harlan J. Bushfield (governor of South Dakota, 1939–1943, and US senator, 1943–1948). ❖ First Lady of South Dakota, was also a US Republican senator in the 80th Congress (Oct 6, 1948–Dec 26, 1948), having been appointed by Governor George T. Mickelson to fill out the term of her late husband; carried out her senate duties in South Dakota, where she concentrated on constituency services, resigning her seat 6 days before the end of Congress so that Karl Mundt, who had won in the November election, could gain seniority by completing the final days of her husband's term.

BUSHNELL, Catherine (1825–1861). *See Hayes, Catherine.*

BUSLEY, Jessie (1869–1950). American actress. Born Mar 10, 1869, in Albany, NY; died April 20, 1950, in New York, NY; m. Ernest Joy. ❖ Made stage debut with Robert B. Mantell's company (1888); had a long and illustrious career, appearing in such plays as *The Bells of Haslemere, Charley's Aunt, The Sporting Duchess, The Admirable Crichton, In the Bishop's Carriage, Pollyanna, Daisy Mayme, Alien Corn, The Great Waltz, The Women* and *The Happiest Years;* also appeared in films.

BUSONI, Anna (1833–1909). Italian pianist. Born Anna Weiss in Trieste in 1833; died 1909; m. Ferdinando Busoni (clarinettist); children: Feruccio Benvenuto Busoni (1866–1924, pianist). ❖ Made debut as a soloist at 14; began giving duet recitals with 12-year-old son; concentrated on teaching in later years. ❖ See also *Women in World History.*

BUSS, Frances Mary (1827–1894). English educator. Born in London, England, 1827; died in London, Dec 24, 1894; dau. of R.W. Buss (painter and etcher who was one of the original illustrators of *Pickwick Papers*). ❖ Pioneer in women's education, attended a school in Camden Town, and continued there as a teacher until she joined her mother in keeping a school in Kentish Town; moved her school to Camden Street (1850), renaming it the North London Collegiate School for Ladies; appeared before the Schools Inquiry Commission (1864), which later singled out her school for exceptional commendation; saw school rehoused and a Camden School for Girls founded; with Dorothea Beale, became famous as the chief leader in the educational reform movement; played an active part in promoting the success of the Girls' Public Day School Company, encouraging the connection of the girls'

schools with the university standard by examinations; worked for the establishment of women's colleges and improved the training of teachers.

BUSSMAN, Gabriele (1959—). West German runner. Born Oct 1959 in Germany. ❖ At Los Angeles Olympics, won a bronze medal in 4 x 400-meter relay (1984).

BUSTA, Christine (1914–1987). Austrian poet. Born April 23, 1914, in Vienna, Austria; died Dec 3, 1987, in Vienna; m. Carl Dimt (musician), 1940 (killed during WWII). ❖ Wrote about her difficult childhood and youth; following WWII, worked as a translator, then a librarian; writings include *De Regenbaum* (1951), *Unterwegs zu älteren Feuern* (1965) and *Immitten aller Vergänglichkeit* (1985). Received Georg Trakl Prize (1954) and Austrian State Prize (1969).

BUSTOS, Crystl (1977—). American softball player. Born Sept 8, 1977, in Canyon Country, California; attended West Palm Beach Community College. ❖ Shortstop, won team gold medals at Sydney Olympics (2000) and Athens Olympics (2004).

BUTALA, Sharon (1940—). Canadian novelist and short-story writer. Born 1940 in Nipawin, Saskatchewan, Canada; attended University of Saskatchewan. ❖ Worked in special education before becoming full-time writer; works include *Country of the Heart* (1984), *Queen of the Headaches* (1985), *The Gates of the Sun* (1986), *Fever* (1990), *Upstream* (1991), the bestselling *The Perfection of the Morning* (1994), and *The Garden of Eden* (1998). Received Canadian Authors Award for Fiction (1992) and Saskatchewan Book Award for Non-Fiction (1994).

BUTCHER, Charlotte (1790–1860). *See Kemp, Charlotte.*

BUTCHER, Joan (d. 1550). *See Bocher, Joan.*

BUTCHER, Rosemary (1947—). British dancer. Born Feb 4, 1947, in Bristol, England; trained at Dartington College of Arts, 1965–69; studied with Dorothy Madden at University of Maryland and at Merce Cunningham Studio in NY. ❖ Launched career with choreography for Scottish Ballet's Moveable Workshop (1974); founded Rosemary Butcher Dance Company (1975); taught and held residencies as choreographer at numerous institutions, including Dunfermeline College, Glasgow (1973–74), Dartington College, Gloucestershire (1980–81), Laban Centre, London, and Surrey University, Guildford.

BUTCHER, Susan (1954—). American sled-dog racer. Born Dec 26, 1954, in Cambridge, Massachusetts; m. David Monson (winner of Yukon Quest). ❖ Was 4-time winner of the Iditarod (1986, 1987, 1988, 1990); set records in 4 other races: Norton Sound 200, Kusko 300, Arctic Coast 200, and John Beargrease Race in Minnesota. ❖ See also Nicki J. Nielsen, *The Iditarod: Women on the Trail* (Wolfdog, 1986); (film) *Alaska's Great Race: The Susan Butcher Story* (1989); and *Women in World History.*

BUTCHILL, Elizabeth (1758–1780). English murderer. Born 1758 in England; hanged at Cambridge, Mar 17, 1780; children: 1. ❖ While working as a servant at Trinity College, gave birth to daughter out of wedlock; threw infant's body in river; was sentenced to death and hanged before a crowd that apparently numbered in the thousands (Mar 17, 1780).

BUTE, countess of. *See Mary (b. 1718).*

BUTE, Mary Ellen (1906–1983). American avant-garde filmmaker. Born in Houston, Texas, 1906; died 1983; attended the Pennsylvania Academy and the Sorbonne; m. Ted Nemuth (director). ❖ One of the most original avant-garde filmmakers of her day, worked with musician and electronics engineer Leon Theremin, in an effort to create "visual music"; began to experiment with optical devices that projected color and images synchronized to musical compositions; made several films using drawings photographed at differing speeds of light; early films included *Rhythm in Light* (1934) and *Spook Sport* (1939); collaborated with husband on *Abstronics,* based on music by Aaron Copland; deciding to direct live-action features, chose as her 1st work, *Passages from Finnegan's Wake,* also titled *Finnegan's Wake,* adapted from a play by Mary Manning. ❖ See also *Women in World History.*

BUTER, Yvonne (1959—). Dutch field-hockey player. Born Mar 18, 1959, in Netherlands. ❖ At Seoul Olympics, won a bronze medal in team competition (1988).

BUTIRSKAYA, Maria (1972—). *See Butyrskaya, Maria.*

BUTLER, Eleanor (c. 1738–1829). Irish diarist and letter writer. Name variations: Ladies of Llangollen; became Lady Eleanor when brother John recovered earldom of Ormonde (1791). Born in Cambrai, France, in 1738 or 1739; died in Llangollen, Wales, June 2, 1829; dau. of Eleanor (Morris) Butler and Walter Butler, *de jure* earl of Ormonde. ❖ One of the celebrated women of Llangollen who lived with Sarah Ponsonby for 50 years in rural Wales in an age when romantic friendship between women and retirement to the countryside were fashionable; left Ireland forever (May 1778), to avoid being sent back to the nunnery in Cambrai; settled with Ponsonby in rural Llangollen in northern Wales, residing in a cottage they called Plas Newydd (New Place); read and studied the classics as well as contemporary literature in English, French, Italian and Spanish; tended a large garden; kept up a voluminous correspondence with the greatest minds of the day; frequently entertained genteel neighbors as well as distinguished persons who went out of their way to visit Llangollen, "the vale of friendship." Tourists still stream to Llangollen to visit Plas Newydd. ❖ See also Elizabeth Mavor, *The Ladies of Llangollen: A Study in Romantic Friendship* (Michael Joseph, 1971); and *Women in World History.*

BUTLER, Eleanor (c. 1915–1997). Irish politician and architect. Name variations: Countess of Wicklow. Born Eleanor Butler, c. 1915, in Dublin, Ireland; died Feb 1997; dau. of Rudolph M. Butler (architect); m. William Howard, 8th earl of Wicklow, 1959. ❖ At 6, contracted polio, remaining partially disabled throughout life; joined the Labour Party; elected a member of the Dublin Corporation (1943); nominated to the Seanad by the Taoiseach (John A. Costello, 1948); served in the Seanad (1948–51); represented Ireland at the Congress of Europe (1948–49); as an architect, was in business with father.

BUTLER, Elizabeth Beardsley (c. 1885–1911). American labor investigator. Born c. 1885; died of tuberculosis, Aug 2, 1911; graduate of Barnard College, 1905; never married. ❖ Was executive assistant at the New Jersey Consumers' League and the New Jersey Child Labor Committee (1905); was assistant secretary at Rand School of Social Science (1907); wrote 2 of the most comprehensive examinations of women's labor conditions in pre-World War I America: *Women and the Trades, Pittsburgh, 1907–1908* (1909) and *Saleswomen in Mercantile Stores, Baltimore, 1909* (published posthumously, 1912). ❖ See also *Women in World History.*

BUTLER, Elizabeth Thompson (1846–1933). English painter. Name variations: Elizabeth Southerden Thompson; Lady Butler. Born Elizabeth Southerden Thompson, Nov 3, 1846, near Lausanne, Switzerland; died Oct 2, 1933, at Gormanston Castle, Co. Meath, Ireland; dau. of Thomas James Thompson and Christiana (Weller) Thompson; sister of Alice Meynell (writer); studied at the Female School of Art, South Kensington (1866–1870), and Giuseppe Bellucci's Academy in Florence (1869); m. Major William Butler, June 11, 1877; children: Elizabeth (b. 1879), Patrick (b. 1880), Richard, Eileen (b. 1883), Martin (b. 1887), and Mary, who died in infancy. ❖ One of the most successful painters of military subjects in 19th century, brought a new realism to the depiction of war in British art; visited the battlefield of Waterloo (1865); exhibited at Society of Women Artists and the Dudley Gallery (1867); received commission for *The Roll Call* (1872); had *Missing* accepted by the Royal Academy (1873), as well as *The Roll Call* (1874), which was exhibited to great acclaim, because its realistic portrayal of the enduring strength of the common British soldier resonated strongly with popular sentiments; traveled extensively (1885–92), including time in Egypt where her husband was serving; toured Palestine (1891) and published *Letters from the Holy Land* (1903); published *From Sketch-Book and Diary* (1909); exhibited watercolors at Leicester Galleries (1912); exhibited at Waterloo Centenary Exhibition held at Leicester Galleries (1915); major works also include *The 28th Regiment at Quatre Bras* (1875), *Balaclava* (1876), *The Defence of Rorke's Drift* (1880), *Scotland for Ever!* (1881), and *"Steady the drums and fifes!"* (1897); her works were reproduced in thousands of prints. ❖ See also *An Autobiography* (1922); and *Women in World History.*

BUTLER, Grace Ellen (1886–1962). New Zealand artist. Name variations: Grace Ellen Cumming. Born Dec 23, 1886, at Invercargill, New Zealand; died Nov 23, 1962, at Wellington, New Zealand; dau. of William Forbes Cumming (carter and contractor) and Jane (Cameron) Cumming; m. Guy Raphael Butler (law clerk), 1911; children: 3 daughters. ❖ Studied art at Canterbury College School of Art; became working member of Canterbury Society of Arts (1915); was known primarily for large landscape paintings around Otira.

BUTLER, Helen May (1867–1957). American composer, conductor, and politician. Name variations: Helen May Spahn, Helen May Young. Born Helen May Butler, May 17, 1867, in Keene, New Hampshire; died June 16, 1957, in Covington, Kentucky; m. John Leslie Spahn, 1902 (div., 1908); married a Mr. Young, c. 1910. ❖ Known as the "Female Sousa," was the 1st American woman to lead a professional concert band; founded Talma Ladies Orchestra (1892) and Talma Ladies Military Band (1896); initiated band tours with manager John Leslie Spahn (1898); led performance at Pan American Exposition in Buffalo, NY (1901); conducted at NY Women's Exposition and White House Concert (1902); conducted at Willow Grove Park, St. Louis World's Fair (1904); composed "Cosmopolitan America" for Republican Convention (1904); conducted at Barnum & Bailey Show (1914); ran for US Senate (1936); compositions include "The Billboard Girl March" (1904) and "What Cheer March" (1904). ❖ See also *Women in World History.*

BUTLER, Ida (1868–1949). American nurse. Born Ida de Fatio Butler, Mar 18, 1868, in Watertown, NY; died Mar 11, 1949, in Hartford, Connecticut; dau. of John Hartwell Butler (major) and Ida de M. Fatio Butler (Civil War nurse); raised by grandfather, John S. Butler (psychiatrist), after mother's death; cousin of Anne Warburton Goodrich (pioneering nurse); Hartford Hospital School of Nursing, diploma, 1901; never married. ❖ Worked at Hartford Hospital in many roles (1902–18), including obstetric department supervisor; during WWI, sent to Lyons, France, to oversee nursing at Hospital Violet and Hospital Holtzman (children's hospitals); returned to US (1919) to direct home for influenza epidemic victims; was director of Red Cross (1936–39).

BUTLER, Josephine (1828–1906). British social reformer. Name variations: Josephine Grey. Born Josephine Elizabeth Grey, April 13, 1828, at Dilston, Northumberland, England; died Dec 30, 1906, at Wooler, Northumberland; dau. of John and Hannah (Annett) Grey; m. George Butler (cleric), 1851 (died 1890); children: 3 sons and daughter Evangeline (died young). ❖ President of the Ladies National Association, who led a successful campaign to repeal the British Contagious Diseases Acts, which subjected women suspected of prostitution to enforced examination and imprisonment; moved to husband's parish in Oxford (1851); was drawn into education issues (1858); took up more social issues after move to Liverpool (1866), bringing many destitute women who were sick and dying to her home, where she nursed them until they regained health or else died; opened a "House of Rest" to look after women who had been discharged from hospital, but were incurably ill and had no place else to go; served as president of North of England Council for Promoting the Higher Education of Women (1867–73); was also instrumental in the establishment of Newnham, the 1st women's college at Cambridge University; served as president of Ladies National Association for the Repeal of the Contagious Diseases Acts, which held women, not men, responsible for the spread of syphilis and gonorrhea (1869–86); became founding member of National Vigilance Association (1885); published the 1st edition of her monthly journal, *Storm Bell,* where she recounted her experiences of rescue work and raised questions about ethical issues (1898); writings include *The Education and Employment of Women* (1868), *On the Moral Reclaimability of Prostitutes* (1870), *Rebecca Jarrett* (1886) and *Personal Reminiscences of a Great Crusade* (1896). In the calendar of the Church of England, Dec 30th is sanctified as Josephine Butler Day, in memory of her work. ❖ See also George and Lucy Johnson, eds., *Josephine E. Butler: An Autobiographical Memoir* (1928); and *Women in World History.*

BUTLER, Lady (1846–1933). See Butler, Elizabeth Thompson.

BUTLER, Margaret Mary (1883–1947). New Zealand sculptor. Born April 30, 1883, in Greymouth, New Zealand; died Dec 4, 1947, at Wellington, New Zealand; dau. of Edward Butler (engineer) and Mary (Delaney) Butler. ❖ Studied sculpture at Wellington Technical School; exhibited at British Empire Exhibition at Wembley, London (1924–25); also exhibited at Salon des Tuileries, Paris (1927), and at salons of the Société des artistes français, Société nationale des beaux-arts, and Galerie Hébrard, Paris; especially noted for busts of Maori figures; contents of studio were directed to National Art Gallery (1950).

BUTLER, Mother (1860–1940). See Butler, Mother Marie Joseph.

BUTLER, Mother Marie Joseph (1860–1940). American founder of the Marymount schools and colleges. Name variations: Mother Butler. Born Johanna Butler, July 22, 1860, in Ballynunnery, Co. Kilkenny, Ireland; died April 23, 1940, in Tarrytown, NY; dau. of John and Ellen (Forrestal) Butler. ❖ Entered convent in Béziers, France, of the Congregation of the Sacred Heart of Mary (1876); taught in convent school at Oporto, Portugal (1879–80), then headed English and French departments at school in Braga, Portugal; appointed superior of Braga convent and school (1893); sent to head congregation's school at Sag

Harbor, Long Island, NY (c. 1903); opened Marymount School in Tarrytown, NY (1908), which was followed by opening of novitiate (1910) and college (1918); founded branches of Marymount in other US locations and abroad; established the Mother Butler Mission Guilds and is credited with the development of retreat movement in US; elected mother general of the Congregation of the Sacred Heart of Mary (1926). ❖ See also Katherine Burton, *Mother Butler of Marymount* (Longmans, 1944).

BUTLER, Mrs. (1809–1893). *See Kemble, Fanny.*

BUTLER, Octavia E. (1947–2006). African-American science-fiction writer. Born Octavia Estelle Butler, June 22, 1947, in Pasadena, California; died April 28, 2006, in Lake Forest Park, Washington; dau. of Laurice Butler (who died when she was an infant) and Octavia M. (Guy) Butler (domestic); Pasadena College, AA, 1968; attended California State University, 1969. ❖ The 1st published African-American female science-fiction writer, was mentored by Harlan Ellison; attended the Clarion Science Fiction Writer's Workshop (1970); wrote the "Patternist" saga, which includes *Patternmaster* (1976), *Mind of My Mind* (1977), *Survivor* (1978), *Wild Seed* (1980) and *Clay's Ark* (1984); also wrote *Kindred* (1979), *Adulthood Rites* (1988), *Parable of the Sower* (1995) and *Lilith's Brood* (2000); major sci-fi writer, her works attack racism, sexism, the class system and hypocrisy. Received Hugo Award (1984) and Nebula Award (1985).

BUTLER, Selena Sloan (1872–1964). African-American child-welfare activist. Born Selena Sloan in Thomasville, Georgia, Jan 4, 1872; died Oct 1964; dau. of Winnie (Williams) Sloan (African-Indian) and William Sloan; graduate of Atlanta Baptist Female Seminary (now Spelman College), 1888; attended Emerson School of Oratory (now Emerson College), 1894; m. Henry Rutherford Butler (doctor), May 3, 1893 (died 1931); children: 1 son. ❖ Taught in Atlanta and edited the *Woman's Advocate,* a monthly paper devoted to the interests of black American women; established the 1st black parent-teacher association in the country and patterned it after the National Congress of Parents and Teachers (1911); developed a state organization, Georgia Colored Parent-Teacher Association (1919), and served as its president for many years; helped form the National Congress of Colored Parents and Teachers (1926), serving as its president. ❖ See also *Women in World History.*

BUTLER-SLOSS, Elizabeth (1933—). British judge. Name variations: Elizabeth Butler Sloss; Elizabeth Havers; Dame Elizabeth Butler-Sloss. Born Ann Elizabeth Oldfield Havers, Aug 10, 1933, in Kew Gardens, Richmond, Surrey, England; dau. of Sir Cecil Havers QC (high court judge); sister of Nigel Havers; attended Wycombe Abbey School; m. Joseph William Alexander Butler-Sloss, 1958; children: 2 sons, 1 daughter. ❖ The 1st woman appointed to the Court of Appeal, was called to Bar by Inner Temple (1955) and practiced as barrister (1955–75); unsuccessfully contested the Conservative seat at Lambeth (1959); served as a divorce registrar (1970–79), as a judge of the High Court, Family Division (1979–88), and as 1st lady Lord Justice of Appeal (1987–99); chaired Cleveland Sex Abuse Inquiry (1987–88); named president of the Family Division (1999); began serving as chancellor of University of the West of England (1993). Appointed Dame of the Order of the British Empire (DBE, 1979).

BUTSOVA, Hilda (1896–1976). English ballet dancer. Name variations: Hilda Boot; Hilda Butsova Mills. Born Hilda Boot, July 11, 1896, in Nottingham, England; died Mar 21, 1976, in White Plains, NY. ❖ At 13, performed with Diaghilev Ballet Russe in London; toured with Anna Pavlova's company and remained with company, serving as Pavlova's understudy and dancing principal roles (1911–29); moved to US (1930); toured with Mikhail Mordkin's company intermittently; appeared at Capitol Theater in New York City, directed by Chester Hale; danced at Capitol with other Pavlova dancers: Ella Dagnova and Joyce Coles; retired to teach (mid-1930s) and was celebrated as a master trainer of Russian classical repertory.

BUTT, Clara (1872–1936). English contralto. Name variations: Madame Clara, Dame Clara. Born Clara Ellen Butt, Feb 1, 1872, in Southwick, Sussex, England; died Jan 23, 1936, at North Stoke, Oxfordshire; m. Robert Kennerley Rumford, June 26, 1900. ❖ Awarded scholarship to Royal College of Music (1890); made debut in Gluck's *Orpheus* (1892); toured Canada and US (1899); sang "Abide with Me" at memorial service for Queen Victoria (1901); was inspiration for songs by British composer, Sir Edward Elgar, including "Land of Hope and Glory" (1901); began recording career (1909); mobilized women for war effort (1914–18); seriously injured (1931), but continued recording; her

concert hall appearances, early recordings, and broadcasting career made her one of the 1st entertainment superstars beloved throughout the world. Named Dame of the British Empire (1920). ❖ See also Winfred Ponder, *Clara Butt: Her Life-Story* (DaCapo, 1978); and *Women in World History.*

BUTTERS, Mary (fl. 1839). Irish woman accused of sorcery. Lived in the town of Carrickfergus, Co. Antrim, Ireland. ❖ Was found guilty of sorcery "to recover . . . a cow, the property of Alexander Montgomery" (1839).

BUTTERWORTH, Mary Peck (1686–1775). American counterfeiter. Born in Rehoboth, Massachusetts, July 27, 1686; died in Rehoboth, Feb 7, 1775. ❖ With Hannah Peck, was accused of organizing a counterfeiting ring involving a dozen or so citizens of Rehoboth, Massachusetts (then Plymouth Colony, c. 1715); when charges were dropped, was set free.

BUTTFIELD, Nancy (1912—). Australian politician. Name variations: Dame Nancy Buttfield. Born Nancy Eileen Holden, Nov 12, 1912, in South Australia, Australia; 2nd dau. of Edward (later Sir) Holden (major founder of the Australian auto industry) and Hilda May Holden; attended Adelaide University; m. Frank Charles Buttfield (company director) Feb 19, 1936; children: 2 sons. ❖ A Liberal, stood unsuccessfully for the federal seat of Adelaide (1954); when a federal senate vacancy was created by the death of Senator George McLeay (1955), was nominated by State Parliament and became South Australia's 1st female Member of Parliament; served as a senator for over 16 years. Named DBE (1972). ❖ See also *Dame Nancy: The Autobiography of Dame Nancy Buttfield* (1992).

BUTTINGER, Muriel (1901–1985). *See Gardiner, Muriel.*

BUTTLE, Mehetabel (c. 1822–1908). *See Newman, Mehetabel.*

BUTTON, Isabel (1863–1921). New Zealand horse trainer, racer and equestrian. Name variations: Isabel Moore, Isabella Moore. Born Oct 9, 1863, in Canterbury, New Zealand; died Feb 7, 1921; dau. of Robert Thomas Button and Anna Mary (Pymar) Button; m. Augustus Frederick Lipscombe Moore, 1911. ❖ Adept at breaking horses, began training them for trotting and steeplechase races; as owner of horses she trained, was also allowed to race them (late 1880s); competed in numerous shows and exhibitions, winning many prizes. ❖ See also *Dictionary of New Zealand Biography* (Vol. 2).

BUTTROSE, Ita (1942—). Australian journalist, publisher, broadcaster and media personality. Name variations: Ita Clare Buttrose. Born Jan 17, 1942, in Sydney, Australia; dau. of Charles Oswald Buttrose and Mary Clare Buttrose; married 1963. ❖ Well-known radio and tv personality, was a founding editor of the magazine *Cleo* (1972–75), editor of *Australian Women's Weekly* (1975–76) and editor-in-chief of both publications (1976–81); served as director of Australian Consolidated Press (1974–81) and publisher of women's publications by Australian Consolidated Press (1977–81); was women's editor for *Daily Telegraph,* then *Sunday Telegraph,* later returning to paper to become Australia's 1st woman editor-in-chief of either daily or Sunday paper (1981); entered radio broadcasting (1983) and was given own show by 2 stations; became presenter of *Woman's Day* on tv (1985); continued to broadcast while returning to print as newspaper columnist; served as chair of National Advisory Committee on AIDS (1984–88); became founder and chief executive of Capricorn Publishing and editor-in-chief of *The Sun Herald* (1988); launched own magazine, *Ita* (1989), editing it until 1994; served as president of National Opera Festival (1995–97); became director of Australian media conglomerate, Terraplanet (2000). Awarded Order of British Empire (OBE, 1979), Officer of Order of Australia (1988), Hartnett Medal (1992), and Centenary Medal (2003).

BUTTS, Mary (1890–1937). British author. Born Mary Francis Butts in Poole, Dorset, England, Dec 13, 1890; died in Sennen, Cornwall, England, Mar 5, 1937; dau. of Mary Jane (Briggs) and Frederick John Butts (naval captain); educated at St. Leonard's School and Westfield College of London University; m. John Rodker (poet), 1918 (sep. 1920); m. Gabriel W. Aitkin (writer), 1930 (sep. 1934); children: (1st m.) Camilla Rodker (b. 1920). ❖ Published *Speed the Plough* (1923), followed by *Ashe of Rings* (1925), and *Armed with Madness* (1928); published autobiography *The Crystal Cabinet,* just prior to her death from a ruptured appendix; though her work was well-respected in her time by other writers, her personal escapades overshadowed her literary reputation. ❖ See also Nathalie Blondel, *Mary Butts: Scenes from the Life* (McPherson, 1997); and *Women in World History.*

BUTUZOVA, Natalya (1954—). Soviet archer. Born Feb 17, 1954, in USSR. ❖ At Moscow Olympics, won a silver medal in double FITA round (1980).

BUTYRSKAYA, Maria (1972—). Russian figure skater. Name variations: Butirskaya or Butirskaia. Born June 28, 1972, in Moscow, Russia; trained with Victor Kudryavtsev and Elena Tchaikovskaya. ❖ At European championships, won a gold medal (1998, 1999, 2002) and a silver (2000, 2001); won the bronze medal at World championships (1998, 2000) and became World champion (1999); placed 4th at Nagano (1998); was 6-time national champion; turned professional; also became a commentator for European TV.

BUXTON, Mary Ann (c. 1795–1888). New Zealand educator and school founder. Name variations: Mary Ann Streetin. Born Mary Ann Streetin, c. 1795 or 1796, in England; died 1888; m. Harry Bridger Buxton, c. 1827 or 1828; children: 5. ❖ Immigrated with family to New Zealand (1839); founded private school in Wellington (1841–78); following husband's death (1847), secured 25,000-acre property on which sons raised sheep (1850s–1870), and owned several properties in Wellington area. ❖ See also *Dictionary of New Zealand Biography* (Vol. 1).

BUZONAS, Gail Johnson (1954—). American synchronized swimmer. Name variations: Gail Johnson; Gail Johnson-Buzonas. Born 1954 in US. ❖ Won 11 national championship titles, including consecutive outdoor solo titles (1972–75) and indoor solo title (1972), indoor and outdoor duet with Teresa Andersen (1972–73), and outdoor duet with Sue Baros (1974); won a gold medal for solo at Pan American games and World championships (1975). Inducted into International Swimming Hall of Fame.

BUZUNOVA, Natalya (1958—). Soviet field-hockey player. Born Mar 1958 in USSR. ❖ At Moscow Olympics, won a bronze medal in team competition (1980).

BYARS, Betsy (1928—). American children's writer. Born Betsy Cromer, Aug 7, 1928, in Charlotte, North Carolina; dau. of George Guy (cotton-mill executive) and Nan (Rugheimer) Cromer; attended Furman University, 1946–48; Queens College, BA, 1950; m. Edward Ford Byars (professor of engineering), June 24, 1950; children: Laurie, Betsy Ann, Nan, Guy. ❖ Prolific writer of children's novels in contemporary realist style, became interested in writing while reading to own children; came to prominence with *The Summer of the Swans* (1970), which was awarded the Newbery Medal; wrote 50 books, including *The Night Swimmers,* winner of the American Book Award (1981) and *Wanted . . . Mud Blossom,* winner of The Edgar for best young people's mystery (1992); produced several popular series: "Bingo Brown," "Blossoms," "Golly Sisters," and "Herculeah Jones"; other writings include *The Eighteenth Emergency* (1973), *Goodbye, Chicken Little* (1979), *The Animal, The Vegetable, and John D Jones* (1982), *Beans on the Roof* (1988) and *Tornado* (1995). Honored with Regina Medal by Catholic Library Association for body of work. ❖ See also autobiography, *Betsy Byars* (Chelsea House, 2002).

BYATT, A.S. (1936—). British novelist and literary critic. Name variations: Antonia Susan Byatt. Born Antonia Susan Drabble, Aug 24, 1936, in Sheffield, Yorkshire, England; dau. of John Frederick Drabble (judge) and Kathleen Marie Bloor Drabble; sister of Margaret Drabble (writer); educated at Newnham College, Cambridge, Bryn Mawr College, and Somerville College, Oxford; m. Ian Charles Rayner Byatt, 1959 (div. 1969); m. Peter John Duffy, 1969; children: 4. ❖ Was a lecturer in literature at University College, London (1972–83), before becoming full-time writer; addresses themes of academic insularity, the challenges facing contemporary women, and the role of art and literature; earned international acclaim for her novel *Possession: A Romance* (1990); other novels include *The Shadow of the Sun* (1964), *The Game* (1967), *The Virgin in the Garden* (1978), *Still Life* (1980), *Angels and Insects* (1992), *Babel Tower* (1996) and *A Whistling Woman* (2002); also wrote and edited works of literary criticism. Received several awards, including Booker Prize for *Possession;* made CBE (1990) and DBE (1999).

BYCKERDYKE, Mary Ann (1817–1901). See Bickerdyke, Mary Ann.

BYE, Karyn (1971—). American ice-hockey player. Born May 18, 1971, in River Falls, Wisconsin; graduate of University of New Hampshire, 1993, and Concordia University, Montreal. ❖ Captained the IIHF Pacific Women's Hockey championship (1996); won a team gold medal at Nagano (1998), the 1st Olympics to feature women's ice hockey; won a team silver medal at World championships (1992, 1994, 1997, 1999, 2000, 2001); won a team silver medal at Salt Lake City Olympics (2002). Named USA Hockey Women's Player of the Year (1995, 1998). ❖ See also Mary Turco, *Crashing the Net: The U.S. Women's Olympic Ice Hockey Team and the Road to Gold* (HarperCollins, 1999); and *Women in World History.*

BYERS, Margaret (1832–1912). Irish educator. Born Margaret Morrow in April 1832 in Rathfriland, Co. Down, Ireland; died in Belfast, Feb 21, 1912; dau. of Andrew Morrow (farmer) and Margaret (Herron) Morrow; attended Ladies' College at Nottingham where she qualified as a teacher; m. Reverend John Byers (Presbyterian minister), Feb 24, 1852 (died 1853); children: John (b. 1853). ❖ Educationalist who founded the Ladies' Collegiate School in Belfast and took a leading part in campaigns to secure equality for women within the Irish education system; taught at the Ladies' Collegiate School in Cookstown, Co. Tyrone (1853–59); opened the Ladies Collegiate School, later Victoria College, in Belfast (1859), which by 1888, won 48 distinctions, more than any other girls' school in Ireland, and 25 more than its nearest competitor, Alexandra College in Dublin; elected president of Ulster Headmistresses' Association (1903); awarded honorary degree by Trinity College, Dublin (1905), the 1st Ulsterwoman to receive such an honor from any university; appointed to the Senate of Queen's University, Belfast (1908); was also a leading member of the Ladies' Temperance Union and secretary of the Belfast Woman's Temperance Association and 1st president of the Irish Women's Temperance Union; played a major part in opening up opportunities to women outside the home. ❖ See also *Women in World History.*

BYINGTON, Spring (1886–1971). American actress. Born in Colorado Springs, Colorado, Oct 17, 1886; died Sept 7, 1971; dau. of Edwin Lee (English teacher) and Helene Byington (physician). ❖ In a career that included 20 Broadway appearances and 75 films, is probably best remembered for starring role as Lily Ruskin in tv series "December Bride," which 1st aired in 1954 after 2 successful years on radio; made Broadway debut as Miss Hey in *Beggar on Horseback* (1924); also appeared in *Be Your Age* (1928), *Ladies Don't Lie* (1929), *Once in a Lifetime* (1932) and *When Ladies Meet* (1932); made screen debut as Marmee in *Little Women* (1933); soon found her niche in supporting roles, playing mostly scatter-brained wives or loving moms; had 1st lead in *Louisa* (1950); nominated for Academy Award for Best Supporting Actress for performance in *You Can't Take It With You;* was also a regular in the "Jones Family" film series (1936–40), which began with *Every Saturday Night;* other films include *Way Down East* (1935), *Mutiny on the Bounty* (1935), *Ah! Wilderness* (1935), *Dodsworth* (1936), *Theodora Goes Wild* (1936), *The Adventures of Tom Sawyer* (1938), *Jezebel* (1938), *The Story of Alexander Graham Bell* (1939), *The Bluebird* (1940), *Meet John Doe* (1941), *The Devil and Miss Jones* (1941), *Roxie Hart* (1942), *Presenting Lily Mars* (1943), *Heaven Can Wait* (1943), *Dragonwyck* (1946), *Angels in the Outfield* (1951) and *Please Don't Eat the Daisies* (1960). ❖ See also *Women in World History.*

BYKOVA, Natalya (1958—). Soviet field-hockey player. Born Aug 17, 1958, in USSR. ❖ At Moscow Olympics, won a bronze medal in team competition (1980).

BYKOVA, Tamara (1958—). Soviet high jumper. Born Dec 21, 1958, in Azov, near Rostov-on-Don, USSR. ❖ Won a gold medal (1983) and silver medal (1987), both for high jump, at World championships; broke 3 world records; at her peak, could not compete in Olympics because of Soviet boycott of Los Angeles Games; at Seoul Olympics, won a bronze medal in the high jump (1988).

BYLUND, Ingamay (1949—). Swedish equestrian. Born Sept 25, 1949. ❖ At Los Angeles Olympics, won a bronze medal in team dressage (1984).

BYNS, Anna (d. 1575). See Bijns, Anna.

BYON KYUNG-JA (1956—). Korean volleyball player. Born Jan 6, 1956, in Korea. ❖ At Montreal Olympics, won a bronze medal in team competition (1976).

BYRAM, Melissa (1973—). See Mills, Melissa.

BYRD, Mary Willing (1740–1814). American letter writer. Born 1740 in Philadelphia, Pennsylvania; died 1814; m. Colonel William Byrd of Virginia, 1761; children: 8. ❖ After husband's death, supported 8 children by turning family plantation into prosperous enterprise; accused of being disloyal to the patriot cause during the American Revolution, wrote to Thomas Jefferson for help; her letters, included in *The Papers of*

William Jefferson, are an eloquent defense of her loyalty to the cause (the charges were dropped).

BYRNE, Charlotte Dacre (c. 1772–1825). *See Dacre, Charlotte.*

BYRNE, Jane (1934—). American politician. Born Jane Margaret Burke in Chicago, Illinois, May 24, 1934; dau. of William Burke (executive with Inland Steel and co-founder of Gordon-Burke Steel) and Katherine (Nolan) Burke; Barat College of the Sacred Heart, BA, 1955; attended University of Illinois and Chicago Teachers College (now Chicago State University); m. William P. Byrne (Marine Corps pilot), Dec 31, 1956 (killed May 1959); m. Jan McMullen (reporter), Mar 17, 1978; children: (1st m.) Katherine Byrne. ❖ Mayor of Chicago who was the 1st woman to head the nation's 2nd largest city; secured a position on the administrative staff of the Chicago Commission of Urban Opportunity (1965); appointed to the Cabinet of Mayor Richard Daley (1968), as commissioner of consumer sales, weights, and measures; became co-chair of the Cook County Democratic Committee and was appointed to the party's National Committee; won election for mayor, with 82% of the vote, a greater margin than even Daley had accomplished (1979); failed in reelection bid (1983). ❖ See also *My Chicago* (Norton, 1992); Bill and Lori Granger, *Fighting Jane: Mayor Jane Byrne and the Chicago Machine* (Dial, 1980); and *Women in World History.*

BYRON, Annabella (1792–1860). *See Milbanke, Anne.*

BYRON, Augusta (1784–1851). *See Leigh, Augusta.*

BYRON, Augusta Ada (1815–1852). *See Lovelace, Ada Byron.*

BYRON, Beverly Butcher (1932—). American politician. Born Beverly Barton Butcher in Baltimore, Maryland, July 27, 1932; attended Hood College, Frederick, Maryland, 1963–64; m. Goodloe E. Byron (US congressional representative, 1971–78); dau.-in-law of Katharine E. Byron (politician). ❖ Worked on husband's campaigns for the Maryland Legislature and US House of Representatives; following his death (1978), was elected to his seat; became the 1st woman to chair an Armed Services subcommittee (1987); also served on the Committee on Interior and Insular Affairs and the Select Committee on Aging; chaired the House Special Panel on Arms Control and Disarmament (1983–86); served as chair of the Maryland Commission on Physical Fitness (1979–89); as a Democrat, served 6 succeeding terms (96th–101st Congresses, Jan 3, 1979–Jan 3, 1993), but was an unsuccessful candidate for renomination (1992). ❖ See also *Women in World History.*

BYRON, Katharine Edgar (1903–1976). American politician. Born in Detroit, Michigan, Oct 25, 1903; died in Washington, DC, Dec 28, 1976; m. William D. Byron (congressional representative, 1939–41); children: 5 sons, including Goodloe E. Byron, who served in US House of Representatives from 1971–78 and was succeeded upon his death by his wife Beverly Butcher Byron. ❖ When husband was killed in a plane crash (1941), was chosen to complete his term in a special election (77th Congress, May 27, 1941–Jan 43, 1943); as a Democrat, served on the Committee on the Civil Service and the Committee on War Claims; in later years, continued her long-term association with the Red Cross. ❖ See also *Women in World History.*

BYRON, Kathleen (1922—). English actress. Born Jan 11, 1922, in London, England; trained for stage at the Old Vic. ❖ Made 1st billed film *The Silver Fleet* (1943); appeared as Sister Ruth in *Black Narcissus;* other films include *Madness of the Heart, The House in the Square, Tom Brown's Schooldays, The Scarlet Thread, Four Days, Young Bess, Profile, Secret Venture, Hammerhead, Private Road, The Abdication, The Elephant Man, Emma* and *Saving Private Ryan.*

BYRON, Kitty (c. 1879–?). English murderer. Born c. 1879 in England. ❖ Twice stabbed her lover, Arthur Reginald Baker, on the street in front of witnesses (Nov 10, 1902), but had public sympathy on her side during trial (Dec); was found guilty of murder, though jury strongly recommended mercy; after a 15,000-name petition was submitted from public for a reprieve, had sentence commuted to life, then reduced to 10 years.

BYRON, Lady (1792–1860). *See Milbanke, Anne.*

BYRON, Marion (1911–1985). American comedic actress. Born Mar 16, 1911, in Dayton, Ohio; died July 5, 1985, in Santa Monica, California; m. Lou Breslow (screenwriter); children: 2 sons. ❖ Made film debut opposite Buster Keaton in *Steamboat Bill, Jr.* (1928); other films include *Broadway Babies of 1929, Song of the West, The Heart of New York, Tenderfoot, Love Me Tonight, Gift of Gab* and *Five of a Kind* (1928–38).

BYRON, Lady Noel (1792–1860). *See Milbanke, Anne.*

BYRON, Patricia (1914–1989). *See Cockburn, Patricia.*

BYSTROVA, Galina (1934—). Soviet pentathlete. Born Feb 1934 in USSR. ❖ At Tokyo Olympics, won a bronze medal in pentathlon (1964).

BYZANTIUM, empress of.
See Eusebia of Macedonia (fl. 300).
See Faustina of Antioch (fl. 300s).
See Helena (c. 320–?).
See Fausta (d. 324).
See Eudocia of Byzantium (d. 404).
See Pulcheria (c. 398–453).
See Verina (fl. 437–483).
See Theodora (c. 500–548).
See Lupicinia-Euphemia (d. 523).
See Constantina (fl. 582–602).
See Ino-Anastasia.
See Fabia-Eudocia (fl. 600s).
See Fausta (fl. 600s).
See Martina (fl. 600s).
See Leontia (fl. 602–610).
See Irene (fl. 700s).
See Irene of the Khazars (fl. 700s).
See Maria (fl. 700s).
See Theodora of the Khazars (fl. 700s).
See Irene of Athens (752–803).
See Theodota (fl. 795).
See Eudocia Decapolita (fl. 800s).
See Eudocia Ingerina (fl. 800s).
See Euphrosyne (fl. 800s).
See Maria of Amnia (fl. 800s).
See Prokopia (fl. 800s).
See Thecla (fl. 800s).
See Theophano of Athens (fl. 800s).
See Theophano, Saint (866–893).
See Zoë Zautzina (d. 896).
See Theodora (early 900s).
See Theodora (late 900s).
See Eudocia Baiane (d. 902).
See Zoë Carbopsina (d. 920).
See Theophano (c. 940–?).
See Helena Lekapena (r. 945–959).
See Helena of Alypia (fl. 980s).
See Catherine of Bulgaria (fl. 1050).
See Zoë Porphyrogenita (980–1050).
See Theodora Porphyrogenita (c. 989–1056).
See Eudocia Macrembolitissa (1021–1096).
See Maria of Alania (fl. 1070–1081).
See Priska-Irene of Hungary (c. 1085–1133).
See Marie of Antioch (fl. 1180–1183).
See Euphrosyne (d. 1203).
See Marie de Courtenay (fl. 1215).
See Irene of Brunswick. (fl. 1300s).
Anne of Savoy (c. 1320–1353).

C

CABALLÉ, Montserrat (1933—). Spanish soprano. Name variations: Caballe. Born April 12, 1933, in Barcelona, Spain; studied at Barcelona Conservatorio del Liceo and with Eugenia Kemeny, Conchita Badia, and Napoleone Annovazzi. ❖ One of the 20th century's greatest prima donnas, awarded Liceo gold medal (1954); appeared in Barcelona, Basel and Vienna (late 1950s); debuted at the Teatro alla Scala (1960), and Mexico City, Chicago, and Metropolitan Opera (1965); debuted at Covent Garden (1970); in one 7-year period, sang 47 different operatic roles, from Mozart to Wagner and Strauss, though Carmen came to dominate her repertoire. ❖ See also *Women in World History.*

CABALLERO, Fernán (1796–1877). See Böhl von Faber, Cecilia.

CABANILLAS, Nuria (1980—). Spanish rhythmic gymnast. Born Aug 9, 1980, in Barcelona, Spain. ❖ Won a team gold medal at Atlanta Olympics (1996).

CABARRUS, Thérésa (1773–1835). See Tallien, Thérésa.

CABELLO, Mercedes (1845–1909). See Cabello de Carbonera, Mercedes.

CABELLO DE CARBONERA, Mercedes (1845–1909). Peruvian novelist. Name variations: Mercedes Cabello. Born in Moquegua, Peru, 1845; died 1909. ❖ Though her early novels are considered sentimental and stylized, later works are praised for effective use of naturalist style; espoused reform in such books as *Sacrificio y recompensa* (1886), *Eledora* (1887), *Los amores de Hortensia* (1888), *Blanca Sol* (1889), *Las Consecuencias* (1890) and *El Conspirador: autobiografía de un hombre público* (1892).

CABETE, Adelaide (1867–1935). Portuguese physician, feminist and essayist. Born 1867 into a working-class family in Portugal; died 1935; at 19, married a sergeant in the Republican army. ❖ One of the leading figures of Portuguese feminism, earned her medical degree (1900) with a thesis on working-class mothers-to-be; with Ana de Castro Osório, founded National Council of Portuguese Women and organized the First Feminist Congress in Lisbon (1924); contributed essays on health care for women and children to magazine *Alma Feminina;* went to Angola (1929) and continued work on health issues; returned to Portugal (1934).

CABLE, Mildred (1878–1952). British missionary. Born Alice Mildred Cable in Guildford, England, Feb 21, 1878; died April 30, 1952 in Shaftsbury, Dorset, England; attended Guildford High School. ❖ Inspired by the China Inland Mission, the organization for which she studied medicine, sailed for China; met Evangeline French in Hwochow (1902), becoming lifelong companions; with Evangeline and Francesca French, ran a girls' school while preparing for a journey through the Gobi Desert to preach the Gospel; traveled the Gobi with them for 16 years (1923–39) which informs their narrative *The Gobi Desert* (1942).

CABOT, Dolce Ann (1862–1943). New Zealand teacher, journalist, feminist. Name variations: Dolce Ann Duncan. Born Nov 25, 1862, at Christchurch, New Zealand; died May 31, 1943, at Christchurch; dau. of Thomas Cabot and Louisa Augusta (Kinkel) Cabot; attended Christchurch Normal School, Canterbury College; m. Andrew Duncan, 1907 (died 1935). ❖ Trained as teacher and took position at Timaru Main School until 1891; served as editor of women's page of *Canterbury Times* (1894–1907); believed to have been the 1st woman in New Zealand appointed to newspaper staff; advocated women's rights and opportunities; also published poetry and short stories. ❖ See also *Dictionary of New Zealand Biography* (Vol. 2).

CABOT, Eliza (1787–1860). See Follen, Eliza.

CABOT, Susan (1927–1986). American actress. Name variations: Susan Cabot-Roman. Born Harriet Shapiro, July 9, 1927, in Boston, Massachusetts; beaten to death by her son, Dec 10, 1986, in Encino, California; m. Martin Sacker, 1944 (div. 1951); m. Michael Roman, 1968 (div. 1983); children: Timothy Scott Roman. ❖ Raised in foster homes; made film debut in *Kiss of Death* (1947); other films include *On the Isle of Samoa, Machine Gun Kelly, Son of Ali Baba, The Enforcer, Gunsmoke, Ride Clear of Diablo, Flame of Araby* and *On the Isle of Samoa.*

CABRERA, Lydia (1899–1991). Cuban-born author and ethnologist. Name variations: (pseudonym) Nena en Sociedad (Little Girl in Society). Born May 20, 1899, in Havana, Cuba; died Sept 19, 1991, in Miami, Florida; dau. of Raimundo Cabrera, well-known lawyer, politician and writer, and Elisa Bilbao; studied art at San Alejandro Academy; pursued a degree in Oriental art at the Louvre in Paris; lover and partner of María Teresa de Rojas (historian); longtime companion of Teresa de la Parra (novelist). ❖ Leading authority on Afro-Cuban culture and religion, particularly santeria, undertook a lengthy study of Cuban-African culture and established contact with the Yorubas (black cubans); published 1st book of fiction *Contes nègres de Cuba* (Black Stories from Cuba, 1936); other works include *Pourquoi contes nègres de Cuba* (Why Black Stories from Cuba, 1954), *El monte* (The Forest, 1954), *Anaforuana* (1975), *Otán Iyebiye* (1986), and a Congolese dictionary.

CABRINI, Frances Xavier (1850–1917). Italian nun and saint. Name variations: Francesca Maria Cabrini (1850–1874); Sister Saveria or Xavier Angelica (1874–1879); Mother Francesca Saveria or Frances Xavier Cabrini (1879–1917). Born Francesca Maria Cabrini, July 15, 1850, at Sant'Angelo Lodigiano in the Lombardy region of Italy; died in Chicago, Illinois, Dec 22, 1917; dau. of Agostino Cabrini (Lombard farmer) and Stella Oldini Cabrini; never married; no children. ❖ Charity entrepreneur and champion of Italian immigrants in the US, taught school in Lombardy (1868–74); became orphanage worker and novice in Codogno (1877); took vows as a nun and promoted to superior (1877); founded Missionary Sisters of the Sacred Heart (1881); immigrated to NY (1889); founded a school in Nicaragua (1891); opened Columbus Hospital in NYC (1892); became naturalized US citizen (1909); named superior for life of the Missionary Sisters of the Sacred Heart (1910); beatified (Nov 1938); became 1st American citizen to be elevated to sainthood in the Roman Catholic Church (July 7, 1946). ❖ See also Lucille P. Borden, *Francesca Cabrini: Without Staff or Scrip* (Macmillan, 1945); Mary Louise Sullivan, MSC. *Mother Cabrini: Italian Immigrant of the Century* (Center for Migration Studies, 1992); and *Women in World History.*

CACCAMISI, Baroness A. (1863–1940). See Marchesi, Blanche.

CACCHI, Paola (1945—). Italian runner. Born Dec 30, 1945, in Italy. ❖ At Munich Olympics, won a bronze medal in the 1,500-meters (1972).

CACCIALANZA, Gisella (1914–1998). American ballet dancer. Name variations: Giselle Caccialanza; Gisella C. Christensen. Born Sept 17, 1914, in San Diego, California; died July 16, 1998, in San Bruno, California; m. Lew Christensen (dancer, died 1984). ❖ Trained and worked with Enrico Cecchetti in Milan (1925–28); toured in US with Albertina Rasch's dance troupes; joined Balanchine's newly formed American Ballet and created roles in his *Serenade* (1934), *Le Baiser de la Fée* (1937), *Ballet Imperial* (1941) and *Four Temperaments* (1946); danced in Ballet Caravan in premieres of *Harlequin for President* (1936), *Promenade* (1936) and *The Soldier and the Gypsy* (1936); danced with husband Lew Christensen at San Francisco Ballet in CA, before retiring to teach and coach.

CACCINI, Francesca (1587–c. 1626). Italian composer, singer and teacher. Name variations: Signorini, La Cecchina. Born in Florence, Italy, Sept 18, 1587; died c. 1626 (some sources cite 1640), possibly in Florence; dau. of Giulio Caccini (c. 1546–1618, revolutionary composer and instrumentalist) and a musical mother (name unknown); sister of Settimia Caccini (c. 1591–c. 1638); m. Giovanni Battista Signorini Malaspina. ❖ Known as "La Cecchina," was proficient on the lute, guitar, and harpsichord; appeared with mother and sister Settimia, taking part in lavish musical productions; also appeared with them in Paris (1604–05); began composing at the prompting of poet Buonarroti; at the Florentine court, served the Medici; wrote *La liberazione di Ruggiero dall' isola d'Alcina,* the 1st known opera by a woman (1625), and the 1st Italian opera to be performed abroad. ❖ See also *Women in World History.*

CÁCERES, Esther de (1903–1971). *Uruguayan poet and essayist.* Name variations: Esther de Caceres. Born 1903 in Montevideo, Uruguay; died 1971. ❖ Worked as attaché in Uruguayan embassy in Washington; wrote poetry noted for its musicality and intensity of feeling; writings include *Las ínsulas extrañas* (1929), *Canción de Esther Cáceres* (1931), *Cruz y éxtasis de la Pasión* (Cross and Ecstasy of the Passion, 1937), *Espejo sin muerte* (Mirror without Death, 1941), *Antología de Esther de Cáceres (1929–1945)* (1945), *Paso de la noche* (Passage of the Night, 1957), *Tiempo y abismo* (Time and Abyss, 1965) and *Canto desierto* (Desert Song, 1969).

CACHAT, Beth (1951—). *American dancer and choreographer.* Born Feb 18, 1951, in Cleveland, Ohio. ❖ Trained in acting and ballet; studied modern dance with Louis Falco, Merce Cunningham, Viola Farber, and others; performed in contemporary works by such choreographers as Kathryn Bernson and Martha Wiseman; created and presented numerous works in and around New York City to critical acclaim; choreographies include *My Grandfather's Nose* (1977), *Blue* (1978), *Long Division* (1978), *Mirage* (1979), *Elegy* (1979), *Rocky Mountain Suite* (1979) and *Wind Chimes* (1980).

CÄCILIE, Fanny (1805–1847). *See Mendelssohn-Hensel, Fanny.*

CADBURY, Dorothy Adlington (1892–1987). *English botanist.* Born Dorothy Adlington Cadbury, Oct 14, 1892, in Birmingham, England; died Aug 21, 1987; dau. of Barrow Cadbury (chair of Cadbury Bros, Ltd., 1922–32) and Geraldine Southall Cadbury (1865–1941); sister of Geraldine Mary "Cherry" Cadbury and Paul Cadbury. ❖ Known for pondweeds expertise and for assembling roughly 400 collections of *Potamogeton* (British species and natural hybrids in Britain) for British Museum; collected and studied wildflowers from youth and joined Wild Flower Society as Warwickshire recorder (1929); became member of Botanical Society of the British Isles (1936); created complete list of flowering plants in Edgbaston Park after joining Birmingham Natural History Society (BNHS, 1950); served as director of Cadbury Bros. in Bournville, Birmingham, until 1952. Hybrid *Potamogeton x. cadburyae* named after her.

CADBURY, Geraldine Southall (1865–1941). *English social reformer.* Name variations: Dame Geraldine Cadbury. Born Geraldine Southall in 1865; died Jan 30, 1941; m. Barrow Cadbury (chair of Cadbury Bros, Ltd., 1922–32); children: Geraldine Mary "Cherry" Cadbury; Paul Cadbury; Dorothy Adlington Cadbury (botanist). ❖ Social activist, long involved in the Birmingham Quaker peace movement. Made DBE (1937). ❖ See also Maggie Goodrich, *Geraldine Cadbury, 1865–1941: The Problem of Deprived and Delinquent Children (Social Reformers)* and Percy W. Bartlett *Barrow Cadbury: A Memoir* (1960).

CADBURY, Rachel (b. 1894). *British pacifist.* Born Rachel Wilson in 1894; m. Paul Cadbury (son of Geraldine Southall Cadbury). ❖ Had a Quaker background; was a VAD nurse during Boer War, serving with Friends Ambulance Unit in Devon (c. 1916–17) and in France (1917–19).

CADDEN, Mamie (c. 1894–1959). *Irish murderer.* Name variations: Marie Anne Cadden. Born c. 1894 in Ireland; died April 20, 1959, in Dundrum, Ireland. ❖ After Helen O'Reilly was found dead in Dublin from a botched abortion (1956), was charged with murder, tried and found guilty; death sentence was commuted to life imprisonment; was transferred to Dundrum Central Criminal Lunatic Asylum (1958).

CADE, Toni (1939–1995). *See Bambara, Toni Cade.*

CADELL, Jean (1884–1967). *Scottish actress.* Born Sept 13, 1884, in Edinburgh, Scotland; died Sept 24, 1967, in London, England; m. P. Percival Clark. ❖ Appeared on stage in England and America for over 50 years; made London debut in *The Chair of Love* (1911); made Broadway debut in *Bunty Pulls the Strings* (1911); other plays include *The Old Lady Shows Her Medals, The Young Person in Pink, The Enchanted Cottage, At Mrs. Beam's, The Importance of Being Earnest* and *Marigold,* as Mrs. Pringle, which she played over 600 times; also appeared on tv and in numerous films.

CADIÈRE, Catherine (b. 1709). *French woman accused of witchcraft.* Name variations: Catherine Cadiere. Born 1709; went to trial for witchcraft in 1731. ❖ See also *Women in World History.*

CADILLA DE MARTÍNEZ, Maria (1886–1951). *Puerto Rican writer, academic, and folklorist.* Name variations: Maria Cadilla de Martinez; Maria Tomasa Cadilla y Colón; Liana Cadilla de Martínez. Born Dec 21, 1886, in Arecibo, Puerto Rico; died Aug 21, 1951, in Arecibo; dau. of Armindo Cadilla y Fernandez (navy official) and Catalina Colón y Nieves; University of Puerto Rico, AB, 1928, AM, 1930; doctorate from Universidad Central (Madrid), 1933; m. Julio Tomas Martínez Mirabal (architect), 1903; children: María, Tomasita. ❖ Memorable figure in Puerto Rican cultural history, was instrumental in focusing attention upon the indigenous Latin culture of her island, and her research, writings, and academic work helped the folk arts of Puerto Rico achieve recognition as an important part of its past; became professor of Hispanic history and literature at University of Puerto Rico (1916); published 1st book, *Cuentos a Lillian* (Stories for Lillian, 1925); doctoral thesis, *La Poesía Popular en Puerto Rico* (Popular Poetry in Puerto Rico), became a standard textbook at the university level; writings include *Cantos y Juegos Infantiles de Puerto Rico* (Puerto Rican Songs and Children's Games, 1938), *Costumbres y Tradicionalismos de mi Tierra* (Customs and Traditions of My Country, 1939), *Raíces de la Tierra* (Roots from the Earth, 1941) and *Rememorando el Pasado Heroico* (Remembering our Historic Past, 1946); served as vice-president of Puerto Rico's Suffrage Association and was also involved in the Insular Association of Women Voters; was the only female member of Academy of History of Puerto Rico. ❖ See also *Women in World History.*

CADILLA Y COLÓN, Maria Tomasa (1886–1951). *See Cadilla de Martínez, Maria.*

CADIZ, duchess of. *See Louisa Carlotta of Naples (1804–1844).*

CADOGAN, Sarah (1706–1751). *Duchess of Richmond.* Name variations: Sarah Lennox. Born Sarah Cadogan, Sept 18, 1706; died Aug 25, 1751; dau. of William Cadogan, 1st Earl Cadogan, and Margaretta Cecilia Munter; m. Charles Lennox, 2nd duke of Richmond, 1719; children: Caroline Lennox (1723–1774), Emily Lennox (1731–1814), Louisa Lennox (1743–1821), Sarah Lennox (1745–1826), George Lennox (died 1895); Charles Lennox (died 1806), 3rd duke of Richmond.

CADUFF, Sylvia (1937—). *Swiss conductor.* Born in Chur, Switzerland, Jan 7, 1937; attended Lucerne Conservatory; studied with Herbert von Karajan in Berlin, becoming a 1st-class conductor during her 3-year apprenticeship. ❖ Was the 1st woman to win the Dimitri Mitropoulos Competition (1966); served as assistant conductor to Leonard Bernstein at NY Philharmonic; returned to Europe and made several guest appearances, including British debut conducting the Royal Philharmonic Orchestra at Royal Festival Hall (1967); was general director of the Orchestra of the City of Solingen, Germany, the 1st European woman to hold such a position. ❖ See also *Women in World History.*

CADY, H. Emilie (1848–1941). *American New Thought healer and writer.* Name variations: Harriette Emilie Cady. Born 1848 in Drysden, Syracuse; died 1941. ❖ Practiced homeopathy in NY (1880s); influenced by New Thought leaders, became interested in faith healing; published regularly in *Unity* (from 1892); writing collections include the Unity textbook, *Lessons in Truth* (1908), *God a Present Help* (1908), and *Miscellaneous Writings* (1916), later titled *How I Used Truth.*

CAEMMERER, Hanna von (1914–1971). *See Neumann, Hanna.*

CAESAR, Doris Porter (1892–1971). *American sculptor of bronze figures.* Born Doris Porter in Brooklyn, New York, 1892; died in Litchfield, Connecticut, 1971: dau. of a lawyer; attended Spence School for girls and Art Students League; studied with George Bridgman and Alexander Archipenko; married, 1913; children: 2 sons, 1 daughter. ❖ Distorted her figure pieces until they were almost "stick-like," an Expressionistic device evident in sculpture groups like *Mother and Child* (1947) and *Descent from the Cross* (1950). Following her death, 40 of her pieces were included in the 4-person show, *Four American Expressionists,* at Whitney Museum (1959).

CAESAR, Mary (1677–1741). *British letter writer and diarist.* Born 1677 in England; died 1741 in England; m. Charles Caesar (Tory MP for Hertford). ❖ Jacobite whose husband was imprisoned in the Tower of London for his involvement in the Gyllenborg plot (1705), kept a journal, a source of information concerning English Jacobite culture and activity; corresponded with Alexander Pope, Jonathan Swift, Matthew Prior, and the 1st earl of Oxford. ❖ See also *Memoirs of Mrs. Mary Caesar, 1705–1741* (Vol. 1).

CAESONIA (d. 41). *See Milonia Caesonia.*

CAFFYN, Kathleen (1853–1926). Irish novelist. Name variations: Mrs. Mannington Caffyn; (pseudonym) Iota. Born Kathleen Goring in 1853 at Waterloo House, Co. Tipperary, Ireland; died 1926; dau. of William and Louisa Hunt Goring; educated at home; had nurses' training at St. Thomas' Hospital; m. Stephen Mannington Caffyn (1850–1896, surgeon, writer, and inventor). ❖ Noted for her skill at characterization and the intense romantic and sensual qualities of her books, wrote 17 novels; lived in Australia with husband (1880–92); following return to Ireland, published 1st novel, *A Yellow Aster* (1893), which was enormously successful; often writing under pseudonym Iota, wrote most of her books after husband's death (1896); works include: *A Comedy in Spasms, Children of Circumstances, A Quaker Grandmother, Poor Max, Anne Mauleverer, The Minx, The Happiness of Jill* and *Dorinda and Her Daughter.*

CAFFYN, Mrs. Mannington (1853–1926). *See Caffyn, Kathleen.*

CAGNEY, Frances (1901–1994). American dancer. Name variations: Billie Vernon; Frances Willard Vernon. Born Frances Willard Vernon, June 19, 1901; died Oct 10, 1994, in Fishkill, NY; m. James Cagney (actor), Sept 28, 1922 (died Mar 30, 1986). ❖ In vaudeville, had a sister act with Wynne Gibson, then toured with husband.

CAGNEY, Jeanne (1919–1984). American stage, screen, radio and tv actress. Name variations: Jean Cagney. Born Jeanne Carolyn Cagney, Mar 25, 1919, in New York, NY; died Dec 7, 1984, in Newport Beach, California; sister of William Cagney (actor-producer) and James Cagney (actor); m. Jack Morrison, 1953. ❖ Made stage debut at Pasadena Playhouse in *Brother Rat* (1938) and NY debut in *I'll Take the High Road* (1943), followed by *The Streets Are Guarded, A Place of Our Own, The Iceman Cometh* and *Accent on Youth;* films include *Rhythm on the River, Golden Gloves, Queen of the Mob, Yankee Doodle Dandy, The Time of Your Life, Don't Bother to Knock, A Lion in the Streets* and *Man of a Thousand Faces.*

CAHAN, Cora (1940—). American modern dancer. Born Feb 26, 1940, in Brooklyn, NY. ❖ Trained with May O'Donnell at High School of Performing Arts and with Norman Walker at Juilliard, and continued to work with both throughout career; danced O'Donnell's role in revivals of her *Suspension* and danced major parts for her in *Brandenburg Concerto No. 5, Pelleas and Melisande* and *Dance Sonata;* briefly danced with companies of Pearl Lang and Helen Tamiris, and joined faculty of Juilliard School (late 1950s); danced lead in Walker's *Meditation of Orpheus* (1964), *The Testament of Cain, The Chanter* (1965), and *Eloges* (1967); served on dance faculty of University of Cincinnati (mid-1960s); worked as administrator and executive director of Eliot Feld Ballet in NY where she helped turn a half-empty building into the prosperous Lawrence A. Wien Center for Dance and Theater; served as president of The New 42nd Street Inc., a non-profit arts organization; choreographed works include *Iphigenia* (1971).

CAHILL, Lily (1885–1955). American actress. Name variations: Lilly Cahill. Born July 17, 1885, in San Antonio, Texas; died July 20, 1955, in San Antonia; m. Brandon Tynan (actor). ❖ Made stage debut on tour with Mrs. Leslie Carter in *Vesta Hearne* (1909); other appearances include *The Concert, Joseph and His Brethren, Under Cover, The Purple Mask, So This is London, Caprice, Chrysalis, Alien Corn* and *First Lady;* made last stage appearance as Vinnie in *Life with Father* (1945); films include *The Failure, Colonel Carter of Cartersville* and *My Sin.*

CAHILL, Mabel E. (1863–?). Irish-American tennis player. Born April 2, 1863, in Ireland; death date unknown. ❖ Moved to US (1880s); won US singles championships (1891, 1892), women's doubles (1891, 1892) and mixed doubles (1892).

CAHILL, Margaret (1905–1995). *See Gorman, Margaret.*

CAHILL, Marie (1870–1933). American actress. Born Dec 20, 1870, possibly in Brooklyn, NY; died Aug 23, 1933, in New York, NY; dau. of Richard and Marie (Grogean) Cahill (both Irish); m. Daniel V. Arthur (business manager), June 18, 1903. ❖ Worked as popular musical-comedy and vaudeville performer for 4 decades; played at Poole's Eighth Street Theatre (NY) in *COD* and had 1st musical-theater comedy role as Patsy in *The Tin Soldier* (1888); performed under direction of managers Augustin Daly and George Lederer; became headliner with

song "Nancy Brown" from *The Wild Rose;* appeared in title role of *The Boys and Betty* (1908), as Buttercup in *HMS Pinafore* (1911), Celeste Deremy in *The Opera Ball* (1912), Polly Bainbridge in *Ninety in the Shade* (1915) and Gloria Wentworth in *The New Yorkers* (1930).

CAHINA (r. ca. 695–703). *See Kahina.*

CAHUN, Claude (1894–1954). French photographer. Born Lucy Schwob in France in 1894; died in Jersey, England, 1954; dau. of Maurice Schwob; niece of Marcel Schwob, son of the publisher of *Le Phare* (The Lighthouse), a newspaper in Nantes, France. ❖ Specializing in Surrealist photographs and photomontages, launched career with 200-page Surrealist text (*Cancelled Confessions*), containing 10 photomontages (1930); included in *Surrealist Exhibition of Objects* at Galerie Charles Ratton in Paris (1934); was also associated with Georges Bataille's group, Contre-Attaque, founded in 1935; later work included illustrations for a book of poems, *The Pick-Axe Heart,* by Lise Deharme. ❖ See also *Women in World History.*

CAI CHANG (1900–1990). Chinese politician. Name variations: Ts'ai Ch'ang, or incorrectly Tsai Chang. Pronunciation: Cai (rhymes with sigh). Born Cai Chang in Hunan province, China, 1900; died Sept 11, 1990, in Beijing, at age 90; dau. of mother Ge Jianhao (Ke chien-hao); sister of Cai Hesen (1890–1931); attended Zhou Nan Girls' Normal School in Changsha; sister-in-law of Xiang Jingyü (1895–1928); m. Li Fuqun (economist and revolutionary), 1923; children: 1 daughter. ❖ One of the 1st female members of the Chinese Communist Party, rose to hold its most important post in the women's movement: chair of the National Women's Federation; attended Collège de Montargis, south of Paris; attended a special school for Asian revolutionaries, University of the Toilers of the East, in Soviet Union (1924–25); like many Communists, held joint membership in both Guomindang and CCP and served in many posts for both parties, rising quickly through the ranks; when Mao Zedong gained full control over the CCP on the Long March (1934–35), became leader of its important women's movement; became the only full female member of the Central Committee (1945); became 1st chair of All-China Women's Federation (1949); was a member of the Central Committee (1928–82). ❖ See also *Women in World History.*

CAI HUIJUE. Chinese swimmer. Born in Shanghai, China; attended Binghamton University. ❖ Won a bronze medal for 4x100-meter relay at Atlanta Olympics (1996); banned from international competition by FINA for failing a drug test (1998).

CAI WENJI (c. 162–239). *See Cai Yan.*

CAI YAN (c. 162–239). Chinese composer and poet. Name variations: Caiyan or Ts'ai Yen; Cai Wenji. Born c. 162, during the time of the Han Dynasty; died c. 239; dau. of the scholar and poet Cai (Ts'ai) I, also known as Cai Yong; widowed c. 192; children: 2 sons. ❖ The 1st Chinese female poet whose life and writings are documented, had been married and widowed before being captured and taken North by the Huns; for next 12 years, was a captive and had two sons by a Hun chieftain; when her family found her and paid a ransom, had to return to China without her boys; though attribution is uncertain, likely wrote *Eighteen verses,* which describes the life she endured—war, barbarism, and grief—meant to be accompanied by lute and Tatar horn. ❖ See also *Women in World History.*

CAIEL or CAÏEL (1860–1929). *See Pestana, Alice.*

CAILLAUX, Henriette (?–1943). French murderer. Born Henriette Rainouard; died 1943; 2nd wife of Joseph Caillaux (1863–1944, member of chamber of deputies, premier of France [1911–1912], French minister of finance). ❖ After *Le Figaro* editor Gaston Calmette went on a 2-month campaign against her husband (1914), printing some 138 articles and cartoons aimed at discrediting the minister's political and personal life, purchased a Browning revolver, visited the newspaper offices of *Le Figaro,* and fired 4 bullets into Calmette, who died that night of his injuries; at her trial, was found innocent of premeditated murder and sent home, shocking the nation and the press. ❖ See also Edward Berenson, *The Trial of Madame Caillaux* (U. of California Press, 1992); and *Women in World History.*

CAIRD, Maureen (1951—). Australian hurdler. Born Sept 29, 1951, in Cumberland, NSW, Australia. ❖ At Mexico City Olympics, age 17, won a gold medal in the 80-meter hurdles (1968); won a silver medal at Commonwealth Games (1970) for 100-meter hurdles.

CAIRD, Mona Alison (1858–1932). British novelist and essayist. Name variations: Alice Mona Caird; Mrs. Mona Hector Caird; (pseudonym)

G. Noel Hatton. Born 1858 in Ryde, Isle of Wight, England; died Feb 4, 1932, in London, England; dau. of an inventor named Hector; m. A. Henryson-Caird, 1877. ❖ Wrote essays on marriage, collected in *The Morality of Marriage* (1891), which linked inequality to marriage and brought criticism from conservatives; also a passionate anti-vivisectionist, wrote *Legalized Torture* and *The Savagery of Vivisection* (1894–95); novels include *A Romance of the Moors* (1891) and *The Daughters of Danaus* (1894).

CAIRNS, Elizabeth (1685–1714). Scottish Dissenting preacher and memoirist. Born 1685 in Scotland; died 1714. ❖ Deeply religious Calvinist with mystical and visionary leanings, worked as shepherd and schoolteacher; kept a journal of her daily existence and religious experiences.

CAJAL, Rosa María (1920—). Spanish novelist. Name variations: Rosa Maria Cajal. Born 1920 in Zaragoza, Spain. ❖ Novels, which are feminist and Existentialist in tone, include *Juan Risco* (1948), *Primera derecha* (1955), and *Un paso más* (1956).

CAJANELLO, duchess of. See Edgren, Anne Charlotte (1849–1892).

CAJU (1871–1920). See Júlia, Francisca.

CALAMAI, Clara (1915–1998). Italian actress. Born Sept 7, 1915, in Prato, Tuscany, Italy; died Sept 21, 1998, in Rimini, Emilia-Romagna, Italy; m. Leonardo Bonzi. ❖ Italy's preeminent star during WWII, made screen debut in *Pietro Micca* (1938), followed by *Ettore Fieramosca, Boccaccio, Regina di Navarra, La Cena delle beffe, L'Adultera, La Resa di Titi* (*The Merry Chase*), *Ultimo amore, Le Notti Bianche* (*White Nights*), *Enrico IV, Aphrodite, Le Streghe* (*The Witch*) and *La Peccatrice;* probably best remembered for performance as Giovanna Bragana in *Ossessione* (1943).

CALAMITY JANE (1852–1903). See Cannary, Martha Jane.

CALDEIRA, Hilma (1972—). Brazilian volleyball player. Name variations: Hilma Aparecida Caldeira. Born Jan 5, 1972, in Brazil. ❖ Won a team bronze medal at Atlanta Olympics (1996).

CALDER, Liz (1938—). English publisher. Name variations: Elizabeth Calder, Liz Baber. Born Elizabeth Nicole Baber in 1938 in London, England; attended Canterbury University, New Zealand; m. Richard Calder (engineer), 1958 (div. 1972). ❖ Co-founder of publishing empire Bloomsbury Plc., one of the few women at top of the publishing profession, was raised in New Zealand; moved to England and taught in Derby; when husband was posted in Brazil, worked as a fashion model there (1964–68); returned to England and managed publicity department at Victor Gollancz (1971–74), where she later served as editorial director (1975–78); joined firm of Jonathan Cape, again serving as editorial director (1979–86); promoted such authors as Julian Barnes, Anita Brookner and Bruce Chatwin and nurtured prize-winning author Salman Rushdie; joined with Nigel Newton to become one of 4 co-founders of Bloomsbury Plc. Publishing (1986), serving as publishing director; known as the "Queen of Literature," has helped establish many prominent authors, including Isabel Allende and Margaret Atwood, and her books have won almost every major award including the Booker, Pulitzer, Whitbread and Nobel Prize; maintains a house in Brazil, where she has organized a literary festival in the resort town of Parati, with the goal of raising the profile of Brazilian authors.

CALDERÓN, Sila M. (1942—). Puerto Rican politician. Name variations: Calderon. Born Sept 23, 1942, in San Juan, Puerto Rico; Manhattanville College (Purchase, NY), BA in government, 1964; attended Graduate School of Public Administration at University of Puerto Rico; m. twice; children: 2 daughters, 1 son. ❖ As a member of Popular Democrat Party, served for 8 years as mayor of San Juan; was elected the 1st woman governor of Puerto Rico (2001); led a successful effort to halt US naval bombing exercises at nearby Vieques Island; opposes US statehood for Puerto Rico.

CALDERÓN DE LA BARCA, Frances (1804–1882). Scottish-American woman of letters and traveler. Name variations: Fanny Calderon. Born Frances Erskine Inglis, Dec 23, 1804, in Edinburgh, Scotland; died Feb 6, 1882, in Madrid, Spain; dau. of William Inglis (prominent attorney) and Jane (Stein) Inglis; m. Angel Calderón de la Barca (aristocratic Spanish civil servant and diplomat), Sept 24, 1838; no children. ❖ Companion to the royal family of Spain, whose observations of Mexico in the age of Antonio López de Santa Anna are considered among the finest of the travel-literature genre; moved with widowed mother and 4 siblings to Boston, where she helped operate the family's private school (1831); moved with family to New York where they established a 2nd school on Staten Island (1837); moved with husband, Angel Calderón de la Barca, to Mexico City, where he was the 1st Spanish diplomat posted to Mexico (1839); stationed in Washington (1844–53); wrote much-respected *Life in Mexico* (1843); after Angel's recall to Spain to serve as foreign minister, forced by revolution to flee to France (1854); returned to Spain (1856), where Angel served as senator while she attended the royal court and wrote her 2nd book, *The Attaché in Madrid* (1856); after death of husband, became tutor to Princess Maria Isabel Francisca, serving in the household of Spain's royal family as educator, friend and confidante (1861); awarded patent of nobility, as the Marquesa de Calderón de la Barca (1876). ❖ See also *Women in World History.*

CALDERON DIAZ, Rosir (1984—). Cuban volleyball player. Born Dec 28, 1984, in Cuba. ❖ Won a team bronze medal at Athens Olympics (2004).

CALDERON MARTINEZ, Mercedes (1965—). Cuban volleyball player. Born Sept 1965. ❖ At Barcelona Olympics, won a gold medal in team competition (1992).

CALDERONE, Mary Steichen (1904–1998). American reformer. Name variations: Mary Steichen; Mary Steichen Martin. Born Mary Steichen in New York City, July 1, 1904; died Oct 24, 1998, in Kennett Square, Pennsylvania; dau. of Edward Steichen (photographer) and Clara (Smith) Steichen; Vassar College, BA, 1925; University of Rochester Medical School, MD, 1939; Columbia University, MA in Public Health, 1941; m. W. Lon Martin, 1926 (div. 1933); m. Frank Calderone, Nov 27, 1941; children: (1st m.) Nell (d. 1935) and Linda; (2nd m.) Francesca and Maria. ❖ Pioneer in the development of responsible sex education for children and adults, became medical director of Planned Parenthood (1953), a position she held until 1964; named 1st executive director of Sex Information and Education Council of the US, Inc. (SIECUS, 1965), a clearinghouse on sexuality, providing individuals and organizations with information on reproduction, premarital sex, masturbation, homosexuality, frigidity, and impotence; became president of SIECUS (1975); retired from active involvement in SIECUS (1982); held a lectureship in sexuality at New York University (1982–88); firmly believed that if ordinary people had access to information relating to human sexuality they would make responsible and rational decisions about sex; is credited with taking information on procreation and sexuality out of the exclusive domain of professional circles and putting it into homes and public schools across America. ❖ See also *Women in World History.*

CALDERWOOD, Margaret (1715–1774). Scottish diarist. Name variations: Margaret Stuart Calderwood. Born Margaret Stuart, 1715, in Scotland; died 1774; dau. of Sir James Stuart and Anne Dalrymple; sister of James Stuart (1713–1780), economist and Scottish nationalist); m. Thomas Calderwood, 1775. ❖ Known chiefly for journals recounting journey through England, Holland, and Belgium en route to join her brother Sir James Stuart, who was living in exile (1745–63) after the 2nd Jacobite rising (he had backed Bonnie Prince Charlie); wrote unpublished novel, *The Adventures of Fanny Roberts,* and unpublished journal about management of husband's estates; journals published as *Letters and Journals of Mrs. Calderwood* (1884).

CALDICOTT, Helen (1938—). Australian pediatrician, anti-nuclear campaigner, conservationist, and orator. Pronunciation: COLD-ee-cot. Born Helen Mary Broinowski, Aug 7, 1938, in Melbourne, Victoria, Australia; dau. of Philip Broinowski (paint factory manager) and Mary Mona Enyd (Coffey) Broinowski (interior designer); attended University of Adelaide Medical School, Bachelor of Medicine and Bachelor of Surgery, 1961, Paediatrics, 1975; lived with family in America (1966–69), where she had a fellowship at Harvard Medical School in Boston; m. William Caldicott (pediatric radiologist), Dec 8, 1962 (div. 1988); children: Phillip (b. 1964); Penelope Mary Caldicott (b. 1965); William (b. 1967). ❖ The brightest star in the anti-nuclear movement, brought about cessation of French atmospheric nuclear testing in the Pacific (1971–72); moved to US (1977), where she was a fellow in cystic fibrosis and an associate in medicine at Children's Hospital Medical Center and an instructor in pediatrics at Harvard Medical School; published *Nuclear Madness: What You Can Do* (1978); resigned as pediatrician (1980); resurrected, and was national president of, Physicians for Social Responsibility (1978–83); founded Women's Party for Survival (WPFS, 1980) and Women's Action for Nuclear Disarmament (WAND, 1980), an influential Washington-based lobby group; published *Missile Envy* (1984); nominated for Nobel Peace Prize (1986); returned to Australia (1986); founded Green Labor political faction within the Australian Labor Party (1988); ran (unsuccessfully) for Parliament (1990); published *If You Love This Planet* (1992). Won British Medical Association Prize for Clinical Medicine (1960) and prize for Surgical Anatomy (1961); received Margaret Mead award for defense of the environment, Gandhi Peace Prize, Thomas Merton Peace Prize, and Boston Ethical Society's Humanist of the Year (1980); UN Association for Australia Peace Medal Award (1985); her Physicians for Social Responsibility won the Nobel Peace Prize (1985); (with Bishop Desmond Tutu and Los Angeles Mayor Tom Bradley) given John-Roger Foundation Integrity Award (1985); won Academy Award for best short documentary, *If You Love This Planet* (1983). ❖ See also autobiography *A Desperate Passion* (1996); and *Women in World History*.

CALDWELL, Anne (1876–1936). American lyricist and composer. Name variations: Anne O'Dea. Born Anne Marsh Caldwell in Boston, Massachusetts, 1876; died Oct 22, 1936; m. James O'Dea. ❖ Prolific Broadway lyricist, collaborated with Jerome Kern on 8 musicals, for which she wrote lyrics and often the librettos, and provided lyrics for one of Kern's collaborations with Otto Harbach, *Criss Cross,* which included the songs "In Araby with You," "You Will, Won't You?" and "I Love My Little Susie"; also collaborated on songs for films *Babes in Toyland* and *Flying Down to Rio.* ❖ See also *Women in World History*.

CALDWELL, Anne Marsh (1791–1874). See Marsh-Caldwell, Anne.

CALDWELL, Marianne (1866–1933). English actress. Born Marianne Lipsett, 1866, in Dominica, West Indies; died May 18, 1933. ❖ Made London debut (1886); appeared in *Mamma, The Profligate, The Cabinet Minister, Magda, The School Girl, The Light that Failed, Billy, As You Like It* and *The Sphinx,* among others; appeared for several seasons with Forbes Robertson's company; engaged by Oscar Asche at His Majesty's Theatre during the run of *Chu Chin Chow* (1916–21).

CALDWELL, Mary Gwendolin (1863–1909). American philanthropist and founder. Name variations: Mamie; Marquise des Monstiers-Mérinville. Born Mary Gwendolin Caldwell in Louisville, Kentucky, 1863; died Oct 5, 1909, aboard the German liner *Kronprinzessin Cecile* outside New York; dau. of William Shakespeare Caldwell and Mary Eliza (Breckinridge) Caldwell; attended Academy of the Sacred Heart, New York; m. François Jean Louis, Marquis des Monstiers-Mérinville, Oct 19, 1896 (sep. 1905). ❖ With sister, became a ward of Roman Catholic friends and also inherited several million dollars when father died (1874); founded what became the Catholic University of America, incorporated in the District of Columbia (1887); renounced her faith (1904). Received Laetare Medal from Notre Dame University (1899). ❖ See also *Women in World History*.

CALDWELL, Sarah (1924–2006). American operatic conductor and impresario. Born Sarah Caldwell in Maryville, Missouri, Mar 6, 1924; died Mar 23, 2006, in Portland, Maine; attended University of Arkansas and New England Conservatory of Music; never married. ❖ Leading figure on the Boston music scene, known for her innovative interpretations of operatic works, entered New England Conservatory of Music to continue violin studies (1942); won a scholarship as a violinist at Berkshire Music Center at Tanglewood (1946); staged Vaughan Williams' *Riders to the Sea* at Berkshire (1947); engaged as assistant to Boris Goldovsky, founder of New England Opera Co. (1947); headed Boston University's opera workshop (1952–60); founded Opera Company of Boston (1958); organized a concert of music by women conductors (1976); became 1st woman to conduct the orchestra of Metropolitan Opera in NY (1976); organized cultural exchanges involving several hundred Soviet and American musicians (1988 and 1991). ❖ See also *Women in World History*.

CALDWELL, Taylor (1900–1985). English-American writer. Name variations: (pseudonym) Max Reiner. Born Janet Miriam Taylor Caldwell, Sept 7, 1900, in Prestwich, Manchester, England; died Aug 30, 1985, in Greenwich, Connecticut; dau. of Anna (Marks or Markham) Caldwell and Arthur Francis Caldwell (commercial artist); University of Buffalo, BA, 1931; m. William Fairfax Coombes (sometimes spelled Combs), May 27, 1919 (div. 1931); m. Marcus Reback (linguist and advisor to Herbert Hoover), May 12, 1931 (died 1970); m. William E. Stancell, June 17, 1972; m. William Robert Prestie, 1978; children: (1st m.) Mary Margaret Coombes Fried; (2nd m.) Judith Ann Reback Goodman (died 1979). ❖ Writer whose historical romances were bestsellers and often adapted as motion pictures, moved to US with family (1907); beginning with *Dynasty of Death* (1938), became a popular romance novelist; was also a founding member of New York State Conservative Party, and her stories often reflect her traditional views;

writings include *The Eagles Gather* (1940), *The Earth Is the Lord's* (1941), (under pseudonym Max Reiner) *Time No Longer* (1941), *Let Love Come Last* (1949), *Tender Victory* (1956), *The Sound of Thunder* (1957), *Dear and Glorious Physician* (1959), *A Prologue to Love* (1961), *The Late Clara Beame* (1963), *A Pillar of Iron* (1965), *Captains and the Kings* (1973), *Glory and Lightening* (1974), (with Jess Stearn) *The Romance of Atlantis* (1975), *Ceremony of the Innocent* (1977), (with Stearn) *I, Judas* (1977), *Bright Flows the River* (1978) and *Answer as a Man* (1981). ❖ See also memoir, *On Growing Up Tough* (Devin-Adair, 1971); Jess Stearn, *In Search of Taylor Caldwell* (Stein & Day, 1981); and *Women in World History*.

CALDWELL, Zoë (1933—). Australian actress and director. Name variations: Zoe Caldwell. Born Sept 14, 1933, in Melbourne, Australia; attended Methodist Ladies College; m. Robert Whitehead (theatrical producer), 1968 (died 2002); children: 2 sons, including Charles Whitehead (producer). ❖ Highly successful stage actress and director, studied dance, elocution and music when young; made theatrical debut at 9 in *Peter Pan* and worked on national radio soap operas as a teenager; was one of the original members of Melbourne's Union Theatre Repertory Co. (1954–57); made British debut at Stratford-upon-Avon (1958); joined Royal Court Co. (1960); helped launch Tyrone Guthrie Theater in Minnesota (1963); made Broadway debut in *The Devils* (1965); won Best Actress Tonys for performances in *Slapstick Tragedy* (1966), *The Prime of Miss Jean Brodie* (1968), *Medea* (1982), and *Master Class* (1995); also worked as theatrical director, most notably for Broadway productions of *Othello* and *Park Your Car at Harvard Yard,* as well as off-Broadway hit *Vita & Virginia;* collaborated with husband on *The Prime of Miss Jean Brodie* and *Medea* and with son Charles on *The Play What I Wrote* (2003); also worked in tv and film, appearing briefly in Woody Allen's *The Purple Rose of Cairo* (1985) and more prominently in *Macbeth* (1961), *Medea* (1983), and as Sarah Bernhardt in *Sarah* (1976). Awarded Order of British Empire (OBE, 1970). ❖ See also Zoë Caldwell, *I Will Be Cleopatra: An Actress's Journey* (Norton, 2001).

CALHOUN, Alice (1900–1966). American actress. Born Alice Beatrice Calhoun, Nov 21, 1900, in Cleveland, Ohio; died June 3, 1966, in Los Angeles, California; m. Mendel B. Silverburg; m. Max C. Chotiner (broker). ❖ Appeared in 52 films as a featured player for Vitagraph and Warner Bros., including *Gentlemen Prefer Blondes, Everybody's Business, Show Girl, Between Friends, The Man Next Door, Angel of Crooked Street, One Stolen Night* and *The Little Minister.*

CALHOUN, Catherine (1875–1958). See Doucet, Catherine.

CALHOUN, Marge (fl. 1950s). American surfer. Born in California; children: Candy and Robin Calhoun (surfers). ❖ Surfing pioneer, won the Makaha International (1958); worked as a stunt woman in movies. Inducted into Surfing Hall of Fame (2003). ❖ See also "Heart of the Sea" (documentary, PBS) and Andrea Gabbard, *Girl in the Curl* (Seal Press).

CALISHER, Hortense (b. 1911). American fiction writer. Born Hortense Calisher, Dec 20, 1911, in New York, NY; dau. of Hedwig (Lichstern) Calisher (German-Jewish émigré) and Joseph Henry Calisher (Jewish manufacturer); Barnard College, BA, 1932; m. Heaton Bennet Heffelfinger (engineer), 1935 (div. 1958); m. Curtis Harnack, 1959; children: (1st m.) Bennet and Peter Heffelfinger. ❖ Published 1st short-story collection, *In the Absence of Angels* (1951); taught at colleges throughout nation; published more than 15 vols. of fiction, including *False Entries* (1961), *The New Yorkers* (1969), *Queenie* (1971), *Herself* (1972), *The Collected Stories of Hortense Calisher* (1975), *On Keeping Women* (1977), *Mysteries of Motion* (1973) and *In the Palace of the Movie King* (1993). ❖ See also memoir, *Kissing Cousins: A Memory* (Weidenfeld & Nicolson, 1988); Kathleen Snodgrass, *The Fiction of Hortense Calisher* (U. of Delaware Press, 1993); and *Women in World History*.

CALKINS, Mary Whiton (1863–1930). American psychologist and philosopher. Born Mary Whiton Calkins in Hartford, Connecticut, Mar 30, 1863; died in Newton, Massachusetts, Feb 26, 1930; dau. of Wolcott (Presbyterian minister) and Charlotte Grosvenor (Whiton) Calkins; graduate of Smith College, 1885; never married; no children. ❖ One of the preeminent psychologists and philosophers of her time, was the 1st woman president of both the American Psychological Association and the American Philosophical Association; though repeatedly denied many of the professional rights and privileges extended to her male counterparts because of her gender, nonetheless rose to the top of her profession; created the paired-associate technique of learning, founded one of the 1st psychological laboratories in the country, and developed a theory of "self psychology," which she detailed in books and numerous published articles; became tutor in Greek at Wellesley College (1887), then instructor in Greek (1889) and instructor in psychology (1891); established 1st psychology laboratory at women's college (1891); appointed associate professor in psychology, Wellesley College (1894); pioneered technique of paired-associate learning (1894–95); appointed associate professor of psychology and philosophy, Wellesley College (1896); completed requirements for PhD in psychology at Harvard University, one of a handful of female graduate students at Harvard (1896); promoted to full professor, Wellesley College (1898); published *An Introduction to Psychology* (1901); published *The Persistent Problem of Philosophy* (1907), *A First Book in Psychology* (1909) and *The Good Man and The Good* (1918); retired from active teaching (1919). ❖ See also *Women in World History*.

CALL, Peggy (1926–1973). *See Castle, Peggie.*

CALLAGHAN, Audrey (1915–2005). English campaigner and fund raiser. Name variations: Lady Callaghan of Cardiff. Born Audrey Elizabeth Moulton, July 28, 1915, in Maidstone, Kent, England; died March 15, 2005; earned an economics degree from London University; m. James Callaghan (prime minister of England, 1976–79), 1938 (died Mar 27, 2005); children: Margaret (Baroness Jay, once leader of the House of Lords, b. 1940), Julia (b. 1943) and Michael (b. 1946). ❖ Though she had considerable influence over husband's campaigns, maintained a low public profile while at No. 10 Downing Street; began career as an alderman on the London borough of Lewisham and on the Greater London Council (1964–70); chaired the board of governors of the Great Ormond Street Hospital for Children (1969–82), then chaired the special trustees (1984–90); became Lady Callaghan (1987).

CALLAHAN, Sophia Alice (1868–1894). Creek novelist. Born 1868 near Sulphur Springs, Texas, of Creek descent; died of pleurisy, Jan 7, 1894, age 26, in Muskogee, Oklahoma; dau. of Samuel Benton Callahan (captain in Confederate Army, of Creek descent) and Sara Elizabeth (Thornberg) Callahan; attended Wesleyan Female Institute in Staunton, VA (1887–88). ❖ Taught at Harrell International Institute and Wealaka School; wrote *Wynema, A Child of the Forest* (1891), one of the earliest novels by a Native American woman, which focuses on Creek culture and women's rights, and defends the Sioux role in events at Wounded Knee (1890).

CALLANDER, Caroline Henrietta (1779–1851). *See Sheridan, Caroline Henrietta.*

CALLAS, Maria (1923–1977). American opera singer. Name variations: Mary, Marianna. Born Maria Cecilia Sophia Anna Kalogeropoulos, Dec 2, 1923, in NY; died in Paris, France, Sept 16, 1977; dau. of Georges (chemist) and Evangelia "Litza" (Dimitriadu) Kalogeropoulos; m. Giovanni Battista Meneghini, 1949. ❖ Family moved from Greece to NY (1923); started musical training (1930); departed for Greece with mother and sister (1937) and studied under Trivella and de Hidalgo; made operatic debut during German occupation of Greece and sang at La Scala, Milan (1951); sang *Norma* for US debut with Chicago Lyric Opera (1954); made debut at Metropolitan Opera (1956); with voice problems plaguing her performances, reduced number of engagements (late 1950s); quit opera altogether (1965) and collaborated, unsuccessfully, with Pier Paolo Pasolini, in *Medea*; taught master classes at Juilliard (1971–72); sang in public for the last time (1973), with Giuseppe di Stefano; with her powers of vocal interpretation, sparked a revival of classical coloratura roles and gave rise to recordings which significantly contributed to opera performance in the 20th century, including *Norma* (1955), *La Sonnambula* (1957), *Lucia di Lammermoor* (1953, 1955), *Medea* (1957), *Cavalleria Rusticana* (1953), *La Gioconda, Tosca* (1953), *Turandot* (1957), *Macbeth* (1952), *Rigoletto* (1955), *La Traviata* (1955), and *Aïda* (1955). ❖ See also Evangelia Callas, *My Daughter Maria Callas* (Arno, 1977); Stephen Linakis, *Diva: The Life and Death of Maria Callas* (Prentice-Hall, 1980); Michael Scott, *Maria Meneghini Callas* (Simon & Schuster, 1991); Arianna Stassinopoulos, *Maria Callas: The Woman Behind the Legend* (Simon & Schuster, 1981); John Ardoin, *The Callas Legacy: A Biography of a Career* (Scribner, 1982); and *Women in World History*.

CALLCOTT, Maria (1785–1842). English writer. Name variations: Maria Dundas; Maria Dundas Graham; Mrs. Graham; Lady Callcott. Born Maria Dundas at Papcastle, near Cockermouth, 1785; died at Kensington, near London, Nov 21, 1842; sister-in-law of John Wall Callcott (composer); m. Thomas Graham (captain in RN), in India, 1809 (died 1822); m. Sir Augustus Wall Callcott (1779–1844, landscape painter), 1827. ❖ Wrote *Journal of a Voyage to Brazil, and Residence there during part of the years 1821, 1822, 1823,* among others.

CALLEN, Maude (1899–1990). African-American nurse-midwife. Name variations: Maude Evelyn Callen. Born May 8, 1899; orphaned at age 7 and raised by an uncle in Quincy, Florida; died Jan 22, 1990; attended Florida A&M College, Georgia Infirmary in Savannah, Tuskegee Institute, and South Carolina Division of Maternal and Child Health (late 1930s); children: 1. ❖ Worked among rural poor in South Carolina; served as Episcopal missionary nurse in rural Pineville, SC; provided nutrition and primary care for residents of Berkeley County (SC); trained midwives and delivered more than 1,000 babies; appointed public health nurse for Berkeley County Health Department (1936) and opened county's 1st venereal disease and prenatal clinics. Inducted into South Carolina Hall of Fame (1990).

CALLENDER, Beverley (1956—). English runner. Name variations: Bev Goddard-Callender. Born Aug 28, 1956, in Barbados. ❖ Won a gold medal for the 4x100-meter relay at Commonwealth Games (1982) and a silver medal in the 4x400-meter relay at World championships (1983); won Olympic bronze medals in the 4x100-meter relay at Moscow (1980) and Los Angeles (1984).

CALLENDER, Hannah (1737–1801). American diarist. Born 1737, probably in Philadelphia, Pennsylvania; raised in Burlington, New Jersey; died 1801; m. Samuel Sansom, 1762. ❖ Traveled widely, visiting Quaker communities in Pennsylvania, NY, and New Jersey; recorded experiences in diary (1757–62), which was published as "Extracts from the Diary of Hannah Callender," in *Pennsylvania Magazine of History and Biography* (1888).

CALLENDER, Marie (1907–1995). American entrepreneur. Born in 1907 in South Dakota; died in Laguna Hills, California, Nov 11, 1995; m. Cal Callender, 1924; children: Donald Callender. ❖ Purchased an old oven and 3 rolling pins and launched her own pie business with husband (1948), wholesaling to local stores in Long Beach; opened a small pie and coffee shop, Marie Callender's, on Tustin Avenue in Orange (1962); throughout 1960s, opened a chain of shops in southern California; by 1985, had 119 restaurants in California and 11 other states. ❖ See also *Women in World History*.

CALLENDER, Sheila (1914–2004). English physician. Born Sheila Theodora Elsie Callender, April 14, 1914, in Sidcup, Kent, England; died Aug 17, 2004; youngest of 4 children of a Scottish general practitioner and surgeon and an Irish mother; St. Andrew's University, MD, 1938, PhD, 1944; University of Oxford, doctorate of science, 1970; m. Ivan Monostori (physician), 1955; no children. ❖ Spent working career at Oxford, after joining Leslie Witts as a house physician in the newly formed Nuffield Department of Clinical Medicine at Radcliffe Infirmary (1942); became May Reader in Medicine (1947), 1st assistant (1954), and clinical reader and consultant physician; elected a fellow of Royal College of Physicians (1962); specialized in blood diseases and helped establish and develop the field of hematology after WWII.

CALLENS, Els (1970—). Belgian tennis player. Born Aug 20, 1970, in Antwerp, Belgium. ❖ Turned pro (1990); won a bronze medal for doubles at Sydney Olympics (2000).

CALLIGARIS, Novella (1954—). Italian swimmer. Born Dec 27, 1954. ❖ At Munich Olympics, won a bronze medal in the 400-meter individual medley, a bronze medal in the 800-meter freestyle and a silver medal in the 400-meter freestyle (1972).

CALLIL, Carmen (1938—). Australian publisher. Name variations: Carmen Therese Callil. Born to parents of Irish-Lebanese descent, Sept 15, 1938, in Melbourne, Australia; father was a barrister and lecturer in French; Melbourne University, BA (1960). ❖ Founder of Virago Press, moved to England (1963); after working for Hutchinson, Batsford, and Andrew Deutsch, founded her own company, Callil Book Publicity; with Ursula Owen and Rosie Boycott, co-founded Virago Press (1972), which was dedicated to the publication of women writers; began reprinting women's works (1978), initially focusing on English authors like Emily Eden, Antonia White, Angela Carter, E.M. Delafield and Margaret Kennedy; appointed managing editor and publishing director of Chatto & Windus, Bodley Head & Cape, when Virago was acquired by Chatto (1982); remained chair and managing director as company changed hands over the course of 11 years; worked as publisher-at-large for Random House (1993–94); also served on board of directors for Britain's Channel 4; writings include *Subversive Sybils: Women's Popular Fiction this Century* (1996), *The Modern Library: The 200 Best Novels in*

English Since 1950 (1998) and *Darquier's Nebula: A Family at War* (2003).

CALLISON, Carole Jo (1938—). American golfer. Name variations: Carole Jo Kabler-Skala; Carole Jo Skala. Born Carole Jo Kabler, June 13, 1938, in Eugene, Oregon; children: 3. ❖ Won USGA Junior Girls' championship (1955); seven-time winner of Oregon state championship (1955–61); joined LPGA tour (1970); won George Washington Classic (1973), Sacramento Union, Peter Jackson, Wheeling Ladies and du Maurier Classic (1974).

CALLOWAY, Blanche (1902–1973). African-American singer and bandleader. Born Feb 2, 1902, in Baltimore, Maryland; died Dec 16, 1973, in Baltimore; sister of entertainer Cab Calloway and band leader Elmer Calloway; attended Morgan State College. ❖ One of the most successful band leaders of 1930s and the 1st black woman to lead an all-male band, began professional career in Baltimore as a singer; joined touring company of *Shuffle Along* (1923); began work as a nightclub vocalist in Chicago (1927); sang with Andy Kirk band at Philadelphia's Pearl Theater (1931); headed her own all-male band—Blanche Calloway and Her Joy Boys (1931–38), then Blanche Calloway and Her Orchestra—which included some of the top musicians of the day, appearing at NY's exclusive black theaters, the Lafayette, Harlem Opera House, and the Apollo; recorded frequently for Victor; became a disc jockey on radio station WMEM out of Miami (1953); founded Afram House, a company specializing in cosmetics and hair preparations for blacks; active in politics, was the 1st black woman in Miami to vote (1958). ❖ See also *Women in World History.*

CALLWOOD, June (1924—). Canadian journalist, feminist and social activist. Born 1924 in Chatham, Ontario, Canada; m. Trent Frayne (journalist), 1944; children: 4. ❖ Founder and co-founder of several homes, safe houses, and social organizations, including Digger House youth hostel, Nellie's hostel for women, PEN Canada, Canadian Civil Liberties Foundation, and Feminists Against Censorship; also worked on behalf of AIDS victims; worked for *Brantford Expositor,* then Toronto *Globe and Mail;* hosted CBC tv's "In Touch" (1975–78), was an interviewer on VisionTV's "National Treasures," and hosted "Caregiving with June Callwood"; writings include *A Woman Doctor, Looks at Life* (1957), *Love, Hate, Fear, Anger and the Other Lively Emotions* (1964), (with Martin Zuker) *The Law is Not for Women!* (1984), *Emotions* (1986), *Twelve Weeks in Spring* (1986) and *June Callwood's National Treasures;* also wrote for *Maclean's.* Received Order of Canada (1986).

CALPURNIA (c. 70 BCE–?). Roman noblewoman, third wife of Julius Caesar. Born c. 70 BCE; death date unknown; dau. of Lucius Calpurnius Piso Caesoninus; sister of Lucius Calpurnius Piso, the "pontifex"; became 3rd wife of Julius Caesar (c. 100–44 BCE), military and political leader of Rome, in 59 BCE. Caesar was also married to Cornelia (c. 100–68 BCE) & Pompeia (c. 87–?BCE). ❖ Roman noblewoman of the late Republic; though marriage to Julius Caesar was entirely political, quickly developed a real affection for him; hearing rumors of his possible assassination (44), tried to prevent him from attending the meeting of the Senate where he would, in fact, be murdered; though she must have been aware of his affair with Cleopatra VII, remained a Caesarian partisan even after her husband's death; also represented an important link between her family and that of Caesar, for her brother Lucius Calpurnius Piso, the "pontifex," long served the interests of Caesar's posthumously adopted son and heir, Octavian (later, Augustus). ❖ See also *Women in World History.*

CALTHROP, Gladys E. (1894–1980). English theatrical designer. Name variations: G.E. Calthrop. Born Gladys E. Treeby in Ashton, Devon, 1894; died 1980; m. Major Everard E. Calthrop. ❖ Began career as stage designer with Noel Coward's *The Vortex* (1924) and continued a long association with him; designed for such plays as *Dick Whittington, On with the Dance, Easy Virtue, Hay Fever, Sirocco, The Cradle Song, The Master Builder, Prite Lives, Autumn Crocus, Cavalcade, Words and Music, Design for Living, Point Valaine, You Can't Take it With You,* and *Present Laughter;* was assistant art director on the classic *Brief Encounter,* suggesting the title; also worked on *In Which We Serve;* wrote novel *Paper Pattern* (1940).

CALTON, Patsy (1948–2005). English politician and member of Parliament. Born Patricia Yeldon, Sept 19, 1948; died of breast cancer, May 29, 2005, in England; attended school in Egypt, then Wymondham College in Norfolk; earned a degree in biochemisty at Umist and postgraduate degree in education from University of Manchester; m. Clive Calton, 1969; children: 2 daughters, 1 son. ❖ Held several positions as a science teacher; representing Liberal Democrats, elected to House

of Commons at Westminster (2001) for Cheadle, ordinarily a Conservative stronghold, by 33 votes; reelected by 4,020 (2005).

CALUB, Dyana (1975—). Australian swimmer. Born Nov 28, 1975, in Bourke, NSW, Australia. ❖ At Pan Pacific Games, won a gold medal for 100-meter backstroke (1999); won a silver medal for 4x100-meter medley relay at Sydney Olympics (2000).

CALVÉ, Emma (1858–1942). Spanish-born soprano. Name variations: Emma Calve. Born Emma de Roquer, Aug 15, 1858, in Décazeville, Spain; died Jan 6, 1942, in Millau; dau. of Spanish father and French mother; trained in Paris, studying with Jules Puget, Mathilde Marchesi, and Rosina Laborde; m. Galileo Gaspari (tenor). ❖ Known as the "Singing Duse" for her dramatic powers, made debut as Marguerite in Gounod's *Faust* in Brussels (1881, 1882); performed at Opéra-Comique in Paris (1880s); debuted at Teatro alla Scala (1887); created Suzel in Mascagni's *L'amico Fritz* in Rome (1891); debuted at Metropolitan Opera (1893); made debut in Boston (1912), then Nice (1914); also created the part of Bianca in Dubois' *Aben Hamlet,* and Massenet's *Navarraise* and *Sapho* were written specially for her; particularly beloved for her portrayals of Santuzza, in Mascagni's *Cavalleria Rusticana,* and of Carmen, a role to which she remains inseparably linked. ❖ See also *Women in World History.*

CALVERT, Carolina L.W. (1834–1872). *See Atkinson, Louisa.*

CALVERT, Catherine (1890–1971). American stage and silent-film star. Born Catherine Cassidy, April 20, 1890, in Baltimore, Maryland; died Jan 18, 1971, in Uniondale, LI, NY; m. Paul Armstrong (playwright, died); m. Col. George Carruthers (Canadian millionaire). ❖ Made NY stage debut in her husband's play *The Deep Purple* (1911), and starred in his *Alias Jimmy Valentine* and *The Escape;* also appeared opposite Otis Skinner in *Blood and Sand;* films include *Behind the Mask, Out of the Night, Dead Men Tell No Tales* and *That Woman;* retired (1923).

CALVERT, Mrs. Charles (1837–1921). English stage actress. Born née Biddles in 1837 (some sources cite 1835) in England; died Sept 20, 1921, in London, England; dau. of James Biddles (well-known provincial actor); m. Charles Alexander Calvert (actor-manager, 1828–1879); children: Leonard Calvert, Alexander Calvert, Cecil G. Calvert (stage actor) and Louis Calvert (actor, 1859–1923). ❖ Made stage debut as a child in *The Stranger,* with Charles and Ellen Kean; for next decade, lived in America; following marriage, appeared at the Prince's, in Manchester, under her husband's management, in many Shakespearean roles (1864–75); after husband's death, appeared at Sadler's Wells in *Rob Roy;* other plays include *Arms and the Man, Saucy Sally, A Royal Family, The Clandestine Marriage, The Rivals, Beauty and the Barge, She Stoops to Conquer* and *A Woman of No Importance;* over the years, toured the US with the companies of Edwin Booth, Lillie Langtry, and Mary Anderson.

CALVERT, Irene (1909–2000). *See Calvert, Lilian.*

CALVERT, Lilian (1909–2000). Northern Ireland politician. Name variations: Irene Calvert. Born Lilian Irene Mercer Earls, Feb 10, 1909, in Belfast, Northern Ireland; died May 19, 2000; dau. of Mary Arnold and John Earls (professor of mathematics at Queen's University); m. Raymond Calvert. ❖ As wartime chief welfare officer, handled the resettlement of evacuated Gibraltarians (1940) and the care of those affected by the bombing of Belfast (1941); an Independent for Queen's University, Belfast, elected to the Northern Ireland House of Commons in a by-election (1945); introduced reforms to education and child welfare laws; resigned over partition (1953).

CALVERT, Louie (c. 1893–1926). English murderer. Name variations: Louisa Jackson. Born c. 1893; executed June 26, 1926; m. Arthur Calvert. ❖ Feigned pregnancy to employer Arthur Calvert and convinced him to marry her; stayed in Leeds at home of Mrs. Lily Waterhouse during her supposed pregnancy; returned to husband with a baby who had been either adopted or borrowed from a woman in a neighboring town and with belongings stolen from Waterhouse; charged with murder after Waterhouse was found beaten to death; convicted at Leeds Assizes; confessed to earlier murder of John William Frobisher; executed at Strangeways Prison.

CALVERT, Patricia (1906–1978). English-born actress. Name variations: Patricia C. Dressler. Born Oct 4, 1906, in London, England; died April 8, 1978, in Tryon, North Carolina; dau. of Violet (Fenton) Calvert and Louis Calvert (actor, 1859–1923); granddau. of Mrs. Charles Calvert; m. John Emery (div.); m. Eric Dressler. ❖ Made NY stage debut in *The Crooked Square* (1923), followed by *Meet the Wife, Stronger than Love,*

Ten Per Cent, Lost Sheep, Lean Harvest, After all, Christopher Comes Across, Nona, Autumn Crocus, Strange Orchestra, May Wine, The Three Sisters and *The Duchess of Malfi.*

CALVERT, Phyllis (1915–2002). English stage, tv, and screen actress. Born Phyllis Bickle, Feb 18, 1915, in Chelsea, London, England; died Oct 8, 2002, in London; m. Peter Murray-Hill (publisher, died 1957); children: son and daughter. ❖ Made stage debut with Ellen Terry in *Crossings* (1925); appeared in such plays as *Flare Path, Peter Pan, Escapade, The Complaisant Lover, Present Laughter, Blithe Spirit, Hay Fever, The Reluctant Debutante, All Over, Dear Daddy, Before the Party, It's Never Too Late, The Rehearsal, A Woman of No Importance* and most notably as Madame Ranevskaya in *The Cherry Orchard* (1971) and Queen Mary in *Crown Matrimonial;* films include *The Man in Grey, Fanny by Gaslight, Madonna of the 7 Moons, They Were Sisters, Mandy* and *Mrs. Dalloway;* on tv, appeared in the series "Kate" and such plays as "Death of a Heart" and "Across the Lake."

CALVET, Corinne (1921–2001). French actress. Born Corinne Dibos, April 30, 1925, in Paris, France; died June 23, 2001, of a cerebral hemorrhage in Los Angeles, California; dau. of a scientist who invented Pyrex glassware; studied criminal law at Sorbonne; m. Jeffrey Stone (div.); m. John Bromfield (actor), 1948 (div. 1953); m. 3 others. ❖ Made film debut in *La Part de l'ombre* (1945), followed by *Rope of Sand, My Friend Irma Goes West, Peking Express, Sailor Beware, What Price Glory, Powder River, The Far Country, So This is Paris, Le Avventure di Giacomo Casanova, Hemingway's Adventures as a Young Man* and *Too Hot to Handle,* among others; tv guest appearances included "Burke's Law," "Studio One," "Batman," and "Starsky and Hutch." ❖ See also autobiography *Has Corinne Been a Good Little Girl?*

CALVILLO, María del Carmen (1765–1856). Mexican rancher. Name variations: Doña María del Carmen Calvillo; Maria Calvillo. Born María del Carmen Calvillo, July 9, 1765, at the Villa of San Fernando de Béxar (now San Antonio, Texas); died Jan 15, 1856; eldest of 6 children of Francisco Xavier Calvillo and Antonia de Arocha; m. Juan Gavino de la Trinidad Delgado (helped overthrow the Spanish in 1811–14), c. 1781 (sep. c. 1814); children: Juan Bautista and José Anacleto; (adopted) Juan José, María Concepción Gortari, and Antonio Durán. ❖ Inherited Rancho de las Cabras (now Rancho de las Cabras State Historic Site, April 15, 1814); could shoot expertly and rope as well as the men; increased land holdings, and built an extensive irrigation system, a granary and sugar mill; held ownership of the land until her death; passed the property on to 2 of her adopted children, María and Antonio.

CALVO DE AGUILAR, Isabel (1916—). Spanish novelist. Born 1916 in Pontevedra, Spain. ❖ Founded Associación de Escritoras Españolas (Association of Spanish Female Writers); works include *El misterio de palacio chino* (1951), *La isla de los siete pecados* (1952), and *La danzarina inmóvil* (1954).

CALYPSO (fl. c. 200 bce). Ancient Greek painter. Name variations: Kalypso. ❖ In his account of women painters, Pliny the Elder mentions the subjects of 3 paintings after Calypso's name; it is possible that Calypso was not a painter at all but actually the subject of a portrait by Irene. ❖ See also *Women in World History.*

CALYPSO ROSE (1940—). Trinidadian calypso singer and feminist. Name variations: McArtha Linda Sandy-Lewis; McArtha Lewis (also seen as McCartha and McArthur [named for Douglas MacArthur]). Born April 27, 1940, in Bethel, Tobago; attended San Juan Government School. ❖ At 9, was sent to live with an aunt in Tobago; attended school in Trinidad; began career at the Original Young Brigade Tent (1957); won Road March Crown with "Tempo" (1977), the 1st female calypsonian to win the national title; won the Calypso Crown for "Her Majesty" and "I Thank Thee" and Road March title for "Soca Jam" (both 1978), the 1st calypsonian to win both crowns in the same year; known as the "Calypso Queen of the World." Received British Empire Medal (1975), Citizens of Liberia Humanitarian award (1986), Sunshine Award (1989), and Trinidad & Tobago Humming Bird Gold Medal (for Culture, 2000).

CALZADA, Alba (1945—). Puerto Rican-American ballet dancer. Born Jan 28, 1945, in Santurce, Puerto Rico. ❖ Studied at American Ballet Center and American Ballet Theater School in New York City; danced featured and principal roles for Ballet San Juan in Puerto Rico, including in *Les Sylphides, Giselle, Swan Lake* and *Coppélia* (mid-1960s); joined Pennsylvania Ballet (1968) where she danced numerous Balanchine solos in repertory including *Scotch Symphony Serenade, Four Temperaments* and

Symphony in C.; performed in revivals of Antony Tudor's *Jardin aux Luxembourg,* and Benjamin Harkavay's *Madrigalesco* and *Time Past Summer.*

CAM, Helen M. (1885–1968). English university professor and historian. Born Helen Maud Cam, Aug 22, 1885, in Abingdon, Berkshire, England; died Feb 9, 1968, in Orpington, Kent, England; dau. of William Herbert Cam (educator and rector) and Kate (Scott) Cam; University of London, BA, 1907, MA, 1909; University of Cambridge, LittD, 1937; never married; no children. ❖ Served as assistant mistress in history at Ladies' College, Cheltenham, then held teaching positions at Royal Holloway College (1912–21); was a lecturer in history at Girton College, Cambridge (1921–29); accepted a post at University of Cambridge (1920), where in addition to lecturing on English medieval constitutional history, she tutored and conducted research; returned to Girton (1940), where she was director of studies in history and law; appointed to a full professorship at Harvard University (1948), the 1st woman to hold such an appointment there; writings include *Local Government in Francia and England, 768–1934* (1912), *Liberties and Communities in Medieval England* (1944), and *Law Finders and Law Makers in Medieval England* (1962). ❖ See also *Women in World History.*

CAMA, Bhikaiji (1861–1936). Indian revolutionary. Born 1861 into a rich Parsi family; died Aug 16, 1936; m. Rustum Cama (well-known solicitor in Bombay). ❖ Called the mother of the Indian revolution, attended the 2nd Internationalist Socialist Congress in Stuttgart, Germany (1907), where she presented the case for India's independence and dared to unfurl the Indian Tricolour with Vande Mataram insignia.

CAMACHO BAQUEDANO, Margarita (1922–1980). *See Paz Paredes, Margarita.*

CAMARGO, Marie-Anne Cupis de (1710–1770). French-Spanish ballerina. Born Marie-Anne de Cupis (or Marie Anne Cuppi) in Brussels, Belgium, of Spanish descent, April 15, 1710; died in Paris, April 20, 1770; dau. of Ferdinand Joseph de Cupis (violinist and dance master); studied with Françoise Prévost. ❖ While young, secured an engagement as *première danseuse* at Brussels, then Rouen; under maternal grandmother's name of Camargo, debuted at Paris Opéra (1726), electrifying the audience with her technical feats and the *entrechat quatre,* up until then reserved for male dancers; at 16, was the rage of Paris; at 23, became mistress of Louis de Bourbon, comte de Clermont, grandson of the great Condé, and at his request lived in retirement (1736–41); resumed career (1741), continuing at the Opéra for 10 more years, appearing in 78 ballets or operas, always to the delight of the public; was the 1st ballet dancer to shorten the skirt to what afterwards became the regulation length. ❖ See also *Women in World History.*

CAMBER, Irene (1926—). Italian fencer. Born Feb 12, 1926. ❖ Won an Olympic gold medal in individual foil at Helsinki (1952) and a bronze medal in team foil at Rome (1960).

CAMBODIA, queen of.
See Mei (d. 1875).
See Kossamak (r. 1955–1960).
See Norodom Monineath Sihanouk (b. 1936).

CAMBRIDGE, Ada (1844–1926). Australian fiction writer and poet. Name variations: Ada Cross; Mrs. George Cross. Born Ada Cambridge, Nov 21, 1844, at Wiggenhall, St. Germains, Norfolk, England; died July 19, 1926, at Elsternwick, Australia; dau. of Thomasine (Emerson) and Henry Cambridge (farmer); m. Reverend George Frederick Cross, April 25, 1870 (died 1917); children: Arthur Stuart (1871–1876); Edith Constance (1873–1884); Vera Lyon (b. 1876); Hugh Cambridge (1878–1902); Kenneth Stuart (1880–1967). ❖ By age 22, deeply religious, had anonymously published 2 volumes of hymns, and had contributed short stories to local magazines and newspapers; following marriage, sailed with husband to Australia for his 1st parish (1870), in Wangaratta; moved to Yackandandah (1872), Ballan (1874), and Coleraine (1877); though frequently bedridden, wrote voluminously; published vol. of poetry *Unspoken Thoughts* (1887), which voiced her increasing doubt in the organized religion her husband represented and the "relentless bonds" of marriage; lived in Melbourne (1884–93), then moved to Williamstown (1893); works include *Hymns on the Litany* (1865), *The Manor House* (poems, 1875), *Thirty Years in Australia* (1903) and *The Hand in the Dark* (1913). ❖ See also Belby and Hadgraft, *Ada Cambridge, Tasma and Rosa Praed* (Oxford U. Press, 1979); Bradstock and Wakeling, *Rattling the Orthodoxies: A Life of Ada*

Cambridge (Penguin, 1991); Audrey Tate, *Ada Cambridge* (Melbourne U. Press, 1991); and *Women in World History.*

CAMBRIDGE, countess of.
See Clifford, Maud (d. 1446).
See Mortimer, Anne (1390–1411).

CAMERON, Agnes Deans (1863–1912). Canadian traveler, educator, and feminist. Born Agnes Deans Cameron, 1863, in Victoria, British Columbia, Canada; died May 13, 1912, and had the largest funeral cortège the city of Victoria had witnessed to date; dau. of Jessie Anderson (schoolteacher from Scotland) and Duncan Cameron (miner and contractor); never married; no children. ❖ Began teaching at Angela College, Victoria (1879); became the 1st high-school teacher in British Columbia (1890) and was appointed the 1st woman principal in the province (1894); moved to Chicago and took up journalism (1906); began 10,000 mile trip from Chicago up the Mackenzie River to the Arctic Circle (1908), accompanied by her niece Jessie Cameron Brown; wrote an account of the journey, *The New North* (1909), which included photographs; also wrote articles and lectured on experiences; was a supporter of equal rights, immigration, and school reform.

CAMERON, Mrs. Alan (1899–1973). *See Bowen, Elizabeth.*

CAMERON, Bessy (c. 1851–1895). Aboriginal teacher. Born in King George Sound, Western Australia, c. 1851; died Jan 12, 1895; attended Annesfield School, Albany; attended a model school in Sydney; m. Donald Cameron, Nov 4, 1868; children: 4 who survived. ❖ Because of father's connections to a government official, received a formal education and had a short teaching career, a rare opportunity for an Aboriginal; became a teacher at Ramahyuck mission (1867), where, in addition to attending classes, she performed housework; final years were spent trying to keep her younger children and her grandchildren from being taken from her to be brought up "white." ❖ See also *Women in World History.*

CAMERON, Donaldina (1869–1968). New Zealand-born mission superintendent and social reformer. Born Donaldina Mackenzie Cameron, July 26, 1869, in Otago Land District on the South Island of New Zealand; died Jan 4, 1968, in Palo Alto, California; dau. of Allan Cameron (sheep rancher) and Isabella Mackenzie; attended Castleman School for Girls and Los Angeles Normal School; never married; no children. ❖ Moved with family to San Joaquin Valley of California (1871); under auspices of Presbyterian Church, began to work with Chinese women at the mission home of Woman's Occidental Board of Foreign Missions (1895), located on the fringe of San Francisco's Chinatown; became superintendent of the home (1900), a position to which she devoted the rest of her professional life; effectively waged a campaign against Chinese female slavery, rescuing thousands of Chinese women and young girls held as slaves in sweatshops and brothels; established a 2nd mission house in Oakland as a refuge for young children (1925). The mission house at 920 Sacramento Street in San Francisco was renamed the Donaldina Cameron House (1942). ❖ See also Mildred Crowl Martin, *Chinatown's Angry Angel: The Story of Donaldina Cameron* (Pacific, 1986); Carol Green Wilson, *Chinatown's Quest: The Life and Adventure of Donaldina Cameron* (Stanford U. Press, 1958); and *Women in World History.*

CAMERON, Dorothy (d. 1958). American dancer. Name variations: Cameron Sisters. Died April 15, 1958. ❖ Teamed with Madeline Gaxton (then known as Madeline Seitz) as the Cameron Sisters at Ned Wayburn Studio in New York City, and 1st appeared as a duo dance team touring the Keith vaudeville circuit (c. 1912); made Broadway debut with Madeline as twin exotic dancers in *Miss Simplicity* (1914); appeared in the film *Maxim's at Midnight* (1915); performed as tandem team on stages at Capitol Theater in New York City and in Wayburn's *Town Topics of 1915* and *So Long Letty* (1916).

CAMERON, Eleanor (1912–1996). Canadian-born children's writer. Born Eleanor Frances Butler, Mar 23, 1912, in Winnipeg, Manitoba, Canada; died Oct 11, 1996, in Monterey, California; dau. of Henry and Florence (Vaughan) Butler; attended University of California at Los Angeles; m. Ian Stuart Cameron, 1934; children: David Gordon Cameron. ❖ Best known for *The Wonderful Flight to the Mushroom Planet* (1954) and the "Julia Redfern" series, also wrote *The Terrible Churnadryne* (1959), *Time and Mr. Bass* (1967), *A Room Made of Windows* (1971), *Court of the Stone Children* (1973), and *The Curse of Casa del Monte* (1975), among others; wrote collection of essays on children's literature, *The Green and Burning Tree* (1969).

CAMERON, Hilda (b. 1912). Canadian runner. Name variations: Hilda Young. Born Aug 14, 1912. ❖ At Berlin Olympics, won a bronze medal in 4x100-meter relay (1936); had a career as a teacher (1932–73).

CAMERON, Julia (c. 1947—). American writer. Born c. 1947 in Libertyville, Illinois; 2nd oldest of 7 children of James (advertising executive) and Dorothy Cameron; graduate of Georgetown University; m. Martin Scorsese (film director), Dec 30, 1975 (div. c. 1978); m. Mark Bryan (div. 1993); children: Domenica Cameron-Scorsese (b. 1976, actress and writer). ❖ Poet, playwright, fiction writer, and essayist, wrote for *Rolling Stone* and the *Village Voice*; wrote the bestselling *The Artist's Way* (1992); other writings include the detective novel *The Dark Room.*

CAMERON, Julia Margaret (1815–1879). British photographer. Born Julia Margaret Pattle in Calcutta, India, June 11, 1815; died in Kalutara, Ceylon (now Sri Lanka), Jan 26, 1879; dau. of James Pattle (official of East India Company) and Adeline (de l'Etang) Pattle; great-aunt of Virginia Woolf and Vanessa Bell; m. Charles Hay Cameron (official in British Civil Service), 1838; children: 5 sons, 1 daughter. ❖ One of the most prominent figures in the history of photography, moved to England (1848), eventually settling on Isle of Wight, next door to Emily and Alfred Tennyson; known for her abundance of wit and her extraordinary gift for capturing the beauty in others, used her home, "Dimbola," to entertain some of the most prominent scientists, artists, and literary figures of Victorian England; took up photography at age 49 (1863); 1st displayed work (1864), at 10th Exhibition of Photographic Society in London, followed by shows in Edinburgh, Dublin, Berlin, Paris and Vienna; focused her camera on the luminaries of her social circle, including Sir John Herschel, Sir Henry Taylor, Charles Darwin, Henry Wadsworth Longfellow, Robert Browning, Ellen Terry, and Tennyson, who posed up to 50 times; her soft-focused portraits, mostly heads or half-lengths, are considered some of the finest contributions to early photography in England; also shot allegorical, religious, and genre pictures, heavily influenced by the Pre-Raphaelites, and illustrated Tennyson's *Idylls of the King* (1874–75); moved to Ceylon (1875). ❖ See also Joanne Lukitsh, *Cameron: Her Work and Career* (1986); and *Women in World History.*

CAMERON, Kate (1874–1965). Scottish artist. Name variations: Katharine Cameron. Born 1874 in Hillhead, Glasgow, Scotland; died 1965 in Scotland; dau. of Sir David Young Cameron (artist); sister of Sir D.Y. Cameron (artist); attended Glasgow School of Art; studied at Colarossi Academy, Paris; m. Arthur Kay (art connoisseur and collector), 1928. ❖ Known for watercolor flower studies and for etchings, studied at Glasgow School of Art, becoming part of generation of Scottish women artists now known as Glasgow Girls, including Annie French and Jessie M. King; worked during early career in arts-and-crafts style of "Glasgow 4" (Charles Rennie Mackintosh, Margaret Mackintosh, Frances Macdonald and Herbert Macnair); best known for later works which demonstrate development of extremely delicate, highly stylized approach, often including butterflies or bumble bees; worked also as illustrator of many books, including children's fairy tales.

CAMERON, Lucy Lyttleton (1781–1858). English writer. Name variations: Lucy Littleton Cameron. Born Lucy Lyttleton Butt in 1781 in Stanford, England; died 1858; eldest dau. of Dr. George Butt; sister of Mary Martha Sherwood (children's writer); m. Rev. C.R. Cameron, 1806. ❖ Went to school in Reading (the same school attended by Jane Austen and Mary Russell Mitford); ran schools at Wick; wrote religious tales for children.

CAMERON, Madeline (1897–1990). *See Gaxton, Madeline.*

CAMERON, Michelle (1962—). Canadian synchronized swimmer. Born Dec 28, 1962, in Calgary, Alberta, Canada; m. Alan Coulter (Olympic volleyball player); children: 3. ❖ Partnered with Carolyn Waldo, won Rome and Spanish Opens (1985), FINA World Cup (1985, 1987), Spanish Open (1986), Commonwealth Games (1986), World championships (1986), Pan Pacific championships (1987) and a gold medal in duet at Seoul Olympics (1988). Received Order of Canada (1989); inducted into International Swimming Hall of Fame (2000).

CAMERON, Robina Thomson (1892–1971). New Zealand nurse. Born April 15, 1892, in Edinburgh, Scotland; died June 28, 1971, in Rotorua, New Zealand; dau. of James Cameron (blacksmith) and Jane (Thompson) Cameron. ❖ Immigrated to New Zealand (1911); trained as nurse at Cook Hospital, Gisborne; joined Queen Alexandra's Imperial Military Nursing Service and worked in Egypt and Palestine during WWI; worked as native-district nurse for Department of Health in Opotiki (1919) and district nurse in Rotorua (1931); served as president of Women's Health League (1937); became nurse inspector (1939); sent to London by Department of Labor to organize immigrant nursing plan (1947). Received Royal Red Cross (1919) and British Empire Medal (1938); Nurse Cameron Memorial Health Centre opened in her honor (1986). ❖ See also *Dictionary of New Zealand Biography* (Vol. 4).

CAMERON, Violet (1862–1919). English stage actress. Name variations: Mrs. De Bensaude. Born Violet Lydia Thompson, Dec 7, 1862; died Oct 25, 1919; cousin of Violet and Florence Lloyd; married D. de Bensaude. ❖ Made stage debut in *Faust and Marguerite* (1871), followed by *The Children in the Wood, Piff-Paff, The Commodore, Morocco Bound, Miami* and *The School Girl*, among others; came to prominence as Germaine in *Les Cloches de Corneville* (1878) and originated the role of Bettina in *The Mascotte* (1880).

CAMERON SISTERS.
See Cameron, Dorothy (d. 1958).
See Gaxton, Madeline (1897–1990).

CAMILLE (1824–1847). *See Plessis, Alphonsine.*

CAMMERMEYER, Margarethe (1942—). American combat nurse and gay-rights activist. Name variations: Grethe Cammermeyer. Born Mar 1942 in Oslo, Norway; dau. of a renowned neuropathologist and a nurse; immigrated to America, 1951; became US citizen, 1960; University of Maryland, BS, 1963; graduate of Army Student Nurse Program, 1963; University of Washington, MA, 1976, PhD, 1991; m. Harvey Hawken, Aug 14, 1965 (div. 1980); lives with Diane Divelbess (university professor and artist); children: 4 sons. ❖ Chief nurse of the Washington National Guard who, discharged from duty on the grounds that she was a homosexual, determined to change the military's prejudiced policy against gays; served in Vietnam as head nurse of an intensive care ward (1967–68) and was awarded a Bronze Star; continued serving in veteran's hospitals; promoted to colonel, was chief nurse of the Washington State National Guard; having served 3 decades as an army nurse, was discharged for admitting in a security clearance interview that she was a lesbian (1991), the highest-ranking officer ever discharged for homosexuality; took her case to court (1994), and the Pentagon was ordered by a federal judge to reinstate her; reported back to the National Guard (1994), serving as chief nurse of the 164th MASH until May 1996; retired (1997). Named Nurse of the Year by Veterans Administration and Woman of the Year by Women's Veterans Association (1985). ❖ See also autobiography, *Serving in Silence* (Penguin, 1994); (film) *Serving in Silence,* starring Judy Davis and Glenn Close (1995); and *Women in World History.*

CAMPAN, Jeanne Louise Henriette (1752–1822). French educator and writer. Born Jeanne Louise Henriette Genet or Genest in Paris, France, 1752; died 1822; dau. of M. Genet or Genest (1st clerk in the foreign office); m. M. Campan; children: 1 son. ❖ By 15, had gained such a high reputation for erudition that she was appointed reader to the aunts of Louis XVI: Adelaide, Victoire, Sophie, and Louise Marie; was appointed first lady of the bedchamber by Marie Antoinette, and continued to be her faithful attendant until the Revolution; after the Terror, established a girls' boarding school at St. Germain, which was patronized by Hortense de Beauharnais; appointed superintendent of the academy founded by Napoleon at Écouen for the education of daughters and sisters of Legion of Honor members; wrote *Mémoires sur la vie privée de Marie Antoinette, suivis de souvenirs et anecdotes historiques sur les règnes de Louis XIV-XV* (Paris, 1823) and the treatise *De l'Education des Femmes.* ❖ See also Jules Flammermont, *Les Mémoires de Madame de Campan* (Paris, 1886); and *Women in World History.*

CAMPANELLI, Pauline (1943–2001). American painter. Born Pauline Eble, Jan 25, 1943, in the Bronx, NY; died of complications from childhood polio, Nov 29, 2001, in Pohatcong Township, New Jersey; dau. of Joseph Eble (professional photographer); attended Ridgewood School of Art; m. Dan Campanelli (painter), 1969. ❖ Painted super-realist still lifes that sold in the hundreds of thousands, including her most popular "Wild Rose Berries"; writings include *Ancient Ways: Reclaiming Pagan Traditions* (1991).

CAMPANINI, Barbara (1721–1799). Italian ballerina. Name variations: La Barbarina; Barberina Campanini; Countess de Campanini or Comtesse de Campanini. Born in Parma, Italy, 1721; died June 7, 1799, in Barschau, Silesia, Prussia; sister of Barbe or Barbet, poet, linguist, musician, painter and actress who married the Marquis d'Argens; studied with Rinaldi Fossano, Neapolitan comic dancer; m. Carlo Luigi Cocceji, also known as Charles-Louis de Cocceji (son of Frederick the Great's chancellor), 1749 (sep. 1759, div. 1788). ❖ At 16,

arrived in France and soon became the mistress of Prince de Carignan, inspector general of the Paris Opéra; made successful debut there in *Les Fêtes d'Herbe, ou Les Talents Lyriques* (1793); next appeared in *Zaide, Reine de Grenade* and *Momus Amoureux;* known for her precision, elevation, and the acrobatic style of the Italian school, executed her *entrechat huit* with ease; made 1st London appearance (1740), at Covent Garden, and became an immediate favorite of the royal family; made a number of appearances at Covent Garden, Académie Royal, Versailles, and Smock Alley Theatre in Dublin; also became mistress of Lord Arundel, Marquis de Thebouville, and Duc de Durfort; the hit of Berlin (1744), was granted the title, Comtesse de Campanini; became mistress of Frederick the Great; later settled down for a quiet life, endowing a convent for Poor Ladies of Good Birth and becoming its prioress until her death. ❖ See also *Women in World History.*

CAMPBELL, Ada (c. 1860–?). *See Irwin, Flo.*

CAMPBELL, Ann Casson (1915–1990). *See Casson, Ann.*

CAMPBELL, Anne (1940—). English politician and member of Parliament. Born Anne Lucas, April 6, 1940; m. Dr. Archie Campbell, 1963. ❖ Served as head, Statistics and Data Processing, National Institute of Agricultural Botany, Cambridge (1983–92); representing Labour, elected to House of Commons for Cambridge (1992, 1997, 2001); lost general election (2005).

CAMPBELL, Beatrice (1922–1979). Irish actress. Born July 31, 1922, in Co. Down, North Ireland; died May 10, 1979, in London, England. ❖ Films include *Silent Dust, Now Barabbas, Last Holiday, The Mudlark, No Place for Jennifer, The Master of Ballantrae, Grand National Night* and *The Cockleshell Heroes.*

CAMPBELL, Beatrice Stella (1865–1940). *See Campbell, Mrs. Patrick.*

CAMPBELL, Betty Becker (1903–1989). *See Becker-Pinkston, Elizabeth.*

CAMPBELL, Cassie (1973—). Canadian ice-hockey player. Born Nov 22, 1973, in Brampton, Ontario, Canada; graduate of University of Guelph. ❖ Won a team gold medal at World championships (1994, 1997, 2001); won a team silver medal at Nagano (1998), the 1st Olympics to feature women's ice hockey; won a team gold medal at Salt Lake City Olympics (2002) and Torino Olympics (2006). Named University of Guelph Sportswoman of the Year (1996).

CAMPBELL, Charlotte C. (1914–1993). American medical mycologist and university professor. Born Charlotte Catherine Campbell in Winchester, Virginia, Dec 4, 1914; died in Boston, Massachusetts, Oct 8, 1993; dau. of Philip Edward and Mary (Ambrose) Campbell; attended Blackstone College, Virginia, 1934, and Ohio State University; George Washington University, BS, 1951; earned a diploma in medical technology from University of Pennsylvania Hospital in Philadelphia; never married; no children. ❖ Served as medical technician in Winchester (1938–41); during WWII, was an instructor in bacteriology and medical mycology at Walter Reed Army Institute of Research, Washington, DC (1941–48), becoming chief of medical mycology (1948); an expert on histoplasmosis and other fungal diseases, was on the faculty of Harvard University (1962–73) and promoted to full professor (1970), despite the fact that she had never been awarded a doctorate; left Harvard for a prestigious post at Southern Illinois University (1973); retired from academic life (1977); served as coordinator of US/USSR Exchange Program in Microbiology (1977–82). Received Rhoda Benham Award from Mycology Society of America and International Society for Human and Animal Mycology Award for distinguished contributions to the field. ❖ See also *Women in World History.*

CAMPBELL, Lady Colin (1857–1911). Irish-English journalist and socialite. Name variations: Gertrude Elizabeth, Lady Colin Campbell; (pseudonym) G.B. Brunefille. Born Gertrude Elizabeth Blood in May 1857; grew up at Thurloe Square, South Kensington, in London, and Brickhill, Co. Clare, Ireland; died Nov 2, 1911; dau. of Edmund Maghlin Blood; m. Lord Colin Campbell (1853–1895, MP for Argyllshire, 1878–85), July 21, 1881 (div. 1884). ❖ Had a liberal upbringing and could speak English, Italian and French; enjoyed the company of royals, politicians, artists and writers; when marriage ended up in divorce courts, accused husband of adultery and cruelty, while he accused her of having 4 co-respondents (it was the longest divorce trial in English legal history); after he died (1895), reestablished her place in society as art critic of *The World* (1889–1903) and *Art Journal;* was also founder and co-editor of *Realm* (1894–1905) and editor of *Ladies Field* (1901–03); under pseudonym G.B. Brunefille, wrote *Topo, A Tale about*

English Children in Italy (1878); also wrote *Etiquette in Society* (1886) and *Darrell Blake, a Study* (1889).

CAMPBELL, Lady Colin (1949—). Jamaican-born writer. Born Georgia Ariana Ziadie in 1949 in Jamaica; dau. of Michael Ziadie (Lebanese emigre) and Gloria Ziadie (Jamaican); m. Lord Colin Ivar Campbell (son of 11th duke of Argyll), Mar 23, 1974 (div. 1975); children: (adopted) 2. ❖ Born with a genital deformity, was brought up as a boy (George William Ziadie) though she was not; had an operation at 21; had a brief and acrimonious marriage; wrote the controversial book on the Princess of Wales, *Diana in Private*, as well as *The Royal Marriages*. ❖ See also autobiography *A Life Worth Living* (1997).

CAMPBELL, Dorothy I. (1883–1945). *See Hurd, Dorothy Iona.*

CAMPBELL, Edith (d. 1945). American stage actress. Name variations: Edith Campbell Faversham; Edith Campbell Walker. Died May 21, 1945, in New York, NY; m. William Faversham (actor), 1925. ❖ Prior to marriage, acted under name Edith Campbell; supported Robert Mantell in Shakespearean repertory; plays include *Mind the Paint Girl, Cinders, Leah Kleschna, Follow Through*, and *The Skin of Our Teeth*; made film debut as Edith Campbell Walker in *Diplomacy* (1916), followed by *A Woman's Way, The Valentine Girl, Hedda Gabler* and *The Sporting Duchess*.

CAMPBELL, Elizabeth Grace (1846–1926). *See Neill, Elizabeth Grace.*

CAMPBELL, Grace MacLennan (1895–1963). Canadian novelist and short-story writer. Name variations: Grace Campbell. Born Grace MacLennan Grant in 1895 in Williamstown, Ontario, Canada, of Highland and Loyalist ancestry; died May 31, 1963; graduate of Queen's University, 1915, with a gold medal in English Literature; m. Rev. Harvey Campbell, 1919 (died 1976); children: 3 sons. ❖ Lived in Saskatchewan, Ontario, Northern Quebec, Montreal and Regina; writings, which often depict lives of Scots Highland settlers in Glengarry, Canada, include *Thorn-Apple Tree* (1942), *The Higher Hill* (1944), *Fresh Wind Blowing* (1947) and *Torbeg* (1953).

CAMPBELL, Harriet Louisa (1829–1906). *See Browne, Harriet Louisa.*

CAMPBELL, Helen Stuart (1839–1918). American writer and sociologist. Name variations: Helen Stuart Weeks Campbell; Helen C. Weeks; wrote under the names Campbell, Weeks (her married name), and several pseudonyms, some of which were male. Born in Lockport, New York, July 4, 1839; died 1918; married a man named Weeks (div. 1871). ❖ Wrote children's books under married name; published widely in newspapers and magazines; served as literary editor of *Our Continent*, Philadelphia (1881–84); turned attention to plight of women workers and the poor, publishing her best-known work, *Prisoners of Poverty* (1886); was also concerned over what she termed "nicotine poisoning" among tobacco industry workers, a view that was far ahead of its time. ❖ See also *Women in World History.*

CAMPBELL, Mrs. J. (1902–1971). *See Campbell, Laurel.*

CAMPBELL, Janet Mary (1877–1954). *See Campbell, Mary.*

CAMPBELL, Jean (b. 1917). *See Erdman, Jean.*

CAMPBELL, Lady Jeanne (1928—). English aristocrat and journalist. Name variations: Jeanne Mailer. Born Jeanne Louise Campbell, Dec 10, 1928; dau. of Sir Ian Douglas Campbell, 11th duke of Argyll, and Janet Gladys Aitken (dau. of Lord Beaverbrook); m. Norman Mailer (novelist), 1962 (div. 1963); m. John Sergeant Cram, 1964; children: (1st m.) Kate Mailer (b. 1962); (2nd m.) Cust Charlotte Cram (b. 1967). ❖ While working as a researcher at *Life* magazine, became involved romantically with Henry Luce.

CAMPBELL, Jeannette (1916–2003). Argentinean swimmer. Born Mar 1916 in Argentina; died Jan 15, 2003; children: Ines, Susie and Roberto. ❖ At Berlin Olympics, won a silver medal in 100-meter freestyle (1936); won the 100-meter freestyle in Brazil (1935), Uruguay (1937), Peru (1938), and Ecuador (1939); was one of the greatest swimmers in South American history.

CAMPBELL, Judy (1916–2004). English actress. Born May 31, 1916, in Grantham, Lincolnshire, England; died June 6, 2004; dau. of J.A. Campbell (playwright) and Mary Fulton (actress); educated at St. Michael's Convent, East Grinstead; m. David Birkin, 1943; children: 1 son and 2 daughters, including Jane Birkin (actress and singer). ❖ Though she could barely sing, launched her career in the *New Faces* revue the night she sang "A Nightingale Sang in Berkely Square" (1940), when her intended script had not arrived; had a 60-year career in the West End, often appearing in plays by Noel Coward.

CAMPBELL, Juliet (1970—). Jamaican runner. Born in 1970 in Jamaica. ❖ Won a bronze medal for 4x100-meter relay at World championships (1993) and silver medals for 200 meters and 4x100-meter relay at Commonwealth Games (1998, 2002).

CAMPBELL, Kate (1899–1986). Australian pediatrician. Born Kate Isabel Campbell at Hawthorn, Melbourne, 1899; died July 12, 1986; dau. of Janet Duncan (Mill) Campbell (schoolteacher) and Donald Campbell (shipping clerk); attended Methodist Ladies' College; University of Melbourne, MB BS, 1922, MD, 1924. ❖ Important voice in health care for children, was medical officer for Victorian Baby Health Centres Association for more than 40 years; was also appointed University of Melbourne's inaugural lecturer in neo-natal pediatrics (1929) and would continue in this capacity until 1965; in private practice as a Collins St. specialist in pediatrics (from 1937), quickly became known for her brilliant diagnostic skills; co-authored the *Guide to the Care of the Young Child* for the Department of Health (1947) which saw 6 editions; had a hand in introducing unrestricted visiting in children's hospitals (1947); discovered the cause of *retrolental fibroplasia*, a disease that results in blindness of premature babies (1951). Awarded DBE (1971). ❖ See also *Women in World History.*

CAMPBELL, Kim (1947—). Canadian prime minister. Name variations: A. Kim Campbell. Born Avril Phaedra Campbell, Mar 10, 1947, in Port Alberni, British Columbia, Canada; attended University of British Columbia and London School of Economics; m. Nathan Divinsky, 1972 (div. 1983); m. Howard Eddy, 1986 (div. 1993). ❖ Lawyer, lecturer, Progressive Conservative, served in the British Columbia legislature for Vancouver–Point Grey riding (1986–88); elected to House of Commons for Vancouver Centre (1988); was minister of state (Indian Affairs and Northern Development, 1989–90), minister of justice and attorney general of Canada (1990–93), minister of national defense (1993), minister of veterans affairs (1993), minister responsible for Federal-Provincial Relations (1993); was the 1st woman and 1st native British Columbian to serve as prime minister of Canada (June 25, 1993–Nov 3, 1993); was the 1st former Canadian prime minister to be given a diplomatic post after leaving office, Canada's consul general in Los Angeles (1996). ❖ See also autobiography *Time and Chance: The Political Memoirs of Canada's First Woman Prime Minister* (Doubleday, 1996).

CAMPBELL, Laurel (1902–1971). New Zealand racehorse trainer. Name variations: Laurel Amy Eva Doyle, Mrs. J. Campbell. Born Laurel Amy Eva Doyle, Mar 15, 1902, in Doyleston, New Zealand; died Jan 3, 1971, in Christchurch, New Zealand; dau. of William John Doyle (storekeeper) and Matilda Jane (McCausland) Doyle; m. James Campbell (jockey), 1929 (div. 1950); children: 1 daughter. ❖ Began career as trainer for Alec Roberts, breeder of Phar Lap, and later entered into partnership with English trainer, Jack Jefferd; became 2nd woman professional racehorse trainer in New Zealand and sometimes raced under name Mrs. J. Campbell; her horses captured many titles, including the Wellington Cup, Melbourne Cup, and the Grand National Steeplechase. ❖ See also *Dictionary of New Zealand Biography* (Vol. 4).

CAMPBELL, Louise (1911–1997). American stage and screen actress. Name variations: Louise McMahon. Born Louise Weisbecker, May 30, 1911, in Chicago, Illinois; died Nov 5, 1997, in Norwalk, Connecticut; m. Horace McMahon (actor). ❖ Appeared on Broadway; films include *Night Club Scandal, Bulldog Drummond's Revenge, Wild Money, Bulldog Drummond Comes Back, The Buccaneer, Bulldog Drummond's Peril, Men with Wings, The Star Maker, Bowery Boy, Anne of Windy Poplars, Bush Pilot, Devil Ship* and *Contract on Cherry Street*.

CAMPBELL, Margaret (1912–1993). *See Margaret, duchess of Argyll.*

CAMPBELL, Margaret A. (1932–1998). *See Howell, Mary.*

CAMPBELL, Maria (1940—). Canadian biographer and folklorist. Name variations: June Stifle. Born June Stifle in 1940 in northern Saskatchewan, Canada, a Métis of Indian, French and Scottish ancestry; grew up in Prince Albert National Park. ❖ Wrote powerful autobiography *Halfbreed* (1973), which describes oppression of Canadian Metis women and celebrates life of her Cree great-grandmother Cheechum; other works include *People of the Buffalo: How the Plains People Lived* (1976), *Little Badger and the Fire Spirit* (1977), *Achimoona* (1985), *The Book of Jessica: A Theatrical Transformation* (1989) and *Stories of the Road Allowance People* (1995). Won Molson Prize for *Halfbreed.*

CAMPBELL, Mary (1877–1954). British medical reformer. Name variations: Dame Mary Campbell, Janet Mary Campbell, Janet Campbell. Born Janet Mary Campbell, 1877, in England; died 1954 in England;

dau. of a banker; graduate of London School of Medicine for Women; trained at Royal Free Hospital, 1902, and at Belgrave Hospital for Children, 1904. ❖ Early state medical officer and reformer, graduated with several qualifications from London School of Medicine, one of the 1st women to be permitted to study medicine; was appointed assistant school medical inspector to London Country Council (1905) and later 1st full-time woman medical officer on board of education; co-founded Medical Woman's Federation (1917), an organization still extant, to represent interests of women medical practitioners and women patients, addressing such concerns as venereal disease, prostitution, birth control and maternal and infant health; served as Britain's 1st woman senior medical officer for maternity and child welfare at Ministry of Health (1919–34); writings include *Physical Welfare of Mother and Children* (1917) and *A Comprehensive Report on Maternity Services* (1945). Awarded Dame of British Empire (DBE, 1924).

CAMPBELL, Mary Katherine (1905–1990). Miss America. Name variations: Mary K. Townley. Born Mary Katherine Campbell, Dec 18, 1905, in Ohio; died June 1990; attended Ohio State University and Ohio Wesleyan; m. Frederick Townley (DuPont executive). ❖ Named Miss Columbus, Ohio (1922); named Inter-City Beauty in Atlantic City, NJ (1922); was the 1st high school graduate to win title Miss America (1922); named Miss America once more (1923), the only woman to win the title twice. ❖ See also Frank Deford, *There She Is* (Viking, 1971).

CAMPBELL, Maude B. (c. 1908–?). American travel pioneer. Born Maude B. Campbell, c. 1908, in Salt Lake City, Utah. ❖ Paid $160 for a round-trip flight from Salt Lake City, UT, to Los Angeles, CA (June 10, 1926); as the only passenger in the open cockpit biplane, received a parachute and emergency instructions.

CAMPBELL, May.
See Irwin, May (1862–1938).
See Pearce, May (1915–1981).

CAMPBELL, Meg (1937—). New Zealand poet. Born 1937 of Maori and Polynesian descent; m. Alistair Te Ariki Campbell (novelist and poet); children: daughters, Maringi and Josie (both singers and writers). ❖ Worked as a librarian and bookseller in Wellington; works include *The Way Back* (1981), *A Durable Fire* (1982) and *The Better Part* (1998).

CAMPBELL, Naomi (1970—). English fashion model. Born May 22, 1970, in Streatham, South London, England; dau. of an unmarried teenage mother of Jamaican and Chinese descent; raised by grandparents; attended Italia Conti Academy of Theatre Arts, London. ❖ Supermodel, was spotted at 15 by a NY modeling agent in London's Covent Garden; appeared on cover of British *Elle* fashion magazine and experienced meteoric rise, becoming model, media star and international celebrity; was 1st black model to appear on covers of *Time* and both British and French *Vogue* (1988); moved to New York (1989) and landed cover of American *Vogue*; recorded album *Babywoman* with Epic Records (1995); appeared in numerous music videos for such artists as Michael Jackson, George Michael and Aretha Franklin; appeared in films *Girl 6*, *Miami Rhapsody* and *Invasion of Privacy*, and guest starred on tv; co-wrote bestselling suspense novel *Swan* and published photo book *Naomi* (1996), to benefit Red Cross Somalia Relief Fund.

CAMPBELL, Mrs. Patrick (1865–1940). English actress. Name variations: Beatrice Tanner; Stella Campbell; Stella Tanner. Born Beatrice Rose Stella Tanner, Feb 9, 1865; died in Pau, France, April 9, 1940; dau. of John and Maria Louisa Romanini Tanner; m. Patrick Campbell, June 21, 1884 (died 1900); m. George Cornwallis-West, April 6, 1914 (sep.); children: (1st m.) Alan Urquhart (b. 1885); Stella Tanner Campbell (b. 1886, actress). ❖ One of the most celebrated of English actresses, passed into literary history when George Bernard Shaw created the role of Eliza in *Pygmalion* for her; made debut as Marie Graham in *In His Power* in Norwood (1886); moving on to Ben Greet's Woodland Co., was soon playing Shakespearean roles, including Rosalind; with Greet's company, made London debut in *The Hunchback* (1889); had 1st major London success as Astrea in *The Trumpet Call* (1890), which ran for 220 performances; became overnight star as Paula in Pinero's *The Second Mrs. Tanqueray* (1893); famed for her wit and bad temper, flourished as one of the great ladies of the English stage (1894–1914), appearing in 43 roles, though not always to critical acclaim, and came to know everyone who mattered; had a triumph in Pinero's *The Notorious Mrs. Ebbsmith* (1895); won universal praise for portrayals of Ratwife, then Rita Allmers, in the same production of *Little Eyolf* (1896); triumphed in *Pelléas et Mélisande* (1899); became manager at the Royalty Theater (1900), staging a number of plays; made 1st visit to US for 6 months of repertory

in which she had a triumphant success in Chicago and NY (1901); had extraordinary success playing Mélisande to Sarah Bernhardt's Pelléas; thereafter, undertook to appear in several of Bernhardt's successes, among them *Fédora*; became increasingly involved with Shaw, who wrote *Pygmalion* for her on a dare (1914); starred in London revival of *Hedda Gabler* (1922); had last important original role as Anastasia Rakonitz in Stern's *The Matriarch* (1929); arrived in Hollywood (mid-1930); appeared in 4 films (1934), but her performance as the pawnbroker in *Crime and Punishment* remains the only true film record of her as an artist. ❖ See also memoir *My Life and Some Letters* (1922); Margot Peters, *Mrs. Pat: The Life of Mrs. Patrick Campbell* (1984); Alan Dent, *Bernard Shaw and Mrs. Patrick Campbell: Their Correspondence* (1952); (play) *Dear Liar*, based on correspondence between Campbell and Shaw; and *Women in World History*.

CAMPBELL, Persia (1898–1974). Australian-American economist. Name variations: Persia Crawford Campbell. Born Persia Crawford Campbell, Mar 15, 1898, in Sydney, Australia; died Mar 2, 1974, in Queens, NY; dau. of Rodolphe Campbell (primary schoolteacher) and Beatrice (Hunt) Campbell; Sydney University, AB, 1918, and AM; London School of Economics, MSc, 1923; also attended Bryn Mawr; m. Edward Rice Jr. (American electrical engineer), 1931 (died 1939); children: son Edward (b. 1933), daughter Sydney (b. 1934). ❖ Was research economist for Industrial Commission of New South Wales and taught economics courses for Workers' Educational Association (1926–30); became US citizen (1937); helped found Consumers' National Federation (1930s), National Association of Consumers (1947), and Consumer Federation of America (1960); worked at Queens College, NY (1939–65), as instructor in economics department, becoming head of department of social sciences (1960) and emeritus professor of economics (1965); worked with United Nations Educational, Scientific, and Cultural Organization (UNESCO, 1940s–50s); appointed 1st consumer counsel of NY (1954); was a member of Consumers Union board of directors (1959–74); conducted radio and tv broadcasts to raise consumer awareness about rights (1962–63); named to President's Council of Economic Advisers (1962, 1964). Wrote *Chinese Coolie Emigration* (1923), *Consumer Representation in the New Deal* (1940) and *Mary Williamson Harriman* (1960).

CAMPBELL, Stella (1865–1940). *See Campbell, Mrs. Patrick.*

CAMPBELL, Stella Patrick (b. 1886). *See Campbell, Stella Tanner.*

CAMPBELL, Stella Tanner (b. 1886). English actress. Name variations: Stella Patrick Campbell. Born Sept 27, 1886, in Norwood, England; dau. of Patrick Campbell and Beatrice Stella (Tanner) Campbell (Mrs. Patrick Campbell, actress, 1965–1940); m. Mervyn Beech, 1911 (died). ❖ Made stage debut in *Abdullah's Garden* (1907); made NY debut with her mother in *The Second Mrs. Tanqueray* (1907); other plays include *The Thunderbolt*, *Pinkie and the Fairies*, *The Prisoner of Zenda*, *The Importance of Being Earnest*, the title role in *The Princess Clementina*, *The Day before the Day*, *The Ware Case*, *Sheila*, *Arms and the Man* and Mrs. Darling in *Peter Pan*.

CAMPBELL, Veronica (1982—). Jamaican runner. Born May 15, 1982, in Trelawny, Jamaica; attended Barton Community College. ❖ Was the 1st woman to win the sprint double at World Junior championships (2000); won a silver medal for 4x100-meter relay at Sydney Olympics (2000); won gold medals for 200 meters and 4x100-meter relay and a bronze medal for 100 meters at Athens Olympics (2004).

CAMPBELL, Violet (1892–1970). English actress. Born April 24, 1892, in Hertfordshire, England; died Jan 3, 1970, in London; m. William Nigel Bruce. ❖ Made stage debut in *When We Were 21* (1915); made London debut in *The Professor's Love Story* (1916), followed by *The Bells*, *The Yellow Ticket*, *Two Jacks and a Jill*, *Dulcy*, *Iris*, *The Last of Mrs. Cheyney*, *The Bridge*, *The Circle*, *The Painted Veil* and *Tomorrow Never Comes*, among others.

CAMPELLO, Marina (1954—). *See Sciocchetti, Marina.*

CAMPION, Jane (1954—). New Zealand film director. Born April 30, 1954, in Wellington, New Zealand; dau. of Edith Campion (b. 1924, actress) and Richard Campion (opera and theater director); sister of Anna Campion (director); Victoria University, BA, 1975; Sydney College of the Arts, BA, 1979; attended Australian School of Film and Television; m. Colin Englert, 1992; children: 1 daughter, 1 son. ❖ One of international cinema's most distinctive talents, began making short films, including *Passionless Moments* (1983), *A Girl's Own Story* (1984) and *Two Friends* (1986), and won the Palme D'Or at Cannes for 1st short film, *Peel* (1986); co-wrote and directed 1st feature film *Sweetie* (1989), which won Georges Sadoul prize for Best Foreign Film (1989) and Australian Critics' Award, among others; followed with *An Angel at My Table* (1990), based on the autobiography of Janet Frame, which reaped several prizes, including Silver Lion at Venice Film Festival (1990); was the 1st woman to win Palme D'Or for feature-length film at Cannes for *The Piano* (1993), which also earned her an Academy Award for Best Original Screenplay and a nomination for Best Director; other films include *Holy Smoke* (1999), *Portrait of a Lady* (1996), *Soft Fruit* (1999) and *In the Cut* (2000).

CAMPION, Sarah (1906–2002). *See Coulton, Mary Rose.*

CAMPLIN, Alisa (1974—). Australian freestyle skier. Born Nov 10, 1974, in Melbourne, Australia. ❖ Won a gold medal for aerials at Salt Lake City (2002), the 1st Australian woman to win a gold medal at the Winter Games, and a bronze medal for aerials at Torino Olympics (2006); won the World Cup aerials (2003) and the FIS Freestyle World championship for aerials (2003). Named (with squash player Sarah Fitz-Gerald) Sport Australia Female Athlete of the Year (2002).

CAMPO ALANGE, countess of (1902–1986). *See Laffitte, María.*

CAMPOAMOR, Clara (1888–1972). Spanish lawyer, politician, and feminist. Born in Madrid, Spain, Feb 12, 1888; died April 30, 1972, in Lausanne, Switzerland; dau. of Manuel Campoamor Martínez and Pilar Rodríguez Martínez. ❖ Worked as a secretary for newspaper *La Tribuna* and translated French for a publishing house; affiliated with Spanish Social Party but was more interested in female suffrage and other women's rights than adherence to a political party; during Second Republic, won election to Constituent *Cortes* (Assembly); also founded the Feminine Republican Union, but her insistence that the Republic grant suffrage alienated many male deputies and left her isolated, even within her own party; failed to win reelection (1933); was part of the investigating commission sent to Oviedo following the brutal suppression of the miners' strike (1934); attempted to stand for election (1936) but no party would support her; when the Civil War began, went into exile (July 1936); published account of events in Spain, *La révolution espagnole vue par une républicaine* (1937); moved to Argentina and abandoned politics; translated French novels into Spanish and wrote several biographies, including one of Juana Ines de la Cruz; moved to Switzerland (1955). ❖ See also (in Spanish) memoir *Mi pecado mortal: el voto feminino y yo* (laSal, 1981); and *Women in World History.*

CAMPONESCHI, Angela (1898–1975). *See Bambace, Angela.*

CAMPS, Miriam (1916–1994). American government official and writer. Born Miriam Camp in Lynn, Massachusetts, 1916; died of lung cancer, age 78, in Little Abingdon, Cambridge, England, Dec 30, 1994; sister of Paul R. Camp and Margaret Schwartz; earned degrees at Mount Holyoke and Bryn Mawr; m. William Anthony Camps (classicist at Cambridge University), 1953. ❖ The 1st woman to serve as vice chair of US State Department's Planning Council (1968–70), joined State Department during WWII, working at US embassy in London; worked for the State Department in Washington, DC (1947–53); writings include *Britain and the European Community* (1964), *What Kind of Europe?* (1965), and *European Unification in the Sixties* (1966). ❖ See also *Women in World History.*

CANAL, Marguerite (1890–1978). French composer, conductor, and teacher. Born in Toulouse, France, Jan 29, 1890; died in Cépet, France, Jan 27, 1978; m. Maxime Jamin. ❖ Began studies at Paris Conservatory under Paul Vidal (1903), eventually earning 1st prizes in harmony, piano accompaniment and fugue; began to write songs, some of them to accompany her own poems; became 1st woman to conduct orchestral concerts in France (at a series held at Palais de Glace, 1917–18); appointed teacher of solfège (music theory) for singers at Paris Conservatory (1919); won Premier Grand Prix de Rome for "Don Juan," dramatic scene for voice and orchestra (1920); wrote one of her most moving works, Sonata for Violin and Piano (1922), followed by *Spleen* (1926), a composition for cello and small ensemble; often set many songs written during this period to the works of French poets, including Baudelaire, Verlaine, Marceline Desbordes-Valmore, and Paul Fort (the song cycle, *Amours tristes*, was set to her own verse and that of other poets); completed a full-scale opera, *Le pays blanc*, based on a Jack London story. ❖ See also *Women in World History.*

CANALE, Gianna Maria (1927—). Italian actress. Name variations: Gianna-Maria Canale; Gianna Canale. Born Sept 12, 1927, in Reggio di Calabria, Calabria, Italy; m. Riccarda Freda (director). ❖ Was a runner-up in the Miss Italy beauty contest; made film debut in *Aquila nera* (1946); other films include *Rigoletto, Il Cavaliere misterioso, Go for Broke, Tradimento, See Naples and Die, The Man from Cairo, Theodora Slave Empress, Madame du Barry, Napoléon, The Sword and the Cross, The Vampires, Hercules, The Mighty Crusaders, The Silent Enemy, The Whole Truth, The Warrior and the Slave Girl, Les Nuits de Raspoutine, Queen of the Pirates, The Secret of Monte Cristo, The Centurion* and *The Lion of St. Mark.*

CANALI, Isabella (1562–1604). *See Andreini, Isabella.*

CANARY, Christa (1962—). American gymnast. Name variations: Christa Canary Deford. Born June 5, 1962. ❖ Won Antibes International (1978), Paris Grand Prix (1979); was the 1st woman to perform a Cuervo in the vault.

CANARY, Martha Jane (1852–1903). *See Cannary, Martha Jane.*

CANDACE. *Like the name pharaoh for earlier Egyptian kings, Candace is a hereditary name of the queens of Meroe, an extensive kingdom in Upper Nubia, ranging from just south of Aswan and the 1st Cataract of the Nile in modern-day Egypt to the north and well into Ethiopia to the south. Pronunciation: KANDA-see.*

CANDEILLE, Julie (1767–1834). French singer, actress, writer and composer. Born Amélie Julie in Paris, France, July 31, 1767; died in Paris, Feb 4, 1834; married to Jean Simons from 1798–1821. ❖ By age 13, had appeared in public as a composer and a pianist; at age 15, sang the title role in Gluck's *Iphigénie en Aulide* (1782); by 18, was an established actress at the Comédie Française; had greatest success as a singer and actress in *Catherine, ou La belle fermière*, which ran for 154 performances and for which she wrote both the text and music (1792–93); also wrote *Bathilde, ou Le duc, Le commissionnaire, La bayadère ou Le Français à Surate, Louise, ou La réconcilliation* and *Ida, ou L'orpheline de Berlin*, a two-act opéra comique (1807); composed music, mainly for the piano, and wrote novels, many on historical topics. ❖ See also *Women in World History.*

CANDLER, Ann (1740–1814). British poet. Name variations: Ann More Candler. Born Ann More in 1740; died 1814; children: 4 (3 died in infancy). ❖ Spent time with her children in Ipswich workhouse as result of husband's alcoholism; was eventually supported by Elizabeth Cobbold and others; wrote poems for Ipswich journal and detailed her life in *Poetical Attempts by Ann Candler, a Suffolk Cottager, with a Short Narrative of Her Life* (1803).

CANDY, Alice (1888–1977). New Zealand teacher and university lecturer. Born Alice Muriel Flora Candy, July 9, 1888, at West Oxford, Canterbury, New Zealand; died May 18, 1977, in Christchurch, New Zealand; dau. of James Candy (blacksmith) and Alice (Hood) Candy; Canterbury College, BA, 1910, MA, 1911. ❖ Taught in several schools (1912–20), and became senior mistress at Chilton St James School, Lower Hutt; appointed assistant lecturer, Canterbury College (1920); helped form Canterbury Women Graduates' Association (1921); became president of Canterbury branch of New Zealand Federation of University Women (1926); was exchange lecturer at Bedford College, University of London (1928–29); appointed warden of Helen Connon Hall for women students (1936); retired as senior university lecturer (1948); member of college council (1954–57). ❖ See also *Dictionary of New Zealand Biography* (Vol. 4).

CANFIELD, Dorothy (1879–1958). *See Dorothy Canfield Fisher.*

CANFIELD, Ella Jean (1918—). Canadian politician. Born Oct 4, 1918, in Westmorland, Prince Edward Island, Canada. ❖ Was the 1st woman to sit in the Prince Edward Island Legislative Assembly (1970); was the 1st woman to be appointed to the Provincial Cabinet (1972–74), as Minister without Portfolio and Minister Responsible for P.E.I. Housing Authority. Awarded Queen's Jubilee Medal (1977).

CANINS, Maria (1949—). Italian cyclist and Nordic skier. Name variations: The Flying Mum. Born June 4, 1949, in La Villa, Alta Badia, Italy. ❖ Won the Tour de France (Tour Feminin, 1985 and 1986) and came in second 3 times; won 2 tours of Norway, 1 tour of Colorado, and 4 tours of the Adriatic; was 6-time road-racing champion and 4-time time-trials champion of Italy; at World championships, won 1 gold, 3 silvers, and 2 bronze medals; as a skier, was World champion in the Winter Triathlon (1997) and Italian champion 15-times at various distances.

CANNARY, Martha Jane (1852–1903). American frontierswoman. Name variations: Calamity Jane; Martha Jane Burk or Burke; Marthy Jane Canary. Born Martha or Marthy Jane Cannary, May 1, 1852, in

Princeton, Missouri; died in Terry, South Dakota, Aug 1, 1903; dau. of Robert and Charlotte Cannary; m. Clinton Burk or Burke (1885?); also had a number of common-law husbands; children: number and names uncertain; one woman, Jane McCormick, claimed Calamity Jane as her mother, though the veracity of this is questioned. ❖ Legendary frontierswoman, known as Calamity Jane, who did exactly as she pleased in her own colorful manner, thus significantly contributing to the lore of the Wild West; moved to Montana after living in Missouri in her early years (1865); mother died (1866); moved to Utah where father died (1867); moved to Wyoming (1868); went on army expeditions (1872–73); with Wild Bill Hickok, came to Deadwood, South Dakota, where Hickok was murdered by Jack McCall (1876); nursed victims of smallpox epidemic in Deadwood (1878); worked as bullwhacker or teamster between Fort Pierre and Black Hills (1879); claimed to have married Clinton Burk (1885), though marriage probably occurred sometime in the 1890s; appeared on stage at the Palace Museum in Minneapolis (1896); appeared at Pan-American Exposition in Buffalo, New York (1901). ❖ See also autobiography *Life and Adventures of Calamity Jane by Herself* (1896); Dora DeFran, *Low Down on Calamity Jane* (Argus, 1981); Doris Faber, *Calamity Jane: Her Life and Legend* (Houghton, 1992); Irma M. Klock, *Here Comes Calamity Jane* (Dakota Graphics, 1979); Ellen Crago Mueller, *Calamity Jane* (Jelm Mountain, 1981); Roberta B. Sollid, *Calamity Jane: A Study in Historical Criticism* (Historical Society of Montana, 1958); Glenn Clairmonte, *Calamity Was the Name for Jane* (Sage, 1959); and *Women in World History*.

CANNON, Annie Jump (1863–1941). *American astronomer.* Born Annie Jump Cannon, Dec 11, 1863, in Dover, Delaware; died in Cambridge, Massachusetts, April 13, 1941; dau. of Wilson Lee (state senator, merchant, and shipbuilder) and Mary Elizabeth (Jump) Cannon; Wellesley College, BS, 1884, MA, 1907; special student in astronomy at Radcliffe College (1895–97). ❖ One of the most famous woman astronomers in the world, who was called the "Census Taker of the Sky," developed the 1st simple spectral classification system, classified more stars than anyone had before (400,000 stellar bodies), and discovered 300 variable stars, 5 novas, and a double star; became assistant astronomer at Harvard College Observatory (1896–1911), curator of astronomical photographs (1911–38), William Cranch Bond Astronomer and Curator (1938–40); developed a simple spectral classification system (1901), that was adopted by the International Solar Union (1910); compiled Henry Draper Catalogues (1911–24); was 1st woman elected an officer of the American Astronomical Society (1912–19). Designated America's leading female scientist by League of Women Voters (1922); was 1st woman to receive honorary doctorate from Oxford University (1925); awarded Henry Draper Gold Medal from National Academy of Sciences (1931); saw 1st Annie Jump Cannon Prize awarded (1934). ❖ See also Bessie Z. Jones and Lyle Boyd. *The Harvard College Observatory: The First Four Directorships, 1839–1919* (Harvard U. Press, 1971); and *Women in World History*.

CANNON, Dyan (1937—). *American actress and director.* Name variations: Diana Cannon, Diane Cannon. Born Samile Diane Friesen, Jan 4, 1937, in Tacoma, Washington; attended University of Washington, Seattle; m. Cary Grant (actor), July 22, 1965 (div. Mar 21, 1968); m. Stanley Fimberg, April 1985 (div. 1991); children: Jennifer Grant (b. 1966, actress). ❖ Made film debut in *The Rise and Fall of Legs Diamond* (1960); received New York Film Critics' Award and nominated for Academy Award, both for Best Supporting Actress, for *Bob and Carol and Ted and Alice* (1969); nominated for Academy Award as director for Best Short Film for *Number One* (1976) and as Best Supporting Actress for *Heaven Can Wait* (1978); other films include *Doctors' Wives* (1971), *The Anderson Tapes* (1971), *The Love Machine* (1971), *Such Good Friends* (1971), *The Last of Sheila* (1973), *Revenge of the Pink Panther* (1978), *Deathtrap* (1982), *Out to Sea* (1997), *That Darn Cat* (1997) and *Kangaroo Jack* (2003); on tv, guest starred on "Ally McBeal" and "The Practice."

CANNON, Frank (1930—). *See Mayhar, Ardath.*

CANNON, Harriet Starr (1823–1896). *American religious leader.* Born May 7, 1823, in Charleston, South Carolina; died April 5, 1896, in Peekskill, New York; orphaned at 12 months, was raised by an aunt in Bridgeport, Connecticut. ❖ Entered New York City's Episcopal Sisterhood of the Holy Communion (1856), becoming a full member (1857); managed a ward at St. Luke's Hospital (1858–63); preferring a more monastic-type rule, left the order with a few other sisters (1863); with that small group, ran the House of Mercy, a rescue house and reformatory for young women, as well as the Sheltering Arms orphanage

and St. Barnabas' House for homeless women and children; after the group founded the Community of St. Mary, the 1st Episcopal religious community in US (1865), was elected its 1st superior (1865) and took her life vows (1867); helped establish many institutions, including St. Mary's School in New York City (1868), St. Gabriel's School in Peekskill (1872), St. Mary's School in Memphis, Tennessee (1873), Kemper Hall in Kenosha, Wisconsin (1878), and St. Mary's Free Hospital for Poor Children in New York City (1870). ❖ See also *Women in World History*.

CANNON, Ida (1877–1960). *American social worker.* Name variations: Ida M. Cannon or Ida Maud Cannon. Born Ida Maud Cannon, June 9, 1877, in Milwaukee, Wisconsin; died July 7, 1960, in Watertown, MA; dau. of Colbert Hanchett Cannon and Sarah Wilma (Denio) Cannon (schoolteacher); sister of Walter Bradford Cannon (physiologist); graduate of City and County Hospital Training School for Nursing, 1898; attended University of Minnesota and Boston School of Social Workers. ❖ Pioneer in medical social work, who encouraged study of the impact of environmental factors on disease, began career as a visiting nurse for St. Paul Associated Charities, St. Paul, MN (1903–06); worked at experimental medical social work department at MA General Hospital (MGH, 1906–07), becoming head worker (1908); served as chief of MGH social service (1915–45), overseeing formal incorporation of department into hospital (1919); created and directed specialized program for medical social work at Boston School for Social Workers (1912–25); wrote *Social Work in Hospitals: A Contribution to Progressive Medicine* (1913) and *On the Social Frontier of Medicine: Pioneering in Medical Social Service* (1952); taught at Boston College School of Social Work (1937–45); helped found American Association of Hospital Social Workers (1918) and was its 2nd president (1920). Received Lemuel Shattuck Award for distinguished service in public health from MA Public Health Association.

CANNON, Josephine J. (1910–1990). *See Johnson, Josephine Winslow.*

CANNON, Ophelia Colley (1912–1996). *See Pearl, Minnie.*

CANO, María (1887–1967). *Colombian political leader.* Name variations: María de los Angeles Cano Márquez; Maria Cano. Born Aug 12, 1887, in Medellín, Colombia; died April 26, 1967, in Medellín. ❖ The most significant Colombian socialist leader of the 1920s, began literary circle Cyrano and founded a magazine by the same name; worked at *El correo liberal* (The Liberal Mail, by 1922); became 1st woman in Columbian history to have leadership position in a political organization, as an organizer of regional representation of Antioquía at Third National Labor Congress (1926); worked on behalf of The Partido Socialista Revolucionario (PSR); founded newspaper *La justicia;* opposed *ley heroica* (law constructed to combat international communism) and supported Nicaraguan rebel leader Sandino in fight for national sovereignty in Nicaragua (1928); imprisoned and charged with conspiracy; made unsuccessful attempt to return to politics (1934).

CANOSSA, Matilda of (1046–1115). *See Matilda of Tuscany.*

CANOVA, Judy (1916–1983). *American comedian and singer.* Born Juliet Canova, Nov 20, 1916, in Jacksonville, Florida; died of cancer, Aug 5, 1983, in Hollywood, California; married twice; children: Diana Canova (b. June 1, 1953, tv actress) and Juliette Canova. ❖ Known for her hillbilly antics and ear-splitting yodel, was part of a family vaudeville team before landing a part on Broadway in Ziegfeld's *Calling All Stars* (1934); hired for a small part in *In Caliente* (1935), stole the film with her rendition of "The Lady in Red"; went on to perform similar humorous bits in such major films as *Thrill of a Lifetime* (1937) and *Artists and Models* (1937); made a string of low-budget films, including *Scatterbrain* (1940), *Puddin' Head* (1941), *Singin' in the Corn* (1946), *Honeychile* (1951), *WAC from Walla Walla* (1952), and *Untamed Heiress* (1954); starred in a successful weekly half-hour radio show. ❖ See also *Women in World History*.

CANSINO, Elisa (b. 1895). *Spanish dancer.* Name variations: Dancing Cansinos. Born 1895, probably in Andalusia, Spain; dau. of Antonio Cansino (dance master) and Carmen Cansino (dancer); sister of Eduoardo, Angel, Paco, José, Antonio II, and Rafael Cansino (all dancers); aunt of Rita Hayworth (actress); children: Gabriel Cansino (1913–1963, dancing teacher). ❖ Toured US on Keith circuit with brother Eduoardo (c. 1910); returned to Spain to teach; danced with brothers Eduoardo and Angel as The Dancing Cansinos, probably in and around New York City; toured extensively throughout life, moving back and forth between US and Spain; played a major role in introducing Spanish and other ethnic dance forms to US.

CANSINO, Rita (1918–1987). *See Hayworth, Rita.*

CANTER-LUND, Hilda M. (1922—). English mycologist, protozoologist, and photographer. Name variations: Hilda Canter Lund. Born Hilda M. Canter, 1922, in Highbury, London; dau. of a gas fitter; Bedford College in London, BS, 1944; University of London, education diploma, 1945; Queen Mary College Department of Botany, PhD, 1948, DSc, 1955; m. Dr. John W.G. Lund (phycologist), 1949. ❖ Known for her expertise on fungi that parasitize freshwater algae and for research on protozoan parasites that kill algae, was appointed mycologist (1948) and later worked as senior principal scientific officer (1976–87) for Freshwater Biological Association (FBA); received Royal Photographic Society fellowship (1965); realized 1st successful isolation of chytrid, *Rhizophydium planktonicum,* with G.H.M. Jaworski; appointed FBA honorary research fellow (1990); with husband, wrote *Freshwater Algae: Their Microscopic World Explored* (1995).

CANTH, Minna (1844–1897). Finnish playwright and author. Name variations: Ulrika Wilhelmina Canth. Born Ulrika Vilhelmina Johansson, Mar 19, 1844, in Tampere, Finland; died May 12, 1897, in Kuopio, Finland; dau. of Gustaf Wilhelm Johannson or Johnson (inspector in a cotton mill, then shopkeeper) and Ulrika Johannson or Johnson; attended a teacher's college at Jyväskylä; m. Johan Ferdinand Canth (natural science instructor and newspaper editor), c. 1864 (died c. 1877); children: 7. ❖ A major representative of the realist school, who was an eloquent advocate for women's rights, began to submit articles to local newspapers after death of husband; completed a folk play, *The Burglary* (1879); became a leading member of the Young Finns (1880s), a movement organized to promote both social reforms and the heightening of national cultural awareness; wrote plays as *The Workman's Wife* (1885) and *Children of Misfortune* (1888); also wrote novellas *Poor Folk* (1886) and *The Sunken Rock* (1887) and short stories "Hanna" and "Poor People" (both 1886) and "Lopo the Peddler" (1889); became the voice of the oppressed in her final plays, *The Vicar's Family* (1891), *Sylvi* (1893) and *Anna-Liisa* (1895). Honored on centenary of her birth with commemorative Finnish postage stamp.

CANTO, Estela (1919–1994). Argentinean novelist and journalist. Born 1919 in Buenos Aires, Argentina; died 1994 in Buenos Aires. ❖ Claimed to have had a love affair with writer Jorge Luis Borges who dedicated his story "El aleph" to her; works include *El retrato y la imagen* (1950), *El hombre del crepúsculo* (1953), *El estanque* (1956) and *Borges a contraluz* (1989).

CANTOFOLI, Ginevra (1618–1672). Italian artist. Born at Bologna in 1618; died 1672; pupil of Elisabetta Sirani. ❖ Paintings were historical in nature and may be seen in several churches in Bologna.

CANTRELL, Lana (1943—). Australian singer. Born Aug 7, 1943, in Sydney, Australia. ❖ Popular international singer in 1970s, was well-known in Australia by the time she was 10; for 4 years, was a regular on tv's "Bandstand" and "In Melbourne Tonight"; moved to US and appeared often on "The Ed Sullivan Show" and "The Tonight Show starring Johnny Carson"; won the International Song Festival with "I'm All Smiles" (1966); nominated for a Grammy for Best New Artist (1967); recorded 7 albums for RCA Victor and had a hit single "Like a Sunday Morning"; retired from performing; became an entertainment lawyer in NY. Received the Order of Australia (2003).

CANTY, Mary Agnes (1879–1950). New Zealand nun and teacher. Born Mar 22, 1879, in Greta, New South Wales, Australia; died Oct 6, 1950, in Auckland, New Zealand; dau. of Daniel Canty (miner) and Bridget (Wade) Canty. ❖ Joined Sisters of Mercy in Auckland (1895) and took vows (1898); helped found New Zealand Mater hospital (1936) and nursing school (1937), serving as nursing school matron until 1973. ❖ See also *Dictionary of New Zealand Biography.*

CAO MIANYING. Chinese rower. Born in China. ❖ Won a silver medal for double sculls at Atlanta Olympics (1996).

CAPANO, Lauri (1960—). *See Merten, Lauri.*

CAPE, Judith (b. 1916). *See Page, P.K.*

CAPÉCIA, Mayotte (1928–1953). Martiniquan novelist. Name variations: Mayotte Capecia. Born 1928 in Martinique; lived later years in France; died 1953. ❖ Wrote *Je suis Martiniquaise* (I Am a Martinican Woman, 1948) and *La Négresse Blanche* (The White Negress, 1950).

CAPELL-CONINGSBY, Catherine (1794–1882). *See Stephens, Catherine.*

CAPELLMANN, Nadine (1965—). German equestrian. Born July 9, 1965, in Aachen, Germany. ❖ Won a gold medal for team dressage at Sydney Olympics (2000), on Farbenfroh.

CAPELLO, Bianca (1548–1587). *See Cappello, Bianca.*

CAPERS, Virginia (1925–2004). African-American actress and singer. Born Eliza Virginia Capers, Sept 22, 1925, in Sumter, South Carolina; died May 6, 2004, in Los Angeles, California; attended Howard University and Juilliard School; children: Glenn S. Capers. ❖ Hired by bandleader Abe Lyman because she could speak Yiddish, logged in many hours on radio; on Broadway, appeared in *Saratoga* (1959), then won a Tony Award for performance as Lena Younger in *Raisin* (1974); films include *Lady Sings the Blues, Trouble Man, The Lost Man, Ferris Bueller's Day Off, The Toy, Pacific Palisades* and *What's Love Got to Do With It;* nominated for Emmy for a performance in episode of "Mannix" (1973), also appeared on "The Untouchables," "Dragnet," "Frank's Place," "Fresh Prince of Bel-Air" and "The Hughleys," among others; founded the Lafayette Players, a Los Angeles repertory company.

CAPERTON, Harriette (c. 1913—). American dancer. Born Harriette Caperton, c. 1913, in Richmond, Virginia. ❖ Toured the Prolog circuit, dancing with Earl Vernon Biddle, and appeared with him at Capitol Theater in New York City (1932); formed team with Charles Columbus—considered 1 of the greatest exhibition and adagio dancers of the time—and performed exhibition waltzes, fox trots, and adagio dances (1935–41); performed acts that incorporated gravity-defying moves and gymnastic routines.

CAPES, Lee (1961—). Australian field-hockey player. Born Oct 3, 1961; sister of Michelle Capes. ❖ At Seoul Olympics, won a gold medal in team competition (1988).

CAPES, Michelle (1966—). Australian field-hockey player. Born Oct 3, 1966; sister of Lee Capes. ❖ At Seoul Olympics, won a gold medal in team competition (1988).

CAPET, Agnes (1260–1327). *See Agnes Capet.*

CAPET, Alice (1150–c. 1197). *See Alice.*

CAPET, Constance (c. 1128–1176). *See Constance Capet.*

CAPET, Gabrielle (1761–1817). French artist. Born Marie Gabrielle Capet, Sept 6, 1761, in Lyon, France; died 1817. ❖ One of the most popular French miniature portraitists of late 18th and early 19th centuries, entered the studio of Adelaide Labille-Guiard in Paris, living in her household from 1782 and caring for Labille-Guiard during her final illness; debuted at Exposition de la Jeunesse (1781), where she would exhibit for 4 years; though she began with pastel and oil portraits, specialized in portrait miniatures starting in 1787, the same year she received a commission to paint the royal princesses; was one of 21 women and 236 men whose works were represented in the Salon (1791), the 1st year it was open to women; continued to exhibit there until 1814; rendered approximately 30 oil paintings, 35 pastel, and 85 miniatures. ❖ See also *Women in World History.*

CAPMANY FARNES, Maria Aurèlia (1918—). Spanish novelist and feminist. Name variations: Maria Capmany; Maria Aurelia Capmany Farnes. Born 1918; read philosophy at University of Barcelona. ❖ Catalan writer, works include *Necessitem morir* (We Must Die, 1925), *L'altre ciutat* (The Other City, 1955), *Tana o la felicitat* (Tana, or Happiness, 1956), *La pluja als vidres* (Rain on the Windowpane, 1963), *Un lloc entre els morts* (A Place among the Dead, 1969), *Vitrines d'Amsterdam* (Showcase of Amsterdam, 1970), *Quim/Quimá* (1971), *El jaqué dela democracia* (The Tuxedo of Democracy, 1972), and *Lo color més blau* (The Bluest Color, 1982); also wrote important feminist studies, including *La dona a Catalunya* (Woman in Catalonia, 1966) and *El femenisme a Catalunya* (Feminism in Catalonia, 1973).

CAPONI, Donna (1945—). American golfer. Name variations: Donna Caponi Young. Born Jan 29, 1945, in Detroit, Michigan; sister of Janet LePera (golfer). ❖ Joined LPGA tour (1965); won USGA Women's Open (1969, 1970); voted *Los Angeles Times'* Woman Golfer of the Year (1970); won Lincoln-Mercury Open (1969); won Bluegrass Invitational (1970, 1973); won Burdine's Invitational, Lady Tara Classic, Colgate European Open (1975); won Portland Classic, Carlton, Mizuno Japan Classic and Australian championship (1976); won Sarah Coventry and Houston Classic (1978); won LPGA championship (1979, 1981); won LPGA National Pro-Am, Colgate-Dinah Shore, and Corning Classic (1980), Desert Inn Pro-Am, American Defender, WUI Classic, Boston

Five Classic (1981); commentator for NBC, TBS, Australian TV, and analyst for The Golf Channel. Inducted into World Golf Hall of Fame and LPGA Tour Hall of Fame.

CAPPA, Benedetta (1897–1977). *See Marinetti, Benedetta Cappa.*

CAPPELLO, Bianca (1548–1587). Grand duchess of Tuscany. Name variations: Bianca Capello; Bianca Bonaventuri; Bianca de Medici. Born in Venice, 1548; died suddenly in Tuscany during colic epidemic, Oct 1587; dau. of Bartolommeo Cappello (Venetian aristocrat); m. Pietro Bonaventuri (clerk), 1563 (died 1572); became 2nd wife of Francesco I also known as Francis I de Medici (1541–1587), grand duke of Tuscany, June 1578; children: (1st m.) Pellegrina Bonaventuri (who m. Ulisse Bentivoglio); (2nd m.) stepdaughter Marie de Medici (c. 1573–1642). ❧ Born into a wealthy family of the Venetian aristocracy, was renowned for her beauty; rebelled against parents' plans for her, and eloped to Florence with a lowly clerk when she was 15 (Nov 1563), causing great consternation in Venice and catching the attention of the Venetian authorities; allowed to remain safely in Florence by Cosimo de Medici, duke of Florence and Tuscany; became mistress of Cosimo de Medici's son and heir, Francesco de Medici, himself already married to Joanna of Austria (1546–1578); when Francesco succeeded his father, her relationship with him became public knowledge, scandalizing Florence; when Joanna died (1578), married him; was unpopular in Florence and especially disliked by the Medici family. ❧ See also *Women in World History.*

CAPPIANI, Luisa (1835—?). Austrian musician, singer and voice teacher. Name variations: Louisa Kapp-Young. Born Luisa Young, 1835, in Austria; educated in Vienna; m. a Mr. Kapp (Austrian counselor), 1847 (died 1850). ❧ Following the death of husband, began a music career under the name Kapp-Young; later, to satisfy 19th-century preference for Italian musicians, fused her name into Cappiani; became a renowned voice teacher. ❧ See also *Women in World History.*

CAPPIELLO, Rosa (1942—). Italian-Australian novelist. Born 1942 in Naples, Italy. ❧ Immigrated to Australia (1971); works include *I Semi Negri* (The Black Seeds, 1977) and *Paese Fortunata* (Oh Lucky Country, 1981). Won Italian Premio Calabria award for *Paese Fortunata.*

CAPPS, Lois (1938—). American politician. Born Jan 10, 1938, in Ladysmith, Wisconsin; Pacific Lutheran University, BS in Nursing; Yale University, MA in Religion; University of California at Santa Barbara, MA in Education; m. Walter Capps (US congressional representative, died 1998); children: Lisa (died 2000) and Laura Capps. ❧ Worked as Elementary District Nurse for the school system of Santa Barbara; representing California, won a special election for a Democratic seat in the 105th US Congress (1998), succeeding her late husband; served on the Committee on Science and Committee on International Relations; reelected (2000, 2002, 2004).

CAPRIATI, Jennifer (1976—). American tennis player. Born Mar 29, 1976, in Long Island, NY. ❧ Turned pro at 14, making the semifinals for singles at Roland Garros (1990), the youngest player to reach that round in a Grand Slam; won a gold medal for singles at Barcelona Olympics (1992); won singles championship at Australian Open (2001, 2002), Roland Garros (2001); competed in semifinals for singles at US Open (1991, 2001, 2003).

CAPRICE, June (1899–1936). American silent-film actress. Born Elizabeth Lawson, Nov 19, 1899, in Arlington, Massachusetts; died Nov 9, 1936, in Los Angeles, California; m. Harry F. Millarde (actor, director). ❧ Juvenile Fox star, appeared in such films as *The Ragged Princess, Miss Innocence, Caprice of the Mountains, A Modern Cinderella, Oh Boy!, The Love Cheat, Rogues and Romance* and *A Damsel in Distress.*

CAPTAIN AND TENNILLE. *See Tennille, Toni.*

CAPTAIN MOLLY. (1751–c. 1800). *See Corbin, Margaret.*

CAPUCINE (1931–1990). French model and actress. Born Germaine Lefebvre, Jan 6, 1931, in Toulon, France; died Mar 17, 1990, in Lausanne, Switzerland, after jumping from the balcony of her 8th-floor apartment; m. Pierre Trabaud, 1950 (div. 1950). ❧ Was a top haute-couture model in Paris; made film debut in *Rendez-vous de juillet* (1949), followed by *Song without End, North to Alaska, Walk on the Wild Side, The Lion, The Pink Panther, What's New Pussycat?, Fellini's Satyricon, Trail of the Pink Panther* and *Curse of the Pink Panther,* among others; close friend of Audrey Hepburn; became more and more reclusive in later years.

CAPUTO, Bonnie (1948—). *See Tiburzi, Bonnie.*

CARABELLA, Flora (1926–1999). Italian actress. Name variations: Flora Mastroianni. Born Feb 15, 1926, in Rome, Italy; died April 19, 1999, in Rome; m. Marcello Mastroianni (actor), 1948 (died Dec 19, 1996). ❧ Appeared in 1st film *I Basilischi* (1963); other films include *Il Messia* (1976), *Casotto* (1977), *A Night Full of Rain* (1978), *In viaggio con papà* (1982), *Donne in un giorno di festa* (1993) and *Quando finiranno le zanzare* (1994).

CARABILLO, Toni (1926–1997). American feminist and historian. Born Virginia Ann Carabillo in Jackson Heights, New York, Mar 26, 1926; died in Los Angeles, California, Oct 28, 1997; dau. of Ann and Anthony Carabillo (pharmacist); graduate of Middlebury College, 1948, and Columbia University, MA, 1949; lived with Judith Meuli (writer). ❧ Joined NOW (1967) and helped launch branches throughout California, serving over the years as president of Los Angeles chapter, national vice president, and board member; also co-edited NOW's national newsletter and newspaper; co-founded Women's Heritage Corp. (1969), publishing *Women's Heritage Calendar and Almanac* and a series of paperbacks, concerning such women as Elizabeth Cady Stanton and Lucy Stone; wrote (with Judith Meuli) *The Feminization of Power* (1988) and (with June Csida) *Feminist Chronicles, 1953–1993* (1993); teamed with Meuli, Eleanor Smeal, Peg Yorkin and Katherine Spillar to create the Feminist Majority Foundation (1987), to encourage women's empowerment by supporting professional women in the private and public sphere, and served as national vice president. ❧ See also *Women in World History.*

CARADUS, Elizabeth (1832–1912). New Zealand suffragist, welfare worker, and shopkeeper. Name variations: Elizabeth Russell. Born Elizabeth Russell, April 26, 1832, in Falkirk, Stirlingshire, Scotland; died Nov 5, 1912, in Auckland, New Zealand; dau. of David and Elizabeth (Adam) Russell; m. James Caradus (ropemaker), 1848 (died 1906); children: 15. ❧ Immigrated with family to New Zealand (1842); managed small shop until 1910; active in moral and social reform issues; member of Women's Christian Temperance Union (WCTU); founding member and vice president of New Zealand branch of Young Women's Christian Association (YWCA). ❧ See also *Dictionary of New Zealand Biography* (Vol. 2).

CARAGIOFF, Olga (1887–1969). *See Oelkers-Caragioff, Olga.*

CARAMAGNO, Denise (1961—). American mountain biker. Born July 5, 1961, in New York, NY. ❧ Pioneered the sport of mountain biking in US; helped found magazine *Fat Tire Flyer.* Inducted into Mountain Biker Hall of Fame (2001).

CARAWAY, Hattie Wyatt (1878–1950). American politician. Born Hattie Ophelia Wyatt in Bakerville, Tennessee, Feb 1, 1878; died in Falls Church, Virginia, Dec 21, 1950; dau. of William Carroll Wyatt and Lucy Mildred (Burch) Wyatt; attended public school; Dickson (Tennessee) Normal College, BA, 1896; m. Thaddeus Horatius Caraway (US Democratic senator), 1902 (died 1931); children: Paul Wyatt, Forrest, and Robert Easley. ❧ Following death of husband (1931), received a courtesy appointment to fill out his unexpired term as US senator; surprised Arkansas politicians by running for a full 6-year term, becoming the 1st woman elected to US Senate (1932); gained the respect of her constituents who elected her to a 2nd term; supported FDR's foreign policy and domestic economic programs; was also attentive to the needs of her largely agricultural constituency, throwing her support behind farm relief and flood control; became the 1st woman to chair a Senate committee, the 1st woman senior senator, and the 1st woman to conduct a Senate committee hearing; during 2nd term, co-sponsored the Lucretia Mott Equal Rights Amendment to the Constitution (1943), thus becoming the 1st woman in the Senate to endorse the measure; after 13 years of service, was defeated in the Arkansas primary by Republican William Fulbright (1944); served on the Federal Employees' Compensation Committee (1946–50). ❧ See also *Women in World History.*

CARBASSE, Louise (1895–1980). *See Lovely, Louise.*

CARBERY, Ethna (1866–1902). *See MacManus, Anna.*

CARBON, Sally (1967—). Australian field-hockey player. Born April 14, 1967. ❧ At Seoul Olympics, won a gold medal in team competition (1988).

CARDALE, Effie (1873–1960). New Zealand social-welfare worker. Born Effie Julia Margaret Cardale, May 20, 1873, in Christchurch, New Zealand; died Oct 19, 1960, in Christchurch; dau. of Alfred (stock owner) and Flora Emily (Coward) Cardale. ❧ Worked on behalf of women and children through various charities funded by Anglican church (1914–55); member of North Canterbury Hospital Board (1929–31); became justice of peace and was appointed conciliator to court and mediated divorce cases (1939). Member of British Empire (1949). ❖ See also *Dictionary of New Zealand Biography* (Vol. 3).

CARDELL-OLIVER, Florence (1876–1965). Australian politician. Name variations: Annie Florence Gillies Cardell-Oliver; Dame Florence Cardell-Oliver. Born May 11, 1876, in Stawell, Victoria, Australia; died Jan 12, 1965; dau. of Annie Thompson and Johnson Wilson; m. Arthur Cardell-Oliver (physician, died 1929); children: 2 sons. ❖ Studied in England; married and returned to Perth with husband (1914); unsuccessfully contested the federal seat of Freemantle (1934); won as Nationalist candidate for the State seat of Subiaco (1936); was the 1st woman in Australia to be appointed to a state cabinet, when she was named Western Australian minister for Health, Supply and Shipping (1949), serving until 1953; was responsible for the introduction of compulsory testing for tuberculosis and the distribution of free milk for schoolchildren, among other initiatives. Awarded DBE (1951).

CARDEN, Joan (1937—). Australian opera singer. Name variations: Joan Maralyn Carden. Born Oct 9, 1937, in Melbourne, Victoria, Australia; dau. of Frank Carden and Ethel Gabriel (Cooke) Carden; attended Trinity College of Music and London Opera Centre. ❖ Renowned soprano, joined the Australian Opera (1971) where she worked as a principal throughout career; made début at London's Covent Garden as Gilda in *Rigoletto* (1974) and went on to make role her own, performing as Gilda with Australian Opera as well; traveled throughout UK and continental Europe, performing widely, including at Glyndeborne Festival (1977) and with Scottish Opera (1978); also performed in US with Metropolitan Opera Tour (1978), at Kennedy Center (1980), and with Miami Opera (1982); best known for performances of Mozart and of the 4 heroines in *The Tales of Hoffmann*. Awarded Office of British Empire (OBE, 1981) and Officer of Order of Australia (AO, 1988).

CÁRDENAS, Nancy (1934–1994). Mexican playwright and director. Name variations: Nancy Cardenas. Born May 29, 1934, in Coahuila, Parras, Mexico; died of breast cancer, Mar 22, 1994; Nacional Autónoma Universidad de Mexico (UNAM), PhD in liberal arts; also attended Center for Cinematographic Studies in Poland. ❖ Renowned playwright and director, fought against homophobia; directed *Claudine, Las amargas lágrimas de Petra Von Kant,* and *El día que pisamos la luna,* among others; also worked in other disciplines, as poet, journalist, and critic; received Best Director Award from Asociación de Críticos de Teatro (ACT), for *El efecto de los rayos gama sobre las caléndulas* (1971), *Aquelarre* (1973), and *Cuarteto* (1976).

CARDINAL, Marie (1929–2001). French novelist. Born Mar 9, 1929, in Algiers, Algeria; died May 9, 2001; studied philosophy in Paris; children: 3. ❖ Best known for her semi-autobiographical, bestselling novel *Les Mots pour le dire* (*The Words to Say It,* 1975), one of the 1st books about the personal experience of psychoanalysis; won the Prix International du Premier Roman for her 1st novel, *Ecoutez la Mer;* other writings, which often focus on women's experiences and explore their relationship to language, include *La Clé sur la porte* (1972), *Une vie pour deux* (1979), *Au pays de mes racines* (1980), *Le passé empiété* (1983), and *Les Grands Désordres* (1987); taught at the universities of Salonika, Lisbon, and Montreal.

CARDINALE, Claudia (1939—). Italian actress. Born April 15, 1939, in Tunis, Tunisia; dau. of Italian parents; m. Franco Cristaldi (producer, writer, div. 1974); m. Pasquale Squitieri (director, writer); children: 2. ❖ Won a beauty contest in Tunis (1957); made film debut in *Les Noces Venetienne* (1958); came to prominence in *Big Deal on Madonna Street,* followed by *Rocco and His Brothers, The Leopard, 8½, Cartouche, Once Upon a Time in the West, The Pink Panther, Circus World, Blindfold, Lost Command, The Professionals, The Hell with Heroes, A Fine Pair, The Red Tent, Conversation Piece, Escape to Athena, The Gift, Fitzcarraldo, Henry IV, History, A Man in Love* and *Son of the Pink Panther,* among others. At Venice, named Best Actress in an Italian film for performance in *Claretta* (1984); given Lifetime Achievement Award at Berlin International Film Festival (2002).

CARDNY, Marion (fl. 1300s). Scottish royal mistress. Dau. of John Cardny; paramour of Robert II (1316–1390), king of Scotland (r. 1371–1390); children: (with Robert II) Alexander Stewart, canon of Glasgow; John Stuart of Arntullie; James Stuart of Kinfauns; Walter Stuart.

CARDUS, Ana (1943—). Mexican ballet dancer. Born May 8, 1943, in Mexico City, Mexico. ❖ Performed with Serge Unger's Ballet Concierto de Mexico in Mexico City until 1960; appeared in performances with a variety of European companies; danced with Ballet International du Marquis de Cuevas, then with Stuttgart Ballet in Germany, creating roles in John Cranko's *l'Estro Armonico* (1963), *Onegin* (1965), *The Interrogation* (1967), and *Quatre Images* (1967), and also in Kenneth Macmillan's *Song of the Earth* (1965); danced in numerous works by choreographer Louis Gai, including *The Stone Flower* (1973) and *Hamlet* (1974), at Hanover State Opera in Germany, where she also served as ballet master.

CARÈRE, Christine (1930—). French actress. Name variations: Christine Carere; Christine Carrère or Carrere. Born July 27, 1930, in Dijon, Côte-d'Or, Burgundy, France; m. Philippe Nicaud (actor). ❖ Made film debut in *Folie douce* (1951), followed by *Olivia, Un Caprice de Caroline Chérie, Sang et Lunière, Cadet Rousselle, Femmes libres, l'Affaire des Poisons, Don Juan, Bonjour Jeunesse, A Certain Smile, Mardi Gras, A Private's Affair, La Nuit des suspectes* and *I Deal in Danger,* among others.

CAREW, Edith Mary (1868–?). English murderer. Born 1868 in England; dau. of John Albert Porch (mayor of Glastonbury); m. Walter Carew, May 1889 (died Oct 22, 1896). ❖ Lived in style with husband Walter in the European quarters of Yokohama (Japan); after he died of arsenic poisoning (1896), was charged with his murder; at her trial, which took place under judicial authority of British Consul (1897), her love letters from a bank clerk were produced; found guilty and sentenced to death, saw sentence commuted to penal servitude for life by British ambassador; confined in Aylesbury Prison in England.

CAREW, Elizabeth (before 1558–c. 1617). See Carey, Elizabeth.

CAREW, Mary (1913–2002). American runner. Born Sept 8, 1913; died July 2002. ❖ At Los Angeles Olympics, won a gold medal in 4x100-meter relay (1932).

CAREW, Ora (1893–1955). American actress. Born Ora Whytock, April 19, 1893, in Salt Lake City, Utah; died Oct 26, 1955, in Hollywood, California; sister of Grant Whytock (actor); m. John C. Howard. ❖ Performed in vaudeville and musical comedies; made film debut in Mack Sennett's Keystone comedies; films include *Too Many Millions* (opposite Wallace Reid), *The Big Town Round-Up* and *After Your Own Heart* (both opposite Tom Mix), and *Go West, Young Man, Go West;* opened a cosmetics shop in Hollywood.

CAREY, Catherine (1529–1569). England's chief lady of the bedchamber during reign of Henry VIII. Name variations: Katherine Carey; Catherine Knollys. Born 1529; died June 18, 1569; dau. of William Carey and Mary Boleyn (d. 1543, sister of Anne Boleyn); m. Sir Francis Knollys; children: Lettice Knollys (c. 1541–1634); William Knollys (1547–1632), comptroller of Queen Elizabeth I's household.

CAREY, Eileen Reynolds (1900–1995). See O'Casey, Eileen.

CAREY, Elizabeth (before 1558–c. 1617). English aristocrat. Name variations: Lady Elizabeth Carey or Carew; Baroness Hunsdon of Hunsdon. Born before 1558; buried Mar 2, 1617 or 1618 at Westminster Abbey; dau. of John Spencer of Althorpe and Katherine Kitson; related to Edmund Spenser who dedicated his *Muiopotmos* to her; m. Sir George Carey, 2nd baron Hunsdon, Dec 29, 1574; m. Ralph Eure, 3rd Lord Eure, after Mar 1612; children: Elizabeth Carey (1576–1635).

CAREY, Elizabeth (1576–1635). English aristocrat. Name variations: Lady Elizabeth Carey; Lady Elizabeth Berkeley. Born May 24, 1576; died April 23, 1635; dau. of George Carey, 2nd baron Hunsdon, and Elizabeth Carey (before 1558–c. 1617); m. Sir Thomas Berkeley, Feb 19, 1595; children: George Berkeley (1601–1658) and Theophila Berkeley (b. 1611). ❖ Was a patron of Thomas Nash, the satirist; possibly wrote *The Tragedie of Marian* (1613); purchased the estate of Cranford, Middlesex (1618).

CAREY, Eva (fl. 1921). American church administrator. Born in US. ❖ As a layperson, elected member of the Bishop's Council of the Protestant Episcopal Church at the annual Diocesan Convention in Boston, MA (1921), the 1st woman to occupy an administrative post in that Church in US.

CAREY, Ida Harriet (1891–1982). New Zealand artist and art teacher. Born Oct 3, 1891, at Taonui, near Feilding, New Zealand; died Aug 23, 1982, at Trevellyn, New Zealand; dau. of Richard Octavius Egerton Carey (farmer) and Elizabeth (Keeble) Carey; studied under J.S.

Watkins, in Sydney, Australia, 1920s. ❖ Elected member of Royal Art Society of New South Wales (1924); produced religious art for St. Peter's Cathedral in Hamilton and work was exhibited widely throughout New Zealand (1930s); taught art privately and at Auckland Training College (1930s); helped establish Waikato Society of Arts (1934) and served as president (1945–48); was a member of Hamilton High School staff (1945–49); painted series of portraits of well-known ballet and theater performers in London (1950s); produced series of portraits of prominent early 20th-century Maori women, which became popular solo exhibition in early 1980s. ❖ See also *Dictionary of New Zealand Biography* (Vol. 4).

CAREY, Mariah (1970—). *American singer and songwriter.* Born Mar 27, 1970, in Long Island, NY; m. Tommy Mottola, June 1993 (div. 1997). ❖ With her 7-octave voice, was the biggest-selling woman musical artist of 1990s, the only artist to have #1 hit every year in that decade; cowrote and coproduced most of her songs; hit singles include "Vision of Love" (1990), "Someday" (1991), "I'll Be There" (1992), "Dreamlover" (1993), "Fantasy" (1995), (with Boyz II Men) "One Sweet Day" (1995), "My All" (1997), and "Heartbreaker" (1999). Albums include *Mariah Carey* (1990), *Emotions* (#1, 1991), *Music Box* (#1, 1993), *Daydream* (#1, 1995), *Butterfly* (#1, 1997), and *Rainbow* (#2, 2000).

CAREY, Mary (c. 1610–c. 1680). *British religious writer.* Born c. 1609, in Berwick, Sussex; died c. 1680 in England; dau. of Sir John Jackson; m. Pelham Carey (son of 4th Lord Hunsdon); m. George Payler (paymaster for parliamentary forces at Berwick), c. 1643; children: 3 who survived infancy. ❖ Wrote *My Lady Carey's Meditation, & Poetry* (1681), a spiritual autobiography in which several poems focus on the deaths of her children.

CAREY, Miriam E. (1858–1937). *American librarian.* Born Feb 21, 1858, in Peoria, Illinois; died Jan 9, 1937, in Cheyenne, Wyoming; dau. of Isaac Eddy (Presbyterian minister); attended Rockford Seminary, 1876, Oberlin College, 1877, and library school of University of Illinois, 1898. ❖ The innovative force in the movement to establish libraries in state institutions throughout US, was appointed supervisor for the Iowa State Institution Libraries, the 1st position of its kind in America (1906), and oversaw the pioneering program, which utilized books as a rehabilitative tool in prison wards, mental hospitals, tuberculosis sanitariums and schools for delinquent children; headed the institutional libraries in Minnesota (1913), where she organized libraries at 18 various institutions across the state. ❖ See also *Women in World History*.

CAREY, Mary (d. 1543). *See Boleyn, Mary.*

CAREY, Olive (1896–1988). *American actress.* Name variations: Olive Golden; Olive Fuller Golden. Born Olive Fuller Golden, Jan 31, 1896, in NYC; died Mar 13, 1988, in Carpinteria, California; sister of Mignonne Golden (actress, 1904–1997); m. Harry Carey (western star), 1916 (died 1947); children: Harry Carey Jr. (b. 1921, actor). ❖ Made screen debut in D.W. Griffith's *The Sorrowful Shore* (1913); other films include *Trader Horn, Rogue Cop, the Cobweb, The Searchers, Two Rode Together, The Alamo, Pillars of the Sky* and *Gunfight at OK Corral.*

CAREY, Rosa Nouchette (1840–1909). *British children's writer.* Born Sept 24, 1840, in London, England; died July 19, 1909, in London; dau. of William Henry Carey (shipbroker) and Maria Jane Wooddill Carey. ❖ Wrote stories and novels for young girls, including *Wee Wifie* (1869), *Nellie's Memories, A Novel* (1880), *Barbara Heathcote's Trial* (1885), *Averil* (1890), *Our Bessie* (1892), *Mollie's Prince* (1898), *The Highway of Fate* (1902), and *The Key of the Unknown* (1909); also wrote *Twelve Notable Good Women of the 19th Century* (1899); stories were often serialized in *Girl's Own Paper.*

CARHART, Georgiana (d. 1959). *American opera singer and media personality.* Died Mar 2, 1959, age 93, in NYC. ❖ Made NY stage debut in *La Folote* (1893); sang in several Gilbert and Sullivan operas; came to prominence late in life as a frequent guest on tv's "Jack Paar Show."

CARIA, queen of. *See Artemisia II (c. 395–351 BCE).*

CARINA (1821–?). *See Howard, Caroline Cadette.*

CARINTHIA, duchess of. *See Maultasch, Margaret (1318–1369).*

CARIOCA, Tahia (c. 1921–1999). *See Karioka, Tahiya.*

CARIOCCA, Taheya (c. 1921–1999). *See Karioka, Tahiya.*

CARISBROOKE, marquise of. *See Mountbatten, Irene (1890–1956).*

CARKEEK, Frances Ann (1840–1916). *See Stewart, Frances Ann.*

CARLÉN, Emilia (1807–1892). *Swedish novelist and feminist.* Name variations: Emilie Smith Flygare-Carlén; Emilia Carlen. Born Emilia Smith in Strömstad, Sweden, Aug 8, 1807; died in Stockholm, Feb 5, 1892; dau. of Rutger Smith (merchant, shipowner, and retired sea captain); m. Axel Flygare (doctor), 1827 (died 1833); m. Johan Gabriel Carlén (lawyer and poet), 1841; children: (1st m.) Edvard Flygare (1820–1853, writer), and 3 others (two died in childhood); (out of wedlock) Rosa Carlén (1836–1883), who was also a popular novelist. ❖ Considered Sweden's 1st regional writer, was noted for her stories of seafarers, fishermen, and smugglers, with whom she came in frequent contact as a child; anonymously published 1st novel, *Waldemar Klein* (1838), which met with great success; moved to Stockholm (1839); produced 1 or 2 novels annually over next 12 years, and her works were widely read; silenced as a writer for a period following death of son (1853–58), took up pen (1858) and continued writing until 1884; her house became a meeting place for Stockholm's literati until death of husband (1875), when she completely retired from the world; most famous tales are *Rosen på Tistelön* (*The Rose of Tistelön,* 1842), *Enslingen på Johanniskäret* (1846, English trans. published as *The Hermit of the Johannis Rock,* 4 vols., 1853), *Jungfrutornet* (*The Maiden's Tower,* 1848), and *Ett köpemanshus i skärgarden* (*The Merchant's House on the Cliffs,* 1859); also wrote *Gustav Lindorm* (1835). Honored by the Swedish Academy (1862). ❖ See also *Women in World History.*

CARLÉN, Rosa (1836–1883). *Swedish novelist.* Name variations: Rosa Carlen. Born in Sweden, 1836; died 1883; dau. of Emilia Carlén. ❖ Published 1st book, *Agnes Tell* (1861), which was well received; followed that with *Tuva* (1862), *Helena, a Woman's History* (1863), *Three Years and Three Days* (1864), and *The Gypsy's Son* (1866), thought to be her best work.

CARLES, Emilie (1900–1979). *French educator, conservationist and writer.* Born Emilie Allais in 1900 in Val-des-Pres, France; died July 29, 1979; dau. of Joseph Allais and Catherine (Vallier) Allais (killed by lightening, 1904); studied in Paris, 1918–20; m. Jean Carles (pacifist), 1928; children: Georges, Janny, Michel. ❖ Activist and autobiographer who spoke eloquently to the urbanized world about the increasingly threatened rural way of life; had a long career as a teacher (1918–62) in the remote Alpine region where she was born; at 77, became a national celebrity with autobiography, *Une Soupe aux herbes sauvages* (*A Soup of Wild Herbs,* 1977).

CARLESCU, Laura Badea (1970—). *See Badea, Laura.*

CARLETON, Claire (1913–1979). *American stage and screen actress.* Name variations: Clara Carlton. Born Sept 28, 1913, in NYC; died Dec 11, 1979, in North Ridge, California; m. Frederick E. Sherman. ❖ Made NY stage debut in *Blue Monday* (1932); had great success in London in *Three Men on a Horse*; films include *A Double Life, Red Light, Born Yesterday, Death of a Salesman, Barkleys of Broadway, Witness to Murder, Buster Keaton Story, Son of Dr. Jekyll, Two of a Kind, Wabash Avenue* and *The Careless Years.*

CARLETON, Mary (1643–1673). *See Moders, Mary.*

CARLETON, Janet (1905–1999). *See Adam Smith, Janet.*

CARLIER, Madeleine (c. 1876–?). *French actress.* Born c. 1876 in France; m. M. Bilitis. ❖ Made stage debut in *Madame Flirt* at the Athénée (Dec 27, 1901); appeared successively at the Rénaissance and the Odéon in such plays as *La Seconde Madame Tanqueray, La Variation,* and the classics; other plays include *Papillon, Les Liasons Dangereuses, Le Bourgeon, La Petite Bouche, Potashe et Perimutter, Le Frère Prodigue, L'Illusionist, La Vie est Belle, Le Divan Noir* and *Monsieur Beverley;* was the beloved of 17-year-old Jean Cocteau (c. 1907) but later ended the relationship. Subject of portraiture: "Madeleine Carlier Seated with a Feather Boa" by Paul Helleu and "Madeleine Carlier" by Paul Robe.

CARLILE. *Variant of Carlisle or Carlyle.*

CARLIN, Cynthia (d. 1973). *American actress and tv producer.* Died Feb 23, 1973, in NYC. ❖ Appeared in numerous Broadway productions and on over 250 radio shows; produced several shows for tv.

CARLINE, Nancy (1909–2004). *English artist.* Born Nancy Mona Higgins, Nov 30, 1909, in London, England; died Oct 18, 2004; dau. of shopkeepers; attended Slade School of Art; studied with Philip Wilson Steer and Victor Polunin; m. Richard Carline (artist and son of artist

George Carline), 1950; children: 1 son, 1 daughter. ❖ Painter of townscapes and landscapes, was a member of the Carline circle; painting "Supper on the Terrace" (1946) hangs in the Tate; had a retrospective at the Camden Centre (1980).

CARLISLE. *Variant of Carlyle.*

CARLISLE, Alexandra (1886–1936). English-born stage actress. Born Alexandra Swift, Jan 15, 1886, in London, England; died April 21, 1936; m. 2nd husband Dr. Albert Pfeiffer (div.); m. 3rd husband J. Elliott Jenkins. ❖ Made London stage debut in *White-washing Julia* (1903); came to prominence as Carlotta in *The Morals of Marcus* (1906), then appeared as Portia in Herbert Beerbohm Tree's revival of *The Merchant of Venice* (1908); made NY debut in *The Mollusc* (1908); other plays include *The Devils, Arséne Lupin, Money, Above Suspicion, Proud Maisie, Driven, David Garrick* and *The Country Cousin,* among others; while appearing in America, seconded the nomination of Warren Harding at the Republican Convention in Chicago (1920). Received gold medal from American Academy of Arts and Letters (1932).

CARLISLE, Anne B. (1902–1981). *See Eline, Marie.*

CARLISLE, Belinda (1958—). American pop vocalist. Name variations: The Go-Go's. Born Belinda Jo Carlinsky, Aug 17, 1958, in Hollywood, California; m. Morgan Mason (son of actor James Mason), 1986; children: Duke Mason (b. 1992). ❖ Formed Go-Go's with Jane Wiedlen, Charlotte Caffey, Gina Shock, and Margot Olaverra; traveled to England with group and recorded minor Brit club hit "We Got the Beat"; began downplaying punk sensibility, replacing Olaverra with Kathy Valentine; hit #1 with debut album *Beauty and the Beat* (1981), which included hit single "Our Lips are Sealed"; released albums *Vacation* (1982), and *Talk Show* (1984); launched successful solo career with album *Belinda* (1986); sang hits "Heaven is a Place on Earth" (1986) and "I Get Weak" (1986); continued to release albums, including *Runaway Horses* (1989), *Live Your Life Be Free* (1991), and *A Woman & a Man* (1997); reunited with Go-Go's for albums *Return to the Valley of the Go-Go's* (1994) and *God Bless the Go-Go's* (2001); played herself on reality tv series "Hell's Kitchen" (2004); lives in Cap d' Antibes, France.

CARLISLE, countess of.
See Hay, Lucy (1599–1660).
See Cavendish, Georgiana (1783–1858).
See Howard, Rosalind Frances (1845–1921).

CARLISLE, Kitty (b. 1910). American actress, classical singer, and arts administrator. Name variations: Kitty Carlisle Hart; Mrs. Moss Hart. Born Catherine Conn (later used mother's maiden name, Catherine Holzman, also seen as Holtzman), Sept 3, 1910, in New Orleans, Louisiana; m. Moss Hart (playwright), Aug 10, 1946 (died 1961); children: Christopher Hart; Cathy Hart. ❖ Made NY debut in title role of a tabloid version of *Rio Rita* (1932); other plays include *Champagne Sec, White Horse Inn, Three Waltzes, Walk with Music,* title role in Benjamin Britten's *The Rape of Lucretia, Anniversary Waltz, Kiss Me Kate* and *On Your Toes;* made Metropolitan Opera debut as Prince Orlovsky in *Fledermaus* (1966); briefly signed with MGM, appearing in *Murder at the Vanities, She Loves Me Not, Here is My Heart, Hollywood Canteen, Radio Days,* and with the Marx Brothers in *Night at the Opera;* was a regular panelist on tv's "To Tell the Truth" (1956–91); was chair of Governor Nelson Rockefeller's Conference on Women (1966) and NY State Council on the Arts; received National Medal of Arts (1991). ❖ See also autobiography, *Kitty* (1988).

CARLISLE, Mary (b. 1912). American actress. Born Feb 3, 1912, in Boston, Massachusetts; stepdau. of Henry J. Kaiser (industrialist); m. James Blakeley (actor, socialite, and 20th Century-Fox exec). ❖ Made film debut in *This Reckless Age* (1932), followed by *Grand Hotel, The Sweetheart of Sigma Chi, Palooka, Girl of My Dreams, It's in the Air, Lady Be Careful, Double or Nothing, Touchdown Army, Beware Spooks, Dance Girl Dance, Rags to Riches, Baby Face Morgan* and *Dead Men Walk,* among others; took over management of Elizabeth Arden salon in Hollywood (1951).

CARLOT. *See Edgren, Anne Charlotte (1849–1892).*

CARLOTA. *Variant of Carlotta.*

CARLOTA (1840–1927). Belgian princess who became empress of Mexico. Name variations: Carlotta, Charlotte, Charlotte of Belgium, Charlotte Saxe-Coburg; Marie Charlotte of Saxe-Coburg. Pronunciation: Car-LOW-ta. Born Marie Charlotte Amelie Augustine Victoire Clementine Leopoldine, June 7, 1840, at Laeken, Belgium; died at castle of Bouchout, Belgium, Jan 19, 1927; dau. of Leopold I (1790–1865), king of the Belgians (r. 1831–1865), and his 3rd wife Princess Louise d'Orléans (1812–1850); m. Archduke Maximilian von Habsburg, July 27, 1857; children: none, except for adoption of son Agustín de Iturbide, 1865. ❖ Belgian princess who accompanied her husband on an ill-fated adventure to Mexico, where she was crowned empress and witnessed royal splendor, civil war, personal tragedy, and ultimately dementia in an attempt to bring monarchical rule to the land of the Aztecs; after marriage to Archduke Maximilian and his appointment as Austrian viceroy of Lombardy-Venetia, began residence in northeastern Italy; with Austrians expelled from Lombardy (1859), relocated to palace of Miramar near Trieste; when agents of Mexican conservative party and of Napoleon III floated inquiries regarding the couple's interest in the throne of Mexico, convinced husband with her enthusiasm (1863); busied herself upon arrival in Mexico City with organizing court life, founding hospitals, and coordinating affairs with French sponsors; when guerrilla actions against the monarchy kept Maximilian and the French from consolidating their hold on the country, was forced to agree to the adoption of a Mexican-born son (to placate the populace); was sent to Europe to negotiate with Napoleon III for further aid, after French expeditionary force began to evacuate Mexico (1867); in Paris, showed signs of severe mental strain; upon hearing of husband's death by firing squad, spent the next 60 years insane, dying as a mental recluse in a Belgian castle (1927). ❖ See also Joan Haslip, *The Crown of Mexico: Maximilian and his Empress Carlota* (Holt, 1971); Richard O'Connor, *The Cactus Throne: The Tragedy of Maximilian and Carlotta* (Putnam, 1971); and *Women in World History.*

CARLOTA JOAQUINA (1775–1830). Queen of Portugal as wife of John VI. Name variations: Carlotta, Charlotte or Joaquina Carlota de Borbon; Charlotte Bourbon; Charlotte of Spain. Born April 25, 1775, in Aranjuez, Spain; died Jan 7, 1830, in Queluz Palace outside Lisbon; dau. of Charles IV, king of Spain (r. 1788–1808), and Maria Luisa Teresa of Parma (1751–1819); sister of Maria Luisa of Lucca and Etruria (1782–1824); betrothed to John, prince of Portugal in 1778; m. Joao VI also known as John VI (died Mar 10, 1826), king of Portugal (r. 1816–1826); children: Teresa of Portugal (1793–1874); António Pio (1795–1801); Maria Isabel of Portugal (1797–1818); Peter IV (b. 1798), king of Portugal (r. 1826) also known as Pedro I, emperor of Brazil (r. 1826–1831); Francisca of Portugal (1800–1834); Isabel Maria (1801–1876); Miguel also known as Michael I (1802–1866), king of Portugal (r. 1828–1834); Maria da Assumpção (1805–1834); Ana de Jesus Maria (1806–1857, who m. Nuno José Sevro de Moura, 1st duke of Loulé). ❖ Renowned for political intrigue, was a leading proponent of conservatism and absolutism against rising tide of liberalism after 1822; became crown princess of Portugal on death of John's older brother (1788); husband declared regent due to insanity of his mother Maria I (1792); fled to Brazil with husband and court because of Napoleonic invasion (1807); initially tried to claim regency of Spanish River Plate territory and then unsuccessfully pressed for right to rule it as empress (1808–12); acclaimed queen of Portugal (1816); after liberal Revolution of 1820 in Portugal, returned to Portugal with John VI (1821); though the liberal constitution required that the royal couple swear allegiance to it, which John did (Nov 1822), absolutely refused, avowing that her religious views prevented her from taking oaths, placing her at the head of the reactionary elements within Portugal; plotted, without success, to have husband declared insane so that son Michael could rule; with Michael, headed "Abrilada" revolt against liberal monarchy (1824); after John VI was succeeded by Maria da Glória (1826), backed her son in his declaration that he was absolute monarch, leading to civil war (1828). ❖ See also Marcus Cheke, *Carlota Joaquina, Queen of Portugal* (Sidgwick & Jackson, 1947); and *Women in World History.*

CARLOTTA. *Variant of Carlota.*

CARLOTTA, queen of Cyprus (1442–1487). *See Charlotte of Lusignan.*

CARLOTTI, Marie-Arlette (1952—). French politician. Born Jan 21, 1952, in Béziers, France. ❖ Member of the Socialist Party National Executive and national secretary (1986–94); elected to 4th and 5th European Parliament (EP, 1994–99, 1999–2004); named vice-president of members from the EP to the Joint Parliamentary Assembly of the Agreement between the African, Caribbean, and Pacific States and the European Union (ACP-EU).

CARLOVNA, Anna (1718–1746). *See Anna Leopoldovna.*

CARLSEN, Agnete (1971—). Norwegian soccer player. Born Jan 15, 1971 in Norway. ❖ Won a team bronze medal at Atlanta Olympics (1996).

CARLSON, Carolyn (1943—). American dancer and choreographer. Born Mar 7, 1943, in Oakland, California; studied with Claire-Lauche Porter at San Francisco Ballet School; attended University of Utah; trained with Alwin Nikolais. ❖ Often compared to Isadora Duncan for innocence and purity in her work, danced with Alwin Nikolais Company in NY (1965–71); performed with Compagnie Anne Béranger (1971–72); choreographed at Paris Opéra Ballet (1973–80); had large impact on European artistic development (1970s–80s), especially in France and Italy, inspiring establishment of *nouvelle dance française* and numerous post-modern Italian companies; was artistic director of Cullberg Ballet in Sweden (1994–95). Choreographed works include *Densité 21.5* (1st performed at Paris Opéra, 1973), *The Year of the Horse* (1978), *Underwood* (1982), *L'Orso e la luna* (1983), *Commedia* (1993), and *Improvisata* (1997). ❖ See also Alain Macaire and Michel Marcelle, *Carolyn Carlson* (1986).

CARLSON, Gretchen (c. 1966—). Miss America and broadcaster. Name variations: Gretchen Carlson Close. Born Gretchen Elizabeth Carlson c. 1966 in Anoka, Minnesota; Stanford University, honors graduate, 1990. ❖ Named Miss America (1989), representing Minnesota, the 1st classical violinist to win title; was host of "Saturday Early Show" for CBS and correspondent for "CBS Evening News." Recognized by National American Women in Radio and Television for 30-part series on domestic violence; received 2 Emmy Awards.

CARLSON, Violet (d. 1997). American actress and vaudevillian. Born in Oak Park, Illinois; grew up in Omaha, Nebraska; died Dec 3, 1997, age 97, in Los Angeles, California; m. Henri Margo (nee Henry Sanderson, vaudevillian), 1941. ❖ Created the part of Gretchen in *The Student Prince* (1924); other musicals include *Spice of 1922, Caroline, The Nightingale, Ruddigore, The Love Call, The Red Robe* and *Sweet Adeline*; also toured in vaudeville and played the Palace.

CARLSTEDT, Lily (1926—). Danish javelin thrower. Born Mar 5, 1926. ❖ At London Olympics, won a bronze medal in the javelin throw (1948).

CARLTON, Clara (1913–1979). *See Carleton, Claire.*

CARLTON, Cousin Mary (1840–1880). *See Fleming, May Agnes.*

CARLTON, Doris (1877–1966). *See McDowell, Claire.*

CARLYLE, Jane Welsh (1801–1866). Scottish letter writer. Name variations: Jane Welsh Baillie; Jane Baillie Welsh; Mrs. Thomas Carlyle; known by close friends and family as Jeannie. Born Jane Baillie Welsh, July 14, 1801, in Haddington, near Edinburgh, Scotland; died in London, April 21, 1866; dau. of John Welsh (country doctor) and Grace Baillie (Welsh) Welsh (despite the same last name, parents were not related); m. Thomas Carlyle (the writer and historian), Oct 17, 1826; no children. ❖ Brilliant conversationalist and letter-writer whose correspondence is filled with entertaining and detailed accounts of her day-to-day experiences and of the many men and women, famous and not so famous, with whom she came into contact; spent childhood and young adult life in Haddington; spent 1st 18 months of married life at Comely Bank in Edinburgh, followed by 6 years at an isolated farmhouse at Craigenputtock in Dumfriesshire; moved to London (1833); made many visits to family and friends in Scotland, Manchester, and near Liverpool and, after Thomas Carlyle had found fame, to country houses of the English aristocracy, especially that of Lord and Lady Ashburton in Hampshire; seriously injured in an accident (1863); wrote on average 116 letters each year. ❖ See also N. Brysson Morrison, *True Minds: The Marriage of Thomas & Jane Carlyle* (Dent, 1974); Osbert Burdett, *The Two Carlyles* (Faber & Faber, 1930); Virginia Surtees, *Jane Welsh Carlyle* (Michael Russell, 1976); Charles R. Sanders, ed. *The Collected Letters of Thomas and Jane Welsh Carlyle* (12 vols., 1970–85), Leonard Huxley, ed. *Jane Welsh Carlyle: Letters to Her Family, 1839–1863* (1924), Townsend Scudder, ed. *Letters of Jane Welsh Carlyle to Joseph Neuberg, 1848–1862* (1931), Trudy Bliss, ed. *Jane Welsh Carlyle: A New Selection of Her Letters* (1949); and *Women in World History.*

CARLYLE, Mrs. Thomas (1801–1866). *See Carlyle, Jane Welsh.*

CARMEN, Gioia (1965—). *See Bruno, Gioia Carmen.*

CARMEN, Janet (1897–1984). *See Carmen, Jewel.*

CARMEN, Jewel (1897–1984). American actress. Name variations: Evelyn Quick, Janet Carmen. Born Florence Lavinia Quick, July 13, 1897, in Danville, Kentucky; died Mar 4, 1984, in San Diego, California; m. Roland West (director), 1918. ❖ Lauded for her performance in *A Tale of Two Cities* (1917), was also star of *The Bat;* other films include *Intolerance, The Half Breed, Flirting with Fate, Les Miserables* and *Nobody;* was often Douglas Fairbanks' leading lady.

CARMEN SYLVA (1843–1916). *See Elizabeth of Wied.*

CARMICHAEL, Amy (1867–1971). Irish-born missionary to India. Name variations: Amy Beatrice Carmichael. Born 1867 in Millisle, Co. Down, Ireland; died 1971 in India; adopted by Robert Wilson in 1887. ❖ Northern Irish-born missionary to India, served briefly as missionary in Japan; with Thomas Walker, worked with Church of England Zenana Missionary Society in Dohnavur, India; founded Dohnavur fellowship, a safety and refuge for temple children (1901); wrote over 35 books which brought word of missionary work and evangelical spirituality to the West, including *Gold Cord* (1932), *Gold by Moonlight* (1935), *God's Missionary* (1957), and *His Thoughts Said . . . His Father Said* (1958). ❖ See also Elisabeth Elliot, *A Chance to Die: The Life and Legacy of Amy Carmichael* (Revell, 1987).

CARMICHAEL, Elizabeth (fl. 1530s). Mistress of James V, king of Scotland. Name variations: Katherine. Dau. of Sir John Carmichael; mistress of James V (1512–1542), king of Scotland (r. 1513–1542); children: (with James V) John Stewart (b. around 1531), prior of Coldinghame.

CARMON, Amalia Kahana (1930—). *See Kahana-Carmon, Amalia.*

CARMONA, Adriana (1972—). Venezuelan taekwondo player. Born Dec 3, 1972, in Venezuela. ❖ Placed 2nd at World championships for +70kg (1993); won a bronze medal for 67kg at Athens Olympics (2004).

CARMONT, Agnes (1829–1906). *See McDonald, Agnes.*

CARNACHAN, Blanche Eleanor (1871–1954). New Zealand teacher. Born Nov 23, 1871, in Cambridge, Waikato, New Zealand; died, Mar 22, 1954, in Auckland, New Zealand; dau. of David Carnachan and Elizabeth (Friars) Carnachan. ❖ Taught at Goodwood School and at Parnell School (early 1900s); began teaching at Epsom School (1917); served as executive member of New Zealand Educational Institute and New Zealand Women Teachers' Association; after retirement, worked with deaf and intellectually handicapped children; became president of Auckland After-care Association, which reorganized as Institute for Care of Backward Children and later became Intellectually Handicapped Children's Society. Awarded British Empire Medal (1940). ❖ See also *Dictionary of New Zealand Biography* (Vol. 4).

CARNAHAN, Suzanne (1921–1952). *See Peters, Susan.*

CARNARVON, countess of (1903–1975). *See Losch, Tilly.*

CARNE, Judy (1939—). English actress. Born Joyce Botterill, April 27, 1939, in Northampton, Northamptonshire, England; m. Burt Reynolds (actor), 1963 (div. 1965); m. Robert Bergman (tv producer), 1970 (div. 1971). ❖ Light comedian, was a regular on the sitcom "The Baileys of Balboa" (1964), then starred in "Love on a Rooftop" (1966); came to prominence as a member of the cast of "Laugh-In," where she introduced the phrase, "Sock it to me!" ❖ See also autobiography, *Laughing on the Outside* (1985).

CARNEGIE, Mrs. Andrew (1857–1946). *See Carnegie, Louise Whitfield.*

CARNEGIE, Caroline (1934—). Duchess of Fife. Born Caroline Cecily Dewar, Feb 12, 1934, in Bardowie Castle, Milngavie, Strathclyde, Scotland; elder dau. of Alexander Dewar, 3rd baron Forteviot, and Cynthia Starkie; m. James Carnegie, 3rd duke of Fife, Sept 11, 1956 (div. 1966); children: Alexandra Carnegie (b. 1959); David Carnegie, earl of Macduff; and one other.

CARNEGIE, Hattie (1886–1956). Austrian-born American fashion designer and retailer. Born Henrietta Kanengeiser in Vienna, Austria, Mar 14, 1886; died in New York City, Feb 22, 1956; m. 3rd husband John Zanft (motion-picture executive); no children. ❖ Immigrated to New York with family (1897); as Hattie Carnegie, opened a business in Manhattan, designing and selling hats, in partnership with a seamstress named Rose Roth (1909); with its success, moved the boutique to 86th Street and Broadway; though she could not sew, branched out from hats to dresses, employing top-notch fashion designers; bought out partner

(1918) and changed the business emphasis from American designs to stylish adaptations of Paris originals; opened shop at 42 East 49th Street; by mid-1920s, was in control of a fashion empire, which lasted until her death; hired highly gifted designers, including Travis Banton, Bruno, Madeleine Vionnet, Jean Louis, Claire McCardell, Norman Norell, Pauline Potter and Pauline Trigére; created both custom-made clothing and high-priced ready-to-wear items which sold in major stores throughout US; her Carnegie suit and little black dress became status symbols. Received Neiman-Marcus Award (1939) and American Fashion Critics' Award (1948). ❖ See also *Women in World History*.

CARNEGIE, Louise Whitfield (1857–1946). American philanthropist. Name variations: Mrs. Andrew Carnegie. Born Louise Whitfield, Mar 7, 1857, New York, NY; died June 24, 1946, in New York, NY; dau. of John William Whitfield (prosperous NY merchant, died 1878) and Fannie (Davis) Whitfield; attended Miss Haines' School; m. Andrew Carnegie (the industrialist and philanthropist), April 22, 1887 (died 1919); children: Margaret Carnegie (b. 1897). ❖ Helped Charles Schwab convince husband to sell out to Morgan syndicate (1901); concerned with international peace, played an important role in formation of the Church Peace Union; continued many of husband's interests after his death; promoted US participation in League of Nations, provided $100,000 to Union Theological Seminary, and supported Near East College Association and Grenfell Mission in Labrador.

CARNEGIE, Maud (1893–1945). Countess of Southesk. Name variations: Maud Duff. Born Maud Alexandra Victoria Georgina Bertha, April 3, 1893, in Richmond upon Thames, Surrey, England; died Dec 14, 1945, in London, England; dau. of Louise Victoria (1867–1931), princess Royal and duchess of Fife, and Alexander Duff, 1st duke of Fife; m. Charles Carnegie, 11th earl of Southesk, Nov 12, 1923; children: James Carnegie (b. 1929), 3rd duke of Fife.

CARNER, JoAnne (1939—). American golfer. Name variations: JoAnne Gunderson; The Great Gundy. Born Joanne Gunderson, April 4, 1939, in Kirkland, Washington; graduate of Arizona State University; m. Don Carner, c. 1965. ❖ Top money-winner whose winnings include: USGA Amateur (1957, 1960, 1962, 1966, 1968); LPGA Burdine (1969); US Open (1971, 1976); Bluegrass Invitational (1971); Desert Inn Classic, Hoosier Open, Dallas Civitan (1974); American Defender Classic, All-American Sports Classic (1975); Orange Blossom Classic (1976); LPGA team championship (with Judy Rankin) and Borden Classic (1977); Colgate Triple Crown (1978, 1979); Peter Jackson Classic (1978); Honda Civic Classic (1979, 1980); Women's Kemper Open (1979); Whirlpool Championship and Sunstar '80 (1980); Lady Keystone Open (1980, 1981); S&H Golf Classic (1981); McDonald's Classic (1982); Chevrolet World Championship (1982, 1983); Henredon Classic (1982); Portland Ping (1983); Corning (1984); and Safeco Classic (1985), making her the oldest winner ever on the LPGA tour. Won 5 Vare trophies. ❖ See also *Women in World History*.

CARNES, Kim (1945—). American singer and songwriter. Born July 20, 1945, in Los Angeles, California; m. Dave Ellingson (musician). ❖ Wrote songs (some with husband) which were covered by such artists as Frank Sinatra, Rita Coolidge, and Barbara Streisand; had #1 single "Betty Davis Eyes," which received a Grammy for Record of the Year (1981); released other hits, including "Draw of the Cards" (1981), "Voyeur" (1982), and "Crazy the Night" (1985); became Nashville-based songwriter. Albums include *Mistaken Identity* (1981), *Rest on Me* (1972), *Kim Carnes* (1976), *Sailin'* (1976), *Voyeur; The Best of You* (1982), *Barking at Airplanes* (1985), *Light House* (1986) and *Gypsy Honeymoon: The Best of Kim Carnes* (1993).

CARNEY, Kate (1870–1950). English music-hall star. Born in 1870; died 1950; dau. of one of the Brothers Raynard (variety performer); m. George Barclay. ❖ Made stage debut at the Albert, Canning Town (1890); known as the Cockney Queen for such songs as "Here's My Love to Ould Ireland," "Three Pots a Shilling," "I Love You in the Sunshine," "Liza Johnson," "Our Threepenny Hop," "When the Summer Comes Again," "Our Village Home in the East," "Janey de Laney," and "Maggie Maguire"; toured in the revue *I Should Say So* (1915).

CARNEY, Winifred (1887–1943). Irish suffragist, socialist and labor organizer. Born in Bangor, Co. Down, Ireland, Dec 4, 1887; died in Belfast, Northern Ireland, Nov 21, 1943; dau. of Alfred and Sarah (Cassidy) Carney; m. George McBride (labor organizer), 1928. ❖ Became involved in the Gaelic League, which was concerned with the revival of the Irish language, and in suffrage and socialist activities; met James Connolly (1912), Ulster provincial secretary of Irish Transport and General Workers Union

(ITGWU), who helped to organize the Textile Workers Union, which functioned as the women's section of the ITGWU; appointed secretary of the Textile Workers Union, responsible for the insurance section; became Connolly's trusted associate and confidante; joined Belfast branch of Cumann na mBan (The Women's League), where she taught first aid and learned rifle-shooting, and the Irish Citizen Army (ICA, 1914); with the rank of adjutant, was with the garrison at General Post Office in Dublin during the Easter Rising (1916); arrested and imprisoned; was Belfast delegate at the Cumann na mBan convention (1917); was nominated for the Victoria Division of Belfast (1918), one of only two women chosen by Sinn Fein to contest the general election, though unsuccessful; when the Irish civil war broke out (1922), supported the republican side and sheltered many republicans in her home, which led to police raids; arrested (July 1922), was released after 3 weeks and fined for possessing seditious papers; continued to work for the ITGWU both in Belfast and Dublin until 1928; joined Northern Ireland Labor Party (1924) and was associated with the radical wing, which later became the Revolutionary Workers Groups. ❖ See also *Women in World History*.

CARNOVSKY, Phoebe (1907–2004). *See Brand, Phoebe.*

CARO, Ana (c. 1590–1650). *See Caro Mallén de Soto, Ana.*

CARO, Margaret (1848–1938). New Zealand dentist, religious and social reformer. Name variations: Margaret Malcolm. Born Margaret Malcolm, Dec 17, 1848, at Richmond, Nelson, New Zealand; died May 19, 1938, in Wellington, New Zealand; dau. of Andrew Malcolm and Margaret (Barrie) Malcolm; m. James (Jacob) Selig Siegfried Caro (physician), 1864 (died 1902); children: 3 sons. ❖ Provided medical and dental services to mining and farming communities; settled in Napier and established dental practice (1909); became Seventh-day Adventist and actively promoted its social causes; supported reforms of Women's Christian Temperance Union (WTCU) and helped establish rescue home for women and children of alcoholics. ❖ See also *Dictionary of New Zealand Biography* (Vol. 2).

CARO, Pauline (1835–1901). French novelist. Born 1835 in France; died 1901; m. Elme-Marie Caro (philosopher). ❖ Published several novels anonymously; works include *Le Péché de Madeleine* (Madeleine's Sin, 1864), *Flamien* (1866), *Histoire de Souci* (The Tale of the Marigold, 1868), *Les Nouvelles Amours de Hermann et Dorothée, Amour de jeune fille* (1892), *Fruits Amers* (Bitter Fruits, 1892), *Complice* (Accomplice, 1893), *Idylle nuptiale* (Wedding Idyll, 1898), and *Aimer c'est vaincre* (Love Conquers All, 1900).

CARO MALLÉN DE SOTO, Ana (c. 1590–1650). Spanish playwright. Name variations: Doña Ana Caro Maillén de Soto; Ana Caro Mallén de Soto; Ana Caro. Born c. 1590; died 1650. ❖ Active in academic circles, writings include *El conde Partinuplés* (Count Partinuplés).

CAROL, Martine (1922–1967). French actress. Name variations: Maryse Arley. Born Maryse Mourer (also seen as Marie Louise Mourer), May 16, 1922, in Biarritz, France; died Feb 6, 1967, in Monte Carlo; m. Steve Crane, 1949 (div. 1954); m. Christian-Jacque (journalist), 1954 (div. 1959); m. André Rouveix, 1959 (div. 1961); m. Mike Eland (British businessman). ❖ Began career on French stage as Maryse Arley; made film debut (1943); attempted suicide by throwing herself off a bridge into the Seine (April 1947); had 1st starring role (1948), in *Les Amants de Vérone*; was France's leading box-office draw and postwar sex symbol (early 1950s); appeared in such notable films as Richard Pottier's *Caroline Chérie* (1951), René Clair's *Les Belles de Nuit* (1952), and Max Ophüls's *Lola Montès* (1955); also appeared in *Adorable Créatures* (1952), *Lucrèce Borgia* (1953), *Madame Du Barry* (1954), and *Nana* (1955); shot last film, *Vanina Vanini*, in Italy (1961).

CAROL, Sue (1906–1982). American actress and talent agent. Born Evelyn Lederer, Oct 30, 1906, in Chicago, Illinois; died Feb 4, 1982, in Hollywood, California; m. Nick Stuart (actor), 1929 (div.); m. 4th husband, Alan Ladd (actor), 1942 (died 1964); children: (4th m.) David Ladd (actor), Alana Ladd (actress). ❖ Appeared in films (1927–37), including *Soft Cushions, The Cohens and Kellys in Paris, Check and Double Check, Graft, In the Line of Duty* and *The Exalted Flapper*; became a leading talent agent, handling Alan Ladd, among others.

CAROLINA. *Variant of Caroline.*

CAROLINA, Queen of the Two Sicilies (1752–1814). *See Maria Carolina.*

CAROLINE. *Variant of Carolina.*

CAROLINE (1768–1821). *See Caroline of Brunswick.*

CAROLINE (1793–1812). Tuscan noblewoman. Born 1793; died 1812; dau. of Ferdinand III, grand duke of Tuscany (r. 1790–1802 and 1814–1824) and Louisa Amelia (1773–1802); sister of Leopold II, grand duke of Tuscany (r. 1824–1859).

CAROLINE (1793–1881). Danish princess. Born in 1793; died in 1881; dau. of Marie Sophie of Hesse-Cassel (1767–1852) and Frederick VI, king of Denmark (r. 1808–1839); married Frederick Ferdinand, prince Oldenburg.

CAROLINE AMELIA AUGUSTA or CAROLINE AMELIA ELIZABETH (1768–1821). *See Caroline of Brunswick.*

CAROLINE AMELIA OF AUGUSTENBURG (1796–1881). Queen of Denmark. Name variations: Caroline Amalie of Augustenborg; Caroline Amelia of Schleswig-Holstein. Born June 22, 1796, in Copenhagen, Denmark; died Mar 9, 1881, in Amalienborg, Copenhagen; dau. of Frederick Christian, duke of Schleswig-Holstein, and Louise Augusta (1771–1843); became 2nd wife of Christian VIII (1786–1848), king of Denmark (r. 1839–1848), May 22, 1815; children: (stepchild) Frederick VII (1808–1863), king of Denmark (r. 1848–1863).

CAROLINE AUGUSTA OF BAVARIA (1792–1873). Bavarian princess. Name variations: Karoline Augusta or Auguste; Charlotta Augusta; Charlotte of Bavaria. Born Feb 8, 1792, in Mannheim; died Feb 9, 1873, in Vienna; dau. of Wilhelmine of Darmstadt (1765–1796) and Maximilian I Joseph, elector of Bavaria (r. 1799–1805), king of Bavaria (r. 1805–1825); m. William I (1781–1864), king of Wurttemberg (r. 1816–1864), June 8, 1808 (annulled 1814); m. Francis I (1768–1835), emperor of Austria, also known as Francis II, the last Holy Roman emperor (r. 1792–1806). Francis' other wives were Maria Teresa of Naples (1772–1807), Elizabeth of Wurttemberg (1767–1790), and Maria Ludovica of Modena (1787–1816).

CAROLINE ELIZABETH (1713–1757). Princess royal. Name variations: Caroline Guelph. Born Caroline Elizabeth in Hanover, Lower Saxony, Germany, June 10, 1713; died at St. James' Palace, London, England, Dec 28, 1757; buried at Westminster Abbey, London; dau. of George II (1683–1760), king of Great Britain and Ireland (r. 1727–1760) and Caroline of Ansbach (1683–1737).

CAROLINE LOUISE OF SAXE-WEIMAR (1786–1816). Duchess of Mecklenburg-Schwerin. Born July 18, 1786; died Jan 20, 1816; dau. of Charles Augustus (b. 1757), duke of Saxe-Weimar and Eis, and Louise of Hesse-Darmstadt (d. 1830); became 2nd wife of Frederick Louis (1778–1819), duke of Mecklenburg-Schwerin; children: Albert of Mecklenburg-Schwerin (b. 1812); Helene Louise of Mecklenburg-Schwerin (1814–1858).

CAROLINE MATILDA (1751–1775). Queen of Denmark. Name variations: Caroline Mathilde; Caroline Guelph. Born July 11, 1751, at Leicester House, St. Martin's, London, England; died of scarlet fever, May 11, 1775, in Celle Castle, Brunswick, Germany; posthumous dau. of Frederick Louis, prince of Wales (eldest son of King George II of Great Britain) and Augusta of Saxe-Gotha (1719–1772); sister of George III, king of England; m. her cousin Christian VII (son of Frederick V of Denmark), king of Denmark and Norway (r. 1766–1808), Nov 8, 1766 (div. 1772); children: (with Christian VII) Frederick VI (b. 1768), king of Denmark and Norway (r. 1808–1839); (with Johann Struensee) Louise Augusta (1771–1843). ❖ Betrothed to Christian VII (Jan 10, 1765); married the mad and profligate Christian by proxy (Oct 1, 1766), in actuality (Nov 8, 1766); formed a romantic and political liaison with the brilliant statesman Count Johann Friedrich von Struensee; following a palace revolt staged by Christian's stepmother and his half-brother, the heir presumptive, learned of her lover's execution and was exiled to Celle in Germany (1772); though a conspiracy was formed to liberate her, died of scarlet fever before rescuers could intervene (1775). ❖ See also Hester W. Chapman, *Caroline Matilda* (Cape, 1971); and *Women in World History.*

CAROLINE MATILDA OF DENMARK (1912–1995). Danish princess. Name variations: Caroline-Matilda Louise Oldenburg; Caroline Mathilde von Schleswig-Holstein-Sonderburg-Glucksburg. Born April 27, 1912; died Dec 12, 1995; dau. of Harald (b. 1876, son of Louise of Sweden and Frederick VIII, king of Denmark), and Helen of Schleswig-Holstein (1888–1962); m. Prince Knud Christian Frederik (b. 1900, son of Christian X, king of Denmark), Sept 8, 1933; children: Elizabeth

Caroline-Matilde (b. 1935); Ingolf Christian Frederik Knud (b. 1940); Christian Frederik Francis (b. 1942).

CAROLINE MATILDA OF SCHLESWIG-HOLSTEIN (1860–1932). Duchess of Schleswig-Holstein. Name variations: Victoria Frederica of Schleswig-Holstein. Born Victoria Fredericka Augusta Mary Carolina Matilda, Jan 25, 1860; died Feb 20, 1932; dau. of Frederick, duke of Schleswig-Holstein-Sonderburg-Augustenburg, and Adelaide of Hohenlohe-Langenburg (1835–1900); m. Frederick Ferdinand (1855–1934), duke of Schleswig-Holstein-Glucksburg (r. 1855–1934), Mar 19, 1885; children: Victoria Adelaide of Schleswig-Holstein (1885–1970); Alexandra Victoria of Schleswig-Holstein (1887–1957, who m. Augustus William, the son of Kaiser Wilhelm II); Helen of Schleswig-Holstein (1888–1962); Karoline-Mathilde of Schleswig-Holstein (b. 1894, who m. Hans, count of Solms-Baruth); Adelaide of Holstein-Schleswig (b. 1899); Wilhelm Fredrich also known as Frederick (1891–1965), duke of Schleswig-Holstein (r. 1934–1965).

CAROLINE OF ANSBACH (1683–1737). Queen of England. Name variations: Wilhelmina Carolina, Caroline the Good, Caroline of Brandenburg-Ansbach or Anspach; Caroline of Wales; princess of Wales. Born Wilhelmina Charlotte Caroline in Ansbach, Germany, Mar 1, 1683; died at St. James' Palace, London, England, Nov 20, 1737; dau. of John Frederick, margrave of Brandenburg-Ansbach (d. 1686) and Eleanor of Saxe-Eisenach (1662–1696); m. George II (1683–1760), king of Great Britain and Ireland (r. 1727–1760), Aug 22, 1705; children: Frederick, prince of Wales (1701–1751, father of George III and husband of Augusta of Saxe-Coburg-Gotha); Anne (1709–1759); Amelia Sophia (1711–1786), Caroline Elizabeth (1713–1757); George (died as an infant); William Augustus (1721–1765), duke of Cumberland (called the Butcher of Culloden); Mary of Hesse-Cassel (1723–1772); Louise of England (1724–1751). ❖ Grew up in Dresden and Berlin; married the Hanoverian prince, George Augustus (1705); took a strong interest in the approaching accession of the Hanoverian dynasty to the British throne; was on friendly terms with the old electress, Sophia (1630–1714), and corresponded with Baron Gottfried von Leibnitz; followed husband and father-in-law, soon to be King George I of England, to London (1714); as princess of Wales, was accessible and accepted, filling a difficult position with tact and success; when squabbles between husband and his unpopular father escalated, sided with husband (1717); driven from court, ostracized by the king, deprived even of the custody of her children, took up residence with husband in London at Leicester House; was surrounded by noted celebrities: Lord Chesterfield, Alexander Pope, John Gay, Lord Hervey and Mary Hervey; became reconciled with George I (1720); on his death (1727), crowned alongside husband; influenced English politics through friend Sir Robert Walpole, a minister whom she kept in power and in control of church patronage; was regent of the kingdom on 4 occasions; complaisant towards the king, flattered his vanity and acknowledged his mistresses, including Henrietta Howard, and retained her influence over him to the end. ❖ See also *Women in World History.*

CAROLINE OF AUSTRIA (1801–1832). Austrian princess. Name variations: Karolina Ferdinanda. Born April 8, 1801, in Vienna; died May 22, 1832, in Dresden; dau. of Maria Teresa of Naples (1772–1807) and Francis I, emperor of Austria (r. 1804–1835), also known as Francis II, Holy Roman emperor (r. 1792–1806); became 1st wife of Frederick Augustus II (1797–1854), king of Saxony (r. 1836–1854), Oct 7, 1819. Frederick Augustus' 2nd wife was Maria of Bavaria (1805–1877).

CAROLINE OF BADEN (1776–1841). Queen of Bavaria and electress of Bavaria. Born July 13, 1776, in Karlsruhe; died Nov 13, 1841, in Munich, Germany; dau. of Amalie of Hesse-Darmstadt (1754–1832) and Charles Louis of Padua, prince of Padua and Baden; became 2nd wife of Maximilian I Joseph, elector of Bavaria (r. 1799–1805), king of Bavaria (r. 1805–1825); children: Maximilian (1800–1803); Elizabeth of Bavaria (1801–1873, who m. Frederick William IV of Prussia); Amalia of Bavaria (1801–1877); Sophie of Bavaria (1805–1872); Maria of Bavaria (1805–1877, who m. Frederick Augustus II of Saxony); Ludovica (1808–1892, who m. Duke Maximilian Joseph of Bavaria); Maximiliana (1810–1821).

CAROLINE OF BIRKENFELD-ZWEIBRUCKEN (1721–1774). Landgravine of Hesse-Darmstadt. Name variations: Caroline of Zweibrücken-Birkenfeld. Born Mar 9, 1721; died Mar 30, 1774; m. Ludwig IX also known as Louis IX (b. 1719), landgrave of Hesse-Darmstadt, Aug 12, 1741; children: Caroline of Hesse-Darmstadt (1746–1821); Frederica of Hesse (1751–1805); Louis I (b. 1753), grand duke of Hesse; Amalie of Hesse-Darmstadt (1754–1832); Natalie of Hesse-Darmstadt (1755–1776).

CAROLINE OF BOURBON (1822–1869). Duchess of Aumâle. Name variations: Caroline de Bourbon. Born April 26, 1822; died Dec 6, 1869; dau. of Leopold (b. 1790), prince of Salerno, and Clementine of Austria (1798–1881); m. Henry (1822–1897), duke of Aumâle, Nov 25, 1844; children: Louis Philippe (b. 1845), prince of Conde; Henry (b. 1852); Franz (b. 1854), duke of Guise; and two other children who died in infancy.

CAROLINE OF BRANDENBURG-ANSBACH (1683–1737). *See Caroline of Ansbach.*

CAROLINE OF BRUNSWICK (1768–1821). Queen of Great Britain and Ireland. Name variations: Caroline Amelia Augusta; Caroline Amelia Elizabeth; Queen Caroline; Caroline Amelia of Brunswick-Wolfenbuttel; Princess of Wales. Born Caroline Amelia Augusta, May 17, 1768, in Brunswick, Lower Saxony, Germany; died at Brandenburg House, Hammersmith, London, England, Aug 7, 1821; buried in Brunswick, Lower Saxony, Germany; 2nd dau. of Charles William Ferdinand Bevern, duke of Brunswick-Wolfenbüttel, and Augusta Guelph (1737–1813), sister of George III, king of England); m. George IV (1762–1821), king of England (r. 1820–1830), April 8, 1795; children: Charlotte Augusta (1796–1817, who m. Leopold I, king of the Belgians); (adopted) William Austin and Edwina Kent. ❖ Fun-loving, vivacious, and out-spoken, was ill-prepared for a future as queen and long-suffering wife of a disreputable monarch; married George, prince of Wales (future King George IV, 1795), who was already illegally wed to Maria Anne Fitzherbert; as soon as a legal heir was conceived, was deserted by husband for his mistresses, who over the years included Lady Jersey, Mary Robinson, Countess von Hardenburg, Anna Maria Crouch, and Lady Melbourne; after giving birth to Charlotte Augusta, princess royale (1796), was granted permission to see her for about 2 hours a week; resided alone at Blackheath, entertaining writers and artists, selling produce from her garden to subsidize the education of 9 local orphans, 2 of whom she adopted; lapsed into rebellious conduct, but the sympathies of the people of England were strongly in her favor; when husband ordered an investigation, was acquitted of any serious offense; left England with adopted children and traveled on the Continent (1814), living principally in Italy; on the accession of the prince to the throne of England as George IV (1820), returned to England to claim her rights as queen; was accused by the openly adulterous George IV of living in sin with Bartolomo Pergami, a chamberlain in the royal household; when a bill to dissolve her marriage was brought into House of Lords, successfully argued her position at the so-called Trial of Queen Caroline (Aug 1820), but was still locked out of Westminster by husband on coronation day (1821); died 3 weeks later. ❖ See also Flora Fraser, *The Unruly Queen: The Life of Queen Caroline* (Knopf, 1996); and *Women in World History.*

CAROLINE OF HESSE-DARMSTADT (1746–1821). Landgravine of Hesse-Homburg. Name variations: Caroline von Hessen-Darmstadt. Born Mar 2, 1746; died Sept 18, 1821; dau. of Ludwig IX, landgrave of Hesse-Darmstadt, and Caroline of Birkenfeld-Zweibrucken (1721–1774); sister of Frederica of Hesse (1751–1805), Grand Duke Louis I, Amalie of Hesse-Darmstadt (1754–1832), and Natalie of Hesse-Darmstadt (1755–1776); m. Frederick Louis V (1748–1820), landgrave of Hesse-Homburg (r. 1751–1820), Sept 27, 1768; children: Frederick VI (b. 1769), landgrave of Hesse-Homburg; Mary of Hesse-Homburg (1785–1846).

CAROLINE OF MECKLENBURG-STRELITZ (1821–1876). Princess of Mecklenburg-Strelitz. Born Jan 10, 1821; died June 1, 1876; dau. of George (b. 1779), duke of Mecklenburg-Strelitz; became 2nd wife of Frederick VII (1808–1863), king of Denmark (r. 1848–1863), June 10, 1841 (div. 1846).

CAROLINE OF MONACO (1957—). Princess of Monaco. Name variations: Caroline Grimaldi. Born Caroline Louisa Marguerite Grimaldi, Jan 23, 1957, in Monaco; eldest child of Rainier III, Prince of Monaco, and Grace Kelly (actress); sister of Albert and Stephanie of Monaco; m. Philippe Junot, June 18, 1978 (div. Oct 9, 1980); m. Stefano Casiraghi (Italian industrialist), Dec 29, 1983 (killed in a power-boat racing accident, 1990); m. Ernst August Hanover, prince of Hanover, Jan 23, 1999; children: (2nd m.) Andrea (b. 1984), Charlotte (b. 1986), and Pierre (b. 1987); (3rd m.) Alexandra (b. 1999).

CAROLINE OF NAPLES (1798–1870). Duchess of Berry. Name variations: Caroline Ferdinande Louise of Naples; Caroline of Naples; Marie

Caroline Ferdinande Louise of Naples; Maria Carolina de Bourbon; Marie-Caroline de Bourbon-Sicile; duchesse de Berry; princess of the Two Sicilies. Born Marie Caroline Ferdinande Louise, Nov 5, 1798; died April 17, 1870; dau. of Francis I, king of Two Sicilies (r. 1825–1830) and Maria Clementina of Austria (1777–1801); m. Charles Ferdinand (1778–1820), duke of Berry (2nd son of Charles X, king of France), 1816; m. Ettore, count Lucchesi-Palli, 1831; children: (1st m.) Louise of Bourbon-Berry (1819–1864), duchess of Parma; Henry V (1820–1883), duke of Bordeaux and count of Chambord (who m. Therese [1817–1886]); (2nd m.) Clementina de Campofranco (b. 1835). ❖ Married Charles Ferdinand, son of Charles X, king of France (1816); husband was assassinated in Paris (Feb 13, 1820); with Legitimists, promoted an unsuccessful attempt at revolution in favor of son Henry, count of Chambord, proclaiming him Henry V, king of France (1832). ❖ See also *Women in World History.*

CAROLINE OF NASSAU (fl. 1730s). Countess of Zweibrucken. Married Christian III, count of Zweibrucken (r. 1733–1735); children: Christian IV (r. 1735–1775), count of Zweibrucken; Frederick Michael (d. 1767).

CAROLINE OF NASSAU-USINGEN (1762–1823). Landgravine of Hesse-Cassel. Name variations: Caroline Polyxena of Nassau-Usingen. Born Caroline Polyxene, April 4, 1762; died Mar 28, 1823; dau. of Charles William, prince of Nassau-Usingen, and Caroline Felizitas of Leiningen-Heidesheim (b. 1734); m. Frederick III, landgrave of Hesse-Cassel, Dec 2, 1786; children: 8, including William, landgrave of Hesse-Cassel (1787–1867); Mary of Hesse-Cassel (1796–1880, who m. George, grand duke of Mecklenburg-Strelitz); Augusta of Hesse-Cassel (1797–1889, who m. Adolphus Guelph, 1st duke of Cambridge).

CAROLINE OF ORANGE (1743–1787). Princess of Nassau-Weilburg. Name variations: Wilhelmina Caroline of Nassau-Dietz. Born Feb 28, 1743; died May 6, 1787; dau. of William IV, prince of Orange (r. 1748–1751), and Anne (1709–1759, dau. of King George II of England and Caroline of Ansbach); m. Charles, prince of Nassau-Weilburg, Mar 5, 1760; children: 9, including Frederick William (1768–1816); Henrietta of Nassau-Weilburg (1780–1857).

CAROLINE OF PARMA (1770–1804). Princess of Parma. Born Nov 22, 1770; died Mar 1, 1804; dau. of Maria Amalia (1746–1804) and Ferdinand I (1751–1802), duke of Parma (r. 1765–1802); m. Maximilian of Saxony (son of Frederick Christian and Maria Antonia of Austria), duke of Saxony (r. 1830–1838), May 9, 1792; children: Frederick Augustus II (1797–1854), king of Saxony (r. 1836–1854); John (1801–1873), king of Saxony (r. 1854–1873); Amalie of Saxony (1794–1870); Maria Josepha of Saxony (1803–1829).

CAROLINE OF SAXONY (1833–1907). Queen of Saxony. Born Caroline Frederica Francisca, Aug 5, 1833; died Dec 15, 1907; dau. of Prince Gustavus Vasa (b. 1799) and Louise of Baden (1811–1854); m. Albert (1828–1902), king of Saxony (r. 1873–1902), June 18, 1853.

CAROLINE OF SICILY (1820–1861). Sicilian princess. Born Feb 29, 1820; died Jan 13, 1861; dau. of Marie Isabella of Spain (1789–1848) and Francis I, king of Two Sicilies (r. 1825–1830); m. Charles of Molina, July 10, 1850.

CARON, Christine (1948—). French swimmer. Name variations: Kiki Caron. Born July 10, 1948. ❖ At Tokyo Olympics, won a silver medal in 100-meter backstroke (1964).

CARON, Kiki (1948—). *See Caron, Christine.*

CARON, Leslie (1931—). French actress and dancer. Born Leslie Claire Margaret Caron, July 1, 1931, in Boulogne-Billancourt, France; dau. of Claude Caron and Margaret Pettibone Caron (dancer as Margaret Petit); m. George A. Hormel (meat-packing heir), 1951 (div. 1954); m. Peter Hall (British producer-director), 1956 (div. 1966); m. Michael Laughlin (producer), 1969 (div. 1980); children: (2nd m.) 2. ❖ Trained with Olga Preobrazhenska; appeared with Roland Petit's Ballets des Champs-Élysées (1947–50) and the Ballet de Paris (1954); made acting debut opposite Gene Kelly in film *American in Paris* (1951); made stage acting debut in Renoir's *Orvet* (1955); debuted in London in title role in *Gigi* (1961), followed by title role in *Ondine*; films include *Gigi, The Doctor's Dilemma, Daddy Long Legs, Man with a Cloak, The Subterraneans, Fanny, Gaby* and *Chocolat*; owns an inn in Villeneuve-sur-Yonne in Burgundy. Won British Film Academy awards for *The L-Shaped Room* (1962) and *Lili* (1953) and Oscar nominations for both.

CARON, Margaret Pettibone (b. around 1904). American theatrical ballet dancer and choreographer. Name variations: Margaret Petit;

Margaret Pettibone; Marguerite Caron. Born Margaret Pettibone, c. 1904, in Seattle, Washington; died in France; m. Claude Caron (wealthy chemist); children: Leslie Caron (b. 1931, actress and dancer). ❖ Studied with Luigi Albertieri, Ivan Tarasoff, and Mikhail Fokine in New York City during adolescence; performed in *What's in a Name* (1920) and *Greenwich Village Follies* (1921); appeared as specialty dancer in *Pin Wheel Revue of 1922* and staged many of her own dances, such as *The Masked Bacchantes;* moved to Paris (1926) and retired from performance career.

CAROSIO, Margherita (1908–2005). Italian soprano. Born June 7, 1908, in Genoa, Italy; died Jan 10, 2005; dau. of Natale Carosio (singing teacher and composer). ❖ One of the leading sopranos at La Scala for over 20 years, who was then considered the best bel canto soprano in Italy, began career in concerts at 14; at 16, made operatic debut as Lucia di Lammermoor at Novi Lugure (1926); sang Musetta and Feodor to Chaliapin's Boris Godunov at Covent Garden (1928); debuted at La Scala as Oscar in *Un Ballo in Maschera,* followed by Philine in *Mignon;* sang Aminta in Italian premiere of *The Silent Woman* and Egloge in the premiere of *Nerone* (1935); was noted for her Aminta in *La Sonnambula,* Norina in *Don Pasquale* and Konstanze in *Entfuhrung,* as well as her Mimi, Adina and Violetta.

CAROTHERS, E. Eleanor (1882–1957). American zoologist. Born Estella Eleanor Carothers, Dec 4, 1882, in Newton, Kansas; dau. of Mary (Bates) Carothers and Z.W. Carothers; Nickerson Normal College, University of Kansas, AB, 1911, AM, 1912; University of Pennsylvania, PhD, 1916. ❖ Was an assistant zoology professor at University of Pennsylvania (1914–36); traveled to southern and southwestern states on scientific expeditions (1915–19); worked as research associate for University of Iowa's Department of Zoology and received Rockefeller Foundation Fund grant to research cytology and physiology of normal cell. Honors include star in American Men of Science (1927), for research on embryos of grasshoppers; was a regular member of Marine Biological Laboratory in Woods Hole, MA (1920–56).

CARPADIOS, Marissa (1977—). Australian softball player. Born Dec 30, 1977, in Brisbane, Australia; attended Griffith University. ❖ Catcher/third base, won a team silver medal at Athens Olympics (2004).

CARPENTER, Connie (1957—). See Carpenter-Phinney, Connie.

CARPENTER, Constance (1904–1992). English actress and singer. Born April 19, 1904, in Bath, Somerset, England; died Dec 26, 1992 in Manhattan of a stroke. ❖ Primarily a stage actress, starred opposite Yul Brynner in *The King and I* (1951–54); also appeared on Broadway in *Charlot Revue* (1925–26), *Oh, Kay!* (1926–27), *A Connecticut Yankee* (1927–28), *Roar Like a Dove* (1964) and *The Incomparable Max* (1971).

CARPENTER, Iris (b. 1906). British journalist and war correspondent. Name variations: Iris Carpenter Akers. Born in England in 1906; dau. of a cinema entrepreneur; m. Charles Scruby (wealthy developer); m. Russell F. Akers Jr. (American colonel), 1946; children: (1st m.) 1 son, 1 daughter. ❖ One of the few women to report the Allied invasion of Europe from D-Day in June 1944 to the surrender of Germany in May 1945, landed 1st writing job as a film critic for a British publication, *The Picture Show* (1924), then signed on with London's *Daily Express;* though she retired from journalism to raise a family (1933), was motivated by the start of WWII to return to the profession; reported on the conflict in several roles, including as a broadcaster for the BBC as well as a print reporter for both *Daily Express* and *Daily Herald;* facing strong discrimination by British military authorities and determined to be a combat reporter, was hired by the *Boston Globe* and accredited with the 1st American Army; her reports from the front lines and hospitals in France and Germany described in graphic prose some of the bloodiest fighting on the Western front, including the Battle of the Bulge and the liberation of Nazi concentration camps; remained in US, working for Voice of America. ❖ See also memoir *No Woman's World* (Houghton, 1946); and *Women in World History.*

CARPENTER, Karen (1950–1983). American singer and drummer. Born in East Haven, Connecticut, Mar 2, 1950; died Feb 4, 1983; sister of Richard Carpenter (1946—); m. Tom Burris (real-estate developer), 1980 (sep.). ❖ Pop singer, known for her pure voice, whose death at age 32 helped bring anorexia nervosa to national consciousness, moved with family to Downey, CA (1963); began playing drums; with brother on piano and Wes Jacobs on bass, became part of The Richard Carpenter Trio; also began to do vocals; with trio, made the finals of the prestigious "Battle of the Bands" at Hollywood Bowl (1966); formed a duo with brother, calling themselves Carpenters, minus the *The;* signed with A&M

records (1969); released single "Close to You," which made #1 on Billboard charts and sold over 1 million copies, followed by "We've Only Just Begun" which went gold (an album featuring both hits sold 5 million copies and grabbed 6 Grammy nominations, including Record of the Year and Album of the Year, 1970); released "For All We Know" ("Love, look at the two of us"), which became another million-selling record (1971); toured US, Europe, Japan and Australia (1970–75); appeared on 1st tv special (1976); other hit singles include "Top of the World," "Rainy Days and Mondays" and "Superstar." ❖ See also Ray Coleman, *The Carpenters: The Untold Story* (HarperCollins, 1994); and *Women in World History.*

CARPENTER, Marion (1920–2002). American photographer. Born Mar 6, 1920; body found in her home, Oct 29, 2002, age 82, in St. Paul, Minnesota; married a Navy officer (div.); married a radio announcer (div.); children: 1 son. ❖ One of the 1st women to be a White House photographer, traveled with and covered President Harry Truman for the International News Photos syndicate; died in obscurity.

CARPENTER, Mary (1807–1877). English philanthropist and social reformer. Born April 3, 1807, in Exeter, England; died June 14, 1877, in Bristol, England; dau. of Lant Carpenter (1780–1840, Unitarian minister) and Anna Penn; sister of William Benjamin (1813–1885, physiologist). ❖ Influential in juvenile delinquency and prison reform, opened 1st Ragged School in Bristol (1846); published the 1st of many works on the subject of delinquent children, *Ragged Schools: Their Principles and Modes of Operation* (1850); organized a conference for reformatory school workers (1851), resulting in the Reformatory Schools Act (1854); opened a reformatory school for boys (1852) and one for girls, Red Lodge (1854); also published 2 books on school reform; left England for India (1866), the 1st of many trips she would undertake over next 10 years, turning to the problems women faced there; became a member of the Bristol Committee for the repeal of the Contagious Diseases Acts. ❖ See also memoir, *Six Months in India* (1868); Jo Manton, *Mary Carpenter and the Children of the Streets* (Heinemann, 1976); and *Women in World History.*

CARPENTER, Mary Chapin (1958—). American singer and songwriter. Name variations: Mary-Chapin Carpenter. Born Feb 21, 1958, in Princeton, New Jersey; graduate of Brown University, 1981; m. Timmy Smith, 2002. ❖ Known for articulate country songs with rock textures, released such hit singles as "Never Had It So Good" (1989), "Quittin' Time" (1990), "Down at the Twist and Shout" (1990), "I Feel Lucky" (1992), "He Thinks He'll Keep Her" (1994), and "Shut Up and Kiss Me" (1994); received multiple Grammy awards, including 4 consecutive awards for best female country vocal; named Best New Female Vocalist by Academy of Country Music (1989); published children's books, including *Dreamland* (1996) and *Halley Came To Jackson* (1998). Albums include *Hometown Girl* (1987), *State of the Heart* (1989), *Shooting Straight in the Dark* (1990), *Come On Come On* (1992), *Stones in the Road* (1994), *A Place in the World* (1996) and *time*sex*love* (2001).

CARPENTER, Maud (d. 1967). English theatrical manager. Died June 16, 1967; dau. of George Carpenter; m. David Farrington. ❖ Was connected with the Liverpool Playhouse from its inception as a repertory theater (Nov 1911), as secretary and assistant manager, then licensee and business manager (1923–39), then manager; characterized in Beryl Bainbridge's novel *An Awfully Big Adventure* and portrayed in the film adaptation by Prunella Scales.

CARPENTER, Thelma (1922–1997). African-American jazz singer and actress. Born Jan 15, 1922, in Brooklyn, NY; died May 14, 1997, in New York, NY. ❖ Began performing at an early age; joined Count Basie (1939), with whom she produced her most memorable recordings, then worked with Teddy Wilson's orchestra; made Broadway debut in *Memphis Bound* (1944), followed by *Inside USA, Shuffle Along, Ankles Aweigh, Bubbling Brown Sugar,* and as Pearl Bailey's replacement in *Hello Dolly!;* films include *Hellzapoppin, The Wiz* and *The Cotton Club;* also recorded with Herman Chittison; albums include "Souvenir" (1998).

CARPENTER-PHINNEY, Connie (1957—). American cyclist. Name variations: Connie Carpenter or Connie Carpenter Phinney. Born Connie Carpenter, Feb 26, 1957, in Madison, Wisconsin; m. Davis Phinney (professional cyclist). ❖ At 14, made US Olympic speed-skating team, finishing 7th in the 1,500 meters at Sapporo (1972); at Los Angeles Olympics, won inaugural Olympic gold medal for cycling (1984), the 1st cycling medal for US in an international event since 1912; won US national championships in road race (1976–78, 1981) and pursuit (1976–78, 1981, 1983); won 4 World championships; won

Coors International Classic (1977, 1981–82) won more national and international cycling titles than any American cyclist, male or female. Inducted into International Women's Sports Hall of Fame (1990).

CARPINTERI, Laura (b. 1910). Italian novelist and painter. Name variations: (pseudonym) Laura Di Falco. Born 1910; grew up in Syracuse. ❖ Studied philosophy in Pisa and taught at teacher-training college in Rome; contributed to *Il Mondo* (1950–66); works include *Paura del giorno* (1954), *Una donna disponibile* (1959), *Tre carte de gioco* (1962), *Le tre mogli* (1967), *Miracolo d'estate* (1971), *L'inferriata* (1976) and *Piazza della quattro vie* (1982).

CARR, Ann (1958—). American gymnast. Born Jan 16, 1958. ❖ Won Pan American Games (1975) and AIAW Division 1 championships (1977, 1978).

CARR, Catherine (1954—). American swimmer. Born May 27, 1954. ❖ Won gold medals for 100-meter breaststroke and 4x100-meter relay at Munich Olympics (1972).

CARR, Emily (1871–1945). Canadian painter. Name variations: Millie. Born Emily Carr, Dec 13, 1871, in Victoria, British Columbia (Canada); died in Victoria, Mar 2, 1945; dau. of Richard and Emily (Sauders) Carr; attended California School of Design (later named Mark Hopkins Institute of Art) in San Francisco, Westminster School of Art in England, and Academie Colarossi in Paris; never married; no children. ❖ Painter of totem poles and forest scenes, who belatedly achieved both international and national recognition as one of her nation's greatest artists, left home for art school in San Francisco (1891); began a period of study and travel in England (1899); left Victoria to study in France (1910); saaw 1st national exhibit of her work (1927); had most productive and creative period of painting (1928–36), rendering such works as *Tanoo, Q.C. Islands* (1913), *Indian Church* (1929), *Blunden Harbour* (1930), *Forest, British Columbia* (1931), and *Above the Gravel Pit* (1936); rejecting traditional methods of painting realistic images, sought to capture the emotions that the objects evoked; suffered serious heart attack, beginning of declining health (1937); published 1st book *Klee Wyck* (1941); other writings include *The Book of Small* (1942), *The House of All Sorts* (1944), *Growing Pains* (1946), *The Heart of a Peacock* (1953), *Pause: A Sketchbook* (1953) and *Hundreds and Thousands: The Journals of Emily Carr* (1966); paintings provide a vivid testimonial to the inherent beauty and mysticalness of nature. Received Governor General's Award for *Klee Wyck* (1942). ❖ See also Maria Tippett, *Emily Carr: A Biography* (Oxford U. Press, 1979); and *Women in World History*.

CARR, Emma Perry (1880–1972). American chemist and university professor. Born July 23, 1880, in Holmesville, Ohio; died 1972 in Evanston, Illinois; dau. of Edmund Cone (physician) and Anna Mary (Jack) Carr; attended Ohio State University, 1898, studying there with William McPherson; attended Mount Holyoke College for 2 years; University of Chicago, BS, 1905, then did advanced work there with Alexander Smith and Julius Steiglitz, receiving PhD in chemistry, 1910. ❖ An influential organic and physical chemist, headed the chemistry department at Mount Holyoke College for over 30 years, building the department into a unique and important research facility; with Dorothy Hahn, initiated a series of group research projects in the application of physical chemistry to organic problems, the most important of which involved the synthesis and analysis of complex organic compounds by absorption spectra of organic compounds; investigating simple unsaturated hydrocarbons, also contributed to the understanding of the carbon-carbon double bond, an important link in chemistry. Was the 1st recipient of Garvan Medal for distinguished service in chemistry by an American woman (1937); shared James Flack Norris Award of the American Chemical Society (1957). ❖ See also *Women in World History*.

CARR, Jean (1921—). See Kent, Jean.

CARR, Lindy (1952—). See Nelson-Carr, Lindy.

CARR, Mary (1874–1973). American actress. Born Mary Kennevan, Mar 14, 1874, in Germantown, Pennsylvania; died June 24, 1973, in Woodland, Hills, California; m. William Carr (actor); children: Stephen, Louella, Maybeth, John, Rosemary and Thomas Carr (director). ❖ Began career on stage, touring extensively with husband's company; appeared in films for over 50 years, including title role in *Mrs. Wiggs of the Cabbage Patch*, as well as *Over the Hill to the Poorhouse, On the Banks of the Wabash, On Your Toes, The Oregon Trail* and *Friendly Persuasion*.

CARR, Philippa (1906–1993). See Hibbert, Eleanor.

CARR, Vikki (1941—). Mexican-American pop singer. Name variations: Florencia Bisenta de Casillas Martinez Cardona. Born Florencia Bisenta de Casillas Martinez Cardona, July 19, 1941, in El Paso, Texas; raised in San Gabriel Valley, California; eldest of 7 children. ❖ Began performing at 4; sang with Pepe Callahan's Mexican-Irish Band in Los Angeles; broke through to solo stardom after debut in Reno with Chuck Leonard Quartet, signing contract with Liberty Records (1961); under name Vikki Carr, recorded "He's a Rebel" (1961), a hit in Australia, followed by "It Must Be Him" which rose to #1 on British pop charts and earned her 3 Grammy nominations (1962); released a string of hits, including the Grammy Award-nominated "With Pen in Hand," as well as "The Lesson" and "For Once in My Life"; signed by Columbia Records (1970), released such favorites as "Love Story," "Live at the Greek," and "Ms. America"; a beloved performer in the Latin world, recorded *Vikki Carr en Español* (1972); was 1st female to regularly guest host for Johnny Carson on "The Tonight Show"; made acting debut on "The Bing Crosby Show" and had guest roles on several other tv programs, performing on stage as well; signed with Columbia Records, Mexico (1980) and released such albums as *Vikki Carr y El Amor*; earned gold and platinum albums for Spanish-language recordings in US, Mexico, Chile, Venezuela, Puerto Rico, Costa Rica, Colombia and Ecuador; won Grammy award for 1st Mariachi recording, *Simplemente Mujer* (1985), and then again for *Cosas de Amor* (1992) and *Recuerdo a Javier Solis* (1995); taped PBS special "The Mexican Americans" (2000); set up the Vikki Carr Scholarship Foundation for Mexican-Americans pursuing higher education (1971).

CARR-BOYD, Ann (1938—). Australian composer. Born in Sydney, Australia, 1938; dau. of Nyora (artist) and Norbert Wentzel (co-founder of the Sydney Symphony Orchestra); studied with Donald Peart at Sydney University. ❖ Won the Sydney Moss Scholarship and went to London where she studied with Peter Racine Fricker and Alexander Goehr; after writing several works, won the Maggs Award in Melbourne for orchestral composition *Gold* (1975), which was premiered by National Training Orchestra; began composing for harpsichord; broadcast a series of programs on women composers on Australian tv (1980s). ❖ See also *Women in World History*.

CARR-COOK, Madge (1856–1933). English actress. Born in Yorks, England, June 28, 1856; died Sept 20, 1933; sister of T. Morton Powell (theatrical manager); m. Charles Robson; m. Augustus Cook (actor); children: (1st m.) Eleanor Robson Belmont (1879–1979). ❖ Made stage debut at 3, appearing as Fleance in *MacBeth;* following many tours within England, moved to US (1887), joining the Lyceum stock company under Daniel Frohman's management; had her 1st taste of fame when she opened as Elvira Wiggs in *Mrs. Wiggs of the Cabbage Patch* (1904); retired from stage (1910). ❖ See also *Women in World History*.

CARRAN, Catherine (1842–1935). New Zealand midwife. Name variations: Catherine McKay, Catherine Patterson. Born Catherine McKay, probably at Putataka, Waikato Heads, New Zealand, 1842; died Nov 6, 1933, at Fortrose, New Zealand; dau. of John Horton McKay and Irihapeti; m. William Carran (ferryman), 1860 (died 1871); m. William Henry Patterson (miner), 1872 (died 1910); children: (1st m.) 3 sons, 3 daughters; (2nd m.) 6 son, 1 daughter. ❖ Followed 1st husband to Kapuka goldfields and served as nurse and midwife to settlers' wives after deaths of 1st and 2nd husbands. ❖ See also *Dictionary of New Zealand Biography* (Vol. 2).

CARRANZA, María Mercedes (1945–2003). Colombian poet, journalist and political activist. Name variations: Maria Mercedes Carranza. Born Mar 24, 1945, in Bogotá, Colombia; committed suicide, July 11, 2003, in Bogotá; dau. of Eduardo Carranza (poet, consular representative) and Rosa Coronado; m. Fernando Garavito; m. Juan Luis Panero, 1977 (div. 1978); children: 1 daughter. ❖ Central figure in contemporary Colombian poetry, influenced by Albert Camus, Simone de Beauvoir, Catalan anarchism, and social movements of 1960s, was a member of the "disenchanted" generation; wrote critically of roles assigned to women in patriarchal society but eschewed the label of feminism, preferring a class-based analysis of social inequality; served as founding director (1986–2003) of private foundation and cultural community center Casa de Poesía Silva (Silva House of Poetry); worked as cultural journalist for *El Siglo* (The Century) in Bogotá, and *El Pueblo* (The People) in Cali, Colombia; served as chief editor of magazine *Nueva Frontera* (New Frontier) for 13 years, and wrote for *Semana* (Week); joined Alianza Nacional M-19 (M-19 National Alliance, 1990) and was 1 of 4 women elected to National Constitutional Assembly, which proclaimed new constitution for Colombia (1991); as political activist, fought for abortion rights, rights of women and children, religious freedom, cultural pluralism, freedom of information, democratization of mass-media ownership, and extradition of Colombians as legal tool against drug traffickers; committed suicide (2003), despairing of deaths of many close friends (including Luis Carlos Galán, presidential candidate assassinated by mafia hitmen in 1989), the kidnapping of her brother Ramiro, and Colombia's descent into civil crisis. Writings include *Tengo miedo* (I Am Afraid, 1983), *Hola soledad* (Hello Solitude, 1987), *Amor y desamor* (Love and Disenchantment, 1994), and *El canto de las moscas* (The Song of the Flies, 1998).

CARRASCO, Heather (1970—). *See Simmons-Carrasco, Heather.*

CARRASCO, Margarita (1909—). *See de Alonso, Carmen.*

CARRÉ, Mathilde (1908–c. 1970). French spy. Name variations: Carre. Born Mathilde-Lucie Bélard in Chateauroux, France, 1908 (some sources cite 1910); studied law at the Sorbonne; m. Maurice Carré (schoolteacher), 1933 (div. 1939). ❖ Triple agent, known as La Chatte ("The Cat"), joined Army Nurse Corps at start of WWII; became leading member of the Interallié spy network; arrested and interrogated by the Germans (Nov 1941); turned against her former comrades and began working for the Gestapo; as a result, the Interallié network was destroyed; arrested in England (June 1942) and returned to France after the war; found guilty of treason and sentenced to death (1949); upon appeal, sentence was reduced to life imprisonment; released (1954) and lived in seclusion under a new identity until her death. ❖ See autobiography *I was "The Cat": The Truth about the Most Remarkable Woman Spy since Mata Hari—by Herself* (trans. by Mervyn Savill, Souvenir Press, 1960); Lauran Paine, *Mathilde Carré, Double Agent* (Hale, 1976); and *Women in World History.*

CARREL, Dany (1935—). French actress. Name variations: Suzanne Chazelle. Born Suzanne Chazelles du Chaxel, Sept 20, 1935, in Tourane, Annam, Indochina. ❖ Made film debut in *Dortoir des grandes* (1953), followed by *Maternité clandestine, Tres hombres van a morir, La Cage aux souris, Les Grandes manoeuvres, La Môme Pigalle, Les Possédées, La Melodía misteriosa, People of No Importance, Club de femmes, Élisa, Porte des Lilas, Escapade, No Escape, La Moucharde, Les Dragueurs, The Enemy General, Carillons san joie, Le Bluffeur, La Pacha, Woman in Chains* and *Les Portes de feu,* among others.

CARREL, Felicite (fl. 1860s). Italian mountaineer. Dau. of J.A. Carrel (Italian guide and mountaineer). ❖ Attempted to climb the Matterhorn (1867). The point she reached is now known as Col Felicite. ❖ See also *Women in World History.*

CARRELET DE MARRON, Marie-Anne (1725–1778). French playwright and painter. Born 1725 in Dijon, France; died 1778. ❖ Was a painter and designer of porcelain before becoming a writer; wrote 8 tragedies and 2 comedies, but only *La Comtesse de Fayel* was published (1770).

CARREÑO, Teresa (1853–1917). Venezuelan pianist and opera singer. Name variations: Teresa Carreno. Born Maria Teresa Carreño in Caracas, Venezuela, Dec 22, 1853; died in New York, NY, June 12, 1917; dau. of Manuel Antonio Carreño (pianist and Venezuelan minister of finance); m. Émile Sauret, 1872; m. Giovanni Tagliapietra, 1875; m. Eugen d'Albert, 1895; m. Arturo Tagliapietra, 1902; children: (1st m.) 2, including Emelita Sauret Tauscher; (2nd m.) 3, including Teresita Carreño Tagliapietra (pianist) and Giovanni Tagliapietra Jr. (baritone singer); (3rd m.) Herta and Eugenia. ❖ Most famous woman pianist of the late 19th century, who also sang operatic roles, conducted an orchestra, and introduced the music of Edward MacDowell and Edvard Grieg to audiences throughout Europe and the Americas, gave 1st piano concert at age 9, in NY, followed by a performance tour of Cuba (1862); performed solo with Boston Philharmonic (1863); performed at White House for Abraham Lincoln (1863); taught Edward MacDowell, the American composer (1872); began operatic career (1872); appeared at 1st Telephone Concert (April 2, 1877); composed *Hymn for Bolivar* (1883); was established as one of Europe's greatest pianists with a series of concerts in Berlin (1889); gave 2nd performance at White House, for Woodrow Wilson (1916). ❖ See also *Women in World History.*

CARRÈRE, Christine (1930—). *See Carère, Christine.*

CARRICK, countess of. *See Marjorie of Carrick (c. 1254–1292).*

CARRIERA, Rosalba (1675–1757). Italian portrait painter. Born in Venice, Italy, Oct 7, 1675; died in Venice, 1757; dau. of Andrea (Venetian clerk) and Alba (Foresti) Carriera (lacemaker); sister-in-law

of Giovanni Antonio Pellegrini (1675–1741). ❖ One of the few women painters to gain international renown during the 18th century, made her name as a miniaturist, before popularizing pastel as a medium for serious portraiture; rendered miniature portraits which gained her entrance into Academy of Saint Luke, Rome (1705); was made an *accademico di merito,* a title reserved for a few special artists; became well recognized in Italy, where she was elected to membership in the academies of Bologna and Florence, as well as Saint Luke's in Rome; visited Paris (1720) and took the city by storm; was made a member of French Academy (1720), despite a 1706 rule forbidding admission of any more women; establishing a fashion for pastel portraits that persisted in France well into the 19th century; influenced artists Maurice Quentin de la Tour, Marie Suzanne Giroust-Roslin, Magdalene Basseporte, and Theresa Concordia Mengs; returned to Venice (1721), where she settled into a quiet life on the Grand Canal and dedicated herself to her work, until she gradually lost her eyesight; works include *Africa* (from the cycle *The Four Continents*), *Abbé Leblond, Cardinal Melchior de Polignac, Woman at Her Dressing Table* and *Portrait of a Man.* ❖ See also *Women in World History.*

CARRIGAN, Sara (1980—). Australian cyclist. Born Sept 7, 1980, in Gunnedah, Australia; attended Griffith University. ❖ Won a gold medal for road race at Athens Olympics (2004). Named Australian Female Road Cyclist of the Year (2002, 2003).

CARRIGHAR, Sally (1898–1985). American writer and naturalist. Born Feb 10, 1898, in Cleveland, Ohio; died Oct 1985 in Carmel, California; graduate of Wellesley College, 1922. ❖ One of the most respected naturalists of her time, was a prolific animal writer; awarded a Guggenheim fellowship for fieldwork in the Arctic; wrote 10 books, including *One Day on Beetle Rock* (1944), *One Day at Teton Marsh* (1947), *Icebound Summer* (1953), *Moonlight at Midday* (1958), *Wild Voice of the North* (1959) and *Wild Heritage* (1965); also wrote for film and radio (1923–28). ❖ See also autobiography, *Home to the Wilderness* (1973).

CARRILHO, Maria (1943—). Portuguese politician. Born Nov 25, 1943, in Beja, Portugal. ❖ Member of the Assembly of the Republic (1995–99) and vice-chair of the parliamentary party of the PS (Partido Socialista, 1995–97); founder and chair of the Portuguese Association for Women's Studies (1993–95); as a European Socialist (PSE), elected to 5th European Parliament (1999–2004) and chaired the Delegation for relations with the countries of South Asia.

CARRILLO DE LA PAZ, Nancy (1986—). Cuban volleyball player. Born Jan 11, 1986, in Cuba. ❖ Won a team bronze medal at Athens Olympics (2004).

CARRINGTON, Dora (1893–1932). English artist. Name variations: Dora Carrington Partridge. Born Dora de Houghton Carrington, Mar 29, 1893, in Hereford, England; committed suicide, Mar 11, 1932, at Ham Spray near Ham, Wiltshire; dau. of Samuel Carrington (civil engineer with East India Railway Co., died Dec 1918) and Charlotte (Houghton) Carrington (governess); attended Slade School of Art, London, 1910–14; m. Ralph Partridge, May 31, 1921; no children. ❖ A serious painter and decorative artist, often neglected by the critics, who lived for nearly half her life with Lytton Strachey; fascinated her friends, many of whom were writers: Katherine Mansfield featured her in a short story, D.H. Lawrence characterized her in *Women in Love* and "None of That," Aldous Huxley used her in *Chrome Yellow,* and Wyndham Lewis in *The Apes of God;* met Strachey (1915) and moved into Tidmarsh Mill with him (1917); began to earn money painting glass pictures and tiles (1924); after Strachey died (Jan 1932), committed suicide 2 months later. Paintings include *Hills in Snow at Hurstbourne Tarrant* (1916), *Giles Lytton Strachey* (1916), *The Mill at Tidmarsh, Berkshire* (1918), *Lady Strachey* (1920), *Farm at Watendlath* (1921), and *Mountain Ranges from Yegen, Andalusia* (c. 1924). ❖ See also Mary Ann Caws, *Women of Bloomsbury: Virginia, Vanessa, and Carrington* (Routledge, 1990); David Garnett, ed. *Carrington: Letters and Extracts from her Diaries* (Cape, 1970); Gretchen Holbrook Gerzina, *Carrington: A Life of Dora Carrington 1893–1932* (John Murray, 1989); film *Carrington,* starring Emma Thompson (1995); and *Women in World History.*

CARRINGTON, Ethel (1889–1962). English actress. Born Ethel McDowell, Mar 29, 1889, in London, England; died June 26, 1962; m. Murray Carrington (actor, div.). ❖ Made stage debut in *Moths* (1907); as a member of F.R. Benson's Company (1907–12), made London debut in *The Piper* (1910); at Stratford, appeared in *Much Ado about Nothing, Merry Wives of Windsor, Merchant of Venice,* as Viola in *Twelfth Night,* Bianca in *The Taming of the Shrew,* and Helena in

A Midsummer Night's Dream; toured Canada and US (1913); other plays include *The Arm of the Law, Stand and Deliver, The 13th Chair* and *Peter Ibbetson.*

CARRINGTON, Joanna (1931–2003). English painter. Name variations: (pseudonym) Reginald Pepper. Born Nov 6, 1931, in Hampstead, England; died Nov 13, 2003; dau. of Noel Carrington (artist); niece of Dora Carrington (artist); studied with Cubist Fernand Léger in Paris; m. Mick Pilcher (designer); m. Christopher Mason (painter, writer, filmmaker), 1966; children: Sophie. ❖ Called "one of the most distinctive and original painters of her generation," had 1st solo show at the Establishment Club's gallery in Soho (1962); taught at Hornsey and Byam Shaw schools of art; began a series of landscapes, still lifes and glowing interiors (1979).

CARRINGTON, Leonora (1917—). English painter. Born in 1917 in Lancashire; dau. of a wealthy textile manufacturer and an Irish mother; attended schools in England, Florence, and Paris; studied at Amedée Ozenfant Academy, London, 1936; lived with Max Ernst for 2 years at St. Martin d'Ardèche; m. Renato LeDuc; m. Enrique "Chiqui" Weisz. ❖ Artist who developed sensibilities that were independent of earlier Surrealist influences, met Surrealist Max Ernst (1937); early paintings, often satirical of the English upper-class society into which she had been born, drew on images from childhood and included magical birds and animals; over time, work matured into a visionary art inspired by Celtic mythology and the ideas and language of alchemical transformation, the image of the white horse became a focal point; wrote "The House of Fear," 1st of her short stories (1937); after Ernst was interned as an enemy alien by the Nazis (1939), fled to Spain, hoping to secure a visa for him; had a breakdown, was institutionalized, then released into the care of a nurse, and escaped to the Mexican consulate (all 1940); for next several years, work was informed by these events; arrived in Mexico (1942); with painter Remedios Varo, became center of a collection of European exiled artists, including Kati Horna, Eva Sulzer, Luis Buñel and Alice Rahon; had exhibitions in Paris (1938, 1947), Amsterdam (1938), and NY (1942); had 1st one-woman exhibition at Pierre Matisse Gallery, NY (1948); painted mural, *The Magic World of the Mayans,* for National Museum of Anthropology (Mexico City, 1963); had retrospective exhibitions at Museo Nacional de Arte Moderno (Mexico Center, 1960) and Center for Inter-American Relations (NY, 1976); paintings include *The Old Maids, Night Nursery Everything, Neighborly Advice, The House Opposite* and *Crookhey Hall* (1947); also wrote short stories and 2 novels, *Down Below* (1944) and *The Hearing Trumpet* (1974). ❖ See also *Women in World History.*

CARROLL, Anna Ella (1815–1894). American writer and political activist. Born Aug 29, 1815, in Somerset Co., Maryland; died Feb 19, 1894 (gravestone misdated as 1893), in Washington DC; dau. of Thomas King Carroll (lawyer and legislator) and Julianna Stevenson; never married; no children. ❖ Writer whose opinions were to influence elections and policy, while her contributions to military strategy would embroil her in controversy, began career by writing promotional material for hire; became involved in the American Party, otherwise known as the "Know-Nothings" (1855); drafted an unwilling Millard Fillmore as the Know-Nothing candidate for president in 1856; as North and South headed toward Civil War, wrote letters and pamphlets for the Union cause and successfully worked to keep her home state of Maryland from seceding; when Breckinridge argued that Lincoln exercised powers that he did not have, and that, in effect, the war was illegal, wrote her highly regarded work, "Reply to Breckinridge," claiming that Lincoln's actions were in defense of the Constitution and the Union and therefore justifiable; also wrote "The War Powers of the General Government," which again supported Lincoln's position and addressed the divisive topic of slavery; during Civil War, assisted the federal government in procuring and delivering military correspondence; reputedly came up with the successful Tennessee Campaign to split the Confederate forces; spent much of her later years seeking recognition and compensation for her written work for the government and her controversial claim that she was sole author of the Tennessee plan. ❖ See also Janet L. Coryell *Neither Heroine nor Fool: Anna Carroll of Maryland* (Kent State U. Press, 1990); and *Women in World History.*

CARROLL, Dee (1925–1980). American actress. Born Betty Jean Marsh, Dec 2, 1925, in Colorado; died April 28, 1980, in Burbank, California. ❖ Appeared in over 100 tv shows and films, including *Airport, Sweet Charity, Uptown Saturday Night, Terminal Man* and *Prisoner of Second Avenue;* had recurring role on tv soap "Days of Our Lives."

CARROLL, Diahann (1935—). African-American actress and singer. Born Carol Diahann Johnson, July 17, 1935, in the Bronx, NY; m. Monte Kay (div.); m. Fredde Glusman, 1973 (div. 1973); m. Robert DeLeon, 1975 (died 1977); m. Vic Damone (singer), 1987 (div. 1996); children: Suzanne Kay (media journalist). ❖ Made Broadway debut in *House of Flowers* (1954); made film debut as Myrt in *Carmen Jones* (1954), followed by *Porgy and Bess, Goodbye Again, Paris Blues, Hurry Sundown, The Five Heartbeats* and *Eve's Bayou,* among others; on tv, starred on "Julia" (1968–71), "The Diahann Carroll Show" (1976), "Roots" (1979), "I Know Why the Caged Bird Sings" (1979), "Sister, Sister" (1982), "Dynasty" (1984–87), "The Colbys" (1985–86), "Lonesome Dove" (1994), "The Court" (2002), and many more. Won Tony Award for performance in *No Strings* (1962); nominated for Oscar for *Claudine* (1974). ❖ See also autobiography, *Diahann.*

CARROLL, Doris Coburn-. *See Coburn, Doris.*

CARROLL, Gladys Hasty (1904–1999). American writer. Born Gladys Hasty, June 26, 1904, in Rochester, New Hampshire; died Mar 28, 1999, in South Berwick, Maine; dau. of Warren V. and Emma Dow Hasty; grew up in South Berwick; graduate of Bates College; m. Herbert A. Carroll, 1925; children: Warren Hasty Carroll (b. 1932). ❖ Wrote over 22 books, including her best-known *As the Earth Turns* (1934), as well as *Come With Me Home* (1960), *Only Fifty Years Ago* (1962), and *The Light Here Kindled* (1967); also wrote for tv and film.

CARROLL, Helen Johns (b. 1914). *See Johns, Helen.*

CARROLL, Heni Materoa (1852/56?–1930). New Zealand tribal leader. Name variations: Heni Materoa, Te Huinga. Born Heni Materoa, Oct 27, 1852 or 1856, at Makauri, New Zealand; died Nov 1, 1930, at Waikanae, New Zealand; dau. of Mikaera Turangi and Ngati Maruhapu; m. James Carroll (Timi Kara), 1881 (died 1926). ❖ One of most influential Maori in Gisborne district, was a generous benefactor of land and money to numerous causes, especially for welfare of women and children (1880s–90s); also helped to raise funds for Maori soldiers serving abroad. Received Order of British Empire (1918). ❖ See also *Dictionary of New Zealand Biography* (Vol. 3).

CARROLL, Madeleine (1906–1987). British actress. Born Marie-Madeleine Bernadette O'Carroll in West Bromwich, Staffordshire, England, Feb 26, 1906; died in Marbella, Spain, Oct 2, 1987; dau. of John and Hélène (Tuaillon) Carroll; Birmingham College, BA; m. British Captain Philip Astley, 1931 (div. 1939); m. Sterling Hayden (actor), 1942 (div.); m. producer-director Henri Lavorel (div.); m. Andrew Heiskell (magazine publisher), 1950 (div. 1965). ❖ Made stage debut in London's West End (1927), playing a minor role in *The Lash;* starred in British film debut, *Guns of Loos* (1928), followed by *The First Born,* which resulted in appearances in a string of British plays and films, including her 1st talkie *The American Prisoner;* other English films include *Young Woodley* (1930), *Escape* (1930), *Madame Guillotine* (1931), *French Leave* (1931), *School for Scandal* (1933), *I Was a Spy* (1933) and *Loves of a Dictator* (1935); came to attention of American audiences in Hitchcock's *Thirty-Nine Steps* (1936); signing with Paramount, made US debut in *The Case Against Mrs. Ames,* followed by *Secret Agent* (1936), *The General Died at Dawn, Lloyds of London* (1936), *The Prisoner of Zenda* (1937), *Cafe Society* (1939), *North West Mounted Police* (1940), *Virginia* (1941), *One Night in Lisbon* (1941), *Bahama Passage* (1942) and *My Favorite Blonde* (1942), among others; appeared on "Madeleine Carroll Reads," a CBS radio show (1942); during WWII, converted her home near Paris into an orphanage for French children, was active in the Allied Relief fund and served as a hospital assistant in overseas branch of American Red Cross; with 3rd husband Henri Lavorel, produced the film *Children's Republic* shown during an International Film Festival at Nice; made American stage debut as Agatha Reed in *Good-bye, My Fancy* (1948); on tv, appeared on "Robert Montgomery Presents" in Somerset Maugham's *The Letter* (1950). Named "Woman of the Year" by National Conference of Christians and Jews (1948). ❖ See also *Women in World History.*

CARROLL, Nancy (1903–1965). American actress and dancer. Born Ann Veronica La Hiff or LaHiff, Nov 19, 1903, in New York, NY; died Aug 6, 1965, in Nyack, NY; sister of Terry Carroll; m. Jack Kirkland (playwright), 1924 (div. 1931); m. Bolton Mallory, 1931 (div. 1934); m. C.H. "Jappe" Groen, 1953; children: Patricia Kirkland Bevan (b. 1925, actress as Patricia Kirkland). ❖ Made Broadway debut in *The Passing Show of 1923* and subsequently appeared in *Mayflowers, Chicago* and *Undesirable Lady;* a leading comedian, was featured in such films as *Abie's Irish Rose,*

Ladies Must Dress, Springtime for Henry, The Dance of Life, Paramount on Parade, After the Dance and *Follow Thru;* on tv, had recurring role as the mother on "The Aldrich Family." Nominated for Academy Award for *The Devil's Holiday* (1930).

CARROLL, Susanna (c. 1669–1723). *See Centlivre, Susanna.*

CARROLL, Vinnette (1922–2002). African-American playwright and director. Born Mar 11, 1922, in New York, NY; grew up in Jamaica; died Nov 5, 2002, in Lauderhill, Florida; dau. of Florence and Edgar Carroll; graduate of Long Island University; New York University, MA in psychology; studied acting with Lee Strasberg and Stella Adler. ❖ The 1st African-American to direct a production on Broadway, was best known for her show *Your Arms Too Short to Box with God;* wrote *Trumpets of the Lord,* an Off-Broadway hit (1963); directed and starred in *Prodigal Son* (1966); as an actress, won an Obie for *Moon on a Rainbow Shawl* (1962) and an Emmy for *Beyond the Blues* (1964); directed the hit musical revue *Don't Bother Me, I Can't Cope* (1972), for which she was the 1st black woman nominated for a Tony Award for direction; was also nominated for 2 other Tonys; was the founder (1967) and artistic director of the Urban Arts Corps in NY and worked in Los Angeles at the Inner City Repertory in Watts.

CARRUTHERS, Kitty (1962—). American pairs skater. Born 1962; adopted by Charley and Maureen Carruthers of Burlington, MA, and named Caitlin Carruthers; sister of Peter Carruthers, who was also adopted; m. Brett Conrad. ❖ With brother Peter, won US nationals (1981, 1982, 1984), Skate America (1983), and a silver medal at Sarajevo Olympics (1984).

CARRUTHERS, Lisa (1970—). *See Powell, Lisa.*

CARSE, Matilda Bradley (1835–1917). American temperance leader. Born Matilda Bradley, Nov 19, 1835, in Saintfield, Ireland; died June 3, 1917, in Park Hill-on-Hudson, NY; dau. of John Bradley (linen merchant) and Catherine (Cleland) Bradley; educated in Ireland; m. Thomas Carse (railroad freight agent), Oct 8, 1861 (died 1870); children: David, Thomas and John Carse. ❖ Came to US (1858), settling in Chicago; after son was run over and killed by a drunken carter (1874), directed efforts largely to temperance cause; served as president of Chicago Central Woman's Christian Temperance Union (1878–1917) which established numerous community services; founded and became president of Woman's Temperance Publishing Association (1880) and issued the weekly journal of the IL WCTU, *Signal,* which merged with national WCTU publication *Our Union* to become *Union Signal* (1882); served as president of Chicago Foundling's Home Aid Society and as the 1st woman member of Cook County Board of Education (1889–90).

CARSON, Ann (d. 1824). American criminal. Born Ann Baker; died in Walnut Street Prison, Philadelphia, Pennsylvania, in April 1824 (some sources cite 1838); m. John Carson; m. Richard Smith. ❖ After 4-to-5-year absence, husband John Carson was presumed to be lost at sea; married Lieutenant Richard Smith in Philadelphia, only to have Carson reappear (c. 1815); after Carson was shot by Smith (Jan 1816), was charged with murder along with Smith; was acquitted, while Smith was sentenced to death; plotted a series of kidnappings (none of which came to fruition) to force Philadelphia governor Simon Snyder to pardon Smith; was imprisoned for the final kidnapping plan, to kidnap the governor himself, during which time Smith was hanged; released, but imprisoned again for counterfeiting; died after contracting typhoid fever while nursing other prisoners in Philadelphia's Walnut Street Prison.

CARSON, Gladys (b. 1903). English swimmer. Born 1903. ❖ At Paris Olympics, won a bronze medal in 200-meter breaststroke (1924).

CARSON, Joan (1935—). Northern Ireland politician. Born Joan Patterson, Jan 29, 1935, in Enniskillen, Co. Fermanagh. ❖ Was a teacher and school principal, Tamnamore Primary School (1982–88); served on the Dungannon Council (1997–2001); as a member of the UUP, elected to the Northern Ireland Assembly for Fermanagh–Tyrone South (1998).

CARSON, Julia (1938—). African-American politician. Born 1938 in Louisville, Kentucky; illeg. dau. of Velma Porter; married and divorced; children: 2. ❖ At age 1, brought to Indianapolis by teenage mother who worked as a housekeeper; elected to Indiana House of Representatives (1972), serving 2 terms; elected to Indiana Senate (1976); served as Center Township Trustee (1990–96); became the 1st woman and the 1st African-American to represent Indianapolis in US Congress (1996); served on Veterans Affairs, Banking and Financial Services and

Transportation and Infrastructure committees; reelected to a 5th term (2004).

CARSON, Rachel (1907–1964). American marine biologist. Born Rachel Louise Carson in Springdale, Pennsylvania, May 27, 1907; died in Silver Spring, Maryland, April 14, 1964; dau. of Robert Warden Carson and Maria Carson; Pennsylvania College for Women in Pittsburgh (became Chatham College), BA, 1929; Johns Hopkins, MA in marine zoology, 1932; never married; children: brought up 2 nieces, then adopted Roger Christie, son of one of the nieces. ❖ Marine biologist who alerted the world to the dangers of chemical pollution and altered its destructive course; intent on studying marine biology (1929), spent the summer before graduate school on a fellowship at Woods Hole Marine Biological Laboratory where she studied the cranial nerves of a turtle; following graduation (1932), found no work in science for 2 years because of gender; began writing 7-minute radio "fish tales" for US Bureau of Fisheries (1935); took a civil-service exam for position of junior aquatic biologist, achieved the highest score, and was assigned to the office of Elmer Higgins, head of the bureau's Division of Scientific Inquiry, her 1st full-time job; moved with mother to Silver Spring, MD; as R.L. Carson, published "Undersea" in *Atlantic Monthly* (1937); published *Under the Sea Wind* (1941), which dazzled critics and marine scientists, then was abruptly forgotten with Japanese bombing of Pearl Harbor; with men at war, was upgraded at US Bureau to assistant to the chief of Office of Information in the Fish and Wildlife Service; became editor-in-chief of Bureau's Information Division; published bestsellers *The Sea Around Us* (1951), which received National Book Award, and *The Edge of the Sea* (1955); aware of the danger of pesticides (1958), began to pore over books and papers; sought to build up an incontrovertible case with thorough research, since she was threatened by lawsuits from corporations before the work was even completed; during the writing, was diagnosed with breast cancer (1960) but told her publisher it was arthritis; after 4 years, completed *Silent Spring* (1961), sounding an alarm about the dangers of pesticide; though she was portrayed as an alarmist, a middle-aged kook, a communist, and a new-age faddist by the chemical and food-processing industry, changed the course of history; died, age 56, 18 months after the publication of *Silent Spring.* Awarded Henry G. Bryant medal of Philadelphia Geographical Society, the 1st conferred on a woman (1952); awarded Presidential Medal of Freedom (1980). The Rachel Carson Seacoast Preserve, a wildlife refuge along the Maine coast, was dedicated (1970). ❖ See also Martha Freeman, ed. *Always, Rachel: The Letters of Rachel Carson and Dorothy Freeman, 1952–1964* (Beacon, 1995); Philip Sterling, *Sea and Earth: The Life of Rachel Carson* (Crowell, 1970); Linda Lear, *Rachel Carson: Witness for Nature* (Holt, 1997); and *Women in World History.*

CARSON, Violet (1898–1983). English actress. Born Sept 1, 1898, in German Street, Ancoats, Manchester, England; died Dec 26, 1983, in Cleveleys, Blackpool, Lancashire, England; m. George Peplow, 1926 (died 1928). ❖ Appeared as the sharp-tongued Ena Sharples on the tv series "Coronation Street" (1960–80); also appeared as Auntie Hemps on "Hilda Lessways" (1950). Awarded OBE (1965).

CARSTENSEN-NATHANSEN, Fritze (1925—). Danish swimmer. Name variations: Fritze Nathansen. Born July 18, 1925. ❖ At London Olympics, won a silver medal in the 4x100-meter freestyle relay (1948).

CARSWELL, Catherine (1879–1946). Scottish biographer and novelist. Born Catherine MacFarlane, Mar 27, 1879, in Glasgow, Scotland; died Feb 18, 1946, in Oxford, England; dau. of George MacFarlane and Mary Anne Lewis MacFarlane; m. Herbert Jackson, 1904 (annul. 1908); m. Donald Carswell, 1915 (died 1940). ❖ Had 1st marriage annulled because of husband's mental illness; met D.H. Lawrence (1914) and would remain his friend until his death (1930); wrote biographies *The Savage Pilgrim: A Narrative of D.H. Lawrence* (1932), *The Life of Robert Burns* (1930), and *The Tranquil Heart: Portrait of Giovanni Boccaccio* (1937); also wrote novels *Open the Door!* (1920) and *Camomile: An Invention* (1922), as well as literary journalism. ❖ See also *Lying Awake: An Unfinished Autobiography* (1950).

CARTAGENA, Teresa de (c. 1420–1470). Spanish nun and writer. Born c. 1420; died 1470. ❖ One of earliest known Spanish women writers, was afflicted with deafness at an early age; studied at University of Salamanca and later became a nun; works include *Arboleda de los enfermos* (c. 1450) and *Admiración operum Dey.*

CARTAMANDIA (fl. 43–69 CE). *See Cartimandua.*

CARTE, Anne (1829/35–?). *See Swift, Anne.*

CARTE, Bridget D'Oyly (1908–1985). English theatrical manager. Name variations: Dame Bridget D'Oyly Carte. Born in 1908; died 1985; educated privately and at Darlington Hall; granddau. of Richard D'Oyly Carte (1844–1901) who, with his father, built the Savoy Theatre in 1876 to present Gilbert and Sullivan operas. ❖ Became manager of D'Oyly Carte Opera Company (1948), presenting operas in England, US and Canada until the copyright expired (1961), the year she endowed the D'Oyly Carte Opera Trust; continued to offer operas until the Arts Council withdrew support (1981); was chair and managing director of Bridget D'Oyly Carte, Ltd., president of the Savoy Company, and director of the Savoy Theatre. Named Dame of the British Empire (DBE, 1975).

CARTEN, Audrey (b. 1900). English actress and playwright. Born Audrey Bicker-Caarten, Jan 6, 1900, in London, England; dau. of Catherine and Edwin Hare Bicker-Caarten; sister of Waveney Carten (writer). ❖ Made London stage debut as Helena in *Midsummer Night's Dream* (1920), followed by *Dear Brutus, Bull-Dog Drummond, The Dancer, The Swallow* and *Happy Families;* with sister, wrote *Happy Families, Q, Fame, Late One Evening, Gay Love, Destination Unknown, Strawberry Leaves* and 2 adaptations, *Mademoiselle* and *My Crime.*

CARTER, Amy (1967—). American first daughter and illustrator. Born Amy Lynn Carter, Oct 19, 1967, in Plains, Georgia; dau. of Jimmy Carter (US president, 1977–81) and Rosalynn Carter; niece of Ruth Carter Stapleton; attended Brown University; Tulane University, MA in art; m. James Wentzel (computer consultant), 1996; children: Hugo James Wentzel (b. July 29, 1999). ❖ Was 9 when she entered the White House; a student activist while in college, was arrested during protests against US policies in South Africa (then under apartheid); illustrated 2 books by her father: *The Little Baby Snoogle-Fleejer* and *Christmas in Plains.*

CARTER, Angela (1940–1992). British novelist. Born Angela Olive Stalker in Eastbourne, England, May 7, 1940; died in London, Feb 16, 1992; dau. of Hugh Alexander Stalker (journalist) and Olive (Farthing) Stalker; attended University of Bristol; m. Paul Carter (industrial chemist), 1960 (sep. 1969); m. Mark Pierce; children: 1 son. ❖ One of the most creative novelists of her generation, whose writings, sensuous in language and rich in imagination, created a strange and dangerously beautiful world; published 1st novel, *Shadow Dance* (1966), followed by *The Magic Toyshop* (1967) and *Several Perceptions* (1969); moved to Japan (1969), taking a job with the English language division of NHK broadcasting company; published *Love* (1971) and *The Infernal Desire Machines of Dr. Hoffman* (1972); came to prominence with *The Passion of New Eve* (1977); examined the issue of pornography in *The Sadeian Woman and the Ideology of Pornography* (1979) and received stellar reviews in US and Britain for *Nights at the Circus* (1985); published last novel *Wise Children* (1991); also wrote plays, screenplays, and children's books; short-story collections include *Fireworks: Nine Profane Pieces* (1974), *The Bloody Chamber and Other Stories* (1979) and *Saints and Strangers* (1986). Won Somerset Maugham Award (1969).

CARTER, Anita (1933–1999). American singer. Born Ina Anita Carter in Maces Springs, Virginia, Mar 31, 1933; died July 29, 1999; dau. of Maybelle Carter (1909–1978) and Ezra Carter; m. Dale Potter (div.); m. Don Davis (div.); m. Robert Wooten (div.). ❖ Accomplished musician, played guitar, autoharp, gitarro and bass, and wrote songs; while singing with Mother Maybelle & the Carter Sisters, also sang duet with Hank Snow on "Blue Island/ Down the Trail of Aching Hearts" (1951); recorded for Columbia (1953–54); joined with Ruby Wright and Rita Robbins to produce several songs for RCA, under the name 'Nita, Rita and Ruby (1955–57). ❖ See also *Women in World History.*

CARTER, Ann Shaw (1922—). American aviator. Born Dec 5, 1922, in Brooklyn, NY. ❖ Trained as a Women's Army Service Pilot (WASP) during World War II; was the 1st woman to be granted her helicopter rating, at the Westchester Country Airport in NY (June 9, 1947); was an original member of the Whirly Girls, the 1st association of women helicopter pilots (formed 1957).

CARTER, Betty (1929–1998). African-American jazz singer. Name variations: Lorene Carter; Lorraine Carter. Born Lillie Mae Jones, May 16, 1929, in Flint, Michigan; died in Brooklyn, NY, Sept 26, 1998; grew up in Detroit; studied piano at Detroit Conservatory; married. ❖ Regarded as one of the few true jazz singers, went professional (1946), using stage name Lorene Carter; while still a teenager, sang with Charlie Parker; toured with Lionel Hampton (1948–51), and Miles Davis (1958–59), as Betty Be-Bop Carter; made an album with Ray Charles (1961) on ABC Paramount label (their duet "Baby, It's Cold Outside," became a jazz classic); toured with Charles in Japan, France and UK (1963–68); started her own company, Bet-Car Records and Lil-Jay Productions, making albums that are now collector's items; had her own trio (1975–80), winning acclaim at Newport Jazz festivals and at Carnegie Hall (1977–78); released *Look What I Got!* (Polygram/Verve) to rave reviews (1988). Presented with National Medal of Arts by President Bill Clinton (1997). ❖ See also *Women in World History.*

CARTER, Carlene (1955—). American rock and country music singer, songwriter, guitar and pianist. Born Rebecca Carlene Smith in Madison, Tennessee, Sept 26, 1955; dau. of June Carter Cash (b. 1929) and Carl Smith; stepsister of Rosanne Cash (1955—); m. Joe Simpkins, 1970 (div.); m. Jack Routh, 1974 (div.); m. Nick Lowe, 1979 (div.). ❖ Began playing piano at 6, studying classical music; at 10, began strumming the guitar after instructions from grandmother Maybelle Carter; recorded 1st album (1977), a collection of piano-based pop songs performed with Graham Parker's band Rumor; recorded albums *Two Sides of Every Woman* (1979) and *Musical Shapes* (1980), and was praised for single "Musical Shapes," a "fusion of rock and country"; toured regularly with the Carter Family (1987–88); co-wrote most of the songs for her album *I Fell in Love* (1990), as well as *Little Love Letters* (1993); released *Little Acts of Treason* (1995). ❖ See also *Women in World History.*

CARTER, Caroline Louise (1862–1937). *See Carter, Mrs. Leslie.*

CARTER, Elizabeth (1717–1806). English intellectual, poet and translator. Name variations: (pen name) Eliza. Born Elizabeth Carter, Dec 16, 1717, in Deal, Kent, England; died in Clarges Street, Piccadilly, Feb 19, 1806; dau. of Nicolas Carter (curate) and Margaret (Swayne) Carter; read Latin, Greek, Hebrew, French, Italian, German, Spanish, Arabic, and Portuguese and was considered to be the most learned member of the Bluestocking Circle; never married. ❖ At 17, began publishing in *Gentlemen's Magazine* (1734); also published *Poems upon Particular Occasions* (1736 or 1738); an expert linguist, translated from the French an attack on Alexander Pope's *Essay on Man* by J.P. de Crousaz (1739); as a result of her work, was introduced to a much larger intellectual and social circle in London, including Lady Mary Coke, Catherine Talbot, Edmund Burke, David Garrick, Samuel Richardson, Horace Walpole and Samuel Johnson; wrote for Johnson's *The Rambler* (1750–52); came to be included among the women intellectuals of the time who were known as "bluestockings," including Hannah More, Elizabeth Vesey, Elizabeth Montagu, and Hester Mulso Chapone; best known for translating the collected works of the Roman Stoic philosopher Epictetus, which took 9 years to complete (1749–58). ❖ See also *Memoirs* (1807); Alice C.C. Gaussen, *A Woman of Wit and Wisdom: A Memoir of Elizabeth Carter* (1906); Catherine Talbot, *Letters between Mrs. Elizabeth Carter and Miss CT* (1808); and *Women in World History.*

CARTER, Elizabeth Eliot (1943—). *See Holland, Cecelia.*

CARTER, Eunice Hunton (1899–1970). African-American lawyer. Born Eunice Hunton, July 16, 1899, in Atlanta, Georgia; died Jan 25, 1970, in New York, NY; dau. of William Alphaeus Hunton (national executive with YMCA) and Addie Waites Hunton; Smith College, AB and AM, 1921; attended Columbia University; m. Lisle Carter (Barbados-born dentist), 1924 (died 1963); children: Lisle Jr. (b. 1925). ❖ Worked with family service organizations (1921–32); graduated in law from Fordham University (1932) and admitted to NY bar (1934); ran unsuccessfully for NY state assembly (1934); appointed secretary of Committee on Conditions in Harlem (1935); serving on staff of Thomas E. Dewey, was the only woman and only black involved with the grand jury investigation into organized crime and was recognized for producing crucial evidence in the case against Lucky Luciano (1935); served as deputy assistant district attorney for NY County (1935–45); returned to private practice (1945); was charter member, legal adviser, and chair of board of trustees of National Council of Negro Women (NCNW); represented NCNW at founding conference of UN (1945); was accredited NCNW observer at UN (until 1952); was adviser for women in public life for German government (1954); retired from active law practice (1952); chaired International Conference of Non-Governmental Organizations at UN's Geneva conference (1955).

CARTER, Helen (1927–1998). American singer and musician. Born Helen Myrl Carter in Maces Springs, Virginia, Sept 12, 1927; died in Nashville, Tennessee, June 2, 1998; first dau. of Maybelle and Ezra Carter; married Glen Jones, 1950; children: Glen Daniel; Kenneth Burton; David Lawrence; Kevin Carter. ❖ Became proficient on accordion, guitar, autoharp, piano and mandolin; sang and played with the

Carter Family and the Carter Sisters; wrote hit song "Poor Old Heartsick Me" (1959). ❖ See also *Women in World History.*

CARTER, Helena (1923–2000). American actress. Born Helen Rickerts, Aug 24, 1923, in New York, NY; died Jan 11, 2000, in Culver City, California; m. Michael Meshekoff. ❖ Began career as a model for Harry Conover; made film debut in *Time Out of Mind* (1947), followed by *Something in the Wind, Intrigue, River Lady, South Sea Sinner, Kiss Tomorrow Goodbye, Fort Worth, Bugles in the Afternoon, The Pathfinder* and *Invaders from Mars,* among others.

CARTER, Janis (1913–1994). American actress. Born Janis Dremann, Oct 10, 1913, Cleveland, Ohio; died July 30, 1994, in Durham, North Carolina; m. Carl Prager, 1942 (div. 1951); m. Julius Stulman, 1956. ❖ Appeared on Broadway in such musicals as *I Married an Angel, DuBarry Was a Lady* and *Panama Hattie;* made film debut in *Cadet Girl* (1941), followed by *Secret Agent of Japan, Who is Hope Schuyler?, I Married an Angel, Girl Trouble, Thunder Birds, Lady of Burlesque, The Missing Juror, The Mark of the Whistler, The Girl in the Case, The Fighting Guardsman, Framed, And Baby Makes Three, Santa Fe* and *Flying Leathernecks,* among others; hosted the NBC quiz show "Feather Your Nest" (1954).

CARTER, Jeanette (1923–2006). American singer and musician. Born Jeanette Carter in Maces Springs, Virginia, July 2, 1923; died Jan 23, 2006, in Kingsport, Tennessee; middle dau. of Sarah Carter (1898–1979) and A.P. Carter; married and divorced twice. ❖ Sang, wrote songs and played the autoharp; began to perform as a soloist during Carter Family radio broadcasts (1938); wrote and recorded with father (mid-1950s); opened the Carter Family "Fold," a performance center in Maces Springs, VA, and the Carter Family Museum; sponsored 1st Annual Carter Family Memorial Festival, held in Hiltons, VA (1975). ❖ See also *Women in World History.*

CARTER, June (1929–2003). See *Cash, June Carter.*

CARTER, Mrs. Leslie (1862–1937). American actress. Name variations: Caroline Louise Carter. Born Caroline Louise Dudley in Lexington, Kentucky, June 10, 1862; died in Santa Monica, California, Nov 13, 1937; m. Leslie Carter (wealthy Chicagoan), May 26, 1880 (div. 1889); m. William L. Payne (actor), July 13, 1906. ❖ After her 9-year marriage to Leslie Carter ended in a sensational divorce in which she was found guilty of adultery, persuaded David Belasco to launch her on a stage career; starred as the central character in his production of *The Ugly Duckling* (1890), followed by the title role in Audran's operetta *Miss Helyett* (1891), which was well received; had major success in *The Heart of Maryland* (1895) and expanded her following by appearing as a prostitute in *Zaza* (1899) and a courtesan in *Du Barry* (1901); peaked in title role of *Andrea* (1905); after split with Belasco, career went into decline until 1921, when she won generous notices as Lady Catherine in Somerset Maugham's *The Circle;* was last seen in NY in *She Stoops To Conquer* (1928); made 1 film, *The Vanishing Pioneer.* ❖ See also *Women in World History.*

CARTER, Lorraine (1929–1998). See *Carter, Betty.*

CARTER, Lorene (1929–1998). See *Carter, Betty.*

CARTER, Maybelle (1909–1978). American guitarist, autoharp player, and singer. Name variations: (nicknamed) Mother Maybelle, Queen Mother of Country Music, and Queen of the Autoharp. Born Maybelle Addington in Nickelsville, Virginia, May 10, 1909; died Oct 23, 1978; dau. of Margaret Addington; m. Ezra J. Carter, Mar 13, 1926; children: Helen Myrl (b. 1927); Valerie June (known as June Carter Cash, b. 1929); Ina Anita (known as Anita Carter, b. 1933). ❖ Popularized country and folk music over a 50-year career with the Carter Family (comprised of Maybelle, her cousin Sarah Carter and Sarah's husband A.P. Carter), the Carter Sisters (Helen, Anita, and June), and as a solo performer; was considered a "musician's musician" because of her unique guitar style, which incorporated the famous "Carter lick"; a living legend in the world of bluegrass and folk music, became the oldest woman listed on the national country charts; recorded over 250 songs, including "Wildwood Flower," "Keep on the Sunny Side," "Will The Circle Be Unbroken," "I'm Thinking Tonight of My Blue Eyes," "John Hardy," "Lonesome Valley," "Engine 143," "Foggy Mountain Top," "Black Jack David," "Rambling Boy," "Bury Me Beneath the Weeping Willow," and "Coal Miner's Blues." Inducted into the Country Music Hall of Fame (1970). ❖ See also Robert K. Krishef, *The Carter Family* (Lerner, 1978); Michael Orgill, *Anchored In Love: The Carter Family Story* (Revell, 1975); and *Women in World History.*

CARTER, Nell (1894–1965). English stage actress. Born Mar 1, 1894, in England; died Mar 21, 1965. ❖ Made stage debut at the Aldwych as Peal-a-Belle in *Blue Bell in Fairyland* (1905); other plays include *The Madras House, Trelawny of the Wells, The Concert, The Schoolmistress, The Alchemist* and *The Country Wife;* joined the Old Vic (1925); made NY debut in *When Crummles Played* (1928); taught at Royal Academy of Dramatic Art.

CARTER, Nell (1948–2003). African-American actress and singer. Born Nell Ruth Hardy, Sept 13, 1948, in Birmingham, Alabama; died Jan 23, 2003, in Beverly Hills, California; m. Georg Krynicki, 1982 (div. 1992); m. Robert Larocque, 1992 (div. 1993); children: daughter Tracy; (adopted) 2 sons. ❖ Made Broadway debut in *Soon,* followed by a turn as Miss Hannigan in 20th-anniversary revival of *Annie* (1997–98); starred as Nell Harper in NBC sitcom "Gimme a Break" (1981–87). Awarded a Tony and Obie for performance in *Ain't Misbehavin'* (1978), which ran on Broadway for 4 years, then was revived with Carter (1988); received 2 Emmy nominations for "Gimme a Break" (1982 and 1983).

CARTER, Rosalynn (1927—). American first lady. Born Eleanor Rosalynn Smith, Aug 18, 1927, in Plains, Georgia; dau. of Wilburn Edgar (auto mechanic) and Frances Alletta "Allie" (Murray) Smith (seamstress); attended Georgia Southwestern College; m. Jimmy Carter (president of US, 1977–81), July 7, 1946; children: John (b. 1947); James Earl III, known as Chip (b. 1950); Donnel Jeffrey (b. 1952); Amy Carter (b. 1967). ❖ At 18, became a navy wife (1946); with husband, returned home to run the family peanut business (1951); ran the warehouse and campaigned when husband ran successfully for a Georgia state senate seat (1962), as well as when he ran successfully for governor of Georgia (1970); while in the governor's mansion, was appointed to Governor's Commission to Improve Services for the Mentally and Emotionally Handicapped and worked with Lady Bird Johnson to start the Georgia Highway Wildflower Program; also pushed for passage of Equal Rights Amendment in Georgia and for judicial reforms for women prisoners; as husband's advisor in his run for the presidency, wrote and delivered speeches, helped make staff decisions, and traveled independently in 40 states (1975–76); as first lady (1977–81), continued to function as a full partner with husband, acting as his emissary on an unprecedented trip to Latin America and envoy to Cambodian refugee camps; toured Central and South America and attended the inauguration of President Jose Lopez Portillo of Mexico; like Eleanor Roosevelt before her, was often considered too influential and powerful, and her attendance at Cabinet meetings, though at husband's invitation, drew criticism; became honorary chair of President's Commission on Mental Health, resulting in the 1st major reform of federal publicly funded mental-health programs since the Community Mental Health Centers Act of 1963; with husband, became active in the Habitat for Humanity housing campaign and the Friendship Force; created the Carter Center's Mental Health Task Force, which she chairs; published a book on care giving, *Helping Yourself Help Others* (1995). ❖ See also memoir, *First Lady from Plains* (Houghton, 1984); and *Women in World History.*

CARTER, Ruth (1929–1983). See *Stapleton, Ruth Carter.*

CARTER, Sarah (1898–1979). American singer and instrumentalist. Born Sarah Dougherty in Flat Woods, Virginia, July 21, 1899; died Jan 8, 1979; dau. of Elizabeth and Sevier Dougherty; m. A.P. (Alvin Pleasant) Carter (bandleader), June 18, 1915 (div. 1933); m. Coy Bayes, 1939; children: (1st m.) Gladys Carter (b. 1919); Jeanette Carter (b. 1923); Joe (b. 1927). ❖ Played autoharp, guitar, banjo and fiddle; initially performed non-professionally with cousin Madge Addington; with husband A.P. and cousin Maybelle Carter, served as lead singer and instrumentalist for the Carter Family; came out of retirement briefly to play a reunion concert and to tour on the folk circuit with Maybelle for a year (mid-1960s). Inducted into the Country Music Hall of Fame (Oct 1970). ❖ See also *Women in World History.*

CARTER, Shirley Verrett (1931—). See *Verrett, Shirley.*

CARTER, Truda (1890–1958). See *Adams, Truda.*

CARTER, Una Isabel (1890–1954). New Zealand cooking teacher and writer. Born Aug 20, 1890, near Marton, New Zealand; died Oct 14, 1954, in London, England; dau. of William Alfred Carter (farmer) and Selina (Brown) Carter; m. Albert David Stanley (secretary), 1924. ❖ Began career giving cooking classes at Wellington Gas Co. (1913); established cooking school (1913); demonstrated art of cooking throughout New Zealand and Australia; writings include *The National*

Cookery Book (1918) and *Home Made Sweets.* ❖ See also *Dictionary of New Zealand Biography* (Vol. 3).

CARTER, Violet Bonham (1887–1969). *See Bonham-Carter, Violet.*

CARTIER, Diana (1939—). American ballet dancer. Born July 6, 1939, in Philadelphia, Pennsylvania. ❖ Trained with Antony Tudor in Philadelphia and at Metropolitan Opera Ballet in New York City; joined Robert Joffrey Ballet (1960) and was a charter member of City Center Joffrey Ballet, performing there until 1970s; featured in Cranko's *Jeu de Cartes* and *Pineapple Poll,* Christensen's *Con Amore,* Flindt's *The Lesson,* Tudor's *Offenbach in the Underworld,* Ailey's *Feast of Ashes,* and Jooss' *The Green Table;* served as ballet mistress at Joffrey Ballet; began teaching at David Howard Dance Center in NY; was guest teacher with National Ballet of Canada, Berlin Opera Ballet, Opera Ballet of Oslo and National Ballet of Mexico; began teaching company classes at American Ballet Theater in NY (1991).

CARTIMANDUA (fl. 43–69 CE). Queen of the Brigantes. Name variations: Cartamandia; Cartumandia. Pronunciation: Car-ti-man-DOO-ah. Married Venutius (div.); m. Vellocatus. ❖ Queen of the Brigantes in central Britain and a Roman ally, ruled Brigantes probably from 43 CE; handed over the British chieftain Caratacus to the Romans (51); divorced husband Venutius and married Vellocatus; was overthrown by Venutius and sought refuge with the Romans (69). ❖ See also *Women in World History.*

CARTLAND, Barbara (1901–2000). British novelist. Name variations: Dame Barbara Cartland; Barbara McCorquodale. Born in Edgbaston, Birmingham, England, July 9, 1901; died in Hertfordshire, England, May 21, 2000; dau. of Bertram Cartland (major in Worcestershire regiment) and Polly (Scobell) Cartland; attended Malvern Girls' College and Abbey House, Netley Abbey, Hampshire, England; m. Alexander George McCorquodale, 1927 (div. 1933); m. Hugh McCorquodale, Dec 28, 1936 (died Dec 29, 1963); children: (1st m.) Raine McCorquodale (who upon marriage became Countess Spencer and the stepmother of Diana Spencer, Princess of Wales); (2nd m.) Ian and Glen. ❖ Destined to see over 600 million copies of her novels in print, began writing career as a gossip columnist for *Daily Express;* after publication of 1st novel, *Jigsaw* (1925), went on to become a prolific author of romance novels, including *The Ruthless Rake* (1975), *The Penniless Peer* (1976) and *The Cruel Count* (1976); also wrote advice books and fictionalized historical biographies, including *The Private Life of Elizabeth Empress of Austria* (1959), *The Private Life of Charles II: The Women He Loved* (1958) and *Josephine, Empress of France* (1961); lent her voice to a number of charitable causes and to England's Conservative Party. Received Gold Medal of City of Paris for Achievement (1988), for selling 25 million books in France; named Dame of the Order of the British Empire (1991). ❖ See also autobiographies *We Danced All Night 1919–1929* (1971), *I Search for Rainbows* (1967), and *I Reach for the Stars* (1995).

CARTLIDGE, Katrin (1961–2002). English actress. Born May 15, 1961, in London, England; died Sept 7, 2002, in London. ❖ Came to prominence in films by Mike Leigh, including *Naked* (1993) and *Career Girls* (1997), for which she won an Evening Standard award for Best Actress; on stage, played a lead role in *Mnemonic* and *Boy Gets Girl;* was also featured in such films as *Before the Rain, Breaking the Waves, Claire Dolan, The Cherry Orchard* and *No Man's Land.*

CARTON, Pauline (1884–1974). Swiss-born actress. Born July 4, 1884, in Geneva, Switzerland; died June 17, 1974, in Paris, France; married. ❖ Appeared in most of the movies of Sacha Guitry; made over 100 films, including *Mademoiselle Mozart, Bonne chance, La Mioche, The House Across the Street, Désiré, Conflit, Marie-Louise, L'armoire volante, Barry, Napoléon, Zaza, The Parisian, Story of a Cheat, Indiscretions, Louise, Private Life of an Actor, The Prize* and *Miquette.*

CARTON, Mrs. Richard (1853–1928). *See Compton, Katherine.*

CARTUMANDIA (fl. 43–69 CE). *See Cartimandua.*

CARTWRIGHT, Julia (1851–1924). British novelist and historian. Name variations: Mrs. Henry Ady. Born Nov 7, 1851, in Northamptonshire, England; died April 24, 1924, in Oxford, England; dau. of Richard Aubrey Cartwright and Mary Fremantle; m. Henry Ady, 1880. ❖ Educated at home; studied French, German, and Italian and taught herself Latin; published novels anonymously for Society for the Promotion of Christian Knowledge; wrote books on art and history, as well as several major biographies; her work on Renaissance art and

women helped establish her as an important scholar of the period; writings include *Sir Edward Burne-Jones, His Life and Work* (1894), *G.F. Watts, Royal Academician, His Life and Works* (1896), *Jean François Millet, His Life and Letters* (1896), *Beatrice d'Este* (1899), *Isabella d'Este* (1902), *Raphael* (1905), *Baldassare Castiglione* (1908), *Hampton Court* (1910) and *Italian Gardens of the Renaissance* (1914); also wrote for journals and magazines.

CARTWRIGHT, Mary L. (1900–1998). English mathematician. Name variations: Mary Lucy Cartwright; M.L. Cartwright. Born Dec 17, 1900; died April 3, 1998; dau. of the rector of Aynho, Northamptonshire; St. Hugh's College, Oxford, mathematics degree, 1923, DPhil, 1930. ❖ The 1st woman mathematician elected as fellow to Royal Society, was also the 1st woman to complete mathematics degree at St. Hugh's College, Oxford (1923); wrote thesis on "Zeros of Integral Functions of Special Types"; worked on complex function theory used in aircraft design, statistical forecasts, and in proof of Fermat's last theorem; during WWII, collaborated with J.E. Littlewood on Val der Pol equation permutations and discovered examples of butterfly effect; published *Integral Functions* (1956); lectured in US and elected mistress of Girton College, Cambridge (1949); served as director of studies of mathematics and mechanical science, lecturer, theory of functions reader, and emeritus reader at University of Cambridge (1933–98). Served as president of Mathematical Association and president of London Mathematical Society; received the Royal Society's Sylvester Medal (1964); named Dame Commander of the Order of the British Empire (1969).

CARTWRIGHT, Peggy (1912–2001). Canadian child actress and dancer. Born Peggy Courtwright, Nov 14, 1912, in Vancouver, B.C., Canada; died June 13, 2001, in Victoria, British Columbia; studied at RADA; m. Bill Walker (actor, died 1992); children: 4. ❖ Appeared briefly in *Birth of a Nation* as a baby; made stage debut in Los Angeles (1919); was the original leading lady of the "Our Gang" troupe, appearing in the first 6 shorts (1922); made London debut in *Cochran's 1930 Revue,* was a principal dancer in *Chelsea Follies,* followed by *For the Love of Mike* and *Half-Holiday;* made NY debut in *Americana* (1932); appeared in the film *Good-Night, Vienna* (1932).

CARUCCIO, Consetta. *See Lenz, Consetta.*

CARUS, Emma (1879–1927). German-born vaudeville and musical-comedy actress and singer. Born Mar 18, 1879, in Berlin, Germany; died Nov 18, 1927; dau. of Carl Carus and Henrietta Rohland Carus (opera singer under the name Henrietta Rolland); m. N.S. Mattson (div.); m. Harry James Everall, June 25, 1905. ❖ Made stage debut in NY (1894); came to prominence as Lady Muriel in *The Giddy Throng* (1900), followed by *King's Carnival, The Wild Rose, Woodland, The Defender, Forty-Five Minutes from Broadway, The Follies of 1907, The Wife Hunters, The Broadway Honeymoon* and *Listen Lester;* introduced Irving Berlin's "Alexander's Ragtime Band" (1911); appeared solely in vaudeville from 1915 on.

CARUS-WILSON, Eleanora Mary (1897–1977). English medieval economic historian. Born Eleanora Mary Carus-Wilson, Dec 27, 1897, in Montreal, Canada; died Feb 1, 1977, in London, England; dau. of Mary L.G. (Petrie) Carus-Wilson and Ashley Carus-Wilson (professor of electrical engineering at McGill University); Westfield College, London, BA, 1921, MA, 1926. ❖ Began academic career as a part-time lecturer at London's Westfield College, where she did research under Eileen Power; during WWII, worked in the Ministry of Food, after which she joined the London School of Economics, becoming a professor of economic history (1948); was at London University (1953–65), where she carried out a major study in medieval trade; was a Ford's lecturer in English history at Oxford (1964–65); writings include *England's Export Trade 1275–1547* (1963); served as president of Economic History Society and Society of Medieval Archaeology (1966–69).

CARVAJAL, Luisa de (1568–1614). Portuguese missionary. Name variations: Carvajal de Mendoza. Born at Jaraicejo in Estremadura, Portugal, Jan 2, 1568; died in London, England, Jan 2, 1614; dau. of Francisco de Carvajal (Portuguese aristocrat) and Maria de Mendoza; never married; no children. ❖ Orphaned at 4 (1572), was taken in with brother by great aunt Maria Chacon, governess of young children of Philip II, king of Spain and soon to be king of Portugal; when Chacon died, lived with maternal uncle, Francisco Hurtado de Mendoza, count of Almazan and viceroy of Navarre, an able public servant in whom religious zeal was carried to the point of inhuman asceticism; under his tutelage, practiced mortifications of the flesh; reaching adulthood, decided to dedicate her life to the conversion of England back to the Catholic faith; devoted her share of the family inheritance to found a college at Louvain for English Jesuits; moved to England (1605); a highly visible missionary, worked among London's poor to win converts, while acting as midwife and nurse; though arrested (1608), was soon released on orders of King James I, who wanted to maintain good relations with Spain; established an underground nunnery at Spitalfields, while under the watch of English authorities; arrested by archbishop of Canterbury (1613); though quickly released, was not allowed to resume missionary work; recalled to Portugal, refused to leave England, but died soon after. In Madrid, *La Vida y Virtudes de la Venerable Virgen Doña Luisa de Carvajal y Mendoza* by the Licentiate Lorenzo Muñoz appeared (1632), a work founded on her own papers, which were collected by Michael Walpole, her English confessor. ❖ See also *Women in World History*.

CARVAJAL, María Isabel (1888–1949). Costa Rican novelist and journalist. Name variations: Maria Isabel Carvajal; (pseudonym) Carmen Lyra. Born María Isabel Carvajal Quesada, Jan 15, 1888, in San José, Costa Rica; died 1949 in Mexico City, Mexico. ❖ Began career as a teacher; spent last years of her life as a Marxist journalist; went into exile in Mexico after the revolution (1948); writings include *Las fantasías de Juan Silvestre* (1918), *En una silla de rodas* (In a Wheelchair, 1918) and *Los cuentos de mi Tía Panchita* (The Stories of My Aunt Panchita, 1920).

CARVAJAL, Mariana de (c. 1620–1680). Spanish novelist and playwright. Name variations: Doña Mariana de Carvajal y Saaveedra or Saaveedra; Mariana de Carvajal y Saavedra. Born into the nobility between 1610 and 1620 in Madrid, Spain; died 1680. ❖ Wrote several plays, now lost, and a collection of 8 novellas, *Navidades entretenidas* (1663).

CARVAJAL DE AROCHA, Mercedes (1902–1994). *See Palacios, Lucila.*

CARVAJAL RIVERA, Magaly Esther (1968—). Cuban volleyball player. Name variations: Magaly Esther Carvajal Rivera; Magaly Carvajal. Born Dec 18, 1968, in Cuba. ❖ One of Cuba's greatest middle blockers, won a team World championship (1994); won a team gold medal at Barcelona Olympics (1992) and at Atlanta Olympics (1996); married a Spaniard and became a citizen of Spain, playing for a team in Tenerife.

CARVALHO, Dinora de (1905—). Brazilian composer, conductor, pianist and professor. Name variations: Dinora Gontijo de Carvalho Murici. Born in Uberaba, Minas Gerais, Brazil, June 1, 1905; dau. of Vincente Gontijo (musician). ❖ At 6, admitted to São Paulo Conservatory to study piano under Maria Machado and Carlino Crescenzo; at 7, gave 1st piano recital and wrote 1st composition, a valse entitled *Serenata ão Luar*, as well as a piano nocturne; with success as a concert pianist, won a scholarship in Europe where she studied with Isidor Philipp; returning to Brazil (1929), studied with Lamberto Baldi and Martin Braunwieser; nominated federal inspector for advanced music education at São Paulo Conservatory (1939); founded and directed the Women's Orchestra of São Paulo, the 1st of its kind in South America (1939); continued to compose, writing many pieces for orchestra. Municipal Theater of São Paulo sponsored the Dinora de Carvalho Festival in which many of her compositions were played (1960); was the 1st woman to be nominated to the Brazilian Academy of Music. ❖ See also *Women in World History*.

CARVALHO, Maria Amália Vaz de (1847–1921). *See Vaz de Carvalho, Maria Amália.*

CARVALHO, Maria Judite de (1921–1998). Portuguese novelist and short-story writer. Born Sept 18, 1921, in Lisbon, Portugal; died 1998; attended University of Lisbon. ❖ Lived in Belgium and France for 6 years; novels, which often concern the struggles of women before the revolution in Portugal, include *Tanta Gente, Mariana* (1959), *As Palavras Poupadas* (1961), *Paisagem sem Barcos* (1963), *Os Armários Vazios* (1966), *A Janela Fingida* (1975), *Além do Quadro* (1983) and *Este Tempo* (1991); also wrote for Lisbon paper *Diário de Notícias*. Awards include International Association of Literary Critics Prize (1995) and Vergílio Ferreira Prize (1998).

CARVALHO, Marie (1827–1895). *See Miolan-Carvalho, Marie.*

CARVEN (b. 1909). French fashion designer. Name variations: Carven Grog. Born Carmen Tommaso in Chateauroux, France, 1909. ❖ Opened fashion house on Champs-Élysees (1944), specializing in clothes for the petite woman; her 50-year career in haute couture was celebrated at the Palais Galliera (2002). Awarded France's highest recognition, Officer of the Legion of Honor.

CARVER, Kathryn (1899–1947). American screen actress. Name variations: Kathryn Hill. Born Aug 24, 1899, in New York, NY; died July 18

(some sources cite July 17), 1947, in Elmhurst, LI, NY; m. Adolphe Menjou (actor), 1928 (div. 1933). ❖ Films include *When Love Grows Cold* (1925), *Beware of Widows* (1927), *Serenade* (1927) and *His Private Life* (1928); retired from films (1934).

CARVER, Louise (1869–1956). American stage and screen actress. Born Louise Spilger, June 9, 1869, in Davenport, Iowa; died Jan 19, 1956, in Los Angeles, California; m. Tom Murray. ❖ Made stage debut in Chicago (1892); best-known stage role was opposite Lew Fields in *The Henpecks* (1912); appeared in Mack Sennett comedies and other silent films, including *The Extra Girl, The Fortune Hunter, The Man from Blankley's, Side Show, Hallelujah I'm a Bum* and *Every Night at Eight*.

CARVER, Lynne (1909–1955). American actress. Name variations: Virginia Reid. Born Virginia Reid Sampson, Sept 13, 1909, in Lexington, Kentucky; died Aug 12, 1955, in New York, NY; m. R.C. McClung, 1935 (div. 1936); m. Nicholas Nayfack (producer), 1937; m. John Burt (annulled 1948). ❖ Made 1st three films as Virginia Reid; later films include *Maytime, The Bride Wore Red, Young Dr. Kildare, Broadway Melody, A Christmas Carol* and *Huckleberry Finn*.

CARVER, Tina (c. 1923–1982). American stage and screen actress. Born c. 1923; died Feb 18, 1982, in Everett, Washington. ❖ Films include *A Bullet for Joey, Inside Detroit, Hell on Frisco Bay, A Cry in the Night* and *See How They Run*.

CARVER-DIAS, Claire (1977–). Canadian synchronized swimmer. Born May 19, 1977, in Burlington, Ontario, Canada. ❖ Won a team bronze medal at Sydney Olympics (2000).

CARY, Alice (1820–1871). American poet, short-story writer and salonnière. Name variations: Patty Lee. Born Alice Patty Lee Cary, April 26, 1820, in Mount Healthy, near Cincinnati, Ohio; died Feb 12, 1871, in New York, NY; dau. of Elizabeth (Jessup) and Robert Cary; sister of poet Phoebe Cary (1824–1871); never married; no children. ❖ Published poetry in local papers (1838–48); with sister Phoebe, was brought to national readership with the help of editors Rufus Griswold and Gamahiel Bailey (1849); moved to Manhattan (1850); joined by Phoebe (1851); worked with Phoebe in what has been described as "unbroken partnership"; served as the earliest president of Sorosis (1868–69), the 1st professional woman's club organized in New York; began regular publication in magazines (*National Magazine, Atlantic Monthly, National Era*), and hosted a popular New York literary salon for 15 years; wrote prose sketches and novels, now almost forgotten, and volumes of verse; writings include *Lyra* (1852), *Poems* (1855), *Ballads, Lyrics, Hymns* (1866), *Lover's Diary* (1868) and *Poetical Works of Alice and Phoebe Cary* (1886).

CARY, Anne (1615–1671). British poet. Name variations: Dame Clementia (or Clementina), O.S.B. Born Anne Cary, 1615, in London, England; died 1671 in Paris, France; dau. of Sir Henry Cary, Viscount Falkland, and Elizabeth Cary (1585–1639, dramatist); sister of Lucy Cary (1619–1650, writer). ❖ Spent childhood in England and was sent to Europe with siblings, in the care of English Benedictine monks; joined order of recusant Benedictines in Flanders and was sent to found the abbey Our Lady of Good Hope in Paris (1652); remained there until death (1671); wrote devotional poetry and songs which can be found in "Glow-Worm Light," *Writings of 17th Century English Recusant Women from Original Manuscripts* (1989). ❖ See also *The Lady Falkland: Her Life*.

CARY, Annie Louise (1841–1921). American contralto. Born Ann Louisa Cary, Oct 22, 1841, in Wayne, Maine; died in Norwalk, Connecticut, April 3, 1921; grew up in Yarmouth and Gorham; graduate of Gorham Seminary, 1860; studied in Milan under Giovanni Corsi, with Pauline Viardot in Baden-Baden, and Giovanni Bottesini in Paris; m. Charles M. Raymond (NY banker), 1882. ❖ One of the most popular contraltos in America in her day, made debut in Copenhagen (1868); made London debut at Covent Garden in Donizetti's *Lucrezia Borgia* (1870); in NY, created the part of Amneris in *Aida* (1873); became the 1st American woman to sing a Wagnerian role in US, undertaking *Lohengrin*; appeared in US premieres of Verdi's *Requiem* (1874), Bach's *Magnificat* (1875) and *Christmas Oratorio* (1877), and Boito's *Mefistofele* (1880). ❖ See also *Women in World History*.

CARY, Diana Serra (b. 1917). *See Montgomery, Peggy.*

CARY, Elisabeth Luther (1867–1936). American art critic. Born in Brooklyn, New York, May 18, 1867; died in Brooklyn, July 13, 1936; educated at home by her father, a newspaper editor; studied painting with local teachers. ❖ Art critic for *The New York Times* for 28 years, began career with 3 translations from the French: *Recollections of Middle Life* by Francisque Sarcey (1893), *Russian Portraits* by E. Melchior de Vogüe (1895), and *The Land of Tawny Beasts* by "Pierre Maël" (Charles Causse and Charles Vincent); started writing and publishing a monthly art periodical, *Script* (1905), which came to the attention of Adolph Ochs, publisher of *The New York Times;* was invited to become the art critic for his newspaper, the 1st position of its kind; writings include *Tennyson: His Homes, His Friends, and His Work* (1898), *Browning, Poet and Man* (1899), *The Rossettis: Dante Gabriel and Christina* (1900), *William Morris, Poet, Craftsman, Socialist* (1902), *Emerson, Poet and Thinker* (1904), *The Novels of Henry James* (1905), *The Art of William Blake* (1907), *Honoré Daumier* (1907), *The Works of James McNeill Whistler* (1907) and *Artists Past and Present: Random Studies* (1909).

CARY, Elizabeth (1586–1639). British poet, dramatist and translator. Name variations: Lady Falkland; Viscountess Falkland. Born Elizabeth Tanfield in 1586 in Oxfordshire, England; died Oct 1639 in London, England; dau. of Lawrence Tanfield and Elizabeth (Symondes) Tanfield; m. Sir Henry Cary, Viscount Falkland, 1602; children: 11, including Elizabeth Cary (b. 1617), Mary Cary (c. 1621–1693), and Anne Cary (1615–1671, writer) and Lucy Cary (1619–1650, biographer). ❖ Prominent woman writer and translator of Renaissance, who was known both for her literary works and conversion to Roman Catholicism (1626); after conversion, husband sought separation and custody of children; spent remainder of life in London in poverty; translations include *The Mirror of the World* (1598–1602) and *The Reply to the King of Great Britain* (1630); poetry includes *Verse Lives of Mary Magdalen, St. Agnes, St. Elizabeth of Portugal* (c. 1630). ❖ See also *The Lady Falkland: Her Life.*

CARY, Lucy (1619–1650). British biographer. Name variations: Dame Lucy Magdalena, O.S.B. Born 1619; died Nov 1, 1650 in Cambrai, Flanders; dau. of Sir Henry Cary, Viscount Falkland, and Elizabeth Cary (1586–1639, dramatist); sister of Anne Cary (1615–1671, writer). ❖ Sent by mother to Flanders with English recusant Benedictines; became Benedictine at English Abbey of Our Lady of Consolation; remained there until death; may be the author of the biography of her mother, *The Lady Falkland: Her Life.* ❖ See also *The Lady Falkland: Her Life.*

CARY, Mary (c. 1621–after 1653). British religious writer. Name variations: (pseudonym) Mary Rande. Born c. 1621; died after 1653. ❖ Brought up Presbyterian but joined millenarian Fifth Monarchist sect; called for equality for women, concern for the poor, and church reform; wrote *A Word in Season to the Kingdom of England* (1647), *The Resurrection of the Witness; and England's Fall from The Mystical Babylon—Rome* (1648), *The Little Horn's Doom and Downfall* (1651), *A New and More Exact Mappe or Description of New Jerusalem's Glory, When Jesus Christ and His Saints with Him Shall Reign on Earth a Thousand Years, and Possess all Kingdoms* (1651), and *Twelve New Proposals to the Supreme Governours of the Three Nations now assembled at Westminster* (1653).

CARY, Mary Ann Shadd (1823–1893). American teacher, journalist, and lawyer. Born Mary Ann Shadd, Oct 9, 1823, in Wilmington, Delaware; died in Washington, DC, June 5, 1893; dau. of black abolitionist Abraham Doros Shadd (shoemaker) and Harriet (Parnell) Shadd; Howard University, LLB, 1883; m. Thomas F. Cary of Toronto, 1856; children: Sarah and Linton. ❖ Champion of the cause of racial integration in Canada and US, taught school in Delaware, Pennsylvania, and New York (1840–51); moved to Canada (1851); wrote *Notes on Canada West* (1852); helped found *Provincial Freeman* (1853), a weekly journal devoted to bettering conditions of North Americans of African descent, and served as de facto editor (1854–58); was, as the *Provincial Freeman* itself reported (1855), "the 1st colored woman on the American continent to establish and edit a weekly newspaper"; served as recruiting officer for black volunteers in Indiana (1863); moved to Washington, DC (1869), and taught next 15 years in public schools; served as public school principal (1872–74); also wrote for the *New National Era* and other journals on a variety of subjects, including women's rights. ❖ See also Jim Bearden and Linda Jean Butler, *Shadd: The Life and Times of Mary Ann Shadd* (NC Press, 1977); and *Women in World History.*

CARY, Phoebe (1824–1871). American poet. Born Phoebe Cary, Sept 4, 1824, in Mount Healthy, near Cincinnati, Ohio; died July 31, 1871, in New York, NY; dau. of Elizabeth (Jessup) and Robert Cary; sister of poet Alice Cary (1820–1871); never married; no children. ❖ In a literary partnership with sister Alice, was less known for her poetry than for

support of her more famous sibling; writings include *Poems and Parodies* (1854), *Poems of Faith, Hope, and Love* (1868) and *Poetical Works of Alice and Phoebe Cary* (1886).

CASA, Lisa Della (b. 1919). *See Della Casa, Lisa.*

CASADESUS, Gaby (1901–1999). French pianist. Born Aug 9, 1901, in Marseilles, France; died Nov 12, 1999, in Paris, France; studied with Louis Diemer at Paris Conservatory; m. Robert Casadesus (1899–1972, pianist); children: son Jean (1927–1972). ❖ Enjoyed a career as a duo-pianist with husband Robert that took them all over the world; recorded Gabriel Fauré's *Ballade* for Piano and Orchestra, one of the 1st to appear in the long-playing format.

CASAGRANDE, Anna (1958—). Italian equestrian. Born April 26, 1958, in Italy. ❖ At Moscow Olympics, won a silver medal in 3-day event team competition (1980).

CASAITITE, Aldona (1949—). *See Neneniene-Casaitite, Aldona.*

CASALINA, Lucia (1677–1762). Italian artist. Born 1677 in Bologna, Italy; died 1762. ❖ Extremely successful portrait painter, whose self-portrait is in the Florentine Gallery.

CASALS, Rosemary (1948—). American tennis player. Name variations: Rosie Casals. Born Sept 16, 1948, in SanFrancisco, California; dau. of Manuel Casals y Bordas (San Salvadorian immigrant); grandniece of cellist Pablo Casals; never married. ❖ With Billie Jean King, won numerous US titles as well as 5 Wimbledon titles; won singles crown at Wills Invitational tournament in New Zealand (1967) and reached the semifinals at US championships (1967, 1968); with King and others, threatened to boycott future tournaments unless there was more parity in prize money for women (1970); was one of the 1st woman players to sign a pro contract and join the pro tour (1968); went on to win more than 30 national titles, becoming one of the world's top money winners. Inducted into International Tennis Hall of Fame (1996). ❖ See also *Women in World History.*

CASANOVA, Danielle (1909–1943). French resistance leader and political activist. Born Vincentella Périni, Jan 9, 1909, in Ajaccio, Corsica; died in Auschwitz, May 10, 1943; dau. of Olivier Périni and Marie Hyacinthe (Versini) Périni; m. Laurent Casanova (1906–1972, militant Communist), Dec 1933. ❖ During WWII, organized Young Communist cadres into effective partisan fighters; during a mass roundup (1942), was arrested along with a large number of other resistance activists; imprisoned and interrogated, 1st in La Santé in Paris and then in the prison of Romainville/ Seine, was deported to Auschwitz (1943); probably the best-known Corsican after Napoleon Bonaparte. ❖ See also Simone Téry, *Danielle: The Wonderful Story of Danielle Casanova* (trans. by Helen Simon Travis, International, 1953); and *Women in World History.*

CASARES, Maria (1922–1996). Spanish-born French actress. Name variations: Maria Casares Quiroga; Casarès. Born Maria Casarès Quiroga in La Coruña, Spain, Nov 21, 1922; died at home outside La Rochelle, Brittany, France, Nov 22, 1996; dau. of Santiago Casares Quiroga, a pro-Republic politician and diplomat; studied acting at Paris Conservatoire. ❖ During WWII, performed at Mathurins theater in Paris, working with director Marcel Herrand; while there, appeared in J.M. Synge's *Deirdre des douleurs* (*Deidre of the Sorrows*) and such existentialist plays as Camus' *La Malentendu* and Sartre's *Le Diable et le Bon Dieu;* starred in important films (1945–49), such as *Les Dames du Bois de Boulogne, Orphée, Les Enfants du Paradis* and *La Chartreuse de Parme;* preferring the stage, returned to theater; excelled at both classical and modern drama and earned distinction as one of France's foremost actresses, appearing in nearly every classic female stage role, from Medea to Lady Macbeth. Won Molière Prize for best comedienne (1988); awarded National Grand Prix of Theater (1990). ❖ See also (memoir in Spanish) *Residente privilegiada* (Editorial Argos Vergara, 1981); (in French) Beatrix Dussane, *Maria Casarés* (Calmann-Lévy, 1953); and *Women in World History.*

CASARETTO, Caroline (1978—). German field-hockey player. Born May 24, 1978, in Germany. ❖ Won a team gold medal at Athens Olympics (2004).

CASE, Adelaide (1887–1948). American professor. Born Adelaide Teague Case, Jan 10, 1887, in St. Louis, Missouri; died June 19, 1948, in Boston, Massachusetts; dau. of Charles Lyman Case and Lois Adelaide (Teague) Case; twin sister of Mary Cushing Case. ❖ Served as librarian in national headquarters of Episcopal Church in NY (1914–16); taught in

New York Training School for Deaconesses (1917–19); served in religious education department, Columbia University Teachers College, as instructor, then assistant professor (1925–29), associate professor (1929–35), professor (beginning 1935) and department chair; served as full professor (1941–48) of Christian education at the Episcopal Theological School in Cambridge, MA (1st woman appointed as full professor in any Episcopal or Anglican seminary) and became department chair (1941). Author of *Liberal Christianity and Religious Education* (1924) and *As Modern Writers See Jesus: A Descriptive Bibliography* (1927).

CASELOTTI, Adriana (1916–1997). American singer and actress. Born May 16, 1916, in Bridgeport, Connecticut; died Jan 19, 1997, in Los Angeles, California; dau. of Guido and Maria Caselotti (opera singer); sister of Louise Caselotti (opera singer); m. 4 times. ❖ Was the voice of Disney's Snow White (1937).

CASELY-HAYFORD, Adelaide (1868–1960). Sierra Leonean writer and educator. Born Adelaide Smith, June 2, 1868, in Sierra Leone, Africa; died Jan 24, 1960, in Freetown, Sierra Leone, Africa; dau. of Anne (Spilsbury) Smith and William Smith Jr. (registrar); educated at Jersey Ladies' College and Stuttgart Conservatory; m. Joseph E. Casely-Hayford (lawyer), Sept 10, 1903; children: Gladys Casely-Hayford (1904–1950), poet). ❖ With sister Emma, established a school in Freetown, the 1st private secondary school for girls in Sierra Leone (1898); campaigned for an Industrial and Technical Training School (ITTS) that would give African girls the skills to support themselves rather than depend on husbands; to increase funds, ventured to US (1920), touring 36 cities and observing African-American schools; opened school (1923) which would remain open until 1940; in England, honored with the King's Silver Jubilee Medal (1935) and Medal of the British Empire (1950).

CASELY-HAYFORD, Gladys (1904–1950). Sierra Leonean poet. Name variations: Aquah Luluah. Born Gladys May Casely-Hayford in 1904 in Axim, Ghana, Africa; died 1950 in Accra, Sierra Leone, Africa; dau. of Adelaide Casely-Hayford (1868–1960) and Joseph E. Casely-Hayford (lawyer and author); educated at Penrhos College, Wales, and Ruskin College in Oxford; m. Arthur Hunter, c. 1936; children: Kobina Hunter (b. 1940). ❖ Taught in mother's Industrial Technical and Training School (ITTS); her poetry, sometimes published under Aquah Luluah, drew critical acclaim, and her writings in Krio, a Sierra Leonean Creole, were revolutionary; poems appeared in a collection, *Take Um So* (1948), and in international magazines, such as the *Atlantic Monthly*.

CASEY, Maie (1892–1983). Australian painter, illustrator, aviator and patron of the arts. Name variations: Lady Maie Casey. Born Ethel Marian Sumner Ryan, Mar 13, 1892, in Melbourne, Australia; died Jan 20, 1893; dau. of Alice Elfrida Sumner and Sir Charles Snodgrass Ryan (1853–1926, surgeon-general); sister of Rupert Ryan; attended St. George's boarding school in Ascot and Westminster School of Art; m. Richard Gardiner Casey (then Australian political liaison officer in London), 1926. ❖ Lived in London (1906–31); with husband's election to Australian House of Representatives, settled in Canberra where she took up flying (1938) and was a founder of the Australian Women Pilots' Association; accompanied diplomat husband to US, when he was posted to Washington DC (1940–42), then Cairo (1942–44), then Calcutta (1944–46); as a painter, was associated with Joan Lindsay, as well as the George Bell School in Melbourne; illustrated Helen Jo Samuel's biography of Ellis Rowan *Wild Flower Hunter* (1961), and her own book, the autobiographical *An Australian Story, 1837–1907* (1962); also wrote *Tides and Eddies* (1966), an account of her early married life, *Rare Encounters* (1980), *Melba Re-visited* (1975), 2 vols. of verse, *From the Night* (1976), and the libretto for a musical based on an episode in the life of Daisy Bates, *The Young Kabbarli* (1972). Awarded Kaiser-I-Hind Medal and Amelia Earhart Medal; made Commander of the Order of St. John of Jerusalem and fellow of Royal Society of Arts; made Companion of the Order of Australia (1982).

CASGRAIN, Thérèse (1896–1981). French-Canadian feminist and antiwar activist. Pronunciation: Ter-ACE CAS-gra. Born Thérèse Forget, July 11, 1896, in Quebec, Canada; died in Quebec, 1981; dau. of Blanche (MacDonald) and Sir Rodolphe Forget (financier and member of Federal Parliament, 1904–17); m. Pierre Casgrain (lawyer and Liberal Member of the Federal Parliament, 1917–40, serving as speaker of the house, 1936–40 and as secretary of state during WWII), 1916; children: Rodolphe, Hélène, Paul, Renée. ❖ Feminist, humanist, pacifist, and social reformer who led the feminist movement in Quebec for 60 years; joined the newly formed Comité provincial pour le Suffrage féminin (Provincial Suffrage Committee, 1921); founded Ligue de la

jeunesse féminine (Young Women's League), which organized young volunteers for social work (1926); also created Fédération des oeuvres de charité canadiennes-françaises (Federation of French-Canadian Charitable Workers); elected president of Provincial Suffrage Committee (1928) which was renamed Ligue des droits de la femme (League for Women's Rights, 1929); saw vote for women finally achieved in Quebec (1940); working to increase female access to the professions and to improve the position of women in law, won the battle over Family Allowance checks (1945); joined Cooperative Commonwealth Federation (1946), a socialist party dedicated to improving the lives of workers, farmers, and the disadvantaged; elected to leadership of Quebec CCF (1951–57); toured Asia and the East (1956); formed Quebec branch of Voice of Women (1961); appointed to Canadian Senate (1970); considered one of the most prominent figures in the Quebec feminist movement. ❖ See also autobiography, *A Woman in a Man's World* (trans. by Joyce Marshall, McClelland & Stewart, 1972); and *Women in World History*.

CASH, June Carter (1929–2003). American country music songwriter, singer, entertainer and actress. Name variations: June Carter. Born Valerie June Carter in Maces Springs, Scott Co., Virginia, June 23, 1929; died May 15, 2003, in Nashville, Tennessee; dau. of Maybelle Carter (1909–1978) and Ezra Carter; m. Carl Smith, 1952 (div.); m. Rip Nix, 1960 (div.); m. Johnny Cash, 1968 (died Sept 12, 2003); children: Rebecca Carlene Smith (b. 1955, later known as Carlene Carter); Rosie Nix Adams (died 2003); John Carter Cash (b. 1970). ❖ The most famous of the Carter Sisters, signed with Columbia (early 1950s) and recorded a number of hits that made the country music charts; left the Carter Sisters and the Grand Ole Opry (1954) and moved to NY to study at Actor's Studio; appeared on tv shows hosted by Tennessee Ernie Ford, Jack Paar, and Garry Moore, as well as episodes of "Jim Bowie," "Gunsmoke," and "Little House on the Prairie"; starred in film *Country Music Holiday* (1958); joined Johnny Cash's touring troupe (1961); coauthored "The Matador" (1963), a huge hit; with Merle Kilgore, co-wrote "Ring of Fire"; with Johnny Cash, released successful duet "It Ain't Me, Babe" (1964) and country music hits "Jackson" and "Guitar Pickin' Man" (1967); married and began touring as a singing team (1968); played Mary Magdalene in film *Gospel Road* (1972). Earned Vocal Group of the Year award from Country Music Association and a Grammy for "If I Were a Carpenter" (1969). ❖ See also autobiographies, *Among My Klediments* (1979) and *From the Heart* (1987); and *Women in World History*.

CASH, Kellye (c. 1965—). Miss America and singer. Name variations: Kellye Cash Sheppard. Born c. 1965; dau. of Roy and Billie Cash (motivational speaker); greatniece of Johnny Cash; married; children: 3. ❖ Named Miss America (1987), representing Tennessee; appeared off-Broadway in *Always . . . Patsy Cline;* recorded album "Living by the Word."

CASH, Rosalind (1938–1995). African-American stage, tv, and screen actress. Born Dec 31, 1938, in Atlantic City, New Jersey; died Oct 31, 1995, in Los Angeles, California. ❖ Was an original member of the Negro Ensemble Co.; made Broadway debut as Mrs. Hoyt in *The Wayward Stork* (1966), followed by many off-Broadway shows, including *Song of the Lusitania Bogey, Ceremonies in Dark Old Men, King Lear* and *Boesman and Lena;* films include *Klute, The Omega Man, The New Centurians, Uptown Saturday Night, Wrong is Right, Amazing Grace* and *The Adventures of Buckaroo Banzai;* was also a regular as Mary Mae Ward on "General Hospital" (1993–95). Nominated for Emmy for PBS "Go Tell It on the Mountain."

CASH, Rosanne (1955—). American country singer. Born May 24, 1955, Memphis, Tennessee; 1st-born dau. of Johnny Cash (country-music legend) and Vivian Liberto; stepdau. of June Carter Cash (singer); stepsister of Rosie Nix Adams and Charlene Carter (both singers); m. Rodney Crowell (country-and-western singer), 1979 (div. 1992); children: 3 daughters. ❖ Crossover singer known for introspective lyrics, joined father's tour as wardrobe assistant after high school; attended Vanderbilt University (1977); studied at Lee Strasberg Theater Institute (1978); recorded 1st album in Germany (1978); released successful US debut album *Right or Wrong* (1980); collaborated with singer-songwriter husband Rodney Crowell on albums *Seven Year Ache* (1981), *Somewhere in the Stars* (1982), *Rhythm and Romance* (1985), and *King's Record Shop* (1987); scored hits with "Seven Year Ache" (1981), "Ain't No Money" (1982), "I Don't Know Why You Don't Want Me" (1985), "Never Be You" (1985) and "Hold On" (1986); topped country charts with cover of The Beatles' "I Don't Want to Spoil the Party" (1979); released self-produced album *Interiors* (1990); used marital breakup with Crowell as material for critically acclaimed album *The Wheel* (1993); published *Bodies of Water* (1996), a book of short stories, and children's book *Penelope Jane; A Fairy's Tale* (2000).

CASH, Swin (1979—). African-American basketball player. Born Swintayla Marie Cash, Sept 22, 1979, in McKeesport, Pennsylvania; graduate of University of Connecticut, 2002. ❖ Forward; member of University of Connecticut's NCCA championship teams (2000, 2002); selected 2nd overall in WNBA draft by Detroit Shock (2002); won a team gold medal at Athens Olympics (2004).

CASHIN, Bonnie (1915–2000). American fashion designer. Born in Oakland, California, Sept 28, 1915; died Feb 3, 2000, in New York, NY; studied painting at Art Students League (NY) and in Paris; mother Eunice was also a fashion designer; father Carl was a photographer. ❖ One of America's most original and successful designers, founded her own firm, Bonnie Cashin Designs, Inc., in Briarcliff Manor, New York (1952); also designed costumes for such films as *Claudia* (1943), *The Eve of St. Mark* (1944), *Laura* (1944), *Keys of the Kingdom* (1944), *A Tree Grows in Brooklyn* (1944), *Junior Miss* (1945), *The House on 92nd Street* (1945), *Fallen Angel* (1945), *Cluny Brown* (1946), *Anna and the King of Siam* (1946), *Claudia and David* (1946), (with Charles LeMaire) *Give My Regards to Broadway* (1948) and (with LeMaire) *The Snake Pit* (1948). Received Neiman-Marcus award (1950) and Coty Award (1961); named Woman of the Year by Lighthouse of the Blind (1961). ❖ See also *Women in World History.*

CASHMAN, Karen. American short-track speedskater. Name variations: Karen Cashman-Lehmann. Born in Quincy, Massachusetts. ❖ Won a bronze medal for the 3,000-meter relay at Lillehammer Olympics (1994).

CASHMAN, Mel (1891–1979). Australian union organizer. Born Ellen Imelda Cashman, Nov 19, 1891, at Gladesville, Sydney; died 1979; dau. of Ellen and Edward (Ned) Cashman (hotel licensee); attended St. Joseph's School, Hunter's Hill. ❖ Begin work at an early age in the clothing trade, then took a job in the printing industry, eventually becoming foreman; 10 years later, lost job upon joining the Women and Girls' Printing Trades Union; became president of the union (1914); when the women's union amalgamated with the men's as the Printing Industry Employee's Union of Australia, was appointed organizing secretary of Women and Girls' Section (1917), and Cardboard Box and Carton Section (1918); also wrote a column for the *Printer;* following one in a series of attempts to limit the voting rights of women union members, resigned her post (1940); was also a Commonwealth arbitration inspector for many years.

CASHMAN, Nellie (1844–1925). American miner and philanthropist. Born in Co. Cork, Ireland, 1844; died Jan 4, 1925, in St. Joseph's Hospital, Victoria; dau. of Patrick and Frances "Fanny" (Cronin) Cashman; grew up in Boston. ❖ Followed gold miners into British Columbia, Canada, where she operated a boarding house while learning mining techniques and geology (early 1870s); for next 50 years, sought out the precious metal in Arizona, Nevada, Mexico, Canadian Yukon, and north of Arctic Circle in Alaska; in addition to successfully prospecting and running mines (at one time she owned 11 mines in the Koyukuk District of Alaska), operated boarding houses, restaurants, and supply depots; exceedingly generous, earned the titles "Angel of Tombstone" and "Saint of the Sourdoughs"; led a dangerous rescue effort to free a group of miners trapped by a severe storm; helped establish Tombstone's 1st hospital and its 1st Roman Catholic Church; also contributed articles to Tucson's *Arizona Daily Star.* ❖ See also Don Chaput, *Nellie Cashman and the North American Mining Frontier* (Westernlore, 1995); and *Women in World History.*

CASILDA (d. about 1007). Moorish saint. Died c. 1007; dau. of Aldemon, Moorish king of Toledo; widowed. ❖ A catechumen (student of Christianity), secretly visited Christian prisoners of her father and brought them food; according to legend, was on her way to the prison with a basket filled with bread and ran into her father; when he insisted on seeing the contents of the basket, lifted the cloth to reveal red roses (the flowers returned to bread as soon as he walked on); diagnosed with an incurable illness, traveled to bathe in Lake St. Vincent, received baptism, and built a small chapel and house by the lake where she passed her years. ❖ See also *Women in World History.*

CASLARU, Beatrice (1975—). Romanian swimmer. Name variations: Beatrice Coada or Coada-Caslaru. Born Beatrice Nicoleta Coada, Aug 20, 1975, in Braila, Romania; m. Eduard Caslaru (her coach). ❖ Won a silver medal for 200-meter indiv. medley and a bronze medal for 400-meter

indiv. medley at Sydney Olympics (2000); at LC European championships, won gold medals for 200-meter breaststroke and 200-meter indiv. medley (2000).

CASLAVSKA, Vera (1942—). Czech gymnast. Name variations: Caslavska-Odlozil; Cáslavská. Born May 3, 1942, in Prague, Czechoslovakia; m. Josef Odlozil (track champion), 1968; children: Radka and Martin Odlozil. ❖ One of the top gymnasts in the world, won 15 World and European championships; won a silver in team all-around in Rome Olympics (1960); won a silver medal for team all-around and gold medals in balance beam, vault, and all-around in Tokyo Olympics (1964); won a silver medal in all-around team and balance beam, gold medals in floor exercises, vault, uneven bars, and all-around at Mexico City Olympics (1968), becoming the 1st woman to win 4 individual gold medals in the summer games; by openly defying Communist authorities, was ostracized until the revolution. Came in 2nd to Emil Zatopek as Czech Olympian of the Century (1999).

CASON, Barbara (1928–1990). American stage, tv, and screen actress. Born Nov 15, 1928, in Memphis, Tennessee; died June 18, 1990, in Hollywood, California; m. Dennis Patrick (actor). ❖ Films include *The Honeymoon Killers, Cold Turkey* and *Exorcist II: The Heretic;* on tv, appeared as Nurse Tillis on "The New Temperatures Rising Show" (1973–74), as Cloris on "Carter Country" (1977–79), and as Ruth Shandling on "It's Garry Shandling's Show" (1986–90).

CASPARY, Vera (1899–1987). American mystery writer, screenwriter and playwright. Born Nov 13, 1899, in Chicago, Illinois; died June 13, 1987, in New York, NY; m. Isadore Goldsmith (film producer), 1949. ❖ Published 1st novel, *The White Girl* (1929); wrote 9 crime novels, including *Laura* (1943); adapted screenplays for *Laura* (1944), *Claudia and David* (1946), *Bedelia* (1946), *A Letter to Three Wives* (1949), *Three Husbands* (1950) and *I Can Get It for You Wholesale* (1951), among others. ❖ See also autobiographical novel, *Thicker Than Water* (1932).

CASPER, Linda Ty (1931—). *See Ty-Casper, Linda.*

CASS, Mama (1941–1974). *See Elliott, Cass.*

CASS, Peggy (1924–1999). American stage and screen comedic actress. Born Mary Margaret Cass, May 21, 1924, in Boston, Massachusetts; died Mar 8, 1999, in New York, NY; m. Eugene Feeny, 1979. ❖ Made Broadway debut in *Touch and Go* (1949); films include *The Marrying Kind, Gidget Goes Hawaiian,* and *If It's Tuesday This Must be Belgium;* was a regular panelist on such tv game shows as "Match Game," "Password," and "To Tell the Truth." Won Tony Award and nominated for Academy Award for portrayal of Agnes Gooch in *Auntie Mame.*

CASSAB, Judy (1920—). Hungarian-Australian artist. Born Aug 15, 1920, in Vienna, Austria, of Hungarian parents (Kaszab); grew up in Hungary; studied in Prague, 1939, and at Budapest Academy, 1945–49; m. John Kampfner, 1938; children: 2 sons. ❖ Migrated to Sydney, Australia, after WWII (1951); primarily a portrait painter, exhibited widely in Australia and Europe; often painted fellow artists and figures from the arts community, including Joan Sutherland and Robert Helpmann, as well as royalty, including Queen Sirikit; expressionistic paintings are in the collections of the Australian National Gallery (Canberra), High Court of Australia, and National Portrait Gallery (London). Received the Rubinstein Portrait Prize (1964, 1965) and the Archibald Prize (1961, 1968); made an Officer of the Order of Australia (1988).

CASSANDANE (fl. 500s BCE). Queen of Persia. Married Cyrus II the Great (c. 590–529 BCE), 1st Persian king; children: possibly Atossa (c. 545–470s BCE); possibly Cambyses II (d. 522 BCE), king of Persia; and possibly Smerdis.

CASSANDRA (possibly fl. around 1200 BCE). Trojan woman. Legendary child of King Priam and Queen Hecuba of Troy, was renowned as their most beautiful daughter; thought to be buried near Amyclae. ❖ Though the historicity of Cassandra's life is questionable, she became a prototype for the historical sibyls (female prophets widely dispersed throughout the Mediterranean world in antiquity). ❖ See also *Women in World History.*

CASSANDRA (1892–1985). *See Tabouis, Geneviève.*

CASSATT, Mary (1844–1926). American artist. Born Mary Stevenson Cassatt in Allegheny City, Pennsylvania, May 22, 1844; died at Château de Beaufresne (Oise), France, June 14, 1926; dau. of Robert Simpson Cassatt (stockbroker and mayor of Allegheny City, PA, died

1891) and Katherine Kelso Johnston Cassatt (died 1895); graduate of Pennsylvania Academy of Fine Arts, 1865; never married; no children. ❖ Grande dame of the Impressionists, moved to Paris (1866); as Mary Stevenson, had 1st painting exhibited in the Salon (1868); spent 2 years in Italy and Spain (1872–74); as Mary Cassatt, exhibited in Salon (1872–76); met Edgar Degas, who asked her to join the Impressionist group (1877); rebelled against the officially sanctioned "true" art accorded the blessing of the French Academy of Fine Arts and exhibited with Impressionists (1879–86); used family members as models for some of her best pictures: women and children were her forte; produced 12 pictures in 1889 alone, placing great emphasis on design and on delicate texture, with landscapes and still life simply serving as background to her individualized figures; painted a series of murals depicting *The Modern Woman* for the Women's Building at Chicago World's Fair (1893); held 1st one-woman show, Paris (1893), which received great acclaim from French critics, who rated *The Boating Party* as one of her best paintings; bought Château de Beaufresne near Mesnil-Théribus (Oise, 1892); named honorary president of Paris Art League (1904); toured Egypt (1910); caused a sensation when *Lady at the Tea Table* was exhibited by Durand-Ruel (1914); lived her adult years in France, receiving little attention in US during lifetime; other paintings include *The Blue Room* (1878), *The Loge* (1879), *Young Women Picking Fruit, Woman Arranging Her Veil* and *Young Girl in Large Hat*. ❖ See also Nancy Hale, *Mary Cassatt* (Addison-Wesley, 1987); Frederick A. Sweet, *Mary Cassatt: Impressionist from Pennsylvania* (U. of Oklahoma Press, 1966); Nancy Mowll Mathews, *Mary Cassatt: A Life* (Villard, 1994); Griselda Pollack, *Mary Cassatt* (Harper & Row, 1980); and *Women in World History*.

CASSIAN, Nina (1924—). Romanian poet, translator and composer. Born Renée Annie Cassian, Nov 27, 1924, in Galati, Romania; m. Vladimir (Jany) Colin (1921–1991, poet), 1943 (div.); m. Al. I. (Ali) Stefanescu (1915–1983), 1948. ❖ Enrolled at Pompilian Institute as a teen, was expelled when fascism took hold in Romania; finished education at a high school for Jewish girls; became a Communist; published 1st verse collection, *La Scala 1/1* (1947); as her popularity rose, her work came under political scrutiny by Romanian government which demanded a stylistic change; rather than comply, turned to translating, writing children's books, and composing music; arrived in US to serve as visiting professor at New York University (1985); shortly thereafter, upon learning that a friend, whose diary contained a copy of her unpublished satirization of President Nicolae Ceausescu, had been imprisoned in Romania, requested and was granted US political asylum (her friend was tortured to death). Works include *Nica fara frica* (Fearless Niki, 1952), *Numaratoarea in versa* (Countdown, 1983), and *Life Sentence* (1990). ❖ See also *Women in World History*.

CASSIDY, Eileen (1932–1995). Irish politician. Born Eileen Foreman, Aug 1932, in Dublin, Ireland; died Oct 6, 1995; m. John B. Cassidy; children: 4 daughters, 3 sons. ❖ Representing Fianna Fáil, nominated to the Seanad by Taoiseach Jack Lynch (1977) and served until 1981.

CASSIDY, Sheila (1937—). English physician and religious author. Name variations: Dr. Sheila Cassidy. Born Sheila Anne Cassidy, 1937, in Lincolnshire, England; dau. of John Reginal Cassidy (Air Vice Marshall who played central role in British telecommunications during WWII); Somerville College, Oxford University, MD. ❖ Immigrated with family to chicken farm in Australia (1949); studied medicine in Sydney then returned to England (1957); qualified as a surgeon at Oxford; went to work in Chile (1971); after bloody overthrow of Salvador Allende by Augusto Pinochet (1973), was arrested by Pinochet police after granting priest's request to treat a wounded guerrilla fighter (1975); returned to England and related experiences of torture and imprisonment in *The Audacity to Believe* (1977); became medical director of St. Luke's Hospice in Plymouth (1982) and then a palliative care physician at Plymouth General Hospital (1993); lectures widely on spirituality and human rights and has written several books on prayer and on the care of suffering and bereaved individuals, including award-winning *Good Friday People* (1991) and *Sharing the Darkness: The Spirituality of Caring* (1992); founded Jeremiah's Journey, a program for helping bereaved children (1996).

CASSIE, Alice Mary (1887–1963). New Zealand feminist and political activist. Name variations: Alice Mary Peters. Born Nov 19, 1887, in Dundee, Scotland; died Mar 17, 1963, at Western Springs, New Zealand; dau. of William Peters (baker) and Mary Ann (Reynolds) Peters; m. Andrew Cassie (plumbing contractor), 1915 (died 1947); children: 2 sons. ❖ Immigrated to New Zealand (1912); became executive member of Auckland branch of New Zealand Labour Party (1927)

and member of New Zealand Section of Women's International League for Peace and Freedom; campaigned for women's access to pensions and protested exclusion of women from unemployment relief (1920s–30s); later active in other social welfare efforts, including working with the blind. ❖ See also *Dictionary of New Zealand Biography* (Vol. 4).

CASSIE, Vivienne (1926—). *See Cassie Cooper, Vivienne.*

CASSIE COOPER, Vivienne (1926—). New Zealand botanist. Name variations: Vivienne Cassie-Cooper; Vivienne Cassie; Vivienne Dellow; Vivienne Cooper. Born Una Vivienne Dellow, Sept 29, 1926, in Auckland, New Zealand; m. Richard Morrison Cassie (professor), 1953 (died); Dr. Robert Cecil Cooper (botanist), 1984; children: (1st m.) 2. ❖ Made 1st regional study of New Zealand marine phytoplankton while working as a New Zealand Oceanographic Institute (NZOI) researcher; studied intertidal ecology of Narrow Neck Reef at University of Auckland (BA, 1947, MA, 1949) and ecology of Hauraki Gulf's marine algae at University of Wellington (PhD, 1955); studied at American institutions including Woods Hole (1960–61); returned to NZOI to study phytoplankton collected at Fuchs Transarctic expedition; studied Lakes Rotorua and Rotoiti's freshwater phytoplankton populations while employed at University of Auckland's Botany Department (1966–74); researched at Scripps Institute of Oceanography to study lead poisoning on algae in culture (1971); was researcher at Mt. Albert Research Centre's Department of Scientific and Industrial Research (DSIR, Botany Division); helped create the 1st International Phycological Congress (1982) at St. Johns, Newfoundland; worked as research associate at Centre for Biodiversity & Ecology Research at University of Waikato, New Zealand. Writings *Microalgae: Microscopic Marvels* (1996); received New Zealand Order of Merit (1997).

CASSON, Ann (1915–1990). English actress. Name variations: Ann Casson Campbell. Born Nov 6, 1915, in London, England; died May 2, 1990, in Hampstead, England; dau. of Sir Lewis Casson (actor and director) and Dame Sybil Thorndike (1882–1976, actress); sister of Christopher Casson (1912–1996, actor), John Casson (1909–1999, actor and producer) and Mary Casson (b. 1914, actress); m. Douglas Campbell. ❖ Made stage debut at the Lyric as Tiny Tim in *A Christmas Carol* (1921); also appeared in *Quality Street, The Young Visiters, Macbeth, Jane Clegg, The Roof, The Way to the Stars, Sanctuary, Night's Candles, Mrs. Warren's Profession, George and Margaret,* and as Perdita in *The Winter's Tale* at Old Vic, among others; often toured with parents and later with her own group; relocated to Stratford, Ontario (1954) and performed there for many years; films include Hitchcock's *Number Seventeen.*

CASSON, Lady Lewis (1882–1976). *See Thorndike, Sybil.*

CASSON, Margaret MacDonald (1913–1999). Scottish architect and designer. Name variations: Lady Margaret Casson; Margaret Troup. Born Margaret MacDonald Troup, Sept 26, 1913, in Huntley, Aberdeenshire, Scotland (some sources cite Pretoria); grew up in Pretoria, South Africa; died Nov 12, 1999, in London, England; dau. of Dr. James MacDonald Troup (medical advisor to president of South Africa); m. Sir Hugh Casson (architect and professor), Nov 9, 1938 (died 1999); children: Carola Casson (b. 1941), Nicola Margaret Casson (b. 1943), Dinah Victoria Casson (b. 1946). ❖ Known for work in architecture, photography, and sciagrams (shadow drawings), was 1 of few women students at Bartlett School of Architecture, University College, London; set up private architectural practice in South Africa (1938–39); returned to Britain (WWII) and worked as senior tutor for Royal College of Art (1952–74); helped to redesign building interior of Royal Society of Arts (1970s); after husband's appointment as Royal Academy's president (1975), assisted as chair of shop and restaurant committee and established Royal Academy's Country Friends; appointed fellow of Royal Academy (1985) and senior fellow of Royal College of Art (1980).

CASSON, Mary (b. 1914). English actress. Born May 22, 1914, in London, England; dau. of Sir Lewis Casson (actor and director) and Dame Sybil Thorndike (1882–1976, actress); sister of Christopher Casson (1912–1996, actor), John Casson (1909–1999, actor and producer) and Ann Casson (1915–1990, actress); m. William Devlin. ❖ Made stage debut at the Lyric as Belinda Cratchitt in *A Christmas Carol* (1921); other plays include *The Admirable Crichton, Quality Street, Peter Pan, Mariners, Jane Clegg, Becket, Strange Orchestra, Mrs. Siddons, The Convict, Rosetti* and *The Master of Thornfield,* as Jane Eyre.

CASTELLANOS, Rosario (1925–1974). Mexican novelist, poet and diplomat. Born in Mexico City, Mexico, May 25, 1925; grew up on her wealthy parents' coffee plantation near town of Comitán close to Mexico-Guatemala border; accidentally electrocuted in Tel Aviv, Israel, Aug 7, 1974; studied at National University; m. Ricardo Guerra, 1958 (div. 1971); children: Gabriel. ❖ One of Mexico's major writers, became aware of both the suffering of the Indian population of Chiapas province and the subordinate position of women in a culture dominated by the concept of *machismo;* while at National University, joined a group of other young writers who came to be known as the "Generation of 1950s"; published long poem "Trajectory of Dust" (1948); wrote master's degree "On Feminine Culture" (1950), now seen as a landmark in history of Mexican feminism; published autobiographical 1st novel, *Balún-Canán* (1957), translated as *The Nine Guardians* (1959), which received the Chiapas Prize (1958); became a successful academic, teaching 1st at Institute of Indian Affairs in Chiapas, then later in Mexico City at National University where she held a chair in journalism (1960–66, 1967–70); continued to explore the world of Chiapas in the novel, *Oficio de tienblas* (*Book of Lamentations,* 1962), considered by many to be her best, and in a collection of short stories, *Los convidados de agosto* (*The Guests of August,* 1964); appointed Mexican ambassador to Israel (1971); her farcical drama, *The Eternal Feminine,* was staged posthumously. Named Mexico's Woman of the Year and received Carlos Trouyet Prize (1967). ❖ See also Myralyn F. Allgood, ed. and trans. *Another Way to Be: Selected Works of Rosario Castellanos* (U. of Georgia Press, 1990); and *Women in World History.*

CASTELLOZA, Na (fl. early 13th c.). French poet. Name variations: Dame Castelloza. Born in Alvernia; flourished around 1212. ❖ One of most famous of *trobairitz* (troubadours), left 3 or 4 songs in Occitan that are extant. ❖ See also W.D. Paden, ed., *The Voice of the Trobairitz* (U. of Pennsylvania Press, 1989).

CASTENSCHIOLD, Thora (1882–1979). Danish tennis player. Born Feb 1882; died Jan 30, 1979. ❖ At Stockholm Olympics, won a silver medal in the singles–indoor courts (1912).

CASTIGLIONE, Virginie, Countess de (1837–1899). Florentine noblewoman. Name variations: Virginia Oldoini or Oldoïni; Contessa Virginie di Castiglione. Born in Florence, Mar 22, 1837; died 1899; dau. of Marchese Filippo Oldoini (diplomat and tutor to Prince Louis Napoleon) and an invalided mother; granddau. of jurist Lamporecchi; cousin of Count Camillo di Cavour; m. the Count Francesco di Castiglione, 1851 (some sources cite 1855); children: (with Castiglione) 1 son; (with Napoleon III) 1 son, known in later life as Dr. Hugenschmidt, a dentist. ❖ To influence Napoleon III, was sent to France as a present from Count Camillo Cavour, an Italian aristocrat and master manipulator of Europe's diplomatic scene, and the chief counsel to the king of Sardinia (1855); was instructed to obtain a Franco-Italian alliance, stipulating that if Austria made war, France would join with Italy in combat; as a beauty and member of the Florentine nobility, easily accessed the French upper strata; by night, plotted French-Italian strategy with Napoleon; by day, carried documents from one embassy to another or drove to the border to deliver information to Cavour; was highly successful. ❖ See also *Women in World History.*

CASTILE, queen of.
See Blanche of Navarre (d. 1158).
See Eleanor of Castile (1162–1214).
See Juana la Loca (1479–1555).

CASTILE AND LÉON, queen of.
See Sancha of Leon (1013–1067).
See Constance of Burgundy (1046–c. 1093).
See Agnes of Poitou (1052–1078).
See Urraca (c. 1079–1126).
See Bertha of Burgundy (d. 1097).
See Berengaria of Provence (1108–1149).
See Ryksa of Poland (d. 1185).
See Beatrice of Swabia (1198–1235).
See Joanna of Ponthieu (d. 1279).
See Yolande of Aragon (d. 1300).
See Constance of Portugal (1290–1313).
See Maria de Molina (d. 1321).
See Maria of Portugal (1313–1357).
See Marie de Padilla (1335–1365).
See Blanche of Bourbon (c. 1338–1361).
See Castro, Juana de (d. 1374).

See Joanna of Castile (1339–1381).
See Eleanor of Aragon (1358–1382).
See Beatrice of Portugal (1372–after 1409).
See Catherine of Lancaster (1372–1418).
See Maria of Aragon (1403–1445).
See Blanche of Navarre (1424–1464).
See Isabel of Portugal (1428–1496).
See Joanna of Portugal (1439–1475).
See Isabella I (1451–1504).

CASTILLO, La Madre (1671–1742). *See Castillo y Guevara, Francisca Josefa del.*

CASTILLO Y GUEVARA, Francisca Josefa del (1671–1742). Colombian abbess, mystic, and spiritual writer. Name variations: Madre Maria Francisca Josefa del Castillo y Guevara; Mother Francisca Josefa of the Conception; La Madre Castillo. Born Maria Francisca Josefa del Castillo y Guevara, Oct 1671, in Tunja, Colombia; died 1742 in Tunja; dau. of Ventura Castillo (Spanish merchant) and Maria Guevara (Colombian noblewoman and descendant of the marqueses of Poza). ❖ Forbidden to marry her cousin, became a nun at 20, after entering the monastery of Santa Clara de Tunja (1689); regarded as great mystic, her writings often compared to St Teresa de Jesús; wrote religious poetry and prose, published posthumously; works include autobiography *Vida de la Venerable Madre Francisca de la Concepción escrita por ella* (1817) and prose manuscript *Sentimientos espirituales* (2 vols, 1843).

CASTLE, Amy (1880–?). New Zealand entomologist. Born May 9, 1880, at Maori Gully, near Greymouth, New Zealand; dau. of Henry Samuel Castle (storekeeper) and Ellen (Wilson) Castle. ❖ Worked as photographic assistant at Dominion Museum in Wellington (1907); assumed responsibility for entomology collection (1913–31); participated in numerous expeditions to collect specimens (1920s); fellow of Entomological Society of London; contributed articles to *New Zealand Journal of Science and Technology* (early 1920s). ❖ See also *Dictionary of New Zealand Biography* (Vol. 4).

CASTLE, Barbara (1910–2002). British political leader and writer. Name variations: Baroness of Blackburn. Born Barbara Anne Betts in Chesterfield, England, Oct 6, 1910; died in Buckinghamshire, May 3, 2002; dau. of Frank Betts (government official) and Annie Rebecca (Farrand) Betts; attended St. Hugh's College, Oxford University; m. Edward (Ted) Castle (journalist), 1944 (died 1979). ❖ The most powerful woman in British politics prior to the appointment of Margaret Thatcher as prime minister, began working life as a journalist; representing Labour Party, elected member of House of Commons for Blackburn, an industrial city in Lancashire (1945), serving uninterruptedly until 1979; spent next few years as parliamentary private secretary to the president of the Board of Trade, working 1st for Sir Stafford Cripps, then for Harold Wilson (1947–51); became a well-known personality on the British political stage, speaking out on unpopular issues; was an alternate British delegate to UN General Assembly (1949–50); elected to national executive committee of Labour Party (1950), a post she would also hold until 1979; served as vice-chair of the national executive committee (1957–58), then chair (1958–59); became honorary president of British Anti-Apartheid Movement (1963); held several important ministerial posts (1964–76); appointed minister of Overseas Development (1964), the only woman minister in Wilson's cabinet, then Minister of Transport (1965), then first secretary of state for Employment and Productivity (1968), in effect serving as national chief of labor relations; had a 2nd distinguished career as a member of European Parliament (1979–89); created life peer (1990) with title of Baroness Castle of Blackburn of Ibstone in the County of Buckinghamshire; detailed the nuts and bolts of cabinet decision-making in *The Castle Diaries 1964–70, The Castle Diaries 1964–76* and *The Castle Diaries 1974–76;* also wrote *Sylvia and Christabel Pankhurst* (1987); in 1990s, was one of the surviving legends of Old Labour, a rare blend of the idealistic and pragmatic elements of politics. ❖ See also autobiography, *Fighting All the Way* (Macmillan, 1993); Wilfred De'ath, *Barbara Castle: A Portrait from Life* (Clifton, 1970); and *Women in World History.*

CASTLE, Irene (c 1893–1969). American dancer. Born Irene Foote, April 7, 1893, in New Rochelle, NY; died in Eureka Springs, Arkansas, Jan 25, 1969; studied dance with Rosetta O'Neill; m. British-born Vernon Blythe Castle (dancer), 1911 (killed in aviation accident in Texas, Feb 15, 1918); m. Robert E. Treman; m. Frederick McLaughlin; m. George Enzinger, 1946; children: 2. ❖ With 1st husband, invented modern social dancing, becoming one-half of the most famous and admired couples of the day; developed and introduced the fox trot, turkey trot, one-step, and Castle Walk, which became standards in ballrooms throughout the nation; performed in Irving Berlin's 1st musical *Watch Your Step* (1914); after husband's death (1918), continued to perform on stage and in films; was a popular figure on the vaudeville circuit (1920s) and started the bobbed-hair fad. ❖ See also memoir, *My Memories of Vernon Castle* (1918); (film) *The Story of Vernon and Irene Castle*, starring Fred Astaire and Ginger Rogers; and *Women in World History*.

CASTLE, Naomi (1974—). Australian water-polo player. Born May 29, 1974, in Sydney, Australia. ❖ Center forward, won a team gold medal at Sydney Olympics (2000).

CASTLE, Peggie (1926–1973). American actress. Name variations: Peggy Castle; Peggy Call. Born Dec 22, 1926, in Appalachia, Virginia; died Aug 11, 1973, in Hollywood, California; m. William McGarry, 1964. ❖ Made film debut in *Mr. Belvedere Goes to College* (1950); other films include *Payment on Demand, Overland Pacific, Wagons West, Son of Belle Starr, Miracle in the Rain* and *Seven Hills of Rome;* had recurring roles on tv series "The Lawman" and "The Outlaws."

CASTLEMAIN, countess of. See Villiers, Barbara (c. 1641–1709).

CASTLENAU, Henriette de (1670–1716). See Murat, Henriette Julie de.

CASTLES, Amy (1880–1951). Australian soprano. Born in Melbourne, Australia, July 25, 1880; died in Melbourne, Nov 19, 1951; studied in London with Mathilde Marchesi. ❖ Made debut in Cologne (1907); toured Australia (1909–10); awarded 4-year contract at Vienna Hofoper (1912), but WWI intervened; eventually gave up an international career and faded into obscurity, but recordings document the brilliance of her voice. ❖ See also *Women in World History*.

CASTRO, Agnes de (c. 1320–1355). See Castro, Inez de.

CASTRO, Fernanda de (1900–1994). Portuguese poet and novelist. Name variations: Maria Fernanda Teles de Castro e Quadros Ferro. Born 1900 in Portugal; died 1994; m. António Ferro (writer and official in Salazar government). ❖ Early work reflected nationalist spirit; writings include *Ante Manhã* (1919), *Maria da Lua* (1945), *Asa no Espaço* (1955), *Urgente* (1989), the autobiographical *A Ilha da Grande Solidão* (1962) and *África Raíz*. Won National Poetry Prize (1970).

CASTRO, Hortensia de (1548–1595). See Castro, Públia Hortênsia de.

CASTRO, Inez de (c. 1320–1355). Spanish paramour. Name variations: Ines de Castro or Inês de Castro; Ines di Castro; sometimes Anglicized as Agnes; called Collo de Garza (Heron's Neck). Born in Spanish Galicia c. 1320 (some sources cite 1327); stabbed to death, Jan 7, 1355, at Coimbra, Spain; daughter, possibly illeg., of Pedro Fernandez de Castro of Castile and Alonca also known as Aldonca or Aldonza Soares de Villadares of Portugal; the reigning house of Portugal directly descended from her brother, Alvaro Perez de Castro; presumably became 3rd wife of Peter I, also known as Pedro I (1320–1367), king of Portugal (r. 1357–1367), probably in 1354; children: (with Peter I) probably Beatrice of Portugal (c. 1347–1381), countess of Albuquerque; Affonso (b. 1348, died young); John, duke of Valencia (c. 1349–1397); Diniz or Denis, count of Villar-Dompardo (c. 1354–1397). ❖ Mistress and probably wife of Peter I of Portugal, was sent to be educated in the palaces of Juan Manuel, duke of Penafiel, as a child; grew up with, and became lady-in-waiting to, her cousin Constance of Castile (1323–1345); moved to Lisbon upon Constance's marriage to Peter, prince of Portugal (1341); became his lover; after Constance died (1345), supposedly married Peter (1354), though this would have been a secret marriage and thus cannot be proven; considered a threat to the throne, was murdered. The love between Inez and Peter became the stuff of legends in their own time, and for several centuries to follow. Around 1558, António Ferreira wrote *Inês de Castro*, the 1st dramatic tragedy in Portuguese. ❖ See also *Women in World History*.

CASTRO, Públia Hortênsia de (1548–1595). Portuguese scholar and orator. Name variations: Publia Hortensia de Castro; Hortensia de Castro. Born 1548 in Portugal; died 1595. ❖ At 17, disguised herself as a man to earn a doctorate in Philosophy and Letters from University of Coimbra; thought to be 1st woman orator in Portugal, also wrote poetry and was considered one of leading intellectuals in the court of Philip II; awarded lifetime pension by the king.

CASTRO, Rosalía de (1837–1885). Galician writer. Name variations: María Rosalía Rita; Rosalía Castro de Murguía; Rosalia de Castro.

Born Feb 24, 1837, in Santiago de Compostela, Spain; died in Padrón, Galicia, Spain, July 15, 1885; dau. of María Teresa da Cruz de Castro y Abadía (of noble family) and José Martínez Viojo (priest); m. Manuel Martínez Murguía, Oct 10, 1858, in Madrid; children: Alejandra (b. 1859); Aurea (b. 1869); twins Gala and Ovidio (b. 1871 or 1872); Amara (b. 1874); Adriano (b. 1875, died in infancy); Valentina (1877–1877). ❖ Best known for her poetry and for her contribution to the revival of the Galician language in Spain, expressed a vivid concern in her work for the sorrows and predicament of her fellow Galicians; began composing verses at age 11 or 12; published 1st book of poetry, *La flor* (The Flower, 1857); enjoyed 1st publicly acclaimed poetry collection *Cantares gallegos* (Galician Songs, 1863), which constituted a crucial turning point for the literary status of the Galician language; published 2nd poetry collection *Follas novas* (New Leaves, 1880); published last poetry collection and book, *En las orillas del Sar* (On the Banks of the River Sar, 1884); is one of the few women as well as one of the few regional writers in Spain to have a position in the literary canon of Spanish literature. Prose includes *La hija del mar* (The Daughter of the Sea, 1859), *Flavio* (1861), *El cadiceño: Descripción de un tipo* (The Man from Cádiz: Description of a Type, 1863), *Ruinas: Desdichas de tres vidas ejemplares* (Ruins: Misfortunes of Three Exemplary Lives, 1866), *El caballero de las botas azules* (The Gentleman of the Blue Boots, 1867), *El primer loco* (The First Madman, 1881), and *Conto gallego: Os dous amigos e a viuda* (Galician Tale: The Two Friends and The Widow, 1923). ❖ See also Kathleen Kulp-Hill, *Rosalía de Castro* (Twayne, 1977); Shelley Stevens, *Rosalía de Castro and The Galician Revival* (Tamesis, 1986); and *Women in World History*.

CASTRO ALVES, Diná Silveira de (1911–1983). Brazilian writer. Name variations: (pseudonym) Dina Silveira de Queiros. Born 1911 in Brazil; died 1983. ❖ Traveled abroad with diplomat husband and promoted Brazilian culture; works include *Floradas na serra* (1939), *A sereia verde* (1941), *A Muralha* (1945), *Margarida La Rocque* (1949), *As noites do morro do encanto* (1956), *Eles herdarão a terra* (1960), *Os invasores* (1965), *Comba Malina* (1969), *Eu venho (Memorial de Cristo I)* (1974), and *Guida, caríssima Guida* (1981); was the 2nd woman elected to Brazilian Academy of Letters.

CASTROVIEJO, Concha (1915–1995). Spanish novelist. Born 1915 in Compostelo, Spain; died 1995. ❖ Lived in exile in Mexico (1939–50); works include *Los que se fueron* (1957) and *Víspera de odio* (1959), both set during Spanish Civil War.

CASULANA, Maddalena (c. 1540–1583). Italian composer. Name variations: Maddalena Mezari. Born c. 1540, in Italy; died c. 1583. ❖ Referred to as "la Casulana Famosa" at performance in Perugia (1582), her extant works include the text of epithalamium composed for marriage banquet of William IV of Bavaria, and 66 madrigals published in 3 vols. (1568, 1570, 1583) and in other collections; gave music lessons to Antonio Molino who dedicated *Dilettovoli madrigali* to her and whose 2nd vol. she had published.

CASWELL, Maude (c. 1880–?). American dancer. Born 1879 in Sacramento, California. ❖ Toured midwestern US in combination shows (mid-1890s); performed for 3 years on Proctor vaudeville circuit, where she was known as the American Girl, Acrobatic Girl, or Athletic Girl; became successful throughout Europe, where she performed for 9 consecutive years on popular stages (1900–09), including Théâtre des Folies-Marigny in Paris; returned to US where she briefly performed on William Morris circuit (1909–11), before retiring from the stage.

CAT, The (1908–c. 1970). See Carré, Mathilde.

CATALÀ, Víctor (1869–1966). See Albert, Caterina.

CATALANI, Angelica (1780–1849). Italian opera singer. Born in Senigallia, Italy, May 10, 1780; died of cholera in Paris, France, June 12, 1849; m. Paul Valabrègue (French diplomat who later became her manager), 1804. ❖ One of the last of the bel cantos, made debut in Venice in Mayr's *Lodoïska* (1797); sang in Rome at La Scala to great success (1802); next appeared in Madrid and Paris to large acclaim; made 1st appearance in London (1806), at the King's Theatre; remained in England for next 7 years and appeared as Susanna in 1st London production of Mozart's *Le nozze di Figaro* (The Marriage of Figaro); with husband, managed Théâtre Italien at the Salle Favart in Paris (1814–18); retired (1828); established a tuition-free singing school for girls in Florence (1830). ❖ See also *Women in World History*.

CATALINA. *Variant of Catherine.*

CATALINA (1403–1439). Duchess of Villena. Born 1403; died Oct 19, 1439, in Saragosa; dau. of Catherine of Lancaster (1372–1418) and Enrique, also known as Henry III (1379–1406), king of Castile (r. 1390–1406); m. Henry of Aragon (1399–1445), duke of Villena, July 12, 1420.

CATALINDA DE ALBRET (c. 1470–1517). See Catherine de Foix.

CATARGI, Marie (fl. 1850s). Mother of the king of Serbia. Name variations: Maria Catargi Obrenovic. Born Adlige Elena Maria Catargiu in Romania; married Milosh of Serbia (died 1861); children: Milan II (I, 1854–1901), prince of Serbia (r. 1868–1882), king of Serbia (r. 1882–1889).

CATARINA. Spanish variant for Catharine or Catherine.

CATCHINGS, Tamika (1979—). African-American basketball player. Born July 21, 1979, in Stratford, New Jersey; attended University of Tennessee. ❖ Forward, was the 2nd Lady Vol to score 2,000+ points and pull down 1,000 rebounds; won team World championship (2002); won a team gold medal at Athens Olympics (2004); in WNBA, played for Indiana Fever. Received an ESPY award as College Player of the Year (2000); named WNBA Rookie of the Year (2002).

CATCHPOLE, Margaret (1762–1819). English pioneer and convict. Born in Nactom, Suffolk, England, Mar 10, 1762; died in Richmond, Australia, May 13, 1819; illeg. dau. of Elizabeth Catchpole and a father unknown, possibly Richard Marjoram; never married; no children. ❖ The 1st female convict to chronicle Australia's early frontier history, was a skilled and accomplished equestrian; in England, became a nurse and cook in the household of John Cobbold; a valued member of the household, was responsible for saving the lives of the Cobbold children on 3 separate occasions; left their service (1795); to aid lover, stole a horse from the Cobbold coach house (May 23, 1797); arrested and sentenced to death; due to intervention of John Cobbold, sentence commuted to transportation for 7 years (1797); escaped Ipswich jail (Mar 25, 1800); recaptured, sentenced to death, and had sentence commuted to transportation for life (1800); deported to Australia (May 27, 1801), arriving (Dec 20, 1801); worked as a cook for James Palmer, the colony's commissary (1802–04); became a well-known midwife; appointed overseer by the Rouse family of a property at Richmond (1804); recorded the Hawkesbury River floods (1806, 1809); pardoned by Governor Macquarie (Jan 31, 1814); for rest of life, farmed and ran a small store in Richmond; for many years, corresponded with Mrs. Cobbold, which formed the basis of Mrs. Cobbold's son's fictionalized account of her life, The History of Margaret Catchpole (1885), as well as a stage play. ❖ See also Women in World History.

CATERINA. Italian variant for Catharine or Catherine.

CATERINA BENINCASA (1347–1380). See Catherine of Siena.

CATERINA CORNARO (1454–1510). See Cornaro, Caterina.

CATERINA DI IACOPO (1347–1380). See Catherine of Siena.

CATERINA SFORZA (1462–1509). See Sforza, Caterina.

CATESBY, Sophia (1849–1926). See Anstice, Sophia.

CATEZ, Elizabeth (1880–1906). See Elizabeth of the Trinity.

CATHARINA. Variant of Catharine or Catherine.

CATHARINE. Variant of Catherine.

CATHER, Willa (1873–1947). American novelist and short-story writer. Name variations: Willa S., Willa Sibert, Wilella. Pronunciation: CATH-er (like rather). Born Dec 7, 1873, in Back Creek Valley (near Winchester), Virginia; died in New York, NY, April 24, 1947; dau. of Charles and Virginia (Boak) Cather; University of Nebraska, Lincoln, BA, 1895; never married; lived in partnership with Edith Lewis, 1908–47; no children. ❖ Writer whose work celebrated the complexities of life in the New World—the American west, midwest, southwest, south, and occasionally the urban east and Canada; moved with family to Webster Co., Nebraska (1883), then settled in Red Cloud (1884); became journalist and published early stories during undergraduate years in Lincoln, Nebraska (1891–95); moved to Pittsburgh, Pennsylvania (1896) to become managing editor of Home Monthly magazine and newspaper columnist; lived with Pittsburgh socialite Isabelle McClung Hambourg (1901–06); taught high school Latin and English, published vol. of poems April Twilights (1903) and stories The Troll Garden (1905); moved to New York City as editor for McClure's Magazine (1906); published 1st novel Alexander's Bridge (1912); left editing to write fiction after successful "second 1st novel" O Pioneers! (1913); other novels include Alexander's Bridge (1912), O Pioneers! (1913), The Song of the Lark (1915), My Antonia (1918), One of Ours (1922), A Lost Lady (1923), The Professor's House (1925), My Mortal Enemy (1926), Death Comes for the Archbishop (1927), Shadows on the Rock (1931), Lucy Gayheart (1935), Sapphira and the Slave Girl (1940); short stories include The Troll Garden (1905), Youth and the Bright Medusa (1920), Obscure Destinies (1932), The Old Beauty and Others (posthumously 1948). Won Pulitzer Prize (1922); received Prix Femina Americaine (1931); elected member of American Academy of Arts and Letters (1938), and National Institute of Arts and Letters (1944). ❖ See also Cather's Not Under Forty (U. of Nebraska Press, 1936); Mildred R. Bennett, The World of Willa Cather (U. of Nebraska Press, 1961); E.K. Brown, Willa Cather: A Critical Biography (U. of Nebraska Press, 1987); Hermione Lee, Willa Cather: Double Lives (Pantheon, 1989); Sharon O'Brien, Willa Cather: The Emerging Voice (Oxford U. Press, 1987); James Woodress, Willa Cather: A Literary Life (U. of Nebraska Press, 1987); Edith Lewis, Willa Cather Living: A Personal Record (Ohio U. Press, 1953); Elizabeth Shepley Sergeant, Willa Cather: A Memoir (Ohio U. Press, 1992); and Women in World History.

CATHERINA. Variant of Catherine.

CATHERINA OF SAXE-LAUENBURG or LUNEBURG (1513–1535). See Katarina of Saxe-Luneburg.

CATHERINE. Variant of Catharine, Katharine, Katherine, or Ekaterina.

CATHERINE (?–305). See Catherine of Alexandria.

CATHERINE (c. 1420–1493). Austrian royal. Name variations: Katharina. Born c. 1420 in Wiener Neustadt; died Sept 11, 1493, at Hochbaden Castle; dau. of Cimburca of Masovia (c. 1396–1429) and Ernest the Iron of Habsburg (1377–1424), duke of Inner Austria.

CATHERINE (1507–1578). Queen of Portugal. Name variations: Catalina; Katherine; Katherina Habsburg. Born Jan 14, 1507, in Torquemada; died Feb 12, 1578 (some sources cite 1577), in Lisbon; dau. of Philip I the Fair also known as Philip the Handsome, king of Castile and Leon (r. 1506), and Juana la Loca (1479–1555); sister of Eleanor of Portugal (1498–1558), Mary of Hungary (1505–1558), Charles V, Holy Roman emperor (r. 1519–1558), Ferdinand I, Holy Roman emperor (r. 1558–1564), and Elisabeth of Habsburg (1501–1526); m. Joao also known as John III (b. 1502), king of Portugal (r. 1521–1557), 1525; children: Alfonso (1526–1526); Mary of Portugal (1527–1545), 1st wife of Philip II of Spain); Isabella (1529–1530); Manuel (1531–1537); Filippe (1533–1539); Diniz (1535–1539); John of Portugal (1537–1554, who m. Joanna of Austria [1535–1573]); Antonio (1539–1540); Isabella (1529–1530); Beatriz (1530–1530).

CATHERINE (1584–1638). Countess Palatine. Name variations: Katarina; Catherine Vasa. Born Nov 19, 1584; died Dec 13, 1638; dau. of Charles IX, king of Sweden, and Anna Maria of the Palatinate (1561–1589); half-sister of Gustavus II Adolphus (1594–1632); aunt of Christina of Sweden (1626–1689), queen of Sweden; m. John Casimir of Zweibrücken (b. 1589), count Palatine, June 11, 1615; children: Charles X Gustavus (1622–1660), king of Sweden (r. 1654–1660); Christina Casimir (who m. Frederick of Baden-Durlach).

CATHERINE, Mother (1793–1858). See Spalding, Catherine.

CATHERINE, Saint (?–305). See Catherine of Alexandria.

CATHERINE I (1684–1727). Empress of Russia. Name variations: Catherine Skavronsky; Marta, Marfa, or Martha Skovoronski (Skavronska or Skavronskii, Skovortskii, Skowronska); Yekaterina Alexseyevna. Born Marta Skovoronski, April 5, 1684, in Marienburg or Jacobstadt, in Swedish controlled province of Livonia, now part of Latvia; died May 6, 1727, in St. Petersburg, Russia; dau. of Samuel Skovoronski and his peasant wife; m. Johann Raabe; m. Peter I the Great (1672–1725), tsar of Russia (r. 1682–1725), Feb 9, 1712; children: 12, including Paul (1704–1707); Peter (1705–1707); Catherine (1706–1708); Anne Petrovna (1708–1728); Elizabeth Petrovna (1709–1762); Margaret (1714–1715); Peter Petrovitch (1715–1719); Natalia (1718–1725). ❖ Born to a peasant family, survived an arduous life before becoming the mistress and finally, rechristened Catherine, the 2nd wife of Peter I the Great; when young, family moved to Latvia (1690s); became prisoner and paramour of General Boris P. Shermatov (1702); became servant and mistress of Alexander D. Menshikov (1704–05); became mistress and companion of Emperor Peter the Great (1705–12); married Peter the Great (1712); after 12 difficult years of marriage, crowned empress-consort (1724); succeeded Peter as empress of Russia (1725–27); made every effort to complete several projects instituted by husband, including opening the Academy of Sciences and financing the expedition of Vitus Bering in the northern Pacific region. ❖ See also Philip Longworth, *The Three Empresses: Catherine I, Anne and Elizabeth of Russia* (Holt, 1973); John Mottley, *History of the Life and Reign of the Empress Catherine of Russia* (London: 1744); and *Women in World History.*

CATHERINE II THE GREAT (1729–1796). Empress of Russia. Born Sophia Augusta Frederika, princess of Anhalt-Zerbst; Catherine Alexeievna, Alekseyevna, or Alekseevna, grand duchess of Russia; Catherine II, empress of All the Russias; (nickname) Figchen. Born in Stettin, Pomerania, April 21, 1729; died of a cerebral stroke in Winter Palace in St. Petersburg, Russia, Nov 6, 1796; dau. of Prince Christian Augustus von Anhalt-Zerbst and Johanna Elizabeth of Holstein-Gottorp (1712–1760); m. Peter Fedorovich, grand duke of Russia, later Peter III, tsar of Russia (r. 1762–1762), Aug 21, 1745, in St. Petersburg; secretly m. her lover, Gregory Potemkin, 1774; children: Paul Petrovich also known as Paul I (b. Sept 20, 1754), tsar of Russia; (with Stanislas Poniatowski, later king of Poland) Anna Petrovna (1757–1758); (with Gregory Orlov) Count Alexei Gregorevich Bobrinski (b. April 11, 1762), and 2 more sons born in 1763 and 1771. ❖ Enlightened despot who seized the throne from husband and ruled Russia as empress and autocrat of All the Russias for over 34 years; selected by Empress Elizabeth Petrovna as a prospective bride for Grand Duke Peter (later Peter III), who was immature, irascible and cruel; began to assert herself and to take an active role in influencing court policies; on death of Elizabeth, crowned with husband (1761); after Peter alienated important segments of Russian society with his open devotion to all things Prussian, publicly chided him; with lover Gregory Orlov, led coup against husband (June 28, 1762); declared empress (June 29, 1762), just a few days before Peter was murdered at Ropsha, though it is certain she did not give the orders (July 5, 1762); crowned in Moscow (Sept 22, 1762); set out to "civilize Russia" through education, laws, and administration, attempting to drag Russia into Age of Enlightenment; made sincere efforts to improve conditions in her empire; assembled a Great Commission of elected delegates from all classes to discuss a new law code (Dec 1766–June 1768); was at war with Turkey (1768–74); crushed the Pugachev Rebellion (1773–74); introduced Charter to the Nobility (April 21, 1785); annexed the Crimea (1783); went to war with Turkey (1787–92), resulting in Russian expansion to the Black Sea and into the Caucasus region and the Balkans; along with Austria and Prussia, partitioned Poland (1772, 1793, 1795); presided over a brilliant court with tact and ease, corresponded with great thinkers and powerful monarchs as equals, and revelled in their admiration; collected art, built palaces, wrote plays and satirical articles, and worked on a comprehensive chronicle of Russian history. ❖ See also John T. Alexander, *Catherine the Great: Life and Legend* (Oxford U. Press, 1989); Dominique Maroger, ed. *The Memoirs of Catherine the Great,* trans. by Moura Budberg (Macmillan, 1955); Zoé Oldenbourg, *Catherine the Great,* trans. by Anne Carter (Pantheon, 1965); Henri Troyat, *Catherine the Great* (Dutton, 1981); (films) *Catherine the Great,* starring Elisabeth Bergner (1934) and *The Scarlet Empress,* starring Marlene Dietrich (1934); and *Women in World History.*

CATHERINE AGNES DE SAINT PAUL, Mere (1593–1671). See *Arnauld, Jeanne Catherine.*

CATHERINE CHARLOTTE OF HILDBURGHAUSEN (1787–1847). Princess of Saxe-Hildburghausen and duchess of Wurttemberg. Name variations: Charlotte of Saxe-Hildburghausen. Born Catherine Charlotte Georgina, June 17, 1787; died Dec 12, 1847; dau. of Duke Frederick and Charlotte (1769–1818), sister of Louise of Prussia; m. Paul Charles Frederick (1785–1852), duke of Wurttemberg, Sept 28, 1805; children: Helene of Wurttemberg (1807–1873), who m. Grand Duke Michael of Russia); Frederick Charles (1808–1870); Paul (1809–1810); Pauline of Wurttemberg (1810–1856); August (1813–1885).

CATHERINE CORNARO (1454–1510). See *Cornaro, Caterina.*

CATHERINE DE BORA (1499–1550). See *Bora, Katharina von.*

CATHERINE DE CLERMONT (fl. 16th c.). French military hero. Fl. 16th century in Clermont, France. ❖ Loyal to the monarchy, commanded her own troops in defense of her estates and successfully brought Clermont back under authority of the French king. ❖ See also *Women in World History.*

CATHERINE DE COURTENAY (d. 1307). Countess of Valois. Name variations: Katherina de Courtenay. Died Jan 3, 1307; dau. of Beatrice of Anjou (d. 1275) and Philipp de Courtenay, titular emperor of Constantinople; became 2nd wife of Charles of Valois, also known as Charles I (1270–1325), count of Valois and duke of Anjou (son of Philip III the Bold, king of France), Feb 8, 1301; children: Jeanne of Valois, countess of Beaumont (b. 1304, who m. Robert III of Artois); stepchildren: Philip VI of Valois (1293–1350), king of France (r. 1328–1350); Jeanne of Valois (c. 1294–1342, mother of Philippa of Hainault).

CATHERINE DE FOIX (c. 1470–1517). Queen of Navarre. Name variations: Catalinda de Albret; Catherine of Navarre; Katherine. Reigned as queen of Navarre, 1483–1517. Born c. 1470; died in 1517; dau. of Madeleine of France (1443–1486) and Gaston de Foix, vicomte de Castelbon and prince of Viane; m. Jean also known as John III, duc d'Albret, king of Navarre, around 1502 (died 1512); children: Henry II d'Albret (1503–1555), vicomte de Béarn, king of Navarre (r. 1517–1555, who m. Margaret of Angoulême [1492–1549]).

CATHERINE DE FRANCE (1428–1446). French princess. Name variations: Catherine Valois; Catherine de Valois. Born 1428; died 1446; dau. of Charles VII (1403–1461), king of France (r. 1422–1461), and Marie of Anjou (1404–1463); sister of Louis XI, king of France (r. 1461–1483); 1st wife of Charles the Bold (1433–1477), count of Charolois, later duke of Burgundy (r. 1467–1477); no children.

CATHERINE DE MEDICI (1519–1589). See *Medici, Catherine de.*

CATHERINE DE RUET (c. 1350–1403). See *Swynford, Catherine.*

CATHERINE FREDERICA OF WURTTEMBERG (1821–1898). Princess of Wurttemberg. Born Aug 24, 1821; died Dec 6, 1898; dau. of Pauline of Wurttemberg (1800–1873) and William I (1781–1864), king of Wurttemberg (r. 1816–1864); m. her cousin Frederick Charles Augustus (1808–1870), Nov 20, 1845; children: William II (1848–1921), king of Wurttemberg (r. 1891–1918, abdicated).

CATHERINE HOWARD (1520/22–1542). See *Howard, Catherine.*

CATHERINE JAGELLO (1525–1583). Queen of Sweden. Name variations: Catherine of Poland; Catherine Jagellonica or Jagiello. Born in 1525; died Nov 16, 1583; dau. of Sigismund I, king of Poland (r. 1506–1548), and Bona Sforza (1493–1557); sister of Sigismund II, king of Poland (r. 1548–1572); m. John III Vasa (1537–1592), duke of Finland and king of Sweden (r. 1568–1592), Oct 4, 1562; children: Zygmunt III also known as Sigismund III (1566–1632), king of Poland (r. 1587–1632), king of Sweden (r. 1592–1599); Isabella (1564–1566); Anna (1568–1625); John (d. 1618). Following Catherine Jagello's death, John III married Gunila Bjelke (Feb 21, 1585) and had one child: John, duke of East Gotland (born April 18, 1589).

CATHERINE LABOURÉ (1806–1875). See *Labouré, Catherine.*

CATHERINE OF ACHAEA (d. 1465). Byzantine royal and member of the powerful Paleologi family. Died in 1465; m. Thomas Paleologus (younger brother of Constantine IX, emperor of Byzantium), despot of Morea (present-day Greece); children: Sophia of Byzantium (1448–1503); and 2 sons.

CATHERINE OF ALEXANDRIA (?–305). Christian martyr and saint. Name variations: Catharine, Katharine, Katherine, Katerin; (Spanish) Catarina; (Italian) Caterina; (Portuguese) Catharina. Born in Alexandria, date unknown; according to tradition, tortured on the wheel and beheaded at Alexandria, Nov 25, 305 CE; dau. of Costus, king of Cilicia, and Sabinella, a Samaritan princess. ❖ Born to royalty, was educated at home, where, because of her great wisdom, her tutors are said to have become her pupils; despite wishes of family to marry, chose to remain a virgin; shortly after baptism, had a religious vision, which sealed her Christian faith; refusing advances of Emperor Maximin Daia, was whipped and imprisoned; while in prison, converted his visiting wife Empress Constance, along with Constance's attendant Porphyrius, to Christianity; after Maximin had his wife and attendant put to death, was condemned to be broken on the wheel; when the wheels broke and saved her, was beheaded; distinguished as the patron saint of philosophers, literature, schools, wheelwrights, spinners, and mechanics, is portrayed with a book, a crown, and a wheel, which represent knowledge, royalty, and her miraculous escape from death. Feast day is Nov 25. ❖ See also *Women in World History.*

CATHERINE OF ARAGON (1485–1536). Queen of England. Name variations: Katherine or Catharine; (Spanish) Catalina. Born Dec 16,

1485, in Spain; died of cancer, Jan 7, 1536, in Kimbolton, England; dau. of Isabella I (1451–1504), queen of Castile, and Ferdinand II, king of Aragon (r. 1479–1516); sister of Juana la Loca (1479–1555); m. Arthur, prince of Wales, 1501 (died 1502); became 1st wife of Henry VIII (1491–1547), king of England (r. 1509–1547), 1509; children: Mary I (1516–1558, queen of England); and a number who were stillborn. ❖ Spanish princess, renowned for her piety, dignity, and strength of character, who was queen of England and wife of Henry VIII for 24 years; was educated at Spanish royal court; betrothed to Henry VIII's older brother Arthur, prince of Wales (1489); married him (1501); a widow after only 5 months of marriage (1502), lived in seclusion and poverty for the following 8 years; married Henry VIII (1509); acted as his regent (1513) and governed the country well in his absence; was a popular queen, well known for her religious piety as well as her patronage of scholars; when Henry became convinced that she was unable to provide him with a son and decided to have the marriage dissolved (1525), confronted him in court and appealed divorce proceedings to Rome (1529); banished from court (1531); was divorced from Henry VIII by Archbishop Cranmer (1533). ❖ See also *Women in World History.*

CATHERINE OF BOLOGNA (1413–1463). Italian saint and artist. Name variations: Caterina da Vigri; Caterina de' Vigri; Caterina dei Vigri. Born Sept 8, 1413, in Bologna, Italy; died at Bologna, Mar 9, 1463; never married; no children. ❖ A revered holy woman, was recognized as much for relationship to God as for artistic works; entered a convent of Poor Clares (Franciscan nuns) in Bologna and eventually became its abbess; painted miniatures on manuscripts produced in the convent scriptorium and worked as a calligrapher; earned a reputation for her great learning and intelligence, also showed talent in the field of music; wrote numerous songs for the nuns to sing during services and played several instruments herself; in later life, began receiving visions, descriptions of which were published for the spiritual benefit of others; canonized (1492). ❖ See also *Women in World History.*

CATHERINE OF BOURBON (d. 1469). Duchess of Guelders. Name variations: Katherina de Bourbon. Died May 21, 1469; dau. of Agnes of Burgundy (d. 1476) and Charles I (b. 1401), duke of Bourbon (r. 1434–1456); m. Adolf (b. 1438), duke of Guelders, Dec 18, 1463; children: Philippa of Guelders (d. 1547).

CATHERINE OF BOURBON (c. 1555–1604). French Huguenot reformer and princess of Navarre. Name variations: Catherine, princess of Navarre; Catherine of Navarre; Catherine de Bourbon; duchesse de Bar; duchess of Bar. Born c. 1555; died in 1604; dau. of Jeanne d'Albret (1528–1572) and Antoine, duke of Bourbon; sister of Henry of Navarre (1553–1610), the future Henry VI, king of France (r. 1589–1610); married the duc de Bar. ❖ Highly educated, spent much of her life in Navarre where she acted as regent for absent brother Henry (1585–93); journeyed to France and remained there until her death (1593); was intent on marrying distant cousin, Comte de Soisson, but Henry questioned his loyalty; instead, had to marry the duc de Bar; though a staunch Huguenot reformer who was against her brother's conversion to Catholicism, became a good friend of her brother's mistress, the Catholic Gabrielle d'Estrées, and championed their marriage; along with Gabrielle, helped promulgate the Edict of Nantes, providing religious freedom and restoring order to France. ❖ See also *Women in World History.*

CATHERINE OF BRAGANZA (1638–1705). Queen of England and regent of Portugal. Name variations: Bragança. Born Catherine Henriqueta de Bragança, Nov 25, 1638, at Vila Viçosa, Lisbon, Portugal; died Dec 1, 1705, at Bemposta Palace, Lisbon; interred at Belém Monastery, Lisbon; dau. of John IV, king of Portugal (r. 1640–1656), and Luisa de Guzmán (1613–1666); sister of Alphonso VI (1643–1683), king of Portugal (r. 1656–1667), and Peter II (1648–1706), king of Portugal (r. 1667–1706); m. Charles II (1630–1685), king of England (r. 1661–1685), May 21, 1662, in Portsmouth; children: 4 failed pregnancies. ❖ Betrothed to Charles II, king of England, while still a child; left the convent where she had received a modest education and traveled to England to meet and marry him (1662); remained in England for next 20 years; was often pregnant but remained childless; found situation unbearable and returned to Portugal; began taking an active role in reign of brother Peter II, now king of Portugal; was named regent in his absence (1704). ❖ See also *Women in World History.*

CATHERINE OF BRITTANY (1428–c. 1476). Princess of Orange. Born 1428; died c. 1476; dau. of Marguerite of Orleans (d. 1466) and Richard of Brittany, count d'Etampes; m. William VIII, prince of Orange, 1438; children: John IV the Good, prince of Orange.

CATHERINE OF BRUNSWICK-WOLFENBUTTEL (1488–1563). Duchess of Saxe-Lüneburg. Name variations: Katharina of Brunswick-Wolfenbüttel. Born in 1488; died June 19, 1563; dau. of Henry I the Elder, duke of Brunswick, and Catherine of Pomerania (d. 1526); m. Magnus, duke of Saxe-Lüneburg, Nov 20, 1509; children: Katarina of Saxe-Lüneburg (1513–1535); Dorothea of Saxe-Lauenburg (1511–1571).

CATHERINE OF BULGARIA (fl. 1050). Byzantine empress. Name variations: Aikaterini. Dau. of King Samuel of Bulgaria; m. Isaac I Comnenus, emperor of Byzantium (r. 1057–1059). ❖ A princess of Bulgaria, married Isaac Comnenus long before he became emperor of Byzantium.

CATHERINE OF BURGUNDY (1378–1425). Duchess of Austria. Name variations: Katharina. Born 1378; died Jan 26, 1425 (some sources cite 1426), in Dijon, France; dau. of Margaret of Flanders (1350–1405) and Philip the Bold (1342–1404), duke of Burgundy (r. 1363–1404); m. Leopold IV (1371–1411), duke of Austria (r. 1386–1411).

CATHERINE OF CLERMONT (fl. 16th c.). *See Catherine de Clermont.*

CATHERINE OF CLEVES (1417–1479). Duchess of Guelders. Name variations: Katherine von Kleve. Born May 25, 1417; died Feb 10, 1479; dau. of Adolf of Cleves (d. 1492) and Beatriz; m. Arnold, duke of Guelders, 1430; children: Adolf (b. 1438), duke of Guelders; Mary of Guelders (1433–1463).

CATHERINE OF CLEVES (fl. 1550s). Duchess of Guise. Name variations: Catherine de Cleves. Fl. in 1550s; m. Henry I of Lorraine le Balafré, 3rd duke of Guise (r. 1550–1588); children: 14, including Charles of Lorraine (1554–1611), 4th duke of Guise; Claude, duke of Chevreuse (who m. Marie de Rohan-Montbazon, duchesse de Chevreuse); Louis, 3rd cardinal of Guise (d. 1621).

CATHERINE OF COURTENAY (d. 1307). *See Catherine de Courtenay.*

CATHERINE OF CUSTRIN (1549–1602). Electress of Brandenburg. Name variations: Catherine von Brandenburg-Kustrin or Cüstrin. Born Aug 10, 1549; died Sept 30, 1602; m. Joachim Frederick (1546–1608), elector of Brandenburg (r. 1598–1608), Jan 8, 1570; children: John Sigismund (1572–1619), elector of Brandenburg (r. 1608–1619); Anna Catherina of Brandenburg (1575–1612, who m. Christian IV, king of Denmark).

CATHERINE OF FRANCE (1401–1437). *See Catherine of Valois.*

CATHERINE OF GENOA (1447–1510). Italian mystic. Name variations: Catherine or Caterinetta Adorno; Catherine Fieschi; Caterinetta Fieschi. Born autumn 1447 in Genoa, northern Italy; died Sept 15, 1510, at Pammatone Hospital, Genoa; dau. of Giacomo Fieschi, viceroy of Naples, and Francesca di Negro; m. Giuliano Adorno, Jan 13, 1463; children: none. ❖ Thwarted in desire to become a nun, continued to deepen her religious fervor into a remarkable mysticism, one side of a "double life," which was combined with an active role in the secular world; as daughter of noble parents in one of Italy's most important cities, demonstrated early that she was more concerned with life of the spirit than bodily pleasures; at age 13, attempted to become a nun (1460); pressured into marriage by family at age 16 (1463); distanced herself from her spiritual impulse, first isolating herself in misery and then attempting to live the social life expected of her (1463–73); received a transforming vision, which she called her "conversion" (1473); devoting herself to life of the spirit, fasted for up to 6 weeks at a time, existing only on salt water and the eucharist; spent hours each day in prayer and continued to receive intimate visions of God and revelations concerning the nature of divine love and sin and other mysteries of her faith, combining this intense spirituality with an active physical life of service to the poor and sick (1473–96); served as director of the Pammatone Hospital in Genoa (1490–96); died age 63, her physical vitality apparently burned away by her consuming love of God (1510). ❖ See also *Life and Doctrine of Saint Catherine of Genoa* (Christian Press, 1907); *Purgation and Purgatory: The Spiritual Dialogue* (Paulist, 1979); *Treatise on Purgatory: The Dialogue* (Sheed & Ward, 1946); Friedrich von Hugel, *The Mystical Element of Religion, as Studied in St. Catherine of Genoa and her Friends,* 2 vols. (Dent, 1908); and *Women in World History.*

CATHERINE OF GORIZIA (fl. late 1300s). Duchess of Bavaria. Fl. in late 1300s; m. John II of Munich (c. 1341–1397), duke of Bavaria

(r. 1375–1397); children: Ernest or Ernst (b. 1373), duke of Bavaria (r. 1397–1438); William II (b. 1375), duke of Bavaria (r. 1397–1435); Sophia of Bavaria (fl. 1390s–1400s), queen of Bohemia.

CATHERINE OF GUISE (1552–c. 1594). Duchess of Montpensier. Name variations: Caterina de Lorraine; Catherine Marie of Lorraine; Catherine Marie de Lorraine. Born 1552; died c. 1594; dau. of Francis (1519–1563), 2nd duke of Guise, and Anne of Ferrara (1531–1607); sister of Henry, 3rd duke of Guise, and Louis, 2nd cardinal of Guise; m. Louis de Bourbon (d. 1582), duke of Montpensier.

CATHERINE OF HABSBURG (c. 1254–1282). German princess. Name variations: Catherine of Hapsburg; Katharina. Born c. 1254; died April 4, 1282, in Landshut; dau. of Rudolf I (1218–1291), Holy Roman emperor (r. 1273–1291), and Anna of Hohenberg (c. 1230–1281); sister of Clementia of Habsburg (d. 1293) and Albert I, Holy Roman emperor (r. 1298–1308, but not crowned); m. Otho of Bavaria, also known as Otto III, duke of Lower Bavaria (r. 1290–1312), king of Hungary (r. 1305–1308).

CATHERINE OF HABSBURG (1533–1572). Queen of Poland. Name variations: Catherine of Austria; Caterina of Austria; Catherine Gonzaga, duchess of Mantua; Catherine of Hapsburg. Born 1533; died 1572; dau. of Ferdinand I, Holy Roman emperor (r. 1558–1564), and Anna of Bohemia and Hungary (1503–1547); sister of Elizabeth of Habsburg (d. 1545), Maximilian II (1527–1576), Holy Roman emperor (r. 1564–1576), and Eleonora of Austria (1534–1594); m. Francesco Gonzaga (1533–1550), 2nd duke of Mantua (r. 1540–1550), 1549 (17-year old Francesco fell into a lake that same year and died of a fever shortly thereafter); 3rd wife of Sigismund II, king of Poland (r. 1548–1572). ❖ See also *Women in World History*.

CATHERINE OF LANCASTER (1372–1418). Queen of Castile and León. Name variations: Catalina; Katherine of Lancaster; Katherine Plantagenet. Born in Hertford, Hertfordshire, England, 1372 (some sources cite 1373); died in Valladolid, Castile and Leon, Spain, June 2, 1418; dau. of Constance of Castile (1354–1394) and John of Gaunt, 1st duke of Lancaster (his 1st wife was Blanche of Lancaster); half-sister of Joan Beaufort (c. 1379–1440), Henry IV, king of England (r. 1399–1413), and Philippa of Lancaster (c. 1359–1415); m. Enrique also known as Henry III (b. 1379), king of Castile and León (r. 1390–1406); children: 4, including Juan also known as John II (1405–1454), king of Castile (r. 1406–1454); Catalina (1403–1439, who m. Henry of Aragon, duke of Villena); Maria of Castile (1401–1458).

CATHERINE OF LORRAINE (fl. 1600s). Duchess of Nevers. Name variations: Catherine or Katherine de Lorraine. Dau. of Charles, duke of Maine; m. Charles II Gonzaga, duke of Nevers (r. 1601–1637); children: 2, including Anne de Gonzaga (1616–1684).

CATHERINE OF MECKLENBURG-SCHWERIN (1692–1733). Duchess of Mecklenburg-Schwerin. Name variations: Yekaterina Ivanova or Ivanovna Romanov. Born July 25, 1692; died June 25, 1733; dau. of Ivan V (1666–1696), tsar of Russia (r. 1682–1689), and Praskovya Saltykova (1664–1723); elder sister of Anna Ivanovna (1693–1740); niece of Peter I the Great; m. Charles Leopold, duke of Mecklenburg-Schwerin, April 19, 1716; children: Anna Leopoldovna (1718–1746).

CATHERINE OF NAVARRE.
See *Catherine de Foix (c. 1470–1517)*.
See *Catherine of Bourbon (c. 1555–1604)*.

CATHERINE OF POLAND (1525–1583). See *Catherine Jagello*.

CATHERINE OF POMERANIA (d. 1426). Danish countess. Name variations: Katharina. Died Mar 4, 1426; dau. of Marie of Mecklenburg and Vratislas of Pomerania (d. 1394); sister of Erik of Pomerania also known as Eric VII, king of Denmark, Norway, and Sweden (r. 1397–1439); m. Johan or John of Bavaria (son of Emperor Rupert), count of Neumarkt, Aug 15, 1407; children: Christopher III of Bavaria (1416–1448), king of Denmark, Norway, and Sweden (r. 1439–1448).

CATHERINE OF POMERANIA (d. 1526). Duchess of Brunswick. Name variations: Katharina of Pommerania. Died 1526; dau. of Sophia of Pomerania and Eric II of Pomerania; m. Henry I the Elder, duke of Brunswick, Aug 1486; children: Catherine of Brunswick-Wolfenbuttel (1488–1563); Henry II the Younger, duke of Brunswick.

CATHERINE OF PORTUGAL (1540–1614). Duchess of Braganza. Name variations: Catarina; Katherine of Portugal. Born Jan 18, 1540, in Lisbon; died Nov 15, 1614; dau. of Duarte, duke of Guimaraes, and Isabella of Braganza (c. 1512–1576); m. Joao also known as John I (1544–1583), duke of Braganza, Dec 8, 1563; children: Theodosius II, duke of Braganza (1568–1630), who m. Anne of Velasquez); Duarte (1569–1627); Alexander of Evora (1570–1608), archbishop of Evora; Filipe (1581–1608); Maria of Braganza (1565–1592); Serafina of Braganza (1566–1604, who m. John Fernandez-Pacheco, duke of Escalona); Cherubina of Braganza (1572–1580); Angelica of Braganza (1573–1576); Maria (1573–1573); Isabella (1578–1582).

CATHERINE OF RICCI (c. 1522–1589). Italian saint and Dominican nun. Name variations: Catherine de Ricci. Born in Florence, Italy, c. 1522; died Feb 2, 1589. ❖ Noted for her wisdom, took the veil among Dominican nuns at Prato, Tuscany (1535); was made perpetual prioress 7 years later, age 25; though they never met, was a great friend of, and correspondent with, St. Philip Neri; canonized (1746). Feast day is Feb 3. ❖ See also *Women in World History*.

CATHERINE OF RUSSIA (1788–1819). Queen of Wurttemberg. Name variations: Catherine Pavlovna, Grand Duchess; Catherine Romanov. Born May 21, 1788; died Jan 19, 1819; dau. of Sophia Dorothea of Wurttemberg (1759–1828) and Paul I (1754–1801), tsar of Russia (r. 1796–1801, son of Catherine II the Great); sister of Alexander I, tsar of Russia; m. George, duke of Oldenburg, Aug 3, 1809; m. William I (1781–1864), king of Wurttemberg (r. 1816–1864), Jan 24, 1816; children: (1st m.) Alexander (b. 1810); Peter (b. 1812), duke of Oldenburg; (2nd m.) Maria (1816–1887, who m. Count Neipperg); Sophia of Wurttemberg (1818–1877, who m. William III, king of the Netherlands).

CATHERINE OF SAXE-LAUENBURG or LÜNEBURG (1513–1535). See *Katarina of Saxe-Lüneburg*.

CATHERINE OF SAXONY (1421–1476). Electress of Brandenburg. Name variations: Katharina of Saxony. Born 1421; died Aug 23, 1476; dau. of Fredrick I the Warlike (b. 1370), elector of Saxony; sister of Anna of Saxony (1420–1462); m. Frederick II the Iron (1413–1471), elector of Brandenburg (r. 1440–1470, abdicated), June 11, 1441; children: Dorothea of Brandenburg (1446–1519); Margaret of Brandenburg (c. 1450–1489).

CATHERINE OF SIENA (1347–1380). Roman Catholic saint. Name variations: Caterina di Iacopo (YAH-co-po) or Giacomo (JAH-co-mo) di Benincasa; Caterina or Catherina Benincasa; St. Catherine (or Katherine) of Siena; Caterina da Siena; also spelled Sienna. Born Catherine di Benincasa in Siena, Italy, 1347; died in Rome, April 30, 1380; dau. of Lapa Piacenti and Iacopo (or Giacomo) di Benincasa (well-to-do wool-dyer); never married; no children. ❖ Though she never officially joined a religious order, held great influence in the balance of powers in Europe and in the direction of the Roman Catholic Church; wrote letters (382 survive) to various European leaders—Bernabò Visconti, John Hawkwood, Joanna I, Elizabeth of Pomerania (1347–1393) and Pope Gregory XI—urging them to end the schism in the church, to stop warring with each other, and to settle their differences (1370–80); wrote the *Dialogue of Divine Providence*, a didactic religious work; undertook commissions at behest of pope; led a religious group in Siena; canonized (1461); declared Doctor of Roman Catholic Church (1970). ❖ See also Mary Anne Fatula, O.P. *Catherine of Siena's Way: The Way of the Christian Mystics*, Vol. 4 (Michael Glazier, 1989); Foster and Ronayne, *I, Catherine: Selected Writings of St. Catherine of Siena* (Collins, 1980); Suzanne Noffke, O.P., ed. *The Letters of St. Catherine of Siena*, 2 vols. (State U. at Binghamton, 1988); and *Women in World History*.

CATHERINE OF SPAIN (1567–1597). Duchess of Savoy. Name variations: Katherine Michela. Born 1567; died 1597; dau. of Philip II (1527–1598), king of Spain (r. 1556–1598), and king of Portugal as Philip I (r. 1580–1598), and Elizabeth of Valois (1545–1568); married Charles Emmanuel I the Great (1562–1630), duke of Savoy (r. 1580–1630); children: Victor Amadeus I (1587–1637), duke of Savoy (r. 1630–1637); Margaret of Savoy (fl. 1609–1612, who m. Francesco IV Gonzaga of Mantua); Philibert, prince of Oneglia; Cardinal Maurice; Thomas Francis, prince of Carignan or Carignano (d. 1656).

CATHERINE OF SWEDEN (c. 1330–1381). Swedish saint. Name variations: Karin. Born in 1330 or 1331 in Sweden; died Mar 24, 1381 at Vadstena (or Wadstena), Sweden; dau. of (Saint) Bridget of Sweden

(1303–1373) and Sir Ulf Gudmarsson, prince of Nericia (knight); m. Count Eggard, a Swedish knight (widowed); no children. ❖ Was the only one of her siblings to follow her mother's religious path so closely; husband, a Swedish noble, did not live long; deciding against remarriage, became her mother's most important ally in religious work; achieved a reputation for herself as equally committed to the faith and to serving others; with mother, traveled across Europe on pilgrimages; became an important political voice in the struggle over returning the pope to Rome from Avignon; after mother's death, remained influential, establishing the Birgittine order of nuns as her mother had wished; later, moved to abbey of Vadstena as a nun, where she became known as a healer and miracle worker; canonized for her crucial reforming work and untiring devotion to serving others. Feast day is Mar 24. ❖ See also *Women in World History.*

CATHERINE OF TARENTO (fl. early 1300s). Empress of Constantinople. Name variations: Catherine of Valois. Possibly dau. of Philip III the Bold, king of France; m. Philipp or Philip of Tarento (d. 1332), prince of Tarent; children: Louis of Tarento; Robert II of Constantinople; Philip II of Constantinople; Margaret Balliol (fl. 1300s, who m. Edward Balliol).

CATHERINE OF VALOIS (fl. early 1300s). *See Catherine of Tarento.*

CATHERINE OF VALOIS (1401–1437). Queen of England. Name variations: Catharine; Catherine de Valois; Katherine of France; Fair Kate of France. Born Catherine, Oct 27, 1401, at the Hôtel de St. Pôl, Paris, France; died of breast cancer, Jan 3, 1437, at Bermondsey Abbey, London, after a lengthy illness; buried in Westminster Abbey; dau. of Charles VI the Mad (1368–1422), king of France (r. 1380–1422), and Isabeau of Bavaria (1371–1435); sister of Isabella of Valois (c. 1389–1409) and Charles VII, king of France (r. 1422–1461); m. Henry V, king of England (r. 1413–1422), at Troyes, France, June 2, 1420 (died Aug 31, 1422); secretly m. Owen Tudor (Owen ap Meredyth ap Tudur) sometime before 1429; children: (1st m.) Henry VI (b. Dec 2, 1421), king of England (r. 1422–1461); (2nd m.) Owen Tudor (1429–1502); Edmund (1430–1456), earl of Richmond; Jasper (c. 1431–1495), earl of Pembroke; Tacinda Tudor (who m. Reginald Grey, Lord Grey de Wilton); Margaret (1436–1436). ❖ Sent to a convent at Poissy when young; chosen as a wife for Henry V (1413), but no dowry could be agreed upon; finally engaged to Henry V after Treaty of Troyes (May 21, 1420); crowned queen of England in Westminster Abbey, London (Feb 24, 1421); joined the extensive procession of mourners at Rouen when husband died (1422); held the title of dowager-queen and publicly supported her son, the child monarch Henry VI, until 1428; maintained a liaison with Welsh commoner Owen Tudor, which was kept secret from the public for many years, even though it led to 4 children; with Owen Tudor imprisoned in Newgate (he would later escape), fell ill and entered Bermondsey Abbey in London to rest and recover; never left the abbey alive; was grandmother of the 1st Tudor monarch, Henry VII. ❖ See also (film) *Henry V,* starring Kenneth Branagh as Henry V and Emma Thompson as Catherine of Valois (1989); and *Women in World History.*

CATHERINE OF VENDÔME (r. 1374–1412). Countess of Vendôme. Name variations: Vendome. Born before 1360 in Vendôme; died 1412 in Vendôme; dau. of Bouchard VI, count of Vendôme, and Jeanne de Castile (r. 1366–1374); sister of Bouchard VII; m. Jean I, duke of Bourbon, before 1374 (d. 1393); children: Louis (c. 1376–1346), later count of Bourbon (who m. Jeanne de Montfort-Laval). ❖ Daughter of the noble house of Vendôme, was married to French noble Jean, duke of Bourbon, to seal an alliance between Bourbon and Vendôme; resided at court of Bourbon until 1374, bearing only one surviving child; upon death of brother Bouchard VII (1374), succeeded as ruler of Vendôme; governed for 38 years. ❖ See also *Women in World History.*

CATHERINE OF WURTTEMBERG (1783–1835). Queen of Westphalia and 2nd wife of Jérôme Bonaparte. Born Sophia Dorothea Frederica Catherine, Feb 21, 1783; died Nov 28, 1835; dau. of Frederick II (1754–1816), duke of Wurttemberg (r. 1797–1802), elector of Wurttemberg (r. 1802–1806), also known as Frederick I, king of Wurttemberg (r. 1806–1816), and Augusta of Brunswick-Wolfenbuttel (1764–1788); m. Jérôme Bonaparte (1784–1860), king of Westphalia, Aug 23, 1807; daughter-in-law of Letizia Bonaparte (1750–1836); sister-in-law of Napoleon I (1769–1821), emperor of France; children: Jérôme Napoléon; Mathilde, princess of Westphalia (1820–1904); Napoléon Joseph also known as Plon-Plon. ❖ See also *Women in World History.*

CATHERINE PARR (1512–1548). *See Parr, Catherine.*

CATHERINE ROMANOV (1878–1959). Russian princess. Name variations: Ekaterina Iurevskaya. Born 1878; died 1959; dau. of Ekaterina Dolgorukova (1847–1922) and Alexander II (1818–1881), tsar of Russia (r. 1855–1881); m. Alexander VI, prince Bariatinsky; m. Serge, Prince Obelensky; children: (1st m.) Andrei (b. 1902); Alexander (b. 1905).

CATHERINE SKOVRONSKY (1684–1727). *See Catherine I of Russia.*

CATHERINE THE GREAT (1729–1796). *See Catherine II the Great.*

CATHERINE VON GEBWEILER (d. around 1340). *See Katharina von Gebweiler.*

CATHERWOOD, Ethel (1910–1987). Canadian track-and-field champion. Name variations: Saskatoon Lily; Ethel Catherwood Mitchell. Born May 2, 1910, in Ontario, Canada; died Sept 18, 1987; grew up in Saskatoon, Saskatchewan. ❖ Set world record (1926); won a gold medal in the high jump at Amsterdam Olympics, setting new Olympic and World record (1928); moved to US (1929), settling in San Francisco, CA, at time of marriage. ❖ See also *Women in World History.*

CATHERWOOD, Mary Hartwell (1847–1902). American author. Born Mary Hartwell, Dec 16, 1847, in Lurav, Ohio; died Dec 26, 1902, in Chicago, Illinois; dau. of Marcus (physician, died 1857) and Phoebe (Thompson) Hartwell (died 1858); reared by maternal grandparents in Hebron, Ohio; graduate of Granville Female College, 1868; m. James Steele Catherwood, Dec 27, 1877; children: son (died in infancy) and Hazel Catherwood (b. 1884). ❖ One of 1st women from the West to earn a living by writing, served as drama critic for *Saturday Review* in Indianapolis, Indiana; served as a founder of Western Association of Writers; writings for adults include *A Woman in Armor* (1875), *Craque-o'-Doom* (1881), *The Romance of Dollard* (1889), *Lazarre* (1901), *Mackinac and Lake Stories* (1899); children's books include *Dogberry Bunch* (1880), *Rocky Fork* (1882) and *Old Caravan Days* (1884).

CATLETT, Elizabeth (b. 1915). African-American sculptor and printmaker. Born in Washington, DC, April 15, 1915; Howard University, BA, 1936; University of Iowa, MFA in sculpture, 1940; m. Charles White (artist), 1941 (div.); m. Francisco Mora (Mexican artist), 1947; children: 3. ❖ Married and moved to NY, where she flourished in the Harlem Renaissance; continued studies in several mediums, working with French sculptor Ossip Zadkine, who would profoundly influence her work, and learning lithography at Art Students League; exhibited around the country, including at Institute of Contemporary Art in Boston and Baltimore Museum of Art; after receiving a Rosenwald fellowship (1946), moved with husband to Mexico, where she worked with Taller de Grafica Popular (TGP), a collaborative of printmakers; executed a series of prints and paintings on theme *The Negro Woman;* earned 1st solo exhibition, at Barnett-Aden Gallery, Washington, DC (1948); became citizen of Mexico; was 1st woman professor of sculpture at Mexico's national university (1959); had 17 one-woman shows, most of them in US (1970s); other works include *Black Woman Speaks, Homage to My Young Black Sisters, Olmec Bather, Black Unity, Target Practice, Homage to the Panthers, Malcolm Speaks for Us, Torres Bodet* and *Vasconcelos;* commissioned to create a bust of Phillis Wheatley (1973); created a 10-foot bronze sculpture of Louis Armstrong for City Park of New Orleans (1975). ❖ See also Samella Lewis, *The Art of Elizabeth Catlett* (Hancraft, 1984); and *Women in World History.*

CATLEY, Ann (1745–1789). English actress and singer. Name variations: Ann Lascelles. Born near Tower Hill, in London, England, 1745; died at Ealing, Dec 14, 1789; studied under Charles Macklin; m. Francis Lascelles (major-general). ❖ Made stage debut at Vauxhall (1762), earning fame and notoriety for her voice, beauty, and idiosyncratic manners; was also immensely popular in Dublin (1763–70); to be "Catleyfied" became synonymous with dressing becomingly. ❖ See also *Women in World History.*

CATO, Nancy (1917–2000). Australian novelist, poet and journalist. Born Mar 11, 1917, in Adelaide, South Australia, Australia; died July 3, 2000, in Noosa, Queensland, Australia; m. Eldred Norman, 1941; children: 3. ❖ Active in Australian literary circles, was a founding member of Lyrebird Writers; best known for her trilogy: *All the Rivers Run* (1958), *Time, Flow Softly: A Novel of the River Murray* (1959) and *Green Grows the Vine* (1960), issued in 1 vol. as *All the Rivers Run* (1978); other works, which capture the spirit of the Australian outback and often feature strong female characters, include *The Darkened Window: Poems* (1950), *But Still the Stream: A Novel of the Murray River* (1962), *Brown Sugar* (1974), *Nin and the Scribblies* (1976), *The Noosa Story: A Study in Unplanned Development* (1979), *The Lady Lost in Time* (1986) and

Marigold (1992). Received Alice Award (1988); made Member of Order of Australia.

CATON-THOMPSON, Gertrude (1888–1985). English archaeologist. Born Feb 1, 1888 (some sources cite 1889), in London, England; died April 18, 1985, in Hereford, Worcester, England; educated at Links School, Eastbourne, and Newnham College, Cambridge; trained at British School of Archaeology in Egypt, studying under Flinders Petrie. ❖ With Elinor W. Gardner, worked on a number of projects in Egypt, especially in Northern Fayum (1924–28); investigations pushed back beginnings of Egyptian culture as far as 5000 BCE, into Neolithic era, and were reported in her book *The Desert Fayum;* traveled to Rhodesia to excavate ruins at Zimbabwe (1928–29); worked on early site of Kharga Oasis in Egypt (1930–33), later publishing *Kharga Oasis in Pre-history,* as well as the tombs of Hureidha in the Hadramaut of southern Arabia (1937–38), which resulted in *The Tombs and Moon Temple of Hureidha, Hadramaut;* was president of British Prehistoric Society, vice-president of Royal Anthropological Institute, governor of Bedford College (University of London), and a fellow of Newnham College (Cambridge); retired (1957).

CATT, Carrie Chapman (1859–1947). American suffragist and pacifist. Born Carrie Clinton Lane, Jan 9, 1859, in Ripon, Wisconsin; died Mar 9, 1947, in New Rochelle, New York; dau. of Lucius (farmer) and Maria (Clinton) Lane; Iowa State Agricultural College (now Iowa State University), BS, 1880; m. Leo Chapman (editor of *Mason City* [Iowa] *Republican*), Feb 12, 1885 (died 1886); m. George Catt (d. 1905), June 10, 1890; no children. ❖ Activist for women's rights and crusader for world peace, who was president of National American Woman Suffrage Association, founder and 1st president of the International Woman Suffrage Alliance, and organizer of the League of Women Voters; began teaching high school in Mason City, Iowa (1881); promoted to principal and city school superintendent (1883); resigned to marry Leo Chapman and became his business partner (1885); widowed (1886); established suffrage clubs in Iowa (1887–90); elected secretary of Iowa Woman Suffrage Association (1889); played major role in successful campaign for woman suffrage in Colorado (1893); served as president of National American Woman Suffrage Association (NAWSA, 1900–04, 1916–20); founded International Woman Suffrage Alliance (1902); traveled to Europe, Africa and Asia, observing conditions of women, speaking, and organizing women's rights groups; helped to found the Woman's Peace Party (1915); while continuing work on the international scene, organized and led the unsuccessful "Victory in 1915" New York suffrage campaign (1915); led the successful "Victory in 1917" campaign (1917); assisted in creating League of Women Voters (1919); founded Committee on the Cause and Cure of War (1925); helped to establish the Protest Committee of Non-Jewish Women Against the Persecution of Jews in Germany (1933); writings include *The Home Defense* (1918), *Then and Now* (1939), *War Aims* (1918), (with Nettie Rogers Shuler) *Woman Suffrage and Politics: The Inner Story of the Suffrage Movement* (1923) and *Women in the Industries and Professions* (1901). Given "Distinguished Service" award of National American Woman Suffrage Association (1920); awarded American Hebrew Medal (1933). ❖ See also Robert Booth Fowler, *Carrie Catt: Feminist Politician* (Northeastern U. Press, 1986); Jacqueline Van Voris, *Carrie Chapman Catt: A Public Life* (Feminist Press, 1987); and *Women in World History.*

CATTANEI, Vannozza (1442–1518). Italian noblewoman. Name variations: Vanozza dei Catanei; Rosa Vanozza. Probably born in Mantua 1442; died Nov 26, 1518; buried in Santa Maria del Populo with the highest honors; mistress of Pope Alexander VI (Rodrigo Borgia) from c. 1468–1482; married Domenico d'Arignano (officer of the church); m. Giorgio san Croce (Apostolic clerk and Venetian scholar), 1480 (died 1486); m. Carlo Canale (protégé of the Gonzaga family), 1486; children: (with Rodrigo Borgia) Cesare (1475–1507); Juan I (1476–1497), 2nd duke of Gandia; Lucrezia Borgia (1480–1519); Geoffredo also known as Joffré (1482–1517); (2nd m.) Ottaviano. ❖ See also *Women in World History.*

CATTANEO, Simonetta (d. 1476). *See Vespucci, Simonetta.*

CATTARINA. *Variant of Catherine.*

CATTERSON, Pat (1946—). American dancer and choreographer. Born Feb 20, 1946, in Indianapolis, Indiana; dau. of ballroom dancers. ❖ Trained in a variety of dance techniques, including modern, jazz and tap, from which she developed a unique style of choreography which has been characterized as "postmodern tap"; received Fulbright scholarship (1995); created works for Dance Theater of Oregon, Ohio University,

and Eglevsky Ballet, among others; was dance consultant on film *I Shot Andy Warhol;* taught on dance faculties of Sarah Lawrence College, UCLA, and Merce Cunningham Studio; taught composition at Juilliard School and LaGuardia High School for Performing Arts in NY.

CATTLE KATE (1861–1889). *See Watson, Ellen.*

CATUNA, Anuta (1968—). Romanian marathon runner. Born Jan 10, 1968, in Lunca Ilvei, Romania. ❖ Won World Cup (1995); won a silver medal at World championships (1995); won New York City marathon (1996), with a time of 2:28:18.

CAUER, Minna (1841–1922). German feminist leader and writer. Born Wilhelmina Theodore Marie Schelle, Nov 1, 1841, in Freyenstein-Ostprignitz, Germany; died in Berlin, Aug 3, 1922; dau. of Alexander Schelle (Lutheran minister) and Juliane (Wolfschmidt) Schelle; m. August Latzel (physician), 1862 (died 1866); passed teaching examinations, 1867; m. Eduard Cauer (educator), 1868 (died 1881); children: (1st m.) son (died in infancy). ❖ Major figure in the history of the political emancipation of German women, spent years of 2nd marriage in Berlin and moved in influential liberal circles; played a key role in transforming the German Academic Alliance, an educational reform organization founded the year before, into a national organization, the Women's Welfare Association (Verein Frauenwohl, 1889); for next 2 decades, would be the leading voice of the left wing of the bourgeois German women's movement, demanding that German women be granted the right to vote; began serving as editor of the journal *Die Frauenbewegung* (1895). ❖ See also (in German) Naumann, Gerlinde, *Minna Cauer: Eine Kämpferin für Frieden, Demokratie und Emanzipation* (1988); and *Women in World History.*

CAUKIN, Esther (1901–1959). *See Brunauer, Esther C.*

CAULFIELD, Joan (1922–1921). American stage, tv and screen actress. Born Beatrice Joan Caulfield, June 1, 1922, in Orange, New Jersey; died June 18, 1991, in Los Angeles, California; m. Frank Ross (producer), 1950 (div. 1960). ❖ Appeared on Broadway in ingenue roles; became a top star for Paramount in such films as *Duffy's Tavern, Monsieur Beaucaire, Blue Skies, Dear Ruth, Welcome Stranger, The Sainted Sisters, Dear Wife, The Lady Says No, The Rains of Ranchipur* and *Pony Express Rider;* starred in tv series "My Favorite Husband" (1953–55) and "Sally" (1957–58).

CAULIER, Madeleine (d. 1712). French soldier. Died in the battle of Denain, July 24, 1712. ❖ French peasant who was noted for her bravery during the siege of Lille, in the War of the Spanish Succession. ❖ See also *Women in World History.*

CAULKINS, Frances Manwaring (1795–1869). American historian. Born April 26, 1795, in New London, Connecticut; died Feb 3, 1869, in New London; dau. of Joshua (died on a trading voyage before her birth) and Fanny (Manwaring) Caulkins (remarried 1807); never married; no children. ❖ Ran girls' school in Norwichtown, Connecticut (1820–29, 1832–34); prepared widely printed inspirational tracts for American Tract Society in NY (1830s–40s); authored 6 Bible studies volumes for children (late 1850s) and verse; published *History of Norwich* (1845), which she rewrote for 2nd edition (1866), and *History of New London* (1852); became 1st woman elected to Massachusetts Historical Society (1849); served as secretary of Ladies' Seaman's Friend Society, New London, CT, for 20 years.

CAULKINS, Tracy (1963—). American swimmer. Born Jan 11, 1963, in Winona, Minnesota; grew up in Nashville, Tennessee; attended University of Florida, 1981–85. ❖ Won 48 titles, becoming the most victorious woman swimmer in history (1981), eclipsing the records of Ann Curtis; won 200-meter and 400-meter indiv. medleys at Pan American Games (1982); won 3 gold medals—the 200-meter indiv. medley, 400-meter indiv. medley, and the 400-meter relay—at Los Angeles Olympics (1984); set NCAA records in 4 indiv. events (200-meter indiv. medley, 400-meter indiv. medley, 100-meter breaststroke and 200-meter butterfly) and 2 relay events (800-meter freestyle and 400-meter freestyle). Was the youngest recipient of the Sullivan Memorial Trophy at 16 (1979); awarded Broderick Cup as outstanding collegiate athlete of year (1983–84); selected by US Olympic Committee as "female athlete of the year" (1984); elected to Women's Sports Hall of Fame (1986); inducted into International Swimming Hall of Fame (1990). ❖ See also *Women in World History.*

CAULLERY, Isabelle (1955—). French politician. Born Aug 17, 1955, in Bordeaux, France. ❖ Representing Union for Europe of the Nations

Group (UEN), elected to 5th European Parliament (1999–2004); named vice-chair of the Committees and Delegation for relations with Belarus.

CAUMONT DE LA FORCE, Charlotte Rose de (1650–1724). *See La Force, Charlotte-Rose de Caumont de.*

CAUQUIL, Chantal (1949—). French politician. Born July 3, 1949, in Montauban, France. ❖ Member of the national leadership of the Lutte Ouvrière Party; representing the Confederal Group of the European United Left/Nordic Green Left (GUE/NGL), elected to 5th European Parliament (1999–2004).

CAUX, Marchioness de (1843–1919). *See Patti, Adelina.*

CAVAGNOUD, Regine (1970–2001). French Alpine skier. Name variations: Régine Cavagnoud. Born June 27, 1970, in La Clusaz, France; died Oct 31, 2001, in Austria, two days after a high-speed training crash. ❖ Placed 10th in combined at Albertville Olympics (1992) and 7th in the downhill at Nagano Olympics (1998); won the super-G at World championships (2001).

CAVALCANTI, Ginevra. *See Medici, Ginevra de.*

CAVALIERI, Caterina (1760–1801). Austrian soprano. Name variations: Katharina or Catherina. Born in Vienna, Austria, Feb 19, 1760; died in Vienna, June 30, 1801. ❖ Best known for performing Mozart's music during his lifetime, had some of music's greatest works written for her by one of the world's most talented composers; with a career based entirely in Vienna, made debut at the Kärntnertortheater in Vienna (1775). Her character fictionalized in Peter Shaffer's *Amadeus.* ❖ See also *Women in World History.*

CAVALIERI, Lina (1874–1944). Italian soprano. Born Dec 25, 1874, in Viterbo, Italy; killed in a bombing raid, Feb 7, 1944, in Florence; m. Prince Alexander Baritinsky, 1890s; m. Winthrop Chandler, 1907; m. French tenor Lucien Muratore (div. 1927); m. Giuseppe Campari. ❖ Began career as a cafe singer before studying with Maddelena Mariani-Masi; debuted in Naples as Mimi in *La Bohème* (1900), and Metropolitan Opera as Fedora (1906); appeared at Covent Garden (1906); performed mostly in Paris, Monte Carlo, and St. Petersburg; achieved great stardom in Russia (1904–13) and was featured at the glamorous international Italian seasons in St. Petersburg; eventually opened a successful beauty salon. ❖ See also autobiography, *Le mie verità* (1936), and an Italian film of her life, *La donna piu bella del mondo,* starring Gina Lollobrigida (1957); and *Women in World History.*

CAVALLAZZI, Malvina (c. 1852–1924). Italian ballet dancer and teacher. Born c. 1852, in Italy; died 1924 in Ravenna, Italy. ❖ Made London stage debut (1879); soon joined Mapleson Opera Troupe in New York City; became prima ballerina at Metropolitan Opera of New York (1884); appeared as mime and character performer at Empire Theatre in London in such roles as Antony in *Cleopatra* (1889) and Dantès in *Monte Christo* (1896); danced in numerous works by Katti Lanner, including *A Dream of Wealth* (1889), *Cécile* (1890), *Orfeo* (1891) and *Versailles* (1892); served as director of Metropolitan Opera Company's ballet school (1909–c. 1913), where her students included Eva Swain, Maria Gambarelli and Queenie Smith; retired (1914).

CAVALLERI, Silvia (1972—). Italian golfer. Born Oct 10, 1972, in Milan, Italy. ❖ Won 10 national titles; won European Amateur (1996–97); won US Women's Amateur (1997); turned pro (1997); placed 3rd at LPGA Corning Classic (2002).

CAVANAGH, Kit (1667–1739). Irish-born English soldier. Name variations: Christian Davies; Christopher Welsh; Mother Ross. Born Christian Cavanagh in Dublin, Ireland, 1667; died in 1739 in England; dau. of a prosperous brewer; m. Richard Welsh (British soldier killed at battle of Malplaquet, 1709); m. Hugh Jones (grenadier with Royal Greys killed in battle, 1710); m. a man named Davies; no children. ❖ When 1st husband was drafted (1692), joined up as a dragoon disguised as a man under name Christopher Welsh (1693); for 10 years, served under John Churchill, duke of Marlborough; after fighting the French in Holland, transferred to husband's cavalry regiment, the Scots Greys, eventually finding him; during War of Spanish Succession, distinguished herself on battlefield (1702 and 1703) and was wounded several times; having suffered a skull fracture at battle of Ramillies (1706), gender was discovered during an ensuing operation; though discharged, was allowed to remain with dragoons as a cook; retired from army (1712) and opened an inn. ❖ See also *The Life and Adventures of Mother Ross* (possibly authored by Daniel Defoe); and *Women in World History.*

CAVANI, Liliana (1933—). Italian director and screenwriter. Born Jan 12, 1933, in Emilia, near Modena, Italy. ❖ Wrote and directed documentaries and dramas for Italian tv; made film debut with *Primo Piano* (1965), followed by *Francesco d'Assisi, Galileo, I Cannibali (Year of the Cannibals), L'Ospite, Il Portiere di notte (The Night Porter), Milarepa, La Pelle, Oltre la porta, The Berlin Affair, Francesco* and *Ripley's Game,* among others; wrote the screenplays for many of her films; also staged operas for tv.

CAVE, Ann (c. 1827–1914). *See Boyce, Ann.*

CAVE, Jane (c. 1754–1813). Welsh poet. Name variations: Jane Winscom. Born c. 1754 of Nonconformist parents; died 1813 in Newport, Monmouthshire, England; m. John Winscom. ❖ Wrote *Poems on Various Subjects* (1783), which was reissued with additions (1789, 1794).

CAVE, Madge (1881–1917). *See Syers, Madge Cave.*

CAVELL, Edith (1865–1915). English nurse and hero. Born Edith Louisa Cavell, Dec 4, 1865, in Swardeston, Norfolk, England; executed by firing squad at the Tir National near Brussels, Belgium, Oct 12, 1915; dau. of Frederick Cavell, vicar of Swardeston, and Louisa Sophia Walming Cavell; studied nursing at the London Hospital; never married; no children. ❖ Nurse and hero of World War I who was executed by the Germans for assisting fugitive Allied soldiers escaping from German-occupied Belgium; served as governess for a Brussels family (1890–95); entered nurses training at London Hospital (1895); appointed matron of nurses training school at Berkendael Medical Institute in Belgium (1907); by 1912, was also matron of St. Gilles Hospital and carried out similar responsibilities at St. Pierre and St. Jean hospitals; changed nursing school into a Red Cross Hospital during WWI (1914); aided Allied soldiers trapped in Belgium (1914–15), as over 200 soldiers passed through her hospital in their flight to freedom; accused of aiding the enemy (1915); refused to defend herself throughout her trial, even admitting guilt (Oct 1915). Her execution aroused widespread indignation around the world; to many, she was a martyr who had resolutely done her duty. ❖ See also Elizabeth Grey, *Friend Within The Gates: The Story of Nurse Edith Cavell* (Houghton, 1961); A.A. Hoehling, *A Whisper of Eternity: The Mystery of Edith Cavell* (Yoseloff, 1957); Helen Judson, *Edith Cavell* (Macmillan, 1941); Rowland Ryder, *Edith Cavell* (Stein and Day, 1975); Jacqueline van Til, *With Edith Cavell in Belgium* (Bridges, 1922); and *Women in World History.*

CAVENDISH, Ada (1839–1895). English actress. Name variations: Mrs. Frank Marshall. Born 1839; died 1895. ❖ Made acting debut at New Royalty (1863); went on to play Juliet, Beatrice, Rosalind, and Lady Teazle on London and NY stage. ❖ See also *Women in World History.*

CAVENDISH, Christiana (1595–1675). Countess of Devonshire. Born 1595; died 1675; dau. of Edward Bruce, Baron Kinloss; m. William Cavendish, 2nd earl of Devonshire (c. 1591–1628, MP for Derby). ❖ Was an ardent supporter of the Royalist cause.

CAVENDISH, Deborah (b. 1920). *See Mitford, Deborah.*

CAVENDISH, Elizabeth (d. 1582). Countess of Lennox. Name variations: Bess of Hardwick. Died in 1582; dau. of Elizabeth Talbot (1518–1608), countess of Shrewsbury, and Sir William Cavendish, 1st earl of Devonshire; m. Charles Stuart, 5th earl of Lennox, 1574 (died April 1576); children: Arabella Stuart (1575–1615).

CAVENDISH, Elizabeth (1619–1689). *See Cecil, Elizabeth.*

CAVENDISH, Elizabeth (1626–1663). British poet and playwright. Name variations: Lady Elizabeth Cavendish. Born 1626 in England; died 1663; dau. of Sir William Cavendish (1592–1676), duke of Newcastle-on-Tyne; stepdau. of writer Margaret Cavendish (1623–1673), duchess of Newcastle; sister of Jane Cavendish (1621–1669) and Henry Cavendish, 2nd duke of Newcastle-on-Tyne. ❖ With sister Jane, wrote a book of poems and 2 plays, *The Concealed Fansyses* and *A Pastoral.*

CAVENDISH, Elizabeth (1759–1824). Duchess of Devonshire. Name variations: Lady Elizabeth Foster; Dearest Bess. Born 1759; died 1824; dau. of Frederick Augustus, bishop of Derry and 4th earl of Bristol (1730–1803), and Elizabeth Davers; m. John Thomas Foster (died 1796); m. Edmund Gibbon, 1787; m. William Cavendish, 5th duke of Devonshire, Oct 19, 1809; children: (1st m.) Frederick (b. 1777); Augustus (b. 1780, who m. Albinia Hobart); (with the duke of Devonshire) Caroline St. Jules (b. 1785, who m. George Lamb); Augustus Clifford (b. 1788, who m. Elizabeth Townshend). ❖ While living in Rome, subsidized editions of Horace and Virgil. ❖ See also *Women in World History.*

CAVENDISH, Lady Frederick (1841–1925). *See Cavendish, Lucy Caroline.*

CAVENDISH, Georgiana (1757–1806). English social patron and duchess of Devonshire. Name variations: Lady Georgiana Spencer. Born Georgiana Spencer in London, England, June 7, 1757; died Mar 30, 1806; eldest dau. of John Spencer, 1st earl Spencer, and Georgiana (Poyntz) Spencer (eldest dau. of Stephen Poyntz); sister of Henrietta Frances Spencer (1761–1821); m. William Cavendish, 5th duke of Devonshire (1748–1811), June 6, 1774; children: Georgiana Cavendish (b. 1783, later countess of Carlisle); Harriet Cavendish (1785–1862, later Lady Harriet Leveson-Gower); William Spencer Cavendish (1790, the marquess of Hartington and later 6th duke of Devonshire, known as "Hart"); (with Charles, 2nd earl Grey) Eliza Courtney (b. 1792 and adopted by 1st earl Grey). ❖ Married at 16 and soon bored, took to gambling within a year of her reign as hostess of Devonshire House and came under spell of Charles James Fox; campaigned for Fox in Westminster election (1784); also took up with Lady Elizabeth Foster (later Elizabeth Cavendish); a reigning queen of society, had portrait painted by Joshua Reynolds and Thomas Gainsborough; was friends with Richard Brinsley Sheridan and Dr. Samuel Johnson. ❖ See also Amanda Foreman, *Georgiana: Duchess of Devonshire* (Random House, 2000); and *Women in World History.*

CAVENDISH, Georgiana (1783–1858). Countess of Carlisle. Name variations: Lady Morpeth. Born 1783; died 1858; dau. of Georgiana Cavendish (1757–1806), and William, 5th duke of Devonshire, June 6, 1774; m. George, Viscount Morpeth (later 6th earl of Carlisle), Mar 21, 1801; children: 5 daughters, 4 sons.

CAVENDISH, Harriet (1785–1862). *See Leveson-Gower, Harriet.*

CAVENDISH, Henrietta (d. 1755). Countess of Oxford and Mortimer. Name variations: Henrietta Holles; Henrietta Harley. Died in 1755; dau. of John Holles (c. 1661–1711), 1st duke of Newcastle; m. Edward Harley (1689–1741), 2nd earl of Oxford and Mortimer, 1713; children: Margaret Cavendish Harley (d. 1785). ❖ Henrietta Street in Cavendish Square, London, was named after her.

CAVENDISH, Isabel (1879–1927). *See Jay, Isabel.*

CAVENDISH, Jane (1621–1669). British poet and playwright. Name variations: Lady Jane Cavendish. Born 1621 in England; died 1669; dau. of Sir William Cavendish (1592–1676), duke of Newcastle-on-Tyne, and Elizabeth Bassett (died c. 1643); stepdau. of writer Margaret Cavendish (1623–1673), duchess of Newcastle; sister of Elizabeth Cavendish (1626–1663) and Henry Cavendish, 2nd duke of Newcastle-on-Tyne. ❖ With sister Elizabeth, wrote a book of poems and 2 plays, *The Concealed Fansyses* and *A Pastoral.*

CAVENDISH, Lucy Caroline (1841–1925). English social and educational reformer. Name variations: Lady Frederick Cavendish, Lucy Cavendish, Lucy Lyttelton. Born Lucy Caroline Lyttelton, Sept 5, 1841, in Worcestershire, England; died April 22, 1925, in England; dau. of George William, 4th Lord Lyttelton (Endowed Schools Commissioner and girls' education advocate) and Mary (Glynne) Lyttelton; sister of Meriel Lyttelton Talbot (1840–1925), Lavinia Talbot (1849–1939), May Lyttelton; also had 8 brothers; m. Lord Frederick Cavendish (MP and 2nd son of Duke of Devonshire), 1864. ❖ Social reformer who campaigned for many causes, including women's education and Home Rule for Ireland, became maid of honor to Queen Victoria (1863); husband assassinated in Phoenix Park, weeks after his acceptance of appointment as secretary for Ireland (1882); served as president of Yorkshire Ladies Council of Education (1885–1912); became member of Royal Commission on Secondary Education (1894) and was also member of Girls Public Day School Trust, founded by father; honored posthumously with founding of Lucy Cavendish College, which focuses on needs of older women students (1965). ❖ See also Sheila Fletcher, *Victorian Girls: Lord Lyttelton's Daughters* (Hambledon & London, 1997).

CAVENDISH, Margaret (1623–1673). English philosopher, duchess of Newcastle, and 1st woman to write about science. Name variations: Duchess of Newcastle upon Tyne. Born Margaret Lucas in Colchester, Essex, England, 1623 (some sources cite 1624); died Dec 15, 1673 (some sources cite 1674) in Welbeck Abbey, Nottinghamshire, England; buried in Westminster Abbey; dau. of Thomas and Elizabeth Lucas; had 3 brothers—including Sir William, Lord John Lucas—and 4 sisters; served in the court of Queen Henrietta Maria; m. William Cavendish (1592–1676), marquis of Newcastle, later duke of Newcastle, Dec 1645. ❖ Published many philosophical works as well as biography and utopian science fiction;

was the 1st woman to attend a meeting of the Royal Society (May 23, 1667). Writings include *Poems and Fancies* (1653), *Philosophical Fancies* (1653, reprinted as *Philosophical and Physical Opinions,* 1655), *Philosophical Letters: or Modest Reflections upon some Opinions in Natural Philosophy Maintained by Several Famous and Learned Authors of This Age* (1655), *Observations Upon Experimental Philosophy* (1666), *Grounds of Natural Philosophy* (1668), *The Description of a New World, Called the Blazing World* (1668) and *The Life of William Cavendish, Duke of Newcastle, to Which Is Added the True Relation of My Birth, Breeding and Life* (1886). ❖ See also Douglas Grant, *Margaret the First: a Biography of Margaret Cavendish, Duchess of Newcastle* (U. of Toronto Press, 1957); Kathleen Jones, *A Glorious Fame: The Life of Margaret Cavendish, Duchess of Newcastle, 1623–1673* (Bloomsbury, 1988); and *Women in World History.*

CAVENDISH, Margaret (1714–1785). *See Bentinck, Margaret.*

CAVENDISH, Mary (d. 1632). *See Talbot, Mary.*

CAVENDISH-BENTINCK, Elizabeth (1735–1825). Marchioness of Bath. Name variations: Viscountess Weymouth; marchioness of Bath. Born July 27, 1735; died Dec 12, 1825, in London, England; dau. of William Bentinck, 2nd duke of Portland, and Margaret Bentinck (1714–1785); m. Sir Thomas Thynne, 1st marquis of Bath, Mar 22, 1759; children: Henrietta Thynne (d. 1813), Louisa Thynne (1760–1832), Sophia Thynne (1763–1791), Sir Thomas Thynne, 2nd marquis of Bath (1765–1837), George Thynne, 2nd baron Carteret of Hawnes (1770–1838), John Thynne, 3rd baron Carteret of Hawnes (1772–1849). ❖ Held the office of Lady of the Bedchamber to Queen Charlotte of Mecklenburg-Strelitz (1761–93), then was Mistress of the Robes (1793–1818).

CAVENDISH-BENTINCK, Nina (c. 1860–?). Countess of Strathmore. Name variations: Lady Strathmore. Born Nina Cecilia Cavendish-Bentinck around 1860; dau. of a Mrs. Scott and Charles Cavendish-Bentinck; m. Claude Bowes-Lyon, 14th earl of Strathmore and Kinghorne, 1881; children: Violet Bowes-Lyon (1882–1893); Mary Bowes-Lyon (b. 1883); Patrick (b. 1884); John (1886–1930); Alexander (1887–1911); Fergus (1889–1915); Rose Bowes-Lyon (b. 1890); Michael (b. 1893); Elizabeth Bowes-Lyon (b. 1900); David (b. 1902). ❖ See also *Women in World History.*

CAWLEY, Evonne Goolagong (b. 1951). *See Goolagong, Evonne.*

CAWLEY, Shirley (1932—). English long jumper. Born April 26, 1932, in UK. ❖ At Helsinki Olympics, won a bronze medal in the long jump (1952).

CAYETANA, Maria del Pilar Teresa (1762–1802). Duchess of Alba. Name variations: María del Pilar Teresa Cayetana de Silva y Alvarez de Toledo, duquesa de Alba de Tormes; also duchess of Montoro. Born June 10, 1762, in Madrid, Spain; died July 23, 1802, in her palace in Madrid; dau. of Francisco de Paula de Silva (1733–1770), duke of Huescar, and Mariana de Silva Bazan y Sarmiento; granddau. of Fernando de Silva y Alvarez de Toledo (1714–1778), 12th duke of Alba, and Bernarda de Toledo Portugal y Fernandez de Cordoba. ❖ The 13th duchess of Alba and one of the most influential women in the court of Charles IV of Spain, was famed for her relationship with Francisco de Goya and the subject of his painting "The Naked Maja"; also had a liaison with politicians Pignatelli and Manuel Godoy, as well as others; found suspiciously dead in her bed at age 40, causing Charles IV to call for an inquiry but nothing was learned; was succeeded by Fitz-James Stuart, duke of Berwick. ❖ See also *Women in World History.*

CAYETANA FITZ-JAMES STUART Y SILVA, Maria del Rosario (1926—). Duchess of Alba. Name variations: Duchess of Alba or Duquesa de Alba de Tormes; duchess of Berwick. Born Maria-Rosario Cayetana FitzJames Stuart Silva y Falco, Mar 28, 1926, in Madrid, Spain; descendant of England's King James II, through his illeg. son James Fitz-James, duke of Berwick (1670–1734), and Arabella Churchill; dau. of Jacobo Fitz-James Stuart y Falco (1876–1953), 17th duke of Alba (ambassador to Britain) and María del Rosario de Silva y Fernández de Córdova, duchess of Medinaceli, Denia, Tarifa and Hijar and marchioness of San Vicente del Barco (1900–1934); m. Luis Martinez de Irujo y Artacoz (1919–1972), duke of Sotomayor; m. Jésus Aguirre y Ortiz de Zárate (publisher, noted intellectual and former Jesuit priest), 1978 (died 2001); children: (1st m.) sons, including Carlos Maria (b. 1948). ❖ Became the duchess of Alba on the death of her father (1953); reputedly the richest person in Spain, held 47 titles of nobility and was 18 times a Spanish Grandee.

CAYLA, Comtesse du (1785–1852). *French royal mistress.* Name variations: Zoe Victoire Talon, Zoé du Cayla; Madame du Cayla. Born Zoé-Victoire Talon at Boullay-Thierry, near Dreux, France, Aug 5, 1785; died at St. Ouen, near Paris, Mar 19, 1852; dau. of Omer Talon. ❖ Was a favorite of Louis XVIII, king of France; following his death (1824), became a patron of agriculture and industry. ❖ See also (in French) Catherine Decours, *La dernière favorite: Zoé du Cayla, le grand amour de Louis XVIII.*

CAYLUS, Marthe M. (1673–1729). *French writer of memoirs.* Name variations: Marquise or Comtesse de Caylus. Pronunciation: KAY-lüs. Born Marie Marguerite Le Valois de Villette de Murçay in Poitou, France, 1673; died in Paris, April 15, 1729; niece of Mme de Maintenon (1635–1719); m. J.-Anne de Tubières (d. 1704), comte de Caylus, 1686; children: son Anne Claude Philippe de Tubières, Comte de Caylus (archaeologist who published *Recueil d'Antiquités Égyptiennes, Étrusques, Grecques, Romaines, et Gauloises* [7 vols. 1752–67]). ❖ A woman of fashion, was one of the brilliant wits and social leaders of the court of Louis XIV; passed her declining years dictating her famous *Souvenirs* (*My Recollections*), which contained valuable insight into the life of the king and were edited (1770) by Voltaire.

CAYVAN, Georgia (1857–1906). *American actress.* Born Georgia Eva Cayvan, Aug 22, 1857 (some sources cite 1858), in Bath, Maine; died Nov 19, 1906, in Flushing, Long Island, NY; dau. of William T. Cayvan and Sophie (Dunham) Cayvan. ❖ Made stage debut at Boston Theatre as Hebe in *H.M.S. Pinafore* (1879); performed in NY as Dolly Dutton in *Hazel Kirke* (1880) and then in title role; appeared as Daisy Brown in *The Professor* (1881), Jocasta in *Oedipus Tyrannus* (1882), and Lisa in *The White Slave* (1882); became leading lady in Daniel Frohman's company at Lyceum Theatre, NY (1887), and originated many roles, including Helen Truman in *The Wife* (1887), Camilla Brent in *Lady Bountiful* (1891), and Lady Noeline in *The Amazons* (1894); retired from the stage (1896).

CAZNEAU, Jane McManus (1807–1878). *American journalist and expansionist.* Name variations: Jane McManus; Jane McManus Storms; (pseudonym) Cora Montgomery. Born Jane Maria Eliza McManus, April 6, 1807, near Troy, NY; died Dec 12, 1878; dau. of William Telemachus McManus and Catharina (Coons) McManus; m. Allen B. (or William F.) Storms, 1825; m. William Leslie Cazneau (died 1876), late 1840s; children: (1st m.) 1 son. ❖ Wrote for Moses Yale Beach's *New York Sun;* traveled with Beach on secret peace mission to Mexico City (1846); provided valuable information to General Winfield Scott about potential routes for his westward move toward Mexico City; became lobbyist for Mexican annexation; backed Narciso Lopez in efforts to free Cuba from Spain and served as editor of pro-Lopez paper *La Verdad;* wrote *The Queen of Islands and the King of Rivers* (1850), which urged Cuban annexation; involved with 2nd husband in attempting annexation of Santo Domingo; with others, formed American West Indian Co. to promote Caribbean colonization; died in the foundering of the *Emily B. Souder* off Cape Hatteras. Other works include *In the Tropics; by a Settler in Santo Domingo* (1863), *The Prince of Kashna: A West Indian Story* (1866) and *Our Winter Eden; Pen Pictures of the Tropics* (1878).

C.E. *See Tonna, Charlotte Elizabeth.*

CEAUSESCU, Elena (1916–1989). *Romanian political leader.* Name variations: Ceauçescu. Pronunciation: Chaow-u-SESH-coo or Shaow-CHESS-coo. Born Elena Petrescu, Jan 7, 1916, in Petresti near Scornicesti in Oltenia region; executed Dec 25, 1989; m. Nicolae Ceausescu, president of Romania (1974–1989), 1944; children: 2 sons, Nicolae (popularly known as Nicu, d. 1996) and Valentin (adopted); and daughter Zoia Ceausescu. ❖ One of the most powerful women in Eastern Europe during final decades of Communist rule, was a key member of a regime of corruption and clan rule that left Romania with a legacy of economic, social and moral devastation, co-ruling for almost 2 decades with husband Nicolae Ceausescu; was a member of central committee of Romanian Communist Party (1965–89); received numerous Romanian and foreign decorations and honorary degrees; arrested along with husband (Dec 1989); found guilty of several offenses by an improvised political tribunal and executed along with him (Dec 25, 1989). ❖ See also Mark Almond, *The Rise and Fall of Nicolae and Elena Ceausescu* (Chapmans, 1992); Edward Behr, *Kiss the Hand You Cannot Bite: The Rise and Fall of the Ceausescus* (Villard, 1991); and *Women in World History.*

CEBOTARI, Maria (1910–1949). *Bessarabian soprano.* Born Maria Cebotari in Kishinev, Bessarabia, Russia, Feb 10, 1910; died June 9, 1949, in Vienna, Austria; m. Count Alexander Virubov (div. 1938); m. Gustav Diessl (film actor); studied at Kishinev Conservatory (1924–29) and at Hochschule für Musik in Berlin with Oskar Daniel. ❖ Made debut at Dresden Staatsoper as Mimi (1931) and sang there until 1936; appeared at Covent Garden (1936, 1947); sang in Berlin (1936–44) and Vienna (1946–49); appeared in 6 films (1933–41); specialized in the music of Richard Strauss, Mozart, Verdi, and Puccini and sang many Russian operas. ❖ See also A. Mingotti, *Maria Cebotari* (Salzburg, 1950); and *Women in World History.*

CECCARELLI, Daniela (1975—). *Italian Alpine skier.* Born Sept 25, 1975, in Frascati, Italy; m. Alessandro Colturi (skiing coach). ❖ Won a gold medal for super-G at Salt Lake City Olympics (2002); became a military policewoman (1999).

CECCHI D'AMICO, Suso (1914—). *Italian screenwriter.* Name variations: Suso D'Amico. Born July 21, 1914, in Rome, Italy; dau. of Emilio Cecchi (1884–1966, producer, writer, director); m. Fedele D'Amico (music critic). ❖ One of Italy's most distinguished screenwriters, launched career as a translator of plays; after WWII, collaborated on screenplay with father for *Mio figlio professore* (*Professor, My Son*); also collaborated with Luigi Zampa on *Vivere in pace* (*To Live in Peace,* 1946), which brought her a Silver Ribbon (Italy's equivalent to an Oscar); wrote the classic neo-realist *Ladri di biciclette* (*Bicycle Thief,* 1948), which won an American Academy Award for Best Foreign Film (1949); had many long-standing collaborations with great Italian directors of her day, including De Sica, Zefferelli and Antonioni; for Visconti, wrote *Bellissima* (1951) and *The Innocent* (1976), and collaborated with director Nikita Mikhalov on film *Dark Eyes* (1989); also wrote social satire and comedy, and worked in tv; other films include *Miracoloe a Milano* (*Miracle in Milan,* 1950), *I vinti* (*The Vanquished,* 1952), *Siamo donne* (*We the Women,* 1953), *Tempi Nostri* (*Anatomy of Love,* 1953), *Senso* (1954), *Le amiche* (*The Girl Friend,* 1955), *Le notti biache* (*White Nights,* 1957), *I magliari* (1959), *Rocco e i suoi* (*Rocco and His Brothers,* 1960), *Salvatore Giuliano* (1962), *Il Gattopardo* (*The Leopard,* 1963), *Taming of the Shrew* (adaptation, 1964), *Gli indifferenti* (*Time of Indifference,* 1964), *Vaghe stelle dell'Orsa* (*Sandra,* 1965), *Lo Straniero* (*The Stranger,* 1967), *Ludwig* (1974), *Cruppo di famiglia in un interno* (*Conversation Piece,* 1974) and *La Slovia* (*The Story,* 1986).

CECIL, Anne (1556–1589). *English poet.* Name variations: Anne Cecil de Vere; Countess of Oxford. Born 1556; died 1588; dau. of William Cecil, Baron Burghley, and Mildred Cooke Cecil (1526–1589, translator); sister of Robert Cecil, 1st Lord of Salisbury (1563–1612); Elizabeth Cecil (b. 1589); m. Edward de Vere, 17th earl of Oxford; children: 5, including Susan de Vere (d. around 1628), Elizabeth de Vere (1584–1626), Bridget de Vere (1584-c. 1631). ❖ May have written 4 epitaphs in sonnet form published as "Four Epitaphs made by the Countess of Oxenford, after the death of younge Sonne, the Lord Bulbecke" in John Soowthern's *Pandora, the Musyque of the Beautie of his Mistresse Diana* (1584), though sonnets may have been the work of Soowthern because of similarity of rhyme scheme and meter to his other poems. Sometimes identified with Shakespeare's Ophelia in *Hamlet.*

CECIL, Anne (d. 1637). *English aristocrat.* Born before 1620; died Dec 6, 1637; dau. of Catherine Howard (d. 1672) and William Cecil, 2nd earl of Salisbury; was 1st wife of Algernon Percy (1602–1668), 10th earl of Northumberland (r. 1632–1668); sister of Elizabeth Cecil (1619–1689); children: Elizabeth Percy (d. 1717, who m. Arthur Capell, 1st/21st earl of Essex); Anne Percy. ❖ Algernon's 2nd wife was Elizabeth Percy (d. 1704).

CECIL, Elizabeth (1619–1689). *Countess of Devonshire.* Name variations: Elizabeth Cavendish. Born in 1619; died Nov 19, 1689; interred in Westminster Abbey; dau. of Catherine Howard (d. 1672) and William Cecil, 2nd earl of Salisbury; sister of Anne Cecil (d. 1637); married William Cavendish, 3rd earl of Devonshire, Mar 4, 1638; children: Anne Cavendish (1648–1703); William Cavendish (b. 1640), 1st duke of Devonshire.

CECIL, Georgiana (1827–1899). *Countess of Salisbury.* Name variations: Georgiana Alderson; Countess of Salisbury; marchioness of Gascoyne-Cecil. Born Georgiana Alderson in 1827 in England; died Nov 20, 1899; dau. of Sir Edward Alderson; m. Robert Arthur Talbot Gascoyne-Cecil (1830–1903), 3rd marquess of Salisbury, July 11, 1857; children: Beatrix Maud Cecil (d. 1950); Gwendolyn Cecil (d. 1945); Fanny Georgina Mildred Cecil (d. 1867); James Gascoyne-Cecil, 4th marquess of

Salisbury (1861–1947), Rupert Cecil (1863–1936), Edgar Gascoyne-Cecil, 1st and last Viscount Cecil of Chelwood (1864–1958), Edward Gascoyne-Cecil (1867–1918); Hugh Gascoyne-Cecil, 1st and last baron Quickswood (1869–1956).

CECIL, Mildred Cooke (1526–1589). British translator. Name variations: Mildred Cooke; Lady Burghley. Born Mildred Cooke in 1526 in Essex, England; died in 1589; eldest dau. of Sir Anthony Cooke and Anne Fitzwilliam Cooke; sister of Anne Cooke Bacon (1528–1610), Elizabeth Russell (1528–1609), and Catherine Killigrew (c. 1530–1583); m. William Cecil, Baron Burghley, 1545; children: Anne Cecil (1556–1589, who married Edward de Vere, 17th earl of Oxford); Robert Cecil, 1st Lord of Salisbury (1563–1612); Elizabeth Cecil (b. 1589). ❖ Learned scholar, said to have translated part of the work of St. Chrysostom but refused to publish it.

CECIL, Sylvia (1906–1983). English actress and singer. Born Dec 27, 1906, in London, England; died Sept 11, 1983. ❖ Made stage debut in Notting Hill as Titania in *A Midsummer Night's Dream* with Clive Currie's company (1914); was a member of the D'Oyly Carte Opera Company (1918–21, 1930, 1936–37), appearing as Yum-Yum in *The Mikado*, Gianetta in *The Gondoliers*, Elsie Maynard in *The Yeomen of the Guard*, Josephine in *H.M.S. Pinafore*, Mabel in *The Pirates of Penzance*, and Patience and Princess Ida; also appeared in *Pacific 1860*, among others; during WWII, toured variety halls with Martyn Green.

CECILIA (c. 154–c. 207). Christian martyr, patron saint of music, and legendary inventor of the pipe organ. Born in Rome; conflicting dates of birth are around 154 or 177 or 207 CE; conflicting dates of death are around 177 or 200 or 230 CE; any of the 3 sets of dates yields a lifespan of 23 years; member of a noble Roman family. ❖ Legend has it that she converted her home into a church where some 400 converts were baptized; compelled to violate her vows of celibacy, was forced to marry the pagan Valerianus, a Roman noble; eventually converted husband and his brother Tiburtius to Christianity (when both refused to make a sacrifice to Jupiter, they were executed); was also given the choice of a sacrifice to the gods or death; chose death, but two attempts to execute her, by suffocation and beheading, failed before the penalty was carried out; canonized in 16th century. Many paintings show her playing the organ, the viola, pedal harp, clavichord, virginal spinet, and viol; composers from time of Henry Purcell in the 17th century composed works in her honor, and many academies and schools of music bore her name, though she was never identified as having been a composer; feast day is Nov 22. ❖ See also *Women in World History*.

CECILIA (c. 1059–1126). Abbess of the Holy Trinity at Caen. Name variations: Cecily. Born c. 1059 (some sources cite 1055) in Normandy, France; died July 30, 1126 (some sources cite 1127), in Holy Trinity Abbey, Caen, Normandy, France; buried in Holy Trinity Abbey, Caen; dau. of Matilda of Flanders (c. 1031–1083) and William I the Conqueror (c. 1027–1087), duke of Normandy (r. 1035–1087), king of England (r. 1066–1087); sister of Adela of Blois (1062–c. 1137). ❖ Elected abbess of the Holy Trinity Abbey at Caen (1112).

CECILIA (1469–1507). English princess. Name variations: Cecily Plantagenet. Born Cecilia, Mar 20, 1469; died Aug 24, 1507, at Quarr Abbey, Isle of Wight, England; 3rd dau. of Edward IV, king of England, and Elizabeth Woodville; betrothed to James IV, king of Scots, 1474; betrothed to Alexander Stewart, 1st duke of Albany, 1482; m. John Welles, 1st viscount Welles, in Dec 1487; m. Thomas Kymbe or Kyne, of the Isle of Wight, 1502; children: (1st m.) 2; (2nd m.) 2. ❖ Became a pawn in England's struggles with Scotland and the War of the Roses; to secure an alliance with Scotland (1474), was betrothed at age 5 to future James IV, son of James III, king of Scots; was 13 when betrothed to James IV's brother, Alexander Stewart, 1st duke of Albany (1482); when uncle Richard, duke of Gloucester, usurped throne as Richard III (1483), sought sanctuary with family in Westminster Abbey; surrendered to uncle (1484); was "taken into favor" by Richard's successor, Henry VII (1486). ❖ See also *Women in World History*.

CECILIA OF BADEN (1839–1891). Princess of Baden. Name variations: Cecily of Baden; Cecily Augusta Zahringen; after marriage became Olga Feodorovna. Born Cecilia Augusta, Sept 20, 1839; died April 12, 1891; dau. of Leopold, grand duke of Baden, and Sophia of Sweden (1801–1875); m. Michael Nicholaevitch (son of Nicholas I of Russia and Charlotte of Prussia), Aug 16, 1857; children: Nicholas (1859–1919); Anastasia Romanova (1860–1922, who m. Frederick Francis III, grand duke of Mecklenburg-Schwerin); Michael (1861–1929); George (1863–1919); Alexander (1866–1933); Sergius (1869–1918); Alexi (b. 1875).

CECILIA OF FRANCE (fl. 1100s). Princess of Antioch. Name variations: Cecilia Capet. Fl. in 1100s; dau. of Bertrada of Montfort (d. after 1117) and Philip I the Fair (1052–1108), king of France (r. 1060–1108); m. Tancred, prince of Antioch (r. 1111–1112).

CECILIA OF MECKLENBURG-SCHWERIN (1886–1954). Duchess of Mecklenburg. Name variations: Cecily von Mecklenburg-Schwerin. Born Sept 20, 1886, in Schwerin, Germany; died May 6, 1954, in Bad Kissingen, Germany; dau. of Anastasia Romanova (1860–1922), and Frederick Francis III, grand duke of Mecklenburg-Schwerin; m. William or Wilhelm also known as Frederick William (1882–1951), crown prince of Prussia, June 6, 1905; children: William Frederick (1906–1940, who m. Dorothea de Salviati); Prince Louis Ferdinand of Prussia (1907–1994, who m. Kira of Russia); Hubert (1909–1950, who m. Magdalene Pauline, Princess Reuss); Frederick (1911–1966, who m. Brigid, Lady Guinness); Alexandrine Irene (1915–1980), princess of Prussia; Cecilia (1917–1975), princess of Prussia (who m. Captain Clyde Kenneth Harris).

CECILIA RENATA OF AUSTRIA (1611–1644). Queen of Poland. Name variations: Cecilia Renata of Hungary; Cecilie Renate; Cecily Habsburg or Hapsburg; Cacilia Renata. Born July 16, 1611, in Graz; died Mar 24, 1644, in Vilna; dau. of Ferdinand II (1578–1637), king of Bohemia and Hungary and Holy Roman emperor (r. 1619–1637), and Maria Anna of Bavaria (1574–1616); sister of Ferdinand III (1637–1657); became 1st wife of Wladyslaw also known as Ladislas IV (1595–1648), king of Poland (r. 1632–1648), tsar of Russia (1610–1634), Sept 13, 1637; children: Casimir Sigismund (b. 1640).

CECILY. *Variant of Cecilia.*

CECILY NEVILLE (1415–1495). *See Neville, Cecily.*

CEDERNA, Camilla (1921–1997). Italian journalist and biographer. Born 1911 in Milan, Italy; died Nov 11, 1997; dau. of an industrial chemist; attended University of Milan. ❖ Major political journalist, who wrote for Italian newspapers, had an enormous impact (her book on president Giovanni Leone, *Giovanni Leone: La carriera du un presidente* [1978], helped ensure his resignation); during WWII, was briefly imprisoned during the siege of Milan (1943); became one of the founders of the Milanese weekly *Europeo* (1945), remaining on the editorial staff for 11 years; became editor and special Rome envoy of the magazine *L'Espresso* (1958), contributing a weekly variety column, "La milanese," followed by the socio-literary column, "Il lato debole" (The weak side); joined the staff of the weekly *Panorama* (1980); writings include *Noi siamo le signore* (1958), *Fellini 8½* (1963), *Maria Callas* (1968), *Il lato debone: Diario italiano* (1977), *Casa nostra: Viaggi nei misteri d'Italia* (1983) and *Il meglio di* (1987). ❖ See also (autobiography in Italian) *Il mondo di Camilla* (1980).

CEDERQVIST, Jane (1945—). Swedish swimmer. Born July 1, 1945. ❖ At Rome Olympics, won a silver medal in the 400-meter freestyle (1960).

CEDERSCHIÖLD, Charlotte (1944—). Swedish politician. Born Sept 28, 1944, in Gävle, Sweden. ❖ Member of the Moderate Party Executive (1990–95), the Stockholm county council (1979–88), and the Riksdag (1988–95); served as vice-chair of the European Union of Women (1993–99); as a member of the European People's Party (Christian Democrats) and European Democrats (EPP), elected to 4th and 5th European Parliament (1994–99, 1999–2004).

CELANO, Margie (1896–1918). *See Dean, Margie.*

CELESTE, Madame (1811–1882). French dancer, actress, and actress-manager. Name variations: Mme Céleste; Celeste-Elliott; Keppler-Elliot. Born Celeste Keppler in Paris, France, Aug 16, 1811; died in Paris, Feb 12, 1882; trained at the Paris Opéra; married a Mr. Elliott in America. ❖ At 15, had an offer from America and made debut at Bowery Theatre in New York City; returning to England (1831), appeared at Liverpool as Fenella in *Masaniello*, and also in London; in US once more (1834–37), was enormously popular; back in England, gave up dancing and now appeared as an actress, 1st at Drury Lane and then at Haymarket; joined Benjamin Webster in the management of the Adelphi (1844); took over sole management of the Lyceum until 1861, the 1st woman to perform "Harlequin" (1850); after a 3rd visit to US (1865–68), retired (1870). Not to be confused with Mlle Celeste (Williams) who toured the US, reaching California, and, it is thought, was not a trained ballet dancer.

CELLA, Karen (1952—). *See Magnussen, Karen.*

CELLI, Faith (1888–1942). English actress. Name variations: Lady Elibank. Born Nov 27, 1888, in Kensington, England; died Dec 16 (some sources cite Dec 27), 1942, in Ascot, England; m. Hon. Arthur Murray. ❖ Made stage debut at the Duke of York as Tootles in *Peter Pan* (1907); other plays include *Priscilla Runs Away, The Man from Mexico, Very Much Married, The Little Café, The Blue Lagoon, Threads, Mixed Doubles, Caroline, Brother Alfred* and *Pygmalion;* came to prominence as Margaret in *Dear Brutus* (1917); films include *The Bump.*

CELLIER, Elizabeth (fl. 1679). British midwife and tract writer. Born Elizabeth Dormer; flourished around 1679; m. Peter Cellier (Frenchman). ❖ Noted London midwife, converted to Catholicism; was arrested for participating in Catholic conspiracy, dubbed the "Meal-Tub Plot" (1679); released after accuser, Thomas Dangerfield, was discredited; published *Malice Defeated* (1680) and other tracts, including *The Matchless Picaro;* also wrote defense of midwives, *To Dr — an answer to his Queries Concerning the Colledge of Midwives* (1688).

CELY, Margery (fl. late 15th c.). British letter writer. Married George Cely. ❖ Cely Papers, the largest archive of a medieval English merchant firm, include her letters to her husband and details of the wool-trading business. ❖ See also Alison Hanham (ed.), *The Cely Letters, 1472–1488* (Oxford U. Press, 1975).

CENCI, Beatrice (1577–1599). See *Beatrice of Cenci.*

CENDRITH (fl. 680s). Queen of Wessex. Name variations: Centhryth; Centhryth of Wessex. Flourished in the 680s; m. Cedwalla, also spelled Caedwalla (c. 659–689), king of Wessex (r. 685–688). ❖ Rounded up the entire pagan population of the Isle of Wight and, with a squadron of armed evangelists, baptized them in 1 day; husband, who was baptized as Peter, died in Rome (689).

CENTENO, Yvette (1940—). Portuguese poet and novelist. Name variations: Yvette Kace Centeno. Born 1940 in Lisbon, Portugal; degree in German philology, University of Lisbon. ❖ Worked as professor at New University in Lisbon; works of poetry include *Opus I* (1966), *Poemas Fracturados* (1967), *Sinais* (1977), *Perto da Terra* (1984), and *Entre Silêncios* (1997); novels include *Quem Se Eu Gritar* (1965), *As Palavras, Que Pena* (1972), *As Muralhas* (1986) and *Três Histórias de Amor* (1994); also wrote several works of criticism including *Literatura e Alquimia* (1987), *Fernando Pessoa: Os Trezentos e Outros Estudos* (1988), and *Hermetismo e Utopia* (1995). Received Jacinto do Prado Coelho Prize (1984) and Poesia da Revista Mulheres Prize (1984).

CENTHRYTH (fl. 680s). See *Cendrith.*

CENTLIVRE, Susanna (c. 1669–1723). British playwright. Name variations: Susan Centlivre; Susanna Carroll; (pseudonym) R.M. Born Susan Freeman around 1669 (some sources cite 1667), probably in Whaplode, England; died Dec 1, 1723, in London; probably dau. of William and Anne Freeman; possibly m. to "nephew of Sir Stephen Fox," date unknown; widowed; m. an army officer named Carroll, who was killed in a duel 18 months later; m. Joseph Centlivre, April 23, 1707. ❖ The "celebrated Mrs. Centlivre" has been acclaimed as one of the best comic playwrights of her age; wrote 19 plays of which 4 became stock pieces: *The Gamester* (1705), *The Busy Body* (1709), *The Wonder: A Woman Keeps a Secret* (1714) and *A Bold Stroke for a Wife* (1718), comedies that continued to be staged in England and US throughout 18th and 19th centuries; was a highly acclaimed writer of the comedy of intrigue, and her plays follow the trends of an age that had moved from bawdy, sexual innuendo to a more decorous approach to love and marriage; other plays include *The Perjur'd Husband, or, The Adventures of Venice* (1700), *The Stolen Heiress, or, The Salamanca Doctor Outplotted* (1702), *Love's Contrivance, or, Le Médecin Malgré Lui* (1703), *The Bassett Table* (1705), *The Platonick Lady* (1706), *A Bickerstaff's Burying: or, Work for the Upholders* (1710), *Marplot: or, The 2nd Part of The Busy Body* (1710), *A Gotham Election* (1715), *A Wife Well Managed* (1715) and *The Cruel Gift: or The Royal Resentment* (1716). ❖ See also F.P. Lock, *Susanna Centlivre* (Twayne, 1979); John Wilson Bowyer, *The Celebrated Mrs. Centlivre* (Duke U. Press, 1952); and *Women in World History.*

CEO, Maria do (1658–1753). See *Maria do Céu.*

CEO, Violante do (1601–1693). See *Violante do Céu.*

CEPLAK, Jolanda (1976—). Slovenian runner. Name variations: Jolanda Steblovnik. Born Sept 12, 1976, in Celje, Slovenia. ❖ Won 4 Grand Prix and 4 Super Grand Prix events (2001–04); at World Indoor championship, placed 2nd for 800 meters (2004); won a bronze medal for 800

meters at Athens Olympics (2004). Named Female Athlete of the Year in Slovenia (2002–2003).

CERDEIRA MORTERERO, Carmen (1958—). Spanish lawyer and politician. Born Sept 27, 1958, in Ceuta, Spain. ❖ Member of the Parliamentary Assemblies of the Council of Europe and of the WEU (1990–93); as a European Socialist, elected to 5th European Parliament (1999–2004).

CERETA, Laura, of Brescia (1469–1499). Italian scholar. Born Laura Cereta in 1469, in Brescia, Italy; died in 1499 and buried at Church of San Domenico in Brescia; dau. of Veronica di Leno and Silvestro Cereta (jurisprudent and humanist); eldest of six children; educated for 2 years at a convent school and then at home by her father; m. Pietro Serina, 1484 (died 18 months later). ❖ From an early age, was involved in public argumentation, orations and debates, and argued that women should be educated; had a great love of learning and a desire to seek the truth; taught philosophy for 7 years at University of Padua; on death of husband, sought solace in religion; wrote 84 pieces comprised mostly of letters, orations, and essays, including one parody of funeral orations.

CERMAKOVA, Jirina (1944—). Czech field-hockey player. Born Nov 17, 1944. ❖ At Moscow Olympics, won a silver medal in team competition (1980).

CERMÍNOVÁ, Marie (1902–1980). See *Toyen.*

ČERNÍNOVÁ Z HARASOVA, Zuzana (1601–1654). Czech letter writer. Name variations: Zuzana Cerninova z Harasova; Zuzana Cerninova z Harasova. Born 1601 in Bohemia; died 1654; m. Jan Černín z Chudenic (noble); children: daughters Eliska and Eva Polyxena married army officers; sons Humprecht and Herman Cernin z Chudenic played significant roles in Bohemia in the counterreformation. ❖ Letters, published frequently since 1869, describe experiences during Thirty Years War (1618–48) and give details about life of a noblewoman managing estates, enduring taxation, dealing with plundering soldiers.

CERRI, Cecilie (1872–1931). Italian ballet dancer. Born Feb 11, 1872, in Turin, Italy; died Jan 17, 1931, in Vienna, Austria. ❖ When young, appeared on stage at Teatro Reggio in Turin; performed in Milan and Florence, where she danced in Manzotti's *Rolla;* worked at Alhambra Theatre in London under Carlo Coppi, for whom she danced principal parts in his *Ali Baba* (1894), *Barbe Bleu* (1895), *Titania* (1895) and *Beauty and the Beast* (1898); performed at Teatro alla Scala in Milan, most notably in Pratesi's *Bracco e Gambrinus* (1904); joined Vienna's Court Opera Ballet where she danced in numerous ballets by Josef Hassreiter, then served as teacher (1907–19).

CERRITO, Fanny (1817–1909). Italian ballerina and choreographer. Name variations: Francesca Cerrito; Fanny St. Léon. Born Francesca Cerrito in Naples, Italy, in May 11, 1817; died May 6, 1909, in Paris; dau. of modest Neapolitans; studied at ballet school of Royal Theaters of Naples; studied with Carlo Blasis; m. dancer and choreographer Arthur Saint-Léon, in April 17, 1845; children: (with Marqués de Bedmar, a Spanish noble) Matilde (b. 1853). ❖ Considered one of the finest ballerina's of the Italian Romantic school, made debut dancing a *pas de deux* in *L'Oroscopo* (1832); subsequently toured Italy and Austria, before becoming prima ballerina at La Scala in Milan; debuted in London (184) to great success; after excelling in Perrot's *Ondine,* in which she also presented some of her own choreography, was asked to dance the *pas de deux* with Fanny Elssler at a Royal Command performance (1843), which led to the sensational *pas de quatre* with Maria Taglioni, Carlotta Grisi, and Lucille Grahn (1844); danced other notable roles in Perrot's ballets, including a goddess in *Le Jugement de Pâris* (1846), Air in *Les Eléments* (1847), and Spring in *Les Quatre Saisons* (1848); made a successful debut at Paris Opera, dancing *La Fille de Marbre* (1847); remained at the Opera, where she starred and also choreographed; retired from dancing (1857), but remained active in the ballet world for another half century. ❖ See also *Women in World History.*

CERVERA, Luisa (1964—). Peruvian volleyball player. Born June 4, 1964, in Peru. ❖ At Seoul Olympics, won a silver medal in team competition (1988).

CÉSAR, Ana Cristina (1952–1983). Brazilian poet and literary critic. Name variations: Ana Cristina Cesar. Born June 2, 1952, in Rio de Janeiro, Brazil; committed suicide, Oct 29, 1983, in Rio de Janeiro. ❖ Studied Theory and Practice of Literary Translation at University of Essex in England; returned to Brazil to work as translator; belonged to 1960s group of poets called "mimeograph generation"; wrote 4 poetical pamphlets published in *A teus pés* (1982); also wrote *Dispersos e esparsos* (1985), *Escritos da Inglaterra* (1988) and *Critica e Tradução* (1999).

CESARI, Welleda (1920—). Italian fencer. Born Feb 15, 1920, in Italy. ❖ At Rome Olympics, won a bronze medal in team foil (1960).

CESPEDES, Alba de (1911–1997). *See De Cespedes, Alba.*

CÉU, Maria do (1658–1753). *See Maria do Céu.*

CEU, Violante do (1601–1693). *See Violante do Céu.*

CEZELLI, Constance de (d. 1617). *See Constance de Cezelli.*

CHA JAE-KYUNG (1971—). Korean handball player. Born Nov 1, 1971, in South Korea. ❖ At Barcelona Olympics, won a gold medal in team competition (1992).

CHA, Theresa Hak Kyung (1951–1982). Korean-American performance artist and essayist. Name variations: Theresa Cha. Born Cha Hak Kyung, Mar 4, 1951, in Pusan, Korea; murdered by a stranger, Nov 5, 1982, age 31, in New York, NY; dau. of Cha Hyung Sang and Huo Hyung Soon (both teachers); attended University of San Francisco; University of California at Berkeley, BA in comparative literature, 1973, BA in art, 1975, MFA in art, 1977; also attended Centre d'Etudes Americaine du Cinema in Paris, 1976. ❖ Performance art pieces include *Barren Cave Mute* (1974), *A Secret Spill* (1974), *A Blé Wall* (1975), *Aveugle Voix* (1975), *Life Mixing* (1975), *Vampyr* (1976), and *Reveille Dans La Brume* (1977); also published mail art series *Audience Distant Relatives* (1978), edited collection of essays *Apparatus? Cinematographic Apparatus: Selected Writings* (1980), and wrote the influential *Dictée* (1982); granted an NEA fellowship (1981) to shoot black-and-white film in Korea. Received Stuart McKenna Nelson Award for the Photographic Medium (1977).

CHABI (fl. 13th c.). Empress of China. Fl. in 13th century; empress-consort and 2nd wife of Kublai Khan (1215–1294, also called Shih-tsu, Mongol founder of China's Yüan dynasty who was one of the most famous rulers of all time). ❖ Khan's 4 wives were: Telegun, Chabi, Tarakhan, and Bayaghuchun; he had at least 12 sons with his wives (Dorji, Chen-chin, Manggala, Nomukhan, Khoridai, Hugechi, A'urugchi, Ayachi, Kokochu, Khudlugh Temur, Toghon, Temechi) and at least 2 daughters (Miao-yen, Hu-tu-lu Chieh-li-mi-shih).

CHABOT, Maria (1913–2001). American patron of Native American art. Born Sept 1913 in San Antonio, Texas; died July 9, 2001, in Albuquerque, New Mexico; studied Spanish and archaeology in Mexico City; married Dana K. Bailey, 1961 (div. 1961). ❖ Moved to Santa Fe, New Mexico (1931); during depression, worked for Works Progress Administration, photographing and documenting Native American and Spanish Colonial arts and crafts; ran a ranch for Mary Cabot Wheelwright for 20 years; was named head of the Indian advocacy group (1936) and began the popular Indian markets on the Plaza in Santa Fe; visited Indian villages to encourage women, especially potters, to participate, including Maria Martinez; was a great friend of Georgia O'Keeffe.

CHABRILLAN, Céleste de (1824–1909). French dancer, courtesan, and writer. Name variations: Comtesse de Moreton de Chabrillan; Celeste or Céleste Mogador, Mme Mogador, La Mogador. Born Céleste Vénard in Paris, France, Dec 27, 1824; died in 1909; dau. of working-class parents; m. Lionel, Comte de Chabrillan, c. 1853 (who had made his fortune in gold fields of Australia in 1852). ❖ Parisian-born courtesan whose 5 volumes of memoirs, *Adieux au Monde* (Goodbye World, 1853–54), scandalized France; also wrote *Les Voleurs d'Or* (1857, later trans. as *The Gold Robbers*), *Sapho* (1858) and *Miss Pewel* (1859). ❖ See also Charlotte Haldane, *Daughter of Paris: The Life Story of Céleste Mogador* (1961); and *Women in World History.*

CHACE, Elizabeth Buffum (1806–1899). American abolitionist and suffragist. Born Elizabeth Buffum, Dec 9, 1806, in Providence, Rhode Island; died Dec 12, 1899, in Central Falls, Rhode Island; dau. of Arnold Buffum (abolitionist) and Rebecca (Gould) Buffum; sister of Sarah Buffum Borden and Rebecca Buffum Spring (who m. Marcus Spring); m. Samuel Buffington Chace (Quaker), June 1828; children: several, including Arnold C. Buffum (chancellor of Brown University) and Elizabeth Buffum (writer known as Lillie Buffum Wyman). ❖ Helped form the Fall River Female Anti-Slavery Society in Rhode Island (1835) and served as vice president; an important antislavery organizer, her home became a way station on the Underground Railroad; served as a founder of National Free Religious Association in Boston, MA (1867), of which

she became vice president (1881); served as vice president of American Anti-Slavery Society (1865–70); with Paulina Wright Davis, organized a Rhode Island association of New England Woman Suffrage Association and served as president (1870–1899); supported American Woman Suffrage Association (1869); worked (unsuccessfully) for woman suffrage amendment in RI and pushed for admission of women to Brown University; published *Anti-Slavery Reminiscences* (1891); was also active in prison reform. ❖ See also Lillie B.C. Wyman and Arthur C. Wyman, *Elizabeth Buffum Chace* (2 vols., 1914).

CHACE, Marian (1896–1970). American dance therapist. Born Marian Chace, Oct 31, 1896, in Providence, Rhode Island; died July 20, 1970, in Washington, DC; dau. of Daniel Champlain Chace (editor and journalism teacher) and Harriet Edgaretta (Northrup) Chace; m. Lester Shafer (dancer), July 29, 1924 (div. 1938); children: Marian Lester Shafer (b. 1925). ❖ Pioneer who was the 1st to use dance as therapy for psychiatric patients in a hospital, began career performing with Denishawn School dancers at NYC concerts (1929, 1930); opened branch of Denishawn School in Washington, DC (1930), serving as director (1930–44), teaching creative dance and dance as therapy for psychiatric patients; as a volunteer at Washington's Saint Elizabeths [*sic*] psychiatric hospital, developed and directed "dance for communication" program (1942–44); worked full-time at Saint Elizabeths, helping patients write and produce theatrical works, such as *Cry for Humanity* and *Hotel Saint Elizabeth*, and training other therapists (1944–66); was dance therapist and head of psychodrama program at Chestnut Lodge psychiatric hospital in Rockville, MD (1946–70); joined faculty of Turtle Bay Music School in NYC (1955), teaching summer dance therapy training workshops (1957–70); was instrumental in founding American Dance Therapy Association, becoming 1st director (1965). Received Oveta Culp Hobby Award (1955) and US Department of Health, Education, and Welfare award (1956).

CHACEL, Rosa (1898–1994). Spanish writer. Name variations: Rosa Clotilde Cecilia María del Carmen Chacel Arimón. Born in Valladolid, northcentral Spain, June 3, 1898; died in Madrid, Aug 3, 1994; dau. of Francisco Chacel Barbero and Rosa Cruz Arimón Pacheco (teacher); studied art in Madrid and Rome; m. Timoteo Pérez Rubio (painter), April 1922 (died 1977); children: Carlos (b. 1930). ❖ Published 1st book, *Estación, ida y vuelta* (*Season of Departure and Return,* 1930); when the Spanish Civil War began, supported the Republic, working in a hospital, and also published a book of sonnets, *A la orilla de un pozo;* left Spain for refuge in France (1936); with outbreak of WWII, moved to Buenos Aires (1940), where her works began to attract critical attention; moved with family to Rio de Janeiro (1964); chief works include novels *Teresa* (1941), *Memorias de Leticia Valle* (*Memoirs of Leticia Valle,* 1946), *Ofrenda a una virgen loca* (1960), *La sinrazón* (1960), *Barrio de Maravillas* (1976), and a compilation of literary criticism, *Los títulos* (1981). Received National Prize for Spanish Letters (1987). ❖ See also autobiographical works: *Desde el amanecer* (1972) and *Alcancía* (1982); and *Women in World History.*

CHACHKOVA, Lioubov (1977—). Russian volleyball player. Name variations: Liubov Shashkova; Lioubov Sokolova; Lyubov Chachkova-Sokolova. Born Dec 4, 1977, in Moscow, Russia. ❖ Made national team debut (1996); won European team championship (1997, 1999, 2001) and World Grand Prix (1997, 1999); placed 3rd at World championships (1998); won a team silver medal at Sydney Olympics (2000) and a team silver at Athens Olympics (2004).

CHACÓN, Dulce (1954–2003). Spanish novelist and poet. Name variations: Dulce Chacon; Dulce Chacón Gutiérrez. Born June 3, 1954, in Zafra, Spain; died Dec 3, 2003; one of twin girls of the Francoite mayor of Zafra, who was a poet; married; children: 2. ❖ Published the 1st of 5 books of poetry (1992); wrote a trilogy, which included *Algún Que No Mate* (Some Love That Doesn't Kill, 1996); published *Cielos de Barro* (Mud Skies, 2000), which won the Azorin Prize; came to prominence with *La Voz Dormida* (The Sleeping Voice, 2002), a novel based on real events, which tells of the women in the prisons of Spain's dictator, Francisco Franco; also wrote *Matadora* (1999), the biography of bullfighter Cristina Sánchez.

CHACÓN NARDI, Rafaela (1926–2001). Cuban poet and historian. Name variations: Rafaela Chacon Nardi. Born 1926; died Mar 11, 2001, in Havana, Cuba; attended University of Havana. ❖ Poetry published in *Viaje al sueño* (1948, 1957) and *De rocío y de humo* (1965); also wrote on art, history and education; works translated into several languages.

CHADD, Elizabeth (1836–1900). *See Pulman, Elizabeth.*

CHADIMOVA, Alena (1931—). Czech gymnast. Born Nov 22, 1931. ❖ At Helsinki Olympics, won a bronze medal in team all-around (1952).

CHADWICK, Ada (1867–1965). *See Pilgrim, Ada.*

CHADWICK, Cassie L. (1859–1907). Canadian swindler. Name variations: Constance Cassandra Chadwick; alias Lydia de Vere. Born Elizabeth Bigley in Strathroy, Ontario, Canada, 1859; died in prison in 1907; dau. of an Ontario railway worker; married Dr. Leroy Chadwick. ❖ Defrauded rich Americans and Ohio banks out of an estimated $2 million. ❖ See also *Women in World History.*

CHADWICK, Florence (1918–1995). American swimmer. Born Florence May Chadwick, Nov 9, 1918, in San Diego, California; died Mar 15, 1995, in San Diego; attended San Diego State College, Southwestern University of Law at Los Angeles, and Balboa Law School, San Diego. ❖ At 13, won 2nd place at National backstroke championship; made 1st swim of the English Channel, from France to England, in 13:20, breaking 1926 record of Gertrude Ederle (1950); major swims include Cape Gris-Nez, France, to Dover, England (1950); English Channel from England to France (1951, 1953); English Channel from England to France in 13:55, 11 minutes faster than existing men's record (1955); Catalina to California coast in 13:47, breaking 1927 record of George Young (1952); Straits of Gibraltar, Dardanelles, Bosporus (1953); served as president of San Diego Stadium Authority and member of the board of directors San Diego Hall of Champions. Elected to International Swimming Hall of Fame (1970). ❖ See also *Women in World History.*

CHADWICK, Helen (1953–1996). English artist. Born May 18, 1953, in Croydon, Surrey, London, England; died suddenly at 42 of heart failure, Mar 15, 1996, in England; attended Brighton Polytechnic, 1976–77, and Chelsea School of Art, 1976–77; m. David Notarius. ❖ One of modern art's most provocative and inspirational figures and one of the most important British artists of late 1980s–90s, worked as lecturer at Chelsea School of Art and at Royal College; a feminist, addressed the roles and images of women in society in many works such as *In the Kitchen* (1977); worked in many disciplines, including mixed media installation and performance art, but used photography as a primary tool; held many acclaimed shows, including exhibitions at ICA (1986) and Serpentine (1994); was one of 1st women to be short-listed for the Turner Prize (1987). Work includes *Ego Geometria Sum* (1983), *Ecce* (1987), *Viral Landscapes* (1988–89), *Meat Abstracts* (1989), *Loop My Loop* (1989), *Self Portrait* (1991), *Piss Flowers* (1991–92), *Cacao* (1994) and *Stilled Lives* (1993).

CHADWICK, Helene (1897–1940). American silent-film actress. Born Nov 25, 1897, in Chadwick, NY; died of injuries from a fall, Sept 4, 1940, in Los Angeles, California; m. William A. Wellman (director, div.). ❖ Made over 50 films, including *Dangerous Curve Ahead, Reno, Why Men Leave Home, Dancing Days, Stolen Pleasures* and *The Rose of Kildare.*

CHAFFEE, Suzy (1946—). American skier. Name variations: Suzy Chapstick (from a popular advertising campaign she endorsed). Born Nov 29, 1946, in Rutland, Vermont. ❖ Influential in the creation of freestyle skiing, was known as the "Mother of the Hotdog"; ranked #1 as US female skier (1967); captained US Olympic ski team at Grenoble (1968); began competing in freestyle, skiing head-to-head with men; was World freestyle champion (1971–73); when International Freestyle Association was formed (1973), saw her concepts become central to the sport; as a member of US Olympic Committee, pushed for acceptance of freestyle skiing.

CHAFIK, Doria (1908–1975). *See Shafik, Doria.*

CHA HAK KYUNG (1951–1982). *See Cha, Theresa.*

CHAI, Ling (1966—). Chinese dissident, human-rights activist and entrepreneur. Born 1966 in China; dau. of military doctors; graduated from Beijing University with a degree in child psychology, 1987; Princeton University, MA; Harvard University, MBA; m. Feng Congde (another leader of the protests, div.); m. Robert A. Maginn Jr. ❖ As a graduate student in child psychology, was elected chief commander of the student protesters in Tiananmen Square, because of her leadership skills and electrifying speeches (1989); called the "Goddess of Democracy," initiated and led the hunger strike during the protests; fled the square on June 4, just before the tanks rolled in; one of the most wanted women in China, hid out for 10 months before escaping to Hong Kong in a nailed-shut crate; came to US by way of France (1990); became an internet entrepreneur in Boston.

CHAIBI, Aïcha. Tunisian novelist. Name variations: Aicha Chaibi. Born in Tunisia. ❖ Wrote *Rachid* (1975), which celebrates Tunisian cultural identity and criticizes European values.

CHAIKINA, Liza (d. 1941). Russian fighter. Name variations: Elizaveta Chaikina; Lisa Chaikina. Died Nov 1941. ❖ A partisan during WWII and secretary of the Young Communist League, was shot by the Nazis; became a hero in Soviet Russia, where a street was named in her honor.

CHAIN, Anne Beloff (1921–1991). *See Beloff-Chain, Anne.*

CHALAMOVA, Yelena (1982—). *See Shalamova, Elena.*

CHALANOZITIS, Angélique (1901–1983). *See Arvanitaki, Angélique.*

CHALKER, Lynda (1942—). English politician. Name variations: Lynda Chalker of Wallasey, Baroness Chalker of Wallasey, Lynda Bates. Born Lynda Bates, April 29, 1942, in England; attended University of Heidelberg, London University, and Central London Polytechnic; m. Eric Chalker, 1967 (div. 1973); m. Clive Landa, 1981. ❖ Conservative politician who rose to a high position in foreign and commonwealth affairs during the Thatcher era, worked in market research before serving in Parliament as an MP for Wallasey (1974–92); served as opposition speaker on social services during Labour administration (1976–79); held under-secretary of state positions at Department of Health and Social Security (1979–82) and Department of Transport (1983–86); promoted to minister of State for Department of Transport (1983–86); moved to Foreign and Commonwealth Office (1986) and was appointed minister for Overseas Development (1989–97); controlled world's 5th largest foreign-aid budget and earned popularity in developing world; had longest consecutive service of any woman minister and was one of only 4 ministers to serve through Conservative Party's longest stretch of power since 1820s; granted life peerage and title Baroness Chalker of Wallasey (1992); employed expertise and connections to serve as Independent Adviser on Africa and Development with World Bank and numerous other business concerns in UK and Southern Africa since leaving office (1997), including Group Five, Ashanti Goldfields and Freeplay Energy Group.

CHALLANS, Mary (1905–1983). *See Renault, Mary.*

CHALLINOR, Hannah (b. 1623). *See Woolley, Hannah.*

CHALLONER, Dorothy (1893–1972). *See Dalton, Dorothy.*

CHALMERS, Angela (1963—). Canadian runner. Born Sept 1963 in Manitoba, Canada; dau. of a Scottish father and Sioux mother. ❖ At Commonwealth Games (1990), was the 1st woman in the history of the Games to win both the 1,500- and 3,000-meter races; at Barcelona Olympics, won a bronze medal in 3,000 meters (1992); was the flag-bearer at the Commonwealth Games (1994); won a gold medal at Grand Prix for 1,500 meters (1994). Received National Aboriginal Achievement Award in Sports (1995)

CHALPAIDA (c. 654–c. 714). *See Alphaida.*

CHAMBEFORT, Marie (fl. 1850—). French daguerreotype photographer. Fl. 1850 in France. ❖ Early itinerant daguerreotype photographer, worked in Département de Saône-et-Loire in France (1850s); best known for her portraits, including *Stephanie Poyet, agée de 7 ans.*

CHAMBERLAIN, Ann Marie (1935—). New Zealand runner. Born Dec 5, 1935. ❖ At Tokyo Olympics, won a bronze medal in the 800 meters (1964).

CHAMBERLAIN, Lindy (1948—). Australian accused of murder. Name variations: Lindy Chamberlain Creighton or Chamberlain-Creighton. Born Alice Lynne Murchinson, Mar 4, 1948, in Whakatane, on the North Island of New Zealand; moved to Victoria, Australia, with family as a baby; attended Launceston Technical College; m. Michael Leigh Chamberlain (cleric), Nov 18, 1969 (div. June 1991); m. Rick Creighton (publisher), Dec 20, 1992; children: (1st m.) Aidan Leigh (b. 1973), Reagan Michael (b. 1976), Azaria Chantel (b. June 11, 1980), Kahlia Shonell (b. Nov 17, 1982, in Darwin Hospital while mother was in the custody of Darwin Prison). ❖ During a family camping trip to Ayers Rock in the Northern Territory of Australia, reported seeing her 9-week-old baby taken by a dingo, a wild Australian dog (Aug 17, 1980); accused of murdering her child, was vilified in the press; with the backing of scientific experts, was convicted of murder and husband named as an accessory; sentenced to life with hard labor; when the child's jacket was found (Feb 1986), was exonerated and released. ❖ See also autobiography *Through My Eyes* (Heinemann, 1990); John Bryson *Evil Angels;* (film) *A Cry in the Dark* (1988), starring Meryl Streep.

CHAMBERS, Anne Cox (1919—). American diplomat. Name variations: Anne Cox. Born Anne Cox, Dec 1, 1919, in Dayton, Ohio; dau. of Margaretta P. (Blair) Cox and James M. Cox (newspaper owner, 3-term governor of Ohio and 1920 Democratic nominee for president, 1870–1957); sister of Barbara Cox Anthony; attended Finch College; m. Robert W. Chambers, Sept 12, 1956; children: James C. Kennedy, Kathy Rayner, and Margaretta (Retta) Taylor. ❖ Grand dame of Atlanta business, inherited newspaper fortune, Cox Communications, along with sister; served as ambassador to Belgium under President Jimmy Carter (1977–81); served as director of the Bank of the South (1977–82) and of Coca-Cola (1981–91). Cox Enterprises was an early investor in the Women's United Soccer Association (WUSA).

CHAMBERS, Charlotte (d. 1821). American diarist. Died in 1821. ❖ Wrote *The Memoir of Charlotte Chambers* (1856), documenting the work of the Bible Society and her life as member of a religious community in Cincinnati, OH (1796–1821).

CHAMBERS, Dorothea Lambert (1878–1960). British tennis player. Name variations: Dorothea Katharine Chambers; Dorothea Lambert-Chambers; Mrs. Robert Lambert Chambers; Dorothea Katherine Douglass. Born Dorothea Katharine Douglass at Ealing, Middlesex, England, Sept 1878; died Jan 1960; m. Robert Lambert Chambers, 1907. ❖ Possibly the most outstanding woman tennis player before WWI, won singles at Wimbledon (1903–04, 1906, 1910–11, 1913–14); was All-England badminton doubles champion (1903) and mixed champion (1904); won a gold medal in singles tennis in London Olympics (1908). ❖ See also *Women in World History.*

CHAMBERS, Norah (1905–1989). Scottish musician and prisoner of war. Born Margaret Constance Norah Hope, April 26, 1905, in Singapore; died June 18, 1989, on Jersey, Channel Islands, England; dau. of James Laidlaw Hope (mechanical engineer) and Margaret Annie Ogilvie (Mitchell) Hope; m. John Lawrence Chambers (civil engineer), Mar 1, 1930; children: Sally Hope (b. 1933). ❖ Studied violin, piano and chamber music at Royal Academy of Music, London, where she played in orchestra under Sir Henry Wood; lived on and off in Malaya, 1st with parents, and later with husband; when Japanese invaded Malaya, trekked through the jungle and arrived in Singapore as evacuation was in progress (1941); evacuated daughter to Perth; was aboard rescue vessel *Vyner Brooke,* which was bombed and sunk; was separated from husband and interned in Japanese prison camp; in attempt to inspire fellow prison-camp internees with will to survive the south Sumatran camps, conceived idea of forming a vocal orchestra to perform orchestral works (1943); with Margaret Dryburgh, worked from memory to transcribe and arrange over 30 miniature classics for 4-part vocal harmonies; after war, returned to Malaya; retired to Jersey in Channel Islands (1952); composed for and directed the choir of St. Mark's Church in St. Helier. Her work in the camp inspired movie *Paradise Road.* ❖ See also *Women in World History.*

CHAMBLIT, Rebekah (d. 1733). American murderer. Executed Sept 27, 1733, in Massachusetts. ❖ Convicted of infanticide, was forced to write *Dying Warning and Advice of Rebekah Chamblit* before execution. The work expresses the desperation of a young woman faced with the birth of illegitimate child.

CHAMBRUN, Comtesse de or Josée de (c. 1911—). See Laval, Josée.

CHAMIE, Tatiana (d. 1953). Russian ballet dancer. Born in Odessa, Russia; died Nov 18, 1953. ❖ Danced with Diaghilev Ballet Russe (early 1920s), where she created roles in Bronislava Nijinska's *Les Biches* (1924), Balanchine's *The Triumph of Neptune* (1926), and Leonid Massine's *Cimarosiana* (1926); danced for brief period with Russian Opera Ballet after Diaghilev's death (1929), and Les Ballets de Boris Kniaseff (c. 1931); earned acclaim for her performances in works by Massine, including *Contes Russes, Beach, Vienna–1814, Rouge et Noir* and *Bacchanale,* all probably performed with Ballet Russe de Monte Carlo; choreographed for ballet Russe de Monte Carlo after retiring from the stage (1943); works of choreography include *Le Petite Sirène* (1938), *Birthday* (1949), *Prima Ballerina* (1950) and *Chez Maxime* (1951).

CHAMINADE, Cécile (1857–1944). French composer and pianist. Pronunciation: SHAH-mee-nod. Born Cécile Louise Stéphanie Chaminade in Paris, France, Aug 8, 1857; died in Monte Carlo, Monaco, April 13, 1944 (some sources cite the 18th); dau. of

Hippolyte Chaminade (manager of a British insurance firm in Paris who played the violin) and a mother who was an amateur pianist; m. Louis-Mathieu Carbonel (music publisher), Aug 29, 1901. ❖ The 1st professional woman composer, made professional debut at Salle Pleyel in Paris (1877); performed her own piano solos and songs at the keyboard at Le Vésinet (1878), introducing a style that would henceforth mark her career; was much in demand as a recitalist; composed an *opéra-comique, La Sévillane* (1st performed in 1882); presented public performance of her 1st full-scale symphonic work, Suite for Orchestra, Op. 20, before National Society of Music in Paris (1881); to help support family, began to focus primarily on more commercial solo piano pieces and songs, which would become her musical legacy; works include a full-length ballet *Callirhoë* (premiered in Marseille, 1888), choral symphony *Les Amazones* (premiered in Antwerp, 1888), and the widely performed *Concertstück for Piano and Orchestra;* became a major star on international touring circuit; was extremely well-received in Great Britain and received Jubilee Medal (1897); also toured France, Belgium, Switzerland, Germany, Austria-Hungary, and less-traveled places including Romania, Bulgaria, Serbia, Greece and Turkey; gave "Chaminade Festivals" (1890s); had stellar reputation in US where by 1898 at least 4 Chaminade Clubs had been founded; was the 1st female composer to receive Chevalier of Legion of Honor from French government (1913); during WWI, ministered to wounded soldiers in Les Sablettes; became recluse at villa near Toloun; her signature piece, *Pas des écharpes,* Op. 37 (*Scarf Dance*), had sold well over 5-million copies by time of her death; was later rescued from obscurity by new recordings of her work by James Galway, Peter Jacobs and Eric Parkin, among others. ❖ See also Laura Kerr, *Scarf Dance: The Story of Cecile Chaminade* (Abelard, 1953); and *Women in World History.*

CHAMORRO, Violeta (1929—). Nicaraguan president. Born Violeta Barrios in Rivas, Nicaragua, Oct 18, 1929; dau. of Carlos Barrios and Amelia (Sacasa) Barrios, members of the landowning elite; m. Pedro Joaquin Chamorro Cardenal (revolutionary), 1950; children: Pedro Joaquin ("Quinto"); Carlos Fernando; Claudia Chamorro; Cristiana Chamorro. ❖ Nicaraguan political leader, president of Nicaragua (1990–96), who was thrust into politics as a result of her husband's assassination and the triumph of the Sandinista revolution; married Pedro Chamorro (1950), publisher of *La Prensa,* who for many years would be involved in an ill-fated rebellion against Somoza and spend months and years in jail; after husband founded a coalition of anti-Somoza elements as the Democratic Union of Liberation (UDEL, 1973), often traveled with him to rural areas where they attended meetings and met with the poor; while in Miami (Jan 10, 1978), learned of husband's assassination; as the new publisher of *La Prensa,* continued to attack the Somoza regime; when he had *La Prensa* building burned (1979), continued to publish in another city; respected by anti-Somoza Nicaraguans as the "noble widow," her honesty and courage in the face of the dictatorship was an inspiration when hopes seemed to fade; when Somoza fled, was asked to join the new Ortega government, dominated by the radical Sandinistas, as a more moderate member of its provisional executive junta; resigned from the junta after only 9 months because of the increasingly militant Ortega administration; became increasingly disenchanted with Sandinista policies, criticizing them caustically in *La Prensa;* after election of Ortega as Nicaraguan president (1984), endured pressure against *La Prensa,* which was frequently shut down; refusing to bow to the pressure, published critiques in other journals; backed by anti-Sandinista forces which had created a coalition of 14 parties calling itself the National Opposition Union (UNO), won the presidential election (1990); acting as both head of state and government, took steps from the 1st day to heal the nation's wounds, calling for a general amnesty for all political crimes, which included those individuals responsible for husband's assassination; by end of her tenure (1996), had achieved significant constitutional reforms, including a permanent prohibition of obligatory military service and guarantees of private property rights. ❖ See also (with Sonia Cruz de Baltodano and Guido Fernandez) *Dreams of the Heart: The Autobiography of President Violeta Barrios de Chamorro of Nicaragua* (Simon & Schuster, 1996); and *Women in World History.*

CHAMOT, Madeleine (1931—). See Berthod, Madeleine.

CHAMPAGNE, Andrée (1939—). Canadian politician. Name variations: Andree Champagne. Born July 17, 1939, in Saint-Hyacinthe, Quebec, Canada. ❖ The 1st woman deputy speaker of the House of Commons, was an actress and pianist before entering politics, appearing frequently in film, tv and theater, including as Donalda in the tv series "Les Belles histoires des Pays-d'en-Haut" (1956) and as Carmen Forcier in "Les As" (1977); was 1st elected to the House of Commons as a Progressive

Conservative member for Saint-Hyacinthe-Bagot (1984); served in the Cabinet as minister of State ([Youth], 1984–86), as assistant deputy chair of the Committee of the Whole House (1986–90), then as deputy speaker and chair of the Committee of the Whole House (1990–93); after defeat of the Conservative government (1993), returned to acting; appeared on the tv series "Juliette Pomerleau" (1999). Sworn to the Privy Council (1984).

CHAMPAGNE, countess of.
See Maud of Normandy (d. 1107).
See Marie de Champagne (1145–1198).
See Maud Carinthia (c. 1105–1160).
See Joan I of Navarre (1273–1305).

CHAMPAGNEUX, Madame (1781–1858). Daughter of Madame Roland. Name variations: Eudora Roland. Born Marie-Thérèse-Eudora de la Platière, Oct 4, 1781; died 1858; dau. of Madame Roland (1754–1793, a journalist) and Jean-Marie Roland de la Platière.

CHAMPAIGNE, countess of. *See Champagne, countess of.*

CHAMPGRAND, Alexandrine Sophie Goury de (1773–1860). *See Bawr, Alexandrine de.*

CHAMPION, Kate (1861–1889). *See Watson, Ellen.*

CHAMPION, Marge (1919—). American actress and dancer. Name variations: Marjorie Bell. Born Marjorie Celeste Belcher, Sept 2, 1919, in Hollywood, California; dau. of Ernest Belcher (ballet coach); half-sister of Lina Basquette (actress); studied ballet with father, tap with Nick Castle, ballet with Vincenzo Celli and modern dance with Hanya Holm; m. Art Babbitt (animator), 1937 (div. 1940); m. Gower Champion (dancer-choreographer), 1947 (div. 1973); m. Boris Sagal (director, died 1981); stepchildren: Katey Sagal, Jean Sagal, and Liz Sagal (all actresses). ❖ Began dancing as a child; was a movement model for Disney's Snow White and for the Blue Fairy in *Pinocchio*; appeared in 3 films as Marjorie Bell, including *Honor of the West* and *All Women Have Secrets* (1939); teamed with Gower Champion (1945) to appear in *Show Boat, Lovely to Look at, Everything I Have Is Yours, Give a Girl a Break, Jupiter's Darling* and *Three for the Show*; other films include *The Party* and *The Swimmer*; choreographed dances for *The Day of the Locust* (1975). Won Emmy for choreography for "Queen of the Stardust Ballroom" (1975).

CHAMPLIN, Jane (1917–1943). American military pilot. Name variations: Jane Deloris Champlin. Born May 14, 1917, in Chicago, Il; grew up in Richmond, Virginia; died June 7, 1943, near Westbrook, Texas; graduate of Arcadia College; St. Louis University, BA, 1937. ❖ Learned to fly (1940); joined Women's Auxiliary Ferrying Squadron; was killed with her instructor Henry S. Aubrey during a training flight in a BT-13, near Westbrook, Texas (June 7, 1943).

CHAMPMESLE, Marie (c. 1642–1698). French actress. Name variations: Marie Desmares; Marie de Champmeslé; La Champmeslé. Born Marie Desmares in Rouen, France, 1642 (some sources cite 1641 or 1644); died in Auteuil, France, May 15, 1698; sister of actor Nicolas Desmares (c. 1650–1714); aunt of actress Christine Desmares (1682–1753); m. Charles Chevillet (1645–1701), who called himself sieur de Champmeslé or lord of Champmeslé, 1666; no children. ❖ Began acting (early 1660s), making 1st appearance in Rouen with Charles Chevillet, known as the lord of Champmeslé; appeared with him in many plays, then married (1666); with husband, moved to Paris to further careers (1669), appearing at the Théâtre du Marais as Venus in Boyer's *Fête de Venus*; had great success at Paris' Hôtel de Bourgogne as Hermione in Racine's *Andromaque*; was also the original Berenice, Monimia, and Phèdre in Racine's works; opened the Comédie Française in Paris (Aug 26, 1680) in *Phèdre*, remaining there with husband as principal players for next 30 years. ❖ See also *Women in World History*.

CHAMPSEIX, Léodile (1832–1900). *See Léo, André.*

CHAN, Erin (1979—). Canadian synchronized swimmer. Born Aug 9, 1979, in Toronto, Ontario, Canada. ❖ Won a team bronze medal at Sydney Olympics (2000).

CHAN, Yau-nui (1873/75?–1940). *See Doo, Unui.*

CHANCELLOR, Joyce (1906—). Irish actress. Born Dec 27, 1906, in Dublin, Ireland; dau. of John William Chancellor and Cicely (Granger) Chancellor; sister of Betty Chancellor (actress who married playwright William Denis Johnston); m. Fred O'Donovan (actor, died 1952). ❖

Made stage debut at the Abbey Theatre, Dublin, as Paquita in *The Kingdom of God* (1923); made London debut as Honor Blake in *Playboy of the Western World* (1925), followed by *Juno and the Paycock, The Plough and the Stars, The White-Headed Boy, The Far-Off Hills, General John Regan* and *The Moon in the Yellow River*, among others; made film *Irish Hearts* (1934).

CHAND BIBI (1550–1599). Indian queen and regent. Name variations: Chand Bibi. Born 1550 (some sources cite 1547) in Ahmadnagar, India; died 1599; dau. of Hussain Nizma Shah of Ahmadnagar and Khonza Humayun; m. Ali Adil Shah (1558–1580) of Bijapur, 1562 (murdered 1580). ❖ Queen of the Muslim kingdom of Bijapur, ruled as regent for her nephew, Ibrahim Adil Shah II, in Bijapur (1580–85); returned to Ahmadnagar; when Murtada Shah, the ruler of Ahmadnagar, died, mustered troops from Bijapur to defend the kingdom and the infant king Bahadur from Akbar's imperial troops, led by his son Murad; during the Mughal siege, defended the fort successfully (1597) and came to be known as Chand Sultana; after fighting valiantly (1599), lost heart during a 2nd siege; in some sources, informed her eunuch that she was going to surrender and was killed by mob who accused her of turning traitor; in other sources, fought bravely to the end and was killed by the troops of Akbar (Ahmadnagar fell into the hands of Akbar in 1600). ❖ See also Hindi film *Sultana Chand Bibi* (1936).

CHAND, Meira (1942—). British novelist and short-story writer. Born Meira Angela Chand in 1942. ❖ Born and educated in London but lived in Japan (1962–97) and India (1971–75); immigrated to Singapore (1997); novels, which often deal with the clash between Eastern and Western cultures, include *The Gossamer Fly* (1979), *Last Quadrant* (1981), *The Bonsai Tree* (1983), *The Painted Cage* (1986), *House of the Sun* (1989), *A Choice of Evils* (1996) and *Far Horizon* (2001); short stories often appear in magazines and anthologies.

CHANDLER, Dorothy Buffum (1901–1997). American newspaper executive and civic activist. Name variations: Buffy. Born Dorothy Buffum in Lafayette, Illinois, May 19, 1901; died July 6, 1997; dau. of Charles Abel (owner of chain of department stores) and Fern (Smith) Buffum; attended Stanford University; m. Norman Chandler (publisher of *Los Angeles Times*, 1944–60), Aug 30, 1922; children: Otis Chandler (publisher of *Los Angeles Times*, 1960–80); Camilla Chandler. ❖ While husband was publisher of Times-Mirror Co., became his administrative assistant (1948); helped establish an afternoon paper, *Los Angeles Mirror*, and worked with the women's department of *Los Angeles Times*; was a director of the company (1955–76); during long involvement in civic affairs, was active with Southern California Symphony Association, served as director of San Francisco Opera Association, raised funds for Los Angeles Philharmonic Orchestra; chaired board of Civic Auditorium and Music Center Association of Los Angeles County, and raised over 18 million to build Los Angeles Music Center, which now houses the Dorothy Chandler Pavilion. ❖ See also *Women in World History*.

CHANDLER, Elizabeth Margaret (1807–1834). American abolitionist and writer. Born Dec 24, 1807, at Centre, near Wilmington, Delaware; died Nov 22, 1834, in Michigan; dau. of Thomas Chandler (Quaker farmer); educated at the Friends' schools in Philadelphia; never married. ❖ Contributed to Benjamin Lundy's paper, the *Genius of Universal Emancipation*. ❖ See also *The Political Works of Elizabeth Margaret Chandler*; and *Women in World History*.

CHANDLER, Helen (1906–1965). American stage and screen actress. Born Feb 1, 1906, in New York, NY; grew up in Charleston, South Carolina; died April 30, 1965, in Hollywood, California; m. Cyril Hume (screenwriter), 1930 (div. 1934); m. Bramwell Fletcher (English actor), 1935 (div. 1940; he was also married to Diana Barrymore); m. Walter Piascik. ❖ Made NY stage debut (1919); other plays include *It's a Bet, Pride and Prejudice, Springtime for Henry, The Show Off, Outward Bound* and *The Wild Duck* (1925), which brought her to prominence; films include *Salute, Mother's Boy, Vanity Street, Outward Bound, Christopher Strong* and *Dracula*.

CHANDLER, Janet (1915–1994). American actress. Born Lillian Guenther, Dec 31, 1915, in Pine Bluffs, Arkansas; died Mar 16, 1994, in Los Angeles, California; m. George E. Barrett, 1935 (div.); m. Joseph A. Kramm (writer, div.). ❖ Films include *The Golden West, The Drunkard, Now or Never* and *Million Dollar Haul*.

CHANDLER, Jennifer (1959—). American diver. Born June 13, 1959, in Langdale, Alabama; attended University of Alabama. ❖ At Montreal

Olympics, won a gold medal in springboard (1976); won gold medal for springboard at Pan American games (1975).

CHANDLER, Mary (1687–1745). British poet and milliner. Born 1687 in Malmsbury, Wiltshire, England; died Sept 11, 1745, in Bath, Gloucestershire, England; dau. of Henry Chandler (Dissenting minister) and Miss Bridgman of Marlborough. ❖ Tended millinery shop in Bath; in spare time, wrote poetry which showed the influence of Alexander Pope and the Roman poet Horace; wrote *A Description of Bath: A Poem* (1733).

CHANDLER, Michelle. Australian basketball player. Born in Australia. ❖ Won a team bronze medal at Atlanta Olympics (1996); played for Bulleen Bloomers.

CHANEL, Coco (1883–1971). French fashion designer. Name variations: Gabrielle Bonheur Chanel. Born Gabrielle Bonheur Chanel, Aug 19, 1883, in Saumur, France; died Jan 10, 1971, in Paris, France; dau. of Albert Chanel (itinerant merchant) and Jeanne (Devolle) Chanel; attended Aubazine Orphanage and Notre Dame Finishing School, Moulins; never married; no children. ❖ Fashion innovator, patron of the arts, entrepreneur, and creator of the little black dress and the Chanel suit, was raised by nuns (1895–1901); employed as a shop assistant, seamstress, and music-hall performer (1901–06); lived with Étienne Balsan at Royallieu (1906–09); moved to Paris (1909); met Arthur Capel, who became her financier and lover (1909); opened a small millinery shop on rue Cambon (1910) to immediate success; opened shop in Deauville (1913); introduced casual sports wear; in Biarritz (1915), opened her 1st *maison de couture*, complete with its own dress-makers and high fashion collections, which she would operate until 1922; created the jersey dress; worked on ballets with Sergi Diaghilev and Pablo Picasso; introduced Chanel no. 5 perfume (1921); had a romance with Grand Duke Dimitri (1922–24) and Duke of Westminster (1924–30); created the little black dress (1926); accepted contract from Samuel Goldwyn (1930); when war was declared, closed House of Chanel (1939); during German occupation, became involved with Hans Gunther Spatz, a German diplomat and suspected Gestapo agent (1940); arrested in Paris for collaboration, moved to Switzerland with Spatz (1946); with Spatz out of her life, made fashion comeback (1954); introduced the Chanel suit (1956); inspired Broadway musical *Coco* (1969). ❖ See also Francis Kenneth, *Coco: The Life and Loves of Gabrielle Chanel* (Gollancz, 1989); Axel Madsen, *Chanel: A Woman of Her Own* (Holt, 1990); Janet Wallach, *Chanel: Her Style and Her Life* (Doubleday, 1998); and *Women in World History.*

CHANEY, Cleva (d. 1967). *See Bush, Frances Cleveland.*

CHANEY, Frances (1915–2004). American actress. Name variations: Frances Lardner. Born Fanya Lipetz, July 2, 1915, in Odessa, Ukraine; died of Alzheimer's disease, Nov 23, 2004, in New York, NY; attended Hunter College and the Neighborhood Playhouse; m. David Lardner (killed by a land mine in Germany, 1944); m. his brother Ring Lardner Jr. (writer), 1946 (died 2000); children: (1st m.) Joseph and Kate Lardner; (2nd m.) James Lardner. ❖ Immigrated with parents to the Bronx as a child; on radio, could be heard on "Topper," "Gangbusters," and "Mr. District Attorney," among others, and was the voice of the character Burma on "Terry and the Pirates" (1937–39, 1943); on tv, was a 10-year regular on "The Edge of Night" (1956–67); career effectively killed when she was placed on the Hollywood blacklist with husband during the McCarthy era; turned to the NY stage for work.

CHANG, Ai-ling (1920–1995). *See Chang, Eileen.*

CHANG CAI (1900–1990). *See Cai Chang.*

CHANG CHIEH (1937—). *See Zhang Jie.*

CHANG, Diana (1934—). Asian-American novelist and poet. Born 1934 in New York, NY; dau. of a Chinese architect and a Eurasian; grew up in China; returned with family to New York after World War II; attended Barnard College. ❖ Professor of creative writing at Barnard College until 1989, came to prominence with publication of *The Frontiers of Love* (1956); served as editor of American Pen and also exhibited paintings in New York galleries; wrote *A Woman of Thirty* (1959), *A Passion for Life* (1961), *The Only Game in Town* (1963), *Eye to Eye* (1974), and *A Perfect Love* (1978), and such poetry collections as *The Horizon is Definitely Speaking* (1982), *What Matisse is After* (1984) and *Earth Water Light* (1991).

CHANG, Eileen (1920–1995). Chinese novelist and short story writer. Name variations: Chang Ai-ling or Zhang Ailing. Born Chang Ai-ling (Zhang Ailing) in Shanghai, Sept 30, 1920, into an elite family; found dead in her apartment in Los Angeles, California, Sept 8, 1995; attended University of Hong Kong, 1938–42; m. Hu Lan Cheng (high official of the pro-Japanese puppet Chinese regime); m. Ferdinand Reyher (screen-writer, died 1967). ❖ One of the greatest writers in modern Chinese literature, studied literature and English at University of Hong Kong, then returned to Shanghai (1942), now under Japanese occupation; made her living by turning out both novels and film scripts; her romance *Love in a Lost City* made her an overnight cultural celebrity; at war's end, disdain for the growing politicization of literature served to isolate her within intellectual circles; found little support for her books, including *Rumors* (essays) and *Strange Stories*, though they would later be held in high esteem; left the mainland for Hong Kong (1952), where a collection of her short stories appeared in print (1954); moved to US (1955), settling in Los Angeles; writing under the name Eileen Chang, published novel *The Rice-Sprout Song*; served as a writer-in-residence at University of California, Berkeley (1960s); having written a novella *The Golden Cangue* (1944), expanded it into the full-length novel, *The Rouge of the North* (1967), now considered her greatest work; because her writing was often viewed in light of the Cold War rather than simply literature, rapidly lost confidence in her abilities; essentially abandoned her own writing, concentrating instead on teaching and working on a translation from the Shanghai dialect into Mandarin Chinese of *The Lives of Shanghai Beauties*, a classic novel of the Qing dynasty; became a recluse. ❖ See also *Women in World History.*

CHANG EUN-JUNG (1970—). South Korean field-hockey player. Born Aug 18, 1970, in South Korea. ❖ Won a team silver medal at Seoul Olympics (1988) and a team silver at Atlanta Olympics (1996).

CHANG HEE-SOOK (1955—). Korean volleyball player. Born Mar 5, 1955, in South Korea. ❖ At Montreal Olympics, won a bronze medal in team competition (1976).

CHANG, Iris (1968–2004). Chinese-American historian. Born Iris Shun-Ru Chang, Mar 28, 1968, in Princeton, New Jersey; grew up in Champaign-Urbana, Illinois; committed suicide, Nov 9, 2004, near Los Gatos, California; dau. of a professor of physics (father) and a microbiologist (mother); graduated in journalism from University of Illinois, 1989; attended Johns Hopkins University; m. Brett Douglas (electronics engineer); children: Christopher. ❖ Because of grandparents who had fled Nanking (1937), was outraged that textbooks contained no mention of the atrocities during the Sino-Japanese war; came to prominence with the international bestseller *The Rape of Nanking: The Forgotten Holocaust of World War II* (1997), having used original documents, interviews and an important diary for her sources; also wrote *Thread of the Silkworm* (1995) and *The Chinese in America* (2003).

CHANG JUI-FANG (b. 1918). *See Zhang Ruifang.*

CHANLER, Margaret (b. 1862). American author. Name variations: Mrs. Winthrop Chanler; Daisy Chanler or Daisy Terry. Born Margaret Terry in Rome, Italy, Aug 6, 1862; dau. of Luther Terry and Louisa Cutler (Ward) Terry; privately educated; awarded diploma in music from St. Cecilia Conservatory, Rome; Nazareth College, DLitt, Rochester, New York; m. Winthrop Chanler, Dec 16, 1886; children: Laura Astor (Mrs. Lawrence Grant White); John Winthrop; Beatrice (Mrs. Pierre Francis Allegaert); Hester Marion (Mrs. Edward Motley Pickman); Marion Winthrop; Gabrielle (Mrs. Porter Ralph Chandler); Hubert Winthrop; Theodore Ward. ❖ Arrived in US (1886); became a great friend of Edith Wharton; wrote memoirs, *Roman Spring* (1934) and *Autumn in the Valley* (1936), which contain observations on Wharton; also translated Gertrud von Le Fort's *Hymns to the Church* (1937). ❖ See also *Women in World History.*

CHANLER, Mrs. Winthrop (b. 1862). *See Chanler, Margaret.*

CHANNING, Carol (1921—). American actress. Born Jan 31, 1921, in Seattle, Washington; only child of George Channing and Adelaide (Glazer) Channing; attended Bennington College in Vermont; m. briefly to novelist Theodore Naidish; m. Alexander Carson (ex-football player from Canada); m. Charles Lowe (her manager), c. 1957 (div. 1998); children: (2nd m.) son, Channing Lowe (who would be adopted by her 3rd husband). ❖ Award-winning actress best known for her roles as Lorelei Lee in *Gentlemen Prefer Blondes* and Dolly Levi in *Hello, Dolly!*, found 1st job on Broadway in her junior year in college; gained stardom with her creation of Lorelei Lee in *Gentlemen Prefer Blondes* (1949); cast as Dolly Levi in *Hello, Dolly!* (1964), a role for which she received the Tony Award as Best Actress in a Musical and which she has since played more than 4,000 times on Broadway and on tour; also appeared on stage in *Lend an Ear, Wonderful Town, Lorelei, Jerry's Girls* and (tour) *Legends*; films include *Paid in Full* (1950), *The First Traveling Saleslady* (1956), *Thoroughly Modern Millie* (1967), *Skidoo* (1968) and *Sgt. Pepper's Lonely Hearts Club Band* (1978). Received Tony Award for Lifetime Achievement (1995). ❖ See also *Women in World History.*

CHANNING, Stockard (1944—). American actress. Born Susan Antonia Williams Stockard, Feb 13, 1944, in New York, NY; attended Chapin and Madeira schools; Radcliffe College, BA in history and literature; m. Walter Channing, 1963 (div. 1967); m. Paul Schmidt, 1970 (div. 1976); m. David Debin, 1976 (div. 1980); m. David Rawle, 1980 (div. 1988). ❖ Won a Tony award for *A Day in the Death of Joe Egg* (1985) and was acclaimed for performance in John Guare's *Six Degrees of Separation* (1990); films include *The Fortune, The Big Bus, The Cheap Detective, Grease, The Fish That Save Pittsburgh, Without a Trace, Heartburn, Meet the Applegates, Married to It, Six Degrees of Separation, Moll Flanders, The First Wives Club, Edie & Pen, The Venice Project, Le Divorce* and *To Wong Foo, Thanks for Everything! Julie Newmar*; on tv, starred in "The Stockard Channing Show" (1980) and began appearing as the first lady, Abbey Bartlet, on "The West Wing" (1999).

CHANTAL, Jane de (1572–1641). See *Chantal, Jeanne de.*

CHANTAL, Jeanne de (1572–1641). French saint and religious community founder. Name variations: Saint Jane Chantal; Jeanne Chantal; Jane de Chantal or Jeanne de Chantal; Jane Frances de Chantal; Madame de Chantal; Jeanne-Françoise, baroness de Chantal; Jeanne de Rabutin-Chantal. Born Jeanne-Françoise Frémiot in Dijon, France, Jan 23, 1572; died in Moulins, France, Dec 13, 1641; dau. of Bénigne Frémiot and Marguerite de Berbisey Frémiot; grandmother of Marie de Sévigné (1626–1696); m. Baron Christophe de Rabutin-Chantal; children: Celse-Bénigne de Rabutin-Chantal (1596–1627, father of Marie de Sévigné); and 5 others, of which 3 survived infancy. ❖ Co-founder, along with Francis de Sales, of the Order of the Visitation of Holy Mary; her many letters survive, providing a detailed picture of the religious ideas and ideals of her age; canonized as a saint of the Roman Catholic church (1767). ❖ See also Émile Bougaud, *St. Chantal and the Foundation of the Visitation,* 2 vols. (Benziger, 1895); Andre Ravier, *Saint Jeanne de Chantal: Noble Lady, Holy Woman* (Ignatius, 1989); Ella Katharine Sanders, *Sainte Chantal, 1572–1641: A Study in Vocation* (Macmillan, 1928); and *Women in World History.*

CHANTAL, Marie de Rabutin (1626–1696). See *Sévigné, Marie de.*

CHANTELS, The.
See *Goring, Sonia.*
See *Harris, Lois.*
See *Landry, Jackie.*
See *Minus, Rene.*
See *Smith, Annette.*
See *Smith, Arlene.*

CHAO NA. Chinese swimmer. Born in China. ❖ Won a silver medal for 4x100-meter relay at Atlanta Olympics (1996).

CHAPELLE, Dickey (1919–1972). American photojournalist. Name variations: Dickey Meyer. Born Georgette Louise Meyer in Shorewood, Wisconsin, 1919; killed near Chu Lai, South Vietnam, Nov 4, 1972; dau. of Edna and Paul Gerhard Meyer; attended Massachusetts Institute of Technology, 1935; m. Tony Chapelle, Oct 2, 1940 (annulled, July 1956); children: (stepson) Ron Chapelle. ❖ The 1st American woman reporter killed in action, became the 1st woman photographer accredited to the Pacific Fleet during WWII and the youngest of all women correspondents (1945); photographed Guam and Okinawan campaigns; back in US, became a staff photographer and associate editor for *Seventeen*, where she quickly grew bored; with husband, traveled through Eastern and Central Europe (1947–53), where she took 10,000 pictures used by a dozen agencies—including CARE, Save the Children and United Nation's Children's Emergency Fund (UNICEF); snuck into Hungary during the revolution (1956), where she was captured, brought to trial (Jan 26, 1957), and sentenced by the Communists to 50 days in prison; crediting the American embassy for her release, returned to US, recognized as something of a Cold War celebrity; covered Algerian War from the side of the FLN (1957), who were rebelling against the French; set out for Cuba to successfully interview Fidel Castro (1958); covered Lebanese Civil War, the marine maneuvers on Crete, and the marines' final assault landing in Beirut (1958); signed up for parachute training (1959) and jumped with the 1st Special Forces of 82nd Airborne; arrived in Vietnam

early in war (1961), when there were fewer than 12 accredited reporters from the West. Received George Polk Award from Overseas Press Club (1962). ❖ See also autobiography *What's a Woman Doing Here?* (Morrow, 1962); Roberta Ostroff, *Fire in the Wind: The Life of Dickey Chapelle* (Ballantine, 1992); and *Women in World History.*

CHAPIN, Anne Morrison (1892–1967). American actress, playwright, and screenwriter. Born Jan 5, 1892; died April 7, 1967, in West Hollywood, California. ❖ Following a successful Broadway career in such plays as *Why Marry?* and *The Bat*, moved to Hollywood (1934); wrote screenplays, including *This Man is Mine, The Big City, Dangerous Corner, Love Takes Flight, High Barbaree, Secret Heart* and *Sailor Takes a Wife.*

CHAPIN, Augusta (1836–1905). American minister. Name variations: Reverend Augusta J. Chapin. Born Augusta J. Chapin in Lakeville, New York, 1836; died in New York, NY, June 30, 1905; received degree from Olivet College; University of Michigan, AM; never married. ❖ Preached 1st sermon (c. 1856), beginning the life of an itinerant minister, who taught school to support her efforts; ordained by Universalists at Lansing, Michigan (1863); received 1st pastorate (1864); ordained by congregations in Iowa, Illinois, Nebraska, and rural New York, finding increased opportunity in remote locations; received 1st honorary doctorate of divinity given to an American woman, from Lombard University in Galesburg, Illinois (1893); was a member of the 1st executive committee of the Association for the Advancement of Women and served as chair of the general committee for women at the Columbian Exposition (1893); retired (1901). ❖ See also *Women in World History.*

CHAPIN, Sallie F. (c. 1830–1896). American temperance reformer. Born Sarah Flournoy Moore, Mar 14, c. 1830, in Charleston, South Carolina; died April 19, 1896, in Charleston; dau. of George Washington Moore and Elizabeth Martha (Vigneron) Simons Moore; sister of writer Georgia Moore De Fontaine; m. Leonard Chapin, Aug 12, 1847; children: adopted Elizabeth Vigneron (dau. of her brother, James O.A. Moore). ❖ Supported Confederacy; served as president of Soldiers' Relief Society, the Ladies' Auxiliary Christian Association in Charleston, SC, and the Ladies' Christian Association; organized Charleston Woman's Christian Temperance Union (1880); elected president of South Carolina WCTU (1883); served as national superintendent of WCTU's Southern Department (1880s); was influential in founding of South Carolina Industrial and Winthrop Normal College (which became a state college for women, Winthrop College).

CHAPLIN, Geraldine (1944—). American actress. Born Geraldine Leigh Chaplin, July 31, 1944, in Santa Monica, California; grew up in England; dau. of Charles Chaplin (actor) and Oona O'Neill Chaplin; attended the Royal Ballet Academy in London; had long-term relationship with Spanish director Carlos Saura; children: Shane and Oona. ❖ Appears in opening scene of her father's *Limelight* (1952); came to prominence in film *Doctor Zhivago* (1965); appeared in over 90 films, including *La Madriguera* (1969), *Z.P.G.* (1972), *Ana y los lobos* (1973), *The Four Musketeers* (1974), *La Banda de Jaider* (1975), *Nashville* (1975), *Buffalo Bill and the Indians* (1976), *Elisa, vida mía* (1977), *Remember My Name* (1978), *A Wedding* (1978), *Le Voyage en douce* (1980), *The Mirror Crack'd* (1980), *The Moderns* (1988), *The Children* (1990), *Chaplin* (1992), *The Age of Innocence* (1993), *Mother Teresa* (1997), *Cousin Bette* (1998), *To Walk with the Lions* (1999) and *The Bridge of San Luis Rey* (2004); also frequently appeared on tv.

CHAPLIN, Lita Grey (1908–1995). American actress. Name variations: Lita Grey. Born Lillita Louise MacMurray, April 15, 1908, in Hollywood, California; died Dec 29, 1995, in Woodland Hills, California; m. Charles Chaplin (actor), Nov 26, 1924 (div. 1938); m. Henry Aguirre (div.); m. Arthur Day (div.); m. Pat Long (div.); children: Sydney Chaplin and Charles Chaplin Jr. (died 1968). ❖ At 12, was Charlie Chaplin's new star in *The Kid* (1921); at 16, became pregnant by him and married him; at 18, was caught up in a bitter divorce in one of the earliest celebrity court cases.

CHAPLIN, Mildred Harris (1901–1944). See *Harris, Mildred*

CHAPLIN, Oona O'Neill (1925–1991). American notable. Born Oona O'Neill, May 14, 1925, in Bermuda; died of cancer, Sept 27, 1991, in Corsier-sur-Vevey, Switzerland; dau. of Agnes Boulton (1893–1968, writer) and Eugene O'Neill (playwright); attended Brearley School, New York; m. Charlie Chaplin (film actor), June 16, 1943 (died 1977); children: Josephine, Christopher, Jane, Eugene, Michael,

Victoria, Annette-Emilie and Geraldine Chaplin (actress). ❖ Well-known daughter of Eugene O'Neill and wife of Charlie Chaplin, was raised primarily by mother after father deserted the family when she was 2; at 17, left NY for Hollywood, hoping to break into acting; fell in love with Charlie Chaplin, age 53; eloped (1943), much to the consternation of her father who disowned her; helped revive husband's interest in work. ❖ See also Jane Scovell, *Oona: Living in the Shadows* (Warner, 1998); and *Women in World History.*

CHAPMAN, Anne Maria (1791–1855). New Zealand missionary. Name variations: Anna Maria Maynard. Born Anna Maria Maynard, Jan 13, 1791, in Oxfordshire, England; died 1855; dau. of Thomas Maynard (butcher) and Sarah (Binfield) Maynard; m. Thomas Chapman (missionary), 1822. ❖ Immigrated with husband to New Zealand (1830); helped to found 1st mission station at Te Koutu, Rotorua; assisted with mission schools, teaching catechism and secular subjects; provided food and medicine to needy; adopted Maori godson. ❖ See also *Dictionary of New Zealand Biography* (Vol. 1).

CHAPMAN, Caroline (c. 1818–1876). American actress. Born c. 1818 in London, England; died May 8, 1876, in San Francisco, California; possibly dau. of William Chapman (actor); possibly illeg. dau. of his son, William B. Chapman, later known in America as Uncle Billy Chapman. ❖ Worked as child actor in NY; made adult debut in NY in *A Husband at First Sight* (1846); won acclaim at Burton's Theatre (1848–52); debuted in California at Maguire's Jenny Lind Theatre (1852); known primarily for roles on CA stage (1850s); joined company at San Francisco Theatre and played opposite a young Edwin Booth in *Hamlet* (1853); ridiculed Lola Montez in burlesque pieces; last major role was in *Death, or the Angel of Midnight.*

CHAPMAN, Edythe (1863–1948). American stage actress. Name variations: Mrs. James Neil. Born Oct 8, 1863, in Rochester, NY; died Oct 15, 1948, in Glendale, California; m. James Neil (actor, died 1931). ❖ Made stage debut (1898); often appeared in productions with husband James Neil; made screen debut (1908), then followed with over 90 films, including *Richelieu, Huckleberry Finn* (as Aunt Polly, 1920), *The County Fair, Double Crossroads* and *Up the River;* retired from film (1930).

CHAPMAN, Lee (1930–1999). *See Bradley, Marion Zimmer.*

CHAPMAN, Marguerite (1918–1999). American actress. Born Mar 9, 1918, in Chatham, NY; died Aug 31, 1999, in Burbank, California; m. G. Bentley Ryan, 1948 (div. 1951); m. J. Richard Bremerkamp (div.); m. Anthony Havelock-Allan (British producer-director, div.). ❖ Began career as a John Powers model in NY; films include *Charlie Chan at the Wax Museum, Appointment in Berlin, Pardon My Past, Mr. District Attorney, Destroyer, Bloodhounds of Broadway* and *The Seven Year Itch.*

CHAPMAN, Maria (1806–1885). American abolitionist. Born Maria Weston in Weymouth, Massachusetts, July 25, 1806; died July 12, 1885, in Weymouth; educated in Europe; m. Henry G. Chapman (liberal merchant), Oct 1830 (died 1842); lived in Paris, 1844–55; children: 3. ❖ Helped found the Boston Female Anti-Slavery Society (1832), editing its annual report *Right and Wrong in Boston,* and occasionally editing William Lloyd Garrison's *Liberator;* was a supporter of the Grimké sisters and wrote the biography of Harriet Martineau (1877). ❖ See also *Women in World History.*

CHAPMAN, Merilyn (1962—). American gymnast. Born April 9, 1962, in California; attended Stanford University; married; children: 3. ❖ Won British Invitational and Far West Invitational (1977).

CHAPMAN, Pansy (1892–1973). New Zealand hospital matron and nursing administrator. Born Pansy Helen Auld Chapman, Nov 24, 1892, at Blacks Point, Reefron, New Zealand; died July 6, 1973, at Auckland, New Zealand; dau. of Hender Chapman (miner) and Elizabeth Ann (Richards) Chapman. ❖ Trained as nurse in Dunedin and Christchurch; administered children's ward at Christchurch Hospital (1917); served as matron of Christchurch Karitane hospital (1920–23); was a member of Wellington branch of Royal New Zealand Society for the Health of Women and Children (Plunket Society); managed out-patient department of Mothercraft Training Centre at Cromwell House, London (1930); appointed acting charge nurse at Auckland branch of Plunket Society (1931–51); advocated for pre-school medical examinations and was instrumental in Plunket Society's institutional success in Auckland. Awarded British Empire Medal (1948). ❖ See also *Dictionary of New Zealand Biography* (Vol. 4).

CHAPMAN, Susan (1962—). Australian rower. Born Sept 17, 1962, in Australia. ❖ At Los Angeles Olympics, won a bronze medal in coxed fours (1984).

CHAPMAN, Sylvia (1896–1995). New Zealand physician, medical superintendent, and welfare worker. Born Sylvia Gytha de Lancey Chapman, Nov 27, 1896, in Dunedin, New Zealand; died Sept 1, 1995, at Bexhill-on-Sea, England; dau. of Frederick Revans Chapman (barrister) and Clara Jane (Cook) Chapman; Victoria University College, 1915; University of Otago, MB, ChB, 1921; University of New Zealand, MD, 1934. ❖ Active in organizations concerned with health, women's issues, and humanitarian work, including Lepers' Trust Board and South Pacific Health Service; provided foundation for discovery of Rh factor from research for her doctoral thesis into perinatal toxaemia; gained practical experience in obstetrics and gynecology at Dublin and Vienna; appointed medical superintendent at St. Helens Hospital, Wellington (1936); advocated educating poor about safe contraception and establishment of free birth-control clinics; was the 1st woman appointed as government nominee to Senate of University of New Zealand; represented Young Women's Christian Association (YWCA) as member and medical adviser of Polish Children's Hospitality Committee during WWII; participated in organization of New Zealand Council of Organisations for Relief Service Overseas (CORSO, 1944); headed medical team sent to Greece when CORSO joined UN's Relief and Rehabilitation Administration (UNRRA, 1945); worked at Dulwich hospital in England and worked with College of General Practitioners before becoming 1st medical supervisor at home for elderly at Bexhill-on-Sea. ❖ See also *Dictionary of New Zealand Biography* (Vol. 4).

CHAPMAN, Tracy (1964—). African-American singer. Born Mar 30, 1964, in Cleveland, Ohio; attended Tufts University, majoring in anthropology and African studies. ❖ Made *Tracy Chapman* debut album for Elektra (1987) which included "Fast Car," "Baby Can I Hold You," and "Talkin' Bout a Revolution"; appeared at the televised tribute to Nelson Mandela (1987), resulting in the sale of 12,000 copies of album in 2 days; won Grammy as Best New Artist (1989); released *Crossroads* (1989) which went platinum; released "Bang Bang Bang" single, followed by the album *Matters of the Heart* and the single "Dreaming on a World" (1992); released *New Beginning* (multi-platinum) and had hit "Give Me One Reason" (1995), for which she won a Grammy for Record of the Year (1997); released *Telling Stories* (2000), followed by *Let It Rain* (2002); appeared in the film *Malcolm X* (1992).

CHAPMAN, Vera (1898–1996). British writer. Name variations: Belladonna Took. Born May 7, 1898, in Bournemouth, Hampshire, England; died May 14, 1996, in Croydon, Surrey, England; dau. of John Frederick Fogerty and Kate Isabella Veronica Morse Fogerty; m. Charles Sydney Chapman, 1924; children: 2. ❖ Began writing at 65; based fiction on Arthurian legends and other medieval tales; founded Tolkien Society; wrote *The Green Knight* (1975), *The King's Damosel* (1976), *King Arthur's Daughter* (1976), *Judy and Julia* (1977), *The Wife of Bath* (1978), *Blaedud the Birdman* (1978) and *Miranty and the Alchemist* (1983).

CHAPMAN, Yvonne (1940—). Australian politician. Born Jan 21, 1940, in Brisbane, Australia. ❖ Representing the National Party, served in Queensland Parliament for Pine Rivers (1983–89); named minister for Welfare Services (1986–87) and minister for Transport and Ethnic Affairs (1989).

CHAPONE, Hester (1727–1801). English writer. Name variations: Hester Mulso. Born Hester Mulso, Oct 27, 1727, in Twywell, Northamptonshire, England; died Dec 25, 1801, in Hadley, Middlesex, England; dau. of Thomas Mulso (farmer and landowner) and Hester (Thomas) Mulso; m. John Chapone (attorney), 1760 (died 10 months later); no children. ❖ Literary figure who challenged conventions of her time to earn recognition as a writer and advocate educational opportunities for women in Georgian England; published 1st poem, "To Peace: Written During the Late Rebellion" (1745), which established her as a literary figure of the day; began writing fiction for *The Rambler* (1750), a well-known journal published by Samuel Johnson; was esteemed for her spirited conversational skills among the literati with whom she socialized, including Elizabeth Carter, Mary Wollstonecraft, Samuel Richardson, Elizabeth Montagu and Catherine Talbot; was among the 1st generation of Bluestockings; widowed (c. 1761); wrote educational treatise for young women, *Letters on the Improvement of the Mind* (1773); also wrote *Miscellanies in Verse and Prose* (1775) and *A Letter to a New-Married Lady* (1777). ❖ See also *Memoirs of Mrs. J.*

Chapone, from Various Authentic Sources (1839); and *Women in World History.*

CHAPUIS, Germaine Poinso- (1901–1981). *See Poinso-Chapuis, Germaine.*

CHARAOUI, Hoda (1879–1947). *See Shaarawi, Huda.*

CHARD-WILLIAMS, Ada (c. 1876–1900). English murderer. Name variations: Mrs. Hewetson; Ada Chard Williams. Born c. 1876 in England; hanged at Newgate, Mar 6 (some sources cite Mar 8), 1900. ❖ Placed advertisement in paper which stated she could find homes for unwanted children; charged Florence Jones £5 to find a home for her daughter, 21-month-old Selina, whose body later washed up on the bank of the Thames; at her trial at Old Bailey (Feb 16–17, 1900), convicted of battering and strangling the child; suspected in the deaths of additional children, was the last woman to be hanged at Newgate (Mar 1900).

CHARDININA-BARSKAYA, Margarita (1903–1938). *See Barskaya, Margarita A.*

CHARDONNET, Michele (1956—). French hurdler. Born Oct 27, 1956, in France. ❖ At Los Angeles Olympics, tied with Kim Turner for a bronze medal in 100-meter hurdles (1984).

CHAREST, Isabelle (1971—). Canadian short-track speedskater. Born Mar 1, 1971, in Rimouski, Quebec, Canada; m. Steve Charbonneau (football player). ❖ Won a silver medal in the 3000-meter relay at Lillehammer Olympics (1994); at World championships, won a gold medal for the 500 meters (1996) and a silver medal (1998); won a bronze medal at Nagano Olympics (1998) and a bronze medal at Salt Lake City Olympics (2002), both for the 3,000-meter relay; was the 1st woman to break 45 seconds in the 500.

CHARISSE, Calliope (c. 1880–1946). Greek interpretive dancer. Born c. 1880 in Greece; died Sept 6, 1946, in US; children: 11, including Noel Charisse (1905–1983), Nico Charisse (1906–1970, who m. Cyd Charisse); Katerina Charisse (who as Kathryn Etienne taught dance), Pierre Charisse (who had a ballroom act with wife Renée); Helen Charisse (who taught in Indianapolis); André Charisse (actor and ballet master), Rita Charisse (1917–1993, dancer); and Nanette Charisse (taught dance). ❖ Toured Greece performing a mix of ballet and Duncan-style dance; moved to Paris at the start of WWI to perform at benefits (with her 11 children) for American soldiers and their families; immigrated to US (1923) and performed, with children, at numerous venues, including the Hippodrome and on the Keith circuit; performed and choreographed works throughout lifetime that were inspired by Isadora Duncan, her children appearing in Greek chitons and shoulder-length hair.

CHARISSE, Cyd (1921—). American actress and dancer. Name variations: Lily Norwood. Born Tula Ellice Finklea, Mar 8, 1921, Amarillo, Texas; aunt of actress Nana Visitor (b. 1957); trained with Adolf Bolm, Nico Charisse, and Bronislava Nijinska; m. Nico Charisse (her ballet instructor), 1939 (div. 1947); m. Tony Martin (singer), 1948. ❖ At 13, joined the Ballet Russe, dancing under the names Maria Istomina and Felia Sidorova; as Lily Norwood, made film debut in a bit part in *Something to Shout About* (1943); as Cyd Charisse, signed with MGM and appeared in *The Harvey Girls* (1946), followed by *Ziegfeld Follies, Till the Clouds Roll By, Fiesta, The Unfinished Dance, On an Island with You, The Kissing Bandit, Words and Music, Singin' in the Rain, The Band Wagon, Easy to Love, Brigadoon, Deep in My Heart, Sombrero, Invitation to the Dance, It's Always Fair Weather* and *Silk Stockings,* among others; partners included Gene Kelly and Fred Astaire; made Broadway debut in *Grand Hotel* (1992). ❖ See also autobiography with husband Tony Martin, *The Two of Us* (1976).

CHARITO (fl. 300s). Byzantine and Roman empress. Fl. around 350; m. Jovian, Byzantine and Roman emperor (r. 363–364).

CHARKE, Charlotte Cibber (1713–1760). British novelist and actress. Name variations: Charlotte Cibber. Born 1713; died 1760; youngest of 12 children of Colley Cibber (actor) and Katherine Cibber (briefly an actress and singer at Drury Lane); m. Richard Charke (violinist), Feb 1730; briefly m. John Sacheverille; children: Katerine "Kitty" Charke. ❖ Led wayward and adventurous life as actress and writer; often appeared in men's clothing and passed as a man on several occasions; finally deserted by family, ended life in poverty; wrote *The Art of Management* (1735), *The Carnival; or, Harlequin Blunderer* (1743), *A Narrative of the Life of Mrs. Charlotte Charke (Youngest Daughter of Colley Cibber, Esq.) Written by Herself* (1755), *The Mercer; or, Fatal Extravagance* (1755), *The Lover's Treat; or, Unnatural Hatred* (1758), *The History of Henry Dumont, Esq.; and Miss Charlotte Evelyn* (1758) and *The History of Charley and Patty: or, The Friendly Strangers* (1760).

CHARLES, Daedra (1969—). American basketball player. Born Nov 22, 1968. ❖ At Barcelona Olympics, won a bronze medal in team competition (1992).

CHARLES, Elizabeth (1828–1896). English author. Name variations: Elizabeth Rundle. Born at Tavistock, Jan 2, 1828; died at Hampstead, Mar 28, 1896; dau. of John Rundle (Member of Parliament); m. Andrew Paton Charles, 1851. ❖ Wrote some 50 books, primarily of a semi-religious nature, the best known being *The Chronicles of the Schönberg-Cotta Family* (1862), about Martin Luther. ❖ See also *Women in World History.*

CHARLES, Eugenia (1919–2005). Dominican prime minister. Name variations: Dame Eugenia Charles. Born Mary Eugenia Charles in Roseau, Dominica, May 15, 1919; died Sept 6, 2005, on the island of Martinique; dau. of wealthy planter and political figure J.B. Charles; studied law at University of Toronto and in England; never married; no children. ❖ Prime minister of island nation of Dominica, and 1st female head of state in the Caribbean, who took a major leadership role in regional and international affairs; born into a successful, well-to-do family, grew up in an environment of relative privilege; sent to best schools in the British Caribbean and to University of Toronto (late 1940s), where she earned a bachelor's degree; qualified as a barrister in Britain (1947); returned to Dominica to open a law practice (1949); entered politics (1968) and then only to protest the passage of a controversial sedition law by the Edward Oliver LeBlanc government; became the chief focus of loyal opposition, creating the Dominica Freedom Party along the way; during years in the opposition, saw her influence on island's politics grow (1968–78); in the wake of violence between various partisan factions, her DFP organization came out on top (1979); elected prime minister (1980), a position she held for 15 years (1980–95); under her leadership, Dominica's government became the most conservative in the region, firmly committed to free enterprise and attracting foreign, particularly American, investment to the island; her greatest moment in terms of international exposure came during the US intervention on the island of Grenada—an effort that she vociferously defended as chair of the newly established Organization of Eastern Caribbean States (1983). ❖ See also *Women in World History.*

CHARLES, Gerda (1914–1996). *See Lipson, Edna.*

CHARLES, Lallie (1869–1919). British photographer. Name variations: Charlotte Charles. Born Charlotte Martin in 1869 in England; died 1919; sister of Beaulah "Bea" Martin (photographer who assisted her). ❖ Leading society photographer of her day, had a studio in Curzon Street; photographed royals, aristocrats, and theatrical personalities.

CHARLES, Suzette (1963—). Miss America and singer. Born with surname DeGaetano, Mar 3, 1963 in Mays Landing, New Jersey; m. Leonard Bley (ophthalmologist and plastic surgeon); children: Hannah and Ilan. ❖ Representing NJ, replaced Vanessa Williams as Miss America, when Williams stepped down amid controversy (July 23, 1984); continued singing career.

CHARLESON, Mary (1890–1961). Irish-born actress. Born May 18, 1890, in Dungannon, Ireland; died Dec 3, 1961, in Woodland Hills, California; niece of actress Kate Price; m. Henry B. Walthall (silent screen star). ❖ Began career as a lead player for Vitagraph; appeared in many early Essanay films, often co-starring with husband, Henry B. Walthall; films include *The Raven, Mr. Barnes of New York, The Road to Strife, Passers-By, His Robe of Honor* and *Human Stuff.*

CHARLESWORTH, Maria (1819–1880). British religious writer. Born Oct 1, 1819, in Suffolk, England; died Oct 18, 1880, in Surrey, England; dau. of John Charlesworth (rector of Flowton, Suffolk); aunt of Florence Louisa Barclay (1862–1921, writer). ❖ Began ministering to poor in father's parish as child; didactic writings, which focus on duties of children and work of missionaries, include *The Female Visitor to the Poor* (1846), *The Light of Life* (1850), *Ministering Children* (1854), *Africa's Mountain Valley* (1858), *Oliver of the Mill: A Tale* (1871) and *Broken Looking Glass* (1880).

CHARLIEU, Louise (c. 1523–1566). *See Labé, Louise.*

CHARLOTTE. *Variant of Carlota.*

CHARLOTTE (1516–1524). French princess. Born 1516; died at age 8 in 1524; dau. of Claude de France (1499–1524) and Francis, duc d'Angoulême, later Francis I, king of France (r. 1515–1547). ❖ Upon her death (1524), her aunt Margaret of Angoulême wrote an essay in her honor.

CHARLOTTE (1769–1818). Duchess of Saxe-Hildburghausen. Born 1769; died 1818; dau. of Charles II Louis Frederick, duke of Mecklenburg-Strelitz, and Frederica of Hesse-Darmstadt; sister of Louise of Prussia (1776–1810); m. Frederick, duke of Saxe-Hildburghausen, 1785; children: Catherine Charlotte of Hildburghausen (1787–1847).

CHARLOTTE (1896–1985). Grand duchess of Luxemburg. Name variations: Duchess of Nassau; Princess of Bourbon-Parma; Countess-Palatine of the Rhine; Countess of Sayn, Königstein, Katzenelnbogen, and Dietz; Burgravine of Hammerstein; Lady of Mahlberg, Wiesbaden, Idstein, Merenberg, Limburg, and Eppstein; Grand Duchess of Luxembourg. Born Charlotte Aldegonde Elise Marie Wilhelmine at the castle Colmar-Berg in northern Luxemburg, Jan 23, 1896; died 1985; 2nd of six daughters of William IV (1852–1912), grand duke of Luxemburg (of the House of Nassau) and Marie-Anne of Braganza (infanta of Portugal); younger sister of Marie Adelaide of Luxemburg; privately educated by tutors; m. Felix, prince of Bourbon-Parma, Nov 6, 1919; children: son Jean or John, grand duke of Luxemburg (b. 1921, who m. Princess Josephine-Charlotte of Belgium in 1953); Elisabeth (b. 1922); Marie Adelaide (b. 1924); Marie Gabrielle (b. 1925); Charles (b. 1927); Alix (b. 1929). ❖ Following German subjugation of Luxemburg, won overwhelmingly in a referendum to rule the country and continue its sovereignty, forcing sister Marie Adelaide to abdicate (Sept 28, 1919); a progressive and advocate of republicanism, encouraged the 1919 emendation of Luxemburg's constitution, which established universal suffrage and proportional representation; during WWII (1940), when Luxemburg once again suffered German occupation, set up a government-in-exile in London, then joined husband and children who had fled to Montreal; frequently broadcast to her nation and made repeated visits to Washington, DC, and London to work closely with Allies; abandoned policy of unarmed neutrality and joined in a customs union with Belgium and the Netherlands (1948); during her popular reign, saw Luxemburg prosper; abdicated in favor of son, who ascended throne as Grand Duke Jean (1964), having ruled her country for 45 years (1919–64). ❖ See also *Women in World History*.

CHARLOTTE (c. 1899–after 1948). See Oelschlagel, Charlotte.

CHARLOTTE, Countess of Derby (1599–1664). See Stanley, Charlotte.

CHARLOTTE, Empress of Mexico (1840–1927). See Carlota.

CHARLOTTE, Queen of Portugal (1775–1830). See Carlota Joaquina.

CHARLOTTE-AGLAE (1700–1761). Duchess of Modena. Name variations: Charlotte d'Orléans; Charlotte of Orleans; Charlotte of Orléans. Born Dec 22, 1700; died Jan 19, 1761; dau. of Françoise-Marie de Bourbon (1677–1749) and Philippe II also known as Philip Bourbon-Orléans (1674–1723), 2nd duke of Orléans (r. 1701–1723); m. Francesco or Francis III, duke of Modena (r. 1748–1780), June 21, 1720; possibly mother of Ercole III Rinaldo (1727–1803), duke of Modena. ❖ Was the subject of a painting by Angelica Kauffmann.

CHARLOTTE AMALIA OF HESSE (1650–1714). Queen of Denmark and Norway. Name variations: Charlotte Amalie of Hesse-Cassel; Charlotte Amelia. Born April 27, 1650, in Cassel; died Mar 27, 1714, in Copenhagen, Denmark; m. Christian V (1646–1699), king of Norway and Denmark (r. 1670–1699), June 25, 1667; children: Frederik or Frederick IV (1671–1730), king of Norway and Denmark (r. 1699–1730); Christian William (b. 1672); Christian (b. 1675); Sophie Hedwig (1677–1735); Christiane Charlotte (1679–1689); Charles (b. 1680); William (b. 1687).

CHARLOTTE AMALIE (1706–1782). Danish princess. Name variations: Charlotte Amalie Oldenburg. Born Oct 6, 1706; died Oct 28, 1782; dau. of Louise of Mecklenburg-Gustrow (1667–1721) and Frederick IV (1671–1730), king of Denmark and Norway (r. 1699–1730).

CHARLOTTE AUGUSTA (1796–1817). Princess of Wales. Born Charlotte Augusta of Wales; Charlotte of Wales, Charlotte Guelph; Princess Charlotte. Born Charlotte Augusta at Carlton House, London, England, Jan 7, 1796; died in childbirth in Esher, Surrey, England, Nov 6, 1817; buried at St. George's Chapel, Windsor, Berkshire, England; dau. of George IV (1762–1821), king of England (r. 1820–1830), and Caroline of Brunswick (1768–1821); m. Leopold of Saxe-Coburg-Saalfeld, also known as Leopold I (b. 1790), king of the Belgians (r. 1831–1865), May 2, 1816; children: a son who died at birth. ❖ See also *Women in World History*.

CHARLOTTE AUGUSTA MATILDA (1766–1828). Princess royal. Name variations: Charlotte Guelph; Charlotte Hanover. Born Charlotte Augusta Matilda, Sept 29, 1766, at Buckingham Palace, London, England; died Oct 6, 1828, at Ludwigsburg Palace, Stuttgart, Germany; buried at Ludwigsburg Palace; dau. of George III (1738–1820), king of England (r. 1760–1820) and Charlotte of Mecklenburg-Strelitz (1744–1818); m. Frederick II (1754–1816), duke of Wurttemberg (r. 1797–1802), elector of Wurttemberg (r. 1802–1806), also known as Frederick I, king of Wurttemberg (r. 1806–1816), May 18, 1797, at Chapel Royal, St. James's Palace; children: Paul of Wurttemberg (b. 1798). Frederick's 1st wife was Augusta of Brunswick-Wolfenbuttel.

CHARLOTTE DE MONTMORENCY (1594–1650). French aristocrat. Name variations: Charlotte of Montmorency; Princesse de Condé or Conde; Princess of Condé. Born Charlotte Marguerite de Montmorency, May 11, 1594, in Pezenas; died Dec 2, 1650, in Chatillon-sur-Loing; m. Henry II de Bourbon, 3rd prince de Condé (1588–1646); children: Louis II de Bourbon, prince de Condé (1621–1686, known as The Great Condé); Anne Geneviève, Duchesse de Longueville (1619–1679); and a son who married Anne-Marie Martinozzi. ❖ An influential member of the French court, was involved with cousin Anne of Austria and Marie de Rohan-Montbazon in the *Conspiration des Dames*, to spoil a matchmaking scheme of Cardinal Richelieu's to better position Gaston, duke of Orléans, brother of Louis XIII, in line for the throne; her son, the Great Condé, was a celebrated French general. ❖ See also *Women in World History*.

CHARLOTTE ELIZABETH (1790–1846). See Tonna, Charlotte Elizabeth.

CHARLOTTE ELIZABETH OF BAVARIA (1652–1722). Duchess of Orleans. Name variations: Elisabeth Charlotte of Orleans; Elizabeth Charlotte of Bohemia; Elizabeth Charlotte of the Palatinate; Elizabeth-Charlotte of Bourbon Orleans; princess of the Palatinate; Madame Palatine. Born in Heidelberg, Baden, May 27, 1652; died in St. Cloud, France, Dec 8, 1722 (some sources cite 1712); dau. of Charlotte of Hesse (1627–1687) and Charles I, Elector Palatine; became 2nd wife of Philip (1540–1701), duke of Orléans (r. 1660–1701, brother of King Louis XIV of France), Nov 16 or 21, 1671, at Metz (died 1701); children: Alexander (b. 1673); Philip or Philippe (b. 1674), 2nd duke of Orleans; Elizabeth-Charlotte (1676–1744, who m. Leopold, duke of Lorraine, and was the mother of Emperor Francis I). ❖ Was married to Louis XIV's brother Philip, duke of Orléans (1671); regally known as Madame after her marriage, became a formidable force in court life, largely because of her flourishing relationship with the king, whom she came to call the "Great Man"; developed a surprisingly good relationship with husband, children, and stepchildren; in addition to her status as one of the best-read members of court, distinguished herself as one of the most prolific letter writers of all time, detailing day-to-day life there, as well as observations on the relatives and courtiers of Louis XIV. ❖ See also *Women in World History*.

CHARLOTTE FREDERICA OF MECKLENBURG-SCHWERIN (1784–1840). Princess of Mecklenburg-Schwerin. Name variations: Charlotte Frederikke; Charlotte of Mecklenburg-Schwerin; Charlotte von Mecklenburg-Schwerin. Born Dec 4, 1784, in Ludwigslust; died July 13, 1840, in Rome, Italy; dau. of Frederick Francis, duke of Mecklenburg-Schwerin, and Louise of Saxe-Gotha (1756–1808); became 1st wife of Christian VIII (1786–1848), king of Denmark (r. 1839–1848), June 21, 1806 (div. 1810); children: Frederick or Frederick VII (b. 1808), king of Denmark (r. 1848–1863).

CHARLOTTE OF BAVARIA (1792–1873). See Caroline Augusta of Bavaria.

CHARLOTTE OF BELGIUM (1840–1927). See Carlota.

CHARLOTTE OF BOURBON (d. 1582). Princess of Orange and countess of Nassau. Born Charlotte Bourbon; Charlotte of Bourbon-Montpensier; Charlotte de Montpensier. Died 1582; possibly dau. of Louis, duke of Montpensier; became 3rd wife of William I the Silent (1533–1584), prince of Orange, count of Nassau (r. 1544–1584), stadholder of Holland, Zealand, and Utrecht (r. 1572–1584); children: Louisa Juliana of Orange (1576–1644); Amalia (who m. Frederick Casimir of Zweibrücken); Elizabeth; Catherine Belgica; Brabantina; Flanderina; Antwerpina. William the Silent's 1st wife was Anna of Egmont (1533–1558); his 2nd was Anna of Saxony (1544–1577); his 4th was Louise de Coligny (1555–1620).

CHARLOTTE OF BRUNSWICK-WOLFENBÜTTEL (1694–1715). German princess. Born Aug 29, 1694; died in childbirth, Nov 2, 1715; dau. of Ludwig Rudolf, duke of Brunswick-Wolfenbüttel; sister of Elizabeth Christina of Brunswick-Wolfenbüttel (1691–1750, the mother of Maria Theresa of Austria); m. Alexis Petrovitch (d. June 1718 while undergoing judicial inquiry authorized by his father Peter I the Great), Oct 25, 1711; children: Natalie (1714–1728); Peter Alexivitch also known as Peter II (1715–1730), tsar of Russia.

CHARLOTTE OF HESSE (1627–1687). Landgrave of Hesse-Cassel. Name variations: Charlotte of Hesse-Cassel. Born Nov 20, 1627, in Cassel, Germany; died Mar 16, 1687, in Cassel; dau. of William V (b. 1602), landgrave of Hesse, and Amelia of Hanau; m. Karl Ludwig also known as Charles I Louis (1617–1680), elector Palatine of the Rhine (r. 1648–1680), Feb 22, 1650 (div.); children: Charles II (1651–1685), elector Palatine of the Rhine; Frederick Simmern; Charlotte Elizabeth of Bavaria (1652–1722); Charlotte Wittelsbach (1659–1696, who m. Meinhard, duke of Leinster). Charles I Louis' 2nd wife was Marie Susanne Louise Raugräfin.

CHARLOTTE OF HESSE-DARMSTADT (1755–1785). Grand duchess of Mecklenburg-Strelitz. Born in 1755; died in 1785, probably in childbirth; dau. of Prince George William, landgrave of Hesse-Darmstadt (1722–1782) and Marie Louise Albertine of Leiningen-Heidesheim; sister of Frederica of Hesse-Darmstadt (1752–1782) who was Charles II's 1st wife and the mother of Louise of Prussia; became 2nd wife of Charles II, grand duke of Mecklenburg-Strelitz, 1784; children: Charles (1785–1837).

CHARLOTTE OF LUSIGNAN (1442–1487). Queen of Cyprus. Name variations: Carlotta; Carlotta, queen of Cyprus; Charlotte of Cyprus. Born Cyprus in 1442; died in Rome, Italy, July 16, 1487; eldest dau. of John II, king of Cyprus (r. 1432–1458), and Helen Paleologina; m. Joao de Coimbra or John of Coimbra also known as John of Portugal (1431–1457), 1456 (murdered); married her 1st cousin Louis of Savoy, count of Geneva; children: none. ❖ On her father's death, became queen of Cyprus (1458); ruled alone for several years before her illeg. half-brother James wrested control of the government from her and established himself as King James II; forced to flee, moved to Rhodes with husband, where she continued to intrigue for her reinstatement until her death. ❖ See also *Women in World History.*

CHARLOTTE OF MECKLENBURG-STRELITZ (1744–1818). Queen consort of England. Name variations: Charlotte Sophia or Charlotte-Sophia. Born a princess, May 19, 1744, in Mirow, Mecklenburg-Strelitz, Germany; died Nov 17, 1818, in Kew Palace, Surrey; interred at St. George's Chapel, Windsor Castle; dau. of Charles Louise Frederick (b. 1708), duke of Mecklenburg-Strelitz and Elizabeth of Saxe-Hildburghausen (1713–1761); m. George III (1738–1820), king of England (r. 1761–1820), Sept 8, 1761; children: George IV (1762–1830), prince of Wales and king of England (r. 1820–1830); Frederick Augustus (1763–1827), duke of York; William IV (1765–1837), duke of Clarence; Charlotte Augusta Matilda (1766–1828); Edward Augustus (1767–1820), duke of Kent; Augusta Guelph (1768–1840); Elizabeth (1770–1840); Ernest Augustus (1771–1851), duke of Cumberland; Augustus Frederick (1773–1843), duke of Sussex; Adolphus Frederick (1774–1850), duke of Cambridge; Mary (1776–1857), duchess of Gloucester; Sophia Matilda (1777–1848); Octavius (1779–1783); Alfred (1780–1782); Amelia (1783–1810). ❖ Following marriage to George III, settled down to quiet living; when husband's violent episodes began (1804), refused to be alone with him. ❖ See also *Women in World History.*

CHARLOTTE OF MEXICO (1840–1927). See *Carlota.*

CHARLOTTE OF MONTMORENCY (1594–1650). See *Charlotte de Montmorency.*

CHARLOTTE OF OLDENBURG (1759–1818). Queen of Sweden. Name variations: Hedwig of Oldenburg. Born Mar 22, 1759; died June 20, 1818; dau. of August, duke of Oldenburg, and Friederike of Hesse-Cassel (1722–1787); m. Karl or Charles XIII (1748–1818), king of Sweden (r. 1809–1818), July 7, 1774; children: Charles XIV John (b. 1763), king of Sweden; Charles Adolf (b. 1798).

CHARLOTTE OF PRUSSIA (1798–1860). Empress of Russia. Name variations: Alexandra Feodorovna; Charlotte Hohenzollern; Louise Charlotte of Prussia. Born July 13, 1798; died Nov 1, 1860; dau. of Frederick William III, king of Prussia (r. 1797–1840), and Louise of Prussia (1776–1810); m. Nicholas I (1796–1855), tsar of Russia (r. 1825–1855), July 13, 1817; children: Alexander II, tsar of Russia (r. 1855–1881); Constantine Nicholaevitch (who m. Alexandra of Saxe-Altenburg); Nicholas Nicholaevitch (1831–1891), grand duke (who m. Alexandra of Oldenburg); Michael Nicholaevitch (who m. Cecilia of Baden); Maria Nikolaevna (1819–1876); Olga of Russia (1822–1892), who m. Charles I of Württemberg); Alexandra Nikolaevna (1825–1844, who m. Frederick William, landgrave of Hesse-Cassel); and two others.

CHARLOTTE OF SAVOY (c. 1442–1483). Queen of France. Name variations: Charlotte d'Savoie. Born 1442 (some sources cite 1439, 1440 or 1445); died Dec 1, 1483 (some sources cite 1515); dau. of Louis I, prince of Piedmont and duke of Savoy, and Anne of Lusignan; sister of Bona of Savoy (c. 1450–c. 1505); became 2nd wife of Louis XI (1423–1483), king of France (r. 1461–1483), in Mar 1451; children: Joachim (b. 1459, died at age four months); Anne of Beaujeu (c. 1460–1522); Francis (1466–1466); Charles VIII (1470–1498), king of France (r. 1483–1498); Francis (1473–1473); Jeanne de France (c. 1464–1505). ❖ See also *Women in World History.*

CHARLOTTE OF SAXE-HILDBURGHAUSEN (1787–1847). See *Catherine Charlotte of Hildburghausen.*

CHARLOTTE OF SAXE-MEININGEN (1860–1919). German princess. Name variations: Charlotte Hohenzollern. Born Victoria Elizabeth Augusta Charlotte, July 24, 1860, in Potsdam, Brandenburg, Germany; died Oct 1, 1919, in Baden-Baden, Germany; dau. of Frederick III (1831–1888), emperor of Germany (r. 1888), and Victoria Adelaide (1840–1901), princess royal (and dau. of Queen Victoria of England); sister of Kaiser Wilhelm II (r. 1888–1918); m. Bernard III (b. 1851), duke of Saxe-Meiningen and Hildburghausen, Feb 18, 1878; children: Feodora of Saxe-Meiningen (1879–1945, who m. Henry III, prince of Reuss), duchess of Saxony.

CHARLOTTE OF VENDÔME (fl. 15th c.). Duchess of Nevers. Name variations: Charlotte of Vendome. Married Engelbert, duke of Nevers; children: Charles I, duke of Nevers (d. 1521).

CHARLOTTE OF WALES (1796–1817). See *Charlotte Augusta.*

CHARLOTTE OLDENBURG (1789–1864). Danish royal. Name variations: Louise Charlotte of Denmark. Born Oct 30, 1789; died Mar 28, 1864; dau. of Frederick (1753–1805), prince of Denmark (son of Frederick V of Denmark and Maria Juliana of Brunswick) and Sophia of Mecklenburg (1758–1794); sister of Christian VIII, king of Denmark (r. 1839–1848); m. William, landgrave of Hesse-Cassel, Nov 10, 1810; children: Caroline Frederica of Hesse-Cassel (1811–1829); Marie Louise Charlotte of Hesse-Cassel (1814–1895, who m. Frederick Augustus, prince of Anhalt-Dessau); Louise of Hesse-Cassel (1817–1898, wife of Christian IX of Denmark); Frederick William (1820–1884), landgrave of Hesse; Augusta Frederica Marie (1823–1889, who m. Charles Frederick, lord of Dalund); Sophie Wilhemina Augusta (1827–1827).

CHARLOTTE SAXE-COBURG (1840–1927). See *Carlota.*

CHARNAS, Suzy McKee (1939—). American science-fiction writer. Name variations: (pseudonym) Rebecca Brand. Born Oct 22, 1939, in New York, NY; Barnard College, BA in economic history, 1961; New York University, MA; m. Stephen Charnas, 1968. ❖ Worked for Peace Corps in Nigeria (1961–62), as high-school teacher in NY, and as a mental-health worker, before becoming a full-time writer; works include *Walk to the End of the World* (1974), *Motherlines* (1980), *The Bronze King* (1985), *The Golden Thread* (1989), *The Furies* (1994), *The Ruby Tear* (1997) and *Music of the Night* (2001).

CHAROLOIS, countess of (d. 1465). See *Isabelle of Bourbon.*

CHARPENTIER, Constance Marie (1767–1841). French painter. Born Constance Marie Blondeau, 1767, in Paris, France; died 1841; trained under famed artist Louis David. ❖ Admired for paintings of family scenes, her most famous painting, *Mademoiselle Charlotte du Val d'Ongres,* was attributed to Louis David until 1950s; exhibited in 10 salons (1795–1819); won gold medal from Musée Royale (1819).

CHARRAT, Janine (1924—). French ballet dancer and choreographer. Name variations: wrongly seen as Jeanine Charrat. Born July 24, 1924, in Grenoble, France. ❖ As a child dancer, appeared as the character Rose Souris in the film *La Mort du Cigne* (1937); performed in Soirée de la Danse series (1941–44); danced with Roland Petit's Ballets des Champs-Élysées in Paris and with Nouveau Ballet de Monte Carlo in Serge Lifar's *Prière* (1946); founded own ballet company, Ballets de France de Janine Charrat (late 1940s), for which she choreographed dances and performed in numerous works including *Les Algues* (1953), *Concerto* (1947), and *Le Massacre des Amazones* (1951); had to retire from stage after her costume caught fire during a tv rehearsal; served as director of Geneva Ballet in Switzerland (1960s), then opened her own dance studio in Paris. Works of choreography include *Jeux de Cartes* (1944), *Theme and Variations* (1948), *La Nuit* (1949), *Heracles* (1953), *Le Jouer de Flute* (1956), *Les Lieux* (1957), *Roi David* (1960), *Pour le Temps Présent* (1963), *Paris* (1964), *Up to Date* (1968), *Firebird* (1969) and *Hyperprisme* (1973).

CHARRIERE, Isabelle de (1740–1805). Dutch-born author of plays, stories, novels and essays. Name variations: Isabelle de Charrière; Zelide or Zélide; Isabella or Isabelle van Tuyll; Abbe de la Tour. Born Isabelle Agnès Elisabeth van Tuyll van Seeroskerken van Zuylen in 1740 at Zuylen, Netherlands; died 1805; dau. of the Lord of Zuylen; m. Charles-Emmanuel de Charriere (mathematician), Feb 17, 1771, in Zuylen; no children. ❖ Works, which were largely romantic reflections on her liaisons, include *Lettres de Mistress Henley* (The Letters of Mistress Henley, 1784), *Lettres neuchâteloises* (Letters from Neuchâtel, 1784), *Lettres trouvées dans des portfeuilles d'emigrés* (Letters from an émigré's Wallet, 1793), and *Trois Femmes* (Three Women, 1797). ❖ See also Geoffrey Scott, *The Portrait of Zélide* (Scribner, 1927); and *Women in World History*.

CHÁRSKAIA, Lidiia Alekséevna (1875–1937). *See Churilova, L.A.*

CHARTERIS, Catherine Morice (1835–1918). Scottish social activist. Name variations: Catherine Anderson. Born Catherine Anderson, 1835, in Aberdeen, Scotland; died in 1918 in Scotland; dau. of Sir Alexander Anderson (Lord Provost of Aberdeen); m. Archibald Hamilton Charteris (minister in Church of Scotland, early and vocal advocate of women's rights, Royal Chaplain), 1863 (died 1908); children: raised husband's nephew, Archibald Charteris. ❖ Activist who promoted Church of Scotland's Women's Guild, women's rights and support for poor families; met husband in Glasgow, where he was working as minister of Park Church; pursued social reform with husband, who demanded wealthy congregation endow funds for territorial outreach and set aside pews for poor; led group of well-to-do women from Park Church to slums of Port Dundas to visit homes and run meetings; founded Order of Deaconesses in Scotland; moved to Edinburgh where husband took post as professor of Biblical Criticism at University of Edinburgh (1868); helped him establish Women's Guild and later became its president, serving until 1906; assisted in launching of husband's *Christian Life and Work* magazine; continued activities into old age, organizing slum missions, Bible classes and mothers' meetings and setting up homes for missionaries' children and deaconesses.

CHARTERIS, Violet (1888–1971). English aristocrat. Name variations: Lady Violet Charteris; Violet Manners. Born Violet Catherine Manners, April 24, 1888, in London, England; died Dec 23, 1971; dau. of Henry John Brinsley Manners, 8th duke of Rutland, and Marion Margaret Violet Lindsay; sister of Marjorie Manners, marchioness of Anglesey, and Lady Diana Manners; studied at Slade School of Art; m. Hugo Francis Charteris, Lord Elcho, Feb 1, 1911 (killed in action in WWI, 1916); m. Guy Holford Benson, July 9, 1921; children: (1st m.) Sir Francis David Charteris, 12th earl of Wemyss (b. 1912) and Martin Charteris, Lord Charteris of Amisfield (1913–1999). ❖ Victorian beauty, was the subject of drawings by John Singer Sargent and George Frederic Watts.

CHARTRAND, Isabelle (1978—). Canadian ice-hockey player. Born 1978 in Canada. ❖ Played for St. Lawrence University; won a gold medal at World championships (2001) and a gold medal at Salt Lake City Olympics (2002).

CHARTRES, countess of.
See Maud of Normandy (d. 1017).
See Maud of Normandy (d. 1107).
See Adela of Blois (1062–c. 1137).
See Marie de Chatillon (r. 1230–1241).

CHARTRES, duchess of.
See Louise Marie of Bourbon (1753–1821).
See Helene Louise of Mecklenburg-Schwerin (1814–1858).
See Françoise d'Orléans (1844–1925).

CHARTROULE, Marie-Amélie (1848–1912). French novelist. Name variations: Marie-Emilie de Chartroule; Marie-Amelie Chartroule de Montifaud; also known as Mrs. Quivogne or Marie Amelie Quivogne de Montifaud; (pseudonym) Marc de Montifaud. Born Marie-Amelie Chartroule, 1848, in France; died in 1912; m. Juan-Francis-Leon Quivogne (writer). ❖ Writings, which were often condemned for licentiousness and anti-clericalism, include *Les Vestales de l'Eglise* (1877), *Les Dévoyés* (1879), *Mme Ducroisy* (1879) and *La Rue Sainte-Amendée* (1881); was imprisoned for 4 months following publication of *Mme Ducroisy*, then wrote a pamphlet in self-defense, *Mme Ducroisy, la presse et la justice.*

CHARVATOVA, Olga (1962—). Czech Alpine skier. Name variations: Olga Charvatova-Krizova. Born June 11, 1962, in Gottwaldov, Czechoslovakia. ❖ Won a bronze medal for downhill at Sarajevo Olympics (1984).

CHASCHINA, Irina (1982—). *See Tchachina, Irina.*

CHASE, Agnes Meara (1869–1963). American botanist. Name variations: Mary Agnes Meara Chase. Born Mary Agnes Meara in Iroquois Co., Illinois, April 20, 1869; died in Bethesda, Maryland, 1963; dau. of Martin J. (railroad engineer) and Mary (Brannick) Meara; m. William Ingraham Chase, 1888 (died 1889). ❖ Lacking formal education, turned a passionate hobby into a distinguished career as a botanist and international authority on grasses; on a plant collecting trip (1898), met bryologist Ellsworth Hill, who instructed her in plant lore and enlisted her as an illustrator; while working for Hill, also illustrated 2 publications for Field Museum of Natural History: *Plantae Utowanae* (1900) and *Plantae Yucatamae* (1904); worked as a meat inspector at Chicago Stockyards for US Department of Agriculture (USDA), before obtaining a position as a botanical artist with Bureau of Plant Industry in Washington, DC (1903), where she became principal scientist in charge of systematic agrostology; was also devoted to a number of reform movements. ❖ See also *Women in World History*.

CHASE, Alison Becker (c. 1948—). American dancer and choreographer. Born c. 1948 in Eolia, Missouri; Washington University in St. Louis, BA in Intellectual History and Philosophy, 1969; University of California at Los Angeles, MA in dance; studied with Murray Louis and Mia Slavenska; children: 3. ❖ Taught modern dance at Dartmouth College (1970–72); was a major influence on Moses Pendleton and Jonathan Wolken, founders of Pilobolus; as one of the inventors of the movement vocabulary of Pilobolus, began performing with the troupe during its 2nd season (1973) and appeared in most all the dances; taught at Yale (1991–97); choreographed numerous works, both solo and in collaboration with Pendleton and Martha Clarke; choreographed for La Scala Opera, Geneva Opera, Ballet du Rhin, and the Rockettes at Radio City.

CHASE, Arline (1900–1926). American film dancer. Born 1900; died of tuberculosis, April 19, 1926, in Sierra Madre, California. ❖ Made featured debut in the Jerome Kern musical *Leave It to Jane* (1918); performed as ballet dancer in 2 Ned Wayburn Midnight matinees: *Century Revue* (1920) and *Ziegfeld Midnight Frolic* (1921); after moving to Hollywood, became Mack Sennett Bathing Beauty and often appeared as an extra in dance scenes and in more significant parts in his romantic comedies.

CHASE, Barrie (1933—). American film dancer and actress. Name variations: Barrie Kaufman. Born Oct 20, 1933, in King's Point, Long Island, NY; dau. of Borden Chase (1900–1971, writer); m. Gene Shacove (div.); m. James Kaufman (dentist); children: 1 son. ❖ As a child, appeared in the film *Scaramouche;* worked with Jack Cole on films *Les Girls* and *Designing Women* (both 1957); appeared in numerous films under contract with 20th Century-Fox, including *Mardi Gras* (1958); also appeared in *Cape Fear* (1962), *It's a Mad Mad Mad Mad World* (1963) and *The Flight of the Phoenix* (1965); was partnered with Fred Astaire on many tv shows, including "An Evening with Fred Astaire" (1958), "Think Pretty" (1964) and "The Fred Astaire Show" (1968).

CHASE, Catherine Jane (1840–1899). *See Sprague, Kate Chase.*

CHASE, Edna Woolman (1877–1957). American editor. Born Mar 14, 1877, in Asbury Park, New Jersey; died Mar 20, 1957, in Sarasota, Florida; dau. of Franklyn and Laura (Woolman) Alloway; m. Francis Dane Chase, 1904 (div.); m. Richard T. Newton (English automotive engineer and inventor), 1921 (died 1950); children: (1st m.) Ilka Chase (1905–1978). ❖ America's "high priestess of fashion" for most of the 1st half of the 20th century, was editor of *Vogue* magazine (1914–29) and editor-in-chief (1929–52). ❖ See also autobiography (with Ilka Chase) *Always in Vogue* (Doubleday, 1954); and *Women in World History*.

CHASE, Elizabeth (1832–1911). *See Allen, Elizabeth.*

CHASE, Elizabeth (1950—). Zimbabwean field-hockey player. Born April 26, 1950. ❖ At Moscow Olympics, won a gold medal in team competition (1980).

CHASE, Ilka (1905–1978). American actress and author. Born April 8, 1905, in New York, NY; died Feb 15, 1978, in Mexico City, Mexico; dau. of Francis Dane (hotel manager) and Edna Woolman Chase (editor *Vogue* magazine); m. Louis Calhern (actor), 1926 (div. 1926); m. William B. Murray (radio executive), July 13, 1935 (div. 1946); m. Norton Sager Brown (physician), Dec 7, 1946; no children. ❖ As an actress, performed in over 20 Broadway plays, most notably as Sylvia Fowler in *The Women* (1936); launched movie career in *Paris Bound* (1929), ultimately appearing in some 30 movies, most notably *Fast and Loose* (1930), *The Animal Kingdom* (1942) and *Now, Voyager* (1942); hosted radio program, "Luncheon at the Waldorf" (1938), later titled "Penthouse Party," which lasted until 1945; as a writer, penned several novels, 2 biographies, and 7 travel books; writings include *In Bed We Cry* (1943), *I Love Miss Tilli Bean* (1946), *New York 22* (1951), *The Island Players* (1956), *The Sounds of Home* (1971) and *The Care and Feeding of Friends* (1973). ❖ See also autobiography *Past Imperfect* (1942) and *Free Admission* (1948); and *Women in World History*.

CHASE, Lucia (1897–1986). American dancer and founder. Name variations: Lucia Chase Ewing. Pronunciation: LOO-shuh. Born Mar 24, 1897, in Waterbury, Connecticut; died Jan 1986, in New York, NY; dau. of Irving Hall Chase (president of Waterbury Watch Co.) and Elizabeth Hosmer (Kellogg) Chase; studied ballet at Vestoff Serova School; studied with Mikhail Mordkin; m. Thomas Ewing Jr., 1926 (died 1933); children: Thomas (died 1963); Alexander Cochran Ewing (chancellor of North Carolina School of the Arts). ❖ Became a principal dancer and founding member of the Ballet Theatre (1940), later to be called the American Ballet Theatre (ABT), intent on developing a world-class American ballet company; during the initial sold-out season, created roles of the Girl in Loring's *The Great American Goof* and Minerva in Tudor's *Judgment of Paris;* made her mark in a number of other performances, including the title role in *Princess Aurora,* the Greedy One in Agnes de Mille's *Three Virgins and the Devil,* the Nurse in *Romeo and Juliet,* and Pallas Athena in *Helen of Troy;* became co-director of the company (1945); dancing career peaked (1960), when she and Nora Kaye performed in Tudor's *Pillar of Fire,* which was considered one of the masterpieces of the company; throughout near 40-year association with ABT, provided generous financial support and guided careers of countless dancers and choreographers. Received Presidential Medal of Freedom (1980). ❖ See also *Women in World History*.

CHASE, Martha (1927–2003). American scientific researcher. Born Nov 30, 1927; died Aug 8, 2003, age 75, in Lorain, Ohio; attended College of Wooster; University of Southern California, PhD, 1964; married briefly. ❖ Was a research assistant for biologist Dr. Alfred D. Hershey at the Cold Spring Harbor Laboratory on Long Island (1952); with Hershey, devised an experiment to determine whether DNA or its associated protein carried the genetic information for infection, grown and development, using a Waring blender (the successful experiment provided one of the foundations of molecular biology, and Hershey would win the Nobel Prize).

CHASE, Mary Agnes Meara (1869–1963). *See Chase, Agnes Meara.*

CHASE, Mary Coyle (1907–1981). American playwright. Born Mary Coyle, Feb 25, 1907, in West Denver, Colorado; died Oct 21, 1981, in Denver; dau. of Frank and Mary (McDonough) Coyle; attended Denver University, 1929–23, and University of Colorado at Boulder, 1923–24; m. Robert Lamont Chase (newspaper reporter), June 7, 1928; children: Michael Lamont, Colin Robert, and Barry Jerome. ❖ Winner of the Pulitzer Prize for the comedy *Harvey* (1945), which contained one of the most famous characters in dramatic literature—a 6′1½ rabbit, and was one of Broadway's 4 longest running shows, 1st worked as reporter for *Rocky Mountain News* (1924–31); was freelance correspondent, International News Service and United Press (1932–36); named runner-up New York Drama Critics Circle Award for *Mrs. McThing* (1951–52); appointed to honorary committee of American National Theater and Academy (ANTA, 1981); during lifetime, worked for numerous social causes; other plays include *Bernardine* (two-act), 1st produced on Broadway, Oct 16, 1952, starring John Kerr, and *Midgie Purvis* (two-act), 1st produced on Broadway in 1961; also wrote novels for children including *Loretta Mason Potts* (1958) and *The Wicked Pigeon Ladies in the Garden* (1968). ❖ See also *Women in World History*.

CHASE, Mary Ellen (1887–1973). American writer and educator. Born Feb 24, 1887, in Blue Hill, Maine; died July 28, 1973, in Northampton, Massachusetts; graduate of University of Maine, 1909; University of Minnesota, PhD 1922. ❖ Worked for 9 years as a schoolteacher, before publishing 1st novel, *His Birthday* (1915); followed this with 2 children's books: *The Girl from the Bighorn Country* (1916) and *Virginia of Elk Creek Valley* (1917); became an instructor at University of Minnesota (1918), then assistant professor (1922); became associate professor at Smith College (1926), then full professor (1929), retiring (1955); novels include *Uplands* (1927), *Mary Peters* (1934), *Silas Crockett* (1935), *Dawn in Lyonesse* (1938), *Windswept* (1941) and *The Plum Tree* (1949). ❖ See also autobiographies *A Goodly Heritage* (1932), *The Goodly Fellowship* (1939), *Recipe for a Magic Childhood* (1951) and *The White Gate: Adventures in the Imagination of a Child* (1954); and *Women in World History*.

CHASE, Pauline (1885–1962). American-born actress. Born May 20, 1885, in Washington DC; died Mar 3, 1962, at Tunbridge Wells, Kent, England; m. Alexander V. Drummond. ❖ Appeared on Broadway in *Belle of New York, The Little Slavey* and *Liberty Belles;* made debut in London with Edna May in *The Girl from Up There* (1901); remained in London where she came to prominence, appearing over 1,000 times in title role in *Peter Pan* for 8 consecutive seasons (1906–14).

CHASE-RIBOUD, Barbara (1936—). African-American novelist and sculptor. Born June 26, 1936, in Philadelphia, Pennsylvania; dau. of Charles Edward Chase and Vivian May Braithwaite Chase; Temple University, BFA, 1957; Yale Graduate School of Art, MFA (1960); m. Marc Eugene Riboud, 1961 (div. 1981); m. Sergio Tosi, 1981; children: 2. ❖ Moved to Paris (1961) and began to show art; came to prominence with *Sally Hemings* (1979), an immediate bestseller; became embroiled in legal battle with director Steven Spielberg over film *Amistad* which she claimed had plagiarized several details from her novel *Echo of Lions* (1989), and settled case for an undisclosed sum (1998); wrote novels, poetry, and essays, including *From Memphis to Peking* (1974), *Albin Michel* (1981), *Valide: A Novel of the Harem* (1986), *Portrait of a Nude Woman as Cleopatra* (1987), *The President's Daughter* (1994), *Egypt's Nights* (1994) and *Hottentot Venus* (2004). Received Janet Kafka Award for Best Novel by an American Woman (1979), Carl Sandburg Poetry Award for Best American Poetry (1988), and Knight of the Order of Arts and Letters of the French Republic (1996).

CHASEN, Maude (1904–2001). American restaurateur. Born Maude Martin, May 20, 1904, in Louisville, Kentucky; died Dec 8, 2001, in Los Angeles, California; m. Dave Chasen (ex-vaudeville performer), 1942 (died 1973); children: Kay MacKay. ❖ Began career overseeing the beauty salons of Saks Fifth Avenue; with husband, ran the popular Chasen's Restaurant in Los Angeles, which catered to celebrities and presidents (1936–95); continued presiding over the restaurant after husband died (1973).

CHAST, Roz (1954—). American cartoonist. Born Nov 26, 1954, in Brooklyn, NY; dau. of George and Elizabeth (Buchman) Chast (both schoolteachers); Rhode Island School of Design, BFA, 1977; m. Bill Franzen (writer), 1984; children: Ian and Nina. ❖ Sold 1st cartoon to *The New Yorker* (1978); soon under contract, her cartoons of suburban mom angst became a *New Yorker* staple, freeing the magazines from the men-in-bars humor or the ladies speaking to their clubs before the potted palms; books include *Childproof: Cartoons about Parents and Children* (1997); also contributed to *National Lampoon* and *Village Voice*.

CHASTAIN, Brandi (1968—). American soccer player. Born Brandi Denise Chastain, July 21, 1968, in San Jose, California; dau. of Robert and Lark Chastain; graduate of Santa Clara University; m. Jerry Smith (soccer coach at Santa Clara). ❖ Defender and forward; at World Cup, won a team gold medal (1991) and scored the winning goal (1999), famously stripping off jersey in celebration to reveal a black sports bra; won a team gold medal at Atlanta Olympics (1996) and a team silver at Sydney Olympics (2000); was a founding member of the Women's United Soccer Association (WUSA); signed with the San Jose CyberRays (2001); won a team gold medal at Athens Olympics (2004). ❖ See also Jere Longman *The Girls of Summer* (HarperCollins, 2000).

CHASTENAY, countess of (1771–1855). *See Chastenay, Victorine de.*

CHASTENAY, Victorine de (1771–1855). French musician, memoirist and essayist. Name variations: Madame de Chastenay; Louise-Marie Victorine de Chastenay de Lenty; Louise Marie Victorine de Lanty;

Comtesse de Chastenay or countess of Chastenay. Born Louise-Marie Victorine de Chastenay de Lenty in 1771; died in 1855; dau. of Erard Louis Guil de Lenty (1748–1830), comte de Chastenay, and Catherine Louise d'Herbouville; sister of Henri Louis de Lenty (b. 1772), comte de Chastenay; never married. ❖ Noblewoman, imprisoned during the Reign of Terror and later known as *citoyenne Victorine,* wrote *Mémoires* and works of botany and history, including *Calandrier de Flore* (1802–03), *Du génie de peuples anciens* (1808), *Les Chevaliers normands en Italie et en Sicile* (1816) and *De l'Asie* (1833); trans. Ann Radcliffe's *The Mysteries of Udolpho* and Oliver Goldsmith's *The Deserted Village.*

CHASTENAY DE LENTY, Louise-Marie Victorine de (1771–1855). *See Chastenay, Victorine de.*

CHÂTEAUBRIANT, Comtesse de (c. 1490–1537). French mistress of King Francis I. Name variations: Madame de Chateaubriant or Chateaubriand; Françoise de Foix. Born c. 1490; died at Châteaubriant, France, Oct 16, 1537. ❖ Was the 1st of many mistresses of Francis I, king of France (r. 1515–1547), but had little, if any, political influence. ❖ See also *Women in World History.*

CHÂTEAUROUX, Marie Anne de Mailly-Nesle, Duchesse de (1717–1744). French mistress of Louis XV. Born 1717; died Dec 8, 1744; 4th dau. of Louis, marquis de Nesle (descendant of one of Mazarin's nieces) and Madame de Nesle (lady-in-waiting to Queen Marie Leczinska); sister of Pauline, marquise de Vintimille (1712–1741), Louise, comtesse de Mailly (1710–1751), and the Duchesse de Lauraguais; m. marquis de la Tournelle. ❖ Upon death of husband (1740), attracted the attention of Louis XV of France; intelligent and ambitious, replaced her sisters Louise and Pauline as titular mistress (1742); treated Queen Marie Leczinska with contempt and drove a wedge in the relationship between king and queen from which it never totally recovered; directed by Richelieu, encouraged the king to pay more attention to affairs of state and joined him on his army campaigns; when Louis became dangerously ill at Metz, pretended that his illness was a passing one and, against his wishes, would not send for the queen; when news of her actions were made known, was booed by the French whenever she appeared in public; retired to her bed with a complete breakdown. ❖ See also Ed. and J. de Goncourt, *La Duchesse de Châteauroux et ses swurs* (Paris, 1879); and *Women in World History.*

CHÂTELET, Émilie du (1706–1749). French scientist, philosopher, and feminist. Name variations: Emilie du Chatelet; Marquise du Chatelet or Chastellet; Marquise du Châtelet-Laumont; Émilie de Châtelet. Pronunciation: SHA-te-let. Born Gabrielle-Émilie Le Tonnelier de Breteuil Dec 17, 1706, in Paris, France; died in Lunéville, France, Sept 7, 1749; dau. of Gabrielle-Anne de Froulay and Louis-Nicholas Le Tonnelier de Breteuil, baron of Preuilly (died 1728); m. Florent-Claude, marquis du Châtelet-Laumont, 1725; children: (with Marquis du Châtelet) Françoise Gabrielle Pauline (b. 1726), Louis Marie Florent (b. 1727), and an unnamed son who died in infancy; (with Marquis de Saint-Lambert) unnamed daughter (b. 1749, who died in infancy). ❖ Scientist who, together with Voltaire and others, served to popularize Newton's ideas throughout continental Europe; met Voltaire who appreciated her brilliant scientific mind, which seems to have formed the basis for his attraction (1733); after government ordered Voltaire's arrest on publication of his *Lettres philosophique* (June 10, 1734), brought him to Cirey, the ancestral château of the du Châtelets (1734), where they lived for next 15 years; began work on *Institutions de physique* (*Institution of Physics*), a modern replacement for Rohault's textbook on physics (1734), which established her reputation as a scientist and a scholar when published (1740); began translation of Bernard Mandeville's *Fable of the Bees* (1735); began work on *Grammaire raisonnée* (1736); entered the French Academy of Sciences essay competition (1737); had dispute with Academy of Science over the dynamic force in matter (1739); began work on *Discours sur le bonheur* (1744); by 1747, was being sought out by young scientists from all over Europe who wanted to study with her; guest at the court of Stanislas Leszczynski, ex-king of Poland (1748); met poet Marquis de Saint-Lambert (1748); completed translation of Isaac Newton's *Principia Mathematica* from Latin into French (1749); from mathematics, algebra and geometry, to physics, metaphysics, moral philosophy, and theology, exhibited a breadth of interest that distinguished her, not only as a true enlightenment scholar, but a scholar for all seasons. ❖ See also Samuel Edwards, *The Divine Mistress: A Biography of Émilie de Châtelet, the Beloved of Voltaire* (McKay, 1970); Nancy Mitford, *Voltaire in Love* (Harper, 1957); Esther Ehrman, *Mme du Châtelet* (Berg, 1986); and *Women in World History.*

CHÂTELET-LOMONT, Gabrielle Emilie du (1706–1749). *See Châtelet, Émilie du.*

CHÂTILLON, Madame de (fl. 1498–1525). *See Louise de Montmorency.*

CHATTERTON, Ruth (1893–1961). American actress. Born Dec 24, 1893, in New York City; died in Redding, Connecticut, Nov 24, 1961; dau. of an architect; m. Ralph Forbes (British actor), 1924 (div. 1932); m. George Brent (actor), 1932 (div. 1934); m. Barry Thomson (actor), 1942 (died 1960). ❖ Best known for her performance in *Dodsworth* (1936), was also a stage star, playwright (*Monsieur Brotonneau*), director and author of 4 novels, most notably *Homeward Borne;* made Broadway debut (1911) in *The Great Name;* triumphed at 20 as the star of *Daddy Long Legs* (1914); went on to become one of Broadway's leading ladies, shunning movie offers until she was well into her 30s; made film debut as Emil Jannings' 2nd wife in *Sins of the Fathers* (1928); won Oscar nominations as Best Actress for *Madame X* (1929) and *Sarah and Son* (1930); other films include *Paramount on Parade* (1930), *The Magnificent Lie* (1931), *Once a Lady* (1931), *Tomorrow and Tomorrow* (1932), *The Crash* (1932) and *Girls' Dormitory* (1936); left Hollywood behind (1937) and made 2 British films before returning to the stage in a London revival of *The Constant Wife,* after which she toured US in *West of Broadway;* also appeared in *Leave Her to Heaven* (1940) and *Idiot's Delight* (1951); a licensed pilot, flew her own plane cross country. ❖ See also *Women in World History.*

CHATTO, Sarah (1964—). *See Armstrong-Jones, Sarah.*

CHATTOPADHYAYA, Kamaladevi (1903–1988). Indian political activist and feminist. Name variations: Kamala Devi Chattopadhyay. Born into a wealthy family in Mangalore, Karnataka, India, 1903; died in Bombay, Oct 29, 1988; educated locally at St. Mary's College before attending Bedford College, London, and the London School of Economics; married and widowed; m. Harindranath Chattopadhyay (poet and dramatist), 1919. ❖ Indian independence leader, feminist and eloquent advocate of Indian cultural and artistic autonomy, joined the independence movement at an early age and was imprisoned many times; quickly became one of the leading women of the national movement, and counted among her friends such leaders as Mahatma and Kasturba Gandhi, Jawaharlal Nehru, and Sarojini Naidu; elected to All-India Congress (1927), becoming organizing secretary and president of All-India Women's Conference; imprisoned (1930, 1932, 1934, 1942); after achievement of Indian freedom (1947), continued to call for social justice; founded the Indian Cooperative Union (1948) to assist refugees uprooted by the partition; established the 1st co-operative at Chattarpur, near Delhi; helped build city of Faridabad; was the leader of many craft organizations in India and internationally; developed the Cottage Industries Emporium; became chair of All-India Handicrafts, Ltd. (1952); helped found the World Crafts Council of which she was senior vice-president; served as president of the Centre of India. ❖ See also memoir *Inner Recesses, Outer Spaces* (Navarang, 1986); and *Women in World History.*

CHATTOPADHYAYA, Sarojini (1879–1949). *See Naidu, Sarojini.*

CHATWIN, Margaret (c. 1881–1937). English actress and singer. Born c. 1881 in Edgbaston, Birmingham, England; died Oct 19, 1937; attended Royal Academy of Music. ❖ Made stage debut in Portsmouth with the D'Oyly Carte company in *The Rose of Persia* (1901), then appeared as the Countess of Newtown in *The Emerald Isle* (1902); was lead player with the Pilgrim Players at Birmingham Rep (1907–12), appearing in about 160 roles; made London debut in *Abraham Lincoln* (1919), followed by *The Immortal Hour, Back to Methuselah, The Farmer's Wife, Arden of Faversham, Six Characters in Search of an Author, The River* and *Heartbreak House,* among others.

CHATZIIOANNOU, Ioanna (1973—). Greek weightlifter. Name variations: Chatzioannou. Born Oct 22, 1973, in Thessalonika, Greece. ❖ Won European champioships (1997) and EU championships (1997, 1999); won a bronze medal for 58–63kg at Sydney Olympics (2000).

CHAUCER, Alice (fl. 1400s). Duchess of Suffolk. Dau. of Thomas Chaucer of Ewelme (son of Geoffrey Chaucer, the writer) and Maud Burghersh; m. Thomas Montacute, 4th earl of Salisbury; m. William de la Pole, duke of Suffolk; children: (2nd m.) John de la Pole, 1st duke of Suffolk.

CHAUCER, Philippa (c. 1348–c. 1387). *See Rouet, Philippa.*

CHAUNCY, Nan (1900–1970). Australian children's writer. Born May 29, 1900, in England; died May 1, 1970; dau. of Charles Edward and

Lilla (Osmond) Masterman; m. Anthony Chauncy, 1938; children: Heather. ❖ Moved with family to Tasmania at age 12; became deeply interested in conservation and, with husband, bought 1,000 acres of bush and established a wildlife sanctuary; also established a girl guides company and promoted Tasmania overseas; wrote 14 children's books, including *They Found a Cave* (1948), *Tiger in the Bush* (1957), *Devils' Hill* (1958) and *Tangara* (1960).

CHAUSSON, Anne-Caroline (1977—). French mountain biker. Name variations: Anne Caroline Chausson. Born Oct 8, 1977, in Dijon, France. ❖ Began racing competitively (1993) and became dominate force in international mountain biking; became 8-time World Downhill champion (Junior: 1993–95; Senior: 1996–2000), 5-time European champion (1994–98), 6-time French national champion (1994–99), VeloNews International Cyclist of the Year (1999), World Dual champion (2000), Downhill and Dual World champion (2000), and 4-time Overall World Cup Downhill champion.

CHAUVET, Marie (1916–1973). Haitian novelist and playwright. Name variations: Marie Vieux. Born Marie Vieux in 1916 in Port-au-Prince, Haiti; died 1973 in Bronxville, NY; dau. of a Haitian father and West Indian mother from the Virgin Islands; m. Aymon Charlier (physician, div.); m. Pierre Chauvet. ❖ One of Haiti's best-known novelists, whose works often depict harsh socio-political conditions there, was exiled to France after criticizing the Duvalier regime; eventually settled in New York; writings include *Fille d'Haïti* (1954), *La Danse sur le volcan* (1957), *Fonds des Nègres* (1961), *Amour* (1968) and *Les Rapaces* (1986). Won Henri Deschamps Prize (1986).

CHAUVIN, Jeanne (1862–1926). French lawyer. Name variations: Mlle Chauvin. Pronunciation: JHAN show-VAN. Born in Jargeau (Loiret), France, Aug 22, 1862; died at Provins (Seine-et-Marne), Sept 28, 1926; sister of Émile Chauvin (1870–1933), prominent deputy (1898–1909) from Seine-et-Marne; never married. ❖ France's 1st woman lawyer, was admitted to the bar (1900). ❖ See also *Women in World History*.

CHAUVIRÉ, Yvette (1917—). French ballet dancer and teacher. Name variations: Yvette Chauvire. Born April 22, 1917, in Paris, France; trained at the Paris Opéra. ❖ One of the great dancers of the 1950s, joined the Paris Opéra Ballet (1930) and became soloist (1941), dancing many major roles in such Serge Lifar ballets as *Alexandre le Grand* (1937) and *Suite en blanc* (1943); moved to Nouveau Ballet de Monte Carlo (1946), creating roles in *Dramma per musica* (1946) and *Chota Rustaveli* (1947); back at the Opéra Ballet (1948–49, 1953–63), created *Mirages* and starred in *Giselle* and *Sleeping Beauty;* traveled widely and guest starred with numerous companies; appointed artistic advisor to Opéra Ballet (1963) and became director of Académie Internationale de Danse, Paris (1970); retired from the stage (1972); featured in the film *La Mort du Cygne* (1937), which was released in US as *Ballerina.* Awarded Légion d'honneur (1946). ❖ See also autobiography (in French) *Je suis Ballerina* (1960).

CHA-VEELA (1845–1936). *See Chona, Maria.*

CHAVEZ-THOMPSON, Linda (1944—). Hispanic-American labor leader. Born Aug 1, 1944, in Lubbock, Texas; 1 of 8 children of sharecroppers; married at 19 and divorced; m. 2nd husband Robert Thompson (died); children: (1st m.) 2. ❖ Rose from the ranks of her union, the American Federation of State, County and Municipal Employees, to be elected executive vice president of the AFL-CIO (Oct 25, 1995); reelected for a 4-year term (1997), the highest-ranking woman in the labor movement; at start of career, served as union secretary for the Laborer's International Union (1967–71); was an International Union representative of AFSCME (1971–73); served in several positions with both the San Antonio Local and Texas Council of AFSCME (1973–95); was international president of AFSCME (1998–96); also served as national vice president of the Labor Council for Latin American Advancement (1986–96); appointed by Bill Clinton to serve on the President's Initiative on Race and as vice chair of the President's Committee on Employment of People with Disabilities.

CHAWAF, Chantal (1943—). French novelist and feminist. Born Sept 1943 in Paris, France, during WWII, when doctors pulled her from her mother's dying body after a shell hit her parents' car; studied classics in Paris; married a Syrian; children: Rayane and Jinane. ❖ Lived in Syria with husband where she had her children, then returned to France; associated at beginning of career with feminist group *Psych et Po;* works, which often explore feminine experience of language and sensuality, include *Retable, La rêverie* (Mother Love/Mother Earth, 1974), *Chair*

chaude (1976), *Rougeâtre* (1978), *Landes* (1980), *La Vallée incarnate* (1984), *L'intérieur de heures* (1987), *L'éclaircie* (1990) and *Le Manteau Noir* (1998); also published literary essays and *Le corps et le verbe: la langue en sense inverse* (1992).

CHAWLA, Kalpana (1961–2003). India-born astronaut. Name variations: KC. Born July 1, 1961, in Karnal, Haryana, India; died Feb 1, 2003, when the space shuttle *Columbia* disintegrated over the southern US; graduated from Tagore School (1976); Punjab Engineering College, India, BS in aeronautical engineering (1982); University of Texas at Arlington, MS in aerospace engineering (1984); University of Colorado, PhD in aerospace engineering (1988); became a US citizen; m. Jean-Pierre Harrison (flying instructor), 1984. ❖ Selected for space program (1994); made maiden shuttle flight STS-87 *Columbia* as mission specialist and prime robotic arm operator (Nov 19–Dec 5, 1997); member of the flight crew of the STS-107 *Columbia* (Jan 16–Feb 1, 2003) who successfully conducted 80 experiments before the mission ended abruptly on reentry, 16 minutes prior to scheduled landing. Held a Certified Flight Instructor's license with airplane and glider ratings and Commercial Pilot's licenses for single- and multi-engine land and seaplanes, and Gliders, and instrument rating for airplanes.

CHAWORTH, Maud (1282–c. 1322). Countess of Lancaster. Born 1282; died before Dec 3, 1322; dau. of Patrick Chaworth and Isabel Beauchamp; m. Henry (1281–1345), earl of Lancaster, 1298; children: Blanche (c. 1305–1380); Maud Plantagenet (c. 1310–c. 1377); Joan (c. 1312–c. 1345); Henry of Grosmont, 1st duke of Lancaster (c. 1314–1361); Isabel (c. 1317–1347); Eleanor Plantagenet (c. 1318–1372); Mary Percy (1320–1362). Henry's 2nd wife was Alice de Joinville.

CHAZAL, Madame (1803–1844). *See Tristan, Flora.*

CHAZAL, Aline-Marie (1825–1869). French dressmaker. Name variations: Aline Chazal; Aline Gauguin. Born 1825 in Paris, France; died July 7, 1869, in Paris; dau. of Flora Tristan (French activist, 1803–1844) and André-François Chazal (lithographer); m. Clovis Gauguin (Republican), 1846 (died 1851); children: Marie Gauguin (b. 1847); Paul Gauguin (artist, 1848–1903). ❖ Was abused sexually by father, for which her mother Flora Tristan brought charges against him and claimed custody (her father would later shoot her mother, though she survived); lived in Lima, Peru, with her children for 4 years (1851–55); opened a dressmaking business in Paris (1861).

CHAZELLE, Suzanne (1935—). *See Carrel, Dany.*

CHEBUKINA, Yelena (1965—). Soviet volleyball player. Name variations: Yelena Ovchinnikova or Ovtchinnikova. Born Oct 11, 1965, in USSR. ❖ At Seoul Olympics, won a gold medal in team competition (1988); at Barcelona Olympics, won a silver medal in team competition (1992).

CHEDID, Andrée (1921—). Egyptian-French poet. Name variations: Andree Chedid. Born 1921 in Cairo, Egypt. ❖ Drew on her life in Egypt and Lebanon for her fiction, often depicting characters coping with domestic or political trauma; published most works in French; poetry includes *Fraternité de la Parole* (1976) and *Cérémonial de la Violence* (1976); novels include *Le Sommeil Délivré* and *La Maison Sans Racines* (1985); short fiction includes *Les Corps et Le Temps* (1978). Received Louis Lajeier and Mallarmé awards for poetry (1976), Royal Belgian Grand Prize for French Literature, and Goncourt Prize for fiction; also awarded honorary doctorate from American University in Cairo (1988).

CHEER, Margaret (d. 1774). *See Hallam, Mrs. Lewis.*

CHEDWORTH, Margaret (fl. 1450). *See Howard, Margaret.*

CHEESEBOROUGH, Chandra (1959—). African-American runner. Born Jan 10, 1959, in Jacksonville, Florida; attended Tennessee State University. ❖ Won a gold medal at Pan American Games (1975) and a gold medal for 100 meters at TAC (1976); at Los Angeles Olympics, won a silver medal in the 400 meters and gold medals in the 4x400-meter relay and the 4x100-meter relay (1984).

CHEESEMAN, Clara (1852–1943). New Zealand novelist and short-story writer. Born 1852; died 1943. ❖ Published short stories in journals (1880s–90s); wrote novel *A Rolling Stone* (3 vols., 1886).

CHEESEMAN, Gwen (1951—). American field-hockey player. Name variations: Gwen Cheeseman Alexander. Born Aug 13, 1951, in Harrisburg, Pennsylvania. ❖ At Los Angeles Olympics, won a bronze medal in team competition (1984).

CHEESEMAN, Sylvia (1929—). *English runner.* Name variations: Sylvia Cheeseman Disley. Born May 19, 1929. ❖ At Helsinki Olympics, won a bronze medal in 4x100-meter relay (1952).

CHEESMAN, Lucy Evelyn (1881–1969). *English entomologist and explorer.* Born 1881 in Westwell, Kent, England; died April 5, 1969. ❖ As curator of insects for Zoological Society of London, provided animal talks for BBC's *Children's Hour* (1920–26); traveled to West Indies, Panama, Galápagos Islands, and South Pacific on St. George's Expedition (1924); went on independent expeditions to New Hebrides, Papua, Cyclops Mountains, Waigeu, Japan, Dutch New Guinea, and New Caledonia; publications include "Biogeographical Significance of Aneityum Island, New Hebrides" (1957), *Everyday Doings of Insects* (1924), *The Great Little Insect* (1924), *Marooned in Du-Bu Cove* (1949), and 2 autobiographies, *Things Worthwhile* (1957) and *Time Well Spent* (1960); contributed more than 50,000 insect specimens to British Museum of Natural History. Made an Officer of the Order of the British Empire (OBE, 1955).

CHEKHOVA or CHEKOVA, Olga.
See Knipper-Chekova, Olga (1870–1959).
See Tschechowa, Olga (1897–1980).

CHELARIU, Adriana (1963—). See Bazon-Chelariu, Adriana.

CHELGREN, Pamela (c. 1949—). *American field operations officer.* Name variations: Pamela Chelgren-Koterba or Pamela Chelgren Koterba. Born c. 1949 in Port Orchard, Washington. ❖ Became the 1st woman officer appointed to the National Oceanic and Atmospheric Administration Corps (1972); served as lieutenant; appointed field operations officer (1977); retired from the NOAA Corps (1995).

CHELLES, abbess of.
See Bertille (d. 705/713).
See Gisela of Chelles (781–814).
See Louise-Adelaide (1698–1743).

CHELSEA, Baroness of (1891–1975). See Stocks, Mary Danvers.

CHEMIS, Annie (1862–1939). *New Zealand dairy worker and government petitioner.* Name variations: Annie Dowd. Born Annie Dowd, May 24 1862, in Co. Kerry, Ireland; died Feb 21, 1939, in Wellington, New Zealand; m. Louis Chemis (laborer), 1880 (died 1898); children: 5. ❖ Immigrated to New Zealand (1878); operated dairy business with husband until land-lease dispute resulted in murder charge against him (1889); after unfortunate circumstances led to husband's conviction, presented petition to Parliament, which resulted in commutation of sentence and nationwide debate regarding reform of criminal justice system (1891); following release of husband and his later suicide, cleaned Parliament buildings and government offices to support herself (1898); became permanent employee (1907–26). ❖ See also *Dictionary of New Zealand Biography* (Vol. 3).

CHEN CHONG (1961—). See Chen, Joan.

CHEN CUITING (1971—). *Chinese gymnast.* Born July 15, 1971, in Changsha, Hunan Province, China. ❖ Won Asian Games (1986, 1990), Chinese Sports Festival and Shenyang International (1987), All-Chinese championships (1988); at World championships, won a bronze medal for team all-around (1989).

CHEN DUANSHENG (1751–1796). *Chinese novelist and poet.* Born in 1751 in Qiantang, Zhejiang Province, China; died in 1796; dau. of scholar-official Chen Yuden; granddau. of scholar-official Chen Zhaolun (1700–1771); sister of Chen Quingsheng and Chen Changsheng (writer); married Fan Tan; children: son and daughter. ❖ Author of verse narrative, *Tale of the After Life* (20 vols., *Zaishengyuan*), which she began writing at age 17 (1768); wrote 64 chapters of the narrative, but stopped writing in autumn of 1770, just after her mother died; wrote 4 more chapters (1784). At Chen's death, the narrative was taken up and completed by Liang Desheng, and finally edited and published by Hon Xiangye.

CHEN HONG. *Chinese softball player.* Born in China. ❖ Won a silver medal at Atlanta Olympics (1996).

CHEN HONG (1968—). *Chinese actress.* Born 1968 in Jiangxi, China. ❖ Popular actress, starred in *Together* (2003) and *Story of Xiangxiang* (1996).

CHEN JIERU (fl. 1920). *Second wife of Chiang Kai-shek.* Name variations: Ch'en Chieh-ju. Fl. around 1920; said to have been a prostitute; became 2nd wife of Chiang Kai-shek (1887–1975), Nov 1921 (marriage lapsed). Chiang's 1st wife was Mao Fumei.

CHEN JING (1975—). *Chinese volleyball player.* Born Sept 3, 1975, in Chengdu, China. ❖ Middle blocker, won a team gold medal at Athens Olympics (2004).

CHEN JING (1968—). *Chinese table tennis player.* Born Sept 20, 1968 in Wuhan, China. ❖ At Seoul Olympics, won a silver medal for doubles and a gold medal for singles (1988); defected to Taiwan; representing Chinese Taipei, won a silver medal at Atlanta Olympics (1996) and a bronze medal at Sydney Olympics (2000), both for singles.

CHEN JINGRONG (1917–1989). *Chinese poet and translator.* Born 1917 in Leshan, China; died 1989. ❖ Translated works by Hans Christian Andersen, Victor Hugo, Rainer Maria Rilke, and Charles Baudelaire; associated with *Jiuye* poets and the writers' united front against the Japanese invasion; served as editor of *Shijie Wenxue.* ❖ See also Shiu-Pang E. Almberg, *The Poetry of Chen Jingrong, A Modern Chinese Woman Poet* (Orientaliska Studier, 1988).

CHEN, Joan (1961—). *Chinese actress.* Name variations: Chen Chong. Born April 26, 1961, in Shanghai, China; became US citizen (1989); dau. of physicians; sister of Chen Chuan, an artist who goes by name of Chase Chenoff; attended Shanghai Film Academy and Shanghai Institute of Foreign Languages; m. Jim Lau, 1985 (div. 1990); m. Peter Hui, 1992; children: Angela Frances (b. 1998) and a 2nd daughter (b. 2000). ❖ As Chen Chong, began making films at 14; was the juvenile star in China of *Little Flower*, for which she received China's Best Actress award, and *Awakening* (1980); came to US to study filmmaking at California State University, Northridge (1981); made 1st US film *Tai-Pan* (1986); as Joan Chen, appeared as the ill-fated bride of Pu-Yi in *The Last Emperor* (1987); was featured as Josie Packard on tv series "Twin Peaks"; other films include *The Night Stalker* (1987), *The Blood of Heroes* (1990), *Turtle Beach* (1992), *You Seng* (1993), *The Hunted* (1995), *Judge Dredd* (1995), *Ziyu fengbao* (1999), *What's Cooking* (2000), *Avatar* (2004) and *Sunflower* (2005).

CHEN JO HSI (1938—). See Chen Ruoxi.

CHEN, Joyce (1918–1994). *Chinese-born American restaurateur.* Born in Beijing, China, 1918; died in Lexington, Massachusetts, Aug 1994; immigrated to US, 1949; married; children: Henry, Stephen and Helen Chen. ❖ Cooking teacher, author, tv personality and restaurateur, who played a major role in introducing Americans to authentic Chinese cuisine, opened the Joyce Chen Chinese restaurant in Cambridge, MA (1958), which began attracting the likes of Julia Child, James Beard, Henry Kissinger and John Kenneth Galbraith; had a tv program on PBS, "Joyce Chen Cooks," published a cookbook (1964), and created a thriving business empire that included a cookware firm, Joyce Chen Products. ❖ See also *Women in World History.*

CHEN LI JU (1981—). *Chinese Taipei archer.* Born April 24, 1981, in Taiwan. ❖ Won a bronze medal for team at Athens Olympics (2004).

CHEN, Lu (1976—). *Chinese figure skater.* Name variations: Last name: Chen; first name: Lu; (nickname) Lulu. Born Nov 24, 1976, in Changchun, Jilin Province, northeast China; dau. of a hockey skater and a ping-pong player; raised in Jilin Province. ❖ Placed 3rd at World championships (1993), 1st (1995), 2nd (1996), and 25th (1997); won a bronze medal at Lillehammer Olympics (1994); finished 1st at the Karl Schafer Memorial figure-skating championship in Vienna, Austria (1997); won a bronze medal at Nagano Olympics (1998). ❖ See also *Women in World History.*

CHEN MUHUA (c. 1940—). *Chinese politician.* Born c. 1940 in China. ❖ Was vice-minister (c. 1971) and then minister of Economic Relations with Foreign Countries (c. 1977); became member of Chinese Communist Party Central Committee (1973) and member of Politburo (1977); was made vice-premier (1978) responsible for health services, birth control program, and population census of 1982; became minister of Foreign Trade (1982), president of People's Bank of China, and director of State Treasury (1985); served as president of All-China Women's Federation.

CHEN RUIQING (1932—). *Chinese scriptwriter and short-story writer.* Born 1932 in China. ❖ Wrote *The Great Northern Wilds* about her 22 years in political exile during Maoist era; also wrote and edited film scripts and worked for Beijing Film Studio after Mao era.

CHEN RUOXI (1938—). **Chinese novelist and short-story writer.** Name variations: Chen Jo Hsi; Chen Jo-hsi. Born 1938 in Taiwan. ❖ Educated at University of Taiwan, Mount Holyoke College, and Johns Hopkins University; taught at University of California, Berkeley; writings, which reflect life in China during the cultural revolution, include *The Execution of Mayor Yin* (1978), *The Old Man and Other Stories* (1986) and *The Short Stories of Chen Ruoxi.*

CHEN SHIH HSIN (1978—). **Chinese taekwondo player.** Born Nov 16, 1978, in Taipai. ❖ Won a gold medal in -49kg at Athens Olympics (2004).

CHEN, Si-Lan (1909—). **Chinese concert dancer.** Name variations: Si Lan Chen; Si-lan Chen; Si-Lan Chen Leyda. Born 1909 in Trinidad, West Indies, of Chinese parents; father was secretary for Sun Yat-sen and foreign minister of the Canton government; m. Jay Leyda (1910–1988, film historian and scholar). ❖ Pioneer in the use of Chinese elements in dance, moved to London (1912), where she studied at Stedman Academy; joined parents in China and worked under well-known actor Mei-Lan Fang; after Chiang Kai-shek took power, fled with family to Moscow (1927), where she studied at Very Maya's school; worked in plastique with Kasyan Goleizovsky, later becoming an important link between his experiments and American dance forms; studied folk dance in Moscow and gained expert knowledge of Uzbec and Turkistani traditions; immigrated to US where she associated with the New Dance League and began giving concert recitals; works of choreography include *Landlord on a Horse* (1938), *Shanghai Sketches* (1938), *Two Chinese Women* (1938), *Chinese Student-Dedication* (1938), *In Conquered Nanking* (1939), and *Uzbec Dance* (1939); appeared in the film *Keys of the Kingdom* (1944), among others. ❖ See also memoirs edited by Sally Banes, *Footnote to History* (Princeton, 1984).

CHEN TIEJUN (1904–1928). **Chinese revolutionary.** Name variations: Ch'en T'ieh-chün or Chen Tieh-chuen, Chen Tieh-chun. Born 1904 in China; died 1928; dau. of a merchant; attended Jihua Girls' School, teacher training school; attended Zangshan University (1925–27); was forced to marry a merchant's son but quit the marriage after the ceremony. ❖ Joined anti-imperialist student demonstrations of May 4, 1919; active in socialist and feminist movements, joined the Communist Party (1926); went underground after the siege of Zangshan University by Chiang Kai-Shek's forces (1927), smuggling weapons and mobilizing a woman's network; lived with Zhen Wenjiang (Chen Wen-chiang), a commander in the Red Guard; betrayed to the nationalists, was tortured and executed.

CHEN XIAOMIN (1977—). **Chinese weightlifter.** Born 1977 in Guangdong Province, China. ❖ Won World championships (1993, 1995, 1996); won Asian championships and a gold medal for 58–63kg at Sydney Olympics (2000).

CHEN YAN (1981—). **Chinese swimmer.** Born in 1981 in Dalian, China. ❖ Won a bronze medal for 4x100-meter relay at Atlanta Olympics (1996); won a gold medal at World championships (1998).

CHEN YANQING (1979—). **Chinese weightlifter.** Born April 5, 1979, in China. ❖ Won a gold medal for 58kg at Athens Olympics (2004).

CHEN YONGYAN (1962—). **Chinese gymnast.** Born Oct 19, 1962, in China. ❖ At World championships, won silver medals in team all-around and balance beam (1981); won Asian Games (1982) and Blume Memorial (1983); at Los Angeles Olympics, won a bronze medal in team all-around (1984).

CHEN YUEFANG (1963—). **Chinese basketball player.** Born May 1, 1963. ❖ At Los Angeles Olympics, won a bronze medal in team competition (1984).

CHEN YUFENG. **Chinese soccer player.** Born in Shandong, China. ❖ Won a team silver medal at Atlanta Olympics (1996).

CHEN YUELING (1968—). **Chinese athlete.** Born April 1, 1968. ❖ At Barcelona Olympics, won a gold medal in 10-kilometer walk (1992).

CHEN ZHEN (1963—). **Chinese handball player.** Born Jan 11, 1963. ❖ At Los Angeles Olympics, won a bronze medal in team competition (1984).

CHEN ZHONG (1982—). **Chinese taekwondo player.** Born Nov 22, 1982, in Henan Province, China. ❖ Won Asian championships (1998, 2000, 2002); won a gold medal for +67kg at Sydney Olympics (2000); won Jeju World championships and World Cup (2001); won a gold medal for 67kg at Athens Olympics (2004).

CHEN ZIHE (1968—). **Chinese table-tennis player.** Born Feb 28, 1968. ❖ At Barcelona Olympics, won a silver medal in doubles (1992).

CHEN ZONGYING (1902–2003). **Chinese revolutionary.** Born Jan 1902 in Hunan Province, China; died May 31, 2003, in Beijing, China; m. Ren Bish (senior lead of the Communist Party), 1926 (died 1950); children: 8, but most did not survive infancy. ❖ Was imprisoned for nearly a year (1931); took part in the Long March of the Chinese Communists (1934–36); like most of the Red Army women, was given a prestigious but hollow appointment after the liberation (1949). ❖ See also Helen Praeger Young, *Choosing Revolution* (2001).

CHENAL-MINUZZO, Giuliana (1931—). **Italian Alpine skier.** Name variations: Giuliana Minuzzo-Chenal; Giuliana Minuzzo. Born Giuliana Minuzzo, Nov 26, 1931, in Italy. ❖ Won a bronze medal for downhill at Oslo Olympics (1952) and a bronze for giant slalom at Squaw Valley Olympics (1960); at Cortina Olympics (1956), took the oath at the opening ceremony, the 1st time the oath was read by a female athlete in the history of the games.

CHENCHIK, Taisiya (1936—). **Soviet high jumper.** Born Jan 30, 1936. ❖ At Tokyo Olympics, won a bronze medal in the high jump (1964).

CHENEY, Amy (1867–1944). *See Beach, Amy Cheney.*

CHENEY, Dorothy Bundy (1916—). **American tennis player.** Name variations: Dodo Cheney. Born Dorothy May Bundy in 1916; dau. of May Sutton (1887–1975) and Thomas Bundy (both tennis players); m. Art Cheney (pilot), 1946. ❖ Won nearly 300 USTA championships over 6 decades; was the 1st American to win the Australian singles title (1938); won US clay court title (1944); ranked 6th in world (1946), won 11 straight Hard Court Singles titles (1957–67) and over 170 national senior championships. At age 80, received the Southern California Tennis Association Lifetime Achievement Award; inducted into International Tennis Hall of Fame (2004).

CHENEY, Ednah Dow (1824–1904). **American abolitionist, suffragist, and author.** Born Ednah Dow Littlehale, June 27, 1824, in Beacon Hill, Boston, Massachusetts; died 1904; m. Seth Wells Cheney (American engraver), 1853 (died 1856); children: 1 daughter. ❖ Helped relocate freed slaves and organized Boston teachers to serve in the South after Civil War; was secretary, then president, of New England Hospital for Women and Children, as well as president of New England Woman's Club and Massachusetts Woman Suffrage Association; authored *Handbook of American History for Colored People* (1866), *Gleanings in the Field of Art* (1881), *Life of Louisa M. Alcott* (1889), and several stories, including "Nora's Return," a sequel to Ibsen's "A Doll's House"; published reminiscences (1902).

CHENEY, Leona Pressler (1904–1982). **American golfer.** Born Leona Pressler, July 1, 1904, in Stockton, Missouri; died Oct 1982 in El Cajon, California. ❖ Reached the quarterfinals of the USGA Women's Amateur 7 times (1927—34); chosen for the Curtis Cup team (1932, 1943, 1936). Honored by the Helms Foundation as the greatest woman amateur in Los Angeles area (1955).

CHENEY, Lynne (1941—). **American writer, educator and government official.** Name variations: Lynne V. Cheney. Born Lynne Ann Vincent, Aug 14, 1941, in Casper, Wyoming; dau. of Wayne Vincent (engineer with the US Bureau of Reclamation) and Edna (Lybyer) Vincent (deputy sheriff); Colorado College, BA, 1963; University of Colorado at Boulder, MA, 1964; University of Wisconsin, PhD in 19th-century British literature, 1970; m. Dick Cheney (vice president of US), Aug 29, 1964; children: Elizabeth and Mary Cheney. ❖ Taught at University of Wyoming, University of Wisconsin and Northern Virginia Community College (1964–70); taught English at George Washington University; published 1st novel *Executive Privilege* (1979), followed by *Sisters* (1981); worked as a researcher and writer for the Maryland Center for Public Broadcasting (1982–83); became a senior editor of *Washingtonian* magazine (1983) and contributed 2 regular columns; also wrote (with husband) *Kings of the Hill* (1983) and (with Victor Gold) *The Body Politic* (1988), as well as *Telling the Truth* (1996) and 2 books for children, *America: A Patriotic Primer* (2002) and *Abigail: An Almanac of Amazing American Women* (2003); served as chair of the National Endowment for the Humanities (1986–93); became a senior fellow of American Enterprise Institute.

CHENG, Chi (1944—). *See Reel, Chi Cheng.*

CHENNAULT, Anna (1923—). **Chinese-born journalist and entrepreneur.** Name variations: Mrs. Claire Lee Chennault; Anna Chan

Chennault. Born Anna Chan, June 23, 1923, in Beijing, China; came to US (1948); became naturalized citizen (1950); 1 of 6 daughters of Y.W. Chan (diplomat) and Bessie (Joung) Chan; niece of Liao Chengzhi, a high-ranking Chinese official; Ling Nan University, BA, 1944; Chungang University (Korea), LittD, 1967; Lincoln University, LLD, 1970; m. Claire Lee Chennault (US general and aviator who trained the Flying Tigers squadron), Dec 21, 1947 (died July 1958); children: Claire Anna and Cynthia Louise Chennault. ❖ Lecturer, writer, fashion consultant, and airlines executive, had a strong impact on Asian-American relations; was a war correspondent for Central News Agency in China (1944–48), the 1st female reporter for the agency, and became a special Washington correspondent (1965); was a feature writer for the *Hsin Ming Daily News* in Shanghai (1944–49); worked with Civil Air Transport in Taipei (1946–57); served as a broadcaster for Voice of America (1963–66); served as vice president of the Flying Tiger Line (1968–76); active in the Republican Party, was a prominent Washington host; served as chair of the Chinese Refugees Relief Committee for President Kennedy, the 1st person of Chinese ancestry to be named to the White House staff; protested the Vietnam War; representing the US, was often an envoy to China; published more than 50 works in Chinese and English. ❖ See also Catherine Forslund, *Anna Chennault: Informal Diplomacy and Asian Relations* (SR Books, 2001).

CHENOWETH, Helen (1938—). American politician. Name variations: Helen P. Chenoweth-Hage. Born Jan 27, 1938, in Topeka, Kansas; attended Whitworth College; m. Nick Chenoweth (div. 1975); m. Wayne Hage (Nevada rancher), 2000; children: (1st m.) 2. ❖ Republican congressional representative from Idaho, moved to Idaho (1964); was a self-employed medical and legal management consultant (1964–75); served as state executive director of the Idaho Republican Party (1975–77); was chief of staff, then campaign manager, to Representative Steven Symms; elected to 104th Congress and 2 succeeding Congresses (Jan 3, 1995–Jan 3, 2001); served as chair of a Resources subcommittee; retired to honor her promise of not more than 3 terms (2000).

CHENOWITH, Alice (1853–1925). *See Gardener, Helen Hamilton.*

CHEPCHUMBA, Joyce (1970—). Kenyan marathon runner. Born Nov 6, 1970, in Kericho, Kenya. ❖ Won the Chicago marathon (1998, 1999), the London marathon (1999), a bronze medal at Sydney Olympics (2000), the Tokyo marathon (2000), and New York City marathon (2002).

CHEPELEVA, Anna (1984—). Russian gymnast. Name variations: Anna Tchepeleva. Born June 26, 1984, in Volzhsky, USSR. ❖ At Sydney Olympics, won a silver medal for team all-around (2000).

CHER (1946—). American pop singer and actress. Name variations: Cher Bono; Cherilyn Sarkisian LaPiere. Born Cherilyn Sarkisian, May 20, 1946, in El Centro, California; dau. of John Sarkisian (Armenian truck driver) and Georgia Holt (b. 1927, actress); adopted by stepfather, Gilbert LaPiere; sister of Georganne LaPiere (b. 1951); m. Sonny Bono (singer, composer and US congressional representative), 1964 (div. June 1975); m. Gregg Allman (musician), 1975 (div. Jan 1979); children: (1st m.) Chastity Bono (b. 1969, activist and singer); (2nd m.) Elijah Blue Allman (b. 1976). ❖ Multifaceted performer known for frequent comebacks, dropped out of high school and left home at 16; sang in sessions for producer David Geffen with future husband Sonny Bono (1963); performed with Sonny as duo Caesar and Cleo; scored many hits during years with Sonny, including "I Got You Babe" (1965), "The Beat Goes On" (1967), and "All I Ever Need is You" (1971); shared spotlight with Bono on tv variety series "The Sonny and Cher Comedy Hour" (1971–74) and appeared solo on tv series "Cher" (1975); released "Take Me Home" (1979), 1st hit single without Sonny; debuted on Broadway in Robert Altman's production of *Come Back to the 5 and Dime, Jimmy Dean, Jimmy Dean* (1982); acclaimed for film roles in *Silkwood* (1983), *Mask* (1985), and *The Witches of Eastwick* (1987); won Academy Award for playing Italian-American widow in *Moonstruck* (1987); continued producing hit singles with "I Found Someone" (1987), "If I Could Turn Back Time" (1989), and "The Shoop Shoop Song" (1990); scored biggest hit of career with "Believe" (1998); returned to screen in *Tea With Mussolini* (1999).

CHEREMISINA, Nina (1946—). Soviet rower. Born Dec 14, 1946. ❖ At Moscow Olympics, won a bronze medal in coxed fours and a silver medal in quadruple sculls with coxswain (1980).

CHEREVATOVA, Olena (1970—). Ukrainian kayaker. Born Mar 17, 1970, in USSR. ❖ Won a bronze medal for K4 500 at Athens Olympics (2004).

CHÉRI, Rose (1824–1861). French comedian. Name variations: Cheri. Born Rose Marie Cizos at Étampes, France, Oct 27, 1824; died at Passy, near Paris, Sept 22, 1861; m. M. Lemoine Montigny, in May 1847. ❖ Celebrated comedian, 1st appeared at the Gymnase (1842); came to prominence in the role of Clarissa Harlowe (1846).

CHERIFF, Farial (1938—). *See Fadia.*

CHERJAZOVA, Lina (1968—). *See Cheryazova, Lina.*

CHERKASOVA, Marina. Russian pairs skater. Name variations: Maria Cherkasova. Born in USSR. ❖ With partner Sergei Shakhrai, won the World championship and a silver medal at Lake Placid Olympics (1980).

CHERKASOVA, Valentina (1958—). Soviet shooter. Born June 22, 1958. ❖ At Seoul Olympics, won a bronze medal in smallbore rifle 3 positions (1988).

CHERNYSHEVA, Liubov (1890–1976). *See Tchernicheva, Lubov.*

CHERNYSHOVA, Lyudmila (1952—). Soviet volleyball player. Born Nov 1952. ❖ Won Olympic silver medal at Montreal (1976) and Olympic gold medal at Moscow (1980), both in team competition.

CHERNYSHOVA, Nadezhda (1951—). Soviet rower. Born Mar 21, 1951. ❖ At Montreal Olympics, won a silver medal in quadruple sculls with coxswain (1976).

CHÉRON, Elisabeth-Sophie (1648–1711). French poet and painter. Name variations: Elizabeth Sophie Cheron; Mme Le Hay. Born Elizabeth-Sophie Chéron in 1648 in Paris, France; died 1711 in Paris; dau. of Henri Chéron; m. Jacques le Hay. ❖ Talented in art, literature and music, was nominated to 2 academies: for her painting, was named a member of Académie Royale de la Peinture et de la Sculpture (1672); for the publication of her collection of psalms and canticle and verse piece, "La Gloire du Val de Grâce" (1694), was named a member of the Paduan Accademia dei Ricovrati (1699); awarded a pension by Louis XIV.

CHERRILL, Virginia (1908–1996). American actress. Name variations: Virginia Cherrill Martini. Born April 12, 1908, in Carthage, Illinois; died Nov 14, 1996, in Santa Barbara, California; m. Irving Adler; m. Cary Grant (actor), 1933 (div. 1935); m. 9th earl of Jersey, 1937 (div. 1946); m. Florian Martini, 1948. ❖ Best remembered for her portrayal of the blind flower girl in Chaplin's *City Lights* (1931); other films include *The Brat, Charlie Chan's Greatest Case, What Price Crime?* and *Troubled Waters;* retired from film (1937).

CHERRINGTON, Te Paea (c. 1877–1937). New Zealand tribal leader. Name variations: Te Paea. Born Te Paea, 1877 or 1878 (baptized, Nov 17, 1878), near Whangarei, New Zealand; died Sept 30, 1937, in Ngararatunua, New Zealand; dau. of Hemi Tonoriri Kingi and Akinihi Ngaro Brown; m. Wiremu Hone Cherrington (Keretene), 1898; children: 6 sons. ❖ Valuable consultant in resolution of land disputes; protected spiritually significant sites; active in numerous Anglican groups, which addressed health and welfare issues. ❖ See also *Dictionary of New Zealand Biography* (Vol. 3).

CHERRY, Addie (c. 1859–1942). American vaudevillian. Born Rose Alma Cherry c. 1859; died Oct 25, 1942; sister of Elizabeth, Jessie, and Effie Cherry. ❖ One of the four Cherry Sisters, known as "the vegetable sisters of the stage," whose act was deemed so awful they sometimes performed behind a screen to keep from being pelted with vegetables; toured for years.

CHERRY, Carolyn Janice (1942—). *See Cherryh, C. J.*

CHERRY, Effie (d. 1944). American vaudeville performer. Died Aug 5, 1944, in Cedar Rapids, Iowa; sister of Elizabeth, Jessie, and Addie Cherry. ❖ One of the Cherry Sisters, toured with her four sisters as the Cherry Sisters in Iowa, Kansas, and Illinois; brought to New York by Oscar Hammerstein (1896) to perform at the Olympia.

CHERRY, Frances (1937—). New Zealand novelist and short-story writer. Born Nov 25, 1937, in Wellington, New Zealand. ❖ Tutored creative writing and established creative writing correspondence school in Wellington; published short stories in magazines and anthologies; works include *The Daughter-in-Law and Other Stories* (1986), *Dancing With Strings* (1989), *The Widowhood of Jacki Bates* (1991) and *Washing Up in*

Parrot Bay (1999); also wrote *In the Dark* (1999) and *Leon* (2000) for children.

CHERRY, Helen (1915–2001). English actress. Born Nov 24, 1915, in Manchester, England; died Sept 27, 2001, in London; m. Trevor Howard (actor), 1944 (died 1988). ❖ Originally employed as a commercial artist, made stage debut in Manchester in *The Vagabond King* (1938); made London debut in *In Town Again* (1940), followed by *The Recruiting Officer, Volpone, The Magistrate, The Two Mrs. Carrolls, Fit for Heroes, The Glass Slipper* and *Bates Wharf;* often appeared in Shakespearean productions in such parts as Helena in *A Midsummer Night's Dream,* Portia in *The Merchant of Venice* and Rosalind in *As You Like It;* made film debut in *The Courtney Affair* (1947), followed by *The Courtneys of Curzon Street, His Excellency, Castle in the Air, High Flight, The Charge of the Light Brigade, Conduct Unbecoming* and *A Gathering of Eagles,* among others.

CHERRY, Neneh (1963—). Swedish-born musician. Born Neneh Mariann Karlsson, Mar 10, 1963, in Stockholm, Sweden; dau. of Moki Cherry (artist) and Ahmadu Jah (percussionist); stepdau. of Don Cherry (jazz trumpeter); stepsister of singer Eagle Eye Cherry; m. Bruce Smith (drummer), divorced; married Cameron McVey (composer and musician); children: at least 2. ❖ Sang with such bands as Nails, the Slits, Rip Rig + Panic, and Float Up CP; released what has been called the 1st alternative rap album, *Raw Like Sushi* (1989), which included the hits "Buffalo Stance" and "Kisses on the Wind"; with 2nd husband, cowrote the album *Homebrew* (1992). Other albums include *Man* (1996).

CHERRYH, C.J. (1942—). American science-fiction writer. Name variations: (r.n.) Carolyn Janice Cherry. Born Sept 1, 1942, in St. Louis, Missouri; University of Oklahoma, BA in Latin, 1964; Johns Hopkins University (Woodrow Wilson fellow), MA in classics, 1965. ❖ Taught Latin and ancient history in Oklahoma public schools (1965–76); works include *The Book of Morgaine* (1979), *Serpent's Reach* (1980), *Voyager in Night* (1984), *Cuckoo's Egg* (1985), *Rimrunners* (1989), *Heavy Time* (1991), *Hellburner* (1992), *Devil to the Belt* (2000) and *Explorer* (2002); published short stories in science-fiction and fantasy magazines and anthologies. Won Hugo Award (1979).

CHERVINSKAYA, Lidiya Davydovna (1907–1988). Russian émigré poet and literary critic. Name variations: Lidia Chervinskaia. Born in Russia in 1907; died in Paris, France, July 1988. ❖ One of the most original and distinguished poets of the Russian emigration of the interwar decades, moved to Paris (early 1920s); published 3 volumes of verse, including *Approaches* (1934), and a large body of essays and criticism; lived for a number of years in Munich, where she worked for Radio Liberty, which broadcast news and cultural programs to the Soviet Union. ❖ See also *Women in World History.*

CHERYAZOVA, Lina (1968—). Uzbekistani freestyle skier. Name variations: Lina Cherjazova, Tcheriazova, Tcherjazova, or Tsjerjasova. Born Nov 1, 1968, in Uzbekistan. ❖ Won the World championship (1993); won a gold medal for aerials at Lillehammer Olympics (1994); was the 1st aerialist to consistently perform successful triple flips.

CHESEBRO, Caroline (1825–1873). *See Chesebrough, Caroline.*

CHESEBROUGH, Caroline (1825–1873). American novelist and short-story writer. Name variations: Caroline Chesebro or Chesebro'. Born Mar 30, 1825, in Canandaigua, New York; died Feb 16, 1873, in Sparkill, Piermont, Richland Co., NY; dau. of Nicholas Goddard Chesebrough and Betsey Kimball Chesebrough; attended Canandaigua Seminary. ❖ At 23, began publishing short stories in magazines; from mid-1860s, taught rhetoric and composition at Parker Collegiate Institute in Brooklyn; novels include *Dream-Land by Daylight* (1852), *The Children of Light* (1853), *Susan, the Fisherman's Daughter* (1855), *Victoria* (1856), *The Sparrow's Fall* (1963) and *The Foe in the Household* (1871).

CHESIMARD, Joanne (1948—). African-American radical and terrorist. Name variations: now goes by the name Assata Shakur; has used such aliases as Barbara Odoms, Mary Davis, Justine Henderson, Joanne Byron, Josephine Henderson, and Joanne Chesterman. Born July 16, 1948, in Brooklyn, NY; aunt of deceased rapper Tupac Shakur; children: 1 daughter. ❖ Was a member of the Black Liberation Army (BLA); while traveling with BLA members James Costan and Clark Squire, was stopped for traffic violation by New Jersey state trooper James Harper (May 2, 1973), who was wounded in an ensuing gun battle, while trooper Werner Foerster, who next arrived on scene, was killed along with Costan; with Squire, was convicted of murder, assault, robbery and

weapons offenses and sentenced to life imprisonment (1977); escaped from Edna Mahan Correctional Facility for Women in Clinton, NJ (1979); made her way to Cuba, which has no extradition treaty with US (1986); took the name Assata Shakur. ❖ See also autobiography *Assata* (1987).

CHESLER, Phyllis (1940—). American psychologist, educator and writer. Born in 1940 in New York, NY; dau. of Lillian Chesler; Bard College, BA, 1963; New York Medical College, Neurophysiology fellowship, 1968; New School for Social Research, MA, 1967, PhD, 1969; children: 1 son. ❖ Bestselling author, controversial activist and one of the founding voices of New Wave Feminism, taught at many colleges within City University of New York system (1969–98); founded Association for Women in Psychology (1969); taught one of the 1st accredited women's studies courses, at Richmond College in New York (1969–70), and established many services for female students at college; gave speech to American Psychological Association (1970), demanding that profession pay $1 million in reparations for women damaged by psychologists who had tranquilized, seduced, hospitalized, raped, electroshocked and lobotomized them; founded National Women's Health Network (1974); wrote about women's issues, including groundbreaking international bestseller *Women and Madness* (1972); earned Nike Prize for distinguished achievement in promoting rights of women (1998); over course of career, moved from far left of political spectrum to far right; turned to religion, beginning study of Torah (1989) and publishing 1st d'var Torah (2000); wrote with Orthodox feminist Rivka Haut, *Women of the Wall: Claiming Sacred Ground at Judaism's Holiest Site* (2002); also wrote *The New Anti-Semitism: The Current Crisis and What We Must Do About It* (2003). Other writings include *About Men* (1978), *Sacred Bond: The Legacy of Baby M* (1988), *Patriarchy: Notes of an Expert Witness* (1994) and *Woman's Inhumanity to Woman* (2003).

CHESNUT, Mary Boykin (1823–1886). American diarist. Born Mary Boykin Miller, Mar 31, 1823, in Statesburg, South Carolina; died Nov 22, 1886, in Camden, South Carolina; dau. of Stephen Decatur Miller (governor, US senator, and US congressional representative) and Mary (Boykin) Miller; m. James Chesnut Jr. (US senator from Camden, South Carolina), June 23, 1840 (died 1885); no children. ❖ Southern intellectual, socialite, and candid diarist of American Civil War, moved to Washington, DC, when husband James was elected to US Senate (1858); moved to Charleston after he resigned his office and departed to assist in the draft of South Carolina's Ordinance of Secession (1860); briefly resided in Montgomery, Alabama, for the Confederate Provisional Congress; began and kept a private diary, later to be published as *A Diary From Dixie,* an insightful view of the inner circle of Confederate society, written in Charleston, Camden, Columbia, Montgomery and Richmond (1861–65); witnessed the attack on Fort Sumpter (April 12, 1861); observed the decline and collapse of Confederate government in Richmond and took flight as a war refugee (1865); revised and re-revised wartime diaries for possible publication (1881–84). ❖ See also Elizabeth Muhlenfeld, *Mary Boykin Chesnut: A Biography* (Louisiana State U. Press, 1981); C. Vann Woodward and Elizabeth Muhlfeld, *The Private Mary Chesnut: The Unpublished Civil War Diaries* (Oxford U. Press, 1984) and *Mary Chesnut's Civil War* (Yale U. Press, 1981); and *Women in World History.*

CHESTER, Betty (1895–1943). English actress and singer. Born Oct 12, 1895, in Torquay, Devon, England; died Jan 11, 1943, in Lisbon, Portugal. ❖ Made stage debut with Clive Currie's Young Shakespearean Players (1914); plays include *Smile* (revue), *Sylvia's Lovers, The Knight of the Burning Pestle, The Rebel Maid, Love's Awakening, Leap Year, By the Way, The Co-Optimists* (in which she sang "Pig Tail Alley"), *My Son John, The Bow-Wows* and *The Clandestine Marriage;* films include *Tell Me Tonight.*

CHESTER, countess of.
See Matilda de Blois (d. 1120).
See Bertrada of Evreux (fl. 1170s).
See Constance of Brittany (1161–1201).
See Ellen of Wales (d. 1253).

CHESTERFIELD, countess of (d. 1667). *See Kirkhoven, Catherine.*

CHESTERTON, Denise (1897–1985). *See Robins, Denise Naomi.*

CHEUNG, Katherine (1904–2003). Chinese-American aviator. Name variations: Katherine Young. Born 1904 in Canton, China; died Sept 2, 2003, in Thousand Oaks, California; earned a degree in piano at Los Angeles Conservatory of Music; also attended University of Southern

California; m. George Young; children: Doris Wong; Dorothy Leschenko. ❖ Immigrated to US (1921); earned pilot's license (1932), the 1st Chinese-American woman to legally pilot a plane; became a stunt flyer; joined the Ninety Nines (1935); retired from flying (1942).

CHEVALIER, Caroline (c. 1832–1917). New Zealand travel writer. Name variations: Caroline Wilkie. Born Caroline Wilkie, c. 1832–1836, in London, England; died 1917; dau. of Frederick Wilkie (artist) and Sarah (Drew) Wilkie; m. Nicholas Chevalier (artist), 1857. ❖ Immigrated to New Zealand to join husband (1866); accompanied husband on difficult journey to west coast (April 1866); believed to have been the 1st European woman to travel there; recorded event in monograph, *Reminiscences of a journey across the South Island in 1866.* ❖ See also *Dictionary of New Zealand Biography* (Vol. 1).

CHEVENIX, Helen (1886–1963). Irish suffragist, labor organizer, and pacifist. Born in Blackrock, Co. Dublin, Nov 13, 1886; died in Dublin, Mar 4, 1963; dau. of Henry Chevenix and Charlotte Sophia (Ormsby) Chevenix; educated at Alexandra College Dublin; Trinity College, University of Dublin, BA, 1909, one of the 1st generation of women to graduate from there; never married. ❖ Joined Irishwomen's Suffrage Federation and met Louie Bennett (1911), who would be a close friend and co-worker until Bennett's death; with Bennett, helped set up the Irish Women's Reform League, which became an affiliated body of the Suffrage Federation; as a pacifist, was active in the Irish section of the Women's International League for Peace and Freedom during WWI; remained active in various pacifist organizations: Fellowship of Reconciliation, Women's International League for Peace and Freedom, and Irish Pacifist League; with Bennett, established Irish Women Workers' Union (1916), serving as assistant secretary, and was subsequently elected president of Irish Trade Union Congress (ITUC); was also an active member of Irish Labor Party and a regular delegate at its annual conferences; after WWII, served as vice-president of Irish Campaign for Nuclear Disarmament; in recognition of her work, was appointed to the consultative Health Council set up by Irish government under the 1953 Health Act; when Louie Bennett died (Nov 1956), succeeded her as general secretary of Women Workers' Union. ❖ See also *Women in World History.*

CHEVIGNÉ, Laure de (1860–1936). French countess and literary inspiration. Name variations: comtesse de Chevigne; Countess of Chevigne. Born 1860 in France; died 1936; children: Marie-Thérèse de Chevigné; grandmother of Marie-Laure de Noailles (1902–1970). ❖ Became the model for Marcel Proust's duchesse de Guermantes in his monumental novel *A la Recherche du Temps Perdu.*

CHEVREUSE, Duchesse de (1600–1679). See *Rohan-Montbazon, Marie de.*

CHEWIKAR, Princess (1876–1947). Egyptian princess. Name variations: Shivakier. Born Oct 25, 1876, in Istanbul, Turkey; died Feb 17, 1947, in Cairo, Egypt; only dau. of Field Marshal H.H. Prince Ibrahim Ahmad Pasha and Vijdan Navjuvan Khanum; m. Prince Ahmad Fu'ad (later Fuad I, king of Egypt), May 30, 1895 (div. May 1898); married thrice more.

CHÉZY, Helmina von (1783–1856). German musician and writer. Name variations: Chezy. Born Wilhelmina Christiane Klencke in Berlin, Germany, Jan 26, 1783; died in Geneva, Switzerland, Jan 28, 1856; married twice; children: 2 sons. ❖ Known for librettos and incidental music, as well as for her Viennese salon, wrote libretto for Carl Maria von Weber's *Euryanthe* and for her own play *Rosamunde* for which Franz Schubert wrote the music; also wrote poetry and the text for E.J.O. von Hettersdorf's *Singspiel Eginhard und Emma;* lived in Austria (1823–33) and received commissions for dramatic and musical work; had wide circle of admirers despite what has been called a strange personality and uneven gifts; held open house for artists and intellectuals in Vienna; writings include *Poems* (1812), *Heart Notes during a Pilgrimage* (1833), and the novel *Emma's Ordeals* (1827). ❖ See also *Women in World History.*

CHI SHU-JU (c. 1983—). Taiwanese taekwondo player. Born c. 1983 in Taipei, Taiwan. ❖ Representing Chinese Taipei, won a bronze medal for -49kg at Sydney Olympics (2000).

CHIANG CH'ING (1914–1991). See *Jiang Qing.*

CHIANG, Fang-liang (1916–2004). See *Chiang, Faina.*

CHIANG, Faina (1916–2004). First lady of Taiwan. Name variations: Chiang Fang-liang. Born Faina Vakhreva, May 15, 1916, in the Urals city of Sverdlovks, Russia; died Dec 15, 2004, in Taipei, Taiwan;

orphaned at a young age and raised by her sister; m. Chiang Ching-kuo (president of Taiwan and son of Chiang Kai-shek), 1935; daughter-in-law of Song Meiling; children: 3 sons, Alan (d. 1989), Hsiao-wu (d. 1991), and Hsiao-yung (d. 1996); daughter Chiang Hsiao-chang. ❖ Met husband while he was in the Soviet Union (1933); returned with him to China (1937); fled to Taiwan with husband and the Nationalists (late 1940s); was first lady of Taiwan (1978–88).

CHIANG KAI-SHEK, Madame (1897–2003). See *Song Meiling.*

CHIANG MEI-LING or MAY-LING (1897–2003). See *Song Meiling.*

CHIAO YIN (1911–1942). See *Xiao Hong.*

CHIAPPA, Imelda (1966—). Italian cyclist. Born May 10, 1966, in Sotto il Monte, Italy. ❖ Won a silver medal for indiv. road race at Atlanta Olympics (1996).

CHIARA. Variant of Clare.

CHIARA DI FAVORONE (c. 1194–1253). See *Clare of Assisi.*

CHIAURELI, Sofiko (1937—). Russian actress. Name variations: Sofico Chiaoureli or Sophico Tsciaourelli. Born May 21, 1937, in USSR; dau. of Veriko Andjaparidze (actress). ❖ Made over 30 films, including *Chveni ezo* (1957), *Ambavi erti kalishvilisa* (1960), *Generali da zizilebi* (1963), *Rats ginakhavs, vegar nakhav* (1965), *Khevsuruli balada* (1965), *Sayat Nova* (1968), *Peristvaleba* (1968), *Ar daidardo* (1969), *Tsutisopeli* (1971), *Aurzari salkhinetsi* (1975), *Natvris khe* (1977), *Ktor me yerking* (1980) and *The Confession* (1990).

CHIBA, Ginko (1938—). Japanese gymnast. Name variations: Ginko Abukawa. Born Ginko Abukawa, Feb 25, 1938. ❖ Won Japanese nationals (1962, 1963); at Tokyo Olympics, won a bronze medal in team all-around (1964).

CHIBÁS, Silvia (1954—). See *Chivás, Silvia.*

CHIBESAKUNDA, Lombe Phyllis (1944—). Zambian lawyer, judge and diplomat. Name variations: Madame L.P. Chibesakunda. Born in 1944 in Zambia. ❖ Trained at National Institute of Public Administration, Lusaka, and then at Gray's Inn, London; became 1st State Advocate in Ministry of Legal Affairs and was parliamentary candidate for Matero constituency and Solicitor-General in Ministry of Legal Affairs; joined diplomatic corps (1974) and became ambassador to Japan (1975) and then Zambian High Commissioner to UK, Netherlands, and Holy See (1978–81); served as chief justice of Zambia (1981–82), then appointed judge of High Court (1982).

CHICA, Elena (1828–1888). Romanian author. Name variations: (pseudonym) Dora d'Istria; Helene Ghica or Elena Ghika. Born in Bucharest, Romania, 1828; died in 1888; received a classical education and acquired an extensive knowledge of modern languages and literature; married Russian Prince Koltzoff- or Kolzow-Massalsky. ❖ At 15, under pseudonym Dora d'Istria, began a translation of the *Iliad,* and not long after wrote several pieces for the theater; published *La Vie Monastique dans l'église Orientale (Monastic Life in the Eastern Church,* 1855); published the 2-vol. *Des Femmes par une Femme (Women, by a Woman,* 1864), which was trans. into Russian, Italian, and English; writings on Albanian poetry gave rise to a nationalistic and literary movement among the Albanians; also wrote the 4-vol. *German Switzerland.*

CHICAGO, Judy (1939—). American artist, educator and feminist. Born Judy Cohen, July 20, 1939, in Chicago, Illinois; University of California, Los Angeles, BA, 1962, MA, 1964; m. Jerry Gerowitz, 1961 (died 1963); m. Lloyd Hamrol; m. Donald Woodman (photographer). ❖ Taught in California and Washington State; became involved in feminist art movement and co-founded Feminist Studio Workshop, Los Angeles; made such films as *Womanhouse* (1972), which attacked traditional views of female sexuality; most famous and controversial work was *The Dinner Party,* done in collaboration with craftswomen in Chicago (1974–79); similarly, worked on *Birth Project* (1980–85); did individual studio work for *Powerplay;* premiered *Holocaust Project: From Darkness to Light* (1993) and *Resolutions: A Stitch in Time* (2000); co-authored with Edward Lucie-Smith, *Women and Art: Contested Territory* (1999) and published *Fragments from the Delta of Venus* (2004), a collection of images based on the erotic writing of Anais Nin. ❖ See also autobiographies *Through the Flower: My Struggle as a Woman Artist* (1975) and *Beyond the Flower: The Autobiography of a Feminist Artist* (1996); Edward Lucie-Smith, *Judy Chicago: An American Vision* (2000).

CHICAGO MAY (1876–1929). See *Churchill, May.*

CHI CHENG REEL (b. 1944). *See Reel, Chi Cheng.*

CHICHESTER, Dehra (1882–1963). *See Parker, Dehra.*

CHICHESTER, Sophia (1795–1847). English radical. Born Sophia Catherine Ford in 1795 in Staffordshire, England; grew up in London; died in 1847; dau. of Francis Ford (Barbados sugar plantation owner and MP for Newcastle-under-Lyme, died 1801) and Mary Anson (granddau. of the first Lord Vernon); sister of Georgiana Welch (1792–1879); became the 3rd wife of Colonel John Palmer Chichester, 1822 (died 1823). ❧ Following husband's death, lived with sister at Ebworth Park; became critical of state and church that upheld unjust marriage laws; corresponded with Richard Carlile and was mentored by the mystic, James Pierrepont Greaves; attempted to enlighten the villagers near Ebworth Park by issuing tracts; financially supported radicals, including Robert Owen and James E. Smith; appointed president of the British and Foreign Society for the Promotion of Humanity and Abstinence from Animal Food (c. 1842); translated *The Phalanstery* from the French (1841).

CHICHIBU SETSUKO (1909–1995). Princess of Japan. Name variations: Princess Chichibu; Chichibu no Miya Setsuko. Born Matsudaira Setsuko in Walton-on-Thames, England, Sept 9, 1909, when her father was attaché at Japanese Embassy in London; at age 8 months, returned to Japan; died Aug 25, 1995; dau. of Matsudaira Tsuneo (diplomat); moved to Washington DC when father was appointed Japanese ambassador to US (1925); educated in Western schools; m. Prince Yasuhito Chichibu (d. 1953, younger brother of Emperor Hirohito), 1928; no children. ❧ Likely the most Westernized member of the Japanese imperial family in her generation, was heavily involved in the restoration of ties of friendship between Britain and Japan following WWII. ❧ See also memoirs *The Silver Drum: A Japanese Imperial Memoir,* trans. by Dorothy Britton (Global, 1996); and *Women in World History.*

CHICK, Harriette (1875–1977). British nutritionist and physiologist. Name variations: Dame Harriette Chick. Born in London, England, Jan 6, 1875; died in Cambridge, England, July 9, 1977; dau. of Samuel Chick (lace merchant and property owner) and Emma (Hooley) Chick; University College, London, PhD, 1904; post-graduate work at hygiene institutes in Vienna and Munich; never married. ❧ One of the key figures in the development of nutritional science in 20th century, made important contributions to public health—particularly by discovering the nutritional origins of a number of diseases including rickets and pellagra—and who was a co-discoverer of the standard Chick-Martin test for disinfectants; with Sir Charles Martin, began a highly productive relationship of 4 decades with the Lister Institute (1905), becoming the director of its division of nutrition (1922); wrote with Margaret Hume and Marjorie MacFarlane, *War on Disease: A History of the Lister Institute* (1971). Named Commander of the British Empire (1932) and Dame of the British Empire (1949). ❧ See also *Women in World History.*

CHICK, Sandra (1947—). Zimbabwean field-hockey player. Born June 2, 1947, in Zimbabwe; identical twin sister of Sonia Robertson (field-hockey player). ❧ At Moscow Olympics, won a gold medal in team competition (1980).

CHIDLEY, Katherine (fl. 1641). British religious writer. Name variations: Katharine Chidley. Fl. around 1641. ❧ Wrote polemical and didactic works, including *The Justification of the Independent Churches of Christ* (1641), *A New Years Gift, or a Brief Exhortation to Mr Thomas Edwards* (1645) and *Good Counsel to Petitioners that they May Declare Their Faith Before They Build Their Church* (1645).

CHIEN-SHIUNG WU (1912–1997). *See Wu, Chien-Shiung.*

CHIEPE, Gaositwe (c. 1924—). Botswanan diplomat and politician. Born Gaositwe Keagakwa Tibe Chiepe, c. 1924 in Serowe, Botswana; sister of Monametsi Chiepe; educated in Botswana, South Africa, and UK. ❧ Worked as education officer in Botswana and became director of Education (1968–69); appointed High Commissioner to UK and Nigeria (1970) and served as diplomat in several European and Scandinavian countries; became minister of Commerce and Industry (1974–77), minister of Mineral Resources and Water Affairs (1977–84), minister of External Affairs (1984), minister of Foreign Affairs (1988), and minister of Education; also served as chair of the Commonwealth Observer Group (2000).

CHIESA, Laura (1971—). Italian fencer. Born Aug 5, 1971, in Torino, Italy. ❧ Won a gold medal at World championships (1994); won a silver medal for épée team at Atlanta Olympics (1996).

CHIESLEY, Rachel (1682–1745). *See Grange, Rachel.*

CHIFFONS, The.
See Bennett, Patricia.
See Craig, Judy.
See Lee, Barbara.
See Peterson, Sylvia.

CHIFLEY, Elizabeth (1886–1962). Australian prime-ministerial wife. Born Elizabeth Gibson McKenzie, Aug 1, 1886, in Bathurst, New South Wales, Australia; died Sept 9, 1962, in Bathurst; m. Ben Chifley (16th prime minister of Australia, 1945–49), June 6, 1914; children: none. ❧ When younger, active in local civic organizations; though said to be charming and gracious, later avoided politics and campaigning because of a spinal disease that increasingly impaired mobility. ❧ See also Christine Wright's *Portrait of a Lady: Elizabeth Chifley* (Mitchell College, 1988).

CHILCOTT, Susan (1963–2003). English soprano. Born July 8, 1963, in Bristol, England; died Sept 4, 2003, in Timsbury, England; adopted and brought up in Somerset; m. David Sigall, Oct 2000; children: (from previous relationship) 1 son (b. around 1999). ❧ Began singing lessons at 6; joined Guildhall School of Music and Drama (1982); made professional debut as Frasquita in Scottish Opera production of *Carmen* (1991); 1st performed outside England at Théâtre Royal de la Monnaie in Brussels, as Ellen Orford in Britten's *Peter Grimes* (1994); became protégée of conductor, Antonio Pappano; made US debut at Santa Fe Opera, playing Donna Elvira in *Don Giovanni* (1996); made Metropolitan Opera debut, playing Helena in Britten's *A Midsummer Night's Dream* (April 2002); made Royal Opera House debut at Covent Garden opposite Plácido Domingo in *Queen of Spades,* playing Lisa (June 2002); last appeared in public with pianist Iain Burnside and actress Fiona Shaw in a Shakespearean evening in Brussels (June 2003); other roles include Hermione in *Wintermärchen* (1999), Desdemona in Verdi's *Otello* (2001), and the Composer in Strauss's *Ariadne auf Naxos.*

CHILD, Joan (1921—). Australian politician. Name variations: Gloria Joan Liles. Born Gloria Joan Liles, Aug 3, 1921, in Melbourne, Australia. ❧ Worked as a trade union liaison officer and research assistant; as a member of the Australian Labor Party (ALP), was elected to the House of Representatives for Henty, Victoria (1974); became the 1st woman to serve as Speaker of the House (Feb 11, 1986–Aug 28, 1989); served in the House (1974–75, 1980–90).

CHILD, Julia (1912–2004). American chef, culinary-arts writer and tv personality. Born Julia Carolyn McWilliams in Pasadena, California, Aug 15, 1912; died April 13, 2004, in Santa Barbara, California; dau. of John and Carolyn (Weston) McWilliams; Smith College, BA, 1934; studied at Cordon Bleu; m. Paul Child (artist-sculptor), Sept 1946 (died May 1994). ❧ Cooking teacher, cookbook author, and tv personality who pioneered the epicurean cooking revolution in US (1960s–70s), taking the mystery out of the preparation of French cuisine; with French chefs Simone Beck and Louisette Bertholle, published *Mastering the Art of French Cooking* (1961); launched PBS cooking show, "The French Chef," which ran for 9 years; published *The French Chef Cookbook* (1968); her 7 subsequent tv programs (including a 2nd series of "The French Chef" and "Baking with Julia"), as well as 6 one-hour videos called *The Way to Cook,* provided the basis for 9 additional cookbooks; with vintner Robert Mondavi, founded American Institute of Wine & Food (1981). Received France's National Order of Merit (1976); won Peabody Award (1966) and Emmy (1966) for "The French Chef" series. ❧ See also Noël Riley Fitch, *Appetite for Life: The Biography of Julia Child* (Doubleday, 1997); and *Women in World History.*

CHILD, Lydia Maria (1802–1880). American author. Born Lydia Maria Francis, Feb 11, 1802, in Medford, Massachusetts; died in Wayland, Massachusetts, Oct 20, 1880; dau. of David Convers Francis (baker) and Susannah (Rand) Francis; sister of Convers Francis (1795–1863, Unitarian minister); m. David Lee Child (1794–1874, Boston lawyer and journalist); children: none. ❧ Author who used her writings to attack slavery and advance the cause of women's rights; taught school in Watertown, Massachusetts; published 1st novel, *Hobomok* (1824), becoming an overnight celebrity in Boston; next published *The Rebels,* a novel about the Revolution, which was the 1st American book to use actual people and events from New England history; founded and wrote most of the *Juvenile Miscellany,* a bi-monthly children's magazine that was the nation's 1st; took up the unpopular cause of abolition with *An Appeal in Favor of that Class of Americans Called Africans* (1833) which, as she expected, proved to be a devastating setback to her literary career but was a spark that helped ignite a movement; took a job in New York as editor of an important abolitionist journal, the *National Anti-Slavery Standard;* edited Harriet Jacobs' *Incidents in the Life of a Slave Girl* and sponsored its publication; wrote numerous volumes of fiction, light verse, children's stories, as well as serious works on abolition, women's history, and comparative religion; writings include *The Frugal Housewife* (1830), *History of the Condition of Women* (2 vols., 1835), *Letters from New York* (1843, Vol. 1, 1845, Vol. 2) and *Correspondence between Lydia Maria Child, Governor Wise and Mrs. Mason* (1860). ❖ See also Helene G. Baer, *The Heart is Like Heaven: The Life of Lydia Maria Child* (U. of Pennsylvania Press, 1964); Deborah Pickman Clifford, *Crusader for Freedom: A Life of Lydia Maria Child* (Beacon, 1992); Carolyn L. Karcher, *The First Woman in the Republic: A Cultural Biography of Lydia Maria Child* (Duke U. Press, 1994); and *Women in World History.*

CHILD-VILLIERS, Margaret Elizabeth (1849–1945). See *Villiers, Margaret Elizabeth Child-.*

CHILDERS, Naomi (1892–1964). American actress. Born Naomi Weston Childers, Nov 15, 1892, in Pottstown, Pennsylvania; died May 9, 1964, in Hollywood, California; m. Luther Reed. ❖ Began career on Broadway; films include *Dust of Egypt, Fathers of Men, The World and Its Women, White Heat, Earthbound, Anselo Lee, Ziegfeld Follies* and *Trial Marriage.*

CHILDRESS, Alice (1916–1994). African-American actress and playwright. Born Alice Herndon Childress, Oct 12, 1916, in Charleston, South Carolina; died Aug 14, 1994, in Astoria, Queens, New York; dau. of Florence Childress; educated at Radcliffe Institute for Independent Study (1968); m. Nathan Woodard (musician), July 17, 1957; children: Jean R. Childress (1935–1990). ❖ Trailblazer for African-American women in drama, moved with mother to Harlem (1921); made acting debut (1940); joined American Negro Theater (ANT, 1941); received Tony nomination for portrayal of Blanche in *Anna Lucasta* (1944); wrote *Florence* (1949), the 1st of 10 plays; wrote *Gold Through the Trees* (1952), the 1st professionally produced play in NY by an African-American woman; other plays include *Trouble in Mind* (1955), *Wedding Band* (1966) and *Gullah* (1984); wrote serialized column, "Here's Mildred," for the newspapers *Freedom* and *Baltimore Afro-American,* which were collected in 1st book, *Like One of the Family . . . Conversations from a Domestic's Life* (1956); probably best remembered for her adolescent fiction, *A Hero Ain't Nothin' but a Sandwich* (1973), later produced as a movie, and *Rainbow Jordan* (1981). ❖ See also LaVinia Delois Jennings, *Alice Childress* (Twayne, 1995); and *Women in World History.*

CHILDRESS, Laura Webb (1941–2001). See *Webb, Laura.*

CHILDS, Lucinda (1940—). American dancer and choreographer. Born June 26, 1940, in New York, NY; Sarah Lawrence College, BA in dance, 1962; trained with Merce Cunningham. ❖ Presented 1st works with Judson Dance Theater, NY (early 1960s) and danced in Judith Dunn's *Acapulco* (1963), James Waring's *Double Concerto* (1964), and Elaine Summers' *Country Houses* (1963); was founding dancer, choreographer and director of Lucinda Childs Dance company, NY (beginning 1973); collaborated with Robert Wilson in production of *Einstein on the Beach* (1976) and *I Was Sitting On My Patio This Guy Appeared I Thought I Was Hallucinating* (1977); choreographed for other companies, including Bavarian State Opera Ballet, Rambert Dance Company, Lyon Opéra Ballet and Paris Opéra Ballet; won Obie Award (1976). Choreographic works include *Pastime* and *Minus Auditorium Equipment and Furnishings* for Judson Dance Theater (1964), *Dance 1–5* to music by composer Philip Glass (1979), *Available Light* (1983), *Four Elements* (1990), *Impromptu* to music by Andrzej Kurylewicz (1993), *Kengier* (1995) and *Hammerklavier* (1996).

CHILSWINTHA. See *Galswintha.*

CHILTRUD (fl. 700s). Frankish princess. Born between 726 and 740; dau. of Charles Martel (c. 690–741), mayor of Austrasia and Neustria (r. 714–741); and Sunnichild (d. 741); m. Odilo, duke of Bavaria, 749; children: Tassilo III, duke of Bavaria.

CHILVER, E.M. (b. 1914). See *Chilver, Sally.*

CHILVER, Sally (1914—). English anthropologist and educator. Name variations: Sally Graves; E.M. Chilver or Mrs. E.M. Chilver. Born Sally Graves in 1914 in England; dau. of Philip Graves, *Times* correspondent; niece of Robert Graves (poet and novelist); m. Richard Chilver, 1938. ❖ Began career as a journalist; with anthropologist Phyllis Kaberry, worked in, and investigated the ethnography of, the Grassfields of Cameroon in

West-central Africa (1958–63), bringing the region to world attention; served as director of Oxford Institute of Commonwealth Studies (1958–61); became principal of Bedford College, London (1964), and Lady Margaret Hall, Oxford (1971).

CHIMAY, Princess de (1773–1835). See *Tallien, Thérésia.*

CHIMNECHILD (r. 662–675). See *Himnechildis.*

CHIN, Tsai (1937—). Chinese actress. Born Zhou Tsai Chin, 1937, in Tianjin, China; raised in Shanghai; dau. of Zhou Xin-Fang (grand master of the Beijing Opera); sister of Michael Chow; paternal aunt of China Chow; was the 1st Chinese student to attend Royal Academy of Dramatic Art (RADA) in London; married and divorced twice. ❖ Came to prominence in London in title role of *The World of Suzie Wong* (1959); learned that parents had been a target of Madame Mao's (Jiang Qing) Cultural Revolution (her mother was beaten to death by the Red Guard, her father died after a lengthy house arrest in 1974); wrote a play for BBC about Madame Mao and portrayed her in 2 plays; after Jiang Qing's fall, was invited back to China to teach and direct; made Hollywood debut to critical acclaim in *The Joy Luck Club* (1993); other films include *The Inn of the Sixth Happiness* (1958), *The Cool Mikado* (1962), *The Face of Fu Manchu* (1965), *The Brides of Fu Manchu* (1966), *You Only Live Twice* (1967), *Red Corner* (1997), *Long Life, Happiness & Prosperity* (2002) and *Memoirs of a Geisha* (2005).

CHINA, empress of.
See *Lü, Hou (r. 195–180 bce).*
See *Wu, Zetian (624–705).*
See *Chabi (fl. 13th c.).*
See *Cixi (1835–1908).*

CHINCHON, Ana, countess of (1576–1639). Spanish countess. Born at Astorga, Castile, 1576; died at Cartagena, Columbia, Dec 1639; dau. of 8th marquis of Astorga; m. Luis de Velasco, marquis of Salinas (twice viceroy of Mexico and once of Peru, died); m. Luis Geronymo de Cabrera, count of Chinchon (viceroy of Peru). ❖ During residence in Lima, was attacked with a tertian ague (form of fever occurring every other day) and was cured by some powdered Peruvian bark that had been sent to her physician by the *corregidor* (chief magistrate) of Loxa; carried a quantity of the bark with her when she set sail for Spain. In honor of her, Linnaeus named the genus of quinine-bearing plants *Cinchona.* ❖ See also *Women in World History.*

CHING HSI KAI (fl. 1807–1810). See *Ching Shih.*

CHING, Laura Blears (c. 1951—). American surfing champion. Name variations: Laura Blears; Laura Blears-Ching. Born Laura Blears, c. 1951, in Hawaii; dau. of Lord James Blears (professional wrestler). ❖ Winner of the women's international surfing championship at Makaha Beach, Hawaii (1972); was the 1st woman to compete against male surfers, Oahu, Hawaii (1973); twice named Hawaii's top woman surfer; competed in longboard events.

CHING SHIH (fl. 1807–1810). Chinese pirate. Name variations: Ching Hsi Kai; Ching Yih Saou. Married Ching Yih (pirate, died in a typhoon 1807). ❖ After husband died, took over his fleet of 500 to 700 junks which were divided into 6 squadrons, each of which flew a flag of a different color as it cruised for victims along its designated stretch of the China coast; possessed abilities as an administrator and businesswoman that equalled her successes as pirate chief; built a pirate fleet of unprecedented size, with some 70,000 to 80,000 men, women, and children under her command in 2,000 vessels. ❖ See also *Women in World History.*

CHING YIH SAOU (fl. 1807–1810). See *Ching Shih.*

CHINGLING SOONG (1893–1981). See *Song Qingling.*

CHINN, May Edward (1896–1980). African-American physician and scholar. Born April 15, 1896, in Great Barrington, Massachusetts; died Dec 1, 1980; only child of William Lafayette Chinn (son of a slave and white plantation owner) and Lulu Ann Chinn (dau. of a Chickahominy Indian mother and slave father); attended New York's Bellevue Medical College (now New York University Medical College) and New York Post-Graduate Hospital Medical School; Columbia University, MA in public health, 1933. ❖ One of the 1st African-American women in New York City to practice medicine, was also the 1st African-American woman to earn a medical degree at Bellevue; served as 1st African-American Harlem Hospital female intern and ambulance crew member; opened private practice in Harlem (1928) and worked night shift at adjacent Edgecombe Sanitorium; became 1st African-American female with admitting privileges to Harlem Hospital (1940); worked with Dr. George Papanicolaou on invention of Pap smear (1928–33); worked at Dr. Elise L'Esperance Strang's cancer clinics (1944–75) and at New York Infirmary for Women and Children (1945–56); founded Susan Smith McKinney Steward Medical Society (1975); retired from medicine (1977).

CHIONIA (d. 304). Saint. Name variations: Chione; Chionia of Thessalonica. Born in Roman Empire; died 304; sister of Agape of Thessalonica and Irene (saints). ❖ With sisters, was accused of being in possession of the Holy Scriptures, a crime punishable by death, and was burned alive. Feast day is April 3. ❖ See also *Women in World History.*

CHIRAC, Bernadette (1933—). French first lady. Born Bernadette Chodron de Courcel, May 18, 1933, in Paris, France; graduate of the Paris Institut d'Etudes Politiques; received a master's in archeology; m. Jacques Chirac (b. 1932, elected president of France in 1995 and reelected 2002), Mar 16, 1956; children: Laurence and Claude Chirac. ❖ Elected to the Sarran (Corrèze) Municipal Council (1971); was deputy to the mayor of Sarran (1977); was founder and president of the Association for the Promotion of the Arts; elected to the Corrèze General Council, the 1st woman to occupy a seat in this Departmental Assembly (1979), then reelected (1992); served as president of the Association Fondation-Hôpitaux de Paris (1994).

CHIRIAEFF, Ludmilla (1924–1996). Latvian ballet dancer and choreographer. Born Jan 10, 1924, in Riga, Latvia; died Sept 22, 1996. ❖ Raised in Berlin, performed as dance soloist at Berlin Opera Ballet; during WWII, was interned in concentration camp (1941); moved to Switzerland at the end of the war and danced with numerous companies, including Lausanne Municipal Theater and Les Ballets des Artes in Geneva; immigrated to Canada and founded Les Ballets Chiriaeff (1950s), later renamed Les Grands Ballets Canadiens de Montreal (1957); choreographed a large repertory for her company as well as numerous short ballets for the French-language CBC; founded École Supérieure de Danse du Québec (1966) and played a major role in developing dance education in public schools throughout Quebec. Works of choreography include *Jeu de Cartes* (1954), *Pierre et le Loup* (1954), *Les Ruses d'Amour* (1955), *Les Noces* (1956), *Dances Symphonique* (1956), *Les Clowns* (1956), *Scherzo Capriccioso* (1957), *Etude* (1959) and *Jeux d'Arlequins* (1963).

CHIRKOVA, Svetlana (1945—). See Tsirkova, Svetlana.

CHIRWA, Vera (1933—). Malawi lawyer and politician. Born in 1933; m. Orton Chirwa (lawyer and politician, died in prison 1992). ❖ With husband, played a prominent role in Malawi's bid for independence from Britain (1964), but political unrest forced them into exile shortly thereafter; while staying in Zambia, was abducted with husband by Malawi security officials (1981), charged with treason, and sentenced to death (later commuted to life in prison); as a result of efforts by Amnesty International, was released (1993).

CHISHOLM, Catherine (1874–1952). See Cushing, Catherine Chisholm.

CHISHOLM, Caroline (1808–1877). British-born philanthropist. Pronunciation: CHIS-um. Born Caroline Jones, May 10, 1808, in Wootton, near Northampton, England; died in London, Mar 25, 1877; dau. of William (yeoman farmer) and Sarah Jones; m. Archibald Chisholm (captain in the forces of East India Co.), Dec 27, 1830; children: Archibald (b. 1836); William (b. 1837); Henry (b. 1839); Sydney (b. 1846); Caroline (b. 1848); Monica (b. 1851). ❖ Known as "The Emigrant's Friend," was a self-appointed advocate of immigrants arriving in the then fledgling colony of Australia, though she never held any official positions; 1st traveled to India to join husband (1832); founded The Female School of Industry for the Daughters of European Soldiers in Madras; traveled to Australia (Mar 1838); established the Female Immigrants Home in Sydney (1841); formed branches to settle immigrants throughout NSW (1842); prosecuted the captain of the ship *Carthaginian* (1842); gave evidence to New South Wales Legislative Council's Select Committee on Immigration (1845); sailed for England (1846); lobbied the Colonial Office on behalf of emigrants; gave evidence before House of Lords committees on the Execution of the Criminal Law and Colonization from Ireland (1847); established Family Colonization Loan Society (1849); traveled to Melbourne (1854); established Shelter Sheds for immigrants on the routes to the Victorian goldfields (1854); fell ill with a kidney disease and moved to Sydney (1857); founded her Educational Establishment for Young Ladies in Sydney (1862); returned to England (1866); bedridden until her death (1871–77); was so charismatic and of such moral and intellectual stature that she managed to break through the barriers that otherwise prevented women from influencing government and social policy. Except for the queen of England, is the only woman to be featured on an Australian bank note. ❖ See also Mary C. Hoban, *Fifty-One Pieces of Wedding Cake: A Biography of Caroline Chisholm* (Lowden, 1973); Margaret Kiddle, *Caroline Chisholm* (Melbourne U. Press, 1957); and *Women in World History.*

CHISHOLM, Linda (1957—). American volleyball player. Born Dec 21, 1957, in Northridge, California; graduate of Pepperdine University, 1981. ❖ At Los Angeles Olympics, won a silver medal in team competition (1984); won 6 of 16 grand slam events.

CHISHOLM, Janet (1929–2004). British spy. Born Janet Anne Deane, May 7, 1929, at Kasuali, near Simla, India; died July 23, 2004; one of 4 daughters of a Royal Engineers officer; attended Wycombe Abbey School and Queen Anne's, Caversham; studied Russian and French; m. Ruari Chisholm (head of M16 station at the Moscow embassy working under diplomatic cover); children: 2 sons, 2 daughters. ❖ Joined British Secret Intelligence Service (SIS or M16) at the Allied Control Commission in West Germany; as a British mother in Moscow who spoke Russian (as well as an officer in M16), worked as a go-between with the Soviet military intelligence agent Colonel Oleg Penkovsky and US and British intelligence, meeting up with Penkovsky while walking her children in the park (the Penkovsky papers were considered one of the greatest Western intelligence coup since WWII).

CHISHOLM, Melanie (1974—). English singer. Name variations: Melanie C, Mel C, Sporty Spice, The Spice Girls. Born Melanie Jayne Chisholm, Jan 12, 1974, in Liverpool, England. ❖ Shot to fame as part of pop-quintet, the Spice Girls, formed in London (1994); released "Wannabe," the 1st debut single by an all-girl band to enter international charts at #1 (1997), followed by *Spice*, which went to #1 in UK charts and was 1st debut album by UK performers to enter US charts at #1 (1997); had other Top-10 singles, including "Say You'll be There" and "2 Become 1"; released smash-hit album *Spiceworld* and film of same name (1997); like other members of the group, took on solo projects after unsuccessful Spice album, *Forever* (2000), releasing albums *Northern Star* (1999) and *Reason* (2003).

CHISHOLM, Shirley (1924–2005). African-American politician. Pronunciation: CHIZ-um. Born Shirley Anita St. Hill, Nov 30, 1924, in the Bedford-Stuyvesant section of Brooklyn, New York; died Jan 1, 2005, in Osmond Beach, Florida; dau. of Charles Christopher St. Hill (laborer) and Ruby (Seale) St. Hill (born in Barbados); Brooklyn College, BA in sociology (1946); Columbia University, MA in education (1953); m. Conrad Chisholm, Oct 8, 1949 (div., Feb 1977); m. Arthur Hardwick Jr., Nov 26, 1977; no children. ❖ The 1st African-American woman elected to US House of Representatives (1968) and 1st African-American woman candidate for the presidency of US (1972), paved the way for the later nominations of both minority and female candidates for national office; spent ages 3 to 11 in Barbados with maternal grandmother (1927–35); served as director of the large Hamilton-Madison Child Care Center in Lower Manhattan (1953–59); began work for the New York City Division of Day Care, and gained recognition as a child-care expert (1959); was active in Democratic Party politics (1950–80), founding, with others, the reform-oriented Unity Democratic Club in Brooklyn (early 1960s); elected to New York State Assembly (1964); won reelection (1965 and 1966); elected to US House of Representatives from Bedford-Stuyvesant section of Brooklyn (1968) and was appointed to the House Education and Labor Committee; served 7 terms, becoming a celebrated advocate of women, minorities, and domestic priorities (retiring in 1982); in Congress, concentrated on issues related to jobs, housing, education and welfare; ran for the Democratic nomination for president of US (1972), the 1st black woman, and only the 2nd woman, to seek the presidency; taught courses on politics, race, and women at Mount Holyoke. ❖ See also memoirs, *Unbought and Unbossed* (Houghton, 1970) and *The Good Fight* (Harper & Row, 1973); and *Women in World History.*

CHITNIS, Leela (1909–2003). Indian actress. Born Sept 9, 1909, in Dharwar, Karnataka, India; died July 14, 2003, in Danbury, Connecticut; dau. of an English professor; married at 16 (div.); children: 4, including Manavendra, Benoy and Raj Chitnis. ❖ Pioneer in the Indian film industry; came to prominence in movies produced by Bombay Talkies, playing romantic leads in such hit films as *Kangan*, *Bandham* and *Jhoola* opposite Ashok Kumar, one of India's top male stars; an intellectual actress and feminist, often took roles that challenged the caste system; moved into character parts with the patriotic film, *Shaheed* (1948); was especially known for portrayal of mothers in such films as *Awaara* (1951); appeared in over 80 films, concluding with *Dil Tujhko Diya* (1985); came to US in later years to be near her family.

CHITTY, Kathleen (1886–1965). *See Hurd-Wood, Kathleen.*

CHITTY, Letitia (1897–1982). English civil engineer. Born July 15, 1897; died Oct 1982; Newnham College, Cambridge, mathematical tripos, 1917, mechanical science tripos, 1921, MA, 1926. ❖ Employed by Admiralty Air Department to study stress on planes (1917–18); worked as research assistant and later as lecturer at Imperial College in London (1934–62); during WWII, did research on stress analysis of experimental airplanes, as well as safety and design of dams, bridges, and shelters; conducted experimental studies for Iraq's Dokan Dam; was 1st woman to earn 1st-class honors at Cambridge University's mechanical sciences tripos, 1st woman to become a member of the Institution of Civil Engineers' Technical Committee, and 1st woman recipient of Telford Gold Medal (1969); elected fellow of Imperial College (1971) and Royal Aeronautical Society.

CH'IU CHIN (c. 1875–1907). *See Qiu Jin.*

CHIUMINA, Olga Nikolaevna (1865–1909). Russian poet and playwright. Name variations: Ol'ga Nikolaevna Chiuminá; Olga Chiumina; (pseudonyms) Optimist, Boycott. Born 1865; died 1909. ❖ Known for her parody of such modernists as Maeterlinck and for her skillful translations of poetry; had verse drama *Temptation* performed at Aleksandrinskii Theatre (1888); later work included fiction, *For Life and for Death* (1895), *For the Sins of the Fathers* (1896) and *Glow of the Footlights* (1898), as well as poetry collections, *New Poems* (1905) and *Autumn Whirlwinds* (1908); published 2 satirical pamphlets on political events of 1905 (1906); best remembered for her collection of verse satires, *In Expectation.*

CHIVÁS, Silvia (1954—). Cuban runner. Name variations: Silvia Chivas or Chibás. Born Sept 10 (some sources cite Sept 30), 1954, in Cuba. ❖ At Munich Olympics, won a bronze medal in the 4x100-meter relay and a bronze medal in the 100 meters (1972).

CHIVERS, Elizabeth (1682–1712). English murderer. Born in Spitalfields, England, 1682; executed Aug 1, 1712; children: Elizabeth. ❖ At 30, began 1st relationship, with a married attorney named Ward (1711); had daughter Elizabeth, but lost Ward's support when his wife discovered the affair and went public with it; drowned infant in a pond; witnesses made citizen's arrest; pled guilty at trial.

CHIYO UNO (b. 1897). *See Uno, Chiyo.*

CHIZHOVA, Nadezhda (1945—). Russian shot putter. Name variations: Nadyezhda. Born Sept 29, 1945, in Usolye-Sibirskoye, USSR. ❖ Won 4 European titles (1966, 1969, 1971, 1974); won a bronze medal at Mexico City Olympics (1968), a gold medal at Munich Olympics (1972), and a silver medal at Montreal Olympics (1976).

CHLADEK, Dana (1963—). Czech-American kayaker. Born Dec 27, 1963, in Decin, Czechoslovakia; grew up in Bloomfield Hills, Michigan; dau. of Stan and Emma Chladek, who were both on the Czech national team; graduate of Dartmouth, 1986; m. Thierry Humeau (French canoeist). ❖ Immigrated to US at 5; won World Cup (1988); placed 1st in Champion International Whitewater Series Overall rankings (1990); won a bronze medal at Barcelona Olympics (1992) and a silver medal at Atlanta Olympics (1996), both for K1 slalom.

CHLOTHILDE. *See Clotilda.*

CHMIELNICKA, Lidia (1939—). Polish volleyball player. Born Mar 8, 1939. ❖ At Mexico City Olympics, won a bronze medal in team competition (1968).

CHO (1809–1890). Queen dowager and regent of Korea. Name variations: Lady Cho. Born Jan 21, 1809; died at the Ghagyong-jon, Kyongbok Palace, June 4, 1890, in Seoul, Korea; dau. of H.E. Cho Man-yong, Prince P'ungyang; m. Crown Prince Hyomong (b. 1809), 1817 (died 1830), posthumously raised to the rank of king as Ik-jong; children: Prince Yi Hwan (b. 1827) who came to the throne as Hon-jong or Honjong, 24th king of the Chosun dynasty (r. 1834–49). ❖ Powerful Queen Dowager of Chosun who, on the death of King Sun-jo (1834), was raised to the rank of Great Queen Regent for her son Honjong (he died in 1849); made Senior Great Queen Regent (1857), during the reign

of Chol-jong; following Chol-jong's death, adopted Kwang-mu to be the son of her late husband and served as his regent (Jan 16, 1864–Mar 29, 1866); purged the Western faction from power during her reign.

CHO EUN-HEE (1972—). South Korean handball player. Born May 20, 1972, in South Korea. ❖ Won a team silver medal at Atlanta Olympics (1996).

CHO EUN-JUNG. South Korean field-hockey player. Born in South Korea. ❖ Won a team silver medal at Atlanta Olympics (1996).

CHO KI-HYANG (1963—). Korean field-hockey player. Born Sept 23, 1963, in South Korea. ❖ At Seoul Olympics, won a silver medal in team competition (1988).

CHO MIN-SUN. South Korean judoka. Born in South Korea. ❖ Won World championship (1993, 1995); won a gold medal for 61–66kg middleweight at Atlanta Olympics (1996) and a bronze medal for 63–70kg middleweight at Sydney Olympics (2000).

CHO YOUN-JEONG (1969—). Korean archer. Born Sept 29, 1969. ❖ At Barcelona Olympics, won gold medals in team round and double FITA round (1992).

CHOATE, Mrs. Allison (b. 1910). American golfer. Born May 18, 1910, in Buffalo, NY; husband died (2002). ❖ Was non-playing captain of the Curtis Cup and World Amateur teams (1975); won USGA's Women Senior Golf championship, A section (1963); won the US Women's Senior Golf Association title (1963–66, 1968–69).

CHOATE, Pearl (1907–1983). American murderer (accused). Name variations: Pearl Choate Birch. Born May 31, 1907, in Texas; died Feb 1983 in Caldwell, Texas; married 7 times, the last to A. Otis Birch of California, 1966 (died 1967). ❖ Worked as a private nurse for elderly Texas millionaires, 7 of whom she married shortly before their deaths, inheriting their riches; served 12 years in prison for the shooting death of 1 husband, which she claimed was in self-defense; after her release, married 95-year-old millionaire A. Otis Birch. Apparently there was some question as to whether or not 59-year-old Pearl had kidnapped him, but a judge found otherwise (1966); suspicions that she played a part in Birch's death some months later could not be proven.

CHODZIESNER, Gertrud (1894–1943). *See Kolmar, Gertrud.*

CHOI AEI-YOUNG (1959—). Korean basketball player. Born July 25, 1959, in South Korea. ❖ At Los Angeles Olympics, won a silver medal in team competition (1984).

CHOI CHOON-OK (1965—). Korean field-hockey player. Born May 15, 1965, in South Korea. ❖ At Seoul Olympics, won a silver medal in team competition (1988).

CHOI EUN-KYUNG. South Korean field-hockey player. Born in South Korea. ❖ Won a team silver medal at Atlanta Olympics (1996).

CHOI EUN-KYUNG (1984—). South Korean short-track speedskater. Born Dec 26, 1984, in South Korea. ❖ Won a gold medal for the 3,000-meter relay and a silver medal for the 1,500 meters at Salt Lake City Olympics (2002); won a silver medal for 1,500 meters and a gold medal for 3,000 meter relay at Torino Olympics (2006).

CHOI IM-JEONG (1981—). South Korean handball player. Born Feb 14, 1981, in South Korea. ❖ Won a team silver at Athens Olympics (2004).

CHOI KYUNG-HEE (1966—). Korean basketball player. Born Feb 25, 1966, in South Korea. ❖ At Los Angeles Olympics, won a silver medal in team competition (1984).

CHOI MI-SOON. South Korean field-hockey player. Born in South Korea. ❖ Won a team silver medal at Atlanta Olympics (1996).

CHOI MIN-KYUNG. South Korean short-track speedskater. Born in South Korea. ❖ Won a gold medal for the 3,000-meter relay at Salt Lake City Olympics (2002).

CHOI, Sook Nyul (1937—). Korean-American children's writer and memoirist. Born 1937 in Pyongyang, North Korea; immigrated to US (1958); graduate of Manhattanville College; children: 2 daughters. ❖ Taught high school in New York City schools; books, which offer a fictionalized account of her childhood escape from North Korea and life in US, include *Year of Impossible Goodbyes* (1991), *Echoes of the White Giraffe* (1993) and *Gathering of Pearls* (1994).

CHOISEUL-MEUSE, Félicité de (fl. 19th c.). French novelist. Name variations: Felicie de Choiseul Meuse; Félicité, comtesse de Chouseul-

Meuse; Félicité de Chouseul-Meuse; Mme de Choiseul-Meuse. Fl. between 1802 and 1818. ❖ Works, which depict erotic relationships, often between women, include *Amélie de Saint-Far, ou la Fatale erreur* (1802), *Entre chien et loup* (1809), *Cécile ou l'élève de la pitié* (1816), and *Les Amants de Charenton* (1818); best-known novel is *Jullie ou j'ai sauvé ma rose* (1807).

CHOJNOWSKA-LISKIEWICZ, Krystyna (1937—). Polish yachtswoman. Born in Warsaw, Poland, 1937; educated as a shipbuilding engineer; married. ❖ The 1st woman to sail solo around the world, arrived in the harbor of Las Palmas, Canary Islands (April 21, 1978), where her epic voyage of over 28,500 miles in her 32-foot yacht *Mazurek* had begun more than 2 years earlier. ❖ See also *Women in World History.*

CHOLMONDELEY, Elizabeth or Anne (1866–1941). *See Arnim, Elizabeth von.*

CHOLMONDELEY, Mary (1859–1925). British novelist. Name variations: (pseudonym) Pax. Born June 8, 1859, in Shropshire, England; died July 15, 1925, in London, England; dau. of the Reverend Richard Hugh Cholmondeley and Emily Beaumont Cholmondeley. ❖ Assumed duties of parent upon death of mother; moved with family to London (1896), where she became a celebrity after the success of *Red Pottage;* writings include *The Danvers Jewels* (1887), *Diana Tempest* (1893), *Red Pottage* (1899), *Notwithstanding* (1909), *Under One Roof: A Family Record* (1918) and *The Romance of His Life and Other Romances* (1921). ❖ See also Percy Lubbock, *Mary Cholmondeley: A Sketch from Memory* (1928).

CHOLMONDELEY SISTERS. *See Anderson, Lea (1959—).*

CHOMS, Wladyslawa Laryssa (1891–1966). Polish rescuer. Name variations: Angel of Lvov. Born in Poland in 1891; died 1966; lived before World War II in Drohobycz (Drogobych), Eastern Galicia; m. Friedrich Choms (major in Polish Army); children: 1 son (pilot in Royal Air Force, killed in combat 1941). ❖ Polish rescuer who saved the lives of many hundreds of Jews and became known as the "Angel of Lvov" during the Holocaust; with husband and son, settled in the city of Lvov (1934); with start of WWII (1939), stayed in Lvov while husband and son left to fight Nazis; starting 1941, during Nazi occupation of Lvov, created a tight circle of Polish women and men who smuggled food to those in need, provided them with medical care, and arranged for the procurement of false identity papers and the subsequent movement of Jews from the ghetto to safer locations within the city; ordered to Warsaw by Polish underground central command (Nov 1943), continued her resistance activities in Warsaw and survived the 1944 uprising. Named "Righteous among the Nations" at Yad Vashem in Jerusalem (1963). ❖ See also *Women in World History.*

CHONA, Maria (1845–1936). Papago medicine woman and basketmaker. Name variations: Cha-veela. Born 1845 in Mesquite Root village, Papago Reservation, Arizona; died 1936; dau. of Jose Marie (chief of Tautaukwani Papago). ❖ Served as medicine woman and basket maker among the Papago of the Southern Arizona Tohono O'Odham tribe; with the aid of anthropologist Ruth Murray Underhill, was the 1st Southwestern Indian woman to publish her life story, *The Autobiography of a Papago Woman* (1936).

CHOPIN, Kate (1850–1904). American writer. Born Katherine O'Flaherty, Feb 8, 1850, in St. Louis, Missouri; died in St. Louis, Aug 22, 1904; dau. of Thomas (merchant) and Eliza (Faris) O'Flaherty (died 1885); m. Oscar Chopin (French Creole and cotton factor [agent]), 1870 (died 1882); children: Jean Baptiste (b. 1871); Oscar Charles (b. 1873); George Francis (b. 1874); Frederick (b. 1876); Felix Andrew (b. 1878); Lelia (b. 1879). ❖ Originally characterized as a local colorist, is now acknowledged as a pioneering American realist, best known for her 1899 novel, *The Awakening;* moved with husband to New Orleans following marriage; moved to Cloutierville, Louisiana (1879); husband died (1882); returned to St. Louis (1884); published love poems (1889); published stories, poems, reviews and articles in literary journals, newspapers, and large circulation magazines (1889–1902); began *At Fault* (1889), which was self-published (1890); published "Desiree's Baby" in *Vogue,* and Houghton Mifflin accepted *Bayou Folk* (1893); published *The Awakening* (1899) which tells of a woman's frustration and diminishment as she discovers that marriage means she is no more than a husband's personal property with no autonomy of her own; published "Polly" in *Youth's Companion* (1902), last publication during her lifetime. ❖ See also Emily Toth, *Kate Chopin* (Morrow, 1990); and *Women in World History.*

CHOPRA, Joyce (1938—). American director and producer. Born in 1938. ❖ Made several documentaries; made feature debut with *Smooth Talk* (1985), which introduced Laura Dern; other films include *Martha Clarke, Light and Dark* and *The Lemon Sisters;* for tv, directed "Murder in New Hampshire: The Pamela Wojas Smart Story" (1991), "Danger of Love: The Carolyn Warmus Story" (1992), "The Disappearance of Nora," "Deadline for Murder: From the Files of Edna Buchanan," "Murder in a Small Town," and "The Last Cowboy," among others.

CHOQUET-BRUHAT, Yvonne (1923—). French mathematical physicist. Name variations: Yvonne Bruhat. Born Dec 29, 1923 in Lille, France; École Normale Supérieure de Sèvres, DSc, 1951; children: 2 daughters; 1 son. ❖ Renowned for work in mathematical physics, including partial differential equations, general relativity, super gravities, and gauge theories, co-wrote *Analysis, Manifolds, and Physics* (1977); worked as researcher at many institutions, including École Normale Supérieure, Centre Nationale de la Recherche Scientifique, Institute for Advanced Study (Princeton, NJ), Faculté des Sciences de Marseilles, Université de Reims (lecturer), and Université Pierre et Marie Curie (Paris); joined Faculté des Sciences de Paris (1960); was the 1st woman elected to French Academy of Sciences (1979); elected to American Academy of Arts and Sciences (1985). Received (with Cornell University's James York) the American Physical Society and American Institute of Physics' Dannie Heineman Prize for Mathematical Physics (2003).

CHORKINA, Svetlana (1979—). *See Khorkina, Svetlana.*

CHOTEK, Sophie (1868–1914). Archduchess of Austria. Born Sophia, countess of Chotek; Sophie of Hohenberg; Sophie von Hohenberg; duchess of Hohenberg, Hohenburg or Hohenbourg. Born in Stuttgart, Germany, Mar 1, 1868; assassinated in Sarajevo, Bosnia, June 28, 1914; dau. of Count Bohuslav Chotek of Chotkova and Wognin and Countess Wilhelmine Chotek; m. Francis Ferdinand, also known as Franz Ferdinand (1863–1914), archduke of Austria (r. 1896–1914); children: Sofie (b. 1901); Max (b. 1902); Ernst (b. 1904). ❖ German-born Austrian aristocrat whose assassination in Sarajevo with husband Archduke Franz Ferdinand triggered the chain of events that hurled the world into the 1st total war in history. ❖ See also Gordon Brook-Shepherd, *Victims at Sarajevo: The Romance and Tragedy of Franz Ferdinand and Sophie* (Harvill, 1984); Hertha Pauli, *The Secret of Sarajevo: The Story of Franz Ferdinand and Sophie* (Appleton-Century, 1965); and *Women in World History.*

CHOUSOVITINA, Oksana (1975—). *See Chusovitina, Oksana.*

CHOUTEAU, Yvonne (1929—). American ballet dancer. Name variations: Yvonne Terekhov. Born Mar 7, 1929, in Vinita, Oklahoma; m. Miguel Terekhov (dancer). ❖ Danced with Ballet Russe de Monte Carlo (1943–44) where she performed in numerous works by Leonid Massine, including *Gaité Parisienne, Seventh Symphony* and *Le Beau Danube,* and in George Balanchine's *Ballet Imperial* and *Mozartiana;* performed pas de deux on tv's "Omnibus" and "Your Show of Shows"; was artist-in-residence with husband at University of Oklahoma; also with husband, served as director of Oklahoma City Civic Ballet (1960s); works of choreography include *Prayer* (c. 1954), *Ballet Brilliante* (c. 1967), and (with Terekhov) *La Bayadère* (c. 1967).

CHOW, Amy (1978—). American gymnast. Born May 15, 1978, in San Jose, California. ❖ At Pan American Games, won gold medal for team all-around and vault, silver for uneven bars, and bronze for all-around (1995); won Budget Invitational (1995), Reese's Cup (1997, 1998), and Bluewater Invitational (2000); at Atlanta Olympics, won a gold medal in team all-around and a silver medal for uneven bars (1996).

CHOW, Tina (1950–1992). Japanese-American jewelry designer. Born Bettina Louise Lutz, April 19, 1950; died of AIDS, Jan 24, 1992; dau. of Mona Lutz (Japanese) and German-American father; sister of Adelle Lutz (costume designer and actress who m. singer David Byrne); m. Michael Chow (restaurateur, owner of Mr. Chow's), 1972 (div. 1990); children: China Chow (b. 1974, actress) and Maximilian (b. 1977). ❖ With sister, had early success modeling for Shiseido cosmetics in Japan; became a major fashion icon (1980s), through her dramatic crystal/bamboo jewelry designs and elegant presence.

CHOWDHURY, Eulie (1923—). Indian architect. Name variations: Born Urmila Eulie Chowdhury in 1923 in Shahjehanpur, Uttar Pradesh, India; University of Sydney, BA, 1947. ❖ Renowned architect, worked in US before returning to native India to work as senior architect on Le

Corbusier's new Punjab capital city, Chandigarh (1951–63); wrote memoir *Memories of Le Corbusier;* served as principal of Delhi School of Architecture (1963–65); returned to work on Chandigarh project as senior architect (1968–70) and as chief architect in charge of 2nd phase of planning (1971–76); worked as chief architect for Harayana State (1970) and of Punjab State (1976–81); retired from public service (1981) and worked in private practice in Chandigarh; was 1st woman elected to Royal Institute of British Architects and Indian Institute of Architects. Buildings include Polytechnic for Women (1960) and Hostel Block for Home Science College of Chandigarh (1970).

CHOY, Elizabeth (b. 1910). Singaporean heroine, politician and educator. Name variations: Betty Choy. Born 1910 in Kudat, northern tip of British North Borneo; m. Choy Khun Heng, 1941 (died 1983); children: (adopted) Bridget, Lynette and Irene. ❖ Came to Singapore (Dec 1929); began career as a teacher at St. Margaret's (then known as Church of England Zenana Mission School); married just before Singapore fell to the Japanese (1941); with husband, ran a canteen for POWs and began passing on food, money, letters and news to them; when Japanese ships were blown up in Keppel Harbor (Double Tenth Massacre, Oct 10, 1943), came under suspicion and husband arrested (Oct 29); lured to the Kempeitai (secret police) quarters on the pretext of seeing her husband, was interrogated and tortured for 193 days but refused to confess to something she had not done; released (May 26, 1944); at war's end, hailed as a heroine; was invited to be a member of the Legislative Council (1951), the only woman member; helped found the Singapore Council of Women; served as principal for the School for the Blind (1956–60); taught at St. Andrew's School (1960–74). Awarded OBE (1946). ❖ See also Zhou Mei, *Elizabeth Choy: More than a War Heroine* (Landmark, 1995).

CHRESTIENNE. *Variant of Christina or Christine.*

CHRÉTIEN, Aline (1936—). Canadian first lady. Name variations: Aline Chretien. Born Aline Chaîné, 1936, in Shawinigan, Quebec, Canada; m. Jean Chrétien (prime minister of Canada, 1993—), Sept 10, 1957; children: France (b. 1958), Hubert (b. 1963), and Michel (b. 1968, adopted).

CHRIST, Lena (1881–1920). *See Pichler, Magdalena.*

CHRISTALLER, Helene (1872–1953). German novelist and short-story writer. Born Jan 31, 1872, in Darmstadt, Germany; died May 24, 1953, in Tugenheim, Germany. ❖ Wrote novels and stories about village life in the Black Forest which achieved popular success; writings include *Frauen* (1903), *Schiffe im Sturm* (1908), *Das Gotteskind* (1910), *Das Geheimnis* (1918), *Berufung* (1928), *Der Menschenbruder* (1931) and *Die Brücke.*

CHRISTEN, Ada (1839–1901). *See Breden, Christiane von.*

CHRISTENSEN, Gisella (b. 1914). *See Caccialanza, Gisella.*

CHRISTENSEN, Inger (1935—). Danish poet, dramatist and novelist. Born Inger Christensen in Jutland, town of Vejle, Denmark, 1935; dau. of a tailor; received teaching diploma, 1958; married to Poul Borum (Danish author) for several years. ❖ Writer who often focuses on how to be free while living in community; writings include (poems) *Lys (Light,* 1962), (poems) *Gras (Grass,* 1963), (novel) *Evighedsmaskinen (The Perpetual Movement Machine,* 1964), (novel) *Azorno* (1967), (poems) *Det (That,* 1969), (play) *Intriganterne (The Schemers,* 1972), (novel) *Det malede værelse (The Painted Room,* 1976), (poems) *Brev i april (Letter in Apr,* 1979), (poems) *Alfabet (Alphabet,* 1981), and numerous essays. Awarded a 3-year stipend from the Danish Art Foundation (1966); received Danish Critics' Award (1969), Golden Laurels (1970), Aarestrup Medal (1973), and Kjeld Abell Prize and Tagea Brandt's Travel Award (1978); became member of the Danish Academy (1978). ❖ See also *Women in World History.*

CHRISTENSEN, Ruby (c. 1910—). *See Asquith, Ruby.*

CHRISTENSEN, Tara Dawn (c. 1972—). *See Holland, Tara Dawn.*

CHRISTIAN (d. 1246). Countess of Aumale. Name variations: Christian de Forz; Christina de Galloway. Died in 1246; dau. of Alan, lord of Galloway, and Margaret (d. 1228), countess of Huntingdon; sister of Devorgilla (d. 1290); aunt of John Balliol, king of Scots (r. 1292–1296); m. William de Forz, 1st count of Aumale, before 1234; children: William de Forz, 2nd count of Aumale (d. 1260).

CHRISTIAN, Linda (1923—). Mexican-born actress. Born Blanca Rosa Welter, Nov 13, 1923, in Tampico, Tamaulipas, Mexico; dau. of a Dutch oilman; sister of Ariadna Welter (actress, 1930–1998); m. Tyrone Power (actor), 1949 (div. 1956); m. Edmund Purdom (actor), 1962 (div. 1963); children: (1st m.) 2 daughters, including Taryn Power (actress). ❖ Made film debut in *Holiday in Mexico* (1946), followed by *Green Dolphin Street, Tarzan and the Mermaids, The Happy Time, Battle Zone, Thunderstorm, The V.I.P.s, The Moment of Truth* and *Bel Ami 2000,* among others.

CHRISTIAN, Meg (1946—). American folk singer. Born 1946 in Lynchburg, Virginia; graduate of University of North Carolina. ❖ Pioneer in women's music, was among the 1st to deal with lesbian and feminist issues in song; began performing around Washington, DC (1969); wrote and sang of the women's movement; with Chris Williamson and others, became a founding member of the women-centered Olivia Records, which released her *I Know You Know* (1975) as its 1st album; other albums include *Face the Music* (1977), *Turning It Over* (1981) and *From the Heart* (1984); hits include "Ode to a Gym Teacher"; later produced 2 CDs, *Fire of My Love* (1986) and *Songs of Ecstasy* (1995).

CHRISTIAN BRUCE (d. 1356). *See Bruce, Christian.*

CHRISTIAN DE PLESSETIS (c. 1250–?). Baroness Segrave. Name variations: Christian Segrave. Born c. 1250; m. John Segrave (1256–1325), 2nd baron Segrave, 1270; children: Stephen Segrave (d. 1325); Margaret Segrave (c. 1280–?).

CHRISTIAN OF SCHLESWIG-HOLSTEIN, Princess (1846–1923). *See Helena.*

CHRISTIANS, Mady (1900–1951). Austrian-born actress. Name variations: Margarete Christians. Born Marguerita or Margarethe Maria Christians in Vienna, Austria, Jan 19, 1900; died in South Norwalk, Connecticut, Oct 28, 1951; dau. of Rudolf Christians (actor) and Bertha (Klein) Christians (opera singer and recitalist, died 1938); m. Sven von Müller (editor of the *Hamburger Fremdenblatt,* div.). ❖ Distinguished actress who fell victim to McCarthyism, moved with family to NY (1912); made stage debut at 16 in a one-act operetta; returned to Vienna (1917) and enrolled in Max Reinhardt's acting class; came to prominence in Tolstoy's *The Light Shines in Darkness* in Berlin; signed long-term contract with Reinhardt and performed at major theaters throughout Europe; following a string of silents, appeared in 2 sound films, the Franz Lehár operettas *Friederike* and *The Black Hussar* (1932); with rise of Nazism, fled to NY (1933); quickly landed major parts in Broadway plays, but most turned out to be flops; appeared in such films as *Escapade* (1935), *Come and Get It* (1936), *Heidi* (1937), *Seventh Heaven* (1937) and *Tender Comrade* (1944); back on Broadway, portrayed Gertrude to Maurice Evans' Hamlet (1938), to wide acclaim, followed by *Heartbreak House, Henry IV,* and as Sara Mueller in *Watch on the Rhine* (1941); starred in *I Remember Mama* (1944), appearing in all 720 performances; co-starred as Edward G. Robinson's wife in Miller's *All My Sons* (1948), a film that incurred the wrath of some conservatives who thought it anti-American; appeared in last film, *A Letter from an Unknown Woman* (1948) and made last stage appearance in Strindberg's *The Father* (1949), before being accused of "un-American activities" (1950), for having joined organizations that assisted refugees and combatted Nazism on American soil during WWII; blacklisted and hounded, died of a stress-induced stroke. ❖ See also *Women in World History.*

CHRISTIE, Agatha (1890–1976). English novelist and dramatist. Name variations: Agatha Christie Mallowan; Lady Mallowan; (pseudonym) Mary Westmacott. Born Agatha Mary Clarissa Miller, Sept 15, 1890, in Torquay, Devon, England; died Jan 12, 1976, at Wallingford, Berkshire; dau. of Frederick Alvah and Clarissa Margaret (Boehmer) Miller; m. Archibald Christie, Dec 24, 1914 (div., April 1928); m. Max Mallowan, Sept 11, 1930; children: (1st m.) Rosalind (b. 1919). ❖ Author of just under 100 books, mainly detective stories and thrillers, who has been translated into more languages than Shakespeare; published 1st novel, *The Mysterious Affair at Styles* at age 30 (1920); introduced Tommy and Tuppence Beresford in 2nd novel, *The Man in the Brown Suit;* published *The Murder of Roger Ackroyd* (1926), which fully established her reputation; had 1st play produced, *Black Coffee* (1930); under pseudonym Mary Westmacott, published 1st serious novel, *Giant's Bread* (1930), and went on to write 5 more novels as Westmacott, all thought to be partially autobiographical; created characters Hercule Poirot and Miss Marple; premiered play *The Mousetrap* in London (Nov 25, 1952), which would make theatrical history by having an unbroken London run for over 40 years; wrote 2 books containing the deaths of Hercule Poirot and Miss Marple, *Curtain* and *Sleeping Murder;* also wrote *Ten Little Indians,*

Murder on the Orient Express, Evil Under the Sun, The ABC Murders and *The Body in the Library,* as well as plays *Murder on the Nile* (1945) and *Witness for the Prosecution* (1953). Named Order of Dame Commander of the British Empire (1971). ❖ See also autobiographies *Come, Tell Me How You Live* (1946) and *An Autobiography* (Collins, 1977); Charles Osborne, *The Life and Crimes of Agatha Christie* (1982); and *Women in World History.*

CHRISTIE, Dorothy (b. 1896). English playwright and screenwriter. Born Dorothy Casson Walker, June 10, 1896, in Lahore; m. Maj.-Gen. Campbell Manning Christie (died). ❖ Began career as a journalist and writer of short stories; with husband, wrote such plays as *Someone at the Door, Family Group* (1935), *Grand National Night* (1946), *His Excellency* (1950), *Come Live with Me* (1951), *Carrington, V.C.* (1953), *The Touch of Fear* (1956) and *A Gazelle in the Park Lane* (1962); screenplays include *Jassy* (1948) and *The Third Key* (1956).

CHRISTIE, Julie (1941—). English actress. Born Julie Frances Christie, April 14, 1941, in Chabua, Assam, India; dau. of Frank St. John Christie (tea plantation manager) and Rosemary (Ramsden) Christie; sister of Clive Christie; attended Brighton Technical College and Central School of Music and Drama; began living with Duncan Campbell (journalist), 1977. ❖ Made professional stage debut with Frinton Repertory in Essex; appeared on tv serial "A is for Andromeda" (1962), which led to breakthrough role in *Billy Liar* (1963); won Academy Award for Best Actress for *Darling* (1965); consolidated career with roles in *Doctor Zhivago* (1965), *Far from the Maddening Crowd* (1967), and *The Go-Between* (1971); became involved in variety of political issues and starred in films highlighting these interests; revived career with *Heat and Dust* (1982) and *Miss Mary* (1986); other films include *Young Cassidy* (1965), *Fahrenheit 451* (1966), *Petulia* (1968), *McCabe and Mrs. Miller* (1971), *Shampoo* (1975), *Heaven Can Wait* (1978), *Hamlet* (as Gertrude, 1996), *Afterglow* (1998), *Troy* (2004), *Finding Neverland* (2004) and *Harry Potter and the Prisoner of Azkaban* (2004); returned to stage in *Old Times* (1995) and *Suzanna Andler* (1998); served as executive producer for film *The Living Dream* (2004).

CHRISTIE, Philippa (b. 1920). See Pearce, Philippa.

CHRISTIE, Susan (c. 1969—). Irish murderer. Born c. 1969. ❖ While a private in the Ulster Defence Regiment (later Royal Irish Regiment), had an affair with Captain Duncan McAllister of Royal Corps of Signals, who was stationed in Armagh, Northern Ireland (1990–91); killed McAllister's wife Penny during a walk in Drumkeeragh Forest, Co. Down, but claimed they had been attacked by an unidentified man (Mar 27, 1991); convicted of murder, was sentenced to 5 years in jail, which was increased to 9 years on appeal (1992); released from prison after 4½ years (Oct 1995); changed identity and disappeared. Events were basis for ITV film, *Beyond Reason* (also called *A Casual Affair,* 1995), which caused considerable controversy and was debated in UK's House of Commons. ❖ See also Nicholas Davies, *A Deadly Kind of Love.*

CHRISTINA. *Variant of Christine.*

CHRISTINA (fl. 1086). English nun of Romsey. Born in Hungary c. 1055; died before 1102; dau. of Agatha of Hungary and Edward the Exile also known as Edward the Atheling (son of King Edmund II); sister of St. Margaret (c. 1046–1093); brought to England in 1057. ❖ Was a nun at Romsey Abbey in Hampshire, where she brought up her niece Matilda of Scotland (1080–1118) and was opposed to Matilda's marriage to Henry I in 1100.

CHRISTINA, Queen (1626–1689). See Christina of Sweden.

CHRISTINA I OF NAPLES, Queen of Spain (1806–1878). See Maria Christina I.

CHRISTINA BERNADOTTE (b. 1943). Swedish royal. Name variations: Christina of Sweden. Born Christina Louise Helen, Aug 3, 1943, at Haga Palace, Stockholm, Sweden; dau. of Gustavus Adolphus (1906–1947), duke of Westerbotten, and Sybilla of Saxe-Coburg-Gotha (1908–1972); sister of Carl XVI Gustavus, king of Sweden; m. Tod Gösta Magnuson, June 15, 1974; children: Carl Gustaf (b. 1975); Tord Oscar (b. 1977); Victor Edmund (b. 1980).

CHRISTINA CASIMIR (fl. 1640–1660). Margravine of Baden-Durlach. Name variations: Christina von Simmern. Fl. from 1640 to 1660; dau. of Catherine (1584–1638), countess Palatine, and John Casimir of Zweibrücken (b. 1589), count Palatine; m. Frederick VI, margrave of Baden-Durlach, May 15, 1640; children: Christine of Baden-Durlach (1645–1705); Frederick VII (1647–1709), margrave of Baden-Durlach; Johanna Elizabeth of Baden-Durlach (1651–1680).

CHRISTINA OF DENMARK (1521–1590). Duchess of Milan. Name variations: Christine, duchesse de Lorraine; Christierna Sforza. Born 1521; died Dec 10, 1590; dau. of Christian II (1481–1559), king of Norway and Denmark (r. 1513–1523), and Elisabeth of Habsburg (1501–1526); niece of Charles V, Holy Roman emperor; m. Francesco Maria Sforza, duke of Milan (r. 1521–1535), May 4, 1534; m. Francis I (1517–1545), duke of Lorraine (r. 1544–1545, son of Renée of Montpensier), July 10, 1541; children: (2nd m.) Charles II the Great, duke of Lorraine (r. 1545–1608, who m. Claude de France [1547–1575]).

CHRISTINA OF HOLSTEIN-GOTTORP (1573–1625). Queen of Sweden. Born April 13, 1573; died Dec 8, 1625; dau. of Adolf (1526–1586), duke of Holstein-Gottorp (r. 1544–1586), and Christine of Hesse (1543–1604); became 2nd wife of Charles IX (1550–1611), king of Sweden (r. 1604–1611), Aug 27, 1592; grandmother of Christina of Sweden; children: Gustavus Adolphus II (1594–1632), king of Sweden (r. 1611–1632, who m. Maria Eleonora of Brandenburg); Marie Elizabeth (1596–1618, who m. John, duke of East Gotland); Charles Philip, duke of Sodermannland (b. 1601). ❖ Charles IX's 1st wife was Anna Maria of the Palatinate (1561–1589).

CHRISTINA OF MARKYATE (1096–1160). English recluse and prioress. Name variations: Saint Theodora, Christina the Recluse. Born Theodora in 1096 in England; died in 1160 in Markyate, England; dau. of Aute of Huntingdonshire (Anglo-Saxon noble). ❖ Recluse and religious visionary for whom a priory was built in Markyate, resisted overtures of Rannulf Flambard, bishop of Durham, from 1099; refused to consummate marriage to a friend of Flambard, a noble named Burthred, citing vow of chastity and intention to become a nun; suffered persecution from family and legal proceedings by Church for sexual rebuff of husband; escaped and ran away, staying with nearby anchoress Alfwen in Flamstead for 2 years; took refuge in cell at Markyate under protection of monk Roger the Hermit at St. Albans, who became her spiritual mentor; eventually released from marital vows by a dejected Burthred; famed as a spiritual advisor, was invited to lead communities in many parts of England and France but took monastic vows instead (1131); 4 years after her arrival, inherited Roger's hut upon his death and was taken under protection of archbishop of York; served as spiritual advisor to Geoffrey of Gorham (aka Geoffrey of Dunstable) who founded community at Markyate for her; took part in Church struggles against King Stephen out of loyalty to Geoffrey; attracted large gathering of women to community, necessitating building of priory (1145); sent embroidery to English Pope Adrian IV (1155); was subject of biography probably written by chaplain serving community (1150s). Her community survived until the reign of Henry VIII. ❖ See also C.H. Talbot ed., *The Life of Christina of Markyate, a Twelfth Century Recluse* (Oxford, 1959).

CHRISTINA OF SARDINIA (1812–1836). Queen of the Two Sicilies. Name variations: Christine of Sardinia. Born Nov 14, 1812; died Jan 31, 1836; dau. of Maria Teresa of Austria (1773–1832) and Victor Emmanuel I (b. 1759), king of Sardinia (r. 1802–1821); m. Ferdinand II of Naples (b. 1810), king of the Two Sicilies (r. 1830–1859), Nov 21, 1832; children: Francis II (1836–1894), king of the Two Sicilies (r. 1859–1860), king of Sicily (r. 1859–1894).

CHRISTINA OF SAXONY (1461–1521). Queen of Norway and Denmark. Name variations: Christine. Born Dec 25, 1461; died Dec 8, 1521; dau. of Ernest (b. 1441), elector of Saxony; sister of Margaret of Saxony (1469–1528); m. John I or Johannes also known as Hans, king of Norway and Denmark (r. 1481–1513), Sept 6, 1478; children: Johann (died young); Ernst (died young); Christian II (b. 1481), king of Norway and Denmark (r. 1513–1523); Elizabeth of Denmark (1485–1555, who m. Joachim I of Brandenburg); Franz (1497–1511). ❖ With husband, arrived to stay in Stockholm palace when Sweden's regent, Sten Sture, was vying for power (Jan 1501); was left in charge of castle after Hans left (Aug), accompanied by his mistress Adele Ironbeard; came under siege (Sept) and held out until garrison of 1,000 had been reduced to 70 defenders; surrendered to Sten Sture (May 6, 1502). ❖ See also *Women in World History.*

CHRISTINA OF SPAIN (1858–1929). See Maria Christina of Austria.

CHRISTINA OF SWEDEN (d. 1122). Grand Princess of Kiev. Name variations: Kristina of Sweden; Kristina Ingesdottir. died Jan 18, 1122 (some sources cite 1120); dau. of Inge I the Elder, co-regent or king of Sweden (r. 1080–1110, 1112–1125), and Helen (fl. 1100s); m. Mstislav I (b. 1076), grand prince of Kiev (r. 1125–1132), 1095; children: Ingeborg of Russia; Malmfrid of Novgorod; Izyaslav II also known as Yziaslav II, prince of Kiev (r. 1146–1154); Rostislav I (d. 1167), prince of Kiev; Marie of Kiev (d. 1179); Irene of Kiev.

CHRISTINA OF SWEDEN (1626–1689). Queen of Sweden. Name variations: Kristina Augusta Wasa; Christina Maria Alexandra Vasa; Christina Alexandra. Pronunciation: VAH-sa. Born Kristina Augusta Wasa, Dec 8, 1626 (Dec 18, by Gregorian calendar now in use), in Stockholm, Sweden; died in Rome, April 19, 1689 (Gregorian); dau. of Gustavus II Adolphus (1594–1632), king of Sweden (r. 1611–1632), and Maria Eleonora of Brandenburg (1599–1655); never married; probably the most important romantic relationship in Christina's life was with Countess Ebba Sparre; no children. ❖ Learned ruler who crossed gender boundaries, supported knowledge and art, and fascinated people with her unconventional ways; on eve of 6th birthday, became queen of Sweden after father died in battle (1632); with instructions left behind by father, was raised as a boy, learning languages, literature, mathematics, astronomy, geography, politics, history and becoming a first-rate rider and an excellent shot; spent several hours a day with Chancellor Axel Oxenstierna, a superb diplomat who headed the High Council of nobles ruling the country during her minority; on 18th birthday, began to reign (1644); as monarch, 1st efforts went toward halting the wars in Europe that her country had been waging all her life; concluded a truce with Denmark; was instrumental in ending the Thirty Years' War by securing the Peace of Westphalia (1648); at 21, came so near death from malarial fever that she resolved to abdicate (1648); convinced the government that she wouldn't marry and persuaded them to declare her cousin Charles heir to the throne; abdicated (1654) and moved to Rome (1655); converted to Catholicism, much to the shock of her former subjects, and became the queen of the arts and sciences, remembered as a patron of artists, astronomers, composers, singers, alchemists, philosophers, actors, and archaeologists; supported the sculptor Bernini, composer Scarlatti, and astronomer Cassini; founded a public theater; led several "academies," where thinkers gathered to discuss philosophical questions; had many Jews for friends, and near the end of her life declared all Jews of the Roman ghetto to be under her protection; left a unique record of a woman who used both privilege and strength of character to challenge the parameters of "woman" in her time. ❖ See also Susanna Åkerman, *Queen Christina of Sweden and Her Circle: The Transformation of a Seventeenth-Century Philosophical Libertine* (Brill, 1991); Georgina Masson, *Queen Christina* (Farrar, 1968); films *Queen Christina,* starring Greta Garbo (1933), and *The Abdication,* starring Liv Ullmann (1974); and *Women in World History.*

CHRISTINA STIGSDOTTIR (fl. 1160s). Queen of Sweden. Name variations: Kristina Stigsdottir. Dau. of Stig Whiteleather and Margaret Knutsdottir (dau. of Knut Lavard, duke of South Jutland, and Ingeborg of Russia); m. Karl Sverkersson, also known as Charles VII, king of Sweden (r. 1161–1167), 1163; children: Sverker II the Younger, king of Sweden (r. 1195–1208); possibly Sophie Karlsson (d. 1252, who possibly m. Henry Burwin II, prince of Mecklenburg-Rostok).

CHRISTINA THE ASTONISHING (c. 1150–c. 1224). French saint. Born c. 1150 into a peasant family in Brusthem, in Liége, France; died c. 1224. ❖ Spent last days in convent of St. Catherine at Saint Trond. Her life comes down from 2 eminent scholars of the time: Thomas de Cantimpré (d. 1270), professor of theology at Louvain, and Cardinal Jacques de Vitry (d. 1244); feast day is July 24. ❖ See also *Women in World History.*

CHRISTINA THE RECLUSE (1096–1160). See *Christina of Markyate.*

CHRISTINE. *Variant of Christina.*

CHRISTINE, Virginia (1920–1996). American character actress. Born Virginia Kraft, Mar 5, 1920, in Stanton, Iowa; died July 24, 1996, in Brentwood, California; m. Fritz Feld (actor), 1940 (died 1993). ❖ Made film debut in *Edge of Darkness* (1942), followed by *The Killers, High Noon, Cyrano de Bergerac, Never Wave at a WAC, Not as a Stranger, Invasion of the Body Snatchers, Judgment at Nuremberg* and *Guess Who's Coming to Dinner,* among others; appeared as Mrs. Olson in Folger's coffee commercials.

CHRISTINE DE PIZAN (c. 1363–c. 1431). Italian intellectual, poet and feminist. Name variations: Chrystyne; Christine de Pisan; Christine of Pisa; Christine of Pisan. Pronunciation: puh-ZAHN. Born between 1363

and 1365 in Venice, Italy; died after 1429, possibly 1431 or 1434, at convent of Poissy, France; dau. of Tommaso di Benvenuto da Pizzano (physician and astrologer); m. Sir Etienne du Castel, 1380; children: 2 sons, including the eldest Jean, and 1 daughter. ❖ One of the most remarkable of all medieval women, was an internationally known writer, historian, scholar, and poet at the French royal court, who argued passionately against the negative views of women propounded by male writers, and urged men and women to respect and admire all women for their many virtues; moved with family to France (c. 1368); married (1380); widowed (1390); began composing poetry (1390); retired to convent of Poissy (1418); finished last known composition, *Song of Joan of Arc* (July 1429). Writings include *One Hundred Ballads, Virelays, Rondeaux* (1390–1400), *Epistle to the God of Love* (1399), *Epistle to Othea* (1400), *The Book of the Mutations of Fortune* (1400–03), *Epistles on the Debate of the "Romance of the Rose"* (1401–03), *The Book of the Way of Long Study* (1402–03), *The Book of the Deeds and Good Customs of the Wise King Charles V* (1404), *The Book of the City of Ladies* (1405), *The Book of the Three Virtues* (*The Treasure of the City of Ladies*) (1405), *The Vision of Christine* (1405), *The Book of Feats of Arms and Chivalry* (1410) and *The Book of Peace* (1412–14). ❖ See also *Women in World History.*

CHRISTINE OF BADEN-DURLACH (1645–1705). Duchess of Saxe-Gotha. Born April 22, 1645; died Dec 21, 1705; dau. of Christina Casimir and Frederick VI, margrave of Baden-Durlach; m. Albert, margrave of Ansbach, Aug 6, 1665; m. Frederick I, duke of Saxe- Gotha, Aug 2, 1681.

CHRISTINE OF BOURBON (1779–1849). Duchess of Genoa. Name variations: Cristina; Maria Christina of Bourbon. Born Jan 17, 1779; died Mar 12, 1849; dau. of Maria Carolina (1752–1814), queen of the Two Sicilies, and Ferdinand IV (1751–1825), king of Naples (r. 1759–1806, 1815–1825), later known as Ferdinand I, king of the Two Sicilies (r. 1816–1825); m. Charles Felix (Carlos Felice) of Sardinia, duke of Genoa (r. 1821–1831) and king of Sardinia, April 6, 1807.

CHRISTINE OF DENMARK (1521–1590). See *Christina of Denmark.*

CHRISTINE OF FRANCE (1606–1663). Duchess and regent of Savoy. Name variations: Christine of Savoy; Christine of Bourbon; Chrestienne or Christina. Born 1606; died 1663 in Savoy; dau. of Henry IV the Great (1553–1610), king of France (r. 1589–1610), and Marie de Medici (c. 1573–1642); sister of Elizabeth Valois (1602–1644, who m. Philip IV, king of Spain), Henrietta Maria (1609–1669, who m. Charles I, king of England), and Louis XIII, king of France (r. 1610–1643); m. Victor Amadeus I (d. 1637), duke of Savoy (r. 1630–1637); children: Francis Hyacinth, duke of Savoy (r. 1637–1638); Henrietta of Savoy (d. 1638); Charles Emmanuel II (1634–1675), duke of Savoy (r. 1638–1675). ❖ Wed Victor Amadeus I, a marriage arranged as part of a political alliance between France and Savoy; when husband died (1637), took over the duchy as regent for son Charles Emmanuel (1638); an effective and capable ruler, quelled a rebellion of the nobles'; ruled for 10 years as regent, and, though technically resigning her authority when son came of age, remained the most influential and powerful figure in Savoy politics for the next 15 years. ❖ See also *Women in World History.*

CHRISTINE OF GANDERSHEIM (d. 919). Abbess of Gandersheim. Name variations: Christina. Died 919; dau. of Ludolf or Liudolf (c. 806–866), count of Saxony, and Oda (806–913); sister of abbesses Gerberga (d. 896) and Hathumoda (d. 874).

CHRISTINE OF HESSE (1543–1604). Duchess of Holstein-Gottorp. Born June 29, 1543; died May 13, 1604; dau. of Philip I, landgrave of Hesse, and Christine of Saxony (1505–1549); m. Adolf (1526–1586), duke of Holstein-Gottorp (r. 1544–1586), Dec 17, 1564; children: Sophie of Holstein-Gottorp (1569–1634); Christina of Holstein-Gottorp (1573–1625); Johann Adolf, duke of Holstein-Gottorp (b. 1575).

CHRISTINE OF HESSE-CASSEL (1933—). Princess of Hesse. Born Christina Marguerite, Jan 10, 1933, in Schloss Kronberg; dau. of Christopher Ernest, prince of Hesse, and Sophia of Greece (b. 1914); m. Andrei or Andrej Karadjordjevic (son of Alexander I, king of Yugoslavia), Aug 1, 1956 (div. 1962); m. Robert Floris van Eyck, Dec 3, 1962 (div. 1986); children: (1st m.) Princess Tatiana Maria (b. 1957, who m. Gregory Thune-Larsen); Christopher, known as Marko (b. 1960); (2nd m.) Helen Sophia van Eyck (b. 1963); Mark Nicholas van Eyck (b. 1966). Andrei's 2nd wife was Kira of Leiningen (b. 1930).

CHRISTINE OF LORRAINE (c. 1571–1637). Grand duchess of Tuscany. Name variations: Christina of Lorraine; Christine de Medici. Born c. 1571; died 1637 (some sources cite 1636); dau. of Claude de France (1547–1575) and Charles II, duke of Lorraine (r. 1545–1608); granddau. of Catherine de Medici (1519–1589); m. Ferdinand I de Medici (1549–1609), grand duke of Tuscany (r. 1587–1609); children: Cosimo II (1590–1620), grand duke of Tuscany (r. 1609–1620, who m. Maria Magdalena of Austria); Eleonora de Medici (1591–1617); Caterina de Medici (1593–1629, who m. Ferdinand also known as Fernando Gonzaga, 6th duke of Mantua); Francesco (d. 1614); Carlo, cardinal (d. 1666); twins Maddalena de Medici (1600–1633) and Lorenzo (1600–1648); Claudia de Medici (1604–1648, who m. Federigo della Rovere, hereditary prince of Urbino, and Leopold of Austrian Tyrol). ❖ Though born and raised in France, was closely linked to the Medici, one of the most powerful patrician families of Italy; raised by grandmother Catherine de Medici, forging a strong bond; was married to the head of the Medici family, 40-year-old Grand Duke Ferdinand I of Tuscany (1587), a talented politician; with husband, supported the political aims of the Medici family, of which they were the most prominent members, and shared the traditional Medici interest in promoting the arts and keeping an opulent court; after husband's death (Feb 1609) and succession of eldest son Cosimo, retained importance at court; when son died (1620), shared the regency with daughter-in-law Maria Magdalena for young Ferdinand II; following Maria's death (1631), was again the undisputed 1st lady of Florence and did not relinquish the reins of government even after grandson had reached adulthood. ❖ See also *Women in World History*.

CHRISTINE OF PISA (c. 1363–c. 1431). See *Christine de Pizan.*

CHRISTINE OF SAVOY (1606–1663). See *Christine of France.*

CHRISTINE OF SAXONY (1505–1549). Landgravine of Hesse. Born Dec 25, 1505; died April 15, 1549; dau. of Barbara of Poland (1478–1534) and George the Bearded, duke of Saxony; m. Philip I, landgrave of Hesse, Dec 11, 1523; children: Agnes of Hesse (1527–1555); William IV the Wise (b. 1532); Barbara of Hesse (1536–1597, who m. George I, stadholder in Mompelgard); Elisabeth of Hesse (1539–1582, who m. Louis VI, elector of the Palatinate); Christine of Hesse (1543–1604); George I the Pious (b. 1547), landgrave of Hesse-Darmstadt.

CHRISTMAN, Elisabeth (1881–1975). American labor leader. Born in Germany, Sept 2, 1881; died in Delphi, Indiana, April 26, 1975; dau. of Henry Christman (laborer) and Barbara (Guth) Christman; educated in a German Lutheran school until age 13 when she began work in a Chicago glove factory; never married; no children. ❖ Labor leader, who sought to address the frequently harsh conditions under which women worked, co-founded Operators Local 1 of the International Glove Workers Union of America (IGWUA, 1902); joined Chicago Women's Trade Union League (WTUL, 1904); elected to WTUL executive board (1910–29), and national executive board (1919), one of the few working-class women who directed day-to-day policies of WTUL; served as treasurer of Local 1 (1905–11) and president (1912–17); served as IGWUA secretary-treasurer (1913–31); was administrator, WTUL Training School for Women Organizers (1914–26); served as chief of women field representatives for National War Labor Board (1917–18); served as NWTUL secretary-treasurer and editor of WTUL monthly journal *Life and Labor Bulletin* (1921–50); became 1st woman appointed to a National Recovery Administration code authority (1934); appointed to the Women's Bureau advisory committee (1940); served as director of Women's Bureau investigation of women's wages in war industries (1942–43). ❖ See also *Women in World History*.

CHRISTODOULOU, Evangelia. Greek rhythmic gymnast. Name variations: Eva Christodoulou. Born in Greece. ❖ Won a bronze medal for team all-around at Sydney Olympics (2000).

CHRISTOFFERSON, Amy Maud (1859–1943). See *Bock, Amy Maud.*

CHRISTOFFERSEN, Birte (1924—). Danish diver. Born Mar 28, 1924, in Denmark. ❖ At London Olympics, won a bronze medal in platform (1948).

CHRISTOFI, Styllou (c. 1900–1954). Cypriot murderer. Born c. 1900 in Cyprus; hanged at Holloway Prison in England, Dec 13, 1954; children: at least 1 son, Stavros. ❖ Acquitted at trial in Cyprus for murdering mother-in-law by ramming a burning torch down the woman's throat (1925); arrived in Hampstead where son Stavros was living with his wife Hella (Bleicher) Christofi and their 3 children (1953); after hitting Hella

with an ash-plate, strangled her to death and attempted to burn the body in the kitchen (1954); tried at Old Bailey and found guilty.

CHRISTOPHER, Mary (1907–1998). See *West, Dorothy.*

CHRISTOPHER, Patricia (c. 1934—). American modern dancer. Born c. 1934, in San Francisco, California; attended Mills College. ❖ Taught modern dance at Juilliard School in New York City (starting 1964); performed with numerous companies and in a range of concert recitals representing modern dance techniques from Humphrey to Limón to Graham; appeared in Ruth Currier's *Quartet, The Antagonists* and *Dangerous World,* Pearl Lang's *Night Flight, Shirah* (1960) and *Appassionata* (1962), Lucas Hoving's *Strange, Wall of Silence* and *Suite for a Summer Day* (1962), Yuriko's *Tragic Memory* (1966), *Five Characters* (1967) and *Automaton* (1968).

CHRISTOU, B. (1941—). See *Farmer, Beverley.*

CHRISTY, Barrett (1971—). American snowboarder. Born Feb 3, 1971, in Buffalo, NY. ❖ Became competitor (1993) and dominant snowboarder; won gold at X Games in Big Air (Winter 1997, Winter 1999, and Summer 1999) and in Slopestyle (Winter 1997); won silver at X Games in Big Air (Winter 1998 and Winter 2001) and Slopestyle (Winter 1998 and Winter 1999) and Superpipe (Winter 2000); won bronze at X Games in Slopestyle (Winter 2000); was member of US Olympic team (1998). Other 1st-place finishes include Mt. Baker Banked Slalom (2001) and Grand Prix in Breckenridge, Colorado (2001).

CHRISTY, June (1925–1990). American jazz singer. Name variations: Sharon Leslie; Misty Miss Christy. Born Shirley Luster, Nov 20, 1925, in Springfield, Illinois; died June 21, 1990, in Sherman Oaks, California; m. Bob Cooper (tenor saxist), 1946; children: 1. ❖ One of the most talented female singers in jazz history, began singing with local bands at 13; worked with Boyd Raeburn and his Orchestra as Sharon Leslie; replacing Anita O'Day (1945), joined the Stan Kenton band and recorded "Tampico," a huge hit, followed by "Shoo Fly Pie and Apple Pan Dowdy"; sang with Kenton until 1948, returning off and on; went solo and recorded numerous albums for Capitol (1950s), including *Something Cool* (1953), *The Misty Miss Christy* (1956), *Fair and Warmer* (1957), *The Song is June* (1958) and *Off Beat* (1960); singles include "My Heart Belongs to Only You"; semi-retired (1960s); made last album *Impromptu* (1977).

CHRODIELDE (fl. 590). French nun and warrior. Fl. 590 in Poitiers, France; never married; no children. ❖ As a child, joined the convent of St. Radegund of Poitiers; began military career (c. 590), when she tried to force the abbess, Leubevere of Cheribert, out of office in an effort to become abbess herself; after several battles, was evicted from convent; took refuge in a cathedral and raised an even larger army, as more people from Poitiers took up her cause; with army, fought the peacekeeping troops of King Childebert of France and was defeated; excommunicated. ❖ See also *Women in World History*.

CHROTRUD (d. 724). Frankish noblewoman. Name variations: Rothrude; Rotrou of Belgium; Rotrude. Died in 724; dau. of St. Leutwinus; m. Charles Martel, mayor of Austrasia and Neustria (r. 714–741); children: Carloman, mayor of Austrasia (d. 754); Pepin III the Short (715–768), mayor of Neustria (r. 741), king of the Franks (r. 747–768); Grifon; Bernard, count of St. Quentin. Charles Martel's 2nd wife was Sunnichild (d. 741).

CHRYSSA (1933—). Greek-born American painter and sculptor. Name variations: Varda Chryssa; also seen as Vardea or Verdea. Born Chryssa Mavromichali, 1933, in Athens, Greece; studied at Académie de la Grande Chaumière in Paris, 1953–54, and California School of Fine Arts in San Francisco, 1954–55. ❖ Famed for pioneering the use of electric light, neon and outdoor signs as an art form known as Luminist or Light Art; at 21, sailed to New York, where she became fascinated with Times Square; worked initially with paintings and metal reliefs for such works as the Cycladic Book series (1955–56), depicting Japanese calligraphy and Roman letters; later works include "Times Square Sky" (1962), "Large Bird Shape" (1973–75), "Chinese Floor Sculpture" (1983), and "The Gates to Times Square" (1966), said to be one of the most important American sculptures of all time.

CHRYSTYNE. Variant of Christine.

CHTYRENKO, Olga. Russian rhythmic gymnast. Born in USSR. ❖ Won a team bronze medal at Atlanta Olympics (1996).

CHU, Julie (1982—). American ice-hockey player. Born Mar 13, 1982 in Fairfield, Connecticut. ❖ Won a team silver medal at World championships (2001); won a team silver medal at Salt Lake City Olympics (2002) and a team bronze at Torino Olympics (2006).

CHUBBUCK, Emily (1817–1854). See Judson, Emily Chubbuck.

CHUDINA, Alexandra (1923–1990). Soviet track-and-field athlete. Born Nov 1923 in USSR; died Oct 28, 1990. ❖ At Helsinki Olympics, won a bronze medal in high jump and silver medals in javelin throw and long jump (1952).

CHUDLEIGH, Elizabeth (1720–1788). English adventurer and bigamist. Name variations: Elizabeth Chudleigh; Mrs. Hervey; Duchess of Kingston; Countess of Bristol; Elizabeth Chudleigh Pierrepont. Born Elizabeth Chudleigh in Devonshire, England, 1720; died in France, 1788; dau. of Colonel Thomas Chudleigh and Harriet (nee Chudleigh); m. Augustus John Hervey, 1747; m. the duke of Kingston, 1769; children: (1st m.) Henry Augustus Hervey (b. 1747, died in infancy). ❖ The only woman in British history to be tried and convicted of bigamy in an open trial before the House of Lords, was long known as an "adventuress" and sexual intriguer at the courts of kings George II and George III; her trial for wrongful marriage to a duke when she was already wife of an earl was the scandal sensation of 1776. ❖ See also Lewis Melville, ed. *The Trial of the Duchess of Kingston* (Hodge, 1927); and *Women in World History*.

CHUDLEIGH, Mary Lee (1656–1710). English poet and essayist. Name variations: Lady Mary Lee Chudleigh. Born Aug 1656 in Devon, England; died Dec 15, 1710; dau. of Richard Lee, Esq., of Winsdale; m. Sir George Chudleigh; children: several, including Eliza Marie, George, and Thomas. ❖ Anonymously published the poem "The Ladies Defence" (1700), an attack at John Sprint, author of *The Bride-Woman's Counsellor*, who advised women to be subservient to their husbands; the year of her death, published *Essays upon Several Subjects*, which included thoughts on knowledge, pride, humility, life, death, fear and grief. ❖ See also *Women in World History*.

CHUGHTAI, Ismat (1915–1991). See Chugtai, Ismat.

CHUGTAI, Ismat (1915–1991). Indian playwright and novelist. Name variations: Ismat Chughtai. Born 1915 in Badayun, UP, India; died 1991; attended Aligarh Muslim University. ❖ Foremost 20th-century Urdu writer, was involved in the Progressive Writers' Association in Lucknow and campaigned for social reform; charged with obscenity for the story "Lihaaf" ("The Quilt," 1944), which explored areas considered taboo, was exonerated by a court in Lahore; works include *Terhi Lakir* (1944) and *The Quilt and Other Stories* (1994).

CHUKANOVA, Olga (1980—). Russian volleyball player. Born June 9, 1980, in USSR. ❖ Placed 3rd at World championships (1998); won a team silver medal at Athens Olympics (2004).

CHUKOVSKAYA, Lidiya (1907–1996). Russian novelist, critic, memoirist, poet and dissident. Name variations: Lydia, Lidija, Lidiia, or Lidia Chukovskaia, Chukovskaja. Pronunciation: LEE-dia Kor-NAY-yevna Choo-KOVE-skaya. Born Lidiya Korneyevna Chukovskaya, Mar 24, 1907 (some sources cite Mar 23), in St. Petersburg, Russia; died in Moscow, Feb 7, 1996; dau. of Kornei Ivanovich Chukovsky or Chukovskii (Russian critic, translator, and popular author of children's verse and fairy tales) and Maria (Borisovna) Chukovsky; m. Tsezar' Vol'pe (critic and editor), c. 1930; m. Matvei Petrovich Bronshtein, also known as Matvey Bronshteyn (astrophysicist), before 1937; children: (1st m.) Elena (b. 1932). ❖ Writer whose work preserves the history of Russian literature and culture and documents the tragedies of Stalinist and post-Stalinist repression in USSR, began working at Leningrad State Publishing House in children's literature branch (1927); during one of Stalin's many purges, 2nd husband was executed under the guise of a 10-year imprisonment "without the right of correspondence" (1938); began to visit Anna Akhmatova, keeping notes of their conversations, especially Akhmatova's thoughts about poetry, abbreviating the most dangerous details in code, memorizing then burning her poems; wrote 1st novel, *Sofia Petrovna*, the only known prose work about the terror written in the Soviet Union between 1939 and 1940, which would be published in Paris as *The Deserted House* (1965); after 1966, had more and more trouble publishing her work, as she was publicly speaking out and writing open letters to defend dissidents such as writer Aleksandr Solzhenitsyn; expelled from Soviet Writers' Union (1974), which removed her books from library shelves and deprived her of the right to publish; began to publish novels in Moscow (1989); writings include *The Decembrist*

Nikolai Bestuzhev: Investigator of Buratia (1950), *In the Editor's Laboratory* (1960), *Hertsen's "Past and Thoughts"* (1966), *The Open Word* (1976), *On This Side of Death* (1978), *The Process of Expulsion* (1979), *Going Under* (1972), *Notes on Anna Akhmatova* (Vol. I, 1976, Vol. II, 1980). Awarded State Prize for Literature (1995), but refused the money because of Russia's handling of Chechnya. ❖ See also memoir *To the Memory of Childhood* (trans. by Eliza Kellogg Klose, Northwestern U. Press, 1988); Beth Holmgren, *Women's Works in Stalin's Time: On Lidiia Chukovskaia and Nadezhda Mandelstam* (Indiana U. Press, 1993); and *Women in World History*.

CHULABHORN, Princess (1957—). Thai chemist. Born July 4, 1957, in Bangkok, Thailand; dau. of Queen Sirikit and King Rama IX; Faculty of Science and Arts at Kasetsart University, BS in organic chemistry, 1979, PhD, 1985; Mahidol University, DPhil, 1985; m. Flight Lieutenant Virayuth Didyasarin (fighter pilot), 1982 (div.); children: Princess Siribhachudhabhorn and Princess Adityadornkitikhun. ❖ Awarded the Einstein Gold Medal (1966); set up the Chulabhorn Research Institute (1987), to promote scientific research in Thailand.

CHUN LEE-KYUNG (c. 1976—). South Korean short-track speedskater. Born c. 1976 in South Korea. ❖ Won gold medals for 1,000 meter and 3,000-meter relay at Lillehammer Olympics (1994); won World overall title (1995–96), then shared the World overall title with Yang Yang (A) (1997); won gold medals for 1,000 meters and 3,000-meter relay and a bronze for 500 meters at Nagano Olympics, the most successful short tracker of all time (1998).

CHUN, Mary (1893/94?–1946). See Van, Chu-Lin.

CHUNG, Connie (1946—). American newscaster. Born Constance Yu-Hwa Chung, Aug 20, 1946, in Washington, DC; University of Maryland, BA in journalism, 1969; m. Maury Povich, 1984; children: (adopted) Matthew Jay Povich, 1995. ❖ Prominent in network news, co-anchored 3 daily newscasts for KNXT-TV in Los Angeles (1976–83); served as anchor and reporter for "NBC Nightly News" (1983–89) and "CBS Evening News with Dan Rather" (1989–95); hosted tv series "Face to Face with Connie Chung" (1990), followed by "Eye to Eye with Connie Chung" (1993); was co-anchor on "20/20" (1998–2002); launched "Connie Chung Tonight" (2002).

CHUNG EUN-KYUNG (1965—). Korean field-hockey player. Born Mar 22, 1965, in South Korea. ❖ At Seoul Olympics, won a silver medal in team competition (1988).

CHUNG, Kyung-Wha (1948—). Korean-born violinist. Name variations: Chung Trio. Born Mar 26, 1948, in Seoul, South Korea; dau. of Lee Won-Suk (mother); sister of Myung-Wha Chung (cellist) and Myung-Whung Chung (pianist and conductor who was appointed music director of Opéra de la Bastille, Paris, 1989); studied with Ivan Galamian at Juilliard School, 1960–67; later coached by Joseph Szigeti; children: Frederick, Eugene. ❖ Famed violinist, one of most sought-after on the international stage, was born into a musical family of 7 children, each of whom received musical instruction and 3 of whom became world-class musicians; began playing violin by age 6; at 12, moved to NY (1960) to study; made debut with New York Philharmonic (1967); made sensational European debut at Royal Festival Hall with André Previn and London Symphony Orchestra playing Tchaikovsky Concerto (1970); appeared in recitals worldwide and with virtually every major conductor and orchestra in North America, Europe and Far East, including London Philharmonic, Berlin Philharmonic, Toronto Symphony Orchestra and Philadelphia Orchestra; recorded extensively with EMI Classics, Deutsche Grammaphon, London/Decca and RCA, earning critical acclaim as well as Gramophone Award for recording of Bartok's Violin Concerto No. 2 (1988); appeared regularly with brother and sister as the Chung Trio; recordings include Mendelssohn *Concerto* (1972), Beethoven's *Piano Trios Op 11 and 97* with Chung Trio (1994), Brahms' *Violin Sonatas* with pianist Peter Frankl (1998), Brahms *Concerto* recorded live with Vienna Philharmonic and Sir Simon Rattle (2000), Vivaldi's *Four Seasons* with St. Luke's Chamber Orchestra (2001). Awarded South Korean government's highest honor, medal of Civil Merit (1972).

CHUNG, Myung-wha (1944—). Korean-born cellist. Name variations: Chung Trio. Born Mar 19, 1944, in Seoul, South Korea; dau. of Lee Won-Suk (mother); sister of Kyung-Wha Chung (violinist), Myung-Whung Chung (pianist). ❖ With an international career spanning 3 decades, appeared as a soloist with major orchestras throughout the world; with sister and brother, as part of the Chung Trio, made recordings for Decca, EMI, Sori, and Deutsche Grammophon; served as Goodwill Ambassador for UNICEF in the Republic of Korea; headed the cello faculty at the Korean national Institute of Arts in Seoul. Awarded South Korean government's highest honor, medal of Civil Merit (1972).

CHUNG SANG-HYUN (1963—). Korean field-hockey player. Born Jan 17, 1963, in South Korea. ❖ At Seoul Olympics, won a silver medal in team competition (1988).

CHUNG SO-YOUNG (1967—). Korean badminton player. Born Mar 4, 1967, in South Korea. ❖ At Barcelona Olympics, won a gold medal in doubles (1992).

CHUNG TRIO.
See Chung, Kyung-Wha.
See Chung, Myung-Wha.

CHÚNGARA, Domitila (1937—). *See Barrios de Chúngara, Domitila.*

CHUNIKHOVSKAYA, Irina (1968—). Soviet yacht racer. Born July 16, 1967, in USSR. ❖ At Seoul Olympics, won a bronze medal in 470 class (1988).

CHUNSINA (fl. 6th c.). Queen of the Franks. Second wife of Chlothar also known as Clothaire, Clotar, or Lothair I (497–561), king of Soissons (r. 511), king of the Franks (r. 558–561); children: Chrammus (d. 560). Lothair I's 1st wife was Guntheuca; his 3rd wife was Ingunde; his 4th was Aregunde (sister of Ingunde); his 5th was Radegund (518–587); his 7th was Vuldetrade.

CHURCH, Ellen (c. 1905–1965). American stewardess. Born c. 1905 near Cresco, Iowa; died 1965. ❖ In early days of air travel, suggested to Boeing Air Transport (BAT) that nurses be placed on airplanes to ease public's fear of flying; as a registered nurse, became the 1st airline stewardess (1930), working BAT's route between Oakland, CA, and Chicago, IL; served as captain in Army Nurse Corps during WWII and received Air Medal. Airport in her hometown of Cresco, Iowa, named Ellen Church Field.

CHURCH, Esmé (1893–1972). English actress, theatrical manager, and director. Name variations: Esme Church. Born Feb 10, 1893, in England; died May 31, 1972, in Quenington, England. ❖ Made stage debut in London as the Maid in *Playgoers* (1913); with Lena Ashwell Players, appeared in some 150 roles (some of them leads), directed, and toured for the troops during WWI (1916–28); joined Old Vic (1928), appearing in such roles as Rosalind in *As You Like It,* Viola in *Twelfth Night,* Katharine in *Henry VIII,* and Lady Macbeth; appeared with Great London Players (1929–31); joined staff of Old Vic as head of the school of acting (1936) and with Lewis Casson was joint-director for Old Vic Mediterranean tour; was director for H.M. Tennant, the Old Vic and CEMA tours and inaugurated the Children's Theater on tour as The Young Vic; appointed director of Bradford's Civic Playhouse (1944), turning it into a renowned non-professional company; as actress, other plays include *The Blue Coast, Rutherford and Son, Dangerous Corner, The Lake, Nurse Cavell, No Way Back* and *Rosmersholm.*

CHURCH, Mrs. Florence (1837–1899). *See Marryat, Florence.*

CHURCH, Marguerite Stitt (1892–1990). American politician. Born Marguerite Stitt in New York City, Sept 13, 1892; died in Evanston, Illinois, May 26, 1990; graduate of Wellesley College, 1914; Columbia University, MA in political science; m. Ralph Church (Illinois state legislator), 1918. ❖ US Republican Congresswoman who served 6 terms; with husband's election to US House of Representatives (1934), campaigned and accompanied him on investigative trips; was active in Republican presidential campaigns (1940, 1944); during and after WWII, made several inspection tours in Europe at husband's request; after his death (Mar 1950), ran for election to his seat; as a member of the Committee on Foreign Affairs, traveled extensively, particularly in Asia, and helped pass the act that placed the federal budget on a system of annual expenditures.

CHURCHILL, Anne (1684–1716). Countess of Sunderland. Born Feb 27, 1684; died April 15, 1716; interred at Brington, Northamptonshire, England; dau. of Sarah Jennings Churchill (1660–1744) and John Churchill (1650–1722), 1st duke of Marlborough (r. 1702–1722); m. Charles Spencer, 3rd earl of Sunderland, Jan 2, 1699; children: Robert (b. 1700); Robert (b. 1701), 4th earl of Sunderland; Charles (b. 1706), 3rd duke of Marlborough; John, known as Jack of Althorp (b. 1708), a member of Parliament; Anne Spencer (d. 1769), viscountess Bateman; Diana Spencer (1708–1735), duchess of Bedford (who m. John Russell, 4th duke of Bedford).

CHURCHILL, Arabella (1648–1714). English mistress of King James II of England. Born 1648; died 1714; eldest dau. of Sir Winston Churchill of Wootton Bassett, Wiltshire (MP), and Elizabeth Drake; sister of John Churchill, duke of Marlborough (1650–1722); had long affair with James II, king of England (r. 1685–1688, deposed); children: (with James II) 5, including Henrietta FitzJames (b. 1667); James Fitzjames, duke of Berwick-upon-Tweed (1670–1734); Arabella (Ignatia) FitzJames (b. 1674) who became a nun at Pontoise; and Henry Fitzjames, duke of Albemarle (d. 1702). ❖ The daughter of a royalist and MP, 1st met James II when she fell off a horse while out hunting (1669); used influence to advance interests of brother John Churchill, 1st duke of Marlborough, who, as a general, would win some of the most renowned battles in European history. ❖ See also *Women in World History.*

CHURCHILL, Caryl (1938—). British playwright. Born Sept 3, 1938, in London, England; dau. of Robert Churchill and Jan Brown Churchill; Lady Margaret Hall, Oxford, BA in English, 1960; m. David Harter, 1961; children: 3. ❖ Lived in Canada (1948–56); wrote 3 plays while a student at Oxford: *Downstairs* (1958), *You've No Need to Be Frightened* (1960), and *Having a Wonderful Time* (1960); after graduating (1961), wrote radio plays for the BBC, including *The Ants* (1962), *Not, Not, Not, Not Enough Oxygen* (1971) and *Schreber's Nervous Illness* (1972); was resident dramatist at Royal Court (1974–75) and, while collaborating with Joint Stock and Monstrous Regiment, wrote such plays as *Light Shining on Buckinghamshire* (1976), *Vinegar Tom* (1976), and *Cloud Nine* (1979); wrote *Serious Money* (1987), *Icecream* (1989), *Mad Forest* (1990), *The Skriker* (1994), *Blue Heart* (1997), *This is a Chair* (1999) and *A Number* (2002). Received 3 Obies (1982, 1983, 1988) and Society of West End Theatre Award (1988).

CHURCHILL, Clarissa (b. 1920). *See Eden, Clarissa.*

CHURCHILL, Clementine (1885–1977). Political partner and wife of British prime minister Winston Churchill. Name variations: Lady Clementine Churchill; Baroness Spencer-Churchill; Lady Clementine Hozier Spencer-Churchill; (nickname) Clemmie. Born Clementine Ogilvy Hozier, April 1, 1885, in London, England; died at her home in London, Dec 12, 1977; dau. of Colonel (Sir) Henry Montague Hozier (career military officer) and Lady Henrietta Blanche Ogilvy (dau. of the 10th earl of Airlie); educated at home, Berkhamsted Girls' School, and Sorbonne, Paris; m. Sir Winston Spencer Churchill, Sept 12, 1908; children: Diana (1909–1963); Randolph (1911–1968); Sarah (1914–1982); Marigold (died at age 3); Mary (b. 1922). ❖ Remembered for her courage, compassion, and service during the dark hours of WWII, was honored for World War I service by King George V (1918); lived with husband at No. 10 Downing Street while he was prime minister (1940–45, 1951–55); appointed chair British Red Cross Aid to Russia (1939); elevated to rank of Dame, Grand Cross Order of the British Empire (1946); widowed (1965); created Baroness Spencer-Churchill (1966). ❖ See also Jack Fishman, *My Darling Clementine: The Story of Lady Churchill* (McKay, 1963); Mary Soames, *Clementine Churchill: The Biography of a Marriage* (Houghton, 1979) and *Family Album* (Houghton, 1982); and *Women in World History.*

CHURCHILL, Consuelo (1877–1964). *See Vanderbilt, Consuelo.*

CHURCHILL, Deborah (1677–1708). British pickpocket and prostitute. Born 1677; hanged at Tyburn, Dec 17, 1708; m. John Churchill (army ensign). ❖ While attempting to pick the pocket of a merchant in Drury Lane, yelled to 3 male confederates for help when the merchant pushed her down, urging them to stab him (1708); of the 4, was the only one caught by officials; tried for murder, was condemned (Feb 26, 1708) but convinced prison authorities that she was pregnant and received a 7-month reprieve until they realized she had lied. ❖ See also *Women in World History.*

CHURCHILL, Diana (1913–1994). English actress. Born Aug 21, 1913, in Wembley, Middlesex, England; died of multiple sclerosis, Oct 8, 1994, in Mississippi; dau. of Joseph H. Churchill and Ethel Mary (Nunn) Churchill; m. Barry K. Barnes, Mar 21, 1938 (died 1965); m. Mervyn Johns (actor), 1976 (died 1992); children: stepmother of Glynis Johns (actress). ❖ Made London stage debut as Nancy Forster in *Champion North* (1931), followed by *The Flight of the Arrow, The Streets of London, The Rivals, The Country Wife, Vintage Wine, Yes and No, The Admirable Crichton, Soldier's Wife, The Vigil, The Desperate Hours, Heartbreak House,* and as Angela Shale in *The Dominant Sex* (both stage and screen); also appeared in numerous Shakespearean productions; films include *Sally Bishop, Scott of the Antarctic, The History of Miss Polly, Housemaster* and *Jane Steps Out.*

CHURCHILL, Diana Spencer (1909–1963). Eldest daughter and least known of the Churchill children. Name variations: Diana Sandys; Mrs. Duncan Sandys. Born Diana Spencer Churchill, July 11, 1909, at Eccleston Square, London, England; died Oct 19, 1963, at Chester Row, London, England; dau. of Sir Winston S. Churchill (prime minister of England) and Lady Clementine Churchill; studied at Royal Academy of Arts; m. John Milner Bailey (1932–1935), Dec 1932; m. Duncan Sandys (1935–1960), Sept 16, 1935; children: (2nd m.) Julian Sandys (b. 1936); Edwina Sandys (b. 1938); Celia Sandys (b. 1943). ❖ Married John Bailey (1932), son of Sir Abe Bailey, a South African gold-mining millionaire and longstanding friend of her father's, but the marriage was not enthusiastically received in the Churchill home and a strained relationship developed between Diana and her mother that lasted most of her life; separated barely a year later and divorced; married Duncan Sandys, a diplomat and politician (1935); during WWII, served in Women's Royal Naval Service (WRNS) and worked as a nurse during London air raids; suffered nervous breakdown (1953), which affected her health for several years; following 2nd divorce (1960), developed a warmer relationship with mother; took a massive overdose of sleeping pills and died. ❖ See also *Women in World History*.

CHURCHILL, Elizabeth (fl. 1625–1650). *See Drake, Elizabeth.*

CHURCHILL, Fanny (1822–1899). Seventh duchess of Marlborough. Name variations: Lady Frances Emily Vane; marchioness of Blandford. Born Frances Anne Emily Vane, April 15, 1822; died April 16, 1899; eldest dau. of Charles William Stewart (b. 1778), 3rd marquis of Londonderry, and Frances Anne Emily Vane-Tempest (d. 1865); m. John Winston Spencer Churchill (1822–1883), 7th duke of Marlborough (r. 1857–1883), July 12, 1843; children: George Charles Spencer Churchill (1844–1892), 8th duke of Marlborough (r. 1883–1892); Frederick (1846–1850); Randolph Henry Spencer Churchill (1849–1895); Charles (1856–1858); Augustus (1858–1859); Cornelia Spencer Churchill (d. 1927, who m. Ivor Bertie Guest, 1st baron Wimborne); Rosamond Spencer Churchill (d. 1920, who m. William Henry Fellowes, 2nd baron de Ramsey); Fanny Spencer Churchill (d. 1904); Anne Emily Spencer Churchill (d. 1923, who m. James Henry Robert, 7th duke of Roxburghe); Georgiana Spencer Churchill (d. 1906); Sarah Isabella Spencer Churchill (d. 1929). ❖ Ruled Blenheim with a firm hand; during Irish potato famine, started a Famine Fund for Ireland's aged and infirm (1877). ❖ See also *Women in World History*.

CHURCHILL, Henrietta (1681–1733). Second duchess of Marlborough. Born July 19, 1681; died Oct 23, 1733; acceded as duchess of Marlborough, 1722; dau. of Sarah Jennings Churchill (1660–1744) and John Churchill (1650–1722), 1st duke of Marlborough (r. 1702–1722); m. Francis Godolphin, 2nd earl of Godolphin, April 23, 1698; children: William, marquess of Blandford; Henrietta Godolphin (d. 1776, who m. Thomas Pelham-Holles, 1st duke of Newcastle); Mary Godolphin (d. 1764, who m. Thomas Osborne, 4th duke of Leeds).

CHURCHILL, Jennie Jerome (1854–1921). American-born nurse and newspaper founder. Name variations: Jennie Jerome; Lady Jennie Jerome Spencer Churchill; Lady Randolph Churchill; Mrs. George Cornwallis-West. Born Jeanette Jerome, Jan 9, 1854, in Brooklyn, NY; died June 29, 1921, in London, England; dau. of Leonard Walter Jerome and Clara (Hall) Jerome; m. Lord Randolph Churchill, 1874; m. George Cornwallis-West, 1900; m. Montague Porch, 1918; children: (1st m.) Winston Spencer Churchill (1874–1965, prime minister); John Strange Churchill (b. 1880). ❖ American-born public figure, wife of Lord Randolph Churchill, and mother of Sir Winston S. Churchill, who was influential in Britain's royal and political affairs for an entire generation; moved with family to Paris (1868); married Lord Randolph Churchill (1874); husband died (1895); served as chair and nurse on hospital ship *Maine* during Anglo-Boer War (1899–1900); founded and edited the *Anglo-Saxon Review* (1899); had 2 plays produced (1914); served on several hospital boards (1915–19). ❖ See also memoirs *Reminiscences of Lady Randolph Churchill* (Century, 1908) and *Small Talks on Big Subjects* (Pearson, 1916); Peregrine Churchill and Julian Mitchell, *Jennie: Lady Randolph Churchill, a Portrait with Letters* (St. Martin, 1974); Ralph G. Martin, *Jennie: The Life of Lady Randolph Churchill*, 2 vols. (Prentice Hall, 1969–71); and *Women in World History*.

CHURCHILL, Marguerite (1909–2000). American actress. Born Dec 25, 1909, in Kansas City, Missouri; died Jan 9, 2000, in Broken Arrow, Oklahoma; m. George O'Brien (cowboy star), 1933 (div. 1948); children: Orin O'Brien (bassist) and Darcy O'Brien (writer). ❖ At 13, made Broadway debut as Molly in *Why Not?*, followed by *The Wild Man of Borneo* and *Skidding*, among others; starred opposite John Wayne in *The Big Trail*, his 1st major film (1930); returned to Broadway in *Dinner at Eight* (1932); other films include *The Valiant, They Had to See Paris, Riders of the Purple Sage, Man Hunt, The Walking Dead* and *Bunco Squad.*

CHURCHILL, Mary (1689–1751). Duchess of Montagu. Born July 15, 1689; died 1751; dau. of Sarah Jennings Churchill (1660–1744) and John Churchill (1650–1722), 1st duke of Marlborough (r. 1702–1722); m. John Montagu, 2nd duke of Montagu.

CHURCHILL, Mary (1922—). Youngest of the Churchill daughters. Name variations: Lady Soames. Born Sept 15, 1922; youngest dau. of Winston Churchill (prime minister) and Lady Clementine Churchill; m. Christopher Soames (MP), Feb 11, 1947; children: 5, including Emma Soames (b. 1949) and Charlotte Soames (b. 1954). ❖ During WWII, worked for Red Cross and Auxiliary Territorial Service in Britain; also accompanied father as an aide on several of his conferences overseas; married Christopher Soames (1946), who was subsequently a Member of Parliament for 16 years; was posted with husband to the Continent, where Christopher served 1st as ambassador to Paris and then as vice president of European Commission in Brussels; was a vice president of Church Army and served as United Kingdom chair of International Year of the Child (1979); wrote *Clementine Churchill: The Biography of a Marriage* (Houghton, 1979). ❖ See also *Women in World History*.

CHURCHILL, May (1876–1929). Notorious Irish-American swindler and bank robber. Name variations: May Latimer; Chicago May; May Churchill Sharp (or Sharpe); May Vivienne Churchill. Born Beatrice Desmond or May Lambert (sources vary) near Dublin, Ireland, in Nov 1876; died in Philadelphia, Pennsylvania, 1929; married an army officer named Sharp (or Sharpe). ❖ Arrived in New York City from Dublin at age 15 (1891); took up residence in the Tenderloin district, where her apparently staggering beauty, combined with schooling in the badger game by confidence artist Max Shinborn, allowed her to blackmail wealthy men; practiced the badger game in many cities, including NY, Chicago, London, Vienna and Paris; though she was in and out of prison, sentences were relatively short until, with 3 others including her infamous lover jewel thief Eddie McManus, robbed American Express Company in Paris (1901), for which she received a 5-year sentence (1902); arrested with lover Cubine Jackson (alias Charlie Smith) for attempted murder of McManus (1907), who had left her, and sentenced to 15 years of which she served 12; after release (1918), wrote her memoirs (*Chicago May, Her Story,* c. 1928) before dying in Philadelphia boardinghouse (1929); a household name in her own day, reportedly bilked wealthy men of $1 million during her career.

CHURCHILL, Odette (1912–1995). *See Sansom, Odette.*

CHURCHILL, Pamela (1920–1997). *See Harriman, Pamela.*

CHURCHILL, Lady Randolph (1854–1921). *See Churchill, Jennie Jerome.*

CHURCHILL, Sarah (1914–1982). English actress and author, painter. Born Sarah Millicent Hermione Churchill in London, England, Oct 7, 1914, at Admiralty House in London, England; died Sept 24, 1982, in London, England; dau. of Sir Winston S. Churchill (prime minister of England) and Lady Clementine Churchill; m. Vic Oliver, 1936 (div. 1945); m. Anthony Beauchamp, 1949 (div. 1955); m. Baron Henry Audley, 1963; no children. ❖ Made acting debut in the chorus of musical *Follow the Sun* in London (Feb 4, 1936); against parent's wishes, ran away to NY and married the show's star (Dec 1936); gave 1st dramatic performance at Mercury Theater playing Lucrezia in *Mandragola* (1939); appeared in such films as *Who's Your Lady Friend?* (1937) and *Spring Meeting* (1941); during WWII, had several dramatic roles on London stage, separated from husband, served in the Women's Auxiliary Air Force (WAAF), and worked in the highly secret photographic intelligence sector at Medmenham, Buckinghamshire; accompanied father to Teheran Conference (1943) and Yalta Conference (1945); after war, resumed career with stage performances in *Gaslight* (1946), *Barretts of Wimpole Street* (1948) and *House of Sand* (1949); made US debut as Tracy Lord in *The Philadelphia Story* (1949) and Broadway debut in *Gramercy Ghost* (1951); appeared in films *When in Rome* (1947), *All Over Town* (1949), *Serious Charge* (1959) and *Royal Wedding* (1951); after 2nd husband committed suicide (1957), entered a period of alcohol abuse and bad publicity that would probably have been ignored had her name not been Churchill; married Baron Henry Audley (1963) but he died of a massive heart attack later that year in Spain; took up painting later in life and became a respected amateur artist. Published 3 books of poetry, the short memoir *A Thread in the Tapestry,* principally about her father (1967), and a longer autobiography, *Keep on Dancing* (1981). ❖ See also *Women in World History.*

CHURCHILL, Sarah Jennings (1660–1744). Duchess of Marlborough. Name variations: Sarah Jennings. Born May 29, 1660, in St. Albans, Hertfordshire, England; died Oct 18, 1744, at Marlborough House in London; dau. of Richard Jennings (Jenyns) and Frances Thornhurst; sister of Frances Jennings (d. 1730); received no formal education; m. John Churchill (1650–1722), 1st duke of Marlborough (r. 1702–1722), Oct 1, 1677 or 1678; children: Harriet (b. Oct 1679, died in infancy); Henrietta Churchill (1681–1733), 2nd duchess of Marlborough; Anne Churchill (1684–1716), countess of Sunderland; John (b. Jan 12, 1686–1703) 1st marquis of Blandford; Elizabeth Churchill (b. Mar 15, 1687–1714), countess of Bridgwater; Mary Churchill (1689–1751), duchess of Montagu; Charles (b. Aug 19, 1690, died in infancy). ❖ Keeper of the Privy Purse for Queen Anne of England and wife of John Churchill, 1st duke of Marlborough, who used her wealth and connections to further the cause of the Whig Party; from age 12 to 17, was attendant at court of Mary of Modena (1662–67); appointed lady of the bedchamber to Anne, princess of Denmark, later Queen Anne (1683); named 1st lady of the bedchamber for Anne (1685); replaced as lady of the bedchamber by Abigail Hill, later Lady Abigail Masham (1700); after William III was succeeded by Queen Anne (1702), appointed Groom of the Stole, Keeper of the Privy Purse, mistress of the robes, and together with her husband was created duke and duchess of Marlborough (1702); created princess of Mindelheim by Emperor Leopold (1704); dismissed from offices in favor of Abigail Masham (1711); husband died (1721); published vindication of herself in *Account of the Conduct of the Dowager Duchess of Marlborough from her 1st Comming to Court to the Year 1710* (1742). ❖ See also David Green, *Sarah, Duchess of Marlborough* (Scribner, 1967); Frances Harris, *A Passion for Government: Life of Sarah, Duchess of Marlborough* (Oxford U. Press, 1991); and *Women in World History.*

CHURILOVA, L.A. (1875–1937). Russian poet and novelist. Name variations: (pseudonym) Lidiia Alekséevna Chárskaia or Lidiia Alekseevna Charskaia or Lydia Alexeevna Charskaya or Lydia Charskaya, Lydia Charskaia, or Lidiia Charskaia, or L.A. Charskaya. Born Lidiya Alexeyevna Churilova in 1875 in Russia; died 1937. ❖ Worked as actress for Aleksandrinskii Theatre (1898–1924); refused permission to publish under own name after 1917 and dismissed by Aleksandrinskii Theatre; wrote novels for children, including *Princess Dzhavakha* (1903), *A Daring Life* (1905), *The Little Siberian* (1910), *Notes of a Boarding School Girl* and *The Foundlings;* English translations of works include *Little Princess Nina* (1924), *Fledglings* (1926), and *The Little Siberian* (1929). Though her work is considered uneven and formulaic by critics, *Princess Dzhavakha* was republished (1990) and immediately sold out.

CHUSOVITINA, Oksana (1975—). Soviet gymnast. Name variations: Chousovitina. Born June 19, 1975, in Bukhara, Uzbekistan; m. Bakhodir Kuranov (wrestler), 1997. ❖ Won US Olympic Cup and World Sports Fair (1990); at World championships, won a gold medal in floor exercises and team all-around and a silver in vault (1991), a bronze in vault (1992, 1993), and a silver in vault (2001); at Barcelona Olympics, won a gold medal in team all-around (1992); won Friendship Classic and Gander Memorial (2001); was the 1st woman to perform a layout full-out on floor exercises.

CHUTE, B.J. (1913–1987). American writer. Name variations: Joy Chute. Born Beatrice Joy Chute in Minneapolis, Minnesota, Jan 13, 1913; died 1987; dau. of William Young Chute (realtor) and Edith Mary (Pickburn) Chute. ❖ Worked as father's secretary for 10 years before she began writing professionally; books include *The Fields Are White* (1950), *The End of Loving* (1953), *Greenwillow* (1956), *Journey to Christmas* (1958) and *The Moon and the Thorn* (1961).

CHUTE, Carolyn (1947—). American novelist. Born Carolyn Penny, June 14, 1947, in Portland, Maine; dau. of Joseph R. and Annie Prindall Penny; attended University of Southern Maine, 1972–78; m. James Hawkes (factory worker), 1963 (div. 1972); m. Michael Chute, 1978; children: (1st m.) Joannah Hawkes Bowie; (2nd m.) Reuben (died). ❖ Dropped out of high school and married at 16; lived in poverty, variously employed as a waitress, chicken factory worker, hospital floor scrubber, potato farmer, teacher, social worker, and school bus driver; wrote a column for *Currier Free Press* (1978–79); wrote the bestselling *The Beans of Egypt, Maine* (1985), followed by *Metal Man*

(1988); also wrote *Letourneau's Used Auto Parts* and *Snow Man* (1999); member of a "no-wing" militia.

CHUTE, Marchette (1909–1994). American children's poet and biographer. Born Marchette Gaylord Chute, Aug 16, 1909, in Hazlewood, Minnesota; died May 6, 1994, in New Jersey; dau. of Edith Mary (Pickburn) Chute and William Young Chute (realtor); University of Minnesota, BA, 1930; never married, no children. ❖ Published 1st book, *Rhymes about Ourselves,* a collection of children's verse (1932); other writings include *Rhymes about the Country* (1941), *The Innocent Wayfaring* (1943), *Geoffrey Chaucer of England* (1946), *Shakespeare of London* (1950) and *Ben Jonson of Westminster* (1953).

CHYTILOVA, Vera (1929—). Czech film director. Born Feb 2, 1929, in Ostrava, Czechoslovakia (Czech Republic); educated at Charles University and Film Faculty, Academy of Music and Art (FAMU), 1957–62; m. Jaroslav Kucera (cinematographer); children: 2. ❖ Widely regarded as one of the best filmmakers in Europe, landed a coveted spot at FAMU, Prague's film school, where she studied directing; leaning heavily on *cinema verité,* often used non-actors and improvisation to lend authenticity to films; riled censors with *Daisies* and *The Fruit of Paradise* (1969); after Soviet invasion of Czechoslovakia (1968), was fired from Barrandov Studios; though not officially blacklisted, was not allowed to work; wrote to Czechoslovakian President Gustav Husak, telling him in effect that she had been censured (1975); allowed to work again, released *The Apple Game* (1976), hailed internationally as the best Czech film in years; was the 1st Eastern European filmmaker to deal with subject of AIDS (*Tainted Horseplay,* 1989); other films include *Panelstory* (1979), *Calamity* (1980), *The Very Late Afternoon of a Faun* (1983), *Prague, the Restless Heart of Europe* (short, 1985), *Wolf's Cabin* (1986), *The Jester and the Queen* (1987), *The Liberator* (short, 1991), *My Inhabitants of Prague Understand Me* (1991) and *Inheritance* (1992). ❖ See also *Women in World History.*

CIALENTE, Fausta (1898–1994). Italian novelist and translator. Born 1898 in Cagliari, Sardinia, Italy; died Mar 1994 in Pangbourne, England; dau. of an army officer and opera singer; m. Enrico Terni (Italian composer), 1921 (sep.). ❖ Moved with husband to Alexandria, Egypt; during WWII, contributed to anti-Fascist broadcasts on Radio Cairo and founded newspaper for Italian prisoners of war, *Fronte Unito;* published 1st novel *Natalia* (1929); other novels include *Cortile a Cleopatra* (1936), *Ballata levantina* (1961), *Un inferno freddissimo* (1966), *Il vento sulla sabbia* (1972) and *Le quattro ragazze Wieselberger* (1976); short-story collections include *Pamela o la bell'estate* (1963) and *Interno con figure* (1976); also translated Louisa May Alcott's *Little Women* and Henry James's *Turn of the Screw,* among others.

CI'AN (1837–1881). Chinese empress and regent. Name variations: Tz'u-an, Cian. Born 1837; died 1881. ❖ A Manchu aristocrat, was senior consort to the Xianfeng (Hsien-feng) emperor; served as regent with Cixi until Ci'an's death (1881), though Cixi had usurped her power long before.

CIANO, Edda (1910–1995). Italian anti-fascist. Name variations: Edda Mussolini. Pronunciation: CHEE-anno. Born in Italy, Sept 1, 1910; died in Rome, Italy, April 8, 1995; eldest of 5 children of Benito Mussolini (1883–1945) and Rachele (Guidi) Mussolini; aunt of Alessandra Mussolini; m. Count Galeazzo Ciano (future Italian foreign minister), 1930 (executed 1944); children: 2. ❖ Her husband, as foreign minister and a member of the Fascist Grand Council, voted against her father following the Allied invasion of Italy, a vote that led to Mussolini's arrest and would eventually topple his regime (1943); when the Germans freed Mussolini (1944), unsuccessfully pleaded with father not to execute husband; renounced her birth name and never used it again.

CIBBER, Charlotte (1713–1760). See Charke, Charlotte Cibber.

CIBBER, Susannah (1714–1766). English singer and actress. Born Susannah Maria Arne in London, England, Feb 1714; died at Westminster, Jan 30, 1766; buried in Westminster Abbey; dau. of a Covent Garden upholsterer; sister of the composer Thomas Arne; married Theophilus Cibber (1703–1758, actor-manager and son of Colley Cibber), 1834 (div.); children: 2 who died in infancy. ❖ Eminent actress and singer, made debut at 18 at the Haymarket in the opera *Amelia* by Lumpé; became the 2nd wife of the notorious Theophilus Cibber who directed her in her 1st success as a tragic actress in Voltaire's *Zaïre* (1736); after having an affair with William Sloper, was the subject of a sensational trial when Theophilus sued for damages; saw career put on hold for 14 years because of the notoriety; returning to the theater (1753), became

Garrick's most famous partner at the Drury Lane. ❖ See also *Women in World History.*

CIBÒ, Caterina (fl. 1533). Duchess of Camerino. Name variations: Catherine Cibo or Cybo. Dau. of Maddalena de Medici (d. 1519) and Franceschetto Cybo, Cibo, or Cibò. ❖ Accompanied Catherine de Medici to France on Catherine's wedding journey (1533).

CIBO or CIBÒ, Maddalena (d. 1519). See Medici, Maddalena de.

CICCIOLINA (1951—). Italian porn star, singer and politician. Name variations: Ilona Staller. Born Nov 26, 1951, in Budapest, Hungary; mother was a midwife; stepfather was an official in the Ministry of the Interior; m. 2nd husband Jeff Koons (American sculptor), 1991 (div. 1992); children: (2nd m.) Ludwig. ❖ Began working for MTI, the Hungarian modeling agency (1964); married and moved to Italy; working with pornographer Riccardo Schicchi, adopted the name Cicciolina and achieved fame with radio show "Voulez vous coucher avec moi?" on Radio Luna (1970s); was the 1st to bare her breasts on Italian tv (1978); elected the leading candidate of the Lista del Sole (Italy's Green Party, 1979); switched to Partito Radicale (1985), opposing nuclear energy and NATO membership; representing Lazio district of Rome, elected to Italian parliament (1987); starred in last porno film (1989); made an unsuccessful bid to run for Parliament in Hungary (2002).

CICELY. *Variant of Cecilia or Cecily.*

CICIERSKA, Margaret. American dancer and choreographer. Born in New York, NY; trained at Juilliard. ❖ Danced for Anna Sokolow's company (1965–69) in such works as *Lyric Suite, Time + 7, Déserts* and *Steps of Silence;* founded her own dance troupe (early 1970s) for which she choreographed *Seascape* (1970), *Harriet* (1971), *Drifts* (1974), *The Shoppers* (1975), *Impromptu* (1975), *Conquest of Mexico* (1976) and *Bugs Bunny* (1976), among others.

CICOT, Christine (1964—). French judoka. Born Sept 10, 1964, in Libourne, France. ❖ Won European championship (1990); won a bronze medal for +72kg heavyweight at Atlanta Olympics (1996); won World championship (1997).

CID, Estela. See Gimenez, Estela.

CIDIE (1880–1961). See Sarfatti, Margherita.

CIEPLY-WIECZORKOWNA, Teresa (1937—). Polish runner and hurdler. Name variations: Teresa Wieczorek. Born Teresa Wieczorkowna, Oct 19, 1937, in Poland. ❖ At Rome Olympics, won a bronze medal in 4 x 100-meter relay (1960); at Tokyo Olympics, won a silver medal in 80-meter hurdles and a gold medal in 4 x 100-meter relay (1964).

CIGNA, Gina (1900–2001). French-Italian coloratura soprano. Name variations: Genevieve Cigna; Genoveffa Sens; Ginette Sens. Born Mar 6, 1900, in Angères, France; died June 26, 2001, in Milan, Italy; dau. of a general in the French army; studied at Paris Conservatory with Emma Calvé, Darclée, and Storchio; m. Maurice Sens (French opera singer), 1923. ❖ Debuted under name Genoveffa Sens at Teatro alla Scala, singing there every season thereafter under her own name (1929–43); debuted at Metropolitan Opera as Aïda (1937); abandoned singing career after an automobile accident (1947); became a voice teacher and taught at the Royal Conservatory in Toronto, Canada (1953–57). ❖ See also *Women in World History.*

CILENTO, Diane (1933—). Australian-born actress and novelist. Born Oct 5, 1933, in Brisbane, Australia; dau. of Sir Ralph West Cilento (authority on tropical medicine) and Lady Phyllis McGlew Cilento (gynecologist); m. Sean Connery (actor), 1962 (div. 1973); m. Anthony Shaffer (playwright), 1985 (died 2001); children: Jason Connery (actor). ❖ Made screen debut in *Wings of Danger* (1952), followed by *The Admirable Crichton, The Truth about Women, Jet Storm, The Naked Edge, Rattle of a Simple Man, The Agony and the Ecstasy, Hombre, Hitler: The Last 10 Days, Duet for Four* and *The Boy Who Had Everything,* among others; made stage debut in Manchester as Juliet (1953); other plays include *The Big Knife, Tiger at the Gates, Less Than Kind, Orpheus Descending, Heartbreak House, Altona, Naked, The Idiot, Collaborators* and the title role in *Miss Julie;* wrote the novels *The Manipulator* and *The Hybrid.* Nominated for Oscar for performance in *Tom Jones* (1963).

CILENTO, Phyllis (1894–1987). Australian medical practitioner, gynecologist and health educator. Name variations: Phyllis McGlew; Lady Phyllis Dorothy Cilento. Born Phyllis McGlew, Mar 13, 1894, in Sydney, Australia; died 1987 in Australia; Adelaide University, MB, BS; m. Sir Raphael "Ralph" West Cilento (medical administrator), 1920; children: Diane Cilento (actress, writer). ❖ Medical practitioner, author and radio broadcaster who stressed importance of nutrition and family planning and worked for rights of women in medical field; did postgraduate work at hospitals and clinics in Malaysia, New Guinea, London, Paris and New York; on marriage, moved to Brisbane; became a prominent member of Queensland women's movement and highly influential in broader areas of public health; served as lecturer in midwifery and obstetrical physiotherapy at University of Queensland; wrote several books on nutrition, vitamin therapy, childbirth education, family planning, prenatal care and childcare; founded Queensland Mothercraft Association (1930) and served as its president (1930–33, 1935–48); served as president of Queensland Medical Women's Association (1938–47); writings include *Square Meals for the Family* (1934) and *Nutrition of the Elderly* (1980). Awarded membership of Order of Australia for life's work. ❖ See also Lady Phyllis Cilento, *My Life* (Methuen, 1987).

ÇILLER, Tansu (1946—). Prime minister of Turkey. Name variations: Ciller. Pronunciation: (CHILL-air). Born in Istanbul, Turkey, 1946; attended American College for Girls, Istanbul; Robert College, degree in economics, 1967; University of New Hampshire, MA in economics; University of Connecticut, PhD in economics; Yale University, postdoctoral studies, 1971; m. banker and businessman Ozer çiller (who took her surname), 1963; children: 2 sons. ❖ Became the 1st woman minister of Turkey (June 14, 1993), the 3rd woman to head a predominantly Muslim country; at Robert College (now Bosporus University), worked her way up the academic ladder, becoming full professor at 36 (1983), the youngest in Turkey; worked as a consultant for World Bank's Chamber of Industry and Trade Board of the State Planning Organization, and as an adviser to Istanbul Metropolitan Municipality (1980s); prepared a report critical of the economic policies of President Turgut Özal and the ruling Motherland Party; after the moderate-right True Path Party's victory (1991), was appointed minister of state for the economy and elected a deputy of the General Assembly, where she introduced a controversial plan to privatize many of Turkey's State Economic Enterprises; conducted an effective populist campaign for prime minister, even without party support (1993); was beset with problems, including renewed hostilities between Turkish government forces and guerrillas affiliated with the Kurdish Worker's Party, and the ethnic conflict between the Azerbaijanis and the Armenians over control of Nagorno-Karabkh; sent armed forces to join UN peacekeeping troops in Bosnia; received a vote of confidence from True Path Party (1993), but her anti-inflation policy was deemed a failure (1994); by 1996, was no longer prime minister but was still the leader of the True Path Party. ❖ See also *Women in World History.*

CIMBURCA OF MASOVIA (c. 1396–1429). Duchess of Inner Austria. Name variations: Cimburgis of Mazovia; Cymbarka; Cymburga. Born between 1394 and 1397; died Sept 28, 1429, in Turnitz near Lilienfeld; 2nd wife of Ernest the Iron of Habsburg (d. 1424), duke of Inner Austria (son of Virida Visconti and Leopold III of Habsburg); children: Friedrich IV the Fair also known as Frederick III (1415–1493), king of Germany and Holy Roman emperor (r. 1440–1493); Margaret of Saxony (c. 1416–1486, who m. Frederick II of Saxony); Albrecht or Albert VI (1418–1463); Catherine (c. 1420–1493).

CIMBURGIS (c. 1396–1429). See Cimburca of Masovia.

CINDERELLA (1878–1958). See Bruce, Mary Grant.

CINEFWINTHA (fl. 7th c.). See Cuneswith.

CINTHIA. *Variant of Cynthia.*

CINTI-DAMOREAU, Laure (1801–1863). French soprano. Name variations: Madame Damoreau; Laure Cinthie Montalant; Mademoiselle Cinti. Born in Paris, France, Feb 6, 1801; died in Chantilly, France, Feb 25, 1863; studied in Paris with Plantade and Catalani. ❖ Made debut as Cherubino in *Le Nozze di Figaro* in Paris (1819); debuted in London (1822); joined the Grand Opéra in Paris where she created lead roles in Rossini's *Le siège de Corinth,* Moïse, *Le Comte Ory* and *Guillaume Tell* (1826); sang to great success in Europe and US; was a professor of singing at the Conservatoire, Paris (1834–56). ❖ See also *Women in World History.*

CINTRÓN, Conchita (1922—). Chilean bullfighter. Name variations: Conchita Cintron de Castelo Branco; Conchita Cintron Verrill. Born in Chile in 1922; dau. of a Puerto Rican father and an Irish-American mother (both US citizens); raised in Peru. ❖ Began to slay bulls on horseback at age 12; in Mexico, made 1st appearance in the arena on foot at age 15 (1937); during career, was gored only twice while mastering over 1,200 bulls; in farewell appearance in Spain, where bullfighting by women on foot was banned, challenged the law by dismounting from her horse and executing a collection of perfect passes, then was arrested for refusing to kill the bull (1949); retired (1951), having opened the way for women bullfighters in other parts of the world. ❖ See also autobiography *Conchita Cintón: Memoirs of a Bullfighter* (Holt, 1968) and Lola Verrill Cintron, *Goddess of the Bullring* (Bobbs-Merrill, 1960).

CIOBANA, Marioara (1962—). See Popescu, Marioara.

CIOCCA, Giovanna (c. 1825–?). Italian ballet dancer. Born c. 1925, probably in Milan, Italy. ❖ Danced at Teatro alla Scala in Milan; traveled to New York City to perform at Park Theater and stayed on to dance in *Giselle, Diana and Endymeon* and *The Magic Flute;* performed at Bowery Theater in NY, partnering with George Washington Smith; with former La Scala Theater dance partner, Giovanni Neri, appeared at the Bowery and the Broadway Theater on numerous occasions; returned to Europe.

CIONCAN, Maria (1977—). Romanian runner. Born June 19, 1977, in Maieru, Romania. ❖ At Golden League in Oslo, placed 1st in 1,500 meters (2002); won a bronze medal for 1,500 meters at Athens Olympics (2004).

CIPRELLI, Jeannie (1958—). See Longo, Jeannie.

CISNEROS, Eleonora de (1878–1934). American mezzo-soprano. Name variations: Eleanor Broadfoot. Born Eleanor Broadfoot in Brooklyn, NY, Nov 1, 1878; died in New York, NY, Feb 3, 1934; studied with Francesco Fanciulli and Adeline Murio-Celli in NY and Angelo Tabadello in Paris; m. Count François de Cisneros. ❖ Appeared for a season at the Metropolitan Opera (1899–1900), claiming to be the 1st American-trained singer to do so; sang Brünnhilde, Ortrud, Venus, Delilah, and Amneris in Turin (1902); performed regularly at Covent Garden (1904–08) and debuted at La Scala (1906). ❖ See also *Women in World History.*

CISNEROS, Evelyn (1958—). American ballet dancer. Born 1958 in Long Beach, California. ❖ Joined company of San Francisco Ballet (1977), where she danced throughout career (1977–99); danced in numerous works by Lew Christensen—then, artistic director—including his *Beauty and the Beast;* performed in Michael Smuin's *A Song for Dead Warriors* (1979) and as Miranda in his *The Tempest* (1980); appeared in Helgi Tomasson's *Confidencias* and *Valses Poeticos* (1990), *Quartette* (1994) and *Two Bits* (1998).

CISNEROS, Sandra (1954—). Mexican-American poet and novelist. Born 1954 in Chicago, Illinois; grew up in Humboldt Park, Illinois; spent many youthful days in Mexico; dau. of a Mexican father and Chicana mother; Loyola University, BA in English, 1976; University of Iowa Writer's Workshop, MA. ❖ Published acclaimed novel *The House on Mango Street* (1984), describing the life of a Mexican-American girl growing up in a working-class Chicago neighborhood, for which she won the Before Columbus Foundation's American Book Award (1985); published a book of poetry *My Wicked, Wicked Ways* (1987); also wrote *Woman Hollering Creek* (1991), which won the PEN Center West Award for Best Fiction; won the prestigious MacArthur Foundation fellowship (1995).

CISSE, Jeanne-Martin (1926—). Guinean diplomat. Name variations: Jeanne Martin Cisse. Born in 1926; married; children: 6. ❖ The 1st woman appointed as a permanent representative to the UN, began career as a teacher (1945), then served as school director; joining the Democratic Party (1959), worked in the Federal Office of the Kinda Region; served as 1st African secretary, 2nd vice-president, and 1st vice-president of National Assembly of Guinea; also served on the Assembly's National and Regional Women's Committees, and as secretary-general of the Conference of African Women (1962–72); was the 1st woman to be appointed a permanent representative to UN (1972) and the 1st woman to preside over UN Security Council; was minister of social affairs in Guinea (1976–84). Awarded Lenin Peace Prize (1975).

CISTERNE, Gabrielle-Anne (1804–1872). See Saint Mars, Gabrielle.

CISTJAKOVA, Galina (1962—). Soviet long jumper. Born July 26, 1962. ❖ At Seoul Olympics, won a bronze medal in the long jump (1988).

CIXI (1835–1908). Manchu empress-dowager of China. Name variations: Tz'u-hsi, and its alternate spellings, Tse-Hi, Tsu-Hsi, Tze Hsi, Tzu Hsi, T'zu Hsi, Tsze Hsi An; Xiaoqin Xian Huanghou; (empress-dowager of the Western Palace); Imperial Concubine Yi; Yehonala; Nala Taihou (empress-dowager Nala); Lao Fuoye (Old Buddha); Venerable Ancestor. Pronunciation: TSE-shee. Born Yehonala, or Yehe Nara, but 1st name at birth not confirmed, Nov 29, 1835, in Taiyuan, Shanxi province, China; died Nov 15, 1908, in Beijing; dau. of a Manchu official, Huizheng; married as lowly ranked concubine of Xianfeng emperor (r. 1851–1861) in 1851 (died 1861): children: one son, T'ung Chih, the Tongzhi emperor (1856–1875). ❖ Ruled de facto 3 times as empress-dowager regent, as co-regent to her son, the Tongzhi emperor (1861–73), and twice as regent to her nephew, the Guangxu emperor (1875–89, 1898–1908); dominated politics for half a century during failed self-strengthening and reform measures to cope with China's critical decline in the backdrop of Western imperialism and internal rebellion; died one day after the death of the legitimate Guangxu emperor and just 3 years before the 2,000-year-old imperial system was overthrown by the Republican Revolution. Has been portrayed as an ignorant, murderous, and ultraconservative woman who epitomized the incompetence of the Chinese empire and exacerbated the difficulties of modernizing initiatives; nevertheless recent scholars, including Luke Kwong and Sue Fawn Chung, have convincingly provided some balanced and positive views of Cixi's historical role. ❖ See also Luke S.K. Kwong, *A Mosaic of the Hundred Days: Personalities, Politics, and Ideas of 1898* (Council on East Asian Studies, Harvard University, 1984); Sterling Seagrave, *Dragon Lady: The Life and Legend of the Last Empress of China* (Vintage, 1992); and *Women in World History.*

CIXOUS, Hélène (1938—). French playwright, novelist, and literary critic. Name variations: Helene Cixous. Born June 5, 1937 in Oran, Algeria; dau. of a French-Jewish colonialist doctor who died when she was young; mother Eve was Austro-German; married, 1959 (div. 1965); children: daughter (b. 1959); son (b. 1962). ❖ Known for her theory of *écriture féminine* which challenges sexual categories and patriarchal hierarchies, became an assistant at the University of Bordeaux (1962); moved to Paris (1965) and became an assistant at the Sorbonne; published 1st book *Le Prénom de Dieu* (God's First Name, 1967); published doctoral thesis *The Exile of James Joyce* (1969); in the aftermath of the student riots (1968), appointed chargé de mission to found the experimental University of Paris VIII at Vincennes (later Saint Denis), where she became a professor of literature; also founded Paris Centre des Recherches en Etudes Féminines (1974), remaining as chair for years, and co-founded *Poétique* (1969); published 1st fiction *Dedans* (Outside, 1969), for which she won the Prix Médicis, and the trilogy *Le Troisième Corps* (The Third Body), *Les Commencements* (Beginnings), and *Neutre* (Neuter, 1970–72); wrote (with Catherine Clément) *La Jeune Née* (1975); also wrote *Limonade tout était si infini* (1982) and *Le livre de Promethea* (1983), among others; theater writing includes *Portrait of Dora* (1976), *Le Nom d'Oedipe: chant du corps interdit* (1978), *La Prise de l'école de Madhubai* (1985), *L'histoire terrible mais inachevée de Norodom Sihanouk, Roi de Cambodge* (1985), and *L'Indiade ou L'Inde de leurs rêves* (1987); other novels include *Angst* (1977) and *Vive l'Orange* (1979); contributed an autobiographical piece to *An Algerian Childhood* (trans. by Marjolin De Yager, 2001). ❖ See also Susan Sellers, ed., *Writing Differences: Readings from the Seminar of Hélène Cixous* (Palgrave Macmillan, 1988); Lynn Penrod, *Hélène Cixous* (Twayne).

CLAFLIN, Tennessee (1846–1923). American securities broker, spiritualist, and crusader for social reform. Name variations: Tennessee Cook, Lady Cook. Born in Homer, Ohio, Oct 26, 1846 (some sources cite 1845); died Jan 18, 1923; dau. of Roxanna (Hummel) Claflin and Reuben Buckman ("Buck") Claflin; sister of Victoria Woodhull (1838–1927) and Utica Claflin Brooker (d. 1873); m. John Bartels; m. Francis Cook (held the title of Visconde de Montserrate bestowed by the king of Portugal, then became a baronet), Oct 1885. ❖ Better known in her youth then sister Victoria, showed signs of having second sight; became a major attraction as a spiritualist, touring the region as "The Wonder Child" and touted by father as a healer; with sister Victoria, became involved with other movements of the time—free love, women's rights, and politics; with help of Commodore Cornelius Vanderbilt, who was infatuated with her, opened Woodhull, Claflin & Co. with Victoria, making them the nation's 1st female brokers (Jan 19, 1870); fueled by tips from Vanderbilt, prospered; issued *Woodhull & Claflin's Weekly*, a journal of opinion; ran unsuccessfully for a seat in NY legislature (1872); in England, met Francis Cook, wealthy widower soon to be a baronet, who was interested in spiritualism; after she informed him that his departed wife was urging him to marry her, became Lady Cook; was known in London society for her lavish parties, contributions to schools and charities, and efforts on behalf of women's suffrage. ❖ See also *Women in World History.*

CLAFLIN, Victoria (1838–1927). *See Woodhull, Victoria.*

CLAIBORNE, Liz (1929—). American fashion designer and business-woman. Name variations: Elizabeth Claiborne Ortenberg. Born Mar 31, 1929, in Brussels, Belgium; dau. of American bank manager; m. Arthur Ortenberg. ❖ Fashion designer and founder of one of world's most successful fashion companies, fled Nazis with family (1939) and was raised in New Orleans; returned to Europe after WWII to study art instead of finishing high school; won fashion design contest sponsored by Harper's Bazaar magazine (1950); took job as design assistant with NY clothing manufacturer and later joined Jonathan Logan as chief designer of junior dresses; left Logan (1976) and established Liz Claiborne, Inc., designing and producing moderately priced sportswear for women; named the fashion industry's 1st Entrepreneurial Woman of the Year (1980); made public stock offering (1981) and began to diversify, adding petite, dress, and shoe divisions and then expanding into menswear, accessories and perfume; built hugely profitable business, listed among Fortune 500 for 1st time in 1986; elected chair and chief executive officer of company in addition to role as president (1987); with husband, founded Liz Claiborne/ Art Ortenberg Foundation which funds environmental projects worldwide; retired from active management of company (1989) and has since lectured at Fashion Institute of Technology and Parsons School.

CLAIRE. *Variant of Clare.*

CLAIRE, Helen (1911–1974). American stage and radio actress and commentator. Born Oct 18, 1911, in Union Springs, Alabama; died Jan 12, 1974, in Birmingham, Alabama; m. Dr. Milton Smith (div.); m. William Snow. ❖ At 13, made stage debut with Eva Le Gallienne's Civic Rep in *Peter Pan,* subsequently appearing in over 100 plays; on Broadway, appeared in *Michael and Mary, Girls in Uniform, Honeymoon, 9 Pine Street, Jezebel, Cat and the Canary, Kiss the Boys Goodbye* and *Lady in Danger;* also had recurring roles on radio serials and was a commentator for Fox Movietone News.

CLAIRE, Ina (1892–1985). American stage and film actress. Born Ina Fagan, Oct 15, 1892, in Washington, DC; died from effects of a stroke at home in San Francisco, California, Feb 21, 1985; m. James Whittaker (critic), 1919 (div. 1925); m. John Gilbert (actor), 1929 (div. 1931); m. William R. Wallace (attorney), 1939 (died 1976). ❖ At 13, went on the road as a vaudeville comedian, accompanied by mother; gained notice in NY with impersonation of Sir Harry Lauder (1909); made Broadway debut in *Jumping Jupiter* (1911); featured in *Ziegfeld Follies* (1915, 1916); firmly established reputation as a comedian in *Polly with a Past* (1917), following that with *The Gold Diggers* (1919), which ran for 2 years; was a Broadway star throughout 1920s; played lead in *The Awful Truth* on Broadway (1922), then starred in film version (1929), her 1st talkie; other Broadway credits include *The Last of Mrs. Cheyney* (1925) and S.N. Behrman's smash hit *Biography* (1932); retired (1954); films include *The Royal Family of Broadway* (1931), *Rebound* (1931), *The Greeks Had a Name for It* (1932), *Ninotchka* (1939), *Stage Door Canteen* (1943) and *Claudia* (1943).

CLAIRMONT, Claire (1798–1879). Mistress of Lord Byron. Born Clara Mary Jane Clairmont, 1798; died 1879; dau. of Mary Jane Vial and an unknown father; stepdau. of William Godwin; stepsister of Mary Shelley (1797–1851); children: (with Lord Byron) daughter Allegra (1817–1822). ❖ At 18, was briefly Lord Byron's mistress in Switzerland (1816) and gave birth to their daughter Allegra (1817); though Byron refused to see her, relentlessly continued her pursuit, and fought with him as to who would bring up the child (Byron won out and installed Allegra in a convent in Italy, where she caught typhus and died); except for a 4-year sojourn as a governess in Russia, lived with Mary Shelley throughout the rest of her life; was celebrated in Percy Shelley's poem "To Constantia Singing." ❖ See also Marion Kingston Stocking, ed., *The Clairmont Correspondence: Letters of Claire Clairmont, Charles Clairmont, and Fanny Imlay Godwin,* Vol. I, 1808–1834, Vol. II, 1835–1879 (Johns Hopkins U. Press, 1996); and *Women in World History.*

CLAIRON, Mlle (1723–1802). French actress. Name variations: La Clairon; Claire Hippolyte Clairon. Born Claire Hippolyte Josèphe Légris de Latude near Condé, in Hainault, France, 1723; died in Paris, Jan 18, 1802 (some sources cite 1803). ❖ Commonly known as La Clairon, made triumphant stage debut at Comédie Français, Paris, as Phèdre (1743); remained at Comédie for 22 years, dividing the honors

with rival Marie Dumesnil; remembered for her natural style, had greatest achievements in the classical roles of tragedy, including Medea, originated many of parts in Voltaire's plays; retired (1765) and taught acting; published a book of memoirs (1799).

CLAMPITT, Amy (1920–1994). American poet. Born in New Providence, Iowa, June 15, 1920; died in Lenox, Massachusetts, Sept 10, 1994; dau. of Pauline (Felt) and Ray Justin Clampitt; Grinnell College, BA with honors, 1941; studied at Columbia University and New School for Social Research. ❖ After college, worked as a secretary and writer at Oxford University Press in NY (1943–51), then as a reference librarian at National Audubon Society (1952–59); became an editor at E.P. Dutton (1977), a post she would hold until 1982; at 63, published 1st major collection of poetry, *The Kingfisher,* which was nominated for National Book Critics Circle Award (1983); other writings include *Multitudes, Multitudes* (1974), *The Isthmus* (1981), *What the Light Was Like* (1985), *Archaic Figure* (1987) and *Westward* (1990). ❖ See also *Women in World History.*

CLANNAD. *See Enya.*

CLAPHAM, Diana (1957—). English equestrian. Born June 8, 1957, in UK. ❖ At Los Angeles Olympics, won a silver medal in 3-day event team competition (1984).

CLAPP, Cornelia Maria (1849–1934). American zoologist. Born Mar 17, 1849, in Montague, Massachusetts; died Dec 31, 1934, at Mount Dora, Florida; dau. of Richard and Eunice Amelia (Slate) Clapp (both teachers); graduate of Mount Holyoke, 1871; Syracuse University, PhB, 1888, PhD, 1889; University of Chicago, PhD, 1896; never married; no children. ❖ Served as faculty member at Mount Holyoke (c. 1873–1916); attended Anderson School of Natural History established by Louis Agassiz; made several walking trips in 1870s; studied chick embryology at MIT (1880s); at Woods Hole, MA, served as investigator, teacher and librarian (1893–1907), corporation member and trustee (1897–1901, 1910); helped organize department of zoology at Mount Holyoke (1896) and became professor of zoology (1904); was one of few women among the 150 most important American zoologists in *American Men of Science* (1906); as professor emeritus, retired from Mount Holyoke (1916). Cornelia Clapp Laboratory at Mount Holyoke was named in her honor.

CLAPP, Louise (1819–1906). American writer and educator. Name variations: Louise Amelia Knapp Smith Clapp or Clappe; Louisa Amelia Knapp Smith; (pseudonyms) Shirley; Dame Shirley. Born Louisa Amelia Knapp Smith, July 28, 1819, in Elizabeth, New Jersey; died Feb 9, 1906, in Hanover Township, outside Morristown, New Jersey; m. Fayette Clapp, c. 1848 (div. 1857); children: (adopted her niece) Genevieve Stebbins. ❖ With husband, lived for 14 months in the Sierra Nevada mountains in 2 gold camps, Rich Bar and Indian Bar (1851–52); known primarily for letters written under pen name "Shirley" to her sister Mary Jane (aka Molly) describing life in the camps (23 of these "Shirley letters" were published serially in *Pioneer* [1854–55]); served as teacher in San Francisco public schools (1854–78); Bret Harte is said to have borrowed material from the "Shirley letters" for his stories.

CLAPP, Louise Brough (b. 1923). *See Brough, Louise.*

CLAPP, Margaret (1910–1974). American educator and historian. Name variations: Margaret Antoinette Clapp. Born Margaret Antoinette Clapp, April 10, 1910, in East Orange, New Jersey; died May 3, 1974, in Tyringham, Massachusetts; dau. of Alfred Chapin Clapp (insurance broker) and Anna (Roth) Clapp; Columbia University, PhD in American history, 1946; never married; no children. ❖ Taught at Todhunter School in New York City (1930–42); was history instructor at City College of New York (1942–44), Douglass College (1945–46), and Columbia University (1946–47); published doctoral dissertation, *Forgotten First Citizen: John Bigelow* (1947), winning Pulitzer Prize (1948); served as Wellesley College's 8th president, tripling the institution's endowment and building new arts center, faculty club, library wing, and dormitories (1949–66); served as president of Lady Doak College in Madurai, India (1966–67); became cultural attaché to India for US Information Agency (1968) and served as 1st woman minister councilor of public affairs—highest-ranking post at USIA (1970–71); edited *The Modern University* (1950).

CLARA. *Variant of Clare.*

CLARA (c. 1194–1253). *See Clare of Assisi.*

CLARA (1697–1744). Italian saint. Name variations: Clara Isabella Fornari. Born Anna Felicia Fornari in Rome, June 25, 1697; died

1744. ❖ Entered the novitiate of the Poor Clares of Todi; a year later, professed her vows and was given the name Clara Isabella; claimed prolonged visitations from St. Clare of Assisi, St. Catherine of Siena, Jesus Christ, and Mary the Virgin. ❖ See also *Women in World History.*

CLARE. *Variant of Clara.*

CLARE (c. 1194–1253). *See Clare of Assisi.*

CLARE, Ada (1836–1874). American author and actress. Name variations: (real name) Jane McElhenney; (stage name) Agnes Stanfield; (pseudonym) Alastor. Born Jane McElhenney, 1836, in Charleston, South Carolina; died Mar 4, 1874, in New York, NY; dau. of James (lawyer) and Joanna (Wilson) McElhenney (died 1847); m. J. Franklin Noyes (actor), Sept 9, 1868; children: (with Louis Moreau Gottschalk) Aubrey (b. 1857). ❖ Made stage debut in amateur production of *The Hunchback* (1855); began publishing poems, sketches, and stories under pen names "Clare" (1855) and then "Ada Clare"; performed in plays in NY including *Love and Revenge* (1855), *The Wife, Hamlet, The Marble Heart, Jane Eyre* (1856), *The Phantom* (1856) and *Anthony and Cleopatra* (1859); wrote regular column for *Saturday Press;* became known as the "Queen of Bohemia" as a member of literary group which included Henry Clapp, Adah Isaacs Menken, and Walt Whitman (who idealized her as the "New Woman"); in San Francisco, CA, wrote for *Golden Era* and *San Francisco Bulletin* (1864); returned to NY (1864) then toured the South under stage name Agnes Stanfield.

CLARE, Amicia de (1220–1283). English noblewoman. Born May 27, 1220; died 1283; dau. of Gilbert de Clare, 5th earl of Hertford, 1st of Gloucester, and Lady Isabel Marshall (1200–1240); m. Baldwin de Reviers, 6th earl of Devon, 1226; m. Robert de Guines, 1247.

CLARE, countess of. *See Clare, Elizabeth de (1295–1360).*

CLARE, Eleanor de (1292–1337). English noblewoman. Name variations: Alienor or Eleanor Despenser; Eleanor Zouche. Born 1292; died 1337; dau. of Gilbert de Clare, 7th earl of Hertford, 3rd earl of Gloucester, and Joan of Acre (1272–1307); m. Hugh Despenser the Younger, 1306 (executed, Nov 24, 1326); m. William Zouche, 1327; children (1st m.) Isabel Despenser; Edward Despenser (d. 1352).

CLARE, Elizabeth de (1295–1360). Countess of Clare. Name variations: Elizabeth de Burgh. Born in England, 1295 (some sources cite 1291); died Nov 4, 1360, in England; 3rd dau. of Joan of Acre, princess of England, and Gilbert de Clare, 9th earl of Clare, 7th earl of Hertford, 3rd earl of Gloucester (1243–1295); m. John de Burgh, lord of Ulster, 1308 (d. 1313); m. Theobald de Verdon, 1316 (d. 1316); m. Roger Damory, baron of Armoy, 1317 (d. 1322); children: (1st m.) William de Burgh, 3rd earl of Ulster (1312–1333); grandmother of Elizabeth de Burgh (1332–1362). ❖ A powerful and wealthy English noblewoman, was the granddau. of King Edward I Longshanks; married the heir of Ulster, John de Burgh (1308), who died 5 years later; when her brother died (1314), shared the vast holdings of the de Clares (probably the wealthiest of the kingdom) with 2 sisters, Margaret de Clare (c. 1293–1342) and Eleanor de Clare (1292–1337); kidnapped and forced to marry Theobald de Verdon, a noble who wanted her rich estates for himself (1316), but he died several months later; the next year, married the knight Roger Damory but he was executed (1322) by order of Lord Hugh Despenser, who had control of the ineffectual King Edward II; was forcibly taken by orders of Despenser and kept confined until she granted him all her holdings in Wales; when Edward III came to the throne and Despenser lost power (1327), was restored to all her proper inheritance; was known to be a generous founder and pious woman. ❖ See also *Women in World History.*

CLARE, Isabel de (c. 1174–1220). Countess of Pembroke. Name variations: Isabel Marshall, countess Strigoil. Born c. 1174; died 1220; interred at Tintern Abbey; dau. of Richard de Clare (b. 1130), 2nd earl of Pembroke, and Aoife (Eva) MacMurrough, countess of Ireland; m. William Marshall (b. 1146), 4th earl of Pembroke, in Aug 1189; children: William Marshall, 5th earl of Pembroke; Richard Marshall, 6th earl of Pembroke; Maud Marshall (d. 1248, who m. William de Warrenne, 6th earl of Warrenne & Surrey); Gilbert Marshall, 7th earl of Pembroke; Sybilla Marshall; Isabel Marshall (1200–1240); Joan Marshall (d. after 1234, who m. Warine de Monchensy, lord of Swanscombe); Eve de Braose; Walter Marshall, 8th earl of Pembroke; Anselme Marshal, 9th earl of Pembroke.

CLARE, Isabel de.
See Avisa of Gloucester (d. 1217).
See Marshall, Isabel (1200–1240).

CLARE, Isabel de (1226–1254). Scottish noblewoman. Name variations: Isobel de Clare. Born Nov 8, 1226; died in 1254; dau. of Gilbert de Clare, 5th earl of Hertford, 1st earl of Gloucester, and Lady Isabel Marshall (1200–1240); m. Robert Bruce (1210–1295), lord of Annandale, May 12, 1240; children: Robert Bruce (1253–1304), earl of Carrick (who m. Marjorie of Carrick); William Bruce; Bernard of Conington and Exton; Richard Bruce.

CLARE, Joan de (c. 1268–after 1322). *See Joan de Clare.*

CLARE, Margaret de (1249–1313). Countess of Cornwall. Name variations: Marguerite de Clere. Born 1249; died Feb 1313; buried at Chertsey Abbey, Surrey, England; dau. of Richard de Clare, 6th earl of Hertford, 2nd earl of Gloucester, and Maud Lacey; m. Edmund Plantagenet, 2nd earl of Cornwall, Oct 6, 1272 (div. 1293).

CLARE, Margaret de (fl. 1280–1322). English noblewoman. Name variations: Margaret de Clare; Margaret de Badlesmere; Marguerite de Clere; Lady Badlesmere. Fl. between 1280 and 1322; dau. of Thomas de Clare, lord of Thomond, and Juliane Fitzgerald; m. Gilbert de Umphraville, 1289; m. Bartholomew Badlesmere (d. 1322), Lord Badlesmere, 1312; children: Elizabeth Badlesmere (fl. 1315–1342); Sir Giles Badlesmere; Maud Badlesmere (d. 1366, who m. John de Vere, 7th earl of Oxford). ❖ Thought to be Lady Badlesmere who was sent to the Tower of London with her children for not permitting Edward II's queen, Isabella of France (1296–1358), to enter her castle with armed troops at Leeds, Kent (fighting ensued and some of the queen's attendants were killed). ❖ See also *Women in World History.*

CLARE, Margaret de (c. 1293–1342). Countess of Cornwall and Gloucester. Born c. 1293; died 1342; dau. of Gilbert de Clare, 7th earl of Hertford, 3rd of Gloucester, and Joan of Acre (1272–1307); granddau. of King Edward I Longshanks; m. Piers Gaveston, earl of Cornwall, 1307; m. Hugh Audley, earl of Gloucester, 1317; children: (2nd m.) Margaret Audley (who m. Ralph Stafford, 1st earl of Stafford).

CLARE, Mary (1894–1970). English stage and screen actress. Born July 17, 1894, in London, England; died Aug 29, 1970, in London; married L. Mawhood (of the Royal Fusiliers). ❖ Appeared in over 400 stage and film productions; made London stage debut (1912); films include *The Life of Lord Byron* (as Lady Caroline Lamb), *The Constant Nymph, The Lady Vanishes, The Citadel, Cavalcade, No Orchids for Miss Blandish, Ladies in Retirement, Macbeth, The Fugitive* and *Oliver Twist.*

CLARE, Maud de (fl. 1230–1250). *See Lacey, Maud.*

CLARE, Saint (c. 1194–1253). *See Clare of Assisi.*

CLARE DEI SCIFFI (c. 1194–1253). *See Clare of Assisi.*

CLARE JOSEPH, Sister (1755–1830). *See Dickinson, Frances.*

CLARE OF ASSISI (c. 1194–1253). Italian saint and abbess. Name variations: St. Clare; St. Clara; Santa Clara d'Assisi; Claire d'Assise; Clare dei Sciffi; Chiara di Favorone. Born 1193 or 1194 in Assisi, Umbria, in Central Italy; died after a long illness, Aug 11, 1253, in Assisi; dau. of Ortolana (who would later join her daughter's convent) and Favorone (or Favarone) Offreduccio (noble and crusader); sister of Agnes of Assisi; was literate in both Italian and Latin. ❖ Founder of the Franciscan nuns, a community that formed a refuge for women desiring to pursue the religious life by renouncing the world; met Francis (later St. Francis of Assisi) and entered religious life (1212); with her official Rule finally approved, became abbess of the Poor Ladies of San Damiano, later known as the Poor Clares or the Clarisses (1215); though the pope did not permit her to adopt poverty as one of her guiding principles; gave much of her energy to changing this policy, and the pope finally acceded (1228); canonized as St. Clare (1255). The Church of St. Clare was built in Assisi (1260). ❖ See also Armstrong and Brady, *Francis and Clare: The Complete Works* (Paulist, 1982); Nesta de Robeck, *St. Clare of Assisi* (Bruce, 1951); and *Women in World History.*

CLARENCE, duchess of.
See Visconti, Violet (c. 1353–1386).
See Neville, Isabel (1451–1476).
See Adelaide of Saxe-Meiningen (1792–1849).

CLARENDON, countess of (d. 1725). *See Hyde, Jane.*

CLARICIA OF AUGSBURG (fl. 1220). German manuscript illuminator. Fl. in 1220 in Augsburg, Germany. ❖ Worked as a manuscript illuminator at the convent of Augsburg, one of the very few women illuminators who actually signed one of her creations, an ornate initial Q in the text of a Psalter.

CLARINDA

See Egerton, Sarah Fyge (c. 1670–1723).
See Maclehose, Agnes (1759–1841).

CLARK. *Variant of Clarke, Clerk, and Clerke.*

CLARK, Arizona Donnie (1872–1935). See Barker, Ma.

CLARK, Barbara Lynne (1958—). Canadian swimmer. Born Sept 24, 1958. ❖ At Montreal Olympics, won a bronze medal in 4x100-meter freestyle relay (1976).

CLARK, Catherine (1870–1927). See Riwai, Kiti Karaka.

CLARK, Catherine Anthony (1892–1977). Canadian children's writer. Born Catherine Smith, 1892, in London, England; died 1977. ❖ Immigrated to Canada (1914); writings, influenced by Native Canadian folklore and the British Columbia wilderness, include *The Golden Pine Cone* (1950), *The Sun Horse* (1951), *The One-Winged Dragon* (1955), *The Silver Man* (1958), *The Diamond Feather; or The Door in the Mountain: A Magic Tale for Children* (1963), *The Man with the Yellow Eyes* (1963) and *The Hunter and the Medicine Man* (1966).

CLARK, Cheryl (1950—). American theatrical dancer and actress. Born Dec 7, 1950, in Boston, Massachusetts. ❖ Danced on scholarship at Harkness Ballet in New York City; appeared in Bob Fosse's *Pippin* (1972) and *Chicago* (1975); on Broadway, danced role of Cassie in *A Chorus Line.*

CLARK, Cora Maris (1885–1967). New Zealand hockey player, coach, and nurse. Born Cora Mildred Maris Clark, Mar 3, 1885, at Auckland, New Zealand; died June 30, 1967, at Auckland; dau. of Richard Maris Clark (insurance manager) and Cora Juliette (Meurant) Clark. ❖ Representative field-hockey player from 1890s, helped to organize, coach, and referee in formative years before establishment of New Zealand's field-hockey association; was the 1st woman to be accredited an umpire by men's association (c. 1914); registered as nurse (1915); worked at Auckland Hospital before becoming private nurse; made life member of New Zealand Women's Hockey Association (1954). ❖ See also *Dictionary of New Zealand Biography* (Vol. 3).

CLARK, Eleanor (1913–1996). American author and travel essayist. Name variations: Eleanor Clark Warren. Born in Los Angeles, California, July 6, 1913; raised in Roxbury, Connecticut; died in Boston, Massachusetts, Feb 16, 1996; dau. of Frederick Huntington (engineer) and Eleanor (Phelps) Clark; attended Rosemary Hall School; graduate of Vassar College, 1934; m. Jan Frankle (Czech secretary to Leon Trotsky), 1937 (div. 1938); m. Robert Penn Warren (1905–1989, author and Pulitzer Prize winner); children: (2nd m.) Rosanna Warren; Gabriel Penn Warren. ❖ In NY, wrote fiction and reviewed for *The New Republic,* worked for the *Partisan Review,* and edited *New Letters in America* for Norton; became a translator for Leon Trotsky while he was in Mexico (1937); worked for Office of Strategic Services in Washington, DC (1943–46); lived in Italy; published 1st book *Rome and a Villa* (1952); married Warren and settled in Fairfield, CT; considered a master stylist, wrote 4 novels (including *The Bitter Box,* 1946, and *Baldur's Gate,* 1970), 3 travel memoirs, children's books, essays, and a memoir about her failing sight, *Eyes, Etc.* Received the National Book Award for *The Oysters of Locmariaquer* (1964). ❖ See also *Women in World History.*

CLARK, Elizabeth Ann (1953—). See Clark, Liddy.

CLARK, Eugenie (1922—). American ichthyologist. Born May 4, 1922, in New York, NY; m. Ilias Papaconstantinou (physician), June 1951 (div. 1967); children: Hera, Aya, Tak, Niki Konstatinou. ❖ Widely known as the "shark lady," awarded scholarship from US Navy and Pacific Science Board to study poisonous fish in South Pacific (1949); traveled to Red Sea to collect poisonous fish; published *Lady with a Spear* (1953), based on work in Pacific and Red Sea; was founding director of Cape Haze Marine Laboratory in Florida (1955–67), where intelligence of sharks was among her primary studies; taught at Hunter College (1953–54), City University of New York (1966–67), and New England Institute for Medical Research (1966–68); served as full professor (1973–92) in Department of Zoology at University of Maryland and became senior research scientist, Professor Emerita, in Department of Biology (1992);

dedicated to conservation, helped make Ras Muhammad into Egypt's 1st national park; conducted more than 70 deep submersible dives and authored more than 160 scientific papers. Four fishes have been named in her honor: *Callogobius clarki* (Goren), Family Gobiidae; *Sticharium clarkae* George and Springer, Family Clinidae; *Enneapterygius clarkae* Holleman, Family Tripterygiidae; *Atrobucca geniae* Ben-Tuvia and Trewavas, Family Scienidae.

CLARK, Georgia Neese (1900–1995). American politician. Name variations: Georgia Neese Gray. Born Jan 27, 1900, in Richland, Kansas; died Oct 26, 1995; dau. of a businessman; Washburn College (now Washington University of Topeka), BA in economics, 1921; m. George M. Clark (theatrical manager), Jan 1929 (div.); m. A.J. Gray, Jan 1953. ❖ The 1st woman treasurer of US (1949), served in that capacity until 1953; spent 1920s in NY pursuing a career in the theater and was with Earl Carroll's company for a time; during Depression, took over father's business interests, replacing him as president of Richland State Bank after his death in 1937; elected to Democratic National Committee (1936), supported election of Truman (1948); served as chair of the advisory council of the Small Business Administration (1967).

CLARK, Helen (1954—). English politician and member of Parliament. Born Helen Dyche, Dec 23, 1954, in UK; m. 2nd husband Alan Clark, 2001. ❖ Representing Labour, elected to House of Commons for Peterborough (1997, 2001); lost general election (2005).

CLARK, Helen Elizabeth (1950—). Prime minister of New Zealand. Born Helen Elizabeth Clark, Feb 26, 1950, in Hamilton, New Zealand. ❖ A modern social democrat, lectured in political studies, Auckland University (1977–81); elected Labour MP for Mt. Albert (1981); guided 4th Labour Government's anti-nuclear policy as chair of the Foreign Affairs and Defence Committee; was Minister of Housing (1987–89) and Conservation (1987–89); became Minister of Health (1989) and Minister of Labour (1989); was deputy prime minister (1989–90), then deputy leader of the opposition (1990–93), the 1st woman to hold both posts; elected prime minister of New Zealand (1999). Awarded Peace Prize of the Danish Peace Foundation (1986).

CLARK, Hilda (1881–1955). British Quaker relief worker, pacifist and physician. Born 1881 in Somerset, England; died 1955 in Somerset; life companion of Edith Pye (1876–1965, nurse and pacifist); dau. of the owner of a shoe factory in Somerset (family was actively involved with Society of Friends); attended The Mount School in York; obtained degrees from London University. ❖ Medical doctor who was involved in the suffragist movement, became Tuberculosis Officer at Portsmouth; with Edmund Harvey, founded Friends War Victims Relief (1914) and was the 1st medical organizer of a team in France; went to Vienna with Edith Pye (1919) to help starving populace and fight TB and rickets; did peace work for League of Nations and Women's International League and became honorary secretary of Women's Peace Crusade; worked with Greek, Austrian and German refugees (1920s–30s) and served on board of directors of International Commission for Refugee Children (1938–45); in later years, helped Soldiers', Sailors' and Airmen's Families Association in Kent.

CLARK, Jearl (1966—). See Miles, Jearl.

CLARK, Joan (1934—). Canadian novelist and children's writer. Born 1934 in Liverpool, Nova Scotia, Canada; attended Acadia University. ❖ Worked as schoolteacher in Maritimes and Alberta; co-founded literary magazine *Dandelion* (1974) and served as president of Writers' Guild of Alberta and Writers' Alliance of Newfoundland and Labrador; writings for children include *Girl of the Rockies* (1968), *Thomasina and the Trout Tree* (1971), *The Leopard and the Lily* (1984), *The Hand of Robin Squires* (1977), *Wild Man of the Woods* (1985), *The Moons of Madeleine* (1987) and *The Dream Carvers* (1995); works for adults include *From a High Thin Wire* (1982), *The Victory of Geraldine Gull: A Novel* (1988), *Swimming Toward the Light: Short Stories* (1990) and *Eiriksdottir: A Tale of Dreams and Luck: A Novel* (1994). Received Canadian Authors Association Award for Fiction (1989), Marian Engel Award (1991), and Geoffrey Bilson Award for Historical Fiction for Young People (1995).

CLARK, Judy (1950—). See Dickinson, Judy.

CLARK, Karen (1972—). Canadian synchronized swimmer. Born April 9, 1972, in Montreal, Quebec, Canada. ❖ Won a team silver medal at Atlanta Olympics (1996).

CLARK, Kate (1870–1927). See Riwai, Kiti Karaka.

CLARK, Kate Emma (1847–1926). New Zealand society leader, artist, writer, and patron of the arts. Name variations: Kate Emma Woolnough. Born Kate Emma Woolnough, May 15, 1847, in Ipswich, Suffolk, England; died Nov 3, 1926, at Auckland, New Zealand; dau. of Henry Woolnough (architect) and Susan (Bonner) Woolnough; m. James McCosh Clark (businessman and mayor), 1875 (died 1898); children: 5. ❖ Worked as researcher for writers before marriage; became society leader of Auckland and was active in numerous charitable organizations; was also painter and patron of music and art; returned to England following husband's several business failures; pursued career as writer and published *A Southern Cross Fairy Tale* (1891), *Persephone and Other Poems* (1894), and *Maori Tales and Legends* (1896); also contributed articles and short stories to newspapers and magazines. ❖ See also *Dictionary of New Zealand Biography* (Vol. 2).

CLARK, Kelly (1983—). American snowboarder. Born July 26, 1983, in Newport, Rhode Island. ❖ Won Jr. World championships (2000); won halfpipe silver medal at Goodwill Games (2000); won a gold medal for halfpipe at Salt Lake City (2002), the 1st Olympic snowboarding gold in US history; won Grand Prix finals (2002); won gold in Superpipe at X Games (Winter 2002); other 1st-place finishes include: USSA Snowboarding championships, Okemo, VT, in Boardercross (2000); Vans Triple Crown, Sierra-at-Tahoe, CA, in Halfpipe (2001); Grand Prix X-NIX Finals, Sunday River, ME, in Boardercross and Halfpipe (2001); and Grand Prix, Mt. Bachelor, OR, in Halfpipe (2002). Given ESPY Award by Women's Sports Foundation (2002).

CLARK, Kitty (1870–1927). See *Riwai, Kiti Karaka.*

CLARK, Laurel (1961–2003). American astronaut and mission specialist. Born Laurel Blair Salton, Mar 10, 1961, in Iowa, but raised in Racine, Wisconsin; died Feb 1, 2003, when Space Shuttle *Columbia* disintegrated over the southern US; University of Wisconsin–Madison, BS in zoology (1983), doctorate in medicine (1987); postgraduate training in pediatrics, Naval Hospital, Bethesda, MD; m. Jonathan Clark (NASA flight surgeon), 1991; children: son Iain Clark. ❖ Captain in the US Navy, served as a submarine medical officer, diving medical officer, and flight surgeon, before being chosen for the US space program (April 1996); member of the flight crew of the STS–107 *Columbia* (Jan 16–Feb 1, 2003) who successfully conducted 80 experiments before the mission ended abruptly on reentry, 16 minutes prior to scheduled landing.

CLARK, Lesley Ann (1948—). Australian politician. Born Aug 10, 1948, in Harwich, England. ❖ Was a lecturer in education at James Cook University; as a member of the Australian Labor Party, served in the Queensland Parliament for Barron River (1989–95, 1998–2004, 2005); named parliamentary secretary to the premier and minister for Trade in Far North Queensland (2001).

CLARK, Liddy (1953—). Australian politician. Name variations: Elizabeth Ann Clark. Born Nov 6, 1953, in Adelaide, Australia. ❖ Actor, director, and producer; as a member of the Australian Labor Party, elected to the Queensland Parliament for Clayfield (2001); named acting deputy speaker (2001).

CLARK, Lynda (1949—). Scottish politician and member of Parliament. Born Feb 26, 1949. ❖ Called to the English Bar (1990); representing Labour, elected to House of Commons for Edinburgh Pentlands (1997, 2001); was advocate general for Scotland, Department for Constitutional Affairs (1999–2005); left Parliament (2005).

CLARK, Mamo (1914–1986). American actress. Name variations: Mamo. Born Dec 6, 1914, in Honolulu, Hawaii; died Dec 18, 1986, in Panorama City, California; m. James Rawley (actor-teacher); children: son. ❖ Cast opposite Clark Gable in *Mutiny on the Bounty* (1935); other films include *The Hurricane, Hawaii Calls, One Million B.C.* and *Girl from God's Country.*

CLARK, Marguerite (1883–1940). American stage and silent-screen actress. Born Helen Marguerite Clark in Avondale, Ohio, Feb 22, 1883; died in New York City, Sept 25, 1940; educated in public schools and in a convent school in St. Martin, Ohio; m. Harry P. Williams (New Orleans businessman), Aug 1918 (died 1936). ❖ One time rival to Mary Pickford, began career on stage, making NY debut in chorus of *The Belle of Bohemia* (1900); came to prominence as Polly in *Mr. Pickwick* (1903); also appeared in *Babes in Toyland, The Pied Piper, Baby Mine* and *Snow White;* signed with Famous Players and had huge success in 1st film, *Wildflower* (1914); one of the most beloved stars of the silent era, went on to perform in such films as *The Goose Girl* (1915), *Molly Make-Believe* (1916), *Snow White* (1917), *Prunella* (1918), *Mrs. Wiggs of the Cabbage Patch* (1918), *All-of-a-Sudden Peggy* (1920) and *Scrambled Wives* (1921); played double roles in 2 films: *The Prince and the Pauper* and *Topsy and Eva.* ❖ See also *Women in World History.*

CLARK, Marjorie (b. 1909). South African hurdler. Born Nov 6, 1909. ❖ At Los Angeles Olympics, won a bronze medal in the 80-meter hurdles (1932).

CLARK, Marjory (1900–1952). See *Hawtrey, Marjory.*

CLARK, Mary Ellen (1962—). American diver. Born Dec 25, 1962, in Newtown Square, Pennsylvania; graduated Pennsylvania State University, 1985. ❖ Won a bronze medal at Barcelona Olympics (1992) and a bronze medal at Atlanta Olympics (1996), both for 10-meter platform.

CLARK, Mary Higgins (1929—). American mystery and suspense writer. Born Mary Higgins, Dec 14, 1929, in New York, NY; dau. of Luke Joseph (restaurant owner) and Nora C. (Durkin) Higgins (buyer); Fordham University, BA in philosophy, 1974; m. Warren F. Clark (airline executive), Dec 26, 1949 (died Sept 26, 1964); m. Raymond Charles Ploetz (attorney), Aug 8, 1978 (annulled); m. John J. Coheeney, Nov 3, 1996; children: (1st m.) Marilyn, Warren, David, Patricia and Carol Higgins Clark (mystery writer). ❖ Began career as a stewardess for Pan-American Airlines (1949–50); served as a radio scriptwriter and producer for Robert G. Jennings (1965–70); was vice president of Aerial Communications for radio programming (1970–80), then became creative director of David J. Clark Enterprises (1980); served as chair of International Crime Writers Congress (1988) and president of Mystery Writers of America (1989); following 1st husband's death, began writing; published 1st novel, *Where Are the Children?* (1975), which was a best-seller, followed by *A Stranger Is Watching* (1978), a 2nd blockbuster that was filmed in 1982; also wrote *A Cry in the Night* (1982), *Stillwatch* (1984), *Weep No More, My Lady* (1987), *Loves Music, Loves to Dance* (1991), *Remember Me* (1994), *Silent Night* (1995) and *Moonlight Becomes You* (1996), among others.

CLARK, Mattie Moss (1925–1994). Gospel singer. Born 1925 in Selma, Alabama; died Sept 22, 1994, in Southfield, Michigan; children: daughters Jackie, Denise, Elbernita (called Twinkie), Dorinda, and Karen became a famed gospel group known as the Clark Sisters. ❖ One of America's leading female choir directors, trained gospel headliners Donald Vails, Rance Allen, and Beverly Glenn; as national minister of music for the Churches of God in Christ, directed many choirs, the most famous of which was the Churches of God in Christ Southwest Michigan State Choir; founded the Clark Conservatory of Music in Detroit. ❖ See also *Women in World History.*

CLARK, Maureen (1952—). See *McTeer, Maureen.*

CLARK, Nancy Talbot (1825–1901). American physician. Name variations: Nancy Talbot; Nancy E. Clark. Born Nancy Talbot, May 22, 1825, in Sharon, Massachusetts; died July 28, 1901, in Haverford, Pennsylvania; dau. of Josiah and Mary (Richards) Talbot; m. Champion W. Clark (dentist), 1845; m. Amos Binney, July 1856; children: (1st m.) 1; (2nd m.) 6. ❖ Taught at Norwood, MA, schools; married and moved to Baltimore, MD; after death of 1st husband and child, was 1st female admitted to Western Reserve University's medical program in Cleveland, OH (graduated 1852); established successful Boston practice, but was rejected from Massachusetts Medical Society; continued medical studies at La Maternité in Paris, France; established free dispensary for women and children (1874). Became 2nd woman to graduate from conventional medical college in US after Elizabeth Blackwell; was 1st woman in US to apply for state medical society membership (MA).

CLARK, Peggy (c. 1916–1996). American lighting designer. Born Margaret Bronson Clark, c. 1916; died June 19, 1996, age 80, in Lexington, Georgia. ❖ Made career debut (1941); designed over 60 Broadway shows, including *Brigadoon, Auntie Mame, Bye Bye Birdie, Paint Your Wagon, Pal Joey, Wonderful Town, Threepenny Opera* and *Medea* (with Judith Anderson); often worked with George Abbott.

CLARK, Petula (1932—). English actress and singer. Name variations: Pet Clark. Born Petula Sally Olwen Clark, Nov 15, 1932, in Ewell, Surrey, England; m. Claude Wolff (French businessman), 1961; children: Bara, Kate, and Patrick. ❖ At age 11, during WWII, became a popular child singer on BBC and in London concert halls and began to appear in films, including *Strawberry Roan, A Medal for the General, I Know Where I'm Going!, London Town, Dance Hall* and *The Runaway*

Bus; with career on the decline, moved to Paris (1958) and gained a reputation as a concert and recording artist, eventually launching such pop hits as "Downtown," "Don't Sleep in the Subway" and "I Know a Place"; appeared in her own tv specials, had her own series "Petula" (1983), portrayed Norma Desmond in West End production of *Sunset Boulevard* (1999), and starred in such films as *Finian's Rainbow, Goodbye Mr. Chips* and *Never Never Land;* had 15 Top-40 hits. Named Commander of the British Empire (1998).

CLARK, Sally (1958–). New Zealander equestrian. Born Sally Dalrymple, 1958, in New Zealand; dau. of Pat Dalrymple (equestrian); m. A.J. Clark, 1994. ❖ Won a silver medal for indiv. eventing at Atlanta Olympics (1996), on Squirrel Hill.

CLARK, Septima Poinsette (1898–1987). African-American educator and civil-rights activist. Born Septima Poinsette, May 3, 1898, in Charleston, South Carolina; died Dec 15, 1987, on John's Island, South Carolina; dau. of Peter Porcher Poinsette (born a slave on the Poinsette plantation, later worked as caterer on a steamship) and Victoria Warren Anderson Poinsette (freeborn in Charleston and reared in Haiti); graduated (12th grade) from Avery Normal Institute, a private school to train black teachers in Charleston, SC, 1916; Benedict College, AB, 1942; Hampton Institute, MA, 1946; m. Nerie David Clark, May 1920 (died of kidney failure, Dec 1925); children: daughter (who died within a month of birth); son, Nerie David Jr. (b. 1925). ❖ A legend of the civil-rights era, was the driving force behind the influential Southern Christian Leadership Conference Citizenship Schools; unable to teach in Charleston public schools because of race, obtained a position at the Promiseland School on John's Island, SC; took a position with Avery Normal School and joined in a political crusade to change the law barring black teachers in Charleston public schools (1919); enrolled in college, earning bachelor's degree (1942) and master's (1946); as a longtime member of NAACP, refused to renounce her affiliation when South Carolina passed a law prohibiting NAACP membership for state or city employees; thus, was fired from teaching job at Henry Archer School (1956); hired as director of education for Highlander Folk School (HFS) in Tennessee for adult literacy programs; taught skills to enable deep South blacks to qualify to vote and become effective citizens in her Citizenship Schools, based at HFS; because of harassment by Tennessee officials at Highlander, her citizenship training was moved to the Southern Christian Leadership Conference (SCLC), where she continued to conduct literacy training programs that substantially increased the rolls of black voters (early 1960s); retired from SCLC (1970); elected to Charleston School Board (1976). The Septima P. Clark Expressway runs through Charleston (1978). ❖ See also autobiographies *Echo In My Soul* (Dutton, 1962) and (with Cynthia Stokes Brown) *Ready from Within* (Wild Trees, 1986); and *Women in World History.*

CLARK, Sharon Stouder (b. 1948). See Stouder, Sharon.

CLARK SISTERS (fl. 1940s). Singing swing specialists of the 1940s. Name variations: Sentamentalists. Born in US. ❖ The four Clark Sisters—Ann, Jean, Peggy, and Mary Clark—starred as "The Sentimentalists" with Tommy Dorsey's orchestra, doing vocals on "Chicago" and "The Sunny Side of the Street"; sang as instrumentalists, delivering the big-band orchestral stylings of the swing years; albums include *Sing, Sing, Sing!* and *The Clark Sisters Swing Again* on Dot Records. ❖ See also *Women in World History.*

CLARKE. *Variant of Clark, Clerk, and Clerke.*

CLARKE, Betty Ross (1896–1947). American silent-film actress. Name variations: Betty Clark Ross; Betty Ross Clark. Born April 19, 1896, in Langdon, North Dakota; died Feb 2, 1947, in Hollywood, California. ❖ Made film debut in *The Very Idea,* followed by over 30 films, including *Brewster's Millions, Mother o' Mine, At the Sign of the Jack O'Lantern, The Man from Downing Street* and *Judge Hardy's Children.*

CLARKE, Edith (1883–1959). American engineer. Born Feb 10, 1883, in Howard Co., Maryland; died Oct 29, 1959, in Olney, Maryland; dau. of a lawyer-farmer; Vassar College, AB in math and astronomy, 1908; civil engineering courses at University of Wisconsin, 1911–12; Massachusetts Institute of Technology, MS in electrical engineering (1919). ❖ Was the 1st woman elected to the Society of Electrical Engineers, the 1st woman to earn a master's degree from the Massachusetts Institute of Technology (MIT), the 1st woman to address the American institute of Electrical Engineers, and the 1st woman to teach electrical engineering in an American university; worked as an electrical engineer for General

Electric (GE) for 23 years, analyzing power transmission problems across the US. ❖ See also *Women in World History.*

CLARKE, Mrs. Edward (1906–1983). See Lutyens, Elisabeth.

CLARKE, Eldece (1965—). Bahamian runner. Name variations: Eldece Clarke-Lewis. Born Feb 13, 1965, in Bahamas; Hampton University (Virginia), BS in Psychology and Sociology; m. Iram Lewis (sprinter). ❖ Known as one of the "Golden Girls," won a silver medal for 4 x 100-meter relay at Atlanta Olympics (1996); won a gold medal for 4 x 100-meter relay at World championships (1999). Received Silver Jubilee Award (1998) and Bahamas Order of Merit (2000).

CLARKE, Eliza or Elizabeth (c. 1764–1824). *See Cobbold, Elizabeth.*

CLARKE, Gillian (1937—). Welsh poet, editor and essayist. Born Gillian Williams, June 8, 1937, in Cardiff, Wales; dau. of Penri Williams and Ceinwin Evans Williams; m. Peter Clarke, 1960; children: 3. ❖ Known for her use of Celtic meter and interest in lives of Welsh rural women, published several translations from Welsh, including *One Moonlit Night* (1991) and *Cusan Dyn Dall* (2000); poetry collections include *Snow on the Mountain* (1971), *Letter From a Far Country* (1982), *Letting in the Rumour* (1989), *The Animal Wall* (1999), and *Owain Glyn Dwr* (2000); poems have been translated into 10 languages.

CLARKE, Grace Julian (1865–1938). American suffragist and clubwoman. Born Grace Giddings Julian, Sept 11, 1865, in Centerville, Indiana; died June 18, 1938, in Irvington, Indiana; dau. of George Washington Julian (abolitionist and Republican US congressional representative) and Laura (Giddings) Julian; m. Charles B. Clarke (attorney and politician), Sept 11, 1887. ❖ Promoted cause of woman suffrage among women's clubs; served as president of Indiana Federation of Women's Clubs (1909–11); served as director and national press chair of General Federation of Women's Clubs (1912–16); helped found Woman's School Commissioner Organization (1910, later Woman's School League) to elect a woman to Indianapolis school board; with Dr. Amelia Keller and others, formed Woman's Franchise League of Indiana; appointed head of women's division of Federal Employment Bureau in Indianapolis by President Woodrow Wilson (1916); worked on behalf of world peace and supported idea of a League of Nations; collected father's *Later Speeches* (1889) and wrote about him in *Some Impressions* (1902) and *George W. Julian* (1923).

CLARKE, Helen (c. 1897–?). American ballroom and theatrical dancer. Born c. 1897 in Omaha, Nebraska. ❖ Appeared in numerous shows at the Princess Theater, including *Nobody Home* (1915), *Love O'Mike* (1917), *Oh, My Dear* (1918) and *La, La Lucille* (1919); worked in clubs around New York City, specializing in Hesitations and one-steps; partnered for ballroom dancing with Quentin Tod.

CLARKE, Helen Archibald (1860–1926). American writer and publisher. Name variations: (joint pseudonym) H.A.C. Born Helen Archibald Clarke, Nov 13, 1860, in Philadelphia, Pennsylvania; died Feb 8, 1926, in Boston, Massachusetts; dau. of Hugh Archibald Clarke (professor of music) and Jane (Searle) Clarke; studied music as a special student at University of Pennsylvania; never married; lived with Charlotte Endymion Porter; no children. ❖ With Charlotte Endymion Porter, founded the literary magazine *Poet Lore;* writings include *Apparitions* (1892), *Browning's Italy* (1907), *Browning's England* (1908), *A Child's Guide to Mythology* (1908), *Longfellow's Country* (1909), *Hawthorne's Country* (1910), *The Poets' New England* (1911) and *Browning and His Century* (1912). ❖ See also *Women in World History.*

CLARKE, Julia (d. 1912). American aviator. Born in Chicago, Illinois; died June 17, 1912, in Springfield, Illinois. ❖ Learned to fly in San Diego, CA, and became 3rd American woman to receive pilot's license; died in crash of her Curtiss biplane at the Illinois State Fairgrounds (1912).

CLARKE, Kathleen (1878–1972). Irish republican activist. Name variations: Mrs. Tom Clarke. Born Kathleen Daly in Limerick, Ireland, April 11, 1878; died in Liverpool, England, Sept 29, 1972; dau. of Edward Daly and Catherine (O'Mara) Daly; m. Thomas J. Clarke (republican revolutionary), July 16, 1901 (died May 3, 1916); children: John Daly, Thomas and Emmet. ❖ Born into a family that had long been prominent in Irish republican circles, remained a dedicated republican throughout life while witnessing the execution of both her husband and her only brother for the sake of the republican cause; moved to NY and married (1901); returned to Dublin (1907); with Aine Ceannt, started Central Branch of Cumann na mBan and was later president (1914); during the

Rising (1916), was arrested and escorted to Dublin Castle; husband and brother were executed; released from detention, set up Irish Republican Prisoners Dependants' Fund (IRPDF), to help families of the hundreds of men and women who had been deported and interned without trial; elected to executive of Sinn Fein Party and became vice-president of Cumann na mBan (1917); arrested with other Sinn Fein leaders, including Eamon de Valera, on suspicion of plotting with the Germans (1918); though no proof was produced and there was no trial, was imprisoned at Holloway Jail in London and not released until Feb 1919, by which time her health had deteriorated seriously; elected an alderman in the municipal elections for Dublin Corporation (1919); elected to Irish republican parliament, the Dail (1921), but rejected the terms for Irish independence demanded by British government; lost Dail seat in general elections (1922); was on 1st executive of Fianna Fail and briefly elected to Irish Parliament in 1927, though she did not take her seat; accepted nomination for Irish senate (1928) where she served until 1936; was again elected to Dublin Corporation (1930); opposed the clauses of de Valera's 1937 constitution which concerned women and was censured by the party; elected the 1st woman Lord Mayor of Dublin (1939); terminated membership in Fianna Fail (1943); stood as a candidate in general election for the new republican party, Clann na Poblachta, but was defeated (1948). ❖ See also *Revolutionary Woman: An Autobiography* (O'Brien, 1991); and *Women in World History.*

CLARKE, Kathy Johnson (1959—). See Johnson, Kathy.

CLARKE, Mae (1907–1992). American actress and dancer. Born Violet Mary Klotz, Aug 16, 1907, in Philadelphia, Pennsylvania; died April 29, 1992, in Woodland Hills, California; m. Lew Brice (brother of Fanny Brice), 1928 (div.); m. Stephen Bancroft, 1937 (div.); m. Herbert Langdon, 1946 (div.). ❖ At 13, began career with a nightclub act; made NY debut as a specialty dancer on the Mark Strand Roof Garden (1924); on Broadway, appeared in *Sitting Pretty, Gay Paree, The Noose* and *Manhattan Mary;* films include *Big Time, Frankenstein, The Man with Two Faces, Waterloo Bridge, Magnificent Obsession, Flying Tigers, And Now Tomorrow, Annie Get Your Gun, Singin' in the Rain, Pat and Mike* and *Thoroughly Modern Millie;* best remembered as the prostitute Molly Malloy in *The Front Page* and for having a grapefruit shoved in her face by James Cagney in *The Public Enemy;* said to be the model for Lorelei Lee in *Gentlemen Prefer Blondes.*

CLARKE, Martha (1944—). American modern dancer and choreographer. Born June 3, 1944, in Baltimore, Maryland. ❖ Danced with Lucas Hoving's concert group in New York City in *Suite for a Summer Day* (1962); performed with Anna Sokolow's company in *Session for Six, Lyric Suite* and *Dreams;* joined acrobatic troupe Pilobolus (1973–79) where she performed in collaborative works, in duets created with Robert Morgan Barnett, and in Sokolow-inspired solos; began collaborating with Barnett and French choreographer Felix Blaska (1979), creating works for chamber company Crowsnest. Choreographies include (with Alison Chase) *Two Bits* (1973), (with Barnett) *Terra Cotta* (1974), (with others) *Ciona* (1975), *Grey Room* (1977), *Wakefield* (1977), (with Blaska) *La Marquese de Solana* (1979) and (with Barnett and Blaska) *Haiku* (1979).

CLARKE, Mary (1924—). American major general. Born Dec 3, 1924, in Rochester, NY. ❖ Began military career in Fort Des Moines, Iowa (1945); served in Woman's Army Corp (WAC) during WWII; became last commander of WAC; was the 1st woman promoted to major general in the US Army (1978); retired at age 56 after 36 years in service (1981); became member of Defense Advisory Committee on Women in the Services (1984).

CLARKE, Mary Anne (c. 1776–1852). English royal mistress. Name variations: Maryanne Clark. Born Mary Anne Thompson, either in London or at Oxford, c. 1776; died at Boulogne, June 21, 1852; dau. of a man named Thompson (impoverished bricklayer); m. a man named Clarke (proprietor of a stonemasonry business), c. 1794. ❖ After liaisons with Sir Charles Milner and Sir James Brudenell, became mistress of Frederick Augustus, duke of York and Albany, 2nd son of King George III (1804); used the duke's position (commander-in-chief of the British army) to sell army commissions, causing a public scandal (1809). ❖ See also *Women in World History.*

CLARKE, Mary Bayard (1827–1886). American author and editor. Name variations: (pseudonyms) Tenella; Stuart Leigh. Born Mary Bayard Devereux, May 13, 1827, in Raleigh, North Carolina; died Mar 30, 1886, in New Bern, North Carolina; dau. of Thomas Pollok Devereux (planter and lawyer) and Catharine Anne (Johnson) Devereux

(died 1836); 1st cousin of Lillie Devereux Blake (writer and suffragist); m. Capt. William John Clarke (veteran of Mexican War and lawyer), April 6, 1848; children: Francis Devereux Clarke, William Edwards Clarke, Thomas Pollok Clarke, and Mary D. Clarke. ❖ Edited 2-vol. *Wood-Notes; or Carolina Carols* (1854), the 1st anthology of NC verse; published patriotic poems during Civil War in *Southern Illustrated News;* after war, published fiction and other prose under pseudonym "Stuart Leigh"; served as assistant editor of *Southern Field and Fireside* and as contributor to *The Old Guard* and *The Land We Love;* known for promoting literary culture of NC. Other works include *Mosses from a Rolling Stone* (verse, 1866) and *Clytie and Zenobia* (narrative poem, 1871).

CLARKE, Mary Cowden (1809–1898). English Shakespearean scholar. Name variations: Mary Cowden-Clarke. Born Mary Victoria Novello in London, England, June 22, 1809; died in Italy, Jan 12, 1898; dau. of Vincent Novello (composer and organist) and Mary Sabilla Hehl; m. Charles Cowden Clarke (literary historian), 1828. ❖ At 15, was a contributor to magazines; worked for 16 years on *Complete Concordance to Shakespeare,* which was published in London (1846) in a large octavo of 860 pages, and remained the standard concordance until end of 19th century; was also editor of the *Musical Times* (1853–56). ❖ See also autobiography *My Long Life* (1896); and *Women in World History.*

CLARKE, Mary Edith (1888–1979). See Scott, Mary Edith.

CLARKE, Mary Frances (1803–1887). Irish-American religious order founder. Born Mar 2, 1803, in Dublin, Ireland; died Dec 4, 1887, in Dubuque, Iowa. ❖ With 4 other religious women, immigrated to America (1833), taught in Philadelphia, Pennsylvania, and organized as the Sisters of Charity of the Blessed Virgin Mary (Nov 1, 1833), of which Clarke served as superior; on invitation of Bishop Matthias Loras and Father Pierre De Smet, traveled to Dubuque with 4 others, becoming the 1st Roman Catholic nuns in Iowa Territory (1833); was influential in opening the St. Mary's Female Academy (1843), the 1st women's college in IA (later known as Mt. St. Joseph College, then Clarke College).

CLARKE, Mary Goulden (d. 1910). English suffragist. Died in Dec 25, 1910, in Manchester, England; dau. of Robert Goulden (owner of calico-printing and bleach works) and Sophia Jane Craine (Crane) Goulden; sister of Emmeline Pankhurst (1858–1928); married. ❖ Became an organizer for the WSPU in Brighton and was arrested for window-breaking on Black Friday; treated roughly by police and bands of toughs, and force-fed in jail for one month, died 2 days after her release. ❖ See also *Women in World History.*

CLARKE, Maryanne (c. 1776–1852). See Clarke, Mary Anne.

CLARKE, Maura (1931—). American nun and martyr. Born Jan 13, 1931, in Queens, NY; killed Dec 2, 1980, in El Salvador. ❖ Joined the Maryknoll sisters (1950); was sent to Nicaragua where she taught school and did pastoral work in Siuna and later Managua (1959–79); following the appeal of Archbishop Romero for help in El Salvador, relocated there (Aug 1980); was slain by National Guardsmen in El Salvador, along with Ita Ford, Dorothy Kazel and Jean Donovan.

CLARKE, Patricia Hannah (1919—). Welsh biochemist. Name variations: Patricia Green; Patricia Hannah Green. Born Patricia Hannah Green, July 29, 1919, in Pontypridd, Wales; m. Michael Clarke, 1940; children: 2 (born 1947 and 1949). ❖ Attended Howells School in Wales on scholarship and Girton College in Cambridge as a Sparke scholar; employed in war work, testing explosives in Woolwich and Swansea Arsenal; joined B.C.J.G. Knight at Wellcome Research Laboratories in Beckenham, Kent (1944–47) to work on *Clostridia* (pathogenic) immunization methods (research results were later published in *Journal of General Microbiology,* 1947); worked with S.T. Cowan at National Collection of Type Cultures to establish micromethods to identify bacteria based on enzyme reactions (1951–53); employed as lecturer (1953–66), as reader (1966–74), and as microbial biochemistry professor (1974–84) at University College in London; revealed illuminating research results on synthesis of permeases and novel enzymes and later on mechanism of gene regulation. Elected as fellow (1976), council member, and vice president (1981–82) to Royal Society.

CLARKE, Rebecca (1886–1979). English composer and violinist. Name variations: (pseudonym) Anthony Trent. Born in Harrow, England, Aug 27, 1886; died in New York, NY, Oct 13, 1979; m. James Friskin (pianist), 1944. ❖ Studied with Sir Frederick Bridge, Sir Charles Stanford, and Lionel Tetris, and at Royal College of Music; submitted compositions under name Anthony Trent, since publishers were more interested in modern compositions by someone presumed to be male; also composed under her own name; founded an all-women's piano quartet, the English Ensemble (1913); won 2nd place at Berkshire Festival in Tanglewood, MA (1919 and 1921); was the only woman among more than 30 composers present at International Society for Contemporary Music in San Francisco (1942) where her Prelude, Allegro, and Pastorale for clarinet and viola was enthusiastically received; had work widely published by Winthrop Rogers and Oxford University Press in UK and by G. Schirmer in US; was particularly known for her chamber music, which favored English musical themes and texts by Shakespeare, William Butler Yeats, and William Blake; toured widely as concert violinist with pianist husband. In recent years, several of her important chamber music compositions, including the Piano Trio, the Viola Sonata, and the Prelude for Viola and Clarinet, have been recorded.

CLARKE, Rebecca Sophia (1833–1906). American children's author. Name variations: (pseudonym) Sophie May. Born Feb 22, 1833, in Norridgewock, Maine; died Aug 16, 1906, Norridgewock; dau. of Asa and Sophia (Bates) Clarke; sister of Sarah Jones Clarke (children's author known as Penn Shirley). ❖ Published 1st story at age 28 in *Memphis Daily Appeal;* under name Sophie May, had great popularity as author of more than 40 vols. for children, including "Little Prudy" series (6 vols., 1863–65) and "Dotty Dimple" series (6 vols., 1867–69); contributed stories to juvenile magazines including *Little Pilgrim* (where "Prudy Parlin" stories 1st appeared) and *Merry's Museum;* took settings for many books from hometown of Norridgewock.

CLARKE, Sara J. (1823–1904). *See Lippincott, Sara Clarke.*

CLARKE, Sarah Jones (1840–1929). American children's author. Name variations: (pseudonym) Penn Shirley. Born Sept 12, 1840, in Norridgewock, Maine; died 1929 in Norridgewock; dau. of Asa and Sophia (Bates) Clarke; sister of Rebecca Sophia Clarke (children's author). ❖ Enjoyed limited success as author of 10 children's books (1886–1902), including "Little Miss Weezy" series (3 vols., 1886–90), "Silver Gate" series (3 vols., 1895–97) and "Boy Donald" series (3 vols., 1900–02).

CLARKE, Shirley (1925–1997). American filmmaker. Born Shirley Brumberg, Oct 2, 1925, in New York, NY; died in Boston, Massachusetts, Sept 23, 1997; attended Stephens College, Bennington College, Johns Hopkins University, and University of North Carolina; m. Bert Clarke (div. 1963); children: Wendy Clarke (b. 1951). ❖ Pioneer of the independent film movement, began career as a choreographer; started to develop what dance critic John Martin dubbed "Cine-Dance" with 1st film *Dance in the Sun* (1953); helped form New American Cinema Group (1960); completed *The Connection* (1960), a look into the underbelly of life, specifically the drug culture, which won a prize at Cannes Film Festival, but took an 18-month battle with the Supreme Court to gain its release; other films include *Bullfight* (1955), *In Paris Parks* (1955), *A Moment in Love* (1957), *Loops* (1958), *Bridges-Go-Round* (1959), *A Scary Time* (1960), *The Cool World* (1964), *Man in the Polar Regions* (1967), *Portrait of Jason* (1967), *24 Frames Per Second* (1977), *Initiation* (1978), *Four Journeys Into Mystic Time* (1980), (with Sam Shepard) *Savage/Love* (1981), *Tongues* (1983), and a portrait of jazz musician Ornette Coleman, *Ornette: Made In America* (1986). Nominated for American Academy Award for Best Short Subject for *Skyscraper* (1959); won Academy Award for Best Documentary for *Robert Frost: A Lover's Quarrel with the World* (1964). ❖ See also *Women in World History.*

CLARKE, Mrs. Tom (1878–1972). *See Clarke, Kathleen.*

CLARKSON, Cecily (1903–1988). *See Pickerill, Cecily.*

CLARY, Désirée (1777–1860). *See Désirée.*

CLARY, Julie (1771–1845). *See Bonaparte, Julie Clary.*

CLASTER, Nancy (1915–1997). American tv pioneer. Name variations: Miss Nancy. Born Mar 7, 1915; died of cancer, April 25, 1997, in Baltimore, Maryland; m. Bert Claster (tv producer); children: Sally Bell (later host of "Romper Room"). ❖ With husband, created the show "Romper Room" on Baltimore's WBAL-TV (1953), which was quickly franchised in other cities; entertained and educated a generation of children as its host, Miss Nancy, until 1964.

CLAUDE. *Variant of Claudia.*

CLAUDE DE FRANCE (1499–1524). French queen. Name variations: Claudia; Queen Claude; Claude Valois; Claude de Valois; Claude de France. Born Oct 14, 1499, in Romorantin, France; died July 20, 1524, in Blois, Anjou, France; eldest dau. of Louis XII (1462–1515), king of France (r. 1498–1515), and Anne of Brittany (c. 1477–1514); sister of Renée of France (1510–1575); m. Francis, duc d'Angoulême, later Francis I, king of France (r. 1515–1547), May 18, 1515; children: (3 sons) Francis (1518–1536); Henry II (1519–1559), king of France (r. 1547–1559); Charles (1522–1545); (4 daughters) Louise (1515–1517); Charlotte (1516–1524); Madeleine of France (1520–1537, who m. James V, king of Scotland in 1537 and died a few months later); Margaret of Savoy (1523–1574). ❖ A favorite daughter of Louis XII, inherited 2 duchys: Milan and Brittany; was treated harshly by husband Francis I and by regent Louise of Savoy (1476–1531). ❖ See also *Women in World History.*

CLAUDE DE FRANCE (1547–1575). French princess and duchess of Lorraine. Name variations: Claudia; Claude of France. Born Nov 12, 1547; died in 1575; dau. of Catherine de Medici (1519–1589) and Henry II (b. 1519), king of France (r. 1547–1559); sister of Francis II, king of France, Elizabeth of Valois, queen of Spain, Charles IX, king of France, Henry III, king of France, Margaret of Valois, and half-sister of Diane de France (1538–1619); m. Charles II, duke of Lorraine (r. 1545–1608); children: Henry I, duke of Lorraine (r. 1608–1624); Christine of Lorraine (c. 1571–1637, who m. Ferdinand I, grand duke of Tuscany); Francis II, duke of Lorraine (r. 1624–1625).

CLAUDE DES ARMOISES (fl. 1400s). French warrior. Fl. in 1400s. ❖ Like Joan of Arc, claimed to have been instructed by God to wear male attire, and to undertake the life of a soldier; had trouble in Germany with the inquisitor of Cologne, then fled to Italy where she fought in the pope's army, killing 2 men; came to France, where she married a knight, Robert des Armoises, and also became mistress of the bishop of Metz; six years after the Maid of Lorraine had died at the stake, appeared as Joan (1436), and many people, convinced that their heroine had not been burned at Rouen, were persuaded that a woman soldier clad like a man could only be Joan of Arc; was received by the town of Orleans (1439), though she was later arrested and tried, only to resume her life as a soldier.

CLAUDE OF FRANCE. *See Claude de France.*

CLAUDEL, Camille (1864–1943). French sculptor. Pronunciation: Klo-DEL. Born Camille Claudel, Dec 8, 1864, in Fère-en-Tardenois, France; died Nov 19, 1943, in Montdevergues, France; dau. of Louis-Prosper Claudel and Louise-Athénaïse (Cervaux) Claudel; sister of Paul Claudel (renowned poet and diplomat); tutored by sculptor Alfred Boucher and Auguste Rodin; never married. ❖ Sculptor, primarily of small-scale works, noted for their detail and expressive quality, explored portraiture, including a bronze bust of her brother (1881) and a terra cotta head entitled *La Vieille Hélène* (1882); began work as an assistant in the studio of Rodin (1885) and started affair; earned praise for her bronze *Bust of Rodin,* exhibited at Salon of 1892, while her image appeared in some of Rodin's most striking works, among them *Thought* and *The Dawn;* received honorable mention for *Sakuntala* at Salon of 1888; had 1st major exhibition (1888–89); exhibited *The Waltz* (1893), generally considered her masterpiece; left Rodin's studio (1893), then broke with him (1898); continued to exhibit (1898–1908), showing *The Age of Maturity,* a marble *Sakuntala, Perseus and the Gorgon, The Gossips, The Wave* and *Deep Thought,* but showed signs of mental instability; committed to asylum at Ville-Evrard by brother (1913); transferred to asylum at Montdevergues (1914), where she spent remaining 3 decades of her life, virtually cut-off from family and friends; began to receive the recognition she had so long been denied (1951). ❖ See also Reine-Marie Paris, *Camille: The Life of Camille Claudel, Rodin's Muse and Mistress* (trans. by Liliane E. Tuck, Seaver, 1988); film *Camille Claudel,* starring Isabel Adjani; and *Women in World History.*

CLAUDEL, Véronique (1966—). French biathlete. Name variations: Veronique Claudel. Born Nov 22, 1966, in France. ❖ Won a gold medal for 3x7.5km relay at Albertville Olympics (1992); won a bronze medal for 4x7.5km relay at Lillehammer Olympics (1994).

CLAUDIA. *Variant of Claude or Clodia.*

CLAUDIA (c. 94–post 45 BCE). *See Clodia.*

CLAUDIA (fl. 26–36 CE). Biblical woman. Name variations: Claudia Procula. Married Pontius Pilate, Roman procurator of Judea during the time of Jesus' ministry and Crucifixion. ❖ While husband ascended judgment seat to hear the accusations against Jesus, sent a message through a servant imploring Pilate to "have nothing to do with that righteous man, for I have suffered much over Him in a dream." ❖ See also *Women in World History*.

CLAUDIA ACTE (fl. 55–69 CE). *See Acte.*

CLAUDIA ANTONIA (27–66 CE). Roman noblewoman. Born 27 CE; died 66 CE; dau. of Tiberius Claudius Nero Germanicus (10 BCE–54 CE), also known as the Roman Emperor Claudius (r. 41–54 CE), and his 2nd wife Paetina; m. Gnaeus Pompey; m. Faustus Cornelius Sulla Felix, also known as Sulla (consul). ❖ Was an imperial pawn throughout her life, because whomever she married guaranteed a close connection to the imperial house with the potential to affect the imperial succession; after Claudia's mother was replaced by Messalina, constituted a threat to the successional aspirations of Britannicus; 1st husband was executed at Messalina's command; 2nd husband was exiled (58) and eventually murdered (62) at Nero's command; refused all subsequent offers of marriage, including Nero's, which led to her death. ❖ See also *Women in World History*.

CLAUDIA DE MEDICI (1604–1648). *See Medici, Claudia de.*

CLAUDIA FELICITAS (fl. 17th c.). Florentine noblewoman. Born in Florence; dau. of Anna de Medici (b. 1616) and Ferdinand, archduke of Austrian Tyrol; granddau. of Claudia de Medici (1604–1648); 2nd wife of Leopold I, Holy Roman emperor (r. 1658–1705). Leopold's 1st wife was Margaret Theresa of Spain (1651–1673); his 3rd was Eleanor of Pfalz-Neuburg (1655–1720). ❖ In the Uffizi Gallery, there is a portrait of Claudia Felicitas dressed as Galla Placidia.

CLAUDIA OF TUSCANY (1604–1648). *See Medici, Claudia de.*

CLAUDIA QUINTA (fl. 220–206 BCE). Roman woman. Fl. between 220–206 BCE. ❖ When the ship conveying the image of the goddess Cybele grounded in the shallows at the mouth of the Tiber River (206) and the oracles announced that only a chaste woman could move the ship, cleared herself from an accusation of faithlessness by dragging it out of the shallows. ❖ See also *Women in World History*.

CLAUDINE (1451–1514). Ruler of Monaco. Born 1451 in Monaco; died 1514 in Monaco; dau. of Catalan Grimaldi, ruler of Monaco; m. Lambert Grimaldi (Genovese noble and cousin); children: John (later John II of Monaco), Lucien, and Augustin. ❖ At 6, succeeded father as ruler on his death (1657); co-ruled with husband when she came of age. ❖ See also *Women in World History*.

CLAUS, Hildrun (1939—). East German long jumper. Born May 13, 1939, in Germany. ❖ At Rome Olympics, won a bronze medal in the long jump (1960).

CLAUSEN, Stefanie (1900–1981). Danish diver. Born April 1900; died Aug 1981. ❖ At Antwerp Olympics, won a gold medal in platform (1920).

CLAUSS-SZÁRVADY, Wilhelmina (1834–1907). Czech pianist. Name variations: Wilhelmine. Born in Prague, Czechoslovakia, Dec 13, 1834; died in Paris, France, Nov 1, 1907. ❖ Studied in Prague; caused a great stir when she began to tour (1849); said by some to be the artistic rival of Clara Schumann; known throughout 19th-century Europe for renditions of Bach and Beethoven, though also played some Chopin.

CLAVERS, Mrs. Mary (1801–1864). *See Kirkland, Caroline Matilda.*

CLAXTON, Kate (1848–1924). American actress. Born Kate Eliza Cone, Aug 24, 1848, in Somerville, New Jersey; died May 5, 1924, in New York, NY; dau. of Josephine (Martinez) Cone and Spencer Wallace Cone (lawyer); m. Isadore Lyon, 1865 (div.); m. Charles A. Stevenson (English actor), Mar 3, 1878 (annulled); children: 6. ❖ Made 1st professional appearance in Chicago as Mary Blake in *Andy Blake* (1869); made NY debut in Augustin Daly's company in *Man and Wife* (1870); after clash with Daly (1873), performed with A.M. Palmer's company for several seasons and earned fame as Louise in *The Two Orphans* (1874), a role she repeated many times throughout career; was on stage (as Louise) during catastrophic fire at Brooklyn Theater (1876) and helped calm audience; achieved leading lady status with *Ferreol* (1876); toured as star in her own company, performing in *The World Against Her, Conscience* and *The Two Orphans*, among others; appeared with 2nd husband in NY in such works as *Double Marriage* and *Bootles' Baby*.

CLAY, Mrs. Clement C. (1825–1915). *See Clay, Virginia Tunstall.*

CLAY, Laura (1849–1941). American suffragist. Born Feb 9, 1849, in White Hall estate near Lexington, Kentucky; died June 29, 1941, in Lexington, Kentucky; dau. of Cassius Marcellus Clay (antislavery advocate and minister to Russia) and Mary Jane (Warfield) Clay (suffragist); attended University of Michigan and State College of Kentucky; never married; no children. ❖ Served as president (1881–1912) of Kentucky Woman Suffrage Association which was reorganized in 1888 as Kentucky Equal Rights Association; was active in numerous reforms, including property rights for married women; elected 1st auditor of National American Woman Suffrage Association (NAWSA, 1895); as strong supporter of states' rights and white political dominance, was opposed to woman suffrage amendment to federal constitution; increasingly isolated in her positions, resigned from NAWSA and Equal Rights Association (1919); supported Democratic Party and ran unsuccessfully for state senate (1923); active in work with Episcopal church in later years, fought for women's admission to diocesan councils and University of the South. ❖ See also Paul E. Fuller, *Laura Clay and the Women's Rights Movement* (U. of Kentucky Press).

CLAY, Theresa (1911–1995). English entomologist. Born Theresa Rachael Clay, Feb 7, 1911, in England; died 1995; married R.G. Searight, 1975. ❖ Known for expertise on bird lice, went on expeditions to Middle East, Africa, and Arctic (1935–38 and 1946–49); volunteered (1938–49) and later hired as full-time staff member (1949) at British Museum (Natural History); responsible for British Museum's *Phthiraptera* and *Apterygota* section; contributed specimens to British Museum from Pakistan and India (1951), western Himalayas (1957), Trinidad and British Guiana (1961) and Malaysia (1974).

CLAY, Virginia Tunstall (1825–1915). American society leader and suffragist. Name variations: Mrs. Clement C. Clay; Virginia Caroline Tunstall Clay-Clopton; Virginia Tunstall Clopton. Born Virginia Caroline Tunstall, Jan 16, 1825, in Nash Co., North Carolina; died June 23, 1915, near Gurley, Alabama; dau. of Dr. Peyton Randolph Tunstall and Ann (Arrington) Tunstall (died 1828); graduate of Nashville Female Academy, 1840; m. Clement Claiborne Clay (US senator), Feb 1, 1843 (died 1882); m. David Clopton (Alabama Supreme Court justice), Nov 29, 1887 (died 1892); no children. ❖ Was among the brightest figures in Washington society while husband served in the Senate; after husband was accused of complicity in Lincoln's assassination, successfully appealed to President Andrew Johnson for his release; became early advocate of woman suffrage in Alabama and served as president of Alabama Equal Rights Association (1896–1900). Her antebellum memoirs, which were put into narrative form by journalist Ada Sterling, were published as *A Belle of the Fifties* (1904).

CLAY-CLOPTON, Virginia Caroline Tunstall (1825–1915). *See Clay, Virginia Tunstall.*

CLAYBURGH, Alma (d. 1958). American opera and concert singer. Died Aug 4, 1958, age 77, in New York, NY. ❖ Retired from grand opera (1931); later sang often on NY concert stages.

CLAYDEN, Pauline (1922—). English ballet dancer. Born 1922 in London, England. ❖ Performed with numerous companies, including the Royal Opera House at Covent Garden, dancing in operas (1938), and with London Ballet and its offspring Ballet Arts and Ballet Rambert (c. 1940); joined Sadler's Wells Ballet (1942), where she created roles in Ninette de Valois' *Prometheus* (1943), Frederick Ashton's *Cinderella* (1948), and performed in company revivals of ballet classics.

CLAYPOLE, Agnes (1870–1954). *See Moody, Agnes Claypole.*

CLAYPOLE, Edith Jane (1870–1915). English physiologist and pathologist. Born Edith Jane Claypole, Jan 1, 1870, in Bristol, England; died from typhoid fever caught during research work, 1915; dau. of Edward Waller Claypole (science professor); twin sister of Agnes Claypole Moody (zoologist, 1870–1954); Buchtel College, BS in biology, 1892; Cornell University, MS, 1893; University of California, MD with pathology specialization, 1904. ❖ Moved to America (1879); taught histology and physiology at Wellesley College (1894–99); began medical training 1st at Cornell University (1899); volunteered at University of California, Berkeley (1912) and later promoted to research associate in pathology department; during WWI, developed typhoid vaccine with Frederick Parker Gay.

CLAYPOOLE, Elizabeth (1752–1836). *See Ross, Betsy.*

CLAYTON, Barbara (1922—). British chemical pathologist. Name variations: Barbara E. Clayton or B.E. Clayton; Dame Barbara Clayton. Born Barbara Evelyn Clayton, Sept 2, 1922; m. William Klyne, 1949 (died 1977). ❖ Pediatrician interested in nutrition, geriatrics, environmental health, published a paper warning of lead's potentially harmful effects to children (1964); as a member of the Royal Commission on Environmental Pollution (1981–96), examined effects of lead and other pollutants (1997); helped to develop national screening program to detect phenylketonuria (PKU), an inherited metabolic disorder which causes brain damage to infants; researched and developed vitamin supplements for stomach disorders of youth; served as University of Southampton's honorary research professor in metabolism. Made Commander of the Order of the British Empire (1983), Dame Commander of the Order of the British Empire (1988); received British Medical Association's Gold Medal (1999).

CLAYTON, Bessie (c. 1878–1948). American vaudeville star. Born c. 1878 in Philadelphia, Pennsylvania; died July 16, 1948, in Long Branch, New Jersey; m. Julian Mitchell (director, div.). ❖ Made Broadway debut in *A Trip to Chinatown* (1891); appeared with Weber and Fields until 1904; was cast as a specialty dancer in Broadway musicals, including *The Belle of Mayfair* (1906) and *Hip! Hip! Hooray!* (1907); after dancing in *Ziegfeld Follies of 1909*, worked in Europe (1910–13), where she performed the staircase dance, a later trademark; had long career as dancer in vaudeville; retired (1924).

CLAYTON, Ethel (1882–1966). American stage and screen actress. Born Nov 8, 1882, in Champaign, Illinois; died June 11, 1966, in Oxnard, California; m. Joseph Kaufman (director, died 1919); m. Ian Keith (actor, div.). ❖ Appeared on Broadway; debuted in one-reel Essanay comedies (1910); became a popular star whose films include *The Young Mrs. Winthrop, Risky Business, The Princess of Broadway, The Merry Widower, Mother Machree, Artists and Models, Lightnin', The Buccaneer* and *Cocoanut Grove.*

CLAYTON, Eva M. (1934—). African-American politician. Born Sept 16, 1934, in Savannah, Georgia; Johnson C. Smith University, BS, 1955; North Carolina Central University, MS, 1962; attended law school at University of North Carolina at Chapel Hill and North Carolina Central University in Durham; married an attorney; children: 4. ❖ Joined Floyd McKissick in the administration of the Soul City project in Warren Co. (1970s); founded her own management and consulting firm, Technical Resources International, specializing in economic development (1981); served as chair of the Warren Co. Board of Commissioners (1982–90); as a Democrat, was elected to Congress to fill a vacancy (1992), the 1st woman to win a Congressional seat from North Carolina and one of the 1st two black members to do so since Reconstruction; was elected president of the Democratic freshman class, the 1st woman to hold that office; reelected for 4 more terms (Nov 1992–Jan 2003), was a member of the House Agriculture Committee and the House Committee on Small Business.

CLAYTON, Jan (1917–1983). American actress and singer. Born Aug 26, 1917, in Tularosa, New Mexico; died Aug 28, 1983, in West Hollywood, California; m. Russell Hayden (actor), 1938 (div. 1943). ❖ Made Broadway debut as Julie in *Carousel* (1945), followed by *Show Boat, South Pacific, Guys and Dolls, Kiss Me Kate, The King and I* and *Follies,* among others; appeared in films and on tv; probably best remembered as the mother in tv's "Lassie."

CLAYTON, Marguerite (1891–1968). American silent-film actress. Born April 12, 1891, in Ogden, Utah; died of injuries from a road accident, Dec 20, 1968, in Los Angeles, California. ❖ Lead player for Essanay (1912–17), films include *The Birthmark, The Prince of Graustark, The Dream Doll, The New Moon, Inside the Cup, What Love Will Do* and *Twin Flappers;* often appeared opposite Broncho Billy Anderson.

CLAYTON, S. Lillian (1876–1930). American nurse. Born 1876 in Kent Co., Maryland; died May 2, 1930; graduate of Philadelphia General Hospital School of Nursing (1896). ❖ Began career at age 16 at Children's Hospital in Philadelphia; collaborated with nurse Ella Crandall in Dayton, Ohio, on Miami Valley Hospital modernization project and directed nursing school (until 1910); worked as Minneapolis City Hospital nursing teacher and administrator (1911–14); became educational director of Illinois Training School for Nurses in Chicago; appointed director of Philadelphia General Hospital School of Nursing (1915) and served for 15 years; appointed nursing director of all hospitals under Philadelphia Department of Health; served as president of American Nurses Association (ANA, 1926–30).

CLEARE, Ivy (1948—). American ballet dancer. Born Mar 11, 1948, in Camden, Minnesota. ❖ Appeared in small roles in New York City Ballet's production of *The Nutcracker;* joined City Center Joffrey Ballet

and danced in almost all repertory works, including Gerald Arpino's *Viva Vivaldi!,* Anna Sokolow's *Opus '65,* and Ruthanna Boris' *Cakewalk;* held principal roles in Arpino works for numerous seasons; retired and turned to dance management.

CLEARY, Beverly (1916—). American children's writer. Born 1916 in McMinnville, Oregon; dau. of Chester Lloyd (farmer) and Mable (Atlee) Bunn (teacher); Chaffee Junior College, AA, 1936; University of California, Berkeley, BA, 1938; University of Washington, BA in Librarianship, 1939; married Clarence T. Cleary (accountant), Oct 1940; children: Marianne Elisabeth; (twins) Malcolm and James. ❖ Served as children's librarian, Public Library, Yakima, WA (1939–40) and post librarian at US Army Hospital, Oakland, CA (1943–45); writings include *Henry Huggins* (1950), *Henry and Beezus* (1952), *Henry and Ribsy* (1954), *Beezus and Ramona* (1955), *Henry and the Paper Route* (1957), *Jean and Johnny* (1959), *The Real Hole* (1960), *Two Dog Biscuits* (1961), *Emily's Runaway Imagination* (1961), *Henry and the Clubhouse* (1962), *Ribsy* (1964), *The Mouse and the Motorcycle* (1965), *Ramona the Pest* (1968), *Runaway Ralph* (1970), *Socks* (1973), *Ramona the Brave* (1975), *Ralph S. Mouse* (1982), and *Ramona Forever* (1984). Received Laura Ingalls Wilder Award from American Library Association (1975), for substantial and lasting contributions to children's literature; received Newbery Honor Book Award from American Library Association for *Ramona and Her Father* (1978) and *Ramona Quimby, Age 8* (1982); received Regina Medal from Catholic Library Association (1980) and Silver Medallion from University of Southern Mississippi (1982); received Newbery Medal, Christopher Award (1984), for *Dear Mr. Henshaw.* ❖ See also memoir *A Girl from Yamhill* (Morrow, 1988).

CLEAVES, Jessica (1948—). African-American vocalist. Name variations: The Friends of Distinction; Earth, Wind & Fire. Born Dec 10, 1948, in Beverly Hills, California. ❖ With The Friends of Distinction, black vocal group formed in 1967, had such hits as "Grazin' in the Grass" (1969), "Going in Circles" (1969), and "Love or Let Me Be Lonely" (1970); replaced Sherry Scott as vocalist for Earth, Wind & Fire, but left the band in 1973. Albums with Friends of Distinction include *Grazin'* (1969), *Highly Distinct* (1969), *Real Friends* (1970) and *Friends and People* (1971).

CLEAVES, Margaret (1848–1917). American physician. Born Margaret Abigail Cleaves, Nov 25, 1848, in Columbus City, Iowa; died Nov 13, 1917, in Mobile, Alabama; dau. of John T. Cleaves (politician and physician) and Elizabeth Stronach; graduate of a medical program at University of Iowa (1873). ❖ Known for work with mentally ill women, became assistant physician at Iowa State Hospital for insane (1873); opened private practice in Davenport, Iowa (1876); was physician at Female Department of Harrisburg State Lunatic Hospital in Pennsylvania (1880–83); after 2 yrs in Europe, directed retreat for women in Des Moines; became 1st woman chair of obstetrics and gynecology at Iowa State Medical Association's annual meeting (1889); established New York ElectroTherapeutic Clinic Laboratory and Dispensary in New York City (1890); taught electrotherapeutics at New York Post-Graduate Medical School and light energy at New York School of Physical Therapeutics.

CLELAND, Ann (1855–1939). *See Millar, Annie Cleland.*

CLELAND, Tammy (1975—). American synchronized swimmer. Name variations: Tammy Cleland-McGregor. Born Oct 26, 1975, in Orlando, Florida. ❖ Won a team gold medal at Atlanta Olympics (1996).

CLELIA. *See Cloelia.*

CLEMENCE OF BARKING (fl. 12th c.). British nun and translator. Flourished in the late 1100s in England. ❖ Benedictine nun, adapted Latin life of Catherine of Alexandria in Anglo-Norman verse as *Vie de sainte Catherine (Life of St. Catherine,* c. 1163–69).

CLEMENCE OF BURGUNDY (d. 1133). *See Clementia.*

CLEMENCE OF HUNGARY (1293–1328). Queen of France. Name variations: Clemence d'Anjou. Born 1293; died 1328; dau. of Charles Martel of Hungary and Clementia of Habsburg (d. 1293); became 2nd wife of Louis X (1289–1316), king of France (r. 1314–1316), Aug 1315; children: John I the Posthumous (1316–1316), king of France (r. 1316). ❖ See also *Women in World History.*

CLÉMENT, Catherine (1939—). French journalist and educator. Name variations: Catherine Clement. Born 1939 in Paris, France. ❖ Influenced by Marxism and psychoanalysis, served as co-editor of journal

L'Arc; psychoanalytical writings include *Claude Lévi-Strauss ou la Structure du malheur* (1970), *Les fils de Freud sont fatigués* (1978) and *Vies et légendes de Jacues Lacan* (1981); feminist works include *La Jeune Née* (with Hélène Cixous, 1975) and *L'Opéra ou la défaite des femmes* (1981); novels include *La Sultane* (1981), *Le Maure de Venise* (1983), *Bleu Panique* (1986), *Theo's Odyssey* and *Martin and Hannah*.

CLEMENT, Elspeth (1956—). Australian field-hockey player. Born June 19, 1956. ❖ At Seoul Olympics, won a gold medal in team competition (1988).

CLEMENT-SCOTT, Margaret (fl. 19th c.). English actress and journalist. Name variations: Mrs. Clement Scott; Margaret Clement Scott. Born Margaret Brandon in England; dau. of Horace Brandon (solicitor); sister of Florence Waller (actress); m. Clement (William) Scott (1841–1904, drama critic), 1893. ❖ Appeared at music halls; edited *The Free Lance* (1904–08) and was drama critic for *John Bull.*

CLEMENT-SCOTT, Mrs. *See Clement-Scott, Margaret.*

CLEMENTIA (d. 1133). Duchess of Lower Lorraine. Name variations: Clemence of Burgundy. Died in 1133; dau. of Guillaume de Bourgogne also known as William I, count of Burgundy, and Etienette de Longwy; married Robert II of Jerusalem, count of Flanders (r. 1093–1111), c. 1090; became 2nd wife of Godfrey I (d. 1139), duke of Lower Lorraine (r. 1106–1139), after 1121.

CLEMENTIA, Dame (1615–1671). *See Cary, Anne.*

CLEMENTIA OF HABSBURG (d. 1293). German royal. Birth date unknown; died after Feb 2, 1293; dau. of Rudolf I (1218–1291), Holy Roman emperor (r. 1273–1291), and Anna of Hohenberg (c. 1230–1281); m. Charles Martel of Hungary; children: Charles Robert of Anjou (1288–1342) also known as Charles I, king of Hungary (r. 1307–1342, who m. Elizabeth of Poland, 1305–1380); Clemence of Hungary (1293–1328).

CLEMENTINA, Dame (1615–1671). *See Cary, Anne.*

CLEMENTINA OF AUSTRIA (1777–1801). *See Maria Clementina of Austria.*

CLEMENTINA OF ZAHRINGEN (fl. 1150s). Countess of Savoy. Fl. in 1150s; dau. of Conrad I, duke of Zahringen; became 1st wife of Henry XII also known as Henry V the Lion (1129–1195), duke of Saxony and Bavaria (r. 1156–1195), around 1150 (div. 1162); m. Humbert III, count of Savoy, around 1164; children: (1st m.) possibly Gertrude of Saxony (c. 1155–1196, who m. Canute VI, king of Denmark). Henry V's 2nd wife was Matilda of England (1156–1189).

CLEMENTINA SOBIESKI (1702–1735). *See Sobieski, Clementina.*

CLEMENTINE OF AUSTRIA (1798–1881). Princess of Salerno. Born Mar 1, 1798; died Sept 3, 1881; dau. of Maria Teresa of Naples (1772–1807) and Francis I (1768–1835), emperor of Austria (r. 1804–1835), also known as Francis II, Holy Roman emperor (r. 1792–1806); sister-in-law of Napoleon Bonaparte; m. Leopold, prince of Salerno, July 28, 1816; children: Caroline of Bourbon (1822–1869); Ludwig Karl also known as Louis Charles (b. 1824).

CLEMENTINE OF BELGIUM (1872–1955). Belgian princess. Born July 30, 1872; died Mar 8, 1955; dau. of Leopold II (b. 1835), king of Belgium (r. 1865–1909), and Maria Henrietta of Austria (1836–1902); m. Prince Victor (son of Prince Napoleon and Clotilde of Savoy), Nov 14, 1901; children: Clotilde (b. 1912); Louis Napoleon (b. 1914).

CLEMENTINE OF ORLEANS (1817–1907). Princess of Saxe-Coburg. Name variations: Clementine Bourbon; Clémentine of Orléans or Clémentine d'Orléans. Born Marie Clémentine Caroline Leopoldine Clotilde d'Orléans, June 3, 1817, in Neuilly-sur-Seine; died Feb 16, 1907, in Vienna, Austria; 2nd dau. of Maria Amalia (1782–1866) and Louis Philippe I (1773–1850), the Citizen King of France (r. 1830–1848); sister of Louise d'Orleans (1812–1850, queen of Belgium); m. Augustus, prince of Saxe-Coburg-Gotha, April 20, 1843; children: Prince Philip of Saxe-Coburg-Gotha (1844–1921); August of Saxe-Coburg-Gotha (1845–1907); Clotilde of Saxe-Coburg-Gotha (1846–1927); Amalie of Saxe-Coburg-Gotha (1848–1894); Ferdinand I (1861–1948), prince of Bulgaria (r. 1887–1908), tsar of Bulgaria (r. 1908–1918). ❖ Was a close friend of Maria II Da Gloria (1819–1853), queen of Portugal.

CLEMM, Virginia (1822–1847). *See Poe, Virginia Clemm.*

CLEMMER, Mary (1831–1884). *See Ames, Mary Clemmer.*

CLEOBULINA OF RHODES (fl. 570 BCE). Greek philosopher and poet. Name variations: Eumetis. Fl. around 570 BCE; dau. of Cleobulus of Rhodes (one of the "Seven Sages" and ruler of Rhodes); children: (son) Thales of Miletos (philosopher and mathematician). ❖ Her fame was so great that she was the subject of a satire, "Cleobulina," by Athenian dramatist Cratinus, and despite his disparagement of the intellectual capabilities of women, Aristotle quotes one of her riddles (written in her usual style of hexameter) in his *Poetics* and his *Rhetoric;* several of her other rhymes survive. ❖ See also *Women in World History.*

CLEOPATRA (b. 354 BCE). Princess of Macedon. Born c. 354 BCE; dau. of Olympias (c. 371–316 BCE) and Philip II, king of Macedon; sister of Alexander III the Great (356–323 BCE), king of Macedon; m. her uncle Alexander (brother of her mother Olympias), king of Epirus.

CLEOPATRA (fl. 1st c. BCE). Egyptian physician and author. Fl. in the 1st century BCE. ❖ Is known from references in the work of Galen. Since Galen confused her with Cleopatra VII of Egypt (in fact, crediting the latter as the author of the texts he cites), it is probable that she lived and worked as a medical authority in Alexandria in the 1st century BCE, and that she was associated with the Ptolemaic court. ❖ See also *Women in World History.*

CLEOPATRA I (c. 210–176 BCE). Queen of Egypt. Born c. 210 BCE in Syria; died in 176 BCE; dau. of Antiochus III, a Seleucid king, and his cousin-wife, Laodice III; m. Ptolemy V Epiphanes, king of Egypt, 196 BCE; children: Ptolemy VI Philometor; Cleopatra II (c. 183–116 BCE); Ptolemy VIII Euergetes II. ❖ Betrothed to Ptolemy V Epiphanes, when both were about 14 (196 BCE); married (193) for the benefit of Antiochus who returned Palestine to Ptolemy as her marriage dower (though she, not her husband, controlled the region's revenues until her death); when Ptolemy V died (180), seized the reigns of power and ruled, without male oversight, as the 1st female regent in Ptolemaic history; reigned supreme—coining money in her own name and generally ruling well. ❖ See also *Women in World History.*

CLEOPATRA II (c. 183–116 BCE). Co-ruler of Egypt. Name variations: Cleopatra II Philometor or Philomater ("Mother-loving"). Born c. 183 BCE; died in 116 BCE; dau. of Ptolemy V Epiphanes and Cleopatra I (c. 210–176 BCE); sister of Ptolemy VI Philometor and Ptolemy VIII Euergetes II; m. brother Ptolemy VI Philometor, 176 BCE (died 145 BCE); m. brother Ptolemy VIII Euergetes II, 144 BCE; children: (1st m.) Ptolemy Eupator; Ptolemy VII Neos Philopator; Cleopatra III Euergetis; Cleopatra Thea; (2nd m.) Ptolemy Memphites. ❖ Co-ruler of Egypt (176–130 BCE and 118–116 BCE) and sole ruler of Upper Egypt (130–118 BCE). ❖ See also *Women in World History.*

CLEOPATRA III (c. 155–101 BCE). Queen of Egypt. Name variations: Cleopatra III Euergetis. Born c. 155 BCE in Egypt; died in 101 BCE; dau. of Ptolemy VI Philometor and Cleopatra II (c. 183–116 BCE); m. her uncle-stepfather Ptolemy VIII Euergetes; children: two sons, Ptolemy IX Philometor Soter II and Ptolemy X Alexander I; three daughters, Cleopatra Selene, Cleopatra IV, and Cleopatra Tryphaena (d. after 112 BCE). ❖ An imperious queen whose career did little to foster the health and well-being of Egypt, had enormous rivalry with her mother. ❖ See also *Women in World History.*

CLEOPATRA IV (c. 135–112 BCE). Queen of Egypt. Born c. 135 BCE; died in 112 BCE; dau. of Ptolemy VIII Euergetes II and Cleopatra III (c. 155–101 BCE); sister of Cleopatra Selene and Cleopatra Tryphaena; m. full brother, Ptolemy IX Philometor Soter II (div. 115 BCE); m. Antiochus IX Philopator Cyzicenus, a Seleucid king, 113 BCE; children: (1st m.) possibly Cleopatra Berenice III. ❖ See also *Women in World History.*

CLEOPATRA V SELENE (c. 40 BCE–?). Queen of Cyrene and Numidia. Name variations: Cleopatra of Cyrene. Born c. 40 BCE; dau. of Cleopatra VII (69–30 BCE, queen of Egypt) and Marc Antony; m. Rome's Mauritanian client king, Juba II, king of Numidia; children: Ptolemy Caesarion. Ruled Cyrene around 33–31 BCE. ❖ See also *Women in World History.*

CLEOPATRA V TRYPHAENA (c. 95–c. 57 BCE). Queen of Egypt. Name variations: Cleopatra VI Tryphaena or Tryphaeana. Born c. 95 BCE; died c. 57 BCE; illeg. dau. of Ptolemy IX Philometor Soter II Lathyros of Egypt and an unknown mother; m. possibly full-brother Ptolemy XII Theos Philopator Philadelphus Neos Dionysus, in 80 BCE; children: possibly 2 sons, Ptolemy XIII and Ptolemy XIV; and 3 daughters, Berenice IV (d. 55

BCE), Arsinoe IV (d. 41 BCE), and Cleopatra VII (69–30 BCE). ❧ Is a shadowy figure throughout most of husband' reign because she maintained a low profile, unlike other women of her line. Since Auletes was a noted womanizer, there is no way to know how many children she had; in lieu of better evidence, it is possible that she was the mother of Cleopatra VII (the identity of whose mother is nowhere revealed), the most famous queen produced by the Ptolemaic dynasty. ❧ See also *Women in World History.*

CLEOPATRA VI TRYPHAENA (c. 95–c. 57 BCE). *See Cleopatra V Tryphaena.*

CLEOPATRA VII (69–30 BCE). Queen of Egypt. Name variations: sometimes known as Cleopatra VI. Born in 69 BCE; committed suicide, Aug 10, 30 BCE; dau. of Ptolemy XII (king of Egypt) and possibly Cleopatra V Tryphaena (c. 95–c. 57 BCE); sister of Ptolemy XIII, Ptolemy XIV, Berenice IV (d. 55 BCE) and Arsinoe IV (d. 41 BCE); m. brother Ptolemy XIII, in 51 BCE; m. brother Ptolemy XIV, in 47 BCE; children: (with Julius Caesar) Ptolemy XV Caesar (Caesarion); (with Marc Antony) twins Alexander Helios and Cleopatra V Selene (b. around 40 BCE) and another Ptolemy (b. 36 BCE). ❧ A mistress of Julius Caesar and eventual wife of Mark Antony, was the last—but certainly not the least—of the Ptolemaic dynasty to rule Egypt; ascended to the throne (51 BCE) as co-ruler with brother-husband, Ptolemy XIII; became lover of Caesar; was pregnant with Caesar's child and married brother Ptolemy XIV (47 BCE); traveled to Rome to be with Caesar (46 BCE), but remained no more than his mistress at the time of his assassination (44 BCE); returned to Egypt; seeing her salvation in Antony, seduced him; with Antony, was in open war against Octavian, concluding in Octavian's victory (31 BCE); along with Antony, forced into suicide (30 BCE). ❧ See also Michael Grant, *Cleopatra* (Macmillan, 1974); Jack Lindsay, *Cleopatra* (Coward, 1970); and *Women in World History.*

CLEOPATRA BERENICE III (c. 115–80 BCE). Queen of Egypt. Name variations: Berenice III; born Berenice but took the name Cleopatra when she married. Born Berenice around 115 BCE; murdered in 80 BCE; dau. of Ptolemy IX Philometer Soter II Lathyros (meaning Ptolemy the Mother Loving; also known by the population of Alexandria as "Physcon," that is, the "Pot-Bellied") and Cleopatra IV or Cleopatra Selene; m. her uncle Ptolemy X Alexander I, 102 or 101 BCE (died 88 BCE); m. her father Ptolemy IX (died 80 BCE); m. Ptolemy XI Alexander II, in 80 BCE; children: (1st m.) one daughter. ❧ Was one of the most beloved Ptolemies of the last century of that dynasty's rule in Egypt; when her increasing unpopular uncle-husband was at last driven from Egypt and killed (88 BCE), remained so popular that her father Ptolemy IX married her to renew his claim to the Egyptian throne; continued a popular joint rule with father-husband until his death (80 BCE); thereafter, ruled Egypt alone for about 6 months before tradition made her marry yet again; was murdered by last husband (Ptolemy XI) after a marriage of only 19 days (he was then killed by an angry mob). ❧ See also *Women in World History.*

CLEOPATRA SELENE (c. 130–69 BCE). Queen of Egypt and Syria. Born c. 130 BCE; died in 69 BCE; youngest dau. of Ptolemy VIII Euergetes II and Cleopatra III Euergetis (c. 155–101 BCE) of Egypt; sister of Cleopatra IV (c. 135–112 BCE) and Cleopatra Tryphaena (d. after 112 BCE); m. Ptolemy IX Philometer Soter II, 115 BCE (div. 107 BCE); m. Antiochus VIII Grypus, 103 BCE (killed 96 BCE); m. Antiochus IX Cyzicenus, in 96 BCE (killed 95 BCE); m. Antiochus X Eusebes Philopator; children: (1st m.) probably 2 sons, possibly Cleopatra Berenice III; (3rd m.) 2 sons, including Antiochus XIII Asiaticus. ❧ Began political career as the pawn of her mother, Cleopatra III. ❧ See also *Women in World History.*

CLEOPATRA THEA (c. 165–121 BCE). Queen of Syria. Born c. 165 BCE; died in 121 BCE; dau. of Ptolemy VI and Cleopatra II (c. 183–116 BCE) of Egypt; probably the older sister of Cleopatra III; m. Alexander Balas, pretender to the Seleucid throne (r. 150–145 BCE), 150 BCE (died 145 BCE); m. Demetrius II Nicator, Seleucid king (r. 145–138), 146 BCE (died 125 BCE); m. Antiochus VII Sidetes (died 129); children: (1st m.) Antiochus VI Epiphanes; (2nd m.) sons Antiochus VIII Philometor Grypus and Seleucus V, and a daughter Laodice (fl. 129 BCE); (3rd m.) Antiochus IX Philopator Cyzicenus (r. 96–95 BCE). ❧ Renewed the link between Ptolemaic and Seleucid interests; as a result, made her mark in Syria, where she wed 3 Seleucid monarchs in succession. ❧ See also *Women in World History.*

CLEOPATRA TRYPHAENA (d. after 112 BCE). Queen of Syria. Condemned to death by Antiochus IX Cyzicenus after 112 BCE; dau. of Ptolemy VIII Euergetes II and Cleopatra III Euergetis (c. 155–101 BCE) of Egypt; sister of Cleopatra IV and Cleopatra Selene; m. Antiochus VIII Grypus, Seleucid king (r. 125–96 BCE); children: Seleucus VI and Antiochus X Eusebes Philopator. ❧ See also *Women in World History.*

CLERK. *Variant of Clark, Clarke, and Clerke.*

CLERKE, Agnes Mary (1842–1907). Irish-born writer. Pronunciation: Clark. Born Agnes Mary Clerke, Feb 10, 1842, in Skibbereen, Co. Cork, Ireland; died Jan 20, 1907, in London; dau. of John William (bank manager) and Catherine Mary (Deasy) Clerke; sister of Ellen Mary Clerke (1840–1906, writer) and Aubrey St. John Clerke; received home schooling by parents; self-study in Italy and London; never married; no children. ❧ Self-taught astronomy writer, contributed significantly to the popular astronomy literature of late 19th and early 20th centuries; with sister, resided in Italy (1867–77); published 1st articles, "Brigandage in Sicily" (concerning the rise of the Mafia) and "Copernicus in Italy," in the *Edinburgh Review* (1877); continued contributing articles to the *Review* until her death; moved with family to London (1877); published most famous work, *A Popular History of Astronomy during the Nineteenth Century* (1885), to rave reviews; became well known in astronomical circles and spent 2 months working at Cape of Good Hope Observatory (1888); made further observations aboard the yacht *Palatine* in the Baltic Sea and incorporated her experiences in *The System of the Stars* (1891); authored a number of popular books, including *The Herschels and Modern Astronomy* and *Modern Cosmogonies*. Awarded Acton Prize (1892); was the 4th woman elected an honorary member of Royal Astronomical Society (1903). ❧ See also *Women in World History.*

CLERKE, Ellen Mary (1840–1906). Irish-born translator. Born Sept 20, 1840, in Skibbereen, Ireland; died Mar 2, 1906; dau. of John William and Catherine Mary Deasy Clerke; sister of Agnes Mary Clerke (1842–1907). ❧ Wrote poetry, novels, and astronomical pamphlets; published her translation of Italian verse, *Fable and Song in Italy* (1899).

CLERMONT, Catherine de (1545–1603). *See Clermont, Claude-Catherine de.*

CLERMONT, Claude-Catherine de (1545–1603). French poet and duchess. Name variations: Catherine de Clermont, duchess and maréchale de Retz; Dame de Dampierre; La Duchesse de Retz and Baronne de Retz; duchess of Retz. Born Claude-Catherine de Clermont, dame de Dampierre, 1545 (some sources cite 1540 or 1543); died in 1603 (some sources cite 1604); m. Jean d'Annebant, maréchal and baron de Retz (for about 15 years); m. the Italian Albert de Gondi (favorite adviser to the queen), 1565, who took the title Baron de Dampierre, Duc de Retz, and became Maréchal of France, 1573. ❧ Well educated in mathematics, philosophy, history, and Latin, translated address of visiting Polish ambassador into French and replied to address in Polish (1573); was one of the few women admitted to the Academie du Palais by Henry III.

CLERMONT, countess of.
See Marie of Hainault (fl. 1300).
See Guzman, Leonora de (1310–1351).
See Maria Theresa of Wurttemberg.

CLERMONT-TONNERRE, duchesse de (fl. 1875–1935). *See Gramont, Elizabeth de.*

CLEUSA, Mother (c. 1931–1998). *See Millet, Cleusa.*

CLEVELAND, duchess of. *See Villiers, Barbara (c. 1641–1709).*

CLEVELAND, Emeline Horton (1829–1878). American physician. Born Emeline Horton in Ashford, Connecticut, Sept 22, 1829; died in Philadelphia, Pennsylvania, Dec 8, 1878; dau. of Chauncey and Amanda (Chaffee) Horton; graduate of Oberlin College, 1853; Female Medical College of Pennsylvania, MD, 1855; advanced training in obstetrics at school of Maternité hospital in Paris, 1860–61; m. Rev. Giles Butler Cleveland, Mar 8, 1854; children: Arthur (b. Feb 10, 1865). ❧ Following a year of private practice in NY's Oneida valley, became a demonstrator of anatomy at the Female Medical College (1856), before being named professor of anatomy and histology, then serving as chief resident (1861–68) and dean (1872–74); was the 1st woman physician on record to practice as a surgeon (1875), with her 1st of several ovariotomies; appointed gynecologist to the department for the insane at Pennsylvania Hospital (1878). ❧ See also *Women in World History.*

CLEVELAND, Frances Folsom (1864–1947). American first lady. Name variations: Frances F. Preston. Born July 21, 1864, in Buffalo, NY; died Oct 29, 1947, in Baltimore, Maryland; only child of Oscar (attorney) and

Emma Cornelia (Harmon) Folsom; graduate of Wells College (NY), 1885; m. (Stephen) Grover Cleveland (US president, 1884–88, 1892–96), June 2, 1886, at the 1st wedding ceremony to take place in the White House (died 1908); m. Thomas Jex Preston Jr. (archeology professor), Feb 10, 1913; children: (1st m.) Ruth Cleveland (1891–1904, died of diphtheria at 12); Esther Cleveland (1893–1980, only presidential child ever born in the White House); Marion Cleveland (b. 1895); Richard Cleveland (1897–1974); Francis Cleveland (b. 1903). ❖ One of the youngest and most popular women to serve as first lady, was 21 when she exchanged vows with Grover Cleveland, 28 years her senior, at the White House (1886); took over the duties of first lady from Cleveland's sister, Rose Elizabeth Cleveland, who had acted as her brother's host for 15 months of his 1st term; possessed such tact, charm and beauty that she quickly won acceptance; lived in NY after husband failed in reelection bid (1888–92); returned to White House (1893) for his 2nd term. ❖ See also *Women in World History.*

CLEVELAND, Rose Elizabeth (b. 1846). American writer. Born in Fayetteville, NY, 1846; dau. of Richard Falley (Presbyterian minister) and Anne (Neal) Cleveland; sister of Grover Cleveland (US president). ❖ After the presidential inauguration of her brother (1885), became the unofficial first lady until 1886; published a book of essays and lectures, *George Eliot's Poetry, and Other Studies* (1885) and a novel, *The Long Run* (1886).

CLEVELAND, Ruth (1891–1904). American first daughter. Born Oct 3, 1891, in New York, NY; died of diphtheria, Jan 7, 1904, at age 12, in Princeton, New Jersey; dau. of Grover Cleveland (US president) and Frances Folsom Cleveland. ❖ Popularly known as Baby Ruth while living in the White House. Curtiss Candy Company renamed their chocolate-nut candy bar from Kandy Kake to Baby Ruth (1921); the company maintained it was named for Ruth Cleveland, though the claim remains controversial, with some believing it was named for baseball slugger Babe Ruth.

CLEVES, Anne of (1515–1557). *See Anne of Cleves.*

CLEVES, duchess of.
See Mary of Burgundy (c. 1400–1463).
See Elizabeth of Nevers (fl. 1460).
See Maria of Julich-Berg (fl. 1515).
See Mary (1531–1581).
See Elizabeth Charlotte of the Palatinate (fl. 1620).

CLEVES, Marie de (1426–1486). *See Marie of Cleves.*

CLEYRE, Voltairine de (1866–1912). *See de Cleyre, Voltairine.*

CLICQUOT, Mme (1777–1866). French entrepreneur. Name variations: Barbe-Nicole Clicquot-Ponsardin; the Widow Clicquot. Born Barbe-Nicole Ponsardin in 1777; died in 1866; dau. of Baron Ponsardin; m. François Clicquot (died); great-grandmother of Anne, Duchesse d'Uzes. ❖ Widowed early, turned an inherited winery into the producer of the world's leading brand of Champagne, "Veuve Clicquot." ❖ See also *Women in World History.*

CLIDAT, France (1932—). French pianist. Born in Nantes, France, 1932. ❖ Studied in Paris with Lazare-Lévy (1948–50), winning a 1st prize at end of her course of study; made prize-winning series of 24 long-playing recordings of Franz Liszt's works; had extensive repertoire, including complete works of eccentric French composer Erik Satie and daunting Third Concerto of Sergei Rachmaninoff.

CLIFF, Clarice (1899–1972). English ceramic designer. Born Jan 20, 1899, in Tunstall, Staffordshire, England; died Oct 23, 1972, in Clayton, Stoke-on-Trent, England; dau. of Harry Cliff and Ann (Machin) Cliff; attended Royal College of Art; m. Arthur Colley Austin Shorter (owner of Newport Pottery factory), 1940 (died 1963). ❖ One of England's most prolific ceramic designers, whose richly colored Art Deco pottery inspired other artists and brought lasting fame, began working at Linguard Webster and Co. pottery factory at 13; moved to firm of Hollinshead & Kirkham, serving as lithographer, and then to A.J. Wilkinson's Newport Pottery Factory (1916); given own studio (1927); launched *Bizarre* wares, initially as scheme for covering poorly-glazed pieces with bright colored triangular patterns and later as highly successful design style; incorporated Art Deco style in pottery design; achieved widespread success with new pottery line (1928); continued to develop Art Deco and floral patterns which met with great success in UK, South Africa, Brazil, Australia, New Zealand and Canada; won prizes at British Industries Fair for many years; was made art director at Newport Pottery (1930); maintained high sales despite Depression and WWII, though war shortages and necessities altered business practices significantly; sold factory to Midwinter's (1964); held 1st artistic exhibition of work outside of trade-show context (1971). ❖ See also Leonard Griffin, Louis K. Meisel and Susan Pear Meisel, *Clarice Cliff, the Bizarre Affair* (Abrams, 1988).

CLIFF, Leslie (1955—). Canadian swimmer. Born Mar 11, 1955, in British Columbia. ❖ At Munich Olympics, won a silver medal in the 400-meter individual medley (1972).

CLIFF, Michelle (1946—). Jamaican novelist. Born Nov 2, 1946, in Jamaica; grew up in Jamaica and US; educated in NY; Warburg Institute at University of London, PhD on Italian Renaissance; lived with Adrienne Rich (poet). ❖ Writings, which are concerned with multiethnic identity and Caribbean diaspora, include *Abeng* (1984), *The Land of Look Behind: Prose and Poetry* (1985), *No Telephone to Heaven* (1987), *Bodies of Water* (1990), *Free Enterprise* (1993), *History as Fiction, Fiction as History* (1994) and *The Store of a Million Items* (1998); also published numerous essays in anthologies.

CLIFF, Theresa (1978—). American inline skater. Name variations: Theresa Marie Cliff. Born June 19, 1978, in Cedar Springs, Michigan. ❖ Raced with Verducci Racing Team (pro team) and Wolverines of Michigan (home team); won 1st gold medal at World championships (1994); won 18th gold medal, breaking record for most gold medals won in women's skating (2000); won 25th gold medal in marathon at World championships.

CLIFFORD, Anna Rawle (c. 1757–1828). *See Rawle, Anna.*

CLIFFORD, Anne (1590–1676). Countess of Dorset, Pembroke, and Montgomery, who was a diarist and biographer. Name variations: Lady Anne Clifford. Born in Yorkshire, England, Jan 30, 1590; died in Westmoreland, England, Mar 22, 1676; dau. of George Clifford, 3rd earl of Cumberland (naval commander and buccaneer), and Margaret (Russell) Clifford (c. 1560–1616); educated by Samuel Daniel, the poet; m. Richard Sackville, Lord Buchhurst, earl of Dorset (claimed the barony of Clifford in 1628), in Feb 1609 (died 1624); m. Philip Herbert, earl of Pembroke and Montgomery, 1630 (died 1650); children: (1st m.) 3 sons, all of whom died in infancy; 2 daughters. ❖ Had 2 unhappy marriages and endured an extensive lawsuit to regain her inheritance; rebuilt her 6 castles, secured a reputation for "bounty and hospitality," continued to defend her rights, and embarked on an extensive family history, including her own autobiography and the biographies of her parents. Her extensive diary, which she kept until her death, was also published (1923). ❖ See also Martin Holmes, *Proud Northern Lady: Lady Anne Clifford 1590–1676* (1975); Vita Sackville-West, ed. *The Diary of Lady Anne Clifford* (1923); George Williamson, *Lady Anne Clifford, Countess of Dorset, Pembroke and Montgomery* (2nd ed., 1967); and *Women in World History.*

CLIFFORD, Betsy (1953—). Canadian alpine skier. Born Oct 15, 1953, in Old Chelsea, Quebec, Canada; dau. of Margaret and John Clifford (both athletes). ❖ At 13, won a Canadian championship; at 14, competed at Grenoble, the youngest skier in Olympic history (1968); at the World championships, won a gold medal in giant slalom (1970) and a silver medal in the downhill (1974); retired at 22.

CLIFFORD, Camille (1885–1970). English actress. Name variations: Camilla Antoinette Clifford; Mrs. Lyndhurst Bruce. Born Camille Clifford Lizzie Caswell Smith in Denmark in 1885; died 1970; m. Hon. Lyndhurst Henry Bruce; m. Capt. J.M.J. Evans, M.C. ❖ Moved to US when quite young and made stage debut in chorus of *The Defender* (1902); made London debut as a Gibson girl in *The Prince of Pilsen* (1904), where she 1st attracted attention; sang "A Gibson Girl" at the Vaudeville (1905), becoming known as the British Gibson girl; had one of the most famous hourglass figures of the Edwardian period.

CLIFFORD, Lady Jane (d. 1679). *See Seymour, Jane.*

CLIFFORD, Josephine (1838–1920). *See McCrackin, Josephine.*

CLIFFORD, Kathleen (1887–1962). American actress and singer. Born Feb 16, 1887, in Charlottesville, Virginia; died Dec 28, 1962, in Long Beach, California; educated in England; married M.P. Illitch. ❖ Billed as "The Smartest Chap in Town," appeared as a male impersonator in vaudeville; replaced Marie Doro in *The Girl from Kelly's* (1904) in Broadway debut; films include *Who is Number One!, Cold Steel, Kick In, Richard the Lion-Hearted* and *Sporting Life.*

CLIFFORD, Lady (d. 1945). *See de la Pasture, Mrs. Henry.*

CLIFFORD, Lucy Lane (1846–1929). *See Clifford, Mrs. W.K.*

CLIFFORD, Margaret (d. 1596). Countess of Derby. Died Sept 29, 1596; dau. of Henry Clifford, 2nd earl of Cumberland, and Eleanor Brandon (c. 1520–1547); m. Henry Stanley, 4th earl of Derby, Feb 7, 1555.

CLIFFORD, Margaret (c. 1560–1616). Countess of Cumberland. Born Margaret Russell c. 1560; died in 1616; youngest dau. of Francis Russell, earl of Bedford; m. George Clifford, 3rd earl of Cumberland, 1577 (sep.); children: Anne Clifford (1590–1676), countess of Dorset.

CLIFFORD, Maud (d. 1446). Countess of Cambridge. Name variations: Maud Neville. Died Aug 26, 1446; dau. of Thomas Clifford, 4th baron Clifford; m. Richard of Conisbrough, 2nd earl of Cambridge, around 1413; m. John Neville, 6th baron Latimer.

CLIFFORD, Rosamund (c. 1145–1176). Mistress of King Henry II of England. Name variations: Rosamond; Rosamonde; "Fair Rosamund." Born c. 1145 in Wales; died at Godstow convent, England, 1176; believed to be the dau. of Sir Walter de Clifford, a Norman knight, of the family of Fitz-Ponce; never married; no children (there is no evidence for the belief that she was the mother of Henry's natural son William Longsword, earl of Salisbury). ❖ Popular figure in legends and ballads, met Henry (1165), probably at her father's castle when he was warring against the Welsh; soon became lovers; was moved to his castle of Woodstock in Oxfordshire; because she was accorded privileges Queen Eleanor of Aquitaine herself was owed, aroused the queen's ire and started the processes by which Eleanor later encouraged rebellion by her sons against their father; remained at Woodstock until about 1176; left Henry and Woodstock for the convent at Godstow, probably due to an ongoing illness; died a young woman. ❖ See also *Women in World History.*

CLIFFORD, Ruth (1900–1998). American actress. Name variations: Ruth Clifford Cornelius; Ruth Cornelius. Born Feb 17, 1900, in Pawtucket, Rhode Island; died Nov 30, 1998, in Woodland Hills, California; m. James A. Cornelius, 1924 (div. 1938). ❖ Universal star of the late 1920s and member of John Ford's stock company; films include *The Savage, The Desire of the Moth, Fires of Youth, The Cabaret Girl* and *Abraham Lincoln.*

CLIFFORD, Mrs. W.K. (1846–1929). English playwright, novelist, and children's writer. Name variations: Lucy Lane Clifford. Born Lucy Lane in 1846 in Barbados; died April 21, 1929, in London, England; dau. of John Lane; m. William Kongdon Clifford (mathematics professor and philosopher), April 7, 1875 (died 1879); children: 2 daughters. ❖ The Clifford home was a gathering place for the likes of Charles Darwin, Herbert Spencer, Thomas Huxley, Henry James, James Russell Lowell, Oliver Wendell Holmes, Leslie Stephen, Violet Hunt and George Eliot; on death of husband, supplemented income with writing; plays include *An Interlude* (with W.H. Pollock), *A Honeymoon Tragedy, Madeline, A Supreme Moment, The Likeness of the Night, A Long Duel, The Seachlight, The Latch, Hamilton's Second Marriage, A Woman Alone* and *Two's Company;* books include *Mrs. Keith's Crime, The Love Letters of a Worldly Woman, The Wild Proxy, A Flash of Summer, Woodside Farm, The Modern Way, Miss Fingal* and *The House in Marylebone;* also wrote children's stories.

CLIFT, Charmian (1923–1969). Australian novelist and short-story writer. Born 1923 in Kiama, New South Wales, Australia; died 1969; m. George Johnston, 1947. ❖ Lived in England and Greece for 14 years before returning to Australia; with husband, wrote *High Valley* (1949), *The Big Chariot* (1953), *The Sponge Divers* (1956), and *Strong Man from Piraeus and Other Stories* (1986); solo, wrote 2 novels, 2 works about experiences in Greece, and 2 collections of essays; wrote weekly column for *Sydney Morning Herald* and adapted husband's novel, *My Brother Jack,* for tv.

CLIFT, Martha (fl. 1930s). American murderer. Born in US. ❖ Went to work at Eva Coo's speakeasy and bordello in Oneonta, NY (1933); with Coo, murdered handyman Harry Wright for insurance money (1934); found guilty of 2nd degree murder (1935), received 20-year sentence (Coo was found guilty of 1st-degree murder and executed).

CLIFTON, Fanny (1815–1895). *See Stirling, Mary Anne.*

CLIFTON, Lucille (1936—). African-American poet and children's writer. Born Lucille Sayles, June 27, 1936, in Depew, NY; dau. of Samuel L. and Thelma Moore Sayles; studied drama at Howard University; entered Fredonia State Teachers College, 1955; m. Fred James Clifton, 1958; children: 6. ❖ Served as poet-in-residence at

Coppin State College, Baltimore (1971–74) and poet laureate of Maryland (1979–82); published 1st volume of poetry *Good Times* (1969), followed by such poetry collections as *An Ordinary Woman* (1974) and *The Terrible Stories* (1996), among others; published *Some of the Days of Everett Anderson* (1970), the 1st of 8 books which feature Anderson as the protagonist; other children's fiction includes *The Black BC's* (1970), *All Us Come Across the Water* (1973), *My Friend Jacob* (1980), *Sonora Beautiful* (1981) and *Three Wishes* (1992); was Distinguished Professor of Humanities at St. Mary's College in Maryland; taught at Columbia University (1995–99). Received Shelley Memorial Prize and Charity Randall Prize; won Emmy award; was short-listed for the Pulitzer Prize for *Good Woman* and *Next* (1988). ❖ See also memoirs *Generations: A Memoir* (1976), *Good Woman: Poems and a Memoir: 1969–1980* (1987), and *Next* (1987).

CLIGNET, Marion (1964—). French cyclist. Born Feb 22, 1964, in Hyde Park, Illinois. ❖ Began riding for France because of disagreement with US cycling authorities (1989); won a silver medal at Atlanta Olympics (1996) and at Sydney Olympics (2000), both for indiv. pursuit.

CLIJSTERS, Kim (1983—). Belgian tennis player. Born June 8, 1983, in Bilzen, Belgium. ❖ Was runner-up for singles at Roland Garros (2001, 2003), US Open (2003), and Australian Open (2004); won doubles championships at Roland Garros (2003) and Wimbledon (2003); won U.S. Open (2005).

CLINE, Aleisha (1970—). Canadian skier and mountain biker. Born Sept 10, 1970, in Kelowna, British Columbia, Canada; m. Shaums March (athlete). ❖ Set a world speed skiing record of 135 miles per hour (1993); won gold in Skier X at X Games (1999, 2001, and 2002); received 1st-place season-end ranking on IFSA Freeskiing World Tour (2001); other 1st-place finishes include: US Open of Freeskiing, Vail, Colorado, in Skiercross (2000); Skiercross World championships, Squaw Valley, CA, in Skiercross (2000); and 24 Hours of Aspen, Aspen, Colorado, in Endurance DH (2001).

CLINE, Genevieve (1879–1959). American judge. Born July 27, 1879 (some sources cite 1878) in Warren, Ohio; died 1959 in Cleveland, Ohio; educated at Spencerian College and Oberlin College; Baldwin-Wallace Law School, LLB, 1921. ❖ Appointed by President Warren Harding, served as appraiser of merchandise at the port of Cleveland (1922–28), the 1st woman to be appointed to such a position at a large port city; appointed to US Customs Court by President Calvin Coolidge, was confirmed (May 25, 1928), the 1st woman appointed as a US federal judge; sat on the Customs Court until her retirement 25 years later.

CLINE, Maggie (1857–1934). American vaudeville performer. Name variations: Mrs. John Ryan; (stage name) Irish Queen. Born Margaret Cline, Jan 1, 1857, in Haverhill, Massachusetts; died June 11, 1934, in Fair Haven, New Jersey; dau. of Patrick (shoe factory foreman) and Ann (Degman) Cline; m. John Ryan (café owner), 1888. ❖ The 1st woman Irish comedy singer, had established herself as a name in NY vaudeville houses by 1880s; by her estimation, sang her most popular song "Throw 'Em Down McCloskey" about 75,000 times over 23 years, along with "Down Went McGinty to the Bottom of the Sea" and "How McNulty Carved the Duck"; billed as "Irish Queen" (from 1881) and once called Brunnhilde of the Bowery, performed in comedy melodrama *On Broadway* (1896); retired (1917).

CLINE, Nancy Lieberman (b. 1958). *See Lieberman-Cline, Nancy.*

CLINE, Patsy (1932–1963). American pop, rock, and country singer. Name variations: Virginia Dick. Born Virginia Patterson Hensley in Winchester, Virginia, Sept 8, 1932; died in a plane crash near Camden, Tennessee, Mar 5, 1963; m. Gerald Cline, 1953; m. Charlie Dick (linotype operator), 1957. ❖ Made singing debut with a local band, Melody Playboys, on WINC; began singing full time at bandleader Bill Peer's Moose Lodge in Brunswick, MD (1952); signed ill-advised contract with Bill McCall and his 4 Star records (1954); became a regular on Connie B. Gay's daily "Town and Country" tv show in Washington DC (1954); made 1st single, "A Church, a Courtroom and Then Goodbye," but response was tepid; reluctantly recorded "Walkin' after Midnight" and sang it on Arthur Godfrey's "Talent Scouts" (1957), launching a crossover hit which pushed the boundaries for women in country music; finally breaking with 4 Star, signed with Decca and had more freedom to choose material; recorded Owen Bradley's arrangement of "I Fall to Pieces" (1960); was severely injured in an auto accident (1961); recorded "Crazy," then "She's Got You," her 3rd smash hit in a row (1961); other songs include "Leavin' on Your Mind," "Blue Moon of Kentucky,"

"Someday (You'll Want Me to Want You)," and "Sweet Dreams (of You)"; over time, her *Greatest Hits* album was No. 1 on *Billboard*'s chart for 165 weeks, going multiplatinum (1992). Inducted into Grammy's Hall of Fame (1995). ❖ See also Margaret Jones, *Patsy: The Life and Times of Patsy Cline* (HarperCollins, 1994); (film) *Sweet Dreams,* starring Jessica Lange (1985); and *Women in World History.*

CLINTON, Chelsea (1980—). American first daughter. Born Feb 27, 1980, in Little Rock, Arkansas; dau. of Bill Clinton (US president, 1992–2000) and Hillary Rodham Clinton (US senator); attended Sidwell Friends school; graduate of Stanford University, 2001; attended University College at Oxford. ❖ Protected by parents, was rarely the subject of media scrutiny while in the White House; went on numerous governmental tours of South Asia, Bosnia and Africa with mother.

CLINTON, Elizabeth Knevet (c. 1574-c. 1630). British writer. Born c. 1574 in England; died c. 1630 in England; dau. of Sir Henry Knevet and Anne Pickering Knevet; m. Thomas Clinton, 1584; children: 18. ❖ Only surviving work is *The Countess of Lincolnes Nurserie* (1622), promoting the benefits of breast-feeding.

CLINTON, Hillary Rodham (1947—). American politician, lawyer and first lady. Born Hillary Diane Rodham, Oct 27, 1947, in Chicago, Illinois; dau. of Hugh and Dorothy Rodham; sister of Hugh and Tony Rodham; Wellesley College, BA, 1969, Yale Law School, JD, 1973; m. William J "Bill" Clinton (governor of Arkansas 1979–81, 1983–93, and president of US, 1992–2000), 1975; children: Chelsea Clinton (b. 1980). ❖ Influential first lady who went on to become US Senator, was born into conservative Republican family in Illinois; moved with husband to Arkansas and established private law practice, specializing in family issues and children's rights; campaigned vigorously for his gubernatorial elections; worked on behalf of children and families during his 2 terms as governor, continuing law practice and founding Arkansas Advocates for Children and Families; campaigned again for husband in 2 successful bids for presidency (1992 and 1996); an unusually active first lady, inspired admiration as well as criticism; served as head of ill-fated Health Care Task Force; led successful efforts to increase immunizations for young children and expand children's health insurance coverage and was an advocate for prenatal care; wrote weekly syndicated newspaper column "Talking It Over" (1995–2000), as well as numerous books, including *It Takes a Village* (1996); became 1st wife of president to appear before a grand jury (1996) for questionable dealings in 1980s real estate, dubbed "Whitewater Affair"; hosted White House Conference on Early Childhood Development and Learning (1997), as well as White House Conference on Child Care; played role in passage of Adoption and Safe Family Act (1997); served as goodwill ambassador abroad, advocating human rights and women's rights; weathered infidelity scandal during husband's presidency; was the 1st former first lady to be elected to US Senate (2000); served on Senate Committees for Environment and Public Works as well as Health, Education, Labor and Pensions and is the 1st New York senator to serve on Senate Armed Services Committee. ❖ See also autobiography *Living History* (2003); Margaret J. Goldstein and Joann Bren Guernsey, *Hillary Rodham Clinton* (Lerner, 2005).

CLISBY, Harriet (1830–1931). Australian doctor and feminist. Born Harriet Jemima Winifred Clisby in 1830 in London, England; died 1931; dau. of a corn merchant; graduate of New York Medical College for Women, 1865. ❖ In Melbourne, began working as editor of *Southern Photographic Harmonia* (1856), a publication written in shorthand; with Caroline Dexter, edited *The Interpreter,* the 1st Australian journal produced by women (1861); moved to NY to study medicine; lectured and was for many years involved with feminist and Christian groups, founding the Women's Educational and Industrial Union in Boston (1871) and L'Union des Femmes in Geneva.

CLISSON, Jeanne de (fl. 1343). *See Jeanne de Belleville.*

CLITHEROW, Margaret (1556–1586). English martyr and saint. Name variations: Margaret Middleton; Pearl of York. Born in 1556 in York, England; died Mar 25, 1586 in England; dau. of Thomas Middleton (sheriff of York, 1564–65); m. John Clitherow (butcher and chamberlain of city), 1571; children: Henry and William (priests); Anne (nun at St. Ursula's, Louvain). ❖ Canonized for defense of priests and adherence to Catholic precepts and practices despite persecution during Reformation; converted to Catholicism (1574); remained in marriage though husband continued to belong to Protestant Church; for harboring priests and celebrating mass, was frequently imprisoned, sometimes for 2 years at a time, but never abandoned activities; arrested (Mar 10, 1586), was arraigned before Judges Clinch and Rhodes and several members of

Council of the North at York assizes (Mar 14); condemned to "peine forte et dure" (to be pressed to death); tormented by ministers, was urged to confess crimes but refused, to avoid implicating her children and servants; was probably with child when sentence was carried out barbarously on Good Friday (1586); canonized by Pope Paul VI (1970). ❖ See also John Mush, "Life and Death of Margaret Clitherow the Martyr of York" in *Troubles of our Catholic Forefathers* (W. Nicholson, 1849).

CLIVE, Ann (c. 1836–1916). *See Evans, Ann.*

CLIVE, Caroline (1801–1873). English author. Name variations: (pseudonym) V; Mrs. Archer Clive. Born Caroline Meysey-Wigley in Brompton Green, London, England, June 24, 1801; died July 13, 1873, at Whitfield, Herefordshire; 2nd dau. of Edmund Meysey-Wigley (MP for Worcester) and Anna Maria Watkins Meysey; m. Reverend Archer Clive (rector of Solihull in Warwickshire), 1840; children: 1 son; 1 daughter. ❖ Under signature V, published 8 vols. of poetry; is best known as the author of *Paul Ferroll* (1855), a sympathetic portrait of a man who murders his wife to marry his 1st love. While writing in her bedroom surrounded by books and papers, was burned to death when her dress caught on fire.

CLIVE, Catherine (1711–1785). *See Clive, Kitty.*

CLIVE, Kitty (1711–1785). English-Irish actress. Name variations: Catherine (Kitty) Raftor; Mrs. Catherine Clive. Born Catherine Raftor, Nov 15, 1711, in London, England; died at Twickenham, near London, Dec 6, 1785; dau. of William Raftor (lawyer) and his wife, the erstwhile Miss Daniel (given name unknown); m. George Clive, 1733; no children. ❖ Leading lady at London's Drury Lane for 40 years, who was particularly noted for her performances in comedy roles, and as a singer; became a member of the company of Drury Lane at 17 (1728); played the lead role in Colley Cibber's *Love is a Riddle* (1729), the beginning of a long, triumphant career as the undisputed mistress of English comedy; having entered a profession that was still widely regarded as disreputable, compelled respect for her qualities as a woman, her shrewdness, her intelligence, and her strength of character, as well as for the art in which she was acknowledged to be supreme; 1st appeared as Nell in *The Devil to Pay,* one of her most famous roles (1730–31); began successful collaboration with Henry Fielding, appearing in his *The Old Debauchees, The Covent Garden Tragedy, The Lottery* and his adaptation of Moliere's *The Miser;* joined Covent Garden company (1744); published *The Case of Mrs. Clive* (1744); returned to Drury Lane (1745–46), remaining there until her retirement, appearing in some of her more popular parts, such as Lady Fanciful in *The Provok'd Wife* and Hoyden in *The Relapse;* appeared for 1st time as Lady Wishfort in Congreve's *The Way of the World,* a role that was to be one of her most celebrated (1757); played Lady Beverly in *The School for Lovers* (1763) and Mrs. Friendly in *The Dupe* (1763); other notable performances were her Widow Blackacre in *The Plain Dealer,* Mrs. Heidelberg in *The Clandestine Marriage,* Lady Fuz in Garrick's *A Peep behind the Curtain,* and Mrs. Winifred in *The School for Rakes;* made final appearance on stage, opposite David Garrick, in *Lethe* (1769); also wrote plays. ❖ See also Percy Fitzgerald, *The Life of Mrs. Catherine Clive* (1888); and *Women in World History.*

CLIVE, Margaret (1735–1817). English baroness. Name variations: Lady Clive; Baroness Clive. Born Margaret Maskelyne in 1735; died Feb 21, 1817; dau. of Edmund Maskelyne; sister of Rev. Nevil Maskelyne (1732–1811, who was appointed Astronomer Royal); m. Robert Clive (1725–1774, 1st baron Clive, clerk of the British East India Co. who turned to soldiering and laid the foundations of an empire), Mar 15, 1752, at Madras, India; children: Edward, 1st earl of Powis (1754–1839), Charlotte, Robert (1769–1833), Rebecca (d. 1795), Elizabeth, Jennifer and Margaretta or Margaret Clive (d. 1814, m. Theodore Walpole Lambert). ❖ At 16, made the long passage round the Cape of Good Hope to India to marry a man she had never seen, a friend of her brother; her correspondence from India (1762–1817) has been published in *Women Writing Home, 1700–1920* (Vol. 2); portrayed by Loretta Young in the film *Clive of India* (1935).

CLIVE, Sarah Ann (c. 1836–1916). *See Evans, Ann.*

CLODIA. *Variant of Claudia.*

CLODIA (c. 94–post 45 BCE). Roman aristocrat. Name variations: Claudia; Clodia Metelli; possibly Lesbia. Born Claudia, probably in Rome, around 94 BCE; date and place of death unknown, probably after 45 BCE; dau. of Appius Claudius Pulcher (consul in 79 BCE) and a mother whose name is not known for certain, but who may have been Metella; m. Quintus Caecilius Metellus Celer (consul in 60 BCE), sometime before 62 BCE (died 59 BCE); no evidence for remarriage; lovers: possibly the poet Gaius Valerius Catullus and Marcus Caelius Rufus; children: possibly Metella. ❖ A fiercely independent woman who was, for a while, at the center of political debate in Rome, influenced politics and patronized literature and the arts during the Roman Republic; became embroiled in political machinations of brother Clodius, which were opposed by her husband; forced to make a choice between husband and brother, supported brother, placing a strain on her marriage; when husband died suddenly (59 BCE), was suspected of poisoning him; began to prize her independence more than her good reputation and was attacked by Cicero in a judicial speech; continued to support her brother's revolutionary schemes and enjoyed a comfortable lifestyle; was caught up in the political machinations of her brother throughout the 50s, though her support began to wane by end of decade; has been called the "first political strategist" among women at Rome. ❖ See also *Women in World History*.

CLODIA (c. 60 BCE–?). **Roman noblewoman.** Name variations: Claudia. Born c. 60 BCE; dau. of Fulvia (c. 85/80–40 BCE) and Publius Clodius; stepdau. of Mark Antony (80–30 BCE); became 1st wife of Octavian (63 BCE–14 CE), later known as Augustus Caesar, emperor of Rome (div.). His 2nd wife was Scribonia; his 3rd was Livia Drusilla (58 BCE–29 CE). ❖ See also *Women in World History*.

CLOE. *Variant of Chloe.*

CLOELIA (c. 508 BCE). **Roman hero.** Name variations: Clelia. Pronunciation: KLOY-lee-ah. No sources identify her date of birth or death, her family connections or any other accomplishment beside the circumstances of her escape in the early years of the Roman Republic. ❖ Semi-historical hero celebrated by ancient Roman writers for leading an escape of women from an Etruscan camp and swimming across the Tiber River. ❖ See also *Women in World History*.

CLOETE, Hestrie (1978—). **South African high jumper.** Name variations: Hestrie Storbeck. Born Aug 26, 1978, in Germiston, South Africa. ❖ Won a silver medal for high jump at Sydney Olympics (2000) and gold medals at World championships (2001, 2003) and Commonwealth Games (2002); won a silver medal at Athens Olympics (2004); won 9 Golden League, 4 Grand Prix, and 5 Super Grand Prix events (2001–04). Named South African Athlete of the Year (1998–2002).

CLOONEY, Rosemary (1928–2002). **American singer and actress.** Born May 23, 1928, in Maysville, Kentucky; died June 29, 2002, in Beverly Hills, California; dau. of Andrew and Frances Clooney; sister of Betty Clooney (singer who died of a brain aneurysm in Aug 1976) and Nick Clooney (actor and tv host); aunt of George Clooney (actor); m. José Ferrer (actor, producer, director), July 13, 1953 (div.); m. Dante DiPaolo (dancer), Nov 7, 1997; children: Miguel Ferrer (b. 1955), Maria Ferrer, Gabriel Ferrer, Monsita Ferrer (b. 1960) and Rafael Ferrer. ❖ One of America's leading popular singers of the 1950s, began career with younger sister Betty as the Clooney Sisters on radio station WLW in Ohio, then worked with bandleaders Barney Rapp and Tony Pastor (1945); made a solo recording with Pastor, "I'm Sorry I didn't Say I'm Sorry When I Made You Cry Last Night," considered "revolutionary" by disc jockeys because of her soft, whispery style; after Betty retired (1949), left Pastor and went out on her own; produced a series of recordings for Columbia, including "Beautiful Brown Eyes" and a duet with Guy Mitchell of "You're Just in Love"; recorded novelty number "Come on-a My House," adapted from an Armenian folksong, which sold a million copies and paved the way for subsequent novelties like "Botcha Me," "Mangos," "Mambo Italiano," and "This Ole House"; made film debut in *The Stars Are Singing* (1953), followed by 4 movies including *White Christmas* (1954); starred in tv series "The Rosemary Clooney Show" (1956) and the variety series "The Lux Show Starring Rosemary Clooney" (1957–58); career waned; went on tour in "Four Girls Four" (1982); known for impeccable phrasing, became more selective and recorded a series of jazz tributes to such composers as Johnny Mercer, Cole Porter, Harold Arlen, Irving Berlin and Jimmy Van Heusen. ❖ See also autobiography (with Raymond Strait) *This for Remembrance*, the basis for tv film "Escape from Madness" (1978); and tv film "Rosie: The Rosemary Clooney Story," with Sondra Locke (1982); and *Women in World History*.

CLOPTON, Virginia Tunstall (1825–1915). *See Clay, Virginia Tunstall.*

CLOSE, Glenn (1947—). **American actress.** Born Mar 14, 1947, in Greenwich, Connecticut; College of William and Mary, BA; m. John Starke (producer, div.); m. Cabot Wade (guitarist), 1969 (div. 1971); m.

James Marlas (venture capitalist), 1984 (div. 1987); children: Annie Maude. ❖ Celebrated activist actress, grew up on 250-acre farm in CT but at 10 moved with parents, followers of Moral Re-Armament movement, to Switzerland and then Zaire, where surgeon father established a clinic; bounced between Africa and Swiss boarding schools until settling in with grandmother in Greenwich, CT; made Broadway debut in *Love for Love* (1974) and later appeared in Broadway musical *Barnum;* made film debut in *The World According to Garp* (1982), earning Oscar nomination; also nominated for Academy Awards for *The Big Chill* (1983), *The Natural* (1984), *Fatal Attraction* (1987) and *Dangerous Liaisons* (1988); other films include *Reversal of Fortune* (1990), *101 Dalmatians* (1996), *Cookie's Fortune* (1999), *Le Divorce* (2003) and *Stepford Wives* (2004); nominated for Obie for *The Singular Life of Albert Nobbs* (1982) and Tony awards for work in Tom Stoppard's *The Real Thing* (1984) and Ariel Dorfman's *Death and the Maiden* (1992); won Tony for performance as Norma Desmond in *Sunset Boulevard* (1995); on tv, appeared in "Stones for Ibarra" (1988), "Sarah, Plain and Tall" (1991) and won Emmy for "Serving in Silence: The Margarethe Cammermeyer Story" (1995); served as executive producer for documentary *Do You Mean There Are Still Cowboys?* (1987).

CLOSE, Gretchen Carlson (c. 1966—). *See Carlson, Gretchen.*

CLOSSER, Louise (1872–1933). *See Hale, Louise Closser.*

CLOTHIER, Hannah (1872–1958). *See Hull, Hannah.*

CLOTHILDE. *Variant of Clotilda or Clotilde.*

CLOTILDA (470–545). **Queen of the Franks and saint.** Name variations: Chlotilda; Chlotilde; Chlothilde; Chrotechildis; Clothild; Clothilda; Clothilde; Clothildis; Clodechildis; Clotilde; Hlotechilde or Hluodhild. Born c. 470 in Lyon (some sources cite 474 or 475); died in June 545 in Tours, France; dau. of Childeric also known as Chilperic II, king of the Burgundians, king of Lyon, and Queen Caretena; sister of Sedeluna; m. Chlodovechs or Clodovic also known as Clovis I (465–511), king of the Franks (r. 481–511), around 490 or 493 (d. 511); children: Ingomer (b. around 494, died young); Clotimir also known as Clodomir or Chlodomer (495–524), king of Orléans (r. 511–524); Childebert I (d. 558), king of Paris (r. 511–558); Chlothar, Clothaire, Clotar also known as Lothair I (497–561), king of Soissons (r. 511), king of the Franks (r. 558–561); and several daughters including Clotilda (other names unknown, possibly died young); great-grandmother of Bertha of Kent (c. 565–c. 616). Thierry, Theodoric or Theuderic I (c. 490–534), king of Reims and Metz (r. 511–534), was the son of Clovis and Amalaberga or a mistress. ❖ Legendary queen, raised in the Catholic faith, a fact that was to play an important role in the future of the Franks; married Frankish pagan king Clovis (493); established a Christian court at the ancient Roman palace in Soissons; converted husband to Christianity (c. 496), which is considered the defining moment of his reign (before him, no Christian monarch ruled over the people who founded France; after him, no pagan monarch did); turned attentions to educating her children, presiding over an increasingly larger and more pious court, and bringing her faith to their subjects; with husband, founded a church in Paris dedicated to the apostles Peter and Paul and formed a friendship with Geneviève of Paris, the spiritual leader of the city; founded monasteries and churches, endowed convents, and gave away her own lands to support these new religious establishments; when her sons warred against each other, suffered the loss of her eldest son, her only daughter, and two of her grandchildren. ❖ See also Godefroi Kurth, *Saint Clotilda*, trans. by V.M. Crawford (Duckworth, 1906); and *Women in World History*.

CLOTILDE. *Variant of Clotilda.*

CLOTILDE (d. 691). **Queen of Neustria, Burgundy, and the Franks.** Fl. around 682 and 683; m. Thierry or Theoderic III (654–691), king of Neustria and Burgundy (r. 673/75–691), king of the Franks (r. 687–691), in 675; children: Clovis III (682–695), king of the Franks (r. 691–695); Childebert III (c. 683–711), king of the Franks (r. 695–711).

CLOTILDE OF SARDINIA (1759–1802). *See Marie Clotilde.*

CLOTILDE OF SAVOY (1843–1911). **Italian princess.** Name variations: Clothilde. Born Mar 2, 1843; died June 25, 1911; dau. of Victor Emmanuel II, king of Italy (r. 1849–1878), and Marie Adelaide of Austria (1822–1855); sister of Maria Pia (1847–1911), queen of Portugal; m. Prince Napoleon Joseph Charles Paul Bonaparte (Plon-Plon), Jan 30, 1859; children: Prince Victor (b. 1862); Louis (1864–1932); Marie Laetitia (1866–1890, who m. Amadeus, king of Spain).

CLOTILDE OF SAXE-COBURG-GOTHA (1846–1927). Archduchess. Name variations: Klothilde. Born July 8, 1846, in Neuilly; died June 3, 1927, in Alcsut, Hungary; dau. of Clementine of Orleans (1817–1907) and Augustus, Prince of Saxe-Coburg-Gotha; m. Archduke Josef Karl Ludwig also known as Joseph Charles Louis (1833–1905), May 12, 1864; children: Maria Dorothea of Austria (1867–1932); Margaret Clementine (1870–1955); Josef August also known as Joseph of Alcsut (1872–1962); Ladislaus or Ladislas (1875–1895); Elisabeth Clotilde (1883–1958); Clotilde (1884–1903).

CLOTSINDA (fl. 6th c.). Queen of the Lombards. Dau. of Ingunde (fl. 517) and Chlothar also known as Clothaire, Clotar, or Lothair I (497–561), king of Soissons (r. 511), king of the Franks (r. 558–561); m. a Lombard king.

CLOUGH, Jemima (1820–1892). English educator. Born Anne Jemima Clough at Liverpool, England, Jan 20, 1820; died in Cambridge, England, Feb 27, 1892; dau. of a cotton merchant; sister of the poet Arthur Hugh Clough. ❖ Helped found the North of England council for promoting the higher education of women, of which she acted as secretary (1867–70) and president (1873–74); when a house for the residence of women students at Cambridge was opened, was chosen as its 1st principal (1871), which led to the building of Newnham Hall (1875), as well as to the establishment of Newnham College for women (1880); for her stewardship of Newnham College, is regarded as one of the foremost leaders of the women's educational movement. ❖ See also Blanche Athena Clough, *Memoir of Anne Jemima Clough* (1897); and *Women in World History.*

CLOUTIER, Suzanne (1927–2003). French-Canadian actress. Name variations: Anne Saint Jean. Born July 10, 1927, in Ottawa, Canada; died of liver cancer, Dec 2, 2003, in Montreal, Quebec; married an eminent Canadian doctor then fled to NY the next day (annulled); m. Peter Ustinov (actor), 1954 (div. 1971); children: 3. ❖ Began career as a Powers model; made film debut in *Temptation* (1946), followed by *Au royaume des cieux* (under name Anne Saint Jean), *Derby Day, Doctor in the House, Romanoff and Juliet* and *Concerto Grosso Modo,* among others; had most important role as Desdemona in Orson Welles' *The Tragedy of Othello* (1952).

CLOUZOT, Vera (1921–1960). Brazilian-born actress. Born Vera Amado Gibson in Brazil in 1921; died Dec 15, 1960; dau. of Gilberto Amado (writer, politician, and cousin of Jorge Amado, who also served as Brazilian representative to UN) and Alice de Rego Barros Gibson; m. Leo Lapara (comedian), 1938; m. Henri-Georges Clouzot, Jan 15, 1950. ❖ With 1st husband, spent several years touring Americas and Europe with a troupe managed by Louis Jouvert, owner of the Athénée in Paris; met French film director Henri-Georges Clouzot and became a "script girl" on the set of *Miquette et sa mère;* was well-known as the female lead in many of his subsequent films, including *La salaire de la peur* (The Wages of Fear, 1952) and *Les diaboliques* (The Fiends, 1954), in which she portrayed Christina Delasalle; having suffered a pulmonary edema (1951), experienced recurring problems thereafter; turned to morphine and other opium derivatives. ❖ See also *Women in World History.*

CLUBB, Elizabeth (1922—). English doctor and expert in natural family planning. Name variations: Elizabeth Mary Fitz-Simon Clubb. Born Elizabeth Mary Fitz-Simon Thomas, Dec 18, 1922; trained at King's College Medical School in London and West London Hospital; m. Dr. John Clubb (physician), 1948; children: Dr. Cecilia Pyper (doctor). ❖ Expert in family planning, had large Oxford-based general practice with husband, then with Dr. Robert Harvard, and later with daughter; served as a Natural Family Planning Service of the Catholic Marriage Advisory Council (CMAC) medical adviser (1953–90); worked as medical director of Natural Family Planning Service of CMAC (later Marriage Care, 1990–97); taught symptothermal method to patients to spread awareness of personal fertility patterns and peaks; obtained university accreditation for nurses for National Health Service (NHS) natural planning courses; was a Royal College of General Practitioners founding member (1953) and elected fellow (1986).

CLUETT, Mrs. (1881–1973). See Peacocke, Isabel Maud.

CLUNE, Deirdre (1959—). Irish politician. Born Deirdre Barry, June 1959, in Cork, Ireland; dau. of Peter Barry (TD, Cork, 1969–97); m. Conor Clune. ❖ Representing Fine Gael, elected to the 28th Dáil (1997–2002) for Cork South Central; defeated in the next general election.

CLUYSENAAR, Anne (1936—). Irish-Belgian poet. Born Anne Alice Andrée Cluysenaar, Mar 15, 1936, in Brussels, Belgium; dau. of John Cluysenaar and Sybil Fitzgerald Cluysenaar; attended Trinity College, Dublin, and University of Edinburgh; m. Walter Freeman Jackson, 1976. ❖ Worked as lecturer at several English, Irish, and Scottish universities; writings include *A Fan of Shadows* (1967), *Moments of Grace* (1980), *Double Helix* (1982) and *Timeslips* (1997); also published works of literary criticism, including *Introduction to Literary Stylistics: A Discussion of Dominant Structures in Verse and Prose* (1976) and *The Missing Subject* (1987).

CLWYD, Ann (1937—). Welsh journalist, politician and member of Parliament. Born Mar 21, 1937, in Denbigh; dau. of Gwilym and Elizabeth Lewis; attended University College of Wales; m. Owen Roberts, 1963. ❖ Journalist and broadcaster, was a member of European Parliament for Mid and West Wales (1979–84); representing Labour, elected to House of Commons for Cynon Valley (1992, 1997, 2001, 2005).

CLYDE, June (1909–1987). American actress. Name variations: Baby Tetrazini. Born June Tetrazini, Dec 2, 1909, in St. Joseph, Missouri; died Oct 1, 1987, in Fort Lauderdale, Florida; niece of actress Leona Hutton (c. 1892–1949); m. Thornton Freeland (film director), 1930. ❖ Starting at age 7, appeared in vaudeville as Baby Tetrazini, followed by stage musicals; made film debut in *Tanned Legs* (1929); other films include *Hit the Deck, Midnight Mystery, The Secret Witness, The Cohens and Kellys in Hollywood, Back Street, A Study in Scarlet, Only Yesterday, Charing Cross Road, School for Husbands, Sealed Lips, Hollywood and Vine* and *The Story of Esther Costello.*

CLYMER, Eleanor (1906–2001). American children's writer. Born Eleanor Lowenton, Jan 7, 1906, to Russian immigrant parents; died May 30, 2001, in Haverford, Pennsylvania; earned degree in English from University of Wisconsin, 1928; m. Kinsey Clymer (journalist, later social worker); children: Adam Clymer (Washington correspondent for *The New York Times*). ❖ Published 58 books (1943–83), including *A Yard for John* (1943), *The Trolley Car Family* (1947), *My Brother Stevie* (1967), *The Tiny Little House* (1964) and *Hamburgers—and Ice Cream for Dessert* (1975).

COACHMAN, Alice (1923—). African-American track-and-field athlete. Born Nov 9, 1923, in Albany, Georgia; m. Frank Davis (div.). ❖ At London Games, won a gold medal for the women's high jump, 5'6½, setting an Olympic record and becoming the 1st African-American woman to win an Olympic gold medal (1948); holds record for most consecutive Amateur Athletic Union (AAU) championships in outdoor high jump (1939–48); was AAU champion at 50 meters (1943–47), 100 meters (1942, 1945, 1946), indoor high jump (1941, 1945, 1946), and indoor 50 meters (1945, 1946). ❖ See also *Women in World History.*

COAD, Nellie (1883–1974). New Zealand teacher and writer. Born Nellie Euphemia Coad, Oct 15, 1883, at New Plymouth, New Zealand; died Sept 6, 1974, at Wickford, Essex, England; dau. of James Hook Coad (brewer) and Annie Venters (McLaughlin) Coad (teacher); Victoria College, MA, 1914. ❖ Became teacher and head of history, civics, and geography department at Wellington Girls' College (1917–38); served on New Zealand Educational Institute, and was vice president of National Council of Women of New Zealand (1921–22); founding president of New Zealand Women Writers' and Artists' Society (1932–34); wrote numerous textbooks, a novel, and a volume of short stories; moved to England during WWII; worked as air-raid warden and lectured Royal Air Force members on history and geography of Pacific region. ❖ See also *Dictionary of New Zealand Biography* (Vol. 3).

COADA, Beatrice (1975—). See Caslaru, Beatrice.

COAKES, Marion (1947—). English equestrian. Name variations: Mrs. David Mould. Born June 1947. ❖ Won Ladies World championship on Stroller (1965); at Mexico City Olympics, won a silver medal in individual jumping on Stroller (1968), the 1st woman to claim an indiv. jumping medal.

COATES, Anne V. (1925—). British film editor. Born in Reigate, England, 1925; attended Bartrum College; m. director Douglas Hickox. ❖ Leaving a career in nursing (1950s) to work in movies, has been associated with numerous major productions for close to 40 years; films include *The Pickwick Papers* (1952), *The Horse's Mouth* (1958), *Tunes of Glory* (1960), *Those Magnificent Men in Their Flying Machines* (1965), *Hotel Paradiso* (1966), *Murder on the Orient Express* (1974), *The Eagle Has Landed* (1976), (also co-producer) *The Medusa Touch* (1978),

Ragtime (1981), *The Pirates of Penzance* (1983), *Greystoke: The Legend of Tarzan* (1984), *Lady Jane* (1986), *Masters of the Universe* (1987), *Listen to Me* (1989), *I Love You to Death* (1990). Won Academy Award for editing *Lawrence of Arabia* (1962) and was nominated for Oscars for *Becket* (1964) and *The Elephant Man* (1980).

COATES, Dorothy Love (1928–2002). African-American gospel singer. Born Dorothy McGriff, Jan 30, 1928, in Birmingham, Alabama; died April 9, 2002, in Birmingham; dau. of a minister; m. Willie Love (singer, div.); m. Carl Coates (singer, died 1999); children: (1st m.) Cassandra Madison and Carletta Criss. ❖ One of the giants in her field, joined the Gospel Harmonettes, a group that had its 1st hit with "I'm Sealed" (1951); continued with the Harmonettes (1950s–60), writing much of the group's material, and enjoying such hits as "You Must Be Born Again," "That's Enough," "I Won't Let Go of My Faith" and "You've Been Good to Me"; formed the Dorothy Love Coates Singers, featuring her sister Lillian; frequently sang at Newport Jazz Festival; appeared in films *The Long Walk Home* (1990) and *Beloved* (1998); wrote songs for such performers as Johnny Cash, Mahalia Jackson, and Ray Charles; also had a substantial role in the civil-rights movement.

COATES, Florence Nicholson (1850–1927). American poet. Born Florence Van Leer Earle, July 1, 1850, in Philadelphia, Pennsylvania; died April 6, 1927, in Philadelphia; m. William Nicholson, 1872 (died); m. Edward H. Coates (Philadelphia financier), Jan 1879. ❖ Began contributing poems to leading magazines (1890s); esteemed more for their craft than originality, works include *Mine and Thine* (1904), *Lyrics of Life* (1909), *The Unconquered Air and Other Poems* (1912), *Poems* (2 vols., 1916) and *Pro Patria* (1917); was elected "poet laureate of Pennsylvania" (1915) by the state Federation of Women's Clubs.

COATES, Gloria (1938—). American composer and programmer. Born Gloria Kannenberg, Oct 10, 1938, in Wausau, Wisconsin; dau. of Natalie Zanon (Italian coloratura) and Roland Kannenberg (state senator); m. Francis Mitchell Coates Jr., 1959 (div. 1969); children: Alexandra Coates (harpist). ❖ Studied music theory with Leonard Siem and began to compose; won apprenticeship at Brookside Playhouse in Petersburg, Pennsylvania; studied with Norwegian opera singer Nene Baalstadand and with Alexander Tcherrepnin; acted with Chicago Stage Guild; conducted choir in Wausau before arriving in NY where she studied voice and art and starred off-Broadway in musical *Dacota*; while continuing to compose, became music, art, and drama critic for *Louisiana State Times* and produced and moderated daily tv program; settled in Munich and organized radio programs for West German Radio about contemporary American music; started German-American Concert Series for Amerika Haus (1971); was guest of Soviet Composers Union at 1st International Festival of New Music in Moscow (1981); as composer, had 58 commissions by 1978; wrote String Quartet No. II for 1972 Olympics in Munich (recorded in 1977 and 1983); worked on orchestral piece based on texts by Leonardo da Vinci; was also visual artist with works in private collections and European exhibits; her most popular work was a music song cycle based on poems by Emily Dickinson. Selected works: *Music on Open Strings* (1974); *Planets* (1974); *Chamber Symphony or Transitions* (1976); *Sinfonietta della Notte* (1982); *L'Anima della Terra* (1982); Symphony No. 3 (1984); *Three Mystical Songs* (1985). ❖ See also *Women in World History.*

COATES, Renee. *See De Marco, Renée.*

COATSWORTH, Elizabeth (1893–1986). American children's writer. Name variations: Elizabeth Beston. Born May 31, 1893, in Buffalo, NY; died Aug 31, 1986, in Nobleboro, Maine; dau. of William T. and Ida (Reid) Coatsworth; Vassar College, BA, 1915; Columbia University, MA, 1916; also attended Radcliffe College; married Henry Beston (author and naturalist), June 18, 1929 (died April 15, 1968); children: Margaret (Mrs. Dorik Mechau), Catherine (Mrs. Richard Barnes). ❖ Began career as a poet with *Fox Footprints* (1923); published 1st book for children, *The Cat and the Captain* (1927); other books include *The Littlest House* (1940), *Bob Bodden and the Good Ship Rover* (1968), *The Lucky Ones: Five Journeys toward a Home* (1968), *Under the Green Willow* (1971), *The Snow Parlor and Other Bedtime Stories* (1971), *Good Night* (1972), *The Wanderers* (1973), *All-of-a-Sudden Susan* (1974) and *Marra's World* (1975). Won Newbery Medal for *The Cat Who Went to Heaven* (1931); received Kerlan Award from University of Minnesota (1975). ❖ See also *A Personal Geography: Almost an Autobiography* (Stephen Greene, 1976) and *Something About the Author.*

COBB, Florence (1895–1977). *See Vidor, Florence.*

COBB, Jerrie (1931—). American aviator and astronaut. Born Geraldyn Menor Cobb, Mar 5, 1931, at Norman, Oklahoma; dau. of William Harvey Cobb (Air Force officer) and Helena Butler Stone Cobb (teacher). ❖ Licensed pilot since 1947, set world records (1956–60); ferried aircraft to South America, Europe and India; was hired as a test pilot by Aero Design and Engineering Co. (1959); won Woman of the Year in Aviation Award (1959); was the 1st American woman to pass NASA astronaut tests, the same rigorous tests, physical and psychological, as the male Mercury astronauts, and was rated higher than many male candidates, especially in adjustment tests (Feb 1960); addressed the House Committee on Science and Astronautics, arguing that women had proven that they were as physically and mentally suitable to be astronauts as men (1962), but NASA officials explained that it would be too complicated to design spacesuits to fit female astronauts and accommodate their biological needs; became a NASA consultant (1960–62); established airlift service to Amazonia, the Jerrie Cobb Foundation (1964); nominated for Nobel Peace Prize (1981). ❖ See also autobiography (with Jane Rieker) *Woman Into Space: The Jerrie Cobb Story* (1963); and *Women in World History.*

COBB, Jewell Plummer (1924—). African-American educator, administrator, and cell biologist. Born Jan 17, 1924, in Chicago, Illinois; dau. of Carriebel (Cole) Plummer (phys ed and dance teacher) and Frank V. Plummer (physician); Talladega College, Alabama, BSC, 1941; New York University, MSC, 1947, PhD, 1950; m. Roy Paul Cobb, 1954 (div. 1967); children: Roy Jonathan Cobb (b. 1957). ❖ Pioneered programs for the inclusion of women and minorities in the sciences; became fellow of National Cancer Institute, Harlem Hospital (1950), investigating the growth of cancer tumors in tissue cultures and studying the effects of chemotherapy on cancer cells; was instructor at University of Illinois (1952), establishing the 1st tissue culture laboratory at the university, and New York University (1955); promoted to assistant professor at New York University (1956), performing extensive research on the pigmentation of cells, particularly the influence of melanin on skin color; was professor of biology at Sarah Lawrence College (1960), then dean (1969); appointed dean of Connecticut College (1969), where she established privately funded scholarship programs for minority and female students in the fields of premedicine and predentistry (the highly successful programs served as pioneering models for 20 similar programs established across America); appointed the only minority member on the National Science Board (1974); appointed dean of biology at Douglass College, Rutgers University (1976); appointed president of California State University at Fullerton (1981); appointed Trustee Professor of the California State College, Los Angeles (1990). ❖ See also *Women in World History.*

COBBE, Frances Power (1822–1904). Irish writer, journalist, and feminist. Born Frances Power Cobbe in Dublin, Ireland, Dec 4, 1822; died at Hengwrt, Wales, April 5, 1904; dau. of Charles and Frances (Conway) Cobbe; never married; no children; lifelong companion of Mary Lloyd. ❖ Prolific writer who wrote and spoke on a wide range of issues but is best known for her work on wife abuse and antivivisection; lived at home with family in Ireland for 36 years; left home after father died (1857); lived and worked with Mary Carpenter (1858–59); moved to London and began writing for several newspapers; published several hundred pamphlets on various reform causes, including wife abuse, suffrage, post-secondary education for women, and antivivisection; founded antivivisection association, Victoria Street Society (1875); left London with companion Mary Lloyd and settled in Wales; founded British Union for the Abolition of Vivisection (1898); writings include *Essays on the Theory of Intuitive Morals* (1855), *Essays on the Pursuits of Women* (1863), (editor) *The Collected Works of Theodore Parker* (14 vols., 1863–66), *Studies New and Old of Ethical and Social Subjects* (1866), "The Rights of Man and the Claims of Brutes," in *Fraser's Magazine* (1870), *Darwinism in Morals, and Other Essays* (1872), and *The Duties of Women* (1881); was an important participant in the middle-class movement for the reform of women's political, economic, and legal rights. ❖ See also autobiography *The Life of Frances Power Cobbe* (2 vols., 1894); and *Women in World History.*

COBBOLD, Elizabeth (c. 1764–1824). British poet. Name variations: Eliza Clarke; Elizabeth Clarke. Born c. 1764; died 1824; m. William Clarke, 1790 (died 1790); m. John Cobbold. ❖ Works include *Poems on Various Subjects* (1783), *Six Narrative Poems* (1781), and the novel *The Sword, or Father Bertrand's History of His Own Time* (1791); also published in magazines and in *The Ladies Fashionable Repository.*

COBBOLD, Hermione (1905–2004). English landowner and charity worker. Name variations: Lady Cobbold. Born Margaret Hermione Millicent Bulwer-Lytton at Knebworth, Aug 31, 1905; died Oct 27, 2004; elder dau. of Victor Alexander George Robert Bulwer-Lytton, 2nd earl of Lytton (1876–1947), and Pamela Chichele-Plowden; granddau. of Edward Bulwer-Lytton (the writer); m. Cameron "Kim" Fromanteel Cobbold, Lord Cobbold (governor of the Bank of England, 1949–61, and lord chamberlain, 1963–71), 1930 (died 1987); children: Jane (died, age 5) and 2 sons, including David, Lord Cobbold. ❖ Landowner and charity worker, played an active role in many voluntary organizations, notably the YMCA; when father was governor of Bengal (1922–27), acted as his viceriene in Delhi when Lord Reading went on leave; inherited Knebworth on the death of her father (1947).

COBBS, Janet (1967—). American volleyball player. Born Feb 22, 1967, in Saint Paul, Minnesota; attended North Dakota State College. ❖ At Barcelona Olympics, won a bronze medal in team competition (1992); was on the US national team (1989–94).

COBERGER, Annelise (1971—). New Zealand Alpine skier. Born Sept 16, 1971, in Christchurch, New Zealand. ❖ Won a silver medal for slalom at Albertville Olympics (1992).

COBHAM, Eleanor (d. 1452). Duchess of Gloucester. Died Aug 7, 1452 (some sources cite 1446); dau. of Reginald Cobham, 2nd baron Cobham; became 2nd wife of Humphrey, duke of Gloucester, 1431 (div. 1441). ❖ Originally the mistress, then wife, of Humphrey, duke of Gloucester (son of King Henry IV); fell in with Roger Bolingbroke, who dabbled in the black art, and was tried for conspiracy to kill Henry VI by magic, so that husband might have the crown; imprisoned (1441) and sentenced to walk the streets for 3 days while bareheaded and carrying a burning candle; was afterward confined to Chester Castle, followed by Peel Castle, where she remained until her death; appears in Shakespeare's play *Henry VI, part 2*. ❖ See also *Women in World History.*

COBIAN, Miguelina (1941—). Cuban runner. Born Dec 13, 1941, in Santiago, Cuba. ❖ Won the 100 meters in the Central American and Caribbean Games (1962, 1966, 1970) and the 200 meters and sprint relay (1970); won the silver medal in the 4x100-meter relay in Mexico City Olympics (1968); retired (1970).

COBOS, Antonia (c. 1920—). American concert dancer and ballet choreographer. Born Phyllis Nahle, c. 1920 in New York, NY. ❖ Studied classical Spanish dance forms in Barcelona, Spain; made 1st solo appearance in concert recital in Paris, where she performed *Spectral Minuet,* among others (1938); created 3 widely acclaimed works: *The Mute Wife* (1944), *Madroñas* (1948) and *The Mikado* (1954); continued to give recitals of Spanish dance.

COBOS, Maria Barea (1966—). *See Barea Cobos, Maria.*

COBURN, Doris (fl. 1970s). American bowler. Name variations: Doris Coburn-Carroll. Lives in Buffalo, NY; children: Cindy Coburn-Carroll (bowler). ❖ Won 3 professional women's bowling titles; became 1st woman in history of bowling to average a score of over 200 for 8 years in a row; bowled perfect 300 game and inducted into NY State Women's Bowling Association Hall of Fame (1975); inducted into WIBC Hall of Fame (1976); with daughter, set Women's International Bowling Congress (WIBC) Doubles record of 1444 (1977); inducted into Greater Buffalo Sports Hall of Fame (1992).

COBURN-CARROLL, Cindy (fl. 1980s). American bowler. Dau. of Frank Coburn and Doris Coburn (bowler); attended Erie Community College and University of Buffalo. ❖ With mother, set Women's International Bowling Congress (WIBC) Doubles record of 1444 (1977); at 19, became youngest woman in history of WIBC to hold nation's high average of 211; became winner of more than 15 professional titles, including WIBC Queen's Tournament; received the Robby's award for sportsmanship (1984); twice won WIBC championship Tournament Doubles event titles with Lucy Giovinco Sandelin; inducted into numerous halls of fame, including Women's All Star Association Hall of Fame (2001) and WIBC Hall of Fame; became 1st daughter to join a mother as inductee in Greater Buffalo Sports Hall of Fame (2001).

COCA, Imogene (1909–2001). American actress and comedian. Born Nov 18, 1909, in Philadelphia, Pennsylvania; died June 2, 2001, in Westport, Connecticut; dau. of Joseph (musical conductor) and Sadie (Brady) Coca (dancer and vaudeville actress); m. Robert Burton (actor-musician), 1935 (deceased); m. King Donovan (actor). ❖ Star of tv's groundbreaking comedy "Your Show of Shows," was thrust into vaudeville at age 14 by father; made NY debut a year later in chorus of *When You Smile;* in early years, worked in nightclubs and vaudeville, including a stint as Leonard Sillman's dancing partner in an act at the Palace; moved on to minor stage roles, until Sillman drafted her for his *New Faces* revue and discovered her flair for comedy (1934); became a regular in Sillman's shows (1935–38), appearing in featured spots in 7 productions; also appeared in *Straw Hat Revue* (1939); following WWII, began to play the better clubs; made tv debut in "Admiral Broadway Revue" (1949); was then partnered with Sid Caesar, Carl Reiner, and Howie Morris for 90-minute weekly revue "Your Show of Shows," which 1st aired Feb 24, 1950; also starred in the series, "Grindle"; back on Broadway, played Letitia Primrose in *On the Twentieth Century* (1978); films include *Under the Yum-Yum Tree.* ❖ See also *Women in World History.*

COCÉA, Alice (1899–1970). Romanian-born French actress and singer. Name variations: Alice Cocea. Born July 28, 1899, in Sinaia, Romania; died July 2, 1970, in Boulogne-Billancourt, Hauts-de-Seine, France. ❖ Moved to Paris (1910); toured with Suzanne Després; made Paris stage debut in *Le Scandale de Monte Carlo* (1916), followed by *Psyché, La Petite Reine, Phi-Phi, Dédé, Le Singe qui parle,* the title role in *La Petite Catherine, La Route des Indies* and *Les Parents Terribles,* among others; films include *Mon gosse de père* (1930), *Delphine* (1931) and *La Ronde* (1964).

COCHELEA, Veronica (1965—). Romanian rower. Name variations: Veronica Cochelea-Cogeanu; Veronica Cogeanu Cochelea; Veronica Cogeanu. Born Veronica Cogeanu, Nov 15, 1965, in Romania. ❖ At Seoul Olympics, won a bronze medal in quadruple sculls without coxswain and a silver medal in double sculls (1988); at Barcelona Olympics, won silver medals in quadruple sculls without coxswain and double sculls (1992); won a gold medal at Atlanta Olympics (1996) and a gold medal at Sydney Olympics (2000), both for coxed eights.

COCHRAN, Angela (1965—). American windsurfer. Born Mar 28, 1965, in Huntington Beach, California; m. Campbell Cochran (windsurfer); children: Sage. ❖ Won World Wave-sailing championships (1989, 1991); was Aloha Classic champion (1989–91); placed 3rd overall in World Cup (1990).

COCHRAN, Barbara (1951—). American Alpine skier. Born Barbara Ann Cochran, Jan 4, 1951, in Claremont, New Hampshire; dau. of Virginia and Gordon S. ("Mickey") Cochran (skier); sister of Marilyn Cochran, Linda Cochran and Robert Cochran (all skiers); attended University of Vermont. ❖ Won a silver medal for slalom at World championships (1970); won a gold medal for slalom at Sapporo Olympics (1972); won US nationals for giant slalom (1969) and slalom (1971); at World championships, placed 2nd for slalom (1970).

COCHRAN, Jacqueline (1906–1980). American aviator and businesswoman. Born May 11, 1906, probably somewhere in northern Florida; died in Indio, California, Aug 9, 1980; orphaned, parents unknown; m. Floyd B. Odlum (financier), May 11, 1936. ❖ One of the world's most famous woman fliers, held the greatest number of speed, distance, and altitude records of any pilot, male or female; was the 1st woman to break the sound barrier, the 1st woman to make a blind landing, and the 1st woman to fly a British bomber; also held practically all the men's records for propeller-driven planes; took flying lessons at Roosevelt Field (1932); was the only American woman entrant in the McRobertson London-to-Melbourne air race (1934); in Bendix Cross-Country Air Race, against world competition, placed 3rd overall (1937), 1st overall (1938), 2nd overall (1946), 3rd overall (1948); set women's national altitude record, international open-class speed record for both men and women, New York-to-Miami Air Race record, and world speed record for 100 and for 2,000 kilometers (1939–40); won 15 Harmon international trophies; during WWII, served as director of women pilots for Women's Airforce Service Pilots (WASPS, 1943–44); commissioned lieutenant colonel in Air Force Reserves (1948), retiring at rank of full colonel (1970); flew Canadian-built Sabrejet F-86 to become the 1st woman to soar faster than the speed of sound (1953); piloting an A3J plane, was the 1st woman to fly at Mach 2, twice the speed of sound (1960); served as president of Fédération Aéronautique Internationale (1958–61), the only woman to have held that office. Awarded Distinguished Service Medal (1945) and Distinguished Flying Cross with two oak-leaf clusters (1969). ❖ See also autobiographies *The Stars at Noon* (Little, Brown, 1954) and (with Maryann Bucknum Brinley) *Jackie Cochran* (Bantam, 1987); and *Women in World History.*

COCHRAN, Linda (1953—). *American gymnast.* Name variations: Lindy Cochran. Born Oct 7, 1953, in Richmond, Vermont; dau. of Virginia and Gordon S. ("Mickey") Cochran (skier); sister of Bob, Marilyn, and Barbara Cochran (all skiers). ❖ Placed 1st in European Cup giant slalom (1975); was the top American finisher at Innsbruck Olympics, placing 6th (1976).

COCHRAN, Marilyn (1950—). *American Alpine skier.* Name variations: Marilyn Cochran Brown. Born Feb 7, 1950, in Richmond, Vermont; dau. of Virginia and Gordon S. ("Mickey") Cochran (skier); sister of Bob, Linda, and Barbara Cochran (all skiers). ❖ At World Cup, won a giant slalom title (1969) and was the 1st American to win the French championship; at World championships, won a bronze medal for combined (1970).

COCHRANE, Elizabeth (1864–1922). *See Seaman, Elizabeth.*

COCKBURN, Alicia (1713–1794). *Scottish poet.* Name variations: Alison Cockburn. Born Alicia Rutherford or Rutherfurd, Oct 8, 1713, in Fairnalee, Selkirkshire, Scotland; died Nov 22, 1794, in Edinburgh; dau. of Robert Rutherfurd; m. Patrick Cockburn, 1731. ❖ An indefatigable letter writer and a composer of parodies, wrote the well-known Scottish ballad, "Flowers of the Forest." There are two versions of the song, one by Cockburn, the other by Jean Elliot; both were based on an ancient Border ballad.

COCKBURN, Catharine Trotter (1679–1749). *English playwright, essayist, poet, and philosopher.* Name variations: Catherine Trotter Cockburn. Born Aug 16, 1679; died May 11, 1749, in Long Horsley, Northumberland; dau. of Scottish parents, her father a naval commander; mostly self-taught at home; converted from Church of England to Roman Catholic Church, then back to Church of England in 1707; m. Patrick Cockburn (cleric), 1708. ❖ At 17, to supplement the family income, wrote 1st play, *Agnes de Castro* (based on Inez de Castro), which was produced at Drury Lane in London; wrote 4 more plays, becoming a popular playwright before age 20; published fictionalized autobiography, *Olinda's Adventures* (1718); an admirer of John Locke's controversial *Essay Concerning Human Understanding,* anonymously published her *A Defense of the Essay of Human Understanding* (1702); also published *A Discourse Concerning a Guide in Controversies,* to explain why she felt compelled philosophically to return to the Church of England (1707); became well known for her artistic and analytic abilities. ❖ See also *Women in World History.*

COCKBURN, Karen (1980—). *Canadian trampolinist.* Born Oct 2, 1980, in Toronto, Ontario, Canada; attended York University. ❖ At World championships, won a gold medal for indiv. and a bronze medal for team (2003); won a silver medal for indiv. at Athens Olympics (2004).

COCKBURN, Patricia (1914–1989). *Scottish artist, conchologist, writer, and traveler.* Name variations: Patricia Arbuthnot; Patricia Byron. Born Patricia Evangeline Ann Arbuthnot, Mar 17, 1914, in Rosscarbery (Co. Cork), Ireland; died Oct 6, 1989; attended Westminster College of Art; m. Arthur Byron (underwriter), 1932 (div. 1939); Claud Cockburn (Communist journalist), 1940 (died 1981); children: (1st m.) 1; (2nd m.) 2. ❖ Respected traveler, journalist and equestrian, mapped languages and took photographs of groups of Pygmies in the Congo for Royal Geographical Society's Sir William Goodenough (1930s); worked as journalist in Ireland; edited the *Week* (later *Private Eye*) and published *The Years of the Week* (1968); created shell pictures. Other publications include *Figures of Eight* (1985), an autobiography.

COCKBURN, Sarah (1864–1956). *See Salmond, Sarah.*

COCKERHAM, Kimberly (c. 1975—). *See Aiken, Kimberly.*

COCKERILL, Kay (1964—). *American golfer.* Born Oct 16, 1964, in San Carlos, California; attended University of California–Los Angeles (UCLA). ❖ Won US Women's Amateur (1986–87); was a member of the World Cup team (1986).

COCTEAU TWINS. *See Fraser, Elizabeth.*

CODINA, Iverna (1918—). *Argentinean poet and novelist.* Born 1918 in Quillota, Chile. ❖ Moved to Argentina as child, growing up in San Rafael; wrote for national and international newspapers and worked on radio; writings include *Canciones de lluvia y cielo* (1946), *La luna ha muerto* (1957), *Detrás del grito* (1962) and *Los guerilleros* (1968).

COE, Dawn (1960—). *Canadian golfer.* Name variations: Dawn Coe-Jones. Born Dawn Coe, Oct 19, 1960, in Campbell River, British Columbia, Canada; m. Jimmy Jones, 1992. ❖ Won Canadian Amateur (1983) and B.C. Amateur twice; won Kemper Open (1992), Palm Beach Classic (1994), and Chrysler-Plymouth Tournament of Champions (1995). Inducted into Canadian Golf Hall of Fame (2003).

COE, Sue (1951—). *English illustrator.* Born 1951 in Tamworth, Staffordshire, England; attended Royal College of Art, 1970–72. ❖ Moved to New York (1972); in her social-protest art, dealt with many issues, including AIDS crisis, the Gulf wars, apartheid, invasion of Grenada, skinheads, and killing animals for food and research; exhibited at Hirshhorn Museum (1994); frequent contributor to *Village Voice, The New Yorker, New York Times, Time* and *Newsweek.*

COETZER, Amanda (1971—). *South African tennis player.* Pronunciation: Coot-ser. Born Oct 22, 1971, in Hoopstad, South Africa. ❖ Turned pro (1988); was a semifinalist for singles at Australian Open (1996, 1997) and Roland Garros (1997); was runner-up for doubles at US Open (1993); retired (2004).

COEUR-BRULANT, Vicomtesse de (fl. 1880s). *See Mannoury d'Ectot, Madame de.*

COFFEE, Lenore (1896–1984). *American screenwriter.* Name variations: Lenore Cowen. Born July 13, 1896, in San Francisco, California; died July 2, 1984, in Woodland Hills, California; m. William Joyce Cowen (English motion picture director), June 8, 1924; children: daughter Toni (b. Jan 29, 1927) and son Garry (b. Feb 2, 1930). ❖ Received 1st screen credit on *The Better Wife* (1919); in a career that spanned 4 decades, wrote for many of the leading ladies of the day, most often for Joan Crawford and Bette Davis; worked on over 80 films, though she received screen credit on about half of them; credited films include *The Light That Failed* (1922), *East Lynne* (1925), *Chicago* (1927), *The Squaw Man* (1931), *The Age of Indiscretion* (1935), *The Way of All Flesh* (1940), *My Son, My Son* (1940), *The Great Lie* (1941), *Old Acquaintance* (1943), *Till We Meet Again* (1944), *Beyond the Forest* (1949), *Sudden Fear* (1952) and *Cash McCall* (1958). Nominated for Academy Award for *Four Daughters* (1938). ❖ See also autobiography *Storyline: Reflections of a Hollywood Screenwriter* (Cassell, 1973); and *Women in World History.*

COFFEY, Ann (1946—). *English politician and member of Parliament.* Born Ann Brown, Aug 31, 1946; dau. of John Brown (MBE) and Marie Brown (nurse); married 1973 (div. 1989); married 1999. ❖ Social worker; representing Labour, elected to House of Commons for Stockport (1992, 1997, 2001, 2005).

COGEANU, Veronica (1965—). *See Cochelea, Veronica.*

COGHEN, Mercedes (1962—). *See Coghen Alberdingk, Mercedes.*

COGHEN ALBERDINGK, Mercedes (1962—). *Spanish field-hockey player.* Name variations: Mercedes Coghen; Mercedes Coghen Alberdingk-Thijn. Born Aug 1962 in Spain. ❖ At Barcelona Olympics, won a gold medal in team competition (1992).

COGHLAN, Gertrude (1876–1952). *English-born actress.* Born Feb 1, 1876, in Hertfordshire, England; died Sept 11, 1952, in Bayside, NY; dau. of Charles Coghlan (playwright); niece of Rose Coghlan (actress, 1852–1932); m. Augustus Pitou Jr. ❖ Made stage debut as Mion in *Diplomacy* in Detroit (1893); made Broadway debut in her father's play, *The Royal Box* (1897), and starred in his play, *Becky Sharp* (1901); other appearances include *The Sword of Justice, The Lion and the Mouse, The Sorceress, The Traveling Salesman* and *Plumes in the Dust;* retired (1937).

COGHLAN, Rose (1852–1932). *English-American actress.* Born Rosamond Maria Coghlan, Mar 18, 1852 (some sources cite 1850) in Peterborough, Lincolnshire, England; died 1932 in Harrison, NY; dau. of Francis (publisher) and Anna Maria (Kirby) Coghlan (both Irish); sister of actor Charles Coghlan (died 1899); aunt of Gertrude Coghlan; naturalized US citizen, 1902; m. Clinton J. Edgerly (Boston attorney), April 1885 (div. 1890); m. John T. Sullivan (Boston actor), June 7, 1893 (div. 1904); no children. ❖ Famed for her mellow voice, made her debut in Scotland at 13 and went on to star on the London stage; arrived in NY (1872); appeared as Countess Zicka in American premiere of *Diplomacy* (1878) and was a great success as Stephanie in *Forget-Me-Not* (1880); worked with Wallack's company (1880–89). ❖ See also *Women in World History.*

COHAN, Ethel Levey (1880–1955). *See Levey, Ethel.*

COHAN, Georgette (b. 1900). *American actress.* Born Aug 26, 1900, in Los Angeles, California; dau. of George M. Cohan (actor, playwright, composer, manager) and Ethel Levey (actress); half-sister of Helen F.

Cohan (actress); m. J. William Souther (died 1925); m. H.W. Rowse (div.). ❖ Made stage debut in Manchester, England, as Dinah in *Mr. Pim Passes By* and London debut in the title role of *Peter Pan* (both 1919); left for US and appeared in vaudeville; made NY stage debut in the title role of her father's play, *Madeleine and the Movies* (1922); also appeared in *Diplomacy* and *The Rivals*.

COHAN, Helen F. (1910–1996). American actress. Born Sept 13, 1910, in New York, NY; died Sept 14, 1996, in Los Angeles, California; dau. of George M. Cohan (actor, playwright, composer, manager) and Agnes Nolan; half-sister of Georgette Cohan (actress). ❖ Appeared on Broadway in *Friendship*.

COHAN, Josephine (1876–1916). American actress and dancer. Name variations: Josephine Niblo. Born 1876 in Providence, Rhode Island; died July 12, 1916, in New York, NY; dau. of Jerry Cohan and Nellie Cohan (performers); sister of George M. Cohan (entertainer and producer); m. Fred Niblo (1874–1948, performer and film director), 1901; children: Fred Niblo Jr. (1903–1973, writer). ❖ At 7, appeared in family act "Four of a Kind"; was the female lead in most of the productions by Sam Harris and brother George M. Cohan, including *The Governor's Son* (1901), *Running for Office* (1903) and *The Yankee Prince* (1908); appeared in numerous acts with husband, including *A Friend of the Family* (1907) and *The Fortune Hunter* (1912); toured Asia with husband (1913–14); retired thereafter due to illness.

COHEN, Harriet (1895–1967). English pianist. Born in London, England, Dec 2, 1895; died in London, Nov 13, 1967; dau. of musicians. ❖ Studied with Tobias Matthay; made 1st solo appearance at 13; toured widely and made a specialty of early keyboard music; highly regarded for her Bach playing; made the 1st recording of the *Piano Quintet* of Sir Edward Elgar; was the major exponent of the complicated piano music of Sir Arnold Bax; though she suffered a hand injury (1948) which cut short her concert career, continued to play with left hand until 1961; wrote memoirs and a book on piano music, *Music's Handmaid;* her romantic relationship with Bax inspired him to compose a number of his best works, including his greatest orchestral composition, *Tintagel*. Made Commander of the Order of the British Empire (1938); Harriet Cohen International Prize Medal was founded (1961). ❖ See also autobiography *A Bundle of Time* (Faber & Faber, 1969); and *Women in World History*.

COHEN, Hildy Parks (1926–2004). See Parks, Hildy.

COHEN, Lona (1913–1993). American spy. Name variations: Helen Kroger. Born Lona or Leontina Petka in US to Polish Catholic parents but became estranged from family at early age; died 1993 in Moscow, Russia; m. Morris Cohen (American-Jewish Communist spy, b. 1910). ❖ Soviet agent with husband Morris Cohen, worked for KGB in US during WWII; said to have been given the secrets of the A-Bomb by American physicist Ted Hall who worked on the Manhattan Project, but never implicated him; lived in England as Helen and Peter Kroger at 45 Cranley Drive in Ruislip (1954–1961), claiming they were Canadian booksellers; worked with fellow spy Gordon Lonsdale; activities monitored by M15 from the home of the Search family across the street; with husband, caught and tried in England (1961), sentenced to 20 years imprisonment; released to the Russians in a prisoner exchange (1969). The story of their English sojourn was dramatized in the play *Pack of Lies* (1983) and its film, and on tv in "Act of Betrayal." ❖ See also Joseph Albright and Marcia Kunstel, *Bombshell: The Secret Story of America's Unknown Atomic Spy Conspiracy*.

COHEN, Myra (1892–1959). New Zealand barber, dental assistant, entertainer, milliner. Born May 12, 1892, in Westland, New Zealand; died Nov 16, 1959, in Wellington, New Zealand; dau. of Charles Cohen (merchant) and Julia (Dimant) Cohen. ❖ Worked as assistant in barber's shop in Reefton at age 13 and was advertised as only woman barber in New Zealand; also became dental assistant before performing in variety shows and comic operas for Pollard's Pierrot and Pierrette Show during World War I; established millinery shop in Blenheim (1928). ❖ See also *Dictionary of New Zealand Biography* (Vol. 3).

COHEN, Rose (1880–1925). Russian-born American author. Born Rahel Gollup in Belarus, April 4, 1880; died under mysterious circumstances, most likely a suicide, in New York, NY, 1925; dau. of Abraham (tailor) and Annie Gollup; immigrated to US (1892). ❖ Writer whose 1918 autobiography *Out of the Shadow* provides a classic account of the lives of Jewish immigrants in New York City at the end of the 19th century. ❖ See also *Women in World History*.

COHEN, Shula (fl. 1960s). Israeli spy. Name variations: Shulamit Kishak-Cohen; Mata Hari of the Middle East; code name: Pearl. Born in Israel; granddau. of a Jewish rabbi; at 15, entered arranged marriage with Joseph Kisak, a prosperous merchant in Lebanon; children: 7. ❖ Smuggled countless Jewish refugees into Palestine (1940s); ran Mossad operations in Beirut (1950s–60s), providing political documents from Lebanon and Syria and rescuing Jews from Syrian torture; after 14 productive years, was caught, convicted and condemned to hang; sentence was commuted to 7-year prison term; exchanged for Lebanese soldiers (1967), opened a flower shop near the King David Hotel in Jerusalem. Received a Simon Wiesenthal Center award (2001). ❖ See also Aviezer Golan, *Shula, Code Name the Pearl* (Delacorte, 1980); Michael Bar-Zohar, *Lionhearts: Heroes of Israel* (1998).

COHEN, Tiffany (1966—). American swimmer. Born June 11, 1966, in Culver City, California; graduate of University of Texas, 1988. ❖ Won the 400-meter US National outdoor title (1981, 1984) and the 800 meters (1984); won National indoor titles at 500, 1,000, and 1,650 yards (1982, 1983) and the 200-meter freestyle (1983); won the 800 and 1,500 meters at Pan American Games (1983); won gold medals for the 400 and 800 meters at Los Angeles Olympics (1984); won the 400-meter and 800-meter freestyles and the 200-meter butterfly at the National outdoor championships (1986).

COHEN, Ze'eva (1940—). Israeli modern dancer and choreographer. Born Aug 15, 1940, in Tel Aviv, Israel. ❖ Worked with Anna Sokolow at Lyric Theater in Tel Aviv; awarded American-Israel Cultural Foundation grant to study at Juilliard School in NY soon after; danced in numerous works by José Limón and Anna Sokolow while in NY, including Sokolow's *Odes* (1964) and *Ballade* (1965); performed with Anna Sokolow Dance Company in Israel (1961–63) and US (1963–68); joined Dance Theater Workshop in NY (1966) and appeared in many works by Jeff Duncan and Deborah Jowitt; founded Ze'eva Cohen Solo Dance Repertory and toured to great acclaim throughout US, Canada, Europe, and Israel for 12 years; choreographed for Boston Ballet, Munich Tanz project, Batsheva Dance Company, Alvin Ailey Repertory Dance Company, and many others; taught classes in dance for actors at HB Studio in NY; served as head of dance studies of Princeton University.

COHN, Fannia (c. 1885–1962). American labor educator and organizer. Born Fannia Mary Cohn in Minsk, Russia, April 5, 1885; died in New York, NY, Dec 24, 1962; dau. of Hyman and Anna Rozofsky Cohn; never married; no children. ❖ Was a member of the illegal Russian Socialist Revolutionary Party (1901–04); immigrated to US (1904); joined International Ladies' Garment Workers Union (ILGWU, 1909); served as member, executive board of the Kimono, Wrappers, and Housedress Workers Union 41 (1909–14) and chair (1911–14); worked as ILGWU organizer in Chicago (1915–16), where she led a number of critical strikes, including the successful 1915 Chicago white goods workers' strike; served as ILGWU vice-president (1916–25), the 1st woman to hold that office; served as executive secretary of the ILGWU education department (1918–62); co-founded Brookwood Labor College and the Workers' Education Bureau (1921); served as member of the board of directors, Brookwood Labor College (1926–28) and vice-president of the College (1932–37). ❖ See also *Women in World History*.

COHN, Marianne (1921–1944). German-Jewish hero of the French resistance. Born in Mannheim, Germany, 1921; killed by a French militia unit, July 8, 1944. ❖ Fled the Nazi regime with parents (1935); settled in France and became an active member of French Jewish resistance movement, dedicating herself to the rescue of Jewish children; smuggled many children to safety in Switzerland; on May 31, 1944, having come to within 200 meters of Swiss frontier, was arrested with her group of 28 children, ranging in age from 4 to 15, and imprisoned in the nearby town of Annemasse; though the resistance worked out an escape plan, refused to participate, arguing that, if she escaped, the children still in German custody would pay for her freedom with their lives (the children were saved). ❖ See also *Women in World History*.

COICY, Madame de (fl. 18th c.). French essayist. Fl. in the 18th century. ❖ Wrote *Les Femmes comme il convient de les voir* (1785), demonstrating the potential of women when given access to education.

COIGNARD, Gabrielle de (c. 1550–1586). French poet. Born c. 1550 in Toulouse, France; died in 1586 (some sources cite 1594); dau. of Jean de Coignard (prosperous lawyer in the Parlement); m. Pierre de Mansencal (president of the Parlement), lord of Miremont, 1570 (died 1573); children: 2 daughters. ❖ Wrote devotional lyrics, elegies, and meditations to help cope with practical and spiritual struggles, none of which was published in her lifetime. Eight years after her death, daughters had her work published in Toulouse as *Oeuvres chretiennes de feue dame G. de C., veuve a feu M. de Mansencal, sieur de Miremont.* ❖ See also Melanie E. Gregg (trans.), *Spiritual Sonnets* (2003), which contains 129 of her poems.

COIGNET, Clarisse (1823–?). French political activist, philosopher, educator and historian. Born in 1823; death date unknown. ❖ Played a significant role in France's political movement, known as "La Morale independante," which began in the 18th century; published a number of works on education; edited the weekly newspaper *La Morale independanta* (1865–70), arguing for secularizing moral education; wrote many historical works, particularly on the history of morals and culture, including historical biographies of Elisa Grimhail Lemonnier (1856) Francis I (1885), Francis Scepau (1886), Victor Considerant (1895), Catherine de Medici (1895) and François de Guise (1895).

COIMBRA, Erika (1980—). Brazilian volleyball player. Name variations: Erika Pereira Coimbra. Born Mar 23, 1980, in Brazil. ❖ Wing spiker, won a team bronze medal at Sydney Olympics (2000); won South American team championship (2001).

COIT, Margaret L. (1919–2003). American biographer and journalist. Name variations: Margaret Coit Elwell. Born 1919 in Norwich, Connecticut; grew up in North Carolina; died March 15, 2003, in Amesbury, Massachusetts; attended University of North Carolina; m. Albert E. Elwell (politician, died 1992). ❖ Won Pulitzer Prize for her biography *John C. Calhoun: American Portrait* (1951); worked as a free-lance reporter for *Boston Globe* and *Lawrence Eagle,* among others; published 7 more historical books, including *Mr. Baruch, Andrew Jackson* and *Sweep Westward, 1829–1849;* for over 30 years, was a professor of English, history, and political science at Fairleigh Dickinson University.

COIT, Mehetabel Chandler (1673–1758). American diarist. Born 1673 in New London, Connecticut; died 1758. ❖ From age 15, kept diary about life in New London, CT, which was published as *Mehetabel Chandler Coit, Her Book* (1895).

COJOCARU, Christiana (1962—). Romanian hurdler. Born Jan 2, 1962. ❖ At Los Angeles Olympics, won a bronze medal in the 400-meter hurdles (1984).

COKE, Alexandra (1891–1984). Countess of Airlie. Born Alexandra Mary Bridget Coke in England; dau. of Thomas William Coke, 3rd earl of Leicester, and Alice Emily White; m. David Ogilvy, 7th earl of Airlie, July 17, 1917; children: Victoria Ogilvy (b. 1918), Margaret Ogilvy (b. 1920), Griselda Ogilvy (1924–1977), David Ogilvy (b. 1926), 8th earl of Airlie, Angus Ogilvy (husband of Princess Alexandra of Kent, 1928–2004) and James Ogilvy (b. 1934).

COKE, Jane Elizabeth (1777–1863). English noblewoman. Name variations: Lady Andover. Born Jane Elizabeth Coke in 1777; died 1863; dau. of Thomas William Coke, known as Coke of Norfolk (Whig member of Parliament for 56 years), and Jane Dutton Coke; sister of Ann Margaret Coke (later viscountess Anson); m. Charles Nevinson Howard, viscount Andover, 1796 (died in a hunting accident, 1800); m. Henry Digby (naval admiral), April 17, 1806; children: (2nd m.) Jane Digby el Mesrab (1807–1881); Edward St. Vincent Digby (b. 1809); Kenelm Digby (b. 1811). ❖ See also *Women in World History.*

COLAÇO, Branca de Gonta (1880–1944). Portuguese poet and literary critic. Name variations: Branca de Gonta Colaco. Born Branca Ribeiro 1880; died 1944; dau. of Tomás Ribeiro (poet); m. Jorge Calaço (1868–1942, painter), 1898. ❖ Poet whose home became an important gathering place for writers and artists; collections, reminiscent of 19th-century poetry, include *Matinas* (1907) and 4 other vols. (1912–26); also published critical works *Poetas de Ontem* (1915) and *Cartas de Camilo Castello Branco a Tomás Ribeiro* (1922).

COLANDER-RICHARDSON, LaTasha (1976—). African-American runner. Name variations: La Tasha Colander. Born La Tasha Colander, Aug 23, 1976, in Norfolk, Virginia; m. Roderick Richardson (army lieutenant), 2000. ❖ Won a gold medal for 4x400-meter relay at Sydney Olympics (2000); won US 400-meter championship (2000, 2001).

COLAR, Sadie Goodson (b. 1900). *See Goodson, Sadie.*

COLBAN, Marie (1814–1884). Norwegian novelist. Born Adolphine (also seen as Adolfine) Marie Schmidt at Christiania, Norway, Dec 18, 1814; died 1884. ❖ At 36, a widow without resources, moved to Paris; wrote stories in her own language (1869–81); published 7 vols. of tales, including *Tre Noveller* (1873), *Tre nye Noveller* (1875), *Jeg lever* (1877) and *Cleopatra* (1880).

COLBERT, Claudette (1903–1996). American actress. Born Claudette Chauchoin in Paris, France, Sept 13, 1903; died in Barbados, July 30, 1996; came to US with family, 1910; dau. of Georges and Jeanne (Loew) Chauchoin; m. Norman Foster (actor), Mar 13, 1928 (div. 1934); m. Joel Pressman (surgeon), 1936 (died 1968); children: none. ❖ Famed for her warmth, dignified bearing, and charm, made 62 films, playing sirens, comic roles, and serious dramatic parts alike; made NY stage debut in *The Wild Westcotts* (1923); scored 1st success in the farce *A Kiss in a Taxi* (1925) and had another in *The Barker* (1927); appeared in 1st silent film, the poorly received *For the Love o' Mike,* directed by Frank Capra; resumed stage career; signed by Paramount, had a hit with *The Lady Lies* (1929); appeared in Biblical epics *The Sign of the Cross* and *Cleopatra;* starred opposite Clark Gable in *It Happened One Night* (directed by Capra), reaping an Academy Award for Best Actress (1934); other films include *Imitation of Life* (1934), *Drums Along the Mohawk* (1939), *Skylark* (1941), *The Palm Beach Story* (1942), *So Proudly We Hail* (1943), *Since You Went Away* (1944) and *Three Came Home* (1950); also co-starred in several films with Fred MacMurray, most notably *The Egg and I* (1947); devoted last professional years to the stage, touring in *The Kingfisher* and *A Talent for Murder;* starred with Rex Harrison in *Aren't We All* (1985). Won Golden Globe for tv role as Mrs. Grenville in "The Two Mrs. Grenvilles" (1987); was included in Kennedy Center Honors (1989). ❖ See also William K. Emerson, *Claudette Colbert* (Pyramid, 1976); and *Women in World History.*

COLBORN, Theodora (1927—). American ecologist and zoologist. Name variations: Theo Colborn. Born Mar 28, 1927; University of Wisconsin, Madison, PhD in zoology, 1985; m. Harry Colborn; children: 4. ❖ Called by many fellow scientists the "Rachel Carson of the 1990s," joined Conservation Foundation (1987); held chair for 3 years with W. Alton Jones Foundation (1990–93); organized groundbreaking conference in Wisconsin, known as Wingspread I, which brought scientists together to discuss effects of chemical pollutants on endocrine systems of wildlife and humans (1991); was lead author, with Dianne Dumanoski and J. Peterson Myers, of *Our Stolen Future: Are We Threatening our Fertility, Intelligence, and Survival?* (1996), which has been published in more than 12 languages; became controversial figure for asserting that even low-dose exposures to commonly used chemicals can cause problems ranging from infertility and low sperm counts to genital malformations and low IQs; served as senior program scientist, and director of Wildlife and Contaminants Program, for World Wildlife Fund.

COLBRAN, Isabella (1785–1845). Spanish soprano. Name variations: Isabella Rossini. Born Madrid, Spain, Feb 2, 1785; died in Castenaso, Bologna, Oct 7, 1845; studied in Madrid with Pareja, in Naples with Marinelli and Crescentini; m. Gioacchino Rossini (Italian composer), 1822. ❖ Made debut in Spain (1806); beloved as a singer in Italy, had a great influence on composer-husband Gioacchino Rossini, who wrote parts for her in many of his operas, including *Elisabetta, regina d'Inghilterra* (1815), *Otello* (1816), *Armida* (1817), *Mosè in Egitto, Ricciardo e Zoraide* (1818), *Ermione, La donna del lago* (1819), *Maometto II* (1820), *Zelmira* (1822) and *Semiramide* (1823); with Rossini, traveled to London to perform in *Zelmira* (1824), but her reputation had outlasted her voice and the appearance was a disaster; retired from the stage. ❖ See also *Women in World History.*

COLBY, Christine (c. 1950—). American ballet and theatrical dancer. Born Feb 27, c. 1950, in Cincinnati, Ohio. ❖ Studied with James Truitte and David McLain at Cincinnati Ballet and was trained in variety of modern dance techniques; danced with Cincinnati Ballet; moved to New York City where she dedicated herself to jazz performance; on Broadway, was principal dancer in Bob Fosse's *Dancin'* and appeared in *Sweet Charity;* danced as a Rockette at Radio City Music Hall; on film, danced in *A Chorus Line, Annie* and *All That Jazz.*

COLBY, Clara Bewick (1846–1916). American suffragist and publisher. Born Clara Dorothy Bewick, Aug 5, 1846, in Gloucester, England; died Sept 7, 1916, in Palo Alto, California; dau. of Thomas and Clara (Willingham) Bewick (died 1855); graduate of University of Wisconsin; m. Leonard Wright Colby (leader of Nebraska National

Guard and state senator), June 23, 1871 (div. before 1904); children: (adopted) Clarence and Zintkala Nuni (Lost Bird, aka Zindka). ❖ Came to US with family (1849); with husband, adopted Sioux Indian baby named Zintkala Nuni (Lost Bird) whom he'd taken from Wounded Knee massacre; served as president of Nebraska Woman Suffrage Association (1885–98); published weekly *Woman's Tribune* (1883–1909), which became known as official organ of National Woman Suffrage Association (NWSA); followed suffrage plan espoused by Francis Minor; served as chair of NWSA's Committee on Industrial Problems Affecting Women and Children (1900–03) and as corresponding secretary of Federal Suffrage Association (founded by Olympia Brown).

COLCLOUGH, Mary Ann (1836–1885). New Zealand teacher, feminist, social reformer, lecturer. Name variations: Mary Ann Barnes, Polly Plum. Born Mary Ann Barnes, Feb 20, 1836, in London, England; died Mar 7, 1885, in Picton, New Zealand; dau. of John Thomas Barnes (carpenter) and Susan Barnes; m. Thomas Caesar Colclough (farmer), 1861 (died 1867); children: 1 daughter, 1 son. ❖ Immigrated to New Zealand (1859); established school for girls in Auckland (1871); advocated for women's rights and social reform through public lectures as Polly Plum. ❖ See also *Dictionary of New Zealand Biography* (Vol. 2).

COLCORD, Joanna Carver (1882–1960). American social worker. Born Joanna Carver Colcord, Mar 18, 1882, on sailing ship near New Caledonia (overseas territory of France) in southwest Pacific Ocean; died April 8, 1960, in Lebanon, Indiana; dau. of Lincoln Alden Colcord and Jane French (Sweetser) Colcord; University of Maine, BS, 1906, MS in biological chemistry, 1909; studied at New York School of Philanthropy (1910–11); m. Frank J. Bruno (social worker and educator), 1950 (died 1955). ❖ Worked for New York Charity Organization Society (1911–25), becoming supervisor of all district offices; served as Red Cross field representative in Virgin islands (1920); served as director of Russell Sage Foundation's Charity Organization Department (1929–44); was a member of the editorial board of *The Survey* (journal for social work, 1932–35); was a consultant to Office of Defense Health and Welfare Services during WWII; retired because of ill-health (1944). Wrote *Broken Homes: A Study of Family Desertion and Its Social Treatment* (1919), *Your Community: Its Provisions for Health, Safety, and Welfare* (1939), and a study of the impact of sailors' language on English idiom, *Sea Language Comes Ashore* (1945).

COLDEN, Jane (1724–1766). American botanist. Name variations: Jenny Colden. Born Mar 27, 1724, in New York, NY; died Mar 10, 1766, in NY, NY; dau. of Cadwallader Colden (surveyor general, lieutenant governor, and acting governor of the Province of New York) and Alice (Christy) Colden; sister of Alice Colden and Alexander Colden, who succeeded his father as surveyor general; m. Dr. William Farquhar, 1759; children: 1 (died in infancy). ❖ Considered to have been "the first lady on either side of the Atlantic" to master the new Linnaean method of plant nomenclature; created *Flora—Nov Eboracensis (Botanic Manuscript)*, a compendium of drawings and descriptions of some 340 plants observed in Ulster Co., possibly the most extensive botanical study of a single area carried out up to that time; corresponded with Dr. Alexander Garden, John Bartram, Peter Collinson, and other leading botanists of the period; contributed to *Edinburgh Essays*. ❖ See also *Women in World History*.

COLDHAM, Marianne (1793–1879). See Williams, Marianne.

COLE, Anna Russell (1846–1926). American philanthropist. Born Anna Virginia Russell, Jan 16, 1846, in Augusta, Georgia; died June 6, 1926, near Nashville, Tennessee; dau. of Henry F. Russell (mayor of Augusta, GA) and Martha (Danforth) Russell; sister of Whitefoord Russell (killed in Civil War); took courses at Wesleyan College and University of Berlin; m. Edmund W. Cole (railroad magnate), Dec 25, 1872; children: Whitefoord Russell (b. 1874) and Anna Russell (b. 1889). ❖ Encouraged husband to help fund the Randal Cole Institute (renamed Tennessee Industrial School), the temperance cause (1887), and Methodist Church missions, among others; after husband's death, provided financial support to Vanderbilt University; entertained several presidents in her Nashville home, Colemere; contributed generously to Southern Sociological Congress; erected classical monument to 4 noted Southern poets; supported Woodrow Wilson's fight for League of Nations.

COLE, Edith (1870–1927). English actress and writer. Born May 27, 1870, in England; died June 7, 1927; m. W.W. Kelly. ❖ Made stage debut in *Jack and the Beanstalk* (1889), followed by *The Two Orphans, The Fires of Youth* (her own play), and *A Royal Divorce;* came to prominence as Frances Vere in *The Worst Woman in London* (1903); wrote *Scarlet and Grey,* concerning Red Cross work during WWI.

COLE, Johnnetta B. (1936—). African-American educator and anthropologist. Name variations: often spelled wrongly as Johnetta. Born Johnnetta Betsch, Oct 19, 1936, in Jacksonville, Florida; attended Fisk University and Oberlin College; Northwestern University, MA and PhD in anthropology. ❖ Taught at Washington State University; became professor of anthropology and Afro-American studies at University of Massachusetts at Amherst, where she also served as associate provost of undergraduate education for 2 years; joined faculty of Hunter College (1984), as professor of anthropology and director of Latin American and Caribbean studies program; became the 1st African-American woman to serve as president of Spelman College (1987) and turned Spelman into a top-rated school (1987–98); named to President Bill Clinton's transition team; was the 1st woman elected to board of directors of Coca-Cola Enterprises; joined faculty of Emory University (1998); wrote *Conversations: Straight Talk with America's Sister President* (Doubleday, 1992).

COLE, Kay (1948—). American dancer and actress. Born Jan 13, 1948, in Miami, Florida. ❖ As a child, appeared on film and tv; toured as Amaryllis with the national company of *The Music Man;* on Broadway, performed in *Bye Bye Birdie* (1960), *Stop the World, I Want to Get Off* and *The Roar of the Greasepaint, the Smell of the Crowd* (1965); danced in film versions of musicals, including *Hair* (1968), *Jesus Christ Superstar* (1971), *Words and Music* (1974) and *A Chorus Line* (1975).

COLE, Margaret (1893–1980). British political activist and writer. Name variations: Dame Margaret Cole; Margaret I. Cole. Born Margaret Isabel Postgate in 1893 in Cambridge, England; died in 1980; dau. of (John) Percival Postgate (1853–1926, classical scholar); granddau. of John Postgate (1820–1881, reformer); educated at Roedean School and Girton College, Cambridge (degree in classics, 1914); m. G.D.H. Cole, also known as Douglas Cole (socialist and scholar), 1918 (died 1949); children: 2 daughters, 1 son. ❖ Leading socialist, joined the Fabian Society's Research Department; with husband, organized a special strike committee in the General Strike of 1926 and was responsible for influencing many future Labour leaders, including Hugh Gaitskell; was a defender of egalitarian education and organized classes for the Workers' Education Association, an organization for which she taught (1925–49); with husband, founded the new Fabian Research Bureau (1935) and wrote *Review of Europe of Today* (1933) and *The Condition of Britain* (1937); was a member of the London County Council (1943–65), of which she was alderman (1952–65); began serving as president of the Fabian Society (1963); also wrote *Makers of the Labour Movement* (1948) and *Beatrice and Sidney Webb* (1955), edited 2 vols. of Beatrice Webb's diaries, and wrote more than 30 critically acclaimed detective novels with her husband. Created OBE (1965) and Dame of the British Empire (DBE, 1970). ❖ See also *Women in World History.*

COLE, Mary (c. 1913—). Irish murderer. Born c. 1913 in Ireland. ❖ At 13, went to work as domestic servant for Michael and Anastasia Flynn in Co. Laois (1926); after 2 Flynn children were found drowned (1927), charged with their murders; at 15, was tried, found guilty, and sentenced to life imprisonment (1928).

COLE, Natalie (1950—). African-American vocalist. Born Stephanie Natalie Maria Cole, Feb 6, 1950, in Los Angeles, California; 2nd child of Nat "King" Cole (singer) and Maria Ellington Cole; sister of actress Carol Cole and actor Nat Kelly Cole (1959–1995, both adopted); m. Marvin Yancy, July 31, 1976 (div. 1980); m. Andre Fischer, Sept 16, 1989 (div. 1995); m. Kenneth H. Dupree, Oct 12, 2001 (div. 2004); children: (1st m.) 1. ❖ As pop, jazz, R&B vocalist, debuted with Grammy-winning album *Inseparable* (1975); was the 1st black singer to win a Grammy in the Best New Artist category; released popular albums throughout 1970s; won multiple Grammys for comeback album *Unforgettable With Love* (1992), a tribute to her father; scored many pop hits, including "This Will Be" (1975), "Our Love" (1978), "I Live for Your Love" (1987), "Unforgettable" (1992), and "Stardust" (1996); made acting debut in tv series "I'll Fly Away" (1993); collaborated with London Symphony Orchestra on holiday album *Snowfall on the Sahara: The Magic of Christmas* (1999); overcame battles with alcohol and drug addiction. ❖ See also autobiography *Angel on My Shoulder* (2000).

COLE, Paula (1968—). American musician. Born April 5, 1968, in Rockport, Massachusetts. ❖ Gained fame as performer in Lilith Fair (late 1990s); released 2nd album, *This Fire* (1996), which earned her 7 Grammy nominations, including the 1st ever nomination of a woman for Best Producer; reached #8 with single "Where Have All the Cowboys Gone" (1997) and earned Grammy for Best New Artist. Other albums include *Harbinger* (1994) and *Amen* (1999).

COLE, Rebecca J. (1846–1922). African-American physician. Born in Philadelphia, Pennsylvania, Mar 16, 1846; died in Philadelphia, Aug 14, 1922; graduate of Institute for Colored Youth, Philadelphia, 1863, and Female Medical College of Pennsylvania (now The Medical College of Pennsylvania), 1867. ❖ The 1st black woman to graduate from the Female Medical College of Pennsylvania, became resident physician at the New York Infirmary for Women and Children, where she worked with the poor, dispensing practical information on infant and family health; later practiced in Columbia, South Carolina, and was a superintendent of the Government House for Children and Old Women in Washington, DC; eventually returned to Philadelphia where she established a practice and served as superintendent of a homeless shelter.

COLEGATE, Isabel (1931—). British historical-fiction writer. Born Sept 10, 1931, in London, England; dau. of Sir Arthur Colegate (MP) and Lady Colegate Worsley; m. Michael Briggs, 1953. ❖ Novels include *The Blackmailer* (1958), *A Man of Power* (1960), *The Great Occasion* (1962), *Orlando King* (1968), *Orlando at the Brazen Threshold* (1971), *Agatha* (1973), *The Shooting Party* (1980), which was filmed with John Gielgud and James Mason (1984), *Deceits of Time* (1988) and *Winter Journey* (1995).

COLELLA, Lynn (1950—). American swimmer. Name variations: Lynn Colella Bell. Born June 13, 1950; sister of Rick Colella (Olympic swimmer); attended University of Washington. ❖ Won 3 gold medals at World University games (1970); won 200-meter breaststroke and 200-meter butterfly at Pan American games (1971); at Munich Olympics, won a silver medal in 200-meter butterfly (1972); won 10 national championships in the 100-meter and 200-meter butterfly and breaststroke.

COLEMAN, Alice Merriam (1858–1936). American church worker. Born Alice Blanchard Merriam, May 7, 1858, in Boston, Massachusetts; died Oct 22, 1936, in Boston, MA; dau. of James Whyte Merriam and Ellen Maria (Blanchard) Merriam; graduate of Bradford (MA) Academy, 1878; m. George William Coleman, June 30, 1891. ❖ Served on board of managers of Woman's Home Missionary Association; switched denomination and joined Gordon's Clarendon Street Church, Boston, MA (1886); served as president of Woman's American Baptist Home Mission Society (1890–1909), until its merger with Woman's Baptist Home Mission Society, then as vice-president, and later president and chair of the board, of the new organization; served as founder and 1st president of interdenominational Council of Women for Home Missions (1908–16).

COLEMAN, Ann Raney Thomas (1810–1897). British memoirist. Born Ann Raney, Nov 5, 1810, in Cumberland, England; died Mar 1897 in Cuero, Texas; dau. of John Raney; m. John Thomas, 1833 (died); m. John Coleman, c. 1848 (div. 1855); children: (1st m.) 3. ❖ Immigrated with family to Texas; took part in Battle of Velasco (1832), but fled Texas with husband and son after Texas War for Independence; became schoolteacher after divorce from 2nd husband, but was reduced to poverty in old age; wrote memoir about frontier life, *A Victorian Lady on the Texas Frontier.*

COLEMAN, Bessie (1892–1926). African-American aviator. Born Jan 26, 1892, in Atlanta, Texas; killed in fall from plane, April 30, 1926, in Jacksonville, Florida; dau. of George (day laborer) and Susan Coleman (domestic worker); spent 1 year at preparatory school of Colored Agricultural and Normal University in Langston, Oklahoma (now Langston University); m. Claude Glenn, Jan 30, 1917, but at no time did she inform her family, reside with Glenn, or use his name. ❖ The 1st African-American woman pilot in the world, was a manicurist in Chicago before she went to France for flight lessons; was issued license by Fédération Internationale Aéronautique (June 15, 1921); returned to France for advance aerobatic lessons (Feb–Aug 1922); gave 1st exhibition flight in the world by a black woman, in New York (Sept 3, 1922); spent the next 4 years touring the US, giving exhibition flights and speaking in theaters, churches, and schools to exhort blacks to seek their future in aviation; performed further flights in Memphis and Chicago (1922), distributed advertising leaflets by air in California (1923); was badly injured in plane crash in Santa Monica (Feb 4, 1923) and hospitalized until May; that same month, gave lecture series on aviation at Los Angeles

YMCA (May 1923). ❖ See also Doris L. Rich, *Queen Bess: Daredevil Aviator* (Smithsonian Institution, 1993); and *Women in World History.*

COLEMAN, Corrine Grad (1927–2004). American feminist. Born Corrine Grad, June 30, 1927, in the Bronx, NY; died July 4, 2004, in New York, NY; New York University, BS and MA; m. Joseph K. Coleman (div. 1977, died 1991); children: Patricia, Amy, Anthony and Nathaniel Coleman. ❖ Was a founding member of the Redstockings, an offshoot of New York Radical Women (1968); a freelance writer, was one of the editors of the Redstockings Manifesto and edited *Feelings: A Journal of Women's Liberation.*

COLEMAN, Fanny (1840–1919). English actress. Born 1840 in England; died Mar 3, 1919. ❖ Popular ingenue and comedy actress in London for many years, was later considered the grandes dames of impersonators; plays include *The Candidate, The Weaker Sex, The Idler, Forgiveness, Lady Windermere's Fan* and *The Case of Rebellious Susan.*

COLEMAN, Georgia (1912–1940). American diver. Born Georgia Coleman, Jan 23, 1912, in St. Maries, Idaho; died Sept 14, 1940. ❖ Won a bronze medal in springboard and silver in platform at Amsterdam Olympics (1928); took US outdoor springboard and platform titles (1929–31); was indoor 3-meter springboard champion (1929–32) and 1-meter champion (1931); was platform silver medalist and springboard gold medalist at Los Angeles Olympics (1932); stricken with polio (1937). Was the 1st woman to perform a 2½-forward somersault.

COLEMAN, Helen (1847–1884). *See Angell, Helen Cordelia.*

COLEMAN, Kit (1864–1915). Canadian journalist. Name variations: Kathleen Coleman. Born Kathleen Blake near Galway in Western Ireland, 1864; died in Hamilton, Ontario, Canada, 1915; m. George Willis (wealthy country squire), 1880 (died 1884); m. Edward Watkins, 1884 (died 1889); m. Theobald Coleman (physician), 1898; children: (2nd m.) son Thady and daughter Pat. ❖ As a concession to Canada's emerging "New Woman" movement, was hired to create a column of recipes and fashion tips for the Saturday issue of *Toronto Mail* (1889); before long, was producing some of the most imaginative and thought-provoking journalism ever seen in Canada; over next 21 years, through her popular and controversial column "Woman's Kingdom," commented on a host of topics, from Canadian politics to fashion trends; initiated Canada's 1st advice to the lovelorn and joined the press corps to cover the Spanish-American War despite a ban on women journalists imposed by US military; interviewed some of the most prominent personalities of her day; helped found the Canadian Women's Press Club and elected its 1st president (1904). ❖ See also Ted Ferguson, *Kit Coleman: Queen of Hearts* (Doubleday, 1978); and *Women in World History.*

COLEMAN, Mary (1914–2001). American judge. Name variations: Mary Stallings Coleman. Born Mary Stallings, June 24, 1914, in Forney, Texas; died Nov 27, 2001, in Ocala, Florida; m. Creighton R. Coleman (Republican politician and judge). ❖ A Republican, served on the probate court (1961–72), where she revised the state's juvenile justice codes; was the 1st woman elected to the Michigan Supreme Court (1972) and the 1st to serve as chief justice (1979–82).

COLEMAN, Mary Sue (1943—). American educator and biochemist. Born Oct 2, 1943, in Kentucky; grew up in Cedar Falls, Iowa; Grinnell College, bachelor's degree in chemistry; University of North Carolina, PhD in biochemistry; m. Kenneth Coleman (political scientist); children: Jonathan. ❖ Served as a member of the biochemistry faculty and as a Cancer Center administrator at University of Kentucky for 19 years, where her research focused on the immune system and malignancies; served as associate provost and dean of research (1990–92) and vice chancellor for graduate studies and research (1992–93) at University of North Carolina at Chapel Hill; served as provost and vice president for academic affairs at University of New Mexico (1993–95); served as president of University of Iowa (1995–2002); became president of University of Michigan (2002); elected to National Academy of Sciences' Institute of Medicine (1997).

COLEMAN, Nancy (1912–2000). American actress. Born Dec 30, 1912, in Everett, Washington; died Jan 18, 2000, in Brockport, Monroe Co., NY; m. Whitney Bolton (studio publicity head). ❖ Made Broadway debut (1941); made film debut in *Dangerously They Live* (1941); also appeared in *Kings Row, Desperate Journey, The Gay Sisters, Edge of Darkness, In Our Time, Mourning Becomes Electra,* and as Anne Brontë in *Devotion,* among others; on tv, had recurring roles on "Edge of Night" and "Ryan's Hope."

COLEN, Eszter H. (1920–1994). *See Haraszty, Eszter.*

COLENSO, Elizabeth (1821–1904). New Zealand missionary, teacher, translator. Name variations: Elizabeth Fairburn. Born Elizabeth Fairburn, 1821, in Kerikeri, New Zealand; died Sept 2, 1904; dau. of William Thomas Fairburn (missionary) and Sarah (Tuckwell) Fairburn; m. William Colenso (printer), 1843; children: 2. ❖ Skilled in homeopathic medicine and Maori language, started missionary school for women and children (1840s); traveled to London and performed philanthropic work (1861); contributed significantly to publication of first Bible in Maori (1868); returned to New Zealand where she taught at Melanesian mission at Norfolk Island (1876–1898). ❖ See also *Dictionary of New Zealand Biography* (Vol. 1).

COLERIDGE, Ethel (1883–1976). English actress. Born Jan 14, 1883, in South Molton, Devon, England; died Aug 15, 1976, in London; dau. of Henry Coleridge-Tucker and Edith Jane (Chant) Coleridge. ❖ Made London stage debut in *My Lady's Dress* (1920); other plays include *Milestone, If, The Balance, The Rising Generation, Fata Morgana, Thark, A Cup of Kindness, Ballyhoo, Laburnum Grove* and *If Four Walls Told*; made film debut in *Rookery Nook* (1930), followed by *Laburnum Grove, Penny Paradise, When We Are Married* and *Piece of Cake*, among others.

COLERIDGE, Georgina (1916–2003). Scottish journalist, magazine editor, and publishing executive. Name variations: Lady Georgina Coleridge; Lady Georgina Hay; Lady G. Born Margaret Georgina Christine Hay, Mar 19, 1916, in East Lothian, Scotland; died Mar 25, 2003; 2nd dau. of William George Montagu Hay, 11th Marquis of Tweeddale, and Marguerite Christine Ralli Einstein; m. Arthur Coleridge (with the war Cabinet), 1941 (died 1988); children: Frances Coleridge (b. 1943). ❖ Joined the circulation department of the National Magazine Company (1937); became a director for special projects for IPC magazines (1971–74); long interested in horseracing, wrote the turf memoir *That's Racing* (1978); served as director of *Country Life* (1962–74); was editor of *Homes and Gardens* (1947–63), then director of its owner, George Newnes Ltd.; was co-founder, with Odette Hallowes and the marchioness of Lothian, of the ongoing Women of the Year lunch (1955); served as president of Women's Press Club (1965–67).

COLERIDGE, Mary Elizabeth (1861–1907). British poet, novelist, and critic. Born in London, England, Sept 23, 1861; died in Harrogate, Yorkshire, England, Aug 25, 1907; dau. of Arthur Duke Coleridge (clerk of the Assize on the midland circuit) and Mary Anne (Jameson) Coleridge; great-great-niece of Samuel Taylor Coleridge; never married; no children. ❖ Published 1st novel, *The Seven Sleepers of Ephesus* (1893), which was highly praised by Robert Louis Stevenson, though it went unnoticed by critics; published 2 collections of poems, *Fancy's Following* (1896) and *Fancy's Guerdon* (1897), both under a pseudonym, which met with more success; had breakthrough with *The King with Two Faces* (1897), a historical romance based on assassination of Gustavus III of Sweden, which established her reputation and was followed by a number of successful novels, mostly historical in nature; also contributed articles to the *Monthly Review, Guardian, Cornhill Magazine* and *Times Literary Supplement.* ❖ See also *Women in World History.*

COLERIDGE, Sara (1802–1852). English writer. Born at Greta Hall, near Keswick, England, Dec 23, 1802; died May 3, 1852, in Regent's Park, London; dau. of Samuel Taylor Coleridge (poet and critic) and Sara Fricker Coleridge (whose sister Edith Fricker married Robert Southey); m. her cousin Henry Nelson Coleridge (1798–1843, lawyer), 1829; children: 4, including Herbert Coleridge (1830–1861). ❖ Translated Martin Dobritzhoffer's *Account of the Abipones* from the Latin (1822) and *Memoirs* of the Chevalier Bayard (1825); published *Pretty Lessons for Little Children* (1834), which was primarily designed for her own children but speedily passed through several editions; wrote her longest and best-known work, the romantic fairy tale *Phantasmion* (1837); edited father's *Aids to Reflection, Notes on Shakespeare and the Dramatists* and *Essays on his own Times.* ❖ See also *Memoirs and Letters of Sara Coleridge* (1873); and *Women in World History.*

COLERIDGE-TAYLOR, Avril (1903–1998). English conductor, composer, and pianist. Born Avril Gwendolen Coleridge-Taylor in South Norwood, England, Mar 18, 1903; died Dec 21, 1998, in England; dau. of Samuel Coleridge-Taylor, distinguished African-British composer. ❖ At 12, wrote 1st composition and won scholarship to attend Trinity College of Music to study piano and composition; learned composition from Gordon Jacob and Alec Rowely and conducting from Sir Henry Wood; founded 2 orchestras—the Coleridge-Taylor Symphony Orchestra (which she conducted, 1946–51) and the Malcolm Sargent Symphony Orchestra; founded and directed the New World Singers, a male voice ensemble; was 1st woman to conduct the H.M. Royal Marine band; conducted BBC Symphony Orchestra and London Symphony Orchestra; wrote compositions, including *Ceremonial March for Independence of Ghana* (1957), *Comet Prelude* (1952), *Symphonic Impression* (1942) and a Piano Concerto in F-minor (1938). ❖ See also *Women in World History.*

COLES, Joyce (b, around 1904). South African theatrical dancer. Born c. 1904 in Cape Town, South Africa. ❖ Danced with Anna Pavlova's company in London (1918–23); partnered with Simon Karaveff in his ballet vaudeville acts in US (c. 1924); engaged as ballerina at Roxy Theater; worked as assistant for Chester Hale and principal ballet soloist at Capitol Theater in NY (1927); danced featured role in *The Dubarry* on Broadway (1932); partnered with Georges Fontana in his ballroom act in London and also toured with act throughout US; returned to NY to dance at Cosmopolitan Opera and Hippodrome Opera until her retirement (late 1930s).

COLET, Louise (1810–1876). French journalist and poet. Born Louise Revoil at Aix, France, Sept 15, 1810; died Mar 8, 1876; dau. of a Provençal family named Revoil; m. Hippolyte Colet (1808–1851, composer and violinist), Dec 5, 1834; children: (with Victor Cousin) Henriette Cousin. ❖ Flaubert's lover and the model for his *Madame Bovary*, published volume of verse, *Fleurs du Midi* (1836), followed by another, *Penserosa* (1839); also wrote *La Jeunesse de Goethe* (1839), a one-act comedy, *Les Funerailles de Napoléon* (1840), a poem, and the novels *La Jeunesse de Mirabeau* (1841) and *Les Coeurs brisés* (1843); won Academie Française poetry prize (1839), only the 5th woman; is known more for her intimate connections with some of her famous contemporaries—Abel Villemain, Gustave Flaubert, and Victor Cousin—than for her own writing; met and began liaison with Flaubert (1846); published scathing novelized accounts of her lover: *Une Histoire de soldat* (*A Soldier's Story,* 1856) and *La Servante* (*The Maidservant,* 1854). ❖ See also Francine du Plessix Gray, *Rage and Fire: A Life of Louise Colet* (Simon and Schuster, 1994); and *Women in World History.*

COLETTE (1381–1447). Flemish religious reformer and saint. Name variations: Saint Colette; Colette of Corbie. Born Nicolette Boelet at Corbie, near Amiens, Jan 13, 1381; died at Ghent, Mar 6, 1447; dau. of Robert Boelet (artisan) and a mother who was dutifully religious. ❖ Of the Franciscan order of the Poor Clares, instituted reforms in its rules and administration; for 3 years, lived in a cell between two buttresses of Notre Dame de Corbie (1402–05), accessed from the church by a grill; after an audience with Pope Benedict XIII, was named superior general of all the convents of Poor Clares; traveled, worked miracles, endured suffering, and collaborated with St. Vincent Ferrer to eradicate schism. The Colettine reform spread through France, Spain, Flanders and Savoy.

COLETTE (1873–1954). French writer. Name variations: Sidonie-Gabrielle Colette; Colette Willy; la baronne de Jouvenel. Born in Saint-Sauveur-en-Puisaye (Yonne), France, Jan 28, 1873; died in Paris, Aug 3, 1954; dau. of Jules-Joseph Colette and Adèle-Eugenie Sidonie ("Sido") Landoy Robineau-Duclos Colette; m. Henry ("Willy") Gauthier-Villars, in Saint-Sauveur, May 15, 1893; m. Henry Bertrand Léon Robert de Jouvenel des Ursins (called "Sidi"), in Paris, Dec 19, 1912; m. Maurice Goudeket, in Paris, April 3, 1935; children: Colette de Jouvenel, known as "Bel-Gazou" (b. 1913). ❖ Novelist, short-story writer, journalist, essayist, memoirist, actress and music-hall performer who created some of the most memorable female characters in literature; using recollections of her school days, began writing 1st of Claudine novels, *Claudine at School,* which sold 40,000 copies in 2 months (1894); wrote 3 more Claudine novels, followed by 2 works based on the female character, Minne; made debut as a mime (1906); became mistress of Marquise Mathilde de Belboeuf, known as Missy (1906), which eventually caused outrage and a near riot at the Moulin Rouge theater; made her living in music halls and the café-concert circuit, in Paris and on tour (1906–11); wrote *Tendrils of the Vine* (1908), about her affair with Missy, and *The Vagabond* (1910), an autobiographical account of her music-hall years, which was nominated for Prix Goncourt; began writing regular articles for leading Paris newspaper, *Le Matin,* using a pseudonym (1910); began writing one of her best works, *Chéri* (1919); acclaimed as one of France's most distinguished writers, was 1st awarded the Legion of Honor (1920); to supplement her income during the depression, opened Institute of Beauty in Paris (1932); issued one of her most original works, *The Cat*

(1933); during WWII, wrote her last fictional work, *Gigi*, later a successful stage play and movie; elected to Academy Goncourt, only the 2nd woman to be so honored (May 1945), then voted president (1948); received star of "Grand Officier" of the Legion of Honor, the highest rank ever accorded a woman; was the 1st Frenchwoman given a State funeral (Aug 7, 1954). ❖ See also memoirs *My Apprenticeships* (1936); Margaret Crosland, *Colette: The Difficulty of Loving* (Bobbs-Merrill, 1973); Johanna Richardson, *Colette* (Dell, 1983); Robert D. Cottrell, *Colette* (Ungar, 1978); Herbert Lottman, *Colette: A Life* (Little, Brown, 1981); Michèle Sarde, *Colette: Free and Fettered* (trans. by Richard Miller, Morrow, 1980); and *Women in World History*.

COLEY, Doris (1941–2000). African-American singer. Name variations: Doris Coley Kenner, Doris Kenner-Jackson; The Shirelles. Born Doris Coley, Aug 2, 1941, in Goldsboro, North Carolina; died of breast cancer, Feb 4, 2000, in Sacramento, California. ❖ With Shirley Owens, Addie "Micki" Harris and Beverly Lee, formed the Shirelles in Passaic, New Jersey (1958), one of the 1st all-girl groups of the rock era; with group, performed their self-written "I Met Him on a Sunday" for Florence Greenberg and was signed to her Tiara label (the song was so popular, it was bought by Decca Records); with group, released the hit "Tonight's the Night" (1960), the 1# pop hit "Will You Love Me Tomorrow?" (1961), as well as "Mama Said," "Soldier Boy," "Foolish Little Girl" and "Baby It's You" (1963); recorded and performed until group split up (late 1960s); sang with group's surviving members, Owens and Lee, at Rhythm and Blues Foundation awards ceremony (1994) and on Dionne Warwick album. Shirelles were inducted into Rock and Roll Hall of Fame (1996).

COLIGNY, Henriette de (1618–1683). French writer and poet. Name variations: Comtesse de la Suze; countess of La Suze. Born Henriette de Coligny in 1618; died 1683; eldest dau. of Gaspard III de Coligny, maréchal de Châtillon (1584–1646, a marshal of France under Louis XIII and nephew of Louise de Coligny); great granddau. of Gaspard II de Coligny (1519–1572), admiral and leader of the Huguenots); m. Thomas Hamilton, earl of Haddington (died 1 year later); m. compte de La Suze. ❖ With Paul Pellisson and others, wrote *Recueil de pièces galantes* (also known as *Recueil La Suze-Pellisson*) in 1663, one of the most popular miscellanies of 17th-century verse and prose; a cosmopolitan beauty who corresponded with Balzac and Saint-Evremond, held a salon which was a kind of extension of Hôtel de Rambouillet.

COLIGNY, Louise de (1555–1620). Princess of Orange and countess of Nassau. Name variations: Luise of Bourbon-Montpensier. Born in 1555 (some sources cite 1546); died at the Château de Fontainebleau, Nov 15, 1620; dau. of Gaspard II de Coligny, Maréchal de Châtillon (1519–1572, an admiral and leader of the Huguenots), and Charlotte de Laval (d. 1568); granddau. of Louise de Montmorency, Madame de Châtillon (fl. 1498–1525); sister of François de Coligny (1557–1591, a follower of Henry IV) and aunt of Gaspard III (1584–1646, a marshal of France under Louis XIII and father of Henriette de Coligny); m. Charles de Téligny (who died in the Massacre of St. Bartholmew); became 4th wife of William I the Silent, prince of Orange, count of Nassau (r. 1544–1584), stadholder of Holland, Zealand, and Utrecht (r. 1572–1584), April 12, 1583 (assassinated in 1584); children: Frederick Henry (1584–1647), prince of Orange (r. 1625–1647, who m. Amelia of Solms); and others. ❖ Born into an important and influential French family; after father and 1st husband were killed along with 3,000 other Huguenots in the infamous St. Bartholomew's Day Massacre (1572), fled France and took refuge in Switzerland; while spending a life in exile away from her children, wrote over 200 letters to her family and influential Protestants asking for help, letters that reflected her suffering; married William I the Silent, prince of Orange (1583), but he was assassinated the following year. ❖ See also P. Marchegay, ed. *Correspondence de Louise de Coligny* (1887); and *Women in World History*.

COLIN, Jean (1905–1989). English actress and singer. Born Mar 24, 1905, in Brighton, England; died Mar 7, 1989, in London. ❖ Appeared in numerous musicals and revues between 1928 and 1946, including *Many Happy Returns, Beauty and the Beast, The Five O'Clock Girl, Here Comes the Bride, La Poupée, It's You I Want, The Babes in the Wood, She Shall Have Music, Tulip Time, Aladdin*; films include *Mad about Money* and *The Mikado* (1938).

COLLEDGE, Cecilia (1920—). English figure skater. Born Nov 28, 1920, in England. ❖ Invented many features of figure skating, including parallel spin, layback, and one-foot axle; was the 1st to perform a double jump in competition; was British national champion (1935–39 and

1946–48); placed 8th at Lake Placid Olympics (1932); won a silver medal at Garmisch-Partenkirchen Olympics (1936), narrowly losing to Sonja Henie who took the gold; won a silver medal at World championship (1935) and a gold medal (1937); immigrated to US (1951) and taught at Skating Club of Boston. Inducted into Figure Skating Hall of Fame (1980).

COLLET, Clara (1860–1948). British feminist and social economist. Name variations: Clara Elizabeth Collet. Born Clara Elizabeth Collet, Sept 10, 1860, in Islington, England; died Aug 3, 1948, in Sidmouth, England; dau. of Jane Collet (1820–1908) and Collet Dobson Collet (1813–1898, editor of *The Diplomatic Review*); sister of Wilfred Collet (governor of Honduras, died 1927); North London Collegiate School, BA, 1880; University College, London, MA in Political Economy, 1886. ❖ The 1st woman fellow at University College, taught at Wyggeston High School in Leicester for 7 years (1878–85); became assistant commissioner to Royal Commission on Labour (1889); worked for Charles Booth in his investigative study on the conditions prevailing then in London, taking up residency in the East End (1888); collaborated with Booth on *Life and Labour of the People of London* (1889); was co-founder of Economic Club at University College (1890); for Labour Department of Board of Trade, became Labour correspondent (1893), then senior investigator (1903); focused on women's employment and influenced government policy on trade and labor; served as council member of Royal Economic Society (1920–41) and Royal Statistical Society (1919–35); was governor of Bedford College; good friend of George Gissing. Writings include *The Economic Position of Educated Working Women* (1890), *Educated Working Women* (1902) and *Women in Industry* (1911). ❖ See also Deborah McDonald, *Clara Collet, 1860–1948* (Woburn, 2003).

COLLETT, Camilla (1813–1895). Norwegian novelist and feminist. Born (Jacobine) Camilla Wergeland, Jan 23, 1813, in Kristiansand, Norway; died Mar 6, 1895; dau. of Nicolai (cleric) and Alette Dorothea (Thaulow) Wergeland; sister of poet Henrik Wergeland (1808–1845); m. Peter Jonas Collett (lawyer), July 14, 1841 (died Dec 1851, age 38); children: Robert (b. 1842), Alf (b. 1844), Oscar (b. 1845), Emil (b. 1848). ❖ Pioneering feminist and Norway's 1st feminist-realist novelist, had 1st meeting with poet Johan Sebastian Welhaven (early 1830), who would be the catalyst for her long battle for open, honest relations between men and women, and for women's rights in society; published 1st independently written article, in *Den Constitutionelle* (1842); published 1st and only novel, *Amtmandens Døttre* (*The District Governor's Daughters*) in 2 parts (1854 and 1855), the 1st Norwegian novel to address social problems directly, which caused an uproar and had a profound effect on the works of such Norwegian writers as Bjørnstjerne Bjørnson, Jonas Lie, Alexander Kielland, and Henrik Ibsen; awarded a literary gold medal (1863); made 1st honorary member of Norsk Kvinnesaksforening (The Norwegian Women's Cause, 1884); her struggle for women's rights not only paralleled, but in many ways helped shape the social and legal developments that enabled Norway to meet the 20th century as a modern European state; writings include "Nogle Strikketøjsbetraktninger" ("Musings while Knitting"—a collection of articles 1st published in *Den Constitutionelle*, 1862), *Fortællinger* (stories, 1860), *I de lange Nætter* (*In the Long Nights*, 1862), *Sidste Blade* (*Last Leaves*, 1868, 1872, 1873), *Fra de Stummes Lejr* (*From the Camp of the Mutes*, 1877) and *Mot Strømmen* (*Against the Current*, I: 1879, II: 1885). ❖ See also *Women in World History*.

COLLETT, Glenna (1903–1989). *See Vare, Glenna Collett.*

COLLEVILLE, Anne-Hyacinthe de Saint-Léger de (1761–1824). French novelist and playwright. Born Mar 26, 1761, in Paris, France; died Sept 18, 1824. ❖ Novels include *Lettres du chevalier de saint Alme et de Mlle de Melcourt* (1781), *Alexandrine ou l'amour est une vertu* (1782), *Mme de M***, ou la rentière* (1802), *Victor de Martigues* (1804), *Salut à MM. Les maris ou, Rose et d'Orsinval* (1806) and *Coralie* (1816); also wrote plays, *Le Bouquet du père de famille* (1783), *Les deux soeurs* (1783) and *Sophie et Derville* (1788).

COLLEY, Anne (1951—). Irish politician. Born July 1951 in Dublin, Ireland; dau. of George Colley (TD, 1961–83); m. General Ormonde. ❖ Was a founder member of the Progressive Democrats; elected to the 25th Dáil (1987–89) for Dublin South; defeated in general election (1989).

COLLEY, Sarah Ophelia (1912–1996). *See Pearl, Minnie.*

COLLIARD, Renée (fl. 1950s). Swiss Alpine skier. Name variations: Renee Colliard. Born in Switzerland. ❖ Won a gold medal for slalom at Cortina Olympics (1956), registering the fastest time in each run and surprising all in her debut as a member of the Swiss team.

COLLIER, Constance (1878–1955). British actress. Born Laura Constance Hardie in Windsor, England, Jan 22, 1878; died in Hollywood, California, April 25, 1955; dau. of C.A. Hardie (actor) and Lizzie (Collier) Hardie (actor); granddau. of Leopoldina Collier, who brought one of the 1st ballet companies to England; m. actor Julian L'Estrange, c. 1905 (died 1918). ❖ Made 1st appearance in *A Gaiety Girl* (1894), which was followed by *The Shop Girl* (1895); wanting to become a serious actress, signed on for a provincial tour in the 2nd company of *An Ideal Husband;* had breakthrough role as Chiara the Gypsy in *One Summer's Day;* engaged by actor-manager Beerbohm Tree (1901), had a resounding success as Pallas Athene in *Ulysses;* while with Tree, played numerous roles, including Mistress Ford in *The Merry Wives of Windsor,* Viola in *Twelfth Night* and Julie de Noirville in *A Man's Shadow,;* made 1st appearance in New York (1908), as Ann Marie in *Samson;* made Hollywood film debut in Griffith's *Intolerance* (1916) and would continue to make infrequent appearances in films through 1940s; collaborated with Ivor Novello on play *The Rat;* returned to NY for *Our Betters* (1928), her 1st comedy role in the States; for next 10 years, traveled back and forth between UK and US, enchanting audiences in hits like *Hay Fever, Dinner at Eight, The Torch Bearers, Aries is Rising* and *Curtain Going Up;* other films include *Macbeth* (1916), *Bleak House* (1920), *Shadow of a Doubt* (1935), *Little Lord Fauntleroy* (1936), *Wee Willie Winkie* (1937), *Stage Door* (1937), *Zaza* (1939), *Susan and God* (1940), *Monsieur Beaucaire* (1946), *The Perils of Pauline* (1947) and *Rope* (1948).

COLLIER, Edith (1885–1964). New Zealand painter. Born Edith Marion Collier, Mar 28, 1885, at Wanganui, New Zealand; died Dec 12, 1964, at Wanganui; dau. of Henry Collier (shopkeeper) Eliza Catherine (Parkes) Collier. ❖ Studied art at Wanganui Technical School and in England and Ireland (early 1900s); painted highly regarded portraits of rural people and their dwellings before producing modern, experimental work; exhibited at Women's International Art Club show (1920), New Zealand Academy of Fine Arts (1927–28), and with The Group (1929, 1931); represented New Zealand at Empire Artists' Exhibition in London (1937); work is collected by Sarjeant Gallery, Wanganui, and Museum of New Zealand Te Papa Tongarewa, Wellington. ❖ See also *Dictionary of New Zealand Biography* (Vol. 4).

COLLIER, Jane (1710–c. 1754). British satirist. Born 1710; died c. 1754. ❖ Anonymously published *Essay on the Art of Ingeniously Tormenting* (1753); with Sarah Fielding, wrote *The Cry: A New Dramatic Fable* (1754).

COLLIER, Jane Annie (1869–1955). New Zealand teacher of the blind. Name variations: Jane Annie Blamires. Born Sept 28, 1869, at Springston, Canterbury, New Zealand; died Oct 13, 1955, in Christchurch, New Zealand; dau. of Titus Close Collier (clerk) and Mary Ann (Nankervis) Collier; Christchurch Normal School; m. Henry Lawrence Blamires (minister), 1900; children: 1 son, 2 daughters. ❖ Taught at Jubilee Institute for the Blind in Auckland, becoming 1st professional teacher to the blind in New Zealand (1891). ❖ See also *Dictionary of New Zealand Biography* (Vol. 2).

COLLIER, Jeanie (c. 1791–1861). New Zealand landholder. Born Jeanie Collier, c. 1791 or 1792, in Fife, Scotland; died Sept 2, 1904; dau. of Robert Collier (soldier) and Antonia (Ewing) Collier. ❖ Immigrated to New Zealand with 3 of her orphaned nephews (1850s); bought land in South Canterbury and became 1st recorded woman run holder in New Zealand. ❖ See also *Dictionary of New Zealand Biography* (Vol. 1).

COLLIER, Jeanne (1946—). American diver. Name variations: Jeanne Sitzberger. Born May 15, 1946; m. Ken Sitzberger (Olympic diver, died 1984). ❖ At Tokyo Olympics, won a silver medal in springboard (1964).

COLLIER, Lesley (1947—). English ballet dancer. Born Mar 13, 1947, in Orpington, Kent, England. ❖ Was principal dancer with Royal Ballet throughout performance career, creating roles in Frederick Ashton's *Jazz Calendar* (1968) and *Enigma Variations* (1968), and in Kenneth Macmillan's *The Four Seasons* (1975); was featured in Jerome Robbins' *Dances at a Gathering* and in Macmillan's *Manon;* often danced in films, including "Hunca Munca" in Ashton's *Tales of Beatrix Potter* (1971); also appeared in *The Dancing Princesses* (1978) and *Stories from a Flying Trunk*

(1979); on tv, danced in "The Nutcracker" (1985) and "Gala Tribute to Tchaikovsky" (1993).

COLLIER, Lois (1919–1999). American stage, tv, radio and screen actress. Born Madelyn Jones, Mar 21, 1919, in Salley, South Carolina; died Oct 27, 1999, in Woodland Hills, California. ❖ Began career on radio and stage; made film debut in *A Desperate Adventure* (1938), followed by *Outlaws of Cherokee Trail, Raiders of the Range, Ladies Courageous, Follow the Boys, Jungle Queen, Rhythm Inn* and *Missile Monsters,* among others; co-starred in tv series "Boston Blackie" (1951–54).

COLLIER, Mary (c. 1690–c. 1762). British poet. Born c. 1690 in England; died c. 1762. ❖ Hoping to rise from poverty through writing, published 2 collections of poetry, *The Woman's Labour: An Epistle to Mr. Stephen Duck* (1739) and *Poems on Several Occasions* (1762), about the oppressive life of working-class women; remained a washerwoman for most of life.

COLLIER, Patience (1910–1987). English actress. Born Rene Ritcher, Aug 19, 1910, in London, England; died July 13, 1987, in London; m. H.O.J. Collier. ❖ Made stage debut (1932); joined Royal Shakespeare Company (1961); films include *Every Home Should Have One, The French Lieutenant's Woman, The Third Secret, Perfect Friday, Think Dirty, House of Cards, Fiddler on the Roof, Countess Dracula* and *The National Health, or Nurse Norton's Affair;* made over 2,000 radio broadcasts.

COLLING, Ann-Sofi (1932—). See Pettersson, Ann-Sofi.

COLLINGE, Patricia (1892–1974). Irish-born actress. Born Sept 20, 1892, in Dublin, Ireland; died April 4, 1974, in New York, NY; m. James Nichols Smith. ❖ Made stage debut in London as Ching-a-Ling in *Little Black Sambo and Little White Barbara* (1904); made NY debut in *The Queen of the Moulin Rouge* (1908); in Chicago, created the title role in *Pollyanna* (1915), opened in NY (1916); other plays include *Tillie, The Rivals, Hedda Gabler, Importance of Being Earnest, She Stoops to Conquer, Dulcy, Becky Sharp, Lady with a Lamp, Arsenic and Old Lace, The Heiress* and *I've Got a Sixpence;* with Margalo Gillmore, wrote *The B.O.W.S.;* films include *Shadow of a Doubt, Tender Comrade, Casanova Brown* and *The Nun's Story.* Nominated for Academy Award for portrayal of Birdie Hubbard in *The Little Foxes* (1941).

COLLINGWOOD, Elizabeth (1924—). English royal. Name variations: Elizabeth Colvin; Elizabeth Lascelles. Born Elizabeth Ellen Collingwood, April 23, 1924, in Wimbledon, London, England; dau. of Sydney Collingwood and Charlotte Annie (Oughterson) Collingwood; married a man named Colvin; became 2nd wife of Hon. Gerald David Lascelles (b. 1924, grandson of King George V and Mary of Teck), Nov 17, 1978; children: Martin David Lascelles (b. 1962). Gerald Lascelles' 1st wife was Angela Dowding.

COLLINGWOOD, Louise (1920–1979). See Allbritton, Louise.

COLLINO, Maria (1947—). Italian fencer. Born Dec 1947 in Italy. ❖ At Montreal Olympics, won a silver medal in individual foil (1976).

COLLINS, Addie Mae (d. 1963). One of the Birmingham Four. Murdered Sept 15, 1963, age 14; sister of Junie Collins Peavy and Sarah Collins Rudolph who was wounded in the bombing. ❖ With Denise McNair (11), Cynthia Wesley (14), and Carol Robertson (14), was in the Sixteenth Street Baptist church basement in Birmingham, Alabama, preparing to attend Sunday school and the monthly Youth Day service, when a bomb went off, killing her and the others (Sept 15, 1963). In separate trials, Robert Chambliss (1977), Thomas E. Blanton (2001) and Bobby Frank Cherry (2002) were convicted of murder for the crime. ❖ See also Spike Lee documentary *4 Little Girls* (1998).

COLLINS, Ann (fl. mid-17th c.). British poet. Flourished in mid-17th century. ❖ Wrote *Divine Songs and Meditations* (1653), the only extant copy of which is in Huntington Library.

COLLINS, Anne (1951—). New Zealand politician. Name variations: Anne Fraser; Anne Cullen. Born Anne Collins, July 20, 1951, in Napier, NZ; m. Bruce Fraser, 1969 (div. 1988); m. Michael Cullen (MP), 1989. ❖ Active in the peace movement in Whakatane; elected Labour MP for East Cape (1984), concerned with education, anti-nuclear, and women's issues; resigned (1990).

COLLINS, Barbara-Rose (1939—). African-American politician. Born April 13, 1939, in Detroit, Michigan; dau. of Lamar and Versa Richardson; majored in anthropology at Wayne State University; married and divorced; children: Cynthia and Christopher. ❖ Served on Region 1 Public School Board, Detroit Public Schools (1971–73), and on Detroit City Council (1982–90); as a Democrat, represented the 13th Congressional District of Michigan in the US House of Representatives (1991–92) and the 15th Congressional District (1992–96); was appointed majority whip-at-large and served as chair of the Postal Operations and Civil Service Subcommittee.

COLLINS, Cardiss (1931—). American politician. Born Cardiss Hortense Robertson in St. Louis, Missouri, Sept 24, 1931; dau. of Finley (laborer) and Rosia Mae (Cardiss) Robertson (nurse); attended Northwestern University; m. George Washington Collins, 1958 (died Dec 8, 1972); children: Kevin. ❖ Elected to fill husband's unexpired Congressional term after his death (1973), went on to become the longest-serving black woman in the history of Congress (Jan 5, 1973–Jan 3, 1997) and devoted herself to providing better living and working conditions in her predominantly black district in Illinois; as evidence of her popularity, ran unopposed in 1988; was the 1st woman and the 1st black to chair the House Government Operations Subcommittee on Manpower and Housing, and the 1st woman to chair the Congressional Black Caucus; was also the 1st black and the 1st woman to serve as a Democratic whip-at-large. ❖ See also *Women in World History.*

COLLINS, Christine (1969—). American rower. Name variations: Christine Smith Collins. Born Christine Smith, Sept 9, 1969, in Darien, Connecticut; graduate of Trinity College, 1991; m. Matt Collins (World champion rower). ❖ With Sarah Garner, won a World championship title (1998) and a bronze medal for lightweight double sculls at Sydney Olympics (2000); won 4 World titles, more than any female rower in US history.

COLLINS, Cora Sue (1927—). American actress and dancer. Born April 19, 1927, in Beckley, West Virginia. ❖ Appeared in Hollywood films as a child, making debut at age 5 in *The Strange Case of Clara Deane* (1932); also appeared in *Jennie Gerhardt, The Sin of Nora Moran, Queen Christina, Evelyn Prentice, Little Men, Anna Karenina, Magnificent Obsession, The Adventures of Tom Sawyer,* and most memorably as Colleen Moore's daughter Pearl in *The Scarlet Letter* (1934), among others; retired from film at age 18.

COLLINS, Diana (1917–2003). English activist and writer. Name variations: Dame Diana Collins. Born Diana Clavering, Aug 13, 1917, at Stutton Hall, Suffolk, England; died May 23, 2003; attended Lady Margaret Hall, Oxford; m. John Collins (cleric and canon of St. Paul's Cathedral, 1949–82), 1939 (died 1982); children: Andrew, Peter, Mark and Richard (died 1991). ❖ With husband, actively campaigned against capital punishment, the nuclear bomb and apartheid; rewrote his speeches, raised funds, bound political wounds, and was co-founder and editor of the *Christian Action* journal; was also active in the Canon Collins Educational Trust for Southern Africa and an important influence in the early stages of the Movement for the Ordination of Women. Made a DBE (1999). ❖ See also memoirs *Partners in Progress* (1992) and *Time and the Priestleys* (1994).

COLLINS, Dorothy (1926–1994). Canadian actress and singer. Born Marjorie Chandler, Nov 18, 1926, in Windsor, Ontario, Canada; died July 21, 1994, in Watervliet, NY; m. Raymond Scott (bandleader), 1952 (div. 1965); m. Ron Holgate, 1966 (div.); children: 3 daughters. ❖ Was a vocalist on tv's "Your Hit Parade" (1950–57, 1958–59) and co-hosted "Candid Camera" (1960); starred in the original cast of *Follies* (1971), for which she was nominated for a Tony.

COLLINS, Eileen (1956—). American astronaut. Born Eileen Marie Collins, Nov 19, 1956, at Elmira, New York; dau. of James E. Collins and Rose Marie Collins; Corning Community College, AS, 1976; Syracuse University, BA, 1978; Stanford University, MS, 1986; Webster University, MA, 1989; m. James Patrick Youngs. ❖ The 1st female pilot of the space shuttle, joined the Air Force (1978); as 2nd female Air Force test pilot, graduated from Air Force Institute of Technology and Air Force Test Pilot School (1985–90); selected by NASA (1990); became the 1st woman to pilot the space shuttle (Feb 3, 1995), when she was second in command of a crew of 6 that made a historical rendezvous with the Russian space station Mir; appointed space shuttle commander of the *Columbia*, the 1st woman to lead the crew of four (1998); was commander of *Discovery* (2005). ❖ See also *Women in World History.*

COLLINS, Ellen (1828–1912). American housing reformer and philanthropist. Born Dec 1828, in New York, NY; died July 8, 1912, in New York, NY; dau. of Joseph B. and Sarah (Mintern) Collins; granddau. of Isaac Collins (Quaker printer). ❖ Joined Woman's Central Association of Relief in NY during Civil War (1861); worked for New York National Freedmen's Relief Association on behalf of Negro education; inspected schools for Negroes in VA with philanthropist Josephine Shaw Lowell (1866); appointed visitor of public charitable institutions in New York County; in housing experiment to provide for needs of the very poor, purchased 3 old tenement houses in Cherry Hill, the Lower East Side (1880), which were fully occupied by renters during her 23 years of ownership.

COLLINS, Gail (1945—). American columnist. Born Gail Gleason, Nov 25, 1945, in Cincinnati, Ohio; Marquette University, BA in journalism, 1969; University of Massachusetts at Amherst, MA in government; also attended Columbia University, 1981–82; m. Dan Collins (senior producer at CBS News). ❖ Was a reporter at UPI in NY (1980–1985), then joined the *New York Daily News* (1985); was a columnist at *Newsday* (1991–95); hired by the *New York Times* to be an editorial writer for the Op-Ed page (1995), began a Public Interests column (1999), then became the 1st woman to head the editorial page at the *Times* (2001); writings include *Scorpion Tongues* (1998) and (with husband) *The Millenium Book* (1991). Won the Meyer Berger Award from Columbia University (1987).

COLLINS, Jackie (1937—). English writer, actress, and producer. Born Jacqueline Jill Collins, Oct 4, 1937, in London, England; dau. of a theatrical booking agent; sister of Joan Collins (actress); m. Wallace Austin, 1959 (div. 1965); m. Oscar Lerman, 1966 (died 1992); children: (1st m.) daughter Tracy; (2nd m.) Tiffany and Rory. ❖ Made film debut in *Barnacle Bill* (1957), followed by *Undercover Girl* and *Intent to Kill*; author of such books as *The Stud, The World is Full of Married Men, Hollywood Wives, Deadly Embrace* and such teleplays as "Lucky/Chances" (1990) and "Lady Boss" (1992).

COLLINS, Janet (1917–2003). African-American ballet dancer. Born Janet Collins, Mar 2, 1917, in New Orleans, Louisiana; died May 28, 2003, in Fort Worth, Texas; dau. of Ernest Lee Collins (tailor) and Alma (de Lavallade) Collins (seamstress); attended Los Angeles City College; never married; no children. ❖ The 1st African-American dancer to find considerable success in ballet, becoming a *premiere danseuse* for the Metropolitan Opera in the 1950s, 1st studied dance in Los Angeles and performed on early tv shows and with various companies; had New York solo concert debut (1949); was principal ballet dancer of Metropolitan Opera (1951–54); gave solo concert tours in US and Canada (1952–55); taught at Marymount College, Harkness House, School of American Ballet, San Francisco Ballet School; set a precedent that began to enlarge the possibilities for African-Americans in the field; works choreographed include *Blackamoor* (1947), *Eine Kleine Nachtmusik* (1947), *Spirituals* (1947), *Protest* (1947), *Après le Mardi Gras* (1947), *Juba* (1949), *Three Psalms of David* (1949), *Moi l'Aime Toi, Chère* (1951), *The Satin Slipper* (1960), *Genesis* (1965), *Cockfight* (1972), *Birds of Peace and Pride* (1973), *Song* (1973), *Fire Weaver* (1973) and *Sunday and Sister Jones* (1973). Received Donaldson Award for best dancer of the Broadway season (1951–52) and Dance Magazine Award (1959). ❖ See also *Women in World History.*

COLLINS, Jennie (1828–1887). American labor reformer. Born 1828 in Amoskeag, New Hampshire; died July 20, 1887, in Brookline, Massachusetts; orphaned when young. ❖ During Civil War, volunteered in military hospitals (Boston, MA); with shopmates in tailoring firm, formed soldiers' relief association; became significant figure in postwar labor movement; worked with New England Labor Reform League; helped found Working Women's League of Boston (1869); accepted invitation of Susan B. Anthony to address National Woman Suffrage Association convention, Washington, DC (1870); opened social center for working girls in Boston called Boffin's Bower (1870), which provided food, lodging, and employment assistance. Wrote *Nature's Aristocracy* (ed. Russell H. Conwell, 1871).

COLLINS, Joan (1933—). English actress and writer. Born Joan Henrietta Collins, May 23, 1933, in London, England; dau. of a theatrical booking agent; sister of Jackie Collins (writer); m. Maxwell Reed, 1952 (div. 1956); m. Anthony Newley (songwriter, performer), 1963 (div. 1970); m. Ron Kass, 1972 (div. 1984); m. Peter Holm, 1985 (div. 1987); m. Percy Gibson (theater manager), 2002; children: Tara Cynara Newley (b. 1963, news anchor in England), Alexander "Sacha" Newley (artist), and Katyana "Katy" Kass (b. 1972). ❖ Made London debut in *A Doll's House* (1946) and Broadway debut as Amanda in *Private Lives* (1991); made film debut in *Lady Godiva Rides Again* (1951), followed by

Land of the Pharoahs, The Virgin Queen, The Girl in the Red Velvet Swing, The Opposite Sex, Island in the Sun, The Bravados, Rally 'Round the Flag Boys and The Road to Hong Kong, among others; when career slumped, starred in horror flicks and such films as The Stud and The Bitch, based on her sister's novels; revived career with part of Alexis Carrington Colby in tv series "Dynasty" (1981–89); wrote novels. Made Officer of the British Empire (OBE). ❖ See also autobiographies Past Imperfect (1978) and Star Quality.

COLLINS, José (1887–1958). English music-hall star. Name variations: Josephine Collins; Jose Collins. Born Josephine Collins, May 23, 1887, in London, England; died Dec 6, 1958, in London; illeg. dau. of music-hall star Lottie Collins; m. Leslie Chatfield (div.); m. Lord Robert Innes-Ker (div.); m. Captain G.B. Kirkland, R.A.M.C. ❖ Made stage debut as a child, appearing with Harry Lauder (1904); best remembered for role of Teresa in The Maid of the Mountains, which ran in London for 1,352 performances; on Broadway, appeared in Vera Violetta (1911), The Whirl of Society, The Rose of Ispahan, The Merry Countess, Alone at Last, Ziegfeld Follies of 1913 and Passing Show of 1914; toured US in vaudeville (1926); made film debut (1915). ❖ See also her reminiscences The Maid of the Mountains (1932).

COLLINS, Josephine (1887–1958). See Collins, José.

COLLINS, Judy (1939—). American folksinger, writer, and filmmaker. Born May 1, 1939, in Seattle, Washington; dau. of Chuck Collins (bandleader); sister of Holly Collins (dancer); studied piano with Antonia Brico; m. Peter Taylor, 1958 (div. 1965); m. Louis Nelson (designer), 1996; children: Clark (b. 1959, committed suicide 1992). ❖ Studied classical piano from age 5 and made public debut at 13 with Denver Symphony Orchestra; began singing folksongs in coffeehouses (late 1950s); released debut A Maid of Constant Sorrow (1961); covered and popularized songs by Joni Mitchell, Leonard Cohen, and Randy Newman; earned mainstream success with singles "Both Sides Now" (1968) and "Send in the Clowns" (1975); acted in New York Shakespeare Festival's Peer Gynt (1969); produced celebrated documentary on Antonia Brico, Antonia: Portrait of the Woman (1974); released albums Wildflowers (1967), Recollections (1969), Judith (1975), Hard Times for Lovers (1979), Fires of Eden (1990), and All on a Wintry Night (2000); inspired Crosby, Stills, and Nash song "Suite: Judy Blue Eyes"; recorded album of Bob Dylan songs (1993); published 1st novel and released accompanying album Shameless (1995); founded own record label Wildflower. Song "Chelsea Morning" inspired first daughter Chelsea Clinton's name. ❖ See also autobiographies, Trust Your Heart (1987) and Singing Lessons: A Memoir of Love, Loss, Hope an Healing (1998).

COLLINS, Kathleen (1942–1988). African-American independent filmmaker and playwright. Name variations: Kathleen Collins Prettyman. Born Kathleen Conwell Collins, Mar 18, 1942, in Gouldtown, New Jersey; died Sept 18, 1988; attended Skidmore College and Middlebury Graduate School of French in Paris; married; children: (from a previous relationship) 1 daughter, and 2 sons. ❖ In short career, wrote 6 plays, all produced, including a production of "The Brothers," which was staged during the American Place Theatre's 1982–83 season; also wrote several short stories and 4 screenplays; filmed The Cruz Brothers and Miss Malloy, followed by her most important work, Losing Ground, possibly the 1st independent film to feature an African-American professional woman as the protagonist; also filmed Gouldtown: A Mulatto Settlement (1988). ❖ See also Women in World History.

COLLINS, Lottie (c. 1866–1910). English popular entertainer. Born c. 1866, probably in London, England; died 1910 in London; children: illeg. daughter José Collins. ❖ Popular music-hall entertainer, gained wide renown for her vigorous rendition of "Ta-ra-ra-Boom-De-ia" in a Christmas presentation of the longtime pantomime Dick Wittington and His Cat at the Tivoli Theater in London (1891); reprised this, her signature song, for variety of venues—almost always to great success—including on tour in US; danced the solo act in short pink dress, with black stockings, petticoats, and enormous hat, adapting the 5 verses of the piece to topical political events.

COLLINS, Margaret (1878–1945). See Collins-O'Driscoll, Margaret.

COLLINS, Pauline (1940—). English actress. Born Sept 3, 1940 in Exmouth, Devon, England; dau. of Irish immigrants; m. John Alderton (actor), 1969; children: 3. ❖ Made tv debut on series "Emergency–Ward 10" (1957); came to prominence as Sarah in 13 episodes of "Upstairs, Downstairs" (1974); starred on "Thomas and Sarah"

(1979); other series include "The Black Tower," "Forever Green" and "The Ambassador"; won a Tony Award and Laurence Olivier Theatre Award for Best Actress for performance in the play Shirley Valentine (1989); films include Shirley Valentine (1989), Paradise Road (1997), and Mrs. Caldicot's Cabbage War (2000). Awarded OBE (2001). ❖ See also memoir Letter to Louise (1992).

COLLINS-O'DRISCOLL, Margaret (1878–1945). Irish politician. Name variations: Margaret Collins, Margaret O'Driscoll. Born Margaret Collins, 1878, in Woodfield, Clonakilty, Co. Cork, Ireland; died June 17, 1945; sister of Johanna Collins and Michael Collins (1890–1922, Irish nationalist); m. Patrick O'Driscoll, 1901 (publisher of small newspaper); children: 5 sons, 9 daughters; grandaunt of Nora Owen and Mary Banotti. ❖ Was principal of Lisavard Girls' School, Clonakilty (1896–22); following shooting of brother Michael (Aug 22, 1922), elected as Cumann na nGaedheal deputy to 4th Dáil for Dublin North; served in the 4th–7th Dáil (1923–33); served as vice-president of Cumann na nGaedheal (1926–27).

COLLINS, Martha Layne (1936—). American politician. Born Martha Layne Hall, Dec 7, 1936, in Bagdad, Kentucky; graduate of University of Kentucky; m. Dr. Bill L. Collins (dentist who was convicted on charges of extortion). ❖ Taught school until 1970; served as clerk of the state Supreme Court (1978–79); a Democrat, served as lieutenant governor (1979–83); was the 1st woman to serve as governor of Kentucky (1983–87, and the 3rd woman in US to be elected governor in her own right; chaired the Democratic National Convention (1984); served as president of St. Catharine College for 6 years.

COLLINS, Marva (1936—). African-American educator. Born Marva Delores Knight, Aug 31, 1936, in Monroeville, Alabama; attended Bethlehem Academy; graduate of Clark College in Atlanta; m. Clarence Collins; children. ❖ Taught in Alabama for 2 years; moved to Chicago (1959); taught in Chicago's public-school system for 14 years (1961–75); opened school on 2nd floor of her home (1975), which became Westside Preparatory School (later Marva Collins Preparatory School); with her methodology, had such success with students formerly labeled uneachable that she came to the attention of the media, appearing on "60 Minutes" and "Good Morning America"; her life was the basis for the CBS movie "The Marva Collins Story," starring Cicely Tyson and Morgan Freeman; with Civia Tamarkin, wrote Marva Collins Way (1982).

COLLOT, Marie-Anne (1748–1821). French sculptor. Born in 1748 in France; died 1821 in France; studied with sculptor Étienne Maurice Falconet; m. Pierre-Étienne Falconet (painter); children: 1 daughter. ❖ Known for her warm portrait busts, produced heads of French enlightenment figures Voltaire and Diderot (1770s) and maintained extensive correspondence with both, as well as with Montesquieu; best known for her affectionate portrait of Étienne Maurice Falconet (1773), accompanied him to Russia when only 18 to work on the monument to Peter the Great in St. Petersburg (1766), one of 18th century's most famous pieces of sculpture which had been commissioned by Catherine the Great; became 1st female member of Imperial Academy of Arts (1767); remained in Russia for 12 years, rendering many busts for members of the court of Catherine the Great as well as Catherine herself; married Falconet's son, painter Pierre-Étienne, to please elder Falconet, and moved with him to England where husband studied with Joshua Reynolds; sculpted many busts in England, including one of Lady Cathcart; unhappy, left to join elder Falconet in The Hague, living on life pension bestowed by Catherine the Great; ceased work abruptly when Falconet suffered paralytic stroke (1783), becoming devoted nurse and companion; is included in many distinguished collections, including those of Louvre museum.

COLLYER, June (1907–1968). American actress. Born Dorothea Heermance, Aug 19, 1907, in New York, NY; died Mar 16, 1968 in Los Angeles, California; sister of Bud Collyer (game-show host); m. Stuart Erwin (actor), 1931 (died 1967). ❖ Made film debut in East Side, West Side (1928); other films include Charley's Aunt, River of Romance, Man from Wyoming, Alexander Hamilton, Cheaters and The Ghost Walks; retired (1934), then co-starred with husband in tv series "The Trouble with Father," later renamed "The Stu Erwin Show" (1950–55).

COLLYER, Marian (d. 1981). See Shockley, Marian.

COLLYER, Mary (d. 1763). English translator and novelist. Name variations: Mary Mitchell Collyer. Born Mary Mitchell, c. 1716, in England;

died 1763 in London, England; m. Joseph Collyer. ❖ Translated texts from German and French, including Pierre Marivaux's *The Virtuous Orphan; or, the life of Marianne, Countess of . . .* (1735), S. Gessner's *The Death of Abel* (1761), and F.G. Klopstock's *Messiah* (1763); also wrote epistolary novel *Felicia to Charlotte* (1744).

COLMAN, Julia (1828–1909). American temperance writer. Name variations: (pseudonym) Aunt Julia. Born Feb 16, 1828, in Northampton, NY; died Jan 10, 1909, in Brooklyn, NY; dau. of Henry Root Colman (Methodist minister) and Livia (Spier) Colman; attended Lawrence College and Cazenovia Seminary. ❖ Served as librarian and literary assistant for Methodist Sunday-School Union and Tract Society, NY; wrote under name Aunt Julia for *Sunday School Advocate;* resigned from Union and Tract Society (1867) to become lecturer and writer on temperance, hygiene and diet; published "Catechisms" on alcohol and tobacco (1872); served in several positions with Women's Christian Temperance Union (WCTU), including chair of leaflet committee, editor of children's page in WCTU magazine, and superintendent of new Department of Temperance Literature (1880–91); published more than 500 temperance materials; writings include *The Boys' and Girls' Illustrated Bird Book* (1857) and *Alcohol and Hygiene* (textbook, 1880).

COLOMBA. *Variant of Columba.*

COLOMBETTI, Bruna (1936—). Italian fencer. Born Jan 27, 1936, in Italy. ❖ At Rome Olympics, won a bronze medal in team foil (1960).

COLOMBI, Marchioness (1846–1920). *See Torriani, Maria Antonietta.*

COLOMBINE (1867–1932). *See Burgos Seguí, Carmen de.*

COLOMER, Mari Pepa (1913–2004). *See Pepa, Mari.*

COLON, Filippa or Felipa (d. 1483). *See Perestrello-Moniz, Filippa.*

COLON, Maria (1958—). Cuban track-and-field athlete. Name variations: María Caridad Colón. Born María Caridad Colón, Mar 25, 1958, in Cuba; m. Angel Salcedo (her coach). ❖ Won gold medals at two Pan American Games; won a gold medal for javelin at Moscow (1980), the 1st Cuban woman to win an Olympic gold medal. ❖ See also *Women in World History.*

COLONIA, Regina Célia (1940—). Brazilian poet and short-story writer. Name variations: Regina Celia Colonia. Born 1940. ❖ Served as consul in Washington, DC; writings include *Canção para o totem* (1975), *Sumaimana* (1976), and *Os leõs da Luziânia* (1985). Won Jabuti Prize for Poetry (1976).

COLONNA, Catherine (d. around 1440). Countess of Montefeltro. Name variations: Cattarina Colonna. Died c. 1440; niece of Pope Martin V; m. Guido Sforza, count of Montefeltro; children: Seraphina Sforza (1434–1478). ❖ See also *Women in World History.*

COLONNA, Vittoria (c. 1490–1547). Italian poet and religious reformer. Name variations: Marchioness of Pescara. Born probably 1490 (some sources cite 1492) in Marino, Italy; died in Rome, Feb 25, 1547; dau. of Fabrizio Colonna (member of the powerful Colonna family and influential soldier) and Agnese da Montefeltro, also known as Anna da Montefeltro (dau. of Federico, duke of Urbino); betrothed at age 4 to Francesco Ferrante d'Avalos (son of an important Spanish family resident in Italy); they were married in 1509; children: none, though she raised her husband's orphaned nephew. ❖ Wrote poetry throughout adult life, basically on religion and philosophy, though most poems were composed after death of husband (1525), who was killed in one of the many battles in which control of the Italian peninsula was being contested; spent rest of life traveling from convent to convent, writing poems, and involving herself in religious matters and in the arts; settled in Benedictine convent of St. Anne in Rome (1544); was active in reform of Catholic Church; her friendships and correspondence with notables of the day, including Lodovico Ariosto, Luigi Alamanni, Pietro Aretino, Cardinal Pietro Bembo, Baldassare Castiglione, and Michelangelo, contributed to her fame; never involved herself directly in publication of poems, though 5 editions appeared in her lifetime (the 1st in 1538). The poems remained popular, with many more editions appearing throughout 16th and 17th centuries. ❖ See also Maud F. Jerrold, *Vittoria Colonna, With Some Account of Her Friends and Her Times* (Dutton, 1906); and *Women in World History.*

COLOVIC, Laura (1971—). *See Flessel, Laura.*

COLQHOUN, Alva (1942—). Australian swimmer. Born Mar 30, 1942. ❖ At Rome Olympics, won a silver medal in 4x100-meter freestyle relay (1960).

COLQUHOUN, Ithell (1906–1988). English painter and poet. Born Oct 9, 1906, in Shillong, Assam, India; died April 11, 1988, in Cornwall, England; educated at Cheltenham College; studied art at Slade School and in Paris. Work in permanent collections: Tate Gallery, V&A Bradford, Cheltenham and Southampton Galleries, Glasgow and London universities. ❖ Joined English Surrealist group (1939), but left the following year when pressured to abandon her work on occultism; her experiments in automatism resulted in *decalcomania, sfumage, frottage*; wrote *The Crying Wind* (1955), *The Living Stones* (1957), the Surrealist occult novel *Goose of Hermogenes* (1961), *Grimoire of the Entangled Thicket* (1973), *Sword of Wisdom* (1975), and travel books on Cornwall and Ireland.

COLT, Ethel Barrymore (1912–1977). American actress and singer. Name variations: Ethel Miglietta. Born April 30, 1912; died May 22, 1977, in New York, NY; dau. of Ethel Barrymore (actress) and Russell Griswold Colt; m. Romeo Miglietta (petroleum executive); children: John Drew Miglietta (actor). ❖ Made professional debut at 18 in a supporting role opposite her mother in *Scarlet Sister Mary* (1930); also appeared in *George White's Scandals, Under Glass, Laura Garnett, L'Aiglon, London Assurance, Orchids Preferred, Whiteoaks, Come of Age, Curtains Up!, Take It from the Top, A Madrigal of Shakespeare* and was featured as Christine Crane in Stephen Sondheim's long-running *Follies* (1971). ❖ See also *Women in World History.*

COLTER, Mary Elizabeth (1869–1949). American architect and designer. Born Mary Elizabeth Jane Colter in Pittsburgh, Pennsylvania, April 4, 1869; died in 1949; graduate of California School of Design, 1890. ❖ One of the few American women architects working before World War I, was an avid student of Native American culture who was employed for 4 decades as a permanent architect and designer for Fred Harvey Co., an enterprise that prospered by providing food, accommodations, and services for the Santa Fe Railroad; designed 6 ancient-looking buildings in Arizona's Grand Canyon, 4 of which have been designated National Historic Landmarks: Hermit's Rest, which stands at the head of Hermit's Trail, Lookout Studio, an eccentric building that hangs over the edge of the canyon wall, Bright Angel Lodge, and The Watchtower, completed in 1935, which remains her masterpiece. ❖ See also Virginia L. Grattan, *Mary Colter, Builder Upon the Red Earth* (Northland Press, 1980); and *Women in World History.*

COLTON, Anita (b. 1919). *See O'Day, Anita.*

COLTON, Elizabeth Avery (1872–1924). American educator. Born Dec 30, 1872, at outpost in Choctaw Nation, Indian Territory; died Aug 15, 1924, in Clifton Springs, NY; dau. of James Hooper Colton (missionary) and Harriet Eloise (Avery) Colton (missionary); sister of Susanne Colton (missionary); Statesville (NC) Female College, BA; attended Mount Holyoke; Columbia University Teachers College, BS, 1903, AM, 1905. ❖ Taught at Queen's College (Charlotte, NC) and Wellesley College (Wellesley, MA); became head of English department at Meredith College (then known as Baptist University for Women) in Raleigh, NC (1908); helped organize Southern Association of College Women (SACW, 1903) and served as chair of committee on standards of colleges (from 1910), secretary (1912–14), and president (1914–19); known for raising standards of college education for women in the South, made detailed survey of women's colleges there and published findings in bulletins, including *The Various Types of Southern Colleges for Women* (1916); her evaluation provided guidelines for accreditation by the SACW.

COLTON, Mary (1822–1898). Australian philanthropist and suffragist. Born Mary Cutting, Dec 6, 1822, in London, England; died July 28, 1898, in Adelaide, Australia; dau. of Hannah and Samuel Cutting; m. John Blackler Colton (later mayor of Adelaide, 1874–75, MP, 1862–87 and twice premier of South Australia), 1844; children: 9. ❖ With widowed father, immigrated to South Australia (1839); worked with husband in the Benevolent and Strangers' Friend Society and for organizations for the blind, deaf and dumb; was one of the principal founders of the Adelaide Children's Hospital (1876); launched the Young Women's Christian Association in Adelaide and served as its president until her death; deeply involved in women's suffrage, helped to organize the South Australian Women's Suffrage League (1888).

COLTRANE, Alice (1937—). American pianist, organist, and harpist. Name variations: Alice McLeod; Lady Trane; Turiya Sagittinanda. Born Alice McLeod in Detroit, Michigan, Aug 27, 1937; sister of Ernie Farrow; m. John Coltrane (musician), c. 1965 (died 1967). ❖ Known for rippling arpeggios and dramatic pauses, began studying classical music at age 7; studied jazz with Bud Powell and gained experience with church groups; developed talents with jazz ensembles of Kenny Burrell, Lucky Thompson, Yusef Lateef, and Johnny Griffin; toured and recorded with Terry Gibbs (1962 and 1963); joined husband John Coltrane's group (1966), replacing McCoy Tyner; after husband's death (1967), went on to lead many ensembles; moved to California (1972); founded retreat for study of Eastern religions, the Vedantic Center (1975); published book of spiritual texts, *Endless Wisdom;* recorded album *Transfiguration* (1978) with Roy Haynes and Reggie Workman; in tribute to husband, performed with quartet that included her sons at New York's Cathedral of St. John the Divine (1987). Musicians who played in her groups included double bass players Cecil McBee and Jimmy Garrison, drummers Rashied Ali, Roy Haynes and Ben Riley, and saxophonists Pharoah Sanders, Joe Henderson, Archie Shepp, Frank Lowe and Carlos Ward. ❖ See also *Women in World History.*

COLUM, Mary Gunning (1884–1957). Irish-born American author. Name variations: Molly Colum. Born Mary Catherine Maguire in Ireland in 1884 (some sources cite 1887); died in New York, NY, Oct 22, 1957; dau. of Charles Maguire and Maria (Gunning) Maguire; m. Padraic Colum (poet and playwright) in 1912; children, none. ❖ Highly regarded literary critic in New York in 1920s, was active in the literary life of Dublin in her early years; with husband and others, founded *The Irish Review,* a journal that quickly became a major voice in Irish intellectual life; with husband, immigrated to US (1914); contributed articles to leading American literary journals, including *Scribner's, Saturday Review, The Nation, The New Republic* and *Yale Review;* as an expert on modern literature, became a regular reviewer for *The New York Times;* appeared monthly in the *Forum* magazine (1933–40); published *From these Roots* (1937), a sweeping interpretation of modern literature that received generally high marks from fellow critics. ❖ See also autobiography, *Life and the Dream* (1947); and *Women in World History.*

COLUMBA OF CORDOVA (d. 853). Spanish nun and saint. Executed in 853 in Cordova, Spain. ❖ During persecution of Catholics by Muslims, purposefully left her convent at Cordova to declare her faith before the cadi's tribunal (Muslim magistrates) and was beheaded. Feast day is Sept 17.

COLUMBA OF RIETI (1467–1501). Italian mystic. Name variations: Angela or Angelella; Columba de Rieti; Colomba da Rieti; called Columba ("dove") because of a miraculous event that took place during her baptism. Born in Rieti, Italy, 1467, in a merchants' family; died May 20, 1501; dau. of Angelo Antonio and Giovanna Guadagnali, called Vanna. ❖ Italian mystic of the Third Order of Penance who promoted a project to reform the religious life for women in the early modern age; took vows at 18; at 21, moved to Perugia, where she founded the nunnery of the Colombe and engaged in social and political reform; according to tradition, when Perugia was struck by the plague (1494), interceded to end the epidemic and saved the population; known as the co-patron of Rieti and Perugia with the title of protector. ❖ See also *Women in World History.*

COLUMBA OF SENS (d. 274?). Spanish saint. Born in Spain; executed around 274. ❖ As a child in Spain (Hispania), heard stories of France (Gaul) and its Christian religion; fled Spain, settling in Sens, a city in northeast France, where she was baptized and welcomed by the populace; when Roman emperor Aurelian passed through Sens on his mission to reconquer Gaul (274), was the only Christian in Sens not put to death, because he was attracted by her beauty and noble origins; spurned him and was beheaded. Legend has it that, as she was about to die, a bear came out of the woods and knelt before her. Feast day is Dec 31. ❖ See also *Women in World History.*

COLUMBINE (1877–1941). See Polson, Florence Ada Mary Lamb.

COLUMBO, Patricia (1957—). American murderer. Born 1957; dau. of Frank and Mary Columbo. ❖ With boyfriend Frank Deluca, murdered her parents and 13-year-old brother Michael in their Illinois home (May 1976); tried with Deluca (1977), found guilty and sentenced to 200–300 years in prison.

COLUMBUS, Filippa or Felipa (d. 1483). See Perestrello-Moniz, Filippa.

COLVILLE, Elizabeth (c. 1571–1600s). Scottish poet. Name variations: Eliz. Melvill; Elizabeth Melville; Lady Colville of Culross; (pseudonyms) M.M., Gentelwoman [sic] in Culross; Ladie Culross yonger. Born Elizabeth Melvill or Melville, c. 1571, in Halhill, Scotland; died in 1600s; dau. of Sir James Melvill or Melville (courtier and diplomat) and Christina Boswell; m. John Colville, 3rd Lord of Culross; children: Alexander Colville (eminent Episcopalian cleric and Hebrew scholar). ❖ Published long allegorical poem "Ane Godlie Dreame" in Scots dialect (1603); also left letters and a sonnet.

COLVILLE, Meg (1918–2004). Scottish lady-in-waiting. Name variations: Lady Meg Colville. Born Margaret Egerton, 1918, in Roxburghshire, Scotland; died June 2004; dau. of John Francis Granville Scrope Egerton, 4th earl of Ellesmere, and Lady Violet Lambton; m. Sir John Rupert Colville (secretary to Winston Churchill), Oct 1948; children: Elizabeth, Alexander, and Rupert. ❖ Served as lady-in-waiting to Princess Elizabeth for 3 years after WWII, then attended the Queen Mother, Elizabeth Bowes-Lyon, for over 10 years.

COLVIN, Brenda (1897–1981). British landscape architect. Born June 8, 1897, in Simla, India; died Jan 27, 1981, in England; educated in Paris. ❖ Pioneer in the field of landscape architecture, studied at Swanley Horticultural College (later absorbed into Hadlow College) and assisted Madeline Agar on the War Memorial Garden in Wimbledon; went into private practice as a landscape architect (1922) and shared an office with Sylvia Crowe; was co-founder of Institute of Landscape Architects, then later secretary (1941–48), vice-president, and president (1951–53); took on projects for War Office, Port of London Authority, and Electricity Generating Board; designed gardens for the Manor House in Sutton Courtenay and elsewhere; is also known for her own garden at Filkins in Gloucestershire; writings include *Trees for Town and Country* (1947) and *Land and Landscape* (1948); was senior partner at Colvin and Moggridge at the time of her death. Received OBE (1973).

COLVIN, Shawn (1956—). American folk-pop singer. Born Shawna Lee Colvin, Jan 10, 1956, in Vermillion, South Dakota; m. Simon Tassano, 1993 (div. 1995); m. Mario Erwin, 1997; children: Caledonia (b. 1998). ❖ Toured with such artists as Suzanne Vega, Richard Thompson, and Bruce Hornsby; wrote song "Orion in the Sky"; released debut album *Steady On* (1989), which earned her a Grammy for Best Contemporary Folk Recording; released album *A Few Small Repairs* (1996), which was nominated for a Grammy for Album of the Year (1997); had Top-10 hit "Sunny Came Home" (*A Few Small Repairs*) which won Grammy awards for both Song and Record of the Year (1997). Albums include *Steady On* (1989), *Fat City* (1992), *Cover Girl* (1994), *Live '88* (1995), *A Few Small Repairs* (1996), *Holiday Songs and Lullabies* (1998) and *Whole New You* (2001).

COLWELL, Rita R. (1934—). American microbiologist. Name variations: Dr. Rita Rossi Colwell. Born Rita Barbara Rossi, Nov 23, 1934, in Beverly, Massachusetts; Purdue University, BS in bacteriology, 1956, MA, 1958, honorary DSc, 1993; dau. of Louis and Louise (DiPalma) Rossi; m. Jack Colwell; children: 2. ❖ Renowned marine biotechnology pioneer known for work using computers to identify bacteria; earned doctoral degree in genetics at University of Washington (1961) and rose from research assistant to associate professor (1959–64); was assistant professor of biology at Georgetown University (1961–64), then associate microbiology professor at University of Maryland (1972) and later served as vice president for Academic Affairs for University of Maryland system (1983–87); served as director of Center for Marine Biotechnology in Maryland (1987–91); elected 11th director of National Science Foundation (1998); served as vice president of International Union of Microbiological Sciences (1986–90), as president of American Society for Microbiology (1984–85), and as chair of board of governors of American Academy of Microbiologists; holds 2 marine biotechnology patents. Received American Association of Microbiologists' Fisher Award (1985), International Biotechnology Institute's Gold Medal (1990), and Czechoslovakian Academy of Sciences' Purkinje Gold Medal Achievement Award (1991), among others.

COLWIN, Laurie (1944–1992). American fiction and food writer. Born June 14, 1944, in New York, NY; died Oct 24, 1992, in New York; dau. of Estelle Snellenberg; educated at Bard College and Columbia University; m. Juris Jurjevics (editor of Soho Press), 1981; children: Rosa Audrey Jurjevics. ❖ Became assistant editor at Dutton; published 1st story in *The New Yorker* (1969), followed by 1st short-story collection

Passion and Affect (1974); as a columnist for *Gourmet,* collected several of her columns in *Home Cooking* (1988); other writings include *Shine on, Bright and Dangerous Object* (1975), *Happy All the Time* (1978), *Family Happiness* (1982), *A Big Storm Knocked It Over* (1993) and *More Home Cooking* (1993). ❖ See also Mickey Pearlman and Katherine Usher Henderson. *A Voice of One's Own* (Houghton, 1990); and *Women in World History.*

COLYER, Evelyn (1902–1930). English tennis player. Name variations: Evelyn Lucy Colyer. Born Aug 16, 1902; died Nov 1930. ❖ At Paris Olympics, won a bronze medal in doubles (1924).

COMAN, Katharine (1857–1915). American economic historian. Born Nov 23, 1857, in Newark, Ohio; died Jan 11, 1915, Wellesley, Massachusetts; dau. of Martha (Seymour) Coman and Levi Parsons Coman (lawyer and abolitionist); University of Michigan, PhB, 1880; lived with Katharine Lee Bates (professor and poet). ❖ At Wellesley College, became professor of political economy and history (1883), then professor of economics and sociology (1900); with Cornelia Warren, organized club for young working girls (Boston, 1890); supported movement to organize College Settlements Association; served as chair of Boston Settlement Committee which opened Denison House in South End; served as president of electoral board and chair of standing committee of national College Settlements Association (1900–07) and as chair of committee on grievances of Women's Trade Union League of Chicago; traveled in Europe to study social insurance programs and published results in *Survey* magazine (and posthumously as *Unemployment Insurance: A Summary of European Systems* [1915]); wrote with Elizabeth Kendall, *The Growth of the English Nation* (1894) and *A History of England for High Schools and Academies* (1899); also wrote *The Industrial History of the United States* (textbook, 1905) and *Economic Beginnings of the Far West* (2 vols., 1912).

COMAN, Otilia (1942—). Romanian writer and activist. Name variations: Otilia Valeria Coman Rusan; (pseudonym) Ana Blandiana. Born Otilia Valeria Coman, Mar 25, 1942, in Timisoara, Romania; dau. of Gheorghe Coman and Ana Coman; earned degree in philology from Cluj University; m. Romulus Rusan (writer), 1960. ❖ Worked as editor on literary journals *Viata Romanaesca* and *Amfitreatru* (1968–74); became librarian at Institute of Fine Arts in Bucharest; poems were banned by Ceausescu's censorship (1980s), and she was denounced for her poem "Motanul Arpagic," which poked fun at the dictator (1988–89); took an active role in the newly formed government until 1990; helped found Alianta Civica; writings include *Cincizeci de poeme* (1970), *Octombrie, Noiembrie, Decembrie* (1972), *Somnul din somn* (The Sleep within the Sleep, 1977), *Ora de nisip* (*The Hour of Sand,* 1983), *Stea de prada* (Star of Prey, 1985), and *Cartea alba a lui Arpagic* (1998); also published children's books and essay collections. Awarded Herder Prize (1969), Romanian Academy Prize (1970), Romanian Writers Union Prize (1969, 1980), and Opera Omnia Prize from Romanian Writers Union (2002).

COMANECI, Nadia (1961—). Romanian gymnast. Born Nov 12, 1961, in Onesti, Romania; m. Bart Conner (Olympic gymnast), April 27, 1996. ❖ Became overall European Champion (1975, 1977, 1979); won Olympic gold medals in all-around, uneven bars, and balance beam as well as team silver and bronze in floor exercise in Montreal (1976), becoming the 1st woman in the history of international gymnastics to score a perfect 10.0, then followed with 6 more; won Chunichi Cup in Japan (1976); won the World Championship (1978); won Olympic gold medals in floor exercises and balance beam, won a silver team medal and silver in the all-around in Moscow (1980); won the all-around, uneven bars, and floor exercise in World University Games (1981); defected to US (1989). ABC's "Wide World of Sports" aired a 90-minute documentary of her return to Romania (Mar 18, 1995). ❖ See also *Women in World History.*

COMBERTI, Micaela (1952–2003). English violinist. Name variations: Mica Comberti. Born Sept 28, 1952, in London, England; died of cancer, Mar 4, 2003; dau. of a German mother and Italian father; studied with Eduard Melkus at the Hochschule für Music in Vienna; studied for 3 years with Manoug Parikian at Royal Academy of Music in London, then under Sandor Vegh in Salzburg; m. Gustav Clarkson (violinist); children: 2 sons, 1 daughter. ❖ Baroque violinist, became involved in England's early music scene (1977); played for a number of ensembles and was a principal player for the English Concert; often recorded Haydn and Mozart with the Salomon String Quartet; also played with harpsichordist Colin Tilney and led the St. James's Baroque Players; taught at

the Guildhall School of Music and Drama, and later at the Royal College and the Royal Academy of Music.

COMBS, Maria Astrologes (1951—). *See Astrologes, Maria.*

COMDEN, Betty (1915—). American playwright, lyricist, screenwriter, and performer. Born Basya Astershinsky Simselyevitch-Simselyovitch Cohen, May 3, 1915, in Brooklyn, NY; dau. of Leo (attorney) and Rebecca (Sadvoransky) Cohen (teacher); New York University, BS, 1938; m. designer Steven Kyle (d. 1979), Jan 4, 1942; children: Susanna Kyle and Alan Kyle (d. 1990). ❖ Best known for her work with Adolph Green, likely the longest collaboration in American musical theater history, produced librettos, screenplays, and lyrics for Broadway and Hollywood for over 50 years; 1st appeared with the Revuers, a satirical group that wrote and performed topical sketches and songs; with Green, wrote book and lyrics for *On the Town* (1944) and screenplay and lyrics for the movie classic *Singin' in the Rain* (1952); for film, also collaborated on *Good News!* (screenplay, 1947), *The Barkleys of Broadway* (screenplay, 1949), *Take Me Out to the Ball Game* (lyrics, 1949), *The Band Wagon* (screenplay, 1953), *It's Always Fair Weather* (screenplay and lyrics, 1955), *Auntie Mame* (screenplay, 1958), and *Bells Are Ringing* (screenplay and lyrics, 1960); for stage, also collaborated on *Wonderful Town* (lyrics, 1953), *Peter Pan* (lyrics, 1954), *Bells Are Ringing* (book and lyrics, 1956), *Say, Darling* (lyrics, 1958), *Subways Are for Sleeping* (1961), *Fade Out—Fade In* (book and lyrics, 1964), *Hallelujah, Baby!* (lyrics, 1967), *Applause* (book, 1970), and *On the Twentieth Century* (book and lyrics, 1978); also appeared in the successful Off-Broadway revue, *A Party with Betty Comden and Adolph Green* (1958). ❖ See also memoirs *Off Stage* (1995); and *Women in World History.*

COMFORT, Anna Manning (1845–1931). American physician. Name variations: Anna Amelia Manning. Born Anna Amelia Manning, Jan 19, 1845, in Trenton, New Jersey; died Jan 11, 1931; dau. of Elizabeth (Price) Manning and Alfred G. Manning (founder and 1st president of Brown University); graduate of New York Medical College and Hospital for Women, 1865; m. George Fisk Comfort (founder of Metropolitan Museum of Art), Jan 19, 1871. ❖ The 1st female practicing physician in the state of CT, was part of the 1st class at New York Medical College and Hospital for Women (1863), which was founded by her aunt, Dr. Clemence S. Lozier; opened Norwich (CT) medical practice (1866); adopted cousin Charlotte Lozier's New York City practice after Charlotte's death (1870); after marriage, moved to Syracuse and established practice in gynecology; studied at medical institutions in Europe (1887 and 1891); retired from Syracuse practice (1901); with husband, wrote *Woman's Education and Woman's Health Chiefly in Reply to Dr. Edward Clarke's "Sex in Education"* (1874).

COMFORT, Bessie Marchant (1862–1941). *See Marchant, Bessie.*

COMINGORE, Dorothy (1913–1971). American actress. Name variations: acted under names Kay Winters and Linda Winters. Born in Los Angeles, California, Aug 24, 1913; died in 1971; attended University of California. ❖ Made the transition from stage to screen under the name Linda Winters; appeared in comedy shorts (mid-1930s), along with an appearance or two with the Three Stooges and in some low-budget Westerns; had breakthrough role in Orson Welles' *Citizen Kane* (1941), playing Kane's pathetic 2nd wife Kate; career ended (1951), when she was blacklisted in the wake of the House Un-American Activities Committee hearings.

COMITONA (fl. 500s). Byzantine courtesan. Name variations: Comito. Born on island of Cyprus, or more likely in Syria, c. 500; dau. of Acacius (guardian of the bears for the Greens at the Hippodrome in Constantinople) and an unnamed actress; sister of Empress Theodora; m. Sittas, c. 528; children: Sophia (c. 525–after 600 CE). ❖ Upon the death of her father when she was a child, began to work on stage with sister Theodora, then later as a mime with sister Anastasia; became known as a prostitute or courtesan (in the context of the time, actress was synonymous with prostitute). ❖ See also *Women in World History.*

COMMINS, Kathleen (1909–2003). Australian journalist. Born Kathleen Mary Commins in 1909 in Parkes, NSW, Australia; died Feb 2003 in Sydney; dau. of Francis Bede Commins (solicitor, killed in WWI) and Nola Commins; University of Sydney, BA, 1931, BEc, 1934; never married; no children. ❖ Was the 1st woman's editor of the University of Sydney magazine, *Hermes;* joined the staff of *The Sydney Morning Herald* (1934), writing columns on sports and politics, and served as assistant to the chief of staff for 21 years, the only woman of her time to be appointed to an executive position there outside the women's pages; retired (1969).

COMNENA, Anna (1083–1153/55). *See Anna Comnena.*

COMPAGNONI, Deborah (1970—). **Italian skier.** Born June 4, 1970, in Bormio, Sondrio, Italy. ❖ Won a gold medal for super-G at Albertville Olympics (1992); won a gold medal in the giant slalom at Lillehammer Olympics (1994); won a gold medal in the giant slalom at World championships (1996); took the World Cup giant slalom race in Cortina and became the 1st Italian woman to win a World Cup title (1996–97), finishing 4th overall; won a gold in slalom and giant slalom at the World championships (1997); won a gold medal for giant slalom and a silver medal for slalom at Nagano Olympics (1998). ❖ See also *Women in World History.*

COMPSON, Betty (1897–1974). **American actress.** Born Eleanor Lucimme Compson, Mar 18, 1897, in Beaver City, Utah; died April 18, 1974, in Glendale, California; m. James Cruze (director), 1925 (div. 1930); m. Irving Weinberg (div.); m. Silvius Jack Gall (died 1962). ❖ Lead player, began career as a vaudeville violinist at 15; signed for Al Christie's comedy shorts (1915); appeared in 78 two-reelers and 35 feature films, including *The Big City, Docks of New York, The Spoilers, The Little Minister, The Miracle Man, To Have and To Hold, Hollwood Boulevard, Mr. and Mrs. Smith* and *Here Comes Trouble;* retired (1948). Nominated for Academy Award for Best Actress for *The Barker* (1928).

COMPTON, Betty (1907–1944). **English-born musical-comedy actress.** Born Violet Halling Compton, 1907, on the Isle of Wight, England; died July 12, 1944, in New York, NY; raised in Canada; m. James J. Walker (mayor of NY, div. 1941); m. Theodore Knappen (consulting engineer); children: (adopted) Mary Ann Walker, James J. Walker. ❖ Made professional debut in *Abie's Irish Rose;* as one of NY's most popular musical-comedy stars, appeared in *Americana, Oh Kay, Hold Everything, Funny Face,* partnering Fred Astaire, and *Fifty Million Frenchman,* among others; probably best known for her romance with Jimmy Walker, the popular married mayor of NY; followed him when he moved to England because of a tax scandal, where she filmed *The Richest Girl in the World* (1935); was portrayed by Anita Gillette in the stage musical *Jimmy* (1969).

COMPTON, Mrs. Edward (1853–1940). *See Compton, Virginia.*

COMPTON, Fay (1894–1978). **English actress.** Born Virginia Lillian Emmeline MacKenzie in London, England, Sept 18, 1894; died Dec 12, 1978; dau. of Edward Compton (actor and founder of Compton Old English Company) and Virginia (Bateman) Compton (actress and dau. of American impresario H.L. Bateman); sister of Viola Compton (actress) and Sir Compton Mackenzie (novelist); m. producer H.G. Pelissier, 1911 (died 1913); m. comedian Lauri de Frece (died 1921); m. actor Leon Quartermaine (div. 1942); m. actor Ralph Michael (div. 1946); children: (1st m.) director Anthony Pelissier. ❖ Born into one of England's long-established theatrical families, made stage debut at 12 in the Christmas play *Sir Philomir or Love's Victory;* made NY debut as Victoria in the musical *Tonight's the Night;* appeared in title role in *Peter Pan* (1917), as Blanche Wheeler in *Fair and Warmer* (1918), in title roles of *Caesar's Wife* (1919) and *Mary Rose* (1920), and in *The Circle* (1921) and *Quality Street* (1921); was Ophelia to John Barrymore's *Hamlet* (1925), repeating the role with Godfrey Tearle (1931) and John Gielgud (1939); later successes included Regan in Gielgud's *King Lear* (1940), Constance of Britagne (Constance of Brittany) in *King John,* Ruth in *Blithe Spirit* (1941) and Martha Dacre in *No Medals* (1941); also portrayed Aunt Ann on tv series, "The Forsyte Saga"; films include *She Stoops to Conquer* (1914), *A Woman of No Importance* (1921), *The Old Wives' Tale* (1921), *A Bill of Divorcement* (1922), *The Loves of Mary Queen of Scots* (1923), *The Mill on the Floss* (1937), *So This Is London* (1939), *Nicholas Nickleby* (1947), *Britannia Mews* (1949), *Othello* (1952), *The Story of Esther Costello* (1957), *The Haunting* (1963), *Uncle Vanya* (1963) and *The Virgin and the Gypsy* (1970). Received Ellen Terry Award for performance in *Family Portrait* (1948); awarded CBE (1975). ❖ See also *Women in World History.*

COMPTON, Katherine (1853–1928). **English stage actress.** Name variations: Mrs. Richard Carton. Born Katherine Compton Mackenzie, 1853, in London, England; died May 16, 1928; dau. of Henry Compton (Mackenzie) and Emmeline Montague Compton (d. 1910); sister-in-law of Virginia Compton (actress); m. R.C. Carton (playwright). ❖ Made London debut in *Our Babes in the Wood* (1877); other plays include *Such is the Law, Imprudence* and *Low Water;* began to appear

exclusively in plays written by husband (1885), including *The Great Pink Pearl, The Treasure, Robin Goodfellow, A White Elepant, Lord and Lady Algy, Wheels within Wheels, The Undercurrent, A Clean Slate, The Rich Mrs. Repton* and *A Busy Day.*

COMPTON, Madge (c. 1892–1970). **English actress.** Born c. 1892 in England; died 1970 in England; m. George Graves (div.); m. Gerald Lawrence (actor, died 1957). ❖ Plays include *The Arcadians, Postal Orders, The Doctor's Dilemma, Monsieur Beaucaire, The Merry Wives of Windsor, Beau Brummel, Richard III, Dear Octopus, The Last of Mrs. Cheyney* and *The Winslow Boy;* films include *Dear Octopus.*

COMPTON, Viola (1886–1971). **English actress.** Born Viola Compton Mackenzie, 1886, in London, England; died April 7, 1971, in Birchington-on-Sea, England; dau. of Edward Compton and Virginia Compton (actors); sister of Ellen Compton (actress), Fay Compton (actress), Viola Compton (actress), and Compton Mackenzie (novelist); m. Henry Crocker; children: Nicholas John Crocker and John Valentine Crocker. ❖ Made stage debut with her parents' company as Charles in *Sydney Carton* (1893); made London debut in *The 18th Century* (1907); other plays include *The School for Scandal, An Impudent Comedian, Show Boat, Follow Through, The Good Companions, Rise and Shine* and *Alice in Wonderland;* with sister Ellen, jointly managed the Repertory Theatre, Nottingham (1920–23), appearing there in numerous lead roles.

COMPTON, Virginia (1853–1940). **American-born actress and theatrical manager.** Name variations: Mrs. Edward Compton; Virginia Frances Bateman. Born Virginia Frances Bateman, Jan 1, 1853; died May 4, 1940; dau. of H(ezekiah) L(inthicum) Bateman; sister of Isabel Emilie Bateman (1854–1934, actress); sister-in-law of Katherine Compton (actress); m. Edward Compton (actor and manager, died 1918); children: Frank Compton, Ellen Compton (actress), Fay Compton (actress), Viola Compton (actress) and Compton Mackenzie (novelist). ❖ Played Ophelia to Henry Irving's Hamlet (1875) and Desdemona to his Othello; following marriage, played leading parts with the Compton Comedy Company, touring the provinces and appearing in London at the Strand (1883 and 1886); assumed control of the company when husband died; opened the Repertory Theatre, Nottingham (1920).

COMPTON-BURNETT, Ivy (1884–1969). **English novelist.** Name variations: I. Compton-Burnett. Born Ivy Compton-Burnett, June 5, 1884, at Pinner, Middlesex, England; died Aug 27, 1969, at Braemar Mansions, London; dau. of James Compton Burnett (homeopathic physician, died 1901) and Katharine (Rees) Compton-Burnett; never married; lived with Margaret Jourdain (writer), from 1919 until Margaret's death in 1951; no children. ❖ Author of psychological thrillers set in an earlier time, whose works are almost entirely composed of dialogue; favorite brother Guy died (1905); published 1st novel, *Dolores* (1911); mother died (1911); endured another loss when brother Noel was killed fighting in France (1916); 2 sisters died, possibly by suicide (1917); found her own unique voice with her 2nd novel, the highly original *Pastors and Masters* (1925); attracted an appreciative, even ardent core of readers and critics; wrote 20 novels which show little influence from other writers, including the novel *Manservant and Maidservant,* published in US (1947) as *Bullivant and the Lambs,* generally conceded to be her most satisfying work; also wrote *Brothers and Sisters* (1929), *Men and Wives* (1931), *More Women Than Men* (1933), *A House and Its Head* (1935), *Daughters and Sons* (1937), *A Family and a Fortune* (1939), *Parents and Children* (1941), *Elders and Betters* (1944), *Two Worlds and Their Ways* (1949), *Darkness and Day* (1950), *The Present and the Past* (1953), *Mother and Son* (1955), *A Father and His Fate* (1957), *A Heritage and Its History* (1959), *The Mighty and Their Fall* (1961) and *A God and His Gifts* (1963), among others. Named Commander of the Order of the British Empire; won James Tait Black Memorial Prize (1956). ❖ See also Charles Burkhardt, *I. Compton-Burnett* (Gollancz, 1965); Elizabeth Sprigge, *The Life of Ivy Compton-Burnett* (Gollancz); Hilary Spurling, *Ivy, the Life of I. Compton-Burnett* (Knopf, 1984); Cicely Grieg, *Ivy Compton-Burnett, A Memoir* (Garnstone, 1972); Pamela Hansford Johnson, *I. Compton-Burnett* (Longmans, 1951); and *Women in World History.*

COMSTOCK, Ada Louise (1876–1973). **American educator.** Name variations: Ada Notestein. Born Dec 11, 1876, in Moorhead, Minnesota; died Dec 12, 1973, in New Haven, Connecticut; educated at University of Minnesota (1892–1894), Smith College, BL, 1897; Columbia University, AM in English, history and education, 1899; m. Wallace Notestein, 1943. ❖ Taught at University of Minnesota for 12 years (1900–12), becoming full professor of rhetoric and dean of women, the only woman in the university to serve as an administrator at that time; became the 1st woman dean of Smith College (1912), serving in that capacity for 11 years; served as the 1st president of American Association of University Women (AAUW, 1921–23); became president of Radcliffe College (1923), where she would develop a much closer working relationship between Radcliffe and Harvard University; also served on the 11-member Wickersham Commission. ❖ See also *Women in World History*.

COMSTOCK, Anna Botsford (1854–1930). American writer and illustrator. Name variations: Anna Botsford. Born Anna Botsford, Sept 1, 1854, on the family farm near Otto, in Cattaraugus Co., New York; died Aug 24, 1930, in Ithaca, New York; dau. of Marvin and Phebe (Irish) Botsford; enrolled in Cornell University, 1875, left to marry her zoology instructor John Henry Comstock, 1878, returned, 1882, graduated, 1885. ❖ The 1st woman professor at Cornell University, leader of the nature-study movement, and author or illustrator of many natural science books, was widely esteemed not only for the 7 science books and the novel she wrote, but for her work in popularizing the study of nature among schoolchildren and their teachers; along with husband, spent entire career at Cornell, except for 3 years at Department of Agriculture in Washington, DC (1879–81); appointed 1st woman assistant professor at Cornell, in nature study (1899), then full professor (1920); her illustrations and wood engravings appeared in John Henry Comstock's *An Introduction to Entomology* (1888) and *A Manual for the Study of Insects* (1895); her engravings were also exhibited at New Orleans (1885), Chicago (1893), Paris (1900) and Buffalo (1901) expositions and won her election to American Society of Wood-Engravers; collaborated with husband on *Insect Life* (1897) and *How To Know the Butterflies* (1904); also wrote *The Handbook of Nature-Study* (1911), as well as *Ways of the Six-Footed* (1903), *How To Keep Bees* (1905), *Dreams of a Heathen Idol* (1906), *The Pet Book* (1914) and *Trees at Leisure* (1916). ❖ See also memoir *The Comstocks of Cornell* (Cornell U. Press, 1953); and *Women in World History*.

COMSTOCK, Elizabeth Leslie (1815–1891). American Quaker minister. Born Elizabeth Leslie Rous, Oct 30, 1815, at Maidenhead, Berkshire, England; died Aug 3, 1891, in Union Springs, NY; dau. of William Rous (shopkeeper) and Mary (Kekwick) Rous; sister of Lydia Rous (Quaker educator and principal of Mount School York in Yorkshire, England); attended Friends' schools in Islington and Croydon; m. Leslie Wright (druggist), April 6, 1848 (died c. 1851); m. John T. Comstock (Quaker humanitarian), 1858 (died 1884); children: (1st m.) Caroline Wright. ❖ Among the most influential Quaker women of her day and credited with helping shape the modern form of Quakerism, immigrated to Belleville, Ontario, Canada (1854), then to US (c. 1858); lived with 2nd husband at Rollin, Lenawee Co., MI, an antislavery settlement, and worked with Underground Railroad; developed ministry and was in high demand throughout US; worked on behalf of such causes as abolition, peace, woman's rights, temperance, and prison welfare; met with lawmakers including President Abraham Lincoln (1864) and President James A. Garfield; worked on behalf of freedmen's relief efforts and served as secretary of Kansas Freedmen's Relief Association.

COMSTOCK, Nanette (1873–1942). American actress. Born July 17, 1873, in Albany, NY; died June 17, 1942; m. Frank Burbeck. ❖ Made stage debut in NY in *A Hole in the Ground* (1887), followed by *Bootles Baby, Shenandoah, Mavourneen, The Family Circle, Charley's Aunt, The Diplomat, The Virginian, Caught in the Rain* and *A Fool There Was*; made London debut succeeding Marie Montrose in *The Girl I Left Behind Me* (1895).

COMYN, Alice (fl. 1318). Baroness Beaumont. Name variations: Alice Beaumont. Flourished around 1318; dau. of Alexander Comyn, 6th earl of Buchan; m. Henry Beaumont, 1st baron Beaumont, around 1311; children: 5, including John Beaumont (1318–1342), 2nd baron Beaumont; Isabel Beaumont (d. 1368, mother of Blanche of Lancaster).

CONAN, Laure (1845–1924). *See Angers, Félicité.*

CONANT, Hannah Chaplin (1809–1865). American religious translator and writer. Born Hannah O'Brien Chaplin, Sept 5, 1809, in Danvers, Massachusetts; died Feb 18, 1865, in Brooklyn, NY; dau. of Rev. Jeremiah and Marcia S. (O'Brien) Chaplin; m. Thomas Jefferson Conant (professor of languages), July 12, 1830; children: 10 or more. ❖ Edited *Mother's Monthly Journal* of Utica, NY (1838–39); contributed works on moral and religious subjects to newspapers and periodicals; published 1st major work, translation from German of *Lea; or, the Baptism in Jordan* by G.F.A. Strauss (1844); published perhaps most

significant work, *The English Bible: History of the Translation of the Holy Scriptures into the English Tongue* (1856).

CONBOY, Sara McLaughlin (1870–1928). American labor leader. Born Sara Agnes McLaughlin, April 3, 1870, in Boston, Massachusetts; died Jan 7, 1928, in Brooklyn, New York; m. Joseph P. Conboy (letter carrier). ❖ Known as Aunt Sara to thousands of workers, was one of the 1st women to rise to prominence in the upper echelons of organized labor; early in career, successfully led the employees in a strike for increased wages and union recognition while working in a Roxbury mill; became an organizer for the United Textile Workers of America, of which she also served as secretary-treasurer (beginning Oct 1915). ❖ See also *Women in World History*.

CONCANNON, Helena (1878–1952). Irish scholar. Born Helena Walsh in Maghera, Co. Derry, Ireland, Oct 28, 1878; died Feb 27, 1952; educated at Loreto College, Dublin, the Royal University of Ireland, the Sorbonne, and the University of Berlin; m. Thomas Concannon (civil servant and prominent figure in Gaelic League), 1906. ❖ Scholar of works on Irish religious and women's history, published 1st book, *Life of St. Columban* (1915); as representative for the National University of Ireland, was a member of the Dail (1933–37), and the Senate (Seanad Eireann, 1937–52); as a member of de Valera's Fianna Fail party, committed herself to unwavering support for its policies; also wrote *The Defence of Gaelic Civilisation* (1919), *Women of '98* (1919), *Daughters of Banba* (1922), *Defenders of the Ford* (1925), *A Garden of Girls* (1928), *White Horsemen* (1930), *Irish Nuns in Penal Days* (1931), *At the Court of the Eucharistic King* (1931), *St. Patrick: His Life and Mission* (1932), *Blessed Oliver Plunket* (1935), *The Queen of Ireland* (1938), *The Cure of La Courneuve* (1944) and *Poems* (1953). Won National University Prize for Historical Research for *The Poor Clares in Ireland* (1929). ❖ See also *Women in World History*.

CONCEICAO, Janina (1972—). Brazilian volleyball player. Name variations: Janina Déia Chagas da Conceição. Born Oct 25, 1972, in Brazil. ❖ Middle blocker; won a team bronze medal at Sydney Olympics (2000).

CONCRETE BLONDE. *See Napolitano, Johnette.*

CONDE, Carmen (1907–1996). Spanish poet and novelist. Name variations: Carmen Conde; Carmen Conde Abellán. Born 1907 in Cartagena, Spain; died 1996 in Madrid, Spain. ❖ Was the 1st woman elected to Spanish Academy (1978); published numerous collections of poetry, including *Júbilos* (1934) and *Ansia de gracia* (1945); also wrote such novels as *En manos del silencio* (1950), *Creció espesa la yerba* (1979), and *Soy la madre* (1980). Received Elisenda de Moncada prize for *Las oscuras raíces* (1953); Premio Internacional de Poesía Simón Bolívar for *Vivientes de los siglos* (1957) and Premio Nacional de Literatura for *Obra Poética* (1967).

CONDE, Felisa (c. 1920—). American modern dancer. Born c. 1920. ❖ Began performing with the Humphrey-Weidman Group (1946), dancing in numerous works by Charles Weidman, including *A House Divided* (1946), *Fables for Our Time* (1947), and *Lynchtown* (1947); partnered with Peter Hamilton in cabaret performances and on tv (c. 1949); joined John Butler Dance Theater (early 1950s) and appeared in such works by Butler as *Ahmal and the Night Visitors* (1953), *The Brass World* (1954) and *The Parliament of Heaven* (1958).

CONDÉ, Maryse (1937—). Guadeloupean novelist. Name variations: Maryse Conde. Born Feb 11, 1937, in Pointe-à-Pitre, Guadeloupe; m. Mamadou Conde, 1959; m. Richard Philcox; children: 4. ❖ Moved to France at 16 to continue studies and then to Ivory Coast to teach; lived in Ghana and Senegal before returning to France (1973); obtained Fulbright scholarship (1982); taught at University of Paris IV and Columbia University; novels include *Heremakhonon* (1976), *Ségou* (2 vols, 1984–85), *Moi Tituba, Sorcière Noire de Salem* (1986), *La Vie scélérate* (1987), *Desirada* (1997) and *Célanire cou-coupé* (2000); plays include *Dieu nous l'a donne* (1972) and *Mort d'Oluwémi d'Ajumoko*. Received Grand Prix Litteraire de la Femme.

CONDÉ, Princesse de.
See Charlotte de Montmorency (1594–1650).
See Brézé, Claire-Clémence de Maillé de (1628–1694).
See Anne Henriette Louise (1647–1723).
See Louise Adelaide de Bourbon (1757–1824).

CONDON, Jane T. (1934–1996). *See Howard, Jane.*

CONDORCET, Sophie Marie Louise, Marquise de (1764–1822).
French salonnière. Name variations: Mademoiselle de Grouchy; Sophie de Grouchy; also known as Grouchette. Born Sophie Marie Louise de Grouchy at the Château Villette, near Meulan, France, in the spring of 1764; died in Paris, Sept 8, 1822; m. Marie Jean Antoine de Caritat, marquis de Condorcet (mathematician), 1778 (died Mar 29, 1794); children: at least one daughter. ❖ With husband, was a fierce defender of Protestants, slaves, and women; shortly after marriage, opened a salon at the Quai di Conti in the Hôtel des Monnaies (her husband was the director there), drawing many foreigners, particularly the English, whose language she spoke fluently; her salon became the "center of an enlightened Europe"; as a republican who called for the monarchy's end and the start of a constitutional government, saw husband killed and property seized by the Royalists (1793). ❖ See also *Women in World History.*

CONE, Carin (1940—). American swimmer. Name variations: Carin Cone Vanderbush. Born Carin Alice Cone, April 18, 1940, in NY; m. Al Vanderbush (football player for Army). ❖ Won US 200-yard backstroke (1955) and 100-yard backstroke (1955–60); won a silver medal for backstroke at Melbourne Olympics (1956); won gold medals at Pan American Games for 100-meter backstroke and medley relay (1959); broke 6 world records; retired (1960). Inducted into International Swimming Hall of Fame (1984).

CONE, Claribel (1864–1929). American art collector. Born Nov 14, 1864, in Jonesboro, Tennessee; died Sept 20, 1929, in Lausanne, Switzerland; dau. of German immigrants; graduate of Woman's Medical College of Baltimore, 1890; advanced training at Johns Hopkins University Medical School in Baltimore. ❖ Served as a pathology teacher at the Woman's Medical College until the school closed in 1910 and her medical career drew to its end; with sister Etta, ran an informal salon that was open to artists, musicians, intellectuals, and professionals; became an art collector with sister, renting an apartment to serve as a private museum to house their collection, which came to include works of Renoir, Manet, Cézanne, Degas and Bonnard. ❖ See also Mary Gabriel, *The Art of Acquiring: A Portrait of Etta and Claribel Cone* (Bancroft, 1999); and *Women in World History.*

CONE, Etta (1870–1949). American art collector. Born Nov 30, 1870, in Jonesboro, Tennessee; died Aug 31, 1949, in Blowing Rock, North Carolina; dau. of German immigrants. ❖ Became interested in the French Impressionists; began purchasing paintings (1896); with sister, became an ardent collector and purchased a Picasso (1905), followed by a Matisse (1906); left the Cone collection, one of the world's great assemblages of modern art, especially the work of Matisse, to the Baltimore Museum of Art, and $400,000 for the new wing to be built for the purpose of housing it. ❖ See also Mary Gabriel, *The Art of Acquiring: A Portrait of Etta and Claribel Cone* (Bancroft, 1999); and *Women in World History.*

CONE, Greta (1911–1990). See Stevenson, Greta.

CONES, Nancy Ford (1869–1962). American photographer. Born Nancy Ford in Milan, Ohio, 1869; died 1962; m. James Cones (photographer), 1897 (died 1939); children: Margaret Cones. ❖ Took 2nd prize in Eastman Kodak's photographic competition (1st prize went to Edward Steichen; 3rd to Alfred Stieglitz); while she photographed celebrated figures such as William Howard Taft, often photographed rural scenes which were utilized in advertising campaigns for Eastman Kodak and Bausch and Lomb and appeared in *Country Life in America* and *Woman's Home Companion*; left behind 4,000 prints and 15,000 glass-plate negatives. ❖ See also *Women in World History.*

CONFORTO, Tracie (1963—). See Ruiz, Tracie.

CONG XUED (1963—). Chinese basketball player. Born May 13, 1963. ❖ Won an Olympic bronze medal at Los Angeles (1984) and a silver medal at Barcelona (1992), both in team competition.

CONKLIN, Jennie (1841–1900). See Drinkwater, Jennie M.

CONKLIN, Mary Washburn (1907–1994). See Washburn, Mary.

CONKLIN, Peggy (1902–2003). American actress. Born Margaret Eleanor Conklin, Nov 2, 1902, in Dobbs Ferry, NY; died Mar 18, 2003, in Naples, Florida; m. James D. Thompson (advertising exec.), 1935 (died 1998); children: Antonia West and Michael Thompson. ❖ Made Broadway debut in the chorus line of *Treasure Girl* (1928); appeared in many major roles, including the female lead of Gabby Maple in Robert Sherwood's *Petrified Forest*, Prudence Kirkland in *The*

Pursuit of Happiness, Ellen Murray in *Yes, My Darling Daughter*, Pam North in *Mr. and Mrs. North* and Flo Owens in *Picnic*; films include *The President Vanishes, The Devil is a Sissy, One Way Ticket, Her Master's Voice* and *Having a Wonderful Time.*

CONLEY, Martha (1948—). See Randall, Marta.

CONLEY, Peggy (1947—). American golfer. Name variations: Peggy Shane Conley. Born June 10, 1947, in Seattle, Washington; attended University of Washington. ❖ At 16, 2 mos., and 14 days, was the youngest to reach the final round of the USGA Women's Amateur championship (1963); named to the Curtis Cup team (1964, 1968); won 4 amateur titles; was the 1st woman to be granted an athletic scholarship at University of Washington (1965); became a free-lance photographer.

CONLEY, Sandra (1943—). English ballet dancer. Born Oct 24, 1943, in Hatfield, England. ❖ Made professional debut with Royal Ballet School's touring company, but soon joined senior troupe (early 1970s) where she became known for her dramatic portrayals of women in modernized 19th-century classics and contemporary works; danced in Frederick Ashton's *Creatures of Prometheus* and *A Month in the Country,* Geoffrey Cauley's *Symphonie Pastorale,* and Kenneth Macmillan's *Anastasia,* among others.

CONN, Elenor (fl. 1980s). American balloonist. Married Sidney Conn (balloonist). ❖ With husband Sidney and a 10-person team, made 1st modern hot-air balloon flight over the North Pole (1980); owner of The Balloon Works.

CONN, Shena. Northern Ireland politician. Born in Belfast, Northern Ireland; m. Douglas Conn. ❖ Representing the Unionist Party for Londonderry, sat in the Northern Ireland Assembly (1973–82).

CONNALLY, Nellie (1919—). American memoirist and first lady of Texas. Born Idanell Brill, 1919, in Austin, Texas; attended University of Texas; m. John Connally (elected governor of Texas, 1962), Dec 21, 1940 (died 1993); children: 4, including Kathleen (committed suicide, 1958). ❖ Was riding in the car with John F. Kennedy in Dallas when he was assassinated and her husband was seriously wounded; close friend of Lady Bird Johnson. ❖ See also memoir (with Mickey Herskowitz and Shawn Coyne) *From Love Field* (2003).

CONNAUGHT, duchess of. See Louise Margaret of Prussia (1860–1917).

CONNAUGHT, queen of. See O'Malley, Grace.

CONNELLY, Ana Paula (1972—). Brazilian volleyball player. Name variations: Ana Paula. Born Feb 13, 1972, in Lavras, Brazil. ❖ Won a team bronze medal at Atlanta Olympics (1996).

CONNELLY, Cornelia (1809–1879). American religious community founder. Born Cornelia Augusta Peacock, Jan 15, 1809, in Philadelphia, Pennsylvania; died April 18, 1879, at St. Leonards-on-Sea, near Hastings, England; dau. of Ralph and Mary (Swope) Peacock; m. Pierce Connelly (curate), Dec 1, 1831 (died 1883); children: 5. ❖ Became Roman Catholic (1835); after having 5 children (2 of whom died), reluctantly acquiesced when husband decided to become a priest (papal approval was granted for permanent suspension of their marriage vows, Mar 1844); took vow of chastity (1845); founded new Order, Society of the Holy Child Jesus, in Derby, England (c. 1846) and was installed as superior; published *Book of Studies* (1863); proclaimed Venerable by Catholic Church (1992). Her Order has spread to 14 countries.

CONNER, Nadine (1907–2003). American actress and lyric soprano. Born Evelyn Nadine Henderson, Feb 20, 1907, in Compton, California; died Mar 1, 2003, in Los Alamitos, California; m. briefly to an ex-college classmate named Conner; m. Laurance Heacock (surgeon), 1939 (died 1987). ❖ Made NY debut at Metropolitan Opera as Pamina in an English version of *Magic Flute* (1941), followed by Forest Bird in *Siegfried,* the 1st of 25 Sophies in *Der Rosenkavalier,* Marzelline in *Fidelio,* the title role in *Carmen,* Mimi in *La Bohème,* and Marguerite in *Faust,* among others; performed a solo in Mahler's Second Symphony for NY Philharmonic (1942), then appeared there annually in the *St. Matthew Passion;* recorded the role of Gretel, with Risë Stevens as Hansel, in *Hansel and Gretel* (1947); made Met farewell (1960).

CONNOLLY, Maureen (1934–1969). American tennis player. Name variations: (nickname) "Little Mo"; Maureen Connolly Brinker. Born Maureen Catherine Connolly, Sept 17, 1934, in San Diego, California; died June 21, 1969, in Dallas, Texas; m. Norman Brinker, 1955;

children: Brenda Lee Brinker (b. 1957); Cynthia Anne Brinker (b. 1960). ❧ Was the youngest national junior champion, youngest male or female to make the national top 10 professional rankings, and 1st and youngest to complete the Grand Slam at the age of 18 (1953); was the 1st woman to complete the Grand Slam, winning all 4 major tournaments in the same calendar year; won the Wightman Cup 9 times; was Wimbledon singles champion (1952, 1953, 1954); won singles championship at US Open (1951, 1952, 1953); won singles title at French Open (1953, 1954); won singles title at Australian Open (1953); with N. Hopman, won the French Open women's doubles (1954); with Julia Sampson, won the Australian women's doubles (1953). Named female athlete of the year 3 times by the Associated Press.

CONNOLLY, Olga Fikotová (b. 1932). See Fikotová, Olga.

CONNOLLY-O'BRIEN, Nora (1893–1981). Irish politician. Name variations: Nora Connolly O'Brien. Born in 1893 in Edinburgh, Scotland; died June 17, 1981; dau. of James Connolly (socialist revolutionary leader executed after the Rising, 1916); m. Seamus O'Brien (former courier for Michael Collins), 1922. ❧ At 3, moved with family to Dublin; moved to US, then Belfast (1910); joined Fianna Éiranna, helped found the Young Republican Party, and organized the Belfast branch of Cumann na mBan; following father's execution, addressed Republican meetings in US; arrested with husband during Civil War and imprisoned; nominated to the Seanad by Taoiseach Sean Lemass (1957), serving for 15 years.

CONNON, Helen (c. 1859–1903). New Zealand teacher and school principal. Name variations: Helen Brown. Born c. 1859 or 1860, in Melbourne, Australia; died Feb 22, 1903, in Rotorua, New Zealand; dau. of George Connon (carpenter) and Helen (Hart) Connon; Canterbury College, BA, 1880; m. John Macmillan Brown, 1886; children: 2 daughters. ❧ First woman to attend and graduate from Canterbury College (1880); taught at Christchurch Girls' High School while still a student (1878), and served as principal (1882–94). ❧ See also *Dictionary of New Zealand Biography* (Vol. 2).

CONNOR, Chris (1927—). American band singer. Born Jan 8, 1927, in Kansas City, Missouri. ❧ Among the most popular vocalists of the 1950s, began singing in late teens; was a vocalist with Bob Brookmeyer's band at University of Missouri; moved to NY (1949); sang with Herbie Fields and Claude Thornhill's group, The Snowflakes; was also a band singer with Stan Kenton (1952–53), recording "All About Ronnie"; went solo (1953) and had 2 singles that reached the charts, "Trust in Me" and "I Miss You So"; also known for her recordings of "Lush Life" and "Lullaby of Broadway"; cut albums with Kenton and Maynard Ferguson (1970s).

CONOLLY, Louisa (1743–1821). See Lennox, Louisa.

CONRAD, Karen (1919–1976). American ballet dancer. Born Aug 18, 1919, in Philadelphia, Pennsylvania; died July 24, 1976, in Atlanta, Georgia; trained with Catherine Littlefield and Alexis Donlinoff; m. Pittman Corry (dancer). ❧ Danced with Littlefield Ballet in Philadelphia (1935–38), later Philadelphia Ballet; performed with Mikhail Mordkin Ballet where she created role of The Flirt in his *Voices of Spring* (1938) and danced in his *Giselle, Les Sylphides* and *Aurora's Wedding*; joined Ballet Theater where she danced featured roles in Antony Tudor's *Gala Performance* and *Jardin aux Lilac*, and created roles in Anton Dolin's *Capriccioso* (1940); with husband, founded Southern Ballet in Atlanta, GA, where she directed and taught classes for the rest of her life.

CONRAD-MARTIUS, Hedwig (1888–1966). German philosopher. Name variations: Hedwig Martius. Born Hedwig Martius in 1888 to a medical family in northern Germany; died 1966; studied with Edmund Husserl at University of Göttingen, 1911–12; University of Munich, PhD, 1913; m. Theodor Conrad, 1912. ❧ One of the 1st women to be a professional academic, became interested in the philosophical movement of phenomenology and participated in the discussion group that became known as the Göttingen Circle; awarded the essay prize from the Philosophische Fakultat at University of Göttingen (1912); was a lecturer, University of Munich from 1949; published in German magazines and abroad. ❧ See also *Women in World History*.

CONRADT, Jody (1941—). American basketball coach. Born May 13, 1941, in Goldthwaite, Texas; graduate of Baylor University with a degree in physical education, 1963. ❧ Began career coaching for no pay at Sam Houston State (1969); moved to the Lady Longhorns of University of Texas (1976) where she remained; had an undefeated national championship team (1986); won 500th game (1988); was the 1st women's coach to have 700 victories (1997); became the 2nd women's basketball coach to win 800 games (2003), the 1st was Pat Summitt; was 6-time National Coach of the Year. Received the Carol Eckman Award (1987); inducted into International Women's Sports Hall of Fame (1995), Naismith Memorial Basketball Hall of Fame (1998) and Women's Basketball Hall of Fame (1999).

CONRAN, Shirley (1932—). British designer and journalist. Born Shirley Ida Pearce, Sept 21, 1932, in Hendon, England; mother-in-law of fashion designer Georgina Godley; attended St. Paul's Girls' School, London, and a finishing school in Switzerland; trained as a painter and sculptor at Southern College of Art, Portsmouth; m. Sir Terence Conran (designer and businessman), 1955 (div. 1962); m. John Stephenson; m. once more; children: (1st m.) Jasper and Sebastian Conran (both designers). ❧ Bestselling author, worked as press officer for Asprey Suchy jewelers and then publicity officer for Conran Group Companies; became fabric designer and director for Conran Fabrics and member of selection committee of Design Centre, London (1961–69); was Home editor for *Daily Mail*, 1st woman's editor of *Observer Colour* magazine, and woman's editor for *Daily Mail*, where she launched "Femail"; wrote column and features for *Vanity Fair* and *Woman's Own*; moved to Monaco (1979); other writings include *Superwoman* (1975), *Lace* (1982), *The Magic Garden* (1983), *Savages* (1987) and *The Amazing Umbrella Shop* (1990); also wrote children's books *Crimson* (1991), *Tiger Eyes* (1994) and *The Revenge of Mimi Quinn* (1998).

CONS, Emma (1838–1912). British housing reformer and founder. Born 1838 in London, England; died 1912 in England; sister of Liebe Cons (contralto); aunt of Lilian Baylis (1874–1937); studied at Art School in Gower Street and Mrs. Hill's school. ❧ Original founder of the Old Vic, who was the 1st to bring Shakespeare and opera to the working classes, joined Ladies Art Guild and taught toy-making at Ragged Schools; restored illuminated manuscripts for John Ruskin and opened watch-engraving shop with other women; restored glass work at Powell's factory and Merton College, Oxford; with Ruskin and Octavia Hill, began restoring slum property in central London; established men's teetotal club, hostel for girls, coffee taverns, and ran creches and clinics for tenants; bought the Royal Victorian Hall near Waterloo Station (1879), reopened it as the Royal Victorian Hall and Coffee Tavern with variety bills and ballad concerts, and eventually turned it into a prestigious theater (Old Vic); lectures at Old Vic led to establishment of Morley College for working people; served as full-time manager of the Old Vic (1894–1912). Worked for women's suffrage, was executive member of Women's Liberal Foundation, founder of Women's Horticultural College, Swanley, and 1 of 3 women on 1st London County Council; traveled to Armenia to report on war atrocities, established silk factory for Armenian refugees in Crete, and visited émigré tenants in Canada.

CONSTANCE. *Variant of Constantia.*

CONSTANCE (d. 305 CE). Roman empress. Martyred in 305 CE; m. Maximin Daia, the Eastern emperor and governor of Egypt and Syria (r. 305–313).

CONSTANCE (c. 321–354). See Constantina.

CONSTANCE (c. 1066–1090). Countess of Brittany. Born c. 1066; died Aug 13, 1090; buried at St. Melans, near Rhedon; dau. of William I the Conqueror, duke of Normandy (r. 1035–1087), king of England (r. 1066–1087), and Matilda of Flanders (c. 1031–1083); m. Alan IV, duke of Brittany, 1086.

CONSTANCE (fl. 1100). Viscountess of Beaumont. Possibly illeg. dau. of Sybilla Corbert and Henry I (1068–1135), king of England (r. 1100–1135); m. Richard, viscount of Beaumont; children: Ermengarde de Beaumont; Raoul VI de Beaumont.

CONSTANCE (c. 1374–1416). Duchess of Gloucester and Kent. Name variations: Constance Plantagenet. Born c. 1374; died Nov 28, 1416; dau. of Edmund of Langley, 1st duke of York, and Isabel of Castile (1355–1392); m. Thomas Despenser, 1st earl of Gloucester, 1379; m. Edmund Holland, 4th earl of Kent; children: (1st m.) 3, including Isabel Despenser (1400–1439) and Richard Despenser, lord Despenser (d. 1414).

CONSTANCE-ANNA OF HOHENSTAUFEN (fl. 13th century). Byzantine empress. Name variations: Anna-Constance of Hohenstauffen; Anna Constanza. Dau. of Frederick II, Holy Roman emperor (r. 1215–1250) and Constance of Aragon (d. 1222); 2nd wife of John III Dukas Vatatzes, Nicaean [Byzantine] emperor (r. 1222–1254); children: Basil Vatatzes. John III's 1st wife was Irene Lascaris (fl. 1222–1235).

CONSTANCE CAPET (c. 1128–1176). Countess of Toulouse. Name variations: Countess of Boulogne. Born c. 1128; died Aug 16, 1176, at Rheims, Champagne, France; dau. of Louis VI, king of France (r. 1108–1137), and Adelaide of Maurienne (1092–1154); m. Eustace IV, count of Boulogne, 1151; m. Raymond V, count of Toulouse, 1154; children: (2nd m.) Raymond VI, count of Toulouse; William; Baldwin; Alesia of Toulouse (who m. Roger, viscount of Beziers); Laura of Toulouse (who m. Odo, count of Comminger).

CONSTANCE DE CEZELLI (d. 1617). French noble and military leader. Name variations: Constance of Leucates. Birth date unknown; died in 1617 in Leucates, a small region located in Languedoc, what is now southern France; m. the lord of Leucates; children: at least one. ❖ During invasion of France by Spanish (1590), was left in charge of defending Leucates when husband was taken prisoner; led defense of the town and tried to arrange for husband's release; when the Spanish refused to free him unless she relinquished Leucates, would not yield the town and he was killed; was awarded position of governor of Leucates by French king Henry IV for her bravery and loyalty.

CONSTANCE ENRIQUES, Enriquez or Henriques (1290–1313). *See Constance of Portugal.*

CONSTANCE JONES, E.E. (1848–1922). British scholar. Born Emily Elizabeth Constance Jones in Wales in 1848; died in 1922; dau. of the squire of the parish of Llangarron; Moral Sciences Tripos at Girton College, Cambridge University, 1880. ❖ Philosopher whose ideas were misrepresented by Bertrand Russell as his own; was a lecturer at Girton College from 1884; served as librarian of Girton College (1890–93); was vice-mistress of Girton College (1896–1903), then mistress (from 1903); served as executive member of the Aristotelian Society (1914–16); published prolifically, particularly on logic. ❖ See also *Women in World History.*

CONSTANCE OF ANTIOCH (1128–1164). Co-ruler of Antioch. Born 1128; deposed 1163; died 1164; dau. of Bohemond or Bohemund II, prince of Antioch (r. 1126–1130), and Alice of Jerusalem; m. Raymond I of Poitiers (d. 1149, son of William IX of Aquitaine), prince of Antioch, around 1140; m. Reginald also known as Reynald of Chatillon (d. 1187), prince of Antioch (r. 1153–1160), 1153; children: (1st m.) Bohemond or Bohemund III the Stammerer, prince of Antioch (r. 1163–1201); Marie of Antioch (d. 1183, who m. Manuel I Comnenus); Philippa of Antioch; (2nd m.) Anne of Chatillon-Antioche (c. 1155–c. 1185, who m. Bela III, king of Hungary). Reynald's 2nd wife was Stephania (d. 1187). ❖ See also *Women in World History.*

CONSTANCE OF ARAGON (d. 1222). Holy Roman empress and queen of Sicily. Died June 23, 1222; dau. of Sancha of Castile and Leon (1164–1208) and Alphonso II (1152–1196), king of Aragon (r. 1164–1196); m. Emeric, king of Hungary (r. 1196–1204); became 1st wife of Frederick II (1194–1250), Holy Roman emperor (r. 1212–1250) and king of Sicily (r. 1197–1250), Feb 1210; children: (1st m.) Ladislas III, king of Hungary (r. 1204–1205); (2nd m.) Henry VII, king of Germany (d. 1242); Constance-Anna of Hohenstaufen (who m. John III Dukas Vatatzes, Nicaean emperor [r. 1222–1254]). Frederick II's 2nd wife was Yolande of Brienne (1212–1228); his 3rd was Isabella of England (1214–1241).

CONSTANCE OF ARAGON (d. 1283). Princess of Aragon. Died 1283; dau. of Iolande of Hungary (1215–1251) and James I (1208–1276), king of Aragon (r. 1213–1276), also known as Jaime the Conqueror of Aragon; married Manuel of Castile, sn de Villena, 1263; children: Alfonso de Castile (b. after 1260); Violante de Castilla (c. 1265–1314).

CONSTANCE OF ARAGON (d. 1327). Duchess of Penafiel. Died Aug 19, 1327, at Château de Garci Munoz; dau. of Blanche of Naples (d. 1310) and Jaime or James II, king of Sicily and Aragon (r. 1291–1327); m. John Manuel or Juan Manuel de Villena "el Scritor" of Castile, duke of Penafiel, April 2, 1312; children: Constance of Castile (1323–1345), queen of Portugal. Juan Manuel's 2nd wife was Blanche de la Cerda (c. 1311–1347).

CONSTANCE OF ARAGON (c. 1350–?). Queen of Sicily. Name variations: Constanza of Aragón. Born c. 1350; dau. of Eleanor of Sicily (d. 1375) and Pedro IV also known as Peter IV the Ceremonious (b. 1319),

king of Aragon (r. 1336–1387); m. Frederick III the Simple, king of Sicily (r. 1355–1377); children: Maria of Sicily (d. 1402).

CONSTANCE OF ARLES (c. 980–1032). Capetian queen of France. Name variations: Constance of Provence. Born c. 980 (some sources cite 973); died July 25, 1032, in Melun; dau. of William, count of Toulouse (William I of Provence); became 3rd wife of Robert II the Pious (972–1031), king of France (r. 996–1031), 1005; children: Hugh (1007–1025); Adela Capet (c. 1010–1079), countess of Flanders (mother of Matilda of Flanders); Henry I (1008–1060), king of France (r. 1031–1060); Robert I (1011–1076), duke of Burgundy (r. 1031–1076). ❖ On husband's death, was determined to put her youngest son Robert I, duke of Burgundy, on the throne of France, rather than the appointed successor, her eldest living son Henry (the conflict weakened the French monarchy). ❖ See also *Women in World History.*

CONSTANCE OF BRITTANY (1161–1201). Duchess of Brittany and countess of Chester. Name variations: Constance de Bretagne; Constance of Britagne. Born in 1161; died in Nantes, Anjou, France, Sept 5, 1201, while giving birth to twins; dau. of Conan IV, duke of Brittany, and Margaret of Huntingdon (c. 1140–1121); m. Geoffrey Plantagenet, duke of Brittany, in July 1181; m. Ranulf de Blondville, 4th earl of Chester, 1187 (div. 1199); m. Guy, viscount of Thouars, 1199; children: (1st m.) Eleanor, the Maid of Brittany (1184–1241); Matilda (1185–1186); Arthur, duke of Brittany (1187–1203); (3rd m.) twins Alice (1201–1221), duchess of Brittany, and Katherine de Thouars (b. 1201, who m. Andrew de Vitre of Brittany).

CONSTANCE OF BURGUNDY (1046–c. 1093). Queen of Castile and Leon. Name variations: Constance Capet. Born 1046; died 1093 (some sources cite 1092); dau. of Robert I (b. 1011), duke of Burgundy, and Helia de Semur; m. Hugh II, count of Chalon-sur-Saone; became 2nd wife of Alphonso VI, king of Leon (r. 1065–1109), king of Castile (r. 1072–1109), May 8, 1081; children: Urraca (c. 1079–1126), queen of Castile and Leon; Elvira (died young).

CONSTANCE OF CASTILE (d. 1160). Queen of France. Born after 1140; died in childbirth, Oct 4, 1160; dau. of Alphonso VII, king of Castile and Leon (r. 1126–1157), and Berengaria of Provence (1108–1149); became 2nd wife of Louis VII (1120–1180), king of France (r. 1137–1180), before Nov 18, 1153; children: Margaret of France (1158–1198, who m. Bela III, king of Hungary) and Alais of France (b. 1160).

CONSTANCE OF CASTILE (1323–1345). Queen of Portugal. Name variations: Constance of Aragon; Constance Manuel; (Spanish) Constance de Castilla. Born 1323; died Nov 13, 1345, in Santarum, during childbirth; dau. of Juan Manuel de Villena, duke of Penafiel, and Constance of Aragon (d. 1327); m. Alphonso XI, king of Castile and Leon, Mar 28, 1325 (annulled 1327); became 2nd wife of Pedro I also known as Peter I (1320–1367), king of Portugal (r. 1357–1367), Aug 24, 1336; children: (2nd m.) Luiz (1340–1340); Maria of Portugal (1343–1367, who m. Fernando also known as Ferdinand of Aragon, marquis of Tortosa); Fernao also known as Fernando or Ferdinand I the Handsome (1345–1383), king of Portugal (r. 1367–1383, who m. Leonora Telles).

CONSTANCE OF CASTILE (1354–1394). Spanish noblewoman and duchess of Lancaster. Name variations: Constanza. Born in Castrojeriz, Castile, 1354; died at Leicester Castle, Leicestershire, England, Mar 24, 1394; dau. of Peter the Cruel, king of Castile and Leon (r. 1350–1369), and Marie de Padilla (1335–1365); became 2nd wife of John of Gaunt, duke of Lancaster, Sept 21, 1371; children: Catherine of Lancaster (1372–1418, who m. Henry III, king of Castile); John (1374–1375).

CONSTANCE OF FRANCE (fl. 1100s). Princess of Antioch and countess of Blois. Name variations: Constance Capet. Born between 1072 and 1092; dau. of Bertha of Holland (1055–1094) and Philip I the Fair (1052–1108), king of France (r. 1060–1108); sister of Louis VI (c. 1081–1137), king of France (r. 1108–1137); m. Bohemond II or Bohemund I of Taranto (d. 1111), prince of Antioch (r. 1098–1111); m. Hugh I, count of Blois, 1104; children: (1st m.) Bohemond or Bohemund II of Antioch (r. 1126–1130).

CONSTANCE OF GERMANY (1154–1198). *See Constance of Sicily.*

CONSTANCE OF HUNGARY (d. 1240). Queen of Bohemia. Name variations: Constantia. Died in 1240; dau. of Anne of Chatillon-Antioche (c. 1155–1185) and Bela III (1148–1196), king of Hungary

(r. 1173–1196); sister of Emeric I, king of Hungary (r. 1196–1204), and Andrew II (1175–1235), king of Hungary (r. 1205–1235); 2nd wife of Ottokar I (d. 1230), king of Bohemia (r. 1198–1230); children: Wenzel also known as Wenceslas I, king of Bohemia (r. 1230–1253); Agnes of Bohemia (1205–1282). ❖ See also *Women in World History.*

CONSTANCE OF LEUCATES (d. 1617). *See Constance de Cezelli.*

CONSTANCE OF PORTUGAL (1290–1313). Queen of Castile and Leon. Name variations: Constance Henriques, Enriques or Enriquez. Born Jan 3, 1290; died Nov 17, 1313, in Sahagun; interred at Valladolid; dau. of Diniz also spelled Dinis or Denis (1261–1325), king of Portugal (r. 1279–1325), and Elizabeth of Portugal (1271–1336); m. Ferdinand IV (1285–1312), king of Castile and Leon (r. 1295–1321), 1301 or 1302; children: Alphonso XI, king of Castile and Leon (r. 1312–1350); Eleanor of Castile (1307–1359); Constanza (c. 1309–c. 1311).

CONSTANCE OF PROVENCE (c. 980–1032). *See Constance of Arles.*

CONSTANCE OF SICILY (1154–1198). Holy Roman empress and queen of Sicily. Name variations: Constance d'Altavilla; Constance of Germany; (German) Konstanz. Born 1154 in Sicily; died Nov 27, 1198, in Germany; dau. of Roger II the Great, king of Sicily (r. 1103–1154), duke of Apulia (r. 1128–1154), and Beatrice of Rethel; m. Henry VI (1165–1197), king of Germany and Holy Roman emperor (r. 1190–1197), king of Sicily (r. 1194–1197), Jan 27, 1186; children: Frederick II (b. 1194), Holy Roman emperor (r. 1215–1250). ❖ Born a princess of the Sicilian royal house, was orphaned at birth; raised at the Sicilian court, where she remained until 1186 when she married the Holy Roman emperor's son, Prince Henry Hohenstaufen of Germany (later Holy Roman Emperor Henry VI); inherited title of queen of Sicily (1189) but a war of succession quickly developed; was finally able to claim the throne as her own (1194); when husband Henry, an extremely severe emperor, died suddenly, fled Germany with son and returned to Sicily. ❖ See also *Women in World History.*

CONSTANCE OF SICILY (d. 1302). Queen of Aragon. Died 1302; dau. of Manfred, king of Naples and Sicily (r. 1258–1266, illeg. son of Frederick II, Holy Roman emperor) and Beatrice of Savoy; m. Pedro III also known as Peter III, king of Aragon (r. 1276–1285), 1262; children: Alphonso III (1265–1291), king of Aragon (r. 1285–1291); Elizabeth of Portugal (1271–1336); Jaime or James II (d. 1327), king of Aragon (r. 1291–1327); Frederick II (1271–1336), king of Sicily (r. 1296–1336). ❖ Spent life seeing that children were established as rulers of Sicily: Alphonso III succeeded to throne of Aragon; James I succeeded to throne of Sicily under her regency and later succeeded to throne of Aragon; Frederick II, appointed a regent in 1291 when James took over Aragon, was elected king of Sicily 4 years later; and daughter Elizabeth of Portugal left the kingdom and married Denis, king of Portugal. ❖ See also *Women in World History.*

CONSTANCE OF STYRIA (1588–1631). Queen of Poland. Name variations: Constance of Austria. Born Dec 24, 1588; died July 10, 1631; dau. of Charles, archduke of Austria, and Mary of Bavaria (1551–1608); sister of Margaret of Austria (c. 1577–1611) and Anna of Styria (1573–1598); became 2nd wife of Zygmunt III also known as Sigismund III, king of Poland (r. 1587–1632), king of Sweden (r. 1592–1599), Dec 11, 1605; children: Casimir V also known as John II Casimir (1609–1672), king of Poland (r. 1648–1668); John Albert also known as Jan Albert (1612–1634), bishop of Warmia and Cracow; Charles Ferdinand (1613–1655), bishop of Breslau; Alexander Charles (1614–1634); Anna Constancia (1619–1651, who m. Philip William, elector of the Palatinate). Sigismund III's 1st wife was Anna of Styria, sister of Constance.

CONSTANCE OF TOULOUSE (fl. 12th century). Queen of Navarre. Dau. of Raymond VI (b. 1156), count of Toulouse, and Beatrice of Beziers; m. Sancho VII (b. after 1170), king of Navarre (1194–1234), after 1195.

CONSTANCIA OR CONSTANTIA. *Variant of Constance.*

CONSTANTIA (c. 293–?). Roman empress. Name variations: Constantina. Born Flavia Valeria Constantia c. 293; died before 330; dau. of Constantius I Chlorus (r. 305–306) and Theodora (fl. 290s); sister of Flavius Dalmatius and Flavius Julius Constantius; half-sister of Constantine I the Great, Roman emperor (r. 306–337); m. C. Valerius Licinius (primary Roman emperor of the East), 312; children: Licinius Caesar. ❖ Became a pawn in her half-brother Constantine's ambitious plan to reunify the entire empire under his sole authority. ❖ See also *Women in World History.*

CONSTANTIA (c. 321–c. 354). *See Constantina.*

CONSTANTIN, Mariana (1960—). Romanian gymnast. Born Aug 3, 1960, in Romania. ❖ Won the silver medal in team all-around at Montreal Olympics (1976). ❖ See also *Women in World History.*

CONSTANTIN-BUHAEV, Agafia (1955—). Romanian kayaker. Name variations: Agafia Buhaev. Born April 19, 1955. ❖ At Los Angeles Olympics, won a gold medal in K4 500 meters (1984).

CONSTANTINA (c. 321–c. 354). Roman empress and saint. Name variations: Constance or Constantia. Born c. 321; died in Bithynia around 354; buried in a mausoleum attached to basilica of St. Agnes; elder dau. of Constantine I the Great (285–337), Roman emperor (r. 306–337), and Fausta (d. 324); sister of Constantius II; m. cousin Hannibalianus, 335 (div. 337); m. Flavius Claudius Constantius Gallus also known as Gallus Caesar, Roman emperor (r. 351–354), 350. ❖ There are 2 versions of the story of Constantina (or there may be 2 daughters of Constantine the Great whose stories have become intertwined); in the 1st, when Magnentius, a senior Roman army officer, usurped the Western emperor Constans, convinced Vetranio, aging Master of the Infantry, to block Magnentius as he progressed eastward; married cousin, Gallus, an Arian Christian like herself; when Constantius II accused Gallus of treason, hurried to Bithynia to plead her husband's case; died there and was buried in a porphyry sarcophagus in a mausoleum attached to the basilica of St. Agnes (d. 304?), a church she had founded; in 2nd version, was a leper who learned of miracles taking place at the tomb of Christian martyr St. Agnes; had a vision from St. Agnes on a pilgrimage to the tomb and was promised a cure if she converted to Christianity; baptized and restored to health, dedicated herself to her new religion and was intent on remaining a virgin; refused General Vulcacius Gallicanus, conqueror of the Persians, who sought her hand in marriage, but eventually took care of, and lived with, his daughters Attica and Artemia near the church of St. Agnes and was buried there. Feast day is Feb 18. ❖ See also *Women in World History.*

CONSTANTINA (fl. 582–602). Byzantine empress. Name variations: Constantia. Fl. between 582 and 602; dau. of Tiberius II Constantine, Byzantine emperor (r. 578–582), and Ino-Anastasia; m. Maurice Tiberius (Mauritius), Byzantine emperor (r. 582–602); children: 9. ❖ Her husband's military reforms would play an important part in saving the empire in future years, but when he gave an unpopular order to his troops campaigning against the Avars north of the Danube, it caused a revolution; fled with husband and their children (husband and children were beheaded but her fate is unknown). ❖ See also *Women in World History.*

CONSTANTINE, Murray (1896–1963). *See Burdekin, Katharine.*

CONSTANTINESCU, Mariana (1956—). Romanian rower. Born July 5, 1956. ❖ At Moscow Olympics, won a bronze medal in coxed eights (1980).

CONSTANZA. *Variant of Constance.*

CONSUELO, Beatriz (c. 1930—). Brazilian ballet dancer. Born c. 1930, in Porto Alegre, Brazil. ❖ Performed with Teatro Municipal in Rio de Janeiro (1949–53), where she danced principal roles in *Giselle, Les Sylphides, Princess Aurora* and *Swan Lake;* danced with Grand Ballet du Marquis de Cuevas (1953–58) in company versions of Leonid Massine's *Gaîté Parisienne* and *Beau Danube,* and in *Les Sylphides, The Sleeping Princess,* and others; taught classes for Serge Golovine's dance troupe in Geneva, Switzerland.

CONTAT, Louise (1760–1813). French actress. Born Louise Françoise Contat in 1760; died in 1813; sister of Marie Contat (1769–1846); m. a nephew of the poet de Parny. ❖ Made her debut at the Comédie Française as Atalide in *Bajazet* (1766); had initial successes, however, in comedy, playing Suzanne in Beaumarchais' *Mariage de Figaro* and lending importance to several other minor parts; as the soubrette in the plays of Molière and Marivaux, found opportunities fitted specifically to her talents.

CONTAT, Marie (1769–1846). French actress. Born Marie Émilie Contat in 1769; died in 1846; sister of Louise Françoise Contat (1760–1813). ❖ French soubrette who was known especially for her roles as the pert servant in the plays of Molière and Jean François Regnard; made debut (1784); retired (1815).

CONTENT, Marjorie (1895–1984). American photographer. Born in New York, NY, 1895; died in Doylestown, Pennsylvania, 1984; m.

Harold Loeb, 1914 (div. 1921); m. Michael Carr (artist and set designer), 1924 (died 1927); m. Leon Fleischman, 1929 (div. 1934); m. Jean Toomer (poet and novelist), 1934 (died 1967); children: (1st m.) Harold Albert (who legally changed his name to James); and Mary Ellen (who legally changed her name to Susan). ❖ Strongly influenced by Alfred Steiglitz and Consuelo Kanaga, specialized in portraits, still lifes, flowers, cityscapes, and landscapes; traveled intermittently in the West to photograph the life of Native Americans; also photographed for the Bureau of Indian Affairs (1933–34).

CONTI, Francesca (1972—). Italian water-polo player. Born May 21, 1972, in Italy. ❖ At World championships, won team gold medals (1998, 2001); goalkeeper, won a team gold medal at Athens Olympics (2004). Voted Most Valuable Goalkeeper of the Thetis Cup (2001).

CONTI, Italia (1874–1946). English actress and acting teacher. Born 1874 in London, England; died Feb 8, 1946; dau. of Luigi Conti and Emily Mary (Castle) Conti; greatniece of Italian soprano Angelica Catalani (1780–1849). ❖ Made stage debut as a juvenile in *The Last Word* (1891), followed by *The Happy Hypocrite* and *Paolo and Francesca*, among others; came to prominence with portrayal of Rosalind in *As You Like It* (1903); other plays include *The Conqueror, Maternité, Hamilton's Second Marriage, Hannele* and *At Santa Lucia*; engaged by Charles Hawtrey at the Savoy to train children and arrange the fairy scenes for *Where the Rainbow Ends* (1911); from then on, ran an actor's training school for children such pupils as Noel Coward, Brian Aherne, Freddie Bartholomew, Anton Dolin, Jack Hawkins, Gertrude Lawrence, Jane Baxter, Elissa Landi and Margaret Lockwood.

CONTI, Princesse de.
See Martinozzi, Anne-Marie (1637–1672).
See Louise-Elisabeth de Bourbon Condé (1693–1775).
See Louise-Diana (1716–1736).

CONTRERAS, Gloria (1934—). Mexican ballet dancer and choreographer. Born Carmen Gloria Roeniger, Nov 15, 1934, in Mexico City, Mexico. ❖ Trained and performed with Nelsy Dambre's company in Mexico City; studied at School of American Ballet in NY; served as ballet master of Taller Coreográfico de la Universidad Autónoma de México (starting 1970) where she staged numerous ballets; choreographed works for a range of companies, including Ballet Nacional, Ballet Clássico de México, Ballet de Camara in Mexico, New York City Ballet, and Joffrey Ballet. Works of choreography include *Moncayo* (1959), *Homanago a Revueltas* (1963), *Vitalitas* (1961), *Isostasy* (1968), *Dances for Women* (1970), *Interludia* (1970), *Opus 32* (1970), *Agua Fuerte* (1970) and *Eiona* (1971).

CONVERSE, Harriet Maxwell (1836–1903). Native American chief. Born Harriet Arnot Maxwell, Jan 11, 1836, in Elmira, NY; died Nov 18, 1903, in New York, NY; youngest of 7 children of Thomas Maxwell (lawyer) and Maria (Purdy) Maxwell; brought up by relatives in Milan, Ohio; m. George B. Clarke (part owner of the Congress Spring in Saratoga, died); m. Franklin Buchanan Converse, 1861; no children. ❖ Made 1st contact with Seneca Nation (1881); composed the ode "The Ho-dé-no-saunee: The Confederacy of the Iroquois" (1885); adopted into the Snipe Clan of Seneca Nation; successfully lobbied to prevent break up of reservations (1891); made member of Seneca Nation (1891); became honorary chief of the Six Nations in Tonawanda, NY (1891), the 1st white woman to be named a Native American chief.

CONVERSE, Hessie (fl. 1892). *See Donahue, Hessie.*

CONWAY, Anne, Viscountess Conway (1631–1679). *See Finch, Anne.*

CONWAY, Marian (c. 1937—). *See McKnight, Marian.*

CONWAY, Jill Ker (1934—). Australian-born memoirist and educator. Born 1934 in Hillston, NSW, Australia; attended Abbotsleigh School; graduate of University of Sydney, 1958; Harvard University, PhD, 1969; m. John Conway (Canadian historian), 1962. ❖ Resided in the Australian outback until the death of her sheep-rancher father (1945); moved to Sydney with mother and brothers; moved to US (1960); taught at University of Toronto (1964–75), serving as vice president (1973–75); became the 1st woman president of Smith College (1975), serving for 10 years; wrote *When Memory Speaks: Reflections on Autobiography* (1998). ❖ See also autobiographies *The Road from Coorain* and *True North* (1994).

CONWAY, Verona (1910–1986). English botanist. Name variations: Verona Margaret Conway. Born Jan 13, 1910, in England; died Dec 19, 1986; attended Newnham College, Cambridge, 1929–33; Girton

College, Cambridge, PhD, 1937; studied under Dr. Harry Godwin; attended Unitarian College, Manchester, 1961–63; m. Eric Swale, 1969. ❖ Known for work on Pennines' blanket bogs and on ecology of sedge, *Cladium mariscus*, was assistant lecturer at University of Sheffield's botany department (1941–46, 1947–49); studied bogs of central Minnesota via American Association of University Women (1946–47); worked at Nature Conservancy (1949–55); served as director of Nature Conservancy Research Centre at Merlewood, Grange-over-Sands, Cumbria (1955–61); became a Unitarian minister (1963).

COO, Eva (d. 1935). Canadian-American murderer. Born in Canada; died in electric chair at Sing Sing, June 27 (some sources cite June 28), 1935. ❖ After moving to US (early 1920s), established speakeasy and bordello in Oneonta, NY, which was a success during Prohibition; when business suffered, murdered handyman Harry Wright for insurance money, with friend Martha Clift (1934); condemned to death and executed in electric chair at Sing Sing (1935). ❖ See also Niles Eggleston, *Eva Coo, Murderess* (North Country Books, 1997).

COOK, Allison (1972—). Australian basketball player. Name variations: Allison Tranquilli. Born Aug 12, 1972, in Melbourne, Australia; m. Andrew Tranquilli (athlete). ❖ Guard for the Goldmark Opals; won a team bronze medal at Atlanta Olympics (1996) and a team silver medal at Athens Olympics (2004); played for Bulleen Bloomers (1998–2000), C.B. Ciudad de Burgos in Spain (2000–01), then signed with MIZO Pecsi VSK in Hungary (2003). Was WNBL MVP (1993) and Spanish League MVP (2001).

COOK, Barbara (1927—). American singer and actress. Born Barbara Nell Cook, Oct 25, 1927, in Atlanta, Georgia. ❖ Began career in musicals on Broadway with debut in *Flahooley* (1950), followed by *Plain and Fancy* and *Candide;* came to prominence as Marion the Librarian in *The Music Man* (1957), for which she won a Tony; also appeared in *The Gay Life, She Loves Me, Something More* and *The Grass Harp;* retired from the stage; made a huge comeback as a cabaret singer; was nominated for a Laurence Olivier Theatre Award (2002) for her performance in *Barbara Cooks Sings Mostly Sondheim* in London.

COOK, Beryl (1926—). English painter. Born 1926 in Surrey, England; m. John Cook (merchant mariner, co-owner of pub), 1946; children: John Cook (b. 1950). ❖ Painter of humorous and penetrating depictions of family, friends and everyday life, left school at 14 and worked in a variety of jobs; was a showgirl in touring production of *The Gypsy Princess* and also worked in fashion industry, which inspired lifelong interest in style; lived with family in Southern Rhodesia (1951–63); moved to Plymouth, where she ran a busy theatrical boarding house in summer months and began to paint; came to prominence with 1st exhibition at Plymouth Arts Centre (1975) and was offered exhibitions at London's Whitechapel and Portal galleries; published 1st book *The Works* (1978); produced many books, among them *Beryl Cook: The Bumper Edition* (2001); had over 15 solo exhibitions; contributed painting *The Royal Couple* to Golden Jubilee Exhibition (2002); expanded into broadcast media when boisterous characters from her paintings starred in *Bosom Pals,* 2-part animated tv series made for BBC (2004). Awarded Order of the British Empire (OBE, 1995).

COOK, Cordelia E. (1919–1996). American combat nurse. Name variations: Cordelia E. Fillmore. Born Mar 7, 1919, in Fort Thomas, Kentucky; died June 19, 1996, in Columbus, Ohio; m. Harold E. Fillmore (US Army captain). ❖ Made 1st lieutenant in Army Nurse Corps; during WWII, nursed wounded soldiers in Italy at a field hospital, which was bombed (1943); was one of the 1st women to receive Bronze Star; injured by artillery fire (1944), received Purple Heart.

COOK, Edith Maud (d. 1910). British aviator and parachutist. Name variations: Spencer Kavanagh; Violet Spenser. Killed in July 1910. ❖ Learned to fly on a Blériot monoplane (early 1910) at the Grahame-White School at Pau, France, under the name Spencer Kavanagh; was already well-known as a parachute jumper under another pseudonym Violet Spenser; was killed while making a descent from a balloon over Coventry.

COOK, Eliza (1818–1889). English poet. Born Dec 24, 1818, in Southwark, England; died at Wimbledon, England, Sept 23, 1889; dau. of Joseph Cook, a London tradesman (brasier). ❖ At 17, published *Lays of a Wild Harp* (1835); published *Melaia and other Poems* (1838), the same year that her poem "The Old Armchair" caught the fancy of working- and middle-class readers on both continents, making her a household name; edited and published *Eliza Cook's Journal* (1849–54). ❖ See also *Women in World History*.

COOK, Freda Mary (1896–1990). New Zealand feminist, political activist, social reformer, journalist, and teacher. Name variations: Freda Mary Pym. Born Nov 9, 1896, at Alvescott, Oxfordshire, England; died Jan 20, 1990, at Titahi Bay, Wellington, New Zealand; dau. of Samuel Arnott Pym (solicitor) and Emma Bertha (Harrison) Pym; attended Lady Margaret Hall, Oxford University, 1919; m. Eric Kingsley Cook (teacher), 1935 (died 1948). ❖ Immigrated to New Zealand (1924); became activity secretary for Young Women's Christian Association (YWCA) in Auckland, Christchurch, and New Plymouth (1926–29); active in League Against Fascism and Working Women's Movement (1930s); was executive member of Wellington women's section of National Unemployed Workers' Movement (1935); relocated to England with husband where they founded alternative news service, General News Service (later Democratic and General News) in London; drove trucks for Women's Army Auxiliary Force during WWII and joined China Campaign Committee; became member of League Against Imperialism and worked for Indian independence; also visited Eastern Europe for Democratic and General News service; contributed articles to New Zealand periodicals, *Working Woman, Woman To-day, Workers' Weekly* and *Tomorrow;* returned to New Zealand and taught at Wellington College and at the Correspondence School (1950s); traveled to India, Russia, and China, and was invited to North Vietnam as the 1st full-time English teacher at university of Hanoi; wrote letters to *New Zealand Monthly Review* (1960s), which assisted New Zealand's antiwar movement; returned to New Zealand and joined Committee on Vietnam; campaigned against apartheid in South Africa as member of Halt All Racist Tours movement (HART) and Citizens' Association for Racial Equality (CARE, 1970s). ❖ See also *Dictionary of New Zealand Biography* (Vol. 4).

COOK, Judith (1933–2004). English anti-nuclear activist and writer. Name variations: Judith Anne Cook. Born Judith Anne Cushing, July 9, 1933, in Manchester, England; died May 12, 2004; m. Douglas Cook, 1952 (toymaker, div.); m. Martin Green, May 8, 2004; children: (1st m.) Gillian, Joanna, Simon and Nicholas. ❖ An early campaigner against nuclear weapons, founded Voice of Women (1962); wrote for *The Guardian* women's page; went to Moscow and Washington with other campaigners to protest nuclear proliferation; from her home in Ding Dong Cottage, wrote books on J.B. Priestley and Daphne du Maurier, but is best remembered for *Who Killed Hilda Murrell?* (1985), about a well-known anti-nuclear activist who was found dead in March 1984; continued her interest in the case with another book and a play; wrote over 30 books, including mysteries and *To Brave Every Danger* (about Mary Bryant).

COOK, Kathryn (1960—). *See Smallwood-Cook, Kathryn.*

COOK, Lady (1846–1923). *See Claflin, Tennessee.*

COOK, Madge Carr (1856–1933). *See Carr-Cook, Madge.*

COOK, Marianne (1930—). *See Koch, Marianne.*

COOK, Mary (1863–1950). Australian prime-ministerial wife. Born Mary Turner, 1863 in Chesterton, Staffordshire, England; died Sept 24, 1950, in Bellevue Hill, Sydney, Australia; m. Joseph Cook (prime minister of Australia, 1913–14), 1885; children: 9. ❖ Taught school for 8 years; migrated with husband to Australia (1891); active with the Parramatta electorate, the New South Wales branch of the Australian Red Cross, and Australia's High Commission in London; promoted the nation's produce and advocated British women's emigration to Australia. Named Dame of the Order of the British Empire (DBE, 1925).

COOK, Myrtle (1902–1985). Canadian runner. Born Jan 1902; died Mar 18, 1985. ❖ At Amsterdam Olympics, won a gold medal in 4x100-meter relay (1928).

COOK, Natalie (1975—). Australian beach volleyball player. Born Jan 19, 1975, in Brisbane, Queensland, Australia. ❖ With Kerri-Ann Pottharst, won a bronze medal at Atlanta Olympics (1966) and a gold medal at Sydney Olympics (2000).

COOK, Rita (1908–1970). *See Angus, Rita.*

COOK, Sheri (1953—). American ballet dancer. Born Jan 10, 1953, in Fort Riley, Kansas. ❖ Made professional debut with Pittsburgh Ballet Theater (1971); joined Royal Winnipeg Ballet in Canada, where she performed the classics as well as more contemporary works, including

Kurt Jooss' *Green Table*, Brian MacDonald's *Pas d'Action*, Michael Smuin's *Pulcinella* and Agnes de Mille's *Rodeo.*

COOK, Stephanie (1972—). Scottish pentathlete. Born Feb 7, 1972, in Irvine, Scotland; graduate of Oxford University in medicine. ❖ Won a gold medal for modern pentathlon at Sydney Olympics (2000), the 1st female British modern pentathlete to qualify for Olympic Games.

COOK, Tennessee (1846–1923). *See Claflin, Tennessee.*

COOKE. *See also Coke and Cook.*

COOKE, Aileen Anna Maria (c. 1861–1951). *See Garmson, Aileen Anna Maria.*

COOKE, Anna Rice (1853–1934). Hawaiian philanthropist. Born Anna Charlotte Rice in Honolulu, Hawaii, Sept 5, 1853; died in Honolulu, Aug 8, 1934; dau. of William Harrison (American missionary) and Mary Sophia (Hyde) Rice (also a missionary); attended Mills' Young Ladies Seminary, Benicia, California; m. Charles Montague Cooke (businessman), April 29, 1874; children: Charles Montague (b. 1874); Clarence Hyde (b. 1876); William Harrison (1879–1880); George Paul (b. 1881); Richard Alexander (b. 1884); Alice Theodora (b. 1888); twins Dorothea (1891–1892) and Theodore Atherton Cooke. ❖ With husband, founded the Aquarium at Waikiki, Rice Hall (dormitory), and the Cooke Library at Punahou School; also founded the Honolulu Academy of Arts (April 8, 1927). ❖ See also *Women in World History*.

COOKE, Elizabeth (1540–1609). *See Russell, Elizabeth.*

COOKE, Emma. American archer. Born in US. ❖ At St. Louis Olympics, won silver medals in double national round and double Columbia round (1904).

COOKE, F. (1864–1953). *See Cooke, Flora.*

COOKE, Flora (1864–1953). American educator. Name variations: F. Cooke or Flora Juliette Cooke. Born Flora Juliette Hannum, Dec 25, 1864, in Bainbridge, Ohio; died Feb 21, 1953, in Chicago, Illinois; dau. of Sumner Hannum and Rosetta (Ellis) Hannum (died 1870); was formally adopted by Charles Cooke and Luella (Miller) Cooke of Youngstown, OH (1881). ❖ Progressive educator who encouraged economic, racial and cultural diversity in the schools, began teaching in rural areas (1884); worked at Hellman Street School, Youngstown, as teacher and principal (1885–89); became teacher at Cook County Normal School, Chicago (1890); authored *Nature Myths and Stories for Little Children* (1895); traveled through US explaining Francis W. Parker's educational theories and was his representative at overseas conferences (1890s); joined Chicago Institute (1899) and, after incorporation into University of Chicago, served as principal of Francis W. Parker School (1901–34); edited 12-vol. series, *The Francis W. Parker Studies in Education* (1912–34); was trustee of Parker school (1934–48); helped found North Shore Country Day School, Winnetka, IL; was a founder and trustee of Graduate Teachers College, Winnetka, and Roosevelt University, Chicago.

COOKE, Hope (1940—). Queen of Sikkim. Name variations: Maharani of Sikkim. Born June 24, 1940, in San Francisco, California; granddau. and ward of Mr. and Mrs. Winchester Noyes; graduate of Sarah Lawrence College in Oriental studies; m. the widowed Crown Prince of Sikkim, Palden Thondup Namgyal (1923–1982), Mar 1963 (later crowned chogyal or king, div. 1980); remarried, 1987; children: Palden and Hope. ❖ While she was on a visit to NY with her children (1975), her husband was placed under house arrest and Sikkim was annexed by India as its 22nd state; became a historian, especially of New York. ❖ See also autobiography *Time Change* (Simon & Schuster, 1980).

COOKE, Katherine (c. 1530–1583). *See Killigrew, Catherine.*

COOKE, Mildred (1526–1589). *See Cecil, Mildred Cooke.*

COOKE, Rose Terry (1827–1892). American author. Born Rose Terry in West Hartford, Connecticut, Feb 17, 1827; died in Pittsfield, Massachusetts, July 18, 1892; m. Rollin H. Cooke, 1873. ❖ Though her 1st published work was a volume of *Poems* (1860), was best known for her fresh and humorous stories, which dealt primarily with New England country life: *Happy Dodd* (1878), *Somebody's Neighbors* (1881), *Rootbound* (1885), *The Sphinx's Children* (1886), *Steadfast* (1889) and *Huckleberries* (1891).

COOKE, Sarah (1912–1996). *See Palfrey, Sarah.*

COOKSON, Catherine (1906–1998). British novelist. Name variations: Catherine Marchant; Dame Catherine Cookson. Born Catherine McMullen, June 20, 1906, in Tyne Dock, South Shields, England; died of a heart ailment in Jesmond Dene, Newcastle, England, June 11, 1998, at age 91; dau. of Catherine Fawcett and a father she never knew; educated at parochial schools; m. Thomas Cookson, June 1940; no children. ❖ Novelist whose books often depict the working-class country or mind-set of Northern England, where she was raised, published over 50 novels, including her 7-novel "Mary Ann" series; her stories have been adapted to stage, screen, tv and radio, and her annual reading figure of 5 million on Britain's lending library charts eclipsed her nearest rival, Agatha Christie; writings include *Kate Hannigan* (1950), *The Round Tower* (1968), *The Cultured Handmaid* (1988), and *Let Me Make Myself Plain* (1988). Awarded Order of the British Empire (OBE, 1985); made Dame Commander of the British Empire (CBE, 1993). ❖ See also autobiography *Our Kate* and memoir, *Catherine Cookson Country* (1986).

COOLBRITH, Ina Donna (1841–1928). American poet. Name variations: began using mother's maiden name Coolbrith in 1862. Born Josephine Donna Smith in Nauvoo, Illinois, Mar 10, 1841; died in Berkeley, California, Feb 29, 1928; niece of Joseph Smith, founder of Mormonism; m. Robert B. Carsley, 1858 (div. 1861). ❖ The 1st white child to cross the Beckwourth Pass through the Sierra Nevada, attended school in Los Angeles, married, quickly divorced, and moved to San Francisco (1862), where she taught school, wrote, and joined the bay area's literary circle; associated with Bret Harte in editing the *Overland Monthly* (1868); also worked as a librarian for the Oakland Public Library (1873–1906) and was named poet laureate of California (1915); poetry collections include *The Perfect Day and Other Poems* (1881) and *Songs of the Golden Gate*.

COOLIDGE, Elizabeth Sprague (1863–1953). American music patron. Born Elizabeth Penn Sprague in Chicago, Illinois, Oct 30, 1864; died in Cambridge, Massachusetts, Nov 4, 1953; dau. of Albert Arnold Sprague (owner of the largest wholesale grocery business in the world) and Nancy (Atwood) Sprague; cousin of Lucy Sprague Mitchell (writer); m. Frederic Shurtleff Coolidge (orthopedic surgeon), 1891; children: Albert Sprague Coolidge (1894–1915). ❖ One of the most generous "angels" in the musical life of the 20th century, whose benefactions greatly assisted many contemporary composers and introduced chamber music to thousands of Americans, began to lose her hearing in the 1890s and for much of her life used hearing aids; endowed the 1st pension fund for the Chicago Symphony Orchestra (1916); sponsored the renowned Berkshire Quartet; built a Temple of Chamber Music near her Pittsfield estate, and sponsored annual South Mountain Chamber Music Festivals (1918–24); in time, sponsored concerts from London to Moscow to Hawaii and occasionally performed as pianist as well; established the Elizabeth Sprague Coolidge Foundation at the Library of Congress (1925); commissioned chamber music and a number of ballet scores from distinguished composers of the day, some of them famous, others barely known. ❖ See also *Women in World History*.

COOLIDGE, Grace Goodhue (1879–1957). American first lady. Born Grace Anne Goodhue, Jan 3, 1879, in Burlington, Vermont; died July 8, 1957, in Northampton, Massachusetts; dau. of Lemira Goodhue and Andrew Issachar Goodhue (engineer and steamboat inspector); graduate of University of Vermont, 1902; trained and taught at Clarke School for the Deaf in Northampton, Massachusetts; m. Calvin Coolidge (president of US), Oct 4, 1905; children: John Coolidge (b. 1906); Calvin Coolidge Jr. (1908–1924). ❖ One of the most glamorous and popular first ladies of the US (1923–29), became a popular cultural leader and a symbol of American womanhood during the Jazz Age, complemented the stern public image of her husband, encouraged and promoted the artistic life of Washington, DC, and gave her charitable energies to the education of the deaf; though her son died while they were in the White House (1924), brought a winning combination of good humor and personal style that made her a popular favorite when media coverage of the White House became more intense. ❖ See also Ishbel Ross, *Grace Coolidge and Her Era* (Dodd, 1962); Lawrence E. Wikander and Robert H. Ferrell, eds. *Grace Coolidge: An Autobiography* (High Plains, 1992); and *Women in World History*.

COOLIDGE, Martha (1946—). American film director. Born Aug 17, 1946, in New Haven, Connecticut; father was professor of architecture at Yale University; attended Rhode Island School of Design, New York's School of Visual Arts, New York University Institute of Film and Television, and Columbia School of Visual Arts; m. Michael Backes.

❖ Successful film director, pursued unsuccessful career as folksinger and acted with a small group in Cheshire, Connecticut, called the Blackfriars; began making documentary films with feminist themes (1960s), including one about her grandmother; worked in children's tv, directing some episodes of "Sesame Street"; gained wider notice with the controversial *Not a Pretty Picture* (1976), which examined traumas of rape victims and drew on her own harrowing experience; came to prominence with surprise hit *Valley Girls* (1983); became 1st female president of Directors Guild of America (2002), after serving as Guild's 1st vice president and as co-chair of Creative Rights Committee; directed *Real Genius* (winner of Grand Prix Award at Paris Film Festival, 1986), *Rambling Rose* (recipient of 3 IFP Independent Spirit Awards and 2 Oscar nominations, 1991), *Introducing Dorothy Dandridge* (winner of 5 Emmys) and *If These Walls Could Talk 2* (nominated for DGA Award); other films include *Lost in Yonkers* (1993), *Angie* (1994) and *The Prince & Me* (2004); for tv, directed "Crazy in Love" (1992), "The Ponder Heart" (2001), "The Flamingo Rising" (2001), as well as episodes of "Sex and the City" (1998).

COOLIDGE, Priscilla. American singer. Name variations: Priscilla Coolidge-Jones; Booker T & Priscilla; Walela. Dau. of a Baptist minister and Cherokee Indian; sister of Rita Coolidge (singer); m. Booker T. Jones (music producer); children: Laura Satterfield (singer). ❖ Voted best female vocalist by Billboard Magazine for 2 consecutive years, has recorded with such artists as Bob Dylan, Luther Vandross, and Robbie Robertson; wrote songs recorded by sister Rita, Willie Nelson, Emmylou Harris, and Maurice White, among others; with sister Rita and daughter Laura Satterfield, formed trio Walela, whose debut album *Walela* includes version of "Amazing Grace" sung in Cherokee (1997). Albums include *Booker T. & Priscilla* (with husband, 1971), and, with Walela, *Unbearable Love* (2000).

COOLIDGE, Rita (1944—). American singer. Name variations: Walela. Born May 1, 1944, in Lafayette, Tennessee; dau. of a Baptist minister and Cherokee Indian; sister of Priscilla Coolidge (singer); m. Kris Kristofferson (singer and actor), 1973 (div. 1980); children: (1st m.) daughter. ❖ Sang with Delaney & Bonnie and Friends; worked as backup singer for Eric Clapton, Boz Scaggs, and Marc Benno, among others; released solo album *Anytime . . . Anywhere* (1977), which went platinum, and had hit singles "Higher and Higher," "We're All Alone" and "The Way You Do the Things You Do"; played cameo roles in husband's films, including *A Star Is Born*; with Kristofferson, earned 2 Grammys for best country duo for work on album *Natural Act* (1979); had '80s hit "All Time High" from film *Octopussy* (1983); with sister Priscilla and niece Laura Satterfield, formed trio Walela whose debut album includes version of "Amazing Grace" sung in Cherokee (1997). Albums include *Rita Coolidge* (1971), *Lady's Not for Sale* (1972), *Cherokee* (1995), *Out of the Blues* (1996), *Thinkin' About You* (1998), and, with Walela, *Unbearable Love* (2000).

COOLIDGE, Susan (1835–1905). See Woolsey, Sarah Chauncey.

COOMBER, Alex (1973—). British skeleton athlete. Born Dec 28, 1973. ❖ Won a bronze medal for indiv. skeleton at Salt Lake City Olympics (2002).

COOMBS, Claire (1974—). English-born Belgian princess. Born Jan 18, 1974, in Bath, England; grew up in Belgium; dau. of Nicholas Coombs (British-born businessman) and Nicole Mertens (Belgian); m. Laurent, prince of Belgium (youngest son of Albert II and Queen Paola), April 12, 2003; children: Louise Sophie Mary (b. Feb 2004). ❖ Was a property surveyor.

COOMBS, Patricia (1926—). American children's writer and illustrator. Born July 23, 1926, in Los Angeles, California; dau. of Donald Gladstone (engineer) and Katherine (Goodro) Coombs; attended DePauw University, 1944, and Michigan State University, 1945–46; University of Washington, BA, 1947, MA, 1950; further study at New York University and New School for Social Research; married C. James Fox (technical writer, editor and sculptor), July 13, 1951; children: Ann and Patricia. ❖ Author and illustrator of the popular "Dorrie and the Witch" series, about a little girl witch who always wears her hat crooked and whose socks never match (though Dorrie is occasionally placed in magical settings, for the most part the situations and emotions described are basically naturalistic); also published *The Lost Playground* (1963), *Lisa and the Grompet* (1970), *Molly Mullett* (1975) and *The Magician and McTree* (1984). *Dorrie's Magic* was named one of *New York Times* 10 best books of the year (1962); *Dorrie and the Haunted House* (1970), *Dorrie and the Birthday Eggs* (1971), *Dorrie and the Goblin* (1972), *Dorrie and* the Fortune Teller (1973), Dorrie and the Witch's Imp (1975) and Dorrie and the Halloween Plot (1976) were all selected as one of the Child Study Association of America's Children's Books of the Year; Mouse Cafe was named one of New York Times 10 best illustrated books of the year (1972).

COONEY, Barbara (1917–2000). American children's writer and illustrator. Born Aug 6, 1917, in Brooklyn, NY; died Mar 14, 2000; dau. of Russell Schenck (stockbroker) and Mae Evelyn (Bossert) Cooney (artist); had a twin brother; Smith College, BA, 1938; also attended Art Students League, 1940; m. Guy Murchie (war correspondent and author), Dec 1944 (div. Mar 1947); m. Charles Talbot Porter (physician), July 16, 1949; children: (1st m.) Gretel Goldsmith, Barnaby; (2nd m.) Charles Talbot Jr., Phoebe. ❖ Author and illustrator who spent most of her life in Maine, won the Caldecott Medal for Chanticleer and the Fox (1959) and Ox-Cart Man (1980); other books written and illustrated include Miss Rumphius (1982), Island Boy (1988) and Hattie and the Wild Waves; also illustrated Margaret Wise Brown's The Little Fir Tree (1954), Edna Mitchell Preston's Squawk to the Moon, Little Goose (1974), Jean Colby's Lexington and Concord, 1775 (1975), Rumer Godden's The Story of Holly and Ivy (1985) and The Owl and the Pussy-Cat, among others. Received the Silver Medallion from University of Southern Mississippi (1975). ❖ See also Twenty-Five Years A-Graying: The Portrait of a College Graduate, a Pictorial Study of the Class of 1938 at Smith College, Northampton, Massachusetts, Based on Statistics Gathered in 1963 for the Occasion of Its 25th Reunion (1963).

COONEY, Cecelia (1904–1969). American bandit. Name variations: Bobbed-Haired Bandit. Born Cecelia Roth in New York, NY, 1904, possibly Feb 12; possibly died Oct 1969 in Kingston NY; m. Edward Cooney (fellow bandit). ❖ Robbed a string of Brooklyn stores with husband to raise money for a child she was carrying (Jan 5–April 1, 1924); while storeowners began to arm themselves in response to their exploits (and those of copycat bandits), became known among authorities, press, and public as the Bobbed-Haired Bandit; at 20 years old, was a highly romanticized figure by time of arrest with husband in Jacksonville, Florida (April 21, 1924); with husband, confessed to 10 armed robberies and served 6 years before being released (1931). At their sentencing, they reportedly thanked the judge and commented on the correctness of sending them to prison.

COONEY, Joan Ganz (1929—). American tv executive. Name variations: Joan Ganz. Born Joan Ganz in Phoenix, Arizona, Nov 30, 1929; dau. of Sylvan C. (banker) and Pauline (Reardan) Ganz; attended Dominican College, San Rafael, California; University of Arizona, BA cum laude, 1951; m. Timothy J. Cooney (treasurer of Equal Employment Council), Feb 1964 (div.); m. Peter G. Peterson (US secretary of commerce and chair of Lehman Brothers), April 26, 1980. ❖ Founder and director of the Children's Tv Workshop (CTW) and the mastermind behind the revolutionary children's show "Sesame Street," worked as a reporter for the Arizona Republic for a year before moving to New York, where she broke into tv as a publicist for NBC and the "US Steel Hour"; produced documentaries for public tv and won an Emmy for "Poverty, Anti-poverty and the Poor" (1966); recommending that all children be given the opportunity to begin schooling at age 4, launched "Sesame Street" (Nov 10, 1969); was president of CTW until 1990, then chair of its executive committee. Awarded National Humanities Medal (2003). ❖ See also Women in World History.

COOPER, Anna J. (c. 1858–1964). African-American educator, scholar, feminist, and writer. Name variations: Annie. Born Anna Julia Haywood Cooper in Raleigh, North Carolina, Aug 10, 1858 or 1859; died in Washington, DC, Feb 27, 1964; dau. of Hannah Stanley (slave) and possibly George Washington Haywood (her owner); attended Saint Augustine's Normal School and Collegiate Institute (now Saint Augustine's College), Raleigh; Oberlin College, AB, 1884, MS in mathematics, 1887; Sorbonne, PhD, 1925; m. George A.C. Cooper, 1877 (died 1879). ❖ The 4th African-American woman to earn a PhD and among the 1st women to do so in France, taught at the Preparatory High School for Colored Youth, later named the Paul Laurence Dunbar High School, in Washington, DC; during a period of racial terrorism (1890s), helped arouse public consciousness of race relations and provided direction in A Voice from the South (1892); in later years, was involved with Washington's Frelinghuysen University, an institution providing adult educational opportunities for blacks. ❖ See also Louise Daniel Hutchinson, Anna J. Cooper, a Voice from the South (Smithsonian, 1981); and Women in World History.

COOPER, Bette (c. 1920—). Miss America. Born Bette Cooper c. 1920 in Hackettstown, New Jersey. ❖ Named "Miss Bertrand Island (NJ)" (1937); named Miss America (1937), though effectively walked away from the title the same day. ❖ See also Frank Deford, There She Is (Viking, 1971).

COOPER, Beverley (1966—). See Cooper-Flynn, Beverley.

COOPER, Charlotte (1871–1966). British tennis player. Name variations: Mrs. A. Sterry; (nickname) "Chattie." Born Ealing, Middlesex, England, Sept 22, 1870; died Oct 10, 1966. ❖ Won singles championships at Wimbledon (1895, 1896, 1898, 1901, and 1908); won a gold medal for singles and mixed doubles-outdoors at Paris Olympics (1900), the 1st woman to win a gold medal at Olympic Games. ❖ See also Women in World History.

COOPER, Christin (1961—). American Alpine skier. Name variations: Christine Cooper; Christin Cooper-Tache. Born Oct 8, 1959, in Sun Valley, Idaho. ❖ At US nationals, placed 1st for slalom (1977), slalom, giant slalom, and overall (1980), and giant slalom (1984); at World championships, won silver medal for giant slalom and slalom and a bronze for combined (1982); placed 2nd in slalom at the World Cup (1981) and 2nd in slalom and giant slalom and 3rd overall (1982); won Olympic silver medal in giant slalom at Sarajevo Olympics (1984); reported for CBS-TV during Nagano games.

COOPER, Cynthia (1964—). African-American basketball player. Born April 14, 1963, in Chicago, Illinois; m. Brian Dyke. ❖ Named to the NCAA Final Four All-Tournament Team (1986); played for US in Goodwill Games (1986, 1990), World championship (1986, 1990), and Pan American Games (1987); played overseas for Segovia in Spain (1986–87); named MVP of the European All-Star Game (1987); played overseas for Alcamo (1994–96) and Parma in Italy (1987–94 and 1996–97); made Italian League All-Star Team (1996); over 1st 10 pro seasons, was leading scorer 8 times and 2nd leading scorer twice; won team gold medal (1988) and bronze medal (1992), playing with the US Olympic teams; was leading scorer (37.5 ppg) in the European Cup (1996); signed with the WNBA's Houston Comets and named MVP during the premiere season; coached the Phoenix Mercury (2001–02). ❖ See also autobiography She Got Game (Warner, 1999); and Women in World History.

COOPER, Diana Duff (1892–1986). English actress. Name variations: Lady Diana Duff Cooper; Lady Duff Cooper; Lady Diana Manners. Born 1892; died 1986; dau. of the 8th duke of Rutland; sister of Lady Violet Charteris; m. Alfred Duff Cooper (1890–1954), 1st viscount Norwich (politician, diplomat, and author), 1919. ❖ As an actress, used stage name of Lady Diana Manners; appeared as the madonna in The Miracle, her most notable role.

COOPER, Dulcie (1903–1981). Australian-born stage and screen actress. Born Nov 3, 1903, in Sydney, Australia; died Sept 3, 1981, in New York, NY. ❖ NY credits include Topsy and Eva, The Joker, Ringside, Singin' the Blues, It Happened Tomorrow, Tobacco Road, Personal Appearance and Angel in the Wings.

COOPER, Edith Emma (1862–1913). British poet and playwright. Name variations: (pseudonyms) Michael Field; Isla Leigh. Born Jan 12, 1862, in Warwickshire, England; died Dec 13, 1913, in Richmond, Surrey, England; dau. of James Robert Cooper and Emma Bradley; niece of Katharine Harris Bradley (1846–1914). ❖ With her aunt, published plays and poetry under joint pseudonym Michael Field; works include The New Minnesinger and Other Poems (1875), Bellerophon and Other Poems (1881), Long Ago (1889), Sight and Song (1892), The Race of Leaves (1901), Borgia: A Period Play (1905), Queen Marianne: A Play (1908), Mystic Trees (1913) and Dedicated: An Early Work of Michael Field (1914).

COOPER, Edna Mae (1900–1986). American actress and pilot. Born July 19, 1900, in Baltimore, Maryland; died June 27, 1986, in Woodland Hills, California; m. Karl Brown (writer, director, cinematographer). ❖ Films include The Folly of Vanity, Grounds for Divorce, Sally, Irene, and Mary, The King of Kings, Code of the Air and George Washington Cohen; was also a well-known pilot (1930s), setting the women's world refueling record.

COOPER, Eileen (1953—). English artist. Born in 1953 in Glossop, Derbyshire, England; attended Goldsmith's College, 1971–74, and Royal College of Art, 1974–77. ❖ Figurative artist, exploring a wide range of emotions from a feminist viewpoint, became visiting lecturer at

Central St. Martin's College of Art; held 1st solo exhibition at Air Gallery, London (1979); held subsequent exhibitions throughout UK, including Blond Fine Art, London (1982, 1983 and 1985), Artspace Gallery, Aberdeen (1985), Castlefield Gallery, Manchester (1986) and Artsite Gallery, Bath (1987), as well as regular exhibitions at Benjamin Rhodes Gallery (from 1988) and Art First, London (from 1998); became visiting lecturer at Royal College of Art and City & Guilds of London Art School (1998). Work includes *Passions* (2002), *Raw Material: Eileen Cooper* (2000) and *Raw Material Part II* (2000).

COOPER, Elizabeth (fl. 1737). British playwright, actress and literary critic. Name variations: Mrs. Cooper. Flourished around 1737. ❖ Wrote two plays, *The Rival Widows, or the Fair Libertine* (1735), which was produced at Covent Garden with her in the lead role on some nights, and *The Nobleman; or; The Family Quarrel* (1736); also compiled an anthology of poetry, *The Muses' Library; or a Series of English Poetry from the Saxons to the Reign of King Charles II* (1737).

COOPER, Gladys (1888–1971). English actress and manager. Name variations: Dame Gladys Cooper. Born Gladys Constance Cooper in Lewisham, England, Dec 18, 1888; died in Henley-on-Thames, Nov 17, 1971; dau. of Charles William Frederick Cooper (journalist who founded *The Epicure* magazine) and Mabel Barnett Cooper; m. Henry Buckmaster (actor), Dec 12, 1908 (div. 1922); m. Sir Neville Charles Pearson (magazine editor and publisher), June 15, 1928 (div., Oct 1936); m. Philip Merivale (actor), April 30, 1937 (died 1946); children: (1st m.) John Buckmaster (actor) and Joan Buckmaster Morley (who m. actor Robert Morley); (2nd m.) Sally Pearson Hardy (who m. actor Robert Hardy). ❖ Actress-manager and musical-comedy star, best known for her roles in drawing-room comedy, who was the most popular actress on the London stage by 1914 and darling of British "Tommies" as they went into battle in WWI; made stage debut in Colchester, as Bluebelle in *Bluebelle in Fairyland* (1905); made London debut as one of the Gaiety Girls; soon one of the most popular young actresses featured on the theatrical cards of the day, starred in such productions as *Our Miss Gibbs* (1908) and *The Dollar Princess* (1909); appeared in 1st serious drama, *The Pigeon* (1912), followed by *Diplomacy* (1913); with Frank Curzon, launched a series of plays in which she starred, such as *Home and Beauty* (1919), *If* (1921), *The Sign on the Door* (1921), *The Second Mrs. Tanqueray* (1922), *Iris* (1925) and *The Last of Mrs. Cheyney* (1925); was the 1st Peter Pan to "fly" on a suspension wire (1923–24); assumed management of Playhouse Theater in London, where she produced 8 plays in 8 years, the 1st being *The Letter,* which was highly successful (1926–34); made NY debut in *The Shining Hour* (1934), then appeared in *Call It a Day* (1935) and *Spring Meeting* (1938); made regular appearances in American films, including *Rebecca* (1940), *Kitty Foyle* (1940), *That Hamilton Woman* (1941), *The Black Cat* (1941), *This Above All* (1942), *The Song of Bernadette* (1943), *The White Cliffs of Dover* (1944), *Mrs. Parkington* (1944), *Valley of Decision* (1945), *The Green Years* (1946), *Green Dolphin Street* (1947), *The Bishop's Wife* (1947), *The Pirate* (1948), *The Secret Garden* (1949), *Madame Bovary* (1949), *Separate Tables* (1958), *The List of Adrian Messenger* (1963), *My Fair Lady* (1964) and *The Happiest Millionaire* (1967); other plays include *Relative Values* (1951–52), *The Chalk Garden* (1955–56) and *A Passage to India* (1962). Nominated for Academy Award for the Best Supporting Actress for *Now Voyager* (1942); named Dame Commander of the Order of the British Empire (1967). ❖ See also autobiography *Gladys Cooper* (1931); and *Women in World History*.

COOPER, J. California (1940s–). African-American playwright and short-story writer. Born Joan California Cooper in Berkeley, California, in 1940s ("A woman who tells her age will tell anything," she once said); children: daughter, Paris A. Williams. ❖ Author of 17 plays anthologized in Eileen J. Ostrow (ed.), *Center Stage* (1981); short-fiction includes *A Piece of Mine* (1984), *Homemade Love* (1986), *Some Soul to Keep* (1987), *The Matter is Life* (1992) and *The Future Has a Past Stories* (2001); also wrote novels *Family* (1991), *In Search of Satisfaction* (1994), *The Wake of the Wind* (1998) and *Some People, Some Other Place* (2004), among others. Named Black Playwright of the Year (1978) for her play *Strangers;* won James Baldwin Writing Award (1988) and American Book Award (1989).

COOPER, Jacqui (1973–). Australian freestyle skier. Born Jan 6, 1973, in Melbourne, Australia. ❖ Won the World aerial championships (1999); won World Cup aerials titles (1999, 2000, 2001); was the 1st woman in the sport to perform a triple twisting triple somersault. Named Australian Skier of the Year (1999, 2000).

COOPER, Jessie (1914–1993). Australian politician. Born in 1914; died in 1993. ❖ The 1st woman elected to South Australia's Legislative Council (1959), served on the Legislative Council for 19 years, though she did not hold a seat.

COOPER, Jilly (1937—). British romance-fiction writer. Born Feb 21, 1937, in Essex, England; dau. of W.B. Sallitt and Mary Elaine Whincup Sallitt; m. Leo Cooper, 1961. ❖ Worked as a reporter on the *Middlesex Independent* (1957–59), before writing popular columns for the *Sunday Times* (1969–82) and *The Mail on Sunday* (1982–85); her popular trilogy—*Riders* (1986), *Rivals* (1988), and *Polo* (1991)—centers around the lives of the upper-middle class; other novels include *Emily* (1975), *Imogen* (1978), and *Pandora* (2002); also wrote nonfiction, including *How to Stay Married* (1969), *The British in Love* (1979), *On Rugby* (1984), *Horse Mania!* (1986), and *How to Survive Christmas* (1986).

COOPER, Kim (1965—). Australian softball player. Born Oct 26, 1965, in Parramatta, NSW, Australia. ❖ Won a bronze medal at Atlanta Olympics (1996).

COOPER, Lillian Kemble (1891–1977). English-born actress and singer. Name variations: Lillian Kemble-Cooper. Born Mar 21, 1891, in London, England; died May 4, 1977, in Los Angeles, California; dau. of Frank Kemble Cooper (actor) and Alice May (Taunton); granddau. of T. Clifford Cooper and Agnes Kemble; sister of Anthony Kemble Cooper (actor), Violet Kemble Cooper (actress), and Greta Kemble Cooper (actress); m. Louis Bernheimer; m. Charles Mackay (actor); m. Guy Bates Post (actor, died 1968). ❖ Made stage debut in London in *The Chocolate Soldier* (1914); came to US (1918) and made NY stage debut in *Hitchy-Koo* (1919); other plays include *The Night Boat, The New Morality, The National Anthem, The Mountebank* and *Our Betters.*

COOPER, Margaret (c. 1807–1877). See Forbes, Margaret.

COOPER, Margaret Joyce (b. 1909). English swimmer. Born April 18, 1909. ❖ At Amsterdam Olympics, won bronze medals in the 100-meter backstroke and 100-meter freestyle and a silver medal in the 4x100-meter freestyle relay (1928); at Los Angeles Olympics, won a bronze medal in the 4x100-meter freestyle relay (1932).

COOPER, Mary Wright (1714–1778). American diarist. Born 1714, near Oyster Bay, NY; died 1778; children: 6. ❖ Kept a journal, which was published as *The Diary of Mary Cooper: Life on a Long Island Farm 1768–1773.*

COOPER, Miriam (1891–1976). American silent-film actress. Born Nov 7, 1891, in Baltimore, Maryland; died April 12, 1976, Charlottesville, Virginia; m. Raoul Walsh (director), 1916 (div. 1926). ❖ Star of Kalem Company (1912–13); appeared in D.W. Griffith films *Intolerance, Home Sweet Home,* and as Margaret Cameron in *Birth of a Nation;* other films include *Evangeline, Serenade* and *Kindred of the Dust;* retired from the screen (1924). ❖ See also autobiography *Dark Lady of the Silents* (Bobbs-Merrill, 1973).

COOPER, Mrs. (fl. 1737). See Cooper, Elizabeth.

COOPER, Priscilla. (1816–1889). See Tyler, Priscilla.

COOPER, Sarah Ingersoll (1835–1896). American educator. Born Sarah Brown Ingersoll in Cazenovia, New York, Dec 12, 1835; died in San Francisco, California, Dec 10, 1896, when her daughter turned on the gas in their San Francisco apartment and asphyxiated them both; cousin of orator and agnostic Robert C. Ingersoll; attended Cazenovia Seminary, 1850–53; Troy Female Seminary, 1854; m. Halsey F. Cooper (editor of Tennessee's *Chattanooga Advertiser*), 1855 (committed suicide 1885); children: 2 daughters, including Harriet Cooper (d. 1896). ❖ Opened the Jackson Street Kindergarten in San Francisco (1879), which led to the organization of the Golden Gate Kindergarten Association; guided the incorporation of 40 kindergartens in San Francisco area, enrolling nearly 3,600 children; helped found and was elected the 1st president of the International Kindergarten Union (1892); was elected 1st president of the Woman's Congress (1895). ❖ See also *Women in World History.*

COOPER, Susan Fenimore (1813–1894). American writer. Name variations: (pseudonym) Amabel Penfeather. Born Susan Augusta Fenimore Cooper, April 17, 1813, in Mamaroneck, New York; died in Cooperstown, New York, Dec 31, 1894; dau. of Susan Augusta (De Lancey) Cooper and James Fenimore Cooper (writer); never married; no children. ❖ Naturalist, author, philanthropist, and biographer of her father, who turned a fine observational eye to describing the particulars of her locale, recording the minutiae of the place observed and demonstrating an acuity of perception in drawing correlations between the natural routine and order and ways of humanity; moved with family from Mamaroneck (NY) to Cooperstown (1813); moved with family to New York City (1817); lived with family in Europe (1826–33); lived with parents, working as her father's amanuensis until his death (1851); under pseudonym Amabel Penfeather, published novel *Elinor Wyllys; or, the Young Folk of Longbridge* (edited by father, 1845), followed by *Rural Hours* (1850), a chronicle of one year's natural cycle at her home near Lake Otsego, which remained in print for almost 40 years and predates its now well-known counterpart, Thoreau's *Walden* (1854), by 4 years; mother died (1854); devoted much time to charitable work including work with the Christ Church Charity House for destitute families; organized the Christ Church Sewing School (1860); helped establish Thanksgiving Hospital in Cooperstown (1868) and Orphan House of the Holy Savior, also in Cooperstown (1871); also wrote "Village Improvement Societies" (1869), "The Magic Place" (1870), "Insect-Life in Winter" (1870), "The Hudson River and Its Early Names," (1880), "A Lament for the Birds" (1893), and "An Outing on Lake Otsego" (1894); contributed to *Appletons' Illustrated Almanac for 1870* (1869); and edited *The Rhyme and Reason of Country Life: or, Selections from Fields Old and New* (1854). ❖ See also *Women in World History.*

COOPER, Susie (1902–1995). English ceramic designer and factory owner. Name variations: Susan Vera Cooper, Mrs. C.F. Barker. Born Susan Vera Cooper, Oct 29, 1902, in Stoke-on-Trent, England; died July 28, 1995, on Isle of Man, England; attended Burslem School of Art, 1919–20; m. Cecil Barker (architect), 1938 (died 1972); children: Tim Barker. ❖ Acclaimed ceramic designer and factory owner, whose tableware and teapots are sought after by collectors, studied under Scottish ceramic designer Gordon Forsyth; joined Gray's Pottery as painter (1922); introduced geometric and banded patterns that were a hallmark art-deco design (1920s); displayed work at British Empire Exhibition at Wembley (1924) and in Paris (1925 and 1937); seeking artistic freedom, set up own firm with brother-in-law Jack Beeson (1929); purchased local earthenware and decorated it with simple patterns of polka dots, animals and flowers, often in muted shades; used lithographic transfers to reduce inconsistency inherent in handpainting and worked closely with Universal Transfer Co. to develop transfer technique to great benefit of pottery industry; received 1st major orders (1935); became highly successful, supplying such London stores as Harrods and Selfridges; became 1st female Royal Designer for Industry (1940) and received many important commissions; during WWII, was briefly forced to shut down after fire in factory, but reopened Crown Works and rebuilt business; expanded product line to include manufacture of fine bone china (1950s); merged Crown Works with RH & SL Plant, becoming part of Wedgewood Group (1966); was senior designer and director for Josiah Wedgewood and Sons until husband's death (1972); moved to Isle of Man (1982), where she continued to work; awarded Order of British Empire (OBE, 1979). Works displayed in numerous artistic exhibitions, including Victoria & Albert Museum, Stoke-on-Trent City Museum & Art Gallery (1987) and Ipswich Museum (1989–90).

COOPER, Vera (1928—). See Rubin, Vera Cooper.

COOPER, Violet Kemble (1886–1961). English-born stage and screen actress. Name variations: Violet Kemble-Cooper. Born Dec 12, 1886, in London, England; died Aug 17, 1961, in Los Angeles, California; dau. of Frank Kemble Cooper (actor) and Alice May (Taunton); granddau. of T. Clifford Cooper and Agnes Kemble; sister of Anthony Kemble Cooper (actor), Lillian Kemble Cooper (actress) and Greta Kemble Cooper (actress); m. Walter Ferris (screenwriter). ❖ Made stage debut in England as Kitty Verdun at Kennington Theater in *Charley's Aunt* (1902); made Broadway debut as Kate Stirling in *The Indiscretion of Truth* (1912); other stage appearances include *Peg o' My Heart, The Wooing of Eve, Dear Brutus, Clair de Lune, School for Scandal, The Apple Cart, Lysistrata* and *Mackerel Skies;* films include *Our Betters, David Copperfield, The Fountain, Romeo and Juliet* and *The Invisible Ray;* stricken with Parkinson's and forced to retire (1943).

COOPER, Vivienne (1926—). See Cassie Cooper, Vivienne.

COOPER, Whina (1895–1994). Maori activist. Name variations: Mrs. Richard Gilbert; Mrs. William Cooper. Pronunciation: SEE-nah KOO-per. Born Josephine Te Wake on the shores of Hokianga Harbor, New Zealand, Dec 9, 1895; died in Panguru, Mar 26, 1994; dau. of Heremia Te Wake, chief of the Hokianga tribes, and Kare Pauro; attended St. Joseph's School for Maori Girls; m. Richard Gilbert, 1916; m. William Cooper, 1940; children: (1st m.) 4; (2nd m.) 2. ❖ Maori leader

and Mother of the People, beloved by both Maoris and whites, who was prominent in native land rights in New Zealand, active in other reform movements, and was known as Dame Whina Cooper toward the end of her life; became a prominent businesswoman, owning several farms and stores; became active in land reform plan instituted by Sir Apirana Ngata (1929); elected president of a New Zealand rugby association, North Hokianga Rugby Union (1947), the 1st woman to hold a position previously occupied exclusively by men; founded the Maori Women's Welfare League (1951); led a 700-mile march to preserve Maori land (1975); honored as a Commander of the British Empire (CBE) for her services to the Maori people (1979); raised to the rank of Dame of the British Empire (DBE, 1981). ❖ See also Michael King, *Whina: A Biography of Whina Cooper* (Hodder & Stoughton, 1983); and *Women in World History.*

COOPER, Mrs. William (1895–1994). See Cooper, Whina.

COOPER, Mrs. Wyatt E. (b. 1924). See Vanderbilt, Gloria.

COOPER, Yvette (1969—). English economist, politician and member of Parliament. Born Yvette Cooper, Mar 20, 1969, in UK; m. Ed Balls, 1998. ❖ Was an economic columnist and lead writer for *The Independent* (1995–97); representing Labour, elected to House of Commons for Pontefract and Castleford (1997, 2001, 2005); named parliamentary secretary, Lord Chancellor's Department; named minister of State, Office of the Deputy Prime Minister (2005).

COOPER-FLYNN, Beverley (1966—). Irish politician. Name variations: Beverley Cooper; Beverley Flynn; Beverly Cooper Flynn. Born Beverley Flynn, June 1966, in Tuam, Co. Galway, Ireland; dau. of Padraig Flynn (TD, Mayo West, 1977–93). ❖ Representing Fianna Fáil, elected to the 28th Dáil (1997–2002), the 1st woman to represent Mayo; returned to 29th Dáil (2002).

COORY, Shirefie (c. 1864–1950). New Zealand retailer and shopkeeper. Name variations: Shirefie Lettoof. Born Shirefie Lahood, c. 1864 or 1865, in Bsharri, Lebanon; died Mar 18, 1950, in Dunedin, New Zealand; dau. of Peter Lettoof (farmer) and Mary (Lahood) Lettoof; m. Anthony Coory, c. 1880 (died 1943); children: 1 daughter. ❖ Immigrated with husband and family to Australia and entered into manufacturing business in Melbourne (c. 1884); relocated to Dunedin, New Zealand (c. 1892); opened shop for premium goods and imported items; established workshop for Lebanese seamstresses to make items for sale. ❖ See also *Dictionary of New Zealand Biography* (Vol. 2).

COOSAPONAKEESA (c. 1690– c. 1763). See Musgrove, Mary.

COPE, Mother Marianne (1838–1918). German-born American nun. Name variations: Barbara Koob; Sister Mary Anna Cope; Marianna; Mother Cope; Mother Marianne of Molokai. Born Barbara Koob in Germany, Jan 23, 1838; died in Hawaii, Aug 9, 1918; dau. of Peter (farmer) and Barbara (Witzenbacher) Koob; attended St. Joseph's Parish School. ❖ Member of the Third Order of St. Francis, who ministered to the lepers of Hawaii for more than 35 years; relocated from Germany to Utica, New York (1839); invested in the habit of a novice (Nov 9, 1862), becoming Sister Mary Anna; pronounced her vows (Nov 19, 1863); appointed temporary superior for Immaculate Conception Convent in Rome, NY (1866), then superior of St. Teresa's and principal of St. Peter's School in Oswego, NY; appointed superior of St. Joseph's Hospital in Syracuse (June 1870); elected 2nd provincial superior of the Sisters of St. Francis (Dec 1877); arrived in Hawaii (Nov 8, 1883); opened the Kapiolani Home for Girls at Kakaako (Nov 1885); arrived in Kalaupapa to live among a thousand lepers (Nov 1888). ❖ See also *Women in World History.*

COPELAND, Lillian (1904–1964). American track-and-field athlete. Born Nov 25, 1904, in New York, NY; died Feb 7, 1964. ❖ Competitor in the shot put, discus, and javelin, won a silver medal at Amsterdam Olympics (1928) and a gold at Los Angeles Olympics (1932), both for discus. ❖ See also *Women in World History.*

COPELAND-DURHAM, Emily (1984—). American wakeboarder. Name variations: Emily Copeland; Emily Copeland Durham. Born Mar 28, 1984, in Denver, Colorado; married Kevin Durham, July 2003. ❖ Credited with working to advance the sport, became competitor (1999); won gold at Gravity Games (2002 and 2003) and silver at X Games (1999 and 2001) in women's wakeboarding; 1st place finishes include: Wakeboard World championship (2001), Vans Triple Crown (2001), US Masters (2001), Pro Wakeboard Tour (2001, 2004), Masters (2002), and Malibu Open (2002).

COPLEY, Clara (d. 1949). Irish entrepreneur. Name variations: Ma Copley. Died in 1949. ❖ Known as Ma Copley, embarked on her career in the world of prize fighting (1930s); started with a boxing booth and later held boxing matches in a large, wooden building in Belfast. ❖ See also *Women in World History*.

COPLEY, Ethel (1883–1950). See Gabain, Ethel Leontine.

COPLEY, Helen (1922–2004). American newspaper publisher and philanthropist. Name variations: Helen K. Copley. Born Margaret Helen Kinney, Nov 28, 1922, in Cedar Rapids, Iowa; died Aug 25, 2004, at her home in La Jolla, California; married 1940s (div. 1951); m. James S. Copley (newspaper publisher), 1965 (died 1973); children: David C. Copley (newspaper publisher). ❖ Prominent philanthropist and powerful publisher, began working at Union Tribune Publishing Co. as a secretary (1953), becoming publisher and chair of Copley Press, Inc., on death of husband (1973); a canny businesswoman, merged her flagship papers, *San Diego Union* and *San Diego Tribune* (1992) into the *The San Diego Union-Tribune*, which became the 3rd-largest newspaper in California; contributed millions to civic causes, including San Diego Symphony, San Diego Museum of Contemporary Art, and the San Diego central animal shelter. Under her tenure, the *Tribune* won 2 Pulitzer prizes.

COPLEY, Mary Singleton (c. 1710–1789). See Pelham, Mary Singleton.

COPPI, Hilde (1909–1943). German anti-Nazi activist. Born Hilde Rake in Berlin, Germany, May 30, 1909; executed at Plötzensee, Aug 5, 1943; m. Hans Coppi (1916–42, Communist and anti-Nazi leader); children: Hans. ❖ Member of the Berlin support group of the "Red Orchestra" spy network, printed pamphlets and took in anti-Nazis on the run from the Gestapo; with husband, established contact with the Schulze-Boysen-Harnack resistance circle; was pregnant when arrested with virtually all members of the "Red Orchestra" (Sept 1942); gave birth to son Hans in prison (Nov 27), then was executed (Aug 5, 1943). ❖ See also *Women in World History*.

COPPIN, Fanny Jackson (1837–1913). African-American teacher and missionary. Name variations: (pseudonym) Catherine Casey. Born Fanny Marion Jackson in 1837 in Washington, DC; died in Philadelphia, Jan 21, 1913; dau. of unknown father and Lucy Jackson, a slave; Oberlin College, AB, 1865; m. Reverend Levi Jenkins Coppin, 1881. ❖ The 1st black woman in the US to head an institution of higher learning, worked as domestic (1851–59); served as principal of the female department and teacher of Greek, Latin, and mathematics, Institute for Colored Youth in Philadelphia (1865–69); served as principal of the Institute (1869–1902); became quite active in the African Methodist Episcopal (AME) Church in subsequent years, serving as national president of its Home and Foreign Missionary Society in South Africa (1902–04); wrote autobiography, *Reminiscences of School Life and Hints on Teaching* (1913). A Baltimore normal school was named in her honor (1909), which became Coppin State College. ❖ See also *Women in World History*.

COPPS, Sheila (1952—). Canadian politician and journalist. Name variations: Sheila Copps Miller. Born Sheila Maureen Copps, Nov 27, 1952, in Hamilton, Ontario, Canada; dau. of Victor K. Copps (14-year mayor of Hamilton) and Geraldine Copps (Hamilton city councillor); attended University of Western Ontario, McMaster University, and University of Rouen; married and divorced. ❖ Began career as a journalist for the *Hamilton Spectator* and *Ottawa Citizen*; as a Liberal for Hamilton Centre riding, elected to the Legislative Assembly of Ontario in the provincial election (1981), serving until 1984; elected to House of Commons (1984), as MP for Hamilton East; served in the Cabinet as deputy prime minister (Nov 1993–June 1997), minister of the Environment (Nov 1993–Jan 1996), minister of Canadian Heritage (Jan 1996–April 1996, June 1996–1997); sworn to the Privy Council (1993); controversial legislator, ran unsuccessfully for party leadership (2003); retired from politics (2004). ❖ See also autobiographies *Nobody's Baby* (1986) and *Worth Fighting For* (2004).

COQUILLARD-ALBRIER, Albertine (c. 1810–1846). French ballet dancer. Name variations: Albertine Coquillard; Albertine Albrier. Born c. 1810, probably in Paris, France; died Feb 20, 1846, in Paris; sister of Fifine and Victorine (both dancers). ❖ Trained at ballet school of Paris Opéra along with younger sisters; danced with the Paris Opéra's company (starting mid-1830s) where her most important role was in Aumer's *Les Pages du Duc de Vendôme*, which she also performed in London (1840); appeared briefly in Naples with Eduoard Carey.

CORAK, Mia (b. 1914). See Slavenska, Mia.

CORALINA, Cora (1889–1985). See Guimarães Peixoto Bretas, Ana Lins do.

CORBAN-BANOVICI, Sofia (1956—). Romanian rower. Name variations: Sofia Banovici. Born Aug 1, 1956. ❖ At Los Angeles Olympics, won a gold medal in quadruple sculls with coxswain (1984).

CORBAUX, Fanny (1812–1883). English artist. Name variations: Fanny Corbeaux. Born Marie Françoise Catherine Doetter Corbaux in 1812; died in 1883. ❖ Staying primarily with portraits, painted small pictures in oil and watercolors; a self-taught artist, was among the 1st to advocate on behalf of women for their admission as students to London's Royal Academy; was also a distinguished Biblical scholar who wrote a series of letters on "The Physical Geography of the Exodus."

CORBERT, Sybilla (fl. 11th century). Mistress of Henry I. Name variations: Corbet. Dau. of Sir Robert Corbert or Corbet; mistress of Henry I, king of England (r. 1068–1135); children: Matilda, duchess of Brittany (fl. 1000s); Sybilla (d. 1122, who m. Alexander I, king of Scots); Constance (who m. Richard, viscount de Beaumont, and was the mother of Ermengarde de Beaumont.

CORBETT, Cicely (1885–1959). See Fisher, Cicely Corbett.

CORBETT, Leonora (1908–1960). English comedic actress. Born June 28, 1908, in London, England; died July 29, 1960, in Vleuten, Holland, Netherlands; m. John Francis Royal. ❖ Made stage debut in *Israel* (1928); other London appearances include *Lady-in-Waiting, Britannia of Billingsgate, The Nelson Touch, Business with America, Beggars in Hell, Between Us Two, Dusty Ermine* and *Sarah Simple;* appeared on Broadway as Elvira in *Blithe Spirit* for 2 years, and as Sybil Bennett in *Park Avenue;* made numerous films, including *Love on Wheels, The Constant Nymph* and *The Price of Folly*.

CORBETT, Marie (1859–1932). British suffragist. Born Marie Gray in Tunbridge Wells, England, 1859; died in 1932; dau. of George (fruit importer and candy manufacturer) and Eliza Gray; m. Charles Corbett (lawyer and the 1st Liberal elected to represent East Grinstead in the House of Commons), 1881; children: Margery Corbett-Ashby (1882–1981); Cicely Corbett Fisher (1885–1959). ❖ Joined the Uckfield Board of Guardians and subsequently became the 1st woman to serve on the Uckfield District Council; a champion of women's rights, was instrumental in founding the Liberal Women's Suffrage Society; with daughters, helped form the Liberal Women's Suffrage Group; also successfully closed down the Uckfield Workhouse and found homes for all the orphans therein. ❖ See also *Women in World History*.

CORBETT, Rita La Roy (1907–1993). See La Roy, Rita.

CORBETT-ASHBY, Margery (1882–1981). British feminist and politician. Name variations: Dame Margery Ashby; Margery Corbett Ashby. Born Margery Corbett at Danehill, Sussex, England, 1882; died at Danehill, Sussex, May 22, 1981; dau. of Charles Corbett (lawyer) and Marie (Gray) Corbett (suffragist); elder sister of Cicely Corbett Fisher (1885–1959); attended Newnham College, Cambridge; attended Cambridge Teachers Training College; m. Brian Ashby (barrister), 1910; children: Michael. ❖ One of the few women to be involved in Britain's earliest suffrage campaigns, had a political career that spanned three-quarters of a century and included 7 thwarted bids for election to the House of Commons; supported mother in work for women's suffrage and made 1st political speech at 16; learned French, German, Italian and Turkish and worked as translator at conferences; read Classics at Newnham College, and continued suffrage work; became organizing secretary of National Union of Women's Suffrage Societies (1907) and represented International Alliance of Women at Versailles Peace Conference and at International Labour Organization; became secretary of the Alliance (1920) and president (1923); resigned from the Alliance after 42 years and traveled as lecturer on pacifism and feminism until age 80. ❖ See also *Memoirs* (1996); and *Women in World History*.

CORBEY, Dorette (1957—). Dutch nurse and politician. Born July 19, 1957, in Eindhoven, Netherlands. ❖ Nurse (1976–88); served as policy adviser, Construction and Timber Union, for FNV (Netherlands Trade Union Confederation, 1993–99); as a European Socialist, elected to 5th European Parliament (1999–2004).

CORBIN, Alice (1881–1949). See Henderson, Alice Corbin.

CORBIN, Hazel (1894–1988). Canadian-American nurse. Born Aug 31, 1894, in Nova Scotia, Canada; died May 18, 1988, in New Smyrna Beach, Florida; graduate of Brooklyn Hospital, 1917. ❖ Known for work as director of New York City's Maternity Center Association (MCA), began there as staff nurse (1918–22), then worked as assistant director (1922) and general director (1923–65); helped to found 1st American school for nurse-midwifery (1931), the Lobenstine Midwifery Clinic and School, which became part of MCA in 1934; contributed to development of nurse-midwife certification programs at, among others, Columbia, Yale, and Johns Hopkins universities. As MCA director, created 1st major World's Fair exhibit on childbearing (1939–40), 1st film on sex education and family life, *From Generation to Generation* (1959), and 1st nationwide tv series on childbearing (1954).

CORBIN, Lucidor (fl. 18th c.). **French writer and political reformer.** Fl. in 18th century. ❖ Creole activist who wrote "Hymne des citoyens de couleurs," set to the tune of the Marseillaise, and a political speech on freedom, "Discours au Temple de la Raison," which were published in *Les Femmes dans la Révolution française* (1982).

CORBIN, Margaret Cochran (1751–c. 1800). **American revolutionary.** Name variations: Captain Molly; Dirty Kate. Born Margaret Cochran, Nov 12, 1751, in what is now Franklin Co., Pennsylvania; died in Highland Falls, New York, c. 1800; dau. of Robert Cochran; m. John Corbin, 1772 (killed 1776); married, 1782. ❖ Father killed by Indians (1756) and mother made captive, never to return; accompanied husband John Corbin to the army; learned the intricate steps of loading and firing; at Fort Washington, during battle, took over gunner's position in place of husband who was killed (Nov 16, 1776); received army pension and became a soldier in the Invalid Corps (1779), remaining in this capacity until the unit was disbanded (April 1783); lived in vicinity of West Point, drawing provisions from the army commissary; eventually settled in what is now Highland Falls, NY; not to be confused with Mary Ludwig Hays McCauley. ❖ See also Edward Hall, *Margaret Corbin: Heroine of the Battle of Fort Washington, 16 Nov 1776* (1932); and *Women in World History*.

CORBIN, Virginia Lee (1910–1942). **American actress.** Born Virginia LaVerne Corbin, Dec 5, 1910, in Prescott, Arizona; died June 5, 1942, in Winfield, Illinois; m. Charles Jacobson; m. Theodore Elwood Krol, 1929 (div. 1937). ❖ Child star of the silents, films include *Babes in the Woods, Treasure Island, The Forbidden Room, Enemies of Children, Wine of Youth* and *Hands Up!*

CORBY, Ellen (1911–1998). **American actress.** Born Ellen Hansen, June 3, 1911, in Racine, Wisconsin; died April 14, 1999, in Woodland Hills, California; m. Francis Corby, 1934 (div. 1944). ❖ Probably best remembered for portrayal of Grandma Walton on "The Waltons" (1972–79), for which she won 3 Emmys (1972, 1974 & 1975); films include *It's a Wonderful Life, Till the End of Time, The Spiral Staircase, Little Women, Harriet Craig, Angels in the Outfield, Shane, Sabrina* and *Vertigo*; suffered a serious stroke (1976). Nominated for Academy Award for performance in *I Remember Mama* (1948).

CORCORAN, Katharine (1857–1943). *See Herne, Katharine Corcoran.*

CORDA, Maria (1898–1975). **Hungarian-born silent-film actress.** Name variations: Antónia Farkas; María Corda. Born May 4, 1898, in Deva, Hungary; died Feb 2, 1975, in Geneva, Switzerland; m. Alexander Korda (Hungarian director and producer), 1919 (div. 1930). ❖ Made film debut as Antónia Farkas (1920); starred in 6 German features in Germany, all directed by her husband (1923–26); accompanied him to Hollywood and made 2 films, *The Private Life of Helen of Troy* (1927) and *Love and the Devil* (1929). Korda eventually married Merle Oberon (1939).

CORDA, Maria (1930—). *See Corday, Mara.*

CORDAY, Charlotte (1768–1793). **French assassin.** Name variations: Marie-Anne-Charlotte de Corday d'Armont. Born Marie-Anne-Charlotte de Corday d'Armont at Champeaux in the Calvados of Normandy, France, July 27, 1768; executed in Paris, July 17, 1793; dau. of Jacques-François de Corday (minor aristocrat) and a mother who died in childbirth when Charlotte was quite young; never married; no children. ❖ Norman whose passion for justice so far exceeded the capacity or will of the Revolution to separate justice from politics that she individually indicted, judged, and executed the radical journalist Jean Paul Marat, by murdering him in his bath; inspired by the eruption of French Revolution (1789), came to sympathize with the faction known as the Girondins, the moderate republicans of her time; upon the fall of that faction from power in Paris (spring 1793) and the arrival of several Girondin leaders in Caen, sensed a major part for herself in the Revolution; traveled to Paris (July 1793) and murdered Jean Paul

Marat, radical editor of *Ami du Peuple,* whom she blamed for the Girondins' fate. She also sought the inevitable martyrdom that must follow upon her act. In her death, she would do for France what she could not do, as a woman, in the political assemblies in Paris. She would, by her sacrifice and by her example, turn her nation away from the murderous, divisive, and populist policies of the Jacobin regime and lead it back to moderate, rational, constitutional government by those of talent and position. Ironically, her violent act only intensified the terroristic policies of the Parisian regime and precluded any peaceful, legislative resolution of the political crisis of the time. ❖ See also Marie Cher, *Charlotte Corday and Certain Men of the Revolutionary Torment* (Appleton, 1929); and *Women in World History*.

CORDAY, Mara (1930—). **American screen actress.** Name variations: Maria Corda. Born Marilyn Watts, Jan 3, 1930, in Santa Monica, California; m. Richard Long (actor), 1957 (died 1974); children: Valerie Long (actress). ❖ Began career in the chorus of *Earl Carroll's Revue* in Hollywood; appeared in such films as *Two Tickets to Broadway, Sea Tiger, The Lady Wants Mink, Sweethearts on Parade, Playgirl, Francis Joins the WACS, The Giant Claw, The Man from Bitter Ridge, Tarantula, Naked Gun, So This is Paris, Sudden Impact* and *The Rookie;* was at one time a contract player for Universal–International.

CORDAY, Paula (1920–1992). *See Corday, Rita.*

CORDAY, Rita (1920–1992). **Swiss actress.** Name variations: began career as Rita Corday (1943), changed to Paule Croset or Paula Croset (1947), then Paula Corday (1950s). Born Jeanne Paule Teipotemarga, Oct 20, 1920, in Switzerland; died Nov 23, 1992, in Century City, California; m. Harold Nebenzal (producer). ❖ Leading lady in mostly low-budget films, including *Hitler's Children, Mr. Lucky, The Falcon Strikes Back, The Body Snatcher, The Falcon in San Francisco, The Exile, The Sword of Monte Cristo, The Black Castle* and *The French Line,* among others.

CORDELIER, Jeanne (1944—). **French novelist.** Born 1944 in Paris, France. ❖ Lived in Sweden for 17 years before returning to rural France; also lived in Vietnam (1997–99), Ethiopia, and Albania; works include *La Dérobade* (1976), based on her experiences as prostitute in Paris, *La Passagère* (1981), *Chez L'Espérance* (1982), *Malparade* (1985), *Sang et plumes* (1987), *La mort de Blanche-Neige* (1993), *La passion selon Gatien* (1995) and *L'Instruit* (2003).

CORDELL, Cathleen (1915–1997). **American stage and screen actress.** Born May 21, 1915, in Brooklyn, NY; died Aug 19, 1997, in Los Angeles, California; trained at Royal Academy of Dramatic Art. ❖ Began career as a juvenile lead in *It's You I Want* at Weston-super-Mare, England (1933); made London debut in *Inside the Room* (1934), followed by *Arms and the Man* and *Design for Living;* made Broadway debut in Maurice Evans' *Richard II* (1937), followed by *Love of a Woman, Golden Wings, Yesterday's Magic, Sheppey, While the Sun Shines* and *The Linden Tree,* among others; made film debut (1938) and was often featured in tv episodes.

CORDIÈRE, La Belle (c. 1523–1566). *See Labé, Louise.*

CORDUA, Beatrice (1943—). **German ballet dancer.** Born Mar 12, 1943, in Hamburg, Germany. ❖ Made professional debut with Hamburg State Opera Ballet (1959); also danced with state ballets in Cologne and Frankfurt; performed numerous ballets and divertissements by American John Neumeier, including *Firebird* (1970), *Rondo* (1970), *Romeo and Juliet* (1971), *Daphnis and Chloe* (1971) and *Sacre du Printemps* (1972).

CORELLI, Marie (1855–1924). **English novelist.** Name variations: Mary MacKay or Mackay; Minnie Mackay. Born Mary Mills in Bayswater, London, England (some sources cite Perth, Scotland), May 1, 1855; died in Stratford-upon-Avon, England, April 21, 1924; dau. of Charles Mackay (1814–1889, poet and journalist) and Mary Ellen Mills; lived with Bertha Vyver in Stratford-upon-Avon. ❖ One of the most popular novelists in late-19th-century England, writing under pseudonym Marie Corelli, 1st published *A Romance of Two Worlds* (1886), a well-written narrative that had a large sale; came to prominence with 3rd book, *Thelma: A Society Novel* (1887); devoted rest of life trying to satisfy the public clamor for similar works, including *Vendetta* (1886), *Ardath: The Story of a Dead Self* (1889), *Barabbas: A Dream of the World's Tragedy* (1893), *The Sorrows of Satan* (1895), *The Mighty Atom* (1896), *Ziska* (1897) and *Temporal Power* (1902). ❖ See also E. Bigland, *Marie Corelli* (1953); Brian Masters, *Now Barabbas was a Rotter: The Extraordinary Life of Marie Corelli* (1978); W.S. Scott, *Marie Corelli* (1955); Bertha Vyver, *Memoirs of Marie Corelli* (1930); and *Women in World History*.

CORI, Gerty T. (1896–1957). American physician and biochemist.
Pronunciation: KOR-ee. Born Gerta Theresa Radnitz, Aug 15, 1896, in Prague, Austro-Hungarian Empire (now Czech Republic); died in St. Louis, Missouri, Oct 26, 1957; dau. of Otto (chemist and businessman) and Martha (Neustadt) Radnitz; German University of Prague Medical School, MD, 1920. m. Carl Ferdinand Cori, Aug 5, 1920; children: Carl Thomas Cori, 1936. ❖ Scientist, known for her research on the metabolism of carbohydrates in animals, who was the 1st woman from America and the 3rd woman worldwide to earn the Nobel Prize; began career as a student assistant at German University of Prague (1917–19); worked as assistant at Children's Hospital of Vienna (1920–22); was assistant pathologist (1922–25) and assistant of biochemistry (1925–31) at New York State Institute for the Study of Malignant Diseases; was assistant professor at University of Buffalo (1930–31); at Washington University School of Medicine, St. Louis, worked as research associate in pharmacology (1931–43), as associate professor of biochemistry (1943), and full professor (1947); provided the decisive influence to study enzymes with husband and was the major contributor to most of the their papers (1938–39); with husband, discovered the enzyme phosphorylase, which breaks down glycogen into the Cori ester (1939), a discovery that led to the enzymatic synthesis of glycogen in a test tube, which was the 1st bioengineering of a large molecule in a test tube, an event of great import because it disproved the thought that large molecules could only be made in living cells; with husband, was awarded the Nobel Prize for medicine (1947) for discovering the enzymes that convert glycogen into glucose and then back again into glycogen (the process by which glycogen is converted to sugar); encouraged women scientists and provided extra support to those who had children. ❖ See also *Women in World History.*

CORINNA (fl. 5th or 3rd c. BCE). Ancient Greek poet of Boeotia. Name variations: Korinna; nicknamed Myia, "Fly." Born in either the 5th or the 3rd century BCE in Tanagra or Thebes in Boeotia; dau. of Acheloodorus and Procatia; pupil of Myrtis(?), another female poet of Boeotia (almost all details of Corinna's career and dates are doubtful or disputed). ❖ Is said to have been the teacher of the lyric poet Pindar and to have defeated him in competition. In antiquity, 5 books of her poetry, perhaps called *weroia,* "Tales" or "Narratives" on mythical subjects were collected; only fragments remain, 3 of which are fairly large and continuous; these are collected (with a translation) in *Greek Lyric IV: Bacchylides, Corinna, and Others* (Harvard U. Press, 1992). ❖ See also *Women in World History.*

CORIO, Ann (1914–1999). American burlesque star. Born Nov 29, 1914, in Hartford, Connecticut; died Mar 1, 1999, in Englewood, New Jersey; dau. of Italian immigrants; m. 3rd husband Michael P. Iannucci (pro football player). ❖ Star attraction in East Coast burlesque houses for many years; wrote, directed, and appeared in *This Was Burlesque,* a musical satire based on her recollections, which opened off-Broadway (1962), transferred to Broadway (1965), and was revived (1981); made 5 films: *Swamp Women, Jungle Siren, Sarong Girl, Call of the Jungle* and *The Sultan's Daughter.* ❖ See also autobiography *This Was Burlesque* (1968).

CORK, countess of. See *Monckton, Mary (1746–1840).*

CORKLE, Francesca (1952—). American ballet dancer. Born Aug 2, 1952, in Seattle, Washington; dau. of Virginia Ryan Corkle (dancer). ❖ Studied at American Ballet Center and City Center Joffrey Ballet; joined Joffrey and remained there throughout career, creating roles in Gerald Arpino's *Confetti* (1970) and *Kettentanz* (1971), and Joffrey's *Remembrances* (1974) and *Postcards* (1980); was featured in majority of company's repertory works including Balanchine's *Square Dance* and Ruthanna Boris' *Cakewalk.*

CORLETT, Yvette (1929—). See *Williams, Yvette.*

CORLISS, Mrs. Charles Albert (1888–1957). See *Parrish, Anne.*

CORMIER, Lucia M. (1909–1993). American politician. Name variations: Lucia Marie Cormier. Born Nov 20, 1909, in Rumford, Maine, of French-Canadian descent; died Jan 26, 1993 in Daytona Beach, Florida; Columbia University, MA. ❖ Taught French at Rumford's Stephens High; won 6 state elections in Maine including election to House of Representatives (1947); became Democratic minority leader in ME legislature (1960), the 1st woman in either party to become a floor leader in ME; unsuccessfully challenged Margaret Chase Smith in 1st all-female race for US Senate (1960), which was so unique she shared the cover of *Time* with Smith.

CORNARO, Caterina (1454–1510). Queen of Cyprus. Name variations: Catherine Cornaro. Born 1454 in Venice; died July 5, 1510, in Asolo, Italy; m. James II the Bastard, king of Cyprus (r. 1460–1473), 1472;

children: James III (b. 1472), king of Cyprus (r. 1473–1474). ❖ Came from the powerful Cornaro family of Venice; at 14, married James II, king of Cyprus (1472); husband died (1473); gave birth to James III, causing a power struggle between her and the Cyprian nobility to control the regency; after 3 years of war, was restored to the throne with aid of her native Venice, though son died soon after; retained position as sole ruler of island for 14 more years, though increasingly as a puppet of the Venetian government; forced to abdicate and deed the island of Cyprus to Venice (1488), returned to Italy and took up residence on her fief of Asolo, where she established a brilliant court. ❖ See also *Women in World History.*

CORNARO PISCOPIA, Elena Lucretia (1646–1684). Italian philosopher and writer. Name variations: Helena. Born Elena Lucretia Cornaro Piscopia in 1646; dau. of John Baptist Cornaro Piscopia (procurator of St. Mark's); University of Padua, PhD, 1678. ❖ Was the 1st woman to receive a doctorate in philosophy (the University of Padua did not award a doctorate to another woman for 70 years). ❖ See also *Women in World History.*

CORNELIA (c. 195–c. 115 BCE). Mother of the Gracchi. Name variations: Cornelia Sempronii. Born c. 195 BCE; died c. 115 BCE; 2nd dau. of Publius Cornelius Scipio Africanus (the Roman victor over Hannibal in the 2nd Punic War) and Aemilia; m. Tiberius Sempronius Gracchus, around 175 (died 154 BCE); children: 12, though only Sempronia, Tiberius Gracchus, the younger, and Gaius Gracchus, survived to adulthood. ❖ Roman wife of Tiberius Sempronius Gracchus (one of the most powerful Romans of his generation), mother of the Gracchi (whose careers sparked the revolution that overthrew the Roman Republic), and one of the most influential political and cultural figures of her day; was personally diligent in the raising of her children and was later actively partisan on both her sons' behalf to a degree that was unprecedented; after sons died, retired to Misenum, where she retained a high social and cultural profile presiding over perhaps the era's most influential literary salon, in the process fostering the Greco-Roman amalgam that would dominate the Mediterranean cultural scene for almost 500 years; came to be remembered more for her refined statements on what it was to be a philhellenic—but intensely patriotic—Roman matron than for the specific policies she and her sons once supported. ❖ See also D. Stockton, *The Gracchi* (Oxford, 1979); and *Women in World History.*

CORNELIA (c. 100–68 BCE). Roman noblewoman and wife of emperor Julius Caesar. Born c. 100 BCE; died in 68 BCE; dau. of Lucius Cornelius Cinna; m. Gaius Julius Caesar (c. 100–44 BCE), Roman emperor, in 84 BCE; children: daughter Julia (d. 54 BCE). ❖ With her marriage to Caesar (84), helped to rehabilitate the political fortunes of Caesar's branch of his ancient family; remained important to Caesar throughout his early political career because she linked her husband's fortunes to her father's political faction; died at a young age. ❖ See also *Women in World History.*

CORNELIA (c. 75–after 48 BCE). Roman noblewoman and wife of Pompey the Great. Born c. 75 BCE; died after 48 BCE; dau. of Metellus Scipio; m. Publius Licinius Crassus, in 55 (died 53 BCE); m. Pompey the Great (106–48 BCE), Roman consul, in 52 BCE. ❖ The daughter of Metellus Scipio, a partisan of the 1st Triumvirate (the political alliance consisting of Julius Caesar, Pompey the Great, and Crassus), was famous for her lineage, education, character, beauty and charm; when the political friendship of Caesar and Pompey the Great deteriorated into civil war, strongly supported Pompey, who doted upon her; when, in an effort to resuscitate his rivalry with Caesar, Pompey made his way to Egypt, witnessed his murder from the deck of the ship that had carried them both to Alexandria. ❖ See also *Women in World History.*

CORNELIA (fl. 1st c. BCE). Roman noblewoman. Fl. in 1st century BCE; dau. of Scribonia and one of her two unknown husbands, possibly Cornelius Scipio; m. Paullus Aemilius Lepidus (consul); children: 2 sons, Paullus and Lepidus. ❖ After her death, the famous poet Propertius was commissioned to write an elegy to help assuage her husband's grief. ❖ See also *Women in World History.*

CORNELISEN, Ann (1926–2003). American writer. Born Nov 12, 1926, Cleveland, Ohio; raised in Chicago, Illinois; died Nov 12, 2003, in Rome, Georgia; earned a degree from Vassar College; married briefly and divorced; no children. ❖ Expatriate American writer, moved to southern Italy after divorce (1954) to pursue archaeology; lived for 20 years in the region of Abruzzi; served as a social worker for the British Save the Children Fund in a poverty-stricken village, resulting in her best-known book, *Torregreca: Life, Death, Miracles* (1969); went from village to village to set up nurseries; also wrote *Vendetta of Silence* (1971), *Women of the Shadows* (1976), *Strangers and Pilgrims* (1980), and the novel, *Any Four Women Could Rob the Bank of Italy* (1983). ❖ See also memoir *Where It All Began: Italy, 1954* (1990).

CORNELIUS, Kathy (1932—). American golfer. Name variations: Katherine Cornelius. Born Oct 27, 1932, in Boston, Massachusetts; attended Florida Southern College; children: Kay Cornelius (golfer). ❖ Won the Southern Amateur (1952); won US Women's Open (1956), runner-up (1965); joined LPGA tour (1957); won Cosmopolitan Open (1959) and Tippecanoe (1961); was co-winner, with Betsy Rawls, of the Zaharias (1962); won the Sealy-Faberge (1973).

CORNELIUS, Ruth (1900–1998). *See Clifford, Ruth.*

CORNELL, Katharine (1893–1974). American actress. Name variations: 1st name often misspelled Katherine. Born Katharine Cornell in Berlin, Germany, Feb 16, 1893; died in Vineyard Haven, Massachusetts, June 9, 1974; dau. of Peter C. Cornell (physician) and Alice Gardner Plimpton Cornell; m. Guthrie McClintic (director), Sept 8, 1921; no children. ❖ Actress of extraordinary range who competed for the title "First Lady of the American Theater" and helped create its Golden Age, a period dominated almost exclusively by great actresses; made debut with Washington Square Players in *Bushido* in NY (1916); came to attention of critics in Broadway production of *A Bill of Divorcement* (1921); began appearing in plays produced by husband, including *The Way Things Happen* (1924); triumphed in title role of Shaw's *Candida* (1924), then starred in *The Green Hat* (1925), *The Letter* (1927), *The Age of Innocence* (1928) and *Dishonored Lady* (1930); had greatest success with *The Barretts of Wimpole Street* (1931); embarked on grand tour of US, giving 225 performances in 77 cities (1933–34), doing more than any other actress to raise the standards of provincial audiences, in an era when theater had largely given way to the motion picture; appeared in *St. Joan* (1936), another triumph; also starred in *Wingless Victory* (1936), *Herod and Mariamne* (1938), *No Time for Comedy* (1939), *The Doctor's Dilemma* (1941), *The Three Sisters* (1942), *Lovers and Friends* (1943), *Antigone* (1946), *Antony and Cleopatra* (1947), *The Constant Wife* (1951), and *Dear Liar* (1959–60); retired (1961). Received Drama League Award for performance as Juliet in *Romeo and Juliet* (1935). ❖ See also memoirs, *I Wanted to Be an Actress* (Random House) and *Curtain Going Up* (1943); Tad Mosel with Gertrude Macy, *The World and Theater of Katharine Cornell* (1978); Guthrie McClintic, *Me and Kit* (Little, Brown, 1955); and *Women in World History*.

CORNELL, Sheila (1962—). American softball player. Name variations: Sheila Douty. Born Feb 26, 1962, in Diamond Bar, California. ❖ Won team gold medals at Atlanta Olympics (1996) and Sydney Olympics (2000).

CORNELYS, Theresa (1723–1797). Italian dancer, singer and madame. Name variations: Madame Cornelys; Teresa Cornelys. Born Teresa Imer in Venice in 1723; died in Fleet Prison, London, Aug 19, 1797; grew up in father's commedia dell'arte troupe; m. Angelo Pompetai (dancer); m. Cornelis di Rigerbosm. ❖ Made English debut as a vocalist in a season of operas by Wilhelm Christof Gluck at the King's Theatre (1746); was appointed "directice des spectacles en Flendres" (Austrian Netherlands); as a noted manager of public assemblies at Carlisle House (Soho, London), organized balls, concerts, and masquerades, and performed as a singer; also provided beautiful ladies of the night at hefty prices at her celebrated "salon," attended by royalty and members of Parliament; accused of presenting dramatic performance without a license, saw house closed down by Magistrate Sir John Fielding as a pretext for further investigation; brought up on charges of running a disorderly house, had to sell the Carlisle House furniture for needed cash; fell into obscurity, and, under name Mrs. Smith, sold donkey's milk at Knightsbridge for some time; was sent to debtor's prison in Fleet Street (1797); died there before a release could be arranged.

CORNESCOU, Irina Soltanovna (1916—). Soviet spy. Name variations: Mademoiselle or Mlle Germaine. Born Oct 1916; dau. of Soltan Cornescou and Marfa Kalidze; graduate of Moscow University with a diploma in French. ❖ Served as assistant to head of French Section at Soviet Ministry for Foreign Affairs (1941–45); at 31, entered Stiepnaya, Soviet Secret Service spy school, and took the name Mademoiselle Germaine; at 41 (1957), went to France where she served as French governess to a Belgian family while working as a master spy; became a Resident Network Operator in Brussels, where she set up an espionage network to gain information about Belgian military and research stations;

arrested with her second-in-command Paul Veken by counter-intelligence agents.

CORNET, Lynda (1962—). Dutch rower. Born Jan 26, 1962. ❖ At Los Angeles Olympics, won a bronze medal in coxed eights (1984).

CORNETT, Leanza (1971—). Miss America and TV host. Name variations: Leanza Cornett Steines. Born June 10, 1971, in Big Stone Gap, Virginia; attended Rollins College; m. Mark Steines (anchor on "Entertainment Tonight"); children: 2 sons. ❖ Named Miss America (1993), representing Florida; brought attention to AIDS epidemic; served as correspondent for "Entertainment Tonight" and "Good Day LA" for KTTV-Los Angeles; hosted "New Attitudes" for Lifetime network and "What's On" for TV Guide channel.

CORNFIELD, Ellen (1948—). American modern dancer. Born Mar 26, 1948, in Washington, DC. ❖ Trained with Merce Cunningham and Carolyn Brown; joined Cunningham company (mid-1970s) and created roles in his *Westbeth* (1975), *Torse* (1976), and *Travelogue* (1977); choreographed and presented own works, including *Performance No. 1* (1980) and *Three Times 3* (1980); founded Cornfield Dance (1989), which performed throughout Japan, in NY, and at Jacob's Pillow, among other venues; held teaching residencies at North Carolina School of the Arts, SUNY Purchase, Ohio State University, and University of California at Berkeley.

CORNFORD, Frances Crofts (1886–1960). British poet. Name variations: Frances Crofts Darwin. Born Frances Crofts Darwin, Mar 30, 1886, in Cambridge, England; died Aug 19, 1960, in Cambridge; dau. of Francis Darwin and Ellen Crofts Darwin; granddau. of Charles Darwin; m. John M. Cornford, 1909; children: 5, including John Cornford (poet who died in Spanish Civil War). ❖ Works of poetry include *Poems* (1910), *Autumn Midnight* (1923), *Mountains and Molehills* (1934), *Collected Poems* (1954) and *On a Calm Shore* (1960); translations include (with E.P. Salaman) *Poems from the Russian* (1943) and (with S. Spender) *Le Dur desir du durer* by Paul Eluard (1950). ❖ See also J. Galassi, ed., *Understand the Weapon, Understand the Wound: Selected Writings of John Cornford with Some Letters of Frances Cornford* (Carcanet, 1976).

CORNIFICIA (b. 160). Roman noblewoman. Born in 160 CE; dau. of Faustina II (130–175 CE) and Marcus Aurelius, Roman emperor (r. 161–180).

CORNIOLEY, Pearl (b. 1914). *See Witherington, Pearl.*

CORNISH, Mary (c. 1899–?). British heroine. Born Mary A.C. Cornish c. 1899. ❖ A 41-year-old London music teacher, was on board the passenger liner SS *City of Benares* (1927), embarking from Liverpool to Canada with 90 evacuee children (Friday, Sept 13, 1940); when the ship was sunk by a German U-boat 4 days later, risked her life protecting the girls in her charge and entertained the children in the lifeboat for 8 days; awarded the George Cross (1941). ❖ See also Elspeth Huxley, *Atlantic Ordeal: The Story of Mary Cornish* (1942).

CORNWALL, Anne (1897–1980). American silent-film actress. Born Jan 17, 1897, in Brooklyn, NY; died Mar 2, 1980, in Van Nuys, California. ❖ Former chorine, began work at Universal as an ingenue; films include *The Knife, The World to Live In, La La Lucille, Her Gilden Cage, Dulcy, Under Western Skies* and *College.*

CORNWALL, countess of.
See Clare, Margaret de (1249–1313).
See Clare, Margaret de (c. 1293–1342).

CORNWALL, duchess of.
See Sancha of Provence (c. 1225–1261).
See Parker-Bowles, Camilla (1947—).

CORNWALL, Evelyn (1947—). *See St. James, Lyn.*

CORNWALLIS, C.F. (1786–1858). English author. Name variations: Caroline Frances Cornwallis. Born in 1786; died at Lidwells, in Kent, Jan 8, 1858; dau. of William Cornwallis (rector of Wittersham and Elham in Kent). ❖ Acquired a thorough knowledge of Latin and Greek and, from an early age, carried on a correspondence with many eminent persons; her initial work, *Philosophical Theories and Philosophical Experience by a Pariah* (1842), was the 1st of a series of 20 "Small Books on Great Subjects," which included the *Connection of Physiology and Intellectual Science, Ragged Schools, Criminal Law, Greek Philosophy* and the *History and Influence of Christian Opinions*; also published *Pericles, a Tale of Athens* (1847).

CORNWALLIS-WEST, Mrs. George (1854–1921). *See Churchill, Jennie Jerome.*

CORNWALLIS-WEST, Maria or Mary (1873–1943). *See Daisy, Princess.*

COROMBONA, Vittoria (c. 1557–1585). *See Accoramboni, Vittoria.*

CORONADO, Carolina (1820–1911). Spanish writer. Name variations: Victoria Carolina Coronado Romero; Carolina Coronado de Perry. Born Dec 12, 1820, in Almendralejo, near Badajoz, Spain; died Jan 15, 1911; dau. of Nicolás Coronado Gallardo and María Antonia Romero; m. Horatio Justus Perry (American diplomat), 1852; children: Carlos Horacio (b. 1853); Carolina (b. 1857); Matilde (b. 1861). ❖ Published 1st poem (1839), in the magazine *El Piloto* of Madrid; came to prominence with publication of her 1st volume of poetry (1843); wrote profusely for periodicals throughout the Hispanic world and US; moved to Madrid and received from the Artistic and Literary Lyceum a crown of gold and laurel at the hands of Queen Isabella II (1848); became a fixture in the city's literary circles; her lyrical poetry was noted for its liberalism and love of nature; also wrote plays and novels. ❖ See also *Women in World History.*

CORRADI, Doris (1922—). English wireless and cipher operator. Born 1922; m. Guy Corradi (British Merchant Navy Service), 1949. ❖ During WWII, lived in London until air raid demolished house (1940); learned Morse code and wireless operations at Women's Auxiliary Air Force (WAAF); worked as morse slip reader at Chicksands; volunteered to help return Japanese ex-prisoners of war; later worked as cipher and teleprinter operator at Government Communications Headquarters (GCHQ) at Eastcote. Member of Radio Society of Great Britain.

CORREA, Deolinda (fl. 1830). Argentinean unofficial saint. Name variations: María Antonia Deolinda Correa; Difunta Correa (the dead Correa); La Difuntita Correa; or simply Difunta. Lived in Andean province of San Juan. ❖ As legend has it, her family was persecuted by the governor of the province and her father and husband were imprisoned (1830s–40s); fled police and began to search for husband; with newborn baby in her arms, died of thirst and exhaustion in the mountains; when passing mule drivers discovered her body days later, her son was alive, still suckling from her breast; was buried there with the inscription "Difunta Correa"; though never officially recognized as a saint, is held in veneration by thousands who make pilgrimages to the village of Vallecito, where a shrine at her gravesite has grown to 17 chapels and is now known as the Sanctuary of Difunta Correa.

CORREIA, Hélia (1939—). Portuguese novelist. Name variations: Helia Correia. Born 1939 in Portugal. ❖ Novels, which sometimes use Gothic themes and techniques to explore inner lives of characters, especially women, include *O Separar das Águas* (1981), *O Número dos Vivos* (1982), and *Montedemo* (1983), which was adapted for the stage and performed in Lisbon (1987).

CORREIA, Natália (1923–1993). Portuguese poet. Name variations: Natalia de Oliveira Correia. Born Aug 13, 1923, on the island of São Miguel in the Azores; died Mar 16, 1993, in Lisbon, Portugal; educated in Lisbon. ❖ Associated with leftist politics, served as an independent representative in Parliament; wrote reviews and articles for most major Portuguese journals; poetry includes *Rio de Nuvens* (1947), *Passaporte* (1958), *O Vinho e a Lira* (1966), *Mosca Iluminada* (1972), *O Dilúvio d a Pomba* (1979), *A Pécora* (1983), *Sonetos Românticos* (1990) and *Memória da Sombra* (1994); novels include *A sua engloba Aventuras de Um Pequeno Herói* (1945), *A Madona* (1968) and *As Núpcias* (1990); edited several critical works and anthologies, including *Surrealismo na Poesia Portuesa* (1973), and wrote several plays, including *O Encoberto;* also was responsible for publishing the controversial *Novas Cartas Portuguesas* (*The Three Marias: The New Portuguese Letters,* 1975), which set off a fire storm.

CORRI, Adrienne (1930—). Scottish stage, tv and screen actress. Born Adrienne Riccoboni, Nov 13, 1930, in Glasgow, Scotland; m. Daniel Massey (actor), 1961 (div. 1967). ❖ Made London stage debut (1948); made film debut in *The Romantic Age* (1949), followed by *Quo Vadis?, The Little Kidnappers, Make Me an Offer, Three Men in a Boat, The Big Chance, The Tell-Tale Heart, Bunny Lake is Missing, A Study in Terror, Doctor Zhivago, Revenge of the Pink Panther* and most memorably as Mrs. Alexander in Kubrick's *A Clockwork Orange* (1971), among others; well-known expert on portrait painting, published a book on Gainsborough.

CORRIDON, Marie (1930—). American swimmer. Name variations: Marie Corridon Mortell. Born Feb 1930 in Norwalk, Connecticut. ❖

At London Olympics, won a gold medal in 4x100-meter freestyle relay (1948).

CORRIGAN, Mairead (1944—). Irish peace activist. Name variations: Máiread Corrigan; Mairead Corrigan Maguire. Born Mairead Corrigan in Belfast, Northern Ireland, Jan 27, 1944; dau. of a window-cleaning contractor and a housewife; m. Jackie Maguire (her deceased sister's husband); children: Luke, Mark, Joanne, Marie Louise, and John. ❖ With Betty Williams, co-founded the Irish Peace People movement of the mid-1970s, the most successful of several early attempts to create a cross-community alliance against terrorism; in a macabre characterization of the entire Ulster nightmare, sister Anne Maguire was taking her young children for a walk on a suburban street (Aug 10, 1976) when a car smashed into them, seriously injuring Maguire and killing all 3 children—Joanne, 8, John (3), and Andrew (6 weeks old); on learning that the terrorist driver of the stolen car was already dead, shot moments before the crash by British soldiers during a running gun-battle, helped to organize the massive public demonstration which took place on the day after the children's funeral, an unusual display of public outrage in that the Catholic women of West Belfast were joined by Protestant women from elsewhere in the city. Received Norwegian People Peace Prize (1976) and Nobel Peace Prize (1976). ❖ See also *Women in World History.*

CORROCK, Susan (1951—). American Alpine skier. Name variations: Susie Corrock-Luby. Born Nov 30, 1951, in Ketchum, Idaho. ❖ Won a bronze medal for downhill at Sapporo Olympics (1972). Inducted into US Ski Hall of Fame (1976).

CORSON, Juliet (1841–1897). American cookery instructor. Born Jan 14, 1841, in Roxbury, Massachusetts; died June 18, 1897, in New York, NY. ❖ Had regular column in *New York Leader* on subjects of interest to women, then became a staff writer for *National Quarterly Review;* became an organizer and secretary of the Free Training School for Women (1873), adding a cooking course (1874); opened the New York Cooking School (1876), which was an instant success; wrote the textbook for the course entitled *Cooking Manual* (1877); worked as editor of *Household Monthly* (1890–91); also wrote *Fifteen Cent Dinners for Families of Six* (1877), *Juliet Corson's New Family Cook Book* (1885) and *Family Living on $500 a Year* (1887), among others. ❖ See also *Women in World History.*

CORSON, Marilyn (1954—). Canadian-American swimmer. Name variations: Marilyn Corson Whitney. Born June 6, 1954, in Ann Arbor, MI; dau. of Bruce Corson and Rose (Mann) Dawson (19122003, swimming coach); granddau. of Matt Mann (University of Michigan swimming coach). ❖ Trained by her mother who coached in Ann Arbor and ran a swimming camp in Ontario for 55 years; swimming for Canada at Mexico City Olympics, won a bronze medal in 4x100-meter freestyle relay (1968).

CORSTON, Jean (1942—). English politician and member of Parliament. Born Jean Parkin, May 5, 1942; m. Christopher Corston, 1961; m. Prof. Peter Townsend, 1985. ❖ Barrister; representing Labour, elected to House of Commons for Bristol East (1992, 1997, 2001); named chair of joint committee on Human Rights (2001); left Parliament (2005).

CORTESA, Valentina (1924—). Italian-born actress. Name variations: Valentina Cortese (Cortesa, in Hollywood films). Born Jan 1, 1924, in Milan, Italy; m. Richard Basehart (actor), 1951 (div. 1960). ❖ Made film debut in Italy in *Orizzonte dipinto* (1940), then played ingenue leads until breakthrough roles of Fantine and Cosette in *I Miserabili* (*Les Miserables,* 1947) and Alida Morrosini in the British film *The Glass Mountain* (1949); had an international career, appearing in such films as Jules Dassin's *Thieves' Highway,* Antonioni's *Le Amiche,* Fellini's *Giulietta degli spiriti,* as well as *House on Telegraph Hill, The Barefoot Contessa, Adriana Lecouvreur, Axel Munthe, Barabbas, The Visit, The Legend of Lylah Clare, The Secret of Santa Vittoria, Madly, The Assassination of Trotsky* and *The Adventures of Baron Munchausen,* among others; also starred in such plays as *Mary Stewart* and *Lulu.* Won Oscar for Best Supporting Actress for performance in Truffaut's *La Nuit Américaine* (1973).

CORTESE, Valentina (1924—). *See Cortesa, Valentina.*

CORTESI, Giuseppina (c. 1800–?). *See Angiolini, Giuseppina.*

CORTESI, Natascia (1971—). *See Leonardi Cortesi, Natascia.*

CORTEZ, Jayne (1936—). African-American poet. Born 1936 in Fort Huachuca, Arizona; m. Ornette Coleman (saxophonist), 1954 (div. 1961); children: son Denardo. ❖ Grew up in Watts section of Los Angeles; moved to New York with son (1967), where she was influenced by activist poets including Amiri Baraka; established publishing company Bola Press (1972); founded band, Firespitters, which combined jazz, funk, and poetry; poetry collections include *Pisstained Stairs and the Monkey Man's Wares* (1969), *Scarifications* (1973), *Festivals and Funerals* (1982), *Poetic Magnetic* (1991), *Coagulations: New and Selected Poems* (1985), *Somewhere in Advance of Nowhere* (1996) and *Jazz Fan Looks Back* (2002). Received Langston Hughes Award and American Book Award.

CORTI, Maria (1915–2002). Italian novelist and literary critic. Born 1915 in Milan, Italy; died Feb 22, 2002. ❖ Was a professor of Italian at University of Pavia; fiction includes *L'ora di tutti* (1962), *Il ballo dei sapienti* (1966), and *Il canto delle sirene* (1989); criticism includes *Metodi e fantasmi* (1969), *Dante a un nuovo crocevia* (1981), and *Percorsi dell'invenzione* (1993). Awarded Premio della Presidenza del Consiglio dei Ministri per la Letteratura (1990).

CORTIN, Hélène (1972—). French rower. Name variations: Helene Cortin. Born 1972 in France. ❖ With Christine Gosse, won World championships (1993, 1994); won a bronze medal for coxless pair at Atlanta Olympics (1996).

CORTINES, Cristina (1939—). *See Gutiérrez-Cortines, Cristina.*

CORTINES, Júlia (1868–1948). Brazilian poet. Name variations: Julia Cortines. Born Júlia Cortines Laxe in 1868; died 1948; grew up in Niterói, Rio de Janeiro; never married. ❖ Became a teacher at 12; traveled in Europe and published weekly column about travels in the newspaper, *O País;* writings include *Versos* (1894).

CORY, Adela Florence (1865–1904). *See Nicolson, Adela Florence.*

CORY, Annie Sophie (1868–1952). British novelist. Name variations: (pseudonyms) Victoria Cross; Vivian or Vivien Cory; Victoria Cory; V.C. Griffin; Bal Krishna. Born Oct 1, 1868, in Punjab, India; died Aug 2, 1952, in Milan, Italy; dau. of Arthur and Elizabeth Fanny Griffin Cory; sister of Adela Florence Nicolson (1865–1904, poet). ❖ One of the most outspoken of the New Woman writers, wrote *The Woman Who Didn't* (1895), *A Girl of the Klondike* (1899), *Anna Lombard* (1901), *Six Women* (1906), *Life's Shop-Window* (1907), *Five Nights* (1908), *The Life Sentence* (1912), *Electric Love* (1929), *A Husband's Holiday* (1932) and *Jim* (1937), among others; her books, celebrated for their treatment of unconventional and exotic themes, have been translated into French, Norwegian and Italian.

CORY, Victoria (1868–1952). *See Cory, Annie Sophie.*

CORY, Vivian or Vivien (1868–1952). *See Cory, Annie Sophie.*

COSBY, Camille (1945—). African-American philanthropist, entrepreneur and foundation executive. Born Camille Olivia Hanks, 1945, in Washington, DC; dau. of Guy and Catherine Hanks; University of Massachusetts, PhD, 1922; m. Bill Cosby (comedian), 1964; children: Erika, Erinn, Ensa, Evin and Ennis Cosby (killed 1997). ❖ Longtime advocate for education and supporter of African-American colleges; with husband, donated $20 million to Spelman College (1988) and over $70 million to others; as husband's business manager, oversees all philanthropic and financial matters; serves as president of COC Productions (for film) and C&J Productions (for stage); produced the documentary *No Dreams Deferred* (1994).

COSGRAVE, Niamh (1964—). Irish politician. Born Oct 9, 1964, in Dublin, Ireland; dau. of Michael Joe Cosgrave (TD); m. Myles Dunne. ❖ Representing Fine Gael, nominated to the Seanad by Taoiseach John Bruton (Casual Vacancy, 1997); campaigned for restitution for people who acquired Hepatitis C from contaminated blood.

COSSEY, Alice Eleanor (1879–1970). New Zealand tailor and union leader. Born Nov 8, 1879, at Drury, Auckland, New Zealand; died Mar 14, 1970, at Drury; dau. of Solomon Cossey (shoemaker) and Martha Bragg (Martin) Cossey. ❖ Successful labor organizer and activist who advocated for higher wages and equal working conditions for women; one of 1st professional female unionists in New Zealand; became secretary of Auckland Tailoresses' Union (ATU, 1917); administered ATU for 38 years without involving it in a strike; made justice of peace (1931). ❖ See also *Dictionary of New Zealand Biography* (Vol. 3).

COSSGROVE, Selina (1849–1929). New Zealand scout leader. Name variations: Selina Robertson. Born Selina Robertson, probably May 21, 1849, at Cairneyhill, Perthshire, Scotland; died Oct 23, 1929, at Christchurch, New Zealand; dau. of William (farmer) and Catherine (Campbell) Robertson; m. David Cossgrove (teacher and scout leader), 1875 (died 1920); children: 3 daughters, 5 sons. ❖ Instructed Maori women in child care, hygiene and health; with husband, was instrumental in establishment of New Zealand's Girl Peace Scouts' Association (c. 1908). ❖ See also *Dictionary of New Zealand Biography* (Vol. 3).

COSSINGTON-SMITH, Grace (1892–1984). *See Smith, Grace Cossington.*

COSSON DE LA CRESSONIÈRE, Charlotte Cathérine (1740–1813). French poet. Name variations: Charlotte Catherine Cosson de La Cressoniere. Born Charlotte Catherine Cosson in 1740 in Mézières, France; died 1813. ❖ Wrote poems on public events, including *Lamentations sur la mort du dauphin* (1766) and *Ode sur l'incendie d l'Hotel-Dieu de Paris* (1773); published ballads and allegories in various journals, including *Mercure de France, Journal des Dames* and *L'Année littéraire;* may have collaborated on essay *De l'éducation physique et morale des femmes* (1799).

COSSOTTO, Fiorenza (1935—). Italian mezzo-soprano. Born April 22, 1935, in Crescentino, Vercelli, Italy; graduate of Verdi Conservatory in Turin, 1956; m. Ivo Vinco (bass singer). ❖ One of the greatest mezzo-sopranos of late 20th-century, made opera debut as Sister Matilde in 1st performance of Poulenc's *Les dialogues des Carmélites* at La Scala (1957); came to prominence at La Scala with *Tosca* (1958), followed by performance as Neris in Cherubini's *Medea,* alongside Maria Callas at Covent Garden (1959); best known for fiery Verdi roles as Azucena, Amneris, Lady Macbeth, and Eboli; also known for *Adriana Lecouvreur, Cavalleria Rusticana, Norma, Favorita, Barbiere di Siviglia* and *Gioconda.*

COSTA, Emília de Sousa (1877–1957). Portuguese biographer and children's writer. Born 1877 in Portugal; died 1957. ❖ Best known for works published in children's series *Biblioteca Infantil* and *Biblioteca des Pequeninos;* translated *Grimm's Fairy Tales;* also wrote biographies and feminist works, including *Idéias Antigas da Mulher Moderna* (1923) and *Olhai a Malícia e a Maldade das Mulheres* (1932); worked as teacher and on behalf of working-class girls.

COSTA, Maria Velho da (1938—). *See Velho da Costa, Maria.*

COSTA, Marlenis (1973—). Cuban volleyball player. Name variations: Marlenys Costa Blanco. Born July 30, 1973, in Cuba. ❖ At Barcelona Olympics, won a gold medal in team competition (1992); won team gold medals at Atlanta Olympics (1996) and Sydney Olympics (2000).

COSTA, Renata (1986—). Brazilian soccer player. Born July 8, 1976, in Paran, Brazil. ❖ Won a team silver medal at Athens Olympics (2004).

COSTANZA. *Variant of Constance and Constanza.*

COSTANZA (1182–1202). Portuguese princess. Born May 1182; died Aug 3, 1202, at Lorvano; dau. of Douce of Aragon (1160–1198) and Sancho I (1154–1211 or 1212), king of Portugal (r. 1185–1211 or 1212).

COSTELLO, Dolores (1905–1979). American actress. Born Sept 17, 1905, in Pittsburgh, Pennsylvania; died Mar 1, 1979, in Fallbrook, California; dau. of Maurice Costello (1877–1950, silent-screen actor) and Mae Costello (c. 1882–1929, actress); sister of Helene Costello (1903–1957, an actress); m. John Barrymore, 1928 (div. 1935); m. John Vruwink (her obstetrician), 1939 (div. 1951); children: (1st m.) John Barrymore Jr. (b. 1932, actor); Dolores Ethel Mae Barrymore (b. 1933). ❖ As a child, was 1st seen in the Vitagraph films with sister Helen (later Helene) that starred their matinee-idol father Maurice Costello (c. 1911); came to prominence as John Barrymore's leading lady in *The Sea Beast* (silent adaptation of *Moby Dick,* 1924); was a headliner (1920s), starring in *Manon Lescaut* (1926), *Bride of the Storm* (1926), *Tenderloin* (1928), *Old San Francisco* (1927), *Madonna of Avenue A* (1929) and *Expensive Woman* (1931), among others; also appeared in *Little Lord Fauntleroy* (1936) and *The Magnificent Ambersons* (1942). ❖ See also *Women in World History.*

COSTELLO, Eileen (1870–1962). Irish politician and folklorist. Name variations: Edith Drury. Born Edith Drury, 1870, in London, England; died Mar 14, 1962; dau. of Welsh father and Limerick mother; m. Dr. Thomas Bodkin Costello (antiquarian), 1903. ❖ Active in the Irish Revival Movement; representing Fine Gael, elected by the Dáil for the 1st to 5th Triennial periods of the Seanad (1922–36); collected a book of Connacht folksongs; organized Red Cross services during WWII; championed the cause of unmarried mothers.

COSTELLO, Helene (1903–1957). American actress. Born June 21, 1903, in New York, NY; died Jan 26, 1957, in Los Angeles, California; dau. of Maurice Costello (1877–1950, silent-screen actor) and Mae Costello (actress); sister of Dolores Costello (1905–1979); m. George Lee LeBlanc (div.); m. John Regan, 1927 (div. 1929); m. Lowell Sherman, 1930 (div. 1932); m. Arturo del Barrio, 1933. ❖ For a short time, had a film career that rivaled her sister's; starred in 1st Vitaphone all-talking feature *Lights of New York* (1928); other films include *The Man on the Box* (1925), *Don Juan* (1926), *In Old Kentucky* (1927), *The Heart of Maryland* (1927), *Midnight Taxi* (1928) and *The Circus Kid* (1928).

COSTELLO, Louisa Stuart (1799–1870). Irish poet, novelist, travel writer, essayist, and miniature painter. Born Louisa Stuart Costello, 1799, in Ireland; died April 24, 1870, in Boulogne, France; dau. of Col. James Francis Costello, army officer, and Elizabeth Tothridge; sister of Dudley Costello (travel writer, died 1865); never married; no children. ❖ One of the most popular writers of her day, especially known for her travel writing; moved to Paris following death of father (1814), where she supported mother and brother by painting miniatures; published 1st collection of poetry *Maid of Cypress Isle* (1815); moved to London (1820); came to prominence with *Songs of a Stranger* (1825); other writings include *Specimens of the Early Poetry of France* (1835), *Falls, Lakes and Mountains of North Wales* (1845), *Tour To and From Venice, by the Vaudois and the Tyrol* (1846), *Memoirs of Anne, Duchess of Brittany* (1855), and 4-vol. *Memoirs of Eminent Englishwomen* (1844); novels include *The Queen's Poisoner, or, France in the Sixteenth Century* (1841) and *The Contrasts of Life* (1848).

COSTELLOE, Ray (c. 1887–1940). *See Strachey, Ray.*

COSTER, Esther (c. 1835–1911). *See Seager, Esther.*

COSTER, Mary (1821–1910). *See Wallis, Mary Ann Lake.*

COTHRAN, Shirley (c. 1953—). Miss America. Name variations: Shirley Cothran-Barret. Born c. 1953 in Denton, Texas; Texas Womans University, PhD in Education; m. Richard K. Barret, 1976; children: David, Julia, John, Mark. ❖ Named Miss America (1975), representing Texas.

COSTIAN, Daniela (1965—). Australian discus thrower. Born April 30, 1965, in Queensland, Australia. ❖ At Barcelona Olympics, won a bronze medal in discus throw (1992); placed 1st in discus in Commonwealth Games (1994); won 7 national titles in discus and 3 in shot put.

COSTIE, Candace (1963—). American synchronized swimmer. Name variations: Candy Costie; Candy Costie Burke. Born Mar 12, 1963, in Seattle, Washington; attended University of Arizona; m. 2nd husband Fred Merrill Jr.; children: 2. ❖ Had 10-year partnership with Tracie Ruiz; at Los Angeles Olympics, won a gold medal in duet, the 1st Olympics which included the sport (1984); won gold in duet and silver in team at Pan American Games (1983) and 4 US national championships in duet.

COSWAY, Maria (1759–1838). English-Italian painter and musician. Name variations: Maria Cecilia Louisa Hadfield Cosway; Maria Hadfield. Born Maria Cecilia Louisa Hadfield, 1759, in Florence, Italy; died Jan 5, 1838, at Lodi, Italy; dau. of English parents; sister of Charlotte Hadfield (who m. William Combe, writer) and George Hadfield (architect); had Roman Catholic convent education; studied in Italy and England; m. Richard Cosway (famous English miniature painter), Jan 18, 1781; children: daughter (died young). ❖ At 19, elected a member of Academy of Fine Arts in Florence; following father's death (1778), moved to England at invitation of her friend Angelica Kauffman, and exhibited at Royal Academy (1781–1801); was also a composer, musician and authority on girls' education; often traveled to Paris and was friends with notables on the French scene, including Jacques-Louis David; met Thomas Jefferson during his tenure as US minister to France (1786) and they would continue to correspond (Jefferson seemed romantically inclined towards her); with husband's financial help, founded a convent school for girls in Lodi; after he died, returned to Italy and her school, which is still flourishing; for her work, was created a baroness of the Austrian Empire by Francis I. ❖ See also Gerald Barnett, *Richard and Maria Cosway: A Biography* and film *Jefferson in Paris.*

COTERA, Martha (1938—). Chicana feminist and civil-rights activist. Born Jan 17, 1938, in Nuevo Casas Grandes, Chihuahua, Mexico; attended college in Texas, earning MA in education; m. Juan Cotera; children: Juan Javier Cotera (murdered in a carjacking, 1997). ❖ At 8, moved to El Paso, Texas, with family; for over 30 years, worked as a librarian and information specialist at city and state libraries in Texas; became a leader in the Chicano movement (1960s) and published *Diosa y Hembra: The History and Heritage of Chicanas in the U.S.;* co-founded the La Raza Unida Party (1970); owned and directed the Chicana Learning and Research Center.

COTES, Sara Jeannette Duncan (d. 1922). *See Duncan, Sara Jeannette.*

COTRUBAS, Ileana (1939—). Romanian soprano. Born Ileana Galati in Romania, June 9, 1939; studied in Budapest with Elenescu and Stroescu. ❖ Made debut in Bucharest (1964); spent 3 years at Frankfurt Opera (1968–71); sang Second Boy in *Die Zauberflöte* (*The Magic Flute,* 1967) and within 2 years was performing at Glyndebourne (1969); appeared at Covent Garden, Paris Opéra, La Scala, and Metropolitan, often in young heroine roles; sang Tatyana, Violetta, Adina, Norina, Amina, Antonia, and Manon, among others; often recorded, especially Mozart; retired (1989). ❖ See also *Women in World History.*

COTTEE, Kay (1954—). Australian sailor. Born Kay McLaren, Jan 25, 1954, in Sydney, Australia; grew up in southern Sydney, Botany Bayside, suburb of Sans Souci; m. Peter Sutton (tv producer); children: son Lee (b. 1993). ❖ Yachtswoman, was the 1st woman to sail nonstop around the world, solo (Nov 1987–June 1988), sailing for 189 days aboard her 38-foot yacht *Blackmore's First Lady,* covering 25,000 nautical miles. Received several honors, including the Australian of the Year Award (1988). ❖ See also memoirs *First Lady* and *All at Sea on Land.*

COTTEN, Elizabeth (c. 1893–1987). African-American folksinger and composer. Name variations: Libba Cotten; Elizabeth Cotton; Sis Nevilles. Born Elizabeth Nevilles, Jan 4 (or 5), 1893 or 1895, in Chapel Hill, North Carolina; died June 29, 1987, in Syracuse, NY; m. Frank Cotten, c. 1910. ❖ Known for composition "Freight Train" and her left-handed, upside-down guitar picking, did not begin performing until age 60; worked as a domestic throughout most of life; after moving to Washington, DC (1940s), met Seeger family and began working in their home; encouraged by Seegers, began to perform publicly (late 1950s); recorded several folk-music albums and appeared at many colleges, festivals and clubs (1958–80s); composed other songs, including "Shake, Sugaree," "Oh, Babe, It Ain't No Lie," "I'm Going Away," and "Washington Blues." Received Burl Ives Award from National Folk Festival Association (1972) and National Endowment for the Arts National Heritage Fellowship Award; was oldest person honored with Grammy Award, for *Elizabeth Cotten Live!* (1984/85?); included among 75 influential African-American women in photo documentary *I Dream a World;* listed among "The 100 Greatest Guitarists of the 20th Century" by *Musician* magazine (1993). ❖ See also *Women in World History.*

COTTEN, Libba (c. 1893–1987). *See Cotten, Elizabeth.*

COTTEN, Sallie Southall (1846–1929). American club woman. Born Sallie Sims Southall, June 13, 1846, in Brunswick Co., Virginia; died May 4, 1929, in Winchester, Massachusetts; dau. of Thomas James Southall and Susannah Swepson (Sims) Southall; m. Robert Randolph Cotten, Mar 14, 1866 (died Aug 1928); children: 9. ❖ Leader in woman's club movement in North Carolina, served as community leader in Pitt County; appointed a "lady manager" of Chicago World's Fair (1893); helped organize North Carolina Federation of Women's Clubs (1902) and served as head until 1913.

COTTENJÉ, Mireille (1933—). Flemish novelist and playwright. Name variations: Mireille Cottenje. Born Nov 18, 1933, in Moeskroen, Netherlands. ❖ Worked as nurse in Zaire; novels, which are often semi-autobiographical, include *Dagboek van Carla* (1968), *Ewige zomer* (*Eternal Summer,* 1969), *Het grote onrecht* (1973), *Lava* (1973), *Kort lang, lang kort* (1974), *Dertien mannen aan tafel* (1978), *De verkeerde minnaar* (1982), *Te klein voor de waarheid* (1987) and *Wisselspoor* (1991).

COTTIN, Marie (1770–1807). *See Cottin, Sophie.*

COTTIN, Sophie (1770–1807). French novelist. Name variations: Sophie Risteau Cottin; Marie Cottin. Born 1770 in Tonneins, Lot-et-Garonne, France; died in Paris, Aug 25, 1807. ❖ Lived turbulent life in Paris and wrote on themes of passion and romance; wrote sentimental novels *Claire d'Albe* (1799), *Amélie Mansfield* (1803), *Malvina* (1804), *Mathilde, ou mémoires tirés de l'histoire des Croisades* (1805) and *Elisabeth ou les exilés de*

Sibérie (*Elizabeth, or the Exiles of Siberia*, 1806), her best-known work; complete edition of her works published in 5 vols (1817).

COTTON, Elizabeth (c. 1893–1987). *See Cotten, Elizabeth.*

COTTON, Lucy (c. 1891–1948). American stage actress. Born Lucy Cotton Magraw, c. 1891, in Houston, Texas; died Dec 12, 1948, of an overdose of sleeping pills, in Miami Beach, Florida; m. Prince Vladimir Eristavi Tchitcherine; m. Charles Hann; m. Lytton Ament; m. Edward L. Thomas. ❖ Broadway appearances include *The Quaker Girl, Up in Mabel's Room, Turn to the Right* and *Lightnin';* made film debut in *The Fugitive* (1910), followed by 11 others.

COTTON, Mary Ann (1822–1873). English murderer. Name variations: Mary Ann Mowbray. Born Mary Ann Robson in East Rainton, near Durham, England, 1822 (some sources cite 1833); hanged at Durham Co. jail, Mar 24, 1873; m. William Mowbray; m. George Ward (also seen as Wade); m. John Robinson; bigamously m. Frederick Cotton (died Sept 19, 1871); children: (1st m.) 5; (3rd m.) 1 and 4 stepchildren; (4th m.) 1 and 2 stepsons; (with an excise officer named Quick-Manning) 1; possibly others. ❖ Britain's 1st female serial killer, used arsenic to poison an estimated 15 to 20 victims while often benefiting from their wills and insurance; ultimately suspected in deaths of husbands (except for John Robinson), her children (possibly as many as 10), a handful of stepchildren, a lover, a sister-in-law, and her own mother; finally charged with murder after death of stepson Charles Edward Cotton; tried at Durham Assizes for his murder, found guilty and hanged (1873).

COTTON, Priscilla (d. 1664). British religious writer. Died 1664; m. Arthur Cotton. ❖ Wrote Quaker pamphlets arguing for social justice, religious tolerance, and equality of women preachers, including *To the Priests and People of England* (with Mary Cole, 1655), *As I was in the Prison-House* (1656), *A Brief Description by way of Supposition* (1659) and *A Visitation of Love unto all People* (1661).

COTTRELL, Dorothy (1902–1957). Australian journalist, novelist and short-story writer. Born Ida Dorothy Wilkinson, July 16, 1902, in Picton, NSW, Australia; died June 30, 1957; dau. of Walter Barwon and Ida C. Wilkinson; attended Royal Art Society; m. Walter MacKenzie Cottrell, May 21, 1922. ❖ Contracted polio as a child and was forever confined to a wheelchair; went to live at Ularunda station near Morven, Queensland, and married the station bookkeeper (1922); serialized 1st novel, *The Singing Gold,* in *Ladies Home Journal* in US (1927); moved with husband to US where she became a successful journalist and writer; writings include *Earth Battle* (1930) and *The Silent Reefs* (1953); also published 2 children's books, including *Wilderness Orphan;* frequent contributor to *Saturday Evening Post.*

COTTRELL, Violet May (1887–1971). New Zealand writer, poet, and spiritualist. Name variations: Violet May Grainger. Born May 17, 1887, in Napier, New Zealand; died May 28, 1971, in Napier; dau. of George William Grainger (civil engineer) and Eliza Jane (Fleetham) Grainger; m. Horace Spencer Cottrell (salesman), 1915 (died 1960); children: 1 daughter, 1 son. ❖ Wrote on numerous subjects, including health, sex and marriage, philosophy, religion, psychology, economics and war; was a spiritualist (1920s–30s) and contributed writings to *Harbinger of Light;* worked at Rehabilitation Board during WWII and joined New Zealand Women Writers' and Artists' Society (1939); composed brief verses on numerous topics from feminist perspective; contributed substantial work to *Daily Telegraph,* including stories, radio plays, poems, and articles featuring New Zealand sites, bird life, and the Maori. ❖ See also *Dictionary of New Zealand Biography* (Vol. 4).

COUCHMAN, Elizabeth (1876–1982). Australian politician. Name variations: Dame Elizabeth Couchman. Born April 19, 1876, at Geelong, Australia; died Nov 18, 1982; dau. of Elizabeth Mary (Ramsay) Tannock and Archibald Tannock (confectioner); University of Western Australia, BA, 1916; m. Claude Couchman (businessman), 1917 (died 1927); no children. ❖ Influential politician, became president of Australian Women's National League (1927); was the 1st woman to be appointed to the Australian Broadcasting Commission (ABC, 1932), a post she would hold for a decade; was a member of the Australian delegation to the League of Nations (1934); as a Liberal, was a member of the State Executive and State Council and served as the party's Victorian vice-president (1949–55). Appointed Dame of the British Empire (DBE, 1961). ❖ See also *Women in World History.*

COUCY, Isabella de (1332–1382). *See Isabella.*

COUCY, Mary de.
See Mary de Coucy (c. 1220–c. 1260).
See Mary de Coucy (fl. 1300s).

COUCY, Philippa de (fl. 1378). *See Philippa de Coucy.*

COUDRAY, Angelique Marguerite Le Boursier du (1712–1789). *See Du Coudray, Angelique.*

COUDREAU, Octavie (c. 1870–c. 1910). French explorer. Born c. 1870 in France; died c. 1910; m. Henri Coudreau (explorer). ❖ With husband, published 6 vols about travels to French Guiana and Pará, Brazil; after husband died during exploration of tributary of Amazon, completed the journey and published *Voyage au Trombetas;* employed by states of Pará and Amazonas, Brazil, to explore Amazon; published *Voyage au Cuminá* and *Voyage au Rio Curua, á la Mapuera, au Maycurú.*

COUGHLAN, Angela (1952—). Canadian swimmer. Born Oct 1952 in Burlington, Ontario, Canada. ❖ At Mexico City Olympics, won a bronze medal in 4x100-meter freestyle relay (1968).

COUGHLAN, Mary (1965—). Irish politician. Born May 1965 in Cranny, Inver, Co. Donegal, Ireland; dau. of Cathal Coughlan (TD, Donegal South West, 1983–86); m. David Charlton. ❖ Representing Fianna Fáil, elected to the 25th Dáil (1987–89) for Donegal South West; returned to 26th–28th Dáil (1989–2002) and 29th Dáil (2002—); spokesperson on educational reform (195–97).

COUGHLIN, Natalie (1982—). American swimmer. Born Aug 23, 1982, in Vallejo, California; attended University of California, Berkeley. ❖ At World championships, won a gold medal for 100-meter backstroke and 4x200-meter freestyle relay (2001) and 4x100-meter freestyle relay (2003); at SC World Cup in New York, placed 1st in 50-, 100- and 200-meter backstroke (2001 and 2002), 50- and 100-meter butterfly and 100-meter indiv. medley (2002); won a bronze medal for 100-meter freestyle, silver medals for 4x100-meter relay and 4x100-meter medley relay, and gold medals for 100-meter backstroke and 4x200-meter freestyle relay at Athens Olympics (2004); was the 1st woman to go under 1 minute for the 100-meter backstroke (2002). Named Women's Sports Foundation Sportswoman of the Year (2003).

COUGHLIN, Paula A. (c. 1961—). American helicopter pilot and whistleblower. Born c. 1961. ❖ Whistleblower on Tailhook, was a Navy lieutenant, helicopter pilot and admiral's aide when she and 26 other women (14 of them officers) were sexually assaulted during a rowdy party by Naval aviators attending a Tailhook Aviators convention (Sept 7, 1991); sought redress through the appropriate channels but hit a stone wall; put career on the line and went public with the help of ABC News to demand that the Navy bring justice to her attackers (June 1992); efforts resulted in Congressional hearings, resignation of secretary of the Navy, and a Pentagon investigation; resigned from the Navy (Feb 1995). ❖ See also tv movie "She Stood Alone: The Tailhook Scandal," starring Gail O'Grady (1995).

COULON, Anne-Jacqueline (fl. 18th c.). French ballet dancer. Flourished in the late 18th century. ❖ One of the most recognized and celebrated dancers of 18th century, performed principal roles in Maximiel Gardel's *Le Déserteur* (1786) and *Alceste* (1786), and Pierre Gardel's *Le Jugement de Paris* (1973); partnered numerous times by Jean D'Auberval and August Vestris.

COULSON, Juanita (1933—). American science-fiction writer and editor. Name variations: (pseudonym) John J. Wells. Born Juanita Ruth Wellons, Feb 12, 1933, in Anderson, Indiana; Ball State University, BS, 1954, MA, 1961; m. Robert Coulson, 1954; children: 1 son. ❖ With Robert Coulson, began editing *Yandro* fan magazine (1953); writings include *Crisis on Cheiron* (1967), *Unto the Last Generation* (1975), *Fear Stalks the Bayou* (1976), *Fire of the Andes* (1979), *The Death God's Citadel* (1980), *Star Sister* (1990), *The Scent of Magic* (1990) and *Cold, Hard Silver* (1994). Won Hugo Award for editing (1965).

COULTER, Jean. Northern Ireland politician. Born Rose Jean Coulter in Shankill, Belfast, Northern Ireland. ❖ Founded the West Belfast Loyalist coalition (1973), opposing the power-sharing Northern Ireland Executive and the proposed Council of Ireland; as an Independent Unionist for West Belfast, sat in the Northern Ireland Assembly (1973–74).

COULTER, Mrs. (1869–1941). *See Millard, Evelyn.*

COULTON, Mary Rose (1906–2002). Australian-English novelist.
Name variations: Mary Rose Alpers; (pseudonym) Sarah Campion.
Born Mary Rose Coulton, June 1, 1906, in Eastbourne, England; died
July 22, 2002, in Auckland, New Zealand; dau. of George Gordon
Coulton (medieval scholar and controversialist) and Rose (Ilbert)
Coulton; m. Antony Alpers (New Zealander writer), 1949; children:
Philip Alpers. ❖ Traveled widely in Europe, Canada, US, South
Africa, New Zealand and Australia; lived in Auckland, New Zealand,
from 1959 until death; published the bestselling *Father,* a biography
of her father (1948); probably best known for her "Burdekin Trilogy"
(*Mo Burdekin* [1941], *Bonanza* [1942], *The Pommy Cow* [1944]), an
Australian classic which evokes 19th-century life in gold-mining towns of
northern Queensland; other works include *Turn Away No More* (1940),
Dr Golightly (1946) and *Come Again* (1951).

COUPAR, Isabella (c. 1842–1919). *See Siteman, Isabella Flora.*

COURAU, Clotilde (1969—). French actress and princess. Name variations: Princess of Venice. Born April 3, 1969, in Levallois-Perret, Hauts-
de-Seine, France; dau. of Jean Claude Courau and Catherine de
Pontavice des Renardières; sister of Christiane, Camille, and Capucine
Courau; m. Emanuele Filiberto di Savoia, prince of Venice, Sept 25,
2003, grandson of the last king of Italy and 2nd in line to Italy's throne if
the monarchy had not been abolished in 1946. ❖ Named one of
European films "Shooting Stars," made film debut in *Le Petit criminel*
(1990); other films include *Map of the Human Heart* (1993), *Élisa*
(1995), *Les Grands ducs* (1996), *Fred* (1997), *Marthe* (1997), *Le Poulpe*
(1998), *Deterrence* (1999), *En Face* (2000) and *Mon idole* (2002).

COURCEL, Nicole (1930—). French actress. Born Nicole Marie-Anne
Andrieux, Oct 21, 1930, in Saint-Cloud, France. ❖ Discovered by
director Jacques Becker, made film debut in uncredited role in *Antoine
et Antoinette* (1947), followed by *Rendez-vous de juillet, La Marie du port,
Marchandes d'illusions, Le Grand pavois, Huis Clos, Le Testament
d'Orphee, Le Vergini di Roma, Sundays and Cybele, The Night of the
Generals* and *The Strangler,* among others; on tv, appeared as Emma
Bovary in "Madame Bovary" (1974), as Béatrice Roussel in the series
"Allô Béatrice" (1984), and as Margrit Steenfort in "Le Destin des
Steenfort" (1999).

COURIC, Katie (1957—). American tv journalist and host. Born
Katherine Anne Couric, Jan 7, 1957, in Arlington, Virginia; dau. of
Elinor and John Couric (journalist); sister of Emily Couric (Virginia
state senator, died Nov 2001); graduate of University of Virginia, 1979;
m. Jay Monahan (tv legal commentator), 1989 (died Jan 24, 1998);
children: 2 daughters, Ellie (b. 1991), Caroline (b. 1995). ❖ Popular
news anchor, began career as a desk assistant for ABC news bureau in
Washington DC (1979); joined CNN as an assignment editor (1980),
becoming the producer of "Take Two"; worked at WTVJ in Miami for 3
years; joined NBC news (1989); won Emmy while working as a reporter
for NBC's local station in Washington, DC (1990); joined NBC's
"Today" as its 1st national correspondent (June 1990), becoming co-
anchor (April 5, 1991); also a contributing anchor for "Dateline NBC."

COURLAND, Anne of (1693–1740). *See Anna Ivanovna.*

COURNOYEA, Nellie J. (1940—). Native Canadian political leader.
Born 1940 in Aldavik, Alberta, Canada; father an immigrant from
Norway; mother an Inupiak from Herschel Island; married with children.
❖ Fighter for aboriginal self-determination, worked at CBC Inuvik for
9 years as an announcer and station manager and was a land-claim
fieldworker for the Inuit Tapiriit Kanatami (ITK); was a founding
member, later administrator and land-rights worker, of the Committee
of Original Peoples' Entitlement (COPE); represented the riding of
Nunakput (1979–95) and served as premier of the Northwest
Territories (1991–95), the 1st Native Woman elected premier in
Canada; was minister of Health and Social Services, minister
Responsible for Northwest Territories Power Corporation, minister of
Renewable Resources, minister of Culture and Communications, minis-
ter of Energy, Mines and Petroleum Resources, minister of Public Works
and Highways, and minister Responsible for Workers' Compensation
Board; became managing director of the Inuvialuit Development
Corporation (1995).

COURT, Hazel (1926—). English actress. Born Feb 10, 1926, in
Birmingham, England; m. Dermot Walsh (actor), 1949 (div. 1963); m.
Don Taylor (actor, director), 1964 (died 1998). ❖ Made film debut as
Miss Grey in *Dreaming* (1944), followed by *Carnival, Meet Me at Dawn,
Dear Murderer, My Sister and I, Ghost Ship, The Curse of Frankenstein,*

The Hour of Decision, The Man Who Could Cheat Death, Breakout and
Roger Corman's *Premature Burial, The Raven* and *The Masque of the Red
Death,* among others.

COURT, Margaret Smith (1942—). Australian tennis player. Name
variations: Margaret Smith; Margaret Court; Mrs. Barry M. Court;
Reverend Margaret Court. Born July 16, 1942, in Albury, NSW,
Australia; attended St. Augustine's Convent, c. 1956, and Albury
Technical College; m. Barry M. Court (yachtsman and wool broker,
later Western Australia agricultural minister), Oct 28, 1967. ❖ Won
Australian singles (1960–66, 1969–71, 1973); won French singles (1962,
1964, 1969, 1970, 1973); won Wimbledon singles (1963, 1965, 1970);
won US singles (1962, 1965, 1969–70, 1973), Australian doubles
(1961–63, 1965, 1969–71, 1973), French doubles (1964–66, 1973),
Wimbledon doubles (1964, 1969), US doubles (1963, 1968, 1970,
1973, 1975), Australian mixed (1963–64), French mixed (1963–65,
1969), Wimbledon mixed (1963, 1965–66, 1968, 1975), US mixed
(1961–65, 1969–70, 1972) and Federation Cup (1963–65, 1968–69,
1971); was the 4th player in history to win the Grand Slam (1970); won
16 out of 18 tournaments and 78 out of 80 singles matches, 8 out of 10
tournaments on Virginia Slims Tour (1972–April 1973); in a much
publicized match, lost to Bobby Riggs, former US tennis professional
(May 1973); won Virginia Slims Trophy (1973); retired (1975).
Inducted into International Tennis Hall of Fame and International
Women's Sports Hall of Fame. ❖ See also autobiographies, *The
Margaret Smith Story* (1965) and *Court on Court: A Life in Tennis*
(1975); and *Women in World History.*

COURTAULD, Katherine (1856–1935). English agriculturalist. Born
July 13, 1856; died July 5, 1935; longtime companion of Mary
Gladstone. ❖ Self-employed farmer, renowned fruit grower, and advocate of women in agriculture, began to manage the 243 acres of Knights
Farm in Colne Engaine, Essex (1878), which was purchased for her by
father; in addition to raising poultry, cattle, sheep and pigs, developed
orchard, expanded farm to 2,000 acres, and taught women pupils; to
train women in agriculture, created Small Holding Colony on 98 acres
near Lingfield, Surrey, with Louisa Wilkins (1920). Became council
member (1900) and chair (1907) of Women's Farming and Gardening
Union (WFGU); donated Courtauld House, near Gower Street,
London, for WFGU's headquarters (1932).

COURTAULD, Louisa (1729–1807). French silversmith. Name variations: Louisa Perina Courtauld; Louisa Ogier. Born Louisa Perina Ogier,
1729; died Jan 12, 1807, in London, England; dau. of silk weaver; m.
Samuel Courtauld (Huguenot goldsmith); children: 8. ❖ Worked as
silversmith and had knowledge of chemistry; lived in London after
marriage; after husband's death (1765), continued family business in
her name until 1769; created pieces and had personal mark registered at
The Goldsmiths' Company (1766–67); received business assistance from
son (1777–80); sold business to John Henderson, later prime warden of
The Goldsmiths' Company (1780).

COURTENAY, Eleanor (c. 1395–1418). *See Mortimer, Eleanor.*

COURTENAY, Gertrude (c. 1504–1558). Marchioness of Exeter. Name
variations: Gertrude Blount. Born Gertrude Blount c. 1504; died Sept
25, 1558; dau. of William Blount, 4th baron Mountjoy, and Elizabeth
Saye; 2nd wife of Henry Courtenay, marquis of Exeter, Oct 25, 1519
(executed 1538 or 1539); children: Edward Courtenay, 1st earl of Devon
(c. 1526–1556). ❖ Devout Roman Catholic, championed Elizabeth
Barton; when husband was sent to the Tower, was also accused of being
an aspirant to the crown and imprisoned in the Tower (1538); attainted
(1539); saw attainder reversed (1553) and became a lady-in-waiting to
Queen Mary I.

COURTENAY, Margaret (fl. 1330). Countess of Devon. Name variations:
Margaret Bohun. Fl. around 1330; dau. of Humphrey Bohun, 4th earl of
Hereford, 3rd of Essex, and Elizabeth Plantagenet (1282–1316, dau. of
Edward I of England); m. Hugh Courtenay (1303–1377), 2nd earl of
Devon; children: Hugh Courtenay (d. around 1374), 3rd baron
Courtenay.

**COURTENAY-LATIMER, Marjorie (1907–2004). South African
ichthyologist and museum curator.** Born Marjorie Eileen Doris
Courtenay-Latimer, Feb 24, 1907, in South Africa; died May 17, 2004,
in East London, South Africa; dau. of a station master on South African
Railways; attended convent school in South Africa; never married; no
children. ❖ Became a curator (1931) and later director of East London
Museum in South Africa; discovered a live coelacanth, previously known

only from fossils, which was provisionally named *Latimeria chalumnae* by ichthyologist J.L.B. Smith in her honor (Dec 22, 1938); worked at museum in Durban (1932) and later at Cape Town's South African Museum; collected bird, plant and shell specimens from Bird Island (1936) for East London Museum; honored by 50th anniversary of coelacanth discovery held at museum on Comoro Islands, and by a limited edition of a South African gold coin with coelacanth design (1998). After her initial discovery, over 200 more found around Comoro Islands and Indonesia by end of 20th century.

COURTHS-MAHLER, Hedwig (1867–1950). German novelist. Name variations: Hedwig Mahler. Born Hedwig Mahler, Feb 18, 1867; died Nov 26, 1950; illeg. dau. of Ernst Schmidt and Henriette Mahler; m. Fritz Courths; children: 2. ❖ Most widely read German novelist of the 20th century, often wrote about heroines who marry wealthy men to achieve happiness; published over 200 works, including *Scheinehe* (1905), *Ich lasse Dich nicht* (1912) and *Es geht hinauf* (1914).

COURTNEIDGE, Cicely (1893–1980). British comedian. Name variations: Dame Cicely Courtneidge. Born Esmeralda Cicely Courtneidge, April 1, 1893, in Sydney, Australia; died April 26, 1980, in London, England; dau. of Robert Courtneidge (actor, manager, and producer) and Rosaline May (Adams) Courtneidge; sister of Rosaline Courtneidge (actress); m. Jack Hulbert (actor), 1915 (died 1978). ❖ Comedian and musical-comedy star, credited half her success to husband Jack Hulbert, her acting partner, producer, and, often times, director (1913–78); at 8, made stage debut as one of the fairies in *A Midsummer Night's Dream* (her only Shakespearean role); made London debut as Rosie Lucas in *Tom Jones* (1907), which was followed by a string of ingenue roles in musical comedies, including *The Pearl Girl* (1913), opposite then newcomer Hulbert; launched a music-hall act (1916) and was an instant success, especially with her male impersonations that she would continue to perform in shows for over 30 years; also became a top draw in the West End with such successes as *Little Revue Starts at Nine O'Clock* (1923), *By the Way* (1925), *Clowns in Clover* (1927), *The House That Jack Built* (1929), *Under Your Hat* (1938), *Hulbert Follies* (1941), *Full Swing* (1942), *Something in the Air* (1943), *Gay's the Word*, in which she sang "Vitality," and *Dear Octopus* (1967); co-starred with husband in movies, but also did several solo films, including 3 of her biggest successes, *Soldiers of the King* (1933), *Things Are Looking Up* (1935) and *The L-Shaped Room* (1962); had 1st solo lead in a straight play, *The Bride and the Bachelor* (1961), followed by *Move Over, Mrs. Markham* (1971). Made Dame of the British Empire (1972). ❖ See also memoirs, *Cicely* (1953); and *Women in World History*.

COURTNEIDGE, Rosaline (1903–1926). English actress. Born Aug 19, 1903, in London, England; died Dec 8, 1926; dau. of Rosaline May (Adams) Courtneidge and Robert Courtneidge (actor, manager, and producer); sister of Cicely Courtneidge (actress); m. Peter Haddon (actor). ❖ Made stage debut in *The Man from Toronto* (1919); made London debut in *Daddies* (1920), followed by *Sweet William, The Thing That Matters, Paddy the Next Best Thing* and *The Sport of Kings;* films include *Oxford Bags*.

COURTNEY, Annie. Northern Ireland politician. Born Northern Ireland. ❖ Began career as a nurse; was mayor of Derry (1993–94); representing SDLP, elected to the Northern Ireland Assembly for Foyle (2000).

COURTNEY, Inez (1908–1975). American actress. Born Mar 12, 1908, in New York, NY; died April 5, 1975, in Neptune, New Jersey. ❖ NY stage credits include *The Wild Rose, Good News* and *Spring is Here;* films include *Song of the Flame, Sunny, The Raven, Magnificent Obsession, Hit Parade, Hurricane, Shop around the Corner* and *The Farmer's Daughter.*

COURTNEY, Kathleen (1878–1974). British suffragist and pacifist. Name variations: Kathleen D'Olier Courtney; Dame Kathleen Courtney. Born Kathleen D'Olier (also seen as d'Olier) Courtney, 1878, in Chatham, England; grew up in Kensington; died Dec 7, 1974, in England; dau. of Alice Margaret Courtney and Major David C. Courtney of the Royal Engineers; attended boarding school in Dresden; studied modern languages at Lady Margaret Hall, Oxford; never married; no children. ❖ Served as honorary secretary of Oxford branch of National Union of Women's Suffrage Societies (1911–14); attended Women's Congress at The Hague (1915) and was co-founder of Women's International League for Peace, serving as its British Section chair for 10 years; worked with Serbian refugees during WWI and with Society of Friends in Europe; became executive member of British League of Nations Union (1928) and vice-chair (1939); lectured in US for Ministry of Information and was in San Francisco for drawing-up of UN Charter; served as vice-chair, chair, and joint-president of British Branch of UN Association. Made CBE (1946) and DBE (1952).

COURTNEY, Patricia (c. 1932–2003). American baseball player. Born c. 1932 in Brooklyn, NY; died July 2003 in Everett, Massachusetts; Bentley College, degree in accounting, 1958. ❖ Signed with the Chicago Colleens (c. 1950); played third base for one season for the All-American Girls Professional Baseball League; worked for IRS (1958–88); was a consultant on film *A League of Her Own* (1992), appearing in the final induction ceremony scene.

COURTRIGHT, Jennie Lee (1848–1925). *See Lee, Jennie.*

COUSIN ALICE (1827–1863). *See Haven, Emily Bradley Neal.*

COUSINS, Margaret (1878–1954). Irish suffragist, theosophist. Name variations: M.E.C.; Gretta. Born Margaret Elizabeth Gillespie, Nov 7, 1878, in Boyle, Co. Roscommon, Ireland; died in Adyar, India, Mar 11, 1954; studied at Royal Academy of Music in Dublin; received Bachelors degree in Music at Royal University of Ireland, 1902; m. James Cousins (poet, teacher, lecturer and government adviser), 1903; no children. ❖ Reformer who immigrated to India, was active in Indian women's and nationalist movements, became the 1st woman magistrate in India, and initiated numerous reforms and improvements for Indian womanhood; early in career, helped organize the Irish Vegetarian Society (1904–05); was one of the 4 founders of the Irish Women's Franchise League (1908); as a suffragist, served 1 month in prison in Holloway jail for stone throwing (1910) and 1 month in Tullamore jail for breaking windows (1913); moved to Liverpool with husband (June 1913); became founder member of Church of the New Ideal (Mar 1914); sailed for India (Oct 1915); served as founder member of Women's Indian Association (July 1917); elected to be the 1st non-Indian member of the Indian Women's University at Poona (1916); appointed foundation head-mistress of the National Girls' School in Mangalore (1919–20); became 1st honorary woman magistrate in Madras (1922); initiated 1st All-Asia Women's Conference at Lahore (1931); addressed mass meeting in New York to protest imprisonment of Gandhi (1932); sentenced to 1 year's imprisonment at Vellore for addressing a public meeting (1932); awarded 5,000 rupees by the Madras government for being a "political sufferer for Indian freedom" (1949); had focused on 3 issues, Irish independence, Indian independence, and women's rights; writings include *The Awakening of Asian Womanhood* (1922), *The Music of Orient and Occident* (1935) and (with James Cousins) *We Two Together* (1950). Awarded Founders' Silver Medal of the Theosophical Society (1928). ❖ See also Cliona Murphy, *The Women's Suffrage Movement and Irish Society in the Early Twentieth Century* (1989); and *Women in World History.*

COUTINHO, Sônia (1939—). Brazilian novelist and short-story writer. Name variations: Sônia Valquíria de Sousa Coutinho; Sonia Coutinho. Born 1939 in Itabuna, Bahia, Brazil. ❖ Studied art history in Madrid and worked as journalist and translator; participated in writing programs in US; awarded Prêmio Jabuti (1976); works include *Do herói inutil* (1966), *Os venenos de Lucrécia* (1978), *O jogo de Ifá* (1980), *Atire em Sofia* (1989), and the study of detective novels by women, *Rainhas do crime: ótica feminina no romance policial* (1994).

COUTTS, Angela Burdett (1814–1906). *See Burdett-Coutts, Angela.*

COUTTS, Connie (1871–1934). *See Ediss, Connie.*

COUTTS, Jane (1858–1944). *See Thomson, Jane.*

COUVREUR, Jessie (1848–1897). Australian novelist. Name variations: (pseudonym) Tasma. Born Jessie Huybers in Highgate, England, 1848; died 1897; m. Charles Fraser (also seen as Frazer, a gambler), 1867 (div. 1883); m. Auguste Couvreur (member of Belgian Parliament, 1864–84, died 1894). ❖ Moved to Tasmania with family (1850s); after 2nd marriage, settled in Brussels and succeeded husband as Brussels correspondent for *The Times;* lectured in France and Belgium and was active in political circles; novels, which often focus on women in unhappy marriages, include *Uncle Piper of Piper's Hill* (1889), *In Her Earliest Youth* (1890), *The Penance of Portia James* (1891), *A Knight of the White Feather* (1892), *Not Counting the Cost* (1895) and *A Fiery Ordeal* (1897); also published *A Sydney Sovereign and Other Tales* (1890) and *Incidents and Scenes in Melbourne Life* (1892).

COUZINS, Phoebe Wilson (1842–1913). American marshall. Born Sept 8, 1942, in St. Louis, Missouri; died Dec 6, 1913, in St. Louis; dau. of John Couzins (US marshall). ❖ The 1st woman awarded a law degree from Washington University School of Law (1871), was admitted to the bar in 4 states but practiced only briefly; with Susan B. Anthony and Elizabeth Cady Stanton, helped form the National Woman Suffrage Association (NWSA) and lectured widely on woman suffrage; succeeded her father as the 1st woman US marshall (1887) and served for 2 years; broke with the suffrage movement (c. 1897).

COUZYN, Jeni (1942—). South African poet. Born 1942 in Johannesburg, South Africa; attended University of Natal. ❖ Moved to England (1966) and then to British Columbia, Canada; despite absence from South Africa, her poems, both lyric and narrative, remain South African in tone and feeling; works include *Flying* (1970), *Monkeys' Wedding* (1972), *Christmas in Africa* (1975), *The Happiness Bird* (1978), *House of Changes* (1979), *Life by Drowning* (1983) and *In the Skin House* (1993).

COVELL, Phyllis (1895–1982). English tennis player. Born May 22, 1895; died Oct 28, 1982. ❖ At Paris Olympics, won a silver medal in doubles (1924).

COVENEY, Malvina (1830–1906). *See Florence, Malvina Pray.*

COVENTRY, Anne (1673–1763). English countess and writer. Name variations: Anne Beaufort; Countess of Coventry. Born 1673; died Feb 17, 1763; dau. of Henry Beaufort, 1st duke of Beaufort; m. Thomas Coventry, 2nd earl of Coventry, May 4, 1691 (died 1710); children: Thomas Coventry, 3rd earl of Coventry (1702-c. 1711). ❖ Wrote *Meditations & Reflections* (1707).

COVENTRY, countess of.
See Coventry, Anne (1673–1763).
See Gunning, Maria (1733–1760).

COVENTRY, Kirsty (1983—). Zimbabwean swimmer. Born Sept 16, 1983, in Harare, Zimbabwe; attended Auburn University in Alabama. ❖ Won a bronze medal for 200-meter indiv. medley, a silver medal for 100-meter backstroke and a gold medal for 200-meter backstroke, with a time of 2:09.19, at Athens Olympics (2004). Named Sports Woman of the Year (2000).

COVENTRY, Pamela (d. 1939). English murder victim. Born c. 1928 in England; found dead near Hornchurch, Essex, Jan 19, 1939. ❖ At age 11 (some sources cite 9), found dead near Hornchurch, Essex (Jan 1939), having been strangled and sexually assaulted; sensational case remains unsolved. A connection was made by police between evidence at scene and 28-year-old suspect Leonard Richardson, but due to insufficient evidence at his trial at Old Bailey (Mar 1939), he was acquitted.

COWAN, Edith (1861–1932). Australian politician. Born Edith Dircksey Brown, Aug 2, 1861, at Glengarry near Geraldton, Western Australia; died June 9, 1932; dau. of Mary Eliza Dircksey (Wittenoom) Brown (teacher) and Kenneth Brown (pastoralist); granddau. of Eliza Brown (d. 1896), colonist who documented Australian colonial life through letters home to family in England; m. James Cowan (police magistrate in Perth), Nov 12, 1879; children: 4 daughters, 1 son. ❖ The 1st woman in Australian Parliament, dedicated her life to social reforms to improve the status of women; served on the North Fremantle Board of Education (among the few public offices open to women at the time); worked with the Ministering Children's League and the House of Mercy for unmarried mothers (Alexandra Home for Women); served as a foundation member of Children's Protection Society and was a pioneer in the field of day nurseries for children of working mothers; appointed a justice of the Children's Court (1915); became one of the 1st women to be appointed justice of the peace (1920); instrumental in the creation of the Western Australian National Council of Women, served as its president (1913–20); after the ban on women in Parliament was removed, defeated the sitting member as an endorsed Nationalist candidate for West Perth, and became the 1st woman to enter Australian Parliament (1921); promoted migrant welfare, infant health centers, sex education in the State's schools, and women's rights, arguing that women should be legally entitled to a portion of their husbands' income; introduced the Women's Legal Status Act, which opened the legal profession to women in Western Australian; defeated in the elections of 1924 and 1927. Awarded OBE for war work (1920). ❖ See also *Women in World History.*

COWAN, Ruth (1901–1993). American journalist. Name variations: Ruth Baldwin Cowan; Baldwin Cowan; Ruth C. Nash. Born June 15, 1901, in Salt Lake City, Utah; died Feb 5, 1993, in Harpers Ferry, West Virginia; only dau. of William Henry Cowan (mining prospector) and Ida (Baldwin) Cowan; graduate of University of Texas at Austin, 1923;

m. Bradley D. Nash (politician), 1956. ❖ Taught at Main Avenue High School in San Antonio (1924–27); as Baldwin Cowan, became a reporter for *San Antonio Evening News* (1928); began working for United Press (UP, 1929), until they discovered that Baldwin Cowan was a woman; joining Associated Press (AP), covered crime in Chicago (1930s); transferred to AP's Washington bureau (1940), then to London (1941); as one of the 1st women war correspondents of WWII (1943), was sent to Algiers with Women's Auxiliary Army Corps; later covered operations in North Africa, invasion of Normandy, liberation of Paris, and Battle of the Bulge.

COWART, Juanita (1944—). African-American pop singer. Name variations: Marvelettes. Born 1944 in Detroit, Michigan. ❖ Was a member of the Marvelettes, a popular Motown group whose songs "Don't Mess With Bill," "Please Mr. Postman," "I Keep Holding On" and "Beachwood 4–5789" reached the top of the charts (early 1960s). Other members included Gladys Horton, Georgia Dobbins, Katherine Anderson. ❖ See also *Women in World History.*

COWDEN, Marilyn Rowe (1946—). *See Rowe, Marilyn.*

COWDEN-CLARKE, Mary (1809–1898). *See Clarke, Mary Cowden.*

COWEN, Donna (c. 1950—). American ballet dancer. Born c. 1950 in Birmingham, Alabama. ❖ Active in apprentice programs of Atlanta Civic, Birmingham, and City Center Joffrey ballets early on; joined the Joffrey where she created roles Gerald Arpino's *Secret Places* (1969) and performed in numerous company revivals, including Frederick Ashton's *The Dream* and John Cranko's *Pineapple Poll.*

COWEN, Lenore (1896–1984). *See Coffee, Lenore.*

COWIE, Bessie Lee (1860–1950). New Zealand temperance reformer, social reformer, lecturer, and writer. Name variations: Betsy Vickery, Bessie Lee. Born Betsy Vickery, June 10, 1860, at Daylesford, Victoria, Australia; died April 18, 1950, at Pasadena, California; dau. of Henry (butcher) and Susan Emma Maunder (Dungey) Vickery; m. Harrison Lee (railway worker), 1880 (died 1908); m. Andrew Cowie (farmer), 1908 (died 1928). ❖ Joined Women's Christian Temperance Union of Australia (WCTU, 1887); appointed editor of WCTU page in *Alliance Record,* colonial superintendent of literature, and public speaker for WCTU; worked as lecturer, temperance organizer, and missionary, from 1896; toured New Zealand as lecturer (1899), and assisted with local campaigns (1902 and 1905); was one of a few women to become world missionary of WTCU (1911); also involved in prison reform and socialist issues; became foundation member of United Labor Party of New Zealand (1912); wrote several poems, articles, booklets, and tracts, including controversial *Marriage and Heredity* (1890), which advocated women's control of their own bodies; moved to Honolulu, Hawaii, and continued to write and lecture until World War II; relocated to California, where she was active in temperance work. ❖ See also *From Nine to Ninety* (c. 1950); and *Dictionary of New Zealand Biography* (Vol. 3).

COWIE, Eliza Jane (1835–1902). New Zealand social-welfare worker. Name variations: Eliza Jane Webber. Born probably Oct 6, 1835, in England; died Aug 18, 1902, in Parnell, New Zealand; dau. of William (surgeon) and Eliza (Preston) Webber; m. William Garden Cowie (bishop), 1869 (died 1902); children: 1 daughter, 5 sons. ❖ Immigrated with husband to New Zealand (1870); performed social-welfare work among Auckland's poor; founded and supervised women's home in Parnell (now St. Mary's Family Centre) in which domestic skills were taught; helped found children's homes in Parnell (1893) and Ponsonby (1896). ❖ See also *Dictionary of New Zealand Biography* (Vol. 2).

COWIE, Helen Stephen (1875–1956). New Zealand physician. Name variations: Helen Stephen Baird. Born Sept 29, 1875, at Hampden, Otago, New Zealand; died July 8, 1956, at Masterton, New Zealand; dau. of James (minister) and Elizabeth (Stephen) Baird; University of Otago, BA, 1890s; Queen Margaret College, Glasgow University, MB, ChB, 1905; m. James Alexander Cowie (physician), 1908 (died 1941); children: 1 daughter, 1 son. ❖ Believed to have been the 1st woman doctor in Southland, specialized in obstetrics and anaesthetics; began general practice in Invercargill but transferred to Masterton to join husband in private practice (c. 1908); went to England during WWI and worked in civilian hospitals; returned to New Zealand at peak of influenza pandemic (c. 1918); retired from medicine (1945). ❖ See also *Dictionary of New Zealand Biography* (Vol. 3).

COWIE, Laura (1892–1969). Scottish actress. Born April 7, 1892, in Aberdeen, Scotland; died Feb 11, 1969; m. John Hastings Turner (actor, died 1956). ❖ Made London debut as Dolly in *The Bridegroom* (1908), followed by *The Great John Ganton, The Seven Sisters,* Hermia in *A Midsummer Night's Dream, King Henry VIII, Romance, Bubbly, Now and Then, The Enchanted Cottage,* title role in John Drinkwater's *Mary Stuart, The Return Journey, Strange Orchestra, Mourning Becomes Electra* and Gertrude in *Hamlet;* films include *Henry VIII, The Vicar of Wakefield, Under Suspicion, The Blind Spot, The Secret of Stamboul* and *The Breadwinner.*

COWL, Jane (1883–1950). American actress and playwright. Name variations: (pseudonym) C.R. Avery; (joint pseudonym with Jane Murfin) Alan Langdon Martin. Born Grace Bailey in Boston, Massachusetts, Dec 14, 1883; died in Santa Monica, California, June 22, 1950; attended Columbia University; m. Adolph Klauber (American theatrical producer), 1908. ❖ Once considered the most beautiful woman on the American stage, made theatrical debut in *Sweet Kitty Bellairs* (1903), while still a schoolgirl; had 1st major role in *Is Matrimony a Failure?* (1910) and went on to star billing in *Within the Law* (1912), which ran for 540 performances; wrote most of her plays, many of which she also starred in, with Jane Murfin, including *Lilac Time* (1917), a moderate hit, and *Smilin' Through* (1919) a Broadway smash; reached peak of career as Juliet in *Romeo and Juliet* (1923), which ran for 856 performances; also triumphed in *Easy Virtue* (1925), *The Road to Rome* (1927) and *Old Acquaintance* (1940); was co-director of the Stage Door Canteen operated by American Theatre Wing during WWII. ❖ See also *Women in World History.*

COWLES, Anna Roosevelt (1855–1931). American socialite. Name variations: Anna Roosevelt; Mrs. William Sheffield Cowles; Mrs. W.S. Cowles; known as Bamie or Auntie Bye. Born 1855; died 1931; dau. of Martha "Mittie" (Bulloch) Roosevelt and Theodore Roosevelt Sr.; sister of Elliott Roosevelt and Theodore Roosevelt (president of US); aunt of Eleanor Roosevelt; married William Sheffield Cowles, 1895 (died 1923); children: William Sheffield Cowles Jr. (1898–1986). ❖ See also *Letters from Theodore Roosevelt to Anna Roosevelt Cowles, 1870–1918* (Scribner, 1924).

COWLES, Betsey Mix (1810–1876). American educator. Born Betsey Mix Cowles, Feb 9, 1810; died July 25, 1876, in Austinburg, Ohio; dau. of Rev. Giles Hooker Cowles (Congregationalist pastor) and Sally (White) Cowles; sister of Edwin Weed Cowles (physician). ❖ Had teaching career which spanned almost 40 years, including several positions in Ohio and NY; began career in public schools (1848); served as superintendent of girls' grammar and high schools, Canton, OH (c. 1950–55) and of schools in Painesville, OH (beginning 1858); worked on behalf of temperance, peace, women's, and abolition causes, including some contribution to the Underground Railroad.

COWLES, Fleur (1910—). American journalist and editor. Born Fleur Fenton in Montclair, New Jersey, Jan 20, 1910; dau. of Matthew (businessman and manufacturer) and Eleanor (Pearl) Fenton; attended School of Fine and Applied Arts, NY; m. Atherton Pettingell (advertising executive), Feb 13, 1932 (div. 1946); m. Gardner Cowles (publishing magnate), Dec 27, 1946 (div. 1955); m. Tom Montague Meyer (English millionaire), Nov 18, 1955. ❖ Magazine editor, journalist, artist, and author who was founding editor of the innovative and short-lived *Flair* magazine; on marriage to Gardner "Mike" Cowles, president of Cowles Magazines, took over the women's department of *Look* magazine; introduced sections on food, fashion, and family problems, and doubled *Look's* advertising core and circulation within 2 years; launched *Flair* (1950), which was distinguished by state-of-the art features, the use of advanced graphic techniques, including a variety of paper stocks and printing processes, and pages of varying sizes, and is now a collectors' item; wrote 16 books, including *Bloody Precedent* (1952), a comparative study of the Argentinean dictatorships of Juan and Evita Perón and their predecessors Manuel and Encarnación de Rosas; moved to England, began to paint professionally (1969), and had over 50 solo shows. ❖ See also memoir, *She Made Friends and Kept Them: An Anecdotal Memoir* (HarperCollins, 1996); *The Best of Flair* (1996); and *Women in World History.*

COWLES, Julia (1785–1803). American diarist. Born Oct 18, 1785, in Farmington, Connecticut; died 1803; dau. of Zenas Cowles and Mary Lewis. ❖ At 11, sent to Sarah Pierce's Female Academy in Litchfield; maintained a diary from then until her death at 18, which was published as *The Diaries of Julia Cowles: A Connecticut Record 1791–1803* (1931).

COWLES, Virginia (1912–1983). American war correspondent. Born Virginia Spencer Cowles in Brattleboro, Vermont, Aug 12, 1912; died in auto accident, Sept 17, 1983, near Bordeaux, France; dau. of Edward Spencer Cowles (author, physician, psychiatrist) and Florence (Jaquith) Cowles; grew up in Massachusetts. ❖ After apprenticing with a column on the *Boston Breeze,* joined the Hearst syndicate, traveling to Europe and the Far East, then arriving in Spain, a week after the battle of Guadalajara (1936); hired by London *Sunday Times* as a roving correspondent, traveled to Berlin (1940) and was in Prague when Czechoslovakia was overrun with Germans; was in Finland when Russia invaded, and interviewed Mussolini in Italy; published the bestseller *Looking for Trouble* (1941), a plea for US to aid Britain. Named to Order of the British Empire (OBE, 1947). ❖ See also *Women in World History.*

COWLES, Mrs. William Sheffield (1855–1931). *See Cowles, Anna Roosevelt.*

COWLEY, Gillian (1955—). Zimbabwean field-hockey player. Born July 1955. ❖ At Moscow Olympics, won a gold medal in team competition (1980).

COWLEY, Hannah (1743–1809). English dramatist. Name variations: Hannah Parkhouse Cowley; (pseudonym) Anna Matilda. Born Hannah Parkhouse in Devonshire, England, 1743; died in Devonshire, Mar 11, 1809; dau. of Philip Parkhouse (bookseller); m. Captain Thomas Cowley (in the East India Company's service), c. 1768. ❖ Wrote *The Runaway,* which was produced by David Garrick to complete success at Drury Lane (Feb 1776); during next 20 years, wrote a number of plays, one of which, the popular *Belle's Strategem* (1780), was frequently revived by Henry Irving and Ellen Terry; also wrote *A Bold Stroke for a Husband* (1783) and, under pseudonym Anna Matilda, contributed sentimental verse to the *World;* revised Aphra Behn's *The Lucky Chance* as *A School for Greybeards* (1786).

COWLEY, Joy (1936—). New Zealand novelist and short-story writer. Name variations: Cassia Joy Cowley. Born Aug 7, 1939, in Levin, New Zealand; dau. of Peter Summers and Cassia Gedge; m. Ted Cowley (div. 1967); m. Malcolm Mason, 1970 (died 1985); m. Terry Coles, 1989; children: 4. ❖ Wrote over 50 works for Price Milburn School Readers System; adult fiction includes *Nest in a Falling Tree* (1967), *Of Men and Angels* (1970), *The Growing Season* (1978) and *Holy Days* (2001); short-fiction collections include *Heart Attack* (1985) and *Joy Cowley Short Stories* (1996); published children's fiction including *The Silent One* (1982) and *The Shadrach Trilogy* (1990–2001). Received Commemoration medal for Services to New Zealand (1990) and New Zealand Women's Suffrage Centennial Medal (1993).

COWPER, Emily, countess of (d. 1869). *See Lamb, Emily.*

COWPER, Mary (1685–1724). English diarist. Name variations: Countess Mary Cowper. Born Mary Clavering in 1685; died 1724; dau. of John Clavering, Esquire, of Chopwell, Durham; m. Lord William Cowper (lord keeper of the Great Seal and later lord chancellor to King George I), 1706; children: several. ❖ Named lady of the bedchamber to Caroline of Ansbach (1714), then princess of Wales; began a diary of her observations of court life, of which only two portions survive: entries from 1714 to 1716, and a section from 1720. ❖ See also *Women in World History.*

COWSILL, Barbara (1929–1985). American musician. Name variations: The Cowsills. Born July 12, 1928; died Jan 31, 1985, in Tempe, Arizona; m. William "Bud" Cowsill; children: at least 7, including Susan Cowsill. ❖ Appeared with her children as the Cowsills, the musical family group directed by husband which became the inspiration for tv series "The Partridge Family"; with Cowsills, had hit singles including "The Rain, the Park, & Other Things" (1968) and theme for rock musical *Hair* (1969). Cowsill albums include *The Cowsills* (1967), *Captain Sad and His Ship of Fools* (1968), *The Cowsills in Concert* (1969) and *On My Side* (1971).

COWSILL, Susan (1960—). American musician. Name variations: The Cowsills. Born May 20, 1960, in Newport, Rhode Island; dau. of Barbara Cowsill (musician) and William "Bud" Cowsill (musical director); m. Peter Holsapple (musician, div. 2000). ❖ Appeared with her mother and brothers as the Cowsills, the musical family group; with Cowsills, had hit single "The Rain, the Park, & Other Things" (1968) and theme for rock musical *Hair* (1969); joined with Vicki Peterson to form duo Psycho Sisters which later joined the Continental Drifters; with several brothers, revived the Cowsills (1994).

COWSILLS, The.
See Cowsill, Barbara.
See Cowsill, Susan.

COX, Alison (1979—). American rower. Born June 5, 1979, in Turlock, California; attended University of San Diego. ❖ Won a gold medal for coxed eights at World championships (2002); won a silver medal for coxed eights at Athens Olympics (2004); won 2 World Cups for coxed eights (2003 and 2004).

COX, Anne (b. 1919). *See Chambers, Anne Cox.*

COX, Annemarie (1966—). Dutch kayaker. Born July 22, 1966. ❖ At Seoul Olympics, won a bronze medal in K2 500 meters (1988).

COX, Crystal (1979—). American runner. Born Mar 28, 1979, in Virginia; attended University of North Carolina; children: Destiny. ❖ Won a gold medals for 4x400-meter relay at Athens Olympics (2004).

COX, Elizabeth Margaret Beath (b. 1932). *See Beath, Betty.*

COX, Gertrude Mary (1900–1978). American statistician. Name variations: Gertrude Cox. Born Jan 13, 1900, in Dayton, Iowa; died of leukemia, Oct 17, 1978; dau. of Emma Cox; Iowa State College, BS, 1929, MA, 1931; attended University of California at Berkeley, 1931–33. ❖ Undertook graduate studies in psychological statistics at UC Berkeley, then returned to Iowa State College as assistant in Statistical Laboratory, helping develop college's statistical laboratory with George Snedecor (1933–40); appointed assistant professor of statistics at Iowa State (1939); as full professor and founding department head in experimental statistics, was at North Carolina State University (1940–65); was editor of *Biometrics Bulletin* and *Biometrics* (1945–55); was founding member of Biometrics Society (1947); was 1st woman elected to International Statistical Institute (1949); with William G. Cochran, published *Experimental Designs,* a classic text (1950); became president of American Statistical Association (1956); served as director of statistics at Research Triangle Institute in Durham (1960–64); elected to National Academy of Sciences (1975); consultant to World Health Organization in Guatemala, US Public Health Service, government of Thailand and Pan American Health Organization, as well as many government committees.

COX, Hazel (b. 1887). American theatrical dancer. Born 1887 in Baton Rouge, Louisiana; sister of Ray Cox (dancer and comedienne). ❖ Made professional debut on stage in Chicago (c. 1906); moved to NY where she was a specialty dancer in *The Skylark* (1910), *The Night Birds* (1912), *The Love Wager* (1912), *Passing Show of 1913* and *Around the Map* (1916), among others; performed exhibition ballroom act with Andrew Brannigan in vaudeville (c. 1915).

COX, Ida (1896–1967). African-American blues singer. Name variations: Velma Bradley; Kate Lewis; Julia Powers; Julius Powers; Jane Smith. Born Ida Prather in Toccoa, Georgia, Feb 25, 1896 (some sources cite 1889); died Nov 10, 1967, in Knoxville, Tennessee; m. Adler Cox of Florida Blossoms Minstrel Show, 1920s; m. Jesse Crump (singer-pianist); reportedly married a 3rd time. ❖ Known as the "Queen without a Crown," launched career touring with her own tent show in the South; began recording for Paramount (1923), becoming one of the most successful blues recording artists in America, with such songs as "Rambling Blues" and "I've Got the Blues for Rampart Street"; brought to NY by John Hammond for legendary concert *From Spirituals to Swing* (1939); wrote many songs that have been preserved on recordings; had an unusually long recording career (1923–40) and made a comeback (1961). ❖ See also *Women in World History.*

COX, Louise H.K. (1865–1945). American painter. Name variations: Louise Howland King Cox; Louise Howland Cox. Born Louise Howland King in San Francisco, California, 1865; died 1945; studied at New York Academy under Kenyon Cox; m. Kenyon Cox, 1892. ❖ Though skilled at decorative work, was considered at her best in her naturalistic portraits of children; elected a member of National Academy of Design; awarded a bronze medal at Paris Exposition (1900).

COX, Lynne (1957—). American long-distance swimmer. Born Jan 2, 1957, in Manchester, New Hampshire; dau. of Estelle Cox (artist) and Albert Cox (radiologist); attended University of California, Santa Barbara. ❖ Moved with family to Los Alamitos, California (1969); set a new English Channel record for both men and women (1972); was the 1st woman to successfully swim Cook Strait (1975); crossed Bering Strait (1987); swam 10 miles across Peru's Lake Titicaca (1992); completed 14-mile swim across Gulf of Aqaba (1994); also swam the Nile, Africa's Cape of Good Hope, and Siberia's Lake Baikal. Inducted into International Swimming Hall of Fame (1992). ❖ See also memoir *Swimming to Antarctica* (Knopf, 2004); and *Women in World History.*

COX, Margaret (1963—). Irish politician. Born Sept 1963 in Birmingham, England. ❖ Representing Fianna Fáil, elected to the Seanad from the Industrial and Commercial Panel: Oireachtas Sub-Panel (1997–2002, 2002—).

COX, Ray (b. 1880). American theatrical dancer and comedienne. Born 1880 in Baton Rouge, Louisiana; sister of Hazel Cox (dancer and actress). ❖ Performed in vaudeville and numerous Broadway shows, including Lew Fields' *The Never Homes* (1911), *The Charity Girl* (1912), *Twin Beds* (1914) and *With Flags Flying* (1916).

COX, Tricia Nixon (1946—). *See Nixon, Tricia.*

COYLE, Grace Longwell (1892–1962). American social worker and educator. Born Grace Longwell Coyle, Mar 22, 1892, in North Adams, Massachusetts; died Mar 9, 1962, in Cleveland. Ohio; dau. of John Patterson Coyle (minister of North Adams Congregational Church, died 1895) and Mary (Cushman) Coyle; Columbia University, PhD in sociology, 1931. ❖ Began career at West Side Settlement, Kingston, PA (1915); joined Young Women's Christian Association (YWCA) as field worker in Pittsburgh, PA (1917); was industrial secretary of YWCA National Board in NY (1918–26), then executive of Laboratory Division (1930); wrote *Social Process in Organized Groups* (1930), *Studies in Group Behavior* (1937) and *Group Experience and Democratic Values* (1948); joined Western Reserve University, Cleveland, as assistant professor of group work at School of Applied Social Sciences (1934), becoming associate professor (1936), then serving as professor (1939–62); served as president of National Conference of Social Work (1940), American Association of Social Workers (1942–44), and Council on Social Work Education (1958–60).

COYLE, Rose (1914–1988). Miss America. Name variations: Rose Schlessinger; Rose Dingler. Born Rose Veronica Coyle, July 30, 1914, in Yeadon, Pennsylvania; died Feb 1988 in Brookhaven, PA; m. Leonard Schlessinger (national general manager of Warner Bros. theaters), Nov 1938 (died); m. Robert Dingler (business executive); children: (1st m.) 1 daughter. ❖ Named Miss Philadelphia (1936), then Miss America (1936). ❖ See also Frank Deford, *There She Is* (Viking, 1971).

COYNE, Colleen (1971—). American ice-hockey player. Born Sept 19, 1971; lived in East Falmouth, Massachusetts. ❖ Won a team gold medal at Nagano (1998), the 1st Olympics to feature women's ice hockey; won a team silver medal at World championships (1992, 1994, 1997) and as assistant coach (2000). ❖ See also Mary Turco, *Crashing the Net: The U.S. Women's Olympic Ice Hockey Team and the Road to Gold* (HarperCollins, 1999); and *Women in World History.*

CRABTREE, Lotta (1847–1924). American actress. Name variations: Lotta. Born Charlotte Crabtree in New York, NY, Nov 7, 1847; died in Boston, Massachusetts, Sept 25, 1924; never married. ❖ When young, began touring mining camps (1855), entertaining with songs, dances and recitations; had 1st legitimate role as Gertrude in *Loan of a Lover* in San Francisco (1858); performed at the Opera House and Eureka theaters billed as "Miss Lotta, the San Francisco Favorite" (1859–60); came to NY prominence in premiere of *Little Nell and the Marchioness;* won enormous success in plays like *Heartsease, Zip* and *Musette;* began touring with her own company (1870), one of the 1st actresses to travel with supporting players instead of relying on local stock companies to supply them; triumphed in London in an adaptation of *The Old Curiosity Shop;* throughout career, was distinguished by a perpetual childlike innocence, no matter how daring her dances or risqué her repartee. ❖ See also *Women in World History.*

CRACIUNESCU, Florenta (1955—). Romanian discus thrower. Born May 1955. ❖ At Los Angeles Olympics, won a bronze medal in discus throw (1984).

CRADDOCK, Augusta (1863–1941). *See Cradock, Mrs. H.C.*

CRADDOCK, Charles Egbert (1850–1922). *See Murfree, Mary N.*

CRADDOCK, Olive (1849–1926). *See Roshanara.*

CRADDOCK, Fanny (1909–1994). English culinary-arts teacher. Born Phyllis Primrose-Pechey, 1909, in England; died Dec 27, 1994, in East Sussex, England; m. Maj. John Cradock. ❖ The 1st celebrity tv cook in Britain, wore evening gowns, dominated her amiable, monocled kitchen partner (husband John), and added glamour to postwar cooking of leftovers; appeared on hundreds of how-to-cook programs (1950s–80s); writings include *The Practical Cook* (1949) and *The Ambitious Cook* (1950); also wrote newspaper columns.

CRADOCK, Mrs. H.C. (1863–1941). English children's writer. Name variations: Augusta Cradock; Mrs. Henry Cowper Cradock. Born Augusta Whiteford in 1863; grew up in Lincolnshire and Northamptonshire; died Oct 15, 1941, in Dorking, England; dau. of an Anglican cleric; m. Henry Cowper Cradock (later vicar of Birstall, then Whitley Lower), 1893 (died 1933); children: A(line) M(ary) Cradock (b. 1905). ❖ One of the most popular writers for young children between the wars, began career as a teacher in Wakefield, Yorkshire; wrote the "Josephine Stories," about a family of dolls, which were illustrated by Honor C. Appleton (the 1st book appeared in 1915); wrote her last book, *Teddy Bear's Farm* (1941).

CRAFT, Ellen (1826–c. 1891). African-American activist. Born Ellen Smith in 1826 in Clinton, Georgia; died c. 1891 in Charleston, South Carolina; dau. of James Smith (slave-master, lawyer, and surveyor) and Maria (Smith's slave); illiterate until adulthood, then attended Ockham School, Ockham, England; m. William Craft, Nov 7, 1850; children: Charles Estlin; William Jr.; Brougham; Ellen Crum; Alfred. ❖ Escaped slave, abolitionist activist and educator, who, for a brief time, was the most famous black woman in the US; was given as a wedding present to half-sister Eliza Collins and moved to Macon, Georgia (1837); escaped slavery masquerading as a white master of her black slave husband (1848); settled in Boston where she was proclaimed a heroine by such noted former slaves as William Wells Brown and Frederick Douglass, as well as Boston abolitionists Wendell Phillips, William Lloyd Garrison and Theodore Parker; active in New England abolitionist work; fled to England after passage of US Fugitive Slave Act (1850); studied three R's and taught sewing at Ockham School (pioneering venture in industrial education), founded by Lord Byron's daughter (Ada Byron Lovelace); appeared with abolitionist groups; returned with family to US (1870); established Woodville plantation and school south of Savannah, Georgia; taught domestic science, reading and arithmetic; moved to Charleston, South Carolina, to live with activist daughter Ellen (1890). ❖ See also William Craft, *Running a Thousand Miles* (1860); and *Women in World History*.

CRAFTER, Jane (1955—). Australian golfer. Born Dec 14, 1955, in Perth (some sources cite Adelaide), Australia. ❖ Was South Australian Girls' champion (1972–74) and South Australian champion (1977); won the New Zealand Amateur (1978) and Belgian Amateur (1980); turned pro (1983); won LPGA Phar-Mor (1990); worked as golf commentator for ESPN and NBC.

CRAIG, Betty (1957—). Canadian rower. Born Sept 26, 1957, in Brockville, Ontario, Canada. ❖ At Los Angeles Olympics, won a silver medal in coxless pairs (1984).

CRAIG, Christine (1943—). Jamaican poet and short-story writer. Born 1943 in Jamaica; graduated with an honors degree in English from University of the West Indies. ❖ Works include *Quadrille for Tigers* (1984); poetry included in *Jamaica Woman: An Anthology of Poems* (1980) and *Creation Fire: A CAFRA Anthology of Caribbean Women's Poetry* (1990); short stories included in *Her True True Name: An Anthology of Women's Writing from the Caribbean* (1989).

CRAIG, Edith (1869–1947). English actress, costume designer, and stage director. Born Dec 9, 1869, later chose to use name Craig; died Mar 27, 1947, near London; illeg. dau. of Edward Godwin and Dame Ellen Terry (actress, 1847–1928); sister of Gordon Craig (stage designer). ❖ Made stage debut at the Court in *Olivia* (1878); made NY debut in title role of *Barbara* (1888); created the role of Proserpine Garnett in *Candida* (1900); designed and made costumes for many London productions; stage managed, directed, and produced over 150 plays, often designing scenery; produced at Everyman (1920–21), York, Leeds, and Letchworth (1923–24); also directed and appeared in film; converted the Elizabethan barn, adjacent to her mother's house in Kent, into a memorial theater, where she directed Shakespearean plays (1929–39). ❖ See also Katharine Cockin, *Edith Craig, 1869–1947* (Continuum, 1998).

CRAIG, Edith (1907–1979). American stage and screen actress. Born Sept 13, 1907; died Mar 2, 1979, in Tenafly, New Jersey. ❖ Made NY stage debut in George White's *Scandals* (1926), followed by *Ziegfeld Follies, Earl Carroll's Vanities* and *Life with Father*; made over 40 films, including *Behind the Headlines, Smashing the Rackets, Love on a Bet, Condemned Woman, Outcasts of Poker Flat* and *The Singing Marine*.

CRAIG, Helen (1912–1986). American stage, radio, tv, and screen actress. Born May 13, 1912, in San Antonio, Texas; died July 20, 1986, in New York, NY; m. John Beal (actor); children: 2 daughters. ❖ Made Broadway debut in *Russet Mantle* (1936); other NY appearances include *New Faces of 1936, Family Portrait, As You Like It, Land's End, The House of Bernarda Alba, Medea, More Stately Mansions,* and Orson Welles' *Julius Caesar;* probably best remembered for her portrayal of the deaf-mute in *Johnny Belinda;* films include *The Snake Pit* and *They Live by Night.*

CRAIG, Isa (1831–1903). *See Knox, Isa.*

CRAIG, Jenny (1932—). American entrepreneur. Born Genevieve Marie Guidroz, Aug 7, 1932, in Berwick, Louisiana; grew up in New Orleans; dau. of Gertrude Acosta and James Yoric Guidroz; m. 2nd husband Sid Craig (franchiser), 1979; children. ❖ After gaining weight during a difficult pregnancy with 2nd daughter Michelle, went to work in fitness clubs, managing, owning and selling them (1959); having signed a 2-year noncompete clause in US over previous franchise, started Jenny Craig, Inc., a weight-management firm, with 2nd husband in Australia (1983); opened centers in US (1985); eventually reached over 780 centers worldwide. ❖ See also autobiography, *The Jenny Craig Story: How One Woman Changes Millions of Lives* (2004).

CRAIG, Mrs. John Dickey (1880–1971). *See Young, Mary Marsden.*

CRAIG, Judy (1946—). American vocalist. Name variations: The Chiffons. Born 1946 in Bronx, NY. ❖ Sang lead vocal as member of the Chiffons, all-girl vocal group with Barbara Lee, Patricia Bennett and Sylvia Peterson, which had international hits in early 1960s; with Chiffons, had such hits as "He's So Fine" (1963), "One Fine Day" (with Carole King on Piano, 1963), "Nobody Knows What's Going On" (1965) and "Sweet Talkin' Guy" (1966).

CRAIG, Lilian (b. 1915). *See Davies, Lilian May.*

CRAIG, May (1888–1975). American journalist. Name variations: Elisabeth May Craig or Elisabeth May Adams Craig. Born Elisabeth May Adams, Dec 19, 1888, in Coosaw Mines, South Carolina; died July 15, 1975, in Silver Spring, Maryland; dau. of Alexander Adams and Elizabeth Ann (Essery) Adams (died 1893); at 6, was adopted by Frances and William Weymouth; attended George Washington University Nursing School; m. Donald A. Craig (journalist, columnist, and chief of Washington bureau of *Washington Times-Herald*), 1909 (died 1936); children: Donald A. Craig (b. 1910) and Betty Adams Craig (b. 1915). ❖ The 1st woman correspondent to participate in the Berlin airlift, to attend Kaesong truce talks in Korea, to be accredited as a war correspondent by US Navy, to live on a combat ship at sea and to fly over the North Pole, began career helping husband with column for Gannett Publishing, "On the Inside in Washington" (1923); worked with Gannett papers, earning byline as political columnist (1931) and writing column "Inside in Washington" (1930s–65), remaining nonpartisan towards political parties; joined American Newspaper Guild (early 1930s); as May Craig, broadcast "Inside Washington" on radio (1940s–65); was a member of Women's National Press Club, serving as president (1943); earned accreditation as war correspondent (1944) and traveled Europe covering WWII; was a frequent panelist on radio and tv broadcasts of "Meet the Press" (1940s–65); was a member of Washington Newspaper Guild, serving as vice president and as president; helped found Eleanor Roosevelt Press Conference Association.

CRAIG, May (1889–1972). Irish actress. Born in Dublin, Ireland, 1889; died in a Dublin nursing home, Feb 8, 1972; m. Vincent Power-Fardy (American), c. 1916 (died 1930); children: 5. ❖ Appeared in original production of John Millington Synge's *The Playboy of the Western World* (1907); joined Abbey Theatre (1916), remained with the company for the rest of her life, and made 6 US tours; best remembered for roles as Mrs. Tancred in Sean O'Casey's *Juno and the Paycock* and Mrs. Henderson in William Butler Yeats' drama about Jonathan Swift, *The Words upon the Windowpane.*

CRAIG, Minnie D. (1883–1965). American politician. Born Minnie D. Davenport, Nov 4, 1883, in Phillips, Maine; died 1965; dau. of Marshall H. Davenport and Anna Prescott Davenport; graduate of Maine Normal School, 1905; m. Edward O. Craig, 1908 (died Mar 12, 1947). ❖ On marriage, moved to Esmond, North Dakota (1909); served 6 terms in the North Dakota House of Representatives (1923–33); was 1st woman elected speaker of a state house of representatives (ND, 1933); served as state president of the Nonpartisan Clubs; served as Republican National Committee woman (1928–32); appointed state worker for the Federal

Emergency Relief Agency (1933); served as chief clerk of the legislative session (1937 and 1939); returned to Phillips, Maine (1959). Papers are located at North Dakota State University's Institute for Regional Studies.

CRAIG, Molly (c. 1917–2004). *Australian Aborigine.* Name variations: Molly Kelly. Born Molly Craig, c. 1917, in Jigalong, a community on the edge of the desert in Western Australia; died Jan 13, 2004, in Jigalong; dau. of Maude, a Mardudjara Aboriginal, and Thomas Craig, white British-born fence inspector of the rabbit-proof fence; sister of Daisy Kadibil; cousin of Gracie Fields; m. Toby Kelly (Aboriginal stockman); children: Annabelle; Doris Pilkington Garimara. ❖ At 14, along with sister Daisy (8) and cousin Gracie (10), was forcibly taken from her settlement in Western Australia by the Australian government for being half-caste (July 1931); with sister and cousin, made a 1,500-mile journey on foot to return to family (Aug–Oct 1931), though Gracie was recaptured and trained as a domestic; after marrying, was removed from settlement again, with her 2 children (1940); escaped once more and returned to Jigalong with baby Annabelle, having had to leave elder daughter Doris behind (Annabelle was taken at age 3 [1943] and raised in a home for "near whites"). ❖ See also Doris Pilkington, *Follow the Rabbit-Proof Fence* (U. of Queensland Press, 1996); (film) *Rabbit-Proof Fence* (2002).

CRAIG, Nell (1891–1965). *American silent-film actress.* Name variations: Nellie R. Craig. Born June 13, 1891, in Princeton, New Jersey; died Jan 5, 1965, in Hollywood, California; m. Fred E. Wright (died 1936). ❖ Starred in Lubin and Essanay films (1913–14); made over 100 films, including *The Queen of Sheba, The Flirt, The Dramatic Life of Abraham Lincoln, A Boy of Flanders, Cimarron, Dark Delusion* and *Consolation Marriage.*

CRAIG, Sandra (1942—). *Australian ballet dancer.* Born Dec 7, 1942, in Adelaide, Australia. ❖ Trained with Royal Ballet and Ballet Rambert in London, England; joined Ballet Rambert (1962), where she created roles for Christopher Bruce's *George Frederic* and *Living Space* (both 1969) and Norman Morrice's *Hazard* (1966) and *Blindsight* (1970).

CRAIGHILL, Margaret (1898–1977). *American physician.* Born Oct 16, 1898, in Southport, North Carolina; died July 1977 in Southbury, Connecticut; dau. of W.E. Craighill (colonel); University of Wisconsin, BA, 1920, MS, 1921; Johns Hopkins University, MD, 1924. ❖ The 1st woman doctor to serve as a US Army Medical Corps commissioned officer, began career as general surgery assistant at Bellevue Hospital (1928–37); appointed dean of Woman's Medical College of Pennsylvania (1940); advocated Sparkman-Johnson Bill (H.R. 1857), which granted female physicians opportunity to serve in US Army Medical Corps after its passage in 1943; joined Women's Army Corps (1943); served as vice chair for Committee on Women Physicians, Procurement and Assignment Service, War Manpower Commission (1941–44); advised on medical issues for 90,000 army women; initiated standard gynecological exams and mental-health screening for women as 1st consultant to Office of the Surgeon General's Women's Health and Welfare Unit (1944); promoted to lieutenant colonel (1945); became chief of service of Menninger Psychiatric Clinic (1949); returned to private practice in Greenwich and New Haven (CT). Awarded Legion of Merit (1945).

CRAIGIE, Cathie (1954—). *Scottish politician.* Born April 14, 1954, in Stirling, Scotland; children: 2. ❖ As a Labour candidate, elected to the Scottish Parliament for Cumbernauld and Kilsyth (1999, 2003).

CRAIGIE, Pearl Mary Teresa (1867–1906). *Anglo-American novelist and dramatist.* Name variations: (pseudonym) John Oliver Hobbes. Born Pearl Richards in Boston, Massachusetts, Nov 3, 1867; died in London, England, Aug 13, 1906; dau. of John Morgan (New York merchant) and Laura Hortense (Arnold) Richards; attended University College, London; m. Reginald Walpole Craigie, Feb 1887 (div. July 1895); children: 1 son. ❖ Moved to London as a child and remained there most of her life; writing under pseudonym John Oliver Hobbes, established a formula with 1st novel, *Some Emotions and a Moral* (1891), from which she seldom digressed; her dramas, like her novels, met with varying degrees of success, including *The Ambassador* (1898), which ran for a full season, mainly due to the witty dialogue; later efforts, with the exception of *The Bishop's Move* (1902), were not nearly as successful; also wrote many miscellaneous essays and sketches; served as president of Society of Women Journalists (1895–96). Writings include *The Gods, Some Morals and Lord Wickenham* (1894), *The School for Saints* (1897), *Robert Orange* (1899), *The Serious Wooing, a Heart's History* (1901), *The*

Vineyard (1903), *Imperial India, Letters from the East* (1903), *Letters from a Silent Study* (1904) and *The Artist's Life* (1904).

CRAIK, Dinah Maria Mulock (1826–1887). *English writer and activist.* Name variations: Miss Mulock; Mrs. Craik. Born Dinah Maria Mulock, April 20, 1826, in Stoke-on-Trent, Staffordshire; died Oct 12, 1887, at Bromley, Kent; dau. of Thomas Samuel (unstable dissenting preacher) and Dinah (Mellard) Mulock (died 1845); educated at Brampton House Academy, with possibly sporadic tutoring by father; m. George Lillie Craik (partner in Macmillan's publishing firm), 1865; children: (adopted) Dorothy. ❖ Victorian who earned her living by writing and who believed in greater freedom of opportunity for women, especially those unmarried; after father lost job, moved with family to Newcastle-under-Lyme (1831); helped mother to keep a school (183?–39); moved with family to London (1839); published verses in *Staffordshire Advertiser* (1841); published 1st novel *The Ogilvies* (1849), a romantic tale which was an instant success; published *John Halifax, Gentleman* (1856), the story of a poor boy rising to middle-class respectability by honesty and hard work, which critics hailed as a masterpiece and which has never been out of print; published *A Woman's Thoughts about Women* (1857); though she continued to write and her novels remained popular (she was demanding £2,000 a novel at height of career), never produced another *John Halifax, Gentleman;* awarded Civil List Pension of £60 per annum (1864) and often used it to help struggling women writers; wrote children's stories throughout life, but the one for which she is best remembered, *The Little Lame Prince*, was not written until 1875; other writings include *Studies from Life* (1861), *A Brave Lady* (1870), *King Arthur: Not a Love Story* (1886), *Hannah* (1871) and *Fifty Golden Years* (1887). ❖ See also Sally Mitchell, *Dinah Mulock Craik* (Twayne, 1983); and *Women in World History.*

CRAIK, Mrs. (1826–1887). See Craik, Dinah Maria Mulock.

CRAIKE, Isabel Annie (1887–1938). See Aves, Isabel Annie.

CRAIN, Jeanne (1925–2003). *American actress.* Born May 25, 1925, in Barstow, California; died of a heart attack, Dec 14, 2003, in Santa Barbara; dau. of George A. (teacher) and Loretta (Carr) Crain; attended University of California, Los Angeles, 1952; m. Paul Frederick Brinkman (former actor under name of Paul Brooks), Dec 31, 1945; children: Paul Jr., Timothy, Jeanine, Lisa and Maria. ❖ Film star (1940s–50s), made debut adorning a swimming pool in *The Gang's All Here* (1943); landed 1st major role (3rd billing) in *Home in Indiana* (1944); of her early films, probably best remembered for starring role in *State Fair* (1945); popularity rose considerably with release of *Margie* (1946) and *Apartment for Peggy* (1948); made 3 films (1949): *A Letter to Three Wives, The Fan* and *Pinky*, the last of which won her an Academy Award nomination; other films include *Leave Her to Heaven* (1945), *Centennial Summer* (1946), *You Were Meant for Me* (1948), *Cheaper by the Dozen* (1950), *People Will Talk* (1951), *Belles on Their Toes* (1952), *Gentlemen Marry Brunettes* (1955), *The Second Greatest Sex* (1955), *The Joker Is Wild* (1957) and *Skyjacked* (1972). ❖ See also *Women in World History.*

CRAMPTON, Mary (c. 1913–1980). See Pym, Barbara.

CRAMPTON, Mary Josephine (c. 1857–1924). See Player, Mary Josephine.

CRANCH, Elizabeth (1743–1811). *American diarist.* Born Nov 21, 1743, in Braintree, Massachusetts; died 1811; niece of Abigail Smith Adams; married a cleric; raised a family in Weymouth. ❖ Wrote *The Journal of Elizabeth Cranch*, during a visit to relatives in Haverhill, MA (1785–86).

CRANCH, Mary Smith (1741–1811). *Sister of Abigail Adams.* Name variations: Mary Smith. Born Mary Smith in 1741; died 1811; dau. of the Reverend William Smith (pastor, 1706–1783) and Elizabeth (Quincy) Smith (1721–1775); sister of Abigail Smith Adams (1744–1818); m. Richard Cranch, 1762; children: 3.

CRANDALL, Ella Phillips (1871–1938). *American nurse.* Born Sept 16, 1871, in Wellsville, New York; died Oct 24, 1938, in New York, NY; graduate of Philadelphia General Hospital School of Nursing, 1897; attended New York School of Philanthropy. ❖ Dedicated to establishing public nursing as a recognized profession with high standards, served on the graduate nursing faculty of Columbia University Teachers College (1910–12); also served on a commission charged with researching the need for organized public-health work (1911), which resulted in National Organization for Public Health Nursing (1912); was its executive secretary for 8 years; served as associate director of American Child Health Association (1922–25); named executive secretary of Payne Fund (1926), a philanthropic foundation that sponsored research in the field of education. ❖ See also *Women in World History.*

CRANDALL, Prudence (1803–1890). American educator and activist.
Born Prudence Crandall, Sept 3, 1803, in Hopkinton, Rhode Island; died in Elk Falls, Kansas, Jan 28, 1890; dau. of farmer Pardon Crandall and Esther (Carpenter) Crandall (both Quakers); attended New England Friends Boarding School in Providence, Rhode Island, 1825–26, 1827–30; m. Calvin Philleo (Baptist minister), Aug 19, 1834. ❖ Anti-slavery educator whose attempt to open a boarding school for African-American girls in Connecticut grew into one of the great race controversies of the antebellum era; taught school in Plainfield, Connecticut (1830–31); opened the exclusive Canterbury Female Boarding School (1831), housed in a large home in the center of town, which quickly became one of the most respected in Connecticut; admitted Sarah Harris, the school's 1st black student (Jan 1833); when leading members of the community complained and threatened to withdraw their children from the school, refused to back down; instead, opened the High School for Young Colored Ladies and Misses, in Canterbury, with 15 students (1833); faced with fanatical opposition, remained unmoved even when local shopkeepers refused to sell her supplies, doctors failed to visit sick children, and the Congregational church barred black students from attending services; was tried under Connecticut's newly passed "Black Law" (1834): "no person shall set up or establish in this state any school, academy, or literary institution, for the instruction or education of colored persons who are not inhabitants of the state . . . without the consent, in writing, 1st obtained of a majority of the civil authority, and also of the select-men of the town"; became a national (and international) *cause célèbre*; convicted but won on appeal; faced with a mounting threat to the safety of the girls after some of the townspeople turned to more overt violence, finally closed the school and moved away (1834); voted a pension of $400 by Connecticut Legislature (1886). ❖ See also Foner and Pacheco, *Three Who Dared: Prudence Crandall, Margaret Douglas, Myrtilla Miner—Champions of Antebellum Black Education* (Greenwood, 1984); Edmund Fuller, *Prudence Crandall: An Incident of Racism in Nineteenth-Century Connecticut* (Wesleyan U. Press, 1971); and *Women in World History.*

CRANE, Caroline Bartlett (1858–1935). American cleric and activist.
Name variations: Caroline Bartlett; Carrie. Born Caroline Julia Bartlett, Aug 17, 1858, in Hudson, Wisconsin; died Mar 24, 1935, in Kalamazoo, Michigan; dau. of Lorenzo Dow Bartlett (riverboat owner-captain) and Julia (Brown) Bartlett; graduated valedictorian from Carthage College in Illinois; studied privately for the ministry under Reverend Oscar Clute, Minnesota Unitarian Conference missionary; also guided by Reverends William Channing Gannett, Samuel McChord Crothers, and Henry M. Simmons; graduate courses in sociology at University of Chicago; m. Augustus Warren Crane (physician and early radiology pioneer), Dec 31, 1896; children: (adopted) Warren Bartlett Crane and Juliana Bartlett Crane. ❖ Social Gospel minister and municipal reformer, known nationally as "America's Housekeeper," instigated reforms nationwide that would help "clean up" America's cities and was the most widely known woman minister of her day; had 1st assignment as a Unitarian minister in Sioux Fall, Dakota Territory (1887), where she expressed a commitment to the Social Gospel, which combined congregational activism with a belief in scientific and social progress; accepted a ministerial position in Kalamazoo, Michigan (1889), a state in which women ministers were not common; had formal ordination (1889); transformed the church into a large, cohesive organization that embraced her enthusiasm for the Social Gospel and renamed it the People's Church; her flock included agnostics, transcendentalists, Christians, Jews, Muslims, Christian Scientists, and anyone else who felt the need to express spirituality through community action; took on additional duties in nearby Grand Rapids and also traveled to England where she was profoundly moved by many urban social problems (1890); one of the nation's most prominent reformers, was active in woman suffrage activities and served on many local and national committees; named to Michigan Women's Hall of Fame (1985). ❖ See also O'Ryan Rickard, *A Just Verdict: The Life of Caroline Bartlett Crane* (New Issues Press, 1994); and *Women in World History.*

CRANE, Eva (1911—). English apiculturalist. Name variations: Eva Widdowson; Dr. Eva Crane. Born Eva Widdowson, 1911, in England; sister of Elsie Widdowson (1906–2000); PhD in nuclear physics; m. James Alfred Crane (Royal Navy officer), 1942 (died 1978). ❖ Known for lifelong devotion to study of honey bees, began career as physicist (1938); worked as 1st director of International Bee Research Association (IBRA, 1949–83); served as editor of *Apicultural Abstracts*

(1950–83), of *Bee World* (1950–83), and of *Journal of Apicultural Research* (1963–82); wrote *Honey: A Comprehensive Survey* (1975), *The Archaeology of Beekeeping* (1983) and *The World History of Beekeeping and Honey Hunting: Bees as a World Resource* (1999); contributed to IBRA's dictionary of beekeeping terms. Named Officer of the Order of the British Empire (1984).

CRANE, Norma (1928–1973). American stage, tv, and screen actress.
Born Nov 10, 1928, in New York, NY; died Sept 28, 1973, in Los Angeles, California; m. Herb Sargent (writer, div.). ❖ On Broadway, appeared in *The Crucible, Bus Stop, Isle of Children* and *Fiddler on the Roof;* films include *Tea and Sympathy, Penelope, They Call Me Mr. Tibbs* and *Fiddler on the Roof.*

CRANSTON, Kate (1850–1934). Scottish tea-room proprietor and patron of arts. Name variations: Catherine Cranston. Born Catherine Cranston in 1850 in Glasgow, Scotland; died 1937 in Glasgow; dau. of George Cranston (hotelier); sister of Stuart Cranston (tea dealer, caterer, tearoom proprietor); m. John Cochrane (businessman), 1892 (died 1917). ❖ Beloved entrepreneur, a trendsetter in turn-of-the-century tearooms and influential patron of designers from Glasgow School of Art, was the daughter of a hotelier with a reputation for innovative hotel management, running a chain of high-class temperance hotels which provided alcohol-free accommodations; followed in his footsteps by opening chain of highly successful tea rooms in Glasgow, providing alternative social environment to pubs; opened 1st tearoom on Argyle St. with brother Stuart (1878), eventually operating 4 tea rooms (1878–1904); commissioned decorative schemes and furniture fittings by such artists as George Walton, Charles Rennie Mackintosh and Margaret Macdonald Mackintosh; organized and ran tea rooms for Glasgow International Exhibitions (1901 and 1911); sold Argyle and Buchanan St. branches upon husband's death (1917); retired (1919); left two-thirds of estate to the poor.

CRANZ, Christl (1914–2004). German Alpine skier. Name variations: Christl Cranz Borchers or Cranz-Borchers. Born July 1, 1914, in Germany; died Sept 28, 2004, near Oberstauffen, Germany; sister of Heinz Rudolf Cranz (skier). ❖ Germany's most-decorated skier, won a gold medal in the combined event at Garmisch-Partenkirchen Olympics (1936), after falling during the downhill and roaring back from 6th place; won more titles (12) than anyone before her—male or female—in the World championships (1934–39): in the downhill (1935, 1937, 1939), the slalom (1934, 1937–39), and the combined (1934–35, 1937–39); opened a children's ski school in Germany (1947).

CRAPP, Lorraine J. (1938—). Australian swimmer. Born 1938 in Australia; m. Bill Thurlow (physician). ❖ The 1st woman to swim the 400-meter freestyle in under 5 minutes, was also the 1st Australian—male or female—to hold world records in all freestyle races at the same time; broke 23 world records and won 9 Australian championships; won 3 gold, 1 silver, and 2 bronze medals at British Empire and Commonwealth Games; won gold medal for 400-meter freestyle and team gold for 4x100-meter freestyle relay at Melbourne Olympics (1956); won a silver for 400-meter freestyle at Rome Olympics (1960). ❖ See also *Women in World History.*

CRAPSEY, Adelaide (1878–1914). American poet. Born Sept 9, 1878, in Brooklyn, NY; died Oct 8, 1914, in Rochester, NY; dau. of Rev. Algernon Sidney Crapsey (Episcopalian pastor) and Adelaide (Trowbridge) Crapsey; graduate of Vassar College, 1901. ❖ Received appointment at Smith College to teach poetics (1911); created the *cinquain* (unrhymed, 5-line iambic stanza). Two works, *Verse* (1915) and *A Study in English Meters* (1918), published posthumously.

CRASKE, Margaret (1892–1990). English ballet dancer and teacher.
Born 1892 in Norfolk, England; died 1990 in Myrtle Beach, South Carolina. ❖ Danced with Diaghilev's Ballets Russes (1920) before she was forced to leave due to foot injury; returned to England where she served as assistant to Italian ballet master Enrico Cecchetti and became the leading exponent in Britain of his teachings; taught Cecchetti method in London for 7 years (1924–1931); traveled throughout India for 7 years following his death; immigrated to US (1939), where she became ballet master of American Ballet Theater in New York City (1947); taught at Metropolitan Opera School, Juilliard School, and Jacob's Pillow; opened Manhattan School of Dance; trained Antony Tudor, Hugh Laing, and Peggy van Praagh; wrote (with C.W. Beaumont) *Theory and Practice of Allegro in Classical Ballet* (1930) and (with Derra De Moroda) *The Practice of Advanced Allegro* (1956).

CRATTY, Mabel (1868–1928). American YWCA leader. Born Mabel Cratty, June 30, 1868, in Bellaire, Ohio; died Feb 27, 1928, in New York, NY; dau. of Charles Campbell Cratty and Mary (Thoburn) Cratty; niece of Isabella Thoburn (Methodist missionary in India); Ohio Wesleyan, BL, 1890. ❖ Concerned with problems facing young working women, immigrants, and minorities, served as general secretary of National Board of YWCA (c. 1906–28); worked to make YWCA a force for social and economic reform.

CRAVEN, Madame Augustus (1808–1891). *See Craven, Pauline.*

CRAVEN, countess of.
See Craven, Elizabeth (1750–1828).
See Brunton, Louisa (c. 1785–1860).

CRAVEN, Elizabeth (1750–1828). British baroness, playwright and novelist. Name variations: Lady Elizabeth Berkeley Craven; Baroness Craven or countess of Craven; Margravine of Anspach or Ansbach. Born Elizabeth Berkeley, Dec 17, 1750, in Middlesex, England; died Jan 12, 1828, in Naples, Italy; dau. of Augustus, 4th earl of Berkeley, and Elizabeth (Drax), countess of Berkeley; m. William Craven, 1767 (died 1791); m. Christian Fredric, margrave of Anspach, 1791. ❖ Renowned for her wit, beauty and intelligence, traveled widely after separation from husband and earned a scandalous reputation for her affair with the margrave of Anspach (their correspondence was published in London in 1786); works include *Modern Anecdotes of the Ancient Family of Kinkvervankdotdarsprackingatchderns: A Tale for Christmas 1799* (1780), *The Arcadian Pastoral* (1782), *The Georgian Princess* (1799) and *Memoirs* (1826).

CRAVEN, Louisa (c. 1785–1860). *See Brunton, Louisa.*

CRAVEN, Margaret (1901–1980). American novelist and journalist. Born Mar 13, 1901, in Helena, Montana; raised in Puget Sound area of Washington; died July 1980 in Sacramento, California; graduate of Stanford University with honors, 1924. ❖ Worked for a San Jose newspaper; at 69, published the acclaimed *I Heard the Owl Call My Name* (1973), about a dying vicar sent to a remote Indian village in British Columbia, which was filmed for tv; also wrote *Walk Gently This Good Earth* (1977) and *Again Calls the Owl* (1980); short stories, published in popular magazines, were collected in *The Home Front* (1981).

CRAVEN, Pauline (1808–1891). French novelist. Name variations: Madame Augustus Craven; Madame Craven; Pauline de la Ferronays. Born Pauline Marie Armande Aglaé de la Ferronays (also seen as de la Ferronnays) 1808 in London, England; died in Paris, April 1 or 2, 1891; m. Augustus Craven. ❖ Wrote 3 biographical and devotional works, *Récit d'une soeur, souvenirs de famille* (1866), *Le Travail d'une âme, étude d'une conversion* (1877) and *Une Année de méditations* (1881); also published novels, *Anne Séverin* (1868), *Fleurange* (1871), *Le Mot de l'Enigme* (1874), *Eliane* (1882) and *Le Valbriant* (1886), as well as historical and biographical studies.

CRAVEN, Sally (b. 1921). *See De Marco, Sally.*

CRAWFORD, Ann, Anne or Annie (1734–1801). *See Barry, Ann Street.*

CRAWFORD, Cheryl (1902–1986). American producer and director. Born in Akron, Ohio, Sept 24, 1902; died in New York, NY, Oct 7, 1986; dau. of Robert K. and Luella Elizabeth (Parker) Crawford; attended Butchel College and Smith College; never married; no children. ❖ Producer in American theater for 50 years, began career as assistant stage manager for Theresa Helburn at the Theatre Guild; with Harold Clurman and Lee Strasberg, formed The Group Theatre (1930) and co-produced several landmark plays, including Sidney Kingsley's Pulitzer prize-winning, *Men In White*, Maxwell Anderson's *Winterset*, and 4 plays by Clifford Odets, one of which was the ground-breaking *Waiting for Lefty* (1931–36); as an independent producer, had 1st hit, a revival of *Porgy and Bess* (1942); also produced *The Little Foxes* (1942), *Watch on the Rhine* (1942), *One Touch of Venus* (1943), *The Tempest* (1945), which had a longer run than any other US production of the play to date, *Brigadoon* (1946), *Paint Your Wagon* (1951), *Yentl* (1975), and 4 of Tennessee Williams' works, including *The Rose Tattoo* and *Sweet Bird of Youth;* with Margaret Webster and Eva Le Gallienne, founded American Repertory Theater; with Strasberg, Elia Kazan, and director Robert Lewis, formed the Actor's Studio (1947). ❖ See also memoirs *One Naked Individual: My Fifty Years in the Theatre* (1977); and *Women in World History.*

CRAWFORD, Cindy (1966—). American supermodel and actress. Born Cynthia Ann Crawford, Feb 20, 1966, in DeKalb, Illinois; dau. of John

and Jennifer Crawford; sister of Jeffrey Crawford (died of Leukemia, 1976); attended Northwestern University; m. Richard Gere (film actor), 1991 (div. 1994); m. Rande Gerber (model, entrepreneur), 1998; children: (2nd m.) Presley and Kaya. ❖ Supermodel, actress and tv presenter, studied chemical engineering at Northwestern University; discovered by photographer Victor Skrebenski, left college for a part-time modeling job in Chicago; moved to New York (1986), becoming top runway and photographic model and one of 1st major supermodels; graced the covers of over 400 magazines in career; produced exercise videos and make-up workbook in addition to modeling work; starred in film *Fair Game* (1995), with Billy Baldwin; other films include *The Simian Line* (2000) and *We Married Margo* (2000); appeared as fashion presenter in MTV show *House of Style* (1989–95); served as advertising spokesperson for numerous companies, including Pepsi and Revlon; activist for breast and ovarian cancer research, cancer caregivers, and Leukemia Society of American; wrote *About Face* (2001).

CRAWFORD, Fiona (1977—). Australian softball player. Name variations: Fiona Hanes. Born Feb 21, 1977, in Sydney, NSW, Australia; attended University of West Sydney. ❖ Second base/shortstop, won a team bronze medal at Sydney Olympics (2000) and a team silver at Athens Olympics (2004).

CRAWFORD, Jane Todd (1763–1842). American patient. Born 1763 in Rockbridge Co., Virginia; died 1842 in Graysville, Indiana; m. Thomas Crawford, 1794. ❖ Diagnosed with an ovarian tumor by Dr. Ephraim McDowell, rode 65 miles on horseback to undergo the 1st successful ovariotomy, which was completed without anesthesia (1809); lived for more than 3 decades after the 26-pound tumor was removed (procedure of great importance to the development of abdominal surgery). Jane Todd Crawford Memorial Hospital in Greensburg, Kentucky, opened in 1962.

CRAWFORD, Jean Ashley (1939—). American golfer. Name variations: Jean Ashley. Born Jan 10, 1939, in Chanute, Kansas; University of Kansas, BS, 1960. ❖ Won the Kansas Women's Amateur twice as Jean Ashley; reached the finals of the USGA Women's championship (1960); won the USGA title (1965); named to the Curtis Cup team (1962, 1966, 1968) and was non-playing captain (1972). Named to Kansas Golf Hall of Fame (1992).

CRAWFORD, Joan (1906–1977). American actress. Name variations: Billie Cassin. Born Lucille Fay LeSueur, Mar 23, 1906, in San Antonio, Texas; died May 10, 1977, in New York, NY; dau. of Thomas (laborer) and Anna Bell (Johnson) LeSueur; m. Douglas Fairbanks Jr., June 3, 1929 (div. 1933); m. Franchot Tone, Oct 11, 1935 (div. 1939); m. Phillip Terry, Sept 20, 1942 (div. 1946); m. Alfred Steele, May 10, 1955 (died April 1959); children: Christina Crawford (adopted June 1940); Christopher (adopted 1942); Cathy (adopted 1947); Cynthia (adopted, 1947). ❖ Hollywood icon who appeared in 80 films, received an Academy Award for *Mildred Pierce,* and whose humble beginnings, haughty manner, and impeccable grooming inspired a generation of young women, made Broadway debut dancing in the chorus of *Innocent Eyes* (1924); had 1st screen role in *Pretty Ladies* (1925); breakthrough came with silent film *Our Dancing Daughters* (1928), which was a huge success; triumphed in the talkie *Paid,* followed by *Grand Hotel* (1932); following a career slump, made a comeback in *Mildred Pierce* (1945); had other major successes with *Sudden Fear* (1952), a thriller that earned her an Academy Award nomination (also nominated for *Possessed* in 1947) and *Whatever Happened to Baby Jane?* (1962); through tenacity and hard work, remained a star for half a century, but reputation took a hit with the book, *Mommie Dearest,* written by daughter Christina (1978). Other films include *Rain* (1932), *Sadie McKee* (1934), *The Last of Mrs. Cheyney* (1937), *The Bride Wore Red* (1937), *Mannequin* (1938), *Strange Cargo* (1940), *Susan and God* (1940), *When Ladies Meet* (1941), *Above Suspicion* (1943), *Humoresque* (1946), *Daisy Kenyon* (1947), *Flamingo Road* (1949), *Harriet Craig* (1950), *Goodbye My Fancy* (1951), *Johnny Guitar* (1954), *Female on the Beach* (1955), *Queen Bee* (1955), *Autumn Leaves* (1956), *The Story of Esther Costello* (1957), *The Best of Everything* (1959), *The Caretakers* (1963), *Straight Jacket* (1964), *I Saw What You Did* (1965), *Berserk* (1967) and *Trog* (1970). ❖ See also autobiography (with Jane Kesner Ardmore) *A Portrait of Joan* (Doubleday, 1962); Shaun Considine, *Bette and Joan: The Divine Feud* (Dutton, 1989); Bob Thomas, *Joan Crawford* (Simon & Schuster, 1978); and *Women in World History.*

CRAWFORD, Julia (1790–1858). *See Crawford, Louise Macartney.*

CRAWFORD, Louise Macartney (1790–1858). Irish poet. Name variations: Louisa Matilda Jane Crawford; also seen as Julia Crawford. Born Louisa Matilda Jane Macartney, 1790, in Co. Cavan, Ireland (some sources cite London); died 1858 (also seen as 1855 and 1860); dau. of a British soldier and naturalist of Luckham Hall, Wiltshire. ❖ Though she wrote several novels, is best remembered for her lyrics to the song "Kathleen Mavourneen" (music written by Frederick Nicholls Crouch), published in *Metropolitan Magazine* in London (1830). Lyrics have also been wrongly attributed to Anne or Annie Crawford, an actress known as Ann Street Barry (1734–1801).

CRAWFORD, Mimi (d. 1966). English actress, singer and dancer. Name variations: Mimi Forde-Pigott; countess of Suffolk. Born Mimi Forde Pigott in England; niece of Lord Chalmers; died in 1966; m. Charles Henry George Howard, 20th earl of Suffolk, Mar 7, 1934 (died May 12, 1941, while detonating a bomb during WWII); children: 3 sons. ❖ Made stage debut as a child in *Pinkie and the Fairies* (1909), followed by *The Happy Family, Yes Uncle, The Midnight Follies, The Nine O'Clock Revue, Stop Flirting, The Monkey House, Vaudeville Vanities, Topsy and Eva* and *The Co-Optimists of 1930,* among others; appeared as La Camargo in *The Dubarry* and danced the solo of "The Blue Danube" in *Die Fledermaus* at Covent Garden (1931).

CRAWFORD, Ruth (1901–1953). American composer and folksong archivist. Name variations: Ruth Crawford Seeger or Ruth Crawford-Seeger. Born Ruth Porter Crawford, July 3, 1901, in East Liverpool, Ohio; died in Chevy Chase, Maryland, Nov 18, 1953; dau. of Clara Alletta (Graves) Crawford (teacher) and Clark Crawford (Methodist minister); American Conservatory of Music in Chicago, BM, 1924, MM, 1927; m. Charles Louis Seeger, 1932; children: Michael, known as Mike Seeger (b. Aug 1933, singer and multi-instrumentalist); Peggy Seeger (b. 1935); Barbara Seeger (b. 1937); Penelope, known as Penny Seeger (b. 1943, singer). ❖ One of the most innovative American composers of 1st half of 20th century, began piano lessons at 6; completed and premiered earliest musical compositions in public performance (1924); was in residence at MacDowell Colony in Peterborough, NH (1929); arrived in NY (1929); studied composition with Charles Seeger (1929–30); became 1st woman awarded Guggenheim fellowship in composition (1930); began collecting, transcribing, and arranging folk songs (1933); moved to Washington, DC, area (1935); gave private piano lessons and taught music in several nursery schools (1935–53); published folksong collections (1948–53). Published compositions include *Four Preludes for Piano* (1932), *Piano Study in Mixed Accents* (1932), *Three Songs for Contralto, Oboe, Piano, and Percussion* (1933), *String Quartet 1931* (1941), *Suite for Wind Quintet* (1969), *Chant* (1971), *Chinaman, Laundryman, and Sacco Vanzetti* (1976) and *Diaphonic Suites* (1972); folksong anthologies include *American Songbag* (1927), *Coal Dust on the Fiddle* (1943), *Anthology of Pennsylvania Folklore* (1949), *Treasury of Western Folklore* (1951) and *Folklore Infantil do Santo Domingo* (1955). ❖ See also Matilda Gaume, *Ruth Crawford Seeger: Memoirs, Memories, Music* (Scarecrow, 1986); and *Women in World History.*

CRAWFORD, Shannon (1963—). Canadian rower. Born Sept 12, 1963; trained at Argonaut Rowing Club in Toronto, Ontario, Canada. ❖ At Barcelona Olympics, won a gold medal in coxed eights (1992).

CRAWFORD ROGERT, Yunaika (1982—). Cuban hammer thrower. Born Nov 2, 1982, in Cuba. ❖ Won bronze medal at Athens Olympics (2004).

CRAWNMORE AND CROMAR, baroness of (1884–1954). *See MacRobert, Rachel.*

CRAYENCOUR, Marguerite de (1903–1987). *See Yourcenar, Marguerite.*

CRAZY BET (1818–1900). *See Van Lew, Elizabeth.*

CREDI, Nadine (1913–2003). *See Talbot, Nadine.*

CREECH, Christine (1944—). *See Grahame, Christine.*

CREED, Clifford Anne (1938—). American golfer. Born Clifford Anne Creed, Sept 23, 1938, in Alexandria, Louisiana; graduate of Lamar Tech. ❖ Won the Louisiana State championship 6 times; won 5 more amateur events; named to the Curtis Cup team (1962).

CREIDER, Jane Tapsubei (c. 1940s—). Kenyan novelist. Born in Kenya in 1940s. ❖ Works include *Two Lives: My Spirit and I* (1986) and *The Shrunken Dream*; with Chet A. Creider, wrote *A Dictionary of the Nandi Language* and several articles and books on Nandi language.

CREIGHTON, Cleva (d. 1967). *See Bush, Frances Cleveland.*

CREIGHTON, Lindy (1948—). *See Chamberlain, Lindy.*

CREIGHTON, Mary Frances (1899–1936). American murderer. Born July 29, 1899, in Rahway, New Jersey; died in electric chair at Sing Sing Prison, July 16, 1936; m. John Creighton; children: 2. ❖ Charged and acquitted with husband for murder of her younger brother by arsenic poisoning (1920s); charged and acquitted for murder of mother-in-law, also by arsenic poisoning; after moving to Long Island with husband, met Everett and Ada Appelgate who moved in with them (1935); after Ada Appelgate died a few months later from arsenic poisoning, was charged with her murder, along with Everett Appelgate (Jan 1936); admitted to giving arsenic to Ada in milk; electrocuted at Sing Sing Prison, as was Everett Appelgate.

CREMER, Erika (1900–1996). German-born Austrian physicist and chemist. Born May 20, 1900, in Munich, Germany; died Sept 21, 1996; University of Berlin, PhD in physical chemistry (1927). ❖ Called the mother of chromatography, worked with eminent chemists Karl Bonhoeffer, George de Hevesy, Michael Polanyi, and Otto Hahn; obtained teaching position at University of Innsbruck in Austria due to labor shortages caused by World War II (1940); developed plans for gas chromatography machine to separate compounds from a gaseous mixture, but much of the information was lost in bombings and air raids during war; after war, continued developing gas chromatography (one important use of which is to measure gases in blood); published results and was appointed professor of chemistry at University of Innsbruck (1951).

CRENNE, Helisenne de (c. 1510–c. 1550). *See Briet, Marguerite de.*

CREPIN, Margit (1945—). *See Otto-Crepin, Margit.*

CREQUY, Renée Caroline de Froulay, Marquise de (1714–1803). French letter writer. Name variations: Marquise de Créqui; Renee de Froulay. Born Renée-Caroline-Victoire Froullay in Oct 19, 1714, at Chateau of Monfleaux, Mayenne, France; orphaned at early age; died 1803; dau. of Lieutenant-General Charles François de Froullay; niece of M. de Bailli de Froullay, ambassador; m. Louis Marie, marquis de Criquy (died 4 years later, 1741); children: 1 son. ❖ Once an intimate of D'Alembert and J.J. Rousseau, became extremely religious with inclinations to Jansenism; formed a great friendship with Sénac de Meilhan (1781); her *Letters to Sénac de Meilhan* (1782–89), which express conservative but tolerant views on women and religion, was published with preface by Sainte-Beuve (1856); was arrested (1793) and imprisoned in the convent of Les Oiseaux until the fall of Robespierre (July 1794). *Souvenirs de la marquise de Créqui* (1834–35) regarded as inauthentic and attributed to a Breton adventurer, Cousin de Courchamps.

CRESCENTII (892–932). *See Marozia Crescentii.*

CRESPÉ, Marie-Madeleine (1760–1796). French ballerina. Name variations: Mlle Théodore; Marie-Madeleine Crespe. Born Marie-Madeleine Crespé (also seen as Crépé), Oct 6, 1760, in Paris, France; died Sept 9, 1796 (some sources cite 1798), in Audenge, France; studied with Jean-Barthélémy Lany; m. Jean Bercher, known as Jean Dauberval or D'Auberval (ballet dancer, 1742–1806), 1782. ❖ Debuted in *Myrtil et Lycoris* at the Paris Opéra (Dec 1777); created the part of Lise in the original production of Dauberval's *La Fille mal gardée* (1789); was also featured in the works of Georges Noverre; an inveterate reader, especially of Jean-Jacques Rousseau's writings, was known as "the philosopher in satin ballet slippers." ❖ See also *Women in World History.*

CRESPIN, Régine (1927—). French soprano. Name variations: Regine Crespin. Born 1927 in Provence, France; studied at Paris Conservatoire. ❖ Made debut in Mulhouse (1950) as Elsa in *Lohengrin*; was particularly noted for her Marschallin in *Der Rosenkavalier*, Sieglinde in *The Ring*, Carmen, Tosca, and performance in Poulenc's *Dialogues des Carmélites*; began taking mezzo-soprano roles (1977). ❖ See also memoir *On Stage, Off Stage* (Northeastern U., 1997).

CRESSON, Edith (1934—). French economist and politician. Born in France in 1934. ❖ France's 1st woman prime minister, joined the Socialist Party (PS, 1975); served as mayor of Thure (1977) and from her seat in the European Parliament (1979) became known as an expert in agriculture; was the 1st woman to head the Ministry of Agriculture (1981–83); served as trade minister (1983–84, 1984–86) and minister for European affairs (1988); appointed prime minister by François Mitterand (1991), but was forced to resign after the Socialist Party's defeat in regional elections (April 1992), only 10 months into her appointment; served on the European Commission, the administrative and executive arm of the European Union (EU, 1995–98). ❖ See also *Women in World History.*

CREWS, Mrs. J.D. (b. 1907). *See Orcutt, Maureen.*

CREWS, Laura Hope (1879–1942). American actress. Born Dec 12, 1879, in San Francisco, California; died Nov 13, 1942, in New York, NY; dau. of John Thomas Crews (carpenter) and Angelena (Lockwood) Crews (actress). ❖ Debuted at 4 in *Bootle's Baby* at Woodward's Theatre, San Francisco (c. 1884); had 1st significant success in NY supporting Eleanor Robson in *Merely Mary Ann* (1904); began lifelong association with Henry Miller in *Joseph Entangled* (1904) and appeared with him in such plays as *The Great Divide* (1906); at height of career, appeared with Theatre Guild in works including *Mr. Pim Passes By* (1922) and *Right You Are if You Think You Are* (1927); had greatest stage success as Mrs. Phelps in *The Silver Cord* (1926); with advent of talking films (1930s), taught diction to stars of the silents; appeared in numerous films and is especially remembered for her role as Aunt Pittypat in *Gone with the Wind* (1939) and as Mme Prudence in *Camille* (1936).

CREYKE, Elizabeth Rose Rebecca (1827–1881). *See Watts Russell, Elizabeth Rose Rebecca.*

CRIMMINS, Alice (1941—). American accused of murder. Born 1941; m. Edmund Crimmins; m. Anthony Grace; children: Alice Marie (known as Missy, d. 1965) and Eddie Jr. (d. 1965). ❖ The subject of one of the most sensational murder cases in New York (1960s), was tried for deaths of her 2 children in court of law and for promiscuous lifestyle in court of public opinion; husband, from whom she was separated, reported their 2 children missing (July 14 1965, 4-year-old Missy was found strangled to death the same day and 5-year-old Eddie was found dead several days later); almost 2 years after killings, was charged with daughter's murder, tried (May 1968) and found guilty of manslaughter; following appeal, was tried again for manslaughter in case of her daughter and, for the 1st time, for murder of her son; found guilty for both deaths, sentenced to life imprisonment; had 1st-degree murder conviction for death of son reversed, as was manslaughter conviction for death of her daughter; saw manslaughter conviction reinstated; paroled (Nov 1977). Crimmins' case—the story of which has appeared in print, tv, film, and on stage—has been controversial, with some maintaining that she was railroaded by police.

CRIPPS, Isobel (1891–1979). Well-known wife of Sir Stafford Cripps. Name variations: Dame Isobel Cripps. Born Isobel Swithinbank in 1891; died 1979; 2nd dau. of Commander Harold William (landowner) and Amy (Eno) Swithinbank; m. Sir Stafford Cripps (1889–1952, British diplomat), 1911; children: son John (editor of the *Countryman*) and 3 daughters, including Peggy (who m. Joe Appiah). ❖ Supported husband's political career and cared for him in his poor health; accompanied him to USSR, where he served as ambassador in Moscow (1940–42); during WWII, served as president of the British United Aid to China Fund; toured China as guest of General Chiang Kai-shek and Madame Chiang (Song Meiling); visited Yenan at invitation of Mao Zedong and was presented with Special Grand Cordon of the Order of the Brilliant Star of China and the award of the National Committee of India in celebration of International Women's Year. Named CBE (1946). ❖ See also *Women in World History.*

CRIPPS, Sarah Ann (c. 1821–1892). New Zealand shopkeeper, postmaster, and midwife. Name variations: Sarah Ann Rigelsford. Born Sarah Ann Rigelsford, c. 1821 or 1822 in London, England; died June 8, 1892, in Wellington, New Zealand; dau. of John Rigelsford (laborer); m. Isaac Cripps (policeman), 1844; children: 10. ❖ Immigrated to Auckland Islands (1852); operated accommodation house and established shop and post office (mid-1850s); served as midwife to growing community of Whareama. ❖ See also *Dictionary of New Zealand Biography* (Vol. 1).

CRISI, Maria (1892–1953). Italian poet and novelist. Name variations: Maria Ginanni. Born 1892 in Naples, Italy; died 1953 in Florence; m. Count Arnaldo Ginanni-Corradini (futurist writer who used Arnaldo Ginna as his pseudonym). ❖ Edited futurist series *Libri di valore;* was a member of the editorial board of the journal *L'Italia Futurista* from its inception in 1916, and director (1916–18); works include *Luci trasversali* (1917), *Montagne trasparenti* (1917) and *Il poema dello spazio* (1919); with Emilio Settimelli, also wrote the play *La macchina.*

CRISLER, Lois (1897–1971). American writer and naturalist. Born Lois Brown in 1897; died June 4, 1971, in Seattle, Washington; m. Herb

"Cris" Crisler (div.); no children. ❖ Writer who, with husband, spent more than 8 years observing and living with wolves and whose observations provided some of the 1st detailed descriptions of their social interactions; taught at the University of Washington; writings include *Arctic Wild* (1958) and *Captive Wild.* ❖ See also *Women in World History.*

CRISPELL, Marilyn (1947—). American pianist. Born Marilyn Braune, Mar 30, 1947, in Philadelphia, Pennsylvania; studied piano at Peabody Institute in Baltimore from age 7, and composition at New England Conservatory in Boston; attended Karl Berger's Creative Music Studio; studied jazz harmony with Charlie Banacos in Boston; married (1969–75). ❖ One of most compelling talents of a generation of pianists, developed distinctive volcanic improvisational style; collaborated frequently with Anthony Braxton, touring with Creative Music Orchestra (1978), becoming member of Anthony Braxton Quartet and recording on Braxton's Composition 98 album (1981); was also a member of Reggie Workman Ensemble and Barry Guy New Orchestra; composed original music drawing initially on Cecil Taylor's dense rhythmic piano playing and then creating more individual style; began leading groups and playing solo (1980s); made several albums on Music & Arts and Leo labels, working with Reggie Workman, Doug James, Andrew Cyrille, Anthony Davis, Tim Berne, Marcio Mattos, Eddie Prevost, and others; continued recording throughout 1990s, yielding many well-regarded albums that included Braxton Quartet bandmates Mark Dresser and Gerry Hemingway, and sessions with Paul Motian, Irene Schweizer, Gary Peacock and Fred Anderson, as well as solo recordings, notably *Live at Mills College* (1995); performed at jazz and avant-garde festivals, occasionally as solo artist; featured in French film *Women in Jazz* by Gilles Corre; released DVD, *Pianist's Guide To Free Improvisation: Taught By Marilyn Crispell* (2002). Albums include *Spirits Hung in Undrawn Sky* (1983), *And Your Ivory Voice Sings* (1985) and *Labyrinths* (1988).

CRIST, Judith (1922—). American film critic and journalist. Born May 22, 1922, in New York, NY; Hunter College, BA; Columbia University, MS. ❖ Joined staff of *New York Herald Tribune* as a reporter and feature writer; became associate drama critic, then editor for the arts, then film critic; was film and theater reviewer on NBC's "Today" (1964–73); writings include *The Private Eye, The Cowboy and the Very Naked Girl* (1968), *Judith Crist's TV Guide to the Movies* (1974) and *Take 22* (1984); served on the adjunct faculty at Columbia University Graduate School of Journalism for over 45 years.

CRISTIANE (1985—). *See Rozeira de Souza Silva, Cristiane.*

CRISTINA (1948—). *See Saralegui, Cristina.*

CRISTINA (1965—). Spanish princess and duchess of Palma. Name variations: Christina or Christine; Cristina Bourbon. Born Cristina Frederica Victoria, June 13, 1965, in Madrid, Spain; dau. of Sophia of Greece (b. 1938) and Juan Carlos I, king of Spain (r. 1975—); m. Inaki Urdangarín y Liebaert (professional athlete), Oct 4, 1997; children: Juan (b. 1999). ❖ Third in line to the Spanish throne, married a Basque commoner in a 13th-century cathedral in Barcelona (1997), the city's 1st royal wedding in over 600 years. ❖ See also *Women in World History.*

CRISTINA, Ines (b. 1875). Italian actress. Born Dec 1875 in Constantinople; dau. of Raffaello Cristina and Cesira (Sabatini) Cristina (actress). ❖ As a child, made stage debut with the company of Davide Mazzanti (1890), followed by Carlo Cola (1891), Michele Fantechie (1891–92), Angelo Pezzaglia (1892), Ettore Paladini and Virgilio Talli (1892–93), Cesare Rossi (1893–94), Paladini and Vittorio Zampieri (1894–95), and Claudio Leigheb and Virginia Reiter; appeared with Eleonora Duse in the film *La città morta* by Gabriele D'Annunzio (1901).

CRISTINA I OF NAPLES (1806–1878). *See Maria Cristina I of Naples.*

CRITCHFIELD, Lee (c. 1909—). American film and vaudeville dancer. Born c. 1909 in Los Angeles, California. ❖ Trained with Ernest Belcher at his Los Angeles school and appeared in many of his films by age 18; performed on live theater stages, vaudeville, and Prologs, mainly with Fanchon and Marco's West Coast Deluxe Theaters; mastered playing Marimbaphone, a combination of marimba and xylophone created by Edward Mills, which she danced upon.

CROCHET, Evelyne (1934—). French pianist. Born in 1934. ❖ Studied with Yvonne Lefébure, Edwin Fischer and Rudolf Serkin; won a 1st prize in Yvonne Lefébure's class at Paris Conservatory (1954); at American debut, partnered with Francis Poulenc in US premiere of his Concerto for

Two Pianos and Orchestra (conducted at Boston Symphony by Charles Munch); made acclaimed recordings of complete piano works of Gabriel Fauré; revealed affinity for lesser-known works of German composers, particularly Franz Schubert.

CROCKER, Betty.
See Husted, Marjorie Child (c. 1892–1986).
See Cumming, Adelaide Hawley (1905–1998).

CROCKER, Fay (1914—). Uruguayan golfer. Born Aug 2, 1914, in Montevideo, Uruguay. ❖ Won the Uruguayan Women's Amateur 20 times; came to US and joined LPGA (1953); won USGA Women's Open (1955), the oldest champion at age 40 and 11 months, in winds that reached 40 mph; won 11 tournaments (1955–60).

CROCKER, Hannah Mather (1752–1829). American feminist. Born Hannah Mather, June 27, 1752, in Boston, Massachusetts; died July 11, 1829, in Roxbury, MA; dau. of Rev. Samuel Mather (1706–1785) and Hannah (Hutchinson) Mather; granddau. of Cotton Mather; m. Joseph Crocker (captain in the Revolution), 1779 (died 1797); children: 10. ❖ Helped organize, and presided over, a women's Masonic Lodge (beginning 1778); published compilation of her writings about the Lodge, *A Series of Letters on Free Masonry* (1815); published the historic *Observations on the Real Rights of Women* (1818), which maintained that the female mind is equal to the male mind.

CROCKER, Lucretia (1829–1886). American educator. Born Dec 31, 1829, in Barnstable, Massachusetts; died Oct 9, 1886, in Boston, MA; dau. of Henry and Lydia E. (Farris) Crocker; graduate of State Normal School at West Newton, 1850. ❖ Responsible for introducing instruction in zoology and mineralogy in Boston public schools, taught geography, mathematics, and natural science at State Normal School in West Newton (MA); served as professor of mathematics and astronomy, Antioch College (1857–59); headed science department of Society to Encourage Studies at Home (1873–76); seated on the Boston School Committee (c. 1874); elected to newly created Board of Supervisors (1876); was the 1st nonscientist elected to the American Association for the Advancement of Science (1880); published *Our World* (1864) and *Methods of Teaching Geography: Notes on Lessons* (1883).

CROCKER, Mary Lou (1944—). American golfer. Name variations: Mary Lou Daniel Crocker. Born Sept 17, 1944, in Louisville, Kentucky. ❖ Won USGA Junior Girls' and Western Junior titles (1962); joined LPGA tour (1966); won the Marc Equity (1973); hampered by a knee injury.

CROCKETT, Jean A. (1919–1998). American banker. Born April 20, 1919, in Tucson, Arizona; died Oct 3, 1998 in Delaware, Pennsylvania. ❖ Served as professor of economics and chair of finance department, Wharton School, University of Pennsylvania; appointed chair of the Regional Federal Reserve Bank in Philadelphia, PA (1981) and served one-year term beginning Jan 1, 1982.

CROCKETT, Rita Louise (1957—). American volleyball player. Born Nov 2, 1957, in San Antonio, Texas. ❖ At Los Angeles Olympics, won a silver medal in team competition (1984). Named US Volleyball Association's Rookie of the Year (1978).

CROCOMBE, Marjorie Tuainekore (fl. 1970s). New Zealand writer. Name variations: Tua'inekore. Born in Rarotonga, Cook Islands, New Zealand. ❖ Helped develop South Pacific Creative Arts Society and played important role in emergence of Oceanian literature; served as director of Extension Services department at University of Rarotonga and director of Centre for Pacific Studies at Auckland University; works include *They Came for Sandalwood* (1964), (with Ron Crocombe) *The Works of Ta'unga: Records of a Polynesian Traveller in the South Seas 1833–1896* (1968), and *If I Live: The Life of Ta'unga* (1977); trans. and edited *Cannibals and Converts: Radical Changes in the Cook Islands* by Maretu (1983).

CROFT, June (1963—). English swimmer. Born June 17, 1963, in UK. ❖ At Moscow Olympics, won a silver medal in 4x100-meter medley relay (1980); at Los Angeles Olympics, won a bronze medal in 400-meter freestyle (1984).

CROFT, Mabel (1887–1958). *See Ballin, Mabel.*

CROFT, Peta-Kaye (1972—). Australian politician. Born Aug 5, 1972, in Mount Isa, Australia. ❖ As a member of the Australian Labor Party, elected to the Queensland Parliament for Broadwater (2001).

CROISE, Jacques (b. 1906). *See Shakhovskaya, Zinaida.*

CROIZETTE, Sophie Alexandrine (1847–1901). French actress. Name variations: Sophie Alexandrine Croisette. Born in St. Petersburg, Russia, Mar 19, 1847, of French parentage; died 1901; educated in the schools of Versailles; her sister married the artist Carlos Duran; married an American banker named Stern, 1885. ❖ Noted French actress, was admitted to the Paris Conservatoire (1867); made debut (1869); was made an associate of the Comédie Française (1873), of which she was the *jeune première;* retired from the stage (1881).

CROKER, Bithia May (c. 1849–1920). Irish novelist and short-story writer. Name variations: Mrs. B.M. Croker; Bithia Mary Croker; Mary Croker. Born Bithia May (or Mary) Sheppard, c. 1849, in Co. Roscommon, Ireland; died Oct 20, 1920, in London, England; dau. of William Sheppard (rector of Kilgefin); m. John Croker (lieutenant-colonel). ❖ Lived in India and Far East with husband before returning to England, and many of her stories deal with upper-class life in India and Ireland; works include *Proper Pride* (1882), *Diana Barrington* (1888), *Married or Single* (1895), *In the Kingdom of Kerry and Other Stories* (1896), *Jason and Other Stories* (1899), *The Happy Valley* (1904), *Fame* (1910), *The Road to Mandalay* (1917) and *The House of Rest* (1921).

CROKER, Mary (c. 1849–1920). *See Croker, Bithia May.*

CROKER, Norma (1934—). Australian runner. Born Sept 11, 1934. ❖ At Melbourne Olympics, won a gold medal in the 4x100-meter relay (1956).

CROLL, Tina (1943—). American modern dancer. Born Aug 27, 1943, in New York, NY. ❖ Studied with some of most notable modern dancers at American Dance Festival (1962–64), including José Limón, Martha Graham, Lucas Hoving, Alvin Ailey, and Louis Horst; performed with Dance Theater Workshop (late 1960s) in works by Jack Moore, Jeff Duncan, Art Bauman, and James Cunningham; represented the women at whom advertising is directed in Bauman's *Burlesque/Black & White* (1967); choreographed own works—solos and group pieces—for Dance Theater Workshop (1965–68); formed dance troupe, Tina Croll and Company; conceived and directed *From the Horse's Mouth* with Jamie Cunningham, a live documentary performance piece which celebrates the "heart and history of dance."

CROLY, Jane Cunningham (1829–1901). English-born American writer and editor. Name variations: Jennie June (journalistic pseudonym, sometimes spelled Jenny June). Born Jane Cunningham, Dec 19, 1829, in Market Harborough, Leicestershire, England; died Dec 23, 1901, in New York City; moved to US in 1841; dau. of Joseph (Unitarian minister) and Jane (Scott) Cunningham; m. David Goodman Croly, Feb 14, 1856; children: Minnie Croly; Viola Croly; Herbert Croly (founding editor of *The New Republic*); Alice Cary Croly; and a son who died in infancy. ❖ Founder of the women's club movement in America, and champion of women's right to work, who syndicated her work and created the 1st newspaper "women's pages"; became 1st woman reporter at a US daily newspaper (*New York Tribune*, 1855); joined *New York Herald* (1856); as the 1st woman syndicated newspaper columnist in America (1857), was published in *New Orleans Picayune, New Orleans Delta, Baltimore American, Richmond Enquirer, Chicago Times, Louisville Journal,* and other periodicals; was chief staff writer for *Mme. Demorest's Mirror of Fashions,* later *Demorest's Monthly Magazine* (1860–87); created 1st "women's pages" in US newspaper (*New York World,* 1862); formed women's club Sorosis (1868), serving as its president (1870, 1875–86); served as editor of *Godey's Lady's Book* (1887–88); was instrumental in the founding of General Federation of Women's Clubs (1889); founded Woman's Press Club of New York City (1889), serving as its president (1889–1901); awarded honorary doctorate by Rutger's Women's College (1892), where she was appointed chair of journalism and literature; was a tireless champion of women's right to work. Writings include *Jennie Juneiana: Talks on Women's Topics* (1869), *Sorosis: Its Origin and History* (1886) and *The History of the Women's Club Movement in America* (1898). ❖ See also *Women in World History.*

CROMPTON, Richmal (1890–1969). *See Lamburn, Richmal Crompton.*

CROMWELL, Bridget (1624–c. 1660). Daughter of Oliver Cromwell. Name variations: Bridget Fleetwood. Baptized Aug 5, 1624, in Huntingdon, England; died soon after the Restoration (1660), date of death unknown; dau. of Oliver Cromwell (English soldier and Lord Protector) and Elizabeth (Bourchier) Cromwell; sister of Mary, Countess of Falconberg (1636–1712); m. General Henry Ireton (1611–1651); m. Charles Fleetwood, (c. 1618–1692), June 8, 1652; children: (1st m.) Bridget Bendish (c. 1650–1726); Jane Ireton;

Elizabeth Ireton; (2nd m.) Anne (died young), possibly others who also died young. ❖ At 22, married Henry Ireton, a soldier and her father's loyal supporter; shortly after Ireton was killed (1652), a victim of Irish warfare, married Charles Fleetwood, who helped Cromwell govern England; after father died, was often torn in her loyalties between her husband and her brothers who were in opposition. ❖ See also *Women in World History.*

CROMWELL, Elizabeth (1598–1665). Lady Protectress. Name variations: Elizabeth Bourchier; though her name was Elizabeth she was called Joan by the cavaliers. Born Elizabeth Bourchier in 1598; died at Northborough Manor, in Northamptonshire, England, the home of her son-in-law John Claypole, 1665; eldest of 6 children of Sir James Bourchier (merchant of the shire of Essex but no relation to the noble Bourchiers of Essex) and Frances Crane Bourchier; m. Oliver Cromwell (1599–1658, Lord Protector), Aug 22, 1620; children: Robert (b. Oct 1621); Oliver (b. Feb 1623); Bridget Cromwell (1624–c. 1660); Richard (Oct 1626–1712); Henry (b. Jan 1628); Elizabeth Cromwell, later Lady Claypole, known as Bettie (July 1629–Aug 6, 1658); Mary Cromwell (1636–1712), countess of Fauconberg; Frances Cromwell (1638–1721), also known as Lady Rich, later known as Lady Russell. ❖ Plump and pretty, endured mockery from scandalmongers and satirists; along with unproven accusations of drunkenness, was seen as a conventional domestic; in reality, was cunning, with the ability to manage her husband and steer him in political affairs. ❖ See also *Women in World History.*

CROMWELL, Mary (1636–1712). Countess of Fauconberg. Name variations: Mary of Falconberg; Mary, countess of Falconberg; Mary Fauconberg. Born Feb 1636 in Ely, England; died 1712 in London, England; dau. of Oliver Cromwell, later Lord Protector of England, and Elizabeth (Bouchier) Cromwell; m. Thomas Belayse, Viscount Fauconberg, Nov 1657 (died 1700); no children. ❖ The 7th of 8 surviving children, had a particularly close relationship with her father, revealed in their letters and in the letters of those who knew them; intelligent and high-spirited, was a valuable political asset to Oliver, concerned with helping him maintain his position. ❖ See also *Women in World History.*

CRONIN, Breeda (1953—). *See Moynihan-Cronin, Breeda.*

CRONIN, Grace Lenczyk (1927—). *See Lenczyk, Grace.*

CRONIN, Mrs. Robert (1927—). *See Lenczyk, Grace.*

CROOK, Jane (1894–1962). *See Devanny, Jean.*

CROOKS, Charmaine (1961—). Jamaican-Canadian runner. Born Aug 8, 1961, in Jamaica; sister of Natty Crooks (high jumper). ❖ Moved to Canada at age 6; at Los Angeles Olympics, won a silver medal in 4x400-meter relay (1984); was Canada's flag bearer at Atlanta Olympics (1996); was an 11-time Canadian champion in the 400 meters and 800 meters and the 1st Canadian woman to break the 2-minute barrier in the 800; at the Commonwealth Games, won a gold medal in 4x400-meter relay (1982) and a silver medal in the 800 meters and a bronze medal in 4x400-meter relay (1994); at the Pan American Games, won a gold medal in the 400 meters (1983).

CROPLEY, Eileen (1932—). English modern dancer. Born 1932 in London, England. ❖ Trained at Martha Graham school in New York City; joined Paul Taylor's company (1966), where she danced for many years, creating a role in his *Orbs,* and dancing in his *Foreign Exchange, Public Domain, Big Bertha, Aureole, Post Meridian* and *Lento,* among others.

CROPPER, Hilary (1941–2004). British business executive. Born Hilary Mary Trueman, Jan 9, 1941, in Bollington, near Macclesfield, Cheshire, England; died Dec 26, 2004; elder dau. of an accountant; read maths at University of Salford; m. Peter Cropper, 1963; children: 2 daughters; 1 son. ❖ One of Britain's pre-eminent businesswomen, served as chair and chief executive of computer-services group Xansa, one of UK's leading providers of IT services, for 17 years; championed women in work by offering home-based and part-time employment. Appointed CBE (1999) and DBE (2004).

CROSBY, Mrs. Bing (1933—). *See Grant, Kathryn.*

CROSBY, Caresse (1892–1970). American-born philanthropist and publisher. Born Mary Phelps Jacob in New York, NY, 1892; died in Rome, Italy, 1970; m. a Peabody; m. Harry Crosby (died); m. a 3rd time. ❖ With 2nd husband Harry Crosby, founded the Black Sun Press, which printed their own poetry, the letters of Henry James and Marcel

Proust to Walter Berry (Caresse's cousin), and the work of writers D.H. Lawrence, James Joyce, Hart Crane, Ezra Pound, and Gertrude Stein; also founded Crosby Continental Editions (1930s), which would introduce American writers to the French, including Kay Boyle, William Faulkner, and Ernest Hemingway; patented and sold a "backless brassiere" to Warner Brothers Corset Company of Bridgeport, CT (1914) and is now considered the 1st to patent a brassiere. ❖ See also memoir, *The Passionate Years* (1953); Anne Conover, *Caresse Crosby: From Black Sun to Roccasinibalda* (Capra); and *Women in World History.*

CROSBY, Dixie Lee (1911–1952). *See Lee, Dixie.*

CROSBY, Elizabeth (1888–1983). American anatomist. Born Elizabeth Caroline Crosby, Oct 25, 1888, in Petersburg, Michigan; died 1983; dau. of Lewis Frederick Crosby and Frances Kreps Crosby; Adrian College, BS in math, 1910; University of Chicago, MS in anatomy, PhD, 1915; children: 2 (adopted). ❖ Mentor to thousands of students, was a world expert of animal nervous systems (vertebrate phylum); in anatomy, served as instructor (1920–26), assistant professor (1926–29), associate professor (1929–36), then 1st female professor (1936–58), and professor emerita (1958–83) at University of Michigan Medical School; took 1-year leave to help University of Aberdeen's Marischal College (Scotland) develop a neuroanatomy department; retired (1958). Was 1st woman recipient of Henry Russell Lectureship (1946); given American Association of Anatomists' Henry Gray Award (1972) and National Medal of Science (1979).

CROSBY, Fanny (1820–1915). American blind poet, hymn writer, and worker in the Mission Movement. Born Frances Jane Crosby in Southeast Putnam Co., New York, Mar 24, 1820; died in Bridgeport, Connecticut, Feb 12, 1915; dau. of John (farmer) and Mercy (Decker) Crosby; attended New York Institution for the Blind, 1835–43; m. Alexander Van Alstyne, Mar 5, 1858 (died 1902); children: 1 (died in infancy). ❖ Blind from infancy, became a popular poet and a prominent figure in American evangelical religious life at end of 19th century; recognized primarily as the author of as many as 9,000 hymns, was also a well-known speaker and devoted mission worker; in later years, was often referred to as "the Protestant saint" or "the Methodist saint," because of the large number of the faithful throughout the world that made pilgrimages to receive her prayers and advice; best known hymns include "Rescue the Perishing," "Jesus the Water of Life Will Give," "Blessed Assurance," "The Bright Forever," "Savior, More Than Life to Me," "Pass Me Not, O Gentle Savior," and her personal favorite "Safe in the Arms of Jesus"; contributed lyrics to 60 or so other songs, some of which went on to become popular favorites of her day, like "Hazel Dell," "There's Music in the Air," and "Rosalie, the Prairie Flower"; writings include *The Blind Girl and Other Poems* (1844), *Monterey and Other Poems* (1851) and *A Wreath of Columbia's Flowers* (1858). ❖ See also Dolores Burger, *Women Who Changed the Heart of the City: The Untold Story of the City Rescue Mission Movement* (Kregel, 1995); Bernard Ruffin, *Fanny Crosby* (United Church Press, 1956); and *Women in World History.*

CROSBY, Kathryn Grant (1933—). *See Grant, Kathryn.*

CROSET, Paule (1920–1992). *See Corday, Rita.*

CROSMAN, Henrietta (1861–1944). American stage and screen actress. Name variations: Henrietta Foster Crosman; Mrs. Sedley Browne. Born Sept 2, 1861, in Wheeling, West Virginia; died Oct 31, 1944, in Pelham Manor, NY; dau. of George H. Crosman and Mary (Wick) Crosman; granddau. of Henrietta Wick (sister of composer Stephen Foster); m. Sedley Browne, 1886 (div. 1896); m. Maurice Campbell, 1896 (died 1942); children: (1st m.) 1 son; (2nd m.) 1 son. ❖ Debuted in NY at Windsor Theatre as Letty Lee in *The White Slave* (1883); in early career, appeared primarily in farce and comedy; received star status in *Mistress Nell* at the Bijou, NY (1990); had particular success in *Sweet Kitty Bellairs* (1903–04), *Sham* (1909) and *The Real Thing* (1911); also appeared in *The Merry Wives of Windsor* (Mistress Page, 1916), *Getting Married* (Mrs. George, 1916), and *Children of the Moon* (Madame Atherton, 1923); gave final stage performance in *Thunder in the Air* (1929); appeared in silent films (1913–27) and talking pictures, including *Pilgrimage* (1933); known as a feminist.

CROSS, Ada (1844–1926). *See Cambridge, Ada.*

CROSS, Amanda (1926–2003). *See Heilbrun, Carolyn.*

CROSS, Mrs. George (1844–1926). *See Cambridge, Ada.*

CROSS, Jessica (b. 1909). American runner. Born April 14, 1909. ❖ At Amsterdam Olympics, won a silver medal in 4x100-meter relay (1928).

CROSS, Joan (1900–1993). British soprano, opera administrator and teacher. Born in London, England, Sept 7, 1900; died in Aldeburgh, Suffolk, Dec 12, 1993. ❖ Was closely identified with the music of Benjamin Britten (1913–1976); created the role of Ellen Orford at world premiere of Britten's opera *Peter Grimes* (1945); also created major roles in other Britten operas, including *Albert Herring, Gloriana* and *The Turn of the Screw*; was a founding member of the English Opera Group; began directing operas at Covent Garden (1946); founded the Opera School (later the London Opera Centre, 1948). Named Commander of the British Empire (1953). ❖ See also *Women in World History*.

CROSS, Mrs. John W. (1819–1880). *See Evans, Mary Anne.*

CROSS, Mary (c. 1623–1698). *See Fisher, Mary.*

CROSS, Mary Ann or Marian (1819–1880). *See Evans, Mary Anne.*

CROSS, Victoria (1868–1952). *See Cory, Annie Sophie.*

CROSS, Zora (1890–1964). Australian poet and journalist. Born Zora Bernice May Cross, May 18, 1890, at Eagle Farm, Brisbane, Australia; died Jan 22, 1964, at Glenbrook in the Blue Mountains; dau. of Mary Louisa Eliza Ann (Skyring) Cross and Ernest William Cross (accountant); m. Stuart Smith (actor), Mar 11, 1911 (div., 1922); had relationship with David McKee Wright (author and journalist); children: (with Wright) 2 daughters; (with another) one son who was adopted by Wright. ❖ Known as a woman much in advance of her time, was responsible for what one biographer called the "first sustained expression in Australian poetry of erotic experience from a woman's point of view"; was a drama critic for *Green Room* and *Lone Hand*, then worked as a columnist for *Brisbane Daily Mail*; published 1st book of poems, *A Song of Mother Love* (1916), followed by *Songs of Love and Life* (1917), which comprised 60 love sonnets; in addition to poetry, published several works of fiction, including *Daughters of the Seven Mile: The Love Story of an Australian Woman* (1924), *The Lute Girl of Rainyvale: A Story of Love, Mystery and Adventure in North Queensland* (1925), *The Victor* (1933) and *This Hectic Age* (1944). ❖ See also *Women in World History*.

CROSS-BATTLE, Tara (1968—). American volleyball player. Name variations: Tara Battle. Born Sept 16, 1968, in Houston, Texas; attended Long Beach State University. ❖ Outside hitter, made the national team (1990); at Barcelona Olympics, won a bronze medal in team competition (1992); named team MVP (1995); competed at Sydney Olympics (2000); won silver medal at World championships and served as team captain (2002).

CROSSLEY, Ada Jemima (1871–1929). Australian singer. Name variations: Ada Crossley, Ada Muecke, Ada Frederick. Born Mar 3, 1871, in Tarraville, Victoria, Australia; died Oct 17, 1929, in Woodlands Park, Great Missenden, Buckinghamshire, England; studied with Sir Charles Santley and Blanche Marchesi; m. Dr. Francis Frederick (throat specialist), 1905. ❖ Known for interpretive skills as contralto singer, began career with 3rd Philharmonic Subscription Concert at Melbourne Town Hall; debuted in Sydney (1892); left for Europe to study after giving farewell concerts in Melbourne, Sydney and Adelaide (1894); made debut at Queens Hall, London (1895); was in great demand for oratorios and festivals throughout Britain after standing in at short notice for Clara Butt; gave 5 command performances for Queen Victoria in 2 years; toured US (1902–03), recording for new Victor's Red Seal series and later became an established international recording artist; had extensive repertoire; returned to Australia for 2 tours with supporting artists (1903–04, 1907–08), including young pianist Percy Grainger; cut back on commitments in later years but still performed at many charity concerts during WWI.

CROSSON, Marvel (1904–1929). American pilot. Born April 27, 1904, in Warsaw, Indiana; died Aug 18, 1929, in Wellton, Arizona. ❖ Made 1st solo flight in San Diego (1923); accompanied brother to Alaska to try bush flying, and became the 1st woman there to earn pilot's license (1927); became stunt flyer and, with brother, founded an air-transport company; became women's altitude record holder (1929); died during the National Women's Air Derby (1929), after jumping from her disabled plane. Accusations were made that Crosson's plane, and the planes of some other women at the Derby, had suffered from tampering or inadequate maintenance to keep them out of the race.

CROTEAU, Julie (1970—). American baseball player. Born Dec 4, 1970, in Berkeley, California. ❖ While in 12th grade, unsuccessfully sued Osborne Park High (Manassas, VA) for not letting girls play varsity baseball; became 1st woman to play NCAA baseball (1989), at 1st base for Division III St. Mary's College in Maryland; served as assistant coach at Massachusetts, becoming 1st woman to coach Division I (1995–96); noted for helping girls and women discover opportunities in baseball. Her college glove is located at the Baseball Hall of Fame in Cooperstown.

CROTHERS, Rachel (1878–1958). American playwright. Born in Bloomington, Illinois, Dec 12, 1878; died in Redding, Connecticut, July 5, 1958; dau. of Eli Kirk (physician) and Marie Louise (dePew) Crothers (physician); graduate of Illinois State Normal School, 1892. ❖ In a career that bridged 4 decades, wrote 24 full-length plays that were produced on the New York stage, making her the most successful and prolific American playwright of early 20th century and an important, though often overlooked, contributor to the emergence of the modern American drama; during WWII, organized American Theatre Wing for War Relief, best known for its Stage Door Canteen, of which she was executive director until the age of 72; principle works include: *Nora* (1903), *Criss Cross* (1904), *The Three of Us* (1906), *Old Lady 31* (1916), (with Kate Douglas Wiggin) *Mother Carey's Chickens* (1917), *Once upon a Time* (1918), *39 East* (1919), *Nice People* (1921), *Everybody* (1921), *Mary the Third* (1923), *A Lady's Virtue* (1925), *Let Us Be Gay* (1929), *As Husbands Go* (1931), *When Ladies Meet* (1932), judged the best work of her career, *Caught Wet* (1932) and *Susan and God* (1937). ❖ See also *Women in World History*.

CROUCH, Anna Maria (1763–1805). English opera singer. Born 1763, probably in London, England; died Oct 2, 1805, in Brighton, England; married to a lieutenant in Royal Navy named Crouch; lived with Irish baritone Michael Kelly, 1784. ❖ Triumphed in the role of Polly Peachum in John Gay's *The Beggar's Opera*; had brief and profitable relationship with George IV (her husband received £400 per annum for not suing him). ❖ See also M.J. Young, *Memoirs of Mrs. Crouch* (London, 1806).

CROUCH, Eliza (c. 1837–1886). *See Pearl, Cora.*

CROW, Sheryl (1962—). American pop singer. Name variations: Sheryl Suzanne Crow. Born Feb 11, 1962, in Kennett, Missouri; earned degree in classical music from University of Missouri. ❖ Started singing in rock groups at 16; taught music at a St. Louis elementary school; sang backup for Michael Jackson on *Bad* tour (1987–88); signed with A&M records (1991); convinced record company to scrap debut album and replace it with *Tuesday Night Music Club* (1994), which earned 3 Grammys; released hit singles "All I Wanna Do" (1994), "If It Makes You Happy" (1996), "Everyday is a Winding Road" (1997), "My Favorite Mistake" (1998) and "Soak Up the Sun" (2002); released albums *Sheryl Crow* (1996), *The Globe Sessions* (1998), *Sheryl Crow and Friends: Live From Central Park* (1999) and *C'mon, C'mon* (2002); played small role in film *The Minus Man* (1999) and sang Cole Porter's "Begin the Beguine" in *De-Lovely* (2004).

CROW, Tamara (1977—). American synchronized swimmer. Born Feb 3, 1977, in St. Louis, Missouri; attended University of California, Berkeley. ❖ Won a team bronze medal at Athens Olympics (2004); sentenced to 90 days in jail for vehicular manslaughter (2003).

CROW DOG, Mary (1953—). Lakota memoirist. Name variations: Mary Brave Bird. Born Mary Ellen Brave Bird, 1953, on the Rosebud Sioux Reservation in South Dakota; m. Leonard Crow Dog (medicine man), 1970s. ❖ Was not only involved with the AIM takeover and siege at the Wounded Knee memorial in South Dakota, but gave birth in the midst of it; under name Mary Brave Bird, with Richard Erdoes, wrote memoir *Ohitaka Woman* (1990), which was reprinted as *Lakota Woman* (1991) then filmed for TNT by Jane Fonda, starring Irene Bedard.

CROWDY, Rachel (1884–1964). English social reformer. Name variations: Dame Rachel Eleanor Crowdy. Born in 1884; died 1964; educated at Hyde Park New College, London; trained as nurse at Guy's Hospital, 1908. ❖ Joined the Voluntary Aid Detachment (VAD, 1911); was a lecturer and demonstrator at the National Health Society (1912–14), then worked with Katharine Furse to establish the Women's Royal Naval Service (WRNS) during WWI; awarded DBE (1919), the same year she was appointed chief of Social Questions and Opium Traffic Section at the League of Nations; was stationed with the International Typhus Commission in Poland (1920–21), then pursued social work in many nations (1931–39); was regions' advisor to the Ministry of Information (1939–46).

CROWE, Catherine Anne (c. 1800–1876). British novelist, short-story writer and translator. Name variations: Catherine Stevens Crowe. Born

Catherine Stevens, c. 1800 in Borough Green, Kent, England; died 1876 in Folkestone, Kent; dau. of John Stevens; m. John Crowe (lieutenant-colonel), 1822. ❖ Wrote realistic novels about working people, as well as works on the supernatural; novels include *Adventures of Susan Hopley; or, Circumstantial Evidence* (1841), *Men and Women; or, Manorial Rights* (1843), *The Story of Lilly Dawson* (1847), *Adventures of a Beauty* (1852) and *Linny Lockwood* (1854); works on the supernatural include *The Night Side of Nature; or, Ghosts and Ghost Seers* (1848) and *Spiritualism and the Age We Live In* (1859).

CROWE, Eleanor (1902–1957). See *Fair, Elinor*.

CROWE, Ellen (c. 1845–1930). New Zealand community leader. Name variations: Ellen Silke. Born Ellen Silke, c. 1845–1847, in Ballandooley, Co. Galway, Ireland; died Jan 24, 1930, in New Zealand; dau. of John Silke (smallholder) and Bridget (Cody) Silke; m. John Crowe, 1868; children: 9. ❖ Immigrated to New Zealand as part of government immigration scheme (1866); joined by several family members (1870s); settled in Irish Catholic area within Southland's Scots Presbyterian population, becoming central figure within community. ❖ See also *Dictionary of New Zealand Biography* (Vol. 1).

CROWE, F.J. (1929—). See *Johnston, Jill*.

CROWE, Mrs. George (1842–1917). See *Bateman, Kate*.

CROWE, Sylvia (1901–1997). British landscape architect and designer. Name variations: Dame Sylvia Crowe. Born Sylvia Crowe, Sept 15, 1901, in Banbury, Oxfordshire, England; died June 30, 1997, in London; dau. of Eyre Crowe (engineer) and Beatrice (Stockton) Crowe; graduate of Swanley Horticultural College, Kent, 1922; studied under Edward White; shared an office with Brenda Colvin. ❖ One of the leading theorists and practitioners in her field in the 20th century, worked as a landscape designer (1926–39), and, after WWII war service, became one of the world's best known landscape architects; created harmonious plans for several of the UK's new cities, and became a leader in landscaping power plants and other industrial facilities, creating realistic and aesthetically pleasing designs that helped alleviate the scars of industry's intrusion into nature; writings include *The Landscape of Power* (1958), *Forestry in the Landscape* (1966), *The Landscape of Forests and Woods* (1978) and *Garden Design*. Received OBE (1967); named Dame Commander of the British Empire (1973). ❖ See also *Women in World History*.

CROWLEY, Honor Mary (1903–1966). Irish politician. Born Honor Mary Boland, Oct 19, 1903, in London, England; died Oct 18, 1966; dau. of John Pius Boland (chief whip of the Irish Party, representing South Kerry at Wstminsiter, 1900–18); m. Fred H. Crowley (TD, South Kerry, 1927–45). ❖ Began career as social worker in London; following death of husband, won a seat in a by-election as a Fianna Fáil representative to the 12th Dáil (1945–48), the 1st woman to represent Kerry; returned to the 13th–18th Dáil for South Kerry (1948–66); was the 1st woman to represent Ireland on a delegation to the Council of Europe in Strasbourg (1954–57).

CROWLEY, Pat (1929—). American actress. Name variations: Patricia Crowley. Born Sept 17, 1929, in Olyphant, Pennsylvania. ❖ Began career as a child model; made film debut in *Forever Female* (1954), followed by *Red Garters, The Square Jungle, Key Witness, The Wheeler Dealers, The Biscuit Eater* and *Off the Wall*, among others; on tv, appeared as Judy Foster on "A Date with Judy" (1952), Emily Fallmont on "Dynasty" (1986), Mary Margaret Scanlon Collins on "Port Charles" (1997—), and starred in the tv series "Please Don't Eat the Daisies" (1965–67).

CROWLEY, Rosemary (1938—). Australian politician. Name variations: Rosemary Anne Crowley. Born in 1938; lived in Adelaide, South Australia, Australia. ❖ The 1st South Australian female member of the Australian Labor Party (ALP) in federal parliament, was appointed senator for South Australia (1983); was also the 1st SA woman to be elected to a federal ministry when she was made minister for Family Services (1993–96) and minister assisting the Prime Minister on the Status of Women (1993–94); retired (2002).

CROZIER, Catharine (1914–2003). American classical musician. Name variations: Catharine Crozier Gleason. Born 1914 in Hobart, Oklahoma; died Sept 19, 2003, in Portland, Oregon; earned artist's diploma at University of Rochester (1941); m. Harold Gleason (music professor, died 1980). ❖ Worked at University of Rochester's Eastman School of Music, joining organ faculty (1939) and serving as chair of organ department (1953–55); made debut at Washington National Cathedral, Washington, DC (1941); played at inaugural concerts of organs at Philharmonic Hall (now Avery Fisher Hall) (1962) and Alice Tully Hall (1975) at Lincoln Center; was artist-in-residence at Trinity Episcopal Cathedral in Portland, OR (1993–2003); edited several editions of Harold Gleason's *Method of Organ Playing*; among the 1st American women to have a touring and recording career, performed throughout US, Canada and Europe; taught master classes across US; performed music by a variety of composers, including Nicolas de Grigny, Marcel Dupré, and Paul Hindemith. Received Performer of the Year Award from NYC chapter of American Guild of Organists (1979).

CRUDGINGTON, Carolyn (1968—). Australian softball player. Name variations: Carolyn Gunderson. Born Aug 18, 1968, in Queensland, Australia. ❖ Pitcher, won a bronze medal at Atlanta Olympics (1996).

CRUFT, Catherine Holway (1927—). English architectural historian and curator. Name variations: Catherine Cruft. Born in 1927 in London, England; attended Edinburgh University. ❖ Leading figure in the conservation of historic architectural sites in UK, amassed extensive knowledge of Scottish architectural history and successfully preserved innumerable archives; worked with Scottish National Building Record (SNBR) and Scots Ancestry Research Society; spent 2 years producing lists of buildings of special interest for Edinburgh with architect Ian Lindsay; became curator of SNBR (1958); developed integrated approach to Monuments Record with architect Colin McWilliam, collecting buildings, photographs, original architectural drawings, survey drawings and biographical material in one central location.

CRUICKSHANK, Margaret Barnet (1873–1918). New Zealand physician. Born Jan 1, 1873, at Palmerston, Otago, New Zealand; died Nov 28, 1918, at Waimate, New Zealand; dau. of George Cruickshank (contractor and farmer) and Margaret (Taggart) Cruickshank; University of Otago, MB, 1897, MD, 1903; further study at universities of Edinburgh and Dublin, 1913. ❖ First New Zealand woman to register as physician and subsequently to engage in general medical practice (1897); organized local work of Waimate Red Cross Fund during World War I. ❖ See also *Dictionary of New Zealand Biography* (Vol. 3).

CRUIKSHANK, Isabella (c. 1842–1919). See *Siteman, Isabella Flora*.

CRUISE O'BRIEN, Maire (b. 1922). See *Mhac An tSaoi, Máire*.

CRUMP, Diane (1949—). American jockey. Born 1949 in Milford, Connecticut; managed thoroughbred horse farms, including training barn at Calumet Farms in Kentucky; later barn manager at Keysville Post Stables in Flint Hill, Virginia. ❖ At 12, moved to Oldsmar, Florida; was the 1st woman to race against men in a US parimutuel race (Feb 7, 1969); was the 1st to ride in a Kentucky Derby (May 2, 1970); forced to retire due to injuries. ❖ See also *Women in World History*.

CRUMPLER, Rebecca Lee (1831–1895). African-American physician. Born Feb 8, 1831 (some sources cite 1833) in Delaware; died Mar 9, 1895, in Hyde Park, Massachusetts; dau. of Absolum Davis and Matilda Webber; m. Arthur Crumpler, post Civil War. ❖ The 1st African-American woman in US to obtain medical degree, was raised and taught nursing skills by an aunt in PA; assisted doctors in Charlestown, MA (1852); graduate of New England Female Medical College in Boston (1864); treated women and children in Boston, then continued studies in "British Dominion"; treated African-Americans in Richmond, VA, via an agreement with Freedmen's Bureau (post Civil War); returned to Boston practice (1869). Writings include *A Book of Medical Discourses* (1883), based on her journals, which offered advice about women and children's health.

CRUSAT, Paulina (1900–1981). Spanish novelist. Born 1900 in Barcelona, Spain; died in Seville, Spain, 1981. ❖ Wrote *Aprendiz de persona* (Apprentice Person, 1956) and *Las ocas blancas* (The White Geese, 1959).

CRUSO, Thalassa (1908–1997). English-born American writer and horticulturalist. Born in London, England, Jan 7, 1908; died in Wellesley, Massachusetts, June 1997; dau. of Antony Alford and Mildred S. (Robinson) Cruso; granted acad. diploma anthropology and archeology, London School of Economics, 1932; m. Hugh O'Neill Hencken, Oct 12, 1935; children: Ala Mary (who m. William S. Reid); Sophia (who m. David L. Stone); Thalassa (who m. Thomas J. Walsh Jr.). ❖ Had her own program, "Making Things Grow" on PBS's WGBH; became a familiar figure as an expert gardener and gardening instructor; was also a columnist for *Boston Sunday Globe* and frequent contributor to *McCall's*, *Country Journal* and *Horticulture;* writings include *Making Things Grow* (1969), *A Small City Garden* (1972), *To Everything There Is a Season* (1973), *The Cape Cod Dunes* (1974) and *Making Vegetables Grow* (1975). ❖ See also *Women in World History.*

CRUTCHLEY, Rosalie (1921–1997). English actress. Born Jan 4, 1921, in London, England; died July 28, 1997, in London; m. Danson Cunningham (div.); m. Peter Ashmore (div.). ❖ Made stage debut at Liverpool Rep in *St. Joan* (1938); made London debut as Angelica in *Love for Love* (1943), followed by *The Circle, The Compelled People, Intimate Relations, All the Year Round, A Doll's House, The Crucible* and *Don Juan,* among others; made film debut in *Take My Life* (1947), followed by *Quo Vadis, Lady with the Lamp, Sons and Lovers, Make Me An Offer, No Love For Johnny, Freud, Wuthering Heights* and *Creatures the World Forgot.* Won Guild television award for Best Actress of the Year (1956).

CRUVELLI, Sofia (1826–1907). German soprano. Born Sophie Crüwell in Bielefeld, Prussia, Mar 12, 1826; died in Monaco, Nov 6, 1907; sister of Friederika Marie Crüwell(1824–1868), a mezzo-soprano; studied in Paris with Bordogni and in Milan with Lamperti; m. Baron Vigier, 1856. ❖ One of the finest dramatic sopranos of her day, had 1st success in Vienna in Oddabella's *Attila* (1847) and later in Paris and London; widely lauded for performance in Verdi's *Les Vêpres siciliennes* at Grand Opera in Paris, which had been written for her (1854); retired on marriage (1856). ❖ See also *Women in World History.*

CRUZ, Agata (1916–1999). *See Machado, Luz.*

CRUZ, Celia (1924–2003). Cuban singer. Born Celia de la Caridad Cruz Alfonso, Oct 21, 1924, in Havana, Cuba; died of a brain tumor, July 16, 2003, at home in Fort Lee, New Jersey; studied at Havana Conservatory of Music; m. Pedro Knight (trumpeter, as well as her director and manager), July 14, 1962. ❖ Known as the "Queen of Salsa," launched singing career on local radio stations (1940s); was lead singer with La Sonora Matancera, a popular orchestra in Cuba (1950–65); toured, headlined at The Tropicana, and had many hit recordings, including "Bemba Colora," "del Cocoye," "Yerbero," "Moderno," and "Burundanga" (which went gold, 1957); defected to US (1959); joined Tito Puente's band (1966). Won a Grammy for album *Celia and Johnny,* recorded with Johnny Pacheco's orchestra (1974). ❖ See also *Women in World History.*

CRUZ, Juana Inés de La (1651–1695). *See Juana Inés de la Cruz.*

CRYER, Ann (1939—). English politician and member of Parliament. Born Ann Place, Dec 14, 1939; m. Bob Cryer (MP for Keighley and Bradford South), 1963 (died 1994); children: John Cryer (MP). ❖ Representing Labour, elected to House of Commons for Keighley (1997, 2001, 2005).

CRYER, Gretchen (1935—). American actress and lyricist. Born Gretchen Kiger, Oct 17, 1935, in Indianapolis, Indiana; dau. of E.W. Kiger Jr.; graduate of DePauw University; Harvard University, MAT degree; m. David Cryer (actor), 1954 (div. 1968); children: Jon Cryer (actor), Robin Cryer (performer) and Shelley Cryer (make-up artist). ❖ With Nancy Ford (composer), wrote book, lyrics and co-starred in *Now is the Time for All Good Men* (1967), *The Last Sweet Days of Isaac* (1970), *Shelter* (1973) and *I'm Getting My Act Together and Taking It On the Road* (1981); also wrote *American Girls Revue* and appeared in *Little Me* (1962).

CRYER, Sarah (1848–1929). New Zealand farmer and benefactor. Born Feb 14, 1848, at Wroughton, Wiltshire, England; died Aug 30, 1929, at Waterford, New Zealand; dau. of Moses Cryer (butcher) and Hannah (Matthews) Cryer. ❖ Immigrated with family to New Zealand (1849); inherited and farmed 67-acre estate at Waterford (1893); generous patron of church, was also active in several benevolent societies. ❖ See also *Dictionary of New Zealand Biography* (Vol. 2).

CRYSTALS, The.
See Alston, Barbara.
See Brooks, Dolores.
See Kennibrew, Dee Dee.
See Love, Darlene.
See Thomas, Mary.
See Wright, Patricia.

CSÁK, Ibolya (b. 1915). Hungarian high jumper. Name variations: Csak or Czak; Ibolya Kádárné. Born Jan 6, 1915, in Budapest, Hungary. ❖ At Berlin Olympics (1936), won a gold medal after a drawn-out duel with England's Dorothy J. Tyler ended in a jump off, because she had less failures at that height than Tyler (had a later rule applied for deciding ties, Tyler would have been the champion).

CSASZAR, Monika (1954—). Hungarian gymnast. Born Nov 17, 1954. ❖ At Munich Olympics, won a bronze medal in team all-around (1972).

CSATANE, Beatrix (1974—). *See Balogh, Beatrix.*

CSIKNE-HORVATH, Klara (1947—). Hungarian handball player. Born Aug 1947. ❖ At Montreal Olympics, won a bronze medal in team competition (1976).

CSILLIK, Margit (b. 1914). Hungarian gymnast. Born Nov 18, 1914. ❖ At Berlin Olympics, won a bronze medal in team all-around (1936).

CSISZTU, Zsuzsa (1970—). Hungarian gymnast and sports commentator. Born Feb 15, 1970, in Hungary. ❖ Placed 2nd in all-around at the Hungarian International (1987) and Champions All (1990); became a well-known tv sports announcer in Hungary. ❖ See also film *Zuzu* (Norwegian documentary about Csisztu as an 8-year-old gymnast).

CSIZMAZIA, Kim (c. 1968—). American multisport athlete. Born c. 1968 in Vancouver, British Columbia, Canada; grew up in Whistler, British Columbia, and Ketchum, Idaho. ❖ Accomplished ice climber, rock climber, skier, mountain biker, and paraglider; in ice climbing, won gold in Difficulty (Winter 1998 and 1999) and Speed (Winter 1998) at X Games; became (1st woman) Ice Climbing World Cup champion (2000), 2-time Courchevel and Ouray champion, W16 climber undefeated in competition, and 1st woman to climb M10; achieved status of top female ice climber in the world; in paragliding, set North American tandem record of 92 miles with Will Gadd (2000); in skiing, won numerous Nordic National championships and titles including Junior Skier of the Year (1987); as mountain biker, was nationally ranked expert and pro rider (1987–89) and state champion in Utah and Idaho; won silver (1996) and gold (1997) in Survival of the Fittest; serves as pilot for Paraglide America Team, competes in endurance competitions, and is partner in Ascending Women (teaching and guiding service in climbing and skiing for women).

CUCCHI, Claudine (1834–1913). Italian ballet dancer. Born Mar 6, 1834, in Monza, Italy; died Mar 8, 1913, in Milan. ❖ Studied and made performance debut at Teatro alla Scala in Milan; appeared at Paris Opéra in Mazillier's *Le Corsaire* (1856) and at the Hoftheater in Vienna in many works by Pasquale Borri; spent a season in St. Petersburg, where she danced in *Giselle, Catarina* and *Esmeralda;* returned to Milan to perform at La Scala once more. ❖ See also Claudina Cucchi, *Venti anni di paloscenio* (Rome, 1904).

CUDDIE, Mary (1823–1889). New Zealand midwife, shopkeeper. Name variations: Mary Parkinson. Born Mary Parkinson, 1823, in Maybole, Ayrshire, Scotland; died June 9, 1889, in New Zealand; dau. of Richard Parkinson (weaver) and Jane (Girvan) Parkinson; m. Thomas Cuddie (weaver), 1844; children: 11. ❖ Immigrated to New Zealand (1848); served as midwife to community; mortgaged family's 34-acre farm to purchase and operate successful grocery shop (1879). ❖ See also *Dictionary of New Zealand Biography* (Vol. 1).

CUDERMAN, Alenka (1961—). Yugoslavian handball player. Born June 13, 1961. ❖ At Los Angeles Olympics, won a gold medal in team competition (1984).

CUDONE, Carolyn (1918—). American golfer. Name variations: Mrs. Philip Cudone. Born Sept 7, 1918, in Oxford, Alabama; m. Philip Cudone. ❖ Member of the Curtis Cup team (1956) and non-playing captain (1970); won the Metropolitan title (1955, 1961–65) and the New Jersey championship (1955–65); dominated the USGA Women's Senior championship for 5 straight years (1968–72).

CUDONE, Mrs. Philip (1918—). *See Cudone, Carolyn.*

CUDWORTH, Damaris (1658–1708). *See Masham, Damaris.*

CUI YONGMEI (1969—). Chinese volleyball player. Born Jan 23, 1969, in China. ❖ Won a team bronze medal at Seoul Olympics (1988) and a team silver at Atlanta Olympics (1996).

CUILIN GE (1930—). *See Ge Cuilin.*

CULLBERG, Birgit (1908–1999). Swedish dancer, choreographer, and director. Born in Nyköping, Sweden, Aug 3, 1908; died Sept 8, 1999, in

Stockholm; dau. of Ella W. Cullberg and Carl Cullberg (bank director); studied at Stockholm University; trained with Kurt Jooss at Jooss-Leeder School at Dartington Hall, England (1935–39); m. Anders Ek (actor), 1942 (sep. 1949, reconciled 1959, later div.); children: Niklas and Mats Ek (both dancers) and Malin Ek (actress and twin to Mats). ❖ Following studies in choreography in England, returned to Sweden (1939) to learn ballet techniques from Lillian Karina and form her own dance group for commercial revues; initial ballets, especially *Propaganda* and *Offensive,* were known for their humor, satire, and behavioral studies; with Ivo Cramér, directed the Swedish Dance Theatre (1946–47); was a resident choreographer of the Royal Swedish Ballet (1952–59) and then served as director and choreographer of Stockholm City Theatre; appointed a member of the artistic council to the Royal Swedish Ballet, where she staged her *Seven Deadly Sins* (1963); dances were a frequent staple of Scandinavian companies as well as of the American Ballet Theatre, New York City Ballet, and Chilean National Ballet, among others; choreographic works include *Miss Julie* (1950), *Medea* (1951), *Moon Reindeer* (1957), *Odysseus* (1959), *The Lady from the Sea* (1960), and the tv ballet "The Evil Queen" (1961), which won the Prix d'Italia, as well as *Salome* (1964), *Romeo and Juliet* (1969), *Bellman* (1971), *Révolte* (1973), *Rapport* (1976), *Peer Gynt* (1976), *At the Edge of the Backwoods* (1977), and *Krigsdanser* (1979). Awarded Swedish King's fellowship (1958) and the Order of Vasa (1961).

CULLEN, Anne (1951—). *Collins, Anne.*

CULLEN, Betsy (1938—). American golfer. Name variations: Mary Elizabeth Cullen. Born Aug 14, 1938, in Tulsa, Oklahoma; University of Oklahoma, degree in phys. ed. ❖ Joined LPGA tour (1962); won Sears Classic (1972), Alamo Open (1973), and Hoosier (1975); became a teaching pro; named LPGA Central Section Teacher of the Year (1996 & 1998); LPGA Master Professional.

CULLEN, Mary Elizabeth (1938—). *See Cullen, Betsy.*

CULLIS, Winifred Clara (1875–1956). British physiologist. Born 1875 in Gloucester, England; died in 1956; attended Newnham College, Cambridge University; University of London, DSc, 1908; never married. ❖ The 1st woman in United Kingdom to serve as a professor of physiology, was a demonstrator in physiology at Royal Free Hospital Medical School (1901), then lecturer and head of physiology department (1908–41); taught at University of Toronto (1908–12); became a reader at University of London (1912), then professor of physiology (1919), and was the 1st holder of Jex-Blake chair of physiology (1926–41); carried out important research in the early part of her career; an ardent feminist, played a leadership role in several organizations, including British Federation of University Women (president, 1925–29) and the International Federation of University Women (president, 1929–32); retired from teaching (1941) but remained active in the field of physiology; headed women's section, British Information Services, New York (1941–43); lectured in Middle East (1944–45); was one of the 1st women to be elected membership in Physiology Society. Awarded CBE (1929). ❖ See also *Women in World History.*

CULMBERGER, Renate (1939—). *See Garisch-Culmberger, Renate.*

CULPEPER, Frances (b. 1634). *See Berkeley, Frances.*

CUM, Hong (c. 1854–1915). *See Lo Keong, Matilda.*

CUMBA JAY, Yumileidi (1975—). Cuban shot putter. Born Feb 11, 1975, in Cuba. ❖ Won a gold medal at Athens Olympics (2004), after Irina Korzhanenko was disqualified for doping; placed 1st in shot put at Grand Prix (2003).

CUMBERLAND, countess of. *See Clifford, Margaret (c. 1560–1616).*

CUMBERLAND, duchess of.
See Brandon, Eleanor (c. 1520–1547).
See Baird, Frances (d. 1780).
See Horton, Ann (1743–1808).
See Frederica of Mecklenburg-Strelitz (1778–1841).
See Thyra Oldenburg (1853–1933).

CUMMING, Adelaide Hawley (1905–1998). American culinary arts expert and tv host. Name variations: Betty Crocker. Born Dieta Adelaide Fish, Mar 6, 1905; died Dec 21, 1998, in Bremerton, Washington; earned a doctorate in speech education at New York University; m. Mark Hawley. ❖ Broadcasting pioneer who was General Mill's living trademark as Betty Crocker (1949–64), hosted CBS's weekly "The Betty Crocker Television Show" (1950), followed

by "The Betty Crocker Star Matinee" on ABC; also appeared on "The Burns and Allen Show"; admitted in later years that she hated to cook.

CUMMING, Dorothy (1899–1983). Australian-born actress. Name variations: Dorothy G. Cummings. Born April 12, 1899, in Burrows, Australia; died Dec 10, 1983, in New York, NY. ❖ Films include *For Wives Only, The King of Kings, In Old Kentucky* and *Our Dancing Daughters.*

CUMMING, Elizabeth (1889–1967). *See Kelso, Elizabeth.*

CUMMING, Grace Ellen (1886–1862). *See Butler, Grace Ellen.*

CUMMING, Kate (c. 1828–1909). Scottish-American hospital administrator and diarist. Born c. 1828 in Edinburgh, Scotland; died June 5, 1909, in Rosedale, Alabama; dau. of David and Jessie Cumming. ❖ When young, immigrated to US with family; nursed wounded in northern Mississippi and Chattanooga, TN, during Civil War; enlisted as matron in Confederate medical department (1862); served in hospitals in Georgia from 1863 until end of war; best known for her diary, which was originally published as *Journal of Hospital Life in the Confederate Army of Tennessee* (1866).

CUMMING, Ruth (c. 1904–1967). American actress and singer. Born c. 1904; died Aug 11, 1967, age 63, in New York, NY; m. James C. Rodis (actor). ❖ Appeared on Broadway in many Gilbert & Sullivan operettas and in numerous films with Harold Lloyd.

CUMMINGS, Alma (b. 1890). American dancer. Born Alma Stappenback, 1890, in San Antonio, Texas. ❖ Dance instructor who danced for 27 hours in the 1st US dance marathon, winning the competition and setting new world record at the Audubon Ballroom, NY (1923).

CUMMINGS, Blondell (c. 1948—). American postmodern dancer. Born c. 1948 in Effingham, South Carolina. ❖ Debuted at Guggenheim Museum in NY with Meredith Monk/The House in *Juice* (1969); performed in other works by Monk, including *Needle-Brain Lloyd and the Systems Kid* (1970), *Vessel* (1971), *Paris/Chacon* (1974), *Venice/Milan* (1976), and *Quarry* (1976); danced with Richard Bull Improvisational Company (late 1960s), in James Cunningham's *Junior Birdsmen* at American Dance Festival (1970), and in Kai Takei's *Light, Part VI* (1971); appeared in film by Yvonne Rainer, *Kristina Talking Pictures* (1976). Choreographed works include *Face on a Barroom Floor* (1976), *Cycle* (1978); *My Red-Headed Aunt from Red Cheek* (1979) and *The Ladies and Me* (1979).

CUMMINGS, Constance (1910–2005). American-born stage and screen actress. Born Constance Halverstadt, May 15, 1910, in Seattle, Washington; died Nov 23, 2005, in Chelsea, London, England; dau. of Dallas Vernon Halverstadt (attorney) and Kate (Logan) Cummings (concert soprano); m. Ben W. Levy (English playwright and producer), 1933 (died 1973); children: 2. ❖ Made stage debut in regional theater (1926) and Broadway debut in the chorus of *Treasure Girl* (1928); made film debut in *The Criminal Code* (1931), followed by *Movie Crazy* (with Harold Lloyd), *Behind the Mask, Night after Night, Broadway Thru a Keyhole, This Man is Mine* and *Remember Last Night?*; on marriage, moved to England (1934) and had an enormously successful career, appearing in such films as *Seven Sinners, Haunted Honeymoon, The Battle of the Sexes, A Boy Ten Feet Tall, Jane Eyre* and *Blithe Spirit,* and on stage in *Sour Grapes, Skylark, The Petrified Forest, The Shrike, The Rape of the Belt, JB, The Cherry Orchard,* and as Regina Conti in *Young Madame Conti,* Emma Bovary in *Madame Bovary,* Katherine in *Goodbye Mr. Chips,* and Mary Tyrone in *Long Day's Journey into Night* (with Laurence Olivier). Won Tony award for performance in *Wings;* awarded Companion of the British Empire (1974).

CUMMINGS, Edith (1899–1984). American golfer. Name variations: Mrs. Curtis Munson; Edith Cummings Munson; The Fairway Flapper. Born Edith Cummings, Mar 26, 1899, in Chicago, Illinois; died Nov 1984 in Washington, DC; dau. of Chicago socialites; m. Curtis Munson (prominent NY engineer), 1934. ❖ Won the USGA Women's Amateur (1923); won the Western Women's Amateur (1924); with her movie-star looks, graced the cover of *Time* (Aug 24, 1924); dropped out of tournament golf (1926). F. Scott Fitzgerald fashioned the character Jordan Baker in *The Great Gatsby* after Cummings.

CUMMINGS, Mrs. Irving (1894–1984). *See Cummings, Ruth.*

CUMMINGS, Marian (c. 1892–1984). American pilot. Born c. 1892 in Seattle, Washington; died June 16, 1984, in Greenwich, Connecticut. ❖ The 1st woman to receive a commercial pilot's license (1932), worked as corporate pilot for husband's law firm; served as captain in the Civil Air Patrol and ferry pilot in Army Air Corps during WWII.

CUMMINGS, Miriam Bridelia (1879–1971). *See Soljak, Miriam Bridelia.*

CUMMINGS, Ruth (1894–1984). American stage and screen actress. Name variations: Ruth Sinclair; Mrs. Irving Cummings; Ruth Sinclair Cummings. Born Ruth Sinclair, April 4, 1984, in Washington DC; died Dec 6, 1984, in Woodland Hills, California; m. Irving Cummings (director, died 1959); children: Irving Cummings Jr. (tv producer). ❧ Made film debut under name Ruth Sinclair; as Ruth Cummings, films include *La Boheme, In Old Kentucky, The Student Prince, Quality Street, Annie Laurie, Our Dancing Daughters, Wyoming* and *Bridge of San Luis Rey.*

CUMMINGS, Vicki (1913–1969). American actress and singer. Born Feb 15, 1913 in Northampton, Massachusetts; died Nov 30, 1969, in New York, NY; m. William H. Gibberson (actor). ❧ Made Broadway debut as June Doyle in *Here Goes the Bride* (1931); other plays include *Furnished Rooms, The Man Who Came to Dinner, Skylark, The Voice of the Turtle, For Love or Money* and *The Butter and Egg Man.*

CUMMINS, Maria Susanna (1827–1866). American writer. Born Maria Susanna Cummins, April 9, 1827, in Salem, Massachusetts; died Oct 1, 1866, in Dorchester, Massachusetts; dau. of Mehitable (Cave) Cummins and David Cummins (lawyer and judge); never married; no children. ❧ At 27, published *The Lamplighter* (1854), which sold 20,000 copies within a month; though her articles and 3 subsequent novels—*Mabel Vaughan* (1857), *El Fureidîs* (1860) and *Haunted Hearts* (1864)—never achieved the same popularity, was financially well-established.

CUMMINS, Peggy (1925—). Welsh actress. Born Dec 18, 1925, in Prestatyn, North Wales; m. Derek Dunnett; children: 2. ❧ Made stage debut in Dublin in *A Month in the Country* (1936), then appeared at the Abbey Theatre in *On Baile's Strand,* among others; made London debut in *Let's Pretend* (1938) and came to prominence as Fuffy Adams in *Junior Miss* (1943); was replaced by Linda Darnell while shooting the film *Forever Amber;* other movies include *Cash on Delivery, Curse of the Demon, Deadly is the Female, Escape, Green Grass of Wyoming, Gun Crazy, Hell Drivers, If This Be Sin, Moss Rose, The Late George Apley* and *That Dangerous Age.*

CUNARD, Emerald (1872–1948). *See Cunard, Maud.*

CUNARD, Grace (c. 1891–1967). American actress, writer, and filmmaker. Born Harriet Mildred Jeffries in Columbus, Ohio, April 8, 1891; died Jan 19, 1967, in Woodland Hills, California; sister of Myna Seymour (Cunard), actress; m. actor Joe Moore (d. 1926, div.); m. Jack Shannon, real name Tyler (actor/stuntman), 1925; no children. ❧ Under stage name Grace Cunard, made debut at 13; accompanied by mother, hired on with a traveling stock company and toured US; made film debut in D.W. Griffith's *The Duke's Plan* (1910); with actor-director Francis Ford, formed a production company, directing and acting in popular action-adventure serials (1914–1925), including *The Purple Mask* (1916) and *A Dangerous Adventure* (1922); other films include *Lady Raffles* (1914), *The Campbells Are Coming* (1915), *Behind the Mask* (1916), *Heroine of San Juan* (1916), *His Majesty Dick Turpin* (1916), *Lady Raffles Returns* (1916), *Phantom Island* (1916), (serial) *Peg O'the Ring* (1916), *Her Western Adventure* (1917), (serial) *The Haunted Island* (1928), *The Masked Angel* (1928), *The Last Man on Earth* (1929), *The Ace of Scotland Yard* (1929), *Resurrection* (1931) and *The Bride of Frankenstein* (1935). ❧ See also *Women in World History.*

CUNARD, Maud (1872–1948). English-American socialite and patron of the arts. Name variations: Lady Maud; Lady Emerald Cunard. Born Maud Alice Burke in San Francisco, California, Aug 3, 1872; died in England, July 10, 1948; father was related to the Irish patriot, Robert Emmett; mother was half French; m. Sir Bache Cunard (grandson of founder of the shipping line), April 1895 (sep. 1911); children; Nancy Cunard (1896–1965). ❧ On marriage, became mistress of the estate Nevill Holt in Leicestershire, England, but after a dalliance with the writer George Moore, ran off with conductor Sir Thomas Beecham and changed her name to Emerald; was the subject of many books and paintings, including a portrait by Marie Laurencin. ❧ See also Daphne Fielding, *Emerald and Nancy: Lady Cunard and her Daughter* (1968); George Moore, *Letters to Lady Cunard, 1895–1933* (1957); and *Women in World History.*

CUNARD, Nancy (1896–1965). English poet, journalist, publisher. Name variations: Nancy Fairbairn. Born Nancy Clara Cunard at Nevill Holt, in Leicestershire, England, Mar 10, 1896; died at Hôpital Cochin in Paris, France, Mar 16, 1965; only dau. of Sir Bache Cunard and Maud Alice (Emerald) Burke Cunard; m. Sydney Fairbairn, Nov 15, 1916 (div., mid-1925); no children. ❧ Aristocrat who crusaded against racial and class oppression and fascist oppression, gained a reputation as a "New Woman"; published *Wheels* (1922), followed by book of poems, *Outlaws* (1921); had affairs with Aldous Huxley and Michael Arlen, who both used her as a character in their novels (was also said to be Hemingway's model for Lady Brett in *The Sun Also Rises*); published *Sublunary* (1923), then *Parallax* (1925), one of her best works which was well-received by critics; established Hours Press in Paris (1928) and issued works that would not appeal to commercial publishers, including the 1st published work of Samuel Beckett; met African-American Henry Crowder who played piano in a jazz group called Eddie South and His Alabamians (1928) and became aware of American racism, segregation, and black culture; to experience firsthand the black experience in America, made 2 trips to US (1931, 1932); met W.E.B. DuBois, Langston Hughes and other eminent blacks whom she persuaded to contribute to an anthology; published *Negro* (1934), which contains 250 contributions from 150 authors and covered all aspects of black culture and history; began work as a correspondent for Associated Negro Press (Chicago), which took her to Geneva, to report on the League of Nations meetings, and to Spain to cover the Civil War (1936–39); also wrote articles for *New Times* (London) and *Manchester Guardian;* spent WWII in London (1941–45); published *Grand Man: Memories of Norman Douglas* (1954) and *G.M.: Memories of George Moore* (1956); began to exhibit signs of mental instability that led to serious altercations involving the police in various countries; declared insane, committed to Holloway Sanatorium, London, for 4 months (1960); ill and muttering incoherently, was taken to Hôpital Cochin where she died 3 days later. ❧ See also memoir *These Were the Hours* (Southern Illinois U. Press, 1969); Anne Chisholm, *Nancy Cunard* (Penguin, 1979); Hugh Ford, *Nancy Cunard: Brave Poet, Indomitable Rebel, 1896–1965* (Chilton, 1968); Henry Crowder, *As Wonderful as All That? Henry Crowder's Memoir of His Affair with Nancy Cunard* (Wild Tree Press, 1987); Daphne Fielding, *Emerald and Nancy: Lady Cunard and her Daughter* (1968); and *Women in World History.*

CUNEBURGA.
See Cyneburg of Gloucester.
See Cyneburg of Mercia.

CUNEGOND. *Variant of Cunegunde or Cunigunde.*

CUNEGUNDA or CUNEGUNDE. *See also Cunigunde.*

CUNEGUNDE (fl. 800s). Queen of Italy. Name variations: Cunegonde or Kunigunda. M. Bernhard or Bernard (c. 797–818), king of Italy (r. 810–818), in 813; children: Pepin II, count of Perrone (b. 817).

CUNEGUNDE (1234–1292). Saint and queen of Poland. Name variations: Kinga. Born 1234; died 1292; dau. of Bela IV, king of Hungary (r. 1235–1270), and Maria Lascaris (fl. 1234–1242); m. Boleslaus or Boleslav V the Chaste, king of Poland (r. 1243–1279).

CUNEGUNDE (d. 1357). Electress of Brandenburg. Name variations: Kunegunda. Died 1357; dau. of Kazimierz also known as Casimir III the Great, king of Poland (r. 1333–1370), and one of his four wives, Aldona of Lithuania (d. 1339), Adelaide of Hesse, Krystryna Rokizanska, or Jadwiga of Glogow; m. Louis VI the Roman, duke of Bavaria, elector of Brandenburg (r. 1350–1365).

CUNEGUNDE (d. after 1370). Duchess of Saxony. Died after 1370; dau. of Ladislas I Lokietek, king of Poland (r. 1306–1333), and Elizabeth of Bosnia (d. 1339); sister of Casimir III, king of Poland (r. 1333–1370), and Elizabeth of Poland (c. 1310–1386); m. Bernard, duke of Swidnica; m. Rudolf, duke of Saxony.

CUNEGUNDE (1465–1520). Duchess of Bavaria. Name variations: Cunigunde, Kunigunde. Born Mar 16, 1465, in Wiener Neustadt; died Aug 8, 1520, in Munich; dau. of Eleanor of Portugal (1434–1467) and Frederick III, king of Germany and Holy Roman emperor (r. 1440–1493); sister of Maximilian I, Holy Roman emperor (r. 1493–1519); m. Albert II, duke of Bavaria.

CUNESWITH (fl. 7th c.). Queen of Essex. Name variations: St. Cinefwintha; St. Cyneswith. Daughter of Penda the Pagan and Cynewise. ❧ After being taken in good faith by King Offa I of Essex, persuaded him to become a monk. Offa I ruled jointly with his brother in 709.

CUNHA, Marcia Regina (1969—). Brazilian volleyball player. Name variations: Márcia Fú (or Fu) Cunha. Born July 26, 1969, in Minas Gerais, Brazil. ❖ Won a team bronze medal at Atlanta Olympics (1996).

CUNIGUNDE (d. 1040?). Saint and Holy Roman empress. Name variations: Cunegunda; Cunigunde of Hungary; Cunigunda of Luxemburg; Kunegunde or Kunigunde. Died Mar 3, 1039, or 1040 (some sources cite 1030 or 1033) in Germany; interred at Bamberg; dau. of Siegfried of Luxemburg (c. 922–998), count of Ardennes (r. 963–998), and possibly Hedwig of Eberhard (930–992); granddau. of Cunigunde of France (c. 900–?); m. Henry II (972–1024), Holy Roman emperor and king of Germany (r. 1002–1024), 1002 or 1003; children: some sources claim that she was the mother of Agatha of Hungary who m. Edward the Atheling (more likely, however, Agatha was the dau. of Cunigunde's brother-in-law Bruno, bishop of Augsburg). ❖ Married Holy Roman emperor Henry II; vowed with husband to remain chaste throughout life together; after several years, was accused by scandalmongers of adultery; according to legend, in an attempt to refute these accusations, requested a "trial by ordeal" and walked unhurt over burning ploughshares (hot irons); after husband's death (1024), entered the Benedictine Convent at Kaufungen, near Cassel, as a nun; canonized (1200). ❖ See also *Women in World History.*

CUNIGUNDE OF BOHEMIA (d. 1321). Bohemian princess. Died 1321; dau. of Cunigunde of Hungary (d. 1285) and Otakar or Ottokar II the Great (b. 1230?), king of Bohemia (r. 1253–1278), duke of Austria and Styria (r. 1252–1276); m. Boleslaw II (div. 1302); children: Euphrosyne or Eufrozyna; Waclaw of Poland (d. 1336); Berta (died after 1341).

CUNIGUNDE OF FRANCE (c. 900–?). Countess of Verdun. Born c. 900; dau. of Ermentrude of France; grandmother of St. Cunigunde (d. 1040?); m. 2nd husband Richwin (b. around 885), count of Verdun, 920; children: Siegfried of Luxemburg (b. around 922), count of Ardennes.

CUNIGUNDE OF HOHENSTAUFEN (fl. 1215–1230). Queen of Bohemia. Name variations: Cunigunda; Kunegund of Staufen; Cunigunde von Hohenstaufen. Dau. of Philip of Hohenstaufen also known as Philip of Swabia (c. 1176–1208), Holy Roman emperor (r. 1198–1208), and probably Irene Angela of Byzantium (d. 1208); sister of Beatrice of Swabia (1198–1235) and Marie of Swabia (c. 1201–1235); m. Wenzel also known as Wenceslas I (1205–1253), king of Bohemia (r. 1230–1253); children: Otakar or Ottokar II (c. 1230–1278), king of Bohemia (r. 1253–1278), duke of Austria and Styria (r. 1252–1276).

CUNIGUNDE OF HUNGARY (d. 1285). Queen of Bohemia. Name variations: Cunigunde of Hungary; Kunegunda of Chernigov. died Sept 9, 1285; dau. of Anna of Hungary (dau. of Bela IV, king of Hungary) and Rastislav, ex-prince of Novgorod; became 2nd wife of Otakar or Ottokar II the Great (c. 1230–1278), king of Bohemia (r. 1253–1278), duke of Austria and Styria (r. 1252–1276), Oct 25, 1261; m. Javisza von Rosenberg, in June 1284; children: (1st m.) Agnes of Bohemia (1269–1297); Wenzel also known as Wenceslas II (1271–1305), king of Bohemia (r. 1278–1305); Cunigunde of Bohemia (d. 1321). Ottokar II's 1st wife was Margaret of Babenberg.

CUNIGUNDE OF SWABIA (fl. 900s). Holy Roman empress. Name variations: Kunigunde. Fl. in 900s; dau. of Berthold, pfalzgraf of Swabia; m. Liutpold of Bavaria, margrave of Bavaria; m. Conrad I, Holy Roman emperor (r. 911–918); children: (1st m.) Arnulf the Bad, duke of Bavaria (r. 907–937); Berthold, duke of Bavaria (r. 938–947); (2nd m.) Cunigunde of Germany (who m. Werner, count of Worms). Liutpold's 1st wife was Hildegarde of Bavaria (c. 840–?).

CUNIGUNDE SOBIESKA (fl. 1690s). Electress of Bavaria. Name variations: Teresa Sobieski; Theresia Sobieska. Fl. 1690s; dau. of Marie Casimir (1641–1716) and Jan III also known as John III Sobieski (1624–1696), king of Poland (r. 1674–1696); m. Maximilian II Emmanuel (1662–1726), elector of Bavaria (r. 1679–1726); children: Charles Albert, elector of Bavaria (r. 1726–1745), later known as Charles VII (1697–1745), Holy Roman emperor (r. 1742–1745). ❖ Maximilian's 1st wife was Maria Antonia (1669–1692). ❖ See also *Women in World History.*

CUNIGUNDES. *Variant of Cunegunde or Cunigunde.*

CUNITZ, Maria (1610–1664). German astronomer. Name variations: Marie Cunitz. Born Maria Cunitz in 1610 in Schweidnitz, Silesia; died 1664 in Pitschen, Silesia; dau. of Dr. Heinrich Cunitz (wealthy physician and landowner); educated by father and tutors; m. Dr. Elias von Löven

(physician and amateur astronomer), 1630; no children. ❖ Devoted her life to correcting the troublesome problems inherent in Johannes Kepler's *Rudolphine Tables* of planetary motion, which were based on the lifelong observations of Tycho Brahe; her mastery of astronomical theory was evident in her work; published her results as *Urania Propitia (Sive Tabulae Astronomicae Mire Faciles,* 1650) in both Latin and German. ❖ See also *Women in World History.*

CUNLIFFE, Stella (1917—). English statistician. Name variations: S.V. Cunliffe. Born Stella Vivian Cunliffe, Jan 12, 1917, in Battersea, England; spent first few years in Singapore; returned with family to Holmwood, then Ashtead, England; dau. of a merchant; London School of Economics, BS in economics, 1938. ❖ Worked at Danish Bacon Co. (1939–44), contributing to wartime food allocation; employed as statistician and later as statistical department head at brewery firm Arthur Guinness Son and Co. (1947–70); served as research unit head (1970–72) and director of statistics (1972–77) of Home Office, and was interested in statistical application to criminology and sociology; was the 1st woman president of Royal Statistical Society (RSS). Named Member of the Order of British Empire (MBE, 1993).

CUNNINGHAM, Agnes (1909–2004). American music publisher and musician. Name variations: Sis Cunningham. Born Agnes Cunningham, Feb 19, 1909, in Watongo, Oklahoma; died June 27, 2004, at a nursing home in New Paltz, NY; middle of 5 children of a schoolteacher and failed farmer; attended Oklahoma State College for Women, Southwestern State College, and Commonwealth College in Mena, Arkansas; m. Gordon Friesen (radical journalist), July 1941 (died 1996); children: Agnes and Jane Friesen. ❖ An icon of radical American folk music, played, sang with, and wrote songs for Woodie Guthrie, including "How Can You Keep On Movin' Unless You Migrate Too?"; was an agitator with the Southern Tenant Farmers' Union (late 1930s); became a member of the Almanac Singers, playing the accordion and singing along with Pete Seeger, Woody Guthrie and John White; with husband, founded the influential folksong magazine *Broadside* (1962), with the 1st issue containing the song "Talking John Birch" by then unknown Bob Dylan (his "Blowin' in the Wind" appeared 5 issues later); published more than 1,000 songs in the magazine. Fifteen albums of Broadside songs were released by Folkways Records; album *The Best of Broadside, 1962–1988: Anthems of the American Underground from the Pages of Broadside Magazine* (2000) was nominated for 2 Grammys. ❖ See also autobiography (with husband) *Red Dust and Broadsides: A Joint Autobiography* (1999).

CUNNINGHAM, Ann (d. 1647). English noble and rebel. Name variations: Lady Ann Cunningham; died 1647 in England. ❖ A member of the lower nobility, was a devoted convert to the strict doctrine of Calvinism; believed that England should be converted to her faith, by force if necessary; rode across the countryside accompanied by other Calvinist women rebels, terrorizing the populace.

CUNNINGHAM, Ann Pamela (1816–1875). American preservationist. Born Aug 15, 1816, at "Rosemont," Laurens Co., South Carolina; died at "Rosemont," May 1, 1875; dau. of Robert and Louisa Cunningham (wealthy plantation owners); educated at Barhamville Institute near Columbia, South Carolina; never married. ❖ American who, through her efforts to preserve George Washington's home at Mount Vernon, began the movement for historic preservation in the US; founded Mount Vernon Ladies Association of the Union, after Congress virtually declined to purchase and preserve the estate (1853); writing as "The Southern Matron," published the 1st of what would prove to be many rousing "Appeals" for the rescue of Mount Vernon (Dec 2, 1853); completed purchase of Mount Vernon (Feb 22, 1859); served as 1st regent of the Ladies Association (1853–74). ❖ See also Thomas Nelson Page, *Mount Vernon and Its Preservation, 1858–1910* (Knickerbocker, 1932); and *Women in World History.*

CUNNINGHAM, Elizabeth Anne. Australian politician. Born in Australia. ❖ As an Independent, elected to the Queensland Parliament for Gladstone (1995).

CUNNINGHAM, Imogen (1883–1976). American photographer. Born Imogen Cunningham in Portland, Oregon, April 12, 1883; died June 24, 1976, in San Francisco, California; dau. of Isaac Burns Cunningham (farmer and businessman) and Susan Elizabeth Burns Cunningham (homemaker); graduated with honors, University of Washington, Seattle, 1907; m. Roi Partridge (etcher), 1915 (div. 1934); children: Gryffyd, Rondall, and Padraic. ❖ Among the most accomplished and original photographers of the 20th century, whose career spanned 7 decades and whose work did not receive recognition until she was well into her 80s; worked in the portrait studio of Edward S. Curtis (1907–09); studied photochemistry in Dresden, Germany (1909–10); set up a portrait studio in Seattle and began to work professionally (1910); moved to Oakland, California (1920); created her extended photographic study of plants and flowers (1921–25); began photographing for *Vanity Fair* magazine (1931); was a founding member of f/64 Group (1932); moved to San Francisco (1947); taught at California School of Fine Arts (1947–50); named a fellow of National Academy of Arts and Sciences (1967); published *Imogen Cunningham: Photographs* (1970); had photo exhibit of her work, Metropolitan Museum of Art (1973); published *Imogen!: Imogen Cunningham Photographs, 1910–1973* (1974). ❖ See also memoir, *After Ninety* (1977); Judy Dater, *Imogen Cunningham: A Portrait* (New York Graphic Co., 1979); and *Women in World History*.

CUNNINGHAM, Kate (1876–1948). *See O'Hare, Kate Richards.*

CUNNINGHAM, Letitia (fl. 1783). American essayist. Fl. in Philadelphia in 1783. ❖ Known for 1 extant essay, *The Case of the Whigs* (1783), which reveals her as well educated and politically insightful.

CUNNINGHAM, Minnie Fisher (1882–1964). American politician and suffragist. Name variations: Minnie Fisher. Born Minnie Fisher in New Waverly, Texas, Mar 19, 1882; died Dec 9, 1964; dau. of Captain Horatio White Fisher and Sallie (Abercrombie) Fisher; obtained teacher's certificate; attended University of Texas Medical Branch, becoming one of the 1st women to graduate in pharmacy in Texas; m. Beverly Jean Cunningham (lawyer), Nov 27, 1902 (died 1927). ❖ Known throughout Texas as "Mrs. Democrat," became president of the Texas Equal Suffrage Association (1915), and was active in the impeachment proceedings of anti-suffrage governor James Ferguson; ran for US Senate (1927), though she only carried her home county in the primary; ran in the primary for governor of Texas (1944), challenging the views of the seated Democratic governor Coke Stevenson. ❖ See also *Women in World History*.

CUNNINGHAM, Roseanna (1951—). Scottish politician. Born 1951 in Glasgow, Scotland. ❖ Was a solicitor; representing SNP, elected Member of Parliament for Perth and Kinross at the by-election (1995) and Perth at the general election (1997); member of the Scottish Parliment (1999).

CUNNINGHAM, Sarah (1918–1986). American actress and theater founder. Born Sarah Lucie Cunningham, Sept 8, 1918, in Greenville, South Carolina; died Mar 24, 1986, in Los Angeles, California; m. John Randolph (actor). ❖ Made Broadway debut in *The Respectful Prostitute* (1948); other plays include *Blood Wedding, The Visit, Toys in the Attic, The Zulu and the Zayda* and *My Sweet Charlie*; with husband, founded the Ensemble Theater.

CUNNINGHAM, Sis (1909–2004). *See Cunningham, Agnes.*

CUNNINGTON, Eveline Willert (1849–1916). New Zealand social reformer, feminist, lecturer, and writer. Name variations: Eveline Willert Leach, Eveline Willert Baines. Born Eveline Willert Leach, April 23, 1849, at Briton Ferry, Glamorgan, Wales; died July 30, 1916, at Sumner, New Zealand; dau. of Robert Valentine Leach (asylum proprietor) and Ann (Willett) Leach; m. Capel Baines (clerk), 1876 (died 1883); m. Herbert James Cunnington (electrical engineer), 1884 (died 1915); children: (1st m.) 2; (2nd m.) 2. ❖ Immigrated to New Zealand (1875); experienced poverty in 1st marriage, which influenced her social and political views; appointed one of 1st women prison visitors (1895–c. 1920); founding member of National Council of Women of New Zealand (1890s); wrote for *Lyttelton Times* and *Maoriland Worker*, and viewed socialism as the expression of Jesus' teachings; campaigned for improved conditions for poor girls and women, education for working class and poor, and prison reform; founded Workers' Educational Association (WEA, 1915). ❖ See also *Dictionary of New Zealand Biography* (Vol. 3).

CUOCO, Joyce (1953—). American ballet dancer. Name variations: Joyce Cuocco. Born May 7, 1953, in Jamaica Plain, Massachusetts. ❖ Appeared on tv as child in "The Danny Kaye Show" (1966), and on Perry Como and Ed Sullivan variety shows; performed under Marc Platt at Radio City Music Hall (c. 1966–68); moved to Germany to dance with Stuttgart Ballet (c. 1968), where she created a role in John Cranko's *The Seasons* (1971) and danced in his *Eugen Onegin* and *Romeo and Juliet*; danced with Bavarian State Theater for short period after Cranko's death; returned to US to dance with Pennsylvania Ballet and appeared in series of works by George Balanchine as well as 19th-century classics.

CUPPI OR CUPIS, Marie-Anne de (1710–1770). *See Camargo, Marie-Anne Cupis de.*

CURCHOD, Suzanne (1739–1794). *See Necker, Suzanne.*

CURCI, Amelita Galli- (1882–1963). *See Galli-Curci, Amelita.*

CURIE, Éve (b. 1904). French journalist. Name variations: Eve Curie; Eve Curie Labouisse or Curie-Labouisse. Born Éve Denise Curie in Paris, France, Dec 6, 1904; dau. of Pierre and Marie (Sklodowska) Curie, both Nobel Prize-winning scientists; sister of Irène Joliot-Curie (1897–1956); graduate of Collège Sevigné; m. Henry Labouisse (American diplomat), Nov 19, 1954; no children. ❖ Writer who traveled more than 40,000 miles covering Allied action during World War II, began career as a concert pianist, then writer and critic of music, films, and books for several French newspapers and journals; wrote biography of her mother, *Madame Curie*, which won the American National Book Award for nonfiction (1937) and the Polonia Restitua and Chevalier de la Legion d'Honneur (1939); forced from France by the Nazi invasion, joined the Free French in London (1940); began travel as a journalist to Allied battlefields around the world (1941); published widely acclaimed writings from the military front (1943); awarded croix de guerre for her wartime service to France (1944); was co-publisher of *Paris-Presse* (1945–49); made 7 lecture tours to US (1939–49); served as special adviser to the secretary general of North Atlantic Treaty Organization (1952–54); posted in Beirut, Caracas, and other cities with her husband. ❖ See also memoir *Journey Among Warriors* (1943); and *Women in World History*.

CURIE, Irène (1897–1956). *See Joliot-Curie, Irène.*

CURIE, Marie (1867–1934). Polish-born scientist. Name variations: Madame Curie; Marie Sklodowska or Sklodovska. Born Marya or Manya Sklodowska in Warsaw, Poland, Nov 7, 1867; died of leukemia, July 4, 1934, in Saint-Gervais, France; dau. of Wladyslaw Sklodowski (high school physics teacher) and Bronislava or Bronislawa Sklodowska (director of a girls' school); began university study at Sorbonne at age 24; m. Pierre Curie (physicist), July 26, 1895; children: Irène Joliot-Curie (1897–1956); Éve Curie (b. 1904). ❖ Research scientist and discoverer of the element radium, who was the 1st woman to win a Nobel prize, the 1st person to win a 2nd Nobel, and ranks with Albert Einstein in scientific influence and achievement during the 20th century; moved to Paris to attend the Sorbonne (1891); awarded 1st for master's examination for physics (1893); awarded 2nd for master's examination in mathematics (1894); began work on dissertation (1894); in a preliminary note to the Academy of Sciences, made her scientifically stunning announcement about the possibility of a powerful new radioactive element, present in ordinary pitchblende, and the Atomic Age was born (1898); awarded Berthelot Medal of the French Academy of Sciences (1902); awarded Davy Medal of the Royal Society of London (1903); shared Nobel Prize for physics with husband Pierre and Henri Becquerel (1903); received Elliott Cresson Medal of Franklin Institute (1909); husband Pierre killed in traffic accident (1906); awarded 2nd Nobel Prize, for chemistry, for isolation of metallic radium (1911); developed medical use of X-ray technology on the wounded of WWI (1914–18); was a member of 85 scientific societies throughout the world; was a member of the French Academy of Medicine; served 12 years on the International Commission on Intellectual Cooperation of the League of Nations; enshrined in France's Pantheon (1995). ❖ See also Éve Curie, *Madame Curie* (Doubleday, 1939); Françoise Giroud, *Marie Curie: A Life* (Holmes and Meier, 1986); Rosalynd Pflaum, *Grand Obsession: Marie Curie and Her World* (Doubleday, 1989); and *Women in World History*.

CURLESS, Ann (1965—). American singer. Name variations: Exposé. Born Oct 7, 1965, in New York, NY. ❖ Was member of vocal trio Exposé which had great success with Latin-tinged dance songs; with Exposé, released multiplatinum debut album *Exposure* (1987) which broke Beatles' record for most Top-10 hits from a debut album. Exposé hits include "Come Go With Me" (1987), "Point of No Return" (1987), "Seasons Change" (1987), and "I'll Never Get Over You (Getting Over Me)" (1993). Exposé albums include *Exposure* (1987), *What You Don't Know* (1989), *Exposé* (1992), and *Greatest Hits* (1995).

CURLEY, Wilma (1937—). American ballet and theatrical dancer. Born April 1, 1937, in Brooklyn, NY. ❖ Appeared at New York City Ballet (mid-1950s), where she created roles in Todd Bolender's *Souvenirs* (1955) and Jerome Robbins' *The Concert, or the Perils of Everybody* (1956); also appeared in Robbins' *New York Export: Opus Jazz* (1958), *Moves* (1959) and *Afternoon of a Faun*; continued to work with Robbins after dance troupe dispersed and in restagings of his ballets throughout US and Europe.

CURRAN, Jacque (1931–1982). *See Mercer, Jacque.*

CURRAN, Margaret (c. 1962—). Scottish politician. Born c. 1962. ❖ As a Labour candidate, elected to the Scottish Parliament for Glasgow Baillieston (1999), becoming minister for Social Justice.

CURRAN, Mary Katharine (1844–1920). *See Brandegee, Mary Katharine.*

CURREY, Louise (1969—). *See McPaul, Louise.*

CURRIE, Cherie (1959—). American singer and actress. Name variations: Cherie Currie Hays. Born Cherie Ann Currie, Nov 30, 1959, in Los Angeles, California; twin sister of Marie Currie (singer); sister of Sondra Currie (actress); m. Robert Hays (actor, div.); children: 1 son. ❖ Sang with all-girl, hard-rock band, The Runaways; joined group after singer and bassist Micki Steele left; with group, signed with Mercury Records and released unsuccessful debut album, *The Runaways* (1976), which proved popular only in Japan, where, along with *Queens of Noise* (1977) and *Live in Japan,* they earned 3 gold records; left Runaways (1977) and released LP, *Messin' With the Boys* (1980), with sister Marie; pursued acting career, appearing in films *Foxes* (1980), *Wavelength* (1983), and *Rich Girl* (1991); released *Young & Wild* (1998), which included material from work with Runaways, as well as from previous solo albums. ❖ See also autobiography, *Neon Angel: The Cherie Currie Story* (1989).

CURRIE, Edwina (1946—). English politician and paramour. Born 1946 in Liverpool, England; attended Oxford University; London School of Economics, MA in economic history; m. Raymond Currie (div. 1997); m. 2nd husband John Jones (retired detective), 1999; children: (1st m.) 2 daughters. ❖ Conservative, began career holding public office in Birmingham; stood for Parliament (1983) and represented a Midlands seat for 14 years (1983–97); said to be one of the most flamboyant politicians of her era, served in Margaret Thatcher's government (1986–88) in the Department of Health; known for her campaigns on heart disease, women's cancer screening and AIDS, resigned over her remark that most of Britain's egg production was infected with salmonella (Dec 1988); published 10 books, including racy novels and *Diaries 1987–1992* (2002), which revealed her 4-year liaison with John Major when both were married to others and serving as ministers in Thatcher's Government (1984–88); also had her own BBC radio program "Late Night Currie."

CURRIE, Ethel Dobbie (1898–1963). Scottish geologist. Born Dec 4, 1898, in Glasgow, Scotland; died Mar 24, 1963. ❖ Appointed assistant curator of Hunterian Museum in Glasgow (1920–62); developed, cared for, and catalogued geological collections at Hunterian Museum; served as a University of Glasgow senior lecturer (1960–62); was the 1st woman president of Geological Society of Glasgow and one of 1st women (of 3) admitted to fellowship of the Royal Society of Edinburgh.

CURRIE, Mary Montgomerie (1843–1905). British baroness, poet, novelist and essayist. Name variations: Mary Singleton; Lady Currie; Baroness Currie of Hawley; (pseudonyms) V; Violet Fane. Born Mary Montgomerie Lamb, Feb 24, 1843, in Sussex, England; died Oct 13, 1905, in Yorkshire, England; dau. of Charles James Saville Montgomerie Lamb and Anna Charlotte Grey Lamb; m. Henry Sydenham Singleton, 1864 (died 1893); m. Sir Philip Henry Wodehouse Currie, later Baron Currie of Hawley, 1894. ❖ Well known in London society, wrote works of gentle satire; poetry collections include *From Dawn to Noon: Poems* (1872), *Denzil Place: A Story in Verse* (1875), *Collected Verses* (1880), and *Under Cross and Crescent: Poems* (1986); novels include *Thro' Love and War* (1886) and *The Story of Helen Davenant* (1889); collections of essays include *The Edwin and Angelina Papers* (1875) and *Collected Essays* (1902).

CURRIE OF HAWLEY, Baroness (1843–1905). *See Currie, Mary Montgomerie.*

CURRIER, Ruth (1926—). American modern dancer and choreographer. Born Jan 4, 1926, in Ashland, Ohio; attended Black Mountain College. ❖ Danced for 12 years with José Limón Company under artistic director Doris Humphrey; created roles in numerous works by Humphrey, including in *Invention* (1949), *Night Spell* (1952), and *Felipe El Loco* (1955); danced in premieres of Limón's *La Malinche* (1949), *Concert Preludes and Fugues* (1950), *There is a Time* (1956) and *Missa Brevis* (1959); formed own company (1961); created numerous works at Bennington College and Sarah Lawrence College; served as artistic director of Limón Company. Works of choreography include *Idyll* (1955), *Triplicity* (1956), *Toccata* (1960), *Resonances* (1961), *Triangle of Strangers* (1966), *Phantasmagoria* (1975) and *Storm Warning* (1976).

CURRY, Andrea Lloyd- (1965—). *See Lloyd, Andrea.*

CURRY, Denise (1959—). American basketball player. Born Aug 22, 1959, in Fort Benton, Montana; attended Davis (CA) High School, 1974–77, and University of California at Los Angeles (UCLA, 1977–81). ❖ Three-time All-American at UCLA (1979, 1980, 1981); joined US national team playing on its East European tour (1982); began 1st of 8 pro seasons for German, French, and Italian clubs (1983); won a team gold medal at Los Angeles Olympics (1984); during collegiate career, scored 3,198 points and held record for most points in a single game at 47; had #12 jersey retired at UCLA (1994). Named USA Basketball Player of the Year (1981); named French Player of the Decade; inducted into Basketball Hall of Fame (1997).

CURRY, Jenny (1984—). American inline skater. Born Jenny Jean Curry, April 4, 1984, in San Luis Obispo, California. ❖ Won gold in Women's Street/Park at X Games (1998) and bronze (1999); other 1st-places finishes in Street include: Sea Otter Classic, Monterey, California (1998); National championships (1998); IISS World Finals, Birmingham, England (1998); NISS-IISS World Woman's Street Tour Point Leader (1998); NISS Paul Mitchell World Point Leader (1999); IISS #1, National Finals, Canberra, Australia (1999).

CURTIN, Elsie (1890–1975). Australian prime-ministerial wife. Born Elsie Needham, Oct 4, 1890, in Ballarat, Victoria, Australia; died June 24, 1975, in Cottesloe, Perth, Western Australia; m. John Curtin (14th prime minister of Australia, 1941–1945), April 21, 1917; children: Elsie (b. 1917); John (b. 1921). ❖ Lived with parents in Cape Town, South Africa (1898–1910); at 17, joined the Social Democratic Federation there; moved back to Australia, settling in Hobart; was an active member of the Labor women's organization; joined husband on official wartime visits to Washington and Ottawa (1944); after husband died in office (July 5, 1945), continued working with the Labor Party for next 20 years. Named Commander in the Order of the British Empire (1970).

CURTIS, Ann (1926—). American swimmer. Name variations: Ann Curtis Cuneo. Born Ann Elisabeth Curtis, Mar 6, 1926, in Rio Vista, California; m. Gordon Cuneo (basketball star), 1949. ❖ Was the 1st woman to swim 100 yards in less than a minute (59.4 seconds); set 4 World freestyle records and 18 American records; won 31 national championships; won gold medals for 400 meter and relay and a silver medal for 100 meters at London Olympics (1948). Was the 1st woman to win the James E. Sullivan Memorial Trophy. ❖ See also *Women in World History.*

CURTIS, Charlotte (1928–1987). American journalist and editor. Born Charlotte Murray Curtis, Dec 19, 1928, in Chicago, Illinois; grew up in Columbus, Ohio; died from breast cancer, April 1987 in Ohio; dau. of Lucile (Atcherson) Curtis (diplomat and the 1st female officer in the Foreign Service) and George Morris Curtis (surgeon); Vassar College, BA in American history, 1950; m. 2nd husband William E. Hunt (neurosurgeon). ❖ Noted writer and editor at the *New York Times,* began career at the *Columbus Citizen* (1951–61); had a 17-year tenure at the Times (1961–78), rising from society reporter for the women's pages (the doyenne of society writing), to style and family editor (1965), to associate editor (1973), to editor of the op-ed page (1974), the 1st woman to have her name listed on the newspaper's senior masthead; writings include *The Rich and Other Atrocities.* ❖ See also Marilyn S. Greenwald, *A Woman of the Times: Journalism, Feminism, and the Career of Charlotte Curtis* (Ohio U. Press, 1999).

CURTIS, Doris Malkin (1914–1991). American geologist. Born Jan 12, 1914, in Brooklyn, New York; died May 26, 1991, in Houston, Texas; Brooklyn College, BS, Columbia University, PhD. ❖ The 1st woman president of the Geological Society of America (1990), spent the majority of her career as a geologist exploring for Shell Oil Company (1942–79); opened her own consulting firm (1979); also taught at Houston's Rice University, was president of the Society of Economic Paleontologists and Mineralogists, and the 1st woman president of the American Geological Institute. ❖ See also *Women in World History.*

CURTIS, Harriot (1881–1974). American golfer and tennis player. Born Harriot S. Curtis, June 30, 1881, in Manchester-by-the-Sea, MA; died Oct 25, 1974, in Manchester-by-the-Sea; sister of Peggy Curtis. ❖ Won USGA championship (1906); donated a trophy, thus beginning the Curtis Cup (1932). ❖ See also *Women in World History.*

CURTIS, Jamie Lee (1958—). American actress. Name variations: Lady Haden-Guest. Born Nov 22, 1958, in Los Angeles, California; dau. of Tony Curtis (actor) and Janet Leigh (actress); sister of Kelly Curtis (actress); attended University of the Pacific; m. Christopher Guest (actor, aka Christopher Haden-Guest), 1984; children: (adopted) Annie and Thomas. ❖ Appeared on tv as teenager, notably in "Operation Petticoat"; had 1st film success with John Carpenter's *Halloween* (1978), followed by a series of horror films, including *The Fog* (1980) and *Halloween II* (1981); came to prominence in comedies, *Trading Places* (1983) and *A Fish Called Wanda* (1988); won a Golden Globe for her performance in *True Lies* (1994); other films include *Perfect* (1985), *Blue Steel* (1990), *Halloween H2O: 20 Years Later* (1998), *Virus* (1999), *The Tailor of Panama* (2001), *Halloween: Resurrection* (2002), *Freaky Friday* (2003) and *Christmas with the Kranks* (2004); on tv, starred in "The Heidi Chronicles" (1995); also writes children's books.

CURTIS, Kathleen Maisey (1892–1994). New Zealand mycologist. Name variations: Lady Rigg, Kathleen Maisey Rigg. Born Aug 15, 1892, in Foxton, Manawatu, New Zealand; died Sept 5, 1994, at Nelson, New Zealand; dau. of Paul Curtis (postmaster) and Mary Emma (Armitage) Curtis; Auckland University College, BA, 1914, MA, 1915; University of London, DSc, 1919; m. Theodore Rigg, 1966 (died 1972). ❖ The 1st New Zealand woman to earn DSc, was also the 1st woman fellow (and senior fellow) at Royal Society of New Zealand and a fellow at Linnean Society of London; head of Department of Mycology at Cawthron Institute, Nelson (1928–52); published numerous biological treatises (1920s–30s). ❖ See also *Dictionary of New Zealand Biography* (Vol. 4).

CURTIS, Margaret (1883–1965). See Curtis, Peggy.

CURTIS, Mary Louise (1876–1970). See Zimbalist, Mary Louise.

CURTIS, Natalie (1875–1921). See Burlin, Natalie.

CURTIS, Nell (1824–1898). See Demorest, Ellen Curtis.

CURTIS, Peggy (1883–1965). American golfer and tennis player. Name variations: Margaret Curtis. Born Margaret B. Curtis, Oct 8, 1883, in Manchester-by-the-Sea, Massachusetts; died Dec 24, 1965, in Boston; sister of Harriot Curtis. ❖ Runner-up in USGA amateur championship (1900, 1905) and winner (1907, 1911, 1912); with Evelyn Sears, won National doubles title in tennis (1908); donated a trophy, thus beginning the Curtis Cup (1932). Received USGA's Bobby Jones Award for sportsmanship; was one of the 1st to be inducted in Women's Golf Hall of Fame (1951). ❖ See also *Women in World History.*

CURTIS, Priscilla (1914–1958). See Lawson, Priscilla.

CURTIS-THOMAS, Claire (1958—). Welsh politician and member of Parliament. Born April 30, 1958; dau. of Joyce Curtis-Thomas; m. Michael Jakub. ❖ Served as dean, Faculty of Business and Engineering, University of Wales College (1996–97); representing Labour, elected to House of Commons for Crosby (1997, 2001, 2005).

CURTRIGHT, Jorja (1923–1985). American actress. Name variations: Jorja Sheldon. Born Aug 14, 1923, in Amarillo, Texas; died May 11, 1985, in Los Angeles, California; m. Sidney Sheldon (novelist and producer); children: daughter. ❖ Films include *Hitler's Madmen, Whistle Stop, Heaven Only Knows, M, Love is a Many Splendored Thing* and *Revolt of Mamie Stover.*

CURZON, Cynthia (1898–1933). See Mosley, Cynthia.

CURZON, Grace Hinds (1878–1958). Wife of Lord Curzon. Name variations: Lady Curzon; Baroness Curzon; Marchioness Curzon of Kedleston; Grace Duggan; Mrs. George Nathaniel Curzon. Born Grace Elvina Trillia Hinds in 1878 in Decatur, Alabama; died June 29, 1958; dau. of Joseph Monroe Hinds (US minister in Brazil); m. Alfred Hubert Duggan of Buenos Aires (died); m. Lord George Curzon (diplomat), Jan 2, 1917 (sep., died 1925); children: (1st m.) Alfred Leo, Hubert and Marcella Duggan. ❖ Upon marriage to Lord George Curzon, became the center of social gatherings at Carlton House; separated, later had an affair with stepson-in-law, Oswald Mosley. ❖ See also *Reminiscences* (Coward, 1955).

CURZON, Irene (1896–1966). Baroness Ravensdale. Born Jan 20, 1896; died 1966; dau. of Mary Leiter Curzon (1870–1906) and Lord George Curzon (1859–1925, diplomat); never married; no children. ❖ Inherited father's secondary title Baroness Ravensdale; devoted her days to women's rights, social causes, music, and travel.

CURZON, Isabel (1879–1927). See Jay, Isabel.

CURZON, Mary Leiter (1870–1906). Vicereine of India. Name variations: Baroness Curzon of Kedleston. Born Mary Victoria Leiter in Chicago, Illinois, May 27, 1870; died in London, England, July 18, 1906; dau. of Levi Z. Leiter (merchant and partner with Marshall Field) and Mary Theresa (Carver) Leiter (granddau. of Judge Samuel Fish); sister of Nancy Leiter, who m. Colin Campbell, and Marguerite Leiter, known as Daisy, who m. the earl of Suffolk; m. diplomat George Nathaniel Curzon (1859–1925), later marquess Curzon of Kedleston, viceroy of India, 1895; children: Irene Curzon, Baroness Ravensdale (1896–1966); Cynthia Curzon Mosley (1898–1933, who m. Oswald Mosley); and Alexandra Curzon Metcalfe (b. 1903). ❖ One of the most famous women of her time, grew up in luxury; married George Curzon; lived in India when he was viceroy (1898–1904); seemingly up to the task of vicereine of India, fulfilled the role with grace and distinction; was in failing health on return to England. ❖ See also Nigel Nicolson, *Mary Curzon* (Harper and Row, 1977); and *Women in World History.*

CURZON, Sarah Anne (1833–1898). British-Canadian essayist. Name variations: Sarah Vincent. Born Sarah Vincent in 1833 in Birmingham, England; died Nov 8, 1898; m. Robert Curzon. ❖ Immigrated with husband to Canada (1862); wrote *Laura Secord, the Heroine of 1812: A Drama, And Other Poems* (1887) and *The Story of Laura Secord, 1813* (1891); also wrote a column on women's issues and essays on education and suffrage for many journals.

CUSACK, Dymphna (1902–1981). Australian novelist and playwright. Name variations: LND; EDC. Born Ellen Dymphna Cusack, Sept 22, 1902, in Wyalong, NSW, Australia; died 1981; dau. of Bridget (Crowley) Cusack and James Cusack (sheep farmer); attended St. Ursula's College, 1917–20; University of Sydney, BA (with honors), 1925, diploma of education, 1925; m. Norman Freehill (journalist and writer); no children. ❖ Taught for nearly 20 years; published 1st book, *Jungfrau* (1936); a progressive, whose many books dealt with social injustice, was a lifelong member of Australia's Communist Party; writings include (with Miles Franklin) *Pioneers on Parade* (1939), (play) *Red Sky at Morning* (1942), *Say No to Death* (1953), *The Sun in Exile* (1955), *Chinese Women Speak* (1958), *Heatwave in Berlin* (1961), *Picnic Races* (1962), *Holidays among the Russians* (1964), *Black Lightning* (1964), (with Florence James) *Four Winds and a Family* (1965), (with T. Inglis Moore and Barrie Ovendeu) *Mary Gilmore: A Tribute* (1965), *Ilyria Reborn* (1966), *The Sun Is Not Enough* (1967), *The Half-Burnt Tree* (1969) and *A Bough in Hell* (1971). Awarded West Australian drama prizes (1942) for *Morning Sacrifice* and (1943) *Comets Soon Pass;* awarded Playwrights' Advisory Board drama prizes (1945) for *Shoulder the Sky* and (1946) *Stand Still Time;* received *Sydney Daily Telegraph* novel award (1948) for *Come in Spinner* (1951); given the Coronation Medal for services to Australian literature (1953); granted the British Arts Council Award for play, *The Golden Girls;* granted a Commonwealth literary fellowship, for *Southern Steel.* ❖ See also autobiography (with husband Norman Freehill) *Dymphna Cusack* (1975); and *Women in World History.*

CUSACK, Margaret Anne (1832–1899). Irish nun, reformer, and writer. Name variations: Sister Mary Frances Clare; the Nun of Kenmare. Born Margaret Anne Cusack near Dublin, Ireland, 1832; died in Warwickshire, England, 1899. ❖ Joined the Anglican sisterhood in London; converted to Roman Catholicism (1858), taking the religious name Sister Mary Frances Clare; conducted the celebrated convent of Poor Clares (1861–84), which she established at Kenmare, Co. Kerry, and organized for the purpose of providing poor girls with an education; established Sisters of Peace (1884), a similar order but with a wider range; embittered in later life, reverted to Anglicanism and attacked Catholicism; writings include *Students' History of Ireland* and *Woman's Work in Modern Society,* as well as works of fiction, such as *Ned Rusheen* (1871) and *Tim O'Halloran's Choice* (1877). ❖ See also autobiography *The Nun of Kenmare* (1889); and *Women in World History.*

CUSHIER, Elizabeth (1837–1932). American physician. Born 1837 in New York; died 1932; longtime companion of Emily Blackwell (physician). ❖ Highly influential American woman physician and surgeon of the 1800s, graduated from Woman's Medical College of the New York Infirmary for Women and Children (1872); studied histology in Zurich; returned to New York Infirmary as obstetrics professor, resident physician, and administrator; opened private practice which offered gynecological surgery; continued work at New York Infirmary after its Woman's Medical College closed (1899); retired and traveled to Europe with Emily

Blackwell, then settled in Montclair, NJ, with summer home in York Cliffs, Maine.

CUSHING, Barbara (1915–1978). *See Paley, Babe.*

CUSHING, Betsey (1908–1998). *See Whitney, Betsey Cushing Roosevelt.*

CUSHING, Catherine Chisholm (1874–1952). American playwright. Name variations: Catherine Chisholm. Born April 15, 1874, in Mount Perry, Ohio; died Oct 19, 1952, in New York, NY. ❖ Was once editor of *Harper's Bazaar;* plays include *The Master of the Inn, Edgar Allan Poe, Glorianna, Pollyanna, Jerry, Sari, Kitty Mackay, Widow by Proxy* and *The Real Thing;* also wrote the book for the musicals *Topsy and Eva* and *Marjolaine* and book and lyrics for *Lassie;* songs include "L'Amour, Toujours, L'Amour," "Chianti," and "John and Priscilla."

CUSHING, Justine B. (b. 1918). American golfer. Name variations: Mrs. Cushing. Born Aug 3, 1918, in Beverly Farms, Massachusetts. ❖ Won the USGA Women's Senior championship (1974).

CUSHING, Mrs. (b. 1918). *See Cushing, Justine B.*

CUSHING, Mary (1906–1978). *See Fosburgh, Minnie Astor.*

CUSHING, Minnie (1906–1978). *See Fosburgh, Minnie Astor.*

CUSHING SISTERS.
See Fosburgh, Minnie Astor (1906–1978).
See Paley, Babe (1915–1978).
See Whitney, Betsey Cushing Roosevelt (1908–1998).

CUSHMAN, Charlotte Saunders (1816–1876). American actress. Born Charlotte Saunders Cushman in Boston, Massachusetts, July 23, 1816; died in Boston, 1876; dau. of Elkanah Cushman (merchant in West Indies trade) and his 2nd wife Mary Eliza (Babbitt) Cushman; sister of actress Susan Cushman; lived with Emma Stebbins for 20 years. ❖ America's 1st great actress, began career as an opera singer, debuting at Boston's Tremont Theater as Countess Almaviva in *The Marriage of Figaro* (1835); when her voice failed to live up to its early promise, turned to acting and made debut as Lady Macbeth at New Orleans' St. Charles Theatre (1836); was hired by the Park Street Theatre in New York (1837), where she played a variety of roles, most notably Meg Merrilees in the popular *Guy Mannering,* and Romeo, the 1st of the male roles that would figure so prominently in her repertoire; took over management of Philadelphia's Walnut Street Theatre (1842), where she became a local favorite; played Lady Macbeth opposite William Macready (1843), a role that would later be considered one of her finest; made triumphant debut in London (1845), starring as Bianca in the tragedy *Fazio;* performed for Queen Victoria, then returned to US (1849) for a 3-year tour, during which she portrayed Cardinal Wolsey in *Henry VIII* and added Hamlet to her repertoire of male roles; gave an emotional farewell performance of Lady Macbeth in NY (1874). ❖ See also Joseph Leach, *Bright Particular Star* (1970); Clara Erskine Clement Waters, *Mrs. Charlotte Cushman* (Osgood, 1882); and *Women in World History.*

CUSHMAN, Pauline (1833–1893). American actress and spy. Name variations: Major Pauline Cushman; Pauline Cushman Fryer. Born in New Orleans, Louisiana, June 10, 1833; died in poverty in San Francisco, California, Dec 7, 1893; father was a dry goods merchant from Spain; mother was from France (both immigrated to US in 1830s); m. Charles Dickinson, late 1850s (died 1861); m. Jere Fryer, 1879 (div. 1888); children: (1st m.) 2, both died young. ❖ Actress who won fame as a Union spy in the Civil War, began stage career at 18 (1851); while appearing as a Southern sympathizer, volunteered as Union spy (1863); caught by Confederate detectives trying to carry sensitive military documents over to the Union lines (1863), was sentenced to hang, then rescued during an advance by Union troops; granted the honorary title of "Major of Cavalry" by the Union army for her work as a spy; recounted experiences in concert halls and on vaudeville stages (1870s); ran hotels in San Francisco and Casa Grande, Arizona (1880s). ❖ See also F.L. Sarmiento, *Pauline Cushman, Union Spy and Scout* (Potter, 1865); and *Women in World History.*

CUSHMAN, Vera (1876–1946). American YWCA leader. Born Vera Charlotte Scott, Sept 19, 1876, in Ottawa, Illinois; died Feb 1, 1946, in Savannah, Georgia; dau. of Samuel Swan Scott (businessman) and Anna Margaret (Tressler) Scott; attended Ferry Hall at Lake Forest, Illinois; graduate of Smith College, 1898; m. James Stewart Cushman (businessman, 1871–1952), Oct 15, 1901. ❖ Active feminist, served on National Board of YWCA (1906–36) and became 1st president of New York YWCA (1912); as chair of War Work Council of YWCA during WWI, worked to establish Hostess Houses at US training camps and in Europe to meet needs of women workers in war zones; received Distinguished Service Medal (1919); served as vice president of World's Council of YWCA (1924–38).

CUSMIR, Anisoara (1962—). *See Stanciu, Anisoara.*

CUSSONS, Sheila (1922–2004). South African poet. Born 1922 in Piketberg, Western Cape, South Africa; died at Nazareth House, Nov 26, 2004, in Vredehoek, South Africa; m. C.J.M. Nienaber (literary critic, div.); m. Joan de Saladrigas (Spanish businessman); children: Juame and Jordi Saladrigas-Cussons. ❖ Celebrated South African poet, studied fine arts at University of Natal in Pietermaritzburg, as well as in London and Amsterdam; on 2nd marriage, moved to Barcelona, Spain, and converted to the Roman Catholic faith (1955); returned to Cape Town, South Africa (1982); after being severely burned in an accident, began to write religious and mystical poems, many illustrated by her own drawings; published 1st poems in the anthology *Stiebeuel* (1946); works include *Plektrum* (1970), *Die Swart Kombuis* (1978), *Verf en Vlam* (1978), *Die Skitterende Wond* (1979), *Die Somerjood* (1980), *Die Woedende Brood* (1981), *Gestaltes 1947* (1982), *Verwikkelde Lyn* (1983), *Membraan* (1984), *Die Heilige Moeder* (1988), *Die Knetterende Woord* (1991), and *Die Asem wat Ekstase is* (2000); also translated stories by Jorge Luis Borges into Afrikaans in *Die Vorm van die Swaard en Ander Verhale;* lived at Nazareth House (1994–2004). Received CNA Prize, Luyt Prize, WA Hofmeyr Prize (twice), and Hertzog Prize.

CUST, Aleen (1868–1937). Irish veterinary surgeon. Born 1868 near Tipperary, Ireland; died Jan 29, 1937; dau. of Sir Leopold Cust (land agent and heir to Sir Edward Cust) and Charlotte Bridgeman Cust (dau. of a vice admiral). ❖ The 1st woman to be admitted to the British Royal College of Veterinary Surgeons (RCVS), used inheritance to study veterinary surgery under name A.I. Custance; enrolled at New Veterinary College (1896), the only female student, and earned a Gold Medal for zoology; applied to take 1st professional exam (April 1897) but was rejected by examination committee due to gender; worked as assistant to William Byrne (Roscommon, Ireland) and took over practice after his death (1910); traveled to Abbeville, France (1915), to help veterinary surgeons in Remount Hospital for horses; after passage of Sex Disqualification (Removal) Act (Dec 23, 1919), finally granted RCVS diploma (1924); endowed RCVS for the Aleen Cust Research Scholarship.

CUSTANCE, Olive (1874–1944). British poet. Name variations: Lady Alfred Douglas; (pseudonym) Opals. Born Feb 7, 1874, in Norfolk, England; died Feb 12, 1944, in East Sussex, England; dau. of Colonel Frederick Hambelton Custance and Eleanor Custance Jolliffe; m. Lord Alfred Douglas (who, as Bosie, had been intimately linked with Oscar Wilde in the infamous libel trial), 1902 (sep. 1911); children: son Raymond (b. 1903). ❖ Poet praised by John Gray, Aubrey Beardsley, and Richard Le Gallienne, wrote *Opals* (1897), *Rainbows* (1902), *The Blue Bird* (1905) and *The Inn of Dreams* (1911).

CUSTER, Elizabeth Bacon (1842–1933). American writer. Name variations: Libbie Bacon. Born Elizabeth Bacon, April 8, 1842, at Monroe, Michigan; died April 4, 1933; dau. of Judge Daniel Bacon and Eleanor Sophia (Page) Bacon; graduate of Young Ladies' Seminary and Collegiate Institute in Monroe; m. George Armstrong Custer (Civil War brigadier general), Feb 9, 1864. ❖ Traveled with husband to frontier posts, socialized with politicians, and actively promoted his career; following husband's death at the battle of Little Bighorn (1876), supported herself by lecturing and writing; championed the memory of her husband and defended his reputation in such books as *Boots and Saddles, or Life in Dakota with General Custer* (1885), *Tenting on the Plains* (1887) and *Following the Guidon* (1890). ❖ See also Shirley A. Leckie, *Elizabeth Bacon Custer: And the Making of a Myth* (U. of Oklahoma Press, 1993) and Arlene Reynolds, ed., *The Civil War Memories of Elizabeth Bacon Custer* (U. of Texas Press, 1994).

CUSTIS, Eleanor "Nellie" Calvert (fl. 1775). Daughter-in-law of Martha Washington. Name variations: Mrs. John Parke Custis; Nellie Custis. Born Eleanor Calvert in Mt. Airy, Maryland; fl. around 1775; m. John "Jacky" Parke Custis, in Feb 1774; children: (1st m.) Martha Parke Custis (who m. Thomas Peter); Eleanor "Nelly" Parke Custis (1779–1852); George Washington Parke Custis (b. 1781), and one other; (2nd m.) 16 children. ❖ Following death of husband, kept 2 of her children, her older daughters, and sent the other 2 to live with in-laws, George and

Martha Washington; later remarried and give birth to 16 more. ❖ See also *Women in World History*.

CUSTIS, Eleanor "Nelly" Parke (1779–1852). Granddaughter of George and Martha Washington who was raised by them at Mount Vernon. Name variations: Eleanor Custis Lewis; Nelly Custis. Born Eleanor Parke Custis in 1779; died in obscurity on her son's farm in the Shenandoah Valley in Mar 1852; dau. of John Parke Custis and Eleanor Calvert Custis; granddau. of George and Martha Washington; m. Lawrence Lewis, Feb 22, 1799 (died 1839); children: Francis Parke Lewis; Agnes Lewis; Angela Lewis (d. 1839); Lorenzo Lewis; and 4 others. ❖ Grew up in the heady atmosphere of the capital, while her step-grandfather George Washington was president of US. ❖ See also *Women in World History*.

CUSTIS, Martha (1731–1802). See *Washington, Martha*.

CUSTIS, Nelly (1779–1852). See *Custis, Eleanor "Nelly" Parke*.

CUTHBERT, Betty (1938—). Australian runner. Name variations: Golden Girl. Born April 20, 1938, in Ermington, Sydney, Australia; twin sister of Marie Cuthbert. ❖ Won gold medals for the 100 meters, 200 meters, and 4x100 meter relay at Melbourne Olympics (1956); won a gold medal for 400 meters at Tokyo Olympics (1964); contracted multiple sclerosis (1981); helped raise funds for research. Named Australia Broadcasting's Sportstar of the Year (1956); given Helms Award (1964). ❖ See also *Women in World History*.

CUTHBERT, Juliet (1964—). Jamaican runner. Born April 9, 1964, in Jamaica; attended University of Texas at Austin. ❖ Won a gold medal at World championships for the 4x100-meter relay (1991); won silver medals in 200 meters and 100 meters at Barcelona Olympics (1992) and a bronze medal for 4x100-meter relay at Atlanta Olympics (1996).

CUTINA, Laura (1968—). Romanian gymnast. Born Sept 13, 1968, in Bucharest, Romania. ❖ Placed 2nd all-around at American Cup and 1st all-around at Romanian Cup (1984); at Los Angeles Olympics, won a gold medal in team all-around and placed 5th all-around (1984); at World championships, won a silver medal for team all-around (1983, 1985).

CUTLER, Hannah Conant (1815–1896). American woman's rights leader. Name variations: Hannah Conant Tracy. Born Hannah Maria Conant, Dec 25, 1815, in Becket, Berkshire Co., Massachusetts; died Feb 11, 1896, in Ocean Springs, MA; dau. of John and Orpha (Johnson) Conant; attended Oberlin College; m. John Martin Tracy (abolitionist, died 1844), 1834; m. Col. Samuel Cutler, 1852; children: (1st m.) 3. ❖ Lectured on woman's rights and introduced Bloomer costume in England; worked for married women's legal rights in several states (late 1850s–early 1860s); opened medical practice; assisted Lucy Stone with organizing American Woman Suffrage Association and served as president (1870–71); writings include *Woman as She Was, Is, and Should Be* (1846), *Phillipia, or a Woman's Question* (1886) and *The Fortunes of Michael Doyle, or Home Rule for Ireland* (1886).

CUTLER, Kate (1870–1955). English actress. Name variations: Mrs. Sydney Ellison. Born Aug 14, 1870, in London, England; died May 14, 1955, in London; m. Sydney Ellison. ❖ Made stage debut in *Pepita* (1888); other plays include *Paul Jones, In Town, A Gaiety Girl, A Model Trilby, The French Maid, Florodora, A Chinese Honeymoon, The Love Birds, A Man's Shadow, A Woman of No Importance, The Ogre, Good for Nothing, Bellamy the Magnificent, The Rivals* and *The Witness for the Defense*, among others; films include *Pygmalion, When Knights were Bold* and *Moscow Nights*.

CUTLER, Robyn (1948—). American modern dancer. Born May 25, 1948, in Atlanta, Georgia. ❖ Studied at Juilliard School in New York City; joined José Limón Dance Company (1962); performed in numerous repertory works, including title role in Limón's *La Malinche*.

CUTPURSE, Moll (c. 1584–1659). See *Frith, Mary*.

CUTRONE, Angela. Canadian short-track speedskater. Born in Canada. ❖ Won a gold medal at Albertville Olympics (1992) and a silver medal at Lillehammer Olympics (1994), both for the 3,000-meter relay.

CUTTER, Kiki (1951—). American Alpine skier. Born Christina Cutter, Jan 1, 1951, in Bend, Oregon. ❖ The 1st American skier, male or female, to win a World Cup title, in slalom (1968); won 1 giant slalom and 3 more slalom World Cups (1968–70); held the American record for most World Cup ski victories. Inducted into Colorado Ski Hall of Fame (2000) and US National Ski Hall of Fame.

CUTTS, Patricia (1926–1974). English actress. Name variations: Patricia Wayne. Born July 20, 1926, in London, England; died Sept 11, 1974, in London, by taking an overdose of sleeping pills; dau. of Graham Cutts (writer-director). ❖ Child actress, then lead player in British films, including *The Man Who Loved Redheads, Merry Andrew* and *The Tingler;* was a panelist on US tv quiz show "Down You Go" (1955–56) and appeared on Broadway in *The Matchmaker, Kean* and *Any Wednesday*.

CUZZONI, Francesca (c. 1698–1770). Italian soprano. Born in Parma, Italy, c. 1698; died in Bologna, 1770; m. Sandoni (harpsichordist); studied with Lanzi. ❖ Made debut in Parma (1716); debuted in London, creating Teofane in Handel's *Ottone* (1723); created several other Handel roles, including Rodelinda, Cleopatra in *Giulio Cesare*, Asteria in *Tamerlano*, and Lisaura in *Alessandro*. ❖ See also *Women in World History*.

CYBO, Maddalena (d. 1519). See *Medici, Maddalena de*.

CYMBARKA OR CYMBURGA (c. 1396–1429). See *Cimburca of Masovia*.

CYNANE (c. 357–322 BCE). See *Cynnane*.

CYNEBURG OF MERCIA (fl. 655). Abbess of Castor. Name variations: Cyniburg; St. Cuneburga. Eldest dau. of Penda, king of Mercia, and Cynewise; married Alcfrith or Alchfrith of Deira, sub-king of Deira and son of King Oswiu of Northumbria, in c. 651; children: at least 6, including St. Cyneburg of Gloucester (c. 660–710), St. Edburga of Gloucester (d. 735), St. Weeda of Gloucester, Eva of Gloucester, St. Rumwold, and Osric of Northumbria (d. 729). ❖ A pious Christian, was responsible with husband for the building of the monastery of Ripon and a smaller one at Stamford; was present at the Conference of Whitby (664); became abbess at Castor, near Peterborough in Northamptonshire, and was probably its founder.

CYNEBURG OF GLOUCESTER (c. 660–710). English abbess. Name variations: St. Cuneburga of Gloucester. Born c. 660; died 710; dau. of Cyneburg of Mercia and Alcfrith or Alchfrith of Deira. ❖ Appointed by brother King Osric as the 1st abbess of the Abbey of St. Peter in Gloucester (now Gloucester Cathedral); fled and went into hiding to avoid a royal marriage; taken in as a servant to a baker, was murdered by his jealous wife who chopped off her head and tossed it in a well; burial spot became a place of pilgrimage.

CYNESWITH (fl. 7th c.). See *Cuneswith*.

CYNETHRYTH (fl. 736–796). Queen of Mercia. Fl. 8th century; m. Offa II, king of Mercia, around 756; children: at least 3, including Eadburgh (c. 773–after 802) and possibly Etheldreda (d. around 840). ❖ One of the most famous queens of the early Middle Ages, had a reputation for cruelty; married King Offa II of Mercia (c. 756) and ruled with him until his death (796), reigning with almost the same powers as a queen-regnant; as queen, oversaw many aspects of the kingdom's administration, passing edicts and legislation, and making foreign-policy decisions; after Offa's death, became an abbess. ❖ See also *Women in World History*.

CYNEWISE (fl. 7th c.). Queen of Mercia. Name variations: Name variations: Cunewise; m. Penda, king of Mercia (r. c. 626–655, d. 655); children: Paeda, king of Middle Anglia; Wulfhere of Mercia, king of Mercia (r. 657–675); Aethelred, king of Mercia (died 704); Merewald; Cyneburg of Mercia, Cuneswith, St. Cunethrith of Castor, Wilburga, Edburga of Bicester and Edith of Aylesbury.

CYNIBURG (fl. 8th c.). English abbess. Name variations: Cyniberg or Kyneburga; fl in 8th century in England. ❖ Abbess of Inkberrow, received a Letter in Latin (c. 740) which is preserved in the Boniface Correspondence; none of her letters are extant.

CYNIBURG (fl. 655). See *Cyneburg of Mercia*.

CYNISCA (fl. 396–392 BCE). Greek horse breeder. Name variations: Kyniska. Pronunciation: coo-NISS-ka. Born in Sparta, birth date unknown, but probably close to that of brother Agesilaus in 444 BCE; dau. of Archidamus or Archidamos II, king of Sparta, and his 2nd wife. ❖ The 1st Greek woman to breed horses and race them in the Olympic chariot races, was owner of the victorious four-colt chariot in the 96th and 97th Olympic games (396 and 392 BCE). ❖ See also *Women in World History*.

CYNNANE (c. 357–322 BCE). Macedonian half-sister of Alexander the Great. Name variations: Cynane. Born c. 357 BCE; died in 322 BCE; dau.

of Philip II, king of Macedonia (r. 359–336 BCE), and Audata (the 1st of Philip's 7 wives); half-sister of Alexander III the Great (356–323 BCE), king of Macedonia; m. Amyntas, around 337; children: (1st m.) Adea (337–317 BCE, later renamed Eurydice). ❖ Attempted to avenge her husband's death and win power following Alexander's death. ❖ See also *Women in World History.*

CYNTHIA (1910–1963). *See Brousse, Amy.*

CYPROS (fl. 28 CE). Biblical woman. Name variations: Cyprus. Dau. of Mariamne the Hasmonian; granddau. of Herod the Great (73–4 BCE); m. Herod Agrippa I; children: Berenice (28 CE–after 80 CE) and Agrippa II. ❖ Her name was a synonym for Aphrodite, the Greek goddess of love.

CYPRUS (c. 90 BCE–?). Mother of Herod. Name variations: Cypros. Born an Arab in Nabatea, a kingdom east of Judea, around 90 BCE; m. Antipater the Idumaean (d. 43 BCE, minister to the Hasmonian queen Alexandra); children: sons Phasael, governor of Jerusalem (d. 40 BCE); Herod the Great, king of Judea (73–4 BCE); Joseph; Pheroras; and a daughter, Salome (c. 65 BCE–10 CE).

CYPRUS, queen of.
See Alice of Champagne (fl. 1200s).
See Plaisance of Antioch (d. 1261).
See Medea (d. 1440).
See Charlotte of Lusignan (1442–1487).
See Cornaro, Caterina (1454–1510).

CYRENE, queen of.
See Pheretima.
See Cleopatra V Selene.

CZAJKOWSKA, Krystyna (1936—). Polish volleyball player. Born April 25, 1936. ❖ Won an Olympic bronze medal at Tokyo (1964) and Mexico City (1968), both in team competition.

CZAK, Ibolya (b. 1915). *See Csak, Ibolya.*

CZARTORYSKA, Isabella (1746–1835). Polish writer, patriot and countess. Name variations: Princess Izabela Czartoryska or Czrtoryska; Countess of Flemming or Fleming. Born Izabela Flemming (also seen as Fleming) in Warsaw, Mar 3, 1746; died at Wysock, Galicia, Austria, June 17, 1835; dau. of Count Jerzy von Flemming (1699–1771) and Antoinette Czartoryska (1728–1746); m. Prince Adam Kazimierz Czartoryski, 1761; children: 2 sons; 3 daughters, including Zofia Czartoryska and Marie Anna Czartoryska (1768–1854, 1st wife of Louis Frederick Alexander, duke of Wurttemberg). ❖ Met Benjamin Franklin, Jean Jacques Rousseau, and Voltaire in Paris (1772); transformed Czartoryski Palace at Pulawy into meeting place for intellectuals; during last partition of Poland, endured her 2 sons being taken by Catherine II the Great as hostages (1795); after the Warsaw insurrection, rebuilt the ruined palace and established Temple of Sybil for Polish antiquities (1796), the 1st Polish museum; wrote 1st popular histories of Poland, including *Pielgrzym w Dobromilu* (A Pilgrim in Dobromil, 1818).

CZEKALLA, Barbara (1951—). East German volleyball player. Born Nov 7, 1951. ❖ At Moscow Olympics, won a silver medal in team competition (1980).

CZERNY-STEFANSKA, Halina (1922–2001). Polish pianist. Born 1922 in Cracow (Krakow), Poland; died July 1, 2001, in Cracow; studied with Alfred Cortot in Paris. ❖ Shared 1st prize with Bella Davidovich at the Chopin Competition in Warsaw (1949); made London debut (1949); best known for her rendering of Chopin, especially her mazurka playing. A celebrated recording of the Chopin E minor Concerto thought to be by legendary Romanian pianist Dinu Lipatti was discovered to be a 1955 recording by Czerny-Stefanska. ❖ See also *Women in World History.*

CZIGANY, Kinga (1952—). Hungarian kayaker. Born Feb 17, 1952. ❖ At Barcelona Olympics, won a gold medal in K4 500 meters (1992).

CZOBEL, Lisa (1906–1992). Hungarian concert dancer. Born April 2, 1906, in Hamburg, Germany. ❖ Danced for many years with Essen Folkwang Dance Theater of Kurt Jooss and with his company in England; with rise of Nazism, worked in Switzerland and England before immigrating to US (early 1940s) where she performed with Trudi Schoop, another exile; appeared in numerous solo recitals (1946–49); as concert dancer, performed with Alexander von Swaine for many years after returning to Europe, appearing mainly in Germany and Switzerland.

CZOPEK, Agnieszka (1964—). Polish swimmer. Born Jan 9, 1964, in Poland. ❖ At Moscow Olympics, won a bronze medal in 400-meter individual medley (1980).

CZRTORYSKA, Izabela (1746–1835). *See Czartoryska, Isabella.*

D

DABROWSKA, Maria (1889–1965). Polish writer. Born Maria Szumska in Russów near Kalisz, Russian Poland, Oct 6, 1889; died in Warsaw, May 19, 1965; dau. of an estate manager; read philosophy and sociology at Lausanne and Brussels; m. Marian Dabrowski (Polish Socialist), 1911 (died 1925). ❖ A leading writer of the school of critical realism, whose masterwork *Noce i dnie* is one of the greatest novels in 20th-century Polish literature, began career as a journalist for *Spolem* (*United*), the journal of the national cooperative movement (1914); besides writings calling for sweeping land reforms, began to publish short stories about rural life, including the collections *Dzieci Ojczyzny* (*Children of the Fatherland,* 1918) and *Galaz czeresni* (*The Cherry Branch,* 1922); worked at Ministry of Agriculture in Warsaw (1918–24); had 1st major critical success with cycle of short stories based on her memories of rural life, *Usmiech dziecinstwa* (*The Smile of Childhood,* 1923), which caught the attention of avant-garde literary circles because of its innovative, essentially Proustian, form of narration; also wrote *Ludzie stamtad* (*Folk from Over Yonder*), collection of short stories published to critical acclaim (1926); in her tetralogy *Nights and Days* (*Noce i dnie,* 1932–34), matched the quality of the great Russian novels by blending realism with an epic story, a panorama of a half-century of Polish history; joined 33 other writers to protest ever-increasing censorship (1964); was unable to complete her 2nd family saga, *Przygody czlowiecka myslacego* (*The Adventures of a Thinking Man*), intended as a sequel to *Nights and Days,* which was published posthumously as a fragment (1970). ❖ See also Zbigniew Folejewski, *Maria Dabrowska* (Twayne, 1967); and *Women in World History.*

DACHÉ, Lilly (1898–1989). French milliner. Name variations: Lilly Dache. Born Oct 10, 1898, in Bèigles, France; died Dec 31, 1989 in Louvecienne, France; m. Jean Despres (became Coty vice president), Mar 31, 1931; children: Suzanne Dache (took over mother's millinery business). ❖ At 15, became an apprentice to Caroline Reboux and Suzanne Talbot; moved to NY (1924), where she worked as a sales clerk at Macy's; ran her own business in NY (1924–69); became known for her draped turbans, cloche hats, visored caps for war workers, snoods, massed flower shapes, and the swagger hat often worn by Marlene Dietrich. Won Neiman-Marcus fashion award (1940); won 1st Coty Award for Millinery (1943). ❖ See also autobiography *Talking Through My Hats* (1946).

DACIER, Anne (1654–1720). French scholar, linguist, and translator. Name variations: Anne LeFèvre, Lefevre, Lefebvre, or Le ferre; Anne Tanneguy Lefèvre; Madame Dacier. Born Anne Lefebvre in Saumur, France, Mar 1654; died in Paris, Aug 17, 1720; dau. of (Latinized) Tanquillus Faber, also known as Tannegui or Tanneguy Lefèvre (1615–1672, humanist, classical scholar) and Madame Lefebvre; m. Jean Lesnier (printer and bookseller); m. André Dacier (scholar), 1683 (died 1722); children: 2 daughters, Henriette-Susanne Dacier and Marie Dacier; 1 son, Jean-Andre. ❖ One of the most accomplished French scholars of the 17th century, moved to Paris, where she began working as a translator, publishing an edition of the works of Callimachus, head of the Alexandrian library; assisted in the preparation of the Delphin editions of the classics; corresponded with Queen Christina of Sweden, among others, and translated several plays of Plautus, the whole of Terence, the *Plutus* and *Clouds* of Aristophanes, Plutarch's *Lives,* and the whole of Anacreon and Sappho; particularly known for her translation of Marcus Aurelius and Homer; was appointed to the Ricrovati Academy in Padua. ❖ See also *Women in World History.*

DA COSTA, Maria Velho (1938—). *See Velho da Costa, Maria.*

DACRE, Anne (1557–1630). *See Arundel, Ann.*

DACRE, Barbarina (1768–1854). English poet, playwright and translator. Name variations: Barbarina Brand; Barbarina Ogle Wilmot; Lady Dacre, Baroness Dacre. Born Barbarina Ogle in 1768; died May 17, 1854, in London, England; dau. of Admiral Sir Chaloner Ogle and Hester Thomas; m. Valentine Henry Wilmot (Guards officer), 1789 (div.); m. Thomas Brand, Baron Dacre (Whig peer), 1819; children: (1st m.) Arabella Sullivan (c. 1796–1839), writer. ❖ Published *Dramas, Translations and Occasional Poems* (1821), which included 4 verse dramas (*Ina, Gonzalvo of Cordova, Pedarias* and *Xarifa*); best known for her translations of Petrarch's sonnets; was also skilled in wax modeling.

DACRE, Charlotte (c. 1772–1825). British Gothic-fiction writer. Name variations: Charlotte Byrne; Charlotte King; (pseudonym) Rosa Matilda. Born Charlotte King, c. 1772 (some sources cite c. 1781 or c. 1782), in England; died Nov 7, 1825 (some sources cite c. 1841), in London, England; the name Dacre was itself a pseudonym; dau. of Jonathan King (notorious London moneylender) and Deborah Lara King; sister of Sophia King Fortnum (writer); m. Nicholas Byrne, 1806; children: 3. ❖ Wrote *Trifles of Helicon* with Sophia King (1798); as Rosa Matilda, published *Confessions of the Nun of St. Omer* (1805); also wrote *Hours of Solitude* (1805), *The Libertine* (1807), *The Passions* (1811), *George the Fourth* (1822) and *School for Friends, or Domestic Tale;* probably best known for *Zofloya; or the Moor: A Romance of the Fifteenth Century* (1806), a feminized version of Gothic novelist Matthew Gregory Lewis' *The Monk,* which was immensely popular and praised by Shelley and Swinburne.

DACRE, Elizabeth (b. before 1566). English aristocrat. Name variations: Elizabeth Howard. Born before 1566; dau. of Thomas Dacre, 4th lord Dacre of Gilsland, and Elizabeth Leyburne; m. William Howard, Lord Howard, Oct 28, 1577; children: 5 sons, including Sir Francis Howard (1588–1660) and Sir Philip Howard.

DACRE, Lady.
See Fiennes, Anne (d. 1595).
See Dacre, Barbarina (1768–1854).

DACRE, Marie (1563–1578). English aristocrat. Name variations: Mary Dacre; Marie Howard. Born on July 4, 1563; died April 7, 1578, at Walden; dau. of Thomas Dacre, 4th lord Dacre of Gilsland, and Elizabeth Leyburne; m. Thomas Howard (later 1st earl of Suffolk), before May 9, 1577.

DACRE, Mary (1563–1578). *See Dacre, Marie.*

DACRE, Winifred (1893–1981). *See Nicholson, Winifred.*

DAENZER, Frieda. *See Dänzer, Frieda.*

DAFOE, Frances (1929—). Canadian figure skater. Born 1929 in Canada. ❖ With partner Norris Bowden, won Canadian National championships (1952–55), North American championships (1953–56), and World Paris championships (1954–55); won a silver medal at Cortina Olympics (1956); retired (1956); became a fashion designer, specializing in figure-skating costumes. Inducted into Canada's Sports Hall of Fame (1955) and Canadian Figure Skating Hall of Fame (1993).

DAFOVSKA, Ekaterina (1976—). Bulgarian biathlete. Name variations: Katerina Dafovska. Born Nov 28, 1975, in Tchepelare, Bulgaria. ❖ Came in 29th in the 15-kilometer competition at Lillehammer Olympics (1994); won a gold medal in 15km at Nagano Olympics (1998), Bulgaria's 1st-ever Winter Olympic gold medal. ❖ See also *Women in World History.*

DAGMAR (1921–2001). American entertainer. Name variations: Jenny Lewis; Jeanne Lewis. Born Virginia Ruth Egnor, Nov 29, 1921, in Huntington, West Virginia; died Oct 9, 2001, in Ceredo, West Virginia; m. Angelo Lewis (div.); m. Danny Dayton (comic, div.); m. Dick Hinds (died 1977). ❖ Was immensely popular as the dumb-blonde character named Dagmar on NBC's "Broadway Open House" (1950–51), a forerunner of "The Tonight Show."

DAGMAR, empress of Russia (1847–1928). *See Marie Feodorovna.*

DAGMAR OF BOHEMIA (d. 1212). Queen of Denmark. Name variations: Margaret of Bohemia. Died May 24, 1212; dau. of Ottokar I (d. 1230), king of Bohemia (r. 1198–1230), and Adela of Meissen; 1st wife of Valdemar also known as Waldemar II the Victorious, king of Denmark (r. 1202–1241), 1205; children: Valdemar or Waldemar the Younger (1209–1231), joint-king of Denmark with his father (r. 1215–1231). ❖ The day after her marriage, petitioned the king to repeal the ploughtax, which was then a heavy burden on the Danes, and begged for the release of all prisoners; having rapidly won the love of the Danes because of her beauty, goodness, and saintly life, was rechristened Dagmar ("the mother of the day") by a grateful nation. ❖ See also *Women in World History*.

DAGMAR OF DENMARK (1847–1928). *See Marie Feodorovna.*

DAGOE, Hannah (d. 1763). Irish-born thief in London. Born in Ireland; died at Tyburn, May 4, 1763. ❖ Already a petty criminal at a young age, moved to London and met a poor widow, Eleanor Hussey, at Covent Garden; after looting Hussey's home, was caught, tried at Old Bailey, and sentenced to death; on day of execution, struggled with executioner, ripped off her clothes—which normally would have gone to executioner as payment—and tossed them to crowd, then threw herself off the cart with such violence that she broke her neck and died instantly.

D'AGOULT, Marie (1805–1876). *See Agoult, Marie d'.*

DAGOVER, Lil (1897–1980). German actress. Born Marta Maria Lillits Seubert (some sources give her name as Marie Antonia Sieglinde Marta Seubert), Sept 30, 1897, in Madioen, Java, Netherlands East Indies; died in Munich, Germany, Jan 30, 1980; dau. of Adolf and Marta (Herf) Seubert; orphaned at 13 and raised by relatives; m. Fritz Daghofer (actor), 1914 (div. 1919); m. Georg Witt. ❖ Major star of stage and screen for over 50 years, appeared in Fritz Lang's *Harakiri* (*Butterfly*) and in the small role of Jane in expressionist film *The Cabinet of Dr. Caligari* (1919); starred in Lang's *Der müde Tod* (*Destiny*, 1921), as well as in a number of films of F.W. Murnau, including *Phantom* (1922) and *Chronik von Grieshuus* (*At the Grey House*, 1925); co-starred with Emil Jannings in *Tartuffe* (1925); appeared in several Swedish films, including *Hans engelska Fru* (*Discord*, 1928); in France, starred in *Le Tourbillon de Paris* (*The Whirlwind of Paris,* 1928), *La Grande Passion* (1929) and *Monte Cristo* (1929); in Hollywood, filmed the successful *The Woman from Monte Carlo* (1931); in early years of Nazi regime, avoided propaganda films, starring instead in such comedies as *Ich heirate meine Frau* (*I'm Marrying My Wife,* 1934) and a German version of *Lady Windermere's Fan* (1935); later on, appeared in propaganda film *Wien 1910* (*Vienna 1910,* 1943), which glorified the career of anti-Semitic mayor Karl Lueger; for work entertaining German troops, received a War Service Cross (1944); having remained relatively untainted by Nazism, was able to resume acting career after 1945; returned to the stage (1950s), receiving raves for leading roles in *Gigi* and *The Madwoman of Chaillot;* also appeared in tv dramatization of *Buddenbrooks* (1957); made over 100 films, including *Die letzte Illusion* (*The Last Illusion,* 1932), *Das Abenteuer der Thea Roland* (*The Adventures of Thea Roland,* 1932), *Die Kreuzersonate* (*The Kreuzer Sonata,* 1937), *Bekenntnisse des Hochstaplers Felix Krull* (*The Confessions of Felix Krull,* 1957), *Karl May* (1961) and *Geschichten aus dem Wienerwald* (*Tales from the Vienna Woods,* 1979). Awarded Cross of Merit of the Federal Republic of Germany (1967). ❖ See also *Women in World History.*

DAHIYAH KAHINAH (fl. 695–703). *See Kahina.*

DAHL, Arlene (1924—). American actress. Born Aug 11, 1924, in Minneapolis, Minnesota; m. Lex Barker (actor), 1951 (div. 1952); m. Fernando Lamas (actor), 1954 (div. 1960); m. Chris Holmes, 1960 (div. 1964); m. Alexis Lichine, 1965 (div. 1969); m. Rounseville W. Schaum, 1969 (div. 1981); m. Marc Rosen, 1984; children: Lorenzo Lamas (b. 1958, actor). ❖ Named Rheingold beer girl (1946); made film debut in *My Wild Irish Rose* (1947), followed by *The Bride Goes Wild, Reign of Terror, Three Little Words, Woman's World, Slightly Scarlet* and *Journey to the Center of the Earth,* among others; wrote a beauty column and marketed lingerie and cosmetics; on tv, appeared as a regular on "One Life to Live."

DAHL, Aslaug. Norwegian cross-country skier. Born in Norway. ❖ Won a bronze medal for 3 x 5 km relay at Sapporo Olympics (1972).

DAHL-WOLFE, Louise (1895–1989). American photographer. Born in San Francisco, California, Nov 19, 1895; died in Allendale, New Jersey, Dec 11, 1989; attended California School of Design (now San Francisco Art Institute); studied painting with Frank Van Sloan; m. Meyer (Mike) Wolfe (sculptor), 1928 (died 1985); no children. ❖ Acclaimed for her color sense and innovative use of naturalistic decors in fashion photography, was probably the foremost female fashion photographer during the early postwar period; began career as a photographer for an interior decorator; moved to a cabin in the Tennessee Smoky Mountains (1932) and produced still lifes and portraits of the mountain people; began working freelance, producing advertising and fashion photographs for *Women's Home Companion* and various department stores, such as Saks Fifth Avenue and Bonwit Teller; became a staff photographer for *Harper's Bazaar* (1936), a post she held until 1958; also worked for *Sports Illustrated* and *Vogue.* ❖ See also *Women in World History.*

DAHLBECK, Eva (1920—). Swedish actress. Born in Saltsjö-Duvnäs, Sweden, Mar 8, 1920; trained at Royal Dramatic Theater, Stockholm; m. Col. Sven Lampell, 1944; children: 2 sons. ❖ Best known for her work in films of Ingmar Bergman, made stage debut (1941); appeared on stage in *Rid i natt* and in its film adaptation (1942); appeared on US tv in "Foreign Intrigue" (1952–55); wrote script for the film *Yngsjömordet* (Woman of Darkness, 1966); also wrote a play, a book of poetry, and more than 10 novels; films include *Ride Tonight* (1942), *Black Roses* (1945), *Eva* (1948), *Unser Dorf* (*The Village,* 1952), *Defiance* (1952), *Secrets of Women* (1952), *Barabbas* (1953), *A Lesson in Love* (1954), *Dreams* (1955), *Smiles of a Summer Night* (1955), *The Counterfeit Traitor* (1962), *All These Women* (1964), *Loving Couples* (1964), *Morianna* (*I the Body,* 1965), *The Cats* (1965), *Les Créatures* (1966), *The Red Mantle* (*Hagbard and Signe,* 1967), *People Meet and Sweet Music Fills the Heart* (1967), and *Tintomara* (1970). Named Best Actress at Cannes Festival for her performance in Ingmar Bergman's *Brink of Life* (1958).

DAHLE, Gunn-Rita (1973—). Norwegian cyclist. Born Feb 10, 1973, in Stavanger, Norway; attended University of Stavanger. ❖ At World championships, placed 1st in cross country (1998, 2000); placed 1st overall in cross country World Cup ranking (2003, 2004); won a gold medal for cross country at Athens Olympics (2004).

DAHLE, Mona (1970—). Norwegian handball player. Born Aug 24, 1970, in Norway. ❖ At Barcelona Olympics, won a silver medal in team competition (1992).

DAHLMO, Marianne. Norwegian cross-country skier. Born in Norway. ❖ Won a silver medal for 4 x 5 km relay at Calgary Olympics (1988).

DAHLSTROM, Gerda (1871–1959). *See Lundequist, Gerda.*

DAHNE, Heike (1961—). East German swimmer. Born Oct 15, 1961. ❖ At Moscow Olympics, won a bronze medal in 800-meter freestyle (1980).

DAHNE, Sabine (1950—). East German rower. Born Feb 27, 1950. ❖ At Montreal Olympics, won a silver medal in coxless pairs (1976).

DAI, Ailian (1916–2006). Chinese dancer. Name variations: Madam Dai Ailian. Born May 10, 1916 in Trinidad, West Indies, of Chinese parents, whose forebears came from Guangdong Province; died Feb 9, 2006, in Beijing, China; studied Chinese culture and language with such masters as Zhang Daqian and Ye Qianyu. ❖ One of China's premier dance icons, had enormous impact by introducing principles and study of Western ballet and modern dance to China and championing Chinese folk dance traditions at home and abroad; took 1st dance lessons in Trinidad; traveled to London (1931) to study ballet and modern dance with Anton Dolin, Kurt Jooss and Rudolphe von Laban; traveled to China after war broke out (1939), giving benefit performances in Hong Kong and on mainland; became 1st principal of Beijing Dance Academy, where students were taught both ballet and Chinese dance; studied ancient dances and recorded traditional choreography; worked with historians to research dances as old as 5,000 years; produced and performed such dances as "Yao Drum" and "The Dumb Shouldering a Lunatic," Tibetan dance "Ba'an Xianzi," Miao dance "Jiarong Wine Party" and Uygur "Dance of Youth" (1940s); became president of National Dance Troupe under People's Republic of China and served as 1st headmistress of Beijing Dance School as well as co-founder and 1st president of Central Ballet Theater (1959); combined Chinese and Western dance to create such masterpieces as "Lotus Dance" and "Flying Apsaras," which won awards at festivals in Berlin (1953) and Warsaw (1955); toured worldwide with National Ballet of China.

DAI HOUYING (1938–1996). Chinese novelist, reformer and educator. Born Mar 18, 1938, in China; murdered in apartment in Shanghai, China, Aug 25, 1996 (the killer, Tao Feng, admitted to murdering her and her niece and stealing Dai's savings). ❖ Was an associate professor in literature at Shanghai University; published 1st novel, *Ren Ah, Ren!* (People, Oh People!), which explored the excesses of the Cultural Revolution; her trilogy (1981–86), which further focused on persecution of intellectuals in China, was comprised of *Stones of the Wall* (1981), *Death of a Poet* (1982), and *Footsteps Echoing in the Void* (1986); was an activist in pro-democracy rallies (1989).

DAI QING (1941—). *Chinese journalist and essayist.* Born Fu Ning in 1941 in China; dau. of a revolutionary; graduate of Harbin Institute of Military Technology (1966). ❖ China's most famous woman journalist, worked as technician before becoming reporter; established China's 1st environmental lobby group and was instrumental in temporarily halting construction of Three Gorges hydroelectric scheme; was jailed for 10 months after Tiananmen Square massacre (1989) and prohibited from writing in China; worked as scholar in residence at Woodrow Wilson International Center for Scholars and received several international awards; wrote series of interviews on important Chinese dissident intellectuals (1980s) and investigative reports on Chinese women for *Series on Women*; edited *Yangtze! Yangtze!* (1989), containing essays opposed to building of Three Gorges Dam.

DAIGLE, Sylvie (1962—). *Canadian short-track speedskater.* Born Dec 1, 1962, in Sherbrooke, Quebec, Canada. ❖ Won a gold medal in the 1,500 meters and silver medals in the 1,000 and 3,000 meters at Calgary Olympics (1988); won a gold medal in 3,000-meter relay at Albertville Olympics (1992); won a silver in the 3,000-meter relay at Lillehammer Olympics (1994).

DAINI NO SANMI (999–after 1078). *Japanese poet.* Name variations: Echigo no Benin. Born Kenshi or Masako in 999; still alive in 1078; dau. of Murasaki Shikibu (c. 973–c. 1015) and Fujiwara no Nobutaka (court official). ❖ Thirty-seven of her poems can be found in imperial anthologies.

DAINTON, Marie (1881–1938). *Russian-born actress.* Born June 30, 1881, in Russia; dau. of Jenny (Dawson) Sharlach and Robert E. Sharlach. ❖ Famed for her imitations of popular actors, made triumphant London debut at Metropolitan Music Hall (1894); also appeared in *The House That Jack Built, Pot-Pourri, The Belle of Bohemia, A Chinese Honeymoon* (over 1,000 performances), *Peggy Machree* (title role), *The Girl Behind the Counter, By George!, I Should Worry, The Eternal Flame* and *Mary Read;* toured the US and often appeared in music halls.

DAISY, Princess (1873–1943). *Welsh-born princess and memoirist.* Name variations: Princess of Pless; Princess Henry of Pless; Mary or Maria Cornwallis-West. Born Maria (also seen as Mary) Theresa Olivia Cornwallis-West, 1873 in Wales; died 1943; dau. of Col. William and Patsy Cornwallis-West (favorite of the prince of Wales, later King Edward VII); sister of Constance Edwina Cornwallis-West (aka Shelagh who was duchess of Westminster, died 1970) and George Cornwallis-West who m. Jennie Jerome Churchill; m. Prince Hans Heinrich of Pless (German prince), 1891 (div.). ❖ See also *Daisy Princess of Pless, By Herself* (1928) and *The Private Diaries of Daisy, Princess of Pless, 1873–1914* (1950).

DAKIDES, Tara (1975—). *American snowboarder.* Born Aug 20, 1975, in Mission Viejo, California. ❖ Won gold in Slopestyle (Winter 1999 and Winter 2000), gold in Big Air (Winter 2000 and Winter 2001), and silver in Big Air (Winter 1999) at X Games; other 1st-place finishes include: Motocross/Boardercross, Mammoth Mountain, California, in BDX/MTX (1997); Vans Triple Crown (make-up event), Mount Seymour, BC, in Big Air (2000); SIMS Invitational World Snowboarding championships, Whistler/Blackcomb, BC, in Big Air (2000); Gravity Games, Mammoth Mountain, CA, in Quarterpipe (2000); Chevy Grand Prix, Northstar, CA, in Triple Air (2000); World Snowboarding championships, Whistler/Blackcomb, BC, in Slopestyle (2001); and Vans Triple Crown, Snow Summit, CA, in Big Air (2001).

DAL, Ingerid (1895–1985). *Norwegian linguist.* Name variations: Ingerid Blanca Juell Dal. Born Aug 2, 1895, in Drammen, near Oslo, Norway; died Feb 17, 1985; attended Kristiana University, 1914–20, and Heidelberg University, 1920–25; University of Hamburg, PhD, 1925; University of Oslo, PhD, 1930. ❖ Had childhood interests in math, philosophy, science and philology; worked as a research assistant (1930–38), as a German linguistics lecturer (1938–39), and as a professor of German philology (1939–65) at University of Oslo; published research papers, which were later combined for *Research into the History*

of the German Language (1972), a book published by the Norwegian General Scientific Committee in honor of Dal's 75th birthday. Honors and awards include fellow of the Norwegian Academy of Sciences (1940), Nansen Foundation Prize (1954), fellow of Norwegian Academy for Language and Literature (1958) and Goethe Gold Medal (1958).

DALASSENA, Anna (c. 1025–1105). *See Anna Dalassena.*

D'ALBERT, Marie-Madeleine Bonafous (fl. 18th c.). *French novelist.* Fl. in 18th-century France; educated at Abbaye de Pentemont. ❖ Raised the ire of the French ruling class with her novel *Tanastés* (1745), which criticized Parisian and court life, and was imprisoned briefly in the Bastille; released (1746), took refuge in a convent for 13 years at Bernadines de Moulins, then at Petit Saint-Chaumont; produced only one other novel, *Confidences d'une jolie femme* (Secrets of a Pretty Woman), a romance from the perspective of a young girl, which was published 30 years after her first (1775).

D'ALBRET, Jeanne (1528–1572). *See Jeanne d'Albret.*

D'ALBRET, Jeanne III (1528–1572). *See Jeanne d'Albret.*

DALDY, Amey (c. 1829–1920). *New Zealand feminist, social reformer, and benefactor.* Name variations: Amey Hamerton, Amey Smith. Born Amey Hamerton, c. 1829 (baptized, June 14, 1829), in Yarwell, Northamptonshire, England; died Aug 17, 1920, at Auckland, New Zealand; dau. of Charles (farmer) and Amey (Bonfield) Hamerton; m. William Henry Smith (shoemaker), 1860 (died 1879); m. William Daldy (merchant and politician), 1880 (died 1903). ❖ Immigrated to New Zealand (1860); became active in social and political issues; as public advocate for equal rights for women, was satirized in political cartoons published in *New Zealand Graphic*; bequeathed large sums of money to several social and political organizations. ❖ See also *Dictionary of New Zealand Biography* (Vol. 2).

DALE, Dana (1916–1977). *See Hayes, Maggie.*

DALE, Daphne (1931–1982). *English ballet dancer.* Born 1931 in Nairobi, Kenya; died July 9, 1982, in New Orleans, Louisiana; after several years of local training, moved to London to study dance with Grace Cone and Olive Ripman. ❖ Appeared 1 season with London Festival Ballet; moved to Rio de Janeiro, where she danced in productions of *Swan Lake, Les Sylphides, Prince Igor,* and others; performed in Gene Kelly's film *Invitation to the Dance* (1954); danced with Grand Ballet du Marquis de Cuevas in Europe; taught at school of Geneva Opera Ballet in Switzerland.

DALE, Esther (1885–1961). *American character actress.* Born Nov 10, 1885, in Beaufort, South Carolina; died July 23, 1961, in Los Angeles, California. ❖ Appeared on Broadway in such plays as *Carrie Nation* and *Picnic;* made over 100 films, including *Crime without Passion, Back Street, Private Worlds, Dead End, The Awful Truth* and *The Egg and I;* also appeared in many of the "Ma and Pa Kettle" series.

DALE, Esther (1932—). *See May, Elaine.*

DALE, Kathleen (1895–1984). *English pianist and journalist.* Born Kathleen Richards in London, England, June 29, 1895; died in Woking, England, Mar 3, 1984; studied piano with Fanny Davies and York Bowen; studied composition with Benjamin Dale; m. Benjamin Dale (1885–1943). ❖ Highly regarded accompanist and chamber-music performer, made many radio broadcasts (1920s–30s); taught at Matthay Piano School and Workers' Educational Association; as a musical scholar, edited and was the 1st to publish Schubert's Piano Sonata in E minor; also wrote newspaper and journal articles and published *Nineteenth-Century Piano Music* (1954). ❖ See also *Women in World History.*

DALE, Margaret (1876–1972). *American stage star.* Born Mar 6, 1876, in Philadelphia, Pennsylvania; died Mar 23, 1972, in New York, NY. ❖ Made NY debut as Mary Faber in *The Master* (1898); starred or was featured in such plays as *Disraeli, The Mummy and the Humming Bird, The Importance of Being Earnest, The Duke of Killiecrankie, If I Were King, Caesar's Wife, Dinner at 8, The Dark Tower, The Old Maid, Tovarich, Dear Octopus, The Late George Apley* and *Lady in the Dark,* appearing opposite the likes of George Arliss, E.H. Sothern, and John Drew; made film debut in *The World and His Wife* (1920), followed by *Disraeli,* among others.

DALE, Margaret (1922—). *English ballet dancer and tv producer.* Born Dec 30, 1922, in Newcastle-on-Tyne, England; dau. of John Howden Bolam and Gladys (Downs) Bolam; m. John Hart. ❖ As a child, made

London debut at Sadler's Wells in the ballet *Casse Noisette* (1937); danced with Sadler's Wells Company (1940–54), beginning with small roles in such ballets as *The Prospect Before Us, The Wanderer* and *Orpheus and Euridice,* graduating to leading classical roles, including *The Sleeping Princess, The Fairy Queen* and as Swanhilda in *Coppelia*; created choreography for several ballets on tv, including "The Great Detective" (1952); joined the BBC as a dancer producer (1954), presenting such ballets as *The Sleeping Beauty.*

DALE, Virginia (1917–1994). American stage, tv, screen actress and dancer. Born July 1, 1917, in Charlotte, North Carolina; died Oct 3, 1994, in Burbank, California. ❖ Made professional debut with sister Frances as the Paxton Sisters, an acrobatic tap and adagio act; appeared as dancing partner of Fred Astaire in *Holiday Inn* (1942); other films include *Idiot's Delight, The Kid from Texas* (as Annie Oakley), *Las Vegas Nights, Dancing on a Dime, Kiss the Boys Goodbye* and *The Hucksters.*

D'ALENÇON, Emilienne. See Alençon, Emilienne d'.

D'ALESSANDRI-VALDINE, Blanche (c. 1862–1948). French ballet dancer. Name variations: Blanche Rostand Valdine. Born Blanche Rostand Valdine, c. 1862, in Paris, France; died July 1948, in Paris; m. dancer D'Alessandri. ❖ Made professional debut as a child in Paris Opéra's London production of *L'Enfant et les Bijoux* (1871); appeared next at age 17 as soloist at Grand Théâtre in Marseilles, France (1879), where her roles included Myrthe and Giselle; moved to Geneva, Switzerland, with husband, and performed with Grand Théâtre de Genève; ended career because of knee injury while performing on tour in New Orleans, LA; returned to Paris and opened dance studio, where her students included Camille Bos, Maura Paiva and Solange Schwarz.

DALEY, Cass (1915–1975). American comedic actress and singer. Born Katharine (also seen as Catherine) Daley, July 17, 1915, in Philadelphia, Pennsylvania; died Mar 22, 1975, in Hollywood, California; m. Frank Kinsella, 1941 (div.); m. Robert Williamson (actor); children: son. ❖ Began career singing in nightclubs; starred in *Ziegfeld Follies of 1936;* films include *The Fleets In, Crazy House, Riding High, Duffy's Tavern, Here Comes the Groom, Red Garters* and *The Spirit is Willing;* was a regular on radio series "The Fitch Bandwagon." Once voted radio's most popular comedienne.

DALI, Gala (1894–1982). Russian-born model and muse. Name variations: Gala Eluard; Gala Eluard Dali. Born Elena Ivanovna Diakonova, Aug 26, 1894, in Kazan, Russia; died June 10, 1982, in Port Lligat, Spain; m. Paul Eluard (French poet), 1917 (div., 1932); m. Salvador Dali (artist), 1934; children: (1st m.) Cécile. ❖ Suffering from tuberculosis, was sent to a Swiss sanatorium (1913); on 1st marriage, became a part of the Surrealist movement in Paris; on 2nd marriage, became the model, muse and companion of husband.

DALIBARD, Françoise-Thérèse Aumerle de Saint-Phalier (d. 1757). French poet and playwright. Name variations: Françoise Dalibard or Francoise Dalibard; (pseudonyms) Mlle S***; Mlle de St. Ph***. Died in 1757. ❖ Works include *Le Portefeuille rendu, ou lettres historiques* (1749), *Les Caprices du sort, ou l'histoire d'Emilie* (1750), *Recueil de poésies* (1751), *La rivale,* which was performed at Théâtre Italien in Paris (1752), and *Murat et Turquia* (1752).

DALIDA (1933–1987). Egyptian-born French singer and dancer. Born Yolande Christina Gigliotti, Jan 17, 1933, in Cairo, Egypt (some sources cite Serrasatra, Calabria, Italy), to Italian parents; committed suicide, May 3, 1987, in Paris, France; dau. of the 1st violinist of the opera in Cairo; m. Julien Morisse, April 8, 1961 (but ran off with painter Jean Sobiesky 3 months later, a relationship that ended in 1963). ❖ Moved to Paris (1956); began using stage name Dalida and established a successful singing and dancing career, often singing French versions of American, British and Italian hits; came to prominence with "Bambino" and "Gondolier"; starred in the French-Egyptian film *Le Sixième Jour* (1986).

DALILA. *Variant of Delilah.*

DALL, Caroline Wells (1822–1912). American author, reformer, and women's rights advocate. Name variations: Caroline H. Dall. Born Caroline Wells Healey in Boston, Massachusetts, June 22, 1822; died in Washington, DC, Dec 17, 1912; m. Charles H.A. Dall (Unitarian minister), Sept 1844 (some sources cite 1843); children: 2, including William Healey Dall (b. 1845, naturalist and author). ❖ Began contributing essays on religion and moral issues to periodicals by age 13; at 15, started one of the 1st nursery schools for working mothers in Boston; at 19, participated in Margaret Fuller's public conversations and

would later recount the experience in *Margaret and Her Friends* (1895); was vice-principal of a girls' school in Georgetown, Washington, DC, for several years; served as a corresponding editor of Paulina Wright Davis' women's-rights monthly, *The Una;* published a collection of her early writings, *Essays and Sketches* (1849); produced an impressive body of work that included histories, biographies, and children's books, all of which were well received; much of her writing focused on the progress of the women's movement; founded the American Social Science Association (1865), of which she served as director and vice president; writings include *Woman's Right to Labor* (1860), *Historical Pictures Retouched* (1860), *Egypt's Place in History* (1868), *Patty Gray's Journey to the Cotton Islands* (3-vol. children's book, 1868–1870), *The Romance of the Association, or, One Last Glimpse of Charlotte Temple and Eliza Wharton* (1875), *My First Holiday, or, Letters Home from Colorado, Utah, and California* (1881), *Barbara Fritchie—a Study* (1892), *Transcendentalism in New England* (1897) and *Fog Bells* (1905). ❖ See also memoir *Alongside* (1900); and *Women in World History.*

DALLAS, Letitia Marion (d. 1917). *See Darragh, Miss.*

DALLAS, Ruth (1919—). New Zealand poet and novelist. Born Sept 29, 1919, in Invercargill, New Zealand. ❖ Involved with literary journal *Landfall* under editorship of Charles Brasch; children's novels include *The Children in the Bush* (1969), *The Wild Boy in the Bush* (1971), and *Shining Rivers* (1979); poetry includes *Country Road and Other Poems 1947–52* (1953), *Shadow Snow* (1968), *Walking on the Snow* (1976), *Holiday Time in the Bush* (1983), and *Collected Poems* (1987). Named CBE (1989). ❖ See also autobiography *Curved Horizon* (1991).

DALLMANN, Petra (1978—). German swimmer. Born Nov 21, 1978, in Germany; attended University of Heidelberg. ❖ Placed 1st at World championships for 4 x 100-meter freestyle relay (2001); won a bronze medal for 4 x 200-meter freestyle relay at Athens Olympics (2004).

DALMIRA, Dorotéia Engrássia Tavareda (c. 1711–1793). *See Silve e Orta, Teresa M. da.*

DAL MONTE, Toti (1893–1975). Italian coloratura soprano. Born Antonietta Meneghel, June 27, 1893; died at Pieve di Soligo in Treviso, Italy, Jan 26, 1975; m. Enzo de Muro Lomanto (singer). ❖ After studying for 5 years with Barbara Marchesio, made debut in *Francesca di Rimini* at Teatro alla Scala (1916); sang Cio-Cio San in *Madama Butterfly* at Teatro Lirico of Milan (1918); engaged by Arturo Toscanini to sing Lucia (1921) and Beethoven's Ninth Symphony (1922) at La Scala, then asked to join the cast permanently; became well known in the world's major opera houses, debuting at Metropolitan Opera as Lucia (1924) and at Covent Garden as Lucia and Rosina (1926); went on a 4-month tour of Australia and New Zealand with Nellie Melba; retired from singing (1949). ❖ See also *Women in World History.*

D'ALPUGET, Blanche (1944—). Australian novelist and biographer. Name variations: Blanche D'Alpuget. Born Jan 3, 1944, in Sydney, Australia; dau. of Lou d'Alpuget (well-known Sydney journalist); married. ❖ Worked as journalist in Australia and UK; lived in Indonesia and Malaysia and continued to write for newspapers; novels include *Monkeys in the Dark* (1980), *Turtle Beach* (1981), which won the Age Book of the Year Award, and *Winter in Jerusalem* (1986); biographies include *Mediator: A Biography of Sir Richard Kirby* (1977) and *Robert J. Hawke: A Biography* (1982), which won the NSW Premier's Award for nonfiction.

DALRYMPLE, Grace (1758–1823). Scottish courtesan. Name variations: Grace Dalrymple Elliot. Born 1758 in Edinburgh, Scotland; died 1823 at Ville d'Avray, Paris, France; dau. of Hew Dalrymple (advocate); m. John Elliott (Scottish physician); had liaison with George IV (1762–1821), king of England (r. 1821–1830); associated with Lord Cholmondeley; children: Georgina Frederica Elliott (b. 1782, who might have been dau. of Cholmondeley). ❖ Made debut into Edinburgh society (1771); married; ran off with Lord Valentia (1774); became mistress of Valentia, Cholmondley, Charles Windham, George Selwyn, and the Prince of Wales (later George IV); on meeting the duke of Orleans (1784), moved to Paris. ❖ See also *Journal of My Life during the Revolution* written by her granddaughter.

DALRYMPLE, Jean (1910–1998). American theatrical publicist, producer, and director. Born in Morristown, New Jersey, Sept 2, 1910; died in New York City, Nov 15, 1998; dau. of George (businessman) and Elizabeth (Collins) Dalrymple; m. Ward Morehouse (drama critic for *New York Sun*), 1932 (div. 1937); m. Major-General Philip de Witt Ginder, Nov 1, 1951 (died 1968); no children. ❖ One of the most respected women in the American theater, was a driving force behind the New York City Center for 3 decades; with Dan Jarrett, toured in a vaudeville act, then collaborated on a play, *Salt Water*, which was produced by John Golden; opened a publicity office in New York (1940), out of which she handled publicity for such hit plays as *The Green Pastures, One Touch of Venus, The Voice of the Turtle* and *Anna Lucasta;* managed and publicized such stars as Lily Pons, Tallulah Bankhead and Mary Martin; produced 1st play, *Hope for the Best* (1945); during long tenure with City Center, produced plays of Shakespeare and Shaw, as well as more contemporary works and musical revivals, including *Porgy and Bess* (1944, 1961). ❖ See also autobiography, *From the Last Row* (White, 1975); and *Women in World History.*

DALRYMPLE, Learmonth White (1827–1906). New Zealand feminist and educational reformer. Baptized at Coupar Angus, Angus, Scotland, July 21, 1827; died Aug 26, 1906, in Dunedin, New Zealand; dau. of William and Janet (Jessie) Taylor Dalrymple; attended Madras College in St. Andrews. ❖ Set out with father, 2 sisters and a brother for New Zealand (1853), settling on a farm at Kaihiku, South Otago; began career as a teacher, during which time she was in touch with Dorothea Beale and Frances Mary Buss, British innovators in girls' education; following their lead, crusaded for secondary education for females in New Zealand; was influential in opening the Otago Girls' High School (1871), which served as a model for 70 later schools; during early discussions about founding a University of New Zealand, successfully petitioned for the admission of women; was also an advocate for preschool and primary education; wrote *The Kindergarten* (1879) and was active in the temperance and suffrage movements as well.

DALTENHEYM, Mme B. (1814–1886). *See Beauvain d'Althenheim, Gabrielle.*

D'ALTHENHEIM, Gabrielle Beauvain (1814–1886). *See Beauvain d'Althenheim, Gabrielle.*

DALTON, Doris (1910–1984). American actress. Born Mar 18, 1910, in Sharon, Massachusetts; died July 30, 1984, in Prout's Neck, Maine. ❖ Made NY debut in the chorus of *Electra* (1932), followed by *The Curtain Rises, Petticoat Fever, The Country Wife, The Fabulous Invalid, The Ryan Girl, Present Laughter, Pal Joey, Seventeen, The Man Who Came to Dinner* and *Take Me Along,* among others; also appeared on radio and tv.

DALTON, Dorothy (1893–1972). American stage and screen actress. Name variations: Dorothy Challoner. Born Sept 22, 1893, in Chicago, Illinois; died April 13, 1972, in Scarsdale, NY; m. Lew J. Cody (vaudevillian, div.); m. Arthur Hammerstein (theatrical manager and producer), 1924; children: daughter. ❖ Began career on stage with a Midwest touring company under the name Dorothy Challoner and later appeared at the Palace with Ted E. Rose as Rose and Challoner; also performed with husband Lew Cody; made NY stage debut in *Aphrodite* (1919), followed by *The Country Wife;* starred in many films (1914–24), including *The Disciple, D'Artagnon, Flame of the Yukon, Vive la France, The Moral Sinner* and *Moran of the Lady Letty.*

DALTON, Dorothy (1922–1973). American gymnast. Born Aug 1922 in US; died May 1973. ❖ At London Olympics, won a bronze medal in team all-around (1948).

DALTON, Judy Tegart (fl. 1960s–1970s). Australian tennis player. Name variations: Judy Tegart. Born Judy Tegart in Australia. ❖ Won Australian doubles championship with Lesley Turner (1964, 1967) and Margaret Smith Court (1969, 1970); won US doubles with Margaret Smith Court (1970) and Rosemary Casals (1971).

DALTON, Katharina (1916–2004). English physician and chiropodist. Name variations: Katharina Kuipers Dalton; Katharina Kuipers Thompson. Born Katharina Dorothea Kuipers, Nov 12, 1916, in London, England; died Sept 17, 2004, in Poole, Dorset, England; dau. of Dutch parents; attended Royal Masonic school; m. Wilfred Thompson (killed in action with RAF in WWII, 1942); m. Tom E. Dalton (minister), 1944 (died 1992); children: (1st m.) 1 son; (2nd m.) 1 son, 2 daughters. ❖ Pioneering doctor, the 1st to define and treat pre-menstrual syndrome (PMS), was initially a chiropodist and wrote *The Essentials of Chiropody for Students* (1938), a successful textbook with 6 editions; began pursuing medical studies at Royal Free Hospital (1943); went into general practice in Wood Green, north London, and later in Edmonton; became interested in and interviewed women about menstrual-cycle stages; produced more than 100 articles and research papers about PMS, postnatal depression, the importance of steady blood

sugar levels, and the dangers of vitamin B-6 overdose; publications include *Depression after Childbirth* (1989) and *The Pre-menstrual Syndrome and Progesterone Therapy* (1984); was a Royal College of General Practitioners founding member; became the 1st woman member of Royal Society of Medicine's general practitioner section (1971). Received Hawthorne Clinical British Medical Association Prize (1954, 1966, and 1976).

DALTON, Louisa (c. 1842–1893). *See Lord, Lucy Takiora.*

D'ALTON, Lucy (c. 1842–1893). *See Lord, Lucy Takiora.*

DALTON, Regina Maria (c. 1764–1845). *See Roche, Regina Maria.*

D'ALVAREZ, Lili. *See Alvarez, Lili de.*

DALY, Mary (c. 1861–1901). Irish murderer. Born c. 1861 in Ireland; hanged Sept 1, 1901 (some sources cite 1903); m. John Daly. ❖ Hanged by William Billington at Tullamore prison for murder of husband John.

DALY, Mary (1928—). American theologian, philosopher and feminist. Born Oct 16, 1928, in Schenectady, NY; College of St. Rose, BA, 1950; Catholic University, MA, 1952; St. Mary's College, Notre Dame, PhD, 1954; received doctorates in theology (1963) and philosophy (1965) from University of Fribourg, Switzerland. ❖ Taught at Fribourg (1959–66), then began teaching at Boston College (1969); works on theology and philosophy include *The Church and the Second Sex* (1985), which looked at gender bias within the church, *Beyond God the Father* (1985), *Pure Lust: Elemental Feminist Philosophy* (1984) and *Gyn/Ecology: The Meta-ethics of Radical Feminism* (1978); her books challenge normative theology and attempt to reconcile feminism and Christianity. ❖ See also autobiography *Outercourse: The Be-Dazzling Voyage* (1993).

DALY, Mary Agnes. Irish murderer. Born in Ireland. ❖ Notorious killer, beat 83-year-old Mary Gibbons with a hammer in Our Lady of the Seven Dolores church, Dublin (Aug 1948); after Gibbons died of her wounds, was charged with murder, found guilty and sentenced to be hanged; appealed and had sentence commuted to life; served 7 years in jail and 10 years in a convent.

DALY, Tyne (1946—). Amrican actress. Name variations: Tyne Daly Brown. Born Ellen Tyne Daly, Feb 21, 1946, in Madison, Wisconsin; dau. of James Daly (actor) and Hope Newell Daly; granddau. of Chief Justice Earl Warren; sister of Timothy Daly (actor); studied at American Musical and Dramatic Academy; m. Georg Stanford Brown, 1966 (div. 1990); children: 3 daughters, including Kathryne Dora Brown (actress) and Alisabeth Brown (potter). ❖ Made NY stage debut in *The Butter and Egg Man* and tv debut in "The Virginian"; came to prominence partnered with Sharon Gless on tv series "Cagney & Lacey" (1981–88); premiered on "Judging Amy" (1999); by 1990, had appeared in over 200 tv shows; films include *Play It As It Lays* (1972), *The Enforcer* (1976), *Zoot Suit* (1982), *The Aviator* (1985), *Vig* (1998) and *The Autumn Heart* (1999); won Tony award for Best Performance by a Leading Actress in *Gypsy* (1990). Won 4 Emmy's for work on "Cagney & Lacey" and an Emmy for Best Supporting Actress for role in "Christy" (1996).

DALYELL, Elsie (1881–1948). Australian pathologist. Born Elsie Dalyell on Dec 13, 1881, in Newtown, Sydney, Australia; died 1948; 2nd dau. of Jean (McGregor) Dalyell and James Melville Dalyell (mining engineer); University of Sydney, MB, 1st class with honors, 1909, degree in chemistry, 1910. ❖ Appointed medical officer at Royal Prince Alfred Hospital (1910); became the 1st woman on the full-time medical-school staff as demonstrator in pathology (1911) and the 1st woman elected to a Beit fellowship (1912); served out her fellowship at the Lister Institute of Preventive Medicine in London.

DALZIEL, Lianne (1960—). New Zealand politician. Born Lianne Dalziel, June 7, 1960, in Papanui, Christchurch, NZ; m. Mike Pannell (union organizer), 1988. ❖ Served as Labour MP for Christchurch Central (1990–96); elected MP for Christchurch East (1999), becoming minister of Commerce, of Immigration, of Senior Citizens, of Responsible for the Law Commission, and associate minister of Justice and of Special Education; was minister for Disability Issues (2001).

D'AMBOISE, Francise (1427–1485). *See Amboise, Francise d'.*

DAME AUX CAMÉLIAS, La (1824–1847). *See Plessis, Alphonsine.*

DAMER, Anne Seymour (1748–1828). English sculptor. Born Anne Conway in 1748 (some sources cite 1749); died May 28, 1828; dau. of Field Marshal Henry Seymour Conway (1721–1795); friend of Nelson,

Walpole, and Napoleon; m. John Damer, 1767 (committed suicide, 1776). ❖ Studied under Ceracchi, acquired technique in the studio of Bacon, and learned the elements of anatomy from George Cruikshank; executed a number of works, including: an 8-foot marble statue in the Registry Office, Edinburgh; two colossal heads in Portland stone, which ornament the keystone of the bridge at Henley-upon-Thames; a statue of George III; a bust of Fox, which she personally presented to her friend Napoleon Bonaparte in 1815; a bust of another friend Lord Horatio Nelson, who sat for the work immediately after his return from the Battle of the Nile; busts of her father, of Sir Humphry Davy, of her mother, and of herself. ❖ See also *Women in World History*.

DAMES DES ROCHES, Les.
See *Roches, Madeleine des (1520–1587)*.
See *Roches, Catherine des (1542–1587)*.

DAMIAN, Georgeta (1976—). Romanian rower. Name variations: Georgeta Andrunache; Georgeta Andrunache-Damian. Born Georgeta Damian, April 14, 1976, in Botosani, Romania. ❖ Won gold medals for coxless pair and coxed eights at Sydney Olympics (2000); at World championships, won gold medals for coxed eights (1997, 1998, 1999) and coxless pair (2001, 2002); won gold medals for coxed eights and coxless pair at Athens Olympics (2004).

DAMIÃO, Elisa Maria (1946—). Portuguese politician. Name variations: Elisa Maria Damiao. Born Sept 10, 1946, in Alcobaça, Portugal. ❖ Served as deputy secretary-general of th UGT (General Worker's Union, 1983) and 1st woman member of the PS National Secretariat (1985–94); member of the Assembly of the Republic (1987); as a European Socialist (PSE), elected to 4th and 5th European Parliament (1994–99, 1999–2004).

D'AMICO, Suso Cecchi (b. 1914). See *Cecchi D'Amico, Suso*.

DAMIEN, Albertine (1937–1967). See *Sarrazin, Albertine*.

DAMITA, Lili (1901–1994). French-born actress. Born Liliane Marie Madeleine Carré in Bordeaux, France, July 19, 1901; died in Miami Beach, Florida, Mar 21, 1994; m. Errol Flynn (actor), 1935; m. Allen Loomis; children: (1st m.) Sean Flynn. ❖ Leading lady who, though celebrated as a popular movie actress, achieved even greater celebrity as a result of her tempestuous marriage to Errol Flynn; became a music-hall star at 16 at the Folies Bergere, soon succeeding Mistinguett as the star of the Casino de Paris revue; acting career flourished in French, German, Austrian, and British silent films (mid-1920s); came to Hollywood; starred opposite Ronald Colman in film version of Joseph Conrad's "Rescue" (1928), followed by *The Bridge of San Luis Rey* (1929), one of Hollywood's last silent films; also appeared in *Fighting Caravans* with Gary Cooper (1931), *Friends and Lovers* (1931), *The Match King* (1932), *This is the Night* with Cary Grant (1932), and *Brewster's Millions* (1935), her last film; by mid-1930s, was an established superstar but ceased filming at time of marriage. ❖ See also *Women in World History*.

DAMO (fl. 6th c. BCE). Pythagorean philosopher. Born in Crotona, Italy; dau. of Pythagoras of Samos (philosopher, mathematician, politician, spiritual leader) and Theano of Crotona (Pythagorean philosopher); sister of Arignote, Myia, Telauges, and Mnesarchus; educated at the School of Pythagoras. ❖ Was a member of her father's sect which ascribed to the precept of metempsychosis and the teaching that earthly life is only a purification of the soul, and stressed moderation and the study of mathematics; though not noted for any works herself, quite likely contributed to the doctrines ascribed to Pythagoras; though the Pythagoreans were expelled from Crotona and she was exceedingly poor, refused to sell her father's writings because he had prohibited the communication of their teachings to strangers. ❖ See also *Women in World History*.

DAMON, Babben. See *Enger, Babben*.

DAMON, Cathryn (1930–1987). American stage, tv, and screen actress. Born Sept 11, 1930, in Seattle, Washington; died May 4, 1987, in Los Angeles, California. ❖ Made Broadway debut in *By the Beautiful Sea* (1954), followed by *Shinbone Alley, Flora the Red Menace, UTBU, Come Summer* and *Last of the Red Hot Lovers;* films include *How to Beat the High Cost of Living* and *She's Having a Baby.* Won an Emmy award for portrayal of Mary Campbell on tv's "Soap."

DAMOREAU, Madame (1801–1863). See *Cinti-Damoreau, Laure*.

DAMPIERRE, Emmanuela del (b. 1913). Duchess of Segovia. Born Emmanuela Vittoria del Dampierre, Nov 8, 1913, in Rome, Italy; dau. of Roger del Dampierre, 2nd duke of San Lorenzo, and Vittoria Emilia di Poggio Suasa; became 1st wife of Jaime (1908–1975), duke of Segovia (renounced claim to throne of Spain, 1939), Mar 4, 1935; m. Antonion Sozzani, Nov 21, 1949; children: (1st m.) Alfonso Jaime (b. 1936), duke of Cadiz; Gonzalo (b. 1937).

DAMSEL OF BRITTANY (1184–1241). See *Eleanor, the Maid of Brittany*.

DAN, Aurora (1955—). Romanian fencer. Born Oct 5, 1955. ❖ At Los Angeles Olympics, won a silver medal in team foil (1984).

DANA, Leora (1923–1983). American stage and screen actress. Born April 1, 1923, in New York, NY; died Dec 13, 1983, in NY, NY; attended Royal Academy of Dramatic Art (1948); m. Kurt Kasznar (actor, div.). ❖ On Broadway, appeared as Alice Russell in *The Best Man,* Mrs. Constable in *In the Summer House* and Elizabeth Edwards in *The Last of Mrs Lincoln* (1972), for which she received a Tony Award; appeared frequently on tv in such shows as "Philco Playhouse" and "Alfred Hitchcock Presents," and as Sylvia on "Another World"; films include *The Group, Kings Go Forth, A Gatherine of Eagles, 3:10 to Yuma* and *Some Came Running.* Won the Clarence Derwent Award for her portrayal of Maman in *The Happy Time* (1950).

DANA, Marie Louise (c. 1876–1946). American actress. Born c. 1876; died Dec 10, 1946, in NY, NY. ❖ Appeared on Broadway in *The Climbers, Honeymooning, The Return of the Vagabond* and *The Naked Genius;* portrayed Sara Delano Roosevelt in *I'd Rather Be Right*.

DANA, Viola (1897–1987). American stage and silent-film actress and dancer. Name variations: Viola Flugrath. Born Virginia Flugrath, June 26, 1897, in Brooklyn, NY; died July 3, 1987, in Woodland Hills, California; sister of Shirley Mason (1900–1979, screen actress) and Edna Flugrath (actress); m. John H. Collins (director), 1915 (died 1918); m. Maurice "Lefty" Flynn (screen cowboy), 1925 (div. 1929). ❖ With sister Shirley, appeared on stage as a child; made screen debut in Edison's *A Christmas Carol* (1910); enjoyed success on stage in title roles of *The Littlest Rebel* (1910) and *Poor Little Rich Girl* (1913); became a leading Metro ingenue in over 50 silents, including *The Drummer Boy, Aladdin's Other Lamp, Flower of the Dusk, Naughty Nanette, God's Law and Man's, The Cossack Whip, Salvation Jane, Rosie O'Grady, Merton of the Movies, Lady Barnacle, The Million Trail* and *The Show of Shows;* danced in many of them.

DANANIR AL BARMAKIYYA (fl. late 8th c.). Arabian singer. Flourished in the late 8th to early 9th centuries; dates of birth and death uncertain. ❖ As a slave, sold to household of Yahya ibn Khalid al-Barmaki, where she was taught music by Ibrahim and Ishaf al-Mausuli, Ibn Jami, Fulaih, and Badhl; singing was admired by Abbasid ruler, Caliph Harun al-Rashid, hero of the *Arabian Nights;* also composed *Kitab mujarrad al-aghani* (Book of Choice Songs). ❖ See also *Women in World History*.

DANCER, Ann (1734–1801). See *Barry, Ann Street*.

DANCING CANSINOS. See *Cansino, Elisa*.

DANCO, Suzanne (1911–2000). Belgian coloratura soprano. Born in Brussels, Belgium, Jan 22, 1911; died Aug 10, 2000, in Fiesole, near Florence, Italy; studied at Brussels Conservatory and with Fernando Carpi in Prague. ❖ Won the International Bel Canto Prize in Venice (1936); debuted at the Genoa Opera as Fiodiligi in Mozart's *Cosi fan tutte* (1941); appeared in Teatro alla Scala (1948), Glyndebourne (1948–51), and Covent Garden (1951); remembered primarily as one of the most aristocratic and accomplished recitalists. ❖ See also *Women in World History*.

DANDO, Jill (1961–1999). British newscaster and journalist. Born in 1961 in Weston-super-Mare, England; murdered April 26, 1999, in Fulham, London, England; engaged to be married to Alan Farthing. ❖ Well-known BBC anchorwoman, began career as a journalist for *Weston & Somerset Mercury;* moved to BBC Radio Devon; joined the BBC's national news operation (1988); became the popular host of "Six O'Clock News," "Breakfast News," "Crimewatch" and "Holiday"; was shot and killed on the steps of her London home by an unemployed loner, Barry George, who was obsessed with guns and celebrity (he was found guilty of the murder, July 2, 2001).

DANDO, Suzanne (1961—). English gymnast. Name variations: Susanne Dando. Born July 3, 1961, in UK; m. Graham Maclean (composer and songwriter). ❖ Placed 1st all-around at British championship and Champions Cup (1980); became a tv presenter.

DANDOLO, Giovanna (fl. 1457). Venetian arts patron. Name variations: Giovanna Dandolo Malipiero. Married Pasquale Malipiero (doge of Venice). ❖ Known as "Empress of Printing" and "Queen of Lace," encouraged Venetian printing industry and supported printing of many books; helped poor writers and promoted lace industry in Burano.

D'ANDREA, Novella (d. 1333). Italian lawyer. Born in Bologna; dau. of Giovanni d'Andrea (professor of canon law at University of Bologna); m. John Caldesimus (lawyer); sister of Bettina d'Andrea (d. 1335, a lawyer and philosopher who taught at University of Padua). ❖ An Italian scholar, is believed to have studied with father at the university and given lectures in his place when he was away; died soon after marriage to another scholar of law, John Caldesimus; her grieving father titled one of his works *Novella super Decretalium* in her memory. Her life was preserved by Christine de Pizan in her *Book of the City of Ladies.*

DANDRIDGE, Dorothy (1923–1965). African-American actress, singer and dancer. Born Dorothy Dandridge, Nov 9, 1923, in Cleveland, Ohio; died by her own hand on Sept 8, 1965; dau. of Cyril and Ruby Dandridge (singer and dancer); m. Harold Nicholas, 1941 (div. 1946); m. Jack Denison, June 22, 1959 (div. 1962). ❖ One of the 1st black actresses to enter the Hollywood mainstream and the 1st to be nominated for an Oscar for Best Actress, appeared in black vaudeville with sister as "The Wonder Kids" throughout the South from age 3; moved with family to Los Angeles (1930); began appearing in nightclubs and revues by late teens, and in small film parts soon after; given lead role in *Carmen Jones* (1954), a lavish, all-black adaptation of the Bizet opera, for which she was nominated for Best Actress; starred in film version of *Porgy and Bess* (1959), for which she won the Golden Globe award for Best Actress; other films include *Bright Road* (1953), *Island in the Sun* (1957), *The Decks Ran Red* (1958), *Tamango* (1959) and *Moment of Danger* (*Malaga*, 1960). ❖ See also autobiography (with Earl Conrad) *Everything and Nothing* (Abelard-Schuman, 1970); Donald Bogle, *Dorothy Dandridge* (Amistad, 1997); (HBO movie) "Introducing Dorothy Dandridge," starring Halle Berry (1999); and *Women in World History.*

DANDRIDGE, Gloria Richardson (1922—). *See Richardson, Gloria.*

DANE, Clemence (1888–1965). English novelist and playwright. Name variations: also wrote under real name Winifred Ashton; acted under Diana Cortis. Born Winifred Ashton, Feb 21, 1888, in Greenwich, London; died Mar 28, 1965, in London; dau. of Arthur Charles (commission merchant) and Florence (Bentley) Ashton; studied art at Slade School. ❖ Began writing after ill health cut short an acting career; her 1st novel, *Regiment of Women* (1917), about life at a girls' school, met with critical acclaim, as did *Legend* (1919) and *Broome Stages* (1931); her 1st play, *A Bill of Divorcement* (1921), had a long run in London and in NY where it provided Katharine Cornell with one of her 1st major roles on Broadway; also teamed with Helen Simpson to write several detective stories and wrote 7 film scripts, including the screenplay for *Anna Karenina* (1935). Received CBE (1953). ❖ See also memoir *London Has a Garden* (1964); and *Women in World History.*

DANGALAKOVA-BOGOMILOVA, Tanya (1964—). Bulgarian swimmer. Name variations: Tanya Bogomilova. Born June 30, 1964. ❖ At Seoul Olympics, won a gold medal in 100-meter breaststroke (1988).

D'ANGEVILLE, Henriette (1795–1871). French mountain climber. Born in 1795; died in Lausanne, Switzerland, 1871; member of the Beaumonts, a prestigious French family (her father was imprisoned during the French Revolution); lived at Ferney, near Geneva, Switzerland. ❖ The 1st woman to organize and undertake her own climb, successfully ascended Mt. Blanc (Sept 1838), at age 44; over next 25 years, made 21 more ascents, climbing the 10,250-ft. Oldenhorn in the Alps at age 69. ❖ See also autobiography, *My Ascent of Mont Blanc;* and *Women in World History.*

D'ANGOULÊME, Margaret or Marguerite (1492–1549). *See Margaret of Angoulême.*

DANIAS, Starr (1949—). American ballet dancer. Born Mar 13, 1949, in Queens, NY. ❖ Danced 1 season with London Festival Ballet; joined City Center Joffrey Ballet in NY, where she appeared in such Arpino pieces as *Trinity* (1970), *Reflections* (1970), *Kettentanz* (1971), *Chabriesque* (1972), and *Sacred Grove on Mount Tamalpais* (1972); also appeared as guest dancer with numerous US and European companies, including American Ballet Theater; danced on Broadway in *On Your Toes* (1983); appeared in the film *A Turning Point* and made guest appearance on tv's "The Love Boat," among others.

DANIEL, Annie Sturges (1858–1944). American physician. Born Annie Sturges Daniel, Sept 21, 1858, in Buffalo, NY; died of arteriosclerosis at home, Aug 10, 1944, in New York, NY; dau. of John M. (coal and wood merchant) and Marinda (Sturges) Daniel; orphaned when young, reared by relatives in Monticello, NY; graduate of Dr. Elizabeth Blackwell's Woman's Medical College of the New York Infirmary for Women and Children, 1879. ❖ For 60 years, served as director of New York Infirmary's Out-Practice department to help the poor, earning the nickname "Angel of the Lower East Side"; specialized in obstetrics, gynecology, and pediatrics; served as investigator for New York State Tenement House Commission (1884) and investigator for Congressional committee looking at tenement sweatshop operations (1892); wrote influential report for a Women's Prison Association (1888) which led to legislation for sex-segregated prisons and the hiring of female matrons for female inmates; was an active suffragist; as a result of her classes, former student S. Josephine Baker later directed the establishment of Bureau of Child Hygiene at New York Department of Health.

DANIEL, Beth (1956—). American golfer. Name variations: Elizabeth Ann Daniel. Born Elizabeth Ann Daniel, Oct 14, 1956, in Charleston, South Carolina; attended Furman University. ❖ Won the USGA Women's Amateur (1975 & 1977); member of the Curtis Cup team (1976 & 1978), and World Cup team (1978); joined LPGA tour (1979) and named Rookie of the Year (1979); won four tournaments (1980), two (1981), five (1982), one (1983), one (1985), four (1989); earned the Vare Trophy (1989), with a record 70.38 average; won the Mazda LPGA championship (1990), along with six other tournaments; set a record for the most consecutive rounds in the 60s with nine (1990); was the 3rd player in LPGA history to cross the $5 million mark in earnings; won the Seagrams Seven Crowns of Sport Award (1981). Named to the LPGA Hall of Fame (1999).

DANIEL, Eleanor (1950—). *See Daniel, Ellie.*

DANIEL, Elizabeth Ann (1956—). *See Daniel, Beth.*

DANIEL, Ellie (1950—). American swimmer. Name variations: Eleanor Daniel. Born June 11, 1950. ❖ At Mexico City Olympics, won a bronze medal in the 200-meter butterfly, silver medal in the 100-meter butterfly, and gold medal in the 4 x 100-meter medley relay (1968); at Munich Olympics, won a bronze medal in the 200-meter butterfly (1972).

DANIEL, Jessie Ames (1883–1972). *See Ames, Jessie Daniel.*

DANIEL, Margaret Truman (1924—). *See Truman, Margaret.*

DANIEL, Reveale O (1590–1652). *See Davies, Eleanor.*

DANIELA (1984—). *See Alves Lima, Daniela.*

DANIELE, Graciela (1939—). Argentinean ballet and theatrical dancer. Born Dec 8, 1939, in Buenos Aires, Argentina. ❖ Performed with ballet companies of Teatro Colón and Teatro Argentine de la Plata in Buenos Aires; moved to New York City and appeared in numerous shows, including *What Makes Sammy Run?* (1964), *Promises, Promises, Here's Where I Belong* and *Coco;* appeared on tv on "The Ed Sullivan Show" and "Bell Telephone Hour"; choreographed for NY's Spanish-language theaters and for theater, tv and film, including Woody Allen's *Mighty Aphrodite* and *Everyone Says I Love You,* which both won Fosse Awards; nominated for 11 Tony and 6 Drama Desk awards for choreography; served as resident director at Lincoln Center Theater in NY. Choreographed for *The Most Happy Fella* (1977), *A History of American Film* (1977), *Alice in Concert* (1980), *The Pirates of Penzance* (1980) and *Cada Noche . . . Tango* (1988).

DANIELI, Cecilia (1943—). Italian industrialist. Born 1943; died of cancer, June 17, 1999, in Udine, Italy; grew up in Buttrio, northeast Italy; 1 of 4 daughters of Luigi Danieli (steel magnate); married Italo Moreschi (lawyer); children: 3. ❖ Known as Italy's First Lady of Steel, began working at family steel company as father's assistant (1965); became general manager (1980); took over control of company as managing director and expanded business internationally (1984); sold steel equipment and mills to many countries, to customers that began to include Krupp of Germany and Mitsubishi of Japan; appointed chair of the board (1991).

DANIELL, Martha (1704–1779). *See Logan, Martha.*

DANIELS, Bebe (1901–1971). American actress. Name variations: Bebe Lyon. Born Phyllis (sometimes cited as Virginia) Daniels in Dallas, Texas, Jan 14, 1901; died 1971; dau. of Melville (Scottish-born manager of a touring theater company) and Phyllis (Griffin) Daniels (Spanish-born actress); m. Benjamin Bethel Lyon, Jr. (actor), June 14, 1930; children: Barbara Bebe Lyon; (adopted) Richard Lyon. ❖ In a career that spanned over 50 years, was on stage at age 4, played juveniles in silents, and made over 200 shorts before appearing in a major film; when Paramount, her studio for 10 years, refused to put her in the talkies, signed with RKO and sang her way into a 2nd series of successful films; when career declined (1930s), traveled to London with husband Ben Lyon, where they enjoyed success on the music-hall circuit and in a popular radio and tv series; films include *The Affairs of Anatol* (1921), *Monsieur Beaucaire* (1924), *Rio Rita* (1929), *The Maltese Falcon* (1931), *Forty-Second Street* (1933), *Counsellor at Law* (1933), *The Return of Carol Dean* (1935), *Life with the Lyons* (1953) and *The Lyons in Paris* (1955). ❖ See also *Women in World History.*

DANIELS, Fay (1906–1959). See *Lanphier, Fay.*

DANIELS, Gladys (1930–2003). See *Daniels, Maxine.*

DANIELS, Isabelle Frances (1937—). African-American runner. Name variations: Isabelle Daniels Holston. Born July 31, 1937, in Jakin, Georgia; attended Tennessee State University; m. Sidney Holston. ❖ Won 7 indoor and 5 outdoor AAU sprint titles; with Tennessee State, won 5 consecutive AAU relays; won a team gold medal at Pan American Games (1955); at Melbourne Olympics, won a bronze medal in the 4 x 100-meter relay (1956); became a physical education teacher and track coach.

DANIELS, Mabel Wheeler (1878–1971). American composer. Born Mabel Wheeler Daniels in Swampscott, Massachusetts, 1878; died in Cambridge, Massachusetts, 1971; graduated *cum laude* from Radcliffe College, 1900; studied orchestration at New England Conservatory of Music; attended Munich's Royal Conservatory, 1902. ❖ Directed the Glee Club at Radcliffe (1911–13), before becoming the musical director at Simmons College in Boston (1913–18); with Marian MacDowell, co-founded the MacDowell Colony in Peterborough, NH; composed several operettas, choral and vocal works, orchestral and chamber music, and the cantata *The Desolate City* (1913), which became one of her more popular works. ❖ See also *Women in World History.*

DANIELS, Martha Catalina (d. 2002). Colombian politician. Name variations: Marta Catalina Daniels Guzman. Died Mar 2, 2002, in Zipacon, Cundinamarca, Colombia; m. Hernando Rodriguez; children. ❖ Liberal Party senator, was tortured and killed by rebels near Bogota, Mar 2, 2002, along with her driver Carlos Lozano and friend Ana Maria Medina; had been trying to win the freedom of Medina's husband, a local politician who was being held hostage by the Revolutionary Armed Forces of Colombia (FARC).

DANIELS, Maxine (1930–2003). English jazz singer. Name variations: Gladys Daniels or Maxine Gladys Daniels; Gladys Lynch. Born Gladys Lynch, Nov 2, 1930, in London, England; died Oct 20, 2003, in Romford, England; sister of Kenny Lynch (singer and entertainer); m. Charlie Daniels, 1950 (died 1993); children: 1 daughter. ❖ After WWII, sang with bands in London; won ITV network's "Youth Takes a Bow" talent contest (1953); earned reputation singing with Denny Boyce Band (1954–56); signed by Bernard Delfont agency, made debut at Chiswick Empire Theatre (1956); sang at clubs, cabarets, and theaters in London, including Churchill's and Palladium; signed contract with Oriole Records (1957) and recorded singles, including "Coffee Bar Calypso" and "Why Should I Care?"; retired from music (1958–66); after return, toured with Pizza Express All Stars and Best of British Jazz; appeared in stage shows, including *Evergreen, The Songs of Irving Berlin* and *Swinging Down Memory Lane*; recorded albums, *A Beautiful Friendship, A Pocketful of Dreams* and *The Memory of Tonight*; toured in *Tribute to Ella Fitzgerald* and *Ladies of Jazz* (1990s); appeared with American entertainers Billy Eckstine, Al Cohn, and Wild Bill Davison.

DANIELS, Sarah (1957—). British playwright. Born Nov 21, 1957, in London, England; dau. of Frank James Daniels and Otome Daniels. ❖ Considered one of most controversial of feminist playwrights (1980s), had many plays premiered at the Royal Court; writings, which examine lesbian themes, violence against women, pornography, and class relations, include *Ripen Our Darkness* (1981), *Ma's Flesh is Grass* (1981), *Penumbra* (1981), *Masterpieces* (1983), *The Devil's Gateway* (1983), *Neaptide* (1986), *Byrthrite* (1986), *The Gut Girls* (1988), *Beside Herself*

(1900), *Head-Rot Holiday* (1992), and *The Madness of Esme and Shaz* (1994). Methuen published *Plays: One* (1991) and *Plays: Two* (1994).

DANILEVSKAIA, N.A. Lappo- (c. 1875–1951). See *Lappo-Danilevskaia, N.A.*

DANILOVA, Alexandra (1903–1997). Russian ballerina. Name variations: (nickname) Choura (pronounced Shura), Shura. Born Alexandra Dionisevna Danilova, Nov 20, 1903, in Peterhof near St. Petersburg, Russia; died in New York, July 12, 1997; dau. of Dionis Danilov and Claudia (Gototzova or Gototsova) Danilova (possibly servants of the imperial court); studied at Imperial Ballet School, 1911–20; m. Giuseppe Massera (engineer), 1931 (died 1935); m. Casimir Kokitch (ballet dancer), 1941 (div. 1948); no children. ❖ One of the leading ballerinas of the 20th century who combined a 4-decade dancing career in Soviet Russia, Western Europe, and the US with a subsequent career as a distinguished teacher; joined Soviet State Ballet (1920); promoted to soloist (1922); joined friends for tour of Germany and remained in Western Europe (1924); joined Diaghilev's Ballets Russes (1925); began love affair with Balanchine (1926); promoted to star ballerina in Diaghilev's troupe (1927); because of death of Diaghilev, saw Ballets Russes dissolved (1929); joined Colonel W. de Basil's Ballets Russes de Monte Carlo (1933); toured US (1933–34); joined new Ballets Russe de Monte Carlo (1938); led the migration of top-ranking ballet talent to the US at start of World War II (1939); became US citizen (1946); left Ballets Russe (1951); continued to dance with distinction through 1950s; formed own ballet troupe (1956); her tours made her the most famous ballerina of the time in America and helped to popularize ballet in much of the country; gave farewell ballet performance (1957); began efforts as choreographer (1958); joined faculty of School of American Ballet (1964); appeared in film, *The Turning Point* (1977); ended teaching career and received Kennedy Center Award (1989); as a performer, was famous for her combination of brilliant technique and visible pleasure in dancing; best known roles include The Street Dancer in *Le Beau Danube,* Swanhilda in *Coppélia,* title role in *The Firebird,* title role in *Giselle,* and Odette-Odile in *Swan Lake.* ❖ See also *Choura: The Memoirs of Alexandra Danilova* (Knopf, 1986); A.E. Twysden, *Alexandra Danilova* (Kamin, 1947); and *Women in World History.*

DANILOVA, Maria (1793–1810). Russian ballet dancer. Born 1793 in St. Petersburg, Russia; died of consumption, Jan 8, 1810, age 17, in St. Petersburg. ❖ Studied with Charles-Louis Didelot at Imperial Ballet; performed with same company throughout short life, creating roles in all Didelot's works at the time, including *Les Amours de Vénus et d'Adonis* (1808) and *Cupid et Psyché* (1810).

DANILOVA, Olga (1970—). Russian cross-country skier. Born June 10, 1970, in Bugulm, Russia. ❖ Finished 6th at Lillehammer in the 5K classical cross-country race (1992); won gold medals for 15 km mass and 4 x 5 km relay and a silver for the Combined 5 km + 10 km pursuit at Nagano Olympics (1998); won a gold medal for 5 km pursuit and a silver medal in 10 km at Salt Lake City Olympics (2002); was given a 2-year ban for failing drug test.

DANILOVA, Pelageya (1918—). Soviet gymnast. Born May 1918. ❖ At Helsinki Olympics, won a silver medal in teams all-around, portable apparatus, and a gold medal in team all-around (1952).

DANINTHE, Sarah (1980—). French fencer. Born June 25, 1980, in France. ❖ Won a bronze medal for épée team at Athens Olympics (2004).

DANN, Mary (d. 2005). Western Shoshone activist. Born in Crescent Valley, Nevada; believed to be in her 80s, died April 22, 2005, of injuries sustained in an accident on an all-terrain vehicle at her Crescent Valley ranch; sister of Carrie Dann. ❖ With litigation and civil disobedience, fought the US government for more than 30 years to reclaim 24 million acres of Western Shoshone ancestral land.

DANNER, Blythe (1943—). American actress. Born Blythe Katherine Danner, Feb 3, 1943, in Philadelphia, Pennsylvania; sister of Harry Danner (opera singer), William Danner (violin expert) and Dorothy Danner (opera director and choreographer); aunt of actresses Hillary Danner and Katherine Moennig; graduate of Bard College, 1965; m. Bruce Paltrow (director), 1969 (died Oct 3, 2002); children: Jake Paltrow (b. 1975, director) and Gwyneth Paltrow (b. 1972, actress). ❖ Began stage career in Boston; won Theater World award for performance in *The Miser* at Lincoln Center (1968); won a Tony award for Best Actress for *Butterflies Are Free* (1970); also nominated for Tony awards for *A Streetcar Named Desire, Betrayal* and *Follies;* starred on tv series

"Adam's Rib" (1973) and "The X Files" (1998), and made frequent appearances in-between; films include *1776* (1972), *Lovin' Molly* (1974), *Hearts of the West* (1975), *The Great Santini* (1979), *Brighton Beach Memoirs* (1986), *Mr. and Mrs. Bridge* (1990), *Alice* (1990), *The Prince of Tides* (1991), *Forces of Nature* (1999), *Meet the Parents* (2000), *Sylvia* (2003) and *Meet the Fockers* (2004).

DANNER, Countess (1815–1874). See Rasmussen, Louise Christine.

DANNER, Margaret (1910–1984). African-American poet. Born Margaret Essie Danner, Jan 12, 1910, in Chicago, Illinois; died 1984; dau. of Caleb Danner and Naomi Danner; attended Loyola, Roosevelt, and Northwestern universities; m. Cordell Strickland; m. Otto Cunningham; children: (1st m.) Naomi. ❖ Worked at *Poetry* magazine (1951–57), becoming 1st African-American assistant editor (1956); was poet-in-residence at Wayne State University (1961) and founded community arts center Booth House (1962); works include *Impressions of African Art Forms* (1960) and *The Down of a Thistle* (1976).

DANTON, Gabrielle (d. 1793). French wife of Danton. Born Antoinette Gabrielle Charpentier; died while giving birth to her 4th son, Feb 17, 1793, in Paris; dau. of an owner of the café du Parnasse; was the 1st wife of the revolutionary Jacques Danton (guillotined, 1794). ❖ Died while husband was on a mission in Belgium (on his return, he dug up her grave in his anguish and had an artist make a molding of her face).

DANTON, Louise (1777–1856). Young French wife of Jacques Danton. Name variations: Sebastienne-Louise Gély; Louise Gély; Louise Dupin. Born Sébastienne-Louise Gély in 1777; died at 80 in Paris, 1856; dau. of Marc-Antoine Gély (Admiralty official); m. Jacques Danton, 1793 (guillotined, 1794); m. Claude-François Dupin (prefect, officer of the Legion of Honor, under Napoleon). ❖ At 16, married Jacques Danton; was widowed a year later. ❖ See also *Women in World History*.

D'ANTREMONT, Marie-Henriette-Anne Payan Delestang, Marquise (1746–1802). See Bourdic-Viot, Marie-Henriette Payad d'Estang de.

D'ANTUONO, Eleanor (1939—). American ballet dancer. Born 1939 in Cambridge, Massachusetts; studied dance with Maria Papporello and E. Virginia Williams. ❖ Began professional career with Ballet Russe de Monte Carlo (c. 1953); joined American Ballet Theatre (ABT) as soloist (1961), becoming principal dancer (1963); won popular and critical acclaim in her 20 years there; was 1st American ballerina to appear as guest artist with Kirov Ballet, in *Giselle* (1978) and *Swan Lake* (1979), and with Chinese companies; served as artistic director for Festival Dance Theatre, artistic advisor to New Jersey Ballet, resident coach and artistic advisor for Nutmeg Ballet, and artistic director for New York International Ballet Competition. Alvin Ailey was among the many leading choreographers who created original roles for her ("Giggling Rapids," in his ballet *The River,* 1970).

DANTZSCHER, Jamie (1982—). American gymnast. Born May 2, 1982, in Canoga Park, California. ❖ Won City of Popes (1996); placed 4th for team all-around at Sydney Olympics (2000).

DANVERS, Magdalene (1561–1627). English patron of the arts. Name variations: Lady Danvers; Lady Magdalene Danvers; Magdalene Herbert. Born 1561; died 1627; m. Richard Herbert (died); m. Sir John Danvers of Wilts (1588–1655); children: (1st m.) Lord Edward Herbert of Cherbury (1583–1648, philosopher and historian); George Herbert (1593–1633, orator). ❖ The mother of George Herbert and close friend of John Donne, was a generous patron of letters. ❖ See also *Women in World History*.

DÄNZER, Frieda. Swiss Alpine skier. Name variations: Frieda Daenzer or Danzer. Born in Switzerland. ❖ Won a silver medal for downhill at Cortina Olympics (1956).

DANZI, Maria Margarethe (1768–1800). German composer and singer. Born Maria Margarethe Marchand in 1768 in Frankfurt am Main, Germany; died in Munich, June 11, 1800; dau. of Theobald Marchand, director of Munich Theater; studied singing with Franziska Lebrun, sister of Franz Danzi; m. Franz Danzi (noted composer), 1790. ❖ Lived with brother Heinrich in Salzburg in home of Leopold Mozart (1781–84), father of Wolfgang Amadeus Mozart, taking lessons in piano and composition; began singing career at Munich Court Opera (1786); became a composer of chamber works as well, including an *Andante and Variations* for keyboard and a set of 3 sonatas for piano and violin; died at age 32. ❖ See also *Women in World History*.

DANZIG, Sarah (1912–1996). See Palfrey, Sarah.

DANZIGER, Paula (1944–2004). American children's writer. Born Aug 18, 1944, in Washington, DC; grew up in Metuchen, New Jersey; died July 8, 2004, in New York, NY, from complications following a heart attack; dau. of Samuel (worked in garment district) and Carolyn (Seigel) Danziger (nurse); Montclair State College, BA, 1967, MA; never married. ❖ Taught in Edison, NJ (1967), Highland Park, NJ (1967–68), Edison, NJ (1968–70), and Lincoln Junior High School, West Orange, NJ (1977–78); became a full-time writer (1978), known for her wit and self-deprecation; published 1st book *The Cat Ate My Gymsuit* (1974), considered a classic of pre-teen years; also wrote *The Pistachio Prescription* (1978), *Can You Sue Your Parents for Malpractice?* (1979), *There's a Bat in Bunk Five* (1980), *The Divorce Express* (1982), *It's an Aardvark-Eat-Turtle World* (1985), *This Place Has No Atmosphere* (1986), *Remember Me to Harold Square* (1987), *Everyone Else's Parents Said Yes* (1989), *Amber Brown Is Not a Crayon* (1993), and (with Ann M. Martin) *Snail Mail No More* (1999), among others.

DAONG KHIN KHIN LAY (1913—). Burmese novelist and short-story writer. Born 1913 in Mandalay, Burma. ❖ Published over 600 novels and short stories and wrote film scripts; founded *Yuwadi Daily Newspaper* and published *Yuwadi Journal* (1946).

DAPHEN (1657–1722). See Fuchs, Anna Rupertina.

DAPHNE (fl. 1789). See Hands, Elizabeth.

D'AQUINO, Iva Toguri (b. 1916). See Toguri, Iva.

D'ARANYI, Adila (1886–1962). See Fachiri, Adila.

D'ARANYI, Jelly (1895–1966). See Aranyi, Jelly d'.

D'ARBLAY, Madame (1752–1840). See Burney, Fanny.

DARBY, Eileen (1916–2004). American photographer. Name variations: Eileen Darby Lester. Born Eileen Darby, May 12, 1916, in Portland, Oregon; died Mar 30, 2004, at a nursing home in Long Beach, NY; attended Marylhurst University; m. Roy Lester, 1944 (died 1976); children: Roy, John, Patric and Virginia Lester Teslik. ❖ Photographer of over 500 Broadway shows and such stars as Olivier, Dietrich, Bankhead, Robeson, the Lunts and Brando; co-founded Graphic House, a photo agency.

DARC or D'ARC, Jeanne (c. 1412–1431). See Joan of Arc.

DARC, Mireille (1938—). American actress. Born Mireille Aigroz, May 15, 1938, in Toulon, France. ❖ Made film debut in *Les Distractions* (1960), followed by *La Bride sur le cou, Virginie, Monsieur, La chasse à l'homme, Galia, Les Bons vivants, Du rififi à Paname, Week End, Madly, The Tall Blond Man with One Black Shoe, La valise* and *Les passagers,* among others.

DARCEL, Denise (1925—). French actress. Born Denise Billecard, Sept 8, 1925, in Paris, France. ❖ Began career as a nightclub singer; made film debut in *Thunder in the Pines* (1948), followed by *Battleground, Tarzan and the Slave Girl, Westward the Women, Dangerous When Wet, Flame of Calcutta, Gamble on Love, Vera Cruz* and *Seven Women from Hell,* among others.

DARCLÉE, Hariclea (1860–1939). Romanian soprano. Name variations: Hariclea Darclee. Born Herclea Hartulari, June 10, 1860, in Braila, Romania; died Jan 10, 1939 in Bucharest, Romania; studied in Bucharest and in Paris with Faure; children: Ion Hartulary-Darclée (1886–1969, composer and conductor). ❖ Famed singer and the 1st Tosca, appeared in the world premieres of Catalani's *La Wally,* Mascagni's *Iris* and Puccini's *Tosca,* which was composed for her.

D'ARCONVILLE, Geneviève (1720–1805). French writer. Name variations: Geneviève-Charlotte d'Arlus; Dame Thiroux d'Arconville. Born Marie-Geneviève-Charlotte d'Arlus in Paris, Oct 17, 1720; died in Paris, France, Dec 23, 1805; at 14, m. Louis-Lazare Thiroux d'Arconville (wealthy advisor to parlement of Paris), Feb 1735; children: 3 sons, including Thiroux de Crosne. ❖ Essayist, novelist, moralist, translator, scientist, and implacable enemy of the French revolution, who lost one of her sons to the guillotine and was in hiding during the worst months of Robespierre's Reign of Terror; charmed the leading figures of the Enlightenment, appearing in the prominent salons of Paris and carrying on an extensive correspondence with such literary and scientific figures as Voltaire, Turgot, Lavoisier, Fourcroy, Anquetil, and Sainte-Palaye; published a French translation of Alexander Monro's *Treatise on Osteology* (1759), followed by many translations of contemporary

English books, including work by Aphra Behn; wrote *A Treatise on Putrefaction* (1766) and carried out extensive research into the medicinal value of the chamomile herb (*Anthemis nobilis*); also wrote biographies and essays; published the 7-vol. *Melange of Literature, Ethics and Physics* (1775) at the start of the ill-fated reign of Louis XVI. ❖ See also *Women in World History.*

D'ARCY, Ella (c. 1856–1937). British short-story writer. Name variations: (pseudonym) Gilbert H. Page. Born c. 1856 in London, England; died Sept 5, 1937, in London England; dau. of Anthony D'Arcy and Sophia Anne Byrne. ❖ Published many stories in literary magazine *The Yellow Book* and assisted its editor John Lane; wrote *Monochromes* (1895), *Modern Instances* (1898) and *The Bishop's Dilemma* (1898); translated *Ariel: The Life of Shelley* by A. Maurois (1924).

D'ARCY, Margaretta (1934—). Irish actress, critic and playwright. Name variations: Margaretta Arden; Margaretta Ruth D'Arcy. Born June 14, 1934, in London, England, of Irish parentage; dau. of Joseph D'Arcy (who fought with the Dublin Brigade in Irish War for Independence) and Marie Billig D'Arcy (Russian-Jewish dau. of immigrants); grew up in Dublin, Ireland; m. John Arden (playwright), 1957; children: 4 sons. ❖ Controversial playwright, whose work and activism often address England-Ireland relations; moved to London (1953); became a member of a special acting group at Royal Court Theatre (1958); wrote most plays with husband John Arden, including *The Happy Haven* (1960), *Friday's Hiding* (1966), *My Old Man's a Tory* (1971), *The Island of the Mighty: A Play on a Traditional British Theme* (1972), *The Non-Stop Connolly Show: A Dramatic Cycle of Continuous Struggle in Six Parts* (1975), *No Room at the Inn* (1976), *The Making of Muswell Hill* (1984) and *The Eleanor Mary Show* (1991); also wrote *Tell Them Everything: A Sojourn in the Prison of Her Majesty Queen Elizabeth II at Art Macha (Armagh)* (1981).

DARE, Grace (1873–1953). *See Bondfield, Margaret.*

DARE, Phyllis (1890–1975). British stage actress. Born Phyllis Dones in Fulham Park Gardens, London, England, Aug 15, 1890; died April 27, 1975; dau. of Arthur Dones (clerk in a divorce court who later managed his daughters' careers) and Haddie Dones; sister of Zena Dare. ❖ Actress who delighted audiences in London's West End and on tour for decades; with sister, made stage debut in the pantomime *Babes in the Wood* (1899); at the Vaudeville Theater in London, charmed audiences in *Bluebell in Fairyland* and *The Catch of the Season;* came to prominence starring in the musical comedy *The Belle of Mayfair* (1906); appeared in *The Arcadians,* which played 809 performances at the Shaftesbury, and in the title role in *Peggy* (1911), from which she recorded "Ladies Beware" for His Master's Voice; was in *Kissing Time* (1919), followed by *The Lady of the Rose, The Street Singer* and *The Maids of the Mountains;* during 1930s and 1940s, appeared in show after show, straight comedies as well as musicals. ❖ See also *Women in World History.*

DARE, Zena (1887–1975). British stage actress. Born Florence Harriette Zena Dones in Fulham Park Gardens, London, England, Feb 4, 1887; died Mar 11, 1975; dau. of Arthur Dones (clerk in a divorce court) and Haddie Dones; sister of Phyllis Dare; m. Maurice Vyner Baliol Brett (2nd son of 2nd Viscount Esher), 1911 (died 1934); children: 1 son, 2 daughters. ❖ One of the most popular actresses in Edwardian England, made stage debut with sister in the pantomime *Babes in the Wood* (1899); as a young girl, appeared in pantomime in Scotland and toured in *An English Daisy;* came to prominence in London in 1st adult role in *The Catch of the Season* (1904); appeared in musicals *Lady Madcap, The Little Cherub, The Girl on Stage,* and in the title role of *Peter Pan;* retired at her peak to marry (1911); returned to the stage, at 39, forming her own company and touring South Africa (1926); enjoyed great success in straight roles, including Mrs. Cheyney in *The Last of Mrs. Cheyney* and roles opposite Noel Coward in *The Second Man* and Ivor Novello in *Proscenium, Careless Rapture* and *King's Rhapsody;* appeared as Lady Caroline in a revival of *Dear Brutus* and the Red Queen in *Alice through the Looking Glass;* was also seen in *Sabrina Fair, Double Image* and *Nude with Violin;* last appearance was as Rex Harrison's mother in *My Fair Lady* (1958–63). ❖ See also *Women in World History.*

DARE, Virginia (b. 1587). American colonial. Born Aug 18, 1587, on Roanoke Island (now North Carolina); date of death unknown; dau. of Ananias Dare (bricklayer) and Elyonor also seen as Ellinor or Elenor (White) Dare (dau. of Governor John White). ❖ Colonial figure and 1st child born of English parents in America; parents were among the 116 pilgrims to accompany cartographer and painter John White on his British expedition to Sir Walter Raleigh's Virginia colony, so named after Queen Elizabeth I, the "Virgin Queen." John White returned to England; when he landed again in 1590, there was no trace of the settlement or its inhabitants; though the fate of the "lost colony" was never determined, Virginia Dare came to symbolize faith in the throes of adversity. ❖ See also *Women in World History.*

DARGAN, Olive Tilford (1869–1968). American poet. Name variations: (pseudonym) Fielding Burke. Born Olive Tilford, Jan 11, 1869, in Kentucky; died Jan 22, 1968, in North Carolina; m. Pegram Dargan, 1898 (died 1915). ❖ Fiction and works of poetry, which reveal ardent socialist sympathies and focus on mine and mill laborers, include *Semiramis* (1904), *Path Flower and Other Verses* (1914), *The Cycle's Rim* (1916), *Lute and Furrow* (1922), *Highland Annals* (1925), *Call Home the Heart* (1932), *Sons of the Stranger* (1947) and *The Spotted Hawk* (1958). Received honorary degree from University of North Carolina (1925).

DARK, Eleanor (1901–1985). Australian writer. Name variations: (pseudonyms) P.O'R. and Patricia O'Rane. Born Eleanor ("Pixie") O'Reilly in 1901 in Sydney, Australia; died in Katoomba, NSW, 1985; dau. of Dowell O'Reilly (poet, short-story writer, and sometime Labor politician) and Eleanor (McCulloch) O'Reilly; m. Eric Payten Dark (physician), 1922; children: Michael. ❖ Novelist, mainly of contemporary fiction, whose historical trilogy brought her fame and fortune; lived most of her 63 years of married life in Katoomba, a small town in the Blue Mountains southwest of Sydney; wrote verse from age 7 but eventually turned solely to prose; published *Slow Dawning* (1932), the 1st and least successful of 10 novels; published the 1st of her historical trilogy, *The Timeless Land* (1941), bringing her international acclaim, followed by *Storm of Time* (1948) and *No Barrier* (1953); published last novel *Lantana Lane* (1959), which closed with a flourish one of the most successful writing careers of an Australian woman writer of her generation; also wrote *Prelude to Christopher* (1934), *Return to Coolami* (1936), *Sun Across the Sky* (1937), *Waterway* (1938) and *The Little Company* (1945). Was twice-winner of Australian Literature Society's gold medal for best novel (1936 and 1938); awarded Order of Australia (1977). ❖ See also C. Ferrier, ed. *As good as a yarn with you: letters between Miles Franklin, Katharine Susannah Prichard, Jean Devanny, Marjorie Barnard, Flora Eldershaw and Eleanor Dark* (Cambridge U. Press, 1992); A. Grove Day, *Eleanor Dark* (Twayne, 1976); and *Women in World History.*

DARK LADY, The (c. 1578–1647). *See Fitton, Mary.*

DARLING, Flora (1840–1910). American writer and society founder. Name variations: Flora Adams Darling. Born Flora Adams, July 25, 1840, in Lancaster, New Hampshire; died Jan 6, 1910, in New York, NY; dau. of Harvey and Nancy Dustin Rowell Adams; attended Lancaster Academy; m. Edward Irving Darling, Mar 12, 1960. ❖ Though she regarded herself as a founder of the Daughters of the American Revolution (DAR), was not considered a founder by the DAR; appointed vice-president general of DAR (1890), was recognized as the force that made DAR a national society; formed other women's patriotic societies; writings include *Mrs. Darling's Letters, or Memories of the Civil War* (1883), *A Social Diplomat* (1889), *A Winning, Wayward Woman* (1889), *Founding and Organization of the Daughters of the American Revolution and Daughters of the Revolution* (1901) and *1607–1907: Memories of Virginia* (1907). ❖ See also her papers, located at the Library of the College of William and Mary.

DARLING, Grace (1815–1842). British hero. Born Grace Horsley Darling at Bamburgh, Northumberland, England, Nov 24, 1815; died at 27 from influenza, Oct 20, 1842; dau. of William (lighthouse keeper) and Thomasin (Horsley) Darling. ❖ Famed hero who, with her father, daringly rescued 9 survivors of the luxury steamer *Forfarshire* when it was wrecked in a violent storm (Sept 1838); was besieged by reporters, who spread her story across the country, often taking liberty with the facts; received medals from the Humane Society, as well as a grant from the treasury, and became the subject of countless biographies, two of which were published in 1839: *Grace Darling, or the Heroine of the Farne Islands,* by G.M. Reynolds, and *Grace Darling, or The Maid of the Isles,* by Jerrold Vernon. ❖ See also Jessica Mitford, *Grace Had an English Heart* (Dutton, 1988); and *Women in World History.*

DARLING, May (1887–1971). American theatrical dancer. Name variations: May Hansen. Born Aug 27, 1887, in Chicago, Illinois; died Mar 23, 1971, in Chicago. ❖ Appeared in numerous productions by William Ziegfeld at La Salle Theater in Chicago; in New York City, performed in several of the earliest *Ziegfeld Follies* and in an interpretive dance act at Hammerstein roof garden theaters.

DARLING, Tonique (1976—). See *Williams, Tonique*.

DARLINGTON, Jennie (c. 1925—). American scientist and explorer. Name variations: Jenny Darlington. Born c. 1925 in US; m. Harry Darlington. ❖ Accompanied husband to Antarctica on *Port of Beaumont* and became one of 1st two women (with Edith Ronne) to set foot there (1947); with Ronne, became one of the 1st two women to overwinter in Antarctica. ❖ See also memoir (with Jane McIvaine) *My Antarctic Honeymoon: A Year at the Bottom of the World* (1956).

DARMESTETER, Mary F. (1856–1944). See *Duclaux, Agnes Mary F.*

DARMOND, Grace (1898–1963). Canadian-born silent-screen actress. Born Nov 20, 1898, in Toronto, Ontario, Canada; died Oct 8, 1963, in Hollywood, California. ❖ At 16, made film debut (1914), then starred in the 1st technicolor feature *The Gulf Between* (1918); made over 50 films, including *When Duty Calls, The Other Man, Valley of the Giants* and *Alimony;* also appeared in serials *The Hope Diamond Mystery, A Dangerous Adventure* and *The Shielding Shadow;* retired from film (1928).

DARNELL, Linda (1921–1965). American actress. Born Monetta Eloyse Darnell in Dallas, Texas, Oct 16, 1921; died from injuries sustained in a house fire in Glenview, Illinois, April 10, 1965; m. Peverell Marley (cinematographer), April 18, 1943 (div. 1951); m. Philip Liebmann, Feb 25, 1954 (div. 1955); m. Merle Roy Robertson (pilot), Mar 3, 1957 (div. 1963); children: Charlotte Mildred, called Lola (adopted, 1948). ❖ With her delicate features, dark hair and eyes, was perfect for the innocent heroines and faithful wives of her early pictures, such as *Daytime Wife* (1939) with Tyrone Power; turned to more sultry roles, beginning with Olga in *Summer Storm* (1944), followed by *Hangover Square* (1945) and *Fallen Angel* (1945); best known roles were in the popular musical *Centennial Summer* (1946) and *Forever Amber* (1947); made several other films for Fox, including *Unfaithfully Yours* (1948), *A Letter to Three Wives* (1949), which was probably the best of the lot, and *No Way Out* (1950); on tv, appeared on "Playhouse 90," "Climax," "77 Sunset Strip," "Rawhide" and the "Jane Wyman Theater." ❖ See also *Women in World History*.

D'ARNELL, Nydia (d. 1970). American musical-comedy star. Died May 15, 1970, age 74, in Southampton, NY; m. Harry A. Bruno. ❖ Played the lead in *Little Nelly Kelly* opposite George M. Cohan; also appeared in *Topsy and Eva* (1924), *Happy Go Lucky* (1926) and *My Maryland*.

DARRAGH, Lydia Barrington (1729–1789). American nurse, midwife and hero. Born Lydia Barrington in Dublin, Ireland, 1729; died in Philadelphia, Pennsylvania, Dec 28, 1789; dau. of John Barrington; m. William Darragh (tutor), Nov 1753 (died 1783); children: 9, of which 5 reached maturity, Charles, Ann, John, William, and Susannah. ❖ Immigrated to America (1753), shortly after her marriage; settling in Philadelphia, joined the Monthly Meeting of Friends and worked as a nurse and midwife; during the British occupation of Philadelphia (Sept 1777–June 1778), learned of the British plan to attack General George Washington at Whitemarsh, 8 miles away; on the morning of Dec 4, made her way to the American camp, where she relayed the information. ❖ See also *Women in World History*.

DARRAGH, Miss (d. 1917). English stage actress. Name variations: Letitia Marion Dallas. Born Letitia Marion Dallas; died Dec 15, 1917. ❖ Made London debut as Mrs. Maydew in *The Queen's Proctor* (1897); came to prominence in the part of Margot Le Gros in *Margot* (1903) and created the title role in *Deirdre* for William Butler Yeats when the play opened at the Abbey Theatre in Dublin (1907); also appeared in Wilde's *Salomé*, Shaw's *Man and Superman* and Shakespeare's *Antony and Cleopatra* (title role).

DARRAS, Danielle (1943—). French politician. Born Dec 22, 1943, in Carency, France. ❖ Member of the Socialist Party National Council and later of National Executive; became deputy mayor of Liévin (1983) and deputy chair of the Pas-de-Calais Departmental Council (1986); elected to 4th and 5th European Parliament (EP, 1994–99, 1999–2004).

DARRÉ, Jeanne-Marie (1905–1999). French pianist. Name variations: Darre. Born in Givet, France, near the Belgian border, July 30, 1905; died Jan 26, 1999, in Port Marly, France; studied with Marguerite Long and Isidor Philipp (1863–1958) in Paris. ❖ Made concert debut (1920); delighted Paris by performing all 5 of the Saint-Saëns concerti in one marathon evening (1926); made triumphant American recital debut (1962); had a long, distinguished teaching career at the Paris Conservatoire, and made many recordings, one of the most distinguished being an acclaimed reading of the Liszt Piano Sonata. ❖ See also *Women in World History*.

DARRIEUX, Danielle (1917—). French actress. Born in Bordeaux, Gironde, France, May 1, 1917; dau. of Jean (ophthalmologist) and Marie-Louise Witkowski Darrieux; m. Henri Decoin (film director), 1934 (div. 1940); m. Porfirio Rubirosa, 1942 (div. 1947); m. Georges Mitsinkides (author), 1948; children: (3rd m.) Mathieu. ❖ In an international career lasting more than 6 decades, appeared in a number of classic films, including *Mayerling* (1936) and *La Ronde* (1950); made film debut at 14 in *Le Bal* (1931); appeared in a highly successful musical, *La Crise est finie* (1934), followed by *Mauvaise Graine* (1934), *Volga en flammes* (1934) and *Le Domino vert* (1935); came to prominence with *Mayerling* (1936), in which she co-starred with Charles Boyer; starred in 1st husband's *Mademoiselle ma mere* and made stage debut in his *Jeux Dangereux* (1937); after the war, had a smashing success on stage in *L'Amour Vient en Jouant,* followed by *La Ronde* (1950), directed by Max Ophüls, and 2 further well-received roles in films directed by Ophüls, as Rosa in *Le Plaisir* (*The House of Pleasure*, 1952), and as Madame Louise de . . . in *The Earrings of Madame de . . .* (1953); other films include *Katia* (1938), *Premier Rendezvous* (1941), *Adieu Chérie* (1945), *Five Fingers* (1952), *Alexander the Great* (1956), *The Young Girls of Rochefort* (1967), *En Haut des marches* (1983), *Une Chambre en ville* (*A Room in Town*, 1982) and *Les Mamies* (1992); appeared on tv in "Plège infernal" (1991) and on Paris stage in *Harold et Maude* (1995). Received Chevalier de la legion d'honneur (1962), the rank of Officier de la legion d'honneur (1977), as well as the film industry's César d'honneur (1985) and the prix de l'Amicale des cadres de l'industrie cinématographique (1987). ❖ See also *Women in World History*.

DARROW, Anna (1876–1959). American physician. Name variations: Annie Darrow. Born Anna Albertina Lindstedt, Sept 16, 1876, in Jasper Co., Indiana; died July 22, 1959; dau. of Per Jon and Emma (Lundin) Lindstedt; Kirksville College of Osteopathy, doctor of osteopathy, 1905; Chicago College of Medicine and Surgery, MD with honors, 1909; m. Charles Ray Darrow (surgeon), 1896 (died 1926); children: Richard Gordon Darrow and Dorothy Anna Darrow. ❖ One of 1st women practicing physicians in the state of Florida, began practicing medicine in Chicago; moved to Florida (1912); as a licensed pharmacist, established a drugstore with husband in the Okeechobee area (1912–22), the 1st woman physician there; cared for Seminole Indians in Florida's Everglades; after husband's death (1926), founded and served on medical staff of Broward General Hospital in Ft. Lauderdale (1927–49); served as charter member of the South Florida Branch of the American Medical Women's Association.

DARSONVAL, Lycette (1912–1996). French ballet dancer. Name variations: Lycette Perron. Born Feb 12, 1912, in Countances, France; died 1996; studied with Albert Aveline and Carlotta Zambelli at Paris Opéra Ballet (starting 1925). ❖ Joined Paris Opéra's ballet company (1930) and created roles in Serge Lifar's *Joan de Zarissa* (1942), *Suite en Blanc* (1942), *Chevallier Errant* (1950) and *Phèdre* (1950); also created principal roles in Aveline's *Elvire* (1937) and *Sylvia* (1941); danced title roles in *Giselle, Salome, Sylvia,* and more; formed own troupe, La Compagnie Lycette Darsonval de l'Opéra de Paris, which began touring extensively (early 1950s); served as director of Paris Opéra Ballet (1957–59) and Ballet de Nice (1962). Works of choreography include *La Nuit Venitienne* (1949), *Combat* (c. 1953) and *Sylvia* (1979).

DARTON, Patience (1911–1996). British nurse and political activist. Name variations: Patience Edney. Born Patience Darton in Orpington, Kent, England, Aug 27, 1911; died in Madrid, Spain, Nov 6, 1996; dau. of a publisher; sister of Hillary Darton; m. Eric Edney (Communist Party official); children: Robert Edney. ❖ Completed training as a midwife at University College Hospital, London; worked in midwifery around Woolwich Arsenal; when civil war broke out in Spain (summer 1936), offered assistance to the Republican forces; like all nurses who worked for the International Brigades in Spain, put in long hours with little rest under dangerous conditions, saving many lives; transferred to the front lines, worked in a primitive hospital dug into a cave, caring as best she could for the rapidly growing number of wounded men; arrived back in London (Dec 1938); joined the British Communist Party; devoted her medical talents to taking care of the Czech refugees, many of them Jewish, who now streamed into the UK after Hitler's annexation of Bohemia and Moravia (Mar 1939); following the war, worked for United Nations Relief and Rehabilitation Agency (UNRRA). ❖ See also *Women in World History*.

DARUSMONT or D'ARUSMONT, Frances (1795–1852). *See Wright, Frances.*

DARVAS, Julia (c. 1919—). **Hungarian ballroom dancer and vocalist.** Name variations: Julia Susslar. Born c. 1919, in Budapest, Hungary. ❖ Used stage name Julia Darvas throughout career; immigrated to Istanbul, Turkey, as a child; appeared in numerous Turkish films, becoming known as the Turkish Shirley Temple; partnered with Nicholas Darvas in acrobatic exhibition ballroom act after WWII (c. 1946); with Nicholas, toured Europe and US, presenting their acrobatic act as half-siblings; separated from Darvas (1960); ceased working in dance, but continued to perform as vocalist in France and New York City for numerous seasons; remained in headlines for many months due to "palimony" suit against Darvas.

DARVAS, Lili (1902–1974). **Hungarian-born actress.** Born in Budapest, Hungary, 1902; died in New York, NY, July 22, 1974; m. Ferenc Molnar (playwright), 1926 (sep. c. 1932, died 1952). ❖ In a career on both sides of the Atlantic that spanned more than 50 years, 1st appeared as Juliet in *Romeo and Juliet* with a repertory theater (1921); soon a star in Hungary, mastered German and made her Vienna debut at the famous Theater in der Josefstadt (1926); worked in Max Reinhardt's theaters in Vienna, Salzburg and Berlin, while her husband Ferenc Molnar wrote several plays for her, including *Delilah, Olympia* and *Still Life;* fled Vienna with the Jewish Molnar because of Nazi occupation of Austria (Mar 1938); arrived in NY, learned English, and began working on Broadway in *The Criminals,* followed by *Soldier's Wife,* which ran for almost a year, and "A Far Country"; also appeared as a celebrated European actress in *Bravo* and as Mme. St. Pé in *The Waltz of the Toreadors* (1958); topped off a distinguished career by starring in the internationally acclaimed Hungarian film *Love* (1971). ❖ See also *Women in World History.*

DARVI, Bella (1927–1971). **Polish-French actress.** Born Bayla Wegier, Oct 28 (also seen as 23), 1927, in Sosnowiec, Poland; died Sept 10, 1971, by turning on gas in stove, in Monte Carlo, Monaco. ❖ Grew up in Paris; spent time in a concentration camp during Nazi occupation; brought to Hollywood by Darryl and Virginia Zanuck; films include *Hell and High Water, The Egyptian, The Racers* and *Les Petites Filles modèles.*

DARWELL, Jane (1879–1967). **American actress.** Born Patti Woodward in Palmyra, Missouri, Oct 15, 1879; died Aug 13, 1967, in Woodland Hills, California; dau. of W.R. Woodward (president of the Louisville Southern Railroad); apprenticed with Chicago Opera House. ❖ Won an Academy Award for Best Supporting Actress for portrayal of Ma Joad in *The Grapes of Wrath;* was a member of the pioneering Lasky Film Co. (1913–15), appearing in the early silent films *Rose of the Rancho, The Master Mind* and *Brewster's Millions;* during a 2-season stint on Broadway, had a role in Sidney Howard's 1st play, *Swords* (1921); other films include *Tom Sawyer* (1930), *Back Street* (1932), *Design for Living* (1934), *Life Begins at 40* (1935), *Captain January* (1936), *Jesse James* (1939), *Gone with the Wind* (1939), *The Ox-Bow Incident* (1942), *Captain Tugboat Annie* (1946), *My Darling Clementine* (1946), *Three Godfathers* (1948), *Caged* (1950), *The Lemon Drop Kid* (1951), *Fourteen Hours* (1951), *Hit the Deck* (1955), *The Last Hurrah* (1958) and *Mary Poppins* (1964). ❖ See also *Women in World History.*

DARWIN, Frances Crofts (1886–1960). *See Cornford, Frances Crofts.*

DARWITZ, Natalie (1982—). **American ice-hockey player.** Born Oct 13, 1982, in Eagan, Minnesota. ❖ Won team silver medals at World championships (1999, 2000, 2001); won a team silver medal at Salt Lake City Olympics (2002) and a team bronze medal at Torino Olympics (2006).

DARYUSH, Elizabeth (1887–1977). **British poet.** Name variations: Elizabeth Bridges. Born Elizabeth Bridges, Dec 5, 1887, in London, England; died April 7, 1977, in London; dau. of Robert Bridges (poet laureate of England) and Monica (Waterhouse) Bridges; m. Ali Akbar Daryush. ❖ Praised by critics as a fine minor poet and best 20th-century practitioner of syllabic verse; spent 4 years in Persia with husband but returned to somewhat reclusive life in England; collections include *Charitessi 1911* (1912), *First Book Verses* (1930), *Second Book Verses* (1932), *The Last Man and Other Verses (Fifth Book Verses)* (1936) and *Seventh Book Verses* (1971); poems include "Flanders Fields," "Still-Life," "Song of a Pentecostal Summer" and "Children of Wealth."

DAS, Kamala (1934—). **Indian poet and journalist.** Name variations: (pseudonym) Madhavi Kutty. Born Mar 31, 1934, in Malabar, Kerala, India; dau. of Nalapat Balamani Amma; married K. Madhava Das. ❖ Served as poetry editor of *Illustrated Weekly of India* and president of Jyotsna Art and Education Academy; helped found Bahutantrika Group of Artists; wrote syndicated column and established own political party; nominated for Nobel prize (1984); works include *Summer in Calcutta* (1965), *The Descendants* (1967), *The Old Playhouse* (1973), *Tonight, This Savage Rite: The Love Poems of Kamala Das and Pritish Nandy* (1979) and *Collected Poems* (1984); novels in Malayalam include *Palayan* (1990), *Neypayasam* (1991) and *Dayarikkurippukal* (1992). ❖ See also autobiography *My Life* (1976).

DASH, countess. *See Saint Mars, Gabrielle (1804–1872).*

DASH, Julie (1952—). **African-American director.** Born Oct 22, 1952, in Long Island City, NY; studied filmmaking at City College of New York and American Film Institute. ❖ The 1st female African-American director to have a movie distributed nationally, won acclaim for film *Daughters of the Dust* (1991); also novelized the film (1997); other films include *Four Women* (1975), *Diary of an African Nun* (1977), *Illusions* (1982), *Praise House* (1991) and *Brothers of the Borderland* (2004); for tv, directed "Funny Valentines" (1999), "Incognito" (1999), "Love Song" (2000) and "The Rosa Parks Story" (2002). ❖ See also *Daughters of the Dust: The Making of an African American Woman's Film* (New Press, 1993).

DASH, Sarah (1945—). **American singer.** Name variations: Patti LaBelle and the Blue Belles (also BlueBelles), Labelle. Born Aug 18, 1945, in Trenton, NJ. ❖ With Patti LaBelle, Nona Hendryx and Cindy Birdsong, formed Patti LaBelle and the Blue Belles (1961), which became known for gospel-laced rock & roll sound; after departure of Birdsong (1967), sang as a trio under name Labelle; with Labelle, had million-selling hit "Lady Marmalade" (Voulez-vous chouchez avec moi ce soir?) which reached #1 (1975); signed to Kirschner label as solo artist (1978), released self-titled album which included disco anthem "Sinner Man" (1979); toured with Keith Richards (1990s). Additional albums include *Oh La La* (1980), *Close Enough* (1981) and *You're All I Need* (1985).

DASHKOFF, Ekaterina (1744–1810). *See Dashkova, Ekaterina.*

DASHKOVA, Ekaterina (1744–1810). **Russian princess, philologist, writer.** Name variations: Princess Katerina or Catherine Dashkof; Ekaterina Vorontsova or Worontsova; wrote articles on moral and ethical problems under the pen-name Rossianka, and a number of dramas have been attributed to her. Pronunciation: KAT-eh-REEN-a Dosh-KOV-a. Born Ekaterina Romanovna Vorontsova, Mar 17, 1744, in St. Petersburg, Russia; died Jan 4, 1810, in Trotskoye, Russia; dau. of prince Roman I. Vorontsov and Marfa Surmina; sister of Elizabeth Vorontsova; m. Prince Michail Dashkov, 1760; children: a 1st son, and Paul (Pavel) and Anastasia. ❖ Confidante of Catherine the Great, who became the 1st woman president of the St. Petersburg Academy of Science and of the Russian Academy; wrote plays and poems, composed music, was a recognized philologist, initiated the publication of the 1st Russian dictionary, held progressive views on education, was an enthusiastic naturalist, and her opinions on architectural monuments and works of art were considered exact and profound, but she never quite mastered the ability to sail safely through the sea of political intrigues that ruled the Russian imperial court; in early years, participated in the palace revolution that brought Catherine the Great to the Russian throne (1762); rejected by Catherine for her outspoken views, left the court in disgrace, and retired with husband to Trotskoye, where he died, leaving her to pay off his debts (1764); granted permission to travel in Europe (1769); accompanied her son to study in Edinburgh (1775); returned to St. Petersburg, and the good graces of Empress Catherine, where she was made director of St. Petersburg Academy of Science (1782); was founder and 1st president of the Russian Academy (1783); unofficially dismissed from academy positions (1794); after Catherine's death, exiled to Novgorod by the tsar (1796); reinstated by the new tsar but rejected invitation to return to academic posts (1801); her memoirs were highly regarded by the famous Russian literary critic and writer, Aleksandr Herzen. ❖ See also Kyril Fitzlyon, ed. and trans., *The Memoirs of Princess Dashkova: Russia in the Time of Catherine the Great* (Duke U. Press, 1995); and *Women in World History.*

DASHWOOD, Elizabeth Monica (1890–1943). **British writer.** Name variations: (pseudonym) E.M. Delafield. Born Edmée Elizabeth Monica de la Pasture, June 9, 1890, in Steyning, Sussex, England; died Dec 2, 1943, in Cullompton, Devon, England; dau. of Elizabeth Lydia Rosabelle (Bonham) de la Pasture (writer of numerous novels under Mrs. Henry de la Pasture, who was later known as Lady Clifford) and Count Henry Philip Ducarel de la Pasture (died 1908); m. Paul

Dashwood (engineer in several British harbor-building projects), July 17, 1919; children: Lionel Dashwood (1920–1940); Rosamund Dashwood (b. 1924). ❖ Well known under pseudonym E.M. Delafield (Anglicization of de la Pasture intended to prevent confusion between herself and her mother), was a highly prolific fiction writer who achieved great success with her Provincial Lady, a character whose popularity earned her a large following in both England and America; published *Zella Sees Herself* (1917); joined the writing staff of *Time and Tide* magazine, where she quickly advanced to an editorial position and wrote *Diary of a Provincial Lady*, which debuted in 1930 and has since become a classic; other writings include *The Pelicans* (1919), *The Optimist* (1922), *Messalina of the Suburbs* (1924), *Mrs. Harter* (1924), *The Provincial Lady Goes Further* (Macmillan, 1932), *The Time and Tide Album* (1932), *General Impressions* (1933), *The Provincial Lady in America* (1934), *Faster! Faster!* (1936), *Straw without Bricks: I Visit Soviet Russia* (1937), *As Others Hear Us: A Miscellany* (1937), *When Women Love* (Harper, 1938), *The Provincial Lady in Wartime* (1940) and *Late and Soon* (1943). ❖ See also Maurice L. McCullen, *E.M. Delafield* (Twayne, 1985); Violet Powell, *The Life of a Provincial Lady* (Heinemann, 1988); and *Women in World History*.

DASIC-KITIC, Svetlana (1960—). Yugoslavian handball player. Name variations: Svetlana Kitic. Born June 1960. ❖ Won an Olympic silver medal at Moscow Olympics (1980) and a gold medal at Los Angeles (1984), both in team competition.

DA SILVA, Ana (1949—). Portuguese-English singer and guitarist. Name variations: The Raincoats. Born 1949 in Portugal. ❖ Helped form English punk band, the Raincoats, in London (1977); with group, made albums *Odyshape* (1981), *The Kitchen Tapes* (1983), and *Moving* (1984), before disbanding (1984); reunited with singer and bassist Gina Birch and toured US East Coast after Nirvana's lead singer, Kurt Cobain, released Raincoats albums on band's label, DGC (1994); also released *Extended Play* (1995) and *Looking in the Shadows* (1996).

DA SILVA, Benedita (1942—). Afro-Brazilian politician and poet. Name variations: Bené da Silva. Born Mar 11, 1942, in Praia do Pinto, Rio de Janeiro, Brazil; 1 of 13 children; m. Newton Aldano da Silva (house painter), 1958 (died 1981); m. Agnaldo Bezerra "Bola" dos Santos (Communist-Christian community leader imprisoned by Brazilian military, died 1988); m. Antonio Luis "Pitanga" Sampaio (Afro-Brazilian actor and secretary of sports for state of Rio de Janeiro); children: (1st m.) 2. ❖ Worked as laborer and domestic servant at young age; earned double degree; taught at community school in shantytown of Chapéu Mangueira, using methods of radical educator Paulo Freire; helped form Women's Association of Chapéu Mangueira, Women's Department of the Federation of Shantytown Associations of the State of Rio de Janeiro (FAFERJ), and Center of Shantytown and Periphery Women (CEMUF); joined Workers' Party of Lula da Silva in early 1980s and quickly moved up ranks; elected to several posts as representative of Workers' Party, including town councillor (1982), federal constitutional representative to Bureau of National Constitutional Assembly (1986), member of Chamber of Federal Deputies (1990) and senator to republic (1st Afro-Brazilian woman, 1994); wrote and co-wrote amendments to constitution guaranteeing rights of women, racial minorities, and prisoners, and contributed to Child and Adolescent Code; participated in several investigations into mass sterilization of women, violence against women, and child and adolescent prostitution; fought for family planning, child care, protection of domestic servants and maternity leave; left senatorial post to become vice governor of Rio de Janeiro (1998), then governor (2002), Brazil's 1st black woman governor; wrote numerous books and articles on Brazilian problems, as well as many poems and an autobiography which was made into documentary film. ❖ See also Benedita da Silva, *Benedita da Silva: An Afro-Brazilian Woman's Story of Politics and Love* (Institute for Food and Development Policy, 1997).

DA SILVA, Fabiola (1979—). Brazilian inline skater. Name variations: Fabiola Oliveira Samoes da Silva; Fabby Da Silva. Born June 18, 1979, in Sao Paulo, Brazil. ❖ One of the best-known female inline skaters in the world, largely responsible for increasing female participation in the sport, began competing in 1996; after placing among top 10 male skaters in ASA Street competition, was responsible for the "Fabiola Rule," which allows women to qualify into men's Vert finals (2000); won gold at X Games in Vert (1996, 1997, 1998, 2000, 2001) and Park (2000); won silver in Vert at X Games (1999) and at Gravity Games in Vert and Street (2001); placed in top 10 of men's Vert competition many times, including X Trial (Grand Prairie, TX, 4th, 2001), B3 Event (Anaheim, CA, 5th,

2001), Latin X (Rio De Janeiro, 2nd, 2002), ASA (Cincinnati, OH, 7th, 2002); sponsored by 50/50, Rollerblade, and Harbinger.

DA SILVE E ORTA, Teresa M. (c. 1711–1793). *See Silve e Orta, Teresa M. da.*

DASKALAKI, Gianna (1955—). *See Angelopoulos-Daskalaki, Gianna.*

DASKAM, Josephine Dodge (1876–1961). *See Bacon, Josephine Dodge.*

DAS NEVES, Hilário (1876–1901). *See Souza, Auta de.*

DASSAULT, Madeleine (1901–1992). French industrialist. Born 1901 as Madeleine Minckès in Salonika, Greece; died July 12, 1992; m. Marcel Bloch (name later changed to Marcel Dassault, aircraft designer and industrialist), July 1919; children: Claude and Serge. ❖ Played a crucial role in advancing husband's career, then controlled their vast business empire after his death; persuaded her father, a French-Jewish furniture merchant, to finance husband's 1st ventures in aviation; by 1950s, husband reigned as the undisputed sovereign of France's aerospace industry; avoided publicity despite husband's international fame, but made headlines when she was kidnapped and held for ransom (May 1964); after husband died (April 1986), actively managed their vast industrial holdings, including fighter aircraft and business jets, electronics, pharmaceuticals (Merieux), Europe 1 Radio, financial and real estate companies, and the Chateau Dassault vineyard. ❖ See also *Women in World History*.

D'ASSISI, Clara (c. 1194–1253). *See Clare of Assisi.*

DAT SO LA LEE (c. 1835–1925). Native American artist. Name variations: Dat-So-La-Lee; Datsolalee; Dabuda; Louisa Kayser (or Kaiser); Big Hips, Wide Hips. Born Dabuda around 1835 in a Washo village near present-day Sheridan, Nevada, near Lake Tahoe (since there is no written record of her birth, contemporary estimates placed her age at death between 75 and 90); died Dec 6, 1925, in Carson City, Nevada; m. Assu of Washo tribe who died of consumption early into their marriage; m. Charley Kayser (Kaiser), 1888, a man of mixed Washo-Miwok blood; children: (1st m.) 2 who died in infancy. ❖ Known as the finest of the Washo basket makers, for whom basketry is an art as well as a craft, her work was not introduced to the world until she reached age 60; began marketing baskets with the help of Abe Cohn (1895); had some featured in the St. Louis Exposition of 1919; created some of her best designs from dreams or visions. Many of her finest works were purchased by private collectors for as much as $10,000, and 20 of the baskets are now housed in the Nevada State Museum. ❖ See also Jane Green Hickson, *Dat-So-La-Lee, Queen of the Washo Basket Makers* (Nevada State Museum, 1967); and *Women in World History*.

DATTA, Naomi (1922—). English bacteriologist. Born Naomi Goddard, Sept 17, 1922; married S.P. Datta, 1943. ❖ Known for research on bacteria, worked as a senior bacteriologist at Public Health Laboratory Service (1947–57); taught microbial genetics at Royal Postgraduate Medical School in London (1957–84); proved that antibiotic resistance could be transferred between bacteria (1st time proven outside of Japan); identified and catalogued drug resistant bacteria; elected fellow to Royal College of Pathologists (1973) and to Royal Society (1985); joined Centre for Genetic Anthropology (1996) to study Y chromosome variation in Greeks, Greek Cypriots, Turks, and Turkish Cypriots.

DAUBECHIES, Ingrid (1954—). Belgian-born American mathematician. Born 1954 in Belgium; dau. of Marcel (civil-mining engineer) and Simone Daubechies (criminologist); Free University of Brussels, BS, 1975, PhD in physics, 1980; m. Robert Calderbank, 1987 (mathematician); children: Michael and Carolyn. ❖ Taught at Free University of Brussels for 12 years (1975–87); while attending conference in Montreal, Canada (1987), made important discoveries about wavelets, then relocated to US soon after; served as technical staff member at Mathematics Research Center of AT&T Bell Laboratories (1987–94), where she became a leading authority on wavelet theory; served as professor in mathematics department at Rutgers University (1991–94); was fellow of John D. and Catherine T. MacArthur Foundation (1992–97); at Princeton University, served as professor in math department and professor and director in Program in Applied and Computational Mathematics (1997–2001); was the 1st woman to win the National Academy of Sciences (NAS) Award in Mathematics (2000) "for fundamental discoveries on wavelets and wavelet expansions and for her role in making wavelets methods a practical basic tool of applied mathematics." Other awards include Louis Empain Prize for Physics (1984), Steele Prize for Exposition from American Mathematical

Society for her book *Ten Lectures on Wavelets* (1994), and Ruth Lyttle Satter Prize in Mathematics from American Mathematical Society (1997).

DAUBIÉ, Julie-Victoire (1824–1874). French essayist. Name variations: Julie Daubie. Born 1824 in Eastern France; died 1874. ❖ Submitted essay on female poverty, *La Femme pauvre au XIXe siècle,* to competition organized by Académie de Lyon (1858); won 1st prize and was encouraged to sit for *baccalauréat* exam; became 1st *bachelière* in France (1862) and later obtained degree from Sorbonne (1871).

D'AUBIGNÉ, Françoise (1635–1719). *See Maintenon, Françoise d'Aubigné, Marquise de.*

DAUDET, Madame Alphonse (1844–1940). *See Daudet, Julia.*

DAUDET, Julia (1844–1940). French poet and essayist. Name variations: Julia Allard-Daudet; Madame Alphonse Daudet; (pseudonym) Karl Steen. Born Julia Allard in 1844 in Paris, France; died 1940 in Chargé, France; m. Alphonse Daudet (1840–1897, writer), 1867; children: Léon Daudet (1867–1942, journalist who married and later divorced Jeanne Hugo, granddau. of Victor Hugo). ❖ Works include *L'Enfance d'une Parisienne* (1883) and *Fragments d'un livre inédit* (1884); published critical articles under pseudonym Karl Stern which were collected in *Impressions de nature et d'Art* (1879).

DAUGAARD, Line (1978—). Danish handball player. Born July 17, 1978, in Herning, Denmark. ❖ Right wing, won a team gold medal at Athens Olympics (2004).

D'AULAIRE, Ingri (1904–1980). Norwegian-American illustrator. Pronunciation: DOH-lair. Born Ingrid Maartenson in Kongsberg, Norway, Dec 27, 1904; died of cancer, Oct 24, 1980, in Wilson, Connecticut; dau. of Per (business executive) and Line (Sandsmark) Maartenson; attended Kongsberg Junior College and Institute of Arts and Crafts, Oslo; Hans Hofman School of Art, Munich; and Academie Scandinave, Academie Gauguin, and Academie Andre L'Hote in Paris; married Edgar Parin d'Aulaire (artist and author) July 24, 1925; children: Per Ola, Nils Maarten. ❖ With husband, arrived in America (1929) and began writing and illustrating picture books on Scandinavian themes; by mid-1930s, had abandoned the idyllic fantasies of their Scandinavian period in favor of epic, heroic portrayals of American history, including *Columbus* (1955).

D'AULNOY, Comtesse (c. 1650–1705). *See Aulnoy, Marie Catherine, Comtesse d'.*

DAUMIER, Sophie (1934–2004). French actress. Born Elisabeth Hugon, Nov 24, 1934, in Boulogne-sur-Mer, France; died of Huntingdon's disease, Dec 31, 2003, in Paris; dau. of Georges Hugon (composer); studied classical dance at Châtelet school in Paris; m. Guy Bedos, 1965; children: son. ❖ Began career dancing with a cancan troupe; came to prominence on stage in *Le Patate* (1957), with Pierre Dux, which ran for 6 years; went on to musicals and light films; with Guy Bedos, became a comic duo at La Nouvelle Eve and Galerie 55; also appeared with him in light comedic films; had to retire because of illness.

DAUNIENE, Tamara (1951—). Soviet basketball player. Born Sept 22, 1951, in USSR. ❖ At Montreal Olympics, won a gold medal in team competition (1976).

DAUNT, Yvonne (b. around 1900). English ballet and interpretive dancer. Born c. 1900 in England. ❖ Trained at Paris Opéra ballet school and performed in company's divertissements, including *Aida, Antar* and *Aphrodite;* held private recitals as interpretive dancer to great success in Paris and London; choreographed numerous works, including *Poland in Chains* (1921), *Poland Free* (1921) and *Mennuet* (1921); appeared in films for brief period.

DAUSER, Sue (1888–1972). American superintendent of Navy Nurse Corps. Born Sue Sophia Dauser in Anaheim, California, Sept 20, 1888; died Mar 1972 in Mount Angel, Oregon; dau. of Francis X. Dauser and Mary Anna (Steuckle) Dauser; attended Leland Stanford University, 1907–09; graduate of California Hospital School of Nursing, Los Angeles. ❖ Joined Naval Reserve as a nurse (1917); during WWI, became chief nurse of US Navy, serving at naval hospitals in Brooklyn, San Diego, and aboard ship; when President Warren G. Harding made his Alaskan cruise on the *Henderson,* tended him aboard ship during his final illness (1923); was named superintendent of Navy Nurse Corps (1939); promoted to the relative rank of captain (1943), equivalent to Florence A. Blanchfield's army rank of colonel, making her the 1st

American woman entitled to wear four gold stripes; outranking all other women commanders in the armed forces, continued her leadership of some 8,000 nurse officers until Nov 1945, when she stepped down as superintendent. ❖ See also *Women in World History.*

DAUTE, Heike (1964—). *See Drechsler, Heike.*

DAUTHENDEY, Elisabeth (1854–1943). German novelist and news-paper correspondent. Born 1854 in St Petersburg, Russia; died 1943; dau. of Karl Dauthendey (court photographer) and Anna Olschwang (died 1855); half-sister of Max Dauthendey (poet). ❖ Works include *Vom neuen Weibe und seiner Liebe: Ein Buch für reife Geister* (Of the New Woman and Her Love Life: A Book for Mature Spirits, 1900); also wrote novellas and fairytales.

D'AUVERGNE, Madame (fl. 1807–1823). *See Sansay, Leonora.*

DAVENPORT, Amelia Mary (1844–1930). *See Randall, Amelia Mary.*

DAVENPORT, Dorothy (1895–1977). *See Reid, Dorothy Davenport.*

DAVENPORT, Fanny (1850–1898). American actress-manager. Born Fanny Lily Gypsy Davenport in London, England, April 10, 1850; died in South Duxbury, Massachusetts, Sept 26, 1898; dau. of Edward L. (actor) and Fanny Elizabeth (Vining) Gill Davenport (English actress); m. Edwin H. Price (actor and later her business manager), July 30, 1879 (div. 1888); m. William Melbourne MacDowell, May 19, 1889. ❖ One of the most popular and successful actress-managers of the late-19th century, was brought to Boston as a child, where she often appeared with her father's company; made NY debut at 11 as King Charles in *Faint Heart Never Won Fair Lady;* had 1st adult role in *Still Waters Run Deep* (1865), then joined a Louisville stock company, where among other roles she portrayed Carline in *The Black Crook,* a play considered by some to be the 1st musical comedy; engaged by Augustin Daly for his Fifth Avenue Theater (1869–77), enjoyed particular success in *Charity* (1874) and *Pique* (1876), which ran for 238 performances; started her own touring company (1877); undertook a wide range of roles, including Shakespeare's heroines as well as more contemporary women like Polly Eccles in *Caste* and Lady Gay Spanker in *London Assurance;* while in London (1882), purchased rights to Sardou's *Fedora,* then toured it with great success for 4 years; later played in 4 additional Sardou plays: *Tosca, Cleopatra* and *Gismonda* and *A Soldier of France.* ❖ See also *Women in World History.*

DAVENPORT, Gwen (1909–2002). American novelist and playwright. Name variations: Gwen L. Davenport. Born Gwen Leys, Oct 3, 1909, in Panama; died Mar 23, 2002, in Louisville, Kentucky; dau. of a Navy doctor; children: 1 daughter, 2 sons. ❖ Published the novel *Belvedere* (1947), which was the basis for the "Mr. Belvedere" films, starring Clifton Webb, and an ABC-TV series.

DAVENPORT, Lindsay (1976—). American tennis player. Born June 8, 1976, in Palos Verdes, California; dau. of Ann (president of the Southern California Volleyball Association) and Wink Davenport (engineer who was a member of the 1968 US Olympic team); m. Jon Leach (investment banker and tennis player), 2003. ❖ Turned pro (1993); won a gold medal for singles at Atlanta Olympics (1996); won 4 North American hard court events, including the US Open, and ranked #1 in the world (1998, 2000, 2004); won Princess Cup in Tokyo and Chase championships (1999); won singles and doubles titles at Wimbledon (1999); held #1 rankings in singles and doubles (2000); won Australian Open (2000).

DAVENPORT, Marcia (1903–1996). American author and music critic. Born Marcia Gluck in New York, June 9, 1903; died in Pebble Beach, California, Jan 16, 1996; dau. of Alma Gluck (lyric soprano) and Bernard Gluck; stepdau. of Efrem Zimbalist (celebrated violinist); University of Grenoble, bachelor's degree; m. Frank D. Clarke, April 1923 (div. 1925); m. Russell W. Davenport (managing editor of *Fortune* and key advisor to Wendell Willkie), May 11, 1929 (died 1954); children: (1st m.) Patricia Delmas Clarke (b. 1924); (2nd m.) Cornelia Whipple Davenport (b. 1934). ❖ Served on editorial staff of *The New Yorker* (1928–31); was a music critic for *Stage* magazine (1934–39) and a radio commentator on Metropolitan Opera broadcasts (1936–37); published 1st book, *Mozart* (1932), to great success; published bestseller, *The Valley of Decision* (1942); following WWII, lived in Prague throughout the postwar crisis in Czechoslovakia, which culminated in the Communist coup d'état and the mysterious death of Jan Masaryk; recounted her experiences in *Too Strong for Fantasy* (1967); also wrote *Of Lena Geyer* (fiction, 1936) and *The Constant Image* (fiction, 1960).

DAVES, Joan (1919–1997). German-born literary agent. Born Liselotte Davidson, Nov 14, 1919, in Berlin, Germany; died of complications from asthma, June 25, 1997, in Bedford Hills, NY; dau. of a Jewish banker who died in Auschwitz; m. Joe H. Kirchberger. ❖ Joined Harper & Row as editor (1942); founded the Joan Daves Agency (1953); gained a reputation for handling authors of serious international fiction and nonfiction; was exclusive agent for Martin Luther King Jr.; also represented Vaclav Haval, Isaac Babel, Herman Hesse, Heinrich Boll, Nelly Sachs, Rachel Carson, Frank O'Connor, and Gabriela Mistral, among others.

DAVEY, Constance (1882–1963). Australian psychologist. Born Constance Muriel Davey at Nuriootpa, South Australia, Dec 4, 1882; died Dec 4, 1963; dau. of Stephen Henry (bank manager) and Emily Mary (Roberts) Davey; educated at country schools; University of Adelaide, BS, 1915, MA, 1918; University College, London, PhD, 1924. ❖ Traveled throughout England, US, and Canada to observe teaching methods for children with special needs; was a psychologist in South Australian Education Department (1924–42), where she established the state's 1st "opportunity class" for children with developmental difficulties; lectured at University of Adelaide (1927–50); as a political activist and feminist, was a 30-year member of the Women's Non-Party Political Association (League of Women Voters), working to see women represented on public boards and commissions; helped draft a bill for the Guardianship of Infants Act (1940), which supported equal parental guardianship; championed reforms in the Children's Court, seeking the right for women to serve as jurors; elected a fellow of British Psychological Society (1950); published *Children and Their Law-makers* (1956). Appointed OBE (1955).

DAVEY, Nuna (1902–1977). English actress. Born Dec 19, 1902, in Kanpur (Cawnpore), India; died Dec 11, 1977, in London, England; m. Gerald Cross. ❖ Made London debut in *The Return* (1922), followed by *77 Park Lane, Mother's Gone A-Hunting, The Streets of London, It Depends What You Mean, The Government Inspector, The Bride Goes West, The Seagull* (as Pauline), *Pygmalion* and *The Visit*; on film, appeared as Mrs. Rolandson in *Brief Encounter*.

DAVEY, Valerie (1940—). English politician and member of Parliament. Born April 16, 1940; m. Graham Davey, 1966. ❖ Teacher; representing Labour, elected to House of Commons for Bristol West (1997, 2001); lost general election (2005).

DAVID, Caroline Edgeworth (1856–1951). English-born educator, feminist, and social reformer. Name variations: Mrs. Edgeworth David, Lady Caroline Edgeworth David; Cara David (the name she preferred). Born Caroline Martha Mallett in Southwold, England, 1856; died in Sydney, Australia, Dec 25, 1951; dau. of Samuel (fisherman) and Pamela (Wright) Mallett; attended St. Edmund National School, Southwold, where she became a pupil-teacher at age 13; won a Queen's Scholarship to Whitelands College, 1874, admitted there 1875 and remained as a lecturer from 1876 to 1882; m. Tannatt William Edgeworth David (knighted 1920), July 30, 1885; children: Margaret (Madge) Edgeworth David (1886–1948, the 1st woman to be elected to the Tasmanian Parliament); Mary (Molly) Edgeworth David (b. 1889); William (Billy) Edgeworth David (b. 1891). ❖ Active in Australia for more than 50 years; departed England for a school administrative post in Australia (1882); served as the 1st principal of Hurlstone Training College for Women, Ashfield, Sydney (1883–85); accompanied a geology expedition headed by husband to the coral island of Funafuti, part of the Ellice Islands in the Pacific Ocean and now named Tuvalu (1897), remaining on the island for 3 months; moved into a close and easy relationship with the Funafutians, especially the women, and immersed herself in their customs, lifestyles and environment; was a founding member of the Feminist Club, a founding member and vice president of the Women's Club, and a founder and president of the Women's National Movement for Reform (1926–28); served as state commissioner of Girl Guides NSW (1928–38); writings include *Funafuti, or Three Months on a Coral Island: An Unscientific Account of a Scientific Expedition* (1899). ❖ See also Mary Edgeworth David, *Passages of Time: an Australian Woman 1890–1974* (U. of Queensland Press, 1975); and *Women in World History*.

DAVID, Catherine (fl. 15th c.). Tried for witchcraft. Name variations: Malavesse. Tried for witchcraft in 1439; m. Jacques Blanc. ❖ Following father's disinheritance of her 3 sisters in her favor, was brought to trial on the word of the sisters, who claimed that their parent's decision had been

made under the influence of a magical potion Catherine had prepared. ❖ See also *Women in World History*.

DAVID, Mrs. Edgeworth (1856–1951). *See David, Caroline Edgeworth.*

DAVID, Elizabeth (1913–1992). English cookery writer. Born Elizabeth Gwynne, Dec 26, 1913, in East Sussex, England; died 1992; studied French history and literature at the Sorbonne; m. Ivor David (career army officer), 1944. ❖ Wrote the bestselling cookery book *A Book of Mediterranean Food* (1950), followed by *French Country Cooking* (1951) and *French Provincial Cooking* (1960); sparked British interest in foreign cuisine and lent stylish writing to the preparation of food and selection of wine; also wrote *Italian Food* (1954), *English Bread and Yeast Cookery* (1977), among others. Granted OBE (1976), CBE (1986), the Order of Chevalier du Mérité Agricole from France (1977), and title of fellow of the Royal Society of Literature. ❖ See also *Women in World History*.

DAVID, Ilisaine Karen (1977—). Brazilian basketball player. Name variations: known as Zaine. Born Dec 17, 1977, in Jundiaí, Brazil. ❖ Won a team bronze medal at Sydney Olympics (2000).

DAVID, Zaine (1977—). *See David, Ilisaine Karen.*

DAVID-NEEL, Alexandra (1868–1969). French explorer. Name variations: Alexandra Neel; attempted career as opera singer under name Alexandra Myriel. Born in Saint-Mandé, France, Oct 24, 1868; died in Paris in 1969; dau. of a radical journalist living in exile in Belgium; m. distant cousin, Philippe Neel (split up within days); children: (adopted) Yongden, a Sikkimese monk and companion on her journeys. ❖ Traveler and expert on Tibetan Buddhism who became the 1st Western woman to visit the forbidden city of Lhasa (over the years, an assortment of travelers had unsuccessfully attempted to penetrate the forbidden land, about which almost nothing was known); lived an unhappy childhood, both at convent school and with her family; briefly attempted career as an opera singer, before taking up journalism and studying Eastern religions; set sail for India (Aug 3, 1911) to embark on a 14-year series of Asiatic journeys, culminating with her visit to Lhasa, in disguise, after facing the icy passes and murderous brigands who infested the border areas (1923); also managed to obtain an interview with the Dalai Lama, then in exile in Darjeeling—the 1st Western woman to be so privileged; returned to France as a hero (1925) and was awarded the coveted Gold Medal of the Geographical Society of France and made a Chevalier of the Legion of Honor; also awarded a silver medal by the Royal Geographical Society of Belgium; immersed in writing about her journeys and studying Buddhism until her death (1969); writings include *My Journey to Lhasa* (1927), *With Mystics and Magicians in Tibet* (1931) and *Tibetan Journey* (1936). ❖ See also *Women in World History*.

DAVIDOVA, Elena (1961—). *See Davydova, Yelena.*

DAVIDOVICH, Bella (1928—). Soviet pianist. Born in Baku, Azerbaijani, in USSR, July 16, 1928; studied with Konstantin Igumnov (1873–1948) as well as with Yakov Flier (1912–1978); children: Dmitry Sitkovetsky (violinist). ❖ Shared 1st prize with Halina Czerny-Stefanska at the Chopin Competition in Warsaw (1949); made 1st appearance in the West with Leningrad Philharmonic (1966); enjoyed a successful career in Soviet Union, particularly as a Chopin specialist, before immigrating to US (1978); excelled at music of Scriabin, especially his Second Sonata; recorded the 4 Chopin Ballades, several Beethoven sonatas, and the Saint-Saëns G minor Concerto, and often performed chamber music with her son, Dmitry Sitkovetsky. ❖ See also *Women in World History*.

DAVIDOW, Ruth (1911–1999). Russian-born American nurse and political activist. Born in Volkavisk, Russia, Sept 11, 1911; died June 28, 1999, in San Francisco; grew up in New York City; m. Fred Keller; children: 1 daughter. ❖ With the start of the civil war in Spain (1936), volunteered to go there as a nurse, working with the medical staff of the American volunteer unit, the Abraham Lincoln Brigade; worked at a front-line hospital during the Ebro offensive of 1938; returning to US, remained active in radical politics and emerged as a leading personality on the West Coast; was active in San Francisco in organizing public protests against racism, sexism, the Vietnam War, and the House Un-American Activities Committee; in 1980s, engaged with groups demanding American initiatives on a nuclear weapons freeze.

DAVIDSON, Lucretia Maria (1808–1825). American poet. Born in Plattsburg, New York, Sept 27, 1808; died in Plattsburg, Aug 27, 1825; dau. of a physician; sister of Margaret Miller Davidson (1823–1838).

❖ Wrote 1st poem, "Epitaph on a Robin," at 9; before she died of tuberculosis at 17, had written 278 poems of various lengths, which were collected and published by Samuel F.B. Morse as *Amir Khan and Other Poems* (1929).

DAVIDSON, Margaret Miller (1823–1838). American poet. Born Mar 26, 1823, in Plattsburg, NY; died at age 15 of tuberculosis in Saratoga, New York, Nov 25, 1838; buried in the village graveyard at Saratoga; dau. of a physician; sister of Lucretia Maria Davidson (1808–1825). ❖ Was only two and a half when her sister died of tuberculosis; also wrote poetry. For a time, the entire nation was enthralled with the romantic tragedy of the frail sisters; their works were published collectively in 1850, along with a biography of Margaret by Washington Irving.

DAVIDSON, Mary Frances (1902–1986). Irish politician. Born c. 1902 in Ireland; died May 29, 1986; dau. of William Davidson. ❖ Clerked for the Irish Labour Party during the Civil War (1922–23); elected to the Seanad from the Industrial and Commercial Panel (1950–51) and from the Oireachtas Sub-Panel (1954–69); was secretary of the Labour Party at time of retirement (1967).

DAVIDSON, Robyn (1950—). Australian author and adventurer. Born 1950 on a cattle station in Queensland, Australia; lived with Salmon Rushdie and Narendra Bhati (prince). ❖ Worked as a waitress in Alice Springs, Australia, to buy camels (1977); published *Tracks,* an account of her 1,700-mile journey across the Australian desert with four camels, which won the Thomas Cook Travel Book award (1980); also wrote essays *Travelling Light,* the novel *Ancestors* (1989), and *Desert Places,* the story of her travels with the Robari, nomads of northwestern India (1996).

DAVIES, Betty (1935—). English fashion designer. Born 1935 in Nottingham, England; attended Guildhall School of Music in London. ❖ Award-winning fashion designer based in Scotland, worked in public relations before founding Campus designers group (1966); was principal designer at Scottish Fashion Group; made use of traditional Scottish fabrics; launched designer label, The Academy Collection (1987) in Glasgow and Paris; won Scottish Style Award (1989) with her collection of Betty Davies Tartan; founded Betty Davies Ltd. in Edinburgh (1992), translating experience as designer in fashion market into practical business clothing; designed uniforms for staff at National Museum of Scotland, Royal Bank of Scotland, Dunfermline Building Society, among others; also worked for private clients, including Evelyn Glennie and Elizabeth Harwood; appointed governor of Edinburgh College of Art (1989).

DAVIES, Betty Ann (1910–1955). English actress and singer. Name variations: Betty-Ann Davies. Born Dec 24, 1910, in London, England; died May 14, 1955, in Manchester, England; m. Alexander Blackford. ❖ Made London debut in the chorus of the revue *Life* (1926); other musicals include *This Year of Grace, Mr. Cinders, Little Accident, Children in Uniform, Babes in the World, After Dark, Nine Sharp, The Little Revue, New Faces of 1940* and *Light and Shade;* made non-musical debut as Wanda Baring in *Morning Star* (1942), then appeared as Olivia in *Night Must Fall,* Elvira in *Blithe Spirit* and succeeded Vivien Leigh as Blanche in *Streetcar Named Desire;* films include *Kipps, Now Barabbas, The History of Mr. Polly, Meet Me Tonight, The Belles of St. Trinian's* and *Alias John Preston.*

DAVIES, Caryn (1982—). American rower. Born April 14, 1982, in Ithaca, NY; attended Harvard University. ❖ Won a gold medal for coxed eights at World championships (2002); won a silver medal for coxed eights at Athens Olympics (2004); won 2 World Cups for coxed eights (2004).

DAVIES, Christian (1667–1739). See Cavanaugh, Kit.

DAVIES, Clara (1861–1943). See Novello-Davies, Clara.

DAVIES, Dorothy Ida (1899–1987). New Zealand pianist and piano teacher. Name variations: Dorothy Ida Lochore. Born Oct 24, 1899, at River Bank, Wanganui, New Zealand; died July 11, 1987, at Whangaparaoa, New Zealand; dau. of David Davies (engineer) and Martha Naomi (Oakden) Davies; New South Wales State Conservatorium of Music, 1924; Royal College of Music, 1931; m. Reuel Anson Lochore (government translator), 1940; children: adopted son. ❖ Served as musician librarian for Radio Broadcasting Company of New Zealand, and pianist for Christchurch Broadcasting Trio (1928); toured Australia and New Zealand as accompanist for singer Therese Behr (late 1930s); broadcast all major Bach works and the complete Schubert and Beethoven sonatas

on New Zealand Broadcasting Service; formed Dorothy Davis Trio with Erika Schorss on violin and Marie Vandewart on cello (1940s); organized numerous lecture recitals at Nelson School of Music; gave master classes at Cambridge Summer School of Music and classes in lieder at Porirua Music School; served on Makara Co. Council and as justice of peace (1950s). British Empire Medal (1975). ❖ See also *Dictionary of New Zealand Biography* (Vol. 4).

DAVIES, Eleanor (1590–1652). British religious writer. Name variations: Lady Eleanor Audeley Davies; Lady Eleanor Douglas or Lady Eleanor Davies Douglas; (pseudonyms) Eleanor Audeley; Reveale O Daniel; The Lady Eleanor. Born Eleanor Touchet, 1590, in Ireland; died July 5, 1652; dau. of George Touchet, Baron Audeley, and Lucy (Mervin) Touchet; m. Sir John Davies (poet and barrister), 1609 (died 1626); m. Sir Archibald Douglas, 1627; children: (1st m.) 3, including Lucy Davies. ❖ "Heard a great voice from heaven" and began prophesying (1625); predicted death of husband and of 1st earl of Buckingham; brought before High Commission for illicit printing, and saw some of her work burned; sentenced by Commission for Causes Ecclesiastical to 2 years in prison; imprisoned again (1637) and committed to Bedlam after defacing tapestries at Cathedral of Lichfield; jailed several more times after 1646; wrote more than 60 prophetic tracts, including *A Warning to the Dragon and all His Angels* (1625), *All the Kings of the Earth* (1633), *Her Appeale* (1641), *Amend, Amend* (1643), *Discovery* (1644), *Great Brittains Visitation* (1645), *Day of Judgement* (1646), *Writ of Restitution* (1648), *For the States* (1649), *Hells Destruction* (1651) and *Tobits Book* (1652). ❖ See also Esther S. Cope, ed., *Prophetic Writings of Lady Eleanor Davies* (U. of Nebraska, 1995).

DAVIES, Elizabeth Valerie (b. 1912). English swimmer. Born June 29, 1912. ❖ At Los Angeles Olympics, won bronze medals in 100-meter backstroke and 4 x 100-meter freestyle relay (1932).

DAVIES, Emily (1830–1921). English educator and founder. Born Emily Davies, April 22, 1830, in Southampton, England; died in London, July 13, 1921; dau. of John (Church of England cleric and headmaster of a private school) and Mary (Hopkinson) Davies; sister of John Llewelyn Davies (vicar); aunt of Margaret Llewelyn Davies; never married; no children. ❖ Principal founder of Girton College, devoted her long life to the struggle for equal rights for women; moved with family from southern England to Gateshead (1839); lived in London (1862–1921); acted as editor of the *Englishwoman's Journal;* edited *Victoria Magazine* (1864–65); involved in suffrage movement (1862–67); deeply committed to women's education, served as member of the London School Board (1870–73); rejected the belief, widespread among the middle and upper classes, that such subjects as Greek, Latin, and mathematics were suitable for young men while young women were intended for nothing more intellectually demanding than music, needlework, and the basics of reading and writing; opened a college to provide women with university-level education (1869); was the main founder of Girton College, near Cambridge (1873); was mistress of Girton (1873–75) and associated with the college for the rest of her life; resumed suffrage activities (1886); served as vice-president of Conservative and Unionist Women's Franchise Association (1912); writings include *The Higher Education of Women* (1866) and *Thoughts on some Questions relating to Women* (1910). ❖ See also Daphne Bennett, *Emily Davies and the Liberation of Women 1830–1921* (Deutsch, 1990); M.C. Bradbrook, *"That Infidel Place": A Short History of Girton College 1869–1969* (Chatto & Windus, 1969); Margaret Forster, *Significant Sisters: The Grassroots of Active Feminism, 1839–1939* (Secker & Warburg, 1984); Megson and Lindsay, *Girton College 1869–1959: An Informal History* (Heffer, 1960); Barbara Stephen, *Emily Davies and Girton College* (Constable, 1927); and *Women in World History.*

DAVIES, Fanny (1861–1934). English pianist. Born June 27, 1861, in Guernsey, Channel Islands, England; died in London, Sept 1, 1934. ❖ One of the most celebrated of English pianists, studied 1st with Karl Reinecke and Oscar Paul, then was tutored by Clara Schumann (1883–85), and is now considered to have been one of her most gifted pupils; specialized in the works of Schumann, Chopin, Brahms, and Beethoven, especially The Fourth Concerto, and played the then almost unknown Elizabethan composers; with Adolf Brodsky, gave 1st performance of Ethel Smyth's violin sonata in Leipzig (1887); believed to be the 1st woman to play piano in a church, gave many recitals at St. Martin-in-the-Fields; was also the 1st musician to give a piano recital in Westminster Abbey (1921); also excelled as a recital accompanist, collaborating with such world-class virtuosos as Pablo Casals. ❖ See also *Women in World History.*

DAVIES, Gwendoline (1882–1951). Welsh philanthropist, art collector, and patron of the arts. Name variations: The Ladies of Gregynog. Born Gwendoline Elizabeth Davies in Llandinam, Montgomeryshire, Wales, Feb 11, 1882; died in Oxford, July 3, 1951; dau. of Edward (1852–98) and Margaret Jones Davies (d. 1888); stepdau. and niece of Elizabeth Jones Davies (1853–1942), the 1st woman magistrate in Montgomeryshire; sister of Margaret Davies (1884–1963) and David Davies (1880–1944, Liberal MP and parliamentary private secretary to David Lloyd George); never married; no children. ❖ Patron of art, fine printing and music, who was one half of The Ladies of Gregynog; with sister, collected art from 1908, was a major benefactor of charities and cultural institutions in Wales (c. 1914–50), ran canteen for allied troops at Troyes and Rouen (1916–18), purchased Gregynog Hall, Montgomeryshire, as an art center (1920), organized concerts and festivals of music and poetry (1921–38), founded Gregynog Press (1922), and founded Gwendoline and Margaret Davies Trusts (1934). Awarded Companion of Honor (1937). ❖ See also *Gregynog* (ed. by Hughes, Morgan, and Thomas, U. of Wales Press, 1977); Dorothy A. Harrop, *A History of the Gregynog Press* (1980); Ian Parrott, *The Spiritual Pilgrims* (Walters, 1969); Lady Eirene White, *The Ladies of Gregynog* (U. of Wales Press, 1985); and *Women in World History.*

DAVIES, Judy Joy (1928—). Australian swimmer and journalist. Born June 1928 in Melbourne, Australia. ❖ Won the bronze medal in the 100-meter backstroke in the London Olympics (1948); held 18 Australian championships; won 3 gold medals at Commonwealth Games (1950); became a sports journalist, covering Olympics (1956–88).

DAVIES, Laura (1963—). English golfer. Name variations: Laurie Davies. Born Oct 5, 1963, in Coventry, England. ❖ Won English Intermediate championship (1983), Welsh Open Stroke Play (1984), and South Eastern (1983–84); member of Curtis Cup team (1984); won US Women's Open (1987); won Tucson Open and Jamie Farr (1988); won Lady Keystone (1989); won Inamori Classic (1991); won McDonald's (1993); won Standard Register PING (1994, 1995, 1997); won Sara Lee Classic (1994); won LPGA championship (1994, 1996); won du Maurier Classic (1996); won PageNet tour (1998); won Los Angeles championship and Philips Invitational (2000); member of the European Solheim Cup team (2000); won Wegmans Rochester International (2001). Named MBE by Queen Elizabeth II (1988) and CBE (2000).

DAVIES, Lilian May (1915—). Duchess of Halland. Name variations: Princess Lilian May of Sweden; Lilian Craig. Born Aug 30, 1915, in Swansea, Wales; dau. of William John Davies and Gladys Mary (Curran) Davies; m. Walter Ivan Craig, Sept 27, 1940 (div.); m. Bertil Gustaf Oscar Bernadotte (1912–1997), prince of Sweden and duke of Halland, Dec 7, 1976. ❖ See also *Women in World History.*

DAVIES, Lillian (1895–1932). English actress and singer. Born Jan 18, 1895, Lynmouth, North Devon, England; died Mar 3, 1932; m. Stephen Wentworth Robinson. ❖ Made London debut in the chorus of *Shanghai* (1918) and subsequently toured music halls with Nelson Keys; came to prominence as Polly Peachum in revival of Gay's *The Beggar's Opera* (1922).

DAVIES, Mandy Rice (b. 1944). *See Rice-Davies, Mandy.*

DAVIES, Margaret (1884–1963). Welsh philanthropist, art collector, and patron of the arts. Name variations: The Ladies of Gregynog. Born Margaret Sidney Davies in Llandinam, Montgomeryshire, Wales, Dec 14, 1884; died in London, Mar 13, 1963; dau. of Edward (1852–98) and Margaret Jones Davies (died 1888); stepdau. and niece of Elizabeth Jones Davies (1853–1942), the 1st woman magistrate in Montgomeryshire; sister of Gwendoline Davies (1882–1951) and David Davies (1880–1944, Liberal MP and parliamentary private secretary to David Lloyd George); never married; no children. ❖ Patron of art, fine printing and music, who was one half of The Ladies of Gregynog (see Davies, Gwendoline); arranged for Gwendoline Davies Bequest to National Museum of Wales (1951), gift to National Library of Wales (1951), gift of Gregynog Hall to University of Wales (1960) and Margaret Davies Bequest to National Museum of Wales (1963). ❖ See also *Gregynog* (ed. by Hughes, Morgan, and Thomas, U. of Wales Press, 1977); Dorothy A. Harrop, *A History of the Gregynog Press* (1980); Ian Parrott, *The Spiritual Pilgrims* (Walters, 1969); Lady Eirene White, *The Ladies of Gregynog* (U. of Wales Press, 1985); and *Women in World History.*

DAVIES, Margaret (1914–1982). Welsh archaeologist and conservationist. Born 1914 in Wales; died Oct 6, 1982; Manchester University, BS and PhD in archaeology; m. Elwyn Davies (chief inspector for Welsh Education Office), 1940 (died 1986). ❖ Researched Bronze Age sites in France and megalithic monuments in North Channel and Irish Sea for dissertation, which was published in *Antiquaries Journal;* elected fellow to Society of Antiquaries (1943); after WWII, nurtured interest in botany and in natural history; was 1st chair of Welsh Committee of the Countryside Commission; served as president of Cardiff Naturalists Club; was a member of Council of the National Museum of Wales; revised *Natural History of Man in Britain,* a book by H.J. Fleur. Made Commander of Order of the British Empire (1973).

DAVIES, Margaret Llewelyn (1861–1944). British activist. Born in Marylebone, England, 1861; died 1944; dau. of John Llewelyn Davies (cleric) and Mary (Crampton) Llewelyn Davies (suffragist); niece of Emily Davies (1830–1921); attended Queen's College, London, and Girton College, Cambridge. ❖ Women's rights advocate, was a member of the Women's Co-operative Guild for 33 years, championing a minimum wage for women co-operative employees, equal divorce rights for women, and improved maternity care and benefits; also helped found International Women's Co-operative Guild (1921) and served as the 1st woman president of Co-operative Congress (1922); writings include *Maternity: Letters from Working Women,* an influential book detailing experiences of childbirth and rearing; was also chair of Society for Cultural Relations with the USSR (1924–28).

DAVIES, Marion (1897–1961). American actress. Born Marion Cecilia Douras, Jan 3, 1897, in Brooklyn, New York; died Sept 22, 1961, in Beverly Hills, California; dau. of Bernard (lawyer and politician) and Rose (Reilly) Douras; m. Horace G. Brown (merchant marine officer), Oct 31, 1951. ❖ Film star of 1920s and 1930s whose relationship with newspaper magnate William Randolph Hearst eclipsed her career, was a gifted comedian and one of the most popular women in Hollywood; made Broadway debut as a hoofer in *Chin-Chin* (1914); at 19, began affair with the 52-year-old Hearst, during the run of *The Ziegfeld Follies of 1916;* from then on, her life and career was dominated by Hearst, who selected her roles, financed her movies and backed each film with favorable publicity from his vast newspaper empire; films include *When Knighthood Was in Flower* (1922), *Lights of Old Broadway* (1925), *The Red Mill* (1927), *Tillie the Toiler* (1927), *Quality Street* (1927), *The Cardboard Lover* (1928), *The Hollywood Revue of 1929* (1929), *Polly of the Circus* (1932), *Peg o' My Heart* (1933), *Going Hollywood* (1933), *Page Miss Glory* (1935), *Cain and Mabel* (1936) and *Ever Since Eve* (1936). ❖ See also autobiography *The Times We Had: Life with William Randolph Hearst* (Bobbs-Merrill, 1975); Fred Lawrence Guiles, *Marion Davies* (McGraw-Hill, 1972); and *Women in World History.*

DAVIES, Martha H. (1900–1995). *See Hill, Martha.*

DAVIES, Moll (fl. 1673). English actress and dancer. Name variations: Mary Davies; Moll Davis. Mistress of Charles II (1630–1685), king of England (r. 1661–1685); children: (with Charles) illeg. daughter known as Mary Tudor (1673–1726), who m. Edward Radclyffe, 2nd earl of Derwentwater, Henry Graham of Levens, and James Rooke). ❖ Was a member of Sir William Davenant's troupe at Lincoln's Inn, when she caught the eye of Charles II, king of England. ❖ See also *Women in World History.*

DAVIES, Patricia (1956—). Zimbabwean field-hockey player. Born Dec 1956. ❖ At Moscow Olympics, won a gold medal in team competition (1980).

DAVIES, Sharron (1962—). English swimmer. Born Nov 1, 1962. ❖ At Moscow Olympics, won a silver medal in the 400-meter individual medley (1980).

DAVIES, Siobhan (1950—). British dancer and choreographer. Name variations: Susan Davies. Born Susan Davies, Sept 18, 1950, in London, England; attended Hammersmith College of Art, 1966–67; studied with Robert Cohan at London School of Contemporary Dance, 1967–71. ❖ Danced with Ballet For All, London (1971); began performing with London Contemporary Dance Theatre (1971), for which she became resident choreographer, then member of directorate upon retiring as dancer (1983–87); founded Siobhan Davies Dance Company (1988); taught at London School for Contemporary Dance and Ballet Moderne de Paris; worked as choreographer in residence and senior research fellow at Roehampton Institute, London (1995–96); received 3 Olivier Awards (1991–96). Works include *Sphinx* (1977), *Then You*

Can Only Sing (1978), *Something to Tell* (1980), *New Galileo* for London Contemporary Dance Theatre (1984), *Signature* for Rambert Dance Company (1990), *Different Trains* (1990), *Make-Make* (1992), *White Bird Featherless* (1992) and *Wild Translations* (1995).

DAVIES, Sonja (1923–2005). New Zealand politician. Born Sonja Vile, Nov 11, 1923, in Wallaceville, NZ, to a 26-year-old unwed mother; died June 12, 2005; married and divorced; m. Charlie Davies (trade unionist, died 1971); children: (with Red Brinson, US marine who died in action during WWII) Penny; (with Charlie Davies) Mark (died 1978). ❖ Socialist, feminist, and activist, served as Labour MP for Pencarrow (1987–93); was an executive member of the World Peace Council, marched against the Vietnam war, and argued for a nuclear-free New Zealand; was also the 1st woman vice-president of New Zealand Federation of Labour, and campaigned for the rights of women and the underprivileged. ❖ See also memoirs *Bread and Roses* (which was adapted for film and dir. by Gaylene Preston) and *Marching On*.

DAVIS, Adelle (1904–1974). American nutritionist. Name variations: (pseudonym) Jane Dunlop. Born Daisie Adelle Davis, Feb 25, 1904, in Lizton, Indiana; died in California, May 31, 1974, of bone cancer; dau. of Charles Eugene Davis and Harriet (McBroom) Davis; graduate of University of California, Berkeley, 1927; University of Southern California, MA in biochemistry, 1938; m. George Edward Leisey, 1946 (div. 1953); m. Frank V. Sieglinger, 1960; children: (1st m.) 2 adopted, George Davis Leisey and Barbara Adelle Leisey. ❖ Pioneering and controversial nutritionist, who was an early proponent of a "health food" diet, established a private nutritional counseling practice (1931); published *Vitality Through Planned Nutrition* (1942); wrote the 1st of her 4 "Let's" books, *Let's Cook It Right* (1947), followed by *Let's Have Healthy Children* (1951), *Let's Eat Right to Keep Fit* (1954), and *Let's Get Well* (1965); called for nutritional reform (1940s) and became the nation's leading advocate of the health benefits of foods grown without pesticides, chemical fertilizers, and extensive refining; became a leading figure in the growing "health food" movement, but her work came under increased scientific criticism, particularly her claims that most social ills were the direct result of poor nutrition (1960s); her lax methodology and the discovery of hundreds of errors in her books called her reputation into question, though she remained a popular media figure and continued to espouse her theories freely. Her "Let's" books, still in print, sold well over 10 million copies in various revisions during her lifetime; *Let's Eat Right to Keep Fit* alone went through 33 hardcover editions before a paperback version finally appeared in 1970. ❖ See also *Women in World History*.

DAVIS, Alice Brown (1852–1935). American Seminole Indian leader. Born Alice Brown, Sept 10, 1852, near Park Hill, Cherokee Nation, in Indian Territory (present-day Oklahoma); died June 21, 1935, in Wewoka, Oklahoma; dau. of Dr. John Frippo Brown (surgeon for the Seminoles during their forced removal from Florida) and Lucy Redbeard Brown (Seminole); m. George Rollin Davis, 1874; children: 11. ❖ Served as interpreter for Seminole delegations in Mexico, interpreter for Seminoles in court, and superintendent of tribal girls' boarding school, Emahaka (1906); appointed chief of Seminoles by President Harding (1922), because a chief's signature was required on deed disposing of Emahaka school property; when she refused to deed property before reimbursement to Seminoles, was removed from office.

DAVIS, Altovise (1935—). See Gore, Altovise.

DAVIS, Angela (1944—). African-American revolutionary and activist. Name variations: Angela Y. Davis. Born Angela Yvonne Davis on Jan 26, 1944, in Birmingham, Alabama; dau. of B. Frank Davis (gas station owner) and Sallye B. Davis (teacher); Brandeis University, BA magna cum laude and Phi Beta Kappa; attended Goethe University, Frankfurt, 1965–67, and University of California at San Diego, 1967–69; m. Hilton Braithwaite, 1980 (div. several years later); no children. ❖ Revolutionary activist, scholar, and Communist who gained fame when prosecutors claimed she had assisted a courtroom rebellion by radical black prisoners; joined Communist Party (July 1968); taught at UCLA (1969–70); convinced they were being targeted because of their political views, became a vocal defender of 3 black radicals, including George Jackson, who had been incarcerated in Soledad Prison and accused of killing a white prison guard, though there was little evidence (early 1970); became involved with Jackson and published a collection of his letters, *Soledad Brother* (1970); when Jackson's younger brother took a gun from her closet and used it in an attempt to free 3 other radical black prisoners from a courtroom in Marin Co. which resulted in 4 deaths, was sought for murder, kidnapping, and conspiracy to commit murder and

rescue prisoners, though she had been nowhere near the courthouse; went underground (Aug 9, 1970), but was arrested (Oct 13, 1970); was acquitted of all charges in a highly publicized political trial (June 4, 1972); served as co-chair of the National Alliance Against Racist and Political Repression (1973); was full-time lecturer, San Francisco State University (1978); was vice-presidential candidate on the Communist Party ticket (1980 and 1984); served on board of directors, National Black Women's Health Project (1983); challenged Communist Party (1991); endorsed Committees of Correspondence (1992); writings include *Women, Race and Class* (1981), *Women, Culture and Politics* (1989) and *Blues Legacies and Black Feminism: Gertrude "Ma" Rainey, Bessie Smith, and Billie Holiday* (1998). Received Lenin Peace Prize (1979). ❖ See also memoir *If They Come in the Morning* (Signet, 1971) and *An Autobiography* (International, 1988); and *Women in World History*.

DAVIS, Bessie McCoy (1888–1931). See McCoy, Bessie.

DAVIS, Bette (1908–1989). American actress. Born Ruth Elizabeth Davis in Lowell, Massachusetts, April 5, 1908; died Oct 6, 1989, in Paris, France; dau. of Harlow and Ruth (Favor) Davis; sister of Barbara ("Bobby") Davis; m. Harlan (Ham) Nelson, Aug 1932 (div. 1938); m. Arthur Farnsworth, Dec 30, 1941 (died Aug 1943); m. William Grant Sherry (ex-Navy man), Nov 29, 1945 (div.); m. Gary Merrill (actor), July 28, 1950; children: (3rd m.) Barbara Davis Sherry (called "B.D."); (4th m.) adopted Margot and William. ❖ Two-time Oscar-winning actress, enjoyed 1st public exposure in summer repertory performances (1927), followed by Broadway appearances (1929–30); after a screentest with Universal, embarked on a 55-year film career (1931–86), and became the reigning queen of American cinema, known for her portrayals of strong-willed females capable of overcoming tragedy and outwitting domineering men; 1st came to the attention of critics as the mean-spirited Mildred in *Of Human Bondage* (1936); awarded Oscar as Best Actress for *Dangerous* (1935) and *Jezebel* (1938); gained popularity with *Now, Voyager* (1942); made over 80 films, including *The Petrified Forest* (1936), *Dark Victory* (1939), *Juarez* (1939), *The Old Maid* (1939), *The Private Lives of Elizabeth and Essex* (1939), *All This and Heaven, Too* (1940), *The Letter* (1940), *The Little Foxes* (1941), *The Man Who Came to Dinner* (1941), *Watch on the Rhine* (1943), *Old Acquaintance* (1943), *Mr. Skeffington* (1944), *The Corn Is Green* (1945), *Beyond the Forest* (1949), *All About Eve* (1950), *Phone Call from a Stranger* (1952), *The Virgin Queen* (1955), *A Catered Affair* (1956), *A Pocketful of Miracles* (1961), *Whatever Happened to Baby Jane?* (1962), *Hush, Hush . . . Sweet Charlotte* (1965), *The Nanny* (1965), *Burnt Offerings* (1976), *Return from Witch Mountain* (1978), *Death on the Nile* (1978) and *The Whales of August* (1987). Was the 1st woman awarded American Film Institute's Lifetime Achievement Award (1977). ❖ See also memoirs (with Michael Herskowitz) *This 'n That* (Putnam, 1987) and *The Lonely Life* (Putnam, 1962); Barbara Leaming, *Bette Davis: A Biography* (Simon & Schuster, 1992); Whitney Stein, *Mother Goddam* (Hawthorne, 1974); James Spada, *More Than a Woman: An Intimate Biography of Bette Davis* (Bantam, 1993); and *Women in World History*.

DAVIS, Clarissa (1967—). African-American basketball player. Name variations: Clarissa Davis-Wrightsil. Born June 4, 1967, in San Antonio, Texas; University of Texas at Austin, BA; m. Jerald Wrightsil. ❖ At Barcelona Olympics, won a bronze medal in team competition (1992). Twice named Naismith Player of the Year; won the Wade Trophy; played in ABL (1996–98); played for WNBA Phoenix Mercury (1999).

DAVIS, Dorothy Hilliard (1917–1994). American aviator. Born Dorothy Hilliard Davis in 1917; died in San Francisco, California, May 25, 1994; dau. of Oscar Harris Davis and "Dottie" Davis; graduated in 1944 from Class 44-W-10, the last group of WASPs to graduate before the organization was deactivated. ❖ Member of the Women's Air Service Pilots (WASP) during World War II, who played a crucial role in the campaign to gain official government recognition for the WASPs as military veterans, which was successfully achieved in 1977. ❖ See also *Women in World History*.

DAVIS, Fanny Jane (1879–1952). See Alda, Frances.

DAVIS, Fay (1872–1945). American actress. Born Dec 15, 1872, in Boston, Massachusetts; died Mar 1, 1945, in Exmouth, England; m. Gerald Lawrence. ❖ Sailed for England, where she joined Charles Wyndham's Company and made stage debut in *A Squire of Dames* (1895); other plays include *The Prisoner of Zenda, As You Like It, The Ambassador, The Masqueraders, In Days of Old, Iris* (title role), *Caesar's Wife, Searchlights* and *Hamlet*; made NY debut in *Imprudence* (1902), followed by *Lady Rose's Daughter, Whitewashing Julia, The Rich Mrs. Repton, Man and Superman* and *The Duel;* in films, appeared in *Enoch Arden* and as Margaret Dishart in *The Little Minister* (1915).

DAVIS, Frances Elliott (1882–1965). African-American nurse. Name variations: Frances Reed Elliott Davis; Frances Elliott Reed. Born Frances Elliott, April 28, 1882, near Shelby, North Carolina; died of a heart attack, May 2, 1965, in Mount Clemens, Michigan, just days before she was to be honored at an American Red Cross national convention; dau. of Emma Elliott (white dau. of a plantation owner) and Darryl Elliott (part black, part Cherokee sharecropper); Knoxville College, TN, teaching degree, 1907; m. William A. Davis (musician), Dec 24, 1921. ❖ The 1st African-American nurse officially enrolled in the American Red Cross (July 1918), was employed by the Reed family who supplied her funds to attend Knoxville College; changing her name to Reed, entered Freedmen's Hospital Training School for Nurses in Washington, DC (1910); worked as private-duty nurse in Washington for 3 years; was the 1st African-American nurse accepted into American Red Cross (ARC) Town and Country Nursing Service course at Columbia University Teachers College; sent to ARC Town and Country Nursing Service in Jackson, TN (July 1917) to offer nursing services; during WWI, worked as ARC Public Health Service nurse in TN (1918); organized and sought funding to create the 1st training school for African-American nurses at Dunbar Hospital in Detroit; awarded Rosenwald fellowship to pursue a bachelors degree at Columbia University Teachers College (1929), but was too ill to accept; served on staff of Eloise Hospital in Wayne Co., Michigan (1945–51).

DAVIS, Gail (1925–1997). American actress. Born Bette Jeanne Grayson, Oct 5, 1925, in Little Rock, Arkansas; died Mar 15, 1997, in Los Angeles, California; attended University of Texas at Austin; m. Bob Davis, 1944 (div. 1952); children: Terrie Davis (b. 1952). ❖ Television's 1st female Western star, appeared on "Annie Oakley" (1953–56); in reality, was an expert equestrian and crack rifle shot. Inducted into National Cowgirl Museum and Hall of Fame (2004).

DAVIS, Gladys (b. 1893). English fencer. Born 1893. ❖ At Paris Olympics, won a silver medal in individual foil (1924).

DAVIS, Hallie Flanagan (1889–1969). *See Flanagan, Hallie.*

DAVIS, Heather (1974—). Canadian rower. Born Feb 26, 1974, in Vancouver, British Columbia, Canada. ❖ Won a bronze medal for coxed eights at Sydney Olympics (2000).

DAVIS, Hilda (1905–2001). African-American educator. Born Hilda Andrea Davis, May 24, 1905, in Washington, DC; died Oct 6, 2001, in Newark, Delaware; dau. of Louis Alexander Davis and Ruth Gertrude (Cooke) Davis; graduate of Howard University, 1925; attended Radcliffe, 1929–31; earned doctorate in human development at University of Chicago. ❖ Signed on as dean of women and assistant professor of English at Shaw University (1932), a liberal arts college in Raleigh, North Carolina, founded for blacks; became director of women's activities and associate professor of English at Talladega College in Alabama (1936), then dean of women (one of the most beloved deans in the south). ❖ See also *Women in World History.*

DAVIS, Jessica (1978—). American rhythmic gymnast. Born April 10, 1978, in Greenbrae, California. ❖ At US nationals, came in 2nd (1993), 3rd (1994), 1st (1995, 1996); won a bronze medal in all-around at Pan American Games (1995).

DAVIS, Joan (1907–1961). American actress and comedian. Born Madonna Josephine Davis in St. Paul, Minnesota, June 29, 1907; died in Palm Springs, California, May 22, 1961; only dau. of LeRoy (train dispatcher) and Nina Davis; m. Serenus (Sy) Wills (comedian), 1931; children: Beverly Wills (b. 1933, actress). ❖ Known for her rubber-faced grimaces, sublime sense of timing, and broad slapstick style, began career in a vaudeville act with comedian Sy Wills; made film debut in *Millions in the Air* (1935); made over 30 films (1937–44), including *Sally, Irene and Mary* (1938), *Hold That Ghost* (1941), *Sun Valley Serenade* (1941), *Two Latins from Manhattan* (1941), *George White's Scandals* (1945), *If You Knew Susie* (1948), *Traveling Saleswoman* (1950), *The Groom Wore Spurs* (1951) and *Harem Girl* (1942); made a reluctant debut on the radio (1941), parodying the popular novelty song "Hey, Daddy," and soon had her own show; formed production company and produced her hit tv show "I Married Joan" (1952–57). ❖ See also *Women in World History.*

DAVIS, Judy (1955—). Australian actress. Born April 23, 1955, in Perth, Australia; attended National Institute of Dramatic Arts (1974–77); m. Colin Friels (actor), 1984; children: Jack and Charlotte Friels. ❖ Began career singing in jazz and pop groups; came to international prominence as Sybylla Melvyn in *My Brilliant Career,* picking up 2 BATFA awards (for Best Actress and Best Newcomer), and helping to kick-start new wave of Australian filmmaking; continued working in Sydney and London theater, while appearing in several modest cinematic efforts, including *Winter of Our Dreams* (1981) and *Heatwave* (1982); nominated for Academy Award for portrayal of Adela Quested in *A Passage To India* (1984); co-starred with husband in *Kangaroo* (1986) and *Hightide* (1987), winning Australian Film Institute's Best Actress award for 2 consecutive years; worked with Woody Allen (*Husbands And Wives,* 1992, and *Deconstructing Harry,* 1997), David Cronenberg (*Naked Lunch,* 1991) and Joel Coen (*Barton Fink,* 1991); portrayed George Sand in James Lapine's *Impromptu* (1991); nominated for Golden Globe for performance as WWII heroine Mary Lindell in *One Against the Wind* (1991); earned Australian Film Institute award for portrayal of schizophrenic in Canadian coming-of-age drama *On My Own* (1992); also appeared in Michael Tolkien's satirical *The New Age* (1994) and political comedy *Children of the Revolution* (1996), as well as in tv biopics about Lillian Hellman (1999) and Judy Garland (2001); won Emmy for "Serving in Silence" (1995); made directorial debut with "Barrymore" for Sydney Theatre Company; nominated for a Helpmann Award for performance in the play *Victory* (2004).

DAVIS, Katharine Bement (1860–1935). American penologist and social worker. Born Jan 15, 1860, in Buffalo, New York; died Dec 10, 1935, in Pacific Grove, California; dau. of Oscar Bill (businessman) and Frances (Bement) Davis; graduate of Rochester Free Academy, 1879; Vassar College, graduated with honors, 1892; attended Columbia University, 1892–93; University of Chicago, PhD in economics, 1900. ❖ Appointed superintendent of the newly opened Reformatory for Women at Bedford Hills, NY (1900), a post she would hold for 13 years; was instrumental in establishing a prison farm, a cottage system of housing, and vocational training courses for the women inmates; pioneered in identifying and separating reformable from repeat offenders; was appointed commissioner of correction for New York City (1914), the 1st woman to serve at a cabinet level in that municipality; was also general secretary and a member of the board of directors of the Bureau of Social Hygiene, a branch of the Rockefeller Foundation (1918–28). ❖ See also *Women in World History.*

DAVIS, Knox (1814–1835). *See Taylor, Knox.*

DAVIS, Lady (1923–1990). *See Davis, Pa Tepaeru Ariki.*

DAVIS, Marguerite (1889–1980). American illustrator of children's books. Born Feb 10, 1889, in Quincy, Massachusetts; died Dec 1980, in Tucson, Arizona; attended Vassar College and Boston Museum of Fine Arts School. ❖ Along with 1927 English translation of Johanna Spyri's *Heidi,* illustrated many books in 25-year career, including Christina Rossetti's *Sing-Song* (1924), Robert Louis Stevenson's *A Child's Garden of Verses* (1924), Louisa May Alcott's *Under the Lilacs* (1928), Laura E. Richards' *Tirra Lirra* (1932), and Elizabeth Coatsworth's *The Littlest House* (1940).

DAVIS, Marion (1876–1955). *See Mitchell, Marion.*

DAVIS, Mary. African-American musician. Name variations: S.O.S. Band. Born in Savannah, Georgia. ❖ Keyboardist and lead singer for pop-funk group, the S.O.S. ("Sounds of Success") Band, which was formed in Atlanta, GA (1977); with group, had smash hit with "Take Your Time (Do It Right) Part 1" from debut album, *S.O.S.* (1980), and released album, *S.O.S. III,* which included popular song, "High Hopes" (1982); with group, released album, *On the Rise* (1983), which included hits "Just Be Good to Me," "Tell Me If You Still Care," and "For Your Love," followed by *Just the Way You Like It* (1984), which included hit title track and "No One's Gonna Love You"; with group, released *Sands of Time* (1986), which included "The Finest" and "Borrowed Love"; left group to pursue solo career (1986); released debut album, *Separate Ways* (1990), which included single, "Don't Wear It Out"; rejoined S.O.S. members, Jason "TC" Bryant and Abdul Raoof, in new incarnation of band (1994), touring frequently.

DAVIS, Mary E.P. (c. 1840–1924). Canadian nurse. Born c. 1840 in New Brunswick, Canada; died June 9, 1924, in Norwood, Massachusetts; dau. of Charlotte (McFarland) Davis and John Davis (British army officer); graduate of Boston Training School for Nurses at Massachusetts General

Hospital, 1878. ❖ Contributor to nursing education, served as superintendent of University of Pennsylvania Hospital and Training School for nurses (1889–99); after attending a nursing convention at World's Fair in Chicago (1893), was a key organizer, later vice president (1894–95) and president (1896), of American Society of Superintendents of Training Schools for Nurses of United States and Canada, now called the National League for Nursing; served as committee chair on periodicals (1899–02) of Nurses' Associated Alumnae of United States and Canada, called the American Nurses Association from 1911; helped establish *American Journal of Nursing* (Oct 1900) and later served as president of its board of directors; helped establish (1903) and later served as president (1911–13) of Massachusetts Nurses Association.

DAVIS, Mary Evelyn (1844–1909). See Davis, Mollie Moore.

DAVIS, Mary Fenn (1824–1886). American spiritualist. Name variations: Mary Fenn; Mary Fenn Love. Born Mary Fenn Robinson, July 17, 1824, in Clarendon, Orleans Co., NY; died July 18, 1886, in West Orange, New Jersey; dau. of Chauncey and Damaris (Fenn) Robinson; m. Samuel G. Love (schoolteacher), 1846 (div.); m. Andrew Jackson Davis (spiritualist known as "Poughkeepsie Seer and Clairvoyant"), 1855 (marriage annulled); children: (1st m.) 2. ❖ With 2nd husband, founded *Herald of Progress* (Spiritualist newspaper) in NY (1860); wrote and lectured on such subjects as Harmonial Philosophy, temperance, and women's rights.

DAVIS, Moll. See Davies, Moll.

DAVIS, Mollie Moore (1844–1909). American poet, regional and children's writer. Name variations: Mollie Evelyn Moore; Mollie Evelyn Moore Davis; Mary Evelyn Davis. Born Mary Eveline Moore, April 12, 1844, in either Ladiga or White Plains, Alabama; died Jan 1, 1909, in New Orleans, Louisiana; dau. of John Moore and Mary Ann (Crutchfield) Moore; m. Major Thomas E. Davis (tobacco merchant, 1835–1917), Oct 20, 1874. ❖ Author of poetry, works for children, plays, and prose works set in Texas and Louisiana; early prose published in *Houston Telegram* and *New Orleans Picayune;* published best-known book, *In War Times at La Rose Blanche Plantation* (1888), and most popular book, *The Price of Silence* (1907); other works include *Minding the Gap* (verse 1967) and *An Elephant's Track and Other Stories* (1897).

DAVIS, Muriel (1941—). See Grossfeld, Muriel Davis.

DAVIS, Nancy (b. 1921). See Reagan, Nancy.

DAVIS, Pa Tepaeru Ariki (1923–1990). Cook Islands traditional leader. Name variations: Lady Davis. Born 1923; died Feb 1990; m. Thomas (Tom) Davis (Pa Tuterangi Ariki), later knighted as Sir Thomas Davis; children: 2 sons. ❖ Received the title of Pa Ariki at age 9; husband became premier of Cook Islands (1978), serving almost uninterruptedly until 1987; was elected president of House of Ariki (1980) and served until her death; with her quiet conciliatory personality, was much respected by Cook Islanders both at home and in New Zealand. Her death was marked by 2 days of official mourning in the Cook Islands, the only such official mourning ever recognized there. ❖ See also *Women in World History.*

DAVIS, Paulina Wright (1813–1876). American feminist, reformer and suffragist. Born Paulina Kellogg, Aug 7, 1813, in Bloomfield, NY; died Aug 24, 1876, in Providence, Rhode Island; dau. of Captain Ebenezer (volunteer in War of 1812) and Polly (Saxton) Kellogg; m. Francis Wright (merchant), Jan 1833 (died 1845); m. Thomas Davis (US congressional representative), April 1849; children: (2nd m.) 2 adopted daughters. ❖ With husband, helped organize an anti-slavery convention held in Utica (Oct 1835) and, as a consequence, suffered a mob attack on their house; joined Ernestine Rose in petitioning the New York legislature for a married women's property law (late 1830s); following husband's death (1845), used her sizable inheritance to continue her reform work; turned her energies to the cause of women's rights, taking the lead in plans for the 1st National Woman's Rights Convention, over which she presided (Oct 1850); began publishing, at her own expense, the monthly periodical *Una* (1853), one of the 1st publications devoted to women's rights; helped found the New England Woman Suffrage Association (1868), of which she was president until 1870. ❖ See also *Women in World History.*

DAVIS, Pauline Elaine (1966—). See Davis-Thompson, Pauline.

DAVIS, Pauline Morton (1887–1955). See Sabin, Pauline Morton.

DAVIS, Pearl (1899–1962). See Adler, Polly.

DAVIS, Rebecca Harding (1831–1910). American novelist. Born Rebecca Blaine Harding, June 24, 1831, in Washington, Pennsylvania; died in Mt. Kisco, New York, Sept 29, 1910; grew up in Huntsville, Alabama, and Wheeling, West Virginia; graduate of Washington (Pennsylvania) Female Seminary, 1848; m. L. Clarke Davis (editor of *Philadelphia Inquirer* and *Philadelphia Public Ledger*), Mar 1863; children: Richard Harding Davis (1864–1916, journalist); and others. ❖ The 1st novelist in the nation to introduce the labor question into fiction, began gaining her reputation for grim reality with *Life in the Iron Mills,* which was 1st published in the *Atlantic Monthly* (April 1861); contributed many short stories and sketches to periodicals, was contributing editor for the *New York Tribune,* and wrote a number of novels, including *A Law Unto Herself* (1878) and *Waiting for the Verdict* (1868), about racism in America; later works include *Dallas Galbraith, Berrytown, Natasqua, Silhouettes of American Life, Kent Hampden* and *Doctor Warrick's Daughters.* ❖ See also *Women in World History.*

DAVIS, Shirley Stobs (1942—). See Stobs, Shirley.

DAVIS, Skeeter (1931–2004). American country-and-western singer. Name variations: Born Mary Frances Penick, Dec 30, 1931, in Dry Ridge, Kentucky; died Sept 19, 2004, in Nashville, Tennessee; m. Ralph Emery (country music deejay), 1960 (div. 1964); m. Joey Stampinato (bassist). ❖ Began career with Betty Jack Davis as one-half of the Davis Sisters (1953); was critically injured in a car wreck and Betty Davis was killed (1953); came to prominence with the hit "The End of the World" (1963); sang on the "Grand Ole Opry" radio show for more than 40 years (1959–2004); other hits include "I'm Saving My Love" and "I Can't Stay Mad at You." ❖ See also autobiography, *Bus Fare to Kentucky* (1993).

DAVIS, Sophia Louisa (1847–1903). See Taylor, Sophia Louisa.

DAVIS, Theresa (1950—). American singer. Name variations: The Emotions. Born Aug 22, 1950, in Chicago, Illinois; cousin of Sheila, Jeanette, and Pamela Hutchinson (fellow Emotions members). ❖ With cousins, had R&B successes as the Emotions (1970s); though not an original member of group, joined when Jeanette Hutchinson left to get married (1970); with Emotions, had such hits as "So I Can Love You" (1969), "Show Me How" (1971), "I Don't Wanna Lose Your Love" (1976), and the #1 "Best of My Love," which was a Grammy winner. Emotions albums include *Untouched* (1970), *Flowers* (1976), *Sunshine* (1977), *Rejoice* (1977), *Come Into Our World* (1979), *New Affair* (1981), *Sincerely* (1984) and *If I Only Knew* (1985).

DAVIS, Varina Howell (1826–1906). American first lady. Name variations: Mrs. V. Jefferson Davis. Born Varina Anne Banks Howell, May 7, 1826, on Marengo plantation in Louisiana, near Natchez, Mississippi; died in New York, NY, Oct 16, 1906; dau. of William Burr Howell and Margaret Louisa (Kempe) Howell of The Briers plantation in Natchez; m. Jefferson Davis (1808–1889), Feb 26, 1845; children: Samuel Emerson (b. 1852); Margaret Howell Davis (b. 1855); Jefferson Davis, Jr. (b. 1857); Joseph Evan Davis (b. 1859); William Howell Davis (b. 1861); Varina Anne Davis, called Winnie Davis (1864–1898). ❖ Bright and well educated, married Jefferson Davis and moved to Brierfield plantation (1845); moved to Washington where husband would eventually serve in US House of Representatives and Senate, and be appointed secretary of war (1845–61); was first lady of the Confederacy (1861–65); traveled in Canada and Europe (1865–77); collaborated with husband in writing *The Rise and Fall of the Confederate Government* (1878–81); moved to New York (1892); completed a 1,638-page book, *Jefferson Davis: Ex-President of the Confederate States: A Memoir by His Wife* (1890); was a close friend of Mary Chesnut. ❖ See also Ishbel Ross, *First Lady of the South: The Life of Mrs. Jefferson Davis* (Harper, 1958); Gerry Van der Heuvel, *Crowns of Thorns and Glory: Mary Todd Lincoln and Varina Howell Davis: The Two First Ladies of the Civil War* (Dutton, 1988); and *Women in World History.*

DAVIS-THOMPSON, Pauline (1966—). Bahamian runner. Name variations: Pauline Elaine Davis. Born Pauline Elaine Davis, July 9, 1966, in the Bahamas; University of Alabama, BA, 1989; m. Mark Thompson (hurdler). ❖ Known as one of the "Golden Girls," won a silver medal for 4 x 100-meter relay at Atlanta Olympics (1996); won a gold medal for 4 x 100-meter relay and a silver medal for 200 meters at Sydney Olympics (2000); won a gold medal for 4 x 100-meter relay at World championships (1999); retired (2000). Given the Silver Jubilee Award (1998) and the Bahamas Order of Merit (2000); won Charley Major Award; inducted into Caribbean Hall of Fame.

DAVISON, Emily (1872–1913). English militant suffragist. Born Emily Wilding Davison in Blackheath, England, 1872; died June 8, 1913; dau. of Charles and Margaret Davison; London University, BA; obtained a 1st at Oxford in English Language and Literature. ❖ Joined the Women's Social and Political Union (WSPU, 1906) and was one of the chief leaders in the WSPU demonstration in London (June 1908); arrested while attempting to hand a petition to Herbert Asquith, then prime minister (1909), spent a month in jail; arrested for trying to enter a London hall where Lloyd George was making a speech, was again imprisoned; once more imprisoned, went on a hunger strike; after being force-fed 49 times, barricaded herself in her cell (public sympathy was on her side); became convinced that the conscience of Parliament would only be awakened by the sacrifice of a life; thus at the Epsom Derby (June 4, 1913), in full view of King George V and Queen Mary of Teck, rushed onto the course wrapped in a WSPU banner, grabbed the reins of Anmer, the king's horse, and was trampled; died 4 days later. ❖ See also Gertrude Colmore, *The Life of Emily Davison* (Women's Press, 1913); Ann Morley and Liz Stanley, *The Life and Death of Emily Davison* (Women's Press, 1988); and *Women in World History*.

D'AVRIL, Yola (1907–1984). French actress. Born April 8, 1907, in Lille, France; died Mar 2, 1984, in Port Hueneme, California. ❖ Made film debut in *The Dressmaker from Paris* (1925); other films include *Orchids and Ermine, American Beauty, The Noose* and *Lady Be Good.*

DAVY, Nadia (1980—). Jamaican runner. Born Dec 24, 1980, in Jamaica. ❖ Won a bronze medal for 4 x 400-meter relay at Athens Olympics (2004).

DAVY, Sarah (c. 1639–1670). British religious writer. Name variations: Sarah Roane Davy. Born Sarah Roane c. 1639; died 1670. ❖ Wrote Baptist conversion narrative *Heaven Realized, or the holy pleasure of daily intimate communion with God* (1670).

DAVYDENKO, Tamara. Belarusian rower. Born in USSR. ❖ Won a bronze medal for coxed eights at Atlanta Olympics (1996).

DAVYDOVA, Anastasia (1983—). Russian synchronized swimmer. Born Feb 2, 1983, in Moscow, USSR. ❖ At World championships, won gold medals for duet (2003) and team (2001 and 2003); with Anastasia Ermakova, won a gold medal for duet at Athens Olympics (2004), as well as a team gold medal.

DAVYDOVA, Yelena (1961—). Soviet gymnast. Name variations: Elena Davydova or Davidova. Born Aug 7, 1961, in Voronezh, Russia; m. Pavel Filatov (boxer). ❖ Won Antibes International (1976), Chunichi Cup (1978), USSR Cup (1980), and USSR nationals (1981); at Moscow Olympics, won gold medals in indiv. and team all-around and bronze medals for floor exercise and balance beam (1980), becoming the 1st female to perform a Tkachev on uneven bars and the 1st to perform an Arabian 1¾ on floor exercise; at World championships, won a gold medal in team all-around, silver in floor exercise, and bronze in all-around (1981); immigrated to Canada (1991).

DAVYS, Mary (1674–1731). Irish playwright and novelist. Born 1674 in Ireland; died 1731 in Cambridge, England; m. Peter Davys (Dublin schoolmaster). ❖ Wrote *The Northern Heiress, or the Humors of York* (1716), *The Reform'd Coquet, or the Memoirs of Amoranda* (1724), *The Works of Mrs. Davys* (1725) and *The Accomplish'd Rake, or the Modern Fine Gentleman* (1727).

DAW, Evelyn (1912–1970). American actress. Born Nov 16, 1912, in Geddes, South Dakota; died Nov 29, 1970, in San Diego, California; m. Stephen Smith (physician). ❖ Best known for role as Rita Wyatt opposite James Cagney in *Something to Sing About.*

DAW, Marjorie (1902–1979). American silent-film actress. Born Marguerite House, Jan 19, 1902, in Colorado Springs, Colorado; died Mar 18, 1979, in Huntington Beach, California; sister of Chandler House (film editor); trained as a opera singer by Geraldine Farrar; m. A. Edward Sutherland (director, div.). ❖ Appeared in juvenile parts in a number of Cecil B. De Mille productions; starred opposite Douglas Fairbanks Sr. in 7 films (1918–19); films include *Joan the Woman, Rebecca of Sunnybrook Farm, A Modern Musketeer, His Majesty the American, The River's End, Dinty, Revelation* and *Topsy and Eva*; retired with advent of sound.

DAWBIN, Annie Maria (1816–1905). Australian diarist. Name variations: Annie Maria Baxter. Born Annie Maria Hadden, Nov 24, 1816, in Exeter, Devonshire, England; died 1905; dau. of Elizabeth (Hall) Hadden and Major William Frederick Hadden; m. Lt. Andrew Baxter, 1834 (died 1855); m. Robert Dawbin. ❖ Stationed with 1st husband in Van Diemen's Land; recorded life experiences in diaries (1834–65), which were later published as *Memories of the Past, by a Lady in Australia* (1873).

DAWES, Dominique (1976—). African-American gymnast. Born Nov 20, 1976, in Silver Spring, Maryland. ❖ At Barcelona Olympics, won a bronze medal in team all-around (1992); at World championships, won silver medals for uneven bars and balance beam (1993); won US Classic (1993), American Classic, US nationals, American Cup and Hilton Challenge (1994); at Atlanta Olympics, won a gold medal for team all-around and a bronze medal for floor exercises (1996), the 1st African-American to win an individual event medal; placed 4th for team all-around at Sydney Olympics (2000).

DAWES, Eva (1912—). Canadian high jumper. Born Sept 17, 1912, in Canada. ❖ At Los Angeles Olympics, won a bronze medal in the high jump (1932).

DAWES, Sophia (1705–1840). *See Feuchères, Sophie, Baronne de.*

DAWIDOWICZ, Lucy (1915–1990). American scholar. Born Lucy Schildkret in New York, NY, June 16, 1915; died in New York, NY, Dec 5, 1990; dau. of Max and Dora (Ofnaem) Schildkret (Polish-Jewish immigrants); sister of Eleanor Schildkret; graduate of Hunter College, 1936; spent a year in Vilna working at YIVO Institute; m. Szymon M. Dawidowicz (Polish-Jewish activist), Jan 1948 (died 1979). ❖ Historian of the Holocaust, whose major work *The War Against the Jews, 1933–1945* (1975) argued that Hitler's ideological goals—the achievement of German racial purity and the annihilation of the Jews—determined his political and military goals, that Nazi Germany's drive towards war and the attempt to achieve world domination came from its murderous campaign against the Jews; also wrote *From that Time and Place: A Memoir 1938–1947* (1989), *The Golden Tradition: Jewish Life and Thought in Eastern Europe* (1967), *The Holocaust and the Historians* (1981) and *The Jewish Presence: Essays on Identity and History* (1977); was associate professor at New York's Yeshiva University. In later years, her political views moved to the neoconservative Right, her religion became Orthodox Judaism, and her former indifference to Zionism metamorphosed to one of being a passionate defender of a militarily strong Israel. ❖ See also *Women in World History*.

DAW KHIN MYO CHIT (1915–2003). Burmese journalist and short-story writer. Born 1915 in Burma; died 2003; Rangoon University, BA. ❖ Worked for independence movement; wrote columns for *Guardian Daily* and *Working People's Daily;* also wrote historical novel, *Anawrahta of Burma*, and short stories for magazines and journals.

DAW MI MI KHAING (1916–1990). Burmese educator. Born 1916 in Minhla, Burma; died 1990; obtained BA (Hons) from Rangoon University and BSc from King's College, London. ❖ Served as principal of a private school (1951–53); became blind after brain tumor, but learned to read and write in Braille; writings in English include *Burmese Family* (1946).

DAWN, Dolly (1916–2002). American big-band singer. Name variations: Billie Starr. Born Theresa Maria Stabile, Feb 3, 1916, in Newark, New Jersey; died Dec 11, 2002, in Englewood, New Jersey; cousin of Dick Stabile (bandleader). ❖ Launched career as Billie Starr; given the name Dolly Dawn, sang with George Hall's orchestra (1935), which broadcast nationally six days a week from the Taft hotel on CBS radio; led a group of 7 carved out of the band called "Dolly Dawn and Her Dawn Patrol"; granted leadership of the band by Hall who became her manager (1941); hit records include "It's a Sin to Tell a Lie," "You're a Sweetheart," "Robins and Roses" and "Little Yellow Basket"; recordings reissued (1976 and 2001). Walter Winchell coined the term "canary" for female singers when referring to her; inducted into Big Band Hall of Fame (1998).

DAWN, Hazel (1891–1988). American musical star. Name variations: The Pink Lady. Born Hazel LaTout, Mar 23, 1891, in Ogden, Utah; died Aug 28, 1988, in New York, NY; m. Charles Groehl (also seen as Gruwell and Gruelle, mining engineer), 1927; children: Hazel Dawn Jr. (actress and singer). ❖ Made triumphant stage debut in London in *Dear Little Denmark* (1909); made sensational NY debut starring as Claudine in hit musical *The Pink Lady* (1911); starred in such musicals as *The Little Café, The Debutante, The Century Girl, Up in Mabel's Room, Getting Gertie's Garter* and *Ziegfeld Follies*; joined Famous Players and made many films, including *One of Our Girls, The Heart of Jennifer, The Sales*

Lady, Devotion, Under Cover and *The Lone Wolf* (1916–27); retired (1931); appeared in *Margie* (1946).

DAWN, Isabel (1905–1966). American actress and screenwriter. Born Oct 20, 1905, in Evansville, Indiana; died June 29, 1966, in Woodland Hills, California; m. Ray Herr. ❖ As an actress, appeared on Broadway and in films; as a writer, wrote such screenplays as *If I Had a Million, Girl of the Golden West, The French Line, Behind the News, Ice-Capades, Lady for a Night, Remember Pearl Harbor* and *Goodnight Sweetheart.*

DAW SAN SAN (1944–1990). Burmese novelist and short-story writer. Name variations: (pseudonym) Moe Moe. Born 1944; died 1990. ❖ Worked as magazine editor; writings include *Lost and Wondering, Ngapali Story, A Thing Called Love, A Hundred Wild Flowers* and *We Live in Burma.* Won 4 National Literary Awards (1974, 1980, 1982, 1986).

DAWSON, Alice Madge (c. 1980–2003). Australian feminist. Born Alice Madge Burton in Echunga, South Australia; Adelaide University, BA; m. David Dawson (teacher and actor), 1934; children: Paddy; (adopted) Sean. ❖ One of the pioneers of the women's movement in Australia, introduced women's studies into the Department of Adult Education at University of Sydney (late 1950s); was also an outspoken advocate for Aboriginal rights and opposed the Vietnam War and nuclear armament.

DAWSON, Elida (1895–1975). *See Webb, Elida.*

DAWSON, Louisa Alice (1856–1926). *See Baker, Louisa Alice.*

DAWSON, Mary Elizabeth (1833–1924). New Zealand social leader and landowner. Name variations: Mary Elizabeth Prebble. Born Mary Elizabeth Prebble, 1833, in Mersham, Kent, England; died Feb 22, 1924, at Waterton, New Zealand; dau. of James (carpenter) and Ann Maria (Gurr) Prebble; m. Andrew Dawson, 1852; children: 12. ❖ Immigrated to Wellington, New Zealand, with family (1840); converted 1,460 acres of swamp into arable and successful farm by draining and stabilizing it with trees (1870s); served as nurse to Waterton community. ❖ See also *Dictionary of New Zealand Biography* (Vol. 1).

DAWSON, Nancy (c. 1735–1767). English theatrical dancer. Born c. 1735 in London, England; died June 9, 1767, in London. ❖ One of the best-known performers of her time, worked in traveling puppet troupe during adolescence; joined Sadler's Wells Theatre company, mainly as specialty dancer and as Columbine in company's harlequinades (c. 1755); performed at Covent Garden in London for 3 seasons (1757–60) and was soon widely known for her specialty, the hornpipe, which she also interpolated in company's version of *The Beggar's Opera* (1759); performed 3 seasons at Drury Lane, appearing in Garrick's production of *The Beggar's Opera.*

DAY, Alice (1905–1995). American silent-film actress. Born Jacquline Alice Newlin, Nov 7, 1905, in Colorado Springs, Colorado; died May 25, 1995, in Orange, California; sister of Marceline Day (actress). ❖ Began film career as one of Mack Sennett's bathing beauties; eventually played leads in silents of 1920s and '30s.

DAY, Ann (c. 1837–?). *See Vitelli, Annie.*

DAY, Doris (1924—). American singer and actress. Born Doris von Kappelhoff in Cincinnati, Ohio, April 3, 1924; m. Al Jorden (trombone player), Mar 1941 (div. 1943); m. George Weidler (saxophone player and brother of Virginia Weidler), 1946 (div. 1949); m. Marty Melcher (producer-manager), April 3, 1951 (died 1968); m. restaurateur Barry Comden (div. 1981); children: (1st m.) Terry Melcher (1942–2004). ❖ One of the most popular film stars of 1950s, began career as a band singer for Bob Crosby; toured with Les Brown's band, introducing song "Sentimental Journey" which became a million seller (1943); replaced Betty Hutton in film *Romance on the High Seas* (1945); embarked on a series of 14 movies for Warner Bros. and was labeled Hollywood's girl-next-door, even though she'd occasionally take on dramatic roles in such films as *Young Man with a Horn* (1950), *Love Me or Leave Me* (1955), and *The Man Who Knew Too Much* (1956), which also produced the Oscar-winning song "Que Sera, Sera"; was also a leading moneymaker for Columbia Records for over 4 years; saw film career peak (1960s) while starring in a series of sophisticated bedroom farces opposite such co-stars as Rock Hudson and James Garner; married her agent Marty Melcher (1951), who managed her earnings; at time of his death (1968), learned that $20 million had been squandered, leaving her heavily in debt, and that she was committed to a tv series, "The Doris Day Show" (1968–73); left show business (1981), devoting herself to the animal-rights movement; other films include *Tea for Two* (1950), *Lullaby*

of Broadway (1951), *On Moonlight Bay* (1951), *By the Light of the Silvery Moon* (1953), *Calamity Jane* (1953), *Young at Heart* (1955), *The Pajama Game* (1957), *Teacher's Pet* (1958), *Please Don't Eat the Daisies* (1960), *Midnight Lace* (1960) and *Send Me No Flowers* (1964). Nominated for Academy Award for *Pillow Talk* (1959). ❖ See also autobiography (with A.E. Hotchner) *Doris Day: Her Own Story* (Morrow, 1976); and *Women in World History.*

DAY, Dorothy (1897–1980). American activist. Born Dorothy Day, Nov 8, 1897, in Brooklyn, New York; died Nov 29, 1980; dau. of John and Grace (Saterlee) Day; m. Barkeley Tobey (div.); married (common law) Forster Batterham; children: (2nd m.) Tamar (b. 1926). ❖ Pacifist and radical who founded the *Catholic Worker* newspaper and ran the movement's New York House of Hospitality, spent her youth as a hard-drinking radical journalist in Greenwich Village, roaming the poorest sections of NY's slums, writing about strikes, hunger, and the struggle of impoverished immigrant workers for living wages; had love affairs with several literary celebrities of her day, including playwright Eugene O'Neill; volunteered for the Anti-Conscription League, which tried to prevent young men from being drafted to fight in WWI; published autobiographical novel, *The Eleventh Virgin* (1924); converted to Catholicism (1927) and became a different kind of radical, as dedicated as before to social justice but now in the context of strict religious orthodoxy; issued 1st *Catholic Worker* (May 1, 1933); decided to live among the poor by running a House of Hospitality, always open, in which hungry men and women were fed, clothed, and sheltered, with no questions asked about their origins or experiences, and no effort to feed them religion before dinner; published *From Union Square to Rome* (1937); jailed with Mexican migrant workers, California (1973). Many American Catholics in the early years of the Catholic Worker movement disliked and mistrusted her, but by the last years of her life in the 1970s she was a widely acclaimed figure, taken by Catholic activists as a prophet and forerunner of the modern church. ❖ See also autobiography, *The Long Loneliness* (1952); Robert Coles, *Dorothy Day: A Radical Devotion* (Addison-Wesley, 1987); William Miller, *Dorothy Day: A Biography* (Harper & Row, 1982); June O'Connor, *The Moral Vision of Dorothy Day: A Feminist Perspective* (Crossroad, 1991); Nancy L. Roberts, *Dorothy Day and the Catholic Worker* (SUNY Press, 1984); and *Women in World History.*

DAY, Edith (1896–1971). American-born musical-comedy star. Born Edith Marie Day, April 10, 1896, in Minneapolis, Minnesota; died May 2, 1971, in London, England; m. Carle E. Carlton (div.); m. Pat Somerset (div.). ❖ Actress, singer, and dancer, made NY stage debut in *Pom-Pom* (1916); starred on Broadway in *Going Up* and gave 670 performances in the title role of *Irene*, in which she introduced the song "Alice Blue Gown"; journeyed to London to appear in the same play and became the toast of the town (1920); briefly returned to NY for *Orange Blossoms* and *Wildflower*, before settling in London and subsequently appearing in *Rose Marie, The Desert Song, Showboat* and *Rio Rita*; was known as the Queen of Drury Lane; made film debut (1917); retired (1930s) but returned to the stage for Noel Coward's *Sail Away* (1962).

DAY, Frances (1907–1984). American-born actress and singer. Born Frances Victoria Schenk, Dec 16, 1907, in New York, NY; died April 1984 in Brighton, England; m. Beaumont Alexander (div.). ❖ Made US cabaret debut, appearing with Texas Guinan; made London cabaret debut (1925); debuted on London stage in *Out of the Bottle* (1932), followed by *Cold Blood, Jill Darling, The Fleet's Lit Up, Du Barry was a Lady, Separate Rooms* and *Latin Quarter*; films include *Such Is the Law, The Girl from Maxim's, Two Hearts in Waltz Time, Dreams Come True, Room for Two* and *Tread Softly.*

DAY, Josette (1914–1978). French actress. Born Josette Dagory, July 31, 1914, in Paris, France; died June 29, 1978, in Paris; m. Marcel Pagnol (playwright, director, div.); m. a Belgian industrialist. ❖ Made film debut at age 5; best known for her roles in films of Marcel Pagnol and Jean Cocteau, including Beauty in *Beauty and the Beast.*

DAY, Lady (c. 1915–1959). *See Holiday, Billie.*

DAY, Laraine (1917—). American actress. Name variations: Laraine Johnson. Born Laraine Johnson, Oct 13, 1917, in Roosevelt, Utah; dau. of Mormons; m. Ray Hendricks (singer), 1942 (div. 1947); m. Leo Durocher (baseball manager), 1947 (div. 1960); m. Michael Grilkhas (also seen as Grilikhes, tv producer), 1960. ❖ Made film debut in *Stella Dallas* (1937); achieved popularity appearing as Nurse Mary Lamont in 7 of MGM's "Dr. Kildare" series; other films include *Border G-Men, The Painted Desert, Sergeant Madden, Tarzan Finds a Son,*

Foreign Correspondent, Mr. Lucky, Journey for Margaret, The Locket, Keep Your Powder Dry, Woman on Pier 13, The High and the Mighty and *House of Dracula's Daughter;* author of *The America We All Love.* ❖ See also memoirs *Day with Giants* (1952).

DAY, Marceline (1907–2000). American silent-film actress. Born Marceline Newlin, April 24, 1907, in Colorado Springs, Colorado; died Feb 16, 2000, in Cathedral City, California; sister of Alice Day (actress); m. Arthur J. Klein; m. John Arthur, 1959. ❖ Starred opposite such actors as Lon Chaney, John Barrymore, Harry Langdon, Stan Laurel, and Buster Keaton; films include *The Beloved Rogue, The Cameraman, The Boy Friend, The White Outlaw* and *Rookies.*

DAYDÉ, Liane (1932—). French ballet dancer. Name variations: Liane Dayde; Liane Daydé-Giraud. Born Feb 27, 1932, in Paris, France. ❖ At 10, made debut dancing a "Golliwog" in Albert Aveline's *Jeux d'Enfants* at Paris Opéra Ballet; joined Paris Opéra's professional company around age 15, performing major role in Aveline's *Elvire* (1948); danced principal roles in numerous works by Aveline and Serge Lifar, including *Snow White* (1951), *Fourberries* (1952) and *Romeo and Juliet* (1955); danced with Grand Ballet du Marquis de Cuevas (late 1950s); was prima ballerina of Grand Ballet Classique de France; appeared with numerous European companies, often in works by Heinz Rosen, and performed in US.

DAYDREAM, Princess (1887–1917). *See Brovar, Anna Iakovlevna.*

DAYKARHANOVA, Tamara (1889–1980). Russian-born actress and acting coach. Born Jan 14, 1889, in Moscow, Russia; died Aug 2, 1980, in Englewood, New Jersey. ❖ Began career with the Moscow Art Theater; came to NY (1929); with Akim Tamiroff and Maria Ouspenskaya, opened a drama school, which she headed until retirement (1971); on Broadway, appeared in *Chauve-Souris, The House of Bernarda Alba, The Emperor's Clothes, Bullfight* and *The Three Sisters.*

DAZIE, Mademoiselle (1882–1952). American dancer. Name variations: Mlle Dazie. Born Daisy Peterkin, Sept 18, 1882, in St. Louis, Missouri; raised in Detroit; died Aug 12, 1952, in Miami Beach, Florida; m. Mark A. Luescher; m. Cornelius Fellowes. ❖ Made debut as a child in vaudeville at Wonderland Theater, Detroit; in NY, appeared in *The Belle of New York* (1900), followed by *Buster Brown* (1905); appeared in leading music halls in London, Paris, Berlin and Vienna, then came to prominence in NY at Wisteria Grove under name La Domino Rouge (1904), a mysterious Russian dancer who did not speak English and performed in a red mask; was principal dancer at Metropolitan Opera (1906) and appeared in other musical comedies, notably as La Sylphide in *La Belle Paree,* Romance in *Maid in America,* and Aphrodasia in *Aphrodite,* among others; in Paris, appeared in *The Follies of 1907* and *1908;* performed in vaudeville with her own dance company (1909–11); starred in film serials, including *The Black Panther's Cub* (1921).

D'COSTA, Jean (1937—). Jamaican poet and children's writer. Born 1937 in Jamaica; educated at University of West Indies, University College, London, and universities of Oxford and Indiana. ❖ Taught literature at University of West Indies; writings include *Sprat Morrison* (1972), *Escape to Last Man Peak* (1975), and (with Barbara Lalla) *Language in Exile: Three Hundred Years of Jamaican Creole* (1990); with Velma Pollard, edited short-story anthology *Over Our Way* (1981).

DEACON, Susan. Scottish politician. Born in Musselburgh, Scotland. ❖ As a Labour candidate, elected to the Scottish Parliament for Edinburgh East and Musselburgh (1999).

DE ACOSTA, Mercedes (1893–1968). American screenwriter. Born Mar 1, 1893, in NY; died May 9, 1968, in New York, NY; dau. of Ricardo de Acosta; m. Abram Poole (painter), May 11, 1920 (div. 1935); no children. ❖ Poet, playwright and scenarist, is best remembered for her liaisons with beautiful and famous women, among them Eleonora Duse, Isadora Duncan, Marie Doro, Alla Nazimova, Eva Le Gallienne, Ona Munson and Marlene Dietrich, as well as Greta Garbo, who was perhaps the great love of her life. ❖ See also memoir *Here Lies the Heart* (Reynal, 1960); Hugo Vickers, *Loving Garbo* (Random House, 1994); and *Women in World History.*

DEAKIN, Pattie (1863–1934). Australian prime-ministerial wife. Born Elizabeth Martha Anne Browne, Jan 1, 1863, in Australia; died Dec 30, 1934, Point Lonsdale, Victoria; m. Alfred Deakin (2nd prime minister of Australia, 1903–04, 1905–08, 1909–10), April 3, 1882; children: Ivy Deakin (b. 1883, as Lady Ivy Brookes, was on the executive council of the National Council of Women, Victoria [1912–40]); Stella Deakin Rivett

(b. 1886, research chemist), and Vera Deakin White (b. 1891). ❖ Active in the delegation lobbying for the Commonwealth of Australia Constitution Bill (1900); participated in the ceremonial opening of the 1st parliament (May 9, 1901); organized a national Exhibition of Women's Work (1907); active in the "Deakinite" Liberal Party. Named Commander of the British Empire (CBE, 1935). ❖ See also Diana Langmore, *Prime Ministers' Wives* (McPhee Gribble, 1992).

DE ALMANIA, Jacqueline Felicia (fl. 1322). Parisian doctor. Name variations: Jacoba Felicie de Almania; Jacqueline Felicie de Almania; Jacoba d'Alamanie. Flourished 1322 in Paris. ❖ One of the most well known of medieval women doctors, practiced medicine in Paris and became involved in a long court battle over her right to practice; when the faculty of the medical school in Paris issued a ban on all physicians working without a license (1322), a move designed to protect the interests of university-trained physicians who were often less knowledgeable than midwives and healers, was arrested, fined, and excommunicated for her violation of the ban; eloquently but unsuccessfully argued her case. ❖ See also *Women in World History.*

DE ALMEIDA, Julia (1862–1934). *See Almeida, Julia Lopes de.*

DE ALONSO, Carmen (1909—). Chilean novelist and short-story writer. Name variations: (pseudonym) Margarita Carrasco. Born Carmen de Alonso in Chile in 1909. ❖ Writes about her homeland of Chile in a slightly revised *criollismo* style; though a true *criollista*'s work would bear and perpetuate the perspective only of its characters, offers a slightly more rounded view; unlike many of her Latin American peers, work is based in realism with a strong narrative flow and story line; writings include *Provena* (1935), *Gleba* (Clod, 1936), *Anclas en la cuidad* (Anchors in the City, 1941), *Y había luz de estrellas* (And Then There Was Starlight, 1950), *Medallones de luna* (Moon Medallions, 1956), and *La Cita* (The City, 1962).

DEAMER, Dulcie (1890–1972). Australian actress, novelist, playwright and journalist. Name variations: Mary Elizabeth Kathleen Dulcie Deamer. Born 1890 in Christchurch, New Zealand; died 1972; m. a business manager and divorced; children: 6. ❖ An overnight sensation at 17 as a writer of popular romance, eventually wrote 6 novels, a collection of short stories, *In the Beginning: Six Studies of the Stone Age and Other Stories* (1909), reprinted with illustrations as *As It Was in the Beginning,* 1929) and 2 vols. of poetry; also wrote plays, including *Easter;* an eccentric, was well known in Sydney Bohemian and literary circles (1920s–30s) and is best remembered for appearing at the Artists Ball in a leopard-skin costume (1923); wrote humorous articles for the *Women's Mirror, Truth* and *Daily Mirror.* ❖ See also autobiography, *Dulcie Deamer: The Queen of Bohemia.*

DEAN, Brenda (1943—). British trade unionist and baroness. Name variations: Baroness Dean of Thornton-le-Fylde. Born April 29, 1943, in Salford, England. ❖ The 1st woman to lead a major craft or industrial trade union, left high school at 16 and became a typist at a local printing firm; became administrative secretary for Manchester Society of Graphic and Allied Trades (SOGAT, 1959) and then assistant branch secretary (1971), branch secretary (1976), general president (1983), and general secretary (1985–91), its highest post; was member of Institute of Advanced Motorists and helped train disabled to drive; came to national attention during the printer's dispute with Rupert Murdoch's News International; became deputy chair of Graphical Paper and Median Union (1991–92); was awarded a life peerage and appointed to the House of Lords (1993), becoming a member of the House of Lords Appointments Commission; served as chair of Housing Corporation; appointed chair of Covent Garden Market Authority (2005).

DEAN, Dora (c. 1872–1950). African-American theatrical dancer. Name variations: Dora Babbige. Born c. 1872 in Covington, Kentucky; died Jan 1950 in Minneapolis, Minnesota. ❖ Had 1st major performance in *The Creole Show* in Boston (1889), where she danced the cakewalk to great acclaim; appeared with dance partner Charles Johnson at vaudeville theaters in NY and throughout Northeast, the 1st black dance duo booked as a "class act"; performed popular act at Madison Square Garden (1895) and toured Europe to great success; split from Johnson and returned to US (1914), where she performed on vaudeville circuits with the successful *Dora Dean and Co.* and *Dora Dean and Her Phantoms;* retired (1920s).

DEAN, Erica (1932—). *See Burstyn, Ellen.*

DEAN, Frances (1908–2000). *See Drake, Frances.*

DEAN, Janet (1949—). English politician and member of Parliament. Born Janet Gibson, Jan 28, 1949; m. Alan Dean, 1968 (died). ❖ Representing Labour, elected to House of Commons for Burton (1997, 2001, 2005).

DEAN, Jennie (1852–1913). African-American missionary and school founder. Name variations: Jane Serepta Dean. Born a slave in 1852 (some sources cite 1854); died 1913; dau. of Charles and Annie Dean (who were owned by the Cushing and Newson families in Prince William Co., Virginia). ❖ Concerned by the flight of black children from rural areas to the cities, encouraged parents to purchase land and keep their children home; helped establish the Mount Calvary Church (1880), which initially had met in the house her father had built; after 12 years of mission work, secured both local and national funding for the establishment of Manassas Industrial School for Colored Youth. ❖ See also *Women in World History*.

DEAN, Julia (1830–1868). American actress. Name variations: Julia Dean Hayne. Born July 22, 1830, in Pleasant Valley (now Cahoonzie) near Port Jervis, Orange Co., NY; died soon after childbirth in NY, Mar 6, 1868, and buried with her infant daughter; dau. of Julia Drake Dean (d. 1832, actress known for her work in Western theaters) and Edwin Dean (actor-manager); niece of Frances Denny Drake (actress); m. Dr. Arthur P. Hayne (son of Senator Robert Y. Hayne of South Carolina), Jan 21, 1855 (div.); m. James G. Cooper (federal official in Utah Territory), 1865; children: (1st m.) Arthur Hayne; Julia Hayne; 2 others died in infancy. ❖ Made NY debut as Julia in *The Hunchback* at Bowery Theatre (1846), a role that would remain her specialty; was also the original Norma in Epes Sargent's *Priestess* and the original Leonora de Guzman, mistress of Alphonso XI, king of Castile, in Boker's tragedy *Leonor de Guzman;* other NY plays include *The Lady of Lyons, The Wife, Jane Shore* and *Love's Sacrifice;* opened in San Francisco at Metropolitan Theatre in *The Hunchback* (1856) and performed primarily in the West for next decade; returned to the East and reestablished career in NY theaters; made last NY appearance at Broadway Theatre (1867).

DEAN, Julia (1878–1952). American stage and screen actress. Born May 13, 1878, in St. Paul, Minnesota; died Oct 17, 1952, in Hollywood, California; niece of Julia Dean (actress, 1830–1868); m. Orme Caldera. ❖ Made NY stage debut in *The Altar of Friendship* (1902), followed by *A Marriage of Reason, The Lily, Bought and Paid For, The Law of the Land, Her Own Money* and *The Magic Melody,* among others; films include *Matrimony, Rasputin the Black Monk, An Honorable Cad, The Curse of the Cat People, O.S.S., The Emperor Waltz* and *People Will Talk.*

DEAN, Laura (1945—). American dancer and choreographer. Born Dec 3, 1945, on Staten Island, NY; graduate of High School of Performing Arts, 1963; trained with Mia Slavenska, Lukas Hoving, Paul Sanasardo, and Merce Cunningham. ❖ Danced for short periods in NY with Paul Taylor Dance Company, Paul Sanasardo, Kenneth King, Meredith Monk, and Robert Wilson (1965–66); received recognition as choreographer for 1-minute solo *Medieval* (1965); founded Laura Dean Dance company (1971), renamed Laura Dean Dancers and Musicians (1976); worked closely with composer Steve Reich for such works as *Stamping Dance* (1971), *Jumping Dance* (1972) and *Walking Dance* (1973); choreographed for Joffrey Ballet, Ohio Ballet, Royal Danish Ballet, and New York City Ballet; taught at University of Texas, University of Rhode Island, and Pratt Institute; received a New York Dance and Performance (Bessie) award. Further works include *An Hour in Silence* (1970), *Drumming* (1975), *Night* (1980, for Joffrey Ballet), *Fire* (1982, for Joffrey), *Space* (1988, for New York City Ballet), *Earth* (1993, for Ohio Ballet), and *Cloud* (1994).

DEAN, Margie (1896–1918). American bandit. Name variations: Margie Celano; (alias) Mrs. Forbes. Born Margie Celano in Paris, France, 1896; died Nov 24, 1918; m. Dale Jones (alias Charles Forbes). ❖ Jailed in Chicago's Joliet Prison for jewelry-store theft; after release, took up with gang of outlaws headed by Frank "Jumbo" Lewis and married fellow gang member Dale Jones; with Lewis-Jones gang, was often driver in the then-new technique of bank robbing with a getaway car; when police followed Dean and Jones's Marmon touring car to gas station in Arcadia, Los Angeles, fired 1st, shooting LA deputy sheriff Michael V. Van Vliet in face; was then killed, along with Jones, when officers honeycombed their automobile with bullets (Nov 24, 1918).

DEAN, Minnie (1844–1895). *See Dean, Williamina.*

DEAN, Priscilla (1896–1987). American actress. Born Nov 25, 1896, in New York, NY; died Dec 27, 1987, in Leonia, New Jersey; dau. of stage actors; m. Wheeler Oakman (actor, div.); m. Lt. Leslie Arnold (flew around the world in 1924). ❖ As a child, began performing in her parents' stock company; was the principal soubrette in Eddie Lyons-Lee Moran comedy series; achieved stardom with serial *The Gray Ghost;* other films include *The Virgin of Stamboul, Under Two Flags, Waltz Time, Babes in Bagdad, East of Suez, The Saint, Lady Windermere's Fan, Anna Karenina* and *Moulin Rouge.*

DEAN, Vera Micheles (1903–1972). Russian-born American writer. Born Vera Micheles in St. Petersburg, Russia, Mar 29, 1903; died in New York City, Oct 10, 1972; dau. of Alexander Micheles (journalist) and Nadine (Kadisch) Micheles (translated English novels into Russian); moved to US (1919); became US citizen (1928); graduated with distinction from Radcliffe College, 1925; Yale University, MA, 1926; Radcliffe, PhD in international relations and international law, 1928; m. William Johnson Dean (attorney), Aug 1929 (died 1936); children: Elinor (b. 1933) and William (b. 1936). ❖ International relations analyst who opposed the worst excesses of McCarthyism to argue for a world peace based on US–Soviet détente; served as research director of Foreign Policy Association (1938–61); was an advisor to the American delegation at the founding conference of the UN in San Francisco (1945); taught at Harvard University, Barnard College, Smith College, University of Rochester, and the Graduate School of Public Administration of New York University; writings include *Europe in Retreat* (1941), *On the Threshold of World Order* (1944), *The Four Cornerstones of Peace* (1946), *The United States and Russia* (1948), *Foreign Policy Without Fear* (1953) and *Roads to Peace* (1962); also contributed to *The New Republic* and *The Christian Century.* Received French Legion of Honor (1947) and Jane Addams Medal (1954). ❖ See also *Women in World History.*

DEAN, Williamina (1844–1895). New Zealand murderer (accused). Name variations: Minnie Dean, Williamina McCulloch. Born Williamina McCulloch, Sept 2, 1844, at Renfrewshire, Scotland; died Aug 12, 1895, at Invergargill jail, New Zealand; dau. of John (engine driver) and Elizabeth (Swan) McCulloch; m. Charles Dean (innkeeper), 1872 (died 1908); children: 1 adopted daughter. ❖ Immigrated to New Zealand as widow with 2 daughters; after marriage, began taking in unwanted babies for payment (c. 1887); convicted of murdering infants for financial gain (1895), was sentenced to death by hanging (the scandal resulted in enactment of child-welfare legislation). ❖ See also *Dictionary of New Zealand Biography* (Vol. 2).

DEAN PAUL, Lady (1880–1932). *See Wieniawska, Irene Regine.*

DEANE, Doris (1900–1974). American actress. Name variations: Dorris Deane. Born Jan 20, 1900, in Wisconsin; died Mar 24, 1974, in Hollywood, California; m. Fatty Arbuckle, whose 1st wife was Minta Durfee (div.). ❖ Appeared in Fatty Arbuckle comedies.

DEANE, Helen Wendler (1917–1966). American histochemist. Name variations: Helen Deane Markham. Born 1917 in Massachusetts; died 1966; Wellesley College, BS; Brown University, PhD, 1944; m. Dr. George Markham, 1947. ❖ Histochemist who worked on fine structure of mammalian tissues, joined department of anatomy at Harvard University (1947); was forced out of Harvard after testifying before McCarthyite House Un-American Activities Committee about strongly held views on social injustice; struggled to find employment after leaving Harvard, experiencing double discrimination as woman in scientific field and an academic falsely labeled as a Communist; was hired as professor of anatomy at Albert Einstein College of Medicine in New York but experienced lapse in employment at this institution as well due to McCarthyite pressures. ❖ See also Ellen W. Schrecker, *No Ivory Tower: McCarthyism and the Universities of New York* (Oxford U. Press, 1986).

DEANE, Martha (1899–1976). *See McBride, Mary Margaret.*

DE ANGELI, Marguerite (1889–1987). American children's author and illustrator. Born Mar 14, 1889, in Lapeer, Michigan: died June 16, 1987, in Philadelphia, Pennsylvania; dau. of Shaddrach George (Eastman representative) and Ruby (Tuttle) Lofft; m. John Dailey de Angeli, April 2, 1910; children: John, Arthur, H. Edward (Ted), Nina, Catherine (died), and Maurice Bower (Maury). ❖ Was a concert and church soloist (1906–20s); illustrated articles for *Country Gentleman;* began writing and illustrating books (1935); won Newbery medal for *The Door in the Wall* (1950); other books include *Yonie Wondernose*

(1945), *Book of Nursery and Mother Goose Rhymes* (1955), *Black Fox of Lorne* (1957), *Marguerite de Angeli's Favorite Hymns* (1963) and the "Ted and Nina" series. Received Regina Medal (1968).

DE ANGELO, Ana Marie (1955—). American ballet dancer. Born 1955 in San Francisco area, California. ❖ Danced professionally with City Center Joffrey Ballet in New York City, appearing in numerous works by Joffrey, Gerald Arpino, and revivals of Frederick Ashton; performed with numerous companies as guest dancer and toured off-season with Stars of the American Ballet and Stars of the World Ballet, among others; danced at Pendleton Festival Ballet (1980); performed revivals of Anna Pavlova's repertory, often dancing Pavlova's parts; choreographed *Le Papillon* (1980), a tribute to Pavlova.

DEANS, Jane (1823–1911). New Zealand social leader and memoirist. Name variations: Jane McIlraith. Born Jane McIlraith, 1823, in Ayrshire, Scotland; died Jan 19, 1911, at Canterbury, New Zealand; dau. of James and Agnes (Caldwell) McIlraith; m. John Deans, 1852 (died 1854); children: 1. ❖ Immigrated to New Zealand with husband (1853); after husband's death, helped promote establishment of Presbyterian church and academy (1857). ❖ See also memoirs, *Letters to My Grandchildren* (1923); and *Dictionary of New Zealand Biography* (Vol. 1).

DEANS, Jeannie (1710–1791). See Walker, Helen.

DEARDURFF, Deena (1957–). American swimmer. Name variations: Deena Deardurff-Schmidt. Born May 1957 in Cincinnati, Ohio; graduate of San Diego State University; m. Bob Schmidt; children: Michael and Tyler. ❖ At Munich Olympics, won a gold medal in the 4 x 100-meter medley relay (1972); became head swimming coach at San Diego State.

DEARIE, Blossom (1926—). American jazz-pop singer and pianist. Born Blossom Dearie, April 28, 1926, in East Durham, NY; m. Bobby Jaspar (Belgian jazz woodwind player), 1956 (died 1963). ❖ Legendary jazz singer, who accompanied herself on piano, alone or with her trio or quartet; early in career, began singing with vocal groups like the Blue Flames (with Woody Herman's band) and the Blue Reys (with Alvino Rey's); moved to Paris (1952) and founded the group The Blue Stars of France, which hit the charts with a French version of "Lullaby of Birdland" (1954); signed with Verve (1956); recorded standards and wrote the song "Blossom's Blues"; formed her own record label, Daffodil Records (1965); had long career in New York supper clubs; albums include *My Gentleman Friend* (1959), *May I Come In?* (1964), *Blossom Dearie Sings* (1974) and *My Favorite Celebrity Is You* (1975); billed as The Jazz Singers, performed at Carnegie Hall with Anita O'Day and Joe Williams.

D'EAUBONNE, Françoise (1920—2005). See Eaubonne, Françoise d'.

DE AYALA, Josefa (1630–1684). Portuguese painter. Name variations: Josefa de Obidos; Josefa Aiala Figueira. Born Josefa Aiala Figueira in 1630, probably in Seville, Spain; died July 22, 1684; dau. of Baltazar Gomes Figueira and Catalina de Ayala y Cabrera. ❖ Living in the Quinta da Capeleira outside the walls of Obidos, became a fixture in her father's studio and early showed artistic talent; at 19, made engravings for the *Estatutos* for University of Coimbra; worked with a broad variety of mediums: oils, watercolors, ceramics, metals, and drawings; also did portraits, including that of the Portuguese queen Marie Françoise of Savoy (1646–1683). ❖ See also *Women in World History*.

DE BAISSAC, Lise (1905–2004). See Villameur, Lise.

DE BANZIE, Brenda (1915–1981). English stage, screen and tv actress. Name variations: Brenda De Banzie, Brenda DeBanza. Born July 28, 1915, in Manchester, England; died Mar 5, 1981, in Maywards Heath, Sussex, England; aunt of Lois de Banzie (b. 1930, actress); m. Rupert Marsh. ❖ Made London debut in *Du Barry Was a Lady* (1942), followed by *Point of Departure*, *Speaking of Murder* and *The Entertainer* (as Phoebe Rice); films include *Hobson's Choice*, *Doctor at Sea*, *The Man Who Knew Too Much*, *The Entertainer*, *The 39 Steps*, *Come September*, *The Mark*, *The Pink Panther* and *A Matter of Innocence*; appeared as Mrs. Dakers on "Walk's End" (1966).

DE BARANDAS, Ana (1806–1856). See Barandas, Ana Eurídice Eufrosina de.

DE BARY, Amy-Catherine (1944—). Swiss equestrian. Born Jan 29, 1944. ❖ At Los Angeles Olympics, won a silver medal in team dressage (1984).

DE BAWR, Baroness (1773–1860). See Bawr, Alexandrine de.

DE BEAUHARNAIS, Hortense (1783–1837). See Hortense de Beauharnais.

DE BEAUHARNAIS, Josephine (1763–1814). See Josephine, Empress.

DE BEAUVOIR, Simone (1908–1986). See Beauvoir, Simone de.

DEBECHE, Jamila (1925—). Algerian novelist. Born 1925 in Ghiras, Algeria. ❖ Worked for women's education and suffrage and founded feminist review *L'Action* (1947); writings include *Leila, jeune fille d'Algérie* (1947) and *Aziza* (1955).

DE BELO, Roseli (1969—). Brazilian soccer player. Name variations: Roseli. Born Sept 7, 1969, in Sao Paulo, Brazil. ❖ Forward or mid-fielder; considered the 1st great star of the Brazilian national team; scored over 200 goals in a career that spanned 15 years (1985–2000); played for Vasco da Gama; played for Washington Freedom (2001); won a team silver medal at Athens Olympics (2004).

DEBENHAM, Cicely (1891–1955). English actress and singer. Born April 17, 1891, in Aylesbury, England; died Nov 7, 1955; m. Guy Ridley. ❖ Made stage debut in *Alice in Wonderland* (1907), followed by *The Arcadians*, *The Mousmé*, *Princess Caprice*, *Oh Oh Delphine!*, *The Night Hawk*, *Ready Money*, *The Light Blues*, *Vivien* (later titled *My Lady Frayle*), *Zig-Zag*, *Who's Hooper?*, *My Girl*, *Patricia* and *Clo-Clo* (title role); made NY debut in *Hammerstein's Nine O'Clock Revue* (1923); appeared as Elsie Pester in the film *Charity* (1919).

DE BENSAUDE, Mrs. (1862–1919). See Cameron, Violet.

DEBERNARD, Danielle (1954—). French Alpine skier. Name variations: Daniele or Danièle Debernard. Born July 21, 1954, in Aime, France. ❖ Won a silver medal for slalom at Sapporo Olympics (1972) and a bronze medal for giant slalom at Innsbruck Olympics (1976); won a World championship for combined (1976).

DEBERTSHÄUSER, Monika. East German cross-country skier. Name variations: Debertshauser or Debertshaeuser. Born in East Germany. ❖ Won a bronze medal for the 4 x 5 km relay at Innsbruck Olympics (1976).

DE BETTIGNIES, Louise (d. 1918). French spy. Name variations: Alice Dubois. Born Louise de Bettignies in Lille, France; died in prison, Sept 27, 1918. ❖ At onset of World War I, fled the German invasion along with many other French refugees (1914); enlisted by the British as a spy, returned to France under name Alice Dubois; posing as a lace peddler, worked out of her hometown of Lille and enlisted some 40 agents; made trips to Holland once a week carrying hidden information; died in prison a few weeks before the end of the war. ❖ See also *Women in World History*.

DE BEUS, Bernadette de (1958—). Dutch field-hockey player. Name variations: Det de Beus. Born Anna Maria Bernadette de Beus, Feb 18, 1958, in Utrecht, Netherlands. ❖ One of her nation's best goalkeepers and the 1st in women's field hockey to wear a mask, won an Olympic gold medal at Los Angeles (1984) and a silver at Seoul (1988), both in team competition; played goal for Holland (1978–88).

DE BLOIS, Natalie (1921—). American architect. Name variations: Natalie De Blois. Born April 2, 1921, in Patterson, New Jersey; dau. of civil engineer; Columbia School of Architecture, BA, 1944; attended École des Beaux-Arts, 1951; children: 4 sons. ❖ Joined fledgling NY architectural firm Skidmore, Owings & Merrill, which was responsible for pioneering modern glass curtain-wall office building (1944); rose at Skidmore from draftsperson to participating associate; worked alongside star architects of firm, such as William Brown, Louis Skidmore, and Gordon Bunshaft; served as senior designer on buildings generally regarded as among the finest examples of the glass-curtain style; made design associate (1968); left Skidmore after 30 years to pursue writing and teaching (1974); addressed hardships and limitations faced by women in architecture and was an active member of American Institute of Architects Task Force on Women; joined Houston firm of Neuhaus & Taylor, as senior project designer (1975); began teaching design studio at University of Texas (1980) and remained as adjunct professor until 1990. Worked as design co-coordinator and senior designer on many well-known buildings such as Terrace Plaza Hotel (Cincinnati, 1948), Connecticut General Life Insurance Company Building (Bloomfield, CT, 1957), Pepsi-Cola Building on Park Avenue (originally Olivetti Building, 1959), Union Carbide Building, Emhart Manufacturing Company Building (1962), and Boots Building (Nottingham, England, 1968). ❖ See also Judith Paine, *Natalie de Blois: Women in American Architecture: A Historic and Contemporary Perspective* (Whitney Library of Design: 1977).

DEBO, Angie (1890–1988). American scholar. Born Angie Elbertha Debo, Jan 30, 1890, near Beattie, Kansas; died in Enid, Oklahoma, Feb 21, 1988; dau. of Edward Peter Debo (farmer) and Lina (Cooper) Debo; graduate of University of Oklahoma, 1918; University of Chicago, MA in history, 1924; University of Oklahoma, PhD in history, 1933; never married; no children. ❖ Prize-winning historian whose works described the tragic fate of North American Indians, especially the Five Tribes of Oklahoma, and whose interest in justice led her to become an activist on their behalf; moved with family to Marshall, Oklahoma Territory (1899); taught in rural schools; taught at West Texas State Teachers College (1924–33); was curator of Panhandle-Plains Historical Museum (1933–34); was an independent scholar (1934–41); served as state director for Oklahoma Federal Writers Project (1941–42); was curator of maps for Oklahoma State University Library (1947–54); was a scholar and activist on behalf of American Indians (1954–81); writings include *And Still the Waters Run* (1940), *The Road to Disappearance* (1941), *Tulsa: From Creek Town to Oil Capital* (1943), *Prairie City* (1944), *Oklahoma: Foot-loose and Fancy-free* (1949), *The Five Civilized Tribes of Oklahoma* (1951), *Indians of the US* (1970) and *Geronimo* (1976). Received John H. Dunning Prize from American Historical Association (AHA) for *The Rise and Fall of the Choctaw Republic* (1934); was the 1st woman to have her portrait hung in the State capital rotunda in Oklahoma City. ❖ See also *Women in World History.*

DE BOISSY, Marquise (c. 1801–1873). See *Guiccioli, Teresa.*

DE BOLIVIA, Yolande (1916–1999). See *Bedregal, Yolanda.*

DEBORAH (fl. 12th c. BCE). Prophet and judge of Israel. Name variations: Deborah the Judge. ❖ Considered to be a historical figure, whose story is told in the book of Judges from the Hebrew Bible; stands out among women in both Jewish and Christian history because of her power, influence, and honor; though details are missing on early life, might have been given special attention when it came to religious education; emerged as a leader who was subject to no one and was responsible for the securing of land for her people. There are 2 accounts of her leadership in book of Judges (chaps. 4 and 5): a prose rendering, which shows the hand of one or more editors, and a piece of poetry (known as "Deborah's Song") that was possibly an eyewitness account and which is one of the oldest examples of extant Hebrew literature. ❖ See also *Women in World History.*

DE BOURBON, Anne Geneviève (1619–1679). See *Longueville, Anne Geneviève de.*

DE BOURBON, Elizabeth (1614–1664). See *Elizabeth de Bourbon.*

DE BRABANT, Marie (c. 1530–c. 1600). See *Marie de Brabant.*

DE BRAY, Yvonne (1889–1954). French stage and screen actress. Born May 12, 1889, in Paris, France; died Feb 1, 1954, in Paris; dau. of Blanche (Lincelle) and Viscomte Gabriel de Bray. ❖ At 8, made stage debut as Little Toto in *Zaza* (1897); other plays include *Le Torrent, Francesca da Rimini, Le vieux coq, La petite peste, La retraite, Le ruisseau, La Barricade, Sherlock Holmes, Princesse d'Amour, Suzette, La Fugitive, Papa, L'accord parfait, Les Flambeaux, La Phalène* and *La Possession,* among others; made film debut in Jean Cocteau's *L'Eternel Retour* (1943), followed by *Imperial Venus, The Eagle Has Two Heads, Les parents terribles* and *The Eternal Return;* made final film *Quand tu liras cette lettre* (1953).

DE BRÉMONT, Anna (1864–1922). South African novelist. Name variations: Comtesse or countess Anna de Bremont. Born Anna Dunphy, 1864, in Cincinnati, OH, of Irish parents; died 1922; married a French count (div.). ❖ Moved to London (1889); immigrated to South Africa; writings, which often reflect goldmining life on Witwatersrand, include novels *The Gentleman Digger: A Study of Johannesburg Life* (1891), *A Son of Africa* (1899, reissued as *Was It a Sin,* 1906), and *The Black Opal* (1981), as well as the short-story collection *The Ragged Edge Tales of the African Gold Fields* (1895); also published poetry collections *Love Poems* (1889) and *Sonnets and Love Poems* (1892), as well as *The World of Music: The Great Composers* (1890).

DE BRIET, Marguerite (c. 1510–c. 1550). See *Briet, Marguerite de.*

DE BRINVILLIERS, Marguerite d' (1630–1676). See *Brinvilliers, Marie de.*

DE BRUIJN, Chantal (1976—). Dutch field-hockey player. Born Feb 13, 1976, in the Netherlands. ❖ Won European championship (2003); won a team silver medal at Athens Olympics (2004).

DE BRUIJN, Inge (1973—). Dutch swimmer. Pronunciation: de Brown. Born Aug 24, 1973, in Barendrecht, Netherlands. ❖ At SC European championships, placed 1st for 50-meter freestyle (1998, 2001), 50-meter butterfly (1998) and 100-meter freestyle (2001); at LC European championships, placed 1st for 50-meter freestyle and 100-meter butterfly (1999); at SC World championships, won a gold medal for 50-meter freestyle; won gold medals for 100-meter butterfly, 100-meter freestyle, and 50-meter freestyle and a silver medal for 4 x 100-meter freestyle relay at Sydney Olympics (2000); at LC World championships, won gold medals for 50-meter freestyle, 100-meter freestyle, and 50-meter butterfly (2001); won bronze medals for 100-meter butterfly and 4 x 100-meter freestyle relay, silver medal for 100-meter freestyle, and gold medal for 50-meter freestyle at Athens Olympics (2004).

DE BRUIN, Michelle (1969—). See *Smith, Michelle.*

DE BRÚN, Bairbre (1954—). Northern Ireland politician. Name variations: Bairbre De Brun. Born Jan 1, 1955, in Dublin, Ireland. ❖ As a member of Sinn Féin, elected to the Northern Ireland Assembly for West Belfast (1998); named minister of Health, Social Services and Public Safety (1999); member of the Sinn Féin National Executive.

DE BRUNHOFF, Cécile (1903–2003). French pianist and teacher. Name variations: Cecile de Brunhoff. Born Cécile de Sabouraud, Oct 10, 1903, in Paris, France; died in Paris, April 7, 2003; dau. of a dermatologist; studied piano at École Normale de Musique under Alfred Cortot; m. Jean de Brunhoff (painter and writer), 1923 (died 1937); children: Thierry (pianist), Mathieu (pediatrician) and Laurent de Brunhoff (b. 1925, writer, painter and illustrator). ❖ Was a piano teacher at École Normale de Musique; created a bedtime story for her son Mathieu about an orphaned elephant, then known as Bébé (1930); husband copied the story down, illustrated it, and it was published as *Story of Babar* (1933), followed by 5 sequels; though the original copy had her name on the title page, demanded that it come off for commercial issue; son Laurent later added 30 more titles.

DEBUCQ DE RIVERY, Aimée de (c. 1762–1817). See *de Rivery, Aimee Dubucq.*

DE BURGH, Aimée (d. 1946). Scottish actress. Born in Aberdeen, Scotland; died April 2, 1946; m. Leon Quartermaine (div.); m. Gilbert Frankau. ❖ Made London debut with Mrs. Patrick Campbell as Lady Betty in *Mrs. Jordan* (1900), followed by *Sapho, Othello, The Light that Failed, The Edge of the Storm, Waste, The Great Young Man, The Greatest Wish, The Three Daughters of M. Dupont* and *The Coming of Gabrielle.*

DE BURGH, Cecily (d. before 1273). See *Balliol, Cecily.*

DE BURGH, Elizabeth.
See *Clare, Elizabeth de (1295–1360).*
See *Elizabeth de Burgh (d. 1327).*
See *Elizabeth de Burgh (1332–1363).*

DE BURGH, Margaret.
See *Margaret de Burgh (d. 1243).*
See *Margaret de Burgh (d. 1259).*
See *Margaret de Burgh (d. 1303).*

DE BURGOS, Julia (1914–1953). Puerto Rican poet and political activist. Name variations: Julia Burgos de Rodriguez, Julia Burgos. Pronunciation: WHO-lee-uh day BOOR-goes. Born Julia Constanza de Burgos, Feb 17, 1914, in Carolina, Puerto Rico; died July 6, 1953, in New York, NY; dau. of Francisco Burgos Hans (farmer) and Paula García de Burgos; granted degree in education from University of Puerto Rico, 1933; took post-graduate studies in languages at University of Havana; m. Rubén Rodríguez Beauchamp, 1934 (div. 1937); m. Armando Marín, 1943; no children. ❖ Legendary poet whose work celebrated Puerto Rican culture, explored woman's experience, and denounced injustice and exploitation; grew up in rural Puerto Rico (1914–27); moved with family to Río Piedras to further education (1928); worked as rural grade-school teacher and social worker (1934–36); published 1st poems in the newspaper *El Imparcial* (1937); published *Poema en veinte surcos* (Poem in Twenty Furrows, 1938), emerging as a mature voice in Puerto Rican poetry; published 2nd book, *Canción de la verdad sencilla* (Song of the Simple Truth, 1939), for which she received Puerto Rican Institute of Literature's award for best book of the year; traveled to New York and then settled in Havana, Cuba (1940); returned to NY (1942); worked as journalist for the weekly *Pueblos Hispánicos* (1943–44); suffered repeated bouts of alcoholism, depression and hospitalization (1946–53); collapsed on Fifth Avenue and died anonymously (1953); posthumous publication of final volume of poetry, *El mar y tú* (The Sea and You, 1954). Received Journalism Prize of the Institute of Puerto Rican Literature (1946). ❖ See also *Women in World History*.

DEBYASUVAN, Boonlua Kunjara (1911–1982). Thai writer. Name variations: (pseudonym) Boonlua. Born Boonlua Kunjara in 1911 in Thailand; died 1982; half-sister of M.L. Bupha Kunjara Nimmanhemin (Sod Dok Mai). ❖ Wrote *Caak Nyng Chiiwid* (1964) and *Tutiyawises;* also wrote essays and translated Thai and English fiction.

DE CAMP, Miss (1774–1838). *See Kemble, Maria Theresa.*

DECAMP, Rosemary (1910–2001). American actress. Name variations: Rosemary De Camp (incorrect). Born Nov 14, 1910, in Prescott, Arizona; died Feb 20, 2001, in Torrance, California; m. John Ashton Shidler, 1941 (died 1998); children: Margaret, Martha, Valerie, and Nita. ❖ Began career on stage and radio; made film debut in *Cheers for Miss Bishop* (1941), followed by *Hold Back the Dawn, Jungle Book, Yankee Doodle Dandy, This is the Army, Rhapsody in Blue, Pride of the Marines, Weekend at the Waldorf, Nora Prentiss, Look for the Silver Lining, The Story of Seabiscuit, On Moonlight Bay, By the Light of the Silvery Moon, So This is Love, Strategic Air Command* and *Saturday the 14th;* on radio, spent 17 years as the voice of Nurse Judy on "Dr. Christian"; on tv, was a regular on "The Bob Cummings Show" (1955–59) and played Marlo Thomas' mother on "That Girl" (1966–70). ❖ See also memoir *Stories from Hollywood* (1991).

DE CARLO, Yvonne (1922–). Canadian-born actress. Name variations: Yvonne DeCarlo (incorrect). Born Peggy Yvonne Middleton, Sept 1, 1922, in Vancouver, British Columbia, Canada; m. Bob Morgan, 1955 (div. 1968). ❖ Was Miss Venice Beach (1938); made film debut in *Harvard Here I Come* (1942), followed by *Deerslayer, The Story of Dr. Wassell, Kismet, Here Come the Waves, Salome—Where She Danced, Frontier Gal, Song of Scheherazade, Brute Force, Black Bart, Casbah, Criss Cross, Calamity Jane and Sam Bass, Buccaneer's Girl, The Desert Hawk, Scarlet Angel, Hurricane Smith, Fort Algiers, The Ten Commandments, Mary Magdalene, McLintock!, Munster Go Home!, The Delta Factor, Won Ton Ton, Liar's Moon* and *Oscar,* among others; appeared in the original Broadway cast of Sondheim's *Follies* (1971) and as Lily Munster on "The Munsters" (1964–66). ❖ See also autobiography *Yvonne* (1987).

DE CARVAJAL, Luisa (1568–1614). *See Carvajal, Luisa de.*

DE CASALIS, Jeanne (1897–1966). South African-born actress, revue comedian, and playwright. Name variations: Jeanne de Casalis. Born Jeanne De Casalis de Pury, May 22, 1897, in Basutoland, South Africa; died Aug 19, 1966, in London, England; m. Colin Clive (English actor, died 1937); m. C.D. Stephenson. ❖ Made professional stage debut in Cannes in *La Poudre aux Yeux* (1919), NY debut in *Afgar* (1920), and London debut in *Deburau* (1921); appeared with Comédie des Champs-Élysées (1923) in *Six Chracters in Search of an Author, Liliom* and *RUR;* in London, came to prominence as Mathilde Fay in *Fata Morgana* (1924); other plays include *The Tidings Brought to Mary, Mixed Doubles, The Snow Man, Arms and the Man, A House of Cards, The Masque of Venice, Payment Deferred* and *The Hollow;* also appeared in revues, vaudeville, and on radio as Mrs. Feather; co-authored (with Colin Clive) *Let's Leave It at That* and (with R.C. Sherriff) *St. Helena;* wrote and directed *Dearly Beloved Wife* and adapted *Froufrou,;* also wrote 2 books: *Things I Don't Remember* and *Never Will She Be Unfaithful;* films include *Nell Gwyn, Jamaica Inn* and *Charley's Big-Hearted Aunt.*

DE CASTRO, Inez (c. 1320–1355). *See Castro, Inez de.*

DECASTRO, Peggy (1921–2004). Hispanic singer. Name variations: DeCastro Sisters; Peggy de Castro. Born Marguerita Dolores Esperanza Fernando DeCastro, Jan 24, 1921, in Cibao, Dominican Republic; died Mar 6, 2004, in Las Vegas, Nevada; father owned a sugar plantation; mother was a former dancer with the Ziegfeld Follies in NY; sister of Cherie and Babette DeCastro; cousin of Olgita DeCastro Marino (died 2000, who had replaced Babette in the act in 1958); m. John Carricaburu (died 2002); children: Gene Lilley. ❖ Eldest of the singing trio, the DeCastro Sisters, gained fame with a nightclub act in Cuba; moved with family to Miami (1945); had hit recording "Teach Me Tonight" (1954), followed by "Boom Boom Boomerang"; with sisters, appeared in Las Vegas nightclubs for years.

DE CASTRO, Públia Hortênsia (1548–1595). *See Castro, Públia Hortênsia de.*

DE CASTRO, Rosalía (1837–1885). *See Castro, Rosalía de.*

DECAUX, Lucile (1887–1973). *See Bibesco, Marthe Lucie.*

DE CESPEDES, Alba (1911–1997). Italian novelist, poet and journalist. Name variations: Alba de Céspedes y Bertini. Born 1911 in Rome, Italy; died Nov 14, 1997, in Paris, France; dau. of Carlos Manuel de Carlos Manuel de Céspedes y Quesada (Cuban ambassador in Italy) and Ana de Quesada; grandddau. of 1st president of Cuba. ❖ Pioneering figure in Italian feminist movement, worked as journalist for *Piccolo, Epoca* and *La Stampa;* imprisoned for anti-fascist activities and work with partisan Radio Bari (1943); founded partisan journal *Il Mercurio* (1944); moved to Paris (1950s) and worked in theater and film, contributing to Antonioni's *Le Amiche;* fiction includes *L'Anima degli altri* (1935), *Concerto* (1937), *Nessuno torna indietro* (1938), *La fuga* (1940), *Dalla parte di lei* (1949), *The Secret* (1952), *Invito a pranza* (1955), *Il rimorso* (1963), and *Nel buio della notte* (1976); published poetry collections *Prigione* (1936) and *Chanson des Filles de Mai* (1969).

DE CHAMBRUN, Josée. *See Laval, Josée.*

DE CHASTENAY, Victorine (1771–1855). *See Chastenay, Victorine de.*

DE CISNEROS, Eleonora (1878–1934). *See Cisneros, Eleonora de.*

DECKER, Mrs. Jay D. (1937–). *See Sander, Anne Quast.*

DECKER, Mary (b. 1958). *See Slaney, Mary Decker.*

DECKER, Sarah Platt (1852–1912). American clubwoman and reformer. Name variations: Sarah Sophia Chase Platt. Born Sarah Sophia Chase, Oct 1, 1852, in McIndoe Falls, Vermont; died July 7, 1912, in San Francisco, California; dau. of Edwin Chase and Lydia Maria (Adams) Chase; m. Charles B. Harris (merchant), Jan 5, 1875 (d. c. 1878); m. James H. Platt (oil refiner), April 16, 1884 (d. 1894); m. Westbrook S. Decker, Dec 3 1899; children: (2nd m.) Harriet Platt. ❖ Worked on behalf of successful Colorado woman suffrage campaign (1893); became president of Woman's Club of Denver (1894); served as vice-president of General Federation of Women's Clubs and served 2 terms as president (1904–08); served on National Child Labor Committee; championed conservation; served as member (1898–1912) and chair of Colorado Board of Charities and Correction.

DE CLARE, Isabel (c. 1174–1220). *See Clare, Isabel de.*

DE CLARE, Matilda (d. 1315). *See Matilda de Burgh.*

DE CLERE. *Variant of de Clare.*

DE CLERMONT, Claude-Catherine (1545–1603). *See Clermont, Claude-Catherine de.*

DE CLEYRE, Voltairine (1866–1912). Political theorist and feminist. Name variations: (pseudonym) Fannie Fern (not to be confused with journalist Sara Payson Willis Parton). Born Voltairine de Claire, Nov 17, 1866, in Leslie, Michigan; died June 12, 1912, in Chicago, Illinois; dau. of Hector Auguste de Claire and Harriet (Clarke) de Claire (seamstress); never married; children: Harry (b. 1890). ❖ Theorist, whose work made a significant contribution to the development of the Anarchist movement in US, believed that all legal and administrative institutions of the state (such as the police and prisons) only seek to exercise an illegitimate power of coercion over the individual; embarked on 1st lecture tour in Michigan (1884); published 1st volume of poems, which she pointedly entitled *The Burial of My Yesterday* (1885); political beliefs began to be focused in aftermath of the Haymarket affair in Chicago in which a bomb killed or injured several policemen, resulting in the execution of 4 anarchists who were widely considered to be innocent of the crime (1886); traveled to Great Britain on lecture tour (1897); with assassination of President McKinley by an anarchist sympathizer (1901), found it increasingly difficult to carry on her work as a lecturer; shot and seriously wounded in Philadelphia (1902), wrote that her attackers actions should be attributed to temporary mental instability and that he should not be sent to prison; traveled to Norway (1903); moved to Chicago where she became involved with International Workers of the World ("Wobblies"); supported peasants after outbreak of Mexican revolution (1911); following her death, her writings were edited by Hippolyte Havel and published as *Selected Works* (1914). ❖ See also Paul Avrich, *An American Anarchist: A Life of Voltairine de Cleyre* (Princeton U. Press, 1978); and *Women in World History*.

DE COIGNARD, Gabrielle (c. 1550–1586). *See Coignard, Gabrielle de.*

DE COLLEVILLE, Anne-Hyacinthe de Saint-Léger (1761–1824). *See Colleville, Anne-Hyacinthe de Saint-Léger de.*

DE COSTA, Ethel Rebecca (1875–1943). *See Benjamin, Ethel Rebecca.*

DE COSTA, Maria Velho (1938—). *See Velho da Costa, Maria.*

DECOSTA, Sara (1977—). American ice-hockey player. Born May 13, 1977, in Warwick, Rhode Island. ❖ Goaltender, played for Providence College; won a team gold medal at Nagano (1998), the 1st Olympics to feature women's ice hockey; won a team silver medal at World championships (2000, 2001); won a team silver medal at Salt Lake City Olympics (2002). ❖ See also Mary Turco, *Crashing the Net: The U.S. Women's Olympic Ice Hockey Team and the Road to Gold* (HarperCollins, 1999); and *Women in World History.*

DE CRAYENCOUR, Marguerite (1903–1987). *See Yourcenar, Marguerite.*

DE CRENNE, Helisenne (c. 1510–c. 1550). *See Briet, Marguerite de.*

DE CRÉQUI, Marquise (1714–1803). *See Crequy, Renée Caroline de Froulay, Marquise de.*

DE DIA, Beatrice (c. 1160–1212). French troubadour. Name variations: Contessa Beatrice de Dia. Born c. 1160, lived in Provence; died 1212; may have married William of Poitiers, count of Valentinois. ❖ Known mainly for writing 4 ballads, all love elegies that still survive, may have been the wife of William of Poitiers and mistress of Rambaud of Orange (Raibaut d'Orange), also a troubadour (some accounts indicate that she may have married the count of Ambrunois and been the mistress of Guillaume Adhermar); her ballads indicate that Rambaud left her in later years, inspiring her to write her most acclaimed ballad, *Plang.* ❖ See also *Women in World History.*

DEDIEU, Virginie (1979—). French synchronized swimmer. Born Feb 25, 1979 in Aix-en-Provence, France. ❖ Won a bronze medal for duet at Sydney Olympics (2000); won European duet championship (2000) and solo championship (2002, 2003); won solo World championship (2003).

DE DURAS, Claire (1777–1828). *See Duras, Claire de.*

DEE, Frances (1907–2004). American actress. Born Frances Marion Dee, Nov 26, 1907, in Los Angeles, California; died Mar 6, 2004, in Norwalk, Connecticut; attended University of Chicago; m. Joel McCrea (b. 1905, actor), 1933 (died Oct 20, 1990); children: Peter, David, and Jody McCrea (actor). ❖ Came to screen prominence starring opposite Maurice Chevalier in *Playboy of Paris* (1930), one of the 1st movie musicals; other films include *June Moon, An American Tragedy, Working Girls, The Strange Case of Clara Deane, The Silver Cord, Little Women, Of Human Bondage, Becky Sharp, The Gay Deception, Come and Get It, Wells Fargo, Four Faces West, Because of You* and *Gypsy Colt;* also appeared in the cult classic *I Walked with a Zombie* (1943).

DEE, Mildred Wiley (1901–2000). *See Wiley, Mildred.*

DEE, Ruby (1923—). African-American actress and civil-rights activist. Born Ruby Ann Wallace, Oct 27, 1923, in Cleveland, Ohio; dau. of Marshall Edward and Emma (Benson) Wallace; Hunter College, BA; m. Ossie Davis (actor), Dec 9, 1948; children: Nora, LaVerne and Guy Davis. ❖ Obie and two-time Drama Desk award winner, known for her dedication in the cause of civil rights, made stage debut with American Negro Theater in *Natural Man* (1941); made Broadway debut as Ruth in Rigsby and Heyward's *South Pacific* (1943); appeared in title role of *Anna Lucasta* (1944); portrayed Ruth Younger in *A Raisin in the Sun* (1959), Lutiebelle in *Purlie Victorious* (1961), and Lena in *Boesman and Lena* (1970); also appeared in Alice Childress' *Wedding Band* (1973); published *Child Glow and Other Poems* (1973) and several plays, including *Twin Bit Gardens* (1976), the musical *Take It from the Top* (1979), and *Zora Is My Name* (1983), about Zora Neale Hurston; also co-authored and starred in the film *Uptight* (1969); other films include *No Way Out* (1950), *The Jackie Robinson Story* (1950), *St. Louis Blues* (1958), *A Raisin in the Sun* (1961), *Take a Giant Step* (1963), *Gone Are the Days!* (*Purlie Victorious,* 1963), *The Balcony* (1963), *The Incident* (1967), *Buck and the Preacher* (1972) and *Do the Right Thing* (1988); received Emmy nomination for performance in episode of "East Side, West Side," and appeared with husband on PBS programs, including "History of the Negro People." Elected to Theater Hall of Fame (1988); was a Kennedy Center Honoree (2004). ❖ See also memoir (with Ossie Davis) *With Ossie and Ruby: In This Life Together* (Morrow, 1998) and *My One Good Nerve* (a collection of verse based on her one-woman show, Wiley, 1998); and *Women in World History.*

DEE, Sandra (1942–2005). American actress. Born Alexandra Zuck, April 23, 1942, in Bayonne, New Jersey; died of kidney disease, Feb 20, 2005, in Thousand Oaks, California; m. Bobby Darin (singer), 1960 (div. 1967); children: Dodd Darin. ❖ Began career as a child model; made film debut in *Until They Sail* (1957), followed by *The Reluctant Debutante, Imitation of Life, Gidget, A Summer Place, Romanoff and Juliet, Tammy Tell Me True, Come September, Tammy and the Doctor, Take Her She's Mine, The Dunwich Horror* and *That Funny Feeling;* retired from films (1983). The song "Look at Me, I'm Sandra Dee" originated in the film *Grease* (1978). ❖ See also Dodd Darin, *Dream Lovers: The Magnificent Shattered Lives of Bobby Darin and Sandra Dee.*

DEELSTRA, Atje (1938—). Dutch speedskater. Name variations: Atje Keulen-Deelstra. Born Dec 31, 1938, in the Netherlands. ❖ At World championships, won a gold medal for small allround (1970, 1972–74); at European championships, won a gold medal for small allround (1972–74); won a silver medal for the 1,000 meters and bronze medals for the 1,500 and 3,000 meters at Sapporo Olympics (1972).

DEER, Ada (1935—). Native American government official. Born Ada Elizabeth Deer, Aug 7, 1935, in Keshena, Wisconsin, a town in the Menominee Indian Reservation; 1st of 9 children of Joseph Deer (Menominee) and Constance Stockton (Wood) Deer (white Quaker); University of Wisconsin at Madison, BA in social work, 1957, the 1st member of her tribe to graduate from that university; Columbia University, MA in Social Work, 1961. ❖ Was an administrative social worker (1958–71); successfully spearheaded the fight to restore the Menominees' status as a federally recognized tribe (1973); became the 1st female chair of her tribe; taught in School of Social Work and in American Indian Studies Program, University of Wisconsin, Madison (1977–93); appointed assistant secretary for Indian Affairs, Department of the Interior (1993), the 1st woman to head the Bureau of Indian Affairs (BIA) and ran the agency until 1997.

DE ERAUSO, Catalina (1592–1635). *See Erauso, Catalina de.*

DE ERGADIA, Joan (fl. 1300s). *See Isaac, Joan.*

DEERING, Olive (1918–1986). American stage, tv, and screen actress. Born Olive Korn, Oct 11, 1918, in New York, NY; died Mar 22, 1986, in New York, NY; sister of Alfred Ryder (actor); m. Leo Penn (actor, div.). ❖ Made Broadway debut in *Girls in Uniform* (1932); other NY plays include *Winged Victory, Daughters of Atreus,* the queen in Maurice Evan's production of *Richard II,* Mollie Malloy in *Front Page, The Devil's Advocate, Marathon '33, Vieux Carre, Ceremony of Innocence* and *Two by Tennessee;* appeared in the film *Ten Commandments;* often appeared on live-tv drama during the "Golden Years."

DEEVY, Teresa (1894–1963). Irish playwright. Born in Ireland in 1894; died 1963. ❖ Was profoundly deaf after contracting Menière's disease in her teens but learned lip-reading; wrote 25 plays of which 6 were performed at the Abbey Theatre (1930–58); also wrote for Irish radio, BBC radio and later tv, and children's stories and reviews; most important plays are *Reapers* (1930), *A Disciple* (1931), *Katie Roche* (1936) and *Wife to Whelan* (1942).

DEFAR, Meseret (1983—). Ethiopian runner. Born Nov 19, 1983, in Addis Ababa, Ethiopia. ❖ At World Indoor championship, placed 1st for 3,000 meters (2004); won a gold medal for 5,000 meters at Athens Olympics (2004).

DEFFAND, Marie Anne de Vichy-Chamrond, Marquise du (1697–1780). French patron of fashion and literature and salonnière. Name variations: Madame du Deffand; Marquise du Deffand; Marie de Vichy-Chamrond. Born Marie Anne de Vichy-Chamrond in 1697; died in 1780; dau. of the Comte de Chamrond; sister of Gaspard de Vichy; aunt of Julie de Lespinasse; m. the Marquis du Deffand, a distant cousin. ❖ Cultivated and intense, engaged in voluminous correspondence with Horace Walpole, Duchesse de Choiseul, and Voltaire; when husband died (1750), regained her dowry and founded a salon; living in a suite attached to Convent of St. Joseph, received guests every day after 6, including the Maréchale de Luxembourg, Duchesse de Choiseul, d'Alembert, Montesquieu, Maupertuis, Beaumarchais, Lady Mary Hervey and George Selwyn; formed rivalry with Julie de Lespinasse; went blind. ❖ See also Benedetta Craveri, *Madame Du Deffand & Her World,* trans. by Teresa Waugh (Godine, 1994); and *Women in World History.*

DEFORD, Christa (1962—). *See Canary, Christa.*

DE FOREST, Marie (1899–1983). *See Mosquini, Marie.*

DE FOREST, Nora (1883–1971). *See Barney, Nora.*

DEFRANCO, Marisa (1955—). Canadian vocalist. Name variations: The DeFranco Family. Born July 23, 1955, in Port Colborne, Canada; sister of Benny, Nino, Tony and Merlina DeFranco. ❖ Vocalist with the DeFranco Family, a Canadian act modeled after the Cowsills, which had year's top single with "Heartbeat—It's a Lovebeat" (1973). DeFranco Family albums include *Heartbeat—It's a Lovebeat* (1973) and *Save the Last Dance for Me* (1974).

DEFRANCO, Merlina (1957—). Canadian vocalist. Name variations: The DeFranco Family. Born July 20, 1957, in Port Colborne, Canada; sister of Benny, Nino, Tony and Marisa DeFranco. ❖ Vocalist with the DeFranco Family, which had year's top single with "Heartbeat—It's a Lovebeat" (1973).

DEFRANCO FAMILY, The.
See DeFranco, Marisa.
See DeFranco, Merlina.

DEFRANTZ, Anita (1952—). African-American rower, lawyer, and Olympic official. Name variations: Anita De Frantz. Born Anita Luceete DeFrantz, Oct 4, 1952, in Philadelphia, Pennsylvania; graduate of Connecticut College; graduate of University of Pennsylvania Law School, 1977. ❖ At Montreal Olympics, won a bronze medal in coxed eights (1976); won a silver medal in coxed fours at World championships (1978); was 6-time national champion; elected the International Olympic Committee's (IOC) 1st female vice president (1977); elected the 1st woman to represent US on IOC (1986); became a member of the IOC Executive. Was only the 2nd American athlete to receive the Bronze Medal of the Olympic Order of the International IOC (1981).

DE FROULAY, Renée (1714–1803). *See Crequy, Renée Caroline de Froulay, Marquise de.*

DE GABRIAK, Cherubina (1887–1928). *See Dmitreva, Elizaveta Ivanovna.*

DEGAETANI, Jan (1933–1989). American mezzo-soprano. Name variations: Jan de Gaetani; Janice Reutz. Born Janice Reutz, July 10, 1933, in Massilon, Ohio; died of leukemia, Sept 15, 1989, in Rochester, New York; studied at Juilliard with Sergius Kagen; m. Thomas DeGaetani (conductor, div.); m. James West (oboist). ❖ Dubbed Queen of Avante-Garde, specialized in modern vocal compositions with the Contemporary Chamber Ensemble; made debut in NY (1958); came to prominence in premiere of George Crumb's *Ancient Voices of Children* in Washington, DC (1970), one of many works written expressly for her by major composers; over 30-year period, collaborated extensively with Crumb, developing new vocal technique, as well as with Gilbert Kalish; collaborated with Peter Maxwell Davies and sang in the premieres of his *Stone Litany* (1973) and *Black Pentecost* (1982); sang in premieres of works by Richard Wernick (*Visions of Wonder and Terror*), William Schuman (*In Sweet Music*) and Elliott Carter; had diverse repertoire, ranging from medieval *Play of Herod* to German lieder, French melodies, and songs of John Dowland, Stephen Foster and Charles Ives; appeared with Chamber Music Society of Lincoln Center and with Speculum Musicae; was professor at Eastman School of Music (1973–89); published *The Complete Sightsinger* (1980), based on her master classes. Recordings include *George Crumb: Ancient Voices of Children* (1971) and *Jan DeGaetani Sings Berlioz, Mahler* (1993).

DE GALARD, Geneviève (1925—). French nurse and heroine. Born Geneviève de Galard-Terraube, April 13, 1925, in Paris, France; dau. of Vicomte Oger de Galard-Terraube (army officer); received baccalaureate degree from a Dominican convent in Toulouse; studied fine arts at École du Louvre, Paris; studied English at the Sorbonne; received state nursing diploma from nurses training school as well as a diploma from Paris School of Social Work; m. paratrooper Captain Jean de Heaulme, May 21, 1957; children: 2. ❖ Hero of the Indo-Chinese war, known as the Angel of Dien Bien Phu, joined the Infirmières Pilotes et Secouristes de L'Air (IPSA), a specially trained corps of airborne pilot-nurses and first-aid workers; began duty in Indochina (1953), as a nurse on a plane that flew into battle zones and brought back wounded French soldiers to Saigon; began flying to Dien Bien Phu in North Vietnam (1954), to evacuate severely wounded soldiers to Hanoi; stranded in Dien Bien Phu, joined the all-male, 30-member medical staff, living and working in extreme conditions and surviving a steady barrage of enemy attacks; risked her life to go out into the fields to attend the long line of wounded. Awarded a Croix de Guerre and the red ribbon of the Legion of Honor (1954); also presented with the Air Medal and the Air Medical Service

Silver Medal from France and the US Medal of Freedom. ❖ See also *Women in World History.*

DE GAULLE, Geneviève (1921–2002). French resistance fighter. Name variations: Genevieve Anthonioz; Geneviève de Gaulle-Anthonioz; Geneviève Anthonioz-de Gaulle. Born in 1921; died Feb 14 2002, in Paris, France; dau. of Xavier de Gaulle, older brother of Charles de Gaulle (president of France); m. Bernard Anthonioz (Resistance fighter), 1946 (died 1994); children: 4. ❖ At 19, following the Nazi occupation of Paris, joined the French underground (1940); arrested (1943), spent 6 months in a French prison, then was deported to Ravensbruck, a Nazi concentration camp in Germany; after the war, helped establish the Association for Deported and Imprisoned Resistance Fighters; was also a witness in the trial of Gestapo chief Klaus Barbie (1987); led the French humantarian organization, ATD Quart Monde. ❖ See also memoir, *The Dawn of Hope: A Memoir of Ravensbruck and Beyond.*

DE GAULLE, Madame (1900–1975). *See de Gaulle, Yvonne.*

DE GAULLE, Yvonne (1900–1979). French first lady. Name variations: Madame de Gaulle. Born Yvonne Charlotte Anne-Marie Vendroux, May 22, 1900, in Calais, France; died Nov 8, 1979, in Val-de-Grâce, Paris; dau. of Jacques and Marguerite (Forest) Vendroux; m. Charles de Gaulle, April 7, 1921 (died Nov 9, 1970); children: Philippe (b. 1921); Elisabeth de Boissieu (b. 1924); Anne de Gaulle (1928–1948). ❖ As German forces advanced toward Calais at outset of WWI, took refuge with family in England (1914); cared for war wounded in Calais (1915–16, 1919–20); married and lived in Paris (1921); moved with Charles, who was promoted to major and placed in charge of 19th Battalion of Light Infantry in Trier, Germany (1927); moved with family to Beirut where Charles was posted (1929); returned to Paris (1931); purchased La Boisserie, an estate in Colombey-les-Deux-Églises, in Haute-Marne department in eastern France (1934); based in Metz where Charles commanded the 507th Tank Regiment (1937); when Germans entered Paris (June 14, 1940), left with family for London where Charles' 1st BBC radio broadcast to France called for resistance against Germany; joined Charles in liberated Algiers (July 1943); after Allied invasion of Normandy (June 6, 1944), rejoined Charles, now head of the Provisional Government, in Neuilly (Sept 1944); when Charles resigned as head of the Provisional Government (1946), moved back to La Boisserie; daughter Anne died of pneumonia (Feb 6, 1948); returned to Paris with recall of Charles to power during Algerian crisis (June 1, 1958); became "first lady" of France upon inauguration of Charles as 1st president of the Fifth Republic (Jan 8, 1959); narrowly survived an assassination attempt in company of husband (Aug 22, 1962); retired to La Boisserie after referendum defeat of husband (April 1969); was, in later years, affectionately known as "Tante Yvonne" (Aunt Yvonne). ❖ See also Marcel Jullian, *Madame de Gaulle* (Paris: Stock, 1982, in French); and *Women in World History.*

DE GAUTIER, Felisa Rincon (1897–1994). *See Gautier, Felisa Rincon de.*

DEGENERES, Ellen (1958—). American comedian. Born Ellen Lee DeGeneres, Jan 26, 1958, in Metairie, Louisiana; dau. of Betty DeGeneres (gay-rights activist); sister of Vance DeGeneres. ❖ Began career as a stand-up comic; was named Best Female Club Standup at Comedy Awards (1991); starred on "Ellen" (1994–98); came out as a lesbian on the show (April 1997), a television 1st that brought cheers and controversy; launched talk show "Ellen: the Ellen DeGeneres Show" (2003), for which she won a daytime Emmy (2004); writings include *My Point . . . And I Do Have One* and *The Funny Thing Is . . .*; was the voice for Dory the Blue Fish in *Finding Nemo* (2003).

DE GENLIS, Stephanie (1746–1830). *See Genlis, Stéphanie-Félicité, Comtesse de.*

DE GIRONDO, Norah (1906–1972). *See Lange, Norah.*

DE GIVRY, Marie-Louise Charlotte de Pellart (1660–1730). *See Fontaines, Marie-Louise-Charlotte de Pelard de Givry, Comtesse de.*

DEGONWADONTI (1941—). *See Brant, Beth.*

DE GOUGES, Olympe (1748–1793). *See Gouges, Olympe de.*

DE GOURNAY, Marie (1565–1645). *See Gournay, Marie le Jars de.*

DE GRAFFENRIED, Clare (1849–1921). American social investigator. Name variations: Mary Clare De Graffenried. Born May 19, 1849, in Macon, Georgia; died April 26, 1921, in Washington, DC; dau. of William Kirkland de Graffenried and Mary Hold (Marsh) de Graffenried; graduate with honors from Wesleyan Female College,

1865. ❖ Became investigator for Bureau of Labor (1886); became 1 of 20 special investigators to serve under 1st commissioner of labor at Department of Labor (1888); primarily investigated labor conditions among women and children, housing conditions, and cost of living; wrote periodical articles based on her statistical findings, the best-known of which was "The Georgia Cracker in the Cotton Mills" (*Century Magazine*, 1891).

DE GROEN, Alma (1941—). Australian playwright. Born Alma Margaret Mathers, Sept 5, 1941, in Foxton, New Zealand; dau. of Archibald Mathers and Eileen Vertongen. ❖ Immigrated to Australia (1964) and traveled to England, France, and Canada; returned to Australia (1973) and worked in theater and tv; works include *The Joss Adams Show, The Sweat-proof Boy* (1972), *The After Life of Arthur Craven* (1973), *Chidley* (1977), *Perfectly All Right* (1977), *Vocations* (1983), *Man of Letters* (1984), *The Rivers of China* (1987) and *The Girl Who Saw Everything* (1993). Received Australian Writers' Guild Award and Premier's Literary Award (NSW and Victoria, 1988).

DEGUTIENE, Irena (1949—). Lithuanian politician. Name variations: Irena Degutienė. Born 1949. ❖ A Conservative (Homeland Union), served as acting prime minister of Lithuania (May 4–May 18, 1999) and as acting prime minister (Oct 27–Nov 3, 1999), after the resignation of Gediminas Vagnorius during a year of political turmoil; became minister of Social Security and Labour (Nov 1999).

DE GUZMAN, Luisa (1613–1666). See Luisa de Guzmán.

DE HAAN, Annemiek (1981—). Dutch rower. Born July 15, 1981, in the Netherlands. ❖ Won a bronze medal for coxed eights at Athens Olympics (2004).

DE HAAN, Carry (1881–1932). See Bruggen, Carry van.

DEHAN, Richard (1863–1932). See Graves, Clotilde Inez Mary.

DEHAVEN, Mrs. Carter (1883–1950). See DeHaven, Flora.

DEHAVEN, Flora (1883–1950). American silent-film actress and dancer. Name variations: Flora De Haven; Flora Parker De Haven; Mrs. Carter DeHaven; Flora Parker. Born Flora Parker, Sept 1, 1883, in Perth Amboy, New Jersey; died Sept 9, 1950, in Hollywood, California; m. Carter DeHaven (actor-director, 1886–1977); children: David DeHaven, Carter DeHaven Jr. (producer); Gloria DeHaven (b. 1924, actress). ❖ At 11, made Broadway debut in *The Telephone Girl* (1901), followed by *Mr. Bluebeard* (1903); appeared with husband in vaudeville, on Broadway in *The Queen of the Moulin Rouge, The Girl and the Wizard* and *Hanky-Panky*, and in a series of light film comedies with music, among them the "Timothy Dobbs" serials; other films include *The College Orphan, The Wrong Door, Twin Beds, The Girl in the Taxi, My Lady Friends* and *Marry the Poor Girl*; performed for 30 years. Portrayed by daughter in the film *Three Little Words* (1950).

DEHAVEN, Gloria (1924—). American actress and singer. Name variations: Gloris De Haven. Born Gloria Mildred DeHaven, July 23, 1924, in Los Angeles, California; dau. of Carter and Flora Parker DeHaven (both actors and dancers); sister of Carter DeHaven Jr. (producer); m. John Payne (actor), 1944 (div. 1950); m. Martin Kimmell, 1953 (div. 1954); m. Richard Fincher, 1957 (div. 1963), remarried 1964 (div. 1968). ❖ As a child, worked the vaudeville circuit with parents; had a bit in Chaplin's *Modern Times* (1936); became a vocalist with Bob Crosby's band; signed with MGM as a starlet and was featured in many musicals, including *Thousands Cheer, Broadway Rhythm, Yes Sir That's My Baby, I'll Get By, Best Foot Forward* and *Summer Stock;* on tv, appeared on "Ryan's Hope." Portrayed her mother in *Three Little Words* (1950).

DE HAVILLAND, Lillian (1886–1975). See Fontaine, Lillian.

DE HAVILLAND, Olivia (1916—). English-born actress. Born Olivia Mary de Havilland, July 1, 1916, in Tokyo, Japan; dau. of Walter and Lillian (Ruse) de Havilland (both British); sister of actress Joan Fontaine (b. 1917); m. Marcus Goodrich (novelist), 1946 (div.); m. Pierre Galante (editor of *Paris-Match*), 1955 (sep.); children: (1st m.) Benjamin; (2nd m.) Gisele. ❖ Made film debut in *A Midsummer Night's Dream* (1935); early roles encompassed a series of demure heroines in films dominated by the studio's top male stars, among them Errol Flynn, with whom she was cast in a number of romantic adventures; won critical acclaim for performance in *Anthony Adverse* (1936); appeared as Melanie in *Gone with the Wind* (1939) and was nominated for an Academy Award; also nominated for her work in *Hold Back the Dawn* (1941); cast in a series of remakes (*Raffles* and *Saturday's Children*) and in a supporting role in *The*

Private Lives of Elizabeth and Essex, brought suit against Warner's for release from her contract, a fight that made it to the Supreme Court of California and resulted in a landmark decision that led to the demise of the repressive studio system (1945); won 1st Oscar as Best Actress for *To Each His Own* (1946); career peaked with portrayal of a mental patient in *The Snake Pit* (1948), which is often considered her most developed role; won her 2nd Oscar for *The Heiress* (1949) and a Golden Globe for tv portrayal of the Dowager empress in "Anastasia: The Mystery of Anna"; other films include *Captain Blood* (1935), *The Charge of the Light Brigade* (1936), *The Adventures of Robin Hood* (1938), *Dodge City* (1939), *They Died with Their Boots On* (1941), *The Male Animal* (1942), *In This Our Life* (1942), *Devotion* (1946), *My Cousin Rachel* (1953), *Not As a Stranger* (1955), *The Light in the Piazza* (1962), *Lady in a Cage* (1964), *Hush Hush Sweet Charlotte* (1965) and *The Swarm* (1978). ❖ See also memoir *Every Frenchman Has One* (1961); Charles Higham, *Sisters: The Story of Olivia de Havilland and Joan Fontaine;* and *Women in World History.*

DE HEIJ, Stella. Dutch field-hockey player. Born in the Netherlands. ❖ Won a team bronze medal at Atlanta Olympics (1996).

DEHNER, Dorothy (1901–1994). American sculptor. Name variations: Dorothy Smith. Born 1901 in Cleveland, Ohio; died in New York, NY, Sept 22, 1994; m. David Smith (artist), 1927 (div. 1951); m. Ferdinand Mann, 1957. ❖ Sculptor of Surrealist and geometric abstractions who was a late bloomer as an artist; started to sculpt in her 50s and went on to become an acclaimed figure in the art world; produced her 1st works of sculpture (1955); began to work in wood, and exhibited at New York's prestigious Willard Gallery (1957); enjoyed a solo exhibition at Jewish Museum in NY (1965); strongly inspired by African art, her sculptures often reproduce the rough surfaces and totemlike quality of the art of Africa; works include *Cenotaph for Li Po* and *Egyptian King.* ❖ See also *Women in World History.*

DE HONDT, Christine (1934—). See Herzberg, Judith.

DE HOYOS, Angela (1940—). Mexican-American poet. Born Jan 23, 1940, in Coahuila, Mexico. ❖ Moved with family to San Antonio, Texas, as child; served as general editor of M&A/Manda Publications and *Huchuetitlan* magazine; poetry explores Hispanic history of Texas and expresses concern for exploited migrant workers in US; writings include *Arise, Chicano and Other Poems* (1975), *Chicano Poems for the Barrio* (1975), *Selecciones* (1976), *Woman, Woman* (1985) and *Linking Roots* (1993).

DÉIA, Maria (c. 1908–1938). See Bonita, Maria.

DE IBÁÑEZ, Sara (1909–1971). Uruguayan poet and educator. Name variations: Sara de Ibanez. Born 1909, near Paso de los Toros, Chambelain, Uruguay; died 1971 in Montevideo. ❖ One of the most distinctive poets of her day, was influenced by the modernist, surrealist, and contemporary religious movements; writings include *Canto* (1940), *Hora ciega* (1943), *Artigas* (1952), *Las estaciones y otros poemas* (1957), *La Batalla* (1967), *Apocalipsis XX* (1970) and *Canto póstumo* (1973).

DEICHMANN, Freya (b. 1911). See von Moltke, Freya.

DEININGER, Beate (1962—). West German field-hockey player. Born Jan 24, 1962, in West Germany. ❖ At Los Angeles Olympics, won a silver medal in team competition (1984).

DEITERS, Julie (1975—). Dutch field-hockey player. Born Sept 4, 1975, in Meudon, Frankrijk, Netherlands. ❖ Won a team bronze medal at Sydney Olympics (2000).

DEI VIGRI, Caterina (1413–1463). See Catherine of Bologna.

DEJANOVIĆ, Draga (1843–1870). Serbian feminist, poet and essayist. Name variations: Draga Dejanović. Born 1843 in Serbia; died 1870. ❖ A leader in the Serbian feminist movement, also worked for the United Serbian Youth Movement; wrote articles on education and politics including "Are Women Capable of Being Equal with Men" (1870); published poems as *Collection* (1869).

DÉJAZET, Pauline-Virginie (1797–1875). French actress. Name variations: Dejazet. Born Aug 30, 1797, in Paris, France; died Dec 1, 1875. ❖ One of the great names in the French theater, 1st appeared on stage at age 5 and subsequently became well-known in vaudeville for her male impersonations; began a 7-year association with the Gymnase (1821), where her male roles became so famous that they were known as "Déjazets"; went to the newly opened Palais-Royal (1831), where she enjoyed 13 years of enormous popularity; appeared at the Variétés and the Gaîté, portraying great ladies and young peasant girls in addition to her repertoire of male roles; became manager of the Folies (1859), which was later renamed the Théâtre Déjazet. ❖ See also *Women in World History*.

DEJERINE, Augusta (1859–1927). *See Klumpke, Augusta.*

DE JESÚS, Carolina Maria (c. 1913–1977). *See Jesus, Carolina Maria de.*

DE JESUS, Clementina (1902–1987). *See Jesus, Clementina de.*

DE JESUS, Gregoria (1875–1943). *See Jesus, Gregoria de.*

DE JONG, Bettie (1933—). Dutch modern dancer. Born May 5, 1933, in Sumatra, Indonesia. ❖ Studied dance in Indonesia and Holland, and with Martha Graham and José Limón in NY after moving to US (mid–1950s); performed professionally for numerous choreographers including John Butler in *Carmina Burana* (1960), Martha Graham in *Clytemnestra* (1961), and Pearl Lang in *And Joy Is My Witness;* joined Paul Taylor Dance Co. (1962), where she created roles in *From Sea to Shining Sea* (1965), *Orbs* (1966), *Lento* (1967), and *Big Bertha* (1973), among others; remained with Taylor throughout career and also served as his rehearsal director.

DE JONG, Dola (1911–2003). Dutch-American journalist, novelist and children's writer. Born Dorothea Rosalie de Jong, Oct 10, 1911, in Arnhem, Netherlands; died Nov 19, 2003, in Los Angeles, California; dau. of S.L. and Lotte (Benjamin) de Jong; m. Jan Hoowij (artist), 1940 (div.); m. Robert H. Joseph (writer), 1946. ❖ Danced with the Royal Dutch Ballet for about 8 years; published 1st book for children at 18; with husband, immigrated to US with advent of WWII (1940); became American citizen (1946) and danced for the Joos ballet; facilitated literary contact between Netherlands and US; adult works include *Dans om het hart* (1939), *En die akker is de wereld* (*And the Field is the World*, 1946, later published as *The Field*), *De thuiswacht* (1954, trans. as *The Tree and Vine*, 1961) and *The House of Charlton Street* (1963); children's books, which were often set during WWII, include *The Level Land* (1943), *Sand for the Sandman* (1944), *The Picture Story of Holland* (1946) and *Return to the Level Land* (1947). Won Edgar Allan Poe award for *The Whirligig of Time* (1964).

DE JONG, Reggie (1964—). Dutch swimmer. Born Jan 7, 1964, in the Netherlands. ❖ At Moscow Olympics, won a bronze medal in 4 x 100-meter freestyle relay (1980).

DE JONG, Xenia (1922—). *See Stad-de Jong, Xenia.*

DE JONGH, Andree (1916—). Belgian resistance leader. Name variations: Andrée de Jongh or dejongh; Dedee or Dédée Jongh. Born 1916 in Schaerbeek, near Brussels, Belgium; dau. of Frederic de Jongh (headmaster and resistance leader who was arrested by the Gestapo in June 1943 and later executed). ❖ Anti-Nazi resistance leader, 1st trained as a nurse; was an artist in Malmédy when the Germans invaded France (1940); moved to Brussels, where, with the help of her father, formed Comet (Comète), an escape network in Belgium for downed airman (the Comet Line helped return about 800 Allied troops to Britain during WWII); caught by the Germans (Jan 1944), was sent to Ravensbruck Concentration Camp; liberated (April 1945); after the war, worked in a leper hospital in Addis Ababa. Awarded the American Medal of Freedom.

DEKANOVA, Vlasta (1909–1974). Czech gymnast. Born Sept 1909; died Oct 16, 1974. ❖ At Berlin Olympics, won a silver medal in team all-around (1936).

DE KEERSMAEKER, Anne Teresa (1960—). Belgian dancer and choreographer. Born June 11, 1960, in Mechelen, Malines, Belgium; trained at Maurice Béjart's Mudra School in Brussels, 1978–80, and at Tisch School of Arts, New York University, 1980s. ❖ Worked with Steve Reich's ensemble in NY (early 1980s); toured Europe with her work *Fase* (1982); presented *Rosas danst Rosas* at Brussels Kaaitheater festival (1983), marking official debut of Rosas dance company; with Rosas, was artist-in-residence at Théâtre de la Monnaie, Brussels (1992); was also artistic director of Performing Arts Research and Training Studio (PARTS) Brussels (1995), a collaboration between La Monnaie and Rosas. Further works include *Elena's Aria* (1984), *Verkommenes Ufer Medeamaterial Landschaft mit Argonauten* (1987), *Ottone, Ottone* (1988), *Stella* (1990), *Kynok* (1994) and *Woud* (1997).

DEKEN, Aagje (1741–1804). Dutch poet and novelist. Name variations: Agathe, Agatha. Born 1741 in the northern Netherlands; died Nov 14, 1804. ❖ Frequent collaborator with Elizabeth Bekker on realistic stories of Dutch life, lived with Bekker for nearly 30 years, collaborating on novels, including the extremely popular works *De Historie van Mejuffrouw Sara Burgerhart* (History of Sara Burgerhart, 1782), *De Historie van den Heer Willem Leevend* (History of William Leevend, 1784–85), *Letters of Abraham Blankaart* (1787), and *Cornelia Wildschut* (1793–96); also produced *Geschrift eener bejaarde vrouw* (Document of an Elderly Woman, 1802). ❖ See also *Women in World History.*

DE KEYSER, Ethel (1926–2004). South African anti-apartheid activist. Born Ethel Tarshish, Nov 4, 1926, in South Africa; died July 16, 2004, in England; dau. of a garment factory owner; sister of Jack Tarshish (jailed for 12 years for anti-apartheid work); m. David de Keyser (div.). ❖ Participated in the underground activities of the African National Congress (ANC), including helping activists flee the country; deported to Britain, spent the rest of her life there pursuing freedom for South Africa; in London, served as executive secretary for the Anti-Apartheid Movement (AAM, 1967–76); worked with Hugh Lewin, to set up SATIS (1973), which dealt with the plight of political prisoners, including Nelson Mandela; became director of the British Defence and Aid Fund for Southern Africa (1981). Awarded OBE (2001).

DE KEYSER, Véronique (1945—). Belgian psychologist and politician. Name variations: Veronique de Keyser. Born Mar 23, 1945, in Brussels, Belgium. ❖ Served as dean of psychology at University of Liège (1990–98); as a European Socialist, elected to 5th European Parliament (1999–2004). Wrote *Human Error Prevention and Well-Being at Work in West Europe and Russia* (Kluwer, 2001) and *L'Erreur humaine.*

DEKKER, Inge (1985—). Dutch swimmer. Born Aug 18, 1985, in Netherlands. ❖ Won a bronze medal for 4 x 100-meter freestyle relay at Athens Olympics (2004).

DEKKERS, Hurnet (1974—). Dutch rower. Born May 8, 1974, in the Netherlands. ❖ Won a bronze medal for coxed eights at Athens Olympics (2004).

DE KLERK, Marike (1937–2001). South African first lady. Born Marike Willemse, Mar 29, 1937, in South Africa; was stabbed and strangled by a 21-year-old security guard at her waterfront apartment complex in Blaauwberg, just north of Cape Town, Dec 4, 2001; attended Potchefstroom University; m. F.W. de Klerk (president of South Africa), 1959 (div. 1998); children: Jan, Willem and Susan Hillocks. ❖ Led the women's wing of the National Party; was South Africa's first lady (1989–94); married to F.W. de Klerk for 39 years, went through a trying divorce after which husband married his mistress, Elita Giorgiades; battled depression the last years of her life. ❖ See also autobiography, *Marike: A Journey Through Summer and Winter.*

DE KOK, Irene (1963—). Dutch judoka. Born Aug 29, 1963. ❖ At Barcelona Olympics, won a bronze medal in half-heavyweight 72 kg (1992).

DE KOONING, Elaine Fried (1918–1989). American artist and art critic. Born Elaine Marie Catherine Fried in Sheepshead Bay, Brooklyn, May 12, 1918; died Feb 1, 1989; dau. of Marie and Charles Fried; attended Leonardo da Vinci Art School and American Artists School; m. artist Willem de Kooning (1905–1997), 1943; no children. ❖ Artist, writer, and wife of Willem de Kooning was a central figure in the emergence of Abstract Expressionism in NY (1940s–50s); though she considered herself 1st and foremost a painter, was also a talented writer whose contributions to *Art News* and other magazines established her as the foremost voice of the New York School; drew and painted continuously, producing still lifes, cityscapes, and portraits, including many of her husband; perfected her own "action painting" technique, consisting of the bold, slashing strokes seen in a series of paintings called "Faceless Men" (1949–56), in which the subjects were recognizable only by their characteristic body stances; became well known as a portrait painter, using as subjects members of her wide circle of friends and admirers, including critic Harold Rosenbert, poets Frank O'Hara and John Ashbery, artist Aristodimos Kaldis, and President John F. Kennedy. ❖ See also *The Spirit of Abstract Expressionism: Selected Writings* (Braziller, 1994); and *Women in World History.*

DE KRÜDENER, Julie (1764–1824). *See Krüdener, Julie de.*

DE LA BARCA, Frances Calderón (1804–1882). *See Calderón de la Barca, Frances.*

DE LA BARRA, Emma (1861–1947). *See Barra, Emma de la.*

DE LA BAUME, Madame (fl. 17th c.). *See Baume, Madame de la.*

DE LA BIJE, Willy (1934—). Dutch ballet dancer. Born June 1, 1934, in Leiden, Holland; m. Jaap Flier. ❖ Danced with Sonia Gaskell's Ballet Recital Group in the Netherlands; joined Netherlands Ballet, where she was featured in productions of *Les Sylphides, Giselle, La Sonnambula,* and more; performed with Netherlands Dance Theater (1959–70), where she appeared in Glen Tetley's *Sargasso* and *The Anatomy Lesson,* Harkavy's *Nocturne,* Job Sander's *Impressions,* and Hans von Manen's *Variomatic,* among others; moved to Australia with husband who served as artistic director of Australian Dance Theater (1973), while she served as ballet master and rehearsal director.

DE LA CERDA, Blanche (c. 1311–1347). Duchess of Penafiel. Born c. 1311; died 1347; dau. of Fernando also known as Ferdinand de la Cerda (b. 1272) and Juana Nunez de Lara (1285–1351); became 2nd wife of John Manuel also known as Juan Manuel "el Scritor," duke of Penafiel, 1328; children: Beatriz (died young); Joanna of Castile (1339–1381). Juan Manuel's 1st wife was Constance of Aragon (d. 1327).

DELAFIELD, E.M. (1890–1943). *See Dashwood, Elizabeth Monica.*

DE LA FONTAINE, Mlle (1655–1738). *See Fontaine, Mlle de la.*

DE LA FORCE, Charlotte-Rose Caumont (1650–1724). *See La Force, Charlotte-Rose de Caumont de.*

DE LA GUERRA, Alejandra (1968—). Peruvian volleyball player. Born Feb 14, 1968, in Peru. ❖ At Seoul Olympics, won a silver medal in team competition (1988).

DE LA GUERRE, Elisabeth-Claude Jacquet (c. 1666–1729). *See Jacquet de la Guerre, Elisabeth-Claude.*

DE LAGUNA, Frederica (b. around 1874). American educator. Born in Oakland, California, c. 1874; dau. of Alexander and Frederica de Laguna; Stanford, AB, 1896, Columbia, AM, 1904. ❖ With Jessica Smith Vance, founded Westlake School for Girls in Los Angeles (1904) and Westlake Junior College (1924), later known as Holmby College.

DE LAGUNA, Frederica (1906–2004). American ethnologist, anthropologist and archaeologist. Name variations: Frederica Annis de Laguna. Born Frederica Annis Lopez de Leo de Laguna, Oct 3, 1906, in Ann Arbor, Michigan; died Oct 6, 2004, in Haverford, Pennsylvania; dau. of Theodore and Grace (Andrus) de Laguna (both philosophers who taught at Bryn Mawr); sister of Wallace de Laguna (geologist); Bryn Mawr College, AB, 1927; Columbia, PhD in Anthropology, 1933. ❖ Studied with Franz Boas, Ruth Benedict, and Gladys Reichard at Columbia; studied in England and France (beginning 1928); accompanied Arctic archaeologist Therkel Mathiassen on the 1st professional excavation in Greenland, on which Inugsuk culture was discovered; conducted research in Alaska (1930–33), which resulted in *The Archaeology of Cook Inlet, Alaska* (1934); conducted anthropological survey (1935), traveling down Tanana and Yukon Rivers, which became foundation of *The Prehistory of Northern North America as Seen from the Yukon* (1947); surveyed social conditions on Pima Indian Reservation, Arizona (1936); became teacher at Bryn Mawr (1938); during WWII, served in WAVES; continued work in Alaska, living in Tlingit village of Angoon (1950) and at Yakutat (1952 and 1954); spent 4 seasons with Athapaskan Atna of Copper River (1954, 1958, 1960, 1968); published 3-vol. *Under Mount Saint Elias* (1972); organized Bryn Mawr's 1st department of anthropology; following retirement from Bryn Mawr, worked in Greenland and as a guest at Alaskan digs. Other works include *Chugach Prehistory* (1956), (with Kaj Birket-Smith) *The Eyak Indians of the Copper River Delta, Alaska* (1938), *The Story of a Tlingit Community* (1960), *Voyage to Greenland: A Personal Initiation into Anthropology* (1977), as well as detective stories.

DE LAGUNA, Grace Mead (1878–1978). American scholar and philosopher. Name variations: Delaguna. Born Grace Mead Andrus, Sept 28, 1878; died Feb 17, 1978; Cornell University, BA, 1903, PhD, 1906; m. Theodore de Laguna; children: Frederica de Laguna (b. 1906, anthropologist); Wallace de Laguna (b. 1910, nuclear scientist). ❖ Spent over 60 years teaching philosophy at Bryn Mawr, as an assistant professor (1912–16), associate professor (1916–28), and professor (from 1928); was cofounder with husband of the Fullerton Philosophy Club (1925); writings include (with Theodore de Laguna) *Dogmatism and Evolution* (1910), *Speech: Its Function and Development* (1927) and *On Existence and the Human World* (1963). ❖ See also *Women in World History.*

DE LA HAYE, Charlotte (1737–1805). *See Montesson, Charlotte Jeanne Béraud de la Haye de Riou, marquise de.*

DE LA HAYE, Ina (1906–1972). Russian-born actress and singer. Name variations: Ina de la Haye. Born Oct 11, 1906, in St. Petersburg, Russia; died Dec 5, 1972, in Tichurst, England; m. Colonel J.V. Delahaye (died). ❖ Made London debut as Gilda in *Calf Love* (1931), followed by *See Naples and Die, Miracle at Verdun, Children in Uniform, Delusion, Tovarich, You Can't Take it With You, Jacobowsky and the Colonel* and *Come Live with Me;* films include *Give Us This Day, Top Secret, Moulin Rouge, Dance Little Lady, Anastasia* and *The Private Life of Sherlock Holmes;* also appeared in concerts.

DE LA HAYE, Nicolaa (1160–1218). *See Haye, Nicolaa de la.*

DE LA HUNTY-STRICKLAND, Shirley (b. 1925). *See Strickland, Shirley.*

DE LAMBERT, Mme. (1647–1733). *See Lambert, Anne Thérèse de Marguenat de Courcelles, marquise de.*

DE LA MORA, Constancia (1906–1950). *See Mora, Constancia de la.*

DE LA MOTTE, Marguerite (1902–1950). American actress. Name variations: Marguerite De LaMotte. Born June 22, 1902, in Duluth, Minnesota; died Mar 10, 1950, in San Francisco, California; m. John Bowers (actor, div.). ❖ Trained as a dancer; starred opposite Douglas Fairbanks in *Mark of Zorro, The Three Musketeers* and *The Iron Mask;* other films include *Pals in Paradise, The Beloved Brute, Arizona, The People vs. Nancy Preston* and *The Unknown Soldier.*

DELAND, Margaret (1857–1945). American writer. Born Margaretta Wade Campbell, Feb 23, 1857, near Allegheny, Pennsylvania; died Jan 13, 1945; dau. of Sample and Margaretta Campbell; studied at Cooper Union in NY, 1875; m. Lorin Fuller Deland, May 12, 1880 (died 1917); no children. ❖ Writer whose popular works often contrast the past with the present, became assistant instructor of drawing and design at Normal College of the City of New York (now Hunter College, 1876); her poem, "The Succory," appeared in *Harper's New Monthly Magazine* (1885); published 1st book, *The Old Garden and Other Verses* (1886); published 1st novel, *John Ward, Preacher* (1888) to great success; following husband's death, did war-relief work in France (1917) and received the Legion of Honor; was among the 1st women elected to National Institute of Arts and Letters (1926); writings include *A Summer Day* (1889), *Florida Days* (1889), *Sidney* (1890), *Philip and His Wife* (1894), *Old Chester Tales* (1899), *Dr. Lavendar's People* (1903), *The Awakening of Helena Ritchie* (1906), *RJ's Mother and Some Other People* (1908), *Around Old Chester* (1915), *The Promises of Alice: The Romance of a New England Parsonage* (1919), *The Kays* (1926), *Captain Archer's Daughter* (1932) and *Old Chester Days* (1937). ❖ See also autobiographical, *If This Be I, As I Suppose It Be* (1935) and *Golden Yesterdays* (1941); and *Women in World History.*

DELANDER, Lois (1911–1985). Miss America. Name variations: Lois Lang. Born on Feb 14, 1911; died Jan 1985 in Evanston, Illinois; attended Chicago School of Industrial Art; m. Ralph Lang (stockbroker); children: 3 daughters. ❖ Named Miss America (1927), representing Illinois. ❖ See also Frank Deford, *There She Is* (Viking, 1971).

DELANEY, Mary Granville (1700–1788). *See Delany, Mary Granville.*

DELANEY, Shelagh (1939—). English playwright. Born in Salford, Lancashire, England, Nov 25, 1939; dau. of Joseph (bus inspector) and Elsie Delaney; children: 1 daughter. ❖ At 18, wrote *A Taste of Honey,* which had a successful run on the West End, was awarded the Charles Henry Foyle New Play Award, transferred to New York and won the New York Drama Critic's Circle Award; adapted her play to film and received a British Film Academy Award for the screenplay (1961); also wrote the play *The Lion in Love* and screenplays for *Charlie Bubbles* (1968) and *Dance with a Stranger* (1985), the story of Ruth Ellis. ❖ See also *Women in World History.*

DELANEY AND BONNIE (1944—). *See Bramlett, Bonnie.*

DELANO, Jane Arminda (1862–1919). American nurse. Born Mar 12, 1862, in Townsend, New York; died April 15, 1919, in Savenay, France; dau. of George and Mary Ann (Wright) Delano; attended Bellevue Hospital Training School for Nurses (NY), 1884–86. ❖ Nurse who unified the workings of the Army Nurse Corps and the Red Cross, began career during a yellow fever epidemic (1887); acted as assistant superintendent of nurses and as an instructor at University of Pennsylvania Hospital School of Nursing (1890–95); named chair of newly formed National Committee on Red Cross Nursing Services (1909), which had been established to create a bridge between the Red Cross and the nursing profession; elected president of American Nurses' Association and named superintendent of Army Nurse Corps (1909); during WWI, administered the flow of 20,000 nurses for duty overseas, as well as large numbers of nurses aides and other workers. ❖ See also *Women in World History*.

DELANOUE, Jeanne (1666–1736). French saint. Born Joan Delanoue. Born in Saumur, in the French province of Anjou, 1666; died in Saumur, 1736; dau. of a merchant. ❖ On father's death, inherited his house and shop and continued the practice of selling cloth, crockery, and religious curios to the faithful on pilgrimage to a nearby shrine; originally a miser, began to help those less fortunate; founded the Sisters of St. Anne and spent rest of life in service to the poor. Feast day is Aug 17.

DELANY, Annie Elizabeth (1891–1995). African-American memoirist. Name variations: Bessie Delany. Born Annie Elizabeth Delany, Sept 3, 1891, in Raleigh, North Carolina; died in Mount Vernon, NY, Sept 25, 1995; dau. of Nanny James Delany and Henry Beard Delany (teacher and Episcopal priest); graduate of St. Augustine's College; Columbia University, DDS, 1923; never married; no children. ❖ As a centenarian, came to national attention with sister with book *Having Our Say: The Delany Sisters' First 100 Years* (1993), an oral history tracing their family life and their achievements as pioneering professionals; also wrote *The Delany Sisters' Book of Everyday Wisdom* (1994). ❖ See also Emily Mann's Broadway play *Having Our Say* (1995); and *Women in World History*.

DELANY, Bessie (1891–1995). See Delany, Annie Elizabeth.

DELANY, Mary Granville (1700–1788). English literary correspondent and artist. Name variations: Mrs. Delany or Delaney; Mary Granville; Mary or Mrs. Pendarves. Born Mary Granville on May 14, 1700, at Coulston, Wiltshire, England; died at Windsor, April 15, 1788; niece of 1st Baron Lansdowne; m. Alexander Pendarves, 1718 (died 1724); m. Patrick Delany or Delaney (Irish cleric), 1743 (died 1768). ❖ A woman of literary tastes, married the eminent preacher Patrick Delany, who became the dean of Down through her influence; while they lived in Delville, near Dublin, began to draw and write, describing the landscapes they encountered on their journeys; also designed and embroidered fabrics; was a close friend of Jonathan Swift and Margaret Bentinck, 2nd duchess of Portland, as well as King George III and Queen Charlotte of Mecklenburg-Strelitz; famed for her "paper mosaic," her major work *Hortus Siccus*, 900 cut-paper depictions of plants, resides in the British Museum; at the time of her death, left behind 6 vols. of autobiography and letters, which present a detailed view of English society in the 18th century. ❖ See also *Women in World History*.

DELANY, Maureen (d. 1961). Irish character actress. Born in Ireland; died Mar 27, 1961, age 73, in London, England. ❖ Was a member of the Abbey Theatre for many years, appearing in such plays as *The Plough and the Stars, The Playboy of the Western World* and *Juno and the Paycock;* US appearances include *God and Kate Murphy* (1959).

DELANY, Sadie (1889–1999). See Delany, Sarah Louise.

DELANY, Sarah Louise (1889–1999). African-American memoirist. Name variations: Sadie Delany. Born Sarah Louise Delany, Sept 19, 1889, in Raleigh, North Carolina; died in Mount Vernon, NY, Jan 25, 1999; dau. of Nanny James and Henry Beard Delany (teacher and Episcopal priest); graduate of St. Augustine's College; attended Pratt Institute; Columbia University, BA, 1920, MEd, 1925; never married; no children. ❖ As a centenarian, came to prominence with sister (1993), with publication of book *Having Our Say: The Delany Sisters' First 100 Years;* also wrote *The Delany Sisters' Book of Everyday Wisdom* (1994); after sister died, wrote *On My Own at 107* (with Amy Hill Hearth, 1997). ❖ See also Emily Mann's Broadway play *Having Our Say* (1995); and *Women in World History*.

DELANY SISTERS, The.
See Delany, Annie Elizabeth.
See Delany, Sarah Louise.

DE LA PARRA, Teresa (1895–1936). See Parra, Teresa de la.

DE LA PASTURE, Elizabeth Bonham (d. 1945). See de la Pasture, Mrs. Henry.

DE LA PASTURE, Mrs. Henry (d. 1945). English novelist and playwright. Name variations: Elizabeth Bonham de la Pasture; Lady Clifford. Born Elizabeth Lydia Rosabelle Bonham in Naples, Italy; died Oct 30, 1945; dau. of Edward Bonham (HM Consul in Calais); m. Count Henry Philip Ducarel de la Pasture (died 1908); m. Sir Hugh Clifford (colonial governor of the Gold Cost, later Nigeria, Ceylon, and the Malay States), 1910 (died 1941); children: 2 daughters, including Elizabeth Monica Dashwood (English novelist under pseudonym E.M. Delafield). ❖ Writer of numerous novels (1900–18), including *The Unlucky Family, The Little Squire, Adam Grigson, Catharine of Calais, The Man from America, Master Christopher* and *Erica;* plays include *Peter's Mother, The Lonely Millionaires, Her Grace the Reformer* and *Deborah of Tod's*.

DE LAPPE, Gemze (1922—). American ballet and theatrical dancer. Born Feb 28, 1922, in Portsmouth, Virginia. ❖ Studied and performed with Mikhail Fokine during her teens; performed in numerous Agnes de Mille projects, most often as leading female dancer, including the original production of *Oklahoma* (1943) and Ballet Theater's productions of *The Harvest According* and *Three Virgins and the Devil;* also toured with De Mille Heritage Dance Theater; danced on Broadway in *The King and I* (1951) and in film version; is considered among the few authentically trained Isadora Duncan dancers.

DE LARA, Adelina (1872–1961). English pianist. Born in Carlisle, England, Jan 23, 1872; died in Woking, England, Nov 25, 1961. ❖ Studied with Clara Schumann and embraced her style and technique, causing her recordings to be valued for their illumination of that earlier world. ❖ See also *Women in World History*.

DE LA RAMÉE, Louise (1839–1908). See Ramée, Louise de la.

DE LA ROCHA, Alicia (b. 1923). See Larrocha, Alicia de.

DE LAROCHE, Baroness (b. 1886). See Deroche, Elise-Raymonde.

DE LA ROCHE, Mazo (1879–1961). Canadian writer. Born Mazo Roche ("de la" added later), Jan 15, 1879, in Toronto, Ontario, Canada; died July 12, 1961; dau. of William and Alberta Lundy Roche; attended the Ontario School of Art in Toronto, Canada, and studied under George Agnew Reid; children: (adopted) Renee and Esme. ❖ Prolific writer, whose chronicles of the Whiteoak family made her one of Canada's most popular writers in early 20th century, is associated with the movement toward greater realism in Canadian fiction; was awarded the *Atlantic Monthly* prize for fiction and received widespread recognition for her 1st Whiteoak novel, *Jalna* (1927); traveled abroad for 1st time and remained in England, making her home there for a number of years (1929); with cousin Caroline Clement, adopted 2 orphaned children of friends (1931); returned to Toronto and re-established a home there (1938); writings include *Explorers of the Dawn* (1922), *Whiteoaks of Jalna* (1929), *Portrait of a Dog* (1930), *Lark Ascending* (1932), *The Master of Jalna* (1933), *Beside a Norman Tower* (1934), *Young Renny* (1935), *Whiteoaks: A Play* (1936), *Whiteoak Harvest* (1936), *The Very House* (1937), *The Sacred Bullock and Other Stories of Animals* (1939), *The Two Saplings* (1942), *Quebec: Historic Seaport* (1944), *The Building of Jalna* (1944), *Return to Jalna* (1946), *Mary Wakefield* (1949), *Renny's Daughter* (1951), *A Boy in the House* (1952), *Variable Winds at Jalna* (1954), *The Song of Lambert* (1955) and *Morning at Jalna* (1960). ❖ See also *Ringing the Changes: An Autobiography* (1957); and *Women in World History*.

DELAROCHE, Suzanne See Avril, Suzanne.

DE LA ROCHEFOUCAULD, Edmée (1895–1991). See La Rochefoucauld, Edmée de.

DE LARROCHA, Alicia (1923—). See Larrocha, Alicia de.

DELARUE-MARDRUS, Lucie (1880–1945). French feminist, poet and novelist. Name variations: Lucie Delarue Mardrus. Born 1880; died 1945. ❖ Belonged to circle of Anna de Noailles and Princess (Yolande) de Polignac that mixed with such luminaries as Gide, Proust, and Rodin; wrote novels, as well as poetry, including *Horizons* (1905), and play *La Prêtresse de Tanit* (1907).

DELARVERIÉ, Stormé (1922—). African-American male impersonator. Name variations: Storme De Larverie or DeLarverie. Born in 1922. ❖ Joined the Jewel Box Revue in which she worked as a male impersonator with 25 female impersonators (1955); sparked the Stonewall Riot (June 1969), after she retaliated against an abusive officer outside the bar. ❖ See also Leslie Feinberg, *Transgender Warriors: Making History from Joan of Arc to RuPaul* (Beacon Press, 1996); (film) *Stormé: The Lady of the Jewel Box* (1987).

DE LA SABLIÈRE, Mme. (1640–1693). See La Sablière, Marguerite de.

DE LA TORRE, Lillian (c. 1902–1993). See McCue, Lillian.

DELAUNAY, Le Vicomte (1804–1855). See Girardin, Delphine.

DE LAUNAY, Mademoiselle (1684–1750). *See Staal de Launay, Madame de.*

DE LAUNAY, Marguerite Jeanne Cordier (1684–1750). *See Staal de Launay, Madame de.*

DELAUNAY, Sonia (1885–1979). Russian-born abstract artist. Name variations: Sonia Terk; Sonia Uhde; Sonia Delaunay-Terk or Terk-Delaunay. Born Sophie Stern, Nov 14, 1885, in Gradzihsk, Ukraine; died Dec 5, 1979, in Paris; dau. of Elie (factory worker) and Anne (Terk) Stern; raised from age five by uncle, Henri Terk (lawyer); attended University in Karlsruhe, Germany, 1903–05; studied at Académie de la Palette in Paris; m. Wilhelm Uhde, 1908 (div. 1910); m. Robert Delaunay, 1910; children: Charles Delaunay (b. 1911). ❖ Abstract artist who was intimately involved in the development of modern art movements, such as Orphism and Dadaism, and largely responsible for the utilization of modern artistic concepts in 20th-century design and fashion; moved to Paris (1905); established studio (1906); painted 1st *Simultaneous Contrasts* (1912); produced 1st simultaneous clothing (1913); opened Casa Sonia and designed costumes for ballet *Cléopatre* (1918); designed costumes for production of *Aïda* (1920); established Atelier Simultané (1924); decorated Boutique Simultanée for International Exhibition of Decorative Arts (1925); published *Sonia Delaunay: Compositions, Couleurs, Idées* (1930); saw portfolio of her works published (1950); had solo exhibition in Paris (1953); appointed Chevalier des Arts and des Lettres (1958); saw 1st major traveling exhibition in North America organized by National Gallery of Canada (1965); published *Colored Rhythms* (1966); received Legion of Honor (1975). Major works: (illustrations) Blaise Cendrars' *La Prose du Transsibérien et de la Petite Jehanne de France* (1913), Tristan Tzara's *Juste Présent* (1961); (lithographs) "10 Origin" (1942), "Album With Six Prints" (1962); (murals) *Les Voyages lointains* (1937), *Portugal* (1937); (paintings) *Le Bal Bullier* (1913), *Rythme coloré* (1946) and *Triptyque* (1963). ❖ See also S. Buckberrough, *Sonia Delaunay: A Retrospective* (1980); A. Cohen, *Sonia Delaunay* (Abrams, 1975) and *The New Art of Colour: The Writings of Robert and Sonia Delaunay* (Viking, 1978); J. Damase, *Sonia Delaunay: Rhythms and Colors* (1972); A. Madsen, *Sonia Delaunay: Artist of the Lost Generation* (1989); E. Morano, *Sonia Delaunay: Art Into Fashion* (1986); and *Women in World History.*

DE LAURETIS, Teresa (1938—). American feminist and educator. Born 1938 in Italy. ❖ Work, influenced by poststructuralist theories, focuses on representations of women in cinema and exclusions of representations of lesbianism in many feminist theories; appointed professor of History of Consciousness at University of California, Santa Cruz; writings include *La Sintassi del desiderio* (1976), *Umberto Eco* (1980), *Alice Doesn't: Feminism, Semiotics, Cinema* (1984), and *Technologies of Gender: Essays on Theory, Film and Fiction* (1987); edited *Feminist Studies/Critical Studies* (1986).

DELAURO, Rosa L. (1943—). American politician. Born Mar 2, 1943, in New Haven, Connecticut; dau. of Ted (aldermen) and Luisa DeLauro (longest serving member on New Haven board of aldermen); Marymount College, BA with honors, 1964; Columbia University, MA in International Politics, 1966; also attended London School of Economics, 1962–63; m. Stanley Greenberg. ❖ Served as executive director of EMILY's List as well as executive director of Countdown '87, the national campaign that successfully stopped US military aid to Nicaraguan Contras; served as chief of staff to US senator Christopher Dodd (1981–87); Democrat, elected to US House of Representatives (1990); served on the House Appropriations Committee; appointed chief deputy whip (1994); reelected (1992, 1994, 1996, 1998, 2000, 2002, 2004).

DE LAVALLADE, Carmen (1931—). American ballet and modern dancer. Born Mar 6, 1931, in Los Angeles, California; m. Geoffrey Holder (dancer, actor, choreographer); children: son. ❖ Performed professionally with Lester Horton's dance company (1950–54), where she created roles in his *Salome* (1950), *Another Touch of Klee* (1951), *Medea* (1951), *Liberian Suite* (1952), and others; danced for Alvin Ailey, John Butler, Donald McKayle, Glen Tetley, and husband Geoffrey Holder; created roles in Agnes de Mille's *Four Marys* (1964), Butler's *Carmina Burana*, McKayle's *Reflections in the Park*, and Ailey's *Roots of the Blues* (1961); was prima ballerina at Metropolitan Opera in NY (1955–56), and New York City Opera Ballet; appeared in numerous films, including *Carmen Jones* (1955), and in several off-Broadway productions, including *Othello* and *Death of a Salesman*; created acclaimed *Les Chansons de Bilitis* (1972) for New York Shakespeare Festival.

DE LA VALLIERE, Louise (1644–1710). *See La Vallière, Louise.*

DE LA VIEUVILLE, Marquise (b. 1731). *See Saint-Chamond, Claire-Marie Mazarelli, Marquise de La Vieuville de.*

DELAY, Dorothy (1917–2002). American violinist and music teacher. Name variations: Dorothy De Lay. Born 1917 in Medicine Lodge, Kansas; died Mar 24, 2002, in Rockland Co., NY; attended Oberlin College and Michigan State University; m. Edward Newhouse (*New Yorker* writer); children: Alison Dinsmore and Jeffrey Newhouse. ❖ The world's foremost violin teacher, had her own concert career, then taught at Juilliard School for over 50 years (1948–2000); traveled the world offering master classes; also taught at Aspen Music School in Colorado in summer; students included Itzhak Perlman, Midori, Gil Shaham and Nigel Kennedy. Received National Medal of Arts from President Clinton (1994). ❖ See also Barbara Lourie Sand, *Teaching Genius: Dorothy DeLay and the Making of a Musician.*

DELAYE, Marguerite (fl. 1569). French war hero. Fl. around 1569 in Montelimar, France. ❖ When Montelimar was put under siege by troops of Huguenot leader Admiral Gaspard de Coligny, was one of its brave defenders, eventually losing one arm during a battle. ❖ See also *Women in World History.*

DEL BENE, Adriana Gabrieli (c. 1755–1799). *See Bene, Adriana Gabrieli del.*

DELBO, Charlotte (1913–1985). French writer. Name variations: Charlotte Dudach. Born Aug 10, 1913, in Vigneux-sur-Seine, Seine-et-Oise, France; father was a civil engineer; died in Paris, 1985; m. Georges Dudach (Marxist intellectual, killed 1942). ❖ Author whose books have been critically acclaimed for providing some of the most profound insights into the Holocaust era and whose masterwork, the trilogy *Auschwitz and After*, has steadily grown in reputation; with husband, was involved in the Communist resistance network during WWII; was arrested (Mar 2, 1942), and husband was executed; deported to Auschwitz-Birkenau (Jan 24, 1943), then transferred to the all-women's camp of Ravensbrück (Jan 1944); a few weeks before collapse of Nazi Germany, was released to Red Cross officials; wrote down her memories of the horrors she and others had experienced (1946), but chose not to publish the manuscript until it had proven it could withstand "the test of time"; wrote a number of plays during next decades; finally published *Aucun de nous ne reviendra* (None of Us Will Return, 1965) as the 1st part of what would be the trilogy *Auschwitz et après* (Auschwitz and After); published 2nd vol., *Une conaissance inutile* (Useless Knowledge, 1970), followed by *The Measure of Our Days* (1971); also wrote *La mémoire et les jours* (Days and Memory, 1985). ❖ See also *Women in World History.*

DELCHEVA, Ina (1977—). *See Deltcheva, Ina.*

DE LEATH, Vaughan (1900–1943). American singer. Name variations: Vaughan DeLeath. Born Sept 26, 1900 (one source cites 1890), in Mt. Pulaski, Illinois; died May 28, 1943, in Buffalo, NY. ❖ Dubbed "First Lady of Radio" and the "Original Radio Girl" after crooning "Swanee River" at Lee Deforest's radio station (1920), became one of the 1st performers on WJZ, NY (1921); composed more than 500 songs and sang on Broadway in *Laugh Clown Laugh* (1923) and *Easy Come, Easy Go* (1925).

DELEDDA, Grazia (1871–1936). Italian novelist. Name variations: Gracia. Pronunciation: de-LEAD-ah. Born Grazia Cosima Deledda, Sept 27, 1871, in Nuoro, Sardinia; died in Rome, Aug 16, 1936; dau. of Giovantonio (Totoni) Deledda (local landowner) and Francesca Cambosa (or Cambosu) Deledda; m. Palmiro Modesani (or Madesani), a civil servant, Nov 4, 1899; children: Sardus (b. 1900), Franz (b. 1904). ❖ Leading Sardinian writer and recipient of the Nobel Prize for Literature who presented, in her most noted works, a profoundly pessimistic view of the human condition; published 1st short story, "Sangue Sardo" ("Sardinian Blood," 1886); published 1st novel, *Fior di Sardegna* (Flower of Sardinia), shortly before the death of her father (1892); enjoyed financial success with novel *Anime oneste* (1895), which gave her a degree of independence; moved to Cagliari, capital of Sardinia (1899); moved to Rome (1900) and wrote *Elias Portolu* (1900), which became the centerpiece of her literary reputation; film version of her 1904 novel *Cenere* appeared (1916); shifted writing themes from Sardinia to psychological introspection (1921), and her bestselling novel *La Madre* (The Mother and the Priest) appeared in English with introduction by D.H. Lawrence (1922); received Nobel Prize for Literature (1926). ❖ See also Mario Aste, *Grazia Deledda: Ethnic Novelist* (Scripta Humanistica, 1990); Carolyn Balducci, *A Self-Made*

Woman: Biography of Nobel-Prize-Winner Grazia Deledda (Houghton, 1975); Bruce Merry, *Women in Modern Italian Literature: Four Studies Based on the Work of Grazia Deledda, Alba De Céspedes, Natalia Ginzburg and Dacia Maraini* (1990); and *Women in World History.*

DE LEEUW, Dianne. Dutch-American figure skater. Dau. of a Dutch mother. ❖ Competing for the Netherlands (held dual American and Dutch citizenships and was at that time residing in Paramount, California), won bronze medals at World championships (1974, 1976) and a gold medal (1975); won a silver medal at Innsbruck Olympics (1976); won the European championship (1976).

DELEHANTY, Megan (1968—). Canadian rower. Born Mar 24, 1968; University of Alberta, BSc, 1990; attended University of British Columbia; University of Pittsburgh, PhD. ❖ At Barcelona Olympics, won a gold medal in coxed eights (1992).

DE LEMPICKA, Tamara (1898–1980). *See Lempicka, Tamara de.*

DE LENCLOS, Ninon (1623–1705). *See Lenclos, Ninon de.*

DE LEPORTE, Rita (c. 1910—). American ballet dancer. Born c. 1910 in New York, NY. ❖ Made professional debut at Metropolitan Opera Ballet in New York City (1922), and danced in *Lakmé, Aida* and *The Bartered Bride,* among others; performed as lead female dancer in Sammy Lee's *Skyscrapers* (1925) at the Opera House in NY; retired at young age (1935).

DE LEVIE, Elka (1905–1979). Dutch-Jewish gymnast. Born Nov 21, 1905, in the Netherlands; died Dec 12, 1979. ❖ At Amsterdam Olympics, won a gold medal for team all-around (1928), the 1st time women's gymnastics was on the Olympic program (no indiv. medals were awarded); was the only Jewish member of the Dutch team to survive the Holocaust.

DELF, Juliet (d. 1962). American vaudeville star. Name variations: Juliet. Died Mar 24, 1962, age 74, in New York, NY; sister of Harry Delf (actor, dancer). ❖ Known professionally as Juliet, was a top headliner in vaudeville (1920s–30s); often played the Palace and the Keith and Orpheum circuits; famed for her imitations.

DEL GIOCONDO, Lisa (1474–?). Florentine woman. Name variations: Mona Lisa; Monna Lisa; Lisa Ghevardini; Mona Lisa de' Gherardini; La Gioconda. Born Lisa Ghevardini in Naples, Italy, 1474; death date unknown; m. Francesco di Zanobi del Giocondo (Florentine merchant), 1495. ❖ A beautiful woman of Florence, whose face inspired one of the most famous paintings in the world, had a platonic friendship with Leonardo da Vinci; after husband commissioned him to paint her portrait (1503), became his subject over and over again. The painting, known as *La Gioconda* or *Mona Lisa,* set a fashion in vitality and subtlety of expression absolutely unrivalled. ❖ See also *Women in World History.*

DELI, Rita (c. 1972—). Hungarian handball player. Born c. 1972 in Hungary. ❖ Won a team silver medal at Sydney Olympics (2000).

DÉLIA (1853–1895). *See Bormann, Maria Benedita Câmara de.*

DELILAH (1200–1000 BCE?). Biblical woman. Name variations: Dalila. ❖ Portrayed in the Old Testament (*Judges 16.4ff.*) as the 3rd romantic interest of the traditional Israelite hero, Samson; as convention has it, was a Philistine beauty from the Wadi Sorek (near modern Gaza) who attracted Samson's amorous attentions; convinced to betray Samson for a monetary reward by some Philistines, did everything within her wiles to bring about his fall. Available evidence suggest that Delilah was probably not a historical figure, but is most accurately seen as an element in a morality tale meant to warn men against beguiling sexuality. ❖ See also *Women in World History.*

DELILLE, Henriette (1813–1862). African-American religious leader. Born a free Creole of color in New Orleans, Louisiana, 1813; died 1862; youngest of 3 children of Jean Baptiste Delille-Sarpy (white creole) and his mistress Marie Joseph "Pouponne" Dias (free woman of color). ❖ Became deeply involved in charitable works; eventually founded the Roman Catholic Sisters of the Holy Family, a society of free black women. ❖ See also Sister Audrey Marie Detiege, *Henriette Delille: Free Woman of Color: Foundress of the Sisters of the Holy Family* (Sisters of the Holy Family in New Orleans, 1976); Sister Mary Francis Hart, *Violets in the King's Garden: A History of the Sisters of the Holy Family of New Orleans* (Sisters of the Holy Family in New Orleans, 1976).

DE LIMA, Clara Rosa (1923—). Trinidadian novelist and short-story writer. Born 1923 in Trinidad; educated in Barbados, Trinidad; attended

Long Island University in US. ❖ Worked as radio journalist; novels include *Tomorrow Will Always Come* (1965), *Not Bad, Just a Little Mad* (1975), *Countdown to Carnival* (1978), *Currents of the Yuna* (1978) and *Kilometre Nineteen* (1980).

DELLA CASA, Lisa (1919—). Swiss lyric soprano. Born in Burgdorf near Berne, Switzerland, Feb 2, 1919; studied with Margaret Haeser in Berne and Zurich; m. Dragan Debeljevic, 1947. ❖ Debuted as Cio-Cio San in Solothurn-Biel (1941) and as Zedenka in Salzburg (1947); made debut in UK at Glyndebourne (1951); was a member of the Vienna State Opera (1947–73); sang at Metropolitan Opera in NY for 15 seasons (1953–68); often sang Mozart, performing and recording Donna Elvira in *Don Giovanni,* the Countess in *Figaro,* and Fiordiligi in *Cosi fan tutte;* also specialized in Richard Strauss, performing Zedenka in *Arabella,* Ariadne in *Capriccio,* Octavian, Sophie, and Marshallin in *Der Rosenkavalier,* and virtually owned the title role of *Arabella,* making complete recordings for Decca (1957) and Deutsche Grammophon (1963). ❖ See also *Women in World History.*

DELLACQUA, Maud (1881–1944). *See Nelson, Maud.*

DELLA ROVERE, Vittoria (d. 1694). *See Medici, Vittoria de.*

DELLA SCALA, Beatrice (1340–1384). Italian noblewoman. Name variations: Regina della Scala; Regina Visconti. Born Beatrice Regina della Scala in 1340 in Vicenza; died June 1384 in Vicenza; dau. of Mastino II della Scala, count of Verona; m. Bernarbò>or Bernabo Visconti, lord of Milan, Aug 1350; children: Marco (d. 1382); Ludovico (d. 1404); Carlo (d. 1404); Thaddaea Visconti (d. 1381); Virida Visconti (c. 1354–1414); Catherine Visconti (c. 1360–1404); Rodolfo (d. 1389); Mastino (d. 1405); Agnes Visconti (c. 1365–1391); Valentina Visconti (d. 1393); Antonia Visconti; Maddalena Visconti (d. 1404); Elizabeth Visconti (d. 1432); Lucia Visconti; Anglesia Visconti. ❖ Born into ruling family of Vicenza and Verona, was married at 10 to Bernabo Visconti, who would become lord of Milan, one of the most powerful men in Italy; was energetic, ambitious, and single-minded in her desire to create in Lombardy an ever larger and more prosperous state ruled by the Visconti; contributed substantially to this goal when she inherited Verona and Vicenza, but was forced to attack and defeat her illeg. brothers before adding the territories to the Visconti state; advised husband on matters of state and often accompanied him on his frequent military campaigns; ruled the territory of Reggio and the cities of Parmigiana and Lunigiana and served as regent of Brescia for her son; gave generously to charities and religious foundations in Milan. ❖ See also *Women in World History.*

DELLA SCALA, Costanza. *See Este, Costanza d'.*

DELLA SCALA, Regina (1340–1384). *See della Scala, Beatrice.*

DELLA SCALA, Verde. *See Este, Verde d'.*

DELLE GRAZIE, Marie Eugenie (1864–1931). Austrian poet. Born 1864 in Austria; died 1931; dau. of a German mother and Venetian father. ❖ Published 1st poetry collection at 17; works include epic poem "Robespierre" (1894) and play *Schlagende Wetter* (1899), which achieved popular success.

DELL'ERA, Antoinetta (1861–?). Italian ballet dancer. Born Jan 24, 1861, in Milan, Italy. ❖ Studied at ballet school of Teatro alla Scala in Milan; danced frequently with Berlin Court Opera from Germany; best known for performances in St. Petersburg, Russia, where she 1st appeared at open-air operetta season; danced with Maryinsky Theater on numerous visits to Russia thereafter; famed for her Sugar Plum Fairy in Lev Ivanov's *The Nutcracker* (1892).

DELLOW, Vivienne (1926—). *See Cassie Cooper, Vivienne.*

DEL MAINO, Agnes (fl. 1420s). Milanese woman. Fl. in 1420s; mistress of Filippo Maria Visconti (1392–1447), duke of Milan (r. 1402–1447); children: (with Filippo) Bianca Maria Visconti (1423–1470). Filippo Visconti was married to Maria of Savoy.

DELMAR, Viña (1903–1990). American playwright, novelist and screenwriter. Born Vina Croter, Jan 29, 1903; died Jan 19, 1990, in Beverly Hills, California; dau. of Charles and Jean (Guran) Croter (both in theater); m. Eugene Delmar, May 10, 1921. ❖ Wrote novels, plays and stories which were often adapted for the screen; screen credits include *Bad Girl* (1931), *Sadie McKee* (134), *Hands Across the Table* (1935), *The Awful Truth* (1937), for which she was nominated for an Academy Award, *Cynthia* (1947) and *About Mrs. Leslie* (1954); plays include *Bad Girl* (1930), *The Rich Full Life* (1945), and *Mid-Summer* (1953), all produced on Broadway; in later years, told the *New York Times* that her work was often written with husband under the single name Viña Delmar.

DEL OCCIDENTE, Maria (c. 1794–1845). See Brooks, Maria Gowen.

DELORIA, Ella (1888–1971). Yankton Sioux linguist and ethnologist. Name variations: Anpetu Waste Win, meaning "Beautiful Day Woman," to commemorate the blizzard that raged on the day of her birth. Born Ella Carla Deloria, Jan 30, 1888, on the Yankton Sioux reservation in South Dakota; died Feb 12, 1971, in South Dakota; dau. of Philip Deloria (Episcopal priest also known as Tipi Sapa or "Black Lodge" of Yankton-French descent) and Mary (Sully) Deloria of Yankton-Irish descent; aunt of Vine Deloria Jr., author of *Custer Died for Your Sins;* attended University of Chicago, 1910–11, and Oberlin College, 1911–13; Columbia University, BS, 1915. ❖ Native American whose research is considered some of the best ever published on her native Sioux (Dakota) culture and whose linguistic translations, including a bilingual collection of Sioux tales, gives a description of Dakota life unparalleled by any other anthropologist; began association with noted anthropologist, Dr. Franz Boas, and worked with him until his death in 1942; awarded Indian Achievement Medal (1943). Writings include *Dakota Texts* (1932), (with Boas) *Dakota Grammar* (1941) and *Speaking of Indians* (1944). *Waterlily,* a novel about the life of a Teton Sioux woman, was written in the early 1940s and published posthumously (1988). ❖ See also *Women in World History.*

DELORME, Marion (c. 1613–1650). French courtesan. Name variations: de Lorme. Born near Champaubert, France, around 1613 (some sources cite 1611); death date established as 1650; dau. of Jean de Lou, sieur de L'Orme (president of the Treasurers of France in Champagne) and Marie Chastelain>; possibly m. Henri Coiffier de Ruzé, marquis de Cinq-Mars. ❖ Legendary courtesan at the time of Louis XIII, was possibly lured into the profession by Jacques Vallée Desbarreaux; soon left him for the successful Henri Coiffier de Ruzé, marquis de Cinq-Mars, whom she may have secretly married; purportedly entertained a who's who of lovers, including Saint-Évremond, the comte de Gramont, and even Cardinal Richelieu; presided over one of the most famous salons of 17th-century Parisian society and was the friend of Ninon de Lenclos. A number of authors used her story, including Alfred de Vigny in the novel *Cinq Mars* (1826), Victor Hugo in the play *Marion Delorme* (1831), Edward Bulwer-Lytton in *Richelieu* (1839), and G. Bottesini in an opera of the same name. ❖ See also *Women in World History.*

DE LOS ANGELES, Victoria (d. 2004). See Los Angeles, Victoria de.

DE LOYNES, Antoinette (fl. 16th c.). See Loynes, Antoinette de.

DE LOYNES, Camille (fl. 16th c.). See Loynes, Camille de.

DELPHY, Christine (1941—). French sociologist, feminist and writer. Born 1941; studied sociology at University of Paris. ❖ Leading proponent of Marxist feminism, began working for Centre National de Recherche Scientifique (CNRS) in Paris (1966); with Simone de Beauvoir, founded journal *Nouvelles question feministes* (New Feminist Issues, 1977); a controversial figure, came to national attention after denouncing Annie Leclerc's *Parole de femme* (1974), effectively splitting the Women's Liberation movement between feminist and class-struggle issues; works include *L'Ennemi principal* (The Main Enemy, 1970) and *Close to Home* (1984); taught at University of Paris X.

DEL RIO, Dolores (1905–1983). Mexican actress. Born Lolita Dolores Asunsolo y Martinez, Aug 3, 1905, in Durango, Mexico; died April 1983; dau. of Jesus and Antonia (Lopez Negrete) Asunsolo; m. Jaime Martinez del Rio, 1921 (died 1928); m. Cedric Gibbons, 1930 (div., Jan 1941); m. Lewis Riley, 1959; children: none. ❖ Film actress of extraordinary versatility who charmed her audiences for better than half a century, was born into an extremely wealthy family in one of the poorest states of northwestern Mexico; moved to Mexico City (1910) to avoid the ravages of Pancho Villa's army; married at age 15 (1921); with husband, spent more time in Paris and US than Mexico; cast in minor roles in several films; after husband died, starred in a critically important film, *Evangeline* (1929), the beginning of an impressive career in Hollywood that lasted throughout 1930s and early 1940s; following a much-publicized falling-out with lover Orson Welles, returned to Mexico to work with film industry there (1943); periodically returned to work in Hollywood but made permanent home in Mexico; became a figure of great repute, not just in film but on stage, where she was an unofficial godmother to a new generation of Mexican actors and actresses; films include *Joanna* (1925), *The Whole Town's Talking* (1926), *What Price Glory?* (1926), *Resurrection* (1927), *The Loves of Carmen* (1927),

Ramona (1928), *Bird of Paradise* (1932), *Flying Down to Rio* (1933), *Wonder Bar* (1934), *Madame Du Barry* (1934), *In Caliente* (1935), *Accused* (1936), *The Man from Dakota* (1940), *Journey into Fear* (1942), *Flor Silvestre* (1943), *Maria Candelaria* (1943), *Bugambilia* (1944), *Los Abandonadas* (1944), *La Otra* (1946), *The Fugitive* (1947), *Historia de una Mala Mujer* (1948), *Dona Perfecta* (1950), *La Cucaracha* (1958), *Cheyenne Autumn* (1964), *C'era Una Volta* ("More Than a Miracle," 1967), *Rio Blanco* (1967) and *The Children of Sanchez* (1978). ❖ See also *Women in World History.*

DELROY, Irene (1898–?). American theatrical dancer. Born Josephine Sanders, 1898, in Bloomington, Illinois; studied interpretive dance and classical ballet. ❖ Performed professionally with Chicago Opera Ballet for 2 years; began vaudeville career thereafter, 1st touring with Charles King in exhibition ballroom act; appeared on Broadway in *Angel Face* (1919), *Ziegfeld Follies of 1927, Here's How* (1928), and *Top Speed* (1929); was a vocalist in *Anything Goes* (1935); films include *Oh, Sailor Behave* (1930).

DEL SOL, Dorina. See Doering, Jane.

DELTA, Penelope (1871–1941). Greek novelist and children's writer. Born Penelope Benaki, 1871, in Alexandria, Greece; died 1941; dau. of Emanuel Benaki. ❖ Writings include *For the Motherland* (1909), *In the Time of Vulgaroktonos* (1911) and *The Secrets of the Swamp* (1937).

DELTCHEVA, Ina (1977–). Bulgarian rhythmic gymnast. Name variations: Ina Delcheva. Born July 20, 1977, in Bulgaria. ❖ Won a silver medal for team all-around at Atlanta Olympics (1996).

DELTEIL, Desha (1892–1965). See Desha.

DE LUCE, Virginia (1921–1997). American theatrical dancer. Name variations: Blue Dove. Born 1921 in Newton, Massachusetts; died 1997 in Charlmont, Massachusetts; m. 3 times, including to Rick Riccardo. ❖ Made professional debut at Leon and Eddie's—a popular Manhattan club—where she performed in conga line; was a lead singer in Roly Rogers band, appearing in numerous shows, movies, hotel cabarets and tv series; sang on "Arthur Godfrey" and other radio shows (1940s–50s); appeared on Broadway in hit musical *New Faces of 1952* and later in Hollywood movie of same name; performed on Broadway in *Who Was That Lady I Saw You With?* (1958); produced several records to little success; lived and worked with Native Americans for numerous years, adopting name of Blue Dove.

DE LUSARRETA, Pilar (1914–1967). See Lusarreta, Pilar de.

DE LUSSAN, Marguerite (1682–1758). See Lussan, Marguerite de.

DE LUSSAN, Zélie (1861–1949). American mezzo-soprano. Name variations: Zelie de Lussan. Born Dec 21, 1861 (some sources cite 1863), in Brooklyn, NY; died Dec 18, 1949, in London, England; dau. of Paul de Lussan and Eugénie de Lussan (singer); m. Angelo Fronani (pianist), 1907 (died 1918). ❖ One of the classic Carmens (a role she is said to have sung some 1,000 times), made concert debut in NY at Chickering Hall (1878); performed with Augustus Harris' Italian Opera Company (Covent Garden, London) and Metropolitan Opera House (NY); toured with several companies; had greatest success in England, where she sang with Royal Opera at Covent Garden (1890–93, 1895–1900, 1902, 1903, 1910); had 3 command performances before Queen Victoria, singing in *Daughter of the Regiment, Carmen* and *Fra Diavolo* (1899–1900).

DEL VANDO, Amapola (1910–1988). Spanish-born stage, tv, and screen actress. Born Feb 1, 1910, in Spain; died Feb 25, 1988, in Lake View Terrace, California; m. Bill Gohl (producer). ❖ Made over 50 films, including *The Snows of Kilimanjaro, Maracaibo, Flying Down to Rio, The Golden Hawk, The Burning Hills, The Appaloosa* and *Justine.*

DELYSIA, Alice (1889–1979). French actress and singer. Born Mar 3, 1889, in Paris, France; died Feb 9, 1979, in Brighton, East Sussex, England; m. Georges Denis (div.); m. René Kolb-Bernard. ❖ Made stage debut at the Moulin Rouge in Paris in the chorus of *The Belle of New York* (1903); made NY debut in *The Catch of the Season* (1905); appeared at Follies-Bergère (1908–09) and in numerous revues at the Olympia; made highly successful London debut in *L'Ingenue* and the revue *Odds and Ends* (1914); other plays include *Carminetta* (title role), *Afgar, As You Were, Mayfair and Montmartre, On With the Dance, Topics of 1923, Princess Charming, Her Past, Mother of Pearl* and *At the Silver Swan;* appeared in the films *She* and *Evensong.*

DELZA, Elizabeth (c. 1903—). American concert dancer. Born c. 1903 in New York, NY; sister of Sophia Delza (expert on Chinese dance who brought Tai Chi Chuan to US); studied at Neighborhood Playhouse and Dalcroze Institute in NY. ❖ Innovative recitalist, joined concert dance movement and presented 1st recitals at Guild Theater; concentrated on teaching, rather than performing, throughout most of life. Works of choreography include *Seven Episodes in The Book of Job* (1933), *Andante with Variations* (1933), *Siciliana* (1934), *Le Tambourin* (1934), *Flammes Soubres* (1934) and *Valse* (1934).

DE MAINTENON, Françoise (1635–1719). *See Maintenon, Françoise d'Aubigné, Marquise de.*

DEMANDOLS DE LA PALUD, Madeleine (fl. 17th century). Accused of witchcraft. Main victim in an episode of possession lasting 1609–1611. ❖ As a young nun in Aix-en-Provence, claimed she had been bewitched by her confessor, Louis Gaufridy; was subjected to several public sessions of exorcism, and the priest was tried and executed; lived a saintly life on her estate as a recluse until Feb 1653, when she found herself accused of bewitchment; held responsible for illness of a neighbor's daughter, was indicted by a tribunal and condemned to life imprisonment. ❖ See also *Women in World History.*

DÉMAR, Claire (1800–1833). French feminist and essayist. Name variations: Claire Demar. Born 1800 in France; drowned herself with lover Perret Delessart, 1833. ❖ Working-class writer associated with Saint-Simonian feminists, expressed radical views on sexual liberation of women; wrote 2 radical feminist works, *Appel d'une femme au peuple sur l'affranchissement de la femme* (1833) and *Ma loi devenir* (1834); her published works and correspondence collected in *Textes sur l'affranchissement de la femme* (1976).

DE MARCO, Renée (c. 1913—). American ballroom dancer and choreographer. Name variations: Marguerite Verney, Renée Verney, Renée LeBlanc, Renée Coates, Renée Verney-Coates; The De Marcos. Born Marguerite Verney, c. 1913, in Burlington, Vermont; niece of George Primrose; studied in Los Angeles with Ernest Belcher; m. Tony De Marco (div. 1939); m. Joe Cassidy; m. Paul Coates; children: Kevin Coates. ❖ Hired by Tony De Marco during adolescence as chorus dancer for Harry Carroll's *Music Box Revue* under name of Marguerite Le Blanc; worked with De Marco for 12 years, appearing in cabarets and such films as *Three Men on a Horse* (1936); danced in Broadway show *Boys and Girls Together* (1940); appeared as solo specialty dancer in a waltz-tap act after breaking from De Marco; choreographed sequences for early tv variety show "Saturday Night Revue" (1952–54).

DE MARCO, Sally (1921—). American ballroom dancer. Name variations: Sally Craven; The De Marcos. Born Ora Lee Allen, Dec 29, 1921, in Roosevelt, Utah; trained in Los Angeles with Ernest Belcher; m. Tony De Marco (dancer), 1944. ❖ Appeared in specialty ballet acts on Broadway; danced in *Boys and Girls Together* (1940), with headline dancers Tony and Renée De Marco; when the couple split, became female lead and continued as Tony De Marco's professional partner for 13 years; with him, appeared in film *Greenwich Village* (1944); still married, retired from performance career (1957).

DE MARILLAC, Louise (1591–1660). *See Marillac, Louise de.*

DEMARINIS, Anne. American musician. Name variations: Sonic Youth. ❖ Briefly performed with influential alternative-rock band, Sonic Youth, as keyboardist (1981–82); performed with numerous other artists, including Glenn Branca and Laurie Anderson; also an accordionist.

DE MARQUETS, Anne (1533–1588). *See Marquets, Anne de.*

DE MARTINEZ, Maria Cadilla (1886–1951). *See Cadilla de Martínez, Maria.*

DE MATTEI, Susan (1962—). American mountain biker. Name variations: Susan DeMattei. Born Oct 15, 1962, in Marin Co., California; attended Chico State University; m. Dave Wiens (mountain biking teammate). ❖ Won a silver medal at World championships (1994); won a bronze medal for cross-country at Atlanta Olympics (1996); retired (1996). Inducted into Mountain Bike Hall of Fame (1997).

DEMBO, Tamara (1902–1993). Russian-born American psychologist. Born into a prosperous Russian-Jewish family in Baku, Azerbaijan, May 28, 1902; died in Worcester, Massachusetts, Oct 17, 1993; studied with Kurt Koffka, Wolfgang Köhler, Kurt Lewin, and Max Wertheimer at University of Berlin, and earned her doctorate in psychology, 1930; never married. ❖ Pioneer of psychological field theory and an important theorist in rehabilitation psychology, developed a method of studying anger that emphasized the importance of understanding the context of each situation; came to US to escape Nazism; taught and carried out research work at a number of American universities including Harvard, spending the final decades of career at Clark University; became one of the world's leading experts on the psychological problems of the handicapped; co-authored *Frustration and Regression: An Experiment with Young Children* (1941). ❖ See also *Women in World History.*

DE MEDICI. *See Medici, de.*

DEMEL, Anna (1872–1956). Austrian entrepreneur. Born in Vienna, Austria, Mar 4, 1872; died in Vienna, Nov 7, 1956; m. Karl Demel. ❖ With husband, was proprietor for more than half a century of Vienna's world-famous Demel's, a pastry shop whose exquisite creations were enjoyed not only by ordinary mortals but also by the exalted nobility who resided a stone's throw down the street in the vast Hofburg complex, the Imperial Palaces of the Habsburg dynasty. ❖ See also *Women in World History.*

DE MELKER, Daisy Louisa (1886–1932). South African murderer. Born June 1, 1886, at Seven Fountains near Grahamstown; hanged in Johannesburg, Dec 30, 1932; m. William Cowle (died 1923); m. Robert Sproat (died Oct 1927); m. Sydney Clarence de Melker, Jan 1931; children: (1st m.) 5, only 1 of whom, Rhodes Cecil Cowle (d. 1932), survived infancy. ❖ A trained nurse, murdered 1st 2 husbands with strychnine, benefitting from their wills; murdered son Rhodes Cecil Cowle with arsenic after he boasted to friends that he would soon come into his inheritance upon reaching age 21; tried on 3 counts of murder in Johannesburg (Oct 1932) and found guilty; hanged without having confessed.

DE MELLO, Theresa (1913–1997). Princess of Hohenzollern. Born Theresa Lisboa Figueria de Mello, June 10, 1913, in Rome, Italy; died Mar 30, 1997, in Madrid, Spain; dau. of Jeronymo de Avellar Figueira de Mello and Candida Riberia Lisboa; m. Andres Bolton, July 3, 1936 (div. 1956); m. Nicholas (1903–1978), prince of Hohenzollern and son of Marie of Rumania, June 13, 1967.

DE MENESES, Juana Josefa (1651–1709). *See Meneses, Juana Josefa de.*

DEMENT, Iris (1961—). American singer, songwriter and guitarist. Born Iris Luella DeMent, Jan 5, 1961, in Paragould, Arkansas; youngest of 14 children of Flora Mae DeMent; m. Elmer McCall (firefighter who became her road manager). ❖ Noted for mix of country and folk music, moved to California with family at age 3; grew up singing gospel; attended college in Kansas City; moved to Nashville (1988); released debut album *Infamous Angel* to rave reviews (1992) and earned even higher praise for 2nd album *My Life* (1994); made acting debut in film *Songcatcher* (2001). Other albums include *The Way I Should* (1996).

DEMENTIEVA, Elena (1981—). Russian tennis player. Name variations: Yelena Dementyeva. Born Oct 15, 1981, in Moscow, Russia. ❖ Won a silver medal for singles at Sydney Olympics (2000); was a semifinalist at US Open (2000).

DEMENTIEVA, Elizaveta (1928—). *See Dementyeva, Yelizaveta.*

DEMENTYEVA, Yelena (1981—). *See Dementieva, Elena.*

DEMENTYEVA, Yelizaveta (1928—). Soviet kayaker. Name variations: Elizaveta Dementieva. Born Mar 1928. ❖ At Melbourne Olympics, won a gold medal in the K1 500 meters (1956).

DE MÉRICOURT, Théroigne (1762–1817). *See Théroigne de Méricourt, Anne-Josèphe.*

DE MERODE, Cleo (1875–1966). *See Mérode, Cléo de.*

DEMERS, Anik (1972—). Canadian skier. Born Jan 1, 1972, in Lac Beauport, Quebec, Canada. ❖ Won gold in Skier X at X Games (2000); other 1st-place finishes include Spring Jam, Squaw Valley, California, in Skiercross (2000) and 24 Hours of Aspen, Aspen, CO, in Endurance DH (2001).

DEMESSIEUX, Jeanne (1921–1968). French composer, organist and pianist. Born in Montpellier, France, Feb 14, 1921; died in Paris, Nov 11, 1968; studied with Magda Tagliaferro, Jean and Noël Gallon, and Marcel Dupré at Paris Conservatoire, graduating with distinction, 1941. ❖ Served as organist at Saint-Esprit Church in Paris (1933–62); appointed professor at Liège Conservatoire in Liege, Belgium (1948); enjoyed an artistically triumphant tour of US (1953); was the

1st woman to play the organ in Westminster Abbey, London. ❖ See also *Women in World History*.

DE MEULAN, Elisabeth (1773–1827). *See Guizot, Pauline.*

DE MILLE, Agnes (1905–1993). American dancer, choreographer, author and lecturer. Name variations: de Mille, De Mille, DeMille. Born Agnes George de Mille in New York, NY, Sept 18, 1905; died in Greenwich Village, Oct 7, 1993; dau. of William Churchill de Mille and Anna Angela (George) de Mille; attended University of California, Los Angeles; studied ballet under Theodore Kosloff, Marie Rambert and Tamara Karsavina; m. Walter Prude, June 14, 1943; children: Jonathan. ❖ Pioneer in the inclusion of American themes, gesture, and body language into classical ballet and the incorporation of classical ballet into musical comedy, whose dances for the Broadway show *Oklahoma!* revolutionized the American musical; made 1st appearance in father's production *The Ragamuffin* (1916) and 1st NY appearance in Mozart's *La Finta Giardiniera* (1927); made concert debut at Guild Theater (1928); appeared with *Grand Street Follies* (1928); choreographed revival of musical *The Black Crook* (1929); choreographed 1st ballet, *Black Ritual* (1940); toured with Agnes de Mille Dance Theater (1953–54); appeared at Covent Garden in *Three Virgins and the Devil* and *Rodeo* (1955); performed with Royal Winnipeg Ballet in her own ballet *The Rehearsal* (1965) and choreographed *The Bitter Weird* for same company; was 1st president of Society for Stage Directors and Choreographers (1965–66); chorographed for such stage musicals as *Hooray for What* (1937), *One Touch of Venus* (1943), *Bloomer Girl* (1944), *Carousel* (1945), *Brigadoon* (1947), *Allegro* (also directed, 1947), *Gentlemen Prefer Blondes* (1949), *Paint Your Wagon* (1951) and *110 in the Shade* (1963); choreographed the ballets *Rodeo* (1942), *Fall River Legend* (1948), *Rape of Lucrecia* (1949), *The Harvest According* (1952), *The Wind in the Mountains* (1965), *The Four Shades* (1965), (also directed) *Come Summer* (1969), *A Rose for Miss Emily* (1971), *Texas Fourth* (1971), *The Informer* (1988) and *The Other* (1992); also wrote 11 books, including *Martha: The Life and Work of Martha Graham* (1991) and her autobiographical works *Dance to the Piper* (1951) and *And Promenade Home* (1957); her letters were published in *Speak to Me, Dance with Me* (1973). Received Tony awards (1947, 1962); elected to Theater Hall of Fame (1973); given Kennedy Center Career Achievement Award (1980) and National Medal of the Arts (1986). ❖ See also Carol Easton, *No Intermissions: The Life of Agnes de Mille* (Little Brown, 1996); and *Women in World History*.

DE MILLE, Beatrice (1853–1923). English-born screenwriter. Name variations: Beatrice C. DeMille; Bebe De Mille. Born Matilda Beatrice Samuel, Jan 30, 1853, in Liverpool, England; died Oct 8, 1923, in Hollywood, California; m. Henry C. De Mille, 1876 (died Feb 10, 1893); children: William C. de Mille (writer) and Cecil B. De Mille (director-producer); grandmother of Agnes de Mille. ❖ Wrote screenplays, scenarios, and stories for such films as *The Storm*, *The Years of the Locust*, *Sacrifice*, *Unconquered*, *Forbidden Paths* and *The Devil-Stone*.

DE MILLE, Mrs. Cecil B. (1874–1960). *See Adams, Constance.*

DE MILLE, Clara (1886–1956). *See Beranger, Clara.*

DE MILLE, Constance (1874–1960). *See Adams, Constance.*

DE MILLE, Katherine (1911–1995). American Actress. Name variations: Katherine De Mille Quinn. Born Katherine Lester in Vancouver, British Columbia, Canada, June 29, 1911; died of Alzheimer's disease, April 27, 1995, in Tucson, Arizona; orphaned as a child; at age 9, adopted by Cecil B. De Mille (1881–1959, the movie director) and Constance (Adams) De Mille (actress); attended the exclusive Hollywood School for Girls; sister of Cecilia De Mille; became 1st wife of Anthony Quinn (actor), 1936 (div. 1963); children: 5. ❖ Appeared in many movies (1930s–40s), including Jack London's *Call of the Wild* (1935) and Helen Hunt Jackson's *Ramona* (1936); retired from acting (1950).

DEMINA, Svetlana (c. 1960—). Russian shooter. Born c. 1960 in Tatarstan, USSR. ❖ Won a silver medal for skeet shooting at Sydney Olympics (2000); won 13 World championships.

DEMING, Dorothy (1893–1972). American nurse and children's writer. Born Dorothy Deming, June 8, 1893, in New Haven, Connecticut; died Jan 1972 in Winter Park, Florida; dau. of Clarence and Mary Bryan (Whiting) Deming; Vassar College, BA, 1914; attended Yale University; graduate of New York City's Presbyterian Hospital School of Nursing, 1920; studied at Henry Street Visiting Nurse Association. ❖ Elected director of Holyoke Visiting Nurse Association (1924); hired as assistant

to director of National Organization for Public Health Nursing (NOPHN, 1927); served as assistant to editor, director general and journal editor of *Public Health Nursing* (1935–42); joined American Public Health Association (1942–52); published the highly successful *Penny Marsh: Public Health Nurse* (1938) and its sequels, which were so popular that high schools created Penny Marsh Clubs for girls who wanted to become nurses; wrote at least 20 fictional novels.

DEMIREVA, Bojanka (1969—). Bulgarian gymnast. Born Nov 23, 1969, in Bulgaria. ❖ Won the Hungarian International (1984) and Golden Sands International (1986); was a bronze medalist at the Chunichi Cup (1985).

DE MIST, Augusta (1783–1832). South African-Dutch diarist. Born 1783 in Kampen, Netherlands; died 1832. ❖ Spent time at Cape, South Africa, and recorded experiences in diary (trans. as *Diary of a Journey to the Cape of Good Hope and the Interior of Africa in 1802 and 1803*); in diary, provides insights into Cape Town life, work of Moravian missionaries, and conflict between Dutch settlers and indigenous inhabitants of Cape.

DEMLEITNER, Elisabeth. West German luge athlete. Born in Germany. ❖ Won a bronze medal for singles at Innsbruck Olympics (1976).

DEMOISELLES DES ROCHES, Les.
See Roches, Madeleine des (1520–1587).
See Roches, Catherine des (1542–1587).

DEMONGEOT, Mylène (1936—). French actress. Name variations: Mylene Demongeot, Mylène-Nicole Demongeot, Mylène Nicole. Born Marie Hélène Demongeot, Sept 29, 1936, in Nice, France; m. Marc Simenon (son of novelist Georges Simenon). ❖ Made film debut in *Les enfants de l'amour* (1953) and come to prominence in *Les sorcières de Salem* (aka *The Witches of Salem* or *The Crucible*, 1957); other films include *Bonjour tristesse*, *Cette nuit-là*, *Upstairs and Downstairs*, *Under Ten Flags*, *Il ratto delle sabine*, *The Singer Not the Song*, *Doctor in Distress*, *Le Bâtard* and *L'homme idéal*; with husband, heads Kangourou Films.

DE MONTIFAUD, Marc (1848–1912). *See Chartroule, Marie-Amélie.*

DEMORELOS, Brenda (1926—). *See Helser, Brenda.*

DEMOREST, Ellen Curtis (1824–1898). American milliner. Name variations: Nell Curtis; Mme. Demorest. Born Ellen Louise Curtis on Nov 15, 1824, in Schuylerville, Saratoga Co., New York; died Aug 10, 1898; dau. of Henry D. (hat manufacturer) and Electa (Abel) Curtis; m. William Jennings Demorest, April 15, 1858; children: William Curtis (b. 1859) and Evelyn Celeste Caradora Louise (b. 1865). ❖ Arbiter of American fashion who democratized the availability of smart women's clothing through the development of paper patterns and was a strong supporter of women's achievements in business; set up a millinery shop in Schuylerville and prospered (1843); moved business to millinery center in Troy, NY, and eventually to New York City (1844); began distributing paper patterns and founded a quarterly fashion catalog *Mirror of Fashions* of which she was editor (1860); continued publishing special fashion publications while the magazine appeared under various titles—*Demorest's Illustrated Monthly* and *Mme. Demorest's Mirror of Fashions* (1865–77), *Demorest's Monthly Magazine* (1878–89), *Demorest's Family Magazine* (1899–99); shifted editorial duties to sons (1882); founded, with other women professionals, the woman's club Sorosis (1868); established, with Susan King, the Woman's Tea Company, to import tea to be sold by gentlewomen (1872). ❖ See also Ishbel Ross, *Crusades and Crinolines: The Life and Times of Ellen Curtis Demorest and William Jennings Demorest* (Harper & Row, 1963); and *Women in World History*.

DEMORGAN, Evelyn (1850–1919). English painter. Name variations: Evelyn De Morgan; Evelyn Pickering, Mary Evelyn Pickering, Mrs. William De Morgan. Born Mary Evelyn Pickering, Aug 30, 1855, in London, England; died May 2, 1919, in London; dau. of Percival Pickering (senior barrister) and Anna Maria Wilhemina Spencer-Stanhope; studied with her uncle, artist John Rodham Spencer-Stanhope; studied at Slade School of Art under Edward J. Poynter; m. William DeMorgan (novelist, potter, designer, important figure in Arts and Crafts movement), 1887. ❖ Successful Pre-Raphaelite painter, sold 1st painting *Tobias and the Angel* (1875) and had 1st exhibition at Dudley Gallery (1876); invited to exhibit at prestigious Grosvenor Gallery in London, met with great success and became a regular exhibitor there; moved into studio in Chelsea; wintered every year in Florence due to husband's health (1890–1914) and flourished in Italian milieu; exhibited frequently, holding show at Leighton House (1902–03), solo exhibition at Bruton Gallery (1906), 25 works at Wolverhampton Art Gallery (1907); influenced by classics, mythology and Renaissance art, was part of Pre-Raphaelite circle that included Edward Burne-Jones, and her paintings reflect his influence; was also influenced by popular Spiritualist movement; collaborated with husband on writings addressing philosophical and spiritual themes, which was published anonymously as *The Result of an Experiment* (1890). ❖ See also Catherine Gordon, ed. *Evelyn De Morgan Oil Paintings* (De Morgan Foundation, 1996).

DEMPSEY, Sister Mary Joseph (1856–1939). American hospital administrator. Born Julia Dempsey, May 14, 1856, in Salamanca, NY; died Mar 29, 1939, in Rochester, NY; dau. of Patrick and Mary (Sullivan) Dempsey. ❖ Took vows as a Franciscan nun (1878); became head nurse at St. Mary's Hospital, Rochester, NY (c. 1889), then served as surgical assistant to Dr. William J. Mayo (1890–1915) and superintendent (1892–1939); founded St. Mary's Hospital School for Nurses (1906); was instrumental in developing relationship between Mayo Clinic and St. Mary's Hospital.

DEMPSTER, Carol (1901–1991). American actress and dancer. Born Dec 9, 1901, in Duluth, Minnesota; raised in Santa Monica, California; died Feb 1, 1991, in La Jolla, California; trained at Los Angeles Denishawn school; m. Edwin S. Larsen, 1929. ❖ Performed with the Denishawn concert groups; starred for D.W. Griffith in *Isn't Life Wonderful* (1924) and *The Sorrows of Satan* (1926); other films include *Dream Street*, *Scarlet Days*, *True Heart Susie*, *The White Rose*, *America*, *Limehouse Nights*, *Sally of the Sawdust* and *That Royle Girl;* also starred opposite John Barrymore in *Sherlock Holmes* and tangoed with Rudolf Valentino at Grauman's (1922); retired (1926).

DENCH, Judy (1934—). British actress. Born Judith Olivia Dench in York, England, Dec 9, 1934; educated at a Quaker school; m. Michael Williams (actor), 1971; children: Tara Williams (b. 1972, actress as Finty Williams). ❖ Appeared on stage in *Hamlet* (1957), *Romeo and Juliet* (1960), *The Cherry Orchard* (1961), *St. Joan* (1966), *Cabaret* (1968), *Major Barbara* (1970), *Pack of Lies* (1983), *Mother Courage* (1984), *A Little Night Music* (1996), *Breath of Life* (2002); on film in *Wetherby* (1985), *Room with a View* (1985), *Henry V* (1990), *Goldeneye* (1995), *Mrs. Brown* (1996), *Shakespeare in Love* (1997), *Tea with Mussolini* (1998), *Iris* (2001), *Chocolat* (2000), *The Shipping News* (2001), *Presenting Mrs. Henderson* (2006). on television in "Talking to a Stranger" (1966), "On Giant's Shoulders" (1979), "Going Gently" (1981), "Love in a Cold Climate" (1980), "Behaving Badly" (1989), "Absolute Hell" (1991), "The Last of the Blonde Bombshells" (1999), and in two long-running series, "A Fine Romance" (with husband, 1980–84) and "As Time Goes By" (1991–2002). Won numerous awards, including Academy Award for *Shakespeare in Love* (1997) and BAFTA awards for *Mrs. Brown* and *Iris;* made Dame Commander of the Order of the British Empire (1988). ❖ See also autobiography *A Great Deal of Laughter* (Futura, 1986); John Miller, *Judi Dench: With a Crack in Her Voice* (rev. ed., Orion, 2002)

DENCH, Patricia (1932—). Australian shooter. Born Mar 8, 1932. ❖ At Los Angeles Olympics, won a bronze medal in sport pistol (1984).

DENDEBEROVA, Yelena (1969—). Soviet swimmer. Born May 4, 1969. ❖ At Seoul Olympics, won a silver medal in 200-meter individual medley (1988).

DENENBERG, Gail (1947—). American golfer. Born Jan 17, 1947, in New York, NY; University of Miami, BA. ❖ Joined LPGA tour (1969); won Sears Classic (1974).

DENEUVE, Catherine (1943—). French actress. Name variations: Sylvie Dorléac. Born Catherine Fabienne Dorléac, Oct 22, 1943, in Paris, France; dau. of actors; sister of Françoise Dorléac (actress, 1942–1967); m. David Bailey (English photographer), 1965 (div. 1972). ❖ One of the grande dames of the French cinema, made film debut at 13 in *Les Collégiennes* (1957); met Roger Vadim (1961) and appeared in his *Le vice et la vertu* (1963); starred in other important films, including Polanski's *Repulsion* (1965), Buñuel's *Belle du jour* (1967) and *Tristana* (1970), Deville's *Benjamin* (1968), and Aldrich's *Hustle* (1975); made over 90 films, including *Les parapluies de Cherbourg* (*Umbrellas of Cherbourg*, 1963), *La chant du monde* (1965), *Les Créatures* (1966), *Les demoiselles de Rochefort* (1967), *Benjamin* (1968), *Manon 70* (1968), *Mayerling* (1968), *Liza* (1972), *L'Agression* (1975), *Le Dernier métro* (*The Last Metro*, 1980), *Le choix des armes* (1981), *Le Choc* (1982), *The Hunger* (1983), *Paroles et musique* (1984), *La Reine blanche* (1991), *Indochine* (1992), for which she earned an Academy Award nomination for Best

Actress, *O Convento* (1995), *Place Vendôme* (1998), *Belle maman* (1999), *Pola X* (1999), *Dancer in the Dark* (2000), *Absolument fabuleux* (2001), *The Musketeer* (2001), and *8 femmes* (*8 Women*, 2002); served as president and director of Films de la Citronille (1971–79) and founded Société Cardeva (1983); on French tv, appeared as the Marquise in miniseries "Les liaisons dangereuses" (2003) and as Marie Bonaparte in "Princesse Marie" (2004).

DENG (r. 105–121). Dowager empress of China. Name variations: Teng. Ruled from 105 to 121; died in 121. ❖ During Eastern or Later Han Dynasty, ruled as dowager queen following death of Emperor He Di (Ho Ti), who ruled from 88 to 105; was regent for infant son from 105 until her death.

DENG, Cora (b. 1900). *See Deng Yuzhi.*

DENG YAPING (1973—). Chinese table tennis player. Born Feb 5, 1973, in Henan Province, China; dau. of a table tennis coach. ❖ By age 15, played at a national level; at Barcelona Olympics, upset top-seeded players to win gold medals in singles and doubles—the 1st double-gold winner in that event in Olympic history (1992); won singles World championships (1991, 1995, 1997); at Atlanta Olympics, won singles and, with partner Qiao Hong, doubles as well (1996).

DENG YINGCHAO (1903–1992). Chinese feminist and revolutionary. Name variations: Deng Yinzhao or Deng Yin-Zhao; Deng Wenxu; Teng Yingchao; Teng Ying-ch'ao; Teng Ying-chao. Pronunciation: Ying (rhymes with ring) Chao (rhymes with now). Born Deng Wenxu in 1903 (some sources say 1904) in the northcentral Chinese province of Henan (Honan); dau. of an officer in the imperial army under the late Qing Dynasty and a mother who became a schoolteacher; education was typical of Chinese students of the time in Beijing and Tianjin; m. Zhou Enlai (Chou Enlai), later premier of Communist China, 1925; children: none of her own, but did adopt. ❖ Most prominent leader of the Chinese women's movement, who was also the revolutionary comrade and wife of Premier Zhou Enlai; joined the radical students' movement, in particular "The Awakening Society," and met Zhou Enlai (1919); joined Socialist Youth League (1924); became member of the new Chinese Communist Party (CCP) and leader in the women's movement (1925); was one of the few women to survive the epochal Long March, the formative event in Chinese Communist history (1934–35); worked in liaison groups between CCP and Chinese Nationalist Party (KMT) throughout Sino-Japanese War (1937–45); continued to direct the woman's movement and held many important offices following the success of the revolution (1949), including a membership on the governing Central Committee of the CCP from 1956; assisted in drafting the Marriage Reform Law of 1950; gave last major policy speech, before the 8th Party Congress (1956); served in many public and ceremonial posts after that time; was perhaps the most honored woman in the People's Republic of China up to the time of her death. ❖ See also Hu Hsing-fen, *Mrs Li Zhifan: A Memoir about Deng Yingchao* (ed. by Israel Epstein and trans. by Li Chaotseng and Deng Guangyin, Hong Kong: Joint Publishing, 1987); and *Women in World History*.

DENG YINZHAO (1903–1992). *See Deng Yingchao.*

DENG YUZHI (1900–1996). Chinese feminist. Name variations: Cora Deng; Teng Yü-chih. Pronunciation: Ding YOU-zhee. Born Deng Yuzhi in Shashi, China, 1900; died in Shanghai, Oct 1, 1996; dau. of a government official; attended Zhou Nan Girls' Middle School, Fuxiang School for Girls, Jinling College in Nanjing, and one year at London School of Economics; married but separated shortly afterward, in 1919; no children. ❖ Radical feminist who took an active role in China's May 4th Revolution of 1919 and, through her work for the Young Women's Christian Association, improved working conditions for women, particularly in factories, while also organizing night schools that became a forum for feminism throughout China; was orphaned at 10 (1910); sent by grandmother to Fuxiang School for Girls, where she joined the YWCA; as president of the student self-government association, became organizer in May 4th Revolution (1919); forced into an arranged marriage, left husband and his family to attend Jinling College in Nanjing (1919); pursued by husband's family, fled to Shanghai where she worked several years for the YWCA; attended London School of Economics (1929–30); returned to China, appointed head of YWCA's Bureau of Labor (1930); began organizing night schools throughout China to raise women's political, social, and feminist consciousness; collaborated with Chinese Communist Party (1930–40s); appeared with Mao Zedong in Tiananmen Square on the occasion of the founding of the People's Republic of China (1949); served in numerous organizations and as general secretary of the YWCA. ❖ See also *Women in World History.*

DENHAM, Isolde (1920—). English actress. Born Oct 30, 1920, in London, England; dau. of Reginald Denham (actor) and Moyna MacGill (actress); half-sister of Angela Lansbury (actress); m. Peter Ustinov (actor), 1940 (div. 1945). ❖ Made stage debut at the King's, Hammersmith, dancing in *Jack and the Beanstalk* (1935), followed by *Rebecca, Murder from Memory, A Month in the Country* and *The Banbury Nose;* also appeared with the Old Vic.

DENIS, Louise (c. 1710–1790). French author. Name variations: Louise Arouet. Born Louise Mignot Arouet c. 1710; died 1790; dau. of Voltaire's oldest brother; m. the middle-class M. Denis, 1738 (died 1744); m. a Sieur du Vivier, 1779. ❖ Wrote several works and a play, "La coquette punie," but her literary work has been largely overshadowed by her relationship with Voltaire. ❖ See also *Women in World History.*

DENIS, María (1916–2004). Italian actress. Name variations: Maria Denis. Born María Esther Beomonte, Nov 22, 1916, in Buenos Aires, Argentina, of Italian parents; died April 15, 2004, in Rome, Italy; married, 1953; children: 1 son, Filippo. ❖ One of the most popular film stars in Mussolini's fascist Italy, moved there as a child; at 16, had a small part in the comedy *Gli Uomini, che mascalzoni!* (*What Scoundrels Men Are!*), then played the lead in *Treno Populare* (1933); within a decade, made 30 films (1933–43), including *1860, Contessa Di Parma, Addio Giovinezza* and *L'Assedio dell'Alcazar;* after war, was accused of being the mistress of the notorious Pietro Koch, chief of police in Rome under the Nazis (though she always denied it); facing charges of collaboration, was forced to retire from film, after starring with Peter Ustinov in *Private Angelo* (1949); became an interior decorator.

DENIS, Michaela (1914–2003). English wildlife filmmaker. Name variations: Machaela Denis Lindsay. Born Michaela Holdsworth, Aug 28, 1914, in London, England; died May 4, 2003, in Nairobi, Kenya; m. Armand Denis (Belgian filmmaker), 1948 (died 1971); became 3rd wife of Sir William Lindsay (former chief justice of Sudan), Aug 1975 (died Oct 1975); no children. ❖ Pioneer filmmaker with husband, brought the life of animals to BBC tv screens; began career as a designer in Paris and NY; known for her white blonde hair and glamorous presentation, was often seen on screen with the animals in such shows as "Filming Wild Animals" (1954), "Filming in Africa" (1955), "On Safari" (1957–59 and 1961–65) and "Safari to Asia" (1959–61); also wrote *Leopard in My Lap* (1957) and *Ride a Rhino* (1960); with husband, built a house near Nairobi, and remained in Kenya after his death; a conservationist, was an outspoken vice-chair of Kenyan branch of The Men of the Trees.

DENISON, Flora MacDonald (1867–1921). Canadian feminist. Name variations: Flora Merrill. Born Flora MacDonald Merrill in 1867 in the wilderness of Northern Ontario, Canada; died May 23, 1921; dau. of George Merrill (teacher); attended a Collegiate Institute in Belleville until age 15; attended a Commercial school in Toronto; m. Howard Denison, Aug 1892; children: Merrill Denison (b. 1893). ❖ Member of the Canadian reform and suffrage movements of the early 20th century, who saw women as equal and autonomous members of society, entitled to the same rights as men, in contrast to the more accepted view of her day, which assumed women and men were fundamentally different in "nature" and, therefore, destined to perform different societal roles; moved to Detroit and began to contribute articles to *Detroit Free Press* (late 1880s); returned to Toronto, began dressmaking career but continued to write (1893); joined suffrage movement (1903); established independent dressmaking shop (1905); began writing a column for *Toronto Sunday World* (1906), a platform for a variety of social issues, mostly related to women; served as president of Canadian Suffrage Association (1910–14); established "Bon Echo," a spiritual retreat in Central Ontario (1916); helped organize the Social Reconstruction Group of the Toronto Theosophical Society (1918); writings include *Mary Melville* (1900), and *Women Suffrage in Canada* (1912). ❖ See also *Women in World History.*

DENISON, Mary Andrews (1826–1911). American novelist. Name variations: (pseudonyms) Clara Vance and N.I. Edson. Born Mary Ann Andrews on May 26, 1826, in Cambridge, Massachusetts; died Oct 15, 1911, in Cambridge; dau. of Thomas Franklin Andrews and Jerusha (Robbins) Andrews; m. Rev. Charles Wheeler Denison (cleric and anti-slavery editor). ❖ Published 1st novel *Edna Etheril, the Boston Seamstress* (1847); wrote about 80 popular novels, including *The Prisoner of La Vintresse* (1860s), *Out of Prison* (1864), *John Dane* (1874), and *That Husband of Mine* (1877), her most popular.

DENIZ, Leslie (1962—). American discus thrower. Born May 25, 1962; attended Arizona State University. ❖ At Los Angeles Olympics, won a silver medal in the discus throw (1984); broke US discus record 5 times (1982–83).

DENMAN, Gertrude (1884–1954). English educator, campaigner for rural life, and birth-control advocate. Name variations: Gertrude Mary Denman; Trudie Denman; Lady Denman. Born Gertrude Mary Pearson, Nov 7, 1884; grew up in London; died June 2, 1954; only dau. of Weetman Dickinson Pearson, 1st Viscount Cowdray (1856–1927), construction magnate); m. Lord Thomas Denman, 3rd baron Denman (1874–1954, 5th governor-general of Australia, 1910–14), Nov 26, 1903. ❖ Inherited father's country estate, Balcombe Place (1905); elected to Women's National Liberal Federation; began working with Bush Nursing Association (1913); served as Women's Institute (WI) chair for Britain (1917–46); served as director for Women's Land Army (1939) and volunteered Balcombe Place for its headquarters; began serving as chair of National Birth Control Association (1930), which was later known as the Family Planning Association; as chair, led committee that produced a report about practical education for women in rural areas (1928). Named Order of the British Empire (1920) and Dame Commander of the Order of the British Empire (1933); honored by the naming of Denman College in Marcham, Abingdon, near Berkshire (1948).

DENMAN, Lady (1884–1954). *See Denman, Gertrude.*

DENMAN, Trudie (1884–1954). *See Denman, Gertrude.*

DENMARK, queen of.
See Lathgertha (b. around 665).
See Thyra (d. 940).
See Gyrid (fl. 950s).
See Sigrid the Haughty (d. before 1013).
See Gunhilda of Poland (d. around 1015).
See Elizabeth of Kiev (fl. 1045).
See Gunhild of Norway (d. 1054).
See Gyde (fl. 1054).
See Ingigerd Haraldsdottir (fl. 1075).
See Bodil of Norway (fl. 1090s).
See Malmfrid of Russia (fl. 1100s).
See Margarethe of Vastergotland (fl. 1100).
See Ulfhild (fl. 1112).
See Frithpoll, Margaret (d. 1130).
See Sophie of Russia (c. 1140–1198).
See Berengaria (1194–1221).
See Leonor of Portugal (1211–1231).
See Dagmar of Bohemia (d. 1212).
See Margaret of Pomerania (d. 1282).
See Mechtild of Holstein (d. 1288).
See Agnes of Brandenburg (d. 1304).
See Ingeborg (d. 1319).
See Elizabeth of Holstein (fl. 1329).
See Euphemia of Pomerania (d. 1330).
See Helvig of Denmark (fl. 1350s).
See Philippa (1394–1430).
See Dorothea of Brandenburg (1430–1495).
See Sophia of Pomerania (1498–1568).
See Elisabeth of Habsburg (1501–1526).
See Sophia of Mecklenburg (1557–1631).
See Anna Catherina of Brandenburg (1575–1612).
See Munk, Kirsten (1598–1658).
See Sophie Amalie of Brunswick-Lüneberg (1628–1685).
See Louise of Mecklenburg-Gustrow (1667–1721).
See Vieregg, Elizabeth Helene.
See Sophia of Bayreuth (1700–1770).
See Louise of England (1724–1751).
See Maria Juliana of Brunswick (1729–1796).
See Caroline Matilda (1751–1775).
See Marie Sophie of Hesse-Cassel (1767–1852).
See Caroline Amelia of Augustenburg (1796–1881).
See Louise of Hesse-Cassel (1817–1898).
See Louise of Sweden (1851–1926).
See Alexandrina of Mecklenburg-Schwerin (1879–1952).
See Ingrid of Sweden (1910—).

DENNAN, Makereti (1873–1930). *See Papakura, Makereti.*

DENNETT, Mary Ware (1872–1947). American feminist and pacifist. Pronunciation: DEN-et. Born Mary Coffin Ware, April 4, 1872, in Worcester, Massachusetts; died in Valatie, New York, July 25, 1947; dau. of George Whitefield Ware (wool merchant) and Livonia Coffin (Ames) Ware; niece of Lucia Ames Mead; attended Boston Museum of Fine Arts; m. William Hartley Dennett, Jan 20, 1900 (div. 1913); children: 3 boys, 2 of whom, Carleton and Devon, survived past childhood. ❖ Birth control advocate, women's suffragist, and pacifist whose 1929 landmark free-speech court case helped redefine the legal definition of obscenity; taught decoration and design, Drexel Institute in Philadelphia (1894–97); opened handicraft shop in Boston (1898); served as councilor, Boston Society of Arts and Crafts (1899–1905); served as field secretary of Massachusetts Woman Suffrage Association (1908–10); named corresponding secretary, National American Woman Suffrage Association (1910–14); served as field secretary, American Union Against Militarism (1916); founded, then directed, National Birth Control League (1915–18) and Voluntary Parenthood League (1919–25); published "The Sex Side of Life: An Explanation for Young People" in the *Medical Review of Reviews* (1918); was editor for *Birth Control Herald* (1922–25); wrote *Birth Control Laws* (1926); won celebrated obscenity case, *US v. Dennett* (1930), which helped to clarify the place of the Bill of Rights in American society; wrote *Who's Obscene?* (1930) and *The Sex Education of Children* (1931); named chair, World Federalists (1941–44). ❖ See also *Women in World History*.

DENNIE, Abigail (1715–1745). American poet. Born Jan 14, 1715; died May 1745. ❖ Brought up in strict Calvinist home; married to escape father and then committed suicide after marriage proved unhappy. One poem is extant, "Lines from a Letter to Her Sister, Jane Colman Turell, Mar 23, 1733."

DENNIS, Clare (1916–1971). Australian swimmer. Name variations: some sources incorrectly cite Claire. Born April 14, 1916; died of cancer, 1971; m. George Golding (Olympic athlete), 1941. ❖ At age 14, won her 1st New South Wales and Australian championships in the 220-yard breaststroke; after breaking the world record at age 15, became the youngest member of the Australian delegation to compete at Los Angeles Olympics (1932), winning the gold medal in the 200-meter breaststroke and breaking the Olympic record at 3:06.3, the only non-American gold medalist in the women's swimming competition; considered the premiere swimmer in her specialty in the world (1931–35); was the 1st Australian swimmer to win a gold medal at British Empire Games (1934).

DENNIS, Mame (1891–1985). See Tanner, Marion.

DENNIS, Sandy (1937–1992). American actress. Born Sandra Dale Dennis in Hastings, Nebraska, April 27, 1937; died in Westport, Connecticut, Mar 2, 1992; attended Nebraska Wesleyan University and University of Nebraska; studied acting at HB Studio and Actors Studio, NY; had 10-year relationship with jazz musician Gerry Mulligan. ❖ Known for her nervous mannerisms and halting speech pattern, often played emotionally uncertain women; made NY debut in *The Lady from the Sea*; emerged as a Broadway star (1960s), winning back-to-back Tony Awards for work in *A Thousand Clowns* (1963) and *Any Wednesday* (1964); later stage appearances included *How the Other Half Loves*, *Absurd Person Singular*, *Same Time Next Year* and *Come Back to the Five and Dime, Jimmy Dean, Jimmy Dean*; films include *Splendor in the Grass* (1961), *Up the Down Staircase* (1967), *The Fox* (1968), *Sweet November* (1968), *The Out-of-Towners* (1970), *Nasty Habits* (1977), *The Three Sisters* (1977), *The Four Seasons* (1981), *Another Woman* (1988) and *Parents* (1989); portrayed Celia in American tv production of "A Hatful of Rain" (1968). Won Academy Award for Best Supporting Actress for *Who's Afraid of Virginia Woolf* (1966). ❖ See also *Sandy Dennis: A Personal Memoir* (ed. by Doug Taylor and Louise Ladd, Papier-Mache, 1997); and *Women in World History*.

DENNISON, Jo-Carroll (c. 1924—). Miss America and producer. Born c. 1924 in Florence, Arizona; m. briefly to Phil Silvers (the comedian); m. Russell Stoneham; children: 2 sons. ❖ Named Miss America (1942), representing Texas; performed on radio, in films and on tv; was an associate producer on several television series; became a partner in the Los Angeles Theatre Company; also a writer. ❖ See also Frank Deford, *There She Is* (Viking, 1971).

DENNY, Arbella (1707–1792). Irish philanthropist, founder, and social reformer. Name variations: Arabella; Lady Arbella Denny. Born Arbella Fitzmaurice in Ireland in 1707; died in Dublin on Mar 18, 1792 (some sources incorrectly cite 1785); dau. of Thomas Fitzmaurice, 1st Earl of Kerry, and Anne (Petty) Fitzmaurice, countess of Kerry; m. Arthur Denny of Tralee, Aug 26, 1727 (died 1742); no children. ❖ Philanthropist who initiated the reform of the Dublin Foundling Hospital and founded the 1st Magdalen Asylum, or home for penitent prostitutes; undertook the reform and improvement of the Dublin Foundling Hospital (1759) and continued to be associated with it until 1778; was a member of the Ladies' Committee of the Dublin Lying-in Hospital (1760); received thanks from the Irish House of Commons for her work at the Foundling Hospital (1764); awarded freedom of the City of Dublin (1765); elected honorary member of the Dublin Society (1766); founded the Magdalen Asylum in Leeson Street, Dublin (1767), the 1st institution of its kind, as well as the 1st charity founded and run by women for women in Ireland; supervised its management until her retirement (1790); paved the way for greater involvement by women in public life. ❖ See also *Women in World History*.

DENNY, Sandy (1947–1978). English singer and songwriter. Name variations: Fairport Convention; Fotheringay. Born Alexandra Elene MacLean Denny, Jan 6, 1947, in Wimbledon, England; died of a brain haemorrhage after falling down a flight of stairs, April 21, 1978, in London, England; m. Trevor Lucas (guitarist), Sept 1973; children: 1. ❖ Among the most popular singer-songwriters in England (early 1970s), wrote "Who Knows Where the Time Goes?" which became title track of Judy Collins gold album; served as lead vocalist for electric folk group Fairport Convention (May 1968–Dec 1969) and recorded 3 albums with them, including *Liege and Lief*; formed group Fotheringay which disbanded in 1970; voted top British female vocalist (1970 and 1971) in *Melody Maker* polls; pursued solo career, usually backed by musicians from Fotheringay and Fairport Convention. Albums include *All Our Own Work* (1968), *Fotheringay* (1970), *Sandy Denny* (1970), *The Northstar Grassman and the Ravens* (1971), *Sandy* (1972), *Rock On* (1972) and *Like an Old Fashioned Waltz* (1973).

DE NOAILLES, Anna (1876–1933). See Noailles, Anna de.

DE NORONHA, Joana See Noronha, Joana de.

DEN OUDEN, Willie (1918–1997). See Ouden, Willemijntje den.

DE NOVALIS, Laura (1308–1348). See Noves, Laura de.

DE NOVES, Laura (1308–1348). See Noves, Laura de.

DENSEN-GERBER, Judianne (1934–2003). American lawyer and psychiatrist. Born Nov 13, 1934, in New York, NY; died of cancer, May 11, 2003, in New York, NY; dau. of Beatrice Densen (heiress of the Densen paperbox fortune) and Gustave Gerber (chemical engineer); graduate of Bryn Mawr College, Columbia Law School and New York University Medical School; m. Michael Baden (NY medical examiner, div. 1997); children: daughters Dr. Sarah Baden and Trissa Baden; son Lindsey Baden. ❖ Founded the drug-treatment program Odyssey House (1966); resigned as executive director (1983); writings include *We Mainline Dreams: The Odyssey House Story* (1971) and the semi-autobiographical *Walk in My Shoes: An Odyssey into Womanlife* (1976).

DENSMORE, Frances (1867–1957). American ethnomusicologist. Born Frances Theresa Densmore in Red Wing, Minnesota, May 21, 1867; died in Red Wing, Minnesota, June 5, 1957; dau. of Benjamin (civil engineer) and Sarah (Greenland) Densmore; sister of Margaret Densmore; attended Oberlin Conservatory of Music. ❖ Pioneer in study of Native American music and a founder of the field of ethnomusicology, made 1st field trip to a Chippewa (Ojibwa) village near Canadian border (1905); published 1st article containing observations, in *American Anthropologist* (1907); aware that transcriptions alone could not convey the spirit of the music, made nearly 2,500 wax cylinder recordings, amassing one of the world's largest collections; over long career, collected songs from more than 30 tribes. ❖ See also *Women in World History*.

DENT, Edith (1863–1948). English botanist. Name variations: Edith Vere Dent. Born Edith Vere Annesley in 1863 in Clifford Chambers, a village near Stratford-on-Avon, England; died Oct 12, 1948; eldest of 6 children of the vicar of Clifford Chambers; m. Robert Wilkinson Dent, 1893; children: 5. ❖ Established Wild Flower Society (1886); published *Wild Flower Diaries* and created and served as editor of *Wild Flower Magazine* (published 3 times annually); during WWI, served as a regional Red Cross president and oversaw VAD detachments. Named Officer of the Order of the British Empire (OBE).

DENTON, Jean (1935–2001). English politician and race-car driver. Name variations: Jean, Baroness of Wakefield; Baroness Denton of Wakefield. Born Jean Moss, Dec 29, 1935, in Yorkshire, England; died

Feb 5, 2001; m. Tony Denton, 1958 (div. 1974). ❖ An avid race-car driver, joined the British Women Racing Driver's Club (1963), was runner-up in the Goodwin Trophy (1967) and won the Embassy Trophy (1966 and 1967); turned professional (1969); joined the Huxford Garage Group as marketing director (1972), moved to Heron Motor Group (1978), and was the 1st woman on the national executive committee of the Institute of Management; became managing director of Herondrive, then external affairs director of Austin Rover Group (1985), making her the most senior woman in the British Motor Industry; served as parliamentary under-secretary of state of Trade and Industries for Consumers' Affairs (1992–93); served as parliamentary under-secretary of state of Northern Ireland responsible to the Depts. of Health and Social Service (1993–95), and the Depts. of Agriculture and Economy as well as spokesperson on all Northern Ireland matters in the House of Lords (1995–97). Named Commander of the British Empire (CBE, 1990); made a life peer as Baroness Denton of Wakefield (1991).

DENTON, Mary Florence (1857–1947). American missionary in Japan. Born Mary Florence Denton, July 4, 1857, in Nevada Co., California; died Dec 24, 1947, in Kyoto, Japan; dau. of Edward Michael Denton and Mary Mehitable (Strobridge) Denton; attended Poston Collegiate School in Oakland, California. ❖ Began association with Doshisha schools in Kyoto, Japan (1888), which continued the rest of her life; largely known for teaching English, the Bible, and Western cooking; served on National Committee of YWCA of Japan; from Japanese government, received sixth class (1933) and third class Order of the Sacred Treasure. ❖ See also Frances Benton Clapp, *Mary Florence Denton and the Doshisha* (Kyoto, 1955).

DENTON, Sandy (1969—). Jamaican-American singer. Name variations: Sandy "Pepa" Denton, "Pepa"; Salt-n-Pepa. Born Nov 9, 1969, in Kingston, Jamaica; m. Anthony "Treach" Criss (rapper with Naughty by Nature), July 24, 1999 (div. 2001); children: 1 son, Tyran (b. 1990); (with Criss) 1 daughter, Egypt (b. Sept 2, 1998). ❖ The 1st female rapper to have 3 platinum albums, formed Salt-n-Pepa with Cheryl "Salt" James (1985) and released platinum debut album, *Hot, Cool and Vicious* (1986), with hit "Push It," which was nominated for Grammy (1988); with James, added Deidre "Dee Dee" "Spinderella" Roper as DJ and released album, *A Salt With a Deadly Pepa* (1988), which went gold, followed by the commercial and artistic smash hit platinum album, *Blacks' Magic* (1990); with group, performed at Bill Clinton's Inaugural Youth Ball (1993), released hit album, *Very Necessary* (1993), and appeared in several films, including *Who's the Man?* (1993) and *Love and a Bullet* (2002); with group, won Grammy for Best Rap Performance (1995), for "None of Your Business," then released moderately successful album, *Brand New* (1997), which featured guest performances by such artists as Queen Latifah and Sheryl Crow.

D'ENTRAGUES, Catherine Henriette de Balzac (1579–1633). See *Entragues, Henriette d'*.

DE OBIDOS, Josefa (1630–1684). See *de Ayala, Josefa*.

DEOTERIA (fl. 535). Queen of Metz (Austrasia). Name variations: Déoteria. Fl. around 535; m. Theodebert or Thibert I (504–548), king of Metz (Austrasia, r. 534–548), in 535; children: Thibaud (d. 555), king of Metz (Austrasia, r. 548–555).

DE PACHECO, Maria (c. 1496–1531). See *Padilla, Maria Pacheco*.

DE PASSE, Suzanne (1946—). African-American producer. Name variations: Suzanne De Passe. Born 1946 in New York, NY; m. Paul Le Mat (actor), 1978 (sep.). ❖ The first lady of Motown, was creative assistant for Berry Gordy and molded the careers of the Jackson 5 and the Commodores, among others; collaborated on screenplay for *Lady Sings the Blues* (1972), earning an Oscar nomination; as president of Motown Productions (1980s), produced a string of Motown specials; formed De Passe Entertainment and produced the miniseries "Lonesome Dove," for which she won an Emmy and Peabody, as well as "Buffalo Girls," "Streets of Laredo," "Zenon: Girl of the 21st Century," and the sitcom "Sister, Sister," among others.

DE PALENCIA, Isabel (1878-c. 1950). See *Palencia, Isabel de*.

DE PAULA, Monica Angelica (1978—). Brazilian soccer player. Name variations: Monica. Born April 4, 1978, in Brazil. ❖ Defender, won a team silver medal at Athens Olympics (2004).

D'EPINAY, Madame (1726–1783). See *Épinay, Louise, Madame la Live d'*.

DE PISAN OR DE PIZAN, Christine (c. 1363–c. 1431). See *Christine de Pizan*.

DE POITIERS, Diane (1499–1566). See *Diane de Poitiers*.

DE POLIAKOFF, Olga See *Poliakoff, Olga*.

DE PORTELA, Noemi Simonetto (1926—). See *Simonetto de Portela, Noemi*.

DE PRADO, Mme (1945—). See *Lacoste, Catherine*.

DE PUISIEUX, Madeleine d'Arsant (1720–1798). See *Puisieux, Madeleine d'Arsant de*.

DE PULSKI, Romola (1891–1978). See *Nijinska, Romola*.

DE PUTTI, Lya (1899–1932). Austro-Hungarian actress and dancer. Name variations: Amalia Janka; Lya de Putti. Born Jan 10, 1899, in Vecsés, Zemplen, Austria-Hungary (now Hungary); died Nov 27, 1931, in New York, NY. ❖ Began career as a dancer in vaudeville in Budapest, then performed in classical ballet in Berlin; made films in Germany for UFA (1921–26), including *Ilona, Othello, Die Fledermaus, Komödianten, Manon Lescaut* and *Variety;* moved to Hollywood (1926) and appeared in such films as *The Prince of Tempters, The Sorrows of Satan, The Heart Thief, Buck Privates* and *The Scarlet Lady;* also appeared in England's *The Informer* (1929).

DE QUEIROS, Raquel (1910–2003). See *Quierós, Raquel de*.

DERAISMES, Maria (1828–1894). French feminist and writer. Pronunciation: der-REM. Born in Paris, France, Aug 15, 1828; died in Paris, Feb 6, 1894; sister of Anna Féresse-Deraismes; never married. ❖ Well-known writer, lecturer, and anti-clericalist, set out to become a writer, producing several comedies collected in *Théâtre chez soi* (1863), as well as some pamphlets and collected articles and speeches, including *Aux femmes riches* (1865), *Nos principes et nos moeurs* (1867), *Ève contre M. Dumas fils* (1867), *Les droits des enfants* (1886), and *Ève dans l'humanité* (1891); also contributed to magazines; gave 1st important lecture at a Free-Thinkers Conference (1866); though she did not speak frequently, became France's most celebrated female orator of the time; with Léon Richer, helped found the weekly *Le Droit des Femmes* (1869), the longest-lived women's publication of its time; also helped found the Association for the Rights of Women (1870), renamed Society for the Amelioration of Woman's Condition (1874); founded and directed *Le Républican de Seine et Oise* (1881–85); played important roles in getting educational reforms for women (1880s), the divorce law (1884), and the right of businesswomen to vote for judges of the commercial tribunals (1894); also was active in such causes as free thinking, anti-vivisection, protection of mothers and children, and societies and homes for mothers; helped organize the Anticlerical Congress (May 15, 1881), participated in National Congress for the Separation of Church and State (1882), and was president of Federation of Free-Thought Groups of Seine-et-Oise; with Richer, began a new stage in the women's movement in France by firmly linking it to political life and issues. ❖ See also *Women in World History*.

DE RANFAING, Élizabeth (d. 1649). See *Ranfaing, Elizabeth of."*

DERBHORCAILL. *Variant of Devorgilla*.

DERBY, countess of.
See *Beaufort, Margaret (1443–1509).*
See *Hastings, Anne (c. 1487–?).*
See *Stanley, Charlotte (1599–1664).*
See *Farren, Elizabeth (c. 1759–1829).*

DERBY, Margaret, countess of. See *Beaufort, Margaret (1443–1509).*

DERCKX, Annemiek (1954—). Dutch kayaker. Born April 12, 1954. ❖ At Los Angeles Olympics, won a bronze medal in K1 500 meters (1984); at Seoul Olympics, won a bronze medal in K2 500 meters (1988).

DEREN, Maya (1908–1961). Russian-born filmmaker. Born Eleanora Derenkowsky in Kiev, Russia, April 29, 1908; died in Queens, New York, Oct 13, 1961; dau. of Marie (teacher) and Alexander (Russian-Jewish psychiatrist called Solomon in some sources) Derenkowsky (name later shortened to Deren); attended L'École Internationale (Geneva), Syracuse University, and New School for Social Research; New York University, BA; Smith College, AM in literature, 1939; married a labor reformer (div. in 1938 after 3 years); m. Alexander Hackenschmied (Czech filmmaker who worked under name Alexander Hammid), 1942 (div.); m. Teiji Ito (composer), 1960. ❖ Director, actress, producer, writer, lecturer and experimental filmmaker often cited as the creator of the 1st film of the American avant-garde and the "choreo-cinema," a collaborative art between the dancer and the camera; films include (with Alexander Hammid) *Meshes of the Afternoon* (1943), *At Land* (1944), *A Study in Choreography for Camera* (1945), *Ritual in Transfigured Time* (1946), *Meditation on Violence* (1948), *The Very Eye of Night* (1959) and *The Witch's Cradle* (released incomplete, 1961); writings include *An Anagram of Ideas on Art, Form and the Film* (1946), *The Divine Horseman: The Living Gods of Haiti* (1953), and *Divine Horsemen: Voodoo Gods of Haiti* (1970); also frequently contributed to magazines; called the "mother of the underground film," paved the way for the future of American independent films. Awarded the 1st Guggenheim fellowship ever bestowed for creative filmmaking (1946); was the 1st woman and the 1st American to win Cannes Grand Prix Internationale for Avant-Garde Film (for *Meshes of the Afternoon*). ❖ See also *Women in World History.*

DE RENNEVILLE, Sophie (1772–1822). *See Renneville, Sophie de.*

DE REUCK, Colleen (1964—). South African runner. Born Colleen Lindeque, April 14, 1964, in Vryheid, Kwazulu, Natal, South Africa; attended University of Port Elizabeth; m. Darren De Reuck, Dec 1988. ❖ Competed in 3 Olympic Games for South Africa; moved to US (1993); won Berlin Marathon (1996); won Cherry Blossom 10m, New Haven Road Race 20k, Quad-City Times Bix 7 mile, Steamboat Classic 4 mile (1997); became US citizen (2000); won bronze medal at World Cross-Country championships (2002).

DE REYES, Consuelo (1893–1948). English theater director and playwright. Born Dec 5, 1893, in Leamington Spa, Warwickshire, England; m. Peter King. ❖ Served as director of the Little Theatre, Citizen House, Bath, and the Everyman Theatre in Hampstead; wrote the chronicle play *Vickie or the Girl Queen* (1935), as well as *The Chief of Kensington, The Widow of Windsor* and *This Year of Grace.* ❖ See also De Reyes' *A Little Theatre and Its Organization.*

DERICKSON, Uli (1944–2005). American flight attendant and hero. Born Ulrike Patzelt, Aug 8, 1944, in Aussig an der Elbe, Czechoslovakia; raised in Bavaria; died of cancer, Feb 18, 2005, in Tucson, Arizona; dau. of Marianne Patzelt; m. Russell G. Derickson (pilot, died 2003); children: Matthew Derickson. ❖ Worked as an au pair in Britain and Switzerland; immigrated to Connecticut (1967); began working for TWA as a flight attendant, then joined Delta; when a pair of Lebanese gunmen skyjacked Flight 847 from Athens to Rome (June 14, 1985), confronted and mollified the terrorists and saved passengers' lives (though 1 man was killed). Was the 1st woman to receive the Silver Cross for Valor from the Legion of Valor, a veterans organization. ❖ See also tv movie "The Taking of Flight 847: The Uli Derickson Story," starring Lindsay Wagner (1988).

DE RIDDER, Alexandra (1963—). *See Simons de Ridder, Alexandra.*

DERIEL, Emily (1974—). American pentathlete. Name variations: Emily de Riel. Born Nov 24, 1974, in Havertown, Pennsylvania. ❖ Won a silver medal at debut of the modern pentathlon at Sydney Olympics (2000).

DERING, Anne (c. 1530–c. 1590). *See Locke, Anne Vaughan.*

DE RIVERY, Aimee Dubucq (c. 1762–1817). French-Turkish sultana. Name variations: de Riverie; Nakshedil Sultana. Born c. 1762 on the French Caribbean island of Martinique; died in Constantinople (now Istanbul), Turkey, 1817; dau. of a noble family; cousin of Josephine Tascher de la Pagerie (Empress Josephine), who m. Napoleon Bonaparte; children: (with Abdul Hamid I) Mahmud II, sultan of the Ottoman Empire (r. 1808–1839). ❖ Born in Martinique; disappeared during a sea voyage (1788) and is said to have reappeared as Nakshedil Sultana in a Turkish Harem of Abdul Hamid I during the period of the Ottoman Empire. ❖ See also *Women in World History.*

DE RIVOYRE, Christine (1921—). French novelist. Born Nov 29, 1921, in Tarbes, France. ❖ Worked as journalist for *Le Monde* and as editor of women's magazine, *Marie Claire;* writings include *La Mandarine* (1957), *Le Petit matin* (1968), *Boy* (1973), *Le Voyage à l'envers* (1977), *Reine-mère* (1985) and *Crépuscule, taille unique* (1989).

DER KOLK, Kirsten van (1975—). *See van Der Kolk, Kirsten.*

DERMAN, Vergie (1942—). South African ballet dancer. Born Sept 18, 1942, in Johannesburg, South Africa. ❖ Trained with Arnold Dover in South Africa before attending Royal Ballet School in London; danced with Royal Ballet throughout career, appearing in classical repertory works that include *The Sleeping Beauty,* and also in numerous contemporary works such as Kenneth Macmillan's *Valses nobles et sentimentals* (1966), *Anastasia* and *Elite Syncopations* (1974), Frederick Ashton's *The Dream* (1964), Glen Tetley's *Field Figures* (1971), and more; performed briefly with Opera Ballet in Berlin (1966–67).

DERMENDZHIEVA, Vanya (1952—). Bulgarian basketball player. Born Dec 3, 1958. ❖ At Moscow Olympics, won a silver medal in team competition (1980).

DERMOÛT, Maria (1888–1962). Dutch novelist. Name variations: Maria Dermout. Born Helena Antonia Maria Elisabeth Ingerman, 1888, in Dutch East Indies, lived in Java and Moluccas; died 1962; married, 1907. ❖ Educated in Netherlands but returned to Dutch East Indies (1905); lived in Java and Moluccas before returning to Netherlands (1933); writings, which are similar to Indonesian stories in style and themes, include *Nog pas gisteren* (1959, trans. as *Days Before Yesterday,* 1960), *De tienduizend dingen* (1955, trans. as *The Ten Thousand Things,* 1983); collected works were published as *Verzameld Werk* (1970 and 1974).

DERNBOURG, Ilona Eibenschütz (1872–1967). *See Eibenschütz-Dernbourg, Ilona.*

DERNESCH, Helga (1939—). Austrian soprano and mezzo-soprano. Born Feb 3, 1939, in Vienna, Austria; studied at Vienna Conservatory (1957–61). ❖ Debuted at the Berne Opera (1961); appeared at Bayreuth (1965–69); debuted at Salzburg (1969), Chicago (1971), Vienna Staatsoper (1972), and Metropolitan (1985); premiered in the operas of Aribert Reimann: *Lear* (1978) and *Troades* (1986). ❖ See also *Women in World History.*

DEROCHE, Elise-Raymonde (1886–1919). French aviator. Name variations: Baroness de Laroche; Baroness de la Roche; Raymonde de Laroche. Born 1886; killed in an airplane accident 1919. ❖ Better known under self-assumed title of Baroness de Laroche, was the 1st woman in the world to be granted a pilot's license; qualified for the brevet (Mar 8, 1910), though she had already flown solo the previous year (Oct 22, 1909). ❖ See also *Women in World History.*

DE ROEVER, Lisanne (1979—). Dutch field-hockey player. Born June 6, 1979, in the Netherlands. ❖ Won European championship (2003); won a team silver medal at Athens Olympics (2004).

DEROIN, Jeanne-Françoise (1805–1894). French feminist. Name variations: Deroin sometimes incorrectly spelled Derouin. Pronunciation: der-RWEN. Born in Paris, France, Dec 31, 1805, to working class parents; died in London, April 2, 1894; m. M. Desroches, 1832; children: 2 daughters, 1 son (d. 1887). ❖ Socialist feminist, prominent in the Revolution of 1848, who was the 1st woman in France to run for national office; became allied with Saint-Simonianism because they favored equality for women (early 1830s); conducted a school for poor children (1840s); during Revolution of 1848, founded clubs as well as daily, weekly, and monthly journals promoting rights for women and workers, including France's 1st feminist daily paper, *La Voix des femmes* (The Women's Voice); ran for the Legislative Assembly (1849); founded the Union of Fraternal Associations of Workers (1849), for which she was arrested and sentenced for subversion (1850); released (1851); because of continuous police surveillance, fled to England (1852) and never returned; published the *Almanach des femmes* (1852–54); corresponded occasionally with feminist and socialist leaders (1850s–80s). ❖ See also *Women in World History.*

DE'ROSSI, Properzia (c. 1490–1530). *See Rossi, Properzia de.*

DE ROTHSCHILD, Baroness Eugene (1908–2003). *See Rothschild, Jeanne de.*

DEROUIN, Jeanne (1805–1894). *See Deroin, Jeanne-Françoise.*

DE ROVER, Jolanda (1963—). Dutch swimmer. Born Oct 10, 1963. ❖ At Los Angeles Olympics, won a bronze medal in 100-meter backstroke and a gold medal in 200-meter backstroke (1984).

DERRICOTTE, Juliette (1897–1931). African-American educator. Born Juliette Aline Derricotte in Athens, Georgia, April 1, 1897; died in Chattanooga, Tennessee, Nov 7, 1931; dau. of Isaac (cobbler) and Laura (Hardwick) Derricotte (seamstress); graduate of Talladega College, 1918; Columbia University, MA in religious education, 1927; never married. ❖ University official whose accidental death triggered a national outrage in the black community (1931); named trustee of Talladega College (1929), the only woman; became dean of women at Fisk University in Nashville, Tennessee (1929); while driving from Nashville to Athens, Georgia (with 3 Fisk students), was grievously injured in an accident about a mile outside Dalton, Georgia; since the local tax-supported hospital did not admit black patients, spent the night at the home of a black woman who provided beds for black patients; died the next day, along with one of the Fisk students. ❖ See also Marion V. Cuthbert, *Juliette Derricotte* (Womans Press, 1933); and *Women in World History.*

DE RUE, Carmen (1908–1986). American actress and child star. Name variations: Baby DeRue; Baby Carmen De Rue; Carmen DeRue. Born Carmen Fay De Rue, Feb 6, 1908, in Pueblo, Colorado; died Sept 28, 1986, in North Hollywood, California. ❖ At age 5, appeared in Cecil B. De Mille's *The Squaw Man* (1914); made close to 200 other films, including Fox "Kiddies" series, Franklin's "Triangle Kiddies," *Carmen's Race for Life, Carmen's Wild Ride, Wash Day, Flirt, Babes in the Woods* and *The Girl with the Champagne Eyes.*

DE RUITER, Wietske. Dutch field-hockey player. Born in the Netherlands. ❖ Won a team bronze medal at Atlanta Olympics (1996).

DE RUTE, Marchesa (1830–1902). See Rute, Mme de.

DERVIS, Suat (1905–1972). Turkish novelist and journalist. Born 1905; died 1972; dau. of a professor of medicine; studied literature in Berlin. ❖ Wrote for German newspapers and magazines; returned to Istanbul (1932) and worked as journalist; with husband, edited socialist literary journal *Yeni Edebiyat* (1940); ceased publishing after imposition of martial law and went to France (1953); returned to Turkey (1963); works include *The Black Book* (1920), *Neither Voice Nor Breath* (1923), *Night of Crisis* (1924), *As the Heart Wills* (1928), *Emine* (1931), *Nothing* (1939), *Like a Madman* (1945) and *Arkara Mahpusa* (1968).

DERVORGILLA. Variant of Devorgilla.

DERYUGINA, Natalya (1971—). Soviet handball player. Born April 23, 1971, in USSR. ❖ At Barcelona Olympics, won a bronze medal in team competition (1992).

D'ERZELL, Catalina (1897–1937). Mexican playwright. Born 1897 in Mexico; died in 1937. ❖ Played important role in Mexican theater movements at start of 20th century; writings include *Cumbres de nieve* (1923), *El pecado de las mujeres* (1925), *La sin honor* (1926), *La razón de la culpa* (1928), *Los hijos de la otra* (1930), *Maternidad* (1937) and *El* (1938).

DERZHINSKAYA, Zeniya (1889–1951). Russian soprano. Born Zeniya Georgiyevna Derzhinskaya in Kiev, Russia, Feb 6, 1889; died in Moscow, June 9, 1951. ❖ Sang at Narodnïy Dom opera house (1913–15), then with the Bolshoi Theater (1916–48); under Václav Suk, created her best roles—Lisa in Tchaikovsky's *The Queen of Spades,* Nastasya in Tchaikovsky's *Sorceress,* and Fevroniya in Rimsky-Korsakov's *The Legend of the City of Kitezh;* was particularly successful portraying Russian women and was also remembered as Mariya in Tchaikovsky's *Mazeppa* and as Marguerite in Gounod's *Faust;* gave a concert performance of *Kitezh* at Paris Opéra to great success (1926); following retirement (1948), taught at Moscow Conservatory until her death. Was made a People's Artists of the USSR (1937). ❖ See also *Women in World History.*

DESAI, Anita (1937—). Indian novelist and short-story writer. Born Anita Muzumdar, June 24, 1937, in Mussoorie, a hill station in Uttar Pradesh, India; dau. of D.N. Mazumdar (Bengali businessman) and Toni Nime (German); Miranda House, Delhi University, BA in English, 1957; m. Ashvin Desai (businessman), 1958; children: 4. ❖ Widely read outside of India and shortlisted 3 times for Booker Prize, won international fame with *Fire on the Mountain* (1977), which won India's National Academy of Letters Award, and *Clear Light of Day* (1980); writings, which often depict lives of anglicized middle class in India, also include *The Peacock* (1963), *Voices of the City* (1965), *Where Shall We Go This Summer?* (1975), *Games at Twilight and Other Stories* (1978), *In Custody* (1984), *Baumgartner's Bombay* (1988), *Journey to Ithaca* (1995), *Fasting, Feasting* (1999), *Diamond Dust* (2000) and *The Zigzag Way* (2004); won Guardian Award for children's fiction for *The Village by the Sea* (1982); taught at Girton, Smith, and Mount Holyoke colleges; became creative writing teacher (one semester a year) at Massachusetts Institute of Technology (1993). Awarded title Padma Shri by the president of India (1988).

DE SALE, Laura (1308–1348). *See Noves, Laura de.*

DES ANGES, Jeanne (fl. 1632). Mother of the Ursulines of Loudun. Fl. 1632 in the small town of Loudun, near Poitiers, France. ❖ As prioress of the convent of the Ursulines, said to have been struck by diabolic possession; when it became an epidemic among her nuns, appeared with them for months before fascinated crowds, in their convulsions and numerous attempts at exorcism (1632–35); successfully struggled with the Demon, which was demonstrated in a series of mystical trials; displayed her palms, marked with red stigmata, to the populace (1635); began performing cures with a holy ointment of her own composition (1638). ❖ See also *Women in World History.*

DE SANT JORDI, Rosa (b. 1910). See *Arquimbau, Rosa Maria.*

DE SARNEZ, Marielle (1951—). French politician. Born Mar 27, 1951, in Paris, France. ❖ Served as secretary-general of the UDF (Union for French Democracy) Group in the National Assembly (1997–98); as a member of the European People's Party (Christian Democrats) and European Democrats, elected to 5th European Parliament (1999–2004).

DESART, Countess of (1857–1933). See *O'Connor, Ellen.*

DESART, Ellen (1857–1933). See *O'Connor, Ellen.*

DESBORDES-VALMORE, Marceline (1785–1859). Romantic French poet and singer. Name variations: Marcelline; Marceline Valmore. Born Marceline Félicité Josèphe Desbordes at Douai, France, June 20, 1785; died July 23, 1859; m. François Prosper Lanchantin (actor known as Valmore), 1817; children: (with Henri Latouche) 1 son; (with Lanchantin) 3 daughters. ❖ Orphaned as a child when French Revolution wiped out most of her family (1789); made debut at age 16 in comic opera; with husband, toured France as actors; wrote Romantic poetry of love and childhood which was praised by Baudelaire and Sainte-Beuve, and Verlaine claimed her as an influence; wrote several stories as well as *Élégies et romances* (Elegies and Romances, 1818), *Élégies et poésies nouvelles* (New Elegies and Poems, 1824), *Les Pleurs* (Tears, 1833), *Pauvres Fleurs* (Poor Flowers, 1839) and *Bouquets et Prières* (Bouquets and Prayers, 1843). Her correspondence was published (1896) and an exhibition at the Bibliothèque Nationale in Paris honored the centenary of her death (1959). ❖ See also *Women in World History.*

DESCAMPS, Marie-Hélène (1938—). French politician. Name variations: Marie-Helene Descamps. Born July 5, 1938, in Monts, France. ❖ Managed Northern France edition of "Téle 7 jours" and "Marie-Claire" (1964–72); served as associate director, "Image September" (1999–2002); chaired the Committee on Finance of the National Assembly (1986–88); head of the press service of UDF and press officer for President Valéry Giscard d'Estaing (1988–96); also press adviser to d'Estaing at the Foundation for Democracy in Europe (1996–99); as a member of the European People's Party (Christian Democrats) and European Democrats, elected to 5th European Parliament (1999–2004). Named Officer of the National Order of Merit; awarded the Chevalier de la Légion d'honneur.

DESCARD, Maria (1847–1927). French novelist. Name variations: (pseudonym) Maryan. Born 1847 in Brest, France; died 1927; dau. of a sea captain; married a sea captain. ❖ Traveled widely and incorporated many experiences into novels; works include *En Poitou* (1878), *Anne du Valmoët* (1880), *Les Chemins de la vie* (1882), *La Cousine Esther* (1889) and *Annie* (1890). Awarded *lauréate* from Academie Française.

DESCLÉE, Aimée Olympe (1836–1874). French actress. Name variations: Aimee Olympe Desclee. Born Nov 18, 1836; died in Paris, Mar 9, 1874. ❖ Excelled in contemporary dramas, *Frou-Frou* and *Diane de Lys.*

DESEO, Suzanne (1913–2003). Hungarian-Australian skier. Name variations: Suzie Deseo. Born Zsuzsanna Rozsa Maria Havasi, 1913, in Budapest, Hungary; m. Lajos Musitz; m. Korel Deseo de Szentvizslo (died 2002); children: Suzanne Davidson. ❖ Won championships in downhill and slalom racing; escaped the Iron Curtain (1949); immigrated to Australia (1950); established Australia's 1st international ski resort: Thredbo Alpine Village.

DESFORGES, Jean Catherine (1929—). English hurdler. Name variations: Jean Desforges Pickering. Born July 1929 in England. ❖ At Helsinki Olympics, won a bronze medal in 4 x 100-meter relay (1952).

DESGARCINS, Magdeleine Marie (1769–1797). French actress. Born Magdeleine Marie Louise at Mont Dauphin (Hautes Alpes) in 1769; died insane in Paris on Oct 27, 1797. ❖ During short career, was an associate of Talma, with whom she almost always appeared; made debut at Comédie Française in *Bajazet* (May 24, 1788), a performance that was so successful that she was immediately made *sociétaire;* followed Talma to the rue Richelieu, which was soon to become the Théâtre de la République (1791), where she triumphed in *King Lear, Otello,* and La Harpe's *Melanie et Virginie;* health soon failed.

DESHA (1892–1965). Yugoslavian-born interpretive dancer. Name variations: Desha Podgorsky; Desha Delteil. Born Desha Podgorsky, 1892, in Yugoslavia; died 1965; trained with Mikhail and Vera Fokine; m. Mario Delteil (dancer). ❖ Danced in Fokine's *Casanova* (1923); known for her bubble dance, appeared on Broadway in *Music in the Air* (1932); was the model for Harriet Whitney Frishmuth's bronze sculpture *Desha* (1927) and Frishmuth's *Roses of Yesterday* (1923); retired from performance career at early age (c. 1934); was teaching classes in Bergerac, Dordogne, France as of 1950.

DE SHANNON, Jackie (1944—). American singer and songwriter. Name variations: Jackie De Shannon or Jackie de Shannon; Sherry Lee; Jackie Dee. Born Sharon Lee Myers, Aug 21, 1944, in Hazel, Kentucky; m. Bud Dain, Jan 29, 1966 (div.); m. Randy Edelman, 1977; children: (2nd m.) 1. ❖ As Sherry Lee, recorded "Baby Honey" (1956); as Jackie Dee, recorded "I'll Be True" (1957); as Jacquie Shannon (with the Cajuns), recorded "Just Another Lie" (1958); as Jackie Shannon, recorded the same song (1959); as Jackie de Shannon, released "So Warm" and "Lonely Girl" (1960), "Needles and Pins" (1963), "He's Got the Whole World in His Hands" (1964), "What the World Needs Now Is Love" (1965), "Will You Love Me Tomorrow" (1966), "Put a Little Love in Your Heart" (also wrote, 1969), "Love Will Find a Way" (1969), "Stoned Cold Soul" (1971); wrote the hit "Bette Davis Eyes"; wrote hundreds of songs, recorded by Brenda Lee, Fleetwoods, Rita Coolidge, Marianne Faithful, Duane Eddy, The Searchers, Cher, and Everly Brothers, among many others.

DESHAYES, Catherine (d. 1680). French poisoner. Name variations: Madame Monvoisin; Catherine Monvoisin; La Voisin. Burned at the stake, Feb 22, 1680; main figure accused in the Affair of the Poisons, lasting 1679–1682. ❖ During the 2nd "Affair of the Poisons" (1679) was incriminated for offering fortunetelling, drugs, poisons and black masses for her numerous clients, members of the higher nobility, as well as ordinary folk; was burned to death in the Place de Grèves. ❖ See also *Women in World History.*

DESHOULIÈRES, Antoinette (1638–1694). French poet. Name variations: Des Houlières, Deshoulières. Pronunciation: DAY-zoo-LYAIR. Born Antoinette du Ligier de la Garde in Paris, France, Jan 1, 1638; died in Paris, Feb 17, 1694; dau. of Melchior du Ligier, sieur de la Garde, maître d'hôtel to the queens Marie de Medici and Anne of Austria (1601–1666); studied poetry with Jean Hesnault; m. Guillaume de Boisguérin, seigneur Deshoulières, 1651; children: Antoinette Thérèse Deshoulières (1662–1718, poet). ❖ Highly visible at the court of Louis XIV and in literary society, won the friendship and admiration of the most eminent literary women and men of her age; her numerous poems included examples of almost all the minor forms, odes, eclogues, idylls, elegies, chansons, ballads, and madrigals; elected to membership of the Academy of the Ricovrati of Padua and of the Academy of Arles. Complete editions of her works were published at Paris (1695 and 1747). ❖ See also *Women in World History.*

DESHPANDE, Shashi (1938—). Indian novelist and short-story writer. Born 1938 in Dharwad, India; dau. of Shriranga; studied law and economics at universities of Bombay and Bangalore, and literature at Mysore University; children: 2. ❖ Did not begin writing until her 30s; short stories appeared in *The Legacy* (1971), *The Miracle* (1986), and *It Was Dark* (1986); novels include *The Dark Holds No Terrors* (1980), *Come Up and Be Dead* (1983), *Roots and Shadows* (1983), *It Was the Nightingale* (1986), and *That Long Silence* (1988). Awarded Thirumathi Rangammal Prize (1984) for *Roots and Shadows.*

DESIDERATA (d. 773). Queen of the Franks. Name variations: Desideria; Ermengarde. Birth date unknown; died in 773; dau. of Desiderius, king of the Lombards, and Queen Ausa; became 2nd wife of Charlemagne (Charles I), king of the Franks (r. 768–814), Holy Roman emperor (r. 800–814), in 770 (annulled 771). Charlemagne had 5 wives: Himiltrude; Desiderata (d. 773); Hildegarde of Swabia (c. 757–783); Fastrada (d. 794); and Luitgarde (d. 800). ❖ Following marriage (770), was repudiated by Charlemagne for reasons unknown (771) and sent back to her family; retired to a monastery founded by parents, where her sister was abbess. ❖ See also *Women in World History.*

DÉSIRÉE (1777–1860). Queen of Sweden. Name variations: Desiree Clary; Bernhardine or Bernardine Eugenie Desiree. Born Bernardiné Eugénie Désirée Clary, Nov 9, 1777, in Marseille, France; died Dec 17, 1860, in Stockholm, Sweden; dau. of François Clary (prosperous merchant of Marseille); sister of Julie Clary Bonaparte (1771–1845); m. Jean Baptiste Jules Bernadotte, also known as Karl XIV Johan or Charles XIV John (1763–1844), king of Sweden (r. 1818–1844), Aug 17, 1798; children: Oscar I (1799–1859), king of Sweden (r. 1844–1859, who m. Josephine Beauharnais [1807–1876]). ❖ Before age 20, was pursued by Napoleon Bonaparte who wanted to marry her, but was forced by father to turn down the proposal; married French soldier Jean Bernadotte (1798), who would rise from the ranks to become one of Napoleon's marshals and later be placed on the throne of Sweden by Napoleon and crowned Charles XIV John; with husband, began the Bernadotte line that continued through the 20th century. ❖ See also film *Desiree,* starring Marlon Brando and Jean Simmons; and *Women in World History.*

DESIREE BERNADOTTE (1938—). Baroness Silfverschiold. Name variations: Désirée of Sweden. Born Désirée Elizabeth, June 2, 1938, at Haga Palace, Stockholm, Sweden; dau. of Gustavus Adolphus (1906–1947), duke of Westerboten, and Sybilla of Saxe-Coburg-Gotha (1908–1972); sister of Carl XVI Gustavus, king of Sweden; m. Niclas, baron Silferschiöld or Silfverschiold, June 5, 1964; children: Carl Otto Edmund (b. 1965); Christina-Louise, baroness Silfverschiold (b. 1966); Helene Ingeborg, baroness Silfverschiold (b. 1968).

DESJARDINS, Marie Catherine (1640–1683). *See Villedieu, Catherine des Jardins, Mme de.*

DESLYS, Gaby (1884–1920). French actress and danseuse. Born Marie-Élise-Gabrielle Caire in 1884 in Marseille, France; died Feb 11, 1920, in Paris. ❖ Around turn of the century, was a well-known vaudeville star in Paris, appearing at Folies-Bergère and the Olympia where she introduced American dancing with partner Harry Pilcer, specializing in whirlwinds and a one-step called the "Gaby Glide"; made 1st appearance in London as the Charm of Paris in *The New Aladdin* (1906), followed by *The Belle of Bond Street* (1914) and *The Passing Show of 1915;* was 1st seen in NY in *Les Debuts de Chichine* (1911), followed by *Vera Violette;* died at 36; was portrayed by Tamara Toumanova in MGM film musical *Deep in My Heart* (1954). ❖ See also *Women in World History.*

DESMARES, Christine (1682–1753). French actress. Born Christine Antoinette Charlotte Desmares in 1682; died 1753; dau. of actor Nicolas Desmares (c. 1650–1714); niece of Marie Champmesle (c. 1642–1698). ❖ A fine actress in both tragedy and ingenue parts, made her debut at the Comédie Française in La Grange Chancel's *Oreste et Pylade* (1699) and was immediately received as *sociétaire;* retired (1721). ❖ See also *Women in World History.*

DESMARES, Marie (c. 1642–1698). *See Champmesle, Marie.*

DESMIER, Eleanor (1639–1722). Countess of Williamsburg. Name variations: Eleanor d'Olbreuse; Eleanore d'Olbreuze. Born Jan 17, 1639; died Feb 5, 1722; dau. of Alexander II Desmier, Seigneur d'Olbreuse; m. George Guelph, duke of Brunswick-Luneburg (elector of Hanover, 1648–1665), duke of Celle (1665–1705), Sept 15, 1665; children: Sophia Dorothea of Brunswick-Celle (1666–1726, who m. George I, king of England). ❖ One of the great beauties of Europe, had a morganatic marriage with George, duke of Brunswick-Luneburg (later, the union was made fully legal by the emperor of Germany).

DESMOND, Astra (1893–1973). English contralto. Born in Torquay, England, April 10, 1893; died in Faversham, England, Aug 16, 1973; studied singing at Royal Academy of Music with Blanche Marchesi; m. Sir Thomas Neame, 1920. ❖ Gave 1st recital in London (1915); though the 1st to sing the title role in Rutland Boughton's opera *Alkestis,* concentrated mainly on concerts and oratorios; introduced many of the works of Edvard Grieg, Edward Elgar, and other modern composers to British audiences; considered an outstanding interpreter of the Angel in Elgar's *The Dream of Gerontius.* Made a Commander of the British Empire (1949); awarded the medal of St. Olav. ❖ See also *Women in World History.*

DESMOND, countess of. *See Fitzgerald, Katherine (c. 1500–1604).*

DESMOND, Eileen (1932—). Irish politician. Born Eileen Harrington, Dec 1932, in Old Head, Kinsale, Co. Cork, Ireland; m. Dan Desmond (TD, Cork South, 1948–61, Mid-Cork, 1961–64); children: 2 daughters. ❖ Began career as civil servant, Dept. of Posts and Telegraphs; following husband's death, won a by-election representing Labour to

17th Dáil for Mid-Cork (1965–65); returned to 18th Dáil (1965–69), then 20th–24th Dáil (1973–87); was a minister for Health and Social welfare (1981–82), 1st woman to hold a senior cabinet portfolio; elected to Seanad (1969–73); retired because of poor health (1987).

DESMOND, Florence (1905–1993). English actress, dancer and impersonator. Born May 31, 1905, in London, England; died Jan 16, 1993, in Guildford, Surrey, England; m. T. Campbell Black; m. Charles Hughesdon. ❖ Made London debut as a dancer in *Babes in the Wood* (1916); spent several years appearing in concert halls, music halls, revues and cabarets with Naunton Wayne; made NY debut in *This Year of Grace* (1928); other plays include *The Student Prince, Savoy Follies, Streamline, Seeing Stars, Let's Raise the Curtain, Funny Side Up, Jack and Jill, Hi-de-Hi, The Apples of Eve,* and *Auntie Mame* (as Vera Charles); films include *Sally in Our Alley, Keep Your Seats Please, Charley Moon, Some Girls Do* and *If the Shoe Fits;* was also an impressionist. ❖ See also autobiography *Florence Desmond* (1953).

DESMOND, Lucy (b. 1889). English gymnast. Born April 17, 1889. ❖ At Amsterdam Olympics, won a bronze medal in team all-around (1928).

DESMOULINS, Lucile (1771–1794). French wife of Camille Desmoulins. Name variations: Lucille. Born Lucile Duplessis in or near Paris in 1771; died on the guillotine in Paris, April 13, 1794; dau. of Madame Duplessis and a wealthy official in French Ministry of Finance; m. Camille Desmoulins (poor law student who, upon outbreak of the Revolution, became a famous activist and journalist), Dec 29, 1790; children: Horace (b. 1792). ❖ Victim of the Terror in the French Revolution whose devotion to her family, particularly her husband Camille Desmoulins, transcended political posturing and evoked a nobility of spirit admirable even to her enemies; supported husband in his shifting political stances and played host to the Jacobins, a circle of his political associates in Paris (1790–94); exerted heroic efforts to secure husband's release upon his arrest by Revolutionary authorities; died by order of the Committee of Public Safety one week after husband was executed (April 1794). ❖ See also *Women in World History.*

DESNOYERS, Marguerite (1663–1719). *See du Noyer, Anne-Marguérite Petit.*

DE SOUSA, May (1887–1948). American musical-comedy actress. Name variations: May DeSousa. Born 1887 in Chicago, Illinois; died Aug 10, 1948, in Chicago; m. E.A. Haines (div.); m. Raymond G. Grant (div.). ❖ Came to prominence on Broadway in *The Tenderfoot, The Wizard of Oz* and *The Land of Nod;* other plays include *A Chinese Honeymoon, Babes in Toyland* and *Lieber Augustin* (renamed *Miss Caprice*); made London debut as Cinderella in the pantomime (1905); was an enormous success in a number of West End productions; also performed in Paris and Berlin.

DE SOUSA, Noémia (1926—). Mozambican poet and journalist. Name variations: Noémia de Sousa; Noemia du Sousa; (pseudonym) Vera Micaia. Born Noémia Carolina Abranches de Sousa in 1926 (some sources cite 1927) in Lourenço Marquez (now Maputo), Mozambique; attended secondary school in Brazil. ❖ Was a politically active journalist in Mozambique under Portuguese colonialism (1950s); published poetry in Mozambican and Portuguese journals; lived with Portuguese husband in Lisbon where she continued writing, protesting Salizar's regime; was forced to seek exile in France (1964), where she wrote under pseudonym Vera Micaia; works are strongly influenced by African-American and Caribbean writing.

DE SOUZA, Mme (1761–1836). *See Souza-Botelho, Adélaïde-Marie-Émilie-Filleul, marquise of.*

DESPARD, Charlotte (1844–1939). English-born Irish feminist and activist. Born Charlotte French in Ripple, Kent, England, June 15, 1844; died Nov 9, 1939, in Belfast, Northern Ireland; dau. of William and Margaret (Eccles) French; sister of Field Marshal Sir John French, commander of British Expeditionary Force in France during WWI, and viceroy of Ireland (died 1925); m. Maximilian Despard (wealthy trader), Dec 20, 1870 (died April 4, 1890); no children. ❖ Activist who embraced a range of causes to which she gave enthusiasm, dedication, and considerable financial support: the plight of the poor, women's suffrage, socialism, Irish independence, and communism; following husband's death (1890), was left a very wealthy widow who wore a black lace mantilla that became something of a trademark; was elected to the Kingston Poor Law Board which supervised the running of the local workhouse (1892); became a socialist and suffragist; joined

Women's Social and Political Union (WSPU) and succeeded Sylvia Pankhurst as secretary (1906); spent 21 days in Holloway Jail after a demonstration outside Houses of Parliament (1907); supported the formation of Women's Freedom League, of which she subsequently became president (1907); when WWI broke out, joined British section of Women's International League for Peace and Freedom; at war's end, stood as a Labor candidate for the British Parliament (Dec 1918) but was defeated; bought Roebuck House in south Dublin (1921), which she shared with Maud Gonne; became involved with the White Cross organization which helped families of Sinn Fein prisoners; after civil war broke out (June 1922), became president of Women's Prisoners' Defence League. ❖ See also Andro Linklater, *An Unhusbanded Life: Charlotte Despard, Suffragette, Socialist and Sinn Feiner* (Hutchinson, 1980); and *Women in World History.*

DESPENSER, Eleanor (1292–1337). *See Clare, Eleanor de.*

DESPENSER, Elizabeth (d. 1408). English noblewoman. Name variations: Elizabeth Fitzalan. Died 1408; dau. of Edward Despenser, 1st baron Despenser, and Elizabeth Burghersh (dau. of Bartholomew, 4th baron Burghersh); m. John Fitzalan, before 1385; children: John Fitzalan (1385–1421); Margaret Fitzalan (b. around 1388).

DESPENSER, Isabel (1400–1439). Baroness Burghersh and countess of Warwick. Name variations: Isabel le Despencer; Isabel Beauchamp. Born July 26, 1400, in Cardiff; died Dec 27, 1439, at Friars Minoresses, London; interred Jan 13, 1439, at Tewkesbury Abbey, Gloucester; dau. of Thomas Despenser, 1st earl of Gloucester, and Constance (c. 1374–1416, dau. of Edmund of Langley); m. Richard Beauchamp, earl of Worcester (d. 1422); m. Richard Beauchamp (1381–1439), 5th (or 13th) earl of Warwick, Nov 26, 1423; children: (1st m.) Elizabeth Beauchamp, baroness Abergavenny; (2nd m.) Henry Beauchamp (c. 1423–1445), 1st duke & 6th earl of Warwick; Anne Beauchamp (1426–1492). ❖ See also *Women in World History.*

DESPOTOVIC, Vesna (1961—). Yugoslavian basketball player. Born April 18, 1961. ❖ At Moscow Olympics, won a bronze medal in team competition (1980).

DESPRÈS, Suzanne (1875–1951). French actress. Born at Verdun, France, 1875; died 1951; studied at Paris Conservatoire; m. Aurelien Lugné-Poë (b. 1870, actor-manager). ❖ Had great success in several plays produced by husband, who was the founder of *L'Œuvre,* a new school of modern drama; later played at the Gymnase and at Porte Saint-Martin; debuted at Comédie Française (1902), where she appeared in important plays, including *Phèdre.* ❖ See also *Women in World History.*

DES ROCHES, Les Dames.
See Roches, Madeleine des (1520–1587).
See Roches, Catherine des (1542–1587).

DESSAUR, C.I. (1931–2002). Dutch writer. Name variations: C.I. Dessaur, Ronnie Dessaur; (pseudonym) Andreas Burnier. Born Catharina Irma Dessaur, July 3, 1931, in The Hague, Netherlands; died Sept 18, 2002, in Amsterdam, Netherlands; m. J.H. Zeylmans van Emmichoven; children: 2. ❖ Was a professor of criminology at Katholieke Universiteit in Nijmegen (1973–88); writings, which focus on homosexuality, transsexuality, and discrimination, include *Een tevreden lach* (1965), *Het jongensuur* (1969), *Die huilende Libertijn* (1970), *De zwembadmentaliteit* (1979), *De literaire salon* (1983), and *De wereld van glas* (1997). Received Lucy B. and C.W. van der Hoogt Prize and Annie Romein Prize (1983).

DESSILAVA (fl. 1197–1207). Tsarina of Bulgaria. Name variations: Princess Dessilava. Fl. between 1197 and 1207; m. Kaloyan, tsar of Bulgaria and 3rd of the Asenid rulers. ❖ See also *Women in World History.*

DESSOFF, Margarethe (1874–1944). Austrian-born choir director. Name variations: Margarete Dessoff. Born 1874 in Vienna, Austria; died 1944; dau. of Otto Dessoff (conductor of the Frankfurt Opera and Vienna Philharmonic). ❖ Conducted 1st public appearance of a woman's chorus (1912); came to US (1919); with Angela Diller, co-founded Adesdi Chorus of women's voices (1924) and A Capella Chorus of mixed voices (1929), which later merged into Dessoff Choirs; directed the choirs in NY (1925–35), pioneering performances of choral works from the pre-Baroque era to the 20th century.

DE STAËL, Germaine (1766–1817). *See Staël, Germaine de.*

D'ESTE. *See Este, d'.*

DE STEFANI, Livia (1913—). Italian novelist and poet. Born 1913 in Palermo, Sicily, Italy; married at 17. ❖ Lived in Rome and wrote for magazines and newspapers; best known for her 1st novel, *La vigna delle uve nere* (The Vineyard of the Black Grapes, 1953); other fiction, often set in the Sicilian countryside, includes *Preludio* (1940), *Gli affatturati* (1955), *Passione di Rosa* (1958), *Viaggio di una sconosciuta e altri raconti* (1963) and *La Signora di Cariddi* (1971).

D'ESTIENNE, Nicole (c. 1544–c. 1596). *See Estienne, Nicole d'.*

DESTINN, Emmy (1878–1930). Czech novelist, composer, and singer. Name variations: Destinnova. Born Ema Pavliná Kittlová or Kittl, Feb 26, 1878, in Prague; died Jan 28, 1930, in Ceske Budjeovice; took stage name in tribute to her teacher, Marie Loewe-Destinn; m. Joseph Halsbach, 1923. ❖ One of the 20th century's greatest sopranos, made debut in role of Santuzza in Mascagni's *Cavalleria rusticana* at Berlin Opera (1898); soon moved to Hofoper where she remained for a decade; was chosen by Cosima Wagner to sing Senta at Bayreuth in *Der Fliegende Holländer* (*The Flying Dutchman*, 1901); debuted at Covent Garden as Donna Anna in Mozart's *Don Giovanni* (1904), then sang the lead role in Giacomo Puccini's opera *Madama Butterfly* at its 1st London performance (1905); created lead role of Richard Strauss' *Salomé* in Paris and Berlin (1907); performed 339 times at the Metropolitan Opera in New York (1908–20); retired to a castle in southern Bohemia (1921), where she wrote a play, a novel, and some poetry. ❖ See also *Women in World History*.

DESTINY'S CHILD.
See Knowles, Beyoncé.
See Luckett, LeToya.
See Roberson, LaTavia.
See Rowland, Kelly.
See Williams, Michelle.

DESTIVELLE, Catherine (1960—). French rock-climber. Born July 24, 1960, in Oran, Algeria; eldest of 6 children; moved with family to Paris in early teens; children: 1 son. ❖ Began climbing at 13 and achieved rapid success; climbed Couzy-Desmaison route on Olan and the Devies-Gervasutti route on Ailefroide (1976) and made ascent of American Direct on Petit Dru (1977) at 17; began competing, entering 1st competition at age 25; climbed still-new 13c route called Chouca at Buoux, France, then the hardest route ever climbed by a woman (1988); experienced incredible success in competition, winning repeatedly, including at Bardonecchia, Italy, for 3 consecutive years, earning title of best female climber (1985–88); was 1st woman to achieve 8a and 8a+ status; retired from competition after 2nd Snowbird Cup (1989) to focus on mountaineering; free-climbed Nameless Tower in Pakistan and solo climbed Bonatti Pillar on Les Drus (1990); opened new route up famous West face of Drus, during 11-day solo-climb (1991); took 17 hours to solo 3,970 meters of North face of Eiger in Bernese Oberland (1992); attempted Latok in Pakistan (1992); achieved winter solo of North Face of Grandes Jorasses and attempted West Pillar of Makalu in Nepal (1993); soloed Bonatti route on North Face of Matterhorn in winter (1994); climbed South West Face of Shishapangma in Tibet, and attempted South Face of Annapurna (1995); suffered accident in Antarctica (1996) but recovered quickly.

D'ESTRAIGUES, Henriette (1579–1633). *See Entragues, Henriette d'.*

D'ESTRÉES, Gabrielle (1573–1599). *See Estrées, Gabrielle d'.*

DE SWIRSKA, Tamara (c. 1890–?). Russian interpretive dancer and pianist. Name variations: Tamara Swirskaya or Svirskaya. Born c. 1890 in St. Petersburg, Russia. ❖ Was a concert pianist before she appeared on stage in dance recitals; performed successfully on Keith circuit and in series of films for Imperial Film Corporation; appeared at London Coliseum in England in *Egyptian Ballet* (1911), *The Temple Dance of Dionysius* (1914), and *Tanagara Suite*, among others; was considered one of the most important—and perhaps earliest—links between opera and classical ballet, and contributed to the establishment of a ballet company in Chicago. Works of choreography include *Let Matin* (1910), *Danse Coquette* (1911), *Faust Ballet* (1911), *Danses Slaves* (1911), *Olympia Ballet* (1914), *Cléopâtre* (1916) and *The Poisoned Flower* (1918).

DE TENCIN, Mme (1685–1749). *See Tencin, Claudine de.*

DETLEF, Karl (1836–1876). *See Bauer, Klara.*

DETTWEILER, Helen (1914–1990). American golfer. Name variations: Helen E. Dettweiler. Born Dec 5, 1914, in Washington DC; died of cancer, Nov 13, 1990, in Palm Springs, California. ❖ Was the 1st woman baseball commentator, broadcasting coast-to-coast for Washington Senators, and the 1st woman to design and build a golf course (Indio, CA); was a member of the WASPs, flying B-17 bombers, during WWII; won Western Open (1939); along with Patty Berg, Babe Zaharias, Betty Jameson, Betty Hicks, and Betty Mims, helped form the LPGA; won the LPGA Teacher of the Year Award (1958). Appeared in film *Pat and Mike* (1952).

D'EU, Maud (d. 1241). *See Maud of Lusignan.*

DEUTSCH, Babette (1895–1982). American poet, novelist, critic and translator. Name variations: Babette Deutsch Yarmolinsky. Born Sept 22, 1895, in New York, NY; died Nov 13, 1982, in New York, NY; dau. of Melanie Fisher and Michael Deutsch; Barnard College, BA, 1917; attended Columbia University; m. Avrahm Yarmolinsky (chief of the Slavonic Division of NY Public Library); children: 2 sons. ❖ Began career teaching at New School for Social Research and publishing poems in *North American Review* and *New Republic*; poetry collections include *Banners* (1919), *Honey Out of the Rock* (1925), *Fire for the Night* (1930), *Epistle to Prometheus* (1932), *One Part Love* (1939), *Animal, Vegetable, Mineral* (1954), and *The Collected Poems of Babette Deutsch* (1969); also translated poems by Rilke, Pushkin, Pasternak, and others, often with husband; wrote works of criticism, *Poetry in Our Time* (1952) and *Poetry Handbook: A Dictionary of Terms* (1957), which were considered standard texts in American universities; critical studies also include *Potable Gold* (1929), *Heroes of the Kalevala, Finland's Saga* (1940), *Walt Whitman, Builder for America* (1941) and *The Reader's Shakespeare* (1946); novels include the semi-autobiographical *A Brittle Heaven* (1926), *In Such a Night* (1927), *Mask of Silenus* (1933) and *Rogue's Legacy* (1942).

DEUTSCH, Helen (1906–1992). American screenwriter. Born in New York, NY, Mar 21, 1906; died in New York, NY, Mar 15, 1992; dau. of Heyman and Ann (Freeman) Deutsch; attended Barnard College; a brief marriage was annulled. ❖ Wrote many prominent screenplays, including *I'll Cry Tomorrow* (1956) and *The Unsinkable Molly Brown* (1964); had initial success as co-writer of the adaptation of Enid Bagnold's *National Velvet*, one of the year's 10 best (1944); won a Golden Globe for screenplay *Lili*; founded and became secretary of the New York Drama Critics Circle; other screenplays include *The Seventh Cross* (1944) and *King Solomon's Mines* (1950). ❖ See also *Women in World History*.

DEUTSCH, Helene (1884–1982). Polish-born psychoanalyst. Born Helene Rosenbach in the town of Przemyśl in Polish Galicia on Ukrainian border of Austro-Hungarian empire (present-day Poland), Oct 9, 1884; died Mar 29, 1982, in Cambridge, Massachusetts; dau. of Wilhelm Rosenbach (lawyer) and Regina (Fass) Rosenbach; University of Munich Medical School, MD, 1912; m. Felix Deutsch, 1912; children: Martin (b. 1917). ❖ Pioneer theoretician in female psychology, whose status as a central figure at the beginning of the psychoanalytic movement is beyond dispute; worked as full-time assistant at the Wagner-Jauregg Clinic for Psychiatric and Nervous Disorders, Vienna (1912–18); was one of the 1st women admitted to Vienna Psychoanalytic Society (1918); as a founding member and director of the Vienna Training Institute, wielded enormous power and influence over the training of analysts and the future direction of psychoanalysis (1925–34); arrived in US (1934); joined the staff of the Boston Psychoanalytic Institute (1934); was a training analyst at the Boston Training Institute (1934–62); was also the 1st major theorist of feminine psychology, devoting numerous books and articles to the subjects of female sexuality and the unique psychological dilemmas posed by motherhood. Writings include *The Psychology of Sexual Functions in Women* (1925), *Psychoanalysis of the Neuroses* (1932), *The Psychology of Women* (Vol. I, 1944, Vol. II, 1945), *Neuroses and Character Types* (1965), *Selected Problems of Adolescence* (1967), *A Psychoanalytic Study of the Myth of Dionysus and Apollo* (1969) and *Confrontations With Myself* (1973). ❖ See also Paul Roazen, *Helene Deutsch: A Psychoanalyst's Life* (Doubleday, 1985); and *Women in World History*.

DEUTSCH, Janszieka (1892–1941). *See Dolly, Jenny.*

DEUTSCH, Roszicka (1892–1970). *See Dolly, Rosie.*

DEUTSCHER, Tamara (1913–1990). Polish-born British editor and writer. Born Tamara Lebenhaft in Lodz, Russian Poland, Feb 1, 1913; died in London, England, Aug 7, 1990; m. Isaac Deutscher (socialist historian, died 1967); children: Martin. ❖ Talented writer and respected intellectual in her own right, played a crucial role in the research and writing of husband's influential books; after his death, edited his manuscripts, including *The Great Purges, Marxism in Our Time,* and *The Non-Jewish Jew and Other Essays;* a democratic socialist, was highly critical of the repressive nature of Soviet regime and was active in British intellectual circles that defended the human rights of dissident elements in the Soviet bloc; published a number of works of her own, including *Not by Politics Alone: The Other Lenin* (1973). ❖ See also *Women in World History.*

DEUTSCHKRON, Inge (1922—). German-Jewish memoirist. Born Ingeborg Deutschkron in Finsterwalde, Germany, Aug 23. 1922; dau. of Martin (teacher) and Ella (Mannhalt) Deutschkron. ❖ Author whose memoirs are considered to be among the most fascinating chronicles of survival to come out of the WWII; writings include *Bonn and Jerusalem: The Strange Coalition* (1970), *. . . denn ihrer war die Hölle: Kinder in Gettos und Lagern* (new ed., 1985), *Milch ohne Honig: Leben in Israel* (1988), *Outcast: A Jewish Girl in Wartime Berlin* (Trans. by Jean Steinberg, Fromm, 1989), *Unbequem—:Mein Leben nach dem Überleben* (1992), *Sie blieben im Schatten: Ein Denkmal für "stille Helden"* (1996). Awarded City of Berlin's Moses Mendelssohn Prize (1994). ❖ See also (documentary) *Daffke: Die vier Leben der Inge Deutschkron (Daffke: The Four Lives of Inge Deutschkron);* and *Women in World History.*

DEUZEWSKA, Malgorzata (1958—). *See Dluzewska, Malgorzata.*

DE VALERA, Sile (1954—). Irish politician. Born Dec 1954 in Dublin, Ireland; granddau. of Éamon de Valera (pres. of Ireland). ❖ Representing Fianna Fáil, elected to 21st Dáil for Dublin Mid-County (1977–81), the youngest member at 22; returned to 25th–28th Dáil for Clare (1987–2002) and the 29th Dáil (2002); named minister of Arts, Heritage, & Gaeltacht and the Islands (1997); member of the joint committee on Women's Rights (1987–89, 1989–92); member of European Parliament (1979–84).

DE VALERA, Sinéad. *See Flanagan, Sinéad.*

DE VALOIS, Ninette (1898–2001). Irish-born choreographer and founder. Pronunciation: VALL-wah. Born Edris Stannus, June 6, 1898, at Baltiboys, Blessington, Co. Wicklow, Ireland; died Mar 8, 2001, in London; dau. of T.R.A. Stannus (lieutenant-colonel) and Lilith (Graydon-Smith) Stannus; m. Dr. Arthur B. Connell, July 1935; no children. ❖ Founder of the Royal Ballet who helped to establish classical ballet in Britain, 1st performed professionally in 1913; danced with Diaghilev's Ballets Russes (1923–25); founded Academy of Choreographic Art, London (1926); hired by Lilian Baylis to work at the Old Vic (1926); worked at Festival Theater, Cambridge (1926–31) and Abbey Theater, Dublin (1927–35); founded Vic-Wells (subsequently Sadler's Wells and Royal) Ballet (1931); founded Sadler's Wells (subsequently Royal) Ballet School (1931); moved company to Royal Opera House, Covent Garden (1946); made 1st American tour (1949); saw Sadler's Wells Ballet given Royal Charter (1956); after 32 years, retired as director of Royal Ballet (1963); was also founder and director, Turkish School of Ballet (1948) and Turkish State Ballet (1956); founder, Iranian National Ballet (1958); patron, Irish Ballet Company (1974); writings include *Invitation to the Ballet* (1937) and *Step by Step* (1977). Named Commander of the British Empire (CBE, 1947); received Chévalier, Légion d'honneur (1950); named Dame of British Empire (DBE, 1951); named a fellow, Royal Academy of Dancing (1963); was 1st woman recipient of Erasmus Prize Foundation Award (1974); granted Companion of Honor (CH, 1982) and Order of Merit (OM, 1992). ❖ See also *Come Dance With Me: A Memoir 1898–1956* (Hamish Hamilton, 1957); Kathrine Sorley Walker, *Ninette de Valois: Idealist without Illusions* (Hamish Hamilton, 1987); "Madam," two-part documentary for Channel Four tv, London (1983); and *Women in World History.*

DEVANNY, Jean (1894–1962). Australian author and political activist. Name variations: Jane, Jenny; Jane Crook. Pronunciation: De-VANE-ee. Born Jane Crook, Jan 7, 1894, in Ferntown, Nelson, New Zealand; died at Townsville, Queensland, Australia, Mar 8, 1962; dau. of William (coal miner) and Jane (Appleyard) Crook; m. Hal Devanny (miner), 1911; children: Karl Devanny (d. 1934); Patricia Devanny; Erin Devanny (d. 1919). ❖ Significant Australian writer during 1st half of 20th century, whose career was marked by the conflict between her devotion to the Australian Communist Party and her strong affiliation with feminism; moved to the New Zealand capital of Wellington (1919); active in

women's branch of New Zealand Labour Party; published 1st novel, *The Butcher Shop* (1926), which was both sexually candid and graphic in describing the brutality to which females were subjected in the society of rural New Zealand (in time, the book was to be banned in Boston as well as a number of countries, including Nazi Germany and Australia); moved to Sydney, Australia (1929); arrested at a workers' march, joined Communist Party (1930); became National Secretary of Australian branch of the Workers International Relief (WIR) and traveled in Germany and the Soviet Union (1931); participated in the northern Queensland sugar-cane strike (1935), resulting in *Sugar Heaven,* about the role of women in the strike (1936); learned of her expulsion from Australian Communist Party (1941); readmitted (1943), resigned (1950), rejoined Communist Party (1957); other writings include *Lenore Divine, Dawn Beloved, Riven* and *Bushman Burke* (1930), *Poor Swine* (1932), *Cindie* (1949), and *Travels in North Queensland* (1951). ❖ See also autobiography *Point of Departure* (1986); *Dictionary of New Zealand Biography* (Vol. 4); and *Women in World History.*

DE VARONA, Donna (1947—). American swimmer. Born April 26, 1947, in San Diego, California; sister of actress Joanna Kerns; m. John Pinto (businessman). ❖ Won gold medals in the 400-meter individual medley and 400-meter freestyle relay at Tokyo Olympics (1964); won 37 national swimming titles; broke 18 national and world records; was the 1st female sports commentator on network tv; co-founded and was president of the Women's Sports Foundation; played an active role in the passage of the Amateur Sports Act and getting Title IX of the Education Amendments of 1972 implemented. ❖ See also *Women in World History.*

DE VAUX, Clotilde (1764–1846). *See Vaux, Clotilde de.*

DE VENDOME, Elizabeth (1614–1664). *See Elizabeth de Bourbon.*

DE VERE. *See Vere.*

DE VERE, Anne.
See Howard, Anne (d. 1559).
See Cecil, Anne (1556–1589).

DE VERE, Philippa. *See Philippa de Coucy.*

DEVEREUX, Frances (d. 1631). *See Walsingham, Frances.*

DEVEREUX, Frances (d. 1674). Duchess of Somerset. Name variations: Frances Seymour. Died April 24, 1674 (some sources cite 1679); dau. of Robert Devereux (b. 1566), 2nd earl of Essex, and Frances Walsingham; m. William Seymour (1587–1660), 2nd duke of Somerset (r. 1660–1660), Mar 3, 1616; children: William (b. 1621); Robert (b. 1624); Henry (b. 1626); Edward; John, 4th duke of Somerset; Frances Seymour (d. 1680); Lady Mary Seymour (d. 1673, who m. Heneage Finch, 3rd earl of Winchelsea); Lady Jane Seymour (d. 1679).

DEVEREUX, Lettice (c. 1541–1634). *See Knollys, Lettice.*

DEVEREUX, Margaret (1571–1633). *See Hoby, Margaret.*

DEVEREUX, Penelope (c. 1562–1607). *See Rich, Penelope.*

DEVERS, Gail (1966—). African-American runner. Born Nov 16, 1966, in Seattle, Washington; grew up near San Diego, California; attended University of California, Los Angeles; m. R.J. Hampton (track-and-field athlete, div.). ❖ Learned she had Graves' disease, a thyroid disorder that compromises the metabolic and nervous systems (1990); at World championships, placed 1st at 100-meter hurdles (1993, 1995, 1999), 100 meters (1993), and 4 x 100-meter relay (1997); at World Indoor championships, placed 1st in 60-meter sprint (1993, 1997, 2004) and 60-meter hurdles (2003); won a gold medal for 100-meter sprint (closest finish ever recorded in Olympic race) at Barcelona Olympics (1992); won gold medals for 100-meter hurdles and 4 x 100-meter relay at Atlanta Olympics (1996). ❖ See also Christina Lessa, *Women Who Win* (Universe, 1998), and tv-movie "Run for the Dream: The Gail Devers Story," (1996).

DEVETZI, Hrysopiyi (1975—). Greek track-and-field athlete. Born Jan 2, 1975, in Alexandroupoli, Greece. ❖ Won Greek championships for triple jump (2002, 2003, 2004); won a silver medal for triple jump at Athens Olympics (2004).

DE VEYRAC, Christine (1959—). French politician. Born Nov 6, 1959, in Toulouse, France. ❖ Named deputy mayor of Toulouse with responsibility for international and European relations (2001); as a member of the European People's Party (Christian Democrats) and European Democrats, elected to 5th European Parliament (1999–2004).

DE VEYRINAS, Françoise (1943—). French politician. Name variations: Francoise de Veyrinas. Born Sept 4, 1943, in Alzonne, France. ❖ Was a member of the National Assembly for Haute-Garonne (1993–95), state secretary for areas with difficulties (1993–95), and 1st deputy mayor of Toulouse; as a member of the European People's Party (Christian Democrats) and European Democrats, elected to 5th European Parliament (1999–2004). Named Knight of the Legion of Honour (1997) and Officer of the Order of Merit (2000).

DEVI, Ashapurna (1909–1995). Indian novelist. Born Feb 8, 1909, in India; lived in Calcutta; died July 13, 1995. ❖ The grande dame of Bengal literature, wrote mostly about lives of middle-class Bengalis; wrote over 175 novels, including *Swarnlatha* and *Bukul Katha,* and 30 short-story collections, as well as 47 children's books; conferred title Padma Shri by the president of India (1976); frequent contributor to *Manushi.* Won the Bengal government Rabindra Award (1966); was the 1st woman to receive the Sahitya Akademi Jnanpith Award (1977), for *Pratham Pratisruti;* given the Gyanpith Award.

DEVI, Gayatri (c. 1897–1995). See Gayatri Devi.

DEVI, Mahasveta (1926—). Indian novelist and playwright. Name variations: Mahasweta or Mahashweta Devi. Born Jan 14, 1926, in Dhaka, present-day Bangladesh; lives in Calcutta; dau. of Manish Ghatak and Dharitri Devi. ❖ Celebrated Bengali writer, was associated with political group Gananatya which performed plays in Bengali villages (1930s–40s); writings, which often address social and political problems, include *Jhansi Rani* (1956), about the rani of Jhansi, and *Agnigarbha* (A Womb of Fire, 1978); works translated into English include *Ek-kori's Dream* (trans. by Lila Majumdar, 1976), *Five Plays* (trans. by Shamik Bandyopadhyay, 1986), *Etoyaa Munda Won the Battle* (trans. by Meenakshi Chatterjee, 1989), *Basia Tudu* (trans. by Gayatri Chakravorty Spivak and Shamik Bandyopadhyay, 1993), and *Breast Stories* (trans. by Spivak, 1997); nonfiction translated into English includes *In Other Worlds: Essays in Cultural Politics* (trans. by Spivak, 1987); received Jnanpith Award (1996) and Magsaysay Award (1997). A collection of her work in Bengali is being published in 40 vols.

DEVI, Maitreyi (1914–1990). Indian poet and social worker. Born Maitreyi Dasgupta, 1914, in Calcutta, India; died 1990; dau. of Surendranath Dasgupta (Hindu professor and philosopher). ❖ Bengali poet and lecturer, had a liberal education provided by father; when Mircea Eliade came to Calcutta to study with him (1930), had her 1st romance, and Eliade was banished from the home; translated her novel, *Na Hanyate* (1974), into English as *It Does Not Die* (1974), which was her response to Eliade's *Bengal Nights,* a novel he had written about their encounter; other works include 4 vols. of poetry as well as books on travel, philosophy, and social reform; also wrote 8 books on the poetry of Rabindranath Tagore; founded the Council for the Promotion of Communal Harmony (1964) and was vice president of the All-India Women's Coordinating Council. Awards include Tagore Medallion (1961) and Soviet Desh Jawaharlal Nehru Prize (1968).

DEVI, Phoolan (c. 1956—). See Phoolan Devi.

DE VILMORIN, Louise (1902–1969). See Vilmorin, Louise de.

DE VITO, Gioconda (1907–1994). Italian-born British violinist. Born in Martina Franca, Lecce, Italy, June 22, 1907; died Oct 14, 1994, in Rome, Italy. ❖ Studied violin at Pesaro, then Rome; won the international violin competition in Vienna (1932); was principal professor of violin at Accademia di St. Cecilia in Rome; went to London to make records (1947) and made concert debut with London Philharmonic Orchestra (1948); married and settled permanently in Great Britain, concertized until retirement (1961). ❖ See also *Women in World History.*

DEVLIN, Bernadette (b. 1947). See McAliskey, Bernadette.

DEVLIN, Judy (1935—). See Hashman, Judy.

DEVOE, Emma Smith (1848–1927). American suffragist. Born Emma Smith, Aug 22, 1848, in Roseville, Illinois; died Sept 3, 1927; m. John "Henry" DeVoe (railroad attorney). ❖ A gifted musician, taught at Eureka College; with husband, moved to Huron, South Dakota (1881), then Tacoma, Washington (1905); as president of the Washington Equal Suffrage Association, led a successful campaign in 1910 to win the vote for women in Washington state; remained active in women's politics until her death. Inducted into the Women's Hall of Fame at Seneca Falls, NY (2000).

DE VOIE, Bessie (b. around 1888). American theatrical dancer. Born c. 1888, in Mt. Clemens, Michigan. ❖ Known for her work as ballet dancer in musicals and comedies, made Broadway debut in the chorus of *The Show Girl* (1902); made 1st ballet appearance in *Mr. Bluebeard* (1903); joined Rogers Brothers' company (1904) and appeared in their comedies *The Rogers Brothers in Paris* (1904) and *In Ireland* (1905); because of publicity received over her involvement in complicated legal battle (c. 1909), was offered larger roles on Broadway, including in *Our Miss Gibbs* (1910) and *Louisiana Lou* (1912); performed frequently in vaudeville throughout New York City.

DEVOLD, Kristin Krohn (1961—). Norwegian Cabinet official. Born Aug 12, 1961, in Ålesund, Norway; Norwegian School of Economics and Business Administration, MS in Business, 1985; attended University of Bergen, 1985–86; married; children: 2. ❖ As a member of the Conservative Party, served in Oslo City Parliament (1991–93); representing Oslo, elected to Parliament (Stortinget, 1993–97, 1997–2001, 2001–05); served as secretary of the Lagting (the presidium, Stortinget, 1993–97); was a member of the Standing Committee on Business and Industry (1993–97), Election Committee (1997–2001), Working Procedures Committee (1997–2001) and chair of the Standing Committee on Justice (1997–2001); appointed minister of defense (Oct 19, 2001); turned Norway's military into a model for small nations; frequently mentioned as a candidate to take over NATO.

DEVON, countess of.
See Courtenay, Margaret (fl. 1330).
See Beaufort, Margaret (c. 1407–?).
See Talbot, Anne.

DEVON, duchess of. See Katherine Plantagenet (1479–1527).

DEVONSHIRE, countess of. See Cavendish, Christiana (1595–1675).

DEVONSHIRE, duchess of.
See Cavendish, Georgiana (1757–1806).
See Cavendish, Elizabeth (1759–1824).
See Mitford, Deborah (b. 1920).

DEVORAN, Dinah (fl. 1696). See Nuthead, Dinah.

DEVORE, Dorothy (1899–1976). American actress. Name variations: Dorothy De Vore. Born Alma Inez Williams, June 22, 1899, in Fort Worth, Texas; died Sept 10, 1976, in Woodland Hills, California; m. Albert Wylie Mather (theater owner), 1926. ❖ Star of the Christie Comedies (1920s); other films include *Know Thy Wife, Forty-Five Minutes from Broadway, The Narrow Street, His Majesty, Bunker Bean* and *The Wrong Mr. Wright.*

DEVORGILLA. *Variant of Dervorgilla.*

DEVORGILLA (1109–1193). Meath princess. Name variations: Dearbhfhorgaill; Dervorgilla. Born 1109; died in religious retirement in Drogheda in 1193; dau. of Muirchertach Mac Lochlainn, king of Meath; m. Tighearnán O'Rourke, king of Bréifne; abducted by Dermot MacMurrough, king of Leinster, 1152. ❖ Was the dau. of the king of Meath, who often aligned with Dermot MacMurrough to retain control over Dublin; married Tighearnán O'Rourke, a long-standing enemy of MacMurrough; abducted by MacMurrough (1152); husband dethroned MacMurrough (1166); was benefactor of the Nuns' Church at Clonmacnoise. ❖ See also *Women in World History.*

DEVORGILLA (d. 1290). Co-founder of Balliol College at the University of Oxford. Name variations: Derbhorcaill; Dervorguilla; Devorgilla de Galloway; Devorgilla Balliol. Died Jan 28, 1290; interred in Sweetheart Abbey, Kirkland; dau. of Margaret (d. 1228) and Alan of Galloway; m. John Balliol, 1233 (died 1269); children: Hugh Balliol (c. 1240–1271, who m. Agnes de Valence); Alan Balliol; Alexander Balliol (d. 1278, who m. Eleanor of Geneva); John Balliol, king of the Scots (c. 1250–1313, r. 1292–1296); Cecily Balliol (d. before 1273, who m. John de Burgh); Ada Balliol (fl. 1256, who m. William Lindsay of Lambarton); Margaret Balliol (c. 1255–?, who m. John Comyn).

DEVOY, Susan (1964—). New Zealand squash player. Name variations: Dame Susan Devoy. Born Susan Elizabeth Anne Devoy in 1964 in Rotorua, New Zealand; children: 4. ❖ One of greatest women squash players of all time (1980s–early 90s), turned professional at 17; moved to England at 18 and settled in Marlow (1982); won British squash championship (1984); earned 1st World Open title (1985); won British Open Squash Championship 8 times, the last time being April 1992 after having lost it in 1991; was ranked 1st in world continuously from 1983 until unexpected retirement (Oct 1992), after achieving 4th World Women's Squash championship (in addition to Australian, British, Hong Kong, Scottish, Irish, Swedish, French and New Zealand titles for same year); named New Zealand Sportswoman of the Year (1985, 1987, 1988, 1993); became chief executive of Sports Bay of Plenty and chair of Halberg Trust. Awarded Member of British Empire (MBE, 1986) and Commander of British Empire (CBE, 1993); became Dame Companion of New Zealand Order of Merit (1998), the youngest New Zealander since Sir Edmund Hillary to receive such a high honor from the queen.

DE VRIES, Dorien (1965—). Dutch yacht racer. Born Dec 7, 1965. ❖ At Barcelona Olympics, won a bronze medal in Lechner (boardsailing, 1992).

DE VRIES, Eva (1934—). See Herzberg, Judith.

DE VRIES, Marta (1934—). See Herzberg, Judith.

DE VRIES, Tineke (1951—). See Bartels, Tineke.

DEVYATOVA, Tatyana (1949—). Soviet swimmer. Born Sept 19, 1948. ❖ At Tokyo Olympics, won a bronze medal in 4 x 100-meter medley relay (1964).

DE WAARD, Elly (b. 1940). See Waard, Elly de.

DEWAR, Phyllis (1915–1961). Canadian swimmer. Name variations: Phyllis Dewar Lowery. Born 1915 in Moose Jaw, Saskatchewan, Canada; died April 1961 in Toronto, Ontario, Canada; sister of Dora Dewar Ellsworth (swimmer). ❖ Won a gold medal in 100-yard freestyle, gold medal in 440-yard freestyle), gold medal in 3 x 100-yard medley relay, and gold medal in 4 x 100-yard freestyle relay at the British Empire games (1934); won the gold medal in 4 x 100-yard freestyle relay at British Empire games (1938).

DE WARRENNE, Isabel. See Isabel de Warrenne.

DEWE, Catharine (1843–1912). See Squires, Catharine.

DEWE, Colleen (1930–1993). New Zealand politician. Born Colleen Dewe, May 30, 1930, in Hokitika, NZ; died May 22, 1993. ❖ Elected National Party MP for Lyttleton (1975–78); lost election to Ann Hercus (1978); chaired Advisory Committee on Women's Affairs (ACWA) for three years (1975–77).

DEWEES, Mary Coburn (fl. 1787–1788). American diarist. Flourished around 1787–88. ❖ Wrote *Mrs. Mary Dewees's Journal from Philadelphia to Kentucky 1781–1788*, about pioneering trip to Kentucky with family, which was published in 1904.

DEWEY, Alice Chipman (1858–1927). American educator. Born Hattie (or Harriet) Alice Chipman, Sept 7, 1858, in Fenton, Michigan; died July 14, 1927, in New York, NY; dau. of Gordon Orlen Chipman (cabinet maker) and Lucy (Riggs) Chipman; grew up with maternal grandparents in Genesee Co., MI; University of Michigan, PhB, 1886; m. John Dewey (philosopher and educator), July 28, 1886; children: Frederick Archibald Dewey, Evelyn Riggs Dewey, Morris (died young), Gordon Chipman Dewey, Lucy Alice Chipman Dewey, and Jane Mary Dewey. ❖ With husband, founded famous elementary school known as Laboratory School (1896), which greatly influenced educational reform during 1st half of 20th century; became principal and director of department of English and literature at Laboratory School (1901); was a strong supporter of feminist movement and lectured in China to promote feminist movement in Chinese education.

DEWHURST, Colleen (1924–1991). Canadian-born actress. Born in Montreal, Quebec, Canada, June 3, 1924; died in South Salem, New York, Aug 22, 1991; dau. of a professional hockey player and a Christian Science practitioner; attended Downer College of Young Ladies (now Lawrence University), Milwaukee, Wisconsin, and NY Academy of Dramatic Arts; m. James Vickery, 1947 (div.); twice m. and twice div. actor George C. Scott; children: (2nd m.) Alexander and Campbell. ❖ Tall, robust, with a throaty voice, was closely identified with the plays of O'Neill; made NY professional stage debut as a walk-on in *Desire Under the Elms* at ANTA (1952); began a long association with Joe Papp, appearing as Lady Macbeth at New York Shakespeare Festival (1957); portrayed Mary Follett in *All the Way Home*, for which she received a Tony Award (1960); appeared as Abbie Putnam in *Desire Under the Elms* (1963), Cleopatra in *Antony and Cleopatra* (1963), Amelia Evans in *Ballad of the Sad Cafe* (1963), Sara in *More Stately Mansions* (1965), Hester in *Hello and Goodbye* (1969), Shen Teh in

The Good Woman of Setzuan (1970), Gertrude in *Hamlet* (1972), Christine Mannon in *Mourning Becomes Electra* (1972), Josie Hogan in *A Moon for the Misbegotten,* for which she received a 2nd Tony Award (1973), and Martha in *Who's Afraid of Virginia Woolf* (1977); portrayed Carlotta O'Neill in one-woman play *My Gene* (1987); had recurring role on tv comedy "Murphy Brown," for which she won 1 of her 3 Emmys; films include *The Nun's Story* (1959), *A Fine Madness* (1966), *Annie Hall* (1977), *Tribute* (1980), *The Boy Who Could Fly* (1986) and *Bed and Breakfast* (1989); was president of Actors' Equity Association (1985–91). ❖ See also (with Tom Viola) *Colleen Dewhurst: Her Autobiography* (Scribner, 1997); and *Women in World History*.

DE WITT, Henriette (1829–1908). See Witt, Henriette de.

DE WITT, Lydia (1859–1928). American pathologist. Born Lydia Maria Adams, Feb 1, 1859, in Flint, Michigan; died Mar 10, 1928, in Winter, Texas; dau. of Oscar Adams and Elizabeth (Walton) Adams; graduate of Ypsilanti Normal College (later Eastern Michigan University), 1886; m. Alton D. De Witt (teacher, d. 1921), June 22, 1878; children: 2. ❖ Served in various positions in pathology department of University of Michigan (c. 1899–1910), as instructor in pathology at Washington University (from 1910), and as assistant city pathologist and bacteriologist in St. Louis department of health; joined staff of Otho S.A. Sprague Memorial Institute (1912), where she conducted experimental research on chemical treatment of tuberculosis; became associate professor in department of pathology at University of Chicago (1918); served as president of Chicago Pathological Society (1924–25).

DE WOLFE, Elsie (1865–1950). American interior decorator. Name variations: Lady Mendl. Born in New York, NY, 1865; died in Paris, France, July 12, 1950; dau. of Stephen de Wolfe (doctor); lived with Elisabeth "Bessie" Marbury (theatrical agent), from 1887 to 1926; m. Sir Charles Mendl (British embassy functionary), Mar 10, 1926. ❖ Known as the Founding Mother of Decorating, rescued interior design from the stuffy Victorian period and remained its arbiter of style for 50 years; turned the design world upside down with her innovations—cotton chintz, mirrors, trellises, painted furniture, and decoupage; was also a legendary character, a master of self-invention, and one of the 1st international celebrities. Awarded Croix de Guerre and later the Legion of Honor from France. ❖ See also Nina Campbell and Caroline Seebohm. *Elsie de Wolfe: A Decorative Life* (Panache, 1992); and *Women in World History*.

DEWSON, Molly (1874–1962). American politician. Name variations: Mary Williams Dewson. Born Mary Williams Dewson in Quincy, Massachusetts, Feb 18, 1874; died in Castine, Maine, Oct 22, 1962; graduate of Wellesley College, 1897; lived with Mary G. Porter. ❖ After serving as president of the Consumers' League of New York (1925–31), was urged by Eleanor Roosevelt to organize the women in the Democratic Party as a viable force; by 1936, was vice-chair of Democratic National Committee, actively lobbying President Roosevelt to appoint more women to Cabinet posts (one result was appointment of Frances Perkins as secretary of labor); also served on President's Advisory Committee on Economic Security, involved in planning the Social Security system; was the 1st woman to serve on the Social Security Board.

DE X, Mademoiselle (1650–1724). See La Force, Charlotte-Rose de Caumont de.

DEXTER, Caroline (1819–1884). Australian feminist. Name variations: Caroline Lynch. Born in Nottingham, England, 1819; died 1884; dau. of a jeweller; educated in England and Paris, France; m. William Dexter (painter), 1843 (died 1860); m. William Lynch (lawyer). ❖ Sailed for Australia (1855); wrote *Ladies' Almanack: The Southern Cross or Australian Album and New Year's Gift* (1857), a book sympathetic to aboriginal culture which chronicled life in Australia; joined with Harriet Clisby to found the *Interpreter* (1861), a radical feminist journal; became a patron of artists and writers. ❖ See also *Women in World History*.

DEXTER, John (1930–1999). See Bradley, Marion Zimmer.

DEY, Courtenay (1965—). See Becker-Dey, Courtenay.

DE ZAYAS Y SOTOMAYOR, Maria (1590–c. 1650). See Zayas Y Sotomayor, Maria de.

DEZURA, Diane (1958—). See Nelson, Diane.

DHABBA THE CAHINA. See Kahina.

D'HAEN, Christine (1923—). Dutch poet and essayist. Name variations: Christine Elodia Maria D'haen. Born Oct 25, 1923, in Sint-Amandsberg,

Netherlands; studied German philology in Ghent and Edinburgh. ❖ Was a teacher in Bruges, then archivist for Gezelle archive; poetry, which draws on classical and Biblical tradition, includes *Gedichten 1946–1958* (1958), *Gezelle, Poems/Gedichten* (1971), *Onyx* (1983), *Mirages* (1989), *Zwarte sneeuw* (1989), *Een brokaten brief* (1992), *Morgane* (1995), *De zoon van de Zon* (1997), *Het gehemeim dat ik draag* (1998), and *Het huwelijk* (2000); made member of Royal Academy of Dutch Linguistics and Literature (1976). Received Anna Bijns Prize (1991).

D'HERICOURT, Jenny Poinsard (1809–1875). *See Hericourt, Jenny Poinsard d'.*

DHOUDA or DHOUDHA (fl. 820–841). *See Dhuoda of Septimania.*

DHUODA OF SEPTIMANIA (fl. 820–843). Frankish noblewoman and writer. Name variations: Dodane; Dhouda; Dhoudha. Flourished between 820 and 841; m. Bernard, count of Septimania, c. 824; children: two sons, including William (b. 826). ❖ Was one of the earliest medieval women writers; though her sons were taken away from her by husband for political purposes, remained a faithful wife and dedicated herself to preserving her estates; recorded a life of loneliness and grief; between 841 and 843, composed a manual of instruction for eldest son, then about 15 and living at the king's court, which is called the *Manual of Dhuoda.* ❖ See also *Women in World History.*

DIACHENKO, Nada (1946—). American modern dancer and choreographer. Born July 31, 1946, in Miami, Florida. ❖ Performed duets with Erick Hawkins in several of his works, including *Here and Now with Watchers, Classic Kite Tails* (1972), and *Greek Dreams with Flute* (1973); appeared in works by Beverly Brown and Lillo Way; danced in recitals by Greenhouse Dance Ensemble, a troupe she later co-directed with Way; taught dance classes at New York University for 10 years and at Erick Hawkins studio for 8; held numerous residencies and gave workshops in injury prevention across US; taught at Princeton, Vassar, North Carolina School of the Arts, as well as in England, Denmark, Germany, and Czech Republic; served as artistic director and choreographer for Nada Diachenko and Dancers and Nada Diachenko-Solo Dance. Works of choreography include *Alighting Aloft* (1972), *Summer Settings* (1973), *For Four* (1977), *Beneath It All* (1978), *Branching* (1979), *Shades of You, Shades of Me* (1979), *Structures* (1980) and *Avian Images* (1981).

DIACONESCU, Camelia (1963—). Romanian rower. Born Feb 1963. ❖ At Los Angeles Olympics, won a silver medal in coxed eights (1984).

DIAKONOVA, Elizaveta (1874–1902). Russian diarist and essayist. Name variations: Elizaveta Aleksandrovna D'iákonova. Born 1874 in Russia; committed suicide in the Swiss Alps, age 28, 1902. ❖ Published stories and articles, including "Women's Education" in *Women's Cause,* but is best known for the posthumously published *The Diary of Elizaveta D'iákonova* (1904–05).

DIALLO, Nafissatou (1941–1982). Senegalese novelist, memoirist and pediatrician. Name variations: Nafissatou Niang Diallo. Born 1941 in Dakar, Senegal; died 1982; dau. of Samba Assane (borough surveyor for Dakar); studied in Toulouse for 2 years; m. Mambaye Diallo, 1961; children: 6. ❖ Worked as pediatrician and midwife at Centre de Protection Maternelle et Infantile; wrote autobiography *De Tilène au Plateau: une enfance dakaroise* (1975, trans. as *A Dakar Childhood,* 1982), one of the 1st literary works published by a Senegalese woman; also wrote 3 works of fiction, *Le Fort maudit* (The Strongly Cursed, 1980), *Awa, le petite marchande* (Awa, The Little Shopkeeper, 1981) and *La Princesse de Tiali* (Princess Tiali, 1987).

DIAMANT, Anita (1917–1996). American literary agent. Name variations: Anita Berke. Born Jan 15, 1917; died Jan 13, 1996, in Weston, Connecticut. ❖ Founded the Anita Diamant Agency (1971); best known for nurturing the career of V.C. Andrews.

DIAMOND, Ann (c. 1827–1881). New Zealand innkeeper, shopkeeper, and midwife. Name variations: Ann Gleeson. Born Ann Gleeson, c. 1827–1831, in Adare, Co. Limerick, Ireland; died April 22, 1881, at Red Jacks, New Zealand; dau. of Patrick (farmer) and Ann (Roberts) Gleeson; m. Patrick Diamond (stonemason), 1859; children: 5. ❖ Immigrated with husband to Melbourne, Australia (1858); sailed to Dunedin, New Zealand (1862); 1st ran boarding house with friends and later settled in Red Jacks community, establishing a successful general store and hotel; served as midwife to community. ❖ See also *Dictionary of New Zealand Biography* (Vol. 1).

DIAMOND, Selma (1920–1985). Canadian-born comedy writer and actress. Born Aug 5, 1920, in Montreal, Quebec, Canada; died May 13, 1985, in Los Angeles, California. ❖ Wrote for many successful tv shows; films include *It's a Mad, Mad, Mad, Mad World, My Favorite Year, Bang the Drum Slowly, The Twilight Zone* and *All of Me;* was a frequent guest on "The Johnny Carson Show." The character Sally (played by Rosemarie) on "Dick Van Dyke Show" said to be based on her; nominated for Emmy as a writer for "Caesar's Hour" (1956) and Outstanding Supporting Actress in a Comedy Series for "Night Court" (1984).

DIANA. *Variant of Diane.*

DIANA (1961–1997). Princess of Wales. Name variations: Lady Diana Spencer. Born Diana Frances Spencer on July 1, 1961, at Park House, Sandringham, Norfolk, England; died in Paris, France, in an automobile accident, Aug 31, 1997; interred at Althorp, Northamptonshire, Sept 6, 1997; dau. of Edward John VIII Spencer (b. 1924), viscount Althorp, and Frances Burke Ruth Roche (Fermoy) Spencer, viscountess Althorp, later known as Frances Shand Kydd; m. Charles Philip Arthur George Windsor (b. 1948), prince of Wales, July 29, 1981; children: William Arthur (b. 1982); Henry Charles (b. 1984). ❖ One of the world's most glamorous and aristocratic women, born to privilege and raised in wealth, bridged the gap between Britain's commoners and an aloof monarchy; known as "the people's princess," embraced charitable causes, aiding the poor and diseased, yet reveled in designer gowns and expensive jewelry; was seen as a beaming member of the international jet-set, yet suffered from debilitating depression; after completing education in private schools, took a job as an assistant in a London kindergarten; married Charles, prince of Wales, royal family's oldest son (July 29, 1981), followed by the birth of two royal sons, Princes William and Harry, during next decade; heard divorce announced in House of Commons (Aug 1996); began dating film producer and financier Dodi al-Fayed; was with al-Fayed in Paris at time of the car crash that claimed both their lives (Aug 1997). ❖ See also Christopher Anderson, *The Day Diana Died* (Morrow, 1998); Andrew Morton, *Diana: Her True Story* (Simon & Schuster, 1992); and *Women in World History.*

DIANDA, Hilda (1925—). Argentine composer, conductor, musicologist, and professor. Born in Córdoba, Argentina, April 13, 1925. ❖ Studied in Buenos Aires under Honorio Siccardi (1942–50); studied conducting with Hermann Scherchen in Venice; invited to join Pierre Schaeffer's Groupe de Recherches Musicales (1958); won Medal of Cultural Merit in Italy (1964); back in Argentina (1967–70), was professor of composition, instrumentation, orchestration, and technical and orchestral conducting at National University's School of Fine Arts in Córdoba; often participated in international festivals as a conductor and composer. ❖ See also *Women in World History.*

DIANE DE FRANCE (1538–1619). French duchess of Montmorency and Angoulême. Name variations: Madame d'Angoulême; Diana of France or Diane of France. Born in Piedmont, Italy, 1538; died Jan 3, 1619; legitimized dau. of Henry II (1519–1559), king of France (r. 1547–1559), and Filippa Duci; m. Orazio Farnese, duke of Castro (son of the duke of Parma), 1553; m. François de Montmorency (d. 1579), governor of Ile-de-France, May 3, 1559. ❖ Though fathered by Henry II of France out of wedlock, was acknowledged by the king, legitimized (1547), and fully accepted as a daughter of France; was also accepted by half-brothers and half-sisters; a beauty and a fine equestrian, was given the duchy of Chastellerault, until she took over Angoulême; after 1st husband was killed in battle at siege of Hesdin, married François de Montmorency, though he was betrothed to Mademoiselle de Piennes; when he was in danger and in need of financial assistance during his conflict with duke of Guise, brought him 50,000 crowns at great risk; was also politically astute and influential at court of brother-in-law Henry IV, who married her half-sister Margaret of Valois (1553–1615).

DIANE DE POITIERS (1499–1566). Duchess of Valentinois and mistress of Henry II. Name variations: Dianne de Poytiers, la grande sénéchale de Normandie; Duchess of Valentinois. Pronunciation: duh Pooah-TEAY. Born Dec 31 (some cite Sept 3), 1499, in province of the Dauphiné, France; died at Anet, Normandy, April 25 (or April 22), 1566; dau. of Jeanne de Bastarnay and Jean de Poitiers, lord of Saint-Vallier and captain of the King's Guard; tutored at home; m. Louis de Brézé, 1515; children: daughters Françoise (b. 1520) and Louise. ❖ French duchess who was married at 15 to a man old enough to be her grandfather, then became, at 37, the mistress of a king who, though young enough to be her son, made her the most powerful woman in France; following death of mother, went to live with the family of the duke of Bourbon (1509); married and moved to Anet (1515); having managed a large estate in the absence of husband, acquired a sound practical sense and knew how to obtain her wants through reason rather then caprice, diplomacy rather than coercion; became mistress of Henry II (1536); ably assisted the queen during her confinements and took charge of the growing nursery; acquired Chenonceau, a jewel of a castle in the Loire Valley (1555); following Henry's death, allowed to return to Anet (1559). ❖ See also Grace Hart Seely, *Diane the Huntress: The Life and Times of Diane de Poitiers* (Appleton-Century, 1936); and *Women in World History*.

DIANE OF FRANCE (1538–1619). See Diane de France.

DIANTI, Laura (fl. 1527). Italian woman of the Renaissance. Mistress of Alfonso I d'Este (1476–1534), 3rd duke of Ferrara and Modena; children: (with Alfonso I) Alfonso d'Este (1527–1587, who m. Giulia della Rovere). Alfonso I d'Este was married to Anna Sforza (1473–1497) and Lucrezia Borgia (1480–1519).

DIAS, Virna (1971—). Brazilian volleyball player. Born Aug 31, 1971, in Natal, Brazil. ❖ Outside hitter, won team World Grand Prix (1994, 1996, 1998); won South American championship (1995, 1997, 2001); won team bronze medals at Atlanta Olympics (1996) and Sydney Olympics (2000).

DIAZ, Abby (1821–1904). American author and reformer. Name variations: Abby Morton Diaz. Born Abigail Morton on Nov 22, 1821, in Plymouth, Massachusetts; died April 1, 1904, in Belmont, Massachusetts; dau. of Ichabod Morton and Patty (Weston) Morton; m. Manuel A. Diaz, Oct 6, 1845; children: 3. ❖ Known as juvenile author and for works on domestic culture, published most famous book *The William Henry Letters* (1870); served as president (1881–92), vice president (1892–1902), and honorary vice president (from 1902) of Women's Educational and Industrial Union of Boston; traveled to help establish similar unions in other cities including Buffalo (NY), Washington (DC), and St. Paul (MN). Other works include *William Henry and His Friends* (1872), *Lucy Maria* (1874), *Domestic Problems* (1884), and *Only a Flock of Women* (1893).

DIAZ, Eileen (1979—). Puerto Rican gymnast. Born Nov 2, 1979, in Rio Piedras, Puerto Rico; dau. of Eileen and Manuel Diaz; sister of Gretchen Diaz (gymnast at University of Arizona); attended University of Georgia, 1999–2002. ❖ At Atlanta, was the 1st female gymnast to represent Puerto Rico at the Olympics and the youngest Puerto Rican Olympian in history (1996); placed 1st all-around at the Puerto Rican nationals (1997), 2nd for vault at the Pan American Games (1997), and 1st for uneven bars at Central American Games (1998).

DIAZ, Jimena (fl. 1074–1100). Spanish hero and wife of El Cid. Name variations: Ximena. Dau. of the count of Oviedo; niece of Jimena Munoz (c. 1065–1128) and Alphonso VI, king of Castile; m. Rodrigo Diaz de Vivar (c. 1043–1099), also known as El Cid Campeador, in 1074; children: twins Maria de Vivar (who m. Peter of Aragon); Cristina de Vivar (mother of Garcia IV the Restorer, king of Navarre); son Diego. ❖ When husband died in Valencia (July 10, 1099), took control of the town and struggled to defend what he had fought so hard to possess; on advice of Alphonso VI, evacuated Valencia and sought refuge in Castile (1102); reinterred husband's body near Burgos, in the Benedictine monastery of San Pedro de Cardeña. ❖ See also *Women in World History*.

DIAZ, Mary F. (c. 1962–2004). American human-rights activist. Name variations: Mary Frances Diaz. Born in Newport News, Virginia; died Feb 12, 2004, age 42, in New York, NY; dau. of Bertha Diaz; graduate of Brown University, 1982; Harvard Graduate School of Education, MA, 1988. ❖ Served as executive director of the Women's Commission for Refugee Women and Children (1994–2003); deployed volunteers in Rwanda, Tanzania, Afghanistan and the Balkans.

DIAZ-BALART, Mirta (c. 1928—). Cuban wife of Castro. Name variations: Mirtha or Mirta Diaz Balart de Nunez. Born Mirta Diaz Balart de Nunez, c. 1928, in Banes, Cuba; dau. of a general; sister of Raphael Diaz Balart (undersecretary to Ramon Hermida, a minister of the interior to Batista); m. Fidel Castro (dictator of Cuba), Oct 12, 1948 (div. 1955); children: son Fidel Jr. (b. Sept 1, 1949). ❖ The only known wife of Fidel Castro, was a student in the Faculty of Philosophy at Havana University when they married (he was still in law school); divorced him

while he was in exile in Mexico (1955); remarried and moved to US, then Spain; went through a long custody battle over son.

DÍAZ LOZANO, Argentina (1912–1999). Honduran novelist and short-story writer. Name variations: Argentina Diaz Lozano. Born 1912 in Santa Rosa de Copán, Honduras; died 1999 in Guatemala. ❖ Works include *Perlas de rosario* (1930), *Luz en la senda* (1935), *Topacios* (1940), *Peregrinage* (1944), *Mayapán* (1950), *Y tenemos que viver* (1963), and *Fuego en la ciudad* (1966).

DIBA, Farah (1938—). See Pahlavi, Farah.

DIBABA, Ejigayehu (1982—). Ethiopian runner. Born June 25, 1982, in Ethiopia. ❖ Placed 1st in 5,000 meters at Golden League in Rome (2004); won a silver medal for 10,000 meters at Athens Olympics (2004).

DIBABA, Tirunesh (1985—). Ethiopian runner. Born Oct 1, 1985, in Ethiopia. ❖ At World championship, placed 1st for 5,000 meters (2003); won a bronze medal for 5,000 meters at Athens Olympics (2004).

DI BONA, Linda (1946—). American ballet dancer. Born June 21, 1946, in Quincy, Massachusetts; m. Robert Brassel (dancer). ❖ Joined Boston Ballet (1965), after having trained there for many years; was engaged during 3-year tenure by Boston and Harkness Ballets; appeared for Harkness in Norman Walker's *Night Song* and *Ballade*, in Ben Stevenson's *Three Preludes*, in Brian MacDonald's *Canto Indio*, in Vincente Nebrada's *Schubert Variations*, and more; made guest appearances with range of companies across US and Canada including in concerts with James Clouser and on tour with Bill Martin-Viscount (c. 1968–70); danced with husband Brassel with Ballet de Wallonie and State Opera Ballet in Basel, Switzerland.

DI CENTA, Manuela (1963—). Italian cross-country skier. Born Jan 31, 1963, in Paluzzo, Italy. ❖ Won a bronze medal for the 4 x 5 km relay at Albertville Olympics (1992); won gold medals for 15 km and 30 km, silver medals for 5 km and Combined 5 km + 10 km pursuit, and a bronze medal for 4 x 5 km relay at Lillehammer Olympics (1994); won a bronze medal for 4 x 5 km relay at Nagano Olympics (1998); won World Cup (1993–94, 1995–96).

DICK, Evelyn (1922—). Canadian murderer. Born Evelyn MacLean, 1922, in Canada; m. 2nd husband John Dick (bus conductor); children: Peter. ❖ Infamous figure in Canadian history, suffered abusive childhood; charged with murder after torso of husband was discovered by children near Hamilton, Ontario (Mar 16, 1946) and police found the body of her infant son encased in cement; found guilty, was sentenced to hang; represented by attorney J.J. Robinette on appeal, saw the verdict overturned with an acquittal (1947); tried separately for murder of her infant, was found guilty of manslaughter; sentenced to life imprisonment, served 11 years; given new identity after release from prison, effectively disappeared. ❖ See also Marjorie Freeman Campbell, *Torso: The Evelyn Dick Case* (MacMillan of Canada, 1974); Brian Vallée, *Torso: The Untold Story of Evelyn Dick* (Key Porter, 2001); (tv documentary) "The Notorious Mrs. Dick" (2001); (tv film) "Torso" (2001).

DICK, Gladys (1881–1963). American physician and microbiologist. Born Gladys Rowena Henry on Dec 18, 1881; died in Palo Alto, California, 1963; Johns Hopkins, MD, 1907; postgraduate work in Berlin; m. George Dick (physician); children: (adopted) Roger Henry Dick and Rowena Henry Dick. ❖ Moved to University of Chicago (1911), where she began working on the etiology, or cause, of scarlet fever, a major public health hazard at the time that killed a quarter of its predominantly young victims; after 10 years of methodical research with husband, isolated hemolytic streptococci, previously considered a secondary invader, as the cause of the disease (1923), then developed a skin test ("the Dick test"), which was distributed throughout the world. ❖ See also *Women in World History*.

DICKASON, Gladys (1903–1971). American labor activist. Name variations: Gladys Marie Dickason. Born Gladys Marie Dickason, Jan 28, 1903, in Galena, Oklahoma; died Aug 31, 1971, in New York, NY; dau. of Simon Milton Dickason and Linnie (Kellerman) Dickason; University of Oklahoma, AB, 1922; Columbia University, AM, 1924; attended London School of Economics; throughout life, had a close relationship with, and was possibly briefly married to, Arthur S. Harrison (building contractor). ❖ Labor economist who saw a similarity between the women's-rights movement and the labor movement in the fight to grant people the power to shape own lives, taught at Hamilton Grange

School in New York City, at economics department at Sweet Briar College in Virginia, and at political science department at Hunter College in NY (1920s–30s); began work with Amalgamated Clothing Workers of America (ACWA, 1933); worked with the industrial committee of National Recovery Administration's Cotton Garment Code Authority (1933–34); was research director of ACWA (1936–54); as special cotton-garment representative, led campaign against Cluett, Peabody & Co., the largest shirt manufacturer in US (1937) and won (1941); campaigned for minimum-wage standards in Fair Labor Standards Act (1938); participated in cotton garment industry national negotiations (1946); led ACWA campaign to raise minimum wage (1948–49); was head of ACWA southern department (mid-1940s) and became ACWA vice president (1946); among other work with US government commissions, visited Japan on US Army sponsorship, speaking to workers and studying role of women in labor movement (1951); honored by National Council of Negro Women for work on behalf of women in labor movement in Japan and US (1951); retired from ACWA (1963).

DICKENS, Helen Octavia (1909–2001). African-American surgeon. Name variations: Helen Henderson. Born Jan 1, 1909, in Dayton, Ohio; died Jan 24, 2001, in Pennsylvania; dau. of Charles Warren Dickens (former slave) and Daisy Jane Dickens (domestic servant); University of Illinois College of Medicine, MD, 1934; University of Pennsylvania Medical School, MS, 1945; m. Purvis Sinclair Henderson (physician), 1943; children: Dr. Jayne Henderson Brown. ❖ Completed residency at Harlem Hospital (1943–46) and was certified by American Board of Obstetric and Gynecology; began serving as director of the Mercy Douglass Hospital Department of Obstetrics and Gynecology in Philadelphia (1948); was the 1st black woman to become a fellow of the American College of Surgeons (1950); became associate dean in the Office for Minority Affairs at University of Pennsylvania (1969).

DICKENS, Monica (1915–1992). British novelist. Born May 10, 1915, in London, England; died Dec 24, 1992, in Reading, England; dau. of Henry Charles Dickens and Fanny Runge Dickens; great-granddau. of Charles Dickens (novelist); m. Roy Stratton (retired US naval officer and writer), 1951 (died 1985). ❖ Worked as nurse during World War II and as reporter after war; was a columnist for *Women's Own* for 2 decades; moved to US with husband and founded American branch of Samaritans to counsel suicidally depressed; returned to England after husband's death; wrote the autobiographical works, *One Pair of Hands* (1939), *One Pair of Feet* (1942), and *My Turn to Make the Tea* (1951); other writings include *Thursday Afternoons* (1945), *Flowers on the Grass* (1949), *Man Overboard* (1958), *The Heart of London* (1961), about alcoholism, *Kate and Emma* (1964), about child abuse, *The House at World's End* (1970), *Enchantment* (1989), *Scarred* (1991), and *Befriending* (1996); her series, *Follyfoot* (1971), *Follyfoot Farm* (1973), *Stranger at Follyfoot* (1976), was serialized for children's tv.

DICKENSCHEID, Tanja (1969—). German field-hockey player. Born June 17, 1969. ❖ At Barcelona Olympics, won a silver medal in team competition (1992).

DICKER-BRANDEIS, Friedl (1898–1944). Austrian-Jewish artist. Name variations: Friedl Dicker; Friedl Brandeisova. Born Friedl Dicker, 1898, in Vienna, Austria; killed 1944 in Auschwitz; studied at Bauhaus, Weimar, with Johannes Itten, Paul Klee, Oskar Schlemmer, and Georg Muche; m. Pavel Brandeis. ❖ Worked in interior, textile and theater design (1921–36); turned from constructivism to still-lifes, landscapes, and portraits (1932–42); deported to Theresienstadt concentration camp (1942); taught art to hundreds of children in the camp; was responsible for much of the 5,000 children's drawings produced at the Theresienstadt (1943–44), a body of work that has become one of the most poignant artifacts of the Holocaust; her own works are now housed at the Simon Wiesenthal Center in Los Angeles.

DICKERSON, Nancy (1927–1997). American journalist. Name variations: Nancy Hanschman. Born Nancy Conners Hanschman in Wauwatosa, Wisconsin, 1927; died in New York, NY, Oct 18, 1997; University of Wisconsin, BA, 1948; m. C. Wyatt Dickerson Jr., Feb 24, 1962 (div. 1983); m. John C. Whitehead (deputy secretary of state); children: (1st m.) 5. ❖ The 1st female correspondent for CBS News, began career producing radio's "The Leading Question" and working as associate producer of tv's "Face the Nation"; as a result of journalistic coups, became 1st woman correspondent for CBS (1960) and was also given a 5-minute radio show, "One Woman's Washington"; became 1st woman to report from the floor of a national convention (1960); moved

to NBC (1963), where she appeared regularly on "The Huntley-Brinkley Report" and "The Today Show," in addition to anchoring her daily news show; covered many of the major events of the decade, including John F. Kennedy's funeral, civil-rights marches on Washington, and Martin Luther King's "I Have a Dream" speech; was a commentator for Fox TV News (1986–91). Won Peabody for documentary "784 Days that Changed America—From Watergate to Resignation." ❖ See also memoir *Among Those Present* (1976); and *Women in World History*.

DICKEY, Mary Adelaide (c. 1884–1959). *See Adelaide.*

DICKEY, Nancy Wilson (1950—). American physician. Born Nancy Wilson, Sept 10, 1950, in Clark, South Dakota; dau. of Ed Wilson; University of Texas Medical School, MD, 1976; m. Franklin Dickey; children: 3. ❖ The 1st female president of American Medical Association (AMA), was 1 of 7 women students in a class of 50 at University of Texas Medical School in Houston, where she completed postgraduate work (1976–79); worked as director of patient education (1979–82), as clinical associate professor (1987–91) and as associate professor (1991–95) at Medical School's Memorial Hospital System Department of Family Practice; served on board of trustees of American Medical Association, as secretary-treasurer (1993–94), as vice-chair of the board (1994–95), and as chair of the board (1995–97); served as president of AMA (1998–99); became president of Texas A&M University System Health Science Center (2002).

DICKEY, Sarah (1838–1904). American educator of freedmen. Born Sarah Ann Dickey, April 25, 1838, near Dayton, Ohio; died Jan 23, 1904, in Clinton, Mississippi; dau. of Isaac Dickey; mother's maiden name was Tryon; graduate of Mount Holyoke Female Seminary, 1869; never married; no children. ❖ Joined staff of United Brethren freedmen's school, Vicksburg, MS (1863); despite threats from Ku Klux Klan, opened the Mount Hermon Female Seminary, a nonsectarian boarding school for African-American girls in Clinton, MS (1875); established Dickeyville settlement which provided land on credit and other assistance to African-Americans (1890s). ❖ See also Helen Griffith, *Dauntless in Mississippi* (Zenger, 1976).

DICKIN, Maria (1870–1951). English reformer and animal activist. Name variations: Marie Elizabeth Dickin. Born Marie Elizabeth Dickin, 1870, in London, England; died Mar 1, 1951; dau. of a Free Church minister; m. 1st cousin Arnold Dickin. ❖ Became a social worker in London's East End (1898); founded People's Dispensary for Sick Animals (PDSA, Nov 1917) and hung a sign, "All animals treated, All treatment free" (it would become England's largest veterinary charity); traveled Britain in a caravan treating animals and setting up clinics (1923); opened PDSA Animals' Sanatorium in Ilford, the 1st of its kind in Europe; introduced the Busy Bees club (1934), to teach children respect for animals. Awarded OBE and CBE.

DICKINSON, Angie (1931—). American actress. Born Angeline Brown, Sept 30, 1931, in Kulm, North Dakota; m. Gene Dickinson, 1952 (div. 1960); m. Burt Bacharach (composer), 1965 (div. 1980); children: daughter. ❖ Won a number of beauty contests; came to prominence in the film *Rio Bravo* (1959), followed by *Ocean's 11*, *The Sins of Rachel Cade*, *Point Blank*, *Rome Adventure*, *Jessica*, *Captain Newman M.D.*, *The Killers*, *The Chase*, *Cast a Giant Shadow*, *Big Bad Mama*, *Dressed to Kill*, *Big Bad Mama II*, *Even Cowgirls Get the Blues* and *Sabrina*, among others; on tv, starred on "Police Woman" (1974–78).

DICKINSON, Anna E. (1842–1932). American orator, abolitionist and feminist. Born Anna Elizabeth Dickinson, Oct 28, 1842, in Philadelphia, Pennsylvania; died Oct 22, 1932, in Goshen, New York; dau. of John (merchant) and Mary (Edmonson) Dickinson; never married; no children. ❖ Popular abolitionist who championed the idea of civil rights for women and blacks, achieved fame for her passionate political speeches, and, with her success, helped dismantle the cultural ideals that restricted women who spoke in public; showed dedication to abolitionism and women's rights at an early age; published an anti-slavery essay at 13 (1855); at 17, delivered 1st public speech on women's rights and within 2 years became the most popular female lecturer on abolition and equality of women in America (1859–61); lectured throughout the Northeast for the Republican Party (1863), which led to a profitable career in political campaigning; continued lecturing throughout the country about civil rights for women and blacks; wrote 1st novel *What Answer?* (1868), followed by *A Paying Investment* (1876), and *A Ragged Register (of People Places and Opinions)* (1879); wrote plethora of plays and debuted as an actress (1876); resumed political campaigning for Republicans (1888). ❖ See also Giraud Chester, *Embattled Maiden:*

The Life of Anna Dickinson (Putnam, 1951); and *Women in World History.*

DICKINSON, Emily (1830–1886). American poet. Born Emily Elizabeth Dickinson, Dec 10, 1830, in Amherst, Massachusetts; died in Amherst, May 15, 1886; dau. of Edward Dickinson (lawyer, businessman, and treasurer of Amherst College) and Emily (Norcross) Dickinson; attended Mt. Holyoke Female Seminary, 1847–1848; never married; no children. ❖ Poet often described misleadingly as a "virgin recluse" and "partially cracked poetess" (her own phrase), who is now widely regarded as one of America's 19th-century geniuses of letters; evaded the religious revivals in her area, noting later in a poem: "I keep [the Sabbath] staying at home" (1844 and 1850); began friendship with Susan Gilbert (1850); wrote "Brother Pegasus" letter to brother Austin on his engagement to Susan (1853); wrote letter: "Sue, you can go or stay" to Susan Gilbert (1854); moved back to the Homestead with family (1855); with Austin and Sue married (1856) and living in The Evergreens next door, exchanged letters between the 2 houses, especially with Sue (1856–86); wrote the "Master" letters during greatest poetic outpouring (1858–60s); workshopped "Safe in their Alabaster Chambers" with Sue (1861); sent her 1st letter to magazine editor Thomas Higginson (April 15, 1862)—"Are you too deeply occupied to say if my Verse is alive?" and a 2nd letter (April 25): "Thank you for the surgery"; wrote Higginson after publication of "A Narrow Fellow in the Grass" (1866): "It was robbed of me... I told you I did not print"; refused Higginson's invitation to visit in Boston, preferring to meet on her terms at her own home (1869); after father died in Boston (1874), wrote Higginson: "His heart was pure and terrible and I think no other like it exists"; her mother was paralyzed from an illness (1875) and died (Nov 1882), followed by Emily's beloved nephew Gilbert Dickinson (1883); fell ill (1884); wrote her last letter (early May 1886): "Little Cousins, Called Back. Emily"; though she refused to publish during her lifetime, wrote about nature and natural phenomena as one who had studied the sciences, and wrote about suicide, madness, and violence, the grave and death, and language, power, and sexual ecstasy with passion and intellect. ❖ See also Martha Dickinson Bianchi, *The Life and Letters of Emily Dickinson* (Houghton, 1924); Richard B. Sewall, *The Life of Emily Dickinson* (Farrar, 1974); Martha Nell Smith, *Rowing in Eden* (U. of Texas Press, 1992); Wendy Barker, *Lunacy of Light: Emily Dickinson and the Experience of Metaphor* (U. of Illinois Press, 1987); John Cody, *After Great Pain: The Inner Life of Emily Dickinson* (Belknap, 1971); Susan Howe, *My Emily Dickinson* (North Atlantic, 1985); play by William Luce, *The Belle of Amherst* (1976); and *Women in World History.*

DICKINSON, Frances (1755–1830). American religious leader. Name variations: Sister Clare Joseph. Born 1755 in London, England; died 1830 in Port Tobacco, Maryland, 1830. ❖ Took final vows at Carmelite convent (Belgium) and assumed name Clare Joseph of the Sacred Heart of Jesus (1773); with Ann Teresa Mathews, co-founded Carmelite convent in Port Tobacco (MD), the 1st Roman Catholic convent in US (1790); upon Mathews' death, succeeded as prioress (1800), serving for 30 years until her own death (1830).

DICKINSON, Judy (1950—). American golfer. Name variations: Judy Clark. Born Mar 4, 1950, in Akron, Ohio; attended Glassboro State College. ❖ Turned pro (1978); won four LPGA tournaments; came in second to Kathy Baker at US Women's Open (1985).

DICKINSON, Amanda America (1849–1893). African-American land-owner. Born in 1849 in Georgia; died 1893 in Georgia; dau. of Julia Frances Lewis, 13-year-old slave who was raped by white plantation owner David Dickson; attended Normal School of Atlanta University, 1876–78; married white 1st cousin, Charles Eubanks, 1866 (div. 1870); m. Nathan Toomer, 1892 (who would later marry Nina Pinchback and father Jean Toomer, the writer); children: Julian Henry and Charles Green Eubanks. ❖ Though legally a slave until 1864, was raised in luxury by father and paternal grandmother; inherited father's fortune (1885), including 17,000 acres of land, which angered his white relations who contested the will; saw will upheld in court. ❖ See also Kent Anderson Leslie, *Woman of Color, Daughter of Privilege: Amanda America Dickson, 1849–1893* (U. of Georgia, 1993).

DICKINSON, Anne (1928—). Northern Ireland politician. Name variations: Anne Letitia Dickson. Born April 1928 in London, England; m. James Johnston Dickson. ❖ Representing the Unionist Party for Carrick, sat in the Northern Ireland House of Commons (1969–72); as an Independent Unionist for South Antrim, sat in the House (1973–74);

was leader of the Unionist Party of Northern Ireland (UPNI, 1976–81), the 1st woman leader of a political party in Northern Ireland.

DICKSON, Barbara (1947—). Scottish singer and songwriter. Born Sept 27, 1947, in Dunfermline, Scotland; m. Oliver Cookson; children: Colm, Gabriel and Archie Cookson. ❖ Versatile tv and stage actress and highly successful pop and folk singer-songwriter, took up piano at 5 and guitar at 12; worked the Scottish folk club circuit (1960s–70s), with such artists as Archie Fisher and Rab Noakes; recorded 3 well-received albums for Decca (early 1970s); moved to northern England and signed with manager Bernard Theobold, a partnership that lasted 30 years; starred in Willy Russell's musical, *John, Paul, George, Ringo... and Bert* at Liverpool's Everyman Theatre (1974); signed with RSO Records and had 1st hit with single "Answer Me" (1976); sang on cast album of *Evita,* and recorded single, "Another Suitcase in Another Hall" (1977) which was a huge hit; signed with CBS Records (1978), scoring another hit with single "January, February" (1980), and her accompanying LP, *The Barbara Dickson Album,* quickly went gold in UK; her collection *All For a Song* shot to top of British charts (1982); played Mrs. Johnstone in Russell musical *Blood Brothers* in West End, earning the 1st of many Best Actress awards from Society of West End Theatres (1983); made sold-out concert tours throughout UK, culminating in shows at London's Royal Albert Hall; returned to folk roots (1990s) and released 15th hit album *The Platinum Collection* (2004); appeared on tv in "Taggart" and "Band of Gold"; with Chris Bond, developed award-winning solo show *The 7 Ages of Woman;* starred in London stage musical *Spend, Spend, Spend* (1999), winning 2nd Laurence Olivier award and Best Actress in Musical at Critics' Circle Awards. Awarded Order of British Empire (OBE, 2001).

DICKSON, Dorothy (1893–1995). American-born actress and ballroom dancer. Born July 25, 1893, in Kansas City, Missouri; died Sept 25, 1995, in London, England; studied at Ned Wayburn Studio in NY; m. Carl Hyson (dancer, div. 1936); children: Dorothy Hyson (1914–1996, actress). ❖ Began career in America as an exponent of ballroom dancing, then appeared in *The Ziegfeld Follies* (1917 and 1918); made London debut dancing with Carl Hyson in *London, Paris, and New York,* and appeared in the title role of the musical *Sally,* introducing and popularizing the Jerome Kern song "Look for the Silver Lining" (both 1921); other plays include *Peter Pan, Patricia, Tip-Toes, Wonder Bar, Casanova, Sunshine Sisters, Diversion, Fine and Dandy, Red Letter Day* and *As Long as They're Happy;* films include *Channel Crossing* and *Sword of Honour;* worked as a dramatic actress from 1938 on; during WWII, was one of the leading figures behind the Stage Door Canteen, a London club frequented by Allied troops.

DICKSON, Eleanor Shaler (1900–1989). *See Shaler, Eleanor.*

DICKSON, Estelle Mae (b. 1923). *See Irwin, Estelle Mae.*

DICKSON, Gloria (1916–1945). American actress. Born Thais Dickerson, Aug 13, 1916, in Pocatello, Idaho; died April 10, 1945, in a fire which destroyed her Hollywood home; m. Perc Westmore (make-up artist), 1938 (div.); m. William Fitzgerald, 1944. ❖ Appeared on stage in stock and touring companies; made film debut in *They Won't Forget* (1937), followed by lead roles in *Gold Diggers in Paris, Waterfront, On Your Toes, King of the Lumberjacks, The Affairs of Jimmy Valentine, Lady of Burlesque* and *Rationing,* among others.

DICKSON, Joan (1921–1994). Scottish cellist. Born Dec 12, 1921, in Edinburgh, Scotland; died Oct 9, 1994, in London, England; sister of Hester Dickson (pianist). ❖ Leading concert cellist and teacher, studied cello with Ivor James; traveled to Paris to study with Pierre Fournier and to Rome and Salzburg to study with Enrico Mainardi; gave recital debut in London (1953); became founding member of Edinburgh Quartet (1953); emerged quickly as leading concerto soloist with all of UK's major orchestras; premiered First Cello Sonata, work written for her, with Ian Hamilton (1958); appeared frequently at London Proms and in duo performances with sister, pianist Hester Dickson; premiered several works with Hester which were written expressly for them; taught at Royal Scottish Academy of Music (1954–81) and at Royal College of Music (1967–81); moved to London, serving as distinguished teacher at various institutions and international master classes; served as chair of European String Teachers Association.

DICKSON, Julia Diana (c. 1810–1895). *See Dickson, Mary Bernard.*

DICKSON, Mary Bernard (c. 1810–1895). New Zealand nun, nurse, and school teacher. Name variations: Julia Diana Dickson, Mary Bernard. Born Julia Diana Dickson, c. 1810 or 1811, at Ipswich,

Suffolk, England; died Aug 5, 1895, in Auckland, New Zealand; dau. of Julia and Richard Lothian Dickson; acquired nursing skills at St. George's Hospital, London, 1850s. ❖ Converted to Catholicism as adult; entered Bermondsey convent of Sisters of Mercy, London, and became nun (1850); was one of five nuns assigned to work under Florence Nightingale at General Hospital, Scutari in the Crimea (1854); joined Auckland community of Sisters of Mercy (1857), performing educational and social work; helped to establish Marist convent in Wellington (1861), and became 1st superior of Sisters of Mercy outside Auckland. ❖ See also *Dictionary of New Zealand Biography* (Vol. 1).

DIDION, Joan (1934—). American novelist and journalist. Born Dec 5, 1934, in Sacramento, California; dau. of Frank Reese Didion (army officer) and Eduene (Jerrett) Didion; University of California at Berkeley, BA, 1956; aunt of actor-director Griffin Dunne and actress Dominique Dunne; m. John Gregory Dunne (writer), Jan 30, 1964 (died Dec 30, 2003); children: (daughter) Quintana Roo (died). ❖ Best known for journalistic essays and for helping to shape New Journalism, worked for *Vogue* magazine for several years (1956–63); collections of her magazine essays are contained in *Slouching Towards Bethlehem* (1968) and *The White Album* (1979); novels include *Run River* (1963), *Play It As It Lays* (1970), *A Book of Common Prayer* (1977) and *The Last Thing He Wanted* (1996); nonfiction includes *Salvador* (1983), *Miami* (1987), *Political Fictions* (2001) and *The Year of Magical Thinking* (2005); also collaborated with husband on several screenplays, including *Panic in Needle Park* (1971), *Play It As It Lays* (1973), *A Star is Born* (1977), *True Confessions* (1982) and *Up Close and Personal* (1995); frequent contributor to *New York Review of Books* and *The New Yorker*. Received Edward MacDowell Medal (1996) and Columbia Journalism Award (1999).

DIDO (fl. 800 BCE). Phoenician princess. Name variations: Elissa. Fl. 800 BCE; dau. of Belus, king of Tyre; sister of Pygmalion; m. Sychaeus also known as Acerbas. ❖ Allegedly founded the city of Carthage. ❖ See also *Women in World History*.

DIDRIKSON, Babe (1911–1956). See *Zaharias, Babe Didrikson.*

DIDUCK, Judy (1966—). Canadian ice-hockey player. Born April 21, 1966, in Sherwood Park, Alberta, Canada; younger sister of NHL defenseman Gerald Diduck. ❖ Won team World championship gold medal (1990, 1992, 1994, 1997); won a team silver medal at Nagano (1998), the 1st Olympics to feature women's ice hockey. Named MV Defensive Player at World championships (1997).

DIEBOLD, Laure (1915–1964). French partisan. Name variations: Mona. Born Laure Mutschler in 1915 in the Bas-Rhin section of Alsace; m. Eugene Diebold (fellow *résistant*), in 1942. ❖ During WWII, adopted the name Mona, became a liaison agent, and was appointed secretary to Jean Moulin, whom she knew as Rex (Sept 1, 1942); following his capture, moved to Paris to work for Moulin's successor Georges Bidault; was arrested with husband and imprisoned at Fresnes (Sept 1943); withstood interrogation so well that she was believed; was sent to Auschwitz (June 1944), then Ravensbrück, then Taucha, near Leipzig; survived the war. Awarded the *Compagnon de la Liberation*. ❖ See also *Women in World History*.

DIEDERICHS, Helene Voigt- (1875–1961). See *Voigt-Diederichs, Helene.*

DIEFENBAKER, Edna Mae (1901–1951). First wife of John Diefenbaker. Born Edna Mae Brower, 1901, in Prince Albert, Saskatchewan, Canada; died Feb 7, 1951; m. John Diefenbaker (prime minister of Canada, 1957–63), June 29, 1929. ❖ Was the 1st wife of John Diefenbaker but died before he took office (his 2nd wife was Olive Diefenbaker).

DIEFENBAKER, Olive (1902–1976). Canadian first lady. Name variations: Olive E. Palmer. Born Olive Evangeline Freeman, 1902, in Roland, Manitoba, Canada; died Dec 22, 1976, in Ottawa; m. Harry Palmer; m. John Diefenbaker (prime minister of Canada, 1957–63), Dec 8, 1953; children: (1st m.) Carolyn (b. 1934).

DIEMER, Emma Lou (1927—). American musician and composer. Born Emma Lou Diemer in Kansas City, Missouri, Nov 24, 1927; studied with Paul Hindemith, Howard Hanson, Roger Sessions, and Ernst Toch; studied at Kansas City Conservatory; awarded a Fulbright fellowship to study composition and piano at Royal Conservatory in Brussels, Belgium; Yale University, BA and MA; Eastman School of Music, PhD in composition. ❖ Composed over 150 pieces for choral groups, orchestras, bands, solo instruments, and chamber groups, and is especially known for her church music. ❖ See also *Women in World History*.

DIENELT, Kerry (1969—). Australian softball player. Born Feb 25, 1969, in Darwin, Australia. ❖ Captain, won bronze medals at Atlanta Olympics (1996) and Sydney Olympics (2000).

DIERS, Ines (1963—). East German swimmer. Born Nov 2, 1963. ❖ At Moscow Olympics, won a bronze medal in 100-meter freestyle, silver medals in 800-meter freestyle and 200-meter freestyle, and gold medals in 400-meter freestyle and 4 x 100-meter freestyle relay (1980).

DIETRICH, Marlene (1901–1992). German-born film actress. Born Maria Magdalena Dietrich in Berlin, Germany, Dec 27, 1901; died in Paris, France, May 6, 1992; dau. of Louis (lieutenant in Royal Prussian police) and Wilhemina (Felsing) Dietrich; m. Rudolph Sieber, 1923; children: Maria Riva (b. 1924, actress and writer). ❖ Actress who was, successively, a notorious Hollywood "love goddess" and rival to Greta Garbo, a hero of the Allied war effort in World War II, a smoky-voiced cabaret singer, and, for the last 20 years of her life, a recluse; began show business career as a chorus girl and was given her 1st substantial film role, *Der kleine Napoleon* (1923); was known only to German-speaking audiences until her discovery by director Josef von Sternberg, who cast her as the female lead in his *Der blaue Engel* (*The Blue Angel*, 1930), an international hit that brought her to Hollywood; continued to work with von Sternberg on a number of films before establishing professional credentials on her own and gaining international celebrity status; refused an offer by Hitler just before World War II to return to Germany; instead, became a US citizen, entertained US troops during the war, and was awarded the National Medal of Freedom for tireless support of the Allied war effort; acting career faded (1950s), though she was much praised for work in smaller roles in such prestigious films as *Judgment at Nuremberg* (1961); rarely appeared in public (1980s), only her voice being heard in the last film in which she participated, the biography *Marlene* (1984). Films include *Morocco* (1930), *Shanghai Express* (1932), *Blonde Venus* (1932), *The Scarlet Empress* (1934), *The Garden of Allah* (1936), *Destry Rides Again* (1939), *Kismet* (1944), *Golden Earrings* (1947), *A Foreign Affair* (1948), *Stage Fright* (1950), *No Highway In the Sky* (1951), *Rancho Notorious* (1952), *Witness for the Prosecution* (1958), *A Touch of Evil* (1958) and *Just a Gigolo* (1979). ❖ See also Maria Riva, *Marlene Dietrich* (Knopf, 1993); Donald Spoto, *Blue Angel: The Life and Death of Marlene Dietrich* (Doubleday, 1992); and *Women in World History*.

DIETZ, Gertrud (b. 1912). See *Fussenegger, Gertrud.*

DIEULAFOY, Jane (1851–1916). French novelist and travel writer. Name variations: Jeanne Rachel Dieulafoy. Born Jeanne Rachel Magre, June 29, 1851, in Toulouse, France; died 1916; m. Marcel Dieulafoy, 1870. ❖ Traveled with husband on diplomatic missions and archeological visits, including excavations in Susa-Persia, and wrote of experiences; wore male clothing while traveling and acquired legal permission to continue to do so in Paris; lectured on Greek and French literature at Théâtre de l'Odéon; travelogues include *La Perse, la Chaldée et la Susiane* (1886); novels include *Parysatis* (1890), *Volontaire* (1892), and *Déchéance* (1897).

DÍEZ GONZÁLEZ, Rosa M. (1952—). Spanish politician. Name variations: Rosa M. Diez Gonzalez. Born May 27, 1952, in Sodupe, Spain. ❖ Member of the Executive Committee of the Basque Socialist Party (within the PSOE); member of the Basque Parliament (two terms) and minister of Trade, Consumer Affairs, and Tourism in the Basque regional government (1991–98); as a European Socialist, elected to 5th European Parliament (1999–2004).

DI FALCO, Laura (b. 1910). See *Carpinteri, Laura.*

DIFRANCO, Ani (1970—). American singer and songwriter. Pronunciation: Ani (ahn-knee). Born Sept 23, 1970, in Buffalo, NY; m. Andrew Gilchrist, May 30, 1998. ❖ Rejected offers from major labels, preferring to release her punk- and funk-inspired folksongs on her own label, Righteous Babe Records; sold 1st album *Ani DiFranco* (1990) from trunk of her car; through Righteous Babe Records, had marketed 2 million of her releases by 1999; had Top-30 releases including albums *Little Plastic Castle* (1998) and *Up Up Up Up Up Up* (1999). Additional albums include *Not So Soft* (1991), *Imperfectly* (1992), *Dilate; More Joy, Less Shame* (1996), *Reveling/Reckoning* (2001), (with Utah Phillips) *Fellow Workers* (1999) and *Evolve* (2003).

DIGBY, Jane (1807–1881). See *Digby el Mesrab, Jane.*

DIGBY, Lettice (c. 1588–1658). English baroness. Name variations: Lady Digby; Baroness Offaley; Baroness Offaly. Born Lettice Fitzgerald c. 1588; died 1658 in England; dau. of Gerald Fitzgerald, earl of

Kildare; m. Lord Robert Digby, of Coleshill, 1608. ❖ Inherited the barony of Offaly from parents; married Lord Robert Digby of Coleshill (1608), becoming one of England's wealthiest and most powerful women through the union of the 2 houses; a prime target for insurgents during the English Civil War, was forced to defend her various castles and manors from mutinous mobs, including Geashill Castle against Irish rebels (1642); was known as a brave warrior.

DIGBY EL MESRAB, Jane (1807–1881). English adventurer. Name variations: Jane Digby; Jane Digby el Mezrab; Jane Digby Law, Lady or Countess Ellenborough; Baroness von Venningen. Born Jane Elizabeth Digby, April 3, 1807, in Norfolk, England; died in Damascus, Syria, Aug 11, 1881; dau. of Jane Elizabeth Coke (Lady Andover, 1777–1863) and Admiral Sir Henry Digby (1763?–1842); m. Edward Law, Lord Ellenborough (div.); m. Baron Karl von Venningen (div.); m. Spiro Theotoky (div.); m. Medjuel el Mesrab (Bedouin sheik); children: (1st m.) Arthur Dudley Law (1828–1830); (with Prince Schwarzenberg) Mathilde Selden; (2nd m.) Heribert von Venningen and Bertha von Venningen; (3rd m.) Leonidas Theotoky. ❖ Condemned by Victorian England for early scandals but revered among Arabs after her marriage to a Bedouin chief, was the female counterpart of the Byronic hero, the sinner who defies the rules; intelligent in all areas except matters of the heart, spoke 9 languages and was considered a talented artist and a magnificent horsewoman; charmed 3 kings, 2 princes, a German baron, an Albanian brigand general and several Bedouin sheiks; was grist for the works of many writers, including Honoré de Balzac and James Michener. ❖ See also Margaret Fox Schmidt, *Passion's Child: The Extraordinary Life of Jane Digby* (Harper, 1976); Mary S. Lovell, *Rebel Heart: The Scandalous Life of Jane Digby* (Norton, 1995); and *Women in World History*.

DI GIACOMO, Marina (1976—). Argentine field-hockey player. Born Marina Emilce di Giacomo, Jan 9, 1976, in Mendoza, Argentina. ❖ Won a team bronze medal at Athens Olympics (2004); placed 1st with team at Pan American Games (2003).

DIGGS, Annie LePorte (1848–1916). American politician and social reformer. Born Annie LePorte in London, Ontario, Canada, Feb 22, 1848; died in Detroit, Michigan, Sept 7, 1916; dau. of Cornelius (lawyer) and Ann Maria (Thomas) LePorte; attended convent and public school in New Jersey, to which the family moved in 1855; m. Alvin S. Diggs (postal clerk), Sept 21, 1873, in Lawrence, Kansas; children: Fred, Mabel, and Esther. ❖ Helped form Kansas Liberal Union, an inclusive group that embraced Unitarians, Universalists, Free Religionists, Socialists, spiritualists, materialists, and agnostics (1881); a few months later, was elected vice president of Free Religious Union; worked for women's suffrage and for the establishment of a cooperative association for farmers and workers; wrote a column on the Farmers' Alliance for Kansas' *Lawrence Journal* and then became an associate editor of the *Alliance Advocate;* was instrumental in turning the Kansas Farmers' Alliance into the political People's (later Populist) Party and became one of its most vocal advocates; spoke at national Populist conventions (1890–92) and worked alongside Mary E. Lease in Populist election campaigns (1894 and 1896); elected president of Kansas Equal Suffrage Association (1899); wrote articles and newspaper stories on reform movements in England and Europe; elected president of Kansas Woman's Press Association (1904); writings include *The Story of Jerry Simpson* (1908) and *Bedrock* (1912). ❖ See also *Women in World History*.

DIGGS, Irene (1906—). African-American anthropologist. Name variations: Ellen Irene Diggs. Born Ellen Diggs, April 13, 1906, in Monmouth, Illinois; died Mar 15, 1998, in Gwynn Oak, Maryland; dau. of Henry Charles and Alice (Scott) Diggs; University of Minnesota, BS, 1928; Atlanta University, MA, 1933, the 1st to be granted there in the field of anthropology; doctorate from University of Havana, 1945. ❖ Pioneering black scholar in African Diaspora and Afro-Latin studies, served as chief research assistant to W.E.B. Du Bois (1933–1943, 1945–1947), editing the *Encyclopedia of the Negro* (1945), and co-founding the influential journal *Phylon: A Review of Race and Culture;* while at University of Havana, traveled extensively throughout Cuba collecting folklore, recording village music, and observing traditional Afro-Cuban dances and rituals; taught at Morgan State College (now University, 1947–76); writings include *Black Chronology: From 4000 B.C. to the Abolition of the Slave Trade* (1983). Received Distinguished Scholar Award from Association of Black Anthropologists (1978). ❖ See also *Women in World History*.

DIGRE, Berit (1967—). Norwegian handball player. Born April 3, 1967, in Norway. ❖ At Seoul Olympics, won a silver medal in team competition (1988).

DIJKSTRA, Sjoukje (1942—). Dutch figure skater. Born June 28, 1942, in Akkrum, the Netherlands. ❖ Placed 12th at Cortina Olympics (1956); won a silver medal at Squaw Valley Olympics (1960); held World championship (1962–64); won 1st Olympic gold medal for the Dutch in Winter Games, at Innsbruck (1964). ❖ See also *Women in World History*.

DI LASCIO, Marilyn (1937—). *See Bell, Marilyn.*

DILKE, Emily (1840–1904). English labor leader. Name variations: Lady Dilke; Emilia Dilke; Frances Dilke; Emily Pattison; Frances Pattison; Emilia Frances Strong. Born Emily Frances Strong in Ilfracombe, Oxfordshire, England, Sept 2, 1840; died in Pyrford Rough, near Woking, England, Oct 24, 1904; dau. of Henry and Emily (Weedon) Strong; aunt of Gertrude Tuckwell; sister-in-law of Dorothy W. Pattison (1832–1878); m. Mark Pattison (1813–1884, rector of Lincoln College, Oxford), Sept 10, 1861; m. Sir Charles Wentworth Dilke (1843–1911, wealthy Liberal member of Parliament), Oct 3, 1885; no children. ❖ Trade union leader, artist, art historian and critic, whose early years and first, extremely unhappy marriage to a man almost 27 years her senior inspired at least 3 novelists, including George Eliot (Mary Anne Evans), who based her character Dorothea Brooke in *Middlemarch* on her; published 1st work, *The Renaissance of Art in France* (1879); had a happy 2nd marriage; joined the Women's Suffrage Union (early 1870s); was a leading member of the Women's Protective and Provident League (WPPL), known as the Women's Trade Union League (WTUL) after 1891 (1875–1904); served as its president (1902–1904); with her impassioned speeches as well as her social and political connections, was instrumental in the phenomenal growth of the WTUL; committed the last 20 years of her life to the trade union cause, seeking the improvement of the conditions of labor for English working women. ❖ See also Betty Askwith, *Lady Dilke: A Biography* (Chatto & Windus, 1969); and *Women in World History*.

DILL, Mary Lou (1948—). American golfer. Born Feb 18, 1948, in Eastland, Texas; graduate of University of Texas, 1971. ❖ Won the USGA Women's Amateur (1967); member of the Curtis Cup team (1968); turned pro (1971).

DILLARD, Annie (1945—). American essayist, novelist and poet. Born Anne Doak, April 30, 1945, in Pittsburgh, Pennsylvania; eldest of 3 daughters of Frank Doak (advertising executive) and Pam (Lambert) Doak; Hollins College, BA, 1967, MA, 1968; m. Richard Henry Wilde Dillard (poet and novelist), June 5, 1965 (div. 1975); m. Gary Clevidence (novelist), April 12, 1980 (div. 1987); m. Robert D. Richardson (scholar-biographer), Dec 10, 1988; children: (2nd m.) Rosie. ❖ Began keeping journals (1971); published 21 of her poems in *Tickets for a Prayer Wheel* (1974); spent 4 seasons living near Tinker Creek in Virginia's Blue Ridge Mountains; used her notebooks to write the bestselling *Pilgrim at Tinker Creek* (1974), for which she won the Pulitzer Prize; other writings include *Holy the Firm* (1977), *Living by Fiction* (1982), *Teaching a Stone to Talk: Expeditions and Encounters* (1982), *Encounters with Chinese Writers* (1984), *The Writing Life* (1989), (novel) *The Living* (1992), and *For the Time Being* (1999); also published numerous essays in journals, magazines, and anthologies; was scholar-in-residence at Western Washington University (1975–79, 1981–82), then became an adjunct professor of English at Wesleyan University. ❖ See also autobiography, *An American Childhood* (1987).

DILLER, Angela (1877–1968). American music educator. Name variations: Mary Angelina Diller. Born Mary Angelina Diller, Aug 1, 1877, in Brooklyn, NY; died May 1, 1968, in Stamford, Connecticut; dau. of William A.M. Diller and Mary Abigail (Welles) Diller. ❖ Taught at Saint John the Baptist School for Girls, NY (1894–99); was 1st recipient of Mosenthal fellowship for musical composition at Barnard College (1899); taught at Music School Settlement in NY (1899–1916), becoming head of theory department; served as head of theory department at David Mannes School of Music (1916–21); with Elizabeth Quaile, co-founded Diller-Quaile School of Music and served as administrator (1921–41), becoming director and part-time teacher, then director emeritus; with Margarethe Dessoff, co-founded Adesdi Chorus (1924) and A Capella Chorus (1929), which later merged into Dessoff Choirs; was visiting instructor at numerous institutions, and lectured in Europe and US (1930–50); received Guggenheim Foundation award to write *The Splendor of Music* (1953); collaborated on music books with

Elizabeth Quaile, Kate Stearns Page and Harold Bauer. Authored *First Theory Book* (1921), *Keyboard Music Study*, Books 1 and 2 (1936–37), and *The Splendor of Music* (1957).

DILLER, Phyllis (1917—). American comedian. Born Phyllis Ada Driver, July 17, 1917, in Lima, Ohio; m. Sherwood Anderson Diller, 1939 (div. 1965); m. Warde Donovan (comic), 1965 (div. 1975). ❖ Nearly 40, with 5 children and an ex-husband called "Fang," became one of the 1st women to attempt stand-up comedy, debuting at the Purple Onion in San Francisco (Mar 1955); appeared regularly on "The Jack Paar Show" and on Bob Hope specials; films include *Boy Did I Get a Wrong Number, Did You Hear the One about the Traveling Saleslady?, The Adding Machine, Pink Motel* and *Wisecracks*; appeared as a piano soloist with 100 symphony orchestras in US; retired from nightclubs (2002).

DILLEY, Dorothy (b. around 1907). American theatrical dancer. Name variations: Dorothy Dilly. Born c. 1907 in Los Angeles area, California; trained by Ernest Belcher in Los Angeles. ❖ Appeared as a child in numerous films; joined *Music Box Revue of 1923*, where she became known for acrobatic ballet numbers; appeared on Broadway in *Kitty's Kisses* (1926), *Oh, Ernest!* (1927), and *Take the Air* (1927); was also known for her musical comedy numbers and popular social dance presentations.

DILLON, Diane (1933—). American artist and illustrator. Born Diane Sorber, Mar 13, 1933, in Glendale, California; dau. of Adelbert Paul (teacher) and Phyllis (Worsley) Sorber (pianist); attended Los Angeles City College, 1951–52, Skidmore College, 1952–53, Parsons School of Design, 1954–56, and School of Visual Arts, 1958; married Leo J. Dillon (artist), Mar 17, 1957; children: Lee. ❖ Was a staff artist at Dave Fris Advertising Agency, Albany, NY (1956–57); illustrated with husband, Erik C. Haugaard's *Hakon of Rogen's Saga* (1963); while collaborating with husband for over 40 years: won Hugo Award from the International Science Fiction Association for illustration of a series of science-fiction book jackets (1971); had books *Behind the Back of the Mountain* and *The Third Gift* included in the American Institute of Graphic Arts Children's Books Show (1973–74); won Balrog Award for Lifetime Contribution to Sci-Fi/Fantasy Art (1982); had Newbery honor book, *The Hundred Penny Box* (1976); won Caldecott medals for *Why Mosquitoes Buzz in People's Ears: A West African Tale* (1976) and *Ashanti to Zulu: African Traditions* (1977); received Hans Christian Andersen Medal (1978) and Lewis Carroll Shelf Award for *Who's in Rabbit's House? A Masai Tale* (1978); and was cited on Books for Young People honor list for illustrations for *The People Could Fly: American Black Folktales* (1986).

DILLON, Halle (1864–1901). See Johnson, Halle.

DILLON, Melinda (1939—). American stage, tv, and screen actress. Born Oct 13, 1939, in Hope, Arkansas. ❖ Came to prominence on stage as the original Honey in *Who's Afraid of Virginia Woolf?* (1962); made film debut in *Un Hombre solo* (1964), followed by *The April Fools, F.I.S.T., A Christmas Story, Harry and the Hendersons, The Prince of Tides, How to Make an American Quilt* and *Magnolia*, among others. Nominated for Oscars in Best Supporting Actress category for *Close Encounters of the Third Kind* and *Absence of Malice*.

DILLWYN, Amy (1845–1935). Welsh industrialist. Born Amy Elizabeth Dillwyn, 1845, in Swansea, Wales; died 1935 in Swansea; dau. of Lewis Dillwyn. ❖ One of 1st female industrialists, inherited the Llansamlet Spelter Works in Swansea which at the time was debt-ridden (1892); declined to file bankruptcy and began managing the works; turned a profit and paid off creditors; her company became one of the largest producers of zinc in Britain; sold the works (1905). ❖ See also David Painting, *Amy Dillwyn* (U. of Wales Press, 1987).

DI LORENZO, Tina (1872–1930). Italian actress. Born Dec 4, 1872, in Turin, Italy; died April 1, 1930; dau. of Amelia Colonnello (famous actress who appeared with Salvini) and Corrado di Lorenzo dei Marchesi di Castellaccio; m. Armando Falconi. ❖ Made stage debut in Naples (1887), then appeared in Florence (1890), soon establishing a stellar reputation in both modern and classical plays; appeared most notably as Paula in *The Second Mrs. Tanqueray*, Margherita in *La Dame aux Camélias*, Mirandolina in *La Locandiera*, Leonore in *Onore*, title role in *Adrienne Lecouvreur*, Suzanne in *Le monde ou l'on s'ennuie* and Evelina Paoli in *Infidele*, among others; toured under the management of Flavio Ando for some years; at the time, reputed to be 2nd only to Eleonora Duse among Italian actresses.

DILOVA, Diana (1952—). Bulgarian basketball player. Born Nov 1952. ❖ Won an Olympic bronze medal at Montreal (1976) and a silver medal at Moscow (1980), both in team competition.

DIMAGGIO, Dorothy (1917–1984). See Arnold, Dorothy.

DI MARIO, Tania (1979—). Italian water-polo player. Born May 4, 1979, in Italy. ❖ At World championship, won team gold medal (2001); driver, won a team gold medal at Athens Olympics (2004).

DIMINA, Mira (c. 1909–1936). See Parker, Madeleine.

DIMITROVA, Blaga (1922—). Bulgarian writer and politician. Born Blaga Nikolova Dimitrova in Biala Slatina, Bulgaria, Jan 2, 1922; studied Slavonic philology in Sofia in 1945 and did graduate work in Moscow, receiving a degree in 1951; m. Iordan Vasilev; children: (adopted) daughter. ❖ Poet, novelist, playwright, political activist, and vice-president of Bulgaria, whose slow evolution from literary Stalinism to dissent is a case study in intellectual disillusionment as well as a chronicle of one writer's moral evolution; was the best-known intellectual dissident in Bulgaria in the closing decade of the Communist regime; novel *Litse* (*Face*) was banned (1980s); elected to Parliament (1990); began to serve as vice-president of Bulgaria (Dec 1991); resigned from that position (June 1993); writings include *Because the Sea is Black: Poems of Blaga Dimitrova* (trans. by Boris and McHugh, 1989), *Journey to Oneself* (trans. by Pridham, 1969); *The Last Rock Eagle: Selected Poems of Blaga Dimitrova* (trans. by Walker and others, 1992). ❖ See also *Women in World History*.

DIMITROVA, Ghena (1941–2005). Bulgarian lyric soprano. Born May 6, 1941, in Beglej, Bulgaria; died June 11, 2005, in Milan, Italy; studied at Sofia Music Academy. ❖ Best known for her Turandot, Abigaille in Verdi's *Nabucco*, and Gioconda, made professional debut at Sofia's National Opera as Abigaille (1965); sang 1st Turandot at Treviso (1975); appeared at Teatro Colón in Buenos Aires (1975–80); made US debut in Dallas as Elvira in Verdi's *Emani* (1981); made debut at Paris Opéra as Verdi's Lady Macbeth (1984).

DIMITROVA, Rositsa (1955—). Bulgarian volleyball player. Born Feb 21, 1955. ❖ At Moscow Olympics, won a bronze medal in team competition (1980).

DIMITROVA, Tanya (1957—). Bulgarian volleyball player. Born Mar 15, 1957. ❖ At Moscow Olympics, won a bronze medal in team competition (1980).

DIMMICK, Mary Scott (1858–1948). See Harrison, Mary Scott.

DIMOCK, Susan (1847–1875). American physician. Born in Washington, North Carolina, April 24, 1847; died in a shipwreck on May 8, 1875; dau. of Henry Dimock (lawyer and newspaper editor) and Mary Malvina Owens Dimock; attended New England Hospital for Women and Children (1866); University of Zurich, MD. ❖ North Carolina's 1st female physician, attended University of Zurich, the only institution at the time that allowed women to study for a medical degree, as one of seven women now considered medical pioneers: Maria Bokova, Nadezhda Suslova, Elizabeth Morgan, Louisa Atkins, Eliza Walker, and Marie Vögtlin; graduating with honors (1871), did additional work in hospitals in Vienna and Paris; served as resident physician at New England Hospital for Women and Children (1872–75, now the Dimock Community Health Center); set sail for Europe on the *Schiller* (April 27, 1875); drowned when the vessel was wrecked on a granite reef off the Scilly Isles. ❖ See also *Women in World History*.

DIMONT, Penelope (1918–1999). See Mortimer, Penelope.

DI MURSKA, Ilma (1836–1889). Croatian soprano. Born Jan 4, 1836, in Zagreb; died in Munich, Germany, Jan 14, 1889; studied in Vienna, then with Mathilde Marchesi. ❖ An opera star of great renown in the 19th century, had a vocal range of over 3 octaves; made debut in Florence as Lady Harriet in *Martha* (1862), then sang in Budapest, Berlin, Hamburg, and Vienna; appeared at Her Majesty's Theater in London (1865–73) with Mapleson's company; sang in 1st Wagner opera heard in London, appearing as Senta in *Der fliegende Holländer*; though particularly known for her interpretation of Queen of the Night, also sang Konstanze, Amina, Marguerite de Valois, Dinorah, and Ophelia. ❖ See also *Women in World History*.

DINAH (fl. 1730 BCE). Biblical woman. Dau. of Jacob and Leah; sister of Simeon and Levi (Genesis 30:21). ❖ In the Old Testament, was the only daughter of Jacob, father of the 12 patriarchs and ancestor of the Israelites, and his 1st wife Leah; was seduced by Shechem, son of Hivite chief Hamor, which led her brothers Simeon and Levi to take revenge by putting the Shechemites to death (Genesis 34). ❖ See also *Women in World History.*

DINESCU, Violeta (1953—). Romanian-born German composer. Name variations: Violeta Dinescu-Lucaci. Born July 13, 1953, in Bucharest, Romania; studied composition, piano, pedagogy and Romanian folk music at Ciprian Porumbescu Conservatory in Bucharest, graduating with honors (1976); attended University of Hiedelberg. ❖ Accomplished composer, received George-Enescu Scholarship and studied composition with Myriam Marbe (1977); taught theory, piano and aesthetics at George Enescu Music School in Bucharest, becoming member of Romanian Union of Composers (1978–82); moved to Germany (1982) and took German citizenship (1989); taught at Academy for Evangelical Church Music in Heidelberg (1986–91), at Academy for Performing Arts in Frankfurt (1989–92) and at Professional Academy for Evangelical Church Music in Bayreuth (1990–94); became full-time professor of applied composition at Carl von Ossietzky University in Oldenburg (1996) and directed many courses at universities in Europe and US; wrote innumerable compositions, generally filtered through Balkan and Transylvanian forms, including *Akrostichon* and *L Ora X* for orchestra, music for F.W. Murnau film *Tabu,* ballets *Der Kreisel* and *Effi Briest* and operas *Hunger and Thirst, Erendira* and *Schachnovelle;* also wrote chamber music for various instruments; served as executive board member of International League of Woman Composers and international director of WOMANSONG in Massachusetts (1990–94); was a correspondent for European and American music journals. Additional works include: (opera) *The 35th of May;* (Pentecostal oratorio) *Pfingstoratorium* based on texts from bible; (orchestral piece) *Anna Perenna;* (solo instrumental sequence) *Satya;* (vocal piece) *Mondnachte.*

DINESEN, Isak (1885–1962). Danish writer. Name variations: Karen Blixen; Karen Blixen-Finecke; (pseudonyms) Pierre Andrézel, Tania B., and Osceola. Born Karen Christentze Dinesen, April 17, 1885, in Rungsted, Denmark; died Sept 7, 1962, in Rungsted; dau. of Wilhelm (army officer and writer under his own name and his Indian name Boganis) and Ingeborg (Westenholz) Dinesen; studied English at Oxford University, 1904; m. Baron Bror Blixen-Finecke (big-game hunter and writer), Jan 14, 1914 (div. 1921). ❖ One of Denmark's most widely acclaimed modern authors, whose exotic and archaic tales set her apart from the literary traditions of her day, was twice nominated for the Nobel Prize; with husband Baron Blixen, managed a coffee plantation in British East Africa (now Nairobi, Kenya, 1913–21); took over management until failing coffee prices forced her to give up the farm (1931); published *Syv Fantastiske Fortaellinger* (*Seven Gothic Tales,* 1934), followed by the autobiographical *Den Afrikanske Farm* (*Out of Africa,* 1937); became one of the founding members of the Danish Academy (Nov 28, 1960); established the Rungsted Foundation, a private institution that purchased her family house and surrounding land and was entrusted with preserving the area as a bird reserve after her death; other writings include *Vinter-Eventyr* (*Winter's Tales,* 1942), (under pseudonym Pierre Andrezel) *Gengaeldelsens Veje* (trans. published as *The Angelic Avengers,* 1946), *Om revtskrivning 23–24 marts 1938* (1949), *Daguerreotypier* (1951), *Babettes Gaestebud* ("Babette's Feast," 1952), *Kardinalens tredie Historie* ("The Cardinal's Third Tale," 1952), *En Baaltale med 14 Aars Forsinkelse* ("Bonfire Speech 14 Years Delayed," 1953), *Sidste Fortaellinger* (*Last Tales,* 1957), *Skaebne-Anekdoter* (*Anecdotes of Destiny,* 1958), *Skygger paa Graesset* (*Shadows on the Grass,* 1961), and *On Mottoes of My Life* (1962). Awarded Ingenio et Arti Medal from King Frederick IX of Denmark (1950). ❖ See also Thorkild Bjornvig, *The Pact: My Friendship with Isak Dinesen* (Louisiana State U. Press, 1974); Thomas Dinesen, *My Sister, Isak Dinesen* (trans. by Joan Tate, M. Joseph, 1975); Linda Donelson, *Out of Isak Dinesen in Africa: The Untold Story* (Coulsong List, 1995); Donald Hannah, *"Isak Dinesen" and Karen Blixen: The Mask and the Reality* (Putnam, 1971); Aage Henriksen, *Isak Dinesen; Karen Blixen: The Work and the Life* (trans. by William Mishler, St. Martin, 1988); Parmenia Migel, *Titania: The Biography of Isak Dinesen* (Random House, 1967); Judith Thurman, *Isak Dinesen: The Life of a Storyteller* (St. Martin, 1982); and *Women in World History.*

DING LING (1904–1985). Chinese writer. Name variations: Ting Ling. Born Jiang Bingzhi in Hunan province in central China in 1904; died 1985; dau. of Jiang Yufeng (Confucian scholar) and Yu Manzhen (Yü Man-chen, early female political activist); attended progressive schools in Hunan, Shanghai and Beijing; m. Chen Ming (writer), 1942; children: (with radical poet Hu Yuepin) a son (b. Nov

1930); (with Communist activist Feng Da) a daughter (b. around 1935). ❖ Leading Chinese writer of the modern era and important figure in Chinese Communist politics, published "Miss Sophia's Diary," which defined her as a writer (1928); joined Chinese Communist Party and rose through the party's literary ranks (1932); kidnapped and held by the Guomindang (1933); after 4 years under house arrest, escaped to the Communist-led base under Mao Zedong (1937); purged and exiled to Manchuria (1957), where she attempted to keep writing while forced to do manual labor; after death of Mao Zedong and emergence of the reform regime of Deng Xiaoping, rehabilitated by the Communists (1978); became an honored figure until her death; walking an uneasy line between her two major roles as Communist Party activist and female writer, became the voice of the many Chinese women caught in their country's difficult transition from the old feudal Confucian society into the modern world; writings available in English translation include "Mengke" (1927), "The Diary of Miss Sophia" (1928), "A Woman and a Man" (1928), "Shanghai, Spring 1930" (1930), "Net of Law" (1932), "Affair in East Village" (1936), "New Faith" (1939), "When I was in Xia Village" (1941), "Thoughts on March 8" (1942), *The Sun Shines over the Sanggang River* (1948), "People Who Will Live Forever in My Heart: Remembering Chen Man" (1949), and "Du Wanxiang" (1978). ❖ See also Tani E. Barlow, with Gary J. Bjorge, *I Myself Am a Woman: Selected Writings of Ding Ling* (Beacon, 1989); Yi-tsi Mei Feuerwerker, *Ding Ling's Fiction: Ideology and Narrative in Modern Chinese Literature* (Harvard U. Press, 1982); and *Women in World History.*

DING MEIYUAN (1979—). Chinese weightlifter. Born 1979 in Liaoning Province, China. ❖ Won University World championships; won World championships (1997, 1999), Asian Games (1998) and Asian championships (2000); won a gold medal for +75kg at Sydney Olympics (2000), while smashing 3 world records and becoming the 1st woman to lift 300kg. Named IWF Best Female Weightlifter (1999).

DING NING (1924—). Chinese actress, director and poet. Born 1924 in China. ❖ Joined Communist revolution (1938) and worked as actress and stage director; also worked at Ministry of Culture; writings include *The Poetic Soul of Youyan* and *An Ox for the Young.*

DINGELDEIN, Margaret (1980—). American water-polo player. Name variations: Margie Dingeldein. Born May 30, 1980, in Merced, California. ❖ Won World championship (2003); driver, won a team bronze medal at Athens Olympics (2004).

DINGLER, Rose (1914–1988). *See Coyle, Rose.*

DINH, Madame (1920–1992). *See Nguyen Thi Dinh.*

DINNERSTEIN, Dorothy (1923–1992). American psychologist. Born April 4, 1923; died in auto accident, Dec 17, 1992. ❖ Distinguished professor of psychology at Rutgers University for many years and one of the founders of feminist psychoanalytic theory, wrote *The Mermaid & the Minotaur: Sexual Arrangements and Human Malaise* (1976).

DINSDALE, Shirley (c. 1928–1999). American ventriloquist. Name variations: Shirley Dinsdale Layburn. Born Oct 31, 1926, in San Francisco, California; died of cancer, May 9, 1999, in Stony Brook, NY; married. ❖ Trained with ventriloquist Edgar Bergen; had own radio show (by 1945); starred with her puppet, Judy Splinters, on "Judy Splinters," on KTLA, Los Angeles (1949–50); won Emmy for "most outstanding television personality" the 1st year the awards were presented (1949); served as the head of the Respiratory Therapy Department of the John T. Mather Memorial Hospital in Port Jefferson, NY (1973–85).

DINWIDDIE, Emily (1879–1949). American housing reformer and social worker. Born Emily Wayland Dinwiddie, Aug 14, 1879, in Greenwood, Virginia; died Mar 11, 1949, in Waynesboro, Virginia; dau. of William and Emily Albertine (Bledsoe) Dinwiddie; never married; no children. ❖ Served as investigator for various agencies including New York Charity Organization Society and Trinity vestry; worked as editor of *Charities Directory* (1903) and inspector for New York City Tenement House Department (1903); hired by Trinity vestry to manage properties, established Trinity Church as model corporate landlord; worked for Red Cross (beginning 1918) and on behalf of children's welfare.

DIOGO, Luisa (1958—). Mozambique politician. Born April 11, 1958, in Mozambique; received MA in finance economics through a correspondence course with University of London, 1992. ❖ Joined the Ministry of Planning and Finance (1980), when Mozambique was in serious economic trouble; served as National Budget Director (1989–92), then World Bank Programme Officer in Mozambique (1993–94); became deputy finance minister (1994); then served as finance minister (1999–2004) and successfully pushed for economic change; became her nation's 1st female prime minister, while retaining her post as finance minister (Feb 17, 2004).

DION, Céline (1968—). French-Canadian singer. Name variations: Celine Dion. Born Céline Marie Claudette Dion, Mar 30, 1968, in Charlemagne, Quebec, Canada; youngest of 14 children; m. René Angélil (manager), Dec 1994; children: René Charles Angelil (b. 2001). ❖ Among the most commercially successful musical artists of 1990s, came to prominence singing "Tale as Old as Time" with Peobo Bryson, the theme song from Disney's *Beauty and the Beast* (1991); had #1 albums *Falling Into You* (1996), which earned a Grammy for Best Pop Album and Album of the Year, and *All the Way ... A Decade of Song* (1999); released hit singles, including "Where Does My Heart Beat Now" (1990) and "My Heart Will Go On" (Love Theme from *Titanic*, 1997), which won an Oscar for Best Original Song (1998); performed in arena built for her in Las Vegas (2003–06). Additional albums include *Incognito* (1987), *Celine Dion* (1982), *The Colour of My Love* (1993), *D'eux* (1995), *Falling Into You* (1996), *S'il Suffisait D'Aimer; These Are Special Times* (1998) and *The Collectors Series, Volume One* (2000).

DIONNE, Annette (1934—). One of the Dionne Quintuplets. Pronunciation: DEE-yon or DEE-yown. Born Marie Lilianne Annette Dionne, May 28, 1934, in Corbeil, in Northern Ontario, Canada; dau. of Oliva and Elzire (Legros) Dionne; studied music at the Marguerite Bourgeois; m. Germain Allard (branch manager of a finance company), 1950s; children: Jean-François (b. Nov 2, 1958); Charles; Eric (b. Sept 1962). ❖ One of Canada's celebrated quints, who was put on display as a major tourist attraction in Ontario during the 1930s. ❖ See also autobiography (with sisters and Jean Yves-Soucy) *The Dionne Quintuplets: Family Secrets* (Canada, 1995); CBC documentary, *The Dionne Quintuplets;* and *Women in World History.*

DIONNE, Cécile (1934—). One of the Dionne Quintuplets. Pronunciation: DEE-yon or DEE-yown. Born Marie Emilda Cécile Dionne, May 28, 1934, in Corbeil, in Northern Ontario, Canada; dau. of Oliva and Elzire (Legros) Dionne; graduated as a nurse from the Hôpital Notre Dame de l'Esperance, Montreal, c. 1956; m. Philippe Langlois (tv technician at CBC), c. 1957 (div.); children: Claude (b. Sept 15, 1958); Bertrand; Elizabeth; Patrice. ❖ One of Canada's celebrated quints. ❖ See also autobiography (with sisters and Jean Yves-Soucy) *The Dionne Quintuplets: Family Secrets* (Canada, 1995); CBC documentary, *The Dionne Quintuplets;* and *Women in World History.*

DIONNE, Deidra (1982—). Canadian freestyle skier. Born Feb 5, 1982, in North Battleford, Saskatchewan, Canada. ❖ Won a bronze medal at FIS World Freestyle championships (2001); won a bronze medal for aerials at Salt Lake City (2002). Voted World Cup female Rookie of the Year (1999–2000).

DIONNE, Émilie (1934–1954). One of the Dionne Quintuplets. Name variations: Emilie Dionne. Pronunciation: DEE-yon or DEE-yown. Born Marie Jeanne Émilie Dionne, May 28, 1934, in Corbeil, in Northern Ontario, Canada; dau. of Oliva and Elzire (Legros) Dionne; died of suffocation, Aug 1954. ❖ One of Canada's celebrated quints. ❖ See also *The Dionne Quintuplets: Family Secrets* (Canada, 1995); CBC documentary, *The Dionne Quintuplets;* and *Women in World History.*

DIONNE, Marie (1934–1970). One of the Dionne Quintuplets. Pronunciation: DEE-yon or DEE-yown. Born Reine Alma Marie Dionne, May 28, 1934, in Corbeil, in Northern Ontario, Canada; dau. of Oliva and Elzire (Legros) Dionne; died Feb 1970; m. Florian Houle (inspector on staff of Quebec government), 1950s (sep. 1966); children: Émilie (b. Dec 24, 1960); Monique. ❖ One of Canada's celebrated quints. ❖ See also *The Dionne Quintuplets: Family Secrets* (Canada, 1995); CBC documentary, *The Dionne Quintuplets;* and *Women in World History.*

DIONNE, Yvonne (1934–2001). One of the Dionne Quintuplets. Pronunciation: DEE-yon or DEE-yown. Born Marie Edwilda Yvonne Dionne, May 28, 1934, in Corbeil, in Northern Ontario, Canada; died of cancer in Montreal, June 23, 2001; dau. of Oliva and Elzire (Legros) Dionne; graduated as a nurse from the Hôpital Notre Dame de l'Esperance, Montreal, around 1956; joined 3 different

convents. ❖ One of Canada's celebrated quints. ❖ See also autobiography (with sisters and Jean Yves-Soucy) *The Dionne Quintuplets: Family Secrets* (Canada, 1995); CBC documentary, *The Dionne Quintuplets;* and *Women in World History.*

DIOSDADO, Ana (1938—). Spanish playwright. Name variations: Ana Isabel Álvarez Diosdado Gisbert. Born May 21, 1938, Buenos Aires, Brazil; dau. of Enrique Diosdado. ❖ One of most important Spanish female playwrights of 1970s and 1980s, writings include *En cualquier lugar, no importa cuando* (1965), *Olvida los tambores* (1970), *El okapi* (1972), *Usted también podrá disfrutar de ella* (1973), *Y de cachemira chales* (1983), *Los ochenta son nuestros* (1986), *Camino de plata* (1990), *La importancia de llamarse Wilde* (1993), and *La última aventura* (1999). Received the Premio Maite, Premio Fastenrath, and Premio Mar del Plata awards.

DIOTIMA OF MANTINEA (fl. 400s BCE). Greek priestess, philosopher, and teacher of Socrates. Fl. 400s BCE ❖ In the *Symposium,* written some time after 389 BCE, Plato puts forth his views of his contemporaries, then uses the character of Socrates (whose own views may have differed) to present a philosophy of love. Plato's Socrates credits Diotima, a priestess of Mantinea, for inspiring his theory. She is said to have argued that the goal of love is immortality, "to give birth in beauty," either through the creation of children or beautiful things. From this, western culture has derived the concept of "Platonic love," an affection that is not based in bodily pleasure. ❖ See also *Women in World History.*

DI PRIMA, Diane (1934—). American playwight and poet. Name variations: Diane DiPrima; Diane di Prima. Born Aug 6, 1934, in Brooklyn, NY; m. Alan Marlowe; m. Grant Fisher (div. 1975); children: 5. ❖ Important female Beat poet, founded Poets Press (1964–69) and Eidolon Editions (1974); with Amiri Baraka, edited *Floating Bear* newsletter (1961–70); writings include *This Kind of Bird Flies Backwards* (1959), *The New Handbook of Heaven* (1963), *Poems for Freddie* (1966), *Earthsong: Poems 1957–59* (1968), and *Revolutionary Letters* (1969).

DIRIE, Waris (1967—). Somalia-born model and women's-rights activist. Name variations: Waris Walsh. Born 1967 into a tribe of herdsmen in Somalia; one of 12 children born to desert nomads; children: son Aleeke. ❖ At 13, escaped being sold into marriage for 5 camels to a man 4 times her age by running away to London where she worked as her uncle's maid; taught herself to read and write; became a top model, including a campaign for Revlon; appeared in the James Bond film, *The Living Daylights* (1987); left the runways to become a UN ambassador, campaigning against female circumcision (1997), having been a victim of the practice at age 5 (her sister died from infection after her circumcision). ❖ See also autobiographies, *Desert Flower: The Extraordinary Journey of a Desert Nomad* (1998), *Desert Dawn* and *Nomad's Daughter.*

DIRKMAAT, Megan (1976—). American rower. Born May 3, 1976, in San Jose, California; attended University of California, Berkeley. ❖ Won a silver medal for coxed eights at Athens Olympics (2004); for coxed eights, won 1 World Cup (2003) and 2 World Cups (2004).

DI ROBILANT, Daisy, Countess (fl. 1922–1933). Italian feminist and activist. Pronunciation: Dee Ro-bee-lan. Little is known about di Robilant apart from the details of her involvement in fascist politics; came from a wealthy Piedmontese noble family; members of her family included such illustrious personalities as the Count Carlo di Robilant. ❖ Worked for the cause of women's and children's rights to welfare benefits both before and during the fascist dictatorship of Benito Mussolini; before arrival of Fascism, was a founder and president of the national Mothers' Aid Society, a charity that provided temporary shelter for homeless, single mothers; believed that the state should enact sweeping welfare reforms to protect citizens from poverty; for years, lobbied successive Italian prewar governments to enact legislation that would help lone mothers care for their children; widely recognized within her own country as a major figure in public life, was appointed to the presidency of the National Council of Italian Women (1931); also served on the governing body of the International Committee for the Protection of Children; appointed director of department on maternity and infancy of International Congress of Women (1934); one of very few women of power and influence within an almost exclusively male-dominated fascist dictatorship, held a number of important government posts and served as a director of welfare and social services for unwed mothers; became disillusioned with fascism's failure to implement reforms effectively;

criticized fascist social policy and was dismissed from high office (1936).
❖ See also *Women in World History.*

DI SAN FAUSTINO, Princess (1898–1963). *See Sage, Kay.*

DISL, Ursula (1970—). German biathlete. Name variations: Uschi Disl. Born Nov 15, 1970, in Bad Tölz, Germany. ❖ Won a silver medal for the 3 x 7.5 km relay at Albertville Olympics (1992); won a silver medal for the 4 x 7.5 km relay and a bronze for 15 km indiv. at Lillehammer Olympics (1994); at World championships, won a gold medal for 4 x 7.5 km relay and silver medals for sprint, indiv. and team (1995); won silver medals for overall at World Cup (1995, 1996, 1997); won a gold medal for the 4 x 7.5 km relay, a silver for the 7.5 km sprint and a bronze for the 15 km indiv. at Nagano Olympics (1998); won a gold medal for the 4 x 7.5 km relay and a silver for the 7.5 km sprint at Salt Lake City Olympics (2002); won a bronze medal for 12.5 km Mass Start at Torino Olympics (2006).

D'ISLES, Marquise (1426–1486). *See Marie of Cleves.*

DISLEY, Sylvia Cheeseman (1929—). *See Cheeseman, Sylvia.*

DISNEY, Lillian (1899–1997). American philanthropist. Born Lillian Bounds in 1899; died in Los Angeles, California, age 98, Dec 16, 1997; dau. of a federal marshal and a homemaker; m. Walt Disney (animator and film producer), 1925 (died 1966); m. John Truyens (real estate developer), 1981; children: (1st m.) Diane Disney; Sharon Disney (d. 1993). ❖ Took a job as a film-frame inker at nascent Disney Studio and married the boss; for the next 41 years, was husband's sounding board; when he showed her his drawing of a mouse named Mortimer, said "How about Mickey?"; helped found the California Institute of the Arts; donated $50 million for an L.A. concert hall.

DISRAELI, Mary Anne (1792–1872). English viscountess. Name variations: Viscountess Beaconsfield; Marianne or Mary Anne Evans. Born Nov 11, 1792, in Exeter, England; died Dec 15, 1872, in Buckinghamshire, England; dau. of John Evans (naval officer, died 1793) and Eleanor (Viney) Evans; m. Wyndham Lewis (wealthy Welsh magistrate and MP), in Jan 1815 (died 1838); m. Benjamin Disraeli (1804–1881, prime minister of England), Aug 1839; no children. ❖ During 20-year marriage to Wyndham Lewis, became a popular hostess—intelligent, charming, outgoing—and excelled in her role as a politician's wife; interested in the welfare of children and the poor, opened a school for the children of Greenmeadow in addition to many other charitable activities; following husband's death, married Benjamin Disraeli (1839), beginning a long and happy union that lasted until her death 32 years later; campaigned for him, criticized and edited his speeches and writings, and hosted his patrons; always had more admirers than critics and counted Queen Victoria as a friend, who honored her with a peerage, as Viscountess Beaconsfield. ❖ See also Mollie Hardwick, *Mrs Dizzy: The Life of Mary Anne Disraeli, Viscountess Beaconsfield* (Cassell, 1972); James Sykes, *Mary Anne Disraeli* (Appleton, 1928); and *Women in World History.*

DISSARD, Marie Louise (b. 1880). French resistance leader. Born 1880 in Toulouse, France. ❖ When Germany invaded France, joined the French resistance at age 60 (1940); worked with Ian Garrow, a British soldier, on an escape route over the Pyrenees; when Garrow was captured and Albert Gueriesse, the new head, was arrested, became the leader of the network; as an elderly woman, was able to travel throughout France to help downed Allied airman escape (during the course of the war, arranged for safe passage for 250 Allied flyers); when her name was discovered by the Nazis, was forced into hiding (Jan 1944) until France was liberated. Awarded American Medal of Freedom.

D'ISTRIA, Dora (1828–1888). *See Chica, Elena.*

DITCHBURN, Ann (c. 1950—). Canadian ballet dancer and actress. Born c. 1950, in Sudbury, Ontario, Canada. ❖ Trained and performed with National Ballet of Canada in Toronto beginning in adolescence (until 1978); held leading roles in company's repertory of contemporary works and several dramatic roles in classical productions by Celia Franca; appeared on film—perhaps her best known performance—as ailing ballerina in *Slow Dancing in the Big City* (1978). Choreographed works include *Listen #1* (1967), *Kisses* (1972) and *Mad Shadows* (1977).

DITLEVSEN, Tove (1917–1976). Danish writer. Born in Copenhagen, Denmark, 1917; committed suicide in Mar 1976; dau. of Ditlev Ditlevsen and Alfrida (Mundus) Ditlevsen; m. four times; 1st husband was editor of *Wild Wheat,* a journal for avant-garde poetry; children: 1 daughter, 2 sons. ❖ Popular writer of poems, short stories, novels and

memoirs, a total of 37 works, which concentrate on life within the family; her novels, which are to some extent autobiographical, fall into two categories: the earlier works are naturalistic depictions of people and places, focusing on childhood; the later novels depict marital problems as universal concerns. ❖ See also *Women in World History.*

DITTMAR, Louise (1807–1884). German philosopher and feminist. Name variations: Luise Dittmar. Born Sept 7, 1807, in the German town of Darmstadt; died July 11, 1884, in the village of Bessungen (now a part of Darmstadt); dau. of Heinrich Karl Dittmar (higher treasury official at the court of Hesse-Darmstadt); never married; no children. ❖ Self-taught German philosopher and feminist active in 1840s who challenged the notion that there were any natural differences between the sexes, and (while also drawing on the Christian tradition) used a critique of Christianity to explore both the ideological oppression of women more generally, and to defend women's rights to sexuality; published 9 books in the space of 5 years (1845–49), including *Bekannte Geheimnisse* (Open Secrets, 1845), *Skizzen und Briefe* (Sketches and Letters, 1845), *Der Mensch und sein Gott* (The Human Being and His God, 1846), *Lessing und Feuerbach* (Lessing and Feuerbach, 1847), and *Vier Zeitfragen* (Four Timely Questions, 1847); founded and edited *Soziale Reform,* one of the 5 women's journals launched in Germany during the revolutions of 1848 and 1849; her work, which includes political satire, religious and mythological history, philosophical and theological exegesis, poetry, and journalism, provides an important example of that peculiar hybrid blend of radical liberalism, pre-Marxist socialism, and humanist Christianity that characterized many utopian visions in 1840's France, England and Germany. ❖ See also *Women in World History.*

DITZEL, Nana (1923–2005). Danish designer. Name variations: Nanna Ditzel. Born Nana Hauberg, Oct 6, 1923, in Copenhagen, Denmark; died June 17, 2005, in Copenhagen; dau. of William Hauberg and Erna (Lytzen) Hauberg; graduated from high school, 1942; graduate of Academy of Arts and Crafts, 1946; m. architect Jörgen Ditzel, c. 1946 (died 1961); m. Knud Heide (German businessman), 1968 (died c. 1986); children: 3 daughters. ❖ With husband Jörgen, gained wide acclaim as designer of jewelry in silver and gold for George Jensen and won the Lunning Prize (1956); after husband's death (1961), continued on her own, designing jewelry, furniture and textiles; set up shop in London (1968); returned to Copenhagen (1986).

DIVER, Jenny (1700–1740). British pickpocket. Name variations: Mary Jones. Born Mary Jones in Ireland in 1700; died on the gallows, Mar 18, 1740, at Tyburn, England; dau. of Harriot Jones (maid); educated in Northern Ireland. ❖ One of the most notorious pickpockets in criminal history, was born out of wedlock and deserted by mother; after living in several foster homes, was taken to Northern Ireland, where an elderly woman cared for her and saw that she had a proper education; as a teenager, moved to London, hoping to make her fortune as a seamstress; became involved with Anne Murphy, den mother to a pack of street thieves; grew so adept that she promptly took over the operation and earned the name Jenny Diver (*diver* being underworld parlance for pickpocket); was said to have repented before her death on the gallows. Immortalized in John Gay's *The Beggar's Opera* (1798) and Brecht's adaptation *The Threepenny Opera* (1928). ❖ See also *Women in World History.*

DIVINYLS. *See Amphlett, Christina.*

DIX, Beulah Marie (1876–1970). American screenwriter and playwright. Name variations: Beulah Marie Dix Flebbe. Born Jan 24, 1876, in Kingston, Massachusetts; died Sept 25, 1970, in Woodland Hills, California; m. G.H. Flebbe. ❖ Plays include *Hugh Gwyeth, Soldier Rigdale, The Making of Christopher Ferringham, The Beau's Comedy, Apples of Eden* and *The Fair Maid of Graystones;* also co-wrote plays with Evelyn Greenleaf Sutherland; wrote or collaborated on over 50 screenplays, including *The Prison without Walls, The Sunset Trail, Wild Youth, The Squaw Man* (scenario and story), *The Affairs of Anatol, Ned McCobb's Daughter* and *Sweater Girl.*

DIX, Dorothea Lynde (1802–1887). American social reformer. Born Dorothea Lynde Dix on April 4, 1802, in Hampden, Maine; died in Trenton, New Jersey, July 18, 1887; dau. of Joseph (Methodist minister) and Mary (Bigelow) Dix; never married. ❖ Reformer who led the crusade to improve treatment of the mentally ill and built hospitals for the insane; at 14, started her 1st school (1816); published *Conversations on Common Things,* the 1st of 6 books (1824); began work as an advocate for the mentally ill (1841); issued public reports, using horrifying tales of mistreatment of the mentally ill to prick the conscience of legislators and citizens, urging them to correct the abuses by building modern facilities for care and treatment of the insane; employed this method successfully in almost every state in the nation, as well as in Europe; served as superintendent of Army Nurses during the Civil War (1861–65); more than any other person in the 19th century, was responsible for pioneering more humane treatment for the mentally ill; over the course of 40-year career, was personally responsible for the creation of 32 asylums in the US, and the improvement and expansion of many more in US, Europe, and Japan. ❖ See also Helen E. Marshall, *Dorothea Dix: Forgotten Samaritan* (U. of North Carolina Press, 1937); Charles Schlaifer and Lucy Freeman, *Heart's Work: Civil War Heroine and Champion of the Mentally Ill, Dorothea Lynde Dix* (Paragon, 1991); Dorothy Clarke Wilson, *Stranger and Traveler: The Story of Dorothea Dix, American Reformer* (Little, Brown, 1975); David L. Gollaher, *A Voice for the Mad: The Life of Dorothea Dix* (Free Press, 1995); and *Women in World History*.

DIX, Dorothy (1861–1951). *See Gilmer, Elizabeth Meriwether.*

DIX, Dorothy (1892–1970). English actress. Born Feb 27, 1892, in London, England; died Jan 1970 in England; m. Jameson Thomas (div.); m. T. Vezey-Strong (div.); m. Roy Clark. ❖ Made London debut in *Monsieur Beaucaire* (1907) and came to prominence in *The White Man* (1908); other plays include *The Conquest, The Three Musketeers, The Rivals, Daddy Long-Legs, Fair and Warmer, Don Q, The Czarina* (title role), *The Cherry Orchard, The Donovan Affair, The Lad* and *Hamlet;* made NY debut in *The Father* (1931); films include *The First Mrs. Fraser* (title role).

DIXIE, Florence (1857–1905). English explorer and writer. Name variations: Lady Florence Dixie. Born Florence Douglas in 1857; died 1905; dau. of Archibald William Douglas (1818–1858), 8th Marquis of Queensberry, and Caroline Margaret Clayton; m. Sir Alexander Dixie, 1875. ❖ Explored Patagonia (1878–79), served as a war correspondent for the *London Morning Post* in the Boer War (1880–81), and was instrumental in securing the liberty of Cetawayo, king of Zululand; in later years, was a champion of women's rights; books include *Across Patagonia, A Defense of Zululand and its King* and *The Child Hunters of Patagonia.*

DIXIE CHICKS
See Lynch, Laura.
See Macy, Robin Lynn.
See Maines, Natalie.
See Robison, Emily.
See Seidel, Martie.

DIXON, Adele (1908–1992). English actress and singer. Name variations: Adèle Dixon. Born June 3, 1908, in Kensington, England; died April 11, 1992, in Manchester, England; m. Ernest Schwaiger. ❖ Made stage debut in *Where the Rainbow Ends* (1921); appeared in numerous Shakespearean roles at the Old Vic (1928–30), including Juliet, Olivia, and Ophelia; other plays include *The Sport of Kings, Leona and Lena, Marriage à la Mode, The Good Companions, Hocus-Pocus, Orders is Orders, Give Me a Ring, Three Sisters, Anything Goes, All Clear, Babes in the Wood* and *The Hasty Heart;* made NY debut in *Between the Devil* (1937); films include *Uneasy Virtue* and *Woman to Woman.*

DIXON, Diane (1964—). African-American runner. Born Sept 23, 1964, in Brooklyn, NY. ❖ Won 5 consecutive TAC indoor 400 titles; won an Olympic gold medal at Los Angeles (1984) and a silver medal at Seoul (1988), both in 4 x 400-meter relay.

DIXON, Jean (1896–1981). American stage and screen actress. Born July 14, 1896, in Waterbury, Connecticut; died Feb 12, 1981, in New York, NY; m. Edward Ely (died 1980). ❖ Made stage debut in France in a Sarah Bernhardt starrer; made Broadway debut in *Wooden Kimono* (1929), followed by *June Moon, George Washington Slept Here, Once in a Lifetime, Heat Lightning, Square Root of Wonderful* and *The Gang's All Here,* among many others; appeared in such films as *The Lady Lies, Sadie McKee, She Married Her Boss, My Man Godfrey, You Only Live Once, Swing High Swing Low* and *Holiday.*

DIXON, Jeane (1918–1997). American astrologer. Name variations: Jeane L. Dixon. Born Jan 3, 1918, in Medford, Wisconsin; grew up in California; died Jan 25, 1997, in Washington, DC; dau. of German immigrants; m. James L. Dixon (California auto dealer, then real estate executive), 1939. ❖ One of the best known American astrologers, had a syndicated newspaper column which was published by more than 800 newspapers worldwide; came to prominence with her prediction

that a young Democratic president, elected in 1960, would die in office; returned to prominence as an adviser to Nancy Reagan; wrote *My Life and Prophecies* (1968), *Reincarnation and Prayers to Live By* (1970), *The Call to Glory* (1972), *Yesterday, Today and Forever* (1976) and *A Gift of Prayer* (1995). ❖ See also Ruth Montgomery, *A Gift of Prophecy: The Phenomenal Jeane Dixon* (1965).

DIXON, Karen (1964—). *See Straker, Karen.*

DIXON, Margaret (1670–1753). Scottish murderer. Born 1670 in Scotland; died 1753; children: at least 1. ❖ Hanged in Edinburgh for murder of her child, was placed in a wooden box to be taken for burial by friends; after they stopped at an inn for refreshments, opened the lid of the box and sat up; because law did not provide for 2nd executions, became a free woman who, as "half-hanged Maggie Dixon," was a local celebrity.

DIXON, Medina (1962—). American basketball player. Born Nov 2, 1962; graduate of Old Dominion, 1985. ❖ At Barcelona Olympics, won a bronze medal in team competition (1992).

DIXON, Reather (1945—). American singer. Name variations: Reather "Dimples" Dixon Turner; The Bobbettes. Born May 1, 1945, in New York, NY. ❖ At 11, became a lead singer of The Bobbettes, the 1st female vocal group with #1 R&B hit and Top-10 hit on pop charts: "Mr. Lee" (1957); with Bobbettes, toured with such artists as Clyde McPhatter and Ruth Brown. Other singles by Bobbettes include "Have Mercy, Baby" (1960), "Dance With Me, Georgie" (1960), and "I Don't Like It Like That, Part 1" (1961).

DIXON, Tina (1976—). American snowboarder. Born May 17, 1976, in Salt Lake City, Utah. ❖ Began competing as snowboarder (1997); received gold at X Games in Big Air (Summer 1997) and Boarder X (Winter 1998); received silver at X Games in Big Air (Summer 1999); other 1st-place finishes in Big Air include USASA State championships (1996) and North American Bud Light Series in California, Oregon, and New Hampshire (all 1997).

DIXON, Victoria (1959—). English field-hockey player. Born Aug 1959. ❖ At Barcelona Olympics, won a bronze medal in team competition (1992).

DIXON JONES, Mary Amanda (1828–1908). American physician. Name variations: Mary Dixon Jones. Born Mary Amanda Dixon, Deb 17, 1828, in Dorchester Co., Maryland; died 1908 in NY; dau. of Noah and Sarah Turner Dixon; graduate of Wesleyan Female College, 1845; studied medicine with Henry F. Askew and Thomas E. Bond Jr., a prominent Baltimore physician; graduate of Hygeio-Therapeutic College in NY, 1862; m. John Q.A. Jones (lawyer), 1854; children: 3, including Charles Jones (physician). ❖ One of the 1st American women physicians to become a successful gynecological surgeon and the 1st American surgeon to perform a successful hysterectomy for fibroid tumors (c. 1887), established successful private practice in Brooklyn, NY; at 44, enrolled at Woman's Medical College of Pennsylvania in Philadelphia, graduating with highest scores in school's history (1873); attended Emeline Cleveland's lectures; completed a 3-month preceptorship with Dr. Mary Putnam Jacobi; employed as chief medical officer of Women's Dispensary and Hospital in Brooklyn (1882); after a trip to Europe to study operations with physician son Charles (1886), performed a new method to successfully remove cancerous uterus (c. 1887); became editor of *Woman's Medical Journal;* involved in the sensational case, People vs. Mary A. Dixon Jones and Charles Dixon Jones, Physicians (1890), which, though unfounded, permanently scarred her reputation; with help of surgeon and microscopist Charles Heitzman, discovered cancer of uterine lining (endothelioma) and cancer of the ovary (gyroma, 1876).

DIZHUR, Bella (b. 1906). Russian poet. Name variations: Bella Abramovna Dizhur. Born 1906 (some sources cite 1903) in Kiev, of assimilated Jewish parents; graduated in biochemistry from Herzen Institute in Leningrad, 1926; children: Ernst Neizvestny (sculptor, b. 1925). ❖ Wrote narrative poem, "Janusz Korczak" (1944), about Polish doctor and orphanage director who chose to go to Treblinka with 200 Jewish orphans in his care; received exit visa (1987) to join sculptor son, Ernst Neizvestny, in New York; poetry published in Russian and English as *Shadow of a Soul* (1990).

DJAHSH, Zaynab bint (c. 590–c. 640). *See Zaynab bint Jahsh.*

DJAMILA (1939—). *See Amrane, Djamila.*

DJEBAR, Assia (1936—). See *Imaleyene, Fatime-Zohra.*

DJUKICA, Slavic (1960—). Yugoslavian handball player. Born Jan 1960 in USSR. ❖ At Los Angeles Olympics, won a gold medal in team competition (1984).

DJURASKOVIC, Vera (1949—). Yugoslavian basketball player. Born Aug 29, 1949. ❖ At Moscow Olympics, won a bronze medal in team competition (1980).

DJURICA, Mirjana (1961—). Yugoslavian handball player. Born Mar 11, 1961, in USSR. ❖ Won an Olympic silver medal at Moscow (1980) and a gold medal at Los Angeles (1984), both in team competition.

DJURKOVIC, Zorica (1957—). Yugoslavian basketball player. Born Sept 14, 1957. ❖ At Moscow Olympics, won a bronze medal in team competition (1980).

DLASTA (fl. 8th c.). See *Valasca.*

DLUGOSZEWSKI, Lucia (1925–2000). American composer, pianist, teacher, poet, and inventor of percussion instruments. Name variations: Lucia Dlugoszevski. Born June 16, 1925, in Detroit, Michigan; found dead in her apartment in Greenwich Village, NY, April 11, 2000; studied under Agelageth Morrison at Detroit Conservatory of Music; attended Wayne State University; studied piano in NY under Grete Sultan, and at Mannes School of Music (1950–51). ❖ Won Tompkins literary award for poetry (1947); was the 1st woman to win the Koussevitzky Prize; taught at New York University and New School for Social Research (1960s); invented over 100 percussion instruments made of plastic, metal, glass and wood, the best known being the timbre piano which has bows and plectra in addition to a keyboard; often composed for these instruments: *Naked Swift Music* used the timbre piano and *Concert of Many Rooms and Moving Space* used 4 unsheltered rattles; often composed for the Erick Hawkins Company. ❖ See also *Women in World History.*

DLUZEWSKA, Malgorzata (1958—). Polish rower. Name variations: Malgorzata Dluzewska-Wieliczko; Deuzewska. Born Aug 1958 in Poland. ❖ At Moscow Olympics, won a silver medal in coxless pairs (1980).

DMITRIEFF, Elizabeth (1851–1910). Russian-French socialist. Name variations: Elisabeth Dmitriev or Dmitrieva. Born in Russia in 1851; died in 1910; dau. of a Russian noble; married a political prisoner. ❖ As a member of the Socialist International, journeyed to London, where she became friends with Karl Marx; during the Paris Commune revolt of 1871, organized the Union of Women for the Defense of Paris and the Care of the Wounded, a branch of the Socialist International; with Communards defeated, escaped to Russia, where she married a political prisoner who had been condemned to Siberia; remained with him in exile until she died.

DMITRIEVA, Elizaveta Ivanovna (1887–1928). Russian poet. Name variations: (pseudonyms) Cherubina de Gabriak; Li Sian Tszy. Born 1887 in Russia; died 1928. ❖ Poems appeared in avant-garde journal *Apollo*, under pseudonym Cherubina de Gabriak (1909, 1910); worked for *Apollo* as translator; with Samuil Marshak, founded children's theater in Krasnodar, then worked at Petrograd's Theatre for Young Spectators (1922), writing children's plays with Marshak; published cycle of poems "The Little House Under the Pear Tree"; during Russia's turmoil, was arrested and sent to Tashkent (1927); most work remains in manuscript.

DMITRIEVA, Valentina (1859–1948). Russian novelist and short-story writer. Name variations: Valentina Ionovna Dmitrieva. Born 1859 in Russia; died 1948; dau. of an educated serf; studied medicine in St Petersburg. ❖ Wrote many realistic short stories and novels about Russian peasant life while exiled in Tver' and Voronezh for revolutionary activities; short novel *Gomochka* (1894), was translated as *Love's Anvil;* fiction often pointed out social and political abuses. ❖ See also autobiography *The Way It Was* (1930).

DOADA (fl. 990–1005). Scottish princess. Name variations: Dovada; (family name) Macalpin. Fl. between 990 and 1005; daughter (or sister) of Malcolm II of Alba (1005–1034), king of Scots (some sources list her as the dau. of Kenneth II); m. Findleach of Moray also known as Findlaech Mac Ruaridh (Macrory), mormaer (ruler) of Moray, c. 1004; children: possibly Macbeth or Machethad, Machetad, Macbethad, often confused with MacHeth in later sources (c. 1005–1057), king of Scotland (r. 1040–1054, who m. Gruoch [Lady Macbeth]). ❖ Possibly the mother of Macbeth. ❖ See also *Women in World History.*

DO AMOR LIMA, Sisleide (1967—). See *Sissi.*

DOAN, Catriona Le May (b. 1970). See *Le May Doan, Catriona.*

DOBBIN, Mrs. G.A. (1873–1922). See *Page, Gertrude.*

DOBBINS, Georgia (1944–1980). African-American pop singer. Name variations: Georgeanna; Georgia Tillman; Marvelettes. Born in 1944 in Detroit, Michigan; died of sickle-cell anemia, Jan 6, 1980, in Detroit; m. Billy Gordon (singer with the Contours). ❖ Was a member of the Marvelettes, a popular Motown group whose songs "Don't Mess With Bill," "Please Mr. Postman," "I Keep Holding On," and "Beachwood 4–5789" reached the top of the charts (early 1960s). Other members included Gladys Horton, Katherine Anderson, Wanda Young, Juanita Cowart. ❖ See also *Women in World History.*

DOBELL, Mrs. Temple (1888–1960). See *Ravenscroft, Gladys.*

DOBERSCHUETZ-MEY, Gerlinde (1964—). East German rower. Name variations: Gerlinde Doberschütz-Mey; Gerlinde Doberschutz. Born Oct 26, 1964, in East Germany. ❖ At Seoul Olympics, won a gold medal in coxed fours (1988).

DOBESOVA, Bozena (1914—). Czech gymnast. Born Oct 1914. ❖ At Berlin Olympics, won a silver medal in team all-around (1936).

DOBLE, Frances (1902–1969). Canadian-born actress. Born June 10, 1902, in Montreal, Quebec, Canada; died Dec 1969 in England; m. Sir Anthony Lindsay Hogg (div.). ❖ Made stage debut in London in *The Man in Dress Clothes* (1922), followed by *As Far as Thought Can Reach* (*Back to Methusalah*), *The Farmer's Wife, Polly Preferred, In the Snare, The Godless, Vaudeville Vanities, Sirocco, The Constant Nymph, Chinese Bungalow* and *Ballerina;* with Lady Eleanor Smith, co-authored *Goosefeather Bed* (1935); also appeared in the films *The Vortex, The Constant Nymph, Dark Red Roses, The Water Gipsies* and *Nine Till Six.*

DOBMEIER, Annette (1968—). German fencer. Born Feb 10, 1968. ❖ At Barcelona Olympics, won a silver medal in team foil (1992).

DOBO, Katica (fl. 1552). Hungarian hero. Name variations: Katalin Dobo or Dóbo. ❖ Great heroine in Hungary, fought the Turks at the 40-day siege at the Castle of Eger (Sept 1552); as the Turks were scaling the walls, dumped buckets of hot soup and boiling water on them, aided by other women.

DOBRANCHEVA, Marina (1961—). See *Logvinenko, Marina.*

DOBRATZ, Erin (1982—). American synchronized swimmer. Born Oct 19, 1982, in Concord, California. ❖ Won a team bronze medal at Athens Olympics (2004).

DOBRAVY OF BOHEMIA (d. 977). Duchess of Poland. Name variations: Dubravka or Dubrawka; family name Premysl. Died 977; dau. of Boleslav or Boleslav I the Cruel, duke of Bohemia (r. 929–967); sister of Boleslav II (d. 999), duke of Bohemia (r. 967–999); m. Mieczislaw also known as Burislaf or Mieszko I (c. 922–992), duke of Poland (r. 960–992); children: Gunhilda of Poland (mother of King Canute the Great of Denmark); Boleslav Chrobry also known as Boleslaw the Brave (c. 967–1025), king of Poland (r. 992–1025); Mieszko; Swietopelk; Lambert. Mieszko I's 2nd wife was Oda of Germany and North Marck.

DOBRE, Aurelia (1972—). Romanian gymnast. Born Nov 6, 1972, in Bucharest, Romania; m. Boz Mofid (gym owner), 1992. ❖ At World championships, earned 5 perfect 10's and became Romania's 1st all-around World champion, placing 1st for all-around, team all-around, and balance beam, and 3rd for vault and floor exercises (1987); at Grand Prix of Rome, placed 1st all-around (1987) and 3rd all-around (1989); at Seoul Olympics, won a silver medal in team all-around (1988); moved to US (1991).

DOBRE-BALAN, Anisoara (1966—). Romanian rower. Name variations: Anisoara Balan. Born July 1966. ❖ Won an Olympic bronze medal at Seoul (1988) and a silver medal at Barcelona (1992), both in quadruple sculls without coxswain.

DOBRITOIU, Elena (1957—). Romanian rower. Born Aug 29, 1957. ❖ At Moscow Olympics, won a bronze medal in coxed eights (1980).

DOBSON, Deborah (c. 1950—). American ballet dancer. Born c. 1950, in Sacramento, California; m. Jonas Kage. ❖ Worked with Sacramento Civic Ballet during adolescence; joined American Ballet Theater (1969), where she created numerous roles including in Alvin Ailey's *Sea-Change* (1972) and Tomm Ruud's *Polyandrion* (1973); was featured in several company premieres including Frederick Ashton's *Les Patineurs,* the Ballet Theater's production of *La Fille Mal Gardée,* and Natalia Makarova's *La Bayadère* (1974); moved to Europe with husband where she danced with Stuttgart Ballet in Germany (1974) and Geneva Ballet in Switzerland, among others.

DOBSON, Emily (1842–1934). Australian philanthropist. Born Emily Lempriere on Oct 10, 1842, at Port Arthur, Van Diemen's Land (Tasmania); died June 5, 1934, in Hobart; dau. of Thomas James (public servant and artist) and Charlotte (Smith) Lempriere; m. Henry Dobson (lawyer, politician, member of the Tasmanian Legislative Assembly, 1891, and premier, 1892–94), on Feb 4, 1868; children: 2 sons, 3 daughters. ❖ Following a typhoid epidemic, organized a petition drive for an improved sewage system and formed the Women's Sanitation Association to educate women on sanitary procedures and to instigate house-to-house visits (1891); was a founding president of the Ministering Children's League (1892) and later worked with the Society for the Protection of Children; was a founding member of the Tasmanian National Council of Women (1899), serving as president (1906–34). ❖ See also *Women in World History.*

DOBSON, Louise (1972—). Australian field-hockey player. Born Sept 1, 1972, in Melbourne, Victoria, Australia. ❖ Midfielder, won a team gold medal at Atlanta Olympics (1996).

DOBSON, Rosemary (1920—). Australian poet. Born on June 18, 1920, in Sydney, Australia; dau. of Arthur Austin Greaves Dobson (civil engineer) and Marjorie Caldwell Dobson; granddau. of a British poet, Austin Dobson; attended University of Sydney; m. Alexander Bolton (publisher who founded Brindabella Press), June 12, 1951; children: Lissant Mary; Robert Thorley; Ian Alexander. ❖ Poet whose verse reflects both the past—in her love of classical civilizations—as well as the modern era with its feminist consciousness, published 1st collection of poetry, *In a Convex Mirror* (1944); won *Sydney Morning Herald* poetry prize for *The Ship of Ice and Other Poems* (1948); explored Europe (1966–71); received prize from Fellowship of Australian Writers (1979); also wrote *Focus on Ray Crooke* (1971), *Three Poems on Water-Springs* (1973), *Greek Coins: A Sequence of Poems* (1977), *Over the Frontier* (1978), and *Summer Press* (1987); edited several anthologies of poetry and has been involved in the translation of Russian works into English, most notably with David Campbell on *Seven Russian Poets: Imitations* (1979). ❖ See also *Women in World History.*

DOBSON, Ruth (1918–1989). Australian diplomat. Name variations: Ruth Lissant Dobson. Born in 1918; died Dec 14, 1989; attended Frensham School where her mother was housemistress; Women's College, BA, 1940. ❖ Became research assistant to Deparment of External Affairs (1943); worked at External Affairs Office, Australian High Commission in London (1946–49); served as 3rd secretary in Geneva (1950–53) and was on the Third Committee of the General Assembly of the UN drafting the convention of the Status of Women; served as 2nd secretary to Information Branch, Canberra (1954–60); elevated to 1st secretary, Australian High Commission, Wellington (1961); assigned to NY as Australian representative at UN General Assembly (1969); served as counselor and deputy head of mission, Australian Embassy in Athens (1971–74); served as ambassador to Denmark (1974–78), the 1st woman career diplomat to be an Australian ambassador; served as ambassador to the Republic of Ireland (1978–81). Awarded OBE (1982).

DOCK, Lavinia L. (1858–1956). American nurse. Born Lavinia Lloyd Dock, Feb 26, 1858, in Harrisburg, Pennsylvania; died April 17, 1956, in Chambersburg, Pennsylvania; dau. of Gilliard and Lavinia Lloyd Bombaugh Dock; graduate of Bellevue Hospital Training School for Nurses in NY (1886). ❖ Contributed to nursing field; advocated women's rights; assisted Jane Delano with yellow fever epidemic in Jacksonville, Florida (1888); began working under Isabel Hampton Robb as assistant superintendent of nurses at the then-new Johns Hopkins Training School for Nurses (Nov 1890); with Robb, attended the Conference of Charities, Correction, and Philanthropy at Chicago World's Fair (1893), which led to creation of American Society of Superintendents of Training Schools for Nurses of US and Canada (later named National League for Nursing) and served as its secretary

(1896–1903); worked at Henry Street Settlement to help NYC poor (1896–1916); with British nurse Ethel Gordon Fenwick, worked to establish the International Council of Nurses (1899) and later served as its secretary (1900–22); provided a model for establishment of the Nurses' Associated Alumnae of US and Canada (1896), renamed the American Nurses Association (1911), the 1st general membership organization for nurses in America; served as contributing editor to *American Journal of Nursing.* Writings include the 1st pharmacology manual for nurses, *Text-book of Materia Medica for Nurses* (1890), which sold over 100,000 copies, *A History of Nursing* (2 vols. 1907, 2 vols. 1912), (with Isabel Stewart) *A Short History of Nursing* (1920) and *Hygiene and Morality* (1910).

DOCKER, Lady (1908–2003). See *Rothschild, Jeanne de.*

DOCKERY, Mary Ann Lake (1821–1910). See *Wallis, Mary Ann Lake.*

DOCKRAY, Marianne (1821–1910). See *Wallis, Mary Ann Lake.*

DOD, Charlotte (1871–1960). British skater, tennis and field-hockey player. Name variations: Lottie Dod. Born Charlotte Dod, Sept 24, 1871, in Cheshire, England; died June 26 or 27, 1960, in Bournemouth, England; grew up in Edgeworth House, in Bebington, Cheshire; sister of William Dod (archer). ❖ British tennis champion, was also the 1st superstar of women's sports as an outstanding skater, tobogganer, golfer, archer, and field-hockey player; won Wimbledon singles championship (1887, 1888, 1891, 1892, 1893); won Wimbledon doubles championship (1886, 1887, 1888); won Wimbledon mixed-doubles championship (1889 and 1892); at 15½, was youngest player ever to play at Wimbledon; was also the 1st woman to complete the Cresta bobsled run at St. Moritz; took the British women's golf championship (1904); won a silver medal for archery at London Olympics (1908). Inducted into International Women's Hall of Fame (1986). ❖ See also Jeffrey Pearson, *Lottie Dod, Champion of Champions;* and *Women in World History.*

DODA (fl. 1040). Duchess of Lower Lorraine. Fl. around 1040; m. Godfrey II the Bearded, duke of Lower Lorraine (r. 1044–1047), duke of Lorraine (r. 1065–1069); children: Godfrey III the Hunchback (d. 1076, who m. Matilda of Tuscany [1046–1115]); Ida of Lorraine (1040–1113, who m. Eustace II, count of Boulogne).

DODA, Carol. American exotic dancer. ❖ Undertook 20 weeks of silicone treatments which increased breast size, then became 1st woman topless entertainer (1964), performing at Condor Night Club in San Francisco for more than 20 years (1964–85); arrested for lewd conduct, was acquitted in 19 minutes (1965); had breasts insured for $1.5 million by Lloyds of London (1965); was earning $700 per week for nude shows by 1972; starred in *The Rise and Fall of the World (As Seen from a Sexual Position)* (1972); received Business Person of the Year Award from Harvard University (1974); designed and launched Champagne & Lace Lingerie Boutique in San Francisco, started fantasy phone line (1986) and eventually owned her own club.

DODANE (fl. 820–843). See *Dhuoda of Septimania.*

DODD, Claire (1908–1973). American actress. Born Dorothy Anne Dodd, Dec 29, 1908, in New York, NY (some sources list Des Moines, IA); died Nov 23, 1973, in Beverly Hills, California; m. Jack Milton Strauss, 1931 (div. 1938); m. H. Brand Cooper, 1942; children: 5. ❖ Began career as a Ziegfeld chorine, appearing in *Whoopee* and *Smiles;* films include *Footlight Parade, Roberta, Babbitt, An American Tragedy, In the Navy* and *Mississippi Gambler;* was Della Street in several Perry Mason features.

DODD, Lynley Stuart (1941—). New Zealand children's writer and illustrator. Born July 5, 1941, in Rotorua, New Zealand. ❖ Taught art at Queen Margaret College; writings include *My Cat Likes to Hide in Boxes* (with Eve Sutton, 1973), *The Nickle Nackle Tree* (1976), *Titimus Trim* (1979), *Druscilla* (with Clarice England, 1980), *The Smallest Turtle* (1982), *The Apple Tree* (1983), *Hairy Maclary from Donaldson Dairy* (1983), *Hairy Maclary's Bone* (1984), *Hairy Maclary's Showbusiness* (1991) and *Sniff-Snuff-Snap!* (1995). Received Choysa Bursary and New Zealand Picture Story Book of the Year Award (1984, 1986, 1988, 1992) for "Hairy Maclary" series.

DODE (b. 586). Frankish noblewoman. Name variations: Doda; Ode de Heristal; Ode of Heristal or Heristol. Born in 586; m. Arnoldus also known as Arnulf, bishop of Metz (d. 639); children: Ansegisal, mayor of Austrasia (r. 632–638).

DODGE, Eva F. (1896–1990). American physician. Born Eva Francette Dodge, July 24, 1896, in New Hampton, New Hampshire; died Mar 1990; dau. of Winnie Josephine (Worthen) Dodge and George Francis Dodge (physician). ❖ The 1st female physician to establish a private practice in Winston-Salem, NC (1932), the 5th woman to earn MD from University of Maryland's Medical School (1925), the 1st woman to serve on University of Maryland's Medical School's rotating internship (1925–26) and residency in obstetrics (1926–27), and the 1st woman (and 2nd professor ever) to become a University of Arkansas Medical School professor emerita, began career as acting professor of obstetrics at Woman's Christian Medical School in Shanghai, China (1928–29); completed postgraduate study in Vienna, Austria (1931); served as obstetrics staff chief at City Memorial Hospital (1934–37), then organized and directed maternity clinics (1933–37); consulted for many organizations, including Alabama Bureau of Maternal and Child Health (1937), Puerto Rico Health Department's Maternal and Child Health Bureau (1940), and US Department of Labor Children's Bureau; served as associate medical director of Planned Parenthood Federation of America in NY (1943–45); worked at University of Arkansas for Medical Science in Little Rock (1945–64); remained active after retirement (June 30, 1964) and took many tours, including a UN tour of family-planning projects in 4 African nations (1969).

DODGE, Grace Hoadley (1856–1914). American social-welfare worker. Born Grace Hoadley Dodge, May 21, 1856, in New York, NY; died Dec 27, 1914, in New York, NY; dau. of William Earl Dodge Jr. and Sarah (Hoadley) Dodge; attended Miss Porter's School in Farmington, Connecticut; never married; no children. ❖ Established Industrial Education Association, NY (1884), which later became Teachers College (1892); established Girls' Public School Athletic League (1905); named president of national YWCA (1906) and worked to unite national and international YWCA.

DODGE, Josephine (1855–1928). American day-nursery proponent and anti-suffragist. Born Josephine Marshall Jewell, Feb 11, 1855, in Hartford, Connecticut; died Mar 6, 1928, in Cannes, France; dau. of Marshall Jewell (governor of Connecticut and minister to Russia) and Esther E. (Dickinson) Jewell; m. Arthur Murray Dodge, Oct 6, 1875 (died 1896); children: 6 sons. ❖ Sponsored the founding of the Virginia Day Nursery in NY (1878); founded Jewell Day Nursery (1888); founded and served as 1st president of Association of Day Nurseries of New York City (c. 1895) and National Federation (later Association) of Day Nurseries (1898); formed and served as president of National Association Opposed to Woman Suffrage (1911).

DODGE, Mabel (1879–1962). See Luhan, Mabel Dodge.

DODGE, Mary Abigail (1833–1896). American writer. Name variations: (pseudonym) Gail Hamilton. Born in Hamilton, Massachusetts, Mar 31, 1833; died in Hamilton, Massachusetts, Aug 17, 1896; dau. of James Brown (farmer) and Hannah (Stanwood) Dodge; graduated from Ipswich Female Seminary, 1850. ❖ Popular essayist, known for her lively, witty, and opinionated style, spent several successful years in the classroom, before moving to Washington, DC (1858), where she became governess to the children of Gamaliel Bailey, editor of the antislavery *National Era*; adopted pen name Gail Hamilton; contributed to *Atlantic Monthly*; published 2 collections of essays, *Country Living and Country Thinking* (1861) and *A New Atmosphere* (1865); worked as assistant editor for the children's magazine *Our Young Folks*; published *Battle of the Books* (1870), a fictionalized account of her break with 1st publisher, Ticknor and Fields of Boston; worked as speechwriter for Congressman James G. Blaine, whose wife was her 1st cousin. Writings include *Skirmishes and Sketches* (1865), *Red Letter Days in Applethorpe* (1866), *Wool Gathering* (1868), *Twelve Miles from a Lemon* (1874), *Sermons to the Clergy* (1876), *The Spent Bullet* (1882), *Biography of James G. Blaine* (1893), and *X-Rays* (1896). ❖ See also H. Augusta Dodge, ed. *Gail Hamilton's Life in Letters* (Vol I and II, Lee & Shepard, 1901); and *Women in World History*.

DODGE, Mary Mapes (1831–1905). American writer. Born Mary Elizabeth Mapes in New York, NY, Jan 26, 1831; died in Onteora, New York, Aug 21, 1905; dau. of James Jay Mapes and Sophia (Furman) Mapes; m. William Dodge (lawyer), Sept 13, 1851; children: James (b. 1852); Harrington (1855–1881). ❖ Author of *Hans Brinker; or, The Silver Skates* and editor of *St. Nicholas*, returned with sons to her family home, Mapleridge, in Waverly, New Jersey, after sudden death of husband of unknown causes (1858); became editor of her father's *United States Journal* (1861); began contributing adult stories to *Harper's New*

Monthly Magazine (1863); published book for boys, *The Irvington Stories* (1864); because of long standing interest in Holland, penned *Hans Brinker; or, The Silver Skates* (1865); inherited her father's considerable debts at the time of his death (1866); began writing for children's periodical, the *Riverside Magazine* (1867); became associate editor of weekly periodical, *Hearth and Home* (1868–73); founded and edited Scribner's children's periodical, *St. Nicholas* (1873); gained steady recognition with publication of foreign editions of *Hans Brinker* as well as 4 more of her books (1870s); lost Waverly property and a great deal of money in legal judgment (1881); lost youngest son to typhoid (1881); in a break from Scribner's, took *Donald and Dorothy* to Roberts Brothers, which published it (1883); purchased a cottage in Onteora, New York, an artists' colony, where she spent her summers (1888); published *The Land of Pluck* and *When Life Is Young* (1894). ❖ See also *Women in World History*.

DODS, Mistress Margaret (1781–1857). See Johnstone, Isobel.

DODUNSKA, Agnes (1873–1947). See Fabish, Agnes.

DOENHOFF, Marion (b. 1909). See Dönhoff, Marion.

DOERDELMANN, Sylvia (1970—). German rower. Name variations: Sylvia Dördelmann. Born April 1970. ❖ At Barcelona Olympics, won a bronze medal in coxed eights (1992).

DOERING, Jane (c. 1922—). American ballet dancer. Name variations: (later stage name) Dorina del Sol. Born c. 1922 in Philadelphia, Pennsylvania; trained at Littlefield School in Philadelphia and later with Mikhail Mordkin at School of American Ballet in NY. ❖ Performed with Ballet Caravan where she created roles in Erick Hawkins' *Show Piece* and Lew Christensen's *Filling Station* (1937); toured briefly with Littlefield Ballet; switched almost entirely to theatrical dance, appearing in Prologs, presentation act houses such as Radio City Music Hall, and on Broadway in the musicals *Early to Bed* (1943) and *Three to Make Ready* (1946), among others; as Dorina del Sol, had secondary career as a Spanish dancer.

DOERR, Harriet (1910–2002). American novelist. Born Harriet Green Huntington, April 8, 1910, in Pasadena, California; died Nov 24, 2002, in Pasadena; dau. of Howard Huntington; granddau. of Henry Edward Huntington (railroad magnate); attended Smith College, 1927; attended Stanford University, 1928–30, BA in European History, 1975; m. Albert Doerr (mining engineer), 1930 (died 1972); children: Michael Doerr (died 1995) and Martha Doerr Toppin. ❖ In her 70s, published 1st novel, *Stones for Ibarra* (1984), the bestselling tome about a small Mexican village which won the American Book Award (an earlier name for the National Book Awards); also wrote *Consider This, Senora* (1993) and *Tiger in the Grass* (1995).

DOERRE, Katrin (1961—). See Dörre, Katrin.

DOERRIE, Doris (1955—). See Dörrie, Doris.

DOERRIES, Jana (1975—). German swimmer. Name variations: Jana Dörries. Born Sept 24, 1975. ❖ At Barcelona Olympics, won a silver medal in 4 x 100-meter medley relay (1992).

DOGONADZE, Anna (1973—). German trampolinist. Born Feb 15, 1973, in Mtskheta, USSR; m. Axel Lilkendey. ❖ Represented Soviet Union (1990), then Georgia (1992–97), then married and received German citizenship (1998); representing Germany, won a gold medal for indiv. at World championships (2001) and a gold medal for indiv. at Athens Olympics (2004).

DOHAN, Edith Hall (1877–1943). American archaeologist. Born Edith Hayward Hall, Dec 31, 1877, in New Haven, Connecticut; died July 14, 1943, in Philadelphia, Pennsylvania; dau. of Ely Ransom Hall (teacher) and Mary Jane (Smith) Hall; Smith College, BA, 1899; Bryn Mawr College, PhD, 1908; m. Joseph M. Dohan (lawyer and gentleman farmer), May 12, 1915; children: David Hayward Warrington Dohan and Katharine Elizabeth Dohan (who m. Denys Page, English classicist). ❖ Went on archaeological expedition to Gournia, Crete, and wrote doctoral dissertation *The Decorative Art of Crete in the Bronze Age* (1907); served as instructor in classical archaeology at Mount Holyoke College (1908–1912); served as assistant curator, associate curator, and curator of the Mediterranean section (beginning 1942) of University Museum at University of Pennsylvania; served review editorship of *American Journal of Archaeology* (1932–43); published most important work *Italic Tomb-Groups in the University Museum* (1942).

DOHERTY, Marie (1914–2003). See Marcus, Marie.

DOHM, Hedwig (1831–1919). German writer and feminist. Born Hedwig Schleh in Berlin, Germany, Sept 20, 1831; died in Berlin, June 1, 1919; m. (Wilhelm) Ernst Dohm (1819–1883, journalist); children: 4 daughters, 1 son. ❖ Influential feminist, published 1st political work, *Was die Pastoren von den Frauen denken* (*What the Clergy Thinks About Women*, 1872), as a response to 2 pamphlets by conservative clerics who argued that access to higher education would harm women both physically and psychologically; also wrote *Die wissenschaftliche Emancipation der Frau* (*The Scientific Emancipation of Women*, 1874), *Der Frauen Natur und Recht* (*The Nature and Rights of Women*, 1876), *Die Antifeministen* (*The Antifeminists*, 1902), and *Die Mütter* (*The Mothers*, 1903); was one of the few German feminists to advocate the vote for women—at a time when the leadership of the German women's movement looked upon this demand as being essentially "premature"; founded the "Deutsche Frauenverein Reform" (1888); also served on the governing board of the Verein "Frauenwohl" (1888–1901); wrote (novelle) *Werde, die Du bist* (*Become Who You Are*, 1894); published a trilogy of novels, *Sibilla Dalmar, Schicksale einer Seele* (*Fates of a Soul*, 1899) and *Christa Roland* (1896–1902). ❖ See also *Women in World History*.

DOHNAL, Darcie. American short-track speedskater. Name variations: Darcie Dohnal Sharapova. Married Anton Sharapov; children: Aleksei (b. 2001). ❖ Won a silver medal for the 3,000-meter relay at Albertville Olympics (1992).

DOHRN, Bernardine (1942—). American radical political activist, lawyer and educator. Born 1942; University of Chicago, BA with honors, MA, JD; m. Bill Ayers (fellow ex-fugitive and University of Illinois professor); children. ❖ As a leader of Students for a Democratic Society (SDS) in opposition to the Vietnam War, became a fugitive (1970) after being indicted on riot charges; led the Weather Underground (1970–80); resurfaced and spent 7 months in prison for refusing to cooperate with a grand jury; became clinical associate professor of law and director/founder of the Children and Family Justice Center at Northwestern University Law School; was also an associate professor at the College of the University of Chicago.

DOI, Takako (1928—). Japanese politician. Born Takako Doi in Kobe, a port city in southwest Japan, Nov 30, 1928; dau. of a physician; granted law degree from Doshisha University, Kyoto, 1958; never married; no children. ❖ As a member of the Socialist Party, captured a seat in the Lower House (1969) and was returned to office in 7 subsequent parliamentary contests; impressing her colleagues with her forceful debating skills, was appointed vice-chair of the party's central executive committee (1983); served as chair of the Social Democratic Party (1986–91), the 1st woman to head a major political organization in Japan; led the Socialists to a stunning victory over the ruling party in the Upper House elections (1989), thus breaking the Liberal Democrats' monopoly on power in that chamber of Parliament; along with her powerful populist message, inspired hundreds of politically inexperienced women to run for political office in the 1989 balloting, and many of them were elected in the wave of "Doi fever" that swept the country. ❖ See also *Women in World History*.

D'OISLY, Rosina (1881–1948). See *Buckman, Rosina*.

DOKIC, Jelena (1983—). Serbian tennis player. Born April 12, 1983, in Belgrade, Yugoslavia. ❖ Representing Serbia and Montenegro, was a semi-finalist for singles at Wimbledon (2000) and runner-up at Roland Garros (2001).

DOK MAI, Sod (1905–1963). See *Nimmanhemin, M.L. Bupha Kunjara*.

DOKOUDOVSKY, Nina (b. 1919). See *Stroganova, Nina*.

DOLBERG, Nola (1895–1994). See *Luxford, Nola*.

DOLE, Elizabeth Hanford (1936—). American politician. Name variations: Mary Elizabeth Hanford, Liddy Dole. Born Mary Elizabeth Hanford, July 29, 1936, in Salisbury, North Carolina; dau. of John Van Hanford (flower wholesaler) and Mary Cathey Hanford (aspiring pianist, church and civic volunteer); Duke University, BA, 1958; attended Oxford University; Harvard University, MA, 1960; Harvard University Law School, JD, 1965; m. Robert J. Dole (US senator, 1969–96, and presidential candidate), 1975. ❖ Republican political organizer and US senator, moved to Washington, DC, as a Democrat (1966), working on issues concerning the handicapped at Department of Health, Education and Welfare; became an independent (1968) and worked in Nixon White House as executive director of President's Committee for Consumer Interests; appointed by Nixon to 7-year term on Federal Trade

Commission, became a Republican (1975), the same year she married Bob Dole; served as 1st woman Secretary of Transportation (1983–87), spearheading efforts to increase automobile safety requirements and raise drinking age to 21; served as Secretary of Labor under George Herbert Bush (1989–90), initiating "Glass Ceiling Study" to identify barriers to senior management opportunities for women and minorities and make recommendations for effective change; took active role in husband's campaigns for office of vice-president (1976) and president (1980, 1984, 1990, 1996); served as president of American Red Cross (1991–2000), the 1st woman president since founder Clara Barton; overhauled disaster relief program for aid organization and implemented program to retool blood collection, processing and distribution system; resigned (1999) to organize own campaign for presidency, but abandoned race before primaries; was successfully elected as Republican to US Senate, representing native North Carolina (2002). Received Raoul Wallenberg Award for Humanitarian Service.

DOLETTI, Joanna Dumitrescu (1902–1963). See *Dumitrescu-Doletti, Joanna*.

DOLGOPOLOVA, Elena (1980—). Russian gymnast. Born Jan 23, 1980, in Volzhky, Russia. ❖ Won Buratino Cup (1996); won a silver medal on vault at Goodwill Games (1998); at Atlanta Olympics, won a silver medal in team all-around (1996).

DOLGORUKAIA, Alexandra (1836–c. 1914). Russian noblewoman who was briefly the mistress of Alexander II. Name variations: Aleksandra Dolgorukaya or Dolgorukova; "La Grande Mademoiselle." Born Alexandra Sergeevna Dolgorukaia in 1836; died c. 1914; dau. of Sergei Dolgorukii; m. General Peter Pavlovich Al'bedinskii (governor-general of the Baltic Region), c. 1861; children: 1 son. ❖ Became lady-in-waiting to Marie of Hesse-Darmstadt (1853), wife of the future tsar of Russia Alexander II; had affair with Alexander, which was encouraged by some conservative members of the court who wanted to break the stabilizing influence Marie had over her weak-willed husband; supported Alexander in his efforts to emancipate the serfs, effectively countering the conservative ploy; is perhaps best known through Ivan Turgenev's novel *Smoke*, whose heroine Irina was modeled after her. ❖ See also *Women in World History*.

DOLGORUKAIA, Natalia Borisovna (1714–1771). Russian memoirist. Name variations: Natal'ia Borisovna Dolgorúkaia, Dolgorukaia or Dolgorukaya. Born Natalia Borisovna Sheremeteva in 1714; died 1771; m. Ivan Dolgorukii (close friend of Peter II), 1730 (executed 1739); children: 2. ❖ Married into the powerful but out-of-favor Dolgoruky family; after husband's execution, moved to Moscow with 2 sons; entered Frolov Convent in Kiev (1758); wrote *Memoirs* (1810) about childhood, controversial marriage, and exile in Siberia, the 1st woman's autobiography in Russia.

DOLGORUKOVA, Catherine (1847–1922). See *Dolgorukova, Ekaterina*.

DOLGORUKOVA, Ekaterina (1847–1922). Russian princess and mistress, then wife, of Alexander II. Name variations: Catherine, Katherine, or Ekaterina Dolgorukova, Dolgorukaia, Dolgorukaja, Dolgoroukov, Dolgoruky; (after 1880) Princess Iurevskaia, Yuriesky, Yourievski, or Yourieffskaia; (nickname) Katia or Katya. Pronunciation: Dol-go-RUK-of-a. Born Ekaterina Mikhailovna Dolgorukova, Nov 2, 1847 (o.s.), in Moscow, Russia; died in Nice, France, Feb 15, 1922 (n.s.); dau. of Mikhail Mikhailovich Dolgorukov (noble landowner) and Vera Gavrilovna (Vishnevskaia) Dolgorukova; educated at Smolny Institute, 1860–65; m. Alexander II (1818–1881), tsar of Russia (r. 1855–1881), July 6, 1880 (o.s.); children: George Iurevskii (1872–1913, who m. Countess Alexandra Zarnekau); Olga Iurevskaia (1873–1925); Boris Iurevskii (b. 1876); Catherine Romanov (1878–1959). ❖ Was mistress of Alexander II (1866–80); had 4 children with him, whom Alexander legitimized by giving them surname Iurevskii (1874) and acknowledged his parentage by assigning them his patronymic of Alexandrovich; her long affair with the tsar—a man 30 years her senior—served to discredit the monarchy, divide the royal family, and isolate Alexander from many of his subjects; following death of Alexander's wife Marie of Hesse-Darmstadt, became his 2nd (morganatic) wife (1880); left Russia after tsar's assassination (1882); spent last 40 years of life in comfortable, self-imposed exile in France; published (under name Victor Laferté) *Alexandre II, Détails inédits sur sa vie intime et sa mort* (1882). ❖ See also Maurice Paléologue, *The Tragic Romance of Alexander II of Russia* (Hutchinson, 1927): Alexandre Tarsaïdzé, *Katia: Wife before God* (Macmillan, 1970); French film *Katia*, starring Danielle Darrieux (1938); and *Women in World History*.

DOLGORUKOVA, Marie (d. 1625). Empress of Russia. Name variations: Dolgoruki. Died of poison, Jan 7, 1625; became 1st wife of Mikhail also known as Michael III (1596–1645), tsar of Russia (r. 1613–1645), Sept 19, 1624.

DOLGORUKY, Catherine (1847–1922). *See Dolgorukova, Ekaterina.*

DOLLEY, Sarah Adamson (1829–1909). American physician. Name variations: Sarah Read Adamson Dolley; Sarah R.A. Dolley. Born Sarah Read Adamson, Mar 11, 1829, in Schuylkill Meeting, Chester Co., Pennsylvania; died Dec 27, 1909, in Rochester, NY; dau. of Mary (Corson) Adamson and Charles Adamson; apprenticed with uncle, Dr. Hiram Corson; graduate of Central Medical College in NY, 1851, the 3rd woman in US to earn a medical degree; m. Lester Clinton Dolley (professor of anatomy and surgery), June 9, 1852 (died 1872); children: 2, including physician Charles Sumner Dolley. ❖ The 1st woman intern at a hospital, began internship at Blockley Hospital in Philadelphia (1851); practiced medicine with husband for 20 years in Rochester, NY; successfully pushed NY state legislation to require a female staff physician at women's institutions; completed postgraduate training in Paris, France (1869–70); after husband's death (1872), taught at Woman's Medical College of Pennsylvania in Philadelphia (1873–74); studied in Paris at Hôpital des Enfants Malades (1875), as well as in Prague and Vienna; served as 1st president of Provident Dispensary Association in Rochester, NY, a dispensary for needy women and children (1886–94); helped found Practitioner's Society, the 1st incorporated society of women physicians (1887), which was renamed Blackwell Medical Society (1906) and fused with 4 medical associations to form Women's Medical Society of New York State (1907).

DOLLY, Jenny (1892–1941). American vaudevillian. Name variations: Yansci Dolly; Janszieka Deutsch; Dolly Sisters. Born Jancsi or Janszieka Deutsch, Oct 25, 1892, in Hungary; died June 1, 1941, in Hollywood, California (suicide); twin sister of Rosie Dolly (1893–1970); m. Jerome Schwartz (div.); m. Harry Fox (actor, div.); m. Bernard W. Vinissky. ❖ With twin sister, taken to NY as a child and made debut as the Dolly Sisters at Keith's Union Square Theater (1909), launching their internationally famous act; made Broadway debut in *The Echo* (1910); other plays include *Ziegfeld Follies, A Winsome Widow, The Merry Countess, Her Bridal Night, Oh Look* and *The Greenwich Village Follies*; apart from her sister, appeared with her 2nd husband, Harry Fox, in vaudeville for some time.

DOLLY, Rosie (1892–1970). American vaudevillian. Name variations: Roszieka, Roszika, or Roszicka Deutsch; Dolly Sisters. Born Roszika Deutsch, Oct 25, 1892, in Budapest, Hungary; died Feb 1, 1970, in New York, NY; twin sister of Jenny Dolly (1893–1941); m. Mortimer Davis (div.); m. 3rd husband Irving Netcher, also seen as Natcher (died 1953). ❖ With twin sister, had an internationally famous act as the Dolly Sisters (1911–27); made Broadway debut in *The Echo* (1910); other plays include *Ziegfeld Follies, A Winsome Widow, The Merry Countess, Her Bridal Night, Oh Look* and *The Greenwich Village Follies*; retired (1927).

DOLLY SISTERS.
See Dolly, Jenny.
See Dolly, Rosie.

DOLMA, Pachen (c. 1933–2002). Tibetan nun and freedom fighter. Name variations: Ani (which means nun) Pachen Dolma. Born Pachen Dolma, c. 1933, in Gonjo in Kham, eastern Tibet; died Feb 2, 2002, in the Tibetan exile community of Dharamsala, India; only surviving child of Pomda Gonor, chieftain of the Lemdha clan. ❖ When young, learned to ride horses and shoot guns; rebelled against an arranged marriage by fleeing on horseback to a monastery and becoming a Buddhist nun; after father died (1958), inherited the leadership of the Lemdha clan; abandoned the religious life to lead the clan in an armed resistance against the invading Chinese army; captured a year later (1959), spent 21 years in prison; released (Jan 1981), continued to fight for Tibetan independence; with the threat of rearrest, fled Tibet (1988); was encouraged to write her autobiography which resulted in *Sorrow Mountain: The Journey of a Tibetan Warrior Nun* (2000).

DOLORES (c. 1890–1975). English-born showgirl. Name variations: Dolores Wilkinson. Born Kathleen Mary Rose, c. 1890, in London, England; died Nov 7, 1975, in Paris, France; m. Tudor Wilkinson (art collector). ❖ Considered one of the most beautiful and most publicized women of the *Ziegfeld Follies*, began career as a model in London for Lucille, Lady Duff-Gordon; also appeared in *Sally;* moved to France on

marriage (1923); arrested for aiding the resistance, was incarcerated throughout WWII by the Nazis.

DOLORES, Mother (1938—). *See Hart, Dolores.*

DOLSON, Mildred (1918—). Canadian runner. Born Aug 13, 1918. ❖ At Berlin Olympics, won a bronze medal in 4 x 100-meter relay (1936).

DOMAN, Amanda (1977—). Australian softball player. Born Oct 24, 1977, in Gladstone, Queensland, Australia. ❖ Infielder, won a team silver medal at Athens Olympics (2004).

DOMANSKA, Janina (1912–1995). Polish-American children's writer and illustrator. Born 1912 in Warsaw, Poland; died Feb 2, 1995, in Naples, Florida; dau. of Wladyslaw Domanski (engineer) and Jadwiga (Muszynska) Domanska (writer); studied at Academy of Fine Arts in Warsaw; m. Jerzy Laskowski (writer), 1953. ❖ During WWII, interned in concentration camp in Western Poland, but rescued by a Polish doctor; immigrated to US (1952), becoming a citizen (1964); worked in NY as a textile designer; translated or wrote and self-illustrated over 22 books and illustrated over 20 books by others; works include *If All the Seas Were One Sea* (1971) and *King Krakus and the Dragon* (1979).

DOMBECK, Carola (1960—). East German gymnast. Born June 25, 1960. ❖ At Montreal Olympics, won a silver medal in vault and a bronze in team all-around (1976). ❖ See also *Women in World History.*

DOMENECH I ESCATE DE CANELLAS, Maria (1877–1952). Spanish short-story writer. Born 1877 in Spain; died 1952. ❖ Worked for reforms in women's education and founded union for Catalan working women; writings include *Contrallum* (1917) and *Confidències* (1946).

DOMERGUE, Faith (1924–1999). American actress. Born June 16, 1924, in New Orleans, Louisiana; died April 4, 1999, in Santa Barbara, California; m. Hugo Fregonese (director, div.). ❖ Once a protégé of Howard Hughes at RKO, films include *Duel at Silver Creek, Cult of the Cobra, It Came from Beneath the Sea, This Island Earth* and *Truck of Thunder.* ❖ See also memoir, *My Life with Howard Hughes* (1972).

DOMESTIC SCIENCE CLUB. *See Macy, Robin Lynn.*

DOMIN, Hilde (1909–2006). German-Jewish novelist and poet. Born July 27, 1909, in Köln, Germany; died Feb 22, 2006, in Germany; studied philosophy in Heidelberg; married Erwin Walter Palm, 1936. ❖ Fled Germany (1932) and completed studies in Florence, Italy (1935); worked as teacher and translator in Dominican Republic (1940–54) until return to Germany; writings, which explore experience of exile, include *Höhlenbilder, Gedichte 1951–1953* (1968), *Da zweite Paradies: Roman in Segmentem* (1968), *Abel steh auf: Gedichte, Prosa, Theorie* (1979), and *Die andalusische Katze* (1971, rev. 1980).

DOMINGUEZ, Josefa Ortiz de (c. 1768–1829). *See Ortíz de Dominguez, Josefa.*

DOMINGUEZ, María Alicia (1908—). Argentinean novelist and short-story writer. Name variations: Maria Alicia Dominguez. Born 1908 in Argentina. ❖ Wrote 30 volumes, including *La Rueca* (1925), *Crepúscules de oro* (1926), *Música de siglos* (1927), *Redención* (1933), *La cruz de la espada* (1942), *Campo de luna* (1944), *Al aire de tu vuelo* (1949), *Siete espadas* (1959) and *Las muchas aguas* (1967).

DOMITIA FAUSTINA (b. 147). Roman noblewoman. Born Nov 30, 147; dau. of Faustina II (130–175 CE) and Marcus Aurelius, Roman emperor (r. 161–180).

DOMITIA LEPIDA (c. 19 bce–?). Roman matron. Fl. at time of Nero; born c. 19 BCE; dau. of Antonia Major (39 BCE–?) and L. Domitius Ahenobarbus (d. 25 CE); sister of Gnaeus Domitius Ahenobarbus; m. M. Valerius Messalla Barbatus (both members of the dynastic Julio-Claudian family); children: Valeria Messalina (c. 23–48). ❖ The sister of Nero's deceased father Gnaeus Domitius Ahenobarbus, was also alleged to be Nero's lover. ❖ See also *Women in World History.*

DOMITIA LONGINA (fl. 80s CE). Roman noblewoman. Married Domitian (51–96), Roman emperor (r. 81–96 CE), in 70; children: all died young. ❖ Was involved in the successful plot to assassinate her husband, the emperor Domitian (96 CE).

DOMITIA LUCILLA. Roman noblewoman. Married M. Annius Verus; children: Marcus Aurelius; Annia Cornificia (who m. C. Ummidius Quadratus).

DOMITIA PAULINA I (fl. 76 CE). Roman noblewoman and mother of Hadrian. Born a Roman matron in Gades (Cadiz) on Atlantic coast 60 miles south of Italica; m. Publius Aelius Hadrianus Afer (d. 85 CE); children: Hadrian (76–138), Roman emperor (r. 117–138); Domitia Paulina II (fl. 80–100 CE).

DOMITIA PAULINA II (fl. 80–100 CE). Roman noblewoman. Fl. 80 to 100 CE; dau. of Domitia Paulina I (fl. 76 CE) and P. Aelius Hadrianus Afer; sister of Hadrian, Roman emperor (r. 117–138); m. L. Julius Ursus Servianus; children: Julia (who m. Cn. Pedanius Fuscus).

DOMITIEN, Elisabeth (1926—). Central African Republic politician. Name variations: Elizabeth Domitien. Born in Central African Republic in 1926. ❖ Africa's 1st female prime minister and the 1st black woman ruler of an independent state, joined the independence movement at 20 and became leader of women's organization for independence; became vice-president of the only legal party, Mouvement d'Evolution Sociale de l'Afrique Noire (Movement for the Social Evolution of Black Africa or MESAN, 1972); was vice-president of the Republic (1975); served as prime minister under Jean-Bédel Bokassa (1974–76) but was placed under house arrest when Bokassa declared himself emperor Bokassa I (1976); arrested after the coup that overthrew the brutal regime of Bokassa (1979), was briefly imprisoned and tried (1980); though not allowed to remain in politics, retained a high profile at home and abroad.

DOMITILLA. See Flavia Domitilla.

DOMNA, Julia (c. 170–217 CE). See Julia Domna.

DOMOLKY, Lidia (1936—). See Sakovitsne-Domolky, Lidia.

DON, Rachel (1866–1941). New Zealand religious and community worker. Name variations: Rachel Hull. Born Rachel Hull, July 23, 1866, at Hokitika, New Zealand; died Sept 4, 1941, in Dunedin, New Zealand; dau. of James Hull (musician and iron molder) and Mary Ann (Walters) Hull; m. William Rae Don, 1890. ❖ Active in Methodist and Presbyterian church work throughout her life; member of Women's Christian Temperance Union of New Zealand (WCTU); lectured, wrote letters, and contributed articles and cartoons to pamphlets on social reform. ❖ See also Dictionary of New Zealand Biography (Vol. 3).

DONADIO, Candida (1929–2001). American literary agent. Born 1929 in Brooklyn, NY; died of cancer, Jan 20, 2001, in Stonington, Connecticut; dau. of Italian immigrants; m. H.E.F. Donahue (critic, div.); m. Henry Bloomstein (writer, div.). ❖ Began publishing career as a secretary at McIntosh & McKee, then moved to Herb Jaffe Associates (1957), where she sold Joseph Heller's 1st novel, Catch-22, and Philip Roth's Goodbye, Columbus; joined Russell & Volkening (1961); had such clients as Thomas Pynchon, William Gaddis, Peter Matthiessen, and Mario Puzo; formed Donadio & Olson; retired (1995).

DONAHUE, Hessie (fl. 1892—). American boxer. Name variations: Hessie Converse. Born in Worcester, Massachusetts; m. Charles Converse (boxing-school owner). ❖ Made sporting history with a punch to the jaw of heavyweight-boxer John L. Sullivan that dropped him to the mat, where he remained unconscious for over a minute (1892), making her one of only two boxers to ever defeat Sullivan, the other being Gentleman Jim Corbett. ❖ See also Women in World History.

DONAHUE, Margaret (c. 1893–1978). American baseball executive. Born c. 1893; died Jan 30, 1978, at Crystal Lake, Illinois. ❖ Became clerk and typist for Chicago Cubs (1919); by 1926, as Cubs' corporate secretary, was major-league baseball's 1st woman executive; became Cubs' vice president (1950).

DONALD, Janet (c. 1819–1892). New Zealand church leader. Name variations: Janet Martin, Janet Main, Janet Mayne. Born Janet Martin, c. 1819–1825, in Wigtownshire, Scotland; died Mar 27, 1892, at Otahuhu, New Zealand; dau. of Andrew Martin (farmer) and Hannah Martin; m. John Main (or Mayne), 1835 (died before 1850); m. Andrew MacKenzie Donald (farmer), 1864; children: (1st m.) 2. ❖ Following death of 1st husband, immigrated to Auckland, New Zealand (1850); with 2nd husband, founded Baptist church at Otahuhu community in Auckland (1878). ❖ See also Dictionary of New Zealand Biography (Vol. 1).

DONALD, Mary Jane (c. 1855–1935). See Longstaff, Mary Jane.

DONALDA, Pauline (1882–1970). Canadian soprano. Born Pauline Lightstone in Montreal, Quebec, Canada, Mar 5, 1882; died in Montreal, Oct 22, 1970; studied with Edmont Duvernoy and Paul Lhérie, and with Clara Lichtenstein at the Royal Victoria College; studied in Paris on a grant from Donald Smith and adopted the name "Donalda" in his honor; m. Paul Seveilhac (French baritone), 1906; m. Mischa Léon (Danish tenor), 1918. ❖ Debuted in Nice (1904) and at Covent Garden (1905); debuted in Canada and US (1906); opened a teaching studio in Paris (1922); taught hundreds of students before returning to Montreal to teach (1937); during WWI, organized the Donalda Sunday Afternoon Concerts in Canada; founded the Opera Guild over which she presided (1942–69). Made an Officer of the Order of Canada (1967). ❖ See also Women in World History.

DONALDSON, Elizabeth (1883–1969). See Wallwork, Elizabeth.

DONALDSON, Margaret Caldwell (1926—). Scottish psychologist. Born in 1926 in Paisley, Scotland; Edinburgh University, BA in French and education, PhD in psychology; completed post-doctoral studies at Geneva and Harvard. ❖ Influential psychologist, was appointed to departments of Education and Psychology at Edinburgh and became professor of developmental psychology (1980); published texts on children's intellectual and linguistic skills which continue to be required reading for students of developmental psychology; covered new ground in A Study of Children's Thinking (1963) and Children's Minds (1978); reinterpreted work of Jean Piaget, paying closer attention to children's thought processes and emphasizing importance of social context; oversaw development of research in developmental psychology and psycholinguistics on extensive scale at Edinburgh University.

DONALDSON, Mary (1921–2003). English politician. Name variations: Dame Mary Donaldson; Lady Donaldson. Born Dorothy Mary Warwick, Aug 29, 1921 in Hampshire, England; died Oct 4, 2003, in Lymington, England; dau. of Reginald George Gale Warwick (ironmonger) and Dorothy Alice Warwick (schoolteacher); m. John Donaldson (lawyer, judge and master of the rolls), 1945; children: 1 son, 2 daughters. ❖ Was the 1st woman elected to the Court of Common Council (1966); became the 1st ever woman Lord Mayor of London (1983–84), a governmental entity established in 1192; also became the 1st woman alderman of the city (1975) and 1st woman sheriff of the city (1981); helped establish the cancer charity BACUP (British Association of Cancer United Patients).

DONALDSON, Mary (1972—). Danish crown princess. Name variations: Crown Princess Mary. Born Mary Elizabeth Donaldson, Feb 5, 1972, in Hobart, Tasmania; grew up in Taroona; dau. of Henrietta Clark Donaldson (college professor, died Nov 20, 1997) and John Dalgleish Donaldson (university chancellor); University of Tasmania, bachelors of commerce and law; m. Frederik (b. 1968), son of Margrethe II and crown prince of Denmark, May 14, 2004. ❖ Australian lawyer and marketing executive, met the prince of Denmark at the Sydney Olympics (2000).

DONALDSON, Norma (1928–1994). African-American stage, tv, and screen actress. Born July 8, 1928, in Harlem, NY; died Nov 22, 1994, in Los Angeles, California. ❖ Best remembered for her stage performance as Adelaide in the all-black revival of Guys and Dolls (1976); also appeared in Purlie, No Place to Be Somebody and Great White Hope; films include The Great White Hope, Nine to Five, Staying Alive and Poetic Justice.

DONALDSON, Viva (1893–1970). New Zealand teacher, nurse, and politician. Name variations: Viva Bedlington. Born Mar 12, 1893, in Auckland, New Zealand; died Aug 2, 1970, in Whangarei, New Zealand; dau. of Percy (surveyor) and Elizabeth Jane (Meldrum) Bedlington; m. James Donaldson (farmer, d. 1941), 1925. ❖ Taught in Whangarei district (1922–23, 1938–49); became obstetric nurse at Glasgow Royal Maternity and Women's Hospital (1923); taught in Canada and US in exchange program until 1925; served on local branch of Plunket Society (1920s); became 1st woman to sit on Whangarei Hospital Board (1927); appointed representative on Auckland Education Board (1929); member of board of governors, Whangarei High School (1929–47); was 1st president of Whangarei branch of Women's Division of New Zealand Farmers' Union (1934); became head teacher at Maunu Children's Health Camp (c. 1949); elected to Whangarei Borough Council (1950); became justice of peace (1954). Received British Empire medal (1956). ❖ See also Dictionary of New Zealand Biography (Vol. 4).

DONA MARIA (c. 1908–1938). See Bonita, Maria.

DONATA (fl. 11th century). Scottish princess. Dau. of Malcolm II MacKenneth (d. 1034), king of Scotland (r. 1005–1034); m. Sigurd the Stout, earl of Orkney, in 1088.

DONATELLA (fl. 1271). Italian painter. Name variations: Donella. Fl. around 1271 in Bologna. ❖ Was listed as a miniatrix, or female miniaturist, in a contract she and her husband (also a miniaturist) negotiated for the sale of their house (1271). ❖ See also *Women in World History.*

DONATH, Ursula (1931—). East German runner. Born July 30, 1931. ❖ At Rome Olympics, won a bronze medal in 800 meters (1960).

DONCHENKO, Natalya (1932—). Russian speedskater. Born 1932 in USSR. ❖ Won a silver medal for the 500 meters at Squaw Valley Olympics (1960); placed 4th at World championships for allround (1960).

DONEGAN, Dorothy (1922–1998). African-American jazz pianist. Born April 6, 1924, in Chicago, Illinois; died May 19, 1998, in Los Angeles, California; studied at Chicago Conservatory and Chicago Musical College; m. John T. McCain, 1948; m. twice more; children: John and Donavan. ❖ More a flamboyant performer than a recording artist, was best known for mixing swing, boogie-woogie, vaudeville, pop, ragtime and Bach in one set; at 14, was playing in the bars of Chicago's South Side; at 17, recorded for Bluebird label (1942); at 18, gave a concert at Orchestra Hall in Chicago, the 1st black performer to do so (1943). Inducted into Big Band and Jazz Hall of Fame (1998).

DONELLA (fl. 1271). See *Donatella.*

DONER, Kitty (1895–1988). American theatrical dancer. Born Sept 6, 1895, in Chicago, Illinois; died Aug 26, 1988. ❖ Trained primarily by parents—vaudeville performers Joe and Kitty—with whom she may have appeared on stage as child; performed in comedy acts *A Night in the Police Station* (1912) and *The Echo* (1914); made Broadway debut in *Ziegfeld Follies of 1914* and remained in NY thereafter; performed frequently and with great popularity at Winter Garden, in such shows as *Dancing Around* (1914), *Robinson Crusoe, Jr.* (1917) and *Sinbad* (1919); performed vaudeville act with brother at Palace and on tour to great success (starting 1920); served as ballet master of Roxy Theater for 15 years (starting 1930s).

DONESCU, Anghelache (1945—). Romanian equestrian. Born Oct 18, 1945, in Romania. ❖ At Moscow Olympics, won a bronze medal in team dressage (1980).

DONG FANGXIAO (1983—). Chinese gymnast. Born Jan 20, 1983, in Hebei, China. ❖ At World championships, won a bronze medal for team all-around (1999); at Sydney Olympics, won a bronze medal for team all-around (2000).

DONGHI, Beatrice Solinas (b. 1923). See *Solinas Donghi, Beatrice.*

DONGUZASHVILI, Tea (1976—). Russian judoka. Born June 4, 1976, in USSR. ❖ Placed 3rd at World championships for +78kg (2003); won a bronze medal for +78kg at Athens Olympics (2004).

DÖNHOFF, Marion, Countess (1909–2002). German journalist and publisher. Name variations: Doenhoff or Donhoff. Born Marion Hedda Ilse, Gräfin Dönhoff, at Schloss Friedrichstein near Loewenhagen, East Prussia, Dec 2, 1909; died Mar 11, 2002, in Hamburg, Germany; dau. of August Count Dönhoff (soldier and diplomat) and Maria Countess von Lepel Dönhoff (once lady-in-waiting to Augusta of Schleswig-Holstein); attended University of Frankfurt am Main; granted doctorate from University of Basel; never married. ❖ Editor-in-chief of *Die Zeit*, Germany's most influential liberal weekly newspaper, served for many years in leading positions; tangentially involved in plot to kill Hitler, was arrested and interrogated but not betrayed; escaped Germany (1945); joined staff of Hamburg's newspaper *Die Zeit* (1946); appointed associate editor in charge of the political section (1955), then general editor-in-chief (1968), then co-owner (1972); became the 1st woman in post-1945 Germany to address a national—indeed international—audience, playing a major role in the reorientation of the foreign policy of the German Federal Republic in the post-Adenauer era; was a major factor in the emergence of West Germany's Ostpolitik which transformed the political landscape of Europe in the 1970s; wrote *Foe into Friend: The Makers of the New Germany from Konrad Adenauer to Helmut Schmidt* (trans. by Gabriel Annan, 1982); is universally acknowledged to be the Grand Old Lady of German journalism. ❖ See also memoir, *Before the Storm: Memories of My Youth in Old Prussia* (Knopf, 1990); and *Women in World History.*

DONHOWE, Gwyda (1933–1988). American stage, tv, and screen actress. Born Oct 20, 1933, in Oak Park, Illinois; stabbed to death by husband who then leapt from the roof of their apartment building, Jan 15, 1988, in New York, NY; m. Norman Kean (theatrical producer),

1958. ❖ Made Broadway debut in *Separate Tables* (1957), followed by *The Shadow Box, Applause, The Flip Side, Paris is Out, Half a Sixpence* and *The Show Off;* films include *The Boston Strangler* and *The Happy Hooker;* on tv, appeared as Isa Fredericks on "Another World" (1981–82).

DONISTHORPE, G. Sheila (1898–1946). English playwright. Born Dec 17, 1898, in London, England; died Sept 1, 1946; m. Frank W. Donisthorpe. ❖ Began career as a pianist; plays include *Children to Bless You!, First Night, Guests at Lancaster Gate, Gaily We Set Out* and *Society Blues.*

DONKOVA, Yordanka (1961—). Bulgarian hurdler. Born Sept 28, 1961. ❖ Won an Olympic gold medal at Seoul (1988) and a bronze medal at Barcelona (1992), both in the 100-meter hurdles.

DONLEVY, Harriet Farley (1813–1907). See *Farley, Harriet.*

DONLON, Mary H. (1894–1977). American editor, lawyer and judge. Name variations: Mary Honor Donlon. Born 1894 in Utica, NY; died Mar 5, 1977, in Tucson, Arizona; dau. of Joseph M. and Mary (Coughlin) Donlon; attended Utica Free Academy; Cornell University, LLB, 1921. ❖ Edited three issues of *Cornell Law Quarterly* (Nov 1919, Jan 1920, Mar 1920); admitted to NY bar (1921); began law practice as partner at Burke and Burke in NY (1928); ran unsuccessfully for congressman-at-large from New York State (1940); active in state and national Republican campaigns, became (1st woman) head of a resolutions subcommittee at Republican National Convention (1944); received lifetime appointment as US Customs Court judge (1955), becoming 1st woman from NY appointed to federal bench.

DONNADIEU, Marguerite (1914–1996). See *Duras, Marguerite.*

DONNELL, Jeff (1921–1988). American actress. Born Jean Marie Donnell, July 10, 1921, South Windham, Maine; died April 11, 1988, in Hollywood, California; attended Yale Drama School; m. Aldo Ray (actor), 1954 (div. 1956); m. three more times. ❖ Played wife of George Gobel in tv series "The George Gobel Show" (1954–58); also appeared in "Matt Helm" series (1975–76) and as Stella Fields on "General Hospital"; appeared in over 50 films, including *My Sister Eileen, A Night to Remember, Tars and Spars, Mr. District Attorney, Skirts Ahoy!, Because You're Mine, Sweet Smell of Success* and *My Man Godfrey.*

DONNELLY, Dorothy (1880–1928). American actress, dramatist, and lyricist. Born Dorothy Agnes Donnelly in New York, NY, Jan 28, 1880; died Jan 3, 1928; dau. of Thomas Lester Donnelly (manager of the Grand Opera House, NY) and Sarah (Williams) Donnelly (actress). ❖ Made 1st appearance as an actress in New York (1898); portrayed Mme. Alvarez in *Soldiers of Fortune* (1901–02) and appeared in title roles of *Kathleen na Houlihan* (1902–03) and *Candida* (1903–04); other roles include Maja in *When We Dead Awaken* (1905), Ruth Jordan in *Little Gray Lady* (1906), Marion Manners in *The Movers* (1907), Jacqueline in *Madame X* (1911), and Anna Markle in *The Song of Songs* (1914); wrote such plays as *Flora Belle* (1916), *Fancy Free* (1918), *Forbidden* (1919) and *Poppy* (1923); best known for writing the book and lyrics to *Blossom Time* (also known as *Lilac Time*) as well as *The Student Prince*, a musical version of *Old Heidelberg* (1924). ❖ See also *Women in World History.*

DONNELLY, Euphrasia (b. 1906). American swimmer. Name variations: Fraze Bungard. Born June 6, 1906, in Indianapolis, Indiana; m. Bruce Ray Bungard, 1934. ❖ At Paris Olympics, won a gold medal in the 4 x 100-meter freestyle relay (1924).

DONNELLY, Geraldine (1965—). Canadian soccer player. Name variations: Geri Donnelly. Born July 9, 1965, in London, England. ❖ At age 8, moved with family to Port Moody, near Vancouver, British Columbia; midfielder; member of Canada's national team (1986–99), played in 72 international games; retired (1999). Named Canadian Player of the Year (1996); received Aubrey Sandford Award (2002).

DONNELLY, Lucy (1870–1948). American teacher. Born Lucy Martin Donnelly, Sept 18, 1870, in Ithaca, NY; died Aug 3, 1948, in Pointe-au-Pic, Quebec, Canada; dau. of Henry D. Donnelly (lawyer) and Abby Ann (Martin) Donnelly (schoolteacher). ❖ Became reader in essay work of English department at Bryn Mawr College (1896); with Helen Thomas (sister of M. Carey Thomas), taught course at Bryn Mawr in descriptive and narrative writing until 1903; served as professor and head of English department, undergraduate and graduate, at Bryn Mawr (1911–36).

DONNELLY, Patricia (c. 1920—). Miss America. Born Mary Patricia Donnelly c. 1920 in Durand, Michigan; married a newspaper editor;

children: 2, both journalists. ❖ Named Miss America (1939), representing Michigan; spent several years with husband Robin as a traveling editor for the Hearst newspaper syndicate. Throat cancer surgery left her unable to speak (1986); subsequent surgery restored voice (1987). ❖ See also Frank Deford, *There She Is* (Viking, 1971).

DONNELLY, Ruth (1896–1982). American comedic actress. Born May 17, 1896, in Trenton, New Jersey; died Nov 17, 1982, in New York, NY; m. Basil de Guichard. ❖ Made Broadway debut as a chorine and subsequently appeared in many George M. Cohan productions, as well as *The Crooked Square, Cheaper to Marry* and *No No Nanette,* among others; made film debut in *The Man Who Lost But Won* (1914), followed by over 90 more films, including *Footlight Parade, Mr. Deeds Goes to Town, Affairs of Annabel, Mr. Smith Goes to Washington, My Little Chickadee, This is the Army, The Bells of St. Mary's, The Snake Pit, The Spoilers* and *Little Miss Broadway.*

DONNER, Vyvyan (1895–1965). American filmmaker and fashion commentator. Born Dec 26, 1895; died June 27, 1965, in New York, NY. ❖ For 30 years, did fashion commentary for Fox Movietone News; produced and directed short subjects; retired (1963).

DONNERS, Wilhelmina (1974—). Dutch field-hockey player. Name variations: Myntje or Mijntje Donners. Born April 2, 1974, in Hertogenbosch, Netherlands. ❖ Won team bronze medals at Atlanta Olympics (1996) and Sydney Olympics (2000); won Champions Trophy (2000) and European championship (2003); forward, won team silver medal at Athens Olympics (2004). Named International Hockey Federation's Player of the Year (2003).

DONNERSMARCK, Countess von (1819–1884). *See Lachman, Therese.*

DONOHOE, Shelagh (1965—). American rower. Born Jan 22, 1965; graduate of University of Massachusetts-Lowell, 1988. ❖ At Barcelona Olympics, won a silver medal in coxless fours (1992); became a coach.

DONOVAN, Anne (1961—). American basketball player and coach. Born Nov 1, 1961, in Ridgewood, New Jersey; attended Old Dominion. ❖ Named to two Kodak All-American teams, the Naismith College Player of the Year, and Champion Player of the Year by the Women's Basketball Coaches Association (all 1983); won team gold medals at Los Angeles Olympics (1984) and Seoul Olympics (1988); was a coach at Old Dominion (1989–95) and East Carolina University (1995–97); coached the ABL Philadelphia Rage (1997–98), WNBA Indiana Fever (2000), and WNBA Charlotte Sting (2001–02), taking the Sting to the WNBA finals; became coach for WNBA Seattle Storm (2002); picked to coach the US 2006 World Championship and 2008 Olympic teams. Inducted into Basketball Hall of Fame (1995).

DONOVAN, Carrie (1928–2001). American fashion journalist. Born Carolyn Gertrude Amelia Donovan, Mar 22, 1928, in Lake Placid, NY; died Nov 12, 2001, in New York, NY; attended Parsons School of Design. ❖ Worked as a fashion editor and writer for *Vogue, Harper's Bazaar* and *New York Times Magazine* (1955–2001); with her over-sized black-rimmed glasses, had second career as a pitchwoman for Old Navy (1997), making 42 ads.

DONOVAN, Jean (1953—). American nun and martyr. Born April 10, 1953, in Westport, Connecticut; died Dec 2, 1980 in El Salvador; dau. of Raymond Donovan (executive engineer) and Patricia Donovan; attended Case Western Reserve University. ❖ Joined Maryknoll Sisters (1979); became Caritas coordinator for the diocesan mission program in El Salvador (July 1979), working in La Libertad, distributing food for the poor and the refugees; stood vigil at the coffin of the assassinated Archbishop Romero (Mar 1980); was slain by National Guardsmen in El Salvador, along with Ita Ford, Dorothy Kazel and Maura Clarke; portrayed by Melissa Gilbert in the tv-movie "Choices of the Heart" (1983).

DONSKA, Maria (1912–1996). Polish-born British pianist and piano teacher. Born in Lodz, Poland, Sept 3, 1912; died Dec 20, 1996; never married; lived with Leonora Speyer (dau. of violinist Leonora Speyer). ❖ A prodigy, began to play the piano at 4; gave 1st performance with an orchestra at 11; studied with Artur Schnabel in Berlin; with Schnabel, fled Berlin when Nazis seized power (1933); returned briefly to Poland to work for Radio Warsaw, but with rising anti-Semitism moved to London (none of her family would survive the Holocaust); began working for BBC by making a series of recordings for broadcasting; studied at Royal College of Music (1936–40), winning several gold medals; became popular with the public during WWII as a performer

at the National Gallery lunchtime concerts; taught piano to advanced pupils at Royal Conservatory of Music (1945–80); gave a much-lauded series of recitals dedicated to the complete Beethoven piano sonatas at London's Royal Festival Hall (1955). ❖ See also *Women in World History.*

DONUSZ, Eva (1967—). Hungarian kayaker. Born Sept 29, 1967. ❖ At Barcelona Olympics, won a bronze medal in K4 500 meters and a gold medal in K2 500 meters (1992).

DONY, Christina Mayne (1910–1995). English botanist. Name variations: Christina Mayne Goodman. Born Christina Mayne Goodman, 1910 in Selly Oak, Birmingham, England; died May 23, 1995; m. John Dony, 1962. ❖ Joined the Botanical Society of the British Isles (1948), serving as membership secretary (1964–74); studied local flora and often collaborated with husband; played hockey and was member of England's national team (3 times); joined Birmingham Natural History Society (1947) and eventually worked as a member of its council and as secretary of its botanical section (7 years); joined Wild Flower Society (1964); with husband, became honorary member of Botanical Society of the British Isles (1975), the 1st wife-husband team in which both members earned the honor; recorded a total of 2,532 flora species. With husband, wrote *The Bedfordshire Plant Atlas* (1976).

DOO, Unui (1873/75?–1940). New Zealand shopkeeper. Name variations: Chan Yau-nui. Born Chan Yau-nui, between 1873 and 1875, in Xinhui, Guangdong province, China; died Aug 18, 1940, in Auckland, New Zealand; dau. of Chan Doon Tai (farmer) and She Hoo Tai; m. Thomas Wong Doo, 1898 (remarried according to New Zealand law, 1915); children: 2 daughters, 3 sons. ❖ Immigrated to New Zealand with husband (1915); helped to manage grocery store that specialized in Chinese imports and served as cultural center for new immigrants. ❖ See also *Dictionary of New Zealand Biography* (Vol. 3).

DOOLITTLE, Hilda (1886–1961). American poet. Name variations: H.D. Born Hilda Doolittle in Bethlehem, Pennsylvania, Sept 10, 1886; died Sept 27, 1961, at Zurich, Switzerland; dau. of Charles Leander Doolittle (professor of astronomy) and Helen Eugenie (Woole) Doolittle; attended Bryn Mawr College, 1905–06; m. Richard Aldington, 1913 (div. 1938): children: Perdita (b. 1919). ❖ Major American poet of 1st half of 20th century who stands as a leading figure—some would say as the founder—of the Imagist movement in American and English poetic writing that flourished from 1912 through World War I; met Ezra Pound (1901), who was later responsible for her nom de plume of "H.D."; moved to Europe (1911); saw 1st important publication as a poet in *Poetry* (1913); became acquainted with Bryher (1918); separated from husband (1919); published collected poems (1925); underwent psychoanalysis with Sigmund Freud (1933–34); lived in England during World War II (1939–45); major works include *Sea Garden* (1916), *Palimpsest* (1926), *Hedylus* (1928), *Red Roses for Bronze* (1931), (war trilogy) *The Walls Do Not Fall* (1944), *Tribute to the Angels* (1945), *Tribute to Freud* (1956), *Bid Me to Live* (1960), *Helen in Egypt* (1961) and (autobiographical) *The Gift* (edited by Jane Augustine, U. of Florida, 1998). Received Brandeis University Creative Arts Award for Poetry (1959) and Award of Merit Medal for Poetry from American Academy of Arts and Letters (1961). ❖ See also Claire Buck, *H.D. and Freud: Bisexuality and a Feminine Discourse* (St. Martin, 1991); Rachel Blau Duplessis, *H.D.: The Career of That Struggle* (Harvester, 1986); Susan Stanford Friedman, *Psyche Reborn: The Emergence of H.D.* (Indiana U. Press, 1981); Janice S. Robinson, *H.D.: The Life and Work of an American Poet* (Houghton, 1982); and *Women in World History.*

DOORN, Marieke van (1960—). *See van doorn, Marieke.*

D'OR, Henrietta (1844–1886). Austrian-born ballet dancer. Born 1844 in Vienna, Austria; died Mar 1886 in Neuilly-sur-Seine, in France; dau. of Louis d'Or (famed ballet teacher). ❖ Trained early on by father in Vienna, made debut at Paris Opéra, partnered by Louis Mérante in *L'Uccelatore* by Lucien Petipa (1867); created principal female role in Petipa's *Le Roi Candaule* soon after (1868); debuted at Maryinsky Theater in Russia around same time, and is thought to have performed at Théâtre de la Monnaie in Brussels.

DORA D'ISTRIA (1828–1888). *See Chica, Elena.*

DORADO GOMEZ, Natalia (1967—). Spanish field-hockey player. Born Feb 25, 1967. ❖ At Barcelona Olympics, won a gold medal in team competition (1992).

DORALDINA (c. 1893–c. 1925). American dancer. Born c. 1893 probably in Chicago, Illinois; died c. 1925. ❖ Studied classical and folk dance with Raphael Vega in Barcelona, where she later performed at Teatro Principal; appeared at Ned Wayburn's Reisenweber's Café in New York City (1916), where she performed specialty dances, including hula, larombe shiver, and harem dance; performed same dances on Keith Circuit, in vaudeville, and on Broadway in such shows as *Step This Way* (1916), *The Red Dawn* (1919) and *Frivolities of 1920;* appeared in early silent films, usually as South Sea islander, including in *The Naulahka* (1918) and *The Passion Fruit* (1921); was one of the 1st female performers to purchase the club in which she appeared, The Montmartre in New York City; helped introduce the hula dance into ethnic dance repertory.

DORAN, Ann (1911–2000). American character actress. Name variations: Ann Lee Doran. Born July 28, 1911, in Amarillo, Texas; died Sept 19, 2000, in Carmichael, California; dau. of Rose Allen (1885–1977, actress). ❖ Made film debut in *Charlie Chan in London* (1934); ultimately appeared in over 1,000 tv shows and 500 films, many uncredited, including *Way Down East, Rio Grande, Blondie, The Green Hornet* (serial), *Mr. Smith Goes to Washington, Meet John Doe, Penny Serenade, My Sister Eileen, The Snake Pit, The Fountainhead, The High and the Mighty, Them, Rebel Without a Cause, A Summer Place* and *The First Monday in October.*

DORCAS (fl. 37 CE). Biblical woman. Name variations: called Tabitha by the Jews. Fl. around 37 CE in Joppa, a Mediterranean seaport town; Dorcas means *gazelle* in Greek. ❖ A Christian widow, sewed and made clothes for the poor; upon her death, grieving friends sent for Jesus' disciple Peter, who laid his hands on her and restored her to life.

DORCHESTER, countess of. *See Sedley, Catharine.*

DÖRDELMANN, Sylvia (1970—). *See Doerdelmann, Sylvia.*

DOREMUS, Sarah Platt (1802–1877). American philanthropist. Born Sarah Platt Haines, Aug 3, 1802, in New York, NY; died Jan 22, 1877, in New York, NY; dau. of Elias Haines (businessman) and Mary Ogden; m. Thomas Doremus, Sept 11, 1821; children: 8 daughters, 1 son, and a number of adoptees. ❖ Became active in benevolent activities for the Greeks suffering under Turkish control (1828); became president of a society to promote the Grande Ligne Mission in Canada, organized and run by Henrietta Feller (1835); began working in the woman's ward of New York City Prison (1840) which led to the formation of the Woman's Prison Association, an organization dedicated to aid recently released women; appointed manager of the City and Tract Society, an organization devoted to evangelizing among the poor (1841), and joined the City Bible Society of New York (1849) which provided them with Bibles; one of the founders of the House and School on Industry (1850), served as president for 10 years and as manager for 8; assisted in the establishment of the Nursery and Child's Hospital of New York State (1855) and during Civil War, helped distribute supplies to hospitals in and around NY. ❖ See also *Women in World History.*

DORFMANN, Ania (1899–1984). Russian-American pianist. Born in Odessa, Russia, July 9, 1899; died in New York, NY, April 21, 1984. ❖ Made 1st public appearance before WWI as an accompanist to Jascha Heifetz; at 12, enrolled at Paris Conservatoire where she studied with Isidor Philipp; left Russia (1920), touring Europe as a concert artist; settled in US (1936) and performed with Arturo Toscanini and his NBC Symphony Orchestra (1939); in last decades of career, taught at Juilliard; became the only woman to record a concerto with Arturo Toscanini and his NBC Symphony, in this case the Beethoven 1st Piano Concerto (1945); also recorded the complete Songs without Words of Felix Mendelssohn. ❖ See also *Women in World History.*

DORFMEISTER, Michaela (1973—). Austrian Alpine skier. Born Mar 25, 1973, in Vienna, Austria. ❖ Began competing on World Cup tour (1992); won a silver medal for the super-G at Nagano Olympics (1998); at World championships, won a silver medal in the downhill and bronze in the super-G (1999) and gold medals in the downhill (2001) and the super-G (2003); won World Cup overall title (2002); won gold medals for downhill and Super–G at Torino Olympics (2006).

DORIA, Clara (1844–1931). *See Rogers, Clara Kathleen.*

DORIA SHAFIK (1908–1975). *See Shafik, Doria.*

DORIO, Gabriella (1957—). Italian runner. Born June 27, 1957, in Italy. ❖ At Los Angeles Olympics, won a gold medal in 1,500 meters (1984).

DORION, Marie (c. 1790–1850). Native American explorer. Name variations: Marie Aioe, Ayvoise, L'Aguivoise; Marie Iowa; Marie Toupin. Born c. 1790 into Iowa tribe; died Sept 5, 1850, near Salem, Oregon; m. Jean Baptiste Toupin, July 19, 1841; children: (with Pierre Dorian or D'Orion) 3 sons; (with man named Venier) daughter (b. around 1819); (with Toupin) son (b. around 1825) and daughter (b. around 1827). ❖ With companion Pierre Dorion, traveled 3,500 miles from St. Louis, MO, to Astoria, OR, the only woman on the famed overland expedition, and gave birth during the journey (Mar 1811–Feb 1812); accompanied a hunting expedition 330 miles east of Astoria (July 1813); with sons, escaped Indian attacks which killed Pierre and all expedition members (Jan 1814); headed for Columbia River with sons, before being trapped by snowstorm; built hut and killed a horse for food, surviving 53 days, then set out when food ran out, becoming snow blind for 3 days before finding help; lived with a man named Venier in Fort Okanogan, Washington (1810s); began relationship with Toupin in Fort Nez Percé, WA (1820s) and lived with him on farm near Salem, OR (1841–50). Was praised in Washington Irving's *Astoria* (1836).

DORLÉAC, Françoise (1942–1967). French actress. Name variations: Francoise Dorleac. Born in Paris, France, Mar 21, 1942 (some sources cite 1941); died in Nice, France, 1967; dau. of Maurice and Renée (Deneuve) Dorléac (both actors); older sister of Catherine Deneuve (actress). ❖ Made screen debut in *Mensonges* 1959, after a short stage career; was at the height of a brilliant international career as a leading lady when she was killed in a fiery automobile crash in Nice, France; at time of death, had just finished shooting *Les Demoiselles de Rochefort* (*The Young Girls of Rochefort*) with sister Catherine Deneuve, the 4th film they had made together; other films include *La Fille aux Yeux d'Or* (*The Girl with the Golden Eyes,* 1961), *Ce Soir ou Jamais* (1961), *Le Jeu de la Vérité* (1961), *Tout l'Or du Monde* (1961), *Arsène Lupin contre Arsène Lupin* (1962), *L'Homme de Rio* (*That Man from Rio,* 1964), *La Chasse a L'Homme* (*Male Hunt,* 1964), *Genghis Khan* (1965), *Where the Spies Are* (1966), *Cul-de-sac* (1966) and *Billion Dollar Brain* (1967).

DORLÉAC, Sylvie (1943—). *See Deneuve, Catherine.*

DORMAN, Loretta (1963—). Australian field-hockey player. Born July 23, 1963. ❖ At Seoul Olympics, won a gold medal in team competition (1988).

DORMAN, Sonya (1924—). American science-fiction writer and poet. Name variations: Sonya Dorman Hess; Sonya Hess. Born Sonya Hess, April 6, 1924; attended agricultural college; married, 1950 (sep.); children: 1 daughter. ❖ Works include novel *Planet Patrol* (1978), and poetry collections *Poems* (1970), *Stretching Fence* (1975), *A Paper Raincoat* (1975), *The Far Traveler* (1980), and *Palace of Earth* (1984); published short stories in magazines and collections. Received Rhysling Award for poetry (1978) and Nebula Award.

D'ORME, Aileen (1877–1939). English actress and singer. Born Feb 14, 1877, in London, England; died Aug 1939; m. George Earle Baker, 1903. ❖ Made stage debut in London in *The Yashmak* (1897), followed by *A Royal Star, The Coquette, San Toy* and *A Country Girl;* retired from the stage on marriage, then returned to score a significant triumph as Alcolom in *Chu Chin Chow* (1916).

DORMER, Daisy (1889–1947). English comedian. Born Jan 16, 1889, in Portsmouth, England; died Sept 13, 1947. ❖ Appeared in major music halls throughout England, introducing such songs as "I'm going I'm Gone," "I Want a Girl," "Mister Johnson," "I Wouldn't Leave My Little Wooden Hut for You," "I Do Like You Susie," and "I Wish I Lived Next Door to You"; appeared in the film *City of Beautiful Nonsense.*

DORMON, Carrie (1888–1971). American botanist, ecologist and writer. Name variations: Caroline Dormon. Born Caroline Coroneos Dormon at Briarwood estate, Louisiana, July 19, 1888; died in Saline, Louisiana, Nov 21, 1971; dau. of James L. Dormon (lawyer and amateur naturalist, died 1909) and Caroline (Trotti) Dormon (writer, died 1907); sister of Virginia Dormon; graduate of Judson College, 1907; never married. ❖ Regarded by many as the foremost authority on wild flowers in southern US, moved with sister to Briarwood, the family home (1918), which would later be recognized by American Horticultural Society as "a sanctuary for the flora of the south"; appointed state chair of conservation for Louisiana Federation of Women's Clubs; gave lectures and wrote newspaper articles, calling for the preservation of a virgin tract of the Kisatchie, called Odom's Falls; with sister Virginia, crusaded to preserve the Kisatchie, resulting in Federal government purchasing 75,589 acres of cutover land for the Kisatchie National Forest (1930); was one of the 1st three women to be elected an associate member of Society of American Foresters; was the only female member of De Soto Commission established by US Congress (1935); published 1st book, *Wild Flowers of Louisiana* (1934), followed by *Flowers Native to the Deep South* (1958), *Natives Preferred* (1965), probably her most popular book, *Southern Indian Boy* (1967), and *Bird Talk* (1969). ❖ See also Fran Holman Johnson, *The Gift of the Wild Things: The Life of Caroline Dormon* (1990); and *Women in World History*.

DORN, Erna (1912–1953). German war criminal. Name variations: (forged identity) Erna Brüser née Scheffler. Born Erna Kaminski, 1912, in Königsberg, East Prussia (modern-day Kaliningrad, Russia); executed in Halle, Oct 1, 1953; dau. of Arthur Kaminski (chief of the Gestapo in Königsberg); m. Erich Dorn (in Nazi SS); children: 2. ❖ Concentration camp guard at Ravensbrück, who was able to avoid punishment for her activities in the Nazi period until 1951 when she was tried and convicted of war crimes in East Germany; under circumstances that are still unclear, was freed from prison during the uprising of June 17, 1953, but recaptured and sentenced to death. ❖ See also *Women in World History*.

DORN, Gertrud (b. 1912). *See Fussenegger, Gertrud.*

DORNEMANN, Luise (1901–1992). German writer and reformer. Name variations: during her years in the United Kingdom, 1936–1947, spelled her name Louise Dornemann. Born in Aurich, Ostfriesland, Feb 23, 1901; died Jan 17, 1992; dau. of a judicial official. ❖ Active in the women's movement during the Weimar Republic, joined the Communist Party of Germany (KPD, 1928); became chair of Unified Organization for Proletarian Sexual Reform and Protection of Mothers (1932); immigrated to United Kingdom (1936); in London, was a member of the Communist-led Allies Inside Germany Council; following WWII, moved to Soviet Occupation Zone (SBZ, 1947) and joined the Socialist Unity Party; became a leader of the state-sponsored women's organization in the German Democratic Republic; wrote a number of well-received history books intended for a broad audience, including biographies of Jenny Marx and Clara Zetkin. ❖ See also *Women in World History*.

DORNEY, Hannah or Joanna (1829–1898). *See Barron, Hannah Ward.*

DORNIK, Polona (1962—). Yugoslavian basketball player. Born Nov 20, 1962. ❖ At Seoul Olympics, won a silver medal in team competition (1988).

DORO, Marie (1882–1956). American actress. Born Marie K. Steward, May 25, 1882, in Duncannon, Pennsylvania; died Oct 9, 1956, in New York, NY; m. Elliot Dexter (actor), 1915 (div.). ❖ Stage and silent-screen star, starred on Broadway in productions of Charles Frohman; films include *Oliver Twist, Common Ground, Diplomacy, The Morals of Marcus, Sally Bishop, The Wood Nymph, The Heart of Nora Flynn, Lost and Won* and *Forget-Me-Nots*.

DORODNOVA, Oksana (1974—). Russian rower. Name variations: Oxana Dorodnova. Born April 14, 1974, in USSR. ❖ Won a bronze medal for quadruple sculls at Sydney Olympics (2000).

DOROTHEA, Princess of Lieven (1785–1857). Russian diplomat. Name variations: Dariya Khristoforovna; Sibyl of Europe. Born Dorothea von Benkendorff in Latvia in 1785 (some sources cite 1784); died 1857; m. Khristofor Andreevich de Lieven, also known as Prince Christoph of Lieven, in 1800 (died 1839). ❖ At an early age, married Prince Christoph of Lieven, ambassador at court of Prussia in Berlin (1811–12); with her penchant for dealing with public affairs combined with her eminent social amenities, was in control of the main springs of political action in Berlin and later succeeded in shaping the opinions of the court of St. Petersburg; when husband was transferred to Britain's court of St. James (1812–34), held a leading position in the highest social and political circles of England; after husband's death, took up residence in Paris (1839–57), where her house became a favorite resort of the chief political, literary, artistic, and social celebrities of that city.

DOROTHEA FREDERICA OF BRANDENBURG-SCHWEDT (1736–1798). *See Sophia Dorothea of Brandenburg.*

DOROTHEA HEDWIG OF BRUNSWICK-WOLFENBUTTEL (1587–1609). Princess of Anhalt-Zerbst. Born Feb 3, 1587; died Oct 16, 1609; dau. of Dorothea of Saxony (1563–1587) and Henry Julius, duke of Brunswick (r. 1589–1613); m. Rudolf, prince of Anhalt-Zerbst, Dec 29, 1605.

DOROTHEA OF BAVARIA (1920—). Member of the Tuscan Branch of the House of Habsburg-Lorraine. Born 1920; m. Gottfried also known as Godfrey (1902–1984); children: Leopold Franz also known as Leopold Francis (b. 1942) and 3 daughters.

DOROTHEA OF BRANDENBURG (1430–1495). Queen of Norway, Denmark, and Sweden. Name variations: Hohenzollern. Born 1430; died Nov 10 or 25, 1495, at Kalundborg, Denmark; dau. of John III the Alchemist, margrave of Brandenburg, and Barbara of Saxe-Wittenberg (c. 1405–1465); sister of Barbara of Brandenburg (1422–1481); m. Christopher of Bavaria also known as Christopher III (1416–1448), king of Norway and Denmark and Sweden (r. 1439–1448), Sept 12, 1445; m. Christian I (1426–1481), king of Denmark, Norway, and Sweden (r. 1448–1481), Oct 26 or 28, 1449; children: (2nd m.) Olaf (1450–1451); Canute (1451–1455); John I, also known as Hans (1455–1513), king of Denmark and Norway (r. 1481–1513); Margaret of Denmark (1456–1486, who m. James III of Scotland); Frederik or Frederik I (1471–1533), king of Norway and Denmark (r. 1523–1533). ❖ At 15, married Christopher III, king of Norway, Denmark, and Sweden; widowed at 18, agreed to marry Count Christian of Oldenburg (Christian I), impoverished heir to crowns of Denmark and Norway, in exchange for his election to the throne.

DOROTHEA OF BRANDENBURG (1446–1519). Duchess of Saxe-Lauenburg. Name variations: Dorothea von Brandenburg. Born 1446; died in Mar 1519; dau. of Catherine of Saxony (1421–1476) and Frederick II the Iron (1413–1471), elector of Brandenburg (r. 1440–1470, abdicated); m. John V of Saxe-Lauenburg, duke of Saxe-Lauenburg, Feb 12, 1464; children: Magnus of Saxe-Lauenburg, duke of Saxe-Lauenburg.

DOROTHEA OF DENMARK (1520–1580). Electress Palatine. Name variations: Dorothea Oldenburg. Born Nov 10, 1520; died Sept 20, 1580; dau. of Christian II (1481–1559), king of Norway and Denmark (r. 1513–1523), and Elisabeth of Habsburg (1501–1526); m. Frederick II (1482–1556), elector Palatine (r. 1544–1556), Sept 26, 1535.

DOROTHEA OF DENMARK (1528–1575). Danish princess. Name variations: Dorothea Oldenburg. Born 1528; died Nov 11, 1575; dau. of Sophia of Pomerania (1498–1568) and Frederik or Frederick I (1471–1533), king of Denmark and Norway (r. 1523–1533); m. Christof von Mecklenburg, Oct 27, 1573.

DOROTHEA OF SAXE-LAUENBURG (1511–1571). Queen of Norway and Denmark. Name variations: Lüneburg or Luneburg. Born July 9, 1511; died Oct 7, 1571, in Sonderburg; dau. of Magnus, duke of Saxe-Lauenburg, and Catherine of Brunswick-Wolfenbuttel (1488–1563); m. Christian III (1503–1559), king of Norway and Denmark (r. 1534–1559), Oct 29, 1525; children: Anna of Denmark (1532–1585); Frederick II, king of Denmark and Norway (r. 1559–1588); Magnus, king of Livonia; Hans also known as Johann or John (1545–1622), duke of Holstein-Sonderburg; Dorothy of Denmark (1546–1617).

DOROTHEA OF SAXONY (1563–1587). Princess of Saxony. Born Oct 4, 1563; died Feb 13, 1587; dau. of Anna of Denmark (1532–1585) and Augustus (1526–1586), elector of Saxony; m. Heinrich Julius also known as Henry Julius, duke of Brunswick (r. 1589–1613), Sept 26, 1585; children: Dorothea Hedwig of Brunswick-Wolfenbuttel (1587–1609, who m. Rudolf, prince of Anhalt-Zerbst). Henry Julius' 2nd wife was Elizabeth of Denmark (1573–1626).

DOROTHEA OLDENBURG (1504–1547). Duchess of Prussia. Born Aug 1, 1504; died April 11, 1547; dau. of Anna of Brandenburg (1487–1514) and Frederick I, king of Norway and Denmark (r. 1523–1533); became 1st wife of Albert (1490–1568), duke of Prussia (r. 1525–1568), July 1, 1526; children: Anna Sophia of Prussia (1527–1591). Albert's 2nd wife was Anne Marie of Brunswick (1532–1568).

DOROTHY OF DENMARK (1546–1617). Duchess of Luneburg. Born June 9, 1546; died Jan 6, 1617; dau. of Dorothea of Saxe-Lauenburg (1511–1571) and Christian III (1503–1559), king of Norway and Denmark (r. 1534–1559); m. William the Younger (1535–1592), duke of Luneburg (1559–1592), Oct 12, 1561; children: Ernest II (b. 1564), duke of Brunswick; Christian (b. 1566), duke of Brunswick; Augustus the Elder (b. 1568), duke of Brunswick; Frederick (b. 1574), duke of Brunswick; George (b. 1582), duke of Brunswick; Sibylle of Brunswick-Luneburg (1584–1652).

DORR, Julia Caroline (1825–1913). American author. Name variations: (pseudonym) Caroline Thomas. Born Julia Caroline Ripley, Feb 13,

1825, in Charleston, South Carolina; died Jan 18, 1913, in Rutland, Vermont; m. Seneca M. Dorr, 1847. ❖ Wrote the novels *Farmingdale* (1854), *Lanmere* (1856), *Sybil Huntington* (1869), and *Expiation* (1873); also wrote an advice book, *Bride and Bridegroom* (1873), and at least 10 volumes of widely popular verse, including *Poems* (1872), *Afternoon Songs* (1885), *Beyond the Sunset: Latest Poems* (1909) and *Last Poems* (1913).

DORR, Rheta Childe (1866–1948). American journalist and feminist. Born Rheta Louise Childe on Nov 2, 1866, in Omaha, Nebraska; died Aug 8, 1948, in New Britain, Pennsylvania; dau. of Edward Payson Childe (druggist and probate judge) and Lucie (Mitchell) Childe (homemaker); attended University of Nebraska, 1884–85; m. John Pixley Dorr (businessman), 1892 (div. 1898); children: son Julian Childe Dorr (1896–1936). ❖ Chronicler and commentator who investigated conditions of women and children in industry and society, and participated in the women's suffrage movement; worked as reporter for New York *Evening Post* (1902–06); wrote for *Everybody's* magazine (1907–09), including a series of articles about the effects of industrialization on women; wrote for *Hampton's* (1910–12), a more aggressive reform magazine; compiled a number of her articles for *Hampton's* into *What Eight Million Women Want* (1910); became editor of National Women's Party newspaper, *The Suffragist* (1914); published *Inside the Russian Revolution* (1917), *A Soldier's Mother in France* (1918) and *Susan B. Anthony* (1928). ❖ See also autobiography, *A Woman of Fifty* (1924); and *Women in World History*.

DÖRRE, Katrin (1961—). East German long-distance runner. Name variations: Katrin Doerre. Born Oct 1961. ❖ At Seoul Olympics, won a bronze medal in the marathon (1988).

DÖRRIE, Doris (1955—). German director, screenwriter and short-story writer. Name variations: Doris Dorrie or Doerrie. Born May 26, 1955, in Hannover, Lower Saxony, Germany; studied drama at University of the Pacific in Stockton, California; attended New School for Social Research in NY, 1973–75; studied at Hochschule für Fernsehen und Film in Munich; m. Helge Weindler. ❖ Made 1st feature, *Straight through the Heart* (1983); came to international prominence with the film *Männer* (*Men*, 1985), the 1st major box-office success for a female director from Germany since the 1960s; other films include *Max und Sandy* (1978), *Paradies* (1986), *Ich und Er* (1988), *Geld* (1989), *Love in Germany* (1989), *Happy Birthday, Türke!* (1992), *Bin ich Schön* (*Am I Beautiful*, 1998), *Erleuchtung garantiert* (*Enlightenment Guaranteed*, 2000) and *Der Fischer und seine Frau* (2005); has also written novels and published 7 vols. of short stories.

DÖRRIES, Jana (1975—). See Doerries, Jana.

DORS, Diana (1931–1984). British actress. Born Diana Fluck in Swindon, Wiltshire, Oct 23, 1931; died in Windsor, Berkshire, England, May 4, 1984; dau. of Albert Edward Sidney Fluck and Winifred Maud Mary (Payne) Fluck; attended London Academy of Dramatic Art; m. Dennis Hamilton (her manager), 1951 (div. 1957); m. Dickie Dawson (British comedian), 1959 (div. 1967); m. Alan Lake (British actor), 1968 (committed suicide, Oct 10, 1984); children: (1st m.) Mark, Gary; (3rd m.) Jason. ❖ Presented by the media as "Britain's answer to Marilyn Monroe," prevailed over personal problems to become well known and admired; made film debut in thriller *The Shop at Sly Corner* (1946); following appearances in formulaic comedies, set out to become a star with help of 1st husband, with such publicity stunts as surfacing at Venice Film Festival wearing a mink bikini (1955); gave best performance in films *A Kid for Two Farthings* (1955) and *Yield to the Night* (1956); marriage collapsed in a blaze of publicity (1957); sold colorful memoirs to British tabloid *News of the World* (1960) and was denounced by archbishop of Canterbury; revived career, appearing on stage at London's Royal Court in *Three Months Gone* (1970); made favorable impression in film *Deep End* (1970); starred on tv series "Queenie's Castle"; appeared as Jocasta in *Oedipus* at Chichester Festival (1974); became a popular guest on countless tv shows; fighting her own battle with weight, hosted a dieting series on breakfast tv and gave advice to the lovelorn on "Good Morning Britain"; other films include *Lady Godiva Rides Again* (1951), *I Married a Woman* (1958), *Scent of Mystery* (1960), *There's a Girl in My Soup* (1970), *Hannie Caulder* (1971), *Theatre of Blood* (1973) and *Steaming* (1984); writings include *Swingin' Dors* (1960), *For Adults Only* (1978), *Behind Closed Dors* (1979) and *Dors by Diana* (1981). ❖ See also Flory and Walne, *Diana Dors: Only a Whisper Away* (Javelin, 1988); and *Women in World History*.

D'ORSAY, Fifi (1904–1983). Canadian actress. Born Yvonne Lussier, April 16, 1904, in Montreal, Canada; died Dec 2, 1983, in Woodland Hills, California; m. Maurice Hill. ❖ Began career on Broadway and in vaudeville; debuted in film opposite Will Rogers in *They Had to See Paris* (1929); with trademark "ooh-la-la" and often typecast as a French "floozy," made 23 films, including *On the Level, Those Three French Girls, Girl from Calgary, The Gangster, What a Way to Go!, Just Imagine, Silk Stockings, Wild and Wonderful* and *Assignment to Kill;* lectured on religion.

DORSET, countess of (1590–1676). See Clifford, Anne.

DORSET, marquise of.
See Holland, Anne (d. 1474).
See Wotton, Margaret.

DORSEY, Lucy (1855–1924). See Iams, Lucy.

DORSEY, Sarah Anne (1829–1879). American prose writer. Born in Natchez, Mississippi, Feb 16, 1829; died in New Orleans, Louisiana, July 4, 1879; owned a plantation called Beauvoir, just outside Biloxi, Mississippi. ❖ A linguist and student of Sanskrit, wrote *Lucia Dare* (1867), *Panola: A Tale of Louisiana* (1877), *Atalie* and *Agnes Graham;* was amanuensis to Jefferson Davis in the preparation of his *Rise and Fall of the Confederate Government.* ❖ See also *Women in World History*.

DORSEY, Susan Miller (1857–1946). American educator. Name variations: Susan Almira Miller Dorsey. Born Susan Almira Miller, Feb 16, 1857, in Penn Yan, NY; died Feb 5, 1946, in Los Angeles, California. ❖ Worked as a teacher and social-welfare worker; served as vice principal at Los Angeles High School (1902–13); appointed assistant superintendent of the LA school system (1913) and superintendent (1920); to honor her 40 years in education, named honorary life president, National Education Association (1934). Susan Miller Dorsey High School (Los Angeles, CA) and Susan Miller Dorsey Hall at Scripps College (Claremont, CA) named in her honor.

DORSTE, Marguerite (d. 1996). See Ganser, Marge.

DORVAL, Marie (1798–1849). French actress. Born Marie Thomase Amélie Delaunay, Jan 6, 1798, in Lorient, France; died May 20, 1849 in Paris, France; dau. of Marie Bourdais (actress); m. Allan Dorval (actor and dance-master), 1813 (died); m. M. Merle (theater director and critic); children: Gabrielle Dorval (b. 1816), Louise Dorval (b. 1817), Caroline Piccini. ❖ Famed for her charm, emotive acting and turbulent love-life, made stage debut at 4; abandoned by father, an actor named Delaunay, in Bourges (1808), was orphaned when mother died in Tours (1813); at 16, married Dorval (1813); moved with family to Paris and began acting in Theater of Saint Martin's (1818), remaining there for 10 years; after husband died, had romantic liaison with composer Piccini and gave birth to daughter Caroline (1821); played role of Thérèse in *Two Convicts* to great acclaim (1822) and was dubbed "First Actress of Paris" after enormous success in *Thirty Years, or the Life of a Player* which also starred Frédérick Lemaître (1827); became involved with Lemaître but left him to marry M. Merle; starred in Alexandre Dumas' play *Antony* (1831), the 1st of many successful collaborations; had affair with Dumas, then became mistress of playwright Alfred de Vigny (1832–38), starring in many of his works, including *Quitte Pour La Peur* (1833) and *Chatterton;* began working in French comedy (1834); is thought to have had love affair with writer George Sand who wrote for Dorval the unsuccessful play *Cosima;* ended relationship with de Vigny with much bitterness, leaving him for Jules Sandeau, former lover of Sand; moved on to work at Odéon (1836–37) and then Gymnasium (1839), only to return to Odéon (1842) to perform in such works as *Lucrèce, Phedre, The Marriage of the Barber* and *Countess of Altemberg;* got involved with comic actor René Luguet who would become husband of daughter Caroline (1842); after giving last great performance at Odéon in *Marie-Jeanne, Woman of the People* (1845); experienced health problems; died in poverty. ❖ See also (in French) Alexandre Dumas, *Les Morts Von Vite* (1861); Anna Gaylor, *Marie Dorval, grandeur et misère d'une actrice romantique* (Flammarion, 1989).

DORZIAT, Gabrielle (1886–1979). French actress. Born Gabrielle Sigrist Moppert, Jan 15, 1886, in Epernay, Marne, France; died Nov 30, 1979 in Biarritz; educated in Paris; studied for the stage with Mlle A. Gerlaut and at Paris Conservatoire. ❖ Made stage debut at Parc Theatre in Brussels as Marianne in Molière's *L'Avare* (1900); in Paris, performed at Gymnase (1901–05), Vaudeville (1905–07), and Sarah Bernhardt Theatre, portraying Yvonne de Chazeau in *Maîtresse de Piano* (1907); made London debut in title role of *Antoinette Sabrier* (1904) and NY debut as Marina de Dasetta in *The Hawk* (1914); generally typed as the intimidating aristocrat, appeared in approximately 70 French, English, and American films, including *L'Infante a la Rose* (1922), *Samson* (1936), *Le Mensonge de Nina Petrovna* (1937), *La Fin du Jour* (1939), *De Mayerling a Sarajevo* (*Mayerling to Sarajevo*, 1940), *Monsieur Vincent* (1947), *Ruy-Blas* (1948), *Manon* (1949), *Little Boy Lost* (1953), *Madame Du Barry* (1954), *Mitsou* (1956), *Gigot* (1962) and *Germinal* (1963). ❖ See also *Women in World History.*

DOSCHER, Doris (1882–1970). American model and actress. Born Jan 24, 1882; died Mar 9, 1970, in Farmingdale, LI, NY; m. H.W. Baum (physician). ❖ Model for many sculptors and the 25-cent piece Miss Liberty; appeared as Eve in *Birth of a Nation* and in other silent films.

DOSS, Nannie (1905–1965). American mass murderer. Born 1905; died of leukemia in prison, 1965; m. at least 4 times; children: at least 2. ❖ Resident of Tulsa, Oklahoma, on a search for the "perfect mate," poisoned to death 4 husbands; also poisoned her mother, 2 children, 2 sisters, and others, for a total of 11 murders; confessed and sentenced to life imprisonment (1964).

DOS SANTOS, Andreia (1977—). Brazilian soccer player. Name variations: known as Maycon. Born April 30, 1977, in Lajes, Brazil. ❖ Forward, won a team silver medal at Athens Olympics (2004).

DOS SANTOS, Adriana (1971—). See *Santos, Adriana.*

DOS SANTOS, Cintia (1975—). Brazilian basketball player. Name variations: Cintia Santos; Cintia dos Santos; Cintia Santos Luz or Cintia Luz; Sintia Silva Santoa; Cintia Tuiu or Cínti Tuiú. Born Jan 31, 1975, in Maúa, Brazil; sister of Silvia Luz and Helen Luz (both basketball players). ❖ Center; won a team silver medal at Atlanta Olympics (1996) and a team bronze medal at Sydney Olympics (2000); drafted by the Orlando Miracle in the 1st round (2000); joined the WNBA Connecticut Sun (2003).

DOS SANTOS, Lucia (1907–2005). See *Lucia, Sister.*

DOS SANTOS AUGUSTO, Rosana (1982—). Brazilian soccer player. Name variations: Rosana. Born July 7, 1982, in Brazil. ❖ Won a team silver medal at Athens Olympics (2004).

D'OSSOLI, Margaret (1810–1850). See *Fuller, Margaret.*

DOSTALOVA, Leopolda (1879–1972). Czech actress. Born in Veleslavin, near Prague, Czechoslovakia (modern-day Czech Republic), Jan 23, 1879; died June 17, 1972; dau. of an actor. ❖ One of the stars of the Prague stage for more than a half-century, made triumphant debut at Prague's National Theater (1901); among her best roles were Sophocles' Antigone and Electra, Shakespeare's Lady Macbeth, Euripides' Medea, Ibsen's Hedda Gabler, and Ferdinand Bruckner's Elizabeth I; also mastered roles by Slavic playwrights, including Slowacki's Balladyna, Ostrovskii's Murzavetskaia (*Wolves and Sheep*), and Tyl's Liudmila (*Dragomiry*); remained a major figure of the Prague stage well into the 1950s. Awarded State Prize of the Czechoslovak Republic (1946). ❖ See also memoirs *Herecka vzpomina* (2nd ed. Prague: Orbis, 1964); and *Women in World History.*

DOSTOEVSKY, Anna (1846–1918). Memoirist and 2nd wife of Russian novelist Fyodor Dostoevsky. Name variations: Dostoevski or Dostoyevsky; Anna Snitkina. Born 1846; died 1918; m. Fyodor or Fedor Dostoevsky, 1867. ❖ Hired by Fyodor Dostoevsky to transcribe his novel *The Gambler*; after marriage, left Russia with husband in order to escape his creditors; spent 3 months in Dresden and Baden, where she suffered a miscarriage, and he indulged his passion for gambling; began a diary in which she described the 1st difficult years of her marriage; with Fyodor, returned to Russia (1871); tended to husband's needs and became an important part of his work; after his death (1881), continued to devote herself to the service of his writings and memory; during final years, transcribed her early diaries, which she used to prepare her memoir *Reminiscences,* published after her death. ❖ See also *Women in World History.*

DOT (1856–1926). See *Dawson, Louisa Alice.*

D'OTTAVIO, Frazia (1985—). Italian rhythmic gymnast. Born Feb 3, 1985, in Chieti, Italy. ❖ Won team all-around silver medal at Athens Olympics (2004).

DOUBROVSKA, Felia (1896–1981). Russian ballet dancer. Born Felizata Dloujnerska, 1896, in St. Petersburg, Russia; died Sept 18, 1981, in New York, NY; trained at Imperial Ballet Academy in St. Petersburg; m. Pierre Vladimiroff (ballet dancer). ❖ One of greatest émigré Russian ballet teachers in US, 1st danced with Maryinsky Ballet (1913–20); joined Diaghilev's Ballets Russes (1920), where she created roles in Nijinska's *Les Noces* (1923), and Balanchine's *Apollon Musagète* (1928) and *Prodigal Son* (1929); after Diaghilev's death (1929), performed with numerous troupes formed by Ballet Russes dancers, including Nijinska's troupe, Monte Carlo Opéra Ballet, Woisikovsky Company, and Balanchine's School of American Ballet; along with husband, served as teacher at American Ballet for the rest of her life.

DOUCE I (d. 1190). Countess of Provence. Born 1190; m. Raymond Berengar I, count of Provence; children: Raymond Berengar II, count of Provence; Berengaria of Provence (1108–1149).

DOUCE OF ARAGON (1160–1198). Queen of Portugal. Name variations: Dulce of Aragon; Dulcia of Barcelona. Born 1160; died Sept 1, 1198, in Coimbra, Portugal; buried at Holy Cross Church, Coimbra; dau. of Raymond Berengar II, count of Provence, and Petronilla (1135–1174), queen of Aragon; m. Sancho I (1154–1211 or 1212), king of Portugal (r. 1185–1211 or 1212), in 1181; children: Theresa Henriques (c. 1176–1250, who m. Alphonso IX, king of Leon); Sancha (c. 1178–1229); Raimundo (1180–1189); Costanza (1182–1202); Alphonso II the Fat (1185–1223), king of Portugal (r. 1211–1223, who m. Urraca of Castile [c. 1196–1220]); Pedro (1187–1258), king of Majorca; Fernando also known as Ferdinand of Portugal (1188–1233, who m. Johanna of Flanders); Henrique (1189–c. 1191); Branca (c. 1192–1240); Berengaria (1194–1221), queen of Denmark; Mafalda (c. 1197–1257).

DOUCET, Catherine (1875–1958). American stage and screen actress. Name variations: Catherine Calhoun. Born Catherine Calhoun, June 20, 1875, in Richmond, Virginia; died June 24, 1958, in New York, NY; m. Paul Doucet. ❖ Made Broadway debut as Marian Thorne in *Brown of Harvard* (1906); other NY appearances include *Cold Feet, The Potters, Miss Lulu Bett, The Royal Family, The Perfect Alibi, Topaze, When Ladies Meet* and *Oh Brother!*; films include *These Three, The Golden Arrow, Poppy, The Longest Night* and *For You Alone.*

DOUDET, Célestine (b. 1817). French murderer (accused). Name variations: Celestine Doudet. Born 1817 in Rouen, France. ❖ Worked as governess for upper-class English families and as wardrobe mistress to Queen Victoria; appointed by English doctor James Loftus Marsden to tutor his 5 daughters (1852), took the girls to Paris to set up small school; after several months, was accused by neighbors of mistreating and starving children; after death of 1 child, was tried for murder and acquitted, but sentenced to 5 years in prison for mistreatment of children.

DOUGALL, Lily (1858–1923). Canadian novelist and essayist. Born 1858 in Montreal, Canada, of Scottish descent; died 1923; studied literature and philosophy at universities of Edinburgh and St. Andrews. ❖ Was the 1st editor of Montreal journal *The Wide World;* came to prominence with 1st novel, *Beggars All* (1891); also wrote *What Necessity Knows* (1893), and *The Mormon Prophet* (1899).

DOUGHERTY, Ellen (c. 1843–1919). New Zealand nurse, pharmacist, and hospital matron. Born c. 1843 or 1844, at Cutters Bay, Marlborough, New Zealand; died Nov 3, 1919, at Carterton, Wairarapa, New Zealand; dau. of Daniel Dougherty (whaler) and Sarah (McAuley) Dougherty. ❖ Completed certificate in nursing (1887); became head of accident and surgery wards at Wellington District Hospital; served as acting matron of Wellington District Hospital, and as matron of Palmerston North Hospital (1893); became registered as pharmacist (1899); was one of 1st state-registered nurses in the world. ❖ See also *Dictionary of New Zealand Biography* (Vol. 2).

DOUGHERTY, Sarah (c. 1817–1898). New Zealand social leader and nurse. Name variations: Sarah McAuley. Born Sarah McAuley, c. 1817 or 1818, in Londonderry, Ireland; died Nov 7, 1898, in Thorndon, New Zealand; dau. of William (farmer) and Elizabeth (Atkin) McAuley; m. Daniel Dougherty (sailor), 1837 (died 1857); children: 7. ❖ At 7, immigrated with family to New Brunswick, Canada; immigrated with husband to Sydney, Australia (1838); returned briefly to Canada before traveling to Bay of Islands, New Zealand, via London (1842); settled at Cutters Bay, Marlborough, where she served as nurse at husband's whaling station; moved to Wellington (1849), establishing boarding house after husband's death. ❖ See also *Dictionary of New Zealand Biography* (Vol. 1).

DOUGHTY, Sue (1948—). English politician and member of Parliament. Born Susan Powell, April 13, 1948; m. David Vyvyan Orchard. ❖ Contested London European Parliament election (1999); representing Liberal Democrats, elected to House of Commons at Westminster (2001) for Guildford; lost general election (2005).

DOUGLAS, Adèle Cutts (1835–1899). American society belle and political hostess. Born Adèle Cutts on Dec 27, 1835, in Washington, DC; died Jan 26, 1899, in Washington, DC; dau. of James Madison Cutts (government clerk and nephew of Dolley Madison) and Ellen Elizabeth O'Neale; attended Madame Burr's School and Academy of the Visitation; m. Stephen A. Douglas (US senator), 1856 (died 1861); m. Robert Williams (military officer); children: (1st m.) Ellen; (2nd m.) Robert, Ellen, Philip, Adèle, James and Mildred Williams. ❖ Attactive and intelligent Washington socialite, met Stephen A. Douglas during election campaign of 1856, soon after he had unsuccessfully campaigned for Democratic presidential nomination against James Buchanan; accompanied husband on political trips and won friends and supporters for him through charm; after husband died (1861), married Captain Robert Williams (1866), a Virginian who had fought with Union Army during Civil War; with Williams and their 6 children, traveled to military posts in West while husband served as adjutant general of Department of Missouri and later Department of the Platte; returned to Washington when husband was assigned to War Department.

DOUGLAS, Aileen Anna Maria (c. 1861–1951). See Garmson, Aileen Anna Maria.

DOUGLAS, Lady Alfred (1874–1944). See Custance, Olive.

DOUGLAS, Amanda Minnie (1831–1916). American author. Born July 14, 1831, in New York, NY; died July 18, 1916, in Newark, New Jersey. ❖ Prolific author of adult novels and books for children, published 1st book, the adult novel In Trust (1866), and then usually at least one book per year (1866–1913); published children series, including 7 "Kathie" books (1868–71) and 10 "Little Girl" books, among earliest historical fiction written for girls.

DOUGLAS, Ann (b. 1901). American concert dancer. Born Mar 12, 1901, in Seattle, Washington; sister of Germaine Ballou. ❖ Trained at Denishawn school in Los Angeles, California, before joining its concert troupe (1919–26); toured with company in Julnar of the Sea (1919) and with St. Denis in her Sonata Tragica (1923), Waltz (1924), Valse à la Loie (1924), and more; joined company on tour of the Orient, performing in same pieces as well as General Wu's Farewell to His Wife (1928) and Impressions of a Wayang Purwa (1928); upon return to US, opened a series of studios with her sister in the Los Angeles area.

DOUGLAS, Catherine (1701–1777). See Hyde, Catherine.

DOUGLAS, countess of.
See Stewart, Isabel (fl. 1371).
See Holland, Anne (fl. 1440–1462).

DOUGLAS, Lady Eleanor (1590–1652). See Davies, Eleanor.

DOUGLAS, Elizabeth (d. before 1451). Countess of Orkney. Name variations: Lady Elizabeth Douglas. Died before 1451; dau. of Margaret Stewart (d. before 1456) and Archibald Douglas, 4th earl of Douglas; m. John Stewart, 3rd earl of Buchan, in Nov 1413; m. Sir Thomas Stewart; m. William Sinclair, 3rd earl of Orkney and Caithness; children: (1st m.) Margaret Stewart, countess of Buchan (who m. George Seton, 1st Lord Seton); (3rd m.) Catherine Sinclair, duchess of Albany (who m. Alexander Stewart, 1st duke of Albany; William Sinclair.

DOUGLAS, Emily Taft (1899–1994). American politician. Born Emily Taft in Chicago, Illinois, April 19, 1899; died in Briarcliff Manor, New York, Jan 28, 1994; dau. of Lorado Taft (sculptor, art teacher, writer, and lecturer) and Ada (Bartlett) Taft; University of Chicago, BA, 1920; attended American Academy of Dramatic Art; m. Paul Howard Douglas (professor of economics and US Senator from Illinois, 1949–66), 1931; children: daughter Jean Douglas. ❖ Began career as an actress; as a Democrat, won Illinois' Representative at Large seat in House of Representatives (1944); during term, served on the Committee on Foreign Affairs and was recognized as a highly qualified specialist in the field; co-sponsored legislation to empower the UN to control arms and outlaw the atomic bomb; also championed federal support for libraries; was among 54 House Democrats ousted in midterm election of 1946; following husband's election to US Senate (1948), served as a representative to UNESCO and as a moderator for American Unitarian Association; in later years, worked for civil-rights movement; wrote several books, including Appleseed Farm (1948), Remember the Ladies (1966) and Margaret Sanger (1970). ❖ See also Women in World History.

DOUGLAS, Helen Gahagan (1900–1980). American actress and politician. Name variations: known as Helen Gahagan from 1900 to 1931, as Helen Gahagan Douglas after 1931. Born Helen Mary Gahagan, Nov 25, 1900, in Boonton, New Jersey; died June 28, 1980; dau. of Lillian Rose (Mussen) and Walter Gahagan (owner of a Brooklyn engineering company); attended Barnard College, 1920–22; m. Melvyn Douglas (actor), 1931; children: Peter and Mary Helen Douglas. ❖ Actress, opera singer, and liberal Democratic Congressional representative, who ran unsuccessfully against Richard Nixon during his infamous campaign; made Broadway debut in lead role in Dreams for Sale (1922); toured extensively throughout US and Canada, becoming a premier stage actress (1922–28); made operatic debut in Ostrava, Czechoslovakia (1928), which was followed by 2 years of successes in that country and in Austria, Germany, and Italy, in the operas Tosca, Aïda, La Gioconda and Manon Lescaut; starred on Broadway opposite Melvyn Douglas in Tonight or Never (1930); married him and moved to Hollywood (1931); made only film, She (1933); was elected to US Congress (1944, 1946, 1948), California's only female Congressional representative between 1920s and 1960s; as a member of the House, was appointed to the influential Foreign Affairs Committee; was a consistent supporter of the New Deal; made biggest contribution with her joint sponsorship of McMahon-Douglas Bill which ensured after the war that control of nuclear research and power would stay in civil rather than military hands; was appointed by Truman as an alternate delegate to the fledgling United Nations (1946), and from its beginnings was a great champion of the UN; was the 1st white representative to hire a black secretary on Capitol Hill and succeeded in abolishing segregation in the House Office Building's cafeteria; as a Democratic candidate for Senate (1950), was defeated by Richard Nixon who, in a speech that became notorious in the annals of both red-baiting and sexism, quipped that she was "pink right down to her underwear"; in later years, was an active member of the Women's International League for Peace and Freedom and of the Committee for a Sane Nuclear Policy, and spoke out against the Vietnam War. ❖ See also memoir A Full Life (Doubleday, 1982); Ingrid Winther Scobie, Center Stage: Helen Gahagan Douglas, A Life (Oxford U. Press, 1992); Greg Mitchell, Tricky Dick and the Pink Lady: Richard Nixon vs. Helen Gahagan Douglas (Random, 1997); and Women in World History.

DOUGLAS, Helyn (c. 1945—). American ballet dancer. Born c. 1945 in Dallas, Texas; trained with Margaret Craske, Vincenzo Celli, Hector Zaraspe, and Maggie Black in New York City. ❖ Danced 1 season with City Center Joffrey Ballet (1967); danced with American Ballet Theater (1968–74) in such classical repertory works as Michael Smuin's Pulcinella Variations, Dennis Nahat's Ontogeny, Eliot Feld's Intermezzo, and more; joined Feld Ballet (1974) and created roles in The Consort (1974) and Half-Time (1978); also performed with a dance troupe for which she choreographed.

DOUGLAS, Isabel (fl. 1371). See Stewart, Isabel.

DOUGLAS, Lizzie (1897–1973). American blues singer, guitarist, recording artist, and club owner. Name variations: Gospel Minnie; Kid; Memphis Minnie; Minnie Douglas; Minnie McCoy; Texas Tessie. Born in Algiers, Louisiana, June 3, 1897 (some sources cite 1896); died in Memphis, Tennessee, Aug 6, 1973; dau. of Abe Douglas and Gertrude Wells; m. Casey Bill Weldon, 1920s; m. Kansas Joe McCoy, 1929–35; m. Little Son Je Ernest Lawlars, 1939. ❖ One of the great blues artists of all time, played banjo and guitar at early age; ran away from home to work as Kid Douglas (1910); toured with Ringling Brothers Circus (1916–20); as Memphis Minnie, made 1st recording on the Columbia label with 2nd husband Joe McCoy (1929); with McCoy, moved to Chicago and formed a blues group (1930); became famous for her Blue Monday parties; continued to record and play Chicago clubs; toured with her own vaudeville troupe throughout South (1940s); retired (1950s). ❖ See also Women in World History.

DOUGLAS, Margaret (b. around 1427). Countess of Douglas and Atholl. Name variations: The Fair Maid of Galloway. Born c. 1427; dau. of Archibald Douglas, count of Longueville and 5th earl of Douglas (c. 1390–1439), and Euphemia Graham (d. 1469); m. William Douglas, 8th earl of Douglas; m. John Stewart (John of Balveny), 1st earl of Atholl.

DOUGLAS, Margaret (1515–1578). Countess of Lennox. Name variations: Lady Margaret Douglas or Douglass; Margaret Lennox. Born at Harbottle Castle, Northumberland, England, Oct 8, 1515; died Mar 7 or

9, 1578 (some sources cite 1577); dau. of Archibald Douglas, 6th earl of Angus, and Margaret Tudor (1489–1541); m. Thomas Howard, Lord Howard; m. Matthew Stuart (1516–1571), 4th earl of Lennox, July 6, 1544; children: (2nd m.) Henry Stuart (b. 1545), Lord Darnley (who m. Mary Stuart, queen of Scots); Charles Stuart (b. 1555), earl of Lennox; and four daughters (names unknown); grandchildren: James VI, king of Scotland (r. 1567–1625), king of England as James I (r. 1603–1625). ❖ Daughter of Margaret Tudor, granddau. of Henry VII, and niece of Henry VIII, whose diplomacy largely contributed to the future succession of her grandson James I to English throne; because of her proximity to the crown, was brought up chiefly at the English court in close association with Princess Mary Tudor (Mary I), who would remain her close friend; was twice discredited: 1st for marriage to Lord Thomas Howard, who died in Tower of London in 1537, and for affair with Sir Charles Howard, brother of Queen Catherine Howard, in 1541; married a Scottish exile, 4th earl of Lennox (1544), who was regent of Scotland (1570–71); during Catholic Mary I's reign, had rooms in Westminster Palace, but on Protestant Elizabeth I's accession, moved to Yorkshire, where her home became a center for Catholic intrigue; successfully maneuvered to have her son Henry Stuart, Lord Darnley, marry Mary Stuart, Queen of Scots (1565); was sent to the Tower (1566) but released after the murder of Darnley the following year; again incurred Elizabeth I's wrath (1574) when son Charles Stuart, earl of Lennox, married Elizabeth Cavendish (d. 1582), dau. of Elizabeth Talbot, countess of Shrewsbury; was sent to the Tower with countess of Shrewsbury and only pardoned after son's death (1577). ❖ See also *Women in World History*.

DOUGLAS, Marjory (d. 1420). Duchess of Rothesay. Born c. 1420; dau. of Archibald Douglas, 3rd earl of Douglas, and Jean also known as Joan Moray; m. David Stewart or Stuart (1378–1402), duke of Rothesay (r. 1398–1402), Feb 1400; m. Walter Haliburton, 1403; children: John, lord Haliburton; Walter; Robert; William.

DOUGLAS, Marjory Stoneman (1890–1998). American environmental activist and writer. Born Marjory Stoneman in Minneapolis, Minnesota, April 7, 1890; died in Miami, Florida, May 14, 1998; dau. of Frank Bryant Stoneman (newspaper publisher) and (Florence) Lillian (Trefethen) Stoneman; graduate of Wellesley College, 1912; m. Kenneth Douglas, 1914 (div. 1919). ❖ One of 20th-century America's earliest and most influential environmentalists, was among the 1st to recognize the crucial role the Everglades play in both the flow of water throughout central and southern Florida and in balancing the state's delicate ecosystem; worked as society editor and occasional general assignment editor at *Miami Herald* newspaper (1915–1918); volunteered for overseas Red Cross (1918–19); served as assistant editor and editorial page columnist at *Miami Herald* (1919–24); worked as fiction writer and essayist (1924–40); served as director, University of Miami Press (1960); founded Friends of the Everglades (1969); saw "Marjory Stoneman Douglas Law" pass (1991); writings include *The Everglades: River of Grass* (1947, rev. ed., 1987), *Road to the Sun* (1952), *Freedom River* (1953), *Hurricane* (1958), *Alligator Crossing* (1959), *Florida: The Long Frontier* (1967) and *Adventures in a Green World: David Fairchild and Barbour Lathrop* (1973). Received Presidential Medal of Freedom (1993); inducted into the Women's Hall of Fame at Seneca Falls, NY (2000). ❖ See also (with John Rothchild) *Voice of the River: The Autobiography of Marjory Stoneman Douglas* (1987); and *Women in World History*.

DOUGLAS, Mary Tew (1921—). British social anthropologist. Born Mary Tew, Mar 25, 1921, in Italy; dau. of Gilbert Charles Tew and Phyllis Twomey Tew; m. James A.T. Douglas (economist), 1951; children: 3. ❖ Conducted fieldwork in southwest Belgian Congo, Zaire (1949–50 and 1953); received PhD from Oxford University (1951) and dissertation published as *The Lele of the Kasai* (1963); began long association with University of London and Professor Daryll Forde (1951); conducted research into ritual dramatization of social patterns; though known for grid and group analysis, is possibly best known for pollution studies, such as *Purity and Danger* (1966); during distinguished academic career, taught at University of Oxford, University of London, Northwestern University, and Princeton University; served as resident scholar and director of culture program at Russell Sage Foundation, NY (1977–81). Other works include *The World of Goods* (with Baron Isherwood, 1979) and *Risk and Culture* (with Aaron Wildavsky, 1982).

DOUGLAS, Minnie (1897–1973). See *Douglas, Lizzie*.

DOUGLAS, O. (1878–1948). See *Buchan, Anna*.

DOUGLAS, Sandra (1967—). English runner. Born April 22, 1967. ❖ At Barcelona Olympics, won a bronze medal in 4 x 400-meter relay (1992).

DOUGLAS, Virginia (c. 1899–1971). See *O'Hanlon, Virginia*.

DOUGLASS, Anna Murray (1813–1882). African-American abolitionist. Name variations: Mrs. Frederick Douglass. Born Anna Murray, 1813, to slave parents Bambarra and Mary Murray; died in 1882 in Washington DC; m. Frederick Douglass (1818–1895, renowned freedom fighter and orator), Sept 15, 1838; children: Rosetta Sprague Douglass (b. 1839), Lewis H. Douglass (b. 1840), Frederick Douglass, Jr. (b. 1842), Charles Remond Douglass (b. 1844), Annie Douglass (1848–1860). ❖ With money she had earned, helped future husband escape slavery (Sept 3, 1838); worked as an abolitionist in Lynn and Boston, Massachusetts; created a way station for runaways in the Underground Railroad in the Rochester (NY) home she shared with husband (his 2nd wife was Helen Pitts Douglass).

DOUGLASS, Dorothea (1878–1960). See *Chambers, Dorothea*.

DOUGLASS, Mrs. Frederick.
See *Douglass, Anna Murray (1813–1882)*.
See *Douglass, Helen Pitts (1838–1903)*.

DOUGLASS, Mrs. Hallam (d. 1774). See *Hallam, Mrs. Lewis*.

DOUGLASS, Helen Pitts (1838–1903). American feminist. Name variations: Mrs. Frederick Douglass. Born Helen Pitts 1838 in Honeoye, NY; died 1903; dau. of Gideon Pitts Jr. (abolitionist and colleague of Frederick Douglass); graduate of Mount Holyoke Seminary; became 2nd wife of Frederick Douglass (1818–1895, freedom fighter and orator), 1884; no children. ❖ Worked on a radical feminist publication, *Alpha*, in Washington DC; became secretary to the widowed-orator Frederick Douglass (his 1st wife was Anna Murray Douglass); a white woman, nearly 20 years younger than her husband, faced a storm of controversy on marriage, and her family stopped speaking to her; after his death, founded the Frederick Douglass Historical and Memorial Association (1900).

DOUGLASS, Margaret (d. 1949). American actress. Died Oct 24, 1949, in New York, NY. ❖ Appeared on Broadway in *Russet Mantle, The Women, Yesterday's Magic, Bloomer Girl* and *The Fatal Weakness;* was one of the founders of the Dallas Little Theatre.

DOUGLASS, Sarah Mapps (1806–1882). African-American educator and abolitionist. Born Sarah Mapps Douglass in Philadelphia, Pennsylvania, Sept 9, 1806; died 1882; dau. of Robert and Grace (Bustill) Douglass; attended the "colored" school founded by her mother and James Forten; m. William Douglass (rector of St. Thomas Protestant Episcopal Church), July 23, 1855 (died 1861). ❖ A leading light in the Philadelphia Female Anti-Slavery Society, which was founded by mother Grace Douglass in 1833, also taught in Philadelphia area most of her life; was a lifelong friend of Angelina E. Grimké and Sarah Moore Grimké. ❖ See also *Women in World History*.

DOUKAS. Variant of *Ducas*.

DOUTY, Sheila (1962—). See *Cornell, Sheila*.

DOUVILLIER, Suzanne (1778–1826). French-born ballet dancer. Name variations: Suzanne Placide or Madame Placide; Suzanne Théodore Vaillande Douvillier. Born Suzanne Théodore Vailland, Sept 28, 1778, in Dole, France; died Aug 30, 1826, in New Orleans, Louisiana; probably the illeg. dau. of Marie Reine Vailland; m. Louis Douvillier (singer and dancer, died 1821). ❖ Brought to US at 14 by Alexandre Placide (1791); made NY debut in *The Bird Catcher* (1792); was leading ballerina for a French company in Charleston, SC (1794–96) and also staged an original ballet of her own, *Echo and Narcissus* (1796); settled with husband in New Orleans, where he was principal singer and she was 1st dancer of the New Orleans stage; as the 1st woman choreographer in America, staged numerous ballets.

DOVADA (fl. 990–1005). See *Doada*.

DOVE, Billie (1900–1997). American actress. Born Lillian Bohny (also seen as Bohney) in New York, NY, May 14, 1900; died Dec 31, 1997, in Los Angeles, California; m. Irving Willat (director), 1923 (div. 1929); m. Robert Kenaston (rancher), 1933 (died 1973); m. John Miller (architect), c. 1974 (div.); children: Robert; (adopted) Gail Adelson. ❖ One of the most beautiful stars of the silent era, was an artist's model and Ziegfeld "showgirl" before entering films; after some bit parts at Cosmopolitan

Studios in New York, left for Hollywood, where she landed a featured role in *Polly of the Follies* (1922); co-starred with Douglas Fairbanks Sr. in one of the early color productions, *The Black Pirate* (1926); starred in many silents and early sound films before retiring (1932), when she left Hollywood to marry a wealthy rancher; returned to the screen only briefly (1962), for a bit part in film *Diamond Head;* other films include *The Stolen Bride* (1926), *Kid Boots* (1926), *American Beauty* (1927), *One Night at Susie's* (1928), *Painted Angel* (1930) and *Blondie of the Follies* (1932).

DOVE, Rita (1952—). American writer. Born Aug 28, 1952, in Akron, Ohio; dau. of Ray A. Dove (1st African-American chemist to break racial barrier in tire and rubber industry) and Elvira Elizabeth (Hord) Dove; Miami University of Ohio, BA in English, 1973; attended Tubingen University; University of Iowa, MFA, 1977; m. Fred Viebahn (German writer, journalist), 1979; children: Aviva Chantal Tamu Dove-Viebahn. ❖ The 1st African-American poet laureate of US (as well as the youngest), published 1st poetry collection *The Yellow House on the Corner* (1980); won Pulitzer Prize for *Thomas and Beulah,* a collection of poems loosely based on grandparents' life (1987); taught creative writing at Arizona State University (1981–89); was writer-in-residence at Tuskegee Institute (1982); served as chair and Commonwealth Professor of English at University of Virginia in Charlottesville; appointed Poet Laureate of US (1993) and Consultant in Poetry at Library of Congress, the highest honor in American letters; collaborated with musicians on various works, such as Alvin Singleton's symphonic piece *Umoja—Each One of Us Counts* for symphony orchestra and narrator (1996), as well as with composers Tania León (1996), Bruce Adolphe (1997) and John Williams (1998); edited anthology *Best American Poetry* (2000); wrote weekly column "The Poet's Choice" for *The Washington Post* (2000–02); appointed Poet Laureate of Virginia (2004); poetry collections include *Grace Notes* (1989), *Mother Love* (1995), *On the Bus with Rosa Parks* (1999) and *American Smooth* (2004); also published (short stories), *Fifth Sunday* (1985), (novel) *Through the Ivory Gate* (1992), (verse drama) *The Darker Face of the Earth* (1994), and *The Poet's World* (1995), a book of laureate lectures.

DOVEY, Alice (1884–1969). American actress and singer. Born Aug 2, 1884, in Plattsmouth, Nebraska; died Jan 12, 1969, in Tarzana, California; m. John E. Hazzard. ❖ Made stage debut in the chorus of *The Strollers* (1903), followed by *Woodland, A Stubborn Cinderella, Old Dutch, The Pink Lady, The Queen of the Movies* and *Very Good Eddie,* among others; made 2 films, *The Commanding Officer* and *The Romantic Journey.*

DOVZAN, Alenka (1976—). Slovenian Alpine skier. Born Feb 11, 1976, in Mojstrana, Slovenia. ❖ Won a bronze medal for combined at Lillehammer Olympics (1994).

DOW, Peggy (1928—). American actress. Born Peggy Josephine Varnadow, Mar 18, 1928, in Columbia, Mississippi; m. Walter Helmerich, 1951 (Oklahoma oil millionaire). ❖ Made film debut in *Undertow* (1949), followed by leads in *Woman in Hiding, Shakedown, The Sleeping City, Harvey, Bright Victory, You Never Can Tell, Reunion in Reno* and *I Want You;* retired from film at time of marriage.

DOWD, Annie (1862–1939). See Chemis, Annie.

DOWD, Nancy (1944—). American screenwriter. Name variations: Nancy N. Dowd; (pseudonyms) Rob Morton; Ernest Morton. Born 1944 in Framingham, Massachusetts; sister of Ned Dowd. ❖ Wrote the screenplay for *Slap Shot* (1977); was a writer on "Saturday Night Live" (1980); as Rob Morton, wrote the screenplay for *Swing Shift* (1984).

DOWDALL, Jane (1899–1974). Irish politician and nurse. Born Jane Doggett, Sept 29, 1899, in Smithfield, Dublin, Ireland; died Dec 10, 1974; m. J.C. Dowdall (senator). ❖ Elected to the Seanad from the Industrial and Commercial Panel (1951–61); was the 1st woman Lord Mayor of Cork (1959–60) and the 1st woman member, Council of State (1964).

DOWDING, Angela (1919—). English royal by marriage. Born April 20, 1919, in Hanwell, England; dau. of Charles Stanley Dowding and Lilian Lawlor; became 1st wife of Gerald Lascelles (b. 1924, grandson of King George V and Mary of Teck), July 15, 1952 (div. 1978); children: Henry Lascelles (b. 1953). Gerald Lascelles' 2nd wife is Elizabeth Collingwood.

DOWLING, Constance (1920–1969). American actress. Name variations: Mrs. Ivan Tors. Born July 24, 1920, in New York, NY; died Oct 28, 1969, in Los Angeles, California; sister of Doris Dowling (actress, b. 1921); m. Ivan Tors (film producer), c. 1955. ❖ On Broadway, appeared in *Panama Hattie, Hold on to Your Hats* and *Strawberries in January;* made film debut (1943), starring in *Knickerbocker Holiday,* followed by *Up in Arms, The Flame* and *Gog.*

DOWLING, Doris (1921–2004). American tv and screen actress. Born May 15, 1921, in Detroit, Michigan; died June 18, 2004, in Los Angeles, California; sister of Constance Dowling (actress); became 7th wife of Artie Shaw, 1952 (div. 1956); m. Robert Blumofe (UA executive), 1956 (div. 1959); m. Leonard Kaufman (publicist), 1960; children: Jonathan Shaw. ❖ Sultry-voiced character actress, 1st appeared on Broadway; made film debut as the hooker in *The Lost Weekend* (1945), followed by *The Blue Dahlia* (1946); unhappy with parts offered in Hollywood, moved to Italy with sister, mingled with the cognoscenti, and filmed the neo-realist *Riso amaro* (*Bitter Rice* 1949); returned to US (1950); other films include *The Crimson Key, The Tragedy of Othello* and *The Party Crashers;* on tv, appeared as Sally Reuters on "Scruples" (1980), among others.

DOWLING, Joan (1928–1954). English actress. Born Jan 6, 1928, in Laindon, Essex, England; died Mar 31, 1954, of asphyxiation in London, England. ❖ Made stage debut as a child dancer in *Waltz without End* (1942), followed by *Panama Hattie, Little Red Riding Hood* (title role), and *Babes in the Wood;* scored a major success as Norma Smith in *No Room at the Inn* (1946); films include *No Room at the Inn, A Man's Affair, Bond Street* and *The Magic Box.*

DOWNES, Mollie Panter- (1906–1997). See Panter-Downes, Mollie.

DOWNEY, June Etta (1875–1932). American psychologist and educator. Born in Laramie, Wyoming, July 13, 1875; died in Trenton, New Jersey, Oct 11, 1932; dau. of Stephen Downey (one of 1st territorial delegates to Congress from Wyoming, who was instrumental in the establishment of University of Wyoming) and Evangeline (Owen) Downey (community organizer); University of Wyoming, BA, 1895; University of Chicago, MA, 1898; University of Chicago, PhD, 1907; never married; no children. ❖ Pioneer in the field of psychology, who was noted for her work in the study of handwriting and personality testing; achieved professorial rank at University of Wyoming (1905); appointed head of department of psychology and philosophy at Wyoming (1908), the 1st woman to head such a department at a state university; wrote over 60 articles and several books, including *Graphology and the Psychology of Handwriting* (1919), *Plots and Personalities* (with Edward E. Slosson, 1922) and *Creative Imagination: Studies in the Psychology of Literature* (1929); served on the council of American Psychological Association (1923–25); was one of the 1st women elected to Society of Experimental Psychologists (1929). ❖ See also *Women in World History.*

DOWNEY, Mrs. Morton (1906–1958). See Bennett, Barbara.

DOWNIE, Dorothy G. (1894–1960). Scottish botanist. Born Sept 16, 1894, in Scotland; died Aug 22, 1960. ❖ The 1st woman to earn a forestry degree at University of Edinburgh (BS, 1919), also studied at Moray House Training College in Edinburgh (1919–20) and at University of Chicago (PhD, 1928) on a Carnegie scholarship; worked as assistant (1920–25 and 1928–29), as lecturer (1929–49) and as reader (1949–60) at University of Aberdeen; focused studies on orchid nutrition.

DOWNIE, Mary Alice (1934—). Canadian children's writer. Name variations: Dawe Hunter. Born Mary Alice Dawe Hunter, Feb 12, 1934 in Alton, Illinois; moved to Canada (1940); dau. of Robert Grant Hunter (research scientist) and Doris Mary (Rogers) Hunter; University of Toronto, BA, 1955; m. John Downie (professor of chemical engineering), 1959; children: Christine and Jocelyn. ❖ Works include *Honor Bound* (with John Downie, 1970), *Scared Sarah* (1974), *The King's Loon* (1979), *The Wicked Fairy-Wife* (1983), *Alison's Ghosts* (with John Downie, 1984), *Cathal the Giant Killer and the Dun Shaggy Filly* (with Jillian Gilliland, 1991), and *Snow Paws* (with Kathryn Naylor, 1996); edited *The New Wind Has Wings: Poems from Canada* (with Barbara Robertson, 1984) and children's history series *Northern Lights.*

DOWNING, Lucy Winthrop (c. 1600–1679). American letter writer. Name variations: Lucy Winthrop. Born Lucy Winthrop, Jan 9, 1600 or 1601, in England; died 1679 in England; sister of John Winthrop (Puritan leader of the Massachusetts Bay Colony); m. Emanuel Downing, 1622. ❖ Moved with family from England to Boston (1638) and then Salem; letters, well written and forthright, give insight into struggles of colonial life; moved with family to Scotland after 1654 and then back to England after husband's death; wrote *Letters of Mrs. Lucy Downing* (1871), detailing conditions for Puritans in England, brother's decision to lead Puritan settlement to Massachusetts Bay Colony, and life in New England colonial community.

DOWNING, Shannon (1972—). *See Dunn, Shannon.*

DOWNING, Virginia (1904–1996). American stage actress. Born Mar 7, 1904, in Washington; died Nov 21, 1996, in New York, NY; m. John Leighton (actor). ❖ Made Broadway debut in *Father Malachy's Miracle* (1937), followed by *Cradle Will Rock, Gift of Time, We Have Always Lived in the Castle* and *Arsenic and Old Lace*, among others; off-Broadway credits include *Juno and the Paycock, Man with the Golden Arm, The Idiot, Medea, Mrs. Warren's Profession, Rimers of Eldritch, Les Blancs, Shadow of a Gunman, All That Fall* and *Richard III*.

DOWNS, Cathy (1924–1976). American actress. Born Mar 3, 1924, in Port Jefferson, LI, NY; died Dec 8, 1976, in Los Angeles, California; m. Robert Brunson (div.); m. Joe Kirkwood Jr. (actor), 1952 (div. 1955). ❖ Appeared in the title role of John Ford's *My Darling Clementine* (1946); other films include *State Fair, The Dolly Sisters, The Sundowners, Triple Cross, The Phantom from 10,000 Leagues, The Amazing Colossal Man, She-Creature* and *Missile to the Moon*.

DOWNS, Deirdre (c. 1980—). Miss America. Born c. 1980; graduate of Samford University; accepted to University of Alabama School of Medicine. ❖ Rhodes Scholar finalist, crowned Miss America (2005), representing Alabama.

DOWRICHE, Anne (before 1560–after 1613). British poet. Born Anne Edgcumbe in Mount Edgcumbe, Cornwall, England, before 1560; died after 1613; dau. of Sir Richard Edgcumbe and Elizabeth Tregian Edgcumbe; m. Hugh Dowriche, 1580. ❖ With husband, committed to the Puritan cause; wrote *The French Historie* (1589), a long poem about the French civil wars of 1500s, which depicts French Protestants (Huguenots) as heroes resisting monarchy and Catholicism.

DOYLE, Avril (1949—). Irish politician. Born Avril Belton, April 18, 1949, in Dublin, Ireland; dau. of Richard Belton, 1969–73); m. Fred Doyle; children: 3 daughters. ❖ Served as mayor of Wexford (1976–77); representing Fine Gael, elected to the 24th Dáil (1982–87) for Wexford; returned to 25th–26th Dáil (1987–1989) and 27th Dáil (1992–1997); was minister of State at the depts. of the Taoiseach, Finance, and Transport, Energy and Communications (1994–97), minister of State at the dept. of Finance with responsibility for the Office of Public Works, and at the dept. of the Environment (1986–87); elected to Seanad from Agricultural Panel (1989–92, 1997) and Member of the European Parliament (MEP, 1999–2004).

DOYLE, Laurel (1902–1971). *See Campbell, Laurel.*

DOYLE, Patricia (d. 1975). American actress and dancer. Died Sept 22, 1975, age 60, in Los Angeles, California; m. Robert Wise (producer-director); children: son. ❖ Appeared in *Grapes of Wrath*, among others.

D'OYLY CARTE, Bridget (1908–1985). *See Carte, Bridget D'Oyly.*

DRABBLE, Margaret (1939—). British novelist and literary critic. Born Margaret Drabble, June 5, 1939, in Sheffield, Yorkshire, England; dau. of John Frederick Drabble and Kathleen Marie (Bloor) Drabble; sister of A.S. Byatt (novelist and critic); m. Clive Smith (actor), 1960 (div. 1975); m. Michael Holroyd (biographer), 1982; children: 3. ❖ Writer of novels, essays, criticism, biographies, short stories, and screenplays, won scholarship to Newnham College, Cambridge, and graduated with starred First in English literature; became an actress and appeared with the Royal Shakespeare Company at Stratford-upon-Avon; published 1st novel, *A Summer Birdcage* (1963), the story of the relationship between 2 sisters; other novels include *The Millstone* (1966), which won the John Llewelyn Rhys Prize, *The Waterfall* (1969), *Jerusalem the Golden* (1967), which won the James Tait Black Memorial Prize, *The Needle's Eye* (1972), *The Realms of Gold* (1975), *The Ice Age* (1977), *The Middle Ground* (1980), *The Peppered Moth* (2001), *The Seven Sisters* (2002) and *The Red Queen* (2004), as well as the triology: *The Radiant Way* (1987), *A Natural Curiosity* (1989) and *The Gates of Ivory* (1991); works of nonfiction include *Arnold Bennett: A Biography* (1974), *For Queen and Country: Britain in the Victorian Age* (1978), and *Angus Wilson: A Biography* (1995); chaired the National Book League (1980–82). Received E.M. Forster Award from American Academy of Arts and Letters (1973); awarded CBE (1980). ❖ See also E.C. Rose (ed.), *Critical Essays on Margaret Drabble* (G.K. Hall, 1985).

DRACOPOULOU, Theony (1883–1968). Greek poet. Name variations: (pseudonym) Myrtiotissa. Born 1883 in Constantinople; died 1968; dau. of the Greek consul. ❖ Worked as actress and elocution teacher in Athens and wrote for literary magazines; writings include *Songs* (1919), *Yellow Flames* (1925), *Children's Anthology* (1930), *Songs of Love* (1932), *Kravges* (1939), and *I'll Never Forget*; translated from French, *Poems of the Countess of Noailles* (1928). Won award from Academy of Athens and National Poetry Prize.

DRAGA (1867–1903). Queen of Serbia. Name variations: Draga Lunyevitza-Mashin; Draga Mashin; Lunjevica-Mashin. Most likely born in 1867 (some sources cite 1865 or 1866); murdered in a palace coup the night of June 10–11, 1903; granddau. of Nikola Panta Lunyevitza; m. Svetozar Mashin (civil servant), 1884 (died 1885); m. Alexander Obrenovich or Obrenovitch, king of Serbia (r. 1889–1903), July 21, 1900. ❖ Queen and consort of King Alexander, whose marriage to him in 1900 constituted a major political scandal, destabilized an already chaotic political landscape, ended the Obrenovich dynasty, and brought about their deaths. ❖ See also Bertita Harding, *Royal Purple: The Story of Alexander and Draga of Serbia* (Harrap, 1937); Cedomilj Mijatovic, *A Royal Tragedy, being the Assassination of King Alexander and Queen Draga of Serbia* (Dodd, 1907); and *Women in World History.*

DRAGILA, Stacy (1971—). American pole vaulter. Born Mar 25, 1971, in Auburn, California. ❖ Placed 1st at Sydney Olympics (2000), the 1st woman to win a gold medal in pole vaulting; at World championships, won a gold medal (2001); did not medal at Athens Olympics (2004).

DRAGO, Eleonora Rossi (1925—). *See Rossi Drago, Eleonora.*

DRAGOICHEVA, Tsola (1893–1993). Bulgarian revolutionary. Name variations: known as the Grand Old Lady of the Bulgarian Communist movement, often called the "Bulgarian La Pasionaria." Born Aug 18, 1893 (some sources cite Aug 22, 1898, as well as 1900), in Biala Slatina, Bulgaria; died May 26, 1993; trained to become a teacher, graduating from the state institute of pedagogy, 1921; children: one son, Chavdar Dragoichev. ❖ The most prominent woman in the history of Bulgarian Communism, whose political career lasted over 60 years and included several death sentences that were never carried out, joined Bulgarian Communist Party (BCP, 1919); during an armed uprising by Communist Party (Sept 1923), was arrested, banned from teaching, and given a 15-year prison sentence; was freed as a result of an amnesty (1924); sentenced to death once more (1925) and freed once more by amnesty (1932); studied at Moscow's Lenin School of the Communist International; returned to Bulgaria (1936); elected to central committee of Bulgarian Communist Party (1937), which during these years was carrying on an underground existence; elected to BCP central committee (1937) and BCP politburo (1940), becoming one of the unchallenged leaders of Bulgarian Communist movement as well as one of the few women politburo members; when Bulgaria became an ally of Nazi Germany and cracked down on its domestic opposition, particularly the Communists (1941), was thrown into a concentration camp; escaped and was sentenced to death in absentia; became Communist representative of Bulgarian Patriotic Front (1942); when Patriotic Front took over reins of government (Sept 1944) with flight of German forces, became the Front's national secretary; as the most powerful woman in Bulgaria, was elected president of the Bulgarian National Women's Union (June 1945); was minister of communications (1947–57); with imposition of a hardline Communist regime, remained in the government Cabinet, but within the party her power was significantly eroded; even so, was unafraid to voice her critiques within party circles; was restored to full membership within the party's politburo (1966). ❖ See also memoirs *The Call of Duty* and *Defeat to Victory: Notes of a Bulgarian Revolutionary;* and *Women in World History.*

DRAGOMIR or DRAGOMIRA. *Variant of Drahomira.*

DRAGONETTE, Jessica (1900–1980). American actress and radio singer. Born Feb 14, 1900, in India; died Mar 18, 1980, in New York, NY; m. Nicholas M. Turner, 1947. ❖ Raised in a convent, having been orphaned as a child; began professional singing career in *The Miracle* (1924), followed by *The Student Prince, Earl Carroll's Vanities* and *The Grand Street Follies;* sang for 22 years on radio's "Cities Service Concerts," "The Philco Hour," "Ford Summer Show," and "Saturday Night Serenade."

DRAHOMIRA OF BOHEMIA (d. after 932). Duchess and regent of Bohemia. Name variations: Drahomire von Stoder; Dragomir or Dragomira. Born in Germany into the Stodoran family; died after

932 in Bohemia; dau. of a chief of the Havolané tribe which lived north of Bohemia in Brandenburg; m. Ratislav, also known as Vratislav I (887–920), duke of Bohemia (r. 912–920); children: 4 daughters, of whom only the name of one (Pribyslava) is known; and 3 sons, Saint Wenceslas (b. around 907), Boleslav I (d. 972), and Spytihnev (died while young). ❖ Was a staunch advocate of the pagan religion of Germany, but husband was a Christian; raised son Boleslav in the pagan religion, though elder son Wenceslas was brought up in the Christian church by his paternal grandmother Ludmila, whom Drahomira despised; when husband died (920) and Ludmila was named regent for 13-year-old Wenceslas, an event which increased the tension between Bohemia's pagan believers and its Christians, quickly became the leader of the pagans and schemed to get rid of Ludmila; assumed the regency for her son after Ludmila was murdered on her orders (920); with outbreak of civil war, was outnumbered, and Wenceslas dismissed her from the government when he came of age at 18; continued to plot against the Christian faction, however, and was in the general vicinity when her son Boleslav murdered Wenceslas (929); fled to the tribe of White Croatians north of Prague. ❖ See also *Women in World History.*

DRAKE, Betsy (1923—). *American actress.* Born Sept 11, 1923, in Paris, France, to American parents; m. Cary Grant (actor), 1949 (div. 1962). ❖ Made film debut in *Every Girl Should be Married* (1948), followed by *Dancing in the Dark, Pretty Baby, The Second Woman, Room for One More, Will Success Spoil Rock Hunter?* and *Intent to Kill,* among others; directed a psychodrama therapy project at UCLA which resulted in her novel *Children, You're Very Young* (1971). Survived the sinking of the *Andrea Doria* cruise ship.

DRAKE, Dona (1914–1989). *American actress.* Name variations: Rita Ray, Rita Rio. Born Rita Novella, Nov 15, 1914, in Miami, Florida; died June 20, 1989, in Los Angeles, California. ❖ Began career as a bandsinger under name Rita Rio; films include *Aloma of the South Seas, Louisiana Purchase, Road to Morocco, Another Part of the Forest, The Girl from Jones Beach, Fortunes of Captain Blood, Valentino* and *Kansas City Confidential.*

DRAKE, Elizabeth (fl. 1625–1656). *English royalist.* Name variations: Elizabeth Churchill. Fl. between 1625 and 1656; dau. of Lady Eleanor Drake (staunch Parliamentarian and dau. of Elizabeth Villiers and Sir John Drake; m. Winston Churchill (West Country lawyer); children: Arabella Churchill (1648–1714); John Churchill (1650–1722), 1st duke of Marlborough (British statesman and general); Charles Churchill (1656–1714). ❖ During English Civil War (1642–51), saw fortunes fall when husband took up arms in defense of crown and Anglican church; with Stuart Restoration (1660), fortunes improved. ❖ See also *Women in World History.*

DRAKE, Fabia (1904–1990). *English stage, tv, and screen actress.* Born Jan 20, 1904, in Herne Bay; died Feb 28, 1990, in London, England; attended Royal Academy of Dramatic Arts; m. Maxwell Turner. ❖ Made stage debut as a small child (1913); had 1st major London role in *Major Barbara* (1921); was long associated with Stratford Memorial Theatre; made Broadway debut in *The Scarlet Lady* (1926); films include *Meet Mr. Penny, Young Wives' Tale, Fast and Loose, All Over the Town, The Good Companions* and *Valmont;* lifelong friend of Laurence Olivier, played Katherine to his Petruchio in grade school.

DRAKE, Frances (1908–2000). *American stage and screen actress.* Name variations: Frances Dean. Born Frances Dean, Oct 22, 1908, in New York, NY; died Jan 18, 2000, in Irvine, California; studied in Canada and England; m. Cecil John Arthur Howard (son of the 19th earl of Suffolk), 1939 (died 1985); m. David Brown, 1992. ❖ Began career as a dancer in London nightclubs, then made stage and film debuts in England as Frances Dean (1933); starred as Yvonne Orlac in the cult horror film *Mad Love* (1935); other films include *The Jewel, The Invisible Ray, Bolero, Les Misérables, The Lone Wolf in Paris* and *The Affairs of Martha;* retired from acting (1942).

DRAKE, Frances Denny (1797–1875). *American actress.* Born Frances Ann Denny, Nov 6, 1797, in Schenectady, NY; died Sept 1, 1875, in Louisville, Kentucky; dau. of John Denny; m. Alexander (Aleck) Drake (comic actor), 1822 (died 1830); m. George Washington Cutter (lawyer, poet); aunt of Julia Dean (1830–1868, actress); children: Julia Drake (actress who married theater magnate Harry S. Chapman and was the mother of actresses Blanche and Ella Chapman), Alexander E. Drake (army colonel), Richard Drake, Samuel Drake (actor and farmer). ❖ Talented stage actress, joined Samuel Drake's company as a teenager and worked with many of Drake's children, including Julia

Drake (mother of famed actress Julia Dean) and future husband Alexander Drake; made stage debut in Cherry Valley, NY, in comedy *The Midnight Hour,* then traveled with company to Lexington, Kentucky, giving performances en route; won considerable fame in Drake's Kentucky theaters; left Kentucky (1819) and went on to perform in Montreal and Boston; made New York City debut as Helen Worrett in *Man and Wife* (1820) and joined Park company; played at Chatham Theater in New York (1824); went West with husband and returned to father-in-law's circuit, making occasional tours in East; after husband died (1830), married George Washington Cutter but soon divorced; achieved star status, performing Shakespeare in New York and receiving warm welcome in England (1833); continued acting throughout 1840s, often alongside daughter Julia Drake. ❖ See also Noah M. Ludlow, *Dramatic Life as I Found It* (1880).

DRAKE, Henry (1901–1968). *See Drake-Brockman, Henrietta.*

DRAKE, Judith (fl. 1696). *British feminist.* Fl. 1696 in England. ❖ Probably wrote *An Essay in Defence of the Female Sex* (1696), and if so, was medical practitioner and sister of prominent physician James Drake and edited his works.

DRAKE-BROCKMAN, Henrietta (1901–1968). *Australian novelist, playwright and historian.* Name variations: Henrietta Drake Brockman; (pseudonym) Henry Drake. Born Henrietta Frances York Jull, July 27, 1901, in Perth, Western Australia; died Mar 8, 1968; dau. of Martin and Roberta Jull (1872–1961, physician); m. Geoffrey Drake-Brockman, commissioner for the far northwest of Australia, Aug 3, 1921. ❖ Novels, which reflect her experience of bush life in Western Australia, include *Blue North* (1934), *Sheba Lane* (1936), *Younger Sons* (1937), *The Fatal Days* (1947), *Sydney or the Bush* (19480, and *The Wicked and the Fair* (1957); plays include *Men Without Wives,* for which she won the New South Wales Sesquicentenary competition; with Walter Murdoch, co-edited *Australian Short Stories.* Named Officer of the Order of the British Empire (1967).

DRANE, Augusta Theodosia (1823–1894). *English writer.* Name variations: Mother Francis Raphael. Born at Bromley, near Bow, England, Dec 29, 1823; died at the Stone convent in Staffordshire, England, April 29, 1894. ❖ Brought up Anglican, was influenced by Tractarian teaching at Torquay and joined Roman Catholic Church (1850); her essay questioning the *Morality of Tractarianism,* published anonymously, was incorrectly attributed to John Henry Newman; following a prolonged stay in Rome, joined 3rd order of St. Dominic (1852), to which she belonged for over 40 years; served as prioress of the Stone convent in Staffordshire (1872–81); books include *The History of Saint Dominic* (1857), *The Life of St. Catherine of Siena* (1880), *Christian Schools and Scholars* (1867), *The Knights of St John* (1858), *Songs in the Night* (1876), and *Three Chancellors* (1859). ❖ See also B. Wilberforce, O.P., ed. *Memoir of Mother Francis Raphael, O.S.D., Augusta Theodosia Drane* (1895).

DRANSFELD, Hedwig (1871–1925). *German politician and social reformer.* Born in Hacheney bei Dortmund, Feb 24, 1871; died in Werl, Westphalia, Mar 13, 1925; dau. of Clemens and Elise (Fleischhauer) Dransfeld; attended teachers' training academy in Paderborn; never married; no children. ❖ Founder of the German Roman Catholic women's movement, taught for a number of years at Paderborn's Ursuline Academy in Werl, Westphalia; published 1st of several volumes of verse (1893); well known in German Catholic literary and social reform circles, became editor of journal *Die christliche Frau* (1905); by 1912, when she became chair of *Katholischer Deutscher Frauenbund* (German Catholic Women's League or KDF), had become the unchallenged leader of German Catholic women; was among the 1st group of German women to be elected to Weimar National Assembly (Jan 1919); as a candidate of the Catholic Center Party, was elected to the Reichstag (1920), where she quickly earned a reputation as one of the most eloquent orators in that political, often turbulent, body; resigned as head of KDF (1924). Was honored on a postage stamp of the German Federal Republic (1988). ❖ See also *Women in World History.*

DRAPER, Dorothy (1888–1969). *American interior decorator.* Born Dorothy Tuckerman, Nov 22, 1888, in New York, NY; grew up in Tuxedo Park; died Mar 1969; dau. of Paul Tuckerman (iron magnate) and Susan (Minturn) Tuckerman; sister-in-law of Ruth Draper (monologist); m. Dr. George Draper (internist and specialist in psychosomatic medicine), 1912 (div. 1929); children: 3. ❖ Opened shop in her house (1925); using bold colors and overscaled patterns, came to prominence with commission to decorate the Hotel Carlyle; achieved the Hall of

Fame for decorating the River Club (1933); also decorated Quitandinha (hotel and casino in Brazil), the Fairmont Hotel in San Francisco, the Hampshire House on Central Park South, and the homes of society's elite, including Mary Lasker and Clare Boothe Luce; retired (1960).

DRAPER, Elisabeth (1900–1993). American interior decorator. Name variations: Elisabeth Low. Born Elisabeth Carrington Frank, 1900, in New York, NY; died July 5, 1993, in New York, NY; dau. of Charles Frank (banker) and Louise Frank; sister of Tiffany Taylor; sister-in-law of Ruth Draper, monologist; attended Miss Spence's School; m. Seth Low (banker), c. 1919 (div. 1929); m. George Draper (internist and specialist in psychosomatic medicine), 1935; children: Seth Low Jr. ❖ Initially trained as a radio operator 1st class and served in that capacity during WWI; with sister, formed interior decorating firm, Taylor & Low; established a business under her own name (1936); decorated many homes, including that of Dwight and Mamie Eisenhower in NY and Gettysburg, PA; also worked on rooms at the White House and Blair House.

DRAPER, Helen (1871–1951). American Red Cross worker. Name variations: Mrs. William K. Draper. Born Helen Hoffman in 1871; died 1951; dau. of Richard Hoffman (noted concert pianist) and Fidelia Lamson Hoffman; sister of Malvina Hoffman (sculptor); m. William K. Draper (died 1926). ❖ During Spanish-American war, headed the New York chapter of the American Red Cross; by marriage, was related to solo performer Ruth Draper.

DRAPER, Margaret (d. around 1800). Massachusetts printer. Died c. 1800 in England; m. Richard Draper (1727–1774). ❖ After death of husband, continued publication of his *Massachusetts Gazette and Boston News-Letter* (1774–1776), the only paper published in MA during the American Revolution's siege of Boston (July 1775–Mar 1776); as a Tory, fled with British army to Halifax (Feb 1776) and then England.

DRAPER, Mary Anna Palmer (1839–1914). American philanthropist and benefactor of astronomy. Name variations: Mrs. Henry Draper. Born Mary Anna Palmer, Sept 11, 1839, in Stonington, Connecticut; died Dec 8, 1914, in New York, NY; dau. of Courtlandt Palmer (merchant, real-estate investor) and Mary Ann (Suydam) Palmer; sister of Courtlandt Palmer Jr. (founder and 1st president of Nineteenth Century Club); m. Henry Draper (professor of physiology and chemistry, astronomer), 1867 (died 1882). ❖ Benefactor and assistant to astronomer husband, helped him to conduct pioneering work in nebular and lunar photography and to take 1st photographs of absorption lines in stellar spectra; from inheritance, funded husband's scientific pursuits and later contributed to research of others; accompanied husband to view and photograph solar eclipse in Rawlins, Wyoming (1878); following husband's death (1882), funded work of E.C. Pickering at Harvard College Observatory, establishing Henry Draper Memorial Fund; enabled Pickering to begin massive program of photographing spectra of stars and classifying these on basis of characteristics, thus compiling *Draper Catalogue of Stellar Spectra* (1890) which classified 10,000 stars and was updated and extended in 11 more vols. (1918–49); visited Harvard observatory regularly and inspected work in progress, giving advice on matters of policy and serving on observatory's visiting committee; contributed as well to National Academy of Sciences, donating Henry Draper Medal (1883). Also known for her knowledge and interest in archeology and for vast collection of archeological artifacts.

DRAPER, Ruth (1884–1956). American actress and monologist. Born Ruth Draper in New York, NY, Dec 2, 1884; died Dec 29, 1956; dau. of William (physician) and Ruth (Dana) Draper; sister of Muriel Draper; never married; no children. ❖ The foremost solo performer of her day, made acting debut in NY, portraying a maid in *A Lady's Name* (1916); never appeared on stage with another performer again; real career began (1918), when she entertained troops of the American Expeditionary Force (AEF) in France during WWI; made formal professional appearance as a solo performer in London (1920) and fame came quickly; invited to give a command performance before George V and Mary of Teck (1926); toured Europe and US (1924–28); regaled audiences for 18 weeks at Comedy Theater in NY (1928–29), a record for a solo performer; toured South Africa (1935), Far East (1938), Latin America (1940), US and Canada (1940–41), Europe and US (1946–56); gave last performances in New York (Dec 25–28, 1956); a humanist who saw and felt the pain of others, depicted her characters with understanding and compassion; over the years, composed 37 skits, featuring some 58 characters; her longest, *Three Women and Mr. Clifford*, took an hour to perform and was, in effect, a one-act play in three scenes; her shortest, *A French Dressmaker*, was accomplished in 4 minutes; others include *Love in the Balkans*, *A Cleaning Woman*, *The Dalmatian Peasant*, *In a Church in Italy*, *The Wives of Henry VIII*, *Three Women in a Court of Domestic Relations*, *The Italian Lesson*, *Vive La France* and *Three Breakfasts*. Named Commander of the Order of the British Empire. ❖ See also Neilla Warren, *The Letters of Ruth Draper* (1979); and *Women in World History*.

DRAVES, Victoria (1924—). American swimmer. Name variations: Vicki or Vickie Draves. Born Victoria Manalo, Dec 31, 1924, in San Francisco, California; dau. of a Filipino father and English mother; had a nonidentical twin sister; m. Lyle Draves (her diving coach), 1946. ❖ Won AAU Outdoor Platform championship (1946–48); won the gold medal in springboard and platform diving at London Olympics (1948), the 1st woman to win both. ❖ See also *Women in World History*.

DRAYTON, Grace Gebbie (1877–1936). American artist and illustrator. Name variations: Grace Gebbie; Grace Gebbie Wiedersheim. Born Grace Gebbie in Philadelphia, Pennsylvania, Oct 14, 1877; died Jan 31, 1936; dau. of George (Philadelphia's 1st art publisher) and Mary (Fitzgerald) Gebbie; sister of Margaret G. Hays (writer); m. Theodore E. Wiedersheim Jr. (div. 1911); m. W. Heyward Drayton III (div. 1923). ❖ One of America's earliest illustrators, developed her 1st cartoon, *Naughty Toodles*, for the Hearst syndicate (1903), followed by her ubiquitous drawings of The Campbell Kids (1905). ❖ See also *Women in World History*.

DREAM 6. See Napolitano, Johnette.

DREAMERS. See Napolitano, Johnette.

DREAM SYNDICATE. See Smith, Kendra.

DREAVER, Mary (1887–1964). New Zealand politician. Name variations: May Bain. Born Mary Bain, Mar 31, 1887, in Dunedin, NZ; died July 19, 1964; m. Andrew Dreaver (butcher), 1911; children: 6, including Alex Dreaver (MP). ❖ Hosted numerous radio programs throughout career; as a Labour candidate, won a by-election for the Waitemata seat for New Zealand House of Representatives (1941); appointed to New Zealand's upper house, the Legislative Council (1946), before it was abolished (1950). Received an MBE (1946) in recognition for her work with Mary Grigg for the Women's Land Service during WWII.

DRECHSLER, Heike (1964—). East German long jumper. Name variations: Heike Daute. Born Heike Daute, Dec 16, 1964, in Gera, East Germany; m. Andreas Drechsler, 1984. ❖ Was a dominant force in the long jump throughout career; at World championships, won a gold for long jump (1983, 1993); at European championships, won a gold for long jump (1986, 1990, 1994, 1998) and 200 meters (1986); won a silver medal for long jump at Seoul Olympics (1988), along with bronze medals for the 200 meters and 100 meters; won a gold medal at Barcelona Olympics (1992) and a gold medal at Sydney Olympics (2000), both for long jump.

DREIER, Katherine Sophie (1877–1952). American artist, suffragist, and social activist. Name variations: frequently misspelled as Drier. Born Sept 10, 1877, in Brooklyn, New York; died Mar 29, 1952, in Milford, Connecticut; dau. of Dorothea Adelheid Dreier and her cousin Theodor Dreier (iron merchant); sister of Mary Elisabeth Dreier and Margaret Dreier Robins; attended Brooklyn Art Students League, 1895–97, Pratt Institute, 1900–01; m. Edward Trumball-Smith, Aug 1911 (annulled 1911); no children. ❖ Served as treasurer, German Home for Recreation for Women and Children (1900–09); sold her 1st art piece, an altar painting for the chapel of St. Paul's school in Garden City, NY; was co-founder and president, the Little Italy Neighborhood Association, Brooklyn (1905); served as a delegate, Sixth Convention of the International Woman's Suffrage Alliance (1911); had 1st exhibit, London (1911); exhibited at the NY Armory Show (1913), the 1st mass showing of modern art on American soil; founded the Cooperative Mural Workshop (1914); chaired the German-American Committee, NYC's Woman's Suffrage Party (1915); was a co-founder of the Society of Independent Artists (1916); with Marcel Duchamp and Man Ray, co-founded Societe Anonyme (1920); held retrospective show, New York Academy of Allied Arts (1933); was instrumental in bringing modern art to America. Published numerous articles and books, including *Five Months in the Argentine: From a Woman's Point of View, 1918 to 1919* (1920), *Western Art and the New Era* (1923), and *Shawn the Dancer* (1933). ❖ See also *Women in World History*.

DREIER, Margaret (1868–1945). *See Robins, Margaret Dreier.*

DREIER, Mary Elisabeth (1875–1963). American labor and women's rights activist. Name variations: frequently misspelled as Drier. Pronunciation: DRY-er. Born Sept 26, 1875, in Brooklyn, New York; died in Bar Harbor, Maine, Aug 15, 1963; dau. of Dorothea Adelheid Dreier and her cousin Theodor Dreier (iron merchant); sister of Margaret Dreier Robins and Katherine Sophie Dreier; lived with Frances Kellor for 45 years; never married; no children. ❖ Did settlement house work at Asacog House, Brooklyn (late 1890s); was a member of the Women's Trade Union League (WTUL, 1904–50), president of the New York WTUL (1906–14); was a member of the NY State Factory Investigating Commission (1911–15); served as delegate-at-large, Progressive Party convention (1912); served as chair of the NYC's Woman Suffrage Party (1916); served as chair of NY State Committee on Women in Industry, Advisory Commission, Council of National Defense (1918–19); was a long-time member of the Industrial Department and National Board, Young Women's Christian Association (YWCA); was an anti-nuclear activist (1950s). ❖ See also *Margaret Dreier Robins: Her Life, Letters and Work* (1950); and *Women in World History.*

DREIFUSS, Ruth (1940—). Swiss politician and economist. Born Jan 9, 1940, in St. Gallen, Switzerland; grew up in Geneva; earned a degree in economics from Geneva University. ❖ A Social Democrat, was elected to the Swiss Federal Cabinet (Mar 1993), serving as interior minister until 2002; was elected, by Parliament, to the 1-year presidential post of the Swiss Confederation (1999), only the 2nd woman and the 1st Jew.

DREMAN, Rebecca (c. 1950—). *See King, Rebecca.*

DRESDEL, Sonia (1909–1976). English actress. Born Lois Obee, May 5, 1909, in Hornsea, Yorkshire, England; died Jan 18, 1976, in Canterbury, Kent, England. ❖ Made stage debut (1931); joined the Old Vic company (1939) and had great success as Hedda in *Hedda Gabler;* films include *This Was a Woman, The Secret Tent, The Fallen Idol, Trials of Oscar Wilde* (as Lady Wilde), *The World Owes Me a Living, Now and Forever* and *Lady Caroline Lamb;* appeared frequently on tv, most notably in "The Pallisers."

DRESDEN, Anna (1906–1943). *See Polak, Anna.*

DRESSEL, Vally (1893—). German swimmer. Born June 3, 1893. ❖ At Stockholm Olympics, won a silver medal in the 4 x 100-meter freestyle relay (1912).

DRESSER, Louise (1878–1965). American stage and screen actress. Born Louise Kerlin, Oct 5, 1878, in Evansville, Indiana; died April 24, 1965, in Woodland Hills, California; m. Jack Norworth (div.); m. John Gardner (singer and actor), 1909 (died 1950). ❖ First appeared in vaudeville (1900), then Broadway musicals; co-starred with Will Rogers in a number of films, including *State Fair, Lightnin'* and *David Harum;* other films include *The Eagle* (opposite Valentino) *Mammy, Cradle Song, The Scarlet Empress, The Girl of the Limberlost* and *Mother Knows Best;* retired (1937). Won Academy Award for performance in *When My Ship Comes In.*

DRESSLER, Marie (1869–1934). American actress. Born Leila Marie Koerber, Nov 9, 1869, in Coburg, Canada; died July 28, 1934, in Santa Barbara, California; dau. of an itinerant music teacher; married twice; no children. ❖ Endearing character actresses of 1930s, joined a stock company at 14 and became a vaudeville headliner; had most successful turn on Broadway as Tillie Blobbs in *Tillie's Nightmare* (1910), in which her rendition of song "Heaven Will Protect the Working Girl" was particularly memorable; signed a film contract with Mack Sennett for a series of "Tillie" movies, the 1st of which co-starred Charlie Chaplin; co-starring with Polly Moran, struck paydirt with film *The Callahans and the Murphys* (1927); made several additional films with Moran, including *Bringing Up Father* (1928); appeared in serious role of Marthy in *Anna Christie* and won Academy Award for Best Actress for performance in *Min and Bill* with Wallace Beery; teamed again with Beery in *Tugboat Annie* (1933); though an unlikely star, was No. 1 box-office attraction in the country for several years; other films include *The Patsy* (1928), *The Vagabond Lover* (1929), *Dinner at Eight* (1933) and *Christopher Bean* (1933). ❖ See also autobiography (with M. Harrington) *My Own Story* (1934); Betty Lee, *Marie Dressler: The Unlikeliest Star* (U. of Kentucky Press, 1997); and *Women in World History.*

DRESSLER, Patricia (1906–1978). *See Calvert, Patricia.*

DREUX, countess of.
See Yolande de Coucy (d. 1222).
See Jeanne I (d. 1346).
See Jeanne II (r. 1346–1355).

DREUX, ruler of. *See Marguerite de Thouars (r. 1365–1377).*

DREVJANA, Alena (1969—). Czech gymnast. Born July 4, 1969, in Opava, Czechoslovakia. ❖ Won Kosice International (1984) and Czech nationals (1986).

DREW, Ellen (1914–2003). American actress. Name variations: Terry Ray. Born Esther Loretta Ray, Nov 23, 1914, in Kansas City, Missouri; died Dec 3, 2003, in Palm Desert, California; m. Fred Wallace (makeup man), 1935 (div. 1940); m. Sy Bartlett (screenwriter), 1941 (div. 1950); m. William T. Walker (Detroit advertising executive), 1951 (div. 1967); m. James Edward Herbert (retired executive), 1971; children: David Bartlett. ❖ Made film debut in *College Holiday* under name Terry Ray (1936); changed name to Ellen Drew (1938), appearing in such films as *Sing You Sinners, If I Were King, Women without Names, Buck Benny Rides Again, Johnny O'Clock* and Preston Sturges' *Christmas in July.*

DREW, Georgiana Emma (1854–1893). American actress. Name variations: Georgiana Emma Drew Barrymore, Georgie. Born in Philadelphia, Pennsylvania, July 11, 1854; died in Santa Barbara, California, July 2, 1893; dau. of John Drew and Louisa Lane Drew (both actors); younger sister of actor John Drew Jr.; m. Maurice Barrymore (1847–1905, actor), Dec 1876; children: actors Lionel (1878–1954), Ethel Barrymore (1879–1959), and John Barrymore (1882–1942). ❖ Made theatrical debut in *The Ladies' Battle* at her mother's Arch Street Theatre in Philadelphia (1872); joined Augustin Daly's repertory company at Fifth Avenue Theatre in NY (1875); excelled in comedy, particularly *The Senator* (1890); contracted tuberculosis; made stage farewell in NY (Feb 1893). ❖ See also Hollis Alpert, *The Barrymores* (Dial, 1964); and *Women in World History.*

DREW, Jane (1911–1996). British architect. Name variations: Dame Jane Beverly Drew; Mrs. Maxwell Fry. Born Joyce Beverly Drew in Thornton Heath, Surrey, England, Mar 24, 1911; died July 27, 1996, at Barnard Castle, Co. Durham; father was a designer and manufacturer of surgical instruments and mother a botanist; graduate of London's Architectural Association School, 1929; m. James Thomas Alliston (architect), 1934 (div. 1939); m. E. Maxwell Fry (architect), 1942 (died 1987); children: (1st m.) twin daughters Jennifer and Sarah Alliston. ❖ One of the world's leading architects, who specialized in the design of structures best suited for tropical climes, is best-known for designs for the New Capital City at Chandigarh, India, and the buildings for the Open University at Milton Keynes, England; went into partnership with husband James Alliston (1934); was soon attracted to modern tendencies in architecture, particularly as exemplified in the Congres International d'Architecture Moderne (CIAM), whose guiding spirit was Le Corbusier; became one of the founding members of the modernist school of British architecture, which was centered around a group naming itself Modern Architectural ReSearch (MARS), the British subsidiary of the international CIAM movement; following divorce (1939), established her own practice; served as chair of "Rebuilding Britain" exhibition held at London's National Gallery (1943); served as assistant town-planning advisor to the Resident Minister for the West African Colonies; married architect Maxwell Fry and started another professional partnership which lasted until his death; with husband, worked in British West African colonies and published *Village Housing in the Tropics,* the 1st of several major works that would be based on their practical experiences in tropical regions; elected president of the Architectural Association (1969); changed the course of British architecture, opening up jobs on all levels for women over a remarkable career lasting almost half a century. Named Dame of the British Empire (1996). ❖ See also *Women in World History.*

DREW, Mrs. John (1820–1897). *See Drew, Louisa Lane.*

DREW, Kathleen M. (1901–1957). *See Drew-Baker, Kathleen M.*

DREW, Louisa Lane (1820–1897). British actress and theater manager. Name variations: Mrs. John Drew. Born Louisa Lane, Jan 10, 1820, at Lambeth Parish, London, England; died in Larchmont, New York, Aug 31, 1897; dau. of Eliza Trentner (actress) and William Haycraft Lane (actor and stage manager); m. Henry Blaine Hunt, 1836 (div. 1846); m. George Mossop; m. John Drew (1827–1862, actor), July 1857; children: (3rd m.) Louisa (whose daughter, actress Georgiana Drew Mendum, was a constant companion to her cousin Ethel Barrymore); John Jr. (1853–1927, actor); Georgiana Drew (1854–1893, actress); (adopted)

Sidney Drew (actor); (adopted) Adine Stevens; grandchildren: actors John, Lionel, and Ethel Barrymore. ❖ Famous as Mrs. John Drew, made stage debut at 12 months, playing a bawling baby; arriving in US with widowed mother and an English stock troupe (1827), made American debut at Walnut Street Theater in Philadelphia, playing the adolescent Duke of York to Junius Brutus Booth's Richard III; with mother, joined various stock companies and toured for next 12 years; managed Mrs. John Drew's Arch Street Theater for 31 years (1862–93), making her one of the 1st women in American history to run an important theater; during tenure, built up one of the most successful repertory companies in the history of American stage—headliners included Edwin Booth, Fanny Davenport, and Helena Modjeska—while distinguishing herself as a major comedy actress, playing Lady Teazle, Peg Woffington, as well as Mrs. Malaprop in *The Rivals*, her most famous portrayal. ❖ See also *Autobiographical Sketch of Mrs. John Drew* (1899); and *Women in World History*.

DREW, Lucille (1890–1925). American actress and director. Name variations: Mrs. Sidney Drew; Lucille McVey; Jane Morrow. Born Lucille McVey, April 18, 1890, in Sedalia, Missouri; died Nov 3, 1925, in Los Angeles, California; m. Sidney Drew (actor and son of Louisa Lane Drew), 1914 (died 1919). ❖ Starred with husband at Vitagraph and Metro; films include *Playing Dead, His Wife's Mother, The Pest, The Professional Patient* and *Payday;* also directed.

DREW, Mrs. Sidney (1890–1925). See Drew, Lucille.

DREW-BAKER, Kathleen M. (1901–1957). English botanist. Name variations: Dr. Kathleen M. Drew; Kathleen M. Baker; Kathleen Drew Baker. Born Kathleen Mary Drew, 1901, in Leigh, Lancashire, England; died 1957; University of Manchester, BS, 1922, MS, 1923, DSc, 1939; m. H. Wright Baker; children: Dr. John Rendle Baker and (Kathleen) Frances Baker Biggs. ❖ A red seaweed (Rhodophyceae) expert, discovered the life cycle of the nori (seaweed), an enormous contribution to the Japanese nori farming industry; was 1st president of British Phycological Society; also studied seaweeds in California and Hawaii; worked as assistant lecturer at University of Manchester's Botany Department (from 1923); studied potential uses of seaweed for manufacture of agar for bacteria cultivation during war years. Monument to her was erected in Sumiyoshi Shrine Park, overlooking the Ariake Sea, in Uto City, Japan (1963).

DREWERY, Corinne (1959—). English singer. Name variations: Swing Out Sister. Born Sept 21, 1959, in Nottingham, England. ❖ With background in fashion design and no professional experience in music, became lead singer for Swing Out Sister, formed in Manchester, England (1985); with group, had hit debut single "Breakout" (1987), which went to #6 in charts, and #1 debut LP, *It's Better to Travel* (1987), which also yielded a minor hit with "Twilight World." Other albums include *Kaleidoscope World* (1989), *Get in Touch With Yourself* (1992) and *Where Our Love Grows* (2004); single hits include "Waiting Game" (1989) and "Am I the Same Girl" (1992).

DREWITZ, Ingeborg (1923–1986). West German novelist and playwright. Born Jan 10, 1923, in Berlin, Germany; died Nov 26, 1986, in Berlin. ❖ Wrote about women's struggles to balance demands of family and public life and was the 1st German to write about concentration camps; works include *Alle Tore waren bewacht* (1951), *Oktoberlicht* (1969), *Gestern war Heute—Hundert Jahre Gegenwart* (1978) and *Eis auf der Elbe* (1982); also wrote *Bettine von Arnim: Romantik, Revolution, Utopie* (1969).

DREXEL, Constance (1894–1956). German-born American journalist. Born in Darmstadt, Germany, Nov 28, 1894; died in Waterbury, Connecticut, Aug 28, 1956; dau. of Theodor and Zela (Audeman) Drexel; attended schools in 4 different countries, including studies at Sorbonne; never married. ❖ Gained notoriety as a broadcaster for Nazi Germany during World War II; moved with family to US when she was one; obtained US citizenship when father became a naturalized American (1898); during WWI, was one of the 1st American women to volunteer her services as a French Red Cross nurse (1914); wrote for the *New York Tribune;* writings clearly revealed a strongly pro-German bias; covered the Paris peace conference and often wrote for European edition of *Chicago Tribune* (1918); believed, as did many others, that the Versailles treaty of 1919 had been harsh and self-defeating as regards the Germans; naïvely allowed herself to carry out assignments for Nazi propaganda agencies (1930s); began broadcasting from Berlin (1940), largely about social and cultural matters; arrested by American troops in Germany and imprisoned for one year (1945); had a treason indictment

against her dismissed for lack of evidence (1948). ❖ See also *Women in World History*.

DREXEL, Katharine (1858–1955). See Drexel, Mary Katharine.

DREXEL, Mary Katharine (1858–1955). American nun, religious founder and saint. Name variations: Mother Mary Katharine; Katharine Drexel. Born Mary Katharine Drexel, Nov 26, 1858, in Philadelphia, Pennsylvania; died in Cornwall Heights, Pennsylvania, at the Motherhouse of the Sisters of the Blessed Sacrament, Mar 3, 1955; dau. of Francis Anthony Drexel (banker from Austria) and Hannah Jane Langstroth; sister of Elizabeth and Louise Drexel; never married; no children. ❖ Particularly interested in relieving the plight of Native Americans, sought to enhance the educational opportunities on the reservations of the American West; traveled to Europe to examine the latest in teaching techniques (1886); meeting with Pope Leo XIII (1887), asked for nuns and priests to work with the Native Americans; was urged by the pope and her local bishop to create her own order; using Sisters of Mercy as a model, entered their novitiate in Pittsburgh (May 6, 1889); took her vows as the 1st sister of the Sisters of the Blessed Sacrament for Indians and Colored People (1891); established a novitiate and motherhouse in Cornwall Heights, Pennsylvania (1892) and the Rules and Constitution for the Order (1894); worked in both urban and rural settings, establishing a boarding school for the Pueblo in Santa Fe, New Mexico, a school for African-American girls in Virginia, a manual arts school in Arizona, and a mission in Harlem, New York, among others; began work to organize a teachers' college (later Xavier University) in New Orleans for African-Americans (1915); was proclaimed a saint by Pope John Paul II (Oct 1, 2000). ❖ See also Katherine Burton, *The Golden Door: The Life of Katharine Drexel* (Kennedy, 1957); Consuela Marie Duffy, *Katharine Drexel: A Biography* (Reilly, 1966); and *Women in World History*.

DREXEL, Wiltrud (1950—). Austrian Alpine skier. Born Aug 16, 1950, in Feldkirch, Austria. ❖ Won a bronze medal for the giant slalom at Sapporo Olympics (1972) and a bronze medal for downhill at World championships (1974); won a World Cup downhill title (1969).

DREYFUSS, Anne (1957—). French modern dancer. Born 1957 in Strasbourg, France. ❖ Performed with jazz ballet troupe of Peter Goss; on European tour, danced with Jennifer Muller's US based company, The Works (1978).

DRIF, Zohra (1941—). Algerian revolutionary and novelist. Name variations: Zohra Drif-Bitat. Born 1941 in Algeria. ❖ As a law student, was a leader with her lover Yacef Saadi of the Algerian National Liberation Front (FLN); was arrested along with Saadi (1957) and sentenced to 20 years hard labor for participating in bomb attacks in battle of Algiers; later worked for women's rights in Algeria; writings include *La Mort de me frères* (1960).

DRINKER, Catherine Ann (1841–1922). American painter. Name variations: Kate; Katherine Ann Janvier. Born Catherine Ann Drinker in 1841; died 1922; dau. of Sandwith Drinker (sea captain in East India trade) and Susan Drinker; aunt of historian Catherine Drinker Bowen; studied art with Dutch painter Adolf van der Whelan at Maryland Institute, and with Thomas Eakins at Pennsylvania Academy; married Thomas Allibone Janvier, 1878. ❖ The 1st woman permitted to teach at the Pennsylvania Academy, was a traditional painter who was fond of historical and Biblical subjects; also earned recognition for her English translations of romantic novels of Provençale. ❖ See also Catherine Drinker Bowen, *Family Portrait* (Little, Brown, 1970); and *Women in World History*.

DRINKER, Elizabeth Sandwith (1734–1807). American diarist. Born Elizabeth Sandwith, 1734, in Philadelphia, Pennsylvania; died 1807; ancestor of writer Catherine Drinker Bowen; m. Henry Drinker; children: 5. ❖ Kept a journal for 50 years (1758–1808), which was later published as *Extracts from the Journal of Elizabeth Drinker* (1889).

DRINKER, Ernesta (1852–1939). American artist's model. Name variations: Etta Beaux. Born Aimeé Ernesta Beaux, Oct 26, 1852, in New York, NY; dau. of Jean Adolphe Beaux (silk manufacturer) and Cecilia Kent (Leavitt) Beaux; sister of Cecilia Beaux (artist); m. Henry Sturgis Drinker (brother of Catherine Ann Drinker and president of Lehigh University), 1879; children: 6, including Catherine Drinker Bowen (1897–1973, writer). ❖ Was the subject of many of her sister's paintings.

DRINKWATER, Jennie M. (1841–1900). American author. Name variations: Jennie Conklin; Jennie Maria Drinkwater Conklin. Born Jennie Maria Drinkwater, April 12, 1841, in Yarmouth, Maine; died April 28, 1900; m. Rev. Nathaniel Conklin, 1880. ❖ Popular writer for young readers, published such works as *Tessa Wadsworth's Discipline* (1879), *Electa* (1881), *Marigold* (1889) and *Looking Seaward* (1893); originated the Shut-In Society (1874), which was incorporated in NY (1885).

DRISCOLL, Clara (1881–1945). American philanthropist and politician. Name variations: Mrs. Henry Sevier. Born in St. Mary's Texas, April 2, 1881; died in Corpus Christi, Texas, July 17, 1945; dau. of Robert (millionaire rancher and businessman) and Julia (Fox) Driscoll; m. Henry Hulme ("Hal") Sevier (founder of newspaper, *Austin American*), July 1906 (div. 1937); no children. ❖ Best remembered for her role in preserving the Alamo Mission in San Antonio, scene of the famous battle of the Texas Revolution of 1836; also established a children's hospital in Corpus Christi (1953); as a Democrat, was heavily involved in state politics; writings include novel *The Girl of La Gloria* (1905), a collection of short stories about Texas, *In the Shadow of the Alamo* (1906), and play *Mexicana* (1906). ❖ See also *Women in World History*.

DRISCOLL, Jean (1966—). American champion wheelchair athlete. Born with spina bifida, Nov 18, 1966, in Milwaukee, Wisconsin; University of Illinois, BA, 1991, MS, 1993. ❖ Won the Boston Marathon's women's wheelchair title for 7 consecutive years (1990–1996), placed 2nd (1998), then won again (2000); won silver medals at Barcelona Olympics (1992) and Atlanta Olympics (1996), both for 800 meters; won 5 Paralympic gold medals. Named Amateur Sportswoman of the Year by Women's Sports Foundation (1991); inducted into Wheelchair Sports (USA) Hall of Fame (2002). ❖ See also autobiography *Determined to Win* (2000) and PBS documentary "Against the Wind."

DRIVER, Senta (1942—). American modern dancer. Born Sept 5, 1942, in Greenwich, Connecticut. ❖ Performed with Paul Taylor's company (1967–73), appearing in his *Aureole, Private Domain, Lento, From Sea to Shining Sea,* and more; founded own dance company, Harry; recognized for integrating allusion and postmodern movement vocabulary, choreographed numerous works, including *Board Fade Excerpt* (1975), *The Kschessinska Variations* (1976), and *Simulcast* (1979).

DRLJACA, Radmila (1959—). Yugoslavian handball player. Born Dec 21, 1959. ❖ At Moscow Olympics, won a silver medal in team competition (1980).

DROBONEGA OF KIEV (d. 1087). *See Maria of Kiev.*

DROESCHER, Mrs. (1902–1964). *See Texidor, Greville.*

DROGENBROEK, Marieke van (1964—). *See van Drogenbroek, Marieke.*

DROITURIÈRE, Marion la (d. 1390). Accused of witchcraft. Name variations: Droituriere or L'Estalee. Burned in 1390. ❖ Along with Margot de la Barre, was sentenced by the judges of the Châtelet in Paris to the pillory and then to be burned at the stake (Aug 9, 1390), for casting a spell on her former lover Ainselin and his wife Agnesot. ❖ See also *Women in World History.*

DROLET, Marie-Eve (1982—). Canadian short-track speedskater. Born Feb 3, 1982, in Chicoutimi, Quebec, Canada. ❖ Was World Jr. champion (2000); won a bronze medal at Salt Lake City Olympics for the 3,000-meter relay (2002).

DROLET, Nancy (1973—). Canadian ice-hockey player. Born Aug 2, 1973, in Drummondville, Quebec, Canada. ❖ Played for Vancouver Griffins; won 4 World championship gold medals with Team Canada (1992, 1994, 1997, 2001); won a team silver medal at Nagano (1998), the 1st Olympics to feature women's ice hockey.

DRONKE, Maria (1904–1987). *See Dronke, Minnie Maria.*

DRONKE, Minnie Maria (1904–1987). New Zealand actor, drama producer and teacher. Name variations: Maria Dronke, Minnie Kronfeld, Maria Korten. Born July 17, 1904, in Berlin, Germany; died Aug 28, 1987, in Lower Hutt, New Zealand; dau. of Salomon Kronfeld (barrister) and Laura (Liebmann) Kronfeld; m. Adolf John Rudolf Dronke (judge, died 1982), 1931; children: 1 son, 1 daughter. ❖ Performed classical roles in Germany (1920s), as Maria Korten; moved to England (1938) and immigrated to New Zealand (1939); privately taught drama and voice production and established studio in Lambton Quay (c. 1951); directed, produced, and performed in plays

(1940s); gave poetry recitals and broadcast series of talks for New Zealand Broadcasting System (1948). Named OBE (1980). ❖ See also *Dictionary of New Zealand Biography* (Vol. 4).

DRONOVA, Nina. Georgian gymnast. Born in Tbilisi, Georgia. ❖ Won the Chunichi Cup (1971, 1974), Champions All (1974), Riga (1975); at World championships, won a gold medal for team all-around (1974).

DROSSIN, Deena (1973—). *See Kastor, Deena.*

DROSTE-HÜLSHOFF, Annette von (1797–1848). German poet and writer. Name variations: Nette; Annette von Droste-Hulshoff. Pronunciation: DROS-te HUELShof. Born Anna Elisabeth Freiin (Baroness) von Droste zu Hülshoff, Jan 10, 1797, at Castle Hülshoff near Münster, Germany; died May 24, 1848, in Meersburg, Germany; dau. of Clemens August, Baron von Droste zu Hülshoff (1760–1826) and Therese (von Haxthausen) von Droste zu Hülshoff (1772–1853); never married; no children. ❖ Commonly considered one of the greatest poets of the German language, whose works are highly regarded for their lyrical brilliance, intricate narrative structures, and insights into the position of women in society, wrote 1st poem (1804); wrote collection of poems for every holiday on the church calendar, *Das geist 'liche Jahr* (*Spiritual Calendar,* 1819), but did not allow publication in her lifetime; published 1st collection of poetry (1838); wrote 18-to-20 ballads (1840–41), which are considered among the very best of the genre and often revolve around the question of guilt and sin; achieved 1st literary success with the criminal novella *Die Juden 'buche* (*The Jew's Beech Tree,* 1842); wrote the prose fragments *Bei uns zu Lande auf dem Lande* (*Out at Our Country Place,* 1841) and *Bilder aus Westfalen* (*Pictures from Westphalia,* 1842); published 2nd collection of poetry (1844); 1st publication of collected works were released posthumously (1860); her *The Jew's Beech Tree,* and many of her poems are required reading in German schools; was also a painter, pianist, and composer. Adorned the new 20DM bill of the Federal Republic of Germany (1990s). ❖ See also Mary Morgan, *Annette von Droste-Hülshoff: A Biography* (Lang, 1984); Edith Toegel, *Emily Dickinson and Annette von Droste-Hülshoff: Poets as Women* (Studia Humanitatis, 1982); and *Women in World History.*

DROUET, Juliette (1806–1883). French actress and paramour. Born Juliette Josephine Guavain, April 10, 1806, in Rillé, France; died 1883; dau. of a tailor and a housemaid; orphaned when young, was reared by an uncle; children: (with Pradier) daughter Claire. ❖ Had relationships with Prince Anatole Demidov and journalist Alphonse Karr; appeared as Princess Negroni in Victor Hugo's *Lucrèce Borgia* at the Porte-Saint-Martin and became his mistress (1833), remaining devoted to him for the rest of her life; went into exile with Hugo to Guernsey, Channel Islands, and acted as his secretary; was the subject of many of his poems; modeled and had an affair with sculptor Jean Pradier and was the inspiration for his "Statue de Strasbourg" in the Place de la Concorde; left a large collection of letters.

DROUIN, Candice (1976—). Canadian snowboarder and skier. Born June 4, 1976, in Toronto, Ontario, Canada. ❖ Won bronze in Boarder X at X Games (Winter 1999).

DROWER, E. S. (1879–1972). English scholar and writer. Name variations: Ethel Stefana Drower; Lady E. S. Drower; Lady Ethel S. Drower; Lady Drower; E.S. Stevens. Born Ethel Stefana May Stevens, Dec 1, 1879; died 1972; children: Margaret S. Drower (Egyptologist). ❖ Best known for book, *The Mandaeans of Iraq and Iran* (1937); also wrote *A Mandaic Dictionary* (1941) and *Peacock Angel* (1941) and translated *The Canonical Prayerbook of the Mandaeans* (1959); as E.S. Stevens, wrote *My Sudan Year.* ❖ See also Margaret Hackforth-Jones, "The Life of Lady E.S. Drower" (ARAM, Vol 11, Issue 1, 1999–2000).

DROWER, Margaret S. (c. 1913—). English egyptologist. Name variations: Margaret Stephana Drower; M.S. Drower; Margaret Hackforth-Jones. Born c. 1913; dau. of E.S. Drower (writer); studied Egyptology at University College in London; m. C. Hackforth-Jones. ❖ Writer, archaeologist, and Egypt specialist, researched in Egypt (2 winters); spent many years in Baghdad; served as lecturer and reader in ancient history (from 1937) and as honorary Department of History and Egyptology research fellow at University College in London; after retirement, assisted BBC with archaeology programs. Publications include several chapters for a revised edition of *Cambridge Ancient History* (1965), as well as a biography on archaeologist Flinders Petrie (1985); as Margaret Hackforth-Jones, wrote "The Life of Lady E.S. Drower" (ARAM periodical, Vol 11, Issue 1, 1999–2000).

DROWN, Julia (1962—). English politician and member of Parliament. Born Julia Drown, Aug 23, 1962; m. Bill Child, 1999. ❖ Representing Labour, elected to House of Commons for South Swindon (1997, 2001); left Parliament (2005).

DRU, Joanne (1923–1996). American actress. Born Joanne LaCock, Jan 31, 1923, in Logan, West Virginia; died Sept 10, 1996, in Beverly Hills, California; sister of Peter Marshall (tv host); m. Dick Haymes (singer), 1941 (div. 1949); m. John Ireland (actor), 1949 (div. 1956). ❖ Began career as model and showgirl; appeared on Broadway in musical *Hold Onto Your Hats* (1940); made film debut in *Abie's Irish Rose* (1946); played lead or second-lead roles in many films, including *Red River, Wagonmaster, All the King's Men, She Wore a Yellow Ribbon, The Pride of St. Louis, Thunder Bay, Sincerely Yours, Durango* and *The Light in the Forest.*

DRUMMOND, Annabella (1350–1401). Queen of Scotland. Name variations: Anabil de Drummond. Born 1350 in Scotland; died Oct 1401 at Scone Palace, Perth, Tayside, Scotland; dau. of Sir John Drummond of Stobhall and Mary Montifex (dau. of Sir William Montifex); m. Sir John Stewart of Kyle, later known as Robert III (1337–1406), king of Scotland (r. 1390–1406), c. 1367; children: Elizabeth Stewart (d. before 1411, who m. James Douglas, Lord of Dalkeith); Margaret Stewart (d. before 1456, who m. Archibald Douglas, 4th earl of Douglas); David Stewart (1378–1402), duke of Rothesay; Robert Stewart (died in infancy); Mary Stewart (d. 1458); Egidia Stewart; James I (1394–1437), king of Scotland (r. 1406–1437). ❖ Born into the petty nobility, married the illegitimately born knight Sir John Stewart of Kyle (c. 1367), whose father became Robert II, king of Scotland; with husband, took over as regents when Robert became ill; became queen of Scotland when husband ascended the throne as Robert III (1390); proved to be an excellent queen; energetic and kind, strongly advocated Scotland's right to be free from English oppression and was involved in all aspects of the administration, including creating legislation; also aided in planning the defense of Scotland upon its invasion by the English (1399). ❖ See also *Women in World History.*

DRUMMOND, Dolores (1834–1926). English-born actress. Born Feb 3, 1834, in London, England; died July 14, 1926; m. W.A. Sprague; children: W.G.R. Sprague (theatrical architect). ❖ Made stage debut in Melbourne, Australia, in *Timour the Tartar* (1856) and London debut as Hermione in *The Winter's Tale* (1874); other plays include *Jo, East Lynne, Elfinella, The Rocket, Dorothy Gray, Proof, Theodora, Sweet Lavender, The Two Orphans* and *Hearts are Trumps.*

DRUMMOND, Flora (1869–1949). Scottish suffragist. Name variations: General Drummond. Born in Scotland in 1869; died in 1949; grew up in the Highlands; married. ❖ Known as "the General" because she wore a uniform and led the drum-and-fife marching band during suffragist parades, arrived in London from Manchester; was spurred into the movement by Christabel Pankhurst's 1905 arrest; a rousing speaker and doer of stunts, was imprisoned 9 times. ❖ See also *Women in World History.*

DRUMMOND, Margaret (d. 1375). Queen of Scotland. Name variations: Margaret Logie. Died after Jan 31, 1375; dau. of Malcolm Drummond; m. Sir John Logie (died); became 2nd wife of David II (1323–1370), king of Scots (r. 1329–1370), Feb 20, 1364 (div., Mar 20, 1370).

DRUMMOND, Margaret (c. 1472–1502). Scottish mistress. Born around 1472; died in 1502; youngest daughter of Lord Drummond; had two sisters, Eupheme and Sybilla; associated with James IV (1473–1513), king of the Scots (r. 1488–1513); children: Margaret Stewart (b. around 1497).

DRURY, Edith (1870–1962). See Costello, Eileen.

DRUSE, Roxana (1846–1889). American murderer. Born 1846; hanged in 1889; lived near Little Falls, NY; m. John Druse; children: at least 2: Mary and John Jr. ❖ With help of daughter, beat husband to death, chopped up body, and boiled remains (1889); was hanged after son told authorities. Daughter received life imprisonment.

DRUSILLA (15–38 CE). Roman noblewoman. Born in 15 CE; died 38 CE; dau. of Germanicus Caesar and Agrippina the Elder; sister of Agrippina the Younger and Julia Livilla; sister and mistress of Caligula. ❖ When she died, Caligula "made it a capital offence to laugh, to bathe, or to dine with one's parents, wives, or children while the period of public mourning lasted," writes Suetonius. Though, in the Roman past, only Julius

Caesar and Augustus had been deified, Caligula deified Drusilla, setting up a shrine for her, complete with priests, and gave her the name "Panthea" to show that she had the qualities of all goddesses. ❖ See also *Women in World History.*

DRUSILLA (c. 37–c. 41 CE). Roman noblewoman. Name variations: Julia Drusilla. Born c. 37 CE; died c. 41 CE; dau. of Caligula (12–41), Roman emperor (r. 37–41), and Milonia Caesonia (d. 41 CE). ❖ Hatred for Caligula was so great that, after he had been assassinated, his wife Milonia Caesonia was killed as well, and his daughter Drusilla's "brains," writes Dio Cassius, "were dashed out against a wall." ❖ See also *Women in World History.*

DRUSILLA (38–79 CE). Herodian noblewoman. Born in 38 CE; died in the eruption of Mount Vesuvius, 79 CE; 3rd and youngest dau. of Herod Agrippa I; sister of Herod Agrippa II and Berenice (28–80 CE); m. Azizus, king of Emesa; children: at least one son. ❖ Induced by Felix, Roman procurator of Judea, to leave her husband Azizus, king of Emesa, to become Felix's adulterous companion; was with Felix when Paul reasoned of "righteousness, temperance, and judgment to come" (Acts 24:24); died with her son in the eruption of Mount Vesuvius.

DRUZHININA, Zinaida (1947—). See Voronina, Zinaida.

DRYBURGH, Margaret (1890–1945). English missionary and prisoner of war. Name variations: Daisy. Born Feb 1890 in Sunderland, northern England; died April 23, 1945, in a Japanese prisoner-of-war camp in Belalau, Sumatra (then Dutch West Indies); dau. of William (Presbyterian minister) and Agnes Dryburgh; studied education and music at Newcastle College, a division of Durham University, BA, 1911; never married. ❖ Presbyterian missionary in China and Singapore who acquired the status of a kind of saint among the women POWs in Sumatra and gained posthumous recognition for her role in creating a repertoire for the vocal orchestra of women; taught at Ryhope Grammar Girls' School, where she led the school choir; worked for Presbyterian Women's Missionary Association in Swatow, South China (1919–25); went to Singapore to work among the Teochow Chinese, whose language she spoke fluently; became the 1st principal of the Kuo Chuan Girls' School on Bishan Street, as well as organist in the Presbyterian Church in Orchard Road; was aboard the *Mata Hari* (Feb 1942) when it was seized by the Japanese in the Banka Strait off Sumatra; was a prisoner of war in a series of camps for women and children in southern Sumatra (1942–45); in the camps, quickly emerged as a religious and social leader whose regular church services as well as her verse, plays, songs and drawings of prison scenes served to inspire those around her; many of her creative works, including poems, drawings and a hymn, have been published in accounts of life in the prison camps. ❖ See also Helen Colijn, *Song of Survival: Women Interned* (Millennium, 1996); and *Women in World History.*

DRYLIE, Patricia (c. 1928–1993). Canadian ballet and theater dancer. Born c. 1928 in Toronto, Canada; died 1993. ❖ Performed in Toronto, Canada, with Boris Volkoff's company; moved to New York City where she was a member of ballet corps at Radio City Music Hall for next 10 years; performed on Broadway in numerous musicals, including *On Your Toes* (1954) and *My Fair Lady* (1956–62), with which she toured extensively throughout Australia and Soviet Union; served as assistant stage manager for numerous Broadway productions, including *Camelot* (1960) and *I Do! I Do!* (1966), and as stage manager for *The Desert Song* (1973); returned to Broadway as performer with *Ballroom* (1978).

DRYSDALE, Ann Meyers (1955—). See Meyers, Ann.

DUANE, Diane (1952—). American science-fiction writer and screenwriter. Born May 18, 1952, in New York, NY; grew up in Roosevelt, LI; attended Dowling College, 1970–71, and Pilgrim State College of Nursing, 1971–74; m. Peter Morwood (Northern Irish writer), 1987. ❖ Was a staff psychiatric nurse at Payne Whitney in NY (1974–76); relocated to California as a writer's assistant (1976–78); published 1st book, *The Door into Fire* (1979); on marriage, moved to UK (1987), then Republic of Ireland (1988); served as a senior writer on BBC's "Science Challenge"; works include "Star Trek" series (1983–2000), several of which were *New York Times* bestsellers, "Young Wizards" series (1983–2003), and the novels *Wounded Sky* (1983), *The Door into Shadow* (1984), *My Enemy, My Ally* (1984), *On Her Majesty's Wizardly Service* (1998) and *Stealing the Elf-King's Roses* (2002); also wrote several books with bestselling author Tom Clancy, including *Virtual Vandals* (1998), *Safe House* (2000) and *Death Match* (2003), and wrote animated and live-action screenplays. Nominated for Emmy for one of the 1st episodes of "Star Trek" ("Where No One Has Gone Before").

DUAYEN, Cesar (1861–1947). *See Barra, Emma de la.*

DU BARRY, Jeanne Bécu, Comtesse (1743–1793). French *maîtresse en titre* to Louis XV. Name variations: Comtesse du Barry; Madame du Barry; Marie Jeanne Bécu. Born Aug 19, 1743, in Vaucouleurs (Meuse), France; guillotined in Paris, Dec 8, 1793; dau. of Anne Bécu (1713–1788, seamstress) and an unknown father but probably a monk, Jean-Baptiste Gomard de Vaubernier; m. Guillaume du Barry (1768–1793); children: none legitimate but possibly an illeg. daughter Marie-Joséphine ("Betsi") Bécu. ❖ Symbolized the brilliance and decadence of the years before the French Revolution; met Jean-Baptiste, Comte du Barry (le Roué, 1763); became Louis XV's mistress and married Guillaume du Barry (1768); presented at court as *maîtresse en titre* (1769); helped bring about the fall of Choiseul (1770); struggled for recognition of her position by Marie Antoinette (1770–72); confined at Abbey of Pont-aux-Dames after Louis XV died (1774–75); returned to Louveciennes (1776); had affair with Henry Seymour (c. 1779–80); was mistress of the Duc de Cossé-Brissac (c. 1780–92); left for England after Cossé-Brissac was lynched (1792); returned and was tried and executed (1793); by any account, was impulsive, frivolous, and unheeding, fatally so, yet was also kind, genuine, and generous; employed her influence to gain recognition, found allies where she could, and asked Louis' help for them, but never used her power to harm others, to imprison, or to kill. ❖ See also André Castelot, *Madame du Barry* (Paris: Perrin, 1989); Joan Haslip, *Madame Du Barry: The Wages of Beauty* (Grove Weidenfeld, 1972); and *Women in World History.*

DU BIEF, Jacqueline. French figure skater. Born in France. ❖ Won a bronze medal at Oslo Olympics (1952); won the World championship (1952).

DU BOCCAGE, Marie Anne Fiquet (1710–1802). *See Bocage, Marie-Anne Le Page du.*

DUBOIS, Alice (d. 1918). *See de Bettignies, Louise.*

DU BOIS, Cora (1903–1991). American cultural anthropologist. Name variations: Cora DuBois. Born Cora Du Bois, Oct 26, 1903, in Brooklyn, NY; died April 7, 1991 in Brookline, Massachusetts; dau. of Jean Jules Du Bois and Mattie (Schreiber) Du Bois; University of California, Berkeley, PhD, 1932. ❖ Served as teaching fellow in Department of Anthropology at University of California, Berkeley (1930–32), then research associate (1932–35); performed ethnographic research with Alfred Kroeber among Wintu Indians in northern California (1932–35); conducted most famous field work in Alor, Indonesia, researching problems in culture-and-personality (1937–39); published landmark study *The People of Alor* (1944); during WWII, served as chief of Indonesian Section of Research and Analysis Branch of Office of Strategic Services; taught at several US colleges, including 15 years at Harvard University; elected president of American Anthropological Association (1968) and of Association of Asian Studies (1969).

DUBOIS, Marie (1937—). French stage and screen actress. Born Jan 12, 1937, in Paris, France. ❖ Leading lady of the French stage, made film debut as Lena in *Shoot the Piano Player* (1960), followed by *Une femme est une femme*, *Le monocle noir*, *Jules et Jim*, *La ronde*, *Les grandes gueules*, *Le voleur*, *Le serpent*, *Antoine et Sébastian*, *Grand Guignol* and *Les enfants du vent*, among others.

DU BOIS, Shirley Graham (1896–1977). *See Graham, Shirley.*

DU BOULAY, Christine (c. 1923—). English ballet dancer. Born c. 1923 in Ealing, Middlesex, England; m. Richard Ellis (dancer). ❖ Performed with Sadler's Wells Ballet during and after WWII (1939–41, 46–52), in such classical works as *The Sleeping Beauty*, *Coppélia* and *Swan Lake*, as well as in numerous works by Frederick Ashton, Robert Helpmann, and Ninette de Valois; performed with Sarah Gate Ballet in Dublin and with International Ballet in London; with husband Richard Ellis, immigrated to US and opened the Ellis-Du Boulay School of Dance in Chicago, where they both taught.

DUBRAWKA (d. 977). *See Dobravy of Bohemia.*

DUBSKY, Countess (1830–1916). *See Ebner-Eschenbach, Marie.*

DUBUISSON, Pauline (1926—). French murderer. Born 1926 in France. ❖ While attending University of Lille as medical student, met athlete Félix Bailley (1946), with whom she had affair; after he ended relationship (1949) and returned to Paris, received word that he was to marry

another; went to Paris and shot him to death before trying to commit suicide by gassing herself (Mar 17, 1951); revived and arrested for his murder, was subject of celebrated case of *crime passionel;* found guilty of murder without premeditation, was sentenced to penal servitude for life.

DUBY-BLOM, Gertrude (1901–1993). Swiss-born Mexican environmental activist. Name variations: Gertrude Duby; Queen of the Rain Forest. Born Gertrude Elisabeth Loertscher in Berne, Switzerland, 1901; died in San Cristóbal de las Casas, Chiapas State, Mexico, Dec 23, 1993; m. Kurt Duby, 1924 (div.); m. Frans Blom (Danish-born American anthropologist), 1950 (died 1963). ❖ Photographer, sociologist and defender of the Lacandón Maya peoples of Chiapas State and their rapidly disappearing rain forest environment; became a political activist, organizing a Social Democratic youth movement in Zurich and working as a journalist for Swiss newspapers in several European countries (late 1920s); moved to Germany (1928) and became an effective public speaker at anti-Nazi rallies; fled Germany for Paris (c. 1935); was arrested (Sept 1939) and spent 5 months in a French detention camp; released because of her Swiss citizenship, immigrated to Mexico (1940); got a job as a journalist for the Ministry of Labor; joined a government expedition to the then-remote Lacandón jungle region near the border with Guatemala (1943); married and moved to Chiapas, setting up the Na-Bolom Center for Scientific Studies with husband (1951); with husband, made a number of expeditions into the Selva Lacandona, the rain forest east of San Cristobal, where they studied flora and fauna and got to know the Lacandón Maya; made countless trips into the rain forest to photograph various Maya tribal groups and the wildlife (1950s–60s); with camera, documented the deforestation of the rain forest by chain saws and bulldozers and the depletion of soil; released photographs of the endangered rain forest, as well as its animals and people to an increasingly sympathetic world. ❖ See also Gertrude Duby-Blom, Alex Harris, and Margaret Sartor, *Gertrude Blom—Bearing Witness* (U. of North Carolina Press, 1984); and *Women in World History.*

DUCAS, Irene (c. 1066–1133). *See Irene Ducas.*

DUCAS, Maria (fl. 1070–1081). *See Maria of Alania.*

DU CAURROY, Mary (1865–1937). *See Russell, Mary du Caurroy.*

DU CHATELET, Gabrielle Emilie (1706–1749). *See Châtelet, Émilie du.*

DUCHÊNE, Gabrielle (1870–1954). French pacifist and feminist. Pronunciation: du-SHEN. Born Mathilde-Denise Laforcade in Paris, France, Feb 26, 1870; died in Zurich, Switzerland, Aug 3, 1954; dau. of Joseph and Rosalie (Maréchal) Laforcade; m. M. Duchêne (landscape architect); children: Suzanne-Henriette Duchêne (Mme. Roubakine, b. 1893). ❖ Activist who was involved in left-wing, feminist, and pacifist organizations for over 50 years; named president of the Labor Section of the National Council of French Women (CNFF, 1913); during WWI, was investigated because of pacifist activities (1915); named secretary-general of the French Section of the International League of Women for Peace and Liberty (LIFPL, 1919); was active in Russian relief during the famine (1920–23); never joined the Communist Party, but intensified her association with Communist front organizations (1927); practiced "realistic" pacifism to counter Hitler's aggression (1934–49); hid from the Gestapo and aided the Resistance (1940–44); was president of the French Section of the LIFPL (1945–54); attended the Congress of Peoples, Vienna (1952). ❖ See also *Women in World History.*

DUCHESNAY, Isabelle (1973—). Canadian-born ice dancer. Born Dec 18, 1973, in Aylmer, Canada. ❖ With brother Paul Duchesnay, skating for France, won the World championship (1991) and a silver medal at Albertville Olympics (1992); turned pro (1992); retired (1996).

DUCHESNE, Rose Philippine (1769–1852). French nun and religious founder. Name variations: Saint Rose Duchesne; Quah-kah-kah-num-ad (Woman-who-prays-always). Born in Grenoble, France, Aug 29, 1769; died in St. Charles, Missouri, Nov 18, 1852; dau. of Pierre François (lawyer and politician) and Rose (Perier) Duchesne; attended Convent of the Visitation, Sainte-Marie-d'en-Haut. ❖ Roman Catholic missionary who founded the US branch of the Society of the Sacred Heart, and is one of three American saints (not native-born); entered the Visitation Order at Convent at Sainte-Marie-d'en-Haut (1788), where she had received education; was ejected from convent during French Revolution and sent home to Grenoble (1792); spent next 10 years teaching and performing charitable work; with peace restored, returned to convent, hoping to reunite the scattered Visitandine nuns; failing this, united the convent with Society of the Sacred Heart (1804); transferred to Paris (1815), founding 1st Sacred Heart convent there; arrived in US (1818), where she established a school in St. Charles, Missouri, the 1st free school west of the Mississippi River for both Catholic and non-Catholic children; built a convent in Florissant, Missouri (1819), which housed a free parish school, an orphanage, a boarding academy, a school for Native American girls, and the 1st novitiate for US members of Sacred Heart Society; relocated to St. Louis (1827), where she presided over an orphanage, academy, and parish school; founded a mission school for Potawatomi Indian girls at Sugar Creek, Kansas (1841); also nursed the sick among the tribe; beatified (May 12, 1940); canonized (1988).

DUCHESS, The (c. 1855–1897). *See Hungerford, Margaret Wolfe.*

DUCHKOVA, Milena (1952—). Czech diver. Born April 25, 1952. ❖ Won a gold medal at Mexico City Olympics (1968) and a silver medal at Munich Olympics (1972), both in platform.

DUCI, Filippa (fl. 16th c.). French royal mistress. Name variations: Filippe Duc. Mistress of Henry II (1519–1559), king of France (r. 1547–1559); children: (with Henry) Diane de France (1538–1619).

DUCKERING, Florence West (1869–1951). American physician. Born Aug 22, 1869, in Sussex, England; died Oct 25, 1951, in Peterborough, New Hampshire; earned medical degree cum laude, Tufts College, 1901. ❖ Served as extern, resident surgeon, and superintendent at Massachusetts Women's Hospital; had medical practice (1903–46); served as assistant surgeon, then senior surgeon, at New England Hospital for Women and Children; became one of 1st two women, with Alice Gertrude Bryant, admitted to the American College of Surgeons (1914); volunteered with American Red Cross and American Women's Hospitals during both world wars; served as volunteer, Medical Service Corps, and as member of Council of National Defense; retired (1946). The Florence W. Duckering Scholarship Fund at Tufts University was established by the bequest of Mary Duckering (1959).

DUCKWORTH, Julia (1846–1895). *See Stephen, Julia Prinsep.*

DUCKWORTH, Marilyn (1935—). New Zealand novelist. Born 1935 in Otahuhu; spent wartime in England; sister of Fleur Adcock (poet); married 4 times. ❖ Works include *A Gap in the Spectrum* (1959), *The Matchbox House* (1960), *A Barbarous Tongue* (1963), *Over the Fence is Out* (1969), *Other Lovers' Children* (1975), *Disorderly Conduct* (1984), which won the New Zealand Book Award for Fiction, *Married Alive* (1985), *Rest for the Wicked* (1986), *Pulling Faces* (1987), *A Message from Harpo* (1989), *Explosions on the Sun* (1989) and *Studmuffin* (1997). Awarded OBE (1987). ❖ See also autobiography, *Camping on the Faultline* (2000).

DUCLAUX, Agnes Mary F. (1856–1944). English poet and critic. Name variations: Mary F. Robinson; Agnes Mary Frances Robinson; A. Mary F. Robinson; Mary Darmesteter. Born Agnes Mary Frances Robinson at Leamington, England, Feb 27, 1856; educated at University College, London; m. James Darmesteter (1849–1894, Oriental scholar); m. Pierre Émile Duclaux (director of the Pasteur institute), 1901 (died 1904). ❖ Followed 1st volume of poetry, *A Handful of Honeysuckle* (1879), with a translation from Euripides, *The Crowned Hippolytus* (1881); wrote some of best verses for *The New Arcadia and Other Poems* (1884) and *An Italian Garden* (1886); also wrote *Life of Ernest Renan* (1897), *End of the Middle Ages* (1888), *Retrospect and Other Poems* (1893), the volume on *Froissart* (1894) in the *Grands écrivains français*, essays on the Brontës, the Brownings and others, for *Grands écrivains d'Outre-Manche* (1901), *Collected Poems, Lyrical and Narrative* (1902), and *The Return to Nature, Songs and Symbols* (1904).

DU COUDRAY, Angélique (1712–1789). French obstetrician. Name variations: Angelique du Coudray; Madame du Coudray; Marguerite le Boursier; Angelique Marguerite Le Boursier du Coudray. Born in Clermont-Ferrand, France, 1712; died in 1789; received training in Paris at the Hôtel Dieu School. ❖ A midwife in France who lent a scientific approach to the field of obstetrics, was licensed as an *accoucheuse*, or midwife (1740); revised and expanded a 1667 midwifery textbook into *Abrégé de l'art des accouchements avec plusiers observations sur des cas singuliers* and began teaching midwifery (1759); when Louis XV provided her with an annual salary for her teaching services in all the provinces, arranged a class of 100 in Auvergne; is said to have trained 4,000 pupils; published her *Oeuvres* (1773). ❖ See also Nina Rattner Gelbart, *The King's Midwife: A History and Mystery of Madame du Coudray;* and *Women in World History.*

DU COUDRAY, Mme (1712–1794). *See Coudray, Angelique du.*

DUCZA, Aniko (1942—). *See Janosine-Ducza, Aniko.*

DUCZYNSKA, Ilona (1897–1978). Austrian-born author and political activist. Name variations: Ilona Polanyi or Polányi. Born Helene Marie Duczynska in Maria Enzersdorf, Lower Austria, 1897; died in Pickering, Canada, April 24, 1978; dau. of Alfred Ritter von Duczynski (railway official of noble Polish descent, died 1907) and Hélen Békássy; enrolled at college of technology in Zurich, Switzerland, 1915; attended Vienna's College of Technology (Technische Hochschule), 1930–36, to complete doctoral work in physics; m. Tivadar Sugár, 1918 (marriage was over within weeks); m. Karl Polányi (Hungarian-born intellectual, activist, and writer), 1922 (died 1964); children: (2nd m.) one daughter, Kári (b. 1923). ❖ Critic of both the passivity of Social Democracy and the brutality of Bolshevism, whose lifelong commitment to Socialism reflected the complexities of Central European political life between the two World Wars; wrote *Der demokratische Bolschewik* (1975) and *Workers in Arms: The Austrian Schutzbund and the Civil War of 1934* (1978). ❖ See also *Women in World History.*

DUDACH, Charlotte (1913–1985). *See Delbo, Charlotte.*

DUDAROVA, Veronika (1916—). Russian orchestra conductor. Name variations: Veronika Borisovna Dudarova. Born Dec 5, 1916, in Baku; studied piano with P.A. Serebriakov at Leningrad Conservatory (1933–37) and conducting at Moscow Conservatory with Leo Ginsburg. ❖ Was the 1st woman to head a major orchestra in the Soviet Union (1947); became chief conductor of Moscow State Symphony Orchestra (1960) and made a large number of recordings for Melodiya, including the folksy Chaikin Concerto for Accordion and Orchestra, and 4 of Tchaikovsky's least-known orchestral works (*The Storm, Fate, The Voyevode,* and the very early *Overture in F major*); conducted the memorial concert for the centennial of Peter Ilyitch Tchaikovsky's death (1993); conducting her newly created Symphony Orchestra of Russia, made a number of highly acclaimed recordings, often of little-known Russian symphonic works, including Miaskovsky's Sixth "Revolutionary" Symphony (1992). Designated a People's Artist of the USSR (1977). ❖ See also *Women in World History.*

DU DEFFAND, Marquise (1697–1780). *See Deffand, Marie Anne de Vichy-Chamrond, Marquise du.*

DUDER, Tessa (1940—). New Zealand children's writer and journalist. Born Nov 13, 1940, in Auckland, New Zealand; dau. of John (doctor) and Elvira (Wycherley) Staveley; attended University of Auckland, 1958–59, 1982–84; m. John Nelson Duder (civil engineer), 1964; children: Lisa, Alexandra, Joanna and Georgia. ❖ Won silver medal in swimming at Cardiff Empire Games (1958) and 1st New Zealand Swimmer of the Year award (1959); worked as journalist in England, Pakistan (1966–70), and New Zealand; writings include *Night Race to Kawau* (1982), *Jellybean* (1985), *Alex* (1987), *Alex in Winter* (1989), and *Songs for Alex* (1992). Received Choysa Bursary for Children's Writers (1985) and Aim Award (1990, 1993); made OBE (1994); received Margaret Mahy Medal (1996).

DUDEVA, Diana (1968—). Bulgarian gymnast. Born July 7, 1968, in Pleven, Bulgaria. ❖ Won Bulgaria's national championship (1985); came in 2nd all-around at Balkan championships and Golden Sands and 1st all-around at Leverskusen Cup (1985); at Europeans, won a bronze medal in all-around (1987); at Seoul Olympics, won a bronze medal in floor exercises (1988), becoming Bulgaria's 1st and only Olympic medalist in women's artistic gymnastics; coaches in Greece.

DUDEVANT, Madame (1804–1876). *See George Sand.*

DUDINSKAYA, Natalya (1912–2003). Russian ballet dancer and choreographer. Name variations: Natalia. Born Natalya Mikhailovna Dudinskaya in Kharkov, Ukraine, Aug 21, 1912; died Jan 29, 2003, in St. Petersburg, Russia; dau. of Natalya Tagliori (ballet dancer and musician); studied dance under mother's tutelage, early 1920s and under ballerina Agrippina Vaganova; attended Leningrad School of Choreography, 1923–31; m. Konstantin Sergeyev (choreographer at the Kirov), c. 1945. ❖ Prima ballerina, choreographer, and instructor at Russia's famed Kirov Ballet (now St. Petersburg Ballet), made debut while still in school as Princess Florine in *Sleeping Beauty;* joined the Kirov (1931); appeared in title role of husband's version of Prokofiev's *Cinderella* (1946); began teaching at the Kirov (1951); retired from dancing (1961); appeared as Carabosse in film version of *Cinderella* (1964); with husband, choreographed *Hamlet* (1970), *Le Corsaire* (1973), and *Beethoven's Appassionata* (1977), among others. Created such roles as the title role in *Laurencia* (1936), Mireille de Poitiers in *Flames of Paris,* Corali in *Lost Illusions,* Pannochka in *Taras Bulba,* title role in *Gayané*, Paragna in *Bronze Horseman* (1949), and Sarie in *Path of Thunder* (1957). Also appeared in *Les Sylphides, Cinderella* (1946), *Raymonda, Don Quixote, La Bayadére, Esmeralda*, and as Titania in *A Midsummer Night's Dream*. ❖ See also *Women in World History*.

DUDLESTON, Penny (1952—). American ballet dancer. Name variations: Penny Dudleston McKay. Born May 26, 1952, in Tacoma, Washington. ❖ At 8, began dance career with Ballet West; trained on scholarship at Juilliard School in New York City; joined New York City Ballet (early 1970s) where she created roles in John Taras' revision of *The Song of the Nightingale* and in Jerome Robbins' *Watermill*, and performed principal roles in repertory works for 5 years; continued to dance principal parts for Ballet West later in career; taught at Brown and Weber universities; founded and directed Wyoming Dance Theater in Jackson Hole; opened Penny Dudleston McKay School of Ballet in Ogden, Utah, where she also served as school director.

DUDLEY, Amy or Amye (c. 1532–1560). See Robsart, Amy.

DUDLEY, Doris (1917–1985). American actress. Born July 7, 1917, in New York, NY; died Aug 14, 1985, in Jacobia, Texas; dau. of Bide Dudley (drama critic for *New York Evening World* and WOR Radio) and Tiney Keplinger Dudley; children: Jackie "Butch" Jenkins (child film star). ❖ Made Broadway debut in *End of Summer* (1935), followed by *The Smiling Visitor, Battle of Angels* and *My Dear Children;* generated headlines when she crashed her plane in Boston and still made it to the theater in time for curtain (1930s).

DUDLEY, Dorothy (fl. 1775). American diarist. Fl. around 1775. ❖ Kept a diary, which records battles and leaders of early years of American Revolution and was published as *Theatrum Majoram . . . The Diary of Dorothy Dudley* (1876).

DUDLEY, Lady Jane (1537–1554). See Grey, Lady Jane.

DUDLEY, Jane (1912–2001). American modern dancer and choreographer. Born April 3, 1912, in New York, NY; died Sept 19, 2001, in London, England; attended University of North Carolina; studied dance in NY with Hanya Holm; m. Leo Hurwitz (filmmaker, div.); children: Tom Hurwitz. ❖ Danced as permanent member of Martha Graham company (1937–44); created numerous roles for Graham's works, including "Ancestress" in *Letter to the World* (1940) and "Sister" in *Deaths and Entrances* (1943); collaborated with New Dance League in New York City where she created such works as *The Dream Ends* (1934), *Songs of Protest* (1937), *Harmonica Breakdown* (1938) and *Cult of Blood* (1938); performed in trio troupe with Sophie Maslow and William Bales until her retirement from performance career (1944); choreographed numerous works for the trio and also for New Dance Group; taught Graham technique at Graham school in NY, for New Dance Group, for Bat-sheva Dance Company in Israel, and at school of London Contemporary Dance Theater. Works of choreography include *In the Life of a Worker* (19334), *My Body, My Carcass* (1937), *The Ballad of Molly Pitcher* (1940), *Dissonance* (1941), *The Lonely Ones* (1946), *Family Portrait* (1953) and *Five Characters and Conclusion* (1979).

DUDLEY, Lettice (c. 1541–1634). See Knollys, Lettice.

DUDLEY-WARD, Penelope (1914–1982). English actress. Name variations: Penelope Dudley Ward; Penelope Ward. Born Aug 4, 1914, in London, England; died Jan 22, 1982, in London; dau. of Winifred (Birkin) and William Dudley Ward; m. Anthony Pelissier (div.); m. Carol Reed (director), 1948. ❖ Made London debut in *Ladies and Gentlemen* (1937), then appeared as Lady Jane in *Victoria Regina;* in NY, starred in *French without Tears, Set to Music* and *Lady Windermere's Fan;* made film debut in *Escape Me Never* (1935), followed by *Moscow Nights, The Citadel, Dangerous Cargo, Convoy, Major Barbara, In Which We Serve, Immortal Battalion, English without Tears* and *Her Man Bilbey*, among others; retired following marriage.

DUDNIK, Olesia (1974—). Ukrainian gymnast. Born Aug 15, 1974, in Zaporozhie, Ukraine. ❖ At European championships, won a gold medal for balance beam (1989); at World championships, won gold medals for vault and team all-around and a silver for balance beam (1989).

DUENHAUPT, Angelika. See Dünhaupt, Angelika.

DUENKEL, Ginny (1947—). American swimmer. Name variations: Virginia Duenkel. Born Virginia Duenkel, Mar 7, 1947, in West Orange, New Jersey; attended University of Michigan. ❖ Won the bronze medal in the 100-meter backstroke and the gold medal in the 400-meter freestyle at Tokyo Olympics (1964).

DUERK, Alene B. (1920—). American naval admiral. Born Mar 29, 1920, in Defiance, Ohio; graduated from Toledo Hospital School of Nursing (1941); Frances Payne Bolton School of Nursing at Western Reserve University, BS, 1948. ❖ Received commission as ensign in US Navy (1943); served stateside and on hospital ship in Pacific; after moving to reserve status, was called to active duty during Korean War (1951); transferred from reserves to regular Navy (c. 1953); taught nursing classes in Navy; became director of nursing at San Diego Naval Hospital Corps School (CA, 1965); served as chief of nursing services at Great Lakes Naval Hospital (1968–70); made head of Navy Nurse Corps (1970); was the 1st woman to be appointed rear admiral in US Navy (1972); retired (1975).

DU FAUR, Emmeline Freda (1882–1935). New Zealand mountaineer and writer. Born Sept 16, 1882, at Croydon, Sydney, Australia; died Sept 11, 1935, at Dee Why, Sydney; dau. of Frederick Eccleston Du Faur (land agent) and Blanche Mary Elizabeth (Woolley) Du Faur. ❖ Regarded as best amateur climber of her time and 1st woman to pursue high-mountain climbing in New Zealand, taught self rock-climbing as young girl and spent holidays in New Zealand, where photographs of Mt. Cook inspired her to learn sport; made numerous 1st assents; most notable climb was 1st grand traverse of all 3 peaks of Mt. Cook (1913); relocated to England (1914); published *The Conquest of Mount Cook* (1915); after death of companion, returned to Australia, where she pursued bush-walking. ❖ See also *Dictionary of New Zealand Biography* (Vol. 3).

DUFF, Alexandra (1891–1959). See Alexandra Victoria.

DUFF, Mary Ann Dyke (1794–1857). English actress. Born Mary Ann Dyke in 1794, in London, England; died Sept 5, 1857, in New York, NY; sister of Elizabeth (Bessie) Dyke Moore and Ann Dyke Murray; m. John R. Duff (actor), 1810 (died 1831); m. Charles Young (actor), 1833 (anulled); m. Joel G. Seaver (lawyer), 1836; children: 10. ❖ One of the foremost tragic actresses of her time, studied dance along with sisters under ballet master at King's Theater; after father died, traveled with mother to Dublin, making stage debut there; sailed for Boston with husband (1810) and performed there and with Philadelphia company of William Warren and William Burke Wood, winning praise for charm but little praise for acting; matured as an actress and increasingly earned plaudits of critics; made New York debut in *Hamlet* (1822) and became enormously popular; played over 200 roles during career, ranging from farce to tragedy, including Queen Katherine in *Henry VIII*, Lady Macbeth, and Hermione in *The Distress Mother;* broke with manager Henry Wallack (1826) and embarked on English tour which was not met with enthusiasm (1828); following 1st husband's death (1831), was forced to appear in popular but inferior plays to make ends meet; had brief and unsuccessful marriage to actor Charles Young (1833) and consequently suffered breakdown resulting in 6-month retirement from stage; returned to acting with some success, performing in Philadelphia, Baltimore and NY; married Joel G. Seaver (1836) and moved with him to New Orleans where Seaver practiced law under name Sevier; continued to make intermittent appearances on stage until 1838; wrote poetry and a religious novel, seeking refuge from successive tragedies in children's lives. ❖ See also Joseph N. Ireland, *Mrs. Duff* (1882).

DUFF, Maud (1893–1945). See Carnegie, Maud.

DUFF, Shiela Grant (1913–2003). See Grant Duff, Shiela.

DUFF COOPER, Diana (1892–1986). See Cooper, Diana Duff.

DUFF-GORDON, Lucie (1821–1869). English translator and travel writer. Name variations: Lady Lucy Duff or Duff Gordon. Born June 24, 1821, in Queen Square, London, England; died July 14, 1869, in Cairo, Egypt; dau. of John Austin (jurist and author) and Sarah Taylor Austin (translator and woman of letters); m. Sir Alexander Duff-Gordon, May 16, 1840; children: Janet Anne Duff-Gordon Ross (1842–1927, writer); Maurice (b. 1849); Urania Duff-Gordon (b. 1858, called Rainie). ❖ With published letters chronicling her years spent in South Africa and Egypt, presented those cultures with keen insight and a rare understanding; spent early childhood in England; traveled to Germany with parents, where she became fluent in the language (1826); as a teenager, attended boarding school in Bromley; made debut in London society (1838); married at 19 (1840); lived in London and translated many important literary and historical works (1840–50), including Barthold Niebuhr's *Studies of Ancient Greek Mythology* (1839), Wilhelm Meinhold's *Mary Schweidler: The Amber Witch* (1844), P.J.A. von Feuerbach's *Narrative of Remarkable Criminal Trials* (1846), A.F.L. de

Wailly's *Stella and Vanessa* (1850), S. D'Arbouville's *The Village Doctor* (1853) and Baron von Moltke's *The Russians in Bulgaria and Roumelia, 1828–1929* (1854); moved with family to Weybridge, where she established a library for working men (1850); moved to Paris (1857); left England for South Africa (1861); moved on to Egypt (1862), where she lived until her death (1869). Published letters: *Letters from the Cape* (published as part of Francis Galton's *Vacation Tourist in 1862–1863*, 1864), *Letters from Egypt, 1863–1865* (1865), *Last Letters from Egypt* (1875). ❖ See also Gordon Waterfield, *Lucie Duff-Gordon in England, South Africa and Egypt* (Dutton, 1937); and *Women in World History*.

DUFF GORDON, Lucy (1862–1935). English-born fashion and theatrical costume designer. Born Lucille Sutherland in London, England, 1862; died in Putney, England, April 1935; dau. of Douglas (engineer) and Lucy (Saunders) Sutherland; sister of writer Elinor Glyn (1864–1943); m. James Wallace (wine merchant), Sept 15, 1884 (div. 1888); m. Sir Cosmo Duff Gordon, May 24, 1900 (d. 1931); children: (1st m.) daughter Esme (who m. Anthony Giffard, viscount Tiverton). ❖ Designer whose clothes were highly popular in London high society from 1890 through WWI; gained fame by designing "personality" dresses for wealthy women in London (1890s); opened The Maison Lucille in London (1898), and branches, known as Lucille Ltd., were established in Paris, NY, and Chicago; designed costumes for London production of *The Merry Widow* (1907); along with husband, survived the *Titanic* disaster (1912) but barely survived the damage to their reputation (as she watched the ship slowly sink, had turned to her secretary aboard the half-filled lifeboat No. 1 and observed, "There is your beautiful nightdress gone"); designed costumes for *Ziegfeld Follies* (1916); film design credits include *The Misleading Lady: The Strange Case of Mary Page* (1916), *Virtuous Wives* (1920), *Way Down East* (1921) and *Heedless Moths;* is often confused with Lady Lucie Duff-Gordon (1821–1869). ❖ See also *Women in World History*.

DUFFERIN, countess of.
See Blackwood, Helen Selina (1807–1867).
See Blackwood, Hariot (fl. 1845–1891).

DUFFERIN, Helen Selina. See Blackwood, Helen Selina.

DUFFERIN, Lady.
See Blackwood, Helen Selina (1807–1867).
See Blackwood, Hariot (fl. 1845–1891).

DUFFY, Martha (c, 1936–1997). American editor. Born c. 1936; died June 1997. ❖ One of the 1st women senior editors, worked at Time for 37 years; began as a researcher, then writer; was arts editor (1974–89), then senior writer and critic.

DUFFY, Maureen (1933—). British novelist and playwright. Born Oct 21, 1933, in Worthing, Sussex, England; dau. of Cahia P. Duffy and Grace (Wright) Duffy. ❖ Writer of novels, plays, poetry, and nonfiction and outspoken defender of gay rights; works include *That's How it Was* (1962), *The Single Eye* (1964), *The Microcosm* (1966), *The Paradox Players* (1967), *The Love Child* (1971), *All Heaven in a Rage* (1973), *Housespy* (1978), *Gor Saga* (1981), *Change* (1987), *First Born* (1989), *Illuminations* (1992), *Henry Purcell* (1994) and *Restitution* (1998); also active in the anti-vivisection cause.

DUFOUR, Marie Armande Jeanne Gacon- (1753–c. 1835). See Gacon-Dufour, Marie Armande Jeanne.

DUFRÉNOY, Adelaïde de (1765–1825). French poet and novelist. Name variations: Adelaïde Dufrénoy or Adelaide Dufrenoy. Born 1765 in Nantes, France; died 1825. ❖ Left France with husband during Revolution and returned 1812; was dubbed the French Sappho because of homoerotic nature of some poems, and her verse was awarded honors by Académie Française (1815); works include *Elégies* (1807), *Etrenne à ma fille* (1815), *La Petite Ménagère* (1816), *Biographie des jeunes demoiselles* (1816), *Les Françaises nouvelles* (1818), *Les Conversations maternells* and *Le Livre des femmes* (1823); also wrote novels and educational texts.

DU FRESNE, Yvonne (1929—). New Zealand novelist and short-story writer. Born 1929 in Takaka, New Zealand. ❖ Grew up in Danish-French Huguenot settlement of Manawatu, often reflected in writing; trained as school music teacher and taught in several schools; work focuses on post-colonial experiences and questions of gender; won PEN International First Book of Prose Award; established residencies for New Zealand writers at Aarhus University in Jutland, Denmark (1999); writings include *Farvel and Other Stories* (1982), *The Book of Ester* (1982), *The Growing of Astrid Westergaard and Other Stories* (1985),

Frédérique (1987), *The Bear From the North* (1989) and *Motherland* (1996).

DUGDALE, Henrietta (1826–1918). Australian feminist. Born Henrietta Augusta Worrell, 1826, in London, England; died June 17, 1918, at Point Lonsdale; dau. of John Worrell; m. a man named Davies (died); m. William Dugdale; m. Frederick Johnson, c. 1905; children: (2nd m.) 1 son, 2 daughters. ❖ Immigrated to Melbourne, Australia, with 1st husband (1852); remarried after his death; led women's rights movement in Victoria and became president of Women's Suffrage Society (1884); campaigned on women's issues and fought for social reform; wrote *A Few Hours in a Far-off Age* (1883), attacking male ignorance; was a secular humanist.

DUGGAN, Eileen May (1894–1972). New Zealand poet and writer. Name variations: Pippa. Born Eileen May Duggan, May 21, 1894, at Tuamarina, near Blenheim, New Zealand; died Dec 10, 1972, in Wellington, New Zealand; dau. of John Duggan (railway worker) and Julia (Begley) Duggan; Victoria University College, BA, 1917, MA, 1918. ❖ The 1st New Zealand poet to gain international reputation, began career teaching at St. Patrick's College, Wellington (1926); became assistant lecturer at Victoria University College (c. 1927); published historical and critical writings, short stories, and weekly column in *New Zealand Tablet*, under pen-name Pippa (late 1920s); lived reclusive life with partner Julia McLeely, publishing poems in *New Zealand Tablet*, and contributing essays to the *Sun*, Christchurch *Press*, Sydney *Bulletin*, London *New English Weekly* and New York *Commonweal*; also published *Poems* (1922), *New Zealand Bird Songs* (1929), *Poems* (1937), *New Zealand Poems* (1940), and *More Poems* (1951). Named OBE (1937) and honorary fellow of Royal Society of Literature (1943). ❖ See also *Dictionary of New Zealand Biography* (Vol. 4).

DUGGAN, Grace Hinds (b. 1878). See Curzon, Grace Hinds.

DUGGAN, Keltie (1970—). Canadian swimmer. Born Sept 7, 1970. ❖ At Seoul Olympics, won a bronze medal in 4 x 100-meter medley relay (1988).

DU GUILLET, Pernette (c. 1520–1545). French poet. Born c. 1520 in Lyons; died 1545. ❖ One of the emancipated women of Lyons, was influenced by poet Maurice Scève, who was in love with her; died at an early age and left behind several short, noteworthy poems.

DÜHRKOP DÜHRKOP, Bárbara (1945—). Spanish politician. Name variations: Barbara Duhrkop Duhrkop or Duehrkop Duehrkop. Born July 27, 1945, in Hannover, Alemania, Germany. ❖ Taught in Sweden (1970–74), then Germany (1974–78), then Spain (1978–87); served as PSE (Socialist Party) Group coordinator (1994–99); as a European Socialist, elected to 4th and 5th European Parliament (1994–99, 1999–2004).

DUIGAN, Suzanne Lawless (1924–1993). Australian botanist and aviator. Name variations: Sue Duigan. Born Suzanne Lawless Duigan, July 7, 1924, in Colac, Australia; died May 1993 in East Melbourne; dau. of Reginald Charles Duigan and Phyllis Mary Duigan; niece of aviator John Duigan; Melbourne University, BSc, MSc in botany; Cambridge, PhD, 1954. ❖ Pioneer palynologist, contributed to the knowledge of Tertiary flora of eastern Australia; became lecturer in botany at Melbourne University (1960), then senior lecturer; collaborated with Isobel Cookson on several papers; took up flying at age 36, gaining pilot's license (1970).

DUIVEKE (c. 1491–1517). See Dyveke.

DUKAKIS, Olympia (1931—). American actress and theater founder. Born June 20, 1931, in Lowell, Massachusetts; dau. of Greek immigrants; cousin of Michael Dukakis (gov. of Massachusetts); sister of actor Apollo Dukakis; m. Louis Zorich (actor), 1962. ❖ Helped found the Charles Playhouse in Boston and, with husband, founded the Whole Theatre company in Montclair, New Jersey, where she acted and directed; made film debut in *Lilith* (1964), followed by *Twice a Man, John and Mary, Made for Each Other, Death Wish, The Wanderers, Working Girl, Steel Magnolias, Dad, Look Who's Talking, In the Spirit, The Cemetery Club, Over the Hill, Mighty Aphrodite* and *Mr. Holland's Opus*, among others; on tv, appeared as Dr. Barbara Moreno on "Search for Tomorrow" (1983), starred in "The Last of the Blonde Bombshells" (2000) and in Armistead Maupin's "Tales of the City" (1993), "More Tales of the City" (1998), "Further Tales of the City" (2001), and "Babycakes" (2003). Won 2 Obies for off-Broadway performances and an Oscar for Best Supporting Actress for *Moonstruck* (1987).

DUKAS. *Variant of Ducas.*

DUKE, Doris (1912–1993). American heiress and philanthropist. Born Nov 22, 1912, in New York, NY; died Oct 28, 1993, at her home in Beverly Hills, California; dau. of James Buchanan Duke (owned American Tobacco Company); attended Brearley School and the Sorbonne; m. James H.R. Cromwell (American sportsman), 1935 (div.); m. Porfirio Rubiroso (Dominican playboy, div.). ❧ Tobacco heiress, one of the richest women in the world, came into her inheritance (1925); focused her philanthropies on animal rights, environment, AIDS, restoration of many old buildings in Newport; lived a somewhat secluded existence in later years. ❧ See also Pony Duke and Jason Thomas, *Too Rich: The Family Secrets of Doris Duke;* Ted Schwarz with Tom Rybak, *Trust No One: The Glamorous Life and Bizarre Death of Doris Duke* (St. Martin, 1997).

DUKE, Patty (1946—). American actress. Name variations: Patty Duke Astin. Born Anna Marie Duke, Dec 14, 1946, in Elmhurst, NY; m. Harry Falk, 1965 (div. 1969); m. Michael Tell, 1970 (annulled 1970); m. John Astin (actor), 1972 (div. 1985); m. Michael Pearce, 1986; children: (3rd m.) 2 sons, Sean Astin and Mackenzie Astin (both actors); (4th m.) (adopted) Kevin Pearce (b. 1988). ❧ In a career guided by managers John and Ethel Ross (who effectively replaced her parents), came to prominence on Broadway as a young Helen Keller in *The Miracle Worker* (1959–61) and in the film of the same name, for which she won an Academy Award (1962); starred on "The Patty Duke Show" (1963–66), the youngest actor to have her own tv series, and won an Emmy; was also in the miniseries "Captains and Kings" (1976), winning another Emmy; won 3rd Emmy portraying Annie Sullivan in "The Miracle Worker" (1979); films include *Billie* (1965), *Valley of the Dolls* (1967), *Me, Natalie* (1969) and *Kimberly* (1999); appeared in numerous tv movies; was president of Screen Actors Guild (SAG, 1985–88); diagnosed with manic-depressive illness (1982), wrote *A Brilliant Madness: Living with Manic Depression Illness* (1992). ❧ See also autobiography, *Call Me Anna* (1987).

DULAC, Germaine (1882–1942). French writer and film director-producer. Name variations: Charlotte Elisabeth Germaine Dulac. Pronunciation: du-LOCK. Born Charlotte Elisabeth Germaine Saisset-Schneider, Nov 17, 1882, in Amiens, France; died July 1942 in Paris; dau. of Captain Pierre-Maurice Saisset-Schneider and Madeleine-Claire Waymel; m. Marie-Louis Albert Dulac (novelist), 1905 (div. 1920). ❧ Feminist journalist and pioneering director-producer whose silent films and theoretical writings were seminal in early avant-garde cinema; 1st worked as a journalist for feminist newspaper *La Française* (1909–13), then turned to cinema; completed 1st film, *Les Soeurs ennemis* (1915); directed 26 films (1915–29), including *Ames de Fous* (1917), *La Fête espagnole,* the 1st film based on a script conceived expressly for the medium (1919), *La Mort du soleil* (1921), *La Souriante Madame Beudet,* considered her masterpiece (1923), *Gossette* (1923), *Le Diable dans la Ville* (1924), *Ame d'artiste* (1925), *Antoinette Sabrier* (1926), *La Coquille et le Clergyman,* considered by cinema historians to be 1st Surrealist film (1927), *L'Invitation au voyage* (1927), *La Princesse Mandane* (1928), and *Etude cinématographique sur une arabesque* (1929); produced and directed newsreels (1929–40); functioned as a major cinema critic and theorist in the area of film esthetics (1930s–40s); served as president of the Fédération des Ciné-Clubs de France, to popularize the new medium; only the 2nd woman film director, was also the 1st to make a personal imprint on the medium, given her key position in the impressionistic school of cinematography; her preeminent position in the early history of European cinema appears unassailed. Named an officer of the Legion of Honor. ❧ See also *Women in World History.*

DULCE. *Variant of Douce.*

DULCE, Sister (b. 1914). *See Pontes, Sister Dulce Lopes.*

DULCE OF ARAGON. *See Douce of Aragon.*

DULCIA. *Variant of Douce.*

DULEY, Margaret (1894–1968). Canadian novelist. Born Sept 27, 1894, in St John's, Newfoundland, Canada; died Mar 22, 1968; dau. of Thomas James Duley and Triphena Soper. ❧ Spent time in England but returned to Newfoundland, where she was active in women's suffrage movement; volunteered for charitable organizations during war and after war at Tuberculosis Sanatorium library in St John's; served as public-relations officer with Red Cross; writings include *The Eyes of the Gull* (1935), *Cold Pastoral* (1939), *Highway to Valour* (1941), *Novelty on Earth* (1943) and *The Caribou Hut* (1949).

DULLEMEN, Inez van (1925—). Dutch novelist and short-story writer. Born Nov 13, 1925, in Amsterdam, Netherlands; dau. of Jo de Wit; m. Erik Vos, 1954. ❧ Traveled extensively in Canada, US, Spain, France, Mexico, India and Kenya, and wrote of experiences in travel letters and stories; works include *Ontmoeting met de andere* (1949), *Luizenjournaal* (1969), *Vroeger is dood* (1976), *De vrouw met de vogelkop* (1979), *Eeuwig dag, eeuwig nacht* (1981), *Na de orkaan* (1983), *Een zwarte hond op my borst* (1983), *Het gevorkte beest* (1986), *Viva Mexico!* (1988) and *Huis van ijs* (1988).

DULLES, Eleanor Lansing (1895–1996). American economist and diplomat. Born June 1, 1895, in Watertown, New York; died in Washington, DC, Oct 30, 1996; dau. of Allen Macy Dulles (Presbyterian minister) and Edith (Foster) Dulles; sister of John Foster Dulles (secretary of state, died 1959), Allen Welsh Dulles (director of Central Intelligence Agency), Margaret Dulles, and Nataline Dulles; Bryn Mawr, degree in social science, 1917; attended London School of Economics and Sorbonne; Radcliffe College, MA, 1924, Harvard University, PhD, 1926; m. David Simon Blondheim (Hebraic scholar), 1932 (committed suicide Sept 1934); children: David Blondheim (b. 1934); (adopted) Ann Blondheim. ❧ Diplomat, author, and expert on international economic issues, who played a significant role in the post-1945 economic reconstruction of West Germany and West Berlin; published dissertation as *The French Franc, 1914–1928: The Facts and Their Interpretation,* to excellent reviews (1929); taught at Simmons College, Bryn Mawr, and University of Pennsylvania; wrote books on the French Franc, the Bank for International Settlements, and the evolution of reparations ideas; became chief of finance division of Social Security Board (1936); joined the State Department as an economics expert (1942); was a prominent member of US delegation to Bretton Woods international monetary conference (1944); was financial attaché of the State Department in Vienna (1945); rejected the idea of imposing a harsh peace on defeated Germany and lobbied for more realistic policies that would create the foundations for postwar social stability and a permanent reconstruction of Europe; became a key policymaker on Germany in the State Department (1948) and special assistant to the Department's Office of German Affairs (1951); advised the American occupying authorities and West German governments on economic reconstruction; joined political science department of Georgetown University (1963); writings include *Berlin: The Wall Is Not Forever* (1967). Received the Federal Republic of Germany's Grand Cross of Merit (1962). ❧ See also *Chances of a Lifetime: A Memoir* (Prentice-Hall, 1980); Leonard Mosley, *Dulles: A Biography of Eleanor, Allen and John Foster Dulles and Their Family Network* (Dial, 1978); and *Women in World History.*

DU MAURIER, Daphne (1907–1989). English writer. Name variations: Lady Daphne Browning; (nickname) Bing. Born May 13, 1907, in London, England; died April 19, 1989, in Par, Cornwall, England; dau. of Gerald du Maurier (actor-manager, died 1934) and Muriel (Beaumont) du Maurier (actress); granddau. of George du Maurier (who wrote *Trilby*); m. Frederick Arthur Montague (Tommy) Browning, July 19, 1932 (died 1965); children: Tessa Browning (b. 1933); Flavia Browning Leng (b. 1937); Christian, called Kit (b. 1940). ❧ Prolific British novelist, biographer, and playwright whose gift was in story-telling and whose imagination moved her to write, works of suspense, mystery, romance, and horror; after father purchased Ferryside in Fowey, Cornwall (1926), found the solitude there to write and used Cornwall as setting for many works (1929); published 1st novel, *The Loving Spirit* (1931), followed by *I'll Never Be Young Again* (1932); following death of father, wrote *Gerald: A Portrait* (1934); had 1st commercial success with *Jamaica Inn* (1936); published the highly successful *Rebecca* (1938); restored and moved into Menabilly (1943), which had provided a model for her fictional Manderley; writings include *The du Mauriers* (1937), *Frenchman's Creek* (1941), *Hungry Hill* (1943), *My Cousin Rachel* (1951), *The Scapegoat* (1957), *The Breaking Point* (1958), *The Infernal World of Branwell Bronte* (1960), *Castle Dor* (1962), *The Glass-Blowers* (1963), *The Flight of the Falcon* (1965), *Vanishing Cornwall* (1967), *The House on the Strand* (1969) and *Rule Britannia* (1972). Won National Book Award (1938), for *Rebecca;* named Dame Commander of the British Empire (DBE, 1969); received Mystery Writers of America Grand Master Award (1977). ❧ See also *Growing Pains* (published in US as *Myself When Young,* 1977); Margaret Forster, *Daphne du Maurier: The Secret Life of the Renowned Storyteller* (Doubleday, 1993); Flavia Leng, *Daphne du Maurier: A Daughter's Memoir* (Mainstream, 1994);

Martyn Shallcross, *The Private World of Daphne du Maurier* (St. Martin, 1992); and *Women in World History*.

DU MAURIER, Lady (1881–1957). *See Beaumont, Muriel.*

DU MAURIER, Muriel (1881–1957). *See Beaumont, Muriel.*

DUMBADZE, Nina (1919–1983). Soviet discus thrower. Born May 23, 1919, in USSR; died April 14, 1983. ❖ At Helsinki Olympics, won a bronze medal in the discus throw (1952).

DUMCHEVA, Antonina (1958—). Soviet rower. Born July 12, 1958, in USSR. ❖ At Seoul Olympics, won a silver medal in quadruple sculls without coxswain (1988).

DUMÉE, Jeanne (fl. 1680). French astronomer. Name variations: Jeanne Dumee. Born in Paris, France; fl. around 1680; widowed at age 17. ❖ Wrote *Entretiens sur l'opinion de Copernic touchant la mobilité de la terre* defending Copernican theories and arguing for women's intellectual equality with men (manuscript held in Bibliothèque Nationale, Paris).

DUMESNIL, Marie Françoise (1713–1803). French actress. Name variations: Mlle Dumesnil. Pronunciation: Du-may-NEL. Born Marie Françoise Marchand in Paris, France, Jan 2, 1713; died at Boulogne-sur-Mer, France, Feb 20, 1803. ❖ Made debut at Comédie Théâtre Français as Clytemnestra in *Iphigénie en Tauride* (1737) to great success; was famed for her portrayals of Athalie, Phèdre, Médéa, Agrippina, and Sémiramis (Sammuramat); continued performing until 1775, when she retired upon a pension. ❖ See also *Women in World History*.

DUMILÂTRE, Adèle (1821–1909). French ballet dancer. Name variations: Adele Dumilatre. Born June 30, 1821, in Paris, France; died May 4, 1909, in Paris. ❖ Studied at school of Paris Opéra with Charles Petit before joining the company (1840); danced title role in *La Sylphide*, one of the 1st dancers to replace famed Maria Taglioni; created roles including Myrthe for *Giselle* (1841) and principal role in *Lady Henriette* by Joseph Mazilier (1844); retired from performance career during her 20s (c. 1848).

DUMITRACHE, Maria Magdalena (1977—). Romanian rower. Born May 3, 1977, in Targoviste, Romania. ❖ Won a gold medal at Sydney Olympics (2000), for coxed eights; won World Rowing championships for coxed eights (1998, 1999, 2000).

DUMITRESCU, Roxana (1967—). Romanian fencer. Born June 27, 1967. ❖ At Barcelona Olympics, won a bronze medal in team foil (1992).

DUMITRESCU-DOLETTI, Joanna (1902–1963). Princess of Hohenzollern. Name variations: Joanna Brana; Joanna Lucie Dumitrescu-Tohani; assumed grandmother's surname Doletti in 1928. Born Joanna Lucy Dumitrescu, Sept 24, 1902, in Bucharest, Romania; died Feb 19, 1963, in Lausanne, Switzerland; dau. of Ion Dumitrescu-Tohani and Nella Theodoru or Teodoru; m. Radu Saveanu, Dec 11, 1924 (div.); m. Nicholas (1903–1978, son of Marie of Rumania), prince of Hohenzollern, Oct 24, 1931; children: Peter.

DUMITRU, Viorica (1946—). Romanian kayaker. Born Aug 4, 1946. ❖ At Mexico City Olympics, won a bronze medal in K1 500 meters (1968); at Munich Olympics, won a bronze medal in K2 500 meters (1972).

DUMM, Edwina (1893–1990). American cartoonist. Born into a newspaper family in Sandusky, Ohio, 1893; died 1990; dau. of Frank Edwin Dumm; attended Art Students League of New York. ❖ Worked as a political cartoonist for a Columbus, Ohio, newspaper; recruited by George Matthew Adams Syndicate to develop a comic strip about a boy and his dog (c. 1918), created *Cap Stubbs and Tippie*, for which she became well known; also drew a dog cartoon called *Sinbad* for *Life* magazine and illustrated a one-column feature, *Alec the Great*, written by her brother; was a strong supporter of women's rights.

DUMMER, Ethel Sturges (1866–1954). American philanthropist. Name variations: Ethel Sturges. Born Ethel Sturges, Oct 23, 1866, in Chicago, Illinois; died Feb 25, 1954, in Winnetka, Illinois; dau. of George and Mary (Delafield) Sturges; m. William Francis Dummer (banker), 1888 (died 1928); children: 4 daughters (b. 1890, 1892, 1895, 1899), 1 son (1902–1902). ❖ Joined National Child Labor Committee and Chicago Juvenile Protection Association (1905); was founding trustee of Chicago School of Civics and Philanthropy (1908); financed 2 University of Chicago lecture series on social problems; financed establishment of Juvenile Psychopathic Institute (1909); financially supported such

scholars as Miriam Van Waters and William I. Thomas; funded Florence Beaman's class for retarded, truant and delinquent boys at Montefiore School, Chicago; financed child development courses at Northwestern University (1940s); rejected forced marriages and legal punishment for prostitution; advocated repeal of state laws discriminating against prostitutes and their children and supported therapeutic detention homes for prostitutes. ❖ See also *Why I think So—The Autobiography of an Hypothesis* (1937).

DUMOLARD, Marie (1816—). French murderer (accused). Name variations: Marie Dumollard. Born 1816 in France; m. Martin Dumolard. ❖ While husband murdered young women over more than a decade, was sometimes rewarded for her complicity with the victims' clothing; was finally apprehended after a potential victim, Marie Pichon, escaped before husband could strangle her (1861); tried at Bourg, while angry mobs cried out for execution (Jan 1862), was found guilty with husband (he was guillotined, she received 20-year prison sentence). Though only 3 corpses were discovered at their cottage near Lyons, they were suspected in as many as 25 murders.

DUMOND, Natalie. *See Natalie, Mlle.*

DUMONT, Brigitte (1944—). French fencer. Born April 25, 1944. ❖ At Montreal Olympics, won a silver medal in team foil (1976).

DUMONT, Carlota (1854–1909). *See Matto de Turner, Clorinda.*

DUMONT, Margaret (1889–1965). American actress and singer. Name variations: Daisy Baker, Daisy Dumont. Born Margaret Baker, Oct 20, 1889, in Brooklyn, NY; died Mar 6, 1965, in Hollywood, California; m. John Moller Jr. (industrialist), 1910. ❖ Best remembered as the society matron foil of the Marx Brothers on stage and screen; films include *A Day at the Races, Animal Crackers, Duck Soup, A Night at the Opera, Anything Goes, Never Give a Sucker and Even Break, The Horn Blows at Midnight* and *Stop You're Killing Me.*

DUNA, Steffi (1910–1992). Hungarian ballet dancer and actress. Name variations: Stephanie Berinde Le Faye. Born Stephanie Berinde (also seen as Berindey), Feb 8, 1910, in Budapest, Hungary; died April 22, 1992, in Beverly Hills, California; m. John Carroll, 1935 (div. 1936); m. Dennis O'Keefe (actor), 1940 (died 1968); children: (1st m.) daughter; (2nd m.) son. ❖ Trained at school of Budapest Opera Ballet where she also performed until 1932; moved to London where she appeared in Noel Coward's *Words and Music*; made Broadway debut in *A Beggar's Opera*; moved to Hollywood, CA, where she appeared in numerous films, often as a Mexican, Spaniard, or Gypsy; was cast in similar roles in musicals including *La Cucaracha* (1936), *The Girl from Havana* (1940) and *Way Down South* (1939).

DUNAVSKA, Adriana (1970—). Bulgarian rhythmic gymnast. Born April 21 (some sources cite April 4), 1970, in Sofia, Bulgaria. ❖ At European championships, came in 4th (1986), 1st (1988), and 2nd (1989); at World championships, won a gold medal for rope and silver for all-around (1987) and a bronze medal for all-around and silvers for ball and ribbon (1989); at Seoul Olympics, won a silver medal in rhythmic gymnastics, all-around (1988); won the Intervision Cup and Bulgarian nationals (1988).

DUNAWAY, Faye (1941—). American actress. Born Dorothy Faye Dunaway, Jan 14, 1941, in Bascom, Florida; dau. of John MacDowell Dunaway (army officer) and Grace April Smith; sister of Mac Dunaway (lawyer); attended University of Florida; Boston University, BFA (1962); trained at Lincoln Center Repertory Theater in NY; m. Peter Wolf (musician with J. Geils Band), 1974 (div. 1979); m. Terry O'Neill, 1983 (div. 1987); children: Liam O'Neill (model). ❖ Leading actress, began career competing in beauty pageants, earning title "Sweetheart of Sigma Chi" at University of Florida; had 1st starring role in *A Man For All Seasons* (1962), just days after graduating from college; appeared in 1st film, *The Happening* (1966); became international film star after Oscar-nominated breakout role in *Bonnie and Clyde* (1967); went on to star in *The Thomas Crown Affair* (1968), *Little Big Man* (1970), *The Three Musketeers* (1973), *The Towering Inferno* (1974) and *Chinatown*, for which she was nominated for another Academy Award (1974); received an Oscar for role in *Network* (1976); other films include *Mommy Dearest* (1981), *Even Cowgirls Get the Blues* (1993), *Drunks* (1996), remake of *The Thomas Crown Affair* (1999) and *The Yards* (2000); returned to Broadway in *Master Class* (1996); wrote, directed, produced and acted in well-received 19-minute *The Yellow Bird* (2001). ❖ See also Faye Dunaway, *Looking for Gatsby: My Life* (Simon & Schuster, 1995).

DUNBAR, Agnes (1312–1369). Scottish hero and countess of Dunbar and March. Name variations: Black Agnes; Agnes of March; Agnes of Dunbar; Lady Randolph or Lady Agnes Randolph. Born 1312 in Scotland; died in 1369 in Scotland; dau. of Sir Thomas Randolph, 1st earl of Moray; m. Patrick (1285–1369, a prominent and powerful Scottish noble), 10th lord of Dunbar and 2nd earl of March, 1324; children: at least 3, including Agnes, later mistress of David II (1323–1370), king of Scotland (r. 1329–1370). ❖ One of Scotland's many female participants in the war against English rule, married Lord Patrick of Dunbar, who was at 1st allied with England but soon switched his allegiance to his native country, no doubt in part due to her influence; became known as an outspoken, bold woman and an inspiration to others as the war against England intensified (1330s); with husband away at war and the earl of Salisbury and his troops at her gates, refused to surrender (Jan 1338); resisted siege for 5 months, refusing all offers to negotiate or surrender; signed a truce with Salisbury, and the English withdrew from Dunbar (June 1338); became a Scottish hero. ❖ See also *Women in World History.*

DUNBAR, Alice (1875–1935). See Dunbar-Nelson, Alice.

DUNBAR, Bridget (c. 1802/27–1899). See Goodwin, Bridget.

DUNBAR, Christine (c. 1350–?). Scottish countess and letter writer. Name variations: Christina Dunbar; Countess of March. Born Christina Seton in Cockburn, England, c. 1350; dau. of Alan and Margaret de Seyton; m. George Dunbar (c. 1338–1420), 10th earl of Dunbar and 3rd earl of March (of the Scottish Marches), c. 1354; children: Janet (who m. Sir William Seton); Sir George of Kilconquhar, earl of Dunbar; Sir Wawan of Newburn, bishop of Moray; Patrick; John; Sir David Dunbar; Elizabeth (who m. David Stewart, earl of Carrick); Margaret. ❖ Her letter written in French to Henry IV, asking for help during exile in England after husband's quarrel with the earl of Douglas (1403), is still extant.

DUNBAR, Diane. American gymnast. Name variations: Diane Dunbar Bijesse. ❖ At Pan American Games, won a gold medal for team all-around and a bronze medal for uneven bars (1975); won the Emerald Empire Cup and Sanlam Cup (1976).

DUNBAR, Dixie (1915–1991). American actress and dancer. Name variations: Christine King. Born Christine Elizabeth Dunbar, Jan 19, 1915, in Montgomery, Alabama; died Aug 29, 1991, in Miami Beach, Florida; m. Jack L. King, 1950. ❖ Made professional debut at Hollywood Restaurant in NY as a tap dancer, then appeared with Harry Richman's band; made NY stage debut in *Life Begins at 8:40;* was a specialty tap and Charleston dancer and juvenile lead in such films as *George White's Scandals, Girls' Dormitory, King of Burlesque, One in a Million, Rebecca of Sunnybrook Farm* and *Alexander's Ragtime Band;* starred on Broadway in *Yokel Boy* (1939); with her Rhythmaires tap chorus, toured with Les Brown and his Band of Renown (1940–41); contracted polio while touring army camps during WWII and was forced to retire.

DUNBAR, Flanders (1902–1959). American psychologist. Name variations: H. Flanders Dunbar or Helen Flanders. Born Helen Flanders Dunbar, May 14, 1902, in Chicago, Illinois; died by drowning in a swimming pool accident, though newspapers suggested suicide, Aug 21, 1959, in South Kent, Connecticut; dau. of Francis William Dunbar and Edith Vaughan (Flanders) Dunbar; Columbia University, PhD in philosophy, 1929; m. Theodor P. Wolfensberger, later Theodore P. Wolfe (psychiatrist), 1932 (div. 1939); m. George Henry Soule, Jr. (economist), 1940; children: (2nd m.) 1 daughter (b. 1941). ❖ Known for her work in psychosomatic medicine for which she coined the term, established a reputation as Dante scholar with publication of doctoral dissertation, *Symbolism in Mediaeval Thought and Its Consummation in the Divine Comedy* (1929); became director of Council for the Clinical Training of Theological Students (1930); participated in study of 1,600 patients at Columbia Presbyterian Hospital, finding connections between personality profiles and ailments, and detecting accident-prone personality (1930s), then published findings in *Psychosomatic Diagnosis* (1943); held appointments in medical and psychiatric departments at Presbyterian Hospital and Vanderbilt Clinic, NY (1931–49); taught at Columbia University's College of Physicians and Surgeons (1931–49) and at New York Psychoanalytic Institute (1942–47); founded journal, *Psychosomatic Medicine,* serving as editor-in-chief (1938–47), and American Psychosomatic Society (1942); was almost killed in automobile accident (1954). Wrote *Mind and Body* (1947), *Your Child's Mind and Body* (1949) and *Psychiatry in the Medical Specialties* (1959).

DUNBAR, Helen Flanders (1902–1959). *See Dunbar, Flanders.*

DUNBAR-NELSON, Alice (1875–1935). African-American poet. Name variations: Alice Dunbar or Alice Moore Dunbar. Born Alice Ruth Moore, July 19, 1875, in New Orleans, Louisiana; died Sept 18, 1935; dau. of Joseph Moore (merchant marine) and Patricia Wright (seamstress); graduate of Straight College (now Dillard University), 1892; m. Paul Laurence Dunbar, Mar 8, 1898 (sep. 1902, died 1906); secretly m. Henry Arthur Callis, Jan 19, 1910 (div. 1911); m. Robert J. Nelson, April 20, 1916 (died 1949); children: (3rd m.) Elizabeth and Bobby Nelson. ❖ Writer who earned popular acclaim as a Harlem Renaissance poet and whose well-known marriage to Paul Laurence Dunbar was not only tumultuous but short-lived; taught school in New Orleans (1892–96); helped found White Rose Home for Girls in Harlem (1897–98); taught and administered at Howard High School, Wilmington, Delaware; wrote for and helped edit the *A.M.E. Church Review* (1913–14); became field organizer for Middle Atlantic States in women's suffrage campaign (1915); toured the South as a field representative of Women's Committee of the Council of National Defense (1918); published poems in *Crisis, Ebony and Topaz, Opportunity, Negro Poets and Their Poems, Caroling Dusk, Harlem: A Forum of Negro Life and Others* (1917–28); coedited and published the *Wilmington Advocate* newspaper (1920–22); began diary (1921); headed the Anti-Lynching Crusaders in Delaware fighting for the Dyer Anti-Lynching Bill (1922); directed the Democratic political campaign from New York headquarters (1924); worked as teacher and parole officer at Industrial School for Colored Girls (1924–28); wrote column "From A Woman's Point of View" (later changed to "Une Femme Dit") in *Pittsburgh Courier* (1926); wrote column "As In a Looking Glass" in *Washington Eagle* (1926–30); wrote column "So It Seems to Alice Dunbar-Nelson" in *Pittsburgh Courier* (1930); served as executive secretary for American Friends Inter-Racial Peace Committee (1928–31); writings include (short stories and poems) *Violets and Other Tales* (1895), (short stories) *The Goodness of St. Rocque and Other Stories* (1899), (edited) *Masterpieces of Negro Eloquence* (1914) and *The Dunbar Speaker and Entertainer* (1920). ❖ See also *Give Us Each Day: The Diary of Alice Dunbar-Nelson* (Norton, 1984); Gloria T. Hull, *Color, Sex, and Poetry: Three Women Writers of the Harlem Renaissance* (Indiana U. Press, 1987); Eleanor Alexander, *Lyrics of Sunshine and Shadow: The Tragic Courtship and Marriage of Paul Laurence Dunbar and Alice Ruth Moore* (New York U. Press, 2002); and *Women in World History.*

DUNCA, Rodica (1965—). Romanian gymnast. Born May 16, 1965, in Baia Mare, Romania; m. Zoltan Papp (choreographer). ❖ Placed 1st team all-around and 5th all-around at World championships (1979) and 1st all-around at Champions All (1980); at Moscow Olympics, won a silver medal in team all-around (1980); at Europeans, won a bronze medal in balance beam (1981).

DUNCAN, Dolce Ann (1862–1943). See Cabot, Dolce Ann.

DUNCAN, Elizabeth (c. 1874–1948). American dance teacher. Born c. 1874 in San Francisco, California; died Dec 1, 1948, in Tubingen, Germany; sister of Raymond, Augustin and Isadora Duncan (dancers). ❖ Was introduced to classical Greek studies and Greek revival theory in dance, philosophy, and music by her mother; moved to Europe with sister Isadora, where they opened boarding school for girls in Grunewald, Germany (c. 1904), and where she trained the 6 Duncan protégés soon to be known as the Isadorables; opened own school in Darmstadt (1900s), where she trained dancers who appeared in annual performances for many years; returned to US briefly during WWI, but was soon back in Germany, where she continued to teach until her death (1948).

DUNCAN, Frances (1942—). *See Duncan, Sandy Frances.*

DUNCAN, Irma (1897–1978). German interpretive dancer and choreographer. Born Dorette Henrietta Ehrich-Grimme, Feb 26, 1897, in Schleswig-Holstein, Germany; died Sept 20, 1978, in Santa Barbara, California. ❖ Trained at Elizabeth and Isadora Duncan's school in Grunewald, Germany, starting age 8, and soon made official debut as Duncan dancer (1905); became a member of Isadora Duncan Dancers, or Isadorables (1918); traveled to US to perform as 1 of 6 Isadorables on Sol Hurok tour; served as director of Duncan school in Soviet Union (1921–30), which toured the West several times (1928–30); moved to US (1930), where she appeared frequently as concert dancer and taught Duncan dance technique to Julia Levien and Anaballe Gamson, among others; choreographed and helped stage numerous works; was considered the best known and most influential of Duncan protégés.

DUNCAN, Isadora (1878–1927). American dancer and choreographer. Born Angela Isadora Duncan, May 27, 1878, in San Francisco; strangled by her shawl in freak accident in Nice, France, Sept 14, 1927; dau. of Mary Isadora (Gray) Duncan (piano and dance teacher) and Joseph Charles Duncan; m. Sergei Esenin (poet), May 22, 1922 (div.); children: (with Gordon Craig) Deirdre; (with Eugene Singer) Patrick Augustus. ❖ The most prominent dancer of her time, who invented the "New System" of improvised movements interpretive of poetry, music, and the rhythms of nature, made NY stage debut in a pantomime called *Mme. Pygmalion* (1896); while giving a series of dances illustrating *The Rubáiyát of Omar Khayyám*, danced with bare arms and legs, something so shocking to Victorian audiences that several walked out (1898); went to London (1899); by 1900, was performing before minor royalty and society matrons; went on dance tours with Loie Fuller troupe in Berlin, Leipzig and Munich (1901); began solo performances in Vienna and Budapest (1902), Berlin, Paris, Vélizy, various German cities (1903); danced to *Tannhäuser* at Bayreuth, met Gordon Craig, and opened her 1st school of the dance at Grünewald, a suburb of Berlin (1904); her most gifted students would henceforth be called "the Isadorables" and go on tour with her; professionally, during next decade, met with nothing but success as tours took her throughout Europe and US; learned that her 2 children, together with their English governess, had drowned when their auto accidentally rolled into the Seine (April 19, 1913); when World War I broke out (1914), transported pupils to the US, installing them in an estate near Tarrytown, NY; accepted an invitation to set up a dance academy in Russia (1921); lived in Nice (1926–27) and gave final performance at Paris' Théâtre Mogator (July 1927); from her flowing garbs that helped revolutionize the dress of women to a platform style that centered on spontaneity, altered dance as an art form. ❖ See also autobiography, *My Life* (1927); Fredrika Blair, *Isadora: Portrait of the Artist as a Woman* (McGraw-Hill, 1986); Walter Terry, *Isadora Duncan: Her Life, Her Art, Her Legacy* (Dodd, 1963); Lilian Loewenthal, *The Search for Isadora* (Princeton, 1993); film *Isadora*, fictionalized account starring Vanessa Redgrave (1969); and *Women in World History*.

DUNCAN, Lois (1934—). American children's writer, novelist and mystery writer. Born Lois Duncan Steinmetz, April 28, 1934, in Philadelphia, Pennsylvania; dau. of Joseph Janney and Lois (Foley) Steinmetz (both magazine photographers); attended Duke University, 1952–53; University of New Mexico, BA (cum laude), 1977; m. 2nd husband, Donald Wayne Arquette (electrical engineer), July 15, 1965; children: (1st m.) Robin, Kerry, Brett; (2nd m.) Donald Jr., Kaitlyn (died 1989). ❖ Writer of youth books, adult novels, magazine articles and short stories, was a 3-time winner during high school years of *Seventeen* magazine's annual short-story contest; served as instructor in department of journalism at University of New Mexico (1971–82); won Seventeenth Summer Literary Award from Dodd, Mead for *Debutante Hill* (1957); won Best Novel Award from National Press Women for *Point of Violence* (1966); was Edgar Allan Poe Award Runner-up for *Ransom* (1967) and *They Never Came Home* (1969); won Zia Award from New Mexico Press Women for *Major Andre: Brave Enemy* (1969); won numerous awards for young adult books, which include *I Know What You Did Last Summer* (1973), *Summer of Fear* (1976), *Killing Mr. Griffin* (1978), *Stranger with My Face* (1981), *The Third Eye* (1984), *Locked in Time* (1985), *The Twisted Window* (1987), and *Don't Look Behind You* (1989); after daughter Kaitlyn was killed in a drive-by shooting (July 16, 1989), wrote the nonfiction book, *Who Killed My Daughter?* (1992). ❖ See also autobiography, *Chapters: My Growth as a Writer* (Little, Brown, 1982).

DUNCAN, Maria Teresa (1895–1987). German interpretive dancer. Born Theresa Kruger, 1895, in Dresden, Germany; died 1987. ❖ Trained with school of Isadora and Elizabeth Duncan in Grunewald, Germany (starting c. 1905); traveled to US to perform as 1 of 6 Isadorables on Sol Hurok tour; returned to Europe (1920), where she performed recitals—mainly Greek dances—with own group Meliconades; created most works based on music interpretation and often dedicated whole concerts to single composers including Schubert and Chopin; retired from performance career for around 3 decades (1940s), but returned to great success with Isadora Duncan Heritage Dance Group (1978), performing—among other works—a demanding Adagio to Beethoven's Seventh Symphony.

DUNCAN, Mary (1895–1993). American actress. Born Aug 13, 1895, in Luttrellville, Virginia; died May 9, 1993, in Palm Beach, Florida; m. Lewis Wood Jr. (annulled); m. Stephen Sanford. ❖ Made stage debut in Chicago in *Toto* and NY debut in *Face Value* (both 1921); other plays include *The Egotist, New Toys, All Wet* and *The Shanghai Gesture*; films include *Four Devils, The River, Through Different Eyes, Our Daily Bread, Kismet, Men Call It Love, Daughter of Luxury, The Age for Love* and *13 Women*.

DUNCAN, Rosetta (1890–1959). American musical-comedy star and songwriter. Name variations: Duncan Sisters. Born Nov 23, 1890, in Los Angeles, California; died Dec 4, 1959, in Acero, Illinois, as a result of injuries from an auto accident; sister of Evelyn Duncan (1893–1972), Vivian Duncan (1902–1986) and Harold Duncan (tennis pro). ❖ With sister Vivian, performed as the Duncan Sisters with Gus Edwards' "Kiddies' Revue" in vaudeville, nightclubs and on Broadway; famed as Topsy in their musical *Topsy and Eva* (1927); other musicals include *Doing Our Bit, She's a Good Fellow* and *Tip Top*; wrote such songs as "Rememb'ring," "Do Re Mi," and "Someday Soon."

DUNCAN, Sandy (1946—). American theater dancer and actress. Born Feb 20, 1946, in Henderson, Texas; attended Lon Morris College; m. Bruce Scott, 1968 (div. 1972); m. Dr. Thomas Calcaterra, 1973 (div. 1979); m. Don Correia, 1980; children: (3nd m.) 2 sons. ❖ Made professional debut performing at Dallas Civic Theater in Texas at age 12; performed in musical revivals at City Center in New York in such shows as *The Music Man, The Sound of Music* and *Finian's Rainbow;* starred on Broadway in *Your Own Thing, Canterbury Tales* (1969) and in revivals of *The Boy Friend* (1970) and *Peter Pan* (1979); on tv, had starring roles in series "Funny Face" (1971), "The Sandy Duncan Show" (1972), "Roots" (1977), "My Little Pony" (1986), "Valerie" (1986) and "The Hogan Family" (1988), among others; guest-starred on "Bonanza" (1971), "The Sonny and Cher Comedy Hour" (1972), "The Muppet Show" (1976), "The Love Boat," "The Tonight Show with Johnny Carson" (1980), "Law & Order" (1995), and many more.

DUNCAN, Sandy Frances (1942—). Canadian children's writer. Name variations: Frances Duncan. Born 1942 in Vancouver, British Columbia, Canada; University of British Columbia, MA in psychology, 1963; children: 2. ❖ Worked as clinical psychologist for 9 years until 1972; writings include *Cariboo Runaway* (1976), *Kap-Sung Ferris* (1977), *The Toothpaste Genie* (1981), *Dragonhunt* (1981), *Finding Home* (1982), *Pattern Makers* (1989), *Listen to Me, Grace Kelly* (1990), and *British Columbia, Its Land, Mineral and Water Resources* (1996). Received GVLF Award and Canadian Children's Book Centre "Our Choice" Award.

DUNCAN, Sara Jeanette (1861–1922). Canadian writer. Name variations: Sara Janet Duncan, S.J. Cotes, Sara Jeanette Duncan Cotes; (pseudonym) Garth Grafton. Born Sara Jeanette Duncan, Dec 22, 1861, in Brantford, Ontario, Canada; died of bronchial pneumonia, July 22, 1922, in Ashtead, Surrey, England; m. Everard Cotes (museum curator), 1890. ❖ Prolific writer of novels and travel diaries, was hired to work on the *Toronto Globe* (1886), the 1st woman to join the editorial staff of a Canadian newspaper; gave love and relationship advice, cooking tips and recipes, and fashion pointers; also wrote for *Washington Post,* Toronto *Globe,* Montreal *Star,* and *The Week* under pseudonym Garth Grafton; undertook around world trip with journalist Lily Lewis (1888), resulting in 1st full-length book *Round the World by Ourselves* (1890); married Calcutta museum curator Everard Cotes and spent next 25 years in India; wrote numerous novels about life and politics in India, including *The Simple Adventures of a Memsahib* (1893); is best known for novel *The Imperialist* (1904) which describes small-town life in Canada; also wrote *A Daughter of Today* (1891), *Hilda: A Story of Calcutta* (1894), *The Story of Sonny Sahib* (1894), *His Honor and a Lady* (1898), *An American Girl in London* (1898) and *The Pool in the Dessert* (1903). ❖ See also Marian Fowler, *Redney: A Life of Sarah Jeanette Duncan* (Penguin London, 1985).

DUNCAN, Sheena (1932—). South African activist. Born Sheena Sinclair in 1932 in Johannesburg, Transvaal, South Africa; dau. of Jean Sinclair (co-founding member of the Black Sash); attended Edinburgh College of Domestic Science (Scotland) where she qualified as a domestic science teacher (1953); m. a Johannesburg architect, 1955; children: 2. ❖ White South African anti-apartheid activist, pacifist, and protester against capital punishment, who was twice-elected national president of the South African women's political group Black Sash which, under her leadership, shifted away from white women standing in silent protest outside government offices to assisting the black community with the convoluted apartheid laws that placed so many restrictions on their daily lives; joined the Black Sash as director of Johannesburg Legal Advice Office (1963); served 1st term as national president of Black Sash (1975–78); served for 3 years as chair of the Johannesburg Diocesan

Challenge Group to eliminate racial discrimination within Anglican church; served 2nd term as national president of Black Sash (1983–86); arrested while praying in front of South African Parliament Building in memory of black mourners killed by police at a funeral (1985); called for international economic sanctions against South Africa (1986); elected vice-president of the South African Council of Churches (1987); organized legal advice centers in churches around the country in conjunction with the Family, Home and Life Division of the South African Council of Churches; appointed to South African Human Rights Commission (1988); as member of South African Council of Churches, called for moratorium on all pending capital punishment executions (1988); reelected National Advice Office Co-Ordinator for Black Sash (1990); appointed member of Independent Board for Inquiry into Informal Repression (1992). ❖ See also Kathryn Spink, *Black Sash: The Beginning of a Bridge in South Africa* (Methuen, 1991); and *Women in World History*.

DUNCAN, Vivian (1902–1986). American actress, composer and songwriter. Name variations: Duncan Sisters. Born June 17, 1902, in Los Angeles, California; died Sept 19, 1986, in Los Angeles; sister of Evelyn Duncan (1893–1972) and Rosetta Duncan (1900–1959) and Harold Duncan (tennis pro); m. Nils Asther (actor), 1930 (div. 1932). ❖ With sister Rosetta, performed as the Duncan Sisters with Gus Edwards' "Kiddies Revue" in vaudeville and on Broadway; famed for the role of Eva in their musical *Topsy and Eva* (1927); appeared in film *It's a Great Life*; wrote such songs as "Rememb'ring," "Do Re Mi," and "United We Stand."

DUNCAN SISTERS.
See Duncan, Rosetta.
See Duncan, Vivian.

DUNCOMBE, Susanna (1725–1812). British poet. Born 1725; died 1812; lived in Canterbury; m. John Duncombe, 1761. ❖ Poems survive only in anthologies; husband praised her now lost allegory in his work *Feminiad* (1754).

DUNDAS, Maria (1785–1842). *See Callcott, Maria.*

DUNEDIN, Maudie (c. 1888–1937). Scottish specialty dancer. Born c. 1888 in Australia, while parents were on tour; died April 9, 1937, in Glendale, California; m. Harry Mallia. ❖ Made debut as a child with her family's acts, The Incredible Dunedins, The Donegan Sisters, and The Variety Girls, where she exhibited trick bicycle and roller skate routines; toured with family's troupes throughout England (1909, 1911, 1914) and in US (1904–15) until she left to appear in solo acts; performed range of specialties on bicycles, skates, and toe shoes to great success at such venues as New York Hippodrome; retired from performance career (1920s); joined husband Harry Mallia on the production end of numerous shows; served as manager for Prologs along West Coast of US for over a dozen years.

DUNFIELD, Sonya Klopfer (c. 1936—). American-born figure skater. Name variations: Sonya Klopfer. Born in US around 1936; m. Canadian skater Peter Dunfield. ❖ Was Ladies' National Figure Skating Champion (1951) and captain of US Olympics team (1952); at World championships, won a bronze medal (1951) and a silver medal (1952); with husband, coached in Canada, mentoring such skaters as Elizabeth Manley, among others. With husband, inducted into Skate Canada Hall of Fame (2001).

DUNHAM, Ethel Collins (1883–1969). American pediatrician. Born Ethel Collins Dunham on Mar 12, 1883, in Hartford, Connecticut; died Dec 13, 1969, in Cambridge, Massachusetts; dau. of Samuel G. Dunham and Alice (Collins) Dunham; lived with Martha May Eliot. ❖ Interned in pediatrics at Johns Hopkins Hospital's Harriet Lane Home (1918); was one of the 1st women house officers at New Haven Hospital and worked in department of pediatrics (late 1910s); became director of New Haven Dispensary's outpatient clinic and head of nursery for newborn babies (1920); was instructor at Yale University's School of Medicine (1920), becoming assistant professor (1924), associate clinical professor (1927), and holding title of lecturer in clinical pediatrics (1935–50); was appointed medical officer in charge of neonatal studies by head of US Children's Bureau (1927); presented report to American Pediatric Society (APS), indicating premature birth as leading cause of death in infants (1933), and was appointed chair of committee on neonatal studies created by APS; became director of Children's Bureau's department of research in child development in Washington, DC (1935); worked with World Health Organization in Geneva,

Switzerland, as consultant to maternal and child health section (1949–51); was 1st woman to win Howland Medal, APS's highest award (1957). Wrote *Premature Infants, a Manual for Physicians* (1948) and *Samuel G. Dunham, Alice Collins Dunham, Their Descendants and Antecedents* (1955).

DUNHAM, Katherine (1909–2006). African-American dancer, choreographer, anthropologist, and social activist. Name variations: (pseudonym) Kaye Dunn. Born Katherine Dunham, June 22, 1909, in Glen Ellyn, Illinois; died May 21, 2006, in New York, NY; dau. of Albert Millard Dunham and Fanny June (Taylor) Dunham; University of Chicago, degree in social anthropology, 1936; m. Jordis McCoo, 1931 (div. 1939); m. John Pratt (costume and set designer), 1939 (died 1986); children: (adopted) Marie-Christine. ❖ Activist dancer who 1st introduced Afro-Caribbean dance to American audiences and created the 1st African-American dance troupe in US; co-founded the Ballet Negre in Chicago (1929) and, later, the Negro Dance Group; traveled to Trinidad, Jamaica, and Haiti (1935–36) and adapted Afro-Caribbean dance rhythms to her own ballets; created the Katherine Dunham Dance Company (1938), which appeared on stage and film to great acclaim (1940s–50s); established the Katherine Dunham Performing Arts Training Center in East St. Louis, Illinois, for urban African-American youth (1967); active in civil-rights movement and social causes, staged a 47-day hunger strike in protest of US treatment of Haitian refugees (1992); choreographed for the stage: *Negro Rhapsody, L'Ag'YA, Tropics, Le Jazz Hot, Tropical Revue, Carib Song, Windy City, Bal Negre, Caribbean Rhapsody, Los Indios, Shango, Bambouche,* and *Aïda* for the Metropolitan Opera Company; choreographed for film: *Carnival of Myth, Star Spangled Banner, Pardon My Sarong, Mumbo, Cakewalk* and *Green Mansions.* ❖ See also memoir, *A Touch of Innocence* (Harcourt, 1959); Ruth Beckford, *Katherine Dunham: A Biography* (Dekker, 1979); and *Women in World History*.

DÜNHAUPT, Angelika. German luge athlete. Name variations: Angelika Dunhaupt or Duenhaupt. ❖ Won a bronze medal for singles at Grenoble Olympics (1968).

DUNIWAY, Abigail Scott (1834–1915). American writer, editor, and businesswoman. Born Abigail Jane Scott (nicknamed Jenny); Oct 22, 1834, in Groveland, Tazewell Co., Illinois; died Oct 11, 1915, in Portland, Oregon; dau. of John Tucker Scott (farmer and sawmill owner) and Ann (Roelofson) Scott; m. Benjamin C. Duniway, Aug 2, 1853 (died 1896); children: Clara Belle Stearns (1854–1886); Willis (1856–1913); Hubert (b. 1859); Wilkie Collins (b. 1861); Claude Augustus (b. 1866); Ralph (b. 1869). ❖ Leader in the women's suffrage movement, immigrated to Oregon via the Oregon Trail with family (1852); published 1st novel, *Captain Gray's Company* (1859); under pseudonym "A Farmer's Wife," was a regular contributor to the *Oregon Farmer* (1859–62); founded and began teaching at Lafayette Union School (1862); opened a millinery shop (1866); helped found Oregon State Equal Suffrage Association (1870); established, then edited, the weekly newspaper, *New Northwest* (1871–86), which exposed injustices toward women; went on 1st lecture tour, in company of suffragist Susan B. Anthony (1871); saw women's suffrage referendum pass in Oregon (1912); also wrote *My Musings* (1875), *David and Anna Matson* (1876), *From the West to the West: Across the Plains to Oregon* (1905), and *Path Breaking: An Autobiographical History of the Equal Suffrage Movement in Pacific Coast States* (1914). ❖ See also Ruth Barnes Moynihan, *Rebel for Rights: Abigail Scott Duniway* (Yale U. Press, 1983); Helen Krebs Smith, *The Presumptuous Dreamers: A Sociological History of the Life and Times of Abigail Scott Duniway (1834–1915)* (Vols I and II, 1974); and *Women in World History*.

DUNKELD, Ada (c. 1145–1206). Countess of Holland. Born c. 1145; died Jan 11, 1206; dau. of Henry Dunkeld, 1st earl of Huntingdon, and Adelicia de Warrenne de (d. 1178); sister of William I (r. 1165–1214) and Malcolm IV (r. 1153–1165), both kings of Scotland; m. Florence also known as Floris III (d. 1190), count of Holland, in 1161 or 1162. ❖ See also *Women in World History*.

DUNKELD, Ada (c. 1195–after 1241). English noblewoman. Born c. 1195; died after 1241; dau. of David Dunkeld, 1st earl of Huntingdon, and Maude of Chester (1171–1233, dau. of Hugh, 3rd earl of Chester); m. Henry Hastings, 1st baron Hastings, before June 7, 1237; children: 3, including Henry Hastings and Eleanor (Hillaria) Hastings.

DUNKELD, Isabel. *See Isabel (fl. 1225).*

DUNKELD, Margaret.
See Margaret, countess of Huntingdon (d. 1228).

See Margaret de Burgh (d. 1259).
See Margaret of Norway (1261–1283).

DUNKLE, Nancy (1955—). American basketball player. Born Jan 10, 1955. ❧ At Montreal Olympics, won a silver medal in team competition (1976).

DUNLAP, Ericka (1982—). Miss America. Born 1982 in Orlando, Florida; youngest of 5 children of a roofing contractor and a nurse; attended University of Central Florida. ❧ The 1st African-American to be crowned Miss Florida, was also crowned Miss America (2003).

DUNLAP, Jane (fl. 1771). American poet. Fl. around 1771. ❧ Published *Poems, Upon Several Sermons, Preached by the Rev'd . . . George Whitefield* (1771), which reflect her devoutness and loyalty to Whitefield's preaching.

DUNLOP, Eliza Hamilton (1796–1880). Australian poet and ethnographer. Born 1796 in Co. Armagh, Ireland; died June 20, 1880, in Wollombi; dau. of Solomon Hamilton (barrister); m. James Sylvius Law (astronomer); m. David Dunlop (police magistrate and protector of Aborigines at Wollombi and Macdonald River), 1823; children: (1st m.) 1 son, 1 daughter; (2nd m.) 4. ❧ Contributed poetry to journals in Ireland; with family, immigrated to Australia (1838); published in Australian newspapers, learned Aboriginal languages and was 1st Australian poet to do transliterations of Aboriginal songs; works include the poem "The Aboriginal Mother" in *The Australian* (1838) and *'The Aboriginal Mother' and Other Poems* (1981); manuscript collection *The Vase* in Mitchell Library, Sydney.

DUNLOP, Florence (c. 1896–1963). Canadian educator. Born in Ottawa, Ontario, Canada, c. 1896; died in Ottawa in 1963; graduate of Ottawa Normal School, 1916; attended Queens University; Columbia University, MA and PhD. ❧ Pioneer in education for children with special needs, began teaching in a rural community in northern Ontario; appointed supervisor of Special Education in Ottawa (1927); worked out a system for the early identification and treatment of both physically and psychologically challenged students; with others, organized International Council for the Study of Exceptional Children; advised US Office of Education in Washington and worked as a consultant in Maryland, Ohio, and California.

DUNLOP, Jane (1904–1964). *See Davis, Adele.*

DUNN, Barbara (c. 1910—). English amateur radio operator. Born c. 1910 in England. ❧ The 1st woman amateur radio operator, earned a radio transmission license (1927) and was the sole female amateur radio operator during a brief period (1927–32); operated an active Essex-based low-power station at Stock with call sign G6YL; served as member of Radio Society of Great Britain; was the 1st woman to earn a Radio Society trophy.

DUNN, Emma (1875–1966). English actress. Born Feb 26, 1875, in Cheshire, England; died Dec 14, 1966, in Los Angeles, California; m. John Stokes (div.). ❧ Appeared in such plays as *Peer Gynt, The Warrens of Virginia, The Easiest Way, Sonny,* and most notably as Katherine Wetherell in *Mother* and Angie in *Old Lady 31;* appeared in over 100 films, including *Mother, Seven Keys to Baldpate, Scattergood Pulls the Strings, Babes on Broadway, The Bridge of San Luis Rey, Life with Father, Mourning Becomes Electra* and *The Woman in White;* had recurring role of Martha Kildare in "Dr. Kildare" series.

DUNN, Gertrude (c. 1932–2004). American baseball and field-hockey player. Born c. 1932; died Sept 29, 2004, in Chester Co., Pennsylvania; attended West Chester University in Pennsylvania. ❧ Led her team to the championship in the All-American Girls Professional Baseball League (1952); immortalized in the film *A League of Their Own* (1992); also played on US national field hockey and lacrosse teams; at age 72, killed when the single-engine plane she was flying crashed at takeoff. Voted Rookie of the Year (1952); was a member of the US Field Hockey Hall of Fame.

DUNN, Josephine (1906–1983). American actress. Born May 1, 1906, in New York, NY; died Feb 3, 1983, in Thousand Oaks, California; m. William P. Cameron, 1925 (div. 1928); m. Clyde Greathouse (div. 1931); m. Eugene J. Lewis, 1933 (div. 1935); m. Allen Carroll Case (son of Frank Case of the Algonquin), 1935 (died 1978). ❧ Debuted in *Fascinating Youth* (1926); also appeared in *Fireman, Save My Child, The Singing Fool, Melody Lane, Safety in Numbers, Two Kinds of Women, Forbidden Company* and *Surrender at Dawn.*

DUNN, Kaye (b. 1909). *See Dunham, Katherine.*

DUNN, Loula Friend (1896–1977). American public-welfare worker. Born May 1, 1896, in Grove Hill, Alabama; died June 1977, in Washington, DC; attended Alabama Polytechnic Institute (now Auburn University) and University of North Carolina; never married; no children. ❧ Taught illiterate children from rural areas in Alabama (1916–17); served as caseworker, Alabama State Child Welfare Dept. (1923–33); served as regional social worker and director of employment in numerous southern states; served as commissioner of Alabama State Department of Public Welfare (1937–50); became the 1st woman director of American Public Welfare Association (1950); served as vice president of American Association of Social Workers (1935–36), Child Welfare League (1940–50), and American Society for Public Administration (1946–47); appointed to federal advisory panel on welfare-benefit coordination (1959).

DUNN, Natalie (1956—). American figure roller skater. Born 1956 in San Antonio, Texas. ❧ One of few female skaters to perform triple Salchow jump and triple Mapes, won 1st skating event at age 7; held national singles title by 16; became 1st woman World champion in figure roller skating (Rome, 1976); defended title in Montreal, Canada (1977); became 3-time world champion and 9-time US national champion by 1979.

DUNN, Nell (1936—). British playwright and novelist. Name variations: Nell Mary Sandford. Born 1936 in London, England; m. Jeremy Sandford, 1956. ❧ A Chelsea heiress, wrote short fiction, novels, documentary, screenplay, and plays; published *Up the Junction* (1963), about working-class life around Clapham Junction in London, which won John Llewellyn Rhys Memorial Prize and was adapted into feature film; also wrote *Talking to Women* (1965), *Poor Cow* (1967), *The Incurable* (1971), *Tear His Head off His Shoulders* (1974), *Living Like I Do* (1976), *The Only Child* (1978), *Steaming* (1981), for which she won Susan Smith Blackburn Prize, *Every Breath You Take* (1988), *The Little Heroine* (1988), *Grandmothers* (1991), *My Silver Shoes* (1996) and *Cancer Tales* (2003).

DUNN, Shannon (1972—). American half-pipe snowboarder. Name variations: Shannon Dunn Downing; Shannon Dunn-Downing. Born Nov 26, 1972, in Carnelian Bay, California; grew up in Arlington Heights, Illinois; m. Dave Downing. ❧ One of the dominant halfpipe competitors in the world, won the 1st bronze medal ever awarded for women's halfpipe snowboarding at Winter Olympics at Nagano (1998); won gold (1997) and silver (1999) in halfpipe, gold in superpipe (2001), and silver in slopestyle (2001) at X Games; became founding member of Boarding for Breast Cancer. Other 1st-place finishes in halfpipe include USSA Super Prix Overall champion (1999), FIS World Cup champion (1999), Gravity Games, Mammoth Mountain, CA (2000), Chevy Grand Prix Overall (2000), and Grand Prix #1 and #2, Mammoth, CA (2001). ❧ See also Christina Lessa, *Women Who Win* (Universe, 1998).

DUNN, Tricia (1974—). American ice-hockey player. Name variations: Tricia Dunn-Luoma. Born Patricia Dunn, April 25, 1974, in Derry, New Hampshire. ❧ Won a team gold medal at Nagano (1998), the 1st Olympics to feature women's ice hockey; won a team silver medal at World championships (1997, 1999, 2000, 2001); won a team silver medal at Salt Lake City Olympics (2002) and a team bronze medal at Torino Olympics (2006). ❧ See also Mary Turco, *Crashing the Net: The U.S. Women's Olympic Ice Hockey Team and the Road to Gold* (HarperCollins, 1999); and *Women in World History.*

DUNN, Velma (1918—). American diver. Name variations: Velma Dunn Ploessel. Born Oct 1918; attended University of Southern California. ❧ At Berlin Olympics, won a silver medal in platform (1936).

DUNNE, Irene (1898–1990). American stage and film actress. Born Irene Marie Dunn in Louisville, Kentucky, Dec 20, 1898; died in Hollywood, California, Sept 4, 1991; dau. of Joseph John Dunn and Adelaide Antoinette (Henry) Dunn; m. Francis J. Griffin (New York dentist), 1927 (died 1965); children: daughter, Mary Frances Griffin (adopted 1936). ❧ Actress who moved easily from serious drama to musicals to "screwball comedy" and was best remembered for her roles in *The Awful Truth, Anna and the King of Siam* and *I Remember Mama,* made stage debut on tour in *Irene* (1920); made NY debut in *The Clinging Vine* (1922); appeared on Broadway in *Yours Truly* (1927), *She's My Baby* (1928); made film debut in *Leathernecking* (1930), followed by *Back Street* (1932), *The Silver Cord* (1933), *Ann Vickers* (1933), *The Age of*

Innocence (1934), Roberta (1935), Magnificent Obsession (1935), Show Boat (1936), When Tomorrow Comes (1939), My Favorite Wife (1940), Penny Serenade (1941), A Guy Named Joe (1943), The White Cliffs of Dover (1944), Life With Father (1947), Never a Dull Moment (1950) and The Mudlark (1950), among others; served as alternate US delegate to United Nations General Assembly in New York (1957–58). Nominated for Academy Award for Best Actress for Cimarron (1931), Theodora Goes Wild (1936), The Awful Truth (1937), Love Affair (1939), and I Remember Mama (1948); received University of Notre Dame's Laetare Medal for her work for Catholic charities; honored for life's work by American Film Institute (1977); awarded Kennedy Center Honors for life achievement (1985). ❖ See also Women in World History.

DUNNE, Jean Gilligan (1951—). American stock specialist. Born Jean Gilligan, 1951; dau. of a senior partner at Gilligan, Will and Company. ❖ Became 1st woman stock specialist on any US stock exchange (1973).

DUNNE, Loula (1896–1977). See Dunn, Loula Friend.

DUNNE, Margaret Abbott (1878–1955). See Abbott, Margaret.

DUNNE, Mary Chavelita (1857–1945). See Bright, Mary Golding.

DUNNETT, Dorothy (1923–2001). Scottish novelist and portrait painter. Name variations: Dorothy Halliday, Lady Dunnett. Born Dorothy Halliday, Aug 25, 1923, in Dunfermline, Fife, Scotland; died Nov 9, 2001, in Edinburgh, Scotland; only child of mining engineer; attended Edinburgh College of Art and Glasgow School of Art; m. Alastair MacTavish Dunnett (journalist, editor of newspaper Record and The Scotsman, and chair of Thomson North Sea Oil), 1946 (died 1998); children: Ninian and Mungo Dunnett. ❖ Prolific writer of more than 20 historical novels and accomplished portrait painter, attended James Gillespie's School for Girls along with novelist Muriel Spark; began career with civil service as press secretary in Edinburgh (1940–55); traveled widely with husband; earned acclaim as portrait painter, exhibiting at Royal Academy, joining Scottish Society of Women Artists (1950s), and rendering portraits of many prominent public figures in Scotland; wrote The Lymond Chronicles, a series of 6 historical romance novels, featuring the fictional Scottish mercenary Francis Crawford of Lymond and including Game of Kings (1961) and Checkmate (1975); beginning with Dolly and the Song Bird (1968), published a series of detective novels under maiden name with enigmatic hero Johnson Johnson; published epic novel about Macbeth, King Hereafter (1982); embarked on 2nd historical set, the House of Niccolò series, with Niccolò Rising (1986); also wrote Caprice and Rondo (1976), Disorderly Knights (1976), Moroccan Traffic (1986) and Gemini (2000), among others. Awarded Officer of British Empire (OBE, 1992); became Lady Dunnett when husband was knighted (1995).

DUNNING, Emily (1876–1961). See Barringer, Emily Dunning.

DUNNOCK, Mildred (1900–1991). American character actress. Born Mildred Dorothy Dunnock, Jan 25, 1900, in Baltimore, Maryland; died in Massachusetts, July 5, 1991; dau. of Walter (president of Dumari Textile Co.), and Florence (Saynook) Dunnock; Goucher College, AB; studied acting with Lee Strasberg and Elia Kazan; m. Keith Urmy (banker); children: Linda McGuire (actress); granddaughter: Patricia McGuire Dunnock (actress). ❖ Excelled in supporting roles for 50 years on stage, screen, and tv; won acclaim for her portrayal of a Welsh schoolteacher in The Corn Is Green (1940), which ran for 477 performances; repeated role in film version (1945); once established, originated a number of memorable roles on Broadway, including Lavinia in Another Part of the Forest and Linda Loman in Death of a Salesman (1949) (repeated the role in 1951 film and 1966 tv adaptation); portrayed Big Mama in Cat on a Hot Tin Roof (1955); played both classical and modern roles with American Shakespeare Festival; directed Graduation on Broadway (1965); made over 25 films and appeared on tv series and specials, including "Studio One," "Kraft Television Theater," and "Philco Playhouse." Nominated for Academy Awards for films Death of a Salesman (1951) and Baby Doll (1956). ❖ See also Women in World History.

DU NOIER, Marguerite (1663–1719). See du Noyer, Anne-Marguérite Petit.

DU NOYER, Anne-Marguérite Petit (1663–1719). French journalist. Name variations: Dame Anne Marguerite Petit Du Noyer; Mme Du Noyer; Marguerite du Noyer; du Noier, Dunoyer, and Desnoyers. Born Anne-Marguérite Petit, 1663, in Nîmes, France; died 1719 (some sources cite 1720). ❖ Writings include Lettres historiques et galants (1704),

Mémoires (1710), Oeuvres mêlées (1711), and Evénements des plus rares, ou l'histoire du S. abbé de Buquoy (1719); also produced periodical La Quintessence des nouvelles historiques critiques et politiques (1716–30).

DU NOYER or DUNOYER, Marguerite (1663–1719). See du Noyer, Anne-Marguérite Petit.

DUNSCOMBE, Adaliza (1867–1943). English optician. Born Adaliza Amelia Clara Mary Elizabeth Emma Frances Dunscombe, July 31, 1867, in London, England; died Dec 1943; dau. of Matthew William Dunscombe (BOA president, 1903–35). ❖ The 1st woman member of the British Optical Association (BOA), worked and trained in father's optical business shop in Bristol; earned optical certificate after passing BOA examination (1899).

DUNSKA, Elzbieta (1934—). See Krzesinska, Elzbieta.

DUNSMORE, Douglas Mary (1789–1873). See McKain, Douglas Mary.

DUNSTER, Elizabeth (d. 1643). See Glover, Elizabeth Harris.

DUNWOODY, Gwyneth (1930—). English politician and member of Parliament. Name variations: Hon. Gwyneth Dunwoody. Born Gwyneth Phillips, Dec 12, 1930; dau. of Baroness Phillips and Morgan Phillips (general sec. of Labour Party); m. Dr. John Elliott Orr Dunwoody, 1954 (div. 1975). ❖ Served as director, Film Production Association of Great Britain (1970–74); representing Labour, elected to House of Commons for Crewe and Nantwich (1992, 1997, 2001, 2005); named chair of Transport committee (2002).

DUPARC, Françoise (1726–1778). French artist. Born in Murcie, Spain, Oct 15, 1726; died in Marseilles, France, Oct 11, 1778; returned to Marseilles from Spain with family (1730); began art studies in father's studio; possibly studied with Jean Baptiste van Loo; daughter and one of several children of Antoine Duparc (sculptor) and Gabrielle Negrela. ❖ Of the 41 paintings that were in her studio at the time of her death, only four remain in the public eye; they are positively attributed to her hand; they were bequeathed in her will to town hall of Marseilles and are now housed in Musée des Beaux-Arts. ❖ See also Women in World History.

DUPIN, Amandine Aurore Lucie (1804–1876). See Sand, George.

DUPLESSIS, Lucile (1771–1794). See Desmoulins, Lucile.

DUPLESSIS, Marie (1824–1847). See Plessis, Alphonsine.

DUPLITZER, Imke (1975—). German fencer. Born July 28, 1975, in Karlsruhe, Germany. ❖ Won a silver medal for épée team at Athens Olympics (2004); at World championships, placed 2nd for team épée (1992, 1993, 1997, 2003) and indiv. épée (2002); had 2nd overall World Cup ranking for indiv. épée (2001–02).

DU PONT, Margaret Osborne (b. 1918). See Osborne, Margaret.

DU PONT, Patricia (1894–1973). American silent-film actress. Name variations: Miss Du Pont; Margaret Armstrong; Patricia DuPont; Patty DuPont. Born April 28, 1894, in Frankfort, Kentucky; died Feb 6, 1973, in Palm Beach, Florida. ❖ Began career as Margaret Armstrong, later Miss Du Pont; films include Foolish Wives, Bonnie May, Brass, So This is Marriage and Mantrap.

DU PRÉ, Jacqueline (1945–1987). English cellist. Name variations: Du Pre. Pronunciation: Du-PRAY. Born Jan 26, 1945, in Oxford, England; died Oct 20, 1987, in London, of multiple sclerosis; dau. of Derek du Pré (accountant) and Iris (Greep) du Pré (pianist and composer); sister of Hilary du Pré (flutist) and Piers du Pré (clarinetist); m. Daniel Barenboim (pianist and conductor), June 15, 1967; no children. ❖ Considered among most talented 20th-century cellists, was especially known for her interpretations of works of Sir Edward Elgar, particularly his Cello Concerto; at 4, became interested in cello (1949); entered Herbert Wallen's Cello School, London, at 6; began studying with William Pleeth at 10; studied with Pablo Casals and then with Mstislav Rostropovich; won Suggia Cello Award (1956); performed for BBC-TV at 12 (1957); won Guildhall's Gold Medal and the Queen's Prize at 15 (1960); made concert debut at Wigmore Hall, London, at 16 (1961); continued to concertize, establishing a worldwide reputation; married and converted to Judaism in Jerusalem (1967); performed often in concert with husband, but began to suffer from major symptoms of multiple sclerosis in her late 20s which destroyed her career; died at 42 (1987). Controversial film Hilary and Jackie (1999), starring Emily Watson as Jacqueline du Pré and Rachel Griffiths as Hilary, was based on Piers and Hilary du Pré's book A Genius in the Family. ❖ See Carol

Easton, *Jacqueline du Pré: A Life* (Summit, 1989); and *Women in World History.*

DUPREE, Minnie (1873–1947). American actress. Born Jan 19, 1873, in LaCrosse, Wisconsin; died May 23, 1947, in New York, NY. ❖ Made NY debut in *Held by the Enemy* (1888); early plays include *Don Juan, The Climbers, Hedda Gabler* and *The Road to Yesterday;* scored triumph in England as Nanny McNair in *The Heart of Maryland* and Kate Brewster in *Way Down East;* later plays include *The Charm School, The Old Soak, Arsenic and Old Lace, Dark Eyes* and *Last Stop;* made film debut in *Two Masters* (1928), followed by *The Young in Heart* and *Anne of Windy Poplars,* among others.

DUPREZ, June (1918–1984). English stage and screen actress. Born May 14, 1918, in Teddington, London, England; died Oct 30, 1984, in London; dau. of Fred Duprez (vaudevillian and actor); m. Dr. F. Guy Beauchamp (div.); m. once more (div. 1965); children: 2 daughters. ❖ Made stage debut at Coventry Repertory; made film debut in *The Crimson Circle* (1936), followed by *The Spy in Black, The Cardinal, The Four Feathers, The Thief of Bagdad, They Raid by Night, None but the Lonely Heart* and *And Then There Were None,* among others.

DUPUIS, Lori (1972—). Canadian ice-hockey player. Born Nov 14, 1972, in Williamstown, Ontario, Canada. ❖ Played at the University of Toronto; won a team silver medal at Nagano (1998), the 1st Olympics to feature women's ice hockey; won team gold medals at World championships (1997, 2000); won a team gold medal at Salt Lake City Olympics (2002).

DUPUREUR, Maryvonne (1937—). French runner. Born May 24, 1937. ❖ At Tokyo Olympics, won a silver medal in 800 meters (1964).

DUPUY, Eliza Ann (1814–1881). American novelist and short-story writer. Name variations: (pseudonym) Annie Young. Born 1814 in Petersburg, Virginia; died 1881 in New Orleans, Mississippi; dau. of Jesse Dupuy and Mary Anne Thompson Sturdivant Dupuy. ❖ Wrote historical melodramas including *Celeste, The Pirate's Daughter* (1845), *The Conspirator* (1850), *All for Love; or, The Outlaw's Bride* (1873) and *The Discarded Wife; or, Will She Succeed?* (1875).

DURACK, Fanny (1889–1956). Australian swimmer. Name variations: Sarah Durack. Born Sarah Durack, Oct 27, 1889, in Sydney, Australia; died of cancer in Stanmore, Australia, Mar 20, 1956; m. Bernard Martin Gately (horse trainer), Jan 22, 1921. ❖ Having paid her own way to get there, won the 100-meter freestyle at Stockholm Olympics (1912), becoming Australia's 1st female Olympic gold medalist; once held every world record in women's swimming, from 100 yards to 1 mile, breaking 12 world records (1912–18); retired (1921). Posthumously inducted into International Swimming Hall of Fame (1967). ❖ See also *Women in World History.*

DURACK, Mary (1913–1994). Australian writer. Name variations: Dame Mary Durack. Born Mary Durack on Feb 20, 1913, in Adelaide, Australia; grew up in the Kimberley region of Western Australia, on a station; died in 1994 in Australia; dau. of Bessie Ida Muriel (Johnstone) and Michael Durack (rancher); sister of Elizabeth Durack (painter and illustrator); educated at Loreto Convent (graduated 1929); m. Horace Clive Miller (airline operator), Dec 2, 1938; children: (Patricia) Mary Miller Millett; Robin Elizabeth Miller Dicks (deceased); Juliana Miller Rowney (deceased); Andrew Clive Miller; Marie Rose Miller Megaw; John Christopher Miller. ❖ Published children's book *Chunuma* (1936), illustrated by sister Elizabeth; wrote for *Western Mail;* though she was also a novelist, greatest success came with her children's books and her biographies of the Durack family, including *Kings in Grass Castles* (1959) and *Sons in the Saddle* (1983); children's books include *Son of Djaro* (1938), *The Way of the Whirlwind* (1941), (poems) *The Magic Trumpet* (1944), (poems) *Kookanoo and Kangaroo* (1963), *To Ride a Fine Horse* (1963), and *Tjakamarra: Boy between Two Worlds* (1977). Awarded Order of the British Empire (OBE, 1966) and Dame of the British Empire (DBE, 1978). ❖ See also *Women in World History.*

DURACK, Sarah (1889–1956). *See Durack, Fanny.*

DURAND, Alice (1842–1903). *See Gréville, Alice.*

DURAND, Catherine (d. 1736). French novelist. Name variations: Cathérine Durand; (married name) Cathérine Bédacier or Catherine Bedacier. Born Catherine Durand in France; died 1736. ❖ Writings include *La Comtesse de Mortane* (1699), *Histoires des amours de Grégoire VII, du duc de Richelieu, de la princesse de Condé et de la Marquise d'Urfé*

(1700), *Les petits soupers de l'été de l'année 1699* (1702), *Les Belles Grèques* (1712), and *Henry, duc des Vandales* (1714).

DURAND, Lucile (1930—). Canadian feminist, novelist, playwright and children's writer. Name variations: Lucille Durand; (pseudonym) Louky Bersianik. Born Lucile Durand, Nov 14, 1930, in Montreal, Quebec, Canada; studied at Université de Montréal and Sorbonne; m. Jean Letarte. ❖ Worked as librarian and scriptwriter for radio and television; awarded Prix de la Province (1966); published poems and feminist essays in magazines and anthologies; works include *Togo apprenti-remorqueur* (1966), *L'Euguélionne: roman triptyque* (1976), *La page de garde* (1978), *Le Pique-nique sur l'Acropole* (1979), *Les Agénésies du vieux monde* (1982) and *Axe et eau* (1984).

DURAND, Marguerite (1864–1936). French actress and feminist journalist. Pronunciation: dew-RAWN. Born Marguerite-Charlotte Durand de Valfère in Paris, France, Jan 24, 1864; died in Paris, Mar 16, 1936; dau. of Anna-Alexandrine-Caroline Durand de Valfère and General Alfred Boucher (Royalist colonel in French army) or possibly Auguste Clésinger (sculptor); m. Georges Laguerre (deputy in Parliament), 1888 (div. 1895); children: (with Antonin Périvier) Jacques Périvier (b. 1896). ❖ Enrolled at Conservatory of Dramatic Art (1879); joined Comédie-Française (1881) and debuted as Marcelle in *Demi-Monde* (1882); for several years, enjoyed a sparkling reputation in plays such as *Les Femmes Savantes* and *Le Mariage de Figaro;* left the stage to marry Georges Laguerre (1886); dubbed "the Madame Roland of Boulangism," played host and was an animating force behind Laguerre's Boulangist tabloid, *La Presse,* where she 1st came in contact with the world of journalism; separated from Laguerre, became a staunch Republican, and joined the prestigious *Le Figaro* (1891), writing a woman-about-town column on fashions, trends, and political gossip; covered the 4th French International Feminist Congress (1896) and came away converted to the feminist cause; established the daily newspaper *La Fronde* (1897), which lasted until 1905 and hugely contributed to the progress of feminism; recruited Séverine, the only top-flight woman journalist in France, and mobilized a large galaxy of collaborators and contributors, including Jane Misme, Jeanne Schmahl, Hubertine Auclert, Clémence Royer, Nelly Roussel, Aline Valette, Dorothea Klumpke, Myriam Harry, Lucie Delarue-Mardrus, and Marcelle Tinayre, among others; was the 1st woman admitted to Union of Newspaper Directors; joined Jacques Stern and William Tournier as co-director of *Les Nouvelles* (1908); ran (illegally) in Paris IX for Parliament (1910), getting 403 write-in votes; after WWI, played the role of *grande dame* of the feminist movement, speaking at banquets promoting women's rights, international disarmament, and the League of Nations; won a personal triumph (1927) when she and Séverine were admitted to the sacrosanct Association of Journalists (*la Maison des journalistes*); became a member of the administrative commission of Republican Socialist Party (1930); before her death, gave the city of Paris her extensive library of feminist documents and history, which grew into The Bibliothèque Marguerite Durand, the most important repository of materials on the history of the women's movement in France and one of the most valuable collections of its kind in the world. ❖ See also *Women in World History.*

DURANT, Ariel (1898–1981). Russian-born American author and historical researcher. Born Ida Appel Kaufman in Prosurov, Russia in 1898; died in Hollywood Hills, California, Oct 25, 1981; brought to New York as an infant; m. Will Durant (historian), 1913 (died 1981); children: Ethel and Louis Durant. ❖ Played a crucial role in the writing of the bestselling 11-vol. series *The Story of Mankind,* 1st as her husband's research assistant, then as his full partner and collaborator; series included *Our Oriental Heritage* (1935), *The Life of Greece* (1939), *Caesar and Christ* (1944), *The Age of Faith* (1950), *The Renaissance* (1953), *The Reformation* (1957), *The Age of Reason Begins* (1961), *The Age of Louis XIV* (1963), *The Age of Voltaire* (1965), *Rousseau and Revolution* (1967) and *The Age of Napoleon* (1975). With husband, awarded the Pulitzer Prize (1968) and Presidential Medal of Freedom (1977). ❖ See also *A Dual Autobiography* (Simon and Schuster, 1977); and *Women in World History.*

DURANTI, Francesca (1935—). Italian novelist. Born 1935 in Genoa, Italy. ❖ Translated short stories of Virginia Woolf; came to international prominence with *La casa sul lago della luna* (*The House on Moon Lake,* 1984); works, which often focus on writers and the writing process, include *La bambina* (1976), *Piazza mi bella piazza* (1978), *Lieto fine* (*Happy Ending,* 1987), *Effetti personali* (*Personal Effects,* 1988), *Ultima stesura* (1991), *Progetto Burlamacchi* (1994), *Sogni Mancini* (1996, trans.

by Duranti as *Left-handed Dreams*), and *Il comune senso delle proporzioni* (2000). Awarded the Premio Bagutta, Premio Martina Franca, Premio Basilicata, Super Campiello, and Città di Milano.

DURAS, Claire de (1777–1828). French duchess, novelist and salonnière. Name variations: Claire Lechat de Kersaint; Claire Kersaint; Duchesse de Duras or Duchess of Duras; Madame de Duras. Born Claire Lechat de Kersaint, 1777 (some sources cite 1778), in Brest; died 1828 in Paris, France; m. Duc de Duras. ❖ Fled France after father was executed during French Revolution; established a salon in London which became meeting places for *émigrés;* married in London, returned to France with husband (1807); writings include *Ourika* (1823), *Edouard* (1825) and *Olivier ou la secret* (1971).

DURAS, duchess of (1777–1828). *See Duras, Claire de.*

DURAS, Marguerite (1914–1996). French author and filmmaker. Name variations: Marguerite Donnadieu. Born Marguerite Donnadieu, April 4, 1914, in Gia-Dinh, near Saigon, French Indochina; died in Paris, France, Mar 3, 1996; dau. of French colonial settlers Henri Donnadieu and Marie Legrand Donnadieu; studied law and political science in Paris; m. Robert Antelme, 1939 (div. 1946); children: (with Dionys Mascolo) son, Jean Mascolo (b. 1947). ❖ One of the most successful and important French literary figures in the 2nd half of the 20th century, whose work crosses traditional boundaries of fiction and autobiography, was born and raised in French Indochina; returned to France with family (1932); chose name Marguerite Duras when 1st book, *Les Impudents,* was published (1943); entered the French Resistance; actively protested against the war in Algeria (1955–60); published over 40 novels, including *Un Barrage contre le Pacifique* (1950, trans. as *The Sea Wall,* 1986), *Le Ravissement de Lol V. Stein* (1964, trans. as *The Ravishing of Lol V. Stein,* 1986), *L'Amant* (1984, trans. as *The Lover,* 1985), *La douleur* (1985, trans. as *The War: A Memoir,* 1987), and *Yann Andréas Steiner* (1992); wrote screenplay for *Hiroshima mon amour* (1960); produced films *Nathalie Granger* (1972), *India Song* (1974), and *Le Camion (The Truck,* 1977). Awarded Goncourt prize for literature for *The Lover* (1984). ❖ See also Marilyn R. Schuster, *Marguerite Duras Revisited* (Twayne, 1993); Leah D. Hewitt, *Autobiographical Tightropes: Simone de Beauvoir, Nathalie Sarraute, Marguerite Duras, Monique Wittig, and Maryse Condé* (U. of Nebraska, 1990); Leslie Hill, *Marguerite Duras: Apocalyptic Desires* (Routledge, 1993); (film) *Cet Amour-là,* starring Jeanne Moreau (2003); and *Women in World History.*

DURBIN, Deanna (1921—). Canadian-born actress and singer. Born Edna Mae Durbin, Dec 4, 1921, in Winnipeg, Manitoba, Canada; studied voice at Ralph Thomas' Academy in Los Angeles, California; m. Vaughn Paul, 1941 (div.); m. Felix Jackson (movie producer), 1945 (div.); m. Charles David (film executive), 1950. ❖ At 14, debuted at MGM in musical short *Every Sunday* (1936); made 1st feature film, *Three Smart Girls* (1936), popularizing the song "Someone to Care for Me," followed by *One Hundred Men and a Girl* (1937); was given a special Academy Award (1938); one of the top box-office attractions during the WWII years, sang for soldiers at USO clubs and appeared on a number of radio shows; retired from film at age 27. Films include: *Mad About Music* (1938), *Spring Parade* (1940), *The Amazing Mrs. Holliday* (1943), *Christmas Holiday* (1944), *Lady on a Train* (1945), *I'll Be Yours* (1947), *Something in the Wind* (1947) and *For the Love of Mary* (1948). ❖ See also *Women in World History.*

DURFEE, Minta (1897–1975). American comedic actress. Name variations: Minta Durfee Arbuckle. Born Araminta Durfee, Oct 1, 1889, in Los Angeles, California; died Sept 9, 1975, in Woodland Hills, California; m. (Roscoe) Fatty Arbuckle, 1908 (div. 1925). ❖ With husband Fatty Arbuckle, joined Mack Sennett's Keystone Company (1913); appeared opposite Charlie Chaplin in many films, including his 1st, *Making a Living;* made other films and appeared in character roles on television into her 80s.

DURGAN, Bridget (c. 1845–1867). Irish-born murderer. Born c. 1845 in Ireland; hanged Aug 30, 1867. ❖ While working as maid in New Market (New Jersey) for William and Mary Ellen Coriell, stabbed Mary Ellen to death in her bed; tried and sentenced to death, was hanged at age 22 before 2,000 spectators.

DURGAUTTI or DURGAVATI (d. 1564). *See Durgawati.*

DURGAWATI (d. 1564). Rani of Gondwana, regent and warrior of India. Name variations: Durgautti or Durgavati; Maharani or Maharanee of Gurrah; Rani of Gondwana. Took own life in battle of Narhi, 1564; dau. of Salwahan, raja of Rath and Mahoba; m. Dalpat Sa

Garha Mandala, raja of Gondwana; children: Bir Narayan. ❖ After Raja Dalpat of Gondwana died, became regent of Gondwana (1548), ruling successfully in name of son Bir Narayan; known as a moderate and skillful monarch, excelled at both diplomacy and conquest; could field a well-equipped army of 20,000 calvary and 1,000 war elephants, along with an indeterminate number of infantry; when Akbar ascended the throne as emperor of the Mughal imperial, was viewed by him as an adversary (1562); sent her minister to negotiate with Emperor Akbar, but this proved unsuccessful; militarily opposing the Mughal expansion, saw Gondwana invaded by Asaf Khan with an army of 50,000 troops (1564); fought bravely but lost and took her own life at battle of Narhi (1564). ❖ See also *Women in World History.*

DURHAM, Dianne (1968—). African-American gymnast. Born June 17, 1968 in Gary, Indiana; m. Tom Drahozal (teacher and coach). ❖ Won US Jr. nationals (1981, 1982) and US nationals (1983), the 1st African-American gymnast to become a national champion; placed 3rd at Chunichi Cup (1983); had to retire from competition due to injuries (1985).

DURHAM, Emily Copeland (1984—). *See Copeland-Durham, Emily.*

DURHAM, Mary Edith (1863–1944). English artist, writer, and anthropologist. Born Dec 8, 1863, in London, England; died Nov 15, 1944; received artist training at Royal Academy schools. ❖ The 1st woman vice president of Royal Anthropological Institute, traveled to Balkans, conducted relief work during Macedonian insurrection (1903), and lobbied British Parliament to alert public to Albanian problems; established Anglo-Albanian Society with Aubrey Herbert; donated Albanian artifacts to Pitt Rivers Museum in Oxford, folk costume collections to Bankfield Museum in Halifax, and photographs and sketches to Royal Anthropological Institute. Publications include *High Albania* (1909), *Some Tribal Origins, Laws and Customs of the Balkans* (1928), illustrations for reptile volumes of *Cambridge Natural History* (1901), and dispatches for *Times* and *Manchester Guardian.*

DURIEUX, Tilla (1880–1971). German actress. Born Ottilie Godeffroy, Aug 18, 1880, in Vienna, Austria; died in West Berlin, Feb 21, 1971; dau. of a professor at Vienna's Museum of Technology and Crafts; m. Eugen Spiro (painter), 1904 (div. 1906); m. Paul Cassirer (1871–1926, art dealer and publisher), 1906 (div. 1926); m. Ludwig Katzenellenbogen (Jewish industrialist), 1930 (killed 1944). ❖ Grand dame of the German stage who introduced the works of George Bernard Shaw to Germany, was regarded as the best exponent of the *femmes fatales* found in the plays of the Expressionists; made stage debut in Olmütz, Austrian Moravia (present-day Olomouc, Czech Republic) in operetta *Der Vogelhändler* (1901); made Berlin debut as Oscar Wilde's *Salomé* (1903); quickly became a star of the Berlin stage; championed playwright Frank Wedekind; appeared in experimental plays by Brecht; was labeled an enemy of traditional German values and therefore of the Nazis who claimed to champion conservative ideals; with 3rd husband Katzenellenbogen, fled Germany (1933) but Nazis killed him (1944); survived in Yugoslavia, joining the partisan forces; returned to Germany (1952); despite age, resumed acting career to great acclaim, starring in the role of Madame Karma in Roussin's *The Clairvoyant;* appeared in film *The Last Bridge* (1954); reigned as the leading actress of the German stage to the end of her long life; writings include *Spielen und Träumen; mit fünf Radierungen von Emil Orlik* (1922), *Eine Tür fällt ins Schloss: Roman* (1928), *Eine Tür steht offen: Erinnerungen* (1954), *Meine ersten neunzig Jahre: Erinnerungen* (1971). Awarded Grand Federal Cross of Merit (1970). ❖ See also *Women in World History.*

DÜRINGSFELD, Ida von (1815–1876). German writer. Name variations: Duringsfeld; Ida von Reinsburg-Duringsfeld; (pseudonym) Thekla. Born at Militsch, in Lower Silesia, Prussia, Nov 12, 1815; died at Stuttgart, Wurttemberg, Oct 25, 1876; m. Otto von Reinsberg, 1845. ❖ Poet, storyteller, and novelist, published her *Poems* (1835) and a cycle of stories entitled *The Star of Andalusia* (1838) under the pseudonym Thekla; pseudonymously or anonymously, issued subsequent volumes annually; published *The Women of Byron* under her own name (1845); her extensive travels gave rise to highly prized works: numerous stories, collections of national songs, descriptions of national usages, including *Proverbs of German and Rumanian Speech* (2 vols., 1872–75) and *The Wedding Book: Usages and Beliefs Regarding the Wedding among the Christian Nations of Europe* (1871); other works include *Skizzenaus der vornehmen Welt* (1842–45) and *Antonio Foscarini* (1850); also wrote eulogistic poem "An George Sand."

DUROCHER, Marie (1809–1893). French-Brazilian obstetrician. Born Marie Josefina Mathilde Durocher, 1809, in Paris, France; died 1893; moved with family to Brazil at age 8; married and widowed young; children: 2. ❖ Influenced by teaching of Marie Boivin, entered medical school at age 24 in Rio de Janiero and received 1st diploma granted there (1834), one of the 1st female doctors in Latin America; practiced for 60 years; elected to titular membership of National Academy of Medicine (1871).

DUROVA, Nadezhda (1783–1866). Russian writer and military leader. Name variations: Nadezha; while serving in the Imperial Russian Army used the name Aleksander Andreievich Aleksandrov. Born Nadezhda Andreevna Durova, Sept 1783, in Kherson, Russia; died Mar 21, 1866, in Elabuga, Russia; dau. of Andrei Vasil'evich Durov and Nadezhda Ivanovna Durova; sister of Vasily Andreievich, Evgeniia Andreievna, and Kleopatra Andreievna; m. V.S. Chernov (jurist), 1801 (sep. 1804); children: 1 son. ❖ The 1st woman to hold officer's rank in the Russian Empire and the 1st to be awarded the Cross of St. George, wrote *The Cavalry Maiden*, which describes her adventures disguised as a man while serving for 9 years in the Russian Imperial cavalry during the Napoleonic Wars; other novels and stories, written in the tradition of European Romanticism, include *Fate's Toy* (1837), *Elena, the Belle of T.* (1837), *Gudishki* (1839), *The Summer House* (1839), *Sulphur Spring* (1839), *Nurmeka* (1839), *Buried Treasure* (1840), *Yarchuk, the Dog Who Saw Ghosts* (1840), and *The Corner* (1840). ❖ See also *The Cavalry Maiden: Journals of a Russian Officer in the Napoleonic Wars* (trans. by Mary Fleming Zirin, Indiana U. Press, 1988); film *Ballad of a Hussar* (1962); and *Women in World History*.

DURR, Françoise (1942—). French tennis player. Name variations: Françoise Durr; (nickname) Frankie. Born a French national, Dec 25, 1942, in Algiers; m. Boyd Browning (American); moved to Phoenix, Arizona. ❖ Was the 1st Frenchwoman in 19 years to win the singles title at Roland Garros (1967); won the German singles title and was a semifinalist at Forest Hills (1967); won the French doubles title, partnering Gail Sherriff (1967, 1970, 1971) and Ann Jones (1968, 1969); won US doubles with Darlene Hard (1969) and Betty Stove (1972); won the French mixed doubles with Jean Claude Barclay (1968, 1971, 1973); retired (1980).

DURRIEU, Edith Mary (1871–1948). See Macfarlane, Edith Mary.

DURRIYAH SHAFIQ (1908–1975). See Shafik, Doria.

DUSE, Eleonora (1858–1924). Italian actress. Born Eleonora Giulia Amalia Duse, Oct 3, 1858, in Vigevano, Italy; died while on tour in Pittsburgh, Pennsylvania, April 21, 1924; dau. of Alessandro (actor) and Angelica Cappelletto Duse; m. Teobaldo Marchetti Checchi, 1881 (estranged after 1885); children: (with Martino Cafiero) son who died within a week of his birth; (with husband) Enrichetta Checchi (b. 1882). ❖ First international stage actress and the most charismatic and honored actress of her time, was renowned for the subtlety, depth, and psychological insights of her stage portrayals; appeared on stage at age 4 in a production of Hugo's *Les Miserables* (1862); joined the company of Cesare Rossi (1879); triumphed in a production of Zola's *Thérèse Raquin* (1879); became prima donna in the Rossi company (1881); became estranged from husband during tour of South America (1885); formed her own company (1886); 1st performed Ibsen's *A Doll's House* (1891); made successful theatrical tours in Russia, Vienna and Berlin (1891–92); performed in US (1893, 1896, 1902); performed in London, including a command performance for Queen Victoria (1895); performed in Ibsen's *Hedda Gabler* (1898); triumphed in her own production of Gabriele D'Annunzio's *Francesca da Rimini* (1904); retired from the stage (1909); made silent film *Cenere* (1916); resumed acting (1921); performed in London and US (1923). ❖ See also Bertita Harding, *Age Cannot Wither: The Story of Duse and d'Annunzio* (Lippincott, 1947); Eva Le Gallienne, *The Mystic in the Theatre: Eleonora Duse* (Bodley Head, 1966); Giovanni Pontiero, ed. and trans. *Duse on Tour: Guido Noccioli's Diaries, 1906–07* (U. of Massachusetts, 1982); Arthur Symons, *Eleonora Duse* (Blom, 1927); William Weaver, *Duse: A Biography* (Harcourt, 1984); and *Women in World History*.

DU SOUSA, Noémia (1926—). See de Sousa, Noémia.

DUSSERRE, Michelle (1968—). American gymnast. Name variations: Michelle Dusserre-Farrell; Michelle Farrell. Born Dec 26, 1968, in Garden Grove, California; m. Matt Farrell. ❖ At Los Angeles Olympics, won a silver medal in team all-around (1984); at US nationals tied for a bronze in uneven bars (1987).

DUSTIN, Hannah (1657–c. 1736). Colonial American hero. Name variations: Hannah Duston or Dustan. Born Hannah Emerson in Haverhill, Massachusetts, Dec 23, 1657 (some sources cite 1659); died in Ipswich, Massachusetts, probably in early 1736; m. Thomas Dustin (or Duston or Dustan), Dec 1677 (died 1732); children: 9. ❖ In King William's War, during a French-incited raid on Haverhill, MA, by a band of Abnakis (Mar 15, 1697), was taken prisoner; with 2 other captives, returned by canoe to Haverhill, carrying the scalps of ten Abnakis (April 21, 1697). ❖ See also *Women in World History*.

DUTILLEUX, Genevieve Joy- (b. 1919). See Joy, Géneviève.

DUTRIEU, Hélène (1877–1961). Belgian aviator. Name variations: Helene Marguerite Dutrieu. Born July 10, 1877, in Tournai, France; died June 25, 1961, in Paris; m. Pierre Mortier (French journalist), 1922 (died 1946). ❖ The 1st Belgian woman pilot, began career as a world-class bicycle racer; received pilot license number 27 (Nov 25, 1910); was the 1st winner of the Coupe Femina (1910) and the 1st female pilot to carry a passenger in flight (April 19, 1910); was the 1st woman to remain airborne for more than an hour; won the King of Italy cup (1911), beating all the male pilots; was the 1st female pilot awarded the French Legion d'Honneur.

DUTT, Toru (1856–1877). Indian poet and translator. Born into family of high-caste Hindus who had converted to Christianity in Calcutta, India, 1856; died 1877 of TB; dau. of Govin Chunder Dutt (justice of the peace); attended a convent in Nice, France. ❖ In an age when few Indian women published, translated French poetry and essays for *A Sheaf Gleaned in French Fields* (1876); also wrote *Le Journal de Mlle. d'Avers* (1879) and *Ancient Ballads and Legends of Hindustan* (1882).

DUTTON, Anne (fl. 1743). American letter writer. Fl. around 1743. ❖ In 1743, published *A Letter from Mrs Anne Dutton . . . to the Rev. Mr G. Whitefield* (Whitefield was a famous preacher of Great Awakening period).

DUVAL, Diane (1914–2001). See Bishop, Julie.

DUVAL, Enna (1818–1892). See Brewster, Anne Hampton.

DUVAL, Helen (1916—). American bowler. Born 1916 in Berkeley, California. ❖ Began bowling (1938) and joined 1st league (1939); began conducting bowling clinics on the West Coast and, after son Richard contracted polio (1954), taught him to bowl while he was in a wheelchair; was a founding member of the women's professional bowling (1959) and a representative for the Bowlers Victory Legion (BVL) Fund, conducting bowling clinic's for American vets; named to the President's Council for Physical Fitness during the Kennedy administration, served for 5 years; won the Phoenix Open and the National championship (1969). Inducted into Women's International Bowling Congress Hall of Fame (1970) and National Bowling Hall of Fame (1993).

DUVALL, Edith (1944—). See McGuire, Edith.

DU VERGER, Susan (before 1625–after 1657). British romance-fiction writer. Name variations: S. Du Verger, Susan Du Vergeere. Born before 1625 in England; died after 1657. ❖ Translated *Admirable Events: Selected out of foure bookes, Written in French by the Right Reverend, John Peter Camus, Bishop of Belley* (1639) and *Diotrephe of A History of Valentines, Written in French by the Right Reverend John Peter Camus, Bishop and Lord of Belley* (1641); may also have been author of *Du Vergers Humble Reflections upon some passages of the right Honourable the Lady Marchioness of Newcastles Olio* (1657).

DUVERNAY, Pauline (1813–1894). French ballet dancer. Born 1813 in Paris, France; died Sept 2, 1894, in Mundford, England. ❖ Performed with Paris Opéra's ballet company (1831–36), creating roles in Coralli's *La Tentation* (1832) and Filippo Taglioni's *Brézilia* (1833), and replaced famed Maria Taglioni in *Nathalie, La Laitière Suisse* and *Robert le Diable*; performed in London in revivals of *The Maid of Cashmere* and Aumer's *The Sleeping Beauty* (1833); a few years later, performed again in London at King's Theatre in Joseph Mazilier's revival of *Le Diable Boiteux* and André Deshayes' *Le Brigand de Terracina* (1836–37); retired (1837).

DUVHOLT, Kristine (1974—). Norwegian handball player. Name variations: Kristine Duvholt Havnås, Havnas or Havnaes. Born Jan 31, 1974, in Tonsberg, Norway. ❖ Won a team silver medal at Barcelona Olympics (1992) and a team bronze at Sydney Olympics (2000).

DUX, Emilienne (b. 1874). French actress. Name variations: Mme Dux. Born Nov 28, 1874, in La Ricamauie, Loire, France; dau. of Claude Deux; m. Émile Duard (div.). ❖ Made stage debut at the Odéon in

Britannicus (1891), remaining there for 6 years, then appeared in leading roles at the Imperial Theater in St. Petersburg for 9 seasons and at the Porte-St.-Martin for 3; plays include *Son Père, L'Otage, Florise, La Vieillesse de Don Juan, Hélène Ardouin, Un Grand Bourgeois* and *Poussiere;* made debut with the Comédie Française as Elmine in *Tartuffe,* followed by *La Bonne Mine, Les Caprices de Marianne, La course du Flambeau, Jeunesse* and *Un ennemi du peuple;* elected a sociétaire (Jan 1919); made London debut as Mme D'Orcieu in *La loi de l'homme* (1908); appeared in film *La Comtesse de Somerive* (1917).

DUXBURY, Elspeth (1909–1967). English actress. Born April 23, 1909, in Mhow, India; died Mar 11, 1967, in London, England; m. John F. Waterhouse. ❖ Made stage debut in Eastbourne as Ann Whitefield in *Man and Superman* (1929) and London debut in *The Pleasure Garden* (1932); appeared at Birmingham Rep (1933–35, 1938, 1946); other plays include *Counsellor-at-Law, Storm Song, The Astonished Ostrich* and *The Taming of the Shrew;* films include *Make Mine Mink, The Yellow Hat* and *The Great St. Trinian's Train Robbery.*

DUYSTER, Willemijn. Dutch field-hockey player. Born in the Netherlands. ❖ Won a team bronze medal at Atlanta Olympics (1996).

D'UZES, Anne, Duchesse (1847–1933). *See Uzès, Anne, Duchesse d'.*

DVORAK, Adelheid (1869–1939). *See Popp, Adelheid.*

DVORAK, Ann (1912–1979). American actress. Name variations: Baby Anna Lehr; Ann McKim. Born Anna McKim, Aug 2, 1912, in New York, NY; died Dec 10, 1979, in Honolulu, Hawaii; dau. of Anna Lehr (silent-screen actress); m. Leslie Fenton (actor), 1932 (div. 1946); m. twice more. ❖ Made film debut as a child in *Ramona* (1916); appeared in over 50 films, including *Sky Devils, Scarface, The Strange Love of Molly Louvain, Three on a Match, G Men, Thanks a Million, Blind Alley, Flame of the Barbara Coast, Gangs of New York, A Life of Her Own* and *The Secret of Convict Lake;* retired (1951).

DWAN, Dorothy (1907–1981). American actress. Name variations: Molly Mills. Born Dorothy Smith, April 26, 1906, in Sedalia, Missouri (took name Dorothy Dwan in honor of director Allan Dwan); died Mar 17, 1981, in Ventura, California; dau. of Nancy Smith (actor's agent); m. Larry Semon (actor). ❖ Often appeared opposite husband; films include *Her Boyfriend, Kid Speed, The Silent Vow, The Perfect Clown* and *McFadden's Flats;* was also in the 1924 version of *The Wizard of Oz.*

DWORKIN, Andrea (1946–2005). American feminist author and activist. Born Sept 26, 1946, in Camden, New Jersey; died April 9, 2005; sister of Mark Dworkin; Bennington College, BA, 1968; lived with activist John Stoltenberg, 1974–2005. ❖ Controversial radical feminist who wrote numerous works on pornography, prostitution, male violence against women, class-based analysis of feminism and other topics, linking sexual issues to broader structures in society; organized grassroots crusade against pornography; co-authored, with feminist lawyer Catharine MacKinnon, Minneapolis and Indianapolis ordinances defining pornography as civil-rights violation against women (later overturned by courts); chronicled anti-pornography crusade in *Take Back the Night: Women on Pornography* (1980) and helped organize Take Back the Night; identified pornography as cause rather than symptom of sexist culture in *Pornography: Men Possessing Women* (1981); taught at many universities including Smith and University of Minneapolis. Selected works: (nonfiction) *Woman Hating: A Radical Look at Sexuality* (1974), *Possessing Women* (1981), *Intercourse* (1988), *Right-Wing Women: The Politics of Domesticated Females* (1991), *Life and Death: Unapologetic Writings on the Continuing War Against Women* (1997) and *Scapegoat: The Jews, Israel, and Women's Liberation* (2000); (short stories) *The New Women's Broken Heart* (1980); (novels) *Ice and Fire* (1986) and *Mercy* (1991); (essays) *Letters from a War Zone: Writings, 1976–1987* (1988). ❖ See also Andrea Dworkin, *Heartbreak: The Political Memoir of a Feminist Militant* (Basic, 2002).

DWORSCHAK, Adelheid (1869–1939). *See Popp, Adelheid.*

DWYER, Ada (1863–1952). American actress. Name variations: Ada Dwyer Russell. Born 1863 in Salt Lake City, Utah; died July 4, 1952; educated in Boston; m. Harold Russell (div.); lived with Amy Lowell (poet), 1914–25; children: Lorna Russell. ❖ Made stage debut in *Alone in London* and was a prominent actress on New York stage for many years; appeared as Doña Julia in *Don Juan* (1891), Mrs. Greenthorne in *Husband and Wife,* and Malka in *The Children of the Ghetto* (1892), reprising performance as Malka for London debut (1899); toured as supporting actress in productions starring Eleanor Robson (Belmont);

toured Australia in title role of *Mrs. Wiggs of the Cabbage Patch* (1908); returned to NY to play Bet in *The Dawn of a To-Morrow* (1909); appeared as Kate Fallon in *The Deep Purple* (1911) and as Grandma in *Blackbirds* (1912); retired from stage (1914). ❖ See also *Women in World History.*

DWYER, Doriot Anthony (1922—). American flutist. Born Doriot Anthony, Mar 6, 1922, in Streator, Illinois; dau. of Edith (Maurer) Anthony and William C. Anthony. ❖ Held position of 1st flutist for Boston Symphony Orchestra (1952–89), the 1st woman to hold a principal chair in a major American symphony orchestra. ❖ See also *Women in World History.*

DWYER, Florence Price (1902–1976). American politician. Born Florence Louise Price in Reading, Pennsylvania, July 4, 1902; died in Elizabeth, New Jersey, Feb 29, 1976; briefly attended University of Toledo in Ohio. ❖ A 16-year veteran of US House of Representatives (1957–73), was elected to New Jersey state assembly (1950), serving as a Republican, won election to Congress (1956); during tenure, concentrated on issues of consumer protection, women's equality, and procedural reform within the House; was a chief sponsor of the act creating the Consumer Protection Agency and a staunch supporter of Equal Rights Amendment; during consideration of Legislative Reorganization Act of 1970, authored an amendment requiring the recording of individual votes; under presidency of Richard Nixon, urged appointment of more women to federal office; retired from politics (1972).

DYACHENKO, Tatyana (1960—). Russian political strategist. Name variations: Tatiana or Tatyana Yeltsin. Born 1960 in USSR; youngest of 2 daughters of Boris Yeltsin (president of Russia, 1990–2000) and Naina Yeltsin; trained as a mathematician; m. 2nd husband Aleksei Dyachenko (aerospace engineer); children: (1st m.) Boris. ❖ A discreet but powerful figure in her father's inner circle, had been a trusted counselor and image manager during his political campaign (1996); while he was president, was appointed by him to the official post of "presidential adviser" with a salary and office in the Kremlin (1998); also policed his use of vodka; at one point, was considered the 2nd most powerful person in Russia; lost her job by order of Putin when her father resigned from office (2000).

DYBENDAHL HARTZ, Trude (1966—). Norwegian cross-country skier. Name variations: Trude Dybendahl. Born Jan 8, 1966, in Norway. ❖ Won a silver medal for 4 x 5 km relay at Calgary Olympics (1988); won a silver medal for 4 x 5 km relay at Albertville Olympics (1992); won a silver medal for 4.5 km relay at Lillehammer Olympics (1994).

DYBKJAER, Lone (1940—). Danish politician. Name variations: Lone Dybkjær. Born May 23, 1940, in Frederiksberg, Denmark. ❖ Social Liberal, was a member of the Folketing (1973–77, 1979–94), serving as minister for the Environment (1988–90), and a member of the Danish delegation to the UN (1984, 1987, and 1992); as a member of the European Liberal, Democrat and Reform Party, elected to 4th and 5th European Parliament (1994–99, 1999–2004). Awarded European gold medal for building preservation (1991).

DYBWAD, Johanne (1867–1950). Norwegian actress and director. Name variations: Johanne Juell. Born Aug 2, 1867, in Bergen, Norway; died 1950 in Norway; dau. of Mathias Juell and Johanne Juell Reimers; m. Vilhelm Dybwad (playwright), 1891 (div.). ❖ Norway's leading actress during a 60-year career, made professional debut in Bergen (1887) and quickly established a reputation for her natural, unaffected style; as lead actress for National Theater in Oslo for 40 years (1899–1939), was especially noted for her work with director Bjørn Bjørnson and for her interpretations of the plays of Ibsen and Shakespeare; began directing regularly (1906) but was sometimes criticized for lack of fidelity to works; retired (1947), receiving Norway's Grand Cross Civil. ❖ See also Carla Waal, *Johanne Dybwad: Norwegian Actress* (Norwegian U. Press, 1967).

DYER, Amelia Elizabeth (1839–1896). English murderer. Born 1839 in England; executed at Newgate, June 10, 1896; married and sep. ❖ Moved to Reading (1895) and took in young children as boarders; after killing 7 of them, was arrested (April 1896) and attempted suicide; at trial, claimed insanity (May 1896) but motive was apparently greed, as she collected boarding fees for the murdered children.

DYER, Louise (1884–1962). *See Hanson-Dyer, Louise.*

DYER, Mary Barrett (c. 1591–1660). American Quaker and religious martyr. Name variations: Dyar. Born Mary Barrett in England c. 1591; hanged June 1, 1660, in Boston (MA) Bay Colony; m. William Dyer; children; 6 survived infancy. ❖ With husband, emigrated from England and settled in the Massachusetts Bay Colony (1635), becoming a member of Boston's 1st Church; after giving birth to a stillborn, deformed child (1637), was cited by authorities as evidence of her unfitness, and that of her midwife Anne Hutchinson, in the eyes of the Lord; when Hutchinson was excommunicated and exiled from the colony (1639), followed her out of the church in a show of support; also excommunicated and banished, moved with family to Rhode Island (Newport) area; lived in England (1652–57); returned to the colonies (1657); in Boston, was hanged for being a Quaker. Inducted into the Women's Hall of Fame at Seneca Falls (2000). ❖ See also Horatio Rogers, *Mary Dyer of Rhode Island the Quaker martyr that was hanged on Boston Common, June 1, 1660* (Preston & Rounds, 1896); Ruth Talbot Plimpton, *Mary Dyer: Biography of a Rebel Quaker* (Branden, 1994); and *Women in World History.*

DYK, Ruth (1901–2000). American suffragist and psychologist. Born Ruth Belcher, Mar 25, 1901, in Portland, Maine; grew up in Newton Center, Massachusetts; died Nov 18, 2000, in Rochester, NY; dau. of Annie Manson Belcher (one of the 1st women admitted to Tufts Medical School) and Arthur Fuller Belcher (lawyer); attended Wellesley College; Simmons College, MA in economics; also attended University of Wisconsin and University of California at Berkeley; m. Walter Dyk (anthropologist, died 1972); children: Timothy Dyke (judge); Penelope Carter. ❖ Worked as a psychiatric social worker with delinquent girls in upstate NY, then as a researcher at the Downstate Medical Center of the State University of New York in Brooklyn; wrote *Anxiety in Pregnancy and Childbirth* (1950), *Psychological Differentiation* (1962), and (with husband) *Left Handed* (1980), an anthropological study of Navajo Indians; an active suffragist in her early years, was campaigning for women in politics at age 99.

DYKE, Eunice (1883–1969). Canadian nurse. Born Eunice Henrietta Dyke, Feb 8, 1883; grew up in Toronto, Ontario, Canada; died Sept 1, 1969, in Toronto; dau. of Jennie (Ryrie) Dyke and Samuel Allerthorn Dyke (pastor); graduate of Johns Hopkins Training School for Nurses, 1909. ❖ Taught kindergarten in a private school; appointed a tuberculosis nurse at Toronto's Department of Health (May 1911); as head (from 1914) of the Toronto Department of Health's Division of Public Health Nurses (renamed Division of Public Health Nursing), revamped division, greatly improved efficiency of nurse visits and created educational training programs for new nurses; also served as a consultant in public health nursing for the League of Red Cross Societies in Paris, France (1924), and created and directed Canada's 1st senior citizen's organization, the Second Mile Club.

DYLEWSKA, Izabella (1968—). Polish kayaker. Name variations: Izabela Dylewska-Swiatowiak. Born Mar 16, 1968. ❖ Won a bronze medal at Seoul Olympics (1988) and a bronze medal at Barcelona Olympics (1992), both in K1 500 meters.

DYMPNA (fl. 650). Martyr and saint. Name variations: Dimpna. Born the dau. of a pagan Irish, British or Armorican king and a Christian princess. ❖ The dau. of a pagan king and a Christian princess, was baptized and instructed in the Christian faith before mother died when Dympna was still young; because she resembled her mother and the king had idolized his wife, is said to have invoked an incestuous lust in her father as she grew up; fled to Antwerp with St. Gerebernus, her confessor; built a site that is now the town of Gheel, and prepared to live as solitaries; discovered by the king, refused to return with him; was beheaded by father. Patron saint of mental illness, epilepsy, possession by the devil, and sleepwalkers. ❖ See also *Women in World History.*

DYNALIX, Paulette (1917—). French ballet dancer. Born Mar 10, 1917, in Grenoble, France. ❖ Trained at school of Paris Opéra with Carlotta Zambelli; danced with Opéra's ballet company throughout career in such repertory works as Balanchine's *Apollo,* as well as numerous works by Serge Lifar including *Les Mirages;* is thought to have been the last female dancer to perform role of Franz in *Coppélia* (upon her retirement [1957], Paris Opéra began to cast only males for the part).

D'YOUVILLE, Marie Marguerite (1701–1771). See Youville, Marie Marguerite d'.

DYROEN-LANCER, Becky (1971—). American synchronized swimmer. Born Becky Dyroen, Feb 19, 1971, in San Jose, California; sister of Suzannah Bianco (synchronized swimmer). ❖ Won a team gold medal at Atlanta Olympics (1996).

DYSART, countess of (1626–1698). See Murray, Elizabeth.

DYSON, Elizabeth Geertruida (1897–1951). New Zealand journalist and magazine editor. Name variations: Elizabeth Geertruida Agatha Weersma, Hedda Weersma, Hedda Lakeman, Hedda Dyson. Born Elizabeth Geertruida Agatha Weersma, Jan 15, 1897, at Ginneken, Netherlands; died Oct 17, 1951, in Auckland, New Zealand; dau. of Tiemen Weersma (army officer) and Joziena Regiena (van Haeften) Weersma; m. Jacobus Maria Lakeman, 1918 (div. 1923); m. Edward Joseph Vernon Dyson (solicitor), 1927; children: (1st m.) 1 son. ❖ Immigrated to New Zealand (c. 1927); served as editor of *New Zealand Woman's Weekly* (1932–48); wrote editorials regularly on national and international social and political issues; broadcast weekly radio variety program (1935). ❖ See also *Dictionary of New Zealand Biography* (Vol. 4).

DYSON, Hedda (1897–1951). See Dyson, Elizabeth Geertruida Agatha.

DYSON, Maureen (1928–1974). See Gardner, Maureen.

DYVEKE (c. 1491–1517). Paramour of Christian II. Name variations: (Dutch) Duiveke; Little Dove. Born c. 1491; died suddenly, possibly poisoned, possibly of appendicitis, summer of 1517, age 26; dau. of Sigbrit Willums (fl. 1507–1523); mistress of Christian II (1481–1559), king of Denmark and Norway (r. 1513–1523). ❖ See also *Women in World History.*

DZERZHINSKA, Sofia (1882–1968). Polish-born Russian revolutionary. Name variations: Zofia Dzierzynska; Sofia Dzerzhinskaia; Zosia Dzerzhinskaya. Born Sofia Sigizmundovna Muszkat in Warsaw, Russian Poland, Dec 4, 1882 (or Nov 22 in the Julian calendar); died in Moscow, Feb 27, 1968; dau. of Zygmunt Muszkat; studied music at Warsaw Conservatory; m. Feliks Dzerzhinsky (close associate of V.I. Lenin and founder of the Cheka—the Soviet secret police), Aug 1910 (died July 1926); children: Jan Dzerzhinsky (worked for the Comintern). ❖ Decorated Soviet revolutionary, was often arrested by Russians in early years, while working for the illegal Social Democracy of the Kingdom of Poland and Lithuania (SDKPiL) in Warsaw; expelled from Russian Poland (1909), settled in Austrian Poland; gave birth to son in prison (1911); after Bolshevik Revolution (Nov 1917), in which husband played a leading role, went to Moscow (1919), working for some time in the People's Commissariat of Education; held posts in Polish Bureau of the Communist Party of the Soviet Union and at Communist University of National Minorities of the West (1920s); also served as executive secretary of the Polish bureau of the Soviet Communist party central committee's department of propaganda and agitation; became editor-in-chief at Moscow's Marx-Engels-Lenin Institute (1929); assumed a post in the executive committee of Communist International (Comintern, 1937); during WWII, served as a director of Radio Kosciuszko, which broadcast to German-occupied Poland, and worked in Moscow headquarters of Bureau of Polish Communists. Awarded Order of Lenin on 3 occasions. ❖ See also *Women in World History.*

DZHANDZHGAVA, Tatyana (1964—). Soviet handball player. Born Feb 25, 1964, in USSR. ❖ Won a bronze medal at Seoul Olympics (1988) and a bronze medal at Barcelona Olympics (1992), both in team competition.

DZHIGALOVA, Lyudmila (1962—). Soviet runner. Born Jan 22, 1962, in USSR. ❖ Won a gold medal at Seoul Olympics (1988) and a gold medal at Barcelona Olympics (1992), both in 4 x 400-meter relay.

DZHUGELI, Medeya (1925—). Soviet gymnast. Born Aug 1925 in USSR. ❖ At Helsinki Olympics, won a silver medal in teams all-around, portable apparatus, and a gold medal in team all-around (1952).

DZIECIOL, Iwona (1975—). Polish archer. Born 1975 in Poland. ❖ Won a bronze medal for teams at Atlanta Olympics (1996).

DZIOUBA, Irina. Russian rhythmic gymnast. Born in USSR. ❖ Won a team bronze medal at Atlanta Olympics (1996).

E

E., Sheila (1957—). *See Escovedo, Sheila.*

EADBURG (d. 751). *See Edburga.*

EADBURGA (d. 751). *See Edburga.*

EADBURGH (d. 751). *See Edburga.*

EADBURGH (c. 773–after 802). **Queen of the West Saxons.** Born Eadburg; Eadburga. Born c. 773; died after 802 in Pavia, Italy; dau. of Offa II, king of West Mercia, and Queen Cynethryth (fl. 736–796); possibly sister of Etheldreda (d. around 840); m. King Brihtric (Beorhtric) of the West Saxons, c. 789 (died 802). ❖ As queen, gained significant power when husband entrusted her with many of the duties of ruling; highly intelligent, was also reportedly ruthless, involved in intrigues and accused of poisoning several court officials whom she disliked; accidentally murdered husband when he drank from a cup of poisoned wine that she had prepared for one of his favorites, of whom she was jealous (802); stole much of the West Saxon treasury and fled to court of Charlemagne, king of the Franks; became an abbess there but was caught with a lover and banished from the kingdom; ended days in Pavia, Italy, probably surviving on charity. ❖ See also *Women in World History.*

EADBURH (d. 751). *See Edburga.*

EADBURH (fl. 9th century). **Saxon noblewoman.** Name variations: Eadburga. Possibly dau. of Wigmund and Elfleda; others say dau. of Coenwulf; m. Ethelred the Great, ealdorman of the Gainis; children: Elswitha (d. 902). ❖ See also *Women in World History.*

EADGIFU. *Variant of Edgifu.*

EADGYTH. *Variant of Edgitha or Edith.*

EADGYTH SWANNESHALS (c. 1012–?). **Mistress of Harold II Godwineson.** Name variations: Edith; Edith of the Swan's Neck; Eadgyth Swan-neck. Born c. 1012; some sources list her as dau. of Emma of Normandy (c. 985–1052) and Ethelred II the Unready, king of England; mistress of Harold II Godwineson (c. 1022–1066), king of England (d. 1066); children: (with Harold) Gyseth (fl. 1070); Godwine; Edmund; Magnus; Gunhild, a nun at Wilton; Ulf (b. Dec 1066). ❖ Found ex-lover Harold II Godwineson on the field where he lay dead after falling at Battle of Hastings (Oct 14, 1066); identified the corpse by birthmarks known only to her and arranged for his burial in Waltham Abbey; because she is also known as Edith of the Swan's Neck, is often confused with Harold's wife Edith (fl. 1063).

EADHILD. *Variant of Edhild.*

EADIE, Helen. **Scottish politician.** Born in Stenhousemuire, Scotland; children: 2 daughters. ❖ As a Labour candidate, elected for Dunfermline East (1999), the 1st candidate to be declared a Labour and Co-operative member of the Scottish Parliament.

EADY, Dorothy (1904–1981). **British-born Egyptian archaeologist.** Name variations: Om Seti; Omm Seti; Omm Sety; Bulbul Abd el-Meguid. Born Dorothy Louise Eady in Blackheath, East Greenwich, London, Jan 16, 1904; died in Araba el-Madfuna near Abydos, Egypt, April 21, 1981; dau. of Reuben Ernest Eady and Caroline Mary (Frost) Eady; m. Imam Abd el-Meguid, 1933 (div. 1936); children: son, Sety. ❖ Noted expert on the civilization of Pharaonic Egypt who believed that she was the reincarnation of an ancient Egyptian temple priestess; in early years, persuaded such eminent Egyptologists as Sir E.A. Wallis Budge to informally teach her the rudiments of the ancient Egyptian hieroglyphs; became a champion of modern Egyptian nationalism as well as of the glories of the Pharaonic age; married an Egyptian, moved to Egypt (1933) and took the name Bulbul Abd el-Meguid; convinced that she was the reincarnation of the young priestess Bentreshyt, who became pregnant by Pharaoh Sety I, began to call herself Omm Sety in Arabic ("Mother of Sety"); took a job with the Department of Antiquities where she revealed a remarkable knowledge of all aspects of ancient Egyptian history and culture; though regarded as highly eccentric, was extremely efficient at studying and excavating ancient Egyptian artifacts; was able to intuit countless details of ancient Egyptian life and rendered immensely useful practical assistance on excavations, where her "memory" enabled them to make important discoveries; writings include *Flowers from a Theban Garden* (1939) and *A Dream of the Past* (1949). ❖ See also "Omm Sety and Her Egypt," BBC documentary by Julia Cave (1981); Jonathan Cott and Hanny El Zeini, *The Search for Omm Sety: A Story of Eternal Love* (Doubleday, 1987); and *Women in World History.*

EAGELS, Jeanne (1894–1929). **American stage actress.** Born Jeannine Eagels in Kansas City, Missouri, June 26, 1894; died in New York, NY, Oct 3, 1929; dau. of Edward (carpenter) and Julia (Sullivan) Eagels; m. Morris Dubinsky (theater troupe manager), c. 1910 (div.); m. Edward Harris Coy (stockbroker and former football star), 1925 (div. 1928); children: (1st m.) 1 son who was put up for adoption. ❖ Best known for her portrayal of Sadie Thompson, made 1st appearance on stage at 7, in a local production of *A Midsummer Night's Dream;* at 15, ran away from home and joined a theater troupe with which she toured the midwest for 2 years; in NY (1911), took small roles in *Jumping Jupiter* (1911), *The "Mind-the-Paint" Girl* (1912), and *Crinoline Girl* (1914); made the 1st of a series of movies (1915) for the fledgling Pathé (NY), while continuing to appear on stage at night; had 1st Broadway hit, *Daddies;* achieved a hard-won dream of stardom as Sadie Thompson in *Rain* (1922), which ran for 2 years on Broadway and toured for an additional 5; made 1st talkie, *The Letter* (1929), followed by *Jealousy* (1929), with Fredric March; died of alcoholism and drug addiction. ❖ See also (film) *Jeanne Eagels,* starring Kim Novak (1964); and *Women in World History.*

EAGLE, Angela (1961—). **British politician and member of Parliament.** Born Feb 17, 1961; twin sister of Maria Eagle (MP). ❖ Representing Labour, elected to House of Commons for Wallasey (1992, 1997, 2001, 2005).

EAGLE, Maria (1961—). **British politician and member of Parliament.** Born Feb 17, 1961; twin sister of Angela Eagle (MP). ❖ Solicitor; representing Labour, elected to House of Commons for Liverpool Garston (1997, 2001, 2005); named parliamentary undersecretary of state, Department for Work and Pensions; named parliamentary undersecretary, Department for Education and Skills (2005).

EAKINS, Susan Hannah (1851–1938). **American painter.** Name variations: Susan Hannah Macdowell. Born Susan Hannah Macdowell in Philadelphia, Pennsylvania, Sept 21, 1851; died in Philadelphia, Dec 27, 1938; dau. of William H. (noted engraver) and Hannah Trimble (Gardner) Macdowell; sister of Elizabeth Macdowell; studied at Philadelphia Academy of Fine Arts (PAFA), 1876–82; m. Thomas Eakins (1844–1916, painter), Jan 19, 1884 (died 1916); no children. ❖ During studies at PAFA, exhibited intermittently and won several prizes, including the Charles Toppan draughtsmanship prize (1882) and the Mary Smith Prize for best PAFA woman artist (1879), an award later bestowed on Cecilia Beaux, Emily Sartain, and Alice Barber Stephens; following marriage, was encouraged by husband and kept a separate studio; primarily a portraitist, specialized in unsentimental domestic scenes depicting one or two subjects sitting while reading or knitting; often used her husband as a subject; long ignored; her 1st solo exhibition—a collection of over 50 oils and watercolors—was held at Pennsylvania Academy of the Fine Arts in 1973, 35 years after her death. ❖ See also *Women in World History.*

EALDGYTH. *Variant of Edith.*

EALDGYTH (fl. 7th c.). *See Edith of Aylesbury.*

EALDGYTH (fl. 1016). **Queen of the English.** Name variations: Algitha; Edith. Fl. around 1016; m. Sigeferth, a Danish thane; m. Edmund II

Ironside (c. 989–1016), king of the English (r. 1016), c. July 1015; children: Edmund (1016–?); Edward the Exile also known as Edward the Aetheling (1016–1057). Her sons were possibly twins. ❖ Following 1st husband's death, married Edmund II Ironside, bringing with her as dowry the submission of Five Boroughs of the Danish Confederacy; because the marriage incurred the wrath of her brother, arranged for murder of her 2nd husband the following year.

EALES, Nellie B. (1889–1989). English zoologist. Name variations: Nellie Barbara Eales. Born April 14, 1889, in England; died Dec 7, 1989; University College, Reading, PhD, 1921, DSc, 1926. ❖ The 1st woman PhD graduate from University College, Reading (later known as Reading University), was a zoology history expert; served as lecturer and senior lecturer in zoology department at Reading (1919–54), where she also catalogued Cole Library's zoology and early medicine collection (1954–89); was president (1948–51) and journal editor (1956–69) of Malacalogical Society of London. Writings include *Transactions of the Royal Society of Edinburgh* (1926), *The Littoral Fauna of Great Britain: A Handbook for Collectors* (1939), *Practical Histology and Embryology* (1940, textbook). The Nellie B. Eales Travel Award for pure and applied zoology students was created in her honor.

EALHSWITH or EALHSWYTH (d. 902). *See Elswitha.*

EAMES, Clare (1896–1930). American actress. Born in Hartford, Connecticut, Aug 5, 1896; died Nov 8, 1930, at 34; dau. of Hayden Eames and Clare (Hamilton) Eames; niece of opera singer Emma Eames; studied for stage under Sarah Cowell Le Moyne and at Academy of Dramatic Art; m. Sidney Howard (1891–1939, Pulitzer Prize-winning playwright), 1922 (sep. 1928, div. Mar 1930); children: Clare Jenness Howard. ❖ Made stage debut at Greenwich Village Theater in *The Big Scene* (1918); attracted considerable attention in title role of John Drinkwater's *Mary Stuart,* then starred in Sidney Howard's 1st play, *Swords* (1921); married Howard and starred in several of his plays, most notably *Ned McCobb's Daughter;* co-starred with James K. Hackett in *Macbeth,* portrayed Hedda Tesman in *Hedda Gabler,* and Proserpine Garnett in *Candida* (1924); appeared as the Empress Carlota in *Juarez and Maximilian* (1926); made London debut as Christina in *The Silver Cord* (1927); after returning to New York (1928), appeared as Nurse Wayland in *The Sacred Flame,* the same role she would play in London (Feb 1929) in her last performance.

EAMES, Emma (1865–1952). Shanghai-born American lyric soprano. Born Emma Hayden Eames, Aug 13, 1865, in Shanghai, China; raised in Maine; died June 13, 1952, in New York, NY; dau. of Emma (Hayden) Eames and Ithama Bellows Eames (lawyer who worked in the international courts of China); aunt of Clare Eames (1896–1930); studied with Clara Munger and Annie Payson Call in Boston and with Mathilde Marchesi in Paris; m. Julian Story (American painter), Aug 1891 (div. 1907); briefly m. Emilio de Gogorza (American opera singer), 1911 (sep.). ❖ Major opera star, made debut starring in Gounod's *Roméo et Juliette* opposite Jean de Reszke at Paris Opéra (1889); after debuting at Covent Garden (1891), sang more than a dozen leading roles in eight seasons there; debuted at Metropolitan Opera (1891) where she would give over 250 performances during 16 seasons (until 1909); performed the 1st Met productions of Mascagni's *Cavalleria rusticana* and *Iris,* and made her way with great assurance into the Wagnerian repertory as early as 1891; taught singing in New York City (1936–52); also made over 50 recordings (1905–11). ❖ See also memoir *Memories and Reflections* (Appleton, 1927).

EAMES, Ray (1912–1988). American architect, abstract artist and industrial designer. Name variations: Ray Kaiser. Born Ray Kaiser, Dec 15, 1912, in Sacramento, California; died Aug 21, 1988, in Venice, CA; studied painting with Hans Hoffman; attended Cranbrook Academy; m. Charles Eames (industrial designer), 1941 (died 1978); children: stepdaughter Lucia Eames (designer). ❖ One of the most important American designers of the 20th century, best known for her groundbreaking contributions to architecture, furniture design, industrial design and photographic arts, spent formative years in New York's modern-art movement (1930s); moved to Cranbrook Academy outside Detroit (1940), where she met Charles Eames and Eero Saarinen; began lifelong artistic and intellectual collaboration with husband and moved with him to California; worked on furniture designs which were picked up by Evans Products (1946) and continue to be manufactured in US and Europe; molded plywood chair which critic Esther McCoy called "chair of the century"; sought to address housing shortage through innovative uses of wartime materials and technologies; with husband, designed and built home in Pacific Palisades (1949), which is now a mecca for architects worldwide due to pioneering use of materials; expanded interest into photography and filmmaking (1950s), creating with husband over 85 short films ranging in subject matter from presidents to sea creatures to complex mathematical and scientific concepts; produced film *The Information Machine* (1957); explored new materials for furniture design, including fiberglass and plastic (1970s) and designed seating for offices, as well as Dulles and O'Hare airports (1960s); also designed numerous textile patterns and magazine covers. ❖ See also Eames Demetrios, *Eames Primer* (Universe, 2001).

EAMES, Virginia (1889–1971). American stage and screen actress. Name variations: Virginia True Boardman; Virginia Boardman. Born May 23, 1889, in Fort Davis, Texas; died June 10, 1971, in Hollywood, California; m. True Boardman (actor, died 1918); children: True Boardman Jr. (tv writer). ❖ Entered films with the Selig Studios in Chicago; appeared in *The Girl of the Limberlost, The Tomboy, Penrod,* and *The House of Intrigue,* among others; often played the mother of Shirley Temple (Black).

EANFLEDA (626–?). Queen of Northumbria. Name variations: Eanfled; Eanflæd; Eanfled of Deira. Born April 17, 626; death date unknown; dau. of Ethelberga of Northumbria (d. 647) and Edwin (Eadwine), king of Northumbria (585?–633); m. Oswy (Oswin, Oswio), king of Northumbria; children: Ecgfrith, king of Northumbia; Elfwine (d. 679); Ostrith (d. 697); Elflaed (d. 714). ❖ Baptized by Bishop Paulinus, was the 1st Northumbrian to receive the rite; along with husband Oswy, continued to champion Christianity and placed their daughter Elflaed under tutelage of Hilda of Whitby; when Elflaed became abbess of Whitby (680), shared the rule with her.

EANGYTH OF WESSEX (fl. 7th c.). *See Engyth.*

EARDLEY, Joan (1921–1963). English painter. Born in May 1921 in Warnham, Sussex, England; died Aug 16, 1963, in Glasgow, Scotland; dau. of William Eardley (army captain) and Irene Morrison; attended Goldsmith College of Art (1938); studied with Hugh Adam Crawford at Glasgow School of Art, graduating with honors (1944); attended Patrick Allen-Fraser School of Art (1947). ❖ Famed 20th-century painter of landscapes, seascapes and studies of children, suffered from intermittent depression throughout life; began to sketch and paint tenement life in Glasgow (1949), becoming so well-known that ill-clothed children came unannounced to pose at her Cochrane Street studio; bought dilapidated Watch House cottage on sea cliffs near the seaside village of Catterline (1950); painted with richer colors and in more experimental and Expressionist style, responding to constant changes of sea, sky and land; showed an affinity with Pollock and de Kooning in later, more abstract work; elected associate to Royal Scottish Academy (RSA, 1955), the youngest person to receive the honor to that date, and later granted full membership (1963); at time of death, was just beginning to be recognized outside Scotland; honored with major retrospective exhibition at Talbot Rice Centre and RSA, Edinburgh (1988); well represented in Scottish National Gallery of Modern Art, Edinburgh. ❖ See also Cordelia Oliver, *Joan Eardley, RSA* (Mainstream, 1988).

EARHART, Amelia (1897–1937). American aviator. Born July 24, 1897, in Atchison, Kansas; lost over the Pacific, July 2, 1937, on a flight between Lae, New Guinea, and Howland Island; dau. of Edwin (lawyer) and Amy (Otis) Earhart; sister of Muriel Earhart Morrisey (1900–1998); attended Columbia University, 1919–20, 1924–25; m. George Palmer Putnam (publisher), Feb 7, 1931; no children. ❖ The world's most famous woman aviator, the 1st woman to cross the Atlantic in an airplane, was also a tireless and effective advocate of commercial aviation and equal rights for women; became the 1st woman to cross the Atlantic by air (1928), though she was actually a mere passenger while two men acted as pilot and mechanic; toured US lecturing on behalf of her convictions and established numerous records for distance and speed flights; set an altitude record in an autogiro, in which she became the 1st person to cross the US and return (1931); was the 1st woman to fly solo across the Atlantic (1932); made the fastest non-stop transcontinental flight by a woman (1932); broke her own transcontinental speed record (1933); was the 1st person to fly solo across the Pacific from Hawaii to California; was the 1st person to fly solo from Los Angeles to Mexico; broke the Mexico City-Newark, NJ speed record (1935); set a speed record for east-west Pacific crossing from Oakland to Honolulu (1937); became one of the ten most famous women in the world in less than a decade; disappeared in the Pacific Ocean on a round-the-world flight (1937). The continual search for a solution to her unexplained disappearance has kept her name legendary in the history of American aviation. ❖ See also memoirs *20 Hrs. 40 Min.* (Putnam, 1929), *The Fun of It* (1932), and *Last Flight* (Harcourt Brace, 1937); Jean Backus, *Letters from Amelia* (Beacon, 1982); Mary S. Lovell, *The Sound of Wings: The Life of Amelia Earhart* (St. Martin, 1989); Doris L. Rich, *Amelia Earhart, a Biography* (Smithsonian Institution Press, 1989); Susan Ware, *Still Missing: Amelia Earhart and the Search for Modern Feminism* (Norton, 1993); Fred Goerner, *The Search for Amelia Earhart* (Doubleday, 1966); and *Women in World History.*

EARLE, Alice Morse (1851–1911). American writer and antiquarian. Born Mary Alice Morse in Worcester, Massachusetts, April 27, 1851; died in Hempstead, Long Island, New York, Feb 16, 1911; dau. of Edwin and Abigail Mason Clary Morse; m. Henry Earle, April 1874; children: 4. ❖ Published 1st book, *The Sabbath in Puritan New England,* at age 40 (1891); authored, edited, and contributed to the publication of 17 books and over 30 articles dealing with various aspects on American colonialism which are considered valuable resources for discovering America's domestic past; utilizing primary source material such as diaries, letters, wills, newspapers, journals, and court records, often focused on the economic and social circumstances of women of the era in such books as *Colonial Dames and Good Wives* (1895), *Diary of Anna Green Winslow; A Boston School Girl of 1771* (1894), *The Life of Margaret Winthrop* (1895) and the most widely read, *Home Life in Colonial Days* (1898); also wrote *Two Centuries of Costume in America, 1620–1820* (1903). ❖ See also *Women in World History.*

EARLE, Sylvia (1935—). See Mead, Sylvia Earle.

EARLE, Victoria (1861–1907). See Matthews, Victoria Earle.

EARLE, Virginia (1875–1937). American actress and singer. Born Aug 6, 1875, in Cincinnati, Ohio; died Sept 21, 1937. ❖ Made stage debut as a member of a juvenile opera company (1888); toured Australia with E.E. Rice management, then US with De Wolf Hopper; made NY debut in *The Passing Show* (1894), followed by *The Merry World, In Gay New York, The Geisha, The Casino Girl, The Girl from Up There, Florodora* and *The Jewel of Asia;* came to prominence in title role of *Sergeant Kitty* (1903); also appeared in vaudeville.

EARLEY, Charity (1917–2002). See Adams, Charity.

EARLY, Martha (1899–1923). See Mansfield, Martha.

EARLY, Penny Ann (c. 1946—). American jockey. Born c. 1946 in California. ❖ The 1st American woman to be licensed as a horse jockey (1968) was scheduled to ride at Churchill Downs, KY, but replaced after male jockeys, in a show of solidarity, threatened a boycott; in retaliation, was signed by Kentucky Colonels of the American Basketball Association, though she had never played basketball (1968–69), and made "cameo" on-court appearance inbounding the ball in a game against Los Angeles Stars (Nov 28, 1969); rode the favorite to victory in the all-women Lady Godiva Handicap, MA (1969).

EARTH, Wind & Fire.
See Cleaves, Jessica (1948—).
See Scott, Sherry (c. 1948—).

EASTERFIELD, Theodora Clemens (1894–1962). See Hall, Theodora Clemens.

EASTERN JEWEL (1906–1948). See Yoshiko Kawashima.

EAST FRANKS, queen of. See Liutgard (d. 885).

EASTLAKE, Elizabeth (1809–1893). English writer. Name variations: Lady Elizabeth Eastlake; Elizabeth Rigby. Born Elizabeth Rigby in Norwich, England, Nov 17, 1809; died Oct 2, 1893; dau. and sister of well-known surgeons; m. Sir Charles Lock Eastlake (1793–1865, English painter and art critic), 1849. ❖ Published 1st article, a criticism of Goethe (1836); as an art critic and woman of letters, was a regular contributor to the *Quarterly Review,* for which she wrote an infamous commentary on *Jane Eyre* and the Brontës; also published *A Residence on the Shores of the Baltic* (1844); edited husband's work and that of her father; also translated many works on art and completed the last volume, *The History of Our Lord in Art,* for Anna Jameson's 4-vol. series, following Jameson's death. ❖ See also *The Journals and Correspondence of Lady Eastlake,* ed. by C. Eastlake Smith (1895); and *Women in World History.*

EASTLAKE-SMITH, Gladys (1883–1941). English tennis player. Born Aug 14, 1883, in UK; died Sept 18, 1941. ❖ At London Olympics, won a gold medal in singles–indoor courts (1908).

EASTMAN, Annis Ford (1852–1910). American minister and feminist. Born Annis Bertha Ford, April 24, 1852, in Peoria, Illinois; died Oct 22, 1910, in Elmira, NY; dau. of George W. (gunsmith) and Catherine (Stehley) Ford; Oberlin College, teaching certificate (1874); m. Samuel Elijah Eastman (preacher), 1875; children: Morgan Eastman, Anstice Ford Eastman, Max Eastman (editor of *The Masses* and *The Liberator*) and Crystal Eastman (social reformer). ❖ Congregational minister and intellectual, moved with husband to his preaching assignment in Swampscott, Massachusetts (1875) and then on to Newport, Kentucky (1878) and Canandaigua, New York (1881); assumed dominant role in family after husband's health deteriorated, forcing him to leave ministry (1886); taught school (1886–87) and preached at parish Church of Brookton, near Ithaca, NY (1887–92); was among the 1st women to be ordained as Congregational minister (1889); moved on to West Bloomfield, NY (1893) where fame as preacher grew; became assistant pastor along with husband at Thomas K. Beecher's Park Church in Elmira, NY (1894), befriending Mark Twain, among others; published collection of sermons, *Have and Give* (1896), for children; became joint pastor with husband of Park Church after Beecher's death (1900); enrolled in Harvard Summer School (1903) and studied with Royce, Palmer and Santayana in attempt to define Christianity intellectually; changed Park Church to Unitarian faith apparently without protest from congregants; began speaking at suffrage conventions and contemplating career in education or social reform, feeling deepening doubt in religion which made ministry difficult.

EASTMAN, Carole (1934–2004). American screenwriter. Name variations: (pseudonyms) Adrien Joyce, A.L. Appling. Born Feb 19, 1934, in Glendale, California; died Feb 13, 2004, in Los Angeles, CA; father was a grip at Warner Bros.; mother was a secretary to Bing Crosby. ❖ Began career as a ballet dancer, then model; wrote the screenplay for *Five Easy Pieces* (1970), including the now-famous chicken-salad scene; was nominated for Academy Awards for the story and screenplay, along with director Bob Rafelson; under name Adrien Joyce, wrote scripts for *The Shooting* (1967), *Model Shop* (1968), and *Puzzle of a Downfall Child* (1970); also wrote *The Fortune* (1975) and *Man Trouble* (1992).

EASTMAN, Crystal (1881–1928). American social activist and feminist. Name variations: Crystal Eastman Benedict. Born Catherine Crystal Eastman, June 25, 1881, in Marlborough, Massachusetts; died July 8, 1928, in Erie, Pennsylvania; dau. of Samuel Elijah Eastman and Annis Ford Eastman (both ordained Congregational ministers); sister of Morgan Eastman, Anstice Ford Eastman and Max Eastman (socialist, writer, editor); Vassar College, BA, 1903; Columbia University, MA, 1904; New York University Law School, LLB, 1907; m. Wallace Benedict (insurance agent), 1911 (div. 1916); m. Walter Fuller (English folk musician manager), 1916 (died 1927); children: Jeffery Eastman Fuller (active in American Civil Liberties Union), Annis Fuller. ❖ Social activist, joined Paul Kellogg in "Pittsburgh Survey," the 1st attempt in US to study effects of industrialism on urban workers; investigated over 1,000 industrial accidents, publishing findings in *Work Accidents and the Law* (1910); as secretary and only female member of New York State Employer's Liability Commission (1909–11), helped to secure passage of worker's compensation laws in NY; with Alice Paul, Lucy Burns and others, co-founded Congressional Union for Woman Suffrage (which later became National Woman's Party) and served as its delegate to International Woman Suffrage Alliance in Budapest (1913); became chair of NY state branch of Woman's Peace Party and member of executive committee of American Union against Militarism, campaigning against impending National Defense Bill and arguing against US entry into WWI in series of articles published in *Survey* and *The New Republic;* was one of the founders of the American Civil Liberties Union (ACLU); joined brother Max on radical journal *Liberator* (1917), acting as managing editor and writing on labor issues and feminism; helped organize Feminist Congress in New York City (1919), calling for voting rights along with equal employment opportunities, birth control, economic independence and sex-blind moral standards; resigned from *Liberator* (1921) and moved to England with 2nd husband; helped found London branch of Woman's Party; active in Conference on Labour Women in Birmingham (1925); returned to US (1927) and continued reform activities despite poor health and news of husband's death. Inducted into the Women's Hall of Fame at Seneca Falls (2000).

EASTMAN, Elaine Goodale (1863–1953). American novelist and poet. Name variations: Elaine Goodale. Born Elaine Goodale in 1863 in Massachusetts; died 1953; sister of Dora Read Goodale (1866–1953, writer); m. Dr. Charles A. Eastman (Santee Sioux writer, sep. 1921). ❖ With sister, wrote *Apple-Blossoms: Verses of Two Children* (1879) at age 15; at 20, began to teach Sioux Indians at Hampton Institute in Virginia; supported missionary schools for education of Native American children and tried to record and preserve Native American history; present at the massacre at Wounded Knee, nursed the wounded, resulting in her article in *Nebraska History* (1945); collaborated with husband on articles and edited his manuscripts. ❖ See also K. Graber, ed., *Sister to the Sioux: The Memoirs of Elaine Goodale Eastman, 1885–1891* (1978).

EASTMAN, Linda. *See McCartney, Linda.*

EASTMAN, Linda A. (1867–1963). American librarian. Born July 17, 1867, in Oberlin, Ohio; died April 5, 1963, in Cleveland, Ohio; dau. of William Harvey Eastman and Sarah (Redrup) Eastman. ❖ The 1st woman to head a metropolitan library system in US, began career as librarian of Cleveland Public Library (CPL, 1918–38); taught public school in Cleveland (1885–92); became assistant at CPL (1892); cofounded Ohio Library Association (1895) and became its 1st woman president (1903); served as assistant librarian and cataloguer in Dayton Public Library (1895–96); became vice-librarian to William H. Brett at CPL, then succeeded him on his death (1918); work at CPL included developing adult-education programs, children's library programs, the open-shelf system, and a book distribution program for those confined to home; served as instructor (1904–18) and professor (1918–37), School of Library Science at Western Reserve University; served as president, American Library Association (1928–29).

EASTON, Florence (1882–1955). English-born Canadian soprano. Name variations: Florence Gertrude Easton. Born Oct 25, 1882, in Middlesborough, England; died Aug 13, 1955, in New York, NY; studied at Royal College of Music in London and in Paris with Haslam. ❖ Made debut in Newcastle as Shepherd in *Tannhäuser* (1903); sang leading roles at the Metropolitan in such operas as *Madama Butterfly, Rigoletto, Parsifal, Elektra, Cavalleria Rusticana* and *Cosi Fan Tutte*; created the role of Aelfrida in Deems Taylor's *The King's Henchman*; retired (1936).

EASTON, Sheena (1959—). Scottish pop star. Born Sheena Shirley Orr, April 27, 1959, in Bellshill, Scotland; naturalized US citizen; m. Sandi Easton, 1978 (div. 1979); m. Robert Light, 1984 (div. 1985); m. Timothy Delarm, 1997 (div. 1998); m. John Minoli, 2002 (div. 2004); children: (adopted) Jake and Skylar. ❖ Released 1st hit single "Modern Girl" (1980), which made Top 10 in England; other hit singles include "Morning Train" (1981), "For Your Eyes Only" (1981), "When He Shines" (1982), "Strut" (1984), and "Sugar Walls" (1984); won Grammy awards for Best New Artist (1982) and Best Mexican/American Performance (for duet with Luis Miguel, "Me Gustas Tal Como Eres," 1985); appeared on tv, in film, and on Broadway in such musicals as *The Man of La Mancha* and *Grease*. Albums include *Sheena Easton* (1981), *You Could Have Been With Me* (1981), *Madness, Money and Music* (1982), *Best Kept Secret* (1983), *A Private Heaven* (1984), *Todo Me Recuerda a Ti* (1984), *Do You* (1985), *No Sound but a Heart* (1987), *The Lover in Me* (1988), *What Comes Naturally* (1991), *No Strings* (1993) and *My Cherie* (1995).

EASTWOOD, Alice (1859–1953). Canadian-born American botanist and naturalist. Born on Jan 19, 1859, in Toronto, Ontario, Canada; died in San Francisco, California, Oct 30, 1953; dau. of Colin Skinner Eastwood and Eliza Jane (Gowdey) Eastwood; never married. ❖ Pioneer in the environmental movement in California, 1st taught at East Denver High School in Colorado; spent summer vacations exploring the high Rockies, identifying wildflowers and collecting specimens for her herbarium; moved to California (1892), settling in San Francisco where she accepted an assistantship at California Academy of Sciences; also founded and directed the California Botanical Club; succeeded Katharine Brandegee as curator of the Herbarium at the Academy (1894); explored little-known regions like the inner south Coast Ranges, where she discovered a number of uncatalogued plants and flowers; accumulated a 1st-rate botanical collection, much of which was destroyed in the San Francisco earthquake; was chosen by the California Academy of Sciences to rebuild its herbarium in Golden Gate Park; served as honorary president of Seventh International Botanical Congress (1950). ❖ See also Michael Elsohn Ross, *Flower Watching with Alice Eastwood* (Carolrhoda, 1997); Carol Green Wilson, *Alice Eastwood's Wonderland: The Adventures of a Botanist* (California Academy of Sciences, 1955); and *Women in World History*.

EATON, Edith (1865–1914). Canadian journalist. Name variations: Sui Sin Far; Edith Maude Eaton. Born Edith Maude Eaton in 1865 in Macclesfield, England, of a Chinese mother and English father; died 1914 in Montreal, Canada; migrated with family to Montreal, Quebec, Canada (c. 1872); sister of Winnifred Babcock (writer). ❖ Wrote *Mrs. Spring Fragrance* (1912); worked as journalist for Montreal papers and published short fiction; lived in Jamaica (1897) and US (1898–1912).

EATON, Margaret O'Neale (c. 1799–1879). *See Eaton, Peggy.*

EATON, Mary (1901–1948). American stage and screen actress, dancer, and singer. Born Jan 29, 1901, in Norfolk, Virginia; died Oct (some sources cite Nov) 10, 1948, in Hollywood, California; sister of Pearl Eaton (1898–1958) and Doris Eaton (b. 1904); studied ballet with Theodore Kosloff, then at Ned Wayburn Studio; m. Millard Webb (div.); m. Eddie Laughton (actor). ❖ As a child actress, made NY stage debut as Tyltyl in *The Blue Bird* (1915) and Broadway debut in *Follow Me* (1916); specializing in a romantic toe dance on point, was featured in *Over the Top, The Royal Vagabond, Kid Boots, The Five O'Clock Girl* and 3 productions of the *Ziegfeld Follies* (1920–22); films include *Cocoanuts, His Children's Children* and *Glorifying the American Girl*.

EATON, Pearl (1898–1958). American theatrical dancer and choreographer. Born Aug 1, 1898, in Norfolk, Virginia; died Sept 10, 1958, in Los Angeles, California; sister of Mary Eaton (1901–1948) and Doris Eaton (b. 1904). ❖ Performed in numerous stock company productions in Norfolk, VA, Washington, DC, and Baltimore, MD, with siblings; moved to New York City to study with Ned Wayburn; appeared in the chorus in several of *Ziegfeld Follies* (1916–23), with featured dance role in *Midnight Frolics*; moved to Hollywood, CA, to work with mentor Elsie Janis at Paramount Studios; choreographed early sound musicals, including *Rio Rita* (1929), *Hit the Deck* (1930), *Paramount on Parade* (1931), and *Dance, Girl, Dance* (1933); danced in such films as *Men of the Night* (1934), *Goin' to Town* (1935), and *Klondike Annie* (1936); worked with Janis in production for many years thereafter.

EATON, Peggy (c. 1799–1879). American socialite. Name variations: Margaret O'Neale or O'Neill Eaton; Peggy O'Neal, or O'Neale; Margaret O'Neale Timberlake Buchignani Eaton. Born Margaret O'Neale in Washington City (present-day Washington DC), Dec 1799; died in Washington, Nov 9, 1879; dau. of William O'Neale (innkeeper) and Rhoda Howell O'Neale (sister of Richard Howell, governor of New Jersey); m. John Bowie Timberlake, July 18, 1816 (died at sea, 1828); m. John Henry Eaton, Jan 1, 1829 (died 1856); m. Antonio Buchignani, June 1859; children: (1st m.) William Timberlake (1817–1818); Virginia Timberlake; Margaret Timberlake Randolph (b. 1824). ❖ Well-known and controversial figure—implicated in the fall of Andrew Jackson's 1st Cabinet, the ascension of Martin Van Buren to the presidency, and the political eclipse of John C. Calhoun—who has been uniformly denied significance in histories of the early republic; grew up in Washington in the Franklin House, an inn for politicians; married John Bowie Timberlake (1816) and continued working in parents' taproom; met Senator John Henry Eaton, a guest at the inn (1818) and formed a 10-year relationship with him while her husband was at sea; following death of husband, married John Henry Eaton (1829); husband appointed secretary of war by President Jackson (1829), beginning "The Petticoat War," where the wives of the administration, led by Floride Calhoun, would not attend events that she attended because of her reputation (1829–31); was defended by Jackson, but rancor escalated, polarizing the president and members of his Cabinet, and husband was forced to resign over the "Eaton affair" (1831); served in Florida as the governor's lady (1834–35) and in Spain as ambassador's wife (1835–40); returned to America (1840); spent final years giving occasional press interviews and being treated as a grande dame of American politics. ❖ See also *The Autobiography of Peggy Eaton* (Scribner, 1932); Queena Pollack, *Peggy Eaton: Democracy's Mistress* (1931); Samuel Hopkins Adams, *The Gorgeous Hussy* (Grosset, 1934); Charles B. Keats, *Petticoat War in the White House: A Novelized Biography of Peggy O'Neill* (Heritage Hall, 1973); Alfred Henry Lewis, *Peggy O'Neal* (1903); Leon Phillips, *That Eaton Woman: In Defense of Peggy O'Neale Eaton* (Barre, 1974); and *Women in World History*.

EATON, Shirley (1937—). English actress. Born Jan 12, 1937, in London, England. ❖ Made film debut in *You Know What Sailors Are* (1954), followed by *Doctor in the House, Three Men in a Boat, Doctor at Large, The Naked Truth, Carry on Sergeant, Carry On Nurse, Carry on Constable, A Weekend with Lulu, Ten Little Indians* and *The Blood of Fu Manchu*; probably best remembered as Jill Masterson, the character who was painted gold in the James Bond film, *Goldfinger* (1964).

EATON, Winnifred (1875–1954). *See Babcock, Winnifred.*

EAUBONNE, Françoise d' (1920–2005). French historian, essayist, poet and feminist. Name variations: Francoise d'Eaubonne. Born Mar 12, 1920 in Toulouse, France; died Aug 3, 2005; children: 2. ❖ Coined term "eco-feminism" and argued that oppression of women is linked to exploitation of nature; writings include *Comme un vol de gerfauts* (A Flight of Falcons, 1947), *Les bergères de l'Apocalypse* (1978), *Le féminisme ou la mort* (1974), and *Féminisme-Ecologie: révolution ou mutation* (1978, trans. 1999); also wrote feminist essays for journals and anthologies.

EAVES, Elsie (1898–1983). American civil engineer. Born May 5, 1898, in Idaho Springs, Colorado; died Mar 27, 1983, in Port Washington, Long Island, NY. ❖ Worked for US Bureau of Public Roads, Colorado State Highway Department, and Denver and Rio Grande Railroad; was the 1st woman admitted to full membership in the American Society of Civil Engineers (ASCE); became manager of *Business News* (1945); worked as adviser to National Commission on Urban Affairs; advised International Executive Service Corps about construction costs in Iran; was the 1st woman admitted to American Society of Cost Engineers (1957) and the 1st to be awarded honorary lifetime membership in ASCE (1979); was charter member of Society of Women Engineers.

EB (c. 610–c. 683). *See Ebba.*

EBADI, Shirin (1947—). Iranian judge. Born 1947 in Hamedan, Iran; grew up in Tehran; Tehran University, MA in Law; m. Javad Tavassolian (also seen as Tavassoliyan) (civil engineer); children: 2 daughters (b. c. 1980, c. 1983). ❖ Winner of Nobel Peace Prize, served as Iran's 1st female judge at Tehran City Court (1975–79) until Islamic revolution, when women judges were banned; practiced law in Tehran, defending rights of women, children, and political dissidents, and taught at Tehran University; after Islamic regime's crackdown on political dissidents, was banned from practicing law for 5 years, but regained license on appeal (2000); became 1st Iranian, and 11th woman, to win Nobel Peace Prize, and 1st female Muslim Nobel laureate (Dec 2003); was recognized several times by Human Rights Watch for work.

EBB (c. 610–c. 683). *See Ebba.*

EBBA (c. 610–c. 683). Northumbrian princess, abbess and saint. Name variations: St. Eb, Ebb, or Ebbe; St. Abb, Aebba, Aebbe; St. Tabbs. Born c. 610 in Northumbria (now England); died c. 683 in Northumbria; dau. of Aethelfrith (king of Bernicia who conquered neighboring Anglian kingdom of Deira and created new united kingdom Northumbria) and Acha (ex-wife of defeated king of Deira); sister of Oswy (king, warrior) and Oswald (king, saint, warrior who invited monks of Iona to set up mission in Northumbria, establishing peaceful Christian kingdom). ❖ Known for founding Ebchester convent and monastery at Coldingham and for contributing to conversion of northern Britons to Christianity; fled to Iona, Scotland, with brothers Oswald and Oswy after father's death in battle against mother's brother, King Edwin (616); converted to Christianity along with brothers, leaving behind traditional religion; received veil from Saint Finan at Lindisfarne; returned to Northumbria after brothers had vanquished foes in battles near Hexham (633); founded convent on river Derwent named Ebchester with help of brother and monks (c. 642); established double monastery for men and women at Coludi (now Coldingham) in marshes of Scotland's Berwickshire; served as holy abbess to Coldingham's nuns until death, basing organization on that of Whitby; after being admonished by priest Adomnan for relaxed state of community, reformed ways of community for short time but later reverted to lax standards; reportedly gave refuge to niece Etheldreda who became nun at Coldingham after separation from husband Ecgfrith; died around 683, shortly before monastery burned down; lives on in name through Ebchester Abbey, Saint Abb's Head (where ruins of fort may indicate site of her monastery), and street and church in Oxford. Feast Day is Aug 25.

EBBE (c. 610–c. 683). *See Ebba.*

EBERHARDT, Isabelle (1877–1904). Swiss-born author, traveler and adventurer. Name variations: (pseudonyms) Nicolas Podolinsky and Si Mahmoud Saadi. Born Isabelle Wilhelmine Marie Eberhardt, Feb 17, 1877, in Geneva, Switzerland; died in Ain Sefra, Algeria, Oct 21, 1904; illeg. dau. of Nathalie Eberhardt de Moerder (Prussian aristocrat) and Alexander Trophimowsky (tutor, scholar and anarchist); m. Slimène Ehnni, Oct 17, 1901; no children. ❖ Traveler who ventured into little-known areas of North Africa in the guise of a Muslim man and who, through her writings, presented an often romanticized vision of Muslim life to her European readers; raised in an eccentric family in Geneva and encouraged to wear male clothing from a young age; traveled to Algeria with mother and contributed essays on North African life to

Parisian magazines (1897); participated in a riot against French colonialism and was forced to return to Geneva to avoid arrest (Mar 1898); after father's death, returned to North Africa (1899); presented herself as a Muslim man, Si Mahmoud Saadi, and traveled to the souf region of Southern Algeria; sojourned briefly in Marseilles and Paris, attempting to launch her career as a writer (1899–1900); returned to Algeria and met future husband, Slimène Ehnni, a non-commissioned officer in the French forces in Algeria; initiated into the Qadryas, a Sufi Islamic order; was almost assassinated by a member of a rival Islamic order (1901); expelled from Algeria (1901) and permitted to return only after securing French citizenship through marriage to Ehnni; working under General Hubert Lyautey, engaged in espionage for French forces planning an incursion into Morocco (1903); killed in a flash flood in Ain Sefra, Algeria (1904), became more famous—and infamous—after her demise than she had ever been during her brief life. Selected publications—in English translation: *The Passionate Nomad* (1987) and *Vagabond* (1988). ❖ See also *The Passionate Nomad: The Diary of Isabelle Eberhardt* (Beacon, 1987); Annette Kobak, *Isabelle: The Life of Isabelle Eberhardt* (Chatto & Windus, 1988); Cecily Mackworth, *The Destiny of Isabelle Eberhardt* (Routledge & Kegan Paul, 1951); and *Women in World History.*

EBERHART, Mignon G. (1899–1996). American writer of mystery, crime, suspense, romance and historical fiction. Born July 6, 1899, in Lincoln, Nebraska; died Oct 8, 1996, in Greenwich, Connecticut; dau. of William Thomas and Margaret Hill (Bruffey) Good; attended Nebraska Wesleyan University, 1917–20; m. Alanson C. Eberhart (civil engineer), Dec 29, 1923 (div.); m. John P. Hazen Perry, 1946 (div.); remarried Alanson C. Eberhart, 1948. ❖ During more than half a century, earned a place as one of the most popular writers in the mystery genre; wrote novel, *The Patient in Room 18* (1929), where her heroine Sarah Keate was one of the genre's 1st female sleuths; published another Keate story, *While the Patient Slept* (1930), which won the Scotland Yard prize; over next 50 years, continued to write exciting, atmospheric murder mysteries and introduced another female serial character, Susan Dare. Several of her novels were adapted as films of the same title, including *While the Patient Slept* and *The White Cockatoo* (both 1935), *Murder by an Aristocrat* (1936), and *The Patient in Room 18* (1938); the novel *Hasty Wedding* was made into a film titled *Three's a Crowd* (1945); *From This Dark Stairway* was filmed as *The Dark Stairway* (1938); *The Great Hospital Mystery* film was based on an unidentified story by Eberhart (1937); *Mystery of Hunting's End* was filmed as *Mystery House* (1938). ❖ See also *Women in World History.*

EBERLE, Abastenia St. Leger (1878–1942). American sculptor. Name variations: Abastenia Saint Leger. Born Mary Abastenia St. Leger in Webster City, Louisiana, 1878; died 1942; grew up in Canton, Ohio, and Puerto Rico; dau. of a physician; studied in Ohio under Frank Vogan and at Art Students League, NY, under Kenyon Cox and George Grey Barnard; also studied in Naples, Italy. ❖ Influenced by the Ash Can School, had a penchant for small bronze sculptures in urban settings; drew many of her subjects from life on NY's Lower East Side; works include *The Girl on Roller Skates, Mowgli, Victory, Little Mother, Dance of the Ghetto Children, The White Slave,* and the very popular, *Windy Doorstep.* ❖ See also *Women in World History.*

EBERLE, Emilia (1964—). Romanian gymnast. Name variations: Trudi Eberle. Born Gertrud Emilia Eberle, Mar 4, 1964, in Arad, Romania; m. Ferenc Kollár (Frank Kollar, judo player). ❖ At Jr. European championships and Romanian nationals came in 1st all-around (1978); at Balkan championships, Europeans, and International Championships of Romania, came in 2nd all-around (1979); at World championships, placed 1st for team all-around and floor exercise and 3rd for uneven bars (1979); at Coca-Cola International, placed 1st all-around (1980); at Moscow Olympics, won a silver medal in the uneven bars and a team silver in all-around (1980); placed 1st all-around at Hapoel Games and 2nd all-around at University Games (1983); defected to Hungary (1989); immigrated to US (1991).

EBERLE, Trudi (1964—). *See Eberle, Emilia.*

EBERLE, Verena (1950—). West German swimmer. Born Nov 13, 1950, in Germany. ❖ At Munich Olympics, won a bronze medal in the 4 x 100-meter medley relay (1972).

EBERT, Henrietta (1954—). East German rower. Born Jan 15, 1954, in East Germany. ❖ At Montreal Olympics, won a gold medal in coxed eights (1976).

EBERT, Joyce (1933–1997). American stage and tv actress. Born Joyce Anne Womack, June 26, 1933, in Munhall, Pennsylvania; died Aug 28, 1997, in Southport, Connecticut; m. Michael Ebert; m. Arvin Brown (director). ❖ Appeared at Long Wharf Theater in New Haven, CT, in 81 productions over a span of 30 years; made NY debut as Julie in *Liliom* (1956); other Broadway credits include *Shadow Box, Watch on the Rhine, Requiem for a Heavyweight,* and *Solitaire/Double Solitaire.*

EBNER, Christine (1277–1355). German nun, writer and mystic. Name variations: Christina von Engelthal. Born 1277 in Nuremberg, Germany; died Dec 27, 1355, in Engelthal, Germany. ❖ At 12, entered the Dominican Convent of Engelthal near Nuremberg; though she had a mysterious illness that recurred yearly, was made mother superior at a young age; became one of most important mystics of her day; wrote *Büchlein von der Gnaden Überlast,* describing mystical experiences of nuns at Engelthal, and *Leben: Geschichte der Christina Ebnerin,* an account of own life as mystic.

EBNER, Margarethe (1291–1351). German writer, nun and mystic. Name variations: Margarata or Margrete Ebner; Blessed Margaret Ebner, Mystic of Medingen. Born 1291 into a wealthy family in Donauworth, Germany; died July 20, 1351, at Medingen, Germany. ❖ Entered Dominican Convent of Maria Medingen (1306); after long and serious illness during which she was sent home to recover (1312–22), began to have visions, revelations and prophecies; was encouraged by Father Heinrich von Nördlingen to write down mystical experiences, which were later published as *Offenbarungen* (1882); beatified by Pope John Paul II (Feb 24, 1979).

EBNER-ESCHENBACH, Marie (1830–1916). Austrian novelist and poet. Name variations: Countess Dubsky; Baroness von Ebner-Eschenbach. Born Countess Dubsky at Castle Zdislavic, in Moravia, Sept 13, 1830; died 1916; dau. of Count Dubsky; m. cousin, Moritz von Ebner-Eschenbach (Austrian field marshal), 1848; no children. ❖ Began career as a playwright; her drama *Maria von Schottland* (Mary Stuart in Scotland) was produced at the Karlsruhe theater (1860), but her next few plays, including *Marie Roland* (Madame Roland), proved less successful; wrote a number of novels depicting the life in Bohemia: *Die Prinzessin von Banalien* (1872), *Bozena* (1876), and *Das Gemeindekind* (Child of the Community, 1887); also wrote of the Austrian aristocracy in *Lotti, die Uhrmacherin* (1883), *Zwei Comtessen* (Two Countesses, 1885), *Unsühnbar* (1890), and *Glaubenslos?* (1893); published the story of a dog, *Krambambuli* (1875), one of her best-known books, and produced a book of *Parables, Fairy Tales and Poems* (1880); became a grande dame of Viennese society. ❖ See also *Women in World History.*

EBNOETHER, Luzia (1971—). Swiss curler. Born Oct 19, 1971, in Switzerland. ❖ Won a silver medal for curling at Salt Lake City Olympics (2002).

EBOLI, princess of (1540–1592). See Mendoza, Ana de.

EBSEN, Vilma (1911—). American tap dancer. Born Vilma Ebsen, 1911, in Belleville, Illinois; sister of Buddy Ebsen (actor and dancer). ❖ Toured throughout Florida with brother Buddy in a tap act (late 1920s); joined him in NY (1929) and performed as tap-dancing team for 12 years; toured in musical show *Whoopee* (1930); gained lasting notoriety through columnist Walter Winchell's persistent praise of appearances at nightclubs including The Cotton Club (early 1930s); opened as tap-team with Buddy at the Palace (1930s); danced on Broadway in *Ziegfeld Follies* (1934); appeared in the film *Broadway Melody of 1936.*

EBTEKAR, Massoumeh (1960—). Iranian vice president. Name variations: Masumeh Ebtekar. Born 1960 in Tehran, Iran; attended school in US; Shahid Beheshti University, BSc in medical technology, 1985; Tarbiat Modarres University, MA in education, MSc in immunology, 1989, and PhD in immunology, 1995. ❖ Named one of the 7 vice presidents of Iran by moderate president Mohammad Khatami (Aug 1997), the 1st woman to serve in a top government post since Iran's 1979 Islamic revolution; was also named to head the Organization for the Protection of the Environment; began serving as editor of the English-language newspaper *Kayhan* (1981).

EBURNE, Maude (1875–1960). Canadian-born character actress. Born Nov 10, 1875, in Bronte-on-the-Lake, Ontario, Canada; died Oct 15, 1960, in Hollywood, California; m. Gene Hill (stage producer, died 1932). ❖ Performed on stage in Canada and in many Broadway productions, including *A Pair of Sixes;* appeared in over 100 films, including *Ruggles of Red Gap, Champagne Waltz, To Be or Not To Be, Bowery to Broadway, Leave It to Blondie* and *Mother Wore Tights.*

ECCLES, Janet (1895–1966). English actress. Born Aug 19, 1895, in Nafferton, East Yorkshire, England; died July 1966; m. F.W.D. Benhall. ❖ Made stage debut in *Jack o' Jingles* (1919), followed by *David Garrick, Mid-Channel, All the King's Horses,* and *The Napoleon of Notting Hill.*

ECCLES, Mary Hyde (1912–2003). American-born viscountess, philanthropist and bibliophile. Name variations: Mary Hyde; Lady Eccles; Viscountess Eccles. Born Mary Morley Crapo, July 8, 1912, in Detroit, Michigan; died Aug 26, 2003, at her home, Four Oaks Farm, in Somerset Co., New Jersey; Vassar College, BS; Columbia University, MA literature; m. Donald Frizell Hyde (lawyer), 1939 (died 1966); m. David Eccles, Viscount Eccles (former Conservative education minister and collector), 1984 (died 1999). ❖ With 1st husband, began collecting ephemera on Samuel Johnson and Oscar Wilde, among others (1941), which grew to become the Hyde Collection, one of the world's finest collections of 18th-century English literature; wrote *The Impossible Friendship: Boswell and Mrs. Thrale* (1972) and *The Thrales of Streatham Park* (1976); published a new edition of Samuel Johnson's letters, called The Hyde Edition (1992–94); with 2nd husband, established the David and Mary Eccles Centre for American Studies at the British Library (1991). ❖ See also *Mary Hyde Eccles: A Miscellany of her Essays and Addresses* (Grolier Club).

ECGWYNN (d. around 901). Saxon woman. Name variations: Ecgwyn. Died c. 901; dau. of a shepherd; mistress of Edward I the Elder (c. 870–924), king of the English (r. 899–924); children: Aethelstan or Ethelstan (895–939), king of the English (r. 924–939); Alfred (died young); Edith (d. 937, who m. Sihtric, king of York).

ECHERER, Raina A. Mercedes (1963—). Austrian politician. Name variations: Mercedes Echerer. Born May 16, 1963, in Linz, Austria. ❖ As Mercedes Echerer, began career as actress on stage and screen (1980); films include *Café de l'union* (1991), *Halbe Welt* (1993), and *Der See* (1996); representing Group of the Greens/European Free Alliance, elected to 5th European Parliament (1999–2004).

ECHOLS, Sheila Ann (1964—). African-American runner. Born Oct 2, 1964, in Memphis, Tennessee. ❖ At Seoul Olympics, won a gold medal in 4 x 100-meter relay (1988); won US championships in 100 meters and long jump (1988).

ECKART, Jean (1921–1993). American set, lighting, and costume designer. Name variations: Jean Levy. Born Jean Levy, Aug 18, 1921, in Glencoe, Illinois; died Sept 6, 1993, in Dallas, Texas; m. William J. Eckart (designer and producer). ❖ Co-designed with husband, *The Scarecrow, Portrait of a Lady, Fiorello!, Damn Yankees, Golden Apple, Li'l Abner, She Loves Me, Mame, Never Too Late, Anyone Can Whistle, Hallelujah Baby, The Fig Leaves are Falling, Norman Is That You?* and *Once Upon a Mattress,* among others; designed costumes for the film *Pajama Game* and sets and costumes for *Damn Yankees* and *The Night They Raided Minsky's;* also designed for tv.

ECKBAUER-BAUMANN, Edith (1949—). West German rower. Name variations: Edith Baumann. Born Oct 27, 1949. ❖ At Montreal Olympics, won a bronze medal in coxless pairs (1976).

ECKBRECHT, Andreas (1894–1985). See Kaus, Gina.

ECKER, Heidemarie Rosendahl (b. 1948). See Rosendahl, Heidemarie.

ECKERSON, Sophia H. (d. 1954). American microchemist, botanist, and plant physiologist. Born Sophia Hennion Eckerson in Tappan, New Jersey; died July 19, 1954, in Pleasant Valley, Connecticut; dau. of Albert Bogert Eckerson and Ann Hennion Eckerson; Smith College, AB, 1905, AM, 1907; University of Chicago, PhD, 1911. ❖ Greatly influenced by Smith professor and mentor William Francis Ganong, served as assistant plant physiologist at University of Chicago (1911–15), then as an instructor (1916–20); worked at the Bureau of Plant Industry (1919–22) and at Cereals Division (1921–22) of the USDA in Washington, DC; served as a charter member of, and employed as a plant microchemist at, Boyce Thompson Institute in NY (1923–40); served as chair of Botanical Society of America's Physiological Section (1935–36); retired (1940); recognized with a star in the publication *American Men of Science* (6th ed.) as one of the 1,000 best scientists in America.

ECKERT (1837–1912). See Kautsky, Minna.

ECKERT, Bärbel (b. 1955). See Wöckel-Eckert, Bärbel.

ECKERT, Cynthia (1965—). American rower. Name variations: Cindy Eckert. Born Oct 27, 1965. ❖ At Barcelona Olympics, won a silver medal in coxless fours (1992).

ECKFORD, Elizabeth (1942—). One of the Little Rock Nine. Born in Little Rock, Arkansas, 1942; served in army as a journalist; earned history degree from Central State College in Ohio; married with 2 sons, including Erin Eckford (killed by police in Little Rock, Dec 2002, who claim he pointed a rifle at them). ❖ Backed by a court order imposing integration, was allowed to attend the all-white Central High School in Little Rock, Arkansas, a defining moment in the civil-rights battle (1957); on arrival at the school, with 8 other black students, was halted by a menacing crowd; 3 weeks later, was escorted into the school by the 101st Airborne paratroopers; became a social worker in Little Rock. ❖ See also *Women in World History.*

ECKHARDT-GRAMATTÉ, S.C. (1899–1974). Russian-born Canadian composer and violinist. Name variations: Sophie or Sophie-Carmen; Sonia Friedman-Gramatté or Gramatte; Sonia de Friedman-Kochevskoy. Born Sophie-Carmen de Friedman, Jan 6, 1899, probably in Moscow; died in Stuttgart, Germany, Dec 2, 1974; dau. of Catherina de Kochevskaya (music instructor) and Nicolas de Friedman; m. Walter Gramatté, Dec 13, 1920 (died of TB, 1929); m. Ferdinand Eckhardt (art historian), 1934. ❖ Wrote *Alphabet Pieces* and *Little Pieces* while not yet a teenager (1905–09); accepted at Paris Conservatoire as violin student where her teachers included Alfred Brun, Guillaume Rémy, Vincent d'Indy, and Camille Chevillard; by 11, was concertizing throughout Europe alternately as pianist and violinist; moved to Berlin with mother and sister (1914) and earned a living for family by playing in cafes; received scholarship sponsored by Franz von Mendelssohn; immersed in composing large works (by 1920); moved to Barcelona (1924) where Pablo Casals became her mentor; commissioned to write piece for Salzburg Festival and the resulting work, *Violin Concerto No. 2* (published 1952), won Composition Prize of the Musikverein (1948); won Austrian State Prize for her Triple Concerto (1950); moved with husband to Winnipeg; wrote *Duo Concertante* for cello and piano for University Music Festival in Saskatoon (1959); known for writing highly individualized music, for innovative approach to teaching violin, and for developing technique for piano called the Natural Piano Technique; won 1st prize in International Competition for Women Composers (1961). The S.C. Eckhardt-Gramatté Competition was named for her. ❖ See also *Women in World History.*

ECKHOFF, Inge (1947—). See Boedding-Eckhoff, Inge.

ECKSTEIN, Therese Schlesinger (1863–1940). See Schlesinger, Therese.

ECKSTORM, Fannie Pearson Hardy (1865–1946). American writer, ornithologist and folklorist. Born Fannie Pearson Hardy, June 18, 1865, in Brewer, Maine; died Dec 31, 1946, in Brewer; dau. of Manly Hardy (fur trader) and Emeline Freeman (Wheeler) Hardy; Smith College, BA, 1888; m. Reverend Jacob Andreason Eckstrom (Episcopal cleric), 1893 (died 1899); children: Katharine Hardy Eckstrom, Paul Frederick Eckstrom. ❖ Expert on Maine history and culture, grew up among hunters, trappers, lumbermen, boatmen and Indian guides of northern and eastern Maine; learned to keep precise trapper's and wildlife records and gained extensive knowledge of Maine birds and animals; was the 1st woman to serve as superintendent of Brewer schools (1889–91); joined father in crusade for preservation of state's big game and rights of native hunters, writing series of articles for *Forest and Stream;* wrote *The Bird Book* (for children) and *The Woodpeckers* (both 1901), as well as *The Penobscot Man* (1904), which recounts exploits of river drivers on Penobscot River, and a biography of woodsman and hunter David Libbey (1907); contributed to *Atlantic Monthly* (1908); began collecting local ballads, co-writing *Minstrelsy of Maine* and *British Ballads of Maine* (both 1929); co-founded Folk-song Society of the Northeast (1930); also wrote *Indian Place-Names of the Penobscot Valley and the Maine Coast* (1941) and *Old John Neptune and Other Maine Indian Shamans* (1945).

ED, Ida (1852–1928). See Boy-Ed, Ida.

EDBERGA (d. 751). See Edburga.

EDBURGA (d. 751). English abbess and saint. Name variations: Bucge, Bugga, Bugge; Eadburg; Eadburga, Eadburgh, Eadburh, Edberga, Edburga or Edburga of Minster-in-Thanet, Edburge; Edburgh of Thanet; Heaburg; Idaberga. Born in Kent, England; died 751 at Minster-in-Thanet Abbey; only dau. of Kenwyn or Centwine, king of Wessex (r. 676–685, died 685) and Engyth. ❖ Benedictine nun and student of Saint Mildred, whom she probably succeeded as abbess of Minster-in-Thanet Abbey (716); secured several royal charters for the abbey and built a new church there; was a friend and correspondent with St. Boniface; with mother, wrote a letter to Boniface describing administrative problems in their religious community; also was a scribe and calligrapher. Feast day is Dec 13.

EDBURGA (d. 960). Nun at Nunnaminster. Born June 15, 960; interred at Pershore Abbey, Worcester, England; dau. of Edgifu (d. 968) and Edward I the Elder (c. 870–924), king of the English (r. 899–924).

EDBURGA OF BICESTER (d. 650). English abbess and saint. Born in England; died July 18, 650, at Aylesbury, Buckinghamshire, England; dau. of pagan warrior king, Penda of Mercia, and Cynewise; sister of Wulfhere of Mercia, king of Mercia (r. 657–675), Wilburga and Edith of Aylesbury. ❖ Abbess of Aylesbury, built a small monastery on land given her by father; with sister, educated their niece, St. Osith.

EDBURGE (d. 751). See Edburga.

EDBURGH OF THANET (d. 751). See Edburga.

EDDY, Bernice (b. 1903). American microbiologist. Born Bernice Eddy, 1903, in Glendale, West Virginia; dau. of Nathan Eddy (physician); University of Cincinnati, PhD in bacteriology, 1927; m. Jerald G. Wooley, 1938; children: Bernice and Sarah. ❖ Began working with the Public Health Service (early 1930s); joined the Biologics Control Division at National Institute of Health (NIH); discovered that batches of a "killed-virus" polio vaccine could actually cause the disease (1950s), but her warnings were ignored and some 200 children contracted polio from a few vaccine batches; with Sarah Stewart, discovered the SE (Stewart-Eddy) polyoma virus, which was shown to cause cancerous tumors in mammals (though the discovery was initially met with widespread skepticism, it was eventually regarded as a major scientific breakthrough); retired at 70 (1973).

EDDY, Helen Jerome (1897–1990). American actress. Name variations: Helen Eddy. Born Feb 25, 1897, in New York, NY; died Jan 27, 1990, in Alhambra, California. ❖ Silent films include *Turn in the Road, Rebecca of Sunnybrook Farm, The Flirt, To the Ladies, The Dark Angel, Quality Street, Camille,* and *13 Washington Square;* had smaller parts in talkies, including *The Bitter Tea of General Yen, Mr. Deeds Goes to Town,* and *Winterset;* retired (1940).

EDDY, Mary Baker (1821–1910). American church founder. Name variations: Mary Glover; Mary Patterson. Born Mary Morse Baker, July 16, 1821, in Bow, New Hampshire; died Dec 3, 1910, in Chestnut Hill, Massachusetts; dau. of Abigail (Ambrose) Baker and Mark Baker (farmer); m. George Washington Glover, 1843 (died 1844); m. Daniel Patterson, 1853 (died 1873); m. Asa Gilbert Eddy, 1877 (div. 1882); children: George Washington Glover II (b. 1844); Ebenezer Foster Eddy (adopted, 1888). ❖ Founder of the Christian Science church and movement, and author of its spiritual textbook *Science and Health with Key to the Scriptures,* was raised in rural New Hampshire; as a child, suffered from chronic health problems; as an adult, experimented with various medical treatments and healing systems; "discovered" religious truths with the power to heal sickness (1866); began to write and teach classes on Christian healing (1866–72); wrote and published *Science and Health* (1872–75); obtained legal charter for Massachusetts Metaphysical College (1881); published several books on Christian Science and founded bimonthly journal (1883–88); dissolved college and moved from Boston to New Hampshire (1889); organized Mother Church of Christian Science in Boston (1892); became pastor emeritus of church and published manual for its operation (1895); successfully battled a series of lawsuits and challenges to her position (1896–1909); returned to live in Boston and founded the *Christian Science Monitor* (1908); was an organizational genius of extraordinary energy, and the church has survived on her strength. ❖ See also autobiography, *Retrospection and Introspection* (1891); Robert Peel, *Mary Baker Eddy: The Years of Discovery* (Holt, 1966), *Mary Baker Eddy: The Years of Trial* (Holt, 1971) and *Mary Baker Eddy: The Years of Authority* (Holt, 1977); Willa Cather and Georgine Milmine, *The Life of Mary Baker G. Eddy and the History of the Christian Science Church* (1909); Susan E. Cayleff, *Wash and Be Healed: The Water Cure Movement and Women's Health* (Temple U. Press, 1987); and *Women in World History.*

EDEBONE, Peta (1969—). Australian softball player. Born Feb 9, 1969, in Kew, Victoria, Australia. ❖ First base and outfielder, won bronze medals at Atlanta Olympics (1996) and Sydney Olympics (2000), and a silver medal at Athens Olympics (2004).

EDELMAN, Marian Wright (1939—). American children's rights advocate. Born Marian Wright, June 6, 1939, in Bennettsville, South Carolina; dau. of Arthur Jerome Wright (minister of Shiloh Baptist Church) and Maggie Leola (Bowen) Wright; Spelman College, BA, 1960; Yale Law School, LLB, 1963; m. Peter Edelman (lawyer, educator and activist), 1968; children: Joshua, Jonah, Ezra. ❖ Founder and president of the Children's Defense Fund, was the 1st black woman admitted to the Mississippi bar (1965); directed the NAACP Legal Defense and Educational Fund office in Jackson, MS; worked with Head Start in MS; served as counsel for the Poor People's March in Washington, DC (1968); founded Washington Research Project; served as director, Center for Law and Education, at Harvard University; founded and became president of the Children's Defense Fund (1973); wrote many books, including *The Measure of Our Success: Loving and Working for Children* (1993), *Lanterns: A Memoir of Mentors* (2000), and *I'm Your Child, God: Prayers for Children* (2002). Received Albert Schweitzer Humanitarian Prize (1987), Presidential Medal of Freedom (2000), and Robert F. Kennedy Lifetime Achievement Award (2000).

EDEN, Barbara (1934—). American tv and screen actress. Born Barbara Jean Moorhead (later used stepfather's name and was known as Barbara Jean Huffman), Aug 23, 1934, in Tucson, Arizona; m. Michael Ansara (actor), 1958 (div. 1972); m. Charles Donald Fegert, 1977 (div. 1983); m. Jon Eicholtz, 1991. ❖ Made film debut in *Back from Eternity* (1956), followed by *Flaming Star, Voyage to the Bottom of the Sea, The Interns,* and *7 Faces of Dr. Lao,* among others; on tv, starred on "How to Marry a Millionaire" (1957–59), "I Dream of Jeannie" (1965–70), and "Harper Valley P.T.A." (1981–82). ❖ See also autobiography *Barbara Eden: My Story* (1986).

EDEN, Clarissa (1920—). British journalist and prime-ministerial wife. Name variations: Clarissa Churchill; Clarissa Spencer-Churchill; Lady Avon. Born Anne Clarissa Spencer-Churchill, June 28, 1920; 3rd child and only dau. of Major John Strange Spencer-Churchill (younger brother of Winston Churchill, died 1947) and Gwendoline Theresa Mary Bertie (dau. of the 7th earl of Abingdon); m. Sir Anthony Eden (prime minister, 1955–57), Aug 14, 1952 (created 1st earl of Avon, 1961, died 1977). ❖ Worked as a journalist; during WWII, worked in the Ministry of Information on *Britansky Soyuznik,* an English-language propaganda newspaper for Russian readers, then the Foreign Office; was feature editor of the London edition of *Vogue* before becoming publicity director for filmmaker Alexander Korda.

EDEN, Emily (1797–1869). English political host and author. Born Mar 4, 1797, in London, England; died Aug 5, 1869, in London, England; dau. of William Eden, 1st Baron Auckland, and Eleanor Elliot Eden; sister of Fanny Eden and George Eden, 2nd Baron Auckland; niece of Lord Minto, early governor-general of India; never married; no children. ❖ Lived with her sister Fanny and brother George in a home that became a meeting place for Whig politicians; in India, presided weekly at official dinners, balls and "At Homes" at Government House in Calcutta; accompanied brother George, the British governor-general of India, on a 2.5-year trip through Northern India (1837–39), a 10-mile-long procession of elephants and soldiers that made up the governor-general's entourage, to impress the Indian rulers in the region with the power of British imperialism; her trenchant and witty letters to her sister describing this trip were published as *Up the Country* (1866); also captured many local rulers in sketches and paintings, which were later published as the highly praised *Portraits of the Princes and People of India;* published 1st novel, a comic work entitled *The Semi-Detached House* (1859), followed by *The Semi-Attached Couple* (1860); paintings and writings depict the splendors and hardships of life in imperial India during 1830s and 1840s. ❖ See also *Women in World History.*

EDER, Elfriede (1970—). Austrian Alpine skier. Name variations: Elfi Eder. Born Jan 5, 1970, in Leogang, Austria. ❖ Won a bronze medal for slalom at World championships (1993) and a silver medal for slalom at Lillehammer Olympics (1994).

EDERLE, Gertrude (1905–2003). American swimmer. Name variations: Trudie or Trudy Ederle. Born Gertrude Caroline Ederle, Oct 23, 1905, in New York, NY; died Nov 30, 2003, in Wyckoff, New Jersey; dau. of Henry Ederle (butcher) and Anna Ederle. ❖ The 1st woman to swim the English Channel, began career winning the Metropolitan New York Jr. 100-meter freestyle championship (1921); won bronze medals for 100-meter and 400-meter freestyle and a gold medal for 4 x 100-meter free-style relay at Paris Olympics (1924); while swimming the English Channel, broke the men's record by 2 hours with a time of 14 hours 31 minutes under horrendous conditions (1926); set many international freestyle swimming records over short and long distances, including 100 meters (1:12.5 on Oct 11, 1923), 150 yards (1:42.5 on Mar 1, 1925), 200 meters (2:45.2 on April 4, 1923), 220 yards (2:46.8 on April 4, 1923), 300 yards (3:58.4 on Feb 28, 1925), 400 meters (5:53.2 on Sept 4, 1922), 440 yards (5:54.6 on Sept 4, 1922), 500 yards (6:45.2 on Sept 4, 1922), 500 meters (7:22.2) and 880 yards (13:19.0 on Sept 4, 1922). ❖ See also *Women in World History.*

EDFLAED (c. 900–?). West Saxon nun. Born c. 900; interred at Wilton Abbey, Wiltshire, England; dau. of Edward I the Elder (c. 870–924), king of the English (r. 899–924), and Elflaed (d. 920).

EDGAR-BRUCE, Tonie (1892–1966). See Bruce, Tonie Edgar-.

EDGELL, Zee (1941—). Caribbean novelist. Born 1941 in Belize, Honduras. ❖ Worked as schoolteacher and as editor of newspaper in Belize City; traveled extensively in US, Middle East, and Africa; served as director of Women's Bureau in Belize; writings include *Beka Lamb* (1982) and *The Festival of San Joaquin* (1997).

EDGER, Kate (1857–1935). New Zealand education reformer, suffragist, and temperance reformer. Name variations: Kate Evans. Born Kate Milligan Edger, Jan 6, 1857, in Berkshire, England; died May 6, 1935, in Dunedin, New Zealand; dau. of Samuel Edger (minister) and Louisa (Harwood) Edger; University of New Zealand, BA, 1877; Canterbury College, MA, 1882; m. William Albert Evans (minister), 1890; children: 3 sons. ❖ Immigrated as a child to New Zealand (1862); became 1st woman in New Zealand to earn university degree (1877); established two major secondary schools for girls; active in suffrage movement and Women's Christian Temperance Union. ❖ See also *Dictionary of New Zealand Biography* (Vol. 2).

EDGEWORTH, Maria (1768–1849). Irish writer. Born on Jan 1, 1768, in Oxon, England; died at family estate, Edgeworthtown, in Co. Longsford, Ireland, May 22, 1849; eldest dau. of Richard Lovell Edgeworth (inventor and educator) and Anna Maria (Elers) Edgeworth; stepdau. of Honora Sneyd Edgeworth, then Elizabeth Sneyd Edgeworth; educated at a girls' boarding school in Derby, England, until 15, then at home by father; never married; no children. ❖ One of the most celebrated authors of her time, best known for her depictions of the Irish peasantry, particularly in her masterpiece *Castle Rackrent,* also made important contributions to the development of the novel, helped create a new children's literature, and made a major contribution to the history of educational thought; lost her mother at age 7; at 15, returned to Edgeworthtown, her family's estate in Ireland, which would soon become one of the most celebrated literary meccas in Europe, a transformation made possible by her collaboration with her father; with father, was a pioneer in the field of experimental education, summarizing findings in *Practical Education* (1798), among others, and becoming the most widely respected authorities on education in early 19th century; published *The Parent's Assistant,* a vol. of children's tales designed to illustrate the educational theories which transformed the fledgling field of children's literature; learned how to instruct without sacrificing art of storytelling; wrote best-known work, *Castle Rackrent* (1800), a humorous short novel about the ruinous mismanagement of an Irish estate by generations of proud but incompetent landlords; wrote several dozen vols. of children's stories, romances, plays, and novels about rural Irish life, including *Letters for Literary Ladies* (1795), *Leonora* (1806), *Tales of Fashionable Life* (6 vols., 1809, 1812), *Memoirs of Richard Lovell Edgeworth* (1820), *Helen* (1834) and *Orlandino* (1848); supervised the Edgeworthtown estate after death of father (1817). ❖ See also Elizabeth Harden, *Maria Edgeworth* (Twayne, 1984); Elisabeth Inglis-Jones, *The Great Maria: A Portrait of Maria Edgeworth* (Greenwood, 1959); James Newcomer, *Maria Edgeworth* (Bucknell U. Press, 1973); and *Women in World History.*

EDGEWORTH DAVID, Mrs. (1856–1951). See David, Caroline Edgeworth.

EDGIFU (902–951). Queen of France and countess of Meaux. Name variations: Eadgifu; Edgiva or Edgive; Ogive or Odgive d'Angleterre. Born 902 (some sources cite 896); died 951; dau. of Edward I the Elder (c. 870–924), king of the English (r. 899–924), and Elflaed (d. 920); m. Charles III the Simple (879–929), king of France (r. 898–923), in 917; m. Herbert of Vermandois, count of Meaux; children: (1st m.) Louis IV (918–954), king of France (r. 936–954).

EDGIFU (d. 968). Queen of the English. Name variations: Eadgifu; Edgiva. Born before 905; died Aug 25, 968; interred at Canterbury Cathedral, Canterbury, Kent, England; dau. of Sigehelm, ealdorman of Kent; became 2nd wife of Edward I the Elder (c. 870–924), king of the

English (r. 899–924), around 905; children: Edgifu (c. 917–?); Edburga (d. 960); Edmund I the Magnificent (921–946), king of the English (r. 939–946); Edred or Eadred (c. 923–955), king of the English (r. 946–955).

EDGIFU (c. 917–?). Queen of Arles. Born c. 917; date of death unknown; dau. of Edward I the Elder (c. 870–924), king of the English (r. 899–924), and Edgifu (d. 968); m. Louis II, prince of Aquitaine and king of Arles (some sources claim that she m. Ebalus the Bastard, count of Poitou).

EDGINTON, May (1883–1957). English playwright, screenwriter, and novelist. Born in 1883; died June 17, 1957, in Rondebosch, Cape Province, South Africa; m. Francis Evans Baily. ❖ With Frank Mandel, wrote the play *His Lady Friends;* with Rudolf Besier, wrote the plays *The Prude's Fall, The Ninth Earl,* and *Secrets;* also wrote plays *Trust Emily, For Better For Worse, Deadlock,* and *Who Knows;* adapted many of her works for the screen, including *His Supreme Moment* (from novel *World without End*), *Creation* (from novel *The Many Who Dared*), and *Three Hours* and *Adventure in Manhattan* (both from novel *Purple and Fine Linen*).

EDGITHA (c. 912–946). West Saxon princess and German empress. Name variations: Eadgyth; Edith. Born c. 912; died Jan 26, 946, in Germany; interred at St. Maurice Cathedral, Magdeburg, Germany; dau. of Edward I the Elder (c. 870–924), king of the English (r. 899–924), and Elflaed (d. 920); stepdau. of Edgifu (d. 968); half-sister of English kings Ethelstan (r. 924–939), Edmund (r. 939–946), and Eadred (r. 946–955); niece of Ethelflaed (869–918) and Elfthrith (d. 929); became 1st wife of Otto I the Great (912–973), king of Germany (936–973), Holy Roman emperor (r. 962–973), and duke of Saxony, in 929 or 930; children: son Liudolf, duke of Swabia; daughter Liutgard of Saxony (d. 953), duchess of Lorraine. (Otto also had an illeg. son William, future archbishop of Mainz, from an early liaison with a Slav woman of noble birth.) ❖ As her wedding gift, was offered the town of Magdeburg, an important commercial crossroad; after Magdeburg was destroyed by the Magyars, rebuilt the town; upon her death, was buried there. ❖ See also *Women in World History.*

EDGIVA. *Variant of Edgifu.*

EDGIVA or EDGIVE (902–951). *See Edgifu.*

EDGREN, Anne Charlotte (1849–1892). Swedish novelist, dramatist, and duchess of Cajanello. Name variations: Anne Charlotte Leffler; Anne Edgren-Leffler; Duchess di Cajanello; (pseudonym) Carlot. Born Anne Charlotte Leffler in Stockholm, Sweden, Oct 1, 1849; died in Naples, Italy, Oct 21, 1892; dau. of C.O. Leffler, sister of Gösta Mittag-Leffler (professor of mathematics at University of Stockholm); m. Gustav Edgren, 1872 (sep. c. 1884, div. 1889); m. Pasquale del Pezzo (Italian mathematician), duke of Cajanello, 1890. ❖ Prominent 19th-century Swedish writer, won an eminent position in the world of letters for her style and realistic portrayal of upper-class life, writings that typically centered around the struggle of a woman's individuality within the confines of her life; published 1st book, a collection of stories entitled *Händelsvis (By Chance)*, under pseudonym "Carlot" (1869); her drama *Skådespelerskan (The Actress)* was produced anonymously and ran for an entire winter in Stockholm (1873); followed this with *Pastorsadjunkten* (*The Curate*, 1876) and *Elfvan* (*The Elf* 1880); published 1st work under her own name, *Ur Lifvet (From Life)*, a series of realistic sketches of upper circles of Swedish society (1882), followed by a 2nd vol. of *From Life* (1883) and a 3rd (1889); also wrote *Hur Man Gör Godt (How We Do Good,* 1885) and *Kampen för Lyckan (The Struggle for Happiness,* 1888), the latter in collaboration with Sophia Kovalevskaya; other plays include *Familjelycka (Domestic Happiness)* and *En Räddande Engel (A Rescuing Angel),* her greatest dramatic success; also published *Kvinlighet och Erotik (Womanliness and Erotics,* 1890) and a biography of her close friend Sophia Kovalevskaya (1892). ❖ See also Ellen Key, *Anne Charlotte Leffler* (Stockholm, 1893); and *Women in World History.*

EDGYTH. *Variant of Edith.*

EDGYTH (fl. 7th c.). *See Edith of Aylesbury.*

EDHILD (d. 946). West Saxon princess. Name variations: Eadhild; Edhilda. Died Jan 26, 946; dau. of Edward I the Elder (c. 870–924), king of the English (r. 899–924), and Elflaed (d. 920); m. Hugh the Great, also known as Hugh the White (c. 895–956), count of Paris and duke of Burgundy, in 926. Hugh the Great's 2nd wife was Hedwig (c. 915–965).

EDIB, Halide (c. 1884–1964). *See Adivar, Halide Edib.*

EDIE, Mildred (1906–1965). *See Brady, Mildred Edie.*

EDINBURGH, duchess of. *See Marie Alexandrovna (1853–1920).*

EDINGER, Tilly (1897–1967). German-born American scientist. Born Johanna Gabrielle Ottilie Edinger in Frankfurt am Main, Germany, Nov 13, 1897; struck by an automobile near her home in Cambridge, May 26, 1967, died of injuries the following day, May 27; dau. of Ludwig Edinger (1855–1918, professor of neurology at University of Frankfurt) and Anna (Goldschmidt) Edinger; sister of Friedrich (Fritz) Edinger and Dorothea (Dora) Edinger; received doctorate from University of Frankfurt, 1921; never married; no children. ❖ Major world figure in vertebrate paleontology, who essentially established the field of paleoneurology, was appointed curator of the vertebrate collection at Frankfurt's Senckenberg Museum (1927); began to study fossil mammal brains from casts made from their cranial cavities, a new area of science for a study of the evolution of animal intelligence which earned her an international scientific reputation; published a major study of fossil brains, *Die fossilen Gehirne* (1929); as a Jew, was dismissed from the museum under the Nazi edicts (1938); arrived at Harvard in US (1940) and became a research associate at Harvard's Museum of Comparative Zoology; except for a year of teaching comparative zoology at Wellesley College, remained at the museum for the rest of her life; published the results of her investigations in a major work, *The Evolution of the Horse Brain* (1948), in which she showed that an enlarged forebrain had evolved several times, independently among advanced mammal groups, and no single evolutionary scale could be seen as embracing all of them; elected president of the Society of Vertebrate Paleontology (1964). ❖ See also *Women in World History.*

EDINGTON, Mary Ann (1897–1949). *See Ellen, Mary Ann.*

EDIP, Halide (c. 1884–1964). *See Adivar, Halide Edib.*

EDISS, Connie (1871–1934). English actress. Name variations: Connie Coutts. Born Aug 11, 1871, in Brighton, England; died April 18, 1934, in London. ❖ Made London debut as Ada Smith in *The Shop Girl* (1896), followed by *My Girl, The Silver Slipper, The Toreador, Peggy, The Sunshine Girl, The Girl on the Film, Not Likely* (revue), *Lord Richard in the Pantry,* and *Tilly of Bloomsbury;* made NY debut with Lew Fields in *The Girl Behind the Counter* (1907); films include *A Warm Corner* and *Night of the Garter;* also appeared in music halls.

EDISSA (fl. 475 BCE). *See Esther.*

EDITH. *Variant of Edgitha.*

EDITH (d. 871). Abbess of Pellesworth. Name variations: Editha, abbess of Polesworth. Died 871; interred at Polesworth Abbey, Warwickshire; dau. of Ecgbert also known as Egbert III (c. 775–839), king of Wessex, Kent, and the English (r. 802–839), and Redburga; sister of Ethelwulf (Æthelwulf), king of Wessex and England (r. 839–858); Ethelstan (d. around 851), king of Kent.

EDITH (c. 912–946). *See Edgitha.*

EDITH (d. 937). Queen of York and abbess of Pellesworth. Name variations: Saint Edith; abbess of Polesworth. Died 937; illeg. dau. of Edward I the Elder, king of the English (r. 899–924), and Ecgwynn (d. around 901); m. Sihtric, king of York, Jan 30, 926 (some sources cite July 30, 925), in Tamworth, Staffordshire, England; children: Amlaib; Gofraid; Olaf Cuarán, king of Dublin and York; possibly Gyda. ❖ Following death of husband, became a nun at Pellesworth Abbey, then transferred to Tamworth Abbey in Gloucestershire where she was elected abbess; canonized as a saint. Feast day is July 15.

EDITH (c. 961–984). West Saxon nun and saint. Name variations: Saint Edith; Eadgyth. Born c. 961 in Kemsing, Kent, England; died Sept 16, 984, in Wilton, Wiltshire, England; illeg. dau. of Edgar (944–975), king of the English (r. 959–975), and Wulfthryth (c. 945–1000, his mistress). ❖ Was raised in the monastery of Wilton, where mother had retired to, and took the veil; remained in the monastery until her death, at 23. Feast day is Sept 16. ❖ See also *Women in World History.*

EDITH (fl. 1009). West Saxon princess. Fl. 1009; dau. of Aethelred or Ethelred II the Unready (c. 968–1016), king of the English (r. 979–1013, deposed, 1014–1016), and Elfgifu (c. 963–1002); m. Eadric or Edric Streona, ealdorman of Mercia (r. 1007–1017), 1009 (executed, Dec 25, 1017); m. Thurkil the Tall; children: (1st m.) daughter (name unknown, who m. Ethelgar and was the mother of Siward and Ealdred); (2nd m.) Harold.

EDITH (c. 1025–1075). Queen of the English. Name variations: Ealdgyth; Eadgyth; Edgyth. Born c. 1025; died Dec 18, 1075, in Winchester, Hampshire, England; interred at Westminster Abbey; dau. of Godwin or Godwine (d. 1053), earl of Wessex, and Gytha; sister of Harald or Harold II Godwineson (c. 1022–1066), king of the English (r. 1066); m. Edward III the Confessor (c. 1002–1066), king of the English (r. 1042–1066), Jan 23, 1045; children: none. ❖ On marriage, received Winchester and Exeter as her morning gift; is said to have planned the murder of Gospatric, one of the king's thegns (1064), at instigation of her brother Tostig, earl of Northumberland; founded a church at Wilton (1065), and on the death of her husband retired there.

EDITH (fl. 1040). Lady Allerdale. Name variations: Ealdgyth. Dau. of Uchtred, earl of Northumberland, and Elfgifu (dau. of Ethelred II the Unready); m. Maldred Dunkeld (brother of Duncan I, king of Scotland), lord of Allerdale; children: Gospatric Dunkeld (b. around 1040), earl of Northumberland; Maldred of Allerdale.

EDITH (fl. 1063). Queen of the English. Name variations: Aldgyth; Algytha; Eadgyth; Ealdgyth. Flourished around 1063; died after 1070; dau. of Aelfgar or Elfgar, earl of Mercia, and Elfgifu (dau. of Morcar and Ealdgyth); m. Griffith also known as Gruffydd ap Llywelyn, ruler of All Wales, around 1050 (killed in 1063); m. Harald or Harold II Godwineson (c. 1022–1066), king of the English (r. 1066), Jan 1066, in London; children: (1st m.) Nesta Ferch; Maredudd, king of Powys; Ithell; (2nd m.) Harold (b. 1066). ❖ Following death of husband at the hands of his own people, married Harold II Godwineson, king of England. When Harold died at the Battle of Hastings (Oct 1066), it was another woman sometimes called Edith, his mistress Eadgyth Swanneshals, who identified his body. ❖ See also *Women in World History.*

EDITH MATILDA (1080–1118). *See Matilda of Scotland.*

EDITH OF AYLESBURY (fl. 7th c.). English nun. Name variations: Saint Edith of Aylesbury; Ealdgyth or Edgyth. Born in Mercia; flourished in mid-7th century; dau. of Penda of Mercia, pagan warrior king, and Cynewise; sister of Wilburga and Edburga of Bicester. ❖ With sister, built a monastery at Aylesbury in Buckinghamshire where they educated their niece St. Osith.

EDITH OF THE SWAN'S NECK (c. 1012–?). *See Eadgyth Swanneshals.*

EDLA (fl. 900s). Swedish mistress. Paramour of Olof or Olaf Sköttkonung or Skötkonung, king of Sweden (r. 994–1022); children: Emund the Old, king of Sweden (r. 1050–1060); Astrid Olafsdottir. Olaf's wife was Astrid of the Obotrites (c. 979–?). ❖ See also *Women in World History.*

EDMOND, Lauris (1924–2000). New Zealand playwright. Name variations: Lauris Dorothy Edmond. Born 1924 in Dannevirke, New Zealand; died Jan 28, 2000. ❖ Worked as speech therapist and English teacher; co-founded Peppercorn Press and served as its poetry editor; writings include *In Middle Air* (1975), *The Pear Tree* (1977), *Wellington Letter: A Sequence of Poems* (1980), *Salt from the North* (1980), *Catching It: Poems* (1983), *Seasons and Creatures* (1986), *Summer Near the Arctic Circle* (1988), *Hot October* (1989), *Bonfires in the Rain* (1991), *An Autobiography* (1994), *Carnival of New Zealand Creatures* (2000), and *Late Song* (2000). Received Katherine Mansfield Memorial Fellowship and Commonwealth Poetry Prize; made OBE.

EDMOND, Wendy (1946—). Australian politician. Name variations: Hon. Wendy Marjorie Edmond. Born April 27, 1946, in Bundaberg, Queensland, Australia. ❖ Began career as a nuclear medicine technologist; as a member of the Australian Labor Party, elected to the Queensland Parliament for Mount Coot-tha (1989); named minister for Health (1998) and minister assisting the premier on Women's Policy (2001).

EDMONDS, Ann (1917–2002). *See Welch, Ann.*

EDMONDS, Emma (1841–1898). Canadian-American nurse and soldier. Name variations: Sarah Edwards; Sarah Emma Evelyn Edmonson; Emma Edmonds; Frank Thompson; Mrs. Sarah Emma E. Seelye. Born Sarah Emma Evelyn Edmonson in Magaguadavic, New Brunswick province, Canada, Dec 1841; died Sept 5, 1898, in La Porte, Texas; dau. of Isaac Edmonson (farmer) and Elizabeth (Betsy) Leeper; attended Oberlin College in Oberlin, Ohio; m. Linus H. Seely (an "e" was added after marriage, creating "Seelye"), April 27, 1867; children: Linus B., Homer, Alice Louise; (adopted) George Frederick, Charles Finney. ❖ Disguised

as a man, joined the Union Army at the outbreak of the American Civil War (1860), serving as a male nurse with the 2nd regiment of Michigan Volunteers; served as a dispatch bearer, then became a spy for the Federal Secret Service, infiltrating the Rebel lines at Yorktown, later infiltrating Rebel headquarters, obtaining information on troop numbers and locations; took part in many battles, including the 2nd Battle of Bull Run, and served as a nurse during the Battle of Antietam; served as orderly to General Poe; though injured, avoided medical care for fear of exposing her gender; was praised as a "strong, healthy and robust soldier" throughout her varied military service; when her health continued to decline and she was under more pressure to seek medical treatment, went "AWOL" from the army (April 1863); following military service, published memoirs, *Nurse and Spy in the Union Army* which became a bestseller at 175,000 copies. ❖ See also Sylvia G.L. Dannett, *She Rode With the Generals* (Nelson, 1960); Bryna Stevens, *Frank Thompson: Her Civil War Story* (Macmillan, 1992); Marian Talmadge and Iris Gilmore, *Emma Edmonds; Nurse and Spy* (Putnam, 1970); and *Women in World History.*

EDMONDS, Helen Woods (1901–1968). *See Kavan, Anna.*

EDMONDS, Sarah (1841–1898). *See Edmonds, Emma.*

EDMONDSON, Barbara Ann (1947—). *See Ferrell, Barbara.*

EDMONDSTONE, Isabel (d. ca. 1410). *See Stewart, Isabel.*

EDMONSON, Sarah E.E. (1841–1898). *See Edmonds, Emma.*

EDMONTON GRADS (1915–1940). Most successful basketball team in Canadian history. Fl. 1915 to 1940. ❖ Edmonton Grads, Alberta, Canada (1915–40), won 502 out of 522 games, competed in 27 games in 4 Olympics, participated in 13 Canadian ladies championships, winning them all, and triumphed in 114 of the 120 games played for the Underwood Trophy (North American championship in ladies' basketball); also played 9 official games against men's teams, winning all but 2. ❖ See also *Women in World History.*

EDMUNDS, Christiana (1835–1907). English poisoner. Born 1835 in England; died in Broadmoor Prison for the Criminally Insane, 1907. ❖ Came from family with mental illness on both sides; fell in love with her married doctor, Dr. Beard, and sent poisoned chocolates (some sources cite cakes) to his wife (Aug 10, 1871), who survived; began employing errand boys to purchase chocolate creams for her; laced these with strychnine and then had boys return them to confectioner, who unknowingly sold them to other customers (4-year-old Sidney Miller died from eating the poisoned sweets); tried for murder of Miller (Jan 1872), found guilty and received death sentence which was commuted to life imprisonment.

EDMUNDS, Elizabeth M. (c. 1941—). American nun, naval officer, and doctor. Name variations: Sister Elizabeth M. Edmunds. Born c. 1941, in Shamokin, Pennsylvania. ❖ As member of the order of the Sisters of Mercy, was the 1st nun to be commissioned as a US Navy officer (lieutenant, 1973); interned (1975) and served as resident at Good Samaritan Hospital, Dayton, OH (1976–78); established family-medicine practice in Reading, PA.

EDNEY, Patience (1911–1996). *See Darton, Patience.*

EDONNE (fl. 8th c.). Queen of the Franks. Married Childebert III (683–711), king of all Franks (r. 695–711).

EDSON, Katherine Philips (1870–1933). American reformer. Born Katherine Philips, Jan 12, 1870, in Kenton, Ohio; died Nov 5, 1933, in Pasadena, California; dau. of William Hunter Philips (surgeon) and Harriet J. Carlin; attended Academy of the Sacred Heart in Clifton, Ohio; studied voice at Chicago music conservatory; m. Charles Farwell Edson (singer, musician and teacher), Oct 8, 1890 (div. 1925); children: Katharine (b. 1892), Philips Josiah (b. 1896) and Charles Farwell (b. 1905). ❖ Active on behalf of woman suffrage, municipal reform, and health issues, worked on the suffrage campaign which successfully won the vote in California (1911); elected to the Los Angeles Charter Revision Commission; was also the 1st woman named to executive committee of National Municipal League (1911); appointed to state central committee of Progressive Party; served as special agent of California Bureau of Labor Statistics (1912); proposed legislation for wage-and-hour reform which was passed (1913); during WWI, served as government mediator and arbiter; appointed to advisory committee on arms limitation by President Harding (1921); served on national board of League of Women Voters (1932–33).

EDSON, N.I. (1826–1911). *See Denison, Mary Andrews.*

EDSTROM, Sonja. Swedish cross-country skier. Name variations: Sonja Edström; Sonja Ruthstrom or Ruthström. Born Sonja Edström in Sweden. ❖ Won bronze medals for 10 km and 3 x 5 km relay at Cortina Olympics (1956); won a gold medal for 3 x 5 km relay at Squaw Valley Olympics (1960).

EDUARDOVA, Eugenia (1882–1980). Russian ballet dancer and teacher. Born 1882 in St. Petersburg, Russia; died Dec 10, 1980, in New York, NY. ❖ Danced with the Maryinksy Ballet (1901–17), where she performed in numerous Petipa ballets, including *Esmeralda, Sleeping Beauty*, and *Halte de Cavalrie;* danced with Anna Pavlova's company; moved to Berlin, where she served as ballet master of Grosse Volksoper and opened own dance studio; forced to leave country (1935), taught briefly in Paris, before moving to US; trained many successful dancers, including Vera Zorina, Alexander von Swaine, Georges Skibini and Yuri Algaroff.

EDVINA, Louise (1878–1948). Canadian soprano. Born Lucienne Juliette Martin, May 28, 1878, in Montreal, Canada; died in London, England, Nov 13, 1948; studied voice with Jean de Reszke; m. James Matthews Buxton, 1898 (died); m. Honorable Cecil Edwardes, 1901 (died); m. Major Nicholas Rothesay Stuart Wortley, 1919 (died). ❖ Made debut as Marguerite in *Faust* at Covent Garden (1908), then performed in Paris, Brussels, Stockholm, Monte Carlo, Chicago, Boston and Montreal; debuted at Metropolitan Opera (1915); made 6 recordings for HMV (1921), including her admired portrayals of Louise and Tosca, which were reissued; retired in Cannes (1926).

EDWARDS, Amelia B. (1831–1892). English author and Egyptologist. Born Amelia Ann Blandford Edwards in London, England, June 7, 1831; died of influenza in Weston-super-Mare, Somersetshire, England, April 15, 1892; dau. of one of the duke of Wellington's officers; cousin of Matilda Barbara Betham-Edwards (1836–1919); educated at home by mother; studied music under Mrs. Mounsey Bartholomew; never married; no children. ❖ At early age, displayed considerable literary and artistic talent; became a contributor to various magazines and newspapers and wrote 8 novels, the most successful of which were *Debenham's Vow* (1870) and *Lord Brackenbury* (1880); visited Egypt (1873–74); learned hieroglyphics and accumulated a considerable collection of Egyptian antiquities; wrote and illustrated *A Thousand Miles up the Nile* (1877), the most comprehensive book on the subject of Egyptian history and hieroglyphics at the time; was largely instrumental in founding the Egypt Exploration Fund (1882), of which she became joint honorary secretary with Reginald Stuart Poole; published *Pharaohs, Fellahs, and Explorers* (1891); bequeathed her valuable collection of Egyptian antiquities to University College, London, together with a sum to found a chair of Egyptology.

EDWARDS, Edna Park (c. 1895–1967). American screen actress. Born c. 1895; died June 5, 1967, age 72, in Hollywood, California. ❖ Child actress who became a leading lady for Tom Mix; retired from the screen and wrote for radio.

EDWARDS, Gloria (1944–1988). African-American actress. Born Aug 7, 1944, in California; died Feb 12, 1988, in Los Angeles, California. ❖ On Broadway, appeared in *What the Wine Sellers Buy* and *Ain't Supposed to Die a Natural Death;* appeared off-Broadway in *Showdown, In New England Winter, One*, and *Black Girl;* performed in film, *Black Girl* (1972).

EDWARDS, Henrietta Muir (1849–1933). Canadian journalist, suffragist, and organizer. Name variations: often listed as one of the Alberta Five also known as the Famous Five. Born Henrietta Muir in Montreal, Quebec, Canada, Dec 19, 1849; died 1933; m. Dr. Oliver C. Edwards, 1876. ❖ As an acclaimed painter of florals and miniatures, founded the Working Girls' Association in Montreal (forerunner of the YWCA, 1875); moved with husband to Fort Qu'Appelle, Saskatchewan (1883), then Ottawa (1890); helped to found the National Council of Women and the Victoria Order of Nurses with Lady Ishbel Aberdeen; moved to Fort Macleod where she compiled a handbook on the legal status of women in Alberta (1903); in later years, acted as the convenor of laws for the National Council of Women and the president of the Alberta Provincial Council; along with Emily Murphy, Nellie McClung, Louise McKinney, and Irene Parlby, launched a court case challenging the historical prohibition of women holding public office which became known as the "persons" case. ❖ See also *Women in World History.*

EDWARDS, India (1895–1990). American political party leader. Born in Chicago, Illinois, 1895; died 1990; moved to Nashville, Tennessee, as a child; attended school in St. Louis, Missouri; married a man named Moffett, 1924 (div. 1931); m. Herbert Edwards (chief of international motion pictures div. of the International Information and Cultural Affairs of the Department of State), 1942; children: (1st m.) India Moffett; John Holbrook Moffett (killed in action, 1944). ❖ Following a 20-year stint as an editorial staff member of the *Chicago Tribune* (1915–42), joined the Democratic National Committee (1944); held the post of executive director of the women's division of the Democratic National Committee; during her tenure, helped to organize a nationwide campaign to publicize the importance of the UN and was effective during the 1948 reelection campaign for Harry S. Truman; following his election, successfully lobbied the president to appoint women to public office, including Georgia Neese Clark, 1st female treasurer of the US, Eugenia Anderson, 1st female ambassador, and Perle Mesta, minister to Luxemburg. ❖ See also *Women in World History.*

EDWARDS, Margaret (1939—). English swimmer. Born Mar 28, 1939, in Great Britain. ❖ Won a bronze medal in the backstroke at the Melbourne Olympics (1956).

EDWARDS, Matilda Betham (1836–1919). See *Betham-Edwards, Matilda.*

EDWARDS, Penny (1928–1998). American actress. Born Millicent Maxine Edwards, Aug 24, 1928, in Jackson Heights, NY; died Aug 26, 1998, in Friendswood, Texas; m. Ralph Winters (casting director); children: Deborah Winters (actress). ❖ Began career as a child actress on NY stage; made film debut in *My Wild Irish Rose* (1947); starred opposite Roy Rogers in many Republic films.

EDWARDS, Sarah (1841–1898). See *Edmonds, Emma.*

EDWARDS, Sarah Pierpont (1710–1758). American mystic. Born Sarah Pierpont, Jan 9, 1710, in New Haven, Connecticut; died Oct 2, 1758, in Philadelphia, Pennsylvania; dau. of James Pierpont (pastor and co-founder of Yale College) and Mary Hooker (granddau. of Reverend Thomas Hooker who founded Hartford); m. Jonathan Edwards (pastor), 1727; children: Sarah, Jerusha, Esther, Mary, Lucy, Timothy, Susannah, Eunice, Jonathan, Elizabeth and Pierpont Edwards. ❖ Puritan mystic, known for her piety and beauty, married Yale graduate and pastor Jonathan Edwards (1727); moved to Northampton parsonage with husband and participated in Northampton revivals (1738), experiencing ecstasies similar to those of St. Teresa of Avila and recording experiences in diary; followed husband to posting in Stockbridge (MA) parsonage and Indian mission, at edge of frontier; a practical pioneer woman, lived resourcefully and fearlessly while caring for 11 children; made home center of hospitality, welcoming guests and caring for soldiers quartered in barracks; had good relations with Native Americans of area as well. ❖ See also Edna Gerstner, *Jonathan and Sarah: An Uncommon Union* (Soli Deo Gloria, 1995).

EDWARDS, Suzanne Zimmerman (b. 1925). See *Zimmerman, Suzanne.*

EDWARDS, Teresa (1964—). African-American basketball player. Born July 19, 1964, in Cairo, Georgia. ❖ Won four team gold medals (1984, 1988, 1996, 2000) and a bronze medal (1992) at Olympic Games; won two gold medals (1986 and 1990) and a bronze medal at World championships (1984); won a gold medal (1987) and bronze medal (1991) at Pan American Games; won two gold medals at Goodwill Games (1986 and 1990); was twice named All-American (1985–86) and USA Basketball Female Athlete of the Year (1987 and 1990); played for Atlanta Glory in the American Basketball League. ❖ See also Christina Lessa, *Women Who Win* (Universe, 1998).

EDWARDS, Torri (1977—). African-American runner. Born Jan 31, 1977, in Fontana, CA. ❖ Won a bronze medal for 4 x 100-meter relay at Sydney Olympics (2000); received a 2-year ban for doping (Aug 2004).

EDWARDS, Tracey (1962—). English yacht racer. Born Sept 5, 1962, in Reading, England. ❖ Renowned sailor, raised over £1 million at age 22 to form Maiden Great Britain Ltd. (1986), which later became Tracey Edwards Associates, dedicated to entering all-woman crews in sailing events; entered boat *Maiden* in 9-month Whitbread Round the World Race with 1st all-woman crew (1990), winning 2 legs and coming in 2nd in class, the best result for a British boat since 1977; organized 2nd all-female crew, raised sponsorship and put together 1st major multi-hull project in Britain, breaking female trans-Atlantic record and male Australia-to-New Zealand record, as well as Channel record which was smashed by average speed of 22.7 knots; was forced to cut short round-the-world attempt when catamaran ran into storm conditions in dangerous waters, losing rig 2,300 miles from nearest land and building makeshift mast which enabled 16-day sail to safety in Chile; created division of company, Tracey Edwards Associates Motivation (1997), which runs leadership and teamwork training seminars; landed biggest sponsorship deal in yachting history, securing £38 million from Qatar in 4-year deal to build new yacht and create 2 round-the-world races. Became 1st woman to receive Yachtsman of the Year Trophy and was awarded MBE for achievements. ❖ See also Tim Madge, *Tracey Edwards: Living Every Second* (Virgin, 2001).

EDWARDS, Valaida (c. 1903–1956). *See Snow, Valaida.*

EFFLATOUN, Inji (1923–1989). *Egyptian feminist and painter.* Name variations: Inge Aflatun. Born in Cairo, 1923, into a family of land-owners; died 1989; sister of Gulpérie Efflatoun Abdalla; introduced to Marxist ideas as a student at a French lycée in Cairo. ❖ A painter, became active in the Communist Party and agitated for women's rights as well as freedom from colonial rule; was imprisoned (1959–64), where she continued to paint, producing such works as *Prison 126* (1960). ❖ See also *Women in World History.*

EFIMOVA, Nina Simonovich (b. 1877). *See Simonovich-Efimova, Nina.*

EFTEDAL, Siri (1966—). *Norwegian handball player.* Born May 22, 1966. ❖ At Barcelona Olympics, won a silver medal in team competition (1992).

EFTHRYTH (d. 929). *See Elfthrith.*

EFUA KOBIRI (fl. 1834–1884). *See Afua Koba.*

EGA, Françoise (1920–1976). *Martiniquan novelist.* Name variations: Francoise Ega. Born 1920 in Martinique; died 1976. ❖ Moved to France (1946) and joined French Air Force; worked in Indochina, Djibouti, and Madagascar; wrote *Les Temps de Madras* (1966) and *Lettres à une Noire* (1978).

EGAMI, Ayano. *Japanese synchronized swimmer.* Born in Japan. ❖ Won a team silver medal at Sydney Olympics (2000).

EGAMI, Yumi (1957—). *Japanese volleyball player.* Born Nov 30, 1957. ❖ At Los Angeles Olympics, won a bronze medal in team competition (1984).

EGERIA (fl. 4th c.). *Christian letter writer.* Name variations: Aetheria, Aiheria or Etheria. Born possibly in northwestern Spain, possibly in the Rhone area of Gaul; strongest evidence says she flourished in the 380s. ❖ Extant fragments of Latin diary describe her 3-year pilgrimage to Jerusalem (*Itinerarium Egeriae*); may have been a Spanish nun.

EGERSZEGI, Krisztina (1974—). *Hungarian swimmer.* Born Aug 16, 1974, in Budapest, Hungary. ❖ At European championships, won a gold medal (1988); won a silver medal for 100-meter backstroke and a gold for 200-meter backstroke at Seoul Olympics (1988); won 2 World titles, breaking world records at 100- and 200-meter backstroke (1991); won gold medals for 400-meter indiv. medley, 200-meter backstroke, and 100-meter backstroke at Barcelona Olympics (1992), the youngest-ever triple champion; won a gold medal for the 200-meter backstroke and a bronze medal for 400-meter indiv. medley at Atlanta Olympics (1996).

EGERTON, George (1857–1945). *See Bright, Mary Golding.*

EGERTON, Sarah Fyge (c. 1670–1723). *British poet.* Name variations: Sarah Fyge; Mrs. Egerton; Mrs. Field or Mrs. Sarah Field; S.F.E.; Clarinda. Born Sarah Fyge, c. 1670, in London, England; died Feb 13, 1723 (some sources cite 1722), in Buckinghamshire, England; dau. of Thomas Fyge and Mary (Beecham or Beacham) Fyge; m. Edward Field, 1687; m. Thomas Egerton, 1690s. ❖ Considered proto-feminist for *The Female Advocate* and for polemic against failure to educate women; entered 2 marriages against her will and became embroiled in public but unsuccessful divorce suit with Egerton; wrote *The Female Advocate: Or, An Answer to A Late Satyr Against the Pride, Lust and Inconstancy of Woman. Written by a Lady in Vindication of her Sex* (1686) in reply to Robert Gould's attack on women (1683); contributed poems to *Luctus Britannici* (1700) and to *The Nine Muses: Or, Poems Written by Nine Several Ladies Upon the Death of the Late Famous John Dryden* (1700).

EGERVÁRI, Márti (1956—). *Hungarian gymnast.* Name variations: Marta or Marti Egervari. Born Aug 1956 in Hungary. ❖ At World championships, won a bronze medal for team all-around (1974); won Hungarian Internationals (1975, 1976); at World Cup, won a bronze medal in all-around and a silver in balance beam (1975) and a bronze in vault (1977); at Montreal Olympics, won a bronze medal in the uneven bars (1976). ❖ See also *Women in World History.*

EGGAR, Samantha (1938—). *English actress.* Born Victoria Samantha Eggar, Mar 5, 1938, in London, England; m. Tom Stern, 1964 (div. 1971). ❖ Appeared on stage in England; made film debut in *The Wild and the Willing* (1961), followed by *Return from the Ashes, Doctor in Distress, Walk Don't Run, Doctor Dolittle, The Molly Maguires, The Lady in the Car with Glasses and a Gun, The Walking Stick, The Light at the Edge of the World, The Seven Percent Solution,* and *Why Shoot the Teacher?,* among others; on tv, co-starred with Yul Brynner as Anna Owens in "Anna and the King" (1972), as Pamela Capwell Conrad in "Santa Barbara" (1987), as Diana Westley in the miniseries "The Secret of Lake Success" (1993), and as Charlotte Devane on "All My Children" (2000). Named Best Actress at Cannes and nominated for an Oscar for performance in *The Collector* (1965).

EGGER, Sabine (1977—). *Austrian Alpine skier.* Born April 22, 1977, in Klagenfurt, Austria. ❖ Placed 5th in slalom at Nagano Olympics (1998) and 4th at World championships (2001); won World Cup in slalom (1998–99).

EGGERTH, Marta (1912—). *Hungarian actress and singer.* Name variations: Mártha Eggerth; Martha Eggerth Kiepura; Marta Eggerth-Kiepura. Born April 17, 1912, in Budapest, Hungary; m. Jan Kiepura (Polish tenor and actor), 1936 (died 1966). ❖ At 11, made stage debut in *The Tales of Hoffmann;* starred in many operettas in Germany and Austria (1930s); after the Anschluss, emigrated from Austria to US (1938); resumed career in Europe following WWII; films include *Der Draufgänger, Bridegroom for Two, Where is the Lady?, Kaiserwalzer, Unfinished Symphony, My Heart is Calling, Casta Diva, Die Blonde Carmen, Das Schloss in Flandern, The Charm of La Bohème, For Me and My Gal, Presenting Lily Mars, Addio Mimi, Das Land des Lächelns* and *Frühling in Berlin.*

EGLAH (fl. 1000 BCE). *Biblical woman.* One of David's wives and mother of his son, Ithream (2 Sam. 3:5; 1 Chr. 3:3). ❖ See also *Women in World History.*

EGLEVSKY, Leda (1915–1989). *See Anchutina, Leda.*

EGMONT, countess of. *See Anna of Egmont (1533–1558).*

EGNOT, Leslie (1963—). *New Zealand yacht racer.* Born Feb 28, 1963, in South Carolina; moved to New Zealand (1973); grew up in Christchurch; sister of Jenny Egnot (sailor); Canterbury University, BA; married. ❖ At Barcelona Olympics, won a silver medal in 470 class (1992); was New Zealand's Women's 470 champion (1985–95) and NZ's Women's keelboat champion (1990, 1991, 1993); won World keelboat championship (1990); also active in Squash and volleyball.

EGOROVA, Irina (1940—). *See Yegorova, Irina.*

EGOROVA, Ludmila (1931—). *See Yegorova, Lyudmila.*

EGOROVA, Lyubov (1880–1972). *Russian ballet dancer and teacher.* Name variations: Lubov or Ljubov Egorova. Born Aug 8, 1880, in St. Petersburg, Russia; died July 18, 1972, in Paris, France. ❖ Trained at school of Imperial ballet in St. Petersburg, Russia; joined Maryinsky Ballet and was featured in numerous classical works, including *Swan Lake, Raymonda,* and *The Sleeping Beauty;* appeared in London with Diaghilev Ballet Russe in role of Lilac Fairy in *The Sleeping Beauty* (1921); retired from performance career (1923) and moved to Paris, where she taught most of the period's notable dancers including André Eglevsky, Janine Charrat, and Igor Youskevitch; founded and directed Les Ballets de la Jeunesse in Paris, where she staged original works as well as numerous Petipa classics. Choreographed works include *La Flamme* (1932), *Visiones Juveniles* (1939), *Afternoon in the Park* (1939) and *Aurora's Wedding* (1949).

EGOROVA, Lyubov (1966—). *Russian cross-country skier.* Name variations: Ljubov or Ljubova Yegorova or Jegorova. Born May 5, 1966, in Tomsk, Russia. ❖ Won silver medals in the 5 km and 30 km and gold medals in the 10 km, 15 km, and 4 x 5 km relay at Albertville Olympics (1992); won a silver medal in the 15 km and gold medals in the 5 km, 10 km, and 4 x 5 km relay at Lillehammer Olympics (1994); at the World championships (1997), won a gold medal in the 5 km but tested positive for doping. ❖ See also *Women in World History.*

EGRESI, Vilma (1936–1979). *Hungarian kayaker.* Born May 7, 1936, in Hungary; died Jan 7, 1979. ❖ At Rome Olympics, won a bronze medal in K2 500 meters (1960).

EGRI, Susanna (1926—). *Hungarian-born ballet dancer and choreographer.* Born Feb 18, 1926, in Budapest, Hungary; trained with Ferenc

Nadési and Sári Bercsik at ballet school of Royal Opera House in Budapest. ❖ One of the leading choreographers in Italy, appeared at opera houses and theaters in Milan, Venice, Turin, and Florence (late 1940s); choreographed opera works for Italian tv, RAI (starting 1949), which were often shown as feature-length films in US and Western Europe; founded own company, I Balletti di Susanna Egri (1953), which later became The EgriBiancoDanza Company (1999), one of Italy's most important dance companies; helped establish renowned Dance Study Center, later developed into Jolanda and Susanna Egri Foundation (1998); served as dancer, choreographer, company director and president of Foundation Centro di Studio della Danza Jolanda e Susanna Egri; served as vice-president of Conseil International de la Danse (UNESCO); received numerous awards, including Prix Italia TV (1963), Viotti d'Oro (1980) and Prix Positano (1999). Works of choreography include *Instananne* (1954), *Chagaliana* for RAI (1954), *Incontro* (1957), *The Four Seasons* (1961) and *Jazz-Play* (1964).

EGUAL, Maria (1698–1735). Spanish playwright. Name variations: Doña Maria Egual. Born 1698 in Castellón, Spain; died 1735 in Valencia, Spain. ❖ Wrote 2 musical comedies, *Los prodigios de Thesalia* and *Triunfo de amor en el aire.*

EGYPT, queen of.
See Mer-neith (fl. c. 3100 BCE).
See Hatshepsut (c. 1515–1468 BCE).
See Tiy (c. 1400–1340 BCE).
See Mutnedjmet (c. 1360–1326 BCE).
See Berenice I (c. 345–275 BCE).
See Arsinoe II Philadelphus (316–270 BCE).
See Berenice II of Cyrene (c. 273–221 BCE).
See Arsinoe III (fl. c. 250–210/05 BCE).
See Cleopatra I (c. 210–176 BCE).
See Cleopatra II (c. 183–116 BCE).
See Cleopatra III (c. 155–101 BCE).
See Cleopatra IV (c. 135–112 BCE).
See Cleopatra Selene (c. 130–69 BCE).
See Cleopatra Berenice III (c. 115–80 BCE).
See Berenice IV (d. 55 BCE).
See Cleopatra VII (69–30 BCE).
See Nazli (1894–1978).
See Nariman (1934–2005).

E. H.
See Hands, Elizabeth (fl. 1789).
See Bethell, Mary Ursula (1874–1945).

EHRE, Ida (1900–1989). German-Jewish actress and theater director. Born in Prerau, Moravia, Austria-Hungary (now Prerov, Czech Republic), July 9, 1900; died in Hamburg, Germany, Feb 16, 1989; trained at Vienna's Academy for Music and the Performing Arts; m. Bernhard Heyde (physician), 1928; children: Ruth Heyde. ❖ A survivor of the Holocaust, was one of only a small number of Jews who chose to remain in Germany after 1945; began professional acting career (1918) in provincial Austrian theaters, appearing in the title role in Goethe's *Iphigenie*; advanced to leading theaters in Bonn, Königsberg, Mannheim and Stuttgart, becoming one of the star performers at Berlin's Lessing Theater; during WWII, incarcerated in a prison camp near Hamburg; after the war, founded the Hamburger Kammerspiele, one of West Germany's most innovative theaters, and became one of the best known and most respected theater personalities in West Germany. ❖ See also *Women in World History.*

EHRENGARDE MELUSINA VON DER SCHULENBURG, baroness Schulenburg (1667–1743). See *Schulenburg, Ehrengard Melusina von der.*

EHRENREICH, Barbara (1941—). American critic and essayist. Born Aug 26, 1941; attended Reed College; Rockefeller University, PhD in biology. ❖ Social critic and essayist, was a regular columnist for *Time* magazine (1991–97); wrote the bestseller *Nickel and Dimed* (2002); often writes an op-ed column for the *New York Times* and is a frequent contributor to *The Progressive*; served as vice chair of the Democratic Socialists of America; also wrote *Fear of Falling* (1989), *The Worst Years of Our Lives* (1990), *Blood Rites* (1991) and *The Snarling Citizen* (1995).

EHRENSVÄRD, Thomasine Gyllembourg (1773–1856). See *Gyllembourg-Ehrensvärd, Thomasine.*

EHRET, Gloria (1941—). American golfer. Name variations: Gloria Jean Ehret. Born Aug 23, 1941, in Allentown, Pennsylvania. ❖ Joined LPGA tour (1965); won LPGA championship (1966); won the Birmingham (1973); played on Senior Women's Golf tour.

EHRHARDT, Anneliese (1950—). East German hurdler. Born June 18, 1950. ❖ At Munich Olympics, won a gold medal in the 100-meter hurdles (1972).

EHRIG, Andrea (b. 1961). See *Schöne, Andrea Mitscherlich.*

EHRLICH, Aline (1928–1991). German freshwater biologist and geologist. Name variations: Aline Buchbinder. Born Aline Buchbinder, Dec 26, 1928, in Berlin, Germany; died Feb 5, 1991; married a man named Ehrlich. ❖ Expert in diatoms, studied zoology, botany, and geology at University of Paris' Faculty of Sciences; worked as biology teacher; conducted research at University of Paris' Geological Department; proficient in German, French, English, Hebrew, and Russian, worked for Geological Survey in Israel (1969–89), where she studied diatom distribution and created an atlas of the diatoms of Israel.

EHRLICH, Ida Lublenski (d. 1986). Russian-born playwright, producer and author. Born in Russia; died Feb 22, 1986, age 99, in Carmel, California. ❖ First play, *Helena's Boys*, produced on Broadway (1924); other plays include *Dr. Johnson, The Magic Carpet*, and *Alice in Fableland*; founded off-Broadway's Everyman's Theater (1940).

EHRLICH, Martha (1899–1923). See *Mansfield, Martha.*

EHRMANN, Marianne (1755–1795). Swiss journalist, novelist and editor. Name variations: Marianne Brentano Ehrmann. Born Marianne Brentano, Nov 25, 1755, in Rapperswil, Switzerland; died Aug 14, 1795, in Stuttgart, Germany; dau. of Franz Xaver Brentano (buyer) and Sebastiana Antonia Corti; niece of Dominik Brentano; briefly married, c. 1777; m. Theophil Friedrich Ehrmann (jurist and writer), 1781. ❖ Worked as governess and actress; helped husband run journal and began publishing poems and fiction in magazines; writings, which challenge traditional notions of womanhood, include *Amalie, eine wahre Geschichte in Briefen* (2 vols, 1787), and *Antonie von Warnstein: Eine Geschichte aus enserem Zeitalter* (2 vols, 1796–98); founded women's magazines, *Amaliens Erholungsstunden* and *Die Einsiedlerin aus den Alpen.*

EIBENSCHÜTZ-DERNBOURG, Ilona (1872–1967). Hungarian pianist. Name variations: Ilona Eibenschütz. Born in Budapest, Hungary, May 8, 1872; died in London, England, May 21, 1967. ❖ As one of the students of Clara Schumann, passed on the unique style of piano playing that could be traced back to early 19th century when the instrument evolved; was directly exposed to thinking of Johannes Brahms, friend and close associate of Schumann's; played many of Brahms' works in public at a time when they were considered both modern and difficult to understand; returned to London to concertize and teach. ❖ See also *Women in World History.*

EICHENBERGER, Sabine. Swiss kayaker. Born in Switzerland. ❖ Won a silver medal for K4 500 meters at Atlanta Olympics (1996); won the World Cup for K1 (2003).

EICHIN, Josefa (1964—). See *Idem, Josefa.*

EIFE, Andrea (1956—). East German swimmer. Born April 12, 1956, in East Germany. ❖ At Munich Olympics, won a silver medal in the 4 x 100-meter freestyle relay (1972).

EIGENMANN, Rosa Smith (1858–1947). American ichthyologist. Born Oct 7, 1858, in Monmouth, Illinois; died Jan 12, 1947, in San Diego, California; m. Carl H. Eigenmann (zoologist), Aug 20, 1887 (died April 24, 1927); children: 5. ❖ The 1st woman ichthyologist of prominence, studied fishes in the San Diego (CA) area; published 1st scientific paper (1880); became 1st woman member of San Diego Society of Natural History and served as recording secretary and librarian; toured Europe with ichthyologist David Starr Jordan and other students (1881); published nearly 20 papers in ichthyology and cryptogamic botany by time of marriage; coauthored 15 scientific papers with husband (1888–93); with husband, was 1st to describe some 150 species of fish.

EIJS, Irene (1966—). Dutch rower. Born 1966 in the Netherlands. ❖ Won a bronze medal for double sculls at Atlanta Olympics (1996).

EIKO (1952—). See *Otake, Eiko.*

EILBER, Janet (1951—). American modern dancer. Born July 27, 1951, in Detroit, Michigan. ❖ Trained in apprenticeship program of Martha Graham studio before graduating into company (1972); performed as principal dancer with Graham company for many years, appearing in such works as *Holy Jungle* (1974), *Adorations* (1975), *The Scarlet Letter*

(1975), *Flute of Pan* (1978) and *Appalachian Spring;* was guest dancer with American Dance Machine; performed in Broadway shows, including in Bob Fosse's *Dancing;* appeared in films *Whose Life Is It, Anyway?, Romantic Comedy,* and *Hard to Hold,* among others; co-founded American Repertory Dance Company; also served as co-artistic director of Martha Graham Trust and incoming artistic director of Martha Graham Dance Company.

EILBERG, Amy (1954—). American rabbi. Born in Philadelphia, Pennsylvania, Oct 12, 1954; dau. of Joshua Eilberg (lawyer who served in US House of Representatives) and Gladys Eilberg (social worker); graduated summa cum laude from Brandeis; earned MA in Talmud from the Jewish Theological Seminary, 1978; graduate degree in social work, Smith College, 1984; m. Howard Schwartz. ❖ The 1st woman to be ordained a rabbi within the Conservative branch of Judaism, completed Talmudic studies (1978) but had to wait until 1985 before Conservative rabbis voted to allow women to be ordained; worked at several posts over next decade including that of chaplain at the Methodist Hospital of Indiana in Indianapolis, as a community rabbi at the Jewish Welfare Federation, and at the Jewish Healing Center in San Francisco, California. ❖ See also *Women in World History.*

EILERS, Angelika (1943–2000). See Mechtel, Angelika.

EILERS, Ludowika (1884–1968). See Jakobsson, Ludowika.

EILERS, Sally (1908–1978). American actress. Born Dorothea Sally Eilers, Dec 11, 1908, in New York, NY; died Jan 5, 1978, in Beverly Hills, California; m. Hoot Gibson (actor), 1930 (div. 1933); m. Harry Joe Brown (producer), 1933 (div. 1943); m. Howard Barney, 1943 (div. 1949); m. John Morse, 1949 (sep 1958); children: Harry Joe Brown Jr. (screenwriter). ❖ Featured in Mack Sennett's *The Goodbye Kiss* (1928); appeared in over 40 films, including *Sailor's Holiday, Long, Long Trail, Show of Shows, Bad Girl, Second Hand Wife, State Fair, Carnival, Strike Me Pink, Lady Behave* and *Stage to Tucson;* retired (1951).

EILIKA OF OLDENBURG (1928—). German duchess. Name variations: Eilika Stephanie, duchess of Oldenburg. Born Eilika Stephanie Elisabeth Thekla Juliana von Holstein-Gottorp, Feb 2, 1928, at Lensahn, Schleswig-Holstein, Germany; dau. of Nicholas, grand duke of Oldenburg, and Helen of Waldeck & Pyrmont; m. Emrich, 7th prince of Leiningen; children: Melita of Leiningen (b. 1951); Karl-Emrich of Leiningen; Andreas of Leiningen; Stephanie of Leiningen (b. 1958).

EILIKA OF OLDENBURG (1972—). German duchess. Name variations: Duchess of Oldenburg. Born Eilika Helene Jutta Clementine von Oldenburg, Aug 22, 1972, at Bad Segeberg, Germany; dau. of Johann Friedrich von Holstein-Gottorp, duke of Oldenburg, and Ilka, countess of Ortenburg; m. George von Hapsburg, archduke of Austria and grandson of Emperor Charles I, Oct 18, 1997.

EINERLING, Gloria (c. 1870–1942). See Mamoshina, Glafira Adolfovna.

EINODER-STRAUBE, Thea (1951—). West German rower. Born June 1951 in Germany. ❖ At Montreal Olympics, won a bronze medal in coxless pairs (1976).

EINSTEIN, Hannah Bachman (1862–1929). American social welfare worker. Name variations: Hannah Bachman. Born Hannah Bachman, Jan 28, 1862, in New York, NY; died Nov 28, 1929 in New York, NY; dau. of Herman S. Bachman (importer and dry goods merchant) and Fanny Bachman (German immigrants); attended New York Chartier Institute and Columbia University; m. William Einstein (woolens manufacturer), 1881; children: William Louis Einstein and Marion Einstein. ❖ Reformer who influenced social welfare policy throughout nation and anticipated federal social security system, began career with the charitable organization Temple Emanu-El Sisterhood; became trustee of United Hebrew Charities of New York, president of Sisterhood (1897) and then president of New York Federation of Sisterhoods (1899); appointed chair of relief committee on dependent children for United Hebrew Charities (1903); founded and became president of Widowed Mothers Fund Association (1909); joined forces with Sophie Irene Loeb to promote "mothers' pension" legislation; as chair of committee on investigation of State Commission on Relief for Widowed Mothers, helped to prepare report which paved way for 1915 Child Welfare Law; went on to chair families committee of New York City's child welfare board (1915–29). Was also founder of Federation of Jewish Women's Organizations.

EINSTEIN-MARíC, Mileva (1875–1948). Serbian mathematician. Name variations: Einstein-Maric. Born Mileva Maríc in Titel, the Serbian part of the former Austro-Hungarian Empire, Dec 19, 1875; died in Zurich, Switzerland, Aug 4, 1948; dau. of a civil servant in Hungarian army and a mother who came from a wealthy family; attended university in Switzerland; m. Albert Einstein, Jan 6, 1903; children: daughter Liserele or Lieserl (b. 1902), whose fate is unknown, and 2 sons, Hans Albert (b. May 14, 1904) and Eduard (b. July 28, 1910). ❖ The 1st wife of Albert Einstein who did the computations for his theory of relativity ($E = mc^2$) and other important papers, but whose contributions went unmentioned after their collaboration ceased, while his scientific contributions never again achieved the level reached during their marriage (mathematics was not known to be Einstein's strong suit); went to Zurich to attend university (c. 1894); met Albert Einstein at the Polytechnic in Zurich (1896); left her studies at the Polytechnic (1901); provided the mathematical calculations for the paper that initially bore her name as co-author, that would later win her husband the Nobel Prize in physics (1905); remained in Zurich after Albert moved to Berlin (1914); received the money awarded with the Nobel Prize (1922). ❖ See also Jürgen Renn and Robert Schulmann, *Albert Einstein/ Mileva Maríc: The Love Letters* (Princeton U. Press, 1992); Andrea Gabor, *Einstein's Wife: Work and Marriage in the Lives of Five Great Twentieth-Century Women* (Penguin, 1996); Michele Zackheim, *Einstein's Daughter: The Search for Lieserl* (Riverhead, 1999); and *Women in World History.*

EIRENE. *Variant of Irene.*

EISE, Ida Gertrude (1891–1978). New Zealand artist and art teacher. Born Sept 9, 1891, in Auckland, New Zealand; died Mar 7, 1978, in Auckland; dau. of Frederick George Eise and Emma Mary Ann (Cox) Eise. ❖ Taught art at New Plymouth Technical College (1915–20); joined staff at Elam in Auckland (1920–56, 1959–60); taught at Auckland Society of Arts (ASA, 1962–76), and exhibited landscapes regularly; served as vice president of ASA Council (1950s–60s), and was one of original elected fellows of ASA. Received Bledsoe Medal (1936 and 1949); received British Empire medal (1976). ❖ See also *Dictionary of New Zealand Biography* (Vol. 4).

EISEMANN-SCHIER, Ruth (c. 1942—). Honduran-born kidnapper. Born c. 1942 in Honduras. ❖ With lover Gary Krist, kidnapped Emory University student Barbara Jean Mackle (Dec 17, 1968) and demanded half a million in ransom; when Mackle was found 80 hours later, buried alive in a plywood box on a remote hillside in Georgia, became 1st woman on FBI's Ten Most Wanted List of fugitives (Jan 1969); arrested in Norman, OK (Mar 1969), was sentenced to 7 years but paroled in 4; deported to Honduras (1972).

EISENBERG, Lea (1883–1973). See Noemi, Lea.

EISENBERG, Mary Jane (1951—). American modern dancer and choreographer. Born Mar 28, 1951, in Erie, Pennsylvania; trained under Laura Foreman, and at studios of Martha Graham and Erick Hawkins. ❖ Performed with company of Louis Falco, most notably in his *Caviar* (1970); appeared in recitals for Jennifer Muller's troupe; danced with Glen Tetley's company; began working as choreographer and dancer with Dance/LA after moving to West Coast (late 1970s); performed in works of Bonnie Brosterman and Spider Kedelsky, among others; taught in dance department of California State University, Long Beach, for 10 years; founded Shale: Mary Jane Eisenberg Dance Company, where she served as artistic and managing director for many years; became managing director for Joe Goode Performance Groupe (1999). Choreographed *Close to Home* (1976), *Apartments* (1977), *Mommy* (1978) and *Train Station* (1980), among others.

EISENBLÄTTER, Charlotte (1903–1944). German anti-Nazi activist. Name variations: Charlotte Eisenblatter or Eisenblaetter. Born in Berlin, Germany, Aug 7, 1903; executed at Plötzensee prison in Berlin, Aug 25, 1944. ❖ Joined an extensive anti-Nazi network led by Robert Uhrig (1933); by the time World War II began (Sept 1939), had become a seasoned underground activist; arrested and sent to Ravensbrück (Feb 1942), the Nazi concentration camp for women; indicted for high treason, was sentenced to death after a farcical judicial procedure (Feb 15, 1944). Honored with a postage stamp issued by the GDR (Sept 3, 1959). ❖ See also *Women in World History.*

EISENHOWER, Julie Nixon (1948—). See Nixon, Julie.

EISENHOWER, Mamie (1896–1979). American first lady. Born Mary Geneva Doud, Nov 14, 1896, in Boone, Iowa; died Nov 1, 1979, in Washington, DC; dau. of John Sheldon (meat packer) and Elivera (Carlson) Doud; m. Dwight David Eisenhower (1890–1969, president of US), July 1, 1916; children: Dwight D. Eisenhower (1921–1924); John Seldon Doud Eisenhower (b. 1923, ambassador and historian). ❖ First lady (1953–61), had no interest in politics and had never voted; developed a self-sacrificing attitude, which left husband "free from personal worries," she said; during WWII, lived in Washington, worked for the USO, and did not see husband for a 3-year stretch; as first lady, did not take on any social or civic causes, preferring to dedicate herself to making the White House comfortable for those who visited; suffered with rheumatic heart problems and from Mèniere's disease, an inner-ear disorder that causes dizziness; often stumbled when walking, which gave rise to rumors of alcoholism. ❖ See also Susan Eisenhower, *Mrs. Ike: Memories and Reflections on the Life of Mamie Eisenhower* (Farrar, Straus, 1996); and *Women in World History.*

EISENSCHNEIDER, Elvira (1924–c. 1944). German anti-Nazi activist. Born on April 22, 1924, in Fischbach near Kirn on the Nahe (county Birkenfeld); death date unknown; studied at Moscow's Institute of International Literature; dau. of Paul Eisenschneider (militant anti-Nazi). ❖ After Nazis had beaten her mother, fled to Soviet Union with mother; received news that father had been arrested by the Nazis (1936); became a militant revolutionary, joining the Komsomol, the Soviet children's organization; volunteered her services to Soviet military authorities (1942), to carry out sabotage assignments in Nazi Germany; parachuted into Nazi territory (summer 1943); captured (spring 1944), after almost a year of successfully carrying out her assignments. Honored with a postage stamp by the GDR (Feb 6, 1961). ❖ See also *Women in World History.*

EISENSTEIN, Judith (1909–1996). American author, musicologist and composer. Born Judith Kaplan, Sept 10, 1909; died Feb 1996 in Bethesda, Maryland; dau. of Rabbi Mordecai Kaplan (founder of the Reconstructionist branch of Judaism); attended Juilliard School; Columbia University Teachers College, BA, 1928, MA, 1932 in music education; School of Sacred Music of Hebrew Union College, PhD; m. Ira Eisenstein (rabbi), 1934. ❖ At 12, became the 1st female to have a bat mitzvah in the US (Mar 18, 1922); taught musical pedagogy and history of Jewish music at Jewish Theological Seminary of America's Teachers Institute; was on the faculty of the School of Sacred Music of Hebrew Union College (1959–79); composed original liturgical music; created and broadcast a 13-hour radio series on the history of Jewish music; wrote the 1st American Jewish songbook for children (1937).

EISENSTEIN, Phyllis (1946—). American science-fiction writer. Born Phyllis Kleinstein, Feb 26, 1946, in Chicago, Illinois; attended University of Chicago, 1963–66; University of Illinois, BA in anthropology, 1981; m. Alex Eisenstein (writer), 1966. ❖ Better known as a writer of fantasy than science fiction, novels include *Born to Exile* (1977), *Sorcerer's Son* (1979), *In the Hands of Glory* (1981), *In the Red Lord's Reach* (1989), *The Book of Elementals* (2002), and *The City in Stone* (2003); also published, with Alex Eisenstein, *Night Lives: Nine Stories of the Dark Fantastic* (2003); co-founded and served as director of Windy City SF Writer's Conference (1972–77); taught creative writing at Columbia College of Chicago and edited anthology *Spec-Lit;* also wrote *Overcoming the Pain of Inflammatory Arthritis,* a disease she suffered from throughout life. Nominated for Nebula and Hugo Awards.

EISINGER, Irene (1903–1994). Viennese-born actress and singer. Born 1903 in Vienna, Austria; died 1994; m. G. Schoenewald. ❖ Made stage debut in Basle, Switzerland (1924), appearing there in opera, operetta, comedy and musical comedy; appeared next in Berlin at the State Opera (under Klemperer), then Prague; appeared in Max Reinhardt's production of *Die Fledermaus* (1930); made debut in England at the Glyndebourne Festival as Despina in *Cosi Fan Tutte* (1934) and London debut in the revue *Follow the Sun* (1936); with England the primary base, appeared in *Lilac Time, Hansel and Gretel, Le Nozze di Figaro* (as Barbarina), *The Laughing Cavalier, The Beggar's Opera* (as Polly), *Diversion,* and *A Night in Venice;* films include *Die Lustigen Weiber von Wien* and *Young Man's Fancy.*

EISLER, Charlotte (1894–1970). Austrian musician. Born Charlotte Demant in Tarnopol, Austria-Hungary (now Ternopol, Ukraine), Jan 2, 1894; died in Vienna, Aug 3, 1970; m. composer Hanns Eisler (1898–1962, div. 1934); children: Georg Eisler (1928–1998, Expressionist painter). ❖ Studied music in Vienna with Anton von Webern and Edward Steuermann; met Hanns Eisler while moving in musical circle of composer Arnold Schönberg; became member of Austrian Communist Party (early 1920s); after onset of Nazi dictatorship in Germany, engaged in underground political work for Communist movement (1930s); fearing Nazi takeover in Austria, immigrated with son to Soviet Union (1936); worked in Moscow at Soviet State Music Publishing House, editing works including vocal compositions of Gustav Mahler; immigrated, 1st to Czechoslovakia, and then to England where she settled in Manchester and resumed musical career; performed as singer and pianist throughout Great Britain; returned to war-devastated Vienna (1946) and received appointment at the municipal Music Conservatory as piano professor; was a mainstay of musical Vienna for next 2 decades, presenting many live concerts and recitals over the radio; with immense knowledge of the 2nd Vienna School of Berg, Schönberg and Webern, became a major link in the chain of Austrian cultural continuity; also regarded as an expert on contemporary British music, particularly that of Benjamin Britten. ❖ See also *Women in World History.*

EISLER, Elfriede (1895–1961). *See Fischer, Ruth.*

EISNER, Lotte (1896–1983). German-born French film critic. Name variations: (during World War II) Louise Escoffier. Born Lotte Henriette Eisner in Berlin, Germany, Mar 6, 1896; died in Paris, France, Nov 26, 1983; dau. of Hugo Eisner (textile merchant) and Margarethe Feodora (Aron) Eisner (died in a concentration camp, 1942); University of Rostock, PhD in art history, 1924; never married; no children. ❖ One of the major film historians of the 20th century, joined the staff of *Film-Kurier* (1927), as Germany's 1st female film critic to work on a full-time professional basis; during her crusade for better German films, met regularly with most of the creative talent including world-renowned film directors like Fritz Lang and G.W. Pabst; following Hitler's rise to power, moved to Paris (1933), where she found work as a film correspondent for a number of French journals as well as English-language periodicals, including *Film Culture, Sight and Sound,* and *World Film News;* collaborated with Henri Langlois to create a film archive and research center, which in later years was to emerge as the world-famed Cinémathèque Française; went underground for 4 years during Nazi occupation of France; worked as archivist and chief curator of Langlois' Cinémathèque Française (1945–74); published a large number of essays and reviews in the journal *Revue du cinéma* (later *Cahiers du cinéma*), starting in 1945; published masterful study of the films influenced by the spirit of German Expressionism (1952), which appeared in an English-language translation as *The Haunted Screen* (1969); also issued definitive studies of the director F.W. Murnau (1964) and Fritz Lang (1977). Award Chevalier des Arts et des Lettres (1967) and Chevalier of the Legion of Honor (1983). ❖ See also (in German) memoirs, *Ich hatte einst ein schönes Vaterland* (*I Once Had a Beautiful Fatherland,* 1984); and *Women in World History.*

EJI (c. 1360–1326 BCE). *See Mutnedjmet.*

EKATERINA. *Variant of Catherine.*

EKBERG, Anita (1931—). Swedish actress. Name variations: Anita Kersten. Born Kerstin Anita Marianne Ekberg, Sept 29, 1931, in Malmö, Sweden; m. Anthony Steel (actor), 1956 (div. 1959); m. Rik Van Nutter (actor), 1963 (div. 1975). ❖ Named Miss Sweden (1950); made film debut in US in *Take Me to Town* (1953), followed by *Blood Alley, Artists and Models, Back from Eternity, Paris Holiday,* and *Screaming Mimi;* frustrated with career, moved to Italy and came to prominence in King Vidor's *War and Peace* (1956) and Federico Fellini's *La dolce vita* (1960) and *Boccaccio '70* (1962); remained in Italy for 10 more years, making 20 films, including Fellini's *Intervista* (1987).

EKEJIUBA, Felicia Ifeoma (1872–1943). *See Okwei of Osomari.*

EKMAN, Kirsten (1933—). Swedish novelist. Born Aug 27, 1933, in Risinge, Östergötland, Sweden; grew up in Katrineholm; graduate of University of Uppsala, 1957. ❖ Was a member of Swedish Academy of Arts and Letters (1978–89); published 1st book, *Trettio meter mord* (1959); writings, which span several genres and often focus on questions of identity, include *Dödslockan* (1963), *Pukehornet* (1967), *Menadarna* (1970), *Häxringarna* (1974, pub. in English as *Witches' Rings*), *Springkällan* (1976), *Änglahuset* (1979), *En stad av ljus* (A Town of Lights, 1983), *Hunden* (1986), *Rövarna i skuleskogen* (1988, pub. in English as *The Forest of Hours*), *Händelser vid vatten* (1993, pub. in English as *Blackwater*), *Gör mig levande igen* (1996) and *Skraplotter* (2003). Received Selma Lagerlöf Prize (1989).

EKSTER, Aleksandra (1882–1949). *See Exter, Alexandra.*

ELAINE (1982—). *See Estrela Moura, Elaine.*

ELASTICA.
See Frischmann, Justine.
See Holland, Annie.
See Matthews, Donna.

ELDER, Anne (1918–1976). Australian dancer and poet. Name variations: Anne MacKintosh Elder; Anne MacKintosh. Born Anne MacKintosh in 1918 in Auckland, New Zealand; died 1976. ❖ Moved to Australia with family at age 3; as Anne MacKintosh, was a well-known ballerina with the Borovansky Ballet; writings include *For the Record* (1972), *Crazy Woman and Other Poems* (1976) and *Small Clay Birds* (1988).

ELDER, Dorothy-Grace. Scottish politician and journalist. Born in Scotland. ❖ As a journalist, wrote columns for the *Scottish Daily Express, Scotland on Sunday*, the *Daily Express* in London, and the *Sunday Mail;* was also an investigative writer for *The Glasgow Herald* and an interviewer and producer for BBC and ITV; an Independent, elected to the Scottish Parliament for Glasgow (1999).

ELDER, Kate (fl. 1881). American legend of the frontier days. Name variations: Kate Fisher. Flourished in 1881. ❖ Known to history as a prostitute and friend of John "Doc" Holliday, who, with his close friend Wyatt Earp, took part in the Gunfight at O.K. Corrall (Oct 1881); was portrayed by Jo Van Fleet in *Gunfight at O.K. Corral,* under the character name of Fisher.

ELDER, Louisine (1855–1929). *See Havemeyer, Louisine.*

ELDER, Ruth (1902–1977). American pioneer. Born Sept 8, 1902, in Anniston, Alabama; died in San Francisco, California, Oct 9, 1977; married 6 times, including to Lyle Womack (div. 1928), C.E. Moody (div.), and Walter Camp Jr. (div.). ❖ Student pilot who enjoyed brief notoriety following her unsuccessful attempt to become the 1st airplane passenger to cross the Atlantic (Sept 1927); setting out with a male pilot from Tampa, Florida, in a plane called the *American Girl,* ran into trouble 250 miles short of the coast of Spain, when an oil leak forced them to deliberately crash in the ocean; was cited for her daring in ceremonies in Paris and at the White House, where she was heralded as the "Miss America of Aviation" but was soon upstaged by Amelia Earhart; went on to an undistinguished movie career.

ELDERS, Joycelyn (1933—). African-American physician. Born Minnie Joycelyn Jones in Schaal, Arkansas, Aug 13, 1933; dau. of Curtis (sharecropper) and Haller Jones; Philander Smith College, BA, 1952; University of Arkansas Medical School, MD, 1960, MS in biochemistry, 1967; m. Oliver Elders (basketball coach); children: 2 sons. ❖ The 1st black woman appointed US surgeon general, was an assistant professor of pediatrics at University of Arkansas Medical School, becoming a full professor (1976) and board certified as a pediatric endocrinologist (1978); appointed director of Arkansas' department of public health (1987); was confirmed as 16th surgeon general (Sept 1993), vowing to become "the voice and vision of the poor and the powerless"; was an outspoken advocate of reproductive rights, contraceptives, safe sex, and the decriminalization of drugs, issues that the American public has not always been comfortable with in open forum; after a series of uncensored statements that embarrassed the White House, was removed from office 15 months into her term. Received the Arkansas Democrat's Woman of the Year award, the National Governors' Association Distinguished Service Award, American Medical Association's Dr. Nathan Davis Award, De Lee Humanitarian Award, and National Coalition of 100 Black Women's Candace Award for Health Science. ❖ See also autobiography (with David Chanoff) *From Sharecropper's Daughter to Surgeon General of the United States* (Morrow, 1996); and *Women in World History.*

ELDERSHAW, Flora (1897–1956). Australian novelist and literary critic. Name variations: (joint pseudonym with Marjorie Barnard) M. Barnard Eldershaw. Born Flora Sydney Patricia Eldershaw in Sydney, Australia, 1897; died Sept 20, 1956; dau. of Henry and Margaret Eldershaw; educated at Wagga Wagga; graduate of Sydney University, 1918; never married but romantically linked with Frank Dolby Davison; no children. ❖ Became hugely successful writing fiction with Marjorie Barnard under the pseudonym M. Barnard Eldershaw; though Barnard was the stronger writer, often edited and created the storyline, and shepherded works to publication, a process that Barnard abhorred; also wrote literary criticism on her own. ❖ See also *Women in World History.*

ELDERSHAW, M. Barnard.
See Barnard, Marjorie.
See Eldershaw, Flora

ELDRED, Pam (c. 1948—). Miss America. Born Pamela Anne Eldred c. 1948 in West Bloomfield, Michigan; attended Mercy College. ❖ Appeared as lead dancer for the Detroit City ballet; named Miss America (1970), representing Michigan. ❖ See also Frank Deford, *There She Is* (Viking, 1971).

ELDREDGE, Sara Willis (1811–1872). *See Fern, Fanny.*

ELDRIDGE, Florence (1901–1988). American actress. Name variations: Mrs. Fredric March. Born Florence McKechnie, Sept 5, 1901, in Brooklyn, NY; died Aug 1, 1988, in Santa Monica, California; dau. of James and Clara Eugenie McKechnie; m. Fredric March (actor), May 30, 1927 (died 1975); children: Penelope and Anthony March (both adopted). ❖ Highly respected actress and half of a famous theatrical couple, made NY debut in the chorus of Jerome Kern's *Rock-a-Bye Baby* (1919); became the toast of Broadway, winning acclaim for performance in *Ambush* (1921), and increasing stature with subsequent roles in *The Cat and the Canary* (1922), *Six Characters in Search of an Author* (1922), and *The Love Habit* (1923); embarked on film career, often starring with husband, notably in *Les Miserables* (1935) and *Mary of Scotland* (1936), but after marriage, put his career first; with husband, also starred in *The Skin of Our Teeth* (1943) and had one of her greatest stage successes as Mary Tyrone in *Long Day's Journey into Night* (1956), for which she received the New York Drama Critics Award for Best Actress. ❖ See also *Women in World History.*

ELEANOR. *Variant of Helena or Leonor.*

ELEANOR, countess of Northumberland (c. 1413–1472). *See Neville, Eleanor.*

ELEANOR, the Maid of Brittany (1184–1241). English royal. Name variations: Damsel of Brittany; Pearl of Brittany; Eleanor of Brittany; Eleanor Plantagenet. Born 1184; died Aug 12, 1241, at Corfe Castle, Dorset, England; buried 1st at St. James's Church in Bristol, before exhumation and reburial at Amesbury, Wiltshire, England; dau. of Geoffrey Plantagenet (1158–1186), duke of Brittany, and Constance of Brittany (1161–1201); granddau. of Eleanor of Aquitaine (1122–1204). ❖ Was the niece of King John of England and sister of Arthur, count of Brittany; because of contention for the throne between Arthur and John (1199–1202), was imprisoned by her uncle John.

ELEANOR BALLIOL.
See Balliol, Eleanor (fl. 1230).
See Balliol, Margaret (c. 1255–?).

ELEANOR D'ARBOREA (c. 1360–c. 1404). Ruler of Sardinia. Name variations: Eleanora of Arborea; Eleanor di Arborea; Leonora. Born c. 1360 in Arborea (on Sardinia); died c. 1404 on Sardinia; dau. of Mariano IV (ruler of Sardinia); m. Brancoleone de Oria (Spanish noble). ❖ After discontented Sardinian citizens rebelled against her brother and killed him (1383), ascended the throne, put down the revolt and restored peace; when an Aragonese army led by Alphonso IV invaded Sardinia, defeated his army and drove it from Sardinia; reigned for another 20 years, restoring economic prosperity and creating a code of law, the Carta de Logu (1421), which remained in effect until the 18th century. ❖ See also *Women in World History.*

ELEANOR DE BOHUN (1366–1399). *See Bohun, Eleanor.*

ELEANOR DESMIER (1639–1722). *See Desmier, Eleanor.*

ELEANOR DE WARRENNE (c. 1250–?). English noblewoman. Name variations: Eleanor Percy; Alianore Plantagenet; Alianore de Warren. Born c. 1250; died after 1282; interred at Sallay; dau. of John de Warrenne (c. 1231–1304), 7th earl of Warrenne and Surrey, and Alice le Brun (d. 1255); m. Henry Percy, 7th baron Percy (d. 1272); children: Henry Percy, 8th baron Percy (d. 1315); John Percy (b. 1270).

ELEANOR GONZAGA.
See Gonzaga, Eleonora (1493–1543).
See Eleonora of Austria (1534–1594).
See Medici, Eleonora de (1567–1611).

ELEANOR I GONZAGA (1598–1655). *See Gonzaga, Eleonora I.*

ELEANOR II GONZAGA (1628–1686). *See Gonzaga, Eleonora II.*

ELEANOR HABSBURG (1498–1558). *See Eleanor of Portugal.*

ELEANOR HABSBURG (1653–1697). Queen of Poland and duchess of Lorraine. Born Eleonore Maria Josefa, May 5, 1653, in Regensburg; died Dec 17, 1697, in Vienna; dau. of Eleonora II Gonzaga (1628–1686) and Ferdinand III (1608–1657), king of Bohemia (r. 1627–1646), king of Hungary (r. 1625), Holy Roman emperor (r. 1637–1657); possibly married Charles V, duke of Lorraine and Bar (r. 1675–1690) and one of the kings of Poland (r. 1669–1690); children: possibly Leopold Joseph (b. Sept 11, 1679), duke of Lorraine.

ELEANOR OF ALBUQUERQUE (1374–1435). Queen of Aragon. Name variations: Leonor of Albuquerque. Born 1474; died Dec 16, 1435 (some sources cite 1455); dau. of Beatrice of Portugal (c. 1347–1318) and Sancho (b. 1373), count of Albuquerque; m. Fernando also known as Ferdinand I of Antequera (b. 1380), king of Aragon (r. 1412–1416); children: Alfonso also known as Alphonso V (1396–1458), king of Aragon (r. 1416–1458); Juan also known as John II of Trastamara (1398–1479), king of Navarre and Aragon (r. 1458–1479); Enrique or Henry (1399–1445); Sancho (1400–1417); Leonora of Aragon (1405–1445, who m. Duarte I, king of Portugal, 1391–1438); Pedro or Peter (1409–1438); Maria of Aragon(1403–1445, who m. John II, king of Leon and Castile).

ELEANOR OF AQUITAINE (1122–1204). Queen of France and England. Name variations: Aliénor. Pronunciation: ACK-ee-taine. Born in 1122 in Bordeaux, France; died at abbey of Fontevrault or Fontevraud, Anjou, France, April 1, 1204; dau. of William X (b. 1099), duke of Aquitaine and Aénor of Châtellerault (d. 1130); sister of Aelith de Poitiers (c. 1123–?); m. Louis VII, king of France (r. 1137–1180), 1137 (marriage annulled 1152); m. Henry Plantagenet, count of Anjou, later Henry II, king of England (r. 1154–1189), in 1152 (died, 1189); children: (1st m.) Marie de Champagne (1145–1198); Alice (1150–c. 1197), countess of Blois; (2nd m.) William (1153–1156); Henry (1155–1183), count of Anjou and duke of Normandy; Matilda of England (1156–1189); Richard I the Lionheart (1157–1199), king of England (r. 1189–1199); Geoffrey (1158–1186), duke of Brittany and earl of Richmond; Eleanor of Castile (1162–1214); Joanna of Sicily (1165–1199); John also known as John Lackland (1166–1216), king of England (r. 1199–1216). ❖ Europe's most famous medieval queen, who wielded power and influence as queen of France and England, was also an important patron of 12th-century troubadour poetry and courtly love literature; became queen of France at age 15 (1137); went on 2nd Crusade with Louis VII (1147); held influential literary court with daughter Marie de Champagne; granted annulment (1152); married Henry II of England (1152); incited her sons to rebel against Henry II (1173); imprisoned under "house arrest" (1173–89); governed as regent for Richard I (1189–94); traveled across Pyrenees at age 78 to obtain marriage alliance; died peacefully at abbey of Fontevrault (1204). ❖ See also Amy Kelly, *Eleanor of Aquitaine and the Four Kings* (Vintage, 1958); M.V. Rosenberg, *Eleanor of Aquitaine* (Houghton Mifflin, 1937); Desmond Seward, *Eleanor of Aquitaine* (Dorset, 1978); D.D.R. Owen, *Eleanor of Aquitaine: Queen and Legend* (Blackwell, 1993); film *The Lion in Winter*, starring Katharine Hepburn as Eleanor of Aquitaine and Peter O'Toole as Henry II (1968); and *Women in World History*.

ELEANOR OF ARAGON (1358–1382). Queen of Castile and Leon. Name variations: Leonor or Leonora of Aragon. Born Feb 20, 1358, in Santa Maria del Puig, Spain; died in Cuellar, Castile and Leon, Spain, Sept 13, 1382; dau. of Peter IV the Ceremonious, king of Aragon (r. 1336–1387), and Eleanor of Sicily (d. 1375); became 1st wife of Juan also known as John I (1358–1390), king of Castile and Leon (r. 1379–1390), June 18, 1375; children: Enrique also known as Henry III (1379–1406), king of Castile and Leon (r. 1390–1406); Fernando also known as Ferdinand I of Antequera (1380–1416), king of Aragon (r. 1412–1416). John I's 2nd wife was Beatrice of Portugal (1372–after 1409).

ELEANOR OF ARAGON (1405–1445). See Leonora of Aragon.

ELEANOR OF AUSTRIA (1498–1558). See Eleanor of Portugal.

ELEANOR OF CASTILE (1162–1214). Queen of Castile. Name variations: Eleanor of England; Eleanor Plantagenet. Born on Oct 13, 1162 (some sources cite 1156), in Domfront, Normandy, France; died Oct 31, 1214, in Burgos, Castile and Leon, Spain; interred at Abbey of Las Huelgas, Burgos, Castile; dau. of Eleanor of Aquitaine (1122–1202) and Henry II, king of England (r. 1154–1189); m. Alfonso or Alphonso VIII (1155–1214), king of Castile (r. 1158–1214, also known as Alphonso III), in Sept 1170; children: Sancho (1181–1181); Berengaria of Castile (1180–1246, who m. Alphonso IX, king of Leon); Sancha (1182–1184); Urraca of Castile (1186–1220, who m. Alphonso II of Portugal); Enrique also known as Henry I (1204–1217), king of Castile (r. 1214–1217); Blanche of Castile (1188–1252, who m. Louis VIII of France); Mafalda of Castile (c. 1190–1204); Fernando (1189–1211); Eleanor of Castile (1202–1244, 1st wife of James I, king of Aragon); Constanza of Castile (c. 1204–1243, who became abbess of Las Huelgas); Henry (died young); Constance (died young). ❖ See also *Women in World History*.

ELEANOR OF CASTILE (1202–1244). Queen of Aragon. Name variations: Leonor. Born 1202; died in Burgos, Castile and Leon, Spain, 1244; dau. of Alphonso VIII, king of Castile, and Eleanor of Castile (1162–1214); became 1st wife of James I (1208–1276), king of Aragon (r. 1213–1276), also known as Jaime the Conqueror of Aragon, Jan 6, 1221 (div., 1229); children: Alfonso of Aragon, infante (d. 1260, who m. Constance de Marsan). James I's 2nd wife was Iolande of Hungary (1215–1251).

ELEANOR OF CASTILE (1241–1290). Queen of England. Name variations: Eleanora of Castile; Eleanor the Faithful. Born in late 1241 in Castile; died at Harby, Nottinghamshire, Nov 28, 1290; dau. of Ferdinand III (1199–1252), king of Castile and Leon (r. 1217–1252) and Joanna of Ponthieu, Countess Aumale (d. 1279); became 1st wife of Edward I Longshanks (1239–1307), king of England (r. 1272–1307), in 1254; children: Eleanor Plantagenet (1264–1297, who m. Alphonso III, king of Aragon); Joan (1265–1265); John (1266?–1271); Katherine (1271–1271); Henry (1267–1274); Joan of Acre (1272–1307), countess of Gloucester; Alphonso (1273–1284); Margaret (1275–1318), duchess of Brabant; Berengaria (1276–c. 1279); Mary (1278–1332, became a nun); Isabel (1279–1279); Alice (1280–1291); Elizabeth (1282–1316), countess of Hereford and Essex; Edward II (1284–1327), king of England (r. 1307–1327, who m. Isabella of France [1296–1358]); Beatrice (c. 1286–?); Blanche (1290–1290). ❖ Paragon of medieval queenship, was an active partner of her husband Edward I, accompanying him to the Holy Land on Crusade, to Gascony and Wales, while also bearing 15 children. ❖ See also *Women in World History*.

ELEANOR OF CASTILE (1307–1359). Queen-consort of Aragon. Name variations: Leonor of Castile; Leonor de Castilla; Infanta of Castile. Born 1307; murdered in 1359 at the Château de Catroheriz; dau. of Ferdinand IV, king of Castile and Leon (r. 1296–1312), and Constance of Portugal (1290–1313); m. Prince Jaime of Aragon, Oct 18, 1319; became 2nd wife of Alfonso or Alphonso IV (d. 1359), king of Aragon (r. 1327–1336), Feb 5, 1329; children: Ferran; Juan (Joan). ❖ Sister of Castilian king Alphonso XI, married Jaime, crown prince of Aragon, who announced that he intended to take religious vows shortly after the wedding; 10 years later, married Jaime's widowed younger brother, Alphonso IV, king of Aragon; dedicated much of her energy to securing properties and power for her 2 sons; became enmeshed in the Castilian civil war between Peter the Cruel and Enrique of Trastámara, siding with Enrique; was assassinated by one of Peter the Cruel's allies. ❖ See also *Women in World History*.

ELEANOR OF CHÂTELLERAULT (d. 1130). See Aénor of Châtellerault.

ELEANOR OF GONZAGA I (1598–1655). See Gonzaga, Eleonora I.

ELEANOR OF GONZAGA II (1628–1686). See Gonzaga, Eleonora II.

ELEANOR OF MONTFORT (1215–1275). English princess, countess of Leicester, and rebel. Name variations: Eleanor of England; Eleanor de Montfort; Eleanor Plantagenet. Born 1215 in Gloucester, Gloucestershire, England; died April 13, 1275, at Montargis convent in France; dau. of John also known as John Lackland, king of England (r. 1199–1216), and Isabella of Angoulême (1186–1246); m. William Marshal, 2nd earl of Pembroke, in 1224 (died 1231); m. Simon V of Montfort (c. 1208–1265), earl of Leicester, Jan 7, 1239 (died 1265); children: Harry or Henry Montfort (1239–1265); Bran; Guy; Amauric; Richard; Eleanor of Montfort (1252–1282). ❖ Married one of her father's baronial supporters, William Marshal of Pembroke, who died when she was 16; married Simon of Montfort, the English noble and leader of the pro-baronial alliance against her brother, King Henry III (1239); was an important aid in Simon's political and military schemes, probably due to her close ties to the house of Simon's enemy, Henry III; when Simon died in battle (1265), was forced to flee for her life, smuggling her children and a personal fortune in gold and jewels to safety in France; retired to a convent at Montargis. ❖ See also *Women in World History*.

ELEANOR OF MONTFORT (1252–1282). Princess of Wales. Name variations: Eleanor de Montfort; (nickname) The Demoiselle. Born 1252 in Kenilworth, Warwickshire, England; died in childbirth in June 1282 in Wales; buried in Llanfaes, Gwynedd, Wales; dau. of Simon of Montfort and Eleanor of Montfort (1215–1275), countess of Leicester; m. Llewellyn ap Gruffydd (Llywelyn III), prince of Wales, Oct 13, 1278; children: Gwenllian (b. 1282). ❖ Born into the chaos of parents' rebellion against King Henry III of England, was only 13 when father died while leading the baronial army at Battle of Evesham; escaped to France with mother and remained at convent of Montargis until about 1276, when she was sent to Wales to marry Welsh prince Llewellyn ap

Gruffydd; captured on ship on which she was sailing and was kept imprisoned for 2 years by Edward I who opposed the marriage; after marriage, used her familial ties to the English royal house and her close relationship with her husband to convince the parties to cease the warring for power over Wales which was destroying lands and families. ❧ See also *Women in World History*.

ELEANOR OF NAVARRE (1425–1479). Queen of Navarre. Name variations: Leonor; Eleanor Trastamara; Eleanor de Foix. Born Feb 2, 1425 (some sources cite 1426), in Aragon; died Feb 12, 1479, in Tudela, Navarre, Spain; dau. of Juan II also known as John II, king of Aragon (r. 1458–1479), and Blanche of Navarre (1385–1441); sister of Blanche of Navarre (1424–1464), queen of Castile and Leon; half-sister of Ferdinand of Aragon (who m. Isabella I [1451–1504]); m. Gaston de Foix also known as Gaston IV, count of Foix, July 30, 1436 (died 1470 or 1472); children: (in order of birth) Maria de Foix; Gaston, prince of Viane or Viana; Jeanne de Foix; Jean; Pierre; Margareta de Foix; Catherine de Foix; Eleanor de Foix; Jaime; Anne de Foix. ❧ On mother's death (1441), her brother Charles, prince of Viana, inherited the small but prosperous kingdom of Navarre, though her father John took over as regent; moved to France to reside on her husband's estates in Foix and gave birth to 10 children; inherited Navarre, when father disinherited Charles; though she was queen in name, was unable to exert the authority of a ruler because her father refused to allow her to govern; when Charles and elder sister Blanche of Navarre (1424–1464) rebelled against their father and demanded Charles' reinstatement, found herself struggling for power; her efforts to secure the throne led to years of warfare and civil strife, while her father retained control of Navarre. ❧ See also *Women in World History*.

ELEANOR OF NORMANDY (fl. 1000s). Countess of Flanders. Born before 1018; dau. of Richard II, duke of Normandy (d. 1027), and Judith of Rennes (c. 982–1018, dau. of Conan I, duke of Brittany); m. Baldwin IV, count of Flanders; children: Baldwin V, count of Flanders.

ELEANOR OF PFALZ-NEUBURG (1655–1720). Holy Roman empress. Name variations: Eleanora of Neuburg; Eleanor of Neuberg; Eleanor Magdalene of Neuburg; Eleanor Magdalene of Neuberg. Born Jan 6, 1655; died Jan 19, 1720; dau. of Elizabeth Amalia of Hesse (1635–1709) and Philip William, elector Palatine; became 3rd wife of Leopold I of Bohemia (1640–1705), Holy Roman emperor (r. 1658–1705), Dec 14, 1676; children: Joseph I (1678–1711), Holy Roman emperor (r. 1705–1711); Maria Elisabeth (1680–1741, stadholder of the Netherlands); Charles VI (1685–1740), Holy Roman emperor (r. 1711–1740); Maria Antonia of Austria (1683–1754, who m. John V, king of Portugal); Maria Magdalena (1689–1743).

ELEANOR OF PORTUGAL (1328–1348). Queen of Aragon. Name variations: Leonor of Portugal; Eleanor Henriques; Enriques or Enriquez. Born 1328; died Oct 29, 1348, age 20, in Teruel, Aragon, Spain; dau. of Beatrice of Castile and Leon (1293–1359), queen of Portugal, and Alphonso IV, king of Portugal (r. 1325–1357); sister of Pedro or Peter I, king of Portugal (r. 1357–1367), and Maria of Portugal (1313–1357, who m. Alphonso XI of Castile); became 2nd wife of Pedro IV also known as Peter IV the Ceremonious (b. 1319), king of Aragon (r. 1336–1387), in 1347; children: none. Peter IV's 1st wife was Marie of Navarre; his 3rd was Eleanor of Sicily (d. 1375).

ELEANOR OF PORTUGAL (1434–1467). Holy Roman empress and queen of Germany. Name variations: Eleanora; Eleonore; Leonor. Born Sept 18, 1434, in Torres Novan Vedras; died Sept 3, 1467, in Wiener-Neustadt from complications of childbirth; dau. of Edward also known as Duarte I, king of Portugal (r. 1433–1438), and Leonora of Aragon (1405–1445); m. Frederick III, king of Germany and Holy Roman emperor (r. 1440–1493), Mar 15, 1452; children: Christopher (b. 1455); Maxmilian I (1459–1519), Holy Roman Emperor (who m. Mary of Burgundy [1457–1482] and Bianca Maria Sforza [1472–1510]); Johann or John (1466–1467); Helen (1460–1461); Cunegunde (1465–1520, who m. Albert II of Bavaria). ❧ Married Frederick III, king of Germany (1452); from the palace-castle at Wiener-Neustadt near the Hungarian border, faced with Frederick the nearly continuous challenge of rebellious German nobles and Turkish expansion into the Balkans; gave birth to Maximilian I, who succeeded his father and established in reality many of the grandiose claims Frederick made for the Habsburg dynasty. ❧ See also *Women in World History*.

ELEANOR OF PORTUGAL (1458–1525). Queen of Portugal. Name variations: Leonor of Portugal. Born May 2, 1458, in Beja; died Nov 17, 1525, in Lisbon; interred in Xabregas; dau. of Beatrice of Beja (1430–1506)

and Fernando also known as Ferdinand, duke of Beja and Viseu; sister of Isabella of Braganza (1459–1521) and Manuel I the Fortunate (1469–1521), king of Portugal (r. 1495–1521); m. Joao II also known as John II (b. 1455), king of Portugal (r. 1481–1495); children: Alfonso or Alphonso of Portugal (1475–1491); Joao (1483–1483). ❧ A patron of the arts, is best known for her patronage of Gil Vicente, a Portuguese dramatist; also guided the publication of the Portuguese translation of Christine de Pizan's *Livre des Trois Vertues*.

ELEANOR OF PORTUGAL (1498–1558). Queen of Portugal and later of France. Name variations: Eléonore; Eleanor Habsburg; Eleanor of Austria; Leonor of Austria. Born in Louvain, Nov 15, 1498; died Feb 25, 1558, near Badajoz on Portuguese border; dau. of Philip I the Fair, king of Castile and Leon, and Juana la Loca (1479–1555); sister of Ferdinand I and Charles V, both Holy Roman emperors, Mary of Hungary (1505–1558), Catherine (1507–1578), Elisabeth of Habsburg (1501–1526); became third wife of Miguel also known as Manuel I the Fortunate (1469–1521), king of Portugal (r. 1495–1521), Nov 24, 1518; became 2nd wife of Francis I (1494–1547), king of France (r. 1515–1547), July 4, 1530; children: (1st m.) Carlos (b. 1520); Maria de Portugal (1521–1577); (2nd m.) none. ❧ See also *Women in World History*.

ELEANOR OF PROVENCE (c. 1222–1291). Queen of England. Name variations: Alianora; Eleanora; Elinor. Date of birth unknown but believed to be 1222, possibly in Nov; place of birth presumed to be Aix-en-Provence, Provence, which is now in France; died at convent of St. Mary, Amesbury, Wiltshire, England, June 24, 1291; her body was buried there Sept 1291; her heart was interred at the church of the Friars Minors in London; dau. of Raymond Berengar or Berenger IV (some sources cite V), count of Provence and Forcalquier (1209–1245) and Beatrice of Savoy (d. 1268); sister of Margaret of Provence (1221–1295), Sancha of Provence (c. 1225–1261), and Beatrice of Provence (d. 1267); m. Henry III (1206–1272), king of England (r. 1216–1272), Jan 14, 1236, at Canterbury, England; children: Edward I Longshanks (1272–1307), king of England (r. 1272–1307); Margaret, Queen of Scots (1240–1275, who m. Alexander III of Scotland); Beatrice (1242–1275), duchess of Brittany; Edmund Crouchback (c. 1245–1296), earl of Lancaster; and Katherine (1253–1257), Richard, John, William and Henry who all died young. ❧ Wife and consort of Henry III, king of England, mother of Edward I, king of England, who unjustly incurred the enmity of her nation; crowned queen of England at Westminster (Jan 20, 1236); during Henry's absence in Gascony, named co-regent with brother-in-law, Richard, earl of Cornwall (1253); after Henry's capture at battle of Lewes, exiled in France (1264); returned to England when Henry regained his throne (Oct 1265); retired to the Convent of St. Mary, Amesbury (1276); took vows as a nun there (1286). ❧ See also *Women in World History*.

ELEANOR OF SAXE-EISENACH (1662–1696). Margravine of Ansbach. Born Eleanor Erdmuthe Louise, April 13, 1662; died Sept 19, 1696; dau. of John George (b. 1634), duke of Saxe-Eisenach, and Johannette of Sayn-Wittgenstein (b. 1632); m. John Frederick, margrave of Ansbach, Nov 14, 1681; children: Caroline of Ansbach (1683–1737, who m. George II, king of England).

ELEANOR OF SICILY (d. 1375). Queen of Aragon. Name variations: Leonor of Sicily. Died 1375; became 3rd wife of Pedro IV also known as Peter IV the Ceremonious (b. 1319), king of Aragon (r. 1336–1387), c. 1349; children: Juan also known as John I the Hunter (b. 1350), king of Sicily and Aragon (r. 1387–1395); Constance of Aragon (c. 1350–?); Martin I the Humane, king of Aragon (r. 1395–1410); Eleanor of Aragon (1358–1382).

ELEANOR OF SOLMS-HOHENSOLMS-LICH (1871–1937). Grand duchess of Hesse-Darmstadt. Born Sept 17, 1871, in Lich, Germany; died in airplane crash, Nov 16, 1937, in Steene, Belgium; m. Ernest, grand duke of Hesse-Darmstadt; children: George and Louis.

ELEANOR OF WOODSTOCK (1318–1355). English princess and duchess of Guelders. Name variations: Eleanor Plantagenet. Born June 18, 1318, in Woodstock, Oxfordshire, England; died April 22, 1355, in Deventer, Netherlands; dau. of Isabella of France (1296–1358) and Edward II (1284–1327), king of England (r. 1307–1327); m. Renaud also known as Rainald or Reginald II the Black Haired, duke of Guelders (aka count of Gelderland), May 1332 (died 1343); children: Renaud III of Guelders (b. 1334); Edward of Guelders (b. 1336). Renaud's 1st wife was Sophia of Malines (d. 1329).

ELEANOR PLANTAGENET (1264–1297). Queen of Aragon. Name variations: Princess Eleanor; Countess of Bar. Born June 17, 1264, at Windsor Castle, Windsor, Berkshire, England; died Oct 12, 1297 (some sources cite 1298), at Ghent, Flanders, Belgium; interred at Westminster Abbey, London; dau. of Edward I Longshanks, king of England (r. 1272–1307), and Eleanor of Castile (1241–1290); m. Alfonso also known as Alphonso III the Liberal (1265–1291), king of Aragon (r. 1285–1291), Aug 15, 1290, at Westminster Abbey; m. Henry de Bar (d. 1302), count de Bar, around 1293 in Champagne, France; children: (2nd m.) Lady Eleanor of Bar; Joan of Bar (b. 1295); Edward I, count of Bar (b. 1294).

ELEANOR PLANTAGENET (c. 1318–1372). Countess of Arundel. Name variations: Eleanor Beaumont; Eleanor Fitzalan. Born between 1311 and 1318 at Grosmont Castle, Gwent, Wales; died Nov 11, 1372, at Arundel Castle, East Sussex, England; dau. of Henry Plantagenet, 3rd earl of Lancaster, and Maud Chaworth (1282–c. 1322); m. John Beaumont, 2nd baron Beaumont; m. Richard Fitzalan, 8th earl of Arundel, 1345; children: (1st m.) Henry Beaumont, 3rd baron Beaumont; (2nd m.) Richard Fitzalan, 9th earl of Arundel; Joan Fitzalan (d. 1419); John Fitzalan; Alice Fitzalan (1352–1416); Thomas Fitzalan, archbishop of Canterbury.

ELEANOR STEWART (1427–1496). See Stewart, Eleanor.

ELEANOR TELLEZ DE MENESES (c. 1350–1386). See Leonora Telles.

ELEANOR TRASTAMARA (d. 1415). Queen of Navarre. Name variations: Leonor of Castile. Died 1415; dau. of Enrique II also known as Henry II, king of Castile and Leon (r. 1369–1379), and Joanna of Castile (1339–1381); m. Charles III, king of Navarre; children: Blanche of Navarre (1385–1441).

ELEANORA. Variant of Leonora.

ELEANORA CHRISTINA (1621–1698). See Ulfeldt, Leonora Christina.

ELEANORA OF REUSS (1860–1917). Queen of Bulgaria. Name variations: Eleanor Reuss. Born Aug 22, 1860; died Sept 12, 1917; dau. of Henry IV (b. 1821), prince Reuss of Köstritz; became 2nd wife of Ferdinand I (1861–1948), king of Bulgaria (r. 1887–1918, abdicated), Feb 28, 1908.

ELEANORA OF TOLEDO (1522–1562). See Medici, Eleonora de.

ELECTRESS PALATINE, Elizabeth (1596–1662). See Elizabeth of Bohemia.

ELEJARDE, Marlene (1950–1989). Cuban runner. Born June 3, 1950, in Havana, Cuba; died April 29, 1989. ❖ Won a silver medal at Mexico City Olympics (1968) and a bronze medal at Munich Olympics (1972), both in the 4 x 100-meter relay.

ELEK-SCHACHERER, Ilona (1907–1988). See Schacherer-Elek, Ilona.

ELEN. Variant of Ellen or Helen.

ELENA. Variant of Helen.

ELENA (1963—). Princess of Spain and duchess of Lugo. Name variations: Elena Bourbon; Helen. Born Elena Maria Isabela Dominica de los Silo, Dec 20, 1963, at Nuestra Señora de Loreto Clinic, Madrid, Spain; dau. of Sophia of Greece (1938—) and Juan Carlos I (b. 1938), king of Spain (r. 1975—); m. Jaime de Maricharlar y de Sáenzde, Mar 18, 1995; children: Felipe Juan Foilon de Todos los Santos (b. 1998).

ELENA GLINSKI (c. 1506–1538). See Glinski, Elena.

ELENA OF MONTENEGRO (1873–1952). Queen of Italy. Name variations: Helena of Italy; Helen of Montenegro; Helena of Montenegro; Helen Petrovitch-Njegos or Petrovich-Njegosh. Born Jan 8, 1873; died 1952; dau. of Queen Milena (1847–1923) and Nicholas (b. 1841), king of Montenegro (r. 1910–1918); m. Victor Emmanuel III (1869–1947), king of Italy (r. 1900–1946, abdicated), Oct 24, 1896; children: Yolanda Margherita (b. 1901); Umberto II (1904–1983), king of Italy (r. 1946); Mafalda of Hesse (1902–1944), who m. Philip of Hesse); Giovanna of Italy (b. 1907, who m. Boris III, king of Bulgaria); Maria (b. 1914).

ELENORA. Variant of Eleanor.

ELEONOR. Variant of Eleanor.

ELEONORA I GONZAGA (1598–1655). See Gonzaga, Eleonora I.

ELEONORA II GONZAGA (1628–1686). See Gonzaga, Eleonora II.

ELEONORA OF AUSTRIA (1534–1594). Duchess of Mantua. Name variations: Eleonora Gonzaga. Born Nov 2, 1534, in Vienna; died Aug 5, 1594, in Mantua; dau. of Ferdinand I, Holy Roman emperor (r. 1558–1564), and Anna of Bohemia and Hungary (1503–1547); sister of Elizabeth of Habsburg (d. 1545), Catherine of Habsburg (1533–1572), and Maximilian II (1527–1576), Holy Roman emperor (r. 1564–1576); m. Guglielmo Gonzaga (1538–1587), 3rd duke of Mantua (r. 1550–1587), duke of Monferrato, in 1561; children: Vincenzo I (1562–1612), 4th duke of Mantua (r. 1587–1612); Margherita Gonzaga (1564–1618); Anna Caterina Gonzaga (1566–1621). ❖ Deeply religious daughter of the Holy Roman emperor, married Guglielmo Gonzaga and had 3 children.

ELEONORA OF ESTE. See Este, Eleonora d'.

ELEONORA OF TOLEDO. See Medici, Eleonora de.

ELEONORE. Variant of Eleanor or Eleanora.

ELEONORE HOHENZOLLERN (1583–1607). Electress of Brandenburg. Born Aug 12, 1583; died Mar 31, 1607; dau. of Maria Eleanora (1550–1608) and Albert Frederick (b. 1553), duke of Prussia; became 2nd wife of Joachim Frederick (1546–1608), elector of Brandenburg (r. 1598–1608), Oct 23, 1603; children: Marie Eleonore (1607–1675). ❖ Joachim Frederick's 1st wife was Catherine of Custrin (1549–1602).

ELEONORE OF SAVOY (d. 1324). French countess. Name variations: Eleonore de Savoie. Died in 1324; dau. of Amadeus V the Great (c. 1253–1323), count of Savoy (r. 1285–1323); possibly half-sister of Anne of Savoy (c. 1320–1353) Byzantine empress; m. William de Chalon, count of Auxerre and Tonnerre, Jan 12, 1292; children: Jeanne of Chalon (1300–1333), countess of Tonnerre; John II, count of Auxerre (b. 1292).

ELEVENTH DAY DREAM. See Bean, Janet Beveridge.

ELFGIFU (c. 914–?). West Saxon princess. Name variations: Aelfgifu or Ælfgifu. Born c. 914; dau. of Edward I the Elder (c. 870–924), king of the English (r. 899–924), and Elflaed (d. 920); possibly m. Conrad, king of Burgundy (some sources cite Boleslav II the Pious, duke of Bohemia); children: (if Boleslav) possibly Boleslav III, duke of Bohemia; (if Boleslav) Jaromir Premysl, duke of Bohemia. Boleslav's 2nd wife was Hemma of Bohemia (c. 930–c. 1005).

ELFGIFU (d. 944). Queen of the English. Name variations: Aelfgifu or Ælfgifu; Saint Aelfgifu. Died 944; became 1st wife of Edmund I the Magnificent (921–946), king of the English (r. 939–946), before 940; children: Edwy also known as Eadwig (c. 940–959), king of the English (r. 955–959); Edgar (944–975), king of the English (r. 959–975); and a daughter (name unknown, who m. Baldwin, count of Hesdin).

ELFGIFU (d. 959). Anglo-Saxon queen. Name variations: Aelfgifu; Elgiva. Died Sept 959 in Gloucester, Gloucestershire, England; dau. of Aethelgifu also spelled Ethelgifu; m. Edwy also known as Eadwig (c. 940–959), king of the English (r. 955–959), c. 955 (marriage annulled). ❖ Because of their blood kinship, was separated from husband King Eadwig by proclamation of Archbishop Odo, a Norman prelate and noble whose half-brother was William I the Conqueror. ❖ See also Women in World History.

ELFGIFU (c. 963–1002). Queen of the English. Name variations: Aelfgifu or Ælfgifu; Elfled, Elfreda, Elgifu. Born c. 963; died Feb 1002, in Winchester, England; dau. of Thored, sometimes referred to as Ethelbert, and Hilda; became 1st wife of Aethelred or Ethelred II the Unready (c. 968–1016), king of the English (r. 979–1013, deposed, 1014–1016), in 985; children: Athelstan or Ethelstan the Atheling (d. 1015); Egbert (d. around 1005); Edmund II Ironside (c. 989–1016), king of the English (r. 1016); Edred (d. around 1012); Eadwig (or Edwy, d. in 1017); Edgar (d. around 1012); Edith (who m. Edric Streona and Thurkil the Tall); Elfgifu (c. 997–?, who m. Uchtred, earl of Northumberland); Wulfhild (who m. Ulfcytel), and two others. Ethelred II's 2nd wife was Emma of Normandy (c. 985–1052).

ELFGIFU (c. 997–?). West Saxon princess and countess of Northumberland. Born c. 997; dau. of Elfgifu (c. 963–1002) and Aethelred or Ethelred II the Unready (c. 968–1016), king of the English (r. 979–1013, deposed, 1014–1016); m. Uchtred, earl of Northumberland (r. around 965–1018); children: Edith (fl. 1040, who m. the brother of Duncan I, king of Scotland).

ELFGIFU OF AELFHELM (c. 1000–1044). See Elfgifu of Northampton.

ELFGIFU OF NORTHAMPTON (c. 1000–1044). Regent of Norway. Name variations: Aelfgifu, Aelgifu, Eligifu, Alfifa, Aelfgifu of Aelfhelm, Aelfgifu of Northumbria; Aelfgiva of Northampton. Born c. 1000 (some sources cite 996) in Northamptonshire, England; died Dec 31, 1044, in England; dau. of Earl Elfheim and Wulfrun of Northamptonshire; mistress and probably wife of Cnut II also known as Canute I the Great (c. 995/998–1035), later king of England (r. 1016–1035), Denmark (r. 1019–1035), and Norway (r. 1028–1035); children: Sven also known as Sweyn (c. 1015–1036), king of Norway (r. 1030–1035); Harald or Harold I Harefoot (c. 1015–1040), king of England (r. 1036–1039 or 1037–1040). ❖ Born into a noble Saxon family, fell in love with King Olaf Haraldson the Stout of Norway who had invaded England to try to win its crown; became his mistress and reigned with Olaf until another invader, Canute I the Great of Denmark, kidnapped her (1013), making her his mistress; reigned with him over England, Denmark, and eventually Norway; appointed regent of Norway (c. 1030); was a far from benevolent ruler, instigating harsh laws and severe punishments for lawbreakers and those disloyal to herself or Canute; after Canute died, fled to England (1036); conducted a successful campaign to popularize son Harald Harefoot as a contender for the kingship. ❖ See also *Women in World History*.

ELFGIFU OF NORTHUMBRIA (c. 1000–1044). *See Elfgifu of Northampton.*

ELFLAED (d. 714). Anglo-Saxon abbess. Name variations: Aelflaed; Aelfled; Aelfflaed; Elfleda; Elflaed; Aelfleda of Whitby; Elfleda of Whitby. Born in Northumbria, date unknown; died in 713 or 714; dau. of Oswin also known as Oswio or Oswy (612?–670), king of Northumbria, and Eanfleda (626–?); granddau. of Ethelberga of Northumbria (d. 647); great granddau. of Bertha of Kent. ❖ Anglo-Saxon abbess of Whitby, the pre-eminent center of learning in Anglo-Saxon England, was a deeply pious Christian who worked hard to ensure that the people of Northumbria adopted Christian beliefs and practices; joining the convent of Whitby, received spiritual guidance from Hilda of Whitby; became renowned as a founder of religious establishments and for her generous acts of charity; is remembered as the founder of the 1st church at Canterbury; succeeded as abbess upon Hilda's death (Nov 17, 680), sharing the rule with her mother Eanfleda. ❖ See also *Women in World History*.

ELFLAED (d. 920). Queen of the English. Name variations: Aelflaed; Aelflaeda; Aelfflaed; Ælfflaed; Elflaeda. Died 920; interred at Winchester Cathedral, London; dau. of Ethelhelm, archbishop of Canterbury, and Elswitha; m. Edward I the Elder (c. 870–924), king of the English (r. 899–924); children: Elfweard, king of the English (d. 924); Edflaed (c. 900–?, became a nun); Edgifu (902–951); Edwin (drowned in 933); Elflaed (c. 905–c. 963); Ethelflaeda (became a nun at Romsey); Ethelhild (son); Edhild (d. 946); Editha (c. 912–946); Elfgifu (c. 914–?).

ELFLAED (c. 905–c. 963). English princess. Born c. 905; died c. 963 in Winchester, England; interred at Wilton Abbey, Wiltshire; dau. of Edward I the Elder (c. 870–924), king of the English (r. 899–924), and Elflaed (d. 920). ❖ Became a nun at Winchester.

ELFLAED (fl. 1030). Queen of Scotland. Name variations: Aelflaed of Northumbria; Sybil. Fl. around 1030; dau. of Ealred, earl of Northumberland, and Efflaed of Bernicia (dau. of Ealdred of Bernicia, lord of Bamburgh); cousin of Siward, earl of Northumberland; m. Duncan I (c. 1001–1040), king of Scots (r. 1034–1040), c. 1030; children: Malcolm III Canmore (1031–1093), king of Scots (r. 1057–1093); Donalbane or Donald III (c. 1033–1099), king of Scots (r. 1093–1098); Maelmuir Dunkeld (b. around 1035).

ELFLEDA. *Variant of Elflaed.*

ELFLEDA or ELFLIDA (869–918). *See Ethelflaed, Lady of the Mercians.*

ELFRIDA (c. 945–c. 1000). *See Elfthrith.*

ELFTHRITH (fl. 7th c.). English abbess and scholar. Name variations: Aelfthryth; Aelfthrith; Aethelfryth; Ethelfryth. Fl. in 7th century. ❖ A renowned scholar, was abbess of Repton which became renowned for the education of its nuns and for the superior schooling given there to lay pupils. ❖ See also *Women in World History*.

ELFTHRITH (d. 929). Countess of Flanders. Name variations: Aelfthrith; Aelfthryth; Aethelfryth; Ælfthryth; Aefthryth; Efthryth; (Lat.) Eltrudis. Birth date unknown; died June 7, 929, in Flanders; buried at St. Peter's Abbey, in Ghent, Flanders, Belgium; dau. of Alfred the Great (848–c. 900), king of the English (r. 871–899) and Elswitha (d. 902); sister of Ethelflaed (869–918); m. Baldwin II (d. 918), count of Flanders (r. 878–918), before 900; children: Arnolph also known as Arnulf I (d. 965), count of Flanders (r. 918–950, 961–964); Adelulf, count of Boulogne; and two daughters (names unknown).

ELFTHRITH (c. 945–1002). Anglo-Saxon queen. Name variations: Aelfthrith, Aelfthryth, Aethelfryth, Elfthryth, Ethelfryth, or Elfrida. Born c. 945 at Lydford Castle, Devon, England; died Nov 17, 1002, at Wherwell Abbey, Hampshire; dau. of Ordgar (ealdorman of Devon); m. Ethelwald (ealdorman of the East Anglians), c. 962; after his death, became 2nd wife of Eadgar or Edgar (944–975), king of the English (r. 959–975), in 965; children: (1st m.) Edmund (b. around 965); Ethelflaeda (c. 963–c. 1016, abbess at Romsey); (2nd m.) Edmund (d. 971); Aethelred or Ethelred II the Unready (968–1016), king of the English (r. 979–1016, who m. Emma of Normandy). ❖ Supposed to have caused the murder of stepson Edward II the Martyr, king of England, at Corfe (978), in order to secure the election of her son Ethelred II the Unready to the throne of England; became a nun (986). ❖ See also *Women in World History*.

ELFTHRYTH. *Variant of Elfthrith.*

ELFWYN (c. 882–?). Queen of Mercia. Name variations: Aelfwyn; Ælfwyn; Elfwynn. Born c. 882; dau. of Ethelflaed (869–918), Lady of the Mercians, and Ethelred II, ealdorman of Mercia; m. a West Saxon noble. ❖ On death of mother, briefly ruled Mercia (June–Dec 918); reign was cut short by her uncle Edward the Elder, who removed her to Wessex.

ELG, Taina (1931—). Finnish actress and dancer. Born Mar 9, 1931, in Impilahti, Finland; trained at Finnish State Opera Ballet. ❖ As a child, performed with the Helsinki company of the Finnish State Opera Ballet; danced with Sadler's Wells and Marquis de Cuevas ballet troupes; made film debut as Elissa in *The Prodigal* (1955), followed by *Diane, Gaby, Les Girls, Imitation General, Watusi, The 39 Steps, The Bacchantes, Hercules in New York,* and *Liebestraum,* among others; appeared as Olympia Buchanan on tv series "One Life to Live" (1980–81); became a naturalized US citizen.

ELGAR, Alice (1848–1920). British author. Name variations: Lady Alice Roberts Elgar; Lady Caroline Alice Elgar; Caroline Alice Roberts. Born Caroline Alice Roberts, Oct 9, 1848, at Bhooj (now Gujerat), India; died in London, April 7, 1920; dau. of Major-General Sir Henry Gee Roberts (hero of Sepoy Mutiny and Sikh Wars) and Julia Maria (Raikes) Roberts; m. Edward Elgar (composer), 1889 (died 1934); children: Carice Elgar (b. 1890). ❖ Wife of Sir Edward Elgar, who served as his inspiration, critic, literary advisor, and music scribe, mastered several foreign languages when young, particularly German; penned both a long poem (*Isabel Trevithoe,* 1879) and a novel (*Marchcroft Manor,* 1882), both of which were published under name Caroline Alice Roberts; began to take violin lessons from Edward Elgar (1886); following marriage, was convinced that her husband was a potential genius, and that her task was to help him achieve the full potentialities of his talents; also provided him with verse for the following works: *Scenes from the Bavarian Highlands, O Happy Eyes, Fly, Singing Bird* and *The Snow,* the latter two being excerpts from her long poem *Isabel Trevithoe;* provided one of the poems, *In Haven (Capri),* for his orchestral song cycle, *Sea Pictures,* which received an enthusiastic reception at its 1899 premiere with Clara Butt as the soloist. ❖ See also Percy M. Young, *Alice Elgar: Enigma of a Victorian Lady* (Dobson, 1978); and *Women in World History*.

ELGIN, countess of (1778–1855). *See Nisbet, Mary.*

ELGIN, Mary (1778–1855). *See Nisbet, Mary.*

ELGIN, Suzette Haden (1936—). American science-fiction writer. Name variations: Suzette Elgin. Born Patricia Anne Suzette Wilkins, Nov 18, 1936, in Louisiana, Missouri; attended University of Chicago, 1954–56; California State University at Chico, BA in French and English, 1967; University of California at San Diego, MA in Linguistics, 1970, PhD, 1973; m. Peter Joseph Haden, 1955 (died); m. George N. Elgin, 1964; children: (1st m.) 2 daughters, 1 son; (2nd m.) 1 son. ❖ Taught linguistics at San Diego State University; retired (1980); was a founding director of Ozark Center for Language Studies and editor of *Lonesome Node;* published 1st novel, *The Communipaths* (1970), starting her "Coyote Jones" series, which includes *Furthest* (1971), *Star-Anchored, Star-Angered* and *Yonder Comes the Other End of Time;* launched her "Ozark" trilogy with *Twelve Fair Kingdoms* (1981); other writings include *At the Seventh Level* (1972) and *Native Tongue* (1984); also wrote books on linguistics including *What is Linguistics?* (1979), *The*

Gentle Art of Verbal Self-Defense (1980), and grammar of invented language Láadan, *A First Grammar and Dictionary of Láadan* (1984).

ELGIVA. *Variant of Elfgifu.*

ELGIVA (fl. 1020). Queen of England. Name variations: Algiva. Married Harold I Harefoot (c. 1015–1040), king of England (r. 1036–1040); children: Elfwin, monk at St. Foi Aquitaine.

ELGOOD, Bonté S. (1874–1960). *See Elgood, Cornelia.*

ELGOOD, Cornelia (1874–1960). English physician. Name variations: Bonté Sheldon Amos; Cornelia Sheldon Amos; Cornelia Bonté Sheldon Amos; Bonté S. Elgood. Born Cornelia Bonté Sheldon Amos in 1874; died 1960 in London, England; dau. of a judge for Egyptian judicial system; sister of Sir Maurice Sheldon Amos (1872–1940, judicial advisor to Egypt's legal system); London University, MD, 1900; m. Major Percy G. Elgood (writer), 1907. ❖ Fluent in Arabic, was hired by International Quarantine Board of Egypt, the 1st woman hired by the Egyptian government (1901); worked in Quarantine Hospitals at El-Tor in Suez for 2 years; after transfer to Alexandria (1902), opened a free clinic for women and children at a government hospital; transferred to Cairo (1906) and hired by the Ministry of Education to improve the education of Egyptian girls, a program that grew from 3 schools in 1906 to 106 schools by 1923 and was implemented nationally; sponsored 6 Egyptian women to study medicine in England; collaborated with the Countess of Cromer's commission to create the 1st free children's dispensaries in Egypt; served on the board of the Victoria Hospital; fled to London during Suez Crisis (1956) and the nationalization of the Suez Canal. Was the 1st woman to receive an honor from an Egyptian agency for public service (Decoration of the Nile, 1923); made Officer of the Order of the British Empire (1918) and Commander of the Order of the British Empire (1939); received a Union des Femmes de France silver medal and a French Medaélle de la Recomissance Française for work for Allied troops in Egypt during WWI.

ELIAS, Rosalind (1930—). American mezzo-soprano. Born on Mar 13, 1930, in Lowell, Massachusetts; studied at New England Conservatory, Boston, and at Academia di Santa Cecilia, Rome. ❖ Debuted at the Metropolitan Opera (1954); sang over 45 roles there; also performed in Europe, including appearances at Glyndebourne and in South America; was a part of Leonard Bernstein's traveling casts; also concertized widely and made many recordings for RCA; remained best known for her role as Erika in *Vanessa,* the Samuel Barber-Gian Carlo Menotti opera.

ELIASSON, Marthe (1969—). Norwegian handball player. Born Sept 27, 1969, in Norway. ❖ At Seoul Olympics, won a silver medal in team competition (1988).

ELIE DE BEAUMONT, Anne Louise (1730–1783). French novelist. Name variations: Anne-Louise Morin-Dumesnil Elie de Beaumont; Madame or Mme Elie de Beaumont. Born Anne Louise Morin du Mesnil in 1730 in Caen, France, into a Huguenot family; died 1783; m. Jean-Baptiste Elie de Beaumont (lawyer at Parlement and advocate of religious tolerance). ❖ Wrote *Lettres du marquis de Roselle* (1764) and completed Madame de Tencin's *Anecdotes de la cour et du règne d'Edouard II* (1776).

ELIGIFU. *Variant of Elfgifu.*

ELINE, Grace (1898—). American theatrical dancer. Born Aug 12, 1898, in Milwaukee, Wisconsin; sister of Marie Eline (1902–1981). ❖ Worked for Thanhouser Studios with sister Marie in New York City where she was known as Thanhouser Juvenile; performed on Broadway as a child in *The Prince of Bohemia* (1909), *The Jolly Bachelors* (1910), *Lady of the Slipper* (1912), and later in *Big Boy* (1926), among others; appeared in vaudeville and clubs with Rudolf Valentino (1915–16), and on tour with Joe Weston in exhibition ballroom act (1917–26); performed with sister once more for series of Prologs (late 1920s), before retiring (mid-1930s).

ELINE, Marie (1902–1981). American child actress. Name variations: Anne B. Carlisle. Born Feb 27, 1902, in Milwaukee, Wisconsin; died Jan 3, 1981, in Longview, Washington; sister of child actress Grace Eline (b. 1898). ❖ Popular child actress, billed as The Thanhouser Kidlet (1909–14, as was Helen Badgley), films include *Jane Eyre, She, Coals of Fire,* and *Uncle Tom's Cabin.*

ELING SOONG (1890–1973). *See Song Ailing.*

ELINOR. *Variant of Eleanor.*

ELION, Gertrude B. (1918–1999). American biochemist and pharmacologist. Pronunciation: ELL-EE-un. Born Gertrude Belle Elion in New York, NY, Jan 23, 1918; died in Chapel Hill, North Carolina, Feb 21, 1999; dau. of Bertha (Cohen) Elion and Robert Elion (dentist); Hunter College, AB, 1937; New York University, MSC, 1941; George Washington University, DSc, 1969; Brown University, DMS, 1969; never married; no children. ❖ Nobel laureate who developed drugs for treatment of leukemia and rejection of transplanted organs and laid the groundwork for the development of AZT in the fight against AIDS; became nursing assistant, New York Hospital (1937); hired as assistant organic chemist, Denver Chemical Co. (1938); became analyst in food chemistry, Quaker Maid Co. (1942); worked as researcher in organic chemistry, Johnson and Johnson (1943); worked as assistant research chemist, Burroughs Wellcome (1944); with George Hitchings, postulated that it might be possible to develop a drug that inhibits the rapid division of cells, such as tumors, protozoa, and bacteria; developed antimetabolite drug designed to block the enzymes essential for the creation of cellular DNA which was approved as 6-mercaptopurine by US Food and Drug Administration (1953); synthesized azathioprine, a modification of 6-mercaptopurine, which proved invaluable in preventing the rejection of transplanted organs (1957); became assistant to the director of the chemotherapy division, Burroughs Wellcome (1963); developed trimethoprim, used to treat AIDS patients who develop pneumocystis carinii, a form of pneumonia which can prove fatal to those with immune-deficiency syndrome; headed experimental therapy, Burroughs Wellcome (1967); served as adjunct professor of pharmacology, University of North Carolina (1973); served as adjunct professor of pharmacology, Duke University (1973); synthesized acyclovir (1975); retired from Burroughs Wellcome as emeritus scientist (1983); was president of the Association for Cancer Research (1983). Awarded Nobel Prize in Physiology and Medicine with George Hitchings and Sir James Whyte Black (1988); received Medal of Honor, American Cancer Society (1990); inducted into National Inventors Hall of Fame (1991), National Women's Hall of Fame (1991), and Engineering and Science Hall of Fame (1992). ❖ See also *Women in World History.*

ELIOT, George (1819–1880). *See Evans, Mary Anne.*

ELIOT, Martha May (1891–1978). American physician and founder. Born April 7, 1891, in Dorchester, Massachusetts; died 1978; dau. of the Reverend Christopher Rhodes Eliot (Unitarian cleric) and Mary Jackson (May) Eliot; Radcliffe, BA, 1913; Johns Hopkins, MD, 1918; lived with Ethel Collins Dunham (1883–1969, noted pediatrician) for 55 years. ❖ Expert on child health who helped found the World Health Organization and UNICEF, spent 30 years working for the US Children's Bureau, earning an international reputation as an expert on child health; was the 1st woman elected president of the American Public Health Association (1947); was one of the few women to join the faculty of Harvard as a full professor (Professor of Maternal and Child Health). ❖ See also *Women in World History.*

ELIOT, Vivienne (1889–1947). English editor and literary inspiration. Born Vivienne Haigh-Wood in 1889; died in 1946; sister of Maurice Haigh-Wood; m. T.S. Eliot (the poet), 1915 (div. 1933). ❖ The inspiration for much of her husband's poetry, was a gifted writer and editor in her own right and the subject of Michael Hasting's play *Tom and Viv;* was committed to an asylum by her brother (1938). ❖ See also Carole Seymour-Jones, *Painted Shadow: The Life of Vivienne Eliot, First Wife of T.S. Eliot, and the Long-Suppressed Truth About Her Influence on His Genius* (Doubleday, 2002).

ELISA. *Variant of Elissa.*

ELISA (fl. 800 BCE?). *See Dido.*

ELISA, Henriqueta (1843–1885). Portuguese poet. Born 1843 in Portugal; died 1885. ❖ Wrote *Lágrimas e Saudades* (1864).

ELISABETA. *Variant of Elisabeth or Elizabeth.*

ELISABETH. *Variant of Elizabeth.*

ELISABETH (1894–1956). Queen of the Hellenes. Name variations: Elisabetha; Elizabeth Hohenzollern; Elizabeth of Greece; Elizabeth of Rumania or Romania. Born Elizabeth Charlotte Josephine Alexandra Victoria, Oct 12, 1894, in Sinaia, Romania; died Nov 15, 1956, in Cannes, France; dau. of Ferdinand I, king of Romania, and Marie of Rumania (1875–1938); m. George II (1890–1947), king of the Hellenes, Feb 27, 1921 (div. 1935); children: none.

ÉLISABETH, Madame (1764–1794). French princess. Name variations: Madame Elisabeth; Elizabeth or Élisabeth de France; Elisabeth of France. Born Élisabeth Philippine Marie Hélène at Versailles, France, May 3, 1764; guillotined May 10, 1794; daughter and last child of Louis the Dauphin (1729–1765) and his 2nd wife Marie Josèphe of Saxony (1731–1767); sister of three kings of France: Louis XVI (r. 1774–1792), Louis XVIII (r. 1814–1824), and Charles X (r. 1824–1830). ❧ Left an orphan at age 3, shared a deep attachment with her brother Louis XVI; demonstrated a generous nature, taking an interest in charitable works; pious, refused all offers of marriage so that she might remain by the side of her brother; from the beginning of French Revolution, was well aware of the gravity of the situation, but refused to leave the king; disguised as a bonneted nurse, accompanied Louis, Marie Antoinette, and the royal children on flight from Versailles (June 20, 1792) and was arrested with them at Varennes; was condemned to death. ❧ See also *Women in World History.*

ÉLISABETH D'AUTRICHE (d. 1545). *See Elizabeth of Habsburg.*

ÉLISABETH DE FRANCE (1764–1794). *See Elizabeth, Madame.*

ÉLISABETH OF AUSTRIA (1554–1592). *See Elizabeth of Habsburg.*

ÉLISABETH OF BELGIUM (1876–1965). *See Elizabeth of Bavaria.*

ÉLISABETH OF HABSBURG (1501–1526). Queen of Denmark and Norway. Name variations: Elisabeth of Hapsburg; Elizabeth of the Netherlands; Isabella or Isabel of Spain; Isabella Habsburg; Ysabeau. Born July 18, 1501; died Jan 19, 1526 (some sources cite 1525); dau. of Juana la Loca (1479–1555) and Philip I the Fair (or Philip the Handsome), archduke of Austria, king of Castile and Leon (r. 1506, son of Maximilian I, Holy Roman emperor); sister of Charles V, Holy Roman emperor (r. 1519–1556), Mary of Hungary (1505–1558), Ferdinand I, Holy Roman emperor (r. 1558–1564), and Eleanor of Portugal (1498–1558); m. Christian II (1481–1559), king of Denmark and Norway (r. 1513–1523), Aug 12, 1515; children: John (b. 1518); twins Maximilian and Philipp (b. 1519); Dorothea of Denmark (1520–1580), who m. Frederick II, elector Palatine); Christina of Denmark (1521–1590), who m. Francesco Maria Sforza, duke of Milan, and Francis I, duke of Lorraine).

ÉLISABETH OF HABSBURG (1554–1592). Austrian archduchess and queen of France. Name variations: Élisabeth d'Autriche; Archduchess Elizabeth; Elizabeth of Habsburg; Elizabeth of Hapsburg; Elisabeth of Austria; Elisabeta; Isabelle d'Autriche; Isabella of Austria; Isabelle; signed her name Isabell; family name sometimes Hapsbourg, Hapsburg. Born July 5, 1554, in Vienna, Austria; died Jan 22, 1592, in Vienna; originally interred in Our Lady of Angels Convent Church, Vienna; remains transferred to crypt of St. Stephen's Cathedral, Vienna, 1782; 2nd dau. of Maximilian II (1527–1576), Holy Roman emperor (r. 1564–1576, son of Holy Roman Emperor Ferdinand I) and Marie of Austria (1528–1603), Holy Roman empress; educated by private tutors; sister of Anne of Austria (c. 1550–1580), Rudolf II, Holy Roman emperor (r. 1576–1612); m. Charles IX (1550–1574), king of France (crowned king of France, May 15, 1560 or 1561, on Oct 22, 1570 (died May 30, 1574). children: Marie Isabelle de France (Oct 27, 1572–April 2, 1578, godchild of Queen Elizabeth I of England). ❧ Supported reformed Catholicism (the "Counter-Reformation") in France and the Habsburg territories of Central Europe; married at 16 to king of France in imperial ceremony at Speyer (Oct 22, 1570); married in royal ceremony in Mezieres, France (Nov 26, 1570); consecrated queen of France at St. Denis (Mar 25, 1571), ceremony officiated by Archbishop of Reims; made ceremonial entry into Paris (Mar 29, 1571); lived at French court during part of the period of the Religious Wars; eclipsed by influence of mother-in-law Catherine de Medici; returned to Central Europe (1575) after death of husband, leaving daughter Marie Isabelle in France; following example of namesake St. Elisabeth, founded a convent (Vienna convent of Poor Clares, Our Lady of Angels) and supported poor and sick; acted as an important patron of the reformed Catholic cause in Central Europe, sponsoring artistic undertakings and the collection of relics; reported to have written a devotional work on the Word of God; collected an appreciable library that she bequeathed to her brother, Emperor Rudolf II. ❧ See also Graham and Johnson, *The Paris Entries of Charles IX and Elisabeth of Austria* (U. of Toronto Press, 1974); and *Women in World History.*

ÉLISABETH OF RUMANIA (1843–1916). *See Elizabeth of Wied.*

ÉLISABETH OF SAXE-ALTENBURG (1826–1896). Duchess of Oldenburg. Born Mar 26, 1826; died Feb 2, 1896; dau. of Joseph,

duke of Saxe-Altenburg, and Amelia of Wurttemberg (1799–1848); sister of Alexandra of Saxe-Altenburg (1830–1911); m. Nicholas Frederick Peter II, duke of Oldenburg, Feb 10, 1852; children: Frederick Augustus (b. 1852), grand duke of Oldenburg; George Ludwig (b. 1855).

ELISHEBA Biblical woman. Name variations: Elizabeth. Dau. of Amminadab; m. Aaron; children: Nadab, Abihu, Eleazar, and Ithamar (Ex. 6:23).

ELISHEVA (1888–1949). *See Bichovsky, Elisheva.*

ELISSA (fl. 800 BCE?). *See Dido.*

ELIZA (1737–1814). *See Moody, Elizabeth.*

ELIZABETH. *Variant of Elisabeth, Isabel or Isabella.*

ELIZABETH (fl. 1st c.). Biblical woman and mother of John the Baptist. Name variations: Elisabeth; Saint Elizabeth. Fl. in 1st century; a descendant of Aaron; m. Zachary also known as Zacharias (priest); children: St. John the Baptist. ❧ After an angel foretold husband about the birth of a son, conceived John the Baptist, who was considered the forerunner of Christ; was 6 months' pregnant when visited by cousin Mary the Virgin; in Mary's presence, felt the child move inside her as if to welcome the Messiah, whom Mary was carrying (Luke 1:39–63). Feast day is on Nov 5. ❧ See also *Women in World History.*

ELIZABETH (1770–1840). English princess, artist, and landgravine of Hesse-Homburg. Name variations: Elizabeth Guelph. Born May 22, 1770, at Buckingham House, London, England; died Jan 10, 1840, at Frankfurt-am-Main, Germany; interred in Mausoleum of Landgraves, Homburg, Germany; dau. of Charlotte of Mecklenburg-Strelitz (1744–1818) and George III (1738–1820), king of England (r. 1760–1820); m. George Ramus (page at the palace); m. Frederick VI, landgrave of Hesse-Homburg, April 7, 1818 (died 1829); children: (1st m.) Eliza Ramus (b. around 1786). ❧ Designed a series of pictures titled *The Birth and Triumph of Cupid* (1795); established a community at Windsor to provide dowries for poor girls (1808); moved to Germany upon marriage (1818); following husband's death 11 years later, set aside £6,000 per year to reduce the debts of her adopted principality. ❧ See also *Women in World History.*

ELIZABETH (1831–1903). Archduchess of Austria. Name variations: Archduchess Elisabeth. Born Jan 17, 1831; died Feb 14, 1903; dau. of Archduke Joseph (b. 1776) and Maria of Wurttemberg (1797–1855); m. Ferdinand (1821–1849), archduke of Austria (r. 1835–1848, abdicated), Dec 4, 1847; children: Maria Teresa of Este (1849–1919, who m. Louis III, king of Bavaria).

ELIZABETH (fl. 1850s). Archduchess of Austria. Fl. around 1850; m. Karl Ferdinand also known as Charles Ferdinand of Austria (1818–1874); children: Friedrich Maria Albrecht (1856–1936, who m. Isabella of Croy-Dulmen); Maria Christina of Austria (1858–1929); Karl Stefan also known as Charles Stephen (1860–1933); Eugen (1863–1954).

ELIZABETH, archduchess (d. 1545). *See Elizabeth of Habsburg.*

ELIZABETH, countess of Sutherland (1765–1839). *See Leveson-Gower, Elizabeth.*

ELIZABETH, empress of Austria (1837–1898). *See Elizabeth of Bavaria.*

ELIZABETH, grand duchess of Russia (1864–1918). *See Ella.*

ELIZABETH, queen of Spain (1602–1644). *See Elizabeth Valois.*

ELIZABETH, saint (1207–1231). *See Elizabeth of Hungary.*

ELIZABETH I (1533–1603). Queen of England. Name variations: Elizabeth Tudor, Good Queen Bess, the Virgin Queen, Gloriana. Born Sept 7, 1533, at Greenwich, England; died Mar 24, 1603, at Richmond upon Thames, Surrey; buried in Westminster Abbey; dau. of Henry VIII, king of England (r. 1509–1547) and his 2nd wife, Anne Boleyn (1507–1536); half-sister of Mary I (1516–1558), queen of England; never married. ❧ Last of the Tudor monarchs, ruled England for 45 years, establishing that island nation as a first-rate power in Europe; inherited throne (1558); appointed William Cecil as principal secretary (1558); had coronation at Westminster Abbey (Jan 15, 1559); with Parliament, devised Elizabethan Settlement of Religion through Act of Supremacy and Act of Uniformity (1559); signed Treaty of Câteau-Cambrésis ending war with France (1559); supported Scottish Reformation and signed Treaty of Edinburgh with Protestant lords (1560); kept her Catholic cousin, Mary Stuart—who had assumed Scottish throne (1561) but was deposed and exiled to England—prisoner (1568–87); suppressed Northern Rebellion of English Catholic nobles (1569) and Ridolfi Plot (1571); branded a heretic and a bastard by Pope Pius V whose bull of excommunication invited English Catholics and European princes to depose her (1570); reluctantly had Mary, Queen of Scots, executed for high treason (1587) after discovering her involvement in several plots; openly aided Dutch Revolt against Spain and licensed English privateers to prey on Spanish ships returning from the Americas (1580s); survived the major crisis of her reign when English naval forces led by Drake, Hawkins, and Howard defeated the Spanish Armada and prevented a Spanish invasion of England (1588); had latter years as queen marred by protracted and expensive war in Ireland (1595–1603), increased tension with Parliament, and betrayal by her last royal favorite, the earl of Essex, whom she had beheaded for leading a rebellion against the Crown (1601). At her death, English throne passed peacefully to Mary Stuart's son, King James VI of Scotland. ❖ See also Conyers Read, *Mr. Secretary Cecil and Queen Elizabeth* (Knopf, 1960); Jasper Ridley, *Elizabeth I: The Shrewdness of Virtue* (Viking, 1987); Ann Somerset, *Elizabeth I* (St. Martin, 1991); Wallace MacCaffrey, *Elizabeth I* (Routledge, 1993); "Elizabeth R," historically faithful 6-part miniseries starring Glenda Jackson (BBC-TV, 1976); and *Women in World History*.

ELIZABETH I OF RUSSIA (1709–1762). *See Elizabeth Petrovna.*

ELIZABETH I PETROVNA (1709–1762). *See Elizabeth Petrovna.*

ELIZABETH II (1926—). Queen of the United Kingdom of Great Britain and Northern Ireland. Name variations: Elizabeth Windsor. Born Elizabeth Alexandra Mary Windsor, April 21, 1926, in London's West End; elder dau. of Albert Frederick Arthur George, 13th duke of York, also known as George VI, king of England (r. 1936–1952), and Elizabeth Bowes-Lyon (b. 1900); sister of Princess Margaret Rose (b. 1930); m. Lieutenant Philip Mountbatten, R.N., duke of Edinburgh (son of Prince Andrew of Greece and Princess Alice of Battenberg), Nov 20, 1947; children: Charles, prince of Wales (b. 1948); Princess Anne (b. 1950); Prince Andrew, duke of York (b. 1960); Prince Edward (b. 1964). ❖ Named Heir Presumptive (1936), after abdication of Edward VIII brought her father to the throne as George VI; acceded to the throne (1952), following death of father; hoping to modernize the monarchy, made herself more accessible to the public as early as 1956; is the 42nd sovereign of England since William I the Conqueror, yet only the 6th woman to occupy the English throne in her own right; predecessors were Mary I, Elizabeth I, Mary II, Anne, and Victoria. ❖ See also Sarah Bradford, *Elizabeth: A Biography of Britain's Queen* (Farrar, 1996); Graham and Heather Fisher *Monarch: A Biography of Elizabeth II* (Salem House, 1985); and *Women in World History*.

ELIZABETH ALEXANDRA OF SAXE-ALTENBURG (1830–1911). *See Alexandra of Saxe-Altenburg.*

ELIZABETH AMALIA OF HESSE (1635–1709). Electress of the Palatinate. Name variations: Elizabeth Amalie von Hesse-Darmstadt. Born Mar 20, 1635; died Aug 4, 1709; m. Philip Wilhelm or Philip William, Elector Palatine of the Rhine, Sept 3, 1653; children: John William (b. 1658), elector of the Palatinate; Charles III Philip (b. 1661), elector of the Palatinate; Maria Sophia of Neuberg (1666–1699); Maria Anna of Neuberg (1667–1740); Eleanor of Pfalz-Neuburg (1655–1720). Philip William's 1st wife was Anna Constancia (1619–1651).

ELIZABETH BOWES-LYON (1900–2002). Queen-consort of England and mother of Elizabeth II. Name variations: Queen Elizabeth; Queen Mum; Duchess of York. Born Lady Elizabeth Angela Marguerite Bowes-Lyon, Aug 4, 1900, in London, England; died Mar 30, 2002, in London; youngest daughter and 9th of 10 children of Claude Bowes-Lyon, 14th earl of Strathmore and Kinghorne, and Nina Cavendish-Bentinck, Lady Strathmore; descendent of Robert Bruce, king of Scotland; m. Albert (d. 1952), duke of York, also known as George VI, king of England (r. 1936–1952), April 26, 1923; children: Elizabeth Alexandra Mary (future queen of England as Elizabeth II, b. April 21, 1926); Princess Margaret Rose (b. 1930). ❖ A commoner, did not follow the usual path to the throne but arrived there by default (1936), when husband Albert, duke of York, became King George VI following the abdication of his brother Edward VIII; often described as a reluctant queen, helped husband (a shy, sensitive man with a debilitating stutter) rise to become a national figurehead; also became the most popular queen-consort in British history. ❖ See also Robert Lacey, *Queen Mother* (Little, Brown, 1987); Ann Morrow, *The Queen Mother* (Stein and Day, 1984); Grania Forbes, *My Darling Buffy: The Early Life of the Queen Mother* (Richard Cohen Books, 1997); and *Women in World History*.

ELIZABETH CAROLINE (1740–1759). English princess. Name variations: Elizabeth Guelph; Elizabeth Caroline Hanover. Born Dec 30, 1740, at Norfolk House, London, England; died Sept 4, 1759, in Kew Palace, Richmond, Surrey, England; buried at Westminster Abbey; dau. of Frederick Louis, prince of Wales, and Augusta of Saxe-Gotha (1719–1772); sister of George III, king of England.

ELIZABETH-CHARLOTTE (1676–1744). Duchess of Lorraine. Born Elizabeth-Charlotte Bourbon-Orleans; Elizabeth Charlotte d'Orleans. Born Sept 13, 1676; died Dec 23, 1744; dau. of Charlotte Elizabeth of Bavaria (1652–1722) and Philip, duke of Orléans (brother of Louis XIV of France); m. Leopold, duke of Lorraine, Oct 25, 1698; children: Leopold; Francis III (b. 1708), duke of Lorraine and Bar, also known as Francis I, Holy Roman emperor; Charles (b. 1712); Elizabeth of Lorraine (1711–1741); Anna Charlotte of Lorraine (1714–1774).

ELIZABETH-CHARLOTTE OF BAVARIA (1652–1722). *See Charlotte Elizabeth of Bavaria.*

ELIZABETH CHARLOTTE OF THE PALATINATE (fl. 1620). Electress of Brandenburg and duchess of Cleves. Fl. around 1620; m. George William (1595–1640), elector of Brandenburg (r. 1619–1640), duke of Cleves and Prussia; children: Frederick William (1620–1688), the Great Elector of Brandenburg (r. 1640–1688).

ELIZABETH-CHARLOTTE OF THE PALATINATE (1652–1722). *See Charlotte Elizabeth of Bavaria.*

ELIZABETH CHRISTINA OF BRUNSWICK-WOLFENBUTTEL (1691–1750). Holy Roman empress. Name variations: Elizabeth Christina of Brunswick-Wolfenbüttel; Elizabeth Christina of Brunswick; Elizabeth of Brunswick; Elizabeth Christine. Born Elizabeth Christine of Brunswick-Lünebrug-Wolfenbüttel, princess of the German house of Brunswick-Wolfenbüttel, Aug 28, 1691, in Wolfenbüttel; died Dec 21, 1750, in Vienna; dau. of Ludwig Rudolf also known as Louis Rudolph, duke of Brunswick-Wolfenbüttel; her younger sister Charlotte of Brunswick-Wolfenbuttel (1694–1715) m. Alexis, son of Peter the Great of Russia; m. Charles VI (1685–1740), Holy Roman emperor (r. 1711–1740); children: Leopold (died in infancy in 1716); Maria Theresa of Austria (1717–1780); Maria Anna (1718–1744) and Maria Amalia (1724–1730).

ELIZABETH CHRISTINA OF BRUNSWICK-WOLFENBUTTEL (1715–1797). Queen of Prussia. Name variations: Elizabeth Christina of Brunswick-Wolfenbüttel; Elizabeth Christine. Born Nov 8, 1715; died Jan 13, 1797; dau. of Antoinetta Amelia (1696–1762) and Ferdinand Albert II, duke of Brunswick-Wolfenbüttel; m. Frederick II the Great, king of Prussia (1712–1786, r. 1740–1786), June 12, 1733; children: none. ❖ See also *Women in World History*.

ELIZABETH CHRISTINE. *See Elizabeth Christina of Brunswick-Wolfenbuttel (1691–1750) or (1715–1797).*

ELIZABETH DE BOURBON (1614–1664). Duchess of Savoy-Nemours. Name variations: Elizabeth Vendôme or Vendome; Elizabeth de Vendome. Born Aug 1614 in Paris, France; died May 19, 1664; dau. of Ceaser (1594–1665), duke of Vendome (and son of Henry IV, king of France, and Gabrielle d'Estrées), and Françoise de Lorraine-Mercoeur (1592–1669); m. Charles Amadeus of Savoy-Nemours, also known as Charles Amedeé of Savoy, 1643 (he was killed in a duel with his brother-in-law, François de Vendome, duke of Beaufort); children: Marie Françoise of Savoy (1646–1683), Jeanne of Nemours (1644–1724).

ELIZABETH DE BURGH (1295–1360). *See Clare, Elizabeth de.*

ELIZABETH DE BURGH (d. 1327). Queen of Scots. Name variations: Ellen; Elizabeth of Ulster. Died Oct 26, 1327, in Cullen, Grampian, Scotland; buried in Dunfermline Abbey, Fife, Scotland; dau. of Richard de Burgh (known as The Red Earl), 2nd earl of Ulster, and Margaret de Burgh (d. 1303); became 2nd wife of Robert I the Bruce, king of Scots (r. 1306–1329), 1302; children: Matilda Bruce (d. 1353); Margaret Bruce (d. 1346); David II (1323–1370), king of Scotland (r. 1329–1370); John Bruce (b. around 1325). ❖ See also *Women in World History*.

ELIZABETH DE BURGH (1332–1363). Countess of Ulster. Born July 6, 1332, in Carrickfergus Castle, Northern Ireland; died April 25, 1363, in Dublin, Ireland; dau. of William de Burgh, the "Brown Earl," 3rd earl of Ulster, and Maud Plantagenet (c. 1310–c. 1377); granddau. of Elizabeth de Clare who was also known as Elizabeth de Burgh (1295–1360); m. Lionel of Antwerp (1338–1368), duke of Clarence, Sept 9, 1352;

children: Philippa Mortimer (1355–1382), countess of Ulster and March. ❖ Was sole heir to earldom of Ulster, when father was murdered by order of his cousins; while still a child, was taken to England by mother; on marriage, her husband could lay claim to the extensive de Burgh estates in Ireland but was unable to enforce those rights during his lifetime. ❖ See also *Women in World History.*

ELIZABETH DE FRANCE (1764–1794). *See Elizabeth, Madame.*

ELIZABETH DE FARNESE (1692–1766). *See Farnese, Elizabeth.*

ELIZABETH DE LA POLE (1444–1503). *See Pole, Elizabeth de la.*

ELIZABETH FARNESE (1692–1766). *See Farnese, Elizabeth.*

ELIZABETH FEODOROVNA (1864–1918). *See Ella.*

ELIZABETH FERRERS (1392–1434). *See Ferrers, Elizabeth.*

ELIZABETH FREDERIKE OF BAYREUTH (fl. 1750). Duchess of Wurttemberg. Fl. around 1750; 1st wife of Karl Eugene also known as Charles Eugene (1728–1793), duke of Wurttemberg (r. 1737–1793).

ELIZABETH HENRIETTA OF HESSE-CASSEL (1661–1683). German noblewoman. Born Nov 8, 1661, in Cassel; died June 27, 1683, in Coln au Der, Spree; dau. of William VI the Just (b. 1629), landgrave of Hesse-Cassel; became 1st wife of Frederick III (1657–1713), elector of Brandenburg (r. 1688–1701), later Frederick I, king of Prussia (r. 1701–1713), Aug 23, 1679; children: Louise Dorothea of Brandenburg (1680–1705). Frederick's 2nd wife was Sophie Charlotte of Hanover (1668–1705).

ELIZABETH HOHENZOLLERN (1815–1885). Grand duchess of Hesse. Name variations: Elizabeth of Prussia; princess of Prussia. Born Mary Elizabeth Caroline Victoria, June 18, 1815; died Mar 21, 1885; dau. of William Hohenzollern and Mary of Hesse-Homburg (1785–1846); m. Charles of Hesse-Darmstadt, Oct 22, 1836; children: Louis IV (1837–1892), grand duke of Hesse-Darmstadt; Henry (b. 1838); Anna of Hesse (1843–1865, who m. Francis II Frederick, grand duke of Mecklenburg); William (b. 1845).

ELIZABETH HOHENZOLLERN (1894–1956). *See Elizabeth, queen of the Hellenes.*

ELIZABETH HOWARD.
See Howard, Elizabeth (1494–1558).
See Tylney, Elizabeth (d. 1497).
See Howard, Elizabeth (d. 1534).
See Howard, Elizabeth (d. 1538).

ELIZABETH MARIA OF THURN AND TAXIS (1860–1881). Duchess of Braganza. Born May 28, 1860, in Dresden; died Feb 7, 1881, in Odenburg; dau. of Maximilian Anton Lamoral, prince of Thurn and Taxis, and Helene of Bavaria (1834–1890); m. Miguel, duke of Braganza, Oct 17, 1877; children: Miguel Maximiliano (b. 1878), duke of Vizeu; Francisco José Gerado (b. 1879); Maria Teresa Carolina (1881–1945, who m. Charles Louis, prince of Thurn and Taxis).

ELIZABETH MUIR or MURE (d. before 1355). *See Muir, Elizabeth.*

ELIZABETH OF ANHALT (1563–1607). Electress of Brandenburg. Born Sept 25, 1563; died Sept 28, 1607; dau. of Joachim Ernst (b. 1536), prince of Anhalt, and Agnes of Barby (1540–1569); became third wife of John George (1525–1598), elector of Brandenburg (r. 1571–1598), Oct 6, 1577; children: Magdalene of Brandenburg (1582–1616); Joachim Ernst (1583–1625), margrave of Ansbach.

ELIZABETH OF ANHALT-DESSAU (1857–1933). Grand duchess of Mecklenburg-Strelitz. Born Elizabeth Mary Fredericka Amelia Agnes, Sept 7, 1857; died July 20, 1933; dau. of Leopold Frederick I, duke of Anhalt-Dessau; m. Adolphus Frederick V, grand duke of Mecklenburg-Strelitz, April 17, 1877; children: Victoria of Mecklenburg-Strelitz (1878–1948); Jutta of Mecklenburg-Strelitz (1880–1946); Adolphus Frederick VI, grand duke of Mecklenburg-Strelitz (1882–1918).

ELIZABETH OF AUSTRIA (c. 1430–1505). *See Elizabeth of Hungary.*

ELIZABETH OF AUSTRIA (1743–1808). Habsburg princess and abbess. Name variations: Maria Elisabeth. Born Maria Elisabeth, Aug 13, 1743, in Vienna; died Sept 22, 1808, in Linz; dau. of Maria Theresa of Austria (1717–1780) and Francis I, emperor of Austria (r. 1804–1835), also known as Francis II, Holy Roman emperor (r. 1792–1806); sister of Marie Antoinette (1755–1793), Maria Carolina (1752–1814),

and Joseph II, Holy Roman emperor (r. 1765–1790). ❖ Was an abbess in Innsbruck.

ELIZABETH OF AUSTRIA (1837–1898). *See Elizabeth of Bavaria.*

ELIZABETH OF BADEN (1779–1826). German princess and empress of All the Russias. Name variations: Elizabeth Louise; Luisa of Baden; Louise of Baden; Tsarina Elizaveta; Yelizaveta Alekseyevna von Baden. Born Luisa of Baden around 1777 in the Rhine Valley of Germany; dau. of Charles Louis of Padua (b. 1755), prince of Padua and Baden, and Amalie of Hesse-Darmstadt (1754–1832); m. Alexander I (1777–1825), tsar of Russia (r. 1801–1825), on Oct 9, 1793; children: Marie (1799–1800); Elizabeth (1806–1808). ❖ See also *Women in World History.*

ELIZABETH OF BAVARIA (fl. 1200s). Princess Palatine. Fl. in 1200s; dau. of Otto II, count Palatine (r. 1231–1253) and Agnes of Saxony, 1st wife of Conrad IV (1228–1254), Holy Roman emperor (r. 1250–1254, not crowned) and king of Jerusalem (r. 1250–1254), king of Naples and Sicily (r. 1250–1254); m. Meinhard IV of Gorizia; children: (1st m.) Conradin, king of Naples and Sicily (r. 1254–1268) and king of Jerusalem (r. 1254–1268).

ELIZABETH OF BAVARIA (1371–1435). *See Isabeau of Bavaria.*

ELIZABETH OF BAVARIA (1801–1873). Bavarian princess. Born Nov 13, 1801; died Dec 14, 1873; dau. of Maximilian I Joseph, elector of Bavaria (r. 1799–1805), king of Bavaria (r. 1805–1825), and Caroline of Baden (1776–1841); twin sister of Amalia of Bavaria (1801–1877); m. Frederick William IV (1795–1861), king of Prussia (r. 1840–1861), Nov 29, 1823.

ELIZABETH OF BAVARIA (1837–1898). Empress of Austria and Hungary. Name variations: Elizabeth of Austria; Elisabeth von Habsburg or Hapsburg; Elisabeth of Austria-Hungary; (nickname) Empress Sisi or Sissi. Born Elizabeth Amélie Eugénie, Dec 24, 1837, at the castle of Possenhofen on Lake Starnberg; died of stab wounds on Sept 10, 1898, in Geneva; dau. of Maximilian Joseph, duke of Bavaria, and Ludovica (1808–1892); m. her cousin Francis Joseph (Franz Joseph I), emperor of Austria (r. 1848–1916), April 24, 1854; children: eldest daughter died in infancy; Gisela (1856–1932); Marie Valerie (1868–1924); crown prince Rudolf (1858–1889, who died at Mayerling). ❖ Intelligent and artistic, married Franz Joseph (1853); her attempts to modify court etiquette, and her extreme love of horses and frequent visits to the imperial riding school, scandalized Austrian society, along with her predilection for all things Hungarian; took little interest in politics, but was one of the most charitable queens; during Seven Weeks' War with Prussia (1866), popularity with Austrian subjects was more than restored by her diligent care of the wounded after the defeat at Königgrätz; never fully recovered from the death of her only son, crown prince Rudolf (1889), who killed his lover Marie Vetsera and committed suicide at Mayerling; as she walked from her hotel to the steamer at Geneva, was stabbed by the anarchist Luigi Luccheni and died within a few hours (1898). ❖ See also A. de Burgh, *Elizabeth, Empress of Austria: A Memoir* (London, 1898); "Sisi," a 26-segment work for Hungarian tv by Márta Mészáros (1992); and *Women in World History.*

ELIZABETH OF BAVARIA (1876–1965). German-born queen of the Belgians, patron of music, and humanitarian. Name variations: Elisabeth, Dowager Queen of Belgium; Elisabeth of Belgium; Elizabeth von Wittelsbach, duchess in Bavaria. Born Elisabeth Valerie Gabrielle Marie von Wittelsbach at Possenhofen Castle, Bavaria, July 25, 1876; died at Château de Stuyvenberg, near Brussels, Nov 23, 1965; buried at Laeken, Brussels, Belgium; dau. of Maria Josepha of Portugal (1857–1943) and Karl Theodor "Gackl" also known as Karl Theodor von Wittelsbach, duke in Bavaria [*sic*]; earned a medical degree from the University of Leipzig; m. Albert (1875–1934), king of the Belgians (r. 1909–1934), Oct 2, 1900; children: Leopold III (b. 1901), king of the Belgians; Charles Theodore (b. 1903); Marie José of Belgium (b. 1906, who married Umberto II of Italy). ❖ One of the most admired European sovereigns of the 20th century, studied nursing, earning a medical degree from University of Leipzig; married Prince Albert and dedicated her energies to learning about the sick and needy of Belgium; shared the sentiments of her egalitarian husband; an accomplished musician, was a patron of the arts; when WWI began with Germany's violation of Belgian neutrality, helped transform the Royal Palace into an emergency hospital for wounded soldiers; waited until last minute before joining retreating Belgian forces; with husband, remained on Belgian soil during war; for next 4 years, spent hours with the wounded soldiers in the La Panne military hospital; after the war, was patron of the World Child Welfare Congress (1958) and took steps to establish a medical foundation specializing in the study, treatment, and prevention of the tropical diseases found in the Congo; when Albert fell to his death while climbing (1934), went into a deep depression; with daughter-in-law Astrid's death in an automobile accident (Aug 1935), effectively became Belgium's only queen; presided over an international music contest for violinists (1937), the *Concours Ysaye,* known later as *Concours Musical International Reine Elizabeth,* one of the musical world's most important festivals; remained in Belgium during WWII and used her position as a German to ameliorate the lives of many Belgians; made a special effort to save as many Jews as possible, wearing in public a five-pointed brooch that resembled the Star of David; after the war, became a unifying element. ❖ See also Theo Aronson, *Defiant Dynasty: The Coburgs of Belgium* (Bobbs-Merrill, 1968); Wanda Z. Larson, *Elisabeth: A Biography: From Bavarian Princess to Queen of the Belgians* (International Scholars, 1997); Alison Nicholas, *Elisabeth, Queen of the Belgians: Her Life and Times* (New Horizon, 1982); and *Women in World History.*

ELIZABETH OF BAVARIA-LANDSHUT (1383–1442). Electress of Brandenburg. Born 1383; died Nov 13, 1442; dau. of Frederick, duke of Bavaria-Landshut; m. Frederick I of Nuremberg (1371–1440), elector of Brandenburg (r. 1417–1440), Sept 18, 1401; children: John the Alchemist III (b. 1406), margrave of Brandenburg; Frederick II (1413–1471), elector of Brandenburg (r. 1440–1470); Albert Achilles (1414–1486), elector of Brandenburg as Albert III (r. 1470–1486); Frederick the Fat (1424–1463), margrave of Brandenburg.

ELIZABETH OF BELGIUM (1876–1965). *See Elizabeth of Bavaria.*

ELIZABETH OF BOHEMIA (1292–1339). Countess of Luxemburg and queen of Bohemia. Born 1292; died Sept 28, 1339; dau. of Wenceslas II (1271–1305), king of Bohemia (r. 1278–1305), and Elizabeth of Poland (fl. 1298–1305); sister of Wenceslas III, king of Bohemia; m. John Limburg also known as John of Luxemburg (1296–1346), count of Luxemburg and king of Bohemia (r. 1310–1346), Aug 31, 1310; children: Bona of Bohemia (1315–1349, who m. John II, king of France); Wenceslas I (b. 1337), duke of Luxemburg and Brabant; Charles IV Luxemburg (b. 1316), Holy Roman Emperor (r. 1347–1378), and John Henry (1322–1375), margrave of Moravia (who m. Margaret Maultasch). ❖ Husband John of Luxemburg was the son of Henry VII of Luxemburg, Holy Roman emperor.

ELIZABETH OF BOHEMIA (1358–1373). Duchess of Austria. Born Mar 19, 1358, in Prague; died Sept 19, 1373, in Vienna; 1st wife of Albrecht also known as Albert III (c. 1349–1395), duke of Austria (r. 1365–1395). Albert's 2nd wife was Beatrice of Brandenburg (1360–1414).

ELIZABETH OF BOHEMIA (1596–1662). Electress Palatine and queen of Bohemia. Name variations: Elisabeth of Bohemia; Elizabeth of England; Elizabeth, Electress Palatine; Elizabeth Stuart, the Winter Queen. Born at Falkland Castle in Fifeshire, Scotland, Aug 15 or 19, 1596; died at Leicester House in Leicester Fields, England, Feb 13, 1662; interred at Westminster Abbey, London; eldest dau. of Anne of Denmark (1574–1619) and James VI (1566–1625), king of Scotland (r. 1567–1625), later king of England as James I (r. 1603–1625); sister of Charles I, king of England (r. 1625–1649); m. Frederick V (d. 1632), Elector Palatine and titular king of Bohemia, on Feb 14, 1613; children: 13, including Frederick Henry (1614–1629, who drowned in the Haarlem Meer); Charles I Louis also known as Karl Ludwig, Elector Palatine (1617–1680, whose daughter Charlotte Elizabeth of Bavaria m. Philippe I, duke of Orléans, and became the ancestor of the elder, and Roman Catholic, branch of the royal family of England); Elizabeth of Bohemia (1618–1680, princess of Palatine, German philosopher, disciple of Descartes); Rupert (1619–1682), duke of Cumberland; Maurice (1620–1654); Louisa (1622–1709), abbess; Edward Simmern (1624–1663, who m. Anne Simmern, "princesse palatine"); Henrietta Maria (1626–1651, who m. Count Sigismund Ragotzki and died childless); Charlotte (1628–1631); Philip (1629–1650); Sophia, electress of Hanover (1630–1714, who m. Ernst August, elector of Hanover, and was mother of George I of England); Gustav (1632–1641). ❖ At 9, was under the care of Lord and Lady Harington at Combe Abbey in Warwickshire, when a failed conspiracy against her father, now known as the Gunpowder Plot, was formed (the plan included kidnapping Elizabeth and making her queen after killing her parents and older brother Henry, heir to the throne); married and moved to Heidelberg and was soon caught up the Thirty Years' War; as ancestor of the Protestant Hanoverian dynasty, secured a prominent place in English

history and has long been regarded as a martyr to Protestantism. ❖ See also *Women in World History.*

ELIZABETH OF BOHEMIA (1618–1680). German philosopher, Princess Palatine, and abbess of Hervorden. Name variations: Elisabeth; Elizabeth of Hervorden; Elizabeth of the Palatinate; Elizabeth Simmern; "La Greque." Born Dec 26, 1618, in Heidelberg, Baden-Wurttemberg, Germany; died Feb 8, 1680 (some sources cite Feb 11, 1681), in Herford, North Rhine-Westphalia, Germany; dau. of Frederic V, king of Bohemia (Elector Palatine, also known as The Winter King) and Elizabeth of Bohemia (1596–1662); 13 brothers and sisters, including Sophia, electress of Hanover (1630–1714); educated by tutors. ❖ Was still a child when her parents were deposed as king and queen of Bohemia; in exile, rejoined parents at the Hague Court; learned music, dancing, art, Latin, as well as sciences, and took to Greek so well that she received the family nickname of "La Greque"; met and became the disciple of the philosopher René Descartes; more than his pupil, influenced him greatly (her questions and criticisms were so provoking that his letters back to her became part of his book *Passions of the Soul*); became abbess of Hervorden Convent in Herford, Westphalia, where she befriended Anna Maria van Schurmann. ❖ See also *Women in World History.*

ELIZABETH OF BOSNIA (c. 1345–1387). Queen and regent of Hungary. Born before 1345; executed Jan 1387; dau. of Stefan Kotromanic of Bosnia (district governor); became 2nd wife of Louis I the Great, king of Hungary (r. 1342–1382) and Poland (r. 1370–1382), betrothed in 1353; children: unnamed daughter (1365–1365); Catherine (1370–1378); Maria of Hungary (1371–1395); Jadwiga (1374–1399), queen of Poland (r. 1384–1399).

ELIZABETH OF BOSNIA (d. 1339). Queen of Poland. Name variations: Elzbieta of Bosnia; some sources cite her as Jadwiga of Wielpolska. Died 1339; possibly dau. of Anna of Plock and Henry V of Zagan; m. Vladislav IV also known as Wladyslaw I the Short or Ladislas I Lokietek (1260–1333), king of Poland (r. 1306–1333); children: Cunigunde (d. after 1370); Elizabeth of Poland (1305–1380); Casimir III (1309–1370), king of Poland (r. 1333–1370).

ELIZABETH OF BRABANT (1243–1261). Princess of Brabant. Born 1243; died Oct 9, 1261; dau. of Sophia of Thuringia (1224–1284) and Henry II (1207–1248), duke of Brabant (r. 1235–1248); m. Albert I, duke of Brunswick-Luneburg, July 13, 1254. ❖ Two years after her death, Albert I married Adelheid of Montferrat (d. 1285), dau. of Boniface III, marquess of Montferrat; Albert and Adelheid had 7 children.

ELIZABETH OF BRANDENBURG (1485–1555). *See Elizabeth of Denmark.*

ELIZABETH OF BRANDENBURG (1510–1558). Duchess of Brunswick. Born Aug 24, 1510; died May 25, 1558; dau. of Elizabeth of Denmark (1485–1555) and Joachim I Nestor (1484–1535), elector of Brandenburg (r. 1499–1535); m. Erik I the Elder (1470–1540), duke of Brunswick (r. 1495–1540), Mar 12, 1525; children: Erik II the Younger (b. 1528), duke of Brunswick; Anne Marie of Brunswick (1532–1568).

ELIZABETH OF BRUNSWICK (1691–1750). *See Elizabeth Christina of Brunswick-Wolfenbuttel.*

ELIZABETH OF BRUNSWICK (1746–1840). Prussian royal. Name variations: Eleonore Christina Ulrica. Born Elizabeth Christine Ulrica, Nov 8, 1746, in Wolfenbüttel, Germany; died Feb 18, 1840, in Stettin; dau. of Charles (b. 1713), duke of Brunswick-Wolfenbüttel, and Philippine Charlotte (1716–1801); became 1st wife of Frederick William II (1744–1797), king of Prussia (r. 1786–1797), on Aug 14, 1765 (div. 1769); children: Frederica of Prussia (1767–1820).

ELIZABETH OF BRUNSWICK-WOLFENBUTTEL (1593–1650). Duchess of Saxe-Altenburg. Born June 23, 1593; died Mar 25, 1650; dau. of Elizabeth of Denmark (1573–1626) and Henry Julius, duke of Brunswick; m. John Philipp, duke of Saxe-Altenburg, Oct 25, 1618; children: Elizabeth Sophie of Saxe-Altenburg (1619–1680). ❖ See also *Women in World History.*

ELIZABETH OF CARINTHIA (c. 1262–1313). *See Elizabeth of Tyrol.*

ELIZABETH OF COURTENAY (d. 1205). French royal. Died 1205; dau. of Reinald, lord of Courtenay, and Hawise de Donjon; m. Peter I de Courtenay (c. 1126–1180), after 1150; children: Peter or Pierre II de

Courtenay (d. 1218), emperor of Constantinople (r. 1216–1217); Alice de Courtenay (d. 1211).

ELIZABETH OF DENMARK (1485–1555). *Electress of Brandenburg.* Name variations: Elizabeth of Brandenburg; Elizabeth Oldenburg. Born 1485; died June 10, 1555; dau. of Christina of Saxony (1461–1521) and John I, also known as Hans (1455–1513), king of Norway and Denmark (r. 1483–1513); m. Joachim I Nestor (1484–1535), elector of Brandenburg (r. 1499–1535), April 10, 1502; children: Joachim II Hektor (1513–1571), elector of Brandenburg (r. 1535–1571); Anna of Brandenburg (1507–1567); Elizabeth of Brandenburg (1510–1558); John of Brandenburg (1513–1571), landgrave of Brandenburg.

ELIZABETH OF DENMARK (1524–1586). *Duchess of Mecklenburg-Güstrow.* Name variations: Elizabeth Oldenburg. Born Oct 14, 1524; died Oct 15, 1586; dau. of Sophia of Pomerania (1498–1568) and Frederick I (1471–1533), king of Denmark and Norway (r. 1523–1533); m. Magnus of Mecklenburg-Schwerin, Aug 26, 1543; m. Ulrich III, duke of Mecklenburg-Güstrow, Feb 16, 1556; children: Sophia of Mecklenburg (1557–1631).

ELIZABETH OF DENMARK (1573–1626). *Duchess of Brunswick.* Name variations: Elizabeth Oldenburg. Born Aug 25, 1573; died June 19, 1626; dau. of Frederick II, king of Denmark and Norway (r. 1559–1588), and Sophia of Mecklenburg (1557–1631); sister of Anne of Denmark (1574–1619); m. Heinrich Julius also known as Henry Julius (1564–1613), duke of Brunswick (r. 1589–1613), April 19, 1590; children: Frederick Ulrich (b. 1591), duke of Brunswick; Elizabeth of Brunswick-Wolfenbuttel (1593–1650, who m. John Philipp, duke of Saxe-Altenburg). Henry Julius' 1st wife was Dorothea of Saxony (1563–1587).

ELIZABETH OF ENGLAND (1596–1662). *See Elizabeth of Bohemia.*

ELIZABETH OF FARNESE (1692–1766). *See Farnese, Elizabeth.*

ELIZABETH OF GERMANY (1409–1442). *See Elizabeth of Luxemburg.*

ELIZABETH OF GORLITZ (c. 1380–c. 1444). *Duchess of Luxemburg.* Name variations: Elizabeth of Görlitz; Elizabeth of Luxembourg, Luxemburg, or Limbourg. Born c. 1380 in Luxemburg; died c. 1444 in Luxemburg; dau. of John of Burgundy and Richarde of Mekelburg; 2nd wife of Antoine or Anthony, duke of Brabant (died 1415); m. John of Bavaria, around 1419; children: (1st m.) John IV, duke of Brabant (r. 1415–1427, who m. Jacqueline of Hainault); Philip, duke of Brabant (r. 1427–1430). ❖ Daughter of ruling house of Luxembourg, married Antoine of Brabant; was ambitious and shrewd, qualities shared with husband; when Holy Roman Emperor Wenceslas IV, who was ruler of Luxemburg, was imprisoned after years of a chaotic reign, claimed the throne of Luxemburg with husband (1412) on grounds that it adjoined their legitimate holdings in Brabant and Limbourg; held the duchy together, co-ruling until husband's death (1415) at battle of Agincourt; ruled alone until c. 1419, when she married Duke John of Bavaria, who assumed the rule of Luxemburg with her; when he died only 6 years later, again ruled alone; outlived both sons and thus was forced to cede the duchy to Philip the Good when she retired (1443). ❖ See also *Women in World History.*

ELIZABETH OF GREECE (1894–1956). *See Elisabeth, Queen of the Hellenes.*

ELIZABETH OF HAINAULT (1170–1190). *See Isabella of Hainault.*

ELIZABETH OF HABSBURG (1293–1352). *Duchess of Lorraine.* Born c. 1293 in Vienna; died May 19, 1352, in Nancy; dau. of Elizabeth of Tyrol (c. 1262–1313) and Albrecht also spelled Albert I of Habsburg (1255–1308), king of Germany (r. 1298–1308), Holy Roman emperor (r. 1298–1308, but not crowned); m. Ferry IV also known as Frédéric or Frederick IV (1282–1328), duke of Lorraine (r. 1312–1328); children: Rodolphe also known as Rudolf (1318–1346), duke of Lorraine (r. 1328–1346); Margareta of Lorraine (who m. John de Chalon and died after 1376). ❖ See also *Women in World History.*

ELIZABETH OF HABSBURG (1501–1526). *See Elisabeth of Habsburg.*

ELIZABETH OF HABSBURG (d. 1545). *Queen of Poland.* Name variations: Élisabeth d'Autriche; Archduchess Elisabeth or Archduchess Elizabeth. Died 1545, possibly poisoned; dau. of Ferdinand I, Holy Roman emperor (r. 1556–1564), and Anna of Bohemia and Hungary (1503–1547); sister of Maximilian II, Holy Roman emperor (r. 1564–1576), Joanna of Austria (1546–1578), Catherine of Habsburg (1533–1572), Anna of Brunswick (1528–1590), Eleonora of Austria (1534–1594), and others; m. Zygmunt

August also known as Sigismund II Augustus (1520–1572), king of Poland (r. 1548–1572); no children.

ELIZABETH OF HABSBURG (1554–1592). *See Elisabeth of Habsburg.*

ELIZABETH OF HABSBURG (1883–1963). *See Elisabeth von Habsburg.*

ELIZABETH OF HARDWICK (1518–1608). *See Talbot, Elizabeth.*

ELIZABETH OF HERVORDEN (1618–1680). *See Elizabeth of Bohemia.*

ELIZABETH OF HESSE-DARMSTADT (1864–1918). *See Ella.*

ELIZABETH OF HOLSTEIN (fl. 1329). *Queen of Denmark.* Name variations: Elizabeth von Holstein. Fl. around 1329; dau. of Henry I (b. 1258), count of Holstein, and Heilwig of Bronkhorst (d. after July 15, 1310); m. Eric, king of Denmark (r. 1321–1326, 1330–1332), 1329 (div. 1331).

ELIZABETH OF HUNGARY (1207–1231). *Hungarian princess and saint.* Name variations: Saint Elizabeth of Hungary; St. Elizabeth of Thuringia; Landgravine of Thuringia. Born June 7, 1207, in Pressburg (Bratislava); died of exhaustion and malnourishment, Nov 19, 1231, at Marburg; dau. of King Andrew II, king of Hungary (r. 1202–1235), and Gertrude of Andrechs-Meran (c. 1185–1213); m. Louis IV also known as Ludwig IV, landgrave of Thuringia, in 1221; children: Hermann (1222); Sophia of Thuringia (1224–1284, some sources note another daughter Sophia born in 1225); Gertrude of Thuringia (b. 1227). ❖ Defied customs of age and class by tireless efforts to care for the sick and poor; at 14, married Ludwig IV, future landgrave of Thuringia (1221); established a hospital for lepers near the castle at Wartburg; in a year of severe famine, distributed food from public granary and ordered all churches and chapels to house the poor (1226); widowed when Ludwig died on crusade (1227); continued to nurse the sick in her small hospital but also supported herself by spinning and expanded her charitable practices by cleaning the houses of the poor; canonized by Pope Gregory IX (1235). ❖ See also Sigmund H. Uminski, *The Royal Beggar: A Story of Saint Elizabeth of Hungary* (The Polish Publication Society of America, 1971); and *Women in World History.*

ELIZABETH OF HUNGARY (fl. 1250s). *Duchess of Lower Bavaria.* Fl. around the 1250s; dau. of Bela IV, king of Hungary (r. 1235–1270), and Salome of Hungary (1201–c. 1270); niece of Elizabeth of Hungary (1207–1231); m. Henry XIII also known as Henry I, duke of Lower Bavaria (r. 1255–1290); children: Otho of Bavaria also known as Otto III, duke of Lower Bavaria (r. 1290–1312), king of Hungary (r. 1305–1308); Louis III of Lower Bavaria (r. 1290–1296); Stephen I of Lower Bavaria (r. 1290–1310).

ELIZABETH OF HUNGARY (1305–1380). *See Elizabeth of Poland.*

ELIZABETH OF HUNGARY (c. 1430–1505). *Queen of Poland.* Name variations: Elizabeth of Austria. Born c. 1429 or 1430 (some sources cite 1436 or 1437); died Aug 30, 1505, in Krakow; dau. of Albert V, king of Hungary (1437) and Bohemia (1438) and Holy Roman emperor as Albert II (r. 1438–1439), and Elizabeth of Luxemburg (1409–1442, dau. of Sigismund); m. Kazimierz also known as Casimir IV Jagiellon (1427–1492), grand duke of Lithuania (r. 1440–1492), king of Poland (r. 1446–1492); children: Ladislas II of Bohemia (1456–1516), king of Bohemia (r. 1471–1516), king of Hungary (r. 1490–1516); John I Albert (1459–1501), king of Poland (r. 1492–1501); Sophie of Poland (1464–1512); Alexander, king of Poland (r. 1501–1506); Sigismund I (1467–1548), king of Poland (r. 1506–1548); Frederick, bishop of Cracow; Barbara of Poland (1478–1534); Jadwiga also known as Hedwig (who m. George, duke of Bavaria); Saint Casimir.

ELIZABETH OF KIEV (fl. 1045). *Queen of Norway.* Name variations: Ellisef or Ellisif; Ellisif Jaroslavna. Born c. 1032; dau. of Jaroslav also known as Yaroslav I the Wise (978–1054), grand prince of Kiev (r. 1019–1054), and Ingigerd Olafsdottir (c. 1001–1050); m. Harald III Hardraade also known as Harald III Haardrada, king of Norway (1015–1066), in 1045; possibly m. Svend II Estridsen (d. 1076), king of Denmark (r. 1047–1074), in 1067; children: (1st m., 2 daughters) Maria Haraldsdottir (who was killed on Sept 25, 1066); Ingigerd Haraldsdottir. ❖ See also *Women in World History.*

ELIZABETH OF KUMANIA (c. 1242–?). *Queen of Hungary.* Name variations: Elizabeth of Kumanien. Born c. 1242; died after 1290; m. Stephen V, king of Hungary (r. 1270–1272); children: Anna of Hungary (who m. Andronicus II Paleologus, emperor of Nicaea); Ladislas IV (1262–1290), king of Hungary (r. 1272–1290); Marie of Hungary (d. 1323, who m. Charles II of Anjou).

ELIZABETH OF LANCASTER (1364–1425). Duchess of Exeter. Name variations: Elizabeth Hastings; Elizabeth Holland; Elizabeth Cornwall. Born in 1364 in Burford, Shropshire, England; died Nov 24, 1425 (some sources cite 1426); dau. of John of Gaunt, 1st duke of Lancaster, and Blanche of Lancaster (1341–1369); sister of Philippa of Lancaster (c. 1359–1415, who m. John I, king of Portugal); sister of Henry IV (r. 1399–1413), king of England (r. 1399–1413); m. John Hastings (1372–1389), 3rd earl of Pembroke, June 24, 1380 (div. 1383); m. John Holland, duke of Exeter, 1386 (died 1400); m. John Cornwall, 1st baron Fanhope; children: (2nd m.) John Holland (1395–1447), duke of Exeter; Constance Holland (1387–1437, who m. Thomas Mowbray, earl of Norfolk, and Sir John Grey); Richard Holland; Edward Holland (b. c. 1399); Alice Holland (c. 1392–c. 1406, who m. Richard de Vere, 11th earl of Oxford); (3rd m.) Constance Cornwall; Sir John Cornwall (b. 1404). ❖ At 22, married John Holland, duke of Exeter; 14 years later (Feb 9, 1400), husband was beheaded at Pleshey at command of Henry IV, king of England. ❖ See also *Women in World History.*

ELIZABETH OF LORRAINE (1711–1741). French royal. Born 1711; died 1741; dau. of Elizabeth-Charlotte (1676–1744) and Leopold, duke of Lorraine; m. Charles Emmanuel III (1701–1773), king of Sardinia (r. 1730–1773). Charles Emmanuel was also married to Louisa Christina of Bavaria.

ELIZABETH OF LUXEMBURG (1409–1442). Queen of Hungary and duchess of Austria. Name variations: Elizabeth of Bohemia; Elizabeth of Germany; Elizabeth of Luxembourg. Born Nov 27, 1409, in Luxembourg; died Dec 19 or 25, 1442, in Ofen (Buda), Hungary; dau. of Sigismund I of Luxemburg (d. 1368), king of Hungary and Poland, also Holy Roman emperor, and Barbara of Cilli; m. Albert V (1404–1439), duke of Austria (r. 1404–1439), king of Germany (r. 1404–1439), Hungary (r. 1437), and Bohemia (r. 1438), also Holy Roman emperor as Albert II (r. 1438–1439), Nov 28, 1421; children: Anne of Austria (1432–1462, who m. William III of Saxony); Elizabeth of Hungary (c. 1430–1505, who m. Casimir IV, king of Poland); Ladislas, later Ladislas V Posthumus, king of Hungary (r. 1444–1457), king of Bohemia (r. 1452). ❖ Married Duke Albert V Habsburg of Austria (1421); through her, husband was elected Holy Roman emperor (as Albert II) and king of Hungary (1437); is most remembered for her career as queen of Hungary; husband died in battle only 2 years after becoming emperor; with help of lady-in-waiting Helene Kottanner, managed to have son crowned king in an effort to secure the throne; also had several powerful foreign allies in her quest, as well as support of the Hungarian people; died with the outcome of the war undecided; son succeed to the Hungarian throne as Ladislas V (1452). ❖ See also *Women in World History.*

ELIZABETH OF NEVERS (fl. 1460). Duchess of Cleves. Fl. around 1460; m. John I, duke of Cleves (r. 1448–1481); children: John II, duke of Cleves (r. 1481–1521); Engelbert, duke of Nevers.

ELIZABETH OF POLAND (1288–1335). *See Ryksa of Poland.*

ELIZABETH OF POLAND (fl. 1298–1305). Queen of Bohemia. Fl. between 1298 and 1305; 3rd wife of Wenceslas II (1271–1305), king of Bohemia (r. 1278–1305); children: Wenceslas III (1289–1306), king of Bohemia (r. 1305–1306); Anna of Bohemia (who m. Henry of Carinthia, king of Bohemia, r. 1306–1310); Elizabeth of Bohemia (1292–1339). Wenceslas II's 1st wife was Judith (1271–1297); his 2nd was Ryksa of Poland (d. 1335).

ELIZABETH OF POLAND (1305–1380). Queen of Hungary. Name variations: Elizabeth Lokietek; Elizabeth of Hungary. Born 1305 in Poland; died 1380 in Hungary (some sources cite 1386); dau. of Elizabeth of Bosnia (d. 1339) and Ladislas I Lokietek (1260–1333), king of Poland (r. 1306–1333); m. Charles Robert of Anjou (1288–1342) also known as Charles I, king of Hungary (r. 1307–1342), in 1320; children: Louis I the Great (b. 1326), king of Hungary (r. 1342–1382), king of Poland (r. 1370–1382); Andrew of Hungary (d. 1345, who m. Joanna I of Naples). ❖ A princess of Polish royal house, was married as a child to Charles Robert of Anjou (who was also known as Charles I, king of Hungary); became well-known for her charity and deep piety; was also interested in science and medicine; when brother Casimir (III) had succeeded their father as king of Poland, died and left the throne to her son Louis (1370), was appointed regent by Louis, retaining the regency until her death; was also influential in upbringing of her powerful granddaughter, Jadwiga (1374–1399), queen of Poland. ❖ See also *Women in World History.*

ELIZABETH OF POLAND (d. 1361). Duchess of Pomerania. Name variations: Elzbieta. Died 1361; dau. of Casimir III the Great, king of Poland (r. 1333–1370) and one of his 4 wives, Aldona of Lithuania (d. 1339), Adelaide of Hesse, Krystryna Rokizanska, or Jadwiga of Glogow; m. Boguslaw also known as Boleslav V of Slupsk, duke of Pomerania; children: Elizabeth of Pomerania (1347–1393).

ELIZABETH OF POMERANIA (1347–1393). Holy Roman Empress. Name variations: Elizabeth von Pommern; Elzbieta of Slupsk. Born 1347 (some sources cite 1335 or 1345); died Feb 14, 1393; dau. of Boleslav V, duke of Pomerania, and Elizabeth of Poland (d. 1361); became 4th wife of Charles IV (1316–1378), Holy Roman emperor (r. 1347–1378), May 1363; children: Anne of Bohemia (1366–1394); Sigismund I (b. 1368), king of Hungary and Bohemia, Holy Roman emperor (r. 1387–1437).

ELIZABETH OF PORTUGAL (1271–1336). Saint and queen of Portugal. Name variations: Isabel or Isabella of Aragon; Isabella of Portugal. Born 1271 in Aragon; died July 4, 1336, in Estremos, Portugal; interred in Coimbra; dau. of Pedro also known as Peter III, king of Aragon, and Constance of Sicily (r. 1282–1302); grandniece of Elizabeth of Hungary (1207–1231); m. Diniz also spelled Dinis or Denis (1261–1325), king of Portugal (r. 1279–1325), in 1280 or 1282; children: Alphonso IV (1291–1357), king of Portugal (r. 1325–1357); Constance of Portugal (1290–1313), later queen of Castile. ❖ An Aragonese princess, married Denis of Portugal (1280); with diplomatic skills and pious nature, was a mediator to various political factions within both the Aragonese and Portuguese royal families, earning her sobriquet "the Peacemaker"; despite mediating role, never played a central part in administration of the kingdom; became increasingly involved in charitable works and acts of personal piety, including extreme fasting; was celebrated throughout Portugal for her generous donations to public works such as hospitals and orphanages; founded a college designed to prepare young women to be farmers; on death of husband, was freed from constraints of marriage and queenship and joined the monastic order of the Poor Clares; embarked on pilgrimages; developed a following of those who believed she was exceptionally gifted and could perform miracles; was not canonized, however, until 1625. ❖ See also *Women in World History.*

ELIZABETH OF RUMANIA.
See Elizabeth of Wied (1843–1916).
See Elisabeth, Queen of the Hellenes (1894–1956).

ELIZABETH OF SAVOY-CARIGNAN (1800–1856). Archduchess of Austria. Name variations: Marie Elizabeth Francesca. Born 1800; died 1856; possibly sister of Charles Albert, king of Sardinia; m. Ranieri also known as Rainer, archduke of Austria; children: Marie Adelaide of Austria (1822–1855).

ELIZABETH OF SAXE-HILDBURGHAUSEN (1713–1761). Duchess of Mecklenburg-Strelitz. Name variations: Elisabeth Albertine, Princess of Saxony-Hildburghausen. Born Elisabeth Albertine, Aug 3, 1713; died June 29, 1761; m. Duke Charles I of Mecklenburg-Strelitz (1708–1752); children: Prince Charles II Louis Frederick of Mecklenburg-Strelitz (father of Louise of Prussia); Charlotte of Mecklenburg-Strelitz (1744–1818, queen to George III).

ELIZABETH OF SAXONY (1830–1912). Duchess of Genoa. Born 1830; died 1912; m. Ferdinando or Ferdinand of Savoy (1822–1855), duke of Genoa; children: Margaret of Savoy (1851–1926).

ELIZABETH OF SCHÖNAU (c. 1129–1164). German mystic. Name variations: Elisabeth von Schönau; Schonau or Schoenau. Born c. 1129; died 1164. ❖ Celebrated German mystic, was a nun at abbey of Schönau in Silesia; told of visions in *Book of the Ways of God* which she dedicated to brother, the canon Egbert. Feast day is June 18. ❖ See also *Women in World History.*

ELIZABETH OF SICILY (fl. 1200s). Queen of Hungary. Fl. in 1200s; m. Ladislas IV, king of Hungary (r. 1272–1290).

ELIZABETH OF SICILY (d. 1349). Duchess of Bavaria. Died Mar 31, possibly 1349; dau. of Lenore of Sicily (1289–1341) and Frederick II, king of Sicily (r. 1271–1296); sister of Peter II, king of Sicily; m. Stephen II (1317–1375), duke of Bavaria (r. 1363–1375), June 27, 1328; children: Stephen III (b. 1337), duke of Bavaria (r. 1375–1413); Frederick (b. 1339), duke of Bavaria (r. 1375–1393); John II (b. 1341), duke of Bavaria (r. 1375–1397). ❖ After 1347, Bavaria was divided into several parts.

ELIZABETH OF SILESIA (fl. 1257). Silesian princess. Fl. around 1257; dau. of Henry II the Pious of Silesia and Anna of Bohemia; m. Przemyslav or Przemysl I of Wielkopolska (1220–1257), king of Poland; children: Przemysl II (1257–1296), king of Poland (r. 1290–1296); Constancia.

ELIZABETH OF THE NETHERLANDS (1501–1526). *See Elisabeth of Habsburg.*

ELIZABETH OF THE PALATINATE (1618–1680). *See Elizabeth of Bohemia.*

ELIZABETH OF THE TRINITY (1880–1906). French Carmelite mystic. Name variations: Elizabeth Catez. Born in Jul, 1880, in Bourges, France; died Nov 9, 1906, in Dijon, France; dau. of Joseph Catez (who had seen much combat in French army and was promoted many times, finally achieving status of Knight of Legion of Honor in 1881) and Marie (Rolland) Catez (dau. of successful military officer); sister of Marguerite Catez. ❖ Nun who held the mystical belief that the trinity dwelled within the soul, lost maternal grandfather and father in same year (1887); moved with mother and sister to an apartment near Dijon overlooking the monastery of Discalced Carmelite Nuns; read Teresa of Avila's *Way of Perfection* and letters of St. Paul and sought guidance from Dominican friar Iréné Vallée; entered Carmelite convent, receiving name Sister Elizabeth of the Trinity at Feast of Epiphany (1902); became very weak (1906) and died from stomach cancer; left behind many writings: summaries of private retreats (including 2 retreats for married sister), prayers (including 1904 devotion to indwelling of Trinity in soul) and extensive correspondence, all of which show deep spirituality which blends tradition of Saint John of the Cross with themes taken from epistles of Saint Paul; beatified by Pope John Paul II (1984). ❖ See also Jennifer Moorcroft, *He Is My Heaven: The Life of Elizabeth of the Trinity* (Institute of Carmelite Studies).

ELIZABETH OF THURINGIA (1207–1231). *See Elizabeth of Hungary.*

ELIZABETH OF THURN AND TAXIS (1903–1976). Saxony royal. Born 1903; died 1976; m. Frederick Christian (1893–1968, son of Louisa Toselli and Frederick Augustus III, king of Saxony), margrave of Meissen; children: Emanuel (b. 1926); Albert (b. 1934).

ELIZABETH OF TYROL (c. 1262–1313). Queen of Germany. Name variations: Elizabeth of Carinthia; Elisabeth of Gorz-Tyrol. Born 1262 or 1263; died Oct 10 or 28, 1313, in Konigsfelden (Aargau, Switzerland); m. Albrecht also known as Albert I of Habsburg (1255–1308), king of Germany (r. 1298–1308), Holy Roman emperor (r. 1298–1308, but not crowned); children: Rudolf III (1281–1307), king of Bohemia and Poland (r. 1306–1307); Agnes of Austria (1281–1364); Friedrich also known as Frederick I (III) the Fair of Austria (1289–1330), king of Germany (r. 1314–1322), (co-regent) Holy Roman emperor (r. 1314–1325); Elizabeth of Habsburg (1293–1352), who m. Frederick IV of Lorraine); Leopold I (1293–1326), duke of Austria and Styria; Catherine (1295–1323); Albrecht also known as Albert II of Austria (1298–1358), duke of Austria; Heinrich also known as Henry (1298–1327); Anna of Habsburg (d. 1327, who m. Hermann of Brandenburg); Otto (1301–1339), duke of Austria, Steiermark and Karten; Guta, also known as Jutta, Jutha, Jeutha, or Bonitas (1302–1329).

ELIZABETH OF ULSTER (d. 1327). *See Elizabeth de Burgh.*

ELIZABETH OF VALOIS (1545–1568). Queen of Spain. Name variations: Elisabeth or Élizabeth of France; Princess Elizabeth of France; Elizabeth of the Peace; Isabel or Isabella of France. Born at Fontainbleau, France, April 2 (some sources cite April 13), 1545; died in childbirth, age 23, in Madrid, Spain, Oct 3, 1568; dau. of Henry II of Valois (1519–1559), king of France (r. 1547–1559), and Catherine de Medici (1519–1589); sister of Claude de France (1547–1575), and Margaret of Valois (1553–1615), as well as Francis II, Charles IX, and Henry III, all kings of France; became 3rd wife of Philip II (1527–1598), king of Spain (r. 1556–1598), and king of Portugal as Philip I (r. 1580–1598), in 1559 or 1560, in Toledo, Spain; children: twin daughters born in 1564 (died at birth); Isabella Clara Eugenia of Austria (1566–1633); Catherine of Spain (1567–1597), duchesse of Savoy; another daughter (b. 1568) died at birth. ❖ See also *Women in World History.*

ELIZABETH OF WIED (1843–1916). Queen of Romania. Name variations: Elisabeth of Rumania or Romania; Elizabeth, Queen of Romania; Elisabeth zu Wied; (pseudonyms) Carmen Sylva and Dito Und Idem. Born Pauline Elizabeth Ottilie Louise (or Luise) in Neuwied, Prussia, Dec 29, 1843; died Mar 3, 1916, in Curtea de Arges, Romania; dau. of Prince Hermann of Neuwied; m. Prince Karl von Hohenzollern also

known as Carol I (1839–1914), king of Romania (r. 1881–1914), Nov 15, 1869; children: Marie (1870–1874). ❖ Talented musician, painter, and writer who produced poems, plays, novels, short stories, essays, collections of adages, and translations, was widely known for cultural interests and voluminous writings; during Russo-Turkish War of 1877–78, tended wounded and established Order of Elizabeth (gold cross on a blue ribbon), to reward others for similar service; founded other charitable societies and helped foster the higher education of women in Romania; put much of the folklore of the Romanian peasantry into literary form; writings include poetry collections *Sappho* (1880) and *Stuerme* (1882) and religious meditations in Romanian *Cuvinte Sufletesci* (1888); received the Prix Botta from French Academy (1888) for her prose aphorisms *Les Pensées d'une reine* (1882); known also for her translations, including German versions of Pierre Loti's romance *Pêcheur d'Islande,* Paul de St. Victor's dramatic criticisms *Les Deux Masques,* and (with Alma Strettell) *The Bard of the Dimbovitza* (English version of Helene Vacarescu's collection of Romanian folksongs, *Lieder aus dem Dimbovitzathal* [1889]); used pseudonym "Dito Und Idem" to indicate joint authorship of several works with her lady-in-waiting Marie Kremnitz, including *Aus zwei Welten* (1884), a novel, *Anna Boleyn* (1886), a tragedy, *Inderlrre* (1888), a collection of short stories, *Edleen Vaughan; or Paths of Peril* (1894), another novel, and *Sweet Hours* (1904), a collection of poems written in English. ❖ See also *Women in World History.*

ELIZABETH OF WITTELSBACH (1540–1594). Electress of Saxony. Born June 30, 1540; died Feb 8, 1594; dau. of Marie of Brandenburg-Kulmbach (1519–1567) and Frederick III the Pious, elector of the Palatinate; m. John Frederick II, elector of Saxony, June 12, 1558. John Frederick's 1st wife was Agnes of Hesse (1527–1555).

ELIZABETH OF WURTTEMBERG (1767–1790). Princess of Wurttemberg. Name variations: Elizabeth Wilhelmine. Born Elizabeth Wilhelmine von Wurttemberg, April 21, 1767; died Feb 18, 1790; dau. of Sophia Dorothea of Brandenburg (1736–1798) and Frederick II Eugene, duke of Wurttemberg (r. 1795–1797); became 1st wife of Francis I (1768–1835) emperor of Austria (r. 1804–1835), also known as Francis II, Holy Roman emperor (r. 1792–1806), Jan 6, 1788; children: Ludovika (1790–1791). ❖ Holy Roman emperor Francis II had four wives: Elizabeth of Wurttemberg (1767–1790), Maria Teresa of Naples (1772–1807), Maria Ludovica of Modena (1787–1816) and Caroline Augusta of Bavaria (1792–1873).

ELIZABETH OF WURTTEMBERG (1802–1864). Princess of Baden. Born Feb 27, 1802; died Dec 5, 1864; dau. of Louis of Wurttemberg and Henrietta of Nassau-Weilburg (1780–1857); niece of Frederick I, king of Prussia; m. William, prince of Baden, Oct 16, 1830; children: four, including Leopoldine (1837–1903).

ELIZABETH OF YORK (1466–1503). Queen of England. Name variations: Elizabeth Plantagenet. Born Feb 11, 1466 (some sources cite 1465), in Westminster, London, England; died in childbirth, Feb 11, 1503 (some sources cite 1502), in Tower of London, England; buried in Westminster Abbey; oldest dau. of Edward IV, king of England, and Elizabeth Woodville; m. Henry VII, king of England (r. 1485–1509), Jan 18, 1486; children: Arthur Tudor (1486–1502), prince of Wales; Margaret Tudor (1489–1541); Henry VIII (1491–1547), king of England (r. 1509–1547); Elizabeth Tudor (1492–1495); Mary Tudor (1496–1533, who m. Louis XII, king of France); Edmund Tudor, duke of Somerset (1499–1500); Edward Tudor (died in infancy); Katherine Tudor (1503–1503). ❖ Following the murder of two younger brothers in Tower of London, became heir to the throne; united the white rose of the Yorks with the red roses of the Lancastrians when she married Henry Tudor (Henry VII), the victorious Lancastrian in the Wars of the Roses (1486). ❖ See also *Women in World History.*

ELIZABETH OF YUGOSLAVIA (1936—). Yugoslavian princess. Name variations: Elizabeth Karadjordjevic or Karageorgevic; Jelisaveta Karadjordjevic. Born April 7, 1936, in Yugoslavia; dau. of Olga Oldenburg (1903–1981) and Paul Karadjordjevic (Prince Paul, regent of Yugoslavia); m. Howard Oxenberg (businessman), 1960 (div. 1966); m. Neil Roxburgh Balfour, 1969 (div. 1978); m. Manuel Ulloa y Elias (1987); children: (1st m.) Catherine Oxenburg (b. 1961, actress) and Christina Oxenburg (b. 1962, writer); (2nd m.) Nicholas Balfour. ❖ Was 4 when family went into exile after a military coup; raised in Kenya, settled in US; formed the Princess Elizabeth of Yugoslavia Foundation to aid war victims in the former Yugoslavia (1990).

ELIZABETH OLDENBURG (1904–1955). Greek princess. Born May 24, 1904; died Jan 11, 1955; dau. of Helena of Russia (1882–1957) and Prince Nicholas (Oldenburg) of Greece (uncle of England's Prince Philip); sister of Marina of Greece (1906–1968) and Olga Oldenburg (1903–1981).

ELIZABETH PETROVNA (1709–1762). Russian empress. Name variations: Elizabeth I of Russia; Elizaveta; Yelizaveta. Pronunciation: Pa-TROV-na. Born Elizabeth Petrovna, Dec 7, 1709 (dates are according to Julian calendar, in use in Imperial Russia, which was 12 days behind Georgian calendar) in Kolomenskoye near Moscow, Russia; died in St. Petersburg, Russia, Dec 25, 1762; dau. of Peter I the Great (1672–1725), tsar of Russia (r. 1682–1725), and Marta Skovoronski or Skavronska (later Empress Catherine I, 1684–1727); educated by tutors, but only superficially and informally; probably secretly m. Aleksei Razumovsky, 1742 or 1744; no children. ❖ Ruled from 1741 to 1761 in a reign marked by Russia's continued development as a major power and an acceleration of Westernization; lived in Moscow and St. Petersburg during early years; consigned to care and upbringing of the Dowager Empress of Ivan V; named to Supreme Privy Council in the will of Catherine I (1727); passed over for throne, retired to self-exile at her estate (1729); led a coup d'état against Regent Anna Leopoldovna (1741); defeated Sweden (1743); founded Moscow University (1755); opposed Prussia in the Seven Years' War (1756). ❖ See also R. Nisbet Bain, *The Daughter of Peter the Great* (Constable, 1899); Robert Coughlan, *Elizabeth and Catherine: Empresses of All the Russias* (Putnam, 1974); Philip Longworth, *The Three Empresses: Catherine I, Anne and Elizabeth of Russia* (Holt, 1972); Tamara Talbot Rice, *Elizabeth: Empress of Russia* (Praeger, 1970); and *Women in World History.*

ELIZABETH PLANTAGENET (1282–1316). Duchess of Hereford and Essex. Name variations: Elizabeth Bohun. Born Aug 1282 in Rhuddlan Castle, Caernarvon, Gwynedd, Wales; died May 5, 1316, in England; dau. of Edward I Longshanks, king of England (r. 1272–1307), and Eleanor of Castile (1241–1290); m. John I, count of Holland and Zeeland, Jan 18, 1297 (died 1299); m. Humphrey Bohun (1276–1322), 4th earl of Hereford, 3rd of Essex, Nov 14, 1320; children: (2nd m.) 10, including John (1306–1335), 5th earl of Hereford, 4th of Essex; Humphrey (c. 1309–1361), 6th earl of Hereford; Edward; William (c. 1312–1360), 1st earl of Northampton; Eleanor Bohun, countess of Ormonde; and Margaret (Bohun) Courtenay.

ELIZABETH-RYKSA (1288–1335). *See Ryksa of Poland.*

ELIZABETH SOPHIE OF SAXE-ALTENBURG (1619–1680). Duchess of Saxe-Gotha. Born Oct 10, 1619; died Dec 20, 1680; dau. of Elizabeth of Brunswick-Wolfenbuttel (1593–1650) and John Philipp, duke of Saxe-Altenburg; m. Ernst I, duke of Saxe-Gotha, Oct 24, 1636; children: Frederick I (b. 1646), duke of Saxe-Gotha; Berharnd I (b. 1649), duke of Saxe-Meiningen; John Ernst (b. 1658), duke of Saxe-Coburg-Saalfeld; Ernst (b. 1655), duke of Saxe-Hilburghausen.

ELIZABETH STUART (1596–1662). *See Elizabeth of Bohemia.*

ELIZABETH STUART (1635–1650). English princess. Name variations: Princess Elizabeth. Born Dec 29 (some sources cite the 28th), 1635, at St. James's Palace in London, England; died at 15 it is said of grief over her father's execution on Sept 8, 1650, at Carisbrooke Castle, Isle of Wight, England; buried at Newport, Isle of Wight; 2nd dau. of Henrietta Maria (1609–1669) and Charles I, king of England; sister of James II and Charles II, kings of England; Mary of Orange (1631–1660); Henry (1640–1660), duke of Gloucester; and Henrietta Anne (1644–1670), duchess of Orléans. ❖ See also *Women in World History.*

ELIZABETH THE GOOD (1386–1420). German saint. Born 1386; died 1420; lived and died at Reute near the Waldsee (Swabia). ❖ A nun of the Franciscan third order, was celebrated for the demonic persecutions she endured. Feast day is Nov 25.

ELIZABETH TUDOR (1533–1603). *See Elizabeth I.*

ELIZABETH VALOIS (1602–1644). Queen of Spain. Name variations: Elizabeth of France; Elizabeth of Valois; Isabel de Borbon; Isabella. Born 1602; died 1644; dau. of Henry IV, king of France (r. 1589–1610), and Marie de Medici (1573?–1642); sister of Henrietta Maria (1609–1669), who m. Charles I, king of England), Christine of France (1606–1663), and Louis XIII, king of France (r. 1610–1643); became 1st wife of Philip IV (1605–1665), king of Spain (r. 1621–1665), in 1615 (some sources cite 1621); children: Maria Teresa of Spain (1638–1683, 1st wife of

Louis XIV of France). Philip IV's 2nd wife was Maria Anna of Austria (1634–1696).

ELIZABETH VON HABSBURG (1837–1898). *See Elizabeth of Bavaria.*

ELIZABETH VON HABSBURG (1883–1963). Austrian archduchess. Name variations: Archduchess Elisabeth Marie; Elisabeth Marie von Habsburg; Erzsi; the Red Archduchess. Born Elizabeth Marie von Habsburg in Laxenburg near Vienna, Sept 2, 1883; died in Vienna, Mar 16, 1963; dau. of Crown Prince Rudolph or Rudolf (1858–1889) of Austria-Hungary and Stephanie of Belgium (1864–1945); m. Otto zu Windischgraetz also known as Otto Windisch-Graetz, prince of Windischgrätz, Jan 23, 1902; m. Leopold Petznek (1881–1956, militant Marxist leader and president of the Parliament of Lower Austria); children: Ernst Ferdinand; Franz Joseph; Rudolf; Stefanie. ❖ At age 5, learned that her father had taken his own life and that of his 17-year-old mistress, Marie Vetsera, in a suicide pact at Mayerling (Jan 1889); married Prince Otto Windisch-Graetz, a man regarded in court circles as being beneath her in social rank (1902); on legally becoming a commoner with demise of Habsburg monarchy (Nov 1918), endured a bitterly contested divorce; found support from the Social Democratic Party, which had long advocated women's rights, including the right to divorce and retain custody of children; joined the party, becoming renowned as the "Red Archduchess." ❖ See also *Women in World History.*

ELIZABETH VON POMMERN (1347–1393). *See Elizabeth of Pomerania.*

ELIZABETH WOODVILLE (1437–1492). *See Woodville, Elizabeth.*

ELIZAVETA. *Variant of Elizabeth.*

ELLA (1864–1918). Princess of Hesse-Darmstadt and grand duchess of Russia. Name variations: after marriage, became known as Elizabeth Feodorovna; Grand Duchess Elizabeth; Elizabeth or Ella Saxe-Coburg. Born Elizabeth Alexandra Louise, Nov 1, 1864, in Darmstadt, in German principality of Hesse-Darmstadt; murdered by Bolsheviks c. July 17, 1918, and thrown down a mine pit in Alapaievsk, Russia, the day after her brother-in-law Tsar Nicholas II, her sister Empress Alexandra Feodorovna, and her nephew and nieces were slaughtered); 2nd dau. of Prince Louis of Hesse-Darmstadt and Princess Alice Maud Mary (1843–1878) of Great Britain; granddau. of Victoria, queen of England (r. 1837–1901); m. Grand Duke Serge of Russia (Sergius Alexandrovitch, son of Tsar Alexander II), June 15, 1884. ❖ Was canonized by the Russian Orthodox Church. ❖ See also Hugo Mager, *Elizabeth, Grand Duchess of Russia* (Carroll & Graf, 1998); and *Women in World History.*

ELLEN. *Variant of Eleanor or Helena.*

ELLEN, Mary Ann (1897–1949). New Zealand women's advocate. Name variations: Mary Ann Edington. Born June 18, 1897, in Glasgow, Scotland; died Aug 19, 1949, at Waikuku Beach, New Zealand; dau. of Edward and Mary Ann (Rogers) Edington; m. Horace Ellen, 1921 (died 1949); children: 2 sons. ❖ Immigrated to New Zealand (1920); was active in Plunket Society and became secretary of Woodend School Committee (1938–40); was founder and served as president of Woodend-Waikuku branch of Women's Division of New Zealand Farmers' Union (1932–36); was active in improving lives of rural women and established union's emergency housekeeper plan to assist mothers at childbirth; was the 1st woman to win seat on North Canterbury Electric Power Board (1935) and served as deputy chair (1944–45); during WWII, chaired Women's War Service Auxiliary; elected to North Canterbury Hospital Board (1947). Received British Empire medal (1946). ❖ See also *Dictionary of New Zealand Biography* (Vol. 4).

ELLEN OF WALES (d. 1253). Countess of Huntingdon and Chester. Name variations: Elen; Helena. Died 1253; dau. of Llywelyn II the Great (1173–1240), ruler of All Wales, and his mistress Tangwystl (some sources cite Joan of England); m. John of Chester (1207–1237), earl of Chester (r. 1232–1237), in 1220 or 1222; m. Robert de Quinci, 1237; children: (2nd m.) Joan de Quinci (d. 1283, who m. Humphrey Bohun); Hawise de Quinci (c. 1250–c. 1295, who m. Baldwin Wake). ❖ See also *Women in World History.*

ELLENBOROUGH, Countess or Lady (1807–1881). *See Digby el Mesrab, Jane.*

ELLERBECK, Anna-Marie (1943—). *See Holmes, Anna-Marie.*

ELLERBEE, Linda (1944—). **American newscaster and tv host.** Born Linda Jane Smith, Aug 14, 1944, in Bryan, Texas; attended Vanderbilt University; m. John David Klein (div.); m. thrice more; children: Joshua and Vanessa. ❖ Outspoken journalist, began career with the Dallas bureau of the Associate Press (1972); worked for WCBS, then was hired to co-anchor NBC's "Weekend" (1979); became host of NBC's "Overnight" (1982), which won the Columbia–duPont Award, then ABC's "Our World"; hosted and produced the highly successful "Nick News" on Nickelodeon channel; formed Lucky Duck Productions to produce shows and specials. ❖ See also memoir *And So It Goes: Adventures in Television.*

ELLERMAN, Winifred (1894–1983). **English novelist and benefactor.** Name variations: Bryher; Winifred Bryher; Annie Winifred Ellerman. Born Annie Winifred Ellerman in 1894; died in 1983; dau. of Sir John Ellerman (shipping magnate) and Hannah Glover; attended Queenwood, a girls' boarding school; m. Robert McAlmon in a marriage of convenience, Feb 1921; m. Kenneth Macpherson in a marriage of convenience. ❖ Preferring to be known as Bryher throughout her life, published a collection of poems, *Region of Lutany* (1914); discovered the Imagist anthologies of Amy Lowell, then published *Amy Lowell: A Critical Appreciation* (1918); published 1st novel, the highly critical *Development* (1920), based on her school years; became a close friend and lived with poet H.D. (Hilda Doolittle); supported other writers, including James Joyce; with 2nd husband Macpherson, started the 1st film magazine, *Close-up,* and produced the 1930 silent *Borderline,* starring Doolittle and Paul Robeson; took over the literary journal *Life and Letters To-day* (1935) and abetted the founding of the *Psychoanalytic Review.* ❖ See also autobiographies, *The Heart to Artemis* (Harcourt, 1962) and *Two Selves* (Contact, 1923); and *Women in World History.*

ELLET, Elizabeth (c. 1812–1877). **American author and historian.** Name variations: Elizabeth Lummis. Born Elizabeth Fries Lummis in Sodus, NY, probably in 1812 (some sources cite 1818); died in NY, June 3, 1877; dau. of William N. Lummis (physician) and Sarah (Maxwell) Lummis; attended Female Seminary, Aurora, NY; m. William H. Ellet (doctor and chemistry professor), c. 1835. ❖ The author of 15 books, a volume of poetry, and numerous magazine articles, was one of the 1st female writers to identify the role of women in the early history of the US; published 1st original work, *Poems, Translated and Original* (1835); best known for *Women of the American Revolution* (1848), a 3-vol. work sketching the lives of 160 women who played a part in, witnessed, or merely commented on, the events of the Revolution; also wrote *Domestic History of the American Revolution* (1850), *Pioneer Women of the West* (1953), and *Queens of American Society* (1867).

ELIBANK, Lady (1888–1942). See Celli, Faith.

ELISHEVA (1888–1949). See Bichovsky, Elisheva.

ELLINAKI, Georgia (1974—). **Greek water-polo player.** Born Feb 1974 in Athens, Greece. ❖ Won team silver medal at Athens Olympics (2004).

ELLIOT, Cass (1941–1974). **American pop singer.** Name variations: Mama Cass. Born Ellen Naomi Cohen in Baltimore, Maryland, Sept 19, 1941; died of heart attack in London, England, July 29, 1974; dau. of Philip Cohen and Beth (Levine) Cohen (pianist); m. James R. Hendricks (singer), 1963 (div.); m. Donald von Weidenman (baron), 1971 (annulled); children: Owen Vanessa Elliot-Kugell (b. 1967). ❖ Ensemble and solo singer whose crystalline contralto played a crucial role in generating the phenomenal success enjoyed by The Mamas and the Papas in mid-1960s; began career singing with 1st husband and Tim Rose in the Big Three, a short-lived but pivotal folk group, recording 2 albums for the FM label, *The Big Three* and *Live at the Recording Studio,* but neither achieved hit status; by summer 1964, her group had evolved into The Mugwumps, which included Dennis Doherty and Zalman Yanovsky; joined with Doherty, John Phillips and Michelle Phillips to form The Mamas and the Papas (1964), releasing the hits "California Dreamin'" and "Monday Monday" (1966), and the album *If You Can Believe Your Eyes and Ears,* which sold more than 1-million copies; with group, had 4 other hit singles, "I Saw Her Again," "Words of Love," "Dedicated to the One I Love," and "Creeque Alley" and a 2nd gold album, *The Mamas and the Papas* (1966–67); when the group disbanded (July 1968), became the most successful solo performer of the individual members of the former group, with album *Dream a Little Dream* (1968) and singles, "California Earthquake," "It's Getting Better," "New World Coming" and "A Song That Never Comes." Inducted into the Rock-and-Roll Hall of Fame (1998). ❖ See also Jon Johnson, *Make Your Own Kind of Music: A Career Retrospective of Cass Elliot* (Music Archives Press, 1987); "The Rolling Stone Interview: Cass Elliot," in *Rolling Stone* (Oct 26, 1968); and *Women in World History.*

ELLIOT, Charlotte. See Elliott, Charlotte.

ELLIOT, Grace (1758–1823). See Dalrymple, Grace.

ELLIOT, Marion. See Styrene, Poly.

ELLIOT, Sarah Barnwell (1848–1928). See Elliot, Sarah Barnwell.

ELLIOT, Wilhelmina (1848–1944). See Bain, Wilhelmina Sherriff.

ELLIOTT, Charlotte (1789–1871). **English hymn writer.** Name variations: Charlotte Elliot. Born Mar 18, 1789, in Clapham, Surrey, England; died Sept 22, 1871, in Brighton, East Sussex, England; grew up in Brighton; dau. of ministers; granddau. of Henry Venn, evangelical leader. ❖ Author of the well-known hymn "Just as I am, without one plea," had dual career in youth as portrait artist and writer of humorous verse, earning nickname "Carefree Charlotte" due to sunny disposition; endured serious illness (1819) and became permanent invalid at 32, sinking into depression; after meeting Genevan evangelist César Malan, was converted to evangelical Christianity and maintained a 40-year correspondence with him; began writing hymns, including "Just as I am, without one plea" (1834) to great success; wrote close to 150 hymns (1834–41), many of which are included in *The Invalid's Hymnbook* (1836); became editor of *The Christian Remembrancer* (1836). Additional works include *Hours of Sorrow* (1836), *Hymns for a Week* (1839) and *Thoughts in Verse on Sacred Subjects* (1869).

ELLIOTT, Cheri (1970—). **American mountain biker.** Name variations: Cherry Elliott. Born April 17, 1770, in Citrus Heights, California. ❖ Won gold in Dual Downhill (Summer 1995) and Speed (Winter 1997), and silver in Dual Slalom (Summer 1995), Speed (Winter 1998), and Downhill (Winter 1998), at X Games; became nationally and internationally famed cyclist, 4-time National champion (BMX), 4-time World champion (BMX), and 4-time NORBA National champion (Mountain biking). With Jennifer Drury, wrote *The Athlete's Guide to Sponsorship* (1996).

ELLIOTT, Gertrude (1874–1950). **American actress.** Born in Rockland, Maine, 1874; died 1950; dau. of Thomas (sea captain) and Adelaide (Hall) Dermot; younger sister of actress Maxine Elliott (1868–1940); m. Sir Johnston Forbes-Robertson (English actor-manager), 1900; children: several, including Diana Forbes-Robertson (author of *My Aunt Maxine: The Story of Maxine Elliott*) and Jean Forbes-Robertson (actress). ❖ Made NY debut (1894); appeared with Nathaniel Goodwin in *In Missoura, The Rivals,* and *Nathan Hale* (1897–99); made London debut as Midge in *The Cowboy and the Lady* (1899); appeared with Johnston Forbes-Robertson, playing Ophelia to his Hamlet; married Forbes-Robertson and often returned to America, where she created the role of Cleopatra in Shaw's *Caesar and Cleopatra,* among others; performed with husband until his retirement (1913), after which she toured under her own management; in one of her last performances in NY (1936), played Gertrude in *Hamlet* opposite Leslie Howard. ❖ See also *Women in World History.*

ELLIOTT, Grace (1758–1823). See Dalrymple, Grace.

ELLIOTT, Harriet Wiseman (1884–1947). **American educator and public official.** Born Harriet Wiseman Elliott on July 10, 1884, in Carbondale, Illinois; died Aug 6, 1947, in Carbondale, IL; dau. of Allan Curtis Elliott and Ann (White) Elliott. ❖ Began teaching at State Normal and Industrial College, Greensboro, NC (1913), becoming professor of history and political science (1921); served as dean of women after the college was renamed Woman's College of University of North Carolina (1935–47); became chair of education department of NC Division of Woman's Committee of Council of National Defense (1918); served on advisory committee of state Emergency Relief Administration (1933–35); served on Democratic National Committee's Women's Division, working to promote New Deal (1935); served as chair of legislative committee of American Association of University Women (1937–40), and as president of North Carolina Social Service Conference (1939–40); was appointed consumer commissioner on National Defense Advisory Commission by President Roosevelt (1940); was consumer division chief and associate administrator of Office of Price Administration and Civilian Supply, but resigned when unsuccessful in campaign for government price controls (April–Nov 1941); appointed to create and head women's division in Treasury Department, directed sale of war bonds and stamps (1942); worked for women's rights, including women's suffrage.

ELLIOTT, Kathryn (1956—). See Keeler, Kathryn.

ELLIOTT, Madge (1896–1955). English actress and dancer. Name variations: Madge Ritchard. Born May 12, 1896, in Kensington, England; died Aug 8, 1955, in New York, NY; m. Cyril Ritchard (actor). ❖ Well known in Britain and Australia, made stage debut in a ballet in Sydney (1912); was subsequently principal dancer in *High Jinks,* among other shows; returned to England (1925) and made London debut in *Better Days;* appeared in many musicals including *Bubbly, Midnight Follies, So This Is Love, Roberta,* and *The Merry Widow;* on Broadway, appeared in *The Relapse.*

ELLIOTT, Margaret Mary (1921–1998). See Gowing, Margaret.

ELLIOTT, Maud Howe (1854–1948). American novelist and historian. Name variations: Maud Howe. Born Maud Howe at Perkins Institute in Boston, Massachusetts, Nov 9, 1854; died in Newport, Rhode Island, Mar 19, 1948; dau. of Samuel Gridley Howe (founder of Perkins Institute for the Blind) and Julia Ward Howe; sister of Laura E. Richards (1850–1943); attended the pioneer Kindergarten of America, established and taught by Elizabeth Peabody; m. John Elliott (artist), Feb 7, 1887. ❖ With sister Laura E. Richards, received 1st Pulitzer Prize for Biography (1917) for a 2-vol. work on their mother, *Julia Ward Howe, 1819–1910* (1916); was a correspondent for several newspapers and also wrote *A Newport Aquarelle* (1883), *The San Rosario Ranch* (1884), *Atalanta in the South* (1886), *Mammon* (1888), *Two in Italy* (1905), *Honor,* and *Phyllida.* ❖ See also autobiography, *Three Generations* (Little, Brown, 1923); and *Women in World History.*

ELLIOTT, Maxine (1868–1940). American actress. Born Jessie Carolyn Dermot in Rockland, Maine, Feb 5, 1868; died in Cannes, France, Mar 5, 1940; dau. of Thomas (sea captain) and Adelaide (Hall) Dermot; older sister of actress Gertrude Elliott (1874–1950); m. George A. McDermott (lawyer and marshal to NY Mayor William R. Grace), c. 1884 (div. 1896); m. Nathaniel C. Goodwin (actor and comedian), Feb 20, 1898 (div. 1908). ❖ Significant figure in the American theater, studied acting with Dion Boucicault; made 1st stage appearance at Palmer's Theater (1890), in *The Middleman,* then did a season each with Rose Coghlan's and Augustin Daly's companies (1894 and 1895); made London debut at Daly's Theater as Sylvia in *Two Gentlemen of Verona* (1895); established herself as a star in *Her Own Way,* written by playwright Clyde Fitch expressly for her (1905); captured the attention of US and English theatergoers and became the toast of British society; opened the Maxine Elliott Theater (1908), thus becoming the 1st woman manager and theater owner in New York; made a few silent films, notably the *Eternal Magdalen* and *Fighting Odds;* from 1925, spent most of her time on the Riviera, where her estate Villa de l'Horizon, near Cannes, was a gathering place for the international social set. ❖ See also Diana Forbes-Robertson, *My Aunt Maxine: The Story of Maxine Elliott* (Viking, 1964); and *Women in World History.*

ELLIOTT, Missy (1971—). American singer and songwriter. Name variations: Melissa Elliott; Missy "Misdemeanor" Elliott. Born Melissa Arnette Elliott, July 1, 1971, in Portsmouth, Virginia. ❖ One of the most influential musical artists in pop and R&B, served as songwriter, producer, and solo artist; worked as writing and producing team with Tim "Timbaland" Mosley; worked as songwriter and/or producer for such artists as Whitney Houston, Mariah Carey, SWV, Jodeci, and Aaliyah; began production company, Gold Mind; released debut solo album *Supa Dupa Fly* (1997) which included hit singles "Sock It 2 Me" and "Beep Me 911"; became 1st hip-hop artist to tour with Lilith Fair; released 2nd album *Da Real World* (1999) which included the hit single "Hot Boyz." Other albums include *Miss E . . . So Addictive.*

ELLIOTT, Rita (1923—). See Yurina, Esfir.

ELLIOTT, Sarah Barnwell (1848–1928). American novelist and suffragist. Name variations: Sarah Elliott; "Miss Sada." Born Sarah Barnwell Elliott, Aug 29, 1848, in Savannah, Georgia; died Aug 30, 1928, in Sewanee, Tennessee; dau. of Stephen Elliott (1st Episcopal bishop of Georgia) and his 2nd wife Charlotte Bull (Barnwell) Elliott; granddau. of Stephen Elliott, botanist and founder of the *Southern Review.* ❖ Writer whose books often contrasted the worthy poor with the privileged classes and often reflected rural life in Southern states, especially Tennessee, wrote such novels as *The Felmeres* (1879), *A Simple Heart* (1887), *Jerry* (1891), *The Durket Sperret* (1898), and *The Making of Jane* (1901); authored short stories, "An Incident" and "Without the Courts," and 3 plays, two of which were performed in London; moved to New York City (1895) and joined Woman's Press Club and Barnard Club, coming under the influence of feminism; moved to Sewanee, TN, to rear children of deceased sister (1902); served as president of Tennessee Equal Suffrage

Association (1912–14); became 1st woman to address Tennessee legislature (1912); participated in Washington march for federal suffrage amendment (1913).

ELLIOTT, Sumner Locke (1881–1917). See Locke, Sumner.

ELLIOTT LYNN, Sophie (1896–1939). See Heath, Sophie.

ELLIS, Alice Thomas (1932—). See Haycraft, Anna Margaret.

ELLIS, Betty (c. 1941—). American soccer official. Born c. 1941. ❖ Began refereeing at local soccer matches (1971); refereed at college, semiprofessional, and professional levels, becoming 1st woman to officiate at professional soccer match (1981), in contest between San Jose Earthquakes (CA) and Edmonton Drillers (Alberta, Canada).

ELLIS, E. (1834–1913). See Wolstenholme-Elmy, Elizabeth.

ELLIS, Edith (c. 1874–1960). American actress and playwright. Born c. 1874 in Coldwater, Michigan; died Dec 27, 1960, in New York, NY; sister of Edward Ellis (actor and playwright); m. H. Furness; children: Ellis Baker (actress). ❖ Began career as an actress; wrote or adapted over 30 plays, including *Mary Jane's Pa, White Collars, Seven Sisters, The Moon and Sixpence, The Dangerous Age* and *The White Villa.*

ELLIS, Ellen (1829–1895). New Zealand novelist. Born Ellen Elizabeth Colebrook, Mar 14, 1829, at Great Tangley Manor near Guildford, Surrey, England; died April 17, 1895, in Auckland, New Zealand; dau. of Mary Ann May and William Colebrook (tenant farmer); m. Oliver Sidney Ellis (builder), Sept 1852 (died 1883); children: John William, Alec (died 1857) and Thomas. ❖ Immigrated with husband and 2 sons to New Zealand (July 1859); sought to gain legal and educational equity for women and Maoris; wrote *Everything is Possible to Will* (1882).

ELLIS, Evelyn (1894–1958). African-American stage and tv actress. Born Feb 2, 1894, in Boston, Massachusetts; died June 5, 1958, in Saranac Lake, NY. ❖ Created the role of Bess in the original production of *Porgy* (1927); also appeared in *Roseanne, Native Son, Deep Are the Roots, The Royal Family, Touchstone,* and the all-black production of *Tobacco Road.*

ELLIS, Florence Hawley (1906–1991). American archaeologist, anthropologist and ethnohistorian. Name variations: Florence M. Hawley; Florence H. Senter. Born Florence M. Hawley in Cananea, Sonora, Mexico, Sept 17, 1906; died in Albuquerque, New Mexico, April 6, 1991; dau. of Fred Graham Hawley and Amy (Roach) Hawley; attended University of Arizona; University of Chicago, PhD; m. Donovan Senter, 1936 (div. 1947); m. Bruce T. Ellis (curator of collections at Albuquerque's Museum of New Mexico); children: (1st m.) Andrea Senter. ❖ Leading authority on the Pueblo Indians of the American Southwest, wrote master's thesis on ceramics fragments that had been excavated in sites near Miami, Arizona (1928); was able to distinguish 3 closely successive stages of pottery, separating 3 sequential types (Early, Middle and Late Gila Polychrome) and making a strong case for the relationships of these artifacts to certain Mexican Indian pottery types; collaborating with father, whose expertise in chemical analysis enabled her to describe in precise terms the pigments of black pottery (carbon, carbon-mineral, and manganese), pioneered in the methodology of Southwestern American archaeology; joined anthropology department of University of Arizona (1928); began to spend several months each summer in New Mexico (1929), where she concentrated on field work at the archaeological site of Chetro Ketl; scientifically established the significance of the stratified variations in ceramics she had observed in the Chetro Ketl East Dump, one of the earliest uses of form statistics (Chi square) in American archaeology; joined the anthropology department at University of New Mexico (1934), remaining there for almost 4 decades; became a strong defender of Indian rights; published *Field Manual of Southwestern Pottery Types* (1936) and *An Anthropological Study of the Navajo Indians* (1974). The Florence Hawley Ellis Museum of Anthropology is situated in Abiquiu, NM. ❖ See also *Women in World History.*

ELLIS, Kathleen (1946—). American swimmer. Name variations: Kathy Ellis. Born Nov 28, 1946. ❖ At Tokyo Olympics, won bronze medals in 100-meter butterfly and 100-meter freestyle, and gold medals in the 4 x 100-meter medley relay and the 4 x 100-meter freestyle relay (1964).

ELLIS, Lucille (c. 1915—). American modern dancer. Born c. 1915 in Arkansas. ❖ Performed at clubs in Chicago, before joining Katherine Dunham Company (1939), where she appeared in *Tropical Pinafore, Rhumba Trio, Cakewalk, Samba,* among others; performed on Broadway in *Cabin in the Sky* (1940); served as assistant to Dunham for many years and ran 2nd Dunham school in New York City.

ELLIS, Mary (1897–2003). American-born stage and screen actress and musical star. Born May Belle Elsas, June 15, 1897 in New York, NY; died Jan 31, 2003, in London, England; m. Edwin Knopf (div.); m. Basil Sydney (actor), 1929 (div.); m. Jock Muir Stewart Roberts (pilot, skier and climber), 1938 (died in a climbing accident, 1950). ❖ Joined the Metropolitan Opera (1918), appearing as Mityl in *Blue Bird;* made musical debut on Broadway in operetta *Rose-Marie* (1924), which was produced by Arthur Hammerstein, written for her by Rudolf Friml, and ran for 558 performances (when, after one year, Ellis left the show to appear in *The Dybbuk*, with a weekly reduction in pay from $500 to $10, Hammerstein made her agree to only sing in US under his management); began to appear in England, often with 3rd husband Basil Sydney; with help of such shows as Jerome Kern's *Music in the Air* and Ivor Novello's *Glamorous Night* and *The Dancing Years,* became known as the queen of London musicals but never sang in US again; also appeared in such dramas as *Strange Interlude, Point Valaine* and *The Browning Version;* films include *All the King's Horses;* on tv, appeared in the Sherlock Holmes tv series starring Jeremy Brett. ❖ See also autobiography *Those Dancing Years* (Murray, 1982).

ELLIS, Mina A. (1870–1956). Canadian explorer and author. Name variations: Mina Hubbard; Mina Benson Hubbard Ellis. Born Mina Benson, April 15, 1870, in Bewdly, Hamilton, Township, Ontario, Canada; killed by a train, May 4, 1956, in Coulston, near London, England; dau. of James Benson and Jane Wood (Irish immigrants); graduated from the Brooklyn (New York) Training School for Nurses, 1899; m. Leonidas Hubbard Jr. (journalist and explorer), Jan 31, 1901; m. Harold Ellis, 1908; children: 3. ❖ While serving as superintendent of the Staten Island Hospital, nursed future husband through typhoid fever (1900); after he perished in Labrador (1903), organized an expedition which successfully crossed the northeastern part of the Labrador Peninsula intent on completing his work (1905); in doing so, became the 1st white person to cross the Great Divide between the Naskaupi and George Rivers; published *A Woman's Way through Unknown Labrador* (1908).

ELLIS, Mrs. (d. 1872). See Ellis, Sarah Stickney.

ELLIS, Norma Millay (d. 1986). See Millay, Norma.

ELLIS, Patricia (1916–1970). American stage and screen actress. Born Patricia Gene O'Brien, May 20, 1916, in Birmingham, Michigan; died Mar 26, 1970, in Kansas City, Missouri; stepdau. of Alexander Leftwich (actor and theatrical producer); m. George T. O'Malley, 1940. ❖ Films include *St. Louis Kid, Elmer the Great, A Night at the Ritz, Romance on the Run,* and *42nd Street.*

ELLIS, Ruth (1927–1955). British murderer. Born in Welsh town of Rhyl, 1927; executed by hanging in North London's Holloway Women's Prison, July 13, 1955; raised in Manchester, England; m. a dentist, 1950 (div.); children: stepson by marriage; daughter, born out of wedlock. ❖ Last woman to be hanged in England, was uneducated with 2 children to support and employed in a London nightclub, when she began a tempestuous affair with racetrack driver David Blakely (1953); a year into their relationship, also became involved with Blakely's friend Desmond Cussen; tried unsuccessfully to terminate her seemingly obsessive relationship with Blakely; on April 10, 1955, took a cab to a local pub, waited for him to emerge, and shot him dead; readily confessed and was sentenced to death by hanging, which brought a storm of protest in England from those opposed to capital punishment (the policy was abolished a year after her hanging). ❖ See also film *Dance with a Stranger,* starring Miranda Richardson (1985); and *Women in World History.*

ELLIS, Sarah Stickney (c. 1799–1872). British novelist and tract writer. Name variations: Mrs. Ellis; Sarah Ellis; Sarah Stickney. Born Sarah Stickney, c. 1799 (some sources cite 1812), in Holderness, Yorkshire, England; died June 16, 1872, in Hoddesdon, Hertfordshire, England; dau. of William Stickney and Esther (Richardson) Stickney; m. William Ellis, 1837. ❖ Wrote novels and conduct manuals on the ideal Victorian woman; writings include *The Negro Slave* (1830), *Pictures of Private Life* (1833–1837) *The Women of England* (1839), *The Daughters of England* (1842), *The Island Queen* (1846), *Social Distinction* (1848), *Fireside Tales for the Young* (1848), *The Mother's Mistake* (1856), *The Brewer's Family* (1863) and *Education of the Heart* (1869).

ELLIS, Terry (1966—). American singer. Name variations: En Vogue; Vogue. Born Sept 5, 1966, in Houston, Texas. ❖ As a member of En Vogue, the R&B girl group known for its four-part harmonies that enjoyed great success in 1990s, had such hits as "Hold On" (1990), "My Lovin' (You're Never Gonna Get It)" (1992), "Free Your Mind" (1992), "Don't Let Go (Love)" (1996), "Whatever" (1997) and "Too Gone, Too Long" (1997); released the critically acclaimed solo album *Southern Gal* (1995). En Vogue albums include *Born to Sing* (1990), *Remix to Sing* (1991), *Funky Divas* (1992, multiplatinum), *Runaway Love* (1993) and *EV3* (1997).

ELLIS-FERMOR, Una Mary (1894–1958). British educator and literary critic. Name variations: U.M. Ellis-Fermor; Una Ellis Fermor or Una Ellis Fermor; (pseudonym) Christopher Turnley. Born Una Ellis-Fermor, Dec 20, 1894, in London, England; died Mar 24, 1958, in London, England; dau. of Joseph Turnley Ellis-Fermor and Edith Mary Katherine Ellis-Fermor. ❖ A major contributor to the study of the English Renaissance, spent most of academic career at Bedford College, University of London, as reader and then professor of English; also taught in US at Yale and Columbia universities; writings include *Christopher Marlowe* (1927), *The Jacobean Drama* (1936), *The Irish Dramatic Movement* (1939), *Masters of Reality* (1942), *The Frontiers of Drama* (1945), and *Shakespeare the Dramatist and Other Papers* (1961).

ELLISIF. See Elizabeth of Kiev (fl. 1045).

ELLISON, Elizabeth Best (1868–1941). See Taylor, Elizabeth Best.

ELLISON, Mrs. Sydney (1870–1955). See Cutler, Kate.

ELLISON, Vanessa (1955—). See Hay, Vanessa Briscoe.

ELLISTON, Daisy (b. 1894). English ballet and theatrical dancer. Born Aug 8, 1894, in London, England; trained with Adeline Genée. ❖ Made debut as child dancer in *The Water Babies* (1902); appeared in numerous musicals and operettas in London's West End and on tour, including *The Merry Widow* (1908), *The Dollar Princess* (1910), *The Girl from Utah* (1913), *Irene* (1921), *The Desert Song* (1927) and *Rio Rita* (1930); appeared in the film, *The Duchess of Seven Dials.*

ELLMAN, Louise (1945—). English politician. Born Louise Rosenberg, Nov 14, 1945; m. Geoffrey Ellman, 1967. ❖ Representing Labour/Co-operative, elected to House of Commons for Liverpool Riverside (1997, 2002, 2005).

ELLMANN, Barbara (1950—). American modern dancer and designer. Born July 11, 1950, in Detroit, Michigan. ❖ Joined James Cunningham and Acme Dance Company (early 1970s), where she performed in Cunningham's *Dancing with Maisie Paradocks* (1974), *Mr. Fox Asleep* (1978), and others; served as Cunningham company's associate director and designed costumes—an integral part of his productions—for numerous works, including *Alexander and the Sheep's Head* (1978), *The Well at the World's End* (1979), *The Attic Window* (1979) and *The Rainbow Bridge* (1979); exhibited artwork, including collages, photography, and graphic art, at numerous venues in New York City.

ELLSTEIN, Sylvia (1908–2003). See Regan, Sylvia.

ELMENDORF, Theresa West (1855–1932). American librarian. Born Theresa Hubble West, 1855, in Pardeeville, Wisconsin; died Sept 4, 1932, in Buffalo, NY; m. Henry L. Elmendorf (librarian). ❖ The 1st woman president of the American Library Association, was known particularly for work in bibliography; began career as assistant librarian at Young Men's Association of Milwaukee, WI (1877); served as deputy librarian (1880–92) and librarian (1892–96) at Milwaukee Public Library, the 1st woman to be elected head of a large public library; served as vice-librarian of Buffalo Public Library, NY (1906–26) and as 1st woman president of American Library Association (1911–12); was among the 1st to be inducted into *Library Journal*'s Hall of Fame (1951). Writings include *The Systematic Catalogue of the Public Library of the City of Milwaukee* (1885), *Books and Articles on the Labor Question in the Milwaukee Public Library* (1887) and *Classroom Libraries for Public Schools* (1923).

ELMHIRST, Dorothy Straight (1887–1968). See Whitney, Dorothy Payne.

EL MOUTAWAKEL, Nawal (1962—). Moroccan runner. Name variations: Moutawakil. Born April 15, 1962, in Casablanca; attended Iowa State University. ❖ Won a gold medal for the women's 1st-ever 400-meter hurdles at Los Angeles Olympics (1984), setting an Olympic record of 54.61 and becoming the 1st Moroccan, 1st African woman, and 1st Islamic woman to win a gold medal. ❖ See also *Women in World History.*

ELMS, Lauris (1931—). Australian mezzo-soprano. Name variations: Lauris Margaret Elms, Mrs. Lauris Margaret Elms de Graaf. Born Oct 20, 1931, in Melbourne, Australia; studied in Paris; children: Deborah de Graaf (clarinetist). ❖ Made debut at Covent Garden in Verdi's *Un Ballo in Maschera* (1957) and became principal resident artist there; appeared with leading Australian companies and is renowned for portrayal of Azucena in Verdi's *Il Trovatore;* toured Australia with Joan Sutherland (1965) and appeared at opening of Sydney Opera House (1973); appeared with all leading Australian companies; made many acclaimed recordings and frequent radio broadcasts and gave regular lieder recitals with pianist Geoffrey Parsons. ❖ See also *The Singing Elms: The Autobiography of Lauris Elms* (Bowerbird, 2001).

ELMY, Elizabeth Wolstenholme (1834–1913). *See Wolstenholme-Elmy, Elizabeth.*

ELOISA (fl. 1727–1745). *See Boyd, Elizabeth.*

ELPHICK, Jeanette (1935–1988). *See Shaw, Victoria.*

ELPHIDE (c. 654–c. 714). *See Alphaida.*

ELPHINSTONE, Eupheme (fl. 1500s.). Mistress of a Scottish king. Mistress of James V (1512–1542), king of Scotland (r. 1513–1542); children: (with James V) Robert Stewart (b. 1533), earl of Orkney.

ELPHINSTONE, Hester Maria (1764–1857). Viscountess Keith. Born in 1764; died in 1857; dau. of Henry and Hester Lynch Piozzi (1741–1821); education directed by Dr. Samuel Johnson; studied Hebrew and mathematics; m. George Keith Elphinstone, Viscount Keith (1746–1823, an admiral).

ELPHINSTONE, Margaret Mercer (1788–1867). Viscountess Keith, comtesse de Flahault, and Baroness Nairne. Born 1788; died 1867; dau. of George Keith Elphinstone, Viscount Keith (1746–1823, an admiral), and Hester Maria Elphinstone (1764–1857); granddau. of Hester Lynch Piozzi (1741–1821); m. the comte de Flahault, in 1817. ❖ Was a confidante of Princess Charlotte Augusta (1796–1817).

EL QALQILI, Kerstin (1976—). *See Kowalski, Kerstin.*

EL SAADAWI, Nawal (1931—). Egyptian feminist, physician, journalist and novelist. Name variations: el Sad'adawi, el-Saadawi, al-Saadawi. Pronunciation: Na-WAA-l el Sa-a-da-we. Born in Kafr Tahla, Egypt, 1931 (some sources cite 1930); Cairo University School of Medicine, MD, 1955; m. 3rd husband, Sherif Hetata (physician); children: daughter Mona Helmi (writer); son Atef Hetata (film director). ❖ Leading contemporary radical feminist, forceful and outspoken critic of women's oppression in the Middle East and globally, whose writings address the impact of misogynist social structures on Egyptian women, especially the sexual abuse Egyptian women undergo, such as the practice of female genital mutilation; practiced medicine in rural and urban areas; promoted to director of Health Education and editor-in-chief of the magazine *Health;* dismissed from her positions (Aug 1971) and blacklisted by the Egyptian government because of her controversial book, *Women and Sex* (1972); practiced medicine part-time and wrote novels depicting the universe of Egyptian women; researched women's neuroses while on the Faculty of Medicine at Ain Shams University (1973–76); served as United Nations' advisor for the Women's Program in Africa (ECA) and the Middle East (ECWA, 1979–80); imprisoned for 3 months (1981) by President Sadat; established the Arab Women's Solidarity Association (AWSA, 1982); fought the banning of AWSA (early 1990s); accepted a visiting professorship at Duke University (1993); served as president of Arab Women's Solidarity Association. Nonfiction works (trans.) include: *The Hidden Face of Eve: Women in the Arab World* (1980), *Memoirs from the Women's Prison* (1983), *My Travels Around the World* (1991); selected fiction (trans.) include: *The Circling Song* (1989), *Death of an Ex-Minister* (1987), *The Fall of the Imam* (1989), *God Dies by the Nile* (1985), *The Innocence of the Devil* (1994), *Memoirs of a Woman Doctor: A Novel* (1989), *Searching* (1991), *She Has No Place in Paradise* (1987), *Two Women in One* (1990), *The Well of Life* (1993) and *Woman at Point Zero.* ❖ See also *Women in World History.*

ELSEETA (1883–1903). American theater ballet dancer. Name variations: Helen Loder Jones. Born Helen Loder Jones, 1883, in Philadelphia, Pennsylvania; died Feb 23, 1903, in Newark, New Jersey. ❖ Made vaudeville debut as a child at age 5; danced on the Keith and roof-garden circuits, appearing at Madison Square Garden and Casino

Roof in NY; appeared on Broadway in *The Sleeping Beauty and the Beast* (1901), her last performance before she died of what is thought to have been a 2nd heart attack; was known to dance barefoot on point, and performed an act that involved jumping from the top of a grand piano to land—on point—on high and middle C of the keyboard.

ELSENER, Patricia (1929—). American diver. Name variations: Patricia Anne Elsener; Patsy Elsener. Born Oct 22, 1929; grew up in San Francisco, California. ❖ At London Olympics, won a bronze medal in springboard and a silver medal in platform (1948).

ELSIE, Lily (1886–1962). English operetta singer and dancer. Born April 8, 1886, in Wortley, near Leeds, England; died Dec 16, 1962, in Sussex, England; niece of Wilfrid Cotton (actor and manager); m. Ian Bullough (div.). ❖ Made stage debut in title role of pantomime *Red Riding Hood* (1896); created the English-language lead part of Sonia in *The Merry Widow* to great acclaim (1907); also starred on London stage in *A Chinese Honeymoon, Lady Madcap, The Dollar Princess, A Waltz Dream, Mauvereen, Pamela, The Count of Luxembourg,* and *The Truth Game.*

ELSNER, Gisela (1937–1992). German novelist. Born May 2, 1937, in Nuremberg, Germany; died May 13, 1992; studied philosophy and theater in Vienna. ❖ Writings, which satirize modern life and portray characters alienated from reality, include *Die Riesenzwerge* (1964), *Der Punktsieg* (1977), *Abseits* (1982), and *Fliegeralarm* (1989). Received Prix Formentor (1964) and Gerrit Engelke Prize of Hanover (1987).

ELSOM, Annie (1867–1962). *See Elsom, Sarah Ann.*

ELSOM, Isobel (1893–1981). English-born actress and singer. Name variations: Isobel Harbord. Born Isobel Reed, Mar 16, 1893, in Chesterton, Cambridge, England; died Jan 12, 1981, in Woodland Hills, California; m. Maurice Elvey (actor and director), 1923 (div.); m. 3rd husband Carl Harbord (actor, died 1958). ❖ Debuted on London stage in chorus of *The Quaker Girl* (1911) and had great success as Lalage Sturdee in *The Outsider* (1923); on Broadway, appeared in *The Mulberry Bush, The Silver Box, Ladies in Retirement, The Innocents, Romeo and Juliet,* and *The First Gentlemen,* among others; films include *Monsieur Verdoux, Ladies in Retirement, Eagle Squadron, Casanova Brown, Of Human Bondage, The Two Mrs. Carrolls, The Ghost and Mrs. Muir, The Paradine Case, The Philadelphians, Desiree, Love is a Many Splendored Thing* and *My Fair Lady;* retired (1964).

ELSOM, Sarah Ann (1867–1962). New Zealand florist. Name variations: Annie Elsom, Annie Read, Sarah Ann Read. Born Sarah Ann Read, Mar 26, 1867, in Dunedin, New Zealand; died Nov 17, 1962, in Christchurch, New Zealand; dau. of William (gardener) and Elizabeth (Martin) Read; m. Edwin Elsom, 1902; children: 2 daughters, 1 son. ❖ As single woman, ran her own successful floristry business in Christchurch, A.&S. Reid (c. 1897–c. 1954). ❖ See also *Dictionary of New Zealand Biography* (Vol. 3).

ELSSLER, Fanny (1810–1884). Austrian ballet dancer. Born in Vienna, Austria, June 23, 1810; died in Vienna, Nov 27, 1884; father was a professional musician and copyist; sister of Thérèse Elssler (1808–1878); cousin of Hermine Elssler (dancer); studied ballet under Jean Aumer and Philippe Taglioni; never married; children: (with Leopold, prince of Salerno) Franz (b. 1827); (with Anton Stuhlmüller) Theresa von Webenau (b. 1833). ❖ At 7, made 1st appearance at the Kärnthner-Thor theater in Vienna; in the early years, almost invariably danced with her sister Thérèse; appeared at the Opéra in Paris (1834), very aware of Maria Taglioni's supremacy on that stage; momentarily eclipsed Taglioni, who, though the finer artist of the two, could not compete with the newcomer's ability to enchant; had developed her staccato, or *taqueté,* style, in contrast to Taglioni's floating, *ballonné* method; her performance of the Spanish *cachucha,* while in the role of Florinda in *Le Diable boiteux* (1836), outshone all rivals; sailed for New York (1840); was greeted by "Elssler mania," received at the White House, and enjoyed 2 years of unblemished success; retired from the stage after farewell performance with Perrot in his *Faust* at La Scala (1845); traveled to St. Petersburg and appeared as an actress in *Giselle* (1848) for 2 years. ❖ See also *Women in World History.*

ELSSLER, Thérèse (1808–1878). Austro-Hungarian ballet dancer. Name variations: Theresa Elssler. Born April 5, 1808, in Vienna, Austria; died Nov 19, 1878, in Merano, Italy; father was a professional musician and copyist; older sister of Fanny Elssler (1810–1884, ballet dancer). ❖ Trained with Friedrich Horschelt and later Jean Aumer, ballet master at Kärnthner-Thor Theater in Vienna; made professional debut at Theater an der Wein in Vienna (1818); appeared frequently in performance with sister Fanny—either as Elssler Sisters or Fanny and

Theresa—with whom she danced en travestie; performed at numerous venues across Europe, including King's Theatre in London, Paris Opéra in France, and theaters in Berlin, Germany; choreographed numerous pas de deux for herself and Fanny as well as full-length ballets; was one of the few female choreographers of Romantic period ballets. Choreography includes *Die Maskerade* (1834), *Pas Styrien* (1834), *La Volière* (1838), *Pas de Châle* (1840), *El Zapateado* (1840) and *La Smolenska* (1840).

ELSTE, Meta (1921—). American gymnast. Name variations: Meta Neuman Elste. Born Oct 16, 1921; grandmother of Kari Elste (gymnast). ❖ At London Olympics, won a bronze medal in team all-around (1948).

ELSTOB, Elizabeth (1683–1756). English Anglo-Saxon scholar. Born in Newcastle, England, 1683; died 1756. ❖ One of the few women scholars of her day, undertook the translation of Madeleine de Scudéry's *Essay on Glory* and the *Anglo-Saxon Homily on the Nativity of St. Gregory* (1709), in which she used the preface to defend the right of women to obtain an education and to engage in theological discussions about the Old English Church; produced a grammar book, *Rudiments of Grammar for the English-Saxon Tongue, First given in English; with an Apology for the Study of Northern Antiquities* (1715); encountered financial difficulties that ended her scholarly pursuits; became governess to the children of Margaret Bentinck, duchess of Portland, remaining there until her death. ❖ See also *Women in World History*.

ELSWITHA (d. 902). Queen of the English. Name variations: Alwitha; Ealhswyth; Ealhswyth; Elswith; Ealhswith of the Gaini. Died Dec 5, 902 (some sources cite 905), at St. Mary's Abbey, Winchester, Dorset; interred at Winchester Cathedral, London; dau. of Ethelred the Great, ealdorman of the Gainis, and Eadburh; m. Alfred the Great (848–c. 900), king of the English (r. 871–899), in 868; children: Edmund (died young); Edward I the Elder (c. 870–924), king of the English (r. 899–924); Ethelweard (880–922); and three daughters, Ethelflaed (869–918), Ethelgeofu (d. around 896), and Elfthrith (d. 929). ❖ Following death of husband (c. 900), became a nun; was reputed to be a saint. ❖ See also *Women in World History*.

ELTHELTHRITH (630–679). Queen of Northumbria and abbess of Ely. Name variations: Aelthelthrith; Aethelthrith; Aethelthryth; Saint Audrey; Ethelreda; Etheldreda; Ethelthrith or Ethelthryth. Born 630 in East Anglia, England; died 679 at convent of Ely; dau. of Saewara and probably Anna (635–654), king of East Anglia; sister of Saint Sexburga (d. 699?) and Withburga and half-sister of Saint Ethelburga (d. 665); m. Tondberht of South Gyrwas, ealdorman of South Gyrwas, also known as Prince Tonbert (died 3 years later); m. Ecgfrith or Egfrid, king of Northumbria, c. 671 (died 685). ❖ Like most young noblewomen, had to marry for parents financial and political benefit; committed from childhood to a religious life, persuaded husband to not consummate union and give up all claims on her as his wife; following his death, retired to a life of prayer until political considerations compelled her to marry Ecgfrith (671), king of Northumbria, though nuptials included a vow to live together as brother and sister; when Ecgfrith began to tire of the arrangement, was advised by St. Wilfrid to abandon the marriage and take up religious pursuits once again; using personal fortune, founded two abbeys on island of Ely (c. 672), one for men and one for women, which she supervised until her death. Feast day is June 23. ❖ See also *Women in World History*.

ELUARD, Nusch (1906–1946). German artist, model, and author. Born Maria Benz, 1906 in Alsace, Mulhouse, France (then annexed by Germany as Mülhausen); died 1946 in Paris; m. Paul Eluard (Surrealist painter), 1934. ❖ Began career as an actress, choosing Nusch as a stage name; moving to Paris (1920), met husband (1930), while working as a model for postcards and serving as a walk-on at the Théâtre Grand Guignol; modeled for Man Ray and Pablo Picasso and created a series of Surrealist photomontages, essentially using the female nude (her collages were published by Editions Nadada, 1978); during WWII, joined the Resistance with husband.

ELVIN, Violetta (1925—). Russian-born ballerina. Name variations: Violette Elvin. Born Violetta Vasilevna Prokhorova, Nov 3, 1925, in Moscow, USSR (now Russia); m. Harold Elvin (div.); m. Siegbert J. Weinberger (div.). ❖ Made stage debut as a child in Moscow, later becoming a soloist with the Bolshoi; evacuated to Tashkent, Central Asia, during the war, appearing there with the Tashkent State Theater (1942); moved to England (1945), making London debut at the Théâtre Royal Opera House as Princesse Florisse in *The Sleeping Beauty* (1946); became a permanent member of Sadler's Wells, appearing there as prima ballerina

in *Swan Lake, Giselle, Sylvia, Cinderella, The Rake's Progress, Checkmate, Ballet Imperial, Tiresias, Le Tricorne, Symphonic Variations, Don Juan,* and *Veneziana*; films include *The Queen of Spades, Twice Upon a Time,* and *Melba*; retired (1956).

ELVIRA (1038–1101). Princess of Castile. Born 1038; died Nov 15, 1101; dau. of Sancha of Leon (1013–1067) and Ferdinand I (c. 1017–1065), king of Castile and Leon (r. 1038–1065). ❖ See also *Women in World History*.

ELVIRA (fl. 1080s). Countess of Toulouse. Fl. in 1080s; died after 1151; dau. of Jimena Muñoz (c. 1065–1128) and Alphonso VI (c. 1030–1109), king of Castile and Leon; sister of Teresa of Castile; m. Raymond IV, count of Toulouse (r. 1088–1105); children: Bertrand de Rouergue, count of Toulouse (r. 1105–1112); Alphonso de Rouergue, count of Toulouse (r. 1112–1114). ❖ See also *Women in World History*.

ELVIRA (d. 1135). Duchess of Apulia and queen of Sicily. Died Feb 8, 1135; illeg. dau. of Zaida (d. 1107) and Alphonso VI, king of Castile and Leon; m. Roger II, king of Sicily (r. 1103–1154), duke of Apulia (r. 1128–1154). Robert II was also m. to Beatrice of Rethel and Sibylle of Burgundy. ❖ See also *Women in World History*.

ELVIRA GONZALEZ OF GALICIA (d. 1022). Queen of Leon and Asturias. Name variations: Geloria. Died Dec 2, 1022; dau. of Menendo, count Gonzalez; m. Alphonso or Alphonso V, king of Leon and Asturias (r. 999–1027), 1015; children: Vermudo III (b. 1010), king of Leon; Sancha of Leon (1013–1067). ❖ See also *Women in World History*.

ELWELL, Margaret L. (1919–2003). *See Coit, Margaret L.*

ELY, Mary (1887–1975). *See Lyman, Mary.*

ELZBIETA. *Variant of Elizabeth.*

EMECHETA, Buchi (1944—). Nigerian novelist. Born Florence Onye Buchi Emecheta, July 21, 1944, in Yaba, near Lagos, Nigeria; dau. of Jeremy Nwabudike Emecheta and Alice Okwuekwu Emecheta; m. Sylvester Onwordi, 1960 (sep. 1966); children: 5. ❖ At 18, moved to England with husband and her 2 children (1962); earned PhD while raising 5 children; endured physical and emotional abuse from husband, who burned 1st manuscript; left husband and became a librarian at the British Museum and a teacher; novels, which are often autobiographical and focus on the position of black women in Britain, include *In the Ditch* (1972), *Second-Class Citizen* (1974), *The Bride Price* (1976), *The Joys of Motherhood* (1979), *Destination Biafra* (1982), *The Rape of Shavi* (1983), *A Kind of Marriage* (1986), *Family Bargain* (1987), and *Gwendolen* (1990); also published children's books.

EMELYANOVA, Inessa (1972—). *See Sargsian, Inessa.*

EMERALD, Connie (1891–1959). English actress. Name variations: Constance Lupino. Born Constance O'Shay, 1891; died Dec 26, 1959; m. Stanley Lupino; children: Ida Lupino (1914–1995, actress, director); Rita Lupino (actress). ❖ Began acting career as a child, appearing at the Shaftesbury Theater in *The Prince of Pilsen* (1904); while still in her teens, toured US for 18 months, followed with a tour of Australia; made last appearance in London (1931), as Jane Howard in *Hold My Hand*.

EMERSON, Ellen Tucker (1811–1831). American wife of Ralph Waldo Emerson. Born Ellen Louisa Tucker in 1811 in Concord, New Hampshire; died of tuberculosis, age 19, Feb 8, 1831, in Massachusetts; m. Ralph Waldo Emerson (philosopher). ❖ Met future husband (1827), became engaged (1828), and married him (Sept 30, 1829).

EMERSON, Ellen Tucker (1839–1909). American daughter of Ralph Waldo Emerson. Name variations: Ella or Nelly Emerson. Born Feb 24, 1839, in Concord, Massachusetts; died 1909; dau. of Ralph Waldo Emerson (1803–1882, Transcendentalist) and Lidian Jackson Emerson (1802–1892); never married. ❖ Was a traveling companion and assistant to her father. ❖ See also *The Letters of Ellen Tucker Emerson.*

EMERSON, Ellen Russell (1837–1907). American ethnologist. Name variations: Mrs. Ellen Emerson. Born Ellen Russell on Jan 16, 1837, in New Sharon, Maine; died June 12, 1907, in Cambridge, Massachusetts; m. Edwin R. Emerson, Feb 1862. ❖ Developed interest in Indian lore and legend as result of childhood meeting with Henry Wadsworth Longfellow; published works include *Indian Myths; or Legends, Traditions, and Symbols of the Aborigines of America Compared with Those of Other Countries, including Hindostan, Egypt, Persia, Assyria and*

China (1884), *Masks, Heads, and Faces, with Some Considerations Respecting the Rise and Development of Art* (1891), and *Nature and Human Nature* (1902).

EMERSON, Faye (1917–1983). American socialite and actress. Name variations: Mrs. Elliott Roosevelt. Born July 8, 1917 in Elizabeth, Louisiana; died Mar 9, 1983, in Devya, Spain; m. William Wallace Crawford, 1938 (div. 1942); m. Elliott Roosevelt (son of Eleanor and Franklin D. Roosevelt), 1944 (div. 1950); m. Skitch Henderson (bandleader), 1951 (div. 1958); m. William Crawford; children: (1st m.) son. ❖ Made Broadway debut in *The Play's the Thing* (1948), followed by *Parisienne, Protective Custody, Back to Methuselah, Mary Stuart,* and *Elizabeth the Queen,* among others; made film debut with *Bad Men of Missouri* (1941); other films include *Destination Tokyo, Between Two Worlds, Secret Enemies, The Very Thought of You, Hollywood Canteen, Hotel Berlin* and *Guilty Bystander;* launched her own talk show "Faye Emerson's Wonderful Town" (1949) and "The Faye Emerson Show" (1950); was such a popular personality in early tv that the name "Emerson" inspired the nickname for the Emmy Awards.

EMERSON, Gladys Anderson (1903–1984). American biochemist and nutritionist. Born in Caldwell, Kansas, July 1, 1903; died in Santa Monica, California, Jan 18, 1984; dau. of Otis and Louise (Williams) Anderson; bachelor's degree in English and chemistry from Oklahoma College for Women, 1925; Stanford University, MA in history; University of California, Berkeley, PhD in biochemistry, 1932; postgraduate study at University of Göttingen; m. Oliver Emerson, biochemist (div. 1940). ❖ One of the outstanding American biochemists of her generation, conducted important research on vitamin E, amino acids, and the B-vitamin complex; became research associate at University of California's Institute of Experimental Biology (1933); with husband and H.M. Evans, isolated vitamin E, enabling it to be created synthetically in the laboratory; became head of the department of animal nutrition at Merck Institute for Therapeutic Research (1942); was entrusted with major research projects at Merck which included investigations of vitamins B-6 and B-12 as well as amino acids; studies contributed to the momentum of later research on the chemotherapy of viral infections; animal investigations, centering largely on the B-complex family of vitamins, yielded important findings, including the fact that vitamin deficiencies could lead to abnormal growth as well as abnormalities of the liver, kidney, eye, skin, and posture; was a research associate with the Sloan-Kettering Institute for Cancer Research in New York City (1950–53), where her research concentrated on the effects of diet and hormones on the growth of tumors; became professor and chair of the department of home economics at the University of California, Los Angeles (UCLA, 1957), then head of the nutrition division at the UCLA School of Public Health (1962), a post she occupied until her retirement (1970); was a member of the food and nutrition board of the National Research Council (1959–64). Received the Garvan Medal (1952). ❖ See also *Women in World History.*

EMERSON, Gloria (1929–2004). American journalist and war and foreign correspondent. Born 1929 in New York, NY; committed suicide, Aug 3, 2004, in New York, NY; dau. of William B. Emerson and Ruth Shaw Emerson; was briefly married to a man named Znamiecki and briefly married to Charles A. Brofferio. ❖ At 28, joined the women's section of *New York Times;* served as a foreign correspondent for the *Times* (1965–72); while working in its London bureau (1969), asked to be sent to Vietnam; freelanced as a journalist for a large number of prominent American newspapers and magazines; covered other trouble spots, including Northern Ireland, El Salvador, Nigeria, the Gaza Strip and Algeria; writings include *Winners and Losers: Battles, Retreats, Gains, Losses, and Ruins from the Vietnam War* (1977), which won the National Book Award, *Some American Men* (1985) and *Gaza: A Year in the Intifada* (1991); also wrote the novel *Loving Graham Greene* (2000). Won a George Polk Award for excellence in foreign reporting (1971); received a Matrix Award.

EMERSON, Hope (1897–1960). American actress. Born in 1897 in Hawarden, Iowa; died April 25, 1960, in Hollywood, California. ❖ Specialized in comedy in early appearances in vaudeville and on Broadway; plays include *Lysistrata, Chicken Every Sunday,* and *Street Scene;* often portrayed a heavy in Hollywood in such films as *Caged, Untamed, Adam's Rib, Dancing in the Dark, Cry of the City, All Mine to Give,* and *Casanova's Big Night;* was the voice of Elsie the Cow in Borden commercials.

EMERSON, Lidian Jackson (1802–1892). American wife of Ralph Waldo Emerson. Name variations: Lydia Jackson Emerson. Born Lydia Jackson, Sept 20, 1802, in Plymouth, Massachusetts; died 1892; m. Ralph Waldo Emerson (1803–1882, Transcendentalist), Sept 14 1835; children: Ellen Tucker Emerson (b. 1839); Edith Emerson (b. 1841); Waldo Emerson (1836–1842); Edward Emerson (b. 1844). ❖ The 2nd wife of Ralph Waldo Emerson, became engaged to him in Jan 1835; though he called her Lidian, was known in his journal as Asia, Queenie, and Queen of Sheba.

EMERSON, Mary Moody (1774–1863). American essayist, diarist, and intellectual. Born Aug 25, 1774, in Concord, Massachusetts; died in Brooklyn, NY, May 1, 1863; dau. of William Emerson (cleric, died 1776) and Phebe (Bliss) Emerson. ❖ Supervised the education and intellectual development of her 4 nephews, the sons of her deceased brother William Emerson (1769–1811); played a crucial role in the intellectual development of her nephew Ralph Waldo Emerson as a Transcendentalist thinker. ❖ See also Phyllis Cole, *Mary Moody Emerson and the Origins of Transcendentalism: A Family History* (Oxford U. Press, 1998); Nancy Craig Simmons, ed. *The Selected Letters of Mary Moody Emerson* (U. of Georgia Press, 1993); and *Women in World History.*

EMERY, Katherine (1906–1980). American stage and screen actress. Born Oct 11, 1906, in Birmingham, Alabama; died Feb 7, 1980, in Portland, Maine; m. Paul Eaton, 1944; children: daughter and son. ❖ Made Broadway debut as Mrs. Klopp in *Carry Nation* (1932); played Karen Wright in *The Children's Hour* for two years (1934–36); films include *Eyes in the Night, Isle of the Dead, The Walls Came Tumbling Down, Chicken Every Sunday,* and *Kid Galahad;* retired (1954).

EMERY, Pollie (1875–1958). English actress. Name variations: Polly Emery. Born May 10, 1875, in Bolton, Lancashire, England; died Oct 31, 1958, in London, England; dau. of Rose and Frank Emery (actor and manager); niece of G.W. Anson. ❖ Made stage debut at Liverpool in *Nine Points of the Law,* then toured South Africa, Australia and New Zealand for many years; made London debut as Sarah in *Trelawny of the Wells* (1898), followed by *Mixed Relations, Our Flat, Lady Huntworth's Experiment, Married by Degrees, The Case of Lady Camber, Who's Hooper?, Sweet William, Hocus Pocus, Tobacco Road,* and *Pericles,* among others; films include *Nothing Else Matters, If Four Walls Told, The Third String* and *A Sister to Assist 'Er.*

EMERY, Winifred (1862–1924). English actress. Born Aug 1, 1862, in Manchester, England; died July 15, 1924; dau. of Samuel Anderson Emery, granddau. of John Emery and great-granddau. of Mackle Emery (all well-known actors in their day); m. Cyril Maude (actor). ❖ Made London debut as a child in *Beauty and the Beast* (1874) and as an adult in *Man Is Not Perfect* (1879); other plays include *Fernande, A Bridal Tour, Mary Stuart* (with Modjeska), *Coralie, The Bells, The Rivals, Olivia* (title role), *Clarissa* (title role), *Lady Windermere's Fan* (title role), *The Little Minister, Money* (as Lady Franklin); also appeared as Beatrice in *Much Ado About Nothing* with Beerbohm Tree; made NY debut with Henry Irving's company as Olivia in *Twelfth Night* (1884).

EMHART, Maria (1901–1981). Austrian Socialist activist and resistance leader. Name variations: name while in the anti-Fascist underground, 1934–1936: Gretl Meyer. Born Maria Raps in Pyhra, Lower Austria, May 27, 1901; died in Bischofshofen, Austria, Oct 9, 1981; dau. of Johann and Maria Kreutzer Raps; attended Social Democratic Workers' University (Arbeiterhochschule); m. Karl Emhart, 1921. ❖ Leader of the anti-Fascist underground (1934–38), began working in one of St. Pölten's textile mills at 14 to help support her family; became a militant trade unionist; joined the Austrian Social Democratic Party (1918); elected to the St. Pölten city council (1932), where she served as one of three women among the 43 representatives; when Dollfuss abandoned democracy (1933), planned for the inevitable suppression of the Social Democratic Party; in a bloody civil war (Feb 1934), oversaw countless details of the battle with government forces; known as St. Pölten's Flintenweib (Musket Moll), quickly became a legend throughout Socialist circles both within Austria and among exiles; arrested with others but released; became a leading personality of the underground Revolutionary Socialists in Lower Austria, living at times in Vienna illegally under the alias Gretl Meyer; arrested (Jan 26, 1935), became internationally celebrated during the show trial of 27 captured leaders of the underground Social Democratic movement (Mar 1936), making an impassioned speech; began by declining the judge's offer to let her sit while she spoke, noting that her tuberculosis had not been taken into account during her 14 months of incarceration and would not now play any role in her decisions; received a sentence of 18 months; at war's end, was the only woman to serve in the Provincial Diet of Salzburg (1945); was elected vice-mayor of Bischofshofen, the 1st woman in the history of Austria to be elected to such a high municipal office (April 1946); held the post for 2 decades, retiring in Aug 1966; elected to the Austrian National Assembly (1953). ❖ See also *Women in World History*.

EMILIA OF ORANGE (1569–1629). Princess of Orange. Born April 10, 1569, in Cologne, Germany; died Mar 16, 1629, in Geneva; dau. of Anna of Saxony (1544–1577) and William I the Silent (1533–1584), prince of Orange, count of Nassau, stadholder of Holland, Zealand, and Utrecht (r. 1572–1584); m. Manuel of Portugal, Nov 17, 1597; children: Manuel II (b. 1600), prince of Portugal; Louis William (b. 1601), prince of Portugal; Maria Belgica (1599–1647), who m. Johan Theodor de Croll); Anna Frisia Luisa (1606–1669); Juliane Katherina (1603–1680); Emilia Luise (1605–1670); Mauritia Eleanora (1609–1674), who m. Georg Friedrich, prince of Nassau-Siegen); Sabine Dorothea (1610–1670). ❖ See also *Women in World History*.

EMIRZYAN, Sirvard (1966—). Soviet diver. Born June 1966 in USSR. ❖ At Moscow Olympics, won a silver medal in platform (1980).

EMMA (fl. 600s). Queen, possibly of Mercia. Fl. in 600s; children: sons St. Ethered, St. Ethelbright, and St. Ermenbert; daughter Ermenburga (fl. late 600s); grandmother of saints Milburg (d. 722?) and Mildred (d. 700?). ❖ See also *Women in World History*.

EMMA (fl. 1080s). Marquise. Fl. in 1080s; dau. of Robert Guiscard (d. 1085), Frankish noble, duke of Apulia and Calabria, count of Sicily (r. 1057–1085), and Sichelgaita of Salerno (1040–1090); m. Odo the marquis; children: possibly Tancred, prince of Antioch (d. 1112). ❖ Some scholars believe that Tancred's mother was the sister, not the daughter, of Robert Guiscard. ❖ See also *Women in World History*.

EMMA (1836–1885). Queen of Hawaii and consort to King Kamehameha IV. Name variations: Emma Rooke; Kaleleokalani or Kaleleonalani. Born Jan 2, 1836, either in Honolulu or at Kawaihae on Kohala coast of island of Hawaii (then called Sandwich Islands); died April 25, 1885, in Honolulu; only child of George Naea and Fanny Kekelaokalani Young; given at birth to childless aunt, Grace Kamaukui Young Rooke and husband Thomas C.B. Rooke (physician), who gave her name of Emma Rooke; attended Royal School in Honolulu; m. King Kamehameha IV (Alexander Liholiho), June 19, 1856 (died Nov 30, 1863); children: Prince Albert Edward Kauikeaouli Leiopapa a Kamehameha (1858–1862). ❖ Intelligent and refined, presided with husband over a stylish royal court and oversaw the establishment of an impressive library filled with English classics (later bequeathed to Honolulu Library, now part of the Library of Hawaii); convinced king to solicit funds for construction of Queen's Hospital, the 1st public hospital in Hawaii (1860); organized the District Visiting Society (1863); was instrumental in establishing the Anglican church in Hawaii, though it was designated as "Hawaiian Reformed Catholic Church"; widowed (1863), left for England to regain health and to stimulate interest in the Anglican mission in Hawaii (1865); came to international prominence, met with crowned heads of Europe and President Andrew Johnson at White House; returned to Honolulu (1866) and concentrated efforts on education, particularly St. Andrew's Priory, an Episcopal school for Hawaiian girls, and a boarding school for boys; became a candidate for the throne when Lunalilo, who had become king after Kamehameha V's death (1872), died without naming a successor (1874); campaigned vigorously but lost to rival Kalakaua. ❖ See also *Women in World History*.

EMMA (1844–1929). See Viola, Emilia Ferretti.

EMMA DE GATINAIS (fl. 1150–1170). Princess of Gwynedd. Dau. of Geoffrey IV, count of Anjou; mother unknown; illeg. half-sister of Henry II, king of England (r. 1154–1189); m. David I, prince of Gwynedd, c. 1174; children: two. ❖ See also *Women in World History*.

EMMA OF BAVARIA (d. 876). Queen of the Germans. Died 876; dau. of Welf of Bavaria and Heilwig; sister of Judith of Bavaria (802–843); m. Louis II the German (804–876), king of the Germans (r. 843–876); children: Carloman of Bavaria (c. 828–880); Louis the Young (b. around 835), king of the East Franks, king of Saxony (r. 876–882); Charles III the Fat (839–887), king of the France (r. 884–887), king of Germany (r. 876–887), Holy Roman emperor as Charles II (r. 881–887); Hildegarde of Bavaria (c. 840–?). ❖ See also *Women in World History*.

EMMA OF BURGUNDY (d. 939). Queen of France. Died 939 (some sources cite 935); dau. of Robert, count of Paris, also known as Robert I (c. 865–923), king of France (r. 922–923), and Beatrice of Vermandois (880–931); sister of Hugh the Great (or Hugh the White), count of Paris and duke of Burgundy (d. 956); m. Raoul also known as Ralph or Rudolf (son of Richard, duke of Burgundy and Aquitaine), duke of Burgundy, king of France (r. 923–936). ❖ An important military figure, supported father while he was king until his death (923); in addition to political skills such as negotiation, organized the defense of Laon in early 10th century; while husband was king, led forces that captured Avalon (931) and conducted a siege against Château Thierry (933), which was surrendered directly to her and not to husband Rudolf. ❖ See also *Women in World History*.

EMMA OF HEREFORD (d. 1100). *See Emma of Norfolk.*

EMMA OF ITALY (948–after 990). Queen of France. Name variations: Emma of France; Emme. Born 948 in Italy; died after 990 in France; dau. of Adelaide of Burgundy (931–999) and Lothair (Lothar), king of Italy; stepdau. of Otto I the Great, king of Germany (r. 936–973), Holy Roman emperor (r. 962–973); m. Lothair or Lothaire (941–986), king of France (r. 954–986), c. 966; children: at least 2 sons, Louis V (c. 967–987), king of France (r. 986–987), and Otto, cleric at Rheims. ❖ Mother of the last of the Carolingians, married Lothair, king of the West Franks, who had begun an aggressive policy of expansion in 956; was an active participant in the administration of the Frankish realm and seemed to play an important role in Lothair's military campaigns; accompanied him on various missions and took charge of the defense of Verdun after they had conquered it; named regent for her young son Louis V after Lothair's death, encountered considerable threat to her power from husband's brother Charles of Lorraine, who wanted to rule; was accused by Charles of committing adultery with a bishop in order to cast doubt on Louis' legitimacy; when Louis died young (987), the last Carolingian ruler of France, retired from political activism. ❖ See also *Women in World History*.

EMMA OF NORFOLK (d. 1100). Countess of Norfolk. Name variations: Emma FitzOsbern; Emma Guader; Emma of Hereford. Born in England; died 1100 in Brittany; dau. of William FitzOsbern and Adeliza of Tosny; m. Ralph Guader, earl of Norfolk, 1075; children: Alan, later earl of Norfolk; Ralph, later lord of Gael and Montfort; Amicia de Waer, countess of Leicester. ❖ When husband revolted against William I the Conqueror and was forced to flee, resulting in a siege of Norwich by the king's troops, was the formidable defender of the town and castle of Norwich; despite the odds, refused to yield to the king's men; orchestrated the defense of the town for so long that the king eventually had to compromise with her to restore peace, agreeing to a safe conduct for Emma to leave England and join her husband in Brittany; with husband and son Alan, also joined the 1st Crusade (1096). ❖ See also *Women in World History*.

EMMA OF NORMANDY (c. 985–1052). Norman queen. Name variations: Imme or Imma; Aelfgifu, Ælfgifu, or Elfgifu; Ælfgifu-Emma; Lady of Winchester. Born c. 985 in Normandy; died Mar 6, 1052, in Winchester, Hampshire, England; buried at Winchester Cathedral, Hampshire; dau. of Duke Richard I of Normandy and Gunnor of Denmark (d. 1031); m. Aethelred or Ethelred II the Unready, king of England (r. 979–1016), in 1002 (died 1016); m. Cnut or Canute I the Great, king of England (r. 1016–1035), Denmark (r. 1019–1035), Norway (r. 1028–1035), in 1017 (died 1035); children: (1st m.) Edward III the Confessor (c. 1005–1066), king of the English (r. 1042–1066); Alfred (d. 1037); Godgifu (c. 1010–c. 1049); (2nd m.) Harthacanute also spelled Hardacnut or Hardicanute (c. 1020–1042), king of Denmark (r. 1039–1042); Gunhild (c. 1020–1038). ❖ Norman queen who married 2 English kings, gave birth to 2 English kings, and remained firmly in the center of the diplomatic and martial activities that rocked the Anglo-Saxon state; married Ethelred II the Unready (1002); because of Viking threat to Anglo-Saxon England, fled to brother's court in Normandy and remained there (1013–17); after husband's death (1016), married Canute the Great (1016), insisting on a mutual agreement that their children by previous unions would be set aside in the line of succession in favor of any offspring they might have together; made many charitable donations to churches throughout England during 2nd husband's reign; on Canute's death (1035), claimed England for son Hardicanute, but claim was ineffectual because he was ruling in Denmark at the time; when stepson Harald Harefoot was recognized as king (1037), lived in exile in Bruges (1037–40); on death of Harald, returned with son Hardicanute to England, where he was crowned king (1040);

following death of Hardicanute and accession of Edward (1042), deprived of properties and wealth by son Edward (1043). ❖ See also *Women in World History.*

EMMA OF PARIS (d. 968). Duchess of Normandy. Died Mar 19, 968; dau. of Hedwig (c. 915–965) and Hugh the Great also known as Hugh the White (c. 895–956), count of Paris and duke of Burgundy; sister of Hugh Capet (939–996), duke of France (r. 956–996), king of France (r. 987–996), 1st of the Capetian kings, who m. Adelaide of Poitou (c. 950–c. 1004); m. Richard I the Fearless (d. 996), duke of Normandy (r. 942–996). Richard the Fearless' 2nd wife was Gunnor of Denmark (d. 1031), mother of Emma of Normandy (c. 985–1052). ❖ See also *Women in World History.*

EMMA OF WALDECK (1858–1934). Queen and regent of the Netherlands. Name variations: Emma of the Netherlands; Emma of Waldeck-Pyrmont. Reigned as queen of the Netherlands (1889–98). Born in Arolsen, Hesse, Germany, Aug 2, 1858; died at The Hague, Netherlands, Mar 20, 1934; dau. of George Victor, prince of Waldeck and Pyrmont, and Helen of Nassau (1831–1888); sister of Helen of Waldeck and Pyrmont (1861–1922); became 2nd wife of William III (1817–1890), king of the Netherlands (r. 1849–1890) and grand duke of Luxemburg, Jan 7, 1879; children: Wilhelmina (1880–1962), queen of the Netherlands (r. 1898–1948). William III's 1st wife was Sophia of Wurttemberg (1818–1877). ❖ See also *Women in World History.*

EMMA OF WERDEN (d. around 1050). Saint. Died c. 1050; dau. of Adela and an unknown father; was a descendant of Widukind, whose defeat and subsequent baptism were celebrated by the order of Pope Hadrian I (r. 772–795); sister of Meinwerk, bishop of Paderborn; m. Count Ludger (d. around 1010); children: son, Imad (also bishop of Paderborn). ❖ After husband died, spent the next 40 years doing good works, using her enormous fortune to improve the lives of the poor and to construct churches in the diocese of Bremen. Feast day is April 19. ❖ See also *Women in World History.*

EMME. *Variant of Emma.*

EMMELIA OF CAPPADOCIA (fl. 300s). Mother of 4 religious leaders. Married Basil (distinguished lawyer and professor of rhetoric in Cappadocia); children: 10, including Macrina (327–379); Peter (bishop of Sebaste); Basil the Great (329–379), bishop of Caesarea (whose authority extended over 11 provinces of Asia Minor); Gregory of Nyssa (335–387, one of the fathers of the Eastern Church); Naucratius (who died young). ❖ See also *Women in World History.*

EMMELMANN-SIEMON, Kirsten (1961—). East German runner. Name variations: Kirsten Siemon. Born April 19, 1961, in East Germany. ❖ At Seoul Olympics, won a bronze medal in 4 x 400-meter relay (1988).

EMMERICH, Anna Katharina (1774–1824). German Augustinian nun and mystic. Name variations: Emmerick; the Nun of Dülmen. Born in Westphalia, 1774; died 1824. ❖ Following an extremely pious youth, became celebrated for her visions of the Passion of Christ, for her revelations, and for bearing the stigmata (wounds of Christ); when poet Clemens Brentano came to the monastery of Dülmen to record her visions (1818), declared that his coming was a fulfillment of the will of God as it had been revealed to her in a vision; beatified by John Paul II (2004). Her life and supernatural experiences were described in a biography by Brentano (Munich, 1852) and in another by Abbé Cazales (Paris, 1870). ❖ See also *Women in World History.*

EMMET, Ellen (1876–1941). *See Rand, Ellen.*

EMMET, Katherine (c. 1882–1960). American actress. Born c. 1882 in San Francisco, California; died June 6, 1960, in New York, NY; m. Alon Bement (artist). ❖ Made stage debut opposite H.B. Warner in *The Ghost Breaker* (1913); created the role of the grandmother in *The Children's Hour* (1934), which she reprised in the revival (1952); other plays include *Jenny, We the People, Ring around Elizabeth, Guest in the House* and *Pygmalion.*

EMMETT, Dorothy Mary (b. 1904). British philosopher. Born Sept 29, 1904; Oxford University, Lady Margaret Hall, BA, 1927, MA, 1931; Radcliffe College, MA, 1930. ❖ Was lecturer in philosophy at University of Durham, King's College (1931–38); lecturer in philosophy of religion at University of Manchester (1938–45); served as Sir Samuel Hall Professor of Philosophy at University of Manchester (1946–66); became professor emeritus at University of Glasgow (1966); writings include *Whitehead's Philosophy of Organism* (1932), *Philosophy and*

Faith (1936), *The Nature of Metaphysical Thinking* (1945), *Alfred North Whitehead, 1861–1947* (1949), *Presuppositions and Finite Truths* (1949), *Function, Purpose and Powers: Some Concepts in the Study of Individuals and Societies* (1958), *Sociological Theory and Philosophical Analysis* (1970), *The Moral Prism* (1979) and *The Effectiveness of Causes* (1984).

EMMONS, Chansonetta Stanley (1858–1937). American photographer and painter. Born Chansonetta Stanley in Kingfield, Maine, Dec 30, 1858; died in Newton, Massachusetts, Mar 18, 1937; dau. of Liberty Solomon (farmer and teacher) and Apphia (French) Stanley; sister of twins F.E. and F.O. Stanley, who created the Stanley Steamer automobile; attended Western State Normal School, Farmington, Maine; studied painting with J.J. Enneking, William Preston Phelps, and J.G. Brown; m. James Nathaniel Whitman Emmons (businessman), Feb 2, 1887; children: Dorothy Emmons (1891–1960, painter and photographer). ❖ One of the few people in the 1st 30 years of the 20th century to photograph the "domestic vernacular," especially in northern New England, was modestly recognized in her time and nearly forgotten by the close of the century; beginning in the 1890s in Kingfield, Maine, photographed the farmyards, barns, gristmills, kitchens, and parlors of neighbors and friends, thus preserving the haunting images of a seemingly innocent and long-forgotten world; limited her professional affiliations to the Guild of Photographers of the Society of Arts and Crafts in Boston and the American Artists' Professional League; exhibited with the Guild for many years (1920s), including at the large Tricentennial Exhibit at the Museum of Fine Arts (1927). ❖ See also Marius B. Péladeau, *Chansonetta: The Life and Photographs of Chansonetta Stanley Emmons, 1858–1937* (Maine Antique Digest, 1977); and *Women in World History.*

EMMS, Gail (1977—). English badminton player. Born July 23, 1977, in Hitchin, Hertfordshire, England. ❖ With Nathan Robertson, won a silver medal for mixed doubles at Athens Olympics (2004) and was ranked No. 1 in the world (2003).

EMNILDE (fl. 986). Third wife of Boleslaw I the Brave. Name variations: Heminilde von Meissen. Fl. around 986; dau. of Rigdag, margrave of Meissen; became 3rd wife of Boleslav Chrobry also known as Boleslaw I the Brave (c. 967–1025), duke of Bohemia (r. 1003–1004), king of Poland (r. 992–1025), in 986 (div.). ❖ See also *Women in World History.*

EMOTIONS, The.
See Davis, Theresa.
See Hutchinson, Jeanette.
See Hutchinson, Pamela.
See Hutchinson, Sheila.
See Hutchinson, Wanda.

EMOTO, Yuko (1972—). Japanese judoka. Born Dec 23, 1972, in Hokkaido, Japan. ❖ Won a gold medal for 56-61kg half-middleweight at Atlanta Olympics (1996); retired (1998).

EMSHWILLER, Carol (1921—). American science-fiction writer. Born Carol Fries, April 12, 1921, in Ann Arbor, Michigan; m. Ed Emshwiller (filmmaker), 1949; children: 2 daughters, 1 son. ❖ Influenced by modern poetry and often seen by critics as experimental within science-fiction genre, wrote such books as *Joy in Our Cause* (1974), *Carmen Dog* (1988), *The Start of the End of It All* (1990), *Ledoyt* (1995), *Leaping Man Hill* (1998), and *The Mount* (2002); published many short stories in magazines and collections, including *Future, Science Fiction Quarterly* and *Fantasy and Science Fiction.*

ENA (1887–1969). Queen of Spain. Name variations: Victoria Eugenie of Battenberg; Victoria Eugenia; Victoria of Battenberg. Born Victoria Eugenia Julia Ena, Oct 24, 1887, at Balmoral Castle, Grampian, Scotland; died April 15, 1969, in Lausanne, Switzerland; dau. of Prince Henry Maurice of Battenberg and Princess Beatrice of England (1857–1944, dau. of Queen Victoria); m. Alphonso XIII (1886–1941), king of Spain (r. 1886–1931), May 1906; children: Alfonso or Alphonso (1907–1938, whose hemophilia forced his abdication and resulted in his death in a motor accident); Jaime, duke of Segovia (1908–1933); Beatriz of Spain (b. 1909); son (1910–1910); Maria Cristina (1911–1996); John Bourbon (b. 1913), count of Barcelona (father of Juan Carlos I, king of Spain); Gonzalo (1914–1934, who also suffered from hemophilia and also died as the result of a motor accident). ❖ Lived a tragic life: 4 sons died young; was dethroned with husband and driven into a life of exile during a republican revolution (1931). On the day of her wedding, as the procession wound through the streets, an anarchist tossed an explosive onto the street: 20 people were killed, 60 wounded (1906). ❖ See also *Women in World History.*

ENCHI, Fumiko (1905–1986). Japanese novelist. Born Oct 2, 1905, in Tokyo, Japan; died of heart failure, Nov 14, 1986; dau. of Ueda Kazutoshi (1867–1937, distinguished Japanese linguist); attended girls's middle school of Japan Women's University, 1918–22; m. Enchi Yoshimatsu (journalist); children: daughter. ❖ Left school after illness and was home-schooled in English, French, and Chinese literature; contributed to *Art for Woman* (1930); writings include *Starved Years, The Waiting Years, Robber of My Brightness, Wounded Wings, A Rainbow and Hell, A Vengeful Spirit, Home Without a Table* (1978), *Like a Loving Child of Chrysanthemums,* and *A Wandering Spirit.* Won Noma Prize for Literature (1958) for *The Waiting Years* and Tanazaki Junichiro Prize.

ENDER, Kornelia (1958—). East German swimmer. Name variations: Kornelia Ender Grummt. Born Oct 25, 1958, in East Germany; moved to West Germany; m. Roland Matthes (swimmer, div. 1982); m. once more. ❖ Won silver medals for the 4 x 100-freestyle relay, 4 x 100-meter medley, and 200-meter indiv. medley at Munich Olympics (1972), the 1st woman to win 4 gold medals at 1 Olympics, all in world-record time; at World championships, won a silver medal for the 200-meter individ. medley (1973), gold medals for the 100-meter freestyle (1963, 1976), a silver medal for 200-meter freestyle (1975), and gold medals for the 100-meter butterfly (1973, 1975); won gold medals for the 100-meter free-style, 200-meter freestyle, 100-meter butterfly, and 4 x 100-meter medley relay and a silver for the 4 x 100-meter freestyle relay at Montreal Olympics (1976); retired (1976). Named World Swimmer of the Year (1973, 1975, 1976); inducted into International Swimming Hall of Fame (1981). ❖ See also *Women in World History.*

ENDERLEIN, Ortrun (1943–). East German luge athlete. Born Dec 1, 1943, in Germany. ❖ Won a gold medal for singles at Innsbruck (1964), when women's luge made its Olympics debut; won World championship (1965, 1967).

ENDICOTT, Lori (1967—). American volleyball player. Born Aug 1967. ❖ At Barcelona Olympics, won a bronze medal in team competition (1992).

ENER, Güner (1935—). Turkish novelist and short-story writer. Name variations: Guner or Guener Ener. Born 1935 in Turkey; studied art in Istanbul and English literature in London and Cambridge. ❖ Writings include *Translations from English* (1966) and *September Tiredness* (1969).

ENFELDT, Monique (1968—). *See Garbrecht-Enfeldt, Monique.*

ENGDAHL, Sylvia (1933—). American science-fiction writer. Name variations: Sylvia Louise Engdahl. Born Nov 24, 1933, in Los Angeles, California; dau. of Amandus J. and Mildred Allen Engdahl (who wrote under the name Mildred Butler); attended Pomona College, 1950, Reed College, 1951, and University of Oregon, 1951–52; University of California at Santa Barbara, AB, 1955; graduate study at Portland State University. ❖ Worked as computer programmer and became computer systems specialist for SAGE Air Defense System; novels include *Journey Between the Worlds* (1970), *Enchantress from the Stars* (1971), *The Far Side of Evil* (1971), *This Star Shall Abide* (1972), *Beyond the Tomorrow Mountains* (1973), and *The Doors of the Universe* (1981); published short stories and the novella "Timescape" in *Anywhere, Anywhen* (1976); also wrote nonfiction works for young adults, including *The Subnuclear Zoo: New Discoveries in High Energy Physics* (1977) and *Our World is Earth* (1979). Won Children's Literature Association Phoenix Award for *Enchantress from the Stars* (1990).

ENGEBERGE. *See Engelberga.*

ENGEL, Marian (1933–1985). Canadian novelist and short-story writer. Born Marian Passmore, May 24, 1933, in Toronto, Ontario, Canada; died 1985; dau. of Frederick Searle (teacher) and Mary (Fletcher) Passmore; McMaster University, BA, 1955; McGill University, MA, 1957; m. Howard Engel (broadcaster), 1962 (div. 1977); children: (twins) William and Charlotte. ❖ Major Canadian writer, also lived in London, Aix-en-Province, Nicosia, and Cyprus; novels include *No Clouds of Glory* (1968), *The Honeyman Festival* (1970), *Joanne* (1975), *Bear* (1976), *The Glassy Sea* (1978), and *Lunatic Villas* (1981); short fiction includes *Inside the Easter Egg* (1975) and *The Tattooed Woman* (1985); also published 2 children's books, *Adventure at Moon Bay Towers* (1974) and *My Name is Not Odessa Yorker* (1977), and nonfiction book *Islands of Canada* (1981). Awards include Governor General's Award for Fiction for *Bear;* made an officer of the Order of Canada (1982). ❖ See also Christi Verduyn and Kathleen Garay, *Marian Engel: Life in Letters* (University of Toronto Press, 2004).

ENGEL, Regula (1761–1853). Swiss memoirist. Born Regula Egli, Mar 5, 1761, in Zurich, Switzerland; died June 25, 1853, in Zurich; m. Colonel Johann Fluri (Florian) Engel; children: 21 (6 died in combat). ❖ Married a French soldier during Napoleonic wars and traveled with him to campaigns in Europe and North Africa, sometimes fighting alongside him; after husband and 2 sons were killed at the Battle of Waterloo (1815), returned to Switzerland and wrote memoirs to make money; writings reprinted as *Frau Oberst Engel: Von Cairo bis Neuyork, von Elba bis Waterloo: Memoiren einer Amazone aus napoleonischer Zeit* (Madame Colonel Engle: From Cairo to New York, from Elba to Waterloo: Memoirs of an Amazon in the Age of Napoleon, 1977).

ENGEL-KRAMER, Ingrid (1943—). East German diver. Name variations: Ingrid Kramer, Krämer or Kraemer. Born July 29, 1943, in Germany. ❖ Won gold medals for platform and springboard diving at Rome Olympics (1960), the 1st woman to win both titles; won a gold medal for springboard and a silver for platform at Tokyo Olympics (1964). ❖ See also *Women in World History.*

ENGELBERGA (c. 840–890). Holy Roman empress. Name variations: Angelberga; Engelbertha; Engeberge; Ingelberg. Born c. 840 in Germany; died c. 890 at convent of Placenza, Italy; dau. of a Frankish noble; m. Louis II le Jeune also known as Louis II the Child (c. 822–875), king of Italy (r. 844), king of Lorraine (r. 872–875), Holy Roman emperor (r. 855–875); children: Ermengarde of Provence; Gisela. ❖ One of the 1st medieval queen-consorts to co-rule openly with her husband, proved to be a capable leader of armies as well as an effective administrator; with husband, led troops into battle in central and southern Italy; was also appointed regent in northern Italy; alienated many Italians with her aggressive policies; though divorced from husband (c. 872) and he remarried, was reinstated as empress a few years before his death (875); banished to Switzerland by his successor, Charles III the Fat, where she remained for some years; eventually, retired to the monastery at Placenza, which she had founded, to live out the last few years of her life. ❖ See also *Women in World History.*

ENGELBERGA OF AQUITAINE (877–917). Duchess of Aquitaine. Born 877; died 917; dau. of Ermengarde of Provence and Boso, king of Provence (r. 879–887); m. William I the Pious, duke of Aquitaine.

ENGELBRETSDATTER, Dorothe (1634–1716). Norwegian poet and hymn writer. Name variations: Dorothe Engelbrechtsdatter. Born in Bergen, Norway, June 16, 1634; died in Bergen, Feb 19, 1716; dau. of Engelbrecht Jörgensen (originally rector of the high school in that city and afterwards dean of the cathedral); educated by father; m. Ambrosius Hardenbeck or Hardenbech (theological writer famous for his flowery funeral sermons who succeeded her father at the cathedral in 1659), in 1652 (died 1683); children: 5 sons, 4 daughters. ❖ The 1st great female writer of hymns in Denmark-Norway, had 9 children, 7 of whom died early; her grief at their deaths was one source of inspiration for her early writings, which she published in Copenhagen as *Själens Sangoffer (The Soul's Song Offering,* 1678), later published in 30 editions; in addition to religious works, her poetry includes occasional, sometimes satirical, verses of a secular nature; after husband's death (1683), wrote a 2nd vol. of hymns, *Taare Offer (Offering of Tears)* published in 1685; was among the 1st to demonstrate publicly that use of the pen as a tool is no male prerogative. ❖ See also *Women in World History.*

ENGELGARDT, Sofia Vladimirovna (1828–1894). Russian novelist and short-story writer. Name variations: Sofia Vladimirovna Engelgárdt, Sof'ia Vladimirovna Èngel'gárdt; (pseudonym) Ol'ga N or Olga N. Born 1828; died 1894; sister of Ekaterina Novosil'tseva, a historian under pseudonym T. Tolycheva. ❖ Stories, which depict the lives of mid-level Muscovite gentry, include "You Can't Escape Your Destined Mate" (1854), "You Can't Please Everyone" (1855), "Fate or Character?" (1861), "In the Homeland" (1870) and "Neither the First Nor the Last" (1883).

ENGELHARD, Jane (1917–2004). American philanthropist and art collector. Born Jane Pinto-Reis Brian, Aug 12, 1917, in Qingdao, China; died Feb 29, 2004, in Nantucket, Massachusetts; dau. of the Brazilian ambassador to China; sister of Brigitte de la Rochefoucauld and Jacque Bemberg; educated at the Couvent des Oiseaux in Paris; m. Fritz Mannheimer (Dutch banker), c. 1933 (died c. 1933); m. Charles Engelhard (wealthy industrialist), 1971; children: Susan O'Connor,

Sophie Craighead, Sally Pingree, Charlene Engelhard and Annette de la Renta. ❖ A fixture in high society, helped Jacqueline Kennedy restore the White House; financed the Charles Engelhard Court in the American Wing of the Metropolitan Museum of Art (1980); was a trustee at the Met (1974–81), then trustee emeritus; also contributed to the Newark Museum and New Jersey Symphony, among other philanthropies.

ENGELHARD, Magdalene Philippine (1756–1831). German poet. Name variations: Magdalena Philippine Engelhard; Philippine Engelhard-Gatterer; Philippine Gatterer. Born Philippine Gatterer, Oct 21, 1756, in Nurnberg, Germany; died Sept 28, 1831, in Blankenburg, Germany; dau. of Johann Christoph Gatterer; children: 10; grandmother of Gabrielle Reuter. ❖ One of the greatest intellects of the German Enlightenment, wrote *Gedichte von Philippine Gatterer* (1778), *Neujahrsgeschenk für liebe Kinder* (1787), and *Neue Gedichte von Philippine Engelhard geborene Gatterer* (1821).

ENGELMANN, Helene. Austrian pairs skater. Born in Austria. ❖ With Karl Mejstrik, won the World championship (1913); with Alfred Berger, won World championships (1922, 1924) and a gold medal at Chamonix Olympics (1924).

ENGELTHAL, Christina von (1277–1355). See Ebner, Christine.

ENGER, Babben. Norwegian cross-country skier. Name variations: Babben Damon-Enger; Babben Enger Damon. Born in Norway. ❖ Won a gold medal for 3 x 5 km relay at Grenoble Olympics (1968).

ENGLAND, Lynndie (1982—). American soldier. Born Lynndie Rana England, Nov 8, 1982, in Ashland, Kentucky; grew up in West Virginia; dau. of Terrie and Kenneth England (rail worker); m. James L. Fike, 2002 (div. 2003); children: Carter Allan England (b. 2004). ❖ Served in US Army reserve; after being photographed smiling, pointing and giving a thumbs-up, became the face of the tortures at Abu Ghraib prison in Baghdad, Iraq (2004); faced a general court martial.

ENGLAND, Maud Russell (1863–1956). New Zealand teacher, feminist, education reformer, and art dealer. Born Dec 30, 1863, in Rugby, Warwickshire, England; died May 12, 1956, at Silverstream, New Zealand; dau. of Russell (army officer) and Emily Alice (Ainsworth) England. ❖ Immigrated to New Zealand (1902); affiliated with Victoria University College (1900s–28); taught at Samuel Marsden Collegiate School (1930s); member of council of Wellington Free Kindergarten Association (1912–52); helped to establish Wellington branch of National Council of Women of New Zealand (1917); established art dealership in Wellington (1930s). ❖ See also *Dictionary of New Zealand Biography* (Vol. 4).

ENGLAND, queen of.
  See Matilda of Flanders (c. 1031–1083).
  See Matilda of Scotland (1080–1118).
  See Matilda, Empress (1102–1167).
  See Adelicia of Louvain (c. 1102–1151).
  See Matilda of Boulogne (c. 1103–1152).
  See Eleanor of Aquitaine (1122–1204).
  See Berengaria of Navarre (c. 1163–c. 1230).
  See Avisa of Gloucester (c. 1167–1217).
  See Isabella of Angoulême (1186–1246).
  See Eleanor of Provence (c. 1222–1291).
  See Eleanor of Castile (1241–1290).
  See Margaret of France (1282–1318).
  See Isabella of France (1296–1358).
  See Philippa of Hainault (1314–1369).
  See Anne of Bohemia (1366–1394).
  See Joanna of Navarre (1370–1437).
  See Isabella of Valois (1389–c. 1410).
  See Catherine of Valois (1401–1437).
  See Margaret of Anjou (1429–1482).
  See Woodville, Elizabeth (1437–1492).
  See Anne of Warwick (1456–1485).
  See Elizabeth of York (1466–1503).
  See Catherine of Aragon (1485–1536).
  See Boleyn, Anne (c. 1507–1536).
  See Seymour, Jane (c. 1509–1537).
  See Parr, Catherine (1512–1548).
  See Anne of Cleves (c. 1515–1557).
  See Mary I (1516–1558).
  See Howard, Catherine (1520/22–1542).
  See Elizabeth I (1533–1603).
  See Anne of Denmark (1574–1619).
  See Henrietta Maria (1609–1669).
  See Catherine of Braganza (1638–1705).
  See Mary of Modena (1658–1718).
  See Mary II (1662–1694).
  See Anne (1665–1714).
  See Caroline of Ansbach (1683–1737).
  See Charlotte of Mecklenburg-Strelitz (1744–1818).
  See Caroline of Brunswick (1768–1821).
  See Adelaide of Saxe-Meiningen (1792–1849).
  See Victoria (1819–1901).
  See Alexandra of Denmark (1844–1925).
  See Mary of Teck (1867–1953).
  See Elizabeth Bowes-Lyon (1900–2002).
  See Elizabeth II (b. 1926).

ENGLE, Hualing (1925—). *See Nieh, Hualing.*

ENGLEHORN, Shirley (1940—). American golfer. Born Shirley Englehorn, Dec 12, 1940, in Caldwell, Idaho. ❖ Won 11 tour titles; won LPGA championship (1970); LPGA Master Professional. Received the Ellen Griffin Rolex Award (1991).

ENGLISH, Ada (c. 1878–1944). Irish politician and physician. Born Adeline English, c. 1878, in Mullingar, Ireland; died 1944; dau. of P.J. and Nora English. ❖ One of the 1st female doctors in Ireland, appointed resident medical superintendent of St. Brigid's Hospital, Ballinasloe, and became a lecturer and examiner on mental disease at University College Galway (1914); an active member of Sinn Féin, was an executive member and founder member of Cumann na mBan branch in Ballinasloe (1915); began work as a medical officer for the Irish Volunteers (1913) and attended at Athenry during the Rising (1916); imprisoned by the British (1920); elected to 2nd Dáil (parliament) for National University of Ireland (1921–22).

ENGLISH, queen of the.
  See Osburga (?–c. 855).
  See Martel, Judith (c. 844–?).
  See Wulfthryth (fl. 860s).
  See Elswitha (d. 902).
  See Elflaed (d. 920).
  See Elfgifu (d. 944).
  See Elfgifu (d. 959).
  See Ethelflaed (d. 962).
  See Edgifu (d. 968).
  See Ethelflaed (d. after 975).
  See Elfthrith (c. 945–1002).
  See Elfgifu (c. 963–1002).
  See Emma of Normandy (c. 985–1052).
  See Elfgifu of Northampton (c. 1000–1044).
  See Ealdgyth (fl. 1016).
  See Elgiva (fl. 1020).
  See Edith (c. 1025–1075).
  See Edith (fl. 1063).

ENGLISH, Sarah (1955—). Zimbabwean field-hockey player. Born Nov 27, 1955, in Zimbabwe. ❖ At Moscow Olympics, won a gold medal in team competition (1980).

ENGQUIST, Ludmila (1964—). Russian-Swedish hurdler. Name variations: Ludmila Narozhilenko. Born Ludmila Narozhilenko, April 21, 1964, in Russia; m. a Russian; m. Johan Engquist (her Swedish agent). ❖ Left Russia to marry; became a Swedish citizen (1996); won a gold medal for the 100-meter hurdles at Atlanta (1996), the 1st female representing Sweden to win an Olympic gold medal in track and field; diagnosed with breast cancer (1999); took up bobsledding and competed at Salt Lake City Olympics (2001) but admitted to taking anabolic steriods.

ENGRACIA. *Variant of Grace.*

ENGYTH (fl. 7th c.). English queen and abbess. Name variations: Eangyth of Wessex; flourished in the early 7th century; m. Kenwyn or Centwine, king of Wessex (r. 676–685, died 685); children: Edburga (d. 751). ❖ Queen of Wessex, was also an abbess; with daughter, corresponded with St. Boniface.

ENHEDUANNA (fl. 2300 BCE). Sumerian poet. Born c. 2300 BCE; dau. of King Sargon I of Agade (2334–2279 BCE). ❖ A high priestess of the moon goddess Inanna, for whom she wrote her famous *The Exhaltation of*

Inanna, is the 1st writer in history whose name and work have been preserved; was revered for generations and her religious poems influenced many later writers. Over 40 poems, recorded on cuneiform tablets, have survived the ages.

ENKE, Karin (b. 1961). *See Kania-Enke, Karin.*

ENNIS, Helena McAuliffe (1951—). *See McAuliffe-Ennis, Helena.*

ENOKI, Miswo (1939—). Japanese pharmacist and feminist. Born 1939 in Japan. ❖ Led radical wing of Japanese feminist movement, Pink Panthers (1970s); formed Japan Woman's Party (1977) but won few votes.

ENRIGHT, Elizabeth (1909–1968). American writer for young people. Born Sept 17, 1909, in Oak Park, Illinois; died June 8, 1968; dau. of Walter J. Enright (political cartoonist) and Maginel Wright; studied at Art Students League of NY, 1927–28, in Paris, 1928, and at Parsons School of Design; m. Robert Marty Gillham (advertiser and tv executive), April 24, 1930; children: Nicholas Wright; Robert II; Oliver. ❖ Began as magazine illustrator but started writing the stories to accompany her drawings and eventually stopped illustrating; wrote books for children and short stories for adults, which appeared in *The New Yorker* and other national magazines and in published collections; was lecturer in creative writing at Barnard College (1960–62), and at writing seminars at Indiana University, University of Connecticut, and University of Utah; won Newbery Medal for *Thimble Summer* (1939) and was runner-up for Newbery (1958), for *Gone-Away Lake;* also wrote *The Saturdays* (1941), *The Four-Story Mistake* (1942), *Then There Were Five* (1944), *The Melendy Family* (1947), *Christmas Tree for Lydia* (1951), *Return to Gone-Away* (1961), *Tatsinda* (1963) and *Zee* (1965), among others. ❖ See also *Doublefields: Memories and Stories* (Harcourt, 1966); and *Women in World History.*

ENRIGHT, Maginel Wright (1881–1916). *See Wright, Maginel.*

ENRíQUEZ DE GUZMÁN, Feliciana (c. 1580–1640). Spanish poet. Name variations: Doña Feliciana Enríquez de Guzmán or Feliciana Enriquez de Guzman. Born c. 1580 in Seville, Spain; died 1640; studied at University of Salamanca. ❖ Wrote *Los jardines y campos sabeos* (1624, 1627), the 1st part of which was performed for Philip IV (1624).

ENSING, Riemke (1939—). New Zealand poet. Born 1939 in Groningen, Netherlands. ❖ Moved with family to New Zealand (1951) and trained as teacher at Ardmore College; was senior tutor in English at Auckland University; writings include *Making Inroads* (1980), *Topographies* (1984), *Spells from Chagall* (1987), *Like I Have Seen the Dark Green Climbing* (1995), *Finding the Ancestors* (1999) and *Talking Pictures* (2000); edited the 1st anthology of New Zealand women poets, *Private Gardens* (1977), among other anthologies; was also published in literary magazines.

ENSLER, Eve (1953—). American playwright. Born May 25, 1953, in New York, NY; graduate of Middlebury College, 1975; m. Richard McDermott, 1978 (div. 1988); children: (legally adopted stepson) actor Dylan McDermott. ❖ Interviewed more than 200 women worldwide, then wrote and performed *The Vagina Monologues,* for which she won an Obie (1997); also wrote *Floating Rhoda and the Glue Man* (1993), *The Depot, Ladies* and *Necessary Targets.*

ENTENMANN, Martha (1906–1996). American entrepreneur. Born Martha Schneider in Hoboken, New Jersey, 1906; died Sept 29, 1996, in West Islip, NY; m. William Entenmann Jr., 1925 (died 1951); children: Robert, Charles, and William. ❖ For more than 50 years (1925–78), ran the prosperous bakery with her sons. ❖ See also *Women in World History.*

ENTERS, Angna (1907–1989). American dancer, painter, and author. Born in New York, NY, April 28, 1907; died in Tenafly, New Jersey, Feb 25, 1989; grew up in Milwaukee, Wisconsin; dau. of Edward and Henriette (Gasseur-Styleau) Enters. ❖ The foremost mime of her day, borrowed money to rent the Greenwich Village theater, sent out handbills, and made New York City debut in a solo mime recital (1926); portrayed over 300 characters in her theater which soon became known as the Theater of Angna Enters; followed this with appearances in London and Paris and a European tour; began to exhibit over 1,000 of her paintings in American galleries (1933) and gave individual exhibitions in 71 leading American and European museums and galleries; wrote many books, often self-illustrated, including volumes of personal reminiscences *First Person Plural* (1937) and *Silly Girl* (1944), the play *Love Possessed Juana* (1939), the screenplays *Lost Angel* (1944) and *Tenth*

Avenue Angel (1948), and nearly 150 dance compositions set to her own music. ❖ See also *Women in World History.*

ENTHOVEN, Gabrielle (1868–1950). English theatrical historian, playwright and activist. Born Gabrielle Romaine, Jan 12, 1868 in London, England; died Aug 18, 1950, in London; dau. of Frances (Tennant) Romaine and William Govett Romaine; m. Charles H. Enthoven (died). ❖ Began career as an actress, appearing with the Old Stagers and Windsor Strollers; plays include *Montmartre, Ellen Young* (with Edmund Goulding), *The Honeysuckle* (adaptation), and *The Confederates* (with H.M. Harwood); presented thousands of playbills, rare engravings, prints, and books related to theater from the earliest times to the Victoria and Albert Museum (1924); was founder and president of the Pioneer Players and councillor of the Stage Society. Served as chief of records for war refugees (1914–15) and Central prisoners of war (1915–20), for which she was awarded Order of the British Empire (OBE).

ENTRAGUES, Catherine Henriette de Balzac d' (1579–1633). *See Entragues, Henriette d'.*

ENTRAGUES, Henriette d' (1579–1633). Marquise de Verneuil. Name variations: Henriette d'Estraigues. Born Catherine Henriette de Balzac d'Entragues in 1579; died 1633; dau. of Charles Balzac d'Entragues and Marie Touchet (who was the mistress of Charles IX); mistress of Henry IV, king of France. ❖ Ambitious and somewhat conniving, was the mistress of Henry IV, king of France, and succeeded in inducing a promise to marry her after death of his other mistress Gabrielle d'Estrées, a promise which led to bitter scenes at court when Henry married Marie de Medici; carried her spite so far as to be deeply compromised in a plot with Marshal Biron against the king (1606); though Biron was convicted of treason and conspiracy with Spain, escaped with only a slight punishment; returned to favor by Henry (1608); seems then to have been involved in the Spanish intrigues which preceded the assassination of the king in 1610.

ENTWHISTLE, Peg (1908–1932). Welsh actress. Born Lillian Millicent Entwhistle, July 1, 1908, in Port Talbot, Wales; died Sept 18, 1932, in Hollywood, California. ❖ Started career on stage; moved to Los Angeles; made film debut in *Thirteen Women* (1932), but came to prominence when she jumped off the letter "H" of the Hollywood sign and was killed instantly (1932).

EN VOGUE.
See Ellis, Terry.
See Herron, Cindy.
See Jones, Maxine.
See Robinson, Dawn.

ENYA (1961—). Irish singer and musician. Name variations: Eithne Ni Bhraonáin; Enya Ni Bhraonáin; Clannad. Born Eithne Ni Bhraonáin on May 17, 1961, in Gaoth Dobhair, Co. Donegal, Ireland; sister of Maire Brennan (b. 1952, singer). ❖ Was a member of her family's musical group Clannad (1979–82); began solo career, mixing classical, New Age, and traditional Irish folk music to produce what has been called an ethereal sound; released debut album *Enya* (1986); released *Watermark* (1988) which included single "Orinoco Flow (Sail Away)" (#1 UK and #24 US) and was followed by other successful albums; had music used in several films; wrote melodies and played all instruments on her recordings; became 2nd bestselling Irish music artist after U2. Other albums include *The Celts* (1987), *Shepherd Moons* (1991), *The Memory of Trees* (1995), *Paint the Sky With Stars: The Best of Enya* (1997), and *A Day Without Rain* (2000).

EPHELIA (fl. 1660s–1680s). British poet and playwright. Name variations: (pseudonym) A Gentlewoman. Born in London, England, but little is known of her life and character. ❖ Major contributor to Restoration poetry, was born by her own account to parents who died young; wrote variety of verse, including political broadsides, verse-essays, elegies, verse-dramas, and verse-epistles; works include *A Poem To His Sacred Majesty. On The Plot. Written by a Gentlewoman* (1678), and *Female Poems On Several Occasions. Written by Ophelia* (1679).

EPHRON, Nora (1941—). American writer and director. Born May 19, 1941, in New York, NY; dau. of Henry (screenwriter) and Phoebe Ephron (screenwriter); sister of Delia Ephron, Hallie Ephron and Amy Ephron; Wellesley College, BA, 1962; m. Dan Greenburg (novelist, div.); m. Carl Bernstein (journalist), 1976 (div. 1980); m. Nicholas Pileggi (journalist, screenwriter), 1987; children: Jacob and Max Bernstein. ❖ Witty, erudite director-screenwriter, began career as a reporter with *New York Post;*

established reputation with caustic comic pieces for *Esquire, New York Magazine,* and *New York Times Magazine,* publishing bestselling collections of essays *Crazy Salad* (1975) and *Scribble Scribble* (1978); made screenplay debut with *Silkwood* (1983), which earned her an Academy Award nomination; wrote novel *Heartburn* (1984), about failed marriage to investigative journalist Carl Bernstein, then adapted the novel for a film starring Meryl Streep and Jack Nicholson (1986); as screenwriter, enjoyed tremendous success with *When Harry Met Sally* (1989), for which she was nominated for a 2nd Academy Award; made directorial debut with *This Is My Life* (1992), co-written with sister Delia, which received critical acclaim but reaped little financial reward; wrote and directed the hits *Sleepless in Seattle* (1993) and *You've Got Mail* (1998); additional works include *Cookie* (1989), *My Blue Heaven* (1990), *Mixed Nuts* (1994), *Michael* (1996) and *Bewitched* (2005).

EPHRON, Phoebe (1914–1971). American playwright and screenwriter. Born Phoebe Wolkind, Jan 26, 1914, in New York, NY; died Oct 13, 1971, in New York, NY; m. Henry Ephron (screenwriter), 1934; children: Nora Ephron (writer-director, b. 1941), Amy Ephron (production executive), Delia Ephron (writer), and one other daughter. ❖ Collaborated with husband on stage comedies, including such hits as *Three's a Family* (1943) and *Take Her She's Mine* (1961); films include *John Loves Mary, Belles on Their Toes, What Price Glory, There's No Business Like Show Business, Daddy Long Legs, Carousel* and *Desk Set.* ❖ See also the Ephrons' *We Thought We Could Do Anything.*

ÉPINAY, Louise-Florence-Pétronille, Madame la Live d' (1726–1783). French literary and social figure. Name variations: Madame d'Epinay; Louise d'Épinay. Born Louise-Florence-Pétronille Tardieu d'Esclavelles on Mar 11, 1726, in Valenciennes (Nord); died in Paris of nephritis and influenza, April 15, 1783; dau. of Louis-Gabriel Tardieu, Baron d'Esclavelles (1665–1736, army officer) and Florence-Angélique Prouveur de Preux (1696–1762); educated at home and in Paris at a convent school, 1737–39; sister-in-law and cousin of Sophie d' Houdetot (1730–1813); m. Denis-Joseph La Live (Lalive) de Bellegarde, later d'Épinay (1724–1782), Dec 24, 1745; children: (with husband) a son, Louis-Joseph (1746–1807) and a daughter, Suzanne-Françoise-Thérèse (1747–1748); (with Claude-Louis Dupin de Francueil) a daughter, Angélique-Louise-Charlotte de Belzunce also seen as Belsunce (1749–1807); a son, Jean-Claude Le Blanc de Beaulieu (1753–1825). ❖ Friend of Voltaire, Rousseau and Diderot, who wrote on education and an autobiographical novel depicting life in the upper classes during the Enlightenment, began a liaison with Dupin de Francueil (1748); obtained a separation of property from husband (1749); through Francueil and Rousseau, met Friedrich Melchior Grimm (1751); ended the liaison with Francueil (1752); began a lifelong liaison with Grimm (1755); lived with Rousseau at The Hermitage (her estate), but he left after a quarrel (1756–67); resided in Geneva and published *Mes Moments heureux* and *Lettres à mon fils* (1757–79); became a close friend of Diderot (1760); began a long correspondence with Abbé Galiani (1769); published the 1st edition of *Conversations d'Émilie* (1774); published 2nd edition of the *Conversations* (1781), which received the Montyon Prize of the Académie Française (1783). An abridged version of her novel, *Mémoires et correspondence de Madame d'Épinay,* published (1818). ❖ See also Francis Steegmuller, *A Woman, a Man, and Two Kingdoms: The Story of Madame d'Épinay and the Abbé Galiani* (Knopf, 1991); Ruth Plaut Weinreb, *Eagle in a Gauze Cage: Louise d'Épinay, femme de lettres* (AMS, 1993); A. Legros, *Madame d'Épinay, Valenciennoise* (Valenciennes, 1920); and *Women in World History.*

ÉPINE, Margherita de l' (c. 1683–1746). Italian soprano. Name variations: Margherita de l' Epine; Francesca Margherita de l'Epine; La Margherita. Born around 1683; died Aug 8, 1746, in London, England; m. Pepusch (poet and composer), c. 1718. ❖ The 1st Italian to have a successful career in England, came to England (1692) and made debut in London with the composer Greber (1702); appeared as Goffredo in *Rinaldo,* created Agilea in *Teseo* and Eurilla in *Il pastor fido* and was the principal rival of Catherine Tofts (1704–18); retired (1719).

EPONINA (40–78). Roman heroine. Wife of Julius Sabinus. ❖ Captured the sympathies of the Roman people with heroic fidelity to her husband, even choosing to die with him when her efforts to save his life failed (he had laid claim to the throne as a descendant of Julius Caesar). ❖ See also *Women in World History.*

EPPES, Maria Jefferson (1778–1804). American first daughter. Name variations: known as Polly in her youth; Mary Jefferson Eppes. Born Mary Jefferson in 1778; died in 1804; dau. of Martha Jefferson (1748–1782) and Thomas Jefferson (1743–1826, 3rd president of US); m. her cousin John Wales Eppes; children: several, including Frances Eppes and Maria Eppes (who died in childbirth at age 25). ❖ Was White House hostess during her father's administration.

EPPLE, Irene (1957—). German Alpine skier. Born June 18, 1957, in Seeg Algäu, Germany; sister of Maria Epple (Alpine skier). ❖ At World championships, won a silver medal for downhill (1978); won a silver medal for giant slalom at Lake Placid Olympics (1980); won the World Cup title for giant slalom and a silver medal for overall (1982).

EPPLE, Maria (1959—). German Alpine skier. Name variations: Maria Epple-Beck or Epple Beck. Born Mar 11, 1959, in Seeg Algäu, Germany; sister of Irene Epple (Alpine skier). ❖ Won a gold medal for giant slalom at World championships (1978); placed 8th in giant slalom at Lake Placid Olympics (1980).

EPSTEIN, Charlotte (1884–1938). American swimmer. Name variations: Eppy Epstein. Born Sept 1884 in New York City; died Aug 27, 1938. ❖ Founded the Women's Swimming Association (WSA), which was largely responsible for gathering the 1st team of American women swimmers to participate in the Antwerp Olympic Games (1920). ❖ See also *Women in World History.*

EPSTEIN, Eppy (1884–1938). See Epstein, Charlotte.

EPSTEIN, Marie (c. 1899–1995). French screenwriter and director. Born Marie-Antoine Epstein in Warsaw, Poland, c. 1899; died in Paris, France, 1995; dau. of Jewish-French father and Polish mother; sister and partner of Jean Epstein (1897–1953); partner of Jean Benoit-Lévy (1888–1959). ❖ One of the most important screenwriter-directors in early avant-garde cinema in France, was often overshadowed by her collaborators, brother Jean Epstein and director Jean Benoit-Lévy; began career as an assistant director and actress in brother's *Coeur fidele* (1923); wrote several screenplays he directed which are considered among his best work; shared a director credit on several films with Benoit-Lévy, including *Ames d'enfants* (1928), *Peau de pêche* (1929), *Maternité* (1929) and *La Maternelle* (1933), one of the best early French sound films; following WWII, made a documentary on atomic energy, *La Grande esperance* (1953), and worked as a film preservationist at Cinémathèque Française where she restored some of her brother's silent films as well as the renowned *Napoleon* by director Abel Gance. ❖ See also *Women in World History.*

EPSTEIN, Selma (1927—). American pianist. Born in Brooklyn, NY, Aug 14, 1927; dau. of Tillie (Schneider) Schectman and Samuel Schectman; studied at Juilliard with Rosina Lhevinne and at Philadelphia Conservatory of Music with Edward Steuermann; m. Joseph Epstein (concert pianist). ❖ Began long concert career with performance at Carnegie Hall at age 15; pioneering contemporary music, concertized in Europe, America, and Australia; became 1st American offered major teaching post at New South Wales Conservatorium; served as a resident recording artist for Australian Broadcasting Company (1972–1975); recorded some unpublished music of Percy Grainger (1st native Australian to achieve worldwide fame as conductor and composer); also performed Grainger's music and founded the American Grainger Society to promote his works; her determination to introduce contemporary composers to music audiences gained her international acclaim. ❖ See also *Women in World History.*

ERAUSO, Catalina de (1592–1635). Spanish soldier and nun. Name variations: Erauzo; Erauzú; Francisco de Erauso; Francisco de Loyola; Alfonso Díaz Ramírez de Guzmán; called La Monja Alférez ("the Nun Ensign"). Pronunciation: Eh-RAU-so. Born Catalina de Erauso on Feb 10, 1592 (some sources cite 1585), in San Sebastián, in northern Spain; disappeared and assumed dead in Mexico at Veracruz, 1635 (some sources cite her survival in Mexico until 1650); dau. of Miguel de Erauso and María Pérez de Galarraga y Arce; attended the Dominican Convent of San Sebastián el Antiguo, to age 15; never married; no children. ❖ One of the most rebellious Spanish women of all time, fled a convent and, disguised as a man, rose to the rank of lieutenant in the Spanish colonial army in South America, then returned to Spain where her exploits were immortalized; escaped the convent dressed as a man and worked as an accountant and page (1607); fled to America as a "cabin boy" and became soldier of fortune in Perú, Bolivia, Chile, and Argentina (beginning 1608); as the legendary "nun-ensign," knifed rivals, killed soldiers, and swashbuckled her way towards acceptance and even popularity in the intolerant Spanish society of the 1600s; revealed in confession that she was a woman (c. 1623); returned to Spain, where she was received by the king and awarded lifelong military pension, then visited the pope (1625); collaborated with Juan Pérez de Montalván in penning drama based on her adventures (c. 1626–27); returned to Mexico (1630). Many of the adventures attributed to her may well be a composite of the lives of several historic personages, but there was a real Catalina de Erauso, and the heart of her story is true. ❖ See also *Lieutenant Nun: Memoir of a Basque Transvestite in the New World* (trans. by Michele and Gabriel Stepto, Beacon, 1995); James Fitzpatrick-Kelly, ed. and trans. *The Nun Ensign* (T. Fisher Unwin, 1908, included are the English translation of Erauso's autobiography, and Juan Pérez de Montalbán's play *La monja alférez* in the original Spanish, with introduction and notes); and *Women in World History.*

ERBESFIELD, Robyn (1963—). American climber. Name variations: Robyn Erbesfield-Raboutou. Born Aug 5, 1963, in Atlanta, Georgia; m. Didier Raboutou; children: Shawn and Brooke. ❖ Dominant force in women's competitive climbing, won competitions including Southeastern Bouldering championships (1986, 1987, and 1988), World Cup (1992, 1993, 1994, and 1995), World championships (1995), US championships (1995), and X Games in Difficulty (1995). Wrote *Sport Climbing with Robyn Erbesfield* (1996).

ERBIL, Leyla (1931—). Turkish novelist and short-story writer. Born 1931 Istanbul, Turkey; studied literature at Istanbul University. ❖ Worked for airline and as translator at various consulates; pioneer in innovative forms of the short story, invented her own syntax to reflect chaos of Turkish society; writings include *Hallaç* (1961), *Gecede* (1968), *Tuhaf Bir Kadin* (1971), *Eski Sevgili* (1977), *Karanligin Gunu* (1985) and *Mektup Asklari* (1988).

ERCIC, Emilija (1962—). Yugoslavian handball player. Born June 14, 1962. ❖ At Los Angeles Olympics, won a gold medal in team competition (1984).

ERDMAN, Jean (1917—). American dancer and choreographer. Name variations: Jean Campbell. Born Feb 20, 1917, in Honolulu, Hawaii; trained with Martha Graham and at Sarah Lawrence College; m. Joseph Campbell (writer and mythologist), 1938 (died Oct 31, 1987). ❖ Danced with Graham company (1938–43), where she created roles in *American Document* (1938), *Every Soul Is a Circus* (1959), and *Punch and Judy* (1941); performed role of "One Who Speaks" in Graham's *Letter to the World* to great acclaim; continued to appear with Graham company as guest dancer for many years; began choreographing own concert works (c. 1940), and staged numerous dance excerpts for theater. Works of choreography include *Departure* (1941), *Ophelia* (1946), *Les Mouches* (1948), *The Blessed Damozel* (1952), *The Coach with Six Insides* (1962), *Hamlet* (1964), *Encounter in the Grove* (1967), *Venerable as an Island is Paradise* (1969), *Gaugin in Tahiti* (1976) and *The Shining Hour* (1980). ❖ See also (video) *Dance and Myth: The World of Jean Erdman* (1990).

ERDMANN, Susi-Lisa (1968—). German bobsledder and luge athlete. Name variations: Susi Erdmann. Born Jan 29, 1968, in Blankenburg/ Harz, Germany. ❖ Won a bronze medal at Albertville Olympics (1992) and a silver medal at Lillehammer Olympics (1994), both for luge singles; placed 4th at Nagano Olympics for luge (1998); with Nicole Herschmann, won a bronze medal for the two-man bobsleigh at Salt Lake City Olympics (2002), the 1st women's bobsleigh competition in Winter Games history; won World championship (1989, 1991, 1997).

ERDOS, Eva. Hungarian handball player. Name variations: Erdös or Erdoes. Born in Hungary. ❖ Won a team bronze medal at Atlanta Olympics (1996).

EREMIA, Alexandra (1987—). Romanian gymnast. Name variations: Alexandra Georgiana Eremia. Born Feb 19, 1987, in Romania. ❖ Won a gold medal for team all-around and a bronze medal for beam at Athens Olympics (2004).

ERICEIRA, Condesa de (1651–1709). See Meneses, Juana Josefa de.

ERICKSON, Hilda (1859–1968). Swedish-American midwife. Name variations: Hilda Anderson Erickson. Born Hilda Andersson, Nov 11, 1859, in Ledsjo, Sweden; died Jan 1, 1968, in Salt Lake City, Utah; dau. of Pehr and Maria Kathrina (Larsson) Andersson; m. John A. Erickson (Swedish immigrant), Feb 23, 1882; children: 2. ❖ One of the last of Utah's immigrant pioneers, came to Utah at age 7; with husband, joined a mission on the Goshute Indian Reservation in Deep Creek Valley, UT (today known as Ibapah, UT, 1883) and was secretary of its Sunday school; studied obstetrics at Deseret Hospital in Salt Lake City (1885); after studies, returned to reservation to help Native American and Euro-American women deliver babies; developed reputation as an excellent

puller of bad teeth; with family, left reservation and purchased Last Chance Ranch (1898), a 320-acre cattle ranch; opened a general store in Grantsville (1925), which she managed for over 21 years; renewed midwifery certificate every year until at least age 90. Commemorations include a bronze monument of Erickson riding sidesaddle in front of Grantsville City Hall.

ERICSSON, Ingela (1968—). Sweden kayaker. Born Sept 27, 1968, in Nyköping, Sweden. ❖ Won a bronze medal for K4 500 meters at Atlanta Olympics (1996).

ERIKSEN, Ann (1971—). Norwegian handball player. Born Ann Cathrin Eriksen, Sept 9, 1971, in Norway. ❖ Won a team bronze medal at Sydney Olympics (2000).

ERIKSEN, Gunn (1956—). Norwegian chef. Born 1956 in Grimstad, Norway; m. Fred Brown, 1984. ❖ Famed chef and restaurateur, 1st trained as a weaver and ceramicist in Ullapool, Scotland; helped future husband open Altnaharrie Inn across Loch Broom from Ullapool (1976); joined him at Inn (1980), married him (1984), and began cooking there despite lack of formal training; became known for incorporating unusual native ingredients, such as nettles, sorrel and hawthorn sprouts, as well as local seafood and imported foods; developed a distinctive cooking style which brought worldwide renown; was also influenced by Scandinavian heritage, creating culinary blends; her restaurant earned 2 stars from Michelin (1994), the only Scottish eatery to receive the honor; built up a devoted clientele and glowing reputation despite isolated location accessible only by boat; was forced to sell inn after 22 years due to severe back problems (2003).

ERIKSEN, Hanne (1960—). Danish rower. Born Sept 20, 1960. ❖ At Los Angeles Olympics, won a bronze medal in quadruple sculls with coxswain (1984).

ERIKSON, Joan (c. 1902–1997). Canadian-born educator and psychological theorist. Born Joan Mowat in Canada, c. 1902; died Aug 3, 1997, in Brewster, Massachusetts; dau. of an Anglican priest; graduate of Barnard College; Columbia University Teachers College, MA; m. Erik Erikson (psychologist), 1930 (died 1994); children: 2 sons, 1 daughter. ❖ Collaborated with husband on the formulation of the eight-cycle theory of human development; after husband's death (1994), continued their work, adding yet a ninth stage of development which appears in a reissue of the book *Life Cycle Completed;* also wrote a book on beading, *The Universal Bead* (1969). ❖ See also *Women in World History.*

ERIKSSON, Agneta (1965—). Swedish swimmer. Born May 3, 1965, in Sweden. ❖ At Moscow Olympics, won a silver medal in 4 x 100-meter freestyle relay (1980).

ERIKSSON, Anna-Lisa. Swedish cross-country skier. Name variations: Anna Lisa Eriksson. Born in Sweden. ❖ Won a bronze medal for 3 x 5 km at Cortina Olympics (1956).

ERIKSSON, Marianne (1952—). Swedish politician. Born May 17, 1952, in Brännkyrka, Sweden. ❖ Teacher; representing the Confederal Group of the European United Left/Nordic Green Left (GUE/NGL), elected to 4th and 5th European Parliament (1994–99, 1999–2004).

ERIKSSON, Michelle Ford- (1962—). See Ford, Michelle.

ERINNA (fl. 7th c. BCE). Ancient Greek composer and poet. Name variations: Lesbia; Erina. Born at Rhodes or Telos around 600 BCE; died at age 19. ❖ Sometimes known as Lesbia because she came from the island of Lesbos; said to love singing so much that her mother chained her to a spinning wheel so that she would spin rather than sing; studied at the art school in Mytilene founded by her friend Sappho and was said to have been her most gifted student; became celebrated Greek poet, whose gifts were regarded by some as greater than Sappho's; died at 19, by which time her poems and compositions were widely admired. Only remaining fragment of her work is a lyric about a female singer named Baucis, later titled "The Distaff" or "The Spindle," which was a lament with recurring cries of sorrow.

ERINNI (1881–1947). See Borgese Freschi, Maria.

ERIPHANIS. Greek poet. Fl. before 4th century BCE. ❖ Greek writer Clearchus in 4th century BCE claims she was the 1st of writer love poetry. Her only extant line was quoted by Greek writer Athenaeus in the 2nd century.

ERISTAVI-XOSTARIA, Anastasia (1868–1951). Georgian novelist. Name variations: Anast'asia Eristav-Khosht'aria or Khoshtaria. Born

1868; died 1951. ❖ Generally regarded as the most distinguished female novelist in Georgian literary history, published 1st novel *Molip'ul gzaze* (*On the Slippery Path*) (1897) to positive reviews, followed by *Be'lis t'riali* (*The Wheel of Fate*, 1901); over next 2 decades, published more novels and short stories that were well received; remained a major figure in Georgian literary circles after the assumption of power by the Bolshevik Party (1921); spent final decades as an honored "living classic" of the nation's literary renaissance. ❖ See also *Women in World History*.

ERLER, Karen Riale (c. 1949—). *See Riale, Karen.*

ERMAKOVA, Anastasia (1983—). Russian synchronized swimmer. Born April 8, 1983, in USSR. ❖ At World championships, won gold medals for duet (2003) and team (2001 and 2003) and a silver for solo (2003) and duet (2001); with Anastasia Davydova, won a gold medal for duet at Athens Olympics (2004), as well as a team gold medal.

ERMAKOVA, Oxana (1973—). Russian fencer. Name variations: Oksana Ermakova. Born April 16, 1973, in Tallinn, USSR. ❖ At World championships, placed 1st for indiv. épée (1993) and team épée (2003); won a gold medal for épée team at Sydney Olympics (2000); won a gold medal for épée team at Athens Olympics (2004).

ERMELOVA, Mariya (1853–1928). *See Ermolova, Mariia.*

ERMENBURGA (fl. late 600s). Queen of Mercia. Name variations: Eormenburga. Dau. of Queen Emma (fl. 600s); m. Merowald or Merwald, king of Mercia; sister of saints Ethered, Ethelbright, and Ermenbert; children: daughters Saint Milburg (d. 722?); Saint Mildred (d. 700?); Mildgyth or Mildgithe; son Mervin or Mervyn. ❖ Was given "48 ploughs of land" as *weregild* (guilt money) by her uncle King Egbert who had had her brothers killed; devoted the land to the founding of a monastery, called Menstrey or Minstre, situated in the Isle of Thanet; sent daughter Mildred to Abbey of Chelles in France, where Mildred took the veil then returned to England as 1st abbess of her mother's newly founded monastery. ❖ See also *Women in World History*.

ERMENGARDE. *Variant of Irmengarde.*

ERMENGARDE (d. 773). *See Desiderata.*

ERMENGARDE (c. 778–818). Queen of France and Holy Roman empress. Name variations: Ermingarde; Irmengard of Hesbain. Born c. 778; died 818; dau. of Count Ingram; became 1st wife of Louis I the Pious (778–840), king of Aquitaine (r. 781–814), king of France (r. 814–840), and Holy Roman Emperor (r. 814–840), in 798; children: Lothair I, Holy Roman emperor (r. 840–855); Pepin or Pippin (d. 838), king of Aquitaine (r. 814–838); Adelaide (c. 794–after 852); Louis II the German (804–876), king of the Germans (r. 843–876); Rotrud (800–841); Hildegard (c. 802–841). Louis I the Pious' 2nd wife was Judith of Bavaria (802–843). ❖ See also *Women in World History*.

ERMENGARDE DE GATINAIS (d. 1147). *See Ermengarde of Anjou.*

ERMENGARDE MELUSINA VON DER SCHULENBURG, baroness Schulenburg (1667–1743). *See Schulenburg, Ehrengard Melusina von der.*

ERMENGARDE OF ANJOU (1018–1076). Duchess of Burgundy. Name variations: Ermengard d'Anjou. Born 1018; died Mar 18, 1076, in Fleury-sur-Ouche; dau. of Fulk III the Black, count of Anjou; m. Geoffrey, count of Gastinois; m. Robert I (1011–1076), duke of Burgundy (r. 1031–1076), c. 1048; children: (1st m.) Geoffrey III the Bearded, count of Anjou; Fulk IV the Rude, count of Anjou; (2nd m.) Hildegard of Burgundy (1050–after 1104). Robert I was also married to Helia de Semur. ❖ See also *Women in World History*.

ERMENGARDE OF ANJOU (d. 1147). Duchess of Brittany. Name variations: Ermengarde of Brittany; Ermengarde de Gatinais. Died in 1147 (some sources cite 1146) in Brittany; dau. of Fulk IV, count of Anjou, and Audearde de Beaugency; m. William IX, duke of Aquitaine, 1088 (div. 1091); m. Alan IV, duke of Brittany, 1091 or 1092 (died 1119); children: (2nd m.) Conan III, duke of Brittany (d. 1148). ❖ During 2nd husband's long absences on crusade (1096–1101, 1112–19), acted as his regent; a successful ruler, gained the approval of many Bretons for her even-tempered sense of justice and attempts to improve their living conditions; when husband died (1119) and their son succeeded as duke of Brittany, continued her work as regent, as he was not yet of an age to rule; rewrote the law code of Brittany, making laws less burdensome on poor Bretons; left Brittany for a pilgrimage to Jerusalem (1131); returned several years later with a more devout religiosity, intent on serving God and helping others do the same; used her wealth to found at least one monastery and donated generously to several local religious houses; earned widespread respect and

was well-remembered by the Bretons for many years after her death. ❖ See also *Women in World History*.

ERMENGARDE OF BEAUMONT (d. 1234). Queen of Scotland. Name variations: Ermengarde Beaumont; Ermengarde de Beaumont. Died Feb 11, 1234 (some sources cite 1233); buried at Balmerino Abbey, Fife, Scotland; dau. of Richard Beaumont, Viscount Beaumont, and Constance (dau. of Sybilla Corbert and Henry I, king of England); m. William I the Lion (1143–1214), king of the Scots (r. 1165–1214), Sept 5, 1186; children: Alexander II (1198–1249), king of Scotland (r. 1214–1249); Margaret de Burgh (c. 1193–1259); Isabel (who m. Robert Bigod, 3rd earl of Norfolk); Marjory (d. 1244). William I the Lion had children with two other women. ❖ See also *Women in World History*.

ERMENGARDE OF BRITTANY (d. 1147). *See Ermengarde of Anjou.*

ERMENGARDE OF CARCASSONNE (d. 1070). Countess of Carcassonne. Died 1070 in Carcassonne, a small but prosperous county in what is now southwestern France; dau. of Roger II, count of Carcassonne; m. Raimond Bernard (French noble); children: unknown. ❖ When brother died leaving no heirs (1067), succeeded him and ruled alone for the next 3 years, until her death. ❖ See also *Women in World History*.

ERMENGARDE OF NARBONNE (c. 1120–c. 1194). Viscountess of Narbonne. Born c. 1120 in Narbonne, a county located in what is now southeast France; died c. 1194 in Narbonne; dau. of Aimery II, viscount of Narbonne; m. at least 3 times, though husbands' identities are uncertain; children: none. ❖ Heiress of Viscount Aimery II of Narbonne, proved herself capable of handling affairs despite her youth after father died; used troops to put down incipient rebellions by her vassals, and repelled Count Alphonse of Toulouse's attempts to take over Narbonne while ostensibly protecting her; fiercely loyal to the pious King Louis VII of France, led her troops to help him put down rebellions by his vassals in southern France; during reign of more than 60 years, became famous as a benevolent and balanced judge in feudal court cases under her jurisdiction; was also renowned as a patron of troubadours, the singer-poets who composed themes on various aspects of love. ❖ See also *Women in World History*.

ERMENGARDE OF PROVENCE (fl. 876). Queen of Provence. Name variations: Ermingarde. Fl. around 876; dau. of Louis II le Jeune also known as Louis II the Child (c. 822–875), king of Italy (r. 844), king of Lorraine (r. 872–875), Holy Roman Emperor (r. 855–875), and Engelberga (c. 840–890); m. Boso, king of Provence (r. 879–887), 876; children: Louis III the Blind of Provence, Holy Roman emperor (r. 901–905); Engelberga of Aquitaine (877–917). ❖ See also *Women in World History*.

ERMENILDA (d. around 700). Queen of Mercia. Name variations: Eormengild of Kent. Died c. 700; dau. of Earconbert also known as Ercombert, king of Kent, and Saint Sexburga (d. 699?); m. Wulfhere, king of Mercia (r. 657–675); children: Saint Werburga (d. 700?, who was also abbess of Sheppey and Ely); Coenred, king of Mercia; Behrtwald. ❖ After being widowed, served as abbess of Sheppey, then of Ely. Feast day is Feb 13.

ERMENSINDE (d. 1247). *See Ermesinde of Luxembourg.*

ERMENTRUDE (d. 869). Queen of France. Died in 869; dau. of Vodon, earl of Orléans, and Engeltrude; became 1st wife of Charles I the Bald, king of France (r. 840–877), known also as Charles II, Holy Roman emperor (r. 875–877), 842; children: Louis II the Stammerer (846–879), king of France (r. 877–879); Judith Martel (c. 844–?); Carloman (d. 874); Charles (c. 847–865), king of Aquitaine; Ermentrude of Hasnon, abbess of Hasnon; Hildegard; Gisele; Rotrude of Poitiers, abbess of St. Radegund; Drogo; Pippin; Lothar. Charles I the Bald's 2nd wife was Richilde of Autun.

ERMENTRUDE (d. 1126). Countess of Maine. Name variations: Aremburg or Heremburge; Ermengarde du Maine. Died 1126; dau. of Elias I, count of Maine, and Matilda of Château du Loir; m. Fulk V (b. 1092), count of Anjou and king of Jerusalem, July 11, 1110; children: 5, including Matilda of Anjou (1107–1154); Sybilla of Anjou (1112–1165); Geoffrey IV, count of Anjou; and Elias II, count of Maine. ❖ See also *Women in World History*.

ERMENTRUDE DE ROUCY (d. 1005). Countess of Burgundy. Name variations: Ermentrude de Rouci; Ermentrude Rheims; Irmtrude. Died Mar 5, 1005; dau. of Renaud or Rainald de Roucy and Alberade of Lorraine (930–973); m. Othon-Guillaume also known as Otto William, count of Burgundy, c. 982 (died 1026); children: Agnes of Aquitaine (c. 995–1068); Gerberga of Burgundy (who m. William II, count of Provence); Matilda of Burgundy (who m. Landeric, count of Nevers); Renaud I (990–1057), 1st count of Burgundy.

ERMESIND OF LUXEMBURG (fl. 1200). Countess of Namur. Name variations: Ermensinde; Ermesinde. Fl. around 1200; dau. of Conrad I, count of Luxemburg (r. 1059–1086); sister of Gilbert, Henry III, and William (all counts of Luxemburg); m. Godfrey, count of Namur; children: Henry IV the Blond also known as Henry IV the Blind, count of Luxemburg (r. 1136–1196). ❖ See also *Women in World History.*

ERMESIND OF LUXEMBURG (d. 1247). Countess and ruler of Luxemburg. Name variations: Ermensinde; Ermesinde; countess of Namur. Reigned (1196–1247); died 1247; dau. of Henry IV the Blind also known as Henry IV the Blond, count of Luxemburg (son of Godfrey, count of Namur, and Ermesind of Luxemburg [fl. 1200]); m. Walram III, duke of Limburg; children: Henry V the Blind also known as Henry V the Blond (1217–1281), count of Luxemburg (r. 1247–1281). ❖ Born into House of Namur, became ruler of principality of Luxemburg (1196), following death of father. ❖ See also *Women in World History.*

ERMINGARDE. *Variant of Ermengarde.*

ERMOLAEVA, Galina. Russian cyclist. Name variations: Ermolayeva; Galina Jermolewa. Born in USSR. ❖ Won the World Championship for sprint (1958, 1959, 1960, 1961, 1963, 1972).

ERMOLEVA, Zinaida (1898–1974). Russian microbiologist. Name variations: Zinaida Vissarionovna Ermol'eva or Ermolaeva; Zinaida Yermolyeva or Yermoleva. Born on Oct 24, 1898, in Frolovo; died in 1974. ❖ "Bacteriochemist" and cholera expert of the Soviet era who is known as "the Mother of Soviet Antibiotics," was a researcher at the Northern Caucasus Bacteriological Institute, then the A.N. Bakh Biochemical Institute of the People's Commissariat for Public Health, then the All-Union Institute of Experimental Medicine; became a noted expert on cholera and, as early as 1931, was able to create a new treatment for infectious diseases, lysozyme; obtained the 1st Soviet samples of penicillin (1942); worked at the Institute of Antibiotics of the USSR Ministry of Public Health (1947–54); obtained laboratory samples of streptomycin (1947); developed a number of Soviet antibiotic agents including interferon, ekmonovicillin, Bicillins, ekmolin, and dipasfen; was editor-in-chief of the journal *Antibiotiki* and Soviet representative to the World Health Organization; elected a corresponding member of the USSR Academy of Medical Sciences (1945), became a full Academician (1965); received the highest scientific honors the Soviet Union bestowed. ❖ See also *Women in World History.*

ERMOLOVA, Mariia (1853–1928). Russian actress. Name variations: Maria Nikolaijevna Yermolova; Maria M. Ermolova; Maria Yermelova, Maria Ermelova. Born Mariia Nikolaevna Ermolova in Moscow, Russia, July 15, 1853; died in Moscow, Mar 12, 1928; dau. of Nikolai Ermolov (prompter at one of Moscow's leading theaters). ❖ One of the greatest stars of the Russian stage for 5 decades, made debut at the Malyi Theater, starring in Lessing's *Emilia Galotti* (1870); quickly became a mainstay of the Malyi; gave stirring portrayals of Katerina in Ostrovsky's *The Thunderstorm* and Laurencia in Lope de Vega's *Fuente Ovejuna;* appeared as Iuliia Tugina in *The Last Victim,* Evlaliia in *Slaves,* Kruchnina in *Guilty Though Guiltless,* and Negina in *Talents and Suitors* (1881), one of her most memorable personas; also performed as Phaedra, Sappho, and Clärchen in Goethe's *Egmont,* as well as several Shakespearean women, including Lady Macbeth (Gruoch); reached the peak of her career in the plays of Friedrich von Schiller, including the title role in *Maria Stuart,* Elizabeth de Valois in *Don Carlos* and, in her greatest success, as Johanna (Joan of Arc) in *Die Jungfrau von Orleans;* her powerful interpretations set a new standard for acting on the Moscow stage. ❖ See also *Women in World History.*

ERNAUX, Annie (1940—). French novelist. Born Sept 1, 1940, in Normandy, France; dau. of a café owner. ❖ Works, which are largely autobiographical, include *Les Armoires vides* (The Empty Cupboards, 1974, trans. as *Cleaned Out,* 1990), *La femme gelée* (1981, trans. as *A Frozen Woman,* 1995), *La Place* (The Square, 1983, a memoir about her father that won the Prix Renaudot, which was trans. by Tanya Leslie as *A Man's Place,* 1984), *Une Femme* (*A Woman's Story,* 1987), a memoir about her mother which was a *New York Times* Notable Book of the Year, *Passion Simple* (1991, trans. by Leslie as *Simple Passion*), *Journal du dehors* (1993), *La honte* (1996, trans. as *Shame,* 1998), *Je ne suis pas sortie de ma nuit* (1997, trans. as *"I Remain in Darkness,"* 1999), *L'événement* (2000,

trans. as *Happening,* 2001), *La vie extérieure* (2000) and the journal, *Se perdre* (2001).

ERNST, Dorothea Tanning (b. 1910). *See Tanning, Dorothea.*

ERNST, Eunice (1926—). *See Ernst, Kitty.*

ERNST, Kitty (1926—). American nurse-midwife. Name variations: Eunice Ernst. Born Eunice Katherine MacDonald, July 21, 1926, in Weston, Massachusetts; awarded a bachelors in education from Hunter College (1957) and an MA in public health from Columbia University (1959); m. Albert T. Ernst; children: 3. ❖ Contributor to the development of education and support programs for nurse-midwives, earned diploma from Waltham Hospital School of Nursing in Massachusetts (1947), then joined its staff; joined Frontier Nursing Service (FNS) as a night nurse for medicine, surgery, and pediatrics in rural Leslie Co., KY (1951); earned nurse-midwife certificate (1951); worked as a FNS public health nurse and nurse-midwife; served as nurse-widwife for Maternity Center Association (MCA) in New York City (1954–58); served as director of Cooperative Birth Center Network (CBCN), later named the National Association of Childbearing Centers (1981–93), becoming Mary Breckinridge chair of Midwifery and Family Nursing there (1991) and director of Consulting Group (1993). Received Maternity Center Association's Carola Warburg Rothschild Award (2003).

ERNSTING-KRIENKE, Nadine (1974—). German field-hockey player. Name variations: Nadine Krienke. Born Feb 5, 1974, in Telgte, Germany. ❖ At Barcelona Olympics, won a silver medal in team competition (1992); won a team gold medal at Athens Olympics (2004).

EROSHINA, Radia. *See Yeroshina, Radya.*

ERRATH, Christine (1956—). East German figure skater. Name variations: Christine Errath-Trettin. Born Dec 29, 1956, in Berlin, East Germany. ❖ Won European championship (1973, 1974, 1975) and World championship (1973, 1974); won a bronze medal at Innsbruck Olympics and a silver medal at World championships (1976).

ERSKINE, Margaret (fl. 1530s). Mistress of James V. Fl. in 1530s; dau. of John, 4th or 12th lord Erskine; mistress of James V (1512–1542), king of Scotland (r. 1513–1542); children: (with James V) James Stuart also seen as James Stewart, earl of Moray (1531–1570, legitimated in 1551); Robert Stuart also seen as Robert Stewart, earl of Orkney (c. 1533–1591, became the abbott of Holyrood House). ❖ The character Lady Sensuality in David Lyndsay's *Satire of the Three Estates* was based on Margaret Erskine. ❖ See also *Women in World History.*

ERSKINE, Mary (1629–1707). Scottish banker and girls' education pioneer. Born in 1629 in Garlet, Clackmannanshire, Scotland; died in 1707 in Scotland; m. Robert Kennedy (writer), 1661 (died 1671); m. James Hair (druggist and apothecary), 1671 (died 1683). ❖ Successful businesswoman and early proponent of girls' education, reverted to maiden name after 2nd husband's death and set up business as a private banker; exceedingly successful, owned extensive rental properties and contributed generously to Edinburgh Merchant Company's foundation of Merchant Maiden Hospital (1694), for purpose of education of daughters of Edinburgh burgesses (Merchant Maiden Hospital became Edinburgh Ladies' College [1869], then Mary Erskine School [1944] and is still extant); was instrumental in founding Trades Maiden Hospital, which unlike similar foundations did not run school but provided boarding and clothing to young women seeking education and training (1704).

ERTL, Martina (1973—). German Alpine skier. Born Sept 12, 1973, in Bad Toelz, Germany; sister of Andreas Ertl (skier). ❖ Won 1st World Cup for giant salom (1991–92); won a silver medal for giant slalom at Lillehammer Olympics (1994); won a silver medal at Nagano Olympics, won a silver medal in the combined (1998) for a German sweep (Katja Seizinger took the gold, Hilde Gerg the bronze); won a gold medal in the combined at World championships (2001); won a bronze medal for combined at Salt Lake City Olympics (2002); became a border patrol officer.

ERTMANN, Dorothea von (1781–1849). *See Von Ertmann, Dorothea.*

ERXLEBEN, Dorothea (1715–1762). German physician. Name variations: Dorothea von Erxleben; Dorothea Leporin-Erxleben. Born Dorothea Christiane Leporin in Quedlinburg, Nov 13, 1715; died in Quedlinburg, June 13, 1762; dau. of Christian Polycarp Leporin (1689–1747, physician) and Anna Sophia (Meinecke) Leporin; sister of Christian Polycarp Leporin; attended University of Halle/Saale; m. Johann Christian Erxleben; children: 2 daughters, 2 sons, including noted physician Johann Christian Polycarp Erxleben (1744–1777), as well as 5 stepchildren. ❖ The 1st woman in Germany to be awarded an MD (June 12, 1754), successfully practiced medicine in Quedlinburg until her death; published *A Thorough Inquiry into the Causes Preventing the Female Sex from Studying* (1742), which advanced a strong case for a nation to take advantage of the talents of its women. ❖ See also *Women in World History*.

ERYTHRO (c. 778–after 839). See Rotrude.

ERZSI VON HABSBURG (1883–1963). See Elizabeth von Habsburg.

ESATO (fl. 10th c. CE). See Judith.

ESAU, Katherine (1898–1997). Russian-born American botanist. Born in Ekaterinoslav, Russia (now Dnepropetrovsk, Ukraine), April 3, 1898; died in Santa Barbara, California, June 4, 1997; dau. of John (mayor of Ekaterinoslav) and Margarethe (Toews) Esau (both Mennonites); attended Moscow's Golitsin Women's College of Agriculture and Berlin's College of Agriculture; University of California at Berkeley, PhD in botany, 1931; never married. ❖ During Revolution, fled Russia with family (1918); in Berlin, studied with noted geneticist Erwin Baur, which led to her certification as an expert in plant breeding; immigrated with family to US, settling in Reedley, California, in which a large number of Mennonites lived as farmers; took a series of jobs including one with a sugar company in Spreckels, a California settlement near Salinas, where she developed a sugar beet that was resistant to curly top disease; was offered a dual position at the University of California at Davis (1932), teaching plant anatomy, systematic botany, morphology of plant crops and microtechnique, and carrying out research projects at the College of Agriculture's experiment station; became internationally recognized for her work in the field of plant anatomy and plant viral diseases; published the classic textbook *Plant Anatomy* (1953); moved to the University of California at Santa Barbara (1963), where she continued her investigations of plant viral diseases; served as president of the Botanical Society of America, which later created the Katherine Esau Award for the most outstanding paper in developmental and structural botany. Awarded National Medal of Science by President George Bush (1989). ❖ See also *Women in World History*.

ESCARDOT, L. (1865–1943). See Karr, Carme.

ESCHENBACH, Marie Ebner (1830–1916). See Ebner-Eschenbach, Marie.

ESCHER, Gitta (1957—). East German gymnast. Born Mar 18, 1957, in East Germany. ❖ At Montreal Olympics, won a bronze medal in team all-around (1976).

ESCHIVA OF IBELIN (fl. late 1100s). Mother of the king of Cyprus. Fl. in late 1100s; 1st wife of Aimery de Lusignan (brother of Guy de Lusignan [d. 1194]) also known as Amalric II, king of Jerusalem (r. 1197–1205), king of Cyprus; children: Hugh I, king of Cyprus (r. 1205–1218). Amalric's 2nd wife was Isabella I of Jerusalem (d. 1205). ❖ See also *Women in World History*.

ESCHIVA OF IBELIN (r. 1282–c. 1284). Queen of Beirut. Reigned (1282–c. 1284); younger dau. of John II of Beirut and Alice de la Roche of Athens; younger sister of Isabella (d. 1282), queen of Beirut; m. Humphrey of Montfort, younger son of Philip of Montfort, lord of Toron and Tyre (died c. 1284); m. Guy de Lusignan (d. 1308, youngest son of Hugh XII;) one son, Roupen. ❖ Became queen of Beirut (1282) upon death of her sister Isabella; is known for her intervention with the Mameluk sultan Qalawun, which resulted in a truce that prevented the Mameluks from attacking Beirut, though the truce was broken under Shujai (1291), who tore down the walls of Beirut and the Castle of the Ibelins and turned the cathedral into a mosque. ❖ See also *Women in World History*.

ESCHSTRUTH, Nataly von (1860–1939). German playwright and novelist. Born 1860 in Germany; died 1939. ❖ Writings include *De Majoratsherr* (1898) and *Die Bären von Hohen-Esp* (1902).

ESCOBAR, Marisol (b. 1930). See Marisol.

ESCOFFERY, Gloria (1923–2002). Jamaican poet and painter. Born Dec 22, 1923, in Jamaica; died April 24, 2002, in Brown's Town, Jamaica; dau. of William T. Escoffery and Sylvia Escoffery. ❖ Studied in Jamaica and then at McGill University, Canada, and Slade School of Fine Arts, England; taught English and worked as journalist; helped establish Brown's Town Community College; exhibited paintings in Jamaica and abroad; works include *Landscape in the Making* (1976); published poetry in *Breaklight* (1972), *Caribbean Voices* (1978), and *The Penguin of Caribbean Verse* (1986); contributed stories, poems, and essays to *Jamaica Journal, BIM, Focus, The Gleaner*, and *Arts Review*. Made Officer of Order of Distinction for services in field of art (1977).

ESCORTS. See Ravan, Genya.

ESCOT, Pozzi (1933—). Peruvian-born composer. Born in Lima, Peru, Oct 1, 1933; dau. of M. Pozzi-Escot (French bacteriologist and diplomat) and a Moroccan mother; tutored at home by Belgian composer André Sas; in US, studied at Reed College, Juilliard, and Hochschule für Musik with Philipp Jarnach. ❖ Admired by Virgil Thomson as "the most interesting and original woman composer now functioning," was appointed to New England Conservatory of Music to teach theory and composition; wrote compositions which became widely known; commissioned by the government of Venezuela to write *Sands,* an orchestral composition for the 400th anniversary of the city of Caracas; known for efforts on behalf of American performers and composers whom she felt were often overlooked in favor of Europeans. ❖ See also *Women in World History*.

ESCOTT, Cicely Margaret (1908–1977). New Zealand novelist, drama teacher, and poet. Born July 9, 1908, at Eltham, London, England; died Aug 15, 1977, in Waitemata Harbour, New Zealand; dau. of Harry Frederick Escott (bank clerk) and Emily (Allen) Escott. ❖ Immigrated to New Zealand with family (1926); returned to London and worked at Times Book Club (1928); wrote several novels, including *Insolence of Office* (1934), *Awake at Noon* (1935) and *Show Down* (1936); returned to New Zealand and taught adult drama classes (1950s–60s); became adjudicator for New Zealand branch of British Drama League, and was on radio arts panel; also wrote volume of poetry, *Separation and/or Greeting,* which was published after her death in 1980. ❖ See also *Dictionary of New Zealand Biography*.

ESCOVEDO, Sheila (1957—). American pop singer and drummer. Name variations: Sheila E. Born Sheila Escovedo, Dec 12, 1957, in Oakland, California; dau. of Juanita and Pete Escovedo (percussionist for band Santana). ❖ The only female Prince protegé with staying power, learned to play drums and other percussion instruments as a child; quit high school to join father's band Azteca; became successful studio percussionist (late 1970s); recorded and toured with Diana Ross, Herbie Hancock, Lionel Richie, and Marvin Gaye (early 1980s); collaborated with Prince on duet "Erotic City" (1984); launched solo act (1984); released album *The Glamorous Life* (1984), which yielded hit title track; released albums *Sheila E. in Romance 1600* (1985), *Sheila E.* (1987), *Sex Cymbal* (1991), and *Writes of Passage* (2001); scored singles hits with "Belle of St. Mark" (1984), "A Love Bizarre" (1985), and "Hold Me" (1987); put solo career on hold to tour with Prince's band the Revolution (late 1980s); suffered collapsed lung (1991); was bandleader on Earvin "Magic" Johnson's late-night talk show (1998).

ESHKOL, Noa (1927—). Israeli dancer and dance notator. Born Feb 28, 1927, in Safed, then Palestine. ❖ Performed in concert recitals (1940s–50s); best known for her work in dance notation and composition theory, developed system now known as Eshkol—or Eshkol-Wachmann—Notation, which can be used for all types of movement study, whether choreographed or not, ballet or folk dance.

ESKENAZI, Roza (c. 1900–1980). Greek popular singer. Name variations: Rosa Eskenazy; Roza Eskenaze. Born in the Ottoman Empire around 1900; died in 1980. ❖ Performer in the *cafe amán* style, whose many recordings brought her as much fame abroad among the Greek diaspora as within Greece itself; at a young age, began career as a *defi* player; performed at the *cafe amáns* of Constantinople where she quickly became one of the most celebrated singers in the Smyrnaic-Rebetic tradition; by the early 1930s, was a superstar in the Greek world; sang in Greek, Turkish, Kurdish, and Ladino (the Spanish-derived language of the Sephardic Jewish diaspora of the Mediterranean); escaped from Greece before Nazi Germany occupied the country (1941); during war years, lived in US but returned to Greece soon after; with her sweet but reedy soprano voice, as expressive as it was pure, made hundreds of recordings. ❖ See also autobiography (in Greek,) written with Kostas Hatzidoulis, *Auta Pou Thymamai* (That Which I Remember, Kaktos, 1982).

ESMAT (d. 1995). Queen of Iran. Name variations: Esmat Dowlatshahi or Dolatshahi. Born Esmat-el-Molouk of Qajar descent; died July 24, 1995; dau. of a Qajar prince, Mojalal-ed-Dowleh (also seen as Mojalal al-Doleh); sister of Ashraf Saltaneh II; became last wife of Reza Shah Pahlavi (1878–1944, shah of Iran), 1923; children: Abdul Reza Pahlavi

(1924–2004), Ahmad Reza Pahlavi (b, 1925), Mahmoud Reza Pahlavi (b. 1926), Fatimeh Pahlevi (b. 1928) and Hamid Reza Pahlavi (b. 1932).

ESMOND, Annie (1873–1945). English actress. Born Sept 27, 1873, in Surrey, England; died Jan 4, 1945. ❖ Made stage debut in Sheffield in *Mother Goose* (1891) and London debut in *Our Flat* (1894); toured with Olga Nethersole in *Sapho* and *Magda*; appeared in NY in *The Catch of the Season* (1905), remaining there until 1914; other London plays include *Damaged Goods, The Flame, Fata Morgana, Doctor Knock, Mr. Pickwick, Little Accident, The Stranger Within, Biography* and *Young Mr. Disraeli;* made film debut in *Dawn* (1917) and subsequently appeared in over 60 films, including *Mr. Pim Passes By, The Outsider, Royal Cavalcade,* and *Dear Octopus,* and as Mrs. Bindle in the "Bindle" series.

ESMOND, Jill (1908–1990). English actress. Name variations: Jill Esmond Olivier. Born Jill Esmond-Moore in London, England, Jan 26, 1908; died July 28, 1990, in Wimbledon, England; dau. of Henry Vernon Esmond and Eva (Moore) Esmond; studied at Royal Academy of Dramatic Art; m. Laurence Olivier (actor), 1930 (div. 1940); children: Tarquin Olivier. ❖ At 14, made stage debut at St. James's Theater as Nibs in *Peter Pan* (1922); appeared as Sorel Bliss at the Ambassador in *Hay Fever* (1925); made 1st NY appearance as Joan Greenleaf in *A Bird in the Hand* (1929), a role she had been playing in London throughout previous year; other stage roles included Sybil Chase in *Private Lives,* Laura Hudson in *Men in White,* Ann Hammond in *Ringmaster,* Olivia in *Twelfth Night,* Blanche Monnier in *I Accuse,* Angela Brent in *Tree of Eden,* and Edith de Berg in *The Eagle Has Two Heads;* appeared in a number of films, including *This Above All, The White Cliffs of Dover, Random Harvest, Journey for Margaret, Casanova Brown* and *A Man Called Peter.*

ESPANCA, Florbela (1894–1930). Portuguese poet and short-story writer. Name variations: Florbela de Alma da Conceição Espanca. Born out of wedlock, Dec 1894, in Vila Viçosa, Portugal; succumbed to an overdose of barbiturates in Matosinhos, Portugal, Dec 7, 1930; married 3 times. ❖ Generally regarded as one of Portugal's foremost women poets, poured her emotions into lyric verse and short stories strongly influenced by the symbolist literature popular at that time, early works which would be published posthumously in 1931; published 1st book of poems, *Livro de mágoas (Book of Woes,* 1919), followed by *Livro de Sóror Saudade (Book of Sister Saudade),* which challenged the puritanism and patriarchy of a conservative society; at the time of her death, was known more for her reputation as a "scandalous woman" than for her work as a writer; within a year, her voice was discovered by a growing number of admirers with publication of 2 books she had been editing, *Charneca em Flor (Flowering Heath)* and *Reliquiae (Relics);* by 1950s, had achieved a towering reputation as not only modern Portugal's greatest female poet, but also as one of that nation's most eloquent advocates of the right of all women to seek personal freedom and happiness. ❖ See also *Women in World History.*

ESPERT, Nuria (1935—). Spanish actress and director. Name variations: Núria Espert; Nuria Espert Romero; Nuria Espert Moreno. Born June 11, 1935, in Barcelona, Spain; m. Armando Moreno. ❖ Began acting at 12; with husband, formed Nuria Espert Company, which traveled worldwide and became renowned for innovative interpretations of modern and classical drama; directed the National Theater in Madrid (1980–81); directed acclaimed production of *The House of Bernarda Alba* in London (1986).

ESPERANZA, Maria (1928–2004). Venezuelan mystic. Name variations: Maria Esperanza de Bianchini. Born Nov 22, 1928, in the village of San Rafael, Barrancas, Monagas State, Venezuela; died Aug 7, 2004, in Ocean Co., New Jersey; m. Geo Bianchini Giani, Dec 8, 1956; children: 7. ❖ Had many visions when young, most especially from Saint Thérèse of Lisieux and Mary the Virgin; reported a visit by Mary in Betania, Venezuela (Mar 25, 1976) where there were later numerous reports of miraculous cures; for some years, experienced spontaneous bleeding from her hands (stigmata).

ESPESETH, Gro (1972—). Norwegian soccer player. Born Oct 13, 1972, in Norway. ❖ Forward; was a stalwart of the Norwegian national team for 10 years; at World Cup, won a team silver (1991) and team gold (1995); won a team bronze medal at Atlanta Olympics (1996) and a team gold medal at Sydney Olympics (2000); played for New York Power; retired (2001). Named to WUSA Global–11 1st team (2001).

ESPíN DE CASTRO, Vilma (1934—). Cuban revolutionary and women's activist. Name variations: Vilma Espín Guillois; Vilma Espín or Espin; Deborah. Pronunciation: Ess-PEEN dav KAH-strow. Born Vilma Espín Guillois in 1934 in Santiago de Cuba; dau. of a lawyer for the Bacardi Rum Company and a mother of French extraction; sister of Nilsa Espín Guillois; earned a degree in chemical engineering at Universidad de Oriente; attended Massachusetts Institute of Technology and studied architecture; m. Raúl Castro, Jan 26, 1959; children: 4 sons. ❖ Long-time president of the Federación de Mujeres Cubanas (Federation of Cuban Women), began her political education with the anti-Batista movement following Batista's coup; was a founding member and leader of the 26th of July Movement in Oriente Province, Cuba (1955–59); after Fidel's brother Raúl established a "second front" in the Sierra Cristal of northern Oriente Province, remained in the Sierra until the triumph of the revolution, working hard to create, among other duties, an administrative network responsible for the maintenance of 11 hospitals and dispensaries, and 100 schools staffed by 26th of July Movement personnel; became Raúl's secretary and served as a translator (1958); married Raúl (Jan 26, 1959), just after Batista fled and Fidel came to power; was a founder and president of the Federación de Mujeres Cubanas (FMC, Federation of Cuban Women, 1960); also worked as chemical engineer for the Ministerio de la Industria Alimenticia (Food Industry Ministry); made an alternate member of the Politburo of the Cuban Communist Party (1980) and a full member (1986); retired from the Politburo (1991); left her mark on the revolution and struck several blows for women's rights in Cuba and in the world. ❖ See also *Women in World History.*

ESPINA, Concha (1869–1955). Spanish writer. Name variations: Concha Espina de Serna. Born Concepción Jesusa Basilisa Tagle y Espina in Santander, Spain, 1869; died in 1955; 7th child of Victor Espina and Ascensión Tagle; m. Ramón de la Serna, 1892 (sep. 1908); children: Ramón; Víctor; José; Josefina de la Maza; Luis. ❖ After separating from husband, moved to Madrid and became a full-time author, the 1st Spanish woman to support herself from her writing; works include the play, *El jayón (The Foundling),* and novels *La esfinge maragata (Mariflor,* 1914) and *El metal de los muertos (Metal of the Dead),* an epic that depicts social conditions among miners in the Río Tinto district, which brought her a nomination for the Nobel Prize; traveled and lectured widely through the Americas and Europe; served as a Spanish cultural emissary to the Caribbean and as vice-president of the Hispanic Society of New York City (1943); received many awards in Spain, including the great cross of Alphonso the Wise. ❖ See also Mary Lee Bretz, *Concha Espina* (Twayne, 1980); (in Spanish) Josefina de la Maza, *Vida de mi madre, Concha Espina* (Magisterio Español, 1969); and *Women in World History.*

ESPINASSE, Mademoiselle de l' (1732–1776). See Lespinasse, Julie de.

ESPINOSA, Judith (1877–1949). Spanish-Dutch ballet dancer and teacher. Born 1877 in England; died 1949; dau. of Léon Espinosa, dancer; sister of Edouard, Mimi and Léa Espinosa. ❖ Grew up in Dutch family of performers, of Spanish descent; performed as prima ballerina at Alhambra Theater, London, under Carlo Coppi; became one of the most distinguished teachers in London.

ESPINOSA, Mimi (1893–1936). Spanish-Dutch dancer. Born 1893 in England; died 1936; dau. of Léon Espinosa, dancer; sister of Edouard, Mimi, Léa Espinosa. ❖ Raised in Dutch family of performers, of Spanish descent; was featured in numerous productions of Oscar Ashe for many years.

ESQUIVEL, Laura (1950—). Mexican novelist and screenwriter. Born Sept 30, 1950, in Mexico City, Mexico; m. Alfonso Arau (Mexican film director), 1975; children: (stepdaughter) Emilia Arau (b. 1964). ❖ Her novel *Como agua para chocolate (Like Water for Chocolate)* topped the bestseller list in Mexico and US (1990) and was translated into 29 languages; adapted it into a screenplay which was filmed by her husband and won Best Picture from the Mexican Picture Awards (1993); also wrote *The Law of Love* and *Between Two Fires.*

ESSEN, Siri von (1850–1912). See von Essen, Siri.

ESSEN, Viola (1926–1969). American ballet dancer. Born Violeta Vassieva Colchagova, 1926, in St. Louis, Missouri; died Jan 1, 1969, in New York, NY. ❖ Trained with Mikhail Mordkin and Mikhail Fokine in New York City, and soon began performing professionally with both of their companies; at 14, danced role of Mythe in *Giselle* to great acclaim for Mordkin Ballet; was featured in Fokine's productions of *Les Sylphides* and *Polovetsian Dances from Prince Igor* (1940); became charter member of Ballet Theater (1940), where she was featured in numerous works until 1950s, including Bolm's *Ballet Méchanique* and Fokine's *Carnaval;* danced intermittently with Ballet International, creating roles in Simon Semenoff's *Memories,* Boris Romanoff's *Prince Goudal's Festival,* and

Edward Caton's *Sebastien* (all 1944); appeared in dramatic roles on stage, and on Broadway in *Follow the Girls* (1944) and *Hollywood Pinafore* (1945).

ESSENTIAL LOGIC. *See Logic, Lora.*

ESSER, Roswitha (1941—). West German kayaker. Born Jan 18, 1941. ❖ Won a gold medal at Tokyo Olympics (1964) and at Mexico City Olympics (1968), both in K2 500 meters.

ESSERMAN, Carol (c. 1945—). American policewoman. Born c. 1945. ❖ Served as plainclothes officer with New York City Police Department; fatally shot Robert L. Greene, alleged numbers runner, becoming 1st woman police officer to kill a suspect in line of duty (1981); indicted by Bronx district attorney and suspended without pay pending trail, was acquitted (1983).

ESSEX, countess of.
See Maud of Mandeville (d. 1236).
See Bohun, Maud (fl. 1275).
See Elizabeth Plantagenet (1282–1316).
See Maud of Lusignan (d. 1241).
See Joan de Quinci (d. 1283).
See Bohun, Alianore (d. 1313).
See Fitzalan, Joan (fl. 1325).
See Fitzalan, Joan (d. 1419).
See Isabel (1409–1484).
See Bourchier, Anne (1512–1571).
See Knollys, Lettice (c. 1541–1634).
See Walsingham, Frances (d. 1631).
See Stephens, Catherine (1794–1882).

ESSEX, Frances (1850–1934). *See French, Alice.*

ESSIPOVA, Annette (1851–1914). Russian pianist. Name variations: Name variations: Annette Essipoff. Born in St. Petersburg, Russia, Feb 13, 1851; died in St. Petersburg, Aug 18, 1914; m. Theodor Leschetizky, 1880 (div. 1892). ❖ Studied with future husband; played throughout Europe and in US; helped Ignace Paderewski early in his career and premiered several of his compositions, including the Concerto and the now ubiquitous Minuet in G; after touring, returned to Russia, where she was the most sought after teacher at the St. Petersburg Conservatory (1893–1908); students included Sergei Prokofiev, Isabelle Vengerova, Simon Barere, Lev Pouishnov, Ignace Hilsberg, and Thomas de Hartmann. ❖ See also *Women in World History.*

ESTAUGH, Elizabeth Haddon (1680–1762). American colonial proprietor. Name variations: Elizabeth Haddon. Born Elizabeth Haddon, May 25, 1680, in Southwark, London, England; died Mar 30, 1762, in Haddonfield, New Jersey; dau. of John Haddon (blacksmith, manufacturer of ship anchors) and Elizabeth (Clark) Haddon; sister of Sarah Haddon; m. John Estaugh (Quaker minister and missionary), 1702 (died 1742); children: (adopted nephew) Ebenezer Hopkins. ❖ Skilled businesswoman and founder of town of Haddonfield, was born into prosperous Quaker family in London; received liberal education in Friends school; experienced religious persecution of family in form of fines levied upon father, leading to his purchase of land in America in an attempt to emigrate, but he was foiled by poor health and business responsibilities; arrived in America to manage 500 acres of his land in Gloucester Co., West Jersey (1701); moved into house on south bank of Cooper's Creek which came to be known as Old Haddonfield; married John Estaugh (1702) in Quaker ceremony; continued to take active role in management of father's properties despite husband's legal status as executive; was frequently left in charge of her family's business concerns as husband traveled extensively as missionary and also suffered bouts of ill-health; moved from Cooper's Creek to new plot of land, founding settlement of New Haddonfield (1713); traveled 3 times to England to visit parents and returned from last visit with nephew Ebenezer Hopkins (1723); founded Friends Meeting House in Haddonfield with grant of land from father (1723); widowed when husband died in British Virgin Islands (1742); published husband's tract *A Call to the Unfaithful Professors of Truth* (1744) with introduction by Benjamin Franklin; became fully vested with property rights after husband's death and administered these with skill. ❖ See also Rebecca Nicholson, *Contributions to the Biography of Elizabeth Estaugh* (1894).

ESTE, Alda d' (fl. 1300s). Ferrarese noblewoman. Name variations: Alda Rangoni. Born Alda Rangoni; m. Aldobrandino II, lord of Ferrara (d. 1326); children: Rinaldo, lord of Ferrara (r. 1317–1335); Niccolo I

(d. 1344); Obizzo III (1294–1352); Elisa d'Este (d. 1329). ❖ See also *Women in World History.*

ESTE, Alda d' (1333–1381). Noblewoman of Mantua. Name variations: Alda Gonzaga. Born 1333; died 1381; legitimated dau. of Lippa d'Este and Obizzo III d'Este (1294–1352), lord of Ferrara; m. Louis also known as Lodovico or Ludovico II Gonzaga (1334–1382), 3rd captain general of Mantua (r. 1369–1382); children: Francesco Gonzaga (1366–1407), 4th captain general of Mantua (r. 1382–1407, who m. Agnes Visconti and Margherita Gonzaga.

ESTE, Anna d' (1473–1497). *See Sforza, Anna.*

ESTE, Anna d', duchess of Guise (1531–1607). *See Anne of Ferrara.*

ESTE, Beata Beatrice I d' (d. 1226). Ferrarese noblewoman. Died 1226; dau. of Azo also known as Azzo VI d'Este (1170–1212), 1st lord of Ferrara (r. 1208–1212), and Leonora of Savoy.

ESTE, Beata Beatrice II d' (d. 1262). Ferrarese noblewoman. Died 1262; dau. of Azzo VII Novello d'Este, lord of Ferrara (d. 1264) and Giovanna d'Este.

ESTE, Beatrice d' (d. 1245). Queen of Hungary. Name variations: Beatrix of Este. Died in 1245; dau. of Aldobrandino I d'Este (d. 1215), podesta of Ferrara; became third wife of Andrew II, king of Hungary (r. 1205–1235), May 14, 1234; children: Istvan also known as Stephen (b. 1235), duke of Slavonia.

ESTE, Beatrice d' (fl. 1290s). Ferrarese noblewoman. Name variations: Beatrice d'Anjou. Second wife of Azzo VIII d'Este, lord of Ferrara (r. 1293–1308).

ESTE, Beatrice d' (d. 1334). Milanese noblewoman. Name variations: Beatrice Visconti. Died 1334; dau. of Giacoma d'Este and Obizzo II d'Este (1247–1293), lord of Ferrara; m. Nino Visconti; m. Galeazzo I Visconti (c. 1277–1328), lord of Milan (r. 1322–1328); children: Azzo Visconti (1302–1339), lord of Milan (r. 1328–1339).

ESTE, Beatrice d' (fl. 1300s). Ferrarese noblewoman. Name variations: Beatrice Gonzaga. Born Beatrice Gonzaga; m. Nicholas also known as Niccolo I d'Este, lord of Ferrara (r. 1317–1344).

ESTE, Beatrice d' (fl. 1350s). Ferrarese noblewoman. Born Beatrice da Camino; m. Aldobrandino III d'Este (1335–1361), lord of Ferrara; children: Obizzo (1356–1388).

ESTE, Beatrice d' (1427–1497). Ferrarese noblewoman. Name variations: Beatrice da Correggio or Correggio; Beatrice Sforza. Born 1427; died 1497; illeg. dau. of Nicholas also known as Niccolo III d'Este (1383–1441), 12th marquis of Ferrara; m. Niccolo da Coreggio; m. Tristano Sforza (d. 1477); children: Niccolo da Correggio (1450–1508, who m. Cassandra Colleoni).

ESTE, Beatrice d' (1475–1497). Duchess of Milan. Name variations: Bianca or Beatrice Sforza; Beatriz; Bice; Duchess of Bari. Born June 29, 1475, in Ferrara, Italy; died in childbirth, Jan 2, 1497, in Milan, Italy; dau. of Ercole I d'Este (1431–1505), 2nd duke of Ferrara and Modena, and Leonora of Aragon (1450–1493); sister of Isabella d'Este (1474–1539) and Alfonso I (1476–1534), 3rd duke of Ferrara, who m. Lucrezia Borgia; m. Louis also known as Ludovico or Lodovico il Moro Sforza (1451–1508), duke of Milan (r. 1479–1500), Jan 17, 1491; daughter-in-law of Bianca Maria Visconti (1423–1470); children: Ercole, duke of Milan (b. 1493, called Maximilian); Francesco Maria (b. 1495), duke of Milan (r. 1521–1535). ❖ Famed for her patronage of artists during the Italian Renaissance; moved to Naples (1477); betrothed (1480); returned to Ferrara (1485); became a trusted companion and political associate of husband; established court at Milan (1491); became duchess of Milan (1494); one of Europe's most admired women, began developing a keen interest in the patronage of up-and-coming painters, sculptors, and poets (1495), who were rewarded handsomely if their work pleased her; corresponded regularly with sister. ❖ See also Julia Cartwright, *Beatrice D'Este, Duchess of Milan: A Study of the Renaissance* (Dent, 1899); and *Women in World History.*

ESTE, Bianca Maria d' (1440–1506). Ferrarese noblewoman. Born 1440; died 1506; illeg. dau. of Nicholas also known as Niccolo III d'Este (1383–1441), 12th marquis of Ferrara; m. Galeotto Pico della Mirandola.

ESTE, Catherine d' (fl. 1700). Duchess of Savoy-Carignan. Flourished in 1700; m. Emmanuel Philibert, duke of Savoy-Carignan (d. 1709); children: Victor Amadeus (d. 1741) and possibly Anna Victoria of Savoy.

ESTE, Costanza d' (fl. 1200s). **Ferrarese noblewoman.** Name variations: Costanza Aldobrandeschi. Dau. of Mambilia d'Este and Azzo VII Novello d'Este, lord of Ferrara (d. 1264); m. Umberto Aldobrandeschi.

ESTE, Costanza d' (fl. 1200s). **Ferrarese noblewoman.** Name variations: Costanza della Scala. Born Costanza della Scala; 2nd wife of Obizzo II d'Este (1247–1293), lord of Ferrara and Modena (r. 1264–1293).

ESTE, Cunegunda d' (c. 1012–1055). **Marquise of Este.** Born c. 1012; died 1055; dau. of Guelph, also known as Welf of Altdorf, and Imagi of Luxemburg (c. 1000–1057); m. Azo also known as Azzo II, marquis of Este; children: Guelph, also known as Welf IV, duke of Bavaria.

ESTE, Eleanora d' (1450–1493). *See Leonora of Aragon.*

ESTE, Eleonora d' (1515–1575). **Italian abbess.** Name variations: Leonora; Leonor d'Este. Born 1515; died 1575; dau. of Lucrezia Borgia (1480–1519) and Alfonso I d'Este, 3rd duke of Ferrara and Modena; niece of Isabella d'Este (1474–1539). ❖ Abbess of the monastery of Corpus Domini in Ferrara.

ESTE, Eleonora d' (1537–1581). **Ferrarese princess.** Name variations: Leonora d'Este; Eleonora of Este. Born June 19, 1537; died Feb 10, 1581; dau. of Renée of France (1510–1575) and Hercules II also known as Ercole II (1508–1559), 4th duke of Ferrara and Modena; sister of Alfonso II (1533–1597), 5th duke of Ferraro and Modena; never married; no children. ❖ Best known as the beloved of Italian poet Torquato Tasso (1544–1595). ❖ See also *Women in World History.*

ESTE, Elisa d' (–1329). **Ferrarese noblewoman.** Name variations: Elisa Bonacolsi. Died 1329; dau. of Alda d'Este and Aldobrandino II, lord of Ferrara (d. 1326); m. Passarino Bonacolsi.

ESTE, Elisabetta d' (fl. 1500). **Ferrarese noblewoman.** Name variations: Elisabetta Pio. Illeg. dau. of Ippolito I d'Este (1479–1520, a cardinal); m. Giberto Pio.

ESTE, Giacoma d' (fl. 1300). **Ferrarese noblewoman.** Name variations: Giacoma de Fieschi. First wife of Obizzo II d'Este (1247–1293), lord of Ferrara (r. 1264–1293); children: Azzo VIII, lord of Ferrara (r. 1293–1308); Aldobrandino II (d. 1326); Francesco (murdered in 1312); Beatrice d'Este (d. 1334). Obizzo's 2nd wife was Costanza d'Este.

ESTE, Giacoma d' (fl. 1300s). **Ferrarese noblewoman.** Name variations: Giacoma de' Pepoli. First wife of Obizzo III d'Este (1294–1352), lord of Ferrara.

ESTE, Gigliola d' Marquesa of Ferrara. Name variations: Gigliola da Carrara. Married Nicholas also known as Niccolo III d'Este (1383–1441), 12th marquis of Ferrara, 1397.

ESTE, Ginevra d' (1414–1440). **Ferrarese noblewoman.** Name variations: Ginevra Malatesta. Born in 1414 (some sources cite 1419); died in 1440; dau. of Parisina (Malatesta) d'Este and Nicholas also known as Niccolo III d'Este (1383–1441), 12th marquis of Ferrara; m. Sigismondo Pandolfo Malatesta (1417–1486); children: Roberto Malatesta (d. 1484). Sigismondo's 2nd wife was Polissena Sforza; his 3rd wife was Isotta degli Atti.

ESTE, Giovanna d' (fl. 1240s). **Ferrarese noblewoman.** Name variations: Joanna. First wife of Azzo VII Novello d'Este, lord of Ferrara (d. 1264); children: Rinaldo d'Este (d. 1251); Beata Beatrice II d'Este (d. 1262). Azzo's 2nd wife was Mambilia d'Este.

ESTE, Giovanna d' (fl. 1280s). **Ferrarese noblewoman.** Name variations: Joanna. Born Giovanna Orsini; 1st wife of Azzo VIII d'Este, lord of Ferrara (r. 1293–1308). Azzo's 2nd wife was Beatrice d'Este (fl. 1290s).

ESTE, Giovanna d' (fl. 1300s). **Ferrarese noblewoman.** Name variations: Giovanna de' Roberti. First wife of Alberto (1347–1393), lord of Ferrara. Alberto's 2nd wife was Isotta d'Este (fl. 1300s).

ESTE, Giulia d'. *See Rovere, Giulia della.*

ESTE, Isabella d' (1474–1539). **Marchioness of Mantua.** Name variations: Isabel, Isabeau; Isabella Gonzaga; Marchioness or Marchesa of Mantua. Born May 18, 1474, in Ferrara, Italy; died Feb 13, 1539, in Mantua, Italy; dau. of Ercole I d'Este (1431–1505), 2nd duke of Ferrara and Modena, and Leonora of Aragon (1450–1493); sister of Beatrice d'Este (1475–1497) and Alfonso I (1476–1534), 3rd duke of Ferrara, who m. Lucrezia Borgia; m. Francesco also known as Gianfrancesco Gonzaga (1466–1519), 4th marquis of Mantua (r. 1484–1519), Feb 11, 1490; children: Eleonora Gonzaga (1493–1543); Margherita (1496–1496); Frederigo also known as Federico (1500–1540), 5th marquis of Mantua (r. 1519–1540); Ippolita Gonzaga (1503–1570, became

a nun); Ercole (1505–1563, a cardinal); Ferrante (1507–1557, prince of Guastalla); Paola Gonzaga (1508–1569, became a nun). Francesco Gonzaga also had two illeg. daughters. ❖ Important leader of the Italian Renaissance as patron of the arts, as well as a politician who worked to advance her family's power and prestige; betrothed (1480); established court at Mantua (1490); corresponded regularly with sister; became a trusted companion and political associate of husband; mastered the endless diplomacies and intrigues which made up Italian politics and seemed to enjoy the responsibilities and burdens of rule; began artistic patronage (1495); during wartime, governed Mantua in husband's place (1495–1519); negotiated with the French in the interests of Milan; became famed across Europe for her patronage of the Renaissance's greatest artists, including Castiglione, Niccolo da Correggio, Bembo, Bellini, Michelangelo, and Titian; commissioned Leonardo da Vinci to sketch portrait (1499); arranged for husband's release from a Venice prison (1509), then continued acting as chief administrator of Mantua when he returned to war; following husband's death (1519), spent the next few years actively involved in the administration of her son's reign; created one of the finest libraries in Europe. ❖ See also Julia Cartwright, *Isabella D'Este: Marchioness of Mantua (1474–1539): A Study of the Renaissance in Two Volumes* (Dent, 1903); George R. Marek, *The Bed and the Throne: The life of Isabella D'Este* (Harper, 1976); and *Women in World History.*

ESTE, Isotta d' (fl. 1300s). **Ferrarese noblewoman.** Name variations: Isotta Albaresani. Second wife of Alberto (1347–1393), lord of Ferrara; children: Nicholas also known as Niccolo III d'Este, lord of Ferrara. Alberto's 1st wife was Giovanna d'Este (fl. 1300s).

ESTE, Isotta d' (1425–1456). **Ferrarese noblewoman.** Name variations: Isotta da Montefeltro; Isotta Frangipani. Born 1425; died 1456; illeg. dau. of Nicholas also known as Niccolo III d'Este (1383–1441), 12th marquis of Ferrara; m. Oddo Antonio da Montefeltro; m. Stefano Frangipani.

ESTE, Lippa d' Ferrarese noblewoman. Name variations: Lippa degli Ariosti. Second wife of Obizzo III d'Este (1294–1352), lord of Ferrara; children: Alda d'Este (1333–1381); Aldobrandino III (1335–1361); Niccolo II Zoppo (1338–1388); Ugo (1344–1370); Alberto (1347–1393).

ESTE, Lucia d' (1419–1437). **Ferrarese noblewoman.** Name variations: Lucia Gonzaga. Born in 1419; died in 1437; dau. of Parisina d'Este and Nicholas also known as Niccolo III d'Este (1383–1441), 12th marquis of Ferrara; m. Carlo Gonzaga.

ESTE, Lucrezia d' Ferrarese noblewoman. Name variations: Lucrezia of Montferrat; Lucrecia. Married Rinaldo d'Este (illegitimate son of Nicholas also known as Niccolo III d'Este [1383–1441], 12th marquis of Ferrara).

ESTE, Lucrezia d' (d. 1516/18). **Ferrarese princess.** Name variations: Lucrezia d'Este Bentivoglio. Born before 1473; died in 1516/18; illeg. dau. of Hercules I also known as Ercole I (1431–1505), 2nd duke of Ferrara and Modena; half-sister of Isabella d'Este (1474–1539) and Beatrice d'Este (1475–1497); m. Annibale Bentivoglio.

ESTE, Lucrezia d' (1535–1598). **Duchess of Urbino.** Name variations: Lucrezia della Rovere. Born 1535; died 1598; dau. of Hercules II also known as Ercole II (1508–1559), 4th duke of Ferrara and Modena, and Renée of France (1510–1575); sister of Eleonora d'Este (1515–1575); m. Francesco Maria II della Rovere, duke of Urbino.

ESTE, Mambilia d' (fl. 1200s). **Ferrarese noblewoman.** Name variations: Mambilia Pelavicino. Second wife of Azzo VII Novello d'Este, lord of Ferrara (d. 1264); children: Costanza d'Este (who m. Umberto Aldobrandeschi). Azzo's 1st wife was Giovanna d'Este (fl. 1240s).

ESTE, Margherita d' (1418–1439). *See Gonzaga, Margherita.*

ESTE, Margherita d' (d. 1452). **Ferrarese noblewoman.** Name variations: Margherita Pio. Died 1452; illeg. dau. of Nicholas also known as Niccolo III d'Este (1383–1441), 12th marquis of Ferrara; m. Galasso Pio.

ESTE, Margherita d' (1564–1618). *See Gonzaga, Margherita.*

ESTE, Maria Beatrice d' (1750–1829). *See Maria Beatrice of Modena.*

ESTE, Mary Beatrice d' (1658–1718). *See Mary of Modena.*

ESTE, Parisina d' (fl. 1400). **Marquesa of Ferrara.** Name variations: Parisina Malatesta. Married Nicholas also known as Niccolo III d'Este (1383–1441), 12th marquis of Ferrara, in 1418; children: Ginevra d'Este (1414–1440); Lucia d'Este (1419–1437). Niccolo III was also m. to

Ricciarda d'Este and had many illegitimate children: Ugo Aldobrandino (1405–1425); Meliaduse (1406–1452); Leonello (1407–1450, who was eventually legitimated and became 13th marquis of Ferrara); Borso (1413–1471, 1st duke of Modena and Ferrara); Alberto (1415–1502); Gurone Maria (d. 1484); Isotta d'Este (1425–1456); Beatrice d'Este (1427–1497); Rinaldo (d. 1503); Margherita d'Este (d. 1452); Bianca Maria d'Este (1440–1506); Baldassare; and others.

ESTE, Pizzocara d' (fl. 1400s). Ferrarese noblewoman. Name variations: Married Sigismondo d'Este (1433–1507); children: Ercole di Sigismondo d'Este (who m. Angela Sforza); Bianca d'Este (who m. Alberigo da San Severino); Diana d'Este (who m. Uguccione di Ambrogio de' Contrari).

ESTE, Ricciarda d' Marquesa of Ferrara. Name variations: Ricciarda da Saluzzo. Married Nicholas also known as Niccolo III d'Este (1383–1441), 12th marquis of Ferrara, in 1431; children: Ercole I (1431–1505), 2nd duke of Ferrara and Modena (who m. Leonora of Aragon [1450–1493]); Sigismondo (1433–1507). Niccolo III was also m. to Parisina d'Este and had many illegitimate children: Ugo Aldobrandino (1405–1425); Meliaduse (1406–1452); Leonello (1407–1450, who was eventually legitimated and became the 13th marquis of Ferrara); Borso (1413–1471, 1st duke of Modena and Ferrara); Alberto (1415–1502); Gurone Maria (d. 1484); Isotta d'Este (1425–1456); Beatrice d'Este (1427–1497); Rinaldo (d. 1503); Margherita d'Este (d. 1452); Bianca Maria d'Este (1440–1506); Baldassare; and others.

ESTE, Taddea d' (1365–1404). Ferrarese noblewoman. Name variations: Thaddaea. Born 1365; died 1404; dau. of Verde d' and Nicholas also known as Niccolo II Zoppo (1338–1388), lord of Ferrara; m. Francesco Novello da Carrara.

ESTE, Verde d' (fl. 1300s). Ferrarese noblewoman. Name variations: Verde della Scala; Virida. Possibly dau. of Mastino II della Scala, count of Verona; possibly sister of Beatrice della Scala (1340–1384); m. Nicholas also known as Niccolo II Zoppo (1338–1388), lord of Ferrara; children: Taddea d'Este (1365–1404, who m. Francesco Novello da Carrara).

ESTE, Virginia d' (b. 1573?). Duchess of Modena. Name variations: Virginia de Medici. Born c. 1573; dau. of Camilla Martelli and Cosimo I de Medici (1519–1574), grand duke of Tuscany (r. 1569–1574); m. Cesare d'Este (1562–1628), duke of Ferrara (r. 1597), duke of Modena (r. 1597–1628).

ESTEFAN, Gloria (1957—). Cuban-American vocalist. Name variations: Gloria Fajardo. Born Gloria Maria Milagrosa Fajardo on Sept 1, 1957, in Havana, Cuba; graduate of University of Miami; m. Emilio Estefan, Jr. (keyboardist), 1978; children: Nayib and Emily Marie. ❖ Moved to Miami when father fled Castro regime (1959); spent early life nursing father, who was injured in Vietnam; joined Emilio Estefan's wedding band, the Miami Latin Boys (1975), which soon became The Miami Sound Machine; sang Spanish vocals on band's debut album (1979) and vocals on Sound Machine's 1st all-English album *Primitive Love* (1985); scored hits with "Conga" (1985), "Bad Boy" (1986), "Words Get in the Way" (1986), "Rhythm is Gonna Get You" (1987), "Anything for You" (1988), and "1-2-3" (1988); followed last Sound Machine album *Let it Loose* (1987) with successful solo album debut *Cuts Both Ways* (1989); reached #1 with solo hit "Don't Wanna Lose You" (1989); broke several vertebrae when tour bus was hit by a tractor-trailer (1990); released 1st solo all-Spanish album *Mi Tierra* (1993); moved into adult contemporary arena with albums *Destiny* (1996) and *Gloria!* (1998); made acting debut in film *Music of the Heart* (1999).

ESTEFANIA OF BARCELONA (fl. 1038). Queen of Navarre. Name variations: Etienette of Barcelona; Estefania of Foix. Fl. c. 1038; dau. of Bernard I, count of Foix, and Gersenda, countess of Bigorre; m. Garcia III, king of Navarre, 1038; children: Sancho IV (1039–1076), king of Navarre (r. 1054–1076); Fernando (who m. Nuna de Biscaya); Raimundo also known as Ramon of Navarre (d. 1084); Cameros; Hermesinda (who m. Fortun Sanchez de Yarnoz); Mayor of Navarre (who m. Guy II, count of Beaune and Mascon); Urraca (who m. Garcia, count of Najera and Granon); Jimena. ❖ See also *Women in World History*.

ESTELITA (1928–1966). See *Rodriguez, Estelita*.

ESTES, Ellen (1978—). American water-polo player. Born Oct 13, 1978, in Novato, California; dau. of Carole and Gary Estes; attended Stanford University. ❖ Center, won a team silver medal at Sydney Olympics (2000) and a team bronze at Athens Olympics (2004); won World championship (2003).

ESTEVE-COLL, Elizabeth (1938—). English university administrator and museum director. Name variations: Dame Elizabeth Esteve-Coll. Born Elizabeth Anne Loosemore Kingdon, Oct 14, 1938, in Ripon, North Yorkshire, England; dau. of Percy Williams Kingdon and Nora Rose Kingdon; graduate of London University, 1976; m. José Esteve-Coll, 1960 (died 1980). ❖ Director of London's Victoria and Albert Museum, became head of learning resources at Kingston Polytechnic (1977) and a university librarian at Surrey University (1982); joined Victoria and Albert (V&A) Museum staff as keeper of national art library (1985); appointed director of museum (1988), the 1st woman director of a national arts collection; upgraded café to attract more visitors and was accused of diminishing the stature of museum by appealing to low-brow desires of public; resigned from museum to become vice-chancellor of University of East Anglia (1995). Awarded Dame of British Empire (DBE, 1995).

ESTHER (fl. 475 BCE). Hebrew queen. Name variations: Edissa. Flourished around 475 BCE; dau. of Abihail; niece of Mordecai; m. Xerxes I (c. 518–465, known in the Biblical text as Ahasuerus or Assuerus), king of Persia (r. 486–465); children: Darius, Hystaspes, and Artaxerxes. ❖ In the ahistorical Old Testament *Book of Esther* (written 2nd century BCE?), is portrayed as an Israelite beauty who became the wife of the Persian king, Xerxes (Ahasuerus in the Biblical text), despite her religious background which was kept hidden from Ahasuerus for a time; her rise is credited to the fall of Ahasuerus' previous wife, Vashti; said to have been the savior of her husband, her uncle, and her people; protected husband against a plot organized by Vashti's partisans; saved her uncle Mordecai and the Israelites from Haman, leading to a general celebration recreated in the feast of Purim. ❖ See also *Women in World History*.

ESTIENNE, Nicole d' (c. 1544–c. 1596). French poet. Name variations: Nicole Estienne; (pseudonym) Olympe. Born Nicole d'Estienne, c. 1544; died c. 1596; dau. of Charles d'Estienne. ❖ Wrote humorous criticism of marriage and men, *Apologie ou défense pour les femmes* (also known as *Misère de la femme Mariée*).

ESTÓPINAL, Renee (1949—). American ballet dancer. Name variations: Renee Estopinal. Born Feb 22, 1949, in Los Angeles, California. ❖ Moved to NY to train at school of American Ballet; began performing professionally with New York City Ballet, where she appeared in numerous repertory works including premiere of *Stravinksy Symphony in C* (1968), Balanchine's *Agon*, as well as *Episodes, Stars and Stripes* and *Chaconne*; performed Theme for Jerome Robbins' *The Goldberg Variations* (1971).

ESTRAIGUES, Henriette d' (1579–1633). See *Entragues, Henriette d'*.

ESTRÉES, Angélique, d' (fl. 16th c.). French abbess. Name variations: Abbess of Maubisson. Dau. of Antoine d'Estrées, marquis of Coeuvres, and Françoise Babou de la Bourdaisière d'Estrées; sister of François-Annibal d'Estrées, bishop of Noyon and constable of France, and Gabrielle d'Estrées (1573–1599). ❖ Had numerous affairs, then joined the Convent of Maubisson, where she became abbess; not only continued to take lovers, but encouraged the young nuns in her charge to do the same, outraging even the lenient church hierarchy of the time; was eventually banished to the Renaissance equivalent of a home for delinquents, where she lived out the remainder of her life under close observation. ❖ See also *Women in World History*.

ESTRÉES, Diane, d' (b. 1572). French author. Name variations: Dame de Balagny. Born in 1572; dau. of Antoine d'Estrées, marquis of Coeuvres, and Françoise Babou de la Bourdaisière d'Estrées; sister of François-Annibal d'Estrées, bishop of Noyon and constable of France, and Gabrielle d'Estrées (1573–1599); 2nd wife of Louis de Balagny, Prince de Cambrai; children: several. ❖ Just a year older than sister Gabrielle and very close to her sister, provided much of what is known about Gabrielle in her book *Memorial to Gabrielle, Duchess of Beaufort*. ❖ See also *Women in World History*.

ESTRÉES, Françoise Babou de la Bourdaisière, Dame d' (fl. 16th c.). Notorious French woman. Name variations: Françoise Babou de la Bourdaisière at the chateau La Bourdaisière near Tours; dau. of Jean Babou (prominent soldier, politician, and diplomat in reign of Henry II); m. Antoine d'Estrées, marquis of Coeuvres; eloped with Antoine, Marquis de Tourzel-Alègre, 1583; children: (with Antoine d'Estrées) 8, including François-Annibal d'Estrées; François-Louis d'Estrées; Françoise d'Estrées; Julienne d'Estrées; Diane d'Estrées (b. 1572); Gabrielle d'Estrées (1573–1599); Angélique d'Estrées; (with Antoine Tourzel-Alègre) one daughter. ❖ After marriage, embarked on a number of casual affairs but then took herself out of circulation to give birth to eight children in as many years, including Gabrielle; at age 40, eloped with Antoine, Marquis de Tourzel-Alègre, a much younger man, and lived openly with him in Picardy, bearing an illegitimate daughter and becoming a symbol of sin for her country neighbors; was murdered with her lover (June 1592). ❖ See also *Women in World History.*

ESTRÉES, Gabrielle d' (1573–1599). French royal mistress. Name variations: Gabrielle d'Estrees; Duchess of Beaufort or Duchess de Beaufort; Duchess d'Etampes or Duchess d'Étampes; Marquise de Monceaux or Marchioness of Monceaux; Dame de Liencourt; Dame de Vandeuil. Born Dec 23, 1573, at Coeuvres, in Picardy (some sources erroneously cite 1565 in the château at la Bourdaisière); died in childbirth of puerperal convulsions, April 10, 1599, in Paris, France; dau. of Antoine d'Estrées, marquis of Coeuvres, and Françoise Babou de la Bourdaisière; sister of François-Annibal d'Estrées, bishop of Noyon and constable of France; m. Nicolas d'Amerval, Sieur de Liencourt (Baron de Benais), June 1592 (div. 1594); mistress of Henry of Navarre also known as Henry IV (1553–1610), king of France (r. 1589–1610); children: (with Henry IV) Caesar, duke of Vendôme; Catherine Henriette de Vendôme, duchess of Elbeuf; Alexander, Chevalier de Vendôme. ❖ Mistress of the king of France who became queen of the realm in all but name; though she was only one of 56 documented mistresses of Henry IV, was the only woman to whom he remained faithful; with Henry, had 3 children, all legitimized by royal decree, and it was only her sudden death at 26 that thwarted their probable marriage; possessed a keen intellect, irresistible charm, and an inborn political savvy, all of which she used to advance Henry's cause of a united France. Historians credit her with promulgating the Edict of Nantes (1598), a decree guaranteeing religious freedom to the Protestants of France, which ended the Wars of the Faith. ❖ See also Adrien Desclozeaux, "Gabrielle d'Estrées" (monograph, 1887); Paul Lewis, [Noel B. Gerson], *Lady of France* (Funk, 1963); and *Women in World History.*

ESTRELA MOURA, Elaine (1982—). Brazilian soccer player. Name variations: known simply as Elaine. Born Nov 1, 1982, in Brazil. ❖ Midfielder, won a team silver medal at Athens Olympics (2004).

ESTRICH, Susan R. (1952—). American lawyer, political activist and feminist. Born 1952 in Lynn, Massachusetts; Wellesley College, BA with highest honors, 1974; Harvard Law School, JD magna cum laude, 1977; m. Marty Kaplan (communications professor); children: 2. ❖ The 1st female president of the *Harvard Law Review* (1976), served as professor in law school at Harvard; served as deputy national issues director for Edward F. Kennedy's presidential campaign (1980), senior policy advisor to Walter F. Mondale (1984), executive director of Democratic National Committee, special counsel to Senate Judiciary Committee, and special assistant to Senator Edward F. Kennedy; appointed manager for Democrat Michael Dukakis's presidential campaign (1987), becoming 1st woman to manage a major presidential campaign; became Robert Kingsley Professor of Law and Political Science at University of Southern California Law School. Writings include *Real Rape* (1987), (co-author) *Dangerous Offenders: The Elusive Target of Justice* (1985), *Getting Away with Murder: How Politics is Destroying the Criminal Justice System* (1998) and *Sex and Power* (2001).

ESTRID. *Variant of Estrith.*

ESTRITH (fl. 1017–1032). Danish princess. Name variations: Astrid; Astrith; Estrid; Margaret of Denmark. Dau. of Sven or Sweyn I Forkbeard, king of Denmark (r. 985–1014), king of England, and Sigrid the Haughty; m. Ulf also known as Wolf (c. 967–1027), jarl of Denmark, c. 1018; 2nd wife of Richard II, duke of Normandy (div.); children: (1st m.) Beorn, earl of England; Asbjorn; Sweyn Ulfson also known as Sweyn Estridson or Svend II (b. around 1019), king of Denmark (r. 1047–1074).

ÉTAMPES, Anne de Pisseleu d'Heilly, Duchesse d' (1508–c. 1580). Duchess and mistress of Francis I. Name variations: Anne d'Heilly; duchess of Etampes. Born Anne de Pisseleu d'Heilly in 1508; died c. 1580; dau. of Guillaume de Pisseleu, sieur d'Heilly (noble of Picardy); m. Jean de Brosse, eventually the duc d'Étampes; mistress of Francis I, king of France (r. 1515–1547). ❖ Came to the French court before 1522 as one of the maids of honor of Louise of Savoy; became mistress of Francis I, probably on his return from captivity at Madrid (1526); pretty, witty and cultured, succeeded in holding the king's favor until his death and had considerable influence over him, especially toward the end of his reign; also co-operated with the king's sister, Margaret of Angoulême, and used her influence to elevate and enrich her family, with the result that her uncle, Antoine Sanguin (d. 1559), was made bishop of Orléans

(1535) and a cardinal (1539); following death of Francis I (1547), was dismissed from court by rival Diane de Poitiers; died in obscurity. ❖ See also *Women in World History.*

ÉTAMPES, countess of. *See Marguerite of Orleans.*

ÉTAMPES, duchess of. *See Estrées, Gabrielle d' (1573–1599).*

ETCHEPARE DE HENESTROSA, Armonía (1914–1994). *See Somers, Armonía.*

ETCHEPARE LOCINO, Armonía (1914–1994). *See Somers, Armonía.*

ETCHERELLI, Claire (1934—). French novelist. Born 1934 in France. ❖ Published *Élise ou la vraie vie* (Elise, or the Real Life, 1967), which won the Prix Femina, then wrote *A Propos de Clémence* (About Clemence, 1971), and *Un Arbre voyageur* (A Travelling Tree, 1978), to form a trilogy; with G. Manceroni and B. Wallon, edited the anthology *Cent poèmes contre le racisme* (1986); in her work, strongly advocated Algerian independence.

ETEYE OF AZEB (fl. 10th c. BCE). *See Sheba, queen of.*

ETHELBERGA. *Variant of Ethelburga.*

ETHELBERGA OF NORTHUMBRIA (d. 647). Queen of Northumbria. Name variations: Aethelburh; Aethelburg; Ethelburga. Died 647; dau. of Bertha of Kent (c. 565–c. 616) and Aethelbert or Ethelbert, king of Kent; sister of Eadbald, king of Kent; m. Edwin (Eadwine) of Northumbria (c. 585–633), 625; children: Ethelhun; Wuscfrea; Ethelthryth; Eanfleda (wife of Oswy, king of Northumbria); grandmother of Elflaed (fl. 640–714), abbess of Whitby. ❖ On marriage, brought a monk named Paulinus to her new kingdom and was instrumental in converting her husband and family members to Christianity, including the king's great-niece Hilda of Whitby. ❖ See also *Women in World History.*

ETHELBURG (fl. 722). Saxon queen. Flourished 722. ❖ As ruler of the Ine tribe, led armies, successfully planned battle strategies, and added territories to her kingdom through her military prowess. ❖ See also *Women in World History.*

ETHELBURGA (d. 665). Saint and abbess. Name variations: Ethelberga; St. Aubierge. Died 665 at Faremoutier, Brie, France; interred at St. Stephen the Martyr Church; dau. of Hereswitha (d. 690) and Anna (635–654), king of East Anglia; half-sister of Sexburga (d. 699?) and Elthelthrith (630–679); niece of Hilda of Whitby. ❖ Was abbess of Faremoutier in Brie, France. Feast day is July 7. ❖ See also *Women in World History.*

ETHELBURGA (d. 676?). Saxon saint and abbess of Barking. Name variations: Aethelburh; Ethelburh; Ethelberga. Died c. 676; sister of Saint Erkonwald. ❖ Served as abbess of a convent at Barking, Essex, and was succeeded by Hildeletha. Feast Day is Oct 11. ❖ See also *Women in World History.*

ETHELBURH (d. 676?). *See Ethelburga.*

ETHELDREDA (d. around 840). Saint. Name variations: Alfrida. Died c. 840; possibly dau. of Offa II, king of Mercia, and Cynethryth (fl. 736–796); possibly sister of Eadburgh (c. 773–after 802). ❖ Lived for some 40 years as a recluse on island of Croyland. Feast day is Aug 2.

ETHELFLAED (869–918). Ruler of Mercia. Name variations: Lady of the Mercians. Originally the Teutonic (Germanic) Æ was used, Aethelflaed or Aethelfleda; this had the value of a short sound before the 11th century, but in some citations was later dropped from common usage, becoming Ethelflaed or Ethelfleda; also Elfleda or Elflida. Born in Wessex in 869; died June 12, 918 (some sources cite 919), in Tamworth, Mercia; eldest dau. of Elswitha (d. 902) and Alfred the Great (848–c. 900), king of the English (r. 871–899); sister of Elfthrith (d. 929); m. Ethelred II, ealdorman of Mercia (r. 879–911), in 886 or 887; children: Elfwyn (c. 882–?). ❖ Constructed a national system of fortifications in partnership with Edward the Elder and contributed to defeat of the Vikings in England; held conference with Alfred and Ethelred II on the subject of the defense of London (898); inherited a portion of the Wiltshire estate of Damerham (899); with husband, leased land in town of Worcester (901); founded monastery of St. Peter and moved the bones of St. Oswald from Northumbria to Gloucester (909); in last years of husband's life, acted as regent and commanded the Mercian army; probably commanded the Mercian contingent during Battle of Tettenhal (909); on death of husband (911), became ruler of Mercia; began building fortresses for defense of Mercia; built fortress at Bremesburh (910); built fortresses of Scargate and Bridgenorth (912) and fortified Tamworth and Stafford (913); fortified Eddisbury and Warwick (914), erected fortresses at Chirbury, Weardburh, and Runcorn (915), and launched expedition against Wales (916); captured the town of Derby (917); defeated Norwegian chieftain Ragnald at 2nd Battle of Corbridge (918); captured Leicester (918); negotiated with Northumbrian Vikings (918). ❖ See also *Women in World History.*

ETHELFLAED (d. 962). Queen of the English. Name variations: Aethelflaeda the Fair; Ethelfled; the White Duck. Died in childbirth in 962 (some sources cite 965) in Wessex, England; interred at Wilton Abbey, Wiltshire; dau. of Ordmaer, an ealdorman, and Ealda; became 1st wife of Edgar the Peaceful (944–975), king of the English (r. 959–975), 959; children: Edward II the Martyr (962–978), king of the English (r. 975–978). ❖ See also *Women in World History.*

ETHELFLAED (d. after 975). Queen of the English. Name variations: Aethelflaed of Domerham. Died after 975; dau. of Elfgar, ealdorman of Wiltshire; 2nd wife of Edmund I the Magnificent (921–946), king of the English (r. 939–946). Edmund's 1st wife was Elfgifu (d. 944).

ETHELFLAEDA (fl. 900s). Abbess of Romsey. Name variations: Aethelflaeda. Fl. in 900s; interred at Romsey Abbey, Hampshire, England; dau. of Edward I the Elder (c. 870–924), king of the English (r. 899–924), and Elflaed (d. 920). ❖ Was a nun at Romsey.

ETHELFLAEDA (c. 963–c. 1016). Abbess at Romsey. Name variations: Aethelflaeda; Ethelfleda. Born c. 963; died c. 1016; dau. of Elfthrith (c. 945–1002) and Edgar (944–975), king of the English (r. 959–975).

ETHELFLED. *Variant of Ethelflaed.*

ETHELFLEDA. *Variant of Ethelfaeda.*

ETHELGEOFU (d. around 896). Saxon princess. Name variations: Aethelgeofu; Ethelgiva. Died c. 896 at Shaftesbury Abbey, Dorset; dau. of Alfred the Great (848–c. 900), king of the English (r. 871–899); and Elswitha (d. 902); sister of Ethelflaed (869–918); never married. ❖ Sometimes referred to as abbess of Shaftesbury.

ETHELMER, Ellis (1834–1913). *See Wolstenholme-Elmy, Elizabeth.*

ETHELREDA (630–679). *See Elthelthrith.*

ETHELREDA (fl. 1090). Queen of Scots. Name variations: Aethelreda. Buried at Dunfermline Abbey, Fife, Scotland; dau. of Gospatric, earl of Northumberland, and Ethelreda; m. Duncan II (c. 1060–1094), king of the Scots (r. 1094), c. 1090; children: William the Noble Dunkeld, earl of Moray.

ETHELSWYTH (c. 843–889). Queen of Mercia. Name variations: Aethelswyth or Æthelswyth. Born c. 843; died in 889; buried at Pavia or Ticino, Italy; dau. of Ethelwulf, king of the English, and Osburga (?–c. 855); sister of Alfred the Great, king of the English (r. 871–899); m. Burghred, king of Mercia, after April 2, 853. ❖ Became a nun on widowhood; died on pilgrimage to Rome and is buried at either Pavia or Ticino.

ETHELTHRITH OR ETHELTHRYTH (630–679). *See Elthelthrith.*

ETHERIA (fl. 4th c.). *See Egeria.*

ETHERIDGE, Melissa (1961—). American musician and singer. Born May 29, 1961, in Leavenworth, Kansas; attended Boston's Berklee College of Music; was a longtime partner of Julie Cypher (director); children: (adopted) Bailey Jean Cypher and Beckett Cypher. ❖ Taught herself guitar starting at age 8; began performing with country group at 12; recorded songs for soundtrack to movie *Weeds* (1987); released debut album *Melissa Etheridge* (1988); won 1st Grammy for single "Ain't It Heavy" (1992); publicly came out as a lesbian (1993); released singles "Like the Way I Do" (1988), "Come to My Window" (1994), "I'm the Only One" (1994) and "I Want to Come Over" (1996); sang and played guitar on such albums as *Brave and Crazy* (1989), *Never Enough* (1992), *Yes I Am* (1993), *Your Little Secret* (1995), *Breakdown* (1999), and *Skin* (2001); released single "Scarecrow," a tribute to slain gay Wyoming college student Matthew Shepard (1999); received significant media attention for longterm relationship with Julie Cypher and for raising two children born to Cypher, both fathered through artificial insemination by musician David Crosby; announced breakup with Cypher (2000).

ETHERINGTON, Marie Susan. *See Tempest, Marie.*

ETHIOPIA, empress of.
See Menetewab (c. 1720–1770).
See Taytu (c. 1850–1918).
See Menen (1899–1962).
See Zauditu (1876–1930).

ETHIOPIA, princess of (1919–1942). *See Tsahai Haile Selassie.*

ETHIOPIA, queen of (fl. 10th c. BCE). *See Sheba, queen of.*

ETHRIDGE, Mary Camille (1964—). American basketball player. Born April 21, 1964, in US. ❖ At Seoul Olympics, won a gold medal in team competition (1988).

ETIENETTE OF BARCELONA (fl. 1038). *See Estefania of Barcelona.*

ETRURIA, queen of (1782–1824). *See Maria Luisa of Etruria.*

ETTEKOVEN, Harriet van (1961—). *See van Ettekoven, Harriet.*

ETTING, Ruth (1896–1978). American pop singer. Born Nov 23, 1896, in David City, Nebraska; died Sept 24, 1978, in Colorado Springs, Colorado; only child of Winifred and Alfred Etting; attended Chicago Academy of Fine Arts; m. Martin "Moe" Snyder, 1922 (div. 1937); m. Myrl Alderman, 1938 (died 1966); children: none. ❖ Known as "the radio canary" during the golden age of network radio in 1920s and 1930s, began singing career shortly after World War I, as a chorus girl in a Chicago nightclub; went on the vaudeville circuit (1924); made New York debut (1927); appeared for 5 consecutive years in The Ziegfeld Follies, where she established her reputation as a so-called "torch singer"; appeared in Broadway musical revues and short films and made her national network radio debut (1930); retired from show business after public scandal involving her ex-husband (1937), but briefly revived her career 10 years later; her life formed the basis of the 1955 film *Love Me or Leave Me;* films include *Roman Scandals* (1933), *The Gift of Gab* (1935), *Hips, Hips, Hooray* (1939), and some 30 musical shorts.

EU, Comtesse d' or Condessa de (1846–1921). *See Isabel of Brazil.*

EUDOCIA (c. 400–460). East Roman empress. Name variations: Aelia Eudocia; Aelia Licinia Eudocia; Athenais; Athenaïs; Athenaïs-Eudokia of Athens; Eudocia Augusta; Eudociae. Born Athenaïs in Athens or Antioch c. 400; died peacefully in Jerusalem on Oct 20, 460; dau. of Leontius (Athenian sophist); educated in Athens by father, and by grammarians Hyperechius and Orion in Constantinople and Jerusalem; m. Theodosius II, East Roman emperor (r. 408–450), June 7, 421; children: Licinia Eudoxia (b. 422); Flaccilla (d. 431); Arcadius (d. before 450). ❖ After death of father Leontius, left Athens for Constantinople; was baptized there and betrothed to Theodosius II (421); though baptized a Christian upon marriage to Theodosius II, is said to have admired classical culture and to have harbored sympathies for learned pagans throughout her life; proclaimed Augusta (423); was thought to have influenced the foundation of the University of Constantinople (425); saw marriage of daughter Licinia Eudoxia to West Roman Emperor Valentinian III (437); made pilgrimage to Jerusalem and restored walls and built fortifications, an episcopal palace, and the church of St. Stephen, in addition to many churches and shelters for pilgrims, the poor, and the elderly (438); visited Antioch, where she addressed the senate (438); fell from favor at court and withdrew to Jerusalem (443). ❖ See also Ioanna Tsatsos, *Empress Athenais-Eudocia: A Fifth Century Byzantine Humanist,* trans. by Jean Demos (Holy Cross Orthodox Press, 1977); and *Women in World History.*

EUDOCIA.
See Licinia Eudoxia (b. 422).
See Fabia-Eudocia (fl. 600s CE).

EUDOCIA (fl. 700s). Wife of Justinian II. Fl. in the 700s; 1st wife of Justinian II Rhinotmetos, Byzantine emperor (r. 685–695 and 705–711). ❖ Her fate is unknown. Justinian's 2nd wife was Theodora of the Khazars. ❖ See also *Women in World History.*

EUDOCIA (fl. 700s). Byzantine empress. Name variations: Eudokia. Third wife of Constantine V, Byzantine emperor (r. 741–775); children: Nicephorus; Christopher; Nicetas; Anthimus; Eudocimus. ❖ With husband, defied the Orthodox tradition that prohibited more than two marriages when she married Constantine V who had been married twice before (his 1st wife was Irene of the Khazars, his 2nd Maria [fl. 700s]); had many children, including a set of twins. ❖ See also *Women in World History.*

EUDOCIA (b. 978). Byzantine royal. Born c. 978 CE; dau. of Constantine VIII, Byzantine emperor (r. 1025–1028), and Helena of Alypia; sister of Zoë Porphyrogenita (980–1050) and Theodora Porphyrogenita (c. 989–1056). ❖ See also *Women in World History.*

EUDOCIA (c. 1260–?). Byzantine princess. Born c. 1260; dau. of Theodora Ducas and Michael VIII Paleologus (1224–1282), emperor of Nicaea (r. 1261–1282); m. John of Trebizond. ❖ See also *Women in World History.*

EUDOCIA ANGELINA (fl. 1204). Byzantine empress. Fl. in 1204; dau. of Alexius III Angelus, Byzantine emperor (r. 1195–1203) and Euphrosyne (d. 1203); m. Stephen of Serbia; m. Alexius V Ducas, Nicaean emperor (r. 1204); sister of Anna Angelina (d. 1210?, who m. Theodore I Lascaris). ❖ See also *Women in World History.*

EUDOCIA BAIANE (d. 902). Byzantine empress. Name variations: Baiana. Born in Phrygia; died in childbirth in 902; became 3rd wife of Leo VI the Wise, emperor of Byzantium (r. 886–912), April 901; no children. Leo VI had 4 wives: Theophano (c. 866–897), Zoë Zautzina (c. 870–c. 899), Eudocia Baiane, and Zoë Carbopsina. ❖ Died one year after marriage to Leo, while giving birth to an infant son who also died. ❖ See also *Women in World History.*

EUDOCIA COMNENA (fl. 1100). Byzantine princess. Fl. in 1100; dau. of Irene Ducas (c. 1066–1133) and Alexius I Comnenus, emperor of Byzantium (r. 1081–1118); sister of Anna Comnena (1083–1153/55). ❖ See also *Women in World History.*

EUDOCIA DECAPOLITA (fl. 800s). Byzantine empress. Name variations: Euxokia Dekapolitissa (meaning "10 cities"). Married Michael III the Drunkard (c. 836–867), Byzantine emperor (r. 842–867), 855. ❖ See also *Women in World History.*

EUDOCIA INGERINA (fl. 800s). Byzantine empress. Name variations: Eudokia Ingerina; Ingerina. Fl. in late 800s; dau. of Inger; probably of Scandinavian descent; became 2nd wife of Basil I the Macedonian, Byzantine emperor (r. 867–886), c. 865; also mistress of Michael III the Drunkard, Byzantine emperor (r. 842–867); children: Leo VI the Wise (b. 866), Byzantine emperor (r. 886–912); Alexander (b. 870), Byzantine emperor (r. 912–913); Stephen (born c. 871). Basil's 1st wife was Maria of Macedonia. ❖ Was the unwitting pawn in several royal power struggles during the Byzantine Empire's Golden Age (843–1025); lowly-born, became the mistress of Michael III (he openly favored her over his wife); remained Michael's mistress for about 10 years, then was given in marriage to co-emperor Basil by Michael, though he kept her as his mistress, an unusual arrangement that lasted for a year, until Michael abruptly turned against Basil and conspired to have him killed; after Basil killed Michael and was sole ruler, became empress. ❖ See also *Women in World History.*

EUDOCIA MACREMBOLITISSA (1021–1096). Byzantine empress. Name variations: Eudoxia, Eudokia Makrembolitissa. Born 1021; died 1096 in Constantinople; dau. of John Macrembolites; m. Constantine X Ducas (d. 1067), Byzantine emperor (r. 1059–1067); m. Romanus IV Diogenes, Byzantine emperor (r. 1068–1071), 1068; children: (1st m.) Michael VII Ducas, Byzantine emperor (r. 1071–1078); Andronicus I, Byzantine emperor; Constantine XII, Byzantine emperor; Zoe Ducas; Theodora Ducas; (with Romanus) 2 sons. ❖ While husband lay dying, swore she would never remarry, and was ordered by him to take over the government and assume regency for young son Michael; called by Psellus "an exceedingly clever woman," revered by her sons, exiled the military leader Romanus IV Diogenes, who was suspected of aspiring to the throne; perceiving, however, that she was incapable of averting the invasions that threatened the eastern frontier, revoked her oath, married Romanus, and dispelled the impending danger; when Romanus was taken prisoner by a Turkish army (1071), was sent to a convent by a reluctant son Michael who feared she would restore Romanus to the throne. In another version of the story, set her cap for Romanus and convinced the patriarch of Constantinople to relinquish the copy of her vow of non-marriage; married Romanus and proclaimed him emperor, much to the dismay of Michael (the accession of Romanus meant the end of the Ducae reign). ❖ See also *Women in World History.*

EUDOCIA OF BYZANTIUM (d. 404). Empress of Byzantium. Name variations: Eudocia Augusta; Eudokia; Eudoxia; Eudoxia the Frank. Died in 404 in Constantinople; dau. of Bauto, Frankish military official; m. Arcadius, emperor of Byzantium (r. 395–408), 395; mother-in-law of Eudocia (c. 400–460); children: Theodocius also known as Theodosius II, East Roman emperor (r. 408–450); and stepdaughters Pulcheria (c. 398–453), Arcadia, and Marina. ❖ Married Arcadius of Byzantium, a union arranged by court official Eutropius; when Arcadius proved to be an incompetent ruler easily dominated by advisors, including Eutropius, used her position to help Eutropius' enemies banish

Eutropius from the empire (399); powerful and intelligent, exerted enormous power over the imperial government; became so important that she was given the title "Augusta" (400), which was usually reserved for a woman ruling in her own name; continued to act as the real ruler of Byzantium until death from a miscarriage. ❖ See also *Women in World History.*

EUDOCIA OF BYZANTIUM (fl. 1181). Lady of Montpellier. Name variations: Eudoxia of Byzantium. Fl. 1180. Granddau. of John II Comnenus, Byzantine emperor (r. 1118–1143), and Priska-Irene of Hungary (c. 1085–1133); niece of Manuel I Comnenus, emperor of Byzantium (r. 1143–1180); m. Guillem also known as William VIII, lord of Montpellier; children: Maria of Montpellier (1181–1213). ❖ See also *Women in World History.*

EUDOKIA. *Variant of Eudocia.*

EUDOXIA. *Variant of Eudocia.*

EUDOXIA GORBARTY OR GORBATY (1534–1581). *See Eudoxia Jaroslavovna.*

EUDOXIA JAROSLAVOVNA (1534–1581). Matriarch of the House of Romanov. Name variations: Eudoxia Yaroslavovna; Eudoxia Gorbarty or Gorbaty. Born 1534; died April 4, 1581; possibly dau. of Alexander Gorbaty; m. Nikita Romanov (1530–1586), 1553; children: Fedor also known as Theodore, the Monk Philaret (1558–1633); Alexander (d. 1602); Michael (d. 1602); Vassili (d. 1602); Ivan; Martha Romanov (who m. Boris Tscherkaski); Irina Romanov (who m. Ivan Godunov in 1601); Euphamia Romanov (who m. Ivan Sitzki); Marpha; Anastasia; Anna Romanov (who m. Ivan Troiekurow). ❖ See also *Women in World History.*

EUDOXIA LOPUKHINA (1669–1731). Empress of Russia. Name variations: Eudoxia Lopukhin; Lapuchin; (nickname) Dunka. Born 1669 (some sources cite 1672); died Sept 7, 1731, in Moscow; dau. of Theodore Lopukhin, a boyar; m. Peter I the Great (1672–1725), tsar of Russia (r. 1682–1725), Jan 27, 1689 (marriage repudiated in 1703; div. 1718; children: Alexis (1690–1718, who m. Charlotte of Brunswick-Wolfenbuttel); Alexander (1691–1692). ❖ Extremely devoted to Russian Orthodox Church, was chosen by Natalya Narishkina to become the bride of her son Tsar Peter I, then 17 (1689); separated after giving birth to 2nd son, who did not survive, refused Peter's demand for a divorce so that he could remarry; ordered to a monastery at Suzdal (1698), where she was given the respect her position as tsarina demanded and found the environment more suited to her retiring nature; when Peter, who still wanted to remarry, accused her of adultery (1718), was forced back to Moscow to answer the charges; compelled to make a public confession, was divorced (1718), then allowed to enter another monastery at Ladoga; when her grandson succeeded as Peter II, was convinced to return to Moscow to act as his regent (1728); ill-prepared by the job's demands, gave up title and retired to a monastery at Moscow. ❖ See also *Women in World History.*

EUDOXIA OF MOSCOW (1483–1513). Russian princess. Name variations: Evdokhiia. Born 1483 (some sources cite 1492); died 1513; dau. of Sophia of Byzantium (1448–1503) and Ivan III the Great (1440–1505), grand prince of Moscow (r. 1462–1505); m. Peter Ibragimovich, prince of Khazan. ❖ See also *Women in World History.*

EUDOXIA STRESHNEV (1608–1645). Empress of Russia. Name variations: Streshneva; Streshniev. Born 1608; died Aug 18, 1645; dau. of Lucas Streshnev and Anne Volkonska; became 2nd wife of Mikhail also known as Michael III (1596–1645), tsar of Russia (r. 1613–1645), Feb 5, 1626; children: Irina Romanov (1627–1679); Pelagia (1628–1629); Alexis I (1629–1676), tsar of Russia (r. 1645–1676); Ivan (1631–1639); Anna Romanov (1632–1692, who m. Boris Morozov); Vassili (1633–1645); Sophie Romanov (1634–1676); Tatiana Romanov; Eudoxia Romanov; Marpha Romanov. Michael's 1st wife was Marie Dolgorukova (d. 1625). ❖ See also *Women in World History.*

EUFEMIA. *Variant of Euphemia.*

EUFROZYNA. *Variant of Euphrosyne.*

EUGENIA (d. around 258). Saint. Died c. 258; dau. of Philip, governor of Egypt. ❖ Lived during reign of Valerian (r. 253–259); converted to Christianity when passing a monastery with servants Hyacinth and Protus; given permission by bishop of Heliopolis to pose as a man and become a monk with Hyacinth and Protus; lived at monastery of Heliopolis for a period of time without being discovered; after leaving monastery, converted entire family and founded a convent of Christian virgins in Africa; later returned to Rome, where she was beheaded because she would not abandon her faith. Feast day is Dec 25. ❖ See also *Women in World History.*

EUGÉNIE (1826–1920). French empress. Name variations: Eugenie de Montijo; Eugénie-Marie, Countess of Teba. Born Marie Eugénie Ignace Augustine de Montijo, May 5, 1826, in Grenada, Spain; died July 11, 1920, in Madrid; dau. of Cipriano Guzman y Porto Carrero, count of Teba (subsequently count of Montijo and grandee of Spain) and Manuela Kirkpatrick (1794–1879, dau. of William Kirkpatrick, US consul at Malaga, a Scot by birth and an American by nationality); sister of Paca (1825–1860), duchess of Alba; educated at convent of the Sacré Coeur and Gymnase Normal, Civil et Orthosomatique; m. Louis Napoleon (Napoleon III), emperor of France (r. 1852–1870), Jan 30, 1853 (died Jan 1873); children: son Napoleon Louis ("Lou-Lou," 1856–1879, known during the empire as prince imperial). ❖ One of the most influential women of her age, reigned as empress of France for 17 years (1853–70); as wife of Napoleon III, was praised for her beauty and credited with transforming the Tuileries Palace into a mecca for European society; as Napoleon's health failed and his politics floundered, grew stronger and more resolute in her attempt to protect the throne; acted as regent during his absence (1859, 1865, 1870) and was generally consulted on significant issues, often sitting in on ministerial councils, where she slowly began to assert herself; persuaded husband to maintain a French army in Rome to protect the unpopular Pope Pius IX, a presence that was greatly resented by the Italian government; was also involved in the attempt by France to establish a puppet state in Mexico, under rule of Maximilian and Carlota; when a crisis broke out between Prussia and France, insisted it was an issue that called for war (1870); within 6 weeks, with Napoleon defeated at Sedan and transported to Germany as a prisoner, was dethroned by a mob; fled to England where she was joined by husband, who died soon after. ❖ See also Comte Fleury, *Memoirs of the Empress Eugenie,* Vols. I and II (Appleton, 1920); David Duff, *Eugenie and Napoleon III* (Morrow, 1978); Harold Kurtz, *The Empress Eugénie, 1826–1920* (1964); Jasper Ridley, *Napoleon III and Eugénie* (1980); and *Women in World History.*

EUGENIE (1830–1889). Swedish princess and composer. Name variations: Eugenie Bernadotte. Born Eugenie Charlotte Augusta Amalia Albertina, April 24, 1830; died April 23, 1889; dau. of Queen Josephine Beauharnais (1807–1876, granddau. of Joséphine and Napoleon), and Oscar I (1799–1859), king of Sweden (r. 1844–1859); sister of kings Charles XV and Oscar II. ❖ Wrote compositions which were largely for piano and voice (many were not heard outside Sweden because they were written in Swedish); was among 1st members of Royal Academy of Music, when women were only beginning to be admitted to the ranks of musicians (until mid-19th century, Sweden had a law prohibiting women from playing the organ); in addition to composing, devoted life to the arts and charitable works. ❖ See also *Women in World History.*

EUGÉNIE HORTENSE (1808–1847). Princess of Hohenzollern-Hechingen. Name variations: Eugenie Hortense de Beauharnais. Born Dec 23, 1808; died Sept 1, 1847; dau. of Amalie Auguste (1788–1851) and Eugene de Beauharnais, duke of Leuchtenburg (d. 1824); m. Frederick-William, prince of Hohenzollern-Hechingen, May 22, 1826. ❖ See also *Women in World History.*

EULALIA (290–304). Roman Christian martyr and saint. Name variations: Eulalia of Barcelona. Born 290; died 304. ❖ Born of Christian parents, was a 14-year-old Roman virgin who was tortured then burned alive for not disavowing her faith during the persecution of Diocletian (there is some confusion as to whether there were 2 Eulalias who died under similar circumstances—Eulalia of Barcelona and Eulalia of Mérida—or if this is one and the same girl). Highly honored in Spain, feast day is Feb 12. ❖ See also *Women in World History.*

EULALIA (1864–1958). Spanish princess and duchess of Galliera. Name variations: Eulalia de Asis de la Piedad, infanta of Spain. Born Mary Eulalia Francesca di Assisi Margaret Roberta Isabel Francesca de Paola Christine Maria de la Piedad, Feb 12, 1864; died March 8, 1958; dau. of Isabella II (1830–1904), queen of Spain, and Francisco de Asiz; m. Anthony or Antoine Bourbon, 4th duke of Galliera; children: Alphonso Bourbon, 5th duke of Galliera (b. 1886); Luis Fernando (1888–1945). ❖ See also *Women in World History.*

EULEVSKAYA, Lolita. *See Milchina, Lolita.*

EULOGIA PALEOLOGINA (fl. 1200s). Byzantine of the Paleologi family. Name variations: Eulogia (Irene) of Byzantium; Irene Paleologina or Palaeologina. Dau. of Andronicus Paleologus and Theodora Paleologina; sister of Michael VIII Paleologus, emperor of Nicaea (r. 1261–1282); children: Maria Paleologina (fl. 1278–1279, who m. Constantine Tich and Ivajlo, both tsars of Bulgaria); Anna Paleologina-Cantacuzene (fl. 1270–1313). ❖ See also *Women in World History.*

EUMETIS (fl. 570 BCE). *See Cleobulina of Rhodes.*

EUN-KYUNG CHUNG (1965—). *See Chung Eun-Kyung.*

EUNICE. Biblical woman. Dau. of Lois; children: Timothy. ❖ A Jew married to a Gentile, was distinguished by her "unfeigned faith"; with her mother, was credited with training Timothy in the Scriptures (2 Tim. 3:15). ❖ See also *Women in World History.*

EUPEN, Marit van (1969—). *See van Eupen, Marit.*

EUPHEMIA (fl. 1100s). Lady Annandale. Name variations: Lady Annandale; Euphemia Bruce. Married Robert Bruce, 2nd Lord of Annandale; children: Robert Bruce, 3rd Lord of Annandale, and William Bruce, 4th Lord of Annandale. ❖ See also *Women in World History.*

EUPHEMIA (1317–after 1336). Duchess of Mecklenburg. Name variations: Euphemia Eriksdottir or Ericsdottir. Born 1317; died after April 10, 1336; dau. of Ingeborg (c. 1300–c. 1360) and Eric Magnusson, duke of Südermannland; sister of Magnus VII Eriksson, king of Norway and Sweden; m. Albert II (1318–1379), duke of Mecklenburg, April 10, 1336; children: Albert (1340?–1412), duke of Mecklenburg and king of Sweden (r. 1365–1388); Henry of Mecklenburg (who m. Ingeborg [1347–1370]); Ingeburg of Mecklenburg (who m. Henry II, duke of Holstein). ❖ See also *Women in World History.*

EUPHEMIA OF KIEV (d. 1139). Queen of Hungary. Died April 4, 1139; dau. of Vladimir II (b. 1053), grand duke of Kiev; m. Koloman also known as Coloman (b. around 1070), king of Hungary (r. 1095–1114), 1104 (div. 1113); children: one daughter (name unknown). ❖ See also *Women in World History.*

EUPHEMIA OF POMERANIA (d. 1330). Queen of Denmark. Name variations: Eufemia; Euphamia of Pommerania. Died July 26, 1330; m. Christopher II (1276–1332), king of Denmark (r. 1319–26, 1330–1332); children: Eric, king of Denmark (r. 1321–1326, 1330–1332); Waldemar IV Atterdag, king of Denmark (r. 1340–1375); Otto, duke of Loland and Estland; Agnes Christofsdottir (d. 1312); Heilwig Christofsdottir; Margaret Christofsdottir (c. 1305–1340). ❖ See also *Women in World History.*

EUPHEMIA OF RUGEN (d. 1312). Queen of Norway. Name variations: Euphamia von Rügen. Died May 1, 1312; dau. of Wizlaw II, prince of Rügen; m. Haakon V Longlegs (1270–1319), king of Norway (r. 1299–1319), 1299; children: Ingeborg (c. 1300–c. 1360); Agnes Haakonsdottir (who m. Hafthor Jonson). ❖ See also *Women in World History.*

EUPHEMIA ROSS (d. 1387). *See Ross, Euphemia.*

EUPHRASIA OF CONSTANTINOPLE (d. around 412). Saint. Died c. 412; dau. of Antigonus; mother's name unknown. ❖ On death of father, became ward of Theodosius I the Great; at 5, was promised in marriage to the son of a wealthy senator; at 7, taken by mother in flight out of Egypt, settled near a convent and received as a nun; following mother's death a short time later, was called upon to honor the marriage promise; wrote the emperor, begging to be released from the betrothal, asking that any possessions left her by parents be disposed of among the orphans, the poor, and the churches, and requesting that her slaves be freed and her farmers released from their debts; when the senate deemed that her religious commitment superseded the marriage agreement, remained in the convent until her death. Feast day is Mar 13. ❖ See also *Women in World History.*

EUPHROSINE. *Variant of Euphrosyne.*

EUPHROSINE (d. 1102). Countess and ruler of Vendôme. Reigned 1085–1102; died in 1102; sister of Count Bouchard III, ruler of Vendôme (1066–1085); m. Geoffroi Jourdain, sire de Previlly. ❖ Became countess and ruler of Vendôme upon death of brother, Count Bouchard III; was succeeded by Count Geoffroi Grisegonella. ❖ See also *Women in World History.*

EUPHROSYNE (c. 790–840). Byzantine empress. Born in Constantinople c. 790; died 840; dau. of Maria of Amnia and

Constantine VI Porphyrogenitus, Byzantine emperor (r. 780–797); granddau. of Irene of Athens (c. 752–802); 2nd wife of Michael II of Amorion, Byzantine emperor (r. 820–29); children: (stepchild) Theophilus. ❖ At a young age, entered the convent on island of Prinkipo where she lived with mother; because of ties to imperial family, was married to emperor Michael II following death of his 1st wife Thecla; as stepmother to future emperor Theophilus (r. 829–842), was involved in his choosing Theodora the Blessed for his wife; favored the restoration of the icons, along with Theodora, in a Byzantium where the use of the icon in religious worship was forbidden; after Theophilus succeeded to the throne, returned to the convent at Prinkipo; when Theophilus later learned she was secretly venerating the icons in her convent with his daughters, including St. Thecla and Anastasia, was prohibited from seeing his daughters again. ❖ See also *Women in World History*.

EUPHROSYNE (d. 1203). Empress of Byzantium. Name variations: Euphrosyne Doukaina Kamatera or Docaina Kamatera; Euphrosine. Died 1203 in Constantinople; m. Alexius III Angelus, emperor of Byzantium (r. 1195–1203); children: Irene (who m. Alexius Paleologus); Anna Angelina (d. 1210?, who m. Theodore I Lascaris, Nicaean emperor); Eudocia Angelina. ❖ Married Alexius, a greedy man whose ambition led him to mutilate and depose his own brother in order to ascend the throne in 1095; co-ruled with him, with authority over many domestic affairs while Alexius concentrated on foreign policy issues; an unpopular empress, was disliked by her subjects for her corrupt politics and lavish lifestyle. ❖ See also *Women in World History*.

EUPHROSYNE (fl. 1200s). Byzantine princess. Fl. in the 1200s; illeg. dau. of Michael VIII, Byzantine emperor (r. 1259–1282); m. Nogaj. ❖ See also *Women in World History*.

EUPHROSYNE OF KIEV (fl. 1130–1180). Queen of Hungary. Name variations: Euphrosine. Dau. of Mstislav, prince of Kiev, and Ljubava Saviditsch (d. 1167); m. Geza II (1130–1161), king of Hungary (r. 1141–1161), 1146; children: Stephen III (c. 1147–1173), king of Hungary (r. 1161–1173); Bela III (1148–1196), king of Hungary (r. 1173–1196). ❖ See also *Women in World History*.

EUPHROSYNE OF OPOLE (d. 1293). Mother of Ladislas I, king of Poland. Died 1293; m. Casimir of Kujawy; children: Leszek II the Black, duke of Cracow; Wladyslaw I the Short also known as Ladislas I Lokietek, king of Poland (r. 1306–1333); Siemowit of Dobrzyn.

EUPRAXIA OF KIEV (c. 1070–1109). *See Adelaide of Kiev.*

EURYDICE (c. 410–350s BCE). Mother of Philip II. Born c. 410 BCE; died in the 350s BCE; dau. of Sirrhas, king of Lyncus in northwestern Macedonia; m. Amyntas III of lower Macedonia, c. 393; m. Ptolemy of Alorus; children: (1st m.) daughter Eurynoe; sons Alexander II, Perdiccas III, and Philip II, all of whom ruled Macedonia. ❖ Was Amyntas' principal wife; on his death, saved the throne for her two living sons against royal pretenders; her most famous son, Philip II, made Macedonia a world power and united the Greek world under his authority. ❖ See also *Women in World History*.

EURYDICE (c. 337–317 BCE). Granddaughter of two Macedonian kings who met Olympias in a decisive battle. Name variations: Adea Eurydice. Born Adea shortly before the accession of Alexander III the Great, her 2nd cousin-uncle-stepbrother-in-law, c. 337 BCE; died in 317 BCE; dau. of Cynnane (who was dau. of Philip II of Macedonia and his Illyrian wife, Audata) and Amyntas (son of Perdiccas and grandau. of Eurydice (c. 410–350s BCE); m. Arrhidaeus (Philip III). ❖ Born shortly before the accession of Alexander III the Great (her father in his youth had been acknowledged Macedon's king and as a result was murdered at Alexander's command to facilitate the latter's accession); raised by her mother to be a soldier; when Alexander died without a viable heir, and when a dual monarchy enthroned Alexander's infant son Alexander IV and his mentally incompetent half-brother Arrhidaeus, pushed to marry Arrhidaeus to lay claim through him to the Macedonian throne; bitter at the murder of her father, fought to destroy Alexander IV and all of those behind him, and, to rule through her husband, independent of aristocratic constraint on her power; handicapped by her gender and her youth, nevertheless took every opportunity to foster her ambitions; in the end, however, was defeated not by her rivals, but by the memory of the dead Alexander the Great, for when she met his mother Olympias (grandmother of Alexander IV) in a decisive battle, her army deserted rather than fight the woman who had given birth to the great Macedonian conqueror; though not entirely to blame for the collapse of the royal dynasty, her conflict with Olympias abetted the disintegration of

Alexander the Great's empire, and led to the murders of her husband and Olympias' grandson, the last two male members of their royal house. ❖ See also *Women in World History*.

EURYDICE (fl. 321 BCE). Macedonian aristocrat and 3rd wife of Ptolemy IV. Name variations: Eurydice I. Fl. c. 321 BCE; dau. of Antipater (Macedonian aristocrat who died in 319 BCE); sister of Phila and Nicaea; m. Ptolemy I Soter, king of Egypt, c. 321 BCE; children: several, including Ptolemy Ceraunus (or Keraunos, d. 279 BCE); daughter Ptolemais (c. 315–?); daughter Lysandra. ❖ The 1st wife of Ptolemy I Soter, was replaced by Berenice I (c. 345–c. 275 BCE), then driven out of Egypt by the year 290 BCE. ❖ See also *Women in World History*.

EURYLEONIS (fl. 368 BCE). *See Bilistiche.*

EURYTHMICS. *See Lennox, Annie.*

EUSEBIA OF BERGAMO (fl. 3rd c.). Saint and martyr. Died the end of 3rd century; niece of St. Domnius. ❖ Feast day is Oct 29.

EUSEBIA OF MACEDONIA (fl. 300 CE). Byzantine empress. Fl. around 300 CE; 2nd wife of Constantius II, Eastern Roman emperor (r. 337–361). ❖ See also *Women in World History*.

EUSTIS, Dorothy (1886–1946). American philanthropist. Born Dorothy Leib Harrison, May 30, 1886, in Philadelphia, Pennsylvania; died Sept 8, 1946, in New York, NY; dau. of Charles Custis Harrison (provost of University of Pennsylvania) and Ellen Nixon (Waln) Harrison; m. Walter Abbott Wood (NY state senator), Oct 6, 1906 (died 1915); m. George Morris Eustis, June 23, 1923 (div.); children: (1st m.) 2 sons. ❖ Established an experimental breeding kennel in Vevey, Switzerland; with 2nd husband and Elliott S. ("Jack") Humphrey, began a research and experimental program that ultimately developed a superior strain of German shepherds which were initially trained for police and army duty in Switzerland; began training guide dogs to assist the blind (1927); divorced from husband, left Switzerland to solicit funds and sponsors to introduce "Seeing Eye" dogs to America (1929); founded the 1st facility in Morristown, NJ; moved to a more permanent location on a 56-acre estate in Whippany, NJ (1932); served as president of the school until 1940, training many of the dogs herself and donating much of her personal fortune to the project. At the time of her death in 1946, The Seeing Eye had provided over 1,300 guide dogs to the blind. ❖ See also *Women in World History*.

EUSTOCHIA (1444–1469). Italian saint. Name variations: Eustocia of Padua. Born Lucrezia Bellini, 1444, in Padua, Italy; died Feb 13, 1469, in Padua. ❖ Entered the monastery of S. Prosdocimo in Padua at 17 for schooling; was ill throughout her life. Some thought she was possessed, but many miracles occurred at her grave and her body remained intact; was canonized (1763).

EUSTOCHIUM (c. 368–c. 419). Early Roman Christian leader and saint. Name variations: St. Julia Eustochium. Born c. 368 in Rome, Roman Empire; died Sept 28, c. 419, in Bethlehem, Palestine; dau. of Toxotius (Roman senator, died c. 380) and St. Paula (347–404); studied under St. Jerome. ❖ Early Christian, sought spiritual guidance with mother Paula from St. Jerome, newly arrived from Palestine (382); counseled to become an ascetic, took vow of virginity in Jerome's celebrated letter *De custodia virginitatie* (384) and followed advice despite objections of her uncle Hymettius and aunt Praetextata; followed Jerome to Palestine with mother and then to Egypt (386), visiting hermits of Nitrian Desert in order to study and imitate way of life; returned to settle permanently in Bethlehem; built 3 nunneries, 1 monastery and 1 hospice near place of Christ's birth; directed nuns with mother, and placed monastery under direction of St. Jerome; fluent in Latin and Greek and able to read Hebrew, assisted St. Jerome in translations and scholarship, influencing many of his writings; on death of mother (404), took over direction of all 3 nunneries; came under attack by mob which pillaged 4 monasteries, killing and mistreating some inmates, probably under instructions from patriarch of Bethlehem; suffered ill-health as result of attacks and died soon after; was succeeded by niece Paula. Feast day is Sept 28.

EUTROPIA (fl. 270–300 CE). Roman empress. Fl. around 270–300; m. Afranius Hannibalianus; m. Maximian, Western emperor of Rome (r. 285/86–305; children: (1st m.) Theodora (fl. 290s); Fausta (d. 324, who m. Constantine I the Great); Maxentius (Western Roman usurper, r. 306–312).

EUTROPIA (fl. 330s). Roman noblewoman. Fl. in the 330s; dau. of Theodora (fl. 290s) and Constantius I, Roman emperor (r. 305–306); m. Nepotianus; children: Nepotianus (usurper, r. 350).

EVAN, Blanche (1909–1982). American concert dancer. Born Jan 28, 1909, in New York, NY; died Dec 15, 1982, in New York, NY. ❖ Studied wide range of modern techniques with Martha Graham, Bird Larson, Hanya Holm, and Harald Kreutzberg, among others; also studied in Soviet Union (c. 1935); associated with New Dance League in New York City and presented many solo recitals; wrote numerous dance articles, including for NY Yiddish-language newspaper *The Call;* taught extensively. Works of choreography include *Two Studies in Despair* (1934), *Contre Tanz* (1934), *On the Fence* (1937), *An Office Girl Dreams* (1937), *Two Women* (1939), *Dream Lives On* (1947) and *Death of a Loved One* (1947).

EVANGELISTA, Linda (1965—). Canadian model. Born May 10, 1965, in St. Catherine's, Ontario, Canada; dau. of Marisa Evangelista; raised in working-class Italian Catholic family; m. Gerald Marie (head of Elite modeling agency, Paris), 1988 (div. 1993). ❖ Supermodel, signed with Elite Model Agency in New York (1980), but did not experience immediate success; moved to Paris and 3 years later got job with *Vogue* magazine; rose to stardom, appearing in advertising campaigns for Alberta Ferretti, American Express, Anne Klein, Barney's, Bloomingdales, Calvin Klein, Chanel, Chloë, Donna Karan, Gianni Versace, Ralph Lauren, and Jones New York, among others; retired from modeling (1997); appeared in music videos and Isaac Mizrahi film *Unzipped* (1995); raised money and awareness for breast cancer research. Received VH1 Fashion Awards' Lifetime Achievement Award (1996).

EVANS, Alice Catherine (1881–1975). American bacteriologist. Born Alice Catherine Evans, Jan 29, 1881, in Neath, Pennsylvania; died Sept 5, 1975, in Alexandria, Virginia; dau. of William Howell Evans and Anne (Evans) Evans (both of Welsh descent); attended Susquehanna Collegiate Institute, 1898–1901; Cornell University, BS in bacteriology, 1909; University of Wisconsin in Madison, MS, 1910; graduate work at George Washington University and University of Chicago. ❖ Scientist who discovered that the consumption of raw milk or handling of infected animals could cause undulant fever (later named brucellosis), a potentially fatal disease that was recognized as a world threat by the late 1920s; began career studying with Dr. E.G. Hastings and Dr. Elmer V. McCollum at University of Wisconsin's College of Agriculture (1910), the 1st woman awarded a scholarship in bacteriology from the University of Wisconsin, Madison; began to work for US Department of Agriculture's Dairy Division of the Bureau of Animal Industry (1910), the 1st woman permanently employed there, where she demonstrated that raw milk could transmit a bacterium, *Bacillus abortus,* which caused disease in cattle and humans (1917), one of the most significant discoveries of the early 20th century; appointed bacteriologist in the Hygienic Laboratory at US Public Health Service (1918), later renamed National Institutes of Health (NIH); studied influenza and epidemic meningitis; caught brucellosis (1922) and struggled with the disease for 23 years; retired from NIH (1945); was one of only 2 women delegates at Pasteur Institute's First International Congress in Microbiology (1930); served as honorary president of Inter-American Committee on Brucellosis (1945–57); wrote almost 100 scientific papers and unpublished memoirs; became the 1st woman president of Society of American Bacteriologists (1928, now called American Society for Microbiology). Pasteurization of milk became mandatory for US dairy industry (1930s).

EVANS, Ann (c. 1836–1916). New Zealand nurse and midwife. Name variations: Ann Clive, Sarah Ann Clive. Born Ann Clive, c. 1832–1840, in Manchester, England; died July 4, 1916, in Hawera, New Zealand; dau. of Robert (railway inspector) and Ann (Regan) Clive; m. Thomas Evans (painter), 1863 (died 1871); children: 5. ❖ Served with Florence Nightingale at Scutari in the Crimea (1854–56); immigrated to New Zealand (1863); after husband's death, relocated to Taranaki and operated store before becoming nurse and midwife to community; opened railway station refreshment rooms (late 1890s). ❖ See also *Dictionary of New Zealand Biography* (Vol. 1).

EVANS, Augusta Jane (1835–1909). *See Wilson, Augusta Evans.*

EVANS, Betty (1925–1979). *See Grayson, Betty Evans.*

EVANS, Dale (b. 1912). *See Rogers, Dale Evans.*

EVANS, Edith (1888–1976). English actress. Name variations: Dame Edith Evans. Born Mary Edith Evans in Belgravia, Westminster, London, Feb 8, 1888; died in Goudhurst, Kent, Oct 14, 1976; dau. of Edward and Caroline Ellen (Foster) Evans; m. George Booth (petroleum engineer), 1925 (died 1935); no children. ❖ One of the greatest actresses of the 20th century, adept at Shakespeare and Shaw and famed for her interpretation of Restoration comedy and her performance as Lady Bracknell in *The Importance of Being Earnest,* made London debut as Cressida in *Troilus and Cressida* (1912); played Lady Utterword in the London debut of Shaw's *Heartbreak House* (1921); thereafter, became well known as an interpreter of Shavian parts and created the roles of the Oracle, the Serpent, and the She-Ancient in his *Back to Methuselah* at Birmingham Rep (1923); came to prominence, however, in Restoration comedy, as Mrs. Millamant in *The Way of the World* (1924); made NY debut as Florence Nightingale in *The Lady with the Lamp* (1931), followed by *Evensong* (1933); won acclaim for the Nurse in Katharine Cornell's production of *Romeo and Juliet* (1934); also appeared on stage as Mrs. Sullen in *The Beaux' Stratagem* (1927, 1930), Madame Ranevsky in *The Cherry Orchard* (1948), title role in *Daphne Laureola* (1949), Helen Lancaster in *Waters of the Moon* (1951), Countess Rosmarin *The Dark is Light Enough* (1954) and Mrs. St. Maugham in *The Chalk Garden* (1956), among numerous others; made screen debut in *The Queen of Spades* (1948), followed by *The Importance of Being Earnest* (1951), *Look Back in Anger* (1959), *The Nun's Story* (1959), *Tom Jones* (1963), *The Chalk Garden* (1964), and *Young Cassidy* (1965), but her most successful film role was in *The Whisperers* for which she was nominated for an Academy Award as Best Supporting Actress (1966); toured with *Edith Evans . . . and Friends* (1973–75). Made Dame Commander of the Order of the British Empire (1946). ❖ See also J.C. Trewin, *Edith Evans* (1954); and *Women in World History.*

EVANS, Elizabeth (1887–1958). *See Risdon, Elisabeth.*

EVANS, Elizabeth Glendower (1856–1937). American social and labor reformer. Born Elizabeth Gardiner in New Rochelle, NY, Feb 28, 1856; died in Brookline, Massachusetts, Dec 12, 1937; dau. of Edward and Sophia (Mifflin) Gardiner; m. Glendower Evans, May 18, 1882 (died 1886); no children. ❖ Devoting her wealth and time to a variety of social and labor reforms, served as trustee, Massachusetts State Reform Schools (1886–1914), where she advocated the case-work approach and vocational training for juveniles in need; was a member of the Massachusetts Consumers' League and the Women's Educational and Industrial Union of Boston (1890s); was a member and officer, Boston Women's Trade Union League (1904–12); was a member of the Massachusetts Minimum Wage Commission (1911–12), leading the fight for the establishment of a minimum wage for women industrial workers; was active in the campaign for women's suffrage (1912–14); sent as a delegate to the International Congress of Women at the Hague (1915); was a co-founder and 17-year board member of the American Civil Liberties Union (1920–37); was on the Sacco-Vanzetti defense committee (1920–27); awarded the 1st annual Ford Hall Forum medal (1933); contributed several articles to *LaFollette's Weekly, The Progressive,* and other periodicals. ❖ See also *Women in World History.*

EVANS, Janet (1971—). American swimmer. Born Aug 28, 1971, in Placentia, California; attended Stanford University and University of Southern California. ❖ Finished 3rd in the 800-meter and 1,500-meter freestyles at Goodwill Games (1986); won gold medals for 400-meter freestyle, 800-meter freestyle, and 400-meter individual medley at Seoul Olympics (1988); won a silver medal for the 400-meter freestyle and a gold medal for the 800-meter freestyle at Barcelona Olympics (1992); won World championship gold medals in the 400-meter freestyle (1991) and 800-meter freestyle (1991, 1994); competed at Atlanta Olympics but did not medal; retired (1996). ❖ See also *Women in World History.*

EVANS, Jillian (1959—). Welsh politician. Born May 8, 1959, in Rhondda, Wales. ❖ Served as spokesperson on Europe and International Affairs for Plaid Cymru (Parti of Wales, 1986–94) and chair (1994–96); representing Group of the Greens/European Free Alliance, elected to 5th European Parliament (1999–2004) from UK.

EVANS, Joan (1934—). American tv and screen actress. Born July 18, 1934, in New York, NY; dau. of Dale Eunson and Katherine Albert Eunson (1902–1970), both screenwriters; m. Kirby Weatherly, 1952. ❖ Made screen debut in *Rosanna McCoy* (1949), followed by *Our Very Own, Skirts Ahoy!, The Outcast, The Flying Fontaines,* and *Walking Target,* among others.

EVANS, Kate (1857–1935). *See Edger, Kate Milligan.*

EVANS, Kathy (1948–2003). English journalist. Name variations: Kathy Bisthawi. Born Katherine Margaret Evans, Oct 24, 1948, in

Wokingham, England; grew up in Abingdon, Oxfordshire; died from breast cancer, Nov 17, 2003; was married and divorced, then married briefly to a Palestinian working for the Syrian Ministry of Information. ❖ Respected Middle East analyst, left for the Middle East at 21; arrived in Beirut (early 1970s) and took a job reporting for the English-language *Daily Star;* covered the Yom Kippur War (1973), Iranian Revolution, the 1st Gulf War, and the career of Osama bin Laden long before others took notice of him; contributed reports to *The Times, The Sunday Times, Guardian Unlimited, Financial Times* and *International Herald Tribune;* campaigned for women's rights in Islamic countries, most especially Afghanistan. Won an Amnesty International Press award (1995).

EVANS, Madge (1909–1981). American stage and screen actress. Name variations: Madge Kingsley; Mrs. Sidney Kingsley. Born Margherita Evans, July 1, 1901, in New York, NY; died April 26, 1981, in Oakland, New Jersey; m. Sidney Kingsley (playwright), 1939. ❖ Began career as child model for Fairy soap; made Broadway debut in *Daisy Mayme* (1926), followed by *The Marquise, Our Betters,* and *Here Come the Clowns,* among others; at 5, made film debut in *The Sign of the Cross,* and appeared in many other silents as well as talking films, including *Hallelujah I'm a Bum, Dinner at 8, Paris Interlude, What Every Woman Knows, David Copperfield, Age of Indiscretion, Hell Below, The Mayor of Hell, Stand Up and Cheer, Pennies from Heaven, The Thirteenth Chair* and *Army Girl;* retired from the screen (1938), from the stage (1943); appeared as a panelist on tv's "Masquerade Party" (1952).

EVANS, Mari (1923—). African-American playwright and poet. Name variations: E. Reed. Born July 16, 1923, in Toledo, Ohio; divorced; children: 2 sons. ❖ Taught at several universities including Purdue, Indiana University, Cornell, Washington University in St. Louis, and State University of New York at Albany; writings include *Where is All the Music* (1968), *I Am a Black Woman* (1970), *Nightstar: 1973–1978* (1981), and *A Dark and Splendid Mass* (1991); children's books include *J.D.* (1973), *I Look at Me!* (1974), *Singing Black* (1976), and *Jim Flying High* (1979); plays and musicals include *Portrait of a Man* (1979), *The Way They Made Beriani* (1979), *Glide and Sons* (1979), and *Eyes* (1979); wrote, produced, and hosted weekly tv program, "The Black Experience" (1970–78).

EVANS, Mary Anne (1819–1880). English novelist. Name variations: Mary Ann Evans; Marian Evans; Marian Evans Lewes; Mary Ann Cross; Mrs. John W. Cross; (nicknames) Polly, Pollian; (pseudonym) George Eliot. Pronunciation: Lewes pronounced Lewis. Born Mary Anne Evans, Nov 22, 1819, in Warwickshire, England; died Dec 22, 1880, in London; dau. of Robert Evans (carpenter turned estate agent) and Christiana (Pearson) Evans; lived as the wife of George Henry Lewes from 1854 until his death on Nov 30, 1878; m. John Walter Cross, May 6, 1880; no children. ❖ Major English writer of the 19th century who, under the pseudonym George Eliot, wrote 7 novels, including *Silas Marner, Middlemarch, Adam Bede,* and *The Mill on the Floss;* her strong links to the people, scenes, and events of her childhood, account for those aspects of her art which have proved the most universally admired and enduring: her ability to portray sympathetically, through her aesthetic of realism, commonplace characters whose psychological needs conflict with social conditions and conventions and with both external and internal moral imperatives; grew up at Chilvers Coton, near Nuneaton; under the influence of evangelical teachers, had a conversion experience at about age 15; left school (1835) during mother's terminal illness; kept house for father after mother's death (1836); though religion dominated her life until age 22, moved with father to Coventry and rejected orthodox religion; translated Strauss' *Das Leben Jesu* (1846); wrote for the Coventry *Herald* and cared for father until his death (1849); settled in London (1851) where she wrote for and served as de facto managing editor of the *Westminster Review;* established friendships with Herbert Spencer and George Henry Lewes; intimacy with Lewes began (1853); translated Feuerbach's *Essence of Christianity* (1854); left England with Lewes for Germany (1854); lived with him as Marian Lewes after their return (1855); liaison caused break with family and scandal to conventional society; wrote her 1st fiction *Scenes of Clerical Life* and assumed George Eliot as pseudonym (1857); subsequently wrote novels, a verse drama, a collection of poetry, and a collection of essays; honored as major novelist and sage in later years; visited by distinguished figures from England, America and Europe; other writings include *Romola* (1863), *Felix Holt, the Radical* (1866) and *Daniel Deronda* (1876). ❖ See also Gordon S. Haight, *George Eliot: A Biography* (Oxford U. Press, 1968); G.S. Haight, ed. *Selections From George Eliot's Letters* (Yale U. Press, 1985); Kerry McSweeney, *George Eliot (Marian Evans): A Literary Life* (St. Martin, 1991); Ruby V. Redinger, *George Eliot: The Emergent Self*

(Knopf, 1976); Ina Taylor, *A Woman of Contradictions: The Life of George Eliot* (Morrow, 1989); Rosemary Ashton, *George Eliot: A Life* (Penguin, 1997); Valerie A. Dodd, *George Eliot: An Intellectual Life* (St. Martin, 1990); Frederick R. Karl, *George Eliot: Voice of a Century* (Norton, 1995); and *Women in World History.*

EVANS, Matilda Arabella (1872–1935). African-American physician, humanitarian, and child advocate. Born Matilda Arabella Evans, May 13, 1872, in Aiken, South Carolina; died Nov 17, 1935, in Columbia, SC; dau. of Anderson and Harriet Evans; attended Schofield Industrial School in Aiken; Oberlin College, BA, 1891; Woman's Medical College of Pennsylvania, MD, 1897; never married; children: adopted 7 who bear her surname. ❖ Pioneer in the battle for health care across the nation and, in particular, for impoverished African-Americans in Columbia, South Carolina; after earning her MD (1897), returned to Columbia, the 1st black woman to practice medicine in that city; ran a busy practice, for white as well as black patients, and opened her home to serve as a hospital; established Columbia Clinic Association, offering free health service and education to the public; also founded the Negro Health Care Association of South Carolina and the Taylor Lane Hospital and Training School for Nurses (later Saint Luke Hospital), the only hospital in the area for black patients; wrote *Martha Schofield: Pioneer Negro Educator* (1916). ❖ See also *Women in World History.*

EVANS, Minnie (1892–1987). African-American painter. Born Minnie Eva Jones, Dec 12, 1892, in Long Creek, North Carolina (her mother was 14 and working as a domestic servant); grew up with grandmother in Wilmington, NC; died Dec 16, 1987, in NC; m. Julius Caesar Evans (valet), Dec 16, 1908; children: 3 sons. ❖ Had only a 6th-grade education, no formal artistic training, and lived in the rural south; began drawing at age 43 (1935); surreal paintings and drawings, which depict religious themes and visions, were exhibited at the Whitney Museum (1975); since then, work has been exhibited worldwide.

EVANS, Nancy (1915–2000). British mezzo-soprano. Born in Liverpool, England, Mar 19, 1915; died Aug 20, 2000; studied vocal music with John Tobin in Liverpool; studied in London with Eva de Reusz and Maggie Teyte; m. Walter Legge (record producer, div.); m. Eric Crozier (opera producer), 1949 (died 1994). ❖ One of the major British singers of her generation, who was closely linked with the music of Benjamin Britten, made London stage debut in the comic opera *The Rose of Persia* (1938); made opera debut as a Flower Maiden and the Voice from on High in *Parsifal;* during WWII, sang on several occasions with John McCormack; alternating with Kathleen Ferrier, created the role of Lucretia in the highly acclaimed premiere of Britten's *The Rape of Lucretia* (1946) at the Glyndebourne Festival, then sang the role alone at Covent Garden's 1st presentation of it (1947); created the role of Nancy in Britten's next opera, *Albert Herring* (1947); over next 2 decades, was one of the leading ensemble members of the English Opera Group, starring in performances not only of Britten's stage works but those of other contemporary composers; sang the solo part in Vaughan Williams' Nativity composition *Hodie* (This Day, 1954) and starred in the world premiere of Malcolm Williamson's opera *The Growing Castle* (1968); also sang Polly Peachum in Britten's *The Beggar's Opera* and starred as Dido in Purcell's *Dido and Aeneas* and as Lucinda Woodcock in *Love in a Village;* in later years, taught vocal master classes at Aldeburgh's Britten-Pears School for Advanced Musical Studies.

EVANS, Renee (1908–1971). American actress and dancer. Born Feb 29, 1908; died Dec 22, 1971, in Hollywood, California; m. John Alban (actor); children: Diane Alban (actress also known as Diane Evans). ❖ Appeared in many Busby Berkeley productions.

EVARTS, Esther (1900–1972). See Benson, Sally.

EVATT, Elizabeth (1933—). Australian lawyer and judge. Born Elizabeth Andreas Evatt, Nov 11, 1933, in Sydney, Australia; dau. of Clive Raleigh Evatt (barrister) and Marjorie Hannah Andreas; niece of Dr. Herbert Vere "Doc" Evatt (influential Labor leader and president of UN General Assembly [1948]); sister of Clive Andreas Evatt and Penelope Alice Marjorie Evatt; University of Sydney, Law Medal, LLB, 1955; Harvard University, LLM, 1956; Inner Temple, 1958; m. Robert Joseph Southan; children: Richard Clive Evatt Southan (died 1984) and Anne Penelope Southan. ❖ Known for working extensively with United Nations and other humanitarian organizations to advance the causes of women's rights and human rights, was the youngest student at University of Sydney Law School and the 1st woman to win a Law Medal (1955), passing the New South Wales Bar exam in the same year; passed English Bar (1958) and worked as barrister in Sydney and London (1958–62), focusing on family law; served as editor and librarian at British Institute of International and Comparative Law (1962–68) and as senior legal officer of Law Commission of England and Wales (1968–73); returned to Australia and was appointed presidential member of Australian Conciliation and Arbitration Commission, dealing with industrial disputes (1973–75); presided over Royal Commission on Human Relationships, dealing with abortion, discrimination and family law (1974–77); served as 1st chief judge of Family Court of Australia (1976–88); served on United Nations Committee on Elimination of Discrimination Against Women, monitoring implementation of non-discrimination statutes (1984–92); served as president of Australian Law Reform Commission, advising commonwealth government on matters of federal law (1988–93); served a 4-year term on UN Human Rights Committee (1997–2001); was also a member of Australian National Commission for UNESCO starting 1993, as well as member of Advisory Board of Peace Research Centre at ANU Research School of Pacific Studies starting 1987; served on board of the Evatt Foundation and also as chancellor of University of Newcastle.

E.V.B. (1825–1916). See Boyle, Eleanor Vere.

EVDOKHIIA. Variant of Eudoxia.

EVDOKIMOVA, Eva (1948—). American ballet dancer. Born Dec 1, 1948, in Geneva, Switzerland, to American parents. ❖ Raised in Germany and England, trained at school of Munich State Opera Ballet under Erna Gerbel, as well as with Maria Fay, Vera Volkova, and Natalia Dudinskaya in Leningrad; performed with Royal Danish Ballet (1966–69); joined German Opera Ballet in Berlin as soloist (1969), and became company's prima ballerina (1973); danced briefly with Ballets Classiques de Monte Carlo (early 1970s); performed as permanent guest artist with London Festival Ballet in England; appeared as guest artist throughout the world, frequently partnering Rudolf Nureyev; served as ballet mistress of Boston Ballet in Massachusetts.

EVDOKIMOVA, Irina (1978—). Kazakhstan gymnast. Name variations: Irina Yevdokimova. Born Aug 14, 1978, in Alma-Ata, Kazakhstan. ❖ At Asian Games, won bronze medals in beam and floor (1994) and bronze medals in beam and floor and silver medal in all-around (1998); won Puerto Rico Cup (1995) and Kazakhstan nationals and Nelli Kim Cup (1998); was one of the 1st female gymnasts to perform a layout front vault.

EVE. Biblical women. Name variations: (Hebrew) hawwâ (life). ❖ Created by God from Adam to be his companion in the Garden of Eden (Book of Genesis); children: Cain, Abel, and Seth, among others. As related in the Book of Genesis (Chapters 2 and 3), was the 1st woman, wife of Adam, and the ancestor of the human race; created from the rib of Adam, was lured by the serpent (Satan) to partake of the forbidden fruit, which she ate, then tempted Adam to do the same. ❖ See also Women in World History.

EVE, Marguerite (1915—). See Patten, Marguerite.

EVELYN, Judith (1913–1967). American actress. Born Mar 20, 1913, in Seneca, South Dakota; died May 7, 1967, in New York, NY; attended University of Manitoba. ❖ Debuted on stage in Winnipeg (1928) and continued career in Canada and England; made 1st NY appearance in Angel Street (1941) to critical praise; other plays include The Overtons, The State of the Union, Craig's Wife, A Streetcar Named Desire, The Shrike and The Country Girl; appeared in films, including The Thirteenth Letter, The Egyptian, Female on the Beach, Hilda Crane, Giant, The Brothers Karamazov, Twilight for the Gods; best remembered for her poignant performance in Rear Window.

EVELYN, Mary (1665–1685). British poet. Born Mary Evelyn, Oct 1, 1665, in Surrey, England; died Mar 1685 in Wiltshire, England; dau. of John and Mary (Brown) Evelyn. ❖ Known for one work published posthumously by father, Mundus Muliebris, or, The Ladies Dressing-Room Unlock'd, and Her Toilets Spread: In Burlesque. Together with the Fop-Dictionary, compiled for the Use of the Fair Sex (1690).

EVEN, Nathalie (1970—). See Lancien, Nathalie.

EVEREST, Barbara (1890–1968). English actress. Born June 9, 1890, in London, England; died Feb 9, 1968, in London. ❖ Made London stage debut in The Voysey Inheritance (1912); had a long and prosperous English stage and tv career; during war and postwar years, appeared on NY stage and in several films (1941–51), including Commandos Strike at Dawn, Mission to Moscow, Jane Eyre, Phantom of the Opera, El Cid, The

Damned, The Uninvited, Valley of Decision, Wanted for Murder and Frieda.

EVERETT, Betty (1939–2001). American vocalist. Born Nov 23, 1939, in Greenwood, Mississippi; died Aug 19, 2001, in Beloit, Wisconsin. ❖ As soul singer, had many hits in 1960s and 1970s, including "The Shoop Shoop Song (It's in His Kiss)" (1964), "Let It Be Me" (duet with Jerry Butler, 1964); honored by Rhythm and Blues Foundation (1996).

EVERETT, Eva (1942—). American ballet dancer. Born June 19, 1942, in Springfield, Illinois. ❖ Danced with Chicago Opera Ballet in numerous works by Ruth Page (1958–64); joined American Ballet Theater in New York City (1964), where she created roles for Michael Smuin's Pulcinella Variations (1968), Eliot Feld's Eccentrique (1971), and Dennis Nahat's Mendelssohn Symphony (1971), among others; also performed in repertory works, including Jerome Robbins' Fancy Free and Antony Tudor's Jardin aux Lilas.

EVERETT, Mary Anne (1818–1895). See Green, Mary Anne Everett Wood.

EVERLEIGH, Aida (1864–1960). American madam. Born Aida Simms, 1864, in Stanardsville, Greene Co., Virginia; died Jan 3, 1960; dau. of George Montgomery Simms (widower and lawyer); sister of Minna Everleigh; attended private schools; married the brother of her sister's husband (div. following year). ❖ With sister, ran the Everleigh Club in the red-light district in the Levee in Chicago, the most successful and most expensive bordello in American history; a business genius, was considered the brains of the operation. ❖ See also Women in World History.

EVERLEIGH, Minna (1866–1948). American madam. Born Minna Simms, 1866, in Stanardsville, Greene Co., Virginia; died Sept 16, 1948; dau. of George Montgomery Simms (widower and lawyer); sister of Ada Everleigh; attended private schools; in early 20s, married an older man named Lester (div. following year). ❖ With sister, ran the Everleigh Club in the red-light district in the Levee in Chicago; with her charm and wit, was the marketing side of the operation because she made good press copy. ❖ See also Women in World History.

EVERLUND, Gurli (1902–1985). Swedish swimmer. Born Oct 13, 1902, in Sweden; died June 10, 1985. ❖ At Paris Olympics, won a bronze medal in the 4 x 100-meter freestyle relay (1924).

EVERS, Meike (1977—). German rower. Name variations: Maria Evers. Born June 6, 1977, in Ratzeburg, Germany. ❖ Won gold medal at World championships for double sculls (1997) and quadruple sculls (1999); won a gold medal for quadruple sculls at Sydney Olympics (2000) and Athens Olympics (2004).

EVERS-SWINDELL, Caroline (1978—). New Zealand rower. Born Oct 10, 1978, in Hastings, New Zealand; twin sister of Georgina Evers-Swindell (rower); attended University of Waikato. ❖ At World championships, won gold medals for double sculls (2002, 2003); won a gold medal for double sculls at Athens Olympics (2004). With sister, received Halberg Award (2001) and Lonsdale Cup (2003).

EVERS-SWINDELL, Georgina (1978—). New Zealand rower. Born Oct 10, 1978, in Hastings, New Zealand; twin sister of Caroline Evers-Swindell (rower); attended University of Waikato. ❖ At World championships, won gold medals for double sculls (2002, 2003); won a gold medal for double sculls at Athens Olympics (2004). With sister, received Halberg Award (2001) and Lonsdale Cup (2003).

EVERS-WILLIAMS, Myrlie (1933—). African-American civil-rights activist. Name variations: Myrlie Evers. Born Myrlie Beasley, 1933, in Vicksburg, Mississippi; raised by grandmother Annie McCain Beasley and an aunt, Myrlie Beasley Polk; attended Alcorn A&M College; graduate of Pomona College; m. Medgar Evers (civil-rights leader and field secretary of the Mississippi NAACP), 1951 (killed June 12, 1963); m. Walter Edward Williams (union activist), 1976 (died Feb 1995); children: (1st m.) 3. ❖ After husband was assassinated by a racist sniper on the family doorstep in Jackson, MS (1963), struggled for over 30 years to convict his obvious killer (and endured hung juries in 2 trials) until the guilty verdict arrived in the trial of white supremacist Byron De La Beckwith (1994); moved to California (mid-1960s); earned a degree in sociology; became women's chair of the Democratic Party in Southern California; named commissioner of Public Works for Los Angeles; elected chair of the NAACP board of directors (1995). ❖ See also memoir (with Melinda Blau) Watch Me Fly: What I Learned on the Way to Becoming the Woman I Was Meant to Be (Little, Brown, 1998); HBO movie "Southern Justice: The Murder of Medgar Evers" (1994).

EVERT, Chris (1954—). *American tennis player.* Name variations: Chris Evert Lloyd; Chris Evert Mill. Born Christine Marie Evert, Dec 21, 1954, in Fort Lauderdale, Florida; sister of Jeanne Evert (tennis player); m. John Lloyd, 1979 (div. 1987); m. Andrew Mill, 1988; children: Alexander, Nicholas and Colton Jack. ❖ Won Wimbledon singles championships (1974, 1976, 1981); won US Open singles (1975–1978, 1980, 1982), Australian Open (1982, 1984), and French Open (1974, 1975, 1979, 1980, 1983, 1985, 1986); won 18 "Grand Slam" singles titles during her career; retired (1989), having won more singles titles and matches than any other player in the history of tennis; has since appeared in various celebrity tours and as a network tv commentator; also active in charity fundraising. Inducted into International Tennis Hall of Fame (1995). ❖ See also *Women in World History.*

EVERTS, Sabine (1961—). *West German heptathlete.* Born Mar 4, 1961, in Germany. ❖ At Los Angeles Olympics, won a bronze medal in the heptathlon (1984).

EVERY, Fan (1877–1948). See Smith, Frances Hagell.

EVERY, Frances Hagell (1877–1948). See Smith, Frances Hagell.

EVERYTHING BUT THE GIRL. See Thorn, Tracey.

EWING, Annabelle (1960—). *Scottish politician and member of Parliament.* Born Aug 20, 1960; dau. of Winnie Ewing (member of Scottish Parliament, MSP); sister of Fergus Ewing (MSP). ❖ Contested Scottish Parliament election and Hamilton South by-election (both 1999); representing SNP, elected to House of Commons at Westminster (2001) for Perth; lost general election (2005).

EWING, Juliana Horatia (1841–1885). *British children's writer.* Born Juliana Horatia Gatty, Aug 3, 1841; died May 13, 1885; dau. of Dr. Alfred Gatty, vicar of Ecclesfield, and Margaret (Scott) Gatty (1809–1873, writer); m. Major Alexander "Rex" Ewing (soldier in the commissariat), June 1, 1867. ❖ Storyteller par excellence, showed a natural sympathy and grace reminiscent of Hans Christian Andersen, an exquisite and careful attention to the details of family life, and a deep identification with her characters; produced a number of children's books with a simple, unaffected style, including *Jackanapes* (1883) and *Lob Lie-by-the-fire, or The Luck of Lingborough, and Other Tales* (1874); was a major contributor to the expansion of Victorian children's literature, which was releasing itself from an explicitly religious mission; other books include *Melchior's Dream and Other Tales* (1862), *Mrs. Overtheway's Remembrances* (1869), *The Brownies* (1870), *A Flat Iron for a Farthing* (1872), *Six to Sixteen* (1875), *Jan of the Windmill* (1876), *Brothers of Pity and Other Tales of Beasts and Men* (1882), *Master Fritz, Rhymes* (1883), *The Blue Bells on the Lea* (1884), *Daddy Darwin's Dovecote* (1884), *"Touch Him If You Dare": A Tale of the Hedge, Rhymes* (1884), *The Story of a Short Life* (1885), *Mary's Meadow and Other Tales* (1886), *Dandelion Clocks* (1887), *Snap-Dragons, and Old Father Christmas* (1888), *Verses for Children,* 3 vols. (1888), *Works,* 18 vols. (1894–96). ❖ See also Elizabeth S. Tucker, *Leaves from Juliana Horatia Ewing's "Canada Home"* (1896); Blom and Blom, eds., *Canada Home: Juliana Ewing's Fredericton Letters 1867–1869* (1983); Marghanita Laski, *Mrs. Ewing, Mrs. Molesworth and Mrs. Hodgson Burnett* (Barker, 1958); Christabel Maxwell, *Mrs. Gatty and Mrs. Ewing* (Constable, 1949); and *Women in World History.*

EWING, Margaret (1945–2006). *Scottish politician.* Born Margaret Anne McAdam, Sept 1, 1945 in Lanark, Scotland; died Mar 21, 2006; m. Fergus Ewing (MSP). ❖ As an SNP candidate, elected Member of Parliament for East Dunbartonshire (1974) and Moray (1987); became a member of Scottish Parliament (1999).

EWING, Winnie (1929—). *Scottish politician.* Name variations: Winifred Margaret Ewing. Born July 10, 1929, in Glasgow, Scotland; m. Stewart Ewing; children: 3, including Annabelle Ewing (b. 1960, MP) and Fergus Ewing (SNP member of Scottish Parliament). ❖ Became a practising solicitor (1956); SNP leader, served as Member of Parliament for Hamilton (1967–70) and Moray and Nairn (1974–79); elected to European Parliment (1975—), eventually becoming vice-president, then a senior member of the European Radical Alliance; served as vice-president of the Scottish National Party (1979–87), then became president (1987); elected to Scottish Parliament (1999).

EXENE (1956—). *American musician, singer, songwriter and poet.* Name variations: Christine Cervenkova, Exene Cervenka, X, Auntie Christ, The Knitters, Original Sinners. Born Christine Cervenkova, Feb 2, 1956, in Chicago, IL; m. John Doe (musician and actor), 1977

(div. 1987); m. Viggo Mortensen (actor), 1987 (div. 1997); children: (2nd m.) 1 son, Henry Mortensen (b. 1988). ❖ Joined John Doe in punk band, X (1977), writing lyrics and singing harmonies; with group, released acclaimed albums, *Los Angeles* (1980) and *Wild Gift* (1981), which showed rockabilly and country influences; gave spoken-word performances and (with Lydia Lunch) released book of poetry, *Adulterers Anonymous* (1982); released spoken-word albums, *Twin Sisters* (with Wanda Coleman, 1985), and *Surface to Air Serpents* (1995); formed country music group, Knitters, performing live and releasing album, *Poor Little Critter On the Road* (1985); appeared in films *Salvation!* (1987) and *Floundering* (1994); released solo albums *Old Wives' Tales* (1989) and *Running Sacred* (1990); founded punk group, Auntie Christ (1996), performing as singer and guitarist, and released album, *Life Could Be a Dream* (1997); with a reunited X, released album *Freedom Is . . .* (2000); founded rock group, Original Sinners, and released eponymous album (2002). Other X albums include *Ain't Love Grand* (1985), *See How We Are* (1987) and *Hey Zeus!* (1993).

EXETER, duchess of.
See Elizabeth of Lancaster (1364–1425).
See Anne Plantagenet (1439–1476).
See Montacute, Anne (d. 1457).
See Neville, Margaret (c. 1377–c. 1424).
See Stafford, Anne (d. 1432).

EXETER, marchioness of (c. 1504–1558). See Courtenay, Gertrude.

EXNER, Judith Campbell (d. 1999). *Presidential paramour.* Born Judith Immoor, New York, NY; grew up in California; died, age 65, of breast cancer, Sept 24, 1999, in Duarte, California; m. William Campbell (actor), 1952 (div. 1958); m. Dan Exner (pro golfer, div.); children: David Bohrer. ❖ After a Senate committee investigating CIA–Mafia connections summoned her to testify, revealed in a magazine interview that she had had an on-going affair with John F. Kennedy while he was in the White House (1988); at the time, was also having a relationship with mob boss Sam Giancana. ❖ See also autobiography *My Story* (1977).

EXPOSÉ.
See Bruno, Gioia Carmen.
See Curless, Ann.
See Jurado, Jeanette.
See Moneymaker, Kelly.

EXTER, Alexandra (1882–1949). *Russian painter and designer.* Name variations: Aleksandra Aleksandrovna Ekster. Born Alexandra Alexandrovna Grigorovich, Jan 19, 1882, in Belostok, Grodno Province, Russia; died at Fontenay-aux-Roses, near Paris, Mar 17, 1949; dau. of Alexander Abramovich Grigorovich (tax official); attended Kiev Art School, 1901–06; m. Nikolai Evgenievich Exter, ca. 1903 (died 1918); m. Georgi Georgievich (George) Nekrasov, Oct 25, 1920 (died 1945); no children. ❖ Abstract artist who was influential in bringing Western trends to her native country and went on to become a noted stage designer, moved with family to Kiev (1886); studied in Paris, had 1st meeting with Cubists, participated in "The Link" exhibition in Kiev (1908); began work as theater designer and returned to Russia from Paris (1914); worked under influence of Malevich and Tatlin (1915–16); set up teaching studio in Kiev (1918); began work as puppet designer (1918–19); joined Vkhutemas and participated in Constructivist 5 x 5=25 exhibit in Moscow (1921); worked as film set designer (1923–24); left Russia for Western Europe (1924); held one-woman exhibit in Berlin and settled in suburbs of Paris (1930); in less than 2 decades, moved from an early interest in the French impressionists to work in such diverse styles as Cubism, Futurism, Suprematism, and finally the politically charged style of Constructivism; though a devotee of such distinguished mentors as Picasso, added a substantial element of originality to the models they set for her; her work in Cubism and other styles, for example, was distinguished by a vivid sense of color that added a heightened emotional content to many of her paintings. ❖ See also *Artist of the Theater: Alexandra Exter: Four Essays on Exhibit at Vincent Astor Gallery. Spring-Summer 1974* (New York Public Library, 1974); M.N. Yablonskaya, *Women Artists of Russia's New Age. 1900–1935* (Thames & Hudson, 1990); and *Women in World History.*

EYBERS, Elisabeth (1915—). *South African poet.* Born Feb 26, 1915, in Klerksdorp, South Africa; studied at University of Witwatersrand; m. Albert Wessels, 1937 (div. 1961); children: 4. ❖ The 1st Afrikaans woman to win the Hertzog Prize (1943), began career as a journalist; writings, which examine the lives of women and draw imagery from religion and mythology, include *Beleidenis in die Skemering* (1936), *Die Stil Avontuur* (1939), *Balans* (1962), *Kruis of Munt* (1973), *Voetpad van*

Verkenning (1978), *Dryfsand* (1985), *Noodluik* (1989), *Respyt* (1993), and *Verbruikersverse/ Consumers' Verse* (1997); compiled English translation of own verse *The Quiet Adventure* (1948). Other awards include CNA Literature Prize (1973), Louis Luyt Prize (1983), and Old Mutual Prize (1989). ❖ See also Ena Jansen, *Afstand en verbintenis–Elisabeth Eybers in Amsterdam* (Amsterdam U. Press, 1998).

EYCK, Margaretha van (fl. 1420s–1430s). Flemish painter. Name variations: Margarete van Eyck. Born at Maeseyck, around 1370, and flourished between 1420 and 1430; buried in the Cathedral of Ghent, along with her brother Hubert; sister of artists Hubert (c. 1366–1426), Jan (c. 1370–c. 1440) and Lambert van Eyck, founders of the Flemish school of painting. ❖ Said to have been a skillful painter, though no picture is known that can be positively ascribed to her; with brothers, reputedly originated the process of oil painting with a drying varnish.

EYLES, Joan M. (1907–1986). English geologist, book collector, and science historian. Name variations: Joan Mary Eyles. Born Joan Mary Biggs, June 15, 1907; grew up in Bridgend, Wales; died June 14, 1986; London University, BS, 1929; m. Victor Ambrose Eyles (geologist), Oct 1931. ❖ Renowned expert on William Smith, father of British geology, studied volcanic rocks in Scotland's southern uplands while doing postgraduate work at King's College, London (1930); joined Geological Society (1931); became book collector after purchase of William Smith's *Geological Map of 1815;* after William Smith's manuscripts were discovered in Oxford museum's attic, began research on Smith's life (1955).

EYLES, Leonora (1889–1960). English novelist, writer and feminist. Name variations: M. Leonora Eyles; Leonora Murray; Mrs. D.L. Murray. Born Margaret Leonora Pitcairn in 1889; died July 27, 1960; m. D.L. Murray, editor of TLS; mother-in-law of Mario Praz (Italian literary critic and essayist). ❖ Columnist and feminist, was a regular contributor to the *Times Literary Supplement* (1930s) and woman's editor of the *Daily Herald* throughout 1920s.

EYMERS, Johanna Geertruid (1903–1988). *See Eymers, Truus.*

EYMERS, Truus (1903–1988). Dutch physicist and museum conservator. Name variations: Johanna Geertruid Eymers; Truus van Cittert; Johann Geertruida (Truus) van Cittert-Eymers. Born Johanna Geertruid Eymers in 1903 in Arnhem, Netherlands; died 1988; studied physics, chemistry, and math at University of Utrecht, PhD, 1935; m. Pieter H. Van Cittert (museum conservator), 1938. ❖ Known for physics research and for work at museum of University of Utrecht, began work there as a laboratory assistant in the physics department (1927–33), where she researched bioluminescence; after marriage (1938), assisted husband at University Museum because marriage status rendered her ineligible for continued paid employment (1938–55); after husband left the position, began serving as director (1955). Writings include doctoral thesis, "Fundamental Principles for the Illumination of a Picture Gallery Together with Their Application to the Illumination of the Museum at The Hague."

EYMERY, Marguerite (c. 1860–1953). *See Vallette, Marguerite.*

EYRE, Agnes (1896–1940). *See Ayres, Agnes.*

EYRE, Laura (1840–1903). *See Suisted, Laura Jane.*

EYSVOGEL, Marjolein (1961—). *See Bolhuis-Eysvogel, Marjolein.*

EYTON, Bessie (1890–1965). American silent-film actress. Born July 5, 1890, in Santa Barbara, California; died Jan 22, 1965, in Thousand Oaks, CA; m. Charles Eyton (director). ❖ Lead player, made film debut with Pathé; joined the Selig studio (1911); films include *The Spoilers, The Crisis, The Heart of Texas Ryan, Cheap Kisses,* and *The Girl of Gold.*

EZEKIEL, Denise Tourover (1903–1980). American humanitarian. Name variations: Denise Tourover. Pronunciation: TOUR-over. Born Denise Levy in New Orleans, Louisiana, May 16, 1903; died in Washington, DC, Jan 16, 1980; dau. of Leopold (New Iberia, Louisiana, dry goods merchant) and Blanche (Cogenheim) Levy; George Washington University School of Law, LLB, 1924; m. Raphael Tourover, Nov 14, 1926 (died Nov 2, 1961); m. Walter N. Ezekiel, Sept 27, 1972; children: (1st m.) Mendelle Tourover. ❖ Hadassah leader who saw the "Teheran Children" to safety and whose outraged voice demanded action from diplomats and presidents on behalf of disenfranchised and oppressed people around the world; moved to Washington, DC (1920); admitted to the Bar of the District of Columbia (1924); began more than 50 years of service through Hadassah as member of Washington, DC, section (1925); elected section president (1936); elected to National Board and chosen as Washington representative (1939); during WWII, served as Hadassah's liaison to diplomats, Congress and the White House to ensure safe passage of European refugees to Palestine; through Hadassah, coordinated food distribution to Israel from the US Agency for International Development (1950–74) and Operation Reindeer (1953); represented Hadassah on State Department's American Food for Peace Council (1960–64); was a member of Actions Committee, World Zionist Organization (1956–76). ❖ See also *Women in World History.*

EZHOVA, Ljudmilla (1982—). Russian gymnast. Name variations: Liudmila Ezhova. Born Mar 4, 1982, in Krasnogorsk, Russia. ❖ Won a gold medal at World championships (2001) and a gold medal at European championships (2002), both for balance beam; won a bronze medal for team all-around at Athens Olympics (2004).

EZZELL, Cheryl (c. 1979—). American inline skater. Name variations: Cheryl Ezzell-Matula or Cheryl Ezzell Matula; Cheryl Matula or Cheryl Matula-Ezzell. Born Cheryl Ezzell, c. 1979, possibly in Texas; married; children: sons (b. 1999 and 2002). ❖ Became Overall World champion inline skater for Banked Track and Road, Perth, Australia (1995); won 12 World championships; retired (1999).

F

F (1783–1850). *See Frohberg, Regina.*

FABARES, Nanette (1920—). *See Fabray, Nanette.*

FABBRI, Flora (c. 1807–c. 1857). Italian ballet dancer. Name variations: Flora Fabbri Bretin. Born c. 1807 in Florence, Italy; died c. 1857; aunt of Alessandro Fabbri (ballet dancer); m. Luigi Bretin (dancer); children: Giovanni Fabbri-Bretin (ballet dancer). ❖ Made professional debut at Teatro la Fenice in Venice; performed throughout Italy for multiple seasons, including Teatro Apollo in Rome, Teatro Comunale in Bologna, and Teatro Comunale in Padua; danced at Paris Opéra (1845–c. 52), where she had principal roles in *Zerline, ou la Corbeilles d'oranges, La Sylphide, Jerusalem* and *Paquita,* among others; danced at London's Covent Garden (1846) in *The Offspring of Flowers* and at Théâtre de la Porte-Saint-Martin in Paris (1855); retired (late 1850s).

FABER, Beryl (d. 1912). English actress. Born in England; died May 1, 1912; sister of C. Aubrey Smith (actor); m. Cosmo Hamilton. ❖ Made professional stage debut in London in *The Masqueraders* (1894), followed by *Iris, His House in Order, Waste, The Subjection of Kezia* (title role), *A Sense of Humor, Mrs. Skeffington* and *The Choice,* among others; with husband, wrote plays and playlets.

FABER, Cecilia Böhl de (1796–1877). *See Böhl von Faber, Cecilia.*

FABIA-EUDOCIA (fl. 600s). Byzantine empress. Name variations: Fabia-Eudocia or Eudokia. Born in Carthage; 1st wife of Herakleos also known as Heraclius I of Carthage, Byzantine emperor (r. 610–641); children: Heraclonas-Constantine, emperor of Byzantium (r. 641). Heraclius I's 2nd wife was Martina. ❖ See also *Women in World History.*

FABIAN, Dora (1901–1935). German writer. Born Dora Heinemann in Berlin, Germany, May 28, 1901; along with Mathilde Wurm, died Mar 31–April 1, 1935; dau. of Hugo Heinemann (Jewish lawyer) and Else (Levy) Heinemann; received doctorate in economics and political science from University of Giessen, 1928; no siblings; m. Walter Fabian (Social Democratic activist), 1924 (div. 1930). ❖ Anti-Nazi activist, writer and journalist, was an active member of the Independent Social Democratic Party while still a schoolgirl; as a gifted public speaker as well as a skilled journalist and writer, became a thorn in the side of the Social Democratic leadership by end of 1920s; expelled from Social Democratic Party for insubordination (1931); with husband and others, formed a new party, the Socialist Workers' Party (Sozialistische Arbeiterpartei or SAP), convinced that only a united German labor movement would be able to stand up against the Nazis; as a militant anti-Nazi, had long been regarded as an enemy to be eliminated; following arrest in Berlin (Mar 1933), sought refuge in Great Britain; became an important source of information on Nazi Germany for leaders of British Left; her work was known to the German Embassy in London, and two highly suspicious "burglaries" took place in the flat she shared with fellow political emigré Mathilde Wurm (1934); along with Wurm, was found dead in her London flat (April 4, 1935), raising questions that remain unsolved to this day. ❖ See also Charmian Brinson, *The Strange Case of Dora Fabian and Mathilde Wurm: A Study of German Political Exiles in London during the 1930's* (Peter Lang, 1997); and *Women in World History.*

FABIAN, Françoise (1932—). Algerian stage and screen actress. Born Michèle Cortès de Leone y Fabianera, May 2, 1932, in Touggourt, Algeria; m. Jacques Becker (director), 1957 (died 1960); m. Marcel Bozzuffi, c. 1963 (died 1988). ❖ Made stage debut in 1950s; made film debut in *Mémoires d'un Flic* (1955); came to prominence in such films as Luis Buñuel's *Belle de jour* (1967) and Eric Rohmer's *Ma nuit chez Maud* (*My Night at Maud's,* 1969).

FABIANI, Linda (1956—). Scottish politician. Born Dec 14, 1956, in Glasgow, Scotland; attended Napier College and Glasgow University. ❖ As SNP delegate, elected to the Scottish Parliament for Central Scotland (1999); became deputy shadow minister for Social Justice.

FABIOLA (d. 399). Saint. Name variations: Saint Fabiola. Died 399; married twice to men unnamed in sources. ❖ Early Christian saint and founder of the 1st public hospital in Rome; made public recantation of sins after the death of 2nd husband; donated large sums of money to the poor and religious institutions and founded a house for the sick in Rome; traveled to Jerusalem (395) and studied Scripture with St. Jerome; returned to Rome at onset of Huns; founded a house for pilgrims in Portus. ❖ See also *Women in World History.*

FABIOLA (1928—). Queen of the Belgians. Name variations: Fabiola de Mora y Aragón; Fabiola of Aragon. Born Fabiola Fernanda Maria de las Victori Antonia Adelaide, June 11, 1928, in Madrid, Spain; dau. of Gonzalo Mora y Fernandez (d. 1954), count of Mora; m. Boudewijn also known as Baudouin I (1930–1993), king of the Belgians (r. 1951–1993), Dec 15, 1960 (died July 31, 1993); no children. ❖ At the time of her engagement to Belgium's Baudouin I, was still living at home with mother and employed as a surgical nurse at a military hospital in Madrid; was extremely religious; her reign was distinguished by her charitable work, which began immediately after her honeymoon when a series of crippling strikes brought the country to a standstill; after a landslide buried one village and a flood destroyed another, was one of the 1st on the scene at both disasters, organizing first aid and giving solace to victims; breaking with tradition, kept no official ladies-in-waiting, and her daily life very much revolved around the king. ❖ See also *Women in World History.*

FABISH, Agnes (1873–1947). New Zealand farmer. Name variations: Agnes Dodunska. Born Agnes Dodunska, Dec 21, 1873, at Gremblin, West Prussia (now Poland); died July 21, 1947, at New Plymouth, New Zealand; dau. of Michael Dodunski and Catharina (Liper) Dodunska; m. Joseph Fabish (originally Fabisz), 1894; children: 7 daughters, 7 sons. ❖ Immigrated to New Zealand with family (1883); was placed in domestic service until marriage; husband worked in sawmill during day, while both cleared and planted land; managed daily routine of farm, planted camellias and fruit trees, and collected honey and cured bacon for market; moved to New Plymouth (1921). ❖ See also *Dictionary of New Zealand Biography* (Vol. 3).

FABRAY, Nanette (1920—). American actress, dancer, and singer. Name variations: Nanette Fabares; Baby Nan or Baby Nanette. Born Ruby Bernadette Nanette Fabares, Oct 27, 1920, in San Diego, California; aunt of Shelley Fabares (actress); m. David Tebet (div.); m. Ranald MacDougall (died). ❖ By age 5, was working in vaudeville with Ben Turpin; by 7, was featured as "Baby Nan" in several *Our Gang* comedies; made Broadway debut in *Meet the People* (1940), followed by *Let's Face It, By Jupiter, Bloomer Girl, High Button Shoes, Make a Wish* and *Mr. President,* among others; appeared often on tv, notably on "Caesar's Hour," "The Carol Burnett Show," and "The Nanette Fabray Show" (1961); films include *Elizabeth and Essex, A Child is Born, The Band Wagon, The Happy Ending* and *Cockeyed Cowboys;* as a hearing-impaired performer, was a prime force in bringing sign language and captioning to tv. Received 3 Emmy Awards, 2 Donaldson awards, and a Tony for *Love Life,* as well as the Eleanor Roosevelt Humanitarian award.

FABRICIUS, Sara (1880–1874). *See Sandel, Cora.*

FABULA (fl. 9th, 8th, or 7th c. BCE). *See Larentia, Acca.*

FABYAN, Sarah (1912–1996). *See Palfrey, Sarah.*

FACCIO, Rina (1876–1960). *See Pierangeli, Rina Faccio.*

FACHIRI, Adila (1886–1962). Hungarian-British violinist. Name variations: Adila d'Aranyi or d'Arányi. Born Adila von Aranyi, Feb 26, 1886, in Budapest, Hungary; died Dec 15, 1962, in Florence; sister of Jelly d'Aranyi (1895–1966), violinist; grandniece of Joseph Joachim (violinist, conductor and composer); studied under Jenö Hubay at Budapest Academy. ❖ Given a Stradivarius by granduncle, made debut in Vienna with Beethoven's Violin Concerto (1906); with sister Jelly, came to prominence performing Bach's concerto for two violins; settled with sister in London (1913). Gustav Holst dedicated his Double Concerto to the sisters. ❖ See also J. Macleod, *The Sisters d'Aranyi* (1969).

FADDEN, Ilma (d. 1987). Australian prime-ministerial wife. Born Ilma Nita Thornber in Mackay, Queensland, Australia; died May 14, 1987, Toowong, Brisbane; m. Arthur Fadden (prime minister of Australia for 40 days in 1941 and acting prime minister for periods totaling 2 years), Dec 27, 1916; children: Gordon (b. 1922), John, Mavis, and Betty Fadden. ❖ Active in state and local political organizations, was also a renowned campaign worker in husband's 9 federal elections.

FADEYEVA, Mariya (1958—). Soviet rower. Born Mar 1958 in USSR. ❖ At Moscow Olympics, won a bronze medal in coxed fours (1980).

FADIA (1943–2002). Egyptian princess. Name variations: Fadia Orloff. Born Dec 15, 1943 at Abdin Palace in Cairo, Egypt; died Dec 28, 2002, in Lausanne, Switzerland; dau. of King Faruk or Farouk I (r. 1936–52) and Farida; sister of King Fuad II; m. Pierre Orloff (Russian), Feb 17, 1965; children: Alexander-Ali Orloff (photographer) and Michael-Shamel Orloff. ❖ At 9, went into exile with family following the Egyptian Revolution; spent most of her life in Switzerland.

FADILLA (b. 159). Roman noblewoman. Name variations: Arria Fadilla. Born 159; dau. of Faustina II (130–175) and Marcus Aurelius, Roman emperor (r. 161–180).

FADIMAN, Annalee (1916–2002). American screenwriter and war journalist. Name variations: Annalee Whitmore; Annalee Whitmore Jacoby; Annalee Jacoby Fadiman or Annalee Whitmore Fadiman. Born Annalee Whitmore, May 27, 1916, in Price, Utah; died Feb 5, 2002, in Captiva, Florida; dau. of Leland Whitmore (bank president) and Anne Sharp Whitmore (librarian); graduate of Stanford, 1937; m. Melville Jacoby (*Time* magazine correspondent), 1941 (killed near Darwin, Australia, during WWII); became 2nd wife of Clifton Fadiman (tv moderator and book reviewer for *The New Yorker*), 1950 (died 1999); children: son Kim, daughter Anne. ❖ While in college, was the 1st woman to be managing editor of the *Stanford Daily* newspaper; moved to Hollywood and co-wrote screenplay for *Andy Hard Meets Debutante* (1940); went to China to report on the war for *Liberty* magazine (1941); became foreign correspondent for *Life* and *Time* magazines and co-authored *Thunder out of China* with Theodore H. White; after the war, appeared on radio quiz show "Information Please."

FADL (d. around 870). Arabian singer and poet. Born in Basra (now Iraq); died in Baghdad, probably in 870 CE. ❖ Much-beloved singer, changed owners several times as a slave before coming to the court of Caliph al-Mutawakki (r. 847–861) of Baghdad and becoming his favorite; an excellent poet, often set her poetry to music; when al-Mutawakki died, was equally prized by his successors, al-Muntasir (r. 861–862) and al-Mutamid (r. 870–892).

FAEHNRICH, Gabriele (1968—). See Fahnrich, Gabriele.

FAGGS, Mae (1932—). African-American track-and-field athlete. Name variations: Mae Faggs Starr. Born Aeriwentha Mae Faggs, April 10, 1932, in Mays Landing, NY; m. Eddie Starr (high school principal). ❖ One of the famed Tigerbelles of Tennessee State University, was the 1st American woman to participate in three Olympics (1948, 1952, 1956); won AAU 200-meters (1954, 1955, 1956); won a silver medal in the 200-meter and a gold medal in the 4x100-meter relay at Pan American Games (1955); won a gold medal in the 4x100-meter relay with a 45.9 time at Helsinki Olympics (1952) and the bronze medal in the 4x100-meter relay with a time of 44.9 in the Melbourne Olympics (1956). ❖ See also *Women in World History*.

FAGIN, Claire (1926—). American nurse. Name variations: Claire Mintzer Fagin. Born Claire Mintzer, Nov 25, 1926, in New York, NY; dau. of Mae (Slatin) Mintzer and Harry Mintzer (grocer); Columbia University Teachers College, MA, 1951; New York University, PhD, 1964; m. Samuel Fagin, 1952. ❖ Contributor to pediatric psychiatric nursing practices in America, studied at Columbia University with Hildegard Peplau, a psychiatric nursing pioneer; wrote doctoral dissertation, "The Effects of Maternal Attendance during Hospitalization on the Behavior of Young Children" (1964), which influenced visiting policies for children; directed a child psychiatric program at NYU; served as chair

and professor of newly opened Herbert L. Lehman College in NY (1969–77); as dean, developed the University of Pennsylvania nursing program into one of the highest-ranking of its kind (1977–92); in interim post, served as 1st woman president of University of Pennsylvania (1993–94), then as professor, dean emerita, and program director of John A. Hartford Foundation's "Building Academic Geriatric Capacity" there.

FAGNAN, Marie-Antoinette (d. 1770). French short-story writer. Born in France; died 1770. ❖ Wrote fairytales, which were infused with parody and irony, including *Kanor, conte traduit du sauvage* (1750), *Miroir des princesses orientales* (1755), *Histoire et aventures de Mylord Pet* (1755) and *Minet-Bleu et Louvette* (1768).

FAHMI, Nariman (1934–2005). *See Nariman.*

FAHMY, Marguérite Laurent (b. around 1900). French woman tried for murder. Born c. 1900; m. Prince Ali Kamel Fahmy Bey. ❖ Following a public argument, shot husband (July 10, 1923), who later died from his injuries; captivated a sympathetic public at her trial, at which she was represented by Sir Edward Marshall Hall and Sir Henry Curtis-Bennett; testified that husband had threatened to kill her and grabbed her by throat; acquitted by jury after less than an hour's deliberation.

FAHNRICH, Gabriele (1968—). East German gymnast. Name variations: Gabriele Fähnrich or Faehnrich. Born April 8, 1968, in Hoyerswerda, East Germany; sister of Carola Fahnrich (gymnast). ❖ Won gold medal for uneven bars at World championship (1985); won Cottbus and Moncada Cup (1985) and GDR Cup (1986); at Seoul Olympics, won a bronze medal in team all-around (1988).

FAILEUBA (fl. 586–587). Queen of Austrasia and queen of Burgundy. Fl. around 586 and 587; m. Childebert II, king of Austrasia (r. 575–595), king of Burgundy (r. 593–595); children: Thibert also known as Theudebert II (586–612), king of Austrasia (r. 595–612); Thierry also known as Theuderic or Theodoric II (587–613), king of Burgundy (r. 595–613), king of Austrasia (r. 612–613).

FAINLIGHT, Ruth (1931—). British-American poet and short-story writer. Name variations: Ruth Sillitoe. Born Ruth Esther Fainlight, May 2, 1931, in New York, NY; dau. of Leslie Alexander Fainlight and Fanny Nimhauser Fainlight; educated in US and England; m. Alan Sillitoe (writer), 1959. ❖ Published many collections of poetry, including *Cages* (1966), *Another Full Moon* (1976), *Sybils and Others* (1980), *The Knot* (1990), *This Time of Year* (1994), *Sugar-Paper Blue* (1997) and *Burning Wire* (2002); translated *All Citizens Are Soldiers* by Lope de Vega (with Alan Sillitoe, 1966), *Navigations* (1983), and *Marine Rose* by Sophia de Mello Breyner Andresen (1987); wrote opera libretti for Royal Opera (1991 and 1993). Received Cholmondeley Award (1994).

FAIR, Elinor (1902–1957). American actress. Name variations: Eleanor Crowe; Lenore Fair. Born Dec 21, 1902, in Richmond, Virginia; died April 26, 1957, in Seattle, Washington; m. William Boyd (cowboy star as Hopalong Cassidy), 1926 (div. 1929). ❖ First appeared in vaudeville, stock, and musical comedies; on screen, often appeared opposite husband; films include *The Volga Boatman, Yankee Clipper, The Miracle Man, Kismet, Gold and the Girl* and *Jim the Conqueror*.

FAIR, Lenore (1902–1957). See Fair, Elinor.

FAIR, Lorrie (1978—). American soccer player. Born Lorraine Ming Fair, Aug 5, 1978, in Los Altos, California; attended University of North Carolina; sister of Ronnie Fair (soccer player for San Diego Spirit). ❖ Won a silver medal at Sydney Olympics (2000); was a founding member of the Women's United Soccer Association (WUSA); signed with Philadelphia Courage (2001).

FAIRBAIRN, Ann (1905–1972). See Tait, Dorothy.

FAIRBAIRN, Joyce (1939—). Canadian politician and journalist. Born Nov 6, 1939, in Lethbridge, Alberta, Canada; Carleton University, BA in journalism, 1961. ❖ Liberal, began career as a journalist, working with the Parliamentary Press Gallery Bureau of United Press International; became legislative assistant to Prime Minister Pierre Trudeau (1970), then served as his Communications Coordinator (1981–83); was appointed to the Senate for Lethbridge Alberta (June 29, 1984); appointed to the Cabinet, as the 1st woman Leader of the Government in the Senate (1993); served as minister with special responsibility for literacy (Nov 4, 1993–June 10, 1997); appointed special advisor for Literacy to the Minister of Human Resources Development (1997).

FAIRBAIRNS, Zöe (1948—). British science-fiction writer and novelist. Name variations: Zoe Ann Fairbairns. Born Dec 20, 1948, in Kent,

England; educated at a convent school in Twickenham and St. Andrews University. ❧ Was writer-in-residence at several schools and universities, including Deakin University in Australia and Sunderland Polytechnic in UK; wrote science-fiction novel *Benefits* (1979); other novels include *Live as Family* (1968), *Down: An Explanation* (1969), and *Here Today* (1984); nonfiction includes *Study War No More* (1974) and, with James Cameron, *Peace Moves: Nuclear Protest in the 1980s* (1984). Awarded Fawcett Prize (1985).

FAIRBANKS, Madeline (1900–1989). American film and musical dancer. Name variations: Fairbanks Twins; Thanhouser Twins; Flying Twins. Born Nov 15, 1900, in New York, NY; died Jan 15, 1989, in New York, NY; sister of Marion Fairbanks. ❧ With twin sister Marion, made professional debut in Winthrop Ames' production of *The Blue Bird* (1910), then appeared on Broadway in *The Piper* (1911), *Mrs. Wiggs of the Cabbage Patch* (1912), and *Snow White* (1912); with Marion, appeared in such Thanhouser Kids series films as *Cousins* (1913), *The Flying Twins* (1915), *The Bird of Prey* (1916) and *The Answer* (1916); performed in *Ziegfeld Follies* (1917–20); performed numerous tandem dance acts on stages and Prologs throughout New York City; back on Broadway, appeared with Marion in *Mercenary Mary* (1925), *Oh, Kay!* (1926), *Allez-oop* (1927), and *Happy* (1927) and performed solo in *The Ritz Revue* (1924).

FAIRBANKS, Marion (1900–1973). American dancer. Name variations: Fairbanks Twins; Flying Twins; Thanhouser Twins. Born Nov 15, 1900, in New York, NY; died Sept 20, 1973; sister of Madeline Fairbanks. ❧ With twin sister Madeline, made professional debut in *The Blue Bird* (1910), then appeared on Broadway in *The Piper* (1911), *Mrs. Wiggs of the Cabbage Patch* (1912) and *Snow White* (1912); with Madeline, appeared in such Thanhouser Kids series films as *Cousins* (1913), *The Flying Twins* (1915), *The Bird of Prey* (1916), and *The Answer* (1916); on Broadway, performed with Madeline in *Ziegfeld Follies* (1917–20), *Mercenary Mary* (1925), *Oh, Kay!* (1926), *Allez-oop* (1927) and *Happy* (1927); appeared solo in *Grab Bag* (1924) and on a tour of *Little Nellie Kelly.*

FAIRBROTHER, Nicola (1970—). English judoka. Born May 14, 1970, in United Kingdom. ❧ At Barcelona Olympics, won a silver medal in lightweight 56kg (1992).

FAIRBROTHER, Sydney (1872–1941). English stage and screen actress. Name variations: Sydney Tapping. Born Sydney Parselle, July 31, 1872, in London, England; died Jan 4, 1941, in London; dau. of Florence Cowell and John Parselle; m. Percy Buckler (died 1897); m. Trevor Lowe (died 1910). ❧ Made stage debut as a walk-on in *A Man's Shadow* (1889); accompanied the Kendals (W.H. and Madge) to America for 2 years; plays include *The Two Little Vagabonds, The Little Minister, The Talk of the Town, David Copperfield* (as Mrs. Macawber), and *The Ghost Train;* appeared as Amanda in *Op o' me Thumb,* Proserpine in *Candida,* Mahbubah in *Chu Chin Chow* (1916–20), Mrs. Badger in *The Young Person in Pink,* and with the elder Fred Emney in the music-hall sketch "A Sister to Assist Her" (1912–14); made film debut in *Under Suspicion* (1916), followed by *It's You I Want, All In, Rose of Tralee, Paradise for Two, Make It Three, Little Dolly Daydream, Nell Gwynne, Chu Chin Chow, The Last Journey, Fame, King Solomon's Mines* and *Dreaming Lips,* among others.

FAIRBURN, Elizabeth (1821–1904). *See Colenso, Elizabeth.*

FAIRCLOUGH, Ellen (1905–2004). Canadian politician and businesswoman. Born Ellen Louks Cook in Hamilton, Ontario, Jan 28, 1905; died Nov 13, 2004, in Hamilton; dau. of Norman Ellsworth (farmer) and Nellie Bell (Louks) Cook; m. David Henry Gordon Fairclough (owner of a printing business), Jan 28, 1931; children: David Fairclough. ❧ The 1st woman in Canada to hold a Cabinet position, opened her own accounting and tax service business (1935); served as vice president of Young Conservative Association (Ontario); elected to Hamilton city council as an alderman (1946); after an unsuccessful run for federal Parliament, elected controller for city of Hamilton (1950); for receiving more votes than any other candidate in municipal polling, automatically became deputy mayor; was elected in a by-election to fill a vacant seat in House of Commons (1950); became the "voice" of the opposition on labor matters; remained a member of the opposition party for 7 years; under John Diefenbaker, was appointed secretary of state (1957), the 1st woman Cabinet minister in Canadian history; named minister of citizenship and immigration (1958), then postmaster general (1962); defeated for reelection (1963), became vice president, director, and secretary-treasurer of Hamilton Trust and Savings Corporation, an institution she helped build from scratch. ❧ See also *Women in World History.*

FAIRE, Virginia Brown (1904–1980). American actress. Born June 26, 1904, in Brooklyn, NY; died June 30, 1980, in Laguna Beach, California. ❧ Won a fan magazine contest (1919); appeared in over 50 films, including *Without Benefit of Clergy, Omar the Tentmaker, Welcome Stranger, Friendly Enemies, The Temptress* and *The Donovan Affair;* also starred opposite John Gilbert in *Monte Cristo,* was the original Tinker Bell in *Peter Pan* (1924), and appeared in several westerns.

FAIRFAX, Beatrice (c. 1873–1945). *See Manning, Marie.*

FAIRFAX, Lettice (1876–1948). English actress. Born Mar 26, 1876, in England; died Dec 25, 1948. ❧ Made stage debut in *Auld Lang Syne* (1893), then succeeded Cissie Loftus in the title role in *Haidée;* came to prominence as Lady Edytha Aldwyn in *A Gaiety Girl* (1894); other plays include *One Summer's Day, The Land of Nod, King John* (with Beerbohm Tree), *Alice-Sit-by-the-Fire, Raffles* and *L'Aiglon;* made NY debut as Millie Grace in *Nine or the Lady in Ostend* (1897).

FAIRFAX, Marion (1875–1979). American playwright and screenwriter. Name variations: Mrs. Tully Marshall. Born Marion Neiswanger, Oct 24, 1875, in Richmond, Virginia; died Oct 2, 1970, in Los Angeles, California; m. Tully Marshall (actor). ❧ Began career as an actress, debuting in Providence (RI) in *The Gay Parisienne* (1896); plays include *The Builders, The Chaperon, The Talker* and *Mrs. Boltay's Daughters;* wrote close to 50 screenplays, including the classic film *The Lost World* (1925); worked closely with director Marshall Neilan on such films as *Freckles, Dinty, The Lotus Eater* and *Bob Hampton of Placer;* head of Marion Fairfax Productions.

FAIRFAX SOMERVILLE, Mary (1780–1872). *See Somerville, Mary Fairfax.*

FAIRFIELD, Cicely (1892–1983). *See West, Rebecca.*

FAIRFIELD, Flora (1832–1888). *See Alcott, Louisa May.*

FAIR GERALDINE, The (c. 1528–1589). *See Fitzgerald, Elizabeth.*

FAIRHURST, Sue. Australian softball player. Born in Queensland, Australia. ❧ Pitcher, won a bronze medal at Sydney Olympics (2000).

FAIR MAID OF BRABANT (c. 1102–1151). *See Adelicia of Louvain.*

FAIR MAID OF KENT (1328–1385). *See Joan of Kent.*

FAIR MAID OF NORWAY (c. 1283–1290). *See Margaret, Maid of Norway.*

FAIROUZ (1935—). *See Fairuz.*

FAIRPORT CONVENTION. *See Denny, Sandy.*

FAIR ROSAMOND or ROSAMUND (c. 1145–1176). *See Clifford, Rosamund.*

FAIRUZ (1935—). Lebanese singer. Name variations: Fairouz. Born Hoda Nouhad Haddad, Nov 21, 1935, in Jabal Alarz, Lebanon; m. Assi Rahbani (composer), July 1954 (died June 21, 1986); children: 3 including Ziad Rahbani (composer). ❧ Arabic pop singer who has "the most beautiful voice in the world," wrote *All Music Guide,* "only Billie Holiday comes close"; appeared in films *Biya el-Khawatim* (1965), *Safar barlek* (1966) and *Bint El-Harass* (1967).

FAIRWAY FLAPPER, The (1899–1984). *See Cummings, Edith.*

FAITH (290–303). Gallic Christian martyr and saint. Name variations: Saint Faith, Saint Foy, Saint Fides, Saint Foi. Born in 290 in Agen, Aquitaine, Gaul (now France), to family of wealthy nobles; died in 303 in Agen. ❧ Child martyr and patron saint of pilgrims, prisoners and soldiers, was tested in faith at 13 by Roman procurator Dacian who visited town during Emperor Diocletian's persecution of Christians and ordered all residents to sacrifice to pagan gods or suffer torture; fled to hills with coreligionists but group was discovered and delivered to Dacian; roasted alive and beheaded after refusing to deny faith; said to have inspired faith and sympathy in townspeople and soldiers alike; after relics were transferred to church in Agen in 5th century, was later enshrined in medieval reliquary in monastery of Conques (855); inspired cult worship throughout Europe and South America; commemorated with dedicated chapels in Westminster Abbey and old St. Paul's Church. Feast day is Oct 6.

FAITHFULL, Emily (1835–1895). English feminist, philanthropist, and businesswoman. Name variations: Faithful. Born at Headley Rectory in Surrey, England, 1835; died in Manchester, England, May 31, 1895; dau. of Ferdinand Faithfull (rector of Headley, near Epsom). ❧ Aware of the lack of opportunities for women in industry, set up her own printing firm in Edinburgh (1857), employing women only; moving to London (1858), became secretary of the 1st Society for Promoting the Employment of Women; founded the Victoria Press (1860); was appointed printer and publisher-in-ordinary to Queen Victoria (1862); started *Victoria Magazine* (1863), a monthly bill for 18 years advocated a woman's right to hold monetary employment; also became involved with publications that her firm printed, including *The Englishwoman's Journal;* published a novel, *Change Upon Change: A Love Story* (1868); became involved in a highly publicized divorce suit between Henry Codrington (later admiral) and Helen Codrington (1864), which permanently tarnished her reputation; resigned from Victoria Press, but joined the Women's Trade Union League and founded the *West London Express* (1877), again staffed by women compositors; also lectured widely and successfully on women's issues both in England and US.

FAITHFULL, Marianne (1946—). English musician, singer and actress. Born Marianne Evelyn Gabriel Faithfull, Dec 29, 1946, in Hampstead, London, England; dau. of Eva, Baroness Erisso of Austria, and Major Glynn Faithfull (professor); m. John Dunbar, 1964 (div. 1970); m. Ben Brierly, 1979 (div. 1986); m. Giorgio Della Terza, 1988 (div. 1991); children: (1st m.) 1 son. ❖ Raspy-voiced singer-songwriter known for caustic lyrics, released hits "As Tears Go By" (1964), "Come and Stay With Me," "This Little Bird," and "Summer Nights" (all 1965) as a teen; began longterm and bumpy relationship with Mick Jagger (1965); co-starred with Alain Delon in *The Girl on the Motorcycle* (1968); played Ophelia in Nicol Williamson's film *Hamlet* (1969); was hospitalized 8 months for heroin addiction (1970); abandoned spotlight (1970–77); signed with Island Records (1979); released acclaimed comeback album *Broken English* (1979); received praise for such albums as *Strange Weather* (1987), *Blazing Away* (1990) and *Vagabond Ways* (2000); became known as interpreter of composer Kurt Weill's work, appearing onstage in his *Seven Deadly Sins* (1989) and *Threepenny Opera* (1991); acted in films *Turn of the Screw* and *Shopping* (both 1994) and *Intimacy* (2001); played God in an episode of "Absolutely Fabulous" (2001). ❖ See also autobiography, *Faithfull* (Little, Brown, 1994).

FAIZ, Alys (1914–2003). English-born journalist in Pakistan. Born Sept 22, 1914, in London, England; died Mar 12, 2003, in Lahore, Pakistan; dau. of a bookseller; sister of Christobel Tasser; m. Faiz Ahmed Faiz (Urdu poet and Lenin peace prizewinner), 1941 (died 1984); children: daughters, Saleema Hashmi (artist and former head of the National College of Arts) and Muneeza Hashmi (tv producer and former general manager of Pakistan Television). ❖ As a teenager, joined Communist Party, then the Free Indian League; worked as unpaid secretary to V.K. Krishna Menon; after India was partitioned (1947), moved to Pakistan and helped resettle refugees; husband was imprisoned for alleged role in the trumped-up Rawalpindi conspiracy (1951–55), resulting in a collection of letters she wrote to him, *Dear Heart* (1986); joined the staff of the country's leading English-language daily, the *Pakistan Times,* and wrote a regular column "Appa Jan"; later wrote for the radical weekly Pakistan paper, *Viewpoint;* began work with the UN children's fund (UNICEF, 1973); was closely engaged with the Pakistan human rights commission since its inception in 1986. ❖ See also memoir, *Over My Shoulder* (1991).

FAJARDO, Demisse (1964—). Peruvian volleyball player. Born July 1, 1964, in Peru. ❖ At Seoul Olympics, won a silver medal in team competition (1988).

FAJARDO, Gloria (1957—). See Estefan, Gloria.

FALCA, Marinella (1986—). Italian rhythmic gymnast. Born May 1, 1986, in Italy. ❖ Won team all-around silver medal at Athens Olympics (2004).

FALCK, Hildegard (1949—). West German runner. Name variations: Hildegarde Falck. Born June 1949 in Germany. ❖ Won a gold medal in the 800 meters and a bronze medal in the 4x400-meter relay at the Munich Olympics (1972).

FALCO, Joao (1892–1958). See Lisboa, Irene.

FALCÓN, Lidia (1935—). Spanish feminist, novelist and playwright. Name variations: Lidia Falcon; Lidia Falcón O'Neill. Born June 13, 1935, in Madrid, Spain; studied dramatic arts and law; earned doctorate in law from Universidad de Barcelona (1961) and doctorate in philosophy from Universidad Autónoma de Madrid (1991). ❖ Founded Spain's 1st Feminist Party (1979), and founded and edited the feminist magazine *Vindicació feminista* (1976–79); writings include *Los hijos de los*

vencidos (1979) and *En el infierno: Ser mujer en las cárceles de España* (1977).

FALCON, Marie Cornélie (1814–1897). French soprano and mezzo-soprano. Name variations: Marie Cornelie Falcon. Born Jan 28, 1814, in Paris; died Feb 25, 1897, in Paris; studied with Bordogni and A. Nourrit at Paris Conservatory. ❖ Debuted at the Paris Opéra (1832); premiered the roles of Valentine in Meyerbeer's *Les huguenots* (1836) and Rachel in Halévy's *La Juive* (1835); lost her voice during a performance (1838) and was forced to retire (1840). Roles that demand a combination of dramatic soprano and dramatic mezzo-soprano are referred to as "falcon," because she sang so many roles that overlapped between the soprano and mezzo-soprano voice.

FALCONBRIDGE, Anna Maria (fl. 1790–1794). British memoirist and abolitionist. Born in Bristol; m. Alexander Falconbridge, 1790; m. Isaac DuBois, 1793. ❖ Accompanied 1st husband to Sierra Leone and gave an account of their travels in her only known work, *Narrative of Two Voyages to Sierra Leone During the Years 1791-2-3* (1794); traveled with 2nd husband to Jamaica before returning to England.

FALCONER, Martha Platt (1862–1941). American social worker. Name variations: Martha Platt, Martha Falconer. Born Martha Platt, Mar 17, 1862, in Delaware, Ohio; died Nov 26, 1941, in East Aurora, NY; dau. of Cyrus Platt (jeweler) and Jeanette (Hulme) Platt; m. Cyrus Falconer (employee of Santa Fe railroad), Mar 21, 1885; children: 1 daughter, 2 sons. ❖ Advocate of rehabilitation, rather than incarceration, of delinquent and homeless young women, who influenced treatment of juvenile delinquency; worked at Illinois Children's Home and Aid Society (1898), becoming assistant superintendent; participated in Chicago Woman's Club, and was among the 1st probation officers of Cook County Juvenile Court; served as superintendent of girls' division of House of Refuge (later Sleighton Farm) in Philadelphia, PA (1906–19); worked in social welfare program of women's New Century Club, and helped found Philadelphia Training School for Social Work; was director of department of protective social measures of American Social Hygiene Association in New York City (1919–24); was executive secretary of Federation Caring for Protestant Children in NY (later Federation of Protestant Welfare Agencies, 1924–27); appointed by Governor Franklin D. Roosevelt as a delegate to International Conference of Social Work in Paris (1928).

FALCONETTI, Renée (1892–1946). French actress and producer. Name variations: Renee Falconetti; Maria Falconetti. Born Renée Maria Falconetti in Sermano, Corsica, 1892; died in Buenos Aires, Argentina, 1946. ❖ Celebrated French stage actress and producer, known for comedy roles, made a single film appearance in Carl Dreyer's silent masterpiece *La Passion de Jeanne D'Arc (The Passion of Joan of Arc,* 1927); immigrated to Buenos Aires before onset of WWII. ❖ See also *Women in World History.*

FALCONIERI, Juliana (1270–1341). Italian saint and religious founder. Name variations: Guiliana. Born 1270 in Florence; died 1341 in Florence; niece of St. Alexis; never married; no children. ❖ Established a new religious community (c. 1285), called the Mantellate Sisters, to pray and worship the Virgin and serve among the poor in her name. Feast day is June 19.

FALCONNET, Françoise-Cécile de Chaumont (1738–1819). French playwright. Name variations: Francoise-Cecile de Chaumont Falconnet. Born 1738 in Nancy, France; died 1819; m. Ambroise Falconnet (member of the judiciary in Paris). ❖ Wrote 2 comedies, *La Folle Enchère* (1771) and *L'Heureuse Rencontre* (1771), as well as *L'Amour à Tempé, pastorale érotique* (1773).

FALETIC, Dana (1977—). Australian rower. Born Aug 1, 1977, in Hobart, Tasmania. ❖ Won World championship for quadruple sculls (2003); won a bronze medal for quadruple sculls at Athens Olympics (2004).

FALK, Ria. West German pairs skater. Name variations: Ria Baron; Ria Falk-Baran. Born Ria Baron in Germany; m. Paul Falk (skater), 1951. ❖ With Paul Falk, won World championships (1951, 1952) and a gold medal at Oslo Olympics (1952).

FALKENBERG, Eugenia (1919–2003). See Falkenburg, Jinx.

FALKENBURG, Jinx (1919–2003). Spanish-born actress and model. Name variations: Jinx Falken; Eugenia Falkenberg. Born Eugenia Lincoln Falkenburg, Jan 21, 1919, in Barcelona, Spain; raised in Chile; died Aug 27, 2003, in Manhasset, NY; dau. of Eugene Falkenburg (engineer) and Marguerite (Crooks) Falkenburg; m. Tex McCrary (writer), June 1945 (sep. 1980s); children: John Reagan McCrary and Kevin Jock McCrary. ❖ Began US career as a fashion model and cover girl; made film debut in *Strike Me Pink* (1936), followed by *Nothing Sacred, The Lone Ranger Rides Again* (serial), *Two Latins from Manhattan, Nine Girls, Cover Girl, Tahiti Nights, The Gay Senorita, Meet Me on Broadway* and *Talk about a Lady,* among others; co-starred with husband on radio's "Tex and Jinx Show," which eventually moved to tv as "Closeup"; was a panelist on "Masquerade Party" (1958). ❖ See also autobiography *Jinx* (1951).

FALKENDER, Marcia (1932—). British political worker. Name variations: Baroness Falkender, Marcia Matilda Williams. Born Mar 10, 1932, in England; attended Northampton High School for Girls; Queen Mary College, University of London, BA in History; m. George Edmund Charles Williams, 1955 (div. 1961); children: (with conservative political journalist Walter Terry) 2 sons. ❖ Fiercely loyal secretary and confidante to Harold Wilson (prime minister of Britain, 1964–70 and 1974–76), began career as secretary to the general secretary of the Labour Party (1955); married and divorced, continued to use married name Marcia Williams in professional life; became Harold Wilson's private secretary (1956) and retained that position until she became political secretary and head of his political office (1964), when Wilson became leader of the Labour Party and prime minister; wielded enormous influence over Wilson, both personally and professionally, and was rumored to have had an affair with him; thought to be the inspiration for tv series *Yes, Minister;* was elevated to the peerage as Baroness Falkender (1974); after retiring from political life, worked as columnist for *Mail on Sunday* (1983–88). ❖ See also memoirs, *Inside No. 10* (1972) and *Downing Street in Perspective* (1983).

FALKENHAYN, Benita von (d. 1935). German baroness and spy. Beheaded, Feb 18, 1935, at Plötzensee prison, Germany. ❖ With friend Renate von Natzner, convicted for spying and became 2 of the last prisoners executed by beheading in Germany.

FALKESTEIN, Beatrice von (c. 1253–1277). Queen of the Romans. Name variations: Beatrix of Falkenburg; queen of Germany. Born around 1253 at Falkenburg Castle, Germany; died Oct 17, 1277; buried at Church of Franciscan Friars Minor, Oxford, Oxfordshire, England; dau. of Theodore von Falkestein, count of Falkenburg, or William de Fauquemont, count of Falkenburg, and Joan van Loon; niece of Conrad, archbishop of Cologne; m. Richard of Cornwall (1209–1272), 1st earl of Cornwall, king of the Romans (r. 1227–1272), on June 16, 1269. Richard of Cornwall's 1st wife was Isabel Marshall (1200–1240); his 2nd was Sancha of Provence (c. 1225–1261).

FALKLAND, Lady (1586–1639). *See Cary, Elizabeth.*

FALKLAND, Viscountess (1586–1639). *See Cary, Elizabeth.*

FALLACI, Oriana (1930—). Italian novelist and journalist. Born June 29, 1930, in Florence, Italy; dau. of Edoardo Fallaci (cabinet maker and politician) and Tosca (Cantini) Fallaci; attended University of Florence; companion of Alexandros Panagoulis (political activist, died May 1, 1976). ❖ Journalist, renowned for political interviews of such figures as Yasir Arafat, Henry Kissinger, Indira Gandhi, Willy Brandt, Mu'ammar Muhammad al-Gaddafi, fought in the underground during WWII; became a reporter for *Il mattino dell'Italia centrale* (1946), then *Epoca* magazine (1951); has been a special correspondent for *Europeo* since 1950s; lectured at various universities including University of Chicago, Columbia, Harvard, and Yale; novels include *Il sesso inutile* (1961, published in English as *The Useless Sex,* 1964), *Penelope alla guerra* (1962, *Penelope at War,* 1966), *Gli antipatici* (1963, *Limelighters,* 1967), *Lettera a un bambino mai nato* (1975, *Letter to a Child Never Born,* 1976), *Un uomo* (1979, *A Man,* 1980), and *Insciallah* (1990, *Inshallah,* 1992); nonfiction includes *I sette peccati di Holly wood* (The Seven Sins of Hollywood, 1958), *Se il sole muore* (1965, *If the Sun Dies,* 1966), and *Intervista con la storia* (1974, *Interview with History,* 1976). Twice received the St. Vincent Prize for journalism; won Prix Antibes (1993) for *Insciallah.* ❖ See also Santo L. Arico, *Oriana Fallaci: The Woman and the Myth* (Southern Illinois U. Press, 1998).

FALLIS, Barbara (1924–1980). American ballet dancer. Born 1924 in Denver, Colorado; died 1980 in New York, NY; m. Richard Thomas (dancer and teacher). ❖ Trained at Vic-Wells Ballet in London, performed with that company thereafter (1938–40); joined Ballet Theater in New York City where she danced for 8 years in such productions as Frederick Ashton's *Les Patineurs,* Antony Tudor's *Shadow of the Wind* and David Lichine's *Helen of Troy;* created feature role for Balanchine's *Waltz Academy* (1944); danced a season with Ballet Alicia Alonso where she performed in repertory of 19th-century works; with New York City Ballet, was featured in Balanchine's *Valse Fantasie* (1953) and *Pas de Dix* (1955), among others; taught with husband Richard Thomas at New York School of Ballet until her death.

FALLON, Trisha (1972—). Australian basketball player. Name variations: Trish Fallon. Born Trisha Nicole Fallon, July 23, 1972, in Melbourne, Victoria, Australia. ❖ Played for Sydney Flames (1992–94, 1996–97); won a team bronze medal at Atlanta Olympics (1996), a team silver at Sydney Olympics (2000) and team silver at Athens Olympics (2004); drafted by Minnesota Lynx of the WNBA (1999), traded to Phoenix Mercury (2000); placed 1st at Oceania chamionships (2003). Was Australia's Women's National Basketball League's MVP (2000).

FÄLTSKOG, Agnetha (1950—). Member of Swedish singing group ABBA. Name variations: Agnetha Ulvaeus; Agnetha Faltskog; in early days, known in Great Britain as Anna. Pronunciation: Ann-yetta. Born Agnetha Ase Faltskog in Jonkoping, Sweden, April 15, 1950; m. Björn Ulvaeus (sep. 1978, div.). ❖ Began singing with bands (1965); had #1 hit single in Sweden (1968) with "I Was So In Love" and other solo hits before and during time with ABBA; started living with Björn Ulvaeus, then songwriter for music entrepreneur Stig Anderson, and appeared in *Jesus Christ Superstar* as Mary Magdalene (1970); scored a hit with Swedish recording of "I Don't Know How to Love Him"; with Frida Lyngstad, Benny Andersson, and Björn Ulvaeus, formed singing group ABBA (acronym of their 1st initials); gained international renown with group when "Waterloo" won Eurovision Song Contest (1974); with ABBA, had more than a dozen Top-40 hits in US, including "Dancing Queen," "Knowing Me, Knowing You," and "Fernando," before split up (1982); released solo albums, *Wrap Your Arms Around Me* (1983), *Eyes of a Woman* (1985) and *I Stand Alone* (1988). ❖ See also *ABBA—The Movie;* and *Women in World History.*

FAMINOW, Cathy. *See Priestner, Cathy.*

FAMOSE, Annie (1944—). French Alpine skier. Born June 16, 1944, in Jurançon, France. ❖ At World championships, won a gold medal for slalom and silver medals for downhill and combined (1966) and a bronze medal for combined (1968); placed 3rd overall at World Cup (1967); won a silver medal for giant slalom and a bronze medal for slalom at Grenoble Olympics (1968).

FAN YUNJIE (1972—). Chinese soccer player. Born April 29, 1972, in Henan, China. ❖ Defender; made 1st appearance on Chinese national team (1992) and has over 100 caps; won a team silver medal at Atlanta Olympics (1996); drafted by WUSA's San Diego Spirit (2001); retired (2002).

FANE, Blanche (1855–1875). *See Whiteside, Jane.*

FANE, Florence (1826–1902). *See Victor, Frances.*

FANE, Margaret (1914–2004). *See Rutledge, Margaret Fane.*

FANE, Violet (1843–1905). *See Currie, Mary Montgomerie.*

FANNIA (fl. mid-1st c.). Roman noblewoman. Fl. mid-1st century; dau. of Thrasea Paetus and Arria Minor; granddau. of Caecina Paetus (Roman senator) and Arria Major (d. 42); m. Helvidius Priscus the Elder (praetor 70); children: (stepson) Helvidius Priscus the Younger. ❖ Sided with husband in his provocative attitude toward Emperor Vespasian (r. 69–79), causing her repeated exile; her stepson continued the cause; returned to Rome after death of Domitian (96). ❖ See also *Women in World History.*

FANNY. *Variant of Frances.*

FANNY.
See Millington, Jean.
See Millington, June.

FANNY, Aunt.
See Gage, Frances D. (1808–1884)
See Allison, Fran (1907–1989).

FANSHAWE, Anne (1625–1680). English Royalist and memoirist. Name variations: Lady Anne Fanshawe. Born Anne Harrison in London, England, Mar 25, 1625; died at Ware Park, Hertfordshire, England, Jan 30, 1680; elder dau. and 4th child of Sir John Harrison (prominent Royalist) and Margaret (Fanshawe) Harrison; m. Sir Richard

Fanshawe (1608–1666, diplomat, author, and relative of her mother), 1644; children: 14, of whom only 5 survived to adulthood. ❖ The *Memoirs* for which she is known were completed in 1676 but would not be published until 1829, almost 150 years after her death; they include a partial narrative of her adventures during the Commonwealth (1649–1660). ❖ See also *The Memoirs of Anne, Lady Halkett and Anne, Lady Fanshawe*; and *Women in World History*.

FANSHAWE, Catherine Maria (1765–1834). English poet. Born in Chipstead, Surrey, England, July 6, 1765; died at Putney Heath, England, April 17, 1834; dau. of John Fanshawe of Shabden, a Surrey squire, and Penelope (Dredge) Fanshawe; never married; no children. ❖ Known for her charm and wit and admired in her own circle, was often visited by the literati of her day but rarely agreed to have her work included in publications; best-known poem, a riddle on the letter H which began "'Twas whispered in heaven, 'twas muttered in Hell," was often attributed to Lord Byron; was a semi-invalid throughout life. ❖ See also *Women in World History*.

FANTHAM, Mrs. H.B. (1880–1963). *See Porter, Annie.*

FANTHORPE, U.A. (1929—). British poet. Born 1929 in Kent, England. ❖ The 1st woman nominated for the post of Oxford Professor of Poetry, frequently gave voice to socially oppressed people such as the mentally ill; often wrote poems for 2 voices, and in readings the 2nd voice was read by lifelong partner Rose Bailey; works include *Side Effects* (1978), *Standing To* (1982), *Voices Off* (1984), *Selected Poems* (1986), *A Watching Brief* (1987), *Neck-Verse* (1992), *Safe as Houses* (1995), *Consequences* (2000) and *Queuing for the Sun* (2003). Received Arts Council Writers' Award (1994), Cholmondeley Award (1995), Forward Poetry Prize (1996), CBE (2001), and Queen's Gold Medal for Poetry (2003).

FARA (d. 667). Frankish saint and religious founder. Name variations: Burgundofara; Saint Fara or Fare. Born in neighborhood of Meaux; died at Evoriac, France, in 667; sister of St. Chagnoaldus (monk of Luxeuil) and St. Faro (bishop of Meaux for 46 years and chancellor for King Clotaire II); never married; no children. ❖ Born into a noble Frankish family, refused to marry and founded a double monastery at Evoriac, later called Faremoutiers, after spending youth in a convent; was elected abbess and served in that capacity for 40 years; leadership qualities and great devotion led the Church to declare her a saint some years after her death. Feast day is April 3. ❖ See also *Women in World History*.

FARAH PAHLAVI. *See Pahlavi, Farah.*

FARBER, Viola (1931–1998). American modern dancer and choreographer. Born Feb 25, 1931, in Heidelberg, Germany; died Dec 24, 1998, in New York, NY. ❖ Trained in ballet by Margaret Craske and Alfredo Corvino, as well as in modern dance technique by Katherine Litz and Merce Cunningham, among others; danced with Cunningham Company (1953–65), where she created roles in his *Five in Space and Time* (1953), *Galaxy* (1956), *Picnic Polka* (1957), *Rune* (1959) and *Crises* (1960), among others; danced in Litz's company (1959) and later for Paul Taylor's company (c. 1965–67); founded Viola Farber Dance Company where she served as artistic director (1968–85); served as artistic director of Centre National de Danse Contemporaine in Angers, France (1981–83); taught at London Contemporary Dance School (1984–87); returned to US (1988), where she directed dance program of Sarah Lawrence College until her death; her works were appreciated for their unique sense of humor. Works of choreography include *Surf Zone* (1966), *Legacy* (1968), *Pop. 11* (1969), *Three Duets* (1969), *Route 6* (1972), *Dinosaur Parts* (1974), *Five Works for Sneakers* (1975), *Sunday Afternoon* (1976), *Turf* (1978) and *Private Relations* (1979).

FARE (d. 667). *See Fara.*

FAREBROTHER, Violet (1888–1969). English actress. Born Aug 22, 1888, in Grimsby, England; died Sept 27, 1969, in Eastbourne, Sussex, England. ❖ Made stage debut in London as a walk-on in *The Great Conspiracy* (1907), followed by *The Piper, Richard III, Sweet Nell of Old Drury* (as Lady Castlemaine), *Much Ado about Nothing* (as Beatrice), *Craig's Wife, Napoleon, Guilty, Othello, Major Barbara, Harvey* and *Where Angels Fear to Tread*, among others; toured with Donald Wolfit in US and Canada; made film debut as Queen Elizabeth in *Richard III* (1917), followed by 21 others.

FARENTHOLD, Frances "Sissy" (1926—). American lawyer and college president. Name variations: Frances Tarlton Farenthold; Sissy Farenthold. Born Frances Tarlton, Oct 2, 1926, in Corpus Christi,

Texas; dau. of Benjamin Dudley and Catherine (Bluntzer) Tarlton; Vassar College, AB, 1946; University of Texas, JD, 1959; Hood College, LLD, 1973; m. George Edward Farenthold, Oct 6, 1950; children: Dudley, George, Emilie, James and Vincent. ❖ Champion of human rights, admitted to Texas bar (1949); served 2 terms in Texas House of Representatives (1968–72), representing Nueces and Kleberg counties; was a Democratic candidate for governor (1972) and the 1st woman to be nominated as a candidate for vice president of the US (1972); was president of Wells College (1976–80), the college's 1st woman president since its founding in 1868; taught at Texas Southern University; served as chair of the National Women's Political Caucus.

FARIAL (1938—). Egyptian princess. Name variations: Farial Cheriff. Born Nov 17, 1938, at the Montazah Palace, near Alexandria, Egypt; dau. of King Faruk or Farouk I (r. 1936–52) and Farida; sister of King Fuad II; m. Samir Cheriff (formerly known as Jean-Pierre Perreten), Jan 25, 1966 (div. and remarried); children: Yasmine Perreten (b. 1967).

FARIDA (c. 830–?). Arabian singer. Born around 830 CE; death date unknown; flourished in the court of Caliph al-Watiq (r. 842–847) and his brother Caliph al-Mutawakki (r. 847–861); m. al-Mutawakki; children: at least one son. ❖ As a slave, was purchased, brought up, and educated by the singer Amr Ibn Bana before she was presented as a gift to Caliph al-Watiq; at his court, studied with Shariyya, another singer, but rivalry began to distance the two; exerted considerable influence at court; when al-Watiq died, belonged to his brother, al-Mutawakki.

FARIDA (1921–1988). Queen of Egypt. Name variations: Farida Favzira. Born Safinaz Khanum, Sept 5, 1921, in Alexandria, Egypt; died in Cairo, Oct 15, 1988; dau. of H.E. Yusuf Zulfikar (sometime ambassador to Iran) and Zainab (sometime lady-in-waiting to Queen Nazli); m. King Faruk or Farouk I (r. 1936–52), Jan 20, 1938 (div. Nov 17, 1948); m. Wahid Nasri, Mar 21, 1953; children: Ahmad Fuad (who succeeded his father as King Fuad II); Farial (b. 1938, who m. Samir Cheriff); Fawzia (1940–2005); Fadia (1943–2003).

FARINA, Mimi (1945–2001). American folksinger and guitarist. Name variations: Mimi Baez; Mimi Baez Farina or Fariña. Born Margarita Mimi Baez, April 30, 1945, in New York, NY; died of lung cancer, July 18, 2001, in Mt. Tamalpais, California; younger sister of Joan Baez (singer); m. Richard Farina (novelist and musician), 1963 (killed 1966); m. Milan Melvin (radio entrepreneur), 1968 (div. 1970). ❖ Moved to California (1963); began working with husband as singing duo (1963); fused rock and folk influences on duo's albums *Celebrations of a Grey Day* (1965) and *Reflections in a Crystal Wind* (1966); retreated from public life after death of 1st husband in motorcycle accident (1966); began performing occasionally with sister (late 1960s); worked as actress with The Committee (early 1970s); helped found Bread and Roses, a charitable organization providing entertainment for prisoners, hospital patients, and institutionalized people (early 1970s); appeared as herself in film *Fools* (1970) and concert documentary *Sing, Sing Thanksgiving* (1974).

FARJEON, Annabel (1919—). English ballet dancer and critic. Born 1919 in Buckleberry, Berkshire, England; dau. of Herbert and Joan Farjeon; niece of Eleanor Farjeon (children's writer). ❖ Performed with Sadler's Wells Ballet in London (mid-1930s–40), where she danced in many premiers including Wells' *Les Sylphides*, Ninette De Valois' *Le Roi Nu* (1938), and Frederick Ashton's *Cupid and Psyche* (1939) and *The Wise Virgins* (1940); retired from performance career during WWII to work as dance critic and journalist; was ballet editor for *New Statesman and Nation* as well as *Evening Standard* (starting 1959); wrote a biography of her aunt Eleanor Farjeon, *Morning Has Broken* (1986).

FARJEON, Eleanor (1881–1965). English children's writer. Name variations: (pseudonyms) Tomfool and Chimaera. Born Feb 13, 1881, in London, England; died June 5, 1965, in Hampstead, London; dau. of Benjamin Leopold Farjeon (novelist) and Margaret Jane (Jefferson) Farjeon (actress and dau. of American actor Joseph Jefferson); sister of Harry and Herbert Farjeon; aunt of Annabel Farjeon (ballet dancer); never married; no children. ❖ One of England's most distinguished writers for children, began career with publication of poems, *Pan-Worship* (1908); wrote *Martin Pippin in the Apple Orchard* (1921), a romantic fantasy combining verse, prose, and folklore; in next 8 years, produced 22 works and also penned daily verses for the *Daily Herald*, using the name Tomfool, as well as a weekly poem for the feminist *Time and Tide*, written under pseudonym Chimaera; collaborated with brother Herbert on many works, including the operetta *The Two Bouquets* (1936), which was produced in London and US, and a children's play, *The Glass Slipper* (1944); also wrote a number of adult books: *Ladybrook*

(1931), *Humming Bird* (1936), *Miss Granby's Secret* (1940) and *Ariadne and the Bull* (1945); in later years, created what are considered her best children's books, some of them reworked from earlier publications, including *Silver-Sand and Snow* (1951) and *The Children's Bells* (1957); also known for the hymn "Morning has broken," recorded by singer Cat Stevens. Received International Hans Christian Andersen Award and Carnegie Medal of Library Association in England (both 1956), for *The Little Bookroom;* won 1st Regina Medal of Catholic Library Association (1959). ❖ See also family memoir, *A Nursery in the Nineties* (1935); and *Women in World History.*

FARKAS, Agnes (1973—). Hungarian handball player. Name variations: Farkás. Born April 21, 1973, in Hungary. ❖ Won a team silver medal at Sydney Olympics (2000).

FARKAS, Andrea (c. 1969—). Hungarian handball player. Name variations: Farkás. Born c. 1969 in Hungary. ❖ Won a team bronze medal at Atlanta Olympics (1996) and a team silver medal at Sydney Olympics (2000).

FARKAS, Antónia (1898–1975). *See Corda, Maria.*

FARKAS, Ruth L. (1906–1996). American diplomat. Born Ruby Ruth Lewis, Dec 20, 1906; died Oct 18, 1996, in New York, NY; Columbia University, MA in sociology, 1932; New York University, doctorate in education; m. George Farkas (founder of Alexander's department stores); children: Robin Farkas. ❖ With husband, contributed $300,000 to Richard Nixon's reelection campaign; was then appointed ambassador to Luxemburg (1973), causing an uproar, despite such appointments being commonplace; served until 1976; established the Role Foundation (1967).

FARLEY, Harriet (1813–1907). American writer and editor. Born Feb 18, 1813 (some sources cite 1815 or 1817), in Claremont, New Hampshire; died Nov 12, 1907, in New York, NY; dau. of Stephen Farley (Congregational minister and school administrator) and Lucy (Sanders) Farley; attended Atkinson Academy in Atkinson, New Hampshire (where her father was the principal); m. John Intaglio Donlevy (engraver and inventor), 1854 (died 1880); children: Inez Donlevy; (stepdau.) Alice Heighes Donlevy. ❖ Took a job in one of the textile mills in Lowell, Massachusetts (1837); became editor of the *Offering* (1842), a journal published by and for the "mill girls," which tended to paint a rosy picture of life in the mill; published *Shells from the Strand of the Sea of Genius* (1847), a collection of homilies, many of which had appeared in the *Offering;* contributed to *Godey's Lady's Book* and published a children's book, *Happy Nights at Hazel Nook* (1853). ❖ See also *Women in World History.*

FARMBOROUGH, Florence (1887–1978). British nurse and diarist. Born in Buckinghamshire, England, April 15, 1887; died in Marple, England, Aug 18, 1978; never married; no children. ❖ As a frontline nurse with the Russian Army during World War I, compiled a diary that chronicled the progressive collapse of morale in the tsar's armed forces, a catastrophe that made all but inevitable the two revolutions of 1917 and radically transformed both Russian and world history; became somewhat of a celebrity when she published *Russian Album 1908–1918* and *With the Armies of the Tsar: A Nurse on the Russian Front, 1914–18* (1970s). ❖ See also *Women in World History.*

FARMER, Beverley (1941—). Australian novelist and short-story writer. Name variations: B. Christou. Born Beverley Anne Farmer, Feb 7, 1941, in Windsor, Melbourne, Australia; only child of Maud Ruby Thomas and Colin Stewart Farmer; Melbourne University, BA, 1960, DipEd, 1961; m. a Greek migrant, 1965. ❖ Lived 3 years with husband in Greece where some stories are set; writings include *Alone* (1980), *Milk* (1983), *Home Time* (1985), *A Body of Water* (1990), *The Seal Woman* (1992), *The House in the Light* (1995), and *Collected Stories* (1996). Received *Canberra Times* Short Story Award (1980) and New South Wales Premier's Award for Fiction (1984).

FARMER, Fannie Merritt (1857–1915). American authority on cooking. Born Mar 23, 1857, in Boston, Massachusetts; died Jan 15, 1915, in Boston; dau. of John Franklin (printer) and Mary Watson (Merritt) Farmer; sister of Cora Farmer; aunt of Wilma Lord Perkins; never married; no children. ❖ After graduating from Boston Cooking School (1889), stayed on as assistant director, then became head of school (1894); gained national recognition with her *Boston Cooking School Cook Book* (1896), which was considered such a risky venture that she paid for 1st edition with her own funds; left Boston Cooking School to open Miss Farmer's School of Cookery (1902); her true interest, however, was in improving health through diet; published *Food and Cookery for the Sick and Convalescent* (1904), which she considered her most important work; also contributed monthly to *The Woman's Home Companion.* ❖ See also *Women in World History.*

FARMER, Frances (1913–1970). American actress. Born Sept 19, 1913, in Seattle, Washington; died of cancer, Aug 1, 1970, in Indianapolis, Indiana; dau. of Lillian (Van Ornum) Farmer and Ernest Farmer; sister of Edith Farmer Elliot; m. Leif Erickson (actor), 1936 (div. 1942); m. Alfred Lobley, 1954 (div. 1957); m. Leland Mikesell, 1958 (div. 1958); no children. ❖ Actress whose tragic life became the subject of the movie *Frances,* made breakthrough film *Come and Get It* (1936); also appeared in *Rhythm on the Range* (1936), *Ebb Tide* (1937), *The Toast of New York* (1937), *Ride a Crooked Mile* (1938), *South of Pago Pago* (1940), *Badlands of Dakota* (1941), *Among the Living* (1941) and *Son of Fury* (1942), among others; was heavily criticized for her involvement in left-wing causes during the so-called "Red Scare" (1930s–40s); also had a profound dislike of the studio system; turned to alcohol and drugs which led to several rebellious incidents well-covered in the tabloid press; eventually declared "mentally incompetent" by court order, spent 11 years in a series of institutions, often under horrific conditions, and was exposed to a number of unproven, experimental treatments before being declared "cured" and released in early 1950s; appeared in only one film after her release, worked at a series of odd jobs, and hosted a local tv show in Indianapolis, Indiana, before the effects of her previous psychiatric treatments and the return of her alcoholism permanently ended her working years. ❖ See also *Will There Really Be a Morning?* (Putnam, 1972); William Arnold, *Shadowland* (McGraw-Hill, 1978); film *Frances,* starring Jessica Lange (1982); and *Women in World History.*

FARMER, Virginia (1898–1988). American stage and screen actress. Born April 18, 1898, in Indiana; died May 19, 1988, in Long Beach, California. ❖ Films include *This Gun for Hire, Lady in the Dark, To Each His Own, Another Part of the Forest, Cyrano de Bergerac* and *The Men;* founded LA chapter of Federal Theater Project (1930s); labeled by House Un-American Activities Committee as an unfriendly witness, saw career hampered; taught at LA Actors Studio.

FARMER-PATRICK, Sandra (1962—). American hurdler. Name variations: Sandra Patrick. Born Aug 18, 1962, in US. ❖ At Barcelona Olympics, won a silver medal in the 400-meter hurdles (1992).

FARNADI, Edith (1921–1973). Hungarian pianist. Born in Budapest, Hungary, Sept 25, 1921; died in Graz, Austria, Dec 14, 1973; studied at the Budapest Academy. ❖ Made debut in Budapest with Beethoven's C major Piano Concerto, which she conducted from the keyboard (1933); after graduation from Budapest Academy at 16, became a faculty member there; engaged in extensive concert tours in Europe; was a noted chamber-music performer and made many recordings, including a large number of works by Liszt.

FARNESE, Elizabeth (1692–1766). Queen of Spain. Name variations: Elizabeth of Farnese or Elizabeth de Farnese, Princess of Parma; Isabel Farnese or Isabella of Parma; Isabella Elizabeth Farnese; (Ital.) Isabel de Farnesio. Born Oct 25, 1692, in Parma, Italy; died July 10, 1766; dau. of Dorothea Sophia of Neuburg and Odoardo also known as Edward Farnese of Parma (eldest son of Ranucci II, duke of Parma); m. Philip V (1683–1746), king of Spain (r. 1700–1724, 1724–1746), Dec 24, 1714; children: Charles IV (1716–1788), king of Naples and Sicily (r. 1735–1759), also known as Charles III, king of Spain (r. 1759–1788); Francisco (b. 1717); Maria Ana Victoria (1718–1781); Philip (1720–1765); Maria Theresa of Spain (1726–1746, who m. Louis le dauphin); Louis or Luis Antonio (b. 1727); Maria Antonia of Spain (1729–1785). ❖ Wielded wide political power during husband Philip V's prolonged periods of insanity and inertia; wed Philip by proxy (1714); while he showed slight interest in anything except the hunt, influenced royal policy; remained Italian and condescending to things Spanish; maneuvered to protect her claims to Parma so they might be passed on to her own sons; when the king refused to conduct or even discuss any matters of state (1727), was named regent for the duration of his illness; after Austrian emperor died (1740) and War of the Austrian Succession erupted, exploited the international chaos to seize Parma, Tuscany, and Plasencia; on Philip's death (1746), was exiled from Madrid; with son Charles named king of Spain (1759), acted as regent until his arrival; provided more energy and direction to the Spanish government than it received from her husband. During her reign, Spain began to recover some of its earlier prosperity and glory but Elizabeth failed to assimilate the interests of Spain and make them her own. ❖ See also *Memoirs of*

Elizabeth Farnesio, the Present Queen Dowager of Spain (T. Gardner, 1746); Edward Armstrong, *Elisabeth Farnese: "The Termagant of Spain"* (Longman, Green, 1892); and *Women in World History.*

FARNESE, Giulia (1474–1518?). Italian noblewoman. Name variations: Julia Farnese. Born 1474; died after 1518; dau. of Pier Luigi Farnese; sister of Alessandro (Alexander) Farnese who later was elected Pope Paul III; m. Orsino Orsini, May 21, 1489; mistress of Alexander VI (Rodrigo or Roderigo Borgia). ❖ A portrait of Giulia Farnese by Luca Longhi shows her with the mythical unicorn, a symbol of Chastity. ❖ See also *Women in World History.*

FARNESE, Isabel (1692–1766). *See Farnese, Elizabeth.*

FARNESE, Julia (1474–1518?). *See Farnese, Giulia.*

FARNHAM, Eliza W. (1815–1864). American philanthropist and writer. Born Eliza Woodson Burhans at Rensselaerville, Albany Co., NY, Nov 17, 1815, of an old Dutch Quaker family; died in New York, NY, Dec 15, 1864; m. Thomas J. Farnham (lawyer and travel writer), 1836 (died 1849); married 2nd time; children: 4. ❖ Took a job in Sing Sing (then called Mt. Pleasant) where for 4 years (1844–48) she was matron of the women's division of the New York State Prison; edited Sampson's *Criminal Jurisprudence* and published *Life in Prairie Land* about her experiences living in the wilderness of Illinois; moved to Boston (1848), where she was connected with the management for the Institution for the Blind; organized a society to aid and protect destitute women, and encouraged the unmarried to emigrate, often escorting them to the Western states; published bestseller, *California, Indoors and Out* (1856), followed by *My Early Days* (1859); worked on her most important book, the 2-vol. *Women and her Era* (1856–64), in which she pleaded the superiority of women based on biology, art, literature, history, religion and philosophy. ❖ See also *Women in World History.*

FARNINGHAM, Marianne (1834–1909). English journalist and educator. Name variations: Mary Ann Hearn; Marianne Farningham Hearn; (pseudonym) Eva Hope. Born Mary Ann Hearn, Dec 17, 1834, in Farningham, Kent, England (Marianne Farningham is a pseudonym); died Mar 16, 1909, in Barmouth, Wales; dau. of Joseph (merchant) and Rebecca (Bowers) Hearn (both members of Eynsford Particular Baptist Church); never married; no children. ❖ Victorian Baptist who was an educationalist, journalist, and lecturer at a time when women were not expected to enter public life; took 1st teaching post in Bristol (1852); contributed poem to 1st issue of *The Christian World* (1857); moved to Northampton as head of the Infant Department of the British School (1859); contributed to the 1st issue of *The Sunday School Times and Home Educator* (1860); left teaching to become a salaried member of staff on *The Christian World* (1867); 1st addressed the annual meeting of the Sunday School Union (1874); gave 1st public lecture in Daventry, Northamptonshire (1877); became editor of *The Sunday School Times* (1885); had post on Northampton school board (1886–91); wrote almost 50 books of poetry and prose, mainly collections of contributions to *The Christian World* and *The Sunday School Times.* ❖ See also memoir *A Working Woman's Life* (Clarke, 1907); Shirley Burgoyne Black, ed. *A Farningham Childhood: Chapters from the Life of Marianne Farningham* (Darenth Valley, 1988); Rev. W. Glandwr-Morgan, *Marianne Farningham in her Welsh Home* (Ellesmere, 1909); and *Women in World History.*

FARNSWORTH, Emma J. (1860–1952). American photographer. Born Emma Justine Farnsworth in Albany, NY, 1860; died in Albany in 1952. ❖ Known for her allegorical and narrative studies, joined the Camera Club of New York and, with help of a fellow club member, published a book of her figure studies, *In Arcadia,* accompanied by classical verse (1892); won close to 30 medals in exhibitions abroad and was the subject of the Camera Club's 2nd solo exhibition (1898).

FARQUHAR, Marilyn (1928—). American cell biologist. Name variations: Marilyn Gist Farquhar. Born Marilyn Gist, July 11, 1928; grew up in Tulare, California; dau. of Brooks Dewitt Gist (insurance agent and writer) and Alta Green Gist (managed a floral shop); University of California, Berkeley, BA, 1949, MA, 1952, PhD, 1955; m. John Farquhar (div.); George Palade, June 7, 1970; children: (1st m.) 2. ❖ Worked as an assistant research pathologist at University of California, Berkeley (1956–58); at Rockefeller University's department of cell biology, served as research associate (1958–62) and professor (1970–73); at University of California, San Francisco, was associate research pathologist (1962–64), associate pathology professor in residence (1964–68), and pathology professor

in residence (1968–70); was professor of cell biology and pathology (1973–87) and the Sterling Professor of Cell Biology and Pathology (1987–89) at Yale University School of Medicine; elected to National Academy of Sciences (1988); recruited with husband George Palade to start a new cellular and molecular medicine division at the University of California, San Diego (1990); elected to American Academy of Arts and Sciences (1991). Received American Society for Cell Biology's E.B. Wilson Medal (1987), American Society of Nephrology's Homer Smith Award (1987), and NIH Merit Award (1988).

FARQUHARSON, Marian Ogilvie (1846–1912). *See Ogilvie Farquharson, Marian.*

FARQUHARSON, Martha (1828–1909). *See Finley, Martha Farquharson.*

FARR, Wanda K. (1895–1983). American cytologist. Name variations: Wanda Kirkbride; Mrs. R.C. Faulwetter. Born Wanda Marguerite Kirkbride, Jan 9, 1895, at New Matamoras, Ohio; died April 1983, possibly in New York City; dau. of Frederick and Clara Nikolaus Kirkbride; Ohio University, BS, 1915; Columbia University, MS, 1918; m. Clifford Harrison Farr, May 28, 1917 (died 1928); m. Roy Christopher Faulwetter (div.); children: (1st m.) Robert Nicklaus Farr (b. July 3, 1920). ❖ Scientist who pioneered X-ray diffraction techniques for plant cell research and discovered the mechanism for cellulose manufacture in plant cells; worked as researcher on plant cells, University of Iowa (1919–24); was research associate, Barnard Skin and Cancer Hospital, St. Louis, Missouri (1925–28); instructed classes at Henry Shaw School of Botany, Washington University, St. Louis (1928); carried on studies on root-hair growth financed by National Academy of Sciences' Bache Fund (1928); was plant physiologist, Boyce Thompson Institute for Plant Research (1928–29); served as associate cotton technologist for US Department of Agriculture (1929–36); served as director, Cellulose Laboratory, Boyce Thompson Institute (1936–40); resolved the scientific mystery surrounding the fundamental component of plant life, cellulose, that had befuddled multitudes of scientists for decades (1939); was research microchemist, American Cyanamid Company (1940–43) and research associate, Celanese Corporation of America (1943–54); worked as research consultant (1954–67); was associate professor of botany, University of Maine (1957–68); worked as researcher, Farr Cytochemical Labs (1960s–70s). ❖ See also *Women in World History.*

FARRALLY, Betty (1915–1989). English ballet dancer. Name variations: Betty Farrally Hey. Born 1915 in Bradford, West Yorkshire, England; trained at Torren School of Dance in Leeds. ❖ Immigrated to Canada with Gweneth Lloyd, where they co-founded a dance school in Winnipeg which evolved into the Winnipeg Ballet, then Royal Winnipeg Ballet; shared artistic direction of company with Lloyd until late 1950s and had a great impact upon the development of dance in Canada.

FARRAND, Beatrix Jones (1872–1959). American landscape architect. Name variations: Beatrix Jones. Born Beatrix Cadwalader Jones, June 19, 1872, in New York, NY; died in Bar Harbor, Maine, Feb 27, 1959; dau. of Frederic Rhinelander Jones and Mary Cadwalader Rawle Jones; paternal niece of Edith Wharton; m. Max Farrand, Dec 17, 1913; no children. ❖ One of the finest landscape architects of her time, internationally known for her knowledge of plants and her keen sense of design, was the only woman founder of the American Society of Landscape Architects; apprenticed at Arnold Arboretum under Charles Sprague Sargent (1892); opened 1st office (1895); given 1st important commission (1896); discharged last commission, a guesthouse for David Rockefeller at Seal Harbor, Maine (1949). Major commissions include Princeton University, Princeton, New Jersey (1913–41), Eolia, estate of Edward S. Harkness, in New London, Connecticut (1919–32, now Harkness Memorial State Park), Dumbarton Oaks, residence of Mildred and Robert Bliss, Washington, DC (1921–47), Yale University, New Haven, Connecticut (1922–45), and Dartington Hall, Ltd., Totnes, Devonshire, England (1933–38). ❖ See also Balmori, McGuire, and McPeck, *Beatrix Farrand's American Landscapes* (Sagapress, 1985); McGuire and Fern, *Beatrix Jones Farrand (1872–1959): Fifty Years of American Landscape Architecture* (1982); Patterson, Roper, and Bliss, *Beatrix Jones Farrand, 1872–1959: An Appreciation of a Great Landscape Gardener* (1960); and *Women in World History.*

FARRAR, Cynthia (1795–1862). American missionary. Born Cynthia Farrar, April 20, 1795, in Marlborough, New Hampshire; died Jan 25, 1862, in Ahmednagar, India; dau. of Phinehas and Abigail (Stone) Farrar; attended Union Academy in Plainfield, NH. ❖ Converted to

Congregational church after attending religious festival in Marlborough, NH (1815); was the 1st unmarried American woman missionary sent overseas, traveling to Mumbai (Bombay), India, to found and run schools for girls (1827); worked for Marathi mission, establishing and directing schools in Mumbai (1827–36) and in Ahmednagar (1839–62), gaining support of prominent city residents.

FARRAR, Eliza Rotch (1791–1870). French-American author. Name variations: Elizabeth or Eliza Ware Rotch, Eliza Ware Rotch Farrar. Born Elizabeth Ware Rotch, July 12, 1791, in Dunkirk, France; died April 22, 1870, in Springfield, Massachusetts; dau. of Benjamin and Elizabeth (Barker) Rotch; m. John Farrar (professor), Oct 10, 1828 (died 1853). ❖ Wrote a popular etiquette book, *The Young Lady's Friend,* which offered rules for women's behavior in various areas of life, rather than emphasizing morality and religion (1836); also wrote *The Children's Robinson Crusoe* (1830), *Lafayette* (1831), *John Howard* (1833), *The Youth's Letter-Writer* (1834), *Congo in Search of His Master* (1854) and *Recollections of Seventy Years* (1865).

FARRAR, Geraldine (1882–1967). American soprano. Born Feb 28, 1882, in Melrose, Massachusetts; died Mar 11, 1967, in Ridgefield, Connecticut; dau. of Sidney Farrar (businessman and outstanding baseball player) and Henrietta (Barnes) Farrar; studied voice with Mrs. John H. Long, Emma Thursby, Trabadello, Francesco Graziani, and Lilli Lehmann; m. Lou Tellegen (actor), c. 1915 (div.). ❖ Debuted at the Berlin Royal Opera as Marguerite in *Faust* (1901); remained the Royal Opera's leading soprano, singing roles that included Gounod's Juliette in *Roméo et Juliette,* Violetta in *La Traviata,* Zerlina in *Don Giovanni,* Gilda in *Rigoletto* and Leonora in *Il Trovatore* (1901–04); debuted at Metropolitan Opera as Juliette in *Roméo et Juliette;* created the roles of the Goose Girl in Humperdinck's *Königskinder* (1910) and Louise in Charpentier's *Julien;* sang 29 roles at the Met, frequently with Enrico Caruso (1906–22) and reigned as the opera house's leading diva; retired from the stage (1922).

FARRAR, Gwen (1899–1944). English actress, singer and instrumentalist. Born July 14, 1899, in London, England; died Dec 25, 1944, in London; dau. of Sir George Farrar and Ella M. (Waylen) Farrar; trained for the cello with Herbert Walenn. ❖ Appeared in concert and on stage for a number of years with Norah Blaney; plays include *Whitebirds, Shake Your Feet, Wonder Bar, After Dinner, Charlot's Char-a-bang!* and *Die Fledermaus;* films include *She Shall Have Music* and *Take a Chance;* was also an expert equestrian. ❖ See also film *Gwen Farrar* (1926).

FARRAR, Margaret (1897–1984). American editor. Born Margaret Petherbridge, Mar 23, 1897, in Brooklyn, NY; died June 11, 1984, in New York, NY; daughter of Henry Wade (executive with National Licorice Company) and Margaret Elizabeth (Furey) Petherbridge; graduate of Berkeley Institute, Brooklyn, 1916; Smith College, BA, 1919; m. John Chipman Farrar (author and co-founder of Farrar, Straus), May 28, 1926; children: John, Alison and Janice Farrar. ❖ Once called the "world's supreme authority on crosswords," was the 1st editor of the much-revered crossword puzzles of *The New York Times* and also collaborated on the 1st *Cross Word Puzzle Book;* before retirement (1968), had edited over 130 collections of puzzles. ❖ See also *Women in World History.*

FARRELL, Eileen (1920–2002). American soprano. Born Feb 13, 1920, in Willimantic, Connecticut; died Mar 23, 2002, in Park Ridge, New Jersey; dau. of Michael John Farrell and Catherine (Kennedy) Farrell (vaudeville performers, known as "The Singing O'Farrells"); studied with Merle Alcock and Eleanor McLellan; m. Robert V. Reagan (NY police officer), 1946 (died 1986); children: Robert V., Kathleen and John Reagan. ❖ As the daughter of ex-vaudeville performers turned music teachers, often shook off the pretentions of the opera world because of her populist bent; made debut as singer on CBS (1941); had own half-hour show, "Eileen Farrell Sings," which lasted for 6 years; made 61 appearances with New York Philharmonic, establishing a record and beginning a long association with that organization (1950–51); sang with the San Carlo Opera in Tampa, Florida (1956); made San Francisco debut in *Il Trovatore* (1957); made Metropolitan Opera debut in Gluck's *Alcestis* and firmly established her as one of America's leading dramatic sopranos (1960); released 3 recordings: Puccini arias, French and German art songs, and American popular songs (1960), but is best remembered for her Carnegie Hall recording of Berg's *Wozzeck* with the New York Philharmonic; served as Distinguished Professor of Music at Indiana University's School of Music (1971–80) and at the University of Maine (1984). ❖ See also *Women in World History.*

FARRELL, Glenda (1904–1971). American stage and screen actress. Born June 30, 1904, in Enid, Oklahoma; died May 1, 1971, in NYC; m. Thomas Richards, 1921 (div. 1929); m. Henry Ross (physician), 1941; children: (1st m.) Tommy Farrell (actor). ❖ Made Broadway debut in *Skidding* (1928); other NY appearances include *Divided Honors, Love Honor and Betray, The Life of Reilly, Stage Door, Masquerade* and *Forty Carats;* debuted in film *Little Caesar* (1931); made over 122 films, including *The Mystery of the Wax Museum, Gold Diggers, Susan Slept Here, Girl in the Red Velvet Swing, Lady for a Day, Johnny Eager* and *Talk of the Town;* was also featured in the "Torchy Blane" series. Won Emmy for performance in "A Cardinal Act of Mercy" on "Ben Casey" (1963).

FARRELL, Hortense (b. 1903). See Alden, Hortense.

FARRELL, M.J. (1904–1996). See Keane, Molly.

FARRELL, Michelle (1968—). See Dusserre, Michelle.

FARRELL, Peggy (1920—). Irish politician. Born Nov 15, 1920, in Bantry, Co. Cork, Ireland; m. Thomas P. Farrell. ❖ Representing Fianna Fáil, nominated to the Seanad by Taoiseach Jack Lynch (1969–73).

FARRELL, Renita (1972—). Australian field-hockey player. Name variations: Renita Garard. Born Renita Farrell, May 30, 1972, in Townsville, Australia. ❖ Midfielder; won team gold medals at Atlanta Olympics (1996) and Sydney Olympics (2000).

FARRELL, Suzanne (1945—). American ballerina. Name variations: Suzanne Ficker. Born Roberta Sue Ficker, Aug 16, 1945, in Cincinnati, Ohio; dau. of Robert and Donna Ficker; studied ballet at University of Cincinnati College Conservatory of Music and School of American Ballet; m. Paul Mejia (dancer), Feb 21, 1969 (div. 1997). ❖ Leading interpreter of the work of choreographer George Balanchine, danced with the New York City Ballet (1961–69), attaining stardom with performance in *Don Quixote* (1965); danced roles in *La Valse, Concerto Barocco, Liebeslieder Walzer, Donizetti Variations, A Midsummer Night's Dream, Invesiana, Glinkaiana, Stars and Stripes, Prodigal Son* and *Symphony in C;* also danced in a trio of new ballets that Balanchine created for her, the romantic *Meditation,* the abstract *Agon* and *Clarinade;* danced with Ballet of the 20th Century (1970–75); returning to New York City Ballet (1975–87), performed in premieres of other Balanchine ballets: *Chaconne, Union Jack, Davidsbündlertänze, Mozartiana* and *Vienna Waltzes,* perhaps the single most successful ballet in the company's history; became a master teacher at Kennedy Center (1993); taught and staged Balanchine ballets for companies in US and abroad. Films include *A Midsummer Night's Dream* (1966) and *Elusive Muse* (1996); appeared on tv in "Dance in America: Choreography by Balanchine" (1977–79). ❖ See also autobiography (with Toni Bentley) *Holding on to the Air* (Summit, 1990); and *Women in World History.*

FARREN, Elizabeth (c. 1759–1829). English actress and countess of Derby. Name variations: Eliza Farren. Born c. 1759 in Cork, Ireland; died at Knowsley Park, Lancashire, April 29, 1829; dau. of George Farren (apothecary and surgeon) and actress mother; m. Edward Stanley, 12th earl of Derby, May 1, 1797; children: 3. ❖ Made 1st London appearance as Miss Hardcastle in *She Stoops to Conquer* (1777); was the original Nancy Lovel in George Colman's *Suicide* and appeared at Drury Lane (1778); was popular with London's upper crust; retired (April 8, 1797), following marriage to earl of Derby; was a rival of Frances Abington. ❖ See also *Women in World History.*

FARREN, Ellen (1848–1904). See Farren, Nellie.

FARREN, Nellie (1848–1904). English actress. Name variations: Ellen Farren; Nelly Farren. Born Ellen Farren in 1848; died in 1904; dau. of Henry Farren (1826–1860, an actor); great-granddau. of actor William Farren (1725–1795); granddau. of actor William Farren (1786–1861). ❖ Descending from a long line of actors, began career at Olympic Theater (1864–1868), then was associated with John Hollingshead's company at Gaiety Theater until her retirement (1891); short and slight, specialized in playing young boys, notably Smike in Charles Dickens' *Nicholas Nickleby* and Sam Willoughby in Tom Taylor's *Ticket-of-Leave Man;* female roles included Lydia Languish in *The Rivals* (1874) and Maria in *Twelfth Night* (1876). ❖ See also *Women in World History.*

FARRENC, Louise (1804–1875). French musician. Born Jean-Louise Dumont in Paris, France, May 31, 1804; died in Paris, Sept 15, 1875; studied with composer Anton Reicha; m. Aristide Farrenc (music publisher, died 1865). ❖ Concert pianist, composer, teacher, and scholar, was the only woman piano teacher at the Paris Conservatoire for over 30 years and the only woman to hold a post of this rank in the 19th century (1842–73); compositions include 3 symphonies and a piano concerto. ❖ See also *Women in World History*.

FARRER, Margaret (1914–1997). English midwife and nursing officer. Name variations: Margaret Irene Farrer. Born Feb 23, 1914 in Rhodesia; died July 25, 1997. ❖ Moved back to England with family at age 13, settling in Devon; was the 1st midwife to serve as deputy chair of Central Midwives Board (CMB, 1973–79); also served on Central Health Services Council, on North East Metropolitan Hospital Board, and on Thames Regional Health Authority; oversaw nursing and midwifery for East End of London as chief nursing officer of Thames Group Hospital Management Committee (1971–74); served as matron of St. Mary's Maternity Hospital, West Croydon, Surrey (1949–56) and of Forest Gate Maternity Hospital (1956–71). Made Officer of the Order of the British Empire (OBE, 1970).

FARRÉS, Carmen (1931–1976). Spanish novelist. Name variations: Carmen Farres; (pseudonym) Carmen Mieza. Born 1931 in Barcelona, Spain; died 1976. ❖ Wrote novels based on her exile in Mexico during Spanish Civil War: *La imposible canción* (The Impossible Song, 1962) and *Una mañana cualquiera* (Any Morning, 1964).

FARRINGTON, Sara Willis (1811–1872). *See Fern, Fanny.*

FARROKHZAD, Forugh (1935–1967). Iranian poet and feminist. Name variations: Farrough, Foroogh, Furogh, or Furugh Farrukhzad or Farrokhzaad or Farrokhzād. Pronunciation: Four-UGH Farroch-ZHAHD. Born Forugh Farrokhzad in Tehran, Iran, Jan 5, 1935; died of injuries sustained in auto accident in Tehran, Feb 14, 1967; dau. of Mohammed Farrokhzad (colonel in Iranian Army) and Turan Vaziri Tabar Farrokhzad; attended Kamalolmolk Technical School; m. Parviz Shapur, 1951 (div. 1954); children: 1 son. ❖ Major Iranian poet and early feminist, who was one of her country's 1st important female writers; published 1st poems in Tehran newspapers and magazines (1953); had nervous breakdown (1954); had love affair with Nader Naderpur, a prominent Iranian poet (1954–56); published 1st collection of poetry, *The Captive* (1955), which candidly featured a female's personal thoughts and feelings, causing an immediate stir; lamented the fact that men had been able to describe their experiences of love in poetry without evoking criticism, and insisted on her right to do the same from a feminine perspective; made 1st trip abroad (1956); published 2nd volume of poetry, *The Wall* (1956), followed by *Rebellion* (1958); became assistant at Ebrahim Golestan's film studio and embarked on a long-standing relationship with Golestan (1958); studied film production in England (1959), then began work as documentary filmmaker (1960); completed documentary film on Iranian lepers, *The House is Black* (1962); worked as a stage actress, appearing in *Six Characters in Search of an Author* (1963); published *Another Birth* (1964); now widely recognized as a major figure on the Iranian literary scene, was the subject of UNESCO film (1965); published *Let Us Believe in the Beginning of the Cold Season* (1974). ❖ See also Michael C. Hillmann, *A Lonely Woman: Forugh Farrokhzad and Her Poetry* (Three Continents Press, 1987); and *Women in World History*.

FARRON, Julia (1922—). English ballet dancer. Born July 22, 1922, in London, England. ❖ Trained at Sadler's Wells Ballet School, then joined the company; remained with Sadler's Wells—later known as Royal Ballet—throughout performance career (1936–61); created roles in numerous works by Frederick Ashton including his *A Wedding Bouquet* (1937), *Cupid and Psyche* (1939), *Sylvia* (1952), *Homage to the Queen* (1958), and *Ondine* (1958); performed in company productions of classic repertory works, *Les Sylphides, Swan Lake* and *Giselle;* created role of Lady Capulet in Kenneth Macmillan's *Romeo and Juliet*.

FARROW, Mia (1945—). American actress. Born Maria de Lourdes Villiers Farrow, Feb 9, 1945, in Los Angeles, California; dau. of John Farrow (director) and Maureen O'Sullivan (actress); sister of John Charles, Prudence, Stephanie and Tisa Farrow; m. Frank Sinatra (singer and actor), 1966 (div. 1968); m. André Previn (conductor), 1970 (div. 1979); children: (with Previn) had twins and 1 other child, then adopted 3 more, including Soon-Yi Previn; (with Woody Allen) had 1 child and adopted 2 others. ❖ Began acting in theater at 17; came to prominence as Allison Mackenzie in tv series "Peyton Place" (1964–66); had major film breakthrough in Roman Polanski's *Rosemary's Baby* (1969); moved to London with Previn and spent season with Royal Shakespeare Company (1975–76); began working with Woody Allen (1981) who created roles for her in such films as *A Midsummer Night's Sex Comedy* (1982), *Zelig* (1983), *The Purple Rose of Cairo* (1985), *Hannah and Her*

Sisters (1987), *Radio Days* (1987), *September* (1987), *Another Woman* (1988), *New York Stories* (1989), *Crimes and Misdemeanors* (1989), *Alice* (1990), *Shadow and Fog* (1992) and *Husbands and Wives* (1992); had infamous breakup after living with Allen for many years (1996); other films include *John and Mary* (1969), *The Great Gatsby* (1974), *Full Circle* (1977), *A Wedding* (1978), *Death on the Nile* (1978), *Hurricane* (1979), *Miami Rhapsody* (1995), *Angela Mooney* (1996) and *Purpose* (2002).

FASSBAENDER, Brigitte (1939—). German mezzo-soprano. Name variations: Fassbander or Fassbänder. Born on July 3, 1939, in Berlin, Germany; studied with father, baritone Willi Domgraf-Fassbaender, at Nuremberg Conservatory (1957–61). ❖ One of the finest female lieder singers on the concert stage, debuted at the Bayerische Staatsoper in Munich (1961); debuted at Covent Garden (1971), Salzburg (1973), Metropolitan Opera (1974); though she preferred concertizing to opera, focused on Wagner in the latter half of career and was associated with many operatic roles; made a Bavarian Kammersängerin, a title awarded a singer of outstanding merit (1970).

FASSETT, Cornelia (1831–1898). American portrait painter. Born Cornelia Adele Strong in Owasco, New York, Nov 9, 1831; died in Washington, DC, Jan 4, 1898; dau. of Captain Walter Strong and Elizabeth (Gonsales) Strong; m. Samuel Montague Fassett (artist and photographer); children: 7. ❖ One of the most successful portrait painters of the mid-19th century, is best known for her *Electoral Commission in Open Session*, which hangs in US Capitol; studied watercolor in New York City with English painter J.B. Wandesforde; with husband, moved to Chicago (1855), where her portraits, which included a number of prominent Chicago citizens, established her reputation; elected an associate member of Chicago Academy of Design (1874); moved with family to Washington, DC (1875), where she painted presidents Ulysses S. Grant, Rutherford B. Hayes, and James A. Garfield. ❖ See also *Women in World History*.

FASSIE, Brenda (1964–2004). South African pop singer. Born Nov 3, 1964; grew up in Langa, a black township outside Cape Town, South Africa; died after an asthma attack, age 39, May 9, 2004, in South Africa; youngest of 9 children of a domestic worker; children: son Bongani. ❖ Called by the *New York Times*, "the piercing siren of the dispossessed under apartheid," was one of Africa's top-selling musicians and South Africa's 1st black pop stars; singing in English, Xhosa, Sotho and Zulu, had such hits as "Weekend Special," "It's Nice to Be with People," "No No No, Senor," "Black President," a tribute to the still imprisoned Nelson Mandela, and "Vulindlela," which was adopted by the African Naitonal Congress for its election campaign (1999); was outspoken about her bisexuality, a subject that was largely taboo.

FASTRADA (d. 794). Queen of the Franks. Name variations: Fastrade. Died Aug 10, 794; dau. of Count Rudolph and Luitgarde; became 4th wife of Charles I also known as Charlemagne (742–814), king of the Franks (r. 768–814), Holy Roman emperor (r. 800–814), in 783; children: Theodrada, abbess of Argenteuil; Hiltrude. ❖ Was married to Charlemagne for 11 years.

FATIMA. *Variant of Fatimah.*

FATIMA, Djemille (c. 1890–1921). Vaudeville dancer. Name variations: La Belle Fatima. Born c. 1890, possibly in Syria; died Mar 14, 1921, in Venice, California. ❖ Made performance debut as a Harem dancer at William and Oscar Hammerstein's Victoria Theater (1913); collaborated with Hammersteins and *The New York Telegraph* in an attempt to ridicule the suppressors of vice; after being arrested by vice squad, dressed demurely for court appearance and was quickly released; toured with Hammerstein act *The Tiger Lillies* (1917); performed same solo act throughout performance career, which consisted of *Dance of the Balkans, A Fantasie, The Algerian Apache as Danced 500 Years Ago* and *Arabian Dance.*

FATIMAH (605/11–632/33). Islamic holy woman. Name variations: Fatima. Namesake of the Fatimid dynasty. Born in Mecca between 605 and 611 CE; died 632 or 633 CE; dau. of the Prophet Muhammad and Khadijah; sister of Zaynab, Umm Kulthum, and Ruqaiyah; m. 'Ali b. Abi Talib, 4th caliph of Islam; children: 2 daughters, Zaynab and Umm Kulthum; 2 sons, Hasan and Husain the Shi'ite martyr, al-Husain b. 'Ali), and possibly a 3rd son named Muhassin who died in infancy. ❖ Most famous and controversial woman from early Islamic history who, though honored by all Muslims as a participant in the 1st two formative decades of Islam, is especially significant to Shi'is of various sects since they trace their legitimacy to Muhammad through her and her descendants; was a courageous woman, who coped with loneliness, poverty, ill-health, and cataclysmic social change, but remained dutiful to her family and devoted to Islam. The principle source of information about Fatimah is the *hadiths,* or "reports." ❖ See also *Women in World History.*

FATTIA, Helen Ritz (c. 1931—). *See Nkrumah, Fathia.*

FAUCIT, Helena Saville (1817–1898). English actress. Name variations: Helen Faucit; Lady Martin, or Mrs. Theodore Martin. Born Helena Saville Faucit in London, England, 1817; died at home near Llangollen, Wales, Oct 31, 1898; dau. of John Saville Faucit (actor); m. Sir Theodore Martin (British poet, translator, and essayist), 1851. ❖ Eminent actress of the 19th-century British stage, made stage debut near London (1833), playing Juliet in *Romeo and Juliet;* in London debut, played Julia in Knowles' *The Hunchback* (1836); over next 15 years, appeared opposite William Macready as Desdemona, Cordelia, Portia, Lady Macbeth, Rosalind, and, of course, Juliet; also portrayed the leading female roles in Bulwer-Lytton's *The Lady of Lyons* (1838), *Richelieu* (1839), and *Money* (1840), as well as Robert Browning's *Strafford* (1842), and *Blot on the Scutcheon* (1843); published *On Some of Shakespeare's Female Characters* (1885). ❖ See also *Women in World History.*

FAUCONBERG, Mary (1636–1712). *See Cromwell, Mary.*

FAUGERES, Margaretta V. (1771–1801). American author. Name variations: Margaretta Van Wyck Bleecker; Peggy Faugeres. Born Oct 11, 1771, in Tomahanick, NY; died Jan 14, 1801, age 29; dau. of Ann Eliza Bleecker (poet and writer, 1752–1783) and John Bleecker; m. Peter Faugeres, July 14, 1792; children: Margaretta Mason. ❖ Taught school in Brunswick and later in Brooklyn; contributed poems to the *New York Magazine* (1790–93); published a book of her mother's writings, *The Posthumous Works of Ann Eliza Bleecker, in Prose and Verse,* to which she added some of her own writings (1793); also wrote *Essays in Prose and Verse* (1795) and *Belisarius: A Tragedy* (1795).

FAUGERES, Peggy (1771–1801). *See Faugeres, Margaretta V.*

FAULK, Mary Lena (1926–1995). American golfer. Born Mary Lena Faulk, April 15, 1926, in Chipley, Florida; died Aug 3, 1995, in Delray Beach, Florida. ❖ Won the USGA Women's Amateur (1953); member of the Curtis Cup team (1954); joined LPGA tour (1955); won Kansas City Open (1956); won 9 other tournaments (1957–64); taught for many years at Georgia's Sea Island Golf Club and Broadmoor Country Club in Colorado Springs. Inducted into the Georgia Golf Hall of Fame (1993).

FAULKNER, Ruawahine Irihapeti (?–1855). Maori woman of mana and landowner. Name variations: Ruawahine, Puihi. Born Ruawahine, of Ngai Tukairangi hapu of Ngai Te Rangi; died Sept 24, 1855, at Tauranga, New Zealand; dau. of Tawaho and Parewhakarau; m. John Lees Faulkner (Yorkshire boatbuilder and trader), 1842; children: 13. ❖ Took name of Irihapeti (Elizabeth) when she adopted Christianity; resided on her land at Otumoetai and established trading post with husband; represented important link to Maori in Tauranga district. ❖ See also *Dictionary of New Zealand Biography* (Vol. 1).

FAULWETTER, Mrs. R.C. (1895–1983). *See Farr, Wanda K.*

FAUNTZ, Jane (1910–1989). American diver. Born Dec 19, 1910; died of acute leukemia, May 1989; m. Edgar Manske. ❖ At Los Angeles Olympics, won a bronze medal in springboard (1932); representing the Illinois Women's Athletic Club (1922–32), won 2 national titles; graced the covers of *Life, Ladies Home Journal* and a Wheaties cereal box.

FAUQUES, Marianne-Agnès Pillement, Dame de (1721–1773). French novelist. Born 1721 in Avignon, France; died 1773. ❖ Forced by family to become a nun, had vows annulled after 10 years and moved to Paris; writings include *Le Triomphe de l'amitié* (1751), *Abbassaï* (1753), *Les Préjugés trop bravés et trop suivis* (1755), *La Dernière guerre des bêtes* (1758), *L'Histoire de Mme la marquise de Pompadour* (1759), *Le danger des préjugés, ou les memoires de Mlle d'Oran* (1774) and *Dialogues moraux et amusants* (1777).

FAUSET, Crystal Bird (1893–1965). African-American politician. Born Crystal Dreda Bird, June 27, 1893, in Princess Anne, Maryland; grew up in Boston; died Mar 28, 1965, in Philadelphia, Pennsylvania; dau. of Benjamin (school principal) and Portia E. (Lovett) Bird; Columbia University Teachers College, BA, 1931; m. Arthur Huff Fauset

(educator), June 1931 (div. 1944). ❖ The 1st African-American woman to be elected to a state legislature, began to speak out about the concerns of the black community and race relations in general, through her association with Young Women's Christian Association (YWCA) and American Friends Service Committee; joined administrative staff of Works Progress Administration (WPA) of Philadelphia and organized the Philadelphia Democratic Women's League (early 1930s); became director of black women's activities for National Democratic Committee (1936); elected to state legislature (1938); resigned to join the WPA as assistant state director of the Education and Recreation Program (1939); was named special consultant to the director of Office of Civilian Defense (1941); helped establish the United Nations Council of Philadelphia (1945) and served as an officer until 1950; attended the founding of the UN in San Francisco (1950). Awarded Meritorious Service Medal from Commonwealth of Pennsylvania (1939 and 1955). ❖ See also *Women in World History.*

FAUSET, Jessie Redmon (1882–1961). African-American writer. Born Jessie Redmon Fauset, April 27, 1882, in Camden, New Jersey; died April 30, 1961, in Philadelphia, Pennsylvania; dau. of Redmon Fauset (minister of African Methodist Episcopal Church) and Annie (Seamon) Fauset; was the 1st black woman to graduate from Cornell University, 1905; also attended the Sorbonne; University of Pennsylvania, MA, 1919; m. Herbert E. Harris (businessman), 1929 (died 1958). ❖ Novelist, journalist, poet, and editor whose wide-ranging literary skills both influenced other writers of the Harlem Renaissance and vividly captured the struggles and successes of black Americans in the early part of 20th century; taught Latin and French in Washington, DC, at the M Street High School (later Dunbar High School, 1906–19); served as literary editor of *Crisis* (1919–26), giving much-needed exposure to young novelists and poets like Nella Larsen and Gwendolyn Bennett; edited, with W.E.B. Du Bois, a children's magazine, *The Brownies' Book* (1920–21); wrote 4 novels: *There Is Confusion* (1924), *Plum Bun* (1929), *The Chinaberry Tree: A Novel of American Life* (1931), *Comedy: American Style* (1933); taught French at DeWitt Clinton High School in NY (1927–44); moved to Montclair, New Jersey, with husband (early 1950s); after his death, moved to Philadelphia (1958), where she died of heart disease (1961). ❖ See also Carolyn Wedin Sylvander, *Jessie Redmon Fauset: Black American Writer* (Whitston, 1981); and *Women in World History.*

FAUST, Lotta (1880–1910). American theatrical dancer. Born Feb 8, 1880, in Brooklyn, NY; died Jan 25, 1910, age 29, in New York, NY. ❖ Made performance debut in *Jack and the Bean Stalk* in Brooklyn (1895); made Broadway debut in *The Man in the Moon* (1899); performed in the chorus of George Lederer shows, including *The Belle of Bohemia* (1900), *The Casino Girl* (1900) and *My Lady* (1900); throughout career, performed as specialty dancer in NY and on tour in such shows as *Sally in Our Alley* (1902), Montgomery and Stone's *Wizard of Oz* (1903), *The Girl from Vienna* (1906) and *The Mimic World* (1908).

FAUSTA (d. 324). Byzantine and Roman empress. Name variations: Flavia. Born Flavia Maxima Fausta; died 324 (some sources cite 326); dau. of Maximian, senior emperor (Augustus) of the Roman West (r. 285/286–305), and Eutropia; sister of Maxentius and Theodora (fl. 290s); m. Flavius Valerius Aurelius Constantinus Magnus, known as Constantine I the Great (285–337), Roman emperor (r. 306–337, the 1st Christian emperor of the Roman Empire, who founded Constantinople), in 307; children: Constantine II (b. 317); Constantius II (b. 323), Roman emperor (r. 337–361); Constans (b. 324); Constantina (c. 321–c. 354); Helena (c. 320–?, who m. Julian, Byzantine emperor). ❖ Married Constantine the Great, a union meant to cement the Western Augusti (307), the triumvirate of her husband Constantine, brother Maxentius, and father Maximian; in separate incidents, her father and brother plotted the overthrow of Constantine and were killed (309 and 312, respectively); elevated to the status of Augusta (Empress); during another personal upheaval which marred imperial peace, was accused of high treason, arrested, and put to death (another source maintains that she was charged with adultery because of a liaison with a palace official). ❖ See also *Women in World History.*

FAUSTA (fl. 600s). Byzantine empress. Fl. in 600s; m. Constantine III (also known as Constans II), Byzantine emperor (r. 641–668); children: Constantine IV (r. 668–685); Heraclius; and Tiberius.

FAUSTA, Cornelia (b. 88 BCE). Roman noblewoman. Born c. 88 BCE; dau. of Lucius Cornelius Sulla (consul, 88–80 BCE, and Roman dictator, 82–79) and his 4th wife Caecilia Metella; m. the praetor C. Memmius (div.); m. Titus Annius Milo (praetor), in 55 BCE. ❖ Was notorious for her marital infidelity but may not have had an unbiased appraisal (historian Sallust is said to have been one of her paramours). ❖ See also *Women in World History.*

FAUSTINA, Anna or Annia Galeria (c. 90–141 CE). See *Faustina I.*

FAUSTINA I (c. 90–141). Roman empress and wife of Antoninus Pius. Name variations: Anna or Annia Galeria Faustina; Faustina Maior; Faustina Mater (Faustina the Mother); Faustina the Elder; titled Augusta (Revered), Pia (Pious), and, after her death, Diva (Deified). Pronunciation: Fow-STEEN-ah. Born c. 90; died 141; dau. of Rupilia Faustina and M. Annius Verus; m. T. Aurelius Fulvus Boionus Antoninus, later the Roman emperor Antoninus Pius (r. 138–161), around 110; children: M. Aurelius Fulvus Antoninus; M. Galerius Aurelius Antoninus; Aurelia Fadilla (date of birth unknown); Faustina II (130–175). ❖ Given the title Augusta by Senate (138); died and was deified by Senate (141); commemorated on surviving coins issued (138–141). ❖ See also *Women in World History.*

FAUSTINA II (130–175). Roman empress and wife of Marcus Aurelius. Name variations: Annia Galeria Faustina; Faustina Minor; Faustina the Younger; (Greek) Faustina Nea (Faustina the Younger); titled Augusta (Revered), Pia (Pious), Mater Castrorum (Mother of the Camp), and, after her death, Diva (Deified). Pronunciation: Fow-STEEN-ah. Born 130; died in 175 in Halala, later renamed Faustinopolis, in Asia Minor; dau. of Roman emperor Antoninus Pius (r. 138–161) and Faustina I (c. 90–141); m. her cousin Marcus Annius Verus, later the emperor Marcus Aurelius (r. 161–180), in 145; children—14: Domitia Faustina (b. 147); the twins T. Aurelius Antoninus and T. Aelius Aurelius (b. 149); Lucilla (Annia Aurelia Galeria Lucilla, b. 150); Faustina III (Annia Aurelia Galeria Faustina, b. 151), T. Aelius Antoninus (b. 152); Fadilla (Arria Fadilla, b. 159); Cornificia (b. 160); her 2nd set of twins T. Aurelius Fulvus (also called Antoninus) and the future emperor L. Aurelius Commodus (b. Aug 31, 161); M. Annius Verus (b. 162); Hadrianus (date of birth unknown); Vibia Aurelia Sabina (b. 166); and an unnamed son (birth date unknown). ❖ Reared in the imperial household (138–145); betrothed in childhood to Lucius Aurelius Commodus (later the co-emperor Verus) but married Marcus Aurelius (April 145); given the title Augusta by the Senate (147); gave birth to 14 children (147–166); accompanied Marcus to war (174); implicated in the revolt of Avidius Cassius (174); died in Halala, later renamed Faustinopolis, in Asia Minor, while accompanying Marcus on campaign, and deified by the Senate (175); commemorated on scores of surviving inscriptions, coin-issues, and statues throughout the Roman Empire (147–176). ❖ See also *Women in World History.*

FAUSTINA III (b. 151). Roman noblewoman. Name variations: Anna Aurelia Galeria Faustina. Born Annia Aurelia Galeria Faustina in 151; dau. of Faustina II (130–175) and Marcus Aurelius, Roman emperor (r. 161–180); possibly m. Cn. Julius Severus.

FAUSTINA MAIOR or MAJOR (c. 90–141 CE). See *Faustina I.*

FAUSTINA OF ANTIOCH (fl. 300s). Byzantine empress. Fl. in 300s; was 3rd wife of Constantius II, Eastern Roman emperor and Byzantine emperor (r. 337–361); children: Constantia Postuma. Constantius II's 1st wife was the dau. of Galla (fl. 320); his 2nd was Eusebia of Macedonia.

FAUSTINA THE ELDER (c. 90–141 CE). See *Faustina I.*

FAUT, Jean (1925—). American baseball player. Born Jan 17, 1925, in East Greenville, Pennsylvania; m. Karl Winsch (baseball player, later manager of South Bend Blue Sox), 1947. ❖ Pitched two perfect games for South Bend Blue Sox in the All-American Girls Baseball League, the 1st and only women's professional baseball organization (1951 and 1953). ❖ See also *Women in World History.*

FAVART, Edmée (1886–1941). French actress and singer. Name variations: Edmee Favart. Born Nov 23, 1886, in Paris, France; died Oct 28, 1941, in Marseille, France. ❖ Made stage debut at the Gaîté Lyrique as Clairette in *La fille de Madame Angot* (1912); played leading roles in numerous comic operas; appeared as Hélène in *Veronique*, Catherine in *La rotisserie de la reine Pedauque*, Cherubin in *Les noces de Figaro*, Colette in *La Basoche*, Delphine in *Cosi Fan Tutte* and Lucienne in *Le Paradis Fermé*; appeared in the film *Mannequins* (1933).

FAVART, Marie (1727–1772). French soprano, actress, and dramatist. Name variations: Madame Favart. Born Marie Justine Benoîte du Ronceray at Avignon, France, June 15, 1727; died in Paris, May 12, 1772; m. Charles Simon Favart (French playwright and librettist), 1745 (died 1792); children: Charles Nicolas Justin Favart (1749–1806). ❖ Made debut at the Opéra-Comique as Mme Chantilly in *Les fêtes publiques* by Charles Simon Favart (1745); appeared in the title role of *La serva padrona* as well as many works with librettos by husband; also collaborated with husband on several librettos; was the subject of Offenbach's 1878 opera *Mme Favart;* sang in Paris at Comédie-Italienne until her death.

FAVART, Marie (b. 1833). French actress. Born Marie Pierette Ignace Pingaud Favart at Beaune, France, Feb 16, 1833. ❖ A noted actress, debuted at Comédie Française (1848); became a member of the Comédie (1854); resigned (1881); toured Russia with Coquelin and played in classic comedy, notably in *Tartuffe* (1883); created many original parts and was especially successful in contemporary drama.

FAVERSHAM, Edith Campbell (d. 1945). See *Campbell, Edith.*

FAVOR, Suzy (1968—). American runner. Name variations: Suzanne Hamilton. Born Suzanne Favor, Aug 8, 1968, in Stevens Point, Wisconsin; attended University of Wisconsin. ❖ Was the 1st athlete to win the NCAA outdoor 1,500 meters 4 times (1988–91); was also 800-meter NCAA champion (1990); won US nationals in outdoor 1,500 meters (1989–91) and indoor 1-mile (1991). Won the Honda Broderick Cup (1990).

FAVRE, Julie Velten (1834–1896). French educator and philosopher. Name variations: Mme. Jules Favre. Born Julie Velten in Wissembourg, France, Nov 5, 1834; died Jan 1896; dau. of a Lutheran pastor and official; obtained teacher's degree from Wissembourg; m. Gabriel Claude Jules Favre (1809–1880, French lawyer and diplomat), 1870. ❖ Served as director of École Normale Superieure de Sevres (1881–96), which allowed young women to receive a broad secondary education; writings include *La Morale des Stoiciens (The Morality of the Stoics,* 1887), *La Morale de Socrate (The Morality of Socrates,* 1887), *Montaigne moraliste et pédagogue (Montaigne as a moralist and a pedagogue,* 1887), *La Morale d'Aristotle (The Morality of Aristotle,* 1888), *La Morale de Ciceron (The Morality of Cicero,* 1889), *La Morale de Plutarque (The Morality of Plutarch).* ❖ See also *Women in World History.*

FAWAZ, Florence (1894–1968). See *Austral, Florence.*

FAWCETT, Joy (1968—). American soccer player. Name variations: Joy Biefeld. Born Joy Lynn Biefeld, Feb 8, 1968, in Inglewood, California; attended University of California, Berkeley; m. Walter Fawcett (software engineer); children: 3 daughters. ❖ Defender; won team gold medals at World Cup (1991, 1999); won a team gold medal at Atlanta Olympics (1996) and a team silver at Sydney Olympics (2000); was a founding member of the Women's United Soccer Association (WUSA); signed with the San Diego Spirit (2001); won a team gold medal at Athens Olympics (2004). Named Female Soccer Athlete of the Year (1988). ❖ See also Jere Longman, *The Girls of Summer* (HarperCollins, 2000).

FAWCETT, Marion (1886–1957). Scottish actress and producer. Born Katherine Roger Campbell, Nov 25, 1886, in Aberdeen, Scotland; m. Dennis Bryan (died). ❖ Made stage debut in Liverpool for Sir Henry Irving's company as a walk-on in *Robespierre* (1899), followed by *An American Tragedy, The Matriarch, The Shanghai Gesture, The Brontës, The Last of Mrs. Cheyney, Dear Octopus, Jane Eyre* and *Separate Tables,* among others; became involved with production (1918) for Repertory Players, Jewish Drama League, Lena Ashwell, and the Opera House, Malta.

FAWCETT, Maisie (1902–1988). Australian botanist. Name variations: Stella Grace Maisie Fawcett. Born in Footscray, Melbourne, Australia, 1902; died 1988; m. Denis Carr (professor), 1950s. ❖ Her research at the Bogong High Plains to examine the effects of grazing animals on plant life (beginning Sept 1941) demonstrated that overgrazing led to soil erosion in both the lower and higher pastures; her recommendations—restrictions on the number of cattle permitted to graze on the land, and the banning of sheep (which did greater damage than cattle to plant life)—helped soil conditions to improve; became a permanent senior lecturer at the University of Melbourne (1952) and visiting fellow at the Australian National University.

FAWCETT, Millicent Garrett (1847–1929). British feminist. Name variations: Millicent Garrett. Born Millicent Garrett in Aldeburgh, England,

June 11, 1847; died Aug 5, 1929, in London; dau. of Newson (well-to-do merchant) and Louisa (Dunnell) Garrett; sister of Louisa Garrett, Agnes Garrett, Alice Garrett, Sam Garrett, and Elizabeth Garrett Anderson; m. Henry Fawcett (Liberal member of Parliament and professor of economics at Cambridge University), 1867; children: Philippa Fawcett (b. 1868, mathematician). ❖ Author, speaker, and political leader who witnessed the formal initiation of the women's suffrage campaign in 1867, led the moderate movement for women's enfranchisement, and lived to see the extension of suffrage to women on equal terms with men in 1928; elected to executive committee of London National Society for Women's Suffrage (1867); gave 1st public speech on women's suffrage (1869); published *Political Economy for Beginners* (1870), a bestseller that set forth liberal economic theory in an accessible fashion; one of the pioneers in establishing the organizational basis for the women's suffrage movement, served as president of National Union of Women's Suffrage Societies (1907–19); appointed a magistrate (1920 and 1925); through her articles and public speaking, was the most well-known figure in the British women's suffrage movement, the president of the largest women's suffrage organization in Britain (the National Union of Women's Suffrage Societies), and one of the most important figures in securing the vote for women; writings include *Women's Suffrage: A Short History of a Great Movement* (1912), *The Women's Victory—and After: Personal Reminiscences, 1911–1918* (1920), *Some Eminent Women of our Times* (1889), *Life of Her Majesty Queen Victoria* (1895), and *Five Famous French Women* (1905); had numerous pamphlets and articles published in periodicals such as *Common Cause, The Englishwoman, Woman's Leader, Contemporary Review, Nineteenth Century*. Awarded Dame Grand Cross of the British Empire (1925). ❖ See also autobiography, *What I Remember* (Putnam, 1925); David Rubinstein, *A Different World for Women: The Life of Millicent Garrett Fawcett* (Ohio State U. Press, 1991); Ray Strachey, *Millicent Garrett Fawcett* (Murray, 1931); and *Women in World History*.

FAWCETT, Philippa (1868–1948). English mathematician and educator. Born April 4, 1868, in England; died June 10, 1948; dau. of Dame Millicent Garrett Fawcett (suffragist) and Henry Fawcett (professor and Liberal MP). ❖ Known for contributions to educational systems of London and South Africa, attained highest honors as math student and later lectured at Newnham College, Cambridge (1887–91); awarded a Marion Kennedy studentship (1891); accompanied mother to South Africa after Boer War; organized elementary schools in Transvaal (1902); set up many secondary schools as well as Furzedown and Avery Hill teacher training colleges as chief assistant to the London County Council's (LCC) director of education (1905–20) and later as LCC's assistant education officer for higher learning (1920–34); organized meetings germane to League of Nations after WWI.

FAWCETT, Quinn (1942—). *See Yarbro, Chelsea Quinn.*

FAWCETT, Stella Grace Maisie (1902–1988). *See Fawcett, Maisie.*

FAWZIA (1921—). Egyptian princess. Born in Alexandria, Egypt, Nov 5, 1921; dau. of King Fuad I, king of Egypt, and Nazli Sabri; became 1st wife of Muhammad Reza Pahlavi also known as Riza I Pahlavi, shah of Iran (r. 1941–1979, deposed), Mar 16, 1939 (div. 1948); m. Colonel H.E. Ismail Hussain Shirin Bey (minister for War and the Navy), 1949; children: (1st m.) Shahnaz Pahlavi (b. 1940); (2nd m.) Nadia (b. 1950) and Muhammad Shirin (b. 1955).

FAWZIA (1940–2005). Egyptian princess. Born April 7, 1940, at the Abdin Palace in Cairo, Egypt; died Jan 27, 2005, in Lausanne, Switzerland; dau. of King Faruk or Farouk I (r. 1936–52) and Farida; sister of King Fuad II; never married; no children.

FAY, Amy (1844–1928). American pianist. Born Amelia Muller Fay in Bayou Goula, Mississippi, May 21, 1844; died in Watertown, Massachusetts, Feb 28, 1928; dau. of Charles (scholar) and Charlotte Emily (Hopkins) Fay (1817–1856, visual artist and pianist); sister of Melusina "Zina" Fay Peirce (1836–1923); never married. ❖ Studied in Berlin with Carl Tausig, Ludwig Deppe, and Theodor Kullak, and was accepted in Franz Liszt's master class; returned to US (1875), settled in Boston, and quickly achieved a major career as a concert artist; her letters home from Berlin were published as *Music-Study in Germany* (1880) and went through 25 editions; with sister Melusina, managed New York Women's Philharmonic Society (1899–1914), an organization that promoted the cause of women in the world of classical music. ❖ See also S. Margaret William McCarthy, ed. *Amy Fay: The American Years, 1879–1916* (1986) and *Amy Fay: America's Notable Woman of Music* (1995); and *Women in World History*.

FAY, Eliza (1756–1816). British letter writer. Born 1756, possibly in Blackheath, Worcestershire, England; died Sept 1816 in Calcutta, India; m. Anthony Fay, late 1770s. ❖ Traveled to India with husband whom she later divorced; attempted several business schemes in India but ended in debt; letters, published posthumously in Calcutta as *Original Letters from India—1779–1815* (1817), give account of Anglo-Indian life.

FAY, Gaby (1893–1973). *See Holden, Fay.*

FAY, Vivien (b. around 1908). American theatrical ballet dancer. Name variations: also seen as Vivian Fay. Born May 13, c. 1908, in Lubbock, Texas. ❖ Trained by Theodore Kosloff, Alexandra Baldina, and Julietta Mendez at Kosloff Studio in San Francisco, CA; made debut in Gus Edwards vaudeville; performed in *Naughty Riquette* in Los Angeles (1926); moved to New York to dance in *Rosalie* (1928); performed specialty dances in numerous productions, including Earl Carroll's *Vanities of 1930* and George White's *Melody* (1933); reentered classical ballet in Albertina Rasch's *The Great Waltz*, where she danced the role of Katti Lanner; appeared in Marx Brothers' film *A Day at the Races* (1937).

FAYE, Alice (1912–1998). American actress. Born Alice Jeanne Leppert on May 5, 1912, in New York, NY; died in Rancho Mirage, California, May 9, 1998; dau. of Charles (police officer) and Alice (Moffat) Leppert; m. Tony Martin (singer), Sept 3, 1937 (div. 1940); m. Phil Harris (bandleader-actor), May 12, 1941; children: Alice Harris Regan (b. 1942) and Phyllis Harris (b. 1944). ❖ Began singing and dancing professionally at 14; landed a job in the chorus of *George White's Scandals* (1931); sang with Rudy Vallee's band and co-starred with him in the film *George White's Scandals* (1934); with signature husky voice, found her niche as the sweet and vulnerable girl-next-door beginning with *Poor Little Rich Girl* (1936); received 1st star billing in 10th film, *Sing, Baby, Sing* (1936); in *Stowaway* (1936), sang one of her most memorable songs, "Goodnight, My Love," which she recorded for Brunswick; hit her stride at Fox with 2 big-budget musicals, *In Old Chicago* and *Alexander's Ragtime Band* (1938); made most memorable films of her career (1940–44): *Lillian Russell* (1940), *Little Old New York* (1940), *Tin Pan Alley* (1940), *That Night in Rio* (1941), *The Great American Broadcast* (1941), *Weekend in Havana* (1941), *Hello, Frisco, Hello* (1943), *The Gang's All Here* (1943), and *Four Jills in a Jeep* (1944); co-starred with husband on the hugely popular Sunday-night radio program "The Phil Harris-Alice Faye Show" (1946–54). ❖ See also *Women in World History*.

FAYE, Julia (1893–1966). American actress. Born Sept 24, 1893, in Richmond, Virginia; died April 6, 1966, in Hollywood, California. ❖ One of Cecil B. De Mille's leading players and his mistress off-screen, appeared in *Male and Female, The Ten Commandments, King of Kings, Union Pacific, Northwest Mounted Police, Samson and Delilah* and *The Last Buccaneer;* retired (1958).

FAYETTE, Madame de La (1634–1693). *See La Fayette, Marie-Madeleine de.*

FAZAN, Eleanor (1930—). English dancer and director. Born May 29, 1930, in Kenya; trained at Sadler's Wells Ballet School in London, England. ❖ Began career as a specialty dancer in London's West End, in such shows as *High Spirits* (1953) and *Intimacy at 8:30* (1954), and also at London's Hippodrome; choreographed musicals and dance acts for *The Lily-White Boys* (1960), *The Lord Chamberlain Regrets* (1961), and *Lulu* (1970), among others; directed musicals, revues and operas at venues that include Covent Garden in London; served as choreographer for numerous films, including *Oh! What a Lovely War* (1969), *Yanks* (1979), *Heaven's Gate* (1980), *Willow* (1988), *St. Ives* (1999) and *Onegin* (1999); also staged operas for tv, and choreographed in theater for *The Broken Heart* (1962), *The Beggars' Opera* (1972), *The Threepenny Opera* (1972), *Habeas Corpus* (1973) and *Twelfth Night* (1974).

FAZEKAS, Mrs. Julius (d. 1929). Hungarian murderer. Died 1929 in Hungary. ❖ Obtained large quantities of arsenic and went into business as poison merchant, supplying many of village's women with arsenic to murder their husbands, lovers, and family members; with chief accomplice Susanna Olah, served approximately 50 clients who may have been responsible for as many as 300 murders (1914–29). Many of the 26 women who were tried in Szolnok received death sentences or life sentences; sources vary as to fate of Fazekas, who either committed suicide by poison to escape punishment or was among those executed.

FAZENDA, Louise (1895–1962). American actress. Born June 17, 1895, in Lafayette, Indiana; died April 17, 1962, in Beverly Hills, California; m. Hal B. Wallis (film producer); children: 1 son. ❖ Hired by Universal (1913); joined Mack Sennett (1915) and became his principal female comedian (1915); other films include *Down on the Farm* (1920) *The*

Beautiful and the Damned (1922), *Gold Diggers* (1923), *No, No, Nanette* (1930) and *The Old Maid* (1939); also had title role in *Tillie's Punctured Romance*, opposite W.C. Fields (1928).

FAZLIC, Jasna (1970—). Yugoslavian table-tennis player. Name variations: Jasna Reed. Born Dec 20, 1970, in Yugoslavia. ❖ At Seoul Olympics, won a bronze medal in doubles (1988); won European championship in doubles (1992); moved to US.

FEALY, Maude (1883–1971). American stage and silent-film actress. Born Maude Hawk, Mar 4, 1883, in Memphis, Tennessee; died Nov 9, 1971, in Woodland Hills, California; dau. of Margaret Fealy (actress and drama instructor, 1865–1955); m. Lewis H. Sherwin, 1907 (div. 1909); m. James Durkin, 1909 (div. 1917); m. John E. Cort Jr., 1920 (annulled 1923). ❖ Made stage debut as a child; made NY debut in *Quo Vadis?*; appeared in every film of Cecil B. De Mille after the advent of sound; was also a drama coach.

FEARN, Anne Walter (1865–1939). American physician. Name variations: Anne Walter, Anne Fearn. Born Anne Walter, May 21, 1865, in Holly Springs, Mississippi; died April 28, 1939, in Berkeley, California; dau. of Harvey Washington Walter (prominent attorney, died 1878) and Martha Fredonia (Brown) Walter; Woman's Medical College of Pennsylvania in Philadelphia, MD (1893); m. John Burrus Fearn (medical missionary), April 21, 1896 (died 1926); children: Elizabeth Fearn (1897–1902). ❖ Headed women's hospital for Woman's Board of Foreign Missions of Methodist Episcopal Church, South, in Suzhou (Soochow), China (1893–96); established 1st coeducational medical school for Chinese students (1895); ran private practice in Suzhou (1896–1907); lived in Shanghai (1908–38), managing own hospital, Fearn Sanatorium (1916–26), working as voluntary clinician at Margaret Williamson Hospital for Chinese Women, and conducting private practice; helped found Shanghai American School (1912); was welfare worker with relief agencies in Shanghai. ❖ See also autobiography, *My Days of Strength* (1939).

FEDDE, Sister Elizabeth (1850–1921). Norwegian-American deaconess. Born Elizabeth Feda (later altered to Fedde), Dec 25, 1850, at Feda, in Flekkefjord, Norway; died Feb 25, 1921, near Egersund, Norway; dau. of Andreas Villumsen Feda and Anne Marie Olsdatter; m. Ola A. P. Slettebö, 1896. ❖ Entered Lutheran deaconess motherhouse in Christiania (Oslo), Norway (1873) and studied religion and nursing; worked as a nurse in Tromsö, in northern Norway (late 1870s–early 1880s); in response to a need for social workers to help Norwegian immigrants, moved to New York City (1883); helped found Voluntary Relief Society for the Sick and Poor (later Lutheran Medical Center) for Norwegians in NY and Brooklyn (1883); when refused support by Christiania motherhouse, opened small hospital to train sisters in Brooklyn (1885) and later began ambulance service for New Yorkers of all nationalities; founded deaconess home in Minneapolis, MN (late 1880s); returned to Norway and settled with husband on farm near Egersund (1896).

FEDELE, Cassandra Fidelis (1465–1558). Italian scholar. Born Cassandra Fidelis Fedele in Venice, Italy, 1465; dau. of Angelo Fedele and Barbara Leoni; educated by Gasparino Borro; m. Giovan Maria Mapelli (doctor from Vicenza). ❖ Well-known for her erudition, became a local celebrity; wrote poetry and was particularly known for her public orations, including her welcome to Bona Sforza, queen of Poland, when the queen arrived in Venice; was forced to marry when the novelty of her public presence faded with her beauty; while returning on a ship from several years in Crete with husband, lost most of her property in a severe storm (1520); after husband died (1520), often had to beg for financial assistance from others; became prioress of the girls' orphanage associated with the Church of S. Domenico di Castello in Venice. ❖ See also *Women in World History.*

FEDEROVA, Nina (1958—). American ballet dancer. Born April 24, 1958, in Philadelphia, Pennsylvania; trained at School of Pennsylvania Ballet and School of American Ballet in NY. ❖ Performed with New York City Ballet during adolescence, creating title role in John Taras' *Daphnis and Chloe* (1975); danced such roles as Sacred Love in Ashton's *Illuminations*, La Bonne Fée in Balanchine's *Harlequinade* and Odette in his *Swan Lake.*

FEDEROVA, Sophia (1879–1963). Russian ballet dancer. Born Sept 28, 1879, possibly in Moscow, Russia; died Jan 3, 1963, in Paris, France; trained at school of Imperial Ballet in Moscow. ❖ Joined Bolshoi Ballet (1899), where she danced title roles in Alexander Gorsky's revivals,

including *Esmeralda* and *La Fille du Pharon;* appeared in early works by Mikhail Fokine, including *Cléopâtre* and *Prince Igor;* performed with the company of Anna Pavlova.

FEDICHEVA, Kaleria (1936—). Soviet ballet dancer. Born July 20, 1936, in Ust-Ijory, Russia; trained at Choreographic Institute in Leningrad (now St. Petersburg). ❖ Joined Kirov Ballet (1955) where she was best known for performances in contemporary repertory including Igor Belsky's *Leningrad Symphony,* Konstantin Sergeyev's *The Distant Planet* and *Hamlet* (1970), and Oleg Vingradov's *Prince of the Pagodas* (1972); immigrated to US (1975).

FEDOROVITCH, Sophie (1893–1953). Russian theatrical designer. Born Dec 15, 1893, in Minsk, Russia; died Jan 25, 1953, in London, England. ❖ Immigrated to England after the Revolution (1920); designed ballets for Frederick Ashton's *Tragedy of Fashion* (1926), *Mephisto Valse* (1934), *Horoscope* (1938), *Symphonic Variations* (1946) and *Valses Nobles et Sentimentales* (1947), among others; designed costumes for numerous 1940s operas, as well as for Andrée Howard's *La Fête Etrange* (1940) and *Veneziana* (1953).

FEDOTKINA, Svetlana (1967—). Russian speedskater. Born July 28, 1967, in USSR. ❖ Won a silver medal for 1,500 meters at Lillehammer Olympics (1994).

FEDOTOVA, Irina (1975—). Russian rower. Born Feb 15, 1975, in USSR. ❖ Won a bronze medal for quadruple sculls at Sydney Olympics (2000).

FEENEY, Carol (1964—). American rower. Born Oct 4, 1964, in Washington. ❖ At Barcelona Olympics, won a silver medal in coxless fours (1992).

FEHER, Anna (1921—). Hungarian gymnast. Born Sept 1921 in Hungary. ❖ At London Olympics, won a silver medal in team all-around (1948).

FEIGENHEIMER, Irene (1946—). American modern dancer and choreographer. Born June 16, 1946, in New York, NY. ❖ Trained by Hanya Holm, Martha Graham, and Merce Cunningham, as well as at school of Metropolitan Opera Ballet in New York City; danced in an array of contemporary concert groups for Anna Sokolow, Don Redlich, Cliff Keuter, and Kathryn Posin; collaborated and choreographed with Barbara Roan and Antony La Giglia for such works as *Continuing Dance Exchange* (1973); taught throughout US. Works of choreography include *Micromaze* (1969), *Solo* (1972), *Stages* (1974), *Travelin' Pair* (1975), *Later Dreams, Part I* (1975), *Time Still* (1977), *Inside Whisper* (1979), *Red and White* (1980) and *Homage* (1980).

FEIGNER, Vera (1852–1942). See Figner, Vera.

FEINSTEIN, Dianne (1933—). American politician. Born Dianne Emiel Goldman, June 22, 1933, in San Francisco, California; dau. of Leon Goldman (surgeon and professor) and Betty Goldman (nurse and model); Stanford University, BA in history (1955); m. Jack Berman (lawyer), 1956 (div. 1959); m. Bertram Feinstein (neurosurgeon); m. Richard C. Blum (chair of Blum Capital Partners), 1980; children: Katherine Feinstein Mariano (former assistant district attorney of San Francisco); (stepdaughters) Annette, Heidi, and Eileen. ❖ A champion of breast cancer research, environmental protection, and gun control, served on California Women's Parole Board (1960–66); elected to San Francisco County Board of Supervisors with more votes than any other candidate (1969), thereby making her the 1st woman to serve as president of the city's legislative body; reelected for 2 additional 4-year terms as supervisor, serving 3 terms as board president; became 1st woman mayor of San Francisco following the assassination of mayor George Moscone and supervisor Harvey Milk (1978); was re-elected twice, balancing city budget with firm hand, and finally left post due to term limits (1978–87); though unsuccessful in her bid, was the 1st woman to be nominated by a major party for governor of California; as a Democrat, became 1st woman elected to US senate from California (1992); reelected (1994, 2000); served on many key senate committees including Judiciary, Appropriations, Energy and Natural Resources as well as Select Committee on Intelligence; sponsored and won passage for major legislation to ban the manufacture, sale and possession of military-style assault weapons (1994) and the Methamphetamine Control Act (1996). Received Woodrow Wilson Award for Public Service (2001); was 1st recipient of American Cancer Society's National Distinguished Advocacy Award (2004).

FEINSTEIN, Elaine (1930—). British poet, novelist and translator. Born Elaine Cooklin, Oct 24, 1930, in Bootle, Lancashire, England; dau. of Isidore and Fay (Compton) Cooklin; educated at Cambridge; m. Arnold Feinstein, 1957. ❖ Writer of poetry, fiction, plays, and biographies, was a lecturer in English literature at Essex University; poetry collections include *In a Green Eye* (1966), *The Magic Apple Tree* (1971), *Some Unease and Angels* (1977), *Badlands* (1987), *Daylight* (1997) and *Gold* (2000); novels include *The Circle* (1973), *The Glass Alembic* (1973), *The Ecstasy of Dr. Miriam Garner* (1976), *All You Need* (1989) and *Dark Inheritance* (2001); also translated poetry from Russian, notably the work of poet Marina Tsvetaeva, about whom she also wrote the biography *A Captive Lion: The Life of Marina Tsvetayeva* (1987). Made fellow of Royal Society of Literature (1981) and awarded Cholmondeley Award for Poets (1990).

FEIST, Margot (b. 1927). See Honecker, Margot.

FEKLISTOVA, Maria (1976—). Russian shooter. Born May 12, 1976, in Izhevsk, Russia. ❖ Won a bronze medal for 50m rifle 3 positions at Sydney Olympics (2000).

FEL, Marie (1713–1794). French soprano. Born in Bordeaux, France, Oct 24, 1713; died in Chailot, France, Feb 9, 1794; sister of Antoine Fel (1694–1771). ❖ Student of Italian singer Mme Van Loo, made her debut at the Paris Opera, as Vénus in the prologue of *Philomèle* (1734); was a regular at the Opera until 1758, performing in over 100 premieres and revivals, including major roles in most of the works of Jean-Phillippe Rameau (1683–1764); also appeared in works by Lully, Campra, Mouret, and Boismortier, and was particularly known for her portrayal of Colette in Rousseau's *Le devin du village;* known to have been the mistress of the librettist Jean-Louis Cahusac and the painter Quentin La Tour.

FELDMAN, Andrea (1948–1972). American actress. Born 1948; died Aug 8, 1972, jumping from a New York City building. ❖ Appeared in such films as Andy Warhol's *Trash* and *Heat*.

FELDMAN, Gladys (1891–1974). American actress. Born Sept 28, 1891; died Feb 12, 1974, in New York, NY; m. Horace Braham (actor). ❖ Made stage debut as a Ziegfeld girl, subsequently appearing in *The Gold Diggers, Merton of the Movies, The Great Gatsby, Mating Season, Counselor-at-Law* and *Lady for a Night;* also appeared in two films and had her own radio show.

FELICE, Cynthia (1942—). American science-fiction writer. Born Cynthia Lindgren, Oct 12, 1942, in Chicago, Illinois; m. Robert Edward Felice, 1961; children: 2. ❖ Works include *Godsfire* (1978), *The Sunbound* (1981), *Water Witch* (1982), *Eclipse* (1982), *Downtime* (1985), *Iceman* (1991), and, with Connie Willis, *Promised Land* (1997); also published short stories and essays.

FELICIA. *Variant of Felicitas.*

FELICIE, Jacoba or Jacqueline (fl. 1322). *See de Almania, Jacqueline Felicie.*

FELICITAS (d. 203). Christian saint and martyr. Name variations: Felicita; Felicitas of Carthage. Executed on Mar 7, 203, in the amphitheater at Carthage; children: at least one. ❖ As a Christian, was put to death by Hilarianus (then governor of Africa) during the games; her last days were detailed in the diary of Perpetua, now known as "The Martyrdom of Saints Perpetua and Felicitas." ❖ See also *Women in World History.*

FELICITAS OF ROME (d. 162?). Saint and Christian martyr. Name variations: (French) Félicités. Died in Rome c. 162; may have been a widow with 7 sons: Januarius, Felix, Philip, Silvanus, Alexander, Vitalis, and Martial. ❖ One of two Christian martyrs named Felicitas, was, according to the ancient *Passions,* tortured and killed with her 7 sons at hands of the Romans under the rule of Emperor Marcus Aurelius, for not renouncing her Christian faith. ❖ See also *Women in World History.*

FELICITY. *Variant of Felicitas.*

FELIX, Allyson (1985—). American runner. Born Nov 18, 1985, in Los Angeles, California; attended University of Southern California. ❖ Won a silver medal for the 200 meters at Athens Olympics (2004).

FÉLIX, Elizabeth (1821–1858). See Rachel.

FÉLIX, Lia (b. 1830). French actress. Name variations: Felix. Born 1830; 3rd dau. of poor Jewish peddlers, Jacques and Thérèse Félix; pupil of her actress sister, Rachel (1821–1858). ❖ Had hardly been tested as an actress when she was asked to take the lead in Lamartine's *Toussaint L'Ouverture* at Porte St. Martin (April 6, 1850); though the play was

not a hit, was favorably received; came to be recognized as one of the best comedians in Paris, but was forced to retire for several years because of poor health; had an enormous success when she reappeared at the Gaiété in title role of Jules Barbier's *Jeanne d'Arc.* ❖ See also *Women in World History.*

FELIX, Maria (1914–2002). Mexican actress. Name variations: María Félix; La Doña. Born María de Los Ángeles Félix Guereña in Alamos, Sonoras, Mexico, May 4, 1914 (some sources cite April 8); died in Mexico City, April 8, 2002; m. Enrique Alvarez, 1931 (div. 1938); m. Augustín Lara (composer), 1943 (div. Oct 1947); m. Jorge Negrete (actor), Oct 18, 1952 (died Dec 5, 1953); m. Alex Berger (French financier), 1956 (died 1974); lived with French painter, Antoine Tzapoff, from mid-1980s; children: (1st m.) Enrique Alvarez Felix (b. 1934, actor). ❖ The leading box-office attraction in the Spanish-speaking world (1940s), worked in Mexico, Spain, Italy, and France where she played La Belle Abbesse in Jean Renoir's *French Cancan* (1955); starred in 47 films including *Doña Barbara* (1943), *Amok* (1944), *Le Mujer de todos* (1946), *Rio Escondido* (*Hidden River,* 1947), *Vertigo* (1947), *Enamorada* (1948), *Mare Nostrum* (1948), *Doña Diabla* (1949), *La Corona negra* (1951), *Messalina* (1951), *La Belle Otéro* (1954), *Faustina* (1956), and *La Fièvre mont à El Pao* (1959), in which she starred with Gérard Philipe; retired to Mexico (1970s). ❖ See also *Women in World History.*

FÉLIX, Rachel (1821–1858). See Rachel.

FELIX, Sylviane (1977—). French runner. Born Oct 31, 1977, in Créteil, France. ❖ At World championships, won a gold medal for 4x100-meter relay (2003); won a bronze medal for the 4x100-meter relay at Athens Olympics (2004).

FELKE, Petra (1959—). East German track-and-field athlete. Born July 30, 1959, in East Germany. ❖ At Seoul Olympics, won a gold medal in the javelin throw (1988).

FELL, Honor (1900–1986). English cell biologist. Name variations: Dame Honor Fell. Born Honor Bridget Fell, May 22, 1900, at Fowthorpe, near Filey, Yorkshire, England; died April 22, 1986; dau. of Colonel William Edwin Fell (minor landowner) and Alice Picksgill-Cunliffe; University of Edinburgh, BS in zoology, 1922, PhD, 1924, and DSc, 1932. ❖ Famed cell biologist, was invited by Tom Strangeway to work at his Cambridge Research Hospital, later named Strangeways Research Laboratory (1923), and pushed to keep the hospital running after Strangeways' death; served as Strangeways Research Laboratory director (1929–70) and research worker (1979–86), and was responsible for its tremendous growth and reputation as a 1st-rate cell biology research center; established societies for cell biology and tissue culture; promoted science among youth; became a fellow of the Royal Society. Made Dame Commander of the Order of the British Empire (1963).

FELL, Margaret (1614–1702). English religious leader. Name variations: Margaret Fox. Born Margaret Askew in 1614 at Marsh Grange, near Dalton, England; died April 23, 1702, at Swarthmoor Hall in Furness; dau. of John Askew (gentry landowner); m. Thomas Fell (barrister at law of Gray's Inn, MP, circuit judge), 1632 (died 1658); m. George Fox (preacher and founder of Society of Friends), Oct 1669 (died 1691); children: (1st m.) Margaret Jr. (b. 1633?); Bridget (b. 1635?); Isabel (b. 1637?); George (b. 1638?); Sarah (b. 1642); Mary (b. 1647); Susannah (b. 1650); Rachel (b. Oct 1653); and 1 child lost in infancy. ❖ Known traditionally as the "nursing mother of Quakerism," an English movement that survived heavy persecution to become a powerful influence in Anglo-American history, converted to Quakerism and began holding Quaker meetings in her home (1652); wrote letters to Cromwell and made 10 visits to kings in London describing persecution of Quakers; imprisoned many times after 1st husband's death for her connection with Quakerism (beginning 1664); wrote several Quaker monographs; founded Swarthmoor Women's Monthly Meeting (1671); traveled throughout England facilitating Quaker meetings; writings include *To Manasseth-ben-Israel* (1656), *A loving salutation to the seed of Abraham* (1656), *The Citie of London Reproved* (1660), *A Call to the Universall Seed of God* (1665), *Women's Speaking Justified* (1666), *Epistle to Charles II* (1666), *A Relation of Margaret Fell, Her Birth, Life, Testimony and Sufferings for the Lord's Everlasting Truth in her Generation* (1690) and *Epistle to Friends Concerning Oaths* (1698). ❖ See also autobiography *A Relation of Margaret Fell: Her Birth, Life, Testimony, and Sufferings for the Lord's Everlasting Truth in Her Generation* (1690); Helen Crosfield, *Margaret Fox of Swarthmoor Hall* (1913); Bonnelyn Young Kunze, *Margaret Fell and the Rise of Quakerism* (Macmillan, 1994); Ishbel

Ross, *Margaret Fell: Mother of Quakerism* (Longman, 1949); and *Women in World History*.

FELLOWES, Anne (1911–1983). *See Mantle, Winifred Langford.*

FELLOWS, Edith (1923—). American actress. Born May 20, 1923, in Boston, Massachusetts; m. Freddie Fields, 1946 (div. 1955); m. Hal Lee, 1962. ❖ Child and teen actress, made film debut in *Madame X* (1929), followed by *Daddy Long Legs, Cimarron, Huckleberry Finn, Emma, Jane Eyre, Mrs. Wiggs of the Cabbage Patch, Pennies from Heaven, Five Little Peppers and How They Grew, Her First Beau* and *Lilith,* among others.

FELTON, Rebecca Latimer (1835–1930). American reformer and journalist. Born Rebecca Ann Latimer, June 10, 1835, in DeKalb Co., near Decatur, Georgia; died June 24, 1930, in Atlanta; dau. of Charles (farmer and businessman) and Eleanor (Swift) Latimer; sister of suffragist Mary Latimer McLendon (1840–1921); graduate of Madison Female College, Georgia, 1852; m. William Harrell Felton (physician, Methodist cleric and politician), Oct 11, 1853 (died 1909); children: 5 (4 of whom died before adulthood). ❖ The 1st woman seated in the US Senate, served as husband's campaign manager and press secretary during his 3 successful runs for Congress (1874, 1876, and 1878); again ran his election campaigns, drafted bills and speeches, and served as a general adviser when he served in Georgia legislature (1884–90); became a public figure in her own right; led several movements, notably those for prison reform; also supported women's rights and was active in Georgia's suffrage movement; was a columnist for the *Atlanta Journal* (1899–1927); helped found the Georgia Training School for Girls (1915); when US senator Thomas Watson died in office, was appointed to fill the unexpired term; took her seat on the Senate floor (Nov 21, 1922), the 1st woman to do so; as planned, relinquished the seat to Watson's elected successor the next day. ❖ See also autobiographies *My Memoirs of Georgia Politics* (1911), *Country Life in Georgia in the Days of My Youth* (1919) and *The Romantic Story of Georgia Women* (1930); John E. Talmadge, *Rebecca Latimer Felton: Nine Stormy Decades* (1980); and *Women in World History*.

FELTON, Verna (1890–1966). American actress. Born July 20, 1890, in Salinas, California; died Dec 16 (also seen as Dec 14), 1966, in North Hollywood, CA; m. Lee Millar; children: son Lee Millar. ❖ Actress in radio, tv, and film, best remembered for recurring roles in two tv series, "December Bride" and "Pete and Gladys"; provided the voices for a number of Disney films: Flora in *Sleeping Beauty,* Gossipy Elephant for *Dumbo,* Fairy Godmother for *Cinderella,* Queen of Hearts for *Alice in Wonderland* and Winnifred for *Jungle Book.*

FEMINA (c. 1819–1902). *See Müller, Mary Ann.*

FENAYROU, Gabrielle (b. 1850). French woman convicted for murder. Born Gabrielle Gibon, 1850, in France; m. Marin Fenayrou. ❖ Had marriage of convenience to druggist Marin Fenayrou, who drank and gambled; also had longterm affair with Louis Aubert until he decided to marry another; told husband of affair and enlisted his help in killing Aubert (May 28, 1882); confessed, as did Marin who did the actual killing; though Marin received death sentence, was sentenced to life in Clermont Prison where she befriended Gabrielle Bompard; pardoned (1903).

FÉNELON, Fania (1918–1983). French singer and activist in the resistance. Name variations: Fanny Goldstein; Fania Fenelon. Pronunciation: FAHN-ya FAY-ne-lawn. Born Fanny Goldstein in Paris, France, Sept 2, 1918; died in Paris, Dec 19, 1983; dau. of Jules Goldstein (engineer and a Jew) and Marie (Bernier) Goldstein (Catholic); graduated from Paris Conservatoire with a 1st in piano, 1934; never married; no children. ❖ Became a music-hall singer following graduation from Paris Conservatoire (1934); joined the French underground after Germany occupied France (1940); arrested as a member of the resistance (1943); sent to the Auschwitz-Birkenau concentration camp and became a member of the orchestra led by Alma Rosé (Jan 1944); liberated from Bergen-Belsen (April 15, 1945); published *Playing for Time,* about her camp experiences (1977), which was dramatized by playwright Arthur Miller for television (1980) and produced on stage in England (1985); her book chronicles the mixture of suffering and solidarity that made up her daily routine as a death-camp prisoner whose very existence depended on her continuing to perform as a musician and thus keep her captors entertained. ❖ See also *Women in World History.*

FENG, Amy (1969—). Chinese-born table-tennis champion. Born April 9, 1969, in Tianjin, China, near Beijing; moved to Wheaton, Maryland, then Augusta, Georgia. ❖ Began playing table tennis at age 9; moved to US (1992); won singles at Polish Open (1985), Chinese World College

championships (1987), Canadian National Exhibition (1992), as well as the North American championship series, Women's Allstar Singles, and the Chinese New Year tournament (all 1994); in US, placed 1st at Southern Open, Pacific Rim Open in Portland, Oregon, and Sun TV Open (all 1992) and was North American champion (1993); was US National champion in singles (1992–95); failed to medal at Atlanta Olympics (1996).

FENG KENG (1907–1931). Chinese poet and short-story writer. Born 1907 in Guangdong Province, China; executed 1931. ❖ Active in leftist politics, joined underground Communist Party (1929); along with 4 other writers (now known as the Five Martyrs), was arrested and executed by the Guomindang near the Longhua temple in the southwest of Shanghai (1931); stories include "The Salt Miner" and "The Child Pedlar"; wrote poetry to protest 1927 massacre of Communists in Shanghai.

FENG KUN (1978—). Chinese volleyball player. Born Dec 28, 1978, in China. ❖ Setter and captain of the Chinese national team, won a team gold medal at Athens Olympics (2004).

FENG YUANJUN (1900–1974). Chinese literary critic and educator. Name variations: Feng Yüan-chün or Yuan-chun. Born Feng Yuanjun, 1900, in Henan, China; died 1974; sister of Feng Yulan, well-known professor of Chinese philosophy; m. Lu Kanru. ❖ Influenced by ideas of May Fourth Movement, wrote fiction that rebelled against tradition; received doctorate in literature from Sorbonne (1935) and became vice-chancellor of Shangdong University; writings include *History of Chinese Poetry, History of Chinese Literature* and *Short History of Chinese Classical Literature* (all with Lu Kanru).

FENG ZHONGPU (1928—). *See Zong Pu.*

FENGER, Thit Jensen (1876–1957). *See Jensen, Thit.*

FENLEY, Molissa (1954—). American postmodern dancer and choreographer. Name variations: Avril Molissa Fenley. Born Nov 15, 1954, in Las Vegas, Nevada. ❖ Grew up in Nigeria and lived in Spain; returned to US where she began to receive dance training at Mills College in California (1975); founded Molissa Fenley and Dancers in New York City (1977) for which she choreographed numerous works over next 10 years, including *Energizer* (1980), *Hemispheres* (1983), and *Geologic Moments* (1986); began focusing choreography on solo pieces created with visual artists and composers (c. 1987), such as *State of Darkness* (1988), *Bardo* (1990), *Sightings* (1993) and *Trace* (1997); choreographed numerous works for other companies, including Ohio Ballet, Australian Dance Theater, Deutsche Oper Ballet of Berlin, and National Ballet School of Canada. Further works of choreography include *Cenotaph* (1985), *Esperanto* (1985), *Feral* for Ohio Ballet (1986), *Separate Voices* (1987), *Provenance Unknown* (1989), *Witches' Float* (1993), *Channel* (1993), *Bridge of Dreams* for Deutsche Oper (1996), *Voices* (1999), *Island* (2000) and *Weathering* (2000).

FENN, Mary (1824–1886). *See Davis, Mary Fenn.*

FENNELL, Nuala (1935—). Irish politician, feminist, and journalist. Born Nuala Campbell, Nov 1935, in Dublin, Ireland; m. Brian Fennell; children: 2 daughters, 1 son. ❖ Was a founding member of the Irish Women's Liberation Movement (1971) and columnist for the *Evening Herald;* as an independent, unsuccessfully contested general election in Dublin South (1977); representing Fine Gael, elected to the 22nd Dáil for Dublin South (1981–82); returned to the 23rd and 24th Dáil (1981–87) and 26th Dáil (1989–92); was minister of State at the Dept. of the Taoiseach and the Dept. of Justice with responsibility for Women's Affairs and Family Law Reform (1982–87); elected to Seanad from Labour Panel (1987–89); member of the joint committee on Women's Rights (1987–89, 1989–92).

FENNING, Elizabeth (1792–1815). English criminal. Name variations: Eliza Fenning. Born 1792; hanged on June 26, 1815. ❖ Accused of attempting to poison the family of her employer, Orlibar Turner, by mixing arsenic in the dumplings (Mar 1815). ❖ See also *Women in World History.*

FENNO, Jenny (c. 1765–?). American poet and spiritual writer. Born c. 1765, possibly in Boston; date of death unknown. ❖ Wrote *Original Compositions in Prose and Verse on Subjects Moral and Religious* (1791).

FENTON, Faith (1857–1936). *See Freeman, Alice.*

FENTON, Lavinia (1708–1760). English actress. Name variations: Duchess of Bolton. Born 1708; died Jan 24, 1760; probably dau. of a naval lieutenant named Beswick; m. Charles Paulet, 3rd duke of Bolton, 1751; children: 3 (all died young). ❖ Made stage debut as Monimia in Otway's *Orphans* (1726) at the Haymarket; joined the company of players at the theater in Lincoln's Inn Fields, where her success and beauty made her the toast of the town; had greatest success as Polly Peachum in Gay's *Beggar's Opera* and appeared as Ophelia in *Hamlet* (both 1728). ❖ See also *Women in World History.*

FENTON, Lizzie Frost (1855–1931). See Rattray, Lizzie Frost.

FENTON, Lorraine (1973—). See Graham-Fenton, Lorraine.

FENWICK, Eliza (1766–1840). British children's writer. Name variations: The Reverend David Blair. Born Eliza Jago, Feb 1, 1766, in Cornwall, England; died Dec 8, 1840, in Rhode Island; dau. of Thomas and Elizabeth Jago; m. John Fenwick, c. 1788; children: 2. ❖ After separation from husband (1800) ran schools, worked as governess, and cared for orphans; moved to US with daughter; works include *Secresy, or the Ruin Upon the Rock* (1795), *Presents for Good Boys* (1805), *Simple Stories in Verse* (1809), and *Rays from the Rainbow: Being an Easy Method for Perfecting Children in the First Principle of Grammar without the Smallest Trouble to the Instructor* (1812). ❖ See also A.T. Webb, ed., *The Fate of the Fenwicks: Letters to Mary Hays, 1798–1828* (1927).

FENWICK, Ethel Gordon (1857–1947). English pioneer of nursing reform. Born Ethel Gordon Manson, 1857, in England; died in 1947; m. Bedford Fenwick (physician), 1887. ❖ Following nursing positions at Nottingham children's hospital and London Hospital, served as matron of St. Bartholemew's Hospital (1881–87); led a group of nurses in the formation of British Nurses' Association (BNA, 1887), of which she was president; with husband, formed the British College of Nurses (1926) and purchased *The Nursing Record,* later called *The British Journal of Nursing;* also started the Matrons' Council of Great Britain and Ireland, a group that lobbied Parliament for state registration of matrons (obtained in 1919). ❖ See also *Women in World History.*

FENWICK, Irene (1887–1936). American stage and screen actress. Name variations: Irene Barrymore. Born Irene Frizzel, Sept 5, 1887, in Chicago, Illinois; died Dec 24, 1936, in Beverly Hills, California; m. Felix Isman, 1909 (div.); m. J.F. O'Brien (div.); m. Lionel Barrymore (actor), 1923. ❖ Made NY debut as Sylvia Futvoye in *The Brass Bottle* (1910), followed by *The Speckled Band, The Importance of Being Earnest, The Million, Hawthorne of the U.S.A., Along Came Ruth* (title role), *The Song of Songs, Payday, The Co-Respondent, Bosom Friends, Mary's Ankle* (title role), and *Laugh Clown Laugh,* among others; made 9 films, including *The Woman Next Door* (1915) and *A Girl Like That* (1917).

FENWICK, Millicent (1910–1992). American politician. Name variations: Millicent Hammond Fenwick. Born Millicent Vernon Hammond in New York, NY, Feb 25, 1910; died Sept 16, 1992, in Bernardsville, New Jersey; dau. of Ogden Haggerty Hammond (financier and state representative) and Mary Picton Stevens Hammond (heiress and humanitarian); studied philosophy under Bertrand Russell at New School for Social Research; m. Hugh Fenwick, 1934 (div. 1945); children: Hugh H. Fenwick; Mary Fenwick Reckford. ❖ US Republican Congresswoman, celebrated for her political independence, occasionally modeled for *Harper's Bazaar* in early years, then began work for *Vogue* (1938); became its war editor (1941), assigning features on the conflict abroad and on the home front; compiled *Vogue's Book of Etiquette,* which sold a million copies (1948); served as councilwoman for Bernardsville, NJ (1958–64); served as New Jersey State Assemblywoman (1969–72); appointed New Jersey director of consumer affairs (1972), where she battled deceptive auto advertising and required funeral homes to itemize their bills in advance; served as US Congressional representative (1974–83); espoused a number of causes, including civil rights, aid for asbestos victims, help for the poor, prison reforms, strip-mining controls, urban renewal, gun control, reduction of military programs, restrictions on capital punishment, and joined Bella Abzug in opposing increased funding for Vietnam; served as US envoy to the United Nations Food and Agriculture Organization (1983–87). ❖ See also memoir *Speaking Up* (Harper, 1982); and *Women in World History.*

FEODORE OF HOHENLOHE-LANGENBURG (1866–1932). Princess of Leiningen. Born Feodore Victoria Alberta, July 23, 1866; died Nov 1, 1932; dau. of Hermann, 6th prince of Hohenlohe-Langenburg, and Leopoldine (1837–1903); m. Emich, 5th prince of Leiningen, July 12, 1894; children: 5, including Charles, 6th prince of Leiningen.

FEODORE OF LEININGEN (1807–1872). Princess of Hohenlohe-Langenburg and half-sister of Queen Victoria. Name variations: Feodora of Hohenlohe-Langenburg. Born Anne Feodorovna Augusta Charlotte Wilhelmina, Dec 7, 1807, in Amorbach, Germany; died Sept 23, 1872, in Baden-Baden, Germany; dau. of Victoria of Coburg (1786–1861) and Emich, 2nd prince of Leiningen; half-sister of Queen Victoria (1819–1901); m. Ernest, 4th prince of Hohenlohe-Langenburg; children: Adelaide of Hohenlohe-Langenburg (1835–1900); Hermann, 6th prince of Hohenlohe-Langenburg (1832–1913).

FEODOROVNA, Alexandra.
See Charlotte of Prussia (1798–1860).
See Alexandra Feodorovna (1872–1918).

FEODOROVNA, Elizabeth (1864–1918). See Ella, Princess of Hesse-Darmstadt.

FEODOROVNA, Marie.
See Sophia Dorothea of Wurttemberg (1759–1828).
See Marie Feodorovna (1847–1928).
See Victoria Melita of Saxe-Coburg (1876–1936).

FEODOROVNA, Olga (1839–1891). See Cecilia of Baden.

FEODOSIA. *Variant of Theodosia.*

FEOFANOVA, Svetlana (1980—). Russian pole vaulter. Born July 16, 1980, in Moscow, Russia. ❖ Was a gymnast for 11 years; at World championships, won a silver medal (2001) and gold medal (2003); at World Indoor championships, won a silver medal (2001) and gold medal (2003); won a silver medal at Athens Olympics (2004).

FERBER, Edna (1885–1968). Pulitzer Prize-winning American author. Born Aug 15, 1885, in Kalamazoo, Michigan; died April 17, 1968, in New York, NY, of cancer; dau. of Jacob and Julia (Foster) Ferber; never married; no children. ❖ Author of novels that examine American values and culture, especially their impact on women; became 1st female reporter for a small Wisconsin newspaper and, later, the *Milwaukee Journal;* published 1st short story (1910) and 1st novel (1911); awarded Pulitzer Prize for *So Big* (1925); remained one of America's most popular authors with such works as *Show Boat* (basis for the groundbreaking musical of the same name), *Cimarron* and *Giant;* other works include *Dawn O'Hara, The Girl Who Laughed* (1911), *Come and Get It* (1935), *Saratoga Trunk* (1941), *Great Son* (1945), and *Ice Palace* (1958); also wrote short stories and plays, including *The Royal Family, Dinner at Eight* and *Stage Door* (all with George S. Kaufman). ❖ See also autobiographies *A Peculiar Treasure* (Doubleday, 1939) and *A Kind of Magic* (Doubleday, 1963); and *Women in World History.*

FERDINAND, Marie (1978—). African-American basketball player. Born Oct 13, 1978, in Miami, Florida; graduate of Louisiana State University, 2001. ❖ Guard, won a team gold medal at Athens Olympics (2004); played in WNBA for Utah Starzz, then San Antonio Silver Stars.

FERGERSON, Mable (1955—). African-American runner. Born Jan 18, 1955, in Los Angeles, California. ❖ At Munich Olympics, won a silver medal in the 4x400-meter relay (1972).

FERGUSA (fl. 800s). Queen of Dalriada. Fl. in 800s; dau. of Fergus, king of Dalriada; maternal niece of 2 kings of the Picts, Kenneth II and Alpin II; m. cousin Eochaid IV, king of Dalriada; children: Alpin, king of Kintyre (d. 834).

FERGUSON, Abbie Park (1837–1919). American educator. Born Abbie Park Ferguson, April 4, 1837, in Whately, Massachusetts; died Mar 25, 1919, in Wellington, South Africa; dau. of John and Margaret Snow Eddy Ferguson. ❖ With Anna Bliss, opened Huguenot Seminary for girls in South Africa (1874); became head of higher department at Huguenot (1875); with Bliss, co-founded Women's Missionary Society (later Vrouwen Zending Bond) at Huguenot; toured South Africa for opportunities for mission work (1887); established branch seminaries at Bethlehem in Orange Free State and at Greytown in Natal; established 1st women's college in South Africa, Huguenot College, which, as Huguenot University College, was incorporated by Parliament into University of South Africa (1916); served as its president (1898–1910); helped establish Women's Interdenominational Missionary Committee. Received honorary degree from Mount Holyoke College (1911).

FERGUSON, Cathy Jean (1948—). American swimmer and coach. Name variations: Cathy Ferguson-Pillar. Born July 17, 1948, in Burbank, California; trained with Peter Daland; attended Glendale

College and Cal State Long Beach; Montana University, MA; United States International University, PhD. ❧ At 16, bested five other world-record holders to win the 100-meter backstroke and also took gold in the 4x100-meter medley relay at Tokyo Olympics (1964); held 5 world records, 10 American records and 13 national titles; retired from competitive swimming at 19 and became a coach at Long Beach and was a professor of physical education there (1976–93). Was only the 3rd woman inducted into the Los Angeles Athletic Club-John Wooden Hall of Fame; also inducted into International Swimming Hall of Fame.

FERGUSON, Christina (c. 1814–1882). See Gregg, Christina.

FERGUSON, Debbie (1976—). **Bahamian runner.** Born Jan 16, 1976, in Nassau, Bahamas; graduated with honors from University of Georgia with a biology/pre-med degree. ❧ Known as one of the "Golden Girls," won a gold medal at Sydney Olympics for 4x100-meter relay (2000); won a gold medal for 4x100-meter relay at World championships (1999) and a gold medal for the 200 meters at Pan American Games (1999); won a bronze medal in the 200 meters at Athens Olympics (2004). Given the Silver Jubilee Award (1998) and the Bahamas Order of Merit (2000).

FERGUSON, Dottie (1923–2003). **Canadian-American baseball player.** Name variations: Dottie Ferguson Key. Born Feb 17, 1923, in Virden, Manitoba, Canada; died May 8, 2003, in Rockford, Illinois; m. Donald L. Key, 1949; children: Dona Ericksen. ❧ Was North American speedskating champion (1939); played pro-baseball for 10 seasons with the Rockford Peaches (1945–55). Inducted into Manitoba Baseball Hall of Fame (1998) and Canadian Baseball Hall of Fame. ❧ See also documentary *A League of Their Own* (1987); inspiration for the character Mae Mordabito portrayed by Madonna in feature film *A League of Their Own* (1992).

FERGUSON, Elizabeth Graeme (1737–1801). **American poet.** Name variations: Elizabeth Graeme, Elizabeth Ferguson or Fergusson; (pseudonym) Laura. Born Elizabeth Graeme, Feb 3, 1737, in Philadelphia, Pennsylvania; died Feb 23, 1801, near Philadelphia; dau. of Thomas (physician) and Ann (Diggs) Graeme; m. Henry Hugh Ferguson (also seen as Fergusson), April 21, 1772; children: raised her niece, poet Anna Young Smith (1756–1780). ❧ Was engaged to William Franklin (c. 1757–59), son of Benjamin Franklin, but did not marry, partly due to political differences; visited London, met prominent literary and scientific personalities, and kept travel journal (1764–65); having gained a literary reputation based on her travel journal and a translation of Fénelon's "Telemachus," held a weekly literary salon; composed "Hymn on the Charms of Creation" (1766) and metrical version of Psalms; though a moderate Whig, faced problems during Revolutionary War due to husband's Loyalist leanings; endured severe financial reverses towards end of life.

FERGUSON, Elsie (1883–1961). **American stage and screen actress.** Born Aug 19, 1883, in New York, NY; died Nov 15, 1961, in New London, Connecticut; m. Fred Hoey (div.); m. Thomas B. Clarke, Jr. (div.); m. Frederic Worlock (div.); m. Victor Egan. ❧ Made NY stage debut in the chorus of *The Belle of New York* (1900); starred on Broadway in *Such a Little Queen* (1909); on stage for over 30 years, was featured in such plays as *The First Lady of the Land, Arizona, The Merchant of Venice, The Moonflower* and *Outrageous Fortune;* known as the "Aristocrat of the Screen," appeared in 22 silent films (1917–21), including *The Rise of Jenny Cushing, Rose of the World, Song of Songs, A Doll's House, Forever, Outcast* and *Footlights;* starred in only one talkie, *Scarlet Pages.*

FERGUSON, Helen (1901–1977). **American press agent.** Name variations: Helen Hargreaves. Born Decatur, Illinois, July 23, 1901; died Mar 1977 in Florida; m. William "Big Bill" Russell (actor); m. Robert L. Hargreaves; no children. ❧ One of Hollywood's best-known publicity agents, got her start playing bit parts in 13 Essanay two-reelers in Chicago; made stage debut (1926); retired from acting (1930) and turned to public relations; managed the Helen Ferguson Publicity Agency, handling such stars as Loretta Young, Clark Gable, Henry Fonda, and Barbara Stanwyck. ❧ See also *Women in World History.*

FERGUSON, June Maston (1928—). See Maston, June.

FERGUSON, Ma (1875–1961). See Ferguson, Miriam A.

FERGUSON, Margaret Clay (1863–1951). **American botanist.** Born in Orleans, NY, Aug 20, 1863; died in San Diego, California, 1951; attended Genesee Wesleyan Seminary in Lima, NY; attended Wellesley College as a special student in botany and chemistry; Cornell University, PhD, 1899. ❧ Served as head of science department at Harcourt Place

Seminary in Gambier, Ohio (1891–93); joined faculty at Wellesley College (1899), where she spent close to 40 years, becoming head of botany department (1902); planned, designed, and raised the money for a botany building and two greenhouses; also studied the genus of higher plants; retired (1938); elected a fellow by the American Association for the Advancement of Science.

FERGUSON, Miriam A. (1875–1961). **American politician.** Name variations: Ma Ferguson. Born Miriam Amanda Wallace in Bell Co., Texas, June 13, 1875; died June 25, 1961, in Austin, Texas; dau. of Joseph Lapsley and Eliza (Garrison) Wallace (well-to-do rancher-farmers); entered Baylor Female College, 1890; m. James Edward Ferguson (politician and governor of Texas), Dec 31, 1899 (died 1944); children: Ouida Wallace Ferguson Nalle and Ruby Dorrace Ferguson. ❧ Texan who was the 1st woman in the US to be elected to a full term as a state governor; husband "Farmer Jim" Ferguson inaugurated governor of Texas (1915), then reelected (1916); husband impeached and removed, having been indicted for embezzlement and misuse of public funds (1917); with husband barred from office, stepped in for him and was elected governor of Texas (1924) and inaugurated (1925); husband set up an office next to hers in the capitol, and, when individuals arrived for an audience with the governor, the secretary would ask which governor the caller wanted to see; lost renomination (1926); lost nomination for governor (1930); won nomination and was elected governor for 2nd term (1932); had a quieter, more productive administration; announced she would not run again (1934); lost nomination for governor (1940); retired to Austin (1944); supported Lyndon B. Johnson candidacy for US senate (1948). ❧ See also Ouida Ferguson Nalle, *The Fergusons of Texas or "Two Governors for the Price of One"* (Naylor, 1946); and *Women in World History.*

FERGUSON, Patricia (1958—). **Scottish politician.** Born 1958 in Glasgow, Scotland; m. William G. Butler. ❧ As Labour delegate, elected to the Scottish Parliament for Glasgow Maryhill (1999); appointed minister for Parliamentary Business (2001), then minister for Tourism, Culture and Sport (2004).

FERGUSON, Sarah (1959—). **Duchess of York.** Name variations: Fergie. Born Sarah Margaret Ferguson, Oct 15, 1959, in London, England; dau. of Ronald Ferguson (polo manager for the queen) and Susan Wright Ferguson Barrantes (died in auto accident, Sept 1998); m. Andrew, duke of York, July 23, 1986 (div. 1996); children: Beatrice (b. Aug 8, 1988); Eugenie (b. Mar 23, 1990). ❧ Controversial and spirited duchess, founded (1993) and serves as chair of Children in Crisis (1993); became spokesperson for Weight Watchers International (1997); served as host of the British tv talk show, "Sarah, Surviving Life" (1998); wrote 4 books in the "Budgie" series, including *Budgie the Little Helicopter* (1989) and *Budgie at Bendick's Point* (1989), and a pair of diet books. ❧ See also autobiography, *Sarah Ferguson: The Duchess of York—My Story* (1996).

FERGUSSON, Elizabeth (1737–1801). See Ferguson, Elizabeth Graeme.

FERGUSSON, Elizabeth (1867–1930). **New Zealand nurse, midwife, and hospital matron.** Born Elizabeth Leila Ralston Fergusson, April 16, 1867, at Balligmorrie, Ayrshire, Scotland; died on Feb 12, 1930, near Wanganui, New Zealand; dau. of James (farmer) and Eliza (Ralston) Fergusson; Obstetrical Society of London, diploma, 1897. ❧ Trained at Briston Royal Infirmary (1894); worked as private nurse (1897–1900); served with Britain's Army Nursing Service Reserve during South African War (1900–02); immigrated to New Zealand (1902); worked at private hospital in Wanganui (1902–07); administered Ruanui Maternity Hospital at Taihape (1907–12); became matron of Bay of Islands Hospital at Kawakawa (1912–14); assumed position of native health nurse for Mangonui district (1914–26); purchased land, built own cottage, and converted horse-drawn ambulance into medical supply vehicle for visits around district. ❧ See also *Dictionary of New Zealand Biography* (Vol. 3).

FERGUSSON, Mary (1914–1997). **Scottish civil engineer.** Name variations: Molly Fergusson. Born Mary Isolen Fergusson, April 28, 1914, in Scotland; died Nov 30, 1997. ❧ The 1st woman fellow of Institution of Civil Engineers, studied civil engineering at University of Edinburgh (1933); rose from indentured employee to senior partner and civil engineer at Blythe and Blythe, a firm in Edinburgh (1948–78); after retirement (1978), encouraged women to become engineers and funded students. Made Officer of the Order of the British Empire (1979).

FERGUSSON, Molly (1914–1997). See Fergusson, Mary.

FERGUSSON, Muriel McQueen (1899–1997). Canadian politician. Born Muriel McQueen in Shediac, New Brunswick, Canada, May 26, 1899; died in Fredericton, New Brunswick, Canada, April 11, 1997; graduate of Mount Allison University, 1921; received law degree from Dalhousie University; married a lawyer (died 1942). ❖ A legislator for 22 years and the 1st woman appointed speaker of the Senate (Dec 14, 1972), is remembered as a wise and witty senator who was devoted to the causes of Canadian women; admitted to New Brunswick Bar (1925); following husband's death (1942), took over his law practice; served as director of the Family Allowance and the Old Age Security Programs in New Brunswick, during which time she was also at the forefront in the battle against sex discrimination in the workplace; was 1st woman elected to the Fredericton City Council and 1st deputy mayor of that city; appointed as a Liberal to the Senate (1953); for over 2 decades, served on various Senate committees dealing with the rights of women and the welfare of all Canadian citizens; served as speaker of the Senate (1972–75); retired (1975).

FERKASINSZKY, Ildiko (b. 1945). See Bobis, Ildiko.

FERLAND, Barbara (1919—). Jamaican poet. Born 1919 in Jamaica. ❖ Moved to England; contributed to BBC radio program "Caribbean Voices" (1950s); published poems in Caribbean Voices (1970).

FERMOR, Arabella (d. 1738). English aristocrat. Name variations: Arabella Perkins. Died 1738; dau. of James Fermor of Tusmore; m. Frances Perkins of Ufton Court, near Reading. ❖ Became the subject of "The Rape of the Lock," a poem by Alexander Pope, when a lock of her hair was stolen by Lord Petre.

FERMOR, Henrietta Louisa (d. 1761). Countess of Pomfret and letter writer. Name variations: Fermour. Born Henrietta Louisa Jeffreys; died Dec 15, 1761; dau. of John, 2nd baron Jeffreys of Wem, Shropshire; m. Thomas Fermor, 2nd baron Leominster (later earl of Pomfret), 1720. ❖ Was lady of the bedchamber to Queen Caroline of Ansbach until 1737; while in Rome, wrote a life of Van Dyck. Her letters were published in Correspondence between Frances, Countess of Hartford (afterward Duchess of Somerset) and Henrietta Louisa, Countess of Pomfret, between . . . 1738 and 1741 (1805).

FERMOR, Una Ellis (1894–1958). See Ellis-Fermor, Una Mary.

FERN, Fanny (1811–1872). American writer and feminist. Name variations: Sara Willis Eldredge; Sara Willis Farrington; Sara Willis Parton; Sara Payson Willis; in childhood, spelled 1st name "Sarah"; name legally changed to Fanny Fern. Born Sara Willis, July 9, 1811, in Portland, Maine; died Oct 10, 1872, in New York, NY; dau. of Nathaniel Willis (printer and publisher of religious and children's periodicals) and Hannah Parker Willis; attended Catharine Beecher's Hartford Female Seminary, 1828–31; m. Charles Eldredge, May 4, 1837 (died 1846); m. Samuel Farrington, Jan 17, 1849 (div. 1853); m. James Parton, Jan 5, 1856; children: (1st m.) Mary Eldredge (died 1845 at age 7); Grace Eldredge (d. 1862); Ellen Eldredge. ❖ Under name Fanny Fern, protested American women's social, political, and economic inequality in both her fiction and her popular weekly newspaper column in New York Ledger; became 1st salaried woman newspaper columnist in America, contributing to both the Olive Branch and another Boston-based newspaper, the True Flag (1852); published bestselling novel, Ruth Hall (1854); wrote column for New York Ledger (1856–72); was a founding member of the women's club Sorosis (1868); a national celebrity and pioneer of reform journalism, was the 1st journalist to regularly champion women's rights in a consumer medium with a large readership; newspaper columns collected and published in book form as Fern Leaves from Fanny's Port Folio (1853), Fresh Leaves (1857) and Caper-Sauce (1872), among others; wrote novels Ruth Hall (1854) and Rose Clark (1856); also wrote children's books, including Little Ferns for Fanny's Little Friends (1853). ❖ See also Joyce W. Warren, Fanny Fern: An Independent Woman (Rutgers U. Press, 1992); Florence Bannard Adams, Fanny Fern, or a Pair of Flaming Shoes (Hermitage, 1966); and Women in World History.

FERN, Fanny (1866–1912). See de Cleyre, Voltairine.

FERNANDEZ, Adriana (1971—). Mexican marathon runner. Born Mar 4, 1971, in Mexico City, Mexico. ❖ Won a gold medal for 5,000 meters at Pan American Games (1995); won McGill Invitational 5,000 meters (1997); placed 2nd at New York City Marathon (1998) and 1st (1999), with a time of 2:25:06.

FERNANDEZ, Alina (1956—). Cuban model, memoirist and first daughter. Name variations: Alina Fernández. Born 1956 (some sources cite 1955) in Cuba; illeg. dau. of Fidel Castro and socialite Naty Revuelta Claws; children: Alina Salgado (b. around 1978). ❖ Was a model and public-relations director for a Cuban fashion company; escaped to Spain (1993), then moved to Miami, Florida; wrote Alina: Memorias de la Hija Rebelde de Fidel Castro, which became a bestseller in Spain (1997) and was translated into English as Castro's Daughter; hosted a daily radio program in Miami on Cuban and Cuban-American issues.

FERNANDEZ, Ana Ivis (1973—). Cuban volleyball player. Name variations: Ana Ibis Fernandez; Ana Ivis Fernandez Valle. Born Aug 3, 1973, in Sancti Spiritus, Cuba. ❖ Placed 1st at World championships (1994, 1998); won team gold medals at Atlanta Olympics (1996) and Sydney Olympics (2000) and a team bronze medal at Athens Olympics (2004).

FERNANDEZ, Beatriz (1964—). See Fernandez, Gigi.

FERNANDEZ, Bijou (1877–1961). American actress. Name variations: Mrs. W.L. Abingdon. Born Nov 4, 1877, in New York, NY; died Nov 7, 1961, in New York, NY; dau. of Mrs. E.L. Fernandez ([nee Price], then a well-known theatrical agent, 1852–1909); m. W.L. Abingdon. ❖ As a child, made stage debut in Girls and Boys (1883); appeared as Puck in Augustin Daly's Midsummer Night's Dream; other plays include The Girl I Left Behind Me, May Blossom, Arms and the Man, Man and Superman and The Prescott Proposals; on death of mother, took over her theatrical agency.

FERNANDEZ, Mrs. E.L. (1852–1909). American theatrical agent. Born 1852 (nee Price); died 1909; m. E(scamillo) L. Fernandez; children: Bijou Fernandez (1877–1961, actress) and probably E.L. Fernandez (1879–1952, actor). ❖ Play-broker and agent, "known to every actor who ever sought an engagement in New York," read her obit in the New York Times (Dec 22, 1909); was also vice-president of the Professional Women's League.

FERNANDEZ, Gigi (1964—). Puerto Rican tennis player. Born Beatriz Fernandez in San Juan, Puerto Rico, Feb 24, 1964; attended Clemson University. ❖ At 12, won Puerto Rico Open doubles; won 3 doubles titles with Martina Navratilova (1985), 3 titles with Lori McNeil (1987), and her 1st major title, the US Open doubles, with Robin White (1988); won US Open doubles title with Navratilova (1990) and French Open with Jana Novotna (1991); joined forces with Natasha Zvereva (1992) to dominate women's doubles (1993–97), winning 20 grand slams and ranking as Doubles Team of the Year (1993–95, 1997); won a gold medal at Barcelona Olympics (1992), competing for US and partnered with Mary Joe Fernandez (no relation); won a gold medal at Atlanta Olympics (1996), paired with Mary Joe Fernandez; retired (1997); came out of retirement, competing for semifinals for doubles at Roland Garros (2004) and making it to 2nd round for singles at Wimbledon (2004). ❖ See also Women in World History.

FERNANDEZ, Isabel (1972—). Spanish judoka. Born Feb 1, 1972, in Alicante, Spain. ❖ Won a bronze medal for 52-56kg lightweight at Atlanta Olympics (1996); won a World championship (1997); won European championships (1998, 1999, 2001); won a gold medal for 52-57kg lightweight at Sydney Olympics (2000).

FERNANDEZ, Lisa (1971—). American softball player. Born Feb 22, 1971, in Long Beach, California; graduate in psychology from University of California, Los Angeles, 1995; dau. of Antonio Fernandez (played semi-pro baseball in Cuba before immigrating to US in 1962) and Emilia Fernandez (native of Puerto Rico who played in several softball leagues). ❖ Considered one of the best all-around players in fast-pitch softball (1990s), won 1st American Softball Association championship at 11; during high school career, pitched 69 shutouts, 37 no-hitters, and 12 perfect games; while at University of California, Los Angeles (UCLA), was a 4-time All-American and a 2-time NCAA champion, breaking 7 UCLA records, topping NCAA record of winning percentages with a .930 average (93–7) and leading the nation in hitting (.510); for Team USA, won 6 games and a gold medal at Pan American Games (1991); played for the Raybestos Brakettes; pitched for the 1st-ever US Olympic women's softball team and won the gold medal at Atlanta (1996); won team World championship (2002); won team gold medals at Sydney Olympics (2000) and Athens Olympics (2004). Won Honda Cup Award (2000); named Women's Sports Foundation Athlete of the Year. ❖ See also Christina Lessa, Women Who Win (Universe, 1998); and Women in World History.

FERNANDEZ, Mary Joe (1971—). *American tennis player.* Name variations: Mary-Joe Fernandez. Born Aug 19, 1971, in Dominican Republic; raised in Miami, Florida, where family settled when she was 6 months old. ❖ At 13, won 1st professional tournament; during 1st full-time year on the women's pro circuit, won 40 out of 50 singles matches and 2 tournaments, including 1st professional tournament championship in the Tokyo Indoors; won a bronze medal for singles and a gold medal, with doubles partner Gigi Fernandez (no relation), at Barcelona Olympics (1992). ❖ See also *Women in World History.*

FERNANDEZ MORALES, Juana (1895–1979). *See Ibarbourou, Juana de.*

FERNÁNDEZ OCHOA, Blanca (1963—). *Spanish Alpine skier.* Name variations: Blanca Fernandez Ochoa. Born April 22, 1963, in Madrid, Spain; sister of Francisco Ochoa (who won a gold medal in slalom at Sapporo). ❖ Placed 6th at Sarajevo Olympics in giant slalom (1984) and 5th at Calgary Olympics for slalom (1988); won a bronze medal for slalom at Albertville Olympics (1992).

FERNANDO, Gilda Cordero (1930—). *Filipino short-story writer.* Born 1930 in the Philippines. ❖ With Alfredo Roces, published a 10-vol. encyclopedia of Philippine history, art, and culture; also published *Streets of Manila* (1977), *Turn of the Century* (1978), and *Jeepney* (1979), about Philippine cultural history.

FERNANDO, Sylvia (1904–1983). *Sri Lankan reformer.* Born 1904 in Colombo, Ceylon (now Sri Lanka); died in Colombo, Sri Lanka, 1983; father was a gynecologist and obstetrician and mother was active in social work; married; children: daughter, Nimali. ❖ Obtained funding for a pilot program for family planning in Ceylon ([Sri Lanka], 1946); opened the 1st family planning clinic (1953), at the De Sousa Hospital for Women; served as head of Family Planning Association (FPA) for next 17 years. ❖ See also *Women in World History.*

FERNECK, Christine (1969—). *German field-hockey player.* Born April 29, 1968. ❖ At Barcelona Olympics, won a silver medal in team competition (1992).

FERNER, Astrid (b. 1932). *See Oldenburg, Astrid.*

FERNER, Ellen Elizabeth (1869–1930). *New Zealand artist, photographer, and community leader.* Name variations: Ellen Elizabeth Aley, Nellie Ferner. Born Sept 13 1869, in Auckland, New Zealand; died Nov 3, 1930, at Remuera, New Zealand; dau. of Alfred (watchmaker and jeweler) and Ellen (Beck) Aley; m. James Ferner, 1890; children: 4. ❖ Skilled portrait painter and photographer of children and advocate for children's welfare and education, founded Play and Recreation Association to organize activities for urban children (1917); helped to establish public parks and reserves in Auckland; appointed as one of first three associate members of Children's Court (1926); became justice of peace (1927); helped to establish Community Sunshine School (1930); served on board of governors of Seddon Memorial Technical College. ❖ See also *Dictionary of New Zealand Biography* (Vol. 4).

FERNER, Nellie (1869–1930). *See Ferner, Ellen Elizabeth.*

FERNIG, Félicité de (c. 1776–after 1831). *French soldier.* Name variations: Felicite de Fernig; Madame Van der Walen. Born at Montagne, Nord, France, c. 1776; died after 1831; m. M. Van der Walen, a Belgian officer; sister of Théophile de Fernig. ❖ With sister, assumed male attire and enlisted in a company of National Guards commanded by father (1792); distinguished herself in battle of Jemappes which was fought between the victorious French and the Austrians; rode in a charge by the side of the Duke of Chartres (afterward Louis-Philippe); married a Belgian officer whose life she had saved; with sister, was celebrated by Lamartine in *Histoires de Girondins.* ❖ See also *Women in World History.*

FERNIG, Théophile de (c. 1779–c. 1818). *French soldier.* Name variations: Theophile de Fernig. Born at Mortagne, Nord, France, around 1779; died in Brussels, Belgium, c. 1818; sister of Félicité de Fernig. ❖ With sister, assumed male attire and enlisted in a company of National Guards commanded by father (1792); distinguished herself in battle of Jemappes; reputedly captured a Hungarian major; with sister, was celebrated by Lamartine in *Histoires de Girondins.* ❖ See also *Women in World History.*

FERRAGAMO, Fiamma (1941–1998). *Italian shoe designer.* Born Fiamma di San Giuliano Ferragamo in Florence, Italy, 1941; died of breast cancer at home in Florence, Sept 28, 1998; dau. of Salvatore Ferragamo (died 1960, founder of Salvatore Ferragamo Italia) and Wanda Ferragamo (chair of Salvatore Ferragamo Italia). ❖ At 16, began working for father's famous shoe company; took over the reins when father died (1960); as a designer, valued elegance and comfort, creating one of the most enduring upscale shoe designs, the "Vara" (1960s); also served on the Italian Environmental Fund board, which preserves historic Italian homes. Accorded the Neiman Marcus Award for Distinguished Service in Fashion (1967).

FERRAIS, Amalia (1830–1904). *Italian ballet dancer.* Born 1830 in Voghera, Italy; died Feb 8, 1904, in Florence, Italy. ❖ Made professional debut at Teatro Reggio in Turin (1844); danced 1 season at Her Majesty's Theatre in London, where she performed in Paul Taglioni's *Les Plaisirs de l'hiver* (1849); returned to Teatro Reggio briefly in Jules Perrot's *Ondine,* then had a 10-year engagement at Paris Opéra; danced principal roles in such Opéra productions as Mazilier's *Marco Spada* (1857), Petipa's *Sacountala* and *Graziosa* (both 1861), and Monplaisir's *La Camargo* (1868) and *Brahma* (1869); retired (1869).

FERRARA, duchess of.
See Leonora of Aragon (1450–1493).
See Borgia, Lucrezia (1480–1519).
See Renée of France (1510–1575).
See Sforza, Anna (1473–1497).
See Rovere, Giulia della.
See Medici, Lucrezia de (c. 1544–1561).
See Gonzaga, Margherita (1564–1618).

FERRARA, marquesa of.
See Este, Ricciarda d'.
See Gonzaga, Margherita (1418–1439).

FERRARI, Carlotta (1837–1907). *Italian pianist, poet, singer, and writer.* Born in Lodia, Jan 27, 1837; died in Bologna, Nov 23, 1907; studied piano and voice under Strepponi and Panzini, and composition under Mazzucato at Milan Conservatory. ❖ At 20, completed 1st opera, *Ugo,* but had to pay the expense of presenting it, as no one would showcase an opera written by a woman; with her work soon in great demand, was commissioned to write a cantata as well as a Requiem mass for the anniversary of the death of King Charles Albert; considered one of the great masters of the canon form, was extremely respected in the musical world; poetry was also highly regarded.

FERRARI, Gabrielle (1851–1921). *French concert pianist and composer.* Born Gabriella Colombari de Montègre in Paris, France, Sept 14(?), 1851; died in Paris, July 4, 1921; studied at conservatories in Naples and Milan; in Paris, studied with Théodore Dubois and H. Ketten; m. Francesco Ferrari (Italian correspondent for *Le Figaro*). ❖ A concert artist, like many composers, was also a well-known pianist; championed by François Leborne and Charles Gounod, concentrated on opera, completing 5 large works; 1st success was *Le dernier amour* (1895), followed by *Le Cobzar.*

FERRARI, Maria Paz (1973—). *Argentinean field-hockey player.* Born Sept 12, 1973, in Argentina. ❖ Won a team silver medal at Sydney Olympics (2000).

FERRARIS, Jan (1947—). *American golfer.* Name variations: Janis Jean Ferraris. Born June 2, 1947, in San Francisco, California; attended Odessa College. ❖ Won USGA Junior (1963) and Western Junior (1963–64); joined LPGA tour (1966) and named Rookie of the Year; won Orange Blossom, Atlanta and Japan opens (1970); retired from tour (1984); became a golf instructor.

FERRARO, Geraldine (1935—). *American politician.* Name variations: Geraldine Zaccaro. Born Geraldine Anne Ferraro in Newburgh, NY, Aug 26, 1935; dau. of Dominick Ferraro (businessman) and Antonetta (Corrieri) Ferraro; Marymount Manhattan College, BA, 1956; Fordham Law School, JD, 1960; m. John A. Zaccaro (real-estate developer), 1960; children: Donna, John Jr. and Laura Zaccaro. ❖ The 1st American woman nominated for vice president, was appointed assistant district attorney, Queens, New York (1975); elected to US House of Representatives (1978), then reelected (1982); given a seat on the powerful House Budget Committee; initiated a pension-equity bill (1981), giving women greater access to their husbands' pension plans and retirement benefits; gained influence in the House and made some powerful allies; named chair of the Democratic Platform Committee (1984); nominated for vice president at Democratic National Convention (1984); proved a tenacious, cool, and enthusiastic politician on the hustings, but her candidacy became jeopardized amidst growing speculation over husband's business practices; ran as unsuccessful candidate for US Senate (1992); served as a public delegate (Feb 1993) and alternate

US delegate to the World Conference on Human Rights held in Vienna (June 1993); appointed US ambassador to the UN Human Rights Commission by President Bill Clinton (1994), serving two years; was vice-chair of the US delegation at the Fourth World Conference on Women held in Beijing (Sept 1955); was co-host of "Crossfire," a political interview program on CNN (1996–98); was a partner in the CEO Perspective Group, a consulting firm that advises top executives (1996–98); ran as unsuccessful candidate for US Senate (1998). ❖ See also autobiography (with Linda Bird Francke) *Ferraro: My Story* (Bantam, 1985) and (with Catherine Whitney) *Framing a Life: A Family Memoir* (Scribner, 1998); and *Women in World History*.

FERRÉ, Rosario (1938—). Puerto Rican author. Name variations: Rosario Ferre. Born 1938 in Ponce, Puerto Rico; dau. of Luis A. Ferré (founder of Puerto Rico's New Progressive Party and governor of the island [1968–72]); studied at University of Puerto Rico with Mario Vargas Llosa; married 1960 and 1972 (div.); children: 3. ❖ Famed for parodies and denunciations of racism, sexism, socioeconomic injustice and colonial and neocolonial subordination of Puerto Rico, began writing poetry and short stories (1970) and went on to also publish children's literature, criticism, essays on feminism, historical books and novels; was a founder and editor of literary magazine *Zona de Carga y Descarga*, intent on publishing young, unknown writers; came to prominence with 1st short story, *La muñeca menor* (The Youngest Doll, 1976); was finalist for National Book Award for *House on the Lagoon* (1995); also wrote short stories *Cuando las mujeres quieren a los hombres* (When Women Love Men, 1972), and novels, *Papeles de Pandora* (Pandora's Papers, 1976), *Sweet Diamond Dust* (1988), *El coloquio de las perras* (The Bitches' Colloquy, 1990) and *Flight of the Swan* (2001); collections of short fiction and poetry include *Fabulas de la garza desangrada* (Fables of the Bled Swan, 1982) and *La batalla de las vírgenes* (The Battle of the Virgins, 1993); published a collection of feminist essays, *Sitio a eros: Trece ensayos literarios* (The Seige of Eros: Thirteen Literary Essays, 1980). ❖ See also Susan S. Hintz, *Rosario Ferré, A Search for Identity* (Peter Lang, 1995).

FERREE, Gertrude (1886–1970). *See Rand, Gertrude.*

FERREIRA, Anne (1961—). French politician. Born Mar 18, 1961, in Saint-Quentin, France. ❖ Schoolteacher (1981–99); served as vice-chair of the Aisne Departmental Council; as a European Socialist, elected to 5th European Parliament (1999–2004).

FERRELL, Barbara (1947—). African-American track-and-field athlete. Name variations: Barbara Ann Ferrell Edmondson. Born July 8, 1947, in Hattiesburg, Mississippi; m. Warren Edmondson. ❖ Set the world record in the 100 meters (1968); won the silver medal in the 100 meters and the gold medal in the 4x100-meter relay in the Mexico City Olympics (1968). ❖ See also *Women in World History*.

FERRER, Concepció (1938—). Spanish politician. Born Jan 27, 1938, in Ripoll, Girona, Catalonia, Spain. ❖ Member of UDC Executive (1978–84, 1987—) and chair (1984–86); served as vice-president of the European Union of Christian Democrats (EUCD, 1983–86), president of the Union of Christian Democratic Women (UCDW, 1987–89), and vice-president of the Christian Democratic International (1998—); as a member of the European People's Party (Christian Democrats) and European Democrats, elected to 4th and 5th European Parliament (1994–99, 1999–2004). Awarded Grand Cross of the Order of Bernardo O'Higgins (Chile) and Commander of the Order of May (Argentina).

FERRER SALAT, Beatriz (1966—). Spanish equestrian. Born Mar 11, 1966, in Barcelona, Spain. ❖ At World Equestrian games, placed 2nd in indiv. dressage and 3rd in team dressage (2002); on Beauvalais, won a bronze medal for indiv. dressage and a silver medal for team dressage at Athens Olympics (2004).

FERRERO, Anna-Maria (1931—). Italian actress. Name variations: Anna Maria Ferrero. Born Anna Maria Guerra, Feb 18, 1931, in Rome, Italy; m. Jean Sorel (actor). ❖ Made film debut in *Il cielo è rosso* (1949), followed by *Il Cristo proibito, Domani è un altro giorno, Fanciulle di lusso, I Vinti, Giuseppe Verdi, Viva la rivista, Napoletani a Milano, La Vedova X, La Rivale, War and Peace, Giovanni dalle bande nere, La notte brava, Il mattatore, Austerlitz, Il Gobbo, Always on Sunday* and *Controsesso*, among others.

FERRERS, Anne (d. 1342). English noblewoman. Died 1342; dau. of William Ferrers, 1st baron Ferrers of Groby, and Margaret Segrave (c. 1280–?); m. Edward Despenser; children: Edward Despenser, 1st baron Despenser.

FERRERS, Elizabeth (1392–1434). Lady Greystoke. Name variations: Lady of Wem or Wemme. Born 1392 (some sources cite 1394); died 1434; interred at Black Friars', York; dau. of Robert Ferrers, 2nd baron Ferrers of Wemme, and Joan Beaufort (c. 1379–1440); m. John Greystoke, 6th Lord Greystoke, c. Oct 28, 1407; children: Ralph Greystoke, Lord Greystoke.

FERRERS, Helen (1869–1943. English actress. Born Helen Finney, 1869, in Cookham, Berkshire, England; died Feb 1, 1943, in London; sister of May Fortescue (actress); m. E.F. Mayeur (actor). ❖ As a schoolgirl, made London debut as Pauline in *Frou-Frou* (1885), then toured with her sister; appeared in such plays as *King John* (as Constance), *Toddles, Pssers-By, Peter Ibbetson, The Freaks, Sacred and Profane Love, Skittles, Tilly of Bloomsbury, Head Over Heels, Poppy, The River, The Student Prince, Gentlemen Prefer Blondes, The Duke of Killicrankie, Peg O' My Heart* and *Sweet Lavender;* made film debut in *Sally in Our Alley* (1931), followed by *Mr. Bill the Conqueror, Love on the Spot, In the Air, Going Straight, The Girl from Maxims, Meet My Sister* and *The Primrose Path,* among others.

FERRERS, Isabel. *See Mowbray, Isabel.*

FERRERS, Mary (d. 1457). English noblewoman. Name variations: Lady of Oversley. Born before 1394; died Jan 25, 1457; dau. of Robert Ferrers, 2nd baron Ferrers of Wemme, and Joan Beaufort (c. 1379–1440); m. Ralph Neville (son of the 1st earl of Westmoreland); children: John Neville of Oversley.

FERRI, Olga (1928—). Argentinean ballet dancer. Born 1928 in Buenos Aires, Argentina. ❖ As a child, trained and danced under Esmee Bulnes at Teatro Colón in Buenos Aires; joined Bulnes' company and danced principal roles in Fokine revivals, including *Les Sylphides,* as well as in classical ballets such as *The Nutcracker, Swan Lake* and *Coppélia;* performed throughout Europe for several years including at Munich State Opera, Berlin State Ballet, and London Festival Ballet; appeared in tv film "The Life and Loves of Fanny Elssler"; returned to Argentina and Teatro Colón (1962), where she served as director after retiring from performance career.

FERRIER, Kathleen (1912–1953). English contralto. Born Kathleen Mary Ferrier, April 22, 1912, at Higher Walton, near Preston, Lancashire, England; died Oct 8, 1953; dau. of William (teacher) and Alice (Murray) Ferrier; m. Albert Wilson, Nov 19, 1935 (annulled 1947); no children. ❖ Born into a musical family, studied the piano from age 9 and had established a reputation as an excellent amateur accompanist before she won a major singing competition at 25 (1937); began to take regular voice lessons; within 5 years, had established her singing career in London and begun to win international acclaim (1937–42); triumphed in premiere of Mahler's *Das Lied von der Erde* at the inaugural Edinburgh Festival (1947); became one of the world's best-known and best-loved singers in the course of an all-too-brief career; from oratorio and folk songs, progressed to the songs of Schubert and Mahler and to the operas of Gluck and Britten; when she was 39, diagnosed with the cancer that would kill her (1951), but her voice was unimpaired; for 2 more years, continued to sing, retaining her infectiously joyous spirit until the end. Recordings include *Orfeo ed Euridice, Das Lied von der Erde, Mahler and Brahms Recital, Bach and Handel Arias* and *The World of Kathleen Ferrier.* ❖ See also Neville Cardus, ed. *Kathleen Ferrier, 1912–1953: A Memoir* (Hamilton, 1954); Maurice Leonard, *Kathleen: The Life of Kathleen Ferrier, 1912–1953* (Hutchinson, 1988).

FERRIER, Susan Edmonstone (1782–1854). Scottish novelist. Born Susan Edmonstone Ferrier in Edinburgh, Scotland, Sept 7, 1782; died Nov 5, 1854, in Edinburgh; dau. of James Ferrier (solicitor and friend of 5th duke of Argyll) and Helen Coutts; aunt of James Frederick Ferrier, Scottish philosopher; never married; no children. ❖ Encouraged by author Lady Charlotte Bury, began a satirical work of manners which resulted in the novel *Marriage*, published anonymously (1818); wrote 2 more unsigned novels, *The Inheritance* (1824) and *Destiny* (1831), which present lively pictures of Scottish life and character; a woman of quick wit and warm heart, was an intimate friend of Walter Scott's, as well as other eminent writers of her day, including Joanna Baillie; complete works were published (1882). ❖ See also *Memoir and Correspondence* (ed. by A. Doyle, 1898); Mary Cullinan, *Susan Ferrier* (1984); and *Women in World History*.

FERRIN, Mary Upton (1810–1881). American women's-rights activist. Name variations: Mary Upton, Mary Ferrin. Born Mary Upton, April 27, 1810, in South Danvers (now Peabody), Massachusetts; died

April 11, 1881, in Marblehead, MA; dau. of Jesse and Elizabeth or Eliza (Wyman) Wood Upton; m. Jesse C. Ferrin (grocer), Dec 2, 1845. ❖ Unhappy in marriage, sought a divorce only to learn that, according to law, "the whole of the wife's personal property" belonged to husband; drew up a petition for amendment of law (1848), then traveled, collected signatures, and submitted the petition annually to the legislature through a friendly legislator (1848–53); as the 1st woman in the state to petition legislature for women's rights, influenced the passage of the liberal married women's property act (1855); authored pamphlet, *Woman's Defence* (1869).

FERRIS, Elizabeth (1940—). English diver. Born Nov 19, 1940, in UK. ❖ At Rome Olympics, won a bronze medal in springboard (1960).

FERRIS, Michelle (1976—). Australian cyclist. Born Sept 24, 1976, in Warmambool, Victoria, Australia. ❖ Won 16 Australian cycling titles; won a silver medal for sprint at Atlanta Olympics (1996); won World Cup sprint (1997) and Track World Cup sprint and time trial (1998); won a silver for sprint at World championships (1999); won a silver medal for 500-meter time trial at Sydney Olympics (2000).

FERRONAYS, Pauline de la (1808–1891). *See Craven, Pauline.*

FERYABNIKOVA, Nelli (1949—). Soviet basketball player. Born May 14, 1949, in USSR. ❖ Won a gold medal at Montreal Olympics (1976) and a gold medal at Moscow Olympics (1980), both in team competition.

FETTI, Lucrina (fl. 1614–1651). Italian painter and nun. Name variations: Giustina Fetti. Born Lucrina or Giustina Fetti in Rome; birth and death dates unknown; sister of painter Domenico Fetti (1589–1623). ❖ Entered Franciscan convent of Sant Orsola, Mantua (1614); created a body of religious work for the convent and its adjacent public church, as well as a group of state portraits of the distinguished women of the convent and the court of Mantua. Paintings include *Deposition*, *Adoration of the Shepherds*, *Adoration of the Magi*, *Annunciation*, *Crowning with Thorns*, *Visitation*, *Agony in the Garden*, *St. Margaret*, *Mary Magdalene* and *St. Barbara* (1619); also painted Margherita Gonzaga, Eleanora I Gonzaga, Eleanora II Gonzaga, and Catherine de Medici. ❖ See also *Women in World History.*

FETZER, Brigitte (1956—). East German volleyball player. Born May 17, 1956, in East Germany. ❖ At Moscow Olympics, won a silver medal in team competition (1980).

FEUCHÈRES, Sophie, Baronne de (c. 1795–1841). Anglo-French courtier and baroness. Name variations: Feucheres; Sophia Dawes. Pronunciation: Fe-SHAR. Born Sophie Dawes or Daws at St. Helens, Isle of Wight, c. 1795; died in London, England, Jan 2, 1841 (some sources cite Dec 1840); m. Baron Adrien Victor de Feuchères, 1818 (sep. 1822). ❖ Went to London as a servant; became mistress of Louis Henri Joseph de Bourbon (1756–1830), last of the Condé princes (1811); eager to improve station, was tutored in modern languages and Greek and Latin; went to Paris with prince who, to prevent scandal, had her married to a major in Royal Guards (1818); became a person of consequence at court of Louis XVIII; when relationship with Condé was revealed, was separated from husband and forbidden from appearing at court; convinced Condé to include her in his will; when he was found hanging dead from his window (Aug 27, 1830), was suspected but there was no evidence of foul play. ❖ See also *Women in World History.*

FEUILLÈRE, Edwige (1907–1998). French actress. Name variations: played minor roles early in career under stage name Cora Lynn. Born Caroline Vivette Edwige Cunati, Oct 29, 1907, in Vesorel, France; died Nov 13, 1998; dau. of Guy (architect) and Berthe (Koenig) Cunati; studied acting at Conservatory of Dijon and at Conservatory of Paris, with Georges Le Roy; m. Pierre Feuillère (actor), 1931 (div.). ❖ The "first lady" of French stage and cinema, excelled both in drama and comedy, playing desirable but heartless femmes fatales; made stage debut at Comédie Française as Suzanne in *Mariage de Figaro* (1931), remaining there until 1933; subsequent roles in French and international theater include Marguerite Gautier in *La Dame Aux Camélias* (1940), the Queen in Cocteau's *L'Aigle à Deux Têtes* (*The Eagle Has Two Heads*, 1946), Clothilde in *La Parisienne* (1957), La Périchole in *Le Carosse du Saint-Sacrement* (1957), title roles in *Phèdre* (1957), *Lucy Crown* (1958), and *Constance* (1960); later plays include Giraudoux's *La Folle de Chaillot* (1965), Williams' *Sweet Bird of Youth* (1971), and Anouilh's *Léocadia* (1984); appeared in such films as *La Fine Combine* (1931), *La Perle* (1932), *Topaze* (1932), *Monsieur Albert* (1932), *Le Miroir aux Alouettes* (1934), *Stradivarius* (1935), *Lucrece Borgia* (1935), *Barcarolle* (1935),

Feu! (1937), *La Dame de Malacca* (1937), *Mayerling to Sarajevo* (1940), *L'Idiot* (1946), *Olivia* (1950), *Let's Make Love* (1968), and *Julia* (1977). Was named a Chevalier of the Légion d'Honneur and honored by French Film Academy with a César Award (1984). ❖ See also autobiography, *Les Feux de la Mémoire* (1977); and *Women in World History.*

FEURY, Peggy (1924–1985). American actress and drama coach. Born Margaret Feury, June 20, 1924, in New Jersey; died Nov 20, 1985, in an auto accident in Los Angeles, California; m. William Traylor (actor); children: Susan Traylor (actress). ❖ Appeared on Broadway in *Enter Laughing*, *Turn of the Screw*, *Peer Gynt*, *The Grass Harp*, *The Three Sisters*, and Franco Zeffirelli's production of *The Lady of the Camellias*; was an artistic director, instructor, and charter member of the Actor's Studio; with husband, moved to LA and founded The Loft Studio, becoming one of the city's most respected acting teachers, coaching such students as Sean Penn and Michelle Pfeiffer.

FEWINGS, Eliza Anne (1857–1940). British-born educational reformer. Born in Bristol, England, Dec 28, 1857; died in Wales, 1940; dau. of Charles and Sarah (Twining) Fewings; trained as a teacher under her brother, headmaster of the King Edward VI Grammar School in Southampton. ❖ Known for her dedication to educational reforms in England and Australia, began teaching career at Roan Girls' School in Greenwich, England; was headmistress of Dr. Williams' Endowed High School for Girls in North Wales (1886–96); also served on the Council of Aberystwyth University College, where she campaigned for and won equal status for women; became headmistress of the Brisbane Girls' Grammar School in Australia (1896); founded the Brisbane State High School for Girls (later known as Somerville House), which by 1903 was the largest girls' school in Queensland; returned to England (1908).

FIACCONI, Franca (1965—). Italian marathon runner. Born Oct 4, 1965, in Rome, Italy. ❖ Won New York City Marathon (1998) with a time of 2:25:17; won Netherlands Marathon (2001) and Trieste Marathon (2001, 2002).

FIAMENGO, Marya (1926—). Canadian poet. Born 1926 in Vancouver, British Columbia, Canada. ❖ Educated and became teacher at University of British Columbia; writings include *Quality of Halves* (1958), *The Ikon: Measured Work* (1961), *Overheard at the Oracle* (1969), *Silt of Iron* (1971), *In Praise of Older Women* (1976) and *North of the Cold Star* (1978).

FIAMMETTA (fl. 1300s). *See Maria dei Conti d'Aquino.*

FIAT, J. (1888–1979). *See Scott, Mary Edith.*

FIBINGEROVA, Helena (1949—). Czech track-and-field athlete. Born July 13, 1949, in Czechoslovakia. ❖ At Montreal Olympics, won a bronze medal in the shot put (1976).

FICHANDLER, Zelda (1924—). American theatrical producer and director. Born Zelda Diamond, Sept 18, 1924, in Boston, Massachusetts; dau. of Harry (scientist and inventor) and Ida (Epstein) Diamond; Cornell University, BA, 1945; George Washington University, MA in dramatic arts, 1950; m. Thomas C. Fichandler (executive director of Arena Stage), Feb 17, 1946; children: 2 sons. ❖ Producer and director who co-founded the Arena Stage in Washington, DC, helping to spawn the nationwide movement that revolutionized theater and cultural life in America; co-founded the Arena Stage (1950) and served as producing director (1952–94); received grant from the Rockefeller Foundation to create a training program for her acting company (1965); involved with founding of Theater Communications Group (TCG, 1961); served as delegate to International Theater Institute Conference in Moscow (1974); served as visiting professor at University of Texas in Austin and Boston University (1970s); assumed position of artistic director of Graduate Acting Program at New York University's Tisch School of the Arts (1984—); was artistic director of the Acting Company (1991–94); directed over 50 plays during her tenure at Arena Stage, including US premiere of Christie's *The Mousetrap* (1955), Lawrence and Lee's *Inherit the Wind*, which toured to Moscow and Leningrad (1973), and US premiere of *The Ascent of Mount Fuji* (1975). Received Helen Hayes Award for best direction of *The Crucible* (1988). ❖ See also *Women in World History.*

FICHTEL, Anja (1968—). German fencer. Name variations: Anja Fichtel-Mauritz or Mauritz-Fichtel. Born Aug 17, 1968, in Tauberbischofsheim, Germany. ❖ Won gold medals in team foil and indiv. foil at Seoul Olympics (1988); won a silver medal at Barcelona Olympics (1992) and a bronze medal at Atlanta Olympics (1996), both for team foil; won 5 medals at World Championships and 20 German championships; retired (1997).

FICK, Sigrid (1887–1979). Swedish tennis player. Born Sigrid Frenckell, Mar 28, 1887, in Sweden; died June 4, 1979. ❖ At Stockholm Olympics, won a bronze medal in mixed doubles-indoor courts and a silver medal in mixed doubles-outdoors (1912).

FICKERT, Auguste (1855–1910). Austrian suffragist leader. Born May 25, 1855, in Vienna, Austria; died June 9, 1910, in Maria Enzersdorf, Lower Austria. ❖ With Rosa Mayreder, Marie Lang and Marianne Hainisch, was founder of the feminist movement in Austria, pioneering the right-to-vote for women movement (1893); a Social Democrat, also pushed for opportunities for women's higher education.

FICKLING, Neva Langley (c. 1934—). See Langley, Neva.

FIDELIA (1652–1732). See Barker, Jane.

FIDELIS (1837–1927). See Machar, Agnes Maule.

FIDES (290–303). See Faith.

FIEBIG, Cora (c. 1934—). American bowler. Born c. 1934; lived in Madison Heights, Michigan; children: daughter Lisa, son Chris. ❖ Won US Team Trials championship (1981) and Team USA Tournament national amateur championship (1986); was a member of the Federation Internationale des Quilleurs (FIQ) American Zone champions team (1981) and the FIQ World champions team (1987); won Women International Bowling Congress (WIBC) Queens championship (1986). Inducted into WIBC Hall of Fame (2003).

FIEBIGER, Christel (1946—). German politician. Born Dec 29, 1946, in Uenze-Brandenburg, Germany. ❖ Agricultural engineer; representing the Confederal Group of the European United Left/Nordic Green Left (GUE/NGL), elected to 5th European Parliament (1999–2004).

FIEDLER, Bobbi (1937—). American politician. Born Roberta Frances Horowitz in Santa Monica, California, April 22, 1937; attended Santa Monica City College, 1955–59. ❖ Began public career as the organizer of a citizens' group called BUSTOP, which opposed busing as a means of desegregating Los Angeles schools; served on Los Angeles School Board (1977–80); won 1st race for US House of Representatives (1980); serving 3 consecutive terms, was a member of the Budget Committee where she advocated fiscal conservatism; voted along party lines on most issues, but parted with Republican colleagues in her support of feminist issues, including the Equal Rights Amendment; made an unsuccessful bid for a Republican Senate seat (1986). ❖ See also Women in World History.

FIEDLER, Ellen (1958—). East German hurdler. Born Nov 26, 1958, in East Germany. ❖ At Seoul Olympics, won a bronze medal in 400-meter hurdles (1988).

FIELD, Betty (1918–1973). American actress. Born Feb 8, 1918, in Boston, Massachusetts; died Sept 13, 1973; only dau. of George Baldwin and Katherine Francis (Lynch) Field; studied at American Academy of Dramatic Arts; m. Elmer Rice (playwright), Jan 12, 1942 (div. 1956); m. Edwin J. Lukas, 1957; children: (1st m.) John, Judith, and Paul. ❖ Made Broadway debut in a one-line part in *Page Miss Glory* (1934); became a popular ingenue in George Abbott productions (1930s); after appearances in Elmer Rice's *Flight to the West* (1940) and *A New Life* (1943), achieved 1st genuine triumph in *Dream Girl* (1945), for which she won New York Drama Critics Circle Award; went on to play ingenue and character roles in both comedies and dramas, including Rice's *Not for Children* (1951), Dorothy Parker's *Ladies of the Corridor* (1953), and *Festival* (1955), as well as the 1st American production of O'Neill's *A Touch of the Poet* (1958); films include *Of Mice and Men* (1940), *Seventeen* (1940), *King's Row* (1942), *The Great Gatsby* (1949), *Picnic* (1956), *Bus Stop* (1956), *Peyton Place* (1957), *Butterfield 8* (1960), *Birdman of Alcatraz* (1962), *Seven Women* (1966) and *Coogan's Bluff* (1968). ❖ See also Women in World History.

FIELD, Ethel Maude (1882–1967). New Zealand community leader. Name variations: Ethel Maude Bryant. Born Dec 20, 1882, in Wellington, New Zealand; died July 5, 1967, at Palmerston North, New Zealand; dau. of Robert and Elizabeth (Bradley) Bryant; m. Walter Fitzgerald Field (farmer, d. 1949), 1905; children: 5. ❖ Founding member of Palmerston North branch of Women's Division of the New Zealand Farmers' Union from 1927, represented group on co-ordinating committee at Massey Agricultural College and convened numerous conferences; involved in Kainga Moe rest home and training center project; active in Polish Children's Camp in Pahiatua; president of Palmerston North women's section of New Zealand National Party (1937); president of Palmerston North National Club; helped found Aokautere branch of the Dominion Federation of New Zealand Country Women's Institutes, and the Free Kindergarten Association in Palmerston North; vice president of National Council of Women of New Zealand. Received Coronation Medal and British Empire Medal (1953). ❖ See also *Dictionary of New Zealand Biography.*

FIELD, Jessie (1881–1971). American educator. Name variations: Jessie Field Shambaugh. Born Celestia Josephine Field, June 26, 1881, in Shenandoah, Iowa; died Jan 15, 1971, in Clarinda, Iowa; dau. of Solomon Elijah Field and Celestia Josephine (Eastman) Field (both educators); attended Western Normal College in Iowa; m. Ira William Shambaugh, 1917; children: Phyllis Ruth Shambaugh (b. 1922); (adopted) William H. Shambaugh. ❖ As superintendent of schools for Page Co., Iowa, established Corn Clubs and Home Clubs in all of the county's 130 schools (the clubs later became a national organization, under name 4-H Club); served as national secretary for Young Women's Christian Association (YWCA) in New York (1912–17). ❖ See also autobiographies *The Corn Lady: The Story of a Country Teacher's Life* (1911) and *A Real Country Teacher: The Story of Her Work* (1922); and *Women in World History.*

FIELD, Joanna (1900–1998). See Milner, Marion.

FIELD, Kate (1838–1896). American writer and actress. Born Mary Katherine Keemle Field, Oct 1, 1838, in St. Louis, Missouri; died in Honolulu, Hawaii, May 19, 1896; dau. of Joseph M. (well-known actor, playwright and one of the founders of New Orleans *Picayune*, died 1856) and Eliza Lapsey (Riddle) Field (actress); educated at Lasell Seminary. ❖ Journalist, columnist, actress, lecturer, and publisher of the weekly *Kate Field's Washington*, stayed 2 years in Florence in early years (1858–59); wrote a column for the Boston *Courier* and then the *Transcript*; subsequently gained much of her reputation with 3-part reminiscence of "The Last Days of Walter Savage Landor" in *Atlantic Monthly* (1861); over next 7 years, wrote other articles concerning her stay in Florence for the *Atlantic*, including "A Study of Elizabeth Barrett Browning"; opened on Broadway as Peg Woffington in *Masks and Faces* (1874), which closed the following night; began writing articles on drama for New York *Tribune*; published *Pen Photographs of Dickens' Readings* and *Eyes and Ears in London*, which met with genuine success; established a literary and critical journal in Washington, with a branch office in New York, which she titled *Kate Field's Washington* (1890), a national weekly review in which she continued her brilliant criticism of literature, the stage, and politics; accepted a commission from Chicago *Times-Herald* to visit Hawaii and study conditions there (1895). Decorated by French government with the Palm of the Academy, the highest honor given to a woman, and named as Officier de l'Instruction Publique. ❖ See also Women in World History.

FIELD, Mary (1813–1885). See Parsons, Mary.

FIELD, Mary (1896–c. 1968). English filmmaker. Born Agnes Mary Field in Wimbledon, England, 1896; died 1968 or 1969; attended Bedford College for Women, London; received MA at Institute of Historical Research; m. Gerald Hankin (Ministry of Education official). ❖ Joined British Instructional Films as education manager (1926), then moved to production side (1927); was a director on acclaimed series *Secrets of Nature* and almost single-handedly invented cinematic techniques still used in nature cinematography; went to work for Gaumont British Instructional Films (GBI, 1933), where she pioneered Britain's nascent children's film industry; after making films for 11 years, headed the Children's Entertainment Division for GBI, while also acting as executive producer on Arthur Rank's Children's Cinema Clubs; chaired Brussel's International Centre for Films for Children (1957); worked as a children's programming consultant for ATV/ABC TV (1959–63); wrote *Good Company: The Story of the Children's Entertainment Film Movement in Great Britain, 1943–1950* (1952). Named CBE (1951). ❖ See also Women in World History.

FIELD, Michael
    See Bradley, Katharine Harris.
    See Cooper, Edith Emma.

FIELD, Mrs. (c. 1670–1723). See Egerton, Sarah Fyge.

FIELD, Pattie H. (b. around 1902). American vice consul. Born c. 1902 in Denver, Colorado; graduate of Radcliffe College. ❖ Appointed US vice consul in Amsterdam, Netherlands (1925), becoming 1st American woman in consular service; resigned to accept a job with the National Broadcasting Company (1929).

FIELD, Rachel Lyman (1894–1942). American writer. Born Sept 19, 1894, in New York City; died Mar 15, 1942, in Beverly Hills, California; dau. of Matthew D. Field (physician) and Lucy (Atwater) Field; attended Radcliffe College as special student, 1914–18; m. Arthur S. Pederson (literary agent), June 20, 1935; children: (adopted) Hannah Pederson. ❖ As a member of George P. Baker's famous "English 47" playwriting workshop, scored 1st success with *Rise Up, Jennie Smith* (1918); for 6 years, worked in the editorial department of the film company Famous Players-Lasky, writing synopses of plays and books; made her mark through her work for young people, which encompassed poems, stories, one-act plays, and most especially her juvenile novels, *Hitty: Her First Hundred Years* (1929) and *Calico Bush* (1931); wrote 1st adult novel, *Time Out of Mind* (1935); achieved greatest popular success with *All This and Heaven Too* (1938), a fictionalized account of her great-aunt, the famous Mademoiselle D. (Mademoiselle Henriette Deluzy-Desportes, later Henriette Field) of Paris, who before her marriage to Henry M. Field was wrongly linked to the infamous murder of the Duchess of Choiseul-Praslin; also wrote *All Through the Night* (1940) and *And Now Tomorrow* (1942). Won Newbery Medal, the 1st awarded to a woman (1929), for *Hitty*. ❖ See also *Women in World History.*

FIELD, Sally (1946—). American actress. Born Nov 6, 1946, in Pasadena, California; dau. of Richard (army captain) and Margaret (Maggie Mahoney) Field (actress); stepdau. of actor Jock Mahoney; attended Columbia Studios Actor's Workshop, 1973–75; m. Steven Craig (screenwriter), 1968 (div. 1975); m. Alan Greisman (producer), 1984 (div. 1993); children: (1st m.) Peter and Eli Craig; (2nd m.) Samuel Greisman. ❖ Had early fame in title role of tv series "Gidget" (1965–66), then gained wider popularity as star of tv sitcom "The Flying Nun" (1967–70); made film debut in *The Way West* (1967) but remained primarily tv star, broadening repertoire with the edgy "Maybe I'll Come Home in the Spring" (1970); had 1st major film role in *Stay Hungry* (1976); won Emmy for performance in tv miniseries "Sybil" (1976); while living with Burt Reynolds, starred opposite him in *Smokey and the Bandit* (1977) and *Hooper* (1978); won Oscar, Golden Globe and Best Actress Prize at Cannes for performance as small-town union leader in *Norma Rae* (1979); won 2nd Oscar and Golden Globe for *Places in the Heart* (1984); formed production company, Fogwood Films (1988), which was responsible for *Steel Magnolias* (1989); starred in *Mrs. Doubtfire* (1993) and *Forrest Gump* (1994); directed tv movie "The Christmas Tree" (1996) and feature film *Beautiful* (2000), starring Minnie Driver; won American Society of Cinematographers' Board of Governors Award (2001). Other films and tv movies include *Absence of Malice* (1981), *Kiss Me Goodbye* (1982), *Murphy's Romance* (1985), *Punchline* (1988), *Soapdish* (1991), *Not Without My Daughter* (1991), *A Woman of Independent Means* (1995) and *Where the Heart Is* (2001). ❖ See also Russell Roberts, *Sally Field* (Mitchell Lane, 2003).

FIELD, Sara Bard (1882–1974). American poet. Name variations: Sara Bard Field Wood. Born Sara Bard Field in Cincinnati, Ohio, 1882; died June 15, 1974, in Berkeley, California; dau. of Annie Jenkins (Stevens) Field and George Bard Field; sister of Mary Field Parton (head of a social settlement in Chicago); moved to Detroit at age 3; m. Albert Ehrgott (minister), 1900 (div. 1914); m. Charles Erskine Scott Wood (liberal activist and lawyer), Jan 20, 1938 (died 1944); children: (1st m.) Albert (1901–1918) and Katherine Louise (b. 1906). ❖ Married a minister many years her senior (1900), who had just been accepted by a Eurasian Baptist Church in Rangoon, Burma; while there, witnessed what she deemed the English-Christian exploitation of the Burmese; because of ill health, returned to America; moved with family to a poor parish in Cleveland, where she and husband continued to mingle with liberals and socialists; moved once more to Portland, Oregon, where she organized the College Equal Suffrage League, helped in the Nevada campaign for suffrage, and traveled throughout the country speaking in the interests of national suffrage; lived in San Francisco with Charles Wood for years before he was free to marry; writings include *The Pale Woman* (1927), *Barabbas* (1932), and *Darkling Plain* (1936).

FIELD, Mrs. Sarah (c. 1670–1723). See Egerton, Sarah Fyge.

FIELD, Sarah (c. 1809–1889). See Greenwood, Sarah.

FIELD, Shirley Anne (1936—). English actress. Born June 27, 1936, in Bolton, England. ❖ Made film debut in *Simon and Laura* (1955), followed by *It's Never Too Late, Horrors of the Black Museum, Once More with Feeling, Peeping Tom, The Entertainer, Saturday Night and Sunday Morning, The Damned, The War Lover, Alfie, House of the Living Dead, My Beautiful Laundrette, Shag* and *Carrington;* on tv, appeared on "Santa Barbara" (1987), "Bramwell" (1995), "Madson" (1996), and "Where the Heart Is" (1997), among others.

FIELD, Sylvia (1901–1998). American stage and screen actress. Name variations: Sylvia Field Truex. Born Harriet Johnson, Feb 14, 1901, in Allston, Massachusetts; died July 31, 1998, in Fallbrook, California; m. Robert J. Froelich (div.); m. Harold LeRoy Moffet (died); m. Ernest Truex (actor, died 1973); children: Sally Moffet (1932–1995, actress); Barry Truex (actor). ❖ Best remembered as Mrs. Wilson on the tv series "Dennis the Menace," made NY stage debut in *The Betrothal* (1919) and enjoyed a long theatrical career; films include *Junior Miss* and *All Mine to Give.*

FIELD, Virginia (1917–1992). English actress. Name variations: Katherine Burke. Born Margaret Cynthia Field, Nov 4, 1917, in London, England; died Jan 2, 1992, in Palm Desert, California; dau. of a British judge and mother who was a cousin of Robert E. Lee; m. Paul Douglas (actor), 1942 (div. 1946); m. Howard Grode, 1947 (div. 1948); m. Willard Parker (actor), 1951. ❖ Made 1st stage appearance in Vienna (1932); made London debut in *This Side of Idolatry* (1933); made Broadway debut in *Panama Hattie* (1941), followed by *The Doughgirls* and *Light Up the Sky;* films include *The Lady is Willing, Lloyds of London, Little Lord Fauntleroy, In Old Chicago, Waterloo Bridge, Dream Girl* and *A Connecticut Yankee in King Arthur's Court;* frequently appeared on tv.

FIELDING, Sarah (1710–1768). English novelist. Born in East Stour, Dorsetshire, England, Nov 8, 1710; died at Bath, England, 1768; dau. of Edmund Fielding (general in the army) and Sarah Gould Fielding (dau. of Sir Henry Gould of Sharpham Park); sister of novelist Henry Fielding (1707–1754); never married; no children. ❖ Published 1st and best-known novel, *The Adventures of David Simple* (1744), which led to *Familiar Letters Between the Principal Characters in David Simple, and Some Others* (1747); published *The Governess: or Little Female Academy* (1749), considered the 1st full-length children's novel in English; created the sequel *David Simple, Volume the Last* (1753); collaborated with life-long friend Jane Collier on *The Cry* (1754); also wrote *The Countess of Dellwyn* (1759), *Ophelia* (1760), and *Cleopatra and Octavia* (1757) and translated Xenophone's *Memoirs of Socrates: With the Defense of Socrates before his Judges* (1762). ❖ See also *Women in World History.*

FIELDS, Annie Adams (1834–1915). American poet, essayist, literary host, and social welfare worker. Born Anne Adams in Boston, Massachusetts, June 6, 1834; died 1915; 2nd wife of James Thomas Fields (partner in Boston publishing firm of Ticknor & Fields and publisher and editor of *Atlantic Monthly*); lived with Sarah Orne Jewett. ❖ Because of keen critical eye, was often consulted by husband in choosing manuscripts for publication; opened home to writers, including Celia Thaxter, Sarah Orne Jewett, Longfellow, Hawthorne, Lowell, and Emerson; was also a leading figure in charity work, founding the Associated Charities of Boston; after husband's death, published a book of poems, *Under the Olive* (1881), as well as *The Biography of James T. Fields* (1884), *Authors and Their Friends* (1896), *Life and Letters of Harriet Beecher Stowe* (1897), and a handbook for charity workers, *The Singing Shepherd* (1896), that sold 22,000 copies in 2 years. ❖ See also M.A. DeWolfe Howe, *Memories of a Hostess* (1922); and *Women in World History.*

FIELDS, Crystal (1969—). American baseball player. Born 1969 in Cumberland, Maryland. ❖ At 11, defeated 7 boys to become 1st girl to win the national Pitch, Hit and Run championship (1980); served as all-star shortstop and outfielder for Cumberland, MD, Little League team, batting .528 in 1979.

FIELDS, Debbi (1956—). American entrepreneur. Name variations: Mrs. Fields. Born Sept 18, 1956, in Oakland, California; children: 5. ❖ On her 1st day in the cookie business, made $75 selling cookies on the streets of Palo Alto; opened Mrs. Fields Chocolate Chippery in Palo Alto (Aug 16, 1977); eventually had outlets in 1,600 locations around the world. ❖ See also autobiography, *One Smart Cookie.*

FIELDS, Dorothy (1904–1974). American lyricist. Born July 15, 1904 in Allenhurst, New Jersey; died Mar 28, 1974, in New York, NY; dau. of Lew Fields (Lewis Maurice Schanfield, legendary vaudeville and music-hall performer) and Rose (Harris) Fields; sister of Herbert Fields, librettist (1898–1958), Joseph Fields, playwright, producer and director, and Frances Fields Friedlander; m. Jack J. Weiner (surgeon), 1925 (div. 1932); m. Eli Lahm (blouse manufacturer), 1939; children: (2nd m.) David (b. 1940) and Eliza Lahm (b. 1944). ❖ Author of such standards as "On the Sunny Side of the Street" and "The Way You Look Tonight," 1st made her mark in mid-1920s; with Jimmy McHugh, wrote "I Can't Give You Anything But Love, Baby," for *Blackbirds of 1928* and "Exactly Like You" and "On the Sunny Side of the Street" for *International Revue* (1929); wrote "Lovely to Look At" for the film *Roberta;* collaborated with Jerome Kern on "A Fine Romance" and "Pick Yourself Up" for *Swing Time;* collaborated with brother Herbert on many screenplays, including *Riviera* and *Love Before Breakfast* (both 1936), and Broadway musical-comedy librettos for such shows as *Let's Face It!, Something for the Boys, Mexican Hayride, Up in Central Park* and *Annie Get Your Gun;* wrote lyrics for Broadway's *A Tree Grows in Brooklyn, By the Beautiful Sea* and *Redhead,;* wrote lyrics for "Hey, Big Spender!," "Where Am I Going?" and "If They Could See Me Now," all for *Sweet Charity* (1966); also co-produced *Seesaw* (1973). Won Academy Award for song "The Way You Look Tonight" from *Swing Time* (1936); won Screen Writers Guild Award for *Annie Get Your Gun* with Herbert Fields (1950); won Tony Award for best lyrics for *Redhead* (1959); was 1st woman elected to Songwriters Hall of Fame. ❖ See also *Women in World History.*

FIELDS, Evelyn J. African-American rear admiral. Norfolk State College (now Norfolk State University), degree in mathematics, 1971. ❖ Began work with National Oceanic and Atmospheric Administration Corps (NOAA) as cartographer in Norfolk, VA (1972); was the 1st woman and 1st African-American to be appointed director of the NOAA Marine and Aviation Operations and director of the NOAA Corps (1999); promoted to rear admiral, upper half; served as 1st woman commanding officer of a NOAA ship and a US government oceangoing vessel; retired (2003).

FIELDS, Gracie (1898–1979). English singer, comedian, impersonator, and actress. Born Grace Stansfield, Jan 9, 1898, in Rochdale, Lancashire, England; died on Italian island of Capri, Sept 27, 1979; dau. of Fred (engineer) and Sarah Jane (Jenny) Bamford Stansfield; m. comedian Archie Pitt (Archibald Selinger), April 21, 1923 (div. 1940); m. Monty Banks (Mario Bianchi), Mar 1940 (died 1950); m. Boris Alperovici, Feb 18, 1952; no children. ❖ Entertainer who rose from poverty to become one of the best beloved performers in the world, made professional debut at the Rochdale Hippodrome (1910); began touring with Archie Pitt (1916); debuted to raves in London's West End, starring in *Mr. Tower of London* (1924); made 1st command performance, recorded 1st record, and took on 1st dramatic role in *S.O.S* (1928); made 1st tour of US (1930); made film debut in *Sally in Our Alley,* from which the song "Sally" went on to become a national hit (1931); made 1st film in Hollywood, *We're Going To Be Rich* (1937); other films include *Sing As We Go* (1934), *Queen of Hearts* (1936), *Holy Matrimony* (1943) and *Paris Underground* (1945); entertained Allied troops (1939–45); went on to appear on tv, most especially in "The Old Lady Shows Her Medals" (1956), and made record albums almost to the year of her death; gave 10th Royal Command performance, 50 years after her 1st one, and her last public performance (1978); was the only music-hall star of 1920s to make a successful transition to the new media of radio and film. Named Commander of the British Empire (1938) and Dame Commander of the Order of the British Empire (1979). ❖ See also *Sing As We Go: The Autobiography of Gracie Fields* (Doubleday, 1961); Burgess and Keen, *Gracie Fields* (Allen, 1980); Joan Moules, *Our Gracie: The Life of Dame Gracie Fields* (Hale, 1983).

FIELDS, Julia (1938—). African-American poet. Born 1938 in Bessemer, Alabama. ❖ Taught high school in Alabama and poetry and writing at Hampton Institute, East Carolina University, Howard University, and North Carolina State University; inspired by Langston Hughes, Georgia Douglas Johnson, and black activists of 1960s, published poetry collections *Poems* (1968), *All Day Tomorrow* (1966), *Slow Coins* (1981), and *The Green Lion of Zion Street* (1988).

FIELDS, Mary (c. 1832–1914). African-American pioneer. Name variations: Black Mary; Stagecoach Mary. Born around 1832 in Hickman Co., Tennessee, and celebrated her birthday on both Mar 15 and May 15; died in Cascade, Montana, Dec 5, 1914; never married; no children. ❖ Former slave, associated with the Ursuline nuns, who was one of the 1st women to drive a US mail coach on a regular route and became a folk hero of the American West; following the Civil War, worked at various jobs along the Mississippi River before finding work at the Ursuline convent in Toledo, Ohio; moved to St. Peter's mission, near Cascade, Montana (1885); forced by the area bishop to leave the mission because of her unruly temper, opened a restaurant in Cascade; was the 2nd woman to drive a US mail coach route (1895–1903); the powerful six-foot woman, became legendary as "Black Mary" and "Stagecoach Mary"; ran a laundry, became mascot and supporter of the Cascade baseball team, and a much-loved citizen. ❖ See also Robert H. Miller, *The Story of "Stagecoach" Mary Fields: Stories of the Forgotten West Series* (Silver Burdett, 1994); and *Women in World History.*

FIELDS, Mrs. (1956—). *See Fields, Debbi.*

FIELDS, Verna (1918–1982). American film editor. Born Verna Hellman, Mar 21, 1918, in St. Louis, Missouri; died Nov 30, 1982, in Encino, California; dau. of Sam Hellman (screenwriter); m. Sam Fields (film editor, died 1954); children: 2. ❖ Began career as a sound editor on tv, working on such series as "Death Valley Days," "Sky King," and "Fury"; edited the full-length feature *Studs Lonigan* (1960), followed by *El Cid* (1961), for which she received a Motion Picture Sound Editing Award; did final edit on *American Graffiti* (1973) and edited Spielberg's *The Sugarland Express* (1974) and *Jaws* (1975), for which she won an Academy Award and a new job as Universal's vice president in charge of feature productions, a post she held until her death. ❖ See also *Women in World History.*

FIENNES, Anne (d. 1595). English noblewoman. Name variations: Fienes; Lady Dacre. Pronunciation: Fines. Died 1595; dau. of Sir Richard Sackville (cousin of Anne Boleyn); m. Gregory Fiennes. ❖ Left money for the building of an almshouse in Chelsea.

FIENNES, Celia (1662–1741). British traveler and writer. Pronunciation: Fines. Born in Newton Toney, near Salisbury, 1662; died in London, 1741; dau. of Nathaniel (member of the Council of State and Keeper of the Great Seal under Cromwell) and Frances (Whitehead) Fiennes; never married; no children. ❖ Born into a prestigious Puritan family, undertook a series of journeys through England (c. 1685–1702); traveling mostly on horseback, recorded in detail the towns she visited, where she stayed, food she ate, observations that provide a valuable source of English economic and social history. Her travel book, *Through England on a Side Saddle in the Time of William and Mary,* was 1st published by a descendant (1888); a modern edition, *The Journeys of Celia Fiennes,* came out in 1947. ❖ See also *Women in World History.*

FIENNES, Virginia (1947–2004). English explorer. Name variations: Ginny Fiennes; Lady Fiennes; Lady Twisleton-Wykeham-Fiennes. Born Virginia Frances Pepper, July 9, 1947, near Lodsworth, West Sussex, England; died Feb 20, 2004, in Exeter, England; dau. of Tom and Janet Pepper; m. Sir Ranulph "Ran" Fiennes (polar explorer), 1970; no children. ❖ The 1st woman invited to join the Antarctic Club (1985) and the 1st woman to be awarded the Polar Medal (1987), originated and inspired the planning and was base leader for husband's more than 30 expeditions in Africa, Arabia and the polar regions; specializing in very low frequency communications, became Britain's most experienced polar radio operator and was instrumental in saving the lives of a group of South African scientists lost near her isolated base; wrote bestselling book, *Bothie, The Polar Dog* (1984), about her beloved Jack Russell terrier, her companion to both north and south poles.

FIESCHI, Catherine (1447–1510). *See Catherine of Genoa.*

FIESCHI, Giacoma de. *See Este, Giacoma d'.*

FIFE, countess of. *See Isabel of Fife (c. 1332–1389).*

FIFE, duchess of.
See Louise Victoria (1867–1931).
See Alexandra Victoria (1891–1959).
See Carnegie, Caroline (b. 1934).

FIFIELD, Elaine (1930–1999). Australian-born ballet dancer. Born Oct 28, 1930, in Sydney, Australia; died May 31, 1999, in Perth, Australia; trained at Sadler's Wells School; m. John Lanchbery (musician, div.); m. Les Farley (plantation owner), 1962; children: (1st m.) Margaret Lanchbery; (2nd. m.) Mary-Louise and Joydie Farley. ❖ Made stage debut at the Embassy, Peterborough, dancing the Polka in *Façade* (1947); with Sadler's Wells (1948–52), debuted as the Swan Queen in *Swan Lake,* then created the principal parts in *Tritsch-Tratsch, Selina, Parures, Valses Nobles et Sentimentales, Etudes, Pineapple Poll, Sirènes, Blood Wedding* and *Reflection;* made NY debut (1952) and toured Germany, Holland, Belgium and Canada; moved to Covent Garden Company (1954), dancing in Frederick Ashton's *Homage to the Queen, Madame Chrysanthème* and *Birthday Offering;* became prima ballerina; returned to Australia to join the Borovansky Ballet, forerunner of the Australian Ballet (1957); briefly retired from dance (1958), settling in Papua New Guinea; appeared as principal artist with the Australian Ballet (1964–66,

1969–71), in featured roles in Rudolf Nureyev's *Raymonda* and Peggy Van Praagh's *Carnaval*. ❖ See also autobiography *In My Shoes* (1967).

FIFTH DIMENSION
See LaRue, Florence.
See McCoo, Marilyn.

FIGES, Eva (1932—). German-born British feminist writer. Born in Berlin, Germany, April 15, 1932; dau of Emil Eduard Unger and Irma Cohen Unger; from age 7, educated in London; graduate of University College; m. John George Figes, 1954. ❖ Worked as an editor and translator before becoming a full-time writer (1967); best known for her book *Patriarchal Attitudes: Women in Society* (1970), which examines the ideology of women's subordination in religious thought, liberal philosophy, capitalist economics, psychoanalysis, and popular custom; examined the lives of British women writers in her *Sex and Subterfuge: Women Novelists to 1850* (1981).

FIGINI, Michela (1966—). Swiss Alpine skier. Born April 7, 1966, in Prato Leventina, Switzerland. ❖ Won a gold medal for downhill at Sarajevo Olympics (1984); at World championships, won a gold medal for downhill (1985) and silver medal for downhill and super-G (1987); won a silver medal for super-G at Calgary Olympics (1988); won World Cup for downhill (1985, 1987, 1988, 1989), giant slalom (1985), super-G (1988), and overall (1985, 1988).

FIGNER, Vera (1852–1942). Russian revolutionary. Name variations: Vera Feigner; Verochka. Pronunciation: VEE-rah FIG-nur. Born July 7, 1852, in Khristoforovka, Kazan Province, Russia; died in USSR, June 15, 1942; dau. of Nikolai Alexandrovich Figner (noble and local justice) and Ekaterina Khristoforovna Figner (dau. of a judge); sister of Olga Figner, Lydia Figner, and Evgenia Figner; attended Rodionovsky Institute at Kazan, 1863–69; attended medical school in Zurich and Bern, Switzerland, 1872–75; m. Aleksei Victorovich Filippov, 1870 (legally sep., 1876); no children. ❖ Revolutionary whose work to free all Russian people led to her involvement in the assassination of Alexander II, and whose trial and ensuing years of imprisonment left an imprint on those who would follow a militant revolutionary path; moved with family to Nikoforovo, where she entered school (1863); left for Swiss universities with husband and sister Lydia (1872); joined the Fritsche group (1872), which espoused socialism and class warfare; after sister Lydia's imprisonment in Moscow for possessing socialist literature, returned to Russia to work for the revolutionaries (1875); passed exams for assistant physician in Yaroslavl (1876); became a member of the populist group Land and Freedom (1879), then joined the more radical insurrectionist group People's Will (1879); collected and stored the dynamite used for the bombing of the Winter Palace (Feb 1880); took control of the People's Will group in Odessa, then recalled to St. Petersburg to become a member of the party's Executive Committee, which made the decisions about targets and the methods to be used (1880); assisted in the assassination of Alexander II (1881); remained the last member of the People's Will Executive Committee at large in Russia (1882); arrested in Kharkov (1883); tried and sentenced in St. Petersburg (1884); incarcerated in the Schlüsselburg fortress (1884–1904); exiled in Russia (1904–06); released after 22 years; lived abroad (1906–15); published *Polnoe sobranie sochinenii v shesti tomakh* (Complete Works in Six Volumes, Moscow, 1929); remained a heroine in textbooks. ❖ See also *Memoirs of a Revolutionist* (International, 1927); and *Women in World History*.

FIGUEIRA, Josefa (1630–1684). *See de Ayala, Josefa.*

FIGUEIREDO, Ilda (1948—). Portuguese politician. Born Oct 30, 1948, in Troviscal-Oliveira do Bairro, Portugal. ❖ Teacher (1968–99); served on the Gaia town council (1983–91), Oporto city council (1994–99), and was a member of the Assembly of the Republic (1979–91); representing the Confederal Group of the European United Left/Nordic Green Left (GUE/NGL), elected to 5th European Parliament (1999–2004).

FIGUERAS-DOTTI, Marta (1957—). Spanish golfer. Born Nov 12, 1957, in Madrid, Spain; dau. of the president of the Spanish Golf Association. ❖ Won European amateur (1975, 1977), Spanish Jr., Spanish and French amateur (1979), Italian amateur and British Open (1982); tied for 2nd at Safeco Classic (1984); won LPGA Hawaiian Ladies Open and JC Penney Classic (1994); is the 1st Spanish woman pro golfer. Named Rookie of the Year by *Golf Digest* (1984).

FIGUEROA, Ana (1907–1970). Chilean educator and diplomat. Born in Santiago, Chile, June 19, 1907; died 1970; dau. of Miguel Figueroa Rebolledo and Ana Gajardo Infante; graduate of University of Chile, 1928; attended Teachers College of Columbia University and Colorado State College; children: Arturo. ❖ Began career as an English and philosophy teacher in various Chilean high schools; named principal of Liceo San Felipe (1938) and assumed the same position at Liceo de Temuco (1939); promoted to general inspector of secondary education (1946), a position of national scope; appointed to United Nations (1948), as a delegate plenipotentiary to the 3rd regular session of the General Assembly; appointed alternate permanent Chilean representative to UN and elected to the Assembly's Trusteeship Committee (1950); elected chair of the Social, Humanitarian and Cultural Committee (1951), the 1st woman chosen to head a General Assembly committee; named Chile's alternate delegate to the Security Council (1952), a position never before filled by a woman.

FIGUES DE SAINT MARIE, Solenne (1979—). French swimmer. Born June 6, 1979, in Villepinte, France. ❖ At World Cup, placed 1st in Berlin for 400-meter freestyle (2001) and in Stockholm for 200-meter freestyle (2002); won a bronze medal for 200-meter freestyle at Athens Olympics (2004).

FIGUEUR, Thérèse (1774–1861). French soldier. Name variations: Theresa or Therese Figueur; Therese Figueur de Lyon; Marie-Thérèse Figueur; Mademoiselle Sans-Gêne. Born Jan 17, 1774, in Talmay, near Dijon, France; died Jan 4, 1861; dau. of François Figueur and Claudine Viard (died Jan 17, 1774); married a gendarme. ❖ At 18, with her uncle in Avignon in charge of the gunnery (1793), dressed as a man and became a soldier to fight the advancing army; served under Dugommier at the siege of Toulon; was taken captive near Marseilles and when her true gender was discovered it took her uncle to save her; later joined the 15th Dragoons (April 4, 1794); fought in the Napoleonic wars, taking part in the Italian campaigns; taken captive (1799), was imprisoned in Turin and later released; joined the 9th Dragoons; called Mademoiselle Sans-Gêne by Napoleon Bonaparte, declined the offer to enter the service of Empress Joséphine; returned to her regiment, fighting in Ulm and Austerlitz; had 4 horses shot out from under her.

FIGULI, Margita (1909–1995). Slovak novelist. Born Oct 2, 1909, in Vysny Kubin, Austria-Hungary (now Slovak Republic); died Mar 27, 1995; dau. of peasants. ❖ Early short stories, written in an impressionist style, were published as *Pokusenie* (*Temptation*, 1937); published what was to become her best-known work, *Tri gastanove kone* (*Three Chestnut Horses*, 1940), a short novel which became a bestseller in Slovakia, appearing in 7 reprint editions during next 7 years; during WWII, after publishing several antiwar stories, including *Oloveny vtak* (*The Leaden Bird*) and *Tri noci a tri sny* (*Three Nights and Three Dreams*), was dismissed from her bank job (1942); spent final years of the war writing a massive historical novel, *Babylon,* which appeared in print in 1946 and was popular with the Slovak reading public, though condemned by Stalinist critics; published what would be her last novel, *Vichor v nas* (*The Whirlwind Within Us,* 1974); also wrote well-received children's books. ❖ See also *Women in World History*.

FIKOTOVÁ, Olga (1932—). Czech-American track-and-field athlete. Name variations: Olga Fikotova; Olga Connolly. Born Olga Fikotová in Prague, Czechoslovakia, Nov 13, 1932; entered School of Medicine at Prague's Charles University; m. Harold Connolly (American gold medalist in 16-pound hammer throw), 1957 (div. c. 1972). ❖ Won a gold medal in discus at Melbourne Olympics (1956); married, became US citizen, and competed for US (1957); qualified for 4 consecutive Olympic Games (beginning 1960); was flag bearer for the US team at Munich Olympics (1972). ❖ See also Olga Connolly *The Rings of Destiny* (McKay, 1968); and *Women in World History*.

FILATOVA, Maria (1961—). Soviet gymnast. Name variations: Masha Filatova. Born July 19, 1961, in Leninsk-Kuznetsk, Siberia, USSR; m. Alexander Kourbatov (Soviet power tumbler); children: Alexandra "Sasha" Kourbatova (gymnast). ❖ Won a gold medal in team all-around in the Montreal Olympics (1976) and a bronze medal in uneven bars; won a gold medal in team all-around at Moscow Olympics (1980); won the World Cup (1977, 1978), Moscow News (1977), Riga International (1976, 1977, 1979), USSR nationals (1977), and Paris Grand Prix (1977, 1979); at World championships, won a gold medal for team all-around and a silver for all-around (1981); coaches in US.

FILBRICH, Sigrun. *See Krause, Sigrun.*

FILIPA. *Variant of Philippa.*

FILIPA DE LENCASTRE (c. 1359–1415). *See Philippa of Lancaster.*

FILIPOVA, Nadya (1959—). Bulgarian rower. Born Oct 19, 1959. ❖ At Moscow Olympics, won a silver medal in coxed fours (1980).

FILIPOVA, Nadya (1959—). Soviet field-hockey player. Name variations: Nadia Filipova. Born Sept 17, 1959, in USSR. ❖ At Moscow Olympics, won a bronze medal in team competition (1980).

FILIPOVIĆ, Zlata (1981—). Bosnian diarist. Name variations: Zlata Filipovic. Born in Sarajevo, Bosnia, 1981; only dau. of Malik (lawyer) and Alica Filipović (biochemist). ❖ Dubbed the Anne Frank of the Bosnian War, began her diary at age 10; with Sarajevo under siege by Bosnian Serbs, her 2-year diary turned into a chronicle of the horrors of war and a young girl's loss of innocence. ❖ See also *Zlata's Diary* (1993); and *Women in World History*.

FILIPPI, Rosina (1866–1930). Italian-born actress and novelist. Born Oct 31, 1866, in Venice, Italy; dau. of Vaneri Filippi and Filippo Filippi (music critic); educated in England; m. H.M. Dowson. ❖ Made stage debut in London in *Doctor Davey* (1883); other plays include *Princess George, The Red Lamp* (with Beerbohm Tree), *Mamma, The Old Lady, Trilby, Sapho, Quality Street, Arms and the Man, Faust* and *Arsène Lupin;* appeared in her own play *The Bennetts* (1901); wrote several novels, including *The Heart of Monica,* and also authored *Inhaling* and *Duologues from Jane Austen.*

FILKINS, Grace (c. 1865–1962). American stage star. Born in Philadelphia, Pennsylvania, c. 1865; died Sept 16, 1962, age 97, in New York, NY; m. Adolph Marix (naval admiral). ❖ Made NY debut in *Josephine Sold by Her Sisters* (1886); other plays include *Love in Harness, The Taming of the Shrew, Mary Lincoln MD, Barbara, The Sorrows of Satan, The Crystal Slipper, The American Widow* and *In the Best of Families;* toured with Helena Modjeska in *Camille* and Otis Skinner in *Prince Otto.*

FILLEUL, Jeanne (1424–1498). French poet. Born 1424 in France; died 1498. ❖ Served as lady-in-waiting to Margaret of Scotland, the daughter of James I of Scotland and abandoned wife of Louis XI. One rondeau is extant.

FILLMORE, Abigail Powers (1798–1853). American first lady. Born Mar 13, 1798, in Stillwater, NY; died Mar 30, 1853, in Washington, DC; only dau. of Lemual (Baptist minister) and Abigail (Newland) Powers; m. Millard Fillmore (US president), Feb 5, 1826; children: Millard Powers Fillmore (1828–1889, lawyer); Mary Abigail Fillmore (1832–1854, often served as White House host). ❖ By the time husband was elected vice president (1849), her health was beginning to fail, and she spent as little time in Washington as possible; was at home in Buffalo when she received news of husband's succession to the presidency following death of Zachary Taylor (1851); joining husband in the White House, delegated many of the social duties to her daughter; took immediate steps to have Congress appropriate modest funds for a library, which she established in the Oval Room; attended inaugural ceremonies for Franklin Pierce (1852), but that day's foul weather is thought to have caused the bronchial pneumonia that took her life. ❖ See also *Women in World History.*

FILLMORE, Caroline C. (1813–1881). See McIntosh, Caroline C.

FILLMORE, Cordelia E. (1919–1996). See Cook, Cordelia E.

FILLMORE, Myrtle Page (1845–1931). American religious leader. Name variations: Mary Caroline Page, Myrtle Page. Born Mary Caroline Page, Aug 6, 1845, in Pagetown, Morrow Co., Ohio; died Oct 6, 1931, near Lee's Summit, Missouri; dau. of Marcus (town founder) and Lucy (Wheeler) Page; m. Charles Fillmore (railroad clerk), Mar 29, 1881 (died 1948); children: 3 sons. ❖ Believing in "practical Christianity" and that prayer could overcome life's problems, worked closely with husband in founding and leading Unity School of Christianity; became interested in faith healing (1886); founded magazine, *Modern Thought* (1889), called *Unity* after 1895, which led to the rise of the Unity School of Christianity, the largest of New Thought movements; founded Unity children's magazine *Wee Wisdom* (1893) and was editor; after WWI, established headquarters, Unity Farm, near Lee's Summit, MO, as the movement flourished. ❖ See also *Letters of Myrtle Fillmore* (1936).

FILOMENA. *Variant of Philomena.*

FILOSOFOVA, Anna (1837–1912). Russian feminist. Name variations: Anna Pavlovna Filosova; Anna Filosova. Born Anna Diagileva, 1837, in St. Petersburg; died 1912. ❖ Born into wealthy family; with Nadezhda Stasova and Mariia Trubnikova, formed philanthropic group and organized housing and work for unmarried women; campaign for women's education led to establishment of courses for women in St Petersburg (1872) and Bestuzhev Advanced Courses (1878); became vice-president of International Council of Women (1899); sided with Constitutional Democrats during Revolution; chaired 1st All-Russian Women's Congress (1908).

FILOSOVA, Anna (1837–1912). See Filosofova, Anna.

FILUMENA. *Variant of Philomena.*

FINAS, Lucette (1921—). French novelist and literary critic. Born 1921 in France. ❖ Experimental novels include *L'Echec* (1958), *Le Meurtrion* (1968), and *Donne* (1976); criticism includes *La Crue* (1972) on Georges Bataille, *Le Bruit d'Iris* (1978), and *La Toise et le vertige* (1986).

FINCH, Anne (1631–1679). Viscountess Conway and English philosopher. Name variations: Lady Anne Conway; Viscountess Conway. Born Dec 14, 1631; died Feb 23, 1679; dau. of Sir Heneage Finch (d. 1631, speaker of the House of Commons); sister of physician John Finch (1626–1682); m. Edward, 3rd viscount Conway, 1651; children: son who died in infancy. ❖ Was knowledgeable of the history of philosophy as well as the contemporary philosophy of Descartes, Hobbes and Spinoza before studying with Platonist Henry More; her intellectual circle grew to include 3 other Cambridge Platonists, Ralph Cudworth, Joseph Glanvill and George Rust, as well as Francis Mercury van Helmont, a Kabbalist philosopher; her only work, *The Principles of the Most Ancient and Modern Philosophy,* was published posthumously, and very likely influenced the philosopher Gottfried Wilhelm Leibniz, who borrowed from her the concept of "monad," which is the basis of his most famous work, *The Monadology.* ❖ See also Marjorie Hope Nicholson, ed. *The Conway Letters: The Correspondence of Anne, Viscountess Conway, Henry More, and their friends, 1642–1684;* and *Women in World History.*

FINCH, Anne (1661–1720). Countess of Winchelsea and English poet. Born Anne Kingsmill at Sydmonton, in Hampshire, England, in April 1661; died at home on Cleveland Row, April 5, 1720; dau. of Sir William and Anne (Haslewood) Kingsmill (d. 1664); m. Heneage Finch (c. 1647–1719, became 4th earl of Winchelsea, 1712, 1st earl of Aylesford, 1714), May 15, 1684. ❖ One of the best women poets produced in England before the 19th century, served as maid of honor to Mary of Modena (1683–1712), becoming devoted to the future queen and loyal to the Stuart monarchy; at husband's family estate in Eastwell Park, established a literary circle which included Katharine Philips, Aphra Behn, Alexander Pope, Nicholas Rowe, and Jonathan Swift; printed only one volume of verse in lifetime, *Miscellany Poems on Several Occasions, Written by a Lady* (1713); is best known for her long Pindaric ode, *The Spleen* (1701), which contained a couplet that was echoed in Pope's *Essay on Man* and in Shelley's *Epipsychidion.* ❖ See also Barbara McGovern, *Anne Finch and Her Poetry: A Critical Biography* (U. of Georgia Press, 1992); and *Women in World History.*

FINCH, Flora (1867–1940). English-born comedic actress. Born June 17, 1867, in London, England; died Jan 4, 1940, in Los Angeles, California; m. Harold March. ❖ Began career on the English stage; moved to US; made film debut in *Mrs. Jones Entertains* (1908); made the 1st of 260 short comedies with screen partner John Bunny (1910), known as "Bunnyfinches," for Vitagraph; when Bunny died (1915), formed Flora Finch Film Company, producing slapstick comedies; retired from acting (1939) following the filming of *The Scarlet Letter.*

FINCH, Jennie (1980—). American softball player. Born Sept 3, 1980, in Bellflower, California; attended University of Arizona. ❖ Pitcher/first base, won World championship (2002); won team gold medal at Athens Olympics (2004).

FINCH, Jennifer (1966—). American rock musician. Name variations: L7. Born Aug 5, 1966, in Los Angeles, California. ❖ Bass player and vocalist in punk-metal rock band L7, was 1st enlisted by Donita Sparks and Suzi Gardner to play bass with drummer Roy Koutsky (1986); with group, released *L7* debut album (1988), added Dee Plakas as drummer (1988), and replaced Koutsky; toured US and Britain as opening act for Nirvana, released *Smell the Magic* (1990) with hit single "Shove/Packin' A Rod," and had major success with *Bricks Are Heavy* (1992), which featured international pop hit "Pretend We're Dead," followed by *Hungry for Stink* (1994); began solo career (1996).

FINDLAY, Ruth (1904–1949). American stage actress. Born 1904 in New York, NY; died July 13, 1949, in New York, NY. ❖ Appeared on

Broadway in *Baby Mine, Rebecca of Sunnybrook Farm, Gypsy, The Prince and the Pauper* and *The Land is Bright*.

FINE, Perle (1908–1988). American abstract artist. Born in 1908; died in New York in 1988; studied at the Art Students League with Kimon Nicoläides and with Hans Hofmann at his Eighth Street School; m. Maurice Berezov (abstract artist). ❖ Had 1st solo exhibition at Willard Gallery (1945), followed by subsequent shows at Nierendorf Gallery (1946 and 1947); joined American Abstract artists, a group of primarily abstractionists devoted to the tradition of cubism, but later found her niche with the Abstract Expressionists movement; was an associate professor of art at Hofstra University (1954–66); unable to work on large canvases because of illness, began a series of collages, combining wood pieces with painted grids (late 1960s), which evolved into gridlike paintings which she called her "Accordment" series.

FINE, Sylvia (1913–1991). American lyricist and composer. Name variations: Sylvia Fine Kaye; Mrs. Danny Kaye. Born Aug 29, 1913, in Brooklyn, NY; died Oct 28, 1991, in New York, NY; m. Danny Kaye (actor), 1940 (died 1987). ❖ Wrote a collection of sketches for the Broadway show *Straw Hat Revue* (1940); wrote many of her songs and musical routines for husband Danny Kaye's films, including *Up in Arms, Wonder Man, The Secret Life of Walter Mitty, The Inspector General, Knock on Wood, The Court Jester* and *The Five Pennies*.

FINE, Vivian (1913–2000). American composer. Born in Chicago, Illinois, Sept 28, 1913; died Mar 20, 2000; dau. of Rose (Finder) Fine and David Fine (both Russian-Jewish immigrants); studied with Djane Lavoie-Herz, Abby Whiteside, Ruth Crawford, and Roger Sessions; m. Benjamin Karp, 1935; children: Margaret (Peggy) Karp; Nina Karp. ❖ Began career as an accompanist for dancers and then composed for ballet; wrote dance scores for Martha Graham, Hanya Holm, and Charles Weidman; wrote 1st large ballet, *The Race of Life,* for Doris Humphrey (1937); served as musical director of the Bethsabee de Rothschild Foundation (1955–61); commissioned by Graham to write *Alcestis* (1960); in addition to works for ballet and dance, composed many pieces for orchestra, chamber and choral groups. Received American Academy-National Institute of Arts and Letters Award (1979).

FINGER, Ute (1958—). See Thimm-Finger, Ute.

FINGERHUT, Arden (1945–1994). American lighting designer. Born 1945; died May 13, 1994, age 48, in North Adams, Massachusetts. ❖ Shows designed for the NY stage include *Da, Bent, Hay Fever, Plenty, Driving Miss Daisy, Julius Caesar* and *King John;* also designed for numerous regional theaters.

FINGERIN, Agnes (d. 1515). German textile merchant. Born in Gorlitz, Germany; died in 1515 in Gorlitz; dau. of a wealthy weaver; married (husband died in 1465). ❖ One of the wealthiest textile merchants in Gorlitz, did a fair amount of traveling, both for business and pleasure; even journeyed to Jerusalem on a pilgrimage; used her considerable wealth to set up a permanent endowment to aid the needy by distributing bread, which remained active for hundreds of years; was remembered by the endowment's name, the *Agnetenbrot* (Agnes-bread). ❖ See also *Women in World History*.

FINI, Leonor (1908–1996). Italian-Argentinean artist. Born in Buenos Aires, Argentina, 1908; died in Paris, France, Jan 18, 1996; dau. of an Argentine father and Italian mother. ❖ Spent childhood with mother in Trieste, Italy; largely self-taught, went to Milan (1925), where she was influenced by artists Carlo Carrà, Achille Funi, and Arturo Tosi; later in Paris, became friendly with painters of the burgeoning Surrealist movement, including Leonora Carrington, Salvador Dali, and Max Ernst; though she occasionally exhibited with the group, never completely aligned herself with their goals; during WWII, lived in Monaco, and then in Rome with artist Stanislau Lepri; returned to Paris (1947), where in addition to painting she illustrated books and designed sets and costumes for theater, opera, and films; her painting continued to evolve, and her female form, with its shaved head and rigid body, became a trademark; achieved cult status in Paris art and theater circles; paintings include *Sphinx philagria* (1945), *Sphinx Regina* (1946), *The Angel of Anatomy* (1949), *The Two Skulls* (1950), *The Emerging Ones* (1958), *Capital Punishment* (1960), *Sfinge la Morte* (1973) and *The Lesson on Botany* (1974).

FINLEY, Martha (1828–1909). American children's writer. Name variations: (pseudonym) Martha Farquharson. Born Martha Finley, April 26, 1828, in Chillicothe, Ohio; died in Elkton, Maryland, Jan 30, 1909; dau. of James Brown Finley (doctor) and his 1st cousin Maria Theresa (Brown) Finley (homemaker). ❖ Author of stories and books for children, in particular the "Elsie Dinsmore" series, one of the best-known characters to appear in American fiction; taught school in Indiana (1851–53) and Pennsylvania (1853); began publishing children's stories with Presbyterian Board of Publication (1853), under such titles as *Ella Clinton; or "By Their Fruits Ye Shall Know Them," Clouds and Sunshine; or the Faith Brightened Pathway* and *Elton, the Little Boy Who Loved Jesus;* during lifetime, would produce nearly 100 didactic books for children; published *Elsie Dinsmore* and 27 subsequent "Elsie" books, all under name Martha Farquharson (1867–1905); was something of a recluse during much of her adult life. ❖ See also *Women in World History*.

FINN-BURRELL, Michelle (1965—). American runner. Name variations: Michelle Bonae Finn; Michelle Finn Burrell. Born Michelle Bonae Finn, May 8, 1965; grew up in Orlando, Florida; m. Leroy Burrell (Olympic gold medalist and coach); children: Cameron and Joshua. ❖ At Barcelona Olympics, won a gold medal in 4x100-meter relay (1992).

FINNBOGADÓTTIR, Vigdís (1930—). President of Iceland. Name variations: Vigdis Finnbogadottir. Born April 15, 1930, in Reykjavik, Iceland; dau. of Finnbogi Rutur (also seen as Ruter) Thorvaldsson (civil engineer and professor at the University of Iceland) and Sigridur Eriksdóttir (nurse and chair of the Icelandic Nurses Association for 36 years); graduate of University of Iceland; attended University of Grenoble and Sorbonne; married, 1953 (div. c. 1962); children: (adopted daughter) Astridur. ❖ Hosted a tv series about theater; directed the Reykjavik Theatre Company (1972–80); became interested in politics (1974), when she helped organize a petition campaign for removal of US naval base at Keflavik; elected president of Iceland (1980); reelected (1984 and 1988), using the largely ceremonial post to promote Icelandic culture and to better the status of women. ❖ See also *Women in World History*.

FINNERAN, Sharon (1946—). American swimmer. Name variations: Sharon Rittenhouse. Born Feb 1946 in Fort Lauderdale, Florida; dau. of Carol Finneran; sister of Mike Finneran (Olympian); trained under Peter Daland; m. Bob Rittenhouse; children: Ariel Rittenhouse (swimmer). ❖ At Tokyo Olympics, won a silver medal in 400-meter individual medley (1964); set 6 World and 13 American records; won 11 national titles (1962–66). Inducted into International Swimming Hall of Fame.

FINNEY, Joan (1925–2001). American politician. Born Feb 11, 1925; died July 28, 2001, in Topeka, Kansas; m. Spencer Finney; children: 3, including Mary Holladay. ❖ The 1st woman to be governor of Kansas, spent 16 years as state treasurer; as a Democrat, served one term as governor (1991–95), but did not seek reelection; lost a US Senate primary (1996).

FINNEY, May (1862–1950). See Fortescue, May.

FINNIAN VON SASS, Florence (1841–1916). See Baker, Florence von Sass.

FINNIE, Jessie (c. 1821–?). New Zealand prostitute. Born in Scotland, c. 1821 or 1822; m. John Finnie (soldier); children: 4. ❖ Immigrated to New Zealand (1849); unable to provide for her family when husband left for California or Australia gold fields, became prostitute in Auckland. ❖ See also *Dictionary of New Zealand Biography* (Vol. 1).

FINNIE, Linda (1952—). Scottish mezzo-soprano. Born in 1952 in Paisley, Scotland; studied with Winifred Busfield at Royal Scottish Academy of Music and Drama. ❖ Successful opera and classical music concert singer with broad repertoire, won 1st Prize at International Ferrier Competition (1974); made debut with Scottish Opera (1976) and won Kathleen Ferrier Prize at international competition in Hertogenbosch, Netherlands (1977); began to sing widely with Welsh and English national operas (1979) and as guest at Covent Garden, Bayreuth, Frankfurt Opera, among others; embarked on successful concert tours in Australia, US, Asia and Europe; especially commended for Wagnerian portrayals as Brangaene, Waltraute, and Fricka; worked with many renowned conductors including Abbado, Maazel, Previn, and Barenboim. Made numerous recordings on Chandos label, including *Mendelssohn: Elijah* (1990), *Prokofiev: Ivan the Terrible* (1991), *Elgar: The Light of Life* (1993), *Tchaikovsky: Eugene Onegin* (2001) and *Ravel: Orchestral Works* (2004).

FINNIGAN, Joan (1925—). Canadian poet. Born Joan MacKenzie 1925 in Ottawa, Canada; attended Carleton University and Queen's University. ❖ Worked as teacher, lecturer, and freelance writer; also wrote children's fiction, screenplays, oral histories, and biographies;

writings include *Through a Glass Darkly* (1957), *Entrance to the Greenhouse* (1968), *It was Warm and Sunny When We Set Out* (1970), *Living Together* (1976), *I Come From the Valley* (1976), *Laughing All the Way Home* (1984), *Wintering Over* (1992), *Down the Unmarked Roads* (1997) and *Second Wind, Second Sight* (1998). Received Centennial Prize for Poetry (1967).

FIOCRE, Eugénie (1845–1908). French ballet dancer. Name variations: Eugenie Fiocre. Born July 2, 1845, in Paris, France; died 1908 in Paris. ❖ Trained at Paris Opéra ballet school and was associated with the company throughout performance career, playing male roles in most performances including that of Cupid in *Néméa* (1864); also created male lead role of Franz in *Coppélia* (1870).

FIORENZA, Elisabeth Schuessler (1938—). American feminist theologian. Name variations: Elisabeth Shussler-Fiorenza or Shüssler-Fiorenza. Born in 1938 in Tschand, Germany; University of Würzburg, BA in Pastoral Theology; University of Münster, Doctorate in Theology. ❖ One of the world's foremost feminist theologians, was an accomplished Biblical scholar at the universities of Würzburg and Münster; immigrated to US; published 1st book on ministries of women in church (1964); worked as associate professor at University of Notre Dame, simultaneously serving as associate editor of *Catholic Biblical Quarterly, Journal of Biblical Literature* and *Horizons;* wrote feminist interpretation of Bible, *In Memory of Her: A Feminist Theological Reconstruction of Christian Origins* (1983), based on liberation theology, which reconstructs the way women actively impacted early Christianity; became Krister Stendahl professor at Harvard Divinity School (1988); an international authority on *The Book of Revelation* and early Christian church structures, was the 1st woman scholar to serve as president of American Society of Biblical Literature; elected to American Academy of Arts and Sciences. Wrote many books in English and German, including *Invitation to the Book of Revelation* (1981), *Bread Not Stone* (1984), *Revelation: Vision of a Just World* (1991), *But She Said: Feminist Practices of Biblical Interpretation* (1992), *Discipleship of Equals: A Feminist Ekklesialogy of Liberation* (1993), *Searching the Scriptures* (2 vols, 1993, 1994), *Jesus: Miriam's Child, Sophia's Prophet: Critical Issues in Feminist Christology* (1994), *The Power of Naming: A Concilium Reader in Feminist Liberation Theology* (1996), *Sharing Her Word* (1998), *Rhetoric and Ethic* (1999), *Jesus and the Politics of Interpretation* (2000) and *Wisdom Ways: Introducing Feminist Biblical Interpretation* (2001).

FIRENZE, Francesca da (fl. 15th c.). Florentine artist and nun. Fl. in 15th century Florence; never married; no children. ❖ Though few artistic works have survived, flourished as an artist in the scriptorium of a Florentine convent; her miniature paintings and manuscript illuminations were well known in Florence, and the money generated from their sale helped support her community. ❖ See also *Women in World History.*

FIRESTONE, Shulamith (1945—). Canadian feminist. Born in Ottawa, Canada, 1945; studied at Art Institute of Chicago. ❖ Active as a student in the civil rights and anti-Vietnam War movements, gained prominence in women's movement through her controversial book, *The Dialectic of Sex: The Case for Feminist Revolution* (1970); during early 1970s, also co-founded and was editor of the journals *Notes from the Second Year* and *Redstockings* and remained active in the New York feminist movement; with Chris Kraus, published *Airless Spaces* (1998).

FIREVA, Tatyana (1982—). Russian runner. Born Oct 10, 1982, in USSR. ❖ Won a silver medal for 4x400-meter relay at Athens Olympics (2004).

FIRM, The. *See Brown, Foxy.*

FIRSOVA, Elena Olegovna (1950—). Russian composer. Name variations: Elena Olegovna Firsova. Born Mar 21, 1950, in Leningrad (now St. Petersburg), Russia; father was an atomic physicist; studied with Alexander Pirumov, Yuri Kholopov and Nikolai Rakov at Moscow Conservatory, 1970–75; m. Dmitri Smirnov (composer), 1972; children: Philip and Alissa. ❖ Moved with family to Moscow (1956); attempted 1st composition at 12; developed emotionally expressive melodic style which was then unfashionable in Soviet music; strongly influenced by mentor Edison Denisov, began setting the writings of Russian poet Osip Mandelstam to music (1970s) and returned to Mandelstam poetry many times during career; produced 1st major orchestral piece *Cello Concerto* (1972); faced criticism from Soviet Composer's Union when her compositions, *Sonata for Solo Clarinet* and *Petrarca's Sonnets*, were performed in Cologne (1979); commissioned by BBC, came to prominence in UK with *Earthly Life*, which premiered in London with the Nash Ensemble

(1986); thereafter, received commissions for 2 additional Mandelstam cantatas for Nash Ensemble, *Forest Walks* (1987) and *Before the Thunderstorm* (1994); served as composer in residence at Bard College in US (1990), St John's College, Cambridge (1992) and Dartington Hall, Devon (1992); served as visiting professor and composer in residence at Keele University (1993–97); began teaching composition at Royal Northern College of Music in Manchester (1999); wrote over 100 compositions for operas, oratorios, cantatas, orchestral works, concertos, chamber ensembles and solos; also wrote for Brodsky Quartet, Manchester Wind Orchestra, Schubert Ensemble, Freden Festival and EXPO 2000 (Hanover).

FIRST, Ruth (1925–1982). White South African journalist, sociologist, and revolutionary activist. Born Heloise Ruth First, May 4, 1925, in Kensington section of Johannesburg, South Africa; killed Aug 17, 1982, in Maputo, Mozambique; dau. of Julius and Matilda First (both radical socialists and Jewish immigrants from the Baltic); University of Witwatersrand, BA, 1946; m. Joe Slovo (Communist defense lawyer and labor organizer), Aug 1949; children: Shawn Slovo (b. 1950); Gillian Slovo (b. 1952); Robyn Slovo (b. 1954). ❖ Activist whose outspoken opposition to the policy of apartheid drew her into political collaboration with Nelson Mandela and eventually led to her murder, joined the Communist Party, was secretary of the Young Communist League and secretary of the Progressive Youth Council (early 1940s); was one of only a handful of whites actively involved in the widespread black miners' strike (1946); exposed slavery-like labor conditions on a potato farm in Bethal, Transvaal, prompting a successful countrywide potato boycott led by African National Congress (1947); along with husband, was "named by the government" and placed on a list of dangerous persons which made it illegal for them to be quoted in print (1950); banned from attending political gatherings (1954); became editor of *Fighting Talk*, a radical political and literary journal (1955); along with Nelson Mandela, Walter Sisulu, and her husband, was among 156 activists arrested and accused of treason in the mammoth Treason Trial (1956); detained in Marshall Prison (1956); acquitted due to insufficient evidence (1958); banned from journalistic activities (1960); arrested and held for 117 days in solitary confinement, the 1st white woman to be detained under the 90-Day Detention Act (1963); with family, including father, went into exile never to return to South Africa (1963); started new career in London, teaching, lecturing, publishing and editing books on politics in southern Africa (1964); named Simon Research Fellow at University of Manchester (1972–73); was lecturer in sociology of under-development at the University of Durham, Durham, England (1973–79); began collaborative work with the Center of African Studies, Eduardo Mondlane University, Maputo, Mozambique, directing the Youth Brigades on a research project studying the lives of migrant Mozambican miners (1977); named director of research and co-director of Center of African Studies (1979–82); killed by letter bomb in her office at the Center for African Studies (1982). ❖ See also memoir *117 Days: An Account of Confinement and Interrogation under the South African Ninety-Day Detention Law* (Monthly Review Press, 1989); film *A World Apart*, starring Barbara Hershey, screenplay by Shawn Slovo (1988); "90 Days," BBC teleplay, based on First's book *117 Days*, in which she appears as herself; and *Women in World History.*

FISCHEL, Edna (1878–1970). *See Gellhorn, Edna.*

FISCHER, Alice (1869–1947). American stage actress. Born Jan 16, 1869, in Indiana; died June 23, 1947, in New York, NY; m. William Harcourt. ❖ Made stage debut in *Nordeck* with Frank Mayo (1887); toured with Joseph Jefferson in *Rip Van Winkle;* had greatest success in title role of *Mrs. Jack* (1902); founded the Twelfth Night Club, NY, and served as president for 20 years.

FISCHER, Ann (1919–1971). American social anthropologist. Name variations: Ann Kindrick Fischer. Born Ann Ruth Kindrick, May 22, 1919, in Kansas City, Kansas; died April 1971; Christian College at Columbia, MO, Adjunct in Arts degree, 1938; Ottawa College in Kansas; University of Kansas at Lawrence, BA, 1941; did graduate work in anthropology at University of Kansas, 1921–42) and Radcliffe, 1946–49; m. James Meredith (briefly); m. John Lyle Fischer (anthropologist), July 9, 1949; children: (2nd m.) Madeleine (Nikko) Fischer and Mary Ann Fischer. ❖ Conducted 1st fieldwork on island of Romonum in Truk lagoon; served as research assistant on Ford Foundation Six Cultures Project (1954–57); with appointment as training assistant at School of Public Health and Tropical Medicine, became 1st anthropologist with fellowship in biostatistics and epidemiology (1959); taught at

Tulane and Newcomb College; worked on behalf of Houma Indians; writings include "Field Work in Five Cultures" (1970).

FISCHER, Annemarie. *See Buchner, Annemarie.*

FISCHER, Annie (1914–1995). Hungarian pianist. Born in Budapest, Hungary, July 5, 1914; died 1995; studied with Ernst von Dohnanyi at Franz Liszt Conservatory in Budapest. ❖ Won 1st prize in Budapest's International Liszt Competition (1933); over the years, mastered an imposing repertoire and was particularly known for her Beethoven and Mozart recordings.

FISCHER, Birgit (1962—). East German kayaker. Name variations: Birgit Schmidt or Schmidt-Fischer. Born Birgit Fischer, Feb 25, 1962, in Brandenburg, Germany; m. Jörg Schmidt (canoeist, div.). ❖ At Moscow, won a gold medal in K1 500 meters (1980), the youngest ever Olympic canoe winner; at World championships, won all 3 events (1981–83, 1985, 1987) as well as K4 500 (1993–95, 1997–98), K1 500 (1993–94) and K2 200, 500 and 1,000 (1997); at Seoul Olympics, won a silver medal in K1 500 and gold medals in K4 500 and K2 500 (1988); at Barcelona Olympics, won a gold medal in K1 500 and a silver medal in K4 500 (1992); at Atlanta Olympics, won a silver medal for K2 500 and a gold medal for K4 500 (1996); at Sydney Olympics, won gold medals for K2 500 and K4 500 meters (2000), only the 5th athlete in history to win gold at 5 Olympic games and the only woman to win a gold medal 20 years apart; won a gold medal for K4 500 and a silver medal for K2 500 at Athens Olympics (2004).

FISCHER, Caroline Auguste (1764–1834). German poet and novelist. Born 1764 in Germany; died 1834; m. Danish court preacher (div.); m. Christian August Fischer (writer), 1808 (sep. soon after); children: (2nd m.) 1 son. ❖ Ran school in Heidelberg and library in Würzburg; writings, which serve as a link between pre-modern and modern German women's literature, include *Honigmonathe* (1802–04).

FISCHER, Greta (1909–1988). Czech-born child welfare worker. Born Greta Fischerova in 1909 in Budisov, Czechoslovakia; died in Jerusalem, Israel, Sept 28, 1988; dau. of Leopold (veterinarian) and Ida (Mayer) Fischerova; trained as a kindergarten teacher in 1920s; graduate of McGill School of Social Work, 1955; never married; no children. ❖ Worker with the Special Child Division of the UN Relief and Rehabilitation Agency (UNRRA) who provided care for hundreds of orphaned and displaced children following WWII; fled Czechoslovakia (1939); worked as a nanny in London, then with Anna Freud in the Wartime Hampstead Nursery; joined UNRRA Team 182 (1945) and was sent to Germany to establish an international children's center; served as chief child welfare officer at Kloster Indersdorf in Germany (1945–47); was a social worker for the Canadian War Orphans Project, Jewish Family and Children's Welfare Bureau in Montreal (1948–53); worked as a social worker in the autistic child program, Montreal Children's Hospital (1956–59); was a child resettlement worker for the American Joint Distribution Committee in Morocco and Israel (1960–62); served as social worker for the thalidomide children's program at Montreal's St. Justine's Children's Hospital (1963–67); established a department of social service at Hadassah Hospital in Israel (1970–80); organized a day center and home-care program for the elderly in Jerusalem (1981–88). ❖ See also *Women in World History.*

FISCHER, Margarita (1886–1975). American silent-screen actress. Name variations: appeared as Margarita Fisher, to avoid the Germanic Fischer, during WWI. Born Feb 12, 1886, in Missoury Valley, Iowa; died Mar 11, 1975, in Encinitas, California; m. Harry A. Pollard (director, 1883–1934). ❖ Made stage debut at age 6; often starred in husband's films, including *The Pearl of Paradise, Miss Jackie of the Navy* and *Uncle Tom's Cabin.*

FISCHER, Mary Ann (1933—). American mother of quintuplets. Born 1933 in Hecla, South Dakota; m. Andrew Fischer; children: 10. ❖ Gave birth to four girls and a boy in Aberdeen, SD (1963), the 1st American woman to successfully give birth to quintuplets; had 5 other children.

FISCHER, Ruth (1895–1961). German-born politician. Name variations: Elfriede Eisler; "Fritzi" Eisler. Born Elfriede Eisler in Leipzig, Germany, Dec 11, 1895; died in Paris, France, Mar 13, 1961; dau. of Rudolf Eisler (1873–1926, professor of philosophy) and Ida Maria (Fischer) Eisler; sister of Gerhart and Hanns Eisler; attended University of Vienna; m. Paul Friedländer (div.); m. Gustav Golke, in a marriage of convenience, c. 1923; m. Edmond Pleuchot (French Marxist) in a marriage of convenience; companion to Arkadi Maximovich Maslow (1891–1941, original name Isaac Yefimovich Tshemerinsky); children: (1st m.) Gerhard Friedländer (mathematics professor). ❖ Founding member of

the Austrian Communist Party who became an anti-Stalinist and was regarded as one of the leading experts on Communism in the Western world, joined Austrian Social Democratic Party soon after start of WWI, gravitating to the movement's left wing; with a handful of radicals, became a founding member of the Austrian Communist Party (1918) and edited women's supplement of Communist newspaper *Die soziale Revolution;* moved to Berlin (1919), where she adopted the name Ruth Fischer; emerged as a major personality in German Communist Party (KPD), having by 1920 secured a post on editorial board of the journal *Die Internationale;* elected to KPD post of director of the party's organization in Berlin-Brandenburg (1921); as leader of the Left Opposition within KPD, became a member of the party's Central Committee (1923); was elected to Reichstag from 2nd electoral district (Berlin) and to Executive Committee of the Comintern (1924); because she tried to keep the Comintern from controlling the KPD, was removed from her post as party leader and summoned to Moscow (1925); remained a Reichstag deputy until spring 1928, heading an anti-Stalinist Left Opposition group challenging the KPD; dropped out of politics (1929); with Franz Heimann, published *Deutsche Kinderfibel (German Children's Primer,* 1933); with Hitler's rise to power (1933), fled to Paris and was stripped of German citizenship by Nazi regime (Aug 1933); sentenced to death in absentia by one of Stalin's purge trials (1936); escaped to US (1939–40) and lived in NY; as an independent scholar and journalist, took an unpopular position during war years by reminding readers of brutality of Stalin's brand of "socialism"; became naturalized US citizen and appeared as a friendly witness before House Committee on Un-American Activities (1947); published *Stalin and German Communism* (1948); served as a consultant to US Department of State; moved to Paris (1955), where she would remain for rest of life, working as a journalist, lecturer and commentator. ❖ See also *Women in World History.*

FISH, Jennifer (1949—). American speedskater. Name variations: Jenny Fish. Born Jennifer Lee Fish, May 17, 1949, in US. ❖ Won a silver medal in a 3-way tie with Dianne Holum and Mary Meyers for the 500 meters at Grenoble Olympics (1968).

FISH, Mamie Stuyvesant (1853–1915). *See Fish, Marian.*

FISH, Maree (1963—). Australian field-hockey player. Born Jan 23, 1963, in Australia. ❖ At Seoul Olympics, won a gold medal in team competition (1988).

FISH, Marian (1853–1915). American society leader. Name variations: Marian Graves Anthon or Marian Graves Anthon Fish, Mamie Stuyvesant Fish; Mrs. Stuyvesant Fish. Born Marian Graves Anthon, June 8, 1853, in Staten Island, NY; died May 25, 1915, at Glenclyffe, Garrison-on-Hudson, NY; dau. of William Henry Anthon (prominent criminal lawyer, died 1875) and Sarah Attwood (Meert) Anthon; m. Stuyvesant Fish (son of Hamilton Fish, Secretary of State to US President Grant), June 1, 1876; children: 3 sons, 1 daughter. ❖ Known for her caustic wit and fondness for practical jokes, gave winter dinner parties in New York City at her home in Gramercy Park (1890s) and on 78th Street (after 1900); threw weekend house parties during spring and fall at the family property, Glenclyffe, in Garrison-on-Hudson, NY; entertained at her house Crossways at Newport (RI) every season (beginning 1889), becoming part of highly fashionable society; became famous for vibrant parties, with entertainment provided by such celebrities as Marie Dressler and Vernon and Irene Castle; supported women's strike for the wrapper and kimono industry and visited Lower East Side tenements, but withdrew because of publicity (1913).

FISH, Mrs. Stuyvesant (1853–1915). *See Fish, Marian.*

FISH-HARNACK, Mildred (1902–1943). *See Harnack, Mildred.*

FISHENDEN, Margaret White (c. 1888–1977). *See White, Margaret.*

FISHER, Aileen (1906–2002). American children's writer. Born Aileen Lucia Fisher, Sept 6, 1906, in Iron River, Michigan; died Dec 2, 2002, in Boulder, Colorado; attended University of Chicago; graduate of University of Missouri School of Journalism, 1927; lived with writer Olive Rabe for 30 years. ❖ Wrote over 100 children's books, including *The Coffee-Pot Face* (1933), *Runny Days, Sunny Days* (1958), *Valley of the Smallest: The Life Story of a Shrew* (1966) and *Out in the Dark and Daylight* (1980).

FISHER, Allison (1968—). English snooker and 9-ball player. Born Feb 24, 1968, in Peacehaven, Sussex, England. ❖ Known as the greatest female competitor at snooker, joined snooker league at 13 and began working with coach Frank Callan; won 1st national title by 15 and 1st World championship by 17; moved to US (1995) and competed in Women's Professional Billiards Association (WPBA) Classic Tour event (1995), placing 9th; won 2 of next 3 Tour events; placed 3rd in her 1st WPA Ladies World championship, going on to win (1996, 1997, 1998); took over 80 national titles and 11 world titles including 36 WPBA Tour Titles, 4 WPA 9-Ball World championship titles, 3 ESPN Ultimate 9-Ball titles and 6 WPBA National championships and US Open titles, a record unequaled in the history of professional billiards; boasts top break of 144 and competition best break of 133 and was 1st woman to make a televised century; served a term as president of WPBA board of directors; returned to top spot in WPBA Tour (2003).

FISHER, Anna L. (1949——). American astronaut. Born Aug 24, 1949, in New York, NY. ❖ Specialized in emergency medicine and worked in Los Angeles (CA) hospitals; selected as astronaut candidate by NASA (1978); completed training and evaluation period (1979); served as mission specialist on her 1st space flight (1984), the 2nd flight of orbiter *Discovery,* during which crew achieved 1st salvage in history by retrieving *Palapa B-2* and *Westar VI* satellites; assigned to Space Station Support Office in Houston, TX (1990); served as branch chief of Operations Planning Branch (1997–98); at Space Station Branch, became deputy for operations/training (1998–99) and then chief; served as Astronaut Office representative on numerous boards; assigned to Shuttle Branch.

FISHER, Cicely Corbett (1885–1959). British suffragist and women's rights activist. Born Cicely Corbett in Danehill, Sussex, England, 1885; died in Danehill, Sussex, 1959; dau. of Charles (lawyer) and Marie (Gray) Corbett (suffragist); younger sister of Margery Corbett-Ashby (1882–1981); attended Sommerville College, Oxford; m. Chambers Fisher (journalist), 1913; no children. ❖ With sister and mother, formed the Liberal Women's Suffrage Group; worked for Clementina Black at Women's Industrial Council, an organization that campaigned for improved pay and working conditions for women; was also active in the Anti-Sweating League; in later years, was active in the Labor Party and the Women's International League. ❖ See also *Women in World History.*

FISHER, Clara (1811–1898). English-born American actress. Name variations: Clara Fisher Maeder. Born July 14, 1811, probably in London, England; died in Metuchen, New Jersey, Nov 12, 1898; dau. of Frederick George Fisher (proprietor of a library and later an auctioneer at Covent Garden); m. James Gaspard Maeder (Irish composer and music teacher), Dec 6, 1834 (died 1876); children: 7, including Frank Chickering, Amelia, James Gaspard, and Frederick George (all connected with the theater) and Clara. ❖ At 6, made London debut as Lord Flimnap in a children's adaptation of Garrick's *Lilliput* at Drury Lane Theater; became a famous child actress, touring Great Britain for a decade in children's parts and serious adult roles; made New York debut as Albina Mandeville in *The Will* (1827); appeared in theaters in every major city in US, playing to overflowing houses (1827–34); repertoire encompassed a wide range of roles, including Cherubino in *The Marriage of Figaro,* Clari in *The Maid of Milan,* Helen Worrett in *Man and Wife,* Gertrude in *The Loan of a Lover,* and Letitia Hardy in *The Belle's Stratagem,* in which she sang her famous song "Buy a Broom"; was appearing as the Singing Witch in *Macbeth* at Astor Place Opera House on the occasion of the famous Astor Place riot (May 10, 1849); appeared as the Nurse in *Romeo and Juliet* for final performance at NY's Booth Theater (1883); gave last performance (1889). ❖ See also *Autobiography of Clara Fisher Maeder* (1897); and *Women in World History.*

FISHER, Dehra Kerr- (1882–1963). See Parker, Dehra.

FISHER, Doris (1915–2003). American songwriter. Born May 2, 1915, in New York, NY; died Jan 15, 2003, in Los Angeles, California; m. Charles Gershenson, 1947 (div.); children: Fredericka Fisher Thea; Ned Gershenson. ❖ Partnered with Allan Roberts (1944), wrote such songs as "You Always Hurt the One You Love" (recorded by the Mills Brothers), "That Ole Devil Called Love" (Billie Holiday), "Into Each Life Some Rain Must Fall" (Ella Fitzgerald) and "Whispering Grass" (Ink Spots); also wrote songs for over 20 films, including *Gilda* ("Put the Blame on Mame").

FISHER, Doris. American entrepreneur. Name variations: Doris F. Fisher. Born in US; graduate of Stanford University, 1953; m. Donald G. Fisher; children: John and Robert Fisher. ❖ With husband, opened the 1st Gap clothing store (1969), in San Francisco, CA; took Gap, Inc. public (1976).

FISHER, Dorothy Canfield (1879–1958). American writer. Name variations: Dolly; Dorothy Canfield; (pseudonym) Stanley Cranshaw. Born Dorothea Frances Canfield, Feb 17, 1879, in Lawrence, Kansas; died in Arlington, Vermont, Nov 9, 1958; dau. of James Hulme Canfield (1883–1959, professor and writer) and Flavia (Camp) Canfield; graduate of Ohio State University, 1899, and Columbia University, 1904; m. John Redwood Fisher; children: Sally (b. 1909) and James Fisher (1913–1945). ❖ Popular novelist, short-story writer, essayist, translator, lecturer, philosopher, educator, historian, and children's book writer in the early 20th century who attacked intolerance in all its forms; was also a member of the editorial board of the Book-of-the-Month for 25 years, an enthusiastic advocate on the virtues of Vermont, and a beloved humanitarian, known for her integrity; writings include *Gunhild* (1907), *A Montessori Mother* (1912), *The Montessori Manual* (1913), *The Bent Twig* (1915), *Self-Reliance* (1916), *Understood Betsy* (1917), *Home Fires in France* (1918), *The Brimming Cup* (1921), *Raw Material* (1923), *The French School at Middlebury* (1923), *The Home-Maker* (1924), *The Deepening Stream* (1930), *Basque People* (1931), *Seasoned Timber* (1939), *Nothing Ever Happens and How It Does* (1940), *American Portraits* (1946), (short stories) *Four-Square* (1949) and *Vermont Tradition* (1953). Elected to National Institute of Arts and Letters. ❖ See also Ida H. Washington, *Dorothy Canfield Fisher: A Biography* (New England Press, 1982); Elizabeth Yates, *The Lady from Vermont: Dorothy Canfield Fisher's Life and World* (Stephen Greene, 1958); Mark J. Madigan, ed. *Keeping Fires Night and Day: Selected Letters of Dorothy Canfield Fisher* (U. of Missouri Press, 1993); and *Women in World History.*

FISHER, Frances Christine (1846–1920). See Tiernan, Frances Fisher.

FISHER, Kate (fl. 1881). See Elder, Kate.

FISHER, M.F.K. (1908–1992). American writer and gastronome. Name variations: Mary Frances Parrish (1939–41); (joint pseudonym with Dillwyn Parrish) Victoria Berne. Born Mary Frances Kennedy, July 3, 1908, in Albion, Michigan; died June 22, 1992, in Glen Ellen, California; dau. of Rex Brenton (newspaper editor) and Edith Oliver (Holbrook) Kennedy; sister of Norah K. Barr; sister-in-law of Anne Parrish (1888–1957); attended Illinois College, Occidental College, University of California, and University of Dijon in France; m. Alfred Young Fisher, 1929 (div. 1938); m. Dillwyn Parrish (writer), 1939 (died 1941); m. Donald Friede (book editor), 1945 (div. 1951); children: Anne (b. 1943); (3rd m.) Mary Kennedy (b. 1946). ❖ One of her century's great prose stylists, changed the manner of culinary writing in America and delighted readers for almost 6 decades; wrote over 2 dozen books, contributed short stories, articles, and some poems to the nation's top magazines, including *Harper's Bazaar, Gourmet, Atlantic Monthly, Wine and Food Quarterly* and *House Beautiful;* writings include *Serve It Forth* (1937), *Consider the Oyster* (1941), *How to Cook a Wolf* (1942), *The Gastronomical Me* (1943), *A Cordiall Water* (1961), *Map of Another Town: A Memoir of Provence* (1964), *With Bold Knife and Fork* (1969), *Among Friends* (1971), *A Considerable Town* (1978), *As They Were* (1982), *Sister Age* (1983), *Spirits of the Valley* (1985), *Dubious Honors* (1988), *Answer in the Affirmative and The Oldest Living Man* (1989), *Boss Dog* (1990), *Long Ago in France: The Years in Dijon* (1991) and *Stay Me, Oh Comfort Me: Journal and Stories, 1933–1945* (1993). ❖ See also Barr, Moran, and Moran, comp. *M.F.K. Fisher: A Life in Letters, Correspondence 1929–1991* (Counterpoint, 1997); Joan Reardon, *M.F.K. Fisher, Julia Child, and Alice Waters: Celebrating the Pleasures of the Table* (Harmony, 1994); and *Women in World History.*

FISHER, Margaret (b. 1689). English thief. Born in 1689 in England. ❖ Worked as prostitute and thief; stole 13 gold guineas from Scottish businessman (Sept 1722) and was tried for the crime at Old Bailey; received death sentence but was pardoned after she was found to be pregnant.

FISHER, Margaret (c. 1874–1958). Australian prime-ministerial wife and suffragist. Born Margaret Jane Irvine, c. 1874, in Gympie, Queensland, Australia; died June 15, 1958; m. Andrew Fisher (prime minister of Australia, 1908–09, 1910–13, and 1914–15), Dec 31, 1901; children: Robert (b. 1902), Margaret (b. 1904), Henry (b. 1906), Andrew (b. 1908), John (b. 1910), and James (b. 1912). ❖ When husband became prime minister, was the 1st wife to manage a prime-ministerial residence; represented Australia at the coronation of George V (1911); while there, walked at the head of Australian and New Zealand contingent at a huge suffrage procession, 40,000 strong.

FISHER, Margarita (1886–1975). See Fischer, Margarita.

FISHER, Mary (c. 1623–1698). American Quaker preacher. Name variations: Mary Bayly, Mary Cross. Born c. 1623 in Yorkshire (perhaps in town of Pontefract), England; died 1698 in Charleston, South Carolina; m. William Bayly (sea captain and Quaker preacher), 1662 (died 1675); m. John Cross (cordwainer), Sept 19, 1678 (died c. 1687); children: number uncertain. ❖ Pioneering missionary, was a convert to Society of Friends (Quakers) under influence of George Fox; became itinerant preacher in England (early 1650s); imprisoned numerous times for rebuking priests, was also publicly flogged in Cambridge (1650s); traveled to Barbados, British West Indies, then Massachusetts Bay Colony in Boston (mid-1650s), intent on missionary work in New England; was sent back to Barbados; reportedly traveled alone to Turkey and met Sultan Mohammed IV ("Great Turk," late 1650s); with 2nd husband and children, migrated to Charleston, SC (1682).

FISHER, Mary (c. 1946—). American AIDS activist. Born Mary Fisher in Detroit, Michigan, c. 1946; dau. of Max Fisher (industrialist and philanthropist); m. Brian Campbell (div.); children: (adopted) Zachary; Max (b. 1988). ❖ Was in her early 40s when she learned that she had contracted AIDS from ex-husband who had recently died (1991); a wealthy Republican, had a great deal of cachet when she spoke before the Republican National Convention (1992), exhorting the nation to stop stigmatizing those who find themselves HIV positive; published *Sleep with the Angels,* a compilation of 25 of her speeches, *I'll Not Go Quietly* (1995) and *My Name Is Mary* (1996). ❖ See also *Women in World History.*

FISHER, Mary Frances Kennedy (1908–1992). See Fisher, M.F.K.

FISHER, Matilda (c. 1825–1907). See Meech, Matilda.

FISHER, Minnie (1882–1964). See Cunningham, Minnie Fisher.

FISHER, Nellie (1920–1994). American dancer and choreographer. Born Ethelwyn Fisher, Dec 10, 1920, in Berkeley, California; died Oct 19, 1994, in Edmonds, Washington. ❖ Moved to New York City and danced for Martha Graham in *American Document* (1938) and *Every Soul Is a Circus* (1939); danced with the corps de ballet at Radio City Music Hall; appeared in *One Touch of Venus* (1943) and *On the Town* (1944), among others; choreographed and staged numerous dances including for *The Best of Burlesque* (1957–58), Russell Patterson's *Sketchbook of 1960* and *The Golden Apple* revival; choreographed for tv series "America Song" (1948–49); appeared on tv in such shows as "All-Star Revue" (1950–53), "Your Show of Shows" (1950–54), where she was often teamed with Jerry Ross, and "Colgate Comedy Hour" (1950–55).

FISHER, Sarah (1980—). American race-car driver. Born Oct 4, 1980, in Commercial Point, Ohio. ❖ Took World Karting Association Grand National championship 3 times between ages 11 and 14; became Circleville Points champion (1993); began racing sprint cars at 15; won 5 of 23 races in North American Midget Auto Racing Series at 18; became youngest driver ever in IRL IndyCar Series (1999); became youngest person ever and 3rd woman to race in Indianapolis 500 at age 19 (2000); had 2nd-place finish at Homestead-Miami (best ever by woman in Indy-style racing, 2001); won MBNA Pole for 2002 Belterra Casino Indy 300 at Kentucky Speedway, as 1st woman to win pole position for major-league open-wheel race in North America.

FISHER, Sarah Logan (1751–1796). American diarist. Born 1751 in Pennsylvania; died 1796. ❖ Member of Philadelphia Quaker family, kept record of her experiences as a Loyalist during American Revolution, which was published as *A Diary of Trifling Occurrences* (1958).

FISK, Sari. Finnish ice-hockey player. Born in Finland. ❖ Won a team bronze medal at Nagano (1998), the 1st Olympics to feature women's ice hockey.

FISKE, Fidelia (1816–1864). American missionary and educator. Born Fidelia Fisk (later altered to Fiske) on May 1, 1816, in Shelburne, Massachusetts; died July 26, 1864, in Shelburne; dau. of Rufus (farmer and cooper) and Hannah (Woodward) Fisk. ❖ Made public profession of faith in Congregational Church (c. 1831); joined faculty of Mount Holyoke Seminary (1842); worked as teacher for Congregational mission to Nestorian Christian sect in Oroomiah, Persia (now Rezaiyeh, Iran), learning Syrian language, organizing boarding seminary for girls, and nursing sick in community (1843–58); returned to US because of ill-health (1858); compiled *Memorial: Twenty-Fifth Anniversary of the Mt. Holyoke Female Seminary* (1862) and published *Recollections of Mary Lyons* (1866); provided material for Thomas Laurie's *Woman and Her*

Saviour in Persia (1863). ❖ See also Daniel T. Fiske, *Faith Working by Love: as Exemplified in the Life of Fidelia Fiske* (1868).

FISKE, Minnie Maddern (1865–1932). American actress. Name variations: Minnie Maddern. Born Marie Augusta Davey, Dec 19, 1865, in New Orleans, Louisiana; died Feb 15, 1932, in Hollis, Long Island, New York; only dau. of Thomas W. Davey (theatrical manager) and Elizabeth "Lizzie" (Maddern) Davey (actress); briefly attended convents in Cincinnati and St. Louis; aunt of Emily Stevens (actress); m. LeGrand White, c. 1882 (div. 1888); m. Harrison Grey Fiske (playwright, manager, and journalist), Mar 19, 1890; children: (adopted 1922) Danville Maddern Davey. ❖ At 3, accompanied father's troupe on tour, 1st appearing on stage in Little Rock, Arkansas, as the young Duke of York in *Richard III*; at 4, made New York debut in *A Sheep in Wolf's Clothing*; billed as "Little Minnie Maddern," became a popular child actress and, at 13, was adding adult roles to repertoire, including the elderly Widow Melnotte in *The Lady of Lyons*; by 1880s, had graduated to ingenue roles and appeared in a variety of popular plays of the decade, including *Fogg's Ferry, Caprice* and *Featherbrain;* on marriage to Harrison Grey Fiske, wealthy young owner of New York *Dramatic Mirror,* retired from the stage (1890); began writing one-act plays, of which *The Rose, The Eyes of the Heart* and *A Light for St. Agnes* became quite popular; returned to the stage as Minnie Maddern Fiske (1893), appearing as the heroine in husband's unsuccessful play *Hester Crewe;* played Nora in *A Doll's House* to critical acclaim (1894); throughout next 2 decades, gained a reputation as a serious actress as well as a champion of Ibsen, starring in *Hedda Gabler* (1903), *Rosmersholm* (1907), *The Pillars of Society* (1910) and *Ghosts* (1927); reached height of popular success, however, in *Tess of the d'Urbervilles* (1897) and *Becky Sharp* (1899). ❖ See also Archie Binns, *Mrs. Fiske and the American Theater* (Crown, 1955); and *Women in World History.*

FISKE, Sarah Symmes (1652–1692). American religious writer. Born 1652 in Charleston, Massachusetts, to Puritans; died 1692; m. Moses Fiske, 1671; children: 14. ❖ In preparation for entry into Puritan church, wrote *A Confession of Faith or, A Summary of Divinity* (1704), which was later published to be read by young persons seeking to enter the church.

FITNAT-KHANIM (c. 1725–1780). Turkish poet. Name variations: Zubeyda Fitnat-Khanim. Born c. 1725 in Turkey; died 1780; dau. of Sheik al-Islam. ❖ Considered the most important woman poet of the Ottoman school, was highly thought of by fellow poets with whom she exchanged odes and repartee; wrote lyric poetry using imagery from traditional Persian verse.

FITSCHEN, Doris (1968—). German soccer player. Born Oct 25, 1968, in Zeven, Germany. ❖ At age 9, began playing for FC Hesedorf; as sweeper, played for 5 different German clubs over 18 years; won team European championships (1989, 1991, 1995, 1997, 2001) and Super Cup (1992); won a team bronze medal at Sydney Olympics (2000); signed with WUSA's Philadelphia Courage (2001), becoming captain and scoring the 1st goal in team history and WUSA competition; retired (2001) with a record of 144 caps for the German national team (1986–2001). Named to European All-Star team (1997) and WUSA Defensive Player of the Year (2001).

FITTKO, Lisa (1909–2005). Austrian-born Jewish resistance leader. Born Lisa Eckstein in Uzhorod (then Austria-Hungary, now Ukraine), Aug 23, 1909; died Mar 12, 2005, in Chicago, Illinois; grew up in Vienna and Berlin; m. Johannes (Hans) Fittko (anti-Nazi journalist), c. 1934 (died 1960). ❖ In partnership with husband, was active in resisting Nazism as exiles, living a precarious existence in Czechoslovakia, then Austria, Switzerland, Netherlands and France (1930s); remained at great risk from the Nazis, who continued to occupy the northern region of France, and met Varian Fry; played a crucial role in saving the lives of almost 1,500 endangered refugees, many of them world-famous artists and intellectuals, including Marc Chagall, Jacques Lipchitz, Max Ernst, Wanda Landowska, Hannah Arendt and André Breton (1940–41), helping them flee Nazi-occupied France over a perilous Pyrenees escape route known as the F-Route (Fittko-Route); with husband, escaped to Cuba (1941), finally settling in US; lived in Chicago and was active in the peace movement. Awarded Distinguished Service Medal, 1st Class, by Federal Republic of Germany (1986). ❖ See also memoirs *Escape Through the Pyrenees* (1991) and *Solidarity and Treason: Resistance and Exile, 1933–1940* (1993); and *Women in World History.*

FITTON, Doris (1897–1985). Australian theatrical producer. Name variations: Dame Doris Fitton. Born in Manila, Philippines, Nov 1897;

died April 2, 1985; dau. of Walter (English accountant, broker, and manufacturer of cigars) and Janet (Cameron) Fitton (Australian); early schooling was in Melbourne; attended Loreto convents in Portland and Ballarat; studied acting with Gregan McMahon and at Melbourne Repertory Theatre; m. Norbert "Tug" Mason (lawyer), 1922; children: 2. ❖ Joined 19 other actors and 100 associated members to launch the Independent Theatre in Sydney (1930), modeled after Stanislavsky's Moscow Arts Theatre; through the theatre's 47-year history, was at the helm, acting variously as director, producer, actress, and drama teacher. Made Dame of the British Empire (DBE, 1981). ❖ See also autobiography *Not Without Dust and Heat: My Life in Theatre* (1981); and *Women in World History.*

FITTON, Mary (c. 1578–1647). English noblewoman. Name variations: Mary Logher or Lougher. Born 1578; baptized June 24, 1578; died 1647; dau. of Sir Edward Fitton the Younger of Gawsworth, Cheshire, England; sister of Anne Fitton who m. John Newdigate; m. Captain W. Polwhele, 1606 or 1607 (died 1609 or 1610); m. a Captain Lougher or Logher (d. 1636); children: (1st m.) 1 son, 1 daughter; (with Sir Richard Leveson) possibly 2 illeg. daughters. ❖ Identified by some as the "dark lady" of Shakespeare's sonnets, became maid of honor to Queen Elizabeth I (c. 1595) and was put under the care of Sir William Knollys, comptroller of the queen's household; with her encouragement, was courted by the married Sir William; became mistress of William Herbert, later the 3rd earl of Pembroke, who was sent to the Fleet in disgrace because of the affair. Arguments in favor of Mary Fitton as the false mistress of Shakespeare's sonnets can be found in Tyler's *Shakespeare's Sonnets* (1890) and his *Herbert-Fitton Theory of Shakespeare's Sonnets* (1898). ❖ See also *Women in World History.*

FITZALAN, Alice (fl. 1285). Countess of Arundel. Name variations: Alice of Saluzzo. Fl. around 1285; m. Richard Fitzalan (1267–1302), 6th earl of Arundel; children: Edmund Fitzalan (1285–1326), 7th earl of Arundel.

FITZALAN, Alice (d. around 1338). Countess of Arundel. Name variations: Alice de Warrenne. Died c. 1338; dau. of William de Warrenne (son of John, 3rd earl of Surrey) and Joan de Vere (dau. of 5th earl of Oxford); m. Edmund Fitzalan, 7th earl of Arundel, in 1305; children: Richard Fitzalan (c. 1313–1376), 8th earl of Arundel; Joan Fitzalan (fl. 1325, who m. John Bohun).

FITZALAN, Alice (1352–1416). Countess of Kent. Name variations: Alice Holland. Born 1352 in Arundel Castle, West Sussex, England; died Mar 17, 1416; dau. of Richard Fitzalan (c. 1313–1376), 8th earl of Arundel, and Eleanor Plantagenet (c. 1318–1372); sister of Joan Fitzalan (d. 1419); m. Thomas Holland, 2nd earl of Kent, April 10, 1364; children: Alianor Holland (c. 1373–1405); Thomas Holland, 3rd earl of Kent; Edmund Holland, 4th earl of Kent; Margaret Holland (1385–1429); Joan Holland (c. 1380–1434); Elizabeth Holland (c. 1383–?); Eleanor Holland (c. 1385–?).

FITZALAN, Amy (fl. 1440). Countess of Ormonde. Name variations: Amy Butler. Fl. around 1440; dau. of John Fitzalan, 11th earl of Arundel, and Maud Lovell; 2nd wife of James Butler (1420–1461), 5th earl of Ormonde.

FITZALAN, Anne. *See Percy, Anne.*

FITZALAN, Eleanor (c. 1318–1372). *See Eleanor Plantagenet.*

FITZALAN, Elizabeth (d. 1385). Countess of Arundel. Name variations: Elizabeth Bohun; Elizabeth de Bohun. Died 1385; dau. of William Bohun, 1st earl of Northampton, and Elizabeth Badlesmere; m. Richard Fitzalan, 9th earl of Arundel, in 1359; children: Thomas Fitzalan (1381–1415), 10th earl of Arundel; Elizabeth Fitzalan (d. 1425); Margaret Fitzalan (who m. Sir Rowland Lenthall); Alice Fitzalan (who m. John Charlton, 4th Lord Charleton of Powis); Richard Fitzalan.

FITZALAN, Elizabeth (d. 1408). *See Despenser, Elizabeth.*

FITZALAN, Elizabeth (d. 1425). Duchess of Norfolk. Name variations: Elizabeth Mowbray. Died 1425; dau. of Elizabeth Fitzalan (d. 1385) and Richard Fitzalan, 9th earl of Arundel; m. William Montacute, before 1378; m. Thomas Mowbray (c. 1362–1399), 1st duke of Norfolk, in 1384; children: (2nd m.) Thomas Mowbray, 7th baron Mowbray (1385–1405); John Mowbray, 2nd duke of Norfolk (1389–1432); Isabel Mowbray; Margaret Mowbray.

FITZALAN, Elizabeth (fl. 1408–1417). English noblewoman. Name variations: Elizabeth Berkeley; Lady Maltravers. Flourished around 1408 to 1417; m. John Fitzalan (1385–1421); children: John Fitzalan (1408–1435), 11th earl of Arundel; William Fitzalan (1417–1487), 13th earl of Arundel.

FITZALAN, Isabel (fl. 1267). *See Mortimer, Isabel.*

FITZALAN, Joan (fl. 1325). Countess of Hereford and Essex. Name variations: sometimes referred to as Alice; Joan Bohun. Flourished around 1325; dau. of Edmund Fitzalan, 7th earl of Arundel, and Alice (de Warrenne) Fitzalan (d. around 1338); sister of Richard Fitzalan (c. 1313–1376), 8th earl of Arundel; aunt of Joan Fitzalan (d. 1419); m. John Bohun, 5th earl of Hereford, 4th of Essex, in 1325.

FITZALAN, Joan (d. 1419). Countess of Hereford, Essex, and Northampton. Name variations: Joan Bohun. Born before 1351; died April 7, 1419; buried in Walden Abbey, Essex, England; dau. of Richard Fitzalan (c. 1313–1376), 8th earl of Arundel, and Eleanor Plantagenet (c. 1318–1372); sister of Alice Fitzalan (1352–1416); m. Humphrey Bohun, earl of Hereford, Essex, and Northampton; children: Eleanor Bohun (1366–1399); Mary de Bohun (1369–1394, 1st wife of Henry IV, king of England). ❖ Her daughter Mary de Bohun married Henry IV, a few years before he became king of England; when John Holland, who was plotting to restore Richard II to the throne, fell into her hands, had him beheaded without trial (1400). ❖ See also *Women in World History.*

FITZALAN, Joan (fl. 1480s). *See Neville, Joan.*

FITZALAN, Katherine (b. around 1520). Countess of Arundel. Name variations: Catherine or Katherine Grey. Born c. 1520; dau. of Thomas Grey (1477–1530), 2nd marquess of Dorset, and Margaret Wotton; m. Henry Fitzalan (1512–1580), 16th earl of Arundel; children: Mary Fitzalan (d. 1557); Joanna Fitzalan Lumley (c. 1537–1576).

FITZALAN, Katherine (fl. 1530s). English noblewoman. Fl. around 1530; dau. of William Fitzalan, 15th earl of Arundel, and Anne Percy; 1st wife of Henry Grey (c. 1517–1554), later duke of Suffolk (created in 1551). Henry Grey m. his 2nd wife Frances Brandon (1525); their daughter was Lady Jane Grey.

FITZALAN, Margaret (b. around 1388). English noblewoman. Name variations: Margaret Roos; Baroness Ros. Born c. 1388; dau. of John Fitzalan (1365–1391) and Elizabeth Despenser (d. 1408); m. William Roos (d. 1414), 7th baron Ros; children: Margaret Roos (who m. Reginald Grey); Thomas Roos, 9th baron Ros (d. 1431).

FITZALAN, Margaret (fl. 1450s). *See Woodville, Margaret.*

FITZALAN, Mary (d. 1557). Countess of Arundel. Name variations: Mary Howard. Died after June 28, 1557; dau. of Henry Fitzalan (1512–1580), 16th earl of Arundel, and Katherine Fitzalan (b. around 1520); m. Thomas Howard, 3rd duke of Norfolk, in 1556; children: Philip Howard, 17th earl of Arundel. Thomas Howard also m. Margaret Audley (d. 1564) after Aug of 1557 and Elizabeth Leyburne (d. 1567).

FITZALAN, Maud (fl. 1200s). English noblewoman. Name variations: Maud de Verdun. Born Maud de Verdun; dau. of Roesia de Verdun; m. John Fitzalan (who, though not known as an earl of Arundel, occupied the castle of Arundel from 1243 to 1267); children: John Fitzalan (d. 1272); grandmother of Richard, 6th earl of Arundel.

FITZALAN, Philippa (1375–1401). *See Mortimer, Philippa.*

FITZCLARENCE, Amelia (1807–1858). Viscountess Falkland. Born Nov 5, 1807 (some sources cite 1803); died July 2, 1858, in London; interred at Hutton-Rudby, Yorkshire; legitimized dau. of William IV (1765–1837), king of England (r. 1831–1837), and Dora Jordan (1761–1816); m. Lucius Bentinck, 10th viscount Falkland, Dec 27, 1830; children: Lucius William (b. 1831); Plantagenet Pierrepoint, 11th viscount Falkland (b. 1836); Byron Charles.

FITZGERALD, Benita (1961—). African-American runner. Name variations: Benita Fitzgerald-Brown; Benita Fitzgerald Mosley. Born July 6, 1961, in Dale City, Virginia; graduate of University of Tennessee with a degree in industrial engineering, 1984; m. Laron Brown; m. Ron Mosley. ❖ Won US Jr. nationals (1978–79) and US nationals (1983), in 100-meter hurdles; won 4 NCAA titles; won a gold medal at Pan American Games (1983); at Los Angeles Olympics, won a gold medal for 100-meter hurdles (1984); became director of US Olympic training centers and president of Women's Sports Foundation (1997); became president of Women in Cable and Telecommunications (2001). Named Hurdler of the Decade by *Track and Field News* (1989).

FITZGERALD, Lady Edward (1773–1831). *See Fitzgerald, Pamela.*

FITZGERALD, Eithne (1950—). *Irish politician.* Born Eithne Ingoldsby, Nov 1950, in Dublin, Ireland; m. John FitzGerald. ❖ Representing Labour, stood unsuccessfully in the general elections (1981, 1982, 1987, 1989); elected to the 27th Dáil (1992–1997) for Dublin South; championed the Ethics in Public Office Act (1995) and Freedom of Information Act (1997); defeated in general elections (1997 and 2002).

FITZGERALD, Elizabeth (c. 1528–1589). *English noblewoman.* Name variations: Lady Elizabeth Fitzgerald; The Fair Geraldine. Born at Maynooth, Ireland, around 1528; died in 1589; youngest dau. of George Fitzgerald, 9th earl of Kildare; m. Sir Anthony Browne (d. 1548); m. Edward Fiennes de Clinton, earl of Lincoln, around 1552. ❖ A member of the household of the Princess Mary (Mary I) and later Queen Catherine Howard, was celebrated in verse by Michael Drayton and Sir Walter Scott, and Henry Howard, earl of Surrey, addressed a series of songs and sonnets to her which were 1st published in Tottel's *Miscellany* (1557). ❖ See also *Women in World History.*

FITZGERALD, Ella (1917–1996). *African-American jazz singer.* Born Ella Jane Fitzgerald, April 25, 1917, in Newport News, Virginia; died in Beverly Hills, California, June 15, 1996; dau. of William and Temperance Williams; m. Benjamin Kornegay, 1935 (annulled 1937); m. Ray Brown (bassist), 1947 (div. 1953); children: (2nd m.) adopted, Ray Brown Jr. ❖ Jazz and pop world's "first lady of song," the most honored female vocalist in modern music history, was discovered by bandleader William "Chick" Webb in Harlem (mid-1930s); made her 1st recording with Webb for Decca, "Love and Kisses" (1935); recorded a song officially titled "If You Can't Sing It, You'll Have to Swing It," though it became better known as "Mr. Paganini" (1936); recorded "A-Tisket, A-Tasket" (1937), which sold 1 million copies, went to #1 on the Hit Parade, and made her a star; became a noted jazz stylist with Dizzy Gillespie's band, known for her "scating" and emotive interpretations of pop and jazz standards; burst on the national charts with her recording of "Lady Be Good" (1947), her 1st major hit built almost entirely around her trademark scat singing; became the cornerstone artist of the most prolific jazz label ever created, Verve Records (1956), recording the classic "Songbook" series, each record dedicated to a particular composer, from Harold Arlen to Duke Ellington to Cole Porter; also often sang with the Oscar Peterson Trio; remained the most popular female vocalist of international stature from the end of World War II to mid-1980s, winning 12 Grammy Awards before retiring because of poor health. Received Honors Medal from the Kennedy Center for the Performing Arts (1984). ❖ See also Sid Colin, *Ella: The Life and Times of Ella Fitzgerald* (Elm Tree, 1986); Geoffrey Fidelman, *The First Lady of Song: Ella Fitzgerald for the Record* (Birch Lane, 1994); Stuart Nicholson, *Ella Fitzgerald: A Biography of the First Lady of Song* (Scribner, 1994).

FITZGERALD, Eugenia Tucker (c. 1834–1928). *American founder of a college society.* Name variations: Eugenia Tucker. Born Eugenia Tucker c. 1824 in Laurens Co., Virginia; died Dec 10, 1928; graduated as valedictorian from Wesleyan College, 1852. ❖ Was primary founder and 1st president of the 1st secret college society for women, the Adelphean Society (later named Alpha Delta Phi, 1904, then Alpha Delta Pi, 1913) at Wesleyan College in Macon, GA (1851).

FITZGERALD, Frances (1950—). *Irish politician.* Born Aug 1950, in Croom, Co. Limerick, Ireland; m. Michael Fitzgerald. ❖ Served as chair of the Council of the Status of Women (1988–92); representing Fine Gael, elected to the 27th Dáil (1992–97) for Dublin South East; returned to 28th Dáil (1997–2002).

FITZGERALD, Frances Scott (1921–1986). *American writer.* Name variations: Scottie; Frances Scott Fitzgerald Lanahan Smith. Born Oct 26, 1921; died June 1986 in Montgomery, Alabama; only child of F. Scott Fitzgerald (novelist) and Zelda Fitzgerald (1900–1948); m. Jack Lanahan (lawyer; div.); m. Grove Smith, 1967; children: 4, including Tim and Eleanor Lanahan (artist and illustrator). ❖ Was a playwright, composer, *Washington Post* columnist, and Democratic insider; as depicted by daughter Eleanor Lanahan, adored her alcoholic father and blocked out her mother's bouts of insanity, but was burdened with their fame. ❖ See also Eleanor Lanahan, *Scottie: The Dau. of . . . : The Life of Frances Scott Fitzgerald Lanahan Smith* (HarperCollins, 1995); and *Women in World History.*

FITZGERALD, Geraldine (1913–2005). *Irish-American actress.* Born in Dublin, Ireland, Nov 24, 1913; died July 17, 2005, in New York, NY; dau. of Edward (attorney) and Edith Fitzgerald; studied at Dublin Art School and Queen's College, London; cousin of Shelah Richards (1903– 1985), actress; m. Edward Lindsay-Hogg (songwriter), 1936 (div., 1946); m. Stuart Scheftel, 1946 (died 1995); children: (1st m.) Michael Lindsay-Hogg (b. 1940, film and theater director); (2nd m.) Susan Scheftel (b. 1948). ❖ Made debut at Gate Theater in Dublin (1932); made NY debut as Ellie Dunn in *Heartbreak House* (1938); appeared as Rebecca in *Sons and Soldiers* (1943), Tanis Talbot in *Portrait in Black* (1945), Jennifer Dubedat in *The Doctor's Dilemma* (1955), Goneril in *King Lear* (1956), Ann Richards in *Hide and Seek* (1957), as well as Gertrude in *Hamlet* at American Shakespeare Festival (1958); also appeared as the Queen in *The Cave Dwellers* (1961), Mary Tyrone in *Long Day's Journey into Night* (1971), Jenny in *The Threepenny Opera* (1972), Felicity in *The Shadow Box* (1977) and Nora Melody in *A Touch of the Poet* (1978); appeared in one-woman show *Songs of the Streets: O'Neill and Carlotta* (1979); made theatrical history as the 1st woman to appear as the Stage Manager in *Our Town,* at Williamstown Festival; founded Everyman Street Theatre; directed *Mass Appeal* at Manhattan Theatre Club (1980) and *The Lunch Girls,* Theatre Row (1981). Films include *The Mill on the Floss* (1936), *Dark Victory* (1939), *Till We Meet Again* (1940), *Watch on the Rhine* (1943), *Ladies Courageous* (1944), *10 North Frederick* (1958), *The Pawnbroker* (1965), *Rachel, Rachel* (1968), *The Last American Hero* (1973), *Harry and Tonto* (1974), *Arthur* (1981), *Pope of Greenwich Village* (1984), *Poltergeist II* (1986) and *Arthur 2* (1988). Nominated for Academy Award for Best Supporting Actress for *Wuthering Heights* (1939). ❖ See also *Women in World History.*

FITZGERALD, Katherine (c. 1500–1604). *Countess of Desmond.* Name variations: The old Countess of Desmond. Born c. 1500; died in 1604; dau. of Sir John Fitzgerald, lord of Decies; became the 2nd wife of Thomas Fitzgerald, 12th earl of Desmond, after 1505 (d. 1534, at 80); children: one daughter. ❖ Legend has it that she lived to be 140, though it is more likely that she lived to be around 104, walking three or four miles to market to the last; stories abounded that she died of concussion after being hit by an apple, sometimes a walnut, sometimes a cherry, that fell from a tree. ❖ See also *Women in World History.*

FITZGERALD, Lillian (d. 1947). *American comedian and singer.* Born in New York, NY; died July 9, 1947, in New York, NY. ❖ First appeared in the chorus in a vehicle for Weber and Fields; later performed in musicals with Eddie Cantor and Ed Wynn; also played vaudeville and nightclubs.

FITZGERALD, Pamela (1773–1831). *Daughter of Mme de Genlis.* Name variations: Lady Edward Fitzgerald. Born 1773 (some sources cite 1776); died in Paris, France, 1831; popularly supposed that she was the illeg. dau. of Stéphanie-Félicité, Comtesse de Genlis (1746–1830) and Louis-Philippe Joseph, duke d'Orléans (Philippe-Egalité); m. Lord Edward Fitzgerald (1763–1798, son of Emily Lennox), Dec 27, 1792. ❖ Brought up as a ward in the Orléans household; journeyed to England (1791); married future Irish rebel Edward Fitzgerald in Tournay (1792) and accompanied him to Ireland where he became politically active, joining the United Irishmen who were openly calling for an independent republic; attended to husband in Newgate Prison after he had been shot, but he died of his wounds (June 4, 1798); left Ireland and eventually remarried, though she retained the name Fitzgerald. ❖ See also *Women in World History.*

FITZGERALD, Penelope (1916–2000). *British novelist.* Name variations: Penelope Knox. Born Penelope Knox, Dec 17, 1916, in Lincoln, England; died April 28, 2000, in London, England; dau. of E(dmund) V(alpy) Knox (witty contributor to *Punch*) and Christina (Hicks) Knox; stepdau. of Mary Shepard, the illustrator; niece of Monsignor Ronald Knox (biblical scholar); received 1st in English at Oxford (1939); m. Desmond Fitzgerald, 1941. ❖ One of England's most distinctive and elegant voices in contemporary fiction, wrote 1st novel at 61; writings include *The Golden Child* (1977), *The Bookshop* (1978), *Offshore* (1979), *Charlotte Mew and Her Friends* (1979), *Human Voices* (1980), *William Morris: The Novel on Blue Paper* (1981), *At Freddie's* (1982), *Innocence* (1986), *The Beginning of Spring* (1988), *The Gate of Angels* (1990), *The Blue Flower* (1995), *Heat Wave* (1996) and *The Means of Escape* (2000). Received Booker Prize for *Offshore* and National Book Critics Circle Award for *The Blue Flower.* ❖ See also her biography of father and uncles, *The Knox Brothers.*

FITZGERALD, Scottie (1921–1986). See *Fitzgerald, Frances Scott.*

FITZGERALD, Zelda (1900–1948). *American writer and dancer.* Name variations: Zelda Sayre (1900–20); Zelda Fitzgerald. Born July 24, 1900, in Montgomery, Alabama; died in a fire at Highland Hospital in Asheville, North Carolina, Mar 11, 1948; dau. of Anthony Sayre (Alabama Supreme

Court judge) and Minnie (Machen) Sayre; m. F. Scott Fitzgerald (novelist), 1920; children: Frances "Scottie" Fitzgerald (1921–1986). ❧ Southern society beauty, the 1st and most famous flapper of "the Jazz Age," whose works were overshadowed by those of husband, novelist F. Scott Fitzgerald; her moment of triumph as a rich, carefree bride was followed by years of disillusionment, alcoholism, and a descent into chronic schizophrenia; began writing articles, many of which were published in *Metropolitan Magazine, McCall's* and *New York Tribune;* conceived a sudden passion for ballet dancing and began to study it with obsessive intensity (1927), even though she was 27; won a few brief dancing engagements in Cannes and Nice; suffered a severe nervous breakdown (1930–31); published novel, *Save Me the Waltz* (1932); for next several years, was in and out of hospitals, suffering recurrent episodes of schizophrenia; with doctors' encouragement, took up painting and had solo exhibition in Manhattan (1934); lived at Highland Hospital, a clinic in Asheville, North Carolina (1936–40, 1947–48). ❧ See also Matthew Bruccoli, ed. *The Collected Writings of Zelda Fitzgerald* (Scribner, 1991); Eleanor Lanahan, ed. *Zelda—An Illustrated Life: The Private World of Zelda Fitzgerald* (Abrams, 1996); Nancy Milford, *Zelda: A Biography* (Harper & Row, 1970); and *Women in World History.*

FITZ-GIBBON, Bernice (c. 1895–1982). American advertising pioneer. Name variations: Mrs. Herman Block. Born c. 1895 in Waunakee, Wisconsin; died in a Wisconsin nursing home, 1982; dau. of William Fitz-Gibbon (dairy farmer) and Nora (Bowles) Fitz-Gibbon; University of Wisconsin, BA, 1918; m. Herman Block (attorney), July 6, 1925; children: Peter and Elizabeth Bowles Block. ❧ Sold advertising for *Register-Gazette* in Rockford, Illinois, and worked for a year at Chicago's Marshall Field; after a summer at Wanamaker's in New York, joined staff of Macy's (1923); during 12 years there, came up with several successful ad campaigns; left for Gimbels (1940); established own small agency, Bernice Fitz-Gibbon, Inc. (1954), and became a member of the board of directors of Montgomery Ward and Co.; contributed many articles to *McCall's, Good Housekeeping, The New York Times Magazine* and *Glamour,* and was in demand as a speaker. ❧ See also memoir *Macy's, Gimbels, and Me* (Simon & Schuster, 1951); and *Women in World History.*

FITZGIBBON, Catherine (1823–1896). *See Irene, Sister.*

FITZGIBBON, Hanorah Philomena (1889–1979). New Zealand nurse, hospital matron, and nursing administrator. Name variations: Nora FitzGibbon. Born Mar 19, 1889, at Arrow Junction, Otago, New Zealand; died May 7, 1979, at Dunedin, New Zealand; dau. of Edmond FitzGibbon (farmer) and Mary (Lynch) FitzGibbon. ❧ First nurse at Karitane Home for Babies in Dunedin (1907), was also one of the first 12 New Zealand nurses to serve in Egypt during World War I; returned to Christchurch Hospital as theater nurse (1919); trained as Plunket nurse in Dunedin (1925); became matron of Karitane Hospital and Mothercraft Home, Auckland (1931); became director of Plunket nursing (1934); collaborated on Plunket childcare manual, *Modern Mothercraft* (1945); was president of New Zealand Registered Nurses' Association (1946–49); helped to establish Dunedin Catholic Nurses' Guild (1937). Received British Empire Medal (1939). ❧ See also *Dictionary of New Zealand Biography* (Vol. 4).

FITZGIBBON, Irene (1823–1896). *See Irene, Sister.*

FITZGIBBON, Nora (1889–1979). *See FitzGibbon, Hanorah Philomena.*

FITZGILBERT, Constance (fl. 12th c.). British arts patron. Name variations: Custance FitzGilbert. Fl. around 1150; m. Ralph FitzGilbert. ❧ Lincolnshire noblewoman who gave Geoffrey of Monmouth's *History of the Kings of England* to a clerk, Gaimar, to translate into French (Gaimar was the 1st to render Anglo-Norman verse chronicle into vernacular).

FITZHAMMON, Amabel (d. 1157). Countess of Gloucester. Died 1157; m. Robert, 1st earl of Gloucester (illeg. son of Henry I and Nesta Tewdwr), in 1109 (died 1147); children: William Fitzrobert, 2nd earl of Gloucester.

FITZHARDINGE, Joan (1912–2003). *See Phipson, Joan.*

FITZHENRY, Mrs. (d. 1790?). Irish actress. Maiden name Flannigan; 1st name is unknown. Died c. 1790; dau. of a man named Flannigan who managed the Ferry Boat tavern in Abbey Street, Dublin; m. a Captain Gregory; m. a man named Fitzhenry (lawyer), c. 1757; children: (2nd m.) 1 son, 1 daughter. ❧ Worked as a seamstress before marrying Captain Gregory who operated a ship trading between Dublin and Bordeaux;

following death of husband by drowning, moved to London and appeared at Covent Garden (1754); had 1st success at Smock Alley Theater in Dublin; appeared at Covent Garden as Lady Macbeth and reprised the role of Hermione in *The Distressed Mother* (1757); appeared in Dublin in Shakespearean roles, as well as in role of Calista in *The Fair Pentitent* (1759–64); worked at the Drury Lane (1765). Her chief rival was Elizabeth Yates.

FITZHERBERT, Maria Anne (1756–1837). Illegal wife of King George IV of England. Name variations: Mary Ann; Mrs. Fitzherbert. Born Maria Anne Smythe in Hampshire, England, July 26, 1756; died Mar 27, 1837, in Brighton, Sussex; dau. of Walter Smythe and Mary (Errington) Smythe; m. Edward Weld of Lulworth Castle, Dorset, 1775 (died 1776); m. Thomas Fitzherbert of Swynnerton, Staffordshire, 1778 (died 1781); m. George IV (1762–1821), king of England (r. 1820–1830), Dec 21, 1785 (marriage declared illegal in 1787); children: (with George IV) 10. ❧ Was secretly wed to George (IV), prince of Wales (Dec 21, 1785); even though the marriage was declared illegal (1787), lived as his wife and gave birth to 10 children; at time of King George IV's death (1830), was among the few who mourned. ❧ See also *Women in World History.*

FITZHUGH, Anne (fl. 1466). Viscountess Lovell. Fl. 1466; dau. of Henry Fitzhugh, 5th Lord Fitzhugh of Ravensworth, and Alice Neville (fl. 1480s, sister of the Kingmaker); m. Francis Lovell, Viscount Lovell, 1466.

FITZHUGH, Louise (1928–1974). American writer and illustrator. Born Louise Perkins Fitzhugh in Memphis, Tennessee, Oct 5, 1928; died in New Milford, Connecticut, Nov 19, 1974; dau. of Millsaps (attorney) and Louise (Perkins) Fitzhugh; attended Southwestern College, Florida Southern College, Bard College, and New York University; studied painting at Art Students League and Cooper Union (NY) and in Bologna, Italy. ❧ Oil paintings were exhibited at several galleries, including Banfer Gallery, New York City (1963); 1st attracted attention with her satiric illustrations for *Suzuki Beane,* written in collaboration with Sandra Scoppettone (1961); published *Harriet the Spy* (1964), now considered a major milestone in children's literature, then published its sequel, *The Long Secret* (1965); collaborated again with Scoppettone on *Bang, Bang, You're Dead* (1969), an antiwar story; wrote *Nobody's Family Is Going to Change* (1974), which would become a tv movie and Broadway musical under title "The Tap Dance Kid." ❧ See also *Women in World History.*

FITZJAMES, Louise (b. 1809). French ballet dancer. Name variations: Louise Fitz-James. Born Louise Fizan, Dec 10, 1809, in Paris, France; date of death unknown; probably a sister of Natalie Fitzjames; trained with Auguste Vestris and Philippe Taglioni. ❧ Performed at Paris Opéra (1832–46); replaced Marie Taglioni in *Robert le Diable* and *Le Dieu et la Bayadère;* created roles in *La Revolte du Serail* (1836) and *La Jolie Fille du Gand.*

FITZJAMES, Natalie (b. 1819). French ballet dancer. Born Natalie Fizan, 1819, in Paris, France; probably a sister of Louise Fitzjames; death date unknown. ❧ Trained at ballet school of Paris Opéra and graduated into company (1837); danced featured roles in numerous works including her debut in *Les Mohicans* (1837) and the premiere of *Giselle* (1841); was 1st dancer to take *Giselle* to Florence, Italy; danced in additional works at Opéra including in Aumer's *La Somnambule* and the role of Fenella in *La Muette di Portici,* a part with which she toured Italy and US.

FITZMAURICE, Mrs. *See Hippisley, E.*

FITZOSBERN, Emma. *See Emma of Norfolk (d. 1100).*

FITZROBERT, Amicia (d. 1225). Countess of Hertford, countess of Gloucester. Name variations: Amicia of Gloucester. Died 1225; dau. of William Fitzrobert, 2nd earl of Gloucester, and Hawise Beaumont (dau. of Robert, 2nd earl of Leicester); m. Richard de Clare, 4th earl of Hertford, about 1180; children: Gilbert de Clare, 5th earl of Hertford, 1st earl of Gloucester (born c. 1180); Richard also known as Roger de Clare; Matilda de Clare (who m. William de Braose and Rhys Gryg).

FITZROY, Charlotte (1664–1717). Countess of Lichfield. Name variations: Charlotte Lee. Born 1664; died 1717 (some sources cite 1718); illeg. dau. of Charles II, king of England, and Barbara Villiers (c. 1641–1709); m. Edward Henry Lee, earl of Lichfield, in 1677 (died 1716).

FITZROY, Isabel (1726–1782). Marquise of Hertford. Born 1726; died 1782; dau. of Charles Fitzroy, 2nd duke of Grafton, and Henrietta Somerset; granddau. of Barbara Villiers; m. Francis Seymour, 1st marquis of Hertford; children: Hugh Seymour (1759–1801).

FITZROY, Mary (c. 1519–1557). Duchess of Richmond. Name variations: Mary Howard. Born c. 1519; died 1557; dau. of Thomas Howard, 2nd or 3rd duke of Norfolk, and Elizabeth Stafford; m. Henry Fitzroy, duke of Richmond, 1533 (died 1536). ❖ Married Henry Fitzroy, duke of Richmond (c. 1533) but never lived with him (he died of poisoning in 1536, rumored to have been administered by Anne Boleyn and her brother); gave evidence incriminating her brother, poet Henry Howard, earl of Surrey, on charges of treason, for conspiring to usurp the throne and having encouraged her to become King Henry VIII's mistress (1546). ❖ See also *Women in World History.*

FITZSIMONS, Lorna (1967—). English politician and member of Parliament. Born Lorna Fitzsimons, Aug 6, 1967; m. Stephen Benedict Cooney, 2000. ❖ Representing Labour, elected to House of Commons for Rochdale (1997, 2001); lost election (2005).

FITZWILLIAM, Fanny Elizabeth (1801–1854). English actress. Born Fanny Elizabeth Copeland in Dover, England, 1801; died in London, Nov 11, 1854; dau. of a theater manager; m. Edward Fitzwilliam (actor). ❖ Was a child actress in Dover, where father managed a theater; appeared at Haymarket (1817); performed at Drury Lane (1821–22) and leased the Sadler's Wells (1832); visited US (1837), appearing to great acclaim in *The Country Girl;* on return to England, appeared in *Green Bushes* and *Flowers of the Forest* at height of fame.

FLACCILLA (c. 355–386). Roman empress. Name variations: Aelia Flavia Flaccilla; Flacilla; named "Augusta" (empress), probably c. 383. Born c. 355 in Spain; died in 386 or 387 in Thrace at a spa where she had retired to take the medicinal waters; aunt of Nebridius; became 1st wife of Theodosius I the Great, emperor of Rome (r. 379–395), between 376 and 378; children: Pulcheria (c. 376–385); Arcadius, emperor of Rome (r. in the East, 395–408); Honorius emperor of Rome (r. in the West, 395–423). ❖ Born and bred in Spain of aristocratic parents whose families had long held Roman citizenship, probably met and married Theodosius I when he went into temporary Spanish exile as a result of the political fall of his father (376–78); had already given birth to Pulcheria and Arcadius by the time she made her way to Constantinople with husband; was a follower of the Nicene Creed whose faith reinforced that of her husband in his war to keep the forces supporting the Arian interpretation of Christianity at bay; actively cared for the sick, orphaned (especially virgin girls), widowed, poor, and hungry, Christian actions that helped to legitimize her husband's authority; was especially praised for her *philandria* (wifely love) and thus became a kind of model for the age's "ideal woman"; was so popular that Theodosius consciously brought her image more into the limelight; was elevated to the status of Augusta (Empress, 383), the 1st woman to hold this title since Fausta (d. 324). Following death of Flaccilla, Theodosius I married Galla. ❖ See also *Women in World History.*

FLACCILLA (d. 431). Roman noblewoman. Name variations: Flacilla. Died in childhood in 431; dau. of Theodosius II, East Roman emperor, and Eudocia (c. 401–460).

FLACHMEIER, Laurie (1959—). American volleyball player. Born Jan 28, 1957, in US. ❖ At Los Angeles Olympics, won a silver medal in team competition (1984).

FLACK, Roberta (1937—). African-American jazz singer and pianist. Born Feb 10, 1937, in Black Mountain (Asheville), North Carolina; dau. of a church organist; Howard University, BA in music; m. Steve Novosel, 1965 (div. 1972). ❖ Best known for the ballad, "Killing Me Softly with His Song" (1973), had 1st major hit with "The First Time Ever I Saw Your Face" (1972), which was included in the soundtrack of the film, *Play Misty for Me;* began career singing and playing jazz in a Washington nightclub; signed with Atlantic Records; sang hit duets with Donny Hathaway, "Where Is the Love?" (1972), "The Closer I Get To You" (1978), "You Are My Heaven" (1980) and "Come Ye Disconsolate," then toured with Peabo Bryson and had hit duet "Tonight, I Celebrate My Love" (1983); other songs include "Feel Like Makin' Love" (1974) and (with Maxi Priest) "Set the Night to Music" (1991); also sang the theme song "Together through the Years" for the tv series "The Hogan Family"; albums include *Will You Love Me Tomorrow, Uh Uh Ooh Ooh, You Make Me Feel Brand New, Bustin' Loose, Chapter Two, Quiet Fire, Blue Lights in the Basement, Live & More, Oasis, Roberta* and *Holiday.*

FLAGG, Elise (1951—). American ballet dancer. Born Dec 23, 1951, in Detroit, Michigan; sister of Laura Flagg (ballet dancer). ❖ Danced with New York City Ballet (1960s–70s) where she was featured in Balanchine's *Western Symphony, Ivesiana* and *A Midsummer Night's*

Dream; performed in Richard Tanner's *Octuor* and in Taras' *The Song of the Nightingale* at Stravinsky Festival (1972).

FLAGG, Fannie (1941—). American actress, comedian and novelist. Born Patricia Neal, Sept 21, 1941, in Birmingham, Alabama; studied acting at the Pittsburgh Playhouse; never married. ❖ Began career as a writer for tv's "Candid Camera" (1964), but was soon given a regular role in front of the camera by Alan Funt (1964–69); was frequently a guest on "Match Game" (1970s); on Broadway, was featured in *The Best Little Whorehouse in Texas* (1980); came to prominence as a writer with her bestselling novel, *Fried Green Tomatoes at the Whistle Stop Cafe* (1987), for which she wrote the screenplay with Carol Sobieski; also wrote *Coming Attractions* (1981), *Daisy Fay and the Miracle Man* (1992) and *Welcome to the World, Baby Girl!* (1998).

FLAGSTAD, Kirsten (1895–1962). Norwegian soprano. Born Kirsten Malfrid Flagstad, July 12, 1895, in Hamar, near Oslo, Norway; died in Oslo, Dec 7, 1962; dau. of Michael (violinist and conductor) and Marie (Nielsen) Flagstad (organist, pianist, and operatic coach); sister of Karen Marie Flagstad Orkel (opera singer); took private singing lessons from Ellen Schytte-Jacobsen in Oslo and Dr. Gillis Bratt in Stockholm; m. Sigurd Hall, 1919 (div. 1930); m. Henry Johansen, 1930; children: (1st m.) Else-Marie Hall (b. 1920). ❖ Considered the greatest Wagnerian soprano of mid-20th century, made debut as Nuri in d'Albert's *Tiefland* at the National Theater in Oslo (1913), where she also sang her 1st Isolde (1932); sang in Bayreuth (1933–34); made US debut at Metropolitan Opera (Feb 1935); returned US after the war; gave farewell performance at Covent Garden with *Tristan* (1951), at the Met in Gluck's *Alceste* (1952), at the Mermaid Theater in London (1953) and at Oslo (Dec 1953); made numerous recordings with Edwin McArthur and Gerald Moore; served as director of the Norwegian State Opera (1958–60). Appeared in *Les Choches de Corneville, En hellig Aften, Vaarnat, Der Evangelimann, I Pagliacci, Der Zigeunerbaron, Die Schöne Galathee, Die Nürnberger Puppe, Abu Hassan, La Belle Hélène, Die Lustigen Weiber von Windsor, Die Zauberflöte, Otello, Un Ballo in maschera, Das höllisch Gold, La Fanciulla del West, Orphée aux enfers, Boccaccio, Carmen, Die Fledermaus, Les Brigands, Sjömandsbruden, Faust, Orfeo ed Euridice, Der Freischütz, Saul og David, Aïda, La Bohème, Tosca, Lohengrin, La Rondine, Die Meistersinger, Jonny spielt auf, Schwanda der Dudelsackpfeifer, Rodelinda, Tristan und Isolde, Die Walküre, Götterdämmerung, Tannhauser, Fidelio, Parsifal, Siegfried, Der fliegender Holländer, Oberon, Alceste* and *Dido and Aneas.* ❖ See also Edwin McArthur, *Flagstad* (Knopf, 1965); and *Women in World History.*

FLAHAUT or FLAHAULT, countess of.
See Souza-Botelho, Adélaïde-Marie-émilie-Filleul, Marquise of (1761–1836).
See Elphinstone, Margaret Mercer (1788–1867).

FLAHERTY, Frances Hubbard (c. 1886–1972). American photographer. Born Frances Hubbard in Cambridge, Massachusetts, c. 1886; died in Dummerston, Vermont, 1972; graduate of Bryn Mawr College, 1905; m. Robert Joseph Flaherty (prospector and supervisor for Canadian Grand Trunk Railway and motion-picture director), Nov 12, 1914 (died 1951); children: Barbara Flaherty (b. 1916); Francis Flaherty (b. 1917); Monica Flaherty (b. 1920). ❖ Assisted on many of husband's films, including the silent *Nanook of the North* (1924), about the life of the Eskimo (Inuit), the 1st documentary that attempted to interpret the lives of its subjects; was co-editor on the film *Moana* (1926), a study of life in the South Seas; also served as photographer on *Man of Aran* (1934) and co-writer of *Louisiana Story* (1948). ❖ See also *Women in World History.*

FLAHERTY, Mary (1953—). Irish politician. Born May 1953, in Dublin, Ireland; m. Alexis Fitzgerald (lord mayor of Dublin); children: 4 sons. ❖ Representing Fine Gael, elected to the 22nd–27th Dáil for Dublin North West (1981–97); was minister of state at the Dept. of Social Welfare and minister of state at the Dept. of Health, with responsibility for Poverty and Family Affairs (1981–82); later focused on welfare of Irish prisoners in Britain.

FLANAGAN, Hallie (1889–1969). American theatrical director and producer. Name variations: Hallie Flanagan Davis. Born Hallie Ferguson in Redfield, South Dakota, April 27, 1889; died in Beacon, NY, July 23, 1969; dau. of Frederic (traveling salesman) and Louisa (Fischer) Ferguson; graduate of Grinnell College, 1911; studied with George Pierce Baker at Harvard theater workshop; m. Murray Flanagan, Dec 25, 1912 (died 1917); m. Philip Davis, April 27, 1934 (died 1940); children: (1st m.) Jack (1914–1922) and Frederic; (stepchildren) Joanne, Jack, and Helen. ❖ Experimental and innovative director, producer, and teacher of American theater, taught English and theater at Grinnell College (1920–25); taught playwriting and dramatic production at Vassar College (1925–34); while serving as director of the Federal Theater of Works Project Administration (1935–39), created innovative and provocative entertainment during an era when political sentiment was shifting toward a conservatism that disparaged liberal expression in the arts; was theatrical director at Vassar College (1940–42); served as dean at Smith College (1942–52); writings include *Shifting Scenes of the Modern European Theatre* (1928), *Arena* (1940), and *Dynamo* (1943). ❖ See also Joanne Bentley, *Hallie Flanagan: A Life In the American Theatre* (Knopf, 1988); and *Women in World History*.

FLANAGAN, Jeanne (1957—). American rower. Born May 8, 1957; attended Florida Tech. ❖ At Los Angeles Olympics, won a gold medal in coxed eights (1984).

FLANAGAN, Sinéad (1878–1975). Irish actress and wife of the 1st president of Ireland. Name variations: Sinead Flanagan; Sinéad de Valera; Sinéad Bean de Valera (means Sinéad, the wife of de Valera). Born Sinéad Flanagan, June 3, 1878; died Jan 7, 1975; attended Irish College, 1909; m. Eamon de Valera (1882–1975, 1st president of Ireland), Jan 1910 (died 1975); children: 2 daughters, Emer de Valera and Máirín de Valera (b. April 1912, professor of Botany at Galway University); and 5 sons, éamonn, Ruairí, Terry, Vivion, and Brian. ❖ Popular and politically active member of the Gaelic League, was one of Eamon de Valera's teachers; married him (Jan 8, 1910); soon after he became head of the Irish government (1932), began to write for children in Irish and English; was unassuming and avoided the limelight. ❖ See also *Women in World History*.

FLANDERS, countess of.
See Martel, Judith (c. 844–?).
See Elfthrith (d. 929).
See Adela Capet (c. 1010–1079).
See Eleanor of Normandy (fl. 1000s).
See Gertrude of Saxony (fl. 1070).
See Joan of Montferrat.
See Margaret of Alsace (c. 1135–1194).
See Teresa of Portugal (1157–1218).
See Maria of Champagne (c. 1180–1203).
See Johanna of Flanders (c. 1200–1244).
See Margaret of Flanders (1202–1280).
See Yolande of Burgundy (1248–1280).
See Margaret of Brabant (1323–1368).
See Margaret of Flanders (1350–1405).
See Marie of Hohenzollern-Sigmaringen (1845–1912).

FLANNER, Janet (1892–1978). American novelist and journalist. Name variations: (pen name) Genêt. Born Mar 13, 1892, in Indianapolis, Indiana; died Nov 7, 1978, in New York, NY; dau. of William Francis Flanner and Mary-Ellen (Hockett) Flanner; attended University of Chicago, 1912–14; m. William Lane Rehm, April 25, 1918 (div. 1926); no children. ❖ Writing under the name Genêt, chronicled the history of Europe for 50 years in her fortnightly "Letter from Paris" for *The New Yorker* magazine; served as assistant drama editor, *Indianapolis Star* (1917–18); moved to New York with husband (1918); moved to Greece with lover Solita Solano (1921); settled in Paris (1922); published *The Cubical City* (1926); published 1st "Letter from Paris" in *The New Yorker* (Oct 10, 1925); lived in New York (1939–44); returned to France (Nov 1944); broadcast for the Blue Network (later ABC) from Paris (1945–46); wrote eloquent, incisive prose, loved women and France, admired traditional European civilization, and hated war and the men who made it; writings collected in *Men and Monuments* (1957), *Paris Journal, 1944–1955* (1965), *Paris Journal, 1956–1964* (1988), *Paris Journal, 1965–1970* (1988) and *Paris Was Yesterday, 1925–1939* (1975). Awarded Legion of Honor (1947); received National Book Award for *Paris Journal, 1944–1965* (1966). ❖ See also Brenda Wineapple, *Genêt: A Biography of Janet Flanner* (Ticknor & Fields, 1989); *Darlinghissima: Letters to a Friend* (ed. by Natalia Danesi Murray, 1985); and *Women in World History*.

FLANNERY, Judy (1939–1997). American triathlete. Name variations: Judith M. Flannery. Born Dec 24, 1939; killed by an automobile while on a bike-training ride, near Poolesville, Maryland, April 2, 1997; children: 5. ❖ Took up running at age 38; in the triathlon, won 6 national age-group titles (1991–96) and 4 World titles (1992, 1994, 1995, 1996); was Columbia Triathlon Master's champion (1989–96) and Duathlon

World champion (1991, 1993–96). ❖ See also (documentary) *Judy's Time*.

FLAT, Pamela (1968—). *See Bileck, Pamela.*

FLAUTRE, Hélène (1958—). French politician. Born July 29, 1958, in Bapaume, France. ❖ Mathematics teacher (1980–92); became a member of the Greens' National Inter-Regional Council (1991); representing Group of the Greens/European Free Alliance, elected to 5th European Parliament (1999–2004).

FLAVIA (d. 324). *See Fausta.*

FLAVIA DOMITILLA (fl. 39). Roman noblewoman. Fl. 39; dau. of Flavius Liberalis (Roman freedman) and a mother who was the dau. of a Roman freedman; m. Titus Flavius Vespasianus (Vespasian), general and emperor of Rome (r. 69–79 CE), in 39; children: Flavia Domitilla (fl. 60); Titus, Roman emperor (r. 79–81); Domitian (51–96), Roman emperor (r. 81–96); grandchildren: Flavia Domitilla (c. 60–96).

FLAVIA DOMITILLA (fl. 60). Roman noblewoman. Fl. around 60; dau. of Flavia Domitilla (fl. 39) and Titus Flavius Vespasianus (Vespasian), general and Roman emperor (r. 69–79 CE); m. Q. Petillius Cerialis Caesius Rufus known as Petillius (partisan of Vespasian), by 60; children: (stepchildren) 2 sons, Rufus and Firmus; daughter Flavia Domitilla (c. 60–96).

FLAVIA DOMITILLA (c. 60–96). Roman noblewoman. Born around 60; executed in 96; dau. of Q. Petillius Cerialis Caesius Rufus, known as Petillius, and Flavia Domitilla (fl. 60 CE); m. T. Flavius Clemens; children: sons T. Flavius Domitianus Caesar and T. Flavius Vespasianus Caesar. ❖ The granddaughter of one emperor (Vespasian) and niece of two others (Titus and Domitian), was about 10 when family began its imperial odyssey; married T. Flavius Clemens, probably early in the reign of Domitian (r. 81–96), which helped to consolidate Flavian power, because Clemens was the grandson of Vespasian's older brother; when the increasingly paranoid Domitian learned of her husband's intellectual interest in an "atheistic" religious doctrine, was exiled to the small island of Pandateria while husband was executed. Following her execution (96), Stephanus, one of her stewards, killed Domitian. ❖ See also *Women in World History*.

FLAVIA VALERIA CONSTANTIA (c. 293–?). *See Constantia.*

FLAVIGNY, Marie de, Comtesse d'Agoult (1805–1876). *See Agoult, Marie d'.*

FLEBBE, Beulah Marie (1876–1970). *See Dix, Beulah Marie.*

FLEESON, Doris (1901–1970). American journalist. Born in Sterling, Kansas, May 20, 1901; died Aug 1, 1970; dau. of William (manager of clothing store) and Helen (Tebbe) Fleeson; University of Kansas, BA, 1923; m. John O'Donnell (political reporter), Sept 28, 1930 (div. 1942); m. Dan A. Kimball (corporate president and former secretary of the navy), Aug 1958 (died July 30, 1970); children: (1st m.) Doris Kimball (b. 1932). ❖ One of the 1st women to gain respect as a Washington political columnist, initially worked as city editor for the *Great Neck* (Long Island) *News;* landed a job as reporter for *New York Daily News,* where she covered crimes, trials, and scandals; won a coveted assignment at the Albany bureau, where she began the political reporting that would become her stock in trade; with 1st husband, was assigned to the *Daily News'* newly opened Washington office (1933), where they co-wrote a provocative political column called *Capital Stuff;* left the paper to become a roving war correspondent for *Woman's Home Companion* (1943), covering the Italian and French fronts during World War II in a series of 10 articles (1943–44); after the war, returned to Washington and wrote a syndicated column for 20 years which was carried in over 100 newspapers; covered the administrations of 5 presidents and never hesitated to criticize or offer advice, her barbs fairly and evenly distributed; sponsored 1st African-American applicant for membership in the Women's National Press Club (1953). ❖ See also *Women in World History*.

FLEETWOOD, Bridget (1624–c. 1660). *See Cromwell, Bridget.*

FLEETWOOD MAC.
See McVie, Christine.
See Nicks, Stevie.

FLEISCHER, Leontine (1889–1974). *See Sagan, Leontine.*

FLEISCHER, Ottilie (1911—). German track-and-field athlete. Name variations: Tilly Fleischer; Tilly Fleischer-Grothe. Born Oct 1911 in

Germany. ❖ Won a bronze medal at Los Angeles Olympics (1932) and a gold medal at Berlin Olympics (1936), both in javelin throw.

FLEISCHER, Tilly (1911—). *See Fleischer, Ottilie.*

FLEISCHMANN, Torrance (1949—). American equestrian. Born July 30, 1949, in US. ❖ At Los Angeles Olympics, won a gold medal in team 3-day event (1984).

FLEISCHMANN, Trude (1895–1990). German-born photographer. Born 1895 in Vienna, Austria, into a well-to-do Viennese-Jewish family; died in Brewster, NY, 1990; studied art history in Paris. ❖ Apprenticed in a Vienna portrait studio before opening her own studio (1920), specializing in portraits of such luminaries as Katharine Cornell, Hedy Lamarr, Bruno Walter, and Tilly Losch; after Germany annexed Austria (1938), moved to US (1940); set up a studio in New York City, where she continued to photograph celebrities, including Lotte Lehmann, Albert Einstein, and Arturo Toscanini; also did fashion spreads for *Vogue* and other publications; retired (1969), moving to Lugano, Switzerland.

FLEISSER, Marieluise (1901–1974). German playwright. Name variations: Fleißer. Born Luise Marie Fleisser in Ingolstadt, Bavaria, Nov 23, 1901; died in Ingolstadt, Feb 1, 1974; dau. of Heinrich Fleisser (jewelry maker and ironmonger) and Anna (Schmidt) Fleisser; sister of Heinrich, Anny, Ella and Jetty Fleisser; attended University of Munich; m. Josef (Bepp) Haindl (tobacco-shop owner), 1935 (died 1958). ❖ Writer, confidante of Bertolt Brecht, and controversial innovator in the area of the *Volksstück* (folkplay), who is now viewed as one of the most important female playwrights of the 20th century; produced a small but original body of work—particularly the plays *Fegefeuer in Ingolstadt* (*Purgatory in Ingolstadt*, 1926) and *Pioniere in Ingolstadt* (*Soldiers in Ingolstadt*, 1929)—that in recent years has been critically reevaluated; was one of the most discussed women writers in the Weimar Republic; saw her books burned by the Nazis and was punished with a publication ban; after a decades-long silence that persisted even after 1945, resumed writing (1960s), enjoying in final years a public recognition; other writings include the novel *Mehlreisende Frieda Geier* (*Frieda Geier, Traveling Flour Saleswoman*, 1929), the Bavarian-dialect comedy, *Der starke Stamm* (*Of Sturdy Stock*) and her collected works (*Gesammelten Werke*) which appeared under the Suhrkamp imprint to enthusiastic reviews (1972). ❖ See also autobiographical story, "A Quite Ordinary Antechamber to Hell" (1963); and *Women in World History.*

FLEMING, Alice (1882–1952). American actress. Born Aug 9, 1882, in Brooklyn, NY; died Dec 6, 1952, in New York, NY. ❖ Played leads for the Percy G. Williams Stock Co.; Broadway appearances include *When We Are Married, Some Daddy, The Pelican* and *One More Honeymoon;* appeared in small roles in over 45 films.

FLEMING, Amalia (1912–1986). Greek bacteriologist and political activist. Name variations: Lady Fleming. Born Amalia Koutsouris, 1912, in Constantinople, Ottoman Empire (now Istanbul, Turkey); died in Athens, Greece, Feb 26, 1986; dau. of Harikios Koutsouris (physician); studied medicine at University of Athens, with a specialty in bacteriology; studied bacteriology at St. Mary's Hospital, London, 1946; m. Manoli Vourekis (architect, div. 1946); m. Sir Alexander Fleming (discoverer of penicillin), 1953 (died Mar 11, 1955); children: (stepson) Robert. ❖ During WWII, joined resistance movement with 1st husband, hiding British and Greek officers and arranging their escape routes to Egypt; arrested by the Italians, was sentenced to death and served 6 months, before advancing British troops caused the Germans to abandon the jail; was the 1st woman physician to work in Alexander Fleming's laboratory (1946); became Lady Fleming when she married Sir Alexander Fleming, discoverer of penicillin (1953); following marriage (1953), resumed joint research work at the Wright-Fleming Institute; actively opposed the military dictatorship that ruled Greece (1967–74); was arrested, tried, and briefly imprisoned (1971), then expelled from the country; continued activities from exile in UK; returned to Greece (1974) to become highly visible in that nation's newly revived democracy; elected to Greek Parliament (1977) and re-elected (1981 and 1985); was also a delegate to the Council of Europe Assembly and chosen 1st chair of the Greek chapter of Amnesty International. ❖ See also *Women in World History.*

FLEMING, countess of (1746–1835). *See Czartoryska, Isabella.*

FLEMING, Dorothy (1899–1985). *See Buchanan, Dorothy.*

FLEMING, Jane (fl. 1550s). English royal mistress. Fl. in 1550s; mistress of Henry II (1519–1559), king of France (r. 1547–1559); children: (with Henry) Henri (b. 1551), Grand Prieur.

FLEMING, Margaret (1803–1811). British writer. Name variations: Marjory, Marjorie, or Marjarie. Born Jan 15, 1803; died at age eight of measles on Dec 19, 1811; dau. of James Fleming of Kirkcaldy, Scotland. ❖ Though she lived only 8 years, is remembered for her charming diary, which was edited and published by Dr. John Brown, as *Pet Marjorie: A Story of Child Life Fifty Years Ago.* ❖ See also *Women in World History.*

FLEMING, May Agnes (1840–1880). Canadian novelist and short-story writer. Name variations: Cousin May Carlton. Born May Early 1840 in New Brunswick, Canada; died of Bright's disease, 1880. ❖ First Canadian woman to achieve success as author of popular romances, wrote *La Masque; or, The Midnight Queen* (1863), *A Mad Marriage* (1875), *Kate Danton; or, Captain Danton's Daughters* (1877), *The Heir of Charlton* (1878) and *Lost for a Woman* (1880), among others.

FLEMING, Mina Stevens (1857–1911). *See Fleming, Williamina Paton.*

FLEMING, Nancy (c. 1941—). Miss America. Born c. 1941 in Montague, Michigan; children: 2. ❖ Named Miss America (1961), representing Michigan; was certified as a University of California Master Gardener, working on habitat restoration and non-toxic gardening alternatives; hosted "Sewing Today" on PBS. ❖ See also Frank Deford, *There She Is* (Viking, 1971).

FLEMING, Peggy (1948—). American figure skater. Born July 27, 1948, in San Jose, California; m. Gregory Jenkins (dermatologist), 1970. ❖ By age 16, had won the 1st of 5 successive US figure skating championships; captured and held the World title for 3 years running (1966–68); won a gold medal at Grenoble Olympics (1968), the 1st American to do so; began competing professionally; starred in several tv specials and major ice shows and continued to serve as a network sports commentator. ❖ See also Elizabeth Van Steenwyck, *Peggy Fleming: Cameo of a Champion* (McGraw-Hill, 1978); Stephanie Young and Bruce Curtis *Peggy Fleming: Portrait of an Ice Skater* (Avon, 1984); and *Women in World History.*

FLEMING, Renée (1959—). American opera singer. Born Feb 14, 1959, in Indiana, Pennsylvania; grew up in Rochester, NY; dau. of music teachers; attended State University of New York at Potsdam and Eastman School of Music; studied at Juilliard; m. Richard Lee Ross (actor), 1989 (div. 2000); children: Amelia and Sage. ❖ Made professional debut in *The Abduction from the Seraglio* (1986); came to prominence as Contessa in *Figaro* (1988) and as Desdemona in *Otello;* won Grammy for Best Classic Vocal Performance for *The Beautiful Voice* (1998); also recorded *Signatures,* among others; appeared in title role of *Rodelinda* at the Met (2004); sang on the soundtrack of *The Lord of the Rings;* wrote *The Inner Voice: The Making of a Singer.*

FLEMING, Rhonda (1922—). American actress. Name variations: Rhonda Fleming Mann. Born Marilyn Louis, Aug 10, 1922, in Hollywood, California; m. Thomas Lane (div. 1948); m. Dr. Lew Morell, 1952 (div. 1956); m. Lang Jeffries, 1960 (div. 1961); m. Hall Bartlett (producer), 1966 (div. 1971); m. Ted Mann (movie theater magnate, owner of Hollywood's Chinese Theatre), 1977 (died 2001). ❖ Appeared in supporting roles in such films *In Old Oklahoma, When Strangers Marry, Since You Went Away, Spellbound, The Spiral Staircase, Adventure Island* and *Out of the Past;* starred in *A Connecticut Yankee in King Arthur's Court, The Eagle and the Hawk, Cry Danger, Those Redheads from Seattle, Yankee Pasha, Queen of Babylon, Slightly Scarlet, While the City Sleeps, Gunfight at O.K. Corral, The Buster Keaton Story, Home before Dark* and *The Crowded Sky,* among others. Established the Rhonda Fleming Mann Resource Center for Women for Cancer at UCLA.

FLEMING, Susan (1908–2002). *See Marx, Susan Fleming.*

FLEMING, Williamina Paton (1857–1911). Scottish-American astronomer. Name variations: Mina Stevens Fleming. Born Williamina Paton Stevens, May 15, 1857, in Dundee, Scotland; died of pneumonia, May 21, 1911, in Boston, Massachusetts; dau. of Robert (artisan) and Mary (Walker) Stevens; attended Dundee public schools, where she also taught, 1871–76; m. James Orr Fleming, May 26, 1877; children: Edward Pickering Fleming (b. Oct 6, 1879). ❖ One of the most eminent women scientists of late 19th century, discovered the stars of extremely high density known as "white dwarfs" and became the 1st American woman elected to the Royal Astronomical Society; immigrated to America, where she was abandoned by husband while pregnant (1878);

took a job as a household servant in home of Edward C. Pickering (1878); hired as temporary employee at Harvard College Observatory by Pickering (1879); made a permanent member of his research staff (1881); began Draper Memorial classification project (1886); developed improved stellar spectra classification system published in the "Draper Catalogue of Stellar Spectra" (1890); spoke about women's work in astronomy at Chicago World's Fair (1893); in 1st board appointment of a woman at Harvard, made observatory's curator of astronomical photographs (1898); helped co-found the Astronomical and Astrophysical Society (1898); elected to Royal Astronomical Society (1906); published study of variable stars (1907); discovered the "white dwarf" stars (1910); was starred in 1st edition of *American Men of Science;* during 30-year career, discovered 10 novae, 59 nebulae, and the "white dwarfs"; also established the 1st photographic standards of magnitude for the measurement of the variable brightness of stars, became the curator of astronomical photographs at the Harvard College Observatory and the 1st woman at Harvard to receive a corporation appointment. ❖ See also *Women in World History.*

FLEMMING, countess of (1746–1835). See *Czartoryska, Isabella.*

FLEMMING, Marialiese (1933—). Austrian politician. Born Dec 16, 1933, in Wiener Neustadt, Austria. ❖ Managed a film company (1973–91); was a member of the Vienna Landtag and municipal council (1973–87) and federal minister for the Environment, Youth and Family Affairs (1987–91); served as federal chair of the Austrian women's movement (1984–91) and president of the European Union of Women; as a member of the European People's Party (Christian Democrats) and European Democrats, elected to 4th and 5th European Parliament (1994–99, 1999–2004).

FLEMMING, Mary (fl. 1540s). Scottish paramour. Name variations: Lady Flemming, Madame de Flemming. Had liaison with Henry II, king of France; children: a boy, known as the Bastard of Angoulême. ❖ Was an attendant for the child Mary Stuart, future queen of Scots; possibly encouraged to seduce the king by political rivals of Diane de Poitiers in an effort to minimize de Poitier's influence; made the mistake of bragging about her coup, causing her removal from court. ❖ See also *Women in World History.*

FLENNIKEN, Carol Sorenson (1942—). See *Sorenson, Carol.*

FLESCH, Colette (1937—). Luxemburg politician. Born April 16, 1937, in Dudelange, Luxemburg. ❖ Served as mayor (1970–89) and deputy mayor of Luxemburg (2000—), secretary-general and chair of the Democratic Party (1980–89), director-general at the European Commission (1990–99), and president of the European Federation of Liberal, Democratic, and Reform parties; was a member of the Luxemburg Chamber of Deputies and European Parliament (1969–80, 1984–90); served as vice-president of the Government, foreign minister, minister for External Trade and Cooperation, minister for Economic Affairs and Small and Medium-Sized Businesses, minister of Justice (1980–84); as a member of the European Liberal, Democrat and Reform Party, elected to 5th European Parliament (1999–2004).

FLESHER, Helen (1871–1947). See *MacGill, Helen.*

FLESSEL, Laura (1971—). French fencer. Name variations: Laura Flessel-Colovic; (nickname) La Guêpe (the wasp). Born Nov 6, 1971, in Pointe à Pitre, Guadeloupe; m. a French journalist, 1996. ❖ Won the Pan American championships (1991–92, 1994); won gold medals for indiv. and team at Atlanta Olympics (1996), in the inaugural épée categories; won a bronze medal for épée indiv. at Sydney Olympics (2000); won a silver medal for épée indiv. and a bronze medal for épée team at Athens Olympics (2004); won 3 World championships (1998–99).

FLETCHER, Alice Cunningham (1838–1923). American anthropologist. Born Alice Cunningham Fletcher, Mar 15, 1838, in Havana, Cuba; died April 6, 1923, at home in Washington, DC; dau. of Thomas (lawyer) and Lucia Adeline (Jenks) Fletcher; attended Brooklyn Female Academy (later Packer Collegiate Institute); never married; no children. ❖ Social scientist who did some of the 1st ethnographic field work among Native Americans, primarily the Omaha, and acted as government agent on the Indian allotment program; began educating herself and lecturing in anthropology (1878); launched ethnographic field work among the Omahas (1881); joined Lake Mohonk Conference of the Friends of the Indian (1883); began work for US government on allotting land on the Omaha, Winnebago, and Nez Perce Reservation (1884); carried on survey for the Senate report on Indian Education and Civilization issued 1888; received the Thaw fellowship in anthropology

at Harvard University and started to devote full time to the science (1890); elected to 1st term as president of Woman's Anthropological Society (1890); informally adopted Francis La Flesche (1891); worked on the World's Columbian Exposition (1893); was founding member of American Anthropological Association (1902); served as president of the Anthropological Society of Washington (1903) and American Folklore Society (1905); was presiding officer of the anthropology section of American Academy of Science; served as chair of American Committee of Archaeological Institute of America (1907); elected vice-president of American Anthropological Association (1908); continued active association with Archaeological Institute of America until 1912; in last 12 years of life, served mostly in the role of a research associate to Francis La Flesche, as his own career as an ethnographer matured. ❖ See also Joan Mark, *A Stranger in Her Native Land* (U. of Nebraska Press, 1988); and *Women in World History.*

FLETCHER, Ann (1833–1903). See *Jackson, Ann Fletcher.*

FLETCHER, Caroline (1906—). American diver. Born Nov 22, 1906. ❖ At Paris Olympics, won a bronze medal in springboard (1924).

FLETCHER, Cleva (d. 1967). See *Bush, Frances Cleveland.*

FLETCHER, Chris (1955—). New Zealand politician. Born Chris Lees, Jan 25, 1955, in Papakura, NZ; m. Angus Fletcher, 1977. ❖ Elected National MP for Eden (1990); elected mayor of Auckland.

FLETCHER, Jennie (1890–1968). British swimmer. Name variations: Jenny Fletcher. Born in Great Britain on Mar 19, 1890; died 1968. ❖ Won a bronze medal in the 100-meter freestyle and a gold medal in the 4x100-meter freestyle relay at Stockholm Olympics (1912). Inducted into International Swimming Hall of Fame (1971).

FLETCHER, Louise (1934—). American actress. Born July 22, 1934, in Birmingham, Alabama; dau. of Robert Fletcher (Episcopal minister) and Estelle Fletcher (both parents were deaf); m. Jerry Bick (film producer), 1962 (div. 1978); children: 2 sons. ❖ Began career on episodic tv; took 10-year, child-raising hiatus before making screen debut in Robert Altman's *Thieves Like Us* (1974); other films include *The Cheap Detective, Exorcist II, Mama Dracula, Strange Invaders, Firestarter, Brainstorm, Flowers in the Attic* and *Shadowzone;* on tv, appeared as Kai Winn on "StarTrek: Deep Space Nine" (1993) and Nora Bloom on "VR5" (1995); active in the cause of civil rights for the deaf. Won Oscar for performance as Nurse Ratched in *One Flew Over the Cuckoo's Nest* (1975) and Emmy for "Picket Fences" (1992).

FLETCHER, Maria (c. 1942—). Miss America. Born Maria Beale Fletcher c. 1942. ❖ Was a Rockette at Radio City Music Hall; named Miss America (1962), representing North Carolina. ❖ See also Frank Deford, *There She Is* (Viking, 1971).

FLETCHER, Mrs. Maria Jane (1812–1880). See *Jewsbury, Maria Jane.*

FLETT, Adelaide (1909–2000). See *McDougall, Adelaide.*

FLEURY, Catherine (1966—). French judoka. Born June 18, 1966. ❖ At Barcelona Olympics, won a gold medal in half-middleweight 61 kg (1992).

FLEXNER, Anne Crawford (1874–1955). American playwright, screenwriter, and novelist. Born Anne Crawford, June 27, 1874, in Georgetown, Kentucky; died Jan 11, 1955, in Providence, Rhode Island; m. Abraham Flexner. ❖ Plays include *Miranda of the Balcony, Mrs. Wiggs of the Cabbage Patch* (adapted for stage and screen from novel of Alice Hegan Rice), *A Lucky Star, The Marriage Game* (adapted from her own novel), *Wanted-an Alibi, The Blue Pearl* (also wrote screenplay), *All Soul's Eve* (also wrote screenplay), *Bravo! Maria* and *Aged 26* (adapted from her own novel).

FLEXNER, Jennie M. (1882–1944). American librarian. Born in Louisville, Kentucky, 1882; died 1944; dau. of Jacob (physician) and Rosa (Maas) Flexner; graduate of Western Reserve Library School. ❖ Headed circulation department at Louisville Free Public Library (1912–28), playing a major role in the development of the library and its work within the community; joined New York Public Library (1928), where she created and ran the institution's 1st readers' advisory service (1929–44). ❖ See also *Women in World History.*

FLIKKE, Julia Otteson (1879–1965). American superintendent of Army Nurse Corps. Born Julia Otteson, Mar 16, 1879, in Viroqua, Wisconsin; died Feb 23, 1965, in Washington, DC; dau. of Solfest and Kristi

Severson Otteson; m. Arne T. Flikke, 1901 (died 1911); graduate of Augustana Hospital's School of Nursing in Chicago, 1915; attended Columbia University Teachers College, 1916. ❖ Married and soon widowed, joined Army Nurse Corps during WWI and was stationed with American Expeditionary Force (AEF) in France; stationed at Walter Reed Hospital in Washington, DC (1925–37), before being assigned to office of surgeon general with rank of captain; became superintendent of Army Nurse Corps with rank of major; promoted to colonel (1942).

FLINDT, Vivi (1943—). Danish ballet dancer. Born Vivi Gelker, Feb 22, 1943, in Copenhagen, Denmark; m. Flemming Flindt (ballet dancer and choreographer). ❖ Trained at Royal Danish Ballet and joined company (mid-1960s); performed in numerous works by husband, including *The Miraculous Mandarin* (1967), *Tango Chicane* (1967), *Sacre du Printemps* (1968), *Trio* (1973), and *Felix Luna* (1973); created title role in Louis' *Cléopâtre* (1976).

FLINT, Caroline (1961—). English politician and member of Parliament. Born Caroline Flint, Sept 20, 1961; m. 2nd husband Phil Cole, 2001. ❖ Representing Labour, elected to House of Commons for Don Valley (1997, 2001, 2005); served as PPS to John Reid as minister without portfolio and party chair; named parliamentary undersecretary, Department of Health (2005).

FLINT, Elizabeth (b. 1909). New Zealand botanist. Born Elizabeth Alice Flint, May 26, 1909; University of New Zealand, MS, 1935; Queen Mary College, University of London, PhD, 1940. ❖ Freshwater algae expert, especially of New Zealand species, studied phytoplankton while at University of New Zealand and algae in London reservoirs while at Queen Mary College; assisted Professor Hannah Croasdale with *Flora of New Zealand;* worked as botany lecturer at University of Leeds (1948–50) and University College, Hull (1950–55), among other institutions; conducted research at Department of Scientific and Industrial Research (DSIR, 1956–74); after retirement, studied group of freshwater algae in New Zealand. Made Officer of the Order of the British Empire (1991); received Prince and Princess of Wales Science Award (1989) and New Zealand Commemoration Medal (1990).

FLINT, Helen (1898–1967). American stage and screen actress. Born Jan 14, 1898, in Chicago, Illinois; died Sept 9, 1967, after being struck by an auto in Washington, DC; m. Harmon Spencer Auguste (div.). ❖ At 17, began career in the chorus of *Ziegfeld Follies;* starred on Broadway in *The Nest, Gentlemen of the Press, The Man Who Came to Dinner* and *Ah Wilderness;* starred or was featured in such films as *Ah, Wilderness, Sea Devils, Little Lord Fauntleroy, Black Legion, The Ninth Guest, Midnight, Manhattan Love Song, Doubting Thomas* and *Riff Raff.*

FLINT, Rachael (1939—). *See Heyhoe-Flint, Rachael.*

FLINTOFF, Debra (1960—). Australian track-and-field athlete. Name variations: Debbie Flintoff-King. Born Debra Flintoff in Kew, Melbourne, Australia, April 20, 1960; m. Phil King (her coach). ❖ Won gold medals at the Commonwealth Games (1982, 1986); won a gold medal in 400-meter hurdles at Seoul Olympics (1988).

FLÖGE, Emilie (1874–1952). Austrian fashion designer and entrepreneur. Name variations: Emilie Floege; Emilie Floge. Born Emilie Louise Flöge in Vienna, Austria, Aug 30, 1874; died in Vienna, May 26, 1952; dau. of Hermann Flöge (exporter) and Barbara Flöge; sister of Helene Flöge Klimt, Pauline Flöge, and Hermann Flöge. ❖ Designer, owner and manager with her sisters of one of Vienna's leading fashion salons, who was considered the most important person in the life of artist Gustav Klimt for over 10 years (1897–1918); served several years of apprenticeship, finally obtaining her master diploma in dressmaking; with sisters, founded and ran a fashion shop registered under the name "Schwestern Flöge" (Flöge Sisters) to enormous success (c. 1910–1938); immortalized in Gustav Klimt's stunning *Art Nouveau* (1902). ❖ See also Wolfgang G. Fischer and Dorothea H. Ewan, *Gustav Klimt and Emilie Flöge: An Artist and His Muse* (Overlook, 1992); and *Women in World History.*

FLON, Suzanne (1918–2005). French actress. Born Jan 28, 1919, in Le-Kremlin-Bicêtre, Val-de-Marne, France; died June 15, 2005; dau. of a railway worker. ❖ Began career as secretary to Edith Piaf; closely associated with Jean Anouilh, created the roles of Ismene in *Antigone,* the female lead in *Romeo and Jeannette* and Joan of Arc in *The Lark* (1953); received 2 Cèsar awards; made film debut in *Capitaine Blomet* (1947), followed by some 50 films, including *Suzanne et ses brigands, La belle image, Moulin Rouge, Mr. Arkadin, The Trial, Le Procès, To Die in Madrid, The Train, Tante Zita, Teresa* (title role), *Le silencieux, Quartet* and *La fleur du mal.* Named Best Actress at Venice Film Festival for

performance in Claude Autant-Lara's *Tu ne tueras point* (Thou Shalt Not Kill, 1961).

FLOOD, Debbie (1980—). English rower. Born Feb 27, 1980, in Harrogate, England; attended Reading University. ❖ Won a silver medal for quadruple sculls at Athens Olympics (2004).

FLORA. *Variant of Florence.*

FLORA OF CORDOVA (d. 851). Saint and martyr of the Roman Catholic Church. Born in Cordova, Spain, of a Mohammedan father and a Christian mother; died Nov 24, 851. ❖ Practiced Christian religion in secret but, following death of parents, was turned over to the authorities (the cadi) by brother; when she would not denounce her religion, was beaten, then returned to brother; escaped and went into hiding; met Maria of Cordova, a Christian woman who was also in hiding after execution of her deacon brother; decided to face the authorities with Maria and was martyred with her. ❖ See also *Women in World History.*

FLORE, Jeanne (fl. early 16th c.). French short-story writer. Fl. in early 16th century. ❖ Used female narrators in stories of scorned lovers, and advocated free love for women; wrote 2 sets of novellas, *Les Comptes amoureux* and *Pugnition de l'Amour contempné* (1530–40).

FLOREA, Elena (1958—). *See Horvat-Florea, Elena.*

FLOREA, Rodica (1983—). Romanian rower. Born May 26, 1983, in Romania. ❖ Won a gold medal for coxed eight at Athens Olympics (2004).

FLOREAL, LaVonna (1966—). *See Martin, LaVonna.*

FLORENCE, duchess of.
  See Medici, Alfonsina de (d. 1520).
  See Medici, Eleonora de (1522–1562).

FLORENCE, Malvina Pray (1830–1906). American theater actress. Name variations: Anna Pray, "Miss Malvina," Malvina Coveney. Born Anna Pray, April 19, 1830, in New York, NY; died Feb 18, 1906, in New York, NY; dau. of Samuel (died 1848) and Anna Lewis Pray; sister of Maria Williams (1828–1911) and Louise Browne (both actresses); m. Joseph Littell (actor), c. 1846 (div.); m. William Jermyn ("Billy") Florence (actor), Jan 1, 1853 (died 1891); m. Howard Coveney (actor and playwright), 1893 (div. c. 1896); children: (1st m.) Mrs. Josephine Shepherd (actress). ❖ Began career as dancer under stage name Miss Malvina in NY (mid-1840s); with Billy Florence, appeared as a team in *The Yankee Gal* (1853), *Ireland As It Is* and *Woman's Wrong;* made several tours of England, becoming one of the 1st American comediennes to perform in Europe (beginning 1856); performed in dramatization of *Dombey and Son* as Susan Nipper (1862), in *The Ticket-of-Leave Man* (1863), in Benjamin E. Woolf's *The Mighty Dollar* (1875), and in *Our Governor* (1885); with husband Billy, announced retirement (1889).

FLORENCE, Mary Sargant (1857–1954). English artist and suffragist. Name variations: Mary Sargant. Born Mary Sargant in 1857 in London, England; died 1954 in England; educated privately in Brighton; studied at Slade School under Alphonse Legros and later studied in Paris; m. Henry Smyth Florence (American musician), 1888 (died 1891). ❖ Exhibited paintings at Royal Academy and New English Art Club, becoming member (1911); executed mural at Chelsea Old Town Hall, depicting celebrities in science, religion and politics; received commissions for works in Oakham Old School and Bournville School Hall; was involved in suffrage movement, National Union for Women's Suffrage Societies and Women's Freedom League; joined Tax Resistance League (1909); contributed to various publications including articles on color theory for *Cambridge Magazine.*

FLORENCE OF CARTAGENA (d. 7th c.). *See Florentina of Cartagena.*

FLORENTINA (d. 7th c.). Spanish saint. Name variations: Florence of Cartagena. Born at Cartagena (Andalusia), around middle of 6th century; died in early 7th century; dau. of Severianus and Turtur; sister of St. Fulgentius, bishop of Ecija, St. Leander, and St. Isidore of Seville. ❖ Of Greco-Roman ancestry on father's side, was a cloistered nun; received a letter from brother St. Leander extolling her virtue; upon death, was laid to rest next to him in the cathedral of Seville.

FLORENTINO, Leona (1849–1884). Filipino poet and playwright. Name variations: Leonora Florentino. Born 1849 in Vigan, Ilocos Sur, Northern Luzon; died 1884. ❖ The 1st woman poet of the Philippines, learned Spanish but wrote in native language Iloko; wrote didactic and satirical works as well as lyrics, love poems, and occasional verse which were published in major newspapers with Spanish translations; work exhibited at *Exposition Internationale* in Paris (1889).

FLORENZI, Marianna Bacinetti (1802–1870). *See Bacinetti-Florenzi, Marianna.*

FLORES, Lola (1924–1995). Spanish stage actress and flamenco singer-dancer. Name variations: Dolores Flores Ruiz. Born Dolores Flores Ruiz, Jan 21, 1924 (some sources cite 1928), in Jerez de la Frontera, Spain; died in Madrid, Spain, May 16, 1995; trained by flamenco guitarists Javier Molina and Sebastián Núñez and by the dancer María Pantoja; m. Antonio González (Gypsy [Roma] guitarist), Nov 1957. ❖ Toured as a team with Manolo Caracol, a great flamenco singer (Caracol sang while Flores danced); appeared in the film *Maringala* (1943); formed her own company, as one of the foremost flamenco performers in the Hispanic world. ❖ See also Tico Medina, *Lola, en carne viva: Memorias de Lola Flores* (Madrid: Ediciones Temas de Hoy, 1990); Francisco Umbral, *Lola Flores: Sociología de la petenera* (Barcelona: DOPESA, 1971); and *Women in World History.*

FLOREY, Margaret (1904–1994). English pathologist. Name variations: Lady Margaret Augusta Florey; Dr. Margaret Jennings. Born Margaret Augusta Fremantle in 1904 in Swanbourne, Buckinghamshire, England; died 1994 in England; dau. of T.F. Fremantle, 3rd Baron Cottesloe; Oxford University, BS (1924); Royal Free Hospital, MD (1934); m. Denys Jennings, 1930 (div. 1946); m. Lord Howard Walter Florey (pathology researcher), 1967 (died 1968). ❖ Scientific collaborator with Oxford research team, who helped develop penicillin as the 1st clinically effective human antibiotic treatment, entered Lady Margaret Hall at Oxford to study English but soon transferred to physiology; received clinical training in medicine at Royal Free Hospital in London and earned MD (1934); joined pathology department of Howard Florey at Oxford (1936); was member of team that demonstrated uses of penicillin during WWII; carried out bacteriological, pharmacological and biological studies, together with Florey, and helped pioneer life-saving development of this potent but non-toxic antibiotic discovered in late 20s by Alexander Fleming; served as lecturer in pathology at Oxford (1945–72); was not acknowledged when Howard Florey, Ernst Chain and Alexander Fleming shared 1954 Nobel Prize for Medicine; continued to work with Florey for 20 years, collaborating on over 30 joint scientific papers; married Florey shortly after death of his wife Ethel (1967).

FLORIDA, duchess of (1770–1826). *See Migliaccio, Lucia.*

FLORMAN, Marianne (1964—). Danish handball player. Born June 1, 1964, in Denmark; attended Roskilde University. ❖ Won a team gold medal at Atlanta Olympics (1996); won team European championships (1994, 1996).

FLORY, Regine (1894–1926). French actress and dancer. Born July 24, 1894, in Marseilles, France; died June 17, 1926, in Paris; dau. of M. Arlaz; educated in Marseilles. ❖ An acrobatic dancer, made stage debut at the Capucines Theater, Paris, in *Avec le Sourire* (1911), followed by *Le Matricule 607, Reine s'Amuse, Non . . . mais . . .* (lead), *Oh! Milord* (lead), and *Hullo Paris,* among others; made London debut as Babette in *Paris Frissons* (1913), remaining there for *The Passing Show, By Jingo if We Do, Vanity Fair* (lead), and *The Beauty Spot;* best-known for specialty act, in which she danced in a gold skirt against a gold background and was billed "The Bas Relief."

FLOSADOTTIR, Vala (1978—). Icelandic pole vaulter. Born Sept 16, 1978, in Iceland; lives in Sweden. ❖ Won a bronze medal at Sydney Olympics (2000), the 1st Icelandic woman to win any medal.

FLOWER, Constance (1843–1931). *See Rothschild, Constance de.*

FLOWER, Eliza (1803–1846). English composer. Born in Essex, England, 1803; died 1846; eldest dau. of Benjamin Flower and Eliza (Gould) Flower; sister of Sarah Flower Adams (1805–1848). ❖ Published political songs and music to *Hymns and Anthems* (1841–46) for South Place Chapel, which included compositions for words by her sister. ❖ See also *Women in World History.*

FLOWER, Lucy (1837–1921). American welfare worker. Born Lucy Louisa Coues, May 10, 1837, probably in Boston, Massachusetts; died April 27, 1921, in Coronado, California; adopted daughter of Samuel Elliott Coues (merchant and reformer) and his 2nd wife, Charlotte Haven (Ladd) Coues; attended Packer Collegiate Institute, Brooklyn, 1856–57; m. James M. Flower (lawyer), Sept 4, 1862 (died 1909); children: 2 sons, 1 daughter. ❖ Helped found the Illinois Training School for Nurses (1880), the 1st school of its kind in Chicago, serving

as president for 11 years and as a director until 1908; served on the Chicago board of education (1891–93), helping establish kindergartens and domestic and manual training classes in the lower grades, and also working to provide better training programs and salaries for teachers; elected by a wide margin as a trustee of the University of Illinois (1894), thus becoming the 1st woman to hold an elective office in the state; helped establish the Chicago Bureau of Charities (1894) and was elected its 1st vice president; helped establish a juvenile court system in Chicago (1899), the 1st of its kind anywhere in the world. ❖ See also *Women in World History.*

FLOWERS, Bess (1898–1984). American actress. Born Nov 23, 1898, in Sherman, Texas; died July 28, 1984, in Woodland Hills, California; m. Cullen Tate (film director), 1923 (div. 1947); m. William S. Holman (studio manager at Columbia, div.); m. once more. ❖ Known as the queen of the Hollywood extras, though the sobriquet is misleading; played leads and featured roles in many films and bits in hundreds of others; film credits include *Irene, The Shadow, Lone Wolf in Paris, Meet John Doe, Song of the Thin Man, It Happened One Night, Ninotchka, You Can't Take It with You, The Great Gatsby, All About Eve, Pal Joey* and *Good Neighbor Sam.*

FLOWERS, Tairia (1981—). American softball player. Name variations: Tairia Mims. Born Tairia Mims, Jan 9, 1981, in Tucson, Arizona; attended University of California, Los Angeles. ❖ Won team gold medal at Athens Olympics (2004).

FLOWERS, Vonetta (1973—). African-American bobsledder. Born Oct 29, 1973, in Birmingham, Alabama. ❖ Had a standout track career at University of Alabama; as a pusher for Bonny Warner, finished in top-10 in all 7 World Cup races (2000–01); as brakeman for Jill Bakken, won a gold medal for the two-man bobsleigh at Salt Lake City Olympics (2002), the 1st black athlete to win a gold medal at the Winter Olympics.

FLOWERTON, Consuelo (1900–1965). American actress and performer. Born Aug 9, 1900; died Dec 21, 1965, in New York, NY; m. Dirk Fock (Dutch composer-conductor); m. Robert E. Cushman; children: Nina Foch (actress). ❖ During WWI, was Howard Chandler Christy's model for the Red Cross poster girl; appeared on stage in *Ziegfeld Follies, Good Morning Dearie, Queen of the Hearth* and *Let 'Em Eat Cake;* films include *Camille* and *The Sixth Commandment;* was a founder of AGVA.

FLÜGGE-LOTZ, Irmgard (1903–1974). German engineer. Name variations: Flugge-Lotz. Born Irmgard Lotz in Germany, July 16, 1903; died 1974; dau. of Oscar (mathematician) and Dora Lotz (dau. of a wealthy family in construction business); graduate of Technische Hochschule in Hanover, 1927, PhD in thermodynamics, 1929; m. Wilhelm Flügge (engineer and professor at Stanford), 1938; became naturalized US citizen, 1954. ❖ Became a research engineer at Aerodynamische Versuchsanstalt at Göttingen, working with Ludwig Prandt; by age 30, had invented the "Lotz" method, a new way of calculating the distribution of the lifting force of airplane wings of disparate sizes; was soon heading her own research program at the institute; though anti-Nazi, worked for Göring's aeronautics research institute throughout World War II; after the war, moved to US with husband (1948), where she became the 1st woman professor of engineering at Stanford (1960); remained at Stanford for the rest of her career, establishing graduate programs in mathematical aerodynamics and hydrodynamics; wrote *Discontinuous Automatic Control* (1953).

FLUGRATH, Leonie (1900–1979). *See Mason, Shirley.*

FLUGRATH, Viola (1897–1987). *See Dana, Viola.*

FLYGARE-CARLÉN, Emilie (1807–1892). *See Carlén, Emilia.*

FLYNN, Beverley (1966—). *See Cooper-Flynn, Beverley.*

FLYNN, Elizabeth Gurley (1890–1964). American radical, labor organizer, and Communist Party official. Name variations: Elizabeth Gurley; Rebel Girl. Born Elizabeth Gurley Flynn, Aug 7, 1890, in Concord, New Hampshire; died Sept 5, 1964, in Moscow, USSR; dau. of Annie Gurley Flynn (seamstress) and Thomas Flynn (civil engineer and mapmaker); m. John Archibald Jones, Jan 1908 (div. 1920); children: John Vincent (1909–1909); Fred (1910–1940). ❖ Inspired countless workers to organize for their rights; played an active role in some of the most violent labor strikes from the early 1900s through the Red Scare of the 1920s and was a Communist Party leader during the heady days of the Popular Front (1930s) and during the anti-communist reaction of the McCarthy era (1950s); when young, settled with family in South Bronx (1900); gave 1st speech before the Harlem Socialist Club, at 15; joined Industrial

Workers of the World (IWW, 1906); led IWW free speech fights in Missoula, MT, and Spokane, WA; arrested twice for conspiracy; was an organizer for the IWW during the Lawrence strike (1912) and Paterson strike (1913); helped found Workers' Defense Union (1918) and American Civil Liberties Union (1920); was active in Sacco and Vanzetti defense movement (1920s); elected to American Communist Party (CPUSA) national committee (1938); elected to CPUSA political bureau (1941); served as delegate to Women's Congress in Paris (1945); indicted by federal government under the Smith Act (1951); imprisoned at federal penitentiary for women at Alderson, West Virginia (Jan 1955–May 1957); elected national chair of CPUSA (1961). Writings include *Thirteen Communists Speak to the Court* (1953), *I Speak My Own Piece: Autobiography of "The Rebel Girl"* (1955), *The Alderson Story: My Life as a Political Prisoner* (1963), and regular columns in the *Daily Worker*, *Sunday Worker* and *Political Affairs*. ❖ See also Rosalyn Fraad Baxandall, *Words on Fire: The Life and Writing of Elizabeth Gurley Flynn* (Rutgers U. Press, 1987); and *Women in World History*.

FLYNN, Jeannie. American aviator. Name variations: Jean Marie Flynn. Born in St. Louis, Missouri; Stanford University, MS, 1992. ❖ Graduated 1st in her Air Force Undergraduate Pilot Training class (1992); as an Air Force lieutenant, became the 1st female combat pilot in US (Feb 10, 1994); by the end of 2002, had logged over 2,000 hours in an F-15E, including 200 hours of combat during Operation Allied Force; became an F-15E instructor pilot.

FLYNN, Keri (1932—). *See Burstyn, Ellen.*

FOCH, Nina (1924—). Dutch-born stage, tv, and screen actress and acting coach. Born Nina Consuelo Maud Fock, April 20, 1924, in Leyden, Holland, Netherlands; raised in New York; dau. of Dirk Fock (Dutch conductor-composer) and Consuelo Flowerton (American actress); m. James Lipton, 1954 (div. 1959); m. Dennis Brite (div. 1963); m. Michael Dewell, 1966 (div. 1993). ❖ Made film debut in *The Wagon Wheels* (1943), followed by *An American in Paris, Scaramouche, Sombrero, Executive Suite, The Ten Commandmants, Cash McCall, Spartacus, Such Good Friends, Mahogany* and *Shadow of a Doubt*, among others; made Broadway debut as Mary McKinley in *John Loves Mary* (1947) and later spent a season with the American Shakespeare Festival Theatre; appeared frequently on tv and was a panelist on several quiz shows; as an acting teacher, worked at USC and the American Film Institute and conducted the Nina Foch Studio in Hollywood.

FOGERTY, Elsie (1865–1945). English drama teacher. Born 1865; died 1945. ❖ Founded (1898) and was principal of the Central School of Speech Training at the Royal Albert Hall. Named Commander of the British Empire (CBE, 1934). ❖ See also *Women in World History*.

FOI (290–303). *See Faith.*

FOIX, Anne de (fl. 1480–1500). Queen of Bohemia and Hungary. Name variations: Anne de Fair. Fl. between 1480 and 1500; possibly dau. of Madeleine of France (1443–1486) and Gaston de Foix, prince of Viane or Viana; possibly sister of Catherine de Foix (c. 1470–1517); m. Vladislav II also known as Ladislas II of Bohemia, king of Hungary (r. 1490–1516), king of Bohemia (r. 1471–1516); children: Louis II, king of Bohemia (r. 1516–1526), king of Hungary (r. 1516–1526); Anna of Bohemia and Hungary (1503–1547, who m. Ferdinand I, Holy Roman emperor, r. 1556–1564).

FOIX, Catherine de (c. 1470–1517). *See Catherine de Foix.*

FOIX, Françoise de (c. 1490–1537). *See Châteaubriant, Comtesse de.*

FOIX, Germaine de (1488–1538). Queen of Aragon and Naples. Born 1488; died 1538; niece of Louis XII, king of France; m. her great-uncle Ferdinand II (1474–1516), king of Aragon (r. 1479–1516), in 1505 (one year after the death of his 1st wife, Isabella I of Castile); children: one son Juan, who died in infancy.

FOIX, Janine-Marie de (fl. 1377). French soldier. Fl. in 1377 in France. ❖ A French peasant, fought for King Charles V of France; as a common footsoldier, held no special place in his army but fought alongside her compatriots for 3 years. ❖ See also *Women in World History*.

FOIX, Margaret de (d. 1258). *See Margaret de Foix.*

FOIX, Marguerite de (fl 1456–1477). *See Marguerite de Foix.*

FOKINA, Vera (1886–1958). Russian ballerina. Born Vera Petrovna (some sources cite Vera Antonova), Aug 3, 1886, in St. Petersburg; died in New York, NY, July 29, 1958; graduate of St. Petersburg Ballet

School, 1904; m. Michel (or Mikhail) Fokine (1880–1942, ballet dancer and choreographer), 1905; children: Vitale Fokine. ❖ Joined Maryinsky Ballet (1904); formally resigned from Maryinsky (1918); settled with husband in New York (1924), where they formed their own company; during 1920s, made many concert appearances in America, while also traveling widely with husband who worked for numerous companies; appeared in hundreds of his works, especially *Daphnis and Cloe, The Dying Swan, Narcisse, Carnaval, Firebird* and *The Thunderbird;* retired from stage (c. 1928).

FOKKE, Annemieke (1967—). Dutch field-hockey player. Born Nov 4, 1967, in the Netherlands. ❖ At Seoul Olympics, won a bronze medal in team competition (1988).

FOLCHEID (fl. 7th c.). Duchess of Bavaria. Married Theodebert of Bavaria, duke of Bavaria; children: Hucbert, duke of Bavaria; Guntrud of Bavaria; Sunnichild (d. 741).

FOLEY, Edna (1878–1943). American nurse. Born Edna Lois Foley, Dec 17, 1878, in Hartford, Connecticut; died Aug 4, 1943; dau. of William R. and Matilda (Baker) Foley; graduate of Smith College (1901) and Hartford Hospital Training School for Nurses (1904). ❖ Became a Chicago Visiting Nurses Association (VNA) superintendent (1912); studied and integrated nurse practices from around the world and elevated VNA's reputation; succeeded Mary Gardner as chief nurse of the American Red Cross Tuberculosis Commission for Italy (1919); chaired meeting that led to establishment of the National Organization for Public Health Nursing (1912) and served as its 1st vice president and as one of its presidents (1920–21); appointed director of the National Society for Study and Prevention of Tuberculosis (1916); appointed director of Chicago Tuberculosis Institute (1931); advocated increased opportunities for African-American nurses. Wrote the popular *Visiting Nurse Manual* (1914).

FOLEY, Jane (1840–1933). *See Te Kiri Karamu, Heni.*

FOLEY, Margaret (c. 1827–1877). American sculptor. Born c. 1827; died in Merano in 1877; grew up in rural Vergennes, Vermont. ❖ Moved to Boston (1848) where she specialized in cameo portraits; moved to Rome and began to work on larger marble medallion portraits (1860), including one of William Cullen Bryant; despite a neurological disorder, won international recognition; her marble fountain base, supported by three children, now resides in Horticulture Center, West Fairmount Park, Philadelphia.

FOLEY, Martha (c. 1897–1977). American editor and writer. Born Martha Foley c. 1897 in Boston, Massachusetts; died of heart disease, Sept 5, 1977, in Northampton, Massachusetts; dau. of Walter Foley and Margaret (McCarthy) Foley; m. Whit Burnett (editor, writer) 1930 (div. 1942); children: David Burnett (b. 1931). ❖ Co-founder and co-editor of the magazine *Story*, worked as a Paris reporter for *New York Herald* (1927); served as European correspondent for *New York Sun* (1929); with husband, was co-editor of *Story* (1931–42); lectured at University of Colorado (1935–36), Columbia University (1936), and New York University (1937); taught at Columbia University (1945–66); dedicated her career to the short-story genre; writings include *The Story of Story Magazine: A Memoir* (1980). ❖ See also *Women in World History*.

FOLGER, Emily (1858–1936). American scholar and collector. Name variations: Emily Jordan or Emily Clara Jordan; Emily Clara Jordan Folger. Born Emily Clara Jordan on May 15, 1858, in Ironton, Ohio; died Feb 21, 1936, in Long Island, NY; dau. of Edward Jordan (lawyer) and Augusta Woodbury (Ricker) Jordan; sister of Mary Augusta Jordan, English scholar and professor at Smith; graduate of Vassar College, 1879; m. Henry Clay Folger (founder of Folger Shakespeare Library), Oct 6, 1885 (died 1930). ❖ With husband, collected manuscripts, folios, and editions of Shakespeare's work, as well as related articles, and recorded purchases in file which later became basis of official catalogue at Folger Shakespeare Library; traveled from NY to Washington to supervise construction of, and installation of, 100,000 items at Folger Library (1930). Folger Shakespeare Library was dedicated on the anniversary of Shakespeare's birth (April 23, 1932).

FOLIGNO, Angela da (1249–1309). *See Angela of Foligno.*

FOLLANSBEE, Elizabeth A. (1839–1917). American physician. Born Dec 9, 1839, in Pillston, Maine; died Aug 22, 1917, in Los Angeles, California; granddau. of Roger Sherman (signer of the Declaration of Independence). ❖ The 1st practicing woman physician in southern CA, was educated in Massachusetts, New York and France; taught at Hillsdale

Seminary and at Green Mountain Institute (Montclair, NJ); was 1 of 1st 2 women admitted to University of California Medical Department (1875); also studied medicine at University of Michigan and at Woman's Medical College of Pennsylvania in Philadelphia (graduated, 1877); interned at New England Hospital (Boston, MA); established a private practice in San Francisco; assisted Dr. Charlotte Brown to revamp the Pacific Dispensary for Women and Children into Women's and Children's Hospital, then the only female-founded West Coast hospital; opened new practice in Los Angeles (1883); was also the 1st woman to be a faculty member of a CA medical school (University of Southern California, pediatrics professor and later appointed professor emerita in 1908).

FOLLAS, Selina. Australian softball player. Born in Southern Australia. ❖ Won a bronze medal at Sydney Olympics (2000).

FOLLEN, Eliza (1787–1860). American abolitionist and children's writer. Name variations: Eliza Cabot or Eliza Lee Cabot; Eliza C. Follen or Eliza Lee Cabot Follen. Born Eliza Lee Cabot, Aug 15, 1787, in Boston, Massachusetts; died Jan 26, 1860, in Brookline, MA; dau. of Samuel (merchant) and Sally, or Sarah (Barrett) Cabot; m. Charles Theodore Christian Follen, Sept 15, 1828 (died 1840); children: 1 son (b. 1830). ❖ Authored children's works, *The Well-Spent Hour* (1827), *Little Songs, for Little Boys and Girls* (1833), *The Pedler of Dust Sticks* and *What the Animals Do and Say* (1858); published *Selections from the Writings of Fénelon* (1829); wrote fictional homilies, *The Skeptic* (1835) and *Sketches of Married Life* (1838), and a biography of husband, *The Works of Charles Follen, with a Memoir of His Life* (5 vols., 1841); published anti-slavery works, *A Letter to Mothers in the Free States* and *Anti-Slavery Hymns and Songs* (1855); edited *Christian Teachers' Manual* (1828–30) and *Child's Friend* (1843–50); served on executive committees of Massachusetts and American anti-slavery societies. The German Christmas tree was 1st introduced in America in the Folger home.

FOLLETT, Barbara (1942—). English politician and member of Parliament. Born Dec 25, 1942; grew up in Cape Town, South Africa; dau. of William Vernon and Charlotte Hubbard; m. Richard Turner, 1963 (div. 1971); m. Gerald Stonestreet, 1971 (div. 1974); m. Les Broer, 1974 (div. 1985); m. Kenneth Martin Follett, 1985. ❖ Representing Labour, elected to House of Commons for Stevenage (1997, 2001, 2005).

FOLLETT, Mary Parker (1868–1933). American management theorist. Born Mary Parker Follett in Quincy, Massachusetts, Sept 3, 1868; died in Boston, Dec 18, 1933; dau. of Charles Allen Follett (skilled tradesman) and Elizabeth Curtis (Baxter) Follett; graduated summa cum laude from Radcliffe College, 1898; involved in longterm relationship for 30 years with Isobel Briggs (died 1926). ❖ Visionary of modern management theory and proponent of democratic governance in organizations, returned to Boston after post-graduate studies in Paris to do social work and social service for 25 years; advised local and national organizations on management issues; pioneered the organization and management of vocational guidance centers in the public schools in Boston, the 1st program of its kind nationally (1917); served as chair of School Houses Sub-Committee to Women's Municipal League of Boston (c. 1909); lectured on business organization and management (1925–33) at annual conferences of the Bureau of Personnel Administration in NY; moved to London (1929), where she continued to study industrial conditions and lecture; lived with Dame Katharine Furse until shortly before Follett's death; her ideas about flatter organizations, participative management, and conflict resolution are ideas whose time came after her; writings include *Creative Experience* (1924) and *Freedom and Coordination* (1949). ❖ See also Elliot M. Fox & L. Urwick, eds. *Dynamic Administration—The Collected Papers of Mary Parker Follett* (Pittman, 1973); Pauline Graham, ed. *Mary Parker Follett—Prophet of Management; A Celebration of Writings from the 1920s* (Harvard Business School, 1995); and *Women in World History.*

FOLLETT, Rosemary (1948—). Australian politician. Born Mar 27, 1948, in Sydney, NSW, Australia; attended Catholic Girls High School (now Merici College) in Canberra; graduate of the Canberra College of Advanced Education. ❖ The 1st woman to lead an Australian state or territory government, was also the 1st woman to attend a Premiers' Conference (1980); moved to Canberra (1952); joined the Ginninderra branch of the Australian Labor Party (ALP, 1975), serving as its president (1983–84); elected women's coordinator for the Australian Capital Territory's (ACT) branch of the ALP (1984); was a member of the ACT House of Assembly (1985–86) and elected ALP ACT branch

president (1987); became ACT's 1st chief minister (1989) and served as chief minister again (1991–95); was a member for Molonglo (1995–96) and Labor leader (1989–91); established the ACT Women's Consultative Council (1989); became the ACT Discrimination Commissioner (1996); portfolio duties included Social Justice, Treasury and Public Service, Attorney-General Law Reform, Consumer Affairs, and Police and Emergency Services.

FOLLIN or FOLLINE, Miriam (1836–1914). *See Leslie, Miriam Folline Squier.*

FOLTOVA, Vlasta (1913—). Czech gymnast. Born Mar 14, 1913. ❖ At Berlin Olympics, won a silver medal in team all-around (1936).

FOLTZ, Clara (1849–1934). American political and social reformer. Born Clara Shortridge in Indiana, possibly in New Lisbon, Henry Co., July 16, 1849; died in Los Angeles, California, Sept 2, 1934; dau. of Elias Willets Shortridge (druggist, minister, and lawyer) and Talitha Cumi (Harwood) Shortridge; attended Howe's Female Seminary, Iowa, 1840–43; briefly attended Hastings College of Law, San Francisco; m. Jeremiah Richard Foltz (businessman), Dec 30, 1864 (widowed or div., 1877); children: 2 sons, 3 daughters. ❖ Pioneering lawyer and the 1st woman to be admitted to the California bar, was also a political and social reformer, particularly in the area of women's rights; was admitted to practice in 20th District Court at San Jose (1878); admitted to the bar of the state supreme court (1879); also served as clerk of the state assembly's judiciary committee (1879–80), the 1st woman so appointed; founded a daily newspaper, the *San Diego Bee* (1887); won admittance to New York bar (1896) and briefly opened an office in New York City; back in California, played an important role in the campaign that secured the vote for women in state elections (1911); published the feminist magazine *New American Woman* (1916–18); was the 1st woman appointed to the State Board of Charities and Corrections (1910), a post she held until 1912; in Los Angeles, was the 1st woman appointed deputy district attorney and served 2 terms; refused an appointment as assistant US attorney general (1921); ran unsuccessfully for California governor (1930).

FONAROFF, Nina (1914–2003). American-born dancer, choreographer and teacher. Born Mar 3, 1914, in New York, NY; died Aug 14, 2003, in London, England; dau. of Mark Fonaroff (violinist); studied ballet with Mikhail and Vera Fokine; studied stage costume and set design in Zurich and painting with George Grosz. ❖ As a soloist in Martha Graham's company (1936–47), created the role of the child in *Punch and the Judy* and one of the Brontë sisters in *Deaths and Entrances* and danced in the premieres of *Letter to the World* and *Appalachian Spring;* taught at the Graham school; also served as assistant to Louis Horst (1937–50); had her own company (1946–53), choreographing such ballets as *Of Tragic Gesture, Yankee Doodle, American Prodigy, Café Chantant* and *Of Wimmin and Ladies;* choreographed *Mr. Puppet* for Alicia Markova and Anton Dolin (1949), among others; taught actors to dance at Neighborhood Playhouse; moved to London, where she taught at the London School of Contemporary Dance (1972–90).

FONDA, Jane (1937—). American actress and activist. Born Jane Seymour Fonda, Dec 21, 1937, in New York, NY; dau. of Henry Fonda (actor) and Frances Seymour Brokaw (socialite, d. 1950); sister of Peter Fonda (actor); aunt of Bridget Fonda (b. 1964, actress); m. Roger Vadim (director), 1965 (div. 1973); m. Tom Hayden (political activist), 1973 (div. 1989); m. Ted Turner (broadcasting magnate), 1991 (div. 2001); children: (1st m.) Vanessa Vadim (b. 1968); (2nd m.) Troy Garity (actor) and (adopted) Mary Fonda. ❖ Made screen debut in *Tall Story* (1960), followed by *Period of Adjustment, Sunday in New York, Any Wednesday, Barefoot in the Park, Walk on the Wild Side, The Chase, Hurry Sundown, Circle of Love, Barbarella, Cat Ballou, Comes a Horseman, California Suite, The Electric Horseman, The China Syndrome, Agnes of God* and *Old Gringo,* among others; as an antiwar activist during Vietnam War, was nicknamed "Hanoi Jane" for supporting the Viet Cong but has since repudiated her stand; launched the aerobic craze with her series of exercise videos. Won Oscars for Best Actress for performances in *Klute* (1971) and *Coming Home* (1978); nominated for Best Actress Oscars for *They Shoot Horses Don't They* (1969), *Julia* (1977), *The Morning After* (1986), and *On Golden Pond* (1981). ❖ See also autobiography, *My Life So Far* (Random House, 2005).

FONSECA, Marchesa de (c. 1768–1799). *See Pimentel, Eleonora.*

FONTAINE, Joan (1917—). English-born actress. Name variations: acted under names Joan Burfield and Joan St. John. Born Joan de Beauvoire de Havilland, Oct 22, 1917, in Tokyo, Japan; dau. of Walter (patent attorney) and Lillian (Ruse) de Havilland (both British); sister of actress Olivia de Havilland (b. 1916); m. Brian Aherne (actor), 1939 (div. 1944); m. William Dozier (producer), 1946 (div. 1951); m. Collier Young (producer-screenwriter), 1952 (div. 1961); m. Alfred Wright Jr. (journalist), 1964 (div.); children: (2nd m.) Deborah; (3rd m.) adopted daughter Marita from Peru. ❖ Made film debut in *No More Ladies* (1935); borrowed the name Fontaine from mother's 2nd husband, and made a series of forgettable pictures, including *A Damsel in Distress* (1937), which she would later recall as aptly named; came to prominence as the 2nd Mrs. de Winter in *Rebecca*, for which she was nominated for an Oscar (1940); won Academy Award for Best Actress for *Suspicion* (1941), and was nominated once more for *The Constant Nymph* (1943); appeared frequently on stage; on tv, played the matriarch in "Dark Mansions"; other films include *Quality Street* (1937), *Gunga Din* (1939), *The Women* (1939), *This Above All* (1942), *Jane Eyre* (1944), *Frenchman's Creek* (1944), *Letter from an Unknown Woman* (1948), *Born to be Bad* (1950), *Ivanhoe* (1952), *Island in the Sun* (1957), *Until They Sail* (1957), *A Certain Smile* (1958), *Voyage to the Bottom of the Sea* (1961) and *Tender Is the Night* (1961). ❖ See also autobiography *No Bed of Roses* (Morrow, 1978); Charles Higham, *Sisters: The Story of Olivia de Havilland and Joan Fontaine;* and *Women in World History.*

FONTAINE, Lillian (1886–1975). English actress. Name variations: Lillian de Havilland; Lilian Fontaine. Born Lillian Ruse, June 11, 1996, in Reading, Berkshire, England; died Feb 20, 1975, in Santa Barbara, California; m. Walter de Havilland (patent attorney, div.); children: Joan Fontaine and Olivia de Havilland (both actresses). ❖ Stage, film actress, and acting coach, appeared in such films as *The Lost Weekend, Time Out of Mind, The Locket, Suddenly, It's Spring, Ivy* and *The Bigamist.*

FONTAINE, Mlle de la (1655–1738). French ballerina. Born 1655; died 1738. ❖ In France, was the 1st premiere ballerina, *la première des premières danseuses,* the "Queen of Dance"; left the stage for a life in the church.

FONTAINES, Marie-Louise-Charlotte de Pelard de Givry, Comtesse de (1660–1730). French novelist. Name variations: Comtesse de Fontaines; Marie-Louise de Fontaines; Marie Louise Charlotte de Pellart de Givry. Born Marie- Louise-Charlotte de Pelard de Givry in 1660; died in 1730; dau. of the marquis de Givry; m. Nicholas de Fontaines (chevalier and maréchal to the king), compte de Fontaines (died 1720); children: Jean Charles, Georges Marie (captain in the cavalry), Charles, Georges Mathieu, René (chevalier of St. Jean of Jerusalem, b. 1704), Anne (lady-in-waiting to the princess de Conty who later m. Jean Pierre, marquis de Fontages), Margueritte Charlotte, and Jacqueline (nun). ❖ Wrote *Histoire de la comtesse de Savoie* (1726) which may have been the source of Voltaire's *Tancrède;* also wrote *Histoire d'Aménophis, prince de Lydie* (1728).

FONTANA, Giovanna (1915–2004). Italian designer. Born Nov 27, 1915, at Traversetolo, southeast of Parma, Italy; died Aug 11, 2004, in Rome; dau. of a dressmaker who owned a dress shop; youngest sister of Zoe (died 1979) and Micol Fontana; children: Giovanni and Roberta. ❖ With sisters, opened 1st dress shop (1943), in Rome; came to prominence designing the wedding dress of Linda Christian for her wedding with Tyrone Power (1949), as well as Margaret Truman's; became associated with celebrities, creating costumes for Audrey Hepburn in *Roman Holiday* (1953) and Ava Gardner in *The Barefoot Contessa* (1954), and the memorable black dress worn by Anita Ekberg in *La Dolce Vita* (1959), among others; eventually created a demand for Italian clothes, moving some of the power of the fashion industry out of France; also designed for Jacqueline Kennedy, Grace Kelly, Kim Novak, Rita Hayworth, Elizabeth Taylor and Soraya.

FONTANA, Lavinia (1552–1614). Italian artist. Name variations: Lavinia Fontana Zappi; Lavinia Fontana de Zappis. Born Lavinia Fontana, Aug 1552, in Bologna, Italy; died in Rome, Italy, Aug 11, 1614; dau. of Prospero Fontana (painter) and Antonia De Bonardis (who came from a printer's family in Parma); m. Giovan Paolo Zappi, 1577; children: Emilia (b. 1578); Orazio (b. 1578); Orazio (b. 1579); Laura (b. 1581); Flaminio (b. 1583); Orazio (b. 1585); Severo (b. 1587); Laodamia or Laudamia (1588–1605); Prospero (b. 1589); Severo (b. 1592); Costanza (b. 1595). ❖ Bolognese painter, mainly of portraits and holy scenes, preferred small formats, representing holy scenes for domestic and private piety, at beginning of career; in following 2 decades, cultivated her real talent, portraiture; had several public commissions; painted the 1.5 meters by 2.5 *Assumption of the Virgin with Saints Peter Crisologus and Cassian* for the Municipal Council in Imola (1584); painted a *Holy Family with the Sleeping Child and Young St. John the Baptist* for the

Escorial monastery (still on the main altar, 1589), considered one of her masterpieces; painted *Birth of the Virgin* (c. 1590, Bologna, church of SS. Trinita), which is considered among her greatest paintings; moved with family to Rome (1603–04), the last step of her successful career; portrayed a number of important people, including Pope Paul V and the Persian ambassador (both portraits have been lost); also painted small paintings on mythological (rather rare in her work) or historical subjects, like the famous Cleopatra (VII) (Rome, Galleria Spada); painted 4 full-length saints (Cecilia, Agnes, Claire, and Catherine of Siena), in the church of Santa Maria della Pace (1611–14); other paintings include *Self-Portrait in the Studio* (1579), *Portrait of the Gozzadini Family* (1584), *Portrait of Lady with Dog* (c. 1584), *Ritratto del frate Panigarola* (1585), *Portrait of a Noblewoman from the Ruini Family* (1593), *Judith and Holophern* (1600), *Conversation-piece* (c. 1600), *The Queen of Sabah Visiting King Solomon* (c. 1600) and *Dressing Minerva* (1613). ❖ See also *Women in World History.*

FONTANGES, Duchesse de (1661–1681). French royal mistress. Name variations: Marie Angélique de Fontanges. Born Marie-Angélique de Scorraille de Roussilles in 1661; died in 1681; mistress of Louis XIV, king of France. ❖ Was created the duchesse of Fontanges by Louis XIV.

FONTANNE, Lynn (1887–1983). British-born actress. Born Lillie Louise Fontanne in Woodford, Essex Co., England, Dec 6, 1887; died July 30, 1983; dau. of Jules Pierre Antoine Fontanne (French designer of printing type) and Frances Ellen (Thornley) Fontanne; studied acting under Ellen Terry (1903–05); m. Alfred Lunt Jr., May 26, 1922; no children. ❖ Star of the American stage who, together with husband Alfred Lunt, formed the most celebrated acting couple in the history of the American theater; made 1st stage appearance in London as a child extra in *Edwin Drood* (1899); made US debut as Harriet Budgeon in *Mr. Preedy and the Countess* in Washington, DC (fall 1910) and then NY (Nov 7, 1910); back in London, appeared in title role in *The Terrorist*, as Ada Pilbeam in *How to Get On*, and in *The Starlight Express* (all 1915); came permanently to US to appear with Laurette Taylor (1916); teamed for 1st time with Alfred Lunt in *Made of Money* at National Theater (1919); had 1st outstanding success in *Dulcy* (1921); with husband, joined the Theater Guild (1924), where their participation in its productions was vital to its success; appeared in well over a dozen Guild productions, both light and serious, including *The Guardsman* (1924, one of their greatest hits), *Arms and the Man* (1925), *Goat Song* (1926), *The Second Man* (1927), *The Doctor's Dilemma* (1927), *Caprice* (1928), *Elizabeth the Queen* (1930), *Reunion in Vienna* (1931), *The Taming of the Shrew* (1935), *Idiot's Delight* (1936), *Amphitryon 38* (1937), and *There Shall Be No Night* (1940); also starred on her own in *Strange Interlude* and *Pygmalion;* filmed screen version of *The Guardsman* (1931), the only film she ever made with husband; later stage successes were *Quadrille* (1952), *The Great Sebastians* (1955) and *The Visit* (1958); after Lunt's death (1977), spent last years between her New York City apartment and retirement home in Genesee Depot, Wisconsin. Received President's Medal of Freedom from Lyndon Johnson (1964); Emmy award (1965). ❖ See also Maurice Zolotow, *Stagestruck: The Romance of Alfred Lunt and Lynn Fontanne* (Harcourt, 1965); and *Women in World History.*

FONTE, Moderata (1555–1592). *See Pozzo, Modesta.*

FONTETTE DE SOMMERY, Mademoiselle (fl. 18th c.). French novelist and essayist. Fl. around 1760 in France. ❖ Essays include *Brochure morale* (1769), *Doutes sur les opinions reçues dans la société* (1782), and *Doutes sur les différents opinions...* (1783); fiction includes *Lettres de Mme la comtesse de L*** à M. le comte de R**** (1785), *Lettres de Mlle de Tourville à Mme. La comtesse de Lenoncourt* (1788), *L'Oreille* (1789) and *Le Rosier et le brouillard* (1791).

FONTEVRAULT, abbess of (fl. 1477). *See Renée de Bourbon.*

FONTEYN, Karen (1969—). Canadian synchronized swimmer. Born Jan 29, 1969, in Calgary, Alberta, Canada. ❖ Won a team silver medal at Atlanta Olympics (1996).

FONTEYN, Margot (1919–1991). British ballerina. Name variations: Peggy Hookham; Margot de Arias. Born Margaret Hookham, May 18, 1919, at Reigate, Surrey, England; died Feb 21, 1991, in Panama City, Panama; dau. of Felix John Hookham (engineer) and Hilda Fontes Hookham; studied ballet at Vic-Wells Ballet School, 1933–34; m. Roberto Arias (Panamanian diplomat), Feb 6, 1955 (died 1989); no children. ❖ Star of the Royal Ballet and one of the world's leading ballerinas, danced especially memorable roles in numerous ballets created for her by choreographer Frederick Ashton in a career that spanned more than 4 decades; made professional debut (1934); at 17, became prima ballerina of Sadler's Wells Company, succeeding Alicia Markova (1936); had 1st great success in the Romantic ballet *Apparitions* (1936); danced the most notable role of the 1st half of her career, Aurora in *The Sleeping Beauty* (1939); emerged as the best-known British ballerina of the era; escaped from German invasion of Holland (1940); toured provinces in reduced ballet company (1939–45); toured US and Canada (1949–50); named president of Royal Academy of Dancing (1954); saw Sadler's Wells Company receive royal charter and become Royal Ballet (1956); toured Australia and New Zealand (1957); began guest status with Royal Ballet (1959); danced 1st performance with Rudolf Nureyev, in *Giselle* (1962), launching the most famous partnership in the ballet world; made triumphal appearance with Nureyev in *Romeo and Juliet* at Covent Garden (1965); over a period of 17 years, danced with Nureyev on a relatively small number of occasions: fewer than 200, but their partnership dominated the dance stage of the era (1962–79); appeared in a 6-part BBC-TV series, "The Magic of Dance" (1980s); also known for Odette-Odile in *Swan Lake*, title role in *Ondine* and Marguerite in *Marguerite and Armand*. Named Dame Commander of the Most Excellent Order of the British Empire (1956). ❖ See also *Autobiography* (Knopf, 1976); Alexander Bland, *Fonteyn and Nureyev: The Story of a Partnership* (Times, 1979); Keith Money, *The Art of Margot Fonteyn* (Reynal, 1965); and *Women in World History*.

FONTYN, Jacqueline (1930—). Belgian composer. Name variations: Jacqueline Schmitt-Fontyn. Born Dec 27, 1930, in Antwerp, Belgium; Royal Chapel of Queen Elisabeth of Belgium, degree in composition; m. Camille Schmitt (composer and organist), 1961 (died 1976). ❖ Award-winning composer, began taking piano lessons at 5 from Ignace Bolotine; studied musical theory and composition in Brussels under Marcel Quinet and continued musical education in Paris with Max Deutsch and in Vienna with Hans Swarowski; served as professor of musical theory at Antwerp Royal Conservatory (1963–70) and later professor of composition at Brussels Conservatory (until 1991); served as visiting professor at conservatories throughout Europe, US, New Zealand and Asia; received commissions from many prestigious sources, including Library of Congress in Washington; became a member of Royal Academy of Sciences, Letters and Fine Arts of Belgium; title of Baroness granted by King of Belgium. Received Oscar Espla Prize in Alicante (1962), 1st Prize at Godak Composition Contest in Mannheim (1961, 1966), 1st Prize of Delta Omicron International Music Fraternity in USA (1965), 1st Prize of Halifax Composition in Canada (1973), Prix Arthur Honegger from Foundation de France.

FOOT, Katherine (c. 1852–?). American cytologist. Born c. 1852 in Geneva, NY; death date unknown; studied at the Marine Biological Laboratory at Woods Hole, 1892. ❖ One of America's most influential early scientists, was a life member of the Marine Biological Laboratory (1921–44); focused research on microscopical observations of the developing eggs of *Allobophora fetida* and often researched with Ella Church Strobell (died 1920); with Strobell, was among the 1st scientists to photograph research samples; received a star by her name—indicating special recognition—in Cattell's *American Men of Science* (1906); also listed in Mozans' *Woman in Science*. Publications include *Cytological Studies*.

FOOT, Philippa (1920—). British philosopher. Born Philippa Ruth Bosanquet, Oct 3, 1920; dau. of a British industrialist and Esther (Cleveland) Bosanquet (American granddau. of President Grover Cleveland); Somerville College, Oxford University, BA, 1942, MA, 1946; married M.R.D. Foot (later professor of history at University of Manchester), 1946 (div.). ❖ Was a lecturer in philosophy, Somerville College (1947), then fellow and tutor (1950–69); was a visiting professor at Cornell University, Massachusetts Institute of Technology, University of California at Berkeley, Princeton University, and City University of New York; was a fellow, Center for Advanced Studies in Behavioral Sciences, Stanford University (1981–82); became senior research fellow, Somerville College (1970); became a professor of philosophy, University of California at Los Angeles (1974); writings include *Virtues and Vices and Other Essays in Moral Philosophy* (1978), *Moral Relativism* (1979), *The Grammar of Goodness* (2000); also published prolifically in philosophical journals, especially on the subject of ethics. ❖ See also *Women in World History*.

FOOTE, Maria (c. 1797–1867). English actress and countess of Harrington. Born, probably at Plymouth, England, c. 1797; died Dec 27, 1867; dau. of Samuel Foote (descendant of the great actor Samuel Foote, 1720–1777); m. Charles Stanhope, 4th earl of Harrington. ❖ Appeared as Amanthis in Elizabeth Inchbald's *The Child of Nature* at Covent Garden (1814), remaining there until 1825; did a stint at the Drury Lane before touring England and Ireland; on marriage, retired from stage, after a relatively notorious career (1831); was as well known for amatory affairs as career. ❖ See also *Women in World History*.

FOOTE, Mary Hallock (1847–1938). American author and illustrator. Born Mary Anna Hallock in Milton, NY, Nov 19, 1847, of English Quaker ancestry; died in Hingham, Massachusetts, June 25, 1938; attended Poughkeepsie (NY) Female Collegiate Seminary and Cooper Institute School of Design for Women; m. Arthur De Wint Foote (mining engineer), 1876. ❖ As a popular illustrator, was a frequent contributor to *Scribner's Monthly*, *Harper's Weekly* and *Century*, but was best known for her stories and drawings depicting the mining life of the West; books include *The Led-Horse Claim* (1883), *John Bodewin's Testimony* (1886), *The Last Assembly Ball* (1889), *The Chosen Valley* (1892), *Coeur d'Alene* (1894); *The Prodigal* (1900), *The Royal Americans* (1910), *The Valley Road* (1915), *Edith Bonham* (1917), and *The Ground Swell* (1919); also produced several collections of short stories, including *In Exile* (1894) and *A Touch of Sun* (1903).

FORBES, Brenda (1909–1996). English-born actress. Born Brenda Taylor, Jan 14, 1909, in London, England; died Sept 11, 1996, in New York, NY; dau. of E.J. Taylor and Mary Forbes (1880–1974, actress); sister of Ralph Forbes (actor who m. Ruth Chatterton); m. Frederic Voight (died); m. Merrill Shepard. ❖ Made stage debut with the Old Vic (1928); made Broadway debut in *The Barretts of Wimpole Street* (1931), which ran for 4 years; other plays in NY include *Lucrece*, *Romeo and Juliet*, *Candida*, *Pride and Prejudice*, *Save Me the Waltz*, *Heartbreak House*, *Ring Round the Moon*, *The Reluctant Debutante*, *The Loves of Cass McGuire*, *The Constant Wife* and *My Fair Lady*; made film debut (1940) and appeared on tv, notably in Cocteau's *La voix humaine*.

FORBES, Esther (1891–1967). American writer. Name variations: Mrs. A.L. Hoskins. Born in Westborough, Massachusetts, June 28, 1891; died in Worcester, Massachusetts, Aug 12, 1967; dau. of William Trowbridge (judge) and Harriette (Merrifield) Forbes (historian and author); attended University of Wisconsin, 1916–18; m. Albert Learned Hoskins Jr., 1926 (div. 1933). ❖ Joined editorial staff of Houghton Mifflin (1919) and worked in spare time on 1st novel, *O Genteel Lady!* (1926); with 2nd book, *A Mirror for Witches* (1928), established her reputation as a historical novelist; focusing on New England in writings, was known for her meticulous research and vibrant, well-drawn characters; reached height of fame with publication of 2 books for children, *Paul Revere and the World He Lived In*, which captured the Pulitzer Prize for History, and *Johnny Tremain*, which won the Newbery Medal (both 1943); also won critical acclaim with children's biography, *America's Paul Revere* (1948); was the 1st woman member of the American Antiquarian Society. ❖ See also *Women in World History*.

FORBES, Joan Rosita (1893–1967). See Forbes, Rosita.

FORBES, Kathryn (1909–1966). See McLean, Kathryn.

FORBES, Margaret (c. 1807–1877). New Zealand innkeeper. Name variations: Margaret Cooper. Born Margaret Cooper, c. 1807, at Fraserburgh, Aberdeenshire, Scotland; died Jan 13, 1877, at Onehunga, New Zealand; dau. of Robert (farmer) and Elizabeth (Ross) Cooper; m. Robert Forbes, 1830 (died 1849); children: 8. ❖ Immigrated to New Zealand with husband and 6 of her children (1841); relocated to Onehunga, where she helped husband operate inn (1844); after husband died before issuance of title deeds and despite much protest, lost most of land to government and was forced to sell liquor license (1857). ❖ See also *Dictionary of New Zealand Biography* (Vol. 1).

FORBES, Margie (1896–1918). See Dean, Margie.

FORBES, Mary (1880–1974). English actress. Born Jan 1 (some sources cite Dec 30, 1883), 1880, in Hornsey, England; died July 23, 1974, in Beaumont, California; m. E.J. Taylor; m. Charles Quartermaine (div.); m. Wesley Wall; children: (1st m.) Brenda Forbes (1909–1996) and Ralph Forbes (both actors). ❖ Began career in music halls; made London debut in *The Two Pins* (1908); had a long and prestigious stage career on both sides of the Atlantic; films include *Sunny Side Up*, *The Brat*, *Farewell to Arms*, *Cavalcade*, *Les Miserables*, *Laddie*, *Anna Karenina*, *Awful Truth*, *You Can't Take It With You*, *Picture of Dorian Gray*, *Terror by Night* and *Earl Carroll Vanities*.

FORBES, Mary Elizabeth (1879–1964). American stage and screen actress and model. Born Nov 8, 1879, Rochester, NY; died Sept 3 (some sources cite Aug 20), 1964, in Hollywood, California. ❖ Was Harrison Fisher's favorite cover girl and also modeled for Charles Dana Gibson; appeared in such plays as *Wildfire, Barbara Frietchie, Earl of Pawtucket, Walls of Jericho, Alias Jimmy Valentine, Trelawny of the Wells, Peter Pan* and *What Every Woman Knows,* and in a few Hollywood silent films.

FORBES, Rosita (1893–1967). English traveler and writer. Name variations: Joan Rosita Forbes. Born Joan Rosita Torr in Swinderley, Lincolnshire, England, 1893; died 1967; dau. of Herbert J. Torr; educated privately; m. Col. Ronald Forbes, c. 1910 (div. 1917); m. Col. Arthur T. McGrath, 1921. ❖ Traversed the world several times during lifetime, turning out novels and nonfiction based on her experiences; began career (1915), driving an ambulance for French Societé de Secours aux Blessés Militaires and winning two medals for valor; travels took her to every country in the world with exception of Tibet and New Zealand, and on one of her trips around the world, covered 30 countries in 13 months; published 1st book *Unconducted Wanderers* (1919); other writings include *The Sultan of the Mountains: The Life Story of Raisuli* (1924), *From Red Sea to Blue Nile* (1925), *Sirocco* (1927), *Conflict: Angora to Afghanistan* (1931), *Ordinary People* (1931), *Forbidden Road: Kabul to Samarkand* (1937), *These Are Real People* (1937), *India of the Princes* (1939), *A Unicorn in the Bahamas* (1940) and *These Men I Knew* (1940).

FORBES-ROBERTSON, Beatrice (1883–1967). English stage actress. Born Sept 11, 1883, in England; died Mar 16, 1967; dau. of Gertrude (Knight) Forbes-Robertson and Ian Forbes-Robertson; m. Swinburne Hale. ❖ Made stage debut as a walk-on in Manchester with Sir Henry Irving's company in *Robespierre* (1899), followed by *Mamma;* then toured with J. Forbes-Robertson, playing Ophelia and Desdemona, as well as Militza in *For the Crown,* among others; also appeared in such plays as *Mademoiselle Mars, Letty* (as Marion Allardyce), *Saturday to Monday,* and as Ophelia in *Hamlet* with Beerbohm Tree; accompanied Ellen Terry on her American tour (1906), making NY debut in *The Good Hope,* and later becoming a member of the New Theatre company in US; lectured on Shakespearean drama in US, Canada, and Great Britain.

FORBES-ROBERTSON, Gertrude. *See Elliott, Gertrude.*

FORBES-ROBERTSON, Jean (1905–1962). English stage star. Name variations: Anne McEwen. Born Mar 16, 1905, in London, England; died Dec 24, 1962, in London; dau. of Sir J(ohnston) Forbes-Robertson (actor-manager) and Gertrude Elliott (1874–1950); sister of Diana Forbes-Robertson (author); niece of Maxine Elliott (1868–1940, actress); m. James Hamilton (div.); m. André Van Gyseghem. ❖ Made stage debut in her mother's company in Natal under name Anne McEwen in *Paddy the Next Best Thing* (1921); debuted in London as Catherine Westcourt in *Dancing Mothers* (1925); starred or featured in numerous plays, including *Uncle Vanya, Don Juan, Berkeley Square,* Juliet in *Romeo and Juliet, The Dybbuk,* title role in *Hedda Gabler, Rosmersholm,* Viola in *Twelfth Night;* often starred at Old Vic and played Peter Pan for 7 seasons (1927–34).

FORBES-SEMPILL, Elizabeth (1912–1965). Scottish aristocrat and physician. Name variations: Elizabeth Forbes Sempill; Dr. Ewan Forbes-Sempill; Sir Ewan Forbes, 20th Lord Sempill. Born Sept 6, 1912, at Craigevar, Aberdeen, Scotland; died Sept 12, 1991, in Scotland; 3rd and youngest dau. of John Forbes-Sempill, 18th Baron Sempill and 9th baronet (died 1934); m. Isabella Mitchell (receptionist and housekeeper), 1952. ❖ Took up a medical practice in Alford (1945) and began dressing as a man; since the titles of the family always passed through the male line, applied to the sheriff of Aberdeen for a warrant for birth re-registration as a male (1952), henceforth known as Dr. Ewan Forbes-Sempill; as a transsexual, married Isabella Mitchell that same year; when brother William died (1965), successfully claimed the titles (Dec 30, 1965).

FORCE, Julia (1860—). American murderer. Born 1860. ❖ Shot sisters Minnie (for her loud humming) and Florence ("a tiresome invalid") with Civil War pistol which belonged to her father (Feb 25, 1893); her trial in Atlanta, Georgia, resulted in a life sentence.

FORCE, Juliana (1876–1948). American art museum administrator. Born Juliana Reiser (later changed name to Rieser), Dec 25, 1876, in Doylestown, Pennsylvania; died in New York, NY, Aug 28, 1948; m. Dr. Willard B. Force. ❖ The 1st director of the Whitney Museum of American Art, ran the Whitney until her death (1930–48).

FORD, Atina (c. 1972—). Canadian curler. Born c. 1972 in Gray, Saskatchewan, Canada. ❖ Won a gold medal for curling at Nagano Olympics (1998); with Team Schmirler, won the World championship (1997).

FORD, Betty (1918—). American first lady. Born Elizabeth Ann Bloomer, April 8, 1918, in Chicago, Illinois; dau. of William Stephenson (industrial supply salesman) and Hortense (Neahr) Bloomer; attended Bennington School of Dance at Bennington College; studied with Martha Graham in NY; m. William C. Warren (furniture dealer), 1942 (div. 1947); m. Gerald Ford (president of US), Oct 15, 1948; children: (2nd m.) Michael Ford (b. 1950); John Ford (b. 1952); Steven Ford (b. 1956); Susan Ford (b. 1957). ❖ In the course of 10 months, went from being wife of House Minority Leader, to being wife of vice-president of US, to being wife of president of US, to being a sought-after first lady (1973–1974); blossomed into a gracious and capable first lady and an outspoken crusader for women's rights (1974–77); made her most significant and lasting contributions to the nation with her courage and honesty in dealing with personal tragedies, 1st breast cancer, then addiction to alcohol and drugs; established the Betty Ford Center in Rancho Mirage, California (1982). ❖ See also autobiographies (with Chris Chase) *Betty: A Glad Awakening* (Doubleday, 1987) and *The Times of My Life* (Harper & Row, 1978); and *Women in World History.*

FORD, Eileen (1922—). American entrepreneur. Born Eileen Otte, May 25, 1922, in New York, NY; dau. of Nathaniel Otte and Loretta Marie (Laine) Otte; Barnard College, BS, 1943; m. Gerard William Ford, known as Jerry Ford (entrepreneur), Nov 20, 1944; children: Gerard William Ford, known as Bill Ford (president of Ford's licensing division); A. Lacey Ford (who m. John Williams); M. Katie Ford (who m. André Balazs and became CEO of Ford Agency, 1995); Margaret Ford, also known as Jamie Ford (who m. Robert Craft). ❖ With husband, started the Ford Model Agency in a Manhattan walkup (1948); revolutionized modeling by establishing standardized fees and acting as agents for models by collecting fees and handling bookings; had flair for spotting charismatic models; discoveries include Lauren Hutton, Jean Shrimpton, Capucine, Jane Fonda, Candice Bergen, Suzy Parker, Christie Brinkley, Jerry Hall, Cheryl Tiegs, Brooke Shields, Ali MacGraw, Penelope Tree, and Christy Turlington. ❖ See also *Women in World History.*

FORD, Elbur (1906–1993). *See Hibbert, Eleanor.*

FORD, Elizabeth Bloomer (b. 1918). *See Ford, Betty.*

FORD, Harriet (c. 1863–1949). American playwright and screenwriter. Born c. 1863 in Seymour, Connecticut; died Dec 12, 1949, in New York, NY; m. Dr. Fordé Morgan. ❖ Following career as an actress, wrote such plays as *The Awakening* (with Caroline Duer), *The Fourth Estate* (with J.M. Paterson), *The Argyle Case, The Dummy, On the Hiring Line, Mr. Lazarus* (with Harvey O'Higgins), *The Greatest Thing in the World* (with Beatrice de Mille), *Christopher Rand* (with Eleanor Robson) and *The Land of the Free* (with Fannie Hurst); also adapted many of her plays for the screen.

FORD, Isabella O. (1855–1924). British feminist. Born in Leeds, England, 1855; died 1924; dau. of Robert (solicitor) and Hannah (Pease) Ford (both Quakers); sister of Bessie Ford. ❖ Began a long campaign to reform conditions for women textile workers in Leeds (1885); joining with Emma Paterson, helped form a Machinists' Society for tailors; established the Leeds Tailoresses' Union and was elected president (1889); with sister Bessie and sister-in-law Helen Cordelia, helped form the Leeds Women's Suffrage Society (1890); helped organize the Leeds branch of the Independent Labor Party (1893); by 1900, had gained a national reputation as a speaker and organizer for the women's movement; also wrote books on the struggle for equality, including *Women's Wages* (1893), *Industrial Women* (1900) and *Socialism* (1904); became a member of the national executive committee of Independent Labor Party (1903); elected to the executive committee of National Union of Women Suffrage Societies (NUWSS, 1907); in later years, put all her effort into the peace movement, serving as a delegate to Women's International League Congress (1919–22). ❖ See also *Women in World History.*

FORD, Ita (1940—). American nun and martyr. Born April 23, 1940, in Brooklyn, NY; killed Dec 2, 1980, in El Salvador; attended Marymount College. ❖ Joined the Maryknoll Sisters (1971); assigned to Chile, lived in the shantytown of Santiago, ministering to the poor (1973–80); following the appeal of Archbishop Romero for help in El Salvador, relocated there (Mar 1980); was slain by National Guardsmen in El Salvador, along with Maura Clarke, Dorothy Kazel and Jean Donovan.

FORD, Jan (1929—). *See Moore, Terry.*

FORD, Judith (c. 1950—). Miss America. Name variations: Judith Ford Nash. Born Judith Anne Ford c. 1950, in Belvidere, Illinois; University of Illinois, BS in phys. ed.; m. Jim Nash (attorney); children: 2 sons. ❖ Was a world-class trampolinist; named Miss America (1969), representing Illinois; served on the President's Council on Physical Fitness and Sports for 8 years. ❖ See also Frank Deford, *There She Is* (Viking, 1971).

FORD, Judy (1929—). *See Moore, Terry.*

FORD, Lita (1958—). English hard-rock musician. Born Carmelita Rosanna Ford, Sept 18, 1958, in London, England; m. Chris Holmes, 1987 (div. 1992); m. Jim Gillette (singer), 1994; children: 2. ❖ Was a member of the all-girl band, the Runaways, with Joan Jett; released solo debut as hard-rock artist *Out for Blood* (1983); as guitarist and singer, broke new ground for women in hard-rock world; became 1st woman inducted into *Circus* magazine's Hall of Fame in 20 years and 1st woman on cover of *Hit Parader;* released hit singles from platinum album *Lita* (1988), including "Kiss Me Deadly" and "Close My Eyes Forever" (duet with Ozzy Osbourne). Additional solo albums include *Dancin' on the Edge* (1984), *Stiletto* (1990), *The Best of Lita Ford* (1992) and *Lita Live* (2000).

FORD, Mary (1924–1977). American pop singer. Born Colleen Summers, July 7, 1924, in Pasadena, California; died Sept 30, 1977; m. Les Paul (guitarist), 1949 (div. 1963); m. Dan Hatfield (contractor). ❖ Was a country-and-western singer on Gene Autry's Sunday night radio program when she met guitarist Les Paul, who changed her singing style and both of their careers; singing with his innovative echo and multiple-track recording techniques (considered years ahead of their time), released 1st record, "Lover" (1949); followed that with a string of hits, including "How High the Moon" and "Vaya Con Dios." ❖ See also *Women in World History.*

FORD, Maude (1888–1963). *See George, Maude.*

FORD, Michelle Jan (1962—). Australian swimmer. Name variations: Michelle Ford-Eriksson. Born July 15, 1962, in Sans Souci, Sydney, Australia. ❖ Won 6 Australian indiv. championships (in the 200-meter butterfly, 200-, 800-, and 1,500-meter freestyle), and one relay championship; won a gold medal at Commonwealth games in Edmonton (1978) and Brisbane (1982); won a bronze medal for the 200-meter butterfly and a gold medal for the 800-meter freestyle at Moscow Olympics (1980). Awarded OBE.

FORD, Patricia (1921—). Northern Ireland politician. Born Patricia Smiles, April 5, 1921; dau. of Lt.-Col. Sir W.D. Smiles (MP, drowned on sinking of *M.V. Princess Victoria*, Jan 31, 1953); m. Dr. Lionel Ford (dean of York and headmaster of Harrow), 1941 (div. 1956); m. Sir Nigel Fisher (MP for Surbiton), 1956. ❖ Representing the Unionist Party, elected to House of Commons at Westminster in a by-election (1953) for North Down, succeeding her father; retired (1955).

FORD, Penny (1964—). African-American rhythm-and-blues singer. Name variations: Pennye Ford; S.O.S. Band. Born Nov 6, 1964, in Cincinnati, Ohio; dau. of Gene Redd Sr. (record executive) and Carolyn Ford (singer); sister of Sharon Redd (singer). ❖ Vocalist with numerous groups, replaced Mary Davis as singer on S.O.S Band and had R&B hit with "I'm Still Missing Your Love" from album, *Diamonds in the Raw* (1987); joined rapper Turbo B. to form duo, Snap! (c. 1989) and released highly successful debut album, *World Power* (1990); had US and UK smash hit with single, "The Power," and had 5 more Top-10 hits in UK; quit Snap! to pursue solo career and released album *Penny Ford* (1993); worked with a number of performers, including Chaka Khan and groups, Soul II Soul and Massive Attack.

FORD, Susan (1957—). American first daughter. Name variations: Susan Ford Bales. Born July 6, 1957, in Washington, DC; dau. of Gerald Ford (president of US) and Betty Ford; m. Charles Vance (Secret Service agent, div. 1988); m. Vaden Bales (attorney), 1989; children: 2 daughters. ❖ Spent adolescence in the White House (1974–77); assisted mother with the Betty Ford Foundation; became a widely recognized speaker on substance abuse and an advocate for breast cancer awareness; replaced mother as board chair of the Betty Ford Center (2005); wrote mystery novels *Double Exposure* and *Sharp Focus.*

FORDE, Eugenie (1879–1940). American silent-film actress. Name variations: Eugenia Forde. Born June 22, 1879, in New York, NY; died Sept 5, 1940, in Van Nuys, California; m. Guy H. Fetters, 1920; children: Victoria Forde (actress) and Eugene Forde (director). ❖ Made film debut in *A Pair of Jacks* (1912); appeared in over 50 movies, including *Uncle Bill, The Outlaw's Bride, Ma's Girls, Pals in Blue, The White Rosette, Lonesome Town, Sis Hopkins, The Road to Divorce* and *Memory Lane.*

FORDE, Florrie (1876–1940). Australian-born comedian and singer. Born Aug 14, 1876, in Melbourne, Australia; died April 18, 1940, in Aberdeen, Scotland; dau. of Francis Lott Flanagan; m. Laurence Barnett. ❖ Made 1st stage appearance in Sydney (1893); made London debut at the Pavilion (1897) and subsequently appeared in all the leading music halls in Great Britain and as principal boy in several pantomimes; popularized such songs as "Down at the Old Bull and Bush," "She's a Lassie from Lancashire," "On a Sunday Afternoon," "Pal o' Mine," "Easy Street," "Waltz Me Round Again Willie," "Has Anybody Here Seen Kelly?," "Flanagan," "Looping the Loop with Lucy" and "Only a Working Girl."

FORDE, Leneen (1935—). Canadian-born governor of Queensland. Born Leneen Kavanagh in Ottawa, Canada; m. Francis Gerard Forde (son of Francis and Vera Forde), 1955 (died 1966); m. Angus McDonald (detective superintendent and district commander of the NSW police force), 1983 (died 1999); children: 5. ❖ Moved to Australia (1954); became a solicitor; chaired the Commission of Inquiry in Abuse of Children in Queensland Institutions (1998–99); served as 22nd governor of Queensland (July 29, 1992–July 29, 1997); was chancellor of Griffith University. Appointed Companion of the Order of Australia (1993).

FORDE, Maude (1888–1963). *See George, Maude.*

FORDE, Phyllis (1858–1946). *See Bruce, Kate.*

FORDE, Vera (1894–1967). Australian prime-ministerial wife. Born Veronica Catherine O'Reilly, 1894, in Wagga Wagga, New South Wales, Australia; died Nov 9, 1967, in St. Lucia, Brisbane; m. Frank (Michael) Forde (prime minister of Australia for 8 days, 1945); children: Mary, Mercia, Clare, and Francis Gerard Forde (who married Leneen Kavanagh Forde, governor of Queensland). ❖ Accompanied the Australian delegation to the conference that established the United Nations (1945); served as host at Australia House in Ottawa, where husband was High Commissioner to Canada (1947–53).

FORDE, Victoria (1896–1964). American actress. Born April 21, 1896, in New York, NY; died July 24, 1964, in Beverly Hills, California; dau. of Eugenie Forde (1879–1940, actress); sister of Eugene Forde; m. Tom Mix (cowboy star), 1918 (div. 1931). ❖ Joined Selig (1915) and starred opposite Tom Mix; films include *The $5,000 Elopement, Local Color, Some Duel, The Cowboy God Forgot* and *Western Blood.*

FORDE-PIGOTT, Mimi (d. 1966). *See Crawford, Mimi.*

FORDER, Annemarie (1978—). Australian shooter. Born Jan 31, 1978, in Queensland, Australia. ❖ Won a gold medal at Commonwealth Games (1998); won a bronze medal for 10m air pistol at Sydney Olympics (2000).

FORDHAM, Julia (1962—). British singer and songwriter. Born Aug 10, 1962, in Portsmouth, Hampshire, England. ❖ Established cult following in US and mainstream success in Japan and Europe as singer-songwriter (late 1980s); albums include *Julia Fordham* (1988), *Porcelain* (1989), *Swept* (1991), *Falling Forward* (1994), *East West* (1997), and *The Julia Fordham Collection* (1999).

FORESTER, Fanny (1817–1854). *See Judson, Emily Chubbuck.*

FORESTIER, Auber (1841–1929). *See Moore, Annie.*

FORGAN, Liz (1944—). Scottish journalist. Name variations: Elizabeth Forgan. Born Elizabeth Anne Lucy Forgan in 1944 in Calcutta, India, where Scottish father was posted in army; attended Benenden School in England, then Oxford University. ❖ One of the most powerful women in British broadcast journalism, worked initially as journalist with English-language newspaper in Tehran and then *Hampstead and Highgate Express* in London; served as chief leader-writer on *Evening Standard* (1974–78); after being appointed women's editor at *The Guardian,* initially saw position as something to be endured but then quickly learned about women's issues and developed strong feminist commitment; became commissioning editor of factual output for Channel 4 Television (1981); introduced controversial programs that allowed broad range of opinion, such as "Right to Reply"; took over the powerful position of Director of Programs (1988); left Channel 4 to become managing director of BBC Network Radio, bringing creative vitality to BBC's 5 national radio stations; left position with BBC because of her opposition to Sir John Birt's ultimately unsuccessful attempt to merge radio and tv into one giant news-gathering source; set up media consultancy. Given Order of British Empire (OBE, 1999).

FORKEL, Karen (1970—). German javelin thrower. Born Sept 24, 1970, in Wolfen, Sachsen-Anhalt, Germany. ❖ At Barcelona Olympics, won a bronze medal in javelin throw (1992).

FORLí, Countess of (1462–1509). See Sforza, Caterina.

FORMAN, Ada (b. around 1895). American concert and theater dancer. Born c. 1895, probably in California. ❖ Danced with Denishawn on tour (1915–16); partnered Ted Shawn in numerous works including *Danse Javanese* (1915), in abstractions such as *Nature Rhythms* (1915), and in exhibition ballroom works such as *Dance Vogue* (1916); left Denishawn to appear solo in vaudeville on the Keith-Albee circuit; performed successfully in Broadway revues, roof garden shows, and in *Greenwich Village Follies of 1922;* also appeared often in London (1920s) to great acclaim.

FORMBY, Margaret (1929–2003). American museum founder. Born in Van Horn, Texas, July 12, 1929; died April 10, 2003, at home in Hereford, Texas; graduate of Texas Tech University; m. Clint Formby; children: Chip, Marshall, Scott Formby and Mary Beth Powell. ❖ Spent nearly 20 years developing the National Cowgirl Hall of Fame which she opened in Hereford in 1975 (it was moved to Fort Worth in 1994). Inducted into Texas Tech Rodeo Hall of Fame (1993) and Cowgirl Hall of Fame (1994).

FÓRMICA, Mercedes (1916—). Spanish novelist. Name variations: Mercedes Formica. Born 1916 in Cádiz, Spain. ❖ Graduated 1945 and practised law; writings, which criticize patriarchal society, include *La ciudad perdida* (1951) and *A instancia de parte* (1955).

FORMIGA (1978—). See Maciel Mota, Miraildes.

FORNALSKA, Malgorzata (1902–1944). Polish revolutionary. Name variations: (underground alias) Jasia. Born June 10, 1902, in Fajslawice, Poland; shot by Nazi captors in Warsaw, Poland, July 26, 1944. ❖ Living in Russia during the revolution, joined the Marxist Social Democratic Party of the Kingdom of Poland and Lithuania (1918); also joined the Red Army; returning to Poland (1921), settled in Lublin where she became a member of Communist Party of Poland (KRPR); as a revolutionary activist, arrested (1922) and sentenced to over 4 years imprisonment; on release, went to Moscow where she worked in the international revolutionary organization, the Communist International; returning to Poland (1934), took a post in the agricultural section of KRPR; arrested (1936), was still in the Warsaw prison when Nazi Germany attacked Poland (Sept 1, 1939); a few days before Warsaw surrendered to German forces, was released and escaped to Bialystok in the newly annexed territories of Soviet Ukraine; worked with Soviet forces behind front lines to establish resistance groups to free Poland from Nazi occupation; parachuted into occupied Poland (1942), immediately joining up with the underground; arrested in Warsaw (Nov 14, 1943) and incarcerated in Pawiak prison; became one of the martyrs celebrated in People's Republic of Poland, with streets, squares and schools named in her honor. ❖ See also *Women in World History.*

FORNARI, Maria Victoria (1562–1617). Italian nun and founder. Born Maria Victoria Fornari, 1562, in Genoa, Italy; died 1617; m. Angelo Strata, 1579 (died 1587); children: 6. ❖ When all her children had grown, entered the religious life; carried out a long-time dream of endowing her native town with a convent consecrated to the honor of the Annunciation of the Blessed Virgin; with several companions, received the white tunic, blue scapular, belt, and cape that would define the order of Celestial Annunciades (1604); served for 6 years as abbess of the convent before retiring from her official duties to live out her life as a nun. ❖ See also *Women in World History.*

FORNAROLI, Cia (1888–1954). Italian ballet dancer and choreographer. Born Oct 16, 1888, in Milan, Italy; died Aug 16, 1954, in New York, NY; m. Walter Toscanini. ❖ Performed as a child at Teatro alla Scala in Milan; joined ballet company of Metropolitan Opera in NY where she danced for 4 seasons (1910–14); danced as prima ballerina at Teatro Principale in Barcelona (1914–16), while also appearing at Teatro Colón in Buenos Aires; returned to La Scala soon after where she remained until 1933; worked on Italian films including *L'Anello di Pierro* (1917), *Nanà* (1918), *Il Castello del Diavolo* (1919), and the 5-part serial *I Setti Pecatti Capitali* (1919–20); directed own company in

San Remo, for which she choreographed numerous works of her own; moved to New York City where she taught classes at dance studios (1943–50) and held tenure as company teacher of Ballet Theater; held large collection of 18th- and 19th- century ballet libretti and materials which were donated to dance collection at New York Public Library upon her death (1954). Choreographed works including *I Carillion Magico* (1919), *Thais* (1920), *Nerone* (1924), *Vecchia Milano* (1928), *Pantea* (1932) and *Vesuvio* (1933).

FORNIA, Rita (1878–1922). American mezzo-soprano. Born Regina Newman in San Francisco, California, July 17, 1878; died in Paris, France, Oct 27, 1922. ❖ Made debut in Hamburg (1901), then joined Henry Savage's Opera Company in US; appeared at Metropolitan Opera (1907–22), often in secondary roles. ❖ See also *Women in World History.*

FORREST, Ann (1895–1985). Danish-born actress. Name variations: Anne Forrest; Anne Kroman. Born Anna Kromann, April 14, 1895, in Sønderho, Denmark; died Oct 25, 1895, in San Diego, California. ❖ Under name Anna Kromann, made film debut in *The Truth of Fiction* (1915) and subsequently appeared in *The Rainbow Trail, The Prince Chap, The Faith Healer, The Man Who Played God, If Winter Comes* and *Ridin' Pretty;* made NY stage debut as Lily Chang in *The Black Cockatoo* (1926), followed by *Quicksand, Gang War, Carnival, Sweet Land of Liberty, The Channel Road* and *The Enemy Within,* among others; scored great success as Frankie in *Frankie and Johnnie* (1930).

FORREST, Catherine Sinclair (1817–1891). See Sinclair, Catherine.

FORREST, Helen (1918–1999). American band singer. Name variations: sang under Helen Trees, Helen Farraday, Fran Helene, Hilda Farrar, and Bonnie Blue. Born April 12, 1918, in Atlantic City, New Jersey; died July 11, 1999, in Los Angeles, California; m. drummer Al Spieldock (div.); m. actor Paul Hogan (div.); m. businessman Charlie Feinman, 1959 (divorced). ❖ Popular singer of the big-band era, was a vocalist for 3 of the top bandleaders of her day: Artie Shaw, Benny Goodman, and Harry James; reached peak of career (early 1940s) with such hits as "I Had the Craziest Dream," "Skylark," "I Cried for You," "I've Heard That Song Before" and "I Don't Want to Walk Without You." ❖ See also *Women in World History.*

FORREST, Lottie Pickford (1895–1936). See Pickford, Lottie.

FORREST, Sally (1928—). American actress and dancer. Born Katherine Sally Feeny, May 28, 1928, in San Diego, California; dau. of amateur ballroom dancers; m. Milo Frank, 1951. ❖ Made film debut as a dancer in *Till the Clouds Roll By* (1947); came to prominence in four Ida Lupino films: *Not Wanted* (1949), *Never Fear* (1950), *Hard Fast and Beautiful* (1951) and *While the City Sleeps (1956);* appeared on Broadway in *The Seven Year Itch.*

FORRESTER, Helen (b. 1919). See Bhatia, June.

FORSBERG, Magdalena (1967—). Swedish biathlete. Name variations: Magdalena Wallin. Born Magdalena Wallin, July 25, 1967, in Oernskoldsvik, Sweden; m. Henrik Forsberg (biathlete), 1996. ❖ Competed at Albertville Olympics in cross-country skiing under maiden name but did not medal (1992); as a biathlete, won 6 consecutive World Cup titles (1997–2002); won 1st of 2 World championship titles (1997); won bronze medals for the 15km indiv. and 7.5km sprint at Salt Lake City (2002); retired (2002).

FORSH, Olga (1873–1961). Russian novelist and short-story writer. Name variations: Ol'ga Dmitrievna Forsh. Born 1873 in Russia; died 1961. ❖ Studied art and taught drawing at high school; historical novels, which often explore moral or psychological conflict, include *Clad in Stone* (1924), *The Contemporaries* (1926), *The Hot Shop* (1926), *The Mad Ship* (1931), *The Symbolists* (1933), *Radischev* (trilogy, 1932–39), and *Pioneers of Liberty* (1953); also wrote film scripts, including *Palace and Fortress,* and plays, including *Copernicus' Death* (1919).

FORSTER, Margaret (1938—). British novelist. Born Margaret Forster, May 25, 1938, in Carlisle, Cumberland, England; dau. of Arthur Gordon Forster and Lilian Hind Forster; Somerville College, Oxford, BA in modern history, 1960; m. Hunter Davies (writer), 1960; children: 3. ❖ Taught in Islington for 3 years; published *Dame's Delight* (1964), followed by the bestselling *Georgy Girl* (1965), which was filmed with Lynn Redgrave; other works include *The Park* (1968), *Fenella Phizackerly* (1970), *The Seduction of Mrs. Pendlebury* (1974), *The Bride of Lowther Fell* (1980), *Significant Sisters: The Grassroots of Feminism 1839–1939*

(1984), *Elizabeth Barrett Browning* (1998), and *Shadow Baby* (1996); worked as nonfiction reviewer for London *Evening Standard* (1977–80).

FÖRSTER-NIETZSCHE, Elisabeth (1846–1935). German writer. Name variations: Elisabeth Nietzsche; Elisabeth Forster-Nietzsche; Lisbeth or Lichen or Eli Förster. Pronunciation: FURstur-NEET-chee. Born Elisabeth Therese Alexandra Nietzsche, July 10, 1846, in Röcken, Saxony; died Nov 8, 1935, at Villa Silberblick, Weimar; dau. of Karl Ludwig Nietzsche (Lutheran pastor) and Franziska (Oehler) Nietzsche; m. Bernhard Förster, May 22, 1885; no children. ❖ Celebrated literary figure, notorious anti-Semite, who wrote books and articles on the life and ideas of her brother, Friedrich Nietzsche, and participated in the founding of the New Germany colony in Paraguay; entertaining Adolf Hitler at the Nietzsche Archive after his accession to power (1933), managed to fix in the popular mind a connection between the philosophy of her brother and Nazism; writings include *Dr. Bernhard Förster's Kolonie Neu-Germania in Paraguay* (Dr. Bernhard Förster's New Germany colony in Paraguay, 1891), *Das Leben Friedrich Nietzsches* (The Life of Friedrich Nietzsche, 2 vols., 1895–1904), *Das Nietzsches-Archiv, seine Freunde und seine Feinde* (The Nietzsche-Archive, his Friends and his Enemies, 1907), *Der junge Nietzsche* (The Young Nietzsche, 1912), *Der einsame Nietzsche* (The Lonely Nietzsche, 1914), *Wagner und Nietzsche zur Zeit ihrer Freundschaft* (Wagner and Nietzsche: Their Times and Their Friendship, 1915), and *Friedrich Nietzsche und die Frauen seiner Zeit* (Friedrich Nietzsche and the Women of His Times, 1935). ❖ See also Ben Macintyre, *Forgotten Fatherland: The Search for Elisabeth Nietzsche* (Farrar, Straus, 1992); Heinz F. Peters, *Zarathustra's Sister: The Case of Elisabeth and Friedrich Nietzsche* (Crown, 1977); "Forgotten Fatherland: The Search for Elisabeth Nietzsche" (2-part, BBC documentary, 1992); and *Women in World History*.

FORSTER-PIELOTH, Kerstin (1965—). East German rower. Name variations: Kerstin Pieloth. Born Nov 1965 in East Germany. ❖ At Seoul Olympics, won a gold medal in quadruple sculls without coxswain (1988).

FORT, Cornelia (1919–1943). American aviator. Born Cornelia Clark Fort, Feb 5, 1919, in Nashville, Tennessee; died in plane crash near Abilene, Texas, Mar 21, 1943; dau. of Rufus E. Fort, Sr. (doctor and insurance executive) and Louise (Clark) Fort; graduate of Sarah Lawrence College; never married; no children. ❖ Member of Women's Auxiliary Ferrying Squadron (WAFS) in World War II and 1st American woman killed on active duty, began flight instruction and became 2nd woman to receive commercial pilot's license (1940); served as private flight instructor and taught in Civilian Pilot Training Program in Colorado and in Hawaii (1941); witnessed Japanese attack on Pearl Harbor from the air (1941); returned to US a celebrity and was asked to recount her experience over and over to newspapers, clubs, and on radio; became 2nd volunteer accepted into WAFS (1942); was included in the 1st WAFS plane delivery from the Piper airplane factory at Lockhaven, Pennsylvania, to Long Island, New York (Oct 22, 1942); assigned to Long Beach, California, to ferry planes to Dallas, Texas (Feb 1943). ❖ See also Rob Simbeck, *Daughter of the Air: The Short Soaring Life of Cornelia Fort* (Atlantic Monthly, 1999); and *Women in World History*.

FORT, Syvilla (c. 1917–1975). American modern dancer and teacher. Born c. 1917 in Seattle, Washington; died Nov 8, 1975, in New York, NY; m. Buddy Philips (tap dancer). ❖ Trained at Cornish School in Seattle, WA, then joined faculty where she associated with John Cage and began choreographing works of her own; joined Katharine Dunham company where she served as ballet master and head of school in New York (1948–55); taught modern dance and theater with husband to many of the black choreographers of her day. Choreographed works include *Bacchanale* (c. 1940), *The Drum Beat* (1942), *Danza* (1958), *The Flies* for theater (1966), *Poetic Suite* (1969) and *Ododo* for theater (1970).

FORTEN, Charlotte (1837–1914). *See Grimké, Charlotte L. Forten.*

FORTEN, Harriet (1810–1875). *See Purvis, Harriet Forten.*

FORTEN, Margaretta (1808–1875). African-American abolitionist and educator. Born in Philadelphia, Pennsylvania, 1808; died Jan 14, 1875; dau. of James Forten (abolitionist) and his 2nd wife Charlotte (Vandine) Forten; sister of Sarah and Harriet Forten (abolitionists); aunt of Charlotte Forten Grimké (1837–1914); educated at home and at school set up by father and Grace Douglass; never married; no children. ❖ Drawn into the abolitionist fold by her upbringing, her community, and her own perceptions of American societal injustices, grew up in a home that was a place of calling for committed opponents to slavery; along with sisters Sarah and Harriet Forten, traveled to New York to attend the Women's Anti-Slavery Convention (1837); participated in drawing up the constitution that formed the Philadelphia Female Anti-Slavery Society, an interracial organization; with a keen interest in promoting the education of black children, ran a successful private school, the Lombard Street Primary School, for more than 30 years, serving as principal from 1845. ❖ See also *Women in World History*.

FORTEN, Sarah (c. 1811–1898). *See Purvis, Sarah Forten.*

FORTESCUE, May (1862–1950). English stage actress. Name variations: May Finney; Miss Fortescue. Born Emily May Finney, Feb 9, 1862, in London, England; died Sept 2, 1950; sister of Helen Ferrers (actress). ❖ Made stage debut with the D'Oyly Carte Opera Company as Lady Ella in the 1st production of *Patience* (1881), then moved with the company for the opening of the Savoy, creating the part of Celia in *Iolanthe* (1882); abandoned career on engagement to Lord Garmoyle; when he broke off engagement, sued for breach of promise, receiving £10,000 and much publicity; plays include *Dan'l Druce Blacksmith, Our Boys, The Blue Bells of Scotland, The Hunchback, The Fortune Hunter, The Cabinet Minister, Bellamy the Magnificent* and *A Man Unknown;* organized her own company and toured for many years in such plays as *Gretchen* (title role), *Moths* and *Pygmalion and Galatea.*

FORTESQUE-BRICKDALE, Eleanor (1872–1945). English painter. Name variations: Mary Eleanor Fortescue-Brickdale, Eleanor Fortescue Brickdale. Born in 1871 in Norwood, Surrey, England; died in 1945 in England; dau. of a successful lawyer; trained at Crystal Palace School of Art under Herbert Bone, 1889–97; attended Royal Academy, 1897–1900. ❖ Famed painter, illustrator and stained-glass artist who revived Pre-Raphaelite style of painting, began exhibiting illustrations and watercolors at Royal Academy (1896) and won a prize for design for academy's dining room (1897); began exhibiting large, set-piece oils such as *The Pale Complexion of True Love* (1899) and other scenes; illustrated many books of poetry and prose; had studio in Kensington (from 1902) and pursued dual career as painter and illustrator of fine color-printed editions of literary texts; taught for some years at Byam Shaw School of Art; traveled extensively in Italy and south of France; employed vibrant colors and chose moral or medieval subjects (including many paintings of fairies) as "second-wave" Pre-Raphaelite painter; painted posters for British government during WWI and was in great demand for stained-glass skills following the war. Was 1st woman to be elected member of Royal Institute of Oil Painters (1902) and the 1st to be associate member of Royal Society of Painters in Watercolor (1903). ❖ See also *Centenary Exhibition of Works by Eleanor Fortescue-Brickdale, 1872–1945, 1 Dec 1972–7 Jan 1973* (Ashmolean Museum, 1972).

FORTH, Sally (1892–1959). *See Tracy, Mona Innis.*

FORTI, Simone (c. 1935—). American postmodernist choreographer. Born c. 1935, in Florence, Italy. ❖ Immigrated with family to US as a child and was raised in Los Angeles, California; trained and began work with Ann Halprin in San Francisco (1956); worked in Dancers' Workshop with Halprin in performance creations and improvisation for 4 years; moved to NY (1959) where she trained and associated with Merce Cunningham, Martha Graham, Robert Whitman, Robert Dunn, and more; began choreographing works of her own (1960) which are now recognized as crucial forerunners to genre of improvisation of 1970s; presented works at Reuben Gallery (1960), equipment piece at Yoko Ono-sponsored event (1961), and numerous other venues throughout New York City. Works of choreography include *Rollers* (1960), *Hangers* (1961), *Platforms* (1961), *Face Tunes* (1967), *Throat Dance* (1968), *The Zero* (1974), *Big Room* (1975), *Red Green* (1975), *Estuary* (1979) and *Home Base* (1979).

FORTIBUS, Isabella de (1237–1293). *See Isabella de Redvers.*

FORTUNE, Louise (1901–1981). *See Lorraine, Louise.*

FORTUNE, Mary (fl. 1866–1910). Australian mystery writer. Name variations: (pseudonyms) W.W., Waif Wander. Wrote between 1866 and 1910; m. Joseph Fortune; m. Percy Rollo Brett, 1858. ❖ Arrived in Australia from Canada and moved to remote goldfield; the 1st woman in Australia to write detective fiction, began with stories in the *Australian Journal*, eventually publishing over 500; pioneered police procedural in fiction; wrote series *The Detective's Album* which was published for more than 40 years; other serialized works include *The Secrets of Balbrooke* (1866), *The Detective's Album: Tales of the Australian Police* (1871), *Navvie's Tales: Retold by the Boss* (1874–75), and *Twenty Six Years Ago,* *or the Diggings from '55* (1882–83). ❖ See also Lucy Sussex, ed., *The Fortunes of Mary Fortune* (Spinifex, 1989).

FORTUYN-LEENMANS, Margaretha Droogleever (1909–1998). Dutch poet and psychiatrist. Name variations: Margaretha Leenmans; (pseudonym) M. Vasalis or Maria Vasalis (Vasalis is Latin for Leenmans). Born Feb 13, 1909, in The Hague, Netherlands; died Oct 16, 1998, in Roden, Netherlands. ❖ Studied medicine and anthropology and worked as a doctor and children's psychiatrist; writings, which achieved popular and critical success, include *Parken en woestijnen* (1940), *Onweer* (1940), *De vogel Phoenix* (1947), *Vergezichten en gezichten* (1954), *Kunstenaar en verzet* (1958). Awarded P.C. Hooft Prize (1982) for complete oeuvre.

FORZ, Avelina de (1259–1274). See Avelina de Forz.

FORZ, Isabella de (1237–1293). See Isabella de Redvers.

FOSBURGH, Minnie Astor (1906–1978). American socialite and philanthropist. Name variations: Mary Cushing; Minnie Astor. Born Mary Benedict Cushing, Jan 27, 1906; died in New York, NY, Nov 4, 1978; dau. of Henry Cushing (neurosurgeon) and Katherine "Kate" (Crowell) Cushing; sister of Betsey Cushing Roosevelt Whitney (1908–1998) and Babe Paley (1915–1978); m. Vincent Astor (b. 1891, real estate tycoon whose 1st wife was Helen Huntington Astor, later Helen Huntington Hull); m. James Whitney Fosburgh (painter); no children. ❖ As a patron of the arts, served as a trustee of the Metropolitan Museum of Art and supported struggling young artists; her salons became famous for their glittering guest lists, which included such notables as composer Leonard Bernstein, playwright Tennessee Williams, and Princess Margaret Rose of England. ❖ See also David Grafton, *The Sisters: The Lives and Times of the Fabulous Cushing Sisters* (Villard, 1992); and *Women in World History.*

FOSHKO, Julia Adler (1897–1995). See Adler, Julia.

FOSSEY, Dian (1932–1985). American primatologist. Name variations: Nyirmachabelli (The Woman Who Lives Alone on the Mountain). Born Jan 16, 1932, in Atherton, California; murdered on Dec 27, 1985, at Karisoke, Rwanda; dau. of George Fossey III (insurance agent) and Kathryn Fossey; attended University of California at Davis, 1950; graduate of San Jose State College, 1954; granted doctorate from Cambridge, 1976; never married; no children. ❖ Controversial primatologist who waged an unrelenting battle to save the mountain gorillas of central Africa, began career directing the Occupational Therapy department at Kosair Crippled Children's Hospital in Louisville, Kentucky (1955–65); went on 1st tour of Africa (1963); with backing of Louis Leakey, left for Africa (1966); set up camp in the Kabara Meadow (1967); escorted off the mountain by soldiers because of outbreak of hostilities in Congo (July 9, 1967); set up Karisoke Research Camp in Rwanda (Sept 24, 1967); except for intermittent periods, which included studies at Cambridge and lecture tours, remained at Karisoke for the rest of her life; attended Darwin College at Cambridge for 3 months (1970); was visiting professor at Cornell in Ithaca, New York (1980–82). ❖ See also autobiography *Gorillas in the Mist* (Houghton-Mifflin, 1983); Harold T.P. Hayes, *The Dark Romance of Dian Fossey* (Simon & Schuster, 1990); Farley Mowat, *Woman in the Mists* (Warner, 1987); film *Gorillas in the Mist,* starring Sigourney Weaver (1989); and *Women in World History.*

FOSTER, Abigail Kelley (1810–1887). See Kelley, Abby.

FOSTER, Autherine (1929—). See Lucy, Autherine Juanita.

FOSTER, Diane (1928—). Canadian runner. Born Sept 13, 1928, in Canada. ❖ At London Olympics, won a bronze medal in 4x100-meter relay (1948).

FOSTER, Dianne (1928—). Canadian actress and director. Born Dianne Laruska, Oct 31, 1928, in Edmonton, Alberta, Canada; m. Joel Murcott, 1954 (div. 1959); children: 2. ❖ Made film debut in *The Quiet Woman* (1950), followed by *The Lost Hours, Bad for Each Other, Drive a Crooked Road, The Bamboo Prison, The Kentuckian, Night Passage, The Deep Six, Gideon's Day, The Last Hurrah* and *Who's Been Sleeping in My Bed?;* frequently appeared on tv and directed the series "Tekkaman the Space Night" (1984).

FOSTER, Elizabeth (1759–1824). See Cavendish, Elizabeth.

FOSTER, Ellen (1840–1910). See Foster, J. Ellen.

FOSTER, Emily Sophia (1842–1897). New Zealand teacher and school principal. Name variations: Emily Sophia Brittan. Born Emily Sophia Brittan, Dec 18, 1842, in Sherborne, Dorsetshire, England; died Dec 30,

1897, at Rangiora, New Zealand; dau. of William Guise Brittan (newspaper editor) and Louisa (Chandler) Brittan; m. Thomas Scholfield Foster (educator), 1882; children: 2 daughters, 1 son. ❖ Immigrated to New Zealand with family (1850); obtained 1st-class teaching certificate (1874); appointed headmistress of girls' division at Christchurch West School (1875); became principal of Christchurch Girls' High School (1894). ❖ See also *Dictionary of New Zealand Biography* (Vol. 2).

FOSTER, Frances (1924–1997). African-American actress, director, and theater founder. Born Frances Brown, June 11, 1924, in Yonkers, NY; died June 17, 1997, in Fairfax, Virginia. ❖ Made NY debut in *Wisteria Trees* (1955), followed by Broadway appearances in *Raisin in the Sun, The River Niger, First Breeze of Summer, Tap Dance Kid* and *Fences* and off-Broadway appearances in *Take a Giant Step* and *Boesman and Lena,* among others; was a founding member and appeared in over 25 productions of Negro Ensemble Company (1967–86); films include *Clockers;* on tv, appeared as Vera on "The Guiding Light" (1985–92, 1993–94).

FOSTER, Gae (b. 1903). American theatrical choreographer. Born 1903 in Bunker Hill, California. ❖ Worked in association with Fanchon and Marco's productions throughout most of career including as performer in *Sunkist* (1920) and assisting Fanchon (starting 1925) as Prolog distributor; began receiving own Prolog credit (1928) for precision team, Gae's Sweet Sixteen, but continued in association with Fanchon and Marco; began serving as dance director and production stage director at Roxy Theater in NY (1933); staged dances for Gae Foster Girls—also known as Roxyettes—on bicycles, unicycles, tricycles, polo sticks, and more, which were considered fierce competition for better known Rockettes; choreographed numerous well-received pieces, such as *Swiss Maid Number* (1939) and *Shawl Dance* (1940); sent her own former dancers to stage further precision dance acts throughout Midwestern theaters.

FOSTER, Gloria (1933–2001). African-American actress. Born Nov 15, 1933, in Chicago, Illinois; died Sept 29, 2001, in New York, NY; studied at Goodman Theater School of Drama; m. Clarence Williams III (actor, div.). ❖ Made NY debut in *In White America* (1963); other plays include *A Hand Is on the Gates, Black Visions, The Cherry Orchard,* and title roles in *Medea* and *Yerma;* films include *The Cool World, Nothing but a Man, The Comedians, Man and Boy* and *The Matrix* (as Oracle). Received an Obie for *In White America* (1963).

FOSTER, Greville (1902–1964). See Texidor, Greville.

FOSTER, Hannah Webster (1758–1840). American author. Born Hannah Webster in Salisbury, Massachusetts, Sept 10, 1758; died in Montreal, Canada, April 17, 1840; m. John Foster (Unitarian minister); children: 6. ❖ Signing herself simply "A Lady of Massachusetts," published *The Coquette; or The History of Eliza Wharton,* a sentimental epistolary novel loosely based on a scandal involving a prominent Connecticut family (1789). The novel reached its peak of popularity between 1824 and 1828, though it was not until the 1866 edition that her name finally appeared on the title page. ❖ See also *Women in World History.*

FOSTER, Jacqueline (1947—). English politician. Born Dec 30, 1947, in Liverpool, England. ❖ Worked in British Airways (BEA) cabin services (1969–81, 1985–99); was a founder member and executive councillor, Cabin Crew '89 (trade union for UK airline crew, 1989–99); held various offices in Conservative Party (1988–99); as a member of the European People's Party (Christian Democrats) and European Democrats, elected to 5th European Parliament (1999–2004), from UK.

FOSTER, J. Ellen (1840–1910). American lawyer and temperance leader. Name variations: Ellen Horton or Judith Ellen Horton; Ellen Avery or Judith Ellen Avery; Judith Ellen Foster or Judith Ellen Horton Foster. Born Judith Ellen Horton, Nov 3, 1840, in Lowell, MA; died Aug 11, 1910, in Washington, DC; dau. of Jotham Horton (Methodist minister) and Judith (Delano) Horton; m. Addison Avery (leather dealer), Mar 14, 1860 (div. late 1860s); m. Elijah Caleb Foster (lawyer), July 1869 (died 1906); children: (1st m.) Mary (1860–1865), William (b. 1863); (2nd m.) Emory (b. 1870), Ellen (1871–1876). ❖ Among the 1st women admitted to the Iowa bar (1872) and possibly the 1st to practice law in the state, was a delegate to the founding convention of National Woman's Christian Temperance Union (WCTU, 1874); was admitted to Iowa Supreme Court (1875); became WCTU's legal adviser and superintendent of Legislation and Petitions (1880); authored several articles and pamphlets, including *The Constitutional Amendment Manual* (1882); opposed WCTU alignment with the Prohibition Party (early 1880s), preferring alliance with Republican Party, and resigned office (1884);

became president of the Iowa WCTU (mid-1880s), led its withdrawal from the National WCTU (1889), and founded the Non-Partisan National WCTU (1890); founded Woman's National Republican Association and served as chair (1888–1910), influencing establishment of more than 1,000 local Republican woman's clubs; traveled with Philippine Commission to Manila to research condition of Filipino women and children (1900); investigated labor conditions of American women and children (1906); as special agent for the Justice Department, reported on treatment of women inmates of federal prisons (1908).

FOSTER, Jodie (1962—). American actress and director. Born Alicia Christian Foster, Nov 19, 1962, in Los Angeles, California; dau. of Lucius and Brandy Foster; sister of Buddy and Connie Foster (both actors); graduate of College Lycée Français, 1980; graduated magna cum laude from Yale University, 1985; children: Charles Foster (b. 1998), Kit Foster (b. 2001). ❖ Began career at age 2; made tv debut on "Mayberry R.F.D." (1968); came to early prominence in *Taxi Driver* (1976), for which she was nominated for an Academy Award; won Academy Award for Best Actress for performance as Sarah Tobias in *The Accused* (1988) and for performance as Clarice Starling in *The Silence of the Lambs* (1991); directed *Little Man Tate* (1991) and *Home for the Holidays* (1995); appeared in *Tom Sawyer* (1973), *Alice Doesn't Live Here Anymore* (1974), *Freaky Friday* (1976), *The Hotel New Hampshire* (1984), *Sommersby* (1993), *Maverick* (1994), *Nell* (1994), *Contact* (1997), *Anna and the King* (1999) and *Panic Room* (2002), among others. ❖ See also Louis Chunovic, *Jodie: A Biography* (1995).

FOSTER, Lillian (d. 1949). American stage actress. Died May 15, 1949, in New York, NY. ❖ Best remembered for performance in *Conscience*; last appeared in *Goodbye My Fancy* (1949).

FOSTER, Margot (1958—). Australian rower. Born Oct 3, 1958, in Australia. ❖ At Los Angeles Olympics, won a bronze medal in coxed fours (1984).

FOSTER, Marie (1917–2003). American civil-rights activist. Born Marie Priscilla Martin on Oct 24, 1917, in Wilcox Co., Alabama; died Sept 6, 2003, in Selma, AL; children: 3. ❖ Returned to high school late in life and went on to college to study dental hygiene; became involved with civil-rights movement and helped in effort to educate African-Americans about voter registration; was beaten by police during voting-rights march in Selma (1965); continued to fight for civil rights into old age, leading fight for housing for poor in Selma, AL.

FOSTER, Susanna (1924—). American actress and singer. Born Suzanne DeLee Flanders Larson, Dec 6, 1924, in Chicago, Illinois; m. Wilbur Evans (actor), 1948 (div. 1956). ❖ An operatic singer as a child, signed with MGM at age 12 but made screen debut at 15 with Paramount in *The Great Victor Herbert* (1939); starred in *The Phantom of the Opera* (1943), *Follow the Boys, Frisco Sal* and *That Night with You*, among others; retired from the screen (1945) and later appeared on stage in operettas with husband.

FOTHERGILL, Dorothy (1945—). American bowler. Born April 10, 1945, in North Attleboro, Massachusetts. ❖ Won WIBC singles and all-events titles (1970); with Mildred Martorella, won WIBC doubles (1971, 1973); named Bowler of the Year (1968 and 1969).

FOTHERGILL, Jessie (1851–1891). British novelist. Name variations: (pseudonym) J.F. Born June 1851 in Cheethem Hill, Manchester, England; died July 28, 1891, in Berne, Switzerland; dau. of Thomas and Anne Coultate Fothergill. ❖ Influenced by Quaker faith, created characters that were often independent and politically liberal; writings include *Healey* (1875), *The First Violin* (1877), *Probation* (1879), *Kith and Kin* (1881), *Borderland: A Country-town Chronicle* (1886), *A March in the Ranks* (1890) and *Oriole's Daughter* (1893).

FOTHERINGAY. *See Denny, Sandy.*

FOUDY, Julie (1971—). American soccer player. Born Jan 23, 1971, in Mission Viejo, California; graduate of Stanford University, 1993; m. Ian Sawyers (head coach of San Jose CyberRays), 1995. ❖ Midfielder; at World Cup, won team gold medals (1991, 1999) and a bronze medal (1995); won a team gold medal at Atlanta Olympics (1996) and a team silver medal at Sydney Olympics (2000); was a founding member of the Women's United Soccer Association (WUSA); signed with the San Diego Spirit (2001), becoming captain; won a team gold medal at Athens Olympics (2004); was one of the most capped players in US history with 211 appearances. Named president of the Women's Sports Foundation (2002). ❖ See also Jere Longman, *The Girls of Summer*

(HarperCollins, 2000), and Christina Lessa, *Women Who Win* (Universe, 1998).

FOULDS-PAUL, June (1934—). *See Paul-Foulds, June.*

FOULGER, Dorothy Adams (1900–1988). *See Adams, Dorothy.*

FOUNTAINE, Margaret (1862–1940). English entomologist. Born Margaret Elizabeth Fountaine, May 16, 1862, in Norfolk, England; died April 21, 1940; dau. of a rector (died 1878); m. Khalil Neimy (interpreter and guide in Damascus). ❖ Independent collector known for her butterfly collections, discovered love of collecting while on vacation in Switzerland (1891); traveled throughout Europe, Asia, Algeria, Middle East, Costa Rica, South Africa, Africa, and Greece; hired future husband as personal guide and interpreter in Damascus; during WWII, after her ship to Trinidad was attacked by a submarine (1939), became ill and died soon after; butterfly specimens totaling over 22,000 were donated to Castle Museum in Norwich and sketchbook and paintings went to the British Museum. Writings include articles in *Entomologist* and extracts from 12 diaries in 2 books titled *Love among the Butterflies: The Travels and Adventures of a Victorian Lady* (1980) and *Butterflies and Late Loves: The Further Travels and Adventures of a Victorian Lady* (1986).

FOUQUÉ, Karoline Freifrau de la Motte (1774–1831). German novelist and short-story writer. Name variations: Karoline von Briest; Karoline Fouque; Caroline de la Motte Fuqué; (pseudonym) Serena. Born Karoline or Caroline Philippine von Briest Oct 7, 1774, in Berlin, Germany; died July 21, 1831, in Nennhausen, Germany; only dau. of Prussian landowner; m. Friedrich Ehrenreich Adolf Ludwig Rochus von Rochow (army officer), 1791, shot himself over gambling debts in 1799; m. Friedrich de la Motte Fouqué (romantic writer), 1803; children: (1st m.) Gustav (b. 1792), Theodor (b. 1794), Klara (b. 1796); (2nd. m.) Marie Luise Caroline de la Motte Fouqué (b. 1803). ❖ Nonfiction includes *Briefe über Zweck und Richtung weiblicher Bildung* (1810) and *Die Frauen in der großen Welt. Bildungsbuch beim Eintritt in das gesellige Leben* (1826); also wrote fairytales, novels, and novellas.

FOURNEAUX, Yvonne (1928—). *See Furneaux, Yvonne.*

FOURQUET, Jeanne (c. 1454–?). *See Hachette, Jeanne.*

FOURQUEUX, Madame de (fl. 18th c.). French novelist. Fl. between 1775 and 1806. ❖ Wrote *Zély* (1775), *Julie de Saint-Olmont* (1805), and *Amélie de Tréville* (1806).

FOURTOU, Janelly (1939—). French politician. Born Feb 4, 1939, in Paris, France. ❖ Elected to Neuilly Municipal Council (1983), responsible for Housing (1989–95) and for Employment (1995—); as a member of the European People's Party (Christian Democrats) and European Democrats, elected to 5th European Parliament (1999–2004).

FOUT, Nina (1959—). American equestrian. Born June 23, 1959, in Middleburg, Virginia. ❖ Won a bronze medal for eventing at Sydney Olympics (2000), on 3 Magic Beans.

FOWKE, Edith (1913–1996). Canadian folklorist. Born Edith Marshall, April 30, 1913, in Lumsden, Saskatchewan, Canada; died Mar 28, 1996, in Toronto, Ontario, Canada; earned degree in English from University of Saskatchewan. ❖ Taught English at York University, Toronto; became Canada's most important folklorist, with such books as *Folk Songs of Canada* (with Richard Johnston, 1954), *Folklore of Canada* (1976), *Folktales of French Canada* (1979), *A Bibliography of Canadian Folklore in English* (1981), *Lumbering Songs from the Northern Woods* (1985) and *Tales Told in Canada* (1986). Appointed member of Order of Canada (1978).

FOWLE, Elida Rumsey (1842–1919). American library founder. Name variations: Elida Barker Rumsey; Elida Fowle or Elida Barker Rumsey Fowle. Born Eliza (later altered to Elida) Barker Rumsey, June 6, 1842, in New York, NY; died June 17, 1919, in Dorchester, Massachusetts; dau. of John Wickliffe Rumsey and Mary Agnes (Underhill) Rumsey; m. John Allen Fowle, Mar 1, 1863; children: 3 daughters (1 adopted), 2 sons. ❖ Civil War relief worker, sang for wounded Union soldiers in hospitals and camps in Washington, DC; with ambulance and driver provided by army, distributed various supplies (early 1860s); with John Fowle, co-founded the Soldiers' Free Library, which also served as recreation center, in Washington (1862); constructed new library building on government land in Washington with authorization from Congress (1863); was a member of Woman's Christian Temperance Union and Daughters of the American Revolution; founded Grandchildren of the Veterans of the Civil War in Dorchester, MA; created library and reading room for neighborhood children (1898); donated Civil War mementos to Dorchester Historical Society.

FOWLER, Katharine (1631–1664). See Philips, Katharine.

FOWLER, Lydia Folger (1822–1879). American physician. Born Lydia Folger in Nantucket, Massachusetts, 1822; died in London, England, 1879; dau. of Gideon (businessman and farmer) and Eunice (Macy) Folger; attended Wheaton Seminary, 1838–39; attended Central Medical College, Syracuse, and later Rochester, NY, 1849–50, MD, 1850; m. Lorenzo Fowler (noted phrenologist), 1844; children: Jessie Fowler. ❧ The 2nd American woman to receive an MD, practiced medicine in NYC, lectured, and became involved in a number of reform causes, including women's rights and temperance (1852–60); moved to London with husband (c. 1864), where she spent the rest of her life engaged in various causes; writings include *Familiar Lessons on Astronomy, Designed for the Use of Children and Youth* (1848), *Familiar Lessons on Phrenology, Designed for the Use of Schools and Families,* and *Familiar Lessons on Physiology, Designed for the Use of Children and Youth in Schools and Families* (1848).

FOWLER, Marjorie (1920–2003). American film editor. Name variations: Marjorie Johnson. Born Marjorie Johnson, July 16, 1920, in Los Angeles, California; died July 8, 2003, in Los Angeles; dau. of Nunnally Johnson (screenwriter); m. Gene Fowler Jr. (film editor and director, died 1998); children: 1. ❧ Nominated for an Academy Award for her work as coeditor on *Doctor Dolittle* (1967); other films include *The Three Faces of Eve* (1957), *Stopover Tokyo* (1957), *Elmer Gantry* (1960), *Separate Tables* (1958), *Take Her, She's Mine* (1963) and *The Strawberry Statement* (1970); often worked in tv (1971–84). Received Lifetime Career Achievement Award from American Cinema Editors (2000).

FOWLER, Tillie (1942–2005). American politician. Born Tillie Kidd, Dec 23, 1942, in Milledgeville, GA; died of a brain hemorrhage, Mar 2, in Jacksonville, FL; dau. of Culver Kidd (Georgia state senator); graduate of Emory University Law School; m. Buck Flowler; children: Tillie and Elizabeth Fowler. ❧ As a Democrat, served in White House as general counsel in Office of Consumer Affairs (1970–71); served on Jacksonville (FL) city council (1985–92); as a Florida Republican, served in US House of Representatives (1993–2001), one of the top-ranking women in her party; served as vice chair of the House Republican Conference, the 5th-ranking GOP leader, and as deputy majority whip for 6 years; was on the Transportation and Infrastructure Committee and Armed Services Committee; as a conservative, championed increased defense budgets but was a moderate on minimum wage and abortion; retired from Congress and chaired the Defense Policy Board Advisory Committee.

FOX, Ann Leah (c. 1818–1890). See Fox, Leah.

FOX, Beatrice (1887–1968). See Auerbach, Beatrice Fox.

FOX, Beryl (1931—). Canadian documentary filmmaker. Born in Canada in 1931. ❧ Began career at Canadian Broadcasting Company (CBC) as a script assistant (early 1960s); produced and directed *The Mills of the Gods* (1965), an hour-long documentary about combat in Vietnam, which was named Film of the Year by Canadian Film Institute and won George Polk Memorial Award; continued to cover Vietnam, the 1st Canadian to do so, with *Saigon* and *Last Reflections on a War: Bernard Fall;* her coverage of black voter registration and race relations in "One More River" and "Summer in Mississippi" contains some of the best documentary footage of the time; left CBC (1966), though she continued to produced documentaries for tv throughout 1970s; began producing feature films for theatrical release (1980s), including *By Design,* starring Patty Duke. ❧ See also *Women in World History.*

FOX, Carol (1926–1981). American opera producer. Born in Chicago, Illinois, June 15, 1926; died in Chicago, July 21, 1981; only dau. of Edward (office supply company executive) and Virginia (Scott) Fox; studied acting at Pasadena Playhouse; studied voice with Edith Mason and Vittorio Trevisan in Chicago and Virgilio Lazarri and Giovanni Martinelli in NY and Italy; coached in operatic repertory by Fausto Cleva; never married. ❧ Credited with restoring Chicago's pre-Depression operatic glory, was the co-founder and general manager of the Lyric Opera of Chicago, often called "La Scala West" because of its international reputation; was largely responsible for the American operatic debut of Maria Callas and many European opera stars, and also helped establish the Lyric's apprentice artist program for American singers. ❧ See also *Women in World History.*

FOX, Caroline (1723–1774). See Lennox, Caroline.

FOX, Caroline (1819–1871). English diarist. Born in Falmouth, Cornwall, England, May 24, 1819; died in Falmouth, Jan 12, 1871; dau. of Robert Were Fox (physicist and mineralogist); sister of Anna Maria Fox (writer). ❧ Began a diary at 16, which covered the period of 1835 to 1871 and was partially published as *Memories of Old Friends* (1881), with a 3rd edition (1882); also translated religious works into Italian; was the friend of John Stuart Mill, Thomas Carlyle, and other noted personages. ❧ See also *Women in World History.*

FOX, Catherine (1977—). American swimmer. Born Dec 15, 1977, in Shawnee Mission, Kansas; attended Stanford University. ❧ Won a gold medal for 4x100-meter freestyle relay at Atlanta Olympics (1996); set an American record in the 100-meter backstroke (52.47) at NCAA championships (1999); was 21-time All-American and 9-time NCAA champion.

FOX, Charlotte Milligan (1864–1916). Irish singer and collector of folksongs. Born Charlotte Milligan, Mar 17, 1864, in Omagh, Co. Tyrone, Ireland; died in London, England, Mar 25, 1916; sister of Alice Milligan (1866–1953); married. ❧ Founded the Irish Folk Song Society (1904); a musician in her own right, toured Ireland, collecting folk songs and airs and recording them on gramophone; published *Annals of the Irish Harpers* from the papers of musician and antiquarian Edward Bunting, which was a standard reference for many years (1911). ❧ See also *Women in World History.*

FOX, Della (1870–1913). American musical star. Born Della May Fox, Oct 13, 1870, in St. Louis, Missouri; died June 15, 1913, in New York, NY; m. Jacob D. Levy (NY diamond broker), 1900. ❧ Briefly the highest paid performer on American variety stage, started theatrical career while still a schoolgirl; made professional debut at 13 in title role of *Editha's Burglar* (1883); made NY debut in *The King's Fool* (1890) and went on to play opposite DeWolf Hopper in the operetta *Castles in the Air* (1890), *Wang* (1891), *Panjandrum* (1893), and *The Lady or the Tiger* (1894); had 1st starring role in *The Little Trooper* (1894), followed by a turn with Lillian Russell in *The Wedding Day* (1897); as Margery Dazzle in the musical *The Little Host* (1898), crossed the continent with her own company, reaching the pinnacle of her popularity; popularized the "Della Fox curl" throughout US. ❧ See also *Women in World History.*

FOX, Dorothy (b. around 1914). American dance satirist. Born c. 1914 in New York, NY. ❧ Trained with Martha Graham, Bird Larson, Charles Weidman, Mary Wigman, and more, in New York City; worked with own dance troupe for brief period in cabarets in Prague and Berlin; returned to NY (1933) where she danced with Charles Walters as an exhibition ballroom and comedy team for 3 years in such shows as *New Faces of 1934, Fools Rush In* and *Jubilee;* performed own dance satire act at St. Moritz Hotel and on Broadway in *Sing Out the News* (1938) and *Lend an Ear* (1941); choreographed for film *Centennial Summer* (1946).

FOX, Elizabeth Vassall (1770–1845). Lady Holland. Name variations: Elizabeth Webster. Born Elizabeth Vassall at Jamaica in 1770; died in 1845; m. Sir Godfrey Webster (div.); m. Henry Richard Vassall Fox, 3rd baron Holland, 1797; children: Henry Edward Fox, 4th and last Lord Holland (who m. Mary Fox). ❧ Presided over the Whig circle at Holland House as Lady Holland; an adroit but slightly haughty host, was censured by Lord Byron in his *English Bards and Scotch Reviewers;* sympathetic to Napoleon, sent a message to him during his exile at Elba and some books for him during his exile at St. Helena.

FOX, Frances (1912–2001). See Rogers, Dale Evans.

FOX, Francine (1949—). American kayaker. Born Mar 16, 1949, in US. ❧ At Tokyo Olympics, won a silver medal in K2 500-meters (1964).

FOX, Jackie (1959—). American musician. Name variations: Jackie Fuchs; The Runaways. Born Dec 20, 1959 in Los Angeles, California. ❧ Bass player with all-girl rock band The Runaways, joined band after departure of singer and bassist, Micki Steele; with group, made such albums as *The Runaways* (1976) and *Queens of Noise* (1977), which were poorly received in US, but proved highly popular in Japan; quit band (mid-1977); executive produced and appears in the documentary *Edgeplay* (2004), about The Runaways.

FOX, Joanne (1979—). Australian water-polo player. Name variations: Jo Fox. Born June 12, 1976, in Melbourne, Australia. ❧ Center back, driver, and shooter, won a team gold medal at Sydney Olympics (2000).

FOX, Kate (c. 1839–1892). Canadian-born spiritualist and medium. Name variations: Catherine or Katie Fox; Kate Fox-Jencken. Probably born in 1839, in Bath, New Brunswick, Canada; died July 2, 1892, in

New York, NY; dau. of John Fox (farmer) and Margaret (Rutan) Fox; sister of Margaret Fox (c. 1833–1893); m. Henry D. Jencken (international lawyer and legal scholar), Dec 14, 1872 (died 1881); children: Ferdinand (b. 1873) and Henry (b. 1875). ❖ Modern spiritualism and mediumism dates from the mid-19th century, the time of the Fox sisters, Kate and Margaret, who quite innocently set into motion a social and religious movement that encompassed millions in America and thousands in Europe and England. ❖ See also *Women in World History.*

FOX, Leah (c. 1818–1890). Canadian-born medium. Born Ann Leah Fox, c. 1818, in New York state; died Nov 1, 1890, in New York, NY; dau. of John Fox (farmer) and Margaret (Rutan) Fox; sister of spiritualists Margaret Fox (c. 1833–1893) and Kate Fox (c. 1839–1892); m. to a man named Fish, 1840s (possibly died); m. Calvin Brown, 1851 (died 1853); m. Daniel Underhill (insurance executive and spiritualist), 1858; children: (1st m.) 3, possibly more. ❖ Managed her sisters during the years of their public demonstrations. ❖ See also *Women in World History.*

FOX, Margaret (1614–1702). *See Fell, Margaret.*

FOX, Margaret (c. 1833–1893). Canadian-born spiritualist and medium. Name variations: Margaretta Fox; Maggie Fox. Possibly born Oct 7, 1833, in Bath, New Brunswick, Canada; died Mar 8, 1893, in Brooklyn, NY; dau. of John Fox (farmer) and Margaret (Rutan) Fox; sister of Kate Fox (c. 1839–1892). ❖ See Fox, Kate. ❖ See also *Women in World History.*

FOX, Mary (b. 1817). Lady Holland. Born Lady Mary Augusta Coventry, 1817; dau. of 8th earl of Coventry and Lady Mary Beauclerk (dau. of 6th duke of St. Albans); m. Henry Edward Fox, 1833 (died 1859); daughter-in-law of Elizabeth Vassall Fox (1770–1845). ❖ Spent early years on the Continent before marrying Henry Edward Fox, son of Elizabeth Vassall Fox and minister plenipotentiary at court of Tuscany; lived primarily in Naples after marriage; after husband died (1859), inherited Holland House in Kensington and St. Ann's Hill near Chertsey; was known as a gracious host to diplomats, distinguished foreigners, and the accomplished. ❖ See also *Women in World History.*

FOX, Mildred (1971—). Irish politician. Born June 1971 in Dublin, Ireland; dau. of Johnny Fox (TD, Wicklow, 1992–95); m. Daryl Tighe. ❖ As an Independent, elected to the 27th Dáil in a by-election (1995–97) for Wicklow following the death of her father; returned to 28th Dáil (1997–2002) and 29th Dáil (2002).

FOX, Paula (1923—). American writer. Born April 22, 1923 in New York, NY; dau. of Paul Harvey Fox (novelist and screenwriter) and Elsie Fox; attended Columbia University; m. Howard Bird (merchant seaman and part-time actor), 1940 (div.); m. Richard Sigerson, 1948 (div.); m. Martin Greenberg (translator and editor), 1962; children: Linda (mother of rock star Courtney Love), Adam (environmental consultant) and Gabriel (zookeeper). ❖ Award-winning fiction writer for children and adults, began career as model, reader for 20th Century-Fox and stringer for small British news service; taught at private schools and a center for delinquents; at 43, published 1st novel, *Poor George* (1967), followed by *Desperate Characters* (1970); won National Book Award for children's book, *A Place Apart* (1980); won Hans Christian Andersen Medal (1978), Newbery Honors for *The Slave Dancer* (1973) and *One-Eyed Cat* (1984), and the Empire State Medal for children's books (1994); also wrote the novels *The Western Coast* (1972), *The Widow's Children* (1976), *A Servant's Tale* (1984), *The God of Nightmares* (1990); other children's books include *Maurice's Room* (1966), *Dear Prosper* (1968), *The Stone-Faced Boy* (1968), *The King's Falcon* (1969), *Blowfish Live in the Sea* (1970), *The Little Swineherd and Other Tales* (1976), *Monkey Island* (1991), *Western Wind* (1993) and *The Eagle Kite* (1995). ❖ See also memoir, *Borrowed Finery* (Harper Collins, 2003).

FOX, Ruby (1945—). American shooter. Born Aug 11, 1945, in US. ❖ At Los Angeles Olympics, won a silver medal in sport pistol (1984).

FOX, Sidney (1910–1942). American stage and screen actress. Born Sidney Leifer, Dec 10, 1910, in New York, NY; died Nov 14, 1942, of a possible overdose of sleeping pills, in Hollywood, California; m. Charles E. Beahan, 1932. ❖ Made stage debut in Johnstown (PA) in *The Big Pond* (1928) and NY debut as Dorothy Donovan in *It Never Rains* (1929), followed by *Lost Sheep*, *The Mask of Kings* (as Marie Vetsera), and *Having a Wonderful Time*; films include *Strictly Dishonorable*, *Murders in the Rue Morgue*, *The Cohens and Kellys in Hollywood*, *Once in a Lifetime*, *Don Quixote*, *Midnight*, *School for Girls*

and *Down to Their Last Yacht.* ❖ See also chapter in *Film Fan Monthly* (July 8, 1971).

FOX, Yolande (1930—). *See Betbeze, Yolande.*

FOX-JERUSALMI, Myriam (1961—). French kayaker. Name variations: Myriam Jerusalmi. Born Myriam Jerusalmi, Oct 24, 1961, in Marseille, France; m. Richard Fox (World Cup winner in K1 slalom). ❖ Won the World Championship for K1 slalom (1993); won a bronze medal for K1 slalom at Atlanta Olympics (1996).

FOY (290–303). *See Faith.*

FOY, Madeline (1903–1988). American vaudevillian. Born Madeline Fitzgerald, Sept 21, 1903, in New York, NY; died July 5, 1988, in Los Angeles, California; dau. of Madeline Morando (Italian ballet dancer) and Eddie Foy (1854–1928, actor); sister of Eddie Foy Jr., Bryan Foy, Charley Foy, Mary Foy, Richard Foy, and Clara Foy. ❖ Following the death of her mother (1918), was put into her father's vaudeville act with siblings so he could keep custody of them. ❖ See also film *The Seven Little Foys* (1955).

FOY, Mary (1901–1987). American vaudevillian. Born Mary Fitzgerald, Aug 15, 1901, in New York, NY; died Dec 13, 1987, in Los Angeles, California; dau. of Madeline Morando (Italian ballet dancer) and Eddie Foy (1854–1928, actor); sister of Eddie Foy Jr., Bryan Foy, Charley Foy, Madeline Foy, Richard Foy, and Clara Foy; m. Lyle Latell. ❖ Following the death of her mother (1918), was put into father's vaudeville act with siblings so he could keep custody of them. ❖ See also film *The Seven Little Foys* (1955).

FOYLE, Christina (d. 1999). British businesswoman. Born Christina Agnes Lillian Foyle; died in London, England, age 88, June 1999; dau. of William (bookseller) and Christina (Tulloch) Foyle; attended Aux Villas Unspunnen, Wilderswil, Switzerland; m. Ronald Batty, 1938 (died 1994). ❖ As managing director of Foyle's Bookshop (W. & G. Foyle, Ltd.) in London, represented the 2nd generation to run one of that city's oldest and most revered businesses; at age 17 (1928), had the idea for the famous Foyle Literary Luncheons, which were inaugurated under her management; ran Foyle's for almost 70 years. ❖ See also *Women in World History.*

FRACCI, Carla (1936—). Italian ballerina. Born Aug 20, 1936, in Milan, Italy. ❖ Began studying at La Scala Ballet School under Vera Volkova and others (1946); graduated into the company (1954); promoted soloist (1956) and principal (1958); the 1st Italian ballerina of the 20th century to win international acclaim, created Juliet in Cranko's *Romeo and Juliet* (1958) and Elvira in Massine's *Don Giovanni* (1959); appeared with London Festival Ballet (1959, 1962), Royal Ballet (1963), Stuttgart Ballet (1965) and Royal Swedish Ballet (1969); became principal guest artist at American Ballet Theatre (1967); had greatest success with Giselle, which was filmed with Erik Bruhn (1969); other great roles included Sylphide and Swanilda; was director of ballet in Naples (1990–91) and in Verona (1995–97); became director of Balletto dell'Opera di Roma.

FRADON, Ramona (1926—). American cartoonist. Born 1926 and raised in Westchester Co., NY; attended Art Students League. ❖ Was one of the few women in 1950s to land a job with a comic-book publisher; during career, drew many of the best-known superheroes, including Superman, Batman, and Plastic Man; took over as artist for Dale Messick's popular "Brenda Starr" comic strip, working with writer Mary T. Schmich (1985). ❖ See also *Women in World History.*

FRAENKEL, Naomi (1920—). Israeli novelist. Born 1920 in Berlin, Germany. ❖ Immigrated to Palestine (1933) and studied at Hebrew University; writings include the trilogy of novels about Jewish-German family, *Saul Ve'Yohana* (Saul and Johana, 1956–67).

FRAGA, Kely (1974—). Brazilian volleyball player. Name variations: Kely Kolasco Fraga. Born Oct 4, 1974, in Belo Horizonte, Minas Gerais, Brazil. ❖ Middle blocker, won a team bronze medal at Sydney Olympics (2000).

FRAGONARD, Marie Anne (1745–c. 1823). French artist. Born Marie Anne (also seen as Anne-Marie) Gérard in Grasse, France, 1745; died in Paris, France, 1823 or 1824; sister of Marguerite Gérard (1761–1837); m. Jean Honoré Fragonard (artist). ❖ A miniaturist and student of husband, was soon eclipsed by her younger sister, who joined the Fragonard household at age 8; exhibited at Salon des Correspondance (1779) but gradually gave up painting to run the household and care for her many children. ❖ See also *Women in World History.*

FRAHM, Pernille (1954—). Danish politician. Born April 1, 1954, in Hillerød, Denmark. ❖ Teacher; member of Socialist People's Party Executive Committee (1990–94); member of the Folketing (1990–94, 1998–99); elected to 5th European Parliament (1999–2004); vice-chair of the Confederal Group of the European United Left/Nordic Green Left.

FRAISSE, Geneviève (1948—). French politician. Name variations: Genevieve Fraisse. Born Oct 7, 1948, in Paris, France. ❖ Representing the Confederal Group of the European United Left/Nordic Green Left (GUE/NGL), elected to 5th European Parliament (1999–2004).

FRALEY, Ingrid (1949—). American ballet dancer. Born Nov 1, 1949, in Paris, France. ❖ Danced for 10 years with both San Francisco Ballet in CA and American Ballet Theater in residence at Washington DC's Kennedy Center; performed best-known role in Michael Smuin's *Pulcinella Variations* (1968) for both companies; appeared as première danseuse at City Center Joffrey Ballet in NY (1975) where her most acclaimed performances included The Ballerina in *Petrouchka*, Fiancée in John Cranko's *Pineapple Poll*, and heroine of the Wallflower Waltz in Ruthana Boris' *Cakewalk;* performed in company productions of Ashton's *Monotones II*, Joffrey's *Remembrances*, and Arpino's *Pas de Deux Holbert* and *Drums, Dreams and Banjos.*

FRAME, Alice (1878–1941). American educator and missionary. Name variations: Alice Brown or Alice Seymour Browne or Alice Seymour Browne Frame. Born Alice Seymour Browne, Oct 29, 1878, in Harpoot, Turkey; died Aug 16, 1941, in Newton, Massachusetts; dau. of Rev. John Kittredge Browne and Leila (Kendall) Browne; m. Murray Scott Frame (missionary), Oct 10, 1913 (died 1918); children: Frances Kendall (1914–1916), Murray Scott (1916–1916), Rosamond (b. 1917). ❖ As secretary of young people's work for Woman's Board of Missions (Congregational), traveled and spoke across US (early 1900s); traveled to Tongzhou (Tungchow), China (1905), and became head of mission's school for girls; was transferred to North China Union Women's College in Beijing (Peking, 1912); was temporarily in charge of Women's College (1919–20); as dean of College (1922–28 and 1930–31), oversaw construction of 9 major buildings; under threat of violence and pressure to resign, oversaw merger of Women's College with Yenching University (1928); served as acting dean of residence at Mount Holyoke College during furlough (1928–29); became secretary of religious education of North China Kung Li Hui (Congregational Church) in Tongzhou (1931); was delegate of China Christian Council to Madras conference of International Missionary Council (1938); returned to US (1941). Awarded DLitt by Mount Holyoke College (1925).

FRAME, Janet (1924–2004). New Zealand writer. Born Janet Patterson Frame, Aug 28, 1924, in Dunedin, New Zealand; died Jan 28, 2004; dau. of Lottie Clarice Godfrey (dental nurse and housemaid) and George Samuel Frame (railway worker); attended Dunedin Training College for teachers and Otago University; never married; no children. ❖ One of the most prolific and innovative of New Zealand's writers, who survived a childhood of poverty and misfortune and many years of incarceration in mental hospitals to write a wealth of novels, poems and short stories, as well as an autobiography; during final year of teacher's training was committed for 6 weeks to Seacliff mental hospital (1945); submitted 1st collection of stories for publication (1945); worked as housemaid and waitress (1946); recommitted to psychiatric hospital, where she stayed for most of the next 8 years, misdiagnosed as schizophrenic (1947); won the Hubert Church award for *The Lagoon and Other Stories* (1951); released from psychiatric hospital (1955); completed 1st novel, *Owls Do Cry*, and traveled to Europe, where she spent 7 years and completed 3 novels and 2 volumes of stories (1957); returned to New Zealand (1964); other writings include *Faces in the Water* (1961), *The Edge of the Alphabet* (1962), *The Reservoir, Stories and Sketches* (1963), *Snowman, Snowman: Fables and Fantasies* (1963), *Scented Gardens for the Blind* (1963), *The Adaptable Man* (1965), *A State of Siege* (1966), (poems) *The Pocket Mirror* (1967), *The Rainbirds* (1968), *Intensive Care* (1970), *Daughter Buffalo* (1972), *Living in the Maniototo* (1979), (selected short stories) *You Are Now Entering the Human Heart* (1983), and *The Carpathians* (1988). ❖ See also her 3-vol. *An Autobiography* which was collected in 1 vol. (Braziller, 1991) and issued separately as *To the Is-Land* (1982), *An Angel at My Table* (1984), and *The Envoy from Mirror City* (1985); authorized biography *Wrestling with the Angel* (2000); (film) *An Angel at My Table*, directed by Jane Campion, starring Kerry Fox; and *Women in World History.*

FRAMPTON, Eleanor (1896–1973). American concert dancer. Born Aug 29, 1896, in Nebraska; died Oct 8, 1973, in Cleveland Heights, Ohio. ❖ Ran own studio in Lincoln, Nebraska, where she trained Charles Weidman for a short period, among others; moved to Los Angeles with Weidman and Helen Hewitt, where they joined Denishawn School (late 1910s); performed group act, The Misses Frampton and Hewitt in The Fantasticks, in non-circuit Midwestern theaters; began creating more innovative pieces for student companies in Cleveland; continued to study with such notable teachers as Mikhail Mordkin, Theodore Kosloff, Adolf Bolm, and Andreas Pavley; upon retirement from stage, worked as dance critic for *The Cleveland Plain Dealer.* Works of choreography include *Greeting Dance* (1934), *Etude* (1934), *Chopin Program* (1934), *Andante* (1936), *Variations on a Theme by Handel* (1937), *Country Dance* (1938), *Years of the Moderns* (1942) and *Suggestions Diabolique* (1949).

FRANCA, Celia (1921—). British ballerina, choreographer and founder. Born in London, England, June 25, 1921; dau. of a British tailor; studied dance at Guildhall School of Music and Royal Academy of Dancing with Marie Rambert; also studied with Stanislas Idzikowski, Judith Espinosa, and Antony Tudor. ❖ Made debut at 15, performing in *The Planets* with the Ballet Rambert; as a member of the Ballet des Trois Arts, choreographed her 1st piece, *Midas* (1939); went on to dance and choreograph with Sadler's Wells, the Metropolitan Ballet, the Ballet Jooss, and other companies; recommended as a founding director of a Canadian classical company by Dame Ninette de Valois (1951), pulled the National Ballet of Canada together in 10 months; remained its director for 24 years, relying on the classics and creating her own ballets when necessary, including *Cinderella* (1968), which won an Emmy (1970), and several versions of *The Nutcracker* (1955 and 1964); with Betty Oliphant, founded the National Ballet School (1959). Received the St. George's Society of Toronto award (1987); was among the 1st to be honored with the Order of Ontario. ❖ See also James Neufield, *Power to Rise: The Story of The National Ballet of Canada* (U. of Toronto Press, 1996); and *Women in World History.*

FRANCE, empress of.
See Josephine (1763–1814).
See Marie Louise of Austria (1791–1847).
See Eugénie (1826–1920).

FRANCE, queen of.
See Ermengarde (c. 778–818).
See Ansgard (fl. 863).
See Ermentrude (d. 869).
See Richilde of Autun (fl. 870).
See Adelaide Judith (fl. 879).
See Theodorade.
See Richilde (d. 894).
See Frederona (d. 917).
See Beatrice of Vermandois (880–931).
See Emma of Burgundy (d. 939).
See Edgifu (902–951).
See Gerberga of Saxony (c. 910–969).
See Emma of Italy (948-after 990).
See Adelaide of Poitou (c. 950–c. 1004).
See Adelaide of Anjou.
See Constance of Arles (c. 980–1032).
See Bertha of Burgundy (964–1024).
See Anne of Kiev (1024–1066).
See Matilda of Germany.
See Bertha of Holland (1055–1094).
See Bertrada of Montfort (d. after 1117).
See Adele of Maurienne (1092–1154).
See Constance of Castile (d. 1160).
See Eleanor of Aquitaine (1122–1204).
See Adele of Champagne (1145–1206).
See Isabella of Hainault (1170–1190).
See Ingeborg (c. 1176–1237/38).
See Agnes of Meran (d. 1201).
See Blanche of Castile (1188–1252).
See Margaret of Provence (1221–1295).
See Isabella of Aragon (1243–1271).
See Marie of Brabant (c. 1260–1321).
See Joan I of Navarre (1273–1305).
See Margaret of Burgundy (1290–1315).
See Jeanne I of Burgundy (c. 1291–1330).
See Clemence of Hungary (1293–1328).

See Jeanne of Burgundy (1293–1348).
See Blanche of Burgundy (1296–1326).
See Mary of Luxemburg (1305–1323).
See Blanche of Boulogne (1326–1360).
See Joan of Evreux (d. 1370).
See Blanche of Navarre (1331–1398).
See Jeanne de Bourbon (1338–1378).
See Isabeau of Bavaria (1371–1435).
See Marie of Anjou (1404–1463).
See Charlotte of Savoy (c. 1442–1483).
See Jeanne de France (c. 1464–1505).
See Anne of Brittany (c. 1477–1514).
See Mary Tudor (1496–1533).
See Eleanor of Portugal (1498–1558).
See Claude de France (1499–1524).
See Maria Teresa of Savoy.
See Medici, Catherine de (1519–1589).
See Elisabeth of Habsburg (1554–1592).
See Louise of Lorraine (1554–1601).
See Medici, Marie de (c. 1573–1642).
See Anne of Austria (1601–1666).
See Maintenon, Françoise d'Aubigne, marquise de (1635–1719).
See Maria Teresa of Spain (1638–1683).
See Marie Leczinska (1703–1768).
See Marie Antoinette (1755–1793).
See Maria Teresa of Savoy (1756–1805).
See Maria Amalia (1782–1866).

FRANCE, Ruth (1913–1968). New Zealand poet and novelist. Name variations: (pseudonym) Paul Henderson. Born June 12, 1913, in Canterbury, New Zealand; died Aug 19, 1968, in Christchurch, New Zealand; dau. of Francis Henry Henderson and Helena Jane Hayes; m. Arnold France, 1934. ❖ Wrote *Unwilling Pilgrim* (1955), *The Race* (1958), *Ice Cold River* (1961) and *The Halting Place* (1961).

FRANCES. *Variant of Francesca.*

FRANCES, Lady Mar (1690–1761). *See Mar, Frances, countess of.*

FRANCES EVELYN, countess of Warwick (1861–1938). *See Greville, Frances Evelyn.*

FRANCES MARY THERESA, Mother (1794–1861). *See Ball, Frances.*

FRANCES OF ROME (1384–1440). Saint. Name variations: St. Frances the Widow. Born in Rome in 1384; died in 1440; dau. of Paul Bussa and Jacobella de' Roffredeschi; m. Laurence Ponziani, a young noble; children: son (b. 1400), son (b. 1404), and daughter (b. 1407). ❖ Born into an illustrious family, was exceptionally pious at an early age; at 11, asked to enter a convent, but was coaxed into marriage with an equally pious noble; had a successful 40-year marriage; though known to treat servants well, imposed mortifications on herself; with sister-in-law Vanozza Ponziani, cared for the sick of Sancto Spirito and gave money to the poor; with husband's approval, founded a monastery for nuns, named the Oblates (1425), and gave them the rule of St. Benedict and statutes of the Olivetan monks; immediately after death, was canonized by Pope Paul V. Feast day is Mar 9. ❖ See also *Women in World History.*

FRANCES XAVIER CABRINI, Mother (1850–1917). *See Cabrini, Frances Xavier.*

FRANCESCA. *Variant of Frances.*

FRANCESCA DA FIRENZE (fl. 15th c.). *See Firenze, Francesca da.*

FRANCESCA DA RIMINI (d. 1285?). Italian noblewoman. Name variations: Francesca Malatesta. Born Francesca da Polenta; slain around 1285; dau. of Bernardino da Polenta; m. Gianciotto (Giovanni) Malatesta. ❖ One of history's ill-starred lovers, fell in love with husband's younger brother Paolo Malatesta; when a 3rd brother informed her husband, was killed along with Paolo in a "crime of honor." The story, immortalized by Dante, has also been the subject of many artists, including Germany's Anselm Feuerbach, Holland's Ary Scheffer, and Italy's Amos Cassioli. ❖ See also *Women in World History.*

FRANCEY, Henriette (b. around 1859). French murderer (accused). Born c. 1859 in France; m. Paul Francey. ❖ Born into wealthy commercial family in Tonnère, was married at 19 to Paul Francey; shot architect Hippolyte Bazard whom she accused of attempted rape (1885); was arrested, charged with murder, and went on trial, where prosecution alleged that murder had been committed to cover up an affair with him; was acquitted after skilled defense by Edgar Demange.

FRANCHI, Anna (1866–1954). Italian journalist and novelist. Born 1866 in Livorno, Italy; died 1954. ❖ Works on art and art history include *Arte ed artisti toscani dal 1850 ad oggi* (1902), *G. Fattori. Studio biografico* (1910), and *I macchiaioli toscani* (1945); historical works include *Caterina de'Medici regina di Francia* (1933) and *Storia della pirateria nel mondo* (1953); other works include *I viaggi di un soldatino di piombo* (1901), *Il figlio della guerra* (1917), *Dono d'amore* (1931), *La mia vita* (1947), and *Polvere del passato* (1953).

FRANCIA, Mirka (1975—). Cuban volleyball player. Name variations: Mirka Francia Vasconcelos. Born Feb 14, 1975, in Cuba. ❖ Won team gold medals at Atlanta Olympics (1996) and Sydney Olympics (2000).

FRANCINE, Anne (1917–1999). American actress and singer. Born Anne Hollingshead Francine, Aug 8, 1917, in Atlantic City, New Jersey; died Dec 3, 1999, in New London, Connecticut. ❖ Began career in nightclubs; best known on Broadway for role of Vera Charles in *Mame*; other plays include *The Great Sebastians, By the Beautiful Sea* and *Tenderloin*; films include *Juliet of the Spirits, Stand Up and Be Counted, Savages* and *Crocodile Dundee*; appeared regularly on "Harper Valley P.T.A." (1981–82).

FRANCIS, Anne (1930—). American actress. Born Sept 16, 1930, in Ossining, NY. ❖ Child model and cover girl for John Robert Powers, appeared in early tv and soap operas and on Broadway as the "young" Gertrude Lawrence in *Lady in the Dark*; made screen debut in *This Time for Keeps* (1948), before starring in *Elopement, Lydia Bailey, Dreamboat, Bad Day at Black Rock, Blackboard Jungle, Don't Go Near the Water, The Crowded Sky* and *Forbidden Planet*, among others; on tv, starred in the series "Honey West" (1965).

FRANCIS, Arlene (1908–2001). American tv personality and actress. Born Arlene Francis Kazanjian in Boston, Massachusetts, Oct 20, 1908; died May 31, 2001, in San Francisco, California; only child of Aram Kazanjian (portrait photographer), and Leah (Davis) Kazanjian; m. Neil Agnew (movie executive), 1935 (div. 1945); m. Martin Gabel (actor-producer), May 14, 1946 (died 1979); children: Peter Gabel. ❖ Had 1st major stage role in *All that Glitters* (1938), followed by featured roles in Orson Welles' Mercury Theater production of *Danton's Death* (1938) and Maxwell Anderson's *Journey to Jerusalem* (1940); early radio assignments included serials and appearances with Jack Benny and Fred Allen; also did soundtrack commentary for fashion newsreels; landed role of Natalia, a Russian lady sniper, in Joseph Fields' comedy *The Doughgirls* (1942), which ran for 18 months; for several years, continued on Broadway and on radio, where her show "Blind Date" became popular and was later transferred to tv; began hosting the "Home" show, the 1st NBC show to be broadcast in color (1954); was the 1st woman to guest-host the "Jack Paar Tonight Show"; became best known, however, as a regular panelist on "What's My Line?" (CBS-TV); briefly had her own tv show, the "Arlene Francis Show," and hosted a radio program, "Arlene Francis at Sardi's"; as late as 1981, was co-hosting the "Prime of Your Life" on WNBC-TV (NY). ❖ See also *Women in World History.*

FRANCIS, Catherine Augusta (1836–1916). New Zealand teacher and headmistress. Name variations: Catherine Augusta Jupp. Born Catherine Augusta Jupp, Sept 16, 1836, in London, England; died Oct 19, 1916, in Wellington, New Zealand; dau. of Edward (tailor) and Catherine (Healy) Jupp; m. George Francis (post office clerk), 1865; children: 2 sons, 2 daughters. ❖ Immigrated with parents to Adelaide, South Australia (1849), and taught school; immigrated to New Zealand with husband and children (1872); established infants' school in Wellington and served as headmistress (1878–1905). ❖ See also *Dictionary of New Zealand Biography* (Vol. 2).

FRANCIS, Clare (1946—). British sailor, yacht racer and novelist. Born Clare Mary Francis, April 17, 1946, in Surbiton, England; attended Royal Ballet School; earned degree in economics at University College, London; m. Jacques Redon; children: 1. ❖ Made solo trip across Atlantic in a 32-foot boat in 37 days; came in 3rd in Round Britain Race (1975); sailed solo to Azores and back (1975); participated in the Observer Royal Western Singlehanded Transatlantic Race and was 1 of 4 women to finish, coming in 13th out of 125 entrants, setting a women's transatlantic record; the 1st woman skipper in the Whitbread Round the World challenge, finished 5th with an 11-member crew; wrote *Come Hell or High Water* (1977), *Come Wind and Weather* (1978) and *The Commanding Sea* (1979); began writing novels which include *Night Sky* (1983), *Wolf Winter* (1987), *Requiem* (1991), *Deceit* (1993), *Betrayal*

(1995), *Keep Me Close* (1999), and *A Death Divided* (2001). Made MBE (1981). ❖ See also *Woman Alone: Sailing Solo Across the Atlantic* (1977).

FRANCIS, Connie (1938—). American pop singer. Born Concetta Marie Franconero, Dec 12, 1938, in Newark, New Jersey; thrice married (thrice divorced). ❖ Shortly before 12th birthday, won 1st place on Arthur Godfrey's tv talent show; appeared on George Scheck's weekly "Star Time" tv show; signed with MGM Records (1955); recorded an uptempo version of "Who's Sorry Now?" (1957) which sold over 1 million copies; over next 5 years, had 25 records in top 100, including "Stupid Cupid" (1958), "My Happiness" (1959), "Lipstick on Your Collar" (1959), "Mama" (1960), and "Vacation" (1962), which she co-wrote; also made 4 films, including *Where The Boys Are,* and starred on her own tv special; became the 1st female singer to have 2 consecutive singles on the charts, "My Heart Has a Mind of Its Own" and "Everybody's Somebody's Fool" (1960); after a performance at Westbury (Long Island) Music Fair, was held at knife point in her hotel room for two-and-a-half hours while being beaten and raped (Nov 7, 1974); thoroughly traumatized by the ordeal, was plagued with emotional problems, which led to 4 years in and out of mental institutions; resumed career (1989). ❖ See also autobiography *Who's Sorry Now?* (St. Martin, 1984); and *Women in World History.*

FRANCIS, Eve (1886–1980). Belgian-born stage and screen actress. Born Aug 24, 1886, in Saint Josse ten Node, Belgium; died Dec 6, 1980, in Neuilly-sur-Seine, France; m. Louis Delluc (director and theorist), 1918 (died 1924). ❖ Star of the Paris stage, made silent film debut in *La dame blonde* (1914), followed by *Le roi de la mer, Le silence, El Dorado, Club de femmes, Antoinette Sabrier, Forfaiture* (also asst. director), *La chair de l'orchidée* and *Adieu poulet,* among others; also worked for Germaine Dulac and Marcel L'Herbier. Named Chevalier of the Legion of Honor. ❖ See also memoirs *Temps héro_ques* (1949).

FRANCIS, Jane Elizabeth (c. 1852–1942). See Harris, Jane Elizabeth.

FRANCIS, Kay (1899–1968). American actress. Born Katherine Edwina Gibbs in Oklahoma City, Oklahoma, Jan 13, 1899; died in New York City, Aug 26, 1968; dau. of Katherine Clinton (vaudeville star); 4 marriages, all ending in divorce, including 3rd husband, actor Kenneth MacKenna (1931–33). ❖ One of the most glamorous and highly paid film stars of 1930s, made film debut as a vamp in *Gentlemen of the Press* (1929), followed by a supporting part in the 1st Marx Brothers film *The Coconuts* (1929); despite a slight speech impediment, typically portrayed stylish, worldly women in romantic melodramas and an occasional comedy; best-known films include *Raffles* (1930), *Trouble in Paradise* (1932), *Cynara* (1932), *The White Angel* (1936), *The Feminine Touch* (1941) and *Four Jills in a Jeep* (1944). ❖ See also *Women in World History.*

FRANCIS, Princess Malee (c. 1802–1848). See Francis, Milly.

FRANCIS, Milly (c. 1802–1848). Native-American Congressional medal awardee. Name variations: Princess Malee (Anglicized to "Milly") Francis. Born Malee Francis, c. 1802, in Alabama; died May 19, 1848, in Creek Nation, near Muskogee, Oklahoma; dau. of Josiah Francis (Chief Hillis Hadjo, "Francis the Prophet") and Creek wife; convert to Baptist Church; married; children: 8. ❖ Dissuaded Creek Indians from executing Georgia militia captive, Captain Duncan McKrimmon (1817); after father's execution (1818), surrendered with family to American military in FL, and later declined proposal of marriage from McKrimmon; was found by Major Ethan Allen Hitchcock living in financial difficulties in Creek Nation near Muskogee, OK (1842); on Hitchcock's recommendation, was voted eligible for Congressional medal and $96 annual pension by Congress for saving life of American soldier (1844), but died before receiving either.

FRANCIS, Paula Marie (1939—). See Allen, Paula Gunn.

FRANCISCA JOSEFA OF THE CONCEPTION, Mother (1671–1742). See Castillo y Guevara, Francisca Josefa del.

FRANCISCA OF PORTUGAL (1800–1834). Duchess of Molina. Born Maria Francisca de Assis, April 22, 1800, in Queluz; died Sept 4, 1834, in Alberstoke Rectory, Gosport, Hampshire, England; dau. of Carlota Joaquina (1775–1830) and Joao or John VI, king of Portugal; m. Charles also known as Don Carlos (1788–1855), duke of Molina, Sept 22, 1816; children: Charles of Molina (1818–1861), count of Montemolin; Johann also known as John of Molina (1822–1887); Ferdinand of Molina (b. 1824).

FRANCISCA OF PORTUGAL (1824–1898). Princess of Brazil. Name variations: Francisca de Braganca. Born Aug 2, 1824, in Rio de Janeiro, Brazil; died Mar 27, 1898, in Paris, France; dau. of Leopoldina of Austria (1797–1826) and Peter IV, king of Portugal (r. 1826), also known as Peter I of Brazil or Pedro I, emperor of Brazil (r. 1822–31); m. François or Francis (1818–1900), duke of Joinville, May 1, 1843; children: Françoise d'Orléans (1844–1925); Peter (b. 1845), duke of Penthievre.

FRANCISCO, Betty (1900–1950). American actress. Born Elizabeth Bartman, Sept 26, 1900, in Little Rock, Arkansas; died Nov 25, 1950, in Corona, CA; sister of Evelyn Francisco (1904–1963, actress). ❖ Films include *Streets of Chance, Broadway, The Gingham Girl* and *Smiling Irish Eyes.*

FRANCO, Carmen Polo de (1902–1988). Spanish first lady. Name variations: María del Carmen Polo y Martínez Valdés de Franco. Born María del Carmen Polo y Martínez Valdés in Oviedo, Spain, 1902; died 1988; m. Francisco Franco (head or Caudillo of the Spanish state), Oct 1923 (died Nov 20, 1975); children: María del Carmen, called Carmencita (who m. Cristóbal Martínez Bordiu). ❖ Wife and adviser of Francisco Franco, dictator of Spain, who played her chosen part well as devoted wife of, depending on one's political inclinations, a hero or rogue; known for her religious conservatism and avarice, was supreme in Spain for 35 years (1939–75). ❖ See also *Women in World History.*

FRANCO, Veronica (1546–1591). Italian poet and courtesan. Born 1546 in Venice, Italy; died 1591; dau. of a cortigiana (courtesan); married a doctor; children: daughter. ❖ Married at early age but became courtesan after husband's death; well educated, was the friend of many influential men in Venice; had a brief liaison with Henry III, king of France; founded charity for courtesans (1575); faced trial for witchcraft (1577) but was acquitted; works include *Terze Rime* (1575) and *Lettere familiari e diversi* (1580). ❖ See also Margaret F. Rosenthal, *The Honest Courtesan: Veronica Franco, Citizen and Writer in Sixteenth-Century Venice* (U. of Chicago Press, 1992); (film) *Dangerous Beauty,* starring Catherine McCormack and Jacqueline Bisset (1998).

FRANCOIS, Elma (1897–1944). Caribbean political activist. Born Elma Constance Francois, Oct 14, 1897, in Overland, on Caribbean island of St. Vincent; died April 17, 1944, from complications of the thyroid, in Port-of-Spain, Trinidad and Tobago; dau. of Stanley and Estina (Silby) Francois (agricultural laborers); lifetime companion: James Barrette; children: Conrad James. ❖ Founder of the National Unemployed Movement and Negro Welfare Cultural and Social Association in the 1930s, and 1st woman charged for sedition in the history of Trinidad and Tobago, migrated from St. Vincent to republic of Trinidad and Tobago, where she worked as a domestic servant (1919); became a member of the Trinidad Workingmen's Association (1920s); with others, founded the National Unemployed Movement (NUM, 1934); participated in NUM "hunger marches" to draw attention to unemployment and destitution (1934); with others, founded the Negro Welfare Cultural and Social Association (NWCSA, 1935); with the NWCSA, led the local agitation against Mussolini's Italian invasion of Ethiopia, then known as Abyssinia (1935–36); with the NWCSA, led the labor disturbances in the north of Trinidad and was charged for sedition (1937); was tried and acquitted after her spirited self-defense (1938); with other members of the NWCSA, was involved in founding the Federated Workers Trade Union, the Public Works and Public Service Workers Trade Union, and the Seamen and Waterfront Workers Trade Union (1937–40); campaigned against local support for and participation in World War II (1939); one of three women out of 25 island citizens named National Heroes of Trinidad and Tobago (Sept 25, 1985). ❖ See also Rhoda Reddock, *Elma Francois, The NWCSA, and the Workers Struggle for Change in the Caribbean* (New Beacon, 1988); and *Women in World History.*

FRANÇOIS, Louise von (1817–1893). German novelist and short-story writer. Name variations: Louise von Francois; (pseudonym) L.v.F. Born June 27, 1817, in Herzberg-Elster, Sachsen, Germany; died Sept 25, 1893. ❖ Writings include novel *Die letzte Reckenburgerin* (1871); also published novellas and stories.

FRANÇOISE D'ORLEANS (fl. 1650). Duchess of Savoy. Name variations: Francoise of Orleans; Mlle de Valois. Fl. around 1650; dau. of Gaston d'Orleans (1608–1660), duke of Orléans (brother of Louis XIII, king of France) and Marguerite of Lorraine; 1st wife of Charles Emmanuel II (1634–1675), duke of Savoy (r. 1638–1675).

FRANÇOISE D'ORLEANS (1844–1925). Duchess of Chartres. Name variations: Francoise d' Orleans; Frances of Orleans; Francisca d'Orleans.

Born Aug 14, 1844; died Oct 28, 1925; dau. of Francisca of Portugal (1824–1898) and François or Francis (1818–1900), duke of Joinville; m. Robert (1840–1910), duke of Chartres, June 11, 1863; children: Mary Oldenburg (1865–1909); Robert (1866–1885); Henry (1867–1901); Margaret of Chartres (b. 1869, who m. Patrice de MacMahon, duke of Magenta); John (1874–1940), duke of Guise.

FRANÇOISE-MARIE DE BOURBON (1677–1749). Countess of Blois and duchess of Orléans. Name variations: Mlle de Blois; Françoise-Marie de Blois; Francoise de Blois. Born May 25, 1677; died Feb 1, 1749; illeg. dau. of Louis XIV, king of France (r. 1643–1715), and Françoise, Marquise de Montespan (1640–1707); m. Philip Bourbon-Orléans (1674–1723), 2nd duke of Orléans (r. 1701–1723), Feb 18, 1692; children: Marie Louise (1695–1719, who m. Charles, duke of Berri); Louise Adelaide (1698–1743); Charlotte-Aglae (1700–1761, who m. Francis III of Modena); Philippe Louis (1703–1752), 3rd duke of Orléans; Louise Elizabeth (1709–1750, who m. Louis I, king of Spain); Philippa-Elizabeth (1714–1734); Louise-Diana (1716–1736). ❖ See also *Women in World History.*

FRANÇOISE OF GUISE (1902–1953). Princess of Greece. Name variations: Francoise of Guise, princess of Guise. Born Dec 25, 1902; died Feb 25, 1953; dau. of Isabella of Orleans (b. 1878) and John (1874–1940), duke of Guise; m. Prince Christopher Oldenburg of Greece (1888–1940), Feb 11, 1929; children: Michael Oldenburg (b. 1939). Christopher Oldenburg's 1st wife was Anastasia Stewart (1883–1923).

FRANDL, Josefine. Austrian Alpine skier. Born in Austria. ❖ Won a silver medal for giant slalom at Cortina Olympics (1956).

FRANK, Anne (1929–1945). Dutch diarist. Born Anneliese Marie Frank on June 12, 1929, in Frankfurt am Main, Germany; died of typhus in the concentration camp at Bergen-Belsen in Mar 1945; dau. of Otto Frank (died 1980) and Edith Frank-Hollander (died in Auschwitz on Jan 6, 1945); sister of Margot Betti Frank (died of typhus in Bergen-Belsen in Mar 1945). ❖ Dutch girl, one of the millions of Jews killed by the Germans, who became a symbol of brutalized innocence through the power of her diary; at 4, moved with family from Frankfurt to Amsterdam, Holland, because of the growing anti-Semitism in Germany (1933); attended the Sixth Public Montessori School (now named the Anne Frank School) for 6 years; on 13th birthday (June 12, 1942), received a diary, a stiff-backed notebook with a red-plaid cover that she called Kitty; went into hiding with family (July 6, 1942), moving into the "Secret Annex" behind father's business at Prinsengracht 263; aided by Miep Gies and Bep Voskuijl, remained in hiding with the van Pels and their son Peter until Aug 4, 1944, until someone tipped off the Germans; 4 days later, was transported to Westerbork; sent on the last transport from the Netherlands to Auschwitz (Sept 3); escaped the selection and was sent to Barracks 29 along with mother Edith and sister Margot; with sister, shipped to Bergen-Belsen (probably Oct 28, 1944); outlived sister by days. Her diary, published as *Het Achterhuis* (The Annex) in the Netherlands (1947), was eventually released in over 50 countries in 55 languages, and the Annex became a museum. ❖ See also *The Diary of a Young Girl: The Definitive Edition* (edited by Otto Frank and Mirjam Pressler, Doubleday, 1995); Miep Gies, with Alison Leslie Gold, *Anne Frank Remembered* (Simon & Schuster, 1987); Willy Lindwer, *The Last Seven Months of Anne Frank* (Random House, 1991); Ruud van der Rol and Rian Verhoeven for Anne Frank House, *Anne Frank, Beyond the Diary: A Photographic Remembrance* (Viking, 1993); (play) *The Diary of Anne Frank,* by Frances Goodrich and Albert Hackett (1955) and *The Diary of Anne Frank,* adapted by Wendy Kesselman from the Goodrich-Hackett script (1997); *Anne Frank Remembered* (winner of an Academy Award for Best Documentary Feature, 1996); *The Last Seven Months of Anne Frank,* documentary by Willy Lindwer (1988); and *Women in World History.*

FRANK, Antje (1968—). German rower. Born June 5, 1968, in Germany. ❖ At Barcelona Olympics, won a bronze medal in coxless fours (1992).

FRANK, Dottie (1941—). American theatrical dancer and opera director. Name variations: Dorothy Danner. Born July 8, 1941, in St. Louis, Missouri. ❖ Made performance debut at St. Louis Municipal Opera in *Annie Get Your Gun* at 15; moved to New York City where she performed in *Once Upon a Mattress* (1959), *Tenderloin* (1960), *Sail Away* (1961) and *No Strings* (1962); appeared as Ernie Flatt Dancer on "The Ed Sullivan Show" and "The Garry Moore Show," among others; also performed in *New Faces of 1968, Irene* (1973), and Michael Bennett's *Ballroom* (1978); served as director for St. Louis Municipal Opera.

FRANK, Jacqueline (1980—). American water-polo player. Born May 1, 1980, in Long Beach, California; attended Stanford University. ❖ Won World championship (2003); won a team bronze medal at Athens Olympics (2004).

FRANK, Margot (1926–1945). Sister of Anne Frank. Born Margot Betti Frank, Feb 1926, in Frankfurt am Main, Germany; died of typhus in the concentration camp at Bergen-Belsen in Mar 1945; dau. of Otto Frank and Edith Frank-Hollander; sister of Anne Frank. ❖ An excellent student and unfailingly polite, was pretty, bookish, and much more introspective than her sociable younger sister. ❖ See also *The Diary of Anne Frank,* a play in two-acts by Frances Goodrich and Albert Hackett (1955); and *Women in World History.*

FRANK, Mary K. (1911–1988). American theatrical producer. Born July 10, 1911, in Ohio; died Nov 20, 1988, in Grand View-on-the Hudson, NY. ❖ On Broadway, produced or co-produced *Tea and Sympathy, Too Late the Phalarope, One More River, Sponono* and *K2;* was president of New Dramatists.

FRANK, Nance (1949—). American skipper. Born 1949 in Key West, Florida. ❖ Became 1st skipper to enter an ocean sailboat race with all-female crew, as skipper of 50-foot sailboat *Ichiban* in 475-mile race from Annapolis, MD, to Newport, RI (June 1991), and came in 8th in fleet of 9, with crew of 12 women; an avid art collector, also co-wrote *Before and After* with Cuban-American artist Mario Sanchez.

FRANK, Rosaline Margaret (1864–1954). New Zealand photographer. Born Dec 21, 1864, in Nelson, New Zealand; died Oct 6, 1954, in Nelson; dau. of Christopher Joseph Frank (carpenter) and Emma Sophia (Haslam) Frank. ❖ Apprenticed to Tyree brothers' studio in Nelson (1886); became manager of studio (1895–1947). Thousands of glass-plate negatives, which document early settlement days, are housed by several organizations, including Alexander Turnbull Library, Nelson Historical Society, and Nelson Provincial Museum. ❖ See also *Dictionary of New Zealand Biography* (Vol. 3).

FRANKAU, Pamela (1908–1967). British novelist and journalist. Name variations: (pseudonym) Eliot Naylor. Born Jan 3, 1908, in London, England; died June 8, 1967, in London; dau. of Gilbert Frankau and Dorothea Drummand (Black) Frankau; m. Marshall Dill Jr., 1945 (div 1961). ❖ At 18, began writing for *Woman's Journal* and later for *Daily Sketch* and *Mirror;* converted to Catholicism (1942); moved to US with husband but after divorce returned to England (1960); writings include *Marriage of Harlequin* (1927), *Born at Sea* (1932), *Fly Now, Falcon* (1934), *Fifty-Fifty and Other Stories* (1936), *Appointment with Death* (1940), *The Willow Cabin* (1949), *The Winged Horse* (1953), *Ask Me No More* (1958) and *Colonel Blessington* (1968).

FRANKEN, Rose (c. 1895–1988). American writer. Name variations: (joint pseudonyms) Franken Meloney and Margaret Grant. Born Rose Dorothy Lewin, Dec 28, 1895, in Gainesville, Texas; died June 22, 1988, in Tucson, Arizona; dau. of Michael and Hannah (Younker) Lewin; attended Ethical Culture School (NY); m. Sigmund Walter Anthony Franken (oral surgeon), 1915 (died 1933); m. William Brown Meloney (author, playwright, and producer), 1937; children: (1st m.) Paul, John, and Peter. ❖ Prolific writer who turned out plays, short-stories, magazine serials, novels, and motion-picture scripts, frequently in collaboration with 2nd husband, William Brown Meloney, was the author of the enormously popular "Claudia" novels, which she also adapted into a hit play, two movies, and a radio serial; also directed her own plays, some of which she co-produced with Meloney; published 1st novel *Pattern* (1925); wrote *Another Language* (1932), which ran for 453 performances on Broadway—a record for a 1st play; began the 1st of her 8 "Claudia" novels (1939), as a series for *Redbook* magazine; wrote the play *Outrageous Fortune* (1943), a serious drama dealing with homosexuality and anti-Semitism, which most reviewers felt was her best theatrical work; also wrote *Soldier's Wife; a Comedy in Three Acts* (1944) and *The Hallams; a Play in Three Acts* (1947). ❖ See also autobiography *When All Is Said and Done* (1963); and *Women in World History.*

FRANKENTHALER, Helen (1928—). American artist. Born Dec 12, 1928, in New York, NY; 1st studied with Mexican painter Rufino Tamayo at the Dalton School; Bennington College, BA, 1949, where she studied with Paul Feeley; studied at Arts Students League in NY and with Hans Hoffmann in Provincetown, MA; m. Robert Motherwell (artist), 1958. ❖ One of the defining artists of American Abstract Expressionism, developed her own approach to painting, despite being strongly influenced by Arshile Gorky and Jackson Pollock; changed the direction of Abstract Expressionism when she began pouring cans of paint onto an unprepared canvas (1952), a style known as "soak stain" which later influenced "color-field painting"; exhibited work in America at the Tibor de Nagy Gallery and Emmerich Gallery, among others, and in Paris (1961, 1963), Milan (1962), London (1964, 1969), Berlin (1969) and Montreal (1971); taught painting and drawing at educational institutions, including New York University, Hunter College, University of Pennsylvania, Yale University, and Princeton University. Had numerous one-woman exhibitions of her work, including retrospectives at the Whitney Museum (1969) and Museum of Modern Art (MoMA, 1989); works *Blue Territory* (1955) and *Arden* (1961) are both at the Whitney. ❖ See also John Elderfield, *Helen Frankenthaler* (Abrams, 1997).

FRANKEVA, Antoaneta (1971—). Bulgarian swimmer. Born Aug 24, 1971. ❖ At Seoul Olympics, won a bronze medal in 200-meter breaststroke and a silver medal in 100-meter breaststroke (1988).

FRANKLAND, Agnes (1726–1783). American hero. Name variations: Lady Agnes Frankland, Lady Agnes Surriage Frankland, Dame Agnes Frankland; Agnes Surriage. Born Agnes Surriage in 1726, in Marblehead, Massachusetts; died April 23, 1783, in Chichester, England; dau. of Edward Surriage and Mary (Pierce) Surriage; m. Charles Henry (Sir Harry) Frankland (English baronet), c. 1755 (died 1768); m. John Drew (banker), Oct 25, 1781. ❖ While working as tavern maid in Marblehead, MA, caught attention, and became ward, of Charles Frankland, customs collector at Boston port (1742); was reared and educated at a fashionable school in Boston; became Frankland's mistress and was shunned by society (c. 1746); after husband inherited baronetcy of Thirsk in North Riding of Yorkshire (1746), visited England with him but was not accepted by his family (1754); in aftermath of severe earthquake in Lisbon, Portugal, frantically hunted for, and found, husband who had been buried by rubble (1755); married him and received acceptance from polite society (mid-1750s). Inspired Oliver Wendell Holmes' ballad, "Agnes," in *Songs in Many Keys* (1862), Edwin Lasseter Bynner's *Agnes Surriage* (1886), and Sir Arthur Quiller-Couch's *Lady-Good-for-Nothing: A Man's Portrait of a Woman* (1910).

FRANKLIN, Alberta (1896–1976). American silent-screen actress. Born May 20, 1896, in California; died Mar 14, 1976, in Mountain View, CA; m. Paul Levy. ❖ Films include *Birth of a Nation, Sunset Strip, Dance of the Seven Veils* and *Devil's Trail;* made several films with Charlie Chaplin, Mary Pickford, and Tom Mix.

FRANKLIN, Ann (1696–1763). New England printer. Born Ann Smith, Oct 2, 1696, in Boston, Massachusetts; died April 19, 1763, in Newport, Rhode Island; sister-in-law of Benjamin Franklin; m. James Franklin, Feb 4, 1723 (died 1735); children: 5. ❖ Probably the 1st woman printer in New England, took over husband's printing business in Newport, RI, after his death (1735); ran business for 13 years (1735–48) and printed *The Rhode-Island Almanack for the Year 1737* and *Acts and Laws* (1745), among others; became colony printer (1736); continued active role in business after son James Franklin Jr. took over (1748); briefly returned to work after son's death (1762) until her own health failed. Approximately 47 works have been attributed to her press between 1735 and 1848.

FRANKLIN, Aretha (1942—). African-American soul singer. Born Aretha Louise Franklin, Mar 25, 1942, in Memphis, Tennessee; dau. of Rev. C.L. Franklin (died from gunshot wounds sustained during a burglary, 1984) and Barbara Franklin; sister of Carolyn (singer) and Erma Franklin (singer, died 2002); m. Ted White, 1961 (div. 1969); m. Glynn Turman, 1978 (div, 1984); children: (1st m.) 4 sons, Clarence, Edward, Kecalf and Teddy. ❖ Legendary singer known as "Lady Soul," was deserted by mother at age 6; toured gospel circuit with father (1950s); made 1st recordings at father's church (1956); signed to Columbia records and moved to New York (1960); earned R&B success with hits "Today I Sing the Blues" (1960) and "Won't Be Long" (1961), while pop success eluded her; signed with Atlantic (1966); reshaped soul music with series of crossover hits that included "Respect" (1967), "Chain of Fools" (1968), "Think" (1968), "Spanish Harlem" (1971), and "Until You Come Back to Me" (1973); appeared on the cover of *Time* (1968); developed flying phobia which limited her touring; had comeback after death of father (1984), with hits "Freeway of Love" (1985) and "Sisters Are Doing It For Themselves" (1986), a duet with the Eurythmics; earned Grammy for duet with George Michael, "I Knew You Were Waiting for Me" (1987); was 1st woman inducted into the Rock and Roll Hall of Fame (1987); hosted tv special "Duets" (1993); collaborated with Lauryn Hill and other contemporary stars on career-revitalizing album *A Rose is Still a Rose* (1999).

FRANKLIN, Christine (1847–1930). *See Ladd-Franklin, Christine.*

FRANKLIN, Deborah (1707–1774). *See Read, Deborah.*

FRANKLIN, Eleanor (1795–1825). English poet. Name variations: Mrs. Eleanor Anne Franklin; Eleanor Anne Porden. Born Eleanor Anne Porden, July 1795; died Feb 22, 1825; m. John Franklin (explorer), 1823. ❖ A poet and invalid, was a magnet to London's literary society; wrote the epic *Coeur de Lion* (1822); the following year, married the explorer John Franklin. Following her death, John Franklin married Jane (Griffin) Franklin. ❖ See also *Women in World History.*

FRANKLIN, Erma (1938–2002). African-American singer. Born Jan 1, 1938, in Shelby, Mississippi; died of cancer, Sept 7, 2002, in Detroit, Michigan; dau. of Rev. Clarence Franklin and Barbara Franklin; sister of Carolyn and Aretha Franklin; graduate of Clark College; attended Wayne State University; children: Sabrina Owens, Thomas Garrett Jr. ❖ Made singing debut at age 5; formed a singing group, The Cleo-Patretts, and recorded for JVB, a small Detroit company; signed wth Epic records, then with Shout; had 1st rhythm-and-blues hit with "Piece of My Heart" (1967), which became a belated hit in the UK (1992), 25 years after it was 1st recorded; with sister Carolyn, sang backup on Aretha's recordings for Atlantic, including "Respect"; for over 30 years, worked for Boysville in Michigan.

FRANKLIN, Irene (1876–1941). American actress. Born June 13, 1876, in New York, NY; died June 16, 1941, in Englewood, New Jersey; m. Burton Green; m. Jeremiah Jarnagin. ❖ Made stage debut as a child; at 15, toured Australia with J.C. Williamson company, remaining there for 3 years; appeared in London variety theaters (1894), then American vaudeville (1895–1907); plays include *The Orchid, The Summer Widowers, Hands Up, The Passing Show of 1917* and *Sweet Adeline;* made film debut as herself in *Actors' Fund Field Day* (1910) and subsequently appeared in *Whipsaw, Timothy's Quest, Along Came Love, Fatal Lady, Wanted–Jane Gardner, Midnight Madonna, Married Before Breakfast* and *Flirting with Fate,* among others.

FRANKLIN, Jane (1712–1794). *See Mecom, Jane Franklin.*

FRANKLIN, Jane (1792–1875). English social reformer and traveler. Name variations: Lady Jane Franklin. Born Jane Griffin in 1792 (some sources cite 1791) in Spitalfields, England; died at Phillimore Gardens, her London home, July 18, 1875; dau. of John Griffin (silk-weaving magnate) and Mary Guillemard (Griffin); educated at boarding school in Chelsea; became 2nd wife of Sir John Franklin (explorer), 1828; children: none. ❖ Gained international fame for relentless efforts to locate and rescue husband's ill-fated Arctic expedition; soon after marriage, traveled and lived in Van Diemen's Land and New Zealand (1828–33); was the 1st woman to travel overland from Melbourne to Sydney in Australia (1829); financed five vessels to the Arctic to search for husband's expedition (1850–57). Awarded Founder's Gold Medal from Royal Geographical Society (1860). ❖ See also Willingham Franklin Rawnsley, *The Life, Diaries and Correspondence of Jane Lady Franklin* (MacDonald, 1923); Francis Woodward, *Portrait of Jane: A Life of Lady Franklin* (Hodder and Stoughton, 1951); and *Women in World History.*

FRANKLIN, Martha Minerva (1870–1968). African-American nurse. Born Oct 29, 1870, in New Milford, Connecticut; died Sept 26, 1968, in New Haven, Connecticut; dau. of Henry J. and Mary (Gauson) Franklin; graduate of Woman's Hospital Training School for Nurses of Philadelphia, 1897; attended Columbia University Teachers College, 1928–30. ❖ The only black woman in her class at the Woman's Hospital Training School for Nurses of Philadelphia (1895–97), worked as a private-duty nurse in her hometown of Meriden, Connecticut, and later in New Haven; though of fair complexion and often mistaken for white, became sensitive to the color barriers in nursing; founded the National Association of Colored Graduate Nurses (NACGN, 1908); served as the organization's president for 2 years, than as permanent historian and honorary president. ❖ See also *Women in World History.*

FRANKLIN, Miles (1879–1954). Australian writer. Name variations: Stella Franklin; (pseudonym) Brent of Bin-Bin. Born Stella Maria Sarah Miles Franklin in Australia at Talbingo, near Canberra, New South Wales, Oct 14, 1879; died in Carlton, near Sydney, Sept 19, 1954; dau. of John Maurice Franklin (grazier and farmer) and Susannah Margaret Lampe Franklin; never married; no children. ❖ One of Australia's most authentic voices, whose 1st novel, the semi-autobiographical *My Brilliant Career* (1901), and later works of fiction and nonfiction brought her enduring fame in the English-speaking world; worked long and toil-laden hours helping parents run a small dairy farm (1889–99); completed 1st and best-known novel, *My Brilliant Career* (1899); moved to Sydney and Melbourne, where she continued writing and became interested in social and economic reform movements (1901); left Australia for US (late 1905), settling in Chicago (1906) where she became secretary of the Women's Trade Union League and helped edit its publication, *Life and Labor;* had 3rd novel, *Some Everyday Folk and Dawn,* published (1909); rejected by publishers for only novel to take place in US, *On Dearborn Street* (1914); moved to England (1915), working with reform groups in London and serving for 6 months (1917–18) as a volunteer with the Scottish Women's Hospital in the Balkans; during the most intense creative period in her life, wrote 6 novels about pioneering days in 19th-century Australia under pseudonym Brent of Bin-Bin, which mystified only strangers to her previous fiction (1925–31); returned to Australia (1932) where she published what is regarded as her masterpiece, *All That Swagger* (1936); devoted the last 18 years of her life to promoting Australian literature; was a prolific but uneven writer who completed some 16 novels, 13 of which were published in her lifetime or after her death. ❖ See also memoir, *Childhood at Brindabella* (1963), as well as *My Brilliant Career* (1901) and *My Career Goes Bung* (1981); Marjorie Barnard, *Miles Franklin: The Story of a Famous Australian* (U. of Queensland Press, 1988); Verna Coleman, *Miles Franklin in America: Her Unknown (Brilliant) Career* (Angus & Robertson, 1981); Colin Arthur Roderick, *Miles Franklin: Her Brilliant Career* (Rigby, 1982); Jill Roe, ed. *My Congenials: Miles Franklin and Friends in Letters* (2 vols. Angus & Robertson, 1993); and *Women in World History.*

FRANKLIN, Rosalind (1920–1958). English chemist and molecular biologist. Born Rosalind Franklin in London, England, July 25, 1920; died in London, April 16, 1958; dau. of Muriel (Waleys) Franklin (involved in socialist movement) and Ellis Franklin (noted educator); graduate of Newnham College, Cambridge, 1941; never married; no children. ❖ Scientist who played a central role in the discovery of the structure of DNA, but was deliberately pushed into the shadows by other self-serving scientists; stayed on at Cambridge after graduation with a research fellowship to Newnham College and went on to study gas-phase chromatography under Professor Ronald Norrish; appointed an assistant research officer of British Coal Utilization Research Association (CURA, 1942), where her work on the structure of coal is still used by scientists; became acquainted with crystallography and molecular biology; published 5 scientific papers, 3 as sole author (1942–46); awarded PhD, Cambridge University (1945); became a researcher at Laboratoire Central des Services Chimique de état, Paris (1947); working with Jacques Méring, was introduced to the techniques of X-ray diffraction and published a series of papers on graphitizing and nongraphitizing carbons; also began to apply X-ray diffraction to biological substances; offered a Turner-Newall Research Fellowship, joined King's College Medical Research Council Biophysics Unit, London (1951), where her research began to stray into the area of DNA X-ray diffraction analysis, as she was the only staff member qualified to undertake such work; research on DNA began to overlap with that of colleague Maurice Wilkins, who was not supportive of women scientists, causing friction; discovered the B form of DNA and produced a significant amount of experimental data on the subject (1951); recognized that 2 states of the DNA molecule existed and defined conditions for the transition; was unaware that Wilkins shared much of her research with Francis Crick and James Watson, who were undertaking similar research at Cambridge (they would publish their findings, which conclusively identified the structure of DNA, with no mention of Franklin, 1953); moved to Birkbeck College, London (1953), where she applied X-ray diffraction techniques to the analysis of the Tobacco Mosaic Virus; recognition of her contribution was largely obscured when Francis Crick, James Watson, and Maurice Wilkins were awarded Noble Prize in Medicine and Physiology (1962). ❖ See also Anne Sayre, *Rosalind Franklin and DNA* (Norton, 1975); and *Women in World History.*

FRANKLIN, Sarah (1743–1808). See Bache, Sarah.

FRANKLIN, Shirley (1945—). African-American politician. Name variations: Shirley Clarke Franklin. Born 1945 in Philadelphia, Pennsylvania; Howard University, BA in sociology; University of Pennsylvania, MA in sociology; children: 3. ❖ Elected mayor of Atlanta, Georgia (2001), the 1st black woman to lead a major Southern city; began career as the city's commissioner of Cultural Affairs (1978); appointed chief administration officer (city manager), then executive officer for operations; was the top-ranking female executive on the Atlanta Committee for the Olympic Games (1991); was vice-chair of the Georgia Regional Transportation Authority (1998).

FRANKLIN, Stella (1879–1954). See Franklin, Miles.

FRANKLYN, Beth (c. 1873–1956). American actress. Born c. 1873; died Mar 5, 1956, age 83, in Baltimore, Maryland. ❖ Appeared on Broadway with Henry Miller in *The Great Divide,* Chauncey Olcott in *Shameen Dhu,* and opposite Frank Craven in a number of plays produced by the John Albaugh Stock Company.

FRANKLYN, Lidije (1922—). Russian dancer. Born Lidije Kocers, May 17, 1922, in USSR; raised in England. ❖ Trained with Kurt Jooss and joined his ballet company (late 1930s); toured US with Jooss Ballet (1941–42) and remained there; performed wide variety of dance styles throughout performance career, but was best known for her Funeral Dance in Agnes de Mille's *Brigadoon;* trained dancers and worked intermittently throughout South America, especially with companies and orchestras in Caracas, Venezuela.

FRANKS, Lucinda (1946—). American writer. Born July 16, 1946, in Chicago, Illinois; dau. of Thomas E. and Lorraine (Leavitt) Franks; Vassar College, BA, 1968. ❖ The youngest person and 1st woman to receive Pulitzer Prize for national reporting (1971), shared prize with Thomas Powers for *The Making of A Terrorist,* 5 articles for UPI about radical activist Diana Oughton; for United Press International, was a journalist in London (1968–72), then NY (1974–74); joined the staff of *New York Times* (1974); writings include *Wild Apples* (novel, 1991) and *Waiting Out a War: The Exile of Private John Picciano* (nonfiction, 1974); also contributed to *The New Yorker* and *Atlantic Monthly.*

FRANKS, queen of the.
See Chunsina.
See Clotilda (470–545).
See Aregunde.
See Ingunde (fl. 517).
See Radegund of Poitiers (518–587).
See Guntheuca (fl. 525).
See Fredegund (c. 545–597).
See Beretrude (d. 620).
See Nanthilde (610–642).
See Bilchilde (d. 675).
See Ragnetrude (fl. 630).
See Balthild (c. 630–c 680).
See Clotilde (d. 691).
See Tanaquille (d. 696).
See Edonne.
See Bertha (719–783).
See Himiltrude.
See Desiderata (d. 773).
See Hildegarde of Swabia (c. 757–783).
See Fastrada (d. 794).
See Luitgarde (d. 800).

FRANKS, Rebecca (c. 1760–1823). American socialite. Name variations: Rebecca Johnson or Lady Rebecca Johnson. Born Rebecca Evans in c. 1760, in Philadelphia, Pennsylvania; died Feb 13, 1823, in Bath, England; dau. of David Franks and Margaret Evans Franks; m. Henry Johnson (British army officer), Jan 12, 1782; children: 2 sons. ❖ Well-known Philadelphia belle, related to powerful colonial families, including the De Lanceys, Hamiltons, Allens, and Penns, who was famed for beauty and wit; though a Loyalist, was later sympathetic to the American cause; moved to England after marriage; became Lady Johnson when husband became baronet after fighting in Irish Rebellion (1818). ❖ See also Max J. Kohler, *Rebecca Franks: An American Jewish Belle of the Last Century* (1894).

FRANTZ, Virginia Kneeland (1896–1967). American physician, surgeon, and researcher. Born Virginia Kneeland in New York, NY, 1896; died 1967; dau. of Yale and Anna Isley Ball Kneeland; graduate of Bryn Mawr College; College of Physicians and Surgeons at Columbia University, MD, 1922; m. Angus MacDonald Frantz (physician), 1920 (div.); children: Virginia Frantz (b. 1924); Angus Frantz, Jr. (b. 1927); Andrew Frantz (b. 1930). ❖ Pioneering woman in the field of medicine, was one of only 5 women in a class of 74 at Columbia University's College of Physicians and Surgeons; became 1st woman to undertake a surgical internship at Columbia-affiliated Presbyterian Hospital (1922); was appointed an assistant surgeon and member of Columbia faculty (1924); specializing in surgical pathology, became one of the 1st women to test the prevailing theory that women physicians were unable to withstand the rigors of surgery; also excelled in research, gaining national renown for work on pancreatic tumors; conducted some of earliest studies on breast disease, including chronic cystic disease and cancer; was one of the 1st to demonstrate that radioactive iodine was effective in treating thyroid cancer (1940); during World War II, discovered that oxidized cellulose used on wounds controlled bleeding and was absorbed into the body; became a full professor at Columbia (1951); served as president of New York Pathological Society (1949 and 1950); was 1st woman president of American Thyroid Association (1961).

FRAPART, Lenora S. (1906–2000). *See Slaughter, Lenora S.*

FRASCA, Mary (d. 1973). American singer and actress. Name variations: La Sorrentina. Died July 24, 1973, in New York, NY. ❖ Films include *The Gang That Couldn't Shoot Straight, Lovers and Other Strangers* and *The Godfather.*

FRASER, Agnes (1877–1968). Scottish actress and singer. Born Agnes Fraser Elder Fraser-Smith, Nov 8, 1877, in Springfield, Fife, Scotland; died July 22, 1968, in London, England; sister of Alec Fraser (actor); m. William Passmore (actor). ❖ Made London debut with the D'Oyly Carte Opera company as Blush-of-Morning during the premiere of *The Rose of Persia* (Nov 1899), followed by *The Emerald Isle, Merrie England, A Princess of Kensington, The Earl and the Girl, The Talk of the Town, The Dairymaids, Queer Fish* and *Ducks and Quacks,* among others.

FRASER, Alexa Stirling (1897–1977). American golfer. Name variations: Alexa Stirling; Mrs. W.G. Fraser. Born Alexandra Williamson Stirling, Sept 5, 1897, in Atlanta, Georgia; died 1977; m. W.G. Fraser (Canadian eye surgeon), 1924; children: 3. ❖ One of the top women amateurs of the early 20th century, won three consecutive USGA Women's Amateur titles (1916, 1919, 1920 [no championships were held in 1917–18 because of WWI]), and was runner-up (1921, 1923, 1925); won the Southern championship (1915, 1916, 1919), the Metropolitan (1922), and Canadian Women's Amateur (1920, 1934). Known as "the girl who beat Bobby Jones" (she was 12, he was 6).

FRASER, Anne (1951—). *Collins, Anne.*

FRASER, Annie Isabel (1868–1939). New Zealand community leader. Name variations: Annie Isabel McLean. Born Sept 21, 1868, in Andersons Bay, Dunedin, New Zealand; died Mar 8, 1939, in Christchurch, New Zealand; dau. of George (merchant) and Isabella (Holmes) McLean; m. Charles Anderson Fraser, 1898 (died 1932); children: 2 daughters. ❖ Helped found Te Waipounamu College for Maori Girls at Ohoka (c. 1918); active in National Council of Women of New Zealand; appointed to Prisons Board (1929); founding member of branch of League of Nations Union of New Zealand in Christchurch (1930s). Received King George V Silver Jubilee Medal and British Empire Medal (1935). ❖ See also *Dictionary of New Zealand Biography* (Vol. 4).

FRASER, Antonia (1932—). British biographer, mystery writer and novelist. Name variations: Antonia Pakenham; Lady Antonia Pinter or Antonia Fraser Pinter. Born Antonia Pakenham, Aug 27, 1932, in London, England; dau. of Francis Aungier Pakenham (writer and politician), 7th earl of Longford, and Elizabeth Harmon Pakenham, known as Elizabeth Longford (historian); sister of Rachel Billington; graduate of Lady Margaret Hall, Oxford, 1953; m. Sir Hugh Charles Fraser, 1956 (div 1977); m. Harold Pinter (playwright), 1980; children: 6. ❖ Popular writer of biographies and fiction, published *Mary, Queen of Scots* (1969) which became a bestseller and won the James Tait Black Memorial Prize; other works include *King Arthur and the Knights of the Round Table* (1954), *Robin Hood* (1957), *Cromwell: Our Chief of Men* (1973), *King James: VI of Scotland, I of England* (1974), *King Charles II* (1979), *The Weaker Vessel* (1984), *Boadicea's Chariot* (1988), *Faith and Treason* (1996), and *Marie Antoinette* (2001); also wrote the "Jemima Shore" series of mysteries, including *Quiet as a Nun* (1977), *A Splash of Red* (1981), *Cool Repentance* (1982), *Jemima Shore at the Sunny Grave and Other Stories* (1991), *The Cavalier Case* (1990) and *Political Death* (1994); served as member of Arts Council of Great Britain, English PEN, and Crimewriters' Association; television series based on her crime novels produced by BBC. Named CBE (1999); awarded Norton Medlicott Medal by the Historical Association (2000).

FRASER, Dawn (1937—). Australian swimmer. Born Dawn Lorraine Fraser, Sept 4, 1937, in Balmain, Sydney, Australia; m. Gary Ware (bookmaker), 1965 (div.). ❖ Won gold medals in the 100-meter freestyle and 4x100-meter freestyle relay and a silver medal in the 400-meter freestyle at Melbourne Olympics (1956); won a gold medal in the 100-meter freestyle and silver medals in the 4x100-meter medley relay and 4x100-meter freestyle relay at Rome Olympics (1960); won a gold medal in the 100-meter freestyle and a silver in the 4x100-meter freestyle relay

at Tokyo Olympics (1964), the 1st Olympian—male or female—to win the same event in 3 consecutive games; held 39 world records (27 indiv. and 12 team); held the record for the 100 meters for 16 years (1956–72); won 30 Australian championships (23 individual and 7 team); won 8 medals (6 gold and 2 silver) for the British Empire and Commonwealth Games. Awarded the OBE. ❖ See also (autobiography) with Harry Gordon, *Below the Surface: The Confessions of an Olympic Champion* (Morrow, 1965); and *Women in World History.*

FRASER, Eliza (c. 1798–1858). Australian heroine. Born Eliza Anne Slack, possibly in Ceylon, c. 1798; died 1858 in Melbourne, Australia; m. Captain James Fraser (died 1836); m. Captain Alexander John Greene, Feb 23, 1837; children: (1st m.) 3. ❖ Pregnant with 4th child, left 3 children in Scotland to accompany ailing husband on a voyage from London to Sydney, Australia (1835); after being set adrift in a longboat with husband and several crew members when their ship, *Stirling Castle,* foundered and sank off New South Wales (May 1836), delivered a "born drowned" baby, which was buried at sea; after 28 days, captured with others by a tribe of Stone Age Aborigines; having witnessed the death of husband who was speared in the back, was made a slave of the tribe and forced to endure ritualistic punishments; was eventually rescued. ❖ See also Michael Alexander, *Mrs. Fraser on the Fatal Shore* (Simon & Schuster, 1971); Patrick White, *A Fringe of Leaves* (1976); Andre Brink, *An Instant in the Wind* (1976); (film) *Eliza Fraser* (1976); and *Women in World History.*

FRASER, Elizabeth (1963—). Scottish vocalist. Name variations: Cocteau Twins. Born Aug 29, 1963, in Grangemouth, Scotland; children: (with musician Robin Guthrie) daughter. ❖ Sang vocals for Cocteau Twins, contemporary pop trio formed in Scotland (1981) which won praise from critics and scored successes, particularly on UK's independent charts; after trio split up (1996), worked with Massive Attack and Craig Armstrong, then launched solo career. Albums with Cocteau Twins include *Garlands* (1982), *Lullabies* EP (1982), *Head Over Heels* (1983), *Four-Calendar Café* (1993), *Twinlights* (1995) and *Milk & Kisses* (1995).

FRASER, Gretchen (1919–1994). Alpine skier. Name variations: Gretchen Kunigk or Kunigk-Fraser; often misspelled Gretchen Frazer. Born Gretchen Kunigk, Feb 11, 1919, in Tacoma, Washington; died Feb 17, 1994, in Sun Valley, Idaho; dau. of William Kunigk and a Norwegian skier; m. Donald Fraser (skier), 1939. ❖ Won the National combined and downhill championships (1941); was National slalom champion (1942); won a silver medal for combined and a gold medal for slalom at St. Moritz Olympics (1948), the 1st American to win a gold medal in skiing since 1924. ❖ See also *Women in World History.*

FRASER, Mrs. Hugh (1851–1922). *See Fraser, Mary Crawford.*

FRASER, Isabella (1857–1932). New Zealand nurse and hospital matron. Born Nov 15, 1857, in Ayrshire, Scotland; died Nov 24, 1932, in Napier, New Zealand; dau. of Charles Fraser (chemist) and Mary (Lyle) Fraser. ❖ Trained as nurse in Scotland (1887); immigrated to Australia with brother and supervised nurses at Melbourne Hospital (1891–93); assumed position of matron of Dunedin Hospital (1893–1911); established 3-year nursing skills training course for medical students at University of Otago Medical School (1894). Fraser medal for proficiency in practical nursing named in her honor (1912). ❖ See also *Dictionary of New Zealand Biography* (Vol. 2).

FRASER, Jane (1924—). *See Pilcher, Rosamunde.*

FRASER, Janet (1883–1945). New Zealand social reformer. Name variations: Janet Henderson Munro, Janet Kemp. Born Janet Munro, Jan 31, 1883, in Glasgow, Scotland; died Mar 7, 1945, in Wellington, New Zealand; illeg. dau. of Mary McLean (housekeeper) and William Munro (iron foundry warehouseman); parents married 4 years later; m. Frederick George Kemp (clerk), Nov 25, 1903 (div. 1919); m. Peter Fraser (prime minister of NZ), 1919; children: (1st m.) Harold. ❖ Immigrated to New Zealand with 1st husband and son (1909); became the 1st secretary of the Wellington women's branch of the NZ Labour Party (1920); served on Wellington Hospital Board (1925–35); appointed one of the 1st women justices of the peace (1926), associate of the Children's Court (1927), and to the Eugenics Board (1929); concerned with health, education and welfare issues, was active in League of Mothers, New Zealand Society for the Protection of Women and Children, Plunket Society and New Zealand Federation of University Women; worked on governmental committee on maternity services, which resulted in measures to provide financial and child-rearing support (1930s); attended conferences worldwide with 2nd husband, before and after he became prime minister (1940); spoke frequently on employment and welfare policies, housing developments, child health, justice systems, and the position of women in the countries she visited; headed Dominion Central Executive of Women's War Service Auxiliary during World War II. ❖ See also *Dictionary of New Zealand Biography* (Vol. 4).

FRASER, Jessie (1867–1934). *See Aitken, Jessie.*

FRASER, Maggie (1866–1951). *See Fraser, Margaret.*

FRASER, Margaret (1866–1951). New Zealand domestic servant and letter writer. Name variations: Maggie Fraser; Margaret Johnston. Born Dec 11, 1866, in Banffshire, Scotland; died Aug 31, 1951, in Totorua, New Zealand; dau. of John (master tailor) and Margaret (Spence) Fraser; m. William (Bill) Crawford Johnston, 1900; children: 3 sons, 1 daughter. ❖ Left Scotland for New Zealand (1887); her many letters record daily life as a domestic worker in late 19th century. ❖ See also *Dictionary of New Zealand Biography* (Vol. 2).

FRASER, Marjory Kennedy (1857–1930). *See Kennedy-Fraser, Marjorie.*

FRASER, Mary Crawford (1851–1922). British travel writer and novelist. Name variations: Mrs. Hugh Fraser. Born Mary Crawford, April 8, 1851, in Rome, Italy; died June 7, 1922; dau. of Thomas Crawford and Louisa Cutler Ward Crawford; sister of Marion Crawford (writer); m. Hugh C. Fraser, 1874. ❖ Best known for travel writings undertaken while traveling in Europe with father and then with diplomat husband; lived in China, Italy, Austria, Chile, and Japan; writings include *A Diplomatist's Wife in Japan* (1899), *A Diplomatist's Wife in Many Lands* (1901) and *Seven Years on the Pacific Slope* (1915); novels include *Palladia* (1896), *The Splendid Porsenna* (1899) and *Gianella* (1909).

FRASER, Mary Isabel (1863–1942). New Zealand teacher, school principal, and education reformer. Born Mar 20, 1863, in Dunedin, New Zealand; died April 18, 1942, in Dunedin; dau. of Hugh Fraser (saddler) and Mary Austin (Graham) Fraser; University of Otago, BA, 1887; MA, 1889. ❖ Taught at several girls' high schools before becoming principal of progressive Wanganui Girls' College (1894–1910). ❖ See also *Dictionary of New Zealand Biography* (Vol. 2).

FRASER, Paula Newby (1962—). *See Newby-Fraser, Paula.*

FRASER, Roslin (1927–1997). English psychiatric nurse. Name variations: Ros Fraser. Born Roslin Margaret Ferguson Fraser, May 21, 1927; died Dec 8, 1997; children: 5. ❖ Contributed to advocacy and development of mental handicap nursing for patients with learning disabilities; studied botany at Edinburgh University; after husband's death, trained as nurse to support large family; worked as psychiatric nurse at Prudhoe Hospital in Northumberland; developed approach to mental handicap nursing as a nursing tutor at Balderton Hospital; played key role in formation of Society for Mental Handicap Nursing at Royal College of Nursing (RCN); joined Womens' National Campaign (1991); began to chair National Alliance of Women's Organisations (1996); represented RCN at United Nations 4th World Conference on Women in Beijing (1995); was 1st psychiatric nurse elected as Royal College of Nursing's deputy president and 1st psychiatric nurse appointed as a mental health commissioner; created 1st published health care organization guide on female genital mutilation for nurses (for RCN).

FRASER, Shelagh (1922–2000). English stage and screen actress and writer. Born Nov 25, 1922, in Purley, Surrey, England; died Sept 13, 2000, in London, England; m. Anthony Squire (div.). ❖ Made London stage debut as Effie in *This Was a Woman* (1944); films include *Staircase, Till Death Do Us Part, In Practice, Star Wars* and *Hope and Glory;* frequently appeared on radio and tv. With Dido Milroy, wrote the play *Always Afternoon;* also wrote children's books.

FRASER, Susan (1966—). Scottish field-hockey player. Born July 15, 1966, in Scotland. ❖ At Barcelona Olympics, won a bronze medal in team competition (1992).

FRASER, Sylvia (1935—). Canadian novelist. Born Sylvia Nicholas, Mar 8, 1935, in Hamilton, Ontario, Canada; dau. of George Nicholas and Gladys Olive Meyers; educated at University of Western Ontario; m. Russell James Fraser, 1959. ❖ Worked as a journalist; was guest lecturer at Banff Centre, writer-in-residence at University of Western Ontario, a member of Canadian cultural delegation to China (1985) and vice-president of Writers' Development Trust; writings include *Pandora* (1972), *The Candy Factory* (1975), *A Casual Affair: A Modern Fairytale* (1978), *The Emperor's Virgin* (1980), *Berlin Solstice* (1984), *My Father's House: A Memoir of Incest and Healing* (1987), *The Book of Strange* (1992), *The Ancestral Suitcase* (1996), *The Rope in the Water: A Pilgrimage to India* (2001) and *The Green Labyrinth: Exploring the Mysteries of the Amazon* (2003).

FRASER, Tamie (1936—). Australian prime-ministerial wife. Born Tamara Margaret Beggs, Feb 28, 1936, in Adelaide, South Australia; m. Malcolm Fraser (prime minister of Australia, 1975), 1956; children: 4. ❖ Deputized for her ailing husband during the crucial election campaign (Dec 1975); was considered an asset on the campaign trail for Liberal Party, taking a prominent role in federal election campaigns (1975, 1977, 1980, and 1983); was the 1st prime-ministerial wife to have an official secretary; thought to have wielded a great deal of power; as 1st president of the Australiana Fund, undertook major renovations to The Lodge (the official prime-ministerial residence, 1978). ❖ See also Christina Hindhaugh's *It Wasn't Meant to be Easy: Tamie Fraser in Canberra* (Lothian, 1986) and Diana Langmore, *Prime Ministers' Wives* (McPhee Gribble, 1992).

FRASER, Mrs. W.G. (1897–1977). *See Fraser, Alexa Stirling.*

FRASER, Wendy (1963—). English field-hockey player. Born April 23, 1963, in UK. ❖ At Barcelona Olympics, won a bronze medal in team competition (1992).

FRASSONI, Monica (1963—). Belgian politician. Born Sept 10, 1963, in Veracruz, Mexico. ❖ Served as secretary-general, Young European Federalists (1987–89) and temporary official, Green Group in the European Parliament (1990–99); elected to 5th European Parliament (1999–2004); co-president of the Green Group and European Free Alliance.

FRATELLINI, Annie (1932–1997). French clown. Born in 1932 in French Algiers, Algeria; died of cancer, June 30, 1997; granddau. of circus performer Paul Fratellini (one of the Fratellini brothers); m. Pierre Etaix (filmmaker). ❖ France's 1st female clown, began career at 14 with the Medrano and Pinder circuses; heralded for her pratfalls, also used a variety of musical instruments, from concertina to vibraphone, in her performances; with husband, founded the Fratellini Circus School, the nation's 1st circus school, and served as its artistic director; as well, directed her own circus, École Nationale du Cirque, in Paris; appeared in feature films, *Le Grand Amour* (1969), Fellini's *The Clowns* (1970) and *Henry and June* (1990).

FRATIANNE, Linda (1960—). American figure skater. Name variations: Linda Maricich. Born Aug 2, 1960, in Northridge, California; m. Nick Maricich. ❖ Placed 8th at Innsbruck Olympics (1976); won US National title four times (1978–81); was World champion (1977, 1979); won a silver medal at Lake Placid Olympics (1980).

FRAZEE, Jane (1918–1985). American actress and singer. Born Mary Jane Frehse, July 18, 1918, in St. Paul, Minnesota; died Sept 6, 1985, in Newport Beach, California; sister of Ruth Frehse (singer and dancer who married Norman Krasna); m. Glenn Tryon (actor-director, div. 1947); m. thrice more. ❖ With sister Ruth, began career singing and dancing in nightclubs as The Frazee Sisters; appeared in 40 films (1940–51), including *Moonlight and Melody, Hellzapoppin, Moonlight in Havana, When Johnny Comes Marching Home, Rosie the Riveter, Ten Cents a Dance* and *Rhythm Inn.*

FRAZER, Gretchen (1919–1994). *See Fraser, Gretchen.*

FRAZIER, Maude (1881–1963). American educator and legislator. Name variations: M. Frazier. Born Maude Frazier, April 4, 1881, near Baraboo, Wisconsin; died June 20, 1963, in Las Vegas, Nevada; dau. of William Henry Frazier and Mary Emma (Presnall) Frazier. ❖ Taught school in various small Nevada towns (1906–21); was deputy state superintendent of public instruction in southern NV (1921–27); was superintendent of Las Vegas Union School District, building schools and laying foundation for largest school district in NV (1927–46); ran unsuccessfully for NV state legislature (1948), but won on 2nd attempt, serving as chair of education committee for 6 terms in legislature, and on ways and means committee (1950–62); as legislator, was instrumental in reorganizing NV state school system (1955), establishing Nevada Southern University (later University of Nevada, Las Vegas), and revising elections laws; was 1st woman to be appointed lieutenant governor in Nevada (1962).

FREAKWATER (1964—). *See Bean, Janet Beveridge.*

FRECHETTE, Sylvie (1967—). Canadian synchronized swimmer. Name variations: Sylvié Fréchette. Born June 27, 1967, in Montreal, Quebec, Canada. ❖ Was a member of the Canadian National Team (1983–92);

won the Commonwealth Games championship (1986, 1990); won the World championship (1991), the only athlete to receive 7 perfect 10's for solo event; at Barcelona Olympics, won a silver rather than gold medal for solo (1992) when a judge mistakenly pushed the wrong button (took 18 months of appeals to change it to gold); won a team silver medal at the Atlanta Olympics (1996). Named female athlete of the year by the Aquatic Federation of Canada (1989–92).

FREDEGAR (c. 547–597). *See Fredegund.*

FREDEGUND (c. 547–597). Merovingian queen. Name variations: Fredegond or Fredegonde or Frédégone; Fredegar; Fredegonda, Fredegunde or Fredegunda; Fredegundis or Fredigundis. Born, presumably in Neustria, c. 547 (some sources cite 545); died 597; dau. of unknown, non-noble parents; became concubine and then 3rd wife of Chilperic I, king of Soissons, king of the Franks (r. 561–584), in 567; children: (with Chilperic) one daughter, Riguntha, and sons Chlodobert (d. 580); Samson (d. 577); Dagobert (d. 580); Theodoric (d. 584); Chlothar also known as Clotaire or Lothair II (584–629), king of Neustria (r. 584–629), king of the Franks (r. 613–629). ❖ Queen whose talent for political intrigue in late 6th-century Gaul resulted in the elevation of her son Lothair II to the position of sole king of the previously divided Frankish territories; was mistress to Chilperic I (prior to 567); engaged in feud with husband's sister-in-law Brunhilda due to Galswintha's murder (567–97); instigated murder of King Sigibert of Austrasia (575); endured deaths of 4 infant sons (577–84) and Chilperic (584); acted as regent for infant son Lothair II upon Chilperic I's death (584). ❖ See also *The Fourth Book of the Chronicle of Fredegar, with its continuations* (Nelson, 1960); and *Women in World History.*

FREDERICA. *Variant of Fredericka or Frederika.*

FREDERICA AMALIE (1649–1704). Duchess of Holstein-Gottorp. Born April 11, 1649; died Oct 30 1704; dau. of Sophie Amalie of Brunswick-Lüneberg (1628–1685) and Frederick III (1609–1670), king of Denmark and Norway (r. 1648–1670); m. Christian Albert, duke of Holstein-Gottorp, Oct 24, 1667; children: Frederick (b. 1671); Christian Augustus (b. 1673), duke of Holstein-Gottorp.

FREDERICA CAROLINE OF HESSE-DARMSTADT (1752–1782). *See Frederica of Hesse-Darmstadt.*

FREDERICA DOROTHEA OF BADEN (1781–1826). Queen of Sweden. Name variations: Frederika von Baden. Born Frederica Dorothea Wilhelmina on Mar 12, 1781; died Sept 25, 1826; dau. of Charles Louis of Padua (b. 1755), prince of Padua and Baden, and Amalie of Hesse-Darmstadt (b. 1754); m. Gustavus IV Adolphus (1778–1837), king of Sweden (r. 1792–1809), Oct 31, 1797 (div. 1812); children: Gustavus of Sweden, prince of Vasa (b. 1799); Sophia of Sweden (1801–1875); Charles Gustavus (b. 1802); Amelia Marie Charlotte (1805–1853); Cecilie (1807–1844, who m. Frederick Augustus, grand duke of Oldenburg).

FREDERICA LOUISE (1715–1784). Margravine of Anspach. Born Sept 28, 1715; died Feb 4, 1784; dau. of Sophia Dorothea of Brunswick-Lüneburg-Hanover (1687–1757) and Frederick William I (1688–1740), king of Prussia (r. 1713–1740); m. Charles William, margrave of Anspach, May 30, 1729; children: Christian Frederick, margrave of Anspach (b. 1736).

FREDERICA LOUISE (1770–1819). Princess of Brunswick-Wolfenbuttel. Born Frederica Louise Wilhelmina on Nov 28, 1770; died Oct 15, 1819; dau. of Wilhelmina of Prussia (1751–1820) and William V, prince of Orange; m. Charles Augustus, prince of Brunswick-Wolfenbuttel, Oct 14, 1790.

FREDERICA OF HESSE (1751–1805). Queen of Prussia. Name variations: Fredericka; Louisa of Hesse-Darmstadt. Born Fredericka Louise, Oct 16, 1751, in Prenzlau, Brandenburg, Germany; died Feb 25, 1805, in Berlin, Germany; dau. of Caroline of Birkenfeld-Zweibrucken (1721–1774) and Ludwig also known as Louis IX, landgrave of Hesse-Darmstadt; became 2nd wife of Frederick William II (1744–1797), king of Prussia (r. 1786–1797), July 14, 1769; children: Frederick William III, king of Prussia (1770–1840); Christine (1772–1773); Frederick Louis Charles (1773–1796, who m. Frederica of Mecklenburg-Strelitz); Frederica Wilhelmina of Prussia (1774–1837, who m. William I, king of the Netherlands); Augusta (1780–1841, who m. William II, elector of Hesse); Charles (1781–1846); William (1783–1851), prince of Prussia; Henry. Frederick William II's 1st wife was Elizabeth of Brunswick (1746–1840).

FREDERICA OF HESSE-DARMSTADT (1752–1782). Duchess of Mecklenburg-Strelitz. Name variations: Frederica of Hesse; Frederika of Hesse; Frederica Caroline of Hesse-Darmstadt. Born Frederica Caroline, Aug 20, 1752; died after premature birth of 11th child, May 22, 1782; dau. of imperial lieutenant field marshal Prince George William, landgrave of Hesse-Darmstadt (1722–1782) and Marie Louise Albertine of Leiningen-Heidesheim (1729–1818); m. Charles II (b. 1741) grand duke of Mecklenburg-Strelitz, Sept 18, 1768; sister of Charlotte of Hesse-Darmstadt (1755–1785), who m. Charles II after Frederica's death; children: Charlotte (1769–1818); Theresa (1773–1839); Louise of Prussia (1776–1810); Frederica of Mecklenburg-Strelitz (1778–1841); George (1779–1860, grand duke of Mecklenburg-Strelitz); and 6 others.

FREDERICA OF MECKLENBURG-STRELITZ (1778–1841). Duchess of Cumberland and queen of Hanover. Name variations: Frederica Caroline of Mecklenburg-Strelitz. Born Mar 2, 1778, in Hanover, Lower Saxony, Germany; died June 29, 1841, in Hanover; interred at Chapel of Schloss Herrenhausen, Hanover; dau. of Charles II Louis Frederick, grand duke of Mecklenburg-Strelitz, and Frederica of Hesse-Darmstadt (1752–1782); sister of Louise of Prussia (1776–1810); m. Frederick Louis Charles (1773–1796), prince of Prussia, Dec 26, 1793 (div. 1796); m. Frederick-William, prince of Salms-Branfels, Jan 10, 1798; m. Ernest Augustus I (1771–1851, son of King George III of England), duke of Cumberland and king of Hanover, Aug 29, 1815; children: (1st m.) two boys who died in infancy; Frederica Wilhelmina Louise (1796–1850, who m. Leopold Frederick, duke of Anhalt-Dessau); (2nd m.) Frederick William Henry (b. 1801); Augusta Louisa of Salms-Branfels (1804–1865, who m. Albert, prince of Schwarzbourg-Roudolstadt); Alexander Frederick (b. 1807); Frederick William (b. 1812); (3rd m.) Frederica (1817–1817, stillborn); another daughter (1818–1818); George V (b. 1819), king of Hanover.

FREDERICA OF PRUSSIA (1767–1820). Prussian princess and duchess of York and Albany. Name variations: Fredericka; Frederica Charlotte, princess royal of Prussia. Born Frederica Charlotte Ulrica Catherine, May 7, 1767, in Charlottenburg, Berlin, Germany; died of water on the lung, Aug 6, 1820, in Oatlands Park, Weybridge, Surrey, England; dau. of Elizabeth of Brunswick (1746–1840) and Frederick William II, king of Prussia (r. 1786–1797); m. Frederick Augustus (1763–1827), duke of York and Albany (son of George III and Charlotte of Mecklenburg-Strelitz), Sept 29, 1791 (sep.).

FREDERICA WILHELMINA OF PRUSSIA (1774–1837). Queen of the Netherlands. Name variations: Wilhelmina of Prussia; Wilhelmina Hohenzollern. Born Nov 18, 1774, in Potsdam, Brandenburg, Germany; died Oct 12, 1837, in The Hague, Netherlands; dau. of Frederick William II, king of Prussia (r. 1786–1797), and Frederica of Hesse (1751–1805); m. William I (1772–1843), king of the Netherlands (r. 1813–1840, abdicated in 1840), Oct 1, 1791; children: William II (1792–1849), king of the Netherlands (r. 1840–1849, who m. Anna Pavlovna); Frederick Orange-Nassau (1797–1881); Charlotte (1800–1806); Marianne of the Netherlands (1810–1883). ❖ Following her death, William I married Henrietta Adrienne in Berlin, Germany (Feb 17, 1841).

FREDERICK, Ada (1871–1929). *See Crossley, Ada.*

FREDERICK, Christine (1883–1970). American household efficiency expert. Name variations: Christine McGaffey; Christine McGaffey Frederick. Born Christine Campbell on Feb 6, 1883, in Boston, Massachusetts; died April 6, 1970, in Newport Beach, California; dau. of William R. Campbell and Mimi (Scott) Campbell; m. Justus George Frederick, 1907 (died 1964); children: 1 son (b. 1908) 3 daughters (b. 1910, 1915, 1917). ❖ Adopted by Wyatt MacGaffey, mother's 2nd husband (1894), and took his last name, but changed spelling later; moved to Long Island and created in-house Applecroft Home Experiment Station, a model efficiency kitchen and laundry, to test home products and appliances (1910); produced film and gave lectures on housekeeping efficiency; became household editor of *Ladies' Home Journal* and established League of Advertising Women, later Advertising Women of NY; wrote *The New Housekeeping* (1913), *Household Engineering: Scientific Management in the Home* (1915) and *Selling Mrs. Consumer* (1929); was household editor for *American Weekly*; wrote articles and lectured in US and Europe (1920s–30s); moved to Laguna Beach, CA (1950); taught interior design courses at Orange Coast College and ran own interior design and decoration business (1950–57); influenced development of standardized work surface heights for comfort.

FREDERICK, Empress (1840–1901). *See Victoria Adelaide.*

FREDERICK, Lynne (1954–1994). English actress. Born July 25, 1954, in Hillingdon, Middlesex, England; died April 27, 1994, in West Los Angeles, California; m. Peter Sellers (actor), 1977 (died 1980); m. David Frost (actor, tv personality), 1981 (div. 1982); m. Barry Unger, 1982 (div. 1991). ❖ Films include *No Blade of Grass, Vampire Circus* and *Voyage of the Damned;* also appeared opposite husband Peter Sellers in *The Prisoner of Zenda.*

FREDERICK, Marcia (1963—). American gymnast. Name variations: Marcia Frederick Blanchette. Born Jan 4, 1963, in Springfield, Massachusetts. ❖ At 15, became 1st American woman to win a gold medal at world gymnastic championships (1978), scoring a 9.95 (with perfect score of 10 from 2 judges) for her performance on uneven bars, executing the 1st Stalder shoot with full pirouette ever completed in competition; was a member of women's Olympic team but could not compete in Moscow because of the US boycott (1980).

FREDERICK, Pauline (1881–1938). American actress. Born Beatrice Pauline Libbey (also seen as Libby), Aug 12, 1881, in Boston, Massachusetts; died Sept 19, 1938, of an asthma attack; m. Frank Mill Andrews, 1909; m. Willard Mack (actor-playwright), 1917 (div. 1920); m. Dr. Charles Rutherford, 1922 (div.); m. Hugh Chisholm Leighton, 1930; m. Col. James A. Marmon, 1934 (died 1934). ❖ Began career as a chorine (1902); became one of the stage's most popular leading ladies; made film debut in *The Eternal City* (1915); was the screen's 2nd, and best known, *Madame X* (1920); lauded for performance in *Smouldering Fires;* other films include *Zaza, The Paliser Case, Bella Donna, Resurrection, Three Women, Mumsie* and *Thank You, Mr. Moto.*

FREDERICK, Pauline (1908–1990). American journalist, tv and radio news reporter and analyst. Name variations: Pauline Frederick Robbins. Born in Gallitzin, Pennsylvania, Feb 13, 1908; died in Lake Forest, Illinois, May 9, 1990; dau. of Matthew P. (official of the Pennsylvania State Department of Labor) and Susan (Stanley) Frederick; American University, BA in political science, MA in international law. ❖ Became a globetrotting war correspondent for North American Newspaper Alliance (1945); covered the Nuremberg trials and "Big Four" conferences in New York and Paris; joined news staff of American Broadcasting Company (ABC), 1946), where she had an early morning radio show and occasionally worked on the evening tv news; shared the United Nations beat (1947); covered Democratic and Republican conventions, presidential campaign, and inauguration (1948–49); covered Korean War as well as revolutions in Africa and Middle East (1950s); rejoined NBC (1953), where she ultimately became a star and the 1st woman to report serious tv news; remained NBC's "man at the UN" for next 21 years; joined National Public Radio as an international affairs analyst (1974) and moderated the presidential debate between Jimmy Carter and Gerald Ford (1976); was the 1st woman elected president of UN Correspondents Association. ❖ See also *Women in World History.*

FREDERICKA. *Variant of Frederika.*

FREDERICKA (1917–1981). Queen of Greece. Name variations: Frederika or Frederica; Fredericka Louise of Brunswick; Queen of the Hellenes. Born Fredericka Louise Thyra Victoria Margaret Sophia Olga Cecily Isabel Christa, April 18, 1917, in Blankenburg, Hanover, Lower Saxony, Germany; died Feb 6, 1981, in Madrid, Spain; dau. of Victoria Louise (1892–1980) and Ernest Augustus of Cumberland, duke of Brunswick-Lüneburg; m. Paul I, king of the Hellenes, Jan 9, 1938 (died Mar 6, 1964); children: Sophia of Greece (b. 1938), queen of Spain; Constantine II (b. 1940), king of Greece (r. 1964–1973); Irene (b. 1942). ❖ Called charitable and charming, was devoted to her adopted country, particularly during and after WWII and during Communist war, when she played a crucial role in the country's rehabilitation; following marriage to Prince Paul, learned the language of Greece and was received into the Greek Orthodox Church; when war broke out (1940), went with family to Crete, then Egypt, finally settling in South Africa; while there, organized the Crown Princess' Relief Fund; returned to Greece (1946), when a plebiscite restored King George II to throne; arrived home to find country devastated and under a new threat from Communists; following death of George (April 1, 1947) and husband's ascension, became queen (1947); with husband, determined to end the war with the Communists and create solidarity between the Greek people and their government; traveled with king throughout Greece, even to the battle front; when peace was restored (1949), embarked on a massive effort to rehabilitate her country, coordinating

philanthropic organizations and taking an active role in establishing hospitals and social institutions to serve the needs of orphaned children; campaigned for a more modern Greek School; when US cut off economic aid to Greece (1962), suffered a sharp decline in popularity along with husband; following his death (1964), had little influence in Greece, now in the grip of conflict; at time of Greek military coup d'état (1967), fled to Rome where she lived in self-imposed exile. ❖ See also autobiography *A Measure of Understanding* (1982); and *Women in World History.*

FREDERICKA LOUISE OF BRUNSWICK (1917–1981). *See Fredericka, Queen of Greece.*

FREDERICKA OF HANOVER (1848–1926). Princess of Hanover. Born Fredericka Sophia Mary Henrietta Amelia Theresa on Jan 9, 1848, in Hanover, Lower Saxony, Germany; died Oct 16, 1926, in Biarritz, France; dau. of George V, king of Hanover, and Mary of Saxe-Altenburg (1818–1907); m. Alphonso, 6th baron von Pawel-Rammingen, April 24, 1880; children: 1.

FREDERICKA OF MECKLENBURG-STRELITZ (1778–1841). *See Frederica of Mecklenburg-Strelitz.*

FREDERIKA. *Variant of Frederica or Fredericka.*

FREDERIKA LOUISE OF BRUNSWICK (1917–1981). *See Fredericka, Queen of Greece.*

FREDERIKA OF HESSE-DARMSTADT (1752–1782). *See Frederica of Hesse-Darmstadt.*

FREDERONA (d. 917). Queen of France. Name variations: Frederuna. Died 917; sister of Bovo, bishop of Chalons; m. Charles III the Simple (879–929), king of France (r. 898–923); children: Gisela Martel (d. 919). Charles' 2nd wife was Edgifu (902–951).

FREDESENDIS (fl. 1000). Frankish noblewoman. Fl. around 1000; 2nd wife of Tancred of Hauteville; children: Robert Guiscard (d. 1085, duke of Apulia and Calabria, count of Sicily, r. 1057–1085); William, count of the Principate (d. 1080); Roger the Great, count of Sicily (r. 1072–1101); Fredesendis (fl. 1050); and others.

FREDESENDIS (fl. 1050). Princess of Capua. Fl. around 1050; dau. of Fredesendis (fl. 1000) and Tancred of Hauteville; m. Richard I, prince of Capua.

FREDRIKSSON, Marie (1958—). Swedish singer. Name variations: Roxette. Born May 30, 1958, in Östra Ljungby, Sweden. ❖ Lead singer, had solo career before forming duo Roxette with singer and guitarist Per Gessle (1986); aiming for international success, wrote and recorded in English; with Gessle, released 2nd album, *Look Sharp!* (1988), which included US #1 pop hits "The Look" and "Listen to Your Heart," and #2 hit "Dangerous"; also had hit single with Roxette, "It Must Have Been Love," used on the soundtrack of the film *Pretty Woman* (1990); with Gessle, released *Joyride,* which included #1 hit title track, began 1st world tour (1991), and released album, *Crash! Boom! Bang!* (1994), which was successful except in US; recorded Roxette hits in Spanish, releasing *Baladas en Español* (1996); after time off for family, released *Stars* (1999) and *Room Service* (2001) with Gessle. Swedish government issued postage stamp in honor of Roxette (1991).

FREED, Amanda (1979—). American softball player. Born Dec 26, 1979, in Fountain Valley, California; attended University of California, Los Angeles. ❖ Pitcher/outfielder, won World championship (2002); won team gold medal at Athens Olympics (2004).

FREEDMAN, Nancy (1920—). American novelist. Name variations: Nancy Mars Freedman; Nancy Mars. Born Lois-Nancy Mars, July 4, 1920, in Evanston, Illinois; dau. of Dr. Hartely Farnum Mars (Chicago surgeon) and Brillie Jellet (Hentermeister) Mars; attended Los Angeles City College; studied art at University of Southern California m. Benedict Freedman (writer), 1941; children: 4. ❖ Began career as an actress as Nancy Mars, touring with Max Reinhardt productions and appearing on radio; wrote several novels with husband Benedict Freedman, including *Back to the Sea* (1942), the bestselling *Mrs. Mike,* which was based on a true story (1947), *Lootville* (1957), *The Apprentice Bastard* (1966), *Prima Donna* (1981), *The Search for Joyful* (2002) and the science-fiction novel *Joshua Son of None* (1974).

FREEMAN, Alice (1857–1936). Canadian columnist. Name variations: (pseudonym) Faith Fenton. Born Alice Freeman in Bowmanville, Ontario, Canada, 1857; died 1936; spent 20 years as a teacher in the Toronto school system. ❖ Pioneer Canadian journalist, led a double life during much of her career, teaching elementary school by day and plying the less respectable trade of reporter by night under name Faith Fenton; covered polite society as well as the down-and-out and once posed as a homeless woman to write an exposé; at age 40, lost teaching job and fled to the Klondike, where she gained notoriety for her stories on the Gold Rush. ❖ See also Jill Downie, *A Passionate Pen: The Life and Times of Faith Fenton* (HarperCollins, 1996); and *Women in World History*.

FREEMAN, Alice E. (1855–1902). *See Palmer, Alice Freeman.*

FREEMAN, Caroline (c. 1855–1914). New Zealand teacher and school principal. Born c. 1855 or 1856, in Yorkshire, England; died Aug 16, 1914, in Christchurch, New Zealand; dau. of William (farmer) and Ann (Holden) Freeman; University of Otago, BA, 1885. ❖ First woman to enroll and graduate from University of Otago (1885); established and co-administered two schools for girls, Girton College, in Dunedin and Christchurch (1886). ❖ See also *Dictionary of New Zealand Biography* (Vol. 2).

FREEMAN, Cathy (1973—). Australian-Aboriginal runner. Born Feb 16, 1973, in Mackay, Australia. ❖ Won the silver medal for the 400 meters in a time of 48.63 at Atlanta Olympics (1996), the 1st Aborigine to earn a medal in an individual event; at World championships, won gold medals for the 400 meters (1997, 1999); lit the cauldron at the Sydney Olympics and won a gold medal for the 400 meters (2000). ❖ See also *A Journey Just Begun.*

FREEMAN, Emma B. (1880–1927). American photographer. Born Emma Belle Richart in Nebraska, 1880; died in San Francisco, California, 1927; m. Edwin R. Freeman (photographer and shop owner), 1902 (div. 1915); m. Edward Blake (bookkeeper), 1925; no children. ❖ Took up photography (c. 1910); did a series of 200 Indian studies, called the Northern California series, which were displayed at the Panama-Pacific International Exposition in San Francisco and widely acclaimed (1915); also made her mark in the male-dominated world of photojournalism with her coverage of the *USS Milwaukee*, when it sank while attempting to salvage the submarine H-3 in Eureka Bay (1916).

FREEMAN, Gillian (1929—). British novelist and screenwriter. Name variations: Eliot George; Elaine Jackson. Born Dec 5, 1929, in London, England; dau. of Jack Freeman and Freda Davids Freeman; m. Edward Thorpe, 1955. ❖ Novels include *The Liberty Man* (1955), *The Leather Boys* (1961), *The Alabaster Egg* (1970), *The Confessions of Elizabeth Von S.* (1978) and *Termination Rock* (1989); screenplays include *The Girl on a Motorcycle* (1969), *That Cold Day in the Park* (1969), *I Want What I Want* (1972), and *Day After the Fair* (1987); also wrote criticism, including *The Undergrowth of Literature* (1967), a study of sexual fantasy.

FREEMAN, Joan (1918–1998). Australian nuclear physicist. Born Jan 7, 1918, in Australia; died Mar 18, 1998; m. John Jelley (scientist), Feb 1958. ❖ Successfully overcame great barriers to excel as a physicist when women were discouraged from the field; on scholarship, attended Sydney University (1936–40); studied at Newnham College, Cambridge and Cavendish Laboratory (PhD, 1949) and worked on a magnetic spectrometer; was senior scientific officer in Nuclear Physics Division at Atomic Energy Research Establishment (AERE) in Harwell (1951–60), then Tandem Group leader (1960–78), and consultant (1978–83); on sabbatical at MIT, met Oxford theoretical physicist and future collaborator, Roger Blin-Stoyle; with Blin-Stoyle, won the British Institute of Physics' Rutherford Medal, the 1st woman to achieve that award; wrote over 80 publications. Awarded honorary doctorate from University of Sydney. ❖ See also autobiography *A Passion for Physics: The Story of a Woman Physicist* (1991).

FREEMAN, Kathleen (1919–2001). American character and comedy actress. Born Feb 17, 1919, in Chicago, Illinois; died Aug 23, 2001, in New York, NY. ❖ Made film debut in *Wild Harvest* (1947), followed by *Bonzo Goes to College, Singin' in the Rain, Artists and Models, Houseboat, Support Your Local Sheriff!, Naked City, A Place in the Sun, The Fly, Point Blank, The Blues Brothers, Dragnet, Innerspace, Gremlins 2, Hocus Pocus* and *Naked Gun 33*, among many others; served as the slapstick foil for Jerry Lewis in 8 of his films; appeared in the tv series "Topper" (1953–54) and "The Beverly Hillbillies" (1969–71). Nominated for Tony award for performance in the musical *The Full Monty.*

FREEMAN, Lucy (1916–2004). American journalist and novelist. Name variations: Lucy Greenbaum Freeman Becker. Born Lucy Greenbaum, Dec 13, 1916, in New York, NY; died Dec 29, 2004, in the Bronx, NY; dau. of Lawrence S. (lawyer) and Sylvia (Sobel) Greenbaum; was a

member of the 1st graduating class at Bennington College; m. William M. Freeman (editor), 1947 (div. 1949); m. Harry J. Becker, 1952. ❖ Pioneered coverage of psychiatry and mental health for the *New York Times;* hired in 1940, was one of the few women on the *Times'* reporting staff; published 1st book *Fight Against Fears* which detailed her own experience in psychoanalysis (1951); wrote 77 books, including mystery novels and memoirs. ❖ See also memoir *The Beloved Prison* (St. Martin, 1989).

FREEMAN, Mary E. Wilkins (1852–1930). American novelist and short-story writer. Name variations: wrote under Mary E. Wilkins Freeman and Mary E. Wilkins. Born Mary Eleanor Wilkins in Randolph, Massachusetts, Oct 31, 1852; died Mar 15, 1930, in Metuchen, New Jersey; dau. of Warren E. Wilkins (architect and storekeeper) and Eleanor (Lothrop) Wilkins; attended Mt. Holyoke Seminary and Mrs. Hosford's Glenwood Seminary in West Brattleboro; m. Charles Manning Freeman (physician), 1902 (sep. 1921); no children. ❖ Once considered the last great genre writer in New England, published novel *Pembroke* (1894), thought by some to be her greatest achievement; writings include *Jane Field* (1893), *Madelon* (1896), *Jerome: A Poor Man* (1897), *The Heart's Highway* (1900), *The Portion of Labor* (1901), *The Debtor* (1905), *"Doc" Gordon* (1906), *By the Light of the Soul* (1906), *The Shoulders of Atlas* (1908), *The Butterfly House* (1912) and *An Alabaster Box;* also wrote *Decorative Plaques* (verse, 1883), *Giles Corey: Yeoman* (play, 1893), and *Once Upon a Time and Other Child Verses* (1897). Awarded Howells medal for distinction in fiction by American Academy of Letters (1926); elected to membership in the National Institute of Arts and Letters. ❖ See also *Women in World History.*

FREEMAN, Mavis (1907—). Australian bacteriologist and biochemist. Name variations: Mavis Louisa Freeman. Born Jan 30, 1907, in Ballarat, Victoria, Australia. ❖ Worked at Walter and Eliza Hall Institute of Medical Research (1928–40, 1946–48); while there, identified the microbe responsible for Q fever with Macfarlane Burnet (1937); during WWII, served in Australian Army Medical Corps, becoming captain, and worked on research to find a safe method for blood transfusion in regions at risk for malaria.

FREEMAN, Mavis (1918—). American swimmer. Born Nov 1918. ❖ At Berlin Olympics, won a bronze medal in 4x100-meter freestyle relay (1936).

FREEMAN, Michele. Jamaican runner. ❖ Won a bronze medal for 4x100-meter relay at Atlanta Olympics (1996).

FREEMAN, Mona (1926—). American actress. Born Monica Freeman, June 9, 1926, in Baltimore, Maryland; m. Pat Nerney, 1945 (div. 1952); m. Jack Ellis, 1961; children: Monie Ellis (actress). ❖ Began career as a young model; made film debut in *National Velvet* (1944), followed by *Our Hearts Were Young and Gay, Till We Meet Again, Junior Miss, Blacky Beauty, That Brennan Girl, Dear Ruth, Mother Wore Tights, The Heiress, The Lady from Texas, Thunderbirds, Angel Face, Battle Cry* and *Hold Back the Night.*

FREEMAN, Muriel (1897—). English fencer. Born in 1897 in UK. ❖ At Amsterdam Olympics, won a silver medal in individual foil (1928).

FREEMAN, Ruth B. (1906–1982). American nurse. Name variations: Ruth Benson Freeman. Born Dec 6, 1906, in Methuen, Massachusetts; died Dec 2, 1982, in Cockeysville, Maryland; dau. of Wilbur Milton Freeman and Elsie (Lawson) Freeman; graduate of Mt. Sinai Hospital School of Nursing (NY); Columbia University, BS, 1934, MA, 1939; New York University, EdD, 1951; m. Anselm Fisher, 1927; children: 1. ❖ Esteemed educator, speaker, author, and nurse, worked as staff nurse at Henry Street Visiting Nurse Service in New York City; taught at New York University (1937–41) and at University of Minnesota School of Public Health (1941–46); was administrator of nursing services at American Red Cross in Washington, DC, and a consultant to National Security Resources Board; invited to establish a nursing program at Johns Hopkins School of Hygiene and Public Health (1950), served as a professor of public health administration (1950–62), professor of public health (1962–71), and professor emerita (1971–82) while there; was president of the National League for Nursing (1955–59).

FREER, Agnes Rand (1878–1972). American poet. Name variations: (pseudonym) Agnes Lee; Mrs. Otto T. Freer. Born Agnes Rand, May 19, 1878, in Chicago, Illinois; died in Ashtabula, Ohio, Dec 1972; dau. of William Henry Rand and Harriet Husted (Robinson) Rand; m. 2nd husband Otto Freer, May 1911 (died 1932); children: Peggy (d. around 1900). ❖ Her books, written under pseudonym Agnes Lee, include

Verses for Children (1901), *The Border of the Lake* (1910), *The Sharing* (1914), *Faces and Open Doors* (1922), and *New Lyrics and a Few Old Ones* (1930); also translated from the French Théophile Gautier's *Enamels and Cameos* and Fernand Gregh's *The House of Childhood;* contributed to many anthologies and magazines.

FREI, Tanya (1972—). Swiss curler. Born May 31, 1972, in Switzerland. ❖ Won a silver medal for curling at Salt Lake City Olympics (2002).

FREIBERGA, Vaira Vike- (1937—). *See Vike-Freiberga, Vaira.*

FREIER, Recha (1892–1984). German-born Zionist. Born Recha Schweitzer in Norden, Ostfriesland, Germany, 1892; died in Jerusalem, 1984; m. Rabbi Moritz Freier (1889–1969); children: Shalhevet, Amud, Zerem and Maayan Freier. ❖ Israeli Zionist leader, teacher, and writer who, as the founder of Youth Aliyah (1933), rescued thousands of young Jews from Nazi Germany; her organization was responsible for the immigration to Palestine of a total of 30,353 youths (1934–48); wrote *Let the Children Come: The Early History of Youth Aliyah* (Weidenfeld & Nicolson, 1961), among others. ❖ See also *Women in World History.*

FREIST, Greta (1904–1993). Austrian-born French artist. Born in Weikersdorf, Lower Austria, July 27, 1904; died in Paris, Sept 19, 1993. ❖ Leading woman artist in Austria (1930s), left Vienna for Paris along with her companion Gottfried Goebel (1936); worked in painting, ceramics and restoration.

FREMANTLE, Anne (1909–2002). English journalist, novelist, essayist and editor. Born Anne-Marie Huth Jackson, June 15, 1909, in Savoie, France; died Dec 26, 2002, in London, England; dau. of a director of the Bank of England; mother was the dau. of Sir Mountstuart Elphinstone Grant Duff, once undersecretary for India; attended Cheltenham Ladies College; studied modern languages at Oxford; postgraduate studies at London School of Economics; m. Christopher Fremantle (2nd son of Lord Cottesloe, died 1978); children: 3 sons. ❖ Began career as a journalist for *The Times, Manchester Guardian, London Mercury* and *The Spectator,* ran unsuccessfully for Parliament as a Fabian socialist; at 33, became a convert to Catholicism; moved to US (1946), took American citizenship, and became an associate editor of *Commonweal;* was also a frequent contributor to *The New York Times,* among others; taught English at Fordham University and City College in NY and religion at New York University; theologically liberal, wrote more than 30 books from novels to ruminations on Protestant mystics and papal encyclicals, including *George Eliot* (1933), *The Medieval Philosophers* (1955), *The Protestant Mystics* (1964), *The Age of Faith* (1965) and *Three-Cornered Heart* (1970); possibly best known for editing *The Wynne Diaries;* eventually returned to England.

FREMAULT, Anita (1915–1970). *See Louise, Anita.*

FRÉMONT, Jessie Benton (1824–1902). American writer. Name variations: Jessie B. Fremont. Born Jessie Ann Benton on May 31, 1824, near Lexington, Virginia; died Dec 27, 1902, in Los Angeles, California; dau. of Thomas Hart Benton (US senator from Missouri) and Elizabeth (McDowell) Benton; m. Lieutenant John Charles Frémont (explorer), Oct 19, 1841; children: Elizabeth (b. 1842), Benton (b. 1848), John Charles (b. 1851), Anne (b. 1853) and Frank Preston Benton (b. 1854). ❖ Outspoken and strong-willed, witnessed and chronicled the changing American scene during final half of 19th century from a woman's perspective; often collaborated with husband on his expedition reports, including his successful tour in Oregon and California (1844), which was printed as a Senate document in an edition of 10,000 copies and widely sold in a commercial edition as well (entitled simply the *Report,* it was said to have influenced Far Western settlement more than any other book); served as husband's ally during his troubled Civil War service, when he was eventually stripped of his command; wrote about his uncompleted campaign in a series of impassioned articles for *Atlantic Monthly,* which were published in book form as *The Story of the Guard: A Chronicle of the War* (1863); produced a flood of reminiscences, travel sketches, and stories for leading magazines; best work was collected in *A Year of American Travel* (1878), *Souvenirs of My Time* (1887), *Far-West Sketches* (1890), and *The Will and The Way Stories* (1891); was also principal author of husband's *Memoirs of My Life* (1887). ❖ See also Ruth Painter Randall, *I Jessie: A Biography of the Girl Who M. John Charles Frémont* (Little, Brown, 1963); Pamela Herr and Mary Lee Spence, eds. *The Letters of Jessie Benton Fremont* (U. of Illinois, 1993); and *Women in World History.*

FREMSTAD, Olive (1871–1951). Swedish-born American mezzo-soprano. Name variations: Olive Fremstadt. Born Anna Olivia Fremstad in Stockholm, Sweden, Mar 14, 1871; died in Irvington, NY, April 21, 1951. ❖ Received early musical training as pianist, organist, and singer in Christiania, Norway (now Oslo); at 12, moved with family to Minneapolis, MN; studied as a contralto in NY (1890) and as a soprano with Lilli Lehmann in Berlin (1893); debuted in grand opera at Cologne (1895), singing the role of Azucena in Verdi's *Il Trovatore;* was a member of the Munich Opera (1900–03) and the Metropolitan Opera (1903–14); was particularly noted for interpretation of Wagnerian roles, which included those of Venus in *Tannhäuser,* Kundry in *Parsifal,* Brünnhilde in both *Siegfried* and *Götterdämmerung,* and Isolde in *Tristan und Isolde;* also sang Carmen in Bizet's *Carmen* and Tosca in Puccini's *La Tosca,* and was celebrated for her performances as Salome in Richard Strauss' opera of the same name. ❖ See also *Women in World History.*

FRENCH, Alice (1850–1934). American author. Name variations: Octave Thanet, Frances Essex. Born Alice French, Mar 19, 1850, in Andover, Massachusetts; died Jan 9, 1934, in Davenport, Iowa; dau. of George Henry French and Frances Wood (Morton) French; lived with Jane Crawford for approximately 50 years. ❖ Writing under pseudonym Octave Thanet, often opposed organized labor and women's suffrage for being against traditional American values; under pseudonym Frances Essex, published 1st short story in newspaper, *Davenport Gazette* (Feb 19, 1871); as Octave Thanet, published 1st notable short story, "Communists and Capitalists," based on railroad strike of 1877, in *Lippincott's Magazine* (Oct 1878); influenced by Social Darwinism, earned reputation as economic theorist with essays on labor and philanthropy; published collections of short stories, *Knitters in the Sun* (1887) and *Otto the Knight* (1891); authored 1st novel, *Expiation* (1890), based on the 1894 Pullman strike, followed by *The Man of the Hour* (1905), and the interventionist novelette *And the Captain Answered* (1917); compiled an edition of Lady Mary Wortley Montagu's letters (1890); received honorary degree from Iowa State University (1911); during WWI, was commander in Motor Car Service and organized Red Cross aid for Europe; served numerous times as president of Iowa Society of Colonial Dames. ❖ See also George L. McMichael, *Journey to Obscurity: The Life of Octave Thanet* (1965).

FRENCH, Annie (1872–1965). Scottish artist. Born 1872 in Glasgow, Scotland; died 1965 in Jersey, England; attended Glasgow School of Art under Fra Newbery, 1896–1902; m. George Wooliscroft Rhead (artist), 1914 (died 1920). ❖ One of the "Glasgow Girls," a group of artists whose most famous work was in illustration with very fine pen-and-ink technique, was schoolmate of Jessie M. King, Margaret and Frances MacDonald and other talented women who made up the group; exhibited for 1st time in Brussels Salon (1903); settled in London and became a prolific exhibitor at Royal Scottish Academy, Royal Glasgow Institute and Royal Academy; was best-known for black-and-white illustrations, many of which appeared in the avant-garde international art journal *The Studio;* painted in watercolor and less frequently in oils; worked in Pre-Raphaelite style with Romantic subjects and often depicted scenes of fairies, then popular; often compared to artist Sir Edward Burne-Jones as well as Aubrey Beardsley, illustrated numerous fairy tales and poems and designed postcards and posters in highly decorative manner, emphasizing unique quality of fine pen-and-ink linear technique; settled in Jersey (late 1950s); work included in permanent collection of Scottish Gallery of Modern Art.

FRENCH, Ashley (1897–1985). *See Robins, Denise Naomi.*

FRENCH, Dawn (1957—). English comedian, actress and writer. Born Oct 11, 1957 in Holyhead, Wales; dau. of Royal Air Force (RAF) pilot; attended Central School of Speech and Drama; m. Lenny Henry (Jamaican-born writer and comedian), 1984; children: (adopted) 1 daughter, Billie. ❖ Best-known for her collaboration with Jennifer Saunders, one of the most successful partnerships in British comedy, 1st worked with Saunders at Comedy Store in London, creating successful double act; came to broader public attention as a regular at the Comic Strip Club (early 1980s); with Saunders, launched successful BBC series "French and Saunders Live" and created and wrote for "Absolutely Fabulous"; independent of Saunders, starred on "Murder Most Horrid" (1991) and then in the long-running BBC comedy "The Vicar of Dibley" (1994–97); returned to stage in Ben Elton's *Silly Cow* (1991) and Sharman MacDonald's *When I Was a Girl I Used to Scream and Shout* (1998); starred in BBC dramas "Tender Loving Care" (1993) and "Sex and Chocolate" (1997); also starred on BBC sitcom "Wild West" (2002–04). ❖ See also Alison Bowyer, *Dawn French: The Biography* (Headline, 2000).

FRENCH, Evangeline (1869–1960). Algerian-born missionary. Name variations: Eva. Born in Algiers in 1869; died in 1960; sister of Francesca French; attended school in Geneva. ❖ Moved to England with family; inspired by the China Inland Mission lectures (1893), converted to Christianity and sailed to Shanghai to begin her work as a missionary; met Mildred Cable in Hezhou (Hwochow, 1902), becoming lifelong companions; with Cable and sister Francesca, ran a girls' school while preparing for a journey through the Gobi Desert to preach the Gospel; traveled the Gobi with them for 16 years (1923–39) which informs their narrative *The Gobi Desert* (1942).

FRENCH, Francesca (1871–1960). Belgian-born missionary. Born in Belgium in 1871; died in 1960; sister of Evangeline French. ❖ Moved to England with family; with sister Evangeline and Mildred Cable, ran a girls' school while preparing for a journey through the Gobi Desert to preach the Gospel; traveled the Gobi with them for 16 years (1923–39) which informs their narrative *The Gobi Desert* (1942).

FRENCH, Heather (1974—). Miss America. Name variations: Heather Henry. Born Heather Renee French, Dec 29, 1974, in Maysville, Kentucky; dau. of a disabled Vietnam vet; graduate of University of Cincinnati; m. Stephen Henry (lt. gov. of Kentucky); children: one. ❖ Named Miss America (2000), representing Kentucky; lobbied Congress on behalf of homeless veterans.

FRENCH, Marilyn (1929—). American novelist and social critic. Born Marilyn Edwards, 1929, in Brooklyn, NY; dau. of E. Charles Edwards (engineer) and Isabel (Hazz) Edwards; Hofstra University, MA; Harvard University, PhD, 1972; m. Robert M. French, Jr., 1950 (div. 1967); children: Jamie and Robert. ❖ Taught at Hofstra for 4 years; was an assistant professor at Holy Cross College (1972–76), and Mellon fellow in English at Harvard (1976–77); published the bestselling *The Women's Room* (1977), now considered one of the most influential works of the modern feminist movement; also wrote *The Bleeding Heart* (1980), *Beyond Power: On Women, Men and Morals* (1986), *Her Mother's Daughter* (1987), *Our Father* (1995) and *Season in Hell* (1998), as well as works of literary criticism, *The Book as World: James Joyce's Ulysses* (1976) and *Shakespeare's Division of Experience* (1981).

FRENCH, Mary (fl. 1703). American poet. Born in Deerfield, Massachusetts. ❖ Captured by Native Americans in Massachusetts, was held prisoner in Canada by the French; addressed "A Poem Written by a Captive Damsel" (1706) to sister, which was 1st published in Cotton Mather's *Good Fetch'd Out of Evil*.

FRENCH, Michelle (1977—). American soccer player. Born Michelle Ann French, Jan 27, 1977, in Fort Lewis, Washington; attended University of Portland; sister of Jamie French (soccer player). ❖ Defender; won a silver medal at Sydney Olympics (2000); signed with Washington Freedom, then San Jose CyberRays.

FRENCH, Ruth (b. 1906). English ballet dancer and teacher. Born 1906 in London, England. ❖ Performed in revues at London's Hippodrome; danced secondary ballerina roles with Anna Pavlova's company, including Myrthe in Ivan Clustine's choreography of *Giselle* and the Blue Bird pas de deux in Pavlova's *The Sleeping Beauty* at Hippodrome in NY (1917); performed in NY in Mikhail Fokine's *The Frolicking Gods* and appeared in *Ziegfeld Follies of 1922*; returned to England where she founded numerous ballet schools and choreographed; published well-known textbooks, *First Steps in Ballet* (1934), *Intermediate Steps* (1947), and *Advanced Steps* (1950).

FRENCH, Valerie (1932–1990). English stage, tv and screen actress. Born Valerie Harrison, Mar 11, 1932, in London, England; died Nov 3, 1990, in New York, NY; m. Michael Pertwee (writer), 1952 (div. 1959); m. Thayer David (actor), 1970 (div. 1975). ❖ Made stage debut in *Treasure Hunt* (1951), London debut (1954), and NY debut in *Inadmissible Evidence* (1965); films include *The Constant Husband, Jubal, The Garment Jungle, The Secret of Treasure Mountain, Decision at Sundown* and *Shalako*; on tv, appeared on "The Nurses" and "All My Children."

FRENI, Mirella (1935—). Italian lyric soprano. Born Mirella Fregni, Feb 27, 1935, in Modena, Italy; studied at Mantua and at Bologna Conservatory with Ettore Campogalliani; m. Leone Magiera; m. Nicolai Ghiaurov (bass), 1981. ❖ Known for her performances of Handel and Mozart, made debut in Modena (1955), Covent Garden (1961), Teatro alla Scala (1962), Metropolitan Opera (1965); appeared at Salzburg (1966–72 and 1974–80); best known for her performance as Tatyana in Tchaikovsky's *Eugene Onegin*, was equally praised for performances of Verdi's *Aida*. ❖ See also *Women in World History*.

FRENKEL-BRUNSWIK, Else (1908–1958). Jewish-Austrian psychologist. Born Else Frenkel in Poland, 1908; died of drug overdose, 1958; dau. of Abraham (bank owner) and Helene (Gelernter) Frenkel; University of Vienna, PhD in psychology; m. Egon Brunswik (psychologist, committed suicide 1955); no children. ❖ Author of *The Authoritarian Personality*, a pioneering synthesis of social psychology and psychoanalysis, which introduced American behaviorists to the nuances of psychoanalysis; was an assistant professor at University of Vienna until Nazi invasion of Austria (1938); fled to US with husband; worked out of University of California at Berkeley as a lecturer and researcher in psychoanalysis, a relatively new subject to American psychologists; became full professor. ❖ See also *Women in World History*.

FRESCHI, Maria Borgese (1881–1947). *See Borgese Freschi, Maria.*

FRETTER, Vera (1905–1992). English zoologist. Born July 5, 1905, in London, England; died Oct 15, 1992; attended Birkbeck College; University of London, BS, 1934, PhD in zoology, 1936. ❖ Mollusks (Prosobranch) expert and marine field naturalist, lectured at Royal Holloway College (1936–45) and at Birkbeck College (1945–55); worked as a reader (1954–70) and as an honorary research associate (1970–92) at University of Reading; was president of Malacological Society; writings include *British Prosobranch Molluscs* (1962, later revised with Alaistair Graham, 1994) and *A Functional Anatomy of Invertebrates* (1976).

FREUD, Anna (1895–1982). Austrian psychoanalyst. Born Anna Freud in Vienna, Austria, Dec 3, 1895; died in London, England, Oct 8, 1982; dau. of Sigmund Freud (founder of psychoanalysis) and Martha Bernays; graduate of Cottage Lyzeum, Vienna, 1912; Clark University, LLD, 1950; Jefferson Medical College, ScD, 1964; University of Sheffield, LLD, 1966; lived with lifelong companion and collaborator, Dorothy Burlingham. ❖ Pioneering psychoanalyst, who commenced analysis with father (1918), began psychoanalyzing adults and children and delivered 1st paper before the Vienna Psychoanalytic Society (1922); met Dorothy Burlingham and became a training analyst at Vienna Psychoanalytic Institute (1925); established the Jackson Nursery for children (1937); immigrated to London (1938); established the wartime nurseries (1941); opened the Hampstead Child Therapy Clinic (1951); for more than 50 years, worked tirelessly to secure the future of psychoanalysis and safeguard its principles with far-reaching effects: her work in ego psychology and child development remain a part of the foundation upon which current psychoanalytic thought is built; in the schools and research centers she established, trained and influenced a generation of future analysts; writings include *The Introduction to Psychoanalysis* (1927), *The Ego and the Mechanisms of Defence* (1936), *Infants Without Families* (1944), *Indications for Child Analysis and Other Essays* (1945–56), *Research at the Hampstead Child Therapy Clinic and Other Papers* (1956–65), *Normality and Pathology in Childhood* (1965), *Problems of Psychoanalytic Technique and Therapy* (1966–70) and *Psychoanalytic Psychology of Normal Development* (1970–80). ❖ See also Robert Coles, *Anna Freud: The Dream of Psychoanalysis* (Addison-Wesley, 1992); Elizabeth Young-Bruehl, *Anna Freud* (Summit, 1988); and *Women in World History*.

FREUND, Gisèle (1912–2000). German-born French photographer. Name variations: Gisele Freund. Born in Berlin, Germany, 1912; died 2000 in Paris; studied sociology and art history, Albert-Ludwigs-Universität Freiburg, Breisgau, Germany, 1932–33; Sorbonne, PhD in sociology and art, 1936; m. Pierre Blum, 1937 (div. 1948). ❖ Became a naturalized citizen of France (1936); was known for her photo portraits, many in color as early as 1938, of literary and artistic greats, including James Joyce, Jean-Paul Sartre, Colette, Virginia Woolf, Elsa Triolet, Sylvia Beach, André Malraux, and Matisse; moved to Lot, France, to escape Nazis (1940–42); was photographer and assistant film producer in Argentina and Chile with Louis Jouvet Theatre Co. (1943–44); worked for France Libre, Argentina (1944–45); lived in New York City (1947–49), then Mexico (1950–52); was a member of Magnum Photos in Paris (1947–54); as a freelance photojournalist for *Life, Weekly Illustrated, Picture-Post* and *Paris Match*, produced photoessays on everyone from unemployed workers to Evita Peron; books include *Photography and Society, The World and My Camera, Three Days with Joyce* and *Gisèle Freund: Photographer*. Honored with Grand Prix National des Arts, France (1980).

FREUNDLICH, Emmy (1878–1948). Austrian politician. Born Emma Kögler in Aussig, Bohemia, Austria-Hungary (now Usti, Czech Republic), June 25, 1878; died in New York, NY, Mar 16, 1948; dau. of Adolf (engineer and mayor of Aussig, died 1895) and Emma Kögler (died 1896); m. Leo Freundlich (Jewish Social Democratic journalist and member of Austrian Reichsrat), 1900 (div. 1912); children: Gertrude and Hertha. ❖ Social Democratic leader and women's rights activist who advocated social reforms in cooperatives, women's suffrage, and adult education; became increasingly active in women's trade union movement in Moravia; moved to Vienna to carry on political and educational work within the Social Democratic movement; as editor of the Austrian women's cooperative society newspaper, increased that journal's circulation to 120,000 copies per printing by 1914; starting in 1915, became one of the leaders of the Social Democratic Kinderfreunde (Friends of Children); also began to work for the government as a specialist in the Ministry of Nutrition (1915); was one of Red Vienna's best-known leaders (1920–34), enjoying a public forum through her writings and lecturing, as a member of the City Council, and as a deputy to the new National Assembly in which she represented Vienna's districts 2, 20 and 21; elected president of International Cooperative Women's Guild (ICWG, 1921), a post she retained until her death; with Nazi annexation of Austria (1938), escaped to London. ❖ See also *Women in World History.*

FREYTAG-LORINGHOVEN, Elsa von (1875–1927). Danish-French poet. Name variations: Baroness von Freytag-Loringhoven. Born in Denmark in 1875; died of asphyxiation in 1927 at age 52. ❖ An advocate of modern art and a published poet in the *Little Review,* also posed for many artists, including William Glackens, Robert Henri, and George Bellows; after the Bolshevik Revolution effectively wiped out her fortune, was found selling newspapers in Germany. ❖ See also *Women in World History.*

FRICIOIU, Maria (1960—). Romanian rower. Born Mar 16, 1960, in Romania. ❖ At Los Angeles Olympics, won a gold medal in coxed fours (1984).

FRICKER, Brenda (1945—). Irish actress. Born Feb 17, 1945, in Dublin, Ireland; m. Barrie Davies. ❖ Had an extensive stage career in Ireland; came to prominence in the film *My Left Foot* (1989); other films include *Angels in the Outfield* (1994), *Moll Flanders* (1996), *Swann* (1996), *Resurrection Man* (1998), *Conspiracy of Silence* (2003), *Veronica Guerin* (2003) and *Inside I'm Dancing* (2004); frequently appears on tv, including the series "Casualty."

FRIDAY, Dallas J. (1986—). American wakeboarder. Born Sept 6, 1986, in Orlando, Florida. ❖ Began competing (2000); won gold (2001) and silver (2000) at X Games in Freeride; won gold (2001) and bronze (2002) at Gravity Games; became World Cup champion (2001); won Pro Wakeboard Tour, Orlando, FL, in Freeride (2002); credited with working to advance the sport.

FRIDAY, Nancy (1937—). American feminist author. Born Aug 27, 1937, in Pittsburgh, Pennsylvania; raised in Charleston, South Carolina; dau. of a financier; Wellesley College, BA; m. Norman Pearlstine (editor in chief of *Time,* Inc.). ❖ Feminist author, worked briefly as reporter for *San Juan Island Times* (1960–61) and as editor of the travel magazine *Islands in the Sun* (1961–63), before turning to freelance writing; worked as journalist in New York, England, Italy and France, contributing to such magazines as *Cosmopolitan* and *Playboy;* produced several popular psychology books beginning with *My Secret Garden* (1973), a compilation of women's sexual desires which sold over 1.5 million copies worldwide; also wrote *Forbidden Flowers* (1975), the bestselling *My Mother/My Self: The Daughter's Search for Identity* (1977), *Men in Love* (1980, *Jealousy* (1985), *Women on Top* (1991), *The Power of Beauty* (1996) and *Our Looks, Our Lives: Sex, Beauty, Power and the Need to Be Seen* (1999).

FRIDESWIDE (d. 735?). English saint and princess. Name variations: Fredeswitha or Fritheswith. Died possibly in 735; was buried in St. Mary's Church, Oxford; her shrine was destroyed in 1538. ❖ According to legend, founded the monastery of St. Frideswide in Oxford, after fleeing persecution by her lover, a king. Feast day is Oct 19.

FRIEBUS, Florida (1909–1988). American actress. Born Oct 10, 1909; died May 27, 1988, in Laguna Niguel, California; dau. of Theodore Friebus. ❖ On Broadway, appeared in *Triple Crossed, The Ivory Door* and *The Lady from the Sea;* also appeared with Eva Le Gallienne's Civic

Rep in *Pride and Prejudice* and *The Primrose Path;* probably best remembered as Mrs. Gillis on the tv series, "The Many Loves of Dobie Gillis."

FRIEDAN, Betty (1921–2006). American writer and feminist. Name variations: Bettye. Pronunciation: FREE-dan. Born Bettye Naomi Goldstein on Feb 4, 1921, in Peoria, Illinois; died Feb 4, 2006, in Washington, DC; dau. of Harry Goldstein (died 1943) and Miriam Horwitz (died 1988); Smith College, BA in psychology, 1942, with honors; attended graduate school at University of California at Berkeley for one year; m. Carl Friedan, June 1947 (div. 1969); children: Daniel Friedan (b. 1948); Jonathon Friedan (b. 1952); Emily Friedan (b. 1956). ❖ Author of *The Feminine Mystique,* the book that launched the feminist movement in the US, who fought for equal rights for women and founded the National Organization for Women (NOW); moved to New York City after father's death (1943); published *The Feminine Mystique* (1963), which turned the world upside down; founded NOW (1966) and became its 1st president; planned and helped organize the historic March for Women's Equality (1970); wrote *It Changed My Life* (1976), followed by *The Second Stage* (1981); served as head of unofficial NOW delegation to final UN Conference for Women in Kenya and accepted an offer from University of Southern California to be joint visiting professor at the School of Journalism and Women's Studies (1985); published *The Fountain of Age* (1993). ❖ See also Sondra Henry and Emily Taitz, *Betty Friedan: Fighter for Women's Rights* (Enslow, 1990); Judith Hennessee, *Betty Friedan: Her Life* (Random House, 1999); and *Women in World History.*

FRIEDBERG, Berta (1864–1944). Russian-Jewish poet and playwright. Name variations: Bertha Friedberg; (pseudonym) Izabella Arkad'evna or Arkadevna Grinévskaia; Izabella Grinevskaia; Isabel or Isabella Grinevskaya. Born Berta Friedberg in 1864 in Grodno, Russia; died in Constantinople in 1944; dau. of A.S. Friedberg (1838–1902, Russian Hebraist) and his 1st wife Mordecai Spector. ❖ Moved to St. Petersburg, where she frequented Jewish literary circles; published 1st novel, *The Orphan* (1888); in Odessa (1890s), worked as translator and also wrote literary criticism; moved to Constantinople (1910); writings, which tended to depict the lives of the Jewish middle class, include *The First Storm* (1895), *The Little Lights* (1900), *Bab* (staged 1904), *Poems* (1904), *Harsh Days* (1909), *Bekha-Ulla* (1912), *Salute to Heroes* (1915), *From the Book of Life* (1915) and *Poems* (1922); also published pamphlet against censorship, *The Right of Books.*

FRIEDERIKE. *Variant of Frederica or Fredericka.*

FRIEDERIKE OF HESSE-CASSEL (1722–1787). Duchess of Oldenburg. Born Oct 31, 1722; died Feb 28, 1787; dau. of Maximilian, prince of Hesse-Cassel; m. August (1711–1785), duke of Oldenburg (r. 1777–1785), Nov 21, 1752; children: Charlotte of Oldenburg (1759–1818), queen of Sweden; Wilhelm, duke of Oldenburg (b. 1754); Luise (1756–1759).

FRIEDL, Ernestine (1920—). American cultural anthropologist. Born 1920 in Hungary; moved to US with family at age 2, settling in the Bronx, NY; Hunter College, BA, 1941; Columbia University, PhD in cultural anthropology, 1950; m. Harry Levy (classicist). ❖ Studied under Ralph Linton and Ruth Benedict at Columbia; performed fieldwork with Chippewa in Wisconsin (1942 and 1943); taught at Wellesley College, Brooklyn College, and Queen's College; conducted fieldwork in Vasilika, Greece, then published *Vasilika: A Village in Modern Greece* (1962); conducted fieldwork with migrants from Vasilika to Athens (1964–65); while in Athens, worked on *Women and Men: An Anthropologist's View* (1975) which examined gender role definition among hunter and gatherer societies and horticultural societies; served as president of American Ethnological Society (1967) and as president of American Anthropological Society (1974–75); served as dean of arts and sciences at Duke University.

FRIEDMAN, Elizabeth (d. 1980). America cryptographer. Born Elizabeth Smith; died in 1980; graduate of Hillsdale College, Michigan, 1915; m. William Friedman (cryptographer), in May 1917; children: John Friedman; Barbara Friedman. ❖ Premier cryptographer who devised a code system for the Office of Strategic Services and deciphered messages from German spies in Allied lands during World War II; while working at Newberry Library in Chicago, obtained a position with the Riverbank Laboratory, a think tank concerned with everything from cryptology to plant genetics; with husband, at the height of World War I (1917), began working on decoding diplomatic messages from unfriendly powers that were sent to Riverbank from the government; began military contract work in Washington, DC (1921); became a "special agent" on loan to Department of Justice to the Coast Guard and Navy (1927), working on liquor and drug smuggling; during World War II, devised a code system for the Office of Strategic Services, and deciphered messages from German spies in Allied lands. ❖ See also *Women in World History.*

FRIEDMAN, Esther Pauline (1918–2002). American syndicated columnist. Name variations: (pseudonym) Ann Landers; Mrs. Jules Lederer; (nickname) Eppie. Born July 4, 1918, in Sioux City, Iowa; June 22, 2002, in Chicago, Illinois; dau. of Abraham (motion-picture exhibitor) and Rebecca (Rushall) Friedman; identical twin of Pauline Esther Friedman (Abigail Van Buren); attended Morningside College, Sioux City; m. Jules William Lederer (businessman), July 2, 1939 (div.); children: Margo. ❖ Known to millions of readers as columnist Ann Landers, moved to Chicago, where she raised her daughter and was active in political and philanthropic causes; entered a contest run by the *Sun-Times* to find a successor to columnist Ruth Crowley, who wrote an advice column under the pen name of Ann Landers (1955); landing the job, launched 1st column (Oct 16, 1955) and was an immediate success; offered insightful, straightforward, and sometimes acerbic replies to questions from readers; wrote such books as *Since You Ask Me* (1961), *Ann Landers Talks to Teen-Agers About Sex* (1964), *Truth is Stranger* (1968), and *Where Were You When President Kennedy Was Shot* (1993). ❖ See also *Women in World History.*

FRIEDMAN, Pauline Esther (1918—). American syndicated columnist. Name variations: (pseudonym) Abigail Van Buren; Mrs. Morton Phillips; (nickname) Popo. Born July 4, 1918, in Sioux City, Iowa; dau. of Abraham (motion-picture exhibitor) and Rebecca (Rushall) Friedman; identical twin of Esther Pauline Friedman (Ann Landers); attended Morningside College, Sioux City; m. Morton Phillips (business-man), July 2, 1939; children: Jeanne and Eddie. ❖ Known to millions of readers as columnist Abigail Van Buren, lived in Minneapolis, Eau Claire, Wisconsin, and San Francisco, where she devoted spare time to charitable causes and politics; launched her own journalistic career by submitting a sample column to *San Francisco Chronicle* (1955); enjoyed the same extraordinary success as her sister; wrote such books as *Dear Abby* (1958), *Dear Teen-Ager* (1959) and *Dear Abby on Marriage* (1962). ❖ See also *Women in World History.*

FRIEDMAN-GRAMATTÉ, Sonia (1899–1974). *See Eckhardt-Gramatté, S.C.*

FRIEDMANN, Roseli (1937—). *See Ocampo-Friedmann, Roseli.*

FRIEDNE-BANFALVI, Klara (1931—). Hungarian kayaker. Name variations: Klara Banfalvi. Born in Hungary. ❖ At Rome Olympics, won a bronze medal in K2 500 meters (1960).

FRIEDRICH, Heike (1970—). East German swimmer. Born April 18, 1970, in East Germany. ❖ Won a gold medal in the 4x100-meter freestyle relay, a gold medal in the 200-meter freestyle, and a silver medal in the 400-meter freestyle at Seoul (1988).

FRIEDRICH, Terry (c. 1949—). *See Meeuwsen, Terry.*

FRIEND, Catherine Mary Ann (1868–1925). *See Adamson, Catherine Mary Ann.*

FRIEND, Charlotte (1921–1987). American microbiologist. Born Mar 11, 1921, in New York, NY; died Jan 13, 1987; dau. of a businessman and pharmacist; Hunter College, BA, 1944), Yale University, PhD, 1950; never married. ❖ Known for research in leukemia and the discovery of the virus that causes leukemia in mice, also claimed that viruses could cause cancers, long before it was discovered that viruses were capable of causing leukemia and cervical cancer; published research results linking viruses to cancers with the help of Peyton Rous, co-editor of the *Journal of Experimental Medicine,* and Ludwik Gross, then a scientist with the 1st and only other research experience with leukemia viruses in mice; mentored by Cornelius P. Rhoads, was associate member (1946–66) and associate professor of microbiology (1952–66) at Sloan-Kettering Institute for Cancer Research; served as a professor and the director of Mt. Sinai School of Medicine's Center for Experimental Cell Biology (1966–87); elected to the National Academy of Sciences (1976). Received Alfred Sloan Award (1954, 1957, 1962), a Hunter College Presidential Medal Centennial Award (1970), a NIH Virus-Cancer Program Award (1974) and the Prix Griffuel (1979).

FRIEND, Florence (1876–1953). *See Mannering, Mary.*

FRIENDS OF DISTINCTION, The.
See Cleaves, Jessica.
See Love, Barbara.

FRIESINGER, Anni (1977—). German speedskater. Name variations: Anna Friesinger. Born Jan 11, 1977, in Germany; dau. of Georg and Janina Friesinger (both speedskaters); sister of Jan and Agnes Friesinger (both speedskaters). ❖ Won a bronze medal in the 3,000 meters at Nagano Olympics (1998); won the European All-Around championships (1999), the World Cup title in the 1,500 meters (2000–01), and the World All-Around championships (2001); at World Single Distance championships, won a gold in the 1,500 and a silver in the 3,000 (2001); won a gold medal for the 1,500 meters at Salt Lake City Olympics (2002) and a gold medal for Team Pursuit and bronze medal for 1,000 meters at Torino Olympics (2006).

FRIETSCHIE, Barbara (1766–1862). American hero. Name variations: Barbara Fritchie. Born Barbara Hauer, Dec 3, 1766, in Lancaster, Pennsylvania; died in Frederick, Maryland, Dec 18, 1862; dau. of German immigrants; m. John Frietschie. ❖ According to legend, defied Confederate troops under General "Stonewall" Jackson as they advanced through Frederick, Maryland, by waving a Union flag from an upper window of her home (Sept 1862). After subsequent investigations, it was determined that Jackson never did pass by her home, but it is possible that a germ of truth was enlarged out of recognition by writers John Greenleaf Whittier (*Barbara Frietchie,* 1863) and Clyde Fitch (*Barbara Frietchie,* a play, 1898). Whittier had Frietschie defiantly yelling to Jackson, after her flag was riddled with bullets, "Shoot, if you must, this old gray head/ But spare your country's flag."

FRIGANZA, Trixie (1870–1955). American comedic actress, dancer, and singer. Born Delia O'Callahan (also seen as Brigit Friganza O'Callaghan), Nov 29, 1870, in Grenola, Kansas; raised in Cincinnati; died Feb 27, 1955, in Flintridge, California; m. W.J.M. Barry; m. Charles A. Goettler. ❖ Made professional debut in Cleveland in *The Prince of Pekin;* with her considerable height and girth, became a dance satirist; appeared in vaudeville and musical comedies, including *The Passing Show of 1912;* films include *Motor Maniac, Gentlemen Prefer Blondes, Thanks for the Buggy Ride, Free and Easy, My Bag O' Trix, The Whole Town's Talking* and *Myrt and Marge;* retired (1939).

FRIGERIO, Marta Lía (1925–1985). Argentinean novelist, short-story writer, socialist and feminist. Name variations: Marta Lynch. Born 1925 in Buenos Aires, Argentina; committed suicide 1985; married a lawyer, 1953. ❖ Social and political writer, participated in government of Arturo Frondisi; wrote articles for *La Nación* and *Clarín,* among others; pulished the novel *La alfombra roja* (The Red Carpet, 1962), about Argentinean politics; other novels include *Al Vencedor* (To the Winner, 1965), *La Señora Ordoñez* (1968), *El cruce del río* (1970), *La penúltima versión de la colorada Villanueva* (1978), *Informe bajo llave* (1983), and the bestselling *No te duermas, no me dejes* (1985).

FRINGS, Ketti (1909–1981). American writer. Name variations: (pseudonym) Anita Kilgore. Born Katherine Hartley, Feb 28, 1909, in Columbus, Ohio; died 1981; dau. of Guy Herbert Hartley (Quaker paper-box salesman) and Pauline (Sparks) Hartley; attended Principia College; m. Kurt Frings (German-born lightweight boxer turned actors' agent), Mar 18, 1938; children: Peter and Kathie. ❖ Playwright, screenwriter and novelist, produced an impressive number of works during 35-year career, but her stage adaptation of Thomas Wolfe's autobiographical novel, *Look Homeward Angel* (1957), remains the work for which she is best known and for which she received the Pulitzer Prize in Drama and New York Drama Critics' Circle Award; following marriage (1938), spent 2 years in Mexico waiting for husband to be allowed to enter US, a hiatus that inspired 1st novel *Hold Back The Dawn* (1940); turned out a series of screenplays, including *Guest in the House* (1944), *The Accused* (1949), *Thelma Jordan* (1949), *The Company She Keeps* (1951), *Because of You* (1952), and adaptations for such plays as *Come Back, Little Sheba* (1952) and *The Shrike* (1955). ❖ See also *Women in World History.*

FRINK, Elisabeth (1930–1993). English sculptor. Name variations: Dame Elisabeth Frink; also seen as Elizabeth Frink. Born in Suffolk, England, Nov 14, 1930; died April 18, 1993; studied at Guildford School of Art, 1947–49, and Chelsea School of Art, 1949–53, under Bernard Meadows and Willi Soukop; m. Michael Jamnet, 1956 (div. 1962); m. Edward Pool, 1968 (div. 1974); m. Alex Csaky, 1975. ❖ During early career, taught at Chelsea School of Art (1953–60) and St. Martin's School of Art (1955–57); lived in France (1967–72); returned to England, living and working in Dorset; exhibited regularly from 1955; is best known for a series of heads, begun in mid-1960s, which reflect her interest in war and the military, though her warriors and soldiers gave way to victims of suffering in mid-1970s; also executed a number of public and religious commissions, including the *Alcock Brown Memorial*, for Manchester Airport (1962), *Horse and Rider* for Dover Street, London, and *Walking Madonna*, for Salisbury Cathedral (1981); illustrated *Aesop's Fables* (1967), *The Canterbury Tales* (1971) and *Odyssey and Iliad* (1974–75). Made a CBE (1969).

FRINTU, Rodica (1960—). Romanian rower. Born Mar 29, 1960, in Romania. ❖ At Moscow Olympics, won a bronze medal in coxed eights (1980).

FRIS, Maria (1932–1961). German ballet dancer. Born 1932, in Berlin, Germany; died May 27, 1961, in Hamburg, Germany. ❖ Performed with range of ballet companies in postwar Europe, including Berlin State Opera Ballet, Gsovsky's Ballet, Frankfurt State Opera, Weisbaden State Ballet, Janine Charat's Ballets de France, and more; committed suicide during a rehearsal with State Opera Ballet in Hamburg, where she jumped from a high-level catwalk onto an empty stage.

FRISCHMANN, Justine (1969—). British singer. Name variations: Elastica. Born Sept 16, 1969, in London, England. ❖ Was a founding member of punk-influenced pop band Elastica which was formed in England (1992), serving as vocalist and guitarist; with band, saw debut album reach #1 in UK (1995) and had hit singles in US, including "Connection" and "Stutter"; released additional albums with Elastica, including *6-Track* (1999) and *The Menace* (2000).

FRISCHMUTH, Barbara (1941—). Austrian novelist and short-story writer. Born July 5, 1941, in Austria; studied Hungarian and Turkish at Graz University and Orientalism in Vienna. ❖ Novels, often semi-autobiographical, focus on experiences of childhood; works include *Klosterschule* (1968), *Bildungsromane: Die Mystifikationen der Sophie Silber* (1976), *Amy oder die Metamorphose* (1978), *Kai und die Liebe zu den Modellen* (1979), *Mörderische Märchen* (1989), *Über die Verhältnisse* (1987), *Einander Kind* (1990), *Hexenherz* (1993), *Donna und Dario* (1997) and *Die Entschlüsselung* (2001).

FRISSELL, Toni (1907–1988). American photographer. Born Antoinette Wood Frissell, Mar 10, 1907, in New York, NY; died April 17, 1988, in Saint James, NY; dau. of Dr. Lewis Fox (medical director of St. Luke's Hospital) and Antoinette Wood (Montgomery) Frissell; m. Francis McNeill Bacon III (broker), 1932; children: son, Varrick Bacon (b. 1933); daughter, Sidney Bacon (b. 1935). ❖ After becoming a fashion photographer for *Vogue* (1933), was the 1st to shoot models outside, in natural sunlight, instead of in the usual studio setting; remained with *Vogue* for 11 years; often used her children and their friends for her photo-illustrated books, notably *A Child's Garden of Verse* (1944); during WWII, received a star and two overseas stripes for her work at the front as a wartime correspondent; worked for *Harper's Bazaar* (1941–50) and for *Life* and *Sports Illustrated* (1950s); photographs and illustrated articles appeared in a number of magazines, including *Collier's, Good Housekeeping, Ladies' Home Journal, Holiday, McCall's, Fortune, This Week* and *Arts and Decoration;* work was included in *Family of Man* exhibition at New York's Museum of Modern Art (1955). ❖ See also *Women in World History.*

FRITCHIE, Barbara (1766–1862). *See Frietschie, Barbara.*

FRITH, Mary (c. 1584–1659). British criminal. Name variations: Moll Cutpurse; Molly Cutpurse; Mary Markham; Molly Frith. Born in London, England, c. 1584; died in 1659; dau. of a shoemaker. ❖ One of Britain's most infamous malefactors, abandoned dresses for breeches and a doublet when young, a costume she wore until her dying day; found her niche as a pickpocket; took to the stage of London's Fortune Theater (c. 1605), belting out bawdy songs, gaining the dubious acclaim as the 1st professional actress in England; after having her hands branded for pickpocketing, moved on to highway robbery, forming her own gang; wounded a notable military figure during a robbery and was jailed and condemned to death; able to bribe her accuser, was freed; opened the Globe Tavern, which soon became a gathering place for criminals, and became a master fence, receiving and selling stolen goods at enormous profit; avoided further confrontations with the law until Feb 1612, when she was arrested, tried, convicted, and punished in a public square, for wearing male attire in public; for next 2 decades, reigned supreme among London criminals. Became immortalized in plays by Thomas Dekker, Thomas Middleton, and Nathan Field. ❖ See also *Women in World History.*

FRITH, Molly (c. 1584–1659). *See Frith, Mary.*

FRITHESWITH (d. 735?). *See Frideswide.*

FRITHPOLL, Margaret (d. 1130). Queen of Norway and queen of Denmark. Born Nov 4, 1130; dau. of Helen (fl. 1100s) and Inge I the Elder, king of Sweden (r. 1080–1110, 1112–1125); m. Magnus III Barelegs, king of Norway (r. 1093–1103), in 1101; m. Niels, king of Denmark (r. 1104–1134), c. 1105; children: (2nd m.) Magnus (b. around 1106); Inge of Denmark (d. around 1121).

FRIULI, countess of (c. 819–c. 874). *See Gisela.*

FRIZZELL, Mary (1913–1972). Canadian runner. Born May 26, 1913, in Canada; died Oct 12, 1972. ❖ At Los Angeles Olympics, won a silver medal in 4x100-meter relay (1932).

FRIZZELL, Mildred (1911—). Canadian runner. Born 1911 in Canada. ❖ At Los Angeles Olympics, won a silver medal in 4x100-meter relay (1932).

FROELICH, Henriette (1768–1833). *See Frölich, Henriette.*

FROEHLICH, Silvia (1959—). East German rower. Name variations: Silvia Fröhlich. Born Feb 24, 1959, in East Germany. ❖ At Moscow Olympics, won a gold medal in coxed fours (1980).

FROELIAN, Isolde (1908–1957). German gymnast. Name variations: Isolde Frölian. Born April 1908 in Germany; died Nov 1957. ❖ At Berlin Olympics, won a gold medal in team all-around (1936).

FROESETH, Hege (1969—). Norwegian handball player. Name variations: Hege Fröseth. Born Dec 20, 1969, in Norway. ❖ At Barcelona Olympics, won a silver medal in team competition (1992).

FROHBERG, Regina (1783–1850). German novelist and short-story writer. Name variations: (pseudonym) F. Born 1783 in Berlin, Germany; died 1850. ❖ Born into Jewish family but converted to Christianity; lived in Vienna and belonged to several literary circles; works include *Schmerz der Liebe* (1810), *Die Entsagung* (1824), *Eigene und fremde Schuld* (1837), and *Vergangenheit und Zukunft* (1840); translations of French plays published as *Theater* (1818).

FRÖHLICH, Sylvia (1959—). *See Froehlich, Silvia.*

FROHMAN, Margaret (1881–1934). *See Illington, Margaret.*

FRÖLIAN, Isolde (1908–1957). *See Froelian, Isolde.*

FRÖLICH, Henriette (1768–1833). German novelist and salonnière. Name variations: Henriette Frolich or Froelich; Frolich. Born 1768 in Germany; died 1833; children: 10. ❖ Her home in Berlin became meeting place for intellectuals and writers; wrote *Virginia oder die Kolonie von Kentucky* (1818–19).

FROLOVA, Inna (1965—). Ukrainian rower. Born June 3, 1965, in USSR. ❖ At Seoul Olympics, representing Soviet Union, won a silver medal in quadruple sculls without coxswain (1988); won a silver medal for quadruple sculls at Atlanta Olympics representing Ukraine (1996).

FROLOVA, Lyudmila (1953—). Soviet field-hockey player. Born July 29, 1953, in USSR. ❖ At Moscow Olympics, won a bronze medal in team competition (1980).

FROLOVA, Nina (1948—). Soviet rower. Born Oct 11, 1948, in USSR. ❖ At Moscow Olympics, won a silver medal in coxed eights (1980).

FROLOVA, Tatiana (1967—). Russian gymnast. Born April 26, 1967, in Bryansk, USSR. ❖ Won Riga (1983, 1984); at World championships, won a gold medal in team all-around (1983).

FROMAN, Jane (1907–1980). American band singer. Born in St. Louis, Missouri, Nov 10, 1907; died in Columbia, MO, April 22, 1980; attended University of Missouri and Cincinnati Conservatory of Music; married twice. ❖ Formally trained, with a strong melodious voice, started career on radio in Cincinnati and with Paul Whiteman in Chicago; established herself in New York (mid-1930s), with successful radio and club appearances as well as recordings (notably, "I Only Have Eyes For You"); appeared on Broadway in *Ziegfeld Follies of 1934* and vaudeville show *Laugh, Town, Laugh* (1942) with Ed Wynn; early movie musicals included *Movie Stars Over Broadway* (1935) and *Radio City Revels* (1938); while on tour entertaining troops during WWII, was seriously injured in a plane crash off coast of Portugal (Feb 1943); underwent numerous operations for badly damaged legs; returned to Broadway in *Artists and Models* (1943) and played New York's Copacabana (1945); had hit recordings, including "I'll Walk Alone," from the movie *Follow The Boys* (1944); dubbed soundtrack for *With a*

Song in My Heart, a film about her life starring Susan Hayward (1952). ❖ See also *Women in World History.*

FROMAN, Margareta (1890–1970). Russian ballet dancer. Name variations: Margareta Frohman. Born Nov 8, 1890, in Moscow, Russia; died Mar 4, 1970, in Boston, Massachusetts. ❖ Trained at school of Bolshoi Ballet in Moscow before joining the company (1915); danced briefly with Diaghilev Ballet Russe on tour in Europe and US (1916–17); rejoined the Bolshoi (1917) where she danced many acclaimed roles, including title role in Mordkin's *The Legend of Aziade;* was also featured in *Coppélia* and *The Sleeping Beauty;* began serving as ballet master of Zagreb Croation National Theater, Opera and Ballet (1921), where she choreographed numerous ballets over next 30 years; training such students as Ana Rojè, Sonja Kastl and Mia Slavenska; moved to US (early 1950s) where she taught at studios in CT until her death. Works of choreography include *Pierrot* (1922), *The Gingerbread Heart* (1924), *Le Boiteau* (1927), *Raymonda* (1927), *The Humpbacked Horse* (1928), *Les Noces* (1932), *Imbrek* (1937) and *Ero Sonoga Svijeta* (Ero, the Joker, c. 1952).

FROMM, Erika (1909–2003). American psychologist. Born Erika Oppenheimer, Dec 23, 1909, in Frankfurt, Germany; died May 25, 2003, in Chicago, Illinois; earned doctorate at University of Frankfurt, 1933; m. Paul Fromm (cousin of psychoanalyst Erich Fromm, died 1987); children: Joan Fromm Greenstone (died 1996). ❖ Moved to Netherlands with rise of Nazism; with husband, moved to US (1938); held a variety of teacher and research positions; joined the faculty of the University of Chicago (1961), where she challenged some of Freud's findings and became an expert in the use of hypnosis; was longtime editor of the journal *Research Developments and Perspectives in Hypnosis;* writings include (with Thomas French) *Dream Interpretation: A New Approach* (1964) and *Hypnotherapy and Hypnoanalysis* (1986) and (with Stephen Kahn) *Changes in the Therapist* (2000), among others.

FROMM, Uta (1969—). See Rohländer, Uta.

FROMM-REICHMANN, Frieda (1889–1957). American psychoanalyst. Name variations: Frieda Reichmann. Born Frieda Reichmann, Oct 23, 1889, in Karlsruhe, Germany; died April 28, 1957, in Rockville, Maryland; dau. of Adolf and Klara (Simon) Reichmann; m. Erich Fromm (social philosopher), Mar 26, 1926 (div. 1942). ❖ Worked at University of Königsberg's psychiatric hospital, becoming instructor (1913–16); was physician-in-charge of Königsberg hospital for soldiers with brain injury (1916–18) and chief of a private psychoanalytic sanitarium in Heidelberg (1924–28); helped found German Psychoanalytic Society's Frankfurt branch (1926) and Psychoanalytic Institute of South-Western Germany (c. 1929); moved to France (1933), and to US (1935), becoming naturalized citizen (1941); worked at Chestnut Lodge psychoanalytic sanitarium in Maryland (1935–57) and was influenced by colleague Harry Stack Sullivan; worked with Washington-Baltimore (later Washington) Psychoanalytic Society as training and supervising analyst (after 1935), serving as president (1939–41); worked with Washington School of Psychiatry (after 1936) and with William Alanson White Institute of Psychiatry, Psychoanalysis, and Psychology, NY (after 1943); wrote *Principles of Intensive Psychotherapy* (1950) and co-wrote "An Intensive Study of Twelve Cases of Manic-Depressive Psychosis" (1954). ❖ See also Gail A. Hornstein, *To Redeem One Person is to Redeem the World* (Free Press).

FROMMATER, Uta (1948—). West German swimmer. Born Dec 12, 1948, in Germany. ❖ At Mexico City Olympics, won a bronze medal in the 4x100-meter medley relay (1968).

FROMME, Lynette (1948—). American murderer and attempted assassin. Name variations: Squeaky Fromme. Born Oct 22, 1948, in Santa Monica, California; dau. of William Millar Fromme and Helen Benzinger Fromme. ❖ Met Charles Manson (1967) and joined Manson commune; arrested for murders of James and Lauren Willett but charges were dropped; pointed .45 Colt automatic at President Gerald Ford in Sacramento (Sept 5, 1975) but, with no bullet in firing chamber, gun never went off; convicted of attempted assassination and sentenced to life imprisonment; made prison break from Alderson Federal Prison for Women (Dec 23, 1987) and recaptured 2 days later; serving sentence in Carswell, Texas. Another attempt was made on Ford's life 17 days later by Sara Jane Moore (Sept 22, 1975), who like Fromme also made prison break from Alderson (1979). ❖ See also Jess Bravin, *Squeaky: The Life and Times of Lynette Alice Fromme* (St. Martin, 1997).

FRÖSETH, Hege (1969—). See Froeseth, Hege.

FROST, Constance Helen (c. 1862–1920). New Zealand physician, bacteriologist, and pathologist. Born 1862 or 1863, in England; died Jan 29, 1920; dau. of Thomas and Mary Ann (Antwis) Frost; University of Otago Medical School, MB, ChB, 1900. ❖ Immigrated with family to New Zealand (c. 1880); after medical residency at Adelaide Hospital, South Australia, established private practice in Mount Eden, New Zealand (1903); became honorary bacteriologist and pathologist at Auckland Hospital (1903); awarded small honorarium (1913), until position finally became full time (1920). ❖ See also *Dictionary of New Zealand Biography* (Vol. 3).

FROST, Phyllis (1917–2004). Australian reformer and humanitarian. Name variations: Dame Phyllis Frost. Born Phyllis Turner in 1917 in Australia; grew up in Brighton, them rural Croydon; died 2004; dau. of Harry and Irene Turner; sister of Elizabeth Turner (the 1st woman superintendent of Royal Children's Hospital) and Nancy Turner (founded the Australian Dietetics Council); attended Melbourne University; m. Glenn Frost (dentist, died 1987); children: Liz, Pauline and Christine. ❖ Began career as a physiotherapist; worked with the Victorian Relief Committee (now VicCare) for over 30 years; helped start the Australian branch of the Freedom from Hunger campaign; gave her approval for the women's prison at Deer Park (2001), later named the Dame Phyllis Frost Centre, the culmination of her many years on the women's prison council.

FROST, Winifred (1902–1979). Irish freshwater biologist. Name variations: Winifred Evelyn Frost. Born Mar 2, 1902, in Ireland; died Aug 1979. ❖ Studied shrimps (euphausids) with Professor James Johnstone at Liverpool University and was awarded a DSc (1945); as assistant inspector of fisheries in Dublin (began 1938), studied trout in the River Liffey; worked as a Freshwater Biological Association (FBA) research scientist in Windermere (1938–79); served as member of Council of the Salmon and Trout Association; elected chair, and later president, of Windermere and District Angling Association; left most of estate to FBA; studied eels in central Africa; contributed to knowledge and history of fish, especially in the Lake District. Writings include (with Margaret E. Brown) *The Trout* (1967).

FROSTIC, Gwen (1906–2001). American nature artist. Born 1906 in Sandusky, Michigan; died April 26, 2001, in Benzonia, Michigan; dau. of Fred (school superintendent) and Sara Frostic; attended Eastern Michigan University and Western Michigan University; never married. ❖ Widely known Michigan artist of block prints, founded Presscraft Papers (1950s) and sold her stationery and postcards for over 50 years. Inducted into the Michigan Women's Hall of Fame (1986).

FROULAY, Renée de (1714–1803). See Crequy, Renée Caroline de Froulay, Marquise de.

FRUELUND, Katrine (1978—). Danish handball player. Name variations: Katrine Fruland or Frülund. Born July 12, 1978, in Randers, Denmark. ❖ Left back, won a team gold medal at Sydney Olympics (2000) and a team gold medal at Athens Olympics (2004).

FRULAND or FRÜLUND, Katrine (1978—). See Fruelund, Katrine.

FRUSTOL, Tone Gunn (1975—). Norwegian soccer player. Name variations: Tone Gunn-Frustol or Frustøl. Born June 21, 1975, in Norway. ❖ Won a team bronze medal at Atlanta Olympics (1996).

FRY, Elizabeth (1780–1845). English social reformer. Born Elizabeth Gurney, May 21, 1780, at Earlham Hall, near Norwich, England; died Oct 12, 1845, at Ramsgate, Kent; dau. of John (wool merchant and banker) and Catherine Bell Gurney (both Quakers); m. Joseph Fry, 1800; children: 11. ❖ Not yet 20, inaugurated a small school at Earlham Hall which provided a rudimentary education to about 70 local children from poor families; adopted lifestyle of a "Plain" Quaker which meant that she relinquished music and dancing and assumed a more simple form of dress (1799); after husband inherited Plashet House, a country estate outside London (1809), began a soup kitchen and did what she could to provide medicines for the sick; becoming an "approved minister" of the Quaker faith (1811), began to travel widely throughout the country to meet and discuss matters of religious concern with other Friends; introduced to the appalling conditions that were then to be found in Newgate, the largest and most notorious of the city's prisons (1813), returned to Newgate and made preparations to establish a school for the child inmates (1817); formed a support committee composed of Quaker friends which was called the Ladies' Association for the Improvement of the Female Prisoners in Newgate (more commonly referred to as the Ladies' Newgate Committee), which helped supervise and fund sewing classes for female inmates and arranged the sale of their work; appeared before a special committee of House of Commons to submit evidence on the state of the nation's prisons and argue for separate women's prisons (1818); in next few years, attempted to improve conditions on transport ships to Australia and to alleviate conditions at the convict settlement in New South Wales; in addition, sought a reform of the death penalty; in her *Observations on the Visiting, Superintendence and Government of Female Prisoners* (1827), put forward the radical proposition that "punishment is not for revenge, but to lessen crime and reform the criminal"; extended her network of prison committees throughout England, Scotland, and Ireland; became a kind of spiritual advisor to many members of the English aristocracy, including young Princess Victoria; made 5 extended tours of France, Germany, and Holland in order to promote the cause of prison reform (1838–43); formulated the 1st plans to put nursing on a professional basis (1840), establishing a training home in London for 20 women (pioneers of the modern nursing profession who became known as the Fry Sisters); advocated the establishment of a new home for the rehabilitation of former prostitutes (1845), which would be known as the Elizabeth Fry Refuge. ❖ See also *Memoir of the Life of Elizabeth Fry* (1847); Georgina King Lewis, *Elizabeth Fry* (1910); Janet Whitney, *Elizabeth Fry* (Harrap, 1937); and *Women in World History.*

FRY, Laura Ann (1857–1943). American artist. Born 1857 in US; died 1943; dau. of William Henry Fry (wood carver and teacher) and Effie Watkin; graduate of Cincinnati School of Design. ❖ Studied drawing, sculpture, wood carving and china painting at Cincinnati School of Design (1872–76); continued studies in Trenton, New Jersey, learning art of throwing, decorating and glazing pottery; went on to study in France and England; was founding member of Cincinnati Art Pottery Club (1879), with Clara Newton and Louise McLaughlin; became 1st employee of Maria Longworth Nichols Storer's Rookwood Pottery (1881); introduced use of atomizer (patented under name "airbrush blending") for applying slips to moist pots, and pioneered underglazing techniques which made "Standard" Rookwood ware the best-known feature of firm's Arts and Crafts pottery; embraced Arts and Crafts movement started by British poet William Morris which sought to return dignity to craft, celebrating simplicity, good design and individual workmanship while also seeking to make decorative art affordable; left Rookwood (1887) to become professor of Industrial Art (1891) and worked at the Lonhuda Pottery in Steubenville, Ohio (1891–94); returned to Rookwood; with 25 others, co-founded Lafayette Art Association in Indiana (1909), now the Art Museum of Greater Lafayette and affiliated with the Smithsonian Institution; helped association hold 1st exhibition (1911).

FRY, Margery (1874–1958). English prison reformer. Born Sara Margery Fry in 1874; died 1958; attended Roedean and Somerville College, Oxford; never married; no children. ❖ Began career as warden of the women's hostel at Birmingham University (1899–1904); during WWI, worked in France for Friends War Victims Relief Committee, after which she became secretary of the Penal Reform League, which was amalgamated (1921) as the Howard League for Penal Reform; served as chair of the league (1919–26), a period also marked by increasing involvement in campaign to abolish capital punishment; appointed a magistrate (1921); served as education advisor to Holloway Prison (1922) and as principal of Somerville College (1926–31). ❖ See also *Women in World History.*

FRY, Mrs. Maxwell (1911–1996). See *Drew, Jane.*

FRY, Shirley (1927—). American tennis player. Name variations: Mrs. K.E. Irvin; Shirley Fry Irvin. Born Shirley June Fry, June 1927, in Akron, Ohio; married K.E. Irvin. ❖ Won the French Open (1951), beating Doris Hart; with Doris Hart, won French Open doubles championship (1950–53), Wimbledon doubles (1951–53) and US Open doubles (1951, 1954); won US Open (1956); with Vic Seixas, won the mixed doubles Wimbledon championship (1956); won Australian singles title (1957). Inducted into International Tennis Hall of Fame (1970).

FRYE, Mary E. (1905–2004). American poet. Born Mary Elizabeth Clark, Nov 13, 1905, in Dayton, Ohio; orphaned at 3; moved to Baltimore at 12; died Sept 15, 2004; m. Claud Frye (ran a clothing business), 1927 (died 1964). ❖ Grew and sold flowers; wrote the well-known 12-line bereavement verse "Do Not Stand at My Grave and Weep" (1932), which circulated privately among the populace. Though she never published or copyrighted the poem, it is often featured at memorial services, especially those brought on by disasters.

FU HAO (fl. 1040 BCE). Queen consort and military general. Name variations: Lady Hao. Pronunciation: FOO HOW. Lived during

China's bronze age, late in the 2nd millennium c. 1040 BCE; consort of Emperor Wu Ding of the Shang dynasty; children: one known son, Xiao Yi, who preceded her in death. ❖ Earliest woman general of the ancient Shang dynasty, whose remarkable activities were known only through oracle bone inscriptions until the 1976 discovery of her tomb. ❖ See also *Women in World History.*

FU MINGXIA (1978—). Chinese diver. Born Aug 16, 1978, in Wuhan, Hubei Province, China. ❖ Won 1st World championship title (1991), the youngest world champion ever (age 12); at Barcelona Olympics, won a gold medal in platform (1992), the youngest Olympic champion ever (age 13); at World championships, won the 10-meter platform gold (1993, 1994) and 3-meter springboard gold (1995); at Atlanta Olympics, won gold medals for 10-meter platform and 3-meter springboard (1996), the 1st woman to win both titles since Ingrid Engel-Kramer, 36 years earlier; at Sydney Olympics, won a gold medal for 3-meter springboard and a silver medal for synchronized 3-meter springboard (2000).

FU YUEHUA (c. 1947—). Chinese reformer. Name variations: Foo Ywehhwa. Born in China. ❖ Suffered a nervous breakdown after her charge that she was raped by the Party Secretary at her work unit was ignored; became one of the major women activists in the Democracy Wall movement (1978–79); at 32, led thousands of peasants and unemployed youth as they marched through Beijing on National Day, protesting conditions (Jan 8, 1979); was arrested during the crackdown against the movement (Jan 18, 1979); though protesters demanded her release, was imprisoned and subsequently disappeared.

FUBUKI, Koshiji (1924–1980). Japanese actress and singer. Born Feb 18, 1924, in Tokyo, Japan; died Nov 9, 1980. ❖ Legendary stage actress, film star and chanson singer, made film debut in *Okaru Kanpei* (1952); also appeared in *Fukeyo haru kaze* (1953), *Pu-san* (1953), *Aijin* (1953), *Mugibue* (1955), *Daigaku no ninkimono* (1958), *Bonchi* (1960) and *Bangkok no yoru* (1966); albums include *Golden Best Series* (2002) and *Takarazuka Daigekijo de Utau* (2005). ❖ See also (in Japanese) Tokiko Iwatani, *Yume no Naka ni Anata ga iru: Fubuki Koshiji Memoriaru* (1999).

FUCHS, Anna Rupertina (1657–1722). German poet. Name variations: (pseudonym) Daphen. Born 1657 in Germany; orphaned when young, grew up in Nuremburg with relatives; died 1722. ❖ Wrote play about Job (1714) and anthology of poems *Poetischer Gedancken-Schatz* (1720); her collection of poems, *Poetische Schriften,* published posthumously (1726).

FUCHS, Jackie (1959—). See *Fox, Jackie.*

FUCHS, Ruth (1946—). East German track-and-field athlete. Name variations: Ruth Fuchs-Gamm. Born Dec 14, 1946, in East Germany. ❖ Won a gold medal at Munich Olympics (1972) and a gold medal at Montreal Olympics (1976), both for javelin throw; also won the European title (1974, 1978) and World Cup (1977, 1979). ❖ See also *Women in World History.*

FUEHRER, Charlotte (1834–1907). See *Führer, Charlotte.*

FUERSTNER, Fiona (1936—). American ballet dancer. Born April 24, 1936, in Rio de Janeiro, Brazil; raised in and around San Francisco, California. ❖ Made performance debut with San Francisco Ballet (1952), where she danced in works by Balanchine and Christensen, among others; moved to New York City to continue dance training at School of American Ballet; also studied with Royal Ballet School in London; danced with Les Grands Ballets Canadiens where she performed in company's classical repertory; danced in numerous repertory pieces of Pennsylvania Ballet (starting mid-1960s), such as John Butler's *Ceremony* (1968) and *Carmina Burana,* Richard Rodham's *Valse Oubliée,* and revivals of Tudor's *Jardin aux Lilas* and Balanchine's *Symphony in C.,* among others; served as ballet mistress of Pennsylvania Ballet for many years and later held the same position at Milwaukee Ballet.

FUERTES, Gloria (1917–1998). Spanish poet. Born in Madrid, Spain, July 28, 1917; died in 1998; youngest of 8 children of working-class parents. ❖ Following Spanish Civil War, published poems and children's stories and read some of her works on the radio; published 1st book of poetry, *Isla ignorada* (1950); continuing to write and publish, co-founded the poetry journal *Arquero* (1952); taught Spanish at Bucknell University on a Fulbright grant (1961–63); returned to Spain, teaching Spanish to foreign students in Madrid's International Institute; published *Poeta de guardia* (1968), one of her best works; began appearing on children's programs on Spanish tv (c. 1970) and was voted both the best writer for children and the children's most popular tv personality; in all, published more than a dozen volumes of poetry and two dozen children's books. ❖ See also *Women in World History*.

FUGARD, Sheila (1932—). South African novelist and poet. Born Sheila Meiring, 1932, in Birmingham, England; m. Athol Fugard (playwright), 1956; children: Lisa Fugard (actress). ❖ Migrated to South Africa (1937); studied speech and drama at University of Cape Town; began career as an actress; with husband, founded Circle Players in Cape Town; novels include *The Castaways* (1972), *Rite of Passage* (1976), and the well-known *A Revolutionary Woman* (1983); her dense and visionary poetry, which explores despair and social injustice, includes *Threshold* (1975) and *Mythic Things* (1981). Received CNA Prize (1972) and Olive Schreiner Prize (1973).

FUGGER, Barbara Baesinger (d. 1497). German textile merchant. Name variations: Barbara Baesinger; Barbara Basinger. Born in Augsburg, Germany; died in 1497 in Augsburg; m. Ulrich Fugger, a textile merchant of Augsburg (died 1469); children: 11, including sons Ulrich, George, and Jacob (who became one of the most successful of all medieval bankers, known as "Jacob the Rich," acting as principal banker to the ruling Habsburgs of Austria), and 8 daughters (names unknown). ❖ Widow who took over the management of the family business and had phenomenal success, eventually dealing internationally in wool and linen. ❖ See also *Women in World History*.

FÜHRER, Charlotte (1834–1907). German midwife. Name variations: Charlotte Heise; Charlotte Fuhrer or Fuehrer. Born Charlotte Heise, 1834, in Hanover, Germany; died Nov 5, 1907, in Montreal, Canada; m. Ferdinand Adolph Führer, May 1853; children: 6. ❖ After marriage, immigrated to US but returned to Germany when the family business in NY failed; studied with an obstetrician at a Hamburg maternity hospital (1856–59); immigrated to Montreal with family (1859) and established a successful midwifery practice; writings include *The Mysteries of Montreal: Being Recollections of a Female Physician* (1881), which warned against out-of-wedlock pregnancies and advocated Victorian values about sexuality.

FUHRMANN, Barbel (1940—). East German swimmer. Born Mar 29, 1940, in East Germany. ❖ At Rome Olympics, won a bronze medal in 4x100-meter medley relay (1960).

FUJII, Raika (1974—). Japanese synchronized swimmer. Born 1974 in Japan. ❖ Won a team bronze medal at Atlanta Olympics (1996) and a team silver medal at Sydney Olympics (2000).

FUJII, Yumiko (c. 1972—). Japanese softball player. Born c. 1972 in Japan. ❖ Won a team silver medal at Sydney Olympics (2000).

FUJIKI, Mayuko (1975—). Japanese synchronized swimmer. Born 1975 in Japan. ❖ Won a team bronze medal at Atlanta Olympics (1996).

FUJIMARU, Michiyo (1979—). Japanese synchronized swimmer. Born April 6, 1979, in Japan. ❖ At World championships, placed 1st in free routine combination (2003); won a team silver medal at Athens Olympics (2004).

FUJIMOTO, Yuko (1943—). Japanese volleyball player. Born Jan 14, 1943. ❖ At Tokyo Olympics, won a gold medal in team competition (1964).

FUKUDA, Hideko (1865–1927). Japanese writer. Name variations: Kageyama Hideko; Fukuda Hideko. Born Hideko Kageyama, 1865, in Okayama, Western Japan; died May 1927; dau. of Katashi (provincial samurai) and Umeko (schoolteacher); left elementary school to become an assistant teacher in 1879; m. Fukuda Yusaku (American-trained scholar), 1892 (died 1900); children: (with Oi Kentaro) 1 son; (with Fukuda Yusaku) 3 sons. ❖ Pioneer in the women's liberation movement during the Meiji era and one of the few women in the early socialist movement, who was editor of Japan's 1st feminist journal and author of the 1st autobiography of a woman to be written in her country; joined women's rights movement after hearing Kishida Toshiko speak (1882); opened a school for girls and women (1883); moved to Tokyo after school closed by authorities (1884); joined group of radical liberal activists, and was arrested and imprisoned for her role as an explosives courier in what became known as the Osaka Incident (1885); became a public figure when she was tried and sent to jail for 10 months (1887); after release from prison, lived with Oi Kentaro, a leader in the radical liberal movement, and gave birth to a son (1890); became a socialist and started school for women (1901); published autobiography *Half My Life*, an immediate success, and began campaign against restrictions against

women in Meiji Civil Code (1904); published the novel *My Reminiscences* (1905), which was less well received; founded feminist magazine *Sekai Fujin* (*Women of the World*, 1907), the project for which she would best be known, though it was later banned by Tokyo court (1909); wrote article for feminist journal *Seito*, advocating the establishment of a community system that would use "all scientific knowledge and mechanical power" for the "equality and benefit of all" (this issue of the journal was also banned, 1913); continued feminist and socialist activities up to year of death (1927). ❖ See also *Women in World History*.

FUKUDA, Patricia (1930—). See Saiki, Patricia Fukuda.

FUKUNAKA, Sachiko (1946—). Japanese volleyball player. Born April 5, 1946, in Japan. ❖ At Mexico City Olympics, won a silver medal in team competition (1968).

FULD, Carrie (1864–1944). American philanthropist. Born Carrie Bamberger, Mar 16, 1864, in Baltimore, Maryland; died July 18, 1944, in Lake Placid, NY; dau. of Elkan Bamberger (businessman) and Theresa (Hutzler) Bamberger (dau. of Moses Hutzler, who founded a well-known Baltimore department store); sister of Louis Bamberger; m. Louis Meyer Frank (co-founder of L. Bamberger & Co., a department store), early 1880s (died 1910); m. Felix Fuld (partner in L. Bamberger & Co.), Feb 20, 1913 (died 1929); no children. ❖ With brother, sold L. Bamberger & Co. to R.H. Macy & Co. for $25 million, just prior to the stock-market crash; donated $5 million to found the Institute for Advanced Study in Princeton, New Jersey (1930), which employed some of nation's finest minds to engage in research and creative scholarship; also made large donations to Beth Israel Hospital in Newark, the American Jewish Joint Agricultural Corporation, the Jewish Day Nursery, and Neighborhood House, a settlement house in the Newark slums. ❖ See also *Women in World History*.

FULHAM, Elizabeth (fl. 1780). See Fulhame, Elizabeth.

FULHAME, Elizabeth (fl. 1780). English chemist. Name variations: Elizabeth Fulham. Married Dr. Thomas Fulhame. ❖ Contributed to research on combustion, reduction of metal salts, and concept of catalysis (considered the foundation of enzymology and biochemistry); studied reduction of metal salts in relation to using metal salts to stain cloth (1780); despite great skepticism of husband and friends, published widely acclaimed book, *An Essay on Combustion, With a View to a New Art of Dying and Painting, Wherein the Phlogistic and Antiphlogistic Hypotheses Are Proved Erroneous* (Nov 5, 1794); highly regarded in US; elected a corresponding member of the Chemical Society of Philadephia.

FULLAM, Augusta Fairfield (1876–1914). English murderer. Born 1876; died May 29, 1914; m. Edward Fullam; children: (with Henry Lovell William Clark) at least 1. ❖ Wife of a military accounts examiner in Agra, India, conspired with lover Dr. Henry Lovell William Clark to murder her husband and Clark's wife; failed to kill husband with arsenic, so Clark murdered him with gelsemine (Oct 19, 1911); with Clark, hired assassins to murder his wife (Nov 17, 1912); turned King's Evidence and was found guilty along with Clark of both killings; sentenced to life in prison, where she gave birth to Clark's child; died in her cell of a heatstroke (Clark was executed, Mar 26, 1913).

FULLANA, Margarita (1972—). Spanish mountain biker. Name variations: Margarita Fullana Riera. Born April 9, 1972, in Manacor, Mallorca, Spain. ❖ Won a bronze medal for cross-country at Sydney Olympics (2000).

FULLER, Amy (1968—). American rower. Born May 30, 1968, in US. ❖ At Barcelona Olympics, won a silver medal in coxless fours (1992).

FULLER, Anne (fl. late 18th c.). British novelist. Flourished in late 1700s; birthplace unknown; died 1790 in Cork, Ireland. ❖ Wrote *Alan Fitz-Osborne: An Historical Tale* (1786), *The Convent, or the History of Sophia Nelson* (1786) and *The Son of Ethelwolf: An Historical Tale* (1789).

FULLER, Crystal Eastman (1881–1928). See Eastman, Crystal.

FULLER, Elizabeth (1775–1856). American diarist. Born 1775 in Princeton, Massachusetts; died 1856; dau. of Rev. Timothy Fuller. ❖ Wrote diary over 2-year period published as *Diary kept By Elizabeth Fuller* (1915), which includes record of domestic life and some poems, possibly written by Fuller.

FULLER, Frances (1826–1902). See Victor, Frances.

FULLER, Frances (1907–1980). American actress and acting teacher. Born Mar 16, 1907, in Charleston, South Carolina; died Dec 18, 1980, in New York, NY; niece of James F. Byrnes (US Supreme Court Justice and governor of South Carolina); m. Worthington Miner (actor, died 1982). ❖ Made Broadway debut as Peggy Grant in *The Front Page* (1928); also appeared in *Café, Five Star Final, The Animal Kingdom, Her Master's Voice, The Country Wife, Stage Door* and *Lady of the Camelias*, among others; appeared in numerus films; served as president and director of American Academy of Dramatic Arts.

FULLER, Ida (1874–1975). First Social Security recipient in America. Born Sept 6, 1874, in Ludlow, Vermont; died Jan 27, 1975, in Brattleboro, Vermont. ❖ Served as clerk for John G. Sargent who later became attorney general under President Calvin Coolidge; retired and became 1st American to receive Social Security check (1940).

FULLER, Iola. *See McCoy, Iola Fuller.*

FULLER, Loïe (1862–1928). American dancer. Name variations: Lois, Loie, La Loïe. Pronunciation: LO-ee. Born Mary Louise Fuller, probably Jan 22, 1862, in Fullersburg, Illinois; died in Paris, France, Jan 1, 1928; dau. of Reuben and Delilah Fuller (singer); m. Colonel William Hayes, May 1889 (div. 1892); lived with Gabrielle Bloch; no children. ❖ Music-hall performer whose innovations with shadows and light brought drama and mystery to the stage, elicited a strong following among French intellectuals, and elevated the level of music-hall entertainment while popularizing the abstract notions of art of the Symbolist and Art Nouveau movements; raised from childhood in vaudeville, stock companies, and burlesque shows; made Paris debut at Folies Bergère (1892); using innovative lighting techniques which became her trademark, created "Fire Dance" (1895); had her own theater at International Exposition in Paris (1900); recorded on film (1904); toured US (1909–10); made honorary member of French Astronomical Society for her artistic uses of light; was known for her endless quest for technological and scientific innovations to enhance her theatrical ideas; works include "Serpentine" (1891), "Butterfly" (1892), "Radium Dance" (1904), "La Tragédie de Salomé" (1907), "Danse Macabre" (1911), "La Feu d'Artifice" (1914), "Le Lys de la Vie" (1920) and "La Mer" (1925). ❖ See also memoir, *Fifteen Years of a Dancer's Life* (1913); Marcia Ewing Current and Richard Nelson Current, *Loie Fuller: Goddess of Light* (Northeastern U. Press, 1997); and *Women in World History.*

FULLER, Lucia Fairchild (1870–1924). American artist. Name variations: Mrs. Henry Brown Fuller. Born Lucia Fairchild in 1870; died 1924; grew up in Madison, Wisconsin; attended Cowles Art School in Boston, studying under Dennis Bunker; studied in NY with William Merritt Chase and H. Siddons Mowbray; m. Henry Brown Fuller (artist), 1893 (sep.); children: 2. ❖ Helped rekindle the dying art of miniature painting, a medium suffering from the advent of photography; co-founded American Society of Miniature Painters (1899), along with William Baer, I.A. Josephi, and Laura Coombs Hill; created a mural for the Woman's Building of the World's Columbian Exposition in Chicago (1893).

FULLER, Margaret (1810–1850). American writer. Name variations: Sarah Margaret Fuller as a child; Margaret Fuller Ossoli, d'Ossoli, or Marchioness Ossoli after her marriage. Born Sarah Margaret Fuller in Cambridgeport, Massachusetts, May 23, 1810; died in a shipwreck off New York harbor, July 19, 1850; dau. of Timothy Fuller (1778–1835, member of US Congress) and Margaret (Crane) Fuller; may have been married to her lover Marquis Giovanni Angelo Ossoli, 1849 or 1850; children: 1 son, Angelo. ❖ Early feminist writer, central figure with the Transcendentalists, and one of the most intellectually gifted American women of the 19th century, was thwarted by her family's poverty and by the restrictions of her gender in early life; taught at Bronson Alcott's Temple School as a Latin and French teacher (1836) and at the Greene Street School in Providence (1837–39); matured into a superb speaker and writer in her 30s; became a central figure in the Transcendentalist Club, befriending Ralph Waldo Emerson, Henry David Thoreau, George and Sophia Ripley, and Elizabeth Palmer Peabody; began "conversations" for educated women, in effect seminars on contemporary issues (1839), which lasted 13 weeks for each of 4 consecutive years, gaining steadily in repute and drawing larger audiences each time; served as the 1st editor of the *Dial*, the Transcendentalists' magazine (1840–42), and was *The Dial's* most prolific contributor throughout its 5-year life; served as a literary critic for Horace Greeley's *New York Tribune* (1844–46); published *Women in the Nineteenth Century* (1845), which marked her as a leading theorist in the cause of American feminism; voyaged to

Europe (1846); as a journalist, covered the Italian republicans and the revolution (1846–49); writings include *Günderode* (trans. of correspondence between Karoline von Günderode and Bettina von Arnim, 1842); *Summer on the Lakes in 1843* (1844), *Papers on Literature and Art* (2 vols., 1846); *Collected Works* (1855) and *Life Without and Life Within* (collection of essays and poems, 1860). ❖ See also Margaret V. Allen, *The Achievement of Margaret Fuller* (Pennsylvania State U. Press, 1979); Charles Capper, *Margaret Fuller: An American Romantic Life* (Oxford U. Press, 1992); Abby Slater, *In Search of Margaret Fuller* (Delacorte, 1978); Madeleine Stern, *The Life of Margaret Fuller* (Greenwood, 1991); Paula Blanchard, *Margaret Fuller: From Transcendentalism to Revolution* (Delacorte, 1978); Ralph Waldo Emerson, W.H. Channing, and J.F. Clarke. *Memoirs of Margaret Fuller Ossoli* (Phillips, Sampson, 1852); Perry Miller, ed. *Margaret Fuller: American Romantic* (Peter Smith, 1969); Joan Von Mehren, *Minerva and the Muse: A Life of Margaret Fuller* (U. of Massachusetts, 1994); and *Women in World History.*

FULLER, Mary (1888–1973). American actress. Born Mary Claire Fuller, Oct 5, 1888, in Washington, DC; died Dec 9, 1973, in a mental hospital in Washington, DC. ❖ Starred in the 1st serial *What Happened to Mary?* (1912), as a leading member of the Edison Company; joined Universal (1914); was in a mental hospital for last 25 years of her life.

FULLER, Meta Warrick (1877–1968). African-American artist. Born Meta Vaux Warrick, June 9, 1877, in Philadelphia, Pennsylvania; died Mar 13, 1968, in Framingham, Massachusetts; dau. of William and Emma Warrick; attended Pennsylvania School of Industrial Arts, 1899; studied 3 years at Academie Colarossi, Paris, and école des Beaux-Arts, Paris, beginning 1899; received instruction from Charles Grafly, Rodin, Gauqui, Rollard, and Raphael Collin in Paris; exhibited several works at L'Art Nouveau, a Paris gallery; attended Pennsylvania Academy of Fine Arts, 1907; m. Liberian-born Solomon Fuller (neurologist and psychologist), 1909; children: 3 sons. ❖ Prolific sculptor and illustrator of the Harlem Renaissance, known for sculptures symbolizing the aspirations of African-Americans as well as works depicting human suffering; exhibited at Paris Salon (1898, 1899, 1903); commissioned to sculpt 150 black figures (called *The Progress of the Negro in America*) for the Jamestown Tercentennial Exposition (1907); saw most of her early sculpture destroyed in a fire in a Philadelphia warehouse (1910); exhibited life-size work, *Awakening Ethiopia*, at the New York Making of America Exposition (1922); invited by W.E.B. Du Bois to sculpt a piece for the 50th anniversary celebration of the Emancipation Proclamation, held in New York (1931); remained active in Boston art circles (1930s); lived and worked at her home in Framingham, Massachusetts, where she also taught students (1929–68); career spanned nearly 9 decades; sculptures include *Crucifixion of Christ in Agony* (c. 1894), *The Wretched* and *Man Carrying a Dead Comrade* (1899–1902), *John the Baptist* (1899), *Head of Medusa* (1903), *Emancipation Group* (1913), *Water Boy* (1914), *Peace Halting the Ruthlessness of War* (1917), *The Talking Skull* (1937), *The Madonna of Consolation* (1961), *The Statue of Jesus on the Cross* (1962), *The Refugee* (1964) and *Bust of Charlotte Hawkins Brown* (1965). ❖ See also *Women in World History.*

FULLER, Minnie Rutherford (1868–1946). American social reformer. Name variations: Minnie Oliver or Minnie Ursula Oliver; Minnie Rutherford; Minnie Ursula Oliver Scott Rutherford Fuller; Minnie Scott. Born Minnie Ursula Oliver, Jan 25, 1868, in Ozark, Arkansas; died Oct 15, 1946, in Brookline, Massachusetts; dau. of James M. and Mattie A. Hale Oliver; attended Sullins College; studied law at universities of Chicago, California, Harvard, and Leipzig; m. Omer H. Scott, 1882 (died c. 1887); m. William B. Rutherford (lawyer), 1889 (div. c. 1909); m. Seabron Jennings Fuller (surgeon), 1915 (died 1932); children: (1st m.) 1 daughter (b. 1882). ❖ Legally trained and admitted to the bar, became national superintendent of Woman's Christian Temperance Union's (WCTU) Department of Juvenile Courts, Industrial Education, and Anti-Child Labor (1907); was president of state WCTU (1913–25) and editor and publisher of WCTU journal, *Arkansas White Ribboner*; successfully led campaign for Arkansas law permitting counties to establish juvenile courts (1911); helped found Arkansas Conference of Charities and Correction (later Conference on Social Welfare, 1912), serving as 1st vice president, then as president (1913–14, 1922–23); helped organize Political Equality League of Little Rock and served as 1st vice president when League grew into Arkansas Woman Suffrage Association (c. 1914); influenced passage of primary-election suffrage for women (1917); was member of Arkansas Women's Democratic Club, becoming 4th District chair (1933); as legislative chair for prominent women's groups, sponsored mother's pension bill, minimum-wage act, and bill admitting women to legal practice; generally credited with passage of laws establishing Girls' Industrial School (1917), equal property rights for women, and equal guardianship of children.

FULLER, Rosalinde (1901–1982). English-born stage actress. Born Feb 16, 1901, in Portsmouth, Hampshire, England; died Sept 15, 1982, in London. ❖ Made Broadway debut in *What's in a Name?* (1920), followed by *Greenwich Village Follies, A Christmas Carol, The Champion, The Farmer's Wife, Patience, Love for Love, The Fountain* and *Murder on Account,* among others; appeared as Ophelia to John Barrymore's Hamlet (1922); made London debut in *The Squall* (1927), followed by *The Stranger in the House, The Enemy, Three Sisters, Unknown Warrior, Death Takes a Holiday* and *Miss Julie,* among others; joined Donald Wolfit's Shakespearean Company, appearing as Portia, Rosalind, Beatrice, Desdemona, and Lady Macbeth (1938–40); appeared in solo performances of her own devising throughout the world. Awarded MBE (1966).

FULLER, Sarah (1836–1927). American educator of the deaf. Born Feb 15, 1836, in Weston, Massachusetts; died in Newton Lower Falls, Massachusetts, Aug 1, 1927; dau. of Hervey (farmer) and Celynda (Fiske) Fuller; never married; no children. ❖ Named principal of the Boston School for Deaf-Mutes (1869), renamed Horace Mann School for the Deaf (1877), the 1st institution of its kind in the country to be operated on a day-school basis, which flourished under her leadership; strongly advocated teaching deaf children to speak, rather than sign, and believed that instruction should begin at the earliest possible age, views that were not always popular with her professional colleagues; invited Alexander Graham Bell to visit the school and teach the new technique of "Visible Speech" to the faculty (1870); united with others to form the American Association to Promote the Teaching of Speech to the Deaf, of which she served as a director from 1896. ❖ See also *Women in World History.*

FULLERTON, Georgiana Charlotte (1812–1885). English novelist and philanthropist. Name variations: Lady Georgiana Charlotte Leveson-Gower; Lady Georgiana Fullerton. Born at Tixall Hall, Staffordshire, England, Sept 23, 1812; died at Bournemouth, England, Jan 19, 1885; youngest dau. of Granville Leveson-Gower, 1st earl Granville (English diplomat) and Harriet Leveson-Gower (1785–1862); m. Alexander Fullerton, 1833. ❖ Sponsored the sisters of St. Vincent de Paul in England and founded the Poor Servants of the Mother of God Incarnate; after converting to Catholicism (1846), wrote various biographies on lives of the saints; also took on translations, principally from the French; writings include *Ellen Middleton* (1844), *Grantley Manor* (1847), *Laurentia* (1861), *Rose Leblanc* (1861), *Too Strange Not to be True* (1864), *Constance Sherwood* (1865), *Life of St. Francis of Rome* (1885), *A Stormy Life* (1867), *Mrs. Gerald's Niece* (1869) and *A Will and a Way* (1881).

FULLERTON, Mary Eliza (1868–1946). Australian poet, author, and socialist. Name variations: (pseudonyms) Alpenstock and Austeal; (pseudonym) "E." Born Mary Elizabeth Fullerton, May 14, 1868, at Glenmaggie, Victoria, Australia; died Feb 23, 1946; dau. of Robert (farmer) and Eliza (Leathers) Fullerton; never married; lived with Mabel Singleton; no children. ❖ Wrote articles, stories, and poems for newspapers, often using the pseudonyms Alpenstock and Austeal; published 1st collection of poems, *Moods and Melodies* (1908); from 1922, lived in England; won a prize for *Two Women* (1923), one of only three novels written under her own name; poetry was often published under the pseudonym "E," (her true identity was the subject of much speculation in literary circles and was only revealed after her death); writings include *The Breaking Furrow* (poetry, 1921), *Bark House Days* (childhood reminiscences, 1921), *The People of the Timber Belt* (novel, 1925), *A Juno of the Bush* (novel, 1930), *The Australian Bush* (a descriptive work, 1928), *Moles Do So Little With Their Privacy* (poetry, 1942) and *The Wonder and the Apple* (poetry, 1946).

FULTON, Catherine (1829–1919). New Zealand diarist, philanthropist, social reformer. Name variations: Catherine Henrietta Elliot Valpy. Born Catherine Henrietta Elliot Valpy, Dec 19, 1829, in England; died 1919; dau. of William Henry Valpy and Caroline (Jeffreys) Valpy; m. James Fulton, 1852 (died 1891); children: 6. ❖ Immigrated with family to Otago, New Zealand (1849); recorded daily life in diaries (1857–1919); actively supported temperance and suffrage movements, co-founding and serving as 1st president of Dunedin branch of Women's Christian Temperance Union (1885); after husband's death, managed family's stud farm at Ravenscliffe. ❖ See also *Dictionary of New Zealand Biography* (Vol. 1).

FULTON, Joan (1926–1987). See Shawlee, Joan.

FULTON, Margaret Barr (1900–1989). English-Scottish occupational therapist. Born Feb 14, 1900, in Manchester, England; died 1989.

❖ Trained at Philadelphia School of Occupational Therapy in PA; was employed at Aberdeen Royal Asylum (1925–63), the 1st occupational instructor in the United Kingdom; served as chair of Scottish Association of Occupational Therapists (SAOT, 1946–49); helped to establish and was elected president of the World Federation of Occupational Therapists (WFOT, 1952); received Order of the British Empire. The Fulton Clinic and Memorial Garden (on site of Royal Cornhill Hospital, formerly the Royal Aberdeen Mental Hospital/Aberdeen Royal Asylum) was opened by H.R.H. Princess Anne (May 12, 1995).

FULTON, Mary Hannah (1854–1927). American medical missionary. Born Mary Hannah Fulton, May 31, 1854, probably in Ashland, Ohio; died Jan 7, 1927, in Pasadena, California; dau. of John S. Fulton (prominent attorney) and Augusta Louise (Healy) Fulton. ❖ Assigned by Presbyterian Board of Foreign Missions, arrived in Guangzhou (Canton), China (1884), joining minister brother Albert and missionary sister-in-law Florence Wishard; with Albert and Florence, established 2 dispensaries in Guangzhou (1887); with Mary Frost Niles, co-founded dispensary in Fati (1891) and established medical practice; worked at Guangzhou Hospital, teaching pediatrics in Cantonese, and directing care of women patients; with Albert, founded Theodore Cuyler Church (1900), David Gregg Hospital for Women and Children, including Julia Mather Training School for Nurses (April 1902), and Hackett Medical College for Women (Dec 1902); retired to Shanghai (1915), and established Cantonese Union Church of Shanghai (Augusta Fulton Memorial Church); retired to Pasadena, CA (1918). ❖ See also memoir, *"Inasmuch": Extracts from Letters, Journals, Papers, etc.*

FULTON, Maude (1881–1950). American actress, playwright, and screenwriter. Born May 14, 1881, in Eldorado, Kansas; died Nov 9, 1950, in Los Angeles, California; m. Robert Ober (div.). ❖ Began career as a stenographer, telegraph operator, and writer of short stories; made acting debut in Aberdeen (SD) in *Lady Windermere's Fan* (1904); spent 4 years in vaudeville, 4 years in musical comedy, then appeared only in drama starting 1915; acted the leading parts in her own plays: *Mary or a String of Beads, The Brat, Sonny, Pinkie, Tomorrow, Punchinello* and *The Humming Bird;* wrote screenplays for *The Brat* (which starred Alla Nazimova) and its remake (which starred Sally O'Neil and was directed by John Ford); other screenplays include *The Humming Bird* (starring Gloria Swanson) and (with Dashiell Hammett) *The Maltese Falcon.*

FULVIA (c. 85/80–40 BCE). Roman aristocrat. Pronunciation: FULL-vee-ya. Born c. 85/80 BCE; died in Greece in 40 BCE; dau. of Marcus Fulvius Bambalio and Sempronia; m. Publius Clodius, in 62 BCE (murdered, Jan 18, 52 BCE); m. Gaius Scribonius Curio, in 52 or 51 BCE (killed in battle, Aug 49 BCE); m. Mark Antony, in 47 or 46 BCE; children: (1st m.) Publius Clodius Pulcher; Clodia (b. around 60 BCE); (2nd m.) Gaius Scribonius Curio; (3rd m.) Marcus Antonius Antyllus; Iullus Antonius. ❖ Ambitious Roman aristocrat who engaged in political and military activities normally reserved exclusively for Roman men; made 1st public appearance on political scene (52 BCE), testifying in court about 1st husband's murder; devoted herself to the advancement of 3rd husband, Marc Antony, and is believed to be the reason for his success; when Antony was on military campaigns in the East, was in Rome gathering support for him against Octavian; led active political life (44–40 BCE), taking on the powers of the consul; led troops against Octavian at Praeneste (41 BCE), commanding husband's troops while he was in Egypt; with her prominence and power, paved the way for the role of a succession of powerful empresses of the Roman Empire. ❖ See also *Women in World History.*

FUMELH, Madame de (fl. 18th c.). French novelist. Fl. in the 18th century. ❖ Wrote *Miss Anysieo ou le Triomphe des moeurs et des vertus* (1788) and *Discours à la nation française.* Her collected works, *Oeuvres diverses,* were published in 1790.

FUNG, Lori (1963—). Canadian rhythmic gymnast. Born Feb 21, 1963, in Vancouver, British Columbia, Canada; m. J.D. Jackson (basketball player) 1991. ❖ Was British Columbia provincial champion (1977–81); at Los Angeles Olympics, won a gold medal in rhythmic gymnastics, all-around (1984); placed 1st in the Four Continents meet (1986); retired from competition (1988); became a coach. Named Member, Order of Canada (1985).

FUNICELLO, Annette (1942—). American tv and screen actress. Name variations: Annette. Born Annette Joanne Funicello, Oct 22, 1942, in Utica, NY; m. Jack Gilardi, 1965 (div. 1981); m. Glen Holt, 1986; children: (1st m.) 3. ❖ Made tv debut as mouseketeer Annette on "The Mickey Mouse Club" (1955); made film debut in *Johnny Tramaine*

(1957), followed by *The Shaggy Dog, Babes in Toyland, Beach Party, Muscle Beach Party, Bikini Beach, How to Stuff a Wild Bikini, Thunder Alley* and *Back to the Beach,* among others; diagnosed with multiple sclerosis (MS, 1987). ❖ See also the tv-movie "A Dream is a Wish Your Heart Makes: The Annette Funicello Story" (1995), starring Eva LaRue.

FUNK, Wally (1939—). American aviator. Name variations: Mary Wallace Funk. Born Jan 31, 1939, in Taos, New Mexico. ❖ A top pilot, became a flight instructor at Fort Sill Army base in Oklahoma at age 20; one of 13 women slated for the "Women in Space" program (1961), passed all the tests the men passed while in training, until NASA abruptly cancelled the program (the world was not yet ready for women astronauts); qualified to fly more than 30 types of planes, continued flight instruction and lectured worldwide; was the 1st woman to become an accident investigator for the National Transportation Safety Board (1974); became a pilot of the Solaris X, an entry in the X-Prize competition (2003). ❖ See also Stephanie Nolen, *Promised the Moon: The Untold Story of the First Women in the Space Race* (2002); Martha Ackmann, *The Mercury 13* (2003).

FUNKENHAUSER, Zita-Eva (1966—). German fencer. Born July 1, 1966, in Germany. ❖ At Los Angeles Olympics, won a gold medal in team foil (1984); at Seoul Olympics, won a bronze medal in individual foil and a gold medal in team foil (1988); at Barcelona Olympics, won a silver medal in team foil (1992).

FUNNELL, Pippa (1968—). British equestrian. Name variations: Philippa Funnell. Born Oct 7, 1968, in Crowborough, East Sussex, England; m. William Funnell (show jumper). ❖ Won European championships (1999, 2001) and a team silver medal for 3-day eventing at Sydney Olympics (2000), all on Supreme Rock; won Rolex Kentucky International 3-day event (2003); won Badminton Horse Trials (2002, 2003); on Primmore's Pride, won a silver medal for team eventing at Athens Olympics (2004). ❖ See also *Pippa Funnell: Road to the Top.*

FUOCCO, Sofia (1830–1916). Italian ballet dancer. Born Maria Brambilla, Jan 16, 1830, in Milan, Italy; died June 4, 1916, in Carate Lario, Lake Como, Italy. ❖ Trained for years with Carlo Blasis; danced at Teatro alla Scala in Milan where she created principal roles in Antonio Cortesi's production of *Gisella* (1843), among others, and appeared in works by Jules Perrot, Carolina Rosati, Carolina Ventu and Marie-Paul Taglioni; made acclaimed debut performance at Paris Opéra in Mazilier's *Betty, ou la Jeunesse de Henry V* (1846) and remained there for 4 more seasons.

FURBISH, Kate (1834–1931). American botanist. Name variations: Catharine Furbish. Born Catharine Furbish, May 19, 1834, in Exeter, New Hampshire; died Dec 6, 1931, in Brunswick, Maine; dau. of Benjamin Furbish (businessman) and Mary A. (Lane) Furbish; studied drawing in Portland, Maine; briefly studied French literature in Paris. ❖ At age 1, moved with family to Brunswick Maine; embarked on life's work (1870), documenting all the flora of her native region; for next 35 years, traveled across Maine and into the wilderness in search of specimens; her exquisite paintings, accurate in every detail, were widely praised by professional botanists; founded the Josselyn Botanical Society of Maine (1895) and later served as its president (1911–12); presented her 16-vol. portfolio drawings, "Illustrated Flora," to Bowdoin College (1908). Two of her plant discoveries bear her name: *Pedicularis Furbishiae* and *Aster cordifolius* L., var. *Furbishiae.* ❖ See also Frank and Ada Graham, *Kate Furbish and the Flora of Maine;* and *Women in World History.*

FURLEY, Matilda (1813–1899). New Zealand shopkeeper, baker, butcher, and innkeeper. Name variations: Matilda Webb. Born Matilda Webb, May 30, 1813, in Gloucestershire, England; dau. of Thomas (woolen mill owner) and Ann (Hill) Webb; m. Samuel Furley, 1835 (died 1878); children: 3. ❖ Learned weaving trade in father's woolen mill (c. 1825); sailed for South Australia with husband (c. 1837), arriving in Auckland, New Zealand (c. 1840/41); with husband, operated general store, small bakery, butcher shop, and trading post (1844); relocated to Onehunga, opening bakery (1854) and establishing inn (1863). ❖ See also *Dictionary of New Zealand Biography* (Vol. 1).

FURLONG, Monica (1930–2003). British journalist, poet, novelist, biographer and feminist. Born Jan 17, 1930, in Harrow, Middlesex, England; died Jan 14, 2003, in Devon, England; dau. of Alfred Gordon Furlong and Freda Simpson Furlong; attended University College London; m. William John Knights, 1953 (div. 1977); children: son and daughter. ❖ Christian feminist who campaigned for ordination of women and rights of homosexuals in Anglican church, began career as a

journalist covering religious issues for *Daily Mail* and later *The Guardian;* also worked as religious programer for BBC (1974–78) and wrote biographies of religious figures, including Thomas Merton and Thérèse of Lisieux; served as moderator of the Movement for the Ordination of Women (MOW, 1982–85); received honorary doctorates from General Theological Seminary of New York and Bristol University; writings include *With Love to the Church* (1965), *God's a Good Man and Other Poems* (1974), *Puritan's Progress: A Study of John Bunyan* (1975), *Divorce: One Woman's View* (1981), *Danger and Delight: Women and Power in the Church* (1991), *The Flight of the Kingfisher* (1996), *Visions and Longings: Medieval Women Mystics* (1996) and *The Church of England: The State It's In* (2000). ❖ See also memoir, *Bird of Paradise* (1995).

FURMAN, Bess (1894–1969). American journalist. Born in Nebraska, Dec 2, 1894; died 1969; dau. of a journalist; m. Robert B. Armstrong, Jr. (reporter), 1932; children: twins, Ruth Eleanor and Robert Furman. ❖ While working for a Nebraska newspaper, came to the attention of Associated Press with her coverage of the 1928 presidential election; during WWII, worked for Office of War Information; covered the White House from the time of the Hoover administration, and knew every prominent woman of her time, including Eleanor Roosevelt; hired by *The New York Times* (1945), worked out of its Washington bureau until 1961; worked as an executive in press relations for Department of Health, Education, and Welfare (1960s); wrote *White House Profile* (1951). ❖ See also autobiography *Washington By-Line: The Personal History of a Newspaperwoman* (Knopf, 1949); and *Women in World History.*

FURNEAUX, Yvonne (1928—). French-born actress. Name variations: Yvonne Fourneaux. Born 1928 in Lille, France. ❖ Made film debut in *Meet Me Tonight* (1952), followed by *24 Hours of a Woman's Life, The Beggar's Opera, The Master of Ballantrae, The House of Arrow, The Dark Avenger, Lisbon, The Mummy, Le Comte de Monte Cristo, I lancieri neri, Io Semiramide, Via Margutta, Leone di Tebe, Le scandale* and *Frankenstein's Great Aunt Tillie,* among others.

FURNERIA OF MIREPOIX (fl. 13th c.). French Albigensian. Fl. in 13th century in France; m. William Roger also known as Guillaume-Roger, count of Mirepoix. ❖ Born into the nobility of southern France, became involved in Albigensianism, or Catharism, a heretical movement sweeping southern France which anticipated many facets of the Protestant Reformation (its adherents denied the truth of the Trinity, materialism, and the rituals of the Catholic service and preached an equality between the sexes); used her wealth to support and protect other Albigensians of fewer means, including providing refuge for them in her castles when Cathars were condemned as heretics. ❖ See also *Women in World History.*

FURNESS, Betty (1916–1994). American actress, broadcast journalist, and consumer advocate. Born Elizabeth Mary Choate, Jan 3, 1916, in New York, NY; died April 2, 1994, in New York, NY; dau. of George (business executive) and Florence (Sturtevant Furness) Choate; m. John Waldo Green (composer and conductor), Nov 26, 1937 (div. 1943); m. radio announcer Hugh B. Ernst (d. 1950); m. Leslie Midgeley (tv producer), Aug 15, 1967; children: (1st m.) Barbara Green. ❖ Worked as a model; appeared in around 35 films, mostly low-budget Bs, except for *Swing Time* and *Magnificent Obsession;* appeared in summer stock and road shows of *Doughgirls* and *My Sister Eileen;* gained fame as on-air spokesperson for Westinghouse, demonstrating refrigerators and vacuum cleaners on live tv commercials (1949–60); became Lyndon Johnson's special assistant for consumer affairs (1967); appointed executive director of New York State Consumer Protection Board and then commissioner of New York City Department of Consumer Affairs; was a consumer specialist on NBC's "Today" show (1970s), answering consumer complaints and later conducting her own investigations. ❖ See also *Women in World History.*

FURNESS, Vera (1921–2002). English chemist and industrial manager. Name variations: V.I. or Vera I. Furness. Born June 2, 1921; died 2002 in Limavady, near Londonderry, Northern Ireland; London University, BS, 1946, MS, 1948, and PhD, 1952. ❖ Employed as development chemist at BX Plastics in Walthamstow as an MA student; worked as research associate and part-time lecturer at Birmingham Technical College (now University of Aston) while doing doctoral research on reactions of hexomethylenetetramine with phenols and dialkylanilines; at Courtaulds in Coventry (1953–81), worked as research chemist (1953–62), Research Division general manager (1970–76), head of Acetate and Synthetic Fibres Laboratory (1964–69), and chair of Steel Cords Ltd. (1976–78); worked to produce Courtelle, an acrylic; visited China, Poland, and Soviet Union to explain technical construction and process of acrylic plants; contributed improvements to production of synthetic fiber that made Courtaulds the most efficient acrylic process in the world. Made Officer of the Order of the British Empire (1971).

FURSE, Judith (1912–1974). English actress and director. Born Mar 4, 1912, in Camberley, Surrey, England; died Aug 29, 1974; dau. of Jean (Evans-Gordon) Furse and Lt. Gen. Sir William Furse; sister of Roger K. Furse (production designer) and Jill Furse (1924–1944, actress); sister-in-law of Margaret Furse (costume designer). ❖ Made stage debut at Sadler's Wells as a walk-on in *King John* (1931), followed by *Distant Point, Goodness How Sad* and *Before the Party*, among others; assisted Theodore Komisarjevsky (1936); directed plays at the Arts Theater (1944–46), including *Anna Christie, The Critic* and *The Lady from the Sea;* also directed *Lady Audley's Secret, Trilby, Intimate Relations* and *Tobias and the Angel;* made acting film debut in *Goodbye Mr. Chips* (1939), subsequently appearing as Elise Batter-Jones in *English without Tears* and Sister Briony in *Black Narcissus,* among many others.

FURSE, Katharine (1875–1952). British military leader. Name variations: Dame Katharine Furse. Born Katharine Symonds, 1875; died 1952; dau. of John Addington Symonds (English scholar); married C.W. Furse, 1900. ❖ Enrolled in the Voluntary Aid Detachment (VAD, 1909), an offshoot of Florence Nightingale's "Naval Nursing Service"; with outbreak of World War I, was tapped as 1st commandant of newly formed Women's Royal Naval Service (WRNS), a special uniformed service for women, organized to provide shore support for the Royal Navy; with Tilla Wallace and Rachel Crowdy, helped organized the WRNS from the ground up, drafting the terms of pay, allowance and regulation, and even designing the uniforms. Awarded a GBE for her outstanding work with the WRNS. ❖ See also *Women in World History.*

FURSE, Margaret (1911–1974). British costume designer for films. Born in 1911; died of cancer, July 7, 1974, at her home in London, England; studied at Central School of Art under Jeanetta Cochrane; m. Roger Furse (artist and set designer); m. editor-critic Stephen Watts. ❖ Began career at Gaumont-British Studios as an assistant designer; credits include such films as *The Mudlark* (1950), *Becket* (1963), *The Lion in Winter* (1967), *Scrooge* (1970), and *Mary, Queen of Scots* (1971), all of which were nominated for an Academy Award; received an Oscar for *Anne of the Thousand Days* (1969); also designed *Oliver Twist* (1948), *The Spanish Gardener* (1956), (with Olga Lehmann) *Inn of the Sixth Happiness* (1958), *Kidnapped* (1960), *Sons and Lovers* (1960), *The Prince and the Pauper* (1962), *A Shot in the Dark* (1964), *Young Cassidy* (1964), *The Three Lives of Thomasina* (1964), *Cast a Giant Shadow* (1965) and *A Delicate Balance* (1973).

FURTADO, Juliana (1967—). American mountain biker. Born April 4, 1967, in New York, NY. ❖ Was a member of the US National Ski team (1980–87); was National Road champion (1989) and Downhill World champion (1992); was 5-time National cross-country champion and 3-time cross-country World Cup champion. Inducted into Mountain Bike Hall of Fame (1993).

FURTSCH, Evelyn (1911—). American runner. Born Aug 16, 1911, in US. ❖ At Los Angeles Olympics, won a gold medal in 4x100-meter relay (1932).

FURTSEVA, Ekaterina (1910–1974). Soviet Cabinet member. Name variations: Catherine. Pronunciation: FURTS-ev-a. Born Ekaterina (or Catherine) Alekseevna Furtseva, Nov 24, 1910 (o.s.) in Vyshnii Volochek, Russia; died Oct 25, 1974, in Moscow; dau. of Aleksei Furtsev (textile worker); attended trade schools in Vyshnii Volochek, Higher Academy of Civil Aviation, 1933–35, Lomonosov Institute of Chemical Technology, 1937–42, Higher Party School (by correspondence), 1948; m. Nikolai Pavlovich Firiubin (diplomat), mid-1930s; children: Svetlana (who married Frol Kozlov) and Margarita. ❖ Soviet government and party official who served as minister of culture for 14 years and was the only woman ever to sit on the Communist Party's ruling Presidium; worked as textile weaver (1925–30); joined Communist Party (1930); served as party organizer and instructor in Komsomol organization (1930–37); served as party official at Lomonosov Institute (1937–42); appointed secretary, Frunze District Party Committee in Moscow (1942–50); became 2nd secretary (1950–54) and then 1st secretary (1954–57) of Moscow City Committee; served as deputy to the USSR Supreme Soviet (1950–62, 1966–74); was a candidate (1952–56) and then full member (1956–74) of the Central Committee of the Communist Party; was a candidate (1956–57) and then full member (1957–61) of the Central Committee's Presidium, the 1st and only woman ever to sit on this, the most powerful body in the Soviet Union; after her dramatic filibuster that helped defeat the "Anti-Party Plot" against Khrushchev

(1957), was at the pinnacle of political power for a period of 3 years; served as a member of the Party Secretariat (1956–60); as minister of culture (1960–74), dramatically expanded Soviet cultural exchanges with other countries; was a member or candidate of the Central Committee for 22 years, of its ruling Presidium for 6 years, and of its Secretariat for 4; her tenure of 14 years as minister of culture was longer than that of almost all of her male ministerial colleagues; was a competent, hard-working and firm-spoken administrator who was politically reliable and ideologically flexible. ❖ See also *Women in World History.*

FURUHJELM, Annie (1854–1937). Finnish suffragist. Born in 1854 in Finland; died 1937; dau. of an admiral. ❖ Began career as a journalist, editing *Nutid,* a monthly, and *Astra,* a women's magazine; as president of the Woman's Alliance Union, attended the International Council of Women in Berlin and the forming of the International Woman Suffrage Alliance (1904), serving as 2nd vice president; was a member of the Finnish Diet under the Russians (1914–19), and then the independent Parliament (1922–29).

FURUKAWA, Makiko (1947—). Japanese volleyball player. Born Jan 22, 1947, in Japan. ❖ At Munich Olympics, won a silver medal in team competition (1972).

FÜRÜZAN (1935—). Turkish novelist and short-story writer. Name variations: Furuzan Selcuk. Born Fürüzan Yerdelen, Oct 29, 1935, in Istanbul, Turkey; m. Turhan Selçuk (cartoonist), 1958 (div.); children: 1. ❖ Received no formal education after elementary school; visited West Germany to write about conditions of Turkish workers (1977); writings, which generally concern the socially alienated, include *Parasiz Yatili* (1971), *Kusatma* (1972), *47 'liler* (1975), *Benim Senemalarim* (1973), *Gecenin Oteki Yuzu* (1982), *Gul Mevsimidir* (1985), and *Berlin'in Nar Cicegi* (1988). Won the Sait Faik short-story prize and Turkish Language Society Prize (1975).

FURY, Bridget (fl. 1850s). See *Swift, Delia.*

FUSAE ICHIKAWA (1893–1981). See *Ichikawa, Fusae.*

FUSAR-POLI, Barbara (1972—). Italian ice dancer. Name variations: Barbara Poli. Born Feb 6, 1972, in Sesto San Giovanni, Milan, Italy; m. Diego Cattani (Olympic short-track champion), June 2000. ❖ With partner Alberto Reani, placed 3rd (1993) and 2nd (1994) at Italian nationals; with partner Maurizio Margaglio, won Cup of Russia (1999, 2000), Sparkassen Cup (2000), Skate America (1999, 2000), as well as the European and World championship (2001), the 1st Italians to win a gold medal at Europeans or Worlds; also won a bronze medal at Salt Lake City Olympics (2002).

FUSAYE ICHIKAWA (1893–1981). See *Ichikawa, Fusae.*

FUSS, Sonja (1978—). German soccer player. Born Nov 5, 1978, in Bonn, Germany. ❖ Played for the University of Hartford Hawks in US; won FIFA World Cup (2003); won a team bronze medal at Athens Olympics (2004).

FUSSENEGGER, Gertrud (1912—). Austrian novelist. Name variations: Gertrud Dietz; Gertrud Dorn; Gertrud Fussenegger-Dorn. Born Gertrud Fussenegger, May 8, 1912, in Pilsen, Austrian Bohemia; studied history, history of art, and philosophy in Munich and Innsbruck; m. Elmar Dietz; m. Alois Dorn, 1950; children: 5. ❖ Writer whose novels have been popular with a conservative reading public since the 1930s, published *Das Haus der dunklen Krüge* (1951), *In deine Hand gegeben* (1954), *Das verschüttete Antlitz* (1957), *Zeit das Raben, Zeit der Taube* (1960), *Ein Spiegelbild mit Feuersäule* (1979) and *Maria Theresia* (1980), among others.

FYGE, Sarah (c. 1670–1723). See *Egerton, Sarah Fyge.*

FYNES, Sevatheda (1974—). Bahamian runner. Born Oct 17, 1974, in Abaco, an island in the northern Bahamas; Michigan State University, BS, 1997. ❖ Known as one of the "Golden Girls," won a silver medal Atlanta Olympics (1996) and a gold medal at Sydney Olympics (2000), both for 4x100-meter relay; won a gold medal for 4x100-meter relay at World championships (1999); Given the Silver Jubilee Award (1998) and the Bahamas Order of Merit (2000).

FYODORENKO, Tatyana (1953—). See *Providokhina-Fyodorenko, Tatyana.*

FYODOROVA, Olga (1983—). Russian runner. Born July 14, 1983, in Sverdlovsk, USSR. ❖ Won a silver medal for 4x100-meter relay at Athens Olympics (2004).

G

G, Miss (1737–1814). *See Moody, Elizabeth.*

GAAL, Franciska (1904–1972). Austro-Hungarian actress and singer. Name variations: Franziska Gaal, Franceska Gaal. Born Fanny Zilveritch, Feb 1, 1904, in Budapest, Austria-Hungary (now Hungary); died Aug 13, 1972, in NYC. ❖ Central European cabaret and stage star, appeared in Hungarian, Austrian and German films between the wars, including *Fräulein Paprika, Gruss und Kuss Veronika, Skandal in Budapest, Spring Parade* and *Katharina;* arrived in Hollywood (1938) to appear in Cecil B. De Mille's *The Buccaneer,* followed by *Paris Honeymoon* and *The Girl Downstairs;* returned to Budapest (1940) to visit ailing mother and was trapped there during WWII; made Broadway debut (1927) and replaced Eva Gabor in *The Happy Time* (1951).

GABAIN, Ethel Leontine (1883–1950). English artist. Name variations: Ethel Copley. Born in 1883 in Le Havre, France; died Jan 30, 1950 in London, England; attended Slade School of Art and Central School of Arts and Crafts and finished studies in Paris; m. John Copley (painter, etcher), 1913. ❖ Portrait painter, won the DeLaszlo Silver Medal for her painting of Flora Robson in the role of Lady Audley (1933); during WWII (1940), was commissioned to create a series of lithographs dealing with the evacuation of children resulting in *The Evacuation of Children from Southend, Sunday 2nd July* (Imperial War Museum); among a small core of women war artists whose paintings were concerned primarily with the home front, also painted women in traditionally male occupations such as *Building a Beaufort Bomber;* elected to both Royal Society of Brittish Artists and Royal Institute of Oil Painters.

GABARRA, Carin (1965—). American soccer player. Name variations: Carin Jennings; Carin Jennings-Gabarra. Born Carin Leslie Jennings, Jan 9, 1965, in East Orange, New Jersey; attended University of California, Santa Barbara; m. Jim Gabarra (soccer player and head coach of Washington Freedom), 1992. ❖ Midfielder; played for 10 years on the national team, becoming the 3rd leading scorer with 53 goals in 97 starts in 117 international appearances; at World Cup, won a team gold medal (1991) and a bronze (1995); won a gold medal at Atlanta Olympics (1996); retired (1997); became head coach at Navy. Awarded the Golden Ball at World Cup tournament top player (1991); became the 2nd woman inducted into US Soccer Hall of Fame (2000).

GABELLANES MARIETA, Nagore (1973—). Spanish field-hockey player. Born Jan 25, 1973, in Spain. ❖ At Barcelona Olympics, won a gold medal in team competition (1992).

GABL, Gertrud (1948–1976). Austrian Alpine skier. Born Aug 26, 1948, in St. Anton, Austria; died from an avalanche in 1976, age 27, while skiing in Arlberg. ❖ Won World Cup overall (1969) and was the 1st Austrian to win a World Cup slalom.

GABOIMILLA. Queen of the South American Amazons of Chile. ❖ Reports of her existence surfaced in the writing of Augustin Zarate, secretary of the Royal Council in Spain, as early as 1543. ❖ See also *Women in World History.*

GABOR, Eva (1919–1995). Hungarian-born actress. Born Feb 11, 1919, in Budapest, Hungary; died from pneumonia on July 4, 1995, in Los Angeles, California; youngest dau. of Vilmos Gabor and Jolie Gabor (1894–1997); sister of Magda Gabor (1914–1997) and Zsa Zsa Gabor (b. 1917); m. Dr. Eric Drimmer (physician), 1939 (div. 1942); m. Charles Isaacs (realtor), 1943 (div. 1950); m. John E. Williams (surgeon), April 9, 1956 (div. 1956); m. Richard Brown (stockbroker), Oct 4, 1959 (div. 1972); m. Frank Jameson (aerodynamics industrialist), 1973 (div. 1983). ❖ Made film debut in *Forced Landing* (1941); made tv debut in *L'Amour the Merrier* (1949); made Broadway debut as Mignonette in *The Happy Time* (1950); appeared on a number of dramatic tv shows, including "Uncle Vanya" in which she played Helena; also made guest appearances on variety shows and had her own tv interview show, "The

Eva Gabor Show" (early 1950s); appeared on Broadway in *Present Laughter* (1958) and replaced Vivien Leigh as Tatiana in *Tovarich* (1963); had secondary roles in such films as *The Last Time I Saw Paris* (1954), *Artists and Models* (1955), *My Man Godfrey* (1957), *Don't Go Near the Water* (1957), *Gigi* (1958), *Youngblood Hawke* (1964), (voice only) *The Aristocrats* (1970), (voice of Miss Bianca) *The Rescuers* (1977) and *The Rescuers Down Under* (1990); was a regular on the tv talk-show circuit; appeared as Lisa Douglas in the CBS-tv series "Green Acres" (1965–71). ❖ See also autobiography *Orchids and Salami* (1954); Peter H. Brown, *Such Devoted Sisters: Those Fabulous Gabors* (St. Martin's, 1985); and *Women in World History.*

GABOR, Georgeta (1962—). Romanian gymnast. Born Jan 10, 1962. ❖ At Montreal Olympics, won a silver medal in team all-around (1976).

GABOR, Jolie (1894–1997). Hungarian matriarch of the infamous Gabors. Name variations: Mama Jolie. Born Jolie Kende, Sept 29, 1894, in Budapest, then Austro-Hungarian Empire (now Hungary); died in Rancho Mirage, California, April 1, 1997; m. Vilmos Gabor, a businessman (div.); children: Magda Gabor (1914–1997); Zsa Zsa Gabor (1917—); Eva Gabor (1919–1995). ❖ Ran a jewelry boutique in Budapest; moved with daughters to Hollywood (c. 1938); managing a string of jewelry boutiques in New York, Palm Beach, London, and Paris. ❖ See also autobiography (with Cindy Adams) *Jolie Gabor* (Mason/Charter, 1975); Peter H. Brown, *Such Devoted Sisters: Those Fabulous Gabors* (St. Martin's, 1985); and *Women in World History.*

GABOR, Magda (1914–1997). Hungarian-born American actress and businesswoman. Born in Budapest, Hungary, June 11, 1914, in Budapest, Hungary; died of kidney failure in Rancho Mirage, California, June 6, 1997; dau. of Vilmos Gabor and Jolie Gabor (1894–1997); sister of Eva Gabor (1919–1995) and Zsa Zsa Gabor (b. 1917); m. Jan de Bichovsky (Royal Air Force pilot), 1937 (div. 1946); m. William Rankin (New York lawyer), 1946 (div. 1947); m. Sidney R. Warren (NY lawyer), 1947 (div. 1950); m. Tony Gallucci (Hungarian noble), 1956 (div. 1957); m. George Sanders (British actor), 1970 (div. 1971); m. Tibor Heltrai, 1972 (div. 1973); no children. ❖ Acted on radio with mother; though she appeared occasionally on tv, never displayed the dramatic ambitions of her sisters; joined mother in managing a string of jewelry boutiques catering to the upscale market in New York, Palm Beach, London, and Paris. ❖ See also Peter H. Brown, *Such Devoted Sisters: Those Fabulous Gabors* (St. Martin, 1985); and *Women in World History.*

GABOR, Zsa Zsa (1917—). Hungarian-born actress. Born Sari Gabor in Budapest, Hungary, Feb 6, 1917; dau. of Vilmos Gabor and Jolie Gabor (1894–1997); sister of Magda Gabor (1914–1997) and Eva Gabor (1919–1995); m. Burhan Belge (press director of the Turkish foreign ministry), 1937 (div. 1941); m. Conrad Hilton (hotelier), April 1942 (div. 1947); m. George Sanders (actor), April 1949 (div. 1954); m. Herbert Hutner (businessman), 1964 (div. 1966); m. Joshua Cosden, Jr. (oil magnate), 1966 (div. 1967); m. Jack Ryan (inventor), 1975 (div. 1976); m. Michael O'Hara (lawyer), 1977 (div. 1982); m. Felipe Alba (Mexican businessman), 1982 (declared invalid); m. Prince Frederick von Anhalt, duke of Saxony, 1986; children: (with Conrad Hilton) one daughter, Francesca Hilton. ❖ The most flamboyant of the Gabor sisters, was a regular on tv, notably as a guest on Jack Paar's late-night program, and as a panelist on the game show "Hollywood Squares"; starred on Broadway in *Forty Carats* (1970); made headlines (1990) when she spent three days behind bars for slapping a traffic officer; films include *Lovely to Look At* (1952), *Moulin Rouge* (1952), *The Story of Three Loves* (1953), *Lili* (1953), *Touch of Evil* (1958), *Queen of Outer Space* (1958), *Pepe* (1960), *Boys' Night Out* (1962), *Arrivederci, Baby* (1966), *A Nightmare on Elm Street 3* (1987), *Dream Warriors* (1987), and (voice only) *Happily Ever After* (1990); wrote *Zsa Zsa Gabor: My Story* (1960),

Zsa Zsa's Complete Guide to Men (1969), *How to Get a Man, How to Keep a Man, and How to Get Rid of a Man* (1971), and *One Lifetime Is Not Enough* (1991). ❖ See also Peter H. Brown, *Such Devoted Sisters: Those Fabulous Gabors* (St. Martin, 1985); and *Women in World History.*

GABRIAK, Cherubina de (1887–1928). *See Dmitreva, Elizaveta Ivanovna.*

GABRIEL-KOETHER, Rosemarie (1956—). East German swimmer. Name variations: Rosemarie Gabriel-Köther. Born Feb 27, 1956, in East Germany. ❖ At Montreal Olympics, won a bronze medal in 200-meter butterfly (1976).

GABRIELLE, La Belle. *See Estrées, Gabrielle de.*

GABRIELLI (d. 1816). *See Meeke, Mary.*

GABRIELLI, Caterina (1730–1796). Italian soprano. Name variations: Catterina; La Cochetta or La Cochettina. Born in Rome, Nov 12, 1730; died in Rome, April 1796; studied with Garcia, Porpora, and Metastasio; sister of Francesca Gabrielli. ❖ Made triumphant debut at Lucca (1747) in Baldasare Galuppi's *Sonfonisba;* beautiful, accomplished and capricious, enjoyed further success in Naples (1750), singing in Jomelli's *Didone;* known for bravura style and her many eccentricities, left Vienna for Sicily (1765) where she was imprisoned for 12 days by the king because she would not sing her role in an opera above a whisper; went to Russia (1768), where she asked for 5,000 ducats as salary at the court of Catherine II the Great; when an astonished Catherine said that the sum was more than she paid a field marshal, replied: "Then let your field-marshals sing for you"; appeared in London for the 1775–76 season, but Londoners were wary of her unconventional behavior; sang with Pacchierotti at Venice (1777) and with Marchesi in Milan (1780). ❖ See also *Women in World History.*

GACIOCH, Rose (1915–2004). American baseball player. Name variations: "Rockford Rosie." Born Aug 31, 1915, in Wheeling, West Virginia; died Feb 9, 2004, in Clinton Township, Michigan. ❖ American pioneer in women's baseball who played right field for the South Bend Blue Sox (1944–45) and the Rockford Peaches (1945–55). Voted to the All-Star team as a pitcher (1952), utility infielder (1953), and pitcher (1954). ❖ See also the film *A League of Their Own* (127 min.), starring Geena Davis, Tom Hanks, Madonna, and Rosie O'Donnell, directed by Penny Marshall, Columbia Pictures, 1992; and *Women in World History.*

GACON-DUFOUR, Marie Armande Jeanne (1753–c. 1835). French novelist and essayist. Name variations: Madame Marie Armande Jeanne d'Humières Gacon Dufour; Mme Gacon Dufour or Gacon-Dufour. Born 1753 in Paris, France; died c. 1835. ❖ Was co-founder of Bibliothèque Agronomique; novels include *L'Homme errant fixé par la raison* (1787), *Le préjugé vaincu* (1787), *Georgeana* (1798), *Melicrete et Zirphile* (1802), and *Les Dangers de la prévention* (1806); wrote essays in defense of women's rights, including *Mémoire pour le sexe féminin contre le sexe masculin* (1787), *Contre le projet de loi de S.M.* (1801), and *De la nécessité de l'instruction pour les femmes* (1805); also edited collections of letters, wrote manuals on domestic and rural economy, and published trade manuals for pastry chefs, soap-makers, and perfumiers.

GADSKI, Johanna (1872–1932). Prussian soprano. Born in Anklam, Prussia, June 15, 1872; died in auto accident, Feb 22, 1932, in Berlin, Germany; studied with Schroeder-Chaloupka in Stettin. ❖ Sang in Germany (1889–95); at 17, debuted in Lortzing's *Undine* at Kroll Opera in Berlin (1894); joined NY's Metropolitan Opera (1900), becoming one of the company's leading Wagnerian sopranos though she performed Mozart and Mahler as well; also a recitalist, was one of the few to include songs by American composers on her program; formed her own Wagnerian touring company (1920s) which performed in Europe and US; made almost 100 recordings, many of which are considered classics. ❖ See also *Women in World History.*

GAFENCU, Liliana (1975—). Romanian rower. Name variations: Gafenku. Born July 12, 1975 in Bucharest, Romania; attended University of Bacau. ❖ Won a gold medal at Atlanta Olympics (1996), a gold medal at Sydney Olympics (2000) and a gold medal at Athens Olympics (2004), all for coxed eights; won World Rowing championships for coxed eights (1997, 1998, 2000).

GAFFNEY, Margaret (1813–1882). *See Haughery, Margaret Gaffney.*

GÁG, Wanda (1893–1946). American artist and writer. Name variations: Wanda Gag. Pronunciation: Gág (rhymes with cog). Born Wanda Hazel Gág on Mar 11, 1893, in New Ulm, Minnesota; died of lung cancer on June 27, 1946, in New York, NY; oldest of seven children (six girls and one boy) of Anton Gág and Lissi Biebl Gág (both artists); studied at the St. Paul Institute of Arts, 1913–1914, Minneapolis School of Art, 1914–1917, Art Students League, New York, 1917–1918; m. Earle Marshall Humphreys, 1930; children: none. ❖ Artist, writer, and translator who was much admired for the melodic style of her self-illustrated children's books; was a teenage illustrator for children's section of the *Minneapolis Journal;* worked as a schoolteacher (1912–13) and commercial artist (1918–23); had major exhibits at Weyhe Gallery, NY (1926, 1930, and 1940 retrospective); wrote and illustrated *Millions of Cats* (1928), which was immediately judged a modern classic, for bridging the fine and commercial arts; illustrated and translated works by the Grimm Brothers: *Tales from Grimm* (1936), *Snow White and the Seven Dwarfs* (1938), *Three Gay Tales from Grimm* (1943), and *More Tales from Grimm* (1947); exhibited in group shows at Museum of Modern Art, New York (1939) and Metropolitan Museum of Art, New York (1943); contributed illustrations and articles to various magazines, including *The Horn Book Magazine;* also wrote and illustrated *The Funny Thing* (1929), *Snippy and Snappy* (1931), *Wanda Gág's Story Book* (1932), *The ABC Bunny* (1933), *Gone is Gone: The Story of a Man Who Wanted to Do Housework* (1935), and *Nothing-at-all* (1941). Received the Kerlan Award, University of Minnesota (1977), in recognition of singular attainments in the creation of children's literature. ❖ See also *Growing Pains: Diaries and Drawings for the Years 1908–1917;* Alma Scott, *Wanda Gág: The Story of an Artist* (University of Minnesota Press, 1949); and *Women in World History.*

GAGE, Frances D. (1808–1884). American reformer and author. Name variations: (pseudonym) Aunt Fanny. Born Frances Dana Barker on Oct 12, 1808, in Marietta, Washington Co., Ohio; died in Greenwich, Connecticut, Nov 10, 1884; dau. of Joseph Barker (farmer and cooper) and Elizabeth (Dana) Barker; m. James L. Gage (lawyer), Jan 1, 1829; children: 8, including Mary Gage. ❖ Wrote for leading journals and spoke to gatherings about women's rights, temperance, and the evils of slavery; became well known for her children's stories, written under name "Aunt Fanny." ❖ See also *Women in World History.*

GAGE, Matilda Joslyn (1826–1898). American feminist. Born Matilda Joslyn in Cicero, New York, Mar 25, 1826; died of an embolism in Chicago, Illinois, Mar 18, 1898; dau. of Dr. Hezekiah Joslyn (physician) and Helen (Leslie) Joslyn; m. Henry H. Gage, 1845; children: Helen Leslie Gage, Thomas Clarkson Gage, Julie L. Gage, and Maud Gage. ❖ Influential 19th-century radical suffragist whose work on behalf of the rights of women has been largely ignored; delivered her 1st public address advocating women's rights in Syracuse, New York (1852); formed the National Woman Suffrage Association with Elizabeth Cady Stanton and Susan B. Anthony and helped found the New York State Woman Suffrage Association (1869); was named president of both state and national suffrage organizations (1875); co-wrote the "Declaration of the Rights of Women" (1876); was a founding member of the Equal Rights Party (1880); co-edited with Stanton and Anthony the 1st three volumes of the *History of Woman Suffrage* (1881–86); formed the Woman's National Liberal Union (1890); published *Woman, Church and State* (1893), which set out to prove that the most egregious wrong ever inflicted upon woman was in the Christian teaching that God did not create her as man's equal (it offended many in the women's movement, particularly members of the Women's Christian Temperance Union); more radical than either Anthony or Stanton, was also the most intellectually daring; while her contemporaries focused on political issues, particularly the vote, concerned herself with the broader sociological and historical aspects of women's issues (1893). ❖ See also *Women in World History.*

GAGE, Susanna Phelps (1857–1915). American embryologist and comparative anatomist. Name variations: Susanna Stewart Phelps Gage; Susanna Stewart Phelps; Mrs. S.H. Gage. Born Susanna Stewart Phelps, Dec 26, 1857, in Morrisville, NY; died Oct 15, 1915; dau. of Mary Austin Phelps (schoolteacher) and Henry S. Phelps (businessman); Cornell University, PhB, 1880; m. Simon Henry Gage (Cornell University professor), Dec 15, 1881; children: Henry Phelps Gage (physicist, inventor, and head of the Optical Laboratory at Corning Glass, 1911–47). ❖ The 1st woman at Cornell University to engage in laboratory work in physics, conducted independent research in embryology and comparative anatomy; engaged in neurological studies at Johns Hopkins University's medical school and at Harvard University's medical school; published work on comparative morphology (of muscle fibers and the brain); illustrated scientific papers for Dr. Burt G. Wilder and for Simon Henry Gage (husband); elected an American Association for the Advancement of Science fellow (1910); was a member of the Association of American Anatomists. Honors include stars in the *American Men of*

Science (2nd edition) and the establishment after her death of Cornell University's Susanna Phelps Gage Fund for Research in Physics by husband and son.

GAGNEUR, Louise (1832–1902). French novelist and feminist. Name variations: Marie-Louise Gagneur. Born Marie-Louise Mignerot, May 25, 1832, in Domblans, France; died 1902; m. Vladimir or Wladimir Gagneur (1807–1889, socialist writer and Chamber deputy); children: Marguerite Gagneur (sculptor, b. 1857). ❖ Outspoken on issues such as rights of women and poverty, wrote *Le divorce* (1872) in favor of divorce law reform which contributed to an eventual law permitting dissolution of civil marriage (1884); published article in *La Constitution* opposing militarism that caused journal to be banned (1872); novels include *Le Calvaire des femmes, La Croisade noire* (1866), *Les Réprouvées* (1867), *Les Crimes de l'amour* (1874), *Un Chevalier de sacristie* (1881), *le Roman d'un prêtre* (1881), and *Le Crime de l'abbé Maufrac* (1882).

GAGNEUR, Marguerite (1857–1945). French sculptor. Name variations: Known as Syamour. Born Aug 10, 1857 at Bréry, France; died May 21, 1945 in Paris, France; dau. of Louise Gagneur (writer) and Vladimir Gagneur; m. Monsieur Gegout (div. Mar 7, 1887); m. Jean Frechout (physician). ❖ Focusing on human rights, was responsible for 18 public monuments, 16 statues and over 200 busts; sculpted such people as Musset, Cipriani, Camille Flammarion, Rene Viviani, Pierre Baudin, Maurice Faure, Voltaire, Marguerite Durand, Clarisse Coignet, Charles Fourier; was a friend of Alfons Mucha.

GAGNEUR, Marie-Louise (1832–1902). *See Gagneur, Louise.*

GAHAGAN, Helen (1900–1980). *See Douglas, Helen Gahagan.*

GAIDINLIU, Rani (1915–1993). Indian freedom fighter. Name variations: Rani Gaidinliu of Nagaland. Born 1915 in Nangkao village of Manipur, India; died Feb 17, 1993, in India; dau. of a poor farmer. ❖ Joined the Indian freedom fighters (1928), when she was just 13; at 16, led the Naga guerrillas against the British in a battle that led to her arrest (1932) and a 15-year imprisonment; released by President Jawaharlal Nehru (1947), later became a social worker in Nagaland.

GAIGEROVA, Varvara Andrianovna (1903–1944). Russian composer, pianist and concertmaster. Born in Oryekhovo-Zuyevo, Russia, Oct 4, 1903; died in Moscow on April 6, 1944; graduated from the Moscow Conservatory, 1927, where she studied piano and composition with the noted composer Nikolai Miaskovsky. ❖ As a child prodigy, began her concert career in her early teens; served as concertmaster of the Bolshoi Theater Orchestra (1936–44) and created an impressive body of compositions reflecting the musical and political ideals of early Soviet society; became interested in the musical heritage of the minority peoples of the Soviet Union, particularly in its southeastern regions. ❖ See also *Women in World History.*

GAILLARD, Lilly. *See Scholz, Lilly.*

GAINES, Chryste (1970—). African-American runner. Born Sept 14, 1970, in Lawton, Oklahoma; graduate of Stanford University (1992); sister of Charletta Gaines (track coach). ❖ Won a gold medal for the 4 x 100-meter relay at Atlanta Olympics (1996); won a bronze medal for the 4 x 100-meter relay at Sydney Olympics (2000); won US outdoor championship for 100 meters (2001); won US indoor championship for 60m (2001, 2002).

GAINES, Irene McCoy (1892–1964). African-American civil-rights activist, civic and social worker. Name variations: Irene McCoy. Born Irene McCoy on Oct 25, 1892, in Ocala, Florida; died April 7, 1964, in Chicago, Illinois; dau. of Charles Vivien McCoy and Mamie (Ellis) McCoy; m. Harris Barrett Gaines, 1914; children: 2 sons (b. 1922, 1924). ❖ During WWI, worked with War Camp Community Service; became industrial secretary for 1st black branch of Young Women's Christian Association, Chicago, IL (1920); was president of Illinois Federation of Republican Colored Women (1924–35); was Republican state central committeewoman for 1st Congressional District (1928); served on President's Housing Commission (1930); worked with Cook Co. welfare department (1930s–1945); was president of Chicago Council of Negro Organizations (CCNO, 1939–53); though unsuccessful, was 1st black woman to run for IL state legislature (1940); with CCNO, led march to Washington to protest employment discrimination against blacks (1941); was historian and recording secretary of National Association of Colored Women's Clubs, and served 2 terms as president (1952–56); founded Chicago and Northern District Association of Club Women and Girls, and served as president.

Received numerous awards, including George Washington Honor Medal from Freedoms Foundation (1958) and Distinguished Alumni Service Award from Fisk University (1959).

GAINES, Myra Clark (1805–1885). American litigant. Name variations: Myra Whitney. Born June 1805, in New Orleans, Louisiana; died Jan 9, 1885, in New Orleans; dau. of Daniel Clark (1st territorial representative for Louisiana to US Congress, 1806–08) and Marie Julie Carrière; m. William Wallace Whitney, Sept 13, 1832 (died 1837); m. Gen. Edmund Pendleton Gaines (commander of Department of the West), April 19, 1839 (died 1849); children: (1st m.) 3. ❖ Learned of parentage as adult and filed suit to be declared legal heir (1835); had claim to legitimacy upheld by US Supreme Court, in one of several rulings related to case (1861); because of outbreak of Civil War and further appeals, died before city of New Orleans paid judgment of $576,707 (1891), 56 years after filing of 1st suit. ❖ See also Nolan B. Harmon Jr., *The Famous Case of Myra Clark Gaines* (Louisiana State University Press, 1946).

GAISUENTA (d. c. 568). *See Galswintha.*

GAITE, Carmen Martín (b. 1925). *See Martín Gaite, Carmen.*

GAL, Jenny (1969—). Dutch judoka. Name variations: Jennifer Gal. Born Nov 2, 1969, in Ukkel, Belgium; sister of Jessica Gal (judoka). ❖ Won a bronze medal for 56–61kg half-middleweight at Atlanta Olympics (1996); won European championship (1995).

GAL, Jessica (1971—). Dutch judoka. Born July 6, 1971, in Amsterdam, Netherlands; sister of Jenny Gal (judoka). ❖ Won European championship for extra-lightweight (1988), half-lightweight (1991) and lightweight (1994, 1996).

GALARD, Geneviève de (b. 1925). *See de Galard, Geneviève.*

GALDIKAS, Biruté (1948—). German-born Canadian primatologist and conservationist. Name variations: Birute Galdikas; Biruté M.G. Galdikas. Pronunciation: bi-ROO-tay GAHL-di-kuhs. Born Biruté Marija Filomena Galdikas on May 10, 1948, in Wiesbaden, West Germany, of Lithuanian heritage; grew up in Toronto, Ontario, Canada; eldest of four children of Anatanas Galdikas (miner) and Filomena Galdikas; attended Elliot Lake High School, in northern Ontario; attended University of British Columbia; BA (summa cum laude), 1966, MA, and PhD from the University of California at Los Angeles (UCLA); m. Rod Brindamour, 1970 (div. 1979); m. Pak Bohap (Dayak tribesman and farmer), 1981; children: (1st m.) son, Binti Paul Brindamour (b. 1976); (2nd m.) Frederick Bohap; Filomena Jane Bohap. ❖ With the backing of anthropologist Louis Leakey, started the Orangutan Research and Conservation Project in Kalimantan, Indonesian Borneo (1971), amassing an extraordinary amount of information about the species; was the 1st scientist to discover that orangutans are not strict vegetarians, and the 1st to document the 8-year birthing cycle of the female; became an Indonesian citizen; serves as a professor extraordinaire at the Universitas Nasional in Jakarta; under a special decree, served as a senior advisor to Indonesia's Ministry of Forestry on orangutan issues (Mar 1996–Mar 1998); won the prestigious Kalpataru award, the highest award given by the Republic of Indonesia for outstanding environmental leadership, the 1st person of non-Indonesian birth and one of the 1st women to be so recognized by the Indonesian government (June 1997); as of 2000, had successfully returned more than 200 orangutans back into the wild. ❖ See also memoir *Reflections of Eden: My Years with the Orangutans of Borneo* (Little, Brown, 1995); Sy Montgomery, *Walking with the Great Apes: Jane Goodall, Dian Fossey, Biruté Galdikas* (Houghton Mifflin, 1992); and *Women in World History.*

GALE, Tristan (1980—). American skeleton athlete. Born Aug 10, 1980, in Salt Lake City, Utah. ❖ Competed as an Alpine skier for 10 years; won a gold medal for indiv. skeleton at Salt Lake City Olympics (2002).

GALE, Zona (1874–1938). American writer. Name variations: Zona Breese. Born Zona Gale on Aug 26, 1874, in Portage, Wisconsin; died of pneumonia on Dec 27, 1938, in Chicago, Illinois; dau. of Charles S. Gale (railroad engineer, died 1929) and Eliza (Beers) Gale (teacher); graduated from the University of Wisconsin, 1895; m. William L. Breese, 1928; children: Leslyn Breese (adopted 1928). ❖ Pulitzer Prize-winning author, regional writer, and political activist, worked for *Evening Wisconsonian;* rose in the newspaper profession, moving to Milwaukee *Journal,* then New York *Evening World* (1901); returned to Portage, Wisconsin (1904); published 1st novel, *Romance Island* (1906) and a collection of stories, *The Loves of Pelleas and Etarre* (1907); had 1st literary success with *Friendship Village* stories (1908), with the same characters appearing in a total of 83 stories over the next 11 years, ending with *Peace in Friendship Village* (1919); published *Birth* (1918), which launched her realistic period, in which she produced her best novels; was involved in Progressive Party activities, woman suffrage, and pacifism (1912–24); won Pulitzer Prize for drama *Miss Lulu Bett* (1921); also wrote *Faint Perfume* (1923); appointed to Board of Regents, University of Wisconsin (1923); named Wisconsin's representative to International Congress of Women (1933); elected to the University of Wisconsin Board of Visitors (1935); brought an acerbic realism to her best work, setting the majority of her stories, novels, and plays in some version of the small town where she spent most of her life; other books include *Preface to a Life* (1926), (short stories) *Yellow Gentians and Blue* (1927), *Portage, Wisconsin and Other Essays* (1928), *Borgia* (1929), *Papa LaFleur* (1933), *Light Woman* (1937), (short stories) *Bridal Pond* (1930), *Old Fashioned Tales* (1933), *Frank Miller of Mission Inn* (1938) and *Magda* (1939). ❖ See also August Derleth, *Still Small Voice: The Biography of Zona Gale* (Appleton-Century, 1940); and *Women in World History.*

GALEANA, Benita (1904–1995). Mexican political activist. Born Sept 10, 1904, in San Jerónimo de Juarez, Guerrero, Mexico; died April 17, 1995; dau. of Genaro Galeana Lacunza; m. Mario Gil; children: 1 daughter. ❖ Political and labor activist who supported worker's rights, 8-hour day, women's rights and redistribution of land; joined Mexican Communist Party (1929) and was arrested and incarcerated more than 50 times for political activities; despite limited literacy skills (self-taught), published autobiographical narrative *Benita* (1940) and collection of short narratives *El peso mocho* (The Damaged Coin, 1979); with husband, raised daughter from another marriage and other girls in need of home; worked on behalf of railroad workers' strike (1958) and supported 1968 students' movement; was outspoken critic of Institutional Revolutionary Party (PRI) government and of Mexico's relationship with US; demonstrated solidarity with Chiapas uprising (1994); remained on cutting edge of Mexican feminism, speaking in support of abortion rights and acceptance of lesbianism. Her Mexico City home was converted by Federal District government into Casa de la Mujer Benita Galeana (Benita Galeana Women's House), a museum, meeting house, archive and women's center (2000).

GALESIA (1652–1732). See Barker, Jane.

GALESWINTHA (d. c. 568). See Galswintha.

GALGÓCZI, Erzsébet (1930–1989). Hungarian novelist and politician. Name variations: Erzsebet Galgoczi. Born 1930 in Györ in western Hungary; died 1989. ❖ Born into extreme poverty but rose to become successful postwar writer; worked as journalist and on films; openly lesbian, served as Member of Parliament until death from cancer; works include *A Közös Bün* (1976), *A törvényen belül* (1980), and *Vidravas* (1984). Won Joszef Attila Prize (1976) and Kossuth Prize (1987).

GALIANA. Moorish princess. Fl. at the time of Moorish Spain; dau. of Gadalfe, king of Toledo. ❖ When Moorish Spain was divided into numerous kingdoms (1031–1492), her father built a palace for her on the banks of the Tagus River; it was so splendid that "palace of Galiana" became a proverb in Spain.

GALIEVA, Roza (1977—). Uzbekistan gymnast. Name variations: Rozaliya or Rozalya Galiyeva. Born April 28, 1977, in Almalyk, Uzbekistan, USSR. ❖ Competed for USSR/CIS until mid-1992, then Uzbekistan (1992–94), becoming a Russian citizen (1995); at World championships, won team all-around (1991); at Barcelona Olympics, won a gold medal in team all-around (1992); won Taipei International (1993); at European championships, won a gold medal on balance beam and silver for team all-around (1996); at Atlanta Olympics, won a silver medal for team all-around (1996); won Russian nationals (1996).

GALIGAÏ, Leonora (c. 1570–1617). Accused of witchcraft. Name variations: Leonora Galigai or Gallegai. Born around 1570; tried and executed in 1617; m. Concino Concini, marshal of Ancre. ❖ Close friend and maid of Marie de Medici, fell victim to the political rivalries between her mistress, the king, and certain lords (1617); was accused of witchcraft and executed on the grounds of cures she took against her constant bad health. ❖ See also *Women in World History.*

GALILEI, Maria Celeste (1600–1634). Italian nun. Name variations: Virginia Galilei. Born Virginia Galilei, 1600, in Padua, Italy; died April 2, 1634, in the convent of San Matteo; illeg. dau. of Galileo Galilei (astronomer and physicist) and Marina Gamba (Galileo's housekeeper); sister of Livia Galilei (1601–1659, known as Sister Arcangela) and Vincenzio Galilei. ❖ Was brought to Florence with sister by their father

(1610); along with sister, was placed in the impoverished convent of San Matteo in nearby Arcetri (1613), after father managed a dispensation from a cardinal friend, since the girls were too young to make the decision; took the veil (1616), choosing the name Sister Maria Celeste; her loving and solicitous letters to her father survive (1623–34). ❖ See also Dava Sobel, *Galileo's Daughter: Letters and Essays.*

GALINA, G.A. (c. 1870–1942). See Mamoshina, Glafira Adolfovna.

GALINDO, Beatriz (1475–1534). Spanish scholar, essayist, and poet. Name variations: Beatrice or Beatrix Galindo; La Latina; M. Francisco Ramírez de Madrid. Born in Salamanca, Spain, 1475; died in Madrid in 1534; buried with her husband at the Convent of Conception Jéronima, which she founded; m. Francisco Ramírez de Madrid, also known as "el Artillero" for his heroism at war in Granada. ❖ Was known particularly for her influence on the Castilian court of Queen Isabella I of Spain, where she educated royals on Latin and the classics and thus helped foster the growth of humanism in Spain; wrote poetry and essays, including the still extant *Comentarios a Aristóteles y notas sabios sobre los antiguos;* founded the Convent of Conception Jéronima, where she and her husband are buried. ❖ See also *Women in World History.*

GALINDO DE TOPETE, Hermila (1896–1954). Mexican revolutionary and feminist. Name variations: Hermila Galindo Acosta de Topete. Born Hermila Galindo Acosta in Ciudad Lerdo, Durango, Mexico, May 29, 1896; died in Mexico City, Aug 19, 1954; dau. of Rosario Galindo and Hermila Acosta de Galindo; attended schools both locally and in Chihuahua and Torreón; m. Manuel de Topete; children: 2 daughters. ❖ The leading woman supporter of the Constitutionalist forces led by Venustiano Carranza, moved to Mexico City at 15 (1911); became private secretary to Carranza (1914); traveled throughout Mexico on behalf of his government during next several years; along with Artemisa Sáenz Royo and several other feminists, founded and became editor of the periodical *La Mujer Moderna* (*The Modern Woman*, 1915); submitted a paper, "Woman in the Future," for Mexico's 1st feminist congress (1916), which proved to be a bombshell by taking a strongly anticlerical line, declaring that the Roman Catholic Church remained a major obstacle to the achievement of feminist goals in Mexico; with other Mexican feminists, successfully pressured Carranza into issuing a new Law of Family Relations (1917); was elected in a stunning upset for the seat of a deputy from Mexico City's 5th electoral district (1917), but was refused the seat because of her gender; wrote five books on various topics linked to the Mexican revolution, as well as a biography of Carranza; retired into private life at age 24. ❖ See also *Women in World History.*

GALITZIN, Amalie von (1748–1806). German princess. Name variations: Princess Gallatzin, Gallitzin, Galitzyn, or Golitsin. Born Amalie von Schmettau in Berlin, Germany, Aug 28, 1748; died in Angelmode, near Munster, Westphalia, Aug 24, 1806; m. Prince Dimitri Alexeivitch Galitzin (1738–1803, Russian diplomat, ambassador to court of France and The Hague).

GALIYEVA, Roza (1977—). See Galieva, Roza.

GALIZIA, Fede (1578–1630). Italian painter. Born in Milan, Italy, 1578; thought to have died of the plague in 1630; dau. of Annunzio Galizia (miniaturist painter). ❖ One of the earliest still-life painters in Italy, was recognized for her talent at 12; by the time she was in her teens, enjoyed an international reputation as a portraitist; among her few authenticated works is a remarkable still life signed and dated 1604. Two other still-life paintings, *Basket of Peaches* and *Still Life with Peaches* (Heusy, Belgium, E. Zurstrassen Collection), have also been attributed to her. ❖ See also *Women in World History.*

GALKINA, Lioubov (1973—). Russian shooter. Born Mar 15, 1973, in Alapayevsk, USSR. ❖ Won a silver medal for 10m air rifle and a gold medal for 50m rifle 3 positions at Athens Olympics (2004); at World Cup Finals, placed 1st for 10m air rifle (2002) and 1st for 50m rifle 3 positions (2003).

GALLA (fl. 320). Byzantine and Roman empress. Fl. around 320; 1st wife of Julius Constantius also known as Constantius II, emperor of Byzantium and emperor of Rome (r. 337–361); children: one daughter and two sons, including Gallus Caesar (b. 325/326–354). Constantius II's 2nd wife was Basilina.

GALLA (c. 365–394). Empress of Rome. Born c. 365; died in childbirth in 394; dau. of Valentinian I, Roman emperor (r. 364–375), and Justina (fl. 350–370); sister of Justa and Grata and emperor Valentinian II; half-sister of Gratian; became 2nd wife of Theodosius I, Roman emperor

(r. 379–395), around 387; children: 3 but only Galla Placidia (c. 390–450), survived infancy. ❖ Was promoted as the emperor's devoted wife and as a Christian whose social activism helped those in society who otherwise could not help themselves; assiduously worked to promote her brother Valentinian II's imperial interests, and as such was an important liaison between the houses of Theodosius and Valentinian. ❖ See also *Women in World History.*

GALLA PLACIDIA (c. 390–450). *See Placidia, Galla.*

GALLAGHER, Ann (1967—). Irish politician. Born Mar 1967 in Donegal, Ireland. ❖ Representing Labour, elected to the Seanad from the Industrial and Commercial Panel: Oireachtas Sub-Panel (1993–97), then the youngest senator.

GALLAGHER, Helen (1926—). American theatrical dancer and actress. Born July 19, 1926, in Brooklyn, NY; m. Frank Wise (sep. 1958). ❖ Trained at School of American Ballet and soon made her debut in replacement cast of *The Seven Lively Arts* (c. 1943); danced in numerous acclaimed works including Balanchine's *Mr. Strauss Goes to Boston* (1945), Jerome Robbins' *Billion Dollar Baby* (1945) and *High Button Shoes* (1947), and Agnes de Mille's *Brigadoon* (1947); featured in numerous Broadway productions including the title role in *Hazel* (1953), *Guys and Dolls* (1955), *Finians' Rainbow* (1955), *Portofino* (1958), *Sweet Charity* (1966), *Mame* (1966) and *No, No, Nanette* (1971), for which she won a Best Actress Tony; appeared in dramatic roles on such soap operas as "Ryan's Hope" (1975–89) and "One Life to Live" (1997) and in the film *Roseland* (1977). Also won a Tony for Best Supporting Actress for *Pal Joey* (1952).

GALLAGHER, Kim (1964–2002). American runner. Name variations: Kimberly Gallagher. Born Kimberly Ann Gallagher, June 11, 1964, in Fort Washington, Pennsylvania; died of a stroke, Nov 18, 2002, in Philadelphia; attended University of Arizona for one year; m. John Corcoran; children: Jessica Smith. ❖ Won TAC championship in 1,500 meters (1984); at Los Angeles Olympics, won a silver medal in 800 meters (1984); at Seoul Olympics, won a bronze medal in 800 meters (1988), battling anemia and an infection of the fallopian tubes; diagnosed with colon cancer (1989) and stomach cancer (1995).

GALLAGHER, Kitty (fl. mid-19th c.). Irish ex-convict and cattle drover. Flourished in the mid-19th century; m. Frank Gallagher; married a 2nd time. ❖ Was the leader of the White Boys, an Irish insurgent group in Ireland during late 18th century; having participated with husband in the Wexford Rebellion (1798), was arrested and transported to New South Wales, where by 1839, they had their own small cattle run; remembered by two landmarks that carry her name: Gallagher's Mountain (near Scone) and Kitty Gallagher's Swamp (near Bundarra). ❖ See also *Women in World History.*

GALLAGHER, Rosie (1970–2003). Irish athlete and geophysicist. Name variations: Rosie or Rosemary Stewart. Born Rosemary Gallagher, Feb 19, 1970, in Derry, Northern Ireland; died of cancer, Aug 2003, in Northern Ireland; attended Thornhill College; Leicester University, BSc in Geophysics, 1991; m. Adrian Stewart, 2002. ❖ A geophysicist, was also one of the founding players of the sport of Rugby in Ulster; played for Ulster Women for several years; won 3 Irish rugby union caps in 1999–2000 season; was 33 when she died.

GALLAND, Bertha (1876–1932). American actress. Born Nov 15, 1876, near Wilkes-Barre, Pennsylvania; died Nov 20, 1932. ❖ Made NY debut as Marie Ottilie in *The Pride of Jennico* (1900); came to prominence as Dorothy in *Dorothy Vernon of Haddon Hall* (1903).

GALLANT, Mavis (1922—). Canadian novelist and short-story writer. Born Mavis de Trafford Young in 1922 in Montreal, Canada, to an English-speaking family; dau. of a painter; m. John Gallant, 1943 (div. 1946). ❖ Worked as journalist for *The Montreal Standard* (1944–50), then became a frequent contributor to *The New Yorker* (publishing 119 pieces as of 1996); spent more than half of her life in Europe, living in Paris since 1960; short-story collections include *The Other Paris: Stories* (1956), *My Heart is Broken: Eight Stories and a Short Novel* (1964), *The Pegnitz Junction: A Novella and Five Short Stories* (1973), *Home Truths: Selected Canadian Stories* (1981), and *In Transit* (1988); novels include *Green Water, Green Sky* (1959) and *A Fairly Good Time* (1970); nonfiction includes *Paris Journals: Essays and Reviews* (1986). Made Officer of Order of Canada and received Governor General's Award (1981).

GALLARDO, Miriam (1968—). Peruvian volleyball player. Born May 2, 1968, in Peru. ❖ At Seoul Olympics, won a silver medal in team competition (1988).

GALLARDO, Sara (1931–1988). Argentinean novelist. Born 1931 in Buenos Aires, Argentina; died 1988. ❖ Works include *Enero* (1958), *Pantalones azules* (1963), *Los galgos, los galgos* (1968), *Teo y la TV* (1974), *La rosa en el viento* (1978), and *El país del humo* (1977).

GALLATIN, Alberta (c. 1861–1948). American actress. Born c. 1861 in America; died Aug 25, 1948, in NYC. ❖ Appeared for over 30 years on stage, earning acclaim as a Shakespearean actress; starred opposite Edwin Booth, Maurice Barrymore, Otis Skinner, and Richard Mansfield.

GALLEGAI, Leonora (c. 1570–1617). *See Galigaï, Leonora.*

GALLI, Caterina (c. 1723–1804). Italian mezzo-soprano. Born in Italy c. 1723; died in London, England, 1804. ❖ Arrived in London (1742), appearing at the King's Theatre in Brivio's *Mandane*; sang for Handel at Covent Garden (1747–54), creating mostly male roles in *Joshua, Solomon* and *Jephtha*; sang in Genoa, Venice, and Naples (1754–63); became companion of the celebrated Martha Ray, a singer and mistress of the earl of Sandwich, who strongly influenced naval appointments; was in attendance when Ray was assassinated by James Hackman (April 7, 1779), while leaving Covent Garden Theatre. ❖ See also *Women in World History.*

GALLI, Rosina (1896–1940). Italian ballet dancer. Born 1896 in Naples, Italy; died April 30, 1940, in Milan, Italy. ❖ Performed at Teatro di San Carlo in Naples and at Teatro alla Scala in Milan; moved to US (1912) for engagement at Philadelphia-Chicago Opera where she worked under Luigi Albertieri; worked as principal dancer at Metropolitan Opera in NY under director Guilio Gatti-Cazzaza and performed in numerous operas and ballets including works by Pauline Verhoeven until 1935; served as ballet mistress there (1919–35) where her students included Miriam Golden, Nora Kaye, and Maria Karnilova.

GALLI-CURCI, Amelita (1882–1963). Italian coloratura soprano. Born Amelita Galli, Nov 18, 1882, in Milan, Italy, of Italian-Spanish ancestry; died Nov 26, 1963, in La Jolla, California; studied harmony, composition, and piano under Vincenzo Appiani at Royal Conservatory in Milan; was mainly a self-taught singer, though she studied briefly with Carignani and Sara Dufes; m. Marquis Luigi Curci, 1910 (div. 1920); m. Homer Samuels (her accompanist), 1921. ❖ Debuted at the Teatro Constanzi, Rome, as Gilda in Giuseppe Verdi's *Rigoletto* (1909); sang in Spain, Italy, Russia, and South America (1910–16); was a sensation at the Chicago Opera, once again as Gilda (1916); recording of "Caro nome" sold 10,000 copies of the 1st edition in Chicago alone; made NY debut singing Myerbeer's *Dinorah*, and was forced to make 24 curtain calls after the "Shadow Song"; sang with Chicago Opera Company (1916–24); enormously popular, debuted at the Met as Violetta in Verdi's *La Traviata* (1920) and remained there until 1930; operatic repertoire also included the roles of Rosina in Rossini's *The Barber of Seville*, Mimi in Puccini's *La Bohème*, Lakmé in Delibes' *Lakmé*, Juliette in Gounod's *Roméo et Juliette* and Elvira in Bellini's *I Puritani*; underwent an operation to remove goiter (1935); forced to retire. ❖ See also *Women in World History.*

GALLI-MARIÉ, Célestine (1840–1905). French mezzo-soprano. Name variations: Celestine Laurence Galli-Marie. Born Célestine Marié d'Isle, Nov 1840, in Paris, France; died Sept 22, 1905, in Vence, France; studied with her father, Felix Mécène Marié d'Isle, in Strasbourg. ❖ Debuted in Strasbourg (1859); appeared in Lisbon (1861) and Rouen (1862); performed at Paris Opéra-Comique (1862–1902), creating several operatic roles including title role in Ambroise Thomas' *Mignon*, Taven and Andrelou in *Mireille* and Dorothée in *Cendrillon*; was most famous, however, for creation of Bizet's *Carmen*, performing this opera over 100 times (1875–83). ❖ See also *Women in World History.*

GALLIENNE, Eva Le (1899–1991). *See Le Gallienne, Eva.*

GALLIERA, duchess of.
See Luisa Fernanda (1832–1897).
See Eulalia (b. 1864).
See Beatrice of Saxe-Coburg (1884–1966).

GALLINA, Juliane (1970—). American brigade commander. Born Aug 3, 1970, in Pelham, NY. ❖ Became 1st woman named brigade commander by US Naval Academy (1991); as midshipman captain, served as leader of 4,300-member brigade and as key liaison between midshipmen and academy officers; serves as Navy lieutenant.

GALLOWAY, Grace Growden (d. 1782). American diarist and poet. Born Grace Growden into wealthy Quaker family in Philadelphia; died 1782; dau. of Lawrence Growden (jurist, 1694–1770); m. Joseph Galloway (colonial politician and lawyer), 1753 (died 1803); children: daughter Betsey. ❖ During American Revolution, her prominent loyalist husband fled with daughter to England, while she remained behind to protect family's estate; kept diary recording her distress on realization that she would receive no help from British government or husband (later published as *Diary of Grace Growden Galloway*, 1931); died without seeing family again.

GALLOWAY, Louise (d. 1949). American actress. Died Oct 10, 1949, in Brookfield, Massachusetts. ❖ Plays include *Way Down East, The Music Master, The Little Princess, Soldier of Fortune, The Gold Diggers, The Clinging Vine, Weak Sisters* and *Lady Alone*; retired (1942).

GALSONDA (d. around 568). *See Galswintha.*

GALSWINTHA (d. around 568). Frankish queen and saint. Name variations: Chilswintha; Gaisuenta; Galsonda; Galeswintha; Queen of the Merovingians. Died c. 568 in Rouen, France; dau. of Athangild also known as Athanagild, king of the Visigoths, and Queen Goiswintha of Spain; sister of Brunhilda (c. 533–613); 2nd wife of Chilperic I, king of Soissons (Neustria), king of the Franks (r. 561–584); no children. ❖ A Visigothic princess, married the polygamous Frankish king Chilperic I, and thereby earned the enmity of Fredegund; humiliated daily by Fredegund and Chilperic's relationship, asked to be returned to her own people, but the king, afraid of losing her large dowry, refused; was strangled in her bed by a pageboy and few doubted Fredegund's guilt; on her death, was mourned deeply, and the Franks began to attribute miracles to her spirit; was regarded as a holy woman for her patient suffering of Chilperic's ill treatment and eventually canonized. ❖ See also *Women in World History.*

GALT, Edith (1872–1961). *See Wilson, Edith Bolling.*

GALTON, Blanche (1845–1936). *See Whiffen, Blanche.*

GALUSHKA, Vera (1945—). Soviet volleyball player. Born April 14, 1945, in USSR. ❖ Won a gold medal at Mexico City Olympics (1968) and a gold medal at Munich Olympics (1972), both in team competition.

GALVÃO, Patricia (1910–1962). Brazilian feminist journalist, poet and novelist. Name variations: (pseudonyms) Pagu; Mara Lobo; GIM. Born 1910 in Sao Joao da Boa Vista, Brazil; died Dec 1962; m. Oswald de Andrade, 1930 (died 1954); m. Geraldo Ferraz. ❖ Worked as journalist for Brazilian and French newspapers, writing on art, drama, literature, and politics; joined Communist party (1930s) and was arrested in Europe and Brazil for political views; wrote *Parque industrial* (1933) and *A famosa revista* (with Geraldo Ferraz, 1945). The Patricia Galvao Institute in Sao Paulo is devoted to raising public awareness about women's rights.

GALVARRIATO, Eulalia (1905–1997). Spanish novelist. Born 1905 in Madrid, Spain; died 1997. ❖ Writings include *Cinco sombras* (1947) and *Raíces bajo el tiempo* (1986).

GALVIN, Sheila (1914–1983). Irish politician. Born Feb 23, 1914, in Cork City, Ireland; died Mar 20, 1983; m. John Galvin (TD, 1956–63); children: Barry Galvin, Carol Galvin Cotter, Mary Galvin Buckley. ❖ Following husband's death, won a by-election representing Fianna Fáil to 17th Dáil for Cork City (1964–65).

GAM, Rita (1928—). American actress and producer. Born April 2, 1928, in Pittsburgh, Pennsylvania; raised in NYC; m. Sidney Lumet (director), 1949 (div. 1954); m. Thomas H. Guinzburg (publisher), 1956 (div. 1963); children: two, including Kate Guinzburg (producer). ❖ Made film debut in *The Thief* (1952), followed by *Night People, Saadia, Sign of the Pagan, Mohawk, King of Kings, Klute, Such Good Friends, Seeds of Evil* and *Midnight*, among others; frequently appeared on tv and made documentary films; bridesmaid and close friend of Grace Kelly. Won a Berlin Festival award for performance in *Huis clos* (*No Exit*, 1962).

GAMBA ADISA (1934–1992). *See Lorde, Audre.*

GAMBARA, Veronica (1485–1550). Italian poet. Name variations: Veronica of Correggio. Born 1485 in Pratalbiono, Italy; died 1550 in Correggio, Italy; m. Gilberto X of Correggio (ruler of that small city-state), 1509 (died 1518); children: 2 sons. ❖ Following husband's death (1518), was left with two young children and the burden of rule; soon proved herself a competent leader, managing the administrative tasks

required with skill; even acted as military leader, fending off at least one invading army; became a great patron of the artists and writers of the early Italian Renaissance, including poets Pietro Bembo and Bernardo Tasso; also composed poems, several of which are extant. ❖ See also *Women in World History.*

GAMBARELLI, Maria (1900–1990). Italian-American theatrical ballet dancer. Born 1900 in Spezia, Italy; died Dec 16, 1990, in Huntington, Long Island, NY; sister of actress Eole Galli. ❖ Immigrated to US as a child; began training at school of Metropolitan Opera Ballet in New York City at age 7; at 13 and 14, performed as soloist at Metropolitan Opera for 2 years; left Metropolitan to become principal dancer at S.L. "Roxy" Rothafel's Roxy Theater in New York City, dancing solos in all Prologs; appeared with "Roxy" at Capitol Theater and served as ballet mistress for Prologs (c. 1922–24); formed Gamby Girls, her own troupe of precision dancers who performed primarily in Prologs on Paramount-Public circuit (c. 1926–31); appeared in films *Hooray for Love* (1935), *Here's to Romance* (1935), and *Santa Barbara Fiesta* (1936), and also in numerous Italian films; choreographed several concert works and solos, as well as acts for Prologs throughout career. Choreographed works including *Snowflakes* (1939), *Rhapsody in Blue* (1939), *Meditation from "Thais"* (c. 1940), *Dance of Valour* (1940), *The Dying Swan* (1940), *The Merry Widow* (1940) and *Figurine* (1941).

GAMBARO, Griselda (1928—). Argentinean playwright and short-story writer. Name variations: Griselda Gámbaro. Born July 28,1928, in Buenos Aires, Argentina. ❖ Moved to Barcelona, Spain, during military dictatorship in Argentina, then returned to Buenos Aires; works of fiction include *Cuentos* (1953), *Madrigal en ciudad* (1963), *Nada que ver con otra historia* (1972), *Dios no nos quiere contentos* (1979), *Lo impenetrable* (1984), and *El mar que nos trajo* (2001); plays include *El desatino* (1965), *Los Siameses* (1967), *El viaje* (1975), *Real envido* (1983), and *Del sol naciente* (1984). Won several awards, including Premio Fondo Nacional de las Artes (1963) and Premio Emecé (1965).

GAMBERO, Anabel (1972—). Argentinean field-hockey player. Born Ana Gambero, July 9, 1972, in Argentina. ❖ Won a team silver medal at Sydney Olympics (2000).

GAMBLE, Jane Jayroe (c. 1947—). *See Jayroe, Jane.*

GAMIN, Judith (1930—). Australian politician. Born July 18, 1930, in Broken Hill, Queensland, Australia. ❖ As a member of the National Party, served in the Queensland Parliament for South Coast (1988–89), then Burleigh (1989–2001).

GAMM, Ruth (1946—). *See Fuchs, Ruth.*

GAMOVA, Ekaterina (1980—). Russian volleyball player. Born Oct 17, 1980, in Tchelyabinsk, Russia. ❖ Made national team debut (1999); won European team championship (1999, 2001) and World Grand Prix (1999, 2002); placed 3rd at World championships (2002); won a team silver medal at Sydney Olympics (2000) and a team silver medal at Athens Olympics (2004).

GAMSON, Annabelle (1928—). American concert dancer. Name variations: Annabelle Gold. Born Aug 6, 1928, in New York, NY. ❖ Trained with Julia Levien, a disciple of Anna and Irma Duncan dance groups; made professional debut at 16 with Katharine Dunham's concert group at Café Society Uptown in New York City; joined Jerome Robbins' road company as understudy in *On the Town*; appeared on Broadway in *Finian's Rainbow* (1947), *Arms and the Girl* (1950), and *Make Mine Manhattan* (1948); moved to Paris for several years with then husband; returned to NY (c. 1955) and soon performed once more on Broadway in *Pipe Dream* (1955), on tv on "The Ed Sullivan Show" and "Lamp Unto My Feet"; appeared in concerts for Anna Sokolow, with American Ballet theater, and Ballet Theater Workshop; stepped back from performance career (1960s) to teach and work with opera companies from time to time; returned to stage with Isadora Duncan revival (1970s) when she presented own choreography in solo concerts and began holding lecture-demonstrations with Julia Levien (1972). Works of choreography include *First Movement* (1976), *Five Easy Pieces* (1976), *Portrait of Rose* (1976), *Dances of Death* (1978) and *Two Dances* (1979).

GAN, Elena Andreevna (1814–1842). Russian author. Name variations: Helena Gan; (pseudonym) Zinaida R-va or Zenaida R-va. Born Helena Andreevna Fadeeva in 1814; died June 1842; dau. of Elena Fadeeva (1788–1860, botanist with international connections); m. Captain (later Colonel) Peter Alekseevich Gan (1798–1873, career military officer), 1830; children: Helena Blavatsky (1831–1891, mystic), son Sasha (who died in infancy, 1833), Vera Zhelikhovskaya (1835–1896, writer), and Leonid (b. June 1840). ❖ One of the Russian Romantics, wrote novels which probed the lot of the intellectual outsider; writings include *Utballa* (1838), *Dzhellaledin* (1843), originally published as *The Moslem* in 1838, *Teofaniia Abbadzhio* (1841), and *A Vain Gift.* ❖ See also *Women in World History.*

GANCHEVA, Lyuba (1912–1974). *See Yazova, Yana.*

GÁNDARA, Carmen (1900–1977). Argentinean novelist and short-story writer. Name variations: Carmen Gandara; Carmen Rodriguez; Carmen Rodriguez Larreta de Gandara. Born 1900 in Argentina; died 1977. ❖ Writings include *El lugar del diablo* (1947), *Los espejos* (1951), and *La figura y el mundo* (1958).

GANDERSHEIM, abbess of.
See Hathumoda (d. 874).
See Gerberga (d. 896).
See Christine of Gandersheim (d. 919).
See Hrotsvitha of Gandersheim (c. 935–1001).
See Gerberga (r. 959–1001).
See Sophia of Gandersheim (975–1039).

GANDHI, Indira (1917–1984). Indian prime minister. Name variations: Indira Nehru Gandhi; (nickname) Indu. Pronunciation: EEN-dee-raa GAAN-dee. Born Indira Priyadarshini Nehru, nicknamed Indu, Nov 19, 1917, in Allahabad, in northern India; assassinated in New Delhi by two Sikhs on Oct 31, 1984; dau. of Jawaharlal Nehru (1889–1964, 1st prime minister of independent India) and Kamala Nehru (1899–1936); grand-dau. of Motilal Nehru (Indian nationalist leader); attended International School, Geneva; St. Mary's Convent, Allahabad; Pupil's Own School, Poona; Somerville College, Oxford (did not complete degree); m. Feroze Gandhi, Mar 26, 1941 (died Sept 1960); children: 2 sons, Rajiv (b. 1944, prime minister of India who was also assassinated on May 21, 1991); Sanjay (1946–1980). ❖ First woman prime minister of independent India who fought against political regionalism, casteism, and religious conservatism to advance her nation to a leading position in Asia; joined the Indian National Congress Party (1938); became a member of the Working Committee of the ruling Congress Party (1955); elected Congress Party president (1959); on father's death, became minister of information and broadcasting (1964); became prime minister of India as a compromise candidate between the right and left wings of the Congress Party (1966); saw a decisive military victory over Pakistan, helped create Bangladesh from East Pakistan, and received Bharat Ratna Award (1971); deprived of seat in Parliament by the High Court of Allahabad, declared emergency to establish authoritarian rule (1975); lost in general elections (1977); saw her supporters split from the Congress Party and form the Congress Party-I (I for Indira); imprisoned for one week (Dec 1978); won general elections to become prime minister again; son Sanjay Gandhi won a seat in Parliament (1980); elected chair of the Non-Aligned movement (1983); assassinated in New Delhi by two Sikh security guards (1984); independent India's 1st woman leader, led her nation for over two decades as prime minister. ❖ See also Mary C. Carras, *Indira Gandhi: The Crucible of Leadership* (Beacon, 1979); Emmeline Garnett, *Madame Prime Minister* (Farrar, Straus, 1967); Zareer Masani, *Indira Gandhi: A Biography* (Crowell, 1975); Nayantara Sahgal, *Indira Gandhi: Her Road to Power* (Ungar, 1982); Pupul Jayakar, *Indira Gandhi: An Intimate Biography* (Pantheon, 1993); and *Women in World History.*

GANDHI, Kasturba (1869–1944). Indian freedom fighter. Name variations: Kasturbai Gandhi; known as Ba. Born 1869 at Porbandar in Gujarat, India; died Feb 22, 1944, in Poona, India; dau. of Gokuladas Makharji (well-to-do businessman); m. Mohandas Gandhi (Indian nationalist and leader), 1882; children: 4 sons, Harilal (b. 1888); Manilal (b. 1892); Ramdas (b. 1897) and Devadas (b. 1900). ❖ At 10, married Mohandas Gandhi; when he decided to observe brahama-charya (vow of chastity), no longer had sexual relations with him; worked alongside husband; joined in the struggle for independence for Indians in South Africa (1897) and was arrested (Sept 1913) and sentenced to 3 months hard labor; later in India, often took husband's place when he was under arrest; following the Quit India movement, joined husband in detention at the Aga Khan's Palace in Poona, where she died.

GANDHI, Sonia (1946—). Indian politician. Name variations: Soniaji. Born Sonia Maino, Dec 9, 1946, in the village of Orbassano, near Turin, Italy; dau. of a building contractor; studied English at Cambridge, 1964; m. Rajiv Gandhi (b. 1944, son of Indira Gandhi and prime minister of India), 1968 (assassinated, May 21, 1991); children: Rahul Gandhi

(politician), daughter Priyanka Gandhi. ❖ Popular politician, met husband while studying at Cambridge; was offered his post within 24 hours of his death but refused it (1991); was elected president of India's Congress Party (1998), then elected to Parliament (1999), representing the seat of Rai Bareilly; won the general election (2005), then stunned the nation when she announced that whe would not become the country's next prime minister.

GANDOLFI, Annapia (1964—). Italian fencer. Born June 24, 1964, in Italy. ❖ At Seoul Olympics, won a silver medal in team foil (1988).

GANDY, Kim A. (c. 1954—). American feminist leader. Born c. 1954; Louisiana Tech University, BS in mathematics, 1973; received a law degree from Loyola University School of Law, 1978; m. Dr. Christopher "Kip" Lornell (ethnomusicologist); children: Elizabeth Cady Lornell and Katherine Eleanor Gandy (b. 1995). ❖ Served as senior assistant district attorney in New Orleans; opened a private trial practice there, litigating many cases seeking fair treatment for women including a successful sex discrimination judgment against the US Air Force; as president of NOW in Louisiana, started 11 chapters there; elected national president of NOW (2001).

GANEURA (d. 470 or 542). *See Guinevere.*

GANGULEE, Aruna (c. 1909–1996). *See Ali, Aruna Asaf.*

GANGULI or GANGULY, Aruna (c. 1909–1996). *See Ali, Aruna Asaf.*

GÁNINA, Maja (1927—). Russian short-story writer. Name variations: Maiya or Maiia Anatolievna Ganina; Majja Ganina. Born 1927 in Moscow, USSR; studied at the Gorky Institute. ❖ Member of Soviet Writers' Union, often spoke out on women's issues; work often focuses on independent female characters, female friendships, and roles for women in Russian society; novella *First Trials* appeared in journal *New World* (1954).

GANNETT, Deborah Sampson (1760–1827). *See Sampson, Deborah.*

GANNON, Kate (d. 1913). *See Wyllie, Kate.*

GANOR, Ganora or Ganore (d. 470 or 542). *See Guinevere.*

GANSER, Marge (c. 1948–1996). American singer. Name variations: The Shangri-Las; Marguerite Dorste. Born Marguerite Ganser, c. 1948; died of breast cancer, July 28, 1996, in Valley Stream, NY; twin sister of Mary Ann Ganser (singer with the Shangri-Las); m. Bill Dorste, 1972 (div.). ❖ With twin Mary Ann, formed one half of the briefly successful Shangri-Las (1964), a group known for teenage, angst-ridden songs; began singing with Mary Ann and sisters Liz and Mary Weiss while at Andrew Jackson High School in Queens, NY; with group, released 1st hit, "Remember (Walkin' in the Sand)," which launched George "Shadow" Morton's Red Bird label (1964), and went on to release the album *Leader of the Pack* (1964), which included #1 hit title track; also released *Shangri-Las '65* (1965) and *I Can Never Go Home Anymore* (1966) and had such hit songs as "Give Him a Great Big Kiss" (1964), "Give Us Your Blessings" (1965) and "Long Live Our Love" (1966); with group, performed concerts in UK and US, then had to disband because of legal and financial problems (late 1960s); reunited with surviving band members, the Weiss sisters, to perform concert (1989), then performed sporadically (1990s).

GANSER, Mary Ann (c. 1948–1971). American singer. Born c. 1948; died of encephalitis, 1971, in New York, NY; sister of Marge Ganser (singer with the Shangri-Las). ❖ With twin Marge, formed one half of the briefly successful Shangri-Las (1964), began singing with Marge and sisters Liz and Mary Weiss while at Jackson High School in Queens; with group, released 1st hit, "Remember (Walkin' in the Sand)," which launched the Red Bird label (1964), and also released the album *Leader of the Pack* (1964), which included #1 hit title track; had such hit songs as "Give Him a Great Big Kiss" (1964), "Give Us Your Blessings" (1965) and "Long Live Our Love" (1966).

GANSKY-SACHSE, Diana (1963—). East German track-and-field athlete. Name variations: Diana Sachse. Born Dec 14, 1963, in East Germany. ❖ At Seoul Olympics, won a silver medal in discus thrower (1988).

GANT, Phyllis (1922—). New Zealand novelist. Name variations: Phyllis Eileen Ferrabee Gant. Born May 16, 1922, in Nhill, Victoria, Australia. ❖ Worked as editor and journalist; writings include *Islands* (1973), *The Fifth Season* (1976), and several short stories.

GANTT, Rosa (1875–1935). American physician and public-health official. Name variations: Love Rosa Hirschmann Gantt; L. Rosa Gantt (also seen as Rosa L. Gantt). Born Love Rosa Hirschmann, Dec 29, 1875, in Camden, South Carolina; died Nov 16, 1935, in Philadelphia, Pennsylvania; dau. of Solomon Hirschmann (merchant) and Lena (Debhrina) Hirschmann; Medical College of South Carolina, MD, 1901, one of the 1st 2 women to graduate from school's 3-year program; m. Robert Joseph Gantt (lawyer), Mar 16, 1905. ❖ Served as secretary (1909–18) of Spartanburg Medical Society; was president of Medical Women's National Association (later American Medical Women's Association) (1931–32); lobbied for state legislation requiring medical inspection of schoolchildren (passed in 1920); organized and headed Spartanburg Health League; sat on board of medical examiners for draft during WWI; served as chair of board of trustees of state reform school for girls (1918–28); was legislative chair of South Carolina Equal Suffrage League (1914–15); in addition to organizational work in public health, practiced as eye, ear, nose, and throat specialist throughout career.

GANZ, Joan (b. 1929). *See Cooney, Joan Ganz.*

GAO E (1962—). Chinese shooter. Born Nov 7, 1962, in Shenyang, China. ❖ Won a bronze medal for double trap at Sydney Olympics (2000) and a bronze medal for double trap at Athens Olympics (2004); placed 1st at World Cup finals (2002, 2003).

GAO FENG (1982—). Chinese judoka. Born Feb 2, 1982, in China. ❖ Won a bronze medal for 48kg at Athens Olympics (2004).

GAO HONG (1967—). Chinese soccer player. Born Nov 27, 1967, in Guangdong, China. ❖ Goalkeeper; won a team silver medal at Atlanta Olympics (1996); played for New York Power (2001); signed with Beijing Chengjian (2003).

GAO JING (1975—). Chinese shooter. Born Feb 19, 1975, in China. ❖ Won a bronze medal for 10m air rifle at Sydney Olympics (2000).

GAO JUN (1969—). Chinese table-tennis player. Born Jan 25, 1969, in Hebei, China; moved to Gaithersburg, Maryland. ❖ At Barcelona Olympics, won a silver medal in doubles (1992); because she married an American and moved to US, had to sit out international competition for 5 years when China objected to change of nationality; was US Open single's champion (1994) and US national champion for singles, doubles and mixed doubles (1996–98).

GAO LING (1979—). Chinese badminton player. Born Mar 14, 1979, in China. ❖ Won a bronze medal for doubles at Sydney Olympics (2000) and a a silver medal for doubles and gold medal for mixed doubles at Athens Olympics (2004); at World championships, won doubles (2001, 2003) and mixed doubles (2001).

GAO MIN (1970—). Chinese diver. Born Sept 7, 1970, in China. ❖ Won a gold medal at Seoul Olympics (1988) and a gold medal at Barcelona Olympics (1992), both in springboard.

GAO YAOJIE (c. 1927—). Chinese gynecologist and AIDS activist. Born c. 1927 in Henan Province, China; m. Guo Jiuming (physician). ❖ Was a professor at the Henan Institute of Traditional Chinese Medicine, an expert on gynecological cancer, a deputy to the 7th People's Congress of Henan Province, and a researcher at the Henan Provincial Research Institute of Culture and History; following retirement, crusaded to help poor farmers in Henan Province who became infected with HIV through selling their blood at illegal collection stations (1990s); began to suspect that up to 100,000 people in Henan might be infected with HIV; put under investigation and warned not to speak out, used her pension to travel remote villages, lecturing, distributing flyers and pamphlets, and dispensing medical care; won the Jonathan Mann Award for Health and Human Rights (2001) but was refused permission to attend the awards ceremony in US; won the Ramon Magsaysay Award for Public Service (2003), Asia's equivalent to the Nobel Prize.

GAO XIUMIN (1963—). Chinese handball player. Born Aug 21, 1963, in China. ❖ At Los Angeles Olympics, won a bronze medal in team competition (1984).

GAPCHENKO, Emma (1938—). Soviet archer. Born Feb 24, 1938, in USSR. ❖ At Munich Olympics, won a bronze medal in double FITA round (1972).

GAPOSCHKIN, Cecilia Payne (1900–1979). *See Payne-Gaposchkin, Cecilia.*

GARAJEWA, Julja. *See Garayeva, Yuliya.*

GARAPICK, Nancy (1961—). Canadian swimmer. Born Sept 24, 1961, in Halifax, Nova Scotia, Canada. ❖ Won a silver medal in 200-meter backstroke and a bronze medal in 100-meter backstroke at World championships (1975); at Montreal Olympics, won bronze medals in 200-meter backstroke and 100-meter backstroke (1976); won 3 silver medals at the World Cup (1979).

GARARD, Renita (1972—). *See Farrell, Renita.*

GARATTI-SAVILLE, Eleanor (1909—). American swimmer. Born June 12, 1909, in US. ❖ At Amsterdam Olympics, won a silver medal in the 100-meter freestyle and a gold medal in the 4 x 100-meter freestyle relay (1928); at Los Angeles Olympics, won a bronze medal in the 100-meter freestyle and a gold medal in the 4 x 100-meter freestyle relay (1932).

GARAUD, Marie-Françoise (1934—). French lawyer and politician. Name variations: Marie-Francoise Garaud; Marie-France Garaud. Born Mar 6, 1934, in Poitiers, France. ❖ Practiced law in Poitiers (1954–57); served as technical adviser in the office of Jean Foyer, minister for Cooperation then minister of Justice (1961–67), special adviser in the office of Georges Pompidou, prime minister (1967–68), technical adviser to the president of the Republic (Georges Pompidou, 1969–74), commissioner of Audit (1974–98), then senior member of the Court of Auditors (1998–99); as an Independent or Non-attached (NI), elected to 5th European Parliament (1999–2004). Elected president of the International Geopolitical Institute (1982).

GARAYEVA, Yuliya. Russian fencer. Name variations: Yulia; Julja Garajewa. Born in USSR. ❖ Won a bronze medal for team épée at Atlanta Olympics (1996).

GARBETT, Cornelia Barns (1888–1941). *See Barns, Cornelia Baxter.*

GARBO, Greta (1905–1990). Swedish actress. Born Greta Louisa Gustafsson on Sept 18, 1905, in Stockholm, Sweden; died in New York on April 15, 1990, of kidney disease; youngest of the three children of Anna and Karl Gustafsson; never married; no children. ❖ Film actress who, despite superstar status, left the film business after *Two-Faced Woman* (1941) and carefully guarded her privacy and the "Garbo mystique"; 1st appeared on film in advertisements for a Stockholm department store for which she worked as a teenager, followed by small parts in studio films while she attended a school of dramatic arts; came under the tutelage of Swedish director Mauritz Stiller, who trained her to act for the camera and gave her a major role in his drama, *The Legend of Gosta Berling*, which was distributed internationally (1924); was subsequently offered a contract by MGM in Hollywood, where she played the mysterious foreign woman in a series of silent films and became America's favorite screen *femme fatale*; silent films include *The Torrent* (1926), *The Temptress* (1926), *Flesh and the Devil* (1926), *Love* (1927), *The Divine Woman* (1928), *The Mysterious Lady* (1928), *A Woman of Affairs* (1928), *Wild Orchids* (1929), *A Man's Man* (1929), *The Single Standard* (1929), and *The Kiss* (1929); survived the transition to "talkies" with *Anna Christie* (1930), which brought her the 1st of 3 Academy Award nominations, elevated her to superstardom, and gave her enough clout to make her the highest-paid woman in America by mid-1930s; her work in both *Anna Karenina* (1935) and in *Camille* (1937), brought her an award from the New York Film Critics as Best Actress as well as Oscar nominations; was also seen in *Romance* (1930), *Susan Lenox—Her Fall and Rise* (1931), *Mata Hari* (1931), *Inspiration* (1931), *As You Desire Me* (1931), *Grand Hotel* (1932), *Queen Christina* (1933), *The Painted Veil* (1934), *Conquest* (1937), *Ninotchka* (1939); after filming *Two-Faced Woman* (1941), turned her back on Hollywood and walked away; for the next 30 years, refused all requests for interviews which perpetuated the mystery she gathered around her like a protective cloak. Was finally given a special Oscar for her "unforgettable screen performances" (1954). ❖ See also Sven Broman, *Garbo on Garbo* (Bloomsbury, 1990); Barry Paris, *Garbo* (Knopf, 1995); Karen Swenson, *Greta Garbo: A Life Apart* (Scribners, 1997); and *Women in World History*.

GARBORG, Hulda (1862–1934). Norwegian writer, dancer and theater instructor. Born in 1862 in Norway; died 1934; m. Arne Garborg (1851–1924, writer). ❖ Pioneer in the folk-dance movement at the beginning of the 20th century, is best known for fueling interest in the bunad tradition, the wearing of Norwegian national costumes; published *Norske Klaebunad* (1903).

GARBOUSOVA, Raya (1909–1997). Georgian-born American cellist. Born in Tiflis (now Tbilisi), Georgia, Sept 25, 1909 (some sources cite

Oct 10, 1905 or 1907); died in De Kalb, Illinois, Jan 28, 1997; father was a professor at the Tiflis Conservatory; studied in Western Europe with Diran Alexanian, Hugo Becker, Julius Klengel, and Felix Salmond, 1925–26; m. Kurt Biss; children: Gregory, Paul. ❖ One of the great cellists of the 20th century, renowned for the lyrical quality of her playing, who inspired major composers including Samuel Barber to write works for her; gave a triumphant Moscow debut (1924); made Berlin debut (1926), followed by a highly successful London debut (1926); after an equally triumphant debut in Paris (1927), studied with Pablo Casals, who invited her to perform as a soloist with his orchestra in Barcelona; made a sensational New York debut (1934); as the clouds of war hung over Europe, settled in US (1939), becoming a US citizen (1946); in Boston, gave world premiere of *Cello Concerto* composed for her by Samuel Barber (April 5, 1946); also introduced works composed for her by Karol Rathaus, Vittorio Rieti, and Gunther Schuller; gave many US as well as world-premiere performances, among which were the cello sonata of Sergei Prokofiev (which she also recorded) and the third sonata for that instrument by Bohuslav Martinu; taught cello at Hartt College at University of Hartford (1970–79), then at Northern Illinois University (1979–91). ❖ See also *Women in World History.*

GARBRECHT-ENFELDT, Monique (1968—). German speedskater. Name variations: Monique Garbrecht; Monique Enfeldt. Born Monique Garbrecht, Dec 11, 1968, in Potsdam, Germany; m. Magnus Enfeldt (Swedish speedskater), 2000. ❖ Won the World sprint title (1991); won a bronze medal for the 1,000 meters at Albertville Olympics (1992); finished 1st in World Cup 1,000-meter standings (1999); won the World sprint title (1999, 2000, 2001); at World Single Distance championships, won the 500 and 1,000 (1999) and the 1,000 (2001); won World Cup title in 500 and 1,000 (1999); won the silver medal in the 500 meters at Salt Lake City Olympics (2002).

GARCEAU, Catherine (1978—). Canadian synchronized swimmer. Born July 1, 1978, in Montreal, Quebec, Canada. ❖ Won a team bronze medal at Sydney Olympics (2000).

GARCIA, Agustina Soledad (1981—). Argentinean field-hockey player. Name variations: Sole García. Born June 12, 1981, in Cordoba, Argentina; dau. of Maria Paula Castelli. ❖ Forward, won a team silver medal at Sydney Olympics (2000) and a team bronze medal at Athens Olympics (2004); won World Cup (2002), and Pan American Games (2003).

GARCIA, Cristina (1948—). *See García-Orcoyen Tormo, Cristina.*

GARCIA, Guadalupe (1878–1963). *See Lupita, Madre.*

GARCÍA, Marta (c. 1945—). Cuban ballet dancer. Born c. 1945 in Havana, Cuba. ❖ Trained at National Ballet of Cuba and with Alicia and Alberto Alonso; joined National Ballet (1960s) where she has danced many principal roles in company's repertory including Giselle; has also danced in contemporary works by national choreographers such as Alberto Mendéz, Iván Tenorio, and José Parés.

GARCIA, Pauline (1821–1910). *See Viardot, Pauline.*

GARCIA, Rosa (1964—). Peruvian volleyball player. Born May 21, 1964, in Peru. ❖ At Seoul Olympics, won a silver medal in team competition (1988).

GARCIA, Sancha (fl. 1230). Spanish abbess of Las Huelgas. Name variations: Sancia. Fl. in 1230 in Las Huelgas, Spain; never married; no children. ❖ A Spanish noblewoman, was one of the last truly powerful abbesses of medieval Europe; her piety, broad learning, and administrative abilities led her to be chosen head of the large abbey of Las Huelgas, putting not only a convent but also several monasteries under her direct control; performed many of the same functions as a priest, including hearing confessions and blessing the nuns. ❖ See also *Women in World History.*

GARCÍA, Sole (1981—). *See Garcia, Agustina Soledad.*

GARCÍA MARRUZ, Fina (1923—). Cuban poet and essayist. Name variations: Josefina C. Garcia Marruz Badia. Born April 18, 1923, in Havana, Cuba; graduated from Social Sciences at Havana University, 1961; sister-in-law of Eliseo Diego (writer); m. Cintio Vitier (poet and critic); children: Sergio and José María Vitier (both composers). ❖ Served on the committee for the magazine *Clavileño* (1943); with Cleva Solís, was one of the two women members of the Origenes group, headed by José Lezama Lima; began work as literary researcher for National Library José Martí (1962) and also worked with others at the

Center of Marti Studies (1977–87), on the complete works of José Martí; writings include *Poemas* (1942), *Transfiguración de Jesús en el Monte* (1947), *Las miradas perdidas 1944–1950* (1951), *Visitaciones* (1970), *Créditos de Charlot* (1990), *Habana de Centro* (1996) and *Darío, Martí y lo germinal americano* (2001). Won the National Literature Prize (1990).

GARCIA-O'BRIEN, Tanya (c. 1973—). American skysurfer. Name variations: Tanya Garcia; Tanya Garcia O'Brien. Born Tanya Garcia, c. 1973; m. Craig O'Brien (her camera flyer). ❖ Began sky-diving (1993); received gold medals in skysurfing: US National championships (1998 and 2000) and World Skysurfing championships (1999 and 2001).

GARCÍA-ORCOYEN TORMO, Cristina (1948—). Spanish politician. Name variations: Cristina Garcia. Born Jan 2, 1948, in Madrid, Spain. ❖ Member (1992–95) and vice-chair (1992–94) of the European Consultative Foru on the Environment; as a member of the European People's Party (Christian Democrats) and European Democrats, elected to 5th European Parliament (1999–2004).

GARDE, Betty (1905–1989). American stage, radio, tv and screen actress. Born Sept 19, 1905, in Philadelphia, Pennsylvania; died Dec 25, 1989, in Sherman Oaks, California; m. Frank Lennon. ❖ Made NY debut as Alma Borden in *Easy Come, Easy Go* (1925); other NY appearances include *The Primrose Path*, *Agatha Sue I Love You*, and as the original Aunt Eller in *Oklahoma!* (1943), repeating the role in many revivals; films include *Call Northside 777*, *Caged* and *The Wonderful World of the Brothers Grimm*; spent many years on radio, primarily with "Lux Radio Theatre" and Orson Welles' Mercury Players, and appeared frequently on tv.

GARDELLA, Tess (1897–1950). Italian-American comedic singer. Name variations: Aunt Jemima. Born 1897 in Wilkes-Barre, Pennsylvania; died Jan 3, 1950, in Brooklyn, NY. ❖ Known professionally as Aunt Jemima (performed in blackface), appeared in nightclubs, vaudeville, George White's *Scandals* and as Queenie in *Showboat* and its revival (1927 and 1932).

GARDEN, Mary (1874–1967). Scottish-born American soprano. Born in Aberdeen, Scotland, Feb 20, 1874; died in Aberdeen, Jan 3, 1967; attended private school in Aberdeen; never married. ❖ Brought to America while still young, lived in Brooklyn, NY, and Chicopee, MA, before family settled in Chicago; studied violin and piano; at 16, began voice lessons with Sarah Robinson Duff; in Paris, studied with Antonio Trabadello and Lucien Fugère and was sponsored by Sybil Sanderson; stepped into title role of *Louise*, when leading soprano took ill, creating a sensation and becoming a permanent member of the Opéra Comique, performing in *La Traviata, La Fille Du Tambour-Major, L'Ouragon* and the world premiere of *Pelléas et Mélisande* by Claude Debussy, which became her signature role; made US debut at Hammerstein's Manhattan Opera House in American premiere of Massenet's *Thaïs* (1907), remaining there until 1910 and appearing in Strauss' *Salome,* stunning audiences as much with her erotic performance of the Dance of the Seven Veils as with her singing (1909); joined Chicago Opera Company, appearing in numerous roles, including Fiora in Italo Montemezzi's *The Love of Three Kings* and the title role in *Monna Vanna,* by Henri Février; became artistic director there (1921–22), the 1st woman to become the director of a major opera company; retired from the stage (1931) at the height of career. ❖ See also autobiography, *Mary Garden's Story* (Simon & Schuster, 1951); and *Women in World History.*

GARDENER, Helen Hamilton (1853–1925). American author, feminist, suffragist, and federal civil service commissioner. Name variations: Alice Chenoweth; Alice Smart. Born Alice Chenoweth in Winchester, Virginia, Jan 21, 1853; died in Washington, DC, July 26, 1925; 3rd daughter and youngest of 6 children of Reverend Alfred G. Chenowith (abolitionist and itinerant Methodist preacher) and Katherine A. (Peel) Chenoweth; graduated from the Cincinnati Normal School, 1873; studied biology at Columbia University; m. Charles S. Smart (school commissioner of Ohio), 1875 (died 1901); m. Colonel Selden Allen Day (retired army officer), April 9, 1902 (died 1919); no children. ❖ Moved to New York with 1st husband (1878), where she lectured in sociology at the Brooklyn Institute of Arts and Science and contributed articles to newspapers; began giving a series of freethinking lectures which were published as *Men, Women and Gods, and Other Lectures* (1885) under pseudonym Helen Hamilton Gardener, which she eventually adopted as her legal name; came to the attention of feminists (1888) with her famed essay "Sex in Brain," a refutation of a widely publicized claim that female brains were inherently and measurably inferior to male brains; achieved greatest popularity with novel *This Your Son, My Lord?* (1890), an attack on legalized prostitution; also wrote a fictional biography of her father, *An Unofficial Patriot* (1884), which is considered by some to be her best work, as well as *Pray You Sir, Whose Daughter?* (1892) and two collections of short stories, *A Thoughtless Yes* (1890) and *Pushed by Unseen Hands* (1892); became vice president of the Congressional Committee of National American Woman Suffrage Association (1917) and was a central figure in steering the federal suffrage amendment to eventual ratification in 1920; was appointed by Woodrow Wilson to US Civil Service Commission (1920), the 1st woman to hold so high a federal position. ❖ See also *Women in World History.*

GARDIE, Anna (c. 1760–1798). Dominican ballet dancer. Born c. 1760, in Santa Domingo, in Dominican Republic; died July 20, 1798, in New York, NY; married a French music copyist. ❖ Immigrated to US (1790s) and soon made American stage debut in Philadelphia, in *La Fôret Noire;* appeared mainly on New York stages for remainder of career including with Old American Company in *Sophia de Brabant or The False Friend* (1794), *Harlequin's Animation or the Triumph of Mirth* (1795), *The Bird Catcher* (1796), and more; was stabbed to death by husband in what was considered murder-suicide (1798).

GARDINER, Antoinette (1941—). Princess of Jordan. Name variations: Tony or Toni Avril Gardiner; HRH Princess Muna or Mona al-Hussein; also seen as Queen Muna or Mona; Muna Hussein. Born Antoinette Avril Gardiner, April 25, 1941, in Chelmondiston, Ipswich, Suffolk, England; dau. of Col. Walter Percy Gardiner and Doris Elizabeth (Sutton) Gardiner; became the 2nd wife of Hussein Ibn Talal (Jordan's King Hussein, r. 1953–1999), May 25, 1961 (div. Dec 21, 1971); children: twin daughters, Zein and Aisha (b. 1968); sons Faisal (b. 1963) and Abdullah II (b. 1962, king of Jordan, r. 1999—). ❖ Was working as a secretary on the set of *Lawrence of Arabia* in the Jordanian desert when she met Hussein; on marriage, converted to Islam and took the name Muna al-Hussein.

GARDINER, Kate (1885–1974). New Zealand mountaineer. Born on Sept 21, 1885, at Wavertree, Lancashire, England; died Jan 29, 1974, in Hastings, New Zealand; dau. of Frederick Gardiner (shipowner) and Alice (Evans) Gardiner. ❖ Internationally recognized premier climber, was the 8th woman to climb Mt Hood (1928); spent summers climbing in New Zealand and remainder of year climbing mountains in Canada and Switzerland; barely survived being stranded during Mt. Tasman climb by sudden storm but returned a year later to successfully be 2nd woman to make ascent (1932–33); worked as commandant of auxiliary convalescent unit in England during World War II. ❖ See also *Dictionary of New Zealand Biography* (Vol. 4).

GARDINER, Lady (1905–1991). *See Box, Muriel.*

GARDINER, Lisa (c. 1896–1958). American ballet dancer and teacher. Born c. 1896, in Washington, DC; died Nov 4, 1958, in Washington, DC. ❖ Toured with company of Anna Pavlova where she worked with Ivan Clustine and Alexander Volinine; performed in *Mecca* on Broadway (1922); trained intermittently with Mikhail Fokine as well as with Roshanara in Indian dance styles; with Mary Day, founded the Washington School of Ballet (1944); also had her own company. Choreographed *The Dance of the Hours* (1936), *An Afternoon in Vienna* (c. 1936) and *Capriccio Espagnol* (c. 1939).

GARDINER, Margaret (1904–2005). English art patron. Born April 22, 1904, in Berlin, Germany, where her Egyptologist father was working; died Jan 2, 2005; dau. of Hedwig and Sir Alan Gardiner; attended Newnham College, Cambridge; children: (with microbiologist J.D. Bernal) son Martin. ❖ Best known as the founder of the Pier Arts Centre in Orkney; often supported such artists and writers as Hepworth, Ben Nicholson, Louis MacNeice, W.H. Auden and Solly Zuckerman. ❖ See also memoirs *Footprints on Malekula* (1987) and *A Scatter of Memories* (1988).

GARDINER, Marguerite (1789–1849). *See Blessington, Marguerite, Countess of.*

GARDINER, Muriel (1901–1985). American psychoanalyst and resistance leader. Name variations: Muriel Buttinger. Born Helen Muriel Morris in Chicago, Illinois, Nov 1901; died in Princeton, New Jersey, Feb 6, 1985; dau. of Edward and Helen Swift Morris (heirs in meat packing industry); graduated from Wellesley College, 1922; attended Oxford University, 1923–25; University of Vienna, MD, 1938; m. Julian Gardiner, May 20, 1930 (div. 1932); m. Joseph Buttinger

(Austrian Socialist leader and writer), Aug 1, 1939; children: (1st m.) Constance Gardiner. ❖ Psychoanalyst who played an important role in the anti-Nazi Austrian Socialist movement (1930s) and who, many feel, was the basis for Lillian Hellman's Julia in *Pentimento;* enrolled at University of Vienna (1932) and was shocked by the accelerating aggressiveness of Viennese anti-Semitism; when the Socialist movement was bloodily suppressed in Austria (Feb 1934), assumed the code name of "Mary" Gardiner and became a member of the Socialist underground, lending her apartment to refugees from the police as well as hiding fugitives in her cottage in Sulz, deep in the Vienna Woods; helped 100s to escape the Nazis (1934–38); after successfully passing her medical examinations at University of Vienna, married and returned to US (1939); with husband, worked to bring as many German and Austrian political and racial refugees to America as possible; after World War II, had a busy psychoanalytical practice, taught at various universities, and published several well-received books in the field of psychology. Received the Cross of Honor 1st Class from Austrian government. ❖ See also *Code Name "Mary": Memoirs of an American Woman in the Austrian Underground* (Yale University Press, 1983); and *Women in World History.*

GARDNER, Ava (1922–1990). American actress. Born Ava Lavinia Gardner on Dec 24, 1922, in Brogden, North Carolina; died of pneumonia at age 67, Jan 25, 1990, at her flat in London, near Hyde Park; youngest of seven children of Jonas Gardner (died 1938) and Mary Gardner; m. Mickey Rooney (actor), 1942 (div. 1943); m. Artie Shaw (musician), 1945 (div. 1947); m. Frank Sinatra, 1951 (div. 1957); no children. ❖ Screen actress, one of MGM's most popular stars, whose candor often had Hollywood wincing; after a trip to New York City to visit eldest sister Beatrice Tarr (1940), was called to MGM casting office for a screen test and sent to Hollywood; appeared in 1st film *H. M. Pullham, Esq.* (1941), but was confined to bit parts and walk-ons until catching the public's attention in *The Killers* (1946), followed by *The Hucksters* (1947) and *One Touch of Venus* (1948); for the next decade, held the position of Hollywood's reigning love goddess, whose escapades and *amours* were the delight of scandal sheets in US and Europe; appeared in *East Side/West Side* (1949), *Show Boat* (1951), *Pandora and the Flying Dutchman* (1951), *The Snows of Kilimanjaro* (1952), and *The Band Wagon* (1953); nominated for an Academy Award for her work in *Mogambo* (1953); moved to Spain (mid-1950s) and lived there for some years while appearing in a number of well-received international film productions, including *Bhowani Junction* (1956), *The Little Hut* (1957), *The Sun Also Rises* (1957), *The Naked Maja* (1959), *On the Beach* (1959), *55 Days at Peking* (1963), *Seven Days in May* (1964), *The Night of the Iguana* (1964), *The Bible* (1966), *Mayerling* (1968), and her signature role in *The Barefoot Contessa* (1954); moved to London (c. 1970); made tv debut in the mini-series "AD" (1985) and had a recurring role as Ruth Galveston in the series "Knots Landing"; other films include *The Life and Times of Judge Roy Bean* (1972), *Earthquake* (1974), *The Blue Bird* (1976), *The Cassandra Crossing* (1951), *The Sentinel* (1977), *City on Fire* (1980), *The Kidnapping of the President* (1980), and *Regina* (1982). ❖ See also *Ava: My Story* (Bantam, 1990); and *Women in World History.*

GARDNER, Briar (1879–1968). *See Gardner, Maria Louisa.*

GARDNER, Edna (1902–1992). *See Whyte, Edna Gardner.*

GARD'NER, Elizabeth Anne (1858–1926). New Zealand teacher, administrator, and writer. Name variations: Elizabeth Anne Milne. Born Elizabeth Anne Milne, Dec 24, 1858, in Allerum, Sweden; died June 5, 1926, at Christchurch, New Zealand; dau. of Henry Alexander Milne (copper mill owner) and Elizabeth (Price) Milne; m. Richard Gard'ner (railroad agent), 1880. ❖ Became skilled in culinary and household arts while in Sweden and introduced study of home science in New Zealand after immigrating with husband (1887); named superintendent of School of Domestic Instruction for Christchurch (1894); when school merged with Christchurch Technical College, served as head of domestic science department (1907–11); was 1st principal of Girls' Training Hostel (1913–16); co-compiled *New Zealand Domestic Cookery Book* and wrote *Recipes for Use in School Cookery Classes.* ❖ See also *Dictionary of New Zealand Biography* (Vol. 3).

GARDNER, Frances (1913–1989). English physician. Name variations: Dame Frances Gardner, Frances Valerie Gardner. Born Frances Violet Gardner in 1913 in England; died 1989 in England; Westfield College London, BS, 1935; London (Royal Free Hospital) School of Medicine for Women, MB, BS, 1940, MD, 1943; m. George Qvist (surgeon), 1958 (d. 1981). ❖ Appointed medical registrar at Royal Free Hospital

(1943–45) and served as clinical assistant in Nuffield Department of Medicine, Oxford (1945–46); became research fellow in medicine at Harvard University (1946) and consultant physician at Royal Free Hospital (1946–78); held consultant posts at Hospital for Women, Mothers' Hospital and Royal National Throat, Nose and Ear Hospital; served as dean of Royal Free Hospital School of Medicine (1962–75) and then as institution's president (1979–89); contributed papers on cardiovascular and other medical subjects to *British Medical Journal, The Lancet* and *British Heart Journal;* served on numerous medical committees, including General Medical Council (1971); honored posthumously by Royal Free Hospital School of Medicine when student residence hall was named after her (2004). Awarded Dame of British Empire (DBE, 1975).

GARDNER, Helen (1878–1946). American art historian. Born Mar 17, 1878, in Manchester, New Hampshire; died June 4, 1946, in Chicago, Illinois; dau. of Charles Frederick Gardner (merchant tailor and Baptist deacon) and Marth Washington (Cunningham) Gardner; sister of Effie Gardner (principal at Brooks Classical School); University of Chicago, AB, 1901, MA in art history, 1917. ❖ Developed art history curriculum (early 1920s) at Art Institute of Chicago where she later went on to become professor and head of art history department (1933); wrote art history textbook *Art Through the Ages* (1926) which was widely used for many years; retired from Art Institute (1943); other writings include *Understanding the Arts* (1932).

GARDNER, Helen (1884–1968). American actress and director. Name variations: Miss Gardner. Born Helen Louise Gardner, Sept 2, 1884; died Nov 20, 1968, in Orlando, Florida; m. Duncan C. Pell, 1902; m. Charles Gaskill (director). ❖ Made film debut with Vitagraph (1911); with husband Charles Gaskill, was the 1st actress to form her own company (1912); directed at Vitagraph and elsewhere; as actress, films include *Becky Sharp, Vanity Fair, Cleopatra, The Strange Story of Sylvia Gray, The Sleep of Cyma Roget* and *Sandra.*

GARDNER, Helen Louise (1908–1986). British literary critic and scholar. Born Helen Louise Gardner, Feb 13, 1908, in London, England; died June 4, 1986, in Oxford; dau. of Charles Henry Gardner and Helen Mary Roadnight Cockman Gardner; St. Hilda's College, Oxford, BA, 1929, MA (1935). ❖ One of most important 20th-century critics, wrote works on English poetry, religion and literature, and poetic interpretation; was a fellow of St. Hilda's (1942–66) and later honorary fellow of Lady Margaret Hall and St. Hilda's; invited to US and delivered lectures including Charles Eliot Norton Lectures at Harvard (1979–80); writings include *The Art of T.S. Eliot* (1949), *The Business of Criticism* (1959), *King Lear* (1967), *Religion and Literature* (1971), *The Waste Land* (1972), *In Defence of the Imagination* (1982), *The Metaphysical Poets* (1985), and *The Noble Moor* (1990); member of Royal Academy, American Academy of Arts and Sciences, and Royal Society of Literature.

GARDNER, Isabella (1915–1981). American poet. Name variations: Isabella Stewart Gardner. Born Isabella Stewart Gardner, Sept 7, 1915, in Newton, Massachusetts; died July 7, 1981, in New York, NY; niece of art collector Isabella Stewart Gardner (1840–1924) and cousin of poet Robert Lowell; attended Foxcroft School; attended Embassy Theatre School; m. 2nd husband Maurice Seymour (div.); divorced 3rd husband (1957); m. 4th husband Allen Tate (poet and critic), 1959 (div. 1966). ❖ Distinguished poet, 1st studied acting at Embassy Theatre School in London under Eileen Thorndike; acted professionally (1939–1944) in both England and US, primarily in character and comedy roles; moved to Chicago with 2nd husband during WWII; turned attention away from theater and towards poetry (1947); became associate editor of nation's most prominent poetry magazine, *Poetry*, working under Karl Shapiro (1951); published 1st book of poems, *Birthdays from the Ocean* (1955), which was received favorably by critics; wrote 2 significant volumes of poetry, *The Looking Glass* (1961) and *West of Childhood* (1965); gave readings throughout US and Europe, often with Allen Tate; published broadside *Salt* (1975); published *That Was Then: New and Selected Poems* (1979), which was nominated for American Book Award; had a strong influence on younger writers, particularly women poets, including Sylvia Plath; published posthumously, *Isabella Gardner: The Collected Poems* (1990). Received 1st Walt Whitman Citation of Merit (1981).

GARDNER, Isabella Stewart (1840–1924). American art collector and socialite. Name variations: Mrs. Jack. Born Isabella Stewart in New York City on April 14, 1840; died in Boston, Massachusetts, July 17, 1924; eldest and one of four children (two girls and two boys) of David (businessman) and Adelia (Smith) Stewart; educated by private tutors and at a small private girls' school in New York; attended a finishing school in Paris; m. John Lowell Gardner (businessman), April 10, 1860 (died 1898); children: one son Jackie, who died at age two. ❖ One of America's most important art collectors, designed and built an elaborate Italian palace, Fenway Court, as a residence and to house her remarkable collection of fine art (1902); upon her death (1924), left Fenway Court to the city of Boston "for the education and enjoyment of the public" which is now known as the Isabella Stewart Gardner Museum; during her life, took delight in shocking conservative Boston society, was painted by paramour John Singer Sargent, enlisted Bernard Berenson to advise and assist her in acquisitions, and surrounded herself with a who's who, including Emma Eames, Nellie Melba, Edith Wharton, Julia Ward Howe, Ignace Paderewski, Henry Irving, Henry James, James Russell Lowell, and Oliver Wendell Holmes. Among American collections, the Gardner Museum has been ranked fourth, after the Metropolitan and the Frick in New York, and the National Gallery in Washington. ❖ See also Morris Carter, *Isabella Stewart Gardner and Fenway Court* (1925); Douglass Shand-Tucci, *The Art of Scandal: The Life and Times of Isabella Stewart Gardner* (HarperCollins, 1997); Louise Hall Tharp, *Mrs. Jack* (Little, Brown, 1965); and *Women in World History.*

GARDNER, Mrs. Jack (1840–1924). *See Gardner, Isabella Stewart.*

GARDNER, Janet (1962—). American musician. Name variations: Janet Patricia Gardner; Vixen. Born Janet Patricia Gardner on Mar 17, 1962, in Juneau, Alaska. ❖ Became lead singer and guitarist for all-girl pop-metal band Vixen (c. 1980); with band, played clubs and military bases, endured numerous personnel changes, and appeared in film *Hardbodies* (1984); playing with a more solid lineup (1987), signed contract with EMI and released debut album *Vixen* (1988), which went gold and included Top-40 hits "Cryin'" and "Edge of a Broken Heart"; also released *Rev It Up* (1990), which included the hit, "How Much Love"; saw band split up (early 1990s), then re-form with minor changes (1997) to release *Tangerine* (1998), only to disband again; joined Jan Kuehnemund and Roxy Petrucci to re-form Vixen with original lineup (2001).

GARDNER, Julia Anna (1882–1960). American geologist. Born in 1882; died in Bethesda, Maryland, 1960; the only child of Charles Henry (physician) and Julia M. (Brackett) Gardner; earned a bachelor's degree from Bryn Mawr, 1905, master's degree, 1907; Johns Hopkins University, PhD in paleontology, 1911; never married; no children. ❖ Taught at Johns Hopkins and did research on invertebrate paleontology at Maryland geological survey; after a brief stint as a volunteer nurse during World War I, joined US Geological Survey (USGS) and remained there for the rest of her career; moved to Texas to study Eocene invertebrates for USGS Coastal Plain division (1920), advancing steadily through the ranks; during World War II, identified the origin of a number of Japanese bombs by analyzing the sand used as ballast in the incendiary balloons, specifically the small shells contained in the sand; following the war, studied the geology of Japan and Pacific Islands, mapping the area for the Office of the Chief of Engineers; served as president of Paleontological Society (1952), and vice president of Geological Society (1953). ❖ See also *Women in World History.*

GARDNER, Kay (1941–2002). American conductor and composer. Name variations: Kay Louise Gardner. Born Kay Louise Gardner, Feb 28, 1941 in Long Island, NY; died Aug 28, 2002 in Bangor, Maine; attended University of Michigan and State University of New York, Stony Brook; m. Colleen Fitzgerald, 1998; children: Jenifer Wilson Smith and Juliana Smith. ❖ Leading authority on curative use of music and sound, helped found feminist and openly lesbian women's band, Lavender Jane (1972), releasing 1973 album with Patches Attom; developed lyrical, improvisational style; produced numerous recordings of original music, including solo flute meditations, music for small ensembles, orchestral compositions and large choral works, including *Amazon* (1994), *Drone Zone* (1996) and *My Mother's Garden* (1998); traveled worldwide with concerts and musical healing workshops; published *Sounding the Inner Landscape: Music as Medicine* (1990) as well as *The Big Book of Relaxation* (1994); had works performed by Kansas City Symphony, National Women's Symphony and Bournemouth Sinfonietta in England, among others; ordained as priestess in Fellowship of Isis by movement's founder Lady Olivia Robertson in Ireland (1998) and then built Temple of Feminine Divine in Bangor. Received Maine Composers' Festival, 1st Prize in Composition (1982), Jane Schliessmann Award for Excellence in Women's Music (1989), honorary doctorate and Maryann Hartman Award from University of Maine (1995).

GARDNER, Margaret (1844–1929). New Zealand landowner and mill owner. Name variations: Margaret McKinley. Born Margaret McKinley, Sept 8, 1844, at Newmains, Lanarkshire, Scotland; died June 19, 1929; dau. of James McKinley (colliery manager) and Mary (McNeil) McKinley; m. George Gleigg Gardner (ship's officer), 1866 (died 1885); children: 10. ❖ Worked as dairy maid in Scotland; immigrated to New Zealand (1863); accumulated large parcels of land, established farm and substantial flour mill (1880s); after husband's death, increased land holdings for farming. ❖ See also *Dictionary of New Zealand Biography* (Vol. 1).

GARDNER, Maria Louisa (1879–1968). New Zealand potter and speech therapist. Name variations: Briar Gardner. Born on July 29, 1879, at Hobsonville, Auckland, New Zealand; died Oct 20, 1968, in Auckland; dau. of John Gardner (farmer) and Louisa (Clark) Gardner; Elam School of Art, 1920s. ❖ First learned to throw pots by watching expert potter work at family's firm and later studied sculpture and Maori design at Elam School of Art (1920s); held exhibition of her pottery at Auckland Society of Arts (1930) which led to many other successful exhibitions and a high demand for her work (1940s); had to abort career because of arthritic hands; became speech therapist working in radio and film in Sydney, Australia. ❖ See also *Dictionary of New Zealand Biography* (Vol. 4).

GARDNER, Mary Sewall (1871–1961). American nurse and social reformer. Born in Newton, Massachusetts, Feb 5, 1871; died Feb 20, 1961, in Providence, Rhode Island; dau. of William Sewall Gardner (superior court judge) and Mary (Thornton) Gardner (descendant of Declaration of Independence signer Matthew Thornton, died 1875); stepdau. of Sarah Gardner, a pioneering woman physician; had half-brother, Charles Thornton Davis; attended Miss Porter's School, in Farmington, Connecticut; graduated from Newport Hospital Training School for Nurses (1905); never married; no children. ❖ Pioneer in the field of public health nursing, who was the force behind the founding of the National Organization for Public Health Nursing; became superintendent of nurses (later director) of the recently created Providence District Nursing Association (PDNA, 1905); with Lillian Wald, founded the National Organization of Public Health Nursing (NOPHN, 1912), serving as its president (1913–16); published the textbook, *Public Health Nursing* (1916), which became the Bible of nurses throughout US, appearing in a series of revised editions and printings until 1947; during World War I, served 1st as director of the American Red Cross' bureau of public health nursing, and then overseas in war-torn Italy; served as chair of the standing committee on public health nursing of the International Council of Nurses (1925–33). Received Walter Burns Saunders medal for distinguished service to nursing (1931); elected to American Nursing Association's Nursing Hall of Fame (1986). ❖ See also *Women in World History*.

GARDNER, Maureen (1928–1974). English track-and-field athlete. Name variations: Maureen Dyson. Born Maureen Angela Gardner, Nov 12, 1928, in Oxford, England; died Sept 1974; m. Geoffrey Dyson (Olympic coach). ❖ Broke the British 80-meter hurdles record, 1st at Chadwick in the National championships, then later in Paris, Luxemburg, and Motspur Park all within one week (1947); won the silver medal in the 80-meter hurdles at London Olympics (1948).

GARDNER, Miriam (1930–1999). See *Bradley, Marion Zimmer*.

GARDNER, Robyn (1964—). See *Grey-Gardner, Robyn*.

GARDNER, Suzi (1960—). American rock musician. Name variations: L7. Born Aug 1, 1960, in Altus, Oklahoma. ❖ Guitarist and singer, joined forces with Donita Sparks (1985); enlisted bassist Jennifer Finch (1986) and drummer Roy Koutsky to form punk-metal rock band L7; with group, released self-titled debut album on Epitaph Records (1988); added Demetra (Dee) Plakas (1988) to band as drummer, replacing Koutsky; toured US and Britain (1988) as opening act for Nirvana; signed with Sup Pop Records and released *Smell the Magic* (1990) and hit single "Shove/Packin' A Rod"; had major success with *Bricks Are Heavy* (1992) on Slash records, featuring international pop hit "Pretend We're Dead"; after Finch went solo (1996), added bass player Gail Greenwood for album *The Beauty Process: Triple Platinum* (1997) which also featured Greta Brinkman; released *Omaha to Osaka, International Pop Underground Convention* (1991), *Virus 100* (1992) and *Slap Happy*; appeared in mockumentary *The Beauty Process* (1998).

GARE, Nene (1919–1994). Australian novelist. Name variations: Doris Violet May Wadham. Born May 9, 1919, in Adelaide, South Australia; died May 29, 1994, in Perth, Western Australia; dau. of John Wadham and Mary Wadham; m. Frank Gare, 1941; children: 3. ❖ Moved with husband to Papua New Guinea (1946–48) and then to banana plantation in Carnarvon, Western Australia; worked as artist and was involved in People for Nuclear Disarmament; published *The Fringe Dwellers* (1961), which was praised for its sensitive account of the life of part-aborigines and filmed (1986); other works include *Green Gold* (1963), *Bend to the Wind* (1978), *A House with Verandahs* (1980), and *An Island Away* (1981); published stories and reviews in *Bulletin, Meanjin, Overland, West Australian* and *Canberra Times*.

GAREAU, France (1967—). Canadian runner. Born April 15, 1967, in Canada. ❖ At Los Angeles Olympics, won a silver medal in 4 x 100-meter relay (1984).

GAREAU, Jacqueline (1953—). French-Canadian marathon runner. Born Mar 10, 1952, in L'Annonciation, Quebec, Canada. ❖ Won National Capital Marathon and Montreal International (1979); placed 3rd in NY City Marathon (1980); won the Boston Marathon (1980), once Rosie Ruiz, who had only run the last half-mile, was eliminated as victor 8 days later; won Los Angeles Marathon (1984).

GAREFREKES, Kerstin (1979—). German soccer player. Born Sept 4, 1979, in Ibbenburen, Germany. ❖ Won FIFA World Cup (2003); midfielder, won a team bronze medal at Athens Olympics (2004).

GARFIELD, Lucretia (1832–1918). American first lady. Name variations: (nickname) Crete. Born Lucretia Rudolph on April 19, 1832, in Garretsville, Ohio; died Mar 13, 1918, in South Pasadena, California; dau. of Arabella Green (Mason) Rudolph and Zebulon Rudolph (founder of Hiram College); attended Geauga Seminary and Hiram College; married James Abram Garfield (1831–1881, later president of US), Nov 11, 1858, in Hiram, Ohio; children: Eliza (1860–1863); Harry Augustus Garfield (1863–1942, president of Williams College and fuel administrator during World War I); James Rudolph Garfield (1865–1950, secretary of the Interior under Theodore Roosevelt); Mary Garfield (1867–1947); Irvin McDowell Garfield (1870–1951); Abram Garfield (1872–1958); Edward (1874–1876). ❖ A private person, who did not socialize easily, held progressive views on women's rights; following husband's inauguration as president (Jan 1881), undertook long hours of research in the Library of Congress, intent on restoring the White House with historical accuracy; was stricken with malaria (May 1881); while recuperating at summer home in Elberon, New Jersey, received news that husband had been gunned down by a disappointed office seeker (July 2, 1881); kept vigil over husband until he died of his wounds (Sept 19, 1881); survived him by 36 years, living comfortably in Mentor, Ohio, meticulously supervising the preservation of his papers and leaving letters revealing early troubled years of their marriage intact. ❖ See also *Women in World History*.

GARFIELD, Viola (1899–1983). American cultural anthropologist. Name variations: Viola Edmundson Garfield. Born Viola Edmundson, 1899; died 1983; dau. of William Henry Edmundson and Mary Louanna (Dean) Edmundson; earned teaching certificate at Bellingham Normal School (now Western Washington University) 1 University of Washington, BA, 1931, MA; Columbia University, PhD, 1939; m. Charles Garfield, 1924. ❖ While working with the Bureau of Indian Affairs, taught Tsimshian children at New Metlakatla (southeastern Alaska); conducted fieldwork at New Metlakatla on Tsimshian marriage patterns; studied with Franz Boas and Ruth Benedict at Columbia University; served as associate professor at University of Washington; published classics of North Pacific ethnography, including works on economics of slavery, Angoon clans, trans-Pacific moieties, and totem poles and mythology; known largely for definitive studies of Tsimshian in British Columbia and Alaska.

GARFIELD, Vivien (1924–2003). See *Alcock, Vivien*.

GARG, Mridula (1938—). Indian novelist and short-story writer. Born 1938 in Calcutta, India. ❖ Wrote primarily in Hindi and translated some works into English; writings include *Uske Hisse Ki Dhoop, Anitya, Kath Gulab, Tukra Tukra Aadmi* and *Ek Aur Ajnabi*. Received Maharaja Veer Singh Award (1975) and Uttar Pradesh Hindi Sansthan Sahitya Bhushan award (1999).

GARIBALDI, Anita (c. 1821–1849). Brazilian-Italian revolutionary. Name variations: Aninha; Annita Bentos. Pronunciation: Gah-ree-BAL-dee. Born Ana Maria de Jésus Riberio da Silva around 1821, in

Morrinhos, Brazil; died at Guiccioli farm, Mandriole, near Ravenna, Italy, Aug 4, 1849; dau. of Bento Ribeiro da Silva de Jesus (peasant) and Maria Antonia; started to learn to read and write a few months before her death; learned to sign her name; m. Manoel Duarte di Aguiar (shoemaker), Aug 30, 1835; m. Giuseppe Garibaldi (Italian nationalist and guerrilla leader), Mar 26, 1842; children (2nd m.): Menotti (b. Sept 16, 1840); Rosita (b. end of 1841 or, according to other sources, 1843 and died young); Teresita or Teresa Garibaldi (b. Nov 1844 or 1845); Ricciotti (b. Feb 24, 1847). ❖ Hero of Brazil and Italy, possessed of exceptional physical and emotional courage, who actively participated in husband Giuseppe Garibaldi's struggles for liberty and national self-determination in South America and Italy; met Garibaldi at Laguna in southern Brazil while he was in exile from Sardinia and had taken up the cause of Brazilian independence (Oct 1839); fought in naval battle of Imbituba (Nov 3, 1839); fought in naval battle and involved in evacuation of Laguna (Nov 15, 1839); caught and escaped; retreated through the mountains of Rio Grande do Sul (late fall-winter, 1840–41), suffering great hardships; with Giuseppe, stayed in Montevideo, Uruguay (1842–47); hearing of nationalist and liberal demonstrations in Italy, sailed for Italy (Jan 1848), intent on uniting the different Italian states into one country (Giuseppe was to follow); arrived in Genoa where she was greeted by cheering crowds, crying, "Long live Garibaldi! Long live the family of our Garibaldi!"; with husband, stayed in Nice, the home of Giuseppe's mother (Apr–Oct 1848); left Genoa with Giuseppe and his volunteers for Livorno (Oct 24, 1848); stayed with husband at Rieti, near Rome (Feb–April 1849); traveled from Nice to Rome, arriving during the siege (June 26, 1849); set out on retreat northward from Rome (July 2, 1849); developed a fever, perhaps malaria, and died. ❖ See also Dorothy Bryant, *Anita, Anita: Garibaldi of the New World* (Ata, 1993); Giuseppe Garibaldi, *Autobiography* (Vols. I and II, translated by A. Werner, Walter Smith & Innes, 1889); *Anita Garibaldi* (Italian film), starring Anna Magnani and Raf Vallone (1954); and *Women in World History*.

GARILHE, Renee (1923—). French fencer. Born June 15, 1923, in France. ❖ At Melbourne Olympics, won a bronze medal in individual foil (1956).

GARISCH-CULMBERGER, Renate (1939—). East German track-and-field athlete. Name variations: Renate Culmberger. Born Jan 24, 1939, in Germany. ❖ At Tokyo Olympics, won a silver medal in the shot put (1964).

GARLAND, Judy (1922–1969). American singer, dancer, and actress. Born Frances Ethel Gumm, June 10, 1922, in Grand Rapids, Minnesota; died in London, England, June 22, 1969, the official coroner's report listing an overdose of sleeping pills as cause of death; youngest of 3 daughters of Frank and Ethel (Milne) Gumm (both vaudeville performers); m. David Rose (musician), 1941 (div. 1945); m. Vincente Minnelli (director), 1946 (div. 1951); m. Sid Luft (producer), 1952 (div. 1957); m. Mark Herron (actor), 1965 (div. 1967); m. Mickey Deans (nightclub owner), 1968; children: (2nd m.) Liza Minnelli (b. 1946); (3rd m.) Lorna Luft (b. 1952); Joseph Luft (b. 1955). ❖ Show-business icon in films and on stage for 3 decades, who had a devoted worldwide following; made stage debut with sisters at age 3 (1925); signed a movie contract with MGM at age 13 (1935); secured position as a Hollywood star at age 17 with portrayal of Dorothy in MGM's musical *The Wizard of Oz* (1939); appeared in a string of lavish MGM musicals to great acclaim; driven by professional and family pressures, began to suffer from depression and anxiety, struggling with addictions to various medications for the rest of her life; films include *Broadway Melody of 1938* (1937), *Everybody Sing* (1938), *Love Finds Andy Hardy* (1938), *Babes in Arms* (1939), *Strike Up the Band* (1940), *For Me and My Gal* (1942), *Presenting Lily Mars* (1943), *As Thousands Cheer* (1943), *Meet Me in St. Louis* (1944), *The Clock* (1945), *The Harvey Girls* (1946), *Ziegfeld Follies* (1946), *Till the Clouds Roll By* (1946), *The Pirate* (1948), *Easter Parade* (1948), *Words and Music* (1948), *In the Good Old Summertime* (1949), *Summer Stock* (1950), *A Star Is Born* (1954), *Judgment at Nuremberg* (1961), *A Child Is Waiting* (1963), *I Could Go on Singing* (1963). ❖ See also Frank Shipman, *Judy Garland* (London: Fourth Estate, 1992); David Shipman, *Judy Garland: The Secret Life of an American Legend* (Hyperion, 1993); (tv movie) "Life with Judy Garland: Me and My Shadows," starring Judy Davis (2001); and *Women in World History*.

GARLICK, Eunice Harriett (1883–1951). New Zealand photographer. Name variations: Harriett Eunice Garlick, Una Garlick. Born on Feb 15, 1883, at Mount Eden, Auckland, New Zealand; died Mar 17, 1951, in Remuera, New Zealand; dau. of Richard Knight Garlick (karui-gum merchant) and Ellen (Green) Garlick. ❖ Initially photographed family and friends and began to receive commissions for portraits and other work (early 1900s); became active in photographic societies, winning many competitions, and gaining recognition for her skill (1920s); saw many of her prints accepted by international salons in London, Paris, Boston, and Vancouver; became associate member of Royal Photographic Society of Great Britain; best remembered for series of portraits of Maori women. ❖ See also *Dictionary of New Zealand Biography* (Vol. 4).

GARLICK, Harriett Eunice (1883–1951). *See Garlick, Eunice Harriett.*

GARLICK, Una (1883–1951). *See Garlick, Eunice Harriett.*

GARMSON, Aileen (c. 1861–1951). New Zealand labor unionist and political activist. Name variations: Aileen Anna Maria Cooke, Aileen Anna Maria Douglas, Aileen Anna Maria Wrack. Born Aileen Anna Maria Douglas, c. 1861–1863, in Co. Cavan, Ireland; died May 30, 1951, in Auckland, New Zealand; dau. of John Douglas (miller) and Bridget (Murphy) Douglas; m. Frederick Garmson (carpenter), 1880 (div. 1898); m. Charles Stephenson Wrack (mariner), 1899 (div. 1917); m. Lindsay Cooke (publican), 1917 (died 1931); children: (1st m.) 1 son and 3 daughters. ❖ Arrived in New Zealand at 17 and worked as domestic servant; active in shearers' union, and member of Knights of Labor at Christchurch (mid-1890s); advocated for working-class women on various issues; ran as Independent Liberal in 1st general election permitting women to participate, campaigning for higher taxes on large estates and free education for all. ❖ See also *Dictionary of New Zealand Biography* (Vol. 2).

GARNER, Helen (1942—). Australian novelist and short-story writer. Born 1942 in Geelong, Victoria, Australia; graduated from University of Melbourne (1965). ❖ Worked as a teacher; writings include *Monkey grip* (1977), *Honour and Other People's Children: Two Stories* (1980), *The Children's Bach* (1984), *Postcards from Surfers* (1985), *Cosmo Cosmolino* (1992), and *My Hard heart: Selected Fictions* (1998); nonfiction includes *La Mama, the Story of a Theatre* (1988) and *The Feel of Steel* (2001); also wrote screenplays including *Two Friends* (1986) and *The Last Days of Chez Nous* (1992). Received National Book Council Award (1978) and New South Wales Premier's Literary Award (1986); also won Walkley Award for feature journalism for controversial story in *Time* magazine on Daniel Valerio case.

GARNER, Peggy Ann (1931–1984). American actress. Born in Canton, Ohio, Feb 3, 1931; died in Woodland Hills, California, Oct 16, 1984; m. Richard Hayes (actor), 1951 (div. 1953); m. Albert Salmi (actor), 1956 (div. 1963); m. Kenyon Foster Brown, 1963 (div. 1968); children: (2nd m.) one daughter, Cass Salmi (died 1995). ❖ Launched into a modeling career before she was 6, arrived in Hollywood at 7; made film debut in *Little Miss Thoroughbred* (1938); appeared in small roles before displaying a mature talent in *The Pied Piper* (1942) and *Jane Eyre* (1944), in which she played the young Jane; was cast in the key role of Francie Nolan in Betty Smith's *A Tree Grows in Brooklyn* (1945), for which she won a special Academy Award as the "outstanding child performer of 1945"; despite consistently good performances and a huge teen following, film career was all but over by early 1950s; made New York stage debut in *The Man* (1950); other films include *Nob Hill* (1945), *Junior Miss* (1945), *Home Sweet Homicide* (1946), *Thunder in the Valley* (1947), *Daisy Kenyon* (1947), *The Sign of the Ram* (1948), *Bomba the Jungle Boy* (1949), *The Big Cat* (1949), *Teresa* (1951), *Black Widow* (1954), *The Cat* (1966), and *A Wedding* (1978). ❖ See also *Women in World History*.

GARNER, Sarah (1971—). American rower. Born May 21, 1971, in Madison, Wisconsin; University of Pennsylvania, 1993. ❖ With Christine Collins, won a World championship title (1998) and a bronze medal for lightweight double sculls at Sydney Olympics (2000).

GARNET, Sarah (1831–1911). American schoolteacher and civil-rights activist. Name variations: Sarah J. Smith Thompson Garnet. Born July 31, 1831, in Queens Co., NY; died Sept 17, 1911, in Brooklyn, NY; dau. of Sylvanus Smith (farmer) and Annie (Springstead) Smith; sister of Susan Maria McKinney Steward (physician); m. Rev. James Thompson (died late 1860s); Rev. Henry Highland Garnet, c. 1879 (died 1882); children: (1st m.) 2. ❖ The 1st black woman to hold rank of principal in the New York public-school system, served as principal of grammar school (now PS 80, 1863–1900); founded and led Equal Suffrage Club, small organization of black women based in Brooklyn, NY; served as delegate to 1st Universal Races Congress (London, 1911).

GARNETT, Constance (1862–1946). English translator. Name variations: C.C. Black. Born Constance Clara Black in Brighton, England, Dec 19, 1862; died Dec 17, 1946, in Edenbridge, England; dau. of David Black (coroner) and Clara (Patten) Black; educated by home tutoring; attended Brighton High School, Newnham College Association for Advanced Learning and Education among Women in Cambridge, 1879–83; m. Edward Garnett (writer and literary critic), 1889; children: David (b. 1892). ❖ Translated Ivan Goncharov's *A Common Story* into English (1894), which began a career that over the span of the next 34 years witnessed the publication of 72 volumes of Russian novels, short stories, and plays in very readable English translations; introduced Dostoevsky and Chekhov to English audiences in addition to translating almost all of the writings of Turgenev and many of those of Tolstoy, Herzen, and Gogol; deserves great credit for stimulating the interest of several generations of English-speaking readers in the classics of Russian literature. ❖ See also Carolyn G. Heilbrun, *The Garnett Family: The History of a Literary Family* (Allen & Unwin, 1961); and *Women in World History*.

GARON, Pauline (1900–1965). Canadian-born actress. Born Sept 9, 1900, in Montreal, Quebec, Canada; died Aug 30, 1965, in San Bernardino, California. ❖ Hailed as the "Perfect Flapper," played the lead in Cecil B. De Mille's *Adam's Rib* (1923); other films include *Sonny, Wine of Youth, The Love of Sunya* and *Her Husband's Secretary*.

GARRETT, Betty (1919—). American stage and screen actress, singer, and dancer. Born May 23, 1919, in St. Joseph, Missouri; raised in NY; trained at Neighborhood Playhouse; m. Larry Parks (actor), 1944 (died 1975); children: Garrett Parks (composer), Andrew Parks (actor). ❖ Made stage debut in Mercury Theater production of *Danton's Death* (1938), followed by *Let Freedom Ring, Something for the Boys* and *Beg Borrow or Steal;* danced with the Martha Graham Company and sang in nightclubs and at resorts; made film debut in *Big City* (1948), followed by *Words and Music, Take Me Out to the Ballgame, Neptune's Daughter, On the Town, My Sister Eileen* and *The Shadow on the Window;* when husband Larry Parks was blacklisted during McCarthy era, her career suffered as well; appeared regularly as Irene Lorenzo on tv's "All in the Family" (1973–75) and Edna Bibish, later Mrs. DeFazio, on "Laverne and Shirley" (1976–81); performed in one-woman autobiographical show *No Dogs or Actors Allowed* (1989). Won Donaldson award for *Call Me Mister* (1946). ❖ See also autobiography (with Ron Rapoport) *Betty Garrett and Other Songs* (1997).

GARRETT, Elizabeth (1836–1917). *See Anderson, Elizabeth Garrett.*

GARRETT, Emma (c. 1846–1893). American educator of the deaf. Born in Philadelphia, Pennsylvania, c. 1846; died in Chicago, Illinois, July 18, 1893, jumping from a hotel window; one of at least 6 children of Henry (businessman) and Caroline Rush (Cole) Garrett; younger sister of Mary Smith Garrett (1839–1925); graduated from Alexander Graham Bell's course for teachers of the deaf at Boston University School of Oratory, 1878; never married; no children. ❖ Began teaching at Pennsylvania Institution for the Deaf and Dumb (1878), at Mount Airy; as a champion of Bell's innovative approach of teaching deaf students to speak and read lips instead of signing, was put in charge of the new Oral Branch of the institution (1881); also began to teach summer courses that year in the techniques of speech instruction for other teachers; addressed the convention of American Instructors of the Deaf and Dumb (1882), urging them to support the new vocal method; after convincing civic leaders from Scranton that the new school for the deaf which they were planning should teach the oral method, was named principal of the new facility, called the Pennsylvania Oral School for Deaf-Mutes (1884); headed a campaign for a new school building (completed in 1888); with sister Mary, established the Pennsylvania Home for the Training in Speech of Deaf Children Before They Are of School Age, which opened with 15 children in temporary quarters (later known as the Bala Home). ❖ See also *Women in World History*.

GARRETT, Mary Elizabeth (1854–1915). American philanthropist. Born Mary Elizabeth Garrett in Baltimore, Maryland, Mar 5, 1854; died in Bryn Mawr, Pennsylvania, April 3, 1915; dau. of John W. Garrett (president of Baltimore & Ohio Railroad); never married; lived with M. Carey Thomas. ❖ At father's death (1884), inherited a 3rd of his considerable fortune, and thereafter devoted her time and money to the advancement of medical education for women and to woman suffrage; raised $100,000 for Johns Hopkins medical school with the provision that women be admitted. ❖ See also *Women in World History*.

GARRETT, Mary Smith (1839–1925). American educator of the deaf. Born in Philadelphia, Pennsylvania, June 20, 1839; died in North Conway, New Hampshire, July 18, 1925; one of at least six children of Henry (businessman) and Caroline Rush (Cole) Garrett; older sister of Emma Garrett (c. 1846–1893); never married; no children. ❖ Ran a private school in Philadelphia to teach deaf children to speak; closed school to join sister Emma in Scranton (1889); with Emma, established the Pennsylvania Home for the Training in Speech of Deaf Children Before They Are of School Age, which opened with 15 children in temporary quarters (later known as the Bala Home); following sister's death (1893), took over as principal at Bala Home and remained there for the next 30 years; through lobbying efforts, obtained passage of laws in 1899 and 1901 requiring the exclusive use of oral methods of instruction in all state institutions for the deaf. ❖ See also *Women in World History*.

GARRETT, Maureen (1922—). British golfer. Born Maureen Ruttle, Aug 22, 1922, in England. ❖ Won French Open (1946); served as president of Ladies Golf Union of Great Britain (1982–84) and vice president (1986). Received USGA's Bobby Jones Award for sportsmanship (1983).

GARRETT, Millicent (1847–1929). *See Fawcett, Millicent Garrett.*

GARRETT-ANDERSON, Elizabeth (1836–1917). *See Anderson, Elizabeth Garrett.*

GARRICK, Mrs. David (1724–1822). *See Veigel, Eva-Maria.*

GARRIGUE, Charlotte (1850–1923). *See Masaryk, Charlotte Garrigue.*

GARRISON, Helen Frances. *See Villard, Frances.*

GARRISON, Lucy McKim (1842–1877). American song collector. Born Lucy McKim, Oct 30, 1842, in Philadelphia, Pennsylvania; died May 11, 1877, in West Orange, New Jersey; m. Wendell Phillips Garrison (son of William Lloyd Garrison, abolitionist). ❖ Attended NJ school run by Grimké sisters and the husband of Angelina Grimké; made musical notations of slave songs while accompanying father, who, as general secretary of a Union relief committee, had been sent to help slaves being freed at the Sea Islands off the South Carolina coast (1861); with husband, gathered 1st collection of slave songs to be published, *Slave Songs of the United States* (1867), on which William Francis Allen and Charles Ware collaborated.

GARRISON, Mabel (1886–1963). American coloratura soprano. Born April 24, 1886, in Baltimore, Maryland; died Aug 20, 1963, in New York, NY. ❖ One of the leading coloraturas of the Metropolitan Opera (1914–22), sang Gilda, Martha, Lucia, Rosina, and Queen of the Night in *The Magic Flute;* was a professor of vocal music at Smith College.

GARRISON, Zina (1963—). African-American tennis player. Name variations: Zina Garrison-Jackson. Born Nov 16, 1963, in Houston, TX; m. Willard Jackson. ❖ Won junior titles at both Wimbledon and US Open (1981); won a gold medal for doubles and a bronze medal for singles at Seoul Olympics (1988); advanced to finals at Wimbledon, becoming the 1st African-American woman to reach Wimbledon finals since Althea Gibson, but lost to Martina Navratilova (1990); established the Zina Garrison Foundation (1988). ❖ See also *Women in World History*.

GARRO, Elena (1916–1998). Mexican playwright, novelist, and journalist. Born Dec 11, 1916, in Puebla, Mexico; died Aug 22, 1998, in Cuernavaca, Mexico; dau. of José Antonio Garro Melendreras and Esperanza Navarro Benítez; m. Octavio Paz (poet and diplomat), 1937 (div.); children: Helena Paz. ❖ Well-known Latin American writer, was one of the 1st to experiment with magic realism, mastering the technique of developing themes within a cyclical time; lived in US (1943–45), France (1946–51), Japan (1952) and Switzerland (1953), due to husband's diplomatic posts, and met anti-fascist intellectuals, writers and artists; returned to Mexico (1953) and earned success as screenwriter, journalist and political activist; wrote film scripts, including *La escondida* (The Hidden Woman), and published a collection of plays, *Un hogar sólido* (A Solid Home, 1958); exiled from Mexico due to activist journalism (1959), especially around rights of indigenous Mexicans; after living in New York and Paris, returned to Mexico (1963) and published novels *Los recuerdos de porvenir* (Recollections of Things to Come, 1963) and *La semana de colores* (The Week of Colors, 1963); identified with 1968 student movement and incorporated events from protests and massacres into political novel *Y matarazo no llamó . . .* (And Matarazo Never Called, 1991), unintentionally alienating those in movement by naming intellectuals involved; moved to US with daughter (1972), due to isolation from Mexican leftist intellectuals, and then to Spain (1974), forced to leave Spain (1980) by estranged husband, who made her departure a condition for his acceptance of Miguel Cervantes prize; moved with daughter to Paris (1980) and worked in Mexican consulate; returned to Mexico (1993) and lived in poverty; received many awards including Xavier Villarrutia Prize (1963) for *Los recuerdos de porvenir*, and Premio Sor Juana Inez de la Cruz (1996) for 2 short novels *Busca mi esquela* (Look for My Death Note, 1996) and *Primer amor* (First Love, 1996). Additional works include: (novels) *Testimonios sobre Mariana* (Testimonies about Mariana, 1981), *Reencuentro de personajes* (Reencounter of Characters, 1981), *La casa junto al río* (The House by the River, 1982), and *Un traje rojo para un duelo* (A Red Dress for a Mourning, 1996); (play) *Felipe Angeles* (1979); (screenplays) *De noche vienes* (You Come at Night) and *Las señoritas Vivanco* (The Vivanco Ladies). ❖ See also Patricia Rosas Lopátegui, *Yo sólo soy memoria* (Ediciones Castillo, 2000).

GARROD, Dorothy A. (1892–1969). English archaeologist and educator. Born Dorothy Annie Elizabeth Garrod, May 5, 1892, in London, England; died Dec 18, 1968; dau. of Sir Alfred Baring Garrod (1819–1907), English physician and professor of therapeutics; sister of Alfred Henry Garrod (1846–1879), a zoologist, and Archibald Edward Garrod (1857–1936), Regius Professor of history of medicine at Oxford; educated in France, where she studied Paleolithic archaeology under Breuil, Begouen, and Peyrony; never married; no children. ❖ Director of studies in archaeology and anthropology at Newnham College at Cambridge, was the 1st woman in any field to be appointed a professor at Cambridge (1939); working in the area of Paleolithic archaeology, directed field investigations in England, Kurdistan, Bulgaria, Gibraltar, and Lebanon; most famous excavation was Mugharet et Tabun in Palestine where evidence was unearthed to provide testimony on the evolution of *Homo neanderthalensis* (Neanderthal man); served in the women's services in both world wars; after WWII, used what she had learned of photographic evaluation to develop aerial photography as a finding tool for archaeology.

GARSENDA (1170–c. 1257). Troubadour and countess of Provence and Forcalquier. Name variations: Garsende; Garsende de Forcalquier; Gersende de Forcalquier; Garsinde of Sabran; Comtesse de Proensa. Born 1170 in southern France; died c. 1257 in Provence; dau. of Garsenda and Bernard de Forcalquier (some sources cite father as Raimund of Sabran); grandmother of Eleanor of Provence (c. 1222–1291); m. Alphonse II, count of Provence (r. 1196–1209), 1193; children: Raymond Berengar V (1198–1245), 4th count of Provence; Garsenda. ❖ One of the female troubadours who flourished in southern France, married Count Alphonse II of Provence, brother to the king of Aragon; when her grandfather took part of her dowry lands away from Alphonse and gave it to Garsenda's sister, found herself in the middle of a bloody war between her family and her husband's family; despite the war, created an important cultural center at her court, where she patronized several male troubadours; when Alphonse died (1209), became regent of Provence, and held the title until her son came of age; retired to an abbey (1225). ❖ See also *Women in World History.*

GARSON, Greer (1904–1996). British actress. Born Eileen Evelyn Garson in London, England, Sept 29, 1904; died of heart failure on April 6, 1996, in Dallas, Texas; only child of George Garson and Nina (Gregor) Garson; educated at the University of London and at the University of Grenoble, France; m. Edward Alec Abbot Snelson, 1933 (div. 1941), m. Richard Ney (actor), 1943 (div. 1947); m. Elijah E. Fogelson, July 15, 1949 (died 1987); no children. ❖ Star of the English stage and the American screen who, despite her Irish origins, became the screen's image of the quintessential Englishwoman; made stage debut with Birmingham Rep; made 1st London appearance in Shakespeare's *The Tempest*; in less than three years (1934–37), starred in 8 popular plays in London: *Golden Arrow* (1934), *Vintage Wine, Accent on Youth, Butterfly on the Wheel, Pages From a Diary, The Visitor, Mademoiselle* and *Old Music* (1937); made tv debut in Shaw's "How He Lied to Her Husband" (BBC, 1937); came to US (1937); made American film debut in *Goodbye Mr. Chips* (1939), which was a great success; portrayed Edna Gladney in *Blossoms in the Dust* (1941), the 1st of 8 films in which she co-starred with Walter Pidgeon; appeared in *Mrs. Miniver* (1942), which established her reputation; became one of the leading members of what was called the MGM Stock company, appearing in such films as *Pride and Prejudice* (1940), *Random Harvest* (1942), *Desire Me* (1947), *Julia Misbehaves* (1948), *That Forsyte Woman* (1949), *The Miniver Story* (1950), *The Law and the Lady* (1951), (as Calpurnia) *Julius Caesar* (1953), *Scandal at Scourie* (1953), *Her Twelve Men* (1954), and *The Happiest Millionaire* (1967). Won Academy Award for Best Actress for *Mrs. Miniver* (1943); nominated for Academy Awards for Best Actress for *Goodbye Mr. Chips* (1939), *Blossoms in the Dust* (1941), *Madame Curie* (1944), *Mrs. Parkington*

(1945), *The Valley of Decision* (1945), and *Sunrise at Campobello* (1961); named honorary Commander of the Order of the British Empire (1984); received Golda Meir Award, Hebrew University of Jerusalem, for her contributions to making educational opportunities available to deserving young people (1988). ❖ See also Michael Troyan, *A Rose for Mrs. Miniver: The Life of Greer Garson* (University of Kentucky Press, 1998); and *Women in World History.*

GARTH, Midi (1920—). American modern dancer and choreographer. Born Jan 28, 1920, in New York, NY. ❖ Trained in modern dance technique by numerous teachers including Sybil Shearer and Elsa Fried; studied choreography with Louis Horst; performed with Shearer in Chicago, Illinois, while teaching at Hull House Settlement and continuing studies in music at Chicago Musical College; choreographed many unconventionally personal works which became known only to a small group of devout admirers. Choreographed works including *Times Casts a Shadow* (1949), *Waking* (1951), *Prelude to Flight* (1951), *Hither Thither* (1952), *Voices* (1954), *Voyages* (1961), *Imaginary City* (1963), *Other Voices* (1966), *Warm Up* (1969), *Impressions of Our Time* (1969), *Open Space* (1976), *Trio* (1976) and *Koto Song* (1978).

GARUFI, Bianca (1920—). Italian novelist and psychoanalyst. Born 1920 in Rome, Italy. ❖ Wrote thesis on Jung and practiced as analyst; co-founded Einaudi publishing house; writings include *Fuoco grande* (with Cesare Pavese, 1959), *Il fossile* (1962), and *Rosa cardinale* (1968).

GARVEY, Amy Jacques (1896–1973). African-American nationalist. Born Amy Jacques in Jamaica, West Indies, 1896; died in Jamaica in 1973; became 2nd wife of Marcus Garvey (1887–1940, black nationalist and founder of the United Negro Improvement Association), 1922; children: Marcus M. Garvey, Jr.; Julius Garvey. ❖ Came to US (1917); working alongside husband, became an activist in her own right; while he was imprisoned for two years for treason (he was later pardoned), worked to keep his message alive, raising money for his defense and publishing the 1st 2 volumes of *Philosophy and Opinions of Marcus Garvey* (1923); served as associate editor of UNIA newspaper *Negro World* (1924–27), and introduced a page called "Our Women and What They Think"; after husband's death (1940), continued to work for black nationalism, becoming a contributing editor to the journal *African;* wrote *Garvey and Garveyism* (1970).

GARVIE, Sheila (fl. 1960s). Scottish murderer. Married Maxwell Robert Garvie (murdered May 1968). ❖ In sensational murder case, was tried with lover Brian Tevendale and one of Tevendale's friends (Alan Peters) for brutal death of her husband (Nov 1968); found guilty along with Tevendale, sentenced to life imprisonment.

GARZONI, Giovanna (1600–1670). Italian painter. Probably born in Ascoli Piceno, Italy, 1600; died in Rome, Italy, in Feb 1670; never married; no children. ❖ At 16, executed an oil painting, *Holy Family;* worked in Venice, Florence, Naples, and Rome; patrons included the Medici, as well as other Italian and Spanish nobility; reached the height of her popularity in Florence where she lived for some time and was able to sell her work for top prices; became quite wealthy and settled in Rome (c. 1654), where she contributed to one of the annual feasts of the Accademia di San Luca, of which she was probably made a member as early as 1633; is best known for her studies of flowers, plants, and animals which are a blend of still-life and scientific drawing, and these include some of the finest botanical studies made in the 17th century; works include *Dish of Broad Beans* (tempera on parchment, Palazzo Pitti, Florence), *Dish of Grapes with Pears and a Snail* (tempera on parchment, Palazzo Pitti, Florence), and *Still Life with Birds and Fruit* (watercolor on Parchment, c. 1640, The Cleveland Museum of Art). ❖ See also *Women in World History.*

GASCH, Marie Manning (1873–1945). See Manning, Marie.

GASCOYNE-CECIL, marchioness of (1827–1899). See Cecil, Georgiana.

GASHE, Marina (b. 1932). See Njau, Rebeka.

GASKELL, Elizabeth (1810–1865). English writer. Name variations: Mrs. Gaskell; Lily; Cotton Mather Mills (early pseudonym). Pronunciation: GAS-kull. Born Elizabeth Cleghorn Stevenson on Sept 29, 1810, at Chelsea, London, England; died Nov 16, 1865, at Alton in Hampshire; dau. of William Stevenson (Unitarian minister, farmer, writer, teacher, keeper of the records of the Treasury) and Elizabeth (Holland) Stevenson; attended school at Barford and Stratford-upon-Avon; m. William Gaskell (Unitarian minister), 1832; children: daughter (stillborn, 1833); Marianne Gaskell (b. 1834); Margaret Emily Gaskell

(b. 1837); Florence Elizabeth Gaskell (b. 1842); William (1844–1845); Julia Bradford Gaskell (b. 1846). ❖ Popular and critically acclaimed English writer of the Victorian period who wrote 6 novels, the authorized biography of Charlotte Brontë, several nouvelles, some 30 short stories, and numerous sketches; spent childhood among deceased mother's family in Knutsford, Cheshire; spent 5 years at boarding school in her teens, then visited family and friends in London, Newcastle, Edinburgh, and Manchester until marrying at age 22 and settling permanently in Manchester; worked with husband on philanthropic and educational projects among Manchester's working class in the early years of marriage, during which she gave birth to 6 children; began writing for publication (1845) after the death of son; published *Mary Barton: A Tale of Manchester Life*, her 1st novel (1848); met Charlotte Brontë, subject of her biography (1850); was a popular and successful writer (1850s–60s) while maintaining a strong family life, cultivating extensive social and professional relationships, enjoying foreign travel, and continuing her philanthropic activities among the poor; died at a new country retreat she had purchased for her and her husband's retirement (1865); was esteemed as a writer who belonged in the distinguished company of Charles Dickens, George Eliot, and Charlotte Brontë in making the 19th century the great period of the English novel; writings include (novel) *Cranford* (1853), (novel) *Ruth* (1853), (novel) *North and South* (1855), (biography) *The Life of Charlotte Brontë* (1857), (novel) *Sylvia's Lovers* (1863), (nouvelle) *Cousin Phillis: A Tale* (1864), (novel) *Wives and Daughters: An Every-day Story* (serialized in the *Cornhill Magazine*, 1864–66). ❖ See also *The Letters of Mrs. Gaskell* (ed. by J.A.V. Chapple and A. Pollard, Manchester University Press, 1966); Angus Easson, *Elizabeth Gaskell* (Routledge & Kegan Paul, 1980); Winifred Gérin, *Elizabeth Gaskell* (Clarendon, 1976); A.B. Hopkins, *Elizabeth Gaskell: Her Life and Work* (John Lehman, 1952); Patsy Stoneman, *Elizabeth Gaskell* (Indiana University Press, 1987); Jenny Uglow, *Elizabeth Gaskell: A Habit of Stories* (Farrar, Straus, 1993); and *Women in World History*.

GASKELL, Sonia (1904–1974). Lithuanian dancer. Born April 14, 1904, in Vilkaviuskis, Lithuania; died July 9, 1974, in Paris, France. ❖ Lived and trained in Israel (then Palestine), Paris, and Amsterdam; founded numerous companies—all predecessors of Dutch National Ballet—including Ballet recital Group (1949), Netherlands Ballet (1954), Amsterdam Ballet (1959); choreographed several dance pieces for companies, including *Ragtime* (c. 1954), *Atles om Een Mantel* (1954), *Sphere* (c. 1956), and *Sonate* (c. 1956); worked as 1st artistic director for Dutch National Ballet (1961–69).

GASKIN, Ina May (1940—). American midwife. Born Ina May, Mar 8, 1940, in Marshalltown, Iowa; graduated from University of Iowa with bachelors, 1962; Northern Illinois University, MA, 1966; m. Steven Gaskin (spiritual leader). ❖ Self-educated midwife considered the "mother of authentic midwifery," began career while traveling throughout US with husband, a spiritual leader (1970); established and worked at the Farm Midwifery Center in an alternative community, the Farm, created by spiritual leader Steven Gaskin's caravan in Summertown (TN); taught English in Kuala Trengganu, Malaysia (1963–65), as a US Peace Corps member; taught English as second language for the Office of Economic Opportunity in San Francisco; learned emergency childbirth and sterile techniques from Dr. Louis La Pere; selected to care for Amish childbirths in TN (1980s) by Dr. John O. William Jr.; established the Farm Midwifery Center's "woman-centered philosophy of childbirth as the norm for national obstetrical care"; served as an editor of *The Birth Gazette*; wrote *Spiritual Midwifery*; her holistic approach to midwifery is supported in *The American Journal of Public Health*.

GASSET, Marie-Claire (1968—). See Restoux, Marie-Claire.

GASTEAZORO, Ana (1950–1993). Salvadoran political activist. Pronunciation: Gas-tee-a-zoro. Born Ana Margarita Gasteazoro Escolande, Oct 10, 1950, in San Salvador, El Salvador; died in San Salvador of breast cancer, Jan 30, 1993; dau. of Ana Marina Escolande (antique dealer) and José Agustín Gasteazoro Mejia (civil engineer); attended primary through high school at American School in San Salvador; studied briefly at Bay State Junior College in Massachusetts and University of Central America in El Salvador; never married; no children. ❖ Political activist in El Salvador during a 12-year "dirty war" waged by the Salvadoran military against the population, joined the National Revolutionary Movement (MNR) and was often sent out of the country for international meetings and conferences, especially those of the Socialist International; with the repression by state security forces and the brazenness of the paramilitary death squads escalating to the point of daily disappearances of student leaders, trade unionists, human-

rights and political activists, and journalists, joined the guerrilla group, Popular Liberation Front (FPL, 1979); was also forced to assume more and more responsibility in the MNR because of the disappearance of so many of her colleagues; was sent to the Socialist International Congress in Madrid (April 1981), where, to protect her identity, gave a keynote speech to the Women's Conference under a pseudonym and in disguise; back in El Salvador, continued double life, working underground for FPL while carrying on "legal" work with MNR; was arrested (May 11, 1981), followed by 11 days of torture after which she signed a false confession, admitting to several "terrorist" activities; the next morning, was presented to the media as a "confessed terrorist," but her life was spared thanks to international pressure; was taken to Ilopango Women's Prison, where she spent 2 years, without charges or a trial (1981–83); inside, joined with the others to form a women's unit of the Committee of Salvadoran Political Prisoners (COPPES), which became an effective force in publicizing the Salvadoran struggle and the cause of women prisoners; released under a mass amnesty for political prisoners (May 1983), went into exile, briefly in Mexico and Cuba before settling in Costa Rica, where she lived until 1992; as the war was winding down, was invited to return to El Salvador as a delegate to the 1st open congress her MNR party had held in many years (1991); invited to run as an MNR candidate in elections (1993), was considering a return to political life in El Salvador when her breast cancer recurred. ❖ See also *Women in World History*.

GATEHOUSE, Eleanor Wright (1886–1973). Australian golfer. Name variations: Nellie Gatehouse. Born Eleanor Wright, 1886, near Geelong, Victoria, Australia; died 1973; m. James Gatehouse, 1909. ❖ Became the 1st Royal Melbourne Women's champion (1906), a title she captured another 10 times over a 30-year span; won 3 Australian championships (1909, 1925, 1928) and 5 Victorian titles; served as president of Australian Women's Golf Union and of Royal Melbourne Associates as well as president of the Royal Society for the Prevention of Cruelty to Children for 7 terms. Nellie Gatehouse azalea was named in her honor.

GATES, Eleanor (1871–1951). American playwright and novelist. Born Sept 26, 1871, in Shakopee, Minnesota; died Mar 7, 1951, in Los Angeles, California; m. Richard Walton Tully (div.); m. Frederick Ferdinand Moore. ❖ Plays include *We are Seven, Apron Strings, The Darling of the World, Out of the West* and *Poor Little Rich Girl* (which was filmed with Mary Pickford [1917] and Shirley Temple Black [1936]); also wrote several novels.

GATES, Nancy (1926—). American screen actress. Born Feb 1, 1926, in Dallas, TX; m. William Hayes (died 1992); children: Jeffrey M. Hayes (producer). ❖ Child actress on radio and tv, made film debut in *Come on Danger* (1942), followed by *The Tuttles of Tahiti, The Great Gildersleeve, The Magnificent Ambersons, Hitler's Children, This Land Is Mine, Member of the Wedding, The Search for Bridey Murphy, Some Came Running* and *Comanche Station*, among others.

GATES, Ruth (1886–1966). American actress. Born Oct 28, 1886, in Denton, TX; died May 23, 1966, in NYC; niece of Edwin Booth; m. Ed Poulter (actor, died 1913). ❖ Made stage debut with David Warfield in *The Music Master*; appearances include *Kiki, Ramshackle Inn, I Remember Mama, Up in Mabel's Room, Pillar to Post* and *Opening Night*.

GATESON, Marjorie (1891–1977). American stage, tv, and screen actress. Born Jan 17, 1891, in Brooklyn, NY; died April 17, 1977, in NYC. ❖ Made Broadway debut in *The Dove of Peace* (1912); other plays include *Fancy Free, Shubert Gaieties, Strange Bedfellows, Midsummer Night's Dream, Sweethearts, Street Scene* and *Show Boat*; made film debut in *The Beloved Batchelor* (1931) and subsequently appeared in over 100 movies, including *Bureau of Missing Persons, Chained, Vogues of 1938, Duke of West Point, Geronimo, 'Til We Meet Again, Back Street* and *The Caddy*; frequently appeared on tv, notably on "One Man's Family" and "The Secret Storm."

GATHERS, Helen (1943—). American singer. Name variations: The Bobbettes. Born Mar 18, 1943, in New York, NY. ❖ At about 12, began singing alto with The Bobbettes, which became the 1st female vocal group with #1 R&B hit and Top-10 hit on pop charts: "Mr. Lee" (1957); with The Bobbettes, toured with artists including Clyde McPhatter and Ruth Brown; left the group (1962). Other singles by The Bobbettes include "Have Mercy, Baby" (1960), "Dance With Me, Georgie" (1960), and "I Don't Like It Like That, Part 1" (1961).

GATICHON, Françoise (b. 1919). See Parturier, Françoise.

GATO, Idalmis (1971—). Cuban volleyball player. Name variations: Idalmis Gato Moya. Born Aug 30, 1971, in Cuba. ❖ Won team gold medals at Barcelona Olympics (1992), Atlanta Olympics (1996), and Sydney Olympics (2000).

GATTERER, Philippine (1756–1831). *See Engelhard, Magdalene Philippine.*

GATTILUSI, Caterina (fl. 1440). Greco-Italian noblewoman. Name variations: Catterina. Fl. around 1440; 2nd wife of Constantine XI Paleologus, emperor of Nicaea (r. 1448–1453). ❖ Died soon after her marriage. ❖ See also *Women in World History.*

GATTILUSI, Eugenia (fl. late 1390s). Greco-Italian noblewoman. Born into the Greco-Italian Gattilusi family, lords of the Isle of Lesbos; fl. in 1390s; m. her cousin John VII Paleologus, emperor of Nicaea (r. 1390). ❖ See also *Women in World History.*

GATTINONI, Fernanda (1906–2002). Italian fashion designer. Born Dec 2, 1906, in Cocquio Trevisago, Lombardy, Italy; died Nov 26, 2002, in Rome, Lazio, Italy. ❖ Worked for the Molineaux fashion house in London; opened her own company in Italy (1945) and was credited with reviving the high-waist, flared-silhouette Empire designs; dressed Audrey Hepburn, Anna Magnani, Kim Novak, Ingrid Bergman, Eva Peron, and Jackie Kennedy, among others. Nominated for Academy Award for her costuming of Hepburn in *War and Peace* (1956).

GATTY, Juliana Horatia (1841–1885). *See Ewing, Juliana Horatia.*

GATTY, Margaret (1809–1873). British author and editor. Name variations: Margaret Scott; (pseudonym) Aunt Judy. Born Margaret Scott in Burnham, Essex, England, June 3, 1809; died at Ecclesfield vicarage in Ecclesfield, Yorkshire, England, Oct 4, 1873; dau. of the Reverend Alexander Scott (1768–1840, chaplain to Horatio Nelson) and Mary Frances (Ryder) Scott (died 1811); m. Reverend Alfred Gatty, D.D. (vicar of Ecclesfield and writer), 1839; children: 10, including daughters, Juliana Horatia Ewing (1841–1885) and Horatia Gatty Eden. ❖ In order to offset the costs of rearing a growing family, began writing; co-authored with husband a biography of her father's life and time with Nelson (1842); published *The Fairy Godmother and Other Tales* (1851); wrote and illustrated *Parables From Nature,* a series of 5 volumes (1855–71); as Aunt Judy, published *Aunt Judy's Tales* (1858), followed by *Aunt Judy's Letters* (1862), *Aunt Judy's Songbook for Children* and *The Mother's Book of Poetry;* established *Aunt Judy's Magazine* (1866), then edited and contributed to the magazine (1866–73); an accomplished botanist, wrote and illustrated *British Seaweeds* (1862) and *History of British Seaweeds* (1863); also published an account of a holiday in Ireland, *The Old Folks From Home,* and edited an autobiography, *The Travels and Adventures of Dr. Wolff the Missionary* (1861); because of ill health, turned editorship of *Aunt Judy's Magazine* over to daughters, Juliana Horatia Ewing and Horatia Gatty Eden (1873). ❖ See also *Women in World History.*

GAUDIN-LATRILLE, Brigitte (1958—). French fencer. Name variations: Brigitte Latrille. Born April 15, 1958, in France. ❖ Won a silver medal at Montreal Olympics (1976), gold medal at Moscow Olympics (1980), and bronze medal at Los Angeles Olympics (1984), all in team foil.

GAUDRON, Mary Genevieve (1943—). Australian lawyer and judge. Name variations: Mary Gaudron, Justice Mary Gaudron. Born Jan 5, 1943 in Moree, New South Wales, Australia; studied at St Ursula's College, Armidale; Sydney University, BA, 1962, Bachelor of Law, 1965. ❖ The youngest ever federal judge and 1st woman to be appointed to the High Court of Australia (1981), passed New South Wales Bar (1968) and was 1st woman appointed to New South Wales Bar Council (1972); argued famed "Equal Pay Case" before Australian Conciliation and Arbitration Commission and scored major victory for women's rights to fair compensation (1973); served as deputy president of Australian Conciliation and Arbitration Commission (1974–80); was appointed 1st chair of Legal Services Commission of New South Wales (1979); was appointed solicitor-general and Queen's counsel of New South Wales (1981), 1st woman to hold those positions; a progressive judge, was appointed to High Court (1987), holding judgeship until 2003; was overlooked for appointment as chief justice (1998) despite status as most senior justice on High Court, generating much criticism of John Howard government; was appointed judge of Administrative Tribunal of International Labor Organization of United Nations in Geneva (2003).

GAUGEL, Heide-Elke (1959—). West German runner. Born July 11, 1959, in Germany. ❖ At Los Angeles Olympics, won a bronze medal in the 4 x 400-meter relay (1984).

GAUGHIN, Lorraine (1924–1974). American writer and actress. Name variations: Lorraine Rivero. Born July 1924, in Seattle, Washington; died Dec 22, 1974, in Los Angeles, California, when fire destroyed her home; dau. of Julian Rivero (actor); children: daughter. ❖ As actress, appeared in *One Million B.C.* and *The Falcon* series; wrote a column for *Hollywood Callboard* and several fan magazines.

GAUGUIN, Aline (1825–1869). *See Chazal, Aline-Marie.*

GAUHAR SHAD (c. 1378–1459). Persian-Afghan queen. Born c. 1378 in Afghanistan; executed in 1459 in Afghanistan; m. Shah Rukh (son and successor of Tamburlaine), 1391 (king of Persia-Afghan, r. 1404–47); children: 2 sons. ❖ Timurid queen, married to Shah Rukh, helped establish the court as the center of a cultural and scientific renaissance; built mosques in Meshed and Herat in northwest Afghanistan; exerted influence even after husband's death until she was executed for supporting her great-grandson against an opposing prince, Abu Sa'id. Her mausoleum is still extant.

GAULLE, Yvonne de (1900–1979). *See de Gaulle, Yvonne.*

GAULT, Alma Elizabeth (1891–1981). American nurse. Born Alma Elizabeth Gault, Sept 28, 1891, in Fernwood, Ohio; died July 12, 1981, in Columbus, Ohio; graduated from the College of Wooster in OH, 1916; dau. of Nancy Emma (Stark) Gault and Davison Stewart Gault. ❖ As a dean (1944–53) of the Meharry Medical College School of Nursing (historically African-American institution in Nashville, TN), created a baccalaureate program (as well as an accredited diploma school of nursing) and successfully pushed for the school to become the 1st "historically black institution" to be a member of the American Association of Collegiate Schools of Nursing; enrolled in the Vassar Training Camp for Nurses (1918) and in the Philadelphia General Hospital School of Nursing (graduated, 1920); worked as a Philadelphia General Hospital head nurse; appointed the Union Memorial Hospital School of Nursing's director (Baltimore); served as the Memorial Hospital's director of Nursing Service (Springfield, IL); at Vanderbilt University (Nashville, TN), was employed as a nursing school associate professor (1953), as an acting dean, and as a dean (1965–67), during which time the 1st African-American nursing student enrolled at Vanderbilt; continued to work after retirement (1959). Honors include the proclamation of May 21, 1967 as "Alma Gault Day" by Nashville's mayor (at the time).

GAUNT, Mary (1861–1942). Australian novelist and short-story writer. Born Feb 20, 1861, in Chiltern, Victoria, Australia; died Jan 19, 1942, in Cannes, France; dau. of William Gaunt; m. Hubert Miller, 1894 (died 1900). ❖ Was one of the 1st 2 women enrolled at University of Melbourne; left penniless after husband's death, moved to London (1901) to make living as writer; traveled extensively, writing of travels, and did not return to Australia; lived in Italy for 20 years and fled to France during WWII; works include *Dave's Sweetheart* (1894), *Kirkham's Find* (1897), and *Deadman's* (1898).

GAUNTIER, Gene (1885–1966). American actress and screenwriter. Born Genevieve Liggett, May 17, 1885, in Kansas City, Missouri; died Dec 18, 1966, in Cuernavaca, Mexico; m. Jack C. Clark (director). ❖ Began stage career in rep and stock; joined the Kalem Company (1907), as its leading lady and principal screenwriter; founded (1912), appeared in, and wrote over 300 films, including screenplay for original *Ben-Hur,* for the Gene Gauntier Feature Players; with husband, made 1st US films abroad; was a combat correspondent during WWI, then a columnist and drama critic; retired to Mexico City (1942).

GAUTAMI, Mahapajapati or Mahaprajapati (fl. 570 BCE). *See Mahapajapati.*

GAUTHIER, Eva (1885–1958). Canadian mezzo-soprano and modern recitalist. Born Ida Joséphine Phoebe Gauthier, Sept 20, 1885, in Ottawa, Canada; died Dec 26, 1958, in NY; studied with Frank Buris, Auguste-Jean Dubulle, Sarah Bernhardt, and Jacques Bouhy; m. Frans Knoote, 1911 (div. 1917). ❖ Made NY recital debut (1917), devoting the program to such modern masters as Ravel, Bartók, Hindemith, Schoenberg, and Stravinsky; gave North American premieres of Stravinsky's *Trois Poésies de la lyrique japonaise* (1917) and *Pribaoutki* (1918); gave some 700 premieres of modern works during a career which also included recording. ❖ See also *Women in World History.*

GAUTHIER, Marguerite (1824–1847). *See Plessis, Alphonsine.*

GAUTHIER, Xavière (1942—). **French novelist and educator.** Name variations: Xaviere Gauthier. Born 1942 in France. ❖ Worked as lecturer at Paris University; scholarly works, which examine and deconstruct Freudian and surrealist versions of female sexuality, include *Surréalisme et sexualité* (1971) and *Dire nos sexualités: contre la sexologie* (1976); published transcripts of interviews with Marguerite Duras, *Les Parleuses* (1974); also wrote novels and essays and edited the feminist journal *Sorcières*.

GAUTIER, Felisa Rincón de (1897–1994). **Puerto Rican political leader.** Born Felisa Rincón in Ceiba in Puerto Rico on Jan 9, 1897; died in San Juan on Sept 16, 1994; eldest daughter and one of eight children of Enrique Rincón Plumey and Rita Marrero Rivera de Rincón; m. Jenaro A. Gautier (lawyer who served as assistant attorney general of Puerto Rico), 1940; no children. ❖ Mayor of San Juan, Puerto Rico, for over 20 years (1946–69), opened her own dress salon in San Juan in her early years; within a short time, had several stores including a flower shop; began political career (1932), the year Puerto Rican women won enfranchisement, when she assumed leadership of San Juan's Liberal Party; became a member of the Popular Democratic Party and worked to organize poor and disadvantaged voters (1938); began serving as president of the party's San Juan committee (1940) and became mayor of the city (1946); was reelected to office unanimously each consecutive term until 1968, when she declined to run; cleaned up existing slums, built new schools and housing projects, and set up a network of neighborhood medical dispensaries linked to the city's hospitals; held a Wednesday open house at city hall, when hundreds of the island's underprivileged visited her to solicit help and personal attention; as a goodwill ambassador, toured Latin America and made frequent trips to US. ❖ See also *Women in World History.*

GAUTIER, Judith (1845–1917). **French writer.** Name variations: Judith Mendès; Judith Walter. Born Louise Judith Gautier in Paris, France, Aug 24, 1845; died Dec 26, 1917; elder dau. of Théophile Gautier (poet, novelist, and journalist) and his mistress Ernesta Grisi (opera singer); attended Notre-Dame de la Miséricorde for two years; tutored in Chinese by Tin-Tun-Ling; niece of Carlotta Grisi (1819–1899); m. Catulle Mendès (poet), April 17, 1866 (judicial sep. July 13, 1878; div. Dec 28, 1896); no children. ❖ An Orientalist and the 1st female member of the Académie Goncourt, wrote novels, short stories, poetry, plays, translations, and criticism; was probably the mistress of Victor Hugo and was undoubtedly the inspiration for Richard Wagner's opera *Parsifal*; was often painted by John Singer Sargent; her salon in Paris and her seaside villa in Brittany were frequented by Pierre Loti (who carried on a correspondence with her in Egyptian hieroglyphs), Charles-Marie Widor, and Anatole France; also had a late-in-life liaison with Suzanne Meyer-Zundel (1904–17); was elected the 1st female member of the Académie Goncourt (1910); her novels *L'Usurpateur* (1875), recognized by the Académie-Français, *Le Dragon impérial* and *Iskender* are considered some of her best works. ❖ See also autobiography (in French) *Le Collier des jours* (2 vols., 1902 and 1903); Joanna Richardson, *Judith Gautier: A Biography* (Watts, 1987); and *Women in World History.*

GAUTIER, Marguerite (1824–1847). *See Plessis, Alphonsine.*

GAUTSCHI, Lynn Vidali (1952—). *See Vidali, Lynn.*

GAVITT, Elmina M. Roys (1828–1898). *See Roys-Gavitt, Elmina M.*

GAVORNIKOVÁ, Lydia Vadkerti- (1932—). *See Vadkerti-Gavorniková, Lydia.*

GAVRILJUK, Nina (1965—). **Russian cross-country skier.** Name variations: Nina Gavriiljuk, Gavrilyuk or Gavriliuk. Born April 13, 1965, in Leningrad (now St. Petersburg), Russia. ❖ Won a gold medal for 4 x 5 km relay at Calgary Olympics (1988), a gold medal for 4 x 5 km relay and bronze medal for 15 km at Lillehammer Olympics (1994), and a gold medal for 4 x 5 km relay at Nagano Olympics (1998); at World championships, placed 1st for relay (1987, 1993, 1995, 1997, 1999, 2001).

GAWENUS, Monika (1954—). *See Pflug, Monika.*

GAXTON, Madeline (1897–1990). **American dancer.** Name variations: Cameron Sisters; Madeline Cameron; Madeline Seitz; Madeline Seitz-Cameron; also seen incorrectly as Madeleine Cameron. Born Madeline Seitz, Jan 24, 1897; died May 15, 1990, in New York, NY; m. William Gaxton (singer, dancer, actor, r.n. William Gaxiola), 1917 (died 1963). ❖ Teamed with Dorothy Cameron as a duo dance act by Ned Wayburn in New York City (c. 1912) and toured the Keith vaudeville circuit; made

Broadway debut with Dorothy in *Miss Simplicity* (1914); appeared in the film *Maxim's at Midnight* (1915); performed as tandem team on stages at Capitol Theater in New York City and in Wayburn's *Town Topics of 1915* and *So Long Letty* (1916); mastered wide range of dance techniques from classical ballet to acrobatic dance to Russian tap dancing; after Dorothy's retirement, continued to perform as specialty dancer in a variety of productions, including *Hit the Deck* (1927) and *Follow Thru* (1929); appeared in comedy with husband William Gaxton.

GAY, Delphine (1804–1855). *See Girardin, Delphine.*

GAY, Gretchen (1925–1965). *Merrill, Gretchen.*

GAY, Lady (1881–1940). *See Glen, Esther.*

GAY, Maisie (1883–1945). **English musical-comedy actress and singer.** Born Jan 7, 1883, in London, England; died Sept 14, 1945, in London. ❖ On stage for over 40 years, appeared in over 30 musicals, including *The Quaker Girl, High Jinks, Sybil, London Calling, Charlot's Revue, Pins and Needles* and *This Year of Grace*; played the lead role of Nan in *A Country Girl* over 1,000 times (1904–07); often appeared on the NY stage and toured America; films include *To Oblige a Lady* and *The Old Man.* ❖ See also reminiscences *Laughing Through Life* (1931).

GAY, Mrs. (c. 1921–1965). *See Merrill, Gretchen.*

GAY, Sophie (1776–1852). **French novelist.** Name variations: Madame Gay. Born Marie Françoise Sophie Nichault de la Valette or de Lavalette in Paris, France, July 1, 1776; died in Paris on Mar 5, 1852; dau. of M. Nichault de la Valette and Francesca Peretti (Italian); m. M. Liottier (exchange broker), 1793 (div. 1799); m. M. Gay (receiver-general of the department of the Roër or Ruhr); children: (2nd m.) Delphine Gay Girardin (1804–1855). ❖ With 2nd husband posted to Aix-la-Chapelle, began to hold a literary salon there and subsequently in Paris; became friends with many celebrated personages, and her salon was frequented by distinguished writers, musicians, actors, and painters of the time, whom she attracted with her intelligence, charm, and beauty; 1st literary effort was a letter written to *Journal de Paris* (1802) in defense of Germaine de Staël's novel *Delphine*; anonymously published 1st novel *Laure d'Estelle* (1802); published *Léonie de Montbreuse* (1813), considered by Sainte-Beuve as her best work, though *Anatole* (1815) was even more highly regarded; following death of husband (c. 1822), began to publish regularly; other works include *Les malheurs d'un amant heureux* (1818), *Un Mariage sous l'Empire (A Marriage during the Empire*, 1832), *La Duchesse de Châteauroux* (1834), *La Comtesse d'Egmont* (1836), *Salons célèbres* (2 vols., 1837), and *Marie de Mancini* (1840); wrote several comedies and opera libretti which met with considerable success, and her play *The Marquis of Pomenars* had a long run; an accomplished musician, also composed both the lyrics and music for a number of songs. ❖ See also memoirs, *Souvenirs d'une Vieille femme* (1834).

GAYATRI DEVI (c. 1897–1995). **Indian-born religious leader.** Name variations: known to her followers as "Ma," short for *mataji*, meaning reverend mother. Born in Bengal, India, possibly in 1897; died in La Crescenta, California, Sept 8, 1995; one of 19 children of a civil lawyer and a housewife; forced into marriage at an early age, was widowed at 19. ❖ Spiritual leader of Ramakrishna Brahma-Vadin, a female religious order rooted in Hinduism, joined her uncle, Swami Paramananda, in US; was ordained at the Massachusetts center which her uncle founded; the 1st Indian woman to teach Americans the Vedanta philosophy, which honors all religions, inherited leadership of the religious communities in La Crescenta, California, and in Cohasset, Massachusetts, after death of uncle (1940); appeared with Mother Teresa at the Conference of World Religions at the United Nations (1975); helped found the Snowmass Religious Leaders' Conference, and, at invitation of the Dalai Lama, taught at Harmonia Mundi Contemplative Congress in Newport Beach (1989).

GAYATRI DEVI (1919—). **Indian political leader.** Born May 23, 1919, in London, England; one of five children of the Maharajah Jitendra Narayan Bhup Bahadur of Cooch Behar (died 1922) and Princess Indiraraje Gaekwar of Baroda; educated by private tutors; attended St. Cyprian's in Eastbourne, England; graduated from Shantiniketan University, Balpur, India, 1936; attended Brilliamount school, Lausanne, Switzerland, and the London College of Secretaries; m. Sawai Man Singh Bahadur (maharajah of Jaipur), May 9, 1940 (died June 1970); children: one son, Maharaj Kumar Singh. ❖ Maharani of Jaipur and member of the Parliament of India, founded three schools: Maharani Gayatri Devi Public School in Jaipur, a sewing school, and a school of arts and crafts, through which she hoped to perpetuate the handicrafts of Jaipur; joined the Swatantra (Freedom) Party (1961), as a rightist opponent of Indira Gandhi's Congress Party, and announced her candidacy for the House of the People, the lower chamber of Indian Parliament; on election day (Feb 1962), received the largest plurality of any candidate in the country; during 1st 5-year term, focused on her home state of Rejasthan; lost bid for a state legislative seat (1967) but was reelected to the national Parliament; when opponents of the Congress Party in Rejasthan protested the return of the party to power (1967), escaped arrest but made clear her support of the uprising; responding to Gandhi's dissolution of Parliament and her call for elections a year ahead of schedule (1971), ran for the opposition from Jaipur and won by 50,000 more votes than her Congress Party opponent; suffered a political blow (Dec 1971), when both houses of Parliament passed a bill that "de-recognized" all former rulers, thus abolishing their privileges, titles, and privy purses, including those of her late husband; served out term in Parliament but admitted that politics was a full-time job for which she did not have the time; in conjunction with her school of arts and crafts, formed a company to export cotton rugs, or *durries,* made by the local weavers. ❖ See also memoir (with Santha Rama Rau) *A Princess Remembers* (Lippincott, 1976); and *Women in World History.*

GAYLE, Crystal (1951—). American country-and-western singer. Born Brenda Gail Webb, Jan 9, 1951, in Paintsville, Kentucky; younger sister of Loretta Lynn (singer); m. Bill Gatzimos, 1970; children: 2. ❖ Recorded 1st hit "I've Cried the Blue (Right Out of My Eyes)" (1970); signed with United Artists (1974), releasing 3 albums and several hit songs, including "This Is My Year for Mexico," "I'll Do It All Over Again," "Wrong Road Again," and her 1st #1 on the charts, "I'll Get Over You" (1974–76); released album *We Must Believe in Magic* (1977), which included the smash hit "Don't It Make My Brown Eyes Blue"; other hits include "Talking in Your Sleep," "Ready for the Times to Get Better," "Half the Way," "If You Ever Change Your Mind," "Too Many Lovers," "The Woman in Me," "Til I Gain Control Again" and "The Sound of Goodbye"; teamed with Eddie Rabbitt for "You and I" (1982); teamed with Gary Morris for "Makin Up for Lost Time" (the love theme from "Dallas") and "Another World."

GAYLE, Newton (1895–1965). See Lee, Muna.

GAYNOR, Gloria (1949—). African-American pop singer. Born Gloria Fowles on Sept 7, 1949, in Newark, New Jersey; m. Linwood Simon, 1979. ❖ Worked as an accountant after high school; joined band in Canada; toured for 18 months with band Soul Satisfiers; formed own band and signed with Columbia Records (early 1970s); scored disco hit with 1st single "Honey Bee" (1973); signed with MGM (mid-1970s); released hit cover of "Never Can Say Goodbye" (1975); reached #1 with signature hit, the disco anthem "I Will Survive" (1979); released albums *Experience Gloria Gaynor* (1975), *Glorious* (1977), *Love Tracks* (1979), *I Am What I Am* (1984), and *Love Affair* (1992). ❖ See also autobiography *I Will Survive: The Book* (1997).

GAYNOR, Janet (1906–1984). American actress. Name variations: (pseudonym) Augusta Louise. Born Laura Augusta Gainor on Oct 10, 1906, in Germantown, Pennsylvania; died Sept 14, 1984, from complications of pneumonia, in Palm Springs, California; dau. of Frank D. and Laura (Buhl) Gainor; educated in public schools in Pennsylvania, Chicago, and San Francisco; m. Jesse Peck (writer), Sept 11, 1929 (div. 1933); m. Gilbert Adrian (costume designer), 1939 (died 1959); m. Paul Gregory, 1964; children: (2nd m.) one son, Robin Gaynor Adrian (b. 1940). ❖ Film and stage star who won the 1st Academy Award for Best Actress; appeared in amateur theatricals as a child; was chosen at age 18 to appear in her 1st "bathing beauty" film; changed professional name to Janet Gaynor before embarking on a successful 15-year career as leading lady in films; appeared in *Sunrise,* still considered the last great silent film before the movies learned to talk, followed by *Seventh Heaven,* in which she co-starred with the man with whom she would do her most popular films, Charles Farrell (both 1927); won the 1st Best Actress Award from the American Academy of Motion Picture Arts and Sciences for her work in *Sunrise, Seventh Heaven* and *Street Angel* (the awards in those early days were often given for cumulative work rather than specific performances, 1928); retired from the business (1939); appeared sporadically on stage and tv through 1981, but devoted most of her time to oil painting and her family; films include *The Johnstown Flood* (1926), *The Shamrock Handicap* (1926), *The Midnight Kiss* (1926), *The Blue Eagle* (1926), *The Return of Peter Grimm* (1926), *Two Girls Wanted* (1927), *Four Devils* (1929), *Christina* (1929), *Lucky Star* (1929), *Sunny Side Up* (1929), *Happy Days* (1930), *High Society Blues* (1930), *The Man Who Came Back* (1931), *Daddy Long Legs* (1931),

Merely Mary Ann (1931), *Delicious* (1931), *The 1st Year* (1932), *Tess of the Storm Country* (1932), *State Fair* (1933), *Adorable* (1933), *Paddy the Next Best Thing* (1933), *Carolina* (1934), *Change of Heart* (1934), *Servants' Entrance* (1934), *One More Spring* (1935), *The Farmer Takes a Wife* (1935), *Small Town Girl* (1936), *Ladies in Love* (1936), *A Star Is Born* (1937), *Three Loves Has Nancy* (1938), *The Young in Heart* (1938), and *Bernadine* (1957). ❖ See also Connie Billips, *Janet Gaynor: A Bio-Bibliography* (Greenwood Press, 1992); and *Women in World History.*

GAYNOR, Mitzi (1930—). American actress, dancer, and singer. Born Franceska Mitzie Gerber (sometimes seen Franceska Mitzi Marlene De Charney von Gerber), Sept 4, 1930, in Chicago, Illinois; m. Jack Bean (talent agent), 1954. ❖ Made stage debut at age 3; made film debut in *My Blue Heaven* (1950); subsequently made a string of musicals for Fox, including *Golden Girl* (1951), in which she played Lotta Crabtree; made a number of hit films at other studios, including *Anything Goes* (1956), with Bing Crosby, *The Joker Is Wild,* opposite Frank Sinatra, and *Les Girls,* co-starring Gene Kelly and Kay Kendall (both 1957); chosen by director Joshua Logan for the coveted role of nurse Nellie Forbush in the film version of *South Pacific* but the movie was a failure and damaged her career; appeared on tv and initiated a nightclub act in which she sang, danced, and performed comedy skits; made 10 tv specials, including "Mitzi and a Hundred Guys." ❖ See also *Women in World History.*

GAYTAN, Andrea. Mexican wakeboarder. Born in Mexico. ❖ Pioneer of women's wakeboarding, won gold (1998), silver (1997), and bronze (1999) at X Games in women's wakeboarding; won gold at Gravity Games (1999); retired from professional competition (1999). Invert trick known as Mexican Roll named after her.

GE CUILIN (1930—). Chinese children's writer. Born 1930 in China. ❖ Labeled a "Rightist" (counter-revolutionary) by the Maoist regime (1957), was rehabilitated (1970s); writings include *The Clever Daughter-in-Law* (1956) and *Little Hero of the Steppes* as well as other tales, plays, and verse for children.

GE FEI (1975—). Chinese badminton player. Born Oct 9, 1975, in Jiangsu, China. ❖ Won a gold medal for doubles at Atlanta Olympics (1996) and at Sydney Olympics (2000).

GE YANG (1916—). Chinese journalist. Born 1916 in China; children: 3 sons; 2 daughters (who have joined her in US). ❖ Co-founder and chief editor of *New Observer,* joined Communist Party and worked for the New China News Agency; founded the *New Observer,* China's leading liberal journal; branded a "Rightist" (counter-revolutionary) because she felt the Communist Party was not democratic, was exiled to a work camp in the countryside (1957) and forced to do hard labor for 10 years; sent to Inner Mongolia for another 10 years, 22 years all told; was rehabilitated (1970s); relaunched the *New Observer* (1980s); at the height of the democracy movement, left China for conference in US on the May Fourth Movement (1989); was to return May 20, the day authorities declared martial law in Beijing; remained in exile in US after the *New Observer* was blamed for inciting the student protests and closed down.

GEAR, Luella (1897–1980). American comedian and actress. Born Sept 5, 1897, in NYC; died April 3, 1980, in NYC; m. Byron Chandler (div.); m. G. Maurice Heckscher (div.); m. Frederick Engel (div.). ❖ Made Broadway debut as Luella in *Love o' Mike* (1917), followed by *The Gold Diggers, Elsie, Poppy, Gay Divorcee, Life Begins at 8:40, On Your Toes, Streets of Paris, My Romance, Sabrina Fair* and *Four Winds;* also appeared in films and on tv.

GEBARA, Ivone (1944—). Brazilian theologian, author and educator. Born Dec 9, 1944, in São Paulo, Brazil; Pontificia Catholic University of São Paulo, doctorate in philosophy (1975); Catholic University of Louvain, Belgium, doctorate in religious sciences (1998). ❖ Feminist theologian and ecofeminist whose work addresses questions of social inequality for women and poor in Latin America, joined Augustinian Congregation of Sisters of Our Lady (1967); influenced by liberation theology and affected by growing strength of conservative forces in Catholic Church as progressive trends weakened; became active teacher and researcher, teaching philosophy and theology for 17 years at Theological Institute of Recife until its closing (1989); worked for 12 years at Department of Research and Assistance, which specialized in theological training of alternative, grassroots ministries; lives and works (since 1973) in lower-income community in northeastern Brazil, providing assistance to poor while continuing scholarly and activist work; believes that church must address social justice and ecology; presents practical guidelines for antiracist, antisexist, antielitist ecofeminist struggle; has taught, consulted and lectured worldwide and on Brazilian radio. Writings include *Teologia a ritmo de mulher* (Theology for Women, 1995), *Teologia ecofeminista: Ensaio para repensar o conhecimento e a religião* (Ecofeminist Theology: Rethinking Knowledge and Religion, 1997), *Le mal au féminin: Réflexions théologiques à partir du féminisme* (The Female Evil: Theological Reflections Based on Feminism, 1999) and *Longing for Running Waters* (1999).

GEBBIE, Grace (1877–1936). *See Drayton, Grace Gebbie.*

GEBHARDT, Evelyne (1954—). German politician. Born Jan 19, 1954, in Montreuil-sous-Bois, France. ❖ Named vice-chair of the Working Party of Social-Democratic Women (1992); as a European Socialist, elected to 4th and 5th European Parliament (1994–99, 1999–2004).

GEBWEILER, Catherine or Katharina von (d. around 1340). *See Katharina von Gebweiler.*

GECZI, Erika (1959—). Hungarian kayaker. Born Mar 10, 1959, in Hungary. ❖ At Seoul Olympics, won a silver medal in K4 500 meters (1988).

GEDDES, Annabella Mary (1864–1955). New Zealand welfare worker and feminist. Name variations: Annabella Mary Webster, Mary Webster, Mary Geddes. Born Annabella Mary Webster, May 19, 1864, at Mangungu on Hokianga Harbor, New Zealand; died Dec 5, 1955, in Remuera, New Zealand; dau. of William Webster (interpreter and saw-miller) and Annabella (Gillies) Webster; m. John McKail Geddes (importer and merchant), 1886 (died 1910); children: 7. ❖ Founding member of Auckland branch of Society for Promotion of Health of Women and Children (later known as Plunkett Society, 1908); served on Auckland committee of New Zealand Society for the Protection of Women and Children; board member of War Relief Association following World War I; established community kitchens and medical relief services after influenza pandemic of 1918; established Hearth Fire Movement (1915); active in reviving National Council of Women of New Zealand in Auckland (1917); lectured on feminist issues until 1920s. ❖ See also *Dictionary of New Zealand Biography* (Vol. 3).

GEDDES, Barbara Bel (b. 1922). *See Bel Geddes, Barbara.*

GEDDES, Jane (1960—). American golfer. Born Feb 5, 1960, in Huntington, NY; attended Florida State. ❖ Turned pro (1983); won US Women's Open (1986); won Boston Five Classic (1986, 1987); won Women's Kemper Open, Jamie Farr Toledo Classic, GNA/Glendale Federal Classic, and LPGA championship (1987); won Jamaica Classic and Atlantic City Classic (1993); won Oldsmobile Classic (1994); won Chicago Challenge (1996).

GEDDES, Janet (fl. 1637). Scottish religious dissenter. Name variations: Jenny. Flourished around 1637. ❖ Is said to have been the originator of a riot in St. Giles' Church, Edinburgh, Scotland (July 23, 1637); reputedly emphasized her protest against the introduction of the English liturgy into Scotland by throwing her folding stool at the head of the officiating bishop.

GEDDES, Mary (1864–1955). *See Geddes, Annabella Mary.*

GEDDES, Wilhelmina (1887–1955). Irish ecclesiastical artist. Born in Drumreilly, Co. Leitrim, Ireland, 1887; died in 1955; attended Methodist College, Belfast; Belfast School of Art; Metropolitan School of Art, Dublin. ❖ One of Dublin's 1st stained-glass artists, was a member of Sarah Purser's Studio of Ecclesiastical Art, An Túr Gloine; completed an 8-paneled window on the theme of the Children of Lir for the Ulster Museum (1929), installed the Great Rose Window in the Cathedral of Ypres in memory of Albert I, king of the Belgians (1938), and designed windows for churches in Ireland, New Zealand, and Canada; also illustrated books and designed book jackets, book plates, stamps and posters.

GEE, Dolly (1897–1978). Chinese-American embezzler. Born 1897 in Canton, China; died 1987; dau. of Charlie Gee (banker). ❖ With father, was placed in charge of Chinatown (NY) branch of French-American Bank (became Bank of America in 1929); earned great acclaim as 1st woman banker in country and was a pillar of the Chinese community; under her direction, branch assets increased from $2 million to $20 million in 3 decades; father retired (1929); just before her own retirement (Dec 1963), confessed to having embezzled more than $300,000 with her father since 1923; served 16 months of 5-year sentence for embezzlement at Terminal Island.

GEE, Helen (1919–2004). American art gallery owner. Born Helen Charlotte Wimmer, April 29, 1919, in Jersey City, New Jersey; dau. of Peter Wimmer; m. Yun Gee (Chinese modernist painter), 1942 (div.); m. Kevin Sullivan (div.); children: (1st m.) Li-lan Gee (artist). ❖ Launched the Limelight photography gallery in Greenwich Village (1954), which became a pioneering blueprint for the showcasing and selling of photography as an art form; closed Limelight (1961) and became an art consultant. ❖ See also memoir *Limelight: A Greenwich Village Photography Gallery and Coffeehouse in the 50's* (University of New Mexico Press, 1997).

GEER, Charlotte (1957—). American rower. Born Nov 13, 1957, in US. ❖ At Los Angeles Olympics, won a silver medal in single sculls (1984).

GEIJSSEN, Carolina (1947—). Dutch speedskater. Name variations: Carry Geijssen. Born Carolina Cornelia Catharina Geijssen, Jan 11, 1947, in Amsterdam, Netherlands; sister of Beppie te-Winkel-Geijssen (skater). ❖ Won Dutch National allround title (1966); won a gold medal for the 1,000 meters and a silver for the 1,500 meters at Grenoble Olympics (1968); won a bronze medal at World championships for small allround (1968); retired (1971).

GEINECKE, Iraida Gustavovna (c. 1895–1990). *See Odoevtseva, Irina.*

GEIRINGER, Hilda (1893–1973). German applied mathematician and statistician. Born Sept 28, 1893, in Vienna; died Mar 22, 1973, in Santa Barbara, California; only daughter and one of two children of Ludwig (textile manufacturer) and Martha (Wertheimer) Geiringer; University of Vienna, PhD in pure mathematics, 1917; m. Felix Pollaczek (mathematician), 1921 (div. 1925); m. Richard von Mises (mathematician and professor at Harvard), Nov 5, 1943 (died 1953); children: (1st m.) one daughter, Magda. ❖ Served as editor of *Fortschritte der Mathematik* (1920); as assistant to Richard von Mises in Institute of Applied Mathematics at University of Berlin (1921–27), was recognized for her outstanding teaching as well as for her important research in probability theory and the mathematical development of plasticity theory, which led to the Geiringer equations for plane plastic deformations (1930); with Hitler's rise (1933), fled to Turkey, where, after learning the language, she obtained a job lecturing at Istanbul University; went to US (1939), where she secured a position as a lecturer at Bryn Mawr College; moved to Massachusetts (1944), to chair the mathematics department at Wheaton College, a position she held until her retirement. ❖ See also *Women in World History.*

GEIRTHRUD. *Variant of Gertrude.*

GEISE, Sugar (1909–1988). American actress. Name variations: Tanya Geise. Born Dec 17, 1909, in Chicago, Illinois; died Oct 30, 1988, in Hollywood, California. ❖ Popular dancer and cabaret performer (1940s); films include *42nd Street, Swing Time, A Day at the Races, Shall We Dance, For Me and My Gal* and *Advance to the Rear.*

GEISE, Tanya (1909–1988). *See Geise, Sugar.*

GEISLER, Ilse. East German luge athlete. Born in Germany. ❖ Won a silver medal for singles at Innsbruck Olympics (1964).

GEISSLER, Ines (1963—). East German swimmer. Born Feb 16, 1963, in East Germany. ❖ At Moscow Olympics, won a gold medal in 200-meter butterfly (1980).

GEISTER, Janet M. (1885–1964). American nurse. Born Janet Marie Louise Sophie Geister, June 17, 1885, in Elgin, Illinois; died Dec 8, 1964, in Evanston, Illinois; dau. of Sophie (Witte) Geister and Jacob Christian Henry Geister. ❖ Fought for improved conditions for private-duty nurses (the largest group of nurses before WWII); graduated from Elgin's Sherman Hospital School of Nursing (1910) and from the Chicago School of Civics and Philanthropy (social work certificate, June 1914); hired (1917) by Julia Lathrop, then the federal Children Bureau's Chief, to investigate the high infant mortality rates in northern Montana; worked on the "Save 100,000 Babies" campaign (1918); employed (Oct 1919) as the National Organization for Public Health Nursing's (NOPHN) Field Secretary; diagnosed with uterine cancer (1921); was the executive secretary (1923–27) of the Foundation Committee on Dispensary Development, an organization that studied NYC dispensaries; revealed the poor work conditions of 1,400 private-duty nurses in an independent survey (results were published in the *American Journal of Nursing*); hired by Lillian Clayton (then ANA president) to serve as director (Aug 1926–Mar 1933) of the American Nurses Association's headquarters; became associate editor of *Trained Nurse and Hospital Review* (June 1933), then editor (1941); wrote "Plain Talk," a column in *Trained Nurse and Hospital Review* and "Candid Comments" for the journal *RN*.

GEISTINGER, Marie (1833–1903). Austrian soprano, actress, and theater manager. Born Maria Charlotte Cäcilia Geistinger in Graz, Styria, Austria, July 26, 1833 (some sources cite July 20, 1828 or 1836); died in Klagenfurt, Carinthia, Austria, Sept 29, 1903; m. August Kormann (1850–1930, actor), 1877 (div. 1881). ❖ Celebrated singer, actress, and theater manager, who helped popularize the stage works of Johann Strauss, Jr., made debut as an adult actress in Munich (1850); performed in Vienna at the Theater in der Josefstadt (1852), with parodies of then-famous Spanish dancer Pepita de Oliva; left Vienna for Berlin (1854), remaining there for several years before moving on to successful engagements in Hamburg and Riga; reigned over the Riga stage (1859–63); accepted an offer from Vienna to star in Jacques Offenbach's *La belle Helene* (1865), becoming the undisputed "Queen of Operetta"; appeared in countless performances of Offenbach (including his *La Grande-Duchesse de Gerolstein* and *Barbe-bleue*), as well as in other composers' works; became co-director of the Theater an der Wien (1869), sharing management responsibilities with Maximilian Steiner; premiered in the 1st indigenous Viennese operetta, Johann Strauss, Jr.'s hit *Indigo oder die vierzig Räuber* (*Indigo or the Forty Thieves*) at the Theater an der Wien (1871); then appeared as Rosalinde in Strauss' *Die Fledermaus* (The Bat, 1874); resigned from the management of the Theater an der Wien (1875), but remained on stage, creating lead roles in the premieres of two more Johann Strauss operettas, *Carneval in Rom* (1873) and *Cagliostro in Wien* (1875); appeared at Vienna's Stadttheater as Queen Elizabeth I in Heinrich von Laube's *Essex*, as well as taking the roles of Medea and Sappho in the play by Grillparzer; also successfully played Beatrice in *Much Ado about Nothing*; toured North America (1880); gave farewell performance in Vienna (1900). ❖ See also *Women in World History*.

GELB, Joan (1901–2001). See Bove, Joan.

GELFMAN, Gesia (d. 1882). Russian revolutionary. Name variations: Guessia or Jessie Helfman or Helfmann. Grew up in Mozyr (Minsk province), Russia; died of peritonitis, Feb 1, 1882; children: daughter (b. Oct 12, 1881). ❖ To avoid an arranged marriage, fled home at 17 and moved to Kiev; enrolled in midwifery courses and joined a group known as the Fritsche, which advocated socialism and class warfare; was imprisoned for serving as an intermediary for those engaged in propagandizing against the government (1875); escaped (1879); following assassination of Alexander II, tsar of Russia, was again arrested (1881) and, though pregnant, condemned to death; after demonstrations in Russia and abroad, had sentence commuted; gave birth in prison but the child was taken from her; died three months later. ❖ See also *Women in World History*.

GELISIO, Deborah (1976—). Italian shooter. Born Feb 26, 1976, in Belluno, Italy. ❖ Won a silver medal for double trap at Sydney Olympics (2000).

GELLER, Margaret Joan (1947—). American astronomer. Born Dec 8, 1947, in Ithaca, NY; dau. of a crystallographer at Bell Laboratories; Princeton University, PhD, 1975. ❖ Was a professor at Harvard University (from 1988) and a senior scientist at the Harvard-Smithsonian Center for Astrophysics (from 1991); with astronomer John Huchra and French graduate student Valerie de Lapparent, created a map of approximately 1,000 galaxies (1980s) which disproved the idea that the universe had a smooth structure, demonstrating instead clusters of star systems (the largest structure they discovered, termed the Great Wall, is comprised of thousands of galaxies); her work was revolutionary in increasing knowledge about the large-scale structure of the universe.

GELLHORN, Edna (1878–1970). American suffragist and community leader. Name variations: Edna Fischel; Edna Fischel Gellhorn. Born Edna Fischel on Dec 18, 1878, in St. Louis, Missouri; died Sept 24, 1970, in St. Louis, Missouri; dau. of Washington Emil Fischel and Martha (Ellis) Fischel; m. George Gellhorn, Oct 21, 1903; children: 3 sons (b. 1904, 1906, 1913), 1 daughter (b. 1908). ❖ Organized charity drives and worked in campaigns to purify city water supply and to inspect milk; joined suffrage movement (1910), serving in Missouri and St. Louis Suffrage Leagues and helping organize "Walkless-Talkless Parade" at Democratic National Convention in St. Louis (1916); worked as regional administrator of President's food program (WWI); was arrangements chair at suffrage convention where League of Women Voters (LWV) was established (1919), and served as 1st LWV vice president and 1st state wing president; led successful lobby by LWV to introduce merit hiring by

MO government (1930s) and to pass new state constitution (1945); helped found Citizens Community on Nuclear Information, and established local units of American Association for the United Nations; was appointed to Missouri Commission on the Status of Women (1964). Received numerous honors, including honorary LLD from Washington University (1964), which established Edna Fischel Gellhorn Professorship of Public Affairs (1968); Edna Gellhorn Award Dinner was sponsored by Women's Political Caucus and National Organization of Women (1973).

GELLHORN, Martha (1908–1998). American writer and journalist. Born Martha Ellis Gellhorn on Nov 8, 1908, in St. Louis, Missouri; died of cancer at her home in London, England, Feb 16, 1998; dau. of Edna Fischel Gellhorn (community activist) and George Gellhorn (gynecologist); attended John Burroughs School, St. Louis, 1923–26; Bryn Mawr College, 1926–29; m. Bertrand de Jouvenel (journalist), in summer 1933 (sep. 1935); m. Ernest Hemingway (novelist), Nov 21, 1940 (div. 1945); m. Thomas Stanley Matthews (editor of *Time*), Feb 4, 1954 (div. 1963); children: (adopted) George Alexander Gellhorn. ❖ The leading female war correspondent of World War II, began writing career with *New Republic* (1929); bartered her way to Europe (1930), settling on Paris' Left Bank and joining the Paris staff of *Vogue*; had special assignments for *St. Louis Post-Dispatch* (1930); returned to US to work as investigator-at-large for Federal Emergency Relief Administration (FERA, 1934); produced semi-autobiographical novel *What Mad Pursuit* (1934), followed by a fictional account of the Depression, *The Trouble I've Seen* (1936), which brought her minor celebrity status; soon had short stories appearing in *The New Yorker* and *Scribner's Magazine*; met Ernest Hemingway in Key West (1936); began covering the civil war in Spain for *Collier's* (1937), plunging her readers into the daily bombing of Madrid with an intensity that Hemingway himself could not capture; broadcasting from Madrid, conveyed the city's quiet stoicism; with onset of World War II (Nov 1939), was sent to Finland by *Collier's* to cover its incipient war with Russia; sent to Asia to report on Japanese offensives and China's ability to resist them (1941); published semi-autobiographical novel *A Stricken Field* and collection of short stories, *The Heart of Another* (both 1940); novel *Liana* made the bestseller list (1943); covered London (1943), the Italian front (1944); three days after D-Day (June 1944), went ashore at Normandy Beach; attached herself to a Polish squadron stationed in the Adriatic, then traveled through France; reported on the Allied invasion of the Netherlands and covered the Battle of the Bulge; immediately after the war, covered Sukarno's rebellion in Java and the Nuremberg trials; resided in Cuernavaca (1948–52); covered Jerusalem trial of Adolf Eichmann; reported on the Vietnam war (1966), with blistering indictments of American military leaders; was a frequent contributor to the *New Republic*, the *Atlantic Monthly*, the *Saturday Evening Post* and *Good Housekeeping*; also wrote (play, with Virginia Cowles) *Love Goes to Press* (1946), *Wine of Astonishment* (1948, reprinted as *The Point of No Return*, 1989), *The Honeyed Peace* (1953), *Two by Two* (1958), *The Face of War* (1959), *His Own Man* (1961), *Pretty Tales for Tired People* (1965), *The Lowest Trees Have Tops* (1967), *The Weather in Africa* (1978), (editor) *The Face of War* (1988), *The Novellas of Martha Gellhorn* (1993). ❖ See also memoirs *Travels with Myself and Another* (Allan Dale, 1983) and *The View from the Ground* (Atlantic Monthly Press, 1988); Carl Rollyson, *Nothing Ever Happens to the Brave: The Story of Martha Gellhorn* (St. Martin's, 1990); and *Women in World History*.

GELMAN, Polina (1919—). Soviet combat navigator. Name variations: Polya. Pronunciation: Puh-LEE-na Vlah-di-MEE-ruv-nuh GEL-mun. Born Polina Vladimirovna Gelman in Oct 1919 in Berdichev, Ukraine, USSR; dau. of Vladimir (tailor) and Yelya (worker) Gelman; undergraduate study in department of history, Moscow State University; trained as Spanish linguist, Military Institute of Foreign Languages; completed graduate dissertation in economics, earning Candidate of Sciences (Economics) degree; m. Vladimir Kolosov (now a retired lieutenant colonel), 1948; children: daughter Galina Kolosov, a historian (b. 1949). ❖ Night-bomber navigator during World War II, who received the Hero of the Soviet Union medal for bravery in combat; moved with family to Gomel, Byelorussia (1920); entered Moscow State University (1938); joined Soviet Air Force (Oct 1941) and was assigned to Marina Raskova's training group, Aviation Group No. 122; as a member of the famous "night witches" bomber regiment of Soviet female aviators, served as navigator with 588th Night Bomber Aviation Regiment (later redesignated 46th Guards, 1942–45); during her three years as a navigator, flew 860 combat missions, nearly all at night, in the rickety old open-cockpit Po-2 biplane, harassing German troops, disrupting the soldiers' rest, and wreaking what damage could be wreaked on military targets near the front lines (of the 46th; 31 women, or about 27% of the flying personnel, were killed in combat); served as military linguist; resigned from military service (1956) with rank of guards major; completed graduate education; served as senior lecturer (docent) and associate professor in department of Political Economy at Moscow Institute of Social Sciences. Awarded Hero of the Soviet Union. ❖ See also *Women in World History.*

GELORIA (d. 1022). *See Elvira Gonzalez of Galicia.*

GELTZER, Ykaterina (1876–1962). Russian ballet dancer. Name variations: Ekaterina or Yekaterina Geltzer. Born Ykaterina Vasilyevna Geltzer, Nov 14, 1876, in Moscow, Russia; died Dec 12, 1962, in Moscow; dau. of Vasily Geltzer (ballet master of Bolshoi Ballet); m. Vasili Tikhomirov. ❖ Prima ballerina who helped preserve the classical technique and repertory of the Imperial Russian Ballet, 1st trained at the Bolshoi with her father who served as ballet master; danced with the Bolshoi's professional company (from 1894) before moving on to Maryinsky troupe in St. Petersburg where she danced principal roles in both older and newer works, including Petipa's *Raymonda* and *La Bayadère,* and the newer Gorsky's *The Goldfish* (1903) and *Salambó* (1910), among others; toured with Maryinsky dancers throughout Western Europe and US, appearing with Vasily Tikhomirov at Alhambra Theatre in London (1911) and as Odette/Odile on Mikhail Mordkin's US tour; rejoined the Bolshoi and danced there as principal ballerina until retirement; created one of her most famous roles, that of Tao-Hoa in *The Red Poppy* (1927).

GEMMEI (c. 661–721). Japanese empress. Name variations: Gemmei-tenno; Empress Gemmyo; Princess Abe or Princess Ahe (name before she became empress). Pronunciation: Gem-may. Birth thought to have been in 661, most likely in Naniwa, then the capital; died in Nara (new capital) in 721 and buried in the tomb, "Nahoyama no Higashi"; dau. of Emperor Tenji and Nuhi; m. Prince Kusakabe; children: Princess Hidaka (680–748), who ruled as Empress Genshō; Emperor Mommu (d. 707). ❖ One of Japan's most able rulers, this Nara Period empress (43rd tennō and 5th of 10 empresses to date in Japanese history) reigned from 707 to 715; politically seasoned and wise, wielded power decisively yet in a spirit of moderation; took steps to further strengthen the authority of the tennō (emperor-empress) and the central government by enforcing laws against peasants who fled their fields and by restricting property ownership of the nobility and Buddhist temples; commissioned the *Kojiki* (chronicle of ancient matters), the 1st written history of Japan. ❖ See also *Women in World History.*

GEMS, Pam (1925—). British playwright. Born Iris Pamela Price, Aug 1, 1925, in Bransgore, in the New Forest, Hampshire, England; dau. of Jim Price and Elsie Mabel (Annetts) Price; attended Manchester University; m. Keith Gems, 1949; children: 4. ❖ Came to prominence with the London production of *Dusa, Fish, Stas and Vi* (1976); other plays, frequently produced on West End, Broadway, and in Stratford, include *Queen Christina* (1977), *Piaf* (1978), *Loving Women* (1985), *The Danton Affair* (1986), a musical adaptation of *The Blue Angel* (1991), *Deborah's Daughter* (1995), and *Stanley* (1996); also adapted works by other writers, including *Uncle Vanya* (1979), *A Doll's House* (1980), *The Cherry Orchard* (1984), *Camille* (1985), *Yerma* (1993), *Ghosts* (1993), and *The Seagull* (1994); wrote the novels *Mrs. Frampton* (1989) and *Bon Voyage, Mrs. Frampton* (1990).

GENAUSS, Carsta (1959—). East German kayaker. Born Nov 30, 1959, in East Germany. ❖ At Moscow Olympics, won a gold medal in K2 500-meters (1980).

GENCER, Leyla (1924—). Turkish soprano and coloratura. Born in Istanbul, Turkey, Oct 10, 1924 (some sources cite 1928); m. Ibrahim Gencer. ❖ Made stage debut in Ankara singing the role of Santuzza (1950); made triumphant Italian debut in Naples in *Cavalleria Rusticana* (1953); engaged by Naples' San Carlo Opera House to sing in both *Madama Butterfly* and *Eugene Onegin* (which she sang in Italian); over the next decades, performed at most of the world's great opera houses, with noted conductors, including the legendary Italian Tullio Serafin who put her on the path as a bel canto singer; by 1956, was appearing regularly at Milan's La Scala Opera House; sang the "Libera me" from Verdi's *Requiem* at La Scala memorial service for Arturo Toscanini (1957); appeared in several world premieres at La Scala, including *Dialogues des Carmélites* by Francis Poulenc (1957) and *Assassinio nella cattedrale* by Ildebrando Pizzetti (1958); became a major figure in the opera world, presenting annual guest appearances at Florence's Maggio musicale and

the San Francisco Opera; sang at Spoleto Festival in one of the rare performances of Sergei Prokofiev's *The Fiery Angel* (1959); made Austrian debut at Vienna State Opera as well as the Salzburg Festival, where her performance of Amelia in Verdi's *Simon Boccanegra* earned raves (1961); by end of career, had a repertory of 72 operas, overwhelmingly Italian but also including such modern works as Prokofiev's *The Fiery Angel* and Benjamin Britten's *Albert Herring*; appeared at Naples' Teatro San Carlo in the title role of Donizetti's long-neglected opera *Caterina Cornaro* (1972); retired from opera (1983) and from concertizing (1992). ❖ See also *Women in World History.*

GENÉE, Adeline (1878–1970). Danish-born ballerina. Name variations: AG; Adelina or Adeline Genee; Dame Adeline Genée; Dame Adeline Genée-Isitt. Pronunciation: Je-NAY or EYE-sit. Born Anina Margarete Kirstina Petra Jensen on Jan 6, 1878, in the Danish village of Hinnerup, in Aarhus, Jutland, the surviving twin in a farm family; died in Esscher, Surrey, April 23, 1970; dau. of Peter Jensen (musician) and Kirsten Jensen (of Norwegian descent); at 8, studied dance with her famous aunt and uncle, dancers Antonia (Zimmermann) Genée and Alexander Genée; m. Frank S.N. Isitt (prosperous businessman from London), June 11, 1910 (died 1939); no children. ❖ The most famous ballerina of her day, who was a major force in the world of dance, elevating the status of the dancer to a new level of respectability and bringing the art of ballet to the masses as well as the cultured elite; won critical acclaim at a young age; made London debut in *Monte Cristo* at the Empire Theatre (1897) and remained at the Empire for next 10 years, appearing as Fairy Good Fortune in *Alaska* (1898), Lizette in *Round the Town Again* (1899), Variations in *Sea-Side* (1900), Queen of Butterfly Land in *Les Papillons* (1901), Swanilda in *Coppelia* (1902), Grand Adagio in *The Roses of England* (1902), Coquette in *The Milliner Duchess* (1903), the Hunting Dance and the Cakewalk in *High Jinks* (1904), the Bugle Boy in *The Bugle Call* (1905), title role in *Cinderella* (1906), and Queen of the Dance in *The Belle of the Ball* (1907); sailed to US to star in a Ziegfeld's *The Soul Kiss* in Philadelphia (1907); returned to US for 2nd tour (1908), performing in 23 theaters in 30 weeks; retired from the stage (1914); one of the most technically perfect dancers, helped found the London Association of Operatic Dancing (later known as the Royal Academy of Dancing, RAD), which meticulously standardized methods of teaching ballet in the British realm, and served as its president for 34 years (1920–54). Named Dame Commander of the British Empire (1950); received "Ingenio et Arti" from king of Denmark; Order of Dannebrog (1953). ❖ See also Ivor Guest, *Adeline Genée—A Lifetime of Ballet Under Six Reigns* (A.& C. Black, 1958); and *Women in World History.*

GENENGER, Martha (1911—). German swimmer. Name variations: also seen as Martha Geneger. Born Nov 11, 1911, in Germany. ❖ At age 14, won the silver medal in the 200-meter breaststroke in the Berlin Olympics (1936).

GENÊT OR GENET (1892–1978). *See Flanner, Janet.*

GENEVIÈVE (c. 422–512). Patron saint of Paris. Name variations: Genevieve; Genevieve of Paris; Genovefa, Genovefae. Born at Nanterre (some sources claim Montriere), near Paris, between 420 and 423, most sources cite 422; died in Paris, Jan 3, 512; dau. of peasants, Severus and Gerontia. ❖ Having attracted the attention of St. Germanicus, entered a convent at 7 and took the veil at 15; moved to Paris; became revered by all, religious or non-religious, for her charity; when Attila and his Huns swept into Gaul (451), is credited with stopping a mass exodus of Parisians by prompting the people to trust in God and urging them to do works of penance, adding that if they did so the town would be spared (Attila left Paris untouched); years later, when the pagan Childeric besieged the city, set out on an expedition with fellow religious women for the relief of the starving people and successfully brought back boats laden with corn; successfully interceded with Childeric for the lives of many of his prisoners; is also credited with the 1st designs for the magnificent church begun by Clovis, and was interred within the structure, which became the Church of St. Geneviève. The church was plundered by the Normans (847), partially restored (1177), revitalized by the construction of murals of her in several wall panels by Puvis de Chavannes (1764), and converted into the Panthéon (1793), where busts of the famous of France are enshrined. Feast day is Jan 3. ❖ See also *Women in World History.*

GENEVIÈVE (1920–2004). French-born singer. Born Ginette Marguérite Auger, April 17, 1920, in Paris, France; died Mar 14, 2004, in Los Angeles, California; dau. of Edouard Roger Auger (prosperous construction contractor) and Marthe Auger; m. Ted Mills (writer, director producer), 1960 (died 2003). ❖ As chanteuse and cook, opened Chez Geneviève, a small nightclub in Montmarte (1949); moved to US (1954) and headlined the Persian Room at the Plaza; was best known, however, for mangling the English language on Jack Paar's "Tonight Show" (1957–62); on stage, appeared in several musical comedies and toured in *Can Can* (1958).

GENEVIÈVE DE BRABANT (fl. 8th c.). French saint. Name variations: Genevieve of Brabant; Genoveva or Genovefa. Possibly fl. in 8th century; m. Siegfried, count of Treves and Brabant; children: son Scherzenreich. ❖ According to legend, was falsely accused of adultery by a servant, Golo; was sentenced by husband to be taken into woods, along with infant son Scherzenreich, and put to death; abandoned in the forest by the executioners, lived in a cave with son in the Ardennes, nourished by red deer; seven years later, was discovered by husband who had been guided by a red deer while out hunting (Siegfried had learned of the treachery of Golo). ❖ See also *Women in World History*.

GENEVIEVE OF NEW FRANCE (1656–1680). See Tekakwitha, Kateri.

GENHART, Cecile Staub (1898–1983). European-born pianist. Born in 1898; died in 1983; studied in Europe with Feruccio Busoni and Emil Frey. ❖ Joined the piano faculty of the Eastman School of Music in Rochester, New York (1924), where she spent her entire career.

GÉNIAT, Marcelle (1879–1959). Russian-born actress. Name variations: Marcelle Geniat. Born Eugenie Martin, 1879, in St. Petersburg, Russia, of French parentage; died Sept 28, 1959, in Paris, France. ❖ Entered Paris Conservatoire (1897); made 1st appearance at the Comédie Française as Pauline in *Frou-Frou* (1899), remaining there for over 12 years in such plays as *Les femmes savantes, Andromaque, Le Médecin malgré lui, Le Luthier de Crémone, Diane de Lys, Le Monde ou l'on s'ennuie, Le Passant, Gringoire, Blanchette, L'Enigme, Simone, Chacun sa Vie, Primerose, Alkestis, La petite amie* and *Bagatelle;* during WWI, served as the head of the Buffon Military Hospital (1914–17); returned to the stage in *Monsieur Beverley* (1917) and subsequently appeared in *La race, Casanova, L'Amirable Crichton* and *Daniel;* made London debut with Sarah Bernhardt in *Daniel* (1921); made over 40 films, including *Crime et châtiment* (as Mme Raskolnikov), *Le voile bleu, La passante, Manon des sources* and *Sophie et le crime;* elected a Societaire of the Comédie Française (1910).

GENLIS, Stéphanie-Félicité, Comtesse de (1746–1830). French writer. Name variations: Countess de Genlis. Born Stéphanie-Félicité Ducrest de Saint-Aubin on Jan 21, 1746, at Champçéry in Burgundy, France; died Dec 31, 1830, in Paris, France; dau. of Pierre-Cèsar Ducrest or du Crest (French noble who squandered most of his family fortune) and Marie-Françoise de Mézière; m. Charles Alexis, Comte Brûlart de Genlis, later Marquis de Sillery, Nov 8, 1763; children: Caroline de Genlis (1764–1783); Pulchérie de Genlis (b. 1766); Casimir (1768–1773); rumored to have given birth to two illeg. daughters with Louis-Philippe Joseph (Philippe-Egalité), Duke d'Orléans: Pamela (1773–1831), the future Lady Edward Fitzgerald; and Hermine (1776–1822). ❖ Prodigious writer of novels and educational treatises who became the 1st woman to serve as the governor of royal princes when she was appointed to direct the education of the children of Philippe, duke d'Orléans; married at 17 (1763); introduced into Parisian society (1765); became lady-in-waiting to the Louise Marie of Bourbon, Duchesse d'Orléans (1769) and governess to her daughters (1777); dominated the social scene at the Palais-Royale and soon became one of the most sought-after women in Paris; made governor of the sons of the Duke and Duchesse d'Orléans (1782), the 1st woman named governor of royal princes; published *Adèle et Theodore ou lettres sur l'éducation* (1782); published *Discours sur l'éducation publique du peuple* (1791), which pushed for universal education of both boys and girls; lived in exile in Europe during the French Revolution (1793–1800); published *Madame de la Vallière* (1804), which was a fantastic success, followed by one of her most enduring works, *Souvenirs de Félicie* (1806); published *Mémoires* (1825), which were praised in literary circles for their "purity of style and natural charm"; all told, published over 100 books and claimed to have brought up and educated 19 children, including Louis-Philippe I, who not only survived the French Revolution but gave his country 18 years of peaceful rule during the tumultuous 19th century. ❖ See also Jean Harmand, *A Keeper of Royal Secrets: Being the Private and Political Life of Mme. de Genlis* (Eveleigh Nash, 1913); Violet Wyndham, *Madame de Genlis: A Biography* (Andre Deutsch, 1958; and *Women in World History*.

GENOA, Catherine of (1447–1510). See Catherine of Genoa.

GENOA, duchess of.
See Christine of Bourbon (1779–1849).
See Elizabeth of Saxony (1830–1912).

GENOVEFA, Genovefae. *Variant of Genevieve.*

GENOVESE, Kitty (1935–1964). American murder victim. Born Catherine Genovese, 1935, in Brooklyn, NY; murdered Mar 13, 1964, in Queens, NY; dau. of Vincent and Rachel Genovese (Italian-Americans). ❖ A 28-year-old bar manager, was returning home from work in the early morning hours when she became a symbol of urban apathy; was attacked and killed by a stranger outside her home in Kew Gardens, Queens, NY, while 38 neighbors looked on from their apartments and did nothing as she screamed for help (the serial killer, Winston Mosely, fled twice when residents turned on their lights but returned when the lights went back off; the attack lasted over 32 minutes). ❖ See also (documentary) *When Will People Help?* (loosely based tv movie) "Death Scream" (1975).

GENOVEVA. *Variant of Genevieve.*

GENSHŌ (680–748). Japanese empress. Name variations: Princess Hidaka or Hitaka (before ascending the throne); Gensho-tenno. Pronunciation: Gen-SHOW. Born in 680 (some sources cite 679), most likely in the Japanese capital Naniwa; died in 748 in Nara, a later capital of Japan; dau. of Empress Gemmei (c. 661–721) and Prince Kusakabe; sister of Emperor Mommu; niece of Empress Jitō (645–702); never married; no children. ❖ Reigned 715–724 as 44th sovereign during Nara Period, the 6th of 10 empresses who have reigned to date in Japanese history; came to throne upon abdication of mother, though Gemmei continued to oversee affairs of state until 721; encouraged continued growth in the arts, sciences, literature, and economic life; promulgated Yōro Code—which established the rule of her family, the imperial clan—throughout Japan (718); also commissioned a 2nd national history of Japan, the *Nihongi*, a meticulous chronicle of Japanese court and aristocratic life to the year 697 (completed in the middle of her reign, in 720); abdicated in favor of nephew Shomu when he reached age 25 (724). ❖ See also *Women in World History*.

GENTH, Lillian (1876–1953). American artist. Born Lillian Mathilde Genth in Philadelphia, Pennsylvania, 1876; died in 1953; dau. of Samuel Genth and Matilda Caroline (Rebsher) Genth; educated privately and in Philadelphia public schools; studied at the Philadelphia School of Design for Women with Elliott Daingerfield, and with James McNeill Whistler in Paris; never married. ❖ A popular artist at dawn of 20th century, was known for her portraits and paintings of the female nude against an Arcadian setting; work can be found in the National Gallery, Washington, DC, Carnegie Institute, Pittsburgh, National Arts Club and Metropolitan Museum of Art, both New York City, Brooklyn Museum, and private collections. ❖ See also *Women in World History*.

GENTILE-CORDIALE, Edera (1920–1993). Italian track-and-field athlete. Born Jan 30, 1920, in Italy; died April 4, 1993. ❖ At London Olympics, won a silver medal in the discus throw (1948).

GENTILESCHI, Artemisia (1593–c. 1653). Italian artist. Name variations: Aertimisiae Gentilescha. Pronunciation: Ar-tee-ME-zha Gente-LESkee. Born in Rome, Italy, July 8, 1593; died in Naples, Italy, around 1653; dau. of Orazio Gentileschi (painter) and Prudentia (Montone) Gentileschi; m. Pietro Antonio di Vincenzo Stiattesi (Florentine artist), in 1612; children: Palmira (or Prudentia), also a painter (b. 1618) and another girl (name unknown). ❖ One of the most celebrated women painters of the 17th century whose artistic influence, traceable from her native Italy to Spain and Holland, was obscured for centuries by the emphasis placed by many art historians upon her personal mores; at 17, painted earliest signed work, *Susanna and the Elders* (1610), which demonstrated an unusual maturity of style; met the man whose name would forever tarnish hers (1611), her tutor Agostino Tassi; was raped by Tassi who then promised to marry her; father sued Tassi for damage and injury as the result of the rape of his daughter (Mar 1612 [according to the law of the time, Artemisia, as the property of her father, had no legal recourse to justice]); on marriage, moved to Florence, where the support of Cosimo II, one of the Medici family, paved the way for her full acceptance into the artistic community; soon became a member of the Florence Accademia del Disegno, the 1st woman to enter since its founding in 1563; painted *Judith and Maidservant with the Head of Holofernes* (1625), which is recognized by art historians as her greatest work; worked in England for King Charles I (1638); moved to Naples (1642), where she was to spend the last decade of her life (though she had excelled at her work, influencing artists across Europe, worked for some of the most important patrons of the day, left paintings recognized both then and now as masterpieces, interest in her for centuries centered upon the details of her personal life, specifically her promiscuity, as evidenced through the rape trial). Paintings include *Judith Beheading Holofernes* (Galleria degli Uffizi, Florence); *Penitent Magdalen; Aurora; Rape of Proserpine; Lucrezia* (Durazzo-Adorno collection); *Cleopatra* (may be misattributed, Palazzo Rossi deposito); *The Portrait of a Condottiere* (or *Portrait of a Papal Knight*); *Esther and Ahasuerus* (Metropolitan Museum of Art, New York); *Annunciation* (1630, Museo di Capodimonte, Naples); *Fame* (1632); *Self-Portrait as the Allegory of Painting; St. Catherine* (1635); *St. Januarius with Lions* (Pozzuoli Basilica, Naples); *Adoration of the Magi* (Pozzuoli Basilica, Naples); *Sts. Proculus and Nicaea* (Pozzuoli Basilica, Naples); *David and Bathsheba* (two versions, one of which is in Columbus Museum of Art); and *Birth of John the Baptist* (Museo del Prado, Madrid). ❖ See also Anna Banti, *Artemisia* (trans. by Shirley D'Ardia Caracciolo, University of Nebraska Press, 1995); Mary D. Garrard, *Artemisia Gentileschi: The Image of the Female Hero in Italian Baroque Art* (Princeton University Press, 1989); and *Women in World History.*

GENTLE, Alice (1889–1958). American operatic soprano. Born Feb 24, 1889; died Feb 28, 1958, in Oakland, California. ❖ Sang with the Metropolitan Opera, San Francisco Opera, and La Scala in Milan.

GENTLEWOMAN, A (fl. 1660s–1680s). *See Ephelia.*

GENTNER, Diana (1936–1977). *See Hyland, Diana.*

GENTRY, Bobbie (1944—). American country-and-western singer. Name variations: Roberta Lee; Roberta Streeter. Born Roberta Lee Streeter on July 27, 1944, in Chickasaw Co., Mississippi; majored in philosophy at University of California at Los Angeles; m. Jim Stafford, 1978 (div.). ❖ Country singer, wrote 1st song at age 7; worked as secretary and Las Vegas showgirl; reached #1 with debut hit "Ode to Billy Joe" (1967), which won 3 Grammys and became her signature tune; released albums *Ode to Billy Joe* (1967), *The Delta Sweetie* (1969), *Fancy* (1970), and *Greatest Hits* (1990); sang hit duet with Glen Campbell on Everly Brothers' "All I Have to Do is Dream" (1970); hosted English tv series "Bobbie Gentry" (1968) and US series "The Bobbie Gentry Show" (1974); appeared frequently on "The Tonight Show Starring Johnny Carson" (1970s); became staple on Las Vegas casino circuit (1970s); sang song "Fancy" on tv series "Six Feet Under" (1991).

GENTRY, Eva (c. 1920—). American modern dancer and choreographer. Name variations: Henrietta Greenhood. Born Henrietta Greenhood, Aug 20, c. 1920, in Los Angeles, California. ❖ Moved to New York City from San Francisco area to train with Hanya Holm, Martha Graham, Doris Humphrey, Charles Weidman; danced in Holm company where she created roles in *Dance of Work and Play, Dance of Introduction, Salutation, The Too Are Exiles* and *Tragic Exodus* (1930s–40s), among others; taught at Clark Center, High School of Performing Arts, and Dance Notation Bureau (1940s–50s), and gave classes in improvisation to stage actors and dancers; began presenting improvised and untitled dance recitals on stage to enthusiastic audiences (c. 1955); worked, taught, and practiced Pilates method. Works of choreography include *So This Is Modern Dancing* (1935), *Quiet* (1949), *New Horizons* (1951), *Three Rhythms Circles* (1955), *The Antenna Bird* (1956), *All the Dead Soldiers* (1967), *Anatomy* (1967), *Going Nowhere* (1967) and *Trumpets, Clap and Syphilis* (1967).

GENTZEL, Inga (1908–1991). Swedish runner. Born April 24, 1908, in Sweden; died Jan 1, 1991. ❖ Won a bronze medal in the 800 meters in Amsterdam Olympics (1928).

GENVILLE, Joan de (fl. 1300). *See Mortimer, Joan.*

GEOFFRIN, Marie Thérèse (1699–1777). French salonnière. Name variations: Geofrin. Pronunciation: Marie Tur-ESS Jeff-RAN. Born Marie Thérèse Rodet in 1699 in Paris, France; died Oct 6, 1777, in Paris; dau. of Pierre Rodet (*valet de chambre* of the French royal court) and the former Mlle Chemineau (dau. of a banker); m. Pierre François Geoffrin, July 19, 1713; children: Marie Thérèse Geoffrin, later the Marquise de la Ferté-Imbault (b. 1715) and a son (b. 1717) who did not survive childhood. ❖ One of the most famous of the 18th-century *salonnières,* whose salon was the intellectual home of influential writers, philosophers, and artists of the period, including the Encyclopedists, many of whom received her financial support; was orphaned at 7, poorly educated, and married off at 15 to a man 33 years her senior; attended salon of the Marquise de Tencin, which opened her intellectual world (1730); established her Paris salon at no. 372 Rue Saint Honoré (1737), which would

remain a gathering place of artists and women and men of letters for more than a quarter century; supported the work of the Encyclopedists, including Diderot, D'Alembert, and many others (1750s–60s); commissioned many works of art, including over 60 paintings (1750–70); was the most important social and literary arbiter of her age; counted among her correspondents the Empress Catherine II the Great of Russia, King Stanislaus Augustus of Poland, and Empress Maria Theresa of Austria; though she acquired great social power and influence, was known chiefly as a generous patron and friend of the poor, epitomizing the spirit of the period of the Enlightenment in which she lived. ❖ See also *Women in World History.*

GEOGHEGAN-QUINN, Máire (1950—). Irish politician. Name variations: Maire Geoghegan; Maire Quinn. Born Sept 5, 1950, in Carna, Co. Galway, Ireland; dau. of John Geoghegan (TD, Galway West, 1954–75); m. John V. Quinn. ❖ Following the death of father, won a by-election representing Fianna Fáil to the 20th Dáil for Galway West (1975–77); returned to 21st–27th Dáil (1977–97); representing the liberal wing of party, supported family planning and, as 1st woman minister of justice (1993–94), helped decriminalize homosexuality; was also minister for Equality and Law Reform (1994), minister for Tourism, Transport & Communications (1992–93), and minister of State at the Department of the Taoiseach (1987–91); nominated to the European Union Court of Auditors (1999); wrote novel *The Green Diamond.*

GEORGATOU, Maria (c. 1983—). Greek rhythmic gymnast. Born c. 1983 in Corfu, Greece. ❖ Won a bronze medal for team all-around at Sydney Olympics (2000).

GEORGE, Carolyn (1927—). American ballet dancer and photographer. Born Sept 6, 1927, in Dallas, TX; m. Jacques D'Amboise (ballet dancer). ❖ Trained with Lew and William Christensen at school of San Francisco Ballet in CA; joined company of New York City Ballet where she danced in Balanchine's *Bourée Fantasque* and *Stars and Stripes* to great acclaim; performed in numerous company premieres, including Jerome Robbins' *Fanfare* (1953) and William Dollar's *The Five Gifts* (1953); worked as photographer, specializing in dance, upon retiring from performance career.

GEORGE, Eliot (1929—). *See Freeman, Gillian.*

GEORGE, Elizabeth (c. 1814–1902). New Zealand innkeeper. Name variations: Elizabeth Rowe. Born Elizabeth Rowe, c. 1814, in England (baptized at Bodmin, Cornwall, April 6, 1814); died April 4, 1902, Onehunga, New Zealand; dau. of Henry Rowe (carrier) and Sarah (Netherton) Rowe; m. Edward George, 1841 (1855); children: 4. ❖ Immigrated to New Zealand (1842); helped to manage Royal Hotel in Onehunga, built by husband (1848); granted a hotel license in her name after husband's death (1855); became the 1st president of Onehunga Ladies' Benevolent Society (1863). ❖ See also *Dictionary of New Zealand Biography* (Vol. 1).

GEORGE, Fanny Lloyd (1888–1972). *See Lloyd George, Frances Stevenson.*

GEORGE, Frances Shayle (c. 1827–1890). *See Shayle George, Frances.*

GEORGE, Gladys (1900–1954). American actress. Born Gladys Anna Clare on Sept 13, 1900, in Patton, Maine; died Dec 8, 1954, in Los Angeles, California; the dau. of an actor and actress; m. Ben Erway (actor), 1922 (div. 1930); m. Edward Fowler, 1933 (div. 1935); m. Leonard Penn (actor), 1935 (div. 1944); m. Kenneth Bradley, 1946 (div. 1950). ❖ Born into a theatrical family, made her debut at 3 and later played vaudeville, stock, and on Broadway; though she made a few silents, is mainly known for the films she made in the 1930s and 1940s; cast as the leading lady or 2nd lead in melodramas, most notable roles were in *Valiant Is the Word for Carrie* (1936), for which she won an Oscar nomination, *The Roaring Twenties* (1939), and *The Way of All Flesh* (1940); played character roles later in her career; other films include *Red Hot Dollars* (1919), *The Woman in the Suitcase* (1920), *The Easy Road* (1921), *The House That Jazz Built* (1921), *They Gave Him a Gun* (1937), *Madam X* (1937), *Marie Antoinette* (1938), *The House Across the Bay* (1940), *The Maltese Falcon* (1941), *The Hard Way* (1943), *Christmas Holiday* (1944), *Minstrel Man* (1944), *Steppin' in Society* (1945), *The Best Years of Our Lives* (1946), *Flamingo Road* (1949), *Bright Leaf* (1950), *Lullaby of Broadway* (1951), *Detective Story* (1951), and *It Happens Every Thursday* (1953).

GEORGE, Grace (1879–1961). American actress. Born Dec 25, 1879, in New York, NY; died May 19, 1961, in NY, NY; educated at Notre Dame Convent in New Jersey; studied at American Academy of Dramatic Arts,

1893; m. William A. Brady, 1897 (died 1950); children: 1 son. ❖ Made NY debut at Standard Theater (1894), as one of the schoolgirls in *The New Boy;* had 1st appearance of note as Juliette in *The Turtle* at Manhattan Theater (1898); appeared as Peg Woffington in *Pretty Peggy* (1903) and subsequently toured in the same part with great success; made London debut at Duke of York Theater as Cyprienne in *Divorçons* (1907); among a long list of appearances, took on many of George Bernard Shaw's plays, portraying Barbara Undershaft in *Major Barbara* (1915) and Lady Cicely Waynflete in *Captain Brassbound's Conversion* (1917); was last seen at the National Theater in New York as Mrs. Culver in *The Constant Wife* (1951). ❖ See also *Women in World History.*

GEORGE, Maude (1888–1963). American actress. Name variations: Maude Ford or Maude Forde. Born Aug 15, 1888, in Riverside, California; died Oct 10, 1963, in Sepulveda, California. ❖ Joined Universal (1915); made 1st many movies for Erich von Stroheim; films include *The Frame-Up, The Devil's Passkey, Roads of Destiny, Foolish Wives, Monte Cristo, The Garden of Eden* and *The Wedding March.*

GEORGE, Maureen (1955—). Zimbabwean field-hockey player. Born Sept 1955 in Zimbabwe. ❖ At Moscow Olympics, won a gold medal in team competition (1980).

GEORGE, Megan Lloyd (1902–1966). See Lloyd George, Megan.

GEORGE, Mlle. (c. 1787–1867). See Georges, Marguerite J.

GEORGE, Muriel (1883–1965). English stage and screen actress. Born Aug 29, 1883, in London, England; died Oct 22, 1965, in England; m. Arthur Davenport; m. Ernest Butcher (div.). ❖ Made stage debut with H.G. Pelissier's *Follies* (1901); following WWI, appeared in variety theaters throughout England for over 12 years singing folk songs; plays include *The Red Light, Aladdin, Music in the Air, Alice in Wonderland, Call it a Day, When We Are Married* and *The Villain of the Piece;* made film debut in *His Lordship* (1932), followed by *Nell Gwyn, Pack Up Your Troubles, The Briggs Family, Cottage to Let, Dear Octopus* and *Simon and Laura.*

GEORGE, Phyllis (1949—). Miss America and TV host. Name variations: Phyllis George Brown. Born Phyllis George, June 25, 1949, in Denton, TX; m. John Brown (gov. of Kentucky; div.). ❖ Named Miss America (1971), representing Texas; became 1st female sportscaster in America and co-anchored "NFL Today" for CBS (1975–84); was the 1st female co-host of "Candid Camera"; became co-anchor of "CBS Morning News" (1985); created and hosted "Spotlight with Phyllis George" for TNN; authored four books. Was the 1st woman to found a chicken company, Chicken by George, now a division of Hormel Foods.

GEORGE, Rosel (1926–1967). See Brown, Rosel George.

GEORGE, Zelma Watson (1904–1994). African-American sociologist, musicologist, and performer. Born 1904 in Hearne, TX; died in Cleveland, Ohio, July 1994; graduated from University of Chicago; received master's and doctoral degrees in sociology at New York University; studied voice at American Conservatory of Music, Chicago; studied pipe organ at Northwestern University. ❖ Worked briefly as a social worker in Evanston, IL, before becoming a probation officer in Chicago; was dean of women at Tennessee State University (1932–37); began research on black music (1935), traveling the country collecting data from libraries and private collections; published "A Guide to Negro Music," an annotated bibliography; sang the lead in a black production of *The Medium,* a folk opera by Gian Carlo Menotti, at the NY's Arena Stage at the Hotel Edison (1950), becoming the 1st black woman to take a white role on Broadway; appointed by President Dwight Eisenhower as the only African-American member of the US delegation to the 15th General Assembly of the UN (1960). ❖ See also *Women in World History.*

GEORGES, Marguerite J. (c. 1787–1867). French actress. Name variations: Mlle George. Born Marguerite Joséphine Weimer (also seen as Wemmer or Weimar) at Bayeux, France, in 1786 or 1787; died in Paris in Jan 1867. ❖ As an ingenue in Amiens, attracted the notice of actress Mlle Raucourt, who brought her to Paris; caused a sensation when she appeared as Clytemnestra which led to successful engagements in other European cities (1808–13); reappeared at the Théâtre Français (1813–17), where the French actor Talma added polish to her style; while connected with the Odéon and the Porte Saint-Martin theaters (1821–47), bolstered her reputation in such roles as Semiramis (Sammuramat), Agrippina the Younger, Lucrezia Borgia, and Catherine de Medici; only

rivalled by Mlle Duchesnois, received costly presents from emperors, princes, and a host of others; yet on retiring from the stage (1849), her poverty impelled her to become a teacher at the conservatory.

GEORGESCU, Elena (1964—). Romanian rower. Name variations: Elena Nedelcu; Elena Georgescu-Nedelcu. Born April 10, 1964, in Bucharest, Romania. ❖ At Barcelona Olympics, won a silver medal for coxed eights (1992); won a gold medal at Atlanta Olympics (1996), a gold medal at Sydney Olympics (2000), and a gold medal at Athens Olympics (2004), all for coxed eights; won World Rowing championships for coxed eights (1990, 1997, 1998, 1999).

GEORGI, Yvonne (1903–1975). German concert dancer. Born Oct 29, 1903, in Leipzig, Germany; died Jan 25, 1975, in Hanover, Germany; trained by Jacques-Dalcroze at the Wigman school in Dresden. ❖ Toured in recitals with Harald Kreutzberg in Europe and US (1926–31), dancing in Kreutzberg's works as well as own solos; served as ballet master at German theaters including Muenster Stadttheater (c. 1924–25), opera of Gera (c. 1925–26), and Theater of City of Hanover (1926–31); immigrated to Netherlands (1938) where she founded own dance troupe; returned to Germany after WWII (c. 1951) where she served as ballet master once more in Düsseldorf (1951–54) and at Landestheater in Hanover where she also directed dance training program (1954–c. 1975); choreographed own works throughout her life starting in her early 20s. Works of choreography include *Der Daemon* (1925), *Don Morte* (1928), *Kassandra* (1928), *Orpheus and Eurydice* (1929), *Le Train Bleu* (c. 1931), *The Creatures of Prometheus* (c. 1939), *Souvenir* (1939), *Les Animaux* (1951), *Die Vier Temperamente* (1952) and *Ruth* (1959). ❖ See also Horst Koegler, *Yvonne Georgi* (1963).

GEORGIA (d. 6th c.). French saint. Name variations: Georgette. Died at beginning of 6th century; lived at Clermont. ❖ According to Gregory of Tours, withdrew from public life as a young girl in order to pray and fast; when she died, a flight of doves, said to be angels, accompanied her body as it was borne in funeral procession, hid in the church roof during the service, reappeared when the procession left for the cemetery, then flew toward the heavens. Feast day is Feb 15. ❖ See also *Women in World History.*

GEORGIEVA, Anka (1959—). Bulgarian rower. Born May 18, 1959, in Bulgaria. ❖ At Moscow Olympics, won a bronze medal in quadruple sculls with coxswain (1980).

GEORGIEVA, Magdalena (1962—). Bulgarian rower. Born Dec 1962 in Bulgaria. ❖ At Seoul Olympics, won a bronze medal in single sculls (1988).

GEORGIEVA, Maya (1955—). Bulgarian volleyball player. Born May 1955 in Bulgaria. ❖ At Moscow Olympics, won a bronze medal in team competition (1980).

GEORGIEVA-PANAYOTOVNA, Kapka (1951—). Bulgarian rower. Born Sept 30, 1951, in Bulgaria. ❖ At Montreal Olympics, won a silver medal in coxed fours (1976).

GEPPI-AIKENS, Diane (c. 1963–2003). American lacrosse coach. Name variations: Diane Aikens. Born Diane Geppi, c. 1963 in Baltimore, Maryland; died June 29, 2003, at her home in Baltimore; dau. of John and Katherine Geppi; graduate of Loyola, 1984; m. Robert Aikens (div.); children: Michael, Jessica, Melissa, and Shannon. ❖ Was a four-year starter as a goalie for Loyola during college years; was Loyal volleyball coach (1984–90) and became lacrosse coach (1989); while battling an inoperable brain tumor which left her paralyzed in a wheelchair, coached the Loyola of Maryland women's lacrosse team to a 1st-place ranking and the semifinals of the NCAA Division I tournament (2003); led Loyola to NCAA tournament 10 times. Named National Lacrosse Coach of the Year (1996, 1997, 2003); received the NCAA Inspiration Award (2003).

GERAGHTY, Agnes (1906–1974). American swimmer. Name variations: Agnes Geraghty McAndrews. Born Nov 28, 1906; grew up in NY; died Mar 1, 1974, in Baldwin, NY. ❖ At Paris Olympics, won a silver medal in 200-meter breaststroke (1924).

GERAGHTY, Carmelita (1901–1966). American actress. Born Mar 21, 1901, in Rushville, Indiana; died July 7, 1966, in NYC; dau. of Tom Geraghty (screenwriter); sister of Maurice and Gerald Geraghty (writers); m. Carey Wilson (MGM writer, died 1962). ❖ Supporting actress in silent and early talkies, appeared in *Passionate Youth, The Great Gatsby, The Last Trail, My Best Girl, This Thing Called Love, The Mississippi Gambler* and *Fifty Million Frenchmen;* retired (1935).

GERALDINE OF ALBANIA (1915–2002). *See Apponyi, Geraldine.*

GERALDINE THE FAIR (c. 1528–1589). *See Fitzgerald, Elizabeth.*

GÉRARD, Marguerite (1761–1837). French artist. Name variations: Marguerite Gerard. Born in Grasse, France, 1761; died in Paris, France, 1837; purportedly one of 17 children of a perfume maker; sister of Marie Anne Fragonard (1745–c. 1823); studied with Jean Honoré Fragonard, her brother-in-law; never married; no children. ❖ The 1st woman in her country to succeed as a genre painter, was 8 when she went to Paris to live with sister Marie Anne Fragonard, a miniaturist who was married to the artist Jean Honoré Fragonard; ultimately became a successful genre painter, even surpassing her mentor, Fragonard, to whom she remained devoted, as he was to her; professional career flourished for nearly 50 years and brought her considerable personal wealth; exhibited regularly, was honored with three medals, and had works purchased by Napoleon and Louis XVIII; emulated the *trompe l'oeil* effect of the 17th-century Dutch masters and also employed a painstaking glazing technique used to eradicate all traces of brushstroke, which can be seen in one of her most famous genre paintings, *The Piano Lesson* (1780s). ❖ See also *Women in World History.*

GERASIMENOK, Irina (1970—). Russian shooter. Born 1970 in USSR. ❖ Won a silver medal for 50m rifle 3 positions at Atlanta Olympics (1996).

GERBAGE or GERBEGA. *Variant of Gerberga.*

GERBERGA (d. 896). Abbess of Gandersheim. Name variations: Gerbega. Died July 24, 896; dau. of Ludolf or Liudolf (c. 806–866), count of Saxony, and Oda (806–913). ❖ Upon sister Hathumoda's death, succeeded her as abbess of Gandersheim; was later replaced by another sister, Christine of Gandersheim.

GERBERGA (r. 959–1001). Abbess of Hildesheim and Gandersheim. Died 1001; dau. of Judith of Bavaria (c. 925–987) and Henry I the Quarrelsome (918–955), duke of Bavaria (r. 947–955). ❖ Became abbess of Gandersheim (959).

GERBERGA OF SAXONY (c. 910–969). Queen and regent of France. Name variations: Gerberge de Saxe. Born in Germany c. 910 (some sources cite 913 or 919); died in France, May 5, 969 (some sources cite 984); dau. of Henry I the Fowler (c. 876–936), Holy Roman emperor (r. 919–936), and Matilda of Saxony (c. 892–968); sister of Otto I the Great (912–973), king of Germany (r. 936–973), Holy Roman emperor (r. 962–973), and Hedwig (c. 915–965); m. Giselbert also known as Gilbert, duke of Lotharingia (Lorraine), 929 (died 931); m. Louis IV (918–954), king of France (r. 936–954), in 939; children: (1st m.) Gerberga of Lorraine (who m. Adalbert, count of Vermandois); (2nd m.) several surviving children, including Lothair (941–986), king of France (r. 954–986); Charles (b. 953), duke of Upper Lorraine; Matilda Martel (943–c. 982). ❖ A Saxon princess, married at 19 but was widowed 2 years later; married Louis IV of France as part of an alliance between Louis and her father; in the tradition of politically active French queens, headed peace delegations and negotiated treaties; widowed again (954), ruled France as regent until son Lothair came of age; was a valiant queen-regent who used her substantial army to stay in power and thus ensure the throne for Lothair. ❖ See also *Women in World History.*

GERBERGE. *Variant of Gerberga.*

GERBERGE OF THE LOMBARDS (fl. mid-700s). Queen of Austrasia. Name variations: Gerberga. Fl. in mid-700s; m. Carloman (c. 751–771), king of Austrasia (r. 768–771); children: several.

GERDRUD. *Variant of Gertrude.*

GERDT, Elizaveta (1891–1975). Russian ballet dancer and teacher. Name variations: Yelisaveta Gerdt. Born April 29, 1891, in St. Petersburg, Russia; died Nov 5, 1975, in Moscow, Russia; dau. of Pavel Gerdt (1844–1917, ballet dancer, mime and teacher). ❖ Trained by father in St. Petersburg and at school of Imperial Ballet; joined Maryinsky Ballet (1908) where she danced numerous principal roles, including The Plum Fairy, Odette/Odile, and Raymonda, always to great acclaim; began concentrating mainly on teaching (as of 1928) and taught in Leningrad (until 1935); taught at the Bolshoi Ballet where students included Ekaterina Maximova, Raissa Struchkova, and Maya Plisetskaya.

GERG, Hilde (1975—). German Alpine skier. Born Oct 19, 1975, in Bad Toelz, West Germany. ❖ Finished 15th overall in World Cup standings (1995–96); finished 3rd overall in World Cup standings and in the top 4 in all 7 World Cup super-G's (1996–97); won a bronze medal for super-G and combined at World championships (1997); finished 7th in World Cup downhill standings (1997); won a gold medal for slalom and a bronze for combined at Nagano Olympics (1998); placed 2nd overall at World Cup (1998–99); coming back after a debilitating injury, won a bronze medal in super-G and placed 6th in downhill at World championships (2001); competed in Salt Lake City Olympics but did not medal (2002).

GERHARDT, Elena (1883–1961). German-born British mezzo-soprano. Born in Leipzig, Germany, Nov 11, 1883; died in London, Jan 11, 1961; m. Fritz Kohl. ❖ Recognized as one of the greatest lieder singers of the 20th century, gave 1st recital (1903); mastered the vast repertory of songs by Brahms, Mendelssohn, Schubert, and Schumann, as well as songs by Richard Strauss and Hugo Wolf, composers who were her contemporaries; toured Germany and Central Europe; made 1st triumphant tour of United Kingdom (1906); concertized in most European countries, including Spain, and in Russia (1907–14); made American premiere in NYC (eventually made 16 tours of US); during WWII, immigrated to Great Britain with husband; continued concert career and began teaching advanced pupils, both through classes at London's Guildhall School of Music and by giving private instruction; made many recordings, including the lieder of Hugo Wolf. ❖ See also *Women in World History.*

GERHARDT, Ida (1905–1997). Dutch poet and translator. Name variations: Ida Gardina Margaretha Gerhardt. Born May 11, 1905, in Gorinchem, Netherlands; died 1997; earned degree in classical languages. ❖ One of most important 20th-century Dutch poets, taught classical languages (1939–63); translations include Lucretius's *De Rerum Natura* and (with Marie H. van der Zeyde) *De Psalmen* (1972) from Hebrew; poetry collections include *Kosmos* (1940), *Vroeg verzen* (1978), *Verzamelde gedichten* (1980), *Dolen en dromen* (1980), *De zomen van het licht* (1983), and *De adelaarsvarens* (1988). Received Marianne Philips Prize (1967) and P.C. Hooft Prize (1979).

GÉRIN-LAJOIE, Marie (1867–1945). French-Canadian educator and feminist. Name variations: Gerin-Lajoie. Pronunciation: Jay-REEN Laj-OO. Born Marie Lacoste on Oct 19, 1867, at Montreal, Quebec, Canada; died Nov 1, 1945, in Montreal, Canada; 1st child of Sir Alexander Lacoste (lawyer and politician who was chief justice of Quebec, 1891–1907) and Marie Louise Globensky; graduate of Hochelaga Convent, Montreal, 1882; m. Henri Gérin-Lajoie (lawyer), 1887; children: Marie Gérin-Lajoie (b. 1890, who founded the Congrégation de Notre Dame du Bon Conseil); Henri (b. 1892); Alexandre (b. 1893); Léon (b. 1895). ❖ The 1st Francophone champion of women's rights in Quebec, studied law; published a brief manual on legal rights, the *Traité de Droit Usuel* (1902), which eventually became widely distributed in schools and colleges throughout Quebec; joined the Montreal Local Council of Women (MCCW); her legal studies had convinced her that women deserved the same legal rights as males, including the right to vote; at the same time, however, consistently rejected the militant tactics of Anglophone feminists and argued instead that change should come about through the existing order of institutions, with emphasis on home and family; with Caroline Béique, co-founded the Fédération Nationale St-Jean-Baptiste (FNSJB, 1907), which acted as an umbrella organization coordinating the activities of 22 affiliated associations; began serving as editor of *La Bonne Parole* (1913), a FNSJB magazine; extended her work by founding the Ligue des Droits de la Femme (League of Women's Rights, 1913); when women were granted provincial voting rights in every province but Quebec (1921), took it upon herself to convince the conference of Quebec bishops that there was nothing in Catholic doctrine that could be interpreted as forbidding women's suffrage, then appealed directly to the Vatican but to no avail; taught part-time at University of Montreal where her lectures on law were enthusiastically received by a new generation of Francophone feminists. Shortly before her death, was awarded a medal by Pope Pius XI in recognition of her work for the welfare of women as well as the prestigious Palmes Académiques by the government of France for her contribution to improving the legal status of women. ❖ See also (in French) Michelle Hulet *Mère Marie Gérin-Lajoie* (Édition Canadiennes, 1979); and *Women in World History.*

GERLITS, Irina (1966—). Soviet basketball player. Born April 29, 1966. ❖ Won a bronze medal at Seoul Olympics (1988) and a gold medal at Barcelona Olympics (1992), both in team competition.

GERLOC (d. 963). Duchess of Aquitaine. Name variations: Gerletta. Born before 912; died 963; dau. of Rolf or Hrolf also known as Rollo (d. 931, the Norse conqueror of Normandy) and Poppa of Normandy; m. William III, duke of Aquitaine; children: William IV, duke of Aquitaine.

GERMAIN, Dorothy V. (1924—). *See Porter, Dorothy Germain.*

GERMAIN, Marie (1776–1831). *See Germain, Sophie.*

GERMAIN, Sophie (1776–1831). French mathematician. Name variations: Marie Germain. Born Marie-Sophie Germain on April 1, 1776, on rue St. Denis, Paris, France; died June 27, 1831, rue de Savoie, Paris, France; buried in Père Lachaise cemetery, Paris; dau. of Marie-Madeleine (Gruguelin) Germain and Ambroise François Germain (prosperous silk merchant, who was elected to the Estates General and later became a director of the Bank of France); self-taught; never married; no children. ❖ Winner of the French Academy of Sciences' gold medal, who, during the Reign of Terror (1793–94), spent the period teaching herself differential calculus; managed to obtain the lecture notes of various professors when the École central des travaux, later known as the École Polytechnique, was established in Paris for the training of mathematicians and scientists (1794), though women were not admitted; under pen name M. le Blanc, began correspondence with J.L. Lagrange (1794), one of the outstanding mathematicians of the 18th century, and Carl Friedrich Gauss, author of the masterpiece *Disquisitiones Arithmeticae* (1804); concerned about Gauss' safety after the French Invasion of Prussia, had her true identity revealed to him (1807); submitted essay to the French Academy of Sciences on vibrating elastic surfaces (1811), but essay was rejected; submitted 2nd essay and received honorable mention (1813); submitted 3rd essay and was awarded grand prize of the French Academy of Sciences (1816); was permitted to attend public sessions of the French Academy of Sciences (1822); diagnosed with breast cancer (1829); proved Pierre de Fermat's Last Theorem; has been called one of the founders of mathematical physics. Writings include *Recherches sur la théorie des surface élastique* (1821), *Recherches sur la nature, les bornes et l'étendue de la question des surface élastique* (1826), *Considération generales sur l'État des sciences et des lettres aux différentes époque de leur culture* (Armand-Jacques Lherbette, ed., 1833), and *Oeuvres philosophiques de Sophie Germain* (H. Stupuy, ed., 1879). ❖ See also Louis L. Bucciarelli and Nancy Dworsky, *Sophie Germain: An Essay in the History of the Theory of Elasticity* (Dordrecht, Holland: D. Riedel, 1980); and *Women in World History.*

GERMAINE, Diane (1944—). American modern dancer and choreographer. Born July 5, 1944, in New York, NY. ❖ After graduating from High School of Performing Arts in New York City, danced with Paul Sansardo Company until 1976, performing in his *Fatal Birds, The Path, Metallics* and *Consort for Dancers,* among others; danced intermittently with companies of Manual Alum and Donya Feuer; served as artistic director of Sansardo company before founding Diane Germaine and Dancers (1975) for which she has choreographed numerous works; staged pieces for companies around the world, including Norsk Opera Ballet of Oslo, Bat-Dor and Kibbutz Dancers in Israel and Chicago Moving Company; is best known for choreography of multi-segmented *Lulu* and *Antipoem* series. Works of choreography include *The Moth* (1967), *Epitaph* (1970), *Ashes* (1972), *Playground* (1975), *For the Public Only* (1976), *Ghosts* (1978), *Hotel Nicaragua* (part of *Antipoem,* 1980), *A Day in the Park* (part of *Lulu,* 1980) and *Random* (part of *Antipoem,* 1980).

GERMAINE, Mlle (1916—). *See Cornescou, Irina Soltanovna.*

GERMANOVA, Silviya (1961—). Bulgarian basketball player. Born Feb 12, 1961, in Bulgaria. ❖ At Moscow Olympics, won a silver medal in team competition (1980).

GERMAN PRINCESS, The (1633–1673). *See Carleton, Mary.*

GERMANY, empress of.
See Margaret Theresa of Spain (1651–1673).
See Augusta of Saxe-Weimar (1811–1890).
See Victoria Adelaide (1840–1901).
See Hermine of Reuss (1887–1947).

GERMANY, queen of.
See Matilda of Saxony (c. 892–968).
See Oda of Bavaria (fl. 890s).
See Richilde (d. 894).
See Edgitha (c. 912–946).
See Adelaide of Burgundy (931–999).
See Theophano of Byzantium (c. 955–991).
See Cunigunde (d. 1040?).
See Bertha of Savoy (1051–1087).
See Adelaide of Kiev (c. 1070–1109).
See Beatrice of Upper Burgundy (1145–1184).
See Constance of Sicily (1154–1198).
See Marshall, Isabel (1200–1240).
See Constance of Aragon (d. 1222).
See Isabella of England (1214–1241).
See Sancha of Provence (c. 1225–1261).
See Anna of Hohenberg (c. 1230–1281).
See Falkestein, Beatrice von (c. 1253–1277).
See Elizabeth of Tyrol (c. 1262–1313).
See Isabella of Aragon (c. 1300–1330).
See Elizabeth of Luxemburg (1409–1442).
See Eleanor of Portugal (1434–1467).

GEROULD, Katharine (1879–1944). American author. Name variations: Katharine Elizabeth Fullerton Gerould. Born Katharine Elizabeth Fullerton, Feb 6, 1879, in Brockton, Massachusetts; died July 27, 1944, in Princeton, New Jersey; dau. (possibly adopted from within the family) of Rev. Bradford Morton Fullerton (Congregational minister) and Julia Maria (Ball) Fullerton; attended Miss Folsom's School in Boston; Radcliffe College, AB, 1900, AM, 1901; m. Gordon H. Gerould (medievalist and professor at Princeton), June 1910; children: Christopher Gerould (writer) and Sylvia Gerould. ❖ Known primarily for her many essays on literary criticism and social and political themes, published collections of essays *Modes and Morals* (1920) and *Ringside Seats* (1937); also contributed stories to *Atlantic Monthly, Harper's* and *Scribner's,* among others; novels include *A Change of Air* (1917) and *The Light That Never Was* (1931).

GERSÃO, Teolinda (1940—). Portuguese novelist and educator. Name variations: Teolinda Gersao. Born 1940 in Coimbra, Portugal; received doctorate in German philology; children: 2. ❖ Taught German and comparative literature at University of Lisbon and New University of Lisbon; spent time in Brazil and Mozambique; writings include *O Silêncio* (1981), *Paisagem com Mulher e Mar ao Fundo* (1981), *Os Guarda-Chuvas Cintilantes* (1984), *O Cavalo de Sol* (1989), *A Casa da Cabeça de Cavalo* (1995), *Os Teclados* (1999), and *Os Anjos* (2000).

GERSCHAU, Kerstin (1958—). East German gymnast. Born Jan 26, 1958, in East Germany. ❖ At Montreal Olympics, won a bronze medal in team all-around (1976).

GERSENDA (fl. 1000). Countess of Bigorre. Fl. around 1000; m. Bernardo, count of Cousserans; m. Bernard I, count of Foix; children: (1st m.) Gilberga (d. 1054); (2nd m.) Estefania of Barcelona (fl. 1038).

GERSENDE DE FORCALQUIER (1170–1257?). *See Garsenda.*

GERSTEN, Berta (c. 1896–1972). Polish-American actress. Name variations: Berta Gerstenman. Born Berta Gerstenman on Aug 20, around 1896, in Cracow, Poland; died Sept 10, 1972, in NY, NY; dau. of Meshe (Kopps) Gerstenman and Avrom Gerstenman; m. Isaak Hershel Finkel (later Irwin Henry Fenn), July 10, 1911 (died 1960); children: 1 son (b. 1912). ❖ Actress who helped launch a Yiddish theater company, portrayed over 150 roles in melodramas, musicals, and comedies (1918–72); immigrated to US (1899); made professional stage debut as the little boy in *Mirele Efros* (1908); worked with Maurice Schwartz at Irving Place Theater and at Yiddish Art Theater (1918–50), becoming leading lady; performed with traveling troupes across North and South America and Europe, and was a leading actress in the Yiddish theater in Warsaw, Poland (late 1930s); appeared in Yiddish plays *Salvation* (1939), *Believe Your Mother* (1941), *Yosele, the Nightingale* (1949), in title role of *Mirele Efros* and as Gertrude in Yiddish version of *Hamlet;* performed in screen versions of *Mirele Efros* (title role, 1939) and of *God, Man, and the Devil* (1950), and in the film *The Benny Goodman Story* (1955); appeared in English language plays *The World of Sholom Aleichem* (1954), as Esther in *The Flowering Peach* (1955), as Sophie Tucker's mother in *Sophie,* and toured with Sir Cedric Hardwicke in *A Majority of One* (1959); appeared on tv (1950s–60s); appeared opposite Jacob Ben-Ami in a dramatization of *In My Father's Court* in NYC (1971–72 season).

GERSTENMAN, Berta (c. 1896–1972). *See Gersten, Berta.*

GERSTER, Etelka (1855–1920). Hungarian singer. Born in Kaschau (Kosice), Hungary, June 15 or 16, 1855; died in Pontecchio, Aug 20, 1920; m. Pietro Gardini (her director), 1877. ❖ Studied with Mathilde Marchesi; debuted at Venice to great success as Gilda in *Rigoletto*

(Jan 1876); toured Europe and visited US, singing at the Academy of Music, NY (1878, 1883, and 1887); reappeared in London (1890); when vocal powers became suddenly impaired, retired from public life; set up a singing school in Berlin and had Lotte Lehmann as one of her pupils. ❖ See also *Women in World History*.

GERT, Valeska (1900–1978). German actress and concert dancer. Born Jan 11, 1900, in Berlin, Germany; died 1978 in Sylt, Germany. ❖ Appeared in films by Jean Renoir and Ernst Pabst, including Pabst's *Threepenny Opera;* worked with Max Reinhardt early on; presented numerous solo dance recitals at her own cabaret club Kohlkoppec in Berlin, in recitals throughout Germany, and in US during WWII; considered greatly influential upon development of US concert dance (1930s); her works were often a form of social commentary. Works of choreography include *Chansonette* (for cabaret), *Music Hall* (for cabaret), *Strip Tease* (1936), *The Famous Pianist* (1940), *To Die* (1940), *La Tragedienne Française* (1940) and *Americana* (1940).

GERTRUD. *Variant of Gertrude.*

GERTRUDE OF ANDRECHS-MERAN (c. 1185–1213). Queen of Hungary. Name variations: Gertrude of Meran. Born c. 1185; murdered in Sept 1213 by nobles; dau. of Bertold or Berchtold III of Andrechs, marquis of Meran, count of Tirol, and duke of Carinthia and Istria, and Agnes of Dedo; sister of Agnes of Meran (d. 1201), Hedwig of Silesia (1174–1243), and Eckembert, bishop of Bamberg; became 1st wife of Andrew II, king of Hungary (r. 1205–1235), before 1203; children: Elizabeth of Hungary (1207–1231) and Bela IV (1206–1270), king of Hungary (r. 1235–1270). Andrew II's 2nd wife was Yolande de Courtenay (d. 1233); his 3rd wife was Beatrice d'Este (d. 1245).

GERTRUDE OF EISLEBEN (1256–1302). *See Gertrude the Great.*

GERTRUDE OF FLANDERS (d. 1117). Duchess of Lorraine. Name variations: Gertrude of Lorraine. Died 1117; dau. of Robert I, count of Flanders (r. 1071–1093), and Gertrude of Saxony (fl. 1070); m. Henry III, count of Louvain, count of Brussels (died 1095); m. Thierry of Alsace, duke of Lorraine; children: (1st m.) 4 daughters (names unknown); (2nd m.) Thierry of Alsace. ❖ Buried 2 husbands, each time increasing her own wealth and individual power; refused to marry again and became a powerful and active widow; became involved in the politics of the Holy Roman Empire, including plotting against the royal family and sending her troops into battle to defeat her enemies. ❖ See also *Women in World History*.

GERTRUDE OF HACKEBORNE (1232–1292). Germany mystic. Born 1232; died 1292; sister of Mechtild of Hackeborne (1241–1298). ❖ A mystic, became abbess of the monastery at Helfta (1251); often confused with Gertrude the Great. ❖ See also *Women in World History*.

GERTRUDE OF HELFTA (1256–1302). *See Gertrude the Great.*

GERTRUDE OF HOHENBERG (c. 1230–1281). *See Anna of Hohenberg.*

GERTRUDE OF LORRAINE (d. 1117). *See Gertrude of Flanders.*

GERTRUDE OF MEISSEN (d. 1117). Duchess of Saxony. Name variations: Gertrude von Meissen. Died Dec 9, 1117; dau. of Ekberts I, margrave of Meissen; m. Henry the Fat, duke of Saxony, margrave in Friesland, around 1090; children: Richensia of Nordheim (1095–1141).

GERTRUDE OF MERAN (c. 1185–1213). *See Gertrude of Andrechs-Meran.*

GERTRUDE OF METZ (d. 1225). German royal. Name variations: Gertrude von Metz. Killed in 1225; dau. of Albert, count of Metz and Dagsburg; became 1st wife of Teobaldo or Theobald I (1201–1253), king of Navarre (r. 1234–1253), also known as Theobald IV of Champagne, in June 1220 (div. 1225).

GERTRUDE OF NIVELLES (626–659). Frankish princess and abbess. Name variations: Saint Gertrude of Nivelles. Born 626 in present-day Belgium; died 659; dau. of Pepin I of Landen, mayor of Austrasia (d. 640), and Ida of Nivelles (597–652, who became a nun at the abbey and was also canonized); sister of Begga (613–698); cousin of Saint Modesta of Trier (d. about 680); never married; no children. ❖ Though parents tried to arrange several marriages for her, refused to wed, declaring that she would live her life with Christ and no mortal man; as a teenager, entered the convent of Nivelles, where she remained the rest of her life and was eventually elected abbess, responsible for the care of both monks and nuns; was canonized several years after death at age 33; had many

miracles attributed to her powers. Feast day is Mar 17. ❖ See also *Women in World History*.

GERTRUDE OF OSTEND (d. 1358). Dutch mystic and saint. Name variations: Gertrude van der Oosten; Saint Gertrude. Died 1358 at the almshouse in Delft. ❖ Was known for having the stigmata or five wounds, for having worked many miracles, and for her ecstasies, in which she would sometimes remain for weeks. Feast day is Jan 6. ❖ See also *Women in World History*.

GERTRUDE OF POLAND (d. 1107). Grand princess of Kiev. Died Jan 4, 1107; dau. of Mieskzo II (990–1034), king of Poland (r. 1025–1034) and Richesa of Lorraine (d. 1067); m. Yziaslav I (Izyaslav), grand prince of Kiev (r. 1054–1078), c. 1043; children: Sviatopolk II (b. 1050), prince of Kiev.

GERTRUDE OF SAXONY (fl. 1070). Countess of Flanders. Fl. around 1070; m. Robert I, count of Flanders (r. 1071–1093); children: Gertrude of Flanders (d. 1117); Robert II, count of Flanders (r. 1093–1111).

GERTRUDE OF SAXONY (1115–1143). Duchess of Bavaria and Saxony. Born April 18, 1115; died April 18, 1143; dau. of Lothair II (b. 1075), Holy Roman emperor (r. 1125–1137), and Richensia of Nordheim (1095–1141); m. Henry the Proud (c. 1100–1139), duke of Bavaria and Saxony, May 29, 1127; children: Henry V the Lion (1129–1195), duke of Bavaria and Saxony.

GERTRUDE OF SAXONY (c. 1155–1196). Queen of Denmark. Name variations: Gertrude of Saxony; Gurtrude. Born c. 1155; died July 1, 1196; dau. of Henry V the Lion (1129–1195), duke of Saxony and Bavaria, and either Matilda of England (1156–1189) or Clementina of Zahringen; m. Knud or Knut also known as Canute VI (1162–1202), king of Denmark (r. 1182–1202), in 1171.

GERTRUDE OF SULZBACH (d. 1146). Holy Roman empress. Died April 14, 1146; dau. of Berengar II of Sulzbach; sister of Bertha-Irene of Sulzbach (d. 1161); m. Conrad III (1093–1152), Holy Roman emperor (r. 1138–1152); children: Henry (1137–1150); Frederick IV (b. around 1145–1167), duke of Rottenburg (r. 1152–1167) and duke of Swabia (who m. Gertrude of Brunswick.

GERTRUDE OF SWABIA (c. 1104–1191). Countess Palatine. Born c. 1104; died in 1191; dau. of Agnes of Germany (1074–1143) and Frederick I, duke of Swabia (d. 1105); m. Hermann, pfalzgraf (count Palatine) of Lotharingen, in 1125.

GERTRUDE THE GREAT (1256–1302). German abbess, saint, and mystic. Name variations: Gertrude of Helfta; Gertrud von Helfta; Gertrude of Eisleben. Born Jan 6, 1256, somewhere in Germany; died Nov 16, 1302 (some sources cite Nov 17, 1301 or 1311), in the monastery of St. Mary at Helfta in Saxony, Germany; there is only speculation regarding her family and heritage; educated in the monastery at Helfta where she learned Latin, church history, and theology. ❖ German nun from the monastery of St. Mary at Helfta in Saxony whose mystical visions and devotion to God earned her the title "the Great," making her the only woman in Germany to be given such an honor; entered the monastery at age 4 or 5; at 25, had her 1st mystical experience (1281); was a recipient of the stigmata (1283), prophetic visions (1292, 1294), and minor miraculous events; began writing the *Legatus* and the *Spiritual Exercises* (1289); recognized as a saint by the Catholic Church though never formally canonized (1677); given the title "the Great" (1738). Feast day is Nov 16. ❖ See also Mary Jeremy Finnegan, *The Women of Helfta: Scholars and Mystics* (University of Georgia Press, 1991); and *Women in World History*.

GERTRUDE VON HELFTA (1256–1302). *See Gertrude the Great.*

GERTSYK, Adelaida (1874–1925). Russian poet and short-story writer. Name variations: Adelaida Kazimirovna Gértsyk; (pseudonym) Sirin. Born 1874 near Moscow, Russia; died 1925; dau. of a Polish noble; sister of Evgenia or Eugenie Gertsyk. ❖ Was close to Moscow symbolists and later the center of literary group that included Marina Tsvetaeva and Sophia Parnok; poetry was influenced by folklore and imbued with mysticism; published *Poems: 1906–1909;* wrote reviews in the symbolist journal *Sales* and published poetry in anthologies and journals; her story cycle about 3 weeks of imprisonment, "Basement Sketches," was published posthumously in Latvian journal (1926).

GERWIN, Celina (1933—). *See Jesionowska, Celina.*

GESELLIUS, Louise or Loja (1879–1968). *See Saarinen, Loja.*

GESHEVA-TSVETKOVA, Vanya (1960—). Bulgarian kayaker. Born April 1960 in Bulgaria. ❖ At Moscow Olympics, won a silver medal in K1 500 meters (1980); at Seoul Olympics, won a bronze medal in K4 500 meters, a silver medal in K2 500 meters, and a gold medal in K1 500 meters (1988).

GESSNER, Adrienne (1896–1987). Austrian actress. Born Adrienne Geiringer in Maria Schutz am Semmering, Austria, July 23, 1896; died in Vienna, June 23, 1987; m. Ernst Lothar. ❖ A distinguished actress and major star on the Vienna stage, before Hitler's minions marched into Austria; with husband, sailed for America (1938); soon appeared on Broadway in such plays as *Another Sun, Claudia* and *Thank You, Svoboda*; also portrayed Aunt Trinka in *I Remember Mama*; returned to Austria, becaming one of the leading actresses of the Burgtheater and Salzburg Festival.

GESTEFELD, Ursula Newell (1845–1921). American religious writer and leader. Born April 22, 1845, in Augusta, Maine; died Oct 22, 1921, in Kenosha, Wisconsin; m. Theodore Gestefeld (editor and reporter); children: 4. ❖ Inspired by Mary Baker Eddy's teaching and writing on Christian Science, published *Ursula N. Gestefeld's Statement of Christian Science* (1888); founded Exodus Club (1897), which grew into New Thought movement; published monthly magazine *Exodus* (1896–1904); served as vice president of New Thought Federation (now International New Thought Alliance). Writings include *The Builder and the Plan: A Textbook of the Science of Being* (1901), *A Chicago Bible-Class* (1891), *How We Master Our Fate* (1897), and *The Breath of Life: A Series of Self-Treatments* (1897).

GESTRING, Marjorie (1922–1992). American diver. Name variations: Margaret Gestring; Marjorie Gestring Bowman. Born Nov 18, 1922; died April 20, 1992. ❖ Won the gold medal in springboard at the Berlin Olympics (1936), the youngest person ever to win an individual medal in any sport (13 years, 9 months).

GETCHELL, Margaret (1841–1880). *See LaForge, Margaret Getchell.*

GETHIN, Grace Norton (1676–1697). British compiler. Born Grace Norton in 1676 in Abbots Leigh, Somerset, England; died Oct 11, 1697; dau. of Sir George Norton and Lady Frances (Freke) Norton; m. Sir Richard Gethin. ❖ Compiled collection of essays, *Reliquiae Gethinianae* (1699), mostly copied from other writers, which were published posthumously by mother.

GETHING, Mary Elizabeth (1865–1948). *See Simpson, Mary Elizabeth.*

GEVA, Tamara (1906–1997). Russian-born actress and dancer. Born Tamara Gevergeva or Gevergeyeva in St. Petersburg, Russia, 1906, of Russian, Swedish, and Italian descent; died at Manhattan home, Dec 9, 1997; studied at State Ballet School of Maryinsky Theatre (Theatre Street School); m. George Balanchine, 1923 (sep. and div. soon after); m. Kapa Davidoff (div.); m. John Emery (div.). ❖ At 16, left Russia with a small company that included George Balanchine and Alexandra Danilova (1924) and danced in recitals in Frankfurt and Ems, Germany; appeared at Empire in London with Balanchine, then toured the Continent with Diaghilev Monte Carlo Ballet (1924); made triumphant American debut with Nikita Balieff's Chauve-Souris company at Cosmopolitan Theater in NY (1927), dancing "Grotesque Espagnole"; turned to musical comedy, appearing in Florenz Ziegfeld's *Whoopee* with Eddie Cantor (1928); performed in 1st straight play, as Lania in *Divine Drudge* (1933); danced Balanchine's ballet *Errante* at 1st performance of the American Ballet (1935), but subsequent career was devoted to musicals, plays, and films; other stage roles included Vera Baranova in *On Your Toes* (1936), Irene in *Idiot's Delight* (1938), and Helen of Troy in *The Trojan Women* (1941); created choreography for film *Spectre of the Rose* and appeared in *Night Plane from Chungking* and *Orchestra Wives.*

GEWENIGER, Ute (1964—). East German swimmer. Born Feb 24, 1964, in East Germany. ❖ At Moscow Olympics, won a gold medal in the 100-meter breaststroke and a gold medal in the 4 x 100-meter medley relay (1980).

GEYER, Francis (1920–1995). *See Harwood, Gwen.*

GEYRA (fl. 980s). Princess of Wendland. Name variations: Geira. Fl. in 980s; dau. of King Burislaf of Wendland; m. Olav I Tryggvason (968–1000), king of Norway (r. 995–1000). ❖ Died 3 years after her marriage. ❖ See also *Women in World History.*

GHALEM, Nadia (1941—). Algerian novelist and poet. Born June 26, 1941, in Oran, Algeria. ❖ Worked as radio and tv reporter; traveled in Africa, Europe, and US and settled in Canada; received MA in communications (1995); writings include *Exil* (1980), *Le Jardin de cristal* (1981), *L'oiseau de fer* (1918), *Ceci est un message enregistré* (1982), *Manon, la Louisiane* (1984), *La villa désir* (1988), *La nuit bleue* (1991), *La rose des sables* (1993), and *Le Huron et le huard* (1995).

GHEENST, Johanna van der (fl. 16th c.). Dutch mistress. Name variations: Johanna Van der Genst. Mistress of Charles V (1500–1558), Holy Roman emperor (also known as Charles I, king of Spain); children: Margaret of Parma (1522–1586).

GHEVARDINI, Lisa (b. 1474). *See del Giocondo, Lisa.*

GHICA, Helene (1828–1888). *See Chica, Elena.*

GHIKA, Elena (1828–1888). *See Chica, Elena.*

GHIKA, Princess (1866–c. 1940). *See Pougy, Liane de.*

GHILARDOTTI, Fiorella (1946—). Italian politician. Born June 25, 1946, in Castelverde, Cremona, Lombardy, Italy. ❖ Served as secretary-general of the Milan CISL confederation (1981–90) and chair of the Lombardy Regional Council (1992–94); named chair of the European Socialist standing committee on women (1997); elected to 4th and 5th European Parliament (1994–99, 1999–2004).

GHISI, Diana (c. 1530–1590). Italian sculptor and engraver. Born around 1530 into a Mantuan family of engravers; died in 1590; dau. of Giorgio Battista Ghisi, called Mantuano (painter, sculptor, architect, and engraver); sister and pupil of Giorgio Ghisi (b. 1524), also an eminent engraver. ❖ Born into a Mantuan family of engravers, executed some plates of great merit. ❖ See also *Women in World History.*

GIACOBBE, Maria (1928—). Italian novelist. Born Aug 14, 1928, in Sardinia, Italy. ❖ Moved to Denmark with husband and became citizen (1962); wrote articles for Italian and European newspapers on art, literature, and culture; also worked for Danish radio and tv; writings include *Il Diario di una maestrina* (1957), *Piccole Cronache* (1961), *Il mare* (1967), *Eurydike* (1970), *Le radici* (1975), *Den dag vi vågner* (1983), *Gli arcipelaghi* (1995) and *Eksil og adskillelse* (2001).

GIACOMO, Marina di (1976—). *See di Giacomo, Marina.*

GIACONI, Luisa (1870–1908). Italian poet. Born 1870 in Florence, Italy; died 1908. ❖ Received diploma from *Accademia delle belle arti*, Florence, and made living copying paintings; work influenced by D'Annunzio and Pre-Rapahelites; writings collected posthumously in *Tebaide* (1909, 1912).

GIANNINI, Dusolina (1900–1986). American soprano. Name variations: Gianini. Born Dec 19, 1900, in Philadelphia, Pennsylvania; died June 26, 1986, in Zurich, Switzerland; dau. of Ferruccio (tenor) and Antonietta (Briglia) Giannini (violinist); sister of Euphemia Giannini (1895–1979), a soprano who taught at the Curtis Institute, and Vittorio Giannini (1903–1966), a composer; studied with her father. ❖ Debuted in Hamburg (1925) and Teatro alla Scala (1928); made NY debut at Metropolitan in *Aida* (1936); returned to Salzburg that same year at the request of Arturo Toscanini to sing Mistress Ford in Verdi's *Falstaff;* sat out WWII teaching in Zurich; retired (1962). ❖ See also *Women in World History.*

GIANONI, Lavinia (1911—). Italian gymnast. Born Jan 31, 1911, in Italy. ❖ At Amsterdam Olympics, won a silver medal in team all-around (1928).

GIANULIAS, Nikki (1959—). American bowler. Name variations: Nicole Gianulias. Born Dec 5, 1959, in Vallejo, California. ❖ Joined the Ladies Pro Bowlers (1979) and was the 1st woman to roll four 800 series on the tour; averaged a record 213.89 pins (1986).

GIAVOTTI, Luigina (1916–1976). Italian gymnast. Born Oct 12, 1916, in Italy; died Aug 4, 1976. ❖ At Amsterdam Olympics, won a silver medal in team all-around (1928).

GIBAULT, Claire (1945—). French orchestra conductor. Born 1945 in Le Mans, France; studied at the conservatory in Le Mans and in Paris. ❖ Served as director of the Orchestre de Chambéry (1976–83) and staff conductor and assistant to John Eliot Gardiner when he was music director of the Opéra National de Lyon (1983–89); also served as director of the Atelier Lyrique et Maîtrise at the Opéra de Lyon until July 1998; served as music director of Musica per Roma (2000–02); was the 1st woman to conduct at La Scala (1995), where she presented the modern opera "La Station Thermale"; has also conducted at Royal

Opera in Covent Garden, Glyndebourne Festival Opera, Edinburgh Festival, Opéra Comique, Nice, Torino and Bologna, among others.

GIBB, Helen (1838–1914). New Zealand farmer, accommodation-house keeper, and postmaster. Name variations: Helen Lindsay. Born Helen Lindsay, July 9, 1838, in Forfarshire, Scotland; died July 30, 1914, in Motunau, New Zealand; dau. of George Lindsay and Helen (McAndrew) Lindsay; m. Stewart Gibb (shepherd), 1863 (died 1867); children: 4. ❖ Immigrated to New Zealand (1863); farmed husband's land following his death and accumulated additional land; established accommodation house when road was built close to farm (1870s); served as postmaster of Cabbage Tree Flat near Motunau (1883–1901). ❖ See also *Dictionary of New Zealand Biography* (Vol. 2).

GIBB, Roberta (1942—). American marathon runner. Name variations: Roberta Gibb Bingay; Bobbi Gibb. Born Nov 2, 1942, in Winchester, Massachusetts; m. William Bingay (runner), 1966. ❖ Applied to Boston Athletic Association (BAA) for an official Marathon number to run in the Boston Marathon (1966), but was turned down on grounds that women could not run the 26.2-mile distance; entered the race unofficially and finished 125th, beating 290 male competitors, though authorities stood firm on their ban of women from the race; ran again (1967), joined by Kathy Switzer; ran again (1968); Boston marathon officials caved (1972).

GIBBONS, Abby Hopper (1801–1893). American philanthropist, abolitionist, and Civil War nurse. Born Abigail Hopper in Philadelphia, Pennsylvania, Dec 7, 1801; died in New York City on Jan 16, 1893; dau. of Isaac Tatum Hopper; attended Friends' schools; m. James Sloan Gibbons (author and abolitionist), 1833; children: six. ❖ Born into a Quaker family, assisted father in the formation of the Isaac T. Hopper Home for discharged prisoners; because of her prominence as an abolitionist and activities in the Manhattan Anti-Slavery Society, her home in New York was sacked in the riots of July 1863; during Civil War, served as a nurse in the Federal camps and hospitals in Washington, DC; helped found the Protestant Asylum for Infants (1871), and it was chiefly through her efforts that the New York State reformatory for women and girls was established by the legislature (1872). ❖ See also *The Life of Abby Hopper Gibbons Told Chiefly through Her Correspondence* (edited by her daughter, 1897).

GIBBONS, E. Joan (1902–1988). English botanist. Born 1902 in Essex, England; died Dec 2, 1988, in Lincolnshire, England; dau. of Rev. Thomas Gibbons. ❖ Joined the Lincolnshire Naturalists' Union at age 18, serving as their botanical secretary for nearly 50 years, beginning in 1936; was also its 1st woman president (1939) and elected for 2nd term after her 1975 publication on Lincolnshire flora; joined the Botanical Society of the British Isles (BSBI, 1946); recorded flora for 2 Lincolnshire vice-counties and created a record of county flora (by 1960); served as a founding member of the Council of the Lincolnshire Naturalists' Trust (1948), which focused on conservation efforts and rescued, among other species, *Iris spuria;* served as the assistant county secretary of Girl Guide Association (28 years) and as a county secretary for handicapped guides; was a Linnean Society fellow (1969–88); was the 1st woman to write a full flora account of an English county, *The Flora of Lincolnshire* (1975).

GIBBONS, Irene (1895–1977). See Taylor, Eva.

GIBBONS, Stella (1902–1989). British writer. Name variations: Stella Webb. Born Stella Dorothea Gibbons on Jan 5, 1902, in London, England; died in Dec 1989 at age 87; eldest child of Telford Charles Gibbons (north London doctor) and Maud Williams; educated at home by governesses until age 13, when she attended the North London Collegiate School; took journalism course at University College, London; m. Allan Bourne Webb (actor and opera singer), 1933; children: a daughter. ❖ Novelist and poet, best known as the author of *Cold Comfort Farm,* worked as a decoder for the British United Press; spent ten years in Fleet Street working on various jobs (literary and drama criticism, fashion writing, special reporting), while doing some creative writing of her own; published 1st novel *Cold Comfort Farm* (1932), a parody of the rural tradition in English literature, which brought her instant fame; over the next 40 years, wrote 25 novels, together with four volumes of poetry, and three collections of short stories (none, however, were to achieve the same success); writings include *The Mountain Beast and Other Poems* (1930), *Bassett* (1934), *Nightingale Wood* (1938), *Christmas at Cold Comfort Farm* (1940), *The Bachelor* (1944), *Gentle Powers* (1946), *Conference at Cold Comfort Farm* (1949), *Collected Poems* (1950), *Here Be Dragons* (1956), *The Charmers* (1965), *Starlight* (1967), *The Snow Woman* (1969), and *The Woods in Winter* (1970). For *Cold Comfort Farm,* received the Femina Vie Heureuse Prize; was elected a fellow of the Royal Society of Literature (1950). ❖ See also *Women in World History.*

GIBBS, Georgia (1920—). American pop singer. Born Fredda Gibson (also seen as Lipson or Gibbons) in Worcester, Massachusetts, Aug 17, 1920; never married. ❖ Began singing career as a young teenager, performing on local radio shows and at clubs; signed with the Jimmy Durante–Garry Moore radio show (it was Moore who dubbed her "Her Nibs, Miss Georgia Gibbs"); had her own bi-weekly show on NBC; recorded "Kiss of Fire," which sold over 2.5 million copies and became her 1st gold record (1953); followed that with 3 additional gold records: "Dance With Me, Henry," "Arrivederci Roma," and "Tweedlee Dee" (which had originally been recorded by African-American LaVern Baker but in the practice of the day was "covered" or rerecorded by a major label with a white singer, this time Gibbs). ❖ See also *Women in World History.*

GIBBS, Lois (1946—). American environmental activist. Name variations: Lois Marie Gibbs. Born June 25, 1946, in Buffalo, NY. ❖ Discovered that her neighborhood in Love Canal, NY, was located on a 20,000-ton chemical waste dump (1978); after her children began experiencing health problems, organized her neighbors into the Love Canal Homeowners Association and began asking government to clean up Love Canal or relocate residents; despite opposition from Occidental Petroleum and at all government levels, won fight to close the hazardous dump when President Jimmy Carter issued order for paid evacuation of the 900 families in neighborhood (1980); founded Citizen's Clearinghouse for Hazardous Waste 1981 [later renamed Center for Health, Environment, and Justice]) to advise others about problems associated with toxic waste and to teach the basics of advocacy. ❖ See also autobiography *Lois Gibbs: My Story* (1981).

GIBBS, Mary Elizabeth (1836–1920). New Zealand social leader. Name variations: Mary Elizabeth Waine. Born Mary Elizabeth Waine, probably on Jan 10, 1836, in Gloucestershire, England; died Oct 21, 1920, at Nelson, New Zealand; dau. of William Waine (baker) and Mary (Craddock) Waine; m. James Gibbs, 1858; children: 5 sons and 4 daughters. ❖ Following death of husband, immigrated with children to New Zealand (1877); active in community affairs and involved in charitable work; considered to have been one of 1st women to serve on a school committee. ❖ See also *Dictionary of New Zealand Biography* (Vol. 2).

GIBBS, May (1877–1969). Australian writer and illustrator. Born Cecilia May Gibbs on Jan 17, 1877, in Lower Sydenham, Kent, England; died in Sydney, Australia, Nov 27, 1969; dau. of Herbert William Gibbs (artist), and Cecilia May Rogers (amateur artist); attended Miss Best's School for Ladies (Perth); Art Gallery of Western Australia; Cope and Nichol Art School (London); Chelsea Polytechnic (London); Henry Blackburn School for Black and White Artists (London); m. Bertram James Ossoli Kelly, April 17, 1919. ❖ Illustrator and author, especially of fantasy for children, who was one of the 1st creators of a popular Australian imagery; arrived in Australia (1881); studied in London; published 1st book *About Us* (1912); moved to Sydney (1913); on the eve of World War I, developed an amusing set of characters—sturdy, down-to-earth creatures of the gum trees—and applied them to bookmarks and magazine covers, and finally a series of stories; published *Tales of Snugglepot and Cuddlepie* (1918); published 7 more books between 1918 and 1953, *Little Ragged Blossom and More About Snugglepot and Cuddlepie* (1920), *Little Obelia and Further Adventures of Ragged Blossom, Snugglepot and Cuddlepie* (1921), *The Story of Nuttybub and Nittersing* (1923), *Two Little Gumnuts—Chucklebud and Wunkydoo, Their Strange Adventures* (1924), *Scotty in Gumnut Land* (1941), *Mr. and Mrs. Bear and Friends* (1943), and *Prince Dande Lion…A Garden Whim Wham* (1953); published weekly comic strips (1924–67); successfully forged a career in the competitive, largely male, field of illustration, while directing her stories to teach her readers a sympathy and understanding for the natural world. ❖ See also J. Lang, *Pathway to Magic: The Story of May Gibbs in Western Australia* (Challenge Bank, 1991); Maureen Walsh, *May Gibbs, Mother of the Gumnuts; Her Life and Work* (Cornstalk, 1985); and *Women in World History.*

GIBBS, Pearl (1901–1983). Aboriginal activist. Name variations: known as Gambanyi (in Ngiyamba). Born in Australia in 1901; died in 1983; dau. of Maggie Brown and stepdau. of Dick Murray; attended school at Yass and Cowra; married a man named Gibbs (English sailor), in the 1920s (separated); children: one daughter and two sons. ❖ From 1937, gained status as a member of the Aborigines' Progressive Association, which campaigned for full citizen rights and an end to the Aborigines

Protection Board; serving as secretary of all-Aboriginal Aborigines' Progressive Association (1938–40), helped unite regionally based factions and spoke frequently for the Committee for Aboriginal Citizen Rights; with Bill Ferguson, helped establish the 1st formal link between Aborigines in two states, by setting up the Dubbo branch of the Australian Aborigines' League (1946); with Faith Bandler, established the Australian Aboriginal Fellowship (1956), which included both Aboriginal and white members, and for which she served as vice president. ❖ See also *Women in World History*.

GIBSON, Althea (1927–2003). African-American tennis player. Born Althea Gibson, Aug 25, 1927, in Silver, South Carolina; grew up in Harlem, New York; died Sept 28, 2003, in East Orange, New Jersey; Florida Agricultural and Mechanical University, BS, 1953; m. Sidney Llewellyn (her coach, div.); m. William A. Darben (businessman), 1965 (div.). ❖ The 1st African-American to win tennis titles as well as the 1st black female to compete on the Ladies Professional Golf tour, was NY paddle tennis champion at 12; won the National Negro Girl's Championships (1944, 1945, 1948–56); broke tennis's color barrier at the US Open (1950) and nearly defeated Wimbledon champion Louise Brough; won the French Open (1956); with her powerful serve, extraordinary speed, and long reach, won women's singles final at Wimbledon (1957), defeating Darlene Hard, and doubles; won the Wightman Cup (1957) and the Babe Didrikson Zaharias Trophy (1957); won national singles championship twice at Forest Hills (1957 and 1958); won singles and doubles at Wimbledon once more (1958); was a member of the Ladies Professional Golf Association tour (1963–67); served on athletic commissions, as tennis coach, and as an associate of Essex Co., NJ, park commission (1970–92). ❖ See also (autobiographies) *I Always Wanted to Be Somebody* (Harper, 1958) and *So Much to Live For* (Putnam, 1968); Tom Biracree, *Althea Gibson* (Chelsea House, 1989).

GIBSON, Catherine (1931—). Scottish swimmer. Born Mar 25, 1931, in Scotland. ❖ At London Olympics, won a bronze medal in the 400-meter freestyle (1948).

GIBSON, Cheryl (1959—). Canadian swimmer. Born July 28, 1959, in Canada. ❖ At Montreal Olympics, won a silver medal in 400-meter individual medley (1976).

GIBSON, Debbie (1970—). *See Gibson, Deborah.*

GIBSON, Deborah (1970—). American pop singer and actress. Born Deborah Ann Gibson, Aug 31, 1970, in Merrick, NY. ❖ Began piano studies as toddler; won songwriting contest at 12; signed with Atlantic Records (1986) and released hit debut album *Out of the Blue* (1987); scored top-5 hits with "Shake Your Love" and "Only in My Dreams" (1987); hit #1 with ballad "Foolish Beat," which made her the youngest person to write, record, and produce a #1 single (1988); released albums *Electric Youth* (1989), *Anything is Possible* (1990), and *Body Mind Soul* (1993); earned chart success with "No More Rhyme" (1989) and "Anything is Possible" (1990); played Sandy in London production of *Grease* (1993); formed her own record label Espiritu (1997); acted in film comedy *My Girlfriend's Boyfriend* (1999) and starred in Norman Lear sitcom "Maggie Bloom" (2000); took over role of "Belle" in *Beauty and the Beast* on Broadway (2000).

GIBSON, Dorothy (1889–1946). American silent-film actress. Born May 17, 1889, in Hoboken, New Jersey; died Feb 17, 1946, in Paris, France; dau. of Leonard and Pauline Gibson; m. Jules Brulatour (executive at Eclair), 1914 (div. 1916). ❖ Began career as a Harrison Fisher model; became a leading lady of the French-American Eclair Moving Picture Company, starring in *Hands Across the Sea* (1911), among many others; with her mother, survived the sinking of the *Titanic* (1911); starred in the silent film *Saved from the Titanic*, a month after her rescue, wearing the same dress she'd worn on the night of the disaster.

GIBSON, Emily Patricia (1863/64?–1947). New Zealand proof-reader, feminist, political activist, writer. Name variations: Emily Patricia Ray. Born Emily Patricia Ray, 1863 or 1864, in Dublin, Ireland; died April 24, 1947, in Auckland, New Zealand; dau. of Edmund Ray (lawyer) and Anna (Thompson) Ray; m. William Edward Gibson (asylum attendant), 1894; children: 3. ❖ Trained as compositor and proofreader in Dublin and worked for 12 years on a London newspaper before immigrating to New Zealand (1891); worked as proofreader for *Auckland Star;* was active in Women's Franchise League; helped establish Auckland Women's Liberal League and revive Auckland Women's Political League (1907); founding member of New Zealand section of Women's International League for Peace and Freedom (WILPF, 1916); member of advisory

board and contributor of articles to *Women To-day* (1937–39); also contributed articles to *Maoriland Worker* until 1946. ❖ See also *Dictionary of New Zealand Biography* (Vol. 3).

GIBSON, Helen (1892–1977). American actress and stuntwoman. Born Aug 27, 1892, in Cleveland, Ohio; died Oct 10, 1977, in Roseburg, Oregon; m. Clifton Johnson; m. Hoot Gibson (cowboy star), 1913 (div. 1920). ❖ One of the earliest serial stars, known for her athleticism and willingness to assume dangerous stunts, replaced Helen Holmes in the title role of *The Hazards of Helen* (1915–16); appeared in over 50 films and became one of Hollywood's top stuntwomen.

GIBSON, Helena Fannie (1868–1938). New Zealand teacher and school principal. Born on July 14, 1868, at Lyttelton, New Zealand; died July 24, 1938, at Christchurch, New Zealand; dau. of Frederick Denhame Gibson and Mary Fox (Rodd) Gibson; sister of Mary Victoria Gibson. ❖ Administered private school for girls, which became Rangi-ruru school (1889–1938). ❖ See also *Dictionary of New Zealand Biography* (Vol. 2).

GIBSON, Irene Langhorne (1873–1956). The original "Gibson girl". Born in Danville, Virginia, 1873; died in 1956; 3rd child of Chiswell Dabney Langhorne (railroad developer) and Nancy Witcher Keene; sister of Nancy Witcher Astor (1879–1964); m. Charles Dana Gibson (1867–1944, one of the top illustrators of his day), 1895; children: daughter Babs. ❖ The beauty of the Langhorne family, modeled for husband as the "Gibson girl" for 20 years; was also a founder of the Protestant Big Sisters and the New York branch of the Southern Women's Educational Alliance; as a delegate, attended 2 Democratic National Conventions. ❖ See also *Women in World History*.

GIBSON, Mary Victoria (1864–1929). New Zealand teacher and school principal. Born on Oct 28, 1864, at Lyttelton, New Zealand; died Sept 1, 1929, in Oamaru, New Zealand; dau. of Frederick Denhame Gibson and Mary Fox (Rodd) Gibson; sister of Helena Fannie Gibson; Canterbury College, BA, 1887, MA, 1888. ❖ Administered Christchurch Girls' High School, 1898–1928; became principal of Waitaki Girls' High School in Oamaru (1928). ❖ See also *Dictionary of New Zealand Biography* (Vol. 2).

GIBSON, Michelle (1969—). American equestrian. Born Feb 25, 1969, in Maryland. ❖ Won a bronze medal for dressage at Atlanta Olympics (1996), on Peron.

GIBSON, Perla Siedle (d. 1971). South African pianist and concert singer. Name variations: The Lady in White. Died 1971; several children, including daughter Joy Liddiard. ❖ A classical pianist and concert singer, was also a volunteer at a dockside canteen at Durban harbor, a South African port for troopships during WWII; known as "The Lady in White," serenaded every convoy—a total of 20,000 ships and 3 million men—that entered port, never missing a day, even after she learned of her own son's death in action while serving in Italy. ❖ See also autobiography *Durban's Lady in White;* and *Women in World History*.

GIBSON, Wynne (1903–1987). American actress, singer, and theatrical agent. Born Winifred Gibson, July 3, 1903, in NYC; died May 15, 1987; m. John Gallaudet, 1927 (div. 1930). ❖ Appeared in a vaudeville with Ray Raymond, then with Frances Willard Vernon (later Frances Cagney, wife of James Cagney) in a sister dance act; made stage debut in the chorus of Lew Fields' *Snapshots of 1921,* followed by *Little Jessie James, When You Smile* and *Jarnegan,* among others; appeared in over 40 films, including *Ladies of the Big House, The Strange Case of Clara Deane* (title role), *The Crosby Case,* and *The Falcon Strikes Back;* retired to become an agent.

GIDDENS, Rebecca (1977—). American kayaker. Born Sept 19, 1977, in Green Bay, Wisconsin; attended Georgia State University; m. Eric Giddens (kayaker). ❖ Won World championship for K1 (2002); won a silver medal in K1 singles at Athens Olympics (2004).

GIDEON, Miriam (1906–1996). American composer. Born in Greeley, Colorado, Oct 23, 1906; died June 18, 1996, in New York, NY; dau. of Henrietta Shoninger and Abram Gideon (professor of philosophy and modern languages); had one sister, Judith; studied at the Yonkers Conservatory of Music with Hans Barth, the pianist, with her uncle, Henry Gideon, and with Felix Fox at Boston University; studied with Marion Bauer, Charles Haubiel, Jacques Pillois, a distinguished French composer, Lazare Saminsky, a well-known Russian composer, and with Roger Sessions at New York University; Columbia University, MA in musicology, 1946; Jewish Theological Seminary, Doctor of Sacred Music in Composition, 1970; m. Frederic Ewen (professor of German literature), 1949. ❖ The 1st woman commissioned to write a complete synagogue service, was probably the most recorded woman composer of her era; taught at Brooklyn College, City College of the City University of New York, the Manhattan School of Music, and the Jewish Theological Seminary; saw *Lyric Piece for Strings* premiered with the London Symphony Orchestra (1944); won the Ernest Bloch Prize for choral music (1948); won the National Federation of Music Clubs National Award to a woman composer (1969); was elected to the American Academy and Institute of Arts and Letters (1975). ❖ See also *Women in World History.*

GIDGET (1941—). *See Kohner, Kathy.*

GIDLEY, Sandra (1957—). English politician and member of Parliament. Born Sandra Rawson, Mar 26, 1957; m. William Arthur Gidley, 1979. ❖ Began career as a pharmacist; served as mayor of Romsey (1997–98); representing the Liberal Democrats, elected to House of Commons at Westminster (2000, 2001, 2005) for Romsey.

GIELGUD, Maina (1945—). English ballet dancer. Born June 14, 1945, in London, England; dau. of Val Gielgud (BBC producer); niece of John Gielgud (actor); trained in London with Nicholas Legat, Stanislav Idzikovsky, and Tamara Karsavina, and in Paris with Paul Goubé, Julie Sedova, Olga Preobrajenska, and others. ❖ Danced with a range of companies throughout Europe, including International Ballet du Marquis de Cuevas, Roland Petit Ballet (1961), Grand Ballet Classique de France (1965), Boris Tonin's Chamber company; joined Ballets du XXième Siècle (1967) where she danced in numerous premieres, including *Beaudelaire* (1968), and also performed in *Ninth Symphony, Four Last Songs, Romeo et Juliette* and *Le Voyage.*

GIES, Miep (b. 1909). Austrian-born Dutch hero. Name variations: Miep Van Santen in Anne Frank's original diary. Born Hermine Santrouschitz in Vienna, Austria, in Feb 15, 1909; adopted by the Nieuwenhuises; m. Jan Gies (known as Henk in the diaries), July 16, 1941 (died 1993). ❖ Holocaust rescuer who aided Anne Frank and her family while they were in hiding; following WWI, was name-tagged, along with scores of other children, and shipped off to an unknown family in the Netherlands, where there were no food shortages, to be brought back to health (1920); remained in the Netherlands with her adoptive parents; known as Miep Van Santen in Anne Frank's diary, began work for the firm of Otto Frank (1933); with husband, aided the Frank family while they hid in the Secret Annex (1942–44); following the publication of Anne Frank's diary, became a frequent speaker, begging for tolerance—tolerance for everyone; wrote (with Alison Leslie Gold) *Anne Frank Remembered* (Simon & Schuster, 1987). ❖ See also *Women in World History.*

GIESLER-ANNEKE, Mathilde Franziska (1817–1884). *See Anneke, Mathilde Franziska.*

GIFFORD, countess of. *See Blackwood, Helen Selena (1807–1867).*

GIFFORD, Frances (1920–1994). American actress. Born Mary Frances Gifford, Dec 7, 1920, in Long Beach, California; died Jan 22 (some sources cite Jan 15), 1994, in Pasadena, California; sister of Frank Gifford (football player); m. James Dunn (actor), 1938 (div. 1941). ❖ Films include *Stage Door, Mr. Smith Goes to Washington, Louisiana Purchase, Cry Havoc, Our Vines Have Tender Grapes, Riding High* and *Nyoka* in the Edgar Rice Burroughs' serial *Jungle Girl;* suffered severe head injuries in an auto accident (1948); retired from the screen (1953); as a result of injuries, was a patient in Camarillo State Hospital (1958–78).

GIGLI, Elena (1985—). Italian water-polo player. Born July 9, 1985, in Empoli, Italy. ❖ Won a team gold medal at Athens Olympics (2004).

GIL YOUNG-AH (1970—). South Korean badminton player. Born April 11, 1970, in South Korea. ❖ Won a bronze medal at Barcelona Olympics (1992) and a silver medal at Atlanta Olympics (1996), both for doubles.

GILBERD, Rehutai (1895–1967). *See Maihi, Rehutai.*

GILBERGA (d. 1054). Queen of Aragon. Name variations: Hermesenda. Died 1054; dau. of Bernardo, count of Cousserans, and Gersenda, countess of Bigorre; m. Ramiro I, king of Aragon (r. 1035–1069), Aug 22, 1036; children: Sancho V (b. 1042), king of Aragon; Garcia of Aragon (d. 1186), bishop of Pamplona; Teresa of Aragon (b. 1037, who m. William VI, count of Provence); Urraca of Aragon (nun); Sancha of Aragon (who m. Pons, count of Toulouse, and Armengol III, count of Urgel).

GILBERT, Anne (1821–1904). Anglo-American dancer and actress. Name variations: Ann Gilbert; Anne H. Gilbert; Mrs. George H. Gilbert. Born Anne Jane Hartley in Rochdale, Lancashire, England, Oct 21, 1821; died in a Chicago hotel, Dec 2, 1904; studied dance in the ballet school of Her Majesty's Theatre, Haymarket; m. George H. Gilbert (dancer and manager), 1846 (died 1866). ❖ Often danced on stage with husband in England; moved to US with husband (1849); joined a Chicago theater company and had 1st success in a speaking part (1857), in role of Wichavenda in Brougham's *Pocahontas;* made Manhattan debut in *Finesse* (1864); was best remembered as old Mrs. Gilbert, one of the famous members of Augustin Daly's Company, which she joined in 1869; a stage star for 47 years, became identified with eccentric elderly women roles, such as Mrs. Candour in *The School for Scandal* and Mrs. Hardcastle in *She Stoops to Conquer;* after Augustin Daly's death, came under Charles Frohman's management; began farewell tour in Clyde Fitch's *Granny* (1904) and died on tour; held a unique position in the American theater due to the esteem, admiration, and affection she enjoyed both on and off the stage. ❖ See also Charlotte M. Martin, ed. *The Stage Reminiscences of Mrs. Gilbert* (1901); and *Women in World History.*

GILBERT, Eliza (1818–1861). *See Montez, Lola.*

GILBERT, Florence Ruth (1917—). *See Gilbert, Ruth.*

GILBERT, Mrs. George H. (1821–1904). *See Gilbert, Anne.*

GILBERT, Georgina Jane (c. 1839–1904). *See Burgess, Georgina Jane.*

GILBERT, Jody (1916–1979). American actress and singer. Name variations: Jodi Gilbert. Born Mar 18, 1916, in Fort Worth, TX; died Feb 3, 1979, in Los Angeles, CA, following an auto accident. ❖ Appeared in over 150 films, including *Ninotchka, Seventeen, Never Give a Sucker an Even Break, Remember the Day, Tuttles of Tahiti, Blondie's Holiday, The Big Fisherman* and *Butch Cassidy and the Sundance Kid.*

GILBERT, Mrs. John (1893–1985). *See Joy, Leatrice.*

GILBERT, Julia (1924–2003). *See Allen, Rosalie.*

GILBERT, Katherine Everett (1886–1952). American philosopher. Born July 29, 1886; died April 28, 1952, in Durham, North Carolina; Brown University, BA, 1908, MA, 1910; Cornell University, PhD, 1912; m. Allan H. Gilbert, 1913; children: 2 sons. ❖ Was editorial assistant at the *Philosophical Review* (1915–19); was a research fellow, University of North Carolina (1922–29); served as acting professor of philosophy, University of North Carolina (1929–30); was a professor of philosophy, Duke University (1930–40), the 1st woman to sit on the Duke faculty as a full professor; was chair of the Department of Aesthetics, Art and Music, Duke University (1942–51); writings include *Maurice Blondel's Philosophy of Action* (1924), *Studies in Recent Aesthetics* (1927), (with Helmut Kuhn) *A History of Esthetics* (1939), *Aesthetic Studies* (1952), and many articles in philosophical journals. ❖ See also *Women in World History.*

GILBERT, Lady (1841–1921). *See Mulholland, Rosa.*

GILBERT, Linda (1847–1895). American prison welfare worker. Born Zelinda Gilbert on May 13, 1847, probably in Rochester, New York; died Oct 24, 1895, in Mount Vernon, New York; one of two daughters of Horace and Zelinda Gilbert; attended St. Mary's Convent, Chicago; never married; no children. ❖ Aided by an inheritance, donated some 4,000 volumes to the Cook County Jail (1864); in NYC, established her own Gilbert Library and Prisoners' Aid Fund (1872); published *Sketch of the Life and Work of Linda Gilbert* (1876). ❖ See also *Women in World History.*

GILBERT, Marie Dolores Eliza Rosanna (1818–1861). *See Montez, Lola.*

GILBERT, Mercedes (1894–1952). African-American stage actress. Born July 26, 1894, in Jacksonville, Florida; died Mar 1, 1952, in NYC. ❖ Appeared on Broadway in original production of *The Green Pastures;* other appearances include *Mulatto, Lace Petticoat, Bamboola, Play Genius Play, How Come Lawd?, The Searching Wind, Carib Song;* also appeared with all-black casts in *Lysistrata* and *Tobacco Road.*

GILBERT, Mrs. R. (1895–1994). *See Cooper, Whina.*

GILBERT, Ronnie (1926—). American singer, activist, actress and author. Born Sept 7, 1926, in Brooklyn, NY; m. Martin Weg (div. 1959); children: daughter, Lisa Weg. ❖ Performed with social activists Lee Hays, Peter Seeger, and Fred Hellerman as The Weavers (1949–52), selling more than 4 million records (1950–52), with such songs as

"Wimoweh," Leadbelly's "Goodnight, Irene," "Tzena, Tzena, Tzena" (Israeli soldiers' tune), "On Top of Old Smokey" (folk ballad), and Woody Guthrie's "So Long (It's Been Good to Know Yuh)" and "Hard, Ain't It Hard"; saw the disbanding of the group after it was blacklisted from tv and many live concerts because of accusations of pro-Communism by the magazine *Counter attack* during the McCarthy era (June 9, 1950); rejoined the group after its revival (1955–63); began a successful solo singing career (1960s), turning to acting as well; recorded with Holly Near (1980s); combined her acting, singing and writing for her play *Mother Jones: The Most Dangerous Woman in America* (1990s). ❖ See also autobiography (with Herbert Haufrecht) *Travelin' on with the Weavers* (Harper and Row, 1966); and *Women in World History.*

GILBERT, Ruth (1908–1984). *See Ainsworth, Ruth.*

GILBERT, Ruth (1917—). New Zealand poet. Name variations: Florence Ruth Gilbert. Born 1917. ❖ Represented in anthology *Private Gardens* (1977); published the poetry collections *The Sunlit Hour* (1945), *Lazarus and Other poems* (1949), *The Luthier* (1966), *Early Poems, 1938–1944* (1988) and *Breathings* (1992), among others.

GILBERT, Ruth (d. 1993). American actress. Died Oct 12, 1993, age 71, in NYC. ❖ Made Broadway debut in *Girls in Uniform* (1932); chosen by Eugene O'Neill to appear in *Ah Wilderness* and *The Iceman Cometh*; was also seen in *Processional* and *Detective Story*; on film, appeared as Alice in *Alice in Wonderland* (1931).

GILBERT, Sandra M. (1936—). American poet and literary critic. Born Dec 27, 1936, in New York, NY; Cornell University, BA; New York University, MA, 1961; Columbia University, PhD, 1968; m. Elliot Gilbert, 1957 (died 1991). ❖ Major feminist critic, taught at several American universities and became professor at University of California, Davis (1989); poetry includes *In the Fourth World* (1979), *The Summer Kitchen* (1983), *Emily's Bread* (1984), and *Poems in Blood Pressure* (1988); wrote several works with Susan Gubar including *The Madwoman in the Attic: The Woman Writer and the Nineteenth-Century* (1979), and *No Man's Land: The Place of the Woman Writer in the Twentieth Century* (2 vols, 1988, 1989); with Gubar, edited *Shakespeare's Sisters: Feminist Essays on Women Poets* (1979), *The Norton Anthology of Literature by Women: the Tradition in English* (1985), and *The Female Imagination and the Modernist Aesthetic* (1986). ❖ See also memoir *Wrongful Death: A Medical Tragedy* (1995), about the death of her husband.

GILBERT, Virne (1912–1987). *See Mitchell, Jackie.*

GILBERTO, Astrud (1940—). Brazilian singer. Name variations: Astrid Gilberto. Born Astrud Evangelina Weinert, Mar 3, 1940, in Salvador, Bahia, Brazil; grew up in Rio de Janeiro; had a German father and Brazilian mother; m. Joao Gilberto, 1960 (div. 1964); children: 2, including Marcelo Gilberto (bassist). ❖ Immigrated to US (1960s); made professional debut with the hit record, "The Girl from Ipanema," backed by Joao Gilberto and Stan Getz (1964); released the beginning *The Astrud Gilberto Album* (1965), as well as *Astrud Gilberto Now* (1972), *That Girl From Ipanema* (1977) and *Astrud Gilberto Plus the James Last Orchestra* (1987); appeared in the films *The Hanged Man* and *Get Yourself a College Girl* and recorded the soundtrack for *The Deadly Affair*; as a songwriter, wrote "Far Away" and "Live Today."

GILBRETH, Lillian Moller (1878–1972). American writer and management theorist. Born Lillian Evelyn Moller on May 24, 1878, in Oakland, California; died of a stroke in Scottsdale, Arizona, Jan 2, 1972; oldest dau. of 9 children of William Moller (partner in a successful retail hardware business) and Annie (Delger) Moller (dau. of a wealthy Oakland real-estate developer); University of California at Berkeley, BA in literature, 1900; University of California at Berkeley, MA in English, 1902; Brown University, PhD in psychology, 1915; earned 13 additional master's and doctoral degrees in science, engineering, letters, and psychology at Rutgers, Brown, Michigan, Syracuse, and Temple, 1928–52; m. Frank Bunker Gilbreth, Oct 19, 1904 (died 1924); children (all have middle names of Bunker or Moller): Anne Gilbreth Barney (who m. Robert E. Barney); Mary Elizabeth (died young); Ernestine Gilbreth Carey (who m. Charles E. Carey); Martha Gilbreth Tallman (who m. Richard E. Tallman); Frank Gilbreth, Jr.; William Gilbreth; Lillian Gilbreth Johnson (who m. Donald D. Johnson); Frederick Gilbreth; Daniel Gilbreth; John (known as Jack) Gilbreth; Robert Gilbreth; Jane Gilbreth Heppes (who m. G. Paul Heppes, Jr.). ❖ Engineer, industrial psychologist, household efficiency expert, pioneer in management theory, inventor of the field of scientific management, and mother of 12 children; was the 1st to introduce the concept of the psychology of

scientific management (1911); with husband, established the consulting engineering firm, Gilbreth, Inc., in Providence, RI, and later in Montclair, NJ, where a laboratory and school of scientific management for managers, educators, and other professionals was located in their home (1910–20); named honorary member of Society of Industrial Engineers (women were not admitted at that time); following husband's death (1924), headed Gilbreth, Inc., and became lecturer at Purdue University, then full professor of management in School of Mechanical Engineering (1935–48), the 1st woman in that position; served as a member of the President's Emergency Committee for Unemployment Relief (1930); honored by *American Women* as one of ten outstanding women of the year (1936); replaced Amelia Earhart as consultant at Purdue on careers for women (1939); made honorary life member of the Engineering Woman's Club (1940); was head of Department of Personnel Relations at Newark School of Engineering (1941–43); served as educational advisor to Office of War Information during WWII and member of Civil Defense Advisory Commission (1951); awarded Gantt Medal by the American Society of Mechanical Engineers (1944); given the American Women's Association Award for Eminent Achievement (1948); appointed visiting professor of management at University of Wisconsin at Madison (1955); was the 1st woman to receive the Hoover Medal for distinguished public service by an engineer; honored by the American Society of Mechanical Engineers with the Gilbreth Medal, awarded during the Gilbreth Centennial marking the 100th anniversary of husband's birth (1968); writings include *The Psychology of Management* (1914), *The Quest for the One Best Way: A Sketch of the Life of Frank Bunker Gilbreth* (1926), *The Home-Maker and Her Job* (1927), *Living with Our Children* (1928), (with Edna Yost) *Normal Lives for the Disabled* (1944), *Management in the Home* (1954). ❖ See also Frank B. Gilbreth, Jr. *Time Out for Happiness* (Crowell, 1970); Frank B. Gilbreth, Jr. and Ernestine Gilbreth Carey *Cheaper by the Dozen* (Crowell, 1948); Edna Yost, *Frank and Lillian Gilbreth: Partners for Life* (Rutgers University Press, 1949); and *Women in World History.*

GILCHRIST, Ann Monroe (1901–1964). *See Strong, Ann Monroe Gilchrist.*

GILCHRIST, Connie (1901–1985). American character actress. Born Rose Constance Gilchrist, Feb 2, 1901, in Brooklyn, NY; died Mar 3, 1985; dau. of Martha Daniels (actress). ❖ Made stage debut in London (1917) and NY debut (1935); made film debut in *Hullabaloo* (1940), followed by *Two-Faced Woman, Tortilla Flat, Thousands Cheer, Junior Miss, The Hucksters, A Woman's Face, The Thin Man Goes Home, Little Women, Houdini, Auntie Mame* and *Some Came Running,* among many others.

GILCHRIST, Ellen (1935—). American novelist and short-story writer. Born Feb 20, 1935, in Vicksburg, Mississippi. ❖ Worked as journalist and radio commentator; writings include *The Land Surveyor's Daughter* (1979), *In the Land of Dreamy Dreams* (1981), *The Annunciation* (1983), *Victory Over Japan* (1984), *Drunk with Love* (1986), *Light Can Be Both Wave and Particle* (1989), *The Blue-Eyed Buddhist* (1990), *I Cannot Get You Close Enough* (1990), and *Net of Jewels* (1992). Won American Book Award for *Victory Over Japan.*

GILDER, Jeannette Leonard (1849–1916). American journalist and novelist. Born Jeannette Leonard Gilder, Oct 3, 1849, in Flushing, NY; died 1916; dau. of Reverend Gilder (minister and Union Army chaplain). ❖ At 15, after father died of smallpox while serving with Union Army during Civil War, found a job to support the family; following a stint at *Newark Morning Register,* moved to NY and became literary editor of *New York Herald;* with brother Joseph, co-founded (1881) weekly literary magazine, *Critic,* which she edited for 25 years (1881–1906); was also author of *The Autobiography of a Tomboy* (1901) and *The Tomboy at Work* (1904).

GILDER, Virginia (1958—). American rower. Born June 4, 1958. ❖ At Los Angeles Olympics, won a silver medal in quadruple sculls with coxswain (1984).

GILDERNEW, Michelle (1970—). Northern Ireland politician. Born Mar 28, 1970, in Northern Ireland. ❖ Was head of Sinn Féin's London Office, press officer, and member of delegation to Downing Street (1997); representing Sinn Féin, elected to the Northern Ireland Assembly for Fermanagh and South Tyrone (1998); elected to House of Commons at Westminster (2001, 2005), for Fermanagh and South Tyrone.

GILDERSLEEVE, Virginia Crocheron (1877–1965). American educator. Born Virginia Crocheron Gildersleeve on Oct 3, 1877, in New York City; died in Centerville, Massachusetts, July 7, 1965; dau. of Henry Alger Gildersleeve (judge) and Virginia (Crocheron) Gildersleeve; attended Brearley School; Barnard College, AB, 1899; Columbia University, AM, 1900; Columbia University, PhD, 1908; never married; lived with Elizabeth Reynard (professor of English at Barnard); no children. ❖ Outstanding educator and dean of Barnard College, during the years of its greatest development, who was also US delegate to the UN conference held at San Francisco in 1945, thereby holding the highest political appointment then given to an American woman; was an instructor in English, Barnard College (1900–07, 1908–10), assistant professor (1910–11), and professor and dean (1911–47); served as US delegate to United Nations conference on international organization in San Francisco (1945); writings include *Government Regulation of the Elizabethan Drama* (1908), *Many a Good Crusade* (1954), and *A Hoard for Winter* (1962). ❖ See also Alice Duer Miller and Susan Myers, *Barnard College: The 1st Fifty Years* (Columbia University Press, 1939); Marian Churchill White, *A History of Barnard College* (Columbia University Press, 1954); and *Women in World History*.

GILETTE OF NARBONNE (fl. 1300). French physician. Fl. around 1300 in Narbonne, France; dau. of Gerard of Narbonne (physician). ❖ Learned medicine from father; after his death, continued treating his patients; was a highly respected doctor, and Giovanni Boccaccio wrote of her in one of his books, calling her *Donna Medica* ("Lady Doctor"); was said to be so renowned that the French king summoned her to treat him, and that she cured him of fistula.

GILIANI, Allessandra (1307–1326). Italian anatomist. Name variations: Alessandra. Born 1307; died Mar 26, 1326. ❖ Pioneered anatomical dissection.

GILKS, Gillian (1959—). English badminton player. Name variations: Gillian Perrin, Gillian Goodwin. Born Gillian Perrin in 1959 in Sutton, Surrey, England; coached by Jake Downey. ❖ Known for dominating women's international badminton in singles, doubles and mixed doubles competition (1970s), won 1st national title while still teenager; won 27 national titles (9 singles, 7 ladies doubles, 11 mixed doubles); won mixed doubles match at Olympic Games Demonstration in Munich (1972); was triple champion at Commonwealth Games (1974); earned record number of caps for England and won 11 All-England championship titles and 12 European championship titles; won 16 world-class events (1984) and silver medal at Uber Cup; held major titles in Australia, Canada, China-Taipei, and Japan; represented England on 111 occasions but was often in conflict with Badminton Association of England, which tried to decide where she would play and with whom. Named Great Britain's Sportswoman of the Year (1974, 1976); introduced into Badminton Hall of Fame (1999). ❖ See also David Hunn, *A Life of Badminton* (Ward Lock, 1981).

GILL, Mary Gabriel (1837–1905). New Zealand prioress. Name variations: Victoria Margaretta Gill. Born Victoria Margaretta Gill, June 22, 1837, in Dublin, Ireland; died April 22, 1905, in Australia; dau. of Andrew Gill (brewer) and Ellen Maria Gill. ❖ Became Dominican nun (mid-1850s); taught and administered schools and training for novices for 17 years; immigrated to Dunedin, New Zealand, as prioress; founded boarding school at Wakari (1874); opened St. Dominick's College (1890); left priory to further Catholic education in West Australian goldmining districts (c. 1899). ❖ See also *Dictionary of New Zealand Biography* (Vol. 2).

GILL, Neena (1956—). English politician. Born Dec 24, 1956, in Ludhiania, India. ❖ Served as principal housing officer, United Kingdom Housing Trust (1983–86), chief executive, Asra Great London Housing Association (1986–90), and chief executive, New London Housing Group (1990–99); adviser to ministers and members of Parliament on social policy issues; as a European Socialist, elected to 5th European Parliament (1999–2004).

GILL, Victoria Margaretta (1837–1905). See Gill, Mary Gabriel.

GILL, Zillah Smith (1859–1937). New Zealand politician. Name variations: Zillah Smith Billany. Born Zillah Smith Billany, May 29, 1859, at Kingston upon Hull, Yorkshire, England; died Aug 17, 1937, at Palmerston North, New Zealand; dau. of Neiles Boynton Billany (shipwright) and Charlotte Ann (Clevelin) Billany; m. Edward Keimig (bookkeeper), 1880s (died 1888); m. Christopher John Gill (joiner), 1894 (died 1930); children: (2nd m.) 1 son. ❖ Member of ambulance brigade

nursing division in Hull, becoming nurse (1898), secretary of nursing division, then superintendent (1912–30); actively involved in labor movement and was elected Social Democratic Party candidate for Palmerston North Hospital and Charitable Aid Board (1915); 1st woman to gain seat, winning 2nd term (1917); elected to national executive of New Zealand Labor Party, and became the 1st woman to seek a seat on Palmerston North Borough Council (1918); founding member of Palmerston North branch of Royal New Zealand Society for the Health of Women and Children (Plunkett Society) (1918). ❖ See also *Dictionary of New Zealand Biography* (Vol. 3).

GILLAN, Cheryl (1952—). English politician and member of Parliament. Born Cheryl Gillan, April 21, 1952; m. John Coates Leeming, 1985. ❖ As a Conservative, elected to House of Commons for Chesham and Amersham (1992, 1997, 2001, 2005); named opposition whip.

GILLARS, Mildred E. (1900–1988). American-born radio broadcaster. Name variations: Axis Sally; Mildred Gillars Sisk. Born Mildred E. Gillars in Portland Maine, 1900; died in Columbus, Ohio, June 25, 1988; attended Ohio Wesleyan College. ❖ Radio personality who was convicted of wartime treason for broadcasting Nazi propaganda from Germany during World War II; in Germany at onset of World War II, worked as an English teacher before taking the radio position that made her an overnight success and would lead to her imprisonment for treason; was tracked down and returned to US where she was tried in federal court (1948); was convicted on a single count of treason and sentenced to 10 to 30 years in the women's federal prison at Alderson, West Virginia; paroled (1961). ❖ See also *Women in World History*.

GILLESPIE, Mother Angela (1824–1887). American educator. Name variations: Eliza Gillespie. Born Eliza Maria Gillespie near Brownsville, Pennsylvania, Feb 21, 1824; died at Saint Mary's Convent in South Bend, Indiana, Mar 4, 1887; attended private school and a girls' school run by the Dominican Sisters in Somerset, Ohio; graduated from the Visitation Academy in Georgetown, Washington, DC, 1842. ❖ After years of charitable work and teaching positions in Lancaster, Ohio, and at Saint Mary's Seminary in Maryland, felt called to the religious life (1853), devoting the remainder of her days to the Sisters of the Holy Cross; became director of studies at Saint Mary's Academy in Bertrand, Michigan, and was made superior of the convent (1855); at the academy (which later became St. Mary's College and was moved to a new site near Notre Dame), strongly believed in full educational rights for women; began publishing *Metropolitan Readers* (1860), a graded textbook series used in elementary through college courses; during Civil War, supervised some 80 nuns who provided nursing services in army hospitals across the country, as well as aboard hospital ships on the Mississippi; began editing *Ave Maria* (1866); when difficulties between American and French branches of her order erupted (1869), became provincial superior of an independent American branch, thus becoming founder of her order in America. ❖ See also *Women in World History*.

GILLESPIE, Eliza (1824–1887). See Gillespie, Mother Angela.

GILLESPIE, Mabel (1877–1923). American labor activist. Born Mabel Edna Gillespie, May 4, 1877, in St. Paul, Minnesota; died Sept 24, 1923, in Boston, Massachusetts; dau. of James and Ida (Scott) Gillespie; orphaned at an early age, raised by an aunt in Concord; attended Radcliffe College, 1898–1900. ❖ Was only person to serve on Minimum Wage Commission, MA, during its existence (1913–19); became organizer and 1st president of the Stenographers' Union (1917); became 1st woman on executive board of MA State Federation of Labor (1918); served on executive board of WTUL (1919–22).

GILLETT, Emma (1852–1927). American lawyer and feminist. Born Emma Millinda Gillette, July 30, 1852, in Princeton, Green Lake Co., Wisconsin; died Jan 23, 1927, in Washington, DC; dau. of Richard J. Gillett and Sara Ann (Barlow) Gillett. ❖ Appointed one of 1st female notaries public in Washington DC by President James Garfield (June 1881); co-founded (1896) and served as dean (1913–23) of Washington College of Law; established Washington Wimodaughsis (1890), woman's club later absorbed into YWCA; co-founded and was president (1921) of Woman's Bar Association of the District of Columbia.

GILLETTE, Genevieve (1898–1986). American landscape architect and conservationist. Born Emma Genevieve Gillette, May 19, 1898, in Lansing, Michigan; died 1986; was the only woman to graduate from the 1st landscape architecture class at Michigan Agricultural College (now Michigan State University), 1920. ❖ Known as Miss Michigan

State Parks, began career landscaping the campuses of Albion College and Ferris State; under the aegis of P.J. Hoffmaster, director of the Department of Conservation, surveyed potential park sites for their biological and scenic value and through her recommendations and persistence was eventually responsible for Sleeping Bear Dunes, Hartwick Pines State Park, Porcupine Mountain State Park and the Detroit area Metroparks, among others.

GILLIAM, Marie (c. 1882–1935). *See La Belle Marie.*

GILLIAN. *Variant of Julia.*

GILLIATT, Penelope (1932–1993). British novelist, short-story writer and film critic. Name variations: Penelope Osborne. Born Penelope Ann Douglass Gilliatt, Mar 25, 1932, in London, England; died May 9, 1993, in London, England; dau. of Cyril Conner and Mary Douglas Conner; m. R.W. Gilliatt, 1954; m. John Osborne (playwright), 1963; children: 1. ❖ Wrote novels and short stories including *One By One* (1965), *Sunday Bloody Sunday* (1971), *Splendid Lives* (1977), *Quotations from Other Lives* (1981), *22 Stories* (1986), and *Lingo* (1990); also wrote theatre and film reviews in England and US for publications such as *Vogue, Observer* and *The New Yorker;* collections of reviews and studies of film include *Jean Renoir: Essays, Conversations, Reviews* (1975), *Jacques Tati* (1976), and *Three-Quarter Face: Reports and Reflections* (1980). Nominated for an Academy Award for her screenplay of *Sunday Bloody Sunday* (1971).

GILLIES, Janet (1864–1947). New Zealand nurse and nursing administrator. Name variations: Janet Speed. Born Janet Speed, Jan 31, 1864, in Wanganui, New Zealand; died July 24, 1947, in Auckland, New Zealand; dau. of James Speed and Janet (Montgomery) Speed; m. David Welsh Gillies (surveyor), 1904 (died 1930). ❖ Trained as nurse at Wellington District Hospital (1887); served in South African War (1899–1902); studied military nursing at Royal Victoria Hospital (1902); elected honorary nursing sister for St John Ambulance District Nursing Guild, home-nursing service for poor (1903); appointed matron in chief, New Zealand Medical Corps Nursing Reserve (1908), but resistance to her leadership forced resignation (1910); her plans to establish army nursing service in New Zealand were eventually implemented during World War I. Awarded King's South Africa Medal (1902). ❖ See also *Dictionary of New Zealand Biography* (Vol. 3).

GILLIG, Marie-Hélène (1946—). French politician. Name variations: Marie-Helene Gillig. Born Mar 15, 1946, in Aire/Adour, France. ❖ Served as deputy mayor of Strasbourg, vice-chair of the Strasbourg Urban Community, and chair of the board of governors of Strasbourg university hospitals; as a European Socialist, elected to 5th European Parliament (1999–2004). Named Knight of the National Order of Merit.

GILLIGAN, Amy (1869–1928). *See Archer-Gilligan, Amy.*

GILLIGAN, Carol (1936—). American psychologist. Born Nov 28, 1936, in New York, NY; Swarthmore College, BA, 1958; Radcliffe College, MA in clinical psychology, 1961; Harvard University, PhD in social psychology (1964); m. James Gilligan; children: 3 sons. ❖ Pioneer feminist psychologist, worked as lecturer at University of Chicago (1965–66); began teaching at Harvard with psychoanalyst Erik Erikson (1967) and became research assistant for Lawrence Kohlberg (1970); criticized Kohlberg's theories on stages of moral development in her groundbreaking book *In a Different Voice: Psychological Theory and Women's Development* (1982); became full professor at Harvard (1986); published *Women, Girls, and Psychotherapy: Reframing Resistance* (1991) and *Meeting at the Crossroads* (1992); served as Pitt Professor of American History at University of Cambridge in England (1992–94); broadened research to include race in *Between Voice and Silence: Women and Girls, Race and Relationship* (1995); appointed to Harvard's 1st gender studies post (Patricia Albjerg Graham chair, 1997); served as coordinator of Harvard Center on Gender and Education; began teaching at New York University's Graduate Schools of Law and Education (2002); wrote play adaptation of *The Scarlet Letter* and published *The Birth of Pleasure* (2002). Received *Ms.* Magazine's "Woman of the Year" award (1983), Grawemeyer Award in Education (1992) and Heinz Award (1997).

GILLILAND, Helen (1897–1942). Irish actress and singer. Born jan 31, 1897, in Belfast, Ireland (now Northern Ireland); died Nov 24, 1942, at sea; m. L.H. Nelles (div.). ❖ Made stage deubt on tour with the D'Oyly Carte Repertory Opera Company (1917), as one of its principal sopranos, then appeared in London as Aline in *The Sorcerer,* Phyllis in *Iolanthe,*

Yum-Yum in *The Mikado,* Casilda in *The Gondoliers,* Patience, and Elsie Maynard in *The Yeoman of the Guard* (1919–20, 1921–22); left to do musical comedy, appearing in *The Red Robe, The Song of the Drum* and *Nina Rosa* (title role); during WWII, was en route to an ENSA engagement for the troops when her ship was torpedoed by the Japanese Navy and sunk in Far Eastern waters with no survivors.

GILLMOR, Frances (1903–1993). American folklorist, scholar, and novelist. Born May 21, 1903, in Buffalo, NY; died Oct 28, 1993; dau. of Abner Churchill Gillmor (businessman) and Annie McVicar Gillmor; University of Chicago; University of Arizona, BA and MA, 1928–1931; Universidad Nacionál Autónoma de México, PhD, 1957. ❖ Had 1st field experience while living with explorers John and Louisa Wade Wetherill on Navajo reservation in Arizona; collaborated with Louisa Wetherill on the classic, *Traders to the Navajos* (1934); taught at University of New Mexico and in English department of University of Arizona; studied in Mexico at Escuela Nacional de Antropologia e Historia and Universidad Nacional Autonoma de Mexico; published *Flute of the Smoking Mirror* about 15th-century Aztec ruler Nezahualcoyotl (1949); published other acclaimed works, including *The King Danced in the Marketplace* (1964); collected folklore of the Southwest; novels include *Thumbcap Weir* (1929), *Windsinger* (1930), and *Fruit Out of Rock* (1940).

GILLMORE, Inez (1873–1970). *See Irwin, Inez Haynes.*

GILLMORE, Margalo (1897–1986). American actress and writer. Born May 31, 1897, in London, England; died June 30, 1986, in New York, NY; dau. of Frank Gillmore (actor); sister of Ruth Gillmore (actress, d. 1976); m. Robert Ross (died 1954). ❖ Made NY debut in *The Scrap of Paper* (1917) and often appeared with the Theatre Guild; other plays include *Her Honor the Mayor, Up from Nowhere, The Famous Mrs. Fair, The Straw, Alias Jimmy Valentine, He Who Gets Slapped, As You Like It, Scaramouche, Outward Bound, Hedda Gabler, The Green Hat, Marco Millions, Berkeley Square* and *The Barretts of Wimpole Street,;* succeeded Helen Hayes in *Mary of Scotland;* co-authored with Patricia Collinge, *The B.O.W.S.* ❖ See also autobiography *Four Flights Up* (1964).

GILLMORE, Ruth (d. 1976). American actress. Died Feb 12, 1976, in Nantucket, Massachusetts; dau. of Frank Gillmore (actor); sister of Margalo Gillmore (actress). ❖ Made stage debut in *The Betrothal* (1919), followed by *No More Frontier* and *The Farmer Takes a Wife.*

GILLOM, Jennifer (1964—). African-American basketball player. Born June 13, 1964, in Abbeville, Mississippi. ❖ Won a team gold medal at FIBA World championships (1986, 2002), Goodwill Games (1986) and Pan American Games (1987); at Seoul Olympics, won a gold medal in team competition (1988); joined the WNBA Phoenix Mercury (1996). Named Kim Perrot Sportsman of the Year (2002).

GILLON, Karen (1967—). Scottish politician. Name variations: Karen Turnbull. Born Karen Turnbull, 1967, in Edinburgh, Scotland; m. James Gillon. ❖ Served as personal assistant to Helen Liddell (MP, 1997); representing Labour for Clydesdale, was the 1st woman elected to the Scottish Parliament.

GILMAN, Caroline Howard (1794–1888). American author. Name variations: Caroline Howard; (pseudonym) Clarissa Packard. Born Caroline Howard on Oct 8, 1794, in Boston, Massachusetts; died Sept 15, 1888, in Washington, DC; dau. of Samuel Howard and Anna (Lillie) Howard; sister of Harriet Howard Fay; married Samuel Gilman (Unitarian minister who wrote the poem "Fair Harvard"), in Dec 1819; children: Caroline Howard Jervey (1823–1877, poet) and Eliza Gilman; as well as 5 other children, 3 of whom died in infancy. ❖ Began publishing *Rose-Bud,* or *Youth's Gazette,* one of the earliest children's magazines in America (1832); renamed it *Southern Rose-Bud* (1833), then *Southern Rose* (1835), gradually developing it into a broader family magazine before ceasing publication (1839); within its pages, serialized her 1st novel *Recollections of a Housekeeper,* under pseudonym Clarissa Packard, followed by its counterpart, *Recollections of a Southern Matron* (1838); in much of her work, sought to ease some of the tensions between North and South on the political front; other books include *The Poetry of Travelling in the US* (1838), (editor) *Letters of Eliza Wilkinson* (1839), *Love's Progress* (1840), and *The Sibyl; or, New Oracles from the Poets* (1849). ❖ See also *Women in World History.*

GILMAN, Charlotte Perkins (1860–1935). American feminist and socialist writer and orator. Name variations: Charlotte Anna Perkins (1860–1884); Charlotte Perkins Stetson (1884–1900); Charlotte Perkins Gilman (1900–1935). Born Charlotte Anna Perkins in Hartford,

Connecticut, July 3, 1860; committed suicide in Pasadena, California, after cancer treatments had proved ineffectual, Aug 17, 1935; dau. of Frederick Beecher Perkins (librarian) and Mary Fitch Westcott; educated at home and at the Rhode Island School of Design; m. Charles Walter Stetson (artist), in May 1884 (separated 1887, div. 1894); m. her cousin George Houghton Gilman (New York lawyer), in June 1900; children: (1st m.) one child, Katherine Stetson (b. 1885). ❖ One of the most active Progressive reformers of the late 19th and early 20th centuries, scandalized most of her contemporaries when she condemned the middle-class family as outmoded and oppressive; moved to Pasadena, California (1888); published her superb short story "The Yellow Wallpaper" (1892), about an unhappy woman with postpartum depression steadily descending into madness; published *In This Our World* (1893); edited, with Helen Campbell, *The Impress,* organ of the Pacific Coast Woman's Press Association (1894); was resident of Jane Addams' Hull House (1895); went on lecture tours (1895–1900); appointed delegate to the International Socialist and Labor Congress in London (1896); published *Women and Economics* (1898), *Concerning Children* (1900), *The Home* (1903), *Human Work* (1904); founded and edited *The Forerunner* (1909–16), for which she wrote a serialized novel, "Herland," about a women's utopia; published *What Diantha Did* (1910); published *The Man-Made World, Moving the Mountain* and *The Crux* (1911); founded, with Jane Addams, the Woman's Peace Party (1915); published *His Religion and Hers* (1923); lived in Norwich, Connecticut (1922–34); diagnosed with cancer (1932). *Unpunished,* a detective novel, was published by The Feminist Press in 1997. ❖ See also *Charlotte Perkins Gilman: An Autobiography* (1935); Polly Wynn Allen, *Building Domestic Liberty: Charlotte Perkins Gilman's Architectural Feminism* (University of Massachusetts Press, 1988); Ann J. Lane, *To Herland and Beyond: The Life and Work of Charlotte Perkins Gilman* (Pantheon, 1990); Sheryl L. Meyering, ed. *Charlotte Perkins Gilman: The Woman and Her Work* (University of Michigan Research Press, 1989); and *Women in World History.*

GILMAN, Elisabeth (1867–1950). American socialist and reformer. Born Elisabeth Gilman, Dec 25, 1867, in New Haven, Connecticut; died Dec 14, 1950, in Baltimore, Maryland; dau. of Daniel Coit Gilman (educator) and Mary Ketcham. ❖ Through father's status in Baltimore society, found early role in social work; founded St. Paul's Guild House, boys' club; helped soldiers overseas during WWI (1917–19), which propelled her toward socialist principals; revived and served as director of Open Forum, a weekly discussion forum that reflected her socialist and labor leanings; ran as Socialist party's candidate for governor of Maryland (1930), US senator (1934, 1938), and mayor of Baltimore (1935); sat on board of League for Industrial Democracy; served as secretary of Maryland Civil Liberties Union; co-founded Christian Social Justice Fund.

GILMER, Elizabeth May (1880–1960). New Zealand community worker, politician, and conservationist. Name variations: Elizabeth May Seddon. Born on Mar 24, 1880, at Kumara, Westland, New Zealand; died Feb 29, 1960, in Wellington, New Zealand; dau. of Richard John Seddon (politician) and Louisa Jane (Spotswood) Seddon; m. Knox Gilmer (dentist), 1907; children: 2 daughters. ❖ Active in numerous welfare and women's organizations, including Wellington branch of Plunket Society, New Zealand Crippled Children Society, Young Women's Christian Association (YWCA), Wellington Social Club for the Blind, Wellington Unemployed Women Workers' Association, Wellington Children's Health Camp Association, National Council of Women of New Zealand, and Victoria League (1930s–40s); served as justice of peace and member of Wellington College board of governors (1934–56), and was a member of Wellington Hospital Board (1938–53); served as Wellington city councillor (1941–53); ran unsuccessfully for Parliament (1935 and 1938); also active in conservation and horticultural groups and was fellow of Royal Horticultural Society, London; served on executive committee of Women's War Service Auxiliary during WWII; member of allocation committee of housing for State Advances Corporation of New Zealand (1948–60). Named OBE (1946) and DBE (1951); received Greek Red Cross and King George V Silver Jubilee Medal (1935) and Coronation Medal (1953). ❖ See also *Dictionary of New Zealand Biography.*

GILMER, Elizabeth Meriwether (1861–1951). American newspaper columnist. Name variations: (pseudonym) Dorothy Dix. Born Elizabeth Meriwether in Woodstock, Tennessee, Nov 18, 1861 (some sources cite 1870); died in New Orleans, Louisiana, Dec 16, 1951; eldest of three children of William Douglas (plantation owner) and Maria (Winston) Meriwether; attended the Female Academy, Clarkesville,

Tennessee, and Hollins Institute in Virginia; m. George O. Gilmer, in Nov 1888 (died 1929 or 1931). ❖ Authored an advice column under the name Dorothy Dix for over 60 million readers throughout the world, fielding questions on every subject from romance to hair removal; began writing a weekly "sermonette" called "Sunday Salad" for *New Orleans Picayune* (1896), which soon evolved into "Dorothy Dix Talks"; lured away from New Orleans, went to work for *New York Journal* (1901), producing 3 advice columns each week for next 15 years while also covering sensational murder trials, vice investigations, and special-interest stories; accepted a contract from Wheeler Syndicate which allowed her to devote herself exclusively to her column (1917), which was published six times weekly until 1949; also wrote 5 books: *Mirandy* (1914), *Hearts à la Mode* (1915), *Mirandy Exhorts* (1922), *My Trip Around the World* (1924), *Dorothy Dix: Her Book,* based on her columns (1926), and *How to Win and Hold a Husband* (1939). ❖ See also *Women in World History.*

GILMORE, Mary (1865–1962). Australian poet, journalist, and social activist. Name variations: Dame Mary Gilmore. Born Mary Jean Cameron at Cotta Walla, near Goulburn, North New Wales, Australia, Aug 16, 1865; died in Sydney in 1962; 1st daughter and eldest child of Donal (Donald) (building contractor) and Mary (Beattie) Cameron; educated at home except for two years at a school in Wagga Wagga, 1875–77; m. William Alexander Gilmore (shearer from Western Victoria), in May 1897; children: William Dysart Cameron Gilmore (1898–1945). ❖ In a literary life that encompassed nearly a century of Australian history, recorded in poetry and prose the social and political changes that transformed her country from a colony into an independent nation; taught school in militant mining town of Silverton, near Broken Hill (1888–89), which aroused her lifelong interest in labor movement; supported William Lane's venture to establish a Utopian socialist settlement in Paraguay; at his request, sailed to South America to teach in the colony of Cosme (1896); now married with a son, returned to Australia (1902); was hired to edit the Women's Page of the *Worker* (1908), a post she held for the next 23 years, launching a wide range of campaigns for social and economic change, causes which included Aboriginal rights, women's rights, improved health care for children and expectant mothers, and the plight of the working man; published 1st volume of poems, *Marri'd and Other Verses* (1910); published perhaps her best collection of verse, *The Wild Swan* (1930), followed by *The Rue Tree* (1931), a volume of mostly religious poems, and *Under the Wilgas* (1932), which emphasized Aboriginal themes; began writing for Communist newspaper *Tribune* (1952), an action prompted by her zeal as a pacifist but causing some controversy; published final volume of poetry at 90, *Fourteen Men* (1954); was a beloved national figure; other poetry includes *The Tale of Tiddley Winks* (1917), *The Passionate Heart* (1918), *The Tilted Cart* (1925), *Battlefields* (1939), *The Disinherited* (1941), and *Pro Patria Australia and Other Poems* (1945). Made a Dame of the British Empire (1937). ❖ See also *Letters of Mary Gilmore* (Melbourne University Press, 1980); reminiscences *Old Days, Old Ways* (1934) and *More Recollections* (1935); and *Women in World History.*

GILMORE, Rebecca. Australian diver. Born in New South Wales, Australia; m. Julie Manuel. ❖ Won a bronze medal for synchronized platform diving at Sydney Olympics (2000).

GILMORE, Virginia (1919–1986). American stage, tv, and screen actress. Born Sherman Virginia Poole, July 26, 1919, in El Monte, California; died Mar 28, 1986, in Santa Barbara, California; m. Yul Brynner (actor), 1944 (div. 1960); children: Rock Brynner. ❖ Made Broadway debut in *Those Endearing Young Charms* (1943), followed by *The World's Full of Girls* and *Dear Ruth;* appeared in over 40 films, including *Pride of the Yankees, Western Union, Orchestra Wives, Close-Up, Walk East on Beacon* and Jean Renoir's *Swamp Water;* taught drama at Yale (1966–68).

GILMOUR, Christina (c. 1824–c. 1911). Scottish woman tried for murder. Born c. 1824; died c. 1911; m. John Gilmour, Nov 27, 1842 (died Jan 11, 1843). ❖ Married John Gilmour at 18 and, despite appearances to contrary, was apparently unhappy during the 6 weeks of their marriage; after husband died of arsenic poisoning (Jan 11, 1843), headed for NY, from which she was returned by authorities to Scotland (Aug 16); admitted to purchasing arsenic in order to take her own life but not life of husband, a position asserted by defense at trial (Jan 1844); freed by verdict of Not Proven, lived another 62 years until death at 87.

GILMOUR, Sally (1921–2004). English ballet dancer. Name variations: Sally Gilmour Wynn. Born Nov 2, 1921, in Malaya; died May 23, 2004, in Sydney, Australia; m. Allan Wynn (Australian cardiologist), 1949 (died 1987); children: 1 daughter, 2 sons. ❖ Grew up in England and was trained in classical ballet by Tamara Karsavina and Marie Rambert; joined Ballet Rambert (1936) where she came to prominence in the title role in *Giselle* (1945) and appeared in numerous works by Andrée Howard, including *Lady into Fox* (1939), *Carnival of Animals* (1943), *The Fugitive* (1944), and *The Sailor's Return* (1947); created roles for Frank Staff in his *Peter and the Wolf* (1940) and for Walter Gore in *Confessional* (1941) and *Winter Night* (1948); remained with Ballet Rambert, performing works by Antony Tudor, Frederick Ashton, and more, until her retirement (1952).

GILOT, Françoise (1922—). French painter and author. Born in France in 1922; dau. of Emile Gilot (founder of Parfums Gilot); attended Catholic boarding school; received a *licence* in literature (equivalent of an AB in an American university) and studied law at Sorbonne; lived with Pablo Picasso (1881–1973) for a decade beginning in 1943; m. Luc Simon (painter), in July 1953 (div.); m. Dr. Jonas Salk (1914–1995, a physician who developed the 1st vaccine against polio), 1970 (died 1995); children: (1st m.) daughter, Aurélia Simon; (with Picasso) Claude Picasso (b. May 15, 1947); Paloma Picasso (b. April 19, 1949). ❖ Having been with Picasso for a decade (1943–53) and having given birth to two children, walked away from the relationship seemingly unscathed, which cannot be said of all the women in his life; went on to become a respected painter in her own right, as well as a poet and author; sat for many Picasso portraits; had a successful showing at la Hune Gallery in Paris (1951), and a full-scale exhibition at Kahnweiler's (1952); moved to Paris (1953); pursued her art in earnest, producing paintings, drawings, and prints that are included in permanent collections of museums throughout US and Europe; with mythology as a recurring theme, exhibited paintings in US (1966 and 1993–94); wrote 9 books, including *Interface: The Painter and the Mask*, *Françoise Gilot: An Artist's Journey* and *Matisse and Picasso: A Friendship in Art*. Awarded the Legion denier in France (1990); received the Jean Cocteau International Style Award (1994). ❖ See also memoir (with Carlton Lake) *Life with Picasso* (McGraw-Hill, 1964); film *Surviving Picasso* (film), based on her memoir (1996); and *Women in World History*.

GILPIN, Laura (1891–1979). American photographer. Born April 22, 1891, in Austin Bluffs, Colorado; died Nov 30, 1979, in Santa Fe, New Mexico; dau. of Frank Gilpin (furniture maker) and Emma (Miller) Gilpin; attended Baldwin School, 1905–07; attended Rosehall, 1907–09; attended New England Conservatory of Music, 1910; attended Clarence H. White School of Photography, 1916–17; never married; lived with Elizabeth "Betsy" Forster (registered nurse), 1946–72 (d. 1972); no children. ❖ Photographer who documented the lives of the southwest Navajo, among other subjects, and gained renown in the last decade of her life, after 70 years in her field; began experimenting with photography (1903); resolving to become a professional photographer, moved to NY to enter Clarence H. White School of Photography (1916); opened a studio in Colorado Springs and obtained a position teaching at Broadmoor Art Academy (1918); worked as a commercial photographer while her reputation spread across US and Europe; began documenting the Navajo of the southwest (1931), developing a great understanding with the Navajo and earning their trust and admiration; presented work from the Yucatan and American southwest to Library of Congress, resulting in the sale of 42 prints, which became part of Library's permanent collection; published 1st book, *The Pueblos: A Camera Chronicle* (1941); moved to Santa Fe, New Mexico (1945); published *Temples in Yucatan* (1948), *The Rio Grande: River of Destiny* (1949), followed by *The Enduring Navaho* (1968), which finally brought her the recognition she had long sought; at end of a life lived largely in obscurity, was hailed by Ansel Adams as "one of the most important photographers of our time." Received Colorado Governor's Award in Arts and Humanities (1977). ❖ See also Martha A. Sandweiss, *Laura Gilpin: An Enduring Grace* (Amon Carter Museum of Western Art, 1986); and *Women in World History*.

GILROY, Beryl (1924–2001). Guyanan children's writer, novelist and educator. Born Aug 30, 1924, in Berbice, Guyana; died April 4, 2001; received BsC from London University and MA from University of Sussex. ❖ Trained as teacher in Guyana and worked for UNICEF; became 1st black head teacher in London and worked at ILEA Centre for Multicultural Education; was founding member of Camden Black Sisters; awarded Greater London Council Creative Writing Prize for Ethnic Minorities; writings include *Frangipani House* (1986), *Boy Sandwich* (1989), and *Steadman and Joanna* (1996); also wrote autobiographical *Black Teacher* (1970).

GILROY, Linda (1949—). English politician and member of Parliament. Born Linda Jarvie, July 19, 1949; m. Bernard Gilroy, 1986. ❖ Representing Labour/Co-operative, contested Devon and East Plymouth (1994) in European Parliament election; elected to House of Commons for Plymouth Sutton (1997, 2001, 2005).

GILYAZOVA, Nailiya (1953—). Soviet fencer. Born Jan 1953 in USSR. ❖ Won a gold medal at Montreal Olympics (1976) and a silver medal at Moscow Olympics (1980), both in team foil.

GIM. See Galvão, Patricia (1910–1962).

GIMBUTAS, Marija (1921–1994). Lithuanian-born archaeologist and educator. Born Marija Alseika in Vilnius, Lithuania, Jan 23, 1921; died of cancer in Los Angeles, California, 1994; dau. of Daniel and Veronica (Janulaitis) Alseika; Vilnius University, MA, 1942; Tubingen University in Germany, PhD in archaeology, 1946; m. Jurgis Gimbutas, 1942; children: 3 daughters. ❖ Immigrated to US (1949) where she undertook post-graduate work at Harvard; joined University of California at Los Angeles (UCLA, 1963) and served as professor of European archaeology there until retirement (1990); during this time, directed 5 major archaeological excavations in southeastern Europe and wrote 20 books and more than 200 articles on European prehistory and folklore; was also considered an authority on Prehistoric incursions of Indo-European-speaking people into Europe and the ways in which they changed society there; most notable writings include *Goddesses and Gods of Old Europe* (1974), *The Language of the Goddess* (1989), and *The Civilization of the Goddess* (1991), in which she posits her most controversial thesis that the world was at peace during the Stone Age, when goddesses were worshipped and societies were centered around women. *The Living Goddess* was published posthumously (1999). ❖ See also *Women in World History*.

GIMENEZ, Estela. Spanish rhythmic gymnast. Name variations: Estela Gimenez-Cid. ❖ Won a team gold medal at Atlanta Olympics (1996).

GINANNI, Maria (1892–1953). *See Crisi, Maria.*

GINESTE, Marie-Rose (1911—). French resistance worker. Born 1911 near Montauban, France. ❖ During WWII, volunteered to take a letter from Monsignor Théas, which condemned the arrest and deportation of the Jews, to priests within 100 km of Montauban, to be read in all the Sunday services; rode her bike for 4 days, delivering the letter; became head of the Maquis in her area, forging documents and harboring Jews within 50 meters of Gestapo headquarters. Recognized by Yad Vashem as Righteous Gentile among the Nations (Oct 24, 1985). ❖ See also Showtime movie "Woman on a Bicycle," starring Sela Ward (1997).

GINEVRA (d. 470 or 542). *See Guinevere.*

GINGER SPICE (1972—). *See Halliwell, Geri.*

GINGOLD, Hermione (1897–1987). British-born actress of stage and screen. Born Hermione Ferdinanda Gingold on Dec 9, 1897, in London, England; died May 24, 1987, in New York, NY; dau. of James (stockbroker) and Kate (Walter) Gingold; attended Rosina Filippi School of the Theatre, London; m. Michael Joseph, a publisher (div.); m. Eric Maschwitz, a program director with the BBC (div.); children: (1st m.) two sons. ❖ At 11, made stage debut and spent early career in serious roles, until finding her niche as a comedian in London in *The Gate Revue* (1939); began appearing in *Sweet and Low* (1943), which, in continually updated versions (*Sweeter and Lower*, *Sweetest and Lowest*), occupied London's Ambassadors' Theater for almost 6 years; made US debut in Cambridge, MA, in revue *It's About Time* (1951) and NY debut in *John Murray Anderson's Almanac* (1953); delighted Broadway audiences as Mrs. Bennet in *First Impressions* (1959), a musical adaptation of *Pride and Prejudice;* traveled back and forth between London and New York stage, and also made memorable appearances in films, notably *Around the World in 80 Days* (1956), *Gigi* (1958), *Bell Book and Candle* (1958), *The Music Man* (1962), and *A Little Night Music* (1977); made numerous tv appearances, often in role of raconteur on talk shows with Steve Allen, Jack Paar, Garry Moore, and Merv Griffin. ❖ See also autobiographies *The World is Square* (1945) and *Sirens Should Be Seen and Not Heard* (1963); and *Women in World History*.

GINNER, Ruby (c. 1886–1978). English interpretive dancer. Born c. 1886, in Cannes, France; died Feb 19, 1978, in Newbury, Berkshire, England. ❖ Among the 1st proponents of Greek revivalist movement in England, presented numerous lecture-demonstrations and recital programs; began to choreograph pieces for her own dance group, The

Grecian Dancers (1913), and a concert group of the Greek Dance Association (1923); created such dances as *Pyrric Dance, Spartan Warrior's Dance* and *Athenian Women in Mourning;* wrote about different forms of Greek dance, presented programs, and performed and lectured long after Greek revivalist movement had died off in other regions.

GINSBURG, Mirra (1909–2000). American writer and translator. Born June 1, 1909, in Bobruisk, Byelorussia (now Belarus); died Dec 26, 2000, in Port Jefferson, NY. ❖ Lived with family in Latvia before immigrating to Canada (1928), then settling in US; specialized in translating Russian and Yiddish works into English; wrote more than 35 books for children, including *Good Morning Chick, The Two Greedy Bears* and *Clay Boy;* also translated Dostoyevsky, Mikhail Bulgakov and Isaac Bashevis Singer.

GINSBURG, Ruth Bader (1933—). American lawyer and supreme court justice. Born Joan Ruth Bader on Mar 15, 1933, in the Flatbush section of Brooklyn, New York; younger of two daughters of Nathan Bader (clothier and furrier) and Celia (Amster) Bader; graduated Cornell University, BA, 1954; attended Harvard Law School, one of only nine women in a class of over 500; graduated Columbia Law School, 1959; m. Martin D. Ginsburg (lawyer), 1954; children: Jane Ginsburg (b. 1955); James Ginsburg (b. 1965). ❖ While at Harvard Law School, was elected editor of the *Harvard Law Review;* transferred to Columbia University Law School, worked on the *Columbia Law Review,* and, upon graduation (1959), tied for 1st place in her class; passed NY bar exam; completing clerkship (1961), worked on Columbia Law School's International Procedure project for two years as well as studying at University of Lund in Sweden; joined faculty of Rutgers University Law School (1963), where the New Jersey chapter of American Civil Liberties Union (ACLU) began to refer sex discrimination cases to her; won 1st major case, *Reed v. Reed,* when US Supreme Court reversed an Idaho law that preferred men over women for executorship of an estate, the 1st time a law was overturned because of a woman's complaint of unfair sexual bias; was hired as founding counsel (1972), then general counsel, to ACLU's Women's Rights Project; also joined staff of Columbia Law School as its 1st tenured female professor; appointed to US Court of Appeals for District of Columbia (1980); during tenure, wrote 300 opinions, mostly taking a moderate position; nominated to US Supreme Court by Bill Clinton (1993), was confirmed by the Senate with a vote of 96-to-3, the 2nd woman to sit on US Supreme Court. ❖ See also *Women in World History.*

GINZBURG, Evgenia (1896–1980). Russian memoirist and essayist. Name variations: Evgeniia Semënovna Gínzburg; Evgeniia Semenova or Evgeniia Semenovna Ginzburg; Eugenia Semyonova Ginzburg. Born 1896 in Russia; died 1980. ❖ Was a professor of history at Kazan University and married to a high Communist official; arrested during one of Stalin's many purges (1937), spent 18 years in labor camps, prison, and exile and wrote of her harrowing experiences in an autobiography which became a bestseller abroad (trans. into English as *Into the Whirlwind* [1967] and *Within the Whirlwind* [1981]), and was finally published in USSR (1980s).

GINZBURG, Lidiia (1902–1990). Russian literary critic. Name variations: Lidiya, Lidia or Lidiia Iakovlevna Gínzburg. Born 1902 in Odessa, Russia; died 1990; attended Leningrad State Institute of History of the Arts. ❖ Influenced by training in formalism, often emphasized connection between art and life; critical works include *On the Lyric* (1960), *On Psychological Prose* (1971), *On the Literary Hero* (1979), *About the Old and the New* (1982), *Literature in the Search for Reality* (1987), and *A Person Seated at a Desk* (1989); selected writings published in English as *Notes from the Leningrad Blockade and Other Writings* (1992).

GINZBURG, Natalia (1916–1991). Italian novelist. Name variations: (pseudonym) Alessandra Tornimparte. Born Natalia Levi on July 14, 1916, in Palermo, Italy; died in Rome on Oct 9, 1991; dau. of Giuseppe Levi (professor of anatomy at University of Palermo) and Lidia (Tanzi) Levi; private study at home to 1927; attended secondary school in Turin, 1927–33; studied briefly at University of Turin, 1933; m. Leone Ginzburg (academic, writer, and anti-Fascist activist), 1938 (tortured to death, 1944); m. Gabriele Baldini (professor of English at the University of Trieste), 1950 (died 1969); children (1st m.) sons Carlo and Andrea, and Alessandra Ginzburg; (2nd m.) Susanna Baldini. ❖ Leading novelist, known for her neorealistic style, whose most memorable works were novels on the difficult relations between the sexes; moved with family to Turin (1919); published 1st short story and saw father arrested by Fascist government (1934); started work as editor at Einaudi publishing house

(1938); followed 1st husband into exile in village of Pizzoli (1940); published 1st novel, *La strada che va in città* (*The Road to the City*), under pseudonym (1942); fled to Rome during period of German occupation, but husband was arrested and handed over to Nazis (1943); on death of husband, took refuge with children in Florence (1944); resumed work with Einaudi (1944); returned to Turin (1945); was a member of Communist Party (1946–51); moved to Rome (1957); lived in England (1959–62); completed 1st play (1965); as a candidate of Sinistra Indipendenza Party, which was positioned on non-Communist left, elected to Italian Parliament (1983) and reelected (1987); other writings include *Tutti i nostri iera* (*All Our Yesterdays,* 1952), *Le voci della sera* (*Voices in the Evening,* 1961), (collection of essays) *Le piccole virtù* (*The Little Virtues,* 1962), *Lessico famigliare* (*Family Sayings,* 1962), and *Serena Cruz, or True Justice* (1990). Won Tempo Literary Prize (1947), Veillon International Prize (1954), Viareggio Prize (1957), Chiancino Prize (1961), and Strega Prize (1963). ❖ See also memoir *Family Sayings* (trans. by D.M. Low, Dutton, 1967); Alan Bullock, *Natalia Ginzburg: Human Relationships in a Changing World* (Berg, 1990); and *Women in World History.*

GIOCONDA, La (b. 1474). See del Giocondo, Lisa.

GIORDANI, Claudia (1955—). Italian Alpine skier. Born Oct 27, 1955, in Milano, Italy. ❖ Won a silver medal for slalom at Innsbruck Olympics (1976); placed 5th for slalom at Lake Placid (1980).

GIORGI, Brigitta (c. 1756–1806). See Banti, Brigitta.

GIORGI, Virginia (1914—). Italian gymnast. Born in 1914 in Italy. ❖ At Amsterdam Olympics, won a silver medal in team all-around (1928).

GIOVANNA. *Variant of Joanna.*

GIOVANNA I OF NAPLES (1326–1382). *See Joanna I of Naples.*

GIOVANNA II OF NAPLES (1374–1435). *See Joanna II of Naples.*

GIOVANNA OF AUSTRIA (1546–1578). *See Joanna of Austria.*

GIOVANNA OF ITALY (1907–2000). Queen of Bulgaria. Name variations: Giovanna di Savoy; Giovanna de Savoi; Joanna of Italy. Born Nov 13, 1907, in the Quirinale Palace, Rome, Italy; died Feb 26, 2000, in Estoril, Portugal; dau. of Victor Emmanuel III, king of Italy (r. 1900–1946), and Elena of Montenegro (1873–1952); m. Boris III (1894–1943), king of Bulgaria (r. 1918–1943), Oct 25, 1930; children: Simon II (Simeon), king of Bulgaria (r. 1943–1946); Marie Louise of Bulgaria (b. 1933). ❖ Became involved in charitable causes and personally financed the building of a children's hospital; during WWII, after Bulgaria joined the Axis, was shocked by Nazi anti-Semitism; with husband, saved many thousands of Bulgarian Jews from concentration camps; lived her last years in exile at Estoril, visiting Sofia only in 1993.

GIOVANNA OF SAVOY (b. 1907). *See Giovanna of Italy.*

GIOVANNI. *Variant of Joan or Joanna.*

GIOVANNI I OF NAPLES (1326–1382). *See Joanna I of Naples.*

GIOVANNI II OF NAPLES (1374–1435). *See Joanna II of Naples.*

GIOVANNI, Nikki (1943—). American poet, essayist and social activist. Born Yolande Cornelia Giovanni, Jr., June 7, 1943, in Knoxville, Tennessee; grew up in Cincinnati, Ohio; Fiske University, BA, 1967; children: 1 son. ❖ Organized Black Arts Festival in Cincinnati; became professor of English and Gloria D. Smith Professor of Black Studies at Virginia Polytechnic and State University; works, which reflect Black Art Movement and focus on politics and race, include *Black Feeling Black Talk* (1968), *Re:Creation* (1970), *Gemini: An Extended Autobiographical Statement on My First Twenty-Five Years of Being a Black Poet* (1971), *My House: Poems* (1972), *A Poetic Equation: Conversations Between Nikki Giovanni and Margaret Walker* (1974), *The Women and the Men* (1975), *Those Who Ride the Night Wind* (1983), *Sacred Cows and Other Edibles* (1988), *Racism 101* (1994), *Shimmy Shimmy Shimmy Like My Sister Kate: Looking at the Harlem Renaissance Through Poems* (1996), *Love Poems* (1997) and *Blues for All the Changes* (1999); has also written for children and young adults and had a bestselling spoken-word album, *Truth Is On Its Way* (1970s).

GIOVE, Missy (1972—). American downhill mountain bike champion. Born Melissa Giove, Jan 20, 1972, in New York, NY. ❖ Became Junior World champion (1990); won World championship (1994); won World Cup overall titles (1996, 1997) and 3 overall NORBA downnill crowns; retired from competition (2003). Other wins include gold in Snow

Mountain Downhill at X Games (1997), Tour of Hawaii (1998), and Visa Downhill National Championship Series, Mammoth Mountain, CA (2000). ❖ See also Christina Lessa, *Women Who Win* (Universe, 1998).

GIOVINCO, Lucy (c. 1958—). *See Sandelin, Lucy Giovinco.*

GIPPIUS, Zinaida (1869–1945). Russian poet, playwright, novelist, short-story writer, critic, and memoirist. Name variations: (spelling) Hippius; Z.N. Gippius, Zinaida or Sinaida Nikolaevna Gippius-Merezhkovskaia, and Zinaida Nikolaevna Merezhkovskaia or Nikolayevna Merezhkovski; (pseudonyms) Anton Krainii (Anthony "The Extreme"), Tovarisch German (Comrade Herman), Lev Pushchin, Roman Arenskii, V. Vitovt, and Anton Kirsha. Pronunciation: Zin-ay-EE-da Nik-a-LI-yev-na GIP-pee-us Me-rezh-KOF-ska-ya. Born Zinaida Nikolaevna Gippius in Belev (district of Tula), Russia, Nov 8, 1869; died in Paris, France, Sept 9, 1945; dau. of Nikolai Gippius (assistant procurator of the St. Petersburg Senate and later chief justice of Nezhin, a district of Chernigov); name of mother unknown; m. Dmitrii Sergeevich Merezhkovskii (the Symbolist writer and philosopher) in Tiflis (Tbilisi), Jan 8, 1889. ❖ An influential figure in Russian Symbolism, whose emigration after 1917 revolution prevented her from receiving the critical attention she deserved until the disintegration of the Soviet Union; initiated the Religious-Philosophical Meetings in St. Petersburg (1901), which played a major role in the Russian religious renaissance at turn of the century; hosted one of the leading literary salons in St. Petersburg and later, in emigration, in Paris; began publication of literary journal, *The New Path* (1903); moved to Paris (1906); returned to Russia (1908); emigrated from Russia to Poland (Dec 24, 1919); left Warsaw for Paris (Oct 20, 1920); organized the literary society, *The Green Lamp*, in Paris (1926); wrote poetry, plays, short stories, novels, memoirs, and literary criticism, though she is best known for her poetry, which is characterized by its religious and metaphysical themes and its innovative versification patterns; was as notorious in her day as she was influential, holding idiosyncratic views of sex and marriage, assuming contradictory gender roles in her life and art, and fostering religious views that were considered heretical. ❖ See also Temira Pachmuss, *Zinaida Hippius: An Intellectual Profile* (Southern Illinois University Press, 1971); and *Women in World History.*

GIPPS, Ruth (1921—). English composer and conductor. Born Feb 20, 1921, in East Sussex, England; one of two children of Bryan Gipps (violinist) and Hélène (Johner) Gipps (pianist); attended Brickwall School for Girls, Northiam; attended "The Gables" (preparatory school for boys where she was allowed to enroll because her brother had also attended); attended Bexhill County School; studied music at Royal College of Music, London; received doctorate in music from Durham University, 1947; m. Robert Baker (clarinetist), in Mar 1941; children: one son, Lance (b. 1947). ❖ Entered Royal College of Music at 15, where she took up the oboe and began to compose seriously; studied composition with R.O. Morris, Gordon Jacob, and Vaughan Williams, whose influence can be heard in her early compositions; during early career, worked as an orchestral oboist and appeared as a concert pianist; through WWII, was a member of Council for the Encouragement of Music and the Arts (CEMA); continued study of conducting with George Weldon and Stanford Robinson; was choirmaster of City of Birmingham Choir (1948–50); abandoned piano to concentrate on conducting (1954); led the London Repertory Orchestra (1955–61), then founded the Chanticleer Orchestra; also built a distinguished teaching record, including a professorship at Trinity College (1959–66), 10 years as a professor of composition at Royal College of Music (1967–77), and a year as a principal lecturer at Kingston Polytechnic (1979); compositions include five symphonies, concertos for violin, piano, violin and viola, and horn, several choral works, and chamber music. Made a Member of the British Empire (MBE, 1981). ❖ See also *Women in World History.*

GIRALDA DE LAURAC (d. 1211). *See Guirande de Lavaur.*

GIRARD, Anise (1928—). *See Postel-Vinay, Anise.*

GIRARD, Patricia (1968—). French track-and-field athlete. Born April 8, 1968, in Pointe-à-Pitre, Guadeloupe. ❖ Won a bronze medal for 100-meter hurdles at Atlanta Olympics (1996); at World championships, won a bronze (1997) and silver (1999), both for 4 x 100-meter relay.

GIRARDIN, Delphine (1804–1855). French author and salonnière. Name variations: Madame Émile de Girardin; Madame de Girardin; Delphine Gay; Delphine de Girardin; Delphine Gay de Girardin; (pseudonyms) Vicomte de Launay or Le Vicomte Delaunay; Charles de Launay. Born Delphine Gay on Jan 26, 1804, in Aix-la-Chapelle, Prussia; died June 29, 1855, in Paris, France; dau. of Sophie Gay (1776–1852, a novelist) and M. Gay (receiver-general of the department of the Roër or Ruhr); m. Émile de Girardin (1806–1881, journalist, economist and editor of *La Presse*), in 1831 ❖ A talented poet and writer, widely considered the queen of Romantic *cénacles* (literary circles), published poetic work, "Le Dévouement des médicins français et des souers de Ste Camille dans la peste de Barceloné," which was crowned by the Académie Français (1822), as well as *Essais poétiques* (1824) and *Nouveaux Essais poétiques* (1825) and the popular book of poetry, "Napoline" (1833); under pseudonym Vicomte de Launay, published a series of witty letters, *Lettres parisiennes* (1843); after marriage, established a salon, welcoming such literary stars as Théophile Gautier, Honoré de Balzac, Alfred de Musset, and Victor Hugo; skills extended to various genres, including short stories, plays, novels, and poetry; produced a collection of short stories, *La Canne de M. Balzac* (1836); other works include *Le Lorgnon* (1831), *Contes d'une vieille fille à ses neveux* (1832), *Le Marquis de Pontanges* (1835), *Il ne faut pas jouer, avec la douleur* (1853), *C'est la faute du mari* (1851), *La Joie fait peur* (1854), and *Le Chapeau d'un horloger* (1854); plays include *Judith* (1843), *Cléopâtre* (1847), *Lady Tartufe* (1853) and the banned *L'Ecole des journalistes* (1839). ❖ See also *Women in World History.*

GIRARDOT, Annie (1931—). French actress. Born Oct 25, 1931, in Paris, France; m. Renato Salvatori (actor, div.). ❖ Made professional stage debut with the Comédie Française (1954), remaining there until 1957; made film debut in *Trieze à table* (1955); came to prominence in Luchino Visconti's *Rocco and His Brothers* (1960); made over 100 films, including *L'autre femme, The Dirty Game, Vivre pour vivre, Storia di una donna, Les novices, Les feux de la Chandeleur, La gifle, La vielle fille, La Mandarine, Juliette et Juliette,* and *Tendre poulet.* Won Venice Film Festival award for performance in *Trois chambres à Manhattan* (1965) and a César (French Oscar) for *Docteur Françoise Gailland* (*No Time for Breakfast,* 1975).

GIRAUD, Liane Daydé- (1932—). *See Daydé, Liane.*

GIRIAT, Madame (b. 1866). French murderer. Born 1866 in France. ❖ Worked as a lady's companion to wealthy Eugénie Fourgère; became involved in a plot (with her lover Henri Bassot and a man named César Ladermann) to rob Fourgère, who was strangled to death, along with her maid, during the attempt (Sept 1902); implicated by Bassot as plot's mastermind, was sentenced to life for killings, as was Bassot (Ladermann shot himself before he could be apprehended).

GIRL OF THE GOLDEN WEST, The (1873–1941). *See Bates, Blanche.*

GIROUD, Françoise (1916–2003). French editor, journalist, and government official. Name variations: Francoise Giroud. Born Françoise Gourdji on Sept 21, 1916, in Geneva, Switzerland; died Jan 19, 2003, in Neuilly; youngest of two daughters of Salih Gourdji (Turkish journalist) and Elda (Faraji) Gourdji (Frenchwoman); attended boarding school in Epinay, France, a suburb of Paris; attended the Lycée Molière and the Collège de Groslay; m. to M. Eliacheff (marriage dissolved); children: a son born out of wedlock, Alain-Pierre Denis (1941–1972); a daughter, Caroline. ❖ Was a "script girl" on Marcel Pagnol's production of *Fanny;* over next 5 years, worked in continuity for dozens of films, including Jean Renoir's *La grand illusion;* became 1st female assistant director in French cinema history (1938); directed several films and continued to write adaptations and dialogue; with Nazi invasion, joined mass exodus from Paris (1940), settling in Lyon, where she worked for *Paris-Soir,* then took the largest newspaper in France, and contributed features and short stories to *7 Days,* a small weekly newspaper; arrested by Gestapo in Paris and imprisoned in Fresnes (1943), was unaccountably freed several months later, shortly before Allied invasion (1944); joined staff of *Elle* (1946), a women's magazine soon known for its daring subject matter, then took over as editor, staying until 1952; with Jean-Jacques Servan-Schreiber, founded *L'Express,* a leftist journal of opinion that would become one of the most widely read and influential journals in the country (1953); when Servan-Schreiber left to fight in Algerian War (1956), took over editorship; except for a brief stint as feature editor of *France-Soir* (1960), remained editor-in-chief of *L'Express* until 1974; also published *Nouveaux portraits* (1954) and *La Nouvelle vague: portraits de la jeunesse* (1958); appointed Secretary of State for the Condition of Women by President Valéry Giscard d'Estaing (1974), called for the elimination of "feminine" jobs, the establishment of free day-care centers, and a revision of the Napoleonic Code, which regarded women as chattel; after serving an appointment as Secretary of Culture, returned to journalism (1979), becoming director of *Revue du Temps Libre;* co-authored (with philosopher Bernard-Henri Lévy) *Women and Men: A Philosophical Conversation* (1993). ❖ See also autobiography *I Give You My Word* (trans. by Richard Seaver, Houghton, 1974); and *Women in World History.*

GISBERT, Teresa (1926—). *See Gisbert Carbonell de Mesa, Teresa.*

GISBERT CARBONELL DE MESA, Teresa (1926—). Bolivian architect, educator and historian. Name variations: Teresa Gisbert. Born Nov 11, 1926, in La Paz, Bolivia; m. José de Mesa; children: 4. ❖ Cultural icon and important researcher in history, art and architecture, specializing in Andean region, taught American art and Bolivian culture and art history at University of San Andrés (1954–70, 1972 and 1975); published with husband, *Historia de la pintura Cuzqueña* (History of Painting in Cuzco, 1962) and *Holguín y la pintura vicereinal en Bolivia* (Holguín and Viceregal Bolivian Painting, 1977); independent of husband, wrote *Iconografía y mitos indíginas en el arte* (Indigenous Iconography and Myths in Art, 1980) and went on to publish many other works, including *Arte textil y mundo Andino* (Textile Art and the Andean World, 1987) and *Manual de historia de Bolivia* (Handbook of Bolivian History, 1994); taught seminars at many universities, including University of Paris, FLACSO (Latin American Social Science Faculty), Culture Institute in Ecuador, Interamerican University in Puerto Rico and Our Lady of La Paz University; served as visiting scholar at Getty Research Institute for the History of Art and the Humanities (1990–91, 1993–94); served as director of National Art Museum in La Paz (1970–76), president of Bolivian Society for History (1983–84), director of Bolivian Cultural Institute (1985–89), and president of International Council on Monuments and Sites (1986–92). Named Woman of the Year (La Paz, 1965); received Order of the Condor of the Andes from Bolivian government (1987), National Cultural Award (Bolivia, 1995), and Antonio José de Sucre Prize (shared with Josep Barnadas, 2004) for study and preservation of national heritage.

GISELA (c. 753–807). Frankish saint. Name variations: Isberge. Born c. 753; died c. 807; dau. of Bertha (719–783) and Pippin also seen as Pepin III the Short (715–768), mayor of Neustria (r. 741), king of the Franks (r. 747–768); sister of Charlemagne, king of the Franks (r. 768–814), Holy Roman emperor (r. 800–814); aunt of Gisela of Chelles (b. 781); some sources claim she married; children: some sources cite Rowland. ❖ The goddaughter of Pope Stephen II, grew up at Aire in Artois where she met St. Venantius who advised her to remain chaste as an offering to God; according to some, turned down all proposals, including Constantine Copronyme and a Welsh or Scottish prince; when father died, was urged by mother to marry a son of the king of the Lombards; refused; founded a Benedictine abbey at Aire and became a nun; lived there for 30 years and was visited occasionally by brother Charlemagne. Feast day is May 21. ❖ See also *Women in World History.*

GISELA (c. 819–c. 874). Frankish countess in the Carolingian dynasty. Name variations: Countess of Friuli. Born c. 819; died after 874; dau. of Judith of Bavaria (802–843) and Louis I the Pious, Holy Roman emperor (r. 814–840); m. Eberhard, count of Friuli, c. 836; children: Uruoch; Adalhard; Rudolf; Berengar I (840–924), Holy Roman emperor (r. 905–924) and king of Italy (r. 888–924); Judith of Fiuli.

GISELA (1856–1932). Princess of Bavaria. Name variations: Princess of Austria Habsburg-Lotharingen. Born July 12, 1856, in Laxenburg; died July 27, 1932, in Munich; dau. of Elizabeth of Bavaria (1837–1898) and Franz Joseph also known as Francis Joseph, emperor of Austria (r. 1848–1916); m. Prince Leopold of Bavaria (1846–1930), April 20, 1873.

GISELA MARTEL (d. 919). Duchess of Normandy. Name variations: Giselle. Died in 919; dau. of Charles III the Simple (879–929), king of France (r. 893–923), and Frederona (d. 917); became 2nd wife of Rollo also known as Robert, duke of Normandy (d. 931), the Norse who conquered Normandy), in 912; children: Adele of Normandy (c. 917–c. 962). Rollo's 1st wife was Poppa of Normandy.

GISELA OF BAVARIA (c. 975–1033). Queen of Hungary. Name variations: Giselle or Grisela, Princess of Bavaria. Born c. 975; died in 1033; dau. of Henry II the Wrangler (951–995), duke of Bavaria (r. 985–995), and Gisela of Burgundy (d. 1006); sister of Henry II (972–1024), Holy Roman emperor (r. 1002–1024); aunt of Agatha of Hungary; m. Stephen I (c. 975–1038), 1st king of Hungary (r. 1000–1038), in 1008 (some sources cite 995); children: eldest son St. Emeric (also known as Imre)

died young (as did all her other children). ❖ See also *Women in World History.*

GISELA OF BURGUNDY (d. 1006). Duchess of Bavaria. Born before 957; died July 21, 1006; dau. of Conrad III of Burgundy and Adelaide of Bellay; m. Henry II the Wrangler (951–995), duke of Bavaria (r. 985–995); children: Henry II (972–1024), Holy Roman emperor (r. 1002–1024); Gisela of Bavaria (c. 975–1033); Bruno, bishop of Augsburg; Brigitta (nun).

GISELA OF BURGUNDY (fl. 1100s). Countess of Burgundy. Name variations: Gisele of Burgundy. Fl. in early 1100s; died after 1133; dau. of William I, count of Burgundy, and Etienette de Longwy; sister of Sibylle of Burgundy (1065–1102) and Bertha of Burgundy (d. 1097); m. Humbert also known as Umberto II of Maurienne, count of Savoy; m. Rainer, marquess of Montferrat; children: (1st m.) Amadeus II, count of Savoy (d. 1148); Adelaide of Maurienne (1092–1154); (2nd m.) Joan of Montferrat (who was 2nd wife of William the Clito, count of Flanders).

GISELA OF CHELLES (781–814). Frankish princess and abbess. Name variations: Gisele, Giselle. Born in 781 at Aachen, France; died c. 814; dau. of Charles I also known as Charlemagne (742–814), king of the Franks (r. 768–814), Holy Roman emperor (r. 800–814), and Hildegarde of Swabia (c. 757–783); never married; no children. ❖ Was instructed by Alcuin of York, one of her father's closest advisors, who praised her as an excellent student, with a quick intelligence and a great love of knowledge; remained at father's court for more than 30 years and never married; entered convent of Chelles and later became its abbess.

GISELA OF SWABIA (d. 1043). Holy Roman empress. Name variations: Gisele of Schwaben. Born c. 1000; died 1043; m. Brunon II, margrave of Saxony; m. Conrad II the Salian (990–1039), Holy Roman emperor (r. 1024–1039), in 1016; children: (1st m.) Ludolphe, margrave of Saxony; (2nd m.) possibly Emelia (who m. Odo II, count of Blois); Henry III (1017–1056), Holy Roman emperor (r. 1039–1056).

GISELLA or GISELLE. *Variant of Gisela.*

GISELLE OF CHELLES (781–814). *See Gisela of Chelles.*

GISH, Dorothy (1898–1968). American actress. Born Dorothy Elizabeth Gish on Mar 11, 1898, in Dayton, Ohio; died of bronchial pneumonia in Rapallo, Italy, June 4, 1968; younger dau. of Mary (McConnell) and James Lee Gish (struggling grocer and candy merchant); sister of Lillian Gish (actress); descendant of Zachary Taylor, 12th president of US; m. James Rennie (actor), Dec 20, 1920 (div. 1935); no children. ❖ Actress whose way with comedy was compared to that of Chaplin and Keaton, debuted as the boy "Little Willie," in the play *East Lynne* at age 5; made New York stage debut as an Irish girl in *Dion O'Dare* (1906); hired as an extra at D.W. Griffith's Biograph Studios (1911); placed under major star contract (1915); revealed great comic gifts in film *Hearts of the World* (1918); made 1st talkie, *Wolves,* for Herbert Wilcox in England; made last professional appearance in the stage play *The Chalk Garden* with her sister (1956); in the talkie era, after she left Griffith, made only 4 films— *Our Hearts Were Young and Gay* (1944), *Centennial Summer* (1946), *The Whistle at Eaton Falls* (1951), and *The Cardinal* (1963); became a recluse soon after; other films include *An Unseen Enemy* (1912), *The Mysterious Shot* (1914), *The Floor Above* (1914), *Liberty Belles* (1914), *Silent Sandy* (1914), *Arms and the Gringo* (1914), *The City Beautiful* (1914), *The Painted Lady* (1914), *Home Sweet Home* (1914), *The Tavern of Tragedy* (1914), *A Fair Rebel* (1914), *The Wife* (1914), *Sands of Fate* (1914), *The Warning* (1914), *The Saving Grace* (1914), *The Sisters* (1914), *The Better Way* (1914), *An Old-Fashioned Girl* (1915), *Her Mother's Daughter* (1915), *Stage Struck* (1917), *Hearts of the World* (1918), *Remodeling Her Husband* (1919), *Orphans of the Storm* (1922), *The Country Flapper* (1922), *Fury* (1923), *The Bright Shawl* (1923), *Romola* (1924), *Night Life of New York* (1925), *The Beautiful City* (1925), (title role) *Nell Gwynn* (1926), *London* (1927), (title role) *Madame Pompadour* (1927). ❖ See also *Women in World History.*

GISH, Lillian (1893–1993). American actress. Born Lillian Diana Gish on Oct 14, 1893, in Springfield, Ohio; died at her home in New York City on Feb 27, 1993; elder dau. of Mary (McConnell) and James Lee Gish; sister of Dorothy Gish (actress); descendant of Zachary Taylor, 12th president of US; attended various schools including the Ursuline Academy in East St. Louis, Missouri; never married, no children. ❖ One of the world's 1st great film stars, debuted in *Convict's Stripes,* starring Walter Huston, at age 5; hired as an extra at D.W. Griffith's Biograph Studios (1911); gained attention in *The Mothering Heart* (1913); appeared as Elsie Stoneman in *The*

Birth of a Nation (1915); established stardom in *Broken Blossoms* (1919), followed by *Way Down East* (1920); made 1st talkie *One Romantic Night* (1930); made tv debut in "The Late Christopher Bean" (1948); made last film *The Whales of August* (1987); other films include *During the Round-Up* (1913), *A Woman in the Ultimate* (1913), *A Modest Hero* (1913), *The Madonna of the Storm* (1913), *Judith of Bethulia* (1914), *The Battle of the Sexes* (1914), *Lord Chumley* (1914), *The Hunchback* (1914), *Home Sweet Home* (1914), *The Rebellion of Kitty Belle* (1914), *The Sisters* (1914), *The Lost House* (1915), *Captain Macklin* (1915), (as Annie Lee) *Enoch Arden* (1915), *Enoch's Wife* (1915), *The Lily and the Rose* (1915), *Daphne and the Pirate* (1916), *Sold for Marriage* (1916), *An Innocent Magdalene* (1916), *Intolerance* (1916), *Diane of the Follies* (1916), *Pathways of Life* (1916), *The House Built Upon Sand* (1917), *Hearts of the World* (1918), *The Great Love* (1918), *The Greatest Thing in Life* (1918), *A Romance of Happy Valley* (1919), *True Heart Susie* (1919), *The Greatest Question* (1919), (directed only) *Remodeling Her Husband* (1920), *Orphans of the Storm* (1922), *The White Sister* (1923), (title role) *Romola* (1924), (Mimi) *La Bohème* (1926), (Hester Prynne) *The Scarlet Letter* (1926), *Annie Laurie* (1927), *The Enemy* (1928), *The Wind* (1928), *One Romantic Night* (1930), *His Double Life* (1933), *The Commandos Strike at Dawn* (1943), *Top Man* (1943), *Miss Susie Slagle's* (1946), *Duel in the Sun* (1947), *Portrait of Jennie* (1949), *The Cobweb* (1955), *The Night of the Hunter* (1955), *Orders to Kill* (Eng., 1958), *The Unforgiven* (1960), *Follow Me Boys!* (1966), *Warning Shot* (1967), *The Comedians* (1967), *A Wedding* (1978), *Hambone and Willie* (1984), and *Sweet Liberty* (1986). Given honorary Academy Award (1970), received American Film Institute's Lifetime Achievement Award (1984). ❖ See also autobiography (with Ann Pinchot) *The Movies, Mr. Griffith and Me* (Prentice-Hall, 1969); Albert Bigelow Paine, *Life and Lillian Gish* (Macmillan, 1932), and *Women in World History*.

GÍSLADÓTTIR, Sólrún. Icelandic politician, feminist and journalist. Name variations: Ingiborg, Ingibjorg or Ingibjörg Solrun Gisladottir; attended University of Iceland. ❖ Was one of the 1st feminists elected to Parliament (1980s); was the 1st woman elected mayor of Reykjavik (1999); representing the Social Democratic Alliance Party, ran unsuccessfully for prime minister (2003).

GISLER, Dany (d. 2003). See Bebel-Gisler, Dany.

GISOLF, Carolina (1910—). Dutch high jumper. Name variations: Carolina Anna Gisolf. Born July 13, 1910, in the Netherlands. ❖ At Amsterdam Olympics, won a silver medal in the high jump (1928).

GISOLO, Margaret (1914–2003). American baseball player. Born Oct 21, 1914 (some sources cite Oct 6, 1915), in Blanford, Indiana; died Feb 17, 2003, in Terre Haute, Indiana. ❖ When American Legion established a national baseball program for youngsters, was accepted on the newly created junior team, the Blanford Cubs, becoming the 1st female in the program (1928); during tournament playoffs, drove in the winning run at the top of the 11th but opposing team protested the game because a girl had played; officials upheld her eligibility and the Cubs went on to win the state championship; soon after, was told by the American Legion that a new rule was put into effect banning girls from junior baseball; went on to play with Rose Figg's American Athletic Girls and the All Star Ranger Girls (1930–34); won gold medals in doubles at Senior Olympics (1989 and 1991).

GITANA, Gertie (1887–1957). English music-hall star. Name variations: Little Gertie Gitana. Born in 1887 in Tunstall, England; died in 1957. ❖ Made stage debut as a child as "Little Gitana"; made London debut (1900) and subsequently appeared in all the leading halls throughout England; popularized such songs as "A Schoolgirl's Holiday," "When the Harvest Moon is Shining," "Silver Bell," "Sweet Caroline," "Queen of the Cannibal Isles," "When I See the Lovelight Gleaming," and "Never Mind."

GITELMAN, Claudia (1938—). American modern dancer and choreographer. Born June 24, 1938, in Iola, Wisconsin. ❖ Trained in modern dance styles of German origin at University of Wisconsin in Madison and later with American modern dancers such as Martha Graham, Louis Horst, and Helen Tamiris; studied under Alwin Nikolais in New York City (1958); performed early on in concert works by Murray Louis; danced in Hanya Holm's *Camelot* on Broadway; taught at numerous universities and institutions (1960s), until she became official faculty member of Nikolais Dance Theater Lab (1971) where she also served as curriculum director; began presenting her own works (1971) and became

recognized as prime dancer from Nikolais school; wrote *Dancing with Principle: Hanya Holm in Colorado, 1941–1983* (2001). Works of choreography include *The Duet* (1971), *Players, Players* (1972), *Addenda* (1973), *Go Suite* (1973), *Notenbuchlein* (1975), *Head* (1976), *Inside Sam* (1977), *Sundy Dances* (1977), *Portraits* (1979) and *Bag* (1980).

GITHA. *Variant of Agatha.*

GITTOS, Marianne (1830–1908). New Zealand missionary and music teacher. Name variations: Marianne Hobbs. Born Marianne Hobbs, July 31, 1830, at Mangungu, Hokianga, New Zealand; died Jan 24, 1908, in Auckland, New Zealand; dau. of John Hobbs (missionary) and Jane (Brogreff) Hobbs; m. William Gittos (missionary), 1857; children: 5 girls and 2 boys. ❖ Became music teacher at parents' mission station at Mangungu, Hokianga; acquired medical skills and assisted husband at mission station at Waingohi, Kaipara, and later at Rangiora (1856); with family, relocated to Auckland and continued missionary work (late-1880s). ❖ See also *Dictionary of New Zealand Biography* (Vol. 2).

GIULIA or GIULIANA. *Variant of Julia or Juliana.*

GIURANNA, Barbara (1902–1998). Italian composer. Born Elena Barbara in Palermo, Italy, Nov 18, 1902; died 1998 in Rome; studied with G.A. Fano, C. De Nardis, and A. Savasta; graduated from Naples Conservatory, 1921; also studied under Giorgio Federico Ghedini; m. Mario Giuranna, the conductor. ❖ The 1st Italian woman composer invited to participate in International Festival of Music (1935) and Festival of International Music in Brussels (1937), made piano debut with Naples Symphonic Orchestra (1923); during Mussolini's regime, became known for such pieces as *X Legio* (1936) and *Patria* (1938); wrote *Tre canti alla Vergine* for soprano, female chorus and small orchestra (1949); composed for *Mayerling*, an opera dealing with suicide pact between crown prince Rudolf and Marie Vetsera, which was staged in Naples (1960); also taught at Rome Conservatory where she became known for her editions of old music; a music consultant to the National Radio, received many prizes and awards.

GIURCA, Elena (1946—). Romanian rower. Born Jan 11, 1946, in Romania. ❖ At Montreal Olympics, won a bronze medal in quadruple sculls with coxswain (1976).

GIUSTINA or GIUSTINE. *Variant of Justina or Justine.*

GIVNEY, Kathryn (1896–1978). American stage and screen actress. Born Oct 27, 1896, in Rhinelander, Wisconsin; died Mar 16, 1978, age 81, in Hollywood, California. ❖ Made NY debut in *Ballyhoo* (1927), subsequently appearing in *Nightstick, The Behavior of Mrs. Crane, Lost Horizons, Life with Father, The Royal Family,* and *This Too Shall Pass,* among others; films include *Lover Come Back, My Friend Irma, Operation Pacific, A Place in the Sun, Three Coins in the Fountain, Daddy Long Legs, Guys and Dolls* and *A Certain Smile.*

GIZYCKA, Eleanor M. (1881–1948). See Patterson, Eleanor Medill.

GKRITSE-MILLIEX, Tatiana (1920—). See Gritsi-Milliex, Tatiana.

GLABE, Karen (1942—). American murderer. Born 1942; m. Kenneth Glabe (killed June 21, 1971); m. Mitchell Link. ❖ With lover Mitchell Link, hired ex-policeman Preston Haig to kill her husband (1971); after husband was stabbed to death by Haig, married Mitchell, while murder remained unsolved; when Haig's wife reported her husband's involvement in the killing (May 1979) and Haig confessed, was tried with Mitchell (July 1980), found guilty and sentenced to 35–45 years.

GLADISCH, Silke (1964—). See Moeller-Gladisch, Silke.

GLADISHEVA, Svetlana (1971—). Russian Alpine skier. Born Sept 13, 1971, in Lvov, Russia. ❖ Won a bronze medal for downhill at World championships (1991); won a silver medal for super-G at Lillehammer Olympics (1994); placed 5th for downhill at Nagano Olympics (1998).

GLADNEY, Edna (1886–1961). American pioneer in modern adoption practice and legislation. Born Edna Browning Kahly, Jan 22, 1886, in Milwaukee, Wisconsin; died in Fort Worth, TX, Oct 2, 1961, from complications due to diabetes; oldest dau. of Maurice Kahly (watchmaker) and Minnie Nell (Jones) Kahly; attended North Texas Female College (later known as Kidd-Key College) and Texas Christian University; m. Samuel William Gladney, 1906 (died 1935); no children. ❖ Personally oversaw more than 10,000 adoptions; at 17, for health reasons, sent to live with an aunt and uncle in Fort Worth, TX; while living in Sherman, TX, helped organize an effort to improve conditions in a county poor farm (which also housed orphans and the mentally and physically handicapped); around 1917, joined board of Texas Children's Home (later The Edna Gladney Home), an organization founded to facilitate adoption of orphans; organized and operated a day-care center for children of working women (1918); due to loss of husband's business, moved to Fort Worth (early 1920s); named superintendent of Texas Children's Home (1927); successfully lobbied Texas legislature to have the label "illegitimate" removed from birth certificates (1933–36); successfully lobbied again for adoption-law revision (1951); featured on tv show "This Is Your Life" (1953); retired (1960). ❖ See also Ruby Lee Piester, *For the Love of a Child—The Gladney Story: 100 Years of Adoption in America* (Eakin Press, 1987); film *Blossoms in the Dust*, starring Greer Garson (1941); and *Women in World History*.

GLADSTONE, Catherine (1812–1900). Welsh prime-ministerial wife. Name variations: Lady Gladstone, Mrs. William E. Gladstone. Born Catherine Glynne, 1812, Hawarden, Flintshire, Wales; died 1900; dau. of Sir Stephen Glynne, local squire; m. William Ewart Gladstone (1809–1898, Liberal prime minister of England, 1868–74, 1880–85, 1886, and 1892–94), in July 1839; children: 8, including John Gladstone (statesman), W.H. Gladstone (died 1891), Agnes Gladstone, Helen Gladstone and Mary Gladstone Drew (died 1927). ❖ Said to be a woman of wit, discretion and charm; with husband, worked for the well-being of prostitutes. ❖ See also Georgina Battiscombe, *Mrs. Gladstone: The Portrait of a Marriage* (1956).

GLADUSE. *Variant of Gladys.*

GLADYS. *Variant of Claudia.*

GLADYS (fl. 1075). Queen of Deheubarth. Married Rhys ap Tewdr or Tewdwr (Tudor), king of Deheubarth; children: 3, including Nesta Tewdr (mistress of King Henry I).

GLADYS (fl. 1100s). Princess of Gwynedd. Fl. in 1100s; dau. of Llywarch ap Trahaearn ap Caradog; 1st wife of Owen Gwynedd, prince of Gwynedd, Wales; children: 2, including Iorwerth Drwyndwn, prince of Gwynedd (d. around 1174); grandchildren: Llywelyn II the Great (1173–1240), Ruler of All Wales.

GLADYS THE BLACK (d. 1251). Welsh princess. Name variations: Gwladus the Dark; Gladys de Braose. Died 1251 in Windsor, Berkshire, England; illeg. dau. of Llywelyn II the Great (1173–1240), Ruler of All Wales, and his mistress Tangwystl; sister of Angharad and Ellen of Wales (d. 1253); m. Reginald de Braose, around 1215; m. Ralph Mortimer, 1230; children: (1st m.) William de Braose; (2nd m.) Roger Mortimer, Lord of Wigmore (d. 1282).

GLANTZ, Margo (1930—). Mexican writer. Name variations: Margarita Glantz Shapiro. Born Margarita Glantz Shapiro on Jan 28, 1930, in Mexico City, Mexico; dau. of Jacobo Glantz (Yiddish poet) and Elizabeth Shapiro (café owner-operator). ❖ Leading cultural and literary figure in Mexico, won many literary prizes, including Magda Donato Prize (1982) for autobiographical novel describing childhood in Mexico City's Jewish immigrant community *Las genealogías* (The Family Tree, 1981), Javier Villarrutia prize for novel *Síndrome de naufragios* (Syndrome of Shipwrecks, 1984), and Premio Sor Juana Inez de la Cruz for novel *El Rastro* (The Sign, 2003); as literary critic, specialized in colonial Latin American literature; wrote essays confronting patriarchal institutions and established norms in Mexico; taught at University of Mexico and several universities in US, including Yale and Harvard; served as director of publications for Mexican Ministry of Public Education (1982–83), as director of literature at National Institute of Fine Arts (1983–86), and as cultural attaché to Mexican embassy in London (1983–86); founded and served on editorial board of journal *Punto de partida* (Starting Point); inducted into Mexican Academy of Languages (1995). Additional works include (novels) *Doscientas ballenas azules* (Two Hundred Blue Whales, 1979), *Apariciones* (Apparitions, 1996), and *Zona de derrumbe* (Destruction Zone, 2001); (nonfiction) *La lengua en la mano* (Tongue in Hand, 1983), *Erosiones* (Erosions, 1984) and *Sor Juana Inez de la Cruz: Saberes y placeres* (Sister Juana Inez de la Cruz: Knowledge and Pleasure, 1996).

GLANVILLE-HICKS, Peggy (1912–1990). Australian-born composer and critic. Name variations: P.G.-H., P. Glanville-Hicks. Born in Melbourne, Australia, Dec 29, 1912; died of a heart attack in Sydney, Australia, June 25, 1990; dau. of Ernest Glanville-Hicks (Anglican minister who went on to several other occupations) and Myrtle (Bailey or, possibly King) Glanville-Hicks (ceramic artist); attended private school in Australia and Royal College of Music, London, 1931–35 (or 1932–36); studied with Nadia Boulanger, 1936–38; m. Stanley Bate, Nov 7,

1938 (div., June 1949); no children. ❖ Distinguished composer, was a key figure in the production and promotion of modern music in US in years following WWII; left Australia for Britain and received Carlotta Rowe Scholarship for Women at the Royal College (1932); made a visit to India with Indira Gandhi (1933); had compositions broadcast on BBC Empire Service (1934); won Octavia Snow Travelling Scholarship (1936); moved back to Australia (1940); settled in US (1942); hired as a music critic for *New York Herald Tribune* and made return visit to Australia (1947); became American citizen (1948); received 1st Guggenheim grant for study in Greece (1956); settled in Athens (1959); suffered temporary blindness due to brain tumor (1969); moved back to Australia (1976); author of five operas and several ballets, was also a skilled composer in numerous other musical genres; major works include (opera) *The Transposed Heads* (1953) and *Nausicaa* (1960), (ballet) *The Masque of the Wild Man* (1958) and *Saul and the Witch of Endor* (1959), and (orchestral pieces) *Concertina da Camera* (1946) and *Letters from Morocco* (1952); distressed by the unwillingness of the music world to accept female composers, signed her works as P. G.-H. or P. Glanville-Hicks throughout career. Received Royal Medal from Queen Elizabeth II (1977). ❖ See also Wendy Beckett, *Peggy Glanville-Hicks* (Angus & Robertson, 1992); and *Women in World History*.

GLASE, Anne-Karin (1954—). German politician. Born July 24, 1954, in Neuruppin, Germany. ❖ Member of the Volkskammer (1990–94) and chair of the Committee on Economic Cooperation; as a member of the European People's Party (Christian Democrats) and European Democrats, elected to 4th and 5th European Parliament (1994–99, 1999–2004).

GLASER, Elizabeth (1947–1994). American AIDS activist. Name variations: Betsy Meyer. Born Elizabeth Ann Meyer in New York, NY, 1947; died of complications from AIDS in Santa Monica, California, Dec 3, 1994; only dau. of Max (businessman) and Edith Meyer (urban renewal planner); graduated from University of Wisconsin, 1969; received MA from Boston University, 1970; m. Hank Koransky, 1971 (div. 1973); m. Paul Michael Glaser (actor and director), Aug 24, 1980; children: Ariel (Aug 4, 1981–1988); Jake (b. Oct 25, 1984). ❖ Given blood transfusions following birth of daughter (1981); learned that she and daughter and son (born 1984) were all HIV positive; because of negative social climate revolving around AIDS, warned to keep it a secret; lost daughter to AIDS (1988); went public and lobbied Washington to obtain more money for pediatric clinical trial units (PCTUs); founded the nonprofit Pediatric AIDS Foundation (PAF, 1988). ❖ See also autobiography (with Laura Palmer) *In the Absence of Angels* (Putnam, 1991); and *Women in World History*.

GLASER, Lulu (1874–1958). American musical-comedy star. Born June 2, 1874, in Allegheny City, Pennsylvania; died Sept 5, 1958, in Norwalk, Connecticut; m. Thomas D. Richards (div.). ❖ Starred in operettas and musical comedies, including *A Madcap Princess, Sweet Ann Page, Miss Dudelsack, Miss Dolly Dollars, The Prima Donna, Dolly Varden, Lola from Berlin, Mlle Mischief, One of the Boys* and *Marooned;* appeared in vaudeville (1912–15); retired (1918).

GLASER, Pease (1961—). American sailor. Name variations: Sarah Glaser. Born Nov 18, 1961, in Springfield, Illinois; Brown University, AB, 1983; m. Jay Glaser, 1990. ❖ With Jennifer Isler, won a silver medal for double-handed dinghy (470) at Sydney Olympics (2000); 3-time North American champion in the Tornado class (1990, 1991, 1994). Named Rolex Yachtswoman of the Year (2000).

GLASER, Sarah (1961—). *See Glaser, Pease.*

GLASGOW, Ellen (1873–1945). American author. Born Ellen Anderson Gholson Glasgow in Richmond, Virginia, April 22, 1873; died in Richmond, Virginia, Nov 21, 1945; 4th dau. and 8th of 10 children of Francis Thomas Glasgow (managing director of Tredegar Iron Works) and Anne Jane (Gholson) Glasgow; educated at home; never married; no children. ❖ Generally recognized in her day as one of America's foremost novelists, anonymously published *The Descendant* (1897), which was embraced by advocates of the new realism in American literature, as were the two novels that followed, *Phases of an Inferior Planet* (1900) and *The Wheel of Life* (1906); with *The Voice of the People* (1900), about the Civil War, embarked on a series of books about Virginia, which included *The Battleground* (1902), *The Deliverance* (1904), *Virginia* (1913), *Vein of Iron* (1935), and *In This Our Life* (1941), for which she received the Pulitzer Prize; also won genuine critical success with *Barren Ground* (1925), a grim tale set in rural Virginia, often considered her best work; wrote three comedies of manners, *The Romantic Comedians* (1926), *They*

Stooped to Folly (1929), and *The Sheltered Life* (1932). Elected to National Institute of Arts and Letters (1932) and received Howells Medal from American Academy of Arts and Letters (1940); given Southern Authors Award (1941). ❖ See also autobiography *The Woman Within* (Harcourt, 1954); Susan Goodman, *Ellen Glasgow: A Biography* (Johns Hopkins University, 1998); Linda W. Wagner, *Ellen Glasgow: Beyond Convention* (University of Texas Press, 1982); and *Women in World History*.

GLASGOW, Josephine (1901–1967). *See Mulvany, Josephine.*

GLASPELL, Susan (1876–1948). American short-story writer, novelist, and playwright. Pronunciation: Glas-pell. Born Susan Keating Glaspell on July 1, 1876, in Davenport, Iowa; died in Provincetown, Massachusetts, of viral pneumonia and a pulmonary embolism, July 27, 1948; 2nd of three children and the only dau. of Elmer S. and Alice (Keating) Glaspell; attended Davenport public schools; Iowa's Drake University, PhB, 1899; graduate study at the University of Chicago, 1903; m. George Cram Cook, April 14, 1913 (died 1924); lived with Norman Matson (writer), 1925–1931; no children. ❖ A founding member and major contributor to the acclaimed Provincetown Players, saw publication of 1st short story (1902); published 1st novel, *The Glory and the Conquered* (1909); published best-known short story, "A Jury of Her Peers," which became the basis of her 1st play, *Trifles*, produced in the inaugural season of the Provincetown Players (1916); wrote *The Verge,* one of the 1st expressionistic plays staged in the US (1922); moved with husband to Greece, where they lived until his death (1922–24); published biography of husband, *The Road to the Temple* (1926); awarded Pulitzer Prize for drama for *Alison's House* (1931); served as director of Midwest Play Bureau of the Federal Theater Project (1936–38); entered a new period of novel writing, lasting almost to the time of her death (1940–48). Plays include (with George Cram Cook) *Suppressed Desires* (1915), *The People* (1916), *Close the Book* (1916), *The Outside* (1916), *A Woman's Honor* (1918), *Tickless Time* (1918), *Bernice* (1920), *The Inheritors* (1921), and *Chains of Dew* (1922); fiction includes *The Visioning* (1911), *Lifted Masks: Stories* (1912), *Fidelity* (1915), *Brook Evans* (1928), *Fugitive's Return* (1929), *Ambrose Holt and Family* (1931), *The Morning is Near Us* (1939), *Cherished and Shared of Old* (1940), *Norma Ashe* (1942), and *Judd Rankin's Daughter* (1945). ❖ See also Veronica Makowsky, *Susan Glaspell's Century of American Women* (Oxford University Press, 1993); Arthur Waterman, *Susan Glaspell* (Twayne, 1966); and *Women in World History*.

GLASS, Bonnie (b. around 1895). American exhibition ballroom dancer. Born Helen Roche, c. 1895, in Roxbury, Massachusetts; m. Graham Glass, 1911 (div. 1914); m. Ben Ali Haggin (society painter), c. 1915. ❖ Appeared as theatrical ballet dancer at roof garden theaters in New York City as a teenager (c. 1910); had brief marriage to Oregon millionaire, closely followed in local press (1911–14); made 1st appearance as Bonnie Glass partnering with Bernardo Rudolf and The James Reese Europe Orchestra again at roof garden theaters and NY cafés, Rector's and Café Montmartre (1914–15); partnered by Clifton Webb soon after and danced with him at Montmartre and on Keith circuit to great success; continued to perform specialty dances including Tipperary Trot, Military Galop, Flirtation Waltz, and more, at clubs, in vaudeville, and on Keith circuit with Rudolf Valentino (1914–15); retired.

GLASS, Joanna (1936—). Canadian playwright. Born Joanna McClelland, 1936, in Saskatoon, Saskatchewan, Canada; m. Alexander Glass, 1959 (div. 1975). ❖ Studied acting at Pasadena Playhouse; received Rockefeller and National Endowment for the Arts grants and Guggenheim fellowship; plays include *Canadian Gothic, American Modern, Artichoke, The Last Chalice, To Grandmother's House We Go* and *Play Memory;* novels include *Reflections on a Mountain Summer* (1974) and *Woman Wanted* (1984).

GLASS, Julie (1979—). American inline skater. Name variations: Julie Brandt; Julie Brandt-Glass. Born Feb 23, 1979, in Grand Rapids, Michigan; m. Doug Glass (former inline racer). ❖ Won gold in Women's Downhill at X Games (summer 1995 and summer 1998); became Downer's Grove champion (1996 and 1998), World Games double gold medalist (1997), World Cup gold medalist (1997), US Olympic Festival double gold medalist (1995), and US Nationals Overall Sprint champion (track and road, 1995 and 1998); took 1st in Bank Track and in Road at Outdoor nationals, Colorado Springs, CO (1999); won the Long Beach marathon (2000) and Berlin marathon (2003).

GLASSE, Hannah (1708–1770). English cook and author. Born Hannah Allgood in London, England, 1708; died in Newcastle in 1770; m. Peter Glasse (solicitor), before 1725; children: eight, four of whom died in infancy. ❖ Won acclaim with *The Art of Cookery made Plain and Easy* (1747), possibly the earliest guide to cookery and meal planning for the English housewife, which remained in print until 1824; also wrote *The Compleat Confectioner* (c. 1770), and *The Servant's Director or Housekeeper's Companion.* ❖ See also *Women in World History*.

GLATSKIKH, Olga (1989—). Russian rhythmic gymnast. Born Feb 13, 1989, in USSR. ❖ Won team all-around gold medal at Athens Olympics (2004).

GLAUM, Louise (1894–1970). American silent-film star. Name variations: The Spider Woman; The Tiger Woman. Born Sept 10, 1894, in Baltimore, Maryland; died Nov 26, 1970, in Los Angeles, California; m. Harry J. Edwards; m. Zachary Harris (director), 1926. ❖ Early in career, worked with Thomas Ince; films include *Hell's Hinges, The Lure of Woman, The Aryan, Lady of the Peacocks, The Idolators, The Lone Wolf's Daughter, Sex* and *I Am Guilty;* ran a drama school in Hollywood.

GLAZCOVA, Anna (1981—). *See Glazkova, Anna.*

GLAZKOVA, Anna (1981—). Belarusian rhythmic gymnast. Name variations: Glazcova or Glazkoya. Born July 29, 1981. ❖ Won a silver medal for team all-around at Sydney Olympics (2000).

GLEASON, Catherine Crozier (1914–2003). *See Crozier, Catharine.*

GLEASON, Kate (1865–1933). American entrepreneur, engineer, and philanthropist. Born in Rochester, New York, Nov 25, 1865; died in Rochester on Jan 9, 1933; dau. of Ellen McDermont Gleason (active suffragist) and William Gleason (toolmaker); sister of Eleanor Gleason; attended Nazareth Convent, Rochester High School, and Cornell University; never married; no children. ❖ Real-estate developer and innovator of low-cost housing, served as secretary and treasurer of Gleason Works (1890–1913); was the 1st female seller of machine tools, including the beveled-gear planer which allowed Gleason Works to monopolize the gear-cutting market; appointed a receiver in the bankruptcy of a machineshop (1914), the 1st female bankruptcy receiver in New York State, and turned it into a hugely successful enterprise; made engineering history by becoming the 1st female member of the American Society of Mechanical Engineering (1914); admitted to Rochester Chamber of Commerce, as one of its 1st female members (1916); was 1st female president of an American bank, the 1st National in East Rochester (1917–19); manufactured low-cost housing, one of the 1st affordable housing projects in the US, applying the principles of mass production and developing prefabricated building methods (1920); left bequest creating the Gleason Fund for educational and charitable causes, which awarded Johns Hopkins University a donation for pioneering research into cancer (1933); another bequest transformed Rochester Mechanics Institute into Rochester Institute of Technology (1933). Elected 1st female member of the Verein Deutscher Ingenieure (1913); elected 1st female member of American Concrete Institute (1919). ❖ See also *Women in World History*.

GLEASON, Lucile (1886–1947). American actress. Name variations: Lucile Webster, Lucile Webster Gleason, Lucile Webster-Gleason, Lucille Gleason. Born Lucille Webster, Feb 6, 1886, in Pasadena, California; died May 18, 1947, in Hollywood, California; m. James Gleason (actor and playwright, 1886–1959); children: Russell Gleason (1908–1945, actor). ❖ On Broadway, starred with husband in shows he had penned, including *Is Zat So?, The Fall Guy* and *The Shannons of Broadway;* made film debut in *The Shannons of Broadway* (1929), followed by *Klondike Annie, Navy Blues, Beloved Brat* and *Stage Door Canteen,* among others; also appeared as Lil Higgins in the series of "Higgins Family" movies, with husband and son. ❖ See also volume of reminiscences written with husband.

GLEASON, Rachel Brooks (1820–1905). American physician. Born Rachel Brooks, Nov 27, 1820, in Winhall, Vermont; died Mar 17, 1905, in Buffalo, NY; sister of Zippie Brooks Wales (Woman's Medical College of Pennsylvania alumna, class of 1873); Central Medical College, MD, 1851; m. Silas O. Gleason, 1844; children: 2, including Adele Gleason (who earned a medical degree from University of Michigan, 1875). ❖ The 4th woman in America to earn a medical degree (Feb 20, 1851), was a classmate of Sarah Adamson Dolley and Lydia Folger Fowler; worked as a teacher until marriage (1844); owned a water cure facility with husband (1847); created the Glen Haven Water Cure near Scott, NY, with husband and 2 others (1847); with husband, created the Elmira Water Cure (Elmira, NY, 1852), which was known as the Gleason Sanitarium (1893–1903) and then the Gleason Health Resort (after 1904); advocated the importance of good nutrition and activity for women's health; funded several female students through medical school; wrote a home medical reference book for women, *Talks to My Patients, Hints on Getting Well and Keeping Well* (1870), as well as articles for such journals as *Water-Cure Journal, Herald of Health* and *Syracuse Medical and Surgical Journal.*

GLEBOVA, Natalya (1963—). *See Shive, Natalya.*

GLEDITSCH, Ellen (1879–1968). Norwegian educator. Born in Mandal, southern Norway, Dec 29, 1879; died June 5, 1968; attended University of Oslo; awarded licentiate at Sorbonne, 1912; studied for a year at Yale University; awarded doctorate from Smith College. ❖ The 1st woman to study at University of Oslo, qualified in pharmacy (1902); worked on radium research as an assistant at Paris laboratory of Marie Curie (1907–12); became professor of inorganic chemistry at University of Oslo, where she held the chair (1929–46); also served as president of International Federation of University Women (1926–29).

GLEESON, Ann (c. 1827–1881). *See Diamond, Ann.*

GLEICHEN, Feodora (1861–1922). English sculptor. Name variations: Lady Gleichen; Countess Gleichen. Born Feodora Georgina Maud Gleichen in London, England, 1861; died 1922; dau. of Prince Victor of Hohenlohe-Langenburg, Count Gleichen (1833–1891, admiral and sculptor) and Laura Williamina (Seymour) Gleichen (dau. of Admiral Sir George Francis Seymour); sister of Lord Edward Gleichen (1863–1937, British general who organized and ran the intelligence bureau in England during WWI); studied with Alphonse Legros. ❖ Took over father's studio in St. James's Palace and became a leading sculptor, exhibiting regularly at Royal Academy; her studio was frequented by members of art world and visiting royalty, including Faisal I, king of Iraq, whose bust was sculpted; designed and carved the Queen Victoria group for the Children's Hospital (Montreal, Canada), Edward VII Memorial (Windsor, England), Florence Nightingale Memorial (Derby, England), and Kitchener Memorial in Khartoum Cathedral (Sudan). Though award was made posthumously, was the 1st woman named to the Royal Society of British Sculptors.

GLEN, Esther (1881–1940). New Zealand children's writer, journalist, and community worker. Name variations: Alice Esther Glen; Lady Gay. Born on Dec 26, 1881, in Christchurch, New Zealand; died Feb 9, 1940, in Christchurch; dau. of Robert Parker Glen (accountant) and Alice Helen (White) Glen. ❖ Wrote children's book *Six Little New Zealanders* (1917) and its sequel *Uncles Three at Kamahi* (1926), the fantasy story *Twinkles on the Mountain* (1920), and *Robin of Maoriland* (1929) for young adults; contributed regularly to Christchurch *Sun* and began children's section (1922); named full-time editor in addition to assisting with women's page and general reporting (1925); established network of clubs for rural children and during depression of 1930s, which sought to ameliorate hardship, and for her efforts became known as Lady Gay; began broadcasting children's classics and scripts on radio (1930s); transferred to Christchurch *Press,* where she produced children's supplements, *Gay Gazette* and *Press Junior.* The New Zealand Library Association's Esther Glen Award in her honor is given to the most distinguished contributions to New Zealand literature for children. ❖ See also *Dictionary of New Zealand Biography* (Vol. 4).

GLENDOWER, Catherine (d. before 1413). *See Mortimer, Catherine.*

GLENDOWER, Margaret (fl. late 1300s). Welsh noblewoman. Name variations: Margaret Hanmer; Margaret Hanmer; Margaret Glyn Dwr. Born Margaret Hanmer; dau. of Sir David Hanmer (one of the justices of the King's Bench), of Hanmer, Clwyd; m. Owen Glendower (c. 1354–1416), c. 1383; children: Catherine Mortimer. ❖ Between 1400 and 1402, her husband waged a guerilla war against Henry IV, king of England, becoming a Welsh hero; her daughter Catherine married Edmund Mortimer who also joined in the rebellion.

GLENN, Alice (1927—). Irish politician. Born Dec 17, 1927, in Dublin, Ireland; m. Brigadier-General William Glenn. ❖ Began career as a dress designer; was the 1st woman elected to the Fine Gael national executive; representing the conservative wing of Fine Gael, elected to the 22nd (1981–82) and 24th Dáil (1982–87) for Dublin Central; at odds with her party over her stance against abortion, divorce and contraception, resigned (Feb 16, 1987).

GLENN, Laura (1945—). American modern dancer. Born Aug 25, 1945, in New York, NY. ❖ Trained with José Limón and Anna Sokolow at Juilliard School in NY; danced with Limón company (1964–72), creating roles in his solo series *Dances for Isadora* (1972) and performing in his *The Winged, Missa Brevis, There Is a Time,* and more; staged his *The Moor's Pavane* for numerous companies worldwide including Royal Danish Ballet, Royal Swedish Ballet, and American Ballet Theater; danced with Contemporary Dance System since institution's original founding and performed there in numerous repertory works by Humphrey and Sokolow, as well as in director Daniel Lewis's *Rasaumovsky* (1975) and *And First They Slaughtered the Angels* (1975); toured with solos by Sokolow, Humphrey, and choreographer Barbara Roan. Works of choreography include *Stages* (1976), *The Stolen Glance* (1977), *Muse* (1978), *Figurings* (1979) and *Flora Chaya* (1980).

GLENN, Mary Willcox (1869–1940). American social-welfare worker. Born Mary Willcox Brown, Dec 14, 1869, in Baltimore, Maryland; died Nov 3, 1940, in New York, NY; dau. of John Willcox Brown (banker) and Ellen Turner (Macfarland) Brown; sister of J. Thompson Brown and Donaldson Brown (industrialists), Eleanor (Brown) Merrill (head of National Society for the Prevention of Blindness); m. John Mark Glenn (lawyer), May 21, 1902. ❖ Served as general secretary (1897–1900) of Henry Watson Children's Aid Society in Baltimore; appointed general secretary of Baltimore Charity Organization Society (1900); was 1st secretary of Arundell Club, Baltimore's 1st woman's club; taught as regular faculty member of New York School of Philanthropy (later New York School of Social Work of Columbia University); elected 2nd female president of National Conference of Charities and Correction (1915); served as chair of executive board (1920–24) and president (1924–36) of Family Welfare Association of America; co-founded Church Mission of Help (later Episcopal Service for Youth) (1911).

GLENNIE, Evelyn (1965—). Scottish percussionist. Born July 19, 1965, in Aberdeen, Scotland; studied timpani and percussion; attended Royal Academy of Music, 1982–85, graduating at 19; studied marimba with Keiko Abe; m. Greg Malcangi (recording engineer), 1994. ❖ One of the world's top international concert and recording musicians and the 1st full-time solo percussionist, played clarinet and piano at 8, though she was already starting to lose her hearing as result of a neurological disorder; at 12, became 80% deaf; learned to feel vibrations of notes, and to distinguish between them with help of different areas of sensitivity throughout body; though fitted with a hearing aid, discarded it, claiming aid "distorted sound"; as a solo percussion artist, had rapid success, winning Grammy for 1st CD, a recording of Bartok's *Sonata for 2 Pianos and Percussion* (1989) and again for collaboration with Bela Fleck (2002); has made over 11 other recordings including *Rhythm Song* (1990), *Shadow Behind the Iron Sun* (2000) and *Oriental Landscapes* (2002); travels worldwide, giving critically acclaimed concerts which include over 50 instruments; performs as soloist with symphony orchestras as well; also plays on non-traditional instruments such as kitchen utensils used in piece *My Dream Kitchen,* written for Glennie by composer Django Bates; has commissioned over 130 additional pieces of music from leading composers; serves as president of Beethoven Fund which provides music-based treatment for hearing-impaired children; co-authored music book series *Beat It;* debuted with New York Philharmonic at Lincoln Center and collaborated with film director Thomas Riedelsheimer on *Touch the Sound,* which won "Critic's Prize" at Locarno International Film Festival (2004). Named Scot of the Year (1982) and Scot's Woman of the Decade (1990); received Hugh Fitz Prize for Percussion (1983), Leonardo Da Vinci Prize (1987); became a fellow of Royal Academy of Music (1992); made Officer of the British Empire (OBE, 1993); received Classic CD Award for *Veni, Veni, Emmanuel* recording (1993), Percussionist of the Year Award (1998), Grammy for Best Classical Crossover Album, *Perpetual Motion* (2002) and Mark Hatfield Leadership Award for Outstanding Services to Deaf Children (2003). ❖ See also Evelyn Glennie, *Good Vibrations* (Hutchinson, 1991).

GLESS, Sharon (1943—). American actress. Born May 31, 1943, in Los Angeles, California; m. Barney Rosenzweig (tv producer), May 4, 1991. ❖ Best known for her role as Christine Cagney on "Cagney and Lacy" (1982–88), also starred on "The Trials of Rosie O'Neill" (1990–92) and was featured on "Queer as Folk" (2000); in early years, was a regular on "Marcus Welby, M.D." (1974–76).

GLIKL OF HAMELN or GLIKL HAML (1646–1724). *See Glückel of Hameln.*

GLINKA, Avdotia Pavlovna (1795–1863). Russian writer. Born in Koutousof, Russia, 1795; died in 1863; m. Fedor Nicolaievich Glinka (1788–1880, Russian poet). ❖ Wrote many popular books of devotion; translated Schiller's *Song of the Bell.*

GLINSKA, Teofila (c. 1765–1799). Polish poet. Born c. 1765 in Poland; died 1799. ❖ Wrote *Hymn Pervanów o smierci* (1785), adapted from Marmontel novel *Incas* and *Sczorse* (1785).

GLINSKAIA, Anna (d. 1553). Russian princess. Name variations: Anna Glinskaya; Anna Stefanovna Glinskis. Born Anna Stefanovna; died 1553; oldest dau. of the Serbian military governor Stefan Yakshich; m. Prince Basil (or Vasili) L'vovich; children: Elena Glinski (c. 1506–1538); as well as sons.

GLINSKI, Elena (c. 1506–1538). Grand princess of Moscow. Name variations: Yelena, Helen or Helena Glinskaya, Glinskaia, or Glinsky; Helene of Glinski; Elena Vasil'evna (patronymic). Pronunciation: Ie-LIE-na Va-SIL'-evna GLIN-skee. Born possibly in Lithuania, or in or near Moscow, c. 1506; died April 3, 1538, in Moscow, Russia, possibly of poisoning; regent of Moscow (1533–38); dau. of Prince Basil (or Vasili) L'vovich Glinskis (also known as Slepyi, meaning the Blind) and Princess Anna Stefanovna Glinskaia; ward of Michael (Mikhail) Glinski, a Lithuanian mercenary; became 2nd wife of Vasili also known as Basil III Ivanovich (1479–1534), grand prince of Moscow (r. 1505–1534), Jan 21, 1526 or 1527; children: Ivan IV the Terrible (1530–1584), tsar of Russia (r. 1533–1584); Yuri of Uglitsch (b. 1533). ❖ Following husband's death, was the main figure in a regency for son Ivan IV the Terrible, comprised of Prince Andrei of Staritsa, Metropolitan Daniil, Prince Michael Glinski, and some major *boyars,* including Moscow's Andrei Shuiski (1533–38); eventually rid herself of princes Andrei of Staritsa and Michael Glinski; oversaw a government that created a single monetary system for Russia, obstructed potential separatist movements, restricted the growth of monastic landholding, focused on construction of fortifications, and established peaceful relations with Lithuania. ❖ See also *Women in World History.*

GLINSKI or GLINSKY, Helen (c. 1506–1538). See *Glinski, Elena.*

GLOCKSHUBER, Margot. German pairs skater. Born in Germany. ❖ With partner Wolfgang Danne, placed 2nd at World championships (1967) and won a bronze medal at Grenoble Olympics (1968).

GLOUCESTER, countess of.
See Fitzhammon, Amabel (d. 1157).
See Beaumont, Hawise (d. 1197).
See Marshall, Isabel (1200–1240).
See Fitzrobert, Amicia (d. 1225).
See Margaret de Burgh (c. 1226–1243).
See Lacey, Maud (fl. 1230–1250).
See Clare, Margaret de (c. 1293–1342).
See Matilda de Burgh (d. 1315).
See Anne of Warwick (1456–1485).

GLOUCESTER, duchess of.
See Joan of Acre (1272–1307).
See Bohun, Eleanor (1366–1399).
See Constance (c. 1374–1416).
See Cobham, Eleanor (d. 1452).
See Walpole, Maria (1736–1807).
See Mary (1776–1857).
See Montagu-Douglas-Scott, Alice (1901–2004).

GLOVER, Amelia (c. 1873—). American theatrical ballet dancer. Born c. 1873, probably in New England; death date unknown. ❖ Made professional debut as young toe dancer with company of Malvina Cavallazzi (Mapleson Italian Opera) in NY (1883); performed as ballet dancer, skirt dancer, and soloist throughout career, often appearing opposite partners who performed Spanish dances.

GLOVER, Elizabeth Harris (d. 1643). Massachusetts printer. Name variations: Elizabeth Dunster; Elizabeth Harris. Born Elizabeth Harris in Bury, Lancashire, England; died Aug 23, 1643, in Cambridge, Massachusetts; m. Jose or Josse Glover (nonconforming minister, died Dec 22, 1638); m. Henry Dunster (1609–1659, cleric and educator and 1st president of Harvard, then known as Cambridge College), June 22, 1641; children: (1st m.) Elizabeth Glover (married Adam Winthrop, son of governor John Winthrop), Sara Glover and 3 stepchildren, Roger, John and Priscilla. Following her death, Henry Dunster married Elizabeth Atkinson (1627–1690) and had 5 children: Dorothy Dunster (b. 1646), David Dunster (b. 1645), Henry Dunster (b. 1650), Jonathan Dunster (b. 1653), and Elizabeth Dunster (b. 1656). ❖ From England, set out for New England with 1st husband (May 16, 1638) who died en route; with permission from New England officials, opened The Cambridge Press near Cambridge College (later Harvard University), which was 1st printing firm in the colonies (1639); printed publications including *The Whole Booke of Psalms* (more commonly known as *Bay Psalm Book*).

GLOVER, Gilman (1823–1877)—. See *Jervey, Caroline Howard.*

GLOVER, Jane Allison (1949—). English conductor. Born May 13, 1949, in Helmsley, Yorkshire, England; St. Hugh's College, Oxford University, BA, DPhil with dissertation on Venetian Baroque opera (1975). ❖ Leading conductor and musicologist, made debut at Wexford Festival Opera (1975), conducting own edition of Cavalli's *Eritrea;* published *Cavalli* (1978); joined Glyndebourne staff (1979), leading Glyndebourne Touring Opera (1981–85), and made festival debut with *Il Barbiere di Siviglia,* the 1st woman to conduct at the festival (1982); worked as tv presenter of BBC programs *Orchestra* (1983) and *Mozart* (1985); became music director (1983) and principal conductor (1993) of London Choral Society; served as artistic director of London Mozart Players, expanding group's repertoire to include contemporary works; toured with Mozart Players throughout UK, Europe and Asia and recorded pieces by Haydn, Mozart and Britten (1984–91); debuted at Proms (1985), Covent Garden (1988) and ENO (*Don Giovanni,* 1989); was principal conductor of Huddersfield Choral Society (1989–96); served as artistic director of Buxton Festival (1992), conducting *L'italiana in Algeri;* made NY debut with Jessye Norman and Orchestra of St. Luke's at Lincoln Center (1994); conducted Monteverdi's *Orfeo* at Lyric Theater of Chicago (2000), *Hippolyte et Aricie* in St. Louis (2001) and at Lincoln Center's "Mostly Mozart" festivals; also conducted operas by Britten and Richard Strauss and premieres by Judith Bingham, David Matthews, Sally Beamish, Roger Steptoe and others; conducted and recorded with Royal Philharmonic and London Philharmonic Orchestras, and conducted London Symphony, Royal Scottish National, Royal Liverpool Philharmonic, Hallé, Bournemouth Symphony, Philharmonia, BBC Symphony, Concert and Philharmonic Orchestras, Hanover Band, Orchestra of St. John's Smith Square and English Chamber Orchestra; recorded extensively with choral groups including BBC Singers; made Australian debut with *Alcina* for Australian Opera.

GLOVER, Julia (1779–1850). Irish actress. Born Julia Betterton or Butterton on Jan 8, 1779, in Newry, Co. Down; died July 16, 1850; m. Samual Glover, c. 1800. ❖ The daughter of an actor, began career as a child actress, appearing in English provinces with father, but was treated poorly by him; had a successful career as the leading comic actress of her day; made last appearance at Drury Lane (July 12, 1850), as Mrs. Malaprop in Sheridan's *The Rivals;* died four days later. ❖ See also *Women in World History.*

GLUBOKOVA, Lidiya (1953—). Soviet field-hockey player. Born Sept 17, 1953, in USSR. ❖ At Moscow Olympics, won a bronze medal in team competition (1980).

GLUCK (1895–1978). British painter. Name variations: Hannah Gluckstein. Born Hannah Gluckstein on Aug 13, 1895, in West Hampstead, London, England; died in Steyning, Sussex, England, Jan 10, 1978; only daughter and 1st of two children of Joseph Gluckstein (founder of the J. Lyons & Co. catering empire) and his 2nd wife Francesca (Hallé) Gluckstein; tutored at home; attended a Dame School in Swiss Cottage; attended St. Paul's Girls' School in Hammersmith; attended St. John's Wood Art School; lived with Edith Shackleton Heald (journalist), 1945–78. ❖ Known particularly for her portraits of women, chose to be known only as Gluck and dressed in men's clothing; included 57 portraits, many of them of sophisticated women, including Romaine Brooks, in 1st one-woman exhibit (1924), at Dorien Leigh Gallery; at subsequent exhibitions (1926, 1932, 1937), her paintings were snatched up by the rich and famous, including Queen Mary of Teck, Sir Francis Oppenheimer, Cecil Beaton, and C.B. Cochran; emerged from near obscurity to present a final one-woman show, a retrospective of 52 paintings held at The Fine Art Society (May 1973), which drew considerable praise from critics and included her last painting, *The Dying of the Light.* ❖ See also Diana Souhami, *Gluck, 1895–1978: Her Biography* (Pandora, 1989); and *Women in World History.*

GLUCK, Alma (1884–1938). Romanian soprano. Born Reba Fiersohn, May 11, 1884, in Bucharest, Romania; died Oct 27, 1938, in NY; studied with Arturo Buzzi-Peccia, Jean de Rezke, and Marcella Sembrich; m. Bernard Gluck, 1902 (div. 1912); m. Efrem Zimbalist (violinist), 1914; children: (1st m.) Marcia Davenport (music critic and author); (2nd m.) Efrem Zimbalist, Jr. (actor). ❖ One of America's 1st recording stars, began career at the Metropolitan Opera, though after 1918 appeared there only in concert; devoted energies to recordings, becoming well known for popular renditions of sentimental songs, though she made some excellent recordings of operatic music, including Ljuba's aria from Rimsky-Korsakov's *The Tsar's Bride*; was the 1st performer to sell 1 million records, with "Carry Me Back to Old Virginny," a megahit which made her a wealthy woman. ❖ See also *Women in World History*.

GLÜCK, Barbara Elisabeth (1814–1894). *See Paoli, Betty.*

GLÜCK, Louise (1943—). American poet. Name variations: Louise Elisabeth Gluck. Born April 22, 1943, in New York, NY; dau. of Daniel Gluck (inventor of the X-acto knife) and Beatrice (Grosby) Gluck; attended Sarah Lawrence College, 1962; graduate of Columbia University, 1965; m. Charles Hertz (div.); m. John Dranow (writer and vice president of New England Culinary Institute), 1977 (div.); children: Noah Benjamin. ❖ Began teaching English at Williams College in Massachusetts (1983); served as poet laureate consultant in poetry of the Library of Congress (2003–2004); poetry includes *Firstborn* (1968), *The House on Marshland* (1975), *Teh* (1976), *The Garden* (1976), *Descending Figure* (1980), *The Triumph of Achilles* (1985), *Ararat* (1990), *The First Five Books of Poems* (1997), *Vita Nova* (1999), *The Seven Ages* (2001), and *The Wild Iris* (1992), for which she won the William Carlos Williams Award and a Pulitzer Prize; nonfiction includes *Proofs and Theories: Essays on Poetry* (1994). Received the Bollingen Prize, National Book Critics Circle Award, and PEN/Martha Albrand Award for Nonfiction.

GLUCK, Rena (1933—). American modern dancer and choreographer. Born Jan 14, 1933, in New York, NY; trained at High School of Performing Arts and Juilliard School in New York City. ❖ Presented the concert recital *Uprooted*—her most recognized work—before immigrating to Israel (1950); worked with and taught for Kibbutz Beit-Alpha in Israel (1950s); became a charter member of the Batsheva Dance Company in Tel Aviv (1964), where she was principal dancer for a season, then worked in administration, as rehearsal assistant and assistant artistic director. Choreographed works include *Man and His Day* (c. 1958), *Games We Play* (1965), *Reflections* (1968), *Time of Waiting* (1971) and *Journey* (1973).

GLÜCKEL OF HAMELN (1646–1724). Early modern Jewish entrepreneur. Name variations: Glueckel or Gluckel of Hameln; Glückel von Hameln or Gluckel von Hameln; Glikl of Hameln or Glikl Haml; Glikl bas Judah Leib. Pronunciation: GLOO-kel. Born 1646 or 1647 in Hamburg, Germany, then part of Holy Roman Empire; died 1724 in Metz, France; dau. of a man named Loeb (trader in jewels) and a mother who made lace before marriage; provided with a Jewish and secular education as evidenced in her references to Torah and Talmud and her capacity for business; m. Chayim of Hameln, 1660 (died 1689); m. Hirz Lévy of Metz, 1700; children: (1st m.) 14, 2 of whom died before reaching adolescence, including Zipporah (b. around 1662); Nathan (b. around 1664); Hannah (b. around 1669); Loeb (b. around 1679); Joseph; Mordecai; Esther; Hendele; Samuel; Moses; Freudchen; and Miriam (b. just before father's death in 1689). ❖ Memoirist whose personal memoirs provide historians with information regarding women, commerce, and Jewish family life in her time period; successfully managed her family's business affairs after death of 1st husband (1689–1700); started writing memoirs as a testament for her children (1690); recorded her last entry, a reference to the eschatological vision of another woman (1719). ❖ See also *The Memoirs of Glückel of Hameln*, trans. by Marvin Lowenthal (Schocken, 1977); and *Women in World History*.

GLUCKSTEIN, Hannah (1895–1978). *See Gluck.*

GLUECK, Eleanor Touroff (1898–1972). American research criminologist. Born Eleanor Touroff in Brooklyn, New York, April 12, 1898; died in Cambridge, Massachusetts, Sept 25, 1972; dau. of Bernard Leo Touroff (real-estate agent) and Anna (Wodzislawski) Touroff; graduated from Hunter College High School, New York City, 1916; Barnard College, New York, AB, 1919; diploma in community organization from New York School of Social Work, 1921; Harvard University, MEd, 1923, EdD, 1925; m. Sol Sheldon Glueck (criminologist and professor of law), April 16, 1922; children: Anitra Joyce Glueck. ❖ Distinguished in the field of research criminology, produced numerous volumes dealing with problems of criminals and juvenile delinquents; joined husband at Harvard (1925), working as a research criminologist in department of social ethics, where he was an instructor; obtained a regular faculty appointment as a research assistant (1930); with husband, did a detailed study of former inmates of Massachusetts Reformatory, publishing findings in the ground-breaking *500 Criminal Careers* (1930), then released follow-up studies as *Later Criminal Careers* (1937) and *Criminal Careers in Retrospect* (1943); did a parallel study at Massachusetts Reformatory for Women, resulting in *Five Hundred Delinquent Women* (1934); with husband, also wrote *One Thousand Juvenile Delinquents; Their Treatment by Court and Clinic* (1934), *Juvenile Delinquents Grown Up* (1940), and *Unraveling Juvenile Delinquency* (1950); became a research associate in criminology at Harvard Law School (1953). ❖ See also *Women in World History*.

GLUECKEL OF HAMELN (1646–1724). *See Glückel of Hameln.*

GLUEMER, Claire von (1825–1906). *See Glümer, Claire von.*

GLÜMER, Claire von (1825–1906). German travel writer and short-story writer. Name variations: Claire von Glumer or Gluemer. Born Oct 18, 1825 in Blankenburg-am-Harz, Germany; died 1906. ❖ Grew up in France; returned to Germany (1848); worked as governess and government reporter; jailed for 3 months for trying to help brother escape from prison; writings include *Fata Morgana* (1848) and *Aus den Pyrenäen* (1845); also wrote many stories and novellas and translated George Sand's autobiography.

GLUSHCHENKO, Tatyana (1956—). Soviet handball player. Born July 12, 1956, in USSR. ❖ At Montreal Olympics, won a gold medal in team competition (1976).

GLUTTING, Charlotte E. (1910–1996). American golfer. Born Jan 29, 1910, in Newark, New Jersey; died Dec 16, 1996, in Andover, New Jersey. ❖ Member of Curtis Cup team (1934, 1936, 1938, 1940); thrice a semifinalist in the USGA Women's Amateur (1932, 1935, 1939); won the Eastern once and the New Jersey State three times.

GLYCATSI, Helene (1916—). *See Ahrweiler, Hélène.*

GLYKATZI, Helene (1916—). *See Ahrweiler, Hélène.*

GLYN, Elinor (1864–1943). Bestselling English novelist, journalist, screenwriter, and social commentator. Name variations: Nellie Sutherland. Pronunciation: Glin. Born Elinor Sutherland, Oct 17, 1864, in Jersey, England; died Sept 23, 1943, in London; dau. of Douglas Sutherland (engineer) and Elinor (Saunders) Sutherland; sister of Lady Lucy Duff Gordon (1862–1935); m. Clayton Glyn, April 27, 1892 (died 1915); children: 2 daughters. ❖ Author whose romantic fiction critiqued European society in late 19th and early 20th centuries with such famous works as the novel *Three Weeks* and the script for film *It*; with mother and sister, moved to Summer Hill near Guelph after death of father (1865); moved to Scotland after remarriage of mother (1871); presented at British court (1896); published *The Visits of Elizabeth* (1900) and *Three Weeks* (1907); lionized on visit to US (1907), plus later visits (1908, 1910); appeared in stage version of *Three Weeks* (1908); conducted affair with Lord Curzon (1908–16); visited Russia (1909–10); served as war correspondent in France, as well as unofficial ambassador to US Army troops (1917); reported on signing of the Treaty of Versailles (1919); visited Egypt at invitation of Lord Milner (1920); worked as screenwriter and consultant in Hollywood (1920–27); returned to England (1929); worked as war correspondent in WWII (1941). ❖ See also autobiography *Romantic Adventure: Being the Autobiography of Elinor Glyn* (Dutton, 1937); Ethrington-Smith and Pilcher, *The "It" Girls: Lucy, Lady Duff Gordon, the Couturiere "Lucile," and Elinor Glyn, Romantic Novelist* (Harcourt, 1986); Anthony Glyn, *Elinor Glyn: A Biography* (Doubleday, 1955); Joan Hardwick, *Addicted to Romance: The Life and Adventures of Elinor Glyn* (Andre Deutsch, 1994); and *Women in World History*.

GLYNNE, Mary (1895–1954). Welsh actress. Name variations: Mary Neilson-Terry. Born Mary Glynne Aitken, Jan 25, 1895, in Penarth, Vale of Glamorgan, Wales; died Sept 19, 1954, in London, England; m. Dennis Neilson-Terry (actor, died 1932); m. John Mandell; children: Hazel Terry (1918–1974, actress). ❖ Made London debut as the Little Stranger in *The Dairymaids* (1908); came to prominence the following year as Little Rosalie in *The Merry Peasant*; scored further success as Cinderella in *The Golden Land of Fairy Tales* (1911), Wendy in *Peter*

Pan (1912), and Felicia Lady Grandison in *Lady Noggs* (1913); other plays include *Disraeli, Tilly of Bloomsbury, Carnival, Then and Now, The Crooked Friday, The Terror, No Other Tiger, The Highwayman* and *Time and the Conways;* films include *The Mystery Road, Inquest, The Lost Chord, Scrooge, Emil and the Detectives* and *The Angelus.*

GNAUCK, Maxi (1964—). East German gymnast. Born Oct 10, 1964, in Berlin, East Germany. ❖ At World championships, placed 2nd in all-around and 1st in uneven bars (1979) and 1st in uneven bars and 3rd in team all-around (1983); at Moscow Olympics, won a silver medal in indiv. all-around (tied with Nadia Comaneci), bronze medals in team all-around and floor exercises, and a gold medal for uneven bars (1980); at Europeans, won a gold medal in all-around (1981) and a silver in all-around and gold for uneven bars (1985); all told, won 27 Olympic, World and European medals. Inducted into International Hall of Gymnastics Fame (2000).

GÖBEL, Barbara (1943—). See Goebel, Barbara.

GODA (c. 1010–c. 1049). See Godgifu.

GODDARD, Arabella (1836–1922). English concert pianist. Born in St. Servan, St. Malo, of English parents, Jan 12, 1836; died at Boulogne, France, April 6, 1922; m. J.W. Davison (critic), 1859. ❖ The most famous pianist in England (1860s–70s), began studies with Friedrich Kalkbrenner at 6; at 17, was the 1st pianist to perform Beethoven's formidable *Hammerklavier Sonata,* in London; played everything from memory, a rare feat at the time; again in London, performed the then rarely heard last 5 piano sonatas of Beethoven (1957–58); was the soloist at inauguration of Royal Albert Hall (1872), playing *Emperor Concerto* of Beethoven; one of the 1st pianists to achieve a world career, left for a 3-year tour (1872), playing in Australia, New Zealand, India, China, and throughout US; retired (1882).

GODDARD, Mary Katherine (1738–1816). American printer, postmaster, and publisher. Born Mary Katherine Goddard on Aug 6, 1738, in either Groton or New London, Connecticut; died in Baltimore, Maryland, Aug 12, 1816; dau. of Dr. Giles (physician and postmaster, c. 1703–Jan 31, 1757) and Sarah (Updike) Goddard (c. 1700–Jan 5, 1770); learned at home and on-the-job training at printer's office; never married; no children. ❖ Printer and publisher, who is best known for making the *Maryland Journal* a successful enterprise; with mother, moved to Providence, Rhode Island, to assist brother in printing *Providence Gazette and Country Journal* (1763), a newspaper that became a vigorous advocate of the American cause against Great Britain; helped brother publish *Pennsylvania Chronicle* (1768–74); with brother spending little time at Philadelphia shop, turned the *Chronicle* into one of the most successful newspapers in the colonies, with 2,500 subscribers by 1770; joined brother at his new shop in Baltimore (1773); managed the print shop and the publication of the *Maryland Journal and Baltimore Advertiser* (1774–84), the 1st newspaper in the city; published books, pamphlets, almanacs, and broadsides; established bookbindery; upheld the freedom of the press by refusing the Baltimore Whig Club's demand that she reveal the author of an unsigned article she had published; served as postmaster for Baltimore (1775–89), the 1st woman postmaster in the US; upon leaving printing business (1784), continued to operate a bookstore to about 1809; published numerous imprints, which includes the 1st official publication of the Declaration of Independence with the names of the signers. ❖ See also *Women in World History.*

GODDARD, Paulette (1905–1990). American actress. Born Pauline Marion Levee (also seen as Levy), June 3, 1905, in Whitestone Landing, Long Island, New York; died of heart failure on April 23, 1990, at her villa in Ronco, Switzerland; m. Edgar James (lumber industrialist), around 1927 (div. 1931); m. Charlie Chaplin (actor, director, producer), 1936 (div. 1942); m. Burgess Meredith (actor), 1944 (div. 1950); m. Erich Maria Remarque (novelist), 1958 (died 1970); no children. ❖ Appeared on stage as Peaches Browning in the Flo Ziegfeld hit *No Fooling* (1926); for Charlie Chaplin, played the waif in *Modern Times* (1936) and was also seen in *The Great Dictator* (1940); briefly danced with Fred Astaire in *Second Chorus* (1941); throughout 1940s, was one of Paramount's top stars, usually cast in vixen roles, though she excelled in comedy; other films include *North West Mounted Police* (1940), *Hold Back the Dawn* (1941), *Nothing but the Truth* (1941), *Reap the Wild Wind* (1942), *Kitty* (1946), *The Diary of a Chambermaid* (1946), *An Ideal Husband* (1948), *Anna Lucasta* (1949), *Vice Squad* (1953), *The Charge of the Lancers* (1954), and *Gli Indifferenti* (*Time of Indifference,* 1964); made final appearance in tv movie "The Snoop Sisters" (1972). Nominated for an Academy Award as Best

Supporting Actress for *So Proudly We Hail* (1943). ❖ See also *Women in World History.*

GODDARD, Sarah Updike (c. 1700–1770). American printer. Born c. 1700, in Cocumscussuc, near Wickford, Rhode Island; died Jan 5, 1770, in Philadelphia, Pennsylvania; dau. of Lodowick Updike and Abigail (Newton) Updike; m. Dr. Giles Goddard, Dec 11, 1735 (died Jan 31, 1757); children: 4, including 2 who survived to adulthood, William Goddard and Mary Katherine Goddard (1738–1816, printer, publisher and postmaster of Baltimore). ❖ Put up money for son William to start Providence, RI's 1st print shop and newspaper, *Providence Gazette* (1762); ran print shop, bookstore, and bookbindery until 1768; joined son in Philadelphia and helped him with print shop there.

GODDARD, Victorine (1844–1935). New Zealand innkeeper. Name variations: Victorine Rogers. Born Victorine Rogers, Oct 5 1844, in New Zealand; died Oct 12, 1935, at Waitara, New Zealand; dau. of John Rogers and Mary (Faul) Rogers; m. Thomas Frederick Goddard (gunsmith and publican), 1861 (died 1879); m. Arthur Dennys Palmer (tea merchant), 1883 (died 1893); children: (1st m.) 9; (2nd m.) 3. ❖ Born to New Zealand Company settlers who had emigrated from Cornwall, England (1843); lost father as young girl, witnessed murder of her mother and testified at trial (1855); co-managed Bell Inn and then Prince of Wales hotels with 1st husband at Bell Block; upon 2nd marriage, moved to Australia, returning to New Zealand after husband's death. ❖ See also *Dictionary of New Zealand Biography* (Vol. 1).

GODDARD-CALLENDER, Bev (1956—). See Callender, Beverley.

GODDEN, Rumer (1907–1998). British novelist and children's writer. Name variations: Mrs. Laurence Foster. Born Margaret Rumer Godden on Dec 10, 1907, in Sussex, England; died at home in Dumfriesshire, Scotland, Nov 8, 1998; 2nd of 4 daughters of Arthur Leigh Godden (employee of a steamship company in India) and Katherine (Hingley) Godden; sister of Jon Godden (novelist and painter); attended Moira House, Eastbourne; studied dancing privately; m. Laurence S. Foster (stockbroker), 1934 (sep. 1941, later div.); m. James Haynes-Dixon, Nov 11, 1949 (died 1973); children: (1st m.) two daughters, Jane and Paula, and a son who died in infancy. ❖ Sent to school in England (1919); returned to India and opened a dancing school in Calcutta; published 1st book, *Chinese Puzzle* (1936), followed by *Black Narcissus* (1939), a story about a community of nuns in the Himalayas, which established her as a popular author and was a huge hit in US; issued 1st children's book, *The Doll's House* (1947); returned to England (1949); extremely versatile, also wrote plays, poems, and translations, and contributed to numerous journals and periodicals; other novels include *The Lady and the Unicorn* (1938), *Rungli-Rungliot: Thus Far and No Further* (1944), *The River* (1946), *An Episode of Sparrows* (1955), *The Greengage Summer* (1958), *The Battle of Villa Fiorita* (1963), *In This House of Brede* (1969), *The Peacock Spring* (1975), and *The Dark Horse* (1981); also wrote over 25 children's books, including *The Mousewife* (1951), *Impunity Jane* (1954), *Mouse House* (1957), *Miss Happiness and Miss Flower* (1961), *Home Is the Sailor* (1964), *The Old Woman Who Lived in a Vinegar Bottle* (1972), *The Rocking Horse Secret* (1977) and *Fu-dog* (1989). Whitbread Award (1973), for *The Diddakoi.* ❖ See also autobiography *A Time to Dance, No Time to Weep* (Beech Tree, 1988) and memoir with sister Jon, *Two Under the Indian Sun* (1966); and *Women in World History.*

GODFREE, Kitty McKane (1896–1992). See McKane, Kitty.

GODFREE, Mrs. L.A. (1896–1992). See McKane, Kitty.

GODFREY, Kathleen (1896–1992). See McKane, Kitty.

GODFREY, Margo (1953—). See Oberg, Margo.

GODFREY, Ruth (1914–1969). See White, Ruth.

GODGIFU (c. 1010–c. 1049). Anglo-Saxon princess. Name variations: Goda. Born c. 1009 or 1010; died before 1049; dau. of Emma of Normandy (c. 985–1052) and Aethelred or Ethelred II the Unready (r. 979–1016); sister of Edward III the Confessor (c. 1005–1066), king of the English (r. 1042–1066); m. Dreux or Drew, count of Mantes and the Vexin; m. Eustache or Eustace II, count of Boulogne (r. 1049–1093), around 1036; children: (1st m.) Ralph the Timid, earl of Hereford (c. 1027–1057); Walter of Mantes, count of Maine (d. around 1063); Fulk of Amiens, bishop of Amiens (b. 1030). Eustace's 2nd wife was Ida of Lorraine (1040–1113).

GODGIFU (c. 1040–1080). *See Godiva.*

GODIN, Tawney (c. 1957—). *See Little, Tawny.*

GODINA, Elena (1977—). **Russian volleyball player.** Born Sept 17, 1977, in Ekaterinburg, Russia. ❖ Made national team debut (1995); won European team championship (1997, 1999) and World Grand Prix (1997, 1999, 2002); won a team silver medal at Sydney Olympics (2000). Named Best Player of Europe (1997).

GODIN DES ODONAIS, Isabel (1728–d. after 1773). **Peruvian explorer.** Born in Riobamba, Peru, 1728; died in Saint-Amand, France, after 1773; m. Jean Godin des Odonais (French naturalist), 1743. ❖ Set out with brothers and a small company to descend the Napo and Amazon rivers in South America (1769), to rejoin husband who had been exploring in Cayenne for past 19 years; when boat was lost and all the others perished, wandered alone in the forest for 9 days; was finally found by some Indians; rejoined husband after nearly 2 decades of separation.

GODIVA (c. 1040–1080). **Anglo-Saxon hero.** Name variations: Godgifu; Lady Godiva. Born c. 1040; died 1080; fl. during reign of Edward the Confessor (1050); sister of Thorold of Bucknall, sheriff of Lincolnshire; m. Leofric, earl of Mercia and lord of Coventry, in Warwickshire (died 1057). ❖ According to legend, was a Saxon woman married to the lord of Coventry; was asked by inhabitants of Coventry, who found themselves so burdened by husband's oppressive taxes that they feared starvation, to intercede for them; in sympathy, petitioned husband, who replied with contempt that he would only agree to reduce the taxes if she rode naked through the town; sent word to the people of the terms of the agreement and asked them to remain in homes and close all windows on appointed day; mounted on a white horse and covered only by her long hair, rode through town, and only one person disobeyed, a tailor afterward known as Peeping Tom. ❖ See also *Women in World History.*

GODLEY, Charlotte (1821–1907). **New Zealand letter writer.** Born Charlotte Griffith Wynne, 1821, probably at Voelas, Denbighshire, North Wales; died Jan 3, 1907, in London, England; dau. of Charles Wynne Griffith Wynne (grandson of the 3rd earl of Aylesford) and Sarah Hildyard; m. John Robert Godley, 1846; children: John Arthur Godley, later 1st baron Kilbracken). ❖ Traveled with husband to New Zealand (1849) prior to arrival of 1st settlers in Christchurch; wrote letters to mother about colonial life; returned to England (1853); letters privately printed as *Letters from Early New Zealand* (1936) and published for centenary of Canterbury settlement (1951).

GODMAN, Trish (1939—). **Scottish politician.** Born 1939. ❖ Serves as Labour delegate to the Scottish Parliament for West Renfrewshire.

GODOLPHIN, Mary (1781–1864). *See Aikin, Lucy.*

GODOWSKY, Dagmar (1897–1975). **Lithuanian-born actress.** Born Nov 24, 1897, in Vilna, Lithuania; died Feb 13, 1975, in NYC; sister of Leo Godowsky (inventor of Kodachrome film); m. Frank Mayo, 1921 (annulled 1928); m. once more. ❖ A vamp of the silent screen; films include *A Sainted Devil* (with Rudolph Valentino), *The Marriage Pit, Story without a Name, Common Law, Virtuous Liars* and *The Price of a Party.*

GODOY ALCAYAGA, Lucila (1889–1957). *See Mistral, Gabriela.*

GODUNOVA, Irene (d. 1603). **Empress of Russia.** Name variations: Irina or Irine Godunov. Pronunciation: Good-un-OV-a. Born Irina Fedorovna Godunova in 1550s, probably in Moscow; died near Moscow, probably of tuberculosis, 1603; dau. of Fedor Ivanovich Godunov (landowner); sister of Boris Godunov, tsar of Russia (r. 1598–1605); m. Fedor I also known as Theodore I, tsar of Russia (r. 1584–1598), 1574 or 1575; children: Theodosia of Russia (1592–1594). ❖ Wife of Theodore I and sister of Boris Godunov, both tsars of Russia, failed to produce a male heir and thus contributed to the termination of the Riurik dynasty and indirectly to the beginning of Russia's terrible civil war, the Time of Troubles; exercised considerable influence over husband and in part, because of her position, saw brother become the real power behind the throne; prior to husband's death, was named co-ruler by him and was included in discussions of state matters, an honor rarely bestowed on women in medieval Russia; following his death, reigned by default until Theodore's burial 10 days later, then renounced any interest in ruling, entered the Novodevichy Monastery outside Moscow, and took the name of Aleksandra. ❖ See also *Women in World History.*

GODUNOVA, Ksenia (1582–1622). *See Godunova, Xenia.*

GODUNOVA, Xenia (1582–1622). **Russian daughter of Boris Godunov.** Name variations: Xenia Godunov; Ksenia or Ksenya Godunov; Olga Borisovna. Pronunciation: Good-un-OV-a. Born Ksenia Borisovna Godunova probably in 1582 in Moscow; died 1622; dau. of Boris Godunov, tsar of Russia (r. 1598–1605), and Maria Skuratova (d. 1605); sister of Theodore II (Feodor), tsar of Russia; had no formal education; never married. ❖ The much-loved daughter of Boris Godunov, who reigned as tsar of Russia at the beginning of the Time of Troubles, could read and write, skills which few Russian women of the time possessed; reputedly was very beautiful, modest and decorous in speech; following father's death (1605), was present when her mother and brother Theodore II were strangled on orders of the 1st False Dmitri (Gregory Otrepiev); according to legend, was then raped by the new tsar and forced to become his mistress, before he bowed to pressure and compelled her to become a nun; taking the name of Olga Borisovna, was exiled to a remote convent in Beloozero. ❖ See also *Women in World History.*

GODWIN, Fanny Imlay (1794–1816). *See Imlay, Fanny.*

GODWIN, Gail (1937—). **American novelist.** Born June 18, 1937, in Birmingham, Alabama; only child of Kathleen May (Krahenbuhl) Godwin (teacher and writer) and Mose Winston Godwin; raised by mother and grandmother in Asheville, NC; attended Peace Junior College, 1955–57; University of North Carolina, BA; University of Iowa, MA, 1968, PhD in English, 1971; m. Douglas Kennedy (photographer), c. 1962 (div. c. 1962); m. Ian Marshall (psychiatrist, div. 1966); lives with longtime companion Robert Starer (composer). ❖ Began career as a journalist with the *Miami Herald* (1959); lived in England for 6 years, where she was eventually a travel consultant for the US Embassy in London (1963–69); attended Iowa Writer's Workshop and published thesis as *The Perfectionists* (1970); came to prominence with *A Mother and Two Daughters* (1982) and *A Southern Family* (1987); other works, which often focus on strong Southern women who seek freedom from feminine stereotypes, include *Glass People* (1972), *The Odd Women* (1974), *Violet Clay* (1978), *The Finishing School* (1985), *Father Melancholy's Daughter* (1991), *The Good Husband* (1994), and *Evensong* (1999). Received the Janet Heidiger Award and Thomas Wolfe Memorial Literary Award.

GODWIN, Mary.
See Wollstonecraft, Mary (1759–1797).
See Shelley, Mary Godwin (1797–1851).

GOEBBELS, Magda (d. 1945). **German wife of Joseph Goebbels.** Born Johanna Maria Magdalena Quandt; committed suicide, May 1, 1945; m. Joseph Goebbels (1897–1945), Reichsminister of propaganda and *gauleiter* of Berlin, Dec 1931; children: Hedda, Heide, Helga, Helmuth, Hilde, Holde. ❖ Because of his many affairs, chose to live apart from husband and forbade him access to their country house in Schwanenwerder; asked Hitler if she could seek a divorce (1938), but was refused; was in Hitler's underground bunker, when he and Eva Braun committed suicide (April 29, 1945); as Russian troops neared, helped an SS doctor poison her 6 children, of whom the eldest was 12, under husband's orders, then committed suicide with him (May 1, 1945). ❖ See also *Women in World History.*

GOEBEL, Barbara (1943—). **East German swimmer.** Name variations: Barbara Göbel. Born April 1943 in Germany. ❖ At Rome Olympics, won a bronze medal in 200-meter breaststroke (1960).

GOEGG, Marie (1826–1899). **Swiss feminist.** Name variations: Marie Gögg. Born Marie Pouchoulin, 1826, in Geneva, Switzerland; died 1899; m. 2nd husband, Armand Goegg (exiled German revolutionary); children: 3. ❖ With husband, participated in International League of Peace and Freedom; called for equality for women in revolutionary movements and establishment of a separate international body for women; founded and ran Association Internationale des Femmes (1868); campaigned successfully for acceptance of women into University of Geneva (1872).

GOEHR-OELSNER, Marlies (b. 1958). *See Göhr, Marlies.*

GOEPPERT-MAYER, Maria (1906–1972). *See Mayer, Maria Goeppert.*

GOERING, Emmy (1893–1973). **German actress.** Name variations: Emmy Göring; Emmy Sonnemann. Born Mar 24, 1893, in Germany; died June 8, 1973, in Munich; became the 2nd wife of Hermann Goering (Nazi air marshal), April 1935 (died Oct 15, 1946); m. Karl Köstlin (div.); children: Edda Goering (b. June 2, 1938). ❖ Was an actress at the

National Theater in Weimar before she met her husband; as Emmy Sonnemann, also appeared in the film *Guillaume Tell* (1934); was active in the social life of Nazi circles; convicted of being a Nazi, was sentenced to 1 year in jail (1948) and banned from the stage for 5 years. Hermann Goering was 1st married to Karin von Kantzow who died in 1931.

GOERMANN, Monica (1964—). Canadian gymnast. Born Sept 1, 1964, in Winnipeg, Canada; dau. of Wolfgang and Elfriede Goermann (gymnastics judge). ❖ At Commonwealth Games, won a team gold medal and silver medal for all-around (1978); at Canadian nationals, placed 1st all-around (1979) and 3rd all-around (1980); won the Pan American Games with 3 gold medals (1979). ❖ See also film "Monica Goermann, Gymnast," National Film Board of Canada (1980).

GOES, Frederica van der. *See van der Goes, Frederica.*

GOETHE, Cornelia (c. 1751–c. 1778). Sister and companion of Goethe. Name variations: Cornelia Goethe Schlosser. Born c. 1751 in Frankfurt am Main, Germany; died in childbirth c. 1778; dau. of Elisabeth Goethe (1730–1808) and Johann Caspar Goethe (jurist); sister of Johann Wolfgang Goethe (1749–1832); married; children: two. ❖ Was the only sibling of poet Goethe, who was attached to her; died at 27, while giving birth to her 2nd child.

GOETHE, Elisabeth (1730–1808). German storyteller and mother of Goethe. Name variations: Elizabeth Göthe. Born Elisabeth Textor in 1730; died Sept 13, 1808; one of 4 daughters of Johann Wolfgang Textor (tailor and mayor); m. Johann Caspar Goethe (jurist), 1748; children: Johann Wolfgang Goethe (1749–1832); Cornelia Goethe (c. 1751–c. 1778), and 5 boys who did not survive infancy. ❖ Was 18 when she married 40-year-old Johann Caspar Goethe, a cultured but cold man, who regarded her as a child to be educated along with their children; known as both light-hearted and practical, had a gift for storytelling and loved spoiling her son, though in later life he treated her with remoteness. ❖ See also *Women in World History.*

GOETSCHL, Renate (1975—). Austrian Alpine skier. Born Aug 6, 1975, in Judenburg, Austria. ❖ Won the World Cup title in the downhill (1997, 1999) and in the super-G and overall (2000); won a bronze medal in downhill and a silver in the combined at Salt Lake City Olympics (2002); placed 3rd at downhill at World championships (2005).

GOETTE, Jeannette (1979—). *See Götte, Jeannette.*

GOETZ, Janina (1981—). German swimmer. Name variations: Janina Kristin Goetz. Born Jan 10, 1981, in Germany. ❖ Won a bronze medal for 4 x 200-meter freestyle relay at Athens Olympics (2004).

GOETZE, Vicki (1972—). American golfer. Name variations: Vicki Goetze-Ackerman. Born Oct 17, 1972, in Mishicot, Wisconsin; m. Jim Ackerman, 1997. ❖ Won US Women's Amateur (1989, 1992); joined LPGA (1993); tied for 2nd at LPGA Corning Classic (2000).

GOFFIN, Cora (1902–2004). English actress. Born Cora Gwynne Poole Goffin, April 26, 1902, in Hampstead, England; died May 10, 2004, aged 102; dau. of actress Cora Poole; m. Emile Littler (theatrical impresario), 1933 (died 1985). ❖ One of Britain's most famous pantomime principal boys and musical-comedy stars, was a household name in 1920s and 1930s; began career at 10 and toured the country as "Little Cora Goffin—The Child Phenomenon"; came to prominence starring in *Alice in Wonderland* (1913), followed by *Little Lord Fauntleroy*; was also noted for roles as Colin in *Mother Goose* and Robin Hood in *Babes in the Wood*; retired from the stage (1940).

GOGEAN, Gina (1977—). Romanian gymnast. Born Gina Elena Gogean, Sept 9, 1977, in Cimpuri, Romania. ❖ At Barcelona Olympics, won a silver medal in all-around team (1992); at European championships, placed 1st for floor exercises, 2nd for vault and all-around (1992), 1st for all-around, vault, balance beam, and 3rd for floor exercise (1994); placed 1st all-around at International Championships of Romania (1992); at Chunichi Cup, placed 1st for balance beam, 2nd for all-around and vault, and 3rd for floor exercise (1993), 1st for all-around and vault, 2nd for uneven bars, balance beam and floor exercise (1994), 1st for vault, 2nd for all-around, uneven bars, and balance beam (1995), and 1st for all-around, vault and floor exercise (1996); at World championships, placed 2nd for all-around and floor exercise, 3rd for balance beam (1993), 1st for vault, 3rd for floor exercise (1994), and 1st for team all-around, balance beam, and floor exercise (1997); at Atlanta Olympics, won a silver medal for all-around and bronze medals for team all-around, vault, and balance beam (1996).

GÖGG, Marie (1826–1899). *See Goegg, Marie.*

GOGGANS, Lalla (1906–1987). American nurse–midwife. Born Lalla Mary Goggans, Feb 24, 1906, in Live Oak, Florida; died July 30, 1987, in Augusta, Georgia; dau. of Juanita (Gardner) Goggans and Joseph Goggans; graduated from Orange General Hospital's nursing school in Orlando, Florida, 1927; College of William & Mary, public health nursing certificate, 1929; Columbia University Teachers College, BS in nursing education and MA, 1949. ❖ Taught classes for African-American lay midwives as a staff public health nurse in Marianna, Florida; appointed Florida Board of Health's District supervisor of nurses (1934) and later worked as its statewide consultant on child and maternal health (1939–42); after earning a New York Maternity Center Association (MCA) nurse-midwifery certificate, worked as an MCA instructor; supervised an emergency program for mothers and infants in America's southwest region for the federal Children's Bureau (from 1944); created a school for maternity nursing and nurse-midwifery in Puerto Rico (1966); appointed a Children's Bureau (Region III) nursing consultant in Charlottesville, VA; retired (1972).

GO-GO'S, The.
See Caffey, Charlotte.
See Shock, Gina.
See Valentine, Kathy.
See Wiedlin, Jane.

GOGOBERIDZE, Lana (1928—). Soviet filmmaker from Georgia. Born in Tbilisi, Georgia, Oct 13, 1928; father was killed by the secret police; mother, a filmmaker, was sent to a labor camp in Arctic Circle during Stalin's Reign of Terror; studied literature at University of Tbilisi; attended VGIK (Moscow Film School), 1959. ❖ One of the most important filmmakers of the Soviet Union, was also a professor of film at Tbilisi Film Institute; made 1st full-length feature, *Pod odnim nebom* (*Under One Sky*), the story of three women from three different periods in Georgian history; released *Neskolko interviu po lichnym voprosam* (*Several Interviews on Personal Questions,* 1979), the 1st of her films to catch the attention of the West; was the 1st president of Kino Women International (KIWI), an organization to further the position of women in film; served as president of International Association of Women Filmmakers (1987); wrote *A Waltz on the Pechora,* a film based on her mother's recollection of her internment (1987). Won Director's Prize at Tokyo International Film Festival for *Krugovorot* (*Turnover,* 1986). ❖ See also *Women in World History.*

GOGOVA, Tanya (1950—). Bulgarian volleyball player. Born April 28, 1950, in Bulgaria. ❖ At Moscow Olympics, won a bronze medal in team competition (1980).

GÖHR, Marlies (1958—). East German track-and-field athlete. Name variations: Marlies Goehr-Oelsner; Marlies Gohr. Born Mar 21, 1958, in East Germany. ❖ One of the fastest runners in the women's 100-meter race in the world (1997–83), but never won an Olympic gold medal in her specialty; held the world record in the 100 with a time of 10.81 and beat the 11-second clock 9 times; won a gold medal in the 4 x 100-meter relay but finished 8th in the 100 meters at Montreal Olympics (1976); won a silver medal in the 100 meters and a gold medal in the 4 x 100-meter relay at Moscow Olympics (1980); won a silver medal in the 4 x 100-meter relay at Seoul Olympics (1988); took the 100 meters at European championships (1978, 1982) and placed 1st in the World Cup (1977).

GOITSCHEL, Christine (1944—). French Alpine skier. Born June 9, 1944, in St. Maxime, France; sister of Marielle Goitschel (skier). ❖ Won a gold medal in the slalom and a silver in the giant slalom at Innsbruck Olympics (1964). ❖ See also *Women in World History.*

GOITSCHEL, Marielle (1945—). French Alpine skier. Born Sept 28, 1945, in St. Maxime, France; sister of Christine Goitschel (skier). ❖ Won a silver medal for slalom and a gold medal for giant slalom at Innsbruck Olympics (1964); won a gold medal for slalom at Grenoble Olympics (1968); won the World championship in the giant slalom and downhill (1966) and the combined (1962, 1964, 1966); won World Cup titles for downhill (1967) and slalom (1967, 1968) and placed 2nd overall (1967). ❖ See also *Women in World History.*

GOKSOER, Susann (1970—). Norwegian handball player. Name variations: Susann Goksor or Goksør; Susann Goksoer Bjerkrheim. Born July 7, 1970, in Oslo, Norway. ❖ Won a silver medal at Seoul Olympics (1988) and a silver medal at Barcelona Olympics (1992), both in team competition; won a team bronze medal at Sydney Olympics (2000).

GOLCHEVA, Nadka (1952—). Bulgarian basketball player. Born Mar 12, 1952, in Bulgaria. ❖ Won a bronze medal at Montreal Olympics (1976) and a silver medal at Moscow Olympics (1980), both in team competition.

GOLDA, Natalie (1981—). American water-polo player. Born Dec 28, 1981, in Lakewood, California; attended University of California, Los Angeles. ❖ Won World championship (2003); defender, won a team bronze medal at Athens Olympics (2004).

GOLDBERG, Lea (1911–1970). German-born Israeli poet, translator, literary critic and scholar. Name variations: Leah. Born in Königsberg, East Prussia, Germany (now Kaliningrad, Russia), May 29, 1911; died in Jerusalem on Jan 15, 1970; dau. of Abraham Goldberg and Cilia (Levin) Goldberg; never married. ❖ One of the best-loved authors in Israel, was a major figure in the literary and intellectual life of Israel for more than three decades; grew up in Kaunas, Lithuania, then Kovno, Russia (until 1918); emigrated from Germany to Palestine (1935), where she worked as a journalist writing literary criticism; taught comparative literature at the Hebrew University, Jerusalem (1952–70); along with Nathan Alterman (1910–1970) and Yehuda Amichai (1924—), remains a representative poetic voice of Israel in the 1st phase of its cultural as well as political independence; writings include (poems) three collections, *Smoke Rings, Letters from an Imaginary Journey* and *Green-Eyed Ear of Corn* (1939–40), (for children) *The Zoo* (1941), *From My Old Home* (1942), (novel) *It Is the Light* (1946), (nature poems) *Al ha-Perihah* (1948, English trans. by Miriam Billig Sivan titled *On the Blossoming*, 1992), *Remnants of Life* (1971), *Light on the Rim of a Cloud: Fourteen Poems* (1972), *Room for Rent* (1972), and *Lady of the Castle: A Dramatic Episode in Three Acts* (1974). Honored by Israeli postage stamp issued on Feb 19, 1991. ❖ See also *Women in World History*.

GOLDBERG, Rose (d. 1966). Yiddish actress. Died Oct 6, 1966, in Brooklyn, NY. ❖ Appeared on the Yiddish stage for over 50 years; retired (1956).

GOLDBERG, Whoopi (1949—). African-American actress. Name variations: Caryn Elaine Johnson. Born Caryn Elaine Johnson on Nov 13, 1949, in New York, NY; dau. of Robert James Johnson (preacher) and Emma Johnson; abandoned by father and raised by mother; sister of Clyde K. Johnson (personal driver for Goldberg); m. Alvin Martin (drug counselor), 1973 (div. 1979); David Claessen (director of photography), 1986 (div. 1988); m. Lyle Trachtenberg (union organizer), 1994 (div. 1995); children: Alexandrea (Alex) Martin (actress). ❖ Stand-up comic, actress and activist, began appearing on stage at 8 with the Hudson Child Guild and Helena Rubinstein's Children's Theatre; had bit parts on Broadway in *Hair* and *Jesus Christ Superstar*; headed West (1975); appeared in Brecht's *Mother Courage* and Marsha Norman's *Getting Out* while honing comedic skills with improv group Spontaneous Combustion; moved to San Francisco and joined improv group Blake Street Hawkeyes; began appearing in one-woman show, changing characters in rapid succession, which caught the eye of director Mike Nichols, who brought it to Broadway (1984–85); made film debut in *The Color Purple* (1985), winning Golden Globe Award and Oscar nomination for Best Actress; won Grammy for *Whoopi Goldberg: Direct from Broadway* (1985); an activist for many causes, often focuses on children's issues, homelessness, human rights, substance abuse and AIDS; co-founded "Comic Relief" with Billy Crystal and Robin Williams (1985) to raise money for the homeless; films include *Jumpin' Jack Flash* (1986), *The Telephone* (1988), *Ghost* (1990), for which she won an Oscar for Best Supporting Actress, *The Player* (1992), *Sister Act* (1992), *Sister Act 2: Back in the Habit* (1993), *Boys on the Side* (1995), *How Stella Got Her Groove Back* (1998), *The Deep End of the Ocean* (1999), *Rat Race* (2001), *Pauly Shore Is Dead* (2004), *Racing Stripes* (2005); on tv, was a regular on "Star Trek: The Next Generation" (early 90s) and starred in "The Whoopi Goldberg Show" (1994, 1996); became 1st woman to host Academy Awards (1994); won Tony Award as producer of musical *Thoroughly Modern Millie* (2002). Won 2 Emmy Awards (1991, 2001), 2 Golden Globe Awards (1985, 1990), BAFTA Award (1990), multiple NAACP Image Awards, Women in Film's Crystal Award (2001) and Kennedy Center Mark Twain Prize for American Humor (2001). ❖ See also William Caper, *Whoopi Goldberg: Comedian and Movie Star* (Enslow, 1999).

GOLDEN, Diana (1963–2001). American skier. Name variations: Diana Golden Brosnihan. Born Mar 20, 1963, in Cambridge, Massachusetts; died of cancer, Aug 25, 2001, in Providence, Rhode Island. ❖ At age 12, lost right leg to cancer; won the World Handicapped championships while a senior in high school; won 4 gold medals and 19 championships; won the Beck Award for being the best American skier in international competition (1986); placed 10th out of 39 in a slalom race as the only disabled skier in the competition (1987); won a gold medal in the giant slalom for disabled skiers at Calgary Olympics (1988). Named Female Skier of the Year by the US Olympic Committee (1988); named US Female Alpine Skier of the Year by *Ski Racing* magazine (1988).

GOLDEN, Olive Fuller (1896–1988). See Carey, Olive.

GOLDFRANK, Esther S. (1896–1997). American cultural anthropologist. Name variations: Esther Schiff Goldfrank. Born May 5, 1896, in New York, NY; died April 23, 1997, in Mamaroneck, NY; dau. of Herman J. Schiff and Matilda Metzger Schiff; Barnard, AB in economics, 1918; m. Walter S. Goldfrank (businessman, d. 1935); m. Karl August Wittfogel (historian and Sinologist), Mar 1940; children: (1st m.) 3 stepsons and 1 daughter. ❖ Became secretary to Franz Boas at Columbia (1919); did fieldwork with Boas and Elsie Clews Parsons at Laguna Pueblo, NM (1921); returned to Laguna (1922) and worked with Boas in Cochiti, NM; wrote *The Social and Ceremonial Organization of Cochiti* (1927); conducted fieldwork at Isleta Pueblo (1924); was among a group of anthropologists who studied the Blackfoot (Blood) Indians of Alberta, Canada, under direction of Ruth Benedict (1939); contradicted Benedict in "Socialization, Personality, and the Structure of Pueblo Society" (1945), which initiated debate concerning configurational approach in anthropology; served as president of American Ethnological Society (1948). Other works include *Changing Configurations in the Social Organization of a Blackfoot Tribe During the Reserve Period* (1945), and *Artist of "Isleta Paintings" in Pueblo Society* (1967). ❖ See also autobiography, *Notes on an Undirected Life as One Anthropologist Tells It* (1978).

GOLDHABER, Gertrude Scharff (b. 1911). See Scharff-Goldhaber, Gertrude.

GOLDIE, Annabel (1950—). Scottish politician. Born 1950 in Glasgow, Scotland. ❖ Became a partner in a law firm (1978); representing the Scottish Conservative and Unionist Party, serves as a Member of the Scottish Parliament for West of Scotland.

GOLDIE AND THE GINGERBREADS. See Ravan, Genya.

GOLDMAN, Emma (1869–1940). Russian-born labor organizer and leading anarchist writer and lecturer. Name variations: (nicknames) Red Emma, Mother of Anarchy. Born June 27, 1869, in Kovno, Lithuania; died May 14, 1940, in Toronto, Canada; dau. of Abraham Goldman (innkeeper and small businessman) and Taube Goldman; m. Jacob Kershner, 1886 (div. 1889); no children. ❖ One of the most radical women in US history, believed in the inherent goodness of the working man and the absolute right of women to equality; was a fiery advocate of personal freedom and a supporter of the anarchist movement which believes that any government, by its very nature, forces people to conform; lived with family in province of Kurland, part of western Russia, then moved to St. Petersburg; immigrated to US (1885); became involved with anarchists (1889); became a passionate speaker who encouraged rebellion and inspired large crowds; attempted to organize female garment workers into unions and obtained food for the unemployed and set up distribution centers; was 1st jailed (1893); studied nursing in Vienna (1895, 1899); arrested several times; began to moderate activities and support less extreme political causes; published *Mother Earth*, an anarchist magazine (1906–17); became active in the birth-control movement (1915); after writing articles decrying American policy during WWI and speaking out repeatedly against conscription, was arrested for antiwar activities (1917) and deported (1919); obtained British passport (1925); lectured against Nazi policies (1932–40); moved to Canada and lectured and wrote until her death. ❖ See also autobiographies and memoirs *Living My Life* (1931), *My Disillusionment in Russia* (1923) and *My Further Disillusionment in Russia* (1924); Richard Drinnon, *Rebel in Paradise: A Biography of Emma Goldman* (University of Chicago Press, 1961); Marian J. Morton, *Emma Goldman and the American Left: "Nowhere at Home"* (Twayne, 1992); and *Women in World History*.

GOLDMAN, Hetty (1881–1972). American archaeologist. Born in New York, NY, Dec 19, 1881; died in Princeton, New Jersey, May 4, 1972; one of four children of Julius Goldman (lawyer) and Sarah (Adler) Goldman; granddau. of founder of investment bank, Goldman, Sachs & Co.; attended Dr. J. Sachs School for Girls, New York (founded by her uncle Julius Sachs); Bryn Mawr College, BA in Greek and English, 1903;

Radcliffe College, MA, 1911, PhD, 1916; attended American School of Classical Studies, Athens, Greece, 1910–12; never married; no children. ❖ The 1st woman to receive the Charles Eliot Norton fellowship to attend the American School of Classical Studies at Athens (1910), undertook 1st dig at Halae, which in addition to revealing classical remains also uncovered some of the earliest traces of Neolithic village occupation in Greece; at Ionia, undertook the 1st of a number of excavations in Asia Minor (1922), under auspices of Harvard's Fogg Museum; became director of excavations for the Fogg (1924) and, for next 3 years, led excavations in Turkey and Greece; published *Excavations at Eutresis in Boeotia* (1931); made 4th major excavation at Tarsus near southeast coast of Turkey; appointed 1st woman professor at Princeton University's Institute for Advanced Studies (1936); retired (1948); published Tarsus research in three volumes: *Excavations at Gözlü Kule Tarsus* (1950, 1956, and 1963). Awarded gold medal for Distinguished Archaeological Achievement from Archaeological Institute of America (1966). ❖ See also *Women in World History*.

GOLDMAN-RAKIC, Patricia S. (1937–2003). American neuroscientist. Born Patricia S. Goldman, April 22, 1937, in Salem, Massachusetts; died July 31, 2003, in New Haven, Connecticut, from injuries sustained from being struck by an automobile; Vassar College, AB, 1959; University of California at Los Angeles, PhD, 1963; m. Dr. Pasko Rakic (neuroscientist). ❖ Joined the faculty of Yale University (1979); a pioneer in the area of brain and memory function, demonstrated that cells in the prefrontal cortex are dedicated to specific memory tasks; also discovered that the loss of dopamine in the prefrontal cortex led to memory deficits; elected to the National Academy of Sciences (1990).

GOLDMARK, Josephine (1877–1950). American social reformer. Born Josephine Clara Goldmark in Brooklyn, New York, Oct 13, 1877; died in Hartsdale, New York, Dec 15, 1950; sister of Pauline Dorothea Goldmark, a welfare worker, and Alice Goldmark who m. Louis D. Brandeis; graduated from Bryn Mawr College, 1898; studied English at Barnard College. ❖ Chaired National Consumer's League committee on legal defense of labor laws, resulting in publication of *Child Labor Legislation Handbook* (1907); with brother-in-law Louis Brandeis, published *Fatigue and Efficiency* (1912), which was instrumental in reducing excessive labor hours in manufacturing; served on committee to investigate Triangle Shirtwaist Fire which killed 146 workers (1912–14); published *Nursing and Nursing Education in the US* (1923), *Pilgrims of '48: One Man's Part in the Austrian Revolution of 1848, and a Family's Migration to America* (1930), *Democracy in Denmark* (1936), as well as a biography of her friend Florence Kelley, *Impatient Crusader* (1953).

GOLDOBINA, Tatiana (1975—). Russian shooter. Born Nov 4, 1975, in Moscow, Russia. ❖ Won a silver medal for 50m rifle 3 positions at Sydney Olympics (2000).

GOLDRING, Winifred (1888–1971). American paleontologist. Born in Albany, New York, 1888; died in Albany, 1971; 4th of 8 daughters of Frederick (florist) and Mary (Grey) Goldring; granted undergraduate and graduate degrees from Wellesley College, 1909 and 1912, respectively; postgraduate study at Columbia and Johns Hopkins universities; never married; no children. ❖ A pioneering woman in the field of paleontology, was hired as a "scientific expert" in the Hall of Invertebrate Paleontology at the New York State Museum (1914); during her long association with the museum, pursued research on a "missing link" between algae and vascular plants and also made Albany's plant collection one of the world's best; served as official state paleontologist of New York (1939–54); elected president of the Paleontological Society (1949) and vice president of Geological Society (1950). ❖ See also *Women in World History*.

GOLDSCHMIDT, Clara (c. 1879–1982). See *Malraux, Clara*.

GOLDSCHMIDT, Madame (1820–1887). See *Lind, Jenny*.

GOLDSMITH, Grace Arabell (1904–1975). American physician, nutritionist, and public-health educator. Born in St. Paul, Minnesota, April 8, 1904; died in New Orleans, Louisiana, April 28, 1975; only child of Arthur William (accountant) and Arabell (Coleman) Goldsmith; attended University of Minnesota; University of Wisconsin, BS, 1925; Tulane University, MD; University of Minnesota, MS in medicine, 1936; never married; no children. ❖ Began teaching at Tulane (1937), where she pursued an interest in vitamin deficiency diseases, then launched a public health campaign on the benefits of nutritionally enriching food; founded a nutritional training program for medical students at Tulane, the 1st of its kind; served as dean of

Tulane School of Public Health and Tropical Medicine (1960s), the 1st woman dean of a school of public health in US; served as president of the American Institute of Nutrition (1965), American Board of Nutrition (1966–67), and American Society for Clinical Nutrition (1972–73). Received AMA's Goldberger Award in Clinical Nutrition (1964). ❖ See also *Women in World History*.

GOLDSTEIN, Jennie (1896–1960). Yiddish-theater actress. Born 1896 in NY; died Feb 9, 1960, in NYC. ❖ Made stage debut as a child; appeared on the Yiddish stage for 57 years in such plays as *The Galician Rabbitzen, The Great Moment, Mother's Wedding Gown, Her Great Secret, Madame Pagliacci* and *Sonitchka;* on Broadway, appeared in *The Number* and *Camino Real*.

GOLDSTEIN, Vida (1869–1949). Australian feminist and politician. Born Vida Jane Mary Goldstein on April 13, 1869, in Portland, Victoria; died April 15, 1949, in South Yarra, Australia; the eldest of five children of Jacob Goldstein (storekeeper and army officer) and Isabella (Hawkins) Goldstein; sister of Bella Goldstein, who married the British socialist H.H. Champion; graduated with honors from Presbyterian Ladies' College, 1886; attended the University of Melbourne; never married; no children. ❖ The 1st woman parliamentary candidate in the British Empire, devoted herself full time to women's suffrage movement; produced feminist journal *The Australian Woman's Sphere* (1900–05); having gained an international reputation, was a representative at Women's Suffrage Conference in Washington, DC (1902); ran unsuccessfully as an independent candidate for the Senate in the federal election (1903), the 1st woman parliamentary candidate in the British Empire; failed in 4 subsequent bids for a parliamentary seat (1910, 1913, 1914, and 1917); launched a new journal *The Woman Voter* (1909), in which she continued to champion for equal marriage and divorce laws, and equal pay and employment opportunities for women; with Rose Scott, opposed party politics, encouraging women to act independently and lobby every political group; visited Britain (1911), where she enjoyed a successful speaking tour and worked as a political organizer for the Women's Social and Political Union; also wrote suffrage articles for both British and international distribution; became increasingly socialistic in her views; also helped found the Women's Peace Army (1915) and represented Australia at a Women's Peace Conference in Zurich (1919).

GOLDTHWAITE, Anne Wilson (1869–1944). American etcher, lithographer, and painter. Born in Montgomery, Alabama, June 28, 1869; died in New York City on Jan 29, 1944; eldest of four children of Richard Wallach Goldthwaite (lawyer) and Lucy Boyd (Armistead) Goldthwaite; studied etching with Charles Mielatz and painting with Walter Shirlaw at National Academy of Design, New York; never married; no children. ❖ One of America's outstanding women artists and a leading regional painter of the South, went to Paris (1906), where she studied with Charles Guérin and Othon Friesz and was one of a group of students who founded Académie Moderne; returning to New York, exhibited in Armory show (1913), which showcased early modernists; taught at Art Students League (1922–44) and was president of New York Society of Women Artists (1937–38); work is exhibited in Congressional Library and in many American museums, including Metropolitan Museum of Art, Art Institute of Chicago, Brooklyn Museum of Art, Whitney Museum, and Worcester (MA) Museum. ❖ See also *Women in World History*.

GOLDWYN, Frances (1903–1976). See *Howard, Frances*.

GOLEA, Eugenia (1969—). Romanian gymnast. Name variations: Geani Golea. Born Mar 10, 1969, in Bucharest, Romania. ❖ Was the 1st gymnast to complete two consecutive layout stepout saltos; at World championships, placed 2nd in team all-around (1985), then 1st in team all-around and 2nd in vault (1987); at Seoul Olympics, won a silver medal in team all-around (1988); joined a Puerto Rican circus (1991–92); coaches gymnastics in US.

GOLIC, Sladjana (1960—). Yugoslavian basketball player. Born Feb 12, 1960. ❖ At Seoul Olympics, won a silver medal in team competition (1988).

GOLIMOWSKA, Maria (1932—). Polish volleyball player. Born Aug 28, 1932, in Poland. ❖ At Tokyo Olympics, won a bronze medal in team competition (1964).

GOLITSIN or GOLITZYN, Princess (1748–1806). See *Galitzin, Amalie von*.

GOLL, Claire (1891–1977). German-French author. Name variations: Claire Studer. Born Clara Aischmann in Nuremberg, Germany, Oct 29, 1891; died in Paris, France, May 30, 1977; m. Heinrich Studer; m. Yvan or Ivan Goll; children: (1st m.) Dorothea Studer. ❖ Best known for her poetry and her autobiography which detailed the literary history of her times, as well as her liaison with poet Rainer Maria Rilke; writings include: *Lyrische Films* (1922), *Eine Deutsche in Paris* (1927), *Der gestohlene Himmel* (1962), *Traumtänzerin: Jahre der Jugend* (1971), and *Ich verzeihe keinem: Eine literarische Chronique scandaleuse unserer Zeit* (trans. by Ava Belcampo, 1978). ❖ See also *Women in World History*.

GOLLNER, Nana (1919–1980). American ballet dancer. Born Jan 8, 1919, in El Paso, Texas; died Aug 30, 1980, in Antwerp, Belgium. ❖ Performed briefly with company of American Ballet while in residence at Metropolitan Opera; danced with Ballets Russe de Monte Carlo of Basil (1935–36) and with the company of René Blum (1936–37), where she created the role in Fokine's *Les Elements* (1937) and danced in numerous of Blum's other works, including *Les Elfes* and *Igrouchka;* danced intermittently with Ballet Theater (1940–50) where she performed in classic repertory works including *Giselle, Sleeping Beauty, Swan Lake, Les Sylphide* and created roles in Balanchine's *Waltz Academy* (1944), Tudor's *Undertow* (1945), and Herbert Ross' *Caprichos* (1950); moved to London (1947) and was 1st American to dance full-length production of *Swan Lake* with Mona Ingelsby's International Ballet; danced 1 more season with Metropolitan Opera Ballet where she performed in Tudor productions of *Faust, La Traviata,* and others; retired from performance career soon after to teach classes in Belgium.

GOLOFSKI, Hannah (c. 1923–1974). See Klein, Anne.

GOLOVKINA, Sofia (1915–2004). Russian ballet dancer and teacher. Name variations: Sofia Nikolaievna Golovkina. Born Oct 13, 1915, in Russia; died Feb 17, 2004. ❖ Graduated from Moscow Bolshoi Ballet School (1933), then danced with the company (1933–59); though she danced such classical roles as Aurora in *Sleeping Beauty* and Kitri in *Don Quixote,* was said to have been better suited for the heroic roles in Soviet ballet, roles with a dramatic or patriotic flavor, such as the Tsar Maiden in *The Humpbacked Horse,* Zarema in *The Fountain of Bakhchisaray,* or Tao Hor in *The Red Poppy;* served as head of the Bolshoi Ballet School (1960–2001), with Natalia Bessmertnova among her students.

GOLUBKINA, Anna (1864–1927). Russian sculptor. Born Anna Semyonovna Golubkina in Zaraysk, in the region of Ryazan, Russia, 1864; died Sept 7, 1927; studied with sculptor S.M. Volnukhin, 1889; studied with painter Sergei Ivanov at Moscow School of Painting, Sculpture and Architecture, 1891; worked in studio of V.A. Beklemishev at Higher Art Institute, part of the St. Petersburg Academy of Fine Art; studied with Italian sculptor Filippo Colarossi, 1895; studied with painter Nikolai Ulyanov, 1901–03; never married; no children. ❖ A pioneering force in Russian art of the early 20th century, set up her own studio in Paris (1897) where she made the acquaintance of Auguste Rodin, who became a lifelong friend and confidante; returned to Moscow and worked in stone, metal, wood, and marble, achieving what she referred to as "the universal" through her use of simple forms and stylization; works include *Old Age, Manka* (1898), and *Walking Man* (1903); arrested and jailed for distributing a document calling for overthrow of the tsar (1907); after release from prison, set up a studio in Moscow where she continued to work for the rest of her life; in the decade before the revolution, became quite famous for her portraits of leading intellectual and literary figures of the day, which included wooden busts of Alexei Mikhailovich Remizov (1911) and Alexei Nikolaevich Tolstoy (1911); arranged a first-of-its-kind exhibition of 150 of her sculptures in Moscow to raise money for war-wounded (1914–15); produced a powerful bust of Tolstoy and also created her last and unfinished work, *Little Birch-tree* (1927). ❖ See also *Women in World History*.

GOLUBNICHAYA, Mariya (1924—). Soviet hurdler. Born Feb 24, 1924. ❖ At Helsinki Olympics, won a silver medal in the 80-meter hurdles (1952).

GOMBELL, Minna (1892–1973). American stage and screen actress. Born May 28, 1892, in Baltimore, Maryland; died April 14, 1973, in Santa Monica, California; m. Howard C. Rumsey; m. Joseph Sefton, Jr. ❖ Made NY stage debut in *Madame President* (1913), followed by *Indestructible Wife, Indiscretion* and *Nancy's Private Affair;* made film debut in *Doctor's Wives* (1931); made over 100 movies, including *The Great Waltz, Hunchback of Notre Dame, Boom Town, Mexican Spitfire, The Best Years of Our Lives* and *Pagan Love Song*.

GÓMEZ, Dolores Ibárruri (1895–1989). *See Ibárruri, Dolores.*

GOMEZ, Elena (1985—). Spanish gymnast. Born Elena Gomez Servera, Nov 14, 1985, in Manacor, Mallorca. ❖ Won gold medal for floor exercises at World championships (2002).

GOMEZ, Madeleine-Angélique, Gabriel de (1684–1770). *See Poisson, Madeleine-Angelique.*

GOMEZ, Madeleine Angelique Poisson, dame de (1684–1770). *See Poisson, Madeleine-Angelique.*

GOMEZ, Sara (1943–1974). Cuban filmmaker. Name variations: Gómez. Born into a middle-class black family in Havana, Cuba, 1943; died June 2, 1974, in Havana; attended Conservatory of Music, Havana. ❖ Studied Afro-Cuban ethnography and worked as a journalist on such publications as *Mella* and Sunday supplement *Hoy Domingo* before turning to filmmaking; was one of two black filmmakers and the only woman to join the newly formed Cuban Film Institute (ICAIC, 1961); worked as an assistant director to Cuban filmmakers Jorge Fraga and Tomas Gutiérrez Alea and to visiting French filmmaker Agnes Varda; made a series of documentary shorts on subjects like mass transit, pre-natal care, and overtime labor before embarking as a director on what would become her 1st and last feature-length film, *One Way or Another,* an effort that won her renown. ❖ See also *Women in World History*.

GOMEZ-ACEBO, Margaret (fl. 20th c.). Spanish heiress who married a Bulgarian royal in exile. Name variations: Margarita Gomez-Acero y Cejuela. Born Margarita Gomez Acebo y Cejuela in Spain; m. Simon also known as Simeon II (b. 1937), king of Bulgaria (r. 1943–46), 1962; children: Kardam of Veliko Turnovo, prince of Bulgaria; Cyril of Preslav, prince of Bulgaria; Kubrat of Panagurishte; Constantine of Vidin, prince of Bulgaria; Kalina of Bulgaria, princess of Bulgaria. Simon II was deposed in 1946, age nine.

GOMEZ BUENO DE ACUÑA, Dora (fl. 1940s). *See Acuna, Dora.*

GÓMEZ DE AVELLANEDA, Gertrudis (1814–1873). Spanish dramatist and poet. Name variations: (nicknames) La Avellaneda, Tula; (pseudonym) La Peregrina. Born María Gertrudis de los Dolores Gómez de Avellaneda y Artega or Arteaga, Mar 23, 1814, at Puerto Príncipe, Cuba; died in Madrid, Spain, Feb 1 (some sources cite Feb 2), 1873; dau. of Francisca de Arteaga y Betancourt and Manuel de Avellaneda (naval officer); m. Pedro Sabater, May 10, 1846 (died Aug 1, 1846); m. Colonel Domingo Verdugo y Massieu (later governor-general of Cuba), April 26, 1855; children: (with poet Gabriel García Tassara) Brenhilde (b. 1845, lived only 9 months). ❖ One of the chief Spanish literary figures of any gender during the 1800s, moved to Seville (1836), where she published poetry under pseudonym "La Peregrina" (the Wanderer); also met and fell in love with Ignacio de Cepeda, who sometimes encouraged her affections but ultimately rejected her; wrote a series of love letters to Cepeda which underlay much of her literary production (1838–45); moved to Madrid (1840), where she quickly established herself among Spain's literary elite; published 1st volume of poetry, *Poesías,* and 1st novel, *Sab* (1841); wrote several successful plays, including *Munio Alfonso* and *El Príncipe de Viana;* wrote prolifically, despite turbulent and scandalous life; premiered 5 plays in Madrid (1852) and another two (1853); also achieved lasting renown among Spanish literary critics as a lyric poet. ❖ See also Hugh A. Harter, *Gertrudis Gómez de Avellaneda* (Twayne, 1981); and *Women in World History*.

GOMIS, Anna (1973—). French wrestler. Born Oct 6, 1973, in Tourcoing, France. ❖ Won World championships for 50kg freestyle (1993), 53kg freestyle (1996), 53kg freestyle (1997, 1999); won a bronze medal for 55kg freestyle at Athens Olympics (2004). Named Female Wrestler of the Year by the IWF (1999).

GOMMERS, Maria (1939—). Dutch runner. Born Sept 26, 1939. ❖ At Mexico City Olympics, won a bronze medal in 800 meters (1968).

GONÇALVES, Delma (1975—). *See Pretinha.*

GONCALVES, Lilian Cristina (1979—). Brazilian basketball player. Name variations: Lílian Cristina Lopes Gonçalves. Born April 25, 1979, in Sorocaba, Brazil. ❖ Won a team bronze medal at Sydney Olympics (2000).

GONCALVES, Olga (1937—). Portuguese novelist and poet. Name variations: Olga Gonçalves. Born in Angola in 1937; educated in Portugal and England. ❖ Novels include *A Floresta em Bremerhaven*

(1975), *Este Verão o Emigrante là-bas* (1978), *Ora Esguardae, Armandina e Luciano* and *O Traficante de Canários* (1988); also published volumes of poetry.

GONCHARENKO, Svetlana (1971—). Russian runner. Name variations: Svetlana Gontcharenko. Born May 28, 1971, in Rostov-on Don, Russia. ❖ Won a bronze medal for 4 x 400-meter relay at Sydney Olympics (2000).

GONCHAROVA, Natalia (1881–1962). Russian painter and stage designer. Name variations: Natalya or Nathalia Gontcharova. Pronunciation: Na-TAL-ya Gan-CHAR-av-ah. Born June 4, 1881, in village of Nechaevo, Russia; died in Paris, France, Oct 17, 1962; dau. of Sergei Goncharov (architect and owner of a linen factory) and Yekaterina Goncharova; attended High School No. 4 in Moscow, 1893–98; studied sculpture at Moscow School of Painting, Sculpture, and Architecture, 1898–1901; m. Mikhail Larionov, 1955; no children. ❖ Drew on a variety of influences from the West but produced her most significant work by tapping the traditions of Russian art; met Larionov at art school (1900); won silver medal for sculpture at school graduation (1901); shifted artistic interest to painting (1902); exhibited in Impressionist style at Salon d'Automne, Paris (1906); presented works in folk tradition at Moscow's Jack of Diamonds exhibit and sued newspaper for accusing her of painting pornography (1910); held one-woman exhibit in Moscow's Artistic Salon (1913); created stage designs for production of *Coq d'Or* in Paris, then returned to Moscow (1914); joined Ballets Russes in Switzerland (1915); toured Spain and Italy as member of Ballets Russes (1916–17); settled in Paris with Mikhail Larionov (1919); created stage design for *Les Noces* (1923) and for *Czar Sultan* and *Fair at Sorochinsk* (1932); became French citizen (1938); produced final theatrical designs (1957); sold collection of her works to Victoria and Albert Museum (1961). Major works include: *Haymaking* (Tretyakov Gallery, Moscow, 1910–11); *Landscape No. 47* (Museum of Modern Art, NY, 1912); *Cats: Rayonist Apprehension in Pink, Black and Yellow* (Solomon R. Guggenheim Museum, NY, 1913); *Scenery and Stage Designs, 1914–1957* (Victoria and Albert Museum). ❖ See also Mary Chamot, *Goncharova: Stage Designs and Paintings* (Oresko, 1979); and *Women in World History*.

GONCHAROVA, Natalia (1988—). Russian diver. Name variations: Natalia Gontcharova. Born Jan 29, 1988, in Voronezh, USSR. ❖ With Julia Koltunova, won a silver medal for 10-meter synchronized platform at Athens Olympics (2004).

GONDWANA, Rani of (d. 1564). *See Durgawati.*

GONG ZHICHAO (1977—). Chinese badminton player. Born Dec 15, 1977, in Hunan, China. ❖ Won a gold medal for singles at Sydney Olympics (2000).

GONNE, Maud (1866–1953). Irish activist, journalist and feminist. Name variations: Maud Gonne MacBride. Pronunciation: Mawd Gone MAK-bride. Born Maud Gonne, Dec 21, 1866, near Aldershot, Surrey, England; died at Roebuck House in Dublin, Ireland, April 27, 1953; eldest dau. of Thomas Gonne and Edith (Cook) Gonne; m. John MacBride, Feb 21, 1903; children (with Lucien Millevoye) Georges (1890–1891) and Iseult Gonne Stuart (b. 1894); (with John MacBride) Sean MacBride (b. 1904). ❖ Devoted over 50 years to Irish political, cultural, and social causes; became involved in Irish nationalist cause (1880s); met with W.B. Yeats (1889); founded *L'Irlande Libre,* Paris (1897); co-founded Irish Transvaal Committee (1899); founded and served as president of Inghinidhe na héireann (Daughters of Ireland, 1900); co-founded Women's Prisoners' Defence League (1922); immortalized in Yeats' poetry. Writings include *Dawn* (1904) and *Yeats and Ireland* (1940). ❖ See also memoir *A Servant of the Queen: Reminiscences* (1938); Nancy Cardozo, *Maud Gonne: Lucky Eyes and a High Heart* (Gollancz, 1979); Samuel Levenson, *Maud Gonne* (Cassell, 1976); Margaret Ward, *Maud Gonne: A Life* (Pandora, 1990); and *Women in World History*.

GONNEVILLE, Marie de (1827–1914). *See Mirabeau, Comtesse de.*

GONOBOBLEVA, Tatyana Pavlovna (1948—). Soviet volleyball player. Born Jan 19, 1948, in USSR. ❖ At Munich Olympics, won a gold medal in team competition (1972).

GONTCHARENKO, Svetlana (1971—). *See Goncharenko, Svetlana.*

GONTCHAROVA, Natalia (1881–1962). *See Goncharova, Natalia.*

GONTCHAROVA, Natalia (1988—). *See Goncharova, Natalia.*

GONWATSIJAYENNI (c. 1736–1796). *See Brant, Molly.*

GONZAGA, Agnes (c. 1365–1391). *See Visconti, Agnes.*

GONZAGA, Alda (1333–1381). *See Este, Alda d'.*

GONZAGA, Anna (1585–1618). Holy Roman empress. Name variations: Anna of Tyrol. Born Oct 4, 1585, in Innsbruck; died Dec 14 or 15, 1618, in Vienna; dau. of Anna Caterina Gonzaga (1566–1621) and Ferdinand II, archduke of Austria; m. Matthias (1557–1619), Holy Roman emperor (r. 1612–1619).

GONZAGA, Anna Caterina (1566–1621). Archduchess of Austria. Name variations: Anna Katharina of Gonzaga-Mantua. Born Jan 17, 1566, in Mantua; died Aug 3, 1621, in Innsbruck; dau. of Eleonora of Austria (1534–1594) and Guglielmo Gonzaga (1538–1587), 3rd duke of Mantua (r. 1550–1587), duke of Monferrato; was 2nd wife of Ferdinand II, archduke of Austria; children: Maria (1584–1649); Anna Gonzaga (1585–1618, who m. Holy Roman Emperor Matthias). Ferdinand II's 1st wife was Philippine Welser.

GONZAGA, Anne de (1616–1684). Countess Palatine. Name variations: Anne Gonzaga; Anne Simmern; princess Palatine. Born in Mantua (Mantova), 1616 (some sources cite 1624); died in Paris, France, July 6, 1684; dau. of Charles II Gonzaga, duke of Nevers (r. 1601–1637) and Catherine of Lorraine (dau. of Charles, duke of Maine); m. Edward Simmern (1624–1663), duke of Bavaria and count Palatine of the Rhine (son of Frederick V of Bohemia and Elizabeth of Bohemia), April 24 or May 4, 1645; children: Louise-Maria (1646–1679, who m. Karl Theodor Otto of Salms); Anne Henriette Louise (1647–1723, who m. Henry Julius, prince of Conde); Benedicte Henriette Philippine (1652–1730, who m. John Frederick, duke of Brunswick-Luneburg).

GONZAGA, Antonia (d. 1538). Noblewoman of Mantua. Name variations: Antonia de Balzo. Died 1538; m. Gianfrancesco Gonzaga (1446–1496), lord of Rodigo; children: Louis also known as Ludovico (d. 1540); Pirro (d. 1529), lord of Bozzolo and S. Martino dall'Argine.

GONZAGA, Barbara (1422–1481). *See Barbara of Brandenburg.*

GONZAGA, Barbara (1455–1505). Duchess of Wurttemberg. Born 1455; died 1505; dau. of Barbara of Brandenburg (1422–1481) and Louis also known as Ludovico Gonzaga (1412–1478), 2nd marquis of Mantua (r. 1444–1478); m. Eberhard, duke of Wurttemberg.

GONZAGA, Caterina (d. 1501). *See Pico, Caterina.*

GONZAGA, Caterina (1593–1629). *See Medici, Caterina de.*

GONZAGA, Catherine (1533–1572). *See Catherine of Habsburg.*

GONZAGA, Cecilia (1426–1451). Noblewoman of Mantua. Born 1426; died 1451; dau. of Paola Gonzaga (1393–1453) and Gianfrancesco Gonzaga (1395–1444), 5th captain general of Mantua (r. 1407–1433), 1st marquis of Mantua (r. 1433–1444).

GONZAGA, Cecilia (1451–1472). Noblewoman of Mantua. Born 1451; died 1472; dau. of Barbara of Brandenburg (1422–1481) and Louis also known as Ludovico Gonzaga (1412–1478), 2nd marquis of Mantua (r. 1444–1478).

GONZAGA, Chiara (1465–1505). Noblewoman of Mantua. Born 1465; died 1505 (some sources cite 1503); dau. of Margaret of Bavaria (1445–1479) and Frederigo also known as Federico Gonzaga (1441–1484), 3rd marquis of Mantua (r. 1478–1484); sister of Elisabetta Montefeltro (1471–1526) and Maddalena Sforza (1472–1490); m. Gilbert de Bourbon-Montpensier; children: Charles de Bourbon, the Constable, who was killed during the sack of Rome in 1527.

GONZAGA, Chiquinha (1847–1935). Brazilian composer. Born Francisca Hedwiges Neves Gonzaga in Rio de Janeiro, Brazil, Oct 17, 1847; died in Rio de Janeiro, Feb 28, 1935. ❖ One of Brazil's most popular and prolific composers, wrote over 2,000 works; was also active in the anti-slave movement. ❖ See also *Women in World History*.

GONZAGA, Dorotea (1449–1462). Noblewoman of Mantua. Name variations: Dorotea Sforza. Born 1449; died 1462 (some sources cite 1469); dau. of Barbara of Brandenburg (1422–1481) and Louis also known as Ludovico Gonzaga (1412–1478), 2nd marquis of Mantua (r. 1444–1478); 1st wife of Galeazzo Maria Sforza (1444–1476), 5th duke of Milan. Galeazzo's 2nd wife was Bona of Savoy (c. 1450–c. 1505).

GONZAGA, Eleonora (1493–1543). Duchess of Urbino. Name variations: Leonora Gonzaga; Eleanora Gonzaga della Rovere; Eleonora della Rovere. Born Dec 1493 in Mantua, Italy; died in 1543 in Gubbio, Italy; dau. of Isabella d'Este (1474–1539) and Francesco also known as Gian Francesco Gonzaga (1466–1519), 4th marquis of Mantua (r. 1484–1519); niece of Elisabetta Montefeltro; m. Francesco Maria della Rovere (nephew of Pope Julius II), duke of Urbino (r. 1508–1538), in Mar 1509; children: Federico (b. 1511); Guidobaldo (b. 1514), duke of Urbino; Ippolita (c. 1516); Guilia; Elisabetta; Guilio (b. 1535), later Cardinal of San Pietro. ❖ At 15, married Francesco, the 16-year old duke of Urbino; formed a close bond with dowager duchess, Elisabetta Montefeltro; because husband, captain in the papal armies, was often absent from Urbino, administered the duchy for many of years with Elisabetta; when husband refused to lead an army in Pope Leo X's invasion of France (1515), had to flee with him to Mantua; appealed to parents to intercede with Leo, but efforts were in vain; with husband, became rulers in exile; when Leo died and was replaced by Hadrian VI, was restored with husband to duchy (1523); with Elisabetta, returned to previous obligations of administration and also undertook the massive rebuilding of Urbino and surrounding towns needed after the destructive wars; also supervised the building of the palatial Villa Imperiale in Pesaro; with husband, was a liberal patron of major artists, including Titian, and encouraged the founding of Urbino's majolica industry (decorative enameled pottery); also continued Elisabetta's patronage of Baldassare Castiglione, author of *Book of the Courtier* (1528), which includes descriptions of the beautiful, intelligent, and gracious duchess, and the elegance and learning celebrated in the court of Urbino under Francesco and Eleonora. ❖ See also *Women in World History.*

GONZAGA, Eleonora (1534–1594). *See Eleonora of Austria.*

GONZAGA, Eleonora (1567–1611). *See Medici, Eleonora de.*

GONZAGA, Eleonora I (1598–1655). Holy Roman empress and queen of Bohemia. Name variations: Eleanor of Gonzaga; Eleanora I Gonzaga; Eleanore de Mantoue Gonzaque. Born Sept 23, 1598, in Mantua; died June 27, 1655, in Vienna; dau. of Eleonora de Medici (1567–1611) and Vincenzo I (1562–1612), 4th duke of Mantua; sister of Margherita Gonzaga, duchess of Lorraine (1591–1632); became 2nd wife of Ferdinand II, king of Bohemia and Hungary (r. 1578–1637), Holy Roman emperor (r. 1619–1637), Feb 4, 1622. ❖ Married Ferdinand II, king of Bohemia and Hungary, whose 1st wife was Maria Anna of Bavaria (1574–1616). Eleonora I's portrait was painted by Lucrina Fetti.

GONZAGA, Eleonora II (1628–1686). Holy Roman empress and queen of Bohemia. Name variations: Eleanor or Eleanora; Eleanora Gonzaga; Eleanor of Gonzaga; Eleonor or Eleonore; Eleonore of Mantua. Born Nov 18, 1628 (some sources cite 1630), in Mantua; died Dec 6, 1686, in Vienna; dau. of Carlo, count of Rethel (1600–1631) and Maria Gonzaga (1609–1660); 3rd wife of Ferdinand III (1608–1657), king of Bohemia (r. 1627–1646), king of Hungary (r. 1625), Holy Roman emperor (r. 1637–1657); children: Eleanor Habsburg (1653–1697). ❖ Was the 3rd wife of Ferdinand III, king of Bohemia, Hungary, and Holy Roman emperor, whose 2nd wife was Maria Leopoldine (1632–1649) and 1st wife was Maria Anna of Spain (1606–1646); her portrait was painted by Lucrina Fetti. ❖ See also *Women in World History.*

GONZAGA, Elisabetta (1471–1526). *See Montefeltro, Elisabetta.*

GONZAGA, Henriette (r. 1564–1601). *See Henrietta of Cleves.*

GONZAGA, Ippolita (1503–1570). Dominican nun. Born 1503; died 1570; dau. of Isabella d'Este (1474–1539) and Francesco also known as Gianfrancesco Gonzaga (1466–1519), 4th marquis of Mantua (r. 1484–1519); never married.

GONZAGA, Ippolita (1535–1563). Noblewoman of Mantua. Born 1535; died 1563; dau. of Isabella Gonzaga (d. 1559) and Ferrante Gonzaga (1507–1557), prince of Guastalla.

GONZAGA, Isabella (1474–1539). *See Este, Isabella d'.*

GONZAGA, Isabella (d. 1559). Princess of Guastalla. Name variations: Isabella of Capua; Isabella da Capua. Died in 1559; m. Ferrante Gonzaga (1507–1557, son of Isabella d'Este [1474–1539]), prince of Guastalla; children: Cesare (1533–1575), prince of Guastalla; Ippolita Gonzaga (1535–1563); Francesco (1538–1566); Giovanni Vincenzo (1540–1591).

GONZAGA, Isabella (1537–1579). Noblewoman of Mantua. Born 1537; died 1579; dau. of Margherita Gonzaga (1510–1566) and Federigo also known as Federico Gonzaga (1500–1540), 5th marquis of Mantua (r. 1519–1540), 1st duke of Mantua (r. 1530–1540).

GONZAGA, Isabella (fl. 1600s). Duchess of Mantua. Name variations: Isabella Gonzaga de Novellara. Fl. in 1600s; m. Vincenzo II (1594–1627), 7th duke of Mantua (r. 1626–1627).

GONZAGA, Leonora (1493–1543). *See Gonzaga, Eleonora.*

GONZAGA, Lucia (1419–1437). *See Este, Lucia d'.*

GONZAGA, Maddalena (1472–1490). *See Sforza, Maddalena.*

GONZAGA, Margaret (fl. 1609–1612). *See Margaret of Savoy.*

GONZAGA, Margherita (d. 1399). Noblewoman of Mantua. Name variations: Margherita Malatesta. Born Margherita Malatesta; died 1399; m. Francesco Gonzaga (1366–1407), 4th captain general of Mantua (r. 1382–1407); children: Gianfrancesco Gonzaga (1395–1444), 5th captain general of Mantua (r. 1407–1433), 1st marquis of Mantua (r. 1433–1444).

GONZAGA, Margherita (1418–1439). Marquesa of Ferrara. Name variations: Margherita d'Este. Born in 1418; died in 1439; dau. of Paola Gonzaga (1393–1453) and Gianfrancesco Gonzaga (1395–1444), 5th captain general of Mantua (r. 1407–1433), 1st marquis of Mantua (r. 1433–1444); m. Leonello d'Este (1407–1450), 13th marquis of Ferrara; children: Niccolo d'Este (1438–1476). Leonello's 2nd wife was Maria of Aragon, marquesa of Ferrara.

GONZAGA, Margherita (1445–1479). *See Margaret of Bavaria.*

GONZAGA, Margherita (1510–1566). Duchess of Mantua. Name variations: Margherita Paleologo of Monferrato or Montferrat; Margaret of Monferrato or Montferrat. Born in 1510; died in 1566; dau. of Guglielmo Paleologo of Montferrat; m. Federigo also known as Federico Gonzaga (1500–1540), 5th marquis of Mantua (r. 1519–1540), 1st duke of Mantua (r. 1530–1540); children: Francesco (1533–1550), 2nd duke of Mantua (r. 1540–1550); Isabella Gonzaga (1537–1579); Guglielmo (1538–1587), 3rd duke of Mantua (r. 1550–1587), duke of Monferrato; Louis also known as Ludovico (1539–1585), duke of Nevers, count of Rethel; Federigo also known as Federico (1540–1565, a cardinal).

GONZAGA, Margherita (1561–1628). Duchess of Sabbioneta. Born 1561; died 1628; dau. of Cesare Gonzaga (1533–1575), prince of Guastalla, and Camilla Borromeo; 2nd wife of Vespasiano (1531–1591), duke of Sabbioneta. Vespasiano's 1st wife was Anna of Aragon (d. 1567).

GONZAGA, Margherita (1564–1618). Duchess of Ferrara. Name variations: Margherita d'Este. Born 1564; died 1618; dau. of Eleonora of Austria (1534–1594) and Guglielmo Gonzaga (1538–1587), 3rd duke of Mantua (r. 1550–1587), duke of Monferrato; m. Alfonso II d'Este (1533–1597), 5th duke of Ferrara and Modena (r. 1559–1597). Alfonso II's 1st wife was Lucrezia de Medici (c. 1544–1561).

GONZAGA, Margherita (1591–1632). Duchess of Lorraine. Born 1591; died 1632; dau. of Eleonora de Medici (1567–1611) and Vincenzo I (1562–1612), 4th duke of Mantua (r. 1587–1612); sister of Eleonora I Gonzaga (1598–1655); niece of Marie de Medici (1573–1642); m. Henry II, duke of Lorraine (r. 1608–1624); children: Nicole (fl. 1624–1625), duchess of Lorraine.

GONZAGA, Margherita (fl. 1609–1612). *See Margaret of Savoy.*

GONZAGA, Maria (1609–1660). Countess of Rethel and regent. Born 1609; died 1660; dau. of Margaret of Savoy (fl. 1609–1612) and Frances also known as Francesco Gonzaga (1586–1612), 5th duke of Mantua (r. 1612); m. Carlo (1600–1631), count of Rethel; children: Carlo II (1629–1695), 9th duke of Mantua (r. 1637–1665); Eleonora II Gonzaga (1628–1686).

GONZAGA, Paola (1393–1453). Marquesa of Mantua. Name variations: Paolo Malatesta. Born 1393; died 1453; m. Gianfrancesco Gonzaga (1395–1444), 5th captain general of Mantua (r. 1407–1433), 1st marquis of Mantua (r. 1433–1444); children: Louis also known as Ludovico Gonzaga (1412–1478), 2nd marquis of Mantua (r. 1444–1478); Carlo (1417–1456); Margherita Gonzaga (1418–1439); Gianlucido (1423–1448); Cecilia Gonzaga (1426–1451); Alessandro (1427–1466).

GONZAGA, Paola (1463–1497). Countess of Gorizia. Born 1463; died 1497; dau. of Barbara of Brandenburg (1422–1481) and Louis also known as Ludovico Gonzaga (1412–1478), 2nd marquis of Mantua (r. 1444–1478); m. Leonhard, count of Gorizia.

GONZAGA, Paola (1508–1569). Nun from Mantua. Name variations: name as a nun might have been Livia. Born 1508; died in 1569; dau. of

Isabella d'Este (1474–1539) and Francesco also known as Gianfrancesco Gonzaga (1466–1519), 4th marquis of Mantua (r. 1484–1519); never married.

GONZALÈS, Eva (1849–1883). French painter. Name variations: Gonzales. Born in Paris, France, 1849; died in Paris in 1883; dau. of Emmanuel (noted novelist) Gonzalès; mother was an accomplished musician; studied with Charles Chaplin and Edouard Manet; m. Henri Guérard (engraver), 1879; children: one son, Jean Raimond. ❖ An early Impressionist, became Manet's model and student, and their friendship would last throughout both their lives; exhibited 3 works, *The Little Soldier* (Villeneuve-sur-Lot, Musée des Beaux-Arts), *The Passer-by*, and a pastel of sister Jeanne Gonzalès in salon of 1870; had a small but loyal following in England and Belgium, as well as France. Manet's portrait of her is in London's National Gallery. ❖ See also *Women in World History*.

GONZÁLEZ, Beatriz (1938—). Colombian artist. Name variations: Beatriz González Aranda; Beatriz Gonzalez. Born Beatriz González Aranda, Nov 16, 1938, in Bucaramanga, Colombia. ❖ Known for her ironic, irreverent and controversial paintings, often described as late pop and kitsch, was initially influenced by abstract impressionists, most notably in series of paintings entitled *Las encajeras* (The Lacemakers, 1960s); began painting images in 3-D (1967) with such works as *Last Supper on a Metal Bed*; her work, which has been featured by the Museo del Barrio (New York City, 1998 and 1997) and in National Museum of Women in the Arts (Washington, DC, 1996), often critiques daily life and political events in Colombia, such as *Mr. President, What an Honor To Be with You at This Historical Moment* (1986), *Camouflaged Apocalypse* (1989), *Cover, Cover* (1994) and *Mothers of Las Delicias* (1996); became curator of art and history collections at National Museum of Bogotá (1993). ❖ See also Marta Calderón, ed., *Beatriz González: Una pintora de provincia* (Carlos Valencia Editores, 1988).

GONZALEZ, Driulis (1973—). See Gonzalez Morales, Driulys.

GONZÁLEZ, Wanda. See Panfil, Wanda.

GONZÁLEZ ÁLVAREZ, Laura (1941—). Spanish politician. Name variations: Laura Gonzalez Alvarez. Born July 9, 1941, in Avilés, Asturias. ❖ Served as president of the Parliament of Asturias (1991) and vice-chair of the GUE/NGL Group (1994); representing the Confederal Group of the European United Left/Nordic Green Left (GUE/NGL), elected to 4th and 5th European Parliament (1994–99, 1999–2004).

GONZALEZ LAGUILLO, Maria (1961—). Spanish field-hockey player. Born Feb 27, 1961, in Spain. ❖ At Barcelona Olympics, won a gold medal in team competition (1992).

GONZALEZ MORALES, Driulys (1973—). Cuban judoka. Name variations: Driulis Gonzalez Morales; Driulis Gonzalez Moreno; Driulis or Driulys Gonzalez. Born Sept 21, 1973, in Cuba. ❖ At Barcelona Olympics, won a bronze medal in lightweight 56kg (1992); won a gold medal for 52–56kg lightweight at Atlanta Olympics (1996); won World championship for 56kg (1995) and 57kg (1999); placed 1st at A Tournament for 5 events (2000–04); won a silver medal for 52–57kg lightweight at Sydney Olympics (2000); won a bronze medal for 63kg at Athens Olympics (2004).

GONZALEZ MORENO, Driulis (1973—). See Gonzalez Morales, Driulys.

GONZALEZ OLIVA, Mariana (1976—). Argentine field-hockey player. Born Mariana Gonzalez Oliva, Mar 12, 1976, in Buenos Aires, Argentina. ❖ Midfielder, won a team bronze medal at Athens Olympics (2004); won World Cup (2002), and Pan American Games (2003); also played for the Rot Weiss Cologne club in Germany.

GOODALE, Elaine (1863–1953). See Eastman, Elaine Goodale.

GOODALL, Jane (1934—). English ethologist and animal-rights activist. Name variations: Baroness Jane van Lawick-Goodall. Born in London, England, April 3, 1934; dau. of Mortimer Herbert Morris-Goodall and Vanne Joseph Goodall; received PhD in ethology from Cambridge University, 1965; m. Baron Hugo van Lawick (wildlife photographer), 1964 (div. 1974); m. Derek Bryceson, 1975 (died of cancer, 1980); children: (1st m.) Hugo Eric Louis, nicknamed "Grub" (b. 1967). ❖ Ethologist responsible for an increased understanding of the chimpanzee, was raised and educated, mostly in Bournemouth, England (1934–52); worked as a secretary in Oxford and London (1952–57); traveled to Nairobi, Kenya, acquiring position as an assistant

secretary to Dr. Louis Leakey (1957–60); researched chimpanzee behavior at Gombe Stream Research Center (1960–71), where, because of her efforts, the refusal to recognize chimpanzees as individuals is no longer dominant—with the preponderance of evidence demonstrating chimpanzees' tool-using capacity, self-recognition in a mirror, and ability to learn and teach each other American Sign Language; lectured at Stanford University and Yale University in US (1970–75); published *In the Shadow of Man* (Houghton Mifflin, 1971); founded Jane Goodall Institute (1977); published *The Chimpanzees of Gombe*, her synthesis on chimpanzee behavior (1986); spends much of her time traveling as a goodwill ambassador on behalf of environmentalism, animal rights, and the earth's dwindling population of chimpanzees. Received National Geographic Society's prestigious Hubbard Medal and was made a Commander of the British Empire (CBE) by Queen Elizabeth II (1995); received honorary doctorates from such schools as Salisbury State University, University of North Carolina, Munich University, and University of Utrecht. ❖ See also memoir *Through a Window: Thirty Years with the Chimpanzees of Gombe* (Weidenfeld & Nicolson, 1990) and (with Phillip Berman) *Reason for Hope: A Spiritual Journey* (Warner, 1999); and *Women in World History*.

GOODBODY, Buzz (1946–1975). British theater director. Name variations: Mary Ann Goodbody. Born Mary Ann Goodbody (known from childhood as "Buzz"), June 25, 1946, in London, England; committed suicide on April 12 (some sources cite the night of the 11th as time of death), 1975, in London; dau. of Marcelle Yvonne (Raphael) Goodbody and Douglas Maurice Goodbody (lawyer); educated at Roedean, Sussex, England; Sussex University, 1962–66, BA; m. Edward Buscombe, 1967 (div. 1971). ❖ Visionary theater director and 1st woman associate director of the Royal Shakespeare Company who pioneered their alternative performance space, The Other Place, hoping to demonstrate that Shakespeare could still communicate intimately, politically, and potently to a 20th-century audience; showed an early interest in theater and wrote, directed, and performed in university drama while at Sussex; was a founding member of the feminist Women's Street Theatre; won an award for her own adaptation and production of Dostoyevsky's *Notes from the Underground* at National Student Drama Festival (1966) and was invited to become personal assistant to John Barton, an associate director of Royal Shakespeare Company (RSC); while working for him, presented "in-house" productions and readings (in the Company's rehearsal room), and devised an anthology for RSC's touring educational program, TheatreGoRound (TGR) entitled *Eve and After* (1967–68); assisted Barton on *Coriolanus* and *All's Well That Ends Well* (1967); was research assistant on *The Merry Wives of Windsor* (1968); appointed assistant director for RSC season at Stratford Festival Theatre (1968–69)—*Henry VIII, Twelfth Night, Women Beware Women, Pericles, The Winter's Tale* and a revival of *The Merry Wives of Windsor*—taking the latter two productions on a tour of Japan and Australia; directed *King John* and *Arden of Faversham* for TGR (1970); directed RSC touring production of Trevor Griffiths' *Occupations* and *The Oz Trial* at London's Aldwych Theatre (1971); was assistant to Trevor Nunn for acclaimed "Romans" season (*Julius Caesar, Titus Andronicus, Coriolanus* and *Antony and Cleopatra*)—taking a much more prominent role when Nunn fell ill during transfer of all 4 plays from Stratford to the Aldwych (1972); appeared in London's West End in the feminist revue *Top Cats* (1973); directed *As You Like It* for Festival Theatre, Stratford (1973); became artistic director of The Other Place (1974) where she subsequently produced *King Lear* and *Hamlet* (1975); committed suicide at age 28 (1975); her legacy of political commitment opened the way to directors, designers, and actors from the fringe, bringing a new vitality and awareness to the RSC. ❖ See also *Women in World History*.

GOODE, Essie (1896–1965). See Robeson, Eslanda Goode.

GOODENOUGH, Florence Laura (1886–1959). American developmental psychologist. Born Florence Laura Goodenough in Honesdale, Pennsylvania, Aug 6, 1886; died in Lakeland, Florida, April 4, 1959; youngest of eight children of Lines Goodenough (farmer) and Alice (Day) Goodenough; attended rural school in Rileyville, Pennsylvania; Millersville (PA) Normal School, B.Pd., 1908; undergraduate degree from Columbia University, 1920, master's, 1921; PhD from Stanford University; never married; no children. ❖ For PhD thesis, devised the "Draw-a-Man" intelligence test, which could determine the level of development by having a child submit a simple drawing of a man, resulting in *Measurement of Intelligence by Drawings* (1926); after working for two years as chief psychologist at Minneapolis Child Guidance Clinic, joined faculty at University of Minnesota (1926) and quickly attained rank of research professor; published *Experimental Child Study* (with John

E. Anderson) and *Anger in Young Children* (1931), scrutinizing the methods used in evaluating children; created Minnesota Preschool Scale (1932), which estimated intelligence in young children; also wrote *The Mental Growth of Children from Two to Fourteen Years, Exceptional Children*, and her classic *Developmental Psychology*. ❖ See also *Women in World History*.

GOODFELLOW, Mrs. (1889–1966). *See Reed, Alma.*

GOODHUE, Sarah Whipple (1641–1681). American religious writer. Born 1641 in Ipswich, Massachusetts; died in childbirth, July 23, 1681; m. Joseph Goodhue; children: 8. ❖ Wrote *A Valedictory and Monitory Writing* (1681) after having premonition that she would die in childbirth, which she did. The text illustrates characteristics of Puritan autobiography as well as her own poetic style.

GOODMAN, Christina Mayne (1910–1995). *See Dony, Christina Mayne.*

GOODMAN, Ellen (1941—). American syndicated columnist. Born April 11, 1941, in Newton, Massachusetts; Radcliffe College, BA (cum laude), 1963; attended Harvard University as a Nieman Fellow, 1973–74; m. Bob Levey (journalist for *Boston Globe*). ❖ Began career as a researcher at *Newsweek*; became a reporter for *Detroit Free Press* (1965), then *Boston Globe* (1967), where she launched her op-ed column "At Large"; was later syndicated in over 450 newspapers; writings include *Turning Points* (1979) and (with Patricia O'Brien) *I Know Just What You Mean: The Power of Friendship in Women's Lives* (2000); collections of columns include *Close to Home* (1979), *At Large* (1981), *Keeping in Touch* (1985), *Making Sense* (1989), *Value Judgments* (1993) and *Paper Trail* (2004). Awarded the Pulitzer Prize for Distinguished Commentary (1980).

GOODMAN, Shirley (1936–2005). African-American rhythm-and-blues singer. Name variations: Shirley Pixley; Shirley and Lee; Shirley; Shirley and Company. Born Shirley Pixley on June 19, 1936, in New Orleans, Louisiana; died July 5, 2005. ❖ With Leonard Lee, formed duo Shirley and Lee, known as "sweethearts of the blues"; with Lee, made $2 demo of "I'm Gone" and was discovered by New Orleans studio owner Cosimo Matassa; with producer Dave Bartholomew, re-recorded "I'm Gone" with Lee, which hit #2 in R&B charts (1952); after few minor successes (early 1950s), had huge hit with "Let the Good Times Roll" and later with "I Feel Good" (1956), but did not become popular with white audiences; split with Lee (1963) and briefly sang with Jesse Hill as Shirley and Jesse; reunited with Lee for Richard Nader's Rock & Roll Revival Show (1972); had smash hit with disco song, "Shame, Shame, Shame" (1975).

GOOD QUEEN BESS (1533–1603). *See Elizabeth I.*

GOODRICH, Annie Warburton (1866–1954). American nurse. Born Annie Warburton Goodrich, Feb 6, 1866, in New Brunswick, New Jersey; died Dec 31, 1954, in Cobalt, Connecticut; dau. of Annie Williams Butler Goodrich and Samuel Griswold Goodrich (insurance executive); granddau. of Dr. John Butler (pioneering psychiatrist); cousin of Ida Butler (1868–1949, nurse). ❖ Nursing education reformer, graduated from New York Hospital's Training School for Nurses (1892); worked as a nursing superintendent at many institutions, including New York Post-Graduate Hospital (1893–1900); taught (part-time) hospital economics at Columbia University's Teachers College (1904–13); served as president of the American Federation of Nurses (1909); inspected nurse training schools for the state of NY (1910–14); invited by Lillian Wald to be the Henry Street Visiting Nurse Service's director of nurses (1917); during WWI, was employed as the chief inspector of US army hospitals; served as dean of the Army School of Nursing (1918–19) and as a professor and 1st woman dean in Yale University's School of Nursing (1923–34); retired to Colchester, Connecticut (1934); writings include *The Social and Ethical Significance of Nursing* (1932). Received National Institute of Social Science Medal (1920), Yale Medal (1953); inducted into American Nurses Association Hall of Fame (1976).

GOODRICH, Edna (1883–1971). American actress. Born Edna Stephens, Dec 22, 1883, in Logansport, Indiana; died May 26, 1971, in NYC; m. Nat C. Goodwin (actor, div.). ❖ Made stage debut in NY in the chorus of *Floradora* (1900); came to prominence as Madame Recamier in *Mam'selle Napoleon* (1903) and subsequently appeared in *The College Widower, When We Were 21, The Genius, The Easterner* and *Evangeline* (title role); often starred opposite husband; films include title roles in *Queen X* and *The Making of Maddalena*, among others.

GOODRICH, Frances (1891–1984). American screenwriter and playwright. Name variations: Frances Hackett. Born in Belleville, New

Jersey, 1891; died of lung cancer on Jan 29, 1984, in New York City; dau. of Henry W. and Madeliene Christie (Lloyd) Goodrich; educated in private school; Vassar College, BA, 1912; attended the New York School of Social Service; m. Henrik Willem van Loon (div. 1929); m. Albert Hackett, Feb 7, 1931; no children. ❖ With husband, produced some of the most enduring screenplays of 20th century, including *The Thin Man* (1934), *Lady in the Dark* (1944), *It's a Wonderful Life* (1946), *Father of the Bride* (1950), and *Seven Brides for Seven Brothers* (1954); also collaborated on five plays, most notable among them, *The Diary of Anne Frank* (1955), for which they won the Pulitzer Prize, New York Drama Critics Circle Award, and Tony Award. ❖ See also *Women in World History*.

GOODRICH, Lucy (1760–1821). *See Wright, Lucy.*

GOODRIDGE, Sarah (1788–1853). American painter. Born in Templeton, Massachusetts, Feb 5, 1788; died in Reading, Massachusetts, 1853; 6th of 9 children of Ebenezer Goodridge (farmer) and Beulah Goodridge; sister of Beulah Goodridge Appleton and Eliza Goodridge Stone (also a miniaturist); attended local schools; briefly attended David L. Brown's drawing school; never married; no children. ❖ One of the most distinguished American miniaturists of the 19th century, produced portraits on ivory of well-known denizens of Boston and Washington, DC; opened a studio in Boston (1820); studied with Gilbert Stuart; was commissioned to paint Daniel Webster, General Henry Lee, and many others. ❖ See also *Women in World History*.

GOODSON, Katharine (1872–1958). English pianist. Born June 18, 1872, in Watford, England; died in London on April 14, 1958; studied at the Royal Academy of Music with Oscar Beringer and in Vienna with Leschetizky; m. Arthur Hinton (1869–1941, composer). ❖ Was popular on concert stages throughout Great Britain; though she played mostly the standard repertory, ventured to perform such novelties as the Delius Concerto.

GOODSON, Sadie (c. 1900—). African-American jazz pianist and singer. Name variations: Sadie Goodson Colar. Born c. 1900; sister of Billie Pierce and Ida Goodson; m. George "Kid Sheik" Colar (trumpeter), c. 1980. ❖ New Orleans jazz pioneer, performed with sisters Ida and Billie as the Goodson Sisters; began playing with New Orleans bands (1920s); also played with the Sammy Rimington Jazzmen; at 93, was still appearing at Preservation Hall.

GOODSPEED, Marjorie (1917–1997). *See Reynolds, Marjorie.*

GOODWIN, Bridget (c. 1802/27–1899). New Zealand gold miner. Name variations: Bridget Dunbar, Little Biddy, Biddy of the Buller. Born in Ireland, c. 1802–1827 (surname may have been Dunbar); died Oct 19, 1899. ❖ Legendary figure only 4 feet tall, who mined for gold at Bendigo and Ballarat in Australia before arriving in New Zealand (mid-1860s); lived and worked with 2 male companions mainly in Buller Gorge area on west coast of New Zealand (1890s). ❖ See also *Dictionary of New Zealand Biography* (Vol. 1).

GOODWIN, Doris Kearns (1943—). American biographer. Born Jan 4, 1943, in Brooklyn, NY; Colby College, BA (magna cum laude); Harvard University, PhD in government; m. Richard Goodwin (speechwriter to presidents Kennedy and Johnson), 1975; children: 3 sons. ❖ After writing an article opposing Lyndon Johnson's foreign policy, became a special assistant to Johnson in the White House (1968); taught a course on the American Presidency for 10 years at Harvard (1969–79); helped Johnson write his memoir *The Vantage Point* (1971); published *Lyndon Johnson & the American Dream* (1977), followed by *The Fitzgeralds & the Kennedys* (1987), both bestsellers; won the Pulitzer Prize for History for her biography of Franklin and Eleanor Roosevelt, *No Ordinary Time* (1996); was a regular panelist on "The News Hour with Jim Lehrer." ❖ See also memoir *Wait Till Next Year* (1997).

GOODWIN, Gillian (1959—). *See Gilks, Gillian.*

GOODWIN, Michelle (1966—). American gymnast. Born April 3, 1966, in US. ❖ Won gold medals in bars and beam at Hungarian International (1982) and won KIPS Invitational (1984).

GOOLAGONG CAWLEY, Evonne (1951—). Australian-Aboriginal tennis player. Name variations: Evonne Cawley; Evonne Goolagong-Cawley. Born Evonne Goolagong, July 31, 1951, in Griffith, New South Wales, Australia; m. Roger Cawley, June 16, 1975. ❖ Won North England and Cumberland Hard Court championships and Welsh, Victorian, Midlands, Queensland, and Bavarian opens (1970); was Australian Hard Court champion in singles, doubles and mixed doubles, and on the winning Federation Cup team (1970); won South African Doubles and French Open, Wimbledon, Dutch Open, and Queensland Open singles (1971); won NSW and South African opens, and was runner-up at Wimbledon (1972); was US Indoors champion, and on the Federation Cup winning team (1973); won Canadian and Italian opens (1973); won Czechoslovakian championship in singles and mixed doubles (1973); won Australian and US opens (1974); was New Zealand Open champion in singles and doubles, and on winning Federation Cup team (1974); was Wimbledon doubles champion and Virginia Slims champion (1974); won Australian Open and was runner-up at Wimbledon (1975); won NSW and Australian opens (1976); was runner-up at Wimbledon (1976); had 15 consecutive victories on Virginia Slims tour (1976); was Sydney Colgate International champion (1977); won NSW and Australian opens (1977); was US Indoor champion (1979); won Wimbledon singles (1980). Awarded MBE by Queen Elizabeth II and named Australian of the Year (1972); named Sun Sportsman of the Year (1974). ❖ See also autobiography *Home! The Evonne Goolagong Story* (Simon & Schuster, 1993) and autobiography with Bud Collins and Victor Edwards *Evonne* (Hart-Davis, MacGibbon, 1975); and Max Robertson, *Wimbledon—Centre Court of the Game* (BBC, 1981); and *Women in World History*.

GOOLD, Maria Vere (1877–1908). French murderer. Name variations: Lady Vere Goold; Marie Vere Goolde; Marie Girodin. Born Marie Girodin, 1877, in France; died at the French penal colony at Cayenne, 1908; married at least 3 times, the last to Sir Vere Goold. ❖ Married twice, was widowed twice, with husbands dying under mysterious circumstances; at 30, married an Irishman who called himself Sir Vere Goold; insolvent from gambling and other excesses in Monte Carlo, borrowed money from a wealthy widow, Mme Emma Levin (1907); as chief plotter, killed Levin with husband, packed the body parts in a trunk, and attempted to mail it from Marseilles to London; after odor from trunk caught attention of clerk, was tried with husband in Monaco; received death sentence (commuted to life imprisonment) while husband received life sentence; within a year, died in the penal colony known as Devil's Island of typhoid fever (1908); husband committed suicide (1909).

GOOSE, Elizabeth (1665–1757). American writer, possibly the legendary Mother Goose. Born Elizabeth Foster in 1665; died 1757; m. Isaac Goose, 1682; children: 6 (2 died in infancy); stepmother to 10. ❖ Much in her life establishes her identity as the real Mother Goose, whose rhymes and stories comprised a book called *Songs for the Nursery, or Mother Goose's Melodies for Children*, published in 1719. ❖ See also *Women in World History*.

GOOSE, Mother (1665–1757). *See Goose, Elizabeth.*

GOOSSENS, Marie (1894–1991). English harpist. Born 1894 in England; died 1991; dau. of Eugene Goossens (conductor); sister of Eugene (conductor and composer), Leon (oboe player, 1897–1988), Adolphe (horn player, 1896–1916) and Sidonie Goossens (harpist). ❖ In early years, appeared with the Goossens Orchestra, formed by her conductor brother Eugene; composed *Harp Music for Beginners* and the theme music for the long-running radio serial "Mrs. Dale's Diary" and arranged *Fourteen Tunes for the Celtic Harp*; often recorded. Appointed OBE (1980). ❖ See also autobiography, *Life on a Harpstring*.

GOOSSENS, Sidonie (1899–2004). English harpist. Born Oct 19, 1899, in Liscard, on Merseyside, England; grew up in Liverpool; died Dec 14, 2004, age 105; dau. of Eugene Goossens (conductor); sister of Eugene (conductor and composer), Leon (oboe player) Adolphe (horn player) and Marie Goossens (harpist); studied with Miriam Timothy; m. Hyam "Bumps" Greenbaum (musical director, died 1942); m. Norman Millar (major in the Black Watch), 1945 (died 1991); no children. ❖ One of the foremost harpists of her time, was also the principal harp for the BBC Symphony Orchestra; in early years, appeared with the Goossens Orchestra, formed by her conductor brother Eugene; began broadcasting (1924); was a founder member of the BBC Orchestra (1930–80), playing under the baton of Toscanini, Beecham and Walter, among others; participated in the premiere of Vaughan Williams' *Serenade to Music*; taught at the Guildhall School for 30 years; made president for life of the United Kingdom Harp Association (1988). Appointed MBE (1974), OBE (1980); awarded the Cobbett Medal (1990).

GOPOVA, Nina (1953—). *See Trofimova-Gopova, Nina.*

GÖPPERT-MAYER, Maria (1906–1972). *See Mayer, Maria Goeppert.*

GORB, Tatyana (1965—). Soviet handball player. Born Jan 18, 1965, in USSR. ❖ Won a bronze medal at Seoul Olympics (1988) and a bronze medal at Barcelona Olympics (1992), both in team competition.

GORBACHEVA, Raisa (1932–1999). Russian sociologist, educator, and first lady. Name variations: Raisa Maximovna; Raisa Gorbachev. Pronunciation: Gor-ba-CHOFF-a. Born Raisa Maximovna Titarenko in Rubtsovsk, USSR, Jan 5, 1932; died of leukemia on Sept 20, 1999, at the Muenster University Clinic in Muenster, Germany; dau. of Maksim Andreevich Titarenko, sometimes rendered Titorenko (railway construction engineer) and Aleksandra (or Shura) Petrovna Paradina Titarenko; attended Moscow State University, 1949–54; Lenin Pedagogical Institute (Moscow), 1964–67; m. Mikhail Sergeevich Gorbachev (lawyer and future head of the Communist Party and the Soviet state), Sept 25, 1953; children: Irina Gorbacheva Virganskaya (b. 1957). ❖ An intelligent, articulate woman, with a PhD in sociology and a successful career as a lecturer at two Soviet universities, who gave up her own career to help her husband, only to be ridiculed for her efforts; was a lecturer (*dotsent*), Stavropol Agricultural Institute (1959–78) and Moscow State University (1979–85); appeared on the cover of *Time* magazine, the 1st Russian woman to be so honored (June 6, 1988); served as vice-president, Soviet Cultural Foundation (1986–91); donated much of her wealth to charity and raised more than $8 million for children's leukemia hospitals. Granted an honorary degree from Northeastern University in Boston (1989). ❖ See also memoir *I Hope: Reminiscences and Reflections* (1991); Urda Jürgens, *Raisa* (trans. from the German by Sylvia Clayton, Weidenfeld & Nicolson, 1990); and *Women in World History*.

GORBANEVSKAYA, Natalya Yevgenevna (1936—). Russian poet and memoirist. Name variations: Natal'ia Evgen'evna Gorbanévskaia or Natalia Evgenevna Gorbanévskaia. Born 1936 in Moscow, Russia; studied philology at Moscow and Leningrad universities; children: 2. ❖ Activist and poet, helped to found the *samizdat* journal *Khronika tekushchikh sobytiy* (*Chronicle of Current Events*, 1968) which was published abroad and detailed cases of state prosecution and civil-rights abuse; as one of the 7 Red Square demonstrators against the Soviet invasion of Czechoslovakia, was arrested (1969) and confined in a psychiatric prison (1970); freed (1972), continued to edit her journal; permitted her poetry collection *Poberezhye* (The Littoral) to be published in US (1973); was allowed to immigrate to Paris (1975), with her 2 children; worked as deputy editor of the Russian-language magazine *Kontinent* and continued to publish poetry.

GORBYATKOVA, Nelli (1958–1981). Soviet field-hockey player. Born June 25, 1958, in USSR; died Aug 1981. ❖ At Moscow Olympics, won a bronze medal in team competition (1980).

GORCHAKOVA, Yelena (1933—). Soviet track-and-field athlete. Born May 17, 1933, in USSR. ❖ Won a bronze medal at Helsinki Olympics (1952) and a bronze medal at Tokyo Olympics (1964), both in javelin throw.

GORDEEVA, Ekaterina (1971—). Russian figure skater. Name variations: Yekaterina Gordeyeva; Katia Gordeeva. Born May 28, 1971, in Moscow, Russia; eldest of two daughters of Alexander Alexeyevich Gordeev (dancer for the Moiseev Dance Company) and Elena (Levovna) Gordeeva (teletype operator for Soviet news agency Tass); m. Sergei Grinkov (skating partner), April 1991 (died Nov 20, 1995); m. Ilia Kulik (Russian skater), June 10, 2002; children: (1st m.) Daria Grinkova; (2nd m.) Elizaveta (b. 2001). ❖ Paired with husband Sergei Grinkov, won 4 World championships and a gold medal at Calgary Olympics (1988) and at Lillehammer Olympics (1994); turned professional (1995). ❖ See also (autobiography) with E.M. Swift *My Sergei: A Love Story* (Warner Books, 1996).

GORDIJN, Gonnelien. *See Rothenberger, Gonnelien.*

GORDIMER, Nadine (1923—). South African writer. Born in Springs, Transvaal, South Africa, Nov 20, 1923; dau. of Isidore Gordimer (Jewish shopkeeper from Lithuania) and Nan (Myers) Gordimer (dau. of a Jewish family from England); attended the University of the Witwatersrand, 1945; m. Gerald Gavron (Gavronsky), Mar 6, 1949 (div. 1952); m. Reinhold Cassirer, Jan 29, 1954; children: (1st m.) one daughter, Oriane Gavron; (2nd m.) one son, Hugo Cassirer. ❖ Nobel-prize winner and one of South Africa's leading writers, who has devoted much of her career to exploring the complex personal undercurrents in her country's political and racial history in the 2nd half of the 20th century; published 1st story (1939); published 1st collection of short stories, *The Soft Voice of the Serpent* (1952); published 1st novel, *The*

Lying Days, and made 1st trip abroad (1953); saw paperback edition of *A World of Strangers* banned in South Africa (1962), as well as *The Late Bourgeois World* (1971) and *The Burger's Daughter* (1979); participated in defense of Alexandra Township (1986); joined African National Congress (1990); delivered the Charles Eliot Norton Lectures at Harvard University (1994); wrote more than 200 short stories and 11 novels, including *Face to Face* (1949), *Occasion for Loving* (1963), *Livingston's Companions* (1971), *July's People* (1981), *A Sport of Nature* (1987), *My Son's Story* (1990), *Jump and Other Stories* (1991), *None to Accompany Me* (1994), *The House Gun* (1998), (collection of essays and lectures) *Living in Hope and History: Notes from Our Century* (1999); presented a vivid and profound picture of sensitive members of the white community in South Africa living in a segregated society that does violence to their moral principles. Won Booker Prize for her novel *The Conservationist* (1974); won Nobel Prize for Literature (1991). ❖ See also Robert F. Haugh, *Nadine Gordimer* (Twayne, 1974); Dominic Head, *Nadine Gordimer* (Cambridge University Press, 1994); Kathrin Wagner, *Rereading Nadine Gordimer* (Indiana University Press, 1994); Judie Newman, *Nadine Gordimer* (Routledge, 1988); and *Women in World History.*

GORDON, Anna Adams (1853–1931). American social reformer. Born in Boston, Massachusetts, July 21, 1853; died in Castile, NY, June 15, 1931; dau. of James Monroe Gordon (bank cashier and treasurer of the American Board of Commissioners for Foreign Missions) and Mary Elizabeth (Clarkson) Gordon; attended Mt. Holyoke Seminary, 1871–72, and Lasell Seminary, Auburndale, MA; never married; no children; lived with Frances Willard. ❖ Became secretary to Frances E. Willard (1877); joined Woman's Christian Temperance Union (1879), serving as vice president (1898–1925); appointed superintendent of juvenile work, World Woman's Christian Temperance Union (1891), and advanced to president (1922); author of several books, including *The Beautiful Life of Frances E. Willard* (1898), and song collections, among them *Young People's Temperance Chorus Book* (1911), *Marching Songs for Young Crusaders* (1916), and *Jubilee Songs* (1923). ❖ See also *Women in World History.*

GORDON, Annie Elizabeth (1873–1951). New Zealand religious leader and welfare worker. Born on July 20, 1873, at Timaru, New Zealand; died May 28, 1951, in Auckland, New Zealand; dau. of George Granville Sutherland Gordon (boatman) and Anna (Eglington) Gordon. ❖ Joined Salvation Army (1896); performed several years of social work throughout Australia before being transferred to New Zealand (1908); appointed matron of women's rescue home and officer in charge of police court work in Christchurch (1908); was 1st Salvation Army officer in Auckland (1917); appointed Auckland's 1st woman probation officer (1921); was 1st woman recipient of Salvation Army's highest honor, Order of the Founder (1945). ❖ See also *Dictionary of New Zealand Biography* (Vol. 3).

GORDON, Beate (1923—). *See Sirota, Beate.*

GORDON, Bridgette (1967—). American basketball player. Born April 27, 1967, in Deland, Florida. ❖ At Seoul Olympics, won a gold medal in team competition (1988).

GORDON, Caroline (1895–1981). American novelist, short-story writer, and critic. Born Caroline Gordon on Oct 6, 1895, on Merry Mont (or Merimont) farm, Todd Co., Kentucky; died April 11, 1981, in San Cristobal de las Casas, Mexico; dau. of James Maury Morris Gordon and Nancy (Meriwether) Gordon (both teachers); Bethany College, West Virginia, BA, 1916; m. Allen Tate, 1946 (div. 1959); rem. Allen Tate, 1946 (div. 1959); children: Nancy Tate (b. Sept 1925). ❖ Major figure in the Southern Renaissance, whose work described the conflict between industrialism and agrarianism, the tension between the pre-Civil War and post-Civil War South, and humankind's struggle to impose order on an unstable world; spent early childhood at Merry Mont farm; at 10, attended father's school of classical studies; after graduation from Bethany College, taught high school in Clarksville, Tennessee; moved to Chattanooga (1920) and worked as a reporter for Chattanooga *News;* after marriage, moved with husband and child to Paris (1928–29); published 1st short story in *Gyroscope* (1929); returned to the South (1930); published 1st novel, *Penhally* (1931); began moving frequently (1937) to fill temporary academic positions, including teaching creative writing at the Women's College of University of North Carolina at Greensboro (1938); moved to Princeton, New Jersey (1939); converted to Catholicism (1947); novels include *Aleck Maury, Sportsman* (1934), *None Shall Look Back* (1937), *The Garden of Adonis* (1937), *Green*

Centuries (1941), *The Women on the Porch* (1944), *The Strange Children* (1951), *The Malefactors* (1956), and *The Glory of Hera* (1972); short stories include "What Music" (1934), "A Morning's Favor" (1935), "The Women on the Battlefield" (1936–37), "Frankie and Thomas and Bud Asbury" (1939), "The Olive Garden" (1945), *The Forest of the South* (1945), "The Waterfall" (1950), "The Feast of St. Eustace" (1954), "A Narrow Heart: The Portrait of a Woman" (1960), "The Dragon's Teeth" (1961), *Old Red and Other Stories* (1963), "Cock-Crow" (1965), "Cloud Nine" (1969), "A Walk With the Accuser (Who is the God of This World)" (1969), "Always Summer" (1971), "The Strangest Day in the Life of Captain Meriwether Lewis as Told to His Eighth Cousin, Once Removed" (1976). ❖ See also Nancylee Novell Jonza, *The Underground Stream: The Life and Art of Caroline Gordon* (University of Georgia Press, 1995); Ann Waldron, *Close Connections: Caroline Gordon and the Southern Renaissance* (Putnam, 1987); Sally Wood, ed. *The Southern Mandarins: Letters of Caroline Gordon to Sally Wood, 1924–1937* (Louisiana State University Press, 1984); and *Women in World History.*

GORDON, Daisy (b. around 1900). *See Lawrence, Daisy Gordon.*

GORDON, Doris Clifton (1890–1956). New Zealand doctor, university lecturer, obstetrician, and women's health reformer. Name variations: Doris Clifton Jolly. Born on July 10, 1890, in Melbourne, Australia; died July 9, 1956, in Stratford, New Zealand; dau. of Alfred Jolly (cleric) and Lucy Clifton (Crouch) Jolly; University of Otago Medical School, MB, ChB, 1916; m. William Patteson Pollock Gordon, 1917; children: 3 sons, 1 daughter. ❖ Practiced medicine jointly with husband (1919); pioneered use in New Zealand of various forms of anaesthesia during childbirth; was instrumental in founding New Zealand Obstetrical Society (1927); organized successful campaign to raise public funds to establish chair in obstetrics at Otago Medical School (1931) and for Queen Mary Maternity Hospital in Dunedin (1938); helped to establish postgraduate school of obstetrics and gynecology at Auckland University College (1947); co-authored *Gentlemen of the Jury* (1937); became 1st woman in Australasia to gain fellowship of Royal College of Surgeons of Edinburgh (1925); elected to British College of Obstetricians and Gynaecologists (1936) and became honorary fellow (1954). MBE (1935). ❖ See also autobiographies, *Backblocks Baby-Doctor* (1955) and *Doctor Down Under* (1957), and *Dictionary of New Zealand Biography* (Vol. 4).

GORDON, Dorothy (1891–1985). *See Jenner, Andrea.*

GORDON, Dorothy (1889–1970). American radio and tv moderator, singer and author. Name variations: Dorothy Lerner Gordon; Dorothy Lerner. Born Dorothy Lerner on April 4, 1889, in Odessa, Russia, while American parents were posted there; died May 11, 1970, New York, NY; dau. of Leo Lerner and Rosa (Schwartz) Lerner; m. Bernard Gordon (lawyer), June 28, 1910; children: 2 sons (b. 1911, 1913). ❖ Gave performances of American traditional songs for children, which later became "Young People's Concert Hour" (1926–41); wrote *Sing It Yourself* (1929), *All Children Listen* (1942), and *You and Democracy* (1951); joined CBS as director of musical programs for classroom radio show, "American School of the Air" (1931), and started dramatic adaptations program, "Children's Corner," writing scripts and performing (1936); joined NBC as consultant, and hosted program "Yesterday's Children" (1940); during WWII, gave news commentaries for children on NY radio station, WQXR; moderated "New York Times Youth Forum" on WQXR (1945–60, when program was taken over by NBC and renamed "Dorothy Gordon Youth Forum"); moderated Youth Forum on Dumont television network (1952–58) and on WNBC-TV in NY (1958–70). Youth Forum won numerous awards, including George Foster Peabody Award for radio broadcasting (1959, 1964, 1966) and Emmy from National Academy of Television Arts and Sciences.

GORDON, Eliza (1877–1938). New Zealand nurse, midwife, welfare worker. Name variations: Leilah Gordon, Eliza Urquhart, Leilah Urquhart. Born on Jan 29, 1877, in Glasgow, Scotland; died June 15, 1938, in Dunedin, New Zealand; dau. of Robert Maurice Urquhart (ship's steward) and Margaret (Wright) Urquhart; m. William Gordon (painter, d. 1905), 1902; children: 2 daughters. ❖ Immigrated to New Zealand with family (1880); worked as attendant at Seacliff Lunatic Asylum (1899); after training as midwife at St Helens Hospital in Dunedin, served as visiting nurse and district agent for Otago for Child Welfare Branch (1917–32). ❖ See also *Dictionary of New Zealand Biography* (Vol. 4).

GORDON, Elizabeth (1765–1839). *See Leveson-Gower, Elizabeth.*

GORDON, Florence LaRue (1944—). *See LaRue, Florence.*

GORDON, Gale Ann (1943—). American navy pilot. Born 1943 in Ohio. ❖ Assigned to Pensacola Naval Air Station (FL) as member of Medical Service Corps; began flight training as only woman in squadron of 999 men (1966); became 1st woman navy pilot to fly solo (1966), in a propeller-driven T-34 trainer.

GORDON, Hannah (1941—). Scottish actress. Born Hannah Cambell Grant Gordon, April 9, 1941, in Newhaven, Edinburgh, Scotland; dau. of William Munro Gordon and Hannah Grant; orphaned at 11, grew up with two uncles and a great aunt in Edinburgh; attended Glasgow College of Music and Art; m. Norman Warwick (cinematographer), 1970 (died 1994); children: Ben Warwick. ❖ Began career at Dundee Rep (1962); made tv debut in "Johnson Over Jordan" (1965); was soon playing leads in BBC's classical serials of "David Copperfield," "Great Expectations" and "Middlemarch"; also appeared in "Abelard and Heloise," "The Orkney Trilogy," "The Exiles" and "Dear Octopus" for Yorkshire Television; appeared as Suzy Bassett on "My Wife Next Door" (1972–73) and as Lady Virginia Bellamy on "Upstairs, Downstairs" (1971–75); films include *Spring and Port Wine* (1970), *Alfie Darling* (1975), *The Elephant Man* (1980), and *Miss Morrison's Ghosts* (1981); played Desdemona opposite Topol's *Othello* at Chichester (1975); in West End, appeared in *The Killing Game* at Apollo, *The Jeweller's Shop* at Westminster (1982), *Can You Hear Me at the Back* at Piccadilly (1979), *The Country Girl* at Apollo (1983) and Moss Hart's *Light Up The Sky* at Old Vic; starred in *Mary Stuart* at Edinburgh Festival (1987) and was lauded for work in *Shirley Valentine* (1989); also narrated "Watercolour Challenge" for Channel 4 (1998).

GORDON, Helen (1934—). Scottish swimmer. Born May 10, 1934, in Scotland. ❖ At Helsinki Olympics, won a bronze medal in the 200-meter breaststroke (1952).

GORDON, Isabella (1901–1988). English zoologist. Born May 18, 1901, in United Kingdom; died May 11, 1988; Imperial College of Science, University of London, PhD; Aberdeen University, DSc, 1928. ❖ World expert on crabs (Malacostraca), crustaceans, and sea spiders (Pycnogonida), was often called the "Grand Old Lady of Carcinology" (study of crabs, lobsters, etc.); studied sea urchin development at Imperial College of Science, University of London (1924–26); on a Commonwealth Fund fellowship, studied at Woods Hole Marine Laboratory in Woods Hole, Massachusetts (July 1926) and at Hopkins Marine Station in California (autumn 1926); worked as an assistant keeper in the British Museum's (Natural History) Crustacean Section from 1928 until retirement; was a founding member of Groupe d'Etudes Carcinologiques (1955), later Colloquia Crustacea Mediterranea; served as a member of the Linnean and Zoological societies; traveled throughout Japan and was an honored guest at Emperor Hirohito's 60th-birthday celebration. Appointed Officer of the Order of the British Empire (1961).

GORDON, Ishbel (1857–1939). *See Aberdeen, Ishbel Maria Gordon, Lady.*

GORDON, Jean (1918—). Canadian politician. Name variations: G. Jean Gordon. Born Mar 6, 1918, in Vancouver, British Columbia, Canada; m. Wilf Gordon; children: Betty. ❖ Was the 1st woman elected to the Yukon Territorial Council (Sept 11, 1967), for Mayo District; served until 1970.

GORDON, Jean Margaret (1865–1931). American social reformer and suffragist. Born c. 1865 in New Orleans, Louisiana; died Feb 24, 1931, in New Orleans; dau. of George Hume Gordon (educator) and Margaret (Galiece) Gordon; sister of Kate M. Gordon (suffragist). ❖ Lobbied to reform Louisiana's child labor laws of 1886 and 1906 and to authorize women factory inspectors; was 1st factory inspector in New Orleans; served as vice president (1909–11) and secretary of Southern states (1912–13) of National Consumers' League; helped create and served as president of board and supervisor of Alexander Milne Home for Girls; was president of Era Club (1903–04) and Louisiana Woman Suffrage Association (1913–20).

GORDON, Julia Swayne (1878–1933). American silent-film actress. Name variations: Julia Swayne-Gordon. Born Sarah Victoria Swayne, Oct 29, 1878, in Columbus, Ohio; died May 28, 1933, in Los Angeles, California. ❖ Began career with the Edison Company; worked at Vitagraph (1909–18); films include *The Battle Hymn of the Republic, A Million Dollar Bid, The Juggernaut, The Battle Cry of Peace, My Old Kentucky Home, Scaramouche, Bride of the Storm* and *It*; best remembered for her performance as Richard Arlen's mother in *Wings*.

GORDON, Kate M. (1861–1932). American suffragist and social activist. Born July 14, 1861, in New Orleans, Louisiana; died Aug 24, 1932, in New Orleans; dau. of George Hume Gordon (educator) and Margaret (Galiece) Gordon; sister of Jean Margaret Gordon (social activist/reformer). ❖ Founded (1896) and was dominant member of Era Club, which was devoted to woman suffrage and other issues, such as improvement of New Orleans' water supply; addressed annual convention (1900) and served as secretary (1901–09) of National American Woman Suffrage; headed Louisiana state suffrage association (1904–13); established, served as president of, and edited monthly publication for Southern States Woman Suffrage Conference (1913–17); spearheaded fight against tuberculosis in New Orleans, culminating in opening of New Orleans Anti-Tuberculosis Hospital (1926); was opposed to 19th Amendment, or any federal voting legislation that would "usurp states rights," and worked with anti-suffragists against its ratification in Louisiana and Tennessee.

GORDON, Kim (1953—). American musician. Name variations: Sonic Youth. Born April 28, 1953, in Rochester, NY; m. Thurston Moore (musician), 1984; children: Coco Hayley Gordon Moore (b. 1994). ❖ Vocalist, bassist, and guitarist, formed the influential avant-garde rock band Sonic Youth, with Thurston Moore and drummer Richard Edson (1981), and released several albums, including *Confusion is Sex* (1983), *Bad Moon Rising* (1985), and *Daydream Nation* (1988), which became a classic; with Sonic Youth, also released acclaimed albums *Goo* (1990), *Dirty* (1992), *Experimental Jet Set, Trash and No Star* (1994), and *Washing Machine* (1995); began performing on guitar rather than bass; with band Free Kitten, released several albums, including *Unboxed* (1994), and *Sentimental Education* (1997); with Sonic Youth, performed at NYC's Lincoln Center (1997); with band, established own label, SYR (1997); released solo album, *SYR 5* (2000); is owner of, and designs for, fashion label X-Girl.

GORDON, Kitty (1878–1974). English star of stage and screen. Born Constance Blades, April 22, 1878, in Folkestone, Kent, England; died May 26, 1974, in Brentwood, LI, NY; dau. of Lt.-Col. Blades; m. Michael Levenston; m. Hon. H.W. Horsley-Beresford (Harry Beresford, actor); m. Ralph Ranlet (also seen as Raulet, died); children: Vera Beresford (actress). ❖ Made London debut in *Kitty Grey* (1901); made NY debut in *Véronique* (1905); appeared in the operetta *The Enchantress* (1911), written expressly for her by Victor Herbert; films include *The Crucial Test, Forget-Me-Not, The Wasp, No Man's Land* and *The Interloper.*

GORDON, Laura de Force (1838–1907). American lawyer, editor, and reformer. Name variations: Laura D. Gordon. Born Laura de Force, Aug 17, 1838, in Erie Co., Pennsylvania; died April 5, 1907, in Lodi, California; m. Dr. Charles H. Gordon, 1862 (div. by 1878). ❖ Made one of the 1st public speeches on equal rights for women in American West (1868); contributed to founding of California Woman Suffrage Society (1870) and served as its president (1877, 1884–94); became editor of woman's department of *Narrow Gauge* (1873), a semi-weekly paper based in Stockton, California; also took on the responsibility of publishing and editing the *Stockton Weekly Leader* (1873) which moved to Sacramento (1875) as *Weekly Leader*; edited Oakland *Daily Democrat* (1878); applied for admission to Hastings College of Law in San Francisco (1878); denied admission, successfully filed suit against the school; was the 2nd woman admitted to California bar (1879); developed a strong reputation as a criminal lawyer and was admitted to practice before US Supreme Court (1885). ❖ See also *Women in World History.*

GORDON, Leilah (1877–1938). *See Gordon, Eliza.*

GORDON, Lucie Duff (1821–1869). *See Duff-Gordon, Lucie.*

GORDON, Lucy Duff (1862–1935). *See Duff Gordon, Lucy.*

GORDON, Margaret (b. around 1900). *See Lawrence, Daisy Gordon.*

GORDON, Maria Ogilvie (1864–1939). *See Ogilvie Gordon, Maria M.*

GORDON, Maria Matilda (1864–1939). *See Ogilvie Gordon, Maria M.*

GORDON, Mary (1882–1963). Scottish-born actress. Born Mary Gilmour, May 16, 1882, in Glasgow, Scotland; died Aug 23, 1963, in Pasadena, California. ❖ Came to US with a touring stage company; made film debut in *Tessie* (1925); appeared in small or uncredited parts in over 250 films, including *The Little Minister, Stage Struck, Kidnapped, When the Daltons Ride* and *My Son My Son;* probably best remembered as Mrs. Hudson, the housekeeper, in the Sherlock Holmes films.

GORDON, Noele (1923–1985). English actress. Born Dec 25, 1923, in East Ham, London, England; died April 14, 1985, in Birmingham; studied at RADA. ❖ Made London debut as Patsy in *Mother's Gone A-Hunting* (1938); came to prominence as Meg Brockie in *Brigadoon* (1949); films include *The Lisbon Story*; on tv, hosted such series as "Lunch Box" (1955) and "Fancy That" (1956) and appeared as Meg Richardson (Mortimer) on "Crossroads" (1964–81).

GORDON, Pinkie (1925—). *See Lane, Pinkie Gordon.*

GORDON, Ruth (1896–1985). American actress and screenwriter. Born Ruth Gordon Jones in Wollaston, Massachusetts, Oct 30, 1896; died Aug 28, 1985, in Edgartown, Massachusetts; dau. of Clinton and Anne Jones; m. Gregory Kelly (actor), 1921 (died 1927); m. Garson Kanin (director and screenwriter), 1942; children: (with producer Jed Harris) one son, Jones. ❖ When a teenager, began appearing in silent films as a bit player; made Broadway debut at 19, as one of the Lost Boys in Maude Adams production of *Peter Pan* (1915); during the next 2 decades, gave several well-received performances in both comedic and dramatic roles in such plays as *Tweedles, Saturday's Children, Hotel Universe, Serena Blandish, They Shall Not Die* and *A Doll's House* and on film in *Abe Lincoln in Illinois* (1939), *Dr. Erlich's Magic Bullet* (1940), *Two-Faced Woman* (1941), and *Action in the North Atlantic* (1943); during a lull in acting career (1940s), turned to writing for the screen and received Academy Award co-nominations for screenplays of such films as *Adam's Rib* and *Pat and Mike*; resumed acting career (1960s), winning a new audience and an Academy Award for work in *Rosemary's Baby* (1968); worked steadily in film and tv, along with publishing three volumes of memoirs and one novel, before her death; other films include *Inside Daisy Clover* (1966), *Where's Poppa?* (1970), *Harold and Maude* (1971), *The Big Bus* (1976), *The Great Houdini* (1976), *Every Which Way But Loose* (1978), *Boardwalk* (1979), *Scavenger Hunt* (1979), *My Bodyguard* (1980), *Any Which Way You Can* (1980), *Don't Go to Sleep* (1982), *Jimmy the Kid* (1983), *The Trouble with Spies* (1984) and *Maxie* (1985). ❖ See also memoirs *Myself Among Others* (1971), *My Side* (Harper & Row, 1976) and *An Open Book* (Doubleday, 1980); and *Women in World History*.

GORDON, Vera (1886–1948). Russian-born actress. Born Vera Nemirov, June 11, 1886, in Edkerternoslav, Russia; died May 8, 1948, in Beverly Hills, California; m. Nathan Gordon. ❖ Immigrated to US at age 7; for a number of years, appeared in the Yiddish theater in NY; as a character actress in motherly roles, best remembered for her performance in the silent-film version of *Humoresque* (1919); also appeared in vaudeville.

GORDON-BAILLE, Mary Ann (1857–?). Scottish swindler. Name variations: Mary Ann Gordon Baille. Born Mary Ann Sutherland Bruce; m. Richard Percival Bodeley Frost. ❖ Leased mansion in Dundee, Scotland, which she used as a front while purchasing expensive goods on credit and then fencing them (1872); traveled widely, through Edinburgh, Vienna, Rome, Paris, Florence, London and Australia, performing confidence scams; stood trial for passing bad checks and received 5-year prison sentence (husband received 18-months); after release, returned to life of crime which resulted in additional arrests and incarcerations.

GORDON-CUMMING, Eka (1837–1924). Scottish travel writer. Name variations: Constance Fredereka Gordon Cumming. Born Constance Fredereka Gordon-Cumming in 1837 in Altyre, Scotland; died in 1924; dau. of Sir William Gordon-Cumming, baronet of Altyre and Gordonstoun, and Elizabeth Maria (Cambell) Gordon-Cumming. ❖ Began travels with visit to married sister in India (1867); was invited to serve as companion to Lady Gordon, whose husband, Sir Arthur Hamilton Gordon, was posted to the crown colony of Fiji (1874); traveled throughout Pacific, including islands of Hawaii, then to California and Sierra Nevada, followed by Egypt, China and Sri Lanka; an accomplished artist, produced over 1,000 paintings of subjects worldwide; wrote 8 very popular books about experiences, illustrated with her paintings, most popular of which were *At Home in Fiji* (1881) and *A Lady's Cruise on a French Man-of-War* (1882); also wrote *From the Hebrides to the Himalayas* (1876), *Fire Fountains* (1883), *In the Hebrides* (1883), *California As I Saw It* (1884), *Granite Crags* (1884), *Two Happy Years in Ceylon* (1892), *Wanderings in China* (1900) and *Memories* (1904).

GORDON-LAZAREFF, Hélène (1909–1988). French journalist. Name variations: Helene Gordon Lazareff. Born 1909 in Rostov-on-the-Don, Russia; died in 1988; m. Paul Radnitz; m. Pierre Lazareff; children: (1st m.) 1 dau; (2nd m.) 1 daughter. ❖ Fled with family to Turkey then Paris during Russian Revolution (1917); studied ethnology and began working as journalist; worked for American women's magazines during WWII; with Françoise Giroud, founded the highly successful *Elle* magazine (1945), which she then directed and edited until 1973; with Pierre Lazareff, wrote *USSR in the Time of Malenkov*; served on French tv advisory council.

GORDON LOW, Juliette (1860–1927). *See Low, Juliette Gordon.*

GORDON-WATSON, Mary (1948—). English equestrian. Name variations: Mary Watson. Born April 1948, in UK. ❖ At Munich Olympics, won a gold medal in team 3-day event (1972); won World championship (1970).

GORE, Altovise (1935—). American modern dancer and theatrical choreographer. Name variations: Altovise Davis. Born Aug 30, 1935; married Sammy Davis, Jr. (actor, dancer and singer), 1970 (died May 16, 1990); children: (adopted) 1. ❖ Trained with Syvilla Fort and danced with her concert group (1950s); performed with Alvin Ailey company in numerous works by Ailey, including *Creation of the World* and *Gillespiana*; created roles for Talley Beatty and his recital group in *Road of the Phoebe Show* (1959) and *Come and Get the Beauty of It Hot* (1960); performed in London in *Golden Boy* (c. 1968), starring Sammy Davis, Jr.; appeared mainly as tv actress thereafter.

GORE, Catherine (1799–1861). English novelist and dramatist. Name variations: Catherine Grace Frances Moody; Mrs. Charles Arthur Gore; (pseudonyms) C.D.; C.F.G.; Albany Poyntz. Born Catherine Grace Frances Moody in East Retford, Nottinghamshire, England, 1799; died at Lyndhurst, Hampshire, England, Jan 29, 1861; dau. of Charles Moody (wine merchant); m. Captain Charles Gore, 1823; children: 10. ❖ Published 1st work, "The Two Broken Hearts" in verse (1822), then 1st novel, *Theresa Marchmont, or The Maid of Honour* (1823); saw popularity rise with *Lettre de Cachet* (1827), *The Reign of Terror* (1827), and *Hungarian Tales* (1829); had greatest success with *Women as They Are; or The Manners of the Day* (1830); during 1830s, produced *Mothers and Daughters* (1831), *The Fair of May Fair* (1832), *The Hamiltons* (1834), *Mrs. Armytage or Female Domination* (1836), and *Stokeshill Place; or The Man of Business* (1837); also wrote her most popular comedy, *The School for Coquettes* (1832), which ran for 5 weeks at the Haymarket; published *Cecil, or The Adventures of a Coxcomb* considered one of her most revealing novels on social life of the upper-middle class (1841); is known to have written over 70 novels, but her prolific use of pseudonyms makes it probable that other uncredited works exist. ❖ See also *Women in World History*.

GORE, Leslie (1946—). American pop vocalist. Born Lesley Sue Goldstein, May 2, 1946, in New York, NY; sister of Michael Gore; graduated from Sarah Lawrence College (1968). ❖ Attended prep school in Englewood, NJ; discovered by Quincy Jones during senior year in high school, signed with Mercury record label and had #1 hit with debut single "It's My Party" (1963); scored 3 Top-5 hits with "She's a Fool," "Judy's Turn to Cry," and "You Don't Own Me" (1963); released hit singles "Maybe I Know" (1964), "Sunshine, Lollipops, and Rainbows" (1965), and "California Nights" (1967); collaborated with Jones until 1967; appeared on tv series "Batman" (1967); recorded unsuccessful album for Motown subsidiary Mowest (1972); reunited with Jones for *Love Me by Name* (1976), which performed well in England; with brother, earned Academy Award nomination for song "Out Here on My Own" from the *Fame* soundtrack (1980); continues to perform in Atlantic City.

GORE-BOOTH, Constance (1868–1927). *See Markievicz, Constance.*

GORE-BOOTH, Eva (1870–1926). Irish poet, pacifist, suffragist and labor activist. Born Eva Selena Gore-Booth on May 22, 1870, at Lissadell, Co. Sligo, Ireland; died in London, England, June 30, 1926; dau. of Sir Henry Gore-Booth (landowner and explorer) and Georgina (Hill) Gore-Booth; sister of Constance Markievicz (1868–1927); educated at home; never married; lived with Esther Roper (suffrage and labor activist); no children. ❖ Activist who campaigned to improve the pay and conditions of women workers in Manchester; traveled with father to the West Indies and America (1894); diagnosed as having tuberculosis (1895); spent some months in Italy (1895–96), where she met Esther Roper; returned home and set up the Sligo branch of the Irish Women's Suffrage and Local Government Association, before settling with Roper in Manchester (1896), where both were associated with the University Settlement, the Manchester and Salford Women's Trade Union Council, the Manchester National Society for Women's Suffrage, the Women's Co-Operative Guild and the Lancashire and Cheshire Women Textile and Other Workers' Representation Committee; published 1st collection, *Poems* (1898); met Christabel Pankhurst (1901); split with Pankhurst on the use of violence in the suffrage campaign (1904); represented the Lancashire Working Women's Societies, the Trade Unions, and Labor Societies in Lancashire in the Women's Franchise Deputation to Prime Minister Campbell-Bannerman (1906); involved in campaigns for barmaids' right to work, for the improvement of florists' assistants' and pit-brow women's working conditions (1908–11); moved to London with Roper (1914); attended trials of conscientious objectors on behalf of the No-Conscription Fellowship (1915–18); was a member of the British organizing committee of the Women's International Congress, held at The Hague (1915); traveled to Dublin following the Easter Rebellion (1916) to visit her sister, Constance Markievicz, one of the rebel leaders, who was condemned to death but reprieved and imprisoned in England; attended the trial in London of Sir Roger Casement and was involved in the unsuccessful campaign for the reprieve of his death sentence (1916); visited Italy (1920–21); diagnosed as having cancer (1924). Writings include *Poems* (1898), *The One and the Many* (1904), *The Three Resurrections and The Triumph of Maeve* (1905), *The Egyptian Pillar* (1907), *The Sorrowful Princess* (1907), *The Agate Lamp* (1912), *The Perilous Light* (1915), *Broken Glory* (1917), *The Sword of Justice* (1918), *The Shepherd of Eternity* (1925), *The House of Three Windows* (1926), *The Inner Kingdom* (1926), *The World's Pilgrim* (1927), *Collected Poems of Eva Gore-Booth* (1929), and *The Buried Life of Deirdre* (1930). ❖ See also Gifford Lewis, *Eva Gore-Booth and Esther Roper: A Biography* (Pandora, 1988); and *Women in World History*.

GORECKA, Halina (1938—). Polish runner. Name variations: Halina Górecka; Halina Gorecka-Richterowna. Born Halina Richter, Feb 1938, in Poland. ❖ Won a bronze medal at Rome Olympics (1960) and a gold medal at Tokyo Olympics (1964), both in 4 x 100-meter relay.

GORENKO, Anna (1889–1966). *See Akhmatova, Anna.*

GORETZKI, Viola (1956—). East German rower. Born Nov 23, 1956, in East Germany. ❖ At Montreal Olympics, won a gold medal in coxed eights (1976).

GORHAM, Kathleen (1932–1983). Australian ballerina. Name variations: danced briefly under the name Ann Somers. Born in Sydney, Australia, 1932; died April 30, 1983; convent educated; studied ballet with Lorraine Norton and Leon Kellaway; m. Robert Pomie (French dancer), around 1958 (div.); m. Barney Marrows; children: (1st m.) one son, Anthony. ❖ At 15, was invited by Edouard Borovansky to join his company in Melbourne; when the company disbanded (1948), joined Ballet Rambert, which was touring Australia at the time; after appearing as a soloist with Roland Petit Company in Paris and performing with Sadler's Wells Theatre Ballet (1951), rejoined Borovansky's new company, performing for 1st time in *Giselle* (1951), the role for which she is best remembered in Australia; also created several new roles before the company once again folded; danced a season with the Grand Ballet du Marquis de Cuevas in Paris and did another brief stint with Sadler's Wells; danced with yet a 3rd Borovansky company (1954–61), creating new roles and performing principal roles in classical ballets; became prima ballerina of the newly formed Australian Ballet (1962), where she played a significant role in the artistic development of the fledgling company; retired (1966); spent later years teaching in Melbourne and Southport, Queensland. ❖ See also *Women in World History*.

GÖRING, Emmy (1893–1973). *See Goering, Emmy.*

GORING, Sonia (1940—). American singer. Name variations: The Chantels. Born 1940 in NY; married. ❖ While in a school choir at St. Anthony of Padua in the Bronx, formed the doo-wop group The Chantels (1956), one of 1st and most well-received girl groups; with Arlene Smith (lead), Lois Harris (1st tenor), Jackie Landry (2nd alto), and Rene Minus, released album *We Are the Chantels* (1958), singing 2nd soprano; has such hits as "Maybe" (1958), which was later covered by Janis Joplin (1969), "Look in My Eyes" and "Well, I Told You" (both 1961); released *The Best of the Chantels* (1990) and appeared with original group in reunion performances.

GORIZIA, countess of. *See Gonzaga, Paola (1463–1497).*

GORKA (fl. 920s). Queen of Poland. Fl. around 920; m. Ziemionslaw, king of Poland (r. 913–964); children: Mieczislaw also known as Burislaf or Mieszko I (c. 922–992), duke of Poland (r. 960–992).

GORMAN, Margaret (1905–1995). Miss America. Name variations: Margaret Cahill. Born Margaret Gorman, Aug 18, 1905; died Oct 15, 1995, in Washington, DC; m. Victor Cahill (real estate executive), mid-1920s (died 1957). ❖ Named Miss Washington, DC (summer 1921); won the Inter-City Beauty Contest in Atlantic City, NJ (1921), forerunner of the Miss America pageant; was the 1st to be named Miss America (1922), the only winner to receive a crown at the conclusion of her year. ❖ See also Frank Deford, *There She Is* (Viking, 1971).

GORMAN, Miki (1935—). Japanese-American marathon runner. Name variations: Michiko Gorman. Born Michiko Suwa, 1935, of Japanese parents in occupied China; m. Michael Gorman (businessman), 1976; children: Danielle Gorman (actress). ❖ Arrived in Pennsylvania on a student visa (1964); became a US citizen; won Boston marathons (1974, 1977), New York City marathons (1976, 1977), and Tokyo marathon. ❖ See also "Marathon Woman: Miki Gorman" (28 min. film), Ellen Freyer Productions (1980).

GORMAN, Shelley (1969—). *See Sandie, Shelley.*

GORMÉ, Eydie (1931—). American pop singer. Name variations: Eydie Gorme. Born Edith Gormezano, Aug 16, 1931, in The Bronx, NY; m. Steve Lawrence (singer), 1957; children: 2, including David Nessim Lawrence. ❖ Began career as a regular on the "Tonight!" Show, starring Steve Allen (1954–57); starred on "The Steve Lawrence–Eydie Gormé Show" (1958) and "Steve and Eydie" (1975); had huge hit single with "Blame It on the Bossa Nova" (1963); albums include *Eydie in Love* (1958), *Gorme Sings Showstoppers* (1958), *Eydie Gormé on Stage* (1959), *I Feel So Spanish* (1961), *Let the Good Times Roll* (1963), *Don't Go to Strangers* (1966), *Softly, As I Leave You* (1967) and *Since I Fell for You* (1981); also recorded with husband.

GORMFALLITH. *Variant of Gormflaith.*

GORMFLAITH (c. 870–925). Irish poet and wife of kings. Name variations: Gormley; Gormfallith; Gormflath; Gormlaith. Born c. 870; died 925; dau. of Flann Sionna, high king of Ireland (r. 879–916); betrothed to Cormac mac Cuilennáin, king-bishop of Cashel; m. King Cerball of Leinster; m. Niall Glúndubh, high king of Ireland (r. 916–919); children: a son. ❖ Twice married, once betrothed, reputedly wrote poetry about husbands (some lyrics survive in the Irish annals and in the Scottish manuscript entitled *The Book of the Dean of Lismore*). ❖ See also *Women in World History*.

GORMFLAITH OF IRELAND (fl. 980–1015). Irish queen. Name variations: Gormfallith; Gormflath; Gormlaith; Gormley; Kormlod. Flourished between 980 and 1015 in Ireland; dau. of King Flann of Leister; m. Olaf Cuaran of Dublin; m. Malachy of Meath (separated 990); m. Brian Boru (c. 941–1014), overlord of all Ireland (separated 1000); children: (with Olaf Cuaran) at least one son, Sitric Silkbeard, king of Dublin. ❖ Extremely well educated, also had a reputation for great beauty; when 1st husband was defeated in battle by Malachy of Meath, left him and married Malachy (c. 990); married 3rd husband, celebrated Irish leader Brian Boru; separated (1000), then declared war on Malachy and Brian Boru and incited rebellion and rioting against their rule.

GORMFLATH. *Variant of Gormflaith.*

GORMLAITH or GORMLEY (fl. 980–1015). *See Gormflaith of Ireland.*

GOROKHOVA, Galina (1938—). Soviet fencer. Born Aug 31, 1938, in USSR. ❖ Won a gold medal at Rome Olympics (1960), silver medal at Tokyo Olympics (1964), and gold medal in Mexico City Olympics (1968), all in team foil; won a bronze medal in individual foil and a gold medal in team foil at Munich Olympics (1972).

GOROKHOVSKAYA, Mariya (1921—). Soviet gymnast. Born Oct 17, 1921, in USSR. ❖ At Helsinki Olympics, won a silver medal in teams all-around, portable apparatus, silver medals in vault, floor exercises, balance beam, and uneven bars, and gold medals in team all-around and individual all-around (1952).

GORR, Rita (1926—). Belgian mezzo-soprano. Born Marguerite Geirnaert, Feb 18, 1926, in Zelzaete, Belgium. ❖ Equally comfortable as a contralto and mezzo-soprano, sang in Strasbourg Opera (1949–52); made debut at Paris Opéra and Opéra-Comique (1952); debuted at Bayreuth (1958), Covent Garden in *Aida* (1959); debuted at Teatro alla Scala as Kundry in *Parsifal* (1960), and Metropolitan Opera (1962); made several recordings, including as Amneris in Verdi's *Aida* with Georg Solti, which may be the finest performance of the part on record. ❖ See also *Women in World History.*

GORRIS, Marleen (1948—). Dutch film director and screenwriter. Born Dec 9, 1948, in Roermond, Limburg, Netherlands; sister of Henk Gorris (history teacher); studied drama at University of Amsterdam. ❖ Wrote screenplay and directed 1st film *De Stilte rond Christine M.* (1982) and did double duty on *Gebroken spiegels* (1984), *The Last Island* (1990) and *Antonia's Line* (1995), which was the Dutch entry for Best Foreign Language at that year's Academy Awards; also filmed *Mrs. Dalloway* (1997), starring Vanessa Redgrave, *The Luzhin Defence* (2000), *Carolina* (2003) and *Barry* (2005).

GORRITI, Juana Manuela (1816–1892). Argentinean novelist. Born 1816 in Argentina; died 1892; m. General Manuel Isidoro Belzú (president of Bolivia, 1848–48, 1848–55), 1831 (sep 1843, died 1865); children: 3. ❖ The 1st woman novelist in Argentina, had to flee with family to Tarija, Bolivia, because father was a rebel in the Argentinean Independence movement (1831); married at 14; husband became president of Bolivia; moved to Lima, Peru, where she taught and held literary evenings with important intellectuals; moved to Buenos Aires (1874) and founded magazine *La Alvorada del Plata;* writings include the novel *La Quena* (The Flute, 1845) and 2 volumes of *Panoramas de la vida* (Views of Life).

GORTON, Bettina (c. 1916–1983). Australian prime-ministerial wife. Born Bettina Edith Brown, c. 1916, in Maine, USA; died Oct 2, 1983; degree in languages from the Sorbonne, Paris; also had an honors degree in Asian Studies; m. John Gorton (19th prime minister of Australia, 1968–71), Feb 15, 1935; children: Joanna (b. 1937), Michael (b. 1938), and Robin (b. 1941). ❖ An American who also became an Australian citizen (1967), was the only prime-ministerial wife who held duel citizenship; ran the family's orchard farm; worked as a research assistant at the Australian National University, compiling an English–Malay dictionary; created the garden of Australian native plants, now named for her, on the grounds of The Lodge (the official prime-ministerial residence); with her Indonesian language skills, made valuable contributions to Australia's relations with neighboring countries.

GO, Shizuko (1929—). Japanese novelist. Born 1929 in Yokohama, Japan. ❖ Awarded Akutagawa Prize for *Requiem* (1972) which reflects her strong aversion to militarism and war; also wrote *Ghost* and *Outside the Fence.*

GO-SAKURAMACHI (1740–1814). Japanese empress. Name variations: Princess Toshi-ko or Toshiko; Go-Sakuramachi-tenno. Born in 1740 (some sources cite 1741); died 1814, age 74; dau. of Emperor Sakuramachi; sister of Emperor Momosono. ❖ Reigned during Edo Period (1762–71) and was the 10th woman to sit on the throne of Japan; upon brother's death (1762), ascended to imperial throne as Empress Go-Sakuramachi but wielded only ceremonial powers; abdicated in favor of nephew Hidehito (1771).

GOSLAR, Hannah (1928—). Childhood schoolmate of Anne Frank, known as Lies Goosens in the original diary. Name variations: Hannah Pick-Goslar or Hannah Goslar Pick; Hanneli Goslar; Lies Goslar; Lies Goosens in original diary. Born Hannah Elisabeth Goslar in Berlin, Germany, 1928; dau. of Hans Goslar (before moving to the Netherlands, was deputy minister for domestic affairs and press secretary of Prussian Cabinet in Berlin) and Ruth Judith Klee (teacher); married; children: 3, including son Chagi (officer in the Israeli army). ❖ Before Germans invaded, lived diagonally across from the Franks and was very close to Anne; with sister and father, became part of a large Nazi roundup (June 20, 1943); was transported from Westerbork to Bergen-Belsen (Feb 15, 1944); met and talked with Anne Frank through the barbed wire; after the war, with the help of Otto Frank, moved to Israel. ❖ See also *Women in World History.*

GOSLAR, Lotte (1907–1997). German dancer and mime. Born Feb 27, 1907, in Dresden, Germany; died Oct 16, 1997, in West Cornwall, Litchfield, Connecticut. ❖ Best known for her dance solo "Grandma Always Danced," left Germany when the Nazis came to power (c. 1934); made NY debut in *The Peppermill* (1937); choreographed Bertold Brecht's production of *Galileo* (1947); was the subject of *Dolly, Lotte, und Maria*, a West German documentary by Rosa von Praunheim concerning Goslar, Dolly Haas, and Maria Piscator (1987).

GOSLING, Mrs. Nigel (1908–2004). See Lloyd, Maude.

GOSPEL MINNIE (1897–1973). See Douglas, Lizzie.

GOSS, Olga May (1916–1994). Australian plant pathologist. Born Olga May Goss in 1916 in Perth, Australia; died 1994; University of Western Australia, BS in zoology, 1937; never married. ❖ An expert plant pathologist, worked as a laboratory assistant at University of Western Australia, Perth (1938–39) and as a demonstrator (1939–43); employed as a plant pathologist in Department of Agriculture in Perth (1947–80), worked on tomato seed treatments, the causes of apple scab, and the culturing of *Rhizobium* for commercial use; became a specialist in plant nematology (study of eelworms) and focused on nematode-resistant peach rootstocks and cereal eelworm; discovered a fungicide that killed the agent responsible for powdery scab in potatoes; created the rust-resistant runner bean known as Westralia; contributed to *Australian Plant Pathology* and *Australian Journal of Agricultural Research* and the handbook *Practical Guidelines for Nursery Hygiene* (1978). Was the 1st woman to be named Australian Nurseryman of the Year (1978).

GOSSE, Christine (1964—). French rower. Born 1964 in France. ❖ With Hélène Cortin, won World championships (1993, 1994); won a bronze medal for coxless pair at Atlanta Olympics (1996).

GOSSE, Sylvia (1881–1968). English artist. Name variations: Laura Sylvia Gosse. Born in 1881 in London, England; died in 1968 in Hastings, England; dau. of Sir Edmund Gosse (critic, poet, essayist and librarian of House of Lords) and Nellie Gosse (painter); attended St. John's Wood School, Royal Academy Schools, 1903–06, and Westminster School of Art. ❖ Engraver, painter of street scenes, interiors and still-lifes in oils, 1st showed work at Allied Artists Association (1909) and enrolled in Walter Sickert's etching class at Rowlandson House (1910); took over for Madeline Knox, teaching beginners and helping Sickert run school; prevented from joining Camden Town Group because of gender, helped found London Group (1913); showed at New English Art Club (from 1911) and at Royal Academy (from 1912); held solo show at Carfax Gallery (1916); elected to Royal Society of British Artists (1929) and Royal Society of Painter-Etchers & Engravers (1936); paintings, which are in permanent collections of British Museum, as well as Ashmolean, Oxford and Tate museums, include *Industry* (1909), *The Doctor* (1914), *Portrait of Walter Sickert* (1924), and *Charlotte Couchée* (1925).

GOSSICK, Sue (1947—). American diver. Born Nov 12, 1947, in California; dau. of Dr. Gustav Gossick; trained with Lyle Draves. ❖ Was a medalist in 21 of 24 national springboard diving championships (1962–68); was a member of US team at Tokyo Olympics, placing 4th; won a gold medal in springboard diving in Mexico City Olympics (1968). Inducted into International Swimming Hall of Fame (1988).

GOSSWEILER, Marianne (1943—). Swiss equestrian. Born May 15, 1943, in Switzerland. ❖ Won a silver medal at Tokyo Olympics (1964) and bronze medal at Mexico City Olympics (1968), both in dressage team.

GOTLIEB, Phyllis (1926—). Canadian poet and science-fiction writer. Born Phyllis Gotlieb, May 25, 1926, in Toronto, Canada; University of Toronto, BA, 1948, MA, 1950; m. Calvin Gotlieb, 1949; children: Leo, Margaret and Jane. ❖ Regarded as the mother of Canadian sf, science-fiction novels include *Sunburst* (1964), *O Master Caliban* (1976), *The Kingdom of the Cats* (1985), *Violent Stars* (1999), and *Mindworlds* (2002); also published poetry, including *Who Knows One?* (1962), *Doctor Umlaut's Earthly Kingdom* (1974), and *The Works: Collected Poems* (1978); short-story collections include *Son of the Morning and Other Stories* (1983) and *Blue Apes* (1995); also published the mainstream novel *Why Should I Have all the Grief?* (1969); edited *Tesseracts 2* (1987) and *Transversions Poetry* (1995–2000).

GÖTTE, Jeannette (1979—). German soccer player. Name variations: Jeannette Goette. Born Mar 13, 1979, in Hagen, Westfalen, Germany. ❖ Won a team bronze medal at Sydney Olympics (2000).

GOTTFRIED, Gesina Margaretha (d. 1828). German serial killer. Born in Germany; beheaded in Germany, 1828. ❖ Used arsenic to poison husband and 2 children, as well as her parents, brother, lover, and many others; was finally apprehended after her employer Rumf, whose whole family she had killed, discovered white powder on his spareribs and alerted authorities; during her trial, confessed to murdering more than 30 people.

GOTTLEIB, Susan (1957—). See Phranc.

GOTTSCHALK, Laura Riding (1901–1991). See Riding, Laura.

GOTTSCHED, Luise Adelgunde (1713–1762). German poet and translator. Name variations: Luise Adelgunde Victorie Gottsched.

Born April 11, 1713, in Danzig, Germany; died June 26, 1762, in Leipzig, Germany; m. Johann Christoph Gottsched (1700–1766, writer and critic); no children. ❖ Worked as husband's secretary and translator but became famous for own comedies and poetry; works include *Die Pietisterey im Fischbein-Rocke* (1736) and *Kleinere Gedichte* (1761); her lifelong friend Henriette von Runckel published letters as *Briefe der Frau Louise Adelgunde Victorie Gottsched gebohnre Kulmus* (1771–72).

GOTTSCHLICH, Stefanie (1978—). German soccer player. Born Aug 5, 1978, in Wolfsburg, Germany. ❖ Won a team bronze medal at Sydney Olympics (2000).

GOTTY, Elizabeth (?–1906). *See Puhiwahine Te Rangi-hirawea, Rihi.*

GOTZ, Daniela (1987—). German swimmer. Born Dec 23, 1987, in Germany. ❖ Won a bronze medal for 4 x 100-meter medley relay at Athens Olympics (2004).

GOUAULT-HASTON, Laurence. French climber and photographer. Name variations: Laurence Gouault Haston; Laurence Gouault; Laurence Haston. Born Laurence Gouault in France; m. Stevie Haston (English climber). ❖ Europe's best woman ice climber and one of the top woman mountain climbers in the world, placed 1st among women at International Ice Climbing contest, Courchevel, France (1993 and 1994); made 1st ascent by a woman of "Fang" grade 6, Vail (1996); made 3rd ascent and 1st female ascent of a grade 7+ (Les compères, Italy, 1997); won silver in Ice Climbing in both Difficulty and Speed at X Games (1997); made 1st snowboard descent of Snow Dome 5000m, Pakistan (1999); made snowboard descent of a 7000m in Tibet (1999). While climbing with husband in Nepal, was cut off and held captive by Maoist rebels, from whom they managed to escape (2002).

GOUDAL, Jetta (1891–1985). Dutch silent-screen actress. Born Julie Henriette Goudeket, July 8, 1891, in Amsterdam, Netherlands (some sources cite Versailles, France); died Jan 14, 1985, in Los Angeles, California; m. Harold Grieve (art director), 1930. ❖ Began career on stage in Europe; arrived in US following WWI and appeared on Broadway; made film debut in *The Bright Shawl* (1923); other films include *The Coming of Amos, The Forbidden Woman, The Road to Yesterday, White Gold, Lady of the Pavements, Paris at Midnight, The Green Goddess, Salome of the Tenements* and *Tarnished Youth;* retired (1933) but was later active in Actor's Equity.

GOUDGE, Elizabeth (1900–1984). British novelist and children's writer. Born April 24, 1900, in Wells, Somerset, England; died April 1, 1984, in Peppard Common near Henley-on-Thames, Oxfordshire, England; dau. of Henry Leighton Goudge (Regius Professor of Divinity, Oxford University) and Ida de Beauchamp (Collenette) Goudge; tutored at home; attended boarding school in Southbourne in Hampshire; attended Reading University Art School for two years; never married; no children. ❖ Began career writing plays, of which only *The Brontës of Haworth* was produced (1932); wrote bestselling *Green Dolphin Street* (1944), a historical romance which won a literary Guild Award and was filmed (1947); other historical novels worth noting are *Gentian Hill* (1949) and *The Child from the Sea* (1970); is also known for her children's fiction, notably *The Little White Horse* (1946), which won the Carnegie Medal, and *The Bird in the Tree* (1940); produced over 40 titles during her career, including novels, short stories, children's books, and nonfiction religious works. ❖ See also autobiography *The Joy of the Snow* (1974); and *Women in World History.*

GOUDVIS, Bertha (1876–1966). South African novelist and playwright. Born Bertha Cinnamon in 1876 in Barrow-in-Furness, Cumbria, England; died 1966. ❖ Arrived in South Africa with first wave of Jewish immigration (1881) and worked with husband as hotelier in South Africa, Southern Rhodesia, and Mozambique; also worked as journalist and wrote 1st story about Matabele Rebellion (1893); works include *A Husband for Rachel* (1924, reprinted as *The Way the Money Goes and Other Plays,* 1925), *Little Eden* (1949), and *The Mistress of Mooiplaas and Other Stories* (1956); extracts from unpublished memoir appeared in *South African Rosh Hashana Annual and Jewish Year Book* (1932), *Jewish Affairs* (1956), and *South African PEN Yearbook* (1956).

GOUEL, Eva (d. 1915). Mistress of Pablo Picasso. Name variations: Eve Gouel; Marcelle Humbert. Died 1915 in Paris, France. ❖ The French mistress of a sculptor named Marcoussis and a friend of Pablo Picasso's mistress Fernande Olivier, went by the name Marcelle Humbert when she 1st took up with Picasso (1911), just as his affair with Olivier was coming to an end; ushered in a relatively tranquil 4-year period in the

artist's life and seems to have been one of the few who escaped his notorious temper. ❖ See also *Women in World History.*

GOUGAR, Helen (1843–1907). American suffragist and temperance reformer. Born Helen Mar Jackson, July 18, 1843, in Litchfield, Hillsdale Co., Michigan; died June 6, 1907, in Lafayette, Indiana; dau. of William Jackson and Clarissa (Dresser) Jackson; m. John D. Gougar (lawyer), Dec 10, 1863. ❖ Known for eloquent speaking style, sarcasm, and wit, lobbied Indiana state legislature to pass amendments on woman suffrage and prohibition (1881); embarked on national lecture tour for suffrage and testified before committee of US Senate; served as president of Indiana state suffrage association; attempted to vote in 1894 election and, when denied, sued election board; unsuccessfully argued her own case against board, after gaining admission to Indiana state bar (1895); after leaving Republican Party, joined National Prohibition Party (1888); became leader member of "broad gauge" faction (1896) which formed Nationalist Party; addressed national conventions of the Populist and National Silver parties and campaigned for presidential candidate William Jennings Bryan; published *Forty Thousand Miles of World Wandering* (1905), based on 10-month trip around world.

GOUGES, Marie Gouze (1748–1793). *See Gouges, Olympe de.*

GOUGES, Olympe de (1748–1793). French playwright and political writer. Name variations: Marie-Olympe de Gouges; Marie Gouze; Marie Gouze Gouges; though she never used her married name Aubry, she was indicted under it in 1793. Pronunciation; OH-lemp de GOOZE. Born Marie Gouze in Montauban, in southwestern France, 1748; executed for crimes against the state in Paris on Nov 3, 1793; dau. of Pierre Gouze (butcher) and Anne-Olympe Mouisset; m. Louis-Yves Aubry, 1765; children: Pierre (b. 1766). ❖ One of the most outstanding advocates for the rights of women during the French Revolution, lived as a courtesan in Paris (1770s); began literary career (1780); saw anti-slavery play accepted by the Comédie Française (1784); saw *The Loves of Chérubin* performed successfully at Théâtre Italien (1786) and *Slavery of Negroes* (*Zamour et Myrza ou l'heureau naufrage*) performed by the Comédie Française, causing an uproar (1789); wrote and published more than two dozen pamphlets many of which had feminist overtones (1790–93); wrote her most famous work, *Déclaration des droits de la femme et de la citoyenne* (*Declaration of the Rights of Woman and the Female Citizen*), a political manifesto which recast the ideals of the revolution so that gender became the central issue (1791); appeared before the legislature in support of *un pauvre* ("a poor man") who was voted relief (1792); defended King Louis XVI in a letter to the National Convention (Dec 1792); despite the obvious danger, wrote *The Three Urns,* attacking Robespierre; arrested for sedition (July 1793); tried and executed by guillotine, according to her obituary, "for sedition and for having forgotten the virtues which befit her sex" (Nov 1793); her voice, however, was never silenced. ❖ See also *Women in World History.*

GOULANDRIS, Niki (1925—). Greek botanical artist and conservationist. Name variations: Niki Kephalia. Born Niki Kephalia in 1925 in Greece; Athens University, MA, 1951; m. Angelos Goulandris. ❖ Recognized for conservation efforts and for botanical illustrations, founded the Goulandris Natural History Museum at Kifissia, near Athens, with husband (1965), becoming its president (1996); illustrated such books as *Wild Flowers of Greece* (1968, by C. Goulimis and W.T. Stearn) and *Peonies of Greece* (by Stearn and P.H. Davies); painted over 800 Greek indigenous plants; served as Greece's deputy minister for Social Services (1974–75), deputy president of Hellenic Radio and Television (1975–81), deputy president of the National Tourism Organization of Greece (1989–91), and president of the Save the Children Association in Greece (1980); served as a British Linnean Academy member; was a member of the 12-member UN Commission for Culture and Development (1993–96) and nominated for the UN's secretary general position (1992). Honors include United Nations Environmental Programme (UNEP) Global 500 Award (1990), Woman of Europe award (1991, given jointly by European Parliament, European Commission, and European Movement), Academy of Athens Award, and France's Légion d'Honneur.

GOULD, Beatrice Blackmar (c. 1899–1989). American journalist and magazine editor. Born Beatrice Blackmar in Emmetsburg, Iowa, probably in 1899; died in Hopewell, New Jersey, Jan 30, 1989; dau. of Harry E. Blackmar (superintendent of public schools) and Mary Kathleen (Fluke) Blackmar; attended public school in Iowa City and Ottumwa; graduated from the University of Iowa; Columbia University, BS in journalism, 1923; m. Charles Bruce Gould (writer and editor), Oct 4, 1923; children: one daughter Sesaly Gould. ❖ With husband, wrote two produced plays, *Man's Estate* (1929) and *The Terrible Turk* (1934), the screenplay for *Reunion* (1936), and coedited the *Ladies' Home Journal* (1936–1962). ❖ See also joint autobiography with husband, *American Story* (1968); and *Women in World History*.

GOULD, Diana (1912–2003). *See Menuhin, Diana.*

GOULD, Helen Miller (1868–1938). *See Shepard, Helen Miller.*

GOULD, Lois (1932–2002). American novelist, essayist and critic. Name variations: Lois Benjamin. Born Lois Regensburg, 1932, in New York, NY; died May 29, 2002, in New York, NY; dau. of Edward S. Regensburg (cigar manufacturer) and fashion designer Jo Copeland; Wellesley College, BA; m. Philip Benjamin (novelist and journalist), 1955 (died 1966); m. Robert E. Gould (psychiatrist), 1967 (died 1998); children: (1st m.) sons, Roger V. Gould (died April 29, 2002) and Anthony Gould. ❖ Bestselling novelist, worked as journalist and university professor at Wesleyan, Northwestern, and New York Universities; wrote a regular column for the *New York Times;* best known for her 1st novel, the partly autobiographical *Such Good Friends* (1970); also wrote *Necessary Objects* (1972), *Final Analysis* (1974), *A Sea-Change* (1976), and *Medusa's Gift* (1991), as well as two books on motherhood *The Case Against Natural Childbirth* (with Waldo L. Fielding, 1962) and *So You Want to be a Working Mother!* (1966), a children's story *X: A Fabulous Child's Story* (1978), and a collection of essays *Not Responsible for Personal Articles* (1978). ❖ See also memoir *Mommy Dressing: A Love Story, After a Fashion* (1998).

GOULD, Sandra (1916–1999). American actress. Born July 23, 1916, in Brooklyn, NY; died July 20, 1999, in Burbank, California; m. Larry Berns (broadcasting executive). ❖ Replaced Alice Pearce as Gladys Kravitz on "Bewitched" (1966–72); films include *Romance on the High Seas, The Ghost and Mr. Chicken,* and *The Barefoot Executive;* on radio, appeared on "My Friend Irma," "Jack Benny," and "Duffy's Tavern."

GOULD, Shane (1956—). Australian swimmer. Name variations: Shane Innes. Born Shane Elizabeth Gould, Nov 23, 1956, in Sydney, New South Wales, Australia; dau. of Shirley Gould (who wrote the 1972 book *Swimming the Shane Gould Way*); m. Neil Innes, 1974. ❖ Won the 100-meter freestyle at New South Wales championships (1972) as well as 13 other Australian indiv. championships and 3 relay championships; won gold medals in the 200-meter freestyle, 400-meter freestyle and 200-meter individ. medley, a silver medal in the 800-meter freestyle, and a bronze medal in the 100-meter freestyle, all at Munich Olympics (1972).

GOULDING, Valerie (1918–2003). Irish politician. Name variations: Lady Valerie Goulding; Valerie Monckton. Born Valerie Hamilton Monckton, Sept 1918, in Kent, England; died July 28, 2003; dau. of Viscount Monckton of Brenchley, England (Conservative minister); m. Sir Basil Goulding, 1939 (died 1982); children: 3 sons, Sir Lingard, Timothy and Hamilton. ❖ Representing Fianna Fáil, nominated to the Seanad by Taoiseach Jack Lynch (1977) and served until 1981; co-founded the Central Remedial Clinic (1951) and was its chair and managing director until 1984. Received a gold medal from Royal College of Physicians of Ireland; won the Lord Mayor of Dublin's award (1990).

GOULET-NADON, Amelie (1983—). Canadian short-track speedskater. Name variations: Amélie Goulet-Nadon. Born Jan 24, 1983, in Montreal, Quebec, Canada. ❖ Won a bronze medal at Salt Lake City Olympics for the 3,000-meter relay (2002).

GOULUE, La (1869–1929). French cancan dancer. Born Louise Weber in 1869; died in Paris in 1929; dau. of a cab driver. ❖ Rose from obscurity to become La Goulue (Greedy Gal), celebrated cancan dancer at the famous Moulin Rouge and one of Paris' last great courtesans; captured the imagination of Henri de Toulouse-Lautrec, who made her the subject of some of his most famous cabaret posters. ❖ See also *Women in World History*.

GOURD, Emilie (1879–1946). Swiss feminist. Born in Switzerland in 1879; died in 1946. ❖ Founded and edited *Le mouvement féministe*, which championed suffrage, education, and legal rights for women; defying Swiss authorities, also organized plebiscites asking for support for women's suffrage during cantonal and national elections; served as president of Swiss Woman's Association (1914–28) and became secretary of International Alliance of Women (1923); also edited a yearbook of Swiss women and wrote a biography of Susan B. Anthony (1920).

GOURNAY, Marie le Jars de (1565–1645). French philosopher, novelist, translator, and literary critic, and salonnière. Name variations: La Dame de Gournay; Marie de Jars; Marie de Gournay de Jars; "the tenth Muse"; "the French Minerva." Born Oct 6, 1565, in Paris, France; died July 13, 1645; dau. of Jeanne de Hacqueville and Guillaume le Jars, Seigneur de Gournay; had two brothers and three sisters; self-educated. ❖ Considered the French Minerva, acted as assistant, editor and representative for Montaigne and was editor of a new edition of his *Essays* (1595); argued that women are equal to men in *Égalité des hommes et des femmes* (1622) and despaired of women's situation in *Grief des dames* (1626); lived a rich intellectual life, corresponding with Cardinal Richelieu, Cardinal du Perron, Madame de Loges, Guez de Balzac, the Du Puy brothers, and Justus Lipsius; though she was thought to be old-fashioned for her allegiance to Renaissance values, had a successful 1st book, *Le Proumenoir de M. de Montaigne* (1594), now considered the 1st French psychological novel; attended Parisian salons and had own salon, which may well have been the place where the French Academy was conceived as a center for intellectual activity. ❖ See also Marjorie Henry Ilsley, *A Daughter of the Renaissance: Marie le Jars de Gournay, her life and works* (Mouton, 1963); and *Women in World History*.

GOURY DE CHAMPGRAND, Alexandrine Sophie (1773–1860). *See Bawr, Alexandrine de.*

GOUVERNEUR, Mrs. Samuel L. (1803–1850). *See Monroe, Maria Hester.*

GOUWS, Ingrid (b. 1948). *See Winterbach, Ingrid.*

GOUZE, Marie (1748–1793). *See Gouges, Olympe de.*

GOVE, Mary (1810–1884). *See Nichols, Mary Gove.*

GOVOROVA, Olena (1973—). Ukrainian triple jumper. Born Sept 18, 1973, in Odessa, Ukraine. ❖ Won a bronze medal at World championships (1997) and at Sydney Olympics (2000).

GOVRIN, Gloria (1942—). American ballet dancer. Born Nov 9, 1945, in Newark, New Jersey. ❖ Trained with Ivan Tarasoff at school of American Ballet in NY, among others; danced with New York City Ballet throughout career, creating roles in numerous works by Balanchine, including *Valses et Variations* (1961), *A Midsummer Night's Dream* (1961), *Clarinade* (1964), *Trois Valses Romantiques* (1967), and *The Nutcracker,* and dancing featured parts in *Symphony in C, Firebird, Orpheus,* and others.

GOWER, Pauline (1910–1947). British aviator. Name variations: Pauline Fahie. Born Pauline Mary de Peauly Gower in 1910; died soon after childbirth on Mar 2, 1947; dau. of Sir Robert Vaughan Gower (politician and member of Parliament); educated by Sacred Heart nuns at a school in Tunbridge Wells; m. William Fahie, in the summer of 1945; children: twin boys, including Michael Fahie (b. 1947). ❖ British Air Transport officer during WWII, began flying at 18 and was a licensed pilot by 20; with pilot Dorothy Spicer, established an air-taxi service; published *Women with Wings* (1938); during WWII, was made commandant of women's section of Air Transport Auxiliary (ATA, 1940), whose pilots performed many war air services, including flying fighter planes from the factory to frontline defense air stations and ferrying home damaged aircraft; was also appointed to the board of British Overseas Airways Corporation (BOAC, 1943), the 1st woman to be appointed to such a position in UK and, possibly, the 1st to serve on the board of a state airline anywhere in the world. ❖ See also Michael Fahie, *A Harvest of Memories: The Life of Pauline Gower M.B.E.* (1999); and *Women in World History*.

GOWING, Margaret (1921–1998). English historian. Name variations: Margaret Mary Gowing. Born Margaret Mary Elliott, April 26, 1921; died Nov 7, 1998; London School of Economics, BS; m. Donald J.G. Gowing, 1944 (died 1969). ❖ An internationally recognized historian of science, was employed at the Board of Trade (1941–45); worked on a project on the history of war as a Cabinet Office researcher (1945–59); served as historian and archivist at UK Atomic Energy Authority (1959–66) and as reader in contemporary history at University of Kent (1966–72); as Linacre College fellow, served as 1st professor of history of science at Oxford University (1973–86); appointed CBE (1981); retired (1986). Best remembered as author (with Louis Arnold) of *Independence and Deterrence* (2 vols., 1974), authoritative history of Britain's nuclear policies from 1945 to 1952, which achieved status of a classic.

GOYETTE, Cynthia (1946—). American swimmer. Name variations: Cynthia Goyette Shroeder. Born Aug 13, 1946, in Detroit, Michigan;

graduate of Wayne State University, 1973, with a BA in Textiles and Fashion Merchandising; m. Bill Shroeder. ❖ At Tokyo Olympics, won a gold medal in 4 x 100-meter medley relay (1964); 5-time NAAU indoor breaststroke champion, was also the only woman swimmer to win 4 consecutive national breaststroke titles.

GOYETTE, Danielle (1966—). Canadian ice-hockey player. Born Jan 30, 1966, in St. Nazaire, Quebec, Canada. ❖ Won a team silver medal at Nagano (1998), the 1st Olympics to feature women's ice hockey; won team gold medals at World championships (1992, 1994, 1997, 2001); won a team gold medal at Salt Lake City Olympics (2002) and a team gold medal at Torino Olympics (2006).

GOYSHCHIK-NASANOVA, Tatyana (1952—). Soviet runner. Name variations: Tatyana Nasanova. Born June 1952 in USSR. ❖ At Moscow Olympics, won a gold medal in 4 x 400-meter relay (1980).

GOZZI, Luisa Bergalli (1703–1779). See Bergalli, Luisa.

GRABAU, Mary Antin (1881–1949). See Antin, Mary.

GRABLE, Betty (1916–1973). American film actress. Name variations: acted under the name of Frances Dean; made a recording under the name of Ruth Haag. Born Ruth Elizabeth Grable in South St. Louis, Missouri, Dec 18, 1916; died in Las Vegas, Nevada, July 2, 1973; youngest of two daughters of Leon Grable (accountant and stockbroker) and Lillian Rose (Hoffman) Grable; attended Mary's Institute, in Missouri, and the Hollywood Profession School; m. Jackie Coogan (actor), Dec 20, 1937 (div. 1940); m. Harry James (bandleader), July 11, 1943 (div. 1965); children: (2nd m.) 2 daughters, Victoria James (b. 1944) and Jessica James (b. 1946). ❖ Legendary Hollywood film actress, appeared in bit parts for years before appearing in the Fred Astaire-Ginger Rogers classic *The Gay Divorcée* (1934), performing a zany number called "Let's Knock Knees"; embarked on her "Betty Co-ed" period with Paramount, playing in a string of "B" features with titles like *College Swing* (1938) and *Campus Confessions* (1938); with career in a slump (1939), appeared in vaudeville and Broadway show *Du Barry Was a Lady*, with show-stopping dance number, "Well, Did You Evah" which led to 20th Century-Fox; replaced Alice Faye in *Down Argentine Way*, then starred with Faye in another rousing musical, *Tin Pan Alley* (1940); went on to make a series of splashy musicals during next decade, among them *Song of the Islands* (1942), *Footlight Serenade* (1942), *Springtime in the Rockies* (1942), *Sweet Rosie O'Grady* (1943), *Four Jills in a Jeep* (1944) and *The Dolly Sisters* (1945); popularity peaked during WWII, when GIs selected her as their number one "pin-up girl"; made a series of pictures with Dan Dailey: *Mother Wore Tights* (1947), *My Blue Heaven* (1950) and *Call Me Mister* (1951); also made radio appearances on such shows as "Lux Radio Theater" and "Suspense"; best known film of 1950s was not a musical at all, but the comedy *How To Marry a Millionaire* (1953); retired from the screen (1955), but often appeared on stage over the years. ❖ See also *Women in World History*.

GRABOWSKI, Halina (1928–2003). Polish soldier. Born Jan 29, 1928, in Poland; died April 23, 2003, in Independence, Ohio. ❖ At 16, was a Polish soldier in the Warsaw Uprising against the Nazis (1944); wounded, became a prisoner of war; moved with husband to Cleveland, Ohio (1952). Awarded Poland's A.K. Cross.

GRABOWSKI, Petra (1952—). East German kayaker. Born Jan 31, 1952, in East Germany. ❖ At Munich Olympics, won a silver medal in K2 500 meters (1972).

GRACE, Patricia (1937—). New Zealand novelist and short-story writer. Name variations: Ngati Toa; Ngati Raukawa; Te Ati Awa. Born 1937 in Wellington, New Zealand; children: 7. ❖ Worked as primary and secondary school teacher; was 1st Maori woman to publish short-story collection in English; writings, which often focus on extended families and problems of race and class, include *Waiariki* (1975), *Mutuwhenua* (1978), *The Dream Sleepers* (1980), *Potiki* (1986), *Electric City and Other Stories* (1987), *Selected Stories* (1991), *The Sky People* (1994), and *Baby No-Eyes* (1998); children's books, with Robyn Kahukiwa, include *The Kuia and the Spider* (1981) and *Watercress Tuna and the Children of Champion Street* (1984). Received New Zealand Book Award for fiction and Scholarship in Letters.

GRACE, Princess of Monaco (1928–1982). See Kelly, Grace.

GRACEN, Elizabeth (1960—). Miss America and actress. Name variations: Elizabeth Ward. Born Elizabeth Ward, April 3, 1960, in Booneville, Arkansas; dau. of James and Patricia (Hampe) Ward; m. a man named Gracen, 1982 (div. 1984); m. Brendan Hughes (actor), 1989

(div. 1994). ❖ As Elizabeth Ward, named Miss America (1982), representing Arkansas; as an actress, appeared in films *Marked for Death, Pass the Ammo* and on tv, most prominently in role of Amanda on "Highlander: The Series" and "Highlander: The Raven." Admitted to having a sexual liaison with President Bill Clinton when he was governor of Arkansas, causing a bit of a stir.

GRADANTE, Anna-Maria (1976—). German judoka. Born Dec 26, 1976, in Wermelskirchen, Germany. ❖ Won a bronze medal for 48 kg extra-lightweight at Sydney Olympics (2000).

GRAEME, Elizabeth (1737–1801). See Ferguson, Elizabeth Graeme.

GRAF, Steffi (1969—). German tennis player. Born Stefanie Maria Graf, June 14, 1969, in Bruhl, Germany; m. Andre Agassi (tennis player), Oct 2001; children: Jaden (b. 2001) and Jaz (b. 2003). ❖ Under father's guidance, began taking tennis lessons at age 4 and became the 2nd youngest player to receive a ranking on turning professional at 13; won 1st Grand Slam title at French Open (1987), the 1st of 6 French Open victories; became the #1-ranked player on the professional circuit and would hold that ranking for 186 consecutive weeks, the longest unbroken #1 ranking in tennis history; swept all 4 Grand Slam tournaments (1988); won a gold medal at Seoul Olympics (1988); on winning the US Open (1995), became the 1st woman to win each of the four Grand Slam singles titles at least 4 times; facing stiff competition from younger players and sidelined several times for injuries, saw her game suffer (late 1990s), although victory at the French Open (1999) added a 22nd Grand Slam singles title to her career; announced retirement from professional tennis (summer 1999). Inducted into International Tennis Hall of Fame (2004). ❖ See also *Women in World History*.

GRAF, Stephanie (1973—). Austrian runner. Born April 26, 1973, in Klagenfurt, Austria. ❖ Won a silver medal for 800 meters at Sydney Olympics (2000) and a silver medal at World championships (2001).

GRAFFENRIED, Mary Clare de (1849–1921). See De Graffenried, Clare.

GRAFFIGNY, Françoise de (1695–1758). French novelist and playwright. Name variations: Françoise de Grafigny. Born Françoise d'Issembourg d' Happoncourt, Feb 13, 1695, in Nancy, France; died Dec 12, 1758, in Paris; dau. of an officer in the Duke of Lorraine's gendarmerie; married and separated. ❖ Suffered abuse in marriage and sought refuge with Émilie du Châtelet and Voltaire after husband's imprisonment for violence against her; her *Lettres d'une Péruvienne* represent an important development in the epistolary novel; other writings include *Le mauvais exemple, nouvelle espagnole* (1745), *Lettres d'une Péruvienne* (1747), *Ziman et Zenise, comédie* (1749), *Cénie* (1751), *La Fille d'Astride* (1759) and *Vie privée de Voltaire et de Mme du Châtelet* (1820).

GRAFIGNY, Françoise de (1695–1758). See Graffigny, Françoise de.

GRAFTON, Garth (1861–1922). See Duncan, Sara Jeanette.

GRAFTON, Sue (1940). American mystery novelist. Born April 24, 1940, in Louisville, Kentucky; dau. of Chip Warren Grafton (municipal bond attorney and writer) and Vivian Boisseau (Harnsberger) Grafton; University of Louisville, BA in English, 1961; m. 3rd husband Stephen F. Humphrey, 1978; children: (1st m.) Leslie Flood Carnes; (2nd m.) Jay and Jamie Schmidt. ❖ Published 1st novel, *Keziah Dane* (1967), then *The Lolly-Madonna War* (1969); wrote for tv movies and episodic; flipping hard-boiled crime novels on their ear, created the sassy, twice-divorced private investigator Kinsey Millhone who lives in Santa Teresa, California, and drives an old VW bug; published the 1st Millhone book, *A is for Alibi* (1982), followed by *B is for Burglar* (1985), *E is for Evidence* (1988), *H is for Homicide* (1991), *K is for Killer* (1994), *N is for Noose* (1998), and *Q is for Quarry* (2002), among others. Received Shamus Award (1985, 1990, 1994) and Anthony Award (1985, 1986, 1990).

GRAHAM, Barbara Wood (1923–1955). American executed at San Quentin. Born 1923; executed for murder in San Quentin by cyanide poisoning, June 3 (some sources cite June 5), 1955; m. 4 times; children: one. ❖ To the final hour, claimed her innocence, but a troubled past and her condemnation by a sensationalized press ensured her execution. ❖ See also film *I Want to Live!*, starring Susan Hayward (1958); and *Women in World History*.

GRAHAM, Bette Nesmith (1924–1980). American entrepreneur. Name variations: Bette Clair McMurray; Bette Clair Nesmith. Born Bette Claire McMurray in Dallas, Texas, 1924; died in 1980; m. Warren Nesmith, 1942 (div.); m. Robert Graham, 1962 (div. 1975); children:

(1st m.) Michael Nesmith (actor and songwriter). ❖ Invented Liquid Paper; sold her invention to the Gillette Corporation for $47.5 million, plus royalties (1970), which allowed her to spend her last years doing charity work. ❖ See also *Women in World History.*

GRAHAM, Elizabeth N. (1878–1966). See Arden, Elizabeth.

GRAHAM, Euphemia (d. 1469). Countess of Douglas. Name variations: Euphemia Douglas; Euphemia Hamilton; Lady Hamilton. Died 1469; dau. of Patrick Graham of Kilpont and Euphemia Stewart (c. 1375–1415), countess of Strathearn; m. Archibald Douglas, 5th earl of Douglas, in 1425; m. James Hamilton, 1st Lord Hamilton; children: (1st m.) 3, including Margaret Douglas (b. around 1427). ❖ See also *Women in World History.*

GRAHAM, Florence (1878–1966). See Arden, Elizabeth.

GRAHAM, Georgia (1900–1988). American modern dancer. Name variations: Geordie or Jeordie Graham. Born Georgia Graham, Mar 1, 1900, in Allegheny, Pennsylvania; grew up in Santa Barbara, California; died 1988; dau. of Dr. George Graham (physician) and Jane Beers Graham; sister of Mary Graham (1896–1949) and dancer Martha Graham. ❖ Studied at Denishawn school in Los Angeles, California, along with sister Martha; performed with touring concert groups of Ruth St. Denis and Ted Shawn (1922–27), where she also created roles in St. Denis' *Sonata Tragica* (1922), *The Spirit of the Sea* (1923), *Waltzes* (1925), and Shawn's *Pas de Quatre* (1925), *Bubble Dance* (1925), and *General Wu's Farewell to His Wife* (1926), among others; was member of company's oriental tour group; performed in numerous early works by sister Martha including *Primitive Mysteries* (1931), *Ceremonials* (1932), and *Six Miracle Plays* (1933); taught at Martha Graham's school and at Neighborhood Playhouse for a number of years.

GRAHAM, Isabella (1742–1814). Scottish-American educator and philanthropist. Born Isabella Marshall, July 29, 1742, in Lanarkshire, Scotland; died in NY, July 27, 1814; m. Dr. John Graham (army surgeon and local widower), 1765 (died 1773); children: 5, including Joan Graham Bethune. ❖ Accompanied husband to Canada where he was a physician with a British army regiment (1767); moved to Antigua when he was transferred (1772); when husband died (1773), was left penniless and pregnant with 5th child; returned to Scotland to live with father and opened a school in their home which expanded into a girls' boarding school in Edinburgh; moved to NY (1789), where she established a successful seminary for young ladies; along with Elizabeth Ann Seton and other women (1797), organized the Society for the Relief of Poor Widows with Small Children and was its director; with daughter Joan Bethune, founded the Orphan Asylum Society (1806).

GRAHAM, Joyce Maxtone (1901–1953). See Maxtone Graham, Joyce.

GRAHAM, Katharine (1917–2001). American newspaper publisher. Name variations: Kay Graham; Mrs. Phil Graham; Katharine Meyer. Born Katharine Meyer on June 16, 1917, in New York City; died July 17, 2001, in Idaho; dau. of Eugene Meyer (owner of the *Washington Post*) and Agnes Elizabeth (Ernst) Meyer (1887–1970, a publisher, journalist and social worker); graduated from the University of Chicago, 1938; m. attorney Philip Graham (attorney and publisher), 1940 (died 1963); children: Elizabeth "Lally" Graham (b. 1944, who writes under married name Lally Weymouth); Donald E. Graham (b. 1945); William Graham (b. 1948); Stephen Graham (b. 1952). ❖ Worked as a journalist in San Francisco before joining staff of *Washington Post*, which her father had purchased some years earlier; married attorney Philip Graham (1940), who eventually became publisher of the family's newspaper and greatly expanded its operations and reputation; following husband's suicide (1963), became publisher and guided the *Post* through its most turbulent period during and after its publication of the notorious "Pentagon Papers" and its investigative reporting of the Watergate affair, the revelations of which led to the resignation of President Richard Nixon (1974); elected 1st female president of the American Newspaper Publishers Association; was the 1st woman to serve on the board of the Associated Press; by the time of her retirement, was one of only two women in the nation leading a Fortune 500 company and had transformed a newspaper that had once been called "a political hack paper" into one of the world's most respected sources of information, known for its carefully considered editorial opinion. ❖ See also autobiography *Personal History* (Knopf, 1997); Carol Felsenthal, *Power, Privilege and the* Post: *The Katharine Graham Story* (Putnam, 1993); and *Women in World History.*

GRAHAM, Kim (1971—). American runner. Born Mar 26, 1971, in Durham, North Carolina; attended Clemson University, 1991–93.

❖ Won a gold medal for the 4 x 100-meter relay at Atlanta Olympics (1996).

GRAHAM, Laurie (1962—). See Rinker, Laurie.

GRAHAM, Lorraine (1973—). See Graham-Fenton, Lorraine.

GRAHAM, Margaret (d. 1380). Countess of Menteith. Name variations: Mary Graham; countess of Albany. Acceded as countess of Menteith, April 29, 1360. Born before 1334; died 1380; interred at Inchmahome Priory, Perthshire; dau. of Sir John Graham of Abercorn and Mary de Menteith (d. 1346), countess of Menteith; m. John Murray, lord of Bothwell, after 1348; m. Thomas, earl of Mar, c. 1354 (div. 1359); m. John Drummond of Concraig, c. 1359; m. Robert Stewart of Fife (c. 1339–1420), 1st duke of Albany (r. 1398–1420), prime minister to his brother Robert III, king of Scotland, and regent to James I, c. Sept 9, 1361; children: (4th m.) Murdoch (b. around 1362), duke of Albany; Isabel Stewart (fl. 1390–1410, who m. Alexander Leslie and Walter of Dirleton); Joan Stewart (who m. Robert Stewart of Lorn, 1st Lord Lorn); Beatrice Stewart (d. around 1424, who m. James Douglas, 7th earl of Douglas); Mary Stewart (who m. William Abernethy); Janet Stewart (betrothed as a child on July 20, 1371, to David, infant son of Sir Bartholomew de Loen and Lady Philippa Mowbray but marriage probably did not take place); Margaret Stewart (who m. John Swinton). Following Margaret Graham's death, Robert m. Muriel Keith and had 5 more children.

GRAHAM, Maria Dundas (1785–1842). See Callcott, Maria.

GRAHAM, Martha (1894–1991). American dancer and choreographer. Born in Allegheny, Pennsylvania, May 11, 1894; died April 1, 1991, in New York City; dau. of Dr. George Graham (physician) and Jane Beers Graham; sister of dancer Georgia Graham; graduated from Santa Barbara High School, 1913; attended Cumnock School of Expression, 1913–16; m. Erick Hawkins, Sept 20, 1948 (div. 1952). ❖ Founder and major leader of the modernist movement in American dance and one of the most famous dancers and choreographers of the 20th century; enrolled in Ruth St. Denis School of Dancing and the Related Arts (the "Denishawn" school of dance, 1916); scored success in title role of Denishawn production of *Xochitl* (1920); performed in Greenwich Village Follies (1924–25); taught at Milton School of Dance (1925); began teaching dancing at the Eastman School of Music (1925); performed 1st solo dance recital (1926); premiered *Revolt* (1927), then *Lamentations* (1930); appeared in performance of *Rite of Spring* with Leopold Stokowski and Philadelphia Orchestra (1930); premiered *Primitive Mysteries* (1931); was 1st dancer to win a Guggenheim fellowship (1932); performed at opening gala of Radio City Music Hall (1932); taught at Bennington College Summer Dance Festival (1934–38); began collaboration with designer Isamu Noguchi in *Frontier* (1935); performed at White House (1937); premiered *American Document* (1938); premiered *Appalachian Spring* at Library of Congress (1944); premiered *Judith* (1951); opened Martha Graham Dance Company and School of Contemporary Dance (1952); toured Europe (1954, 1963), then Asia and Israel (1955); premiered *Episodes* in joint dance program with George Balanchine (1959); retired from performing (1970). Awarded Presidential Medal of Freedom (1976), the 1st dancer and choreographer to be so honored; received Kennedy Center Honors (1984), the Knight of the French Legion of Honor (1984), and the Order of the Precious Butterfly with Diamond from Japan (1990). ❖ See also *The Notebooks of Martha Graham* (Harcourt, 1973); Agnes De Mille, *Martha: The Life and Work of Martha Graham* (Random House, 1991); Kathilyn Solomon Probosz, *Martha Graham* (Dillon Press, 1995); Ernestine Stodelle, *Deep Song: The Dance Story of Martha Graham* (Schirmer, 1984); Don McDonagh, *Martha Graham: A Biography* (Praeger, 1973); Walter Terry, *Frontiers of Dance: The Life of Martha Graham* (Crowell, 1975); and *Women in World History.*

GRAHAM, Mrs. (1785–1842). See Callcott, Maria.

GRAHAM, Nancy. See Ludington, Nancy.

GRAHAM, Mrs. Phil (b. 1917). See Graham, Katharine.

GRAHAM, Rose (1879–1974). New Zealand innkeeper. Name variations: Rose McBride. Born Rose McBride, Sept 25, 1879, at Gillespies Beach, South Westland, New Zealand; died Feb 3, 1974, in Christchurch, New Zealand; dau. of Archibald McBride (innkeeper and shopkeeper) and Margaret (McGrath) McBride; m. James William Graham, 1907 (died 1921); children: 2 daughters and 1 son. ❖ Managed Franz Josef Glacier

Hotel at Waiho with husband (1911–47); performed all cooking, housekeeping, and laundry duties and eventually developed 6-room inn into hotel for 120 guests. ❧ See also *Dictionary of New Zealand Biography* (Vol. 3).

GRAHAM, Sheila (1904–1988). English-born gossip columnist. Born Lily Sheil, Sept 15, 1904, in London, England; died Nov 17, 1988, in Palm Beach, Florida; m. Trevor Westbrook (div. 1946); m. John Graham Gillam (div.); m. Stanley Wojtkiewkz, 1953 (div. 1956). ❧ Brought up in an orphanage; became a London showgirl and model; moved to US (1933); launched a Hollywood gossip column (1935); wrote *The Real Scott Fitzgerald, The Rest of the Story, College for One, The Garden of Allah, How to Marry Super Rich, Confessions of a Gossip Columnist* and *Hollywood Revisited;* served as the model for the heroine of Fitzgerald's *The Last Tycoon.* ❧ See also autobiography *A Stage of Heat* (1972) and memoir *Beloved Infidel* (1958), recounting the four years she lived with F. Scott Fitzgerald (1936–40), later filmed with Gregory Peck and Deborah Kerr (1959).

GRAHAM, Shirley (1896–1977). African-American playwright and composer. Name variations: Shirley Graham Du Bois. Born Shirley Lola Graham, Nov 11, 1896, in Indianapolis, Indiana; died Mar 27, 1977, in Peking, China; dau. of the Rev. David Graham and Etta B. Graham; Oberlin College, BA and MA in music; m. Shadrach McCants, 1918 (div. 1927); m. W.E.B. Du Bois (writer and founder of NAACP), 1951 (died 1963); children: 2. ❧ Directed Negro United at Federal Theater, Chicago; founded civil-rights magazine *Freedomways* (1960); moved with husband to Ghana after continuous harassment from US officials (1961); left Ghana after coup and moved with son to Cairo, where she continued work on behalf of liberation causes; writings include *Tom-Tom* (1932), *Dust to Earth* (1940), *It's Morning* (1940), *His Day is Marching On* (1971), and *Zulu Heart* (1974); also wrote biographies of Phillis Wheatley, Frederick Douglass, George Washington Carver, Booker T. Washington, Gamal Abdel Nasser, Julius Nyerere, Jean Baptiste du Sable, and Paul Robeson.

GRAHAM, Wilhelmina Barns- (1912–2004). *See Barns-Graham, Wilhelmina.*

GRAHAM-FENTON, Lorraine (1973—). Jamaican runner. Name variations: Lorraine Fenton; Lorraine Graham; Lorraine Fenton-Graham. Born Lorraine Graham, Sept 8, 1973, in Mandeville, Jamaica. ❧ Won silver medals for 400 meters and 4 x 400-meter relay at Sydney Olympics (2000); at World championships, won a silver medal for the 400 and a gold medal for 4 x 400-meter relay (2001).

GRAHAME, Christine (1944—). Scottish politician. Name variations: Christine Creech. Born in 1944 in Burton-on-Trent. ❧ Became a solicitor (1986); stood as a prospective candidate for Tweeddale, Ettrick and Lauderdale (1992) and later as European candidate for South of Scotland; serves as SNP member of the Scottish Parliament for South of Scotland.

GRAHAME, Gloria (1924–1981). American actress. Born Gloria Grahame Hallward on Nov 28, 1924, in Pasadena, California; died of cancer in New York, NY, Oct 5, 1981; dau. of Michael (industrial designer) and Jean (MacDougall) Hallward (actress); attended Hollywood High School; m. Stanley Clements (actor), 1945 (div. 1948); m. Nicholas Ray (director), 1948 (div. 1952); m. Cy Howard, 1954 (div. 1957); m. Tony Ray (her stepson); children: (2nd m.) Tim Ray; (3rd m.) Paulette Howard; (4th m.) 2. ❧ At 9, began performing with the Pasadena Community Playhouse; made Broadway debut (1943) and was signed to an MGM contract within a year; with her seductive voice and pouty mouth, played wayward women with enormous success (1950s), winning an Academy Award as Best Supporting Actress for her role in *The Bad and the Beautiful* (1952); was also memorable in *The Big Heat* (1953) and as the "can't-say-no girl" in the musical *Oklahoma!* (1955); made over 40 films, including *Blonde Fever* (1944), *It's a Wonderful Life* (1946), *It Happened in Brooklyn* (1947), *Crossfire* (1947), *Song of the Thin Man* (1947), *Merton of the Movies* (1947), *The Greatest Show on Earth* (1952), *Macao* (1952), *Sudden Fear* (1952), *Man on a Tightrope* (1953), *The Big Heat* (1953), *Not as a Stranger* (1954), *The Cobweb* (1955), *The Man Who Never Was* (1956), *Odds Against Tomorrow* (1959), *Chilly Scenes of Winter* (1979), *A Nightingale Sang in Berkeley Square* (1979), *Melvin and Howard* (1980). ❧ See also Peter Turner, *Film Stars Don't Die in Liverpool* (Grove, 1986); and *Women in World History.*

GRAHAME, Margot (1911–1982). English-born stage and screen actress. Born Margaret Clark, Feb 20, 1911, in Canterbury, Kent, England; grew up in South Africa; died Jan 1, 1982, in London; m. Francis Lister, 1934 (div. 1936); m. Alan McMartin, 1938 (div. 1946); m. Augustus Dudley Peters, 1958 (died 1972). ❧ Made stage debut in Johannesburg as Sally Jellyband in *The Scarlet Pimpernel* (1926); made London debut in *A Cup of Kindness* (1929) and film in *Rookery Nook* (1930), followed by *Stamboul, Illegal, Sorrell and Son, The Broken Melody, The Informer, The Three Musketeers, Crime over London, Counterfeit, The Buccaneer, The Crimson Pirate, The Beggar's Opera* and *Saint Joan,* among others.

GRAHAME JOHNSTONE, Anne (1928–1998). English illustrator. Born June 1, 1928, in England; died of cancer, May 25, 1998, in England; dau. of Capt E. Grahame Johnstone and Doris Zinkeisen (designer); niece of Anna Zinkeisen (painter); twin sister of Janet Grahame Johnston (illustrator); never married. ❧ With sister, illustrated over 100 books, including Dodie Smith's *One-Hundred and One Dalmations* and works by J.M. Barrie, Charles Kingsley, Hans Christian Andersen, and the Brothers Grimm; on death of sister (1979), illustrated editions of *Peter Pan* and *The Water Babies* and wrote and illustrated two books about Santa Claus; specialized in period costume.

GRAHAME JOHNSTONE, Doris (1898–1991). *See Zinkeisen, Doris.*

GRAHAME JOHNSTONE, Janet (1928–1979). English illustrator. Born June 1, 1928, in England; died in an accident in 1979; dau. of Capt E. Grahame Johnstone and Doris Zinkeisen (designer); niece of Anna Zinkeisen (painter); twin sister of Anne Grahame Johnston (illustrator); never married. ❧ With sister, illustrated over 100 books, including Dodie Smith's *One-Hundred and One Dalmations, The Starlight Barking,* and *The Midnight Kittens,* and Paul Gallico's *Manxmouse, The Man Who was Magic* and *Miracle in the Wilderness;* specialized in animals and birds.

GRAHN, Judy (1940—). American novelist and poet. Born 1940 in Chicago, Illinois; raised in New Mexico. ❧ Writer whose poetry and criticism focus on experiences of ordinary women and lesbian history and mythology, wrote *The Common Woman* (1969), *The Work of a Common Woman* (1980), *The Queen of Wands* (1982), *Another Mother Tongue: Gay Words, Gay Worlds* (1984), *The Highest Apple: Sappho and the Lesbian Poetic Tradition* (1985), *The Queen of Swords* (1987), *Mundane's World* (1988), *Really Reading Gertrude Stein* (1989), and *Blood, Bread, and Roses: How Menstruation Created the World* (1993).

GRAHN, Lucile (1819–1907). Danish ballerina. Born Lucina Alexia Grahn in Copenhagen, Denmark, June 30, 1819; died in Munich, Germany, April 1, 1907; dau. of a Norwegian officer and his Jutland wife; m. Friederich Young (tenor), 1856 (died 1884); no children. ❧ At 10, became the protégée of August Bournonville, head of Royal Ballet School; at 16, danced starring role in Bournonville's *Waldemar* and a year later appeared in his *La Sylphide,* becoming the toast of Copenhagen; set out for France (1837), where she became a student of Jean-Baptiste Barrez, director of Paris Opéra's ballet school, before being summoned back to Copenhagen; granted permission to perform in Germany, moved on independently to Paris, ignoring a number of summonses from Copenhagen; granted a permanent dismissal from the Danish Royal Ballet without pension (1838), which left her free to pursue her career wherever she saw fit; never again returned to her homeland; at Paris Opéra, thrilled Paris audiences with performance in *La Sylphide;* career at the Opéra ended prematurely (1840), with a knee injury; debuted in St Petersburg in *Giselle* (1843), then went on to Milan, Italy, where she made some 40 appearances in *Elda assia Il Patto degli Spiriti* by Bernardo Vestris (1844); career reached its zenith during a 5-year period in England, beginning with modest debut in *Lady Henrietta,* a triumph in *Eoline* (1844), and an appearance in Perrot's famous *Le Pas de Quatre,* considered one of the 1st "abstract" ballets; now a star of substantial magnitude, shunned Paris and returned instead to Germany, where she fell in love, married, and retired (1856); later at Munich Hoftheatre, choreographed a number of ballets, including the *divertissements* for Richard Wagner operas. ❧ See also *Women in World History.*

GRAINÉ. *Variant of Grace.*

GRAINGER, Katherine (1975—). Scottish rower. Born Nov 12, 1975, in Glasgow, Scotland; attended Edinburgh University. ❧ Won a silver medal for quadruple sculls at Sydney Olympics (2000); at World championships, won a gold medal for coxless pair (2003); won a silver medal for coxless pair at Athens Olympics (2004).

GRAINGER, Violet May (1887–1971). *See Cottrell, Violet May.*

GRAJALES, Mariana (1808–1893). Afro-Cuban revolutionary. Name variations: Mariana Grajales de Maceo; Mariana Grajales y Cuello. Born in Santiago de Cuba, June 26, 1808; died in exile in Kingston, Jamaica, Nov 28, 1893; dau. of José Grajales and Teresa Grajales (free blacks); m. Fructuoso Regüeyferos y Hecheverria, 1831 (died 1840); became the common-law wife of Marcos Maceo (Venezuelan immigrant and farmer who fought for independence), then legally married, July 1851 (killed 1869); children: (1st m.) 4; (2nd m.) 9, including General Antonio Maceo Grajales (1845–1896), the Cuban revolution's "Titan of Bronze" ❖ Championed rights of both slaves and free blacks during her nation's struggle against Spanish rule; is universally regarded by Cubans as "Madre de la Patria" (Mother of the Nation). Honored by Cuba in many ways, including two postage stamps issued on Mar 8, 1969, and on Nov 27, 1993. ❖ See also *Women in World History.*

GRAMATICA, Emma (1875–1965). Italian stage and screen actress. Born Mar 22, 1875, in Borgo San Donnino (now Fidenza, Emilia-Romagna), Italy; died Nov 8, 1965, in Ostia Lido, Italay; sister of Irma Gramatica (actress). ❖ Well-known star, appeared in *Le Détour, La Marche Nuptiale, Le Voleur, Bonne Fille, L'Enchantement, Le Scandale, La Patronne, La Meilleure des femmes, Le Lys, Père et Fils, Francillon* and *I Figli D'Ercole;* toured with Eleonora Duse and Ermete Zacconi in *La Società Equivoca* and *La Gioconda* (1899); also toured for several years with Tina di Lorenzo and Flavio Ando and was subsequently a leading lady with Zacconi; made over 25 films.

GRAMATICA, Irma (1873–1962). Italian actress. Born Nov 25, 1873, in Fiume, Italy; died Oct 14, 1962, in Tavarnuzze, Italy; sister of Emma Gramatica (actress); m. Arnaldo Cottin Ando. ❖ Made stage debut with Cesare Rossi (1887); starred with Eleonora Duse (1896) and later opposite Ermete Zacconi, Raspantini, and Enrico Reinach; teamed with Virgilio Talli and Oreste Calabresi to play leads in a number of plays; also appeared in films.

GRAMATTÉ, S.C. Eckhardt (1899–1974). *See Eckhardt-Gramatté, S.C.*

GRAMCKO, Ida (1924–1994). Venezuelan poet, playwright and short-story writer. Born Oct 9, 1924, in Puerto Cabello, Venezuela; died May 2, 1994; sister of Elsa Gramcko; received degree in philosophy. ❖ Participated in *Viernes* group which included Luz Machado, Ana Enriqueta Terán, and Enriqueta Arvelo Larriva; works, which draw on folklore and legend and seek to express universal themes, include *La vara mágica* (The Magic Wand, 1948), *Poemas* (1952), *Poemas de una psicótica* (Poems of a Psychotic, 1964), and *Lo maximo murmura* (The Loudest Murmur, 1965); was Venezuelan ambassador to USSR (1948) but is most celebrated for her literary achievements.

GRAMMONT, countess of. *See Hamilton, Elizabeth (1641–1708).*

GRAMONT, Elizabeth de (fl. 1875–1935). French memoirist. Name variations: Duchesse de Clermont-Tonnerre, Duchesse de Gramont. Born c. 1875; died after 1935; dau. of duc de Gramont; m. the Duc de Clermont-Tonnerre; children: Béatrix Clermont-Tonnerre. ❖ Published memoirs in 4 volumes in Paris (1928–35) which became a cause celebre. ❖ See also *Women in World History.*

GRANA. *Variant of Grace.*

GRANAHAN, Kathryn E. (1894–1979). American politician. Born Kathryn Elizabeth O'Hay on Dec 7, 1894, in Easton, Pennsylvania; died July 10, 1979, in Norristown, Pennsylvania; interred in Gethsemane Cemetery, Easton, Pennsylvania; dau. of James B. O'Hay and Julia (Reilly) O'Hay; attended public school in Easton, Pennsylvania, and Mount St. Joseph Collegiate Institute in Chestnut Hill, Philadelphia, Pennsylvania; m. William T. Granahan (politician who served 4 terms in US House of Representatives), Nov 20, 1943 (died May 25, 1956). ❖ US Democratic Congresswoman from Pennsylvania (Nov 6, 1956–Jan 3, 1963), worked for Pennsylvania state auditor general (1940–43); following husband's death (1956), replaced him as the Democratic candidate for the 84th Congress and was elected to fill out his term, the 1st woman to represent a Philadelphia district; early in tenure, served on Committee on the District of Columbia, Committee on Government Operation, and Committee on Post Office and Civil Service; as chair of a subcommittee on postal operations (1959), spent much of her congressional career fighting for tougher pornography laws; served in 84th–87th Congresses, but her congressional seat was eliminated (1963), following the census; served as treasurer of US (1963–65). ❖ See also *Women in World History.*

GRANATA, Maria (1921—). Argentinean journalist, poet and novelist. Born 1921 in Buenos Aires, Argentina. ❖ Worked as journalist for newspapers and magazines including *Conducta, La Nación* and *Selecta;* also wrote children's books; writings include *Umbral de tierra* (1942), *Color humano* (1966), *Los viernes de la eternidad* (1971), *Los tumultos, El jubiloso exterminio* and *El sol de los tiempos.*

GRANATO, Cammi (1971—). American ice-hockey player. Born Catherine Granato, Mar 25, 1971, in Downers Grove, Illinois; sister of Tony Granato (hockey player for San Jose Sharks); graduated from Providence College, 1993; attended graduate school at Concordia University, Montreal, Canada. ❖ Led US in scoring at the IIHF Pacific Women's Hockey championship (1996); named Outstanding Forward at the Pacific Women's Hockey championship (1996); named USA Hockey Women's Player of the Year (1996); was leading scorer at the Women's World championship (1997); earned a place on the Women's World championship All-Tournament Team; scored 256 goals in career before Nagano; won a team gold medal at Nagano (1998), the 1st Olympics to feature women's ice hockey; won team silver medals at World championships (1990, 1992, 1994, 1997, 1999, 2000, 2001); won a team silver medal at Salt Lake City Olympics (2002). ❖ See also Mary Turco, *Crashing the Net: The U.S. Women's Olympic Ice Hockey Team and the Road to Gold* (HarperCollins, 1999) and Christina Lessa, *Women Who Win* (Universe, 1998); and *Women in World History.*

GRANCHAROVA, Zoya (1966—). Bulgarian gymnast. Born May 6, 1966, in Bulgaria. ❖ At World championships, won a bronze medal in floor exercises (1981), the 1st medal won by a female Bulgarian gymnast at Worlds; tied for 1st at American Cup (1982).

GRAND, Sarah (1854–1943). *See MacFall, Frances E.*

GRANDE, Constance Alice (1872–1922). *See Barnicoat, Constance Alice.*

GRANDE MADEMOISELLE, La.
See Montpensier, Anne Marie Louise d'Orléans, Duchesse de (1627–1693).
See Dolgorukaia, Alexandra (1836–c. 1914).

GRANDIN, Ethel (1894–1988). American silent-film actress. Born Mar 3, 1894, in NYC; died Sept 28, 1988, in Woodland Hills, California; m. Ray C. Smallwood (director-cinematographer), 1912 (died 1964). ❖ Dubbed The Imp of the IMP Company, starred in the 1st two-reel film produced in Los Angeles; other films include *Blazing Trail, Jane Eyre, Beyond Price, Garments of Truth* and *The Hunch;* formed her own company with husband and starred in *The Adopted Daughter, The Burglar and the Mouse,* and *His Doll Wife;* retired (1922).

GRANDISON, Katharine (fl. 1305–1340). Countess of Salisbury. Fl. between 1305 and 1340; m. William Montacute (1301–1343), 1st earl of Salisbury; children: Philippa Montacute (who m. Robert Mortimer, 2nd earl of March); William de Montacute, 2nd earl of Salisbury (d. 1361, who m. Joan of Kent); John. ❖ Defended the castle of Wark in Northumberland against the Scots for several months (1341). The siege was eventually raised by the arrival of Edward III of England's troops. ❖ See also *Women in World History.*

GRANDMA MOSES (1860–1961). *See Moses, Anna "Grandma."*

GRANDVAL, Marie Felicia (1830–1907). French composer. Name variations: Clemence de Reiset; Vicomtesse de Caroline Blangy; Clemence Vaigrand; Maria Felicita de Reiset; Maria Reiset de Tesier. Born at Chateau de la Cour-de-Bois, Saint-Remy des Monts, Sarthe, Jan 20, 1830; died in Paris on Jan 15, 1907; studied under Saint-Saëns and received instruction from Chopin. ❖ One of the foremost woman composers of her era, began studying music at 6 and studied composition under Friedrich von Flotow; also received instruction from Chopin and studied two years with Camille Saint-Saëns; as a composer, used many names for a number of operas produced in Paris; began to use her own name (1869); wrote oratorios, large choral pieces, chamber music, and symphonies.

GRANDY, Maria (1937–1998). American ballet dancer and teacher. Born Jan 28, 1937, in Portland, Oregon; died of cancer, Mar 28, 1998; m. Seymour Schorr. ❖ Danced with the Robert Joffrey Theater Ballet (1957–58); became a coach in the Joffrey apprentice program (1966), then associate director and director of Joffrey II; staged ballets by Joffrey, Massine and Tudor for the Vienna State Opera Ballet, the Royal Ballet of Flanders and Ottawa Ballet Theater.

GRANGE, Rachel (1682–1745). Scottish imprisoned noblewoman. Name variations: Lady Rachel Grange, Lady Rachel Chiesley, Lady

Rachael Chiesley, Lady Rachel Chicely, Lady of St. Kilda. Born Rachel Chiesley, 1682, in Dalry, Scotland; died in June 1745, on Island of Skye, Scotland; dau. of John Chiesley of Dalry; m. James Erskine (lawyer, lord justice clerk of Court of Session, and later Lord Grange, MP), 1699; children: Christopher, Robert, James, John, Mary, Jean, Rachel. ❖ Born into family with disagreeable streak (her father shot a man, 1689), had a miserable marriage exacerbated by husband's supposed infidelities and her drinking and temper; separated from husband (1730), began stalking him, employing spies to watch his visits to London and intercept his mail; suspecting husband of taking part in the Jacobite uprising of 1715 with his brother earl of Mar, threatened to expose him (1731); was seized and kept on the Island of Hesker (1732–37), then on St. Kilda (1737–43); was "buried" in sham funeral staged by husband to explain disappearance; made contact with friends through a letter but a rescue attempt failed; was transferred to Assynt in Sutherland and finally to Isle of Skye; wrote account of abduction and mistreatment which was presented to the marquis of Brute by John Francis, earl of Mar, and ultimately published in *Scots Magazine* (Nov 1817); died on Isle of Skye after 14 years in captivity.

GRANGER, Josie (1853–1934). American ballet and theatrical dancer. Born 1853 in Baltimore, Maryland; died July 6, 1934, in Freeport, Long Island, NY; m. Pat Rooney I (1848–1892, Irish eccentric dancer and comedian); children: Katherine Rooney, Pat Rooney II (1880–1962, vaudevillian), and Mathilda (Mattie) Rooney, Josie Rooney and Julia Rooney (who performed in vaudeville as The Rooney Sisters). ❖ Made professional debut in a production of the popular show *The Black Crook* (c. 1870); danced in operettas and extravaganzas, including *Humpty Dumpty* in the Tony Devere company; toured with husband for 20 years, performing in a number of his vaudeville acts, including *The Miner's Bowery* and *Lord Rooney;* continued on tour with company for several years, even after his death.

GRANGER, Michele (1970—). American softball player. Born Jan 15, 1970, in Anchorage, Alaska; attended University of Tennessee. ❖ Pitcher, won a team gold medal at the Pan American Games, with 57 strikeouts, 4 shutouts, and 1 perfect game (1995); won a team gold medal at Atlanta Olympics (1996).

GRANHOLM, Jennifer M. (1959—). American politician. Name variations: Jennifer Mulhern Granholm. Born Feb 5, 1959, in Vancouver, British Columbia, Canada; dau. of Civtor Ivar (banking consultant) and Shirley Alfreda (Dowden) Ivar; University of California at Berkeley, BS in political science, 1984; Harvard Law School, JD, 1987; m. Daniel Granholm Mulhern (writer), May 23, 1986; children: 3. ❖ Immigrated with family to US at age 3; grew up in San Francisco Bay Area; became US citizen; served as editor-in-chief of *Harvard Civil Rights/ Civil Liberties Law Review;* began career as judicial law clerk for Judge Damon Keith of US Circuit Court of Appeals in Detroit; admitted to Michigan bar; served as federal prosecutor in US Attorney's Office in Detroit (1990–94); appointed Wayne County Corporation counsel (1994); elected the 1st female attorney general in Michigan (1998) and established the state's 1st high-tech crime unit to prosecute internet crimes; elected the 1st female governor of Michigan (Nov 2002).

GRANIA. *Variant of Grace.*

GRANN, Phyllis (1937—). English-born publisher. Born Sept 2, 1937, in London, England; dau. of Solomon and Louisa (Bois-Smith) Eitingon; Barnard College, BA cum laude, 1958; m. Victor Grann, Sept 26, 1962; children: Alison, David and Edward. ❖ Began career as Nelson Doubleday's secretary at Doubleday (1958–60); was an editor at William Morrow & Co. (1960–62) and David McKay (1962–70); served as senior editor at Simon & Schuster (1970–76), where she was made editor-in-chief of Pocket Books (1974); joined Putnam Berkley as editor-in-chief of G.P. Putnam's Sons (1976); named president and publisher of the Putnam Berkley Group (1984), then CEO (1987) and chair (1991); was one of the most powerful women in publishing, heading the American operations of the Penguin Putnam Group (1996–2001); became vice-chair of Random House (2001); edited such authors as Tom Clancy, Scott Berg, Dick Francis, Robin Cook, Art Buchwald, Lawrence Sanders, Dean Koontz, and Elizabeth Taylor.

GRANT, Amy (1960—). American singer. Born Amy Lee Grant, Nov 25, 1960, in Augusta, Georgia; dau. of Burtonn Paine Grant and Gloria Grant; attended Vanderbilt University; m. Gary Chapman, 1982 (div. 1999); m. Vince Gill (country singer), 2000; children: (1st m.) Matt, Millie and Sara; (2nd m.) Corrina. ❖ Youngest of four daughters, grew up in Nashville; landed deal with Christian label Word records (1975),

singing gospel songs; recorded 1st album *Amy Grant* (1977); became an extremely successful Christian vocalist, releasing such albums as *My Father's Eyes* (1979), *Never Alone* (1980), *Age to Age* (1982) and *Lead Me On* (1988); moved onto pop charts with album *Unguarded* (1985); performed hit duet with Peter Cetera on "The Next Time I Fall" (1986); hit #1 on pop charts with single "Baby, Baby" from album *Heart in Motion* (1991); had success with singles "Like I Love You" and "Takes a Little Time" from album *Behind the Eyes* (1997); released Christmas albums *Home for Christmas* (1992) and *A Christmas to Remember* (1999); made acting debut as blind cellist in tv movie "A Song from the Heart" (1999); was subjected to controversy when she divorced Chapman and subsequently married country music star Vince Gill.

GRANT, Ann (1955—). Zimbabwean field-hockey player. Born May 1955 in Zimbabwe. ❖ At Moscow Olympics, won a gold medal in team competition (1980).

GRANT, Anne (1755–1838). Scottish poet, essayist, and writer. Name variations: Mrs. Grant of Laggan; Anne MacVicar; Anne MacVicar Grant. Born Anne MacVicar in Glasgow, Scotland, Feb 21, 1755; died of the flu in Edinburgh on Nov 8, 1838; dau. of Duncan MacVicar (British army officer) and Catherine Mackenzie; m. James Grant (army chaplain), 1779 (died 1801); children: 12, 8 reached adulthood but only 1, J.P. Grant, survived her. ❖ Grew up among Dutch and British colonists in American colony of Albany (1757–68) and spent a good deal of time with Catherine Van Rensselaer Schuyler, wife of General Philip Schuyler; back in Scotland, following death of husband (1801), published *Poems,* a book by subscription, then published *Letters from the Mountain* (1807), which brought her acclaim; published *Memoirs of an American Lady: Sketches of Manners and Scenery in America as They Existed Previous to the Revolution* (1808), followed by *Essays on the Superstitions of the Highlanders of Scotland* (1811) and "Eighteen Hundred and Thirteen, a Poem" (1814). ❖ See also J.P. Grant, ed. *Memoirs and Letters* (1844); and *Women in World History.*

GRANT, Forrestina (Forrest) Elizabeth (1860–1936). *See Ross, Forrestina Elizabeth.*

GRANT, Jane (1895–1972). American feminist. Born May 29, 1895; died Mar 1972 in Litchfield, Connecticut; 1st wife of Harold W. Ross (publisher), Mar 27, 1920 (div. 1929); m. Richard Harris (editor of *Fortune*), 1939. ❖ One of the founders of the New York Newspaper Women's Club and a charter member of the Algonquin set, was the 1st full-fledged female reporter for *The New York Times;* with 1st husband, co-founded *The New Yorker* and was instrumental in getting him to include Janet Flanner's letters from Paris; refusing to give up her birth name after marrying, was an organizing force behind the formation of the Lucy Stone League. ❖ See also autobiography *Ross, The New Yorker and Me* (1968).

GRANT, Julia (1826–1902). American first lady. Born Julia Boggs Dent on Jan 26, 1826, in St. Louis, Missouri; died Dec 14, 1902, in Washington, DC; 5th of 8 children of Colonel Frederick Dent (planter) and Ellen (Wrenshall) Dent; m. Ulysses Simpson Grant (1822–1885), president of US, 1869–1877), Aug 22, 1848, in St. Louis, Missouri; children: Frederick Dent Grant (1850–1912, served as police commissioner of New York City and ambassador to Austria-Hungary); Ulysses Grant, Jr. (1852–1929, became a prominent lawyer in Republican affairs); Jesse Root Grant (1858–1934, became a lawyer and wrote a book about his father); Ellen Grant, known as Nellie (1855–1922, who m. Englishman Algernon Charles Frederick Sartoris, son of Adelaide Kemble, at the White House in 1874). ❖ Followed husband to forlorn army posts in St. Louis, Detroit, and New York, managing his meager wages and attempting to ward off his growing drinking problem; at start of Civil War, moved family to City Point to be near husband's headquarters and to provide him with the moral support he had come to depend upon; contributed to war effort by tending to the wounded and sewing uniforms; referred to her 8 years in the White House as "a feast of cleverness and wit" (1869–77), though it was a difficult time for husband; with husband, undertook the complete remodeling of White House; her receptions were known for informality and inclusiveness; in final years, befriended Varina Howell Davis, widow of Jefferson Davis, and supported Susan B. Anthony and the suffragists. ❖ See also *The Personal Memoirs of Julia Dent Grant* (ed. by John Y. Simon, Southern Illinois University Press, 1988); and *Women in World History.*

GRANT, Kathryn (1933—). American actress. Name variations: Kathy Grant, Kathryn Grant Crosby, Mrs. Bing Crosby. Born Olive Kathryn Grandstaff, Nov 25, 1933, in Houston, Texas; m. Bing Crosby (singer),

1957 (died 1977); children: Harry and Nathaniel Crosby and Mary Frances Crosby (actress who appeared on "Dallas"). ❖ Won numerous beauty contests; made film debut in *Arrowhead* (1953), followed by *Forever Female, Rear Window, The Phenix City Story, Mister Cory, Five Against the House, Storm Center, Guns of Fort Petticoat, Operation Mad Ball, The 7th Voyage of Sinbad, Anatomy of a Murder* and *The Big Circus*, among others; appeared on tv specials with husband. ❖ See also *Bing and Other Things* and *My Life with Bing*.

GRANT, Lee (1927—). American actress, director, and writer. Name variations: Lyova Rosenthal. Born Lyova Haskell Rosenthal, Oct 31, 1927, in NYC; m. Arnold Manoff (writer), 1951 (div. 1960); m. Joseph Feury (producer), 1962; children: Dinah Manoff (b. 1958, actress). ❖ At 4, made stage debut at the Metropolitan Opera in *L'Orocolo;* on Broadway, won the Critics' Circle Award for *Detective Story* (1949), then named Best Actress at Cannes and nominated for a Best Supporting Oscar for debut performance in the film version (1951); blacklisted in the McCarthy era after refusing to testify against 1st husband before the House Un-American Activities Committee (HUAC, 1951) and rarely worked in film or tv for the next decade; directed an adaptation of Strindberg's *The Stronger* to excellent reviews, followed by *Tell Me a Riddle*, and others. Nominated for Academy Awards for *The Landlord* (1970) and *Voyage of the Damned* and won Best Supporting Actress for *Shampoo* (1975); won an Emmy for performance in the recurring role of Stella Chernak on "Peyton Place" (1966); received an Oscar for Best Feature-Length Documentary, *Down and Out in America* (1987) and the Directors Guild Award for CBS's "Nobody's Child" (1986); granted Women in Film's 1st Lifetime Achievement award (1989).

GRANT, Pauline (1915—). English ballet dancer and theatrical choreographer. Born June 29, 1915, in Mosely, Birmingham, England. ❖ Studied interpretive dance with Ruby Ginner and classical ballet with Antony Tudor and Vera Volkova; at 25, began serving as ballet master of Neighborhood Theater in Kensington (1940); toured with ENSA; performed in *A Night in Venice* in London (1944); staged numerous dances for London's West End musicals and operettas, including *Merrie England* (1945) and *The Babes in the Woods* (1950); worked on ice-shows, revues at Palladium Theatre, and as resident choreographer for Royal Shakespeare Company; held tenure position with Festival Opera of Glyndebourne and with English National Opera at Covent Garden; worked on film *Moll Flanders* (1965) and tv series "The Julie Andrews Show" (1972).

GRANT, Rhoda (1963—). Scottish politician. Born 1963 in Stornoway, Scotland. ❖ Serves as Labour member of the Scottish Parliament for Highlands and Islands; is a member of the Petitions and Rural Development Committees.

GRANT, Valentine (1881–1949). American actress. Born Feb 14, 1881, in Indiana; died Mar 12, 1949, in Orange County, California; m. Sidney Olcott (director). ❖ Replaced Gene Gauntier in husband Sidney Olcott's films, but thought to be a mediocre substitute; films include *Bold Emmett, Ireland's Martyr, The Melting Pot, The Innocent Lie* and *The Belgian.*

GRANT, Zilpah (1794–1874). American educator. Name variations: Zilpah Polly Grant; Zilpah Polly Grant Banister. Born Zilpah Polly Grant, May 30, 1794, in Norfolk, Connecticut; died in Newburyport, Massachusetts, Dec 3, 1874; attended Female Academy of Byfield, Massachusetts; m. William B. Banister (lawyer and politician), Sept 1841 (died 1853). ❖ Always of frail health, grew up under intense pressure, having to aid widowed mother in holding on to family farm; taught at Female Seminary in Byfield, MA, and at a girls' school in Winsted, Connecticut; named a preceptor at Adams Female Academy in East Derry, NH (1824), invited friend Mary Lyon to teacher there and the school flourished.

GRANT DUFF, Shiela (1913–2004). English journalist. Born May 11, 1913, in London, England; died Mar 19, 2004; dau. of Adrian Grant Duff (killed in WWI) and Ursula Grant Duff; granddau. of Sir John Lubbock, 1st Lord Avebury, and Sir Mountstuart Elphinstone Grant Duff; attended St. Margaret Hall, Oxford; m. Noel Newsome, 1942 (div. 1950); m. Micheal Sokolova (who changed his name to Sokolov Grant), c. 1952 (died 1998); children: 2 daughters, 3 sons. ❖ Visited Germany with Goronwy Rees (1932); worked in Paris; became the only full-time British journalist in Prague (1936), writing for *The Observer* and *The Spectator;* returning to England (1937), became an adviser to Winston Churchill on Czechoslovakia; critical of Britain's appeasement of

Germany, wrote 2 influential books in support of a free Czechoslovakia, the bestselling *Europe and the Czechs* (1938) and *A German Protectorate: The Czechs under Nazi Rule* (1940); became editor of the Czech section of the BBC's European Service; had a relationship with Adam von Trott (their letters were published as *A Noble Combat*, 1988). ❖ See also memoir *The Parting of Ways* (1982).

GRANT OF LAGGAN, Mrs. (1755–1838). See Grant, Anne.

GRANTZOW, Adele (1845–1877). German ballet dancer. Born Jan 1, 1845, in Brunswick, Germany; died after a leg amputation complicated by typhus, June 7, 1877, in Berlin, Germany. ❖ Made professional debut during adolescence with State Opera in Brunswick, Germany, where her father Gustav was ballet master; performed briefly with Hanover Opera Ballet; moved to Paris where she trained with Mme. Dominique-Venettozza, while performing intermittently at Russian theaters; danced leading roles at Moscow Bolshoi in Saint-Léon's *Fiametta* and *Le Poisson doré* (1865–66); made Paris Opéra debut in revival of *Giselle* (1866) and performed in *Néméa, Don Giovanni* (1866), *La Source* (1867), among others; created role for Saint-Léon in St. Petersburg in his *Le Lys* (1870); continued to commute between Russia and Paris.

GRANUAILE or GRANY. Variant of Grace.

GRANVILLE, Bonita (1923–1988). American actress and producer. Name variations: Bonita Granville Wrather; (nickname) Bunny. Born Feb 2, 1923, in New York City; died of cancer on Oct 11, 1988; buried in Holy Cross Cemetery; m. Jack Wrather (Texas oil millionaire), 1947 (died 1984); children: Molly Wrather; Linda Wrather; Jack Wrather; Christopher Wrather. ❖ At 9, made film debut in *Westward Passage* (1932); at 13, nominated for Best Supporting Actress for performance in *These Three* (1936); best remembered for portrayal of Nancy Drew, based on the series about the girl detective; retired from acting (1950s); became an executive in husband's business empire, the Wrather Corporation; with Wrather's company, was associate producer, then producer, of "Lassie" tv series (1954–71, syndicated 1971–74); other films include *Cavalcade* (1933), *Ah, Wilderness* (1935), *Maid of Salem* (1936), *Plough and the Stars* (1936), *Garden of Allah* (1936), *Quality Street* (1937), *Angels Wash Their Faces* (1939), *Escape* (1940), *The People vs. Dr. Kildare* (1941), *H. M. Pulham, Esq.* (1941), *Now Voyager* (1942), *Andy Hardy's Double Life* (1942), *Hitler's Children* (1943), *Andy Hardy's Blonde Trouble* (1944), *Love Laughs at Andy Hardy* (1946), *Strike It Rich* (1948), *Guilty of Treason* (1950), and *The Lone Ranger* (1956). ❖ See also *Women in World History.*

GRANVILLE, Christine (1915–1952). Polish secret agent during World War II. Name variations: Countess Krystina Skarbek. Born Countess Krystina Skarbek in Poland in 1915; murdered by a spurned suitor in London in 1952; m. George Gizycki. ❖ Was named "Miss Poland" during teens; when the war broke out, offered services to British Intelligence; smuggled Poles and other Allied officers out of Poland; also carried out several missions in the Balkans before being sent to France (1944); often parachuted into Southern France, where, as a courier, maintained contact with French Resistance and Italian partisans. Was awarded the George Medal and an OBE by British government. ❖ See also *Women in World History.*

GRANVILLE, Louise (1895–1968). Australian-born actress. Born Sept 29, 1895, in Sydney, Australia; died Dec 22, 1968, in Woodland Hills, California; m. Joe Rock (actor-producer), 1922; children: son and daughter. ❖ Was a leading lady for John Ford, before moving to Vitagraph (1918), where she appeared in 25 films; retired (1922).

GRANVILLE, Mary (1700–1788). See Delany, Mary Granville.

GRANVILLE-BARKER, Helen (d. 1950). English playwright, poet, and novelist. Name variations: Helen Gates Huntington; Helen Granville Barker. Born Helen Gates in England; died Feb 16, 1950; m. Archer Milton Huntington; m. Harley Granville-Barker (Shakespearean director), 1918 (died 1946). ❖ Plays include *The Solitary Path, The Days That Pass, Folk Songs from the Spanish, Ada, The Sovereign God, An Apprentice to Truth, The Moon Lady, Marsh Lights, Eastern Red, The Cup of Silence, Living Mirrors, Come Julia* and *Moon in Scorpio;* collaborated with husband Harley Granville-Barker in translating several plays from the Spanish, notably *The Romantic Young Lady, The Kingdom of God, The Lady from Alfaqueque, Fortunato, A 100 Years Old, The Women Have Their Way, Wife to a Famous Man, The Two Shepherds,* and *Take Two from One.*

GRANVILLE-BARKER, Lillah (1875–1960). *See McCarthy, Lillah.*

GRASEGGER, Käthe. German Alpine skier. Name variations: Kathe Grasegger. Born in Germany. ❖ Won a silver medal for combined at Garmisch-Partenkirchen Olympics (1936); won bronze medals for downhill and combined and a silver for slalom at World championships (1937).

GRASSO, Ella (1919–1981). American politician. Born Ella Rosa Giovanna Oliva Tambussi in Windsor Locks, Connecticut, May 10, 1919; died in Hartford, Connecticut, Feb 5, 1981; dau. of Giacomo (baker) and Maria (Oliva) Tambussi; attended St. Mary's in Windsor Locks; graduated from the Chaffee School, Windsor; Mt. Holyoke College, BA, magna cum laude, 1940, MA, 1942; m. Thomas A. Grasso (educator), Aug 31, 1942; children: Suzanne Grasso; James Grasso. ❖ Elected to serve in Connecticut's General Assembly (1952); during 2nd term, became Democratic floor leader; served as secretary of state (1956–68), becoming one of the most popular political figures in Connecticut, mainly due to her involvement with citizens' concerns; elected to US Congress (1970 and 1972), where she compiled a liberal voting record, though she opposed abortion; also served on Education and Labor Committee and Veterans Affairs Committee, and took part in drafting the Comprehensive Employment and Training Act; elected governor of Connecticut (1974), the 1st woman to become an American governor on her own and not as husband's successor; successful in belt-tightening, turned the budget deficit into a surplus within 4 years and was reelected for a 2nd term (1978); elected chair of Democratic Governors' Conference (1979). ❖ See also *Women in World History.*

GRATCHEVA, Tatiana (1973–). Russian volleyball player. Name variations: Tatyana. Born Feb 23, 1973, in Ekaterinburg, Russia. ❖ Made national team debut (1992); won European team championship (1993, 1997, 1999, 2001) and World Grand Prix (1997, 1999, 2002); won a team silver medal at Sydney Olympics (2000).

GRATZ, Rebecca (1781–1869). Jewish-American founder. Born in Philadelphia, Pennsylvania, Mar 4, 1781; died Aug 27, 1869, in Philadelphia, Pennsylvania, where she lived most of her life; dau. of Michael Gratz (merchant, originally from Silesia) and Miriam (Simon) Gratz of Lancaster, Pennsylvania; attended the Young Ladies Academy in Philadelphia and possibly another unnamed women's school, but largely educated through her own eager and extensive reading in literature and history; never married. ❖ Founder of five charitable, religious, and educational organizations for needy women and children, who permanently shaped religious education and women's activities in American Jewish life; founded Female Association (1801), Philadelphia Orphan Asylum (1815), Female Hebrew Benevolent Society, the 1st independent Jewish women's charitable society (1819), the 1st Hebrew Sunday School (1838), and the 1st American Jewish Foster Home (1855), all in Philadelphia; surmounted the grief caused by the deaths of many family members and loved ones, confronted Christian evangelists who tried to convert her from Judaism, and became a leader in education, charity, religion, and cultural life in Philadelphia. ❖ See also Dianne Ashton, *Unsubdued Spirits: Rebecca Gratz and the Domestication of American Judaism* (Wayne State University Press, 1998); Rollin G. Osterweis, *Rebecca Gratz: A Study in Charm* (1935); David Philipson, ed. *The Letters of Rebecca Gratz* (1929); and *Women in World History.*

GRAU, Shirley Ann (1929–). American author. Born July 8, 1929, in New Orleans, Louisiana; dau. of Adolph E, Grau and Katherine (Onions) Grau; Newcomb College, BA, 1950; attended Tulane University; m. James Kern Feibleman (teacher); children: 4, including Ian James. ❖ Known for exploring characters who were isolated in some way from others, received critical attention for *The Black Prince and Other Stories* (1955); published 1st novel *The Hard Blue Sky* which was noted for characterization and lyricism (1958); other writings include *The House on Coliseum Street* (1961), *The Condor Passes* (1971), *The Wind Shifting West* (1973), *Evidence of Love* (1977), and *Nine Women* (1985). Won Pulitzer Prize for *The Keeper's of the House* (1964).

GRAU, Sigrun (1965–). *See Wodars, Sigrun.*

GRAVENSTIJN, Deborah (1974–). Dutch judoka. Born Aug 20, 1974, in Tholen, Netherlands. ❖ Placed 2nd at World championships for 57kg (2001); won a bronze medal for 57kg at Athens Olympics (2004).

GRAVES, Beryl (1915–2003). English editor and literary inspiration. Born Beryl Antoinette Pritchard, Feb 22, 1915, in Hampstead, London, England; died Oct 27, 2003, on the island of Majorca, Spain; dau. of Sir Harry Pritchard (president of the Law Society); attended Queen's College

and Oxford; m. Alan Hodge (writer), 1938 (div.); became 2nd wife of Robert Graves (poet), 1950 (died 1985); children: William, Lucia, Juan and Tomás. ❖ The literary inspiration for many of Robert Graves' love poems, lived with him (and had 3 children with him) before marrying; collaborated with husband on 2 of his translations, *The Cross and the Sword* and *The Infant with the Globe;* with Dustan Ward, edited a scholarly edition of husband's poems in 3 volumes (1995–99).

GRAVES, Carie (1953–). American rower. Born June 27, 1953; attended University of Wisconsin. ❖ Won a bronze medal at Montreal Olympics (1976) and a gold medal at Los Angeles Olympics (1984), both in coxed eights.

GRAVES, Clotilde Inez Mary (1863–1932). Irish novelist and playwright. Name variations: (pseudonym) Richard Dehan. Born June 3, 1863, in Buttevant, Co. Cork, Ireland; died Dec 3, 1932; dau. of Major W. H. Graves. ❖ Presented 1st play *Nitocris* (four acts) at Drury Lane (1887), then was commissioned to write the pantomime *Puss in Boots;* plays include *Rachel, Katherine Kavanagh, Dr. and Mrs. Neill, A Maker of Comedies, A Mother of Three, A Matchmaker, The Bishop's Eye, St. Martin's Summer* (with Lady Colin Campbell), *The Lovers' Battle, The Bond of Ninon, A Tenement Tragedy, The Other Side* and *The General's Past;* also wrote novels *Between Two Thieves, The Head Quarter Recruit, The Man of Iron, That Which Hath Wings, The Just Steward* and *The Pipers of the Market Place.*

GRAVES, Nancy (1940–1995). American sculptor, painter, and filmmaker. Born Nancy Stevenson Graves on Dec 23, 1940, in Pittsfield, Massachusetts; died in 1995 in New York City; one of two daughters of Walter L. Graves (assistant director of a museum) and Mary B. Graves (secretary and volunteer worker); attended Miss Hall's School, Pittsfield, and the Northfield School for Girls; Vassar College, BA in English literature, 1961; Yale University, BFA and MFA; m. Richard Serra (sculptor), 1965 (div. 1970); no children. ❖ Was a Fulbright-Hayes fellow in France (1965); lived and worked in Florence, Italy (1966); had solo exhibitions throughout world (1968–95); best remembered for 3 life-sized Bactrian, or two-humped, camels that comprised her 1st major solo exhibition at Whitney Museum (1969); participated in numerous group shows (1970–95); was a resident at the American Academy, Rome, Italy (1979); designed set and costumes for experimental dance *Lateral Pass* (1983); also created paleontological sculptures using bones and other parts of animals; produced bronze sculptures using directly cast objects (1980–95); made several short films. Work represented in numerous museums, galleries, and private collections, including Whitney Museum and Museum of Modern Art, New York City; Chicago Art Institute; Museum of Fine Arts, Houston, Texas; Neue Galerie, Cologne, West Germany; and National Gallery of Canada, Ottawa. ❖ See also Thomas Padon (catalogue), *Nancy Graves: Excavations in Print, A Catalogue Raisonné* (1996); and *Women in World History.*

GRAVES, Sally (b. 1914). *See Chilver, Sally.*

GRAVES, Valerie (1930–1999). *See Bradley, Marion Zimmer.*

GRAY (1920–2003). *See Gray, Oriel.*

GRAY, Coleen (1922–). American actress. Born Doris Jensen, Oct 23, 1922, in Staplehurst, Nebraska. ❖ Made film debut in *State Fair* (1945), followed by *Kiss of Death, Nightmare Alley, Fury at Furnace Creek, Father Is a Bachelor, Riding High, Kansas City Confidential, Sabre Jet, Arrow in the Dust, Death of a Scoundrel, The Vampire* and *Johnny Rocco,* among others; co-starred in tv series "Window on Main Street" (1961–62) and appeared as Diane Hunter on "Days of Our Lives" (1967–68).

GRAY, Dolores (1924–2002). American actress and singer. Born June 7, 1924, in Chicago, Illinois; died June 26, 2002, in NYC; m. Andrew Crevolin (div.). ❖ Began singing in San Francisco supperclubs at age 14; sang on Rudy Vallee's radio program (1940); made Broadway debut with Bea Lillie in *Seven Lively Arts* (1944), followed by a triumphant London run as Annie Oakley in *Annie Get Your Gun* (1947–50); films include *Lady for a Night, Mr. Skeffington, It's Always Fair Weather, Kismet, The Opposite Sex* and *Designing Woman.* Introduced her signature song "Here's That Rainy Day" in *Carnival in Flanders* for which she won a Tony award (1954).

GRAY, Dulcie (1919–). English stage, tv, and screen actress and writer. Born Dulcie Winifred Bailey, Nov 20, 1919, in Kuala Lumpur, Malaya (now Malaysia); m. Michael Denison (actor), 1939 (died 1998). ❖ Made

London debut as Maria in *Twelfth Night* (1942); stage credits include Alexandra Giddens in *The Little Foxes*, the title role in *Dear Ruth*, Agnes in *The Four Poster*, Marion Field in *Love Affair* (which she wrote), the title role in *Candida* (breaking long-run records), and Lady Utterwood in *Heartbreak House*,; frequently appeared with husband on stage, screen and tv, including the highly successful "Howard's Way" (1985); films include *Madonna of the 7 Moons*, *They Were Sisters*, *My Brother Jonathan*, *The Glass Mountain* and *Angels One Five*; wrote 24 books, mostly crime novels and co-wrote, with husband, *The Actor and His World*. Named Commander of the British Empire (CBE, 1983).

GRAY, Eileen (1878–1976). Irish designer. Born Kathleen Eileen Moray Smith (her surname was changed to Gray following her mother's inheritance of the Scottish title of Baroness Gray), Aug 9, 1878, at Brownswood, Enniscorthy, Ireland; died in Paris, France, Oct 31, 1976; dau. of James Maclaren Smith (artist) and Eveleen (Pounden) Smith; educated at home and at private schools abroad; studied art at the Slade School of Fine Arts, London, and at the École Colarossi and the Académie Julian, Paris; never married; no children. ❖ Designer, best known in the 1920s for her lacquerwork and furniture, and pioneering architect, whose work achieved belated recognition during final years of her life; settled in Paris (1902); began to study the craft of lacquer under Charles in London and Sougawara in Paris (1907); exhibited at Salon des Artistes Décorateurs (1913); received 1st commissions from Jacques Doucet (1914); commissioned to redecorate and furnish Mme Mathieu-Lévy's Paris apartment, in the process developing her "block" screens (1919); opened Galerie Jean Désert as a retail outlet for her work (1922); exhibited at Salon des Artistes Décorateurs (1923); built her 1st house, E. 1027 (1926–29); was founder member of Union des Artistes Modernes (1929); designed and built 2nd house, Tempe à Pailla (1932–34); invited by Le Corbusier to show at his Pavillon des Temps Nouveaux at Paris Exposition Internationale (1937); completed 3rd house, Lou Pérou (1958); exhibited in Graz and Vienna (1970); her screen, "Le destin," achieved a record price for 20th-century furniture at auction in Paris, and work exhibited at the RIBA Heinz Gallery, London (1972); over 90 years old, now found herself celebrated by critics and her work avidly sought by museums and private collectors; appointed a Royal Designer for Industry (1972); elected honorary fellow of Royal Institute of the Architects of Ireland (1973); work exhibited in New York, Los Angeles, Princeton and Boston (1975); work exhibited at Victoria and Albert Museum, London and at Museum of Modern Art, New York (1979). ❖ See also Peter Adam, *Eileen Gray, Architect-Designer: A Biography* (Thames & Hudson, 1987); Philippe Garner, *Eileen Gray: Design and Architecture 1878–1976* (Benedikt Taschen, 1993); J. Stewart Johnson, *Eileen Gray: Designer, 1879–1976* (Debrett's Peerage for Victoria and Albert Museum, 1979); and *Women in World History*.

GRAY, Elizabeth Janet (1902–1999). *See Vining, Elizabeth Gray.*

GRAY, Eve (1900–1983). English actress and singer. Name variations: Eve Grey. Born Fanny Evelyn Garrett, Nov 27, 1900, in Handsworth, Birmingham, England; died May 23, 1983, in Mere, Wiltshire, England. ❖ Brought up in Australia, where she made stage debut and had 1st success, as Phyllis Benton in *Bull-Dog Drummond* (1922); made London debut as Madeleine in *Madame Pompadour* (1924); other plays include *None But the Brave*, *Easy Come Easy Go*, *The Flying Fool*, *Sexton Blake*, *The Limping Man*, *The Quitter* and *The Night Hawk*; made film debut in *The Silver Lining* (1927), followed by *Poppies of Flanders*, *Moulin Rouge*, *The Loves of Robert Burns*, *Midnight*, *Scrooge*, *They Didn't Know*, *The Happy Family*, *The Angelus* and *One Good Turn*, among others.

GRAY, Felicity (b. 1914). *See Andreae, Felicity.*

GRAY, Georgia Neese (1900–1995). *See Clark, Georgia Neese.*

GRAY, Gilda (1901–1959). Polish dancer and actress. Born Marianna Michalska, Oct 24, 1901, in Krakow, Poland; died of a heart attack in Dec 22, 1959, in Hollywood, California. ❖ At 7, immigrated to America (1908); starred in a number of silents (1923–36); is credited with inventing the dance-craze, the shimmy; films include: *Lawful Larceny* (1923), *Aloma of the South Seas* (1926), *Cabaret* (1928), *The Devil Dancer* (1928), *Piccadilly* (U.K., 1929), *Rose Marie* (1936), and *The Great Ziegfeld* (1936).

GRAY, Hanna Holborn (1930—). American educator. Born Hanna Holborn in Heidelberg, Germany, Oct 25, 1930; 2nd child and only dau. of Hajo Holborn (European historian and educator) and Annemarie (Bettmann) Holborn; immigrated to US, 1934; naturalized citizen, 1940; Bryn Mawr College, Bryn Mawr, Pennsylvania, AB, 1950; attended St. Anne's College, Oxford University, as a Fulbright Scholar, 1950–51; Harvard University, PhD, 1957; m. Charles Montgomery Gray (educator), June 19, 1954; no children. ❖ Began teaching career at Harvard University, quickly advancing to the rank of assistant professor of history; moved with husband to Chicago (1960), where he was an associate professor at University of Chicago; after a year as research fellow at Newberry Library, also joined the university faculty as an assistant professor of history; by 1964, had obtained tenure and been promoted to associate professor; with husband, edited *Journal of Modern History*; served as 1st woman dean of arts and sciences at Northwestern University (1972–74); became provost of Yale (1974), the 1st woman in that post, then acting president (1977); served as president of University of Chicago (1978–93), the 1st woman to serve as chief executive officer of a major American coeducational institution. ❖ See also *Women in World History*.

GRAY, Harriet (1897–1985). *See Robins, Denise Naomi.*

GRAY, Hiria (1870–1943). *See Kokoro-Barrett, Hiria.*

GRAY, Lorna (1918—). *See Booth, Adrian.*

GRAY, Macy (1970—). African-American pop vocalist. Born Natalie Renee McIntyre on Sept 9, 1970, in Canton, Ohio; m. Tracy Hinds, 1996 (div. 1998); children: 3. ❖ Quirky vocalist known for raspy voice and unusual wardrobe, took stage name Gray from a family friend; moved to L.A at 17 (1987); attended film school at UCLA; began singing jazz standards in local bars; recorded album for Atlantic records that was never released (1994); hosted open-mike nights at popular LA coffeehouse; worked with producer Andrew Slater on 1st released album, the triple-platinum *On How Life Is* (1999); scored hit with Grammy-winning single "I Try" (2000); released follow-up album *The Id* (2001); composed song "My Nutmeg Phantasy" for film *Spider-Man* (2002) and theme song to tv series "Miss Match" (2003); acted in films *Training Day* (1991) and *Wicked Prayer* (2004).

GRAY, Mary Sophia (c. 1830–1911). *See Hinerangi, Sophia.*

GRAY, Nadia (1923–1994). Russian-Romanian stage, tv, and screen actress. Name variations: Nadja Grey, Nadia Grey. Born Nadia Kujnir-Herescu, Nov 27, 1923, in Bucharest, Romania (some sources cite Berlin); died June 13, 1994, in NYC. ❖ Fled to Paris after Communist takeover of Romania (1947); films include *The Spider and the Fly*, *Valley of the Eagles*, *Puccini*, *La Dolce Vita*, *Candide*, *The Naked Runner*, *Two for the Road* and *Rue Haute*.

GRAY, Nicolete (1911–1997). British art historian and designer of lettering. Born Nicolete Mary Binyon in Stevenage, Hertfordshire, July 20, 1911; died in London on June 8, 1997; one of 3 daughters of Laurence Binyon (1869–1943, poet and literary critic) and Cicely Margaret (Powell) Binyon; had two sisters; graduate of St. Paul's School, 1929; studied history at Lady Margaret Hall, Oxford University; m. Basil Gray (assistant keeper in British Museum), 1933; children: 2 sons, 3 daughters, including Camilla Gray Prokofiev (Russian art historian, died 1971). ❖ Organized the 1st international exhibition of abstract art held in England (1936); published *Nineteenth Century Ornamental Types and Title Pages* (1938), followed by *Rossetti, Dante and Ourselves* (1947); published essay collection, *Lettering on Buildings* (1960); taught lettering at Central School of Art and Design (1964–81); wrote last book *A History of Lettering: Creative Experiment and Letter Identity* (1976); designed and carved the tombstone of Agatha Christie and the façade lettering of Sotheby's. Was 1st woman member of the Double Crown, a previously all-male club of printers and typographers. ❖ See also *Women in World History*.

GRAY, Oriel (1920–2003). Australian playwright. Name variations: Gray; Oriel; Holland; Oriel Holland. Born Oriel Holland Bennett, Mar 26, 1920, in Sydney, Australia; died June 30, 2003, in Heidelberg, Melbourne, Australia; dau. of Benjamin Bennett and Ida Bennett; m. John Gray (actor), 1940; children: (1st m.) Stephen (b. 1945); (with John Hepworth) Peter and Nicholas. ❖ Joined Communist Party at 18, prompted by the horrors of the Spanish Civil War and the rise of Nazi Germany; worked as actress at New Theatre; wrote plays for theater as well as radio and tv; wrote the play *Lawson* (produced 1943), an adaptation of Henry Lawson short stories; wrote the pioneering feminist play, *The Torrents* (1955), for which she won the Playwright's Advisory Board Competition; won J.C. Williamson Play Competition for *Burst of Summer* (1959); also wrote *My Life is My Affair* (1947) and *Had We But World Enough* (1950); worked on the ABC-tv series "Bellbird" for 11 years. ❖ See also memoir *Exit Left: Memoirs of a Scarlet Woman* (1985).

GRAY, Sally (1916—). English actress. Name variations: Constance Stevens. Born Constance Vera Stevens, Feb 14, 1916, in Holloway, England; m. Dominick Geoffrey Edward Browne, 4th Baron Oranmore and Browne, 2nd Baron Mereworth, 1950 (died 2002). ❖ At 10, made London stage debut as Ella in *All God's Chillun;* films include *School for Scandal, Checkmate, Cheer Up, Cafe Colette, The Saint in London, Suicide Squadron, They Made Me a Fugitive, Silent Dust* and *Escape Route;* retired on marriage.

GRAY, Teresa Corinna Ubertis (1877–1964). Italian novelist and poet. Name variations: (pseudonym) Teresah. Born 1877 in Frassineto, Italy; died 1964. ❖ Writings include *Il campo delle ortiche* (1897), *Il libro di Titania* (1909), *Piccoli eroi della grande guerra* (1915), *L'ombra sul muro* (1921), *Dobbiamo vivere la nostra vita* (1941), and *La luna* (1942).

GRAYSON, Betty Evans (1925–1979). American softball pitcher. Name variations: Betty Evans. Born Betty Evans, Oct 9, 1925, in Portland, Oregon; died July 9, 1979. ❖ Played 17 years as an amateur, with a record of 465 wins and 91 losses, and 3 as a pro with the Chicago Queens. ❖ See also *Women in World History.*

GRAYSON, Georgina (1926—). *See Jones, Elizabeth Marina.*

GRAYSON, Kathryn (1922—). American actress and singer. Born Zelma Kathryn Hedrick, Feb 9, 1922, in Winston-Salem, North Carolina; m. John Shelton (actor), 1940 (div. 1946); m. Johnny Johnston (singer-actor), 1947 (div. 1951). ❖ A petite brunette, with a heart-shaped face and a coloratura voice, was headed for an operatic career when she was offered a movie contract by Louis B. Mayer; made an auspicious debut in *Andy Hardy's Private Secretary* (1941), in which she sang an aria from an opera; captured attention in next movie, *The Vanishing Virginians* (1942), with a lilting rendition of "The World Was Made for You"; teamed in 2 films with Mario Lanza: *That Midnight Kiss* (1949) and *The Toast of New Orleans* (1950); appeared opposite Howard Keel in the hit remake of *Show Boat* (1951), followed by a remake of *Roberta,* retitled *Lovely to Look At* (1952), and *Kiss Me Kate* (1953), perhaps the best of her brief career; made tv debut in "Shadows of the Heart" on the "General Electric Theater" series (1955), for which she was nominated for an Emmy; also appeared on the concert stage and in the operas *Madame Butterfly, La Bohème* and *La Traviata* (1960). ❖ See also *Women in World History.*

GRAYSON, Shirley (1923–1985). *See Hall, Grayson.*

GRAZIE, Marie Eugenie delle (1864–1931). *See Delle Grazie, Marie Eugenie.*

GRAZIELE (1981—). *See Nascimento Pinheiro, Graziele.*

GREATOREX, Eliza (1820–1897). Irish-American artist. Born Eliza Pratt in Ireland, Dec 25, 1820; died 1897; m. Henry W. Greatorex (composer and organist), 1849; studied in NY and Paris. ❖ Arrived in NY (1840); produced many landscape paintings but later devoted herself to etching and pen-and-ink work, for which she is chiefly remembered; elected associate of the National Academy (1868). Publications include *The Homes of Oberammergau, Summer Etchings in Colorado* and *Old New York from the Battery to Bloomingdale.*

GREAVES, Mary Ann (1834–1897). New Zealand prostitute. Born in 1834, in Leicestershire, England; died Feb 18, 1897, at Christchurch, New Zealand. ❖ Immigrated to Canterbury, New Zealand, from Tasmania (1859); worked as prostitute and served several terms of imprisonment for drunkenness, solicitation, vagrancy, and larceny. ❖ See also *Dictionary of New Zealand Biography* (Vol. 2).

GRÉCO, Juliette (1926—). French actress and singer. Name variations: Juliette Greco. Born Feb 7, 1926, in Montpellier, Hérault, Languedoc-Roussillon, France; m. Philippe Lemaire, 1953 (div. 1956); m. Michel Piccoli (actor), 1966 (div. 1977); m. Gérard Jouannest, 1988. ❖ Sang in Paris cafés (1940s); made film debut in *Au royaume des cieux* (1949), followed by *Orpheus, The Green Glove, Paris Does Strange Things, La Châtelaine du Liban, L'homme et l'enfant, The Sun Also Rises, Bonjour tristesse, The Naked Earth, Whirlpool, Crack in the Mirror, The Night of the Generals* and *Jedermanns Fest,* among others.

GREDAL, Eva (1927–1995). Danish politician and government official. Name variations: Eva Wilhelmsson Gredal. Born Feb 19, 1927, in Copenhagen, Denmark; died Aug 2, 1995, in Stege, Denmark; dau of Albert Victor Michael Wilhelmsson Tuure (1903–1976) and Mary Rigmor Larsen (1903–1992); married Kaj Otto Gredal, 1949 (died 1992); children: Niels Otto (b. 1950), Jens Mikael (b. 1954), Anne

Sofie (b. 1957) and Julie Eva (b. 1967). ❖ Served as chair of National Social Advice Association (1959–67); was vice-chair of National Association of Women (1967–71); elected to Parliament by a Copenhagen constituency (1971), served as Minister for Social Affairs (1971–73, 1977–78), until a change in government prompted resignation; elected to European Parliament (1979).

GREECE, queen of.
See Amalie (1818–1875).
See Olga Constantinovna (1851–1926).
See Sophie of Prussia (1870–1932).
See Elisabeth (1894–1956).
See Manos, Aspasia (1896–1972).
See Fredericka (1917–1981).
See Anne-Marie Oldenburg (b. 1946).

GREELEY-SMITH, Nixola (1880–1919). American journalist. Name variations: Nixola Smith. Born April 5, 1880, in Chappaqua, NY; died Mar 9, 1919, in New York, NY; dau. of Nicholas Smith (lawyer) and Ida Lillian (Greeley) Smith; granddau. of Horace Greeley (editor); sister of Horace Greeley Smith (bacteriologist) and Ida Lillian (actress); m. Andrew Watres Ford (editor), April 1, 1910. ❖ Reputedly published 1st work at age 12, with a play in the New York *World;* hired by Joseph Pulitzer at *St. Louis Post-Dispatch;* spent majority of career with Pulitzer's *Evening World,* in NY (from 1901); specialized in emerging form of popular journalism; was especially successful with women's-interest articles; established reputation for personal interviews, including one with Sarah Bernhardt (published Oct 11, 1916).

GREEN, Alice Stopford (1847–1929). *See Stopford Green, Alice.*

GREEN, Anna Katharine (1846–1935). American writer. Name variations: Anna Katharine Green Rohlfs; Mrs. Rohlfs. Born in Brooklyn, New York, Nov 11, 1846; died in Buffalo, New York, April 11, 1935; dau. of James Wilson (lawyer) and Katharine Ann (Whitney) Green; attended public school in Brooklyn and Buffalo, New York; Ripley Female College (now Green Mountain College), Poultney, Vermont, BA, 1866; m. Charles Rohlfs (actor turned designer), in Nov 1884; children: a daughter and two sons. ❖ Writer, credited with developing the American detective story, whose fictional detective Ebenezer Gryce anticipated the later Sherlock Holmes by nearly a decade; published 1st book, *The Leavenworth Case* (1878), which turned out to be a runaway hit, selling over 150,000 copies, followed by *A Strange Disappearance* (1880) and *Hand and Ring* (1883); other books include *Marked "Personal"* (1893), *The Doctor, His Wife, and the Clock* (1895), *That Affair Next Door* (1897), *Agatha Webb* (1899), *The Circular Study* (1900), *The House in the Mist* (1905), *The Millionaire Baby* (1905), *The Amethyst Box* (1905), *The Woman in the Alcove* (1906), *The Chief Legatee* (1906), *The House of the Whispering Pines* (1910), *Initials Only* (1911), *The Mystery of the Hasty Arrow* (1917), and *The Step on the Stair* (1923).

GREEN, Anne Catherine (c. 1720–1775). American printer. Name variations: Anne Catherine Hoof Green. Born Anne Hoof c. 1720, probably in Holland, Netherlands; probably came to US as a child; died Mar 23, 1775, probably in Annapolis, Maryland; m. Jonas Green (printer), April 25, 1738 (died 1767); children: 14, including Rebecca, Mary, William (died 1770), Frederick, Samuel and Augusta. ❖ After death of husband (1767), continued printing of his *Maryland Gazette;* issued volumes of *Acts* and *Votes and Proceedings* of provincial assembly (1767); maintained printing business with assistance from son William until his death and then from son Frederick; received formal appointment as provincial printer (1768); issued *Deputy Commissary's Guide* by Elie Vallette (1774); made 1st printing of *Letters from a Pennsylvania Farmer* by John Dickinson in *Maryland Gazette.*

GREEN, Constance McLaughlin (1897–1975). American writer, historian, and educator. Born Constance Winsor McLaughlin, Aug 21, 1897, in Ann Arbor, Michigan; died in 1975; 1 of 6 children of Andrew Cunningham McLaughlin (historian and college professor) and Lois Thompson (Angell) McLaughlin; graduated from University High School, Chicago, Illinois, 1914; attended University of Chicago; Smith College, BA, 1919; Mount Holyoke College, MA in history, 1925; Yale University, PhD, 1937; m. Donald Ross Green (textile manufacturer), Feb 14, 1921 (died Nov 1946); children: 1 son, 2 daughters. ❖ Won Yale's Edward Eggleston Prize in History (1938); published dissertation, *Holyoke, Massachusetts: A Case History of the Industrial Revolution in America* (1939); was a history instructor at Smith College (1939–42) and chief historian for Army Ordinance Corps (1948–51); worked as a historian at Office of the Secretary of Defense; named head of Washington history project (1954), which culminated in *Washington, Village and Capital, 1800–1878* (1962), bringing her critical acclaim and a Pulitzer Prize in History; produced a 2nd and longer companion volume, *Washington, Capital City 1879–1950* (1963); other books include *History of Naugatuck, Connecticut* (1949), *Eli Whitney and the Birth of American Technology* (1956), and *American Cities in the Growth of the Nation* (1957). ❖ See also *Women in World History.*

GREEN, Debbie (1958—). American volleyball player. Born June 25, 1958, in US. ❖ At Los Angeles Olympics, won a silver medal in team competition (1984).

GREEN, Debora (c. 1951—). American murderer (accused). Born c. 1951; studied at University of Kansas Medical School; m. Duane Greene; m. Michael Farrar. ❖ Accused of setting fire to home and killing 2 of her 3 children (1995); also accused of attempting to poison husband; received 40-year sentence with no chance of parole.

GREEN, Dorothy (1886–1961). English stage actress. Born June 30, 1886, in Hertfordshire, England; died Jan 14, 1961, in London; m. Alfred A. Harris. ❖ Made London debut as Lady Diana in *The Philosopher's Stone* (1908), followed by *Colonel Smith, The Hartley Family, Stand and Deliver, Lucky Jim, Misalliance, The Rivals* (Mrs. Malaprop), *The Way of the World* (Mrs. Marwood), *King Lear* (as Goneril), and *The School for Scandal* (Lady Sneerwell), among others; made NY debut as Beatrice in *Much Ado about Nothing* (1913); often appeared at Stratford-on-Avon in such Shakespearean roles as Viola, Imogen, Ophelia, and Portia, and with the Old Vic; can be seen in the film *The Informer* (1929).

GREEN, Dorothy (1892–1963). Russian-born silent-screen actress. Born 1892 in St. Petersburg, Russia; died Nov 16, 1963, in NYC; m. Norman November (lawyer). ❖ Films include *A Parisian Romance, The American Way, The Grouch, The Lesson, The Good-Bad Wife, Souls Aflame, The Devil at His Elbow,* and the serial *Patria.*

GREEN, Dorothy (1915–1991). Australian poet and literary critic. Born Dorothy Auchterlonie in Co. Durham, England, 1915; died 1991; m. H.M Green, 1944. ❖ Worked as journalist, editor, and reader for ABC News Service (1942–49); lectured English, Australian, and American literature at Monash University, Australian National University, and Australian Defence Force Academy; poetry includes *Kaleidoscope* (1940), *The Dolphin* (1967), and *Something to Someone* (1984); nonfiction includes *Ulysses Bound: Henry Handel Richardson and Her Fiction* (1973), *The Music of Love, Critical Essays on Literature and Life* (1984), and *Descent of Spirit: Writing of E. L. Grant Watson* (1990); also revised husband's *A History of Australian Literature* (1984–85). Awarded Medal of Order of Australia.

GREEN, Edith Starrett (1910–1987). American politician. Born Edith Starrett in Trent, South Dakota, Jan 17, 1910; died in Tulatin, Oregon, April 21, 1987; dau. of James Vaughn Starrett and Julia (Hunt) Starrett (both schoolteachers); grew up in Oregon; attended Willamette University and University of Oregon, BS, 1939; graduate studies at Stanford University; m. Arthur N. Green (businessman), Aug 19, 1933; children: James S. Green; Richard A. Green. ❖ As a Democrat from Oregon's 3rd District, elected to US Congress (1954) and appointed to Committee on Education and Labor in freshman year; during House tenure (Jan 3, 1955–Dec 31, 1974), served on various committees, including Committee on Appropriations; played a central role in enactment of the National Defense Education Act (1958); authored Higher Education Facilities Act (1963), Equal Pay Act (1963), and Higher Education Act (1972), which included Title IX; was also responsible for 1st federal program for undergraduate scholarships; at successive Democratic National Conventions, seconded presidential nominations for Adlai Stevenson (1956) and John F. Kennedy (1960); appointed to Presidential Committee on the Status of Women; was co-chair of Democrats for Gerald Ford (1976). ❖ See also *Women in World History.*

GREEN, Elizabeth Shippen (1871–1954). American illustrator and watercolorist. Born in Philadelphia, Pennsylvania, 1871; died in Philadelphia in 1954; studied art at the Pennsylvania Academy with Thomas Eakins, Robert Vonnoh, and Thomas Anshutz; studied with Howard Pyle at Drexel Institute, 1894; m. Huger Elliott (architect and teacher), 1911 (died 1951); no children. ❖ Known as an excellent draftswoman and a brilliant colorist, sold 1st illustration to *Philadelphia Times,* after which began to contribute to popular journals, including *Ladies' Home Journal, Saturday Evening Post* and *Harper's Weekly;* at one point, shared a studio-home with Violet Oakley and Jessie Willcox Smith; strongly influenced by Art Nouveau and the Pre-Raphaelite movement, illustrated over 20 books and was the 1st woman staff member of *Harper's* magazine. ❖ See also *Women in World History.*

GREEN, Grace Winifred (1907–1976). New Zealand radio broadcaster and journalist. Born on Feb 13, 1907, in Christchurch, New Zealand; died May 25, 1976, in Christchurch; dau. of William James Green (grocer and trade unionist) and Bridget Teresa (Barrett) Green. ❖ Worked as announcer with small private radio station (1929), later with New Zealand's 1st commercial radio station, 3ZM (1932), and then with government-owned commercial station 3ZB; as the only woman announcer among 12 men, became senior announcer and was known for audience participation quiz shows and patriotic fund-raising functions; served as women's editor of *Christchurch Star* (1962–74). ❖ See also *Dictionary of New Zealand Biography* (Vol. 4).

GREEN, Henrietta (1834–1916). See Green, Hetty.

GREEN, Hetty (1834–1916). American financier. Born Henrietta Howland Robinson on Nov 23, 1834, in New Bedford, Massachusetts; died July 3, 1916, in New York City; 1st of two children and only dau. of Edward Mott Robinson (whaler and foreign trader) and Abby Slocum (Howland) Robinson; attended Eliza Wing school in Sandwich and a private school in Boston run by Reverend Charles Russell Lowell and his wife Anna Cabot (Jackson) Lowell; m. Edward Green (partner in a foreign trade company), July 11, 1867 (sep. 1885, died 1902); children: Edward Henry Green (b. 1868); Sylvia Ann Green (b. 1871). ❖ Regarded at time of her death as the wealthiest woman in the world, became sole heir of the Howland fortune (1865); married a millionaire (1867); devoted herself to the management of her fortune, purchasing government bonds, railroad stocks, and real estate; when husband went bankrupt (1885), refused to underwrite his debts; separated, though she remained on good terms with him until his death; contrary to later gossip, provided well for her children; in later years, became distrustful and tight-fisted, dressing in rags, seeking health care in free clinics, and haggling with shopkeepers over small purchases. ❖ See also Boyden Sparkes and Samuel Taylor Moore, *The Witch of Wall Street: Hetty Green* (Doubleday, 1935); Charles Slack, *Hetty: The Genius and Madness of America's First Female Tycoon* (Ecco, 2004); and *Women in World History.*

GREEN, Janet (1914–1993). English actress, playwright and screenwriter. Born July 4, 1914, in Hitchin, Hertfordshire, England; died Mar 30, 1933, in Beaconsfield, Buckinghamshire; m. John McCormick (producer-writer). ❖ Began career as actress; wrote screenplay for *The Clouded Yellow* (1951), followed by *The Good Beginning, Lost, The Long Arm, Eyewitness, Cast a Dark Shadow, The Gypsy and the Gentleman, Sapphire, Midnight Lace, Victim, Life for Ruth,* and *7 Women,* among others; sometimes collaborated with husband.

GREEN, Lucinda (1953—). British equestrian. Name variations: Lucinda Prior-Palmer. Born Lucinda Prior-Palmer in London, England, Nov 7, 1953; dau. of a cavalry general; m. David Green (Australian Olympic rider), 1981; children: 2. ❖ A specialist in three-day eventing, won team gold in the European Junior Championships (1971); won Badminton Horse Trials on 6 different horses: Be Fair (1973), Wideawake (1976), George (1977), Killaire (1979), Regal Realm (1983), and Beagle Bay (1984); was runner up at Badminton Horse Trials (1978, 1980); won individual on Be Fair and team runner up in European championships (1975); won individual on George and team winner in European championships (1977); won individual on Regal Realm and was team winner at World championships (1982); was Olympic team captain and won team silver on Regal Realm (1984); won team gold in Burghley's European championships (1985) on Regal Realm. ❖ See also *Women in World History.*

GREEN, Mary Anne Everett (1818–1895). British historian. Name variations: Mary Anne Everett Wood. Born Mary Anne Everett Wood, July 19, 1818, in Sheffield, Yorkshire, England; died Nov 1, 1895, in London; dau. of Robert Wood (Methodist minister); m. George Pycock Green (painter), 1846. ❖ Educated at home until family's move to London (1841) where she spent time in British Museum reading history; learned several languages and became respected scholar; spent 40 years editing calendars of state papers published in 41 volumes; works include *Letters of Royal and Illustrious Ladies of Great Britain, from the Commencement of the Twelfth Century to the Close of the Reign of Queen Mary* (1846), *Lives of the Princesses of England, from the Roman Conquest* (1849–1855), and *Elizabeth, Electress Palantine and Queen of Bohemia* (1855).

GREEN, Mitzi (1920–1969). American stage and screen actress. Name variations: Little Mitzi. Born Elizabeth Keno, Oct 22, 1920 in The Bronx, NY; died May 24, 1969, in Huntington Beach, California; dau. of Joseph and Rosie Green (vaudevillians); m. Joseph Pevney (actor), 1942; children: four. ❖ Made stage debut in vaudeville with parents at age 4 at the Orpheum, St. Louis; was a child film star of Paramount early talkies (1929–35) in such parts as Becky Thatcher in *Tom Sawyer* and the title role in *Little Orphan Annie;* made Broadway debut as Billie Smith in *Babes in Arms* (1937); also starred in *Billion Dollar Baby* and on tour in *Gypsy.*

GREEN, Mrs. (d. 1791). See Hippisley, Jane.

GREEN, Olive (1874–1911). See Reed, Myrtle.

GREEN, Patricia Hannah (b. 1919). See Clarke, Patricia Hannah.

GREEN, Mrs. Stopford (1847–1929). See Stopford Green, Alice.

GREEN, Tammie (1959—). American golfer. Born Dec 17, 1959, in Somerset, Ohio; m. Bill Parker, 1998. ❖ Won 7 LPGA titles, including du Maurier Classic (1989) and Corning Classic (1998). Named LPGA Rookie of the Year (1987).

GREEN, Vera Mae (1928–1982). African-American social and applied anthropologist. Born Sept 6, 1928, in Chicago, Illinois; died Jan 17, 1982; graduate of William Penn College; Columbia University, MA in anthropology, 1955; University of Arizona, PhD, 1969; never married. ❖ Worked in social-welfare jobs in Chicago (early 1950s) before studying anthropology at Columbia University; served in international community development with United Nations; became one of the 1st African-American anthropologists to study interethnic relations in Caribbean and 1st to study Dutch Caribbean as culture area; joined staff of Rutgers University (1972) where she went on to serve as chair of the Department of Anthropology and director of Latin American Institute; explored diversity of black families and culture in America and the Caribbean; served as president of Association of Black Anthropologists (1977–79). Works include *Migrants in Aruba* (1974) and *International Human Rights* (as co-editor, 1980).

GREENAWAY, Kate (1846–1901). English illustrator of children's books. Born Mar 17, 1846, in Hoxton, London, England; died Nov 6, 1901, in Frognal, Hampstead, London, of breast cancer; dau. of John Greenaway (engraver and woodcut maker) and Elizabeth (Jones) Greenaway; studied at the Finsbury School of Art, the National Art Training School, Heatherley's School of Art, and Slade School of Art; never married; no children. ❖ Illustrator whose particular style proved widely influential, making her a household name at home and abroad and spawning a host of imitators; published 1st book illustration, *Infant Amusements, or How to Make a Nursery Happy* (1867); began working for the greeting-card industry, where her shrewd instinct for popular taste led to the development of a successful style which depicted a romantic vision of children in historical dress, set against a plain background with an ornate border; achieved success when 1st edition of *Under the Window* sold out within a few weeks (1879); published *Kate Greenaway's Birthday Book* (1880), which reassured her position as a leading illustrator when sales reflected its critical and popular acclaim; with the exception of one year, produced the Kate Greenaway *Almanack* (1883–97); was one of the primary influences on children's illustration and children's publishing in general. ❖ See also Rodney Engen, *Kate Greenaway: A Biography* (MacDonald Futura, 1981); M.H. Spielmann and G.S. Layard, *Kate Greenaway* (Adam & Charles Black, 1905); and *Women in World History.*

GREENAWAY, Margaret (fl. 15th c.). English merchant. Flourished in England in the 15th century; husband was dealer in biscuits and baked goods with the East India Company. ❖ Established herself as a businesswoman in the highly competitive area of international commerce; after husband died, maintained his business and supported herself well for many years.

GREENBAUM, Dorothea Schwarcz (1893–1986). American sculptor and activist. Born Dorothea Schwarcz in Brooklyn, New York, June 17, 1893; died in 1986; dau. of Maximilian Schwarcz (importer who died in the sinking of the *Lusitania*, 1915); attended New York School of Design for Women and Art Students League; m. Edward Greenbaum (lawyer), 1926; children: 2 sons. ❖ Began career as one of the Fourteenth Street School painters; following marriage, took up sculpture; beginning with clay modeling, gradually expanded to stone carving, then hammered lead; her sculpture *Sleeping Girl* (1928) was in the Chicago Century of Progress Exposition (1933); at Weyhe Gallery in Manhattan, had 1st one-woman exhibition; helped found Artist's Equity, an organization concerned with improving rights and economic opportunities for artists; other works include *Fascist* (c. 1938), *Girl With Fawn* (1936) and *Drowned Girl* (1950). ❖ See also *Women in World History.*

GREENE, Angela (1879—). English tennis player. Born in 1879. ❖ At London Olympics, won a silver medal in singles–indoor courts (1908).

GREENE, Angela (1921–1978). Irish actress. Born Aug 23, 1921, in Dublin, Ireland; died Feb 9, 1978, in Los Angeles, California. ❖ Model and actress; made film debut (1943) and subsequently appeared in over 50 films, including *The Time the Place the Girl, Stallion Road, Love and Learn, At War with the Army, The Graduate* and *Futureworld.*

GREENE, Belle da Costa (1883–1950). American librarian and bibliographer. Born in Alexandria, Virginia, Dec 13, 1883; died in New York, NY, May 10, 1950; 2nd daughter and 3rd of 5 children of Richard and Genevieve (Van Vliet) Greene; attended local schools in Princeton, New Jersey; never married; no children. ❖ Began career at Princeton University library; was hired to oversee collection of rare books and manuscripts of banker J. Pierpont Morgan (1905); when Morgan's son converted the library into an incorporated and endowed educational institution (1924), was named its director; for the next 24 years, worked to establish the library as a center for scholarly research; retired (1948). ❖ See also *Women in World History.*

GREENE, Catharine Littlefield (1755–1814). American inventor. Name variations: Katherine or Catherine, and Caty (KAY-tee). Born Catharine Littlefield, possibly with "Ray" as a middle name, Dec 17, 1755, on Block Island, Rhode Island; died Cumberland Island, Georgia, Sept 2, 1814; dau. of John Littlefield landowner and deputy of the General Assembly) and Phebe (Ray) Littlefield; mostly self-taught; m. Nathanael Greene (leading general in Revolutionary army), July 20, 1774 (died 1786); m. Phineas Miller, 1796 (died 1803); children: (1st m.) George Washington Greene (1776–1793), Martha Greene (Patty, b. 1777), Cornelia Lott Green (b. 1778), Nathanael Ray Greene (b. 1780), Louisa Catharine Greene (b. 1784), and Catharine Greene (1785–1785). ❖ Renowned participant in the political society of Revolutionary America who, with Eli Whitney and Phineas Miller, invented the cotton gin; married Nathanael Greene, set up housekeeping in Coventry, RI (1774); began a series of journeys to join husband in Continental Army (1775–83); returned home with husband (1783); moved with family to Mulberry Grove, Georgia (1785); filed a claim of indemnity on husband's behalf versus Federal government (1787); with Eli Whitney and Phineas Miller, invented the cotton gin (1793), providing the impetus for bringing it into being and making effective contributions to its design; patent rights of gin sold to South Carolina legislature (1802). ❖ See also John F. and Janet Stegeman, *Caty: A Biography of Catharine Littlefield Greene* (University of Georgia Press, 1985); and *Women in World History.*

GREENE, Catharine Ray (d. 1794). American letter writer. Died 1794 in Warwick, Rhode Island. ❖ Met Benjamin Franklin in early twenties and began lifelong correspondence with him and his sister Jane Franklin Mecom; letters published as *Benjamin Franklin and Catharine Ray Greene: Their Correspondence 1755–1790* (1949).

GREENE, Cordelia A. (1831–1905). American physician. Born Cordelia Agnes Greene, July 5, 1831, in Lyons, NY; died from surgery complications, Jan 28, 1905, in New York, NY; dau. of Phila (Cooke) Greene and Jabez Greene (sanitarium owner); never married; children: 6 (adopted), including Edward Greene (physician). ❖ One of 1st women medical school graduates in America, read an article about Elizabeth Blackwell that inspired a career in medicine; attended Female (later, Woman's) Medical College of Pennsylvania in Philadelphia (1854–55 and 1857–58) and Western Reserve University in Cleveland (graduated, 1856); was the chief assistant at the Water-Cure, her father's sanitarium in Castile, NY; practiced at Clifton Springs (NY) Sanitarium with Dr. Henry Foster (1859–65); after father's death, served as the Water-Cure's director until 1905 and renamed the business as the Castile Sanitarium (closed in 1954). Was a classmate of Marie Zakrzewska at Western Reserve University, where their entire medical class consisted of only 4 woman.

GREENE, Gertrude Glass (1904–1956). American painter and sculptor. Born Gertrude Glass in Brooklyn, New York, 1904; died in 1956; attended the Leonardo da Vinci Art School, New York; m. Balcomb Greene (painter), 1926; no children. ❖ Set up a studio in NY (1931); for next 15 years, sculpted in abstract, non-representative forms; was also active in bringing together other experimental artists and helped organize the American Abstract Artists Association, the Artists Union, and the

Sculptors Guild; works include the wood reliefs, *Construction in Blue* (1935), *Construction in Grey* (1939), and *White Anxiety* (1943–44).

GREENE, Katherine (1755–1814). See Greene, Catherine Littlefield.

GREENE, Maud (1495–1529). See Parr, Maud.

GREENE, Nancy (1943—). Canadian alpine skier. Name variations: Nancy Greene Raine. Born Nancy Catherine Greene, May 11, 1943, in Ottawa, Ontario, Canada; grew up in Rossland, British Columbia; sister of Liz Greene (skier); m. Al Raine (skier and coach), 1969. ❖ Won World Cup overall (1967, 1968); won a gold medal in giant slalom and a silver medal in slalom at Grenoble Olympics (1968); was 6-time Canadian champion and 3-time US champion; won 14 World Cup races; retired and established the Nancy Greene Ski League to train children (8–13) for competition (1968); operates Nancy Greene's Cahilty Lodge in Sun Peaks, British Columbia. Named Canada's Athlete of the Year (1967 and 1968); named Officer of the Order of Canada; inducted into Canadian Sports Hall of Fame and US Sports Hall of Fame. ❖ See also *Women in World History.*

GREENE, Sarah Pratt (1856–1935). American novelist. Name variations: Sarah Pratt McLean Greene; Sally McLean. Born Sarah Pratt McLean, July 3, 1856, in Simsbury, Connecticut; died Dec 28, 1935, in Lexington, Massachusetts; dau. of Dudley Bestor McLean (farmer) and Mary (Payne) McLean; sister of George Payne McLean (governor of Connecticut and US Senator); m. Franklin Lynde Greene, July 28, 1887; children: 2 sons (died in infancy). ❖ Gained notoriety for 1st novel, *Cape Cod Folks* (1881), having used real names of local people she depicted; published numerous subsequent books which were not as successful, though *Vesty of the Basins* (1892), her 2nd-most-popular book, earned some critical praise. Additional works include *Towhead: The Story of a Girl* (1883), *Some Other Folks* (1884), *Lastchance Junction* (1889), *Leon Pontifex* (1890), *The Moral Imbeciles* (1898), *Flood-Tide* (1901), and *Winslow Plain* (1902).

GREENER, Dorothy (1917–1971). English-born actress, singer, and comedian. Born Oct 16, 1917, in Gateshead, England; died Dec 6, 1971, in NYC. ❖ Moved to US as a child; made NY stage debut in the revue *Come What May* (1950); also appeared in *The Girls against the Boys, Razzle Dazzle, Shoestring Revue, Leave it to Jane* and *War Games;* often appeared in cabarets and on tv drama and variety shows.

GREENER, Rhona (1901–1931). See Haszard, Rhona.

GREENFIELD, Elizabeth Taylor (c. 1819–1876). Black concert artist and teacher. Name variations: The Black Swan. Born Elizabeth Taylor around 1819 in Natchez, Mississippi; died Mar 31, 1876, in Philadelphia, Pennsylvania; dau. of slaves; her father's surname was Taylor and her mother's name was given as Anna Greenfield; taught herself to play guitar, harp and piano; studied voice briefly in Philadelphia and in England; never married; no children. ❖ The 1st American singer to win critical acclaim for her performances both in the US and in Europe, was born into slavery; freed in infancy; taken by former owner to Philadelphia; inherited a substantial portion of her estate but the will was contested (1845); traveled to Buffalo, NY, to perform at the residence of Electa Potter (1851); made professional debut in Buffalo (Oct 1851); toured extensively (1851–53), receiving press coverage and positive reviews at nearly all of her recitals; traveled to England for further study and concertizing (1853); received one of the highest honors possible for any musician, a command performance before Queen Victoria, an unprecedented event; went on to become the 1st African-American performer to win praise from British audiences and the press; returned to US (summer 1854); concertized extensively and taught (1854–74); organized and directed the Black Swan Opera Troupe in Philadelphia (1860s), one of the earliest efforts to involve African-Americans in the performance of standard operatic literature; became increasingly active in her church, Shiloh Baptist, where she directed the choir. ❖ See also autobiography *The Black Swan* (1869); William S. Young, ed. *The Black Swan at Home and Abroad, or a Biographical Sketch of Miss Elizabeth Taylor Greenfield, the American Vocalist* (1855).

GREENFIELD, Meg (1930–1999). American journalist. Born Dec 27, 1930, in Seattle, Washington; died of lung cancer, May 13, 1999, in Washington, DC; dau. of Lewis and Lorraine (Nathan) Greenfield; Smith College, BA, summa cum laude, 1952; Fulbright Scholar, Newnham College, Cambridge (England) University, 1952–53; never married; no children. ❖ Longtime columnist for *The Washington Post,* worked for 11 years on the old *Reporter* magazine before joining the *Post* (1968) as an editorial writer; served as deputy editor of the editorial page

(1970–79), then editor (1979–99); was also a columnist for *Newsweek* magazine (1974–99). Won Pulitzer Prize for editorials on social policy (1978). ❖ See also *Women in World History.*

GREENHOOD, Henrietta (b. 1920). See Gentry, Eva.

GREENHOUGH, Dorothy (1875–1965). English figure skater. Name variations: Dorothy Greenhough Smith or Greenhough-Smith. Born in 1875; died May 1965. ❖ At London Olympics, won a bronze medal in singles (1908).

GREENHOW, Rose O'Neal (c. 1817–1864). American socialite and spy. Name variations: Wild Rose, Rebel Rose. Born around 1817 in Port Tobacco, Maryland; drowned on Oct 1, 1864, in the Cape Fear River near Wilmington, North Carolina; dau. of John O'Neal (Maryland planter); had little formal education, but was tutored by South Carolina Senator John C. Calhoun; m. Robert Greenhow (Virginia doctor, lawyer and linguist), 1835 (died 1854); children: Florence, Gertrude, Leila, and Rose Greenhow. ❖ Washington socialite, confidante of Senator John C. Calhoun and President James Buchanan, who was a daring Confederate spy during Civil War; with intelligence and vivacity, established herself as the most influential woman in Washington during James Buchanan's presidency (1857–61); moved with ease in the highest social circles and counted among her intimates many of the city's elite, including diplomats, senators, congressional representatives, cabinet secretaries, generals, and US presidents; organized an effective spy ring and supplied military information to the Confederate government (1861), providing information which assured an overwhelming Southern victory at Battle of Bull Run; arrested for espionage and imprisoned (Aug 1861); released from prison and deported to the South (June 1862); sent by President Jefferson Davis on a diplomatic and intelligence mission to England and France (Aug 1863); became engaged to 2nd Earl of Granville in London (1864); boarded the blockade runner *Condor,* carrying secret dispatches and gold for the Confederacy (Aug 1964); drowned in a storm off Wilmington, North Carolina (Oct 1864). ❖ See also memoirs, *My Imprisonment and the 1st Year of Abolition Rule in Washington* (1863); Ishbel Ross, *Rebel Rose: Life of Rose O'Neal Greenhow, Confederate Spy* (Harper & Brothers, 1954); and *Women in World History.*

GREENOUGH, Alice (d. 1995). See Orr, Alice Greenough.

GREENSILL, Nina Agatha Rosamond (1879–1965). See Barrer, Nina Agatha Rosamond.

GREENWAY, Isabella Selmes (1886–1953). American politician. Name variations: Isabella Selmes Ferguson Greenway King. Born Isabella Selmes on Mar 22, 1886; died Dec 18, 1953, at her home at the Arizona Inn, of congestive heart failure; dau. of Tilden Russell Selmes (rancher and lawyer, died 1895) and Martha Macomb (Flandrau) Selmes; attended Miss Chapin's and Miss Spence's schools, New York City; m. Robert H. Munro Ferguson, July 15, 1905 (died 1922); m. John Campbell Greenway (mining engineer), Nov 4, 1923 (died 1926); m. Harry Orland King (industrialist), April 22, 1939; children (1st m.) Robert and Martha; (2nd m.) John Selmes. ❖ Congresswoman, cattle rancher, airline operator, hotel owner, and community activist, homesteaded in New Mexico and served as chair of Women's Land Army of New Mexico (1911–21); bought ranch near Williams, Arizona, then moved to Tucson and opened the Arizona Hut, a rehabilitation workshop for veterans, among other community activities (1927); served as national Democratic committeewoman from Arizona (1928–32), campaigning for Al Smith (1928); co-founded G & G commuter airline (1929–30); founded Arizona Inn, resort hotel (1930); achieved national prominence when she seconded Franklin Roosevelt's nomination at Democratic convention, then campaigned for him (1932); elected congresswoman-at-large in special election (1933); easily re-elected (1934), serving until 1937; adamantly opposed to America's entry into the European war and Roosevelt's 3rd term, was active in the Democrats for Willkie movement (1940); served as chair of American Women's Voluntary Services (1941). ❖ See also *Women in World History.*

GREENWELL, Dora (1821–1882). British religious writer. Born Dec 6, 1821, in Greenwell Ford, Lanchester, Durham, England; died Mar 29, 1882, in Clifton, England; dau. of William Thomas Greenwell and Dorothy (Smales) Greenwell. ❖ Began publishing poetry out of financial need, and focused, in later poetry, on religious and mystical themes; prose works include essays, published in *North British Review* and elsewhere on social issues and on rights of women, animals, the insane, and children; writer of hymns, poetry, theological essays, biographies, and dramatic monologues; works include *Poems* (1848), *The Patience of Hope*

(1860), *Two Friends* (1862), *Carmina Crucis* (1869), *Songs of Salvation* (1873), *Camera Obscura* (1876), and *Selections from the Prose of Dora Greenwell* (ed. W.G. Hanson, 1952).

GREENWOOD, Charlotte (1890–1978). American comedic dancer and actress. Name variations: Letty Greenwood. Born Frances Charlotte Greenwood, June 25, 1890, in Philadelphia, Pennsylvania; died Jan 18, 1978, in Beverly Hills, California; m. Cyril Ring (actor and brother of Blanche Ring) (div. 1922); m. Martin Broones (musician), 1924 (died 1971). ❖ Known for her long legs and high kicks, made professional debut in the chorus of *The White Cat* (1905); toured vaudeville; had major career on Broadway in such plays as *The Passing Show of 1912, So Long Letty, She Knew What She Wanted, Music Box Revue, I Remember Mama* and *Out of This World;* films include *Flying High, Star Dust, Down Argentine Way, Moon over Miami, Springtime in the Rockies, Peggy, Oklahoma!* (as Aunt Eller, 1955), and *The Opposite Sex.* ❖ See also autobiography *Never Too Tall.*

GREENWOOD, Edith. American nurse. Name variations: Lt. Edith. Greenwood. Born in North Dartmouth, Massachusetts. ❖ With Pvt. James Ford, successfully evacuated all patients at a military hospital in Yuma, Arizona, after a fire broke out (April 17, 1943); for her heroism, became 1st woman to receive the Soldier's Medal (June 21, 1943).

GREENWOOD, Ellen Sarah (1837–1917). New Zealand teacher and social worker. Born probably on Feb 19, 1837, in Surrey, England; died Nov 29, 1917, in Wellington, New Zealand; dau. of John Danforth Greenwood (surgeon) and Sarah (Field) Greenwood. ❖ Immigrated with family to New Zealand (1843); served as governess in Auckland before returning to New Zealand (1868); opened day school in Taranaki Place (1871–83); with sisters, helped establish The Terrace School for girls in Wellington; through community work with Wellington Ladies' Christian Association, helped establish home for unmarried, destitute, and sick women, and home for orphaned girls and young women. ❖ See also *Dictionary of New Zealand Biography* (Vol. 2).

GREENWOOD, Grace (1823–1904). *See Lippincott, Sara Clarke.*

GREENWOOD, Joan (1921–1987). British actress. Born in London, England, Mar 4, 1921; died in London in Feb 1987; dau. of Sydney Barnshaw (artist) and Ida (Waller) Greenwood; attended St. Catherine's, Bramley, Surrey; attended the Royal Academy of Dramatic Arts; m. André Morell (actor), May 16, 1960 (died 1978); children: one son. ❖ Stage, screen, and tv actress, made London stage debut as Louisa in *The Robust Invalid* (1938); made film debut in *John Smith Wakes Up* (1940); after a two-year stage tour as Wendy in *Peter Pan* (1941), played title role in *Lysistrata* (1957), Hattie in *The Grass is Greener* (1958), title role in *Hedda Gabler* (1960), Hedda in *The Irregular Verb To Love* (1961); title role in *Hedda Gabler* (1964), Olga in *Oblomov* (1964), Mrs. Rogers in *The Au Pair Man* (1969), Lady Kitty in *The Circle* (1970), and Miss Madrigal in *The Chalk Garden* (1970), among others; made NY stage debut in T.S. Eliot's *The Confidential Clerk* (1954); films include *Kind Hearts and Coronets* (1949), *Flesh and Blood* (1950), *The Man in the White Suit* (1951), *The Importance of Being Earnest* (1952), *Moonfleet* (1955), *Stage Struck* (1958), *Mysterious Island* (1961), *Tom Jones* (1963), *The Moon-Spinners* (1964), *The Hound of the Baskervilles* (1978), *The Water Babies* (1979), *Wagner* (1983), and *Little Dorritt* (1987). ❖ See also *Women in World History.*

GREENWOOD, Marion (1909–1980). American-born painter. Born in Brooklyn, New York, 1909; died in Woodstock, New York, 1980; sister of Grace Greenwood (artist); left high school at 15 to study with John Sloan and George Bridgman at Art Students League, New York; studied at the Académie Colarossi, Paris, France; m. Robert Plate; no children. ❖ Known primarily for her powerful murals; career reflects a progression of styles, beginning with the revolutionary fervor of her early work in Mexico (worked on group mural at the central market and civic center in Mexico City [the Mercado Rodríguez]), through the restrained and classical murals commissioned by the Federal Art Project (1930s), and culminating in her later independent murals which represent a freer, almost expressionistic, quality. ❖ See also *Women in World History.*

GREENWOOD, Sarah (c. 1809–1889). New Zealand artist, letter writer, and teacher. Name variations: Sarah Field. Born Sarah Field, c. 1809 (baptized, Dec 20, 1809), in Lambeth, London, England; dau. of John Field (wax chandler) and Mary Ann (Jones) Field; m. John Danforth Greenwood (physician), 1831; children: 13. ❖ After poor health forced her husband to retire from his London practice, settled with family near Paris, France, returning to England to raise capital to purchase shares in

New Zealand Company (1842); immigrated to New Zealand to settle their land (1843); recorded pioneer life in letters and sketches of Nelson district; with two of her daughters, opened boarding school for girls (1866). ❖ See also *Dictionary of New Zealand Biography* (Vol. 1).

GREER, Bettejane (1924–2001). *See Greer, Jane.*

GREER, Germaine (1939—). Australian literary critic and feminist. Born Jan 29, 1939, near Melbourne, Australia; dau. of Eric Reginald Greer and Margaret May Mary (Lanfracan) Greer; Melbourne University, BA in English and French Literature; Cambridge University, PhD, 1967; m. Paul de Feu, 1968. ❖ Became lecturer at University of Warwick before writing 1st book; published *The Female Eunuch* (1970) which became a bestseller in Europe and US and launched her career as a controversial feminist speaker, critic, and writer who would be both praised and excoriated by feminists; other works include *The Obstacle Race: The Fortunes of Women Painters and Their Work* (1979), *Sex and Destiny: The Politics of Human Fertility* (1984), *Shakespeare* (1986), *The Madwoman's Underclothes: Essays and Occasional Writings* (1987), *Daddy, We Hardly Knew You* (1989), *The Change: Women, Aging and Menopause* (1992), and *The Whole Woman* (1999).

GREER, Jane (1924–2001). American actress and singer. Name variations: Bettejane Greer. Born Bettejane Greer, Sept 9, 1924, in Washington DC; died Aug 24, 2001, in Los Angeles, California; m. Rudy Vallee (crooner), 1943 (div. 1944); m. Edward Lasker, 1947 (div. 1963); children: 3 sons, including Alex (writer) and Lawrence Lasker (producer). ❖ Began career singing with big bands, most notably Enric Madriguera's orchestra in the Latin Club Del Rio in Washington, DC; sang on radio; made film debut as Bettejane Greer in *Two O'Clock Courage* (1945), then as Jane Greer in Howard Hughes's *Dick Tracy* (1945); other films include the *film noir* classic *Out of the Past,* as well as *The Falcon's Alibi, The Big Steal, They Won't Believe Me, The Prisoner of Zenda, The Clown, Run for the Sun, The Man of a Thousand Faces* and *Against All Odds.*

GREET, Clare (1871–1939). English actress. Born June 14, 1871, in England; died Feb 14, 1939, in London, England. ❖ Made West End debut as Hetty in *The Love Letter* (1894), followed by *The Duchess of Dantzic, Major Barbara, Hannele, The Naked Truth, The Lower Depths, Jane Clegg, Androcles and the Lion, The Wild Duck, Keeping Up Appearances, The Rotters, Time to Wake Up* (as Mary Scattergood), and *Outward Bound,* among others; films include *Many Waters, Third Time Lucky, Murder, Lord Camber's Ladies, Mrs. Dane's Defence, Little Friend* and *Jamaica Inn.*

GREEVES, Marion Janet (1894–1979). Northern Ireland politician. Born Marion Janet Cadbury, 1894, in England; died in 1979; m. William E. Greeves (member of Cadbury chocolate-manufacturing family). ❖ As an Independent, elected to the Northern Ireland Senate (1950–58).

GREEVY, Bernadette (1939—). Irish mezzo-soprano. Born in Dublin, Ireland, Aug 29, 1939; 6th of 7 children of Josephine (Miller) and Patrick Joseph Greevy; educated at Holy Faith Convent, Clontarf, Dublin and at Guildhall School of Music, London; studied privately with Helene Isepp and later with Nadia Boulanger in Paris; married Peter A. Tattan, 1965 (died Mar 1983); children: one son (b. 1967). ❖ Made professional debut in Dublin (1961) and performed at the Wexford Festival in Mascagni's *L'Amico Fritz* (1962); made London debut at Wigmore Hall (1964); returned to Wexford in Massenet's *Hérodiade* and also sang Laura in Ponchielli's *La Gioconda* in Dublin and Geneviève in Debussy's *Pelléas et Mélisande* at Covent Garden; forged fruitful working relationships with Hungarian conductor Tibor Paul and Radio Eireann Symphony Orchestra in Dublin, and with Sir John Barbirolli and the Hallé Orchestra in Manchester (1960s); with Barbirolli, performed works with which she became particularly associated, notably Mahler's *Lieder eines fahrenden Gesellen* and the Angel in Elgar's *Dream of Gerontius;* best known for her recordings of Elgar and Mahler, also made several recordings of French songs, including Berlioz and Duparc; created roles in works by leading Irish composers: Bodley's *Meditations on lines from Patrick Kavanagh* (1971), *A Girl* (1978) and *The Naked Flame* (1987), Boydell's *A Terrible Beauty is Born* (1965), and Victory's requiem cantata *Ultima Rerum* (1984); gave the 1st in what was to be a regular series of master classes at National Concert Hall in Dublin (1984).

GREFF, Kaye (1951—). *See Hall, Kaye.*

GREGG, Christina (c. 1814–1882). New Zealand accused murderer and farmer. Name variations: Christina Ferguson, Christina Langstreth.

Born Christina Ferguson, c. 1814/15, in Scotland; died Nov 17, 1882, at Riccarton, New Zealand; dau. of John Ferguson (carpenter) and Helen Ferguson; m. James Gregg (quarryman), 1842 (died 1859); children: 1. ❖ Immigrated to New Zealand (1842); established farm with husband in Riccarton; found guilty by coroner's jury of wilful murder after husband's sudden death (Edmund Langstreth, whom she later married, was also detained but not charged); declared not guilty by Supreme Court (1859). ❖ See also *Dictionary of New Zealand Biography* (Vol. 1).

GREGG, Virginia (1916–1986). American stage, tv and screen actress. Born Virginia Gregg Burket, Mar 6, 1916, in Harrisburg, Illinois; died Sept 15, 1986, in Encino, California; m. Jaime Del Valle (died 1981); children: three sons. ❖ Had an active career in radio; films include *Body and Soul, Journey to Nowhere, Spencer's Mountain, I'll Cry Tomorrow, Operation Petticoat, Casbah* and *Love is a Many Splendored Thing.* Was the off-screen voice of Norman Bates' mother in *Psycho.*

GREGO, Melania (1973—). Italian water-polo player. Born June 19, 1973, in Italy. ❖ At World championships, won team gold medals (1998, 2001); driver, won a team gold medal at Athens Olympics (2004).

GRÉGOIRE, Colette Anna (1931–1966). Algerian poet. Name variations: Colette Anna Gregoire; Colette Anna Gregoire-Melki; married name Melki; (pseudonym) Anna Greki. Born 1931 in Algeria; died in childbirth in 1966. ❖ Studied in Paris but returned to Algeria and was arrested, tortured, and imprisoned for 1 year; deported to France; poetry describes prison experience and focuses on Algerian independence struggle.

GREGOR, Nora (1901–1949). Austrian stage and screen actress. Born Eleonora Hermina Gregor, Feb 3, 1901, in Görz, Istrien, Austria-Hungary (now Gorizia, Italy); died Jan 20, 1949, in Santiago, Chile; m. Mitja Nikish; m. Prince Ernst Ruediger von Starhemberg (political figure); children: Prince Heinrich Starhemberg (1934–1997, producer, director, and actor). ❖ Made stage debut in Graz, Austria, then appeared at the Volksbühne an das Raimund Theater and the Burgtheater, both in Vienna, and with Max Reinhardt in Berlin; made silent film debut in *The Schauspielerin des Kaisers* (1921) and 1st talkie in the title role in *Olympia* (1930); after the annexation of Austria by the Nazis (1938), immigrated with family to Switzerland, then Chile.

GREGORIA-ANASTASIA (fl. 640s). Byzantine empress. Fl. around 640s. Married Heraclonas-Constantine, Byzantine emperor (r. 641).

GREGORY, Augusta (1852–1932). Irish playwright, patron, folklorist, and theater founder. Name variations: Lady Gregory. Born Isabella Augusta Persse on Mar 15, 1852, at Roxborough, Co. Galway, Ireland; died at Coole Park, Co. Galway, Ireland, May 23, 1932; dau. of Dudley Persse (landowner) and Frances (Barry) Persse; educated at home; m. Sir William Gregory (MP, 1st as a Conservative [1842–47] then as a Liberal [1852–71] and governor of Ceylon), Mar 4, 1880 (died 1892); children: Robert (1881–1918). ❖ Co-founder of the Abbey Theater in Dublin, married Sir William Gregory (1880), who owned Coole Park, a neighboring estate; with husband, over next 12 years, spent most of her time either at their house in London or traveling abroad; published 1st writing, *Arabi and his Household* (1882); became increasingly interested in history and folklore and learned the Irish language; had meeting with W.B. Yeats (1894); began to support self-government for Ireland; was responsible for 1st performances of Irish Literary Theater (1899); collaborated with Yeats on plays, *Cathleen ni Houlihan* and *The Pot of Broth* (1901–02); published *Cuchulain of Muirthemne* (1902) and *Gods and Fighting Men* (1904), the 1st books to render Irish mythology into an Irish idiom; co-founded and served as director, Abbey Theater (1904); for the next 10 years, wrote over 20 plays—comedies, historical dramas, adaptations from Molière—of which the most successful were *Spreading the News* (1904), *Kincora* (1905), *Hyacinth Halvey* (1906), *The Rising of the Moon* (1907), *The Workhouse Ward* (1908), and *MacDonogh's Wife* (1912); was manager for 1st US tour of Abbey (1911–12); had friendship with Sean O'Casey (1924). ❖ See also *Seventy Years: Being the Autobiography of Lady Gregory. The Coole Edition of the Works of Lady Gregory* (Colin Smythe, 1974); Elizabeth Coxhead, *Lady Gregory: A Literary Portrait* (Secker & Warburg, 1966); Mary Lou Kohfeldt, *Lady Gregory: The Woman Behind the Irish Renaissance* (Andre Deutsch, 1985); Ann Saddlemyer and Colin Smythe, eds. *Lady Gregory: Fifty Years After* (Barnes & Noble, 1987); and *Women in World History.*

GREGORY, Cynthia (1946—). American ballerina. Born Cynthia Kathleen Gregory on July 8, 1946, in Los Angeles, California; only child of Konstantin Gregory (dress manufacturer) and Marcelle (Tremblay) Gregory; studied ballet with Michel Panaieff, Robert Rossellat, Carmelita Maracci, and Jacques D'Amboise; m. Terrence S. Orr (dancer), May 14, 1966 (div. 1975); m. John Hemminger (rock-music manager and promoter), 1976 (died 1984); m. Hilary B. Miller (investment banker), in Dec 1985; children: a stepdaughter, Amanda Hemminger, and a son, Lloyd Miller. ❖ Acclaimed for her technical virtuosity and dramatic appeal, gained international stardom as a principal dancer with New York's American Ballet Theater (ABT), where she was best known for her individualized interpretations of the leading roles in classical ballets, particularly *Swan Lake;* enrolled in the San Francisco Ballet School and danced as an apprentice with the company's corps de ballet; became an official member of the company (1961), dancing 1st solo in *The Nutcracker;* joined ABT and was elevated to soloist (1966), then principal dancer (1967); distinguished herself in works like *Undertow, Miss Julie* and *Intermezzo;* danced Swanilda in *Coppélia* (1977) to acclaim; performed as a guest artist with other companies, among them the Stuttgart Ballet and the state opera ballets of Zurich, Vienna, and Munich; toured with her own troupe in "Cynthia Gregory: A Celebration of Twenty-Five Years of Dancing." ❖ See also *Women in World History.*

GREGORY, Lady.
See Stirling, Mary Anne (1815–1895).
See Gregory, Augusta (1852–1932).

GREIFFENBERG, Catharina Regina von (1633–1694). Austrian poet and baroness. Name variations: Baroness von Greiffenberg. Born Catharina Regina von Greiffenberg, Sept 7, 1633, in Burg Seyssenegg bei Amstetten, Lower Austria; died April 10, 1694, in Nuremberg, Germany; m. Baron Hans Rudolph von Greiffenberg, 1664. ❖ Father died (1641); married uncle who had acted as benefactor; after husband's death (1677), fled persecution of Protestants in Austria for Nuremberg and became established poet; writings include *Geistliche Sonnette/Lieder und Gedichte* (1662), *Tugend-Übungen sieben Lustwehlender Schäferinnen* (1675), and *Sieges-Seule der Buße und des Glaubens* (1675).

GREIG, Dorothy Margaret (1922–1999). See Greig, Margaret.

GREIG, Margaret (1922–1999). English applied mathematician. Name variations: Dorothy Margaret Greig; Margaret Hannah or M. Hannah. Born Dorothy Margaret Hannah, Feb 11, 1922; died June 10, 1999; graduated from Newnham College, Cambridge, 1943; University of Leeds, MS and PhD, 1950; m. W.A. Greig, 1948; children: 3 sons and 1 daughter. ❖ An applied mathematician who worked on the mathematical analysis of the control factors of the Ambler Superdraft process (employed in the worsted spinning industry), began career working for the Air Warfare Analysis Section, Ministry of Defence (from 1943); was a lecturer at the University of Leeds' Department of Textile Industries (1948–59); lectured at an International Wool Conference (and in Australia) on the Ambler Superdraft system; was a Constantine Technical College senior lecturer (1959–64); taught as a University of Durham lecturer and senior lecturer in mathematics (1964–86); served as a higher degree board member of the Council for National Academic Awards (CNAA) for Mathematical Sciences. Received Textile Institute's Warner Memorial Medal (1959), for work on the Ambler Superdraft system.

GREIG, Marion (1954—). American rower. Born Feb 22, 1954. ❖ At Montreal Olympics, won a bronze medal in coxed eights (1976).

GREIG, Teresa Billington (1877–1964). See Billington-Greig, Teresa.

GREINER-PETTER-MEMM, Simone (1967—). German biathlete. Name variations: Simone Greiner, Simone Petter, Simone Memm. Born Sept 15, 1967, in Jena, Germany. ❖ Won a silver medal for 4 x 7.5 km relay at Lillehammer Olympics (1994).

GREKI, Anna (1931–1966). See Grégoire, Colette Anna.

GREKOVA, I. (1907–2002). See Venttsel, Elena Sergeevna.

GRENARD, Lizz (1965—). American climber. Name variations: Liz Grenard. Born Feb 14, 1965, in Michigan. ❖ Wildlife biologist, won bronze in Ice Climbing (Speed) at X Games (Winter 1998); served on 2nd-place team at The Adventure Eco Challenge.

GRENFELL, Helen L. (b. 1868). American educator and penologist. Born Helen Loring in Valparaiso, Chile, 1868; m. Edwin I. Grenfell, 1889. ❖ After serving as superintendent of schools, was made state superintendent of public instruction in Colorado; during 3 terms (1899–1905), greatly increased school revenues and revised and annotated school laws; was commissioner of Colorado State Penitentiary and Reformatory, with full control of penal institutions of the state, the only woman at the time to hold such an office (1909–14).

GRENFELL, Joyce (1910–1979). British actress and writer. Born Joyce Irene Phipps in London, England, Feb 10, 1910; died Nov 30, 1979, in London; only daughter and one of two children of Paul Phipps (architect) and Nora (Langhorne) Phipps (sister of Nancy Astor); attended schools in Claremont, Esher, and Surrey, England; attended Royal Academy of Dramatic Art, London; m. Reginald Pascoe Grenfell (chartered accountant), Dec 12, 1928; no children. ❖ Known for her impersonations of somewhat daffy aristocratic women, began contributing light verse to *Punch;* became a radio critic for London Sunday *Observer* (1935); made professional stage debut in *The Little Revue* (1939) and went on to play in 3 subsequent editions; also appeared in *Diversion* (1940) and *Diversions No. 2;* during WWII, joined a troupe of entertainers touring the battlefields; appeared in Noel Coward's revue *Sigh No More* (1945), followed by the revues, *Tuppence Coloured* (1947) and *Penny Plain* (1953); appeared regularly in films, usually in brief but memorable roles, including *Stage Fright* (1950), *Laughter in Paradise* (1951), *The Pickwick Papers* (1952), *Genevieve* (1953), *The Million Pound Note* (*Man With a Million,* 1954), *The Belles of St. Trinian's* (1954), *The Pure Hell of St. Trinian's* (1960), *The Americanization of Emily* (1964), and *The Yellow Rolls-Royce* (1964); opened in *Joyce Grenfell Requests the Pleasure* (1954), consisting of songs and monologues of her own composition; evolved into a solo performer, touring extensively in US, Canada, Australia, New Zealand with great success; continued to appear on tv (including "Ed Sullivan Show" in US), and wrote light verse and humorous essays for British and American periodicals. Awarded OBE for her war work (1946). ❖ See also *Women in World History.*

GRENVILLE, Honora (c. 1495–1566). *See Lisle, Honora Grenville.*

GRÈS, Alix (1910–1993). French fashion designer. Name variations: Germaine Krebs; Alix Barton; Madame Alix Gres. Born Germaine Barton, 1910; died in southern France, Nov 24, 1993; married M. Krebs; children: daughter Ann Grès. ❖ Under professional name of Madame Grès, was prominent on French fashion scene for 50 years; known for her independent approach to design and her respect for the figure of the wearer, created well-cut clothes that pleased clients as well as fashion commentators and columnists; was president of the Federation Française de la Couture for many years; clothed such clients as Grace Kelly, Marlene Dietrich, and Jacqueline Kennedy. ❖ See also *Women in World History.*

GRESE, Irma (1923–1945). German war criminal. Name variations: Griese. Born 1923; hanged in Hamelin, Germany, Dec 13, 1945. ❖ Known as the "beast of Belsen," supervised and brutalized females at the concentration camps of Ravensbrück, Auschwitz and Bergen Belsen during WWII; was convicted of war crimes. ❖ See also *Women in World History.*

GRESS, Elsa (1919–1989). Danish playwright, memoirist and feminist. Name variations: Elsa Gress Wright. Born 1919 in Denmark; died 1989 (some sources cite 1988); m. Clifford Wright (1919–1999, American painter), 1956. ❖ Independent and forthright speaker in public debates, wrote memoirs *Mine mange hjem* (1965), *Fuglefri og fremmed* (1971), and *Compania I-II* (1976), as well as plays, scripts, and work on feminism including *Det uopdagede kon* (1964) in response to Simone de Beauvoir's *The Second Sex;* with husband, established the artist colony Decenter in Marienborg on the Island of Mon, north of Copenhagen.

GRESSER, Gisela (1906–2000). American chess champion. Born Gisela Kahn, 1906, in Detroit, Michigan; died Dec 4, 2000, in New York, NY; attended Radcliffe College; m. William Gresser (lawyer and musicologist), 1927 (died 1992); children: Ion and Julian. ❖ Pioneer in women's chess, entered her 1st competition in 1940; won her 1st US Women's Chess championship (1944); was 9-time national champion as well as a championship challenger at Women's World Chess championships (1949 and 1950); became the 1st American woman to achieve a master's rating. Was the 1st woman inducted into the US Chess Hall of Fame.

GRESSHÖNER, Maria (1908–1942). *See Osten, Maria.*

GRÉTRY, Lucile (1772–1790). French composer of opera. Name variations: Lucile Gretry. Born Angélique-Dorothée-Louise Grétry in Paris, France, July 15, 1772; died in Paris in Mar 1790; dau. of André Ernest Modeste Grétry (composer). ❖ At 13, composed the vocal parts, as well as the bass and a harp accompaniment for *Le mariage d'Antonio* which her

father later orchestrated; also composed *Toinette et Louis.* ❖ See also *Women in World History.*

GRETKIEWICZ, Jadwiga (1912–1990). *See Wajs, Jadwiga.*

GREUTER, Helen Wright (1914–1997). *See Wright, Helen.*

GRÉVILLE, Alice (1842–1903). French novelist and journalist. Name variations: Alice Greville; Alice Durand; Alice Marie Celeste Fleury Durand-Greville; Alice Durand; (pseudonym) Henry Gréville. Born Alice Marie Céleste Fleury in 1842, in Paris, France; died 1903 in France; dau. of a professor of French at University of St Petersburg; m. Emile-Alex Durand (1838–1914, professor of French). ❖ Well educated, lived 15 years in Russia, returning to France (1872); novels and nonfiction, which reflect fascination with Russian culture, include *Les Koumiassine* (1877), *Les Epreuves de Raissa* (1877), *Instruction morale et civique des jeunes filles* (1881), *Un Violon Russe* (1889), and *Louk Loukitch* (1890).

GREVILLE, Frances Evelyn (1861–1938). Countess of Warwick, British philanthropist, and social leader. Name variations: Daisy Warwick; Lady Brooke. Born Frances Evelyn Maynard in 1861; died 1938; granddau. of Viscount Maynard; m. Charles Greville, Lord Brooke (who became 5th earl of Warwick in 1893), 1881 (died 1923); children: Mercie Greville (actress under stage name Nancie Parsons, b. 1904). ❖ A celebrated beauty of enormous wealth, inherited estates of grandfather when she was just a child; following marriage, became a member of the "Marlborough House Set," the prominent social circle of the prince of Wales (future King Edward VII), with whom she reportedly had a long affair (1890s); founded various organizations for the welfare of the poor, as well as a home for crippled children in Warwick; became an active socialist, establishing schools for rural children (1890s) and eventually founding Lady Warwick College, an agricultural institution for training young women in horticulture; served as editor of *Women's Agricultural Times* and published pamphlets and several books; lectured on Socialism in London and US; joined Labor Party; made an unsuccessful bid as a candidate for Warwick and Leamington (1923), losing to relative, Sir Anthony Eden. ❖ See also autobiographies, *Life's Ebb and Flow* (1929) and *Afterthoughts* (1931); and *Women in World History.*

GREVILLE, Henry (1842–1903). *See Gréville, Alice.*

GREVILLE, Julia (1979—). Australian swimmer. Born Feb 18, 1979, in Perth, Western Australia. ❖ Won a bronze medal for 800-meter freestyle relay at Atlanta Olympics (1996).

GREVILLE, Mercy (1904–1968). *See Parsons, Nancie.*

GREW, Mary (1902–1971). English actress. Born Aug 1902, in London, England; died Mar 20, 1971; m. Victor Sheridan. ❖ Made stage debut in *We Moderns* (1925); other plays include *The Donovan Affair, The Combined Maze* (as Violet Usher), *A Family Man, Before Breakfast, Justice, Loyalties, The Father, Typhoon, Ghosts* (as Regina), *Street Scene* and *100 Years Old.*

GREW, Mary A. (1813–1896). American abolitionist and suffragist. Born Sept 1, 1813, in Hartford, Connecticut; died Oct 10, 1896, in Philadelphia, Pennsylvania; dau. of the Rev. Henry Grew and Kate Merrow; lived for many years with close friend Margaret Burleigh. ❖ Served as corresponding secretary for Female Anti-Slavery Society until 1870; elected to executive committee of Pennsylvania Anti-Slavery Society and was co-editor of its publication, *Pennsylvania Freeman;* served as delegate to World's Anti-Slavery Convention (London, 1840), where neither she nor other women delegates were allowed to enter the convention floor, an event which pushed her toward the issue of women's rights; served as president of Pennsylvania Woman Suffrage Association (1869–92) and American Woman Suffrage Association (1887); helped found New Century Club of Philadelphia (1877), an important early woman's club.

GREY, Anne (d. 1474). *See Holland, Anne.*

GREY, Beryl (1927—). English ballerina. Born Beryl Elizabeth Groom in Highgate, London, England, June 11, 1927; attended theater schools; early dance training with Madeleine Sharpe in Bromley; studied at Sadler's Wells Ballet school under Nicholas Sergevev, Ninette de Valois and Vera Volkova; m. Sven Svenson (Swedish osteopath), 1950; children: Ingvar. ❖ One of Britain's most admired ballerinas, debuted as Odette/Odile in full-length *Swan Lake* on 15th birthday; subsequently danced nearly every major ballet role, including most all of the classical and modern ballets from *Giselle* to *Ballet Imperial;* also created many new roles, including the memorable Winter Fairy in Frederick Ashton's *Cinderella;* resigned from Royal Ballet (1957) to freelance; was the 1st foreign ballerina to be a guest artist with Bolshoi Ballet in Moscow (1957); was the 1st Western dancer to appear with Beijing (Peking) and Shanghai ballets (1964); was appointed director of Arts Educational School in London (1966); served as artistic director of London Festival Ballet (1968–80); also became a great favorite in Sweden, where she made regular guest appearances with Royal Swedish Ballet. ❖ See also memoirs *Red Curtain Up* (1958) and *Through the Bamboo Curtain* (1966); David Gillard, *Beryl Grey* (1977).

GREY, Catherine (c. 1540–1568). *Countess of Hertford and Pembroke.*
Name variations: Lady Katherine Grey; Lady Catherine Seymour; countess of Pembroke. Born c. 1540 or 1541 in England; died Jan 22, 1568, in Cockfield, Suffolk, England; dau. of Henry Grey, marquis of Dorset (later duke of Suffolk) and Frances Brandon (1517–1559, granddau. of King Henry VII); younger sister of Lady Jane Grey (1537–1554); m. Henry Herbert, 2nd earl of Pembroke, May 21, 1553 (div. before 1554); m. Edward Seymour, 2nd earl of Hertford, in Nov 1560; children: (2nd m.) Edward Seymour (b. 1561, Viscount Beauchamp); Thomas Seymour (b. 1563). ❖ At 17, was in line for the throne of England but was excluded because of actions of her sister, Lady Jane Grey (1554); secretly married Edward Seymour without royal approval (1560); was sent to the Tower of London by Elizabeth I; remained in some sort of custody for the rest of her life. ❖ See also *Women in World History.*

GREY, Denise (1896–1996). *French actress of stage and film.* Born Jeanne Marie Laurentine Edouardine Verthuy in Sept 17, 1896, in Turin, Italy; died Jan 13, 1996, in Paris, France; children: Suzanne Grey (b. 1917, actress). ❖ Had a career that spanned 9 decades; began as a leading can-can dancer in Follies Bergères; appeared in over 90 films, including *Les Bleus de l'amour* (1918), *Monsieur Hector* (1940), *Boléro* (1942), *Rome Express* (1949), *Le Père de Mademoiselle* (1953), *Julietta* (1953), *Poison d'avril* (1954), *Carve Her Name with Pride* (1958), *La Bonne soupe* (1963), *Les Saison du plaisir* (1988), and *Cin Cin* (1991); was an actress playing grandmother roles when she retired at 95.

GREY, Elizabeth (1437–1492). *See Woodville, Elizabeth.*

GREY, Elizabeth (fl. 1482–1530). *6th Baroness Lisle.* Born c. 1482; some sources cite death in 1525; dau. of Edward Grey (b. 1462), 1st viscount L'Isle or Lisle, and Elizabeth Talbot (d. 1487); m. Edmund Dudley (c. 1462–1510), chancellor of the Exchequer; m. Arthur Plantagenet (d. 1541), Viscount L'Isle or Lisle (son of King Edward IV and his mistress Elizabeth Lucy), before April 1533; children: (1st m.) John Dudley (c. 1502–1553), earl of Warwick and duke of Northumberland; Andrew Dudley; Jerome Dudley; Elizabeth Dudley (who m. William, 7th baron Stourton); (2nd m.) Frances Plantagenet; Elizabeth Plantagenet; Bridget Plantagenet.

GREY, Elizabeth (1505–1526). *5th Baroness Lisle.* Name variations: Baroness L'Isle. Born 1505; died 1526 (some sources cite 1519); dau. of John Grey, 4th viscount Lisle, and Muriel Howard (d. 1512); m. Charles Brandon, later duke of Suffolk (annulled); m. Henry Courtenay, marquis of Exeter, after June 11, 1515; children: Edward Courtenay, earl of Devon. ❖ As heir, was betrothed to Charles Brandon, who was given the title Viscount Lisle, but refused to marry him when he came of age.

GREY, Elizabeth (1581–1651). *Countess of Kent.* Name variations: Elizabeth Talbot. Born Elizabeth Talbot in 1581; died Dec 7, 1651; dau. of Gilbert Talbot (b. 1552), 7th earl of Shrewsbury, and Mary Cavendish; m. Henry Grey, 7th earl of Kent. ❖ Rumored to be secretly married to jurist John Selden, who had been a steward to her deceased husband; published a collection of culinary recipes as well as *A Choice Manuall, or Rare and Select Secrets in Physick and Chyrurgery.*

GREY, Elizabeth (d. 1818). *Countess of Gainsborough.* Died Sept 20, 1818; dau. of George Grey (b. 1767) and Mary Whitbread; m. Charles Noel, 1st earl of Gainsborough, May 13, 1817; children: Charles George Noel, 2nd earl of Gainsborough (b. on Sept 5, 1818).

GREY, Elizabeth (d. 1822). *Countess Grey.* Died May 26, 1822; dau. of George Grey; m. Charles Grey, 1st earl Grey, June 8, 1762; children: Charles Grey, 2nd earl Grey (b. 1764); Henry George Grey (b. 1766); George Grey (b. 1767).

GREY, Eve (1900–1983). *See Gray, Eve.*

GREY, Frances (1517–1559). *See Brandon, Frances.*

GREY, Lady Jane (1537–1554). **Teenaged usurper of the English throne.**
Name variations: Lady Jane Dudley. Born Oct 1537 at Bradgate, Leicestershire, England; executed Feb 12, 1554, in Tower of London; eldest surviving dau. of Henry Grey (d. 1554), marquis of Dorset (later duke of Suffolk), and Frances Brandon (1517–1559, granddau. of King Henry VII); sister of Lady Catherine Grey (c. 1540–1568) and Mary Grey (1545–1578); m. Lord Guildford Dudley, May 21, 1553; no children. ❖ Reigned for 9 days before being executed in the Tower of London; lived out brief life as a pawn of her ambitious parents and their political connections at court; entered the service of Queen Catherine Parr (1546); coerced into marrying Lord Dudley by his father, the duke of Northumberland (1553); with the death of the king, proclaimed queen by Northumberland without her knowledge; convicted of high treason against Queen Mary I and executed (1554). ❖ See also Alison Plowden, *Lady Jane Grey and the House of Suffolk* (Watts, 1986); Hester Chapman, *Lady Jane Grey: The Nine Days Queen* (Little, Brown, 1962); Mary Luke, *The Nine Days Queen* (William Morrow, 1986); David Mathew, *Lady Jane Grey: The Setting of the Reign* (Eyre Methuen, 1972); films *Lady Jane Grey,* starring Nova Pilbeam (1936) and *Lady Jane,* starring Helena Bonham Carter (1985); and *Women in World History.*

GREY, Jane (1883–1944). *American stage actress.* Born May 22, 1883, in Middlebury, Vermont; died Nov 9, 1944, in NYC; m. Ricardo Martin. ❖ Made stage debut in *Rose of the Rancho* with Belasco Stock Company, Los Angeles (1907); made Broadway debut as Lulu Wheeler in David Belasco's *Is Matrimony a Failure?;* appeared opposite John Barrymore in *Kick In;* other plays include *The Concert, The Conspiracy, Cordelia Blossom, The Tempest* (as Miranda), *De Luxe Annie* (title role), and *The Skin Game.*

GREY, Josephine (1828–1906). *See Butler, Josephine.*

GREY, Katherine (1873–1950). *American stage actress.* Born Katherine Best, Dec 27, 1873, in San Francisco, California; died Mar 21, 1950, in Orleans, Massachusetts; m. Paul Arthur (div.); m. John Mason. ❖ Made stage debut in San Francisco for Augustin Daly; made NY debut in *The Golden Widow* (1889); on Broadway, appeared in *Shore Acres, Shenandoah, Arms and the Man, Dr. Jekyll and Mr. Hyde* (with Richard Mansfield), *The Royal Box, You Never Can Tell, Candida* (with Arnold Daly), *The Shadow, The Straw* and *Bright Star;* retired (1940).

GREY, Lita (1908–1995). *See Chaplin, Lita Grey.*

GREY, Louisa (c. 1842–1893). *See Lord, Lucy Takiora.*

GREY, Maria Georgina (1816–1906). *English writer.* Name variations: Maria Shireff. Born Maria Georgina Shirreff in 1816 in England; died in 1906 in England; dau. of rear admiral; sister of Emily Shirreff; m. cousin William Thomas Grey, 1841. ❖ Pioneer of women's education, was educated by governesses, then undertook self-education with sister Emily; lived abroad and learned several languages; with Emily, wrote *Passion and Principle* (1841) and *Thoughts on Self-Culture Addressed to Women* (1850), laying out arguments for women's education and criticizing ways in which women were trained to be dependent; became proponent of Friedrich Froebel and promoted Froebel Society of which Emily was president; published *Intellectual Education and Its Influence on the Character and Happiness of Women* (1858); with Emily, founded National Union for Promoting the Higher Education of Women (1871) which created Girl's Public Day School Company (1872), enabling schools to be owned by trusts and controlled by a board rather than private individuals; established 38 day schools for middle-class girls (mostly along suburban rail routes into London), including Croydon school; created template for future girls' education efforts, notably Church Schools Company and Girls' High Schools; founded Maria Grey College (1878) which is still extant as Twickenham campus of Brunel University; her efforts bore fruit in the form of policy changes allowing women greater access to University of London (1878), Cambridge (1881) and some schools at Oxford (1879). Also wrote *Love and Sacrifice* (with Emily, 1868), *Journal of a Visit to Egypt* (1869), *The Education of Women* (1871) and *Old Maids: A Lecture* (1875).

GREY, Mary (1545–1578). *English noblewoman.* Name variations: Lady Mary Keys or Keyes. Born 1545 (some sources cite 1540); died April 20, 1578, in London, England; dau. of Henry Grey, marquis of Dorset (later duke of Suffolk) and Frances Brandon (1517–1559, granddau. of King Henry VII); sister of Catherine Grey (c. 1540–1568) and Lady Jane Grey (1537–1554); m. Thomas Keyes, Aug 10, 1565. ❖ Born a dwarf, retained position at court despite the behavior of sisters, until she too married in secret (summer 1565); a month after wedding, was placed in custody of a married couple in Buckinghamshire, while husband was incarcerated until his death in 1571; died penniless, age 33.

GREY, Nadja (1923–1994). *See Gray, Nadia.*

GREY, Nan (1918–1993). American stage, tv, and film actress. Born Eschal Miller, July 25, 1918, in Houston, Texas; died July 25, 1993, in San Diego, California; m. Jack Westrope, 1939 (div. 1950); m. Frankie Laine (singer), 1950. ❖ Made film debut in *Firebird* (1934), followed by *Babbitt, Dracula's Daughter, Three Smart Girls, Tower of London, The Invisible Man Returns* and *House of Seven Gables,* among others; invented a cosmetic mirror for the near-sighted.

GREY, Robyn (1964—). *See Grey-Gardner, Robyn.*

GREY, Takiora (c. 1842–1893). *See Lord, Lucy Takiora.*

GREY, Virginia (1917–2004). American actress. Born Mar 22, 1917, in Los Angeles, California; died of heart failure, July 31, 2004, in Woodland Hills, California; dau. of Ray Grey (director of silent comedies). ❖ At 10, made film debut as Eva in *Uncle Tom's Cabin* (1927); completed schooling and returned to films as an adult; appeared in such movies as *Secret Valley, Test Pilot, Idiot's Delight, Broadway Serenade, The Women, Idaho, Flame of the Barbary Coast, Portrait in Black, Back Street, Madame X* and *Airport.*

GREY-GARDNER, Robyn (1964—). Australian rower. Name variations: Robyn Gardner. Born Sept 6, 1964. ❖ At Los Angeles Olympics, won a bronze medal in coxed fours (1984).

GRICHINA, Oxana (1968—). *See Grishina, Oksana.*

GRIEG, Nina (1845–1935). Norwegian singer. Born Nina Hagerup, Nov 24, 1845, in Bergen, Norway; died Dec 9, 1935, in Copenhagen; dau. of Herman Hagerup and Madame Werligh (Danish actress); studied with Carl Helsted; married Edvard Grieg (composer), June 11, 1867 (died 1907). ❖ With husband, gave highly successful joint concerts throughout Europe, performing his work many times and becoming the most sensitive interpreter of his songs.

GRIER, Pam (1949—). African-American actress. Born Pamela Suzette Grier, May 26, 1949, in Winston-Salem, North Carolina; dau. of Clarence Grier (Air Force mechanic) and Gwendolyn Samuels (nurse); cousin of actor Roosevelt Grier; attended University of California at Los Angeles. ❖ One of the 1st important female action heroes who often played a strong woman out for revenge, made film debut in Roger Corman's *The Big Doll House* and *The Big Bird Cage* (both 1971); for AIP, starred in *Coffy* (1973), *Scream Blacula Scream* (1973), *Foxy Brown* (1974), *Friday Foster* (1975), and *Sheba, Baby* (1975); on tv, was a regular on "Miami Vice" (1984) and "The L Word" (2004); relaunched career starring in Quentin Tarantino's *Jackie Brown* (1997); other films include *Something Wicked This Way Comes* (1983), *Above the Law* (1988), *Mars Attacks!* (1996), *In Too Deep* (1999), *Jawbreaker* (1999), *Ghosts of Mars* (2001) and *Bones* (2001).

GRIERSON, Constantia (c. 1706–c. 1732). Irish poet. Born c. 1706 in Graiguenamanagh, Co. Kilkenny, Ireland; died c. 1732 in Dublin, Ireland; m. George Grierson, c. 1726. ❖ Translated *Virgil* (1724), *Terence* (1727), and *Tacitus* (1730); poems appear in M. Barber, *Poems on Several Occasions* (1734), L. Pilkington, *The Memoirs of Mrs Laetitia Pilkington 1712–50. Written by Herself* (1748–1754), and G. Colman and B. Thornton (eds.), *Poems by Eminent Ladies* (1755). ❖ See also R. Lonsdale, ed., *Eighteenth-Century Women Poets* (1989).

GRIERSON, Mary (1912—). English botanical artist. Name variations: Mary Anderson Grierson. Born Sept 27, 1912, in UK. ❖ Began her long career working as a Women's Auxiliary Air Force (WAAF) freelance botanical artist (1940); during WWII, was employed as a military aerial photography interpreter (1940–45); served as a Hunting Surveys Ltd. cartographical draftswoman (1946–60); served as a Royal Botanical Gardens, Kew, staff artist (1960–72); particularly interested in endangered species, displayed work at the Royal Society, Linnean Society, British Museum, Royal Horticultural Society and abroad in America, the Netherlands, South Africa and Israel; a frequent visitor to Kauai, illustrated Peter Green's *A Hawaiian Florilegium* (1996). Published illustrations include *Mountain Flowers* (A.J. Huxley, 1967) and *Orchidaceae* (P.F. Hunt, 1974); designed stamps for the "British Flora" series (1967); received the Gold Medal of the Royal Horticultural Society (1966, 1969, 1973) and Linnean Society fellow (1967).

GRIESE, Irma (1923–1945). *See Grese, Irma.*

GRIEVE, Agnes (Nancy) (c. 1830–1903). *See Harrold, Agnes.*

GRIEVE, Elizabeth Harriet (1735–?). English swindler. Born 1735 in UK. ❖ By falsely claiming to have relatives in British court—including Lord North, Lady Fitzroy and Lord Guildford—received money from tradesmen who believed she could secure government posts for them; exposed as fraud and taken to court (1774), was sent to America for life; vanished during American Revolution.

GRIFFIES, Ethel (1878–1975). English actress. Born Ethel Woods, April 26, 1878, in Sheffield, England; died Sept 9, 1975, in London, England; dau. of Samuel Rupert Woods and Lillie Roberts Woods (actors); m. Walter Beaumont (actor, died 1910); m. Edward Cooper (actor), 1917 (died 1956). ❖ Character actress with long career, made stage debut at age 3 in the Lake District in *East Lynne* (1881) with acting parents; made Broadway debut in *Havoc* (1924); other plays include *Pygmalion, Loose Ends, Druid Circle, The Cherry Orchard, Lady Dedlock, The Royal Family, Autumn Garden, Ivanov* and *The Natural Look;* appeared in over 100 US and British films, including *Waterloo Bridge, Manhattan Parade, Of Human Bondage, Alice in Wonderland, Bulldog Drummond Strikes Back, Anna Karenina, Irene, A Yank in the R.A.F., How Green Was My Valley, Jane Eyre, Saratoga Trunk, The Birds* and *Billy Liar.*

GRIFFIN, Eleanore (1904–1995). American screenwriter. Name variations: Eleanor Griffin. Born April 29, 1904, in St. Paul, Minnesota; died July 26, 1995, in Woodland Hills, California. ❖ Films include *St. Louis Blues, A Man Called Peter, Imitation of Life, Third Man on the Mountain, Back Street, Good Morning Miss Dove* and *One Man's Way.* Won Academy Award for Best Original Story for *Boys Town* (1938).

GRIFFIN, Ellen (1918–1986). American golfer. Born Dec 19, 1918; died Oct 1986 in Randleman, North Carolina. ❖ With Betty Hicks and Hope Seignious, founded Women's Professional Golf Association (WPGA, 1944); one of the best-known women's golf-teaching professionals in American history, taught physical education at University of North Carolina–Greensboro for 28 years; achieved master professional status and was recognized as one of the six most outstanding teachers in US (1976). Ellen Griffin Rolex Award inaugurated in her honor (1989).

GRIFFIN, Elsie Mary (1884–1968). New Zealand teacher and social reformer. Born on Nov 1, 1884, at Lawrence, Otago, New Zealand; died May 3, 1968, in Auckland, New Zealand; dau. of Cornelius Griffin (minister) and Mary (Brown) Griffin; Auckland University College, MA, 1906. ❖ Became botany mistress at Auckland Girls' Grammar School (1906); elected secretary of Young Women's Christian Association (YWCA) in Dunedin (1912–15); traveled to US to study social work methods (1915–17); modernized YWCA in New Zealand and was appointed national general secretary (1924); was instrumental in forming numerous groups dedicated to women's issues. ❖ See also *Dictionary of New Zealand Biography* (Vol. 3).

GRIFFIN, Jane (1680–1720). English murderer. Born 1680; hanged 1720; married. ❖ London housewife who, in what has been described as momentary madness, stabbed her maid to death with a butcher knife.

GRIFFIN, Marion Mahony (1871–1961). *See Mahony, Marion.*

GRIFFIN, V.C. (1868–1952). *See Cory, Annie Sophie.*

GRIFFIN, Mrs. Walter Burley (1871–1961). *See Mahony, Marion.*

GRIFFING, Josephine White (1814–1872). American reformer. Born Josephine Sophia White on Dec 18, 1814, in Hebron, Connecticut; died Feb 18, 1872, in Washington, DC; dau. of Joseph White, Jr. and Sophia (Waldo) White (sister of portrait painter Samuel Lovett Waldo); reared by stepmother Mary (Waldo) White (her mother's sister); m. Charles S.S. Griffing (machinist), Sept 16, 1835 (died 1880); children: Emma (b. 1841), Helen (b. 1849), and Josephine Cora (b. 1857); 2 others died in childhood. ❖ Made home in Litchfield, OH, a station on the Underground Railroad; served as paid agent of Western Anti-Slavery Society (1851–55) and as president of Ohio Woman's Rights Association (beginning 1853); after Civil War, worked in Washington, DC, on behalf of freedmen; served as 1st vice-president of American Equal Rights Association and as corresponding secretary for National Woman Suffrage Association.

GRIFFITH, Corinne (1894–1979). American actress and film star of the silent era. Born in Texarkana, Texas, Nov 24, 1894; died July 13, 1979, in Santa Monica, California; attended Sacred Heart Academy, New Orleans; m. Webster Campbell (actor-director), 1920 (div. 1923); m. Walter Morosco (producer), 1933 (div. 1934); m. George Preston

Marshall (owner of Washington Redskins and a laundry empire), 1936 (div. 1958); m. Danny Scholl, 1965 (marriage dissolved after 33 days). ❖ Called "The Orchid Lady of the Screen" because of her delicate beauty, signed with Vitagraph (1916); starred in numerous silents, including *The Last Man* (1916), *Thin Ice* (1919), *The Bramble Bush* (1919), *The Garter Girl* (1920), *Island Wives* (1922), *The Common Law* (1923), *Six Days* (1923), *Lilies of the Field* (1924), *Mademoiselle Modiste* (1926), *The Lady in Ermine* (1927), *Three Hours* (1927), *The Garden of Eden* (1928), *Outcast* (1928), and *Saturday's Children* (1929); career ended abruptly with the talkies; wrote 6 books, the most popular being *Papa's Delicate Condition* (1952), which was adapted for the screen. Nominated for an Academy Award for *The Divine Lady* (1929). ❖ See also *Women in World History.*

GRIFFITH, Elizabeth (c. 1720–1793). Welsh-Irish playwright and novelist. Born in Glamorganshire, Wales, c. 1720; died in Millicent, Nass, Co. Kildare, Ireland, Jan 5, 1793; dau. of Thomas Griffith (well-known Dublin actor-manager) and Jane (Foxcroft) Griffith (dau. of a Yorkshire cleric); m. Richard Griffith, c. 1752; children: two. ❖ Born in Wales, brought up in Ireland, was educated and trained by actor-manager father for the theater; made acting debut with Thomas Sheridan's Dublin company (1749); moved to London (1753) and minor roles at Covent Garden; when husband's business failed (1750s), published her courtship letters, *A Series of Genuine Letters between Henry and Frances,* by subscription to support the family (1757); with their success, wrote 1st comedy, *The Platonic Wife,* an adaptation of a play by Marmontel (1765), then wrote *The School for Rakes,* an adaptation of Beaumarchais' *Eugénie,* which opened at Drury Lane with Kitty Clive in lead (Feb 1769); wrote other plays and 3 successful novels. ❖ See also D. Eshelman, *Elizabeth Griffith: A Biographical and Critical Study* (1949); and *Women in World History.*

GRIFFITH, Emily (c. 1880–1947). American teacher and school founder. Born Feb 10, c. 1880, in Cincinnati, Ohio; died June 19, 1947, in Pinecliffe, Colorado; dau. of Andrew Griffith and Martha (Craig) Griffith. ❖ Hired as substitute teacher, then as regular teacher in Denver, Colorado's Central School; twice appointed deputy state superintendent of schools (1904 and 1910); persuaded school board and local community to allow her to open Denver Opportunity School, a free daytime and evening school for children and adults (1916); served as principal of the school (1916–33), which was later renamed Emily Griffith Opportunity School (1934). Griffith's school, which realized her vision of education and social work as entwined, was an immediate success; though it spawned some imitators, her program remained essentially unique, owing at least largely to its founder's personality. ❖ See also Elinor Bluemel, *Emily Griffith and the Opportunity School of Denver* (1954); Fletcher H. Swift and John W. Studebaker, *What Is This Opportunity School?* (1932).

GRIFFITH, Florence (1959–1998). *See Joyner, Florence Griffith.*

GRIFFITH, Linda (1884–1949). *See Arvidson, Linda.*

GRIFFITH, Nanci (1953—). American folksinger and writer. Born Nanci Caroline Griffith, July 6, 1953, in Seguin, Texas. ❖ Began playing guitar and singing in bars at 14; graduated from University of Texas and taught kindergarten briefly; began recording for independent labels (1970s); signed with MCA (1980s) and gained moderate success with 1st album, *Lone Star State of Mind* (1987); reached #1 in Ireland with cover of Julie Gold's "From a Distance" (1987); signed with Elektra Records (1990); won a Grammy for album *Other Voices, Other Rooms* (1993), which featured covers of songs by Bob Dylan, John Prine, and Emmylou Harris; ventured into classical music, recording album *Dust Bowl Symphony* with London Symphony Orchestra (1999); also writes novels and short stories; maintains strong Irish fan base.

GRIFFITH, Phyllis (c. 1922—). English archer. Born c. 1922 in UK. ❖ In 1986, set a world record in archery in Hosworthy, England: scored 31,000 in 76 Portsmouth Rounds over a 24-hour period; she was 64 at the time.

GRIFFITH, Yolanda (1970—). African-American basketball player. Born Mar 1, 1970, in Chicago, Illinois; attended Palm Beach Junior College (1989–91) and Florida Atlantic (1993–94); children: Candace. ❖ Forward; played professionally in Germany (1993–97); drafted by Long Beach Sting Rays of ABL (1997); drafted by Sacramento Monarchs in 1st round (1999); won a team gold medal at Sydney Olympics (2000) and a team gold medal at Athens Olympics (2004). Named WNBA Most Valuable Player (1999).

GRIFFITH-JOYNER, Florence (1959–1998). *See Joyner, Florence Griffith.*

GRIFFITHS, Ann (1776–1805). Welsh hymn-writer and mystic. Born Ann Thomas in 1776; died in 1805; grew up in parish of Llanfihangel-yng-Ngwynfa, Montgomery, Wales; dau. of John Thomas (country poet); m. Thomas Griffiths, 1804; children: 1 (died in infancy, 1805). ❖ Converted to the Methodist Fellowship (1796) and her home became a center for Methodist preaching; composed hymns that were never written down, but have survived because they were recorded from the memory of her maidservant and published in *Casgliad o Hymnau* (A Collection of Hymns). ❖ See also *Women in World History.*

GRIFFITHS, Jane (1954—). English politician and member of Parliament. Born Jane Griffiths, April 17, 1954; m. Andrew Tattersall, 1999. ❖ Served as Asia editor, BBC Monitoring (1984–97); representing Labour, elected to House of Commons for Reading East (1997, 2001); left Parliament (2005).

GRIFFITHS, Martha Wright (1912–2003). American politician. Born Martha Edna Wright on Jan 29, 1912, in Pierce City, Missouri; died April 22, 2003, in Armada, Michigan; dau. of Charles Elbridge (mail carrier) and Nelle (Sullinger) Wright; attended Pierce City public schools; University of Missouri at Columbia, BA, 1934; University of Michigan Law School at Ann Arbor, LLB, 1940; m. Hicks George Griffiths of Schenectady, NY (lawyer), Dec 28, 1933; no children. ❖ US congressional representative (D-Michigan) who sponsored the Equal Rights Amendment and worked for more equitable laws in the areas of welfare, pensions, credit, and health care; admitted to Michigan Bar (1941); joined legal department of American Automobile Insurance Company (1941–42); served as contract negotiator for Army Ordnance in Detroit during World War II; went into law partnership with husband and G. Mennen Williams (1946); served as state representative (1949–52); served as recorder and judge, Recorder's Court, Detroit (1953–54); as a member of the US House of Representatives (1955–74), was the 1st woman appointed to the Joint Economic Committee (JEC, 1961) of the House and the Senate, which influenced the all-important congressional budget; served on the Ways and Means Committee, the 1st woman member of that influential committee, where she spent more time on the tax code than on any other issue, and quickly saw that it discriminated against women; pushed for Civil Rights Act of 1964, successfully demanding an amendment that included "sex" as well as race, color, religion, and national origin; was lieutenant governor of Michigan (1982–90) and scholar-in-residence, University of Missouri (1990–91). Awarded 29 honorary degrees; received Alice Paul Award, National Women's Party (1983); named Michigan Woman of the Year (1990); inducted into National Women's Hall of Fame (1993). ❖ See also Emily George, *Martha W. Griffiths* (University Press of America, 1982); and *Women in World History.*

GRIFFITHS, Michelle (1973—). *See Brogan, Michelle.*

GRIFFITTS, Hannah (1727–1817). American poet and letter writer. Born 1727 in Philadelphia, Pennsylvania; died 1817 in Philadelphia; dau. of Thomas Griffitts and Mary Norris; never married. ❖ Talented and well-educated daughter of wealthy Quaker family, wrote many well-crafted letters and poems but chose not to publish (manuscripts held in Library Company of Philadelphia).

GRIFITHS, Bella (1912–1974). *See Judge, Arline.*

GRIGG, Mary (1897–1971). New Zealand politician. Name variations: Mary Polson; Lady Polson. Born Mary Cracroft Wilson, Aug 18, 1897, in Culverden, North Canterbury, NZ; died Dec 22, 1971; educated in London; m. Arthur Grigg (MP), 1920 (killed in Libya 1941, during WWII); m. William Polson (MP), 1943; children: (1st m.) three. ❖ As a result of MP husband's death, accepted an invitation to stand for Mid-Canterbury (1941), becoming the 1st National Party woman MP; lectured; with Hilda Ross, wrote National Party's women's policy for 1949 election. Received an MBE (1946) in recognition for her work with Mary Dreaver for the Women's Land Service during WWII.

GRIGNAN, Françoise-Marguerite de Sévigné, Countess de (1646–1705). French intellectual. Name variations: Francoise de Sevigne. Born Oct 10, 1646; died Aug 16, 1705; 1646; dau. of Marie de Sévigné (1626–1696) and Henri, Marquis de Sévigné (1623–1651); educated at Sainte-Marie at Nantes; m. François Adhémar de Monteil de Grignan, count de Grignan, 1668; children: one son and a number of daughters, including Pauline de Simiane. ❖ As a disciple of the French philosopher René Descartes, became known as a *femme philosophe;* lived with husband in Provence, and corresponded a great deal with her mother who was renowned as a woman of letters—the primary scholarly medium of the time. ❖ See also *Women in World History.*

GRIGORAS, Anca (1957—). *Romanian gymnast.* Born Nov 8, 1957, in Bucharest, Romania. ❖ At European championships, won a bronze medal for beam (1973); won Balkan championships (1975), FISU Invitiational (1978); at Montreal Olympics, won a silver medal in team all-around (1976).

GRIGORAS, Cristina (1966—). *Romanian gymnast.* Born Cristina Elena Grigoras, Feb 11, 1966, in Romania. ❖ Won a silver medal at Moscow Olympics (1980) and gold medal at Los Angeles Olympics (1984), both in team all-around; at European championships, won a gold medal for vault, silver medals for all-around and uneven bars, and a bronze for floor exercises (1981); won Balkan championships, Champions All, and International Championship of Romania (1981).

GRIGORESCU, Claudia (1968—). *Romanian fencer.* Born Jan 1968. ❖ At Barcelona Olympics, won a bronze medal in team foil (1992).

GRIGORIEVA, Tatiana (1975—). *Russian-Australian pole vaulter.* Name variations: Tatyana. Born Oct 8, 1975, in St. Petersburg, Russia. ❖ Won a silver medal at Sydney Olympics (2000) and a gold medal at Commonwealth Games (2002).

GRIGSBY, Etta (1897–1994). *See Nichols, Etta Grigsby.*

GRIGSON, Jane (1928–1990). *English food writer.* Born Heather Mabel Jane McIntyre, Mar 13, 1928, in Gloucester, England; died Mar 24, 1990, in Wiltshire, England; dau. of town clerk of Sunderland; Newnham College, Cambridge University, degree in English (1949); m. Goeffrey Grigson (poet and critic, died 1985); children: Sophie Grigson (food critic, cookbook writer and star of tv cooking shows, who published compilation of mother's recipes in *The Enjoyment of Food,* 1992). ❖ One of the leading food writers of her generation, began career with translations of *Pinocchio* (1959) and Beccaria's *Of Crimes and Punishments* (1963), sharing John Florio Prize with Kenelm Foster (1966); traveled to France, then wrote 1st cookbook, *Charcuterie and French Pork Cooking* (1967); worked as culinary correspondent for *Observer Colour Magazine* (1968–90), later publishing *Good Things* (1984) and *Food with the Famous* (1991), based on a highly successful series; published *Fish Cookery* (1973) and *English Food* (1974), both influenced by North Country traditions; also wrote *The Mushroom Feast* (1975); though influenced by Elizabeth David, developed her own style. Voted Cookery Writer of the Year (1977) for *English Food;* received Glenfiddich Writer of the Year award (1978) and André Simon Memorial Fund Book award for *Vegetable Book* (1978) and *Fruit Book* (1982).

GRILLET, Louise Hortense (1865–1952). *French novelist.* Name variations: also seen as Louise-Hortense Grille; Mme Rougeul; (pseudonym) Camille Pert. Born 1865 in France; died 1952. ❖ Wrote sentimental romance novels including *Amoureuses* (1895), *Les Florifères* (1898), *Nos amours, nos vices* (1901), *Les Amours perverses de Rosa Scari* (1905), *Une Liaison coupable* (1907), *Passionnette tragique* (1914), and *Amour vainqueur* (1917).

GRILLO, Gabriela (1952—). *West German equestrian.* Name variations: Gabriella Grillo. Born Aug 19, 1952, in Mülheim, Germany. ❖ At Montreal Olympics, won a gold medal in team dressage (1976).

GRILLO, Joann (1939–1999). *American mezzo-soprano.* Born May 14, 1939, in New York, NY; died Feb 1, 1999, in Brooklyn, NY; m. Richard Kness (dramatic tenor). ❖ Began career with the Brooklyn Opera Company (early 1960s); over 20 years, sang in nearly 300 performances with the Metropolitan Opera, making Met debut as Rosette in *Manon* (1963); with husband, founded Ambassadors of Opera and Concert Worldwide.

GRIMALDI, Caroline (1957—). *See Caroline of Monaco.*

GRIMALDI, Stephanie (1965—). *See Stephanie of Monaco.*

GRIMES, Tammy (1934—). *American actress and singer.* Born Jan 30, 1934, in Lynn, Massachusetts; m. Christopher Plummer (actor), 1956 (div. 1960); m. Jeremy Slate, 1966 (div. 1967); children: Amanda Plummer (b. 1957, actress). ❖ Made NY debut replacing Kim Stanley as Chérie in *Bus Stop* (1955); originated the title role in *The Unsinkable Molly Brown* (1960) for which she received a Tony and NY Drama Critics award; other plays include *Rattle of a Simple Man, The Only Game in Town* and *Private Lives;* appeared in such films as *Three Bites of the Apple,*

Play It as It Lays, The Runner Stumbles, Can't Stop the Music and *Backstreet Justice;* starred on "The Tammy Grimes Show" (1966).

GRIMKÉ, Angelina E. (1805–1879). *American abolitionist, feminist, writer and lecturer.* Name variations: Angelina Emily Grimké or Grimke; Nina; Angelina Grimké Weld. Pronunciation: GRIM-kay. Born Angelina Emily Grimké on Feb 20, 1805, in Charleston, South Carolina; died in Hyde Park, Massachusetts, Oct 26, 1879; daughter and youngest child of Honorable John Faucheraud (judge of the Supreme Court of South Carolina) and Mary (Smith) Grimké; sister of Sarah Moore Grimké (1792–1873, abolitionist); attended Charleston Academy for Girls; m. Theodore Dwight Weld (abolitionist), May 14, 1838; children: Charles Stuart Weld (b. 1839); Theodore Weld (b. 1841); Sarah Grimké Weld (b. 1844). ❖ Southern-born abolitionist who campaigned for the extinction of slavery and worked toward resolution of the question of woman's rights, was expelled from Charleston Presbyterian Church, primarily because of her position on slavery (May 1829); accepted into Philadelphia Society of Friends (Mar 1831); published 1st antislavery writing, *Appeal to the Christian Women of the Southern States,* condemning slavery as a violation of human, natural, and Biblical laws, and calling on Southern women to work toward the abolition of the slave system (1836); attended Antislavery Convention of American Women in Philadelphia (May 1837); with sister, undertook New England speaking tour against slavery (1837–38); addressed legislative committee of Massachusetts Assembly (Feb 1838); with husband, wrote *American Slavery As It Is: Testimony of a Thousand Witnesses* (1839); elected to central committee of Women's Rights Convention, Worcester, Massachusetts (1850); retired from schoolteaching (1867). ❖ See also Gerda Lerner, *The Grimké Sisters from South Carolina: Rebels Against Slavery* (Houghton Mifflin, 1967); Katharine Du Pre Lumpkin, *The Emancipation of Angelina Grimké* (University of North Carolina Press, 1974); Gilbert H. Barnes and Dwight L. Dumond, eds. *Letters of Theodore Dwight Weld, Angelina Grimké Weld and Sarah Grimké, 1822–1844* (2 vols., Peter Smith, 1965); and *Women in World History.*

GRIMKÉ, Angelina Weld (1880–1958). *African-American poet and writer.* Name variations: Angela Weld Grimke. Born Feb 20, 1880, in Boston, Massachusetts; died June 10, 1958, in New York, NY; dau. of Archibald Henry Grimké (nephew of Sarah Moore Grimké and Angelina E. Grimké) and Sarah (Stanley) Grimké; attended Carlton Academy in Northfield, Minnesota, and Cushing Academy in Ashburnham, Massachusetts; graduated from Boston Normal School of Gymnastics, 1902; never married; no children. ❖ Wrote 1st drama, *Rachel* (1920), which reflects her growing awareness of, and anger at, the racial problems of the times; also wrote the play *Mara;* began teaching in Washington D.C. (1902); spent summers as a student at Harvard (1906–10); retired from teaching (1926) due to ill health; moved to New York to work on her writing (1930), but produced nothing, spending last years as a recluse in her New York apartment; her poetry, which appeared in the Norfolk *Country Gazette, The Boston Globe, Boston Transcript* and *Opportunity,* included "The Grave in the Corner" (1893), "To Theodore Weld on His Ninetieth Birthday" (1893), "Street Echoes" (1894), "Longing" (1901), "El Beso" (1909), "To Keep the Memory of Charlotte Forten Grimké" (1915), and "To Dunbar High School" (1923). ❖ See also *Women in World History.*

GRIMKÉ, Charlotte L. Forten (1837–1914). *African-American abolitionist, teacher, poet.* Name variations: Charlotte Grimke; Charlotte L. Forten; also wrote as Miss C.L.F. and Lottie. Born Charlotte Lottie Forten on Aug 17, 1837, in Philadelphia, Pennsylvania; died July 22, 1914, in Washington, DC, of a cerebral embolism; dau. of Mary Virginia (Woods) Forten (died 1840) and Robert Bridges Forten (sailmaker and political activist); tutored at home until age 16; attended integrated public schools in Salem, MA: Higginson Grammar School and Salem Normal School (1853–56); prepared for teaching career at Salem Normal School, graduated in 1856; m. Reverend Francis James Grimké (nephew of Sarah Moore Grimké and Angelina E. Grimké), Dec 19, 1878; children: Theodora Cornelia (1880–1880). ❖ Intellectual, from the well-known, politically active Forten family of Philadelphia, whose *Journal,* published after her death, is a rare account of a free, educated black woman's response to the racist culture which she hoped to change; at 16, began keeping diary; accepted an offer, the 1st to a black person, to teach at Epes Grammar School in Salem, MA (June 1856); taught contraband slaves held by Northern troops in Port Royal, South Carolina (Aug 1862–May 1864); moved to Boston and worked as secretary of Teachers Committee of New England Branch of the Freedmen's Union Commission (Oct 1865); taught at Shaw Memorial School in Charleston, South Carolina (1871–72); taught at M Street

School, a preparatory high school in Washington, DC (1872–73); worked as 1st-class clerk in Fourth Auditor's Office of US Treasury in Washington, DC (1873–78); moved with husband to Jacksonville, Florida, where he was pastor of Laura Street Presbyterian Church (1885–89); moved back to Washington, DC, when husband took over pastorship of Fifteenth Street Presbyterian Church (1889); became a founding member of the National Association of Colored Women (1896); was a connecting link between two aristocratic and socially-active families, the Fortens and the Grimkés, both of which were influential in the antislavery movements of the 19th century. ❧ See also *The Journals of Charlotte Forten Grimké* (ed. by Brenda Stevenson, Oxford UP, 1988); and *Women in World History*.

GRIMKÉ, Sarah Moore (1792–1873). American abolitionist, feminist, educator, and writer. Name variations: Sally Grimke. Pronunciation: GRIM-kay. Born Sarah Moore Grimké on Nov 26, 1792, in Charleston, South Carolina; died in Hyde Park (now in Boston), Massachusetts, Dec 23, 1873; dau. of the Honorable John Faucheraud Grimké (1752–1819), judge of Supreme Court of South Carolina) and Mary (Smith) Grimké; sister of Angelina E. Grimké (1805–1879); received education at home, attending brother Thomas Grimké's tutored lessons; never married; no children. ❧ Southern-born teacher who lectured, wrote, and campaigned on the issues of women's rights and abolition; became godmother to youngest sister (1805); accompanied father to Philadelphia and New Jersey, nursing him through a fatal illness (1819); moved to Philadelphia (1821); accepted into Philadelphia Society of Friends (1823); underwent training as abolitionist agent in New York City (1836); attended Anti-Slavery Convention of American Women (1837); with sister, engaged in antislavery speaking tour throughout New England (1837–38); while on the speaking tour, wrote 12 "letters" which appeared in the *New England Spectator* (1837) and were published collectively (1838) as *Letters on the Equality of the Sexes and the Condition of Woman*, making her one of the 1st Americans to be published in support of women's rights; moved to New Jersey and retired to private life (1839); concluded teaching career (1867); writings include *Epistle to the Clergy of the Southern States* (1836) and *Address to Free Colored Americans* (1837). ❧ See also Gerda Lerner, *The Grimké Sisters from South Carolina: Rebels Against Slavery* (Houghton Mifflin, 1967); Gilbert H. Barnes and Dwight L. Dumond, eds. *Letters of Theodore Dwight Weld, Angelina Grimké Weld and Sarah Grimké, 1822–1844* (2 vols., Peter Smith, 1965); and *Women in World History*.

GRIMM, Cherry Barbara (1930–2002). New Zealand science-fiction writer. Name variations: (pseudonym) Cherry Wilder. Born Cherry Barbara Lockett, Sept 3, 1930, in Auckland, New Zealand; died Mar 14, 2002, in Wellington, New Zealand; m. A.J. Anderson, 1952; m. H.K.F. Grimm, 1963; children: 2. ❧ Lived in Australia (1954–76) and wrote reviews for *Sydney Morning Herald* and *The Australian* (1964–74); wrote *The Luck of Brin's Five* (1977), *The Nearest Eye* (1980), *Second Nature* (1982), *The Tapestry Warriors* (1983), *A Princess of the Chameln* (1984), *Yorath the Wolf* (1984), *The Summer's King* (1986), *Cruel Designs* (1988), *Signs of Life* (1996), and *The Wanderer* (2001).

GRIMSHAW, Beatrice (c. 1870–1953). Irish writer. Born in Cloonagh, Co. Antrim, Ireland, 1870 (some sources cite 1871); died in Bathurst, New South Wales, 1953; educated at Margaret Byers' Ladies' Collegiate College, Belfast, and in Caen and London. ❧ Began career as a journalist in Dublin (1891); edited *Social Review* (1895–99); went to the Pacific (1903), working as a tour promoter and eventually settling in New Guinea; commissioned by Australian government to publicize the region, wrote *In the Strange South Seas* (1907), which was illustrated with her photographs, *From Fiji to the Cannibal Islands* (1907), and *The New New Guinea* (1910); was also inspired to write 10 volumes of short stories and some 40 romance and adventure novels, among which *When the Red Gods Call* (1911) is perhaps the best known; an avid cyclist, surpassed the women's world 24-hour record by 5 hours. ❧ See also *Women in World History*.

GRIMSTON, Elizabeth (d. 1603). See Grymeston, Elizabeth Bernye.

GRINBERG, Maria (1908–1979). Soviet pianist. Born in Odessa, Crimea, Sept 6, 1908; died in 1979; studied with Konstantin Igumnov and Felix Blumenfeld. ❧ One of the most respected pianists of the Soviet era, was essentially a Romantic performer, equally at ease in the rhetoric of César Franck's *Symphonic Variations* or the acerbic modernity of Dmitry Shostakovich's 1st Piano Concerto; a celebrated Beethoven performer, recorded all 32 of his sonatas.

GRINDER, Martha (1815–1866). American poisoner. Born 1815; lived in Pittsburgh, Pennsylvania; hanged Jan 19, 1866; married. ❧ While supposedly nursing her neighbor, a Mrs. Caruthers (also seen as Carothers), poisoned the woman with arsenic; confessed to the murder and the murder of Jane R. Buchanan; her demeanor on the gallows was later reported in the press to be "unexpectedly calm."

GRINEVSKAIA, Izabella (1864–1944). *See Friedberg, Berta.*

GRINGS, Inka (1978—). German soccer player. Born Oct 31, 1978, in Dusseldorf, Germany. ❧ Won a team bronze medal at Sydney Olympics (2000).

GRINHAM, Judith (1939—). British swimmer. Name variations: Judy Grinham. Born Judith Brenda Grinham, Mar 6, 1939, in Neasden, England. ❧ At age 17, won a gold medal for 100-meter backstroke at Melbourne Olympics (1956), the 1st English woman to win an Olympic gold medal for swimming in 32 years; won European championship and Commonwealth Games, both for 100-meter backstroke (1958); broke 5 World records. Inducted into International Swimming Hall of Fame. ❧ See also autobiography *Water Babe* (Oldbourne Book, 1960); and *Women in World History*.

GRINI, Kjersti (1971—). Norwegian handball player. Born Sept 7, 1971, in Oslo, Norway. ❧ Won a team bronze medal at Sydney Olympics (2000).

GRIPE, Maria (1923—). Swedish writer. Born July 25, 1923, in Vaxholm, Sweden; graduated from Stockholm University; m. Harold Gripe (painter, illustrator, founder of Swedish Toy Theater Museum); children: Camila. ❧ Renowned writer of novels for children and young adults, wrote initially in traditional narrative style and about traditional subjects in such works as *Hugo and Josephine* (1960); went on to address such themes as alcoholism, imprisonment, jealousy, birth, maladjustment, death and loneliness, using realist style; experimented with voice, narrating 5 novels about the character Elvis Karlsson from a child's point of view (1972–79); incorporated supernatural elements within a realistic framework in such works as *The Glass-blower's Children* (1964), *The Chafer Flies at Dusk* (1978) and *The Shadow Across the Stone Bench* (1982); also wrote *Josephine* (1961), *In the Time of the Bells* (1965), Hugo (1966), *The Land Beyond* (1967), *Night Daddy* (1968), *Julia's House* (1971), *Elvis and His Secret* (1972), *Elvis and His Friends* (1973), *The Green Coat* (1974) and *Agnes Cecelia* (1981). Received Nils Holgersson Prize for *Hugo and Josephine* (1963) and Hans Christian Andersen Medal (1974).

GRIPPENBERG, Alexandra (1859–1913). *See Van Grippenberg, Alexandra.*

GRISCOM, Frances C. (1880–1973). American golfer. Born Frances C. Griscom, 1880, in Philadelphia, Pennsylvania; died Mar 30, 1973. ❧ Won USGA Women's Amateur (1900); as expert trapshooter and avid fisherman, also drove a Red Cross ambulance during WWI.

GRISELA. *Variant of Gisela.*

GRISELDA (fl. 11th c.). Marquise of Saluzzo. Name variations: Griseldis; Griselidis, marquise de Saluses; Grissel. Fl. in 11th century; m. Walter, marquis of Saluces or Saluzzo; children: a son and a daughter. ❧ Said to have been the wife of the marquis of Saluzzo, was noted for the patience with which she submitted to the most cruel ordeals as a wife and mother; her misfortunes were contained in the writings of Petrarch, Chaucer, Boccaccio (*Decameron*) and many others. ❧ See also *Women in World History*.

GRISELDIS or GRIZZELL. *Variant of Griselda.*

GRISHCHENKOVA, Alla (1961—). Soviet swimmer. Born Aug 27, 1961, in USSR. ❧ At Moscow Olympics, won a bronze medal in 4 x 100-meter medley relay (1980).

GRISHINA, Oksana (1968—). Russian cyclist. Name variations: Oxana Grichina. Born Nov 27, 1968, in USSR. ❧ Won a silver medal for the sprint at Sydney Olympics (2000).

GRISHUK, Pasha (1972—). Russian-Ukrainian ice dancer. Name variations: Oksana Grishuk, Gritchuk, Gritschuk, or Gritshuk. Born Mar 17, 1972, in Odessa, Ukraine. ❧ With partner Evgeny Platov, placed 4th at Albertville Olympics, won a gold medal at Lillehammer Olympics (1994), beating out Torvill & Dean, and a gold medal at Nagano Olympics (1998), the only woman in Olympic ice dancing history to win successive gold medals; also won 26 successive competitions (1988–

98), including 4 World championships; began skating with Alexandr Zhulin (1998); went solo (1999); tired of being mistaken for Oksana Baiul, changed her name to Pasha (1998).

GRISI, Carlotta (1819–1899). Italian ballerina. Born June 28, 1819, in Visinada, Italy; sister of Ernesta Grisi; died May 20, 1899, in St. Jean, Switzerland; cousin of Giulia Grisi (1811–1869) and Giuditta Grisi (1805–1840); studied ballet and singing at Milan's school of La Scala and joined the corps de ballet at age 10; children: (with Jules Perrot) one daughter, Marie-Julie; (with Prince Léon Radziwill) one daughter Ernestine. ❖ At 14, while performing in Naples, met dancer and choreographer Jules Perrot who became her teacher and later her lover; debuted with him at Renaissance Theater in Paris (1840), in a gypsy comedy-ballet, *Le Zingaro*, in which she both sang and danced; contracted by Paris Opéra (1841), 1st appeared there in Donizetti's *La Favorita* with Lucien Petipa; inspired Gautier to write the ballet *Giselle* for her (1841), which became her most famous role, though she was notable in *La Péri* (1843), *La Esmeralda* (1844), and *Paquita* (1846); was also one of the celebrated quartet in Perrot's *Pas de Quatre* (1845); made several triumphant tours throughout Europe and her debut at Saint Petersburg Imperial Theater in *Giselle* (1850); may have been the 1st ballerina to have used a boxed slipper for dancing on point. ❖ See also Serge Lifar, *Carlotta Grisi* (1941); and *Women in World History*.

GRISI, Giuditta (1805–1840). Italian mezzo-soprano. Born on July 28, 1805, in Milan, Italy; died May 1, 1840, in Robecco d'Oglio near Cremona; dau. of Gaetano Grisi, one of Napoleon's Italian officers, and a mother who was also a singer; sister of soprano Giulia Grisi (1811–1869); cousin of ballerina Carlotta Grisi (1819–1899); studied with Josephina Grassini (1773–1850), the contralto, who was also her aunt, and at the Milan Conservatory; married Count Barni, 1833. ❖ Debuted in Rossini's *Bianca e Faliero* in Vienna (1825); sang in Florence, Parma, Turin and Venice as well as in London and Paris (1832); created roles in a number of operas, the most important being Romeo in Bellini's *I Capuleti ed i Montecchi*; retired (1839).

GRISI, Giulia (1811–1869). Italian soprano. Born May 22, 1811, in Milan, Italy; felled by a severe cold while on tour, died in Berlin of inflammation of the lungs at the Hotel du Nord, Nov 25 (some sources cite the 29th), 1869; dau. of Gaetano Grisi, one of Napoleon's Italian officers, and a mother who was also a singer; niece of Josephina Grassini (1773–1850), a contralto; cousin of ballerina Carlotta Grisi (1819–1899); sister of mezzo-soprano Giuditta Grisi (1805–1840); studied with Giuditta as well as Filippo Celli and Pietro Guglielmi; also studied with Marliani in Milan and Giacomelli in Bologna; married Count de Melcy, April 24, 1836 (divorced); lived with her singing associate, the tenor Mario, Marchese di Candia (some sources say they were married in 1856); children: (with Mario) 3 daughters. ❖ One of the great prima donnas of her time, made her stage debut in Bologna as Emma in Rossini's *Zelmira* (1828); created the role of Adalgisa in *Norma* in Milan (1831); appeared in Paris as Semiramide in Rossini's opera and had a great success (1832); appeared in London as Ninetta in *La Gazza Ladra* (1834), but 1st great London success was in Donizetti's *Anna Bolena*; the first in line of great dramatic coloraturas, performed in Paris for 18 seasons and London for 26; was also known for her rivalry with Pauline Viardot. ❖ See also *Women in World History*.

GRISWOLD, Denny (1908–2001). American editor and public relations expert. Name variations: Denny G. Sullivan. Born Denny Griswold, Mar 23, 1908, in New York, NY; died Feb 7, 2001, in New York, NY; m. Glenn Griswold (publisher, died 1950); m. J. Langdon Sullivan (investment manager). ❖ Became founder of *Public Relations News* (1944), 1st public relations weekly in the world, and served as editor for almost 40 years; served in numerous public relations and journalistic positions including at *Forbes* (managing editor), *Business Week*, National and Mutual Broadcasting, Conde Nast Publishing, J. Walter Thomas, and Edward L. Bernays public relations firm; became a founder of Women Executives and the International Women's Forum; served on many boards and received more than 100 honors and awards. Author of *The Public Relations Handbook* (1948).

GRITCHUK, Gritschuk, or Gritshuk, Oksana (1972—). See *Grishuk, Pasha*.

GRITSI-MILLIEX, Tatiana (1920—). Greek poet, novelist and short-story writer. Name variations: T. Gritsi or T. Gritsi-Milliex; Tatiana Gkritis- or Gkritse-Milliex; Tatiana Gritsi Milliex; Tatjana or Tatiana Milliex. Born 1920 in Athens, Greece; m. Roger Milliex (director of studies at Institut Français in Athens), 1935. ❖ Joined the left-wing

resistance movement, EAM (1941); after the war, worked in the Centre for Asia Minor Studies (1952–59); while living with husband in Cyprus (1959–71), was deprived of Greek citizenship; returned to Athens (1974); worked for Greek women's movement and represented Greece at international women's conference; worked for radio and wrote for Greek and Cypriot newspapers; writings include *Thision Square* (1947), *Lacerations* (1981), and *Retrospectives* (1982).

GRIZODUBOVA, Valentina (1910–1993). Russian aviator. Born Valentina Stepanovna Grizodubova on Jan 18, 1910, in Kharkov; died April 28, 1993, in Moscow; dau. of aviator and aircraft designer S.V. Grizodubov. ❖ Completed flying-club training and began work in the civil air fleet (1929); assumed command of the 101st Long-Range Air Group (later the 31st Guards Bomber Group) which lent support to partisan detachments (1942); with Polina Osipenko and Marina Raskova, flew 3,717 miles nonstop from Moscow to the Soviet east coast near Japan (1938), a journey one-third longer than Amelia Earhart's solo flight, and crash landed, spending 10 days in the Siberian *taiga* until rescued. Awarded Order of Lenin, Order of the Red Banner of Labor, Order of the Patriotic War 1st class, and Order of the Red Star. ❖ See also Bruce Myles, *Night Witches: The Untold Story of Soviet Women in Combat* (Presidio, 1981); and *Women in World History*.

GRIZZEL. *Variant of Griselda.*

GROEN, Alma de (1941—). See *De Groen, Alma.*

GROENER, Lissy (1954—). German politician. Name variations: Lissy Gröner. Born May 31, 1954, in Langenfeld, Germany. ❖ Joined the Social Democratic Party (SPD, 1971); served as vice-president of the Socialist International; as a European Socialist, elected to 4th and 5th European Parliament (1994–99, 1999–2004).

GROENEWOLD, Renate (1976—). Dutch speedskater. Born Oct 8, 1976, in the Netherlands. ❖ Won bronze medals for all-around at European championships (2000, 2002, 2003) and World championships (2001); won silver medals for the 3,000 meters at Salt Lake City Olympics (2002) and Torino Olympics (2006).

GROES, Lis (1910–1074). Danish politician. Name variations: Anne Lisbeth Groes. Born Anne Lisbeth Toersleff, Nov 2, 1910, in Denmark; died Mar 12, 1974; dau. of P. Madsen Lindegaard (1867–1918) and Signe Andrea Toersleff (1879–1975, headmistress); m. Ebbe Groes, Oct 15, 1936; children: Mette, Niels, Arne, Lise, Inge, Uffe, Birta, Thyge and Eske. ❖ Social Democrat, served as minister of Trade, Industry and Shipping (1953–57); was also chair of the Association of Consumers.

GROESBEEK, Maria (1937–1970). South African poisoner. Born 1937; hanged Nov 13, 1970; m. Christiaan Buys, 1953 (murdered 1969); m. Gerhard Froesbeek, June 11, 1969. ❖ During 17 years of marriage to Christiaan Buys, moved approximately 15 times and was physically abused; when he refused to give her a divorce so that she could marry his friend Gerhard Froesbeek, began purchasing ant poison containing arsenic (Feb 1969); after he took ill (Feb 14) and died from arsenic poisoning (Mar 28), married Froesbeek (June 11) but was arrested with him for murder; took full responsibility, saying she'd just wanted to make her husband sick enough for him to agree to the divorce; tried at Bloemfontein (Nov 1969) and found guilty.

GROG, Carven (b. 1909). See *Carven.*

GROGAN, JoAnne (1938—). See *Brackeen, JoAnne.*

GROGGER, Paula (1892–1984). Austrian novelist and short-story writer. Born July 12, 1892, in Öblarn, Styria, Austria; died Jan 1, 1984 in Öblarn; studied at the teacher's training college of the Ursuline nuns in Salzburg, 1912–14. ❖ Spent many years as a needlework teacher; works include novel *Das Grimmingtor* (The Grimming Gate, 1926), story *Das Gleichnis von der Weberin* (1929) and play *Die Hochzeit* (The Wedding, 1937); also wrote *Bauernjahr* (Farmer's Year), *Die Reise nach Salzburg* (The Journey to Salzburg) and *Sieben Legenden* (Seven Legends).

GROMOVA, Lyudmila (1942—). Soviet gymnast. Born Nov 1942 in USSR. ❖ At Tokyo Olympics, won a gold medal in team all-around (1964).

GROMOVA, Maria (1984—). Russian synchronized swimmer. Born July 20, 1984, in USSR. ❖ At World championships, won team gold medals (2001, 2003); won a team gold medal at Athens Olympics (2004).

GROMOVA, Vera (1891–1973). Russian paleontologist. Name variations: Vera Issacovna Gromova; V.I. Gromova. Born Mar 8, 1891, in St. Petersburg, Russia; died Jan 21, 1973. ❖ Recognized for research on fossil ungulates, earned a degree in vertebrate zoology (1918); served as head of the osteological section of the Academy of Sciences' Zoological Museum in Moscow (1919–42); employed (1942–60) and later served as the head of mammals laboratory (from 1946) at the Academy of Sciences' Paleontological Institute in Moscow; interested in the development of horses, investigated the relationship between long-term skeletal and climate changes.

GRONBEK, Maja (1971—). Danish handball player. Name variations: Grønbæk. Born Jan 30, 1971, in Denmark. ❖ Won a team gold medal at Sydney Olympics (2000).

GRONDAHL, Agathe (1847–1907). See Backer-Grondahl, Agathe.

GRÖNFELDT BERGMAN, Lisbeth (1948—). Swedish politician. Name variations: Gronfeldt or Groenfeldt. Born Sept 20, 1948, in Göteborg, Sweden. ❖ Served as chair of executive of Gothenburg Moderate Party women's association (1980–82); member of Gothenburg City Council (1979–2000) and Gothenburg City Executive, Board, municipal commissioner (1992–2000); as a member of the European People's Party (Christian Democrats) and European Democrats (EPP), elected to 5th European Parliament (1999–2004). Awarded Gothenburg city order of merit (2000).

GROODY, Louise (1897–1961). American actress and dancer. Born Mar 26, 1897, in Waco, Texas; died Sept 16, 1961, in Canadensis, Pennsylvania; trained by Ned Wayburn; m. William Harrigan (div.); m. W. F. McGee (div.); m. John Graham Looftbourrow (AP editor). ❖ Musical-comedy star, began career as a dancer in the chorus of *Around the Map* (1915), then partnered Hal Skelly in *Fiddlers Three* (1918) and *Night Boat* (1920); came to prominence in such shows as *No No Nanette* (title role), *Hit the Deck* and *One Kiss.*

GROOT, Chantal (1982—). Dutch swimmer. Born Oct 19, 1982, in Netherlands. ❖ At SC World Cup in Rio de Janeiro, placed 1st in 50-meter and 100-meter freestyle (2002); won a bronze medal for 4 x 100-meter freestyle relay at Athens Olympics (2004).

GROSHEVA, Yelena (1979—). Russian gymnast. Name variations: Elena Grosheva. Born April 12, 1979, in Yaroslavl, Russia. ❖ Placed 3rd at Goodwill Games (1994) and 2nd at Russian Cup (1996), both in all-around; at Atlanta Olympics, won a silver medal in team all-around (1996); placed 1st in all-around at Moscow Stars and won a team silver in all-around at World championships (1997). ❖ See also Soviet film *Are You Going to the Ball?* (1987).

GROSHKOVA, Tatiana (1973—). Russian gymnast. Born Dec 16, 1973, in Moscow, Russia. ❖ Placed 1st in floor exercises at Tokyo Cup (1989), 3rd all-around at USSR nationals (1989), and 1st all-around at Avignon (1990); won a silver medal in floor exercises at European championships and came in 2nd all-around at Moscow News (1990).

GROSMAN, Haika (1919–1996). See Grossman, Haika.

GROSSETÊTE, Françoise (1946—). French politician. Name variations: Francoise Grossetete. Born May 17, 1946, in Lyon, France. ❖ Served as federal secretary, Loire Republican Party (1984–94); was deputy mayor of Saint Etienne; member of the policy bureau and national secretary for equal opportunities, Démocratie libérale (DL), and national vice-chair of the DL party; as a member of the European People's Party (Christian Democrats) and European Democrats, elected to 4th and 5th European Parliament (1994–99, 1999–2004).

GROSSFELD, Muriel Davis (1941—). American gymnast. Name variations: Muriel Davis. Born Muriel Davis, 1941, in Indianapolis, Indiana; m. Abie Grossfeld (gymnast), 1960. ❖ Won 17 US national championships (1957–66), including all-around (1957 and 1963); was a member of US Olympic teams (1956, 1960, 1964); became a well-known coach.

GROSSINGER, Jennie (1892–1972). American hotel executive and philanthropist. Born in Baligrod, Austria, June 16, 1892; died in Ferndale, New York, Nov 20, 1972; eldest daughter and oldest of three children of Asher Selig (estate overseer) and Malka (Grumet) Grossinger; attended public school in New York City; m. Harry Grossinger (laborer in a garment factory), May 25, 1912 (died 1964); children: one child (b. 1913, died in infancy); Paul Grossinger (b. around 1915); Elaine Grossinger (b. 1927). ❖ One of the world's great hostesses, was a guiding force behind America's premiere resort, the opulent Grossinger's Hotel, located on 700 acres in New York's Catskill Mountains and catering to a largely Jewish clientele; migrated with family to America (1900); moved to Catskill Mountains with family (1914), where they took in summer boarders, most of whom were fellow Jewish immigrants from New York City who were looking for low-cost vacations in the country; built a new wing, adding six rooms and providing for 20 guests (1915), and so on; served as host and business manager and somehow retained the hotel's family-run ambiance even as it expanded into a year-round luxury resort; charity work focused on the Jewish homeland of Israel, where she helped to build a convalescent home and a medical center. ❖ See also Joel Pomerantz, *Jennie and the Story of Grossinger's* (Grosset & Dunlap, 1970); Richard Grossinger, *Out of Babylon: Ghosts of Grossinger's* (Frog, 1997); Tania Grossinger, *Growing up at Grossinger's* (McKay, 1975); and *Women in World History.*

GROSSMAN, Edith (1936—). American translator. Born Mar 22, 1936, in Philadelphia, Pennsylvania; University of Pennsylvania AB, MA; New York University, PhD; married and divorced; children: 2 sons. ❖ Foremost translator of Latin American fiction and poetry, work includes Mayra Montero's *Deep Purple,* Alvaro Mutis's *The Adventures and Misadventures of Maqroll,* Mario Vargas Llosa's *The Feast of the Goat,* Cervantes's *Don Quixote,* and Gabriel Garcia Marquez's *Love in the Time of Cholera* and *Living to Tell the Tale.*

GROSSMAN, Haika (1919–1996). Polish-Jewish resistance leader and Israeli politician. Name variations: Chaika or Chaike Grosman or Grossman; Chayke; Haikah; Haike; Haykah; Jaika; Khaya. Born in Bialystok, Poland, Nov 20, 1919; died at Kibbutz Evron, Israel, May 26, 1996; had two sisters and one brother; m. Meir Orkin; children: 2 daughters. ❖ In Poland, was a leader of the Jewish resistance in Bialystok and Vilna during WWII, where exploits earned her a place in Jewish history; a Zionist from earliest years, immigrated to Israel (1948); was elected to Israeli Knesset (parliament) as a representative of the far-left Mapam Party (1968); became a member of Kibbutz Evron, a settlement affiliated to the Hashomer Hatzair movement; re-elected several times; during her tenure (1968–81 and 1984–88), served in the social affairs committee and was known as a fiery orator; spoke out in favor of a Palestinian state in the West Bank and Gaza; served as the Knesset's deputy speaker (1987–88); wrote *The Underground Army: Fighters of the Bialystok Ghetto* (trans. by Shmuel Beeri, Holocaust Library, 1988). ❖ See also *Women in World History.*

GROSSMAN, Josephine Juliet (1923–1997). See Merril, Judith.

GROSSMANN, Edith Searle (1863–1931). New Zealand teacher, novelist, journalist, and feminist. Name variations: Edith Howitt Searle. Born Edith Howitt Searle, Sept 8, 1863, in Victoria, Australia; died Feb 27, 1931, in St Heliers Bay, Auckland, New Zealand; dau. of George Smales Searle (newspaper editor) and Mary Ann Beeby; Canturbury College, BA, 1884, MA, 1885; m. Joseph Penfound Grossmann; children: 1 son. ❖ Immigrated with family to New Zealand (1878); taught at Wellington Girls' High School (1885–90); a feminist, was involved in suffrage movement (1890s); wrote novels *Angela, a Messenger* (1890), *In Revolt* (1893), *A Knight of the Holy Ghost* (1907), and *The Heart of the Bush* (1910) and biography *Life of Helen Macmillan Brown* (1905); contributed to British and New Zealand newspapers and journals (1897–1918). ❖ See also *Dictionary of New Zealand Biography* (Vol. 2).

GROSSMANN, Judith (1931—). Brazilian poet and short-story writer. Born 1931. ❖ Worked as professor of literature in Bahia; writings include *Linhagem de rocinante* (1959), *Omeio de pedra* (1970), and *A noite estrelada* (1977).

GROSSMITH, Mrs. Lawrence (1880–1928). See Blythe, Coralie.

GROTE, Harriet (1792–1878). English writer and biographer. Born Harriet Lewin near Southampton, England, July 1, 1792; died at Shiere, near Guildford, Surrey, Dec 29, 1878; m. George Grote (1794–1871, English historian who wrote a *History of Greece,* and member of Parliament [1831–41]), in 1820 (died 1871). ❖ Following husband's death, published his biography, *The Personal Life of George Grote* (1873); had also written *The Life of Ary Scheffer* (1860).

GROTELL, Maija (1899–1973). Finnish potter. Born Aug 19, 1899, in Helsingfors, Finland; studied with Alfred William Finch at Central School of Industrial Art; also studied State College of Ceramics at Alfred University in NY, working with school's founder Charles F. Binns. ❖ Innovative, award-winning potter, moved to US to study, then found work at Inwood Studios in Manhattan; went on to teach at

Union Settlement and Henry Street Settlement while exhibiting ceramics; was the 1st art instructor at School of Ceramic Engineering at Rutgers University (1936–38); with architect Eliel Saarinen, sculptor Carl Milles, weaver Marianne Strengell and designer Charles Eames, served on faculty of Cranbrook Academy of Art outside Detroit (1938–66), eventually becoming head of ceramics department; conducted extensive glaze research which was put to use in architectural designs of Eliel and Eero Saarinen; employed layers of bold pattern and vivid color in work and mastered the use of colored and textured glazes; work can be seen in permanent collections of 21 museums, including American Craft Museum and Metropolitan Museum of Art in New York, Detroit Institute of Arts, Art Institute of Chicago, Cleveland Museum of Art and Cranbrook Academy of Art Museum, as well as in many private collections. Won 25 major exhibition awards over 30-year career, including diploma from Barcelona International Exposition (1929), silver medal at Paris International (1937) and Charles Fergus Binns Medal from Alfred University (1961). ❖ See also Jeff Schlanger and Toshiko Takaezu, *Maija Grotell: Works Which Grow from Belief* (Studio Potter, 1996).

GROTHAUS, Gisela (1955—). West German kayaker. Born Feb 20, 1955, in Germany. ❖ At Munich Olympics, won a silver medal in K1 slalom (1972).

GROTHE, Tilly (1911—). See Fleischer, Ottilie.

GROUCHY, Mlle de (1764–1822). See Condorcet, Sophie Marie Louise, Marquise de.

GROULT, Benoîte (1921—). French novelist and essayist. Name variations: Benoite Groult. Born 1921 in Paris, France; sister of Flora Groult. ❖ With sister, wrote such novels as *Journal à quatre mains* (1962), *Le féminin pluriel* (1965), and *Il etait deux fois* (1967); also wrote novel *Le part des choses* (1972) and feminist works, including *Ainsi soit-elle* (1975) and *Le Féminisme au masculin* (1977); with Claude Servan Schreiber, founded *F. Magazine* (1978) and contributed regular column.

GROULT, Flora (1925—). French novelist. Born 1925 in Paris, France; sister of Benoîte Groult. ❖ With sister, wrote the novels *Journal à quatre mains* (1962), *Le féminin pluriel* (1965), and *Il etait deux fois* (1967); also wrote *Belle ombre, Le coup de la reine d'Espagne, Maxime ou la déchirure* and *Memoires de moi.* Won Prix Gallia for *Il etait deux fois* (1968).

GROVÉ, Henriette (1922—). South African novelist and playwright. Name variations: Henriette Grove; (pseudonym) Linda Joubert. Born 1925 near Potchefstroom, Orange Free State, South Africa. ❖ First short stories appeared in anthology *Kwartet* (1957); other novels and stories include *Roosmaryn en Wynruit* (1962), *Jaaringe* (1966), *Winterreis* (1971), and *In die Kamer was 'n Kas* (1989); plays include *Die Jaar* (1958), *Halte 49* (1962), *Toe hulle die Vierkleur of Rooigrond gehys het* (1975), and *Ontmoeting by Dwaaldrif* (1981); children's books include *Die Verlore Skoentjie* (1948) and *Bimbo en Prins* (1950); works often express longing to escape middle-class convention. Awarded CNA Prize and Hertzog Prize.

GROZA, Maria (1918—). Romanian economist and feminist. Born 1918 in Déva, Romania; educated at Bucharest Academy of Economics. ❖ As a civil servant, worked in the Ministry of Foreign Affairs (1948–55); became lecturer in Economics at the Academy of Economics and wrote on education and women's issues; served as secretary of National Council of Women (1958–64) and vice-president (1965–75); became deputy minister of Social Affairs; served as UN delegate and chaired UNESCO and UN conferences; was rapporteur-général at World Conference for International Women's Year (1975); became deputy minister of Foreign Affairs (1980).

GROZDEVA, Maria (1972—). Bulgarian shooter. Born Maria Zdravkova Grozdeva, June 23, 1972, in Sofia, Bulgaria; m. Valeri Grigorov (her trainer). ❖ Won a bronze medal at Barcelona Olympics (1992) and a bronze medal at Atlanta Olympics (1996), both for air pistol; won a gold medal for 25m pistol at Sydney Olympics (2000); won a bronze medal for 10m air pistol and a gold medal for 25m pistol at Athens Olympics (2004); won a World championship and 6 European titles.

GROZDEVA, Svetlana (1959—). Soviet gymnast. Born Jan 29, 1959, in USSR. ❖ At Montreal Olympics, won a gold medal in team all-around (1976).

GRUAIDH (fl. 11 c.). Countess of Moray. Dau. of Aedh, mormaer (ruler) of Moray; maternal granddau. of Gruoch (Lady MacBeth); m. William

Dunkeld, earl of Moray (son of Duncan II, king of Scots); children: 6, including William Dunkeld, Lord of Egremont.

GRUBB, Sarah Lynes (1773–1842). British letter writer and minister. Name variations: Sally Lynes. Born Sarah Lynes, April 13, 1773, in Wapping, London, England; died Mar 16, 1842, in Suffolk, England; dau. of Mason Lynes and Hannah (Holdway) Lynes; served as a nanny to Sarah Pim Grubb (sister-in-law of Sarah Tuke Grubb); m. John Grubb (Quaker minister and cousin of Sarah Pim Grubb), 1803 (died 1841). ❖ Grew up in devout Quaker family and began preaching as Sally Lynes in meeting at 17; began itinerant ministry in England, Ireland, Scotland, and Wales; a gifted preacher, favored Quietism and individual spirituality over dogmatic orthodoxy in Quaker faith.

GRUBB, Sarah Tuke (1756–1790). British religious writer. Born Sarah Tuke, June 20, 1756, in York, England; died Dec 8, 1790, in Cork, Ireland; dau. of William Tuke and Elizabeth Tuke; m. Robert Grubb, 1782. ❖ Began preaching to Quaker congregations at 22; after marriage, continued traveling and preaching throughout Britain; assisted in girls school established by father in York and founded, with husband, finishing school for girls in Clonmel, Ireland; after 1787, visited several Quaker communities in Europe before sudden death at 34. Writings include *A Serious Meditation: or, A Christian's Duty Fully Set Forth* (1790) and *Some Account of the Life and Religious Labours of Sarah Grubb. With an Appendix containing an Account of the Schools at Ackworth and York, Observations on Christian Discipline, and Extracts from Many of Her Letters* (1792).

GRUBER, Lilo (1915–1992). German ballet dancer and choreographer. Born Jan 3, 1915, in Berlin, Germany; died in 1992. ❖ Studied modern dance with Mary Wigman, among others, and classical ballet with numerous teachers throughout Berlin; performed with small German dance company until 1945; served as ballet master of Opera Ballet in Greiswald, Germany (starting 1945), and later in Leipzig; became ballet master of East Berlin State Opera (1955) where she staged numerous original works as well as the city's 1st *Giselle* and *Swan Lake;* remained with East Berlin Opera until retirement (1970). Choreographed works include *Gayanne* (1955), *Coppélia* (1955), *Lysistrata* (1959), *Romeo and Juliet* (1963), *Spartacus* (1964), *Giselle* (1966), *Ballad of Gluck* (1967) and *Swan Lake* (1967).

GRUBER, Ruth (1911—). American journalist, photographer and lecturer. Name variations: Ruth Ellen Gruber. Born 1911 in Philadelphia, Pennsylvania; graduate of Oberlin College. ❖ Did doctoral study in Cologne, Germany (1931); launched career as a journalist (1932); commissioned by *New York Herald Tribune* to write a series on women under communism and fascism; during WWII, was asked by Harold Ickes, secretary of the interior, to secretly escort a group of 1,000 Jewish refugees from Italy to America; escorted her group to Fort Ontario, near Oswego, NY, and, with much effort, effectively lobbied Congress to let them remain after the war; covered the tragic story of the refugee ship *Exodus* (1946); working for UPI, was a foreign correspondent in Rome, Brussels, London, Belgrade, Warsaw, and Vienna; writings include *Upon the Doorposts of Thy House* (1994) and *Virtually Jewish* (1994). ❖ See also tv series "Haven," starring Natasha Richardson (2001).

GRUBEROVÁ, Edita (1946—). Czechoslovakian soprano. Name variations: Edita Gruberova. Born in Bratislava, Czechoslovakia, 1946. ❖ Considered one of the finest coloratura singers of her generation, studied in Prague and Vienna before making her debut with the Slovak National Theater; performed at the Vienna State Opera, Bayreuth, Frankfurt Opera, and, in America, at the Chicago Lyric Opera.

GRUCHALA, Sylwia (1981—). Polish fencer. Name variations: Sylvia Gruchala. Born Nov 6, 1981, in Gdansk, Poland. ❖ Won a silver medal for team foil at Sydney Olympics (2000) and a bronze medal for indiv. foil at Athens Olympics (2004); at World championships, placed 1st for team foil (2003); placed 3rd overall in World Cup ranking (2002–03, 2003–04).

GRUDNEVA, Yelena (1974—). Soviet gymnast. Born Feb 21, 1974, in USSR. ❖ At Barcelona Olympics, won a gold medal in team all-around (1992).

GRUENBERG, Sidonie (1881–1974). American educator and writer. Name variations: Sidonie Matsner, Sidonie Matsner Gruenberg. Born Sidonie Matzner or Matsner, June 10, 1881, near Vienna, Austria; died Mar 11, 1974, in New York, NY; dau. of Idore Matzner and Augusta Olivia (Bassechés) Matzner; m. Benjamin Charles Gruenberg, 1903 (died 1965); children: 3 sons (b. 1907, 1910, 1915), 1 daughter (b. 1913). ❖ Wrote *Your Child Today and Tomorrow* (1912), *The Wonderful Story of How You Were Born* (1952), and *The Encyclopedia of Child Care and Guidance* (1954); worked with Child Study Association of America (previously Federation of Child Study), serving as director (1924–50); served as chair of National Council of Parent Education; taught parent education leadership courses at Columbia University and New York University (1928–37); during WWII, was adviser to US Children's Bureau; was special consultant to Doubleday on education and children's literature (after 1950).

GRUMBACH, Argula von (1492–after 1563). German religious writer. Born Argula von Stauffer in 1492 in Bavaria, Germany; died after 1563; m. Friedrich von Grumbach, 1516 (died c. 1530); had a brief 2nd marriage; children: 4. ❖ Bavarian noblewoman who corresponded with Martin Luther and wrote letters and tracts promoting ideas of Reformation; wrote to University of Ingolstadt challenging faculty to debate her views (1523), causing husband to lose his job; imprisoned briefly (1563) because of her religious views.

GRUMBACH, Doris (1918—). American novelist and biographer. Born July 12, 1918, in New York, NY; m. Leonard Grumbach, 1941; longtime partner of Sybil Pike (book dealer); children: 4. ❖ During WWII, served in the WAVES; worked as professor of English before becoming columnist and editor at *The New Republic;* wrote nonfiction column for *The New York Times Book Review* and taught literature at American University; with partner Sybil Pike, opened Wayward Books in Washington DC and then in Maine; fiction includes *The Spoil of Flowers* (1962), *The Short Throat, The Tender Mouth* (1964), *Chamber Music* (1979), *The Missing Person* (1981), *The Ladies in Waiting* (1984), *The Magician's Girl* (1987), and *The Book of Knowledge* (1995); also wrote biography of Mary McCarthy, *The Company She Kept* (1967). ❖ See also memoirs *Coming into the End Zone* (1991), *Extra Innings* (1993), *Fifty Days of Solitude* (1994) and *Life in a Day* (1996).

GRUMMT, Kornelia (1958—). *See Ender, Kornelia.*

GRUND, Barbara (1814–1894). *See Paoli, Betty.*

GRUNDIG, Lea (1906–1977). German-Jewish artist. Born Lea Langer in Dresden, Germany, Mar 23, 1906; died while on a Mediterranean cruise on Oct 10, 1977; dau. of Moses Baer Langer and Judita (Händzel) Langer; attended Dresden Academy of Fine Arts; had sisters Marie and Klara; m. Hans Grundig (artist), 1928 (died 1958); no children. ❖ Graphic artist of the later years of the Weimar Republic who became one of the most honored artists of the German Democratic Republic; joined the German Communist Party (KPD, 1926); after Hitler came to power (1933), was banned from earning a living as an artist because she was a Jew; purchased a copper-plate etching press with husband and printed approximately 150 engravings (1933–38), which depicted the harsh realities of working-class life in Nazi Germany, including sets titled "Women's Lives," "Under the Swastika," "The Jew is to Blame," "War Threatens!" and "On the Spanish War"; arrested and imprisoned (spring 1938); with help of exit papers, immigrated to Palestine where her family had settled (1941); created another series of graphics entitled "In the Valley of Death" (1942–43), which appeared in print as *Im Tal des Todes* (1947); created "Never Again!," "Ghetto," and "Ghetto Revolt" (1945–48); returned to hometown of Dresden, now in East Germany, and reunited with husband whom she had not seen since May 1938 (Feb 1949); appointed 1st female chaired professor of graphics and drawing at Dresden Academy of Fine Arts (1949), a post she held until retirement (1967); published autobiography, *Gesichte und Geschichte (Faces and History,* 1958), a GDR bestseller that went through 10 printings; elected a member of the German Academy of the Arts (1961) and president of League of German Artists (Verband Bildender Künstler Deutschlands, 1964); elected a member of the Socialist Unity Party's Central Committee (1967); work brought to the attention of art world with one-woman shows in Berlin and New York (1996–97). Received the GDR National Prize, 1st Class (1967). ❖ See also *Women in World History.*

GRUNERT, Martina (1949—). East German swimmer. Born May 17, 1949, in East Germany. ❖ At Mexico City Olympics, won a silver medal in 4 x 100-meter freestyle relay (1968).

GRUNSVEN, Anky van (1968—). *See van Grunsven, Anky.*

GRUOCH (fl. 1020–1054). Queen of Scotland. Name variations: Lady Macbeth or Lady MacBeth. Born around 1015; flourished around 1020 to 1054; dau. of Beoedhe also known as Bodhe or Boite (who was probably the son of King Kenneth II or Kenneth III); granddau. of either King Kenneth II (971–995) or Kenneth III (997–1005); married Gillacomgain or Gillacomgan, mormaer (ruler) of Moray; m. Macbeth or MacBeth also known as Machethad, Machetad, Macbethad, and often confused with MacHeth in later sources (c. 1005–1057), king of Scotland (r. 1040–1057), after 1032; children: (1st m.) Lulach (1032–1058, known as the Fool or the Simple), mormaer of Moray and king of Scots (r. 1057–1058, who m. Finnghuala of Angus). ❖ The historical "Lady Macbeth" (though she would not have been called this), married Gillacomgain who had been involved in the murder of his uncle Findlaech MacRuaridh, mormaer of Moray, in 1020, and had donned the title; when husband was killed, possibly by Macbeth, who was the son of Findlaech, married Macbeth; with the death of the king of Scotland, Duncan I, possibly at the hand of Macbeth, was inaugurated as queen of Scots and Macbeth was made king; fled to Moray with husband with Malcolm III at their heels (1054); suffered severely from the pen of William Shakespeare. ❖ See also *Women in World History.*

GRUSHEVSKI, Agraphia (1662–1681). Russian empress. Born Agraphia Simeonova Grushevski in 1662; died July 14, 1681; dau. of Simeon Grushevski; m. Feodor also known as Theodore III (1661–1682), tsar of Russia (r. 1676–1682); children: Ilya Feodorovich Romanov (1681–1681).

GRUSON, Flora (1922–2002). *See Lewis, Flora.*

GRUYCHEVA, Stoyanka (1955—). *See Kurbatova-Gruycheva, Stoyanka.*

GRYMESTON, Elizabeth Bernye (d. 1603). British poet. Name variations: Elizabeth Bernye Grymeston; Elizabeth Grimston; Elizabeth Bernye. Born Elizabeth Bernye; died 1603; dau. of Martin Bernye and Margaret Flynte Bernye; m. Christopher Grymeston. ❖ Raised in Catholic environment but, like father, fined for recusancy; had a knowledge of Italian, Latin, and Greek; only extant work is *Miscelanea, Meditations, Memoratives* written for son Bernye.

GSOVSKY, Tatiana (1901–1993). Soviet ballet dancer and choreographer. Name variations: Tatiana Issatchenko. Born Mar 16, 1901, in Moscow, Russia; died Sept 9, 1993, in Berlin, Germany; m. Victor Gsovsky. ❖ Trained at Irma Duncan's studio in Moscow and with Olga Preobrazhenska; served as ballet master of company in Krasnoder (late 1910s); served in same capacity for Berlin State Opera Ballet (1922–45), and for the State Opera of East Berlin after WWII (1945–52); moved to West Berlin where she founded Berlin Ballet (1955); choreographed and staged works at numerous theaters including in Munich, Milan, and at Teatro Colón in Buenos Aires; considered of great importance for development of ballet in Germany, combined trends from expressionist and modern dance with traditional opera ballet genres and companies. Works of choreography include *Bolero* (1946), *Romeo and Juliet* (1947), *Don Quixote* (1949), *Rondo vom Goldenen Kalb* (1952), *Der Idiot* (1952), *Ballade* (1955), *Agon* (1958), *The Sleeping Beauty* (1960), *Goyescas* (1961), *Orpheus* (1961) and *Les Climats* (1963).

GU JUN (1975—). Chinese badminton player. Born Jan 3, 1975, in Jiangsu, China. ❖ Won a gold medal for doubles at Atlanta Olympics (1996) and at Sydney Olympics (2000).

GU XIAOLI (1971—). Chinese rower. Born Mar 28, 1971. ❖ At Barcelona Olympics, won a bronze medal in double sculls (1992).

GUACCI, Giuseppina (1807–1848). Italian poet. Name variations: Maria Guiseppa Guacci Nobile; Giuseppina Guacci Nobile. Born Maria Giuseppina Guacci, June 20, 1807, in Naples, Italy; died Nov 25, 1848; dau. of Giovanni Guacci (printer) and Saveria Tagliaferri; m. Antonio Nobile (astronomer), 1835. ❖ Published selected poetry, *Rime* (1832), which addressed Neapolitan women and was noteworthy for its scientific references; rewrote *Canto delle Sirene. Rime.*

GUADAGNINO, Kathy Baker (1961—). *See Baker, Kathy.*

GUAN DAOSHENG (1262–1319). Chinese artist and poet. Name variations: the Lady Guan; Lady Kuan; the Lady Kuan Tao-sheng; the Lady Kuan Tao-jen; Kuan Fu-jen; Wu Hsing Chün fu-jen; Wei Kuo fu-jen; Zi Zhongji. Born in 1262 in Wuxing (Wu Hsing), Zhejiang (Chekiang) province, in Central China; died of beriberi near Linqing (Lin Ch'ung), Shandong (Shantung) province, May 29, 1319; dau. of Guan Shen (Kuan Shen); mother was a member of the Zhou clan; had two sisters; lived during the Yuan Dynasty (1279–1368); m. Songxue also seen as Chao Meng-fu, Zhao Mengfu, or Zhao Meng (1254–1322, painter and calligrapher), 1289; children, two sons, including Zhao Yong, and two daughters (some sources cite 9 children). ❖ The greatest woman painter and calligrapher in the history of China, matched, perhaps even excelled, her husband's level of brilliance, when he served Emperor Kublai Khan and four of his successors as painter and calligrapher (1287–1322); during reign of Emperor Renzong (r. 1312–1321), created an extended calligraphic work, the Thousand Character Classic; though she had produced many highly praised works of calligraphy, as well as paintings of landscape, birds, plum blossoms, orchids, rocks, and Buddhist figures done in the traditional Song style, dared to venture into creating important works depicting bamboo, then a masculine preserve; mastered the art of monochrome black-ink (*mozhu*) resulting in her treatise, *The Bamboo in Monochrome*, which remains a classic account of artistic philosophy and technique; became famed as a bamboo artist throughout China; several masterpieces attributed to her brush have survived the centuries, including "Bamboo Groves in Mist and Rain" (dated 1308, National Palace Museum, Taipei, Taiwan). ❖ See also *Women in World History*.

GUAN WEIZHEN (1964—). Chinese badminton player. Born June 3, 1964, in China. ❖ At Barcelona Olympics, won a silver medal in doubles (1992).

GUANHUMAR or GUANHUMARA (d. 470 or 542). *See Guinevere.*

GUARD, Elizabeth (1814–1870). New Zealand hostage. Name variations: Elizabeth Parker. Born Elizabeth Parker, Dec 3, 1814, in New South Wales, Australia; died July 16, 1870, in New Zealand; dau. of Stephen and Harriott Parker; m. John (Jacky) Guard, 1830; children: 8. ❖ While on journey to Sydney, was driven ashore off coast with family and captured by Maori; survived attacks and lived with tribal chief as a wife until rescued by British troops and husband, who had been released earlier (1834). ❖ See also *Dictionary of New Zealand Biography* (Vol. 1).

GUASTALLA, duchess of. *See Bonaparte, Pauline (1780–1825).*

GUAY, Lucie (1958—). Canadian kayaker. Born Dec 12, 1958, in Canada. ❖ At Los Angeles Olympics, won a bronze medal in K4 500 meters (1984).

GUBAIDULINA, Sofia (1931—). Russian composer. Name variations: Sofiya or Sofia Gubaydulina. Pronunciation: Goo-BUY-doo-LEEN-ah. Born Sofia Asgatovna Gubaidulina in Chsistopol, Tatar Soviet Socialist Republic, USSR, Oct 24, 1931; dau. of a Tatar and a mother of mixed Russian, Polish and Jewish blood; studied at Kazan Music Academy, Kazan Conservatory, and Moscow Conservatory; never married; no children. ❖ Considered by some critics to be the most important woman composer of the 20th century and perhaps of all time, studied piano under Maria Piatnitskaya and theory under Nazib Zhiganov at Kazan Music Academy (1946–49); studied composition at the Kazan Conservatory with Albert Leman and piano with Leopold Lukomsky and Grigory Kogan (1949–54); studied at Moscow Conservatory with Nikolai Peiko and Vissarion Shebalin, beginning 1954; composed more than 20 film scores in order to support herself; after years of working in obscurity, began to gain international attention in the 1980s and to have her works played by major orchestras outside the Soviet Union; her "Offertorium" was performed by the New York Philharmonic (1984); was invited to hear her work performed at Boston's Symphony Hall (1988); major works include (orchestra) "Fazelija" (1956), (mezzo-soprano, male chorus, orchestra) "Night in Memphis" (1968), (piano) "Musical Tog," (B, small orchestra) "Rubaiyant" (1969), (orchestra) "Fairy Tale," (small orchestra) "Concordanza" (1971), (cello, small orchestra) "Detto II," (soprano, piano) "Roses" (1972), (percussion, harpsichord-cello) "Humore e silenzio" (1974), (soprano, alto, tenor, bass, two choirs, orchestra) "Laudatio pacis" (1975), (percussion, orchestra) "Percussio per Pekarsky," (orchestra, jazz band) Concerto (1976), (7 percussion) "Misterioso" (1977), (organ, percussion) "Detto I" (1978), (piano, small orchestra) "Introitus," (4 percussion) "Jubilatio," (cello, organ) "In croce" (1979), (3 trombone, 3 percussion, harp, harpsichord-cello, cello-piano) "Descensio," (cello, accordion, string orchestra) "The Seven Words" (1982), (soprano, bass, 2 violin, 2 viola, 2 cello, double bass, tape) "Perception" (1983), (viola, bassoon, piano) "Quasi Hoquetus," (7 percussion) "In the Beginning was Rhythm," (unaccompanied chorus) "Homage to Marina Tsvetaeva" (1984), (orchestra) Stimmen . . . verstummen (1986), and (8 instruments) "Homage to T.S. Eliot" (1987). ❖ See also *Women in World History*.

GUDA (fl. late 12th c.). German nun and artist. Fl. in the late 12th century in Westphalia, Germany; never married; no children. ❖ Worked in the *scriptoria* of her convent at Westphalia; left her mark on a homiliary (book of sermons) for which she prepared the miniatures and decorated the ornate capital letters by painting a portrait of herself standing within a capital D. ❖ See also *Women in World History*.

GUDE, Franziska (1976—). German field-hockey player. Born Mar 19, 1976, in Göttingen, Germany; attended University of Cologne. ❖ Was the junior German fencing champion (1992); won a team gold medal for field hockey at Athens Olympics (2004). Named German Hockey's Player of the Year (2000).

GUDEREIT, Marcia (c. 1966—). Canadian curler. Born c. 1966 in Hudson Bay, Saskatchewan, Canada. ❖ Won a gold medal for curling at Nagano Olympics (1998); with Team Schmirler, won the World championship (1993, 1994, 1997), the only 3-time winner in the history of the sport. ❖ See also *Gold on Ice* (Coteau Books, 1989).

GUDULA OF BRUSSELS (d. 712?). Patron saint of Brussels. Fl. in Brussels; died c. 712; dau. of Count Witgar and Amalberga of Brussels; greatniece of Pepin I of Landen, king of the Franks; goddaughter and disciple of Gertrude of Nivelles (626–659); never married; no children. ❖ A Frankish noblewoman, was sent to the Belgian convent at Nivelles for education, then returned to father's court; took a vow of virginity and refused to marry; gave her fortune to the poor and lived an ascetic lifestyle; was thought to be able to effect miracles, even of curing lepers, and influenced many others by her self-mortification and humility; canonized some years after her death. Feast day is Jan 8.

GUDZ, Lyudmila (1969—). Soviet handball player. Born Sept 10, 1969, in USSR. ❖ At Barcelona Olympics, won a bronze medal in team competition (1992).

GUDZINEVICIUTE, Daina (1965—). Lithuanian shooter. Born 1965 in Lithuania. ❖ Won a gold medal at Sydney Olympics (2000), the 1st year that women's trap shooting was held as a separate event.

GUEBHARD, Caroline Rémy (1855–1929). *See Séverine.*

GUEDEN, Hilde (1915–1988). Austrian soprano. Name variations: Hilde Güden. Born Hilde Geiringer on Sept 15, 1915, in Vienna, Austria; died Sept 17, 1988, in Klosterneuburg, Austria; dau. of Fritz Geiringer and Frida (Brammer) Geiringer (both musicians); studied with Wetzelsberger at the Vienna Conservatory; studied dramatics at the Max Reinhardt School and ballet at the Vienna State Opera. ❖ Made debut in Zurich (1939), Bavarian Staatsoper in Munich (1941), and Rome (1942); appeared in Salzburg as Zerlina (1947); made Covent Garden debut (1947) and Metropolitan Opera debut (1951); served as an associate of the Vienna Staatsoper until 1972; made an Austrian Kammersängerin (1951).

GUEILER TEJADA, Lydia (1921—). Bolivian politician, diplomat and president. Name variations: Lidia Gueiler. Born in 1921 in Bolivia. ❖ Was a member of Parliament (1956–64), then lived in exile for 15 years; served as subsecretary for Agriculture and president of Camera de Diputados (1978); was acting president of the Congress and acting deputy head of state (1978–79), Bolivia's 1st woman president; deposed in a coup by a military faction with strong ties to the drug trade, lived in exile in France (1980–82); following another coup, served as ambassador to West Germany (1983–83), then Venezuela (1983–86 and 1993—).

GUELDERS, countess of.
See Marguerite de Brabant (c. 1192–?).
See Katherine of Holland (d. 1401).

GUELDERS, duchess of.
See Sophia of Malines (d. 1329).
See Eleanor of Woodstock (1318–1355).
See Marie of Guelders (1325–1399).
See Catherine of Bourbon (d. 1469).
See Catherine of Cleves (1417–1479).

GUELLOUZ, Souad (1937—). Tunisian novelist and educator. Born 1937 in Tunisia. ❖ Taught French at schools in Tunis; writings include *La Vie simple* (1975) and *Les Jardins du nord* (1982).

GUENEVERE (d. 470 or 542). *See Guinevere.*

GUENHUMARE (d. 470 or 542). *See Guinevere.*

GUENIÈVRE (d. 470 or 542). *See Guinevere.*

GUENTHER, Sarah (1983—). German soccer player. Born Jan 25, 1983, in Germany. ❖ Won a team bronze medal at Athens Olympics (2004).

GUEORGUIEVA, Diliana (1965—). Bulgarian rhythmic gymnast. Born Feb 18, 1965, in Pazardjik, Bulgaria; m. Vladimir Klintcharov (pentathlete). ❖ Won the gold medal in all-around at World championships

(1983 and 1985); placed 3rd at European championships (1984); coached the New Zealand National team.

GUÉRIN, Eugénie de (1805–1848). French poet and diarist. Name variations: Eugenie Guerin. Born Jan 11(?), 1805, at Château du Cayla, near Albi, in southern France; died May 31, 1848, in Languedoc; sister of Georges Maurice de Guérin (1810–1839, poet); never married; no children. ❖ Following brother's death (1839), labored constantly to see his work published; her own work, *Reliquiae d'Eugénie de Guérin*, was published for private circulation (1855) and G.S. Trébutien edited *Journal et Fragments d'Eugénie de Guérin* (1862). ❖ See also *Women in World History*.

GUÉRIN, Mother Theodore (1798–1856). American religious order founder. Name variations: Sister Theodore or Mother Theodore; Mother Theodore Guerin. Born Anne-Thérèse Guérin on Oct 2, 1798, in Étables, Côtes-du-Nord, France; died May 14, 1856, at Saint Mary-of-the-Woods, near Terre Haute, Indiana; dau. of a naval officer. ❖ As Sister Theodore, took final vows with Sisters of Providence at Ruillé-sur-Loir, France (1825); served as superior at the order's school in Rennes; transferred to Soulaines (1833); with 5 fellow nuns, arrived in Indiana to establish the convent of St. Mary-of-the-Woods near Terre Haute (1840), the 1st academy for girls in Indiana, which opened in 1841 and later became Saint Mary-of-the-Woods College (1909); served 16 years as superior of this American branch of the Sisters of Providence.

GUERIN, Veronica (1960–1996). Irish journalist. Born in Dublin, Ireland, 1960; killed in Dublin on June 26, 1996; attended parochial schools in Dublin; m. Graham Turley (builder), 1985; children: one son, Cathal. ❖ Ireland's leading investigative reporter, was in the middle of an ongoing crusade against the nation's crime lords when she was gunned down, gangland-style; ran her own public relations firm for several years before moving into journalism (1990); began as a freelancer for Dublin's *Sunday Business Post* and *Sunday Tribune;* joined *Sunday Independent* as an investigative reporter (1994). Received International Press Freedom Award from the Committee to Protect Journalists (1995). ❖ See also Emily O'Reilly, *Veronica Guerin: The Life and Death of a Crime Reporter* (Vintage, 1999); (film) *Veronica Guerin,* starring Cate Blanchett; and *Women in World History*.

GUERRA CABRERA, Patricia (1965—). Spanish yacht racer. Born July 21, 1965, in Las Palmas, Grand Canary, Spain. ❖ At Barcelona Olympics, won a gold medal in 470 class (1992).

GUERRE, Elisabeth-Claude Jacquet de la (c. 1666–1729). *See Jacquet de la Guerre, Elisabeth-Claude.*

GUERRERO (1867–1928). *See Guerrero, Maria.*

GUERRERO, Maria (1867–1928). Spanish actress and theatrical impresario. Name variations: María Ana de Jesús Guerrero. Born April 17, 1867; died Jan 23, 1928; eldest child of Ramón Guerrero (prosperous merchant) and Casilda Torrijo; studied with Teodora Lamadrid; m. Fernando Díaz de Mendoza (actor), Jan 10, 1896; children: Luis Fernando, Carlos. ❖ Made debut (1885) under direction of Emilio Mario at Teatro de la Princesa and later moved with him to Teatro de Comedia, where she appeared in light comedies; soon insisted on appearing in important dramatic plays, both in classical Spanish plays and new works written by José Echegaray, Benito Pérez Galdós, Jacinto Benavente, and Juan Eduardo Marquina; with father, formed a company, remodeled Madrid's Teatro Español, and hired Fernando Díaz de Mendoza as a male lead; with husband, built the huge Teatro Cervantes in Buenos Aires. ❖ See also *Women in World History*.

GUERRERO MENDEZ, Belem (1974—). Mexican cyclist. Born Mar 8, 1974, in Mexico City, Mexico. ❖ Placed 2nd in points race at World championships (1998); won 2 World Cups for points race (2001 and 2002); in World Cup ranking, placed 1st overall for points race (2001, 2002, 2004); won a silver medal for points race at Athens Olympics (2004).

GUERRINI, Josefa (1964—). *See Idem, Josefa.*

GUESNERIE, Charlotte-Marie-Anne Charbonnière, de La (1710–1785). *See La Guesnerie, Charlotte Charbonnier de.*

GUEST, Lady Charlotte (1812–1895). Welsh industrialist, educator, and linguist. Name variations: Lady Charlotte Bertie; Lady Charlotte Schreiber. Pronunciation: Bartie. Born Lady Charlotte Elizabeth Bertie on May 19, 1812, at Uffington House, near Stamford, Lincolnshire, England; died at Canford Manor, Dorset, England, Jan 15, 1895; dau. of

Albermarle Bertie, 9th earl of Lindsey (former army general and member of Parliament for Stamford, 1801–09) and Charlotte Susanna Elizabeth (Layard), Lady Lindsey; no formal schooling, educated at home by governesses; married Josiah John Guest, July 29, 1833 (he became Sir John Guest in 1838; died 1852); m. Charles Schreiber, April 10, 1855; children: (1st m.) Charlotte Maria Guest (b. 1834); Ivor Bertie Guest (b. 1835); Katherine Gwladys Guest (b. 1837); Thomas Merthyr Guest (b. 1838); Montague John Guest (b. 1841); Augustus Frederick Guest (b. 1840); Arthur Edward Guest (b. 1841); Mary Enid Evelyn Guest (b.1843); Constance Rhiannon Guest (b. 1844); Blanche Vere Guest (b. 1847). ❖ Translator of Welsh medieval tales, *The Mabinogion,* and renowned collector of ceramics and fans, moved to South Wales on marriage (1833), living next to the Dowlais ironworks run by her husband; taught herself Welsh; published English translation of 12 medieval Welsh tales (1849); produced a lavish 3-volume illustrated edition of the tales which she called *The Mabinogion;* developed works schools; on husband's death, took over the running of the Dowlais Iron Company, the world's largest ironworks (1852); became (with 2nd husband) a leading collector of 18th-century china and fans; also wrote *Fans and Fan Leaves: English* (1888), *Fans and Fan Leaves: Foreign* (1890), and *Playing Cards of Various Ages and Countries* (3 vols., 1892, 1893, 1895). ❖ See also Revel Guest and Angela V. John, *Lady Charlotte: A Biography of the Nineteenth Century* (Weidenfeld & Nicolson, 1989); Earl of Bessborough, *The Diaries of Lady Charlotte Guest* (John Murray, 1950) and *Lady Charlotte Schreiber 1853–1891* (John Murray, 1952); Montague Guest, ed. *Lady Charlotte Schreiber's Journal: Confidences of a Collector of Ceramics and Antiques* (Bodley Head, 1911); and *Women in World History*.

GUEST, C.Z. (1920–2003). American socialite, horticulturist and columnist. Name variations: Cornelia Guest; Mrs. Winston Guest. Born Lucy Douglas Cochrane, Feb 19, 1920, in Boston, Massachusetts; died Nov 8, 2003, in Old Westbury, NY; dau. of Alexander Lynde Cochrane (investment banker); m. Winston Frederick Churchill Guest (heir to the Phipps steel fortune, international polo player and cousin of Winston Churchill), 1947 (died 1982); children: Alexander (b. 1954), Cornelia (b. 1963). ❖ Renowned gardening expert and icon of fashion, had a rebellious streak; soon after her debutant season, became a showgirl in the *Ziegfeld Follies* (1944) and posed nude for Diego Rivera; became the center of the social set, befriending Truman Capote, Cecil Beaton, Andy Warhol, Jacqueline Kennedy, Ernest Hemingway, and the Duke and Duchess of Windsor; began a gardening column for *New York Post* (1976) which was later syndicated in 350 newspapers; published *First Garden* (1976) and *Tiny Green Thumbs* (2000), for children; launched her own sportswear line (1986).

GUEST, Irene (1900–1979). American swimmer. Born July 22, 1900; died in 1979. ❖ Won a silver medal for the 100-meter freestyle and a gold for the 4 x 100-freestyle relay at Antwerp Olympics (1920).

GUETHLIEN, Christa (1961—). *See Kinshofer, Christa.*

GUETTE, Catherine de la (1613–1676). French memoirist. Name variations: Catherine Meurdrac de la Guette; Madame de la Guette. Born Catherine Meurdrac in 1613 in France; died 1676 in The Hague, Netherlands; sister of Marie Meurdrac; married (husband died 1665); children: 10. ❖ Born into family of nobility and trained in martial arts, expressed preference for war over domestic life and motherhood; though a royalist, married a rebel and remained loyal to him; dressed as a man to act as emissary between rebels (*frondeurs*) and royalists; after husband's death (1665), received support from William of Orange; wrote *Mémoires de Mme de la Guette* (1681) which give insight into French civil wars (1648–53).

GUEVARA, Ana (1977—). Mexican runner. Name variations: Ana Gabriela Guevara. Born Mar 4, 1977, in Nogales, Mexico. ❖ Had 7 1st-place finishes in the Golden League (2003); placed 1st in the 400 meters at World championships (2003); placed 1st in the Grand Prix for 400 meters (2001 and 2003); won World Athletics Final for 400 meters (2002, 2003); won a silver medal for 400 meters at Athens Olympics (2004). Named Central American and Caribbean Confederation's Female Athlete of the Year (2003); named Latin American Sportswoman of the Year (2002 and 2003).

GUFFEY, Emma (1874–1970). *See Miller, Emma Guffey.*

GUFLER, Edith (1962—). Italian shooter. Born in 1962 in Italy. ❖ At Los Angeles Olympics, won a silver medal in air rifle (1984).

GUGGENHEIM, Mrs. Daniel (1863–1944). *See Guggenheim, Florence Shloss.*

GUGGENHEIM, Florence Shloss (1863–1944). American philanthropist. Name variations: Mrs. Daniel Guggenheim. Born Florence Shloss on Sept 3, 1863; died May 13, 1944; m. Daniel Guggenheim (1856–1930); sister-in-law of Irene and Olga Guggenheim; children: M. Robert Guggenheim (1885–1959); Harry Frank Guggenheim (1890–1971); Gladys Eleanor Guggenheim (1895–1980, who m. Roger W. Straus, founder of Farrar, Straus & Giroux, and would serve as president of the Daniel and Florence Guggenheim Foundation). ❖ During WWI, sold $4 million worth of war bonds; with husband, established the Daniel and Florence Guggenheim Foundation for "the promotion, through charitable and benevolent activities, of the well-being of man throughout the world" (1924); became its president on death of husband (1930); opened her mansion, Hempstead House, to war orphans (1940), then deeded the place to Institute of Aeronautical Sciences; sponsored the Guggenheim Concerts in NY and was treasurer of the Women's National Republican Club (1921–38).

GUGGENHEIM, Irene (1868–1954). American art collector and philanthropist. Name variations: Mrs. Solomon Guggenheim; Irene Rothschild. Born Irene Rothschild in NY, NY, Dec 16, 1868; died in NY, Nov 25, 1954; dau. of Henry Rothschild (merchant and broker); m. Solomon R. Guggenheim (1861–1949), 1895; sister-in-law of Olga H. and Florence S. Guggenheim; children: Eleanor May Guggenheim (b. 1896, who m. Arthur Stuart, earl of Castle Stewart); Gertrude R. Guggenheim (1898–1966); Barbara Josephine Guggenheim (1904, who m. John R. Lawson-Johnston, Fred E. Wettach, Jr., and Henry Obre).

GUGGENHEIM, Olga H. (1877–1970). American philanthropist and organization executive. Name variations: Mrs. Simon Guggenheim. Born Olga H. Hirsh, Sept 23, 1877; died 1970; dau. of Barbara (Steiner) Hirsh and Henry Hirsh (NY realtor and diamond merchant); m. Simon Guggenheim (1867–1941, US senator and philanthropist), Nov 24, 1898; sister-in-law of Irene and Florence S. Guggenheim; children: John Simon Guggenheim (1905–1922); George Denver Guggenheim (1907–1939, committed suicide with a hunting rifle). ❖ Was an early member of the board of The Museum of Modern Art and benefactor of the museum collections; with husband, established the John Simon Guggenheim Memorial Foundation (1925); when husband died, succeeded him as president of the foundation and remained in that position for many years; left the bulk of her estate, $40 million, to that foundation. ❖ See also *Women in World History.*

GUGGENHEIM, Peggy (1898–1979). American art patron and collector. Born Marguerite Guggenheim in 1898 in NY, NY; died Dec 23, 1979, in Venice, Italy; dau. of Benjamin Guggenheim (partner in American Smelting and Refining Company who died on the *Titanic*) and Florette (Seligman) Guggenheim; niece of Irene Guggenheim and Solomon R. Guggenheim of the Guggenheim Museum in NY; m. Laurence Vail (writer), May 1922 (div. July 1930); m. Max Ernst (artist), Dec 1941 (div. 1946); children: (1st m.) Sindbad Vail (1923–1986); Pegeen Vail (1925–1967, who m. Jean Helion and Ralph Rumney). ❖ Celebrated for amassing one of the world's foremost collections of 20th-century art and for subsidizing artists Jackson Pollock and Robert Motherwell, among others, was also renowned for her flamboyant and colorful lifestyle. ❖ See also autobiographies, *Out of This Century* (1946) and *Confessions of an Art Addict* (1960); and *Women in World History.*

GUGGENHEIM, Mrs. Simon (1877–1970). *See Guggenheim, Olga H.*

GUGGENHEIM, Mrs. Solomon. *See Guggenheim, Irene.*

GUGGENHEIMER, Mrs. Charles S. (b. 1882). *See Guggenheimer, Minnie.*

GUGGENHEIMER, Minnie (1882–1966). American music patron and philanthropist. Name variations: Minna Schafer; Minna Guggenheimer; Mrs. Charles S. Guggenheimer. Born Minna Schafer in NY, NY, Oct 22, 1882; died May 23, 1966; dau. of Samuel and Sophie (Schwab) Schafer; m. Charles S. Guggenheimer, April 22, 1903 (died 1953); children: Elizabeth (1905–1912); Sophie Guggenheimer Untermeyer; Randolph Guggenheimer (who m. Elinor Coleman [Guggenheimer]). ❖ Became the patron of the outdoor concerts at the Lewisohn Stadium at NY's City College, raising the initial $10,000 needed for funding; eventually began to appear during intermissions to address the audiences, becoming known as the "Mrs. Malaprop of 20th-century America," for her amusing mispronunciations and unique sense

of humor; sat on board of directors of NY Philharmonic Symphony. Received ribbon of French Legion d'Honneur (1951), National Arts Club award (1959), Music Award of NY presented by Mayor Robert F. Wagner (1960), and Gold Medal of the 100 Year Association (1961). ❖ See also *Women in World History.*

GUGLIELMA OF MILAN (d. 1282). Leader of a heretical Italian sect. Died c. 1282 in Milan; never married; no children. ❖ As a young woman, became the center of a new heretical religious movement (c. 1271); was a mystic as well as a prophet, and found numerous supporters for her special calling, especially Mayfreda de Pirovano, who was to become her pope in the new church they wanted to create; believed that she was the embodiment of the Holy Spirit, and that only through a woman's intervention, and thus through all women, would humanity be saved; was accused by Milanese authorities of heresy and other crimes, but managed to survive over a decade, gaining more followers every year.

GUGLIELMINETTI, Amalia (1881–1941). Italian writer. Born in Turin, Italy, April 4, 1881; died in Turin on Dec 4, 1941; dau. of Pietro Guglielminetti and Felicita (Lavezzato) Guglielminetti; had a brother Ernesto and sisters Emma and Erminia; never married. ❖ Author whose erotic poetry and novels created a sensation in the 1st four decades of 20th century; published *Voci di giovinezza* (Voices of Youth, 1903), which received enthusiastic reviews, followed by another volume of verse, *Le vergini folli* (Mad Virgins, 1907); a striking figure in Turin's literary world, was romantically involved with many men, but her most important love affair took place while she was in her early 20s, with poet Guido Gozzano; with publication of 3rd volume of verse, *Le seduzioni* (Seduction, 1909), continued to enhance her image as a woman who celebrated sensuality; published 1st collection of short stories, *I volti dell'amore* (The Faces of Love, 1913), followed by 4 subsequent collections (1915–24); wrote only two novels, but it was the 2nd, *La rivincita del maschio* (*The Male's Return-Match*), that evoked outrage from a local morality league (1923); wrote comedies for the theater, including *Nei e cicisbei* (Beauty Marks and Gallants, 1920); founded and edited literary journal, *Le Seduzioni* (Seduction, 1926–28); published last book, *I serpenti di Medusa* (*Medusa's Serpents,* 1934); remained active as a journalist; also published 4 children's books. ❖ See also *Women in World History.*

GUIBAL, Brigitte (1971—). French kayaker. Born Feb 15, 1971, in Mendes (Lozère), France. ❖ Won a silver medal for K1 slalom at Sydney Olympics (2000); won World championship (1997).

GUIBERT, Elisabeth (1725–1788). French poet and playwright. Born 1725 in France; died 1788. ❖ Works include *La Coquette Corrigée, Le Rendezvous* and *Les triumvirs* (published in 1 volume as *Poésies et oeuvres diverses,* 1764), *Les Filles à marier* (1768), *Le sommeil d'Amynthe* (1768), *Pensées détachées* (1771), and *Les philéniens ou le patriotisme* (1775); poems also published in periodical *Almanach des Muses*; received royal pension.

GUIBERT, Louise-Alexandrine, Comtesse de (d. 1826). French novelist. Died 1826 in France. ❖ After husband's death, edited his works and published her own, including *Margaretha, comtesse Rainsford* (1797), *Agatha ou la religieuse anglaise* (1797), *Fedaretta* (1803), and *Leçons sur la nature* (1806); edited *Lettres de Mlle de Lespinasse au comte de Guibert, 1773–1776* (1809); her correspondence was published as *Lettres inédites* (1887).

GUICCIARDINI, Isabella (fl. 16th c.). Florentine townswoman. Fl. in early 16th century in Florence, Italy. ❖ Represents the life of wealthy townswomen in the last years of the Middle Ages; with husband, a local governor, often away on business, was left with the responsibility of maintaining the family's large estates and managing their agricultural business; soon revealed her business acumen and her administrative abilities.

GUICCIOLI, Teresa (c. 1801–1873). Italian noblewoman. Name variations: Countess Guiccioli; Marquise de Boissy. Pronunciation: GWEE-cho-lee. Born Teresa Gamba in Italy c. 1801; died in Rome, Mar 26, 1873; dau. of Count Gamba; m. Count Guiccioli, c. 1817; m. Marquis de Boissy, 1851. ❖ Best known for her relationship with Lord Byron, married Count Guiccioli when she was 16 and met Byron a few months later; maintained relations with Byron until his death; published in French, *My Recollections of Lord Byron* (1868).

GUIDACCI, Margherita (1921–1992). Italian poet. Born April 25, 1921, in Florence, Italy; died June 19, 1992, in Rome, Italy; received degree from University of Florence in Italian literature. ❖ Taught English and American literature in high schools before teaching at University of

Macerata and University of Maria Assunta in Vatican; writings, which often explore themes of pain, death, and alienation but also reflect strong religious faith, include *La sabbia e l'angelo* (1946), *Morte del rico* (1955), *Paglia e polvere* (1961), *Nerosuite* (1970), *Terra sensa orologi* (1973), *Il vuoto e le forme* (1977), *Inno alla gioia* (1983), *Poesie per poeti* (1987), and *A Book of Sybils* (1989); translated writers from Latin, Spanish, and English and wrote critical studies.

GUIDI, Rachele (1891–1979). Italian wife of Benito Mussolini. Name variations: Rachele Mussolini. Born Rachele Guidi in Romagnol, Italy, 1891; died Oct 1979; dau. of peasants; attended school to 2nd grade; m. Benito Mussolini (1883–1945, Fascist dictator and prime minister of Italy), c. 1916; children: Edda Ciano (1910–1995); Vittorio Mussolini (b. 1916); Bruno Mussolini (b. 1918); Romano Mussolini (b. 1927, who with his 1st wife had daughters Rachele Mussolini and Alessandra Mussolini, an Italian politician); Anna Maria Mussolini (b. 1929). ❖ Never used husband's name, preferring to call herself Rachele Guidi; had to share him with journalist Margherita Sarfatti for a number of years (he would later be machine-gunned to death with another lover, Clara Petacci); though indifferent to ideology, was loyal to husband, in power and out, though she never deigned to interfere in matters of state; during husband's entire 20-year political tenure, did not set foot in his office; instead, stayed home and raised the children. ❖ See also *Women in World History.*

GUIDO, Beatriz (1924—). Argentinean novelist, playwright, screenwriter and short-story writer. Born 1924 in Rosario, Santa Fe, Argentina; died Mar 4, 1988, in Madrid, Spain; studied philosophy and literature in Buenos Aires, Rome and Paris; m. (Leopoldo) Torre Nilsson (screenwriter and director), 1959 (died 1979). ❖ One of the best-known writers in Argentina, was honored with a postal stamp (2002); appointed Argentinean Cultural Attaché to Spain (1984); writings include *La casa del ángel* (1954), *La caída* (1956), *El secuestrado* (1958), *Fin de fieste* (1958), *La mano en la trampo* (1961), and *Homenaje a la hora de la siesta*; also wrote screenplays for *Insomnes* (1984). *La mano en la trampo* made into film by husband and won 1st prize at Cannes Film Festival (1961).

GUIDOSALVI, Sancia (fl. early 12th c.). Spanish sculptor. Name variations: Sancha. Fl. in early 12th century in Spain. ❖ Was a sculptor of great talent, though her only known work still extant is a large silver cross with figures carved in relief. ❖ See also *Women in World History.*

GUIDRY, Carlette (1969—). American runner. Name variations: Carlette Guidry-White. Born Carlette Guidry, Sept 4, 1968, in Houston, Texas; m. Mon White (div.). ❖ At Barcelona Olympics, won a gold medal in 4 x 100-meter relay (1992).

GUIDUCCI, Armanda (1923–1992). Italian poet and literary critic. Born 1923 in Naples, Italy; died 1992; received degree in philosophy from University of Milan. ❖ Became active in politics and edited several cultural periodicals; with Franco Fortini, Luciano Amodio, and Roberto Guiducci, launched literary-political journal *Ragionamenti* (1955); contributed to newspapers and worked for Swiss television; works include *Poesie per un uomo* (1965), *Il mito Pavese* (1967), *La donna non è gente* (1977), *La letterature della nuova Africa* (1979), *A colpi di silenzio* (1982), and *A testa in giù* (1984).

GUIFFRAIS, Magali (1932—). See *Nöel, Magali.*

GUGGENBERGER, Louisa S. (1845–1895). See *Bevington, L.S.*

GUGGISBERG, Lady (1871–1964). See *Moore, Decima.*

GUIGOVA, Maria (1947—). Bulgarian rhythmic gymnast. Born April 24, 1947, in Bulgaria. ❖ At World championships, won gold medal with hoop (1967) and all-around (1969, 1971, 1973), accumulating 13 World medals; named president of the Bulgarian Rhythmic Gymnastics Federation (1982).

GUILBERT, Yvette (1865–1944). French cabaret singer. Pronunciation: Eve-ETT Geel-BEAR. Born Emma Laure Guilbert on Jan 29, 1865, in Paris, France; died Feb 3, 1944, at Aix-en-Provence, of heart failure; dau. of Hippolyte Guilbert (shopkeeper) and Albine (Lubrez) Guilbert (seamstress); attended private school in Paris, 1873–77; married Max Schiller (impresario), June 22, 1897; children: none. ❖ Collector, scholar, and performer of historic French folk songs, survived an impoverished childhood to become France's most famous cabaret singer in the 1890s, delivering her melodies in a half-sung, half-spoken fashion that led critics to describe her as a *diseuse* (reciter, or teller of songs) rather than as a pure singer; began employment as model and saleswoman (1881); became protégé of circus impresario Charles Zidler (1885); made

theatrical debut in Paris (1887); began career in concert cafés in Montmarte, becoming one of the leading performers of the *chanson* or traditional French song (1889); her gloves, which became her signature garment, were featured prominently in the cartoon images that Toulouse-Lautrec produced of her after her fame was established; became an international star as well; her tour of the US (1895–96) was followed by triumphal visits to the capitals of Europe (1897–99); produced a number of novels and several sets of autobiographical works starting with *Struggles and Victories* (1910); founded a school for working-class children (1910); was a wartime resident in US (1915–18) and opened "School of the Theater" in New York (1919); returned to France (1922); began a column of personal opinion and observation, with the title of *Guilbertinages* (1930), that appeared at irregular intervals for years in the newspaper *Paris Soir;* awarded Legion of Honor (1932); fled Paris for Aix-en-Provence in face of German invasion (1940), but did not survive the war. ❖ See also autobiographies *La Chanson de ma vie* (1927, published in English as *The Song of My Life*) and *The Astonished Passer-by* (1929); Bettina Knapp and Myra Chipman, *That Was Yvette: The Biography of Yvette Guilbert, The Great Diseuse* (Holt, Rinehart and Winston, 1964); Gustave Geffroy, *Yvette Guilbert* (trans. by Barbara Sessions, Walker, 1968); and *Women in World History.*

GUILD, Nancy (1925–1999). American actress. Born Oct 11, 1925, in Los Angeles, California; died Aug 16, 1999, in East Hampton, LI, NY; m. Charles Russell (actor, div. 1950); m. Ernest Martin (Broadway producer), 1953 (div. 1975); m. John Bryson, 1978 (div. 1995). ❖ Films include *Somewhere in the Night, Give My Regards to Broadway, Abbott and Costello Meet the Invisible Man* and *Francis Covers the Big Town.*

GUILLARD, Charlotte (d. 1556). French printer. Died 1556 in France; m. Berthold Rembolt (printer, died 1518); m. Claude Chevallon (printer), 1520. ❖ The 1st famous woman printer, developed an interest in printing in 1500; after death of 2nd husband (1540), assumed control of his Soliel d'Or print shop in Paris; put her own imprint on Soliel d'Or books and was recognized for commitment to beauty and accuracy; printed such publications as a Latin Bible, *Erasmus's Testament,* and *Works of St. Gregory* (2 vols); completed and printed the writing of a Greek lexicon which had been begun by scholar Bogard.

GUILLELMA DE ROSERS (fl. 1240–1260). Provençal troubadour. Name variations: Guillelma of Rougiers. Flourished between 1240 and 1260 in southern France. ❖ Apparently met her lover, the troubadour Lanfrancs Cigala, when he visited Provence; exchanged at least one tenson with him which still survives, in which they debate the loyalty a lover owes his lady.

GUILLEMETE, Mary (d. 1262). See *Guzman, Mayor de.*

GUILLEMETE DU LUYS (fl. 1479). French physician. Fl. in 1479 in Paris. ❖ A skillful surgeon of Paris, gained widespread admiration and respect; was not, however, university trained, for the masters of medicine at University of Paris did not allow women to study there; eventually won the position of royal surgeon in the household of King Louis XI of France. ❖ See also *Women in World History.*

GUILLEMOT, Agnès (1931—). French film editor. Name variations: Agnes Guillemot. Born Agnès Perché, 1931, in Roubaix, Nord, Nord-Pas-de-Calais, France; m. Claude Guillemot (director). ❖ Editor of several landmark New Wave films; films include *Une femme est une femme, Le petit soldat, Les Carabiniers, Le Mépris, Bande à part, Masculin féminin, Made in U.S.A., La Chinoise, Week End, Sympathy for the Devil, Les Gauloises bleues, Baisers volés, L'enfant sauvage, Cousin Cousine, La diagonale du fou, La Lumière du lac, Every other Weekend, Nord* and *Romance.*

GUILLET, Pernette du (c. 1520–1545). See *du Guillet, Pernette.*

GUILLÓ, Magdalena (1940—). Spanish novelist. Name variations: Magdalena Guillo. Born 1940 in Spain. ❖ Wrote in Catalan and Castilian; works include *En una vall florida al peu de les espases* (1977), *Entre el ayer y el mañana* (1984), *Un sambenito para el señor Santiago* (1986).

GUIMARÃES, Elina (1904–1991). Portuguese writer and lawyer. Name variations: Elina Guimarães. Born 1904 in Portugal; died 1991. ❖ Writings on women's rights include *Dos Crimes Culposos, A Lei em que Vivemos, Coisas de Mulheres* and *Mulheres Portuguesas Ontem e Hoje* (1979); also wrote articles for *Diário de Noticias* and other journals. Awarded Portuguese Order of Liberty (1985).

GUIMARÃES PEIXOTO BRETAS, Ana Lins do (1889–1985). Brazilian poet and short-story writer. Name variations: Cora Coralina. Born Ana Lins do Guimarães Peixoto, Aug 20, 1889, in Goiás, Brazil; died April 10, 1985, in Goiânia, Brazil; dau. of Francisco de Paula Lins dos Guimaraes Peixoto (appeals court judge) and Jacita Luiza do Couto Brandao; m. Cantidio Tolentino Brêtas (lawyer), 1911 (died 1934); children: Paraguacu, Eneias, Cantidio, Jacintha, Isis and Vicencia. ❖ Lived in village of Goiás Velho; poetry reflects oral traditions derived from troubadours; works include *O cântico da volta* (1956), *Poemas dos becos de Goiás e estórias mais* (1965), *O vintém de cobre, as confissões de Aninha* (1982), and *Meu livro de cordel* (1982).

GUIMARD, Marie Madeleine (1743–1816). French dancer. Born in Paris, France, Oct 10, 1743 (some sources cite Dec 27, 1743); died in Paris on May 4, 1816; illeg. dau. of an inspector of a Paris cloth factory; m. Jean Etienne Despréaux (choreographer and poet), in Aug 1789; children: (with Benjamin de Laborde) daughter, also named Marie-Madeleine Guimard (1763–1779). ❖ Star of Paris Opéra for 25 years, known as much for her love affairs as her dancing, secured a place in the corps de ballet of the Comédie-Française at 15 (1758); 1st appeared at the Opéra as Terpsichore in *Les Fêtes Grecque et Romaines* (1762), replacing Marie Allard; became première danseuse (1763) and went on to perform in many ballets, including *Le Premier Navigateur, Ninette à la Cour, La Fête de Mirza, Le Déserteur, La Chercheuse d'Esprit* and *Les Caprices de Galatée*, perhaps her best work; had a 10-year liaison with Benjamin de Laborde, 1st gentleman-in-waiting to Louis XV; also became the mistress of the Prince de Soubise, then the bishop of Orléans; retired from dance to marry (1789). ❖ See also *Women in World History.*

GUINAN, Texas (1884–1933). American actress and entertainer. Name variations: Mary Louise Cecelia Guinan; Mayme Guinan; Marie Guinan. Pronunciation: GUY-nan. Born Mary Louise Cecelia Guinan on Jan 12, 1884, in Waco, Texas; died Nov 5, 1933, after intestinal surgery, in Vancouver, British Columbia; dau. of Michael Guinan and Bridget "Bessie" Duffy Guinan; m. John J. Moynahan, Dec 2, 1904; no children. ❖ Star of vaudeville and silent films until the Roaring '20s, when Prohibition cast her as reigning queen of New York City nightclubs, where her outsized personality and heart took in everyone within reach; appeared on Broadway stage and in vaudeville (1909–17, 1929–33); appeared in at least 37 films (1917–33), creating a new role for women, a self-reliant heroine, a gunslinger, in such movies as *The Heart of Texas* (1919), *South of Santa Fe* (1919), *Girl of the Rancho* (1920), *The Lady of the Law* (1920), *The Code of the West* (1921); also appeared in *Queen of the Night Clubs* (1929) and *Broadway Thru a Keyhole* (1933); hosted several New York City nightclubs (1923–29), the El Fey, the Texas Guinan Club, the Del Fey, the 300 Club, Club Intime, and Salon Royale, opening with her signature, "Hello, Suckers!" ❖ See also Louise Berliner, *Texas Guinan: Queen of the Nightclubs* (University of Texas Press, 1993); and *Women in World History.*

GUINEVERE (d. 470 or 542). Queen of Britain and wife of King Arthur. Name variations: Ganor, Ganora or Ganore; Ganeura, Ginevra, Genievre, Guenever, Guanhumara, Guanhumar, Guenevere, Guenhumare, Gueniévre, Gwenhwyfar (modern: Jennifer). Pronunciation of Guinevere in Modern English is, roughly, "Gwineveer." Born either as a member of a noble Roman family in post-Roman Britain, or as a Pictish princess during the period of the Saxon invasions in the 400s; died in either 470 or 542; m. King Arthur, or Arthur, war leader of the British, and according to some traditions had from one to three sons, sometimes referred to as Lohot and/or Amhar or Amr; many other traditions leave her childless. ❖ Far from being a medieval queen, is more appropriately positioned in history as one of the last of the great figures of the ancient world; resides in the realm of historical and archaeological speculation even though nearly all scholars have come to accept her existence; became Arthur's archivist, administered his lands during his absence, and may have assumed the role of high priestess; died not long after Arthur's death in battle either in 470 or 542 CE, after having either retired to an abbey or after having returned to her people in Scotland; may have been buried either in Glastonbury, England, or at Meigle, Scotland. ❖ See also Norma Lorre Goodrich, *Guinevere* (HarperCollins, 1991); and *Women in World History.*

GUINEY, Louise Imogen (1861–1920). American poet. Name variations: often signed poetry L.I.G. Born Jan 7, 1861, in Roxbury, Massachusetts; died in Chipping Camden, England, Nov 2, 1920; dau. of General Patrick Robert Guiney (Union army general) and Jenny Guiney; attended Convent of the Sacred Heart in Providence, Rhode Island; never married; no children. ❖ With the success of her poetry

collection *Songs at the Start* (1884), became a recognized poet at 23; had articles published in *The Atlantic,* was a frequent contributor to juvenile magazine *Wide Awake,* and became a popular member of the literati; was also a salon attendee at home of Louise Chandler Moulton and a prodigious correspondent who had many epistolary friendships; published another collection of poetry, *A Roadside Harp* (1893); wrote short biography of Irish patriot Robert Emmet (1904); known as the "Laureate of the Lost," her prose often revived forgotten figures in such books as *A Little English Gallery* (1894) and *Happy Ending* (1909); published *Matthew Arnold's Sohrab and Rustum and Other Poems* (1899) and *The Martyrs' Idyl and Shorter Poems* (1899); for her last 7 years, while living in England, worked on *Recusant Poets 1535–1745,* concerning poets of the Catholic underground hiding from parliamentary persecution, which would be published posthumously (1939); wrote over 30 books. ❖ See also Henry G. Fairbanks, *Laureate of the Lost: Louise Imogen Guiney* (Magi, 1972); Eva Mabel Tenison, *Louise Imogen Guiney, Her Life and Works, 1861–1920* (Macmillan, 1923); and *Women in World History.*

GUINNESS, Heather (1910—). English fencer. Name variations: J. Heather Guinness or Judy Heather Guinness. Born Aug 14, 1910, in UK. ❖ At Los Angeles Olympics, won a silver medal in individual foil (1932).

GUION, Connie M. (1882–1971). American physician. Pronunciation: GUY-on. Born Connie Myers Guion, Aug 29, 1882, in Lincolnton, North Carolina; died at NY Hospital-Cornell Medical Center, April 29, 1971; dau. of Benjamin Simmons Guion (civil engineer and farmer) and Catherine Coatesworth (Caldwell) Guion; graduated from Wellesley College, 1906, and Cornell University Medical College, 1917; never married; no children. ❖ Clinical educator in NY for 50 years, broke many barriers for women in medicine, becoming the 1st woman to be appointed professor of clinical medicine in US (1946) and 1st female physician to have a hospital building named for her in her lifetime (1958). ❖ See also *Women in World History.*

GUION, Madame (1648–1717). *See Guyon, Jeanne Marie Bouviéres de la Mothe.*

GUIRANDE DE LAVAUR (d. 1211). French noblewoman and warrior. Name variations: Giralda de Laurac. Died in 1211 in Lavaur, France; sister of Aimery de Montréal. ❖ A Cathar, was known to be educated, gentle and charitable; defended her castles against attacks by the armies of 3 bishops (1211); eventually had to give in to the superior military forces of Simon de Montfort. ❖ See also *Women in World History.*

GUISE, countess of. *See Marie of Guise (d. 1404).*

GUISE, duchess of.
See Isabelle of Lorraine (1410–1453).
See Jeanne de Laval (d. 1498).
See Antoinette of Bourbon (1494–1583).
See Morata, Fulvia Anne of Ferrara (1531–1607).
See Catherine de Cleves (fl. 1550s).
See Isabella of Orleans (b. 1878).

GUISEWITE, Cathy (1950—). American cartoonist. Born 1950 in Dayton, Ohio; grew up in Midland, Michigan; University of Michigan, BA in English, 1972. ❖ Was an advertising writer for Campbell-Ewald (1972–73), then Norman Prady Ltd (1973–74); served as vice president of W.B. Doner & Co. (1977); began cartoon strip "Cathy," about the trials and tribulations of a single career woman, for Universal Press Syndicate (1976); by 2005, was syndicated in over 1,400 newspapers worldwide; published a number of "Cathy" books. Won an Emmy for Outstanding Animated Program for her 1st animated special "Cathy" (1987); received Reuben Award (1993).

GUIZOT, Pauline (1773–1827). French novelist. Name variations: Madame Guizot; Elisabeth de Meulan. Born Élisabeth Charlotte Pauline de Meulan, Nov 2, 1773, in Paris, France; died Aug 1, 1827, in Paris; m. François Pierre Guillaume (F.P.G.) Guizot (historian and statesman), 1812. ❖ Began writing to support mother and siblings after father's ruin during the Revolution; works, which advocate the domestic education of women, include *La Chapelle d'Ayton* (1800), *Les enfants* (1812), *L'Ecolier* (1821), and *Nouveaux contes* (1823); also wrote prize-winning treatise on women's education *Lettre de famille sur l'éducation domestique* (1826).

GÜLABAHAR (fl. 1521). Ottoman sultana. Name variations: Gulabahar or Gulbehar; Gülfem or Gulfem. Fl. 1521; born a Montenegrin or

Albanian or Crimean; consort of Suleiman also seen as Suleyman, Ottoman sultan (r. 1520–1566); children: (with Suleiman) Mustafa or Mustapha (governor of Mansia).

GULACSY, Maria (1941—). Hungarian fencer. Born April 27, 1941, in Hungary. ❖ At Mexico City Olympics, won a silver medal in team foil (1968).

GULBADAM (c. 1522–1603). See *Gulbadan.*

GULBADAN (c. 1522–1603). Indian historian. Name variations: Gulbadan Banu Begum; Gulbadan Begum; Gulbadam. Born Gulbadan Begam bint Babur Badshah in 1522 or 1523 in Kabul, Afghanistan; died 1603; dau. of Babar (Babur, 1483–1530), the 1st Mughal emperor of India; sister of Humayun (emperor, died 1556); niece of Akbar (emperor). ❖ The 1st Indian woman historian, wrote *Humayun Nama* (c. 1580) which gives insight into lives of the first 2 Mughal emperors; at 5, moved with family to northern India; grew up in her father's court and that of her half-brother Humayan; married before 17, had one son; when brother was driven out of India, spent over 7 years at Kabul as a captive of another half-brother who was fighting Humayan; lived the rest of her life at the Mughal court of Akbar, 1st in Agra, then in Sikri.

GULBEHAR (fl. 1521). See *Gülabahar.*

GULBRANDSEN, Ragnhild (1977—). Norwegian soccer player. Born Ragnhild Oren Gulbrandsen, Feb 22, 1977, in Trondheim, Norway; dau. of Stephanie and Odd Gulbrandsen (soccer pro); sister of Thorstein Gulbrandsen (her coach). ❖ Won a team gold medal at Sydney Olympics (2000); signed with WUSA's Atlanta Beat (2002).

GULBRANDSEN, Solveig (1981—). Norwegian soccer player. Born Jan 12, 1981, in Norway. ❖ Won a team gold medal at Sydney Olympics (2000).

GULBRANSON, Ellen (1863–1947). Swedish soprano. Born Ellen Nordgren on Mar 4, 1863, in Stockholm, Sweden; died in Oslo, Norway, Jan 2, 1947; trained in Stockholm and in Paris under Mathilde Marchesi and Blanche Marchesi. ❖ Known for her interpretation of Wagnerian roles, made her debut in Stockholm as Amneris in *Aïda* (1889) and later played Ortrud and Aïda; 1st sang Brunnhilde at Bayreuth (1896); also performed in Paris, Moscow, Berlin, Vienna, St. Petersburg, Amsterdam, and other European cities, as well as Covent Garden; her favorite roles were Kundry and Brunnhilde; retired (1915).

GULFEM or GÜLFEM (fl. 1521). See *Gülabahar.*

GULICK, Alice Gordon (1847–1903). American missionary. Name variations: Alice Winfield Gordon Gulick. Born Aug 8, 1847, in Boston, Massachusetts; died Sept 14, 1903, in London, England; dau. of James Monroe Gordon (cashier) and Mary Elizabeth (Clarkson) Gordon; sister of Anna Adams Gordon (temperance reformer); m. Alvah Baylies Kittredge (tutor), Oct 3, 1870 (died Oct 4, 1870); m. the Rev. William Hooker Gulick, Dec 12, 1871; children: (2nd m.) 3 daughters, 4 sons. ❖ Moved to Spain with 2nd husband to be missionaries (1871); opened small boarding school for young women, the Colegio Norte Americano (1877); encouraged by school's success, established nondenominational higher-education institution for girls, International Institute for Girls in Spain (1892). ❖ See also Elizabeth Putnam Gordon, *Alice Gordon Gulick, Her Life and Work in Spain* (1917).

GULICK, Charlotte Vetter (1865–1928). American cofounder of Camp Fire Girls. Born Charlotte Vetter, Dec 12, 1865, in Oberlin, Ohio; died July 28, 1928, in South Casco, Maine; m. Luther Halsey Gulick, 1887 (died 1918); children: Louise (1888–1941), Frances (1891–1936), Charlotte (1892–1909), Katherine (1895–1968), Luther (b. 1897, died in infancy), and John Halsey (1899–1980). ❖ Established Wohelo (later renamed Luther Gulick Camp), a summer camp for girls in Maine; with husband and William Chauncey Langdon, founded Camp Fire Girls (1910), which was officially incorporated (1912) and by 1913 had more than 60,000 members; established Camp Fire Girls magazine, *Wohelo,* and served as its 1st editor; served as 1st president of Directors of Girls' Camps.

GULLA, Alejandra (1977—). Argentine field-hockey player. Born Alejandra Laura Gulla, July 4, 1977, in Lomas de Zamora, Argentina. ❖ Forward, won a team bronze medal at Athens Olympics (2004); won Champions Trophy (2001) and Pan American Games (2003).

GULLEN, Augusta Stowe (1857–1943). Canadian physician. Name variations: Augusta Stowe. Born Augusta Stowe, July 27, 1857, in Mount Pleasant, Ontario, Canada; died Sept 25, 1943, in Toronto, Canada; dau.

of Emily Jennings Stowe (1831–1903, 1st Canadian woman to practice medicine in Canada) and John Stowe; m. John Benjamin Gullen (physician), 1883. ❖ The 1st female physician to graduate from a Canadian University (Victoria College in Coburg, Canada, 1883), worked as an anatomy demonstrator, as a professor of pediatrics (1900–06), and as the only female staff member at Woman's Medical College in Toronto; ran a private home medical practice in Toronto; delivered the 1st child born at Western Hospital (1896), which was cofounded by her husband in Toronto; created the Women's Board of Western Hospital to improve the hospital's resources; appointed the University of Toronto Senate's Medical Professional Representative (1910). As an active suffragist, followed mother's footsteps and served as the Dominion Women's Enfranchisement Association President (1903–07) and later as a president of its successor, the Canadian Suffrage Association (1907–11).

GULLICK, Barbara (c. 1904–1986). See *Welch, Barbara.*

GULLIVER, Julia Henrietta (1856–1940). American scholar. Born July 30, 1856; died July 25, 1940; Smith College, BA, 1879, PhD, 1888; postgraduate study at the University of Leipzig, 1892–1893. ❖ Served as president of Rockford College (1902–1919); writings include *Studies in Democracy* (1917). ❖ See also *Women in World History.*

GULLVÅG, Harriet (b. 1922). See *Holter, Harriet.*

GULYASNE-KOETELES, Erzsebet (1924—). Hungarian gymnast. Name variations: Erzsebet Koeteles. Born Nov 1924 in Hungary. ❖ At London Olympics, won a silver medal in team all-around (1948); at Helsinki Olympics, won a bronze medal in teams all-around, portable apparatus, and a silver medal in team all-around (1952); at Melbourne Olympics, won a silver medal in team all-around and a gold medal in teams all-around, portable apparatus (1956).

GUMMEL-HELMBOLDT, Margitte (1941—). East German track-and-field athlete. Name variations: Margitta Gummel. Born June 29, 1941, in Germany. ❖ Won a gold medal at Mexico City Olympics (1968) and a silver medal at Munich Olympics (1972), both in shot put.

GUND, Agnes (1938—). American art historian, collector, philanthropist, educator, and administrator. Born 1938 in Cleveland, Ohio; dau. of George Gund; m. Albrecht Saalfield, c. 1966 (div.); m. Daniel Shapiro, 1987; children: (1st m.) David Saalfield; Catherine Saalfield; Anna Saalfield; Jessica Saalfield. ❖ On father's death (1966), became a millionaire; attended Fogg Museum at Harvard University where she earned a master's; elected to Museum of Modern Art's (MOMA) board of trustees (1976); founded Studio in a School project (1977), which brought artists into public schools to teach art; became president of MOMA (1991). Received National Medal of Arts award, presented by President Bill Clinton (1998). ❖ See also *Women in World History.*

GUNDA, Saida (1959—). Soviet javelin thrower. Born Aug 30, 1959, in USSR. ❖ At Moscow Olympics, won a silver medal in the javelin throw (1980).

GÜNDERRODE, Karoline von (1780–1806). German poet. Name variations: Günderode, Gunderode, Gunderrode; sometimes used the pseudonym Tian. Born in Karlsruhe, Germany, Feb 11, 1780; committed suicide at Winkel on the Rhine, July 26, 1806; grew up as one of several daughters of a moderately affluent widow. ❖ Prompted by mother, entered a kloster for well-born spinsters but was unhappy there; soon found that travel and visits to friends, especially close friend Bettine von Arnim, freed her; had many strong attachments and a natural tendency toward melancholy and mysticism, which colored her poetry; at 26, committed suicide with a dagger. *Gedichte und Phantasien* (Poems and Fancies) was published the year of her death (1806), as was *Poetic Fragments.* ❖ See also *Women in World History.*

GUNDERSEN, Trude (1977—). Norwegian taekwondo player. Born in 1977 in Norway. ❖ Won a silver medal for 57–67kg at Sydney Olympics (2000).

GUNDERSON, Carolyn (1968—). See *Crudgington, Carolyn.*

GUNDERSON, JoAnne (b. 1939). See *Carner, JoAnne.*

GUNDRADA (d. 1085). See *Gundred.*

GUNDRED (d. 1085). Countess of Surrey. Name variations: Gundrada; Gundrada de Warenne or Warrenne. Died 1085; dau. of Gerbod of St. Omer, advocate at St. Bertin; married William de Warenne

(c. 1055–1088), 1st earl of Surrey (r. 1088–1088); children: William de Warenne, 2nd earl of Warenne and Surrey (r. 1088–1138); Reynald; Editha de Warenne (who m. Gerard, baron de Gournay, and Drew de Monceaux). ❖ Cofounded Lewes Priory with husband (1077).

GUNHILD (c. 1020–1038). Norman princess. Name variations: Gunhilda or Gunnhildr. Born c. 1020; died July 18, 1038, on Adriatic Coast; dau. of Emma of Normandy (c. 985–1052) and Cnut also known as Canute the Great (c. 994–1035), king of England (r. 1016–1035), king of Denmark (r. 1019–1035), king of Norway (r. 1028–1035); m. Henry III (1017–1056), king of Germany (r. 1039–1056), Holy Roman emperor (r. 1039–1056), June 10, 1036. Henry III's 2nd wife was Agnes of Poitou (1024–1077), whom he married in 1043.

GUNHILD OF NORWAY (d. 1054). Queen of Denmark. Name variations: Gunnhild Sveinsdottir. Died in 1054; dau. of Svein, earl of Ladir, and Holmfrid Ericsdottir; m. Anund Jakob of Sweden, king of Sweden (r. 1022–1050); 1st wife of Svend II Estridsen (d. 1076) also known as Sweyn Estridsen, king of Denmark (r. 1047–1074). ❖ There are 16 children attributed to Svend II who had 4 wives or paramours (Gunhild of Norway, Gyde, Elizabeth of Kiev, and Thora Johnsdottir); any one of the 4 could be the mother of Svend's royal offspring: Harald Hén, king of Denmark (r. 1074–1080), St. Knud or Canute the Holy, king of Denmark (r. 1080–1086), Oluf or Olaf Hunger, king of Denmark (r. 1086–1095).

GUNHILDA OF DENMARK (d. 1002). Danish princess. Name variations: Gunhild Haraldsdottir. Killed on Nov 13, 1002; dau. of Harald Bluetooth (c. 910–985), king of Denmark (r. 940–985) and Gyrid; sister of Thyra of Denmark (d. 1000) and Sven or Sweyn I Forkbeard, king of Denmark (r. 985–1014), king of England (r. 1014); m. Jarl Pallig or Palig, ealdorman in Devon.

GUNHILDA OF POLAND (d. around 1015). Polish princess. Name variations: Gunhild of Poland; Sygryda Swietoslawa. Died around 1015; dau. of Mieszko I, duke of Poland, and Dobravy of Bohemia (d. 977); m. and was 1st wife of Sven or Sweyn I Forkbeard (b. 965), king of Denmark (r. 985–1014), around 990 (div. in 1000); children: (2nd m.) Canute the Great (c. 994–1035), king of England (r. 1016–1035), king of Denmark (r. 1019–1035), king of Norway (r. 1028–1035); Thyra (d. 1018); possibly Harald (d. 1019), king of Denmark (r. 1014–1018). ❖ Polish princess and sister to Duke (later King) Boleslav Chrobry, became consort and mistress of Sweyn I Forkbeard, king of Denmark; when Sweyn married Sigrid the Haughy, had to leave Sweyn's court, and took her son Canute—then no more than two or three—to the court of her brother.

GUNN, Mrs. Aeneas (1870–1961). See Gunn, Jeannie.

GUNN, Elizabeth Catherine (1879–1963). New Zealand physician, health camp founder, and public health administrator. Born on May 23, 1879, in Dunedin, New Zealand; died Oct 26, 1963, in Wellington, New Zealand; dau. of William Gunn (dentist) and Elizabeth Jane (Melton) Gunn; University of Otago, 1903; University of Edinburgh, 1908. ❖ Joined nascent school medical service (1912); served as captain in New Zealand Medical Corps (1915–17); traveled to Britain and visited schools and child-welfare institutions (1917); rejoined school medical service in Manawatu district (1918); introduced innovative health programs and founded children's health-camps movement (1919); became director of Health Department's Division of School Hygiene (1937–40). Member of British Empire (1951). ❖ See also *Dictionary of New Zealand Biography* (Vol. 3).

GUNN, Jeannie (1870–1961). Australian novelist. Name variations: Mrs. Aeneas Gunn. Born Jeannie Taylor on June 5, 1870, in Carlton, Victoria, Australia; died June 9, 1961, in Hawthorn, Victoria, Australia; m. Aeneas Gunn, 1901 (died 1903). ❖ During WWI, became active in welfare work for soldiers and continued work for returned soldiers and sailors; writings include *The Little Black Princess* (1905) and *We of the Never Never* (1908); also wrote *My Boys—A Book of Remembrances* (2000) about soldiers of Anglo-Boer War, Boxer Rebellion, and WWI. Received OBE (1939) for contribution to Australian literature and work for disabled soldiers.

GUNN-FRUSTOL, Tone (1975—). See Frustol, Tone Gunn.

GUNNARSSON, Martine (1927—). American shooter. Born Mar 30, 1927, in US. ❖ At Tokyo Olympics, won a bronze medal in free rifle–300 meters, 3 positions (1964).

GUNNARSSON, Susanne (1963—). Swedish kayaker. Name variations: Susanne Gunnarsson-Wiberg. Born Sept 8, 1963, in Längbros, Sweden.

❖ At Los Angeles Olympics, won a silver medal in K4 500 meters (1984); at Barcelona Olympics, won a silver medal in K2 500 meters (1992); with Agneta Andersson, won a gold medal for K2 500 meters at Atlanta Olympics (1996); won the K1 title and the K2 title (with Asa Eklund) at World championships (1998).

GUNNELL, Sally (1966—). British runner. Born in Chigwell, England, July 29, 1966; married Jonathan Bigg (runner). ❖ Immensely popular in England, placed 1st for 400 meters (1986), 1st for 400-meter hurdles (1990, 1994) and 1st for 4 x 400-meter relay (1990, 1994) at Commonwealth Games; won European Indoor championships (1989), European Cup (1993, 1994, 1996, 1997), Goodwill Games (1994), European championships (1994), World Cup (1994), and the World championship (1993); won a gold medal for the 400-meter hurdles and a bronze for the 4 x 400-meter relay at Barcelona Olympics (1992); was #1 in *Track & Field News World* rankings (1993, 1994). ❖ See also *Women in World History*.

GUNNESS, Belle (1860–c. 1908). Norwegian-American murderer. Born in Norway in 1860; may have died in a house fire in 1908; m. Mr. Gunness (farmer); 3 children. ❖ A Norwegian immigrant, settled with husband on a farm outside of La Porte, Indiana; was involved in at least 13 murders, beginning with husband. ❖ See also *Women in World History*.

GUNNHILD. Variant of Gunhild.

GUNNHILD (fl. 1150s). Norwegian consort. Fl. around 1150s; had liaison with Sigurd II Mund also known as Sigurd II Mouth (1133–1155), king of Norway (r. 1136–1155); children: Sverre also known as Sverri (c. 1152–1202), king of Norway (r. 1177–1202); Cecilia Sigurdsdottir (who m. Folkvid and Baard of Rein and was the mother of Inge II, king of Norway); Eric.

GUNNHILDR. Variant of Gunhild.

GUNNING, Elizabeth (1734–1790). Duchess of Hamilton and Argyll. Name variations: Elizabeth Hamilton. Born 1734; died May 20, 1790; dau. of John Gunning of Castle Coote, Co. Roscommon, Ireland; sister of Maria Gunning (1733–1760); m. James, 6th duke of Hamilton, 1752; m. John Campbell, marquis of Lorne, afterward 5th duke of Argyll, 1759; children: Lady Charlotte Bury (1775–1861).

GUNNING, Elizabeth (1769–1823). English author. Name variations: Elizabeth Gunning Plunkett. Born 1769; died in Suffolk, England, July 20, 1823; dau. of John and Susannah Minifie Gunning (c. 1740–1800); m. Major James Plunkett.

GUNNING, Louise (1879–1960). American musical-comedy star. Born April 1, 1879; died July 24, 1960, in Sierra Madre, California; m. Oscar Seiling. ❖ Starred in light opera and Shubert musicals for 7 years, including *A Day and a Knight, Flower Girl, Tom Jones, The American Maid* and *Mr. Pickwick;* best remembered for role of Princess Stephanie in *The Balkan Princess.*

GUNNING, Maria (1733–1760). Countess of Coventry. Name variations: Maria, Countess of Coventry. Born 1733; died Oct 1, 1760; dau. of John Gunning of Castle Coote, Co. Roscommon, Ireland, a poor Irish squire; sister of Elizabeth Gunning (1734–1790); m. George William, 6th earl of Coventry, 1752. ❖ With sister Elizabeth Gunning, went to London (1751) and both were pronounced "the handsomest women alive"; was painted a number of times, and there are many engravings of these portraits in existence.

GUNNING, Susannah Minifie (c. 1740–1800). English author. Name variations: Susannah Minifie; Mrs. Gunning. Born Susannah Minifie c. 1740; died in London, England, Aug 28, 1800; dau. of James Minifie; m. John Gunning (colonel of the 65th regiment of foot and lieutenant-general), 1768; sister of Margaret Minifie; sister-in-law of Elizabeth Gunning (1734–1790) and Maria Gunning (1733–1760); children: Elizabeth Gunning Plunkett (1769–1823). ❖ At 23, published *Histories of Lady Frances S... and Lady Caroline S...* (1763), a collaboration with sister Margaret Minifie; followed this work with 3 more, *Family Pictures* (1764), *The Picture* (1766), also written with sister, and *The Hermit* (1770); when daughter Elizabeth Gunning (Plunkett) reached adulthood, contested husband's marriage partner for the girl and was turned out of the house, along with daughter; issued a public letter to duke of Argyll stating her innocence of any deception (there was an intrigue involving a forged letter) and the news became fodder for the press; took advantage of scandal in novels *Anecdotes of the*

Delborough Family (1792) and *Memoirs of Mary* (1793), and a poem "Virginius and Virginia" (1792). ❖ See also *Women in World History.*

GUNNOR OF CRÊPON (d. 1031). *See Gunnor of Denmark.*

GUNNOR OF DENMARK (d. 1031). Duchess of Normandy. Name variations: Gunnor of Crêpon; Gunnora of Crepon; sometimes referred to as Gunhilda. Birth date unknown; died 1031; 2nd wife of Richard I the Fearless (d. 996), duke of Normandy (r. 942–996); children: Richard II (d. 1027), duke of Normandy (r. 996–1027); Robert, archbishop of Rouen (d. 1037); Mauger, earl of Corbeil; Emma of Normandy (c. 985–1052); Hawise of Normandy (d. 1034, who m. Geoffrey I, duke of Brittany); Maud of Normandy (d. 1017, who m. Odo I, count of Blois, Champagne, and Chartres). Richard I the Fearless' 1st wife was Emma of Paris (d. 968).

GUNNORA OF CREPON (d. 1031). *See Gunnor of Denmark.*

GUNTHER, Erna (1896–1982). American cultural anthropologist. Name variations: Erna Gunther Spier. Born Erna Gunther, Nov 9, 1896, in Brooklyn, NY; died Aug 1982, in Kitsap, Washington; dau. of Casper Gunther (jeweler) and Susannah (Ehren) Gunther; graduate of Barnard College, 1919; attended Columbia University, MA, 1920, PhD, 1928; m. Leslie Spier (anthropologist), 1921 (div. 1931); children: sons Robert and Christopher. ❖ Dissertation published as *A Further Analysis of the First Salmon Ceremony* (1928); performed most intensive investigations with Puget Sound Salish (1922–23), the Klallam (1924–25), and the Makah of western Washington (1930–35); made 1st scientific collection of Puget Sound folklore (1925); received 1st full-time academic appointment, with University of Washington (c. 1930); published most popular work, "Ethnobotany of Western Washington" (1945); served as chair of anthropology and director of Washington State Museum at University of Washington; resigned from Washington (1966) and became chair of anthropology at University of Alaska, Fairbanks; known for work with Native Americans of Northwest Coast and for promoting arts and crafts of Northwest Indians.

GUNTHEUCA (fl. 525). Queen of the Franks. Fl. around 525; m. Chlodomer, Clodomir, also known as Clotimir (495–524), king of Orléans (r. 511–524); his brother Chlothar, Clothaire, Clotar or Lothair I (497–561), king of Soissons (r. 511), king of the Franks (r. 558–561); no children. Lothair's 2nd wife was Chunsina; his 3rd was Ingunde; his 4th was Aregunde (sister of Ingunde); his 5th was Radegund (518–587); his 7th was Vuldetrade.

GUNTRUD OF BAVARIA (fl. 715). Queen of the Lombards. Fl. around 715; dau. of Theodebert, duke of Bavaria, and Folcheid; sister of Sunnichild (d. 741, who m. Charles Martel, king of the Franks); m. Liutprand, king of the Lombards, in 715.

GUO DANDAN (1977—). Chinese freestyle skier. Born Aug 5, 1977, in Manchuria, China. ❖ In aerials, won 1st ever world cup ski event for China (1997).

GUO JINGJING (1981—). Chinese diver. Born Oct 15, 1981, in Hebei, China; attended Beijing University. ❖ Won 3-meter springboard at Asian Games (1998); won FINA Grand Prix Superfinal for 3-meter springboard (1999); won silver medals for 3-meter springboard and synchronized 3-meter springboard at Sydney Olympics (2000); won FINA Grand Prix Superfinal (2000, 2001), for 3-meter springboard; won World championships for 3-meter springboard and 3-meter synchronized springboard (2001 and 2003); won a gold medal for 3-meter springboard and a gold medal for 3-meter synchronized springboard at Athens Olympics (2004).

GUO YUE (1988—). Chinese table tennis player. Born July 17, 1988, in China. ❖ At the Austrian Open, was the youngest player to win a Pro Tour Title (2002); won a bronze medal for doubles at Athens Olympics (2004); won team World championship (2004); ranked 1st on ITTF Pro Tour (2003, 2004).

GUPPY, Eileen M. (1903–1980). English geologist. Born May 24, 1903, in UK; died Mar 8, 1980; Bedford College, University of London, BS, 1923. ❖ The 1st woman geologist employed by the Geological Survey of Great Britain (1943), was also its 1st woman employee to be made a Member of the Order of the British Empire (1966); after WWII, demoted from assistant geologist (1943–45) to a senior experimental officer due to sexism; was a Petrographical Department assistant (1927–43), an assistant geologist (1943–45) and a senior experimental officer (1945–66) for the Geological Survey of Great Britain. Writings include *Chemical Analyses of Igneous Rocks, Metamorphic Rocks and Minerals* (1931 and 1956) and *Rock Wool* (1945 and 2nd edition, 1949).

GURAIEB KURI, Rosa (1931—). Mexican composer. Born in Matias Romero (Oaxaca), Mexico, May 20, 1931, into a Lebanese family who had settled there; studied piano, theory, and harmony under Michel Cheskinoff at the National Conservatory in Beirut; did advanced work at the Conservatory of Mexico under Juan Pablo Moncayo and Salvador Ordones Ochoa; studied with Professor Simmonds at Yale University School of Music, returning to Mexico to study advanced composition techniques with Carlos Chavez at National Conservatory of Mexico. ❖ Composed chamber, vocal, and piano works which were performed at music forums and festivals throughout Mexico; based some of her works, including her 2nd String Quartet, *Hommage a Gibran* (1982), on her Lebanese heritage.

GURENDEZ, Lorena (1981—). Spanish rhythmic gymnast. Name variations: Lorena Gurendez Garcia. Born May 7, 1981, in Vitoria, Spain. ❖ Won a team gold medal at Atlanta Olympics (1996).

GUREVICH, Liubov (1866–1940). Russian historian and literary critic. Name variations: Liubov' Iakovleva Gurévich. Born 1866 in Russia; died 1940; never married; children: Elena. ❖ With Akim Volynskii, worked as publisher and co-editor of *Northern Herald* (1891–98), publishing fiction by Chekhov and Tolstoy, as well as women writers like Maria Krestovskaya, Zinaida Gippius, Olga Shapir and Lou Andreas-Salome; wrote literary and theater criticism collected in *Literature and Aesthetics* (1912); also published pamphlets on rights of working women, *The 9th of January* (1906) and *Why Women Must Be Given All Rights and Freedom* (1906); met Stanislavski and later edited his theoretical writings and collaborated on his memoirs *My Life in Art* (1926); published *The Actor's Art: On the Nature of the Actor's Artistic Experiences on Stage* (1927) and *The History of Russian Theatrical Life* (1939); translated writers including Bashkirtseff, Spinoza, Maupassant, Stendhal, Proust, and Hauptmann.

GUREYEVA, Lyudmila (1943—). Soviet volleyball player. Born Feb 12, 1943, in USSR. ❖ At Tokyo Olympics, won a silver medal in team competition (1964).

GURIE, Sigrid (1911–1969). American-born actress. Born Sigrid Gurie Haukelid, May 18, 1911, in Brooklyn, NY; raised in Norway and Belgium; died Aug 14, 1969, in Mexico City, Mexico; dau. of Norwegian parents; twin sister of Knut Haukelid (leader in the Norwegian resistance whose story is told in *The Heroes of Telemark*); m. Thomas Stewart, 1935 (div. c 1938); m. Dr. Lawrence Spangard, 1939 (div. 1948); m. Lynn Abbott, 1958 (div. 1961). ❖ Moved back to Norway (1912); brought to Hollywood by Samuel Goldwyn and billed as the Norwegian Garbo (1936); made film debut in *The Adventures of Marco Polo* (1937), followed by *Algiers, The Forgotten Woman, Rio, Three Faces West, Dark Streets of Cairo, Voice in the Wind, Enemy of Women* and *Sofia*, among others.

GURINA, Elena. Russian gymnast. Born in USSR. ❖ Won Coca-Cola International and Ontario Cup (1978) and Paris Grand Prix and Tunis International (1981).

GURLEY, Elizabeth (1890–1964). *See Flynn, Elizabeth Gurley.*

GURNEY, Eliza (1801–1881). American Quaker minister. Name variations: Eliza Paul Kirkbride Gurney, Eliza Kirkbride. Born April 6, 1801, in Philadelphia, Pennsylvania; died Nov 8, 1881, in West Hill, New Jersey; dau. of Joseph Kirkbride and Mary (Paul) Kirkbride; m. Joseph John Gurney (banker/minister), Oct 21, 1841 (died 1847). ❖ Traveled US, Canada, England, and Scotland (from 1832) with Hannah Backhouse, an English Quaker minister; was recognized as a minister of the gospel by Quaker Monthly Meeting of Darlington, in England (1841); embarked with husband on traveling ministry to France and Switzerland and ministered to heads of state such as Louis Philippe I, Citizen King of France; after husband's death, continued to work as traveling minister in US and Europe; visited with President Abraham Lincoln (1862).

GURNEY, Hilda (1943—). American equestrian. Born Sept 10, 1943, in US. ❖ At Montreal Olympics, won a bronze medal in team dressage (1976).

GURNEY, Nella Hooper (1838–1887). American Brahmin. Name variations: Ellen Gurney. Born Ellen Hooper in 1838; died in 1887; dau. of Robert William Hooper and Ellen Sturgis Hooper (1812–1848); sister of

Clover Adams (1843–1885); m. Ephraim Whitman Gurney (1829–1886, Harvard professor); no children.

GURNEY, Rachel (1920–2001). English actress. Born Rachel Gurney Lubbock, Mar 5, 1920, in Eton, Buckinghamshire, England; died Nov 24, 2001, in Holt, Norfolk, England; dau. of a school housemaster and a concert pianist; attended Webber Douglas Academy of Dramatic Art; m. Denys Rhodes, 1946 (div. 1950); children: 1 daughter. ❖ Best known as Lady Marjorie Bellamy in tv series "Upstairs, Downstairs," worked steadily in the theater in modern and classical roles, including Portia in *Merchant of Venice* (1955) and Hermione in *A Winter's Tale* (1965); made US debut in *You Never Can Tell* (1977) and appeared on Broadway in *The Dresser* (1981) and *Breaking the Code* (1987).

GURO, Elena (1877–1913). Russian poet and playwright. Name variations: Elena Genrikhovna or Genrichovna Guró; Elena G. Guro. Born Elena Genrichovna Guro in 1877 in St. Petersburg, Russia; died 1913 in Usikirko, Finland; trained as a painter. ❖ Influenced by Russian futurists and by Russian and western Symbolists like Andrei Bely, Aleksandr Blok, and Friedrich Nietzsche, and by novelist Knut Hamsun, was the only woman to gain prominence as a Russian Futurist writer; influenced several Russian writers including Cherubina de Gabriak (Elizaveta Dmitreva) and Mariia Shkapskaia; works include *Hurdy-Gurdy* (1905, 1914), *Autumnal Dream* (1912), and *The Little Camels of the Sky* (1914).

GUROVA, Elena (1972—). Russian gymnast. Born Dec 30, 1972, in Moscow, Russia. ❖ Won Cottbus Cup (1985), Chunichi Cup (1987), and World Sports Fair (1987, 1988); at World championships, won a silver for team all-around (1987); was the 1st female to perform a double-twisting layout Yurchenko vault in competition.

GURR, Donna Marie (1955—). Canadian swimmer. Name variations: Donna-Marie Gurr. Born Feb 18, 1955, in British Columbia, Canada; coached by Howard Firby and Derek Snelling. ❖ Was national champion in the 100-meter and 200-meter backstroke (1969–72); won 5 gold medals at the British championships (1969) and 3 gold medals at the Pan American Games (1971); at Munich Olympics, won a bronze medal in 200-meter backstroke (1972). Received the Order of Canada (1976); inducted into the British Columbia Sports Hall of Fame (1987).

GURRAH, rani of (d. 1564). *See Durgawati.*

GURYEVA, Yelena (1958—). Soviet field-hockey player. Born Nov 29, 1958, in USSR. ❖ At Moscow Olympics, won a bronze medal in team competition (1980).

GUSAKOVA, Maria. Russian cross-country skier. Name variations: Mariya or Marija Gusakova or Gussakowa. Born in USSR. ❖ Won a gold medal for 10 km and a silver medal for 3 x 5 km relay at Squaw Valley Olympics (1960); won a bronze medal for 10 km at Innsbruck Olympics (1964).

GUSENBAUER, Ilona (1947—). Austrian high jumper. Born on Sept 16, 1947, in Majdan, Austria. ❖ Won a bronze medal at Munich Olympics (1972); is also a painter.

GUSEVA, Elina (1964—). Soviet handball player. Born Jan 20, 1964, in USSR. ❖ Won a bronze medal at Seoul Olympics (1988) and a bronze medal at Barcelona Olympics (1992), both in team competition.

GUSEVA, Klara (1937—). Russian speedskater. Name variations: Klara Nesterova-Guseva. Born Klara Ivanovna Guseva, Mar 8, 1937, in USSR. ❖ Won the gold medal for the 1,000 meters at Squaw Valley Olympics (1960); placed 4th for the 3,000 meters at Innsbruck Olympics (1964).

GUSEVA-ORENBURGSKAIA, Gloria (c. 1870–1942). *See Mamoshina, Glafira Adolfovna.*

GUSHI-KADARE, Elena (1943—). *See Kadaré, Elena.*

GUSHINGTON, Impulsia (1807–1867). *See Blackwood, Helen Selina.*

GUSHTEROVA, Vangelia (1911–1996). Bulgarian prophet. Name variations: Aunt Vanga; Vanga Gushterova. Born in Macedonia in 1911; died in Rupite, Bulgaria, Aug 11, 1996. ❖ Blinded in a windstorm at 12, was a visionary who drew her powers from an ancient city buried under her village in southwestern Bulgaria; by the time she was a teenager, reputation had spread throughout the nation; called "Aunt Vanga," ministered to politicians and peasants, reputedly diagnosing the sick and even locating missing persons; dreamed of an "ancient horseman" who foretold the Nazi march into the Balkans (1941); consulted from her modest house in Rupite, where hundreds stood in line outside her door

almost daily; was estimated to have administered to over one million believers by the time she died.

GUSMAO, Luisa de (1613–1666). *See Luisa de Guzman.*

GUSTAFSON, Elisabet (1964—). Swedish curler. Name variations: Elisabet Johansson. Born May 2, 1964, in Sweden. ❖ Was 4-time World champion (1992, 1995, 1998, 1999); won a bronze medal for curling at Nagano Olympics (1998); placed 6th at Salt Lake City Olympics (2002); retired (2002).

GUSTAFSON, Zadel Barnes (1841–1917). *See Barnes, Zadel.*

GUSTAFSSON, Tina (1962—). Swedish swimmer. Born Sept 30, 1962, in Sweden. ❖ At Moscow Olympics, won a silver medal in 4 x 100-meter freestyle relay (1980).

GUSTAFSSON, Toini (1938—). Swedish cross-country skier. Name variations: Toini Rönnlund, Roennlund, Rønnlund, or Ronnlund. Born Jan 17, 1938, in Soumisalmi, Sweden. ❖ Won a silver medal for 3 x 5 km relay at Innsbruck Olympics (1964); won gold medals for 5 km and 10 km and a silver medal for 3 x 5 km at Grenoble Olympics (1968); at World championships, won a silver medal (1962) and a bronze medal (1966).

GUSTAVO, Roseli (1971—). Brazilian basketball player. Name variations: Roseli do Carmo Gustavo. Born July 25, 1971, in Araraquara, Brazil. ❖ Won a team silver medal at Atlanta Olympics (1996).

GUSTAVSON, Linda (1949—). American swimmer. Name variations: Linda McGuire. Born Nov 30, 1949, in Soquel, Santa Cruz Co., California; attended Michigan State University; m. Tim McGuire, 1972; children: 2. ❖ At Mexico City Olympics, won a silver medal in 400-meter freestyle, a bronze medal in 100-meter freestyle, and a gold medal in 4 x 100-meter freestyle relay (1968); helped launch the Santa Cruz City Schools program for teenage moms and taught in the program for over 25 years.

GUSTERSON, Bridgette (1973—). Australian water-polo player. Born Feb 7, 1973, in Perth, Western Australia; sister of Danielle Woodhouse (water-polo player). ❖ Won a team gold medal at Sydney Olympics (2000). Named Western Australia Sportswoman of the Year (1999).

GUSTILINA, Diana (1974—). Russian basketball player. Born April 21, 1974, in Vladivostok, USSR. ❖ Won a team bronze medal at Athens Olympics (2004); placed 2nd at World championships (2002) and 1st at European championships (2003).

GUTA or GUTTA. *Variant of Judith and Jutta.*

GUTHEIL-SCHODER, Marie (1874–1935). German soprano. Born in Weimar, Germany, Feb 16, 1874; died in Bad Ilmenau, Thuringia, Oct 4, 1935. ❖ Made debut in Weimar (1891); engaged by Mahler at the Vienna Staatsoper (1900); appeared there until 1926; coached by Richard Strauss for her roles in *Elektra* and *Der Rosenkavalier*, was also known for her many roles in Mozart operas; an adventurous singer, performed in Arnold Schoenberg's avant-garde vocal work *Erwartung* when it premiered in Prague (1924); after retirement from the stage, continued her career as a teacher and director in Vienna and Salzburg.

GUTHKE, Karin (1956—). East German diver. Born Nov 23, 1956. ❖ At Moscow Olympics, won a bronze medal in springboard (1980).

GÜTHLEIN, Christa (1961—). *See Kinshofer, Christa.*

GUTHRIE, Janet (1938—). American auto racer. Born Janet Guthrie, Mar 7, 1938, in Iowa City, Iowa; dau. of Jean Ruth (Midkiff) Guthrie and William Lain Guthrie; University of Michigan, BSc in physics, 1960. ❖ The 1st woman to qualify for, and race in, the Indianapolis 500, moved from Iowa City to NY, Atlanta, and then Miami (1941); started flying at 13, soloed at 16, and had commercial pilot's license by 19; worked at Republic Aviation in the aerospace division, Long Island, NY; granted competition license from Long Island Sports Car Club (1962); granted license from Sports Car Club of America (1963); applied to be one of the 1st scientist-astronauts (1965); worked as a physicist and non-professional auto racer; participated in 24-hour International Manufacturer's Championship at Daytona (1966); successfully finished in 9 consecutive runnings of Daytona 24-hour, Sebring 12-hour, and Watkins Glen 500 endurance races (1964–70); was 2nd in class at Watkins Glen race (1965); was 2nd in class at Sebring race (1967); won Governor of Florida's Award at Sebring (1968); took a job as technical editor for Sperry Rand (1968); was 1st in class at Sebring 12-hour race (1970); participated in North Atlantic Road Racing championship (1973); did public relations work for Toyota (1975); became 1st woman to enter and pass rookie test at Indianapolis 500 trials (1976); was 1st woman to compete in a NASCAR (National Association for Stock Car Auto Racing) superspeedway race (1976); competed in 4 Indy-car races at other tracks; was 1st woman to qualify for, and race in, the Indianapolis 500 (May 1977); finished 9th in Indianapolis 500 (1978). ❖ See also Ross R. Olney, *Janet Guthrie, 1st Woman to Race at Indy* (Harvey House, 1978); and *Women in World History*.

GUTHRIE, Mary Jane (1895–1975). American zoologist and cancer researcher. Born Mary Jane Guthrie, Dec 13, 1895, in New Bloomfield, Missouri; died Feb 22, 1975; dau. of Lula Ella (Lloyd) Guthrie and George Robert Guthrie; University of Missouri, AB, 1916, AM, 1918; Bryn Mawr College, PhD, 1922. ❖ Researcher in the etiologies (causes) of cancers, was influenced by Dr. Florence Peebles, esteemed marine biology researcher; at Bryn Mawr College, worked as a demonstrator (1918–20), biology instructor (1920–21) and biology fellow (1921–22); at University of Missouri, served as an assistant zoology professor (1922–27), associate zoology professor (1927–37), zoology professor (1937–51) and Zoology Department chair (1939–50); was on the editorial board of *Journal of Morphology* (1944–47); researched the cultivation of ovaries in vitro (and the causes of certain cancers) as a Detroit Institute of Cancer research associate (1951–61); was on the faculty of the Wayne State University Biology Department (1950–61); officially retired (1961); served as a Women's Auxiliary of the Pontiac General Hospital president (1965–67); was a member (1966–70), president-elect (1968–69) and president (1969–70) of the Michigan Association of Hospital Auxiliaries' State Board. Publications include *Laboratory Directions in General Zoology* (1925–58), an accompanying manual for the textbook *General Zoology* (1927–57); honors include stars in many editions of *American Men of Science*, later titled *American Men and Women of Science*.

GUTIÉRREZ-CORTINES, Cristina (1939—). Spanish politician. Name variations: Cristina Gutierrez-Cortines. Born Dec 17, 1939, in Madrid, Spain. ❖ Was a professor of art history (1995–99); served as minister of Education and Culture, Murcia Regional Government (1995–99); as a member of the European People's Party (Christian Democrats) and European Democrats, elected to 5th European Parliament (1999–2004).

GUTIÉRREZ DE MENDOZA, Juana Belén (1875–1942). Mexican revolutionary, journalist and feminist. Born in Durango state in 1875; died in Mexico City on July 13, 1942; dau. of Santiago Gutierrez; children: two daughters. ❖ Became a teacher (1901); was an active member of the Precursor movement which spoke out against the oppressive regime of Porfirio Diaz; with fellow teacher Elisa Acuña y Rossetti, founded weekly newspaper, *Vésper* (1901), which called for sweeping social reforms; contributed essays to *Excélsior*, one of Mexico City's leading opposition newspapers; arrested with Acuña y Rossetti, was thrown into women's prison at Belén (1904); remained incarcerated for 3 years and was then exiled; as a supporter of Emiliano Zapata, organized and commanded his "Victoria" regiment (1914); served as editor of a journal, *La Reforma*, advocating liberation of the Indian masses; served another prison term, after having been captured by government forces; began publishing *El Desmonte* (1919), and later a biweekly magazine entitled *Alma Mexicana: Por la Tierra y Por la Raza* (1935). ❖ See also *Women in World History*.

GUTRIDGE, Molly (fl. 1778). American poet. Fl. in 1778; lived in Marblehead, Massachusetts. ❖ Wrote broadside poem "A New Touch on the Times" which mentions effect of war on community of Marblehead.

GUTSU, Tatyana (1976—). Russian gymnast. Name variations: Tatiana Gutsu. Born Tatiana Constantinovna Gutsu, Sept 5, 1976, in Odessa, Ukraine; one of 4 sisters. ❖ Won the Jr. European championships (1990), European Cup, Moscow News, and USSR Cup (1991), and European championships (1992); was also 1st all-around at the Moscow Stars (1991 and 1992); won gold medals for all-around indiv. and all-around team, a bronze medal for floor exercises and a silver medal for uneven bars at Barcelona Olympics (1992).

GUTTERIDGE, Helena Rose (1879–1960). British-born suffragist, labor leader, and politician. Name variations: Nell. Born Helen Rose Gutteridge on April 8, 1879 (some sources cite 1880, but 1879 is documented), in Chelsea, London, England; died of cancer on Oct 1, 1960, in Vancouver, British Columbia, Canada; dau. of Charles Henry Gutteridge (blacksmith) and Sophia (Richardsson) Gutteridge; attended Holy Trinity Church School and Regent Street Polytechnic School; also

Royal Sanitary Institute, earning a South Kensington Department of Education certificate for teaching and sanitary science; m. Oliver Fearn, Oct 11, 1919 (div., Dec 21, 1928); no children. ❖ Activist who championed women's rights in British Columbia and was influential in securing mother's pensions and the minimum wage for women; left home at 14; began career as tailor; was a London suffragist (1908–11); immigrated to Vancouver, British Columbia, Canada (1911); founded the radical British Columbia Woman's Suffrage League; co-edited the woman-suffrage page in the *B.C. Federationist* (1913–15); served as secretary of the United Suffrage Societies (1915 and 1916); served as secretary of the Vancouver City Central Woman's Suffrage Referendum Campaign Committee (1916); was a member of the Pioneer political Equality League and the Vancouver Council of Women; served the Vancouver Trades and Labor Council as 1st woman Council executive and as organizer, secretary-treasurer, business agent, statistician, vice-chair and trustee; helped to organize women laundry and garment workers; was a member of tailor's union; was a correspondent for the *Labor Gazette* (1913–21); served as chair of the Women's Minimum Wage League (1917); was an active supporter of the Mother's Pension Act; was the 1st woman "alderman" for Vancouver (1937), reelected (1939), defeated (1940); served as chair of the Vancouver Town Planning and Parks Committee (1937); was an active campaigner for improved housing, revision of tax laws and assistance for destitute women; worked as a poultry farmer (1921–32); served as supervisor of the welfare office of Japanese internment camp at Slocan City during World War II; served as chair of the Women's International League for Peace; was active in the Socialist Party of Canada as chair of the Economic Planning Commission. ❖ See also *Women in World History*.

GUY, Alice (1875–1968). See Guy-Blaché, Alice.

GUY, Rosa (1925—). Trinidadian novelist. Born Rosa Cuthbert, Sept 1, 1925, in Trinidad, West Indies; dau. of Henry Cuthbert and Audrey (Gonzales) Cuthbert; moved to US (1932); attended New York University; m. Warner Guy (died); children: Warner Guy, Jr. ❖ Grew up in Harlem and left school at 14 to support family; studied theater at New York University; co-founded and was president of the Harlem Writers' Guild and worked for black liberation; writings include *Bird at My Window* (1966), *The Friends* (1973), *Ruby* (1976), *The Disappearance* (1979), *A Measure of Time* (1983), *New Guys Around the Block* (1986) and *And I Heard a Bird Sing* (1987).

GUY-BLACHÉ, Alice (1875–1968). French-born film director. Name variations: Alice Guy; Alice Guy Blache; Alice Guy Blaché. Pronunciation: blah-SHAY. Born Alice Guy on July 1, 1875 (some give the year as 1873 but her daughter maintained that 1875 was correct) at Saint-Mondé, France; died Mar 24, 1968, in a nursing home in New Jersey; dau. of Emile Guy (bookshop owner) and Madame Guy; attended convent schools at Viry and Ferney, France; studied briefly in Paris; studied typing and stenography; m. Herbert Blaché-Bolton (known as Herbert Blaché after moving to the US), 1907 (div. 1922); children: daughter Simone Blaché (b. 1908), son Reginald (b. 1912). ❖ First woman film director and probably the 1st director to produce a story film, who was a pioneer in motion-picture production in France and the US, spent early years with her family in Chile; sent to France for schooling; later returned with family to live in France; after father's death, found employment as secretary to Léon Gaumont in a company that sold film and photographic equipment; directed 1st story film *La Fée aux choux* (*The Cabbage Fairy*, 1896); promoted to head of film production for Gaumont where she directed some 400 films, including the 1st sound films using Gaumont's Chronophone; married (1907) and accompanied husband to US when he was transferred to Gaumont's New York operation; resumed film directing after birth of her daughter; was president and director-in-chief of Solax Company (1910–14) where she directed or supervised production of more than 300 films; was vice-president of Blaché Features founded in 1913; was director of US Amusement Corporation founded in 1914; directed several films for Popular Plays and Players; lectured on film at Columbia University (1917); returned to France following her divorce; awarded Legion of Honor for pioneer work in French film industry (1955); spent final years with daughter in US. Films include *La Vie du Christ* (1906), *An Interrupted Elopement* (1911), *Greater Love Hath No Man* (1911), *The Detective's Dog* (1912), *Canned Harmony* (1912), *The Girl in the Armchair* (1912), *Fra Diavolo* (1912), *Dick Whittington and His Cat* (1913), *A House Divided* (1913), *Matrimony's Speed Limit* (1913), *The Tigress* (1914), *The Heart of a Painted Woman* (1915), *The Great Adventure* (1918), and *Tarnished Reputations* (1920). ❖ See also *The Memoirs of Alice Guy Blaché* (trans.

by Roberta and Simone Blaché, ed. by Anthony Slide, Scarecrow, 1986); and *Women in World History*.

GUY-QUINT, Catherine (1949—). French politician. Born Sept 1, 1949, in Poitiers, France. ❖ Member of the Socialist Party national council (1990–99) and national bureau (1997–99); elected to 5th European Parliament (1999–2004). Named Knight of the National Order of Merit.

GUY-STÉPHAN, Marie (1818–1873). French or Spanish ballet dancer. Born 1818, place uncertain; died Aug 21, 1873, possibly in Paris. ❖ Made professional debut in Madrid (1840), and soon went on to perform title role in the 1st production of *Giselle* in Spain (c. 1844); performed in numerous works by Marius Petipa and was often partnered with him; moved to Paris (1853) where she made her Paris Opéra debut in Mazilier's *Aelia et Mysis;* performed at Théâtre Lyrique and at Théâtre de la Gaîté around same time; created roles including in Saint-Léon's *Néméa, ou l'Amour vengé* (1864).

GUYARD OR GUYART, Marie (1599–1672). *See Marie de l'Incarnation.*

GUYON, Jeanne Marie Bouviéres de la Mothe (1648–1717). French religious leader. Name variations: Jean Marie Guyon; Jeanne Marie Bouviéres de la Mothe; Jeanne-Marie Bouvier de la Mothe; Jeanne Marie de la Motte-Guyon; Madame Guion or Madame Guyon. Born April 13, 1648, in the town of Montargis, 50 miles south of Paris, France; died June 9, 1717, age 69; dau. of Claude Bouviéres de la Mothe, Seigneur de la Mothe Vergonville (widower whose 1st wife was Marie Ozon) and Jeanne le Maistre de la Maisonfort (widow of Etienne Ravault); m. Jacques Guyon (1625–1676), Mar 21, 1664; children: Armand-Jacques Guyon (b. May 21, 1665); Armand-Claude Guyon (b. Jan 8, 1668, d. Oct 20, 1670); Marie-Anne Guyon (b. 1669, d. June 4, 1672); Jean-Baptiste-Denys Guyon (b. May 31, 1674); Jeanne-Marie Guyon, later countess of Vaux (b. Mar 21, 1676). ❖ Catholic aristocrat who, despite rigorous opposition and persecution, devoted her life to the pursuit of spiritual union with God through faith and prayer; spent most of early years in convents where she received a rudimentary education; lived at home until marriage at age 15 (1659–1663), but did not meet wealthy, 38-year-old husband, who had been selected by her father, until 3 days before the wedding; despite her long cherished ambition to become a nun, was attracted by the idea of comfort and independence; found herself a virtual prisoner, however, of husband and mother-in-law; became increasingly spiritual and, after birth of 1st two children, underwent a religious "conversion" (1668), from which time she dedicated her life to God;, widowed at age 28 (1676); though 2 of her children had died in infancy, was left with 3 others; felt called to go on a mission to Geneva, to convert the Protestants there and left Paris (July 1681), renouncing her possessions and giving up her sons to the care of her stepmother; thwarted in plans to get to Geneva, traveled with her little daughter and a maid to Gex, Thonon, Turin and Grenoble, speaking to small groups and individuals about religion, particularly the importance of faith and prayer; also began to write devotional works; because her doctrines were regarded with increasing suspicion by church and state authorities, was confined in the Convent of the Visitation for most of the year under suspicion of Quietism (1688); was rearrested (Dec 1695) and imprisoned in the castle of Vincennes for 9 months; was then transferred to a convent near Paris where she was kept for 2 years; was sent to the fortress prison of the Bastille (June 1698), where she spent more than 4 years in solitary confinement; released (Mar 1703) and was banished to Blois, in custody of her son, Armand-Jacques. ❖ See also Thomas Taylor Allen, trans. *Autobiography of Madame Guyon* (2 vols., Kegan Paul, 1898); Thomas C. Upham, *Life and Religious Opinions and Experience of Madame de la Mothe Guyon* (2 vols., Harper, 1862); and *Women in World History*.

GUZENKO, Olga (1956—). Soviet rower. Born July 17, 1956, in USSR. ❖ At Montreal Olympics, won a silver medal in coxed eights (1976).

GUZMAN, Eleonore de (d. 1512). Duchess of Braganza. Died Nov 2, 1512; dau. of Isabel de Velasco and Juan Alfonso de Guzman, duke of Medina Sidonia; m. Jaime or James (1479–1532), duke of Braganza, in 1502; children: Toeodosio or Theodosius (1510–1563), duke of Braganza. James 2nd wife was Joana de Mendoza.

GUZMAN, Leonora de (1310–1351). Countess of Clermont, mistress of Castilian king Alphonso XI, and mother of Henry II of Trastamara. Name variations: Leonor de Guzmán; La Favorita. Born 1310; died 1351; dau. of Pedro Martínez de Guzmán and Beatriz Ponce de León; m. Juan de Velasco (died 1328); mistress of Alphonso XI (1311–

1350), king of Castile (r. 1312–1350); children: (with Alphonso XI) Pedro (b. 1330); Sancho (b. 1331); Enrique II also known as Henry II Trastamara (1333–1379), king of Castile (r. 1369–1379); Fadrique (b. 1333); Fernando (1336–c. 1342); Tello (1337–1370), count of Castaneda; Juan (1341–1359); Pedro (1345–1359); Juana (who m. Fernando de Castro and Felipe de Castro). ❖ Born into a Castilian noble family, was married to Juan de Velasco, whose death left her a widow by 1328; with her beauty and bearing, attracted Alphonso XI, king of Castile, and had 10 children with him (though he was married to Maria of Portugal); apparently bright and able, participated energetically in Alphonso's rule, and he often sought her advice on political matters; when he died, accompanied his body to Sevilla, performing the role of grieving widow; refused to enter Sevilla, however, rightly fearing for her own safety; was imprisoned by the long-humiliated Maria and executed. ❖ See also *Women in World History*.

GUZMAN, Luisa de (1613–1666). *See Luisa de Guzman.*

GUZMAN, Mayor de (d. 1262). Mistress of Alphonso X. Name variations: Mary de Guzman; Mary Guillemete or Guillemette. Born Mayor Guillen de Guzman; died 1262; dau. of Guillen Prez de Guzman and Maria Gonsalez Giron; mistress of Alphonso X the Wise (1221–1284), king of Castile and Leon (r. 1252–1284); children: Beatrice of Castile and Leon (1242–1303). (One source also places Sancho IV, king of Castile and Leon, as a son of de Guzman).

GWEN. *Variant of Winne.*

GWENDDOLEN or GWENDOLEN. *Variant of Winifred.*

GWENDDYD. *Variant of Winnie.*

GWENFREWI. *Variant of Winifred.*

GWENHWYFAR or GWENHWYFER (d. 470 or 542). *See Guinevere.*

GWENLLIAN OF WALES (fl. 1137). Welsh princess and hero. Fl. around 1137 in Gwynedd, Wales; dau. of Gruffydd ap Cynan, king of Gwynedd; m. Gruffydd ap Rhys, king of Deheubarth; children: Maredudd and Rhys. ❖ A Welsh patriot and warrior, served as a link between her royal brothers and husband Gruffydd, leading to their alliance against Henry III of England; led her own army into battle in southern Wales and was eventually killed on the battlefield; became a symbol of Welsh spirit and patriotism for many years. ❖ See also *Women in World History*.

GWENT, Gwenynen (1802–1896). *See Hall, Augusta.*

GWLADUS. *Variant of Gladys.*

GWYNEDD, princess of (fl. 1173). *See Marared.*

GWYNETH. *Variant of Wenefrid or Winifred.*

GWYNN, Nell (1650–1687). English comedy actress and mistress of Charles II. Name variations: Gwyn or Gwynne. Born Eleanor Gwynn, Feb 2, 1650, in England (authorities are unsure whether in London, Oxford, or Hereford); died Nov 14, 1687; dau. of Helena and Thomas or James Gwynn (common soldier); children: (with Charles II) Charles Beauclerk (1670–1726, later duke of St. Albans); James Beauclerk, earl of Plymouth (d. 1680). ❖ One of the most popular figures of Restoration England and one of its best-known royal mistresses, whose remarkable popularity has endured into modern times; arose from lowly origins to become a favorite of Charles II and, with her quick wit, held his affections from about 1669 until his death in 1685, bearing him 2 sons who were eventually raised to the English peerage. ❖ See also Peter Cunningham, *Nell Gwyn* (Grolier, 1892); Roy MacGregor-Hastie, *Nell Gwyn* (Robert Hale, 1987); B. Bevan, *Nell Gwyn* (1969); and *Women in World History*.

GWYNNE, Anne (1918–2003). American screen actress. Born Marguerite Gwynne Trice, Dec 10, 1918, in Waco, Texas; died Mar 31, 2003, in Woodland Hills, California; m. Max Gilford, 1945; children: Gwynne Gilford (b. 1946, actress). ❖ Made film debut in *Unexpected Father* (1939), followed by westerns, then B horror flicks; films include *The Black Cat, Jail House Blues, Weird Woman, Murder in the Blue Room, House of Frankenstein, The Glass Alibi, The Ghost Goes Wild, Killer Dill, Dick Tracy Meets Gruesome, The Enchanted Valley, Blazing Sun, Breakdown, Phantom of the Jungle* and *Teenage Monster.*

GWYNNE-VAUGHAN, Helen (1879–1967). British botanist. Name variations: Dame Helen Gwynne-Vaughan. Born Helen Charlotte Isabella Fraser in London, England, Jan 21, 1879; died Aug 26, 1967; attended

Cheltenham Ladies' College and King's College, London; BS in Botany, 1904; DS, 1907; m. D.T. Gwynne-Vaughan (professor of botany), 1911 (died 1915). ❖ Founded University of London Suffrage Society with Louisa Garrett Anderson; became head of botany department at Birkbeck College in London (1909); during WWI, served as joint chief controller of Women's Army Auxiliary Corps in France, then as a commandant in Women's Royal Air Force (1918–19); returned to Birkbeck (1921); served as a member of the Royal Commission on Food Prices (1924); during WWII (1939–42), served as 1st director of Auxiliary Territorial Service; taught at Birkbeck College (1942–44); published many scientific studies and two textbooks on fungi. Created Dame of the British Empire (DBE, 1919) and Dame Grand Cross of the Order of the British Empire (GBE, 1926). ❖ See also autobiography, *Service with the Army* (1942).

GYARMATI, Andrea (1954—). Hungarian swimmer. Born May 15, 1954, in Hungary. ❖ At Munich Olympics, won a bronze medal in 100-meter butterfly and a silver medal in 100-meter backstroke (1972).

GYARMATI, Olga (1924—). Hungarian track-and-field athlete. Born Oct 5, 1924, in Hungary. ❖ At London Olympics, won a gold medal in the long jump (1948).

GYDE (fl. 1054). Queen of Denmark. Name variations: Guda Anundsdottir. Dau. of Anund Jakob, king of Sweden (r. 1022–1050); became 3rd wife of Svend II or Sweyn Estridsen, king of Denmark (r. 1047–1074), around 1054 (div.). ❖ There are 16 children attributed to Svend II who had 4 wives or paramours (Gunhild of Norway, Gyde, Elizabeth of Kiev, and Thora Johnsdottir); any one of the 4 could be the mother of Svend's royal offspring: Harald Hén, king of Denmark (r. 1074–1080), St. Knud or Canute the Holy, king of Denmark (r. 1080–1086), Oluf or Olaf Hunger, king of Denmark (r. 1086–1095).

GYE, Mrs. W.E. (1893–1983). See Mann, Ida.

GYENGE, Valeria (1933—). Hungarian swimmer. Born April 1933, in Hungary. ❖ At Helsinki Olympics, won a gold medal in the 400-meter freestyle (1952).

GYLLEMBOURG-EHRENSVÄRD, Thomasine (1773–1856). Danish author and baroness. Name variations: Baroness or Countess Thomasine Gyllembourg. Pronunciation: Gullem-BORG AY-rens-verd. Born Thomasine Christine Buntzen, Nov 9, 1773, in Copenhagen, Denmark; died in Copenhagen, July 2, 1856; m. Peter Andreas Heiberg (writer), 1789 (div. 1800); m. Swedish baron Karl or Carl Frederik Gyllembourg-Ehrensvärd, Dec 1801 (died 1815); children: (1st m.) Johan Ludvig Heiberg (writer). ❖ One of Denmark's 1st great women writers and one of its 1st realists, initially attracted notice because of her great beauty; before age 17, married famous writer Peter Andreas Heiberg; the following year, gave birth to son Johan Ludvig Heiberg, who would become an acclaimed poet and critic; after husband was exiled for liberalism, obtained a divorce (1800); married Swedish baron Carl F. Ehrensvärd (1801) who, as a political fugitive, had taken refuge in Denmark and adopted the name Gyllembourg, having been implicated in assassination of Sweden's Gustavus III; followed son to Kiel (1822), where he was appointed professor; returned with him to Copenhagen (1825); when son married legendary actress Johanne Luise Heiberg (1831), lived with them as part of an intense *menage à trois;* published 1st novel *Familien Polonius (The Polonius Family)* in son's newspaper *Flyvende Post* (1827); with a style considered by critics to be clear, sparkling, and witty, published the immensely popular *En Hverdags historie (Everyday History),* followed by 3 volumes of *Old and New Novels* (1833–34), *New Stories* (1835–36), *Montanus the Younger* (1839), *Ricida* (1839), *One in All* (1840), *Near and Far* (1841), *A Correspondence* (1843), *The Cross Ways* (1844), and *Two Generations* (1845); brought out a library edition of her collected works in 12 volumes (1849–51), but her literary identity remained a secret, even from closest friends, until the day she died. ❖ See also *Women in World History.*

GYLLING, Jane (1902–1961). Swedish swimmer. Born April 6, 1902, in Sweden; died Mar 10, 1961. ❖ At Antwerp Olympics, won a bronze medal in 4 x 100-meter freestyle relay (1920).

GYNT, Greta (1916–2000). Norwegian-born actress and dancer. Name variations: Grete Woxholt; Mrs. Moore. Born Margrethe Thoresen Woxholt, Nov 15, 1916, in Slemdal, near Oslo, Norway; died April 2, 2000, in London, England; sister of Gil Woxholt (famed underwater photographer); m. Christopher Mann (div.); m. Wilfred Anthony John Orchard (div.); m. Noel James Trevenen Holland; m. Frederick Moore (died 1983). ❖ Made stage debut in Oslo in *The Chat-Noir Revue* (1931), followed by the lead in *Sissener's Bar;* made London debut as a principal dancer in *A Midsummer Night's Dream* (1936), eventually playing leads in such plays as *Under Suspicion, The Painted Smile, Lysistrata, Last Train South* and *Under Your Hat;* films include *To-Morrow We Live, Mr. Emmanuel, London Town, Take My Life, Dear Murderer, Easy Money, The Calendar, Soldiers Three, Bulldog Sees It Through* and *See How They Run.*

GYÖRGY-TOTH, Beatrix. See Toth, Beatrix.

GYP (1850–1932). See Martel de Janville, Comtesse de.

GYRID (fl. 950s). Queen of Denmark. Name variations: Gyrid Olafsdottir. Fl. in 950s; m. Harald Bluetooth (c. 910–985), king of Denmark (r. 940–985); children: Haakon; Gunhilda of Denmark (d. 1002); Thyra of Denmark (d. 1000); Sven or Sweyn I Forkbeard, king of Denmark (r. 985–1014), king of England (r. 1014).

GYRING, Elizabeth (1906–1970). Austrian composer. Born in Vienna, Austria, 1906; died in New York City, 1970; received musical education in Vienna. ❖ By mid-1930s, had received public performances for a number of her compositions, including concert premieres played by virtuoso members of both the Vienna and Berlin Philharmonic orchestras; with rise of Nazis, immigrated to US (1938); in US, composed in virtually all forms, including a symphony, military marches (a genre rarely practiced by contemporary women composers), organ works, and several cantatas set to patriotic texts. ❖ See also *Women in World History.*

GYSETH (fl. 1070). English princess. Name variations: Gytha. Fl. in 1070; dau. of Harold II Godwineson, king of England (r. 1066), and Eadgyth Swanneshals; m. Vladimir II Monomakh or Monomach, grand prince of Kiev (r. 1113–1125), around 1070; children: Mstislav I, grand prince of Kiev (r. 1125–1132); Yaropolk I, grand prince of Kiev (r. 1132–1139); Maria of Kiev (d. 1146, who m. Leo Diogenes of Byzantium); Yuri Dolgoruki, grand prince of Kiev (r. 1154–1157).

GYTHA. Variant of Agatha.

GYTHA (fl. 1022–1042). Countess of Wessex. Name variations: Agatha; Countess of Kent. Born in Denmark; fl. around 1022 to 1042; died after 1069 in Flanders; dau. of Thorgils Sprakalegg; granddau. of Thyra of Denmark (d. 1000); great-granddau. of Harald Bluetooth, king of Denmark (r. around 940–985); m. Godwin (b. around 987), earl of Wessex and Kent, before 1042 (died 1053); children: Harald or Harold II Godwineson (c. 1022–1066), king of the English (r. 1066); Tostig (c. 1026–1066), earl of Northumberland; Edith (c. 1025–1075), queen of England; Sveyn, earl of Mercia; Gyrth (d. 1066), earl of East Anglia; Leofwine (d. 1066), earl of Kent; Alfgar (monk at Rheims); Wulfnoth; Edgiva; Elgiva (d. around 1066); Gunhilda (d. 1087, a nun at Bruges or St. Omer in France); and possibly Driella (who m. Donnchad, king of Munster).

GYULAI-DRIMBA, Ileana (1946—). Romanian fencer. Born June 12, 1946, in Romania. ❖ Won a bronze medal at Mexico City Olympics (1968) and a bronze medal at Munich Olympics (1972), both in team foil.

GYUROVA, Ginka (1954—). Bulgarian rower. Born April 15, 1954, in Bulgaria. ❖ Won a silver medal at Montreal Olympics (1976) and a silver medal at Moscow Olympics (1980), both in coxed fours.

GYUROVA, Krasimira (1953—). Bulgarian basketball player. Born Oct 26, 1953, in Bulgaria. ❖ At Montreal Olympics, won a bronze medal in team competition (1976).

H

HAACKER, Kathrin (1967—). East German rower. Born April 3, 1967, in East Germany. ❖ Won a gold medal at Seoul Olympics (1988) and a bronze medal at Barcelona Olympics (1992), both in coxed eights.

HAAG, Ruth (1916–1973). See Grable, Betty.

HAAKULOU (c. 1798–1853). See Kapule, Deborah.

HAALAND, Sara (c. 1964—). See Ballantyne, Sara.

HAAS, Christl (1943–2001). Austrian Alpine skier. Born Sept 19, 1943, in Kitzbühel, Austria; suffered heart attack while swimming in the sea at Manavgat, Antalya, Turkey, and drowned, July 8, 2001. ❖ Won a gold medal at Innsbruck Olympics (1964) and a bronze medal at Grenoble Olympics (1968), both for downhill; at World championships, won a gold medal for downhill (1962) and a silver medal for combined (1964).

HAAS, Dolly (1910–1994). German-born actress. Name variations: Dolly Hirschfeld. Born Dorothy Clara Louise Haas, April 29, 1910, in Hamburg, Germany; died Sept 16, 1994, in New York, NY; m. John Brahm, 1937 (div. 1941); m. Al Hirschfeld (theatrical caricaturist), 1943 (died 2003); children: Nina Hirschfeld (b. 1945, whose 1st name appears in all her father's drawings). ❖ Made film debut in Eine Stunde Glück (1930), followed by 15 more films, making her a popular star in Germany; made NY debut in Circle of Chalk (1941), followed by War and Peace, Crime and Punishment, Threepenny Opera, Brecht on Brecht, and Lute Song (replacing Mary Martin); became US citizen (1940s); appeared in such English-speaking movies as Broken Blossoms, Spy of Napoleon, and I Confess; was the subject of Dolly, Lotte, und Maria, a West German documentary by Rosa von Praunheim concerning Haas, Lotte Goslar, and Maria Piscator (1987).

HAAS, Monique (1906–1987). French composer and pianist. Born in Paris, France, Oct 20, 1906; died in Paris, June 9, 1987. ❖ Known for her fine recordings of major works, studied piano with Lazare-Lévy, receiving a first prize in his class (1927); also studied with Robert Casadesus and Rudolf Serkin; made New York debut (1960) with Charles Munch and the Boston Symphony Orchestra; performed and recorded with Igor Stravinsky, Paul Hindemith, Georges Enesco, Pierre Fournier, Paul Paray, Ferenc Fricsay and Eugen Jochum. Recording of Debussy's Etudes won the coveted Grand Prix du Disque award (1954).

HAAS-HEYE, Libertas (1913–1942). See Schulze-Boysen, Libertas.

HAASE, Helga (1934–1989). East German speedskater. Name variations: Helga Haase-Obschernitzki. Born Helga Obschernitzki, June 9, 1934, in Danzig-Schidlitz, Germany; died June 16, 1989; m. Helmut Haase (her trainer), 1955. ❖ Won a gold medal for the 500 meters (the 1st female Olympic speedskating champion) and a silver medal for the 1,000 meters at Squaw Valley Olympics (1960); at World championships, placed 3rd in 500 and 1,000 meters (1962); won 9 National allround championships.

HAASE, Mandy (1982—). German field-hockey player. Born June 25, 1982, in Germany. ❖ Won a team gold medal at Athens Olympics (2004).

HABBABA (d. 724). Arabian singer. Birth date unknown; died 724. ❖ Exerted great influence in the court of Yazid II (r. 720–724) of the Eastern Caliphate (whose capital was modern-day Baghdad in Iraq). ❖ See also Women in World History.

HABERSATTER, Brigitte (1954—). See Totschnig, Brigitte.

HABETS, Marie-Louise (1905–1986). Dutch nun. Name variations: Marie Habets. Born in Netherlands, Jan 14, 1905; died May 1986 in Kapaa, Kauai, Hawaii; lived with Kathryn Hulme (1900–1981, writer). ❖ Met Kathryn Hulme, then director of relocation camps in Bavaria, while nursing at a UN refugee camp in Germany following WWII; as the 2 became close friends, told Hulme of her 17 years in the Congo as a nun and her subsequent defection from the convent to work for the Belgian Resistance; her life was the basis for The Nun's Story. ❖ See also Women in World History.

HABLÜTZEL-BÜRKI, Gianna (1969—). Swiss fencer. Name variations: Buerki or Bürki or Burki; Habluetzel-Buerki or Hablutzel-Burki. Born Gianna Bürki on Dec 22, 1969; m. Christoph Hablützel, 1997. ❖ Won a silver medal for indiv. épée and team épée at Sydney Olympics (2000).

HABSBURG, Elisabeth von (1837–1898). See Elizabeth of Bavaria.

HACHETTE, Jeanne (c. 1454–?). French military hero. Name variations: Jeanne Laisne, Lainé, Laine; Jeanne Fourquet. Born Jeanne Laisne, Lainé, or Fourquet, Nov 14, c. 1454, in Beauvais, France; date of death unknown; there is no precise information about family or origin; married Colin Pilon, a French bourgeois. ❖ Gained the sobriquet "Hachette" when she led a troop of French women armed with hatchets and swords against the Burgundian soldiers of Charles the Bold, duke of Burgundy, who were besieging Beauvais (June 27, 1472); was rewarded by the grateful King Louis XI. ❖ See also Georges Vallat, Jeanne Hachette (Abbeville, 1898); and Women in World History.

HACHIN-TRINQUET, Pascale (1958—). French fencer. Name variations: Pascale Trinquet. Born Aug 11, 1958, in France. ❖ Won a gold medal in team foil and a gold medal in individual foil at Moscow Olympics (1980) and a bronze medal in team foil at Los Angeles Olympics (1984).

HACK, Maria (1777–1844). English author of children's books. Born Maria Barton, Nov 10, 1777, in Carlisle, Cumberland, England; died Jan 4, 1844; dau. of Quakers; sister of Bernard Barton (poet and friend of Charles Lamb); married Stephen Hack (Chichester merchant), 1800; children: several. ❖ Following husband's death, moved to Southampton where she joined the Church of England; published popular books which were morally instructional, including Winter Evenings (1818), Grecian Stories (1819), and English Stories (1820, 1825).

HACKER, Marilyn (1942—). American poet. Born Nov 1942 in the Bronx, NY. ❖ Lesbian poet, whose writings focus on the relationships between women, include Separations (1976), Taking Notice (1980), Assumptions (1985), Love, Death and the Changing of the Seasons (1986), Going Back to the River (1990), Winter Numbers (1994), and Desesperanto: Poems 1990–2002 (2003); also translated Claire Malroux's Edge as well as Venus Khoury-Ghata's poetry published in Here There Was Once a Country (2001) and She Says (2003); edited The Kenyon Review (1990–94). Won the National Book Award for Presentation Piece (1975); won Lenore Marshall Poetry Prize (1999).

HACKETT, Frances (1891–1984). See Goodrich, Frances.

HACKETT, Jeanette (c. 1898–1979). American vaudeville dancer and choreographer. Born c. 1898, probably in New York, NY; died Aug 16, 1979, in New York, NY; m. John Steele (tenor). ❖ As a child, made vaudeville debut in Nora Bayes' starrer The Songs You Love where she performed hula dance (1907), and intermittently toured with brother Albert in their own act for 8 years; performed in other feature acts including Jules Garrison's After the Play (1908–10); performed solo dance act (late 1910s), before making official NYC debut at 18; launched Jeanette Hackett Chorus for which she created precision line dances; staged numerous acts for husband John Steele who introduced "A Pretty Girl Is Like a Melody" in the Ziegfeld Follies.

HACKETT, Joan (1942–1983). American actress and activist. Born Joan Ann Hackettm May 1, 1942, in New York, NY; died of cancer, Oct 8, 1983, in Encino, California; dau. of John (postal clerk) and Mary (Esposito) Hackett; graduate of St. Jean Baptiste School, NYC; studied acting with Mary Welch and at Lee Strasberg's Actors' Studio; m. Richard Mulligan (actor), Jan 3, 1966 (div. 1973). ❖ Made NY debut at Sheridan Square Playhouse in *A Clearing in the Woods* (1959); distinguished herself on stage as Chris in *Call Me by My Rightful Name* (1961), for which she received an Obie and the Vernon Rice Award, and in film as Dottie Renfrew in the movie adaptation of Mary McCarthy's *The Group*; successfully combined stage career with films, numerous tv appearances, and political activism, especially in regard to the women's movement; other films include *Will Penny* (1968), *Assignment to Kill* (1968), *Support Your Local Sheriff* (1969), *Rivals* (1972), *The Last of Sheila* (1973), *The Terminal Man* (1974), *Mackintosh and T.J.* (1975), *Treasure of Matecumbe* (1976) and *One Trick Pony* (1980). Nominated for Academy Award for *Only When I Laugh* (1981) and an Emmy for an episode of "Ben Casey" (1962). ❖ See also *Women in World History*.

HACKFORTH-JONES, Margaret (c. 1913—). See Drower, Margaret S.

HACKLEY, E. Azalia Smith (1867–1922). African-American singer, choir director, and advocate of African-American music and musicians. Born Emma Azalia Smith in Murfreesboro, TN, June 29, 1867; died in Detroit, Michigan, Dec 13, 1922; received a Bachelor of Music from University of Denver, 1900; m. Edwin Henry Hackley (lawyer and newspaper editor), 1894 (sep. 1909). ❖ Became music director of Episcopal Church of the Crucifixion, a black congregation in Philadelphia (1901); as a skilled choral director, organized the 100-member People's Chorus (later known as the Hackley Choral, 1904), which helped launch careers of a number of black performers, including contralto Marian Anderson and tenor Roland Hayes; set out to advance black music and musicians (1907), raising money through concerts and private solicitations to aid African-Americans who wanted to study abroad; began a series of lecture tours (1910); published a selection of her lectures in *The Colored Girl Beautiful* (1916); focused on traditional Negro folk music in later lectures; produced a series of community folk concerts in black churches and schools across US (1916). The E. Azalia Hackley Memorial Collection of Negro Music, Dance, and Drama was established in Detroit Public Library (1943). ❖ See also *Women in World History*.

HADAREAN, Vanda (1976—). Romanian gymnast. Born Vanda Maria Hadarean, May 3, 1976, in Cluj, Romania; m. Mariana Bagiu (basketball player). ❖ Placed 1st team all-around and 3rd all-around at Balkan championships and 3rd all-around at European championships (1992); at Barcelona Olympics, won a silver medal in team all-around (1992).

HADDING, Annette (1975—). German swimmer. Born Dec 3, 1975, in Germany. ❖ At Barcelona Olympics, won a bronze medal in 4 x 100-meter freestyle relay (1992).

HADDON, Eileen (1921–2003). South African journalist and activist. Born Mar 9, 1921, in Boksberg, South Africa; died July 6, 2003; attended University of Witswatersrand; m. Michael Haddon, 1942 (died 1996); children: Bryan (b. 1945), Timothy (b. 1948). ❖ Fought against segregation in South Africa and oppression in Rhodesia; with the advent of the apartheid era, moved to Southern Rhodesia with family (1948); with husband, established the Interracial Association (1950s) and supported the United Rhodesia Party; prepared papers on key issues for the National Democratic Party and nationalist movements; joined the staff of the progressive *Central African Examiner* (1960), becoming its editor (1962); after husband was imprisoned for 3 years by Smith's Rhodesia Front government, moved with family to Zambia (1969), where she worked as publications officer for University of Zambia (1971–77).

HADDON, Elizabeth (1680–1762). See Estaugh, Elizabeth Haddon.

HADEN, Sara (1897–1981). American screen actress. Born Nov 17, 1897, in Galveston, TX; died Sept 15, 1981, in Woodland Hills, California; dau. of Charlotte Walker (actress); m. Richard Abbott (actor), 1921 (div. 1948). ❖ Appeared on Broadway (1920s); made film debut in *Spitfire* (1934); appeared in over 70 films, including *Anne of Green Gables, Way Down East, Magnificent Obsession, Captain January, Little Miss Marker, Poor Little Rich Girl, The Shop Around the Corner* and *Woman of the Year*; also appeared in recurring role of Aunt Milly in "Andy Hardy" series.

HADEN-GUEST, Lady (b. 1958). See Curtis, Jamie Lee.

HADEWIJCH (fl. 13th c.). Flemish Christian beguine, mystic and writer-poet. Name variations: Hadewijch of Brabant; Hadewijch or Hadewych of Antwerp; Suster Hadewych; Adelwip. Pronunciation: HAD-e-vitch. Born c. 1200 in or near Antwerp in the duchy of Brabant (Belgium); died c. 1260. ❖ Became the mistress of a group of young beguines (women who lived a semi-religious life) and wrote a series of letters, poems, and accounts of her visions for their instruction; had her

authority called into question and her pupils sent away; possibly exiled from the community for her teachings, scholars speculate, and spent the rest of her life caring for others in a hospital or other service-oriented institution; wrote 31 Letters, 14 visions, 45 poems in stanzas, and 16 couplet poems which were published together in 1 volume, *The Complete Works of Hadewijch*. ❖ See also John Giles Milhaven, *Hadewijch and Her Sisters: Other Ways of Loving and Knowing* (SUNY, 1993); and *Women in World History*.

HADEWYCH OF ANTWERP or BRABANT (fl. 13th c.). See Hadewijch.

HADFIELD, Maria (1759–1838). See Cosway, Maria.

HADICE TURHAN (1627–1683). Sultana. Name variations: Turhana Sultana; Turkan Sultan. Probably born in Russia in 1627; died in Constantinople, 1683; consort of Ibrahim, Ottoman sultan (r. 1640–1648); children: Mohammed IV (1641–1691, also seen as Mahomet, Mehemmed, Mehmed, Mehmet, Mohammed, and Muhammed), Ottoman sultan (r. 1648–1687). ❖ After Kösem refused to relinquish the reins of power as valide sultan when Mohammed IV ascended to the throne, had her assassinated (1651) and ruled in the name of her son until her death in 1683, which ended the Reign of Women. ❖ See also *Women in World History*.

HADID, Zaha (1950—). Iraqi-born architect. Born Oct 31, 1950, in Baghdad, Iraq; dau. of Mohammed Hadid (politician, economist) and Wajeeha Sabonji; American University of Beirut, BS, 1971; graduate of Architectural Association School in London, 1977. ❖ Award-winning architect of modernist-deconstructivist school, moved to London to study; partnered with Rem Koolhaas and Elia Zenghelis at Office for Metropolitan Architecture (OMA); taught at Columbia, Yale, Harvard, University of Chicago, Hochschule füür Bildende Küünste in Hamburg, University of Applied Arts at Vienna; designed an apartment building at Eaton Place, London (1980), which won the Architectural Design Gold Medal (1982); came to international prominence with 1st prize at Peak Competition in Hong Kong (1982); opened her own office (1985); best known for designing Vitra Fire Station and the LFone Pavilion in Weil am Rhein, Germany (1993–99), housing project for IBA-Block 2, Berlin (1993), Cardiff Bay Opera House (1994), Mind Zone at Millennium Dome in London (1999), Center for Contemporary Arts, Rome (1999), Bergisel Ski-jump in Innsbruck, Austria (1999), and the Rosenthal Center for Contemporary Art in Cincinnati (2002); paintings and drawings included in permanent collections of Museum of Modern Art, Getty Center in Los Angeles, and Deutsches Architektur Museum in Frankfurt. Made fellow of American Institute of Architecture; named Commander of British Empire (2002); was the 1st woman to become laureate of the prestigious Pritzker Architecture Prize (2004).

HADING, Jane (1859–1933). French actress. Born Jeanne Alfrédine Tréfouret, Nov 25, 1859, at Marseilles, France; died Dec 31, 1933; dau. of an actor; married Victor Koning (1842–1894, manager of Gymnase theater), 1884 (div. 1887). ❖ One of the leading actresses of her day in France, America, and England, made 1st stage appearance at 3, as Little Blanche in *Le bossu*; performed in Algiers and Cairo; had an excellent voice and, on return to Marseilles, sang in operetta and acted in *Ruy Blas*; made Paris debut in *La Chaste Suzanne* at Palais Royal and appeared in an operetta at the Renaissance; enjoyed great success at the Gymnase in *Le Maître de forges* (1883); toured America with Benoît Coquelin (1888) and on her return furthered the success of Henri Lavedan's *Le Prince d'Aurec* at the Vaudeville; later repertoire included Alexandre Dumas *fils'* *Le Demi-monde* and *La Princesse Georges*, Alfred Capus' *La Châtelaine* (1902) and Maurice Donnay's *Retour de Jerusalem*.

HADITONO, Susi Susanti (1971—). See Susanti, Susi.

HADLEY, Jane (1911–1964). See Barkley, Jane Hadley.

HADWIG. Variant of Hedwig.

HADWISA. Variant of Avisa, Hadwig, or Hedwig.

HADWISA OF GLOUCESTER (c. 1167–1217). See Avisa of Gloucester.

HADWISA OF NORMANDY (d. 1034). See Hawise of Normandy.

HAEBLER, Ingrid (1926—). Austrian pianist. Born in Vienna, Austria, June 20, 1926. ❖ A specialist in the Austrian classical and Romantic school, has long been admired for her interpretations of Mozart and Haydn; has also championed the often neglected Schubert piano sonatas; became a member of the faculty of the Salzburg Mozarteum (1969). ❖ See also *Women in World History*.

HAESAERT, Clara (1924—). Flemish poet. Name variations: Claire Haesaert-Weyens; Claire Marie José Haesaert-Weyens. Born Mar 9, 1924, in Hasselt, Netherlands. ❖ Worked at Ministry of Education and Culture; co-founded literary journal *De Meridiaan* (1951–60) and Brussels Art Center, Taptoe; writings include *De overkant* (1953), *Omgekeerde volgorde* (1961), *Onwaarschijnlijk recht* (1967), *Medeplichtig* (1981), *Bevoorrechte getuige* (1986), *Levenslang het vermoeden* (1993) and *Voorbij de laatste vijver* (1995).

HAESEBROUCK, Ann (1963—). Belgian rower. Born Oct 18, 1963, in Belgium. ❖ At Los Angeles Olympics, won a bronze medal in single sculls (1984).

HAFFENDEN, Elizabeth (1906–1976). British costume designer. Name variations: Liz Haffenden. Born in Croydon, England, 1906; died 1976. ❖ Began designing costumes for British films (1933) and eventually became head of costume department at Gainsborough Studios; designed for both American and British films, and won Academy Awards for *Ben Hur* (1959) and *A Man for All Seasons* (1966); other films include *Beau Brummel* (1954), *Bhowani Junction* (1956), *Moby Dick* (1956), *The Amorous Adventures of Moll Flanders* (1965), *Half a Sixpence* (1967), *Chitty Chitty Bang Bang* (1968), *The Prime of Miss Jean Brodie* (1969) and *Fiddler on the Roof* (1971). ❖ See also *Women in World History*.

HAFSA (d. 1534). Ottoman sultana. Name variations: Hafsa Sultana; Hafsa Hatun. Died Mar 1534; possibly a Tatar princess from the Crimea, or a Circassian or Georgian woman from the Caucasus; consort of Selim I the Grim, Ottoman sultan (r. 1512–1520); children: Suleyman or Suleiman I the Magnificent (1494/95–1566), Ottoman sultan (r. 1520–1566); and daughters Sah and Hatice. ❖ Set a precedent for women's public buildings in the Ottoman Empire; shortly after son's accession to the throne, built the largest mosque complex ever constructed, with two minarets, an honor which had heretofore been reserved only for the sultan. ❖ See also *Women in World History*.

HAFSAH (fl. 7th c.). Wife of Muhammad. Name variations: Hafsa. Dau. of 'Umar ibn al-Khattab (who would succeed Muhammad as caliph 'Umar [634–644]). ❖ Widow who had lost her husband at the Battle of Badr, married Muhammad (625). ❖ See also "Wives of Muhammad" in *Women in World History*.

HAGAN, Ellen (1873–1958). Swedish feminist, journalist and speaker. Born 1873; died 1958; married to the governor of Gävleborg County. ❖ Devoting life to feminist causes, founded Uppsala Suffrage Society (1903) and served on Central Board of the Federation for Women's Suffrage (1903–22); after WWI, became president of Federation of Liberal Women in Sweden; was editor of women's journal *Tiderarvet* (1920s) and a member of the International Alliance Committee (1922–32); during WWII, worked as an executive with "Help for Norway." Awarded the Order of the Star of the North (1953).

HAGAR (fl. 3rd, 2nd, or 1st c. BCE). Biblical woman. Fl. in the 3rd, 2nd, or 1st century BCE; born in Egypt; children: (with Abraham also known as Abrahim) Ishmael. ❖ As related in Genesis, was the Egyptian slave of Sarah, wife of Abraham; since Sarah was unable to have children, was given by Sarah to Abraham, so that his line might continue; upon becoming pregnant, mocked Sarah for her barrenness; on being treated poorly by Sarah, ran away; was stopped by an angel who told her to return to Sarah and that she would give birth to a son and name him Ishmael, and that through Ishmael her descendants would be "too numerous to be counted"; returned to Sarah and Abraham and, in due course, gave birth to Ishmael; through her son, became the ancestress of all Arabs.

HAGE, Helen P. (1938—). See Chenoweth, Helen.

HAGEL, Hansel Mieth (1909–1998). See Mieth, Hansel.

HAGEL, Johanna M. (1909–1998). See Mieth, Hansel.

HAGEN, Birgit (1957—). West German field-hockey player. Born June 6, 1957, in Germany. ❖ At Los Angeles Olympics, won a silver medal in team competition (1984).

HAGEN, Jean (1923–1977). American stage and screen actress. Born Jean Shirley Verhagen, Aug 3, 1923, in Chicago, Illinois; died Aug 29, 1977, in Woodland Hills, California; m. Tom Seidel, 1947 (div. 1965); children: two. ❖ Began career on radio; made Broadway debut in *Swan Song* (1946), subsequently appearing in *Another Part of the Forest, Ghosts, Born Yesterday,* and *The Traitor*; films include *Side Street, Adam's Rib, Asphalt Jungle, Carbine Williams, The Big Knife, The Shaggy Dog, Sunrise at Campobello,* and *Dead Ringer*; appeared on television as Danny Thomas' original wife in "Make Room for Daddy" (1953–57); probably best remembered, and nominated for an Oscar, for her performance as Lina Lamont in *Singin' in the Rain*.

HAGEN, Nina (1955—). East German pop singer and actress. Born Nina Catherina Hagen, Mar 11, 1955, in East Berlin, Germany; dau. of Eva Maria Hagen (actress) and Hans Oliva (writer); children: Cosma Shiva Hagen and Otis. ❖ With Reinhard Lakomy's band, sang Tina Turner and Janis Joplin covers (1972); relocated to West Berlin (1976); formed Nina Hagen Band with other German performers and recorded successful debut album; appeared with Lene Lovich in film *Cha Cha* (1979); scored gold record with her group's 2nd German album *Unbehagen* (1979); gained US dance club success with Giorgio Moroder-produced album *Fearless* (1983); offered unusual covers of "Spirit in the Sky" and "My Way" on album *Nana Hagen in Ekstasy* (1985); released albums *Revolution Ballroom* (1993), *14 Friendly Abductions* (1996), and *Return of the Mother* (2000); was subject of Peter Sempel's documentary *Nina Hagen: Punk + Glory* (1999); emphasizes extraterrestrials and spirituality in work.

HAGEN, Uta (1919–2004). German-born actress and acting teacher. Pronunciation: OO-ta; Hagen rhymes with noggin. Born Uta Thyra Hagen, June 12, 1919, in Göttingen, Germany; died Jan 14, 2004, in New York, NY; dau. of Oskar Fran Leonard Hagen (professor of art history) and Thyra A. (Leisner) Hagen; attended Royal Academy of Dramatic Art, London, and University of Wisconsin, 1936–1937; m. José Ferrer (actor), Dec 8, 1938 (div. 1948); m. Herbert Berghof (actor, director, teacher), Jan 25, 1951 (died 1990); children: Leticia Ferrer (actress). ❖ One of America's first ladies of the theater, came to US (1925); joined Eva Le Gallienne's Civic Rep, playing Ophelia in *Hamlet* at Cape Playhouse (1937); made Broadway debut at 19, as Nina in Theatre Guild production of *The Seagull*; co-starred with 1st husband José Ferrer in several successful plays, including the comedy *Vickie* (1942) and *Othello* (1943), starring Paul Robeson; learned a new style of acting (1947) and began teaching at HB studios, which she would remain associated with until her death; appeared as Georgie in *The Country Girl* (1950), for which she won her 1st Tony Award; starred in *Saint Joan* (1951), directed by Margaret Webster; won a 2nd Tony for portrayal of Martha in *Who's Afraid of Virginia Woolf?* (1962); during 1950s, because of her liberal views and earlier relationship with Paul Robeson, was blacklisted, making it impossible for her to work in movies or tv; some 20 years later, finally ventured into films, appearing in *The Other* (1972), followed by *The Boys from Brazil* (1978) and *Reversal of Fortune* (1990); appeared off-Broadway in title role in *Mrs. Klein* (1995); set forth theories in 2 books, *Respect for Acting* (1973) and *A Challenge for the Actor* (1991), which have become standard references for students and professionals; also wrote *Love for Cooking* (1976). ❖ See also autobiography *Sources* (1983); and *Women in World History*.

HAGENBAUMER, Eva (1967—). German field-hockey player. Born Jan 1967 in Germany. ❖ At Barcelona Olympics, won a silver medal in team competition (1992).

HAGERUP, Inger (1905–1985). Norwegian poet, playwright, prose writer and children's author. Born in Bergen, Norway, 1905; died 1985; m. Anders Hagerup; children: Helge and Klaus (both writers). ❖ Worked as a governess in the far north of Norway, then moved to Oslo, where she earned her living as a secretary, proof-reader, and left-wing journalist; during German occupation of Norway, wrote the patriotic poem for which she is best remembered, "Aust-Vågøy, March 1941" which concerns German reprisals on local inhabitants after an Allied raid on Lofoten Islands; spent latter years of WWII in exile in Sweden; worked on the short-lived newspaper *Friheten* (Freedom), which was then the 2nd-largest newspaper in Norway, and on the women's periodical *Kvinnen og Tiden* (Women and Current Affairs, 1945–55); as a writer of children's poetry, followed the tradition of English nonsense verse; collaborating with Norwegian artist-illustrator Paul René Gauguin (grandson of Paul Gauguin), produced 3 classics; also published 3 volumes of autobiography (1960s).

HAGGARD, Lilias Rider. See Rider Haggard, Lilias.

HAGGE, Marlene Bauer (1934—). American golfer. Name variations: Marlene Bauer. Born Marlene Bauer, Feb 16, 1934, in Eureka, SD; younger sister of golfer Alice Bauer who was the 1st woman to win the L.A. Open. ❖ At 15, won the 1st USGA Junior Girls' championship, the Western Junior Girls' championship, the Helms Award, and was named Associated Press Athlete of the Year (1949); turned pro (1949); won her 1st LPGA tournament, the Sarasota Open (1952), in what was to be the beginning of 25 official career victories; won 7 LPGA titles and finished among the top 10 in earnings for 8 seasons. ❖ See also *Women in World History*.

HAGGITH (fl. 1000 BCE). **Biblical woman.** The 5th wife of David, Israelite king (r. 1010–970 BCE); children: Adonijah.

HAGGRÉN, Maria (1880–1943). *See Jotuni, Maria*.

HAGIWARA, Yoko (1920—). **Japanese novelist and essayist.** Born 1920 in Tokyo, Japan; dau. of Hagiwara Sakutaro (well-known poet). ❖ Works, which often explore her family relationships, include *My Father, Hagiwara Sakutaro* (1959), *A Flower in Heaven–Miyoshi Tatsuji* (1966), and *The House Twisted by Nettles* (1973). Won Essayist Club Prize (1960), Tamura Toshiko Prize, and Shincho Prize for Literature.

HAGLUND, Maria (1972—). **Swedish kayaker.** Born May 6, 1972, in Sweden. ❖ At Barcelona Olympics, won a bronze medal in K4 500 meters (1992).

HAGMAN, Lucina (1853–1946). **Finnish educator.** Born 1853; died 1946. ❖ Ahead of her time as a feminist and a champion of the co-educational movement, was head of a co-educational school in Finland (1886–99); founded the Finnish New School in Helsinki (1899), remaining its director until 1938; also founded and was chair of Finland's Women's Association and served in Parliament (1907–14); became an honorary professor (1928); writings include bio-bibliographies of Fredrika Bremer and Minna Canth (*Minna Canthin elämänkerta*, 1906–11).

HAGN, Johanna. **German judoka.** Born in Germany. ❖ Won a bronze medal for +72 kg heavyweight at Atlanta Olympics (1996); won World championship (1997).

HAGOOD, Margaret (1907–1963). **American sociologist.** Name variations: Margaret Loyd Jarman; Margaret Loyd Jarman Hagood or Margaret Jarman Hagood; Marney Hagood. Born Margaret Loyd Jarman, Oct 26, 1907, in Newton County, Georgia; died Aug 13, 1963, in San Diego, California; dau. of Lewis Wilson Jarman and Laura Harris (Martin) Jarman; m. Middleton Howard Hagood, 1926 (div. 1936); children: 1 dau. (b. 1927). ❖ Taught at National Park Seminary in College Park, Maryland (early 1930s); joined Institute for Research in Social Sciences at University of North Carolina (UNC) as graduate fellow (1935), and after graduation (1937), joined sociology department at UNC and became research associate at Institute; authored *Mothers of the South* (1939) and *Statistics for Sociologists* (1941); with sociologist Harriet Herring, and photographers Marion Post and Dorothea Lange, created photographic exhibit of farming life at UNC (1940); worked at US Department of Agriculture's Bureau for Agricultural Economics (1942–52) and became head of Farm Population and Rural Life Branch of Agricultural Marketing Service (1952); became president of Population Association of America (1954) and of Rural Sociological Society (1956); retired (1962). Created "level-of-living index" for all US counties.

HAHN, Anna Marie (1906–1938). **German-American serial killer.** Name variations: Arsenic Anna. Born 1906 in Germany; executed in Ohio, Dec 7, 1938; m. Phillip Hahn, 1924; children: 1 son. ❖ Immigrated to US with family, settling in Cincinnati (1929); a self-proclaimed nurse, took care of elderly men; killed them by poison for their money; convicted of the murder of 78-year-old Jacob Wagner, was the 1st woman to be executed in the electric chair in Ohio (Dec 7, 1938); may have been responsible for as many as 15 murders.

HAHN, Birgit (1958—). **West German field-hockey player.** Born June 29, 1958, in Germany. ❖ At Los Angeles Olympics, won a silver medal in team competition (1984).

HAHN, Dorothy (1876–1950). **American organic chemist.** Born Dorothy Anna Hahn, April 9, 1876, in Philadelphia, PA; died Dec 10, 1950, in South Hadley, Massachusetts; dau. of Carl J. Hahn and Mary (Beaver) Hahn; Yale University, PhD, 1916; had 2 longtime companions: Margaret Morriss of Pembroke College, Brown University, and Dorothy Foster of Mount Holyoke English department. ❖ Served as professor of chemistry and biology at Pennsylvania College for Women in Pittsburgh (1899–1906); was professor of biology at Kindergarten College, also in Pittsburgh (1904–06); studied organic chemistry at University of Leipzig, in Germany (1906–07); served as professor of organic chemistry at Mount Holyoke College (1916–41). Authored or served as adviser for more than 30 published papers in *Journal of the American Chemical Society*; co-authored with Arthur M. Comey, A

Dictionary of Chemical Solubilities, Inorganic (1921), and with Treat B. Johnson, a translation and enlargement of Ferdinand Henrich's *Theories of Organic Chemistry* (1922).

HAHN, Emily (1905–1997). **American writer.** Name variations: Mickey Hahn. Born in St. Louis, Missouri, Jan 14, 1905; died in New York, NY, Feb 18, 1997; dau. of Isaac Newton Hahn and Hannah (Schoen) Hahn; was the 1st woman at University of Wisconsin to obtain a degree in mining engineering; m. Charles Boxer; children: Carola Boxer Vecchio (b. 1941); Amanda Boxer. ❖ A confirmed world traveler and cosmopolitan writer, 1st taught geology at Hunter College in NY (1929); became a regular contributor to *The New Yorker*; published 1st book, *Seductio Ad Absurdum* (1930); sailed for equatorial Africa (1930); published diary and notes of her stay in a Pygmy region of Belgian Congo (now Republic of Congo) as *Congo Solo* (1933); published 1st novel, *Beginner's Luck* (1931); visited Shanghai (1935), settling there as the permanent China correspondent of *The New Yorker*, wrote 10 books on China, including 2 children's books, 2 cookbooks, and *The Soong Sisters* (1941); published 54 books ranging from novels (5 in all), histories (of love, bohemianism in America, and the Philippines), biographies (including studies of Fanny Burney and Mabel Dodge Luhan), and children's books (11 in all, including *Around the World with Nellie Bly*, 1959); became increasingly interested in zoology, especially primates, producing a number of books in that area, including *Eve and the Apes*, which told of women who owned or worked with apes, including Belle Benchley. ❖ See also Ken Cuthbertson, *Nobody Said Not to Go: The Life, Loves, and Adventures of Emily Hahn* (Faber & Faber, 1998); and *Women in World History*.

HAHN, Helen or Helena Andreyevna Fadeyev (1814–1842). *See Gan, Elena*.

HAHN, Helene B. (c. 1940—). **American attorney and motion-picture executive.** Born c. 1940 in New York, NY; Hofstra University, BA; Loyola University, JD, 1975. ❖ Served as instructor in entertainment law at Loyola University (LA) and attorney with ABC-TV; admitted to the bar (1975); became staff attorney in legal department of Paramount Pictures (1977), then senior vice president (by 1983); became senior vice president of business and legal affairs for Walt Disney (1984), the 1st woman to head business and legal areas of a major motion picture studio; moved to Dreamworks (1994).

HAHN, Madame (1814–1842). *See Gan, Elena*.

HAHN, Yelena Andreyevna Fadeyev (1814–1842). *See Gan, Elena*.

HAHN-HAHN, Ida, Countess von (1805–1880). **German author.** Name variations: Gräfin Hahn-Hahn; Countess Hahn-Hahn. Born Ida Marie Luise Sophie Friederike Gustave von Hahn at Tressow, in Mecklenburg-Schwerin, Germany, June 22, 1805; died in Mainz, Germany, Jan 12, 1880; dau. of Graf (Count) Karl Friedrich von Hahn (1782–1857); m. cousin Count Adolf von Hahn, 1826 (div. 1829). ❖ Published 1st novel *Aus der Gesellschaft* (1838); produced novels on subjects similar to those of contemporary George Sand, but they were less critical of social institutions and involved the aristocracy; saw her patrician airs parodied by Fanny Lewald in *Diogena* (1847); turned to Catholicism (1850) and justified her conversion in the polemical work *Von Babylon nach Jerusalem* (*From Babylon to Jerusalem*, 1851); retired to a convent at Angers (1852), but soon left, taking up residence at Mainz where she founded a nunnery; lived there without joining the order and continued to write; for many years, wrote novels that were popular among the aristocracy, including *Sigismund Forster* (1843), *Cecil* (1844), *Sibylle* (1846) and *Maria Regina* (1860). ❖ See also *Women in World History*.

HAIG, Emma (1898–1939). **American theatrical ballet dancer.** Born Jan 21, 1898, in Philadelphia, PA; died June 10, 1939, in Beverly Hills, California. ❖ Made NY debut in *Passing Show of 1914*; was among most successful ballet dance specialists on Broadway; performed at Winter Garden in *The Midnight Girl* and *The Whirl of the World*; appeared in *Ziegfeld Follies of 1916*, where she danced as Anna Pavlova in satire of Ballet Russe, and in *Miss 1917, Hitchy-Koo of 1918* and *Music Box Revue of 1920*; appeared mainly in soubrette roles thereafter, including in *Our Nell* (1923), *Tell Me More* (1925), and *The Girl Friend*, in London (1927).

HAIG, Margaret (1883–1958). *See Rhondda, Margaret*.

HAIGNERÉ, Claudie (1957—). **French astronaut.** Name variations: Claudie Haignere; Claudie André-Deshays or Andre-Deshays. Born Claudie André-Deshays, May 13, 1957, in Le Creusot, France; graduate of Faculté de Médicin and Faculté des Sciences; certificates in biology and sports medicine, 1981, aviation and space medicine, 1982, and rheumatology, 1984; diploma in biomechanics, 1986, and PhD in neuroscience, 1992; married Jean-Pierre Haigneré (astronaut); 1 daughter. ❖ Rheumatologist and expert in neuroscience, became the 1st Frenchwoman in space (1996), serving as the crew engineer during 10 days on Mir, studying the effect of weightlessness on the human body; became the 1st woman to qualify as a Soyuz Return Commander (1999); with 2 others, delivered the Soyuz TM-33 to the International Space Station (Oct 2001); appointed France's Minister for Research and New Technologies (June 2002).

HAINAULT, countess of.
See Margaret of Alsace (c. 1135–1194).
See Maria of Champagne (c. 1180–1203).

HAINAULT AND HOLLAND, countess of.
See Philippine of Luxemburg (d. 1311).
See Jeanne of Valois (c. 1294–1342).
See Joanna of Brabant (1322–1406).
See Margaret of Holland (d. 1356).
See Maud Plantagenet (1335–1362).
See Margaret of Burgundy (c. 1376–1441).
See Jacqueline of Hainault (1401–1436).

HAINES, Helen (1872–1961). American librarian. Born Helen Elizabeth Haines, Feb 9, 1872, in New York, NY; died Aug 26, 1961, in Altadena, California; dau. of Benjamin Reeves Haines and Mary (Hodges) Haines. ❖ Joined publisher Richard R. Bowker as assistant (1892), becoming managing editor of *Library Journal* (1896); worked with American Library Association (ALA), becoming recorder (1896) and 2nd vice president (1906); resigned from *Journal* and ALA because of ill-health (1908) and moved to California; wrote book reviews for *Pasadena News,* then *Pasadena Star-News* (1910–50); taught training class at Los Angeles Public Library (beginning 1914); joined faculty of School of Library Science at University of Southern California (USC); wrote *Living With Books: The Art of Book Selection* (1935) and *What's in a Novel?* (1942); taught at USC and summer classes at Columbia University (1937–50); helped found Intellectual Freedom Committee of California Library Association (1940) and served as its chair for 10 years. Received ALA's Lippincott Award (1951).

HAINES, Janine (1945–2004). Australian politician. Born May 8, 1945, in Tanunda, South Australia, Australia; died Nov 20, 2004, in Adelaide, SA, from a long-standing neurological condition; attended Adelaide University; married Ian Haines; children: Bronwyn and Melanie. ❖ The 1st Australian Democrat senator (1977–78), was later appointed leader of the Australian Democrats (1986), the 1st female leader of an Australian parliamentary political party; became the most successful third-party leader in Australian history (1990), winning 12.6% support for the Democrats; helped push the landmark Sex Discrimination Act; wrote *Suffrage to Sufferance: 100 Years of Women in Politics.* Became a Member of the Order of Australia (2001).

HAINISCH, Marianne (1839–1936). Austrian feminist and founder. Born Marianne Perger in Baden bei Wien, Lower Austria, Mar 25, 1839; died in Vienna, May 5, 1936; dau. of Josef Perger; attended an elite finishing school, Vienna's Institut Betty Fröhlich; m. Michael Hainisch; children: Marie Hainisch; Michael Hainisch (1858–1940, 1st president of Republic of Austria, 1920–28); Wolfgang Hainisch. ❖ Doyenne of the Austrian women's movement, who was a champion of higher education for women and a leader of the world peace movement; began to view the issue of the economic and social advancement of women in terms of more basic reforms, particularly in the area of women's education; called for the creation of grammar schools for girls (1870); campaigned to create equal opportunities for Austrian women in both secondary and higher education; represented Austrian women at international women's conference in London (1899); became the acknowledged leader of the Austrian women's movement; a political moderate, rejected radical feminism as well as the class-warfare ideology and Marxist militancy of the emerging Social Democratic movement; became president of League of Austrian Women's Associations (Bund österreichischer Frauenvereine, 1902), an umbrella organization that by 1914 could boast of 90 constituent groups with 40,000 members; as a pacifist, called on members of the League's constituent organizations to render humanitarian assistance on all levels during WWI; retired from full-time leadership of League of Austrian Women's Associations (1918); announced the founding of the Austrian Women's Party (Österreichische Frauenpartei, 1929). ❖ See also *Women in World History.*

HAISLETT, Nicole (1972—). American swimmer. Born Dec 16, 1972, in St. Petersburg, FL; graduate of University of Florida in jouralism, 1997. ❖ At Barcelona Olympics, won gold medals in 200-meter freestyle, 4x100-meter freestyle relay, and 4x100-meter medley relay (1992); was also 5-time US champion and won the 100-meter freestyle event at World championships (1991). Received the Honda-Broderick award as the nation's top collegiate female swimmer (1994).

HAJKOVA, Jirina (1954—). Czech field-hockey player. Born Jan 31, 1954, in Czechoslovakia. ❖ At Moscow Olympics, won a silver medal in team competition (1980).

HAKANSON, Ulla (1937—). Swedish equestrian. Born Nov 1937 in Sweden. ❖ Won a bronze medal at Munich Olympics (1972) and a bronze medal at Los Angeles Olympics (1984), both in team dressage.

HALABY, Lisa (b. 1951). See Noor, al-Hussein.

HALAMOVÁ, Masa (1908–1995). Slovak poet. Name variations: Masa Halamova. Born Aug 28, 1908 in Blatnici, Slovakia; died July 17, 1995 in Bratislava. ❖ Influenced by traditional oral poetry, Slovak symbolism, and proletarian poetry, wrote *Dar* (The Present, 1929), *Červený mak* (The Red Poppy, 1932), and *Smrt' tvoju žijem* (I Am Your Living Death, 1966); also translated works from Russian, Czech, and Serbian.

HALBERT, Kate (d. 1913). See Wyllie, Kate.

HALBSGUTH, Ruth (1916—). German swimmer. Born Dec 9, 1916, in Germany. ❖ At Berlin Olympics, won a silver medal in 4x100-meter freestyle relay (1936).

HALCOMBE, Edith Stanway (1844–1903). New Zealand painter, community leader, and farmer. Name variations: Edith Stanway Swainson. Born Edith Stanway Swainson, on April 27, 1844, in Wellington, New Zealand; died c. June 14, 1903, at mouth of Waitotara River, New Zealand; dau. of William Swainson (naturalist and artist) and Anne (Grasby) Swainson; m. Arthur William Follett Halcombe, 1863 (died 1900); children: 8. ❖ Paintings and drawings depict the changing landscape of the bush from wilderness to grazing land and townland (1860s); provided nursing services to new immigrants and worked to establish community institutions (1870s); acquired and developed herd of Jersey cows, which contributed to dairy industry in New Zealand. ❖ See also *Dictionary of New Zealand Biography* (Vol. 2).

HALDANE, Charlotte (1894–1969). British novelist and journalist. Name variations: (pseudonym) Charlotte Franklyn. Born Charlotte Franken in Sydenham, London, England, April 27, 1894; died in London, Mar 16, 1969; dau. of Joseph Franken and Mathilde (Saarbach) Franken; had a sister Elizabeth; niece-in-law of Elizabeth Sanderson Haldane (1862–1937); m. Jack Burghes, 1918; m. J(ohn) B(urdon) S(anderson) Haldane (1892–1964, geneticist and biochemist), 1926; children: (1st m.) Ronald John McLeod Burghes (b. 1919). ❖ Significant personage in modern Britain's intellectual and cultural history, remains best known for her 1st novel, *Man's World* (1926), a dystopia in which the state advances its goals, namely the progressive development of the white race, by highjacking scientific advances for its patriarchal, nationalist and racist imperatives; during WWI, published 1st short story in *The Bystander* (1916); worked as social editor and freelance reporter for *Daily Express* and *Sunday Express* (1919); one of the 1st newswomen on Fleet Street, was known for her well-argued articles championing married women who like herself carried the burden of supporting war-wounded husbands and young children; published *Motherhood and Its Enemies* (1928); with 2nd husband, became increasingly active in British Communist Party (1933); published novels, including the essentially autobiographical *Youth Is a Crime* (1934); during WWII, was the 1st British woman war correspondent to be assigned to the Russian front, later publishing *Russian Newsreel: An Eye-Witness Account of the Soviet Union at War* (1942); on return to England, severed ties to British Communist Party, unlike husband; succeeded George Orwell as "talks producer" in Indian Section of BBC Eastern Service (1943); worked for BBC well into the 1950s; published a life of Marcel Proust (1951); wrote a number of finely crafted biographical studies, including well-received volumes on Marie d'Agoult, Mozart, Alfred de Musset, and Madame de Maintenon. ❖ See also autobiography *Truth Will Out* (1951); Judith Adamson, *Charlotte Haldane: Woman Writer in a Man's World* (Macmillan, 1998); and *Women in World History.*

HALDANE, Elizabeth S. (1862–1937). Scottish philosopher and social worker. Born Elizabeth Sanderson Haldane, May 27, 1862; died Dec 24, 1937; dau. of Robert Haldane and Mary Elizabeth Burdon-Sanderson; granddau. of James Alexander Haldane (1768–1851, religious writer);

sister of J(ohn) S(cott) Haldane (1860–1936, physiologist and philosopher) and Richard Burdon, Viscount Haldane (1856–1928, diplomat, lawyer, and philosopher); aunt of J(ohn) B(urdon) S(anderson) Haldane (1892–1964, geneticist), Charlotte Haldane (1894–1969), and novelist Naomi Mitchison (1897–1999). ❧ After studying nursing and working under Octavia Hill, became vice-chair of territorial nursing service; was also manager for some years of Edinburgh Royal Infirmary; politically active as a lifelong liberal, became the 1st woman justice of the peace in Scotland (1920); while known for her nursing work and for having advanced the field of social welfare (she established and supported the Auchterarder Institute and Library), is particularly known for her contributions to philosophy; despite lack of university training, published several biographies and translations of philosophy (her translation with Frances Simon of *Hegel's Lectures on the History of Philosophy* is still the standard); also wrote *Descartes: His Life and Times* (1905), which was probably responsible for her receiving the 1st honorary LLD given to a woman by St. Andrew's University (1911). ❧ See also memoir *From One Century to Another: The Reminiscences of Elizabeth S. Haldane* (Maclehose, 1937).

HALDIMAND or HALDIMOND, Jane (1769–1858). *See Marcet, Jane.*

HALE, Barbara (1921—). American actress. Born April 18, 1921, in DeKalb, Illinois; m. Bill Williams (actor), 1946 (died 1992); children: Jody, Juanita and William Katt (actor). ❧ Appeared as Della Street in tv series "Perry Mason" (1957–66); films include *First Yank into Tokyo, The Boy with Green Hair, The Window, Jolson Sings Again, And Baby Makes Three, Lorna Doone, A Lion Is in the Streets, Unchained, Airport* and *Big Wednesday.* Won an Emmy (1959).

HALE, Binnie (1899–1984). English comedic actress and revue star. Born Beatrice Mary Hale-Monro, May 22, 1899, in Liverpool, England; died Jan 10, 1984, in Hastings, England; dau. of Belle Reynolds Hale and J. Robert Hale (actor); sister of actor Sonnie Hale (1902–1959); sister-in-law of Evelyn Laye, then Jessie Matthews; m. Jack Raine (div.). ❧ Made London stage debut in *Follow the Crowd* (1916); other plays include *Houp La!, Fair and Warmer, The Kiss Call, Just Fancy, Jumble Sale, My Nieces, The Dippers, Katinka, Puppets, The Odd Spot, No No Nanette, Sunny, Nippy, Bow Bells, Crazy Month, Home and Beauty, Magyar Melody* and *One Two Three*; made film debut in *This is the Life* (1933), followed by *The Phantom Light, Hyde Park Corner, Love from a Stranger* and *Take a Chance.*

HALE, Clara (1905–1992). African-American social activist and child-care worker. Name variations: Mother Hale; Clara McBride. Born Clara McBride, April 1, 1905, in Philadelphia, PA; died Dec 18, 1992, in New York, NY; graduated from high school in Philadelphia; m. Thomas Hale (died 1932); children: Lorraine Hale (executive director of Hale House); Nathan Hale; Kenneth Hale. ❧ Devoted most of her life to the disenfranchised mothers and children of New York City's Harlem, 1st as the foster mother of 40, and then as the founder of Hale House, a home for babies, many born addicted to drugs and alcohol and, later, those born HIV-positive. Received honorary doctorate in humane letters from John Jay College of Criminal Justice. ❧ See also *Women in World History.*

HALE, Ellen Day (1855–1940). American painter and printmaker. Born Ellen Day Hale, 1855, in Worcester, Massachusetts; died 1940; dau. of Edward Everett Hale (author and cleric) and Emily Baldwin Perkins; sister of Philip Leslie Hale and sister-in-law of Lilian Westcott Hale (both painters); grandniece of Harriet Beecher Stowe; granddau. of Sarah Preston Hale (writer and translator) and niece of Susan Hale (writer and painter) and Lucretia Peabody Hale (writer); studied with William Rimmer, William Morris Hunt and Helen Knowlton; attended Pennsylvania Academy of Fine Arts, 1878; lived with Gabrielle Clements (artist). ❧ Had 1st major exhibition at Centennial Exposition in Philadelphia (1876); studied in France (1881–82); exhibited at the Royal Academy in London (1882); works also exhibited at Chicago Columbian Exposition (1893) and Appalachian Exposition (1910), among others; wrote *A History of Art* (1888); while father was chaplain of US Senate (1904–09), served as his hostess in Washington DC.

HALE, Georgia (1905–1985). American silent-film actress. Born June 24, 1905, in St. Joseph, Missouri; died June 7, 1985, in Hollywood, CA. ❧ Starred in Josef von Sternberg's *The Salvation Hunters* (1925), followed by her most memorable role, the subject of Charlie Chaplin's hallucinations in *The Gold Rush*; also appeared as Myrtle Wilson in *The Great Gatsby* (1926); retired from screen with advent of sound.

HALE, Keron (1873–1945). *See Lyttelton, Edith Joan.*

HALE, Lilian Westcott (1881–1963). American painter. Born Lilian Westcott, 1881, in Hartford, Connecticut; died 1963; sister-in-law of Ellen Day Hale (painter); studied at Hartford Art School and School of the Museum of Fine Arts in Boston; m. Philip Leslie Hale (painter and critic); children: Nancy Hale (1908–1988, writer). ❧ Influential member of the Boston School, exhibited in major shows throughout US; best known for her charcoal, pencil and silverpoint drawings; paintings include *The Convalescent* (1906) and *Lavender and Old Ivory* (1915), *Child with Yarn* (1923) and *The Sailor Boy*; also painted portraits, still lifes and landscapes. Won gold medal at Panama-Pacific Exhibition (1915).

HALE, Louise Closser (1872–1933). American actress and author. Name variations: Louise Closser. Born Louise Closser on Oct 13, 1872, in Chicago, Illinois; died of heat prostration, July 26, 1933, in Los Angeles, CA; attended American Academy of Dramatic Arts in NY and Emerson College in Boston; m. Walter Hale (actor and artist), Aug 1899 (died 1917). ❧ One of the most popular character actresses on US stage, made debut in *In Old Kentucky* in Detroit (1894); had Broadway success in *Candida* (1903); made London debut in *Mrs. Wiggs of the Cabbage Patch* in her most popular role as Miss Hazy (1907); published 1st novel *A Motor Car Divorce* (1906); other writings include *Her Soul and Her Body* (novel, 1912), *We Discover New England* (travel book, 1915), and *An American's London* (travel book, 1920); appeared in such films as *The Hole in the Wall* (1929), *Daddy Long Legs* (1931), *Platinum Blonde* (1931), *Rasputin and the Empress* (1932), *Shanghai Express* (1932), and *Dinner at Eight* (1933).

HALE, Lucretia Peabody (1820–1900). American writer. Born Sept 2, 1820, in Boston, MA; died June 12, 1900, in Belmont, MA; 2nd dau. and 3rd of 11 children (7 of whom survived infancy) of Nathan Hale (lawyer and owner-editor of *Boston Daily Advertiser*) and Sarah Preston (Everett) Hale (writer); sister of writer Edward Everett Hale (1822–1909) and artist Susan Hale (1833–1910); aunt of Ellen Day Hale (painter); attended Susan Whitney's dame school; attended Elizabeth Palmer Peabody's school; graduated from George B. Emerson School for Young Ladies; never married; no children. ❧ A descendent of patriot Nathan Hale, grew up in a distinguished literary family; spent much time at home due to ill health; collaborated with brother Edward Everett Hale on 1st novel, *Margaret Percival in America* (1850); when family fell upon hard times (1851), turned to writing in earnest; began publishing articles in *Atlantic Monthly* (1858); over the next several years, produced a novel, *Struggle for Life* (1861), and several books of devotional readings; gained reputation with her whimsical sketches about the Peterkins, beginning with "That Lady Who Put Salt in Her Coffee," published in *Our Young Folks* (April 1868); eventually filled 2 books with subsequent stories, *The Peterkin Papers* (1880) and *The Last of the Peterkins* (1886), both of which were extremely popular; became involved in various educational and charitable causes. ❧ See also *Women in World History.*

HALE, Mamie O. (1911–c. 1968). African-American nurse and midwife. Name variations: Mamie Odessa Hale. Born 1911 in Pennsylvania; died c. 1968. ❧ Developed innovative training programs for lay midwives that greatly decreased African-American maternal mortalities in rural Arkansas; studied at Tuskegee School of Nurse-Midwifery for Colored Nurses in Alabama; was an Arkansas State Board of Health public health nurse (1942–45) for the Crittendon County Health Department; created programs for granny midwives (experienced midwives with no formal training) as the midwife consultant for the Arkansas Health Department's Maternal and Child Health Division (1945–50); taught 7-session midwifery courses and granted certificates in 4 Arkansas state counties; advocated the importance of public support for midwives.

HALE, Maria Selina (1864–1951). New Zealand tailor, labor activist, government official. Born on May 23, 1864, in Glasgow, Scotland; died on Mar 5, 1951, in Waitati, New Zealand; dau. of Joseph Hale and Margaret (Forrest) Hale. ❧ After 4-year apprenticeship, was employed by merchant tailor; active in Dunedin Tailoresses' Union from 1898, elected secretary of national federation of tailoresses' unions (1901); helped to prepare cases for arbitration, beginning 1900; managed Dunedin office of Department of Labor's Women's Branch (1908); advocated for domestic training program for women; worked as factory inspector for Dunedin (1919). ❧ See also *Dictionary of New Zealand Biography* (Vol. 3).

HALE, Mother (1905–1992). *See Hale, Clara.*

HALE, Nancy (1908–1988). American novelist and short-story writer. Born 1908; died 1988; dau. of Philip Leslie Hale and Lilian Westcott Hale (both painters); niece of Ellen Day Hale (painter). ❖ Studied art in Boston, MA, later wrote for *Vogue* magazine and *The New Yorker,* and was assistant editor for *Vanity Fair;* became 1st woman reporter at *New York Times* (1935); works include *The Young Die Good* (1932), *Prodigal Woman* (1942), *The Sign of Jonah* (1950), *Dear Beast* (1959), *The Pattern of Perfection* (1960), *The Life in the Studio* (1969), *Mary Cassatt* (1975) and *The Night of the Hurricane* (1978).

HALE, Ruth (1886–1934). American journalist and women's rights advocate. Born 1886 in Rogersville, TN; died Sept 18, 1934, in New York, NY; dau. of Richard Hale and Annie Riley Hale; attended Hollins Institute in Roanoke, Virginia, and Drexel Academy of Fine Arts in Philadelphia; m. Heywood Campbell Broun (1888–1939, columnist), June 6, 1917 (div. Nov 17, 1933); children: Heywood Hale Broun (1918–2001, writer and tv commentator). ❖ At 18, became journalist with Hearst Bureau in Washington, DC; served as drama critic and sports writer for *The Philadelphia Public Ledger,* writer for *The New York Times* (1915–16); during WWI, was a correspondent for Paris edition of *The Chicago Tribune;* was on editorial staff of *Equal Rights,* as drama critic for *Vogue* and *Vanity Fair;* founded the Lucy Stone League (1920) which fought on behalf of married women's rights to use their maiden names.

HALE, Sarah Josepha (1788–1879). American novelist, poet, editor, and women's-rights advocate. Name variations: Used "Cornelia" as a pseudonym very early in her publishing career; sometimes signed articles "S.J.H." or "The Lady Editor." Born Sarah Josepha Buell, Oct 24, 1788, in Newport, New Hampshire; died April 30, 1879, in Philadelphia, PA; dau. of Gordon and Martha (Whitlesey) Buell (farmers and innkeepers); m. David Hale, Oct 23, 1813 (died 1822); children: David (b. 1815); Horatio (b. 1817); Frances Ann (b. 1819); Sarah Josepha (called Josepha, b. 1820); William (b. 1822). ❖ The editor of *Godey's Lady's Book,* the most popular American magazine of the mid-19th century, rose to national fame and influence while maintaining her belief in a separate sphere for women in American life, while staunchly supporting women's education and property rights; served as editor of *The Ladies' Magazine* in Boston (1828–36); published the volume of children's verse, *Poems for Our Children* (1830), that contained the poem for which she is best-remembered, "Mary's Lamb" ("Mary had a little lamb . . ."); was editor of *Juvenile Miscellany* in Boston (1834–36); was editor of *Godey's Lady's Book* in Philadelphia (1837–87); pushed to make Thanksgiving a formally recognized holiday (1846); published 900-page women's biographical dictionary (1853); edited more than 30 children's books, household advice manuals, and volumes of verse, including *Flora's Interpreter; or, The American Book of Flowers and Sentiments* (1832) and *The Ladies' Wreath: A Selection from the Female Poetic Writers of England and America* (1837). ❖ See also Ruth E. Finley, *The Lady of Godey's: Sarah Josepha Hale* (Lippincott, 1931); Patricia Okker, *Our Sister Editors: Sarah J. Hale and the Tradition of Nineteenth-Century American Women Editors* (U. of Georgia Press, 1995); and *Women in World History.*

HALE, Sarah Preston (1796–1866). American writer, translator and columnist. Born Sarah Preston Everett, 1796, in Dorchester, Massachusetts; died 1866; sister of Edward Everett (1794–1865, Unitarian minister, member of US House of Representatives, 1825–35, and US senate, 1852–53, governor of Massachusetts, 1836–40, and president of Harvard); m. Nathan Hale (lawyer and owner-editor of *Boston Daily Advertiser*), 1815; children: 11, including Lucretia Peabody Hale (writer, 1820–1900), Edward Everett Hale (writer, 1822–1909), Charles Hale (politician and diplomat, 1831–1882) and Susan Hale (painter, 1833–1910). ❖ With husband, published the *Boston Daily Advertiser.* ❖ See also Diaries, 1850–1862, in Sophia Smith Collection at Smith College.

HALE, Sue Sally (1937–2003). American polo player. Born Sue Sally Jones, 1937; grew up in Southern California; died April 29, 2003, at her ranch in Coachella, California; dau. of Grover Jones (1893–1940, screenwriter) and Susan Avery (ballerina); stepdau. of Richard Talmadge (stuntman and actor); m. Alex Hale (div. 1976); children: son Trails Hale; daughters Dawn Hale, Stormie Hale (polo player) and Sunny Hale (top-ranked polo player). ❖ Broke American polo's gender barrier by gaining membership in the US Polo Association, the sport's national governing body (1972), having competed in matches for 2 decades as A. Jones while disguised as a man; coached polo teams at Cal Poly–San Luis Obispo and at El Toro Marine Corps Air Station in Santa Ana.

HALE, Susan (1833–1910). American essayist and lecturer. Born 1833 in Boston, MA; died in 1910; youngest of 11 children of Nathan Hale (editor and publisher) and Sarah Preston (Everett) Hale (translator); sister of writers Edward Everett Hale (1822–1909) and Lucretia Peabody Hale (1820–1900). ❖ Began reviewing books at 17 and wrote reviews, essays, and newspaper travel letters throughout life; writings include *A Family Flight Through Spain* (1883), *Self-Instructive Lessons in Painting* (1885), *The Story of Mexico* (1889) and *Men and Manners of the Eighteenth Century* (1898). ❖ See also *Letters of Susan Hale* (1918).

HALE, Una (1922–2005). Australian lyric soprano. Born Nov 18, 1922, in Adelaide, Australia; died Mar 4, 2005; dau. of Unitarian minister; attended Royal College of Music; m. Martin Carr (stage director), 1960; children: 2 sons. ❖ Joined Carl Rosa Opera Co. and was featured in such roles as Marguerite in *Faust,* Violetta in *La traviata,* Micaela in *Carmen,* Mimi in *La bohème* and Donna Anna in *Don Giovanni;* joined Covent Garden Co. as a principal (1954), where she was best known for her Eva in *Die Meistersinger* and Marschallin in *Der Rosenkavalier;* created the role of Naomi in Berkeley's *Ruth* and was the 1st English-speaking soprano to sing Cressida in Walton's *Troilus and Cressida;* was Ariadne in Australian premiere of *Ariadne auf Naxos;* retired (1965).

HALEIN, Kathinka (1801–1877). See Zitz, Kathinka.

HALEY, Margaret A. (1861–1939). American educator. Born Margaret Angela Haley in Joliet, Illinois, Nov 15, 1861; died in Chicago, Jan 5, 1939; attended public and convent schools. ❖ A prominent figure in Chicago politics (1900–1930s), was president of the National Federation of Teachers (1902) and instrumental in securing election of Ella Flagg Young as superintendent of Chicago schools (1910). ❖ See also autobiography *Battleground* (U. of Illinois Press, 1982); and *Women in World History.*

HALICARNASSUS, queen of.
See Artemisia I (c. 520–? BCE).
See Artemisia II (c. 395–351 BCE).

HALICKA, Antonina (1908–1973). Russian geologist. Name variations: Antonina Jaroszewicz. Born Antonina Jaroszewicz, Feb 13, 1908, in Maly Loswid, near Vitebsk, Russia (now Belarus); died Dec 30, 1973; Stefan Batory University, MS, 1935, PhD, 1939. ❖ Quaternary geology specialist, graduated from and worked as an assistant lecturer and researcher at Stefan Batory University in Vilnius, Lithuania (1930–39); mapped parts of Lithuania as a Lithuanian Geological Service prospecting group leader (1940–45); worked as a Polish government employee in Warsaw (1945–47); served as the deputy director (1947) and director (1950–73) of Museum of the Earth in Warsaw, Poland, which later became part of Polish Academy of Sciences; with funding from a Polish National Culture Fund grant (1937), studied volcanic activity and quaternary deposits in Italy, Finland and Sweden; edited and contributed over 40 papers to *Transactions of the Earth Museum;* contributed to the 1st Congress of Polish Science (1950); organized a bilateral Soviet-Polish symposia in Warsaw (1969) and in Leningrad (St. Petersburg, 1972); was a member of several organizations, including Polish Committee of the International Museal Union and International Commission on the History of Geological Sciences (1972). Honors include a Polish Gold Cross (for post-WWII reconstruction contributions to Poland) and membership to the Polish Academy of Science.

HALIDE EDIB (c. 1884–1964). See Adivar, Halide Edib.

HALIM, Tahiya (1919–2003). Turkish-Egyptian painter. Born Sept 9, 1919, in Cairo, Egypt, into an Egyptian family of Turkish descent; died May 24, 2003 in Cairo, Egypt; studied with the Syrian Youssef Trabulsy, 1939–40, the Greek Alecco Jerome, 1941–43, and her future husband, 1943–45; attended the Julian Academy; m. Hamed Abd Allah (painter and teacher). ❖ Legendary realist who portrayed Egyptian daily and national life, exhibited paintings throughout the world; her work is included in the permanent collections of the Guggenheim Museum (NY), National Museum (Stockholm) and Modern Art Museum (Cairo); paintings include *From the Window, The Latin Quarter* and *A Garden in Paris* (1949–52), *War, Compositions* and *Human Suffering* (1952–62) and *Ceremonies of the Nubian Marriage, The High Dam Rejoices,* and *This Land is Ours* (1962–72).

HALIMI, Gisèle (1927—). French lawyer and feminist. Name variations: Gisele Halimi. Born Gisèle Zeiza Elisa Taieb in La Goulette, Tunisia, in 1927; attended a lycée in Tunis; obtained a degree in law and philosophy from the University of Paris, 1948; m. Paul Halimi; m. Charles Faux; children: 3 sons. ❖ A practicing lawyer since 1956, gained recognition as the lawyer for Algerian National Liberation Front (FLN) and as counsel for Algerian nationalist Djamila Boupacha (1960); founded Choisir (1971), a feminist group organized to protect the women who had signed the *Manifeste des 343*, admitting to receiving illegal abortions; campaigned for passage of the contraception and abortion laws that were eventually framed by Simone Veil (1974); also served as representative on many cases involving women's issues, and attracted national publicity for her part in the Bobigny abortion trial (1972); authored *La cause des femmes* (1973) and initiated and contributed to the collective work *Le Programme commun des femmes* (1978), which addressed women's medical, educational, and professional problems; elected as an Independent Socialist to the National Assembly (1981).

HALKET, Elizabeth (1677–1727). *See Wardlaw, Elizabeth.*

HALKETT, Anne (1622–1699). English royalist and author. Name variations: Lady Halkett; Anna Halkett. Born Anne Murray, Jan 4, 1622 (some sources cite 1623), in London, England; died April 22, 1699; dau. of Thomas Murray and Jane (Drummond) Murray; m. Sir James Halkett, 1656; children: 1 survived infancy. ❖ Assisted royalist Colonel Joseph Bampfield in the escape of James, duke of York, 2nd son of Charles I, from prison (1648); when James later became king as James II, was given a pension as a reward; continued her royalist activity by nursing soldiers after the battle of Dunbar (1650); after marriage and motherhood, wrote "The Mother's Will to her Unborn Child" and began teaching children of the nobility; left several volumes after her death, mostly religious works and an autobiography, which records political events of the time along with her own experiences and beliefs. ❖ See also *Women in World History.*

HALKIA, Fani (1979—). Greek hurdler. Born Feb 2, 1979, in Larisa, Greece. ❖ Won European Cup for 400-meter hurdles (2004); won a gold medal for 400-meter hurdles at Athens Olympics (2004).

HALL, Adelaide (1904–1993). African-American jazz singer and actress. Born Oct 20, 1904, in Brooklyn, NY; died Nov 7, 1993, in London, England; m. Bert Hicks, 1925 (died 1962). ❖ One of the few African-American performers of the mid-20th century to earn success both in US and Europe, was probably best known for her rendition of "Digga Digga Do" from *Blackbirds,* and for collaboration with Duke Ellington on "Creole Love Call," in which she sang a wordless instrumental solo; on stage, appeared in *Shuffle Along* (1922), *Runnin' Wild* (1923), *Blackbirds of 1928* (1928), and *Kiss Me Kate* (1951); also appeared in such films as *Dancers in the Dark* (1932) and *Dixieland Jamboree* (1935); with husband, settled in England (1938) and ran several successful nightclubs until his death (1962); appeared at Newport Jazz Festival (1979). ❖ See also *Women in World History.*

HALL, Anna Maria (1800–1881). Irish author. Name variations: Mrs. S.C. Hall. Born Anna Maria Fielding, Jan 6, 1800, in Dublin, Ireland; died Jan 30, 1881, in East Moulsey, Surrey, England; m. Samuel Carter Hall, in 1824. ❖ At 15, moved to England with mother; at 29, published a collection of stories, *Sketches of Irish Character* (1829); wrote 9 novels, including *The Buccaneer* (1832), *Marian: or A Young Maid's Fortunes* (1840), *Light and Shadows of Irish Character* (1838), *The White Boy* (1845) and *Can Wrong be Right?* (1862); published 2 plays, *Tales of the Irish Peasantry* (1840) and *Midsummer Eve, a Fairy Tale of Love* (1848); collaborated with husband on several works; also edited *Sharpe's London Magazine* and *St. James's Magazine*; helped found several benevolent institutions, including the Brompton Consumption Hospital, The Governesses' Institution, the Home for Decayed Gentlewomen and the Nightingale Fund; was also active in temperance and women's-rights movements.

HALL, Anne (1792–1863). American artist. Born in Pomfret, Connecticut, May 26, 1792; died in New York, NY, Dec 11, 1863; 6th of 11 children of Dr. Jonathan (physician) and Bathsheba (Mumford) Hall; received art instruction from Samuel King; studied oil painting with Alexander Robertson; never married; no children. ❖ Painter of miniature portraits and figures on ivory, had 1st exhibitions at American Academy of Fine Arts in New York (1817 and 1818); the first woman admitted to the newly formed National Academy of Design (1827), was elected to full membership (1833) and exhibited regularly in the Academy's annual shows; specializing in portraits of women and children, which she painted as single figures or groups, received numerous commissions from prominent New York families. ❖ See also *Women in World History.*

HALL, Augusta (1802–1896). Patron of Welsh culture. Name variations: Lady Llanover; (pseudonym) Gwenynen Gwent. Born Augusta Waddington, Mar 21, 1802; died Jan 17, 1896; m. Benjamin Hall (1802–67, member of Parliament, 1832–37), in 1823; children: Augusta. ❖ Became patron of the Welsh Manuscripts Society; collaborated on a collection of Welsh melodies; established a factory to make the triple harp; assisted D. Silvan Evans in producing his famous Welsh dictionary; edited *The Autobiography & Correspondence of Mary Granville, Mrs. Delany* (1861–62); wrote and illustrated a recipe book containing color plates of traditional Welsh female costumes (1867); was also a patron of *Y Gymraes* (The Welshwoman), the 1st women's periodical in the Welsh language. ❖ See also *Women in World History.*

HALL, Cara Vincent (1922—). New Zealand concert pianist. Name variations: Cara Kelson. Born Cara Vincent Hall, Oct 16, 1922, in Christchurch, New Zealand; dau. of George Francis Hall (accountant) and Gladys Amelia (Vincent) Hall; sister of Charles Stanley Vincent; educated at Fendalton and Elmwood schools, Christchurch, and Wellington East Girls' College; graduate of Royal Academy of Music, London, where she studied piano with Vivian Langrish; studied in Paris with Lazare-Levy and Olivier Messiaen (early 1950s); m. Robert Natahaniel Kelson (political scientist, academic, and author), May 7, 1955; children: Stanley Crispin Kelson (b. Feb 11, 1957). ❖ Played a central role in bringing the story of the vocal orchestra of women POWs in Sumatra to the world's attention; performed on first radio broadcasts (1935); gained the LRSM and awarded a scholarship to study at Royal Academy of Music in London (1937); performed extensively around the world (1940s–50s), and became especially known in New Zealand, where she performed solo in concert halls, in recitals and concertos with the New Zealand Symphony Orchestra, and on radio and in film. ❖ See also "Women POW's of Sumatra" in *Women in World History.*

HALL, Dorothy Gladys (1927—). *See Manley, Dorothy.*

HALL, Edith Hayward (1877–1943). *See Dohan, Edith Hall.*

HALL, Elisa (1900–1982). Guatemalan novelist. Born 1900 in Guatemala; died 1982. ❖ Wrote 2 historical novels about Spanish conquerors of Guatemala, *Semilla de mostaza* (1938) and *Mostaza* (1939).

HALL, Elizabeth Hazel (1901–1991). *See Lissaman, Elizabeth Hazel.*

HALL, Ella (1896–1982). American silent-film actress. Born Ella August Hall, Mar 17, 1896, in New York, NY; died Sept 3, 1982, in Los Angeles, CA; dau. of May Hall (actress); m. Emory Johnson (actor, div.); children: Richard Emory (1919–1994, actor) and Ellen Hall (1922–1999, actress). ❖ Silent star at Universal, most notably in Lois Weber's *The Jewel*; other films include *The Spy, The Bugler of Algiers, The Charmer, The Third Alarm, The Heart of Rachael* and *The Flying Dutchman.*

HALL, Elsie (1877–1976). Australian composer. Born in Toowoomba, Australia, June 22, 1877; died in Wynberg, South Africa, June 27, 1976. ❖ By 9, had performed Beethoven's Third Concerto in public; in London, attracted the attention of George Bernard Shaw; in Berlin, studied with Ernst Rudorff (1840–1916) and won the prestigious Mendelssohn Prize; during WWII, entertained Allied troops in North Africa and Italy; a veteran of many world tours, settled in South Africa, where she performed concertos into her 90s.

HALL, Emma Amelia (1837–1884). American prison reformer and administrator. Born Feb 28, 1837, in Raisin Township, Lenawee County, Michigan; died Dec 27, 1884, in Albuquerque, New Mexico; dau. of Reuben Lord Hall (farmer and schoolteacher) and Abby Wells (Lee) Hall. ❖ Hired as teacher at House of Shelter, women's workshop and rehabilitation facility in Detroit, MI, by prison reformer Zebulon Reed Brockway, and served as matron (1871–74); worked as matron at 2 other state institutions; established a new, experimental reform school for girls in Adrian, Michigan, and served as its 1st superintendent (1881–84); became missionary teacher to Native Americans in New Mexico (1884).

HALL, Evelyne (1909–1993). American runner. Name variations: Evie Hall; Evie Adams. Born Evelyne R. Hall, Sept 10, 1909, in Minneapolis, Minnesota; died April 1993 in Oceanside, California. ❖ At Los Angeles Olympics, won a silver medal in 80-meter hurdles (1932); was AAU outdoor 80-meter hurdles champion (1930); won indoor 50-meter hurdles (1931, 1933, 1935); became a coach.

HALL, Geraldine (1905–1970). American stage and screen actress. Born Jan 31, 1905, in Illinois; died Sept 18, 1970, in Woodland Hills, California; m. Porter Hall (actor). ❖ Films include *Captive City, Big*

Carnival, Secret of the Incas, The Proud and the Profane, Ace in the Hole and *Five Against the House.*

HALL, Grayson (1923–1985). American stage, tv, and screen actress. Name variations: Shirley Grayson. Born Shirley Grossman, Sept 18, 1923, in Philadelphia, PA; died Aug 7, 1985, in New York, NY; m. Sam Hall (writer), 1953; children: Matthew Hall (writer). ❖ Made off-Broadway debut in *Man and Superman* (1953), followed by *The Balcony, La Ronde, Six Characters in Search of an Author, The Last Analysis, The Screens, What Every Woman Knows, Happy End,* and *Madwoman of Chaillot;* appeared on Broadway in *Subways Are for Sleeping, Leaf People, Happy End,* and *Suicide,* among others; films include *That Darn Cat;* probably best known for her role as Dr. Julia Hoffman on tv's long-running "Dark Shadows." Won Oscar and Golden Globe award for film *Night of the Iguana* (1964).

HALL, Juanita (1901–1968). African-American singer and actress. Born Juanita Long, Nov 6, 1901, in Keyport, NJ; died Feb 29, 1968, in Bayshore, NY; attended Juilliard School of Music; m. Clement Hall (actor, died 1920s). ❖ Best remembered for portrayal of Bloody Mary in hit musical *South Pacific,* in which her renditions of "Bali H'ai" and "Happy Talk" contributed largely to the show's success (1949); made professional debut in chorus of *Show Boat* (1928); played countless small roles in dramatic and musical productions both on and off-Broadway; formed group, the Juanita Hall Choir (1935); went on to play Madame Tango in *House of Flowers* (1954) and Madame Liang in *Flower Drum Song* (1958); also performed in the film versions of *South Pacific* and *Flower Drum Song.* Won Tony Award for *South Pacific.* ❖ See also *Women in World History.*

HALL, Katie Beatrice (1938—). American politician. Born Katie Beatrice Green, April 3, 1938, in Mound Bayou, Mississippi; dau. of Jeff Louis Greene and Bessie Mae (Hooper) Greene; Mississippi Valley State University, BS, 1960; Indiana University, MS, 1968, postgraduate, 1972; m. John H. Hall, Aug 12, 1957; children: 2. ❖ Was a member of Indiana State House of Representatives; served in Indiana State Senate (1976–82); also chaired Lake County Democratic Committee (1978–80); as a US Democratic Congresswoman from Indiana, served one full term in House of Representatives (Nov 2, 1982–Jan 3, 1985); during tenure, was a member of the Committee on Post Office and Civil Service and the Committee on Public Works and Transportation; introduced bill that made the birthday of Martin Luther King Jr. a federal holiday (1983); failed in 2 subsequent bids to win nomination to Congress (1986, 1990). ❖ See also *Women in World History.*

HALL, Kaye (1951—). American swimmer. Name variations: Kaye Hall Greff. Born May 15, 1951, in Tacoma, Washington; attended University of Puget Sound. ❖ At Mexico City Olympics, won a bronze medal in 200-meter backstroke, a gold medal in 100-meter backstroke, and a gold medal in 4x100-meter medley relay (1968); became the 1st woman to break the 60-second barrier in the 100-yard backstroke (Dec 1967). Inducted into International Swimming Hall of Fame (1979).

HALL, Lydia E. (1906–1969). American nurse. Name variations: Lydia Eloise Hall; Lydia Williams. Born Lydia Williams, Sept 21, 1906, in New York, NY; died Feb 27, 1969, at Queens Hospital; dau. of Anna Ketterman Williams and Louis U. Williams (surgeon); graduate of New York Hospital School of Nursing, 1927; Columbia University Teachers College, MA, 1942; m. Reginald A. Hall, 1945. ❖ Pioneer in nurse-led care, was a nurse in Pennsylvania and New York; worked at New York Metropolitan Life Insurance Company's Life Extension Institute (1930–35) and on research staff of New York Heart Association (1935–40); was a supervisor for Visiting Nurse Association of New York (1941–47); began developing a Columbia University academic program to teach nurses to be consultants (1950); was project director, then administrative director, of the Loeb Center for Nursing and Rehabilitation, the 1st institution where nurses were in charge rather than doctors and which focused on patients' emotional well-being as well as physical.

HALL, Marguerite Radclyffe (1880–1943). *See Hall, Radclyffe.*

HALL, Natalie (1904–1994). American actress and singer. Name variations: Natalie Rowe. Born Sept 23, 1904, in Providence, RI; died Mar 4, 1994, in Edgecombe, Maine; m. Barry Mackay; m. Edward C. Rowe. ❖ Made Broadway debut in *Iolanthe* (1926), followed by *Three Little Girls, Through the Years, Music in the Air, Music Hath Charms* and *Otello,* among others.

HALL, Radclyffe (1880–1943). English novelist, poet, and champion of lesbian rights. Name variations: Radclyffe Hall; John or Johnny Hall. Born Marguerite Antonia Radclyffe-Hall, Aug 12, 1880, in Bournemouth, England; died Oct 7, 1943, in London; dau. of Radclyffe Radclyffe-Hall and Mary Jane (Marie) Diehl Sager; educated by governesses; never married; no children; lived with Una Troubridge for 28 years. ❖ Author of *The Well of Loneliness,* arguably the most famous novel about love between women ever written, which was instantly banned on two continents upon its publication (1928), figured in an obscenity trial, sold over 1 million copies and saw translation into 11 languages by the time of her death; wrote 1st book of poems (1906); published 1st novel, *The Forge* (1924); won the Prix Femina and James Tait Black Prize for *Adam's Breed* (1926). ❖ See also Michael Baker, *Our Three Selves: A Life of Radclyffe Hall* (GMP, 1985); Lillian Faderman, *Chloe Plus Olivia* (Viking, 1994); Vera Brittain, *Radclyffe Hall: A Case of Obscenity?* (Femina, 1968); R. Lovat Dickson, *Radclyffe Hall at the Well of Loneliness* (Collins, 1975); Una Troubridge, *The Life and Death of Radclyffe Hall* (Hammond, 1961); and *Women in World History.*

HALL, Rosetta Sherwood (1865–1951). Canadian-American physician and missionary. Name variations: Rosetta Sherwood. Born Rosetta Sherwood on Sept 19, 1865, in Liberty, NY; died April 5, 1951, in Ocean Grove, NJ; dau. of Rosevelt Rensler Sherwood and Phoebe (Gildersleeve) Sherwood; m. William James Hall (missionary doctor), June 27, 1892 (died 1894); children: son (b. 1893), dau. (1895–1898). ❖ Interned at Nursery and Children's Hospital on Staten Island and worked at Methodist Deaconess's Home in NYC (late 1880s); joined (Methodist) Woman's Foreign Missionary Society and went to Seoul, Korea (1890); founded Baldwin Dispensary School (later Lillian Harris Memorial Hospital) in Seoul (early 1890s); through marriage, became a Canadian citizen (1892); worked for Korea mission, was examining physician to children's mission in NY, and advisor to medical students at International Medical Missionary Union, NYC (1895–97); worked in Pyong Yang, Korea (1897–1917), serving as head of Institute for the Blind and the Deaf; built Edith Margaret Memorial Wing of Women's Dispensary (1899, destroyed by fire 1906) and Women's Hospital of Extended Grace (1908); worked in Seoul (1917–33), helping found Women's Medical (Training) Institute (1928); wrote, lectured and practiced medicine in NY (1933–43); designed braille-like system for reading Korean alphabet. Received certificate of merit from Japanese Government General (1915).

HALL, Ruby Bridges (b. 1954). *See Bridges, Ruby.*

HALL, Ruby Violet (1912–1981). *See Scott, Ruby Payne.*

HALL, Mrs. S.C. (1800–1881). *See Hall, Anna Maria.*

HALL, Theodora Clemens (1902–1980). New Zealand doctor. Name variations: Theodora Clemens Easterfield. Born on June 12, 1902, at Wellington, New Zealand; died on Dec 19, 1980, in Auckland, New Zealand; dau. of Thomas Hill Easterfield (chemistry professor) and Anna Maria Kunigunda (Büchel); University of Otago, MB, ChB, 1926; m. Richard John Burnside Hall (surgeon), 1932; children: 3 daughters. ❖ Appointed specialist physician, Cook Hospital, Gisborne (1934); became visiting physician to Bay of Islands Hospital at Kawakawa (1958); made fellow of Royal Australasian College of Physicians (1974). ❖ See also *Dictionary of New Zealand Biography* (Vol. 4).

HALL-MILLS. *See Mills, Eleanor (1888–1922).*

HALLAM, Isabella (1746–1826). *See Mattocks, Isabella.*

HALLAM, Mrs. Lewis (?–1774). English-born actress. Name variations: Margaret Cheer. Little is known about Hallam, including given name, date of birth or family, or place of death; died 1774; m. Lewis Hallam (actor, died 1756); David Douglass (actor), 1756; children: (1st m.) 4, including Isabella Mattocks (actress). ❖ Became regular member of "Mr. [William] Hallam's Company of Comedians" (1745); with theater troupe, moved from England to American colonies (1752); made US debut as Portia in *Merchant of Venice* (Williamsburg, VA, Sept 15, 1752); other roles included Lady Anne in *Richard III,* Lady Percy in *Henry IV,* Indiana in *The Conscious Lovers,* Angelica in *Love for Love* and Gertrude in *Hamlet.*

HALLAREN, Mary A. (1907–2005). American army officer. Born Mary Agnes Hallaren, May 4, 1907, in Lowell, Massachusetts; died Feb 13, 2005, in McLean, Virginia; attended Boston University; graduate of Lowell State Teachers College (now Univ. of Massachusetts at Lowell). ❖ Entered Officer Candidate School of Women's Army Auxiliary

Corps (1942); served in various capacities in Women's Army Corps (WAC) including director of all WAC personnel in European Theater (appointed 1945), deputy director of WAC (appointed 1946), and (as colonel) director of WAC (1947–53); was the 1st woman to be sworn into active duty with the regular army when the Women's Armed Services Integration Act took effect (June 12, 1948); retired from army (1960); served as director of Women in Community Service division of US Labor Department (beginning 1965); championed permanent status for women in the military after WWII. Decorated with the Bronze Star; inducted into National Women's Hall of Fame (1996). ❖ See also Tom Brokaw, *The Greatest Generation*.

HALLÉ, Lady (c. 1838–1911). *See Neruda, Wilma.*

HALLIDAY, Dorothy (1923–2001). *See Dunnett, Dorothy.*

HALLIDAY, Margaret (1956—). **New Zealand-born Australian racer.** Born 1956 in New Zealand. ❖ Became the 1st woman to win an Australian national motor sport Grand Prix when she partnered boyfriend Doug Chivas to win the Grand Prix of the Mount Panorama circuit for 1000cc motorcycle sidecars (April 1984); with this victory, was also the 1st woman in the world to win a national motor sport Grand Prix.

HALLIWELL, Geri (1972—). **English singer.** Name variations: Geraldine Halliwell, Ginger Spice, The Spice Girls. Born Geraldine Estelle Halliwell, Aug 6, 1972, in Watford, Hertfordshire, England. ❖ Shot to fame as part of pop-quintet, the Spice Girls, which was formed in London (1994); in early career, worked as go-go dancer and host on Turkish game show; invited to join Bob and Chris Herbert's group Touch; with other members of the Herbert band, left and formed Spice Girls; with group, released single "Wannabe," the 1st debut single by all-girl band to enter UK charts at #1, then went #1 in 22 other nations, including US (1997); with group, released debut album, *Spice,* which went to #1 in UK charts and became 1st debut album by UK performer to enter US charts at #1 (1997); with Spice, had other Top-10 singles, including "Say You'll Be There" and "2 Become 1"; released smash-hit album, *Spiceworld,* and film of same name (1997); took over as manager of Spice Girls, but quit group soon after, citing friction (May 1998); became goodwill ambassador for United Nations (Fall 1998); pursued solo music career, releasing several albums, including *Schizophonic* (1999) and *Official & Exclusive* (2001); appeared in film *Fat Slags* (2004). ❖ See also Geri Halliwell, *If Only* (Doubleday Canada, 1999).

HALLOWELL, Anna (1831–1905). **American welfare worker and educational reformer.** Born Nov 1, 1831, in Philadelphia, PA; died April 6, 1905, in Philadelphia; dau. of Quakers, Morris Longstreth and Hannah Smith (Penrose) Hallowell. ❖ Served on the board of Home for Destitute Colored Children; did relief work with freed slaves; joined others to establish Society for Organizing Charitable Relief and Repressing Mendicancy (1878) which later became Society for Organizing Charity; served on the Society's Committee on the Care and Education of Dependent Children, which was reorganized as Children's Aid Society, becoming a member of its 1st board of directors (1883); beginning 1879, established free kindergartens in poor neighborhoods; as the 1st woman to be chosen as a member of the board of public education, introduced training courses for kindergarten teachers into the Philadelphia Normal School for Girls; oversaw rehabilitation of the James Forten School (1890); founded the Civic Club, an organization of upper-class women working for social reform. ❖ See also *Women in World History.*

HALLOWES, Odette (1912–1995). *See Sansom, Odette.*

HALLS, Ethel May (1882–1967). **American actress.** Name variations: Ethel Mae Halls; Ethel Halls. Born Nov 20, 1882, in California; died Sept 16, 1967, in Woodland Hills, CA. ❖ Began career as a Floradora girl; appeared in films of Mary Pickford and Rudolph Valentino.

HALONEN, Tarja (1943—). **Finnish politician and trade union lawyer.** Born Tarja Kaarina Halonen, Dec 24, 1943, in Helsinki, Finland; University of Helsinki, Master of Laws degree, 1968; m. longtime companion, Pentti Arajarvi, Aug 2000; children: 1 daughter. ❖ Served as social affairs secretary and general secretary of National Union of Finnish Students (1969–70); served as lawyer for the Central Organization of Finnish Trade Unions SAK (1970–74); joined the Social Democratic Party (1971); served as parliamentary secretary to the prime minister (1974–75); was a member of Helsinki City Council (1977–96); was a Member of Parliament (1979–2000); was chair of the Parliamentary Social Affairs Committee (1984–87); served as minister at the Ministry of Social Affairs and Health (1987–90), as minister of Justice (1990–91), as minister for Nordic Cooperation (1989–91), as minister for Foreign Affairs (1995–2000); became Finland's 1st female president (Jan 3, 2000).

HALPERT, Edith Gregor (c. 1900–1970). **Russian-American art collector and dealer.** Born April 25, c. 1900, in Odessa, Russia; died Oct 6, 1970, in New York, NY; dau. of Gregor and Frances (Lucom) Fivoosiovitch; attended National Academy of Design; m. Samuel Halpert, 1918 (div. 1930); m. Raymond Davis, 1939 (div.). ❖ Moved to America (1906); opened Downtown Gallery of Contemporary Art in Greenwich Village to provide an outlet for modern American artists (1926), showcasing the works of Stuart Davis, Charles Demuth, Arthur Dove, Yasuo Kuniyoshi, John Marin, Ben Shahn, Charles Sheeler, Niles Spencer, Max Weber and William Zorach; began to collect forgotten pieces of Americana and introduced American folk art to Downtown Gallery; introduced the concept of municipal art exhibits to many of America's larger cities; was the 1st to present an exhibition of black artists in a commercial art gallery in US; established the Edith Gregor Halpert Foundation which lobbied for the rights of artists to control their own work. ❖ See also *Women in World History.*

HALPRIN, Ann (1920—). **American dancer.** Born Anna Schumann, July 13, 1920, in Winnetka, Illinois; trained at Humphrey-Weideman Studio; m. Lawrence Halprin; children: Daria Halprin (actress who starred in *Zabriskie Point* and was married to actor Dennis Hopper, 1972–76). ❖ World-renowned director of the San Francisco Dancer's Workshop and originator of public "Happenings," was noted for collaborative approach and innovative choreography; founded experimental dance workshop with Wellard Lathrop in San Francisco (1940s); held summer schools attended by leading choreographers; works include *The Prophetess* (1955), *Birds of America* (1957), *Four-Legged Stool* (1961), *Paradise and Changes* (1967), and *Dance by the People of San Francisco* (1976).

HALSE ROGERS, Lady. *See Trevor-Jones, Mabel.*

HALSINGLAND, duchess of. *See Madeleine (b. 1982).*

HALSTEAD, Nellie (1910–1991). **English runner.** Born Sept 19, 1910, in UK; died 1991. ❖ At Los Angeles Olympics, won a bronze medal in 4x100-meter relay (1932).

HALTVIK, Trine (1965—). **Norwegian handball player.** Born Mar 23, 1965, in Trondheim, Norway. ❖ Won a team silver medal at Seoul Olympics (1988) and a team bronze at Sydney Olympics (2000).

HAMA, Keiko (1947—). **Japanese volleyball player.** Born Nov 7, 1947, in Japan. ❖ Won a silver medal at Mexico City Olympics (1968) and a silver medal at Munich Olympics (1972), both in team competition.

HAMAGUCHI, Kyoko (1978—). **Japanese wrestler.** Born Jan 11, 1978, in Tokyo, Japan; dau. of Heigo Hamaguchi. ❖ Won World championships for 72kg freestyle (1997, 1998, 1999, 2002, 2003) and a bronze medal for 72kg freestyle at Athens Olympics (2004); won Asian championship for 72kg freestyle (2004).

HAMALAINEN, Marja-Liisa (1955—). *See Kirvesniemi, Marja-Liisa.*

HAMANN, Conny (1969—). **Danish handball player.** Born Sept 16, 1969, in Denmark. ❖ Debuted on national team (1989); won a team gold medal at Atlanta Olympics (1996); won team European championships (1994, 1996); retired (1996).

HAMBROOK, Sharon (1963—). **Canadian synchronized swimmer.** Born Mar 28, 1963, in Canada. ❖ At Los Angeles Olympics, won a silver medal in duet (1984).

HAMER, Fannie Lou (1917–1977). **African-American civil-rights activist.** Name variations: Fannie Hamer. Born Fannie Lou Townsend, Oct 6, 1917, in central Mississippi, probably Montgomery County; moved to Sunflower County near Ruleville at age 2, where she remained; died Mar 14, 1977, in Mound Bayou, MS; 20th child of Jim and Ella Townsend (cotton sharecroppers); only completed 6th grade, due to field labor as a child; later taught basic literacy to adults in SNCC's "freedom school" project; taught black studies classes at Shaw University, Raleigh, NC; m. Perry "Pap" Hamer, 1944; children: (adopted 1950s) Dorothy Jean Hamer (d. 1967) and Vergie Hamer; (adopted granddaughters) Lenora and Jacqueline. ❖ Activist whose challenges to racist codes in the Deep South hastened political reforms and the enfranchisement of black citizens (1960s); unsuccessfully attempted to register to vote (Aug 1962); lost job and home, began fugitive existence (autumn 1962); returned to

Ruleville for 2nd registration bid which was successful (Dec 1962); became SNCC fieldworker (1963); arrested in Winona, MS, when co-workers tried to integrate bus terminal (June 1963) and severely beaten in Winona jail; entered primary election contest against incumbent Jamie Whitten (Mar 20, 1964); helped establish Mississippi Freedom Democratic Party (MFDP, April 16, 1964); defeated in primary election by Whitten (June 2, 1964); elected delegate to Democratic National Convention at MFDP state convention (Aug 6, 1964); led MFDP delegation in challenge to white Mississippi delegation at Democratic National Convention (Aug 22, 1964); joined in filing challenge to seating of Mississippi congressional delegation (Dec 4, 1964); spoke out against war in Vietnam (1965); participated with Martin Luther King, Stokely Carmichael, and other leaders in Meredith March through Mississippi (June 1966); attended Democratic National Convention in Chicago as a member of the integrated Loyalist democratic party delegation (Aug 1968); criticized that delegation for its domination by male delegates; helped found National Women's Political Caucus (July 1971); ran unsuccessful campaign for Mississippi senate (fall 1971); appointed delegate to Democratic national convention in Miami Beach (July 1972). ❖ See also Kay Mills, *This Little Light of Mine: The Life of Fannie Lou Hamer* (Dutton, 1993); and *Women in World History.*

HAMERTON, Amey (c. 1829–1920). *See Daldy, Amey.*

HAMES, Mary (1827–1919). New Zealand dressmaker and farmer. Name variations: Mary Maddox. Born Mary Maddox on May 14, 1827, in Herefordshire, England; died April 3, 1919, in Russell, New Zealand; dau. of Richard Maddox (shoemaker) and Priscilla (Bowker) Maddox; m. Charles Hames (tailor and schoolteacher), 1851 (died 1906); children: 6. ❖ Immigrated to New Zealand on free land scheme (1864); helped frail husband clear timber and light bush; helped sustain family by working as dressmaker and domestic servant in Auckland, and later by selling butter and cheese from cow she had purchased; had accumulated 1,000 acres of rolling pasture at time of her death. ❖ See also *Dictionary of New Zealand Biography* (Vol. 1).

HAMILL, Dorothy (1956—). American figure skater. Born Dorothy Stuart Hamill, July 26, 1956, in Chicago, Illinois; m. Dean Paul Martin, Jan 8, 1982 (div.); m. Dr. Kenneth Forsythe, 1987 (sep 1995); children. ❖ Won US National championship (1974, 1975, 1976); won the World championship and an Olympic gold medal at Innsbruck (1976), one of only three American women to win the US National championship, World championship, and Olympic gold medal in the same year; was World Professional Figure Skating champion (1984–87); appeared as a product spokesperson, an Ice Capades headliner; was a tv performer-producer, president of Dorothy Hamill Enterprises, and executive producer of *Cinderella . . . Frozen in Time.* ❖ See also autobiography *Dorothy Hamill, On and Off the Ice* (Knopf, 1983); and *Women in World History.*

HAMILTON, Mrs. Alexander (1757–c. 1854). *See Hamilton, Elizabeth Schuyler.*

HAMILTON, Alice (1869–1970). American toxicologist and social reformer. Born Feb 27, 1869 in New York, NY; died Sept 22, 1970, in Hadlyme, Connecticut; dau. of Gertrude Pond Hamilton (1840–1917) and Montgomery Hamilton (1843–1909, businessman); sister of classical scholar Edith Hamilton (1867–1963) and artist Norah Hamilton (b. 1873); attended Fort Wayne College of Medicine, 1890–1891, University of Michigan Medical School, 1892–93, University of Leipzig, Germany, 1895–96, and Johns Hopkins Medical School, 1896–97; never married; no children. ❖ Groundbreaking practitioner of industrial toxicology and leading American social reformer of 19th and 20th centuries, began teaching at Woman's Medical School of Northwestern University in Chicago (1896); joined Jane Addams' Hull House (1897); was appointed to Illinois Occupation Disease Commission and became a special agent for US Bureau of Labor, for whom she would conduct various surveys of American industries (1910); joined Jane Addams' Women's Peace Party (1915) and attended International Congress of Women at The Hague; became assistant professor of industrial medicine at Harvard Medical School (1919); commenced a 10-year career as medical consultant to General Electric Company (1923); served on Health Committee of Council of League of Nations (1924–28) and on President Hoover's Research Committee on Social Trends (1930–32); retired from Harvard (1935); worked on her last major study of the dangerous trades, in this case, a survey of the viscose rayon industry (1937–38); gave annual lectures about industrial toxicology at Women's Medical College of Pennsylvania (1937–43);

traveled to Frankfurt, Germany, as a representative of Department of Labor at 8th International Congress on Occupational Accidents and Diseases (1938); became president of National Consumers' League (1944). Received Lasker Award (1947) and Knudsen Award (1953); given Elizabeth Blackwell Citation of New York Infirmary (1954); honored with establishment of Alice Hamilton Fund for Occupation Medicine at Harvard School of Public Health (1959). ❖ See also autobiography, *Exploring the Dangerous Trades* (1943); Barbara Sicherman, *Alice Hamilton: A Life in Letters* (Harvard U. Press, 1984); and *Women in World History.*

HAMILTON, Amy Gordon (1892–1967). *See Hamilton, Gordon.*

HAMILTON, Anne (1636–1716). Duchess of Hamilton. Born Dec 24, 1636 (some sources cite 1634); died Oct 17, 1716; dau. of James Hamilton (b. 1606), 1st duke of Hamilton, and Mary Hamilton (1613–1638); m. William Douglas (1635–1694), 1st earl of Selkirk, 3rd duke of Hamilton (r. 1660–1694), April 29, 1656; children: James Douglas-Hamilton (1658–1712), 4th duke of Hamilton; William Hamilton; Charles Hamilton (1662–1739), 2nd earl of Selkirk; John Hamilton (1665–1744), 3rd earl of Selkirk; Archibald Douglas-Hamilton (1673–1754), governor of Jamaica); George Hamilton, 1st earl of Orkney (r. 1696–1737); Basil Hamilton (1671–1701); Mary Hamilton (1657–died before 1683); Catherine Hamilton (d. 1707, who m. John Murray, 1st duke of Atholl); Susannah Hamilton (d. 1736, who m. Charles Hay, 3rd marquess of Tweeddale); Margaret Hamilton (d. 1731). ❖ Because of her petition, husband William Douglas, royal commissioner under William III, became 3rd duke of Hamilton.

HAMILTON, Anne (1766–1846). English lady-in-waiting. Name variations: Lady Anne Hamilton. Born 1766; died 1846; dau. of Archibald, 9th duke of Hamilton; sister of Lord Archibald Hamilton (1770–1827). ❖ Accompanied Queen Caroline of Brunswick on her return to England from exile (1820); her book, *Secret History of the Court,* was published under her name without her consent.

HAMILTON, Anne Heggtveit (1939—). *See Heggtveit, Anne.*

HAMILTON, Betsey (1757–c. 1854). *See Hamilton, Elizabeth Schuyler.*

HAMILTON, Carrie (1963–2002). American actress and singer. Born Carrie Louise Hamilton, Dec 5, 1963, in New York, NY; died Jan 20, 2002, in Los Angeles, CA; dau. of Joe Hamilton (producer) and Carol Burnett (actress, singer); sister of Jody Hamilton and Erin Hamilton (singer); m. Mark Templin, 1994 (div. 1998). ❖ Was a member of the rock band Big Business; made tv debut in "Love Lives On" (1985), followed by "Hostage," "Tokyo Pop," and "A Mother's Justice," and appeared as Reggie Higgins on "Fame" (1986–87); films include *Shag: The Movie* and *Checkered Flag*; starred as Maureen on national tour of *Rent* and collaborated with mother on play *Hollywood Arms* which premiered in Chicago (2002). Won Women in Film Award at Latino Film Festival for her short "Lunchtime Thomas" (2001).

HAMILTON, Catherine (1738–1782). English harpsichordist and composer. Name variations: Lady Catherine Hamilton. Born Catherine Barlow 1738 in Wales; died outside Naples of bilious fever, Aug 25, 1782; buried in Pembrokeshire; m. Sir William Hamilton (envoy to Naples), in 1758; no children. ❖ Was highly esteemed for her proficiency on the pianoforte and the harpsichord, but only one of her works as a composer, a minuet in C major, is extant; following her death, husband married Emma Hamilton. ❖ See also *Women in World History.*

HAMILTON, Cecilia (1837–1909). *See Jamison, Cecilia.*

HAMILTON, Cicely (1872–1952). English author, playwright, actress, and suffragist. Name variations: Cicely Hammill. Born June 15, 1872, in Kensington, London, England; died Dec 5, 1952, in London, England; dau. of Captain Denzil Hammill and Maude Piers Hammill (Irish); never married. ❖ As an actress, appeared in G.B. Shaw's *Fanny's First Play* (1911) and J.M. Barrie's *The Twelve-Pound Look* (1913); began writing novels and detective mysteries but soon turned to plays; developing feminist themes, had 1st major success with *Diana of Dobson's* (1908); co-founded, with Bessie Hatton, the Women Writers' Suffrage League (1908), an arm of the National Union of Suffrage Societies; other plays include *How the Vote was Won* (1909), *The Pageant of Great Women* (1909), *Marriage as a Trade* and *The Child in Flanders* (1917), and *The Old Adam* (1925); throughout WWI, lived in France, working as a military hospital administrator, and became a pacifist; wrote *Senlis* (1917) and *William: An Englishman* (1919), an antiwar novel that won the Femina Vie Heureuse Prize; after the war, continued to promote pacifism, writing *Theodore Savage* (1922), and returned to her feminist views as a journalist and commentator (1920s). ❖ See also autobiography *Life Errant* (1935); and *Women in World History*.

HAMILTON, Clara Decima (1909–1983). *See Norman, Decima.*

HAMILTON, Decima (1909–1983). *See Norman, Decima.*

HAMILTON, duchess of.
See Hamilton, Mary (1613–1638).
See Hamilton, Anne (1636–1716).
See Gunning, Elizabeth (1734–1790).
See Marie of Baden (1817–1888).

HAMILTON, Edith (1867–1963). Scholar of the ancient classical world.
Born Edith Hamilton, Aug 12, 1867, in Dresden, Germany, of American parents; died May 31, 1963, in Washington, DC; dau. of Montgomery Hamilton and Gertrude Pond Hamilton; sister of industrial reformer Alice Hamilton (1869–1979) and artist Norah Hamilton (b. 1873); Bryn Mawr College, BA, MA, 1894; studied classics in Germany at University of Leipzig, 1895; 1st female classics student at University of Munich; never married; lived with Doris Reid; children: adopted Dorian Reid in later life. ❖ Achieved fame as an essayist on the ancient world, communicating her passion to her students as well as readers with *The Greek Way* (1930); served as headmistress of Bryn Mawr School in Baltimore (1906–22); after retirement, began 2nd career as essayist on the classics, 1st in NY City (1924–43), then Washington, DC (1943–63); was actively involved in the arts until her death at age 95; also wrote *The Roman Way* (1932), *Mythology* (1942), *Witnesses to the Truth: Christ and His Interpreters* (1948), *The Echo of Greece* (1957), and (coedited with Huntington Cairns) *Collected Dialogues of Plato* (1961). ❖ See also Doris Reid, *Edith Hamilton: An Intimate Portrait* (Norton, 1967); and *Women in World History*.

HAMILTON, Elizabeth (c. 1480–?). Countess of Lennox. Born c. 1480; dau. of James Hamilton, 1st Lord Hamilton (d. 1479), and Mary Stewart (d. 1488, dau. of James II of Scotland and Mary of Guelders); m. Matthew Stewart, 2nd earl of Lennox; children: John Stewart, 3rd earl of Lennox (murdered by royal architect James Hamilton of Finnart in 1536).

HAMILTON, Elizabeth (1641–1708). Countess of Grammont. Name variations: La Belle Hamilton. Born 1641, probably in County Tyrone, Ireland; died 1708; dau. of Sir George Hamilton, 1st baronet and governor of Nenagh (d. 1679); sister of Anthony Hamilton (c. 1646–c. 1720, author of *Mémoires du Comte de Grammont*); m. Philibert, comte de Grammont, 1663 (died 1707). ❖ One of the most brilliant and beautiful women at the court of Charles II of England, married the gambler and libertine Philibert, count of Grammont (1663), at instigation of her Royalist brother Anthony Hamilton, and moved to France the following year. After her death, her husband's memoirs (*Mémoires du Comte de Grammont*), a French classic about the amorous intrigues at the court of Charles II, appeared anonymously (1713); the 1st half of the book was supposedly dictated to Anthony Hamilton by the count; the 2nd half was presumed to be the creation of Anthony Hamilton. ❖ See also *Women in World History*.

HAMILTON, Elizabeth.
See Villiers, Elizabeth (c. 1657–1733).
See Gunning, Elizabeth (1734–1790).

HAMILTON, Elizabeth (1758–1816). Reformist writer. Name variations: (pseudonym) Almeria. Born July 21, 1758, in Belfast, Ireland; died July 23, 1816, in Harrogate, Yorkshire, England; dau. of Charles Hamilton and Katherine Mackay Hamilton; never married. ❖ Reform-minded author, whose writings espouse a moderate feminism and were infused with a decidedly Episcopalian sense of charity, argued for the education of women and for charity toward the needy; began to collaborate with scholar brother Charles Hamilton, an "Orientalist" who worked to reform British attitudes toward colonial possession (1766); published 1st novel *Translation of the Letters of a Hindoo Rajah* (1796), in homage to brother; lampooned radical feminists in *Memoirs of Modern Philosophers* (1800), though she shared many of the same views as Wollstonecraft, who argued for equal access to learning for women; wrote popular "domestic" novel *The Cottagers of Glenburnie* (1808), a commercial success in the social-realism vein.

HAMILTON, Elizabeth Jane (1805–1897). Canadian midwife. Name variations: Elizabeth Jane Soley; Aunt Jenny. Born Elizabeth Jane Soley in 1805 in Lower Truro, Nova Scotia, Canada; died Oct 1897, in Brookfield, Nova Scotia; dau. of Mary Soley and William Soley; m. Robert Hamilton, 1825; children: 7. ❖ Offered care to the Canadian communities of Brentwood, Middle Stewiacke, Hilden, Pleasant Valley, Brookfield, Alton and Forest Glen; after experience as a nurse, began a midwife career at age 46 (July 1851); traveled by horseback or by foot through extreme weather to deliver babies; attended a total of 776 births and maintained detailed patient records; retired at 88 (1893).

HAMILTON, Elizabeth Schuyler (1757–c. 1854). American promoter of husband Alexander Hamilton. Name variations: Betsey Hamilton; Mrs. Alexander Hamilton. Born Elizabeth Schuyler in 1757; died c. 1854; dau. of General Philip Schuyler and Catherine Van Rensselaer Schuyler (1734–1803); m. Alexander Hamilton (1755–1804, American statesman and US secretary of the treasury), Dec 14, 1780; children: Philip (d. 1801); Angelica Hamilton; Alexander Hamilton; James Alexander Hamilton; John Church Hamilton; William Stephen Hamilton; Eliza Hamilton; Philip Hamilton (named for 1st child who was killed in a duel in 1801). ❖ Remained a shadowy figure until husband's death (1804), when she emerged as one of his most ardent champions; described as a sickly woman, given to nervous attacks, was beleaguered by a long succession of pregnancies, during which she gave birth to 8 children and suffered numerous miscarriages; saw marriage further strained by Alexander's infidelities, one of the most notable being a liaison with Maria Reynolds; during 50 years of widowhood, busied herself with elevating husband's reputation. ❖ See also *Women in World History*.

HAMILTON, Emma (1765–1815). Paramour of Admiral Lord Horatio Nelson. Name variations: Emily or Emma Hart; Amy, Emy, Emma, or Emily Lyon. Born Amy Lyon in spring 1765 (some sources cite April 26), in Denhall, Cheshire, England; died in Calais, France, Jan 15, 1815; dau. of Henry Lyon (blacksmith) and Mary Kidd Lyon (domestic servant); m. Sir William Hamilton, 1791; had liaison with Lord Horatio Nelson, 1799–1805; children: (father unknown) Emily (b. 1782); (with Nelson) Horatia Nelson (b. 1801) and Emma Nelson (died in infancy, 1804). ❖ One of the most famous women in British history, was mistress and subsequently wife to the British ambassador to the court of Naples, then became involved in a passionate and scandalous love affair with Admiral Lord Horatio Nelson, the greatest naval leader in British history; started work as domestic servant in Cheshire (1777); was mistress of Sir Harry Featherstonhaugh (1781) and Charles Greville (1782–86); moved to Italy (1786); was mistress of Sir William Hamilton (1786–91), then married him (1791); began love affair with Nelson (1799); returned to England (1800); learned of the death of Hamilton (1803) and death of Nelson (1805); imprisoned for debt (1813); fled to France (1814). ❖ See also Flora Fraser, *Beloved Emma: The Life of Emma, Lady Hamilton* (Weidenfeld & Nicolson, 1986); Colin Simpson, *Emma* (Bodley Head, 1983); Nora Lofts, *Emma Hamilton* (Coward, 1978); Susan Sontag, *The Volcano Lover* (Farrar, Straus, 1992); film *That Hamilton Woman*, starring Vivien Leigh (1941); film *The Nelson Affair* (titled in England *Bequest to the Nation*), with Glenda Jackson (1973); and *Women in World History*.

HAMILTON, Frances (d. 1730). *See Jennings, Frances.*

HAMILTON, Gail (1833–1896). *See Dodge, Mary Abigail.*

HAMILTON, Gordon (1892–1967). American social worker. Name variations: Amy Gordon Hamilton. Born Amy Gordon Hamilton on Dec 26, 1892, in Tenafly, NJ; died Mar 10, 1967, in British Columbia, Canada; dau. of George Hamilton and Bertha (Torrance) Hamilton. ❖ Worked for Red Cross Home Service in Colorado Springs, CO (1917–20); worked as caseworker and as researcher for Charity Organization Society (COS) in NYC (1920–23); taught at New York School of Social Work (1923–57); worked as associate director of social service and as adviser on research at Presbyterian Hospital in NYC (1925–32); wrote *Medical School Terminology* (1927), *Theory and Practice of Social Casework* (1940), and *Psychotherapy in Child Guidance* (1947); worked with federal relief agencies and helped establish 1st Federal Emergency Relief Administration training program during Great Depression; tried unsuccessfully to create nonsectarian refugee organization, then joined Board of Christian Refugees, worked with Church World Service, and was staff member and consultant for United Nations Relief and Rehabilitation Administration (after WWII); was research consultant to Jewish Board of Guardians (1947–50); was 1st editor-in-chief of journal, *Social Work*

(1956–62); received many honors, including Florina Lasker Award (1958); suffered from respiratory ailments through life.

HAMILTON, Hariot (fl. 1845–1891). See Blackwood, Hariot.

HAMILTON, Hervey (1897–1985). See Robins, Denise Naomi.

HAMILTON, Lady (1765–1815). See Hamilton, Emma.

HAMILTON, Margaret (1902–1985). American actress. Born Margaret Brainard Hamilton, Sept 12, 1902, in Cleveland, Ohio; died May 16, 1985, in Salisbury, Connecticut; dau. of Walter Jones Hamilton (attorney) and Jennie (Adams) Hamilton; obtained teaching certificate from Wheelock Kindergarten Training School (now Wheelock College), Boston, 1923; studied acting and pantomime with Maria Ouspenskaya and Joseph Moon; m. Paul Boynton Meserve (landscape architect), June 13, 1931 (div. 1938); children: 1 son, Hamilton. ❖ In a career that spanned more than 50 years, and included 75 films and as many stage plays, will forever be identified with the dual role of Mrs. Gulch and Wicked Witch of the West in film *The Wizard of Oz* (1939); ran a nursery school for several years; made NY stage debut as Helen Hallam in *Another Language* (1932); performed in dozens of live dramatic tv productions, including "The Man Who Came to Dinner" (1954), "The Devil's Disciple" (1955), "The Trial of Lizzie Borden" (1957), and "The Silver Whistle" (1959); had on-going roles in soap operas "Secret Storm" and "As the World Turns"; also made mark in tv commercials, especially as Cora for Maxwell House; stage credits encompassed comedy, drama, and musicals and included performances on Broadway, off-Broadway, stock, and regional theater, appearing as Mrs. Zero in *The Adding Machine* (1956), Clara in *Save Me a Place at Forest Lawn* (1963), Grandma in *The American Dream* (1962), Dolly Tate in *Annie Get Your Gun*, Aunt Eller in *Oklahoma!*, and Parthy Ann Hawks in *Show Boat*; other films include *Broadway Bill* (1934), *The Farmer Takes a Wife* (1935), *Way Down East* (1935), *These Three* (1936), *Nothing Sacred* (1937), *The Adventures of Tom Sawyer* (1938), *My Little Chickadee* (1940), *State of the Union* (1948), *The Red Pony* (1949), *The Beautiful Blonde from Bashful Bend* (1949), *People Will Talk* (1951), *Comin' Round the Mountain* (1951), *Paradise Alley* (1962) and *Brewster McCloud* (1970). ❖ See also *Women in World History.*

HAMILTON, Mary (1613–1638). Duchess of Hamilton. Name variations: Margaret Fielding; Mary Fielding. Born Mary Fielding in 1613; died May 10, 1638; dau. of William Fielding, 1st earl of Denbigh, and Susan Villiers; m. James Hamilton (1606–1648), 1st duke of Hamilton, in 1630 (beheaded in 1648 for leading a Scottish army into England); children: Anne Hamilton (1636–1716); Charles Hamilton, earl of Arran; Susannah Hamilton. ❖ Lady-of-the-bedchamber to Queen Henrietta Maria, was praised by poet Edmund Waller in "Thyrsis Galatea."

HAMILTON, Mary (1705–?). English cross-dresser. Born 1705 in UK; married to 14 women. ❖ Dressed as man and married 14 women; once her gender was revealed, had charges brought against her by 14th wife, Mary Price (exact nature of charges apparently remain unclear); though court did not find her guilty of bigamy (which under the law presupposed heterosexual unions), was found to be "an uncommon notorious cheat" and sentenced to be whipped in the towns in which she had made marriages (Taunton, Glastonbury, Wells, and Shipton-Mallet).

HAMILTON, Mary (1739–1816). British novelist. Name variations: Lady Mary Hamilton. Born Mary Leslie in 1739; died in 1816. ❖ Lived with 2nd husband in France and published 4 novels; was a friend of Sir Herbert Croft, an English scholar and linguist, and French writer Charles Nodier.

HAMILTON, Mary (1882–1966). Scottish feminist, politician, journalist, and author. Born Mary Agnes Adamson, July 8, 1882, in Glasgow, Scotland; died Feb 10, 1966, in England; dau. of Robert Adamson (professor of logic and metaphysics at Glasgow University) and Daisy (Duncan) Adamson (1st woman student at Newnham College, Cambridge); honors degree from Newnham College, Cambridge; m. Charles Hamilton (professor of logic and metaphysics), 1905. ❖ Joined the Independent Labor Party; following WWI, began writing for *Time and Tide* and was later a journalist for *The Economist*; was elected as Labor MP for Blackburn (1929); during term, served as parliamentary private secretary to Clement Attlee; also served on Royal Commission on the Civil Service, where she supported equal pay for men and women; though defeated in the general election (1931), remained in public eye, serving as a governor of the BBC (1932–36), and as a member of the London County Council (1937–40); during WWII, headed the American Division of the Ministry of Information; also wrote biographies of such Labor figures as Margaret Bondfield and Arthur Henderson. Made Commander of British Empire (CBE, 1949). ❖ See also memoirs *Remembering My Good Friends* (1944) and *Uphill all the Way* (1953); and *Women in World History.*

HAMILTON, Mollie (1908–2004). See Kaye, M.M.

HAMILTON, Nancy (1908–1985). American lyricist. Born July 27, 1908, in Sewickley, Pennsylvania; died Feb 18, 1985, in New York, NY. ❖ One of the 1st successful female lyricists, wrote sketches and lyrics for such Broadway revues as *One for the Money, New Faces of 1924, Two for the Show* and *Three to Make Ready.*

HAMILTON, Suzanne (1968—). See Favor, Suzy.

HAMILTON, Tara (1982—). American wakeboarder. Born Jan 16, 1982, in Lantana, Florida. ❖ Dominant force in women's wakeboarding, began competing (1997); won gold (1997 and 2000) and bronze (1998 and 2001) at X Games; received silver at Gravity Games (1999, 2001, and 2003) and World championships (2000); other 1st-place finishes include Women's Professional Tour Overall champion (1997, 1998), World champion (1997, 1998), Wakeboard World Cup champion (1998, 1999), Vans Triple Crown Women's Overall champion (1998, 1999), US National champion (1998, 1999); and Masters champion (1998, 1999).

HAMILTON, Virginia (1936–2002). African-American children's writer and biographer. Name variations: Virginia Hamilton Adoff. Born Virginia Esther Hamilton, Mar 12, 1934, in Yellow Springs, Ohio; died Feb 19, 2002, in Dayton, OH; attended Antioch College, Ohio State University and New School for Social Research; m. Arnold Adoff (poet), 1960; children: Leigh Hamilton Adoff and Jaime Levi Adoff. ❖ Internationally known writer, was the 1st children's author to receive a MacArthur Foundation "genius" grant (1995); writings, which reflect influence of oral storytelling and focus on African-American history, include *Zeely* (1967), *The House of Dies Drear* (1968), *The Planet of Junior Brown* (1971), *M.C. Higgins, The Great* (1974), for which she won a National Book Award and the Newbery Award, *Sweet Whispers, Brother Rush* (1982), *The Magical Adventures of Pretty Pearl* (1983), *Willie Bea and the Time the Martians Landed* (1983), *The People Could Fly* (1985), *A Little Love* (1985), *Many Thousand Gone: African Americans from Slavery to Freedom* (1993), *The Pizza Place* and *Back to Your Room*; biographies include *W.E.B. DuBois: A Biography* (1972) and *Paul Robeson: The Life and Times of a Free Black Man* (1974). Received Edgar Allan Poe Award (1968), Laura Ingalls Wilder Medal (1995), Coretta Scott King Award and Hans Christian Andersen Medal.

HAMILTON RUSSELL, Lady (1875–1938). See Scott, Margaret.

HAMILTRUDE (fl. 700s). See Himiltrude.

HAMLETT, Dilys (1928–2002). English stage and screen actress. Born Mar 31, 1928, in Tidworth, Hampshire, England; died Nov 7, 2002, in Kirkcaldy, Fife, Scotland; dau. of Sidney Hamlett (MBE) and Mary Jane (Evans) Hamlett; m. Casper Wrede (director). ❖ Made London stage debut in *The Innocents* (1952), followed by *Danton's Death, Brand, A Passage to India, The Miracle Worker, Peer Gynt, Measure for Measure, Othello, Little Eyolf, Long Day's Journey into Night, As You Like It* (as Rosalind), and *Thomas and the King*; films include *Diagnosis Murder, The Wolves of Willoughby Chase*, and *Hollow Reed*; on tv, appeared on "Hedda Gabler," "The Moving Finger," "Gaudy Night," "The Rainbow" and "Harnessing Peacocks"; helped found Manchester's Royal Exchange Theatre (1976).

HAMLIN, Shelley (1949—). American golfer. Born Shelley Hamlin, May 28, 1949, in Fresno, California. ❖ Member of the Curtis Cup team (1968, 1970); won National Collegiate championship while at Stanford University; was four-time California state champion; turned pro (1972); won the Japan Classic (1975) and Patty Berg Classic (1978); served as LPGA president (1980–81). First recipient of Dr. DeDe Owens Spirit of Golf Award (2000).

HAMM, Margherita (1867–1907). Canadian journalist and author. Name variations: Margaret Hamm. Born Margaret Hamm, April 29, 1867, in St. Stephen, New Brunswick, Canada; died Dec 17, 1907, in New York, NY; dau. of Rufus La Fayette Hamm (owner of lumber business) and Martha Almenia (Spencer) Hamm; educated at Convent of the Sacred Heart in Carleton, Nebraska; attended Emerson College of Oratory, 1889–90; m. William E.S. Fales (vice-consul in China), Oct 14, 1893 (div. 1902); m. John Robert McMahon (journalist), Aug 1, 1902;

children: Arlina Douglas McMahon (b. 1903). ❖ While still young, moved with family to Bangor, Maine; worked for *Boston Herald* as a reporter before moving to NY; in Korea when the Sino-Japanese war broke out (1894), scored a journalistic coup by presenting firsthand accounts of events to a variety of newspapers in America, including the attack on the palace at Seoul, the assassination of Queen Min, and the declaration of war; edited *Journalist*, a trade weekly (1894–95); also headed the women's department of New York *Evening Mail and Express*; left the *Evening Mail* to cover the Spanish-American war (1898); wrote several books, including 3 relating to the Spanish-American War: *Manila and the Philippines* (1898), *Puerto Rico and the West Indies* (1899) and *Dewey, the Defender* (1899). ❖ See also *Women in World History*.

HAMM, Mia (1972—). American soccer player. Born Mariel Margaret Hamm, Mar 17, 1972, in Selma, Alabama; dau. of William Hamm (pilot in US Air Force) and Stephanie Hamm (ballerina); graduate of University of North Carolina, 1994; m. Christiaan Corey (Marine Corps pilot), Dec 17, 1994 (div.); married Nomar Garciaparra (baseball player), 2004. ❖ Forward; became leading scorer in world—male or female—with 108 goals (May 16, 1999); was a member of US national team (1987–99); was 4-time member of NCAA women's soccer championship team (1989–93); won World Cup team championships (1991, 1999); set NCAA single-season scoring record of 59 goals, 33 assists for 92 points (1992); won a gold medal at Atlanta Olympics (1996), having led US national team in scoring with 9 goals, 18 assists for 27 points in 23 games (1996); won a silver medal at Sydney Olympics (2000); was a founding member of Women's United Soccer Association (WUSA); signed with the Washington Freedom (2001); won a team gold medal at Athens Olympics (2004). Named ACC tournament MVP (1989, 1992), ACC Player of the Year (1990, 1992, 1993), and National Player of the Year (1992–94); received Mary Garber Award as ACC Female Athlete of the Year (1993, 1994); named US Soccer Female Athlete of the Year (1993–98); received Honda Broderick Cup as Most Outstanding Female Athlete in all college sports (1994); named MVP of the US Cup (1995); named Women's Sports Foundation Athlete of the Year (1997); won ESPN Award (1998). ❖ See also autobiography, with Aaron Heifetz *Go for the Goal* (HarperCollins, 1999); Matt Christopher, *On the Field with . . . Mia Hamm* (Little, Brown, 1998); Jere Longman *The Girls of Summer: The U.S. Women's Soccer Team and How It Changed the World* (HarperCollins, 2000).

HAMMARBERG, Gretchen. American wakeboarder. Trained in Idaho. ❖ Competed as gymnast; competed at semi-pro level in wakeboarding, winning 1st place in Northwest Sessions stops in Sandpoint, Idaho, Kalispell, Montana, Bellevue and Olympia, Washington; finished 3rd in nation as semi- pro at World Wakeboarding championships in Orlando, FL (2000); took 2nd in men's amateur division in INT Tour Stop in Boulder, CO.

HAMMARSTROM, Marianne (1908–1998). *See Strengell, Marianne.*

HAMMER, Barbara (1930–1994). *See Avedon, Barbara Hammer.*

HAMMERER, Resi (1925—). Austrian Alpine skier. Born 1925 in Austria. ❖ Won a bronze medal for the downhill at St. Moritz Olympics (1948). The Resi Hammerer shop in Vienna began selling women's sportswear in 1958.

HAMMERSTEIN, Dorothy (1899–1987). Australian-born interior decorator and actress. Name variations: Dorothy Blanchard; Dorothy Jacobson; Mrs. Oscar Hammerstein. Born Dorothy Blanchard, June 7, 1899, in Australia; died Aug 3, 1987, in New York, NY; m. Oscar Hammerstein II (librettist), 1929 (died 1960). ❖ An interior decorator in NY, appeared on Broadway in *Charlot's Revue* and toured US and Canada understudying Beatrice Lillie.

HAMMERSTEIN, Elaine (1897–1948). American stage and screen actress. Born June 16, 1897, in Philadelphia, PA; died Aug 13, 1948, in auto accident in Tijuana, Mexico; dau. of Arthur Hammerstein (theatrical manager and producer); m. James Walter Kays; m. Alan Crosland. ❖ Made stage debut in *High Jinks*; films include *The Moonstone, Broadway Gold, The Mad Lover, The Argyle Case, Her Man, The Country Cousin, Reckless Youth, Souls for Sale* and *Ladies of Leisure.*

HAMMERSTEIN, Mrs. Oscar (1899–1987). *See Hammerstein, Dorothy.*

HAMMON, Mary (c. 1633–?). American colonial woman tried for lesbianism. Born in Massachusetts. ❖ In 1649, as a citizen of Plymouth in the Massachusetts Bay Colony, was charged with "lude

behavior upon a bed."; recorded as being 16 years old at the time, was acquitted of the charges. ❖ See also *Women in World History*.

HAMMOND, Blodwen (1908–1973). American anthropologist. Born Feb 3, 1908; died Nov 1973 in Redwood City, California. ❖ With Mary Thygeson Shepardson, published *The Navajo Mountain Community* (Shepardson and Hammond, 1970) and performed fieldwork on Bonin Islands, Japan (1971).

HAMMOND, Dorothy (c. 1876–1950). English actress. Born Dorothy Plaskitt, c. 1876 in London, England; died Nov 23, 1950, in London; m. Sir Guy Standing; children: Kay Hammond (actress). ❖ Made stage debut as a walk-on in *The Prisoner of Zenda*, followed by *The Storm, The Royal Necklace, Mademoiselle Mars* (as Eliza Bonaparte), *Mrs. Leffingwell's Boots, Time is Money,* and *The Butterfly on the Wheel,* among others; in America, appeared opposite Richard Mansfield in *Julius Caesar* (as Portia), *Monsieur Beaucaire* (as Lady Mary), and *Dr. Jekyll and Mr. Hyde* (as Agnes).

HAMMOND, Joan (1912–1996). New Zealand-born soprano and golfer. Name variations: Dame Joan Hammond. Born May 24, 1912, in Christchurch, New Zealand; died Nov 26, 1996; dau. of Samuel and Hilda (Blandford) Hammond; studied at Sydney Conservatory. ❖ Debuted in Sydney (1929) before going to London to study with Dino Borgioli; made operatic debut at the Vienna Staatsoper (1938); was a member of the Carl Rosa Opera Company (1942–45); made Covent Garden debut (1949); her recording of "O, my beloved father" from Puccini's *Gianni Schicchi* sold over 1 million copies (1969); retired from singing (1971); became artistic director of the Victoria Opera and head of vocal studies at Victorian College of the Arts; had also played golf, winning the New South Wales (NSW) jr. championship (1929, 1930), the NSW Champion of Champions twice, and the NSW ladies' championship (1932, 1934, 1935). Received the Sir Charles Santley award (for musician of the year) from the Worshipful Company of Musicians in London (1970); made a Dame of the British Empire (DBE, 1974). ❖ See also autobiography, *A Voice, A Life* (1970); and *Women in World History*.

HAMMOND, Kathleen (1951—). American runner. Born Nov 2, 1951, in US. ❖ At Munich Olympics, won a bronze medal in 400 meters and a silver medal in 4x400-meter relay (1972).

HAMMOND, Kay (1909–1980). British actress. Born Dorothy Katherine Standing in London, England, Feb 18, 1909; died May 5, 1980; dau. of Guy Standing (actor) and Dorothy Standing (actress); attended Banstead in Surrey; studied at Royal Academy of Dramatic Art; m. John Selby Clements (actor-manager), c. 1945; no children. ❖ Made stage debut as Amelia in *Tilly of Bloomsbury* (1927); played a progression of bit parts until 1st starring role in *French Without Tears* (1936), which ran for 2 years; had a 2nd 2-year run as the original Elvira in Noel Coward's *Blithe Spirit*, which she also filmed (1945); following marriage, often performed with husband; forced to retire from the stage for 2 years because of ill health, made a triumphant return opposite husband as Mrs. Sullen in *The Beaux' Stratagem* (1949); was also seen in *The Rape of the Belt* (1957), *Gilt and Gingerbread* (1959) and *The Marriage Go Round* (1959), after which she retired from the stage. ❖ See also *Women in World History*.

HAMMOND, Virginia (1893–1972). American stage and screen actress. Born Aug 20, 1893, in Staunton, Virginia; died April 6, 1972, in Washington DC. ❖ Made NY debut in *Arsene Lupin* (1909); also appeared in *What the Doctor Ordered, The Arab, If I Were King, You Can't Take It With You, The Man Who Came to Dinner, Winged Victory, Craig's Wife, Life with Mother* and *Crime and Punishment*; films include *The Discard, Cabin in the Cotton* and *Romeo and Juliet.*

HAMNETT, Katherine (1952—). British fashion designer. Born 1952 in Gravesend, Kent, England; dau. of a diplomat; attended Cheltenham Ladies' College; studied fashion design at St. Martin's School of Art; children: 2 sons. ❖ Known for anti-establishment approach, use of utilitarian fabrics, and clothing with loose, simple lines, 1st partnered with Anne Buck for their Tuttabankmen label (1969–74); after bankruptcy, began freelancing in UK, Europe, and US; with backing from Peter Bertelson, started new company which became extremely profitable (1979); environmentally concerned, tends to use natural fibers; is also active in the peace movement. Received Designer of Year Award from British Fashion Council (1984) and British Knitting and Clothing Export Council award (1988).

HAMNETT, Nina (1890–1956). British artist. Born in Tenby, South Wales, Feb 14, 1890; died 1956; eldest dau. of George (army officer) and Mary Hamnett; attended Dublin School of Art, Pelham School of

Art; studied at London School of Art under Frank Brangwyn, John Swan, and William Nicholson; m. Roald Kristian (artist), Oct 12, 1914 (sep. but never div.); children: 1 son (1915–1915). ❖ One of London's most promising avant-garde painters (1915–28), whose flamboyant personality and bohemian lifestyle eclipsed her standing in the modern art movement; enjoyed a close association with artists Roger Fry, who hired her in 1913 to work in his Omega Workshop, and Walter Sickert, who wrote the preface for her 1st solo exhibition in 1918; known as the "Queen of Bohemia," became absorbed with social life and drinking for a period of 10 years beginning in 1932, virtually abandoning her art; returned to work (1940s–50s), producing some of her most poignant drawings; though she painted still lifes and landscapes, is best known for her illuminating portraits, which include likenesses of some of Walter Sickert, Osbert and Edith Sitwell, Ossip Zadkine, Amedeo Modigliani, Frank Dobson, Henri Gaudier-Brzeska, Rupert Doone, Anthony Powell, and Lytton Strachey; also drew witty and highly praised line illustrations, some of which appeared in Osbert Sitwell's *The People's Album of London Statues* (1928). ❖ See also autobiographies *Laughing Torso* (1932) and *Is She a Lady?* (1955); and *Women in World History*.

HAMPE, Jutta (1960—). See Behrendt-Hampe, Jutta.

HAMPER, Geneviève (c. 1889–1971). American actress. Name variations: Mrs. Robert B. Mantell; Genevieve Hamper. Born c. 1889 in Greenville, Michigan; died Feb 13, 1971, in New York, NY; m. Robert B. Mantell (Shakespearean actor, 1854–1928); m. John Alexander (actor). ❖ Starred in Shakespearean plays opposite husband Robert Mantell (1916–28); retired (1933).

HAMPSHIRE, Margaret (1918–2004). British educator. Born Grace Margaret Hampshire, July 9, 1918, in England; died June 6, 2004; attended Malvern Girls' College; read history at Girton College, Cambridge. ❖ Began career at Board of Trade; was head of the government relations department at the textiles firm Courtaulds; served as principal of Cheltenham Ladies' College (1964–79); while respecting its traditions, restructured the school and modernized its system; was also governor of Alice Ottley School in Worcester (1979–92); actively promoted the education of women.

HAMPSHIRE, Susan (1938—). English actress and writer. Born May 12, 1938, in London, England; m. Pierre Granier-Deferre (French director), 1967 (div. 1974); m. Eddie Kulukundis (Greek ship owner and impresario), 1981. ❖ Made London stage debut as Cynthia in *Expresso Bongo* (1958), followed by *Follow that Girl, The Ginger Man, Past Imperfect,* and *The Circle,* among others; films include *Night Must Fall, Rogan, A Room in Paris, Living Free, Neither the Sea nor the Sand, Dr, Jekyll and Mr. Hyde, Roses and Green Peppers* and *Paris in the Month of August;* on tv, starred in "David Copperfield," "The Pallisers" and "The Barchester Chronicles." Won Emmy awards for performance as Fleur in "The Forsyte Saga," Sarah, duchess of Marlborough, in "The First Churchills," and Becky Sharp in "Vanity Fair"; received Order of the British Empire (OBE, 1995) for dyslexia causes. ❖ See also memoir *Susan's Story* about dealing with her dyslexia, and *The Maternal Instinct.*

HAMPSTEAD, Hariata Whakatau (1836–1885). See Pitini-Morera, Hariata Whakatau.

HAMPTON, Hope (1897–1982). American actress and socialite. Born Mae Elizabeth Hampton, Feb 19, 1897, in Houston, TX; died Jan 23, 1892, in New York, NY; m. Jules Brulatour, 1923 (died 1946). ❖ Dubbed the "Duchess of Park Avenue," was more of a socialite than an actress; films include *Modern Salome, Love's Penalty, The Light in the Dark, The Gold Diggers, The Truth about Women* and *The Unfair Sex;* retired from film to pursue a modest opera career.

HAMPTON, Isabel Adams (1860–1910). See Robb, Isabel Hampton.

HAMPTON, Mabel (1902–1989). African-American gay-right's activist. Name variations: Mabel M. Hampton. Born May 2, 1902, in Winston-Salem, North Carolina; raised by grandmother; died Mar 11, 1989, in New York, NY; lived with partner Lillian Foster, 1932–78 (died 1978). ❖ Black lesbian pioneer, was orphaned at 2, raised by grandmother until age 7, then raped by an uncle at 8; began career dancing in all-women's troupe at Coney Island; was one of the sisters of the Harlem Renaissance; throughout life, collected memorabilia to document her history and the world around her as a black woman and as a lesbian; donated these artifacts to the Lesbian Herstory Archives; appeared in the films *Silent Pioneers* and *Before Stonewall.*

HAN AILI (1937—). Chinese short-story writer. Born 1937 in Japanese-occupied Shanghai, China; graduate of Beijing University. ❖ Wrote scripts for classical Chinese opera; published collection of short stories about cruelty of cultural revolution, *Swept Away* (1979).

HAN HWA-SOO (1963—). South Korean handball player. Born Feb 3, 1963, in Korea. ❖ At Los Angeles Olympics, won a silver medal in team competition (1984).

HAN HYUN-SOOK (1970—). South Korean handball player. Born Mar 17, 1970, in South Korea. ❖ At Seoul Olympics, won a gold medal in team competition (1988).

HAN KEUM-SIL (1968—). South Korean field-hockey player. Born Jan 24, 1968, in South Korea. ❖ At Seoul Olympics, won a silver medal in team competition (1988).

HAN OK-KYUNG (1965—). South Korean field-hockey player. Born Sept 27, 1965, in South Korea. ❖ At Seoul Olympics, won a silver medal in team competition (1988).

HAN PIL-HWA (1942—). North Korean speedskater. Born Jan 21, 1942, in Nampo (when Korea was occupied by Japan). ❖ Won a silver medal for the 3,000 meters at Innsbruck Olympics (1964), the only North Korean speedskater to ever win an Olympic medal; won a bronze medal for the 3,000 meters at World championships (1966); placed 9th in the 3,000 at Sapporo Olympics (1972), the last race of her career; coached; became a member of the North Korean Parliament (1998).

HAN SUN-HEE (1973—). South Korean handball player. Born June 9, 1973, in South Korea. ❖ Won a team silver medal at Atlanta Olympics (1996).

HAN, Suyin (1917—). Chinese author and physician. Name variations: Elizabeth Chou; Chou Kuang Hu; Zhou Guanghu; Elizabeth Comber. Born Chou Kuang Hu or Zhou Guanghu, Sept 12, 1917, in Peking (Beijing), China; dau. of Y.T. Chou (Chinese) and Marguerite (Denis) Chou (Belgian); attended Yenching University in Peking; University of Brussels, BSc; London University, MB, BS, 1948; m. General Pao H. Tang (Bao Dang), 1938 (died 1947); m. Leonard F. Comber, Feb 1, 1952 (div. c. 1962); m. Vincent Ruthnaswamy, 1964; children: (dau.) Yung Mei (adopted 1941). ❖ Took the pseudonym Han Suyin while writing 1st book, *Destination Chungking* (1942); wrote the largely autobiographical novel, *A Many-Splendored Thing* (1952), which was a huge success and established her international literary reputation; accepted assistantship in Obstetrics and Gynecology Department of Queen Mary Hospital in Hong Kong (1949); lived in numerous countries but spent most of early to middle years in China; during 1950s, was suspected of being an American spy by the Chinese despite her earnest medical work for her compatriots and was simultaneously blacklisted as a Communist in US; other books include *. . . And the Rain My Drink* (1956), *From One China to the Other* (1956), *The Mountain is Young* (1957), *Four Faces* (1960), *The Crippled Tree* (1965), *A Mortal Flower* (1966), *Birdless Summer* (1967), *The Morning Deluge: Mao Tse Tung and the Chinese Revolution, 1893–1954* (1972), *The Enchantress* (c. 1985), and two novellas, *Cast But One Shadow* (1962) and *Winter Love* (1963). ❖ See also memoir *My House Has Two Doors* (Putnam, 1980); and *Women in World History.*

HAN XUE (1981—). Chinese swimmer. Born Sept 21, 1981, in Beijing, China. ❖ Won a bronze medal for 4x100-meter relay at Atlanta Olympics (1996).

HAN YAQIN (1963—). Chinese rower. Born Aug 18, 1963, in China. ❖ At Seoul Olympics, won a bronze medal in coxed eights (1988).

HANAFIN, Mary (1959—). Irish politician. Born June 1959 in Thurles, Co. Tipperary, Ireland; dau. of Des Hanafin (senator, 1969–93, 1997); m. Eamon Leahy. ❖ Representing Fianna Fáil, elected to the 28th Dáil (1997–2002) for Dún Laoghaire; appointed minister of State at the Dept. of Health and Children (2000); returned to 29th Dáil (2002).

HANAFORD, Phebe Ann (1829–1921). American Universalist minister, author, and feminist. Born Phebe Ann Coffin, May 6, 1829, in Siasconset, Nantucket Island, Massachusetts; died June 2, 1921, in Rochester, NY; dau. of George W. Coffin and Phebe Ann (Barnard) Coffin; m. Dr. Joseph Hibbard Hanaford, Dec 2, 1849 (sep. 1870); lived with Ellen E. Miles (Universalist author); children: Howard and Florence Hanaford. ❖ Wrote 14 books, including *Lucretia the Quakeress* (1853), and a collection of poems *From Shore to Shore* (1870); also contributed to numerous periodicals, published small volumes for children and biographies of Abraham Lincoln (1865) and George Peabody (1870); though raised a Quaker, turned to Universalism; began preaching (1865); edited a monthly Universalist magazine, *Ladies' Repository,* and a Sunday-school paper, *Myrtle* (1866–68); ordained in Hingham, Massachusetts (1868), took charge of the parish at Waltham, MA, then, after separating from husband, began her service at First Universalist Church of New Haven, CT (1870); also served as chaplain of Connecticut house and senate; moved to Church of the Good Shepherd in Jersey City, NJ (1874); assumed role of pastor of Second Church in New Haven (1884); also active in women's rights issues, published *Women of the Century* (1876) which was revised as *Daughters of America* (1882). ❖ See also *Women in World History.*

HANAN, Susanna (1870–1970). New Zealand governess, singer and social-welfare worker. Name variations: Susanna Murray. Born Susanna Murray, July 1, 1870, at Wallacetown, New Zealand; died on Feb 12, 1970, in Dunedin, New Zealand; dau. of John Murray (dairyman) and Louisa (Boddy) Murray; m. Josiah Alfred Hanan (lawyer), 1902 (died 1954); children: 2 sons. ❖ Worked as governess throughout 1890s; gained reputation as talented singer and pianist in Southland area (1880s); following marriage, became interested in numerous social causes, including infant-welfare movement; founding member of Invercargill branch of Society for the Health of Women and Children (Plunket Society) (1910–25); also active in New Zealand Free Kindergarten Union (1912); helped to establish Southland branch of British Red Cross Society during WWI; with husband, represented New Zealand at coronation of George VI (1937). ❖ See also *Dictionary of New Zealand Biography* (Vol. 3).

HANAU, Marthe (c. 1884–1935). French swindler. Born in Paris, France, c. 1884; died in Paris, July 19, 1935; m. Lazare Bloch (businessman), 1908 (div.); no children. ❖ Confidence woman, hatched a scheme to capitalize on France's postwar money woes by opening an investment house (1925), where she also published the famous *Gazette du Franc,* a tipster's sheet; as her stature grew, hired a new editor for the *Gazette,* respected journalist Pierre Audibert; by 1928, was presiding over the Compagnie Générale Financière et Foncière; with hundreds under her employ, advised 60,000 investors (mostly schoolteachers, clergy, retirees, and small business owners); bilked 150 million francs from victims, 7 of whom took their own lives; arrested and on trial for 2 years (1928–31), was seen as a martyr by many of her clients; pronounced guilty (1931), was sentenced to 2 years in prison and fined; after a series of appeals, imprisoned once more (1933) where she poisoned herself 6 months later. ❖ See also *Women in World History.*

HANBURY, Elizabeth (1793–1901). British philanthropist. Born 1793; died 1901; dau. of Quakers; m. Cornelius Hanbury, 1826; children: Charlotte Hanbury (1830–1900), who worked side by side with her mother and later established a mission in Tangier for improving lives of Moorish prisoners. ❖ Accompanied Elizabeth Fry on her prison rounds (early 1800s) and advocated prison reform; was also an active abolitionist.

HANBURY, Felicity (1913–2002). *See Peake, Felicity.*

HANCOCK, Cornelia (1840–1927). American Civil War nurse, housing reformer and educator of freedmen. Born Feb 8, 1840, at Hancock's Bridge, NJ; died Dec 31, 1927, in Atlantic City; dau. of Thomas Y. Hancock and Rachel (Nicholson) Hancock. ❖ Served as field nurse in Gettysburg (1863); in Washington, DC, cared for contraband Negroes from the South (1863); continued as field nurse near Brandy Station, VA, and at corps hospital in City Point, VA (1964); started school for freedmen outside Charleston, SC, under auspices of Friends' Association for the Aid and Elevation of the Freedmen (1866), which later became Laing School where she remained as principal (until 1875); joined in founding Philadelphia Society for Organizing Charitable Relief and Repressing Mendicancy (1878), soon renamed Society for Organizing Charity, where she served as superintendent (1879–c. 1888); active in establishment of Children's Aid Society (1883) and board member thereof (until 1895); helped reform and improve living conditions in "Wrightsville," an isolated slum settlement outside Philadelphia primarily inhabited by immigrant refinery workers (late 1880s). ❖ See also Henrietta S. Jaquette, ed., *South after Gettysburg: Letters of Cornelia Hancock, 1863–1868* (1956).

HANCOCK, Florence (1893–1974). British trade unionist. Name variations: Dame Florence Hancock. Born in Chippenham, Wilshire, England, 1893; died 1974; 1 of 14 children of a woolen weaver; attended Chippenham Elementary School until age 12; m. John Donovan (unionist), 1964. ❖ Devoted life to upholding the rights of England's laboring class; with merging of the Workers' Union with the Transport and General Workers' Union (1929), was sent to Bristol as a woman's officer, a post she held until 1942; was elected to the general council of the Trades Union Congress (1935), which at the time controlled 7,500,000 organized workers; elected president of the Congress (1947), one of only two women to ever hold that British labor post; during WWII, served as an advisor to the Ministry of Labor on women's war work; was also governor of the BBC (1955–62) and director of Remploy (1958–66). Named Dame of the British Empire (DBE, 1951). ❖ See also *Women in World History.*

HANCOCK, Joy (1898–1986). American naval officer. Born Joy Bright in Wildwood, NJ, May 4, 1898; died in Bethesda, Maryland, Aug 20, 1986; dau. of William Henry Hancock (banker and one-time lt. governor of New Jersey) and Priscilla (Buck) Hancock; attended Catholic University, Washington, DC; m. Charles Gray Little (naval aviator), Oct 9, 1920 (killed 10 months later in crash of dirigible ZR-2 in England); m. Lt. Commander Lewis Hancock Jr. (naval aviator), June 3, 1924 (killed in crash of dirigible USS *Shenandoah,* 1925); no children. ❖ The 3rd and last director of the WAVES, began 35-year career with US Navy (1918) by enlisting in Naval Reserve during WWI; took a position at Navy Department's Bureau of Aeronautics in Washington; began pilot's training, receiving civil license (1928); rejoined Bureau of Aeronautics, where for 8 years she headed its editorial and research section; became a lieutenant in the newly created Women's Naval Reserve (1942), then called Women Accepted for Volunteer Emergency Services (WAVES); named assistant director of the WAVES, then director, with rank of captain (1946); had a leading role in the preparation and promotion of what finally emerged as the Women's Armed Services Integration Act (1948), under which the Navy was authorized to offer regular commissions to women; was one of the 1st 8 women to receive a commission in the Navy, at which time she was accorded the permanent rank of lieutenant commander and appointed assistant to chief of Naval Personnel, with temporary rank of captain; retired (1953). ❖ See also autobiography, *Lady in the Navy* (1972); and *Women in World History.*

HANDA, Yuriko (1940—). Japanese volleyball player. Born Mar 31, 1940, in Japan. ❖ At Tokyo Olympics, won a gold medal in team competition (1964).

HANDAYANI, Lilies (1965—). Indonesian archer. Born April 15, 1965, in Indonesia. ❖ At Seoul Olympics, won a silver medal in team round (1988).

HANDEL-MAZZETTI, Enrica von (1871–1955). Austrian novelist. Name variations: Baroness Enrika von Handel-Mazzetti; (pseudonym) Marien Kind. Born Enrica Ludovica Maria Freiin von Handel-Mazzetti in Vienna, Austria, Jan 10, 1871; died in Linz, Austria, April 8, 1955; dau. of Heinrich von Handel-Mazzetti and Irene Cshergö de Nemes-Tacskánd von Handel-Mazzetti; never married. ❖ Wrote many novels reflecting the religious struggles that convulsed Central Europe in 16th and 17th centuries; by 1890, was publishing short stories in Vienna's semi-official newspaper, the *Wiener Zeitung;* also wrote plays; published *Meinrad Helmpergers denwürdiges Jahr* (*Meinrad Helmperger's Memorable Year,* 1900), followed by *Jesse und Maria* (1906), which many critics consider her best novel; wrote a large number of novels over next half-century—all based on lives of saints; in 2 novels, *Die arme Margaret* (*Poor Margaret*) and *Stephana Schwertner,* depicted religious conflicts in 17th-century Austria; like most Austrian intellectuals, rallied to the national cause when WWI began (1914); already famous, became even more popular while serving as vice-president of Austrian Red Cross; her literary skills entered a period of decline after 1918, with 1 exception, 1934 novel *Die Waxenbergerin* (*The Woman of Waxenberg*). Honored by Austria with commemorative postage stamp on the centenary of her birth (1971). ❖ See also *Women in World History.*

HANDL, Irene (1901–1987). English comedic actress. Born Dec 27 (also seen as 26), 1901, in Maida Vale, London, England; died Nov 29, 1987, in London. ❖ Hugely popular comedic actress of stage, tv and screen; films include *The Italian Job, I'm All Right Jack, On a Clear Day You Can See Forever, The Private Life of Sherlock Holmes, A Kid for Two Farthings, The Belles of St. Trinian's, The Hound of the Baskervilles, The Key, School for Scoundrels, Two Way Stretch, Make Mine Mink* and *A Weekend with Lulu.* Wrote 2 bestselling novels, *The Sioux* (1965) and *The Gold Tip Pfitzer* (1966).

HANDLER, Ruth (1916–2002). American businesswoman. Born Ruth Moskowicz (shortened to Mosko), Nov 4, 1916, in Denver, Colorado; died April 27, 2002, in Los Angeles, CA; dau. of Polish immigrants;

m. (Issadore) Elliott Handler, c. 1940; children: Barbara Handler and Ken Handler. ❖ With husband, founded Mattel Toys; created the Barbie doll (1959); helped run Mattel for 30 years; became an advocate for breast cancer awareness. ❖ See also autobiography *Dream Doll: The Ruth Handler Story* (Longmeadow, 1997); and *Women in World History.*

HANDS, Elizabeth (fl. 1789). British poet. Name variations: (pseudonyms) E.H.; Daphne. Flourished c. 1789 in Coventry, England; m. a blacksmith, c. 1785. ❖ Worked as domestic servant; wrote poetry protesting perceptions of rural workers, which was published as *The Death of Annon. A Poem. With and Appendix: containing Pastorals, and other Poetical Pieces* (1789).

HANDY, Dora Keen (1871–1963). See Keen, Dora.

HANDZLIC, Jean (d. 1963). American opera singer. Died July 9, 1963, age 41, in The Bronx, NY. ❖ Sang with NYC Center Opera and San Francisco Opera; appeared on Broadway in *The Mikado* and *How to Succeed in Business without Really Trying.*

HANDZOVÁ, Viera (1931–1997). Slovak novelist and short-story writer. Name variations: Viera Handzova. Born May 12, 1931, in Kokava near Rimavicou, Slovakia; died June 14, 1997 in Bratislava; studied Russian and Slovak at Bratislava University. ❖ Worked as editor and freelance writer; works include *Madlenka* (1957), *Zrieknite sa prvej lásky* (Renounce Your First Love, 1965), *Lebo sme vedeli, čo činíme* (Because We Knew What We Were Doing, 1969), and *Kamaráti do zlého počasia* (Friends for Bad Weather, 1977).

HANEL, Birgitte (1954—). Danish rower. Born April 25, 1954, in Denmark. ❖ At Los Angeles Olympics, won a bronze medal in quadruple sculls with coxswain (1984).

HANES, Fiona (1977—). See Crawford, Fiona.

HANEY, Carol (1924–1964). American dancer and choreographer. Born in New Bedford, Massachusetts, Dec 24, 1924; died in New York, NY, May 10, 1964; m. actor Larry Blyden (div.); children: 2. ❖ Launched career in Hollywood where she danced in nightclubs with Jack Cole and assisted Gene Kelly in choreographing the movie musicals *An American in Paris* (1951), *Singin' in the Rain* (1952), and *Brigadoon* (1954); also danced with Bob Fosse in film *Kiss Me Kate* (1953); had 1st major role on Broadway in musical hit *Pajama Game* (1954), in which she dazzled in dance number "Steam Heat"; went on to choreograph the stage musicals *Flower Drum Song* (1961), *Bravo Giovanni* (1962), *She Loves Me* (1963), *Jennie* (1963) and *Funny Girl* (1964); also choreographed Garry Moore's tv show.

HANHAM, Eliza (c. 1812–1891). See Wohlers, Eliza.

HANI, Motoko (1873–1957). Japanese journalist. Name variations: Matsuoka Moto (birth name). Pronunciation: HA-nee Moe-toe-koe. Born Matsuoka Moto, Sept 8, 1873, in Hachinobe, Aomori Prefecture, Japan; died 1957; granddau. of Matsuoka Tadataka (former samurai); dau. of a lawyer was adopted into her mother's family, taking the name Matsuoka; attended Daiichi Kōtō Jogakkō (Tokyo First Higher Girls' School) and Meiji Jogakkō (Meiji Girls' School); married, 1896 (div. 1897); m. Hani Yoshikazu, 1880 (died 1955); children: daughters Setsuko (1903–1987) and Keiko (b. 1908). ❖ Japan's 1st female newspaper reporter, was a member of the premiere graduating class of the Tokyo First Higher Girls' School (1891); working at the *Hōchi,* became 1st female newspaper reporter in Japan (1897); edited and published *Fujin no tomo* (Woman's Friend), Japan's longest-surviving women's publication (1906–57); co-founded a private, co-educational school, Jiyū Gakuen (1921); had a profoundly spiritual, rather than a political, perspective. ❖ See also *Women in World History.*

HANIM, Latife (1898–1975). Turkish feminist and first lady. Born Latife Hanim in 1898; died 1975; m. Mustafa Kemal Atatürk (1881–1938, Turkish officer who created the modern secular Turkish republic), 1922; children: none. ❖ The well-educated daughter of a wealthy family in Izmir, married the progressive Mustafa Kemal Atatürk (1922); considered a modern woman, tried to assert herself and control her husband's carousing; for her efforts, was divorced by Kemal with the old Islamic method of repeating 4 times the phrase, "I divorce thee." ❖ See also *Women in World History.*

HANIM, Leyla (1850–1936). Turkish composer, pianist, poet, and writer. Name variations: Leyla Saz. Born in Istanbul, Turkey, 1850; died in Istanbul, Dec 6, 1936; dau. of Ishmal Pasha; m. Shiri Pasha (governor of various provincial capitals and prime minister). ❖ Grew up

in the Ottoman court where her father was the court physician; from age 7, studied piano with an Italian pianist; mastered all details of traditional Turkish music under tutelage of Medini Aziz Efendiu and Astik Aga; created an artistic circle of women in which Turkish and Western literature and music were cultivated; composed 200 instrumental and vocal compositions; also contributed many articles about the lives of women to Turkish journals. ❖ See also *Women in World History.*

HANIM, Nigar (1862–1918). Turkish poet and memoirist. Name variations: Nigâr; Nigar binti Osman; (pseudonym) Uryan Kalp. Born 1862 in Turkey; died 1918. ❖ Divorced after short marriage, began to travel widely in Europe; hosted celebrated Tuesday salon in Turkish capital attended by many intellectuals; best known poet of the late Ottoman period, published *Efsus* (1886) and her must successful work, *Aksi Seda* (1900); letters published as *Weakness of a Heart* (1901); son published an edition of her notebooks and diaries (1959).

HANISCH, Cornelia (1952—). West German fencer. Born June 12, 1952, in Frankfurt, West Germany. ❖ Won a gold medal for team foil and a silver medal for indiv. foil at Los Angeles Olympics (1984).

HANKA, Erika (1905–1958). Austrian ballet dancer and choreographer. Born May 18, 1905, in Vinkovci, Croatia; died May 16, 1958, in Vienna, Austria; trained at Wigman school in Dresden. ❖ Performed as member of Jooss Ballet in Germany (1935–38) where she danced in major roles in *The Green Table, A Ball in Old Vienna,* and *Pavanne,* among others; appeared at opera houses throughout Germany, including Cologne, Essen, Marburg, and Dusseldorf; staged *Joan von Zarissa* at Vienna Staatsoper (1941); served as ballet mistress there (1941–58), choreographing and staging numerous works. Choreography includes *Festa Romantica* (1945), *Hoellische G'Schichte* (1949), *Homeric Symphony* (1950), *The Moor of Venice* (1955), *Hotel Sacher* (1957) and *Medusa* (1958).

HANKE, Henriette (1785–1862). German novelist. Name variations: Henriette Wilhelmine Hanke. Born in 1785 in Jauer, Germany; died 1862; 3rd wife of Gottfried Hanke (Protestant pastor). ❖ Wrote 126 collections of stories and novels; works were popular enough to support Hanke and 5 children after her husband's death.

HANKE, Suzanne (1948—). German ballet dancer. Born Mar 30, 1948, in Altdöbern, Germany. ❖ Trained as a child in gymnastics, later studied dance at Stuttgart Ballet school; joined Stuttgart Ballet (1966) where she created roles in John Cranko's *Eugene Onegin* (1969) and in *Taming of the Shrew* (1969), danced featured roles in *Romeo and Juliet, Opus One,* and *Swan Lake,* and appeared in numerous works by Balanchine, Neumeier, and others.

HANKFORD, Anne (d. 1457). See Montacute, Anne.

HANKFORD, Anne (1431–1485). Countess of Ormonde. Name variations: Anne Hankeford. Born 1431; died Nov 13, 1485; dau. of Sir Richard Hankford and Anne Montacute (d. 1457); m. Thomas Butler, 7th earl of Ormonde (r. 1477–1515), before July 11, 1445; children: Anne Butler (b. 1462, who m. Sir James St. Leger and Ambrose Griseacre); Margaret Butler (1465–1539, who m. Sir William Boleyn). Thomas Butler later m. Lore Berkeley.

HANKIN, Simone. Australian water-polo player. Born in NSW, Australia. ❖ Center forward, won a team gold medal at Sydney Olympics (2000).

HANKS, Jane Richardson (b. 1908). American anthropologist. Born Jane Richardson, Aug 2, 1908, in Berkeley, CA; dau. of Leon Josiah Richardson (professor of Latin at UC, Berkeley); University of California, Berkeley, AB, 1930; Columbia University, PhD, 1943; m. Lucien Mason Hanks Jr. (anthropologist and psychologist); children: 3 sons. ❖ Mentored by Alfred Kroeber, became his research assistant (1934); studied Kiowa Indians in Oklahoma (1935); performed research among Blackfoot in Alberta, Canada; during WWII, worked on Margaret Mead's study of food habits of national minorities; with husband, joined pioneering Bang Chan project in Thailand (early 1950s); became research associate at Cornell Research Center, Bangkok; served as associate director of Bennington-Cornell Survey of Hill Tribes of North Thailand (1960s); with husband, made regional study in Chiengrai province, Thailand (1963–64); served as Peace Corps consultant on Thailand (1964 and 1966); made significant contributions to ethnology of North American Indians and Southeast Asia.

HANKS, Nancy (1783–1818). American mother of Abraham Lincoln. Born 1783; died 1818; became 1st wife of Thomas Lincoln (carpenter), June 12, 1806; children: Sarah Lincoln (d. 1828); Abraham Lincoln

(b. Feb 12, 1809, 16th US president); a son who died in infancy. ❖ Known for her intellect and exemplary character, left an indelible impression on her son Abraham; died when he was 9. ❖ See also *Women in World History.*

HANKS, Nancy (1927–1983). American public official. Born Dec 31, 1927, in Miami Beach, Florida; died Jan 7, 1983, in New York, NY; dau. of Bryan Cayce Hanks and Virginia (Wooding) Hanks; attended University of Colorado, 1946, and Oxford, 1948; Duke University, AB magna cum laude, 1949. ❖ Served as assistant to Nelson A. Rockefeller (beginning 1953) and as executive secretary of Special Studies Project of Rockefeller Brothers Fund (1956–69); became president of Associated Councils of the Arts (1968); as chair of National Endowment for the Arts (1969–77) and National Council on the Arts, was known for increasing funding to the endowment, subsidizing national tours, and providing grants to artists working in inner cities.

HANNA. *Variant of Ann, Anna, or Anne.*

HANNA, Carmel (1946—). Northern Ireland politician. Born April 26, 1946, in Warrenpoint, Co. Down, Northern Ireland. ❖ Began career as a nurse, then became active in the civil-rights movement; representing SDLP, elected to the Northern Ireland Assembly for South Belfast (1998); named minister of Employment and Learning (2001).

HANNAH. *Variant of Ann, Anna, or Anne.*

HANNAH (fl. 11th c. BCE). Biblical woman. Name variations: Anna; Hannah is possibly an abbreviation of Hananiah. Fl. in 11th century BCE; 1 of 2 wives of Elkanah of Ephraim, the Levite (Elkanah's other wife was Peninnah); children: Samuel the prophet, as well as 3 other sons and 2 daughters. ❖ The better beloved of the 2 wives of Elkanah, an Ephraimite from Ramathaim-zophim, was long childless; on an annual visit to Shiloh, vowed to God that she would dedicate a son to his service, if only she could conceive; gave birth to Samuel, who, because of her vow, was raised at Shiloh by the site's chief priest Eli; according to Old Testament's *First Book of Samuel* 2.1-10, authored a prayer in which God is proclaimed the source of victory, justice, fertility and legitimacy, as well as the source of humility for the proud and exaltation for the meek; in the *Talmud*, is considered 1 of 7 important prophetesses, and her prayer is recited in the 1st day service of Rosh Hashana as an example of a successful plea put before God.

HANNAH, Margaret (1922–1999). *See Greig, Margaret.*

HANNAH, Marjory Lydia (1890–1930). *See Nicholls, Marjory Lydia.*

HANNAM, Edith (1878–1951). English tennis player. Born Nov 22, 1878, in UK; died Jan 16, 1951. ❖ At Stockholm Olympics, won a gold medal in singles–indoor courts and a gold medal in mixed doubles–indoor courts (1912).

HANNAN, Cora (c. 1912—). Australian track-and-field athlete. Born c. 1912 in Adelaide, NSW, Australia; sister of Vida Hannan (track-and-field athlete); descendant of Paddy Hannan, founder of Kalgoorlie; m. Buckland C. Day, 1943. ❖ Was the 1st Australian national champion for shot put and discus (1933); also excelled in high jump and hurdling; competed at all 7 nationals (1930–40).

HANNEN, Lynley (1964—). New Zealand rower. Born Aug 27, 1964, in Dunedin, New Zealand; m. Bill Coventry (Olympic rower); children: 4 sons. ❖ At Seoul Olympics, won a bronze medal in coxless pairs with Nicola Payne (1988); won 14 New Zealand titles; became a doctor.

HANNON, Camilla (1936—). Irish politician. Born Camilla Begley, July 21, 1936, in Ballymotte, Co. Sligo, Ireland; m. Joseph Hannon. ❖ Representing Fianna Fáil, nominated to the Seanad by Taoiseach Charles J. Haughey (1982–83).

HANOLD, Paula (1962—). *See Weishoff, Paula.*

HANOVER, electress of.
See Sophia (1630–1714).
See Sophia Dorothea of Brunswick-Celle (1666–1726).

HANOVER, Mary Ann (Marion) (1835–1905). *See Hatton, Marion.*

HANOVER, queen of.
See Frederica of Mecklenburg-Strelitz (1778–1841).
See Mary of Saxe-Altenburg (1818–1907).

HANRAHAN, Barbara (1939–1991). Australian painter, novelist and short-story writer. Born Sept 6, 1939, in Adelaide, South Australia; died in Adelaide, Dec 1, 1991; studied at Adelaide Teachers' College, South Australian School of Arts, and Central School of Art, London. ❖ Taught at South Australia School of Art (1963–66), Falmouth College of Art in Cornwall, England (1966–67) and Portsmouth College of Art (1967–70); held over 20 solo exhibitions in Australia, England, and Italy; writings include *The Scent of Eucalyptus* (1973), *The Albatross Muff* (1977), *The Peach Groves* (1979), *Dove* (1982), *Kewpie Doll* (1984), *Dream People* (1987), *A Chelsea Girl* (1988), *Flawless Jade* (1989) and *Good Night, Mr. Moon* (1992).

HANSBERRY, Lorraine (1930–1965). African-American dramatist, essayist and social activist. Born May 19, 1930, in Chicago, Illinois; died of cancer, Jan 12, 1965, in New York, NY; youngest of 4 children of Charles and Nannie Hansberry; attended University of Wisconsin through sophomore year; m. Robert Nemiroff (musician), 1953 (div. 1964); children: none. ❖ Began writing plays and short stories while working as a journalist in NYC for the progressive African-American newspaper, *Freedom,* founded by Paul Robeson; her 1st play, *Raisin in the Sun,* starring Sidney Poitier and Ruby Dee, opened on Broadway to great acclaim and earned her a New York Drama Critics' Circle Award, the 1st given to a black playwright (1959); saw 2nd play, *The Sign in Sidney Brustein's Window,* produced (1964); also wrote tv drama, poetry and literary and social criticism while taking an active and vocal part in civil-rights and "Black Power" movements (1960s); at her death at 35, left behind an impressive body of unpublished work—unproduced plays, a film script, and a collection of essays. Much of this output reached its audience through efforts of her husband who published her unfinished autobiography as *To Be Young, Gifted and Black,* and shortly afterward adapted it for off-Broadway; he then produced *Les Blancs* on Broadway (1970) and brought a Tony-winning musical version of *Raisin in the Sun* to the stage (1974), which has since been revived several times and adapted for tv (1989). ❖ See also Anne Cheney, *Lorraine Hansberry* (Twayne, 1984); and *Women in World History.*

HANSCHMAN, Nancy (1927–1997). *See Dickerson, Nancy.*

HANSCOM, Adelaide (1876–1932). American photographer. Born in Empire City, Oregon, 1876; died in California, 1932; studied at Mark Hopkins Institute of Art, San Francisco; m. Gerald Leeson (mining engineer and former Canadian Mountie), 1907 (died 1915); children: 2. ❖ Took over Laura Adams' portrait studio (1902), where she photographed many of the area's most prominent families; partnered with Blanche Cumming to establish Hanscom and Cumming (1904); exhibited widely throughout California (1904–07) and contributed photographs to magazines; lost most of her prints and negatives in San Francisco earthquake (1906); moved to Seattle, where she established a studio. ❖ See also *Women in World History.*

HANSEN, Anja (1973—). Danish handball player. Born Anja Byrial Hansen, Nov 1, 1973, in Denmark. ❖ Won a team gold medal at Atlanta Olympics (1996); won team European championships (1994, 1996); retired (1997).

HANSEN, Christina Roslyng (1978—). Danish handball player. Name variations: Christina Roslyng. Born July 10, 1978, in Denmark. ❖ Won a team gold medal at Sydney Olympics (2000).

HANSEN, Jacqueline A. (c. 1949—). American marathon runner. Born c. 1949 in Granada Hills, California. ❖ Won Boston Marathon (1973); beame 1st woman in history to run a sub-2:40 marathon (2:39.19 in 1975); won 12 of her 1st 15 marathons; won 2 World champion titles in 150 and 5,000 meters; lobbied Olympic Committee to add more distances for women in Olympics.

HANSEN, Juanita (1895–1961). American silent-screen star. Name variations: Wahnetta Hanson; Juanita Parsons. Born Mar 3, 1895, in Iowa; died Sept 26, 1961, in West Hollywood, CA. ❖ Began career as a Mack Sennett bathing beauty; films include *The Patchwork Girl of Oz, The Mediator, The Jungle Princess* and *Glory*; succeeded Pearl White at Pathe as "queen" of their serials, starring in *The Secret of the Submarine, The Phantom Foe* and *The Yellow Arm*; career suffered because of drug addiction and ended when her face was severely scarred by boiling water.

HANSEN, Julia Butler (1907–1988). American politician. Born Julia Caroline Butler, June 14, 1907, in Portland, Oregon; died May 3, 1988, in Cathlamet, Washington; dau. of Don C. Butler and Maude (Kimball) Butler; attended Oregon State College, 1924–26; University of Washington, AB, 1930; m. Henry A. Hansen, July 15, 1939; children: David Kimball Hansen. ❖ During 43-year political career, which included elective offices on local, state, and federal levels, served 7 consecutive terms as US Democratic congresswoman (Nov 8, 1960–Dec 31,

1974); 1st settled in Cathlamet, WA, where she entered politics (1938), winning election to city council and serving until 1946; was a member of state house of representatives (1939–60), serving as speaker pro tempore for 5 years (1955–60); elected to fill a vacancy in 86th US Congress, was simultaneously elected to 87th; chaired the Subcommittee on Interior and Related Agencies of the Committee on Appropriations; initiated joint resolutions calling for a national traffic safety agency and an independent Federal Maritime administration; introduced legislation for a joint Congressional committee to investigate crime, for construction of a Veterans' hospital in Vancouver, WA, and for regulation of dairy imports; during war in Vietnam, urged Lyndon Johnson to seek mediation through the UN and also supported UN peace-keeping forces. ❖ See also *Women in World History.*

HANSEN, Lone Smidt (1961—). See *Nielsen, Lone Smidt.*

HANSEN, May (1887–1971). See *Darling, May.*

HANSEN, Pia (1965—). Swedish shooter. Born Sept 25, 1965, in Hassleholm, Sweden. ❖ Won a gold medal for double trap at Sydney Olympics (2000), breaking the Olympic record with 148 targets.

HANSEN, Trine. Danish rower. Born in Denmark. ❖ Won a bronze medal for single sculls at Atlanta Olympics (1996).

HANSFORD JOHNSON, Pamela (1912–1981). See *Johnson, Pamela Hansford.*

HANSHAW, Annette (1910–1985). American pop and jazz vocalist. Name variations: recorded under Gay Ellis, Dot Dare, and Patsy Young. Born in New York City, Oct 18, 1910; died 1985; m. Herman Rose. ❖ Belonged to a cadre of radio stars popular during 1920s–30s, making guest appearances on Maxwell House "Show Boat" and with Glen Gray's band on "Camel Caravan"; recorded with such legendary jazz artists as Benny Goodman, Eddie Lang, Red Nichols, Tommy Dorsey, and Jack Teagarden, often adding a "That's all" tag at end; retired at 23 (1934); in 8-year singing career, made many recordings, among which the collection album *It Was So Beautiful* (Halcyon) provides the best example of her talent, with "Give Me Liberty or Give Me Love" and "I'm Sure of Everything but You" considered standouts. ❖ See also *Women in World History.*

HANSKA, Éveline, Countess (1801–1882). Polish-born patron. Born Eveline Hanska; Madame Hanska; Madame Balzac. Born Éveline Rzewuska, 1801, in Poland; died 1882; m. Count Hanska (died 1841); m. Honoré Balzac (writer), 1850 (died 1850). ❖ Wealthy Polish countess, sent a letter of admiration to French novelist Honoré Balzac (1832), signing it *L'Étrangère* (The Stranger); after an 18-year correspondence that led to a liaison, married Balzac shortly before he died. The letters are contained in *Lettres à l'Étrangère* (1899–1906, 2 vols.).

HANSON, Beverly (1924—). American golfer. Name variations: Mrs. Sfingi. Born Dec 5, 1924, in Fargo, North Dakota. ❖ Won USGA Women's Amateur (1950); member of the Curtis Cup team (1950); won inaugural LPGA championship (1955); won 14 other LPGA tournaments (1951–60).

HANSON, Brooke (1978—). Australian swimmer. Born Mar 18, 1978, in Manly, Australia. ❖ Won 10 World Cup events (2001–03); won a gold medal for 100-meter breaststroke at Athens Olympics (2004).

HANSON, Christilot (1947—). See *Boylen, Christilot.*

HANSON, Elizabeth Meader (1684–1737). American writer. Born 1684 in New Hampshire; died 1737. ❖ Taken captive by French and Native American raiders (1724), wrote account of her captivity, *God's Mercy Surmounting Man's Cruelty* (1728).

HANSON, Gladys (1883–1973). American actress. Born Gladys Snook, Sept 5, 1883, in Atlanta, Georgia; died Feb 23, 1973, in Atlanta; m. Charles Emerson Cook (playwright and producer). ❖ Made NY debut as Ophelia to E.H. Sothern's Hamlet in *The Spoilers* (1907); also appeared in *The Queen's Husband, Richelieu, If I Were King, The Builder of Bridges, Evensong, Raffles, The Trojan Women, Our American Cousin, Mecca* and *The Brown Danube*; retired from stage (1939).

HANSON, Jean (1919–1973). British biophysicist and zoologist. Born Emmeline Jean Hanson, Nov 14, 1919, in Derbyshire, England; died Aug 10, 1973; educated at Burton-upon-Trent High School for Girls and Bedford College, London, 1st class, zoology, 1941; King's College, PhD. ❖ Worked at Strangeways Laboratory during WWII; joined Biophysics Research Unit at King's College, London (1948); studied electron microscopy (1953–54), working on muscular contraction and other problems at Massachusetts Institute of Technology (MIT); returned to England to rejoin Biophysics Unit and continued her study of molecular aspects of contraction mechanism of muscle; was a professor of biology at London University (1966) and director of Muscle Biophysics Unit, King's College (1970–73).

HANSON, Luise V. (1913–2003). American entrepreneur. Born Luise Voss, June 7, 1913; died Oct 19, 2003, in Stuart, Florida; m. John K. Hanson, Nov 14, 1935 (died 1996). ❖ With husband, established Winnebago Industries as well as Manufacturers Bank and Trust in Forest City, Iowa; donated $4.5 million for a library at Waldorf College in Forest City (2003).

HANSON, Marla (c. 1962—). American fashion model. Born c. 1962 in Indepence, Missouri; attended college in Dallas; New York University School of the Arts, BA. ❖ Was a promising young model when 2 men, hired by a rejected admirer, attacked her and slashed her face 15 times with a razor (June 5, 1986); became a speaker for National Victims' Center. ❖ See also tv movie "The Marla Hanson Story" (1991).

HANSON, Wahnetta (1895–1961). See *Hansen, Juanita.*

HANSON-DYER, Louise (1884–1962). Australian-born arts patron and music publisher. Name variations: Louise Berta Mosson; Louise Dyer. Born Louise Berta Mosson in Melbourne, Australia, 1884; died 1962; studied at Royal College of Music, London; m. James Dyer; m. 2nd time to a man named Hanson, 1939. ❖ Founded British Music Society of Melbourne (1921); moved to Paris and founded Éditions du Oiseau-Lyre, a music-publishing house (early 1930s); released complete editions of works of obscure composers, and issued some of the 1st "long-playing" recordings of the music of Italian composer Claudio Monteverdi and Baroque composer George Handel, among others.

HANSTEEN, Aasta (1824–1908). Norwegian artist, author, lecturer, polemicist, and pioneer of women's rights. Born Dec 10, 1824, in Kristiania, Norway; died April 13, 1908; dau. of Professor Christopher Hansteen and Johanne (Borch) Hansteen. ❖ Successful portrait painter, exhibited at Paris Exhibition of 1855; became interested in New Norwegian language movement (*Landsmål*) and published 1st book on the subject (1862), followed by poems written in New Norwegian; influenced by John Stuart Mill's *On the Subjection of Women*, gave lectures in Scandinavian capitals and many Norwegian cities, culminating in book, *Kvinden skapt i Guds billede* (Woman Created in God's Image); spent 1880s in US, where she participated in women's struggle in Boston and Chicago, and took up portrait painting again; returning to Norway after 9 years, was hailed for her pioneering work for women; immortalized by Henrik Ibsen in the character of Lona Hassel in his play *Samfundets Støtter* (*Pillars of Society*) and by Gunnar Heiberg in his play *Tante Ulrikke* (Aunt Ulrikke). ❖ See also *Women in World History.*

HANSTEEN, Kirsten (1903–1974). Norwegian politician and resistance leader. Born Kirsten Moe in Lyngen, Troms county, in the far north of Norway, 1903; died 1974; m. Viggo Hansteen (1900–1941), 1930. ❖ First woman member of the Norwegian ministry, became a Norwegian politician and member of Communist Party; married Oslo barrister Viggo Hansteen (1930), one of the 1st 2 anti-fascist members of the Norwegian Resistance movement to be executed during the German Occupation of Norway; during the war, edited *Kvinnefronten* (The Women's Front), an organ of women's Resistance which changed its name to *Kvinnen og Tiden* (Women and Current Affairs) after the liberation; was given the post of consultative Cabinet minister in Prime Minister Einar Gerhardsen's coalition government of June–Nov 1945; represented Akershus county in the Norwegian Storting (Parliament), 1945–49).

HANWAY, Mary Ann (c. 1755–c. 1823). British novelist. Name variations: Mary Anne Hanway. Born c. 1755; died c. 1823 in London, England; m. Hanway Balack Hanway, 1788. ❖ Wrote *A Journey to the Highlands of Scotland With Occasioned Remarks on Dr. Johnson's Tour, by a Lady* (1776), *Ellinor, or the World as It Is: A Novel in Four Volumes* (1798), *Andrew Stuart, or the Northern Wanderer: A Novel in Four Volumes* (1800), *Falconbridge Abbey: A Devonshire Story in Five Volumes* (1809), and *Christabelle, the Maid of Rouen: A Novel Founded on Facts in Four Volumes* (1814).

HAO, Lady (fl. 1040 BCE). See *Fu Hao.*

HAPGOOD, Mrs. Hutchins (1872–1951). See *Boyce, Neith.*

HAPGOOD, Isabel (1850–1928). American author and translator. Born Isabel Florence Hapgood, Nov 21, 1850, in Boston, MA; died June 26, 1928, in New York, NY; dau. of Asa and Lydia (Crossley) Hapgood; attended Oread Collegiate Institute, 1863–65, and Miss Porter's School in Connecticut, 1865–68. ❖ Offered the English-speaking world the 1st direct translations of Russian classics (prior to her, English-speaking readers read Russian literature translated from the French); began career with translations of Tolstoy's *Childhood, Boyhood, Youth,* Gogol's *Taras Bulba* and *Dead Souls,* and a collection of *The Epic Songs of Russia* (1886); traveled through Russia (1887–89); published Tolstoy's *What to Do?* (1887), *Sevastopol* (1888) and *Life* (1888); also published Sophia Kovalevskaya's *Recollections of Childhood* (1895), Petr Sergeenko's *How Count L.N. Tolstoy Lives and Works* (1899), 2 translations of Maxim Gorky, *Foma Gordyeeff* and *Orloff and His Wife* (1901), a 16-volume edition of *The Novels and Stories of Ivan Turgenev* (1903–04), Nikolai Leskov's *The Steel Flea* (1916) and *The Cathedral Folk* (1924), and Ivan Bunin's *The Village* (1923); also wrote her own books on people and culture of Russia, starting with *Russian Rambles* (1895); published *Service Book of the Holy Orthodox Catholic Apostolic (Greco-Russian) Church* (1906), which was used by Orthodox churches in America; was a correspondent, reviewer, and editorial writer for New York *Evening Post* and the *Nation* for 22 years; also translated French, Italian, and Spanish classics. ❖ See also *Women in World History.*

HAPGOOD, Neith Boyce (1872–1951). See Boyce, Neith.

HAPPE-KREY, Ursula (1926—). West German swimmer. Name variations: Ursula Krey. Born Oct 20, 1926, in Germany. ❖ At Melbourne Olympics, won a gold medal in 200-meter breaststroke (1956).

HAPSBURG, Elisabeth von (1837–1898). See Elizabeth of Bavaria.

HARA, Kazuko (1935—). Japanese composer, librettist, singer, and professor. Born in Tokyo, Japan, Feb 10, 1935; studied composition under Professor Romijiro Ikenouchi at Tokyo Teijutsu Daigaku Faculty of Music, graduating 1957; studied in Paris at École Normale with Henri Dutilleux (1962) and L'Academie International d'Été in Nice with Alexander Tcherepnin (1963); also explored Gregorian chant under Father R.F.J. Mereau; m. Hiroshi Hara (composer). ❖ Awarded 2nd prize of the NHK and Mainichi Music Contest (1955); received the Takei Prize (1967) and Ataka Prize; wrote orchestral pieces and operas, including *The Case Book of Sherlock Holmes* and *The Merry Night.* ❖ See also *Women in World History.*

HARA, Setsuko (1920—). Japanese actress. Born June 17, 1920, in Yokohama, Japan; sister-in-law of Hisatora Kumagai (director). ❖ At 17, made screen debut in *The Samurai's Daughter* (1937), followed by *Pastoral Symphony, Hot Wind, No Regret for Our Youth, Temptation, Late Spring, Blue Mountains, The Idiot, Early Summer, Repast, Tokyo Story, Tokyo Twilight, A Woman's Secret, Akibiyori* (*Late Autumn*) and *Chushingura* (*The Loyal 47 Ronin*); often directed by Yasujiro Ozu.

HARADA, Saho (1982—). Japanese synchronized swimmer. Born Nov 5, 1982, in Japan. ❖ At World championships, placed 1st in free routine combination (2003); won a team silver medal at Athens Olympics (2004).

HARADA, Yasuko (1928—). Japanese novelist. Born 1928 in Japan. ❖ Works include *An Elegy* (1956), *Kazi no Tiride* (1983), *Yameru Oka,* and *Kita no Hayashi.*

HARALAMOW, Ingrid. Swiss kayaker. Name variations: Ingrid Haralamow-Raimann; Ingrid Raimann. ❖ Won a silver medal for K4 500 meters at Atlanta Olympics (1996).

HARAND, Irene (1900–1975). Austrian leader. Born Irene Wedl, Sept 6, 1900, in Vienna, Austria; died Feb 3, 1975, in New York, NY; dau. of a modestly well-to-do Roman Catholic father and a Lutheran mother; attended School of the Desmoiselles Diwisch for 2 years; m. Frank Harand, 1919; children: none. ❖ Viennese who attacked the evils of Nazism, anti-Semitism, and religious intolerance, helped found Sterreichische Volkspartei (Austrian Peoples Party) with Moritz Zalman (1930); published 1st pamphlet, *So? oder So?*; began newspaper *Gerechtigkeit* (Justice) and founded the Movement Against Anti-Semitism, Racial Hatred and Glorification of War, known as the Harand Movement (1933); published *Sein Kampf* to refute Hitler's *Mein Kampf* (1935); gave speeches warning against the Nazi menace throughout Europe and US (1936); saw *Sein Kampf* published in American and French editions (1937); began publication of French-language edition of *Gerechtigkeit* in Brussels (1937); immigrated to US

(1938); gave anti-Nazi speeches in US and Canada and founded Austrian-American League to assist Austrian refugees fleeing Nazi rule (1938–45); became director of women's division of Anti-Nazi League of NY and began work at Austrian Institute of NY (1943). Honored by Israel as one of the "Righteous Among the Nations" (1969); honored by lord mayor of Vienna (1971); ashes given place of honor in Vienna's Central Cemetery (1975); municipal housing project in Vienna named in her honor (1990). ❖ See also *Women in World History.*

HARAREET, Haya (1931—). Israeli stage and screen actress. Name variations: Haya Hararit. Born Sept 20, 1931, in Haifa, Israel; m. Jack Clayton (director). ❖ Acted on stage with Israel's Cameri (Chamber) Theater; came to international prominence as Esther in *Ben-Hur* (1959); films include *Hill 24 Doesn't Answer, The Secret Partner, The Interns, La Legenda di Fra' Diavolo, The Last Charge* and *Our Mother's House.*

HARARI, Manya (1905–1969). Russian-born publisher. Born Manya Benenson in Baku, Russia (now Azerbaijan), April 8, 1905; died in London, England, Sept 24, 1969; dau. of Grigori Benenson and Sophie (Goldberg) Benenson; m. Ralph Andrew Harari (1892–1969), 1925; children: Michael. ❖ Co-founder of the influential Harvill Press, who was co-translator of Pasternak's *Dr. Zhivago*; played a crucial role in bringing dissident works of Russian literature to the attention of the Western reading public. ❖ See also *Memoirs 1906–1969* (Harvill, 1972); and *Women in World History.*

HARARIT, Haya (1931—). See Harareet, Haya.

HARASZTY, Eszter (1920–1994). Hungarian-American colorist, stylist, and designer of textiles. Name variations: Eszter H. Colen. Born Sept 28, 1920, in Hungary; died of non-Hodgkin's lymphoma in Malibu, CA, Nov 24, 1994. ❖ Known for Iceland poppy motif replicated on textiles, ceramics, and stained glass, had her own design studio in NY City; before coming to US (1946), was a costume designer in Hungary, then shifted focus to home design; won 5 gold medals from Association of Interior Designers for her textile designs; work is in the permanent collections of New York Museum of Modern Art, Victoria and Albert Museum in London, and Le Chateau Dufresne in Montreal.

HARB, Helen Hicks (1911–1974). See Hicks, Helen.

HARBORD, Isobel (1893–1981). See Elsom, Isobel.

HARBOTTLE, Mrs. John (1933—). See Lesser, Patricia.

HARBOTTLE, Patricia Lesser (1933—). See Lesser, Patricia.

HARBOU, Thea von (1888–1954). See von Harbou, Thea.

HARCOURT, Johanna (d. 1488). Duchess of Lorraine. Died Nov 1488; dau. of William Harcourt; became 1st wife of Rene II, duke of Lorraine (r. 1480–1508), Sept 9, 1471 (div. 1485).

HARD, Darlene (1936—). American tennis player. Born Jan 6, 1936, Los Angeles, CA; graduate of Pomona College, Claremont, CA. ❖ Among the top tennis players in the world (1955–64), reached finals of Wimbledon singles and won both the women's doubles and mixed doubles, with America's Althea Gibson and Australia's Mervyn Rose, as respective partners (1957); won Wimbledon mixed doubles while teamed with Rod Laver (1959); won French Open (1960); won US doubles titles for 5 consecutive years (1958–62), often partnered with Maria Bueno; won US singles title (1960, 1961), and was ranked #1 among US women's tennis players (1960–63). ❖ See also *Women in World History.*

HARDCASTLE, Sarah (1969—). English swimmer. Born April 9, 1969, in UK. ❖ At Los Angeles Olympics, won a bronze medal in the 800-meter freestyle and a silver medal in the 400-meter freestyle (1984).

HARDEN, Cecil Murray (1894–1984). American politician. Born in Covington, Indiana, Nov 21, 1894; died in Lafayette, IN, Dec 5, 1984; attended University of Indiana at Bloomington; m. Frost R. Harden (automobile dealer), Dec 1914. ❖ Five-term US Republican congresswoman from Indiana (Jan 2, 1949–Jan 3, 1959), chaired the Fountain County Republican Party (1938–50); served as Republican national committeewoman from Indiana and was an at-large delegate to Republican national convention (1948, 1952, 1956, 1968); though narrowly elected to 6th District seat for US Congress (1948), was ultimately reelected to 4 additional terms; during tenure, served on Committee on Veterans' Affairs, Committee on Expenditures in Executive Departments, Committee on Government Operations, and Committee on Post Office and Civil Service; after losing reelection bid (1958), was appointed special assistant for women's affairs to Postmaster

General Arthur E. Summerfield, a post she held until Mar 1961; served on National Advisory Committee for White House Conference on Aging (1970). ❖ See also *Women in World History.*

HARDENBROOK, Margaret (d. 1690). *See Philipse, Margaret Hardenbrook.*

HARDENNE, Justine (1982—). *See Henin-Hardenne, Justine.*

HARDEY, Mary Aloysia (1809–1886). American religious. Name variations: Sister Aloysia; Mother Mary Aloysia Hardey. Born Mary Ann Hardey on Dec 8, 1809, in Piscataway, Maryland; died June 17, 1886, in Paris, France; dau. of Frederick William Hardey and Sarah (Spalding) Hardey. ❖ Took final vows with Society of the Sacred Heart as Sister Aloysia (1833); established the order's 1st convent in the East, on Houston Street in New York (1841) which later became the College of the Sacred Heart, then Manhattanville College, having moved to the outskirts of NY; served as its superior (1842–64); over the next 27 years, also established 16 other houses for the order; was made assistant general of the order (1871). ❖ See also Mary Garvey, *Mary Aloysia Hardey* (1910); Margaret Williams, *Second Sowing: The Life of Mary Aloysia Hardey* (1942).

HARDIE, Kelly (1969—). Australian softball player. Born Nov 21, 1969, in Perth, Western Australia. ❖ Won a bronze medal at Sydney Olympics (2000).

HARDIN, Lil (1898–1971). *See Armstrong, Lil Hardin.*

HARDING, Ann (1902–1981). American actress. Born Dorothy Walton Gatley, Aug 7, 1902, in Fort Sam Houston, Texas; died Sept 1, 1981, in Westport, Connecticut; dau. of Captain George G. (career army officer) and Elizabeth (Crabbe) Gatley; attended Bryn Mawr College for 1 year; m. Harry Bannister (actor), Oct 22, 1926 (div. 1932); m. Werner Janssen (symphony conductor), Jan 13, 1937 (div. 1962); children: (1st m.) Jane Bannister. ❖ Known for her blonde elegance and aristocratic manner, made NY debut as Madeline Morton in *Inheritors* (1921) and Broadway debut as Phyllis Weston in *Like a King* (1921); came to prominence in title role in *The Trial of Mary Dugan* (1927), which ran for 310 performances; signed with Pathé (1929), which later merged with RKO, starring in *Holiday* (1930) and receiving an Academy Award nomination as Best Actress; played a vulnerable divorcée in *Westward Passage* (1932) opposite Laurence Olivier; co-starred with Richard Dix in *The Conquerors* (1932); appeared in *The Animal Kingdom* (1932), as well as the 1st film version of Rachel Crothers' play *When Ladies Meet* (1933); made London stage debut in 1st West End production of *Candida* (1937); other films include *Paris Bound* (1929), *Condemned* (1929), *The Girl of the Golden West* (1930), *East Lynne* (1931), *Westward Passage* (1932), *The Fountain* (1934), *Enchanted April* (1935), *Peter Ibbetson* (1935), *Love From a Stranger* (1937), *Mission to Moscow* (1943), *The Magnificent Yankee* (1951), *The Man in the Gray Flannel Suit* (1956) and *Strange Intruder* (1956). ❖ See also *Women in World History.*

HARDING, Florence K. (1860–1924). American first lady. Born Florence Kling, Aug 15, 1860, in Marion, Ohio; died Nov 21, 1924, in Marion; 3rd child and 1st dau. of Amos Kling (banker) and Louisa (Bouton) Kling; m. Henry A. "Pete" De Wolfe, Mar 1880 (div. 1886); m. Warren Gamaliel Harding (29th US president), July 8, 1891; children: (1st m.) Marshall Eugene De Wolfe (1880–1914). ❖ First lady who was the driving force behind husband, filled in at his *Marion Star* newspaper when he was ill and stayed on for 14 years; was closely involved in all his successful campaigns: for state senator, lieutenant governor, US senator, then president; moving into the White House (1921), exhausted her frail health with a lively social calendar; served as husband's key advisor, frequently visited injured veterans at Walter Reed Hospital, was involved in many charities, and agitated for women's rights; as the image of his administration began to be tarnished by scandals, put out what fires she could; when husband died suddenly and mysteriously, made one final effort to protect his name by destroying private papers. ❖ See also Carl Sferrazza Anthony, *Florence Harding* (Morrow, 1998); and *Women in World History.*

HARDING, Jan (1925—). English science educator. Name variations: Jan Ansell. Born Jan Ansell, May 10, 1925, in England; Royal Holloway College, University of London, BS, 1946; Chelsea College, London, MEd, 1971, PhD, 1975; m. Arthur Harding. ❖ Explored gender inequalities in the classroom, in science and beyond; created the International Gender and Science and Technology Association (GASAT) with Professor Jan Raat of Eindhoven University in Netherlands (1981); taught as a St. Elphin's School science teacher in

Darley Dale (1947–59); employed as a tutor (1966–75) at Trent Park College, later part of Middlesex Polytechnic (now Middlesex University); was head of Centre for Science and Mathematics Education's Chemistry Section at Chelsea College, University of London (1975–85); served as an equal opportunities consultant (from 1985); elected a Royal Society of Arts fellow (1991); was the 1st visiting scholar to the then newly created University of Melbourne Education Faculty (1994); attended the Nongovernmental Organization Forum at UN Fourth World Conference on Women in Beijing (1995); wrote *Switched Off: The Science Education of Girls* (1983).

HARDING, Phyllis (b. 1907). English swimmer. Born Dec 15, 1907, in UK. ❖ At Paris Olympics, won a silver medal in 100-meter backstroke (1924); competed in the next 3 Olympiads, the 1st woman to compete in 4 Olympics; held the World record in 200-meter backstroke (1932–35). Inducted into International Swimming Hall of Fame (1995).

HARDING, Rebecca Blaine (1831–1910). *See Davis, Rebecca Harding.*

HARDING, Tanya (1972—). Australian softball player. Born Jan 23, 1972, in Brisbane, Queensland, Australia. ❖ Pitcher and first baseman, won bronze medals at Atlanta Olympics (1996) and Sydney Olympics (2000) and a team silver medal at Athens Olympics (2004).

HARDING, Tonya (1970—). American figure skater. Born Tonya Maxine Harding, Nov 12, 1970, in Portland, Oregon; m. Jeff Gillooly, 1990 (div. 1993); m. Michael Smith, 1995 (div.). ❖ Placed 2nd at World championships (1991), 1st at Skate America and US nationals (1991), becoming 1st woman in world to complete the Triple Axle in competition; placed 4th at Albertville Olympics (1992); after husband took her competitor Nancy Kerrigan out of competition with a blow to the knee (Jan 6, 1994), won the US nationals (but later stripped of title), then placed 8th at Lillehammer Olympics; pled guilty to hindering the investigation of the attack on Kerrigan, was given 3-years' supervised probation and fined $100,000; banned for life by US Figure Skating Association.

HARDINGE, Belle Boyd (1844–1900). *See Boyd, Belle.*

HARDWICK, Elizabeth (1916—). American novelist and essayist. Born July 27, 1916, in Lexington, Kentucky; dau. of Eugene and Mary Ramsey Hardwick; University of Kentucky, MA, 1939; m. Robert Lowell (poet), July 28, 1949 (div. 1972); children: Harriett Winslow Lowell. ❖ A professor at Columbia School of the Arts, was also a literary critic for *Partisan Review*; co-founded the *New York Review of Books* (1963); novels include *The Ghostly Lover* (1945), *The Simple Truth* (1955), and *Sleepless Nights* (1979); also wrote *A View of My Own: Essays in Literature and Society* (1962), *Seduction and Betrayal: Women and Literature* (1974), which was nominated for the National Book Award, and *Bartleby in Manhattan and Other Essays* (1983); was the editor for 18 volumes of *Rediscovered Fiction by American Women* (1977).

HARDY, Anna Eliza (1839–1934). American painter. Born Jan 26, 1839, in Bangor, Maine; died Dec 15, 1934, in Jamaica Plain, Massachusetts; dau. of Jeremiah Pearson Hardy (painter) and Catherine Sears Wheeler. ❖ Was given instruction in art primarily by father and shared his Bangor studio until his death (1888); in career almost 8 decades long, her single theme of paintings was still life.

HARDY, Barbara (1924—). Welsh educator and literary critic. Born June 27, 1924, in Swansea, Wales; dau. of Maurice Nathan and Gladys Nathan; University of London, BA, MA; m. Ernest Dawson Hardy. ❖ Taught at universities in Japan, England, France, Soviet Union, US, Canada, and Scandinavia; published reviews and essays in journals and newspapers; writings include *The Novels of George Eliot: A Study in Form* (1959), *Charles Dickens: The Later Novels* (1968), *Tellers and Listeners: The Narrative Imagination* (1975), *Forms of Feeling in Victorian Fiction* (1985), and *Shakespeare's Storytellers: Dramatic Narration* (1997).

HARDY, Catherine (1930—). African-American track-and-field athlete. Born Feb 8, 1930, in Carrollton, Georgia. ❖ Won a gold medal in the 4 x 100-meter relay in the Helsinki Olympics (1952); won AAU indoor 50 yards (1951) and AAU outdoor double (1952).

HARDY, Daphne (1917–2003). *See Henrion, Daphne Hardy.*

HAREL, Marie (fl. 1790). French inventor of Camembert cheese. Fl. in 1790 in the town of Camembert, Normandy, France. ❖ Is credited with inventing Camembert cheese during French Revolution, when a resistant priest took refuge at her Beaumoncel Manner in Camembert, gave her a secret recipe to improve her cheese, and she readily heeded his advice (1790); was posthumously awarded the French government's *palmes académiques* (1927).

HAREVEN, Shulamit (1930–2003). Israeli novelist, poet and activist. Name variations: Shulamith Hareven. Born Shulamit Riftin, Feb 14, 1930, in Warsaw, Poland; died Nov 26, 2003; m. Alouph Hareven, 1954; children: Itai Hareven; Gail Hareven (b. 1959, novelist). ❖ Renowned Israeli novelist and outspoken voice for peace in the Middle East, arrived in Israel (1940); served in the Hagana underground; was a combat medic during siege of Jerusalem (1947–48); helped create Israel Army Radio; assisted refugees; served as correspondent during War of Attrition (1968–70) and Yom Kippur War (1973); was the 1st woman elected to Hebrew Language Academy; nominated by French magazine *L'Express* as one of the 100 women "who move the world"; was long a spokesperson for the Peace Now movement; writings include (poetry) *Predatory Jerusalem* (1962), (short stories) *In the Last Month* (1966), (essays) *The Vocabulary of Peace* (1995) and novellas, *The Miracle Hater* (1983), *Prophet* (1989) and *After Childhood* (1994).

HAREWOOD, countess of.
See Mary, Princess (1897–1965).
See Lascelles, Patricia (b. 1926).
See Stein, Marion (b. 1926).

HARFORD, Lesbia (1891–1927). Australian poet. Name variations: Lesbia Keogh. Born Lesbia Venner Keogh, April 9, 1891, in Brighton, Melbourne, Australia; died July 5, 1927, in Melbourne; graduated in Arts and Law from University of Melbourne, 1916; m. Pat Harford (artist), 1920 (sep. 1921). ❖ Lawyer and labor activist with the IWW, was born with a congenital heart defect and later suffered from TB; wrote novel *The Invaluable Mystery*; her poems published posthumously by Nettie Palmer as *Poems* (1941) and later as *The Poems of Lesbia Harford* (ed. Drusilla Modjeska and Marjorie Pizer, 1985). ❖ See also (play) *Earthly Paradise* (1991).

HARGREAVES, Alison (1962–1995). English-born mountain climber. Born 1962 in Belper, Derbyshire, England; died on Pakistan's K2, Aug 13, 1995; dau. of John and Joyce Hargreaves (both mathematicians); lived in Spean Bridge, Scotland; m. James Ballard (climber), 1988; children: To (b. 1989); Kate (b. 1991). ❖ Was the 1st from Britain to ascend the Kangtega in the Khumbu Nepal region of the Himalayas (1986); was the 1st in one season to conquer the 6 major Alpine north faces, including the Eiger and the Matterhorn (1988); entered the record books as the 1st woman, and 2nd climber, to reach the 29,028-foot summit of Mount Everest, the world's highest peak, alone and without supplementary oxygen (1995); disappeared with 5 other climbers while scaling Pakistan's K2 (Aug 13, 1995). ❖ See also *Women in World History*.

HARINGA, Ingrid (1964—). Dutch cyclist and speedskater. Born July 11, 1964, in the Netherlands. ❖ As a speedskater, placed 4th at World Spring championships (1989); as a cyclist, won the 1st Amsterdam RAI Derny race (1991), which became a men's race; won a bronze medal in the 1,000-meter sprint at Barcelona Olympics (1992) and a silver medal for points race and bronze medal for sprint at Atlanta Olympics (1996).

HARINGTON, Lucy (c. 1581–1627). See Russell, Lucy.

HARJO, Joy (1951—). Native American poet and musician. Born Joy Harjo Foster, May 9, 1951, in Tulsa, Oklahoma, of Muscogee Creek, Cherokee, French and Irish ancestry; dau. of Allen W. Foster and Wynema Baker Foster; at 19, took name of maternal grandmother Naomi Harjo; University of New Mexico, Institute of American Indian Arts, BA, 1976; Iowa Writers' Workshop, MFA, 1978; attended College of Santa Fe, 1982; children: Phil and Rainy Dawn. ❖ Poet who draws on Native American history, mythology and contemporary culture, began publishing in feminist journals including *Conditions*; taught at Institute of American Indian Arts, Arizona State University, University of New Mexico, University of Colorado, University of Hawaii and University of California at Los Angeles; took up saxophone and formed the band, Joy Harjo and Poetic Justice, recording *Letter from the End of the Twentieth Century* (1997); as solo artist, recorded *Native Joy For Real* (2004); served as consultant for Native American Public Broadcasting and National Indian Youth Council and as director of National Association of Third World Writers; worked as editor of *High Plains Literary Review, Contact II,* and *Tyuonyi*; poetry collections include *The Last Song* (1975), *What Moon Drove Me to This* (1979), *She Had Some Horses* (1983), *Secrets from the Center of the World* (1989), *In Mad Love*

and War (1990), *The Woman Who Fell from the Sky* (1994), *A Map to the Next World: Poetry and Tales* (2000) and *How We Became Human* (2002); wrote screenplays *Origin of Apache Crown Dance* (1985) and *The Beginning*. Received Lifetime Achievement Award from Native Writer's Circle of Americas, American Book Award and Delmore Schwartz Memorial Award for *In Mad Love and War,* Poetry Society of America's William Carlos Williams Award, American Indian Distinguished Achievement Award, Josephine Miles Award and Academy of American Poetry Award. ❖ See also Laura Coltelli and Joy Harjo, *The Spiral of Memory: Interviews* (U. of Michigan Press, 1996).

HARKIN, Kathryn (1918–1986). See Mostel, Kate.

HARKNESS, Anna M. Richardson (1837–1926). American philanthropist. Born Anna M. Richardson in Dalton, Ohio, Oct 25, 1837; died in New York, NY, Mar 27, 1926; dau. of James and Anna (Ranck) Richardson; m. Stephen Vanderburg Harkness (businessman), Feb 13, 1854 (died 1888); children: Jennie A. Harkness (died young); Charles William Harkness (b. 1860); Florence Harkness (b. 1864); Edward Stephen Harkness (b. 1874). ❖ When husband, having amassed a fortune by investing in Standard Oil, died suddenly (1888), shared an inheritance of over $150 million with children; embarked on a philanthropic career that would dominate the rest of her life; early charities centered on religious and welfare agencies, including Fifth Avenue Presbyterian Church, missions of the Presbyterian Church, New York Association for Improving the Condition of the Poor, and State Charities Aid Association; broadened philanthropic interests to include education, medical research, and cultural institutions (1916); gave $3 million to Yale University to build the Harkness Triangle (1917); also contributed to other educational institutions, among them Hampton and Tuskegee; in NY, gave to New York Public Library, Museum of Natural History, and Metropolitan Museum of Art, and donated a 22-acre site in upper Manhattan to Columbia University for Columbia-Presbyterian Medical Center; established the Commonwealth Fund (1918), a non-profit foundation with an endowment of $20 million. ❖ See also *Women in World History*.

HARKNESS, Georgia (1891–1974). American scholar and theologian. Born Georgia Elma Harkness, April 21, 1891, in Harkness, NY; died at Pomona Valley Community Hospital, Aug 21, 1974; dau. of Joseph Warren Harkness (farmer) and Lillie (Merrill) Harkness; Cornell University, AB, 1912; Boston University, MA, 1920, MRE, 1920, PhD, 1923; lived with Verna Miller; never married; no children. ❖ One of the most prominent female Protestant theologians during 20th century, piled up a number of "firsts": 1st woman participant of the Fellowship of Younger Christian Thinkers, 1st woman member of American Theological Society, 1st full-time woman professor of theological studies at an American seminary, and 1st major woman theologian to be part of the worldwide Protestant ecumenical circle; taught Latin and French at a high school in Schuylerville, NY (1912–14) and Scotia, NY (1915–18); was an instructor at English Bible, Boston University School of Religious Education (1919–20); was a member of faculty, Elmira College, advancing to rank of professor of philosophy (1922–37); served as associate professor of religion, Mount Holyoke College (1937–39); was a professor of applied theology, Garrett Biblical Institute (1939–50); was a professor of applied theology, Pacific School of Theology at Berkeley (1950–61); writings include *The Church and the Immigrant* (1921), *Conflicts in Religious Thought* (1929), *John Calvin: The Man and His Ethics* (1931), *The Resources of Religion* (1936), *Religious Living* (1937), *The Recovery of Ideals* (1937), *The Glory of God* (1943), *The Dark Night of the Soul* (1945), *Prayer and the Common Life* (1948), *The Gospel and Our World* (1949), *Foundations of Christian Knowledge* (1955), *The Church and the Faith* (1962), *The Fellowship of the Holy Spirit* (1966), *Christian Ethics* (1967) and *The Ministry of Reconciliation* (1971). ❖ See also Rosemary Skinner Keller, *Georgia Harkness: For Such a Time as This* (Abington, 1992); and *Women in World History*.

HARKNESS, Mary Stillman (1874–1950). American philanthropist. Born Mary Emma Stillman, July 4, 1874, in Brooklyn, NY; died June 6, 1950, in New York, NY; 3rd of 4 daughters of Thomas Edgar (lawyer) and Charlotte Elizabeth (Greenman) Stillman; m. Edward Stephen Harkness (1874–1940, capitalist, benefactor of Harvard University, and trustee of Metropolitan Museum of Art), Nov 15, 1904 (died 1940); dau.-in-law of Anna M. Richardson Harkness (1837–1926); no children. ❖ Gave $1 million for a convalescent facility in Port Chester, NY, to be operated in conjunction with Columbia-Presbyterian Medical Center; funded several buildings for Connecticut College for Women in New London, and the restoration program of Marine Historical

Association at Mystic, CT; following husband's death (1940), made monetary gifts of over $3 million to Columbia-Presbyterian Medical Center, Bennett Junior College, and Oberlin College, and also supported New York United Hospital Fund, Red Cross, YWCA, and Boy Scouts; her summer mansion on Long Island Sound, known as Eolia, with grounds landscaped by Beatrix Jones Farrand, now comprises Harkness Memorial State Park in Waterford, Connecticut. ❖ See also *Women in World History*.

HARKNESS, Rebekah (1915–1982). American composer, sculptor, dance patron, and philanthropist. Name variations: Betty Harkness. Born Rebekah Semple West, April 17, 1915, in St. Louis, Missouri; died June 17, 1982, in New York, NY; 1 of 3 children of Allen Tarwater (stockbroker) and Rebekah Cook (Semple) West; graduated from Fermata, a finishing school in Aiken, SC, 1932; m. Charles Dickson Pierce, June 10, 1939 (div. 1946); m. William Hale Harkness (attorney and businessman), Oct 1, 1947 (died Aug 1954); m. Benjamin H. Kean (physician), 1961 (div. 1965); m. Niels Lauersen (physician), 1974 (div. 1977); children: (1st m.) Allen Pierce (b. 1940); Anne Terry Pierce (b. 1944); (2nd m.) Edith Harkness. ❖ Once one of the wealthiest women in America, was well known during 1960s as a generous philanthropist and patron of the arts; created a dance empire that included the 40-member Harkness Ballet, a ballet school and home for the company called Harkness House, and a refurbished 1,250-seat theater which presented the Harkness Ballet as well as other dance companies to NY audiences; also sponsored construction of a medical research building at New York Hospital and supported a number of medical research projects. ❖ See also Craig Unger, *Blue Blood* (Morrow, 1988); and *Women in World History*.

HARLAND, Georgina (1978—). English pentathlete. Born April 14, 1978, in Canterbury, England. ❖ At World championships, placed 1st for relay (1999, 2001) and 1st for team (2003, 2004); placed 1st overall for World Cup ranking (2001); placed 1st at World Cup Final in Athens (2003); won bronze medal at Athens Olympics (2004).

HARLAND, Marion (1830–1922). See Terhune, Mary Virginia.

HARLEM BRUNDTLAND, Gro. See Bruntland, Gro Harlem.

HARLEY, Brilliana (c. 1600–1643). British royal who sided with the Puritans. Name variations: Lady Brilliana Harley. Born between 1598 and 1600, most sources cite 1600; died while besieged at Brampton Bryan Castle, 1643; dau. of Edward (later 1st Viscount Conway, MP, secretary of state, and governor of Isle of Wight); became 3rd wife of Sir Robert Harley, 1623. ❖ During English Civil Wars, was accused of aiding the enemies of King Charles I; by mid-1643, found herself besieged at Brampton Bryan Castle in Shropshire by a Royalist army of 700; debilitated by a long illness, possibly pregnant, and deserted by many of her servants, held out for 6 weeks until parliamentary forces came to her aid, forcing the besiegers to withdraw; died a few weeks later, however, when the Cavaliers returned. Her letters, written from 1625 to 1643, were published in 1854.

HARLEY, Henrietta (d. 1755). See Cavendish, Henrietta.

HARLEY, Katherine (1881–1961). American golfer. Name variations: Mrs. H. Arnold Jackson; Kate Harley. Born Nov 13, 1881, in Fall River, Massachusetts; died May 2, 1961, in Pinehurst, North Carolina; m. H. Arnold Jackson, 1913. ❖ Played for the Redlands (CA) Country Club; won USGA Women's Amateur (1908, 1914); won the Women's Eastern (1914, 1921).

HARLEY, Margaret Cavendish (1714–1785). See Bentinck, Margaret.

HARLOW, Jean (1911–1937). American screen actress. Born Harlean Carpenter, Mar 3, 1911, in Kansas City, Missouri; died June 7, 1937, age 26, from complications of kidney disease at Good Samaritan Hospital in Los Angeles, CA; dau. of Jean (Harlow) Carpenter and Mont Clair Carpenter; m. Charles McGrew, 1927 (div. 1929); m. Paul Bern, 1932 (committed suicide, 1932); m. Harold Rosson, 1933 (div. 1934); no children. ❖ Star who rose above her "blonde bombshell" image to become a fine screen comedian; at 16, eloped with a wealthy young businessman (1927); eventually moved to Los Angeles and found part-time work as a walk-on in features and comedy shorts; given 1st important role in *Hell's Angels* (1930) but confined to vulgar, blatant roles until signing with MGM (1932), when her acting ability in both dramatic and comedic roles became apparent; developed into one of Hollywood's superstars (early 1930s), playing opposite such actors as Clark Gable and Spencer Tracy; fell seriously ill while shooting *Saratoga* (1937); other films include

The Saturday Night Kid (1929), *The Secret Six* (1931), *The Public Enemy* (1931), *Goldie* (1931), *Platinum Blonde* (1931), *Three Wise Girls* (1932), *Red-Headed Woman* (1932), *Red Dust* (1932), *Hold Your Man* (1933), *Bombshell* (1933), *Dinner at Eight* (1934), *The Girl from Missouri* (1934), *Reckless* (1935), *China Seas* (1935), *Riffraff* (1936), *Wife vs. Secretary* (1936), *Suzy* (1936), *Libeled Lady* (1936) and *Personal Property* (1937). ❖ See also David Stenn, *Bombshell: The Life and Death of Jean Harlow* (Doubleday, 1993); and *Women in World History*.

HARLOWE, Sarah (1765–1852). English actress. Born 1765; died 1852; m. Francis Godolphin Waldron (1744–1818, actor-writer). ❖ Following a triumph at Sadler's Wells, appeared at Covent Garden (1790); also performed at Haymarket, Drury Lane, and the English Opera House before retirement (1826); was best known for performances as Lucy in *The Rivals*, Widow Warren in *Road to Ruin*, Miss MacTab in *Poor Gentleman* and old Lady Lambert in *Hypocrite*.

HARMAN, Harriet (1950—). English politician and feminist. Name variations: Rt. Hon. Harriet Harman. Born July 30, 1950, in London, England; attended York University; m. Jack Dromey (TGWU official), 1982; children: 3. ❖ Worked as a lawyer at Brent Law Center in London; was legal officer for National Council for Civil Liberties (1978–82); representing Labour, elected to House of Commons for Camberwell and Peckham in a by-election (1982); was the 1st Labour frontbencher to take maternity leave; reelected (1987, 1992, 1997, 2001); became secretary of state for Social Security (1997); named solicitor general, Law Officers' Department (2001); wrote *The Century Gap* (1993).

HARMAN, Katie Marie (c. 1980—). Miss America. Born in Gresham, Oregon c. 1980; attended Portland State University. ❖ Named Miss America (2002), representing Oregon.

HARMON, Ellen Gould (1827–1915). See White, Ellen Gould.

HARMS, Emilie von Berlepsch (1755–1830). See Berlepsch, Emilie von.

HARNACK, Mildred (1902–1943). American-born spy. Name variations: Mildred Fish-Harnack. Born Mildred Fish in Milwaukee, Wisconsin, Sept 16, 1902; executed in Berlin, Germany, Feb 16, 1943; grew up in Wisconsin; attended University of Giessen; m. Arvid Harnack (1901–1942). ❖ Anti-Nazi activist and member of the "Red Orchestra" spy network which supplied the Soviets with important data, including the schedule for Hitler's attack on the USSR; with husband, a key leader of the spy organization, was arrested (Sept 7, 1942); received a sentence of 6 years' imprisonment from Reich War Tribunal, but when Hitler was apprised of the punishment he demanded that the judgment be annulled and a new tribunal rule again; sentenced to death. ❖ See also *Women in World History*.

HARNED, Virginia (1872–1946). American stage actress. Born Virginia Hickes, May 29, 1872, in Boston, MA; died April 29, 1946, in New York, NY; m. E.H. Sothern (actor), 1896 (div. 1910); m. William Courtenay. ❖ Starred opposite 1st husband E.H. Sothern in *Hamlet* and many other plays; created title role in *Trilby* in Boston (1895); appeared as Jane Shore in *The Lady Shore*, Marguerite Gautier in *Camille*, as well as the title roles in *Anna Karenina*, *Josephine* and Pinero's *Iris*.

HARNEY, Mary (1953—). Irish politician. Born Mar 11, 1953, in Ballinasloe, Co. Galway, Ireland. ❖ Was the 1st woman to become auditor of the Historical Society in Trinity College; nominated to the Seanad by Taoiseach Jack Lynch (1977–81), becoming the youngest member of that house; representing Fianna Fáil, served as TD in the 22nd–25th Dáil (1981–1989) for Dublin South West; quit Fianna Fáil (1985) and was instrumental in establishing the Progressive Democrat (PD) Party (Dec 21, 1985); returned to 26th–28th (1987–2002) and 29th (2002—) Dáil as a Progessive Democrat; on the formation of the Fianna Fáil–Progressive Democrat coalition government, appointed minister of State with responsibility for the Office of the Protection of the Environment; appointed deputy leader of the PDs and spokesperson on Justice, Equality and Law Reform (Feb 1993), then became leader of the PDs, the 1st woman to lead a party in the Dáil; appointed minister for Enterprise, Trade and Employment. Chosen *Irish Independent* Woman of the Year (1993).

HAROLD, Erika (c. 1980—). Miss America. Born c. 1980 in Urbana, Illinois; University of Illinois, Phi Beta Kappa. ❖ Named Miss America (2003), representing Illinois; was contracted to lecture on empowering youth against violence, often chose abstinence as her topic instead, to the delight of conservatives and the chagrin of those at pageant headquarters.

HARPER, Edith (1883–1947). *See Wickham, Anna.*

HARPER, Frances E.W. (1825–1911). American educator, writer, lecturer, abolitionist, and human-rights activist. Name variations: Frances Watkins Harper. Born Frances Ellen Watkins, Sept 24, 1825, in Baltimore, Maryland; died Feb 11, 1911, and buried in Eden Cemetery, Philadelphia, PA; m. Fenton Harper, Nov 22, 1860 (died May 1864); children: Mary Harper and 3 stepchildren. ❖ Popular 19th-century African-American poet, aligned herself with those who shared her concerns about slavery, education, temperance, women's rights, and morality, issues often reflected in her literary work; after mother died (1828), was raised and educated by uncle, Reverend William Watkins, headmaster of Watkins Academy; published a volume of poetry and prose, *Forest Leaves*; was 1st woman instructor at Union Seminary (later Wilberforce) in Ohio (1851); taught in York, Pennsylvania (1852); was hired as lecturer for Maine Anti-Slavery Society (1854); was lecturer and agent for the Pennsylvania Anti-Slavery Society (1858); was such a powerful public figure that she was enlisted to help frame the constitution for the new Ohio State Anti-Slavery Society (1858); spoke at the 11th Annual Woman's Rights convention in New York (1866); writings include *Poems on Miscellaneous Subjects* (1854), *Sketches of Southern Life* (1872), and *Iola Le Roy, or the Shadows Uplifted* (1892). ❖ See also *Women in World History.*

HARPER, Ida Husted (1851–1931). American journalist and women's-rights advocate. Born Ida Husted, Feb 18, 1851, in Fairfield, Indiana; died of a cerebral hemorrhage in Washington, DC, Mar 14, 1931; finished high school at 17 and entered Indiana University as a sophomore; left after 1 year to become principal of a high school in Peru, Indiana; m. Thomas Winans Harper (lawyer and friend of labor leader Eugene V. Debs), 1871 (div. 1890); children: Winnifred Harper (writer). ❖ Soon after marriage, began a 12-year stint, writing for the Terre Haute *Saturday Evening Mail* under a male pseudonym; launched a weekly column, "A Woman's Opinions," under her own name (1883); joined Indiana suffrage society (1887); with daughter, moved to Indianapolis and worked for the *Indianapolis News*; a few years later, moved to California where she continued writing for the *News* while doing publicity for Susan B. Anthony's campaign for California state suffrage (1896); began writing a popular column for *Harper's Bazaar* (1909); published 2-volume *Life and Work of Susan B. Anthony* (1898); added a 3rd volume (1908) and volumes 5 and 6 (1922); also assisted Anthony in 4th volume of *History of Woman Suffrage.*

HARPER, Valerie (1940—). American actress. Born Aug 22, 1940, in Suffern, NY; m. Richard Schaal (actor), c. 1964 (div. 1978); m. Tony Cacciotti (actor), 1987. ❖ Began career dancing with corps de ballet at Radio City Music Hall; appeared on Broadway in *Dear Liar, Story Theatre* and *Metamorphosis,* among others; came to prominence as Mary's sidekick on tv series "Mary Tyler Moore" (1970–74), then starred in its spinoff "Rhoda" (1974–78) and "Valerie" (1986–87); films include *Chapter Two* (1979) and *The Last Married Couple in America* (1980).

HARRADEN, Beatrice (1864–1936). English novelist and suffragist. Born Jan 24, 1864, in Hampstead, London, England; died May 5, 1936, in Barton-on-Sea, Hampshire, England; dau. of Samuel and Rosalie (Lindstedt) Harraden; attended Cheltenham Ladies' College, Dresden, and Queens College and Bedford College, London; London University, BA, 1883. ❖ Contributed short stories to *Blackwood's Magazine*; published children's book, *Things Will Take a Turn* (1891); issued most successful book, *Ships That Pass in the Night* (1893), which sold more than 1 million copies; other writings include (short stories) *In Varying Moods* (1894), *Hilda Stafford* (1897), *Untold Tales of the Past* (1897) and *The Fowler* (1899); was also active in the women's suffrage movement and a prominent member of the Women's Social and Political Union.

HARRIET. *Variant of Henrietta.*

HARRIGAN, Lori (1970—). American softball player. Born Sept 5, 1970, in Nevada; attended University of Nevada. ❖ Pitcher, won a team gold medal at World championships (2002); won team gold medals at Atlanta Olympics (1996), Sydney Olympics (2000) and Athens Olympics (2004).

HARRIGAN, Nedda (1899–1989). American actress. Name variations: Nedda Logan; Hedda Harrigan. Born Grace Harrigan, Aug 24, 1899, in New York, NY; died April 1, 1989, in NYC; sister of William Harrigan

(actor, 1894–1966); m. Walter Connolly (actor), 1923 (died 1940); m. Josh Logan (director, producer), 1945 (died 1988); children: (1st m.) Ann Connolly. ❖ Made NY debut in *Josephine* (1918); other plays include *Becky Sharp, Merry Andrew, The Squall, Ceiling Zero, Charley's Aunt,* and *Dracula*; also appeared in films; founded the Stage Door Canteen (1942); served as president of the Actors Fund of America (1979–89).

HARRIMAN, Daisy (1870–1967). *See Harriman, Florence Jaffray.*

HARRIMAN, Florence Jaffray (1870–1967). American social reformer, politician, and diplomat. Name variations: Daisy Harriman; Mrs. J. Borden Harriman. Born Florence Jaffray Hurst, July 21, 1870, in New York, NY; died in Washington, DC, Aug 31, 1967; dau. of Francis William Jones Hurst (head of steamship company) and Caroline Elise Jaffray Hurst (died 1873); m. J(efferson) Borden Harriman, Nov 18, 1889 (died 1914); children: Ethel Borden Harriman Russell (1898–1953). ❖ Social reformer and Democratic Party activist, was US minister to Norway at time of Nazi invasion; served as manager of New York State Reformatory for Women at Bedford (1906–18); co-founded Colony Club with Anne Morgan and Elisabeth Marbury, New York's first women's social club, and served as president (1907–16); helped found women's welfare committee of National Civic Federation, and toured South to report on child-labor conditions; was only woman member of Federal Industrial Relations Commission (1913–14); served as chair of Committee of Women in Industry of the Advisory Committee of the Council of National Defense (1917); organized Red Cross Motor Corps, served as assistant director of transportation in France (1918); was a delegate to Inter-Allied Women's Council (1919); co-founded Women's National Democratic Club (1922) and was its president (1922–30); served as Democratic Committeewoman, Washington, DC (1924–36); served as US minister to Norway (1937–40), the 2nd woman to head an American legation; appointed vice-chair of White Committee to Defend America by Aiding the Allies (1941). Granted Great Cross of St. Olav, highest honor of Norway (1942); received Presidential Medal of Freedom from John F. Kennedy (1963). ❖ See also memoirs *From Pinafores to Politics* (Holt, 1923) and *Mission to the North* (Lippincott, 1941); and *Women in World History.*

HARRIMAN, Mrs. J. Borden (1870–1967). *See Harriman, Florence Jaffray.*

HARRIMAN, Mary (1851–1932). American philanthropist. Name variations: Mary Averell Harriman. Born Mary Williamson Averell, July 22, 1851, in New York, NY; died Nov 7, 1932, in NY; dau. of William John Averell (businessman) and Mary Laurence (Williamson) Averell; m. Edward Henry Harriman, Sept 10, 1879 (died 1909); children: 6, including Cornelia Harriman, Mary Harriman Rumsey (1881–1934) and William Averell Harriman (b. 1891, governor of NY and ambassador to Soviet Union). ❖ Became sole beneficiary of husband's estate which was estimated at $70 million (1909); established Eugenics Records Office under biologist Charles B. Davenport (1910), later transferred to Carnegie Institution; granted 10,000 acres and endowment of $1 million to NY as Harriman State Park (1910); established and financed Training School for Public Service (1911), pioneering venture in public administration; commissioned survey *Modern Philanthropy: A Study of Efficient Appealing and Giving* (1912); served on Women's Advisory Committee of National War Council and American National Red Cross (WWI); after WWI, supported many young artists with interest and money, including Albert Herter and Malvina Hoffman; founded and served as president of American Orchestral Society (1920); received gold medal for "great service to the music-loving people of New York" from National Institute of Social Sciences (1925).

HARRIMAN, Mary (1881–1934). *See Rumsey, Mary Harriman.*

HARRIMAN, Pamela (1920–1997). British-born socialite, politician and diplomat. Born Pamela Digby, Mar 20, 1920, in Farnborough, England; died Feb 5, 1997, in Paris, France; dau. of Lord Edward Kenelm Digby, 11th Baron Digby, and Constance Pamela Alice (Bruce) Digby; m. Randolph Churchill, 1939 (div. 1945); m. Leland Hayward (theatrical producer), 1960 (died 1971); m. W. Averell Harriman (governor of NY and presidential advisor), c. 1972 (died 1986); children: (1st m.) Winston Churchill (b. 1940). ❖ In a time when women had little power, gained wealth and power through 3 marriages; devoted later years to politics, and is credited with helping to put the Democratic Party back on its feet after years of Republican rule; served as US ambassador to France (1993–97), surprising legions of doubters on both sides of the Atlantic by overcoming her image as socialite and dilettante and establishing herself as a powerful and capable American presence in Paris. ❖ See also Sally Bedell Smith, *Reflected Glory* (Simon & Schuster, 1996); Christopher Ogden, *Life of the Party* (Little, Brown, 1994); and *Women in World History*.

HARRINGTON, Baroness (1460–1530). *See Bonville, Cecily.*

HARRINGTON, countess of. *See Foote, Maria (c. 1797–1867).*

HARRINGTON, Penny (c. 1943—). **American police chief.** Born c. 1943 in Lansing, Michigan. ❖ Joined staff of Woman's Protective Division of Police Bureau in Portland, Oregon (1965); filed successful civil-rights complaint against city for sexist language in police-department documents (1971); became police officer in Portland and filed more than 40 complaints before becoming 1st woman appointed police chief of a major US city (Portland, 1985); after disputes with the mayor, union heads, and city commission, resigned as police chief (1986); became founder and chair of National Center for Women and Policing's Advisory Board; testified before US Civil Rights Commission on gender issues in law enforcement.

HARRINGTON, Sara (1941—). *See Leland, Sara.*

HARRIOT. *Variant of Henrietta.*

HARRIS, Addie (1940–1982). **African-American singer.** Name variations: Micki Harris; The Shirelles. Born Jan 22, 1940, in Passaic, NJ; died of heart attack, June 10, 1982, during live performance of Shirelles in Atlanta, GA. ❖ Began singing in high school in Passaic, NJ, with Shirley Owens, Doris Coley, and Beverly Lee as the Shirelles (1958), one of the 1st few all-girl groups of rock era; with group, wrote and performed "I Met Him on a Sunday" which was bought by Decca; released hit song, "Tonight's the Night" (1960), followed by #1 pop hit, "Will You Love Me Tomorrow?" (1961), then "Baby It's You" (1963), "Mama Said," "Soldier Boy" and "Foolish Little Girl." Inducted into Rock and Roll Hall of Fame (1996).

HARRIS, Barbara (1930—). **African-American suffragan bishop.** Born Barbara Clementine Harris in Philadelphia, Pennsylvania, June 12, 1930; dau. of Walter Harris (steelworker) and Beatrice (Price) Harris (classical pianist); attended Villanova University, 1977–79, and Hobart and William Smith College; m.; no children. ❖ The 1st woman bishop in the history of the Episcopal Church, joined the Sun Oil Company in Philadelphia (1968), where she eventually became a public-relations executive; worked for African-American and women's rights (1960s); when ordination became a possibility for women, began studying for the ministry; ordained to the diaconate (1978) and as a priest (1980), age 50; elected suffragan (assistant) bishop of the Massachusetts diocese of the Episcopal Church (1988). ❖ See also *Women in World History*.

HARRIS, Barbara (1935—). **American actress.** Born Sandra Markowitz, July 25, 1935, in Evanston, Illinois; dau. of Oscar Harris and Natalie Densmoor (pianist); attended Wright Junior College, University of Chicago and Goodman School of the Theatre; m. Paul Sills (actor, div.). ❖ With Ed Asner, Mike Nichols and Elaine May, among others, began career as a founding member of Chicago's improv troupe Second City (1960); appeared with the troupe on Broadway and was nominated for a Tony; starred on Broadway in *On a Clear Day You Can See Forever, Oh Dad Poor Dad* and *Mother Courage,* and won a Tony Award for her performance in *The Apple Tree* (1967); films include *A Thousand Clowns* (1965), *Who is Harry Kellerman and Why Is He Saying Those Terrible Things about Me?* (1971), *Plaza Suite* (1971), *Nashville* (1975), *Family Plot* (1976), *Freaky Friday* (1976), *North Avenue Irregulars* (1979), *The Seduction of Joe Tynan* (1979), *Peggy Sue Got Married* (1986) and *Grosse Pointe Blank* (1997).

HARRIS, Barbara (1945—). **African-American rhythm-and-blues singer.** Name variations: Barbara Ann Harris, The Toys, Rhythm & Babs. Born Barbara Ann Harris, Aug 18, 1945, in Elizabeth, NJ; m. Kenneth Wiltshire (musician); children: 7. ❖ With June Monteiro and Barbara Parritt, formed all-girl group The Toys in Jamaica, NY (early 1960s); with trio, had huge hit in US with single "A Lover's Concerto," based on Bach's "Minuet in G," eventually selling 1 million copies; also had hits, "Attack" (1966) and "Sealed With a Kiss" (1968); appeared in film, *It's a Bikini World* (1967); after group disbanded (1968), began performing in NYC clubs; released solo album, *Barbara Now* (1998); continues to perform with own band, Rhythm & Babs, in NJ.

HARRIS, Beverly (1947—). *See Messenger-Harris, Beverly.*

HARRIS, Charlotte (1819–?). **English murderer.** Born 1819 in UK. ❖ Tried for killing husband, was found guilty of premeditated murder and received death sentence (1848); execution was delayed due to her pregnancy; saw sentence commuted to life imprisonment during delay, when the Home Secretary received in excess of 40,000 signatures from Society for the Abolition of Capital Punishment seeking reprieve.

HARRIS, Christie (1907–2002). **Canadian children's writer.** Born Christie Irwin, Nov 21, 1907, in Newark, NJ; died Jan 5, 2002, in Vancouver, British Columbia, Canada; m. Thomas Harris, 1932; children: 5. ❖ Moved with family to British Columbia (1908) and later attended University of British Columbia; writings, which draw on folklore and legend and often reflect experiences of aboriginal peoples, include *Cariboo Trail* (1957), *Once Upon a Totem* (1963), *Raven's Cry* (1966), *Mouse Woman and the Vanished Princesses* (1976), *Mystery at the Edge of Two Worlds* (1978), *Mouse Woman and the Muddleheads* (1979), *The Trouble with Princesses* (1980), and *The Trouble with Adventures* (1982). Received Book of the Year Medal and Vicky Metcalf Award.

HARRIS, Claire (1937—). **Canadian poet and essayist.** Born 1937 in Trinidad; studied at University College, Dublin, and University of West Indies. ❖ Moved to Canada (1966) and taught English; began writing during stay in Nigeria, where she also earned degree in Communications from University of Lagos; co-founded Alberta magazine *blue buffalo* (1983); writings include *Fables from the Women's Quarters* (1984), *Translation into Fiction* (1984), *The Conception of Winter* (1989), *Drawing Down a Daughter* (1992), *Dipped in Shadow* (1996), and *She* (2000).

HARRIS, Corra May (1869–1935). **American novelist.** Born Corra May White, Mar 17, 1869, in Middleton, Georgia; died Feb 9, 1935, in Atlanta, Georgia; dau. of Tinsley Rucker White (planter) and Mary Elizabeth Matthews; m. Lundy Howard Harris (Methodist minister), Feb 8, 1887 (committed suicide 1910); children: 3 (2 of whom died at infancy). ❖ Published letter defending the South's racial views in the *Independent* (NY, 1899); gained literary recognition with "A Circuit Rider's Wife" published 1st as serial in *Saturday Evening Post* (1909), then in book form (1910); published an average of 1 novel per year for almost 2 decades, including *Eve's Second Husband* (1911), *A Circuit Rider's Widow* (1916), and *The Happy Pilgrimage* (1927); wrote a series of articles on women of various European countries (1911) and on conditions behind WWI battle lines (1914) for *Saturday Evening Post*; received honorary degrees from Oglethorpe University (1921), University of Georgia (1927), and Rollins College (1927); writings include popular romances, largely autobiographical works, and critiques of Methodist Church and Georgia towns.

HARRIS, Dionna (1968—). **American softball player.** Born Mar 4, 1968, in Wilmington, Delaware. ❖ Won a team gold medal at Atlanta Olympics (1996).

HARRIS, Edna Mae (1910–1997). **African-American actress.** Born Sept 29, 1910, in Harlem, NY; died Sept 15, 1997, in New York, NY. ❖ One of the best black actresses of the 1930s–40s, began career on stage, appearing in *The Green Pastures* (1930), then reprised the role of Zeba in the film version (1936); other films include *Fury* (1936), *The Garden of Allah* (1936), *Bullets or Ballots* (1936), *Spirit of Youth* (1938), *Paradise in Harlem* (1939), *Murder on Lenox Avenue* (1941), *Night and Day* (1946), *Fall Guy* (1947) and *Take Me Out to the Ball Game* (1949); served as mistress of ceremonies at Harlem's Apollo Theatre (1940s).

HARRIS, Elizabeth (d. 1643). *See Glover, Elizabeth Harris.*

HARRIS, Emily Cumming (c. 1836–1925). **New Zealand teacher, artist, diarist.** Born on Mar 28, 1836 or 1837, in Plymouth, Devonshire, England; died on Aug 5, 1925, in Nelson, New Zealand; dau. of Edwin Harris (civil engineer, surveyor, and artist) and Sarah (Hill) Harris (school administrator). ❖ Studied art in Tasmania and Melbourne, Australia (1860s); returned to Nelson to assist mother and sisters in running school; taught music, dancing, and drawing; kept diary that detailed colonial life; prize-winning watercolors of botanical subjects and landscapes exhibited throughout Australia and New Zealand; published *New Zealand Flowers, New Zealand Ferns, New Zealand Berries,* and illustrated children's book, *Fairyland in New Zealand,* by Sarah Moore (1890). ❖ See also *Dictionary of New Zealand Biography* (Vol. 2).

HARRIS, Emmylou (1947—). **American singer.** Born April 2, 1947, in Birmingham, Alabama; grew up outside Washington, DC; attended University of North Carolina; m. Tom Slocum, 1969 (div.); m. Brian Ahern, 1977 (div. 1983); m. Paul Kennerley, 1985 (div. 1993); children:

Mika and Meghann. ❖ Credited with bringing folk-rock to country, began influential collaboration with Gram Parsons (early 1970s); topped country charts with "If I Could Only Win Your Love" (1975), "Together Again" (1976), and "Sweet Dreams" (1976); began focusing on pure country material on album *Blue Kentucky Girl* (1979); sang duet with Roy Orbison, "That Lovin' You Feeling Again" (1980); had 8 gold albums by early 1980s, including *Roses in the Snow*; released series of country hits, including "Beneath Still Waters" (1980), "On Our Last Date (1983), and "Pledging My Love" (1984); recorded albums *Trio* and *Trio II* with Dolly Parton and Linda Ronstadt (1987 and 1999); broke away from Nashville scene with Grammy-winning album *Wrecking Ball* (1995); executive-produced and sang on tribute to Gram Parsons *Return of the Grievous Angel* (1999); critically acclaimed for solo work and collaborations with great artists.

HARRIS, Jackie. American singer. Name variations: Snap! Born Jacqueline Arlissa Harris in Pittsburgh, PA; cousin of Durron Maurice Butler (known as Turbo B.). ❖ With cousin Turbo B., sang as the duo Snap!, filling in for Penny Ford before being replaced by Paula Abdul.

HARRIS, Jane Elizabeth (c. 1852–1942). New Zealand writer, lecturer, and spiritualist. Name variations: Jane Elizabeth Francis, Jane Elizabeth Roberts, Jenny Wren. Born Jane Elizabeth Francis, in 1852 or 1853, in London, England; died on Sept 18 (1942, in Paeroa, New Zealand; dau. of Harriett Francis and Adelbert Sevyney Frantz; m. Thomas Harris (market gardener), 1873 (died 1887); m. Charles Nathaniel Roberts (teacher), 1900; children: 7. ❖ Immigrated with family to Auckland, New Zealand (1866); published newspaper stories under pseudonym Jenny Wren; became successful medium and lecturer, writing inspirational pieces for *Harbinger*; published volume of poetry, *Leaves of Love* (1890). ❖ See also *Dictionary of New Zealand Biography* (Vol. 2).

HARRIS, Joan (1920—). English ballet dancer and teacher. Born Mar 26, 1920, in London, England. ❖ Danced with Anglo-Polish Ballet for 1 season (1941); performed with International Ballet for 4 years, dancing featured roles in 19th-century classics; joined Sadler's Wells (1945), where she danced in *The Catch* (1946), *The Gods Go-a-Begging* and *The Sleeping Beauty*, among others; worked on many ballet films (1950s) as camera assistant and ballet master including *Red Shoes* (1948) and *Tales of Hoffmann*; appeared in such films as *The Killing Fields* (1984) and *The Manhattan Project* (1986), and worked on production of *Silent Scream* (1980).

HARRIS, Julie (1921—). British costume designer. Born in London, England, in 1921; studied at Chelsea Polytechnic. ❖ Worked for the court dressmaker Reville, before joining film industry (1945), as an assistant in design department under Elizabeth Haffenden at Gainsborough Studios; designed for over 75 films, including *Once Upon a Dream* (1948), *Quartet* (1949), *Under Capricorn* (1950), *Trio* (1951), *Hotel Sahara* (1952), *Made in Heaven* (1953), *Cast a Dark Shadow* (1956), *Simon and Laura* (1956), *It's a Wonderful World* (1957), *The Gypsy and the Gentleman* (1958), *Whirlpool* (1959), *Sapphire* (1960), *The Greengage Summer* (1961), *All Night Long* (1962), *The Chalk Garden* (1964), *A Hard Day's Night* (1965), *Carry on Cleo* (1965), *The Whisperers* (1968), *Goodbye Mr. Chips* (1970), *The Private Life of Sherlock Holmes* (1972), and *Live and Let Die* (1975). Won Academy Award for black-and-white design for film *Darling* (1965); also received Society of Film and Television Arts (SFTA) awards for *Psyche, Help!, The Wrong Box, Casino Royale* and *The Slipper and the Rose*. ❖ See also *Women in World History.*

HARRIS, Julie (1925—). American actress. Born in Grosse Pointe Park, Michigan, Dec 2, 1925; dau. of William Pickett Harris (investment banker) and Elsie (Smith) Harris; attended Yale University School of Drama, 1944–45, and Actors Studio, NY; m. Jay I. Julien (lawyer and producer), Aug 1946 (div. 1954); m. Manning Gurian (stage manager), Oct 21, 1954 (div. 1967); m. William Erwin Carroll (writer), April 27, 1977; children: (2nd m.) Peter Alston Gurian. ❖ Esteemed actress who received an unprecedented 10 Tony nominations and 5 Tony Awards; made Broadway debut in *It's a Gift* (1945); had breakthrough role as Frankie Addams in *The Member of the Wedding* (1950), recreating the role on film, for which she was nominated for an Academy Award (1952); triumphed again as Sally Bowles in *I Am a Camera* (1951), winning 1st Tony award; starred as Saint Joan in *The Lark* (1955), winning 2nd Tony as Best Actress; further distinguished herself as a nun in *Little Moon of Alban* (1960), vaudevillian in *Marathon '33* (1963), and divorcee in *Forty Carats* (1968), for which she received another Tony Award; received 4th Tony for portrayal of Mary Todd Lincoln in *The Last of Mrs. Lincoln*

(1972) and 5th for portrayal of Emily Dickinson in one-woman show *The Belle of Amherst* (1976); films include *East of Eden* (1955), *I Am a Camera* (1955), *Requiem for a Heavyweight* (1962), *The Haunting* (1963), *Harper* (1966), *Reflections in a Golden Eye* (1967), *The People Next Door* (1970), *The Hiding Place* (1975), *Voyage of the Damned* (1976), *The Bell Jar* (1979), and *Gorillas in the Mist* (1988); on tv, won Emmys for 2 roles on NBC's "Hallmark Hall of Fame": Brigid Mary in *Little Moon of Alban* (1958) and Queen Victoria in *Victoria Regina* (1961); also appeared regularly as Lilimae Clements on "Knots Landing." ❖ See also *Women in World History.*

HARRIS, Lois (1940—). American singer. Name variations: Lois Harris Powell; The Chantels. Born 1940. ❖ Sang with Arlene Smith, Sonia Goring, Jackie Landry, and Rene Minus in their Bronx (NY) parochial school choir and became top soprano for their doo-wop group The Chantels (formed 1956), one of 1st and most well-received girl groups; released albums, *We Are the Chantels* (1958) and *The Best of the Chantels* (1990); appeared with original group in reunion performances (1990s). Chantels biggest hit was "Maybe" (1958) which was later covered by Janis Joplin (1969); other hits include "Look in My Eyes" and "Well, I Told You" (both 1961).

HARRIS, Lucy (1955—). *See Harris, Lusia Mae.*

HARRIS, Lusia Mae (1955—). African-American basketball player. Name variations: Lucy Harris. Born Feb 10, 1955, in Minter City, Mississippi; m. George Steward. ❖ Was a 3-time All-American at Delta State University (1975, 1976, 1977), averaging 25.9 points per game; was also Delta State's 1st black homecoming queen; at Montreal Olympics, won a team silver medal (1976); was 1st woman drafted by a men's professional basketball team. Won Broderick Award (1977) and Honda Broderick Cup.

HARRIS, Marjorie Silliman (1890–1976). American philosopher. Born June 6, 1890, in Virginia; died Mar 1976, in Wethersfield, Connecticut; dau. of George Wells and Elizabeth Silliman Harris; Mount Holyoke College, BA, 1913; Susan Linn Sage Scholarship in Philosophy and PhD, Cornell University, 1921. ❖ Was an instructor in philosophy, University of Colorado (1921–22); at Randolph-Macon Women's College, served as adjunct professor of philosophy (1922–25), associate professor (1925–30), professor (1930–58), and professor emeritus and chair of philosophy (1934–58); wrote for *Journal of Philosophy* and *Philosophical Review*, concentrating on French philosophers, Henri Bergson and Auguste Comte, and on Argentinean philosopher Francisco Romero.

HARRIS, Mary Belle (1874–1957). American prison administrator. Born Aug 19, 1874, in Factoryville, Pennsylvania; died Feb 22, 1957, in Lewisburg, PA; only dau. of John Howard (Baptist minister and president of Bucknell University) and Mary Elizabeth (Mace) Harris; Bucknell University, AB in music, 1893, AM in Latin, 1894; earned PhD in Sanskrit and Indo-European comparative philology from University of Chicago, 1900; studied archaeology and numismatics at Johns Hopkins University. ❖ Believing that prisons should teach employable skills and rehabilitate, dedicated herself to prison reform; served as superintendent of women and deputy warden of Workhouse on Blackwell's Island (now Roosevelt Island), NYC (1914–18); assumed superintendent's post at State Reformatory for Women in Clinton, NJ (1918); served as superintendent of State Home for Girls in Trenton, NJ (1919–24), a juvenile institution notorious for its dangerous inmates, and was successful in establishing a system of self-government; became 1st superintendent of Federal Industrial Institution for Women (1928), a model institution. ❖ See also *Women in World History.*

HARRIS, Micki (1940–1982). *See Harris, Addie.*

HARRIS, Mildred (1901–1944). American silent-screen star. Name variations: Mildred Harris Chaplin. Born in Cheyenne, Wyoming, Nov 29, 1901; died of pneumonia in Hollywood, California, July 20, 1944; m. Charlie Chaplin (actor), 1917 (div. 1920); m. Eldridge F. McGovern (div. 1929); m. William P. Fleckerstein (Minneapolis brewer); children: (2nd m.) 1 son. ❖ At 9, made film debut; at 11, was hired by Vitagraph to play children's roles in a number of films, including D.W. Griffith's *Enoch Arden*; by 13, was starring as Dorothy in silent film *The Patchwork Girl of Oz*; became 1st wife of Charlie Chaplin at 18; until she died of pneumonia, at 43, appeared as a juvenile, ingenue, or bit player in over 40 films, 6 of them directed by Lois Weber.

HARRIS, Patricia Roberts (1924–1985). American lawyer and politician. Born May 31, 1924, in Mattoon, Illinois; died of cancer,

Mar 23, 1985; dau. of Bert Roberts (railroad waiter) and Chiquita Roberts; graduate of Howard University (summa cum laude); completed graduate work in industrial relations at University of Chicago; George Washington University Law School, JD, 1960; m. William Beasley Harris (Washington attorney), 1955; no children. ❖ The 1st African-American woman to achieve ambassadorial rank, occupant of 2 Cabinet-level positions in the administration of President Jimmy Carter, and dean of Howard University Law School, was active in civil-rights campaigns (1940s–60s); appointed ambassador to Luxemburg (1965); served as professor of law and later dean of Law School at Howard University; served as secretary of Housing and Urban Development (HUD) and later as secretary of Health, Education, and Welfare in the Carter Administration; held a variety of Democratic Party positions, including temporary chair of credentials committee (1972); ran unsuccessfully for mayor of District of Columbia (1982); served as full-time professor at George Washington National Law Center; known for her political savvy, was also regarded as a tough, productive administrator. ❖ See also *Women in World History.*

HARRIS, Phoebe (1755–1786). British criminal. Born 1755; died 1786 (some sources cite 1788), one of the last persons in England executed by hanging and burning at the stake. ❖ A coiner for most of her short life (a term for melting coins and selling them as gold or silver for profit), was caught and sentenced to death; became almost as well known for her execution as for her crimes, since she was 1st hanged, then burned in front of a throng of 20,000. ❖ See also *Women in World History.*

HARRIS, Renee (1885–1969). American theatrical producer. Name variations: Mrs. Renee Harris. Born June 15, 1885; died Sept 2, 1969, in New York, NY; m. Henry B. Harris (producer, lost on the *Titanic*, 1912); m. Lester B. Consolly; m. L. Marvin Simmons; m. Zach C. Barber. ❖ Was Broadway's first female producer; as owner of the Hudson Theater, gave the 1st Broadway roles to Barbara Stanwyck and Judith Anderson. A *Titanic* survivor, left the ship in the last lifeboat.

HARRIS, Rosemary (1927—). English actress. Born Sept 19, 1927, in Ashby, Suffolk, England; grew up in India; graduate of Royal Academy of Dramatic Art; m. Ellis Rabb (actor-director), 1959 (div. 1967); m. John Ehle (novelist), 1967; children: Jennifer Ehle (actress who won a Tony Award for Best Actress for *Waiting in the Wings*, 2000). ❖ Award-winning actress, made Broadway debut in the short-lived *Climate of Eden* (1952) but won Theatre World Award; starred in *The Seven Year Itch* in London (1953), then appeared with Bristol Old Vic; returned to NY with Old Vic as Cressida in Guthrie's modern-dress version of *Troilus and Cressida* (1956); joined Chichester Festival for inaugural season (1962), then appeared in Olivier's acclaimed production of *Uncle Vanya* (1963); won Tony award for *The Lion in Winter* (1966), Drama Desk Award for *Merchant of Venice* and *Streetcar Named Desire* (1966), and London Evening Standard Award for *Plaza Suite* (1969); nominated for Tonys for *Old Times, The Royal Family, Heartbreak House, Pack of Lies, Hay Fever, A Delicate Balance* and *Waiting in the Wings*; films include *Beau Brummell* (1954), *The Boys from Brazil* (1978), *Crossing Delancey* (1988), *Tom & Viv* (Oscar nomination, 1994), *Hamlet* (1996), *My Life So Far* (1999), *Sunshine* (1999), *Spider-Man* (2002), *Spider-Man 2* (2004) and *Being Julia* (2004).

HARRIS, Sylvia (d. 1966). American theatrical producer. Died Nov 11, 1966, in New York, NY; m. Joseph Harris (producer). ❖ Partner in the Broadway firm of Fryer, Carr & Harris, was associated with such plays as *Make a Million, Tovarich, Mame* and *Sweet Charity.*

HARRIS, Venita (1922—). See VanCaspel, Venita.

HARRISON, Anna Symmes (1775–1864). American first lady. Born Anna Symmes, July 25, 1775, in Morristown, NJ; died Feb 25, 1864, in North Bend, Ohio; 2nd dau. of John Cleves (chief judge of New Jersey Supreme Court) and his 1st wife Anna (Tuthill) Symmes; attended Clinton Academy in East Hampton, NY, and Miss Graham's School in NYC; m. William Henry Harrison (9th US president), Nov 25, 1795; children: 6 sons, 4 daughters (son John Scott Harrison was the only child to outlive her and was the father of Benjamin Harrison, 23rd president of US). ❖ Wife of William Henry Harrison, was the only first lady not to assume any of her duties, due to husband's death one month after his inauguration; having been forbidden to accompany husband to Washington because of her own serious illness, also missed his elaborate state funeral. ❖ See also *Women in World History.*

HARRISON, Barbara Grizzuti (1934–2002). American essayist. Born Barbara Grizzuti, Sept 14, 1934, in Jamaica, Queens, NY; died April 24, 2002, in New York, NY; m. W. Dale Harrison, 1960 (div. 1968); children: Josh and Anna Harrison. ❖ Spent years as a Jehovah's Witness; came to prominence with *Visions of Glory: A History and a Memory of Jehovah's Witness* (1978), about her years spent working at the religion's national headquarters in NY; also wrote *Unlearning the Lie: Sexism in Schools* (1969), *Italian Days* (1989), which won the American Book Award, and the novel *Foreign Bodies* (1984); was a frequent contributor to *Ms.* ❖ See also *An Accidental Autobiography* (1996).

HARRISON, Beatrice (1892–1965). English cellist. Born in Roorkee, India, Dec 9, 1892; died in Smallfield, Surrey, England, Mar 10, 1965; dau. of Colonel John Harrison (officer in Royal Engineers) and Annie Harrison (singer); sister of violinist May Harrison (1891–1959), pianist Margaret Harrison and Monica Harrison; at 11, began studying under W.E. Whitehouse at Royal College of Music. ❖ Premier cellist (1920s–30s), world renowned as "The Lady of the Nightingales," was the 1st female cellist to play in Carnegie Hall and the 1st woman and 1st cellist to win the Mendelssohn Medal (1907); concertized with sister May Harrison, causing a sensation when they revived a seldom-heard Brahms Double Concerto; possibly finest achievement was her performance with Sir Edward Elgar (1919); played often at London's popular Promenade Concerts; gave last performance on tv (1958), playing a cello solo which Roger Quilter had written for her. ❖ See also *Women in World History.*

HARRISON, Mrs. Burton (1843–1920). *See Harrison, Constance Cary.*

HARRISON, Caroline Scott (1832–1892). American first lady. Name variations: Carrie; Caroline Lavinia Scott. Born Caroline Lavinia Scott, Oct 10, 1832, in Oxford, Ohio; died Oct 25, 1892, in Washington, DC; dau. of Mary Potts (Neal) Scott and John Witherspoon Scott (Presbyterian minister, professor, and founder and president of Oxford Seminary); attended Oxford Seminary; m. Benjamin Harrison (23rd US president), Oct 20, 1853; children: Russell Harrison (1854–1936, member of Indiana House and Senate); Mary Scott Harrison (1858–1930, later Mrs. J. Robert McKee); daughter (died at birth, 1861). ❖ When husband was elected to Senate (1881), became one of Washington's most popular hostesses; on husband's election, moved into White House with a large extended family (1889) and undertook an extensive renovation with a meager budget; sorted and identified china from past administrations, providing the basis for the White House china collection; had a conservatory built so that plants from White House could be used for receptions; lent her progressive views and support to a number of local charities; helped raise funds for Johns Hopkins University medical school, on condition that they admit women; served as 1st president general of the National Society of Daughters of the American Revolution (1890), when the Sons of the American Revolution would not allow women to join; became ill during last year of husband's term and died in White House at age 60. Three years after her death, Benjamin Harrison married her niece, Mary Scott Dimmick (Harrison). ❖ See also *Women in World History.*

HARRISON, Constance Cary (1843–1920). American writer. Born April 25, 1843, in Lexington, Kentucky; died Nov 21, 1920, in Washington, DC; dau. of Archibald and Monimia (Fairfax) Cary (dau. of 9th lord of Fairfax); m. Burton Harrison (lawyer and private secretary to Jefferson Davis), 1867 (died 1904); children: sons, Francis Burton, Fairfax, and Archibald. ❖ During Civil War, published 1st book, *Blockade Correspondence,* a fictional account of letters between "Secessia" in Baltimore and "Refugitta" in Richmond; moved to NY; published several novels, magazine stories and historical sketches; for the most part, her novels dealt with Southern life, including *Flower de Hundred: The Story of a Virginia Plantation* (1890), *Belhaven Tales* (1892), and *A Daughter of the South, and Shorter Stories* (1892); wrote a gentle satire of NY society for one of her better-known books, *The Anglomaniacs* (1890), and satirized Americans in Europe in *Good Americans* (1898). ❖ See also memoirs, *Recollections Grave and Gay* (1911); and *Women in World History.*

HARRISON, Elizabeth (1849–1927). American educational reformer, author, and lecturer. Born Sept 1, 1849, in Athens, Kentucky; died Oct 31, 1927, in San Antonio, Texas; dau. of Isaac Webb and Elizabeth Thompson (Bullock) Harrison; studied with Halsey Ives, director of St. Louis Art Museum (1882); studied with Susan E. Blow and Maria Kraus-Boelté; studied abroad with Henrietta Breyman Schrader in Berlin and Baroness von Marenholtz-Bülow in Dresden. ❖ On a visit to Chicago, became interested in the fledgling kindergarten movement; with Alice Harvey Whiting Putnam, founded the Chicago Kindergarten Club, which became the Chicago Kindergarten Training School (1887), then Chicago Kindergarten College and finally the National College of Education; writings include *Montessori and the Kindergarten, A Vision of Dante* (1891), *In Storyland* (1895), *Two Children of the Foot Hills* (1900), *Some Silent Teachers* (1903), *Misunderstood Children* (1908), *Offero, the Giant* (1912), *When Children Err* (1916) and *The Unseen Side of Child Life* (1922). ❖ See also *Women in World History*.

HARRISON, Gwen (b. 1907). *See Meredith, Gwen.*

HARRISON, Hazel (1883–1969). African-American concert pianist. Born Hazel Lucille Harrison, May 12, 1883, in La Porte, Indiana; died April 28, 1969, in Washington, DC; dau. of Hiram Harrison(pianist-choir director) and Olive Jane (Woods) Harrison; studied with Victor Heinze; studied with Hugo van Dalan (Berlin) and Ferruccio Busoni (Italy); m. Walter Bainter Anderson, Sept 1, 1919 (div. 1920s); m. Allen Moton, 1950s (div.). ❖ Made professional debut as a soloist with Berlin Philharmonic, under direction of August Scharrer, the 1st appearance with a European orchestra by an American who had not studied outside US; impressed German critics; fame grew as she criss-crossed America on recital tours (1920s); championed contemporary European, German, Russian and Polish composers, and frequently included works by black composers as well as variations of Strauss waltzes and Bach organ works in recitals; despite immense praise, was denied access to many of the mainstream concert halls in America because of her race; performed with Minneapolis Symphony under Eugene Ormandy (1932) in a concert at Tuskegee Institute and appeared with Hollywood Bowl Symphony under direction of Izeler Solomon (1949); taught piano at School of Music at Tuskegee Institute (1931–37), then served as head of piano faculty at Howard University (1938–55). ❖ See also *Women in World History*.

HARRISON, Jane Ellen (1850–1928). English classical scholar. Born in Cottingham, East Yorkshire, England, Sept 9, 1850; died April 15, 1928, in London, England; dau. of Charles Harrison and Elizabeth Hawksley Nelson Harrison; attended Cheltenham College; graduate of Newnham College, Cambridge, 1874–79; never married; no children. ❖ Known for innovative use of archaeology in the interpretation of Greek religion, received numerous academic awards; while a lecturer in classical archaeology at Newnham (1880–98), served as vice president of Hellenic Society (1889–96); wrote numerous books, including *Myths of the Odyssey in Art and Literature* (1882), *The Mythology and Monuments of Ancient Greece* (1890), *Prolegomena to the Study of Greek Religion* (1903), *Themis* (1912), *Ancient Art and Ritual* (1913), and *Epilogomena to the Study of Greek Religion* (1921); took up study of Russian with Hope Mirrlees, collaborating on 3 books on Russian language and literature, including *The Book of the Bear* (1927), a series of translations.

HARRISON, Jane Irwin (1804–1846). White House hostess. Born Jane Findlay Irwin, 1804; died 1846; dau. of Archibald Irwin and Mary (Ramsey) Irwin; daughter-in-law of Anna Symmes Harrison (1775–1864) and William Henry Harrison (president of US); m. William Henry Harrison Jr., 1824; children: 2 sons. ❖ Accompanied father-in-law William Henry Harrison to Washington when mother-in-law was forbidden to travel because of illness; along with aunt and namesake, Jane Findlay, began to set up the White House when William Harrison died; accompanied the president's body back to North Bend, Ohio, where she died 5 years later.

HARRISON, Joan (c. 1908–1994). British movie producer, screenwriter, and scenarist. Born Joan Mary Harrison in Guildford, Surrey, England, June 20, 1908; died Aug 14, 1994, in London; dau. of Walter Harrison (newspaper publisher) and Maelia (Muir) Harrison; spent a year at Sorbonne; St. Hugh's College at Oxford, BA. ❖ Took a secretarial position with movie director Alfred Hitchcock (1933), moving quickly from secretary to scriptreader; collaborated on screen adaptation of *The Girl Was Young* (1937); received 1st screen credit for work on adaptation of Daphne du Maurier's *Jamaica Inn* (1939); accompanied Hitchcock to Hollywood (1939), where she worked on *Rebecca* (1940), *Foreign Correspondent* (1940), a film for which she wrote her 1st full script, *Suspicion* (1941), and *Saboteur* (1942); left Hitchcock to concentrate on screenwriting (1941); became an associate producer at Universal Studios, a rare opportunity for a woman, working on many pictures, including *Shadow of a Doubt, Ride the Pink Horse* (1947) and *Circle of Danger* (1951). ❖ See also *Women in World History*.

HARRISON, Joan (1935—). South African swimmer. Born Nov 29, 1935, in South Africa. ❖ At Helsinki Olympics, won a gold medal in the 100-meter backstroke (1952).

HARRISON, June (1925–1974). American actress. Born Dec 23, 1924, in Chicago, Illinois; died Mar 10, 1974, in Hollywood, CA; m. George Campeau; children: 4. ❖ Began career as a child actress; appeared in such films as *Girl of the Golden West, Sun Valley Serenade, Citizen Saint* and the "Jiggs and Maggie" series, including *Bringing Up Father*.

HARRISON, Kathleen (1892–1995). English character actress of stage, tv, and screen. Born Feb 23, 1892, in Blackburn, Lancashire, England; died Dec 7, 1995; m. John Henry Back, 1916 (died 1960). ❖ Trained at RADA, then married and lived in Argentina for 8 years; best known for her cockney portrayals, made stage debut in Eastbourne in *The Constant Flirt* (1926) and London debut in *The Cage* (1927), followed by *Badger's Green, Line Engaged, Night Must Fall, The Corn is Green, Flare Path, The Winslow Boy* and *Nude with Violin*, among others; appeared in over 80 films, including *Hobson's Choice, Line Engaged, I Killed the Court, Oliver Twist, Scrooge, Pickwick Papers,* "The Huggetts" series, and as the cook, Mrs. Terence, in *Night Must Fall*; on tv, starred on "Mrs. Thursday" (1966).

HARRISON, Marguerite (1879–1967). American journalist, adventurer and spy. Born Marguerite Elton Baker, Oct 1879, in Baltimore, Maryland; died July 16, 1967; dau. of Bernard Nadal Baker (founder of Atlantic Transport Lines); sister of Elizabeth Baker (Ritchie); attended Radcliffe College; m. Thomas Bullitt Harrison, 1901 (died 1915); m. Arthur Middleton Blake (actor), 1926 (died 1949); children: Thomas Bullitt Harrison II. ❖ One of the earliest correspondents in US as well as an American spy, was left penniless with a young son to support following death of 1st husband (1915); signed on as assistant society editor at *Baltimore Sun* and was soon promoted to music and drama critic and columnist of "Overheard in the Wings," a weekly feature of interviews with visiting artists; during WWI, covered role of women in war effort; under auspices of Military Intelligence Division (MID), was 1st English-speaking woman reporter to reach Berlin after the armistice (1918); began operating in Russia as a secret agent, carrying credentials from the *Sun* (1919); arrested by Russian police, agreed to become a counterspy; attempted to placate captors with bland reports, while smuggling information to US; spent 10 months in Lubianka (1920–21), the 1st American woman ever held in a Bolshevik prison; eventually succumbed to TB and was freed through intervention of American Relief Administration; a few years later, ventured to Chita, capital of southeastern Siberia, and was again arrested; sent to Lubianka, was rescued once more; with Blair Niles, Gertrude Mathews Selby, and Gertrude Emerson, formed the Society of Woman Geographers (1925); published her best work, *Asia Reborn* (1928). ❖ See also memoirs *Marooned in Moscow* and *Unfinished Tales from a Russian Prison*; autobiography *There's Always Tomorrow* (1935); and *Women in World History*.

HARRISON, Mary St. Leger (1852–1931). *See Kingsley, Mary St. Leger.*

HARRISON, Mary Scott Dimmick (1858–1948). Second wife of Benjamin Harrison. Name variations: Mary Scott Lord; Mary Scott Dimmick; Mary Lord Dimmick; Mary Lord Harrison; Mary Dimmick Harrison. Born Mary Scott Lord, April 30, 1858, in Honesdale, Pennsylvania; died Jan 5, 1948, in New York, NY; dau. of Russell Farnham (chief engineer and general manager of Delaware & Hudson Canal Company) and Elizabeth (Mayhew) Scott (sister of Caroline Scott Harrison); m. Walter Erskine Dimmick, Oct 22, 1881 (died 1882); m. her uncle Benjamin Harrison (23rd US president), April 6, 1896; children: (2nd m.) Elizabeth Harrison (1897–1955, who became a successful lawyer and m. James Blaine Walker Jr., grandnephew of James G. Blaine). ❖ Widowed at 24, invited by aunt Caroline Scott Harrison to live in White House and serve as her social secretary; after aunt's death, married uncle, ex-president Benjamin Harrison, though Benjamin's children disapproved of the union and did not attend the ceremony; widowed again at 43; during WWI, served as chair of the NY City division of War Camp Community Service and was active in Republican Party affairs.

HARRISON, May (1891–1959). English violinist. Born in Roorkee, India, Mar 1891; died in South Nutfield, Surrey, England, June 8, 1959; dau. of Colonel John Harrison (officer in Royal Engineers) and Annie Harrison (singer); sister of cellist Beatrice Harrison (1892–1965), Margaret Harrison and Monica Harrison; studied at Royal College of Music and in St. Petersburg; studied with Leopold Auer, Enrique Fernandez Arbos and Sergei Achille Rivarde. ❖ Known for her recordings of Delius as well as for her concerts, was awarded a scholarship to Royal College of Music at 10; made London debut with Sir Henry Wood conducting at St. James' Hall (1904), which led to many private concerts and recitals in Spain; with sister Beatrice, played the Brahms' Double Concerto in London (1911), then toured throughout European capitals; was often a soloist at London's popular Promenade Concerts; taught at the Royal College of Music (1935–47). ❖ See also *Women in World History*.

HARRISON, Ruth (1911–1974). American exhibition ballroom dancer. Born 1911 in Omaha, Nebraska; died Aug 12, 1974, in New York, NY. ❖ Performed as specialty dancer before meeting dance partner Alex Fisher, while both were performing with Chicago Civic Opera (1927); appeared as exhibition ballroom team (Harrison and Fisher) in vaudeville and Prologs throughout NYC, with instant success; appeared with Fisher on Broadway in *Strike Me Pink* (1934), *Ziegfeld Follies* (1936 and 1937) and *Priorities of 1943*; continued to work in nightclubs, cabarets, and bars, and appeared regularly at Radio City Music Hall; performed frequently on tv on "Ed Sullivan Show" and appeared in films *Hollywood Party* (1934) and *Moulin Rouge* (1953).

HARRISON, Susie Frances (1859–1935). Canadian poet, short-story writer, and pianist. Name variations: (pseudonym) Seranus. Born Susie Riley on Feb 24, 1859, in Toronto, Canada; died 1935; m. J.W.F. Harrison. ❖ Pianist and singer of French-Canadian folk songs, composed and wrote songs and an opera; writings include *Crowded Out! and Other Sketches* (1886), *Canadian Birthday Book* (1887), *Pine, Rose, and Fleur de Lis* (1891), *The Forest of Bourg-Marie* (1898), *In Northern Skies and Other Poems* (1912) and *Ringfield* (1914).

HARROLD, Agnes (c. 1830–1903). New Zealand innkeeper, nurse, and midwife. Name variations: Agnes (Nancy) Grieve. Born Agnes (Nancy) Grieve, c. 1830 or 1831, in Hudson's Bay, Canada; died July 7, 1903, on Stewart Island, New Zealand; dau. of James Grieve (bowsman) and an Amerindian mother; m. James Harrold (fisherman), 1847; children: 2. ❖ Immigrated to New Zealand (1848); moved to Stewart Island, where husband opened 3 fishing stations while she ran the large boarding house built by husband (1861); fostered several children over years and served as nurse and midwife to community. ❖ See also *Dictionary of New Zealand Biography* (Vol. 1).

HARROP, Loretta (1975—). Australian triathlete. Born July 17, 1975, in Brisbane, Australia. ❖ Was a national swimming champion (1986–90); placed 1st in Olympic Distance in Montreal (1999); won a silver medal at Athens Olympics (2004); won 2 World Cups (2002) and 1 World Cup (2004).

HARROWER, Elizabeth (1928—). Australian novelist. Born 1928 in Sydney, Australia; grew up in Newcastle. ❖ Lived in London (1951–59) and on return to Australia worked for Australian Broadcasting Commission; wrote reviews for *Sydney Morning Herald*; works include *Down in the City* (1957), *The Long Prospect* (1958), *The Catherine Wheel* (1960), and *The Watch Tower* (1966). Won Patrick White Literary Award (1996). ❖ See also John Hetherington, *Forty-Two Faces* (1962).

HARROWER, Kristi (1975—). Australian basketball player. Born May 4, 1975, in Bendigo, Australia. ❖ Point guard; won a team silver medal at Sydney Olympics (2000) and a team silver at Athens Olympics (2004); won a team bronze medal at World championships (2001); played for Adelaide Lightning, Melbourne Tigers and Australian Opals; played for Phoenix Mercury of the WNBA (1998–99), then Minnesota Lynx (1999–03); suffered a torn ACL (2001); also played for Aix en Provence in France (2000–01).

HARRY, Deborah (1945—). American singer and actress. Name variations: Debbie Harry; Blondie. Born July 1, 1945, in Miami, Florida. ❖ Groundbreaking rocker known for deadpan delivery, once worked as Playboy bunny; began music career with folk-rockers, Wind in the Willows; gained fame as front woman for Blondie, new-wave band founded in 1975 with long-time partner Chris Stein; sang lead vocals on group's *Parallel Lines* (1978), *Eat to the Beat* (1979), *Autoamerican* (1980), and successful comeback effort *No Exit* (1999); released solo albums *KooKoo* (1981), *Rockbird* (1986), and *Debravation* (1993); collaborated with New York underground group the Jazz Passengers (1990s); played quirky leads and supporting roles in films *Union City* (1979), *Videodrome* (1982), *Hairspray* (1988), *Heavy* (1995), *Cop Land* (1997), and *My Life Without Me* (2003); performed frequently for AIDS charities; recognized for early support of rap music; inducted into Rock and Roll Hall of Fame (2006).

HARRY, Myriam (1869–1958). Palestinian-born French author. Name variations: Mme. Perrault-Harry. Born Maria Rosette Shapira in the Old City of Jerusalem, April 1869; died in Neuilly-sur-Seine, France, Mar 10, 1958; dau. of Moses Wilhelm Shapira (bookseller and antiquarian) and Rosette Jockel Shapira; m. Emile Alfred Paul Perrault. ❖ Significant literary figure in pre-1914 Paris, who was awarded the 1st Prix Fémina; after father committed suicide (1884), moved to Germany with rest of family; began to publish in major magazines and newspapers, including *Berliner Tageblatt*; moved to Paris; as Myriam Harry, published *Passage de Bedouins* (1899), followed by a series of novels set in French Indo-China; though all of these works received good reviews, writings began to be regarded seriously only with the publication of the literary sensation *La Conquête de Jérusalem*, which was awarded the Prix Fémina (1904); went on to publish at least 35 novels, escapist works with a stereotypical view of non-Europeans as the Other for a middle-class reading public. ❖ See also *Women in World History*.

HARSANT, Florence Marie (1891–1994). New Zealand temperance reformer, nurse, and writer. Name variations: Florence Marie Woodhead; (pseudonyms) Quick Silver, Trouser Button, Virgo. Born Florence Marie Woodhead, Sept 19, 1891, at New Plymouth, New Zealand; died June 19, 1994, in Thames, New Zealand; dau. of Ambler Woodhead (teacher) and Catherine (Davy) Woodhead; m. Horace Henry Harsant (farmer), 1919 (died 1974); children: 3 sons, 2 daughters. ❖ Trained in basic nursing skills at Anglican mission at Whakarewarewa (c. 1907); became national Maori membership organizer for Women's Christian Temperance Union of New Zealand (1913); wrote and printed leaflets in Maori on hygiene and health care and nursed Maori during influenza pandemic (1918); managed post office at Matata, Bay of Plenty, during WWII; established public library in her home; under pseudonyms, contributed short stories to periodicals, including *New Zealand Dairy Exporter* and *Straight Furrow*. ❖ See also *Dictionary of New Zealand Biography* (Vol. 3).

HARSHAW, Margaret (1909–1997). American soprano and mezzo-soprano. Born May 12, 1907, in Narberth, Pennsylvania; died Sept 5, 1997, in Libertyville, Illinois; studied at Juilliard. ❖ Best known as a Wagnerian singer (Brünnhilde, Kundry, an Isolde), was also highly regarded for her performances in Mozart and Verdi operas; served as Distinguished Professor of Voice at Indiana University.

HARSTICK, Sara (1981—). German swimmer. Born Sept 8, 1981, in Hildesheim, Germany. ❖ Won a bronze medal for 800-meter freestyle relay at Sydney Olympics (2000) and a bronze medal for 4x200-meter freestyle relay at Athens Olympics (2004).

HART, Alice (fl. late–19th c.). British-born social activist. Married Ernest Hart (physician). ❖ With husband, established the Donegal Famine Fund as well as the Donegal Industrial Fund to revive the cottage industries.

HART, Almira (1793–1884). See Phelps, Almira Lincoln.

HART, Annie (d. 1947). American singer and comedian. Died June 13, 1947, in Fair Haven, NJ. ❖ Made stage debut in *The Black Crook*; performed in vaudeville, burlesque, and musical comedy; retired after appearing in *Memory Lane*.

HART, Dolores (1938—). American actress and nun. Name variations: Mother Dolores. Born Dolores Hicks, Oct 20, 1938, in Chicago, Illinois; dau. of Bert Hicks (actor); niece of Mario Lanza. ❖ Films include *Loving You*, *Wild is the Wind*, *King Creole*, *Lonelyhearts*, *The Plunderers*, *Where the Boys Are*, *Francis of Assisi*, *Sail a Crooked Ship*, and *Come Fly with Me*; left Hollywood (1963) to become a Benedictine cloistered nun at Regina Laudis in Bethlehem, Connecticut, and is now prioress. Nominated for Tony Award for Best Featured Actress for performance in *The Pleasure of His Company* (1959).

HART, Doris (1925—). American tennis player. Born Doris J. Hart, June 1925, in St. Louis, Missouri. ❖ Won Australian singles title (1949); won French Open singles title (1950, 1952); won French Open doubles championship with P.C. Todd (1948) and with Shirley Fry (1950–53); won singles championship at Wimbledon (1951); won US Open (1954, 1955); won US Open doubles championships with Shirley Fry (1951, 1954); won US Open mixed doubles with Frank Sedgman (1951–52), and with Vic Seixas (1953–55); won Italian singles (1951, 1953); won South African singles and doubles (1952). ❖ See also *Women in World History*.

HART, Edith Tudor (1908–1978). See Tudor-Hart, Edith.

HART, Emma (1787–1870). See Willard, Emma Hart.

HART, Flo (c. 1896–1960). American theatrical dancer. Name variations: Florence Hart. Born c. 1896; died Mar 30, 1960, in Germantown,

Pennsylvania. ❖ Appeared in almost all editions of *Ziegfeld Follies* where she received celebrity status due to her starlet beauty; once career peaked, worked as actress in stock company of Poli theaters (starting c. 1916); made 3 films then retired from performing (mid-1920s); worked as public health nurse.

HART, Jane (1920—). American aviator and feminist. Name variations: Janey Hart. Born Jane Briggs, 1920, in Detroit, Michigan; dau. of Walter O. Briggs (auto industrialist and owner of Detroit Tigers); m. Phil Hart (US senator from Michigan, died 1976); children: 8. ❖ The 1st licensed female helicopter pilot in Michigan, was one of 13 women slated for the "Women in Space" program (1961); passed all the tests the men passed while in training, but NASA abruptly cancelled the program (the world was not yet ready for women astronauts); lobbied Congress for women astronauts; was a founder of the National Organization for Women (NOW). ❖ See also Stephanie Nolen, *Promised the Moon: The Untold Story of the First Women in the Space Race* (2002); Martha Ackmann, *The Mercury 13* (2003).

HART, Judith (1924—). British politician. Name variations: Lady Hart; Dame Judith Constance Mary Hart, Baroness Hart of South Lanark. Born Constance Mary Judith Ridehalgh in Burnley, Lancashire, England, 1924; attended London School of Economics; m. Dr. Anthony Hart, 1946; children: 2 sons. ❖ As Labour Party candidate, became a member of Parliament (1959), elected by Scottish constituency of Lanark; held a number of ministerial posts (1964–71), including joint parliamentary under-secretary of state at Scottish Office (1964–66), minister of state for Commonwealth Affairs (1966–67), minister of social security (1967), and paymaster-general (1968); trained as a sociologist, was also minister of overseas development (1969–70, 1974–75, and 1977–79) and particularly outspoken about United Kingdom's moral responsibility to third world countries, a subject she also explored in *Aid and Liberation: A Socialist Study of Aid Policies* (1973); starting in 1969, also served as a member of the Labour Party National Executive, and chaired the industrial policy sub-committee and the finance and economic sub-committee. ❖ See also *Women in World History.*

HART, Julia Catherine (1796–1867). Canadian novelist. Born Julia Beckwith, 1796, in Fredericton, New Brunswick, Canada; died 1867; m. George Henry Hart, 1820. ❖ Author of the 1st novel about British North America by a person born there, ran a girls' boarding school in Kingston and then traveled with husband to US (1824–31); works, which reflect colonial life and history, include *St Ursula's Convent; or, The Nun of Canada* (1824) and *Tonnewonte; or, The Adopted Son of America*; also wrote unpublished novel *Edith; or, the Doom.*

HART, Kitty Carlisle (b. 1910). See Carlisle, Kitty.

HART, Lady (b. 1924). See Hart, Judith.

HART, Margie (1916—). American striptease dancer. Born Margaret Bridget Cox, 1916, in Edgerton, Missouri. ❖ At 16, made stage debut at Rialto Theater in Chicago, Illinois, from whence she embarked upon 30-year career as a burlesque dancer; headlined her own revues *The Heartbreakers* at Old Howard in Boston, MA; performed on Broadway in *Wine, Women and Song* (1942), but show was soon closed for indecency; appeared in film *The Lure of the Islands* (1942).

HART, Marie (c. 1882–1935). See La Belle Marie.

HART, Mary (1919–1978). See Roberts, Lynne.

HART, Mrs. Moss (b. 1910). See Carlisle, Kitty.

HART, Nancy (c. 1735–1830). Legendary hero of the American Revolution. Name variations: Aunt Nancy. Born Ann Morgan in either Pennsylvania or North Carolina, c. 1735; died near Henderson, Kentucky, 1830; dau. of Thomas Morgan and Rebecca (Alexander) Morgan; m. Benjamin Hart; children: Morgan, John, Thomas, Lemuel, Mark, Sukey (Sally), Benjamin, and Keziah. ❖ Reputedly 6 feet tall, solidly built, and at ease with a rifle, made her reputation as a stalwart defender of the Whig cause during fierce fighting in the Georgia colony in what came to be called the "War of Extermination," when she captured a band of Tories. ❖ See also *Women in World History.*

HART, Nancy (c. 1846–1902). Confederate spy. Possibly born in 1846, probably in Virginia; died 1902; m. Joshua Douglas (soldier turned farmer), c. 1862. ❖ Sharpshooter and excellent equestrian during Civil War, was still in teens when brother-in-law died in battle, prompting her to join a group of pro-Southern guerrillas dubbed the Moccasin Rangers; when Rangers disbanded (1862), took to the mountains and began spying on Union troops; caught, arrested, and taken to Union-occupied town of Summersville (1863); killed her guard and escaped, returning with 200 Confederate horse soldiers who swept the town clean of Union troops. ❖ See also *Women in World History.*

HART, Pearl (c. 1875–c. 1924). Canadian-born stagecoach robber. Born in Ontario, Canada, c. 1875; died in Kansas City, Missouri, c. 1924; married a man named Hart. ❖ With an unsuccessful mining prospector named Joe Boot, held up the stagecoach outside Globe, Arizona, netting $431 from 4 men aboard, whom they allowed to escape (1897); carted off to jail, became something of a celebrity; served 1 year of 5-year sentence at Yuma Territorial Prison, receiving a pardon by the governor (1902); oddly distinguished as the last person to rob a stagecoach in America. ❖ See also *Women in World History.*

HARTE, Betty (c. 1882–1965). American silent-film actress. Born Daisy May Light, c. 1882, in Lebanon, Pennsylvania; died Jan 3, 1965, in Sunland, California. ❖ Was the 1st leading lady for Selig Polyscope Co. (1909) and appeared in many films opposite Hobart Bosworth; made 40 films, including *The Roman, Boots and Saddles, A Woman's Triumph* and *The Pride of Jennico*; retired from screen (1917).

HARTEL, Lis (1921—). Danish equestrian. Name variations: Lis Hartel-Holst; Liz Hartel. Born Mar 14, 1921, in Denmark. ❖ Stricken with polio (1944); finished 2nd at the Scandinavian Riding championship (1947); though paralyzed below the knees, won a silver medal for indiv. dressage on Jubille at Helsinki Olympics (1952), the 1st year women were allowed to compete, and at Melbourne Olympics (1956). ❖ See also *Women in World History.*

HARTIGAN, Anne Le Marquand (1931—). Irish poet, playwright and painter. Born 1931 in England; grew up there; dau. of an Irish mother and Jersey farmer; children: 6. ❖ Moved to Ireland (1962); paintings and batiks exhibited in Ireland and abroad; plays performed at Dublin Theater Festival; poetry includes *Long Tongue* (1982), *Return Single* (1986), *Now is a Moveable Feast* (1993), and *Immortal Sins*; plays include *Beds* (1982), *La Corbière* (1986), *Jersey Lilies* and *The Secret Game.*

HARTIGAN, Grace (1922—). American painter. Born in Newark, New Jersey, Mar 28, 1922; dau. of Matthew Hartigan and Grace (Orvis) Hartigan; studied privately with Isaac Lane Muse, 1942–46; m. Robert Jachens, May 10, 1941 (div. 1947); m. Harry Jackson (artist), Mar 1949 (annulled 1950); m. Robert Keene (gallery owner), 1958 (div. 1960); m. Dr. Winston H. Price (epidemiologist), Dec 24, 1960 (died 1981); children: (1st m.) Jeffrey. ❖ A disciple of Jackson Pollock and Willem de Kooning, emerged from New York School of abstract expressionists to become the most visible woman painter in US during late 1950s; was the only woman represented in Museum of Modern Art's exhibition, "Twelve Americans" (1956), and in its international touring show, "The New American Painting (1958–59)"; works were purchased by MoMA, Metropolitan Museum of Art, and Whitney; though her popularity waned with Minimalism and Pop art movements of 1960s and 1970s, was rediscovered with the arrival of the "new figurative" and new expressionist painting of 1980s; works include *Secuda Esa Bruja* (1949), *The King Is Dead* (1950), *Bathers* (1953), *The Persian Jacket* (1952), *Grand Street Brides* (1954), *Masquerade* (1954), *Sweden* (1959), *Dido* (1960), *William of Orange* (1962), *Mountain Woman* (1964), *Reisterstown Mall* (1965), *Saint George and the Dragon* (1970), *Another Birthday* (1971), *Autumn Shop Window* (1972), *Lexington Market* (1980), *Theodora* (1983) and *West Broadway* (1989). ❖ See also Robert Saltonstall Mattison, *Grace Hartigan: A Painter's World* (1990); and *Women in World History.*

HARTLAUB, Geno (1915—). German novelist. Name variations: G. Hartlaub. Born June 1915 in Germany; dau. of Gustav Friedrich Hartlaub and Félicie Hartlaub; sister of Felix Hartlaub (1913–1945, writer historian). ❖ Works include *Noch im Traum* (1943), *Anselm, der Lehrling* (1947), *Der Mond hat Durst* (1963), and *Lokaltermin Feenreich* (1972).

HARTLEY, Blythe (1982—). Canadian diver. Born May 2, 1982, in Edmonton, Canada; attended University of Southern California. ❖ At World championships, won Canada's 1st world title in the 1-meter springboard (2001); with Emilie Heymans, won a bronze medal for 10-meter synchronized platform at Athens Olympics (2004).

HARTLEY, Donna-Marie (1955—). English runner. Born May 1955 in UK. ❖ At Moscow Olympics, won a bronze medal in 4x400-meter relay (1980).

HARTLEY, Margaret. English gymnast. Born in UK. ❖ At Amsterdam Olympics, won a bronze medal in team all-around (1928).

HARTLEY, Mariette (1940—). American stage, tv, and screen actress. Born Mary Loretta Hartley, June 21, 1940, in Weston, Connecticut; granddau. of John B. Watson (behavioral psychiatrist); dau. of Paul (artist and ad exec) and Polly (Watson) Hartley; m. John Seventa, 1960 (div. 1962); m. Patrick Boyriven (producer-director), 1974 (div. 1996); children: Justine Boyriven (actress and singer); Sean Boyriven (producer). ❖ Studied with Eva Le Gallienne, then performed on stage with the Shakespeare Festivals in CT and NY; made film debut in *Ride the High Country* (1962), followed by *Drums of Africa, Marnie, Marooned, Barquero, The Return of Count Yorga, Skyjacked, The Magnificent Seven Ride, Improper Channels, O'Hara's Wife* and *Encino Man*; came to prominence with Polaroid commercials opposite James Garner; on tv, was a regular on "Peyton Place," "Goodnight Beantown," and "WIOU," host of CBS's "Morning Program," and appeared in such tv movies as "No Place to Hide," "M.A.D.D.," and "Silence of the Heart"; co-founded a suicide prevention foundation. Won Emmy for performance on "The Incredible Hulk" (1978). ❖ See also autobiography *Breaking the Silence* (1990).

HARTMAN, Elizabeth (1941–1987). American stage and screen actress. Born Dec 23, 1941, in Youngstown, Ohio; died June 10, 1987, by jumping out her 5th-floor apartment window in Pittsburgh, PA. ❖ Made Broadway debut in *Our Town* (1969); films include *The Group, You're a Big Boy Now, The Fixer, The Beguiled, Walking Tall* and (voice only) *The Secret of NIMH*. Won L.A. Critics Award for performance in national company of *Morning's at Seven*; nominated for Oscar for Best Actress for *A Patch of Blue* (1965).

HARTMAN, Grace (1907–1955). American actress and dancer. Name variations: Grace Barrett. Born Grace Barrett, Jan 7, 1907, in San Francisco, CA; died Aug 8, 1955, in Van Nuys, CA; m. Paul Hartman (dancer, div.); m. Norman Abbott. ❖ With 1st husband, appeared as The Hartmans in many Broadway shows, including *Red Hot and Blue, You Never Know, Top-Notchers, Keep 'Em Laughing* and *Tickets Please.* Won a Tony Award as Best Actress in a Musical for *Angels in the Wings* (1948).

HARTMANN, Ingrid (1930—). West German kayaker. Born July 23, 1930, in Germany. ❖ At Rome Olympics, won a silver medal in K2 500-meters (1960).

HARTMANN, Pamela B. (1906–1994). See Bianco, Pamela.

HARTWIG, Brigitta (1917–2003). See Zorina, Vera.

HARTWIG, Julia (1921—). Polish poet, essayist and translator. Born in Lublin, Poland, Aug 14, 1921; m. Artur Adam Miedzyrzecki (writer and critic, b. 1922). ❖ Major contemporary poet in Poland, published *Wolne rece* (Unconstrained Hands, 1967) and *Obcowanie* (Relations, 1987); became an active member of Polish PEN Club (1956), promoting international cultural exchanges; travel to France resulted in a number of books and articles on French writers, including Gerard de Nerval, Max Jacob, and Guillaume; travel to US resulted in *Dzienik Amerykanski* (American Journal, 1980); with demise of Communism in Poland (1989), became a leading personality of a reborn Polish Writers' Association. ❖ See also *Women in World History.*

HARTZ, Trude (1966—). See Dybendahl Hartz, Trude.

HARUKO (1850–1914). Empress of Japan. Name variations: Princess Haru; Princess Haruko; Shōken Kōtaigō; Empress Dowager Shōken; Meiji empress. Born Ichijō Haruko, May 28, 1850; died of Bright's disease at Numadzu Palace, April 9, 1914; 3rd dau. of Prince Ichijō Tadaka (Kuge or noble attached to imperial court and member of house of Fujiwara); m. Mutsuhito (1852–1912, son of Emperor Komei), emperor of Japan (r. 1867–1912), Feb 9, 1869 (died July 29, 1912); children: none, but she adopted Yoshihito Haru-no-miya (1879–1926, son of a secondary wife of Mutsuhito, who, as Emperor Taisho, reigned as emperor of Japan, 1912–1926, and also adopted 4 daughters. ❖ Member of Fujiwara clan, married Mutsuhito 2 years after he had succeeded his father as emperor of Japan and 4 months after his coronation; a beautiful and elegant woman, was as progressive as husband; often wore Western dress at court occasions; appeared in public, loved art and literature, wrote poetry, and was a generous patron of female education, the Red Cross Society, and other philanthropic enterprises; by example, raised the status of women in Japan.

HARUP, Karen-Margrete (1924—). Danish swimmer. Name variations: Karen Margrethe Harup. Born Nov 20, 1924, in Denmark. ❖ At London Olympics, won a silver medal in the 4x100-meter freestyle

relay, a silver medal in the 400-meter freestyle, and a gold medal in the 100-meter backstroke (1948).

HARVEY, Antje (1967—). German biathlete. Name variations: Antje Misersky. Born May 10, 1967, in Magdeburg, Germany. ❖ Won a gold medal for 15km and silver medals for 7.5km and 3x7.5km relay at Albertville Olympics (1992); won a silver medal for 4x7.5km relay at Lillehammer Olympics (1994); won the World championship (1995).

HARVEY, Ethel Browne (1885–1965). American cell biologist and embryologist. Name variations: Ethel Browne. Born Ethel Browne in Baltimore, MD, 1885; died in Falmouth, Massachusetts, 1965; dau. of Bennet Bernard Browne (physician) and Jennie (Nicholson) Browne; attended Bryn Mawr Preparatory School; Woman's College of Baltimore (later Goucher College), AB; Columbia University, AM, 1907, PhD, 1913; m. Edmund Newton Harvey (biology professor), 1916; children: Edmund Newton Harvey Jr. (b. 1916); Richard Bennet Harvey (b. 1922). ❖ Pioneering scientist recognized for her work on cell division, held a 3-year post at New York University as an instructor in biology (1928–31), but spent most of her career at Princeton, where she received neither salary nor compensation; during summers, worked out of office shared with husband at Woods Hole Marine Biology Laboratory on Cape Cod; published over 100 papers, the best-known of which is "Parthenogenetic Merogony of Cleavage without Nuclei in *Arbacia punctulata,*" a complex treatise published in *Biological Bulletin* (1936), documenting her experiments with cell division in sea urchin eggs; though it was then believed that the cell nucleus was generally the part of a cell that "directed" cell division and embryo development, discovered that the nuclei could be removed from the cells, yet continue to divide. Made a trustee of the Woods Hole Laboratory; elected a fellow of American Association for the Advancement of Science and the New York Academy of Science. ❖ See also *Women in World History.*

HARVEY, Georgette (c. 1882–1952). African-American actress. Born c. 1882 in St. Louis, Missouri; died Feb 17, 1952, in New York, NY. ❖ Appeared in *Running Wild, Porgy, Five Star Final, Savage Rhythm, Porgy and Bess, Stevedore, Mamba's Daughters, Morning Star* and *Anna Lucasta*; was last seen in *Lost in the Stars* (1949).

HARVEY, Leisha (1947—). Australian politician. Name variations: Leisha Teresa Harvey. Born April 4, 1947, in Germany. ❖ Representing the National Party, served in Queensland Parliament for Greenslopes (1983–89); named minister for Health (1987–89).

HARVEY, Lilian (1906–1968). British-born German film actress. Born Lilian Muriel Helen Pape, Jan 19, 1906, in Muswell-Hill, England; died in Cap d'Antibes, France, July 27, 1968; dau. of Walter Bruno Pape; m. Valeur Larsen, 1953. ❖ For some years Germany's closest equivalent to an international star, moved to Germany with family at 8; studied dance with Mary Zimmermann; at 16, joined a Viennese dance company; made film debut in *Der Fluch* (The Curse, 1925) which led to 11 more leading film roles in Vienna; by 1926, appeared opposite Willy Fritsch in filmed operetta *Die keusche Susanne* (Chaste Susanne); in all, made 14 films with Fritsch); made French- and English-language versions of her films with advent of talkies; invariably cast as the girl next door, had a great success with *Liebeswalzer* (Waltz of Love) and followed that with a bigger hit *Die drei von der Tankstelle* (*The Three from the Filling Station*) (1930); starred in *Der Kongress tanzt* (*The Congress Dances,* 1931) and in 4 Hollywood films (1933–35), including *Let's Live Tonight,* and the English film *Invitation to the Waltz* (1935), then returned to a now-Nazified Germany; appeared in *Schwarze Rosen* (*Black Roses*), *Fanny Elssler, Sieben Ohrfeigen* (*Seven Slaps*), *Capriccio,*; made last film in Nazi Germany *Frau am Steuer* (*Woman at the Wheel,* 1939); went to Paris on eve of WWII; when Germany conquered France (June 1940), fled to Spain, then South America, then Los Angeles, but could not rekindle career at war's end. ❖ See also *Women in World History.*

HARVEY, Mary (1965—). American soccer player. Born June 4, 1965, in California. ❖ Goalkeeper; at World Cup, won a team gold medal (1991); won a gold medal at Atlanta Olympics (1996); established US Soccer's Athletes' Council.

HARVEY, P.J. (1969—). English guitarist, songwriter, and singer. Born Polly Jean Harvey, Oct 9, 1969, in Yeovil, Somerset, England. ❖ Publicity shy vocalist known for provocative lyrics, grew up on a sheep farm; formed band PJ Harvey with two Yeovil friends (1991); released debut album *Dry* (1992); displayed dynamic vocal skills on singles "Dress," "Happy and Bleeding," and "Sheela-Na-Gig";

collaborated with American producer Steve Albini on band's 2nd album *Rid of Me* (1993); began adding glam touches to her austere stage image; disbanded band (mid-1990s); dueted with then-lover Nick Cave on his album *Murder Ballads* (1996); released solo albums *To Bring You My Love* (1995), *Is This Desire?* (1998), *Stories From the City, Stories From the Sea* (2000).

HARVIE ANDERSON, Betty (1913–1979). Scottish politician. Name variations: Baroness Skrimshire of Quarter Renfrewshire East; Rt. Hon. Margaret Harvie Anderson. Born Margaret Harvie Anderson, Aug 12, 1913, in Scotland; died of bronchitis, Nov 7, 1979; married. ❖ Conservative, was elected MP for Renfrewshire East (1959); became member of Committee of Backbench MPs; the 1st woman to occupy the speaker's chair (1970), kept order even through turbulent times, such as passage of Industrial Relations Act (1970–71) and Common Market debates; served as deputy chair of Ways and Means (1970–73); was appointed Privy Councillor (1974); created Baroness Skrimshire of Quarter of Renfrewshire (1979) and took seat in Upper House after 20 years as MP; died 1 week later.

HARWOOD, Elizabeth (1938–1990). English concert soprano. Name variations: Elizabeth Jean Harwood; also seen as Elisabeth Harwood. Born May 27, 1938, in Barton Seagrave, England; died June 21, 1990, in Ingatestone, England; attended Royal Manchester College of Music (1955–60); m. Julian A.C. Royle, 1966; children: Nicholas Royle. ❖ Best remembered for interpretations of Mozart and Strauss, made debut in *Die Zauberflöte* at Glyndebourne (1960); won Kathleen Ferrier Prize (1960), allowing her to spend year in Milan studying with Verdi expert, Lina Pagliughi; joined Sadler's Wells Opera (1961); won Verdi Prize of Busseto (1963); toured Australia with Sutherland Williamson Company (1965), alternating with Joan Sutherland in leading roles; performed at Aix-en-Provence Festival and made debut at Covent Garden in *Arabella* (1967); sang regularly at Glasgow's Scottish Opera (1967–74), where she appeared in internationally acclaimed production of *Cosi fan tutte* (1967); appeared regularly for conductor Herbert von Karajan at Salzburg Festival (from 1969); made debut at Milan's La Scala (1972) and Metropolitan Opera (1975), returning to NY for 1977–78 season; gave final operatic performance for The Buxton Festival (1983); toured New Zealand (1983), Australia (1986) and British Columbia (1988); particularly associated with Handel's *Messiah*, performing it over 100 times beginning at age 16.

HARWOOD, Gwen (1920–1995). Australian poet. Name variations: Gwendoline Nessie Harwood; (pseudonyms) Francis Geyer, Walter Lehmann, T.F. Kline, and Miriam Stone. Born June 8, 1920, in Taringa, Brisbane, Australia; died Dec 1995 in Hobart, Tasmania, Australia; m. William Harwood, 1945. ❖ Writings of lyrical intensity, which often explore personal experience, include *Poems* (1963), *Selected Poems* (1976), *The Lion's Bride* (1981), *Bone Scan* (1988), *Blessed City* (1990), *Night Thoughts* (1992) and *Present Tense* (1995); also wrote stories, essays, reviews, and libretti. Received J.J. Bray Award, Age Book of the Year award, Patrick White Literary Award, Robert Frost Award, and honorary Doctorate of Letters from University of Tasmania (1988); made Officer of the Order of Australia (1989).

HARZENDORF, Christiane (1967—). German rower. Born Dec 28, 1967, in Germany. ❖ At Barcelona Olympics, won a bronze medal in coxed eights (1992).

HASBROUCK, Lydia Sayer (1827–1910). American editor and reformer. Born Lydia Sayer, Dec 20, 1827, in Warwick, NY; died Aug 24, 1910, in Middletown, NY; dau. of Benjamin (farmer) and Rebecca (Forshee) Sayer; attended Central College; m. John Whitbeck Hasbrouck (editor and publisher of Middletown *Whig Press*), July 1856; children: Daisy (1857–1859); Sayer (b. 1860); Burt (b. 1862). ❖ Invited to participate in a lecture tour about dress reform (1856), soon became editor of feminist periodical *Sibyl*; served as president of National Dress Reform Association (1863–64); also championed medical training for women, increased educational opportunities, and women's suffrage; after NY enacted a law permitting women to vote for and hold school offices (1880), was elected to Middletown board of education, the 1st American woman to hold an elected office. ❖ See also *Women in World History*.

HASE, Dagmar (1969—). German swimming champion. Born Dec 22, 1969, in Quedlinburg, Germany. ❖ At Barcelona Olympics, won silver medals in the 4x100-meter medley relay and 200-meter backstroke and a gold medal in the 400-meter freestyle (1992); won silver medals for 400- and 800-meter freestyle and 800-meter freestyle relay and a bronze medal for 200-meter freestyle at Atlanta Olympics (1996).

HASEGAWA, Itsuko (1941—). Japanese architect. Born 1941 in Yaizu City, Shizuoka, Japan; graduate of Kanto Gakuin University, 1969; attended Tokyo Institute of Technology, 1971–79. ❖ One of the most famous women in Japanese architecture, 1st worked at Kikutake Architect and Associates (1969–71); set up Itsuko Hasegawa Architectural Design Studio in Tokyo (1976) and Itsuko Hasegawa Atelier (1979); received Design Prize from Architectural Institute of Japan for Bizan Hall Project (1986) and also earned Japan Cultural Design Award for residential projects; won 1st prize for Shonandai Cultural and Community Center in Fujisawa (1987); designed Nagoya Design Exhibition Pavilion (1989), Shiogama Lifelong Learning Center, Namekawa Housing Project, Cona Village in Amagasaki (1990), Picture-Book Museum in Oshima (1994), Sumida Cultural Factory (1994), Kirishima Art Center (1995) and Miurart Village in Matsuyama (1997); elected fellow of Royal Institute of British Architects (1997); taught at Waseda University, Tokyo Institute of Technology, Niigata University, Tokyo Denki University (1995) and Harvard University. ❖ See also I. Hasegawa, K. Miyamoto, M. Kira, T. Furodoi, *Itsuko Hasegawa: Island Hopping–Crossover Architecture* (Nai, 2001).

HASEGAWA, Tomoko (1963—). Japanese shooter. Born Aug 23, 1963, in Japan. ❖ At Seoul Olympics, won a silver medal in sport pistol (1988).

HASELBACH, Anna Elisabeth (1942—). Austrian politician. Born Dec 6, 1942 in Berlin, Germany. ❖ Social Democrat, employed by the SPÖ federal women's secretariat (1977–87); elected to the Bundesrat or Austrian Parliament by the provincial diet of Vienna (1987); served as president (Jan 1, 1991–June 10, 1991, July 1, 1995–Dec 31, 1995, Jan 1, 2000–June 30, 2000, and May 23, 2004–Dec 31, 2004) and as vice-president (1996–99, 2000–01, 2001–04, 2005).

HASELDEN, Frances Isabella (c. 1841–1936). New Zealand teacher. Born 1841 or 1842, in London, England; died July 9, 1936, in Remuera, New Zealand; dau. of Charles Haselden and Maria Simpson (Moore) Haselden. ❖ Immigrated with family to New Zealand (1860 or 1861); served briefly as governess in Auckland; taught at country schools before being appointed headmistress of Kauaeranga Girls' School, which became one of the most important schools in Auckland; was highest-paid female public schoolteacher in New Zealand (1888); retired when school became coeducational and position required a male head teacher. ❖ See also *Dictionary of New Zealand Biography* (Vol. 2).

HASENJAGER-ROBB, Daphne (1929—). South African runner. Born July 1929 in South Africa. ❖ At Helsinki Olympics, won a silver medal in the 100 meters (1952).

HASHEMI, Aquila al- (1953–2003). *See Hashimi, Aquila al-.*

HASHEMI, Faezeh (1963—). Iranian politician. Name variations: Faezeh Rafsanjani; Faezeh Hashemi Bahremani. Born Faezeh Rafsanjani, 1963, in Iran; dau. of Ali Akbara Hashemi Rafsanjani (former president of Iran); attended Al-Zahra University and Islamic Azad University; married to the son of a prominent ayatollah; children: 2, including daughter Mona. ❖ Pioneer in the reformist movement and one of Iran's most popular politicians, once called for women to unveil, ride bikes in public, and run for president; was a member of Parliament from Tehran constituency; as vice president of Iran's National Olympic committee (1990), promoted the cause of Muslim women in sports; founded and served as president of the Federation of Islamic Countries' Women's Solidarity and Sports (1991); founded Iran's only women's daily *Zan* (Woman), which was banned in 1999.

HASHEPSOWE (c. 1515–1468 BCE). *See Hatshepsut.*

HASHIGUCHI, Miho (1977—). Japanese gymnast. Born Dec 29, 1977, in Aichi, Japan. ❖ Won Japanese nationals (1995); placed 12th team all-around at Atlanta Olympics (1996).

HASHIMI, Aquila al- (1953–2003). Iraqi politician and diplomat. Name variations: Akila al-Hashemi or Hashimi; Aqila al-Hashemi or Hashemi. Born 1953 in Najaf, Iraq; died Sept 25, 2003, in Baghdad; law degree from Baghdad University; Sorbonne, PhD in French literature; never married; no children. ❖ Born into a secular Shia family, became member of Baathist government; served as aide to Iraqi deputy prime minister Tariq Aziz, directed UN oil-for-food program at Iraqi Foreign Ministry, and served as director of international relations (before Mar 2003); for 2 decades, worked for regime of Saddam Hussein; after overthrow of Hussein (2003), was only member of his regime to be appointed by US government to Iraq's interim governing council, 1 of 3 women;

known for her determination to help Iraqi women, was shot by unidentified gunmen in Baghdad (Sept 20, 2003) and in coma for 5 days; had been expected to become Iraq's ambassador to United Nations.

HASHIMOTO, Seiko (1964—). Japanese speedskater. Born Oct 5, 1964, in Japan. ❖ Won a bronze medal at World Sprint championships (1989); at World championships, won a silver (1990) and a bronze (1992), both for all-around; won a bronze medal for the 1,500 meters at Albertville Olympics (1992), the 1st Japanese woman to medal in speedskating at Winter Games; also appeared in cycling events in Seoul and Barcelona Olympics; won a seat in the Japanese Parliament, Upper House (1995).

HASHMAN, Judy (1935—). American badminton player. Name variations: Judith Hashman, Judy or Judith Devlin, Judy Devlin-Hashman. Born Judith Devlin, Oct 22, 1935, in Winnipeg, Canada; dau. of Joseph "Frank" Devlin (former English singles champion and her badminton coach); sister of Susan Devlin Peard (badminton player); m. Dick Hashman (coach), 1960; children: 2 sons. ❖ The greatest player in history of women's badminton, won every junior title by 13, including 6 consecutive singles titles (1949–54); won 1st major adult title at 14 (women's doubles championships, playing with sister Susan) and played in 1st US national championship at 17; was member of US national lacrosse team (1954); won 56 national championships (1954–67) in US, Canada and England, including 12 US seniors national titles, 10 All-England championships and Dutch, German, Irish, Jamaican, Scottish and Swedish titles; was a member of US Uber Cup team (1957–69); became naturalized citizen of England (1970); wrote *Badminton a Champion's Way* (1969), *Starting Badminton* (1977) and *Winning Badminton* (1981). Inducted into Helms National Badminton Hall of Fame (1963) and International Women's Sports Hall of Fame (1995).

HASHMAT (1925—). *See Sobti, Krishna.*

HASKIL, Clara (1895–1960). Romanian pianist. Born in Bucharest, Romania, Jan 7, 1895; died in Brussels, Belgium, Dec 7, 1960; studied in Vienna with Ernst von Dohnanyi, at Paris Conservatory with Alfred Cortot, and in Berlin with Ferruccio Busoni. ❖ A child prodigy, made debut in Bucharest at 9; began concert career (1910); played with a number of renowned artists, including violinist Georges Enesco, pianist Théophile Ysaÿe, and cellist Pablo Casals; also soloed with major symphony orchestras throughout Europe and America; was known as a superb chamber-music performer; made a number of recordings, particularly of key works of Beethoven, Chopin, Mozart, and Schubert. ❖ See also *Women in World History.*

HASLAM, Anna (1829–1922). Irish feminist. Born Anna Maria Fisher in Youghal, County Cork, Ireland, April 1829; died Nov 1922; dau. of Abraham Fisher (corn miller) and Jane (Moore) Fisher; educated at Newtown School, Waterford, and Quaker School, Ackworth, Yorkshire; m. Thomas Haslam, 1854 (died 1917); no children. ❖ Founder of 1st women's suffrage society in Dublin, had a career spanning well over half a century which was dedicated to the betterment of women's condition; was a founder member of the Irish Society for the Training and Employment of Educated Women (1861); campaigned for repeal of Contagious Diseases Acts (1869–86); was a founder member of Association of Schoolmistresses and Other Ladies Interested in Irish Education (1882); founded the Dublin Women's Suffrage Association, later the Irish Women's Suffrage and Local Government Association (1876), of which she was secretary (1876–1913) and life-president (1913–22). ❖ See also *Women in World History.*

HASLAM, Juliet (1969—). Australian field-hockey player. Born May 31, 1969, in Adelaide, Australia. ❖ Halfback/midfielder; won team gold medals at Atlanta Olympics (1996) and Sydney Olympics (2000).

HASLER, Marie (1945—). New Zealand politician. Born Marie Hasler, July 7, 1945, in Dublin, Ireland; married. ❖ Elected National MP for Titirangi (1990), becoming Minister of Cultural Affairs.

HASLER, Sabine (1967—). *See Wehr-Hásler, Sábine.*

HASLETT, Caroline (1895–1957). British engineer. Name variations: Dame Caroline Haslett. Born Caroline Haslett, Aug 17, 1895, in Sussex, England; died Jan 4, 1957; eldest dau. of Robert Haslett (railroad engineer) and Caroline Sarah (Holmes) Haslett; attended Haywards Heath High School, Sussex; never married; no children. ❖ Leader in opening the engineering industry to British women, trained to be a general, then electrical, engineer; became secretary of the newly formed Women's Engineering Society (1919); also founded and edited the society's journal, *The Woman Engineer,* when the society founded the Electrical Association for Women (1924), became its director, watching it grow from a one-room office to an organization with 90 branches and over 10,000 members by the time she left post (1956); was also editor of its organ *Electrical Age.* Created Dame of the British Empire (DBE, 1947). ❖ See also *Women in World History.*

HASOUTRA (1906–1978). American dancer. Name variations: Ryllis Barnes, Ryllis Barnes Simpson. Born Sept 24, 1906, in Shanghai, China; died Feb 18, 1978, in New York, NY. ❖ Raised in Shanghai by American parents, became involved in Oriental dance; returned to US and began performing on Broadway in such shows as *The Perfect Fool* (1921), *Spices of 1923,* and *Passing Show of 1923;* performed on tour with Dora Duby throughout Europe and Asia, where acts included *The Snake Dancer, Burma,* and *The Golden Idol* (1926–33); appeared as concert dancer in recital accompanied on piano by Louis Horst; retired from performance career (c. 1940) and worked for US State Department as foreign service officer (1940s–72).

HASSALL, Joan (1906–1988). British wood engraver. Born in London, England, Mar 3, 1906; died Mar 6, 1988, in England; dau. of John Hassall (artist and art school proprietor) and Constance (Brooke-Webb) Hassall; sister of Christopher Hassall (1912–1963, noted biographer, poet, playwright, and librettist); attended Froebel Educational Institute; studied art at Royal Academy, 1927–33, and London County Council School of Photo-Engraving and Lithography, 1931; never married; no children. ❖ The 1st woman elected Master of the Art Workers' Guild, illustrated such works as Francis Brett Young's *Portrait of a Village* (1937), Elizabeth Gaskell's *Cranford* (1940), Robert Louis Stevenson's *A Child's Garden of Verses* (1946), Mary Webb's *Fifty-One Poems* (1946), Mary Russell Mitford's *Our Village* (c. 1947), the Opie's *Oxford Nursery Rhyme Book* (1955), Richard Church's *Small Moments* (1957), Jane Austen's *Sense and Sensibility* and *Mansfield Park* (1958, 1959), and *The Poems of Robert Burns* (1965); work appears in numerous institutions, including British Museum, Victoria and Albert Museum, National Gallery of Canada, and National Gallery of Victoria (Melbourne). ❖ See also *The Wood Engravings of Joan Hassall* (Oxford University Press, 1960); and *Women in World History.*

HASSAN, Margaret (1944–2004). Iraqi relief worker. Born Margaret Fitzsimons, 1944, in Dublin, Ireland; died c. Nov 14, 2004, in Iraq; attended Leicester University; m. Iraqi-born Tahseen Ali Hassan (economist), 1961; no children. ❖ Moved to Iraq (1972); taught English to Iraqis, converted to Islam, learned fluent Arabic, and became an Iraqi citizen; was director of studies at British Council in Baghdad and a vocal critic of UN sanctions; while serving as director of Care International during war in Iraq, was abducted at gunpoint in Baghdad (Oct 19, 2004), held hostage, appeared in 3 harrowing videos, then killed.

HASSE, Faustina (c. 1700–1781). *See Bordoni, Faustina.*

HASSE, Ute (1963—). West German swimmer. Born Sept 16, 1963, in Germany. ❖ At Los Angeles Olympics, won a silver medal in the 4x100-meter medley relay (1984).

HASSELQVIST, Jenny (1894–1978). Swedish ballet dancer and actress. Born July 31, 1894, in Stockholm, Sweden; died June 8, 1978, in Stockholm. ❖ Trained with Royal Swedish Ballet until she joined its company (1910); performed in numerous works restaged by Mikhail Fokine for Swedish Ballet while in residence; performed own dance recitals intermittently (starting c. 1918); became member of Ballets Suédois (1920) where she danced numerous leads in works by Jean Borlin, including *Jeux, Les Vierges Folles* and *La Nuit de Saint Jean;* taught classes at own studio in Stockholm and for Royal Swedish Ballet; appeared in numerous silent films, including *The Ballet Girl* (1918), *Sumurun* (1921), and *Gösta Berling Saga* (1924).

HASSO, Signe (1910–2002). Swedish-born actress. Born Signe Larsson on Aug 15, 1910, in Stockholm, Sweden; died June 7, 2002, in Los Angeles, CA; m. Harry Hasso (Swedish director), 1936 (div. 1944); m. William Langford (died 1955); children: 1 son (killed in motorcycle accident, 1954). ❖ Stage actress while still in her teens, made film debut in Sweden in *House of Silence* (1933); soon moved to starring roles (1930s); discovered by Hollywood (1942), appeared in American movies throughout next decade, most often playing strong-willed women; films include *Journey for Margaret* (1942), *Assignment in Brittany* (1943), *Heaven Can Wait* (1943), *The Story of Dr. Wassell* (1944), *The Seventh Cross* (1944), *Johnny Angel* (1945), *The House on 92nd Street* (1945), *A Double Life* (1948), *Crisis* (1950), *The Black Bird* (1975), and *I Never Promised You a Rose Garden* (1977); later career included stage, screen, and tv appearances in US and Europe, and a tour in *Cabaret*; also wrote lyrics for several Swedish songs.

HASTINGS, Agnes (fl. 1340s). *See Mortimer, Agnes.*

HASTINGS, Anne (b. 1355). *See Manny, Anne.*

HASTINGS, Anne (c. 1487–?). Countess of Derby. Born c. 1487; dau. of Edward Hastings of Hungerford, Lord Hastings; m. Thomas Stanley, 2nd earl of Derby, in 1507; children: Edward Stanley, 3rd earl of Derby (1509–1572, who m. Dorothy Howard); Margaret Stanley.

HASTINGS, Anne (d. after 1506). Countess of Shrewsbury. Died after 1506; interred at St. Peter's, Sheffield; dau. of Catherine Neville (fl. 1460) and William Hastings, 1st Lord Hastings; m. George Talbot, 4th earl of Shrewsbury, before June 27, 1481; children: Henry Talbot; Francis Talbot, 5th earl of Shrewsbury (b. 1500).

HASTINGS, Caroline (1841–1922). American physician. Born Caroline Eliza Hastings, 1841, in Barre, Massachusetts; died July 19, 1922, at Massachusetts Homeopathic Hospital, MA; dau. of Mary (Bassett) Hastings and Emery Hastings. ❖ Esteemed educator and physician; graduated from New England Female Medical College in Boston (1868) and established a private practice; was a special anatomy lecturer (1873), an embryology assistant demonstrator and lecturer (1874–77), an anatomy lecturer and demonstrator (1878–79) and an anatomy professor (1880–86) at Boston University Medical School, a coeducational institution that absorbed the New England Female Medical College in 1873; worked with Civil War nurse Mary Jane Safford to offer lectures on women's dress reform; established and was president of Boston's 1st women's medical society, the Twentieth Century Club; while on Boston School Committee, implemented the 1st American free school lunch program for poor children.

HASTINGS, Denise (1958—). English golfer. Name variations: Denise Ann Hastings. Born Mar 24, 1958, in England. ❖ Turned pro (1978); founder member of WPGA (1979); head teaching pro at Abbotsley Golf & Country Club, Cambridgeshire.

HASTINGS, Elizabeth (1682–1739). British philanthropist. Name variations: Lady Elizabeth Hastings. Born 1682; died 1739; dau. of Theophilus Hastings, 7th earl of Huntingdon (1650–1701, lord-lieutenant of Leicester and Derby). ❖ Noted philanthropist whose father was imprisoned for attempting to seize Plymouth for King James II (1688) and on suspicion of treason (1692); founded scholarships at Queen's College, Oxford, and supported charities at Ledsham and in Isle of Man; a friend of William Law, author of *Serious Call,* was likened to Aspasia in the *Tatler* by Richard Steele and William Congreve.

HASTINGS, Flora (1806–1839). English aristocrat. Name variations: Lady Flora Hastings; Lady Flora Elizabeth Hastings. Born Flora Elizabeth Rawdon Hastings, 1806; died 1839; dau. of Francis Rawdon Hastings (1754–1826), 1st marquis of Hastings (soldier, diplomat and governor-general of Bengal); never married. ❖ Involved in a well-publicized scandal; unmarried at 30, served as lady of the bedchamber to Victoria of Coburg, mother of Queen Victoria; became the butt of rumors that she was having an affair with Sir John Conroy (1837); incurred Victoria's wrath, since the newly crowned queen had antipathy towards Conroy (as well as her mother); aroused whispers that she was carrying Conroy's child when she began to increase in girth; ordered to be examined by a physician, learned that her distended midsection was the result of abdominal tumor; died age 33, not long after the press-fueled public furor. ❖ See also *Women in World History.*

HASTINGS, Selina (1707–1791). English religious leader. Name variations: Countess of Huntingdon; Selina Hastings Huntingdon; Selina Huntington; Selina Shirley. Born Selina Shirley, Aug 24, 1707, at Stanton Harold, Leicestershire, England; died June 17, 1791, in London; dau. of Washington Shirley, 2nd earl of Ferrers, and Lady Mary Shirley (Lady Ferrers); m. Theophilus Hastings, 9th earl of Huntingdon, June 3, 1728; children: 7, including Francis (b. 1729); George (b. 1730); Elizabeth Hastings (b. 1731); Ferdinando (b. 1732); Selina Hastings (b. 1737); Henry (b. 1739). ❖ Founder of a sect of Calvinistic Methodists, underwent a profound spiritual conversion to Methodism (1738); joined John Wesley's Methodist society in London (1739); emerged as a major figure in Wesleyan movement; with death of husband (1746), devoted herself to an evangelical life, an existence that became a cycle of short crises of faith and periods of extreme ill health (documented in her copious correspondence), followed by renewed faith and activism; concentrated efforts on converting the upper classes to

Methodism; appointed Methodist clerics as chaplains in towns she held as countess, and with her own funds established over 60 chapels, forming a religious network called "The Countess of Huntingdon's Connexion"; founded Trevecca House, a college for training preachers in Brecknockshire, Wales (1768); tried unsuccessfully to reconcile Methodist factions of George Whitefield and John Wesley after the 2 leaders split over issues of doctrine. ❖ See also Boyd S. Schlenther, *Queen of the Methodists* (Durham Academic Press, 1997); Helen Wright, *Lady Huntington and Her Circle* (American Tract Society, 1853); *The Life of the Countess of Huntingdon* (2 vols., 1844); and *Women in World History.*

HASTON, Laurence. *See Gouault-Haston, Laurence.*

HASWELL, Susanna (1762–1824). *See Rowson, Susanna.*

HASZARD, Rhona (1901–1931). New Zealand artist. Name variations: Rhona Haszard, Rhona McKenzie, Rhona Greener. Born Alice Gwendoline Rhona Haszard, Jan 21, 1901, at Thames, New Zealand; died Feb 21, 1931, in Wellington; dau. of Henry Douglas Morpeth Haszard (surveyor) and Alice Elizabeth Vaughan (Wily) Haszard; Canterbury College School of Art, 1919; m. Ronald James McKenzie (art master), 1922 (div. 1925); m. Herbert Leslie Greener, 1925. ❖ Member of New Zealand Academy of Fine Arts (1921); exhibited series of oils of Wanganui with Canterbury and Auckland art societies (1920s); traveled with 2nd husband to Channel Islands and France, then studied at Académie Julian; exhibited widely and gained recognition in France and Britain before accompanying husband to Egypt (late 1920s); exhibited at Galérie Paul in Cairo (1930). Following her death, husband exhibited collection of her work, generating much publicity and interest; her subjects were primarily landscapes, still-life studies, and portraits. ❖ See also *Dictionary of New Zealand Biography* (Vol. 4).

HASZARD, Patricia (1923–2000). *See Moyes, Patricia.*

HATASU (c. 1515–1468 BCE). *See Hatshepsut.*

HATCH, Annia (1978—). Cuban-American gymnast. Born June 14, 1978, at Guantanamo, Cuba; came to US, 1997; became a US citizen, 2001; married. ❖ Placed 1st in the vault at US nationals (2004); won silver medals for vault and team all-around at Athens Olympics (2004); with husband, owns Stars Academy.

HATCHEPSOUT, Hatchepsu, or Hatchepsut (c. 1515–1468 BCE). *See Hatshepsut.*

HATCHER, Orie Latham (1868–1946). American pioneer in vocational guidance. Born Dec 10, 1868, in Petersburg, Virginia; died April 1, 1946, in Richmond; dau. of William Eldridge and Oranie Virginia (Snead) Hatcher; graduate of Richmond Female Institute, 1884; Vassar College, AB, 1888; University of Chicago, PhD in English literature, 1903. ❖ Began teaching at Richmond Female Institute (1889), where she became a professor of history, English language and literature; was instrumental in the institute's transformation into Woman's College of Richmond (1894); joined Bryn Mawr College faculty as a reader in English (1903); became chair of it's department of comparative literature (1910), then associate professor of comparative and English literature (1912); resigned from Bryn Mawr (1915) to assume presidency of Virginia Bureau of Vocations for Women, an organization she helped found; published *Occupations for Women* (1927), *Rural Girls in the City for Work* (1930) and *A Mountain School* (1930). ❖ See also *Women in World History.*

HATFIELD, Juliana (1967—). American folksinger and musician. Born July 27, 1967, in Wiscasset, Maine; studied piano; attended Boston's Berklee College of Music. ❖ Formed college-rock band, Blake Babies (1986); sang and played guitar on band's albums *Earwig* (1989), *Sunburn* (1990), and *Innocence and Experience* (1993); formed own band, Juliana Hatfield Three, releasing albums *Hey Babe* (1992) and *Only Everything* (1995); released additional solo CDs *Bed* (1998) and *Beautiful Creature* (2000); reunited with Blake Babies for album *God Bless the Blake Babies* (2001) and subsequent tour.

HATHAWAY, Anne (1556–1623). English wife of William Shakespeare. Name variations: Anne Shakespeare. Born in Shottery, near Stratford, 1556 (some sources cite 1557); died 1623; dau. of Richard Hathaway (farmer) and his 1st wife (name unknown); m. William Shakespeare, 1582; children: Susanna (b. 1583); (twins) Judith and Hamnet Shakespeare (b. 1585). ❖ On father's death, was left a marriage portion in his will; was 26 and pregnant when she married 18-year-old William Shakespeare; became estranged from him probably 3 or 4 years after the marriage and probably because of his decision to seek a career on the stage. ❖ See also *Women in World History.*

HATHAWAY, Sibyl (1884–1974). Dame of Sark. Born Sibyl Mary Collings on Channel Island of Guernsey, England, Jan 13, 1884; died home on Sark, July 14, 1974; dau. of William Frederick Collings and Sophia Wallace Collings; m. Dudley John Beaumont (died); m. Robert Woodward Hathaway, 1929 (died); children: 4 sons, 3 daughters. ❖ The 22nd individual to succeed to the seigniory of the 4th largest of the Channel Islands (in the English Channel), stood firmly on her traditional feudal rights, keeping her domain intact during a 5-year Nazi occupation and taking measures to keep the 20th century at bay; held feudal dominion over Sark (1927–74). ❖ See also autobiography *Dame of Sark* (Coward, 1962); William Douglas-Home, *The Dame of Sark: A Play* (French, 1976); and *Women in World History.*

HATHEBURG (fl. 906). Princess of Saxony. Dau. of Erwin of Saxony; became 1st wife of Henry I the Fowler (c. 876–936), Holy Roman emperor (r. 919–936), in 906; children: Thangmar (d. July 28, 938). Henry's 2nd wife was Matilda of Saxony (c. 892–968).

HATHERLY, Ana Maria (1929—). Portuguese poet and literary critic. Born 1929 in Oporto, Portugal. ❖ Participated in avant-garde group *Poesia Experimental* (1960s) and wrote *Po. Ex.* (1981), containing theories of the movement; writings include *Um Ritmo Perdido* (1958) and *A Cidade das Palavras* (1988).

HATHUMODA (d. 874). First abbess of Gandersheim. Name variations: Hathumonda. Died Nov 29, 874; dau. of Oda (806–913) and Liudolf (c. 806–866), count of Saxony; sister of Gerberga (d. 896).

HATICE (fl. 1500–1536). Sister of Suleiman. Name variations: Hatice Sultana. Born in Trebizond, a Black Sea caravan city in Asia Minor (present-day Turkey); dau. of Selim I the Grim (r. 1512–1520) and Hafsa Hatun (d. 1534); sister of Suleiman or Suleyman I, Ottoman sultan (r. 1520–1566); sister-in-law of Roxelana. ❖ Thought to have married Ibrahim Pasha, Suleiman's grand vizier (prime minister, May 1524), who was later executed by her brother (1536).

HATO, Ana Matawhaura (1907–1953). New Zealand tribal singer. Name variations: Ana Black, Ana Raponi. Born on Dec 30, 1907, in Ngapuna, Rotorua, New Zealand; died on Dec 8, 1953, at Rotorua; dau. of Hato Mae Ngamahirau and Riripeti Te Opehoia Eparaima; m. Arthur Black (div.); m. Pahau Raponi (laborer, d. 1942), 1931. ❖ Popular singer of Maori songs, recorded one of her performances for Parlophone Company from Australia (1929) which led to further recordings in Australia; organized many concerts during WWII to help Maori soldiers. Some recordings were released on compact disc, *Music in New Zealand* (1996). ❖ See also *Dictionary of New Zealand Biography* (Vol. 4).

HATSHEPSOUT (c. 1515–1468 BCE). *See Hatshepsut.*

HATSHEPSUT (c. 1515–1468 BCE). Female pharaoh of Egypt's 18th Dynasty. Name variations: Hatasu; Hatchepsout; Hatchepsut; Hatshepset; Hatshepsout; Hashepsowe; throne name was Ma-Ka-Re or Makare. Born c. 1515 BCE; died c. 1468 BCE; eldest daughter and only surviving child of Thutmose I and Queen Ahmose; m. half-brother Thutmose II; children: daughter Neferure; possibly a 2nd daughter; (stepson) Thutmose III. ❖ Among the greatest female figures known from the ancient world and one of the greatest of the pharaohs of ancient Egypt, served as regent for a designated heir, later ousted him from power, then reigned for 20 more years in an era that saw significant political, cultural and economic achievements; left many monuments, making her one of the best-documented personalities from ancient Egypt's 3,000-year history. Her temple at Deir el Bahri remained in use as the most important focal point for annual religious celebrations on the West Bank for centuries. ❖ See also Joyce Tyldesley, *Hatchepsut: The Female Pharaoh* (Viking, 1996); and *Women in World History.*

HATTESTAD, Stine Lise. Norwegian freestyle skier. Name variations: Stine-Lise; Stine Hattestad Bratsberg. Born in Norway. ❖ Won a bronze medal for moguls at Albertville Olympics (1992); won a gold medal for moguls at Lillehammer Olympics (1994).

HATTESTAD, Trine (1966—). Norwegian javelin thrower. Name variations: Trine Solberg-Hattestad. Born Elsa Katrine Solberg, April 18, 1966, in Lorenskog, Norway; m. Anders Hattestad. ❖ Won a bronze medal at Atlanta Olympics (1996) and a gold medal at Sydney Olympics (2000); won gold medals at World championships (1993, 1997) and European championships (1994).

HATTON, Fanny (c. 1870–1939). American playwright and screenwriter. Born c. 1870 in Chicago, Illinois; died Nov 27, 1939, in New York, NY; dau. of Rev. de Witt Clinton Locke; m. Frederick Hatton (drama editor and critic). ❖ With husband, served as drama editor and critic for *Chicago Herald* and wrote such plays as *Years of Discretion, The Song Bird, Squab Farm, Upstairs and Down, Lombardi Ltd., The Indestructible Wife, The Walk-Offs, The Checkerboard, We Girls, Treat 'Em Rough, Love Honor and Betray* and *The Great Lover,* many of which were adapted for the screen; as well, adapted stories and wrote titles for over 50 silent films.

HATTON, G. Noel (1858–1932). *See Caird, Mona.*

HATTON, Marion (1835–1905). New Zealand suffragist. Name variations: Mary Ann (Marion) Hanover. Born Mary Ann Hanover, probably Sept 8, 1835, in Preston, Somersetshire, England; died June 6, 1905, in Dunedin, New Zealand; dau. of Robert Hanover (victualler) and Elizabeth (Stenner) Hanover; m. Joseph Hatton, 1855; children: 5 sons, 1 daughter. ❖ Established first lodge of Good Templars in Amsterdam (late 1850s); introduced various tactics, including circulation of petitions, to centers of Women's Franchise League (WFL, early 1890s); after women had won right to vote in New Zealand, continued to advocate on behalf of women's rights, especially legal equality; served as president of WFL. ❖ See also *Dictionary of New Zealand Biography* (Vol. 2).

HATTORI, Michiko (1968—). Japanese golfer. Born 1968 in Nagoya, Japan; attended University of Texas (1987–91). ❖ Won US Women's Amateur (1985), the 1st Asian to win the event.

HATVANY, Lili (1890–1967). Hungarian-American screenwriter and playwright. Name variations: Lily Hatvany. Born Mar 23, 1890, in Hungary; died Nov 12, 1967, in New York, NY; became a naturalized US citizen; m. twice, div. twice; children: daughter. ❖ Screenplays include *My Kingdom for a Cook, Lucky Number* and *Tonight or Never,* starring Gloria Swanson, adapted from Hatvany's hit stage play, starring Melvyn Douglas and Helen Gahagan Douglas.

HATZ, Elizabeth (1952—). Swedish architect. Born June 20, 1953, in Lund, Sweden; graduate of London's Architectural Association (1977). ❖ Worked in Paris for 2 years before returning to Sweden to join large practice of Berg Arkitektkontor in Stockholm (1979); became leading member of firm's design team, working initially on headquarters of Kodak in Gothenburg (1979–82); taught at Royal Technical High School of Architecture in Stockholm (1983–86) and took on projects of increasing prestige and size; helped create celebrated Stockholm Globe (1989), world's largest spherical building, as well as adjoining glass-encased building, The Triangle, which houses administrative offices; belongs to National Swedish Board of Architects and was elected to board of ATHENA, Swedish Women Architects Association (1987).

HATZIMICHALI, Angeliki (1895–1956). Greek writer and folklorist. Born in Greece, 1895; died 1956; dau. of a professor of Greek literature. ❖ Devoted life to the study and preservation of traditional Greek culture, both Byzantine and modern folk; living among peasants in countryside, observed and recorded daily life, customs, and handicraft techniques; was instrumental in establishment of professional schools for preservation of traditional crafts as well as workshops where immigrant women from Asia Minor could practice their native crafts; organized 1st exhibit of folk art in Greece (1921); writings were widely published in folk-art journals in Greece and abroad.

HATZLER, Clara (fl. 1452). German scribe. Fl. in Augsburg, Germany. ❖ Successful scribe was not affiliated with a convent as most women scribes were, but practiced professionally to support herself in growing town of Augsburg; remained in business for 24 years.

HAUCK, Amalia Mignon (1851–1929). *See Hauk, Minnie.*

HAUCKE, Countess von (1825–1895). *See Hauke, Julie von.*

HAUG, Jutta D. (1951—). German politician. Born Oct 8, 1951, in Castrop-Rauxel, Germany. ❖ Became a member of the Social Democratic Party (SPD) Executive (1999); as a European Socialist, elected to 4th and 5th European Parliament (1994–99, 1999–2004).

HAUGEN, Tone (1964—). Norwegian soccer player. Born Feb 6, 1964, in Norway. ❖ Won a team bronze medal at Atlanta Olympics (1996); played for Nikko in Japan (1994–96).

HAUGENES, Margunn (1970—). Norwegian soccer player. Born Jan 25, 1970, in Norway. ❖ Midfielder; won a team gold medal at Sydney Olympics (2000); played for England's Fulham (2002).

HAUGHERY, Margaret Gaffney (1813–1882). Irish-born American philanthropist and businesswoman. Born Margaret Gaffney near Killeshandra, Co. Cavan, Ireland, 1813; died in New Orleans, Louisiana, Feb 9, 1882; dau. of William Gaffney (tenant farmer) and Margaret (O'Rourke) Gaffney; m. Charles Haughery, Oct 10, 1835 (died 1836); children: Frances (died in infancy). ❖ Known as the "Bread Woman of New Orleans," immigrated to Baltimore with family (1818); moved to New Orleans with husband (1835); following his death (1836), assisted the Sisters of Charity at Poydras Orphan Asylum, where she also lived; with saved earnings, purchased a pair of cows to start a dairy; soon could finance a new orphanage, New Orleans Female Orphan Asylum, for the Sisters of Charity (1840); over the years, helped establish and maintain 11 such institutions; turning attention to a small bakery, transformed it into largest export business in New Orleans; continued to live modestly while conducting her philanthropy. A statue of Haughery, inscribed simply "Margaret," was unveiled in a New Orleans park bearing her name (1884). ❖ See also *Women in World History.*

HAUGHTON, Aaliyah (1979–2001). *See Aaliyah.*

HAUGHTON, Eleanor (1922–1987). *See Leacock, Eleanor Burke.*

HAUK, Minnie (1851–1929). American dramatic soprano. Name variations: Minnie Hauck. Born Amalia Mignon Hauck in New York, NY, Nov 16, 1851; died at Villa Tribschen, Switzerland, Feb 6, 1929; studied with Achille Errani; m. Baron Ernst von Hesse-Wartegg. ❖ The 1st internationally acclaimed opera singer to emerge from US, became a musical sensation in NY (1862), singing in homes of social elite; made operatic debut in *La Sonnambula* at Brooklyn Academy of Music (1866); made Manhattan debut at Winter Garden as Prascovia in *L'Étoile du Nord* (1866); in Paris, appeared as Amina in *La Sonnambula* and became France's darling; sang in major opera houses of London, The Hague, and Russia; debuted in Vienna as Marguerite in *Faust* (1870); sang mostly in Vienna and Berlin (1870–80), starring in, among other operas, Goetz's *Taming of the Shrew*; mastered German, adding dozens of roles to repertory; in Budapest, sang role of Maria in *Hunyadi László* in the original Magyar; sang title role of Carmen in French at Théâtre de la Monnaie in Brussels (1878), then performed *Carmen* in London in Italian (1879), both to great success; mastered new roles, including Berlioz' rarely performed *La Damnation de Faust*; made final NY appearance, at Metropolitan Opera (1891); founded Minnie Hauk Grand Opera Co. (1891) for American tour, appearing in Mascagni's new opera *Cavalleria Rusticana*; retired (1896). ❖ See also autobiography *Memories of a Singer* (Arno reprint, 1977); and *Women in World History.*

HAUKE, Julie von (1825–1895). Countess of Hauke. Name variations: Countess von Haucke. Born Julie Theresa in Poland in 1825; died 1895; dau. of Maurice von Hauke and Sophia Lafontaine; became morganatic wife of Alexander of Hesse-Darmstadt, Oct 1851 (died 1888); grandmother of Louis Mountbatten, earl Mountbatten of Burma; children: Mary of Battenberg (1852–1923); Louis of Battenberg, 1st marquess of Milford Haven (1854–1921, who m. Victoria of Hesse-Darmstadt); Alexander I, prince of Bulgaria (1857–1893); Henry of Battenberg (1858–1896, who m. Beatrice, dau. of Queen Victoria); Francis of Battenberg (1861–1924).

HAUKOVÁ, Jiřina (1919—). Czechoslovakian poet. Name variations: Jirina Haukova. Born 1919 in Moravia, Czechoslovakia. ❖ Works, which echo modernist poets but are also Surrealist and mystical in tone, include *Přisluní* (1943), *Země nikoho* (1970), and *Motýl a smrt* (1990); writing was banned (1970s–80s).

HAUPTMANN, Anna (1898–1994). German-born American wife. Born Anna Schoeffler, 1898, in Markgröningen, near Stuttgart, Germany; died in New Holland, Pennsylvania, Oct 10, 1994; came to US, 1923; married Bruno Richard Hauptmann (executed April 1936 as the murderer of the Lindbergh baby); children: son, Manfred. ❖ For almost 6 decades, fought to clear husband's name in what was called by contemporaries "the crime of the century." By the time of her death, some doubts about his guilt had been raised by a number of well-researched and soberly argued books. ❖ See also Ludovic Kennedy. *The Airman and the Carpenter: The Lindbergh Kidnapping and the Framing of Richard Hauptmann* (Penguin, 1986).

HAUSERMAN, Cindy Noble- (1958—). *See Noble, Cindy.*

HAUSHOFER, Marlen (1920–1970). Austrian novelist and feminist. Born Maria Helene Frauendorfer, April 11, 1920, in Fraünstein, Austria; died Mar 21, 1970; dau. of Heinrich and Maria Frauendorfer; m. Manfred Haushofer. ❖ Writings include *Die Tapetentür* (The Door in the Wallpaper, 1957), *Die Wand* (The Wall 1958), *Das fünfte jahr* and *Schreckliche Treue.*

HAUSSET, Nicole Colleson du (1713–1801). French memoirist. Name variations: Nicole Colleson du Haussay; Madame du Hausset. Born 1713 in Vitry-le-François, France; died 1801. ❖ Married into aristocracy; after husband's death, entered royal household as lady's maid to Duchesse de Pompadour; wrote *Mémoires* (1809), which give a picture of the private lives of Louis XV and Mme de Pompadour.

HAUTALA, Heidi Anneli (1955—). Finnish politician. Born Nov 14, 1955, in Oulu, Finland. ❖ Elected to 4th and 5th European Parliament (1994–99, 1999–2004); left Parliament (Mar 25, 2003); was 1st vice chair of the Green Group in the EP.

HAUTVAL, Adelaide (1906–1988). French physician and Holocaust survivor. Name variations: Haidi Hautval. Born in Hohwald im Elsass, Germany (now Le Hohwald, Alsace, France), Jan 1, 1906; died Oct 17, 1988; dau. of a Protestant pastor; received medical degree in psychiatry from University of Strasbourg. ❖ A doctor, began managing a home for handicapped children in Le Hohwald (1938); worked in a clinic in southwestern France during Nazi occupation (mid-1940); while detained at demarcation line (April 1942), admonished some Germans for their treatment of a Jewish family and was jailed; offered release on condition she retract comments, refused; was deported to Auschwitz (Jan 1943); ignored orders from Nazi doctors on 4 separate occasions, refusing to participate in medical experiments on Jewish prisoners and rejecting SS commands to participate in sterilization of women; instead, practiced medicine as best she could, saving lives, then was transferred to Ravensbrück (Aug 1944); presented damning testimony against Nazi doctors at Nuremberg. Recognized as "Righteous Among the Nations" by Israel's Yad Vashem (April 1965). ❖ See also memoires *Médecine et crimes contre l'Humanité* (1991); and *Women in World History.*

HAVEL, Olga (1933–1996). First lady of the Czech Republic. Name variations: Olga Havlova. Born Olga Splíchalová in Prague, Czechoslovakia, 1933; died in Prague, Jan 27, 1996; m. Václav Havel (playwright, then president of Czech Republic), 1964. ❖ Beloved first lady, supported husband throughout his early career as playwright at Theatre on the Balustrade, where she also worked; after Soviet invasion (1968), saw him through his 20-year rise from leader in dissident movement to president of the country; gave strength to him during his years of imprisonment, which he documented in *Letters to Olga*; as first lady, founded and headed Committee of Good Will, which merged with the Olga Havel Foundation, to carry out work with the mentally and physically handicapped and spearhead a campaign to prevent the spread of AIDS; nominated by the Czech Republic as the European woman of the year (1995). On her death, tens of thousands stood in line to pay their respects.

HAVEMEYER, Mrs. Henry O. (1855–1929). *See Havemeyer, Louisine.*

HAVEMEYER, Louisine (1855–1929). American art collector. Born Louisine Waldron Elder in Philadelphia, PA, 1855; died of heart disease, Jan 6, 1929; dau. of George W. Elder (sugar refiner); m. Henry Osborne Havemeyer (mogul in sugar industry), 1883 (died 1907); children: Adaline Havemeyer Frelinghuysen (b. 1884); Horace Havemeyer (b. 1886); Electra Havemeyer Webb (1888–1960, also a collector). ❖ Convinced husband to collect paintings; joined hands with Mary Cassatt for purchasing expeditions; tracked and stored their vast collection—which included Greco's *View of Toledo*, Goya's *Women on a Balcony*, Manet's *Le Bal de l'Opéra*, Daumier's *Third Class Carriage*, and Courbet's *Landscape and Deer*—in 5th Avenue mansion; continued collecting after husband's death (1907); a feminist, lectured in support of enfranchisement and better education for women; bequeathed 142 works of art from "The H.O. Havemeyer Collection" to Metropolitan Museum of Art. ❖ See also *Women in World History.*

HAVEN, Alice B. (1827–1863). *See Haven, Emily Bradley Neal.*

HAVEN, Emily Bradley Neal (1827–1863). American author and editor. Name variations: Alice Neal; Alice B. Haven; (pseudonyms) Alice G. Lee and Cousin Alice. Born Emily Bradley, Sept 13, 1827, in Hudson, NY; died of consumption, Aug 23, 1863, in Mamaroneck, NY; dau. of George (died 1830) and Sarah (Brown) Bradley (Quaker); at age 6, adopted by her mother's brother, J. Newton Brown, a Baptist minister;

went by the name Alice most of her life; m. Joseph C. Neal (editor), Dec 1846 (died July 17, 1847); m. Samuel L. Haven (NY broker), Jan 1, 1853; children: 2 daughters, 2 sons. ❖ Published a children's column under name Cousin Alice in *Neal's Saturday Gazette and Lady's Literary Museum*; writings include *Helen Morton's Trial* (1849), *The Gossips of Rivertown* (1850), series of "Home Books" for children for D. Appleton & Co. (1852–59), *The Good Report* (memoir, 1867), and *Home Studies* (1869).

HAVER, June (1926–2005). American film actress. Born June Stovenour in Rock Island, Illinois, June 10, 1926; died July 4, 2005, in Brentwood, California; dau. of Fred and Marie Stovenour; attended high school in Hollywood; m. Jimmy Zito (musician), Mar 1947 (div. 1949); m. Fred MacMurray (actor), June 28, 1954; children: (with MacMurray) adopted twins, Katie and Laurie, 1956. ❖ Star of post-WWII musicals, made 2 musical film shorts before signing with 20th Century-Fox; made feature-film debut in *The Gang's All Here* (1943), then was cast with Betty Grable in *The Dolly Sisters* (1945); also starred in *Three Little Girls in Blue* (1946), *Oh, You Beautiful Doll!* (1949), *Look for the Silver Lining* (1949), in which she played Marilyn Miller, *The Daughter of Rosie O'Grady* (1950), and *I'll Get By* (1950); left Hollywood to enter Sisters of Charity convent in Leavenworth, Kansas (1952), but left after a few months, reportedly due to ill health; married and retired from career. ❖ See also *Women in World History.*

HAVER, Phyllis (1899–1960). American silent-film actress. Born Phyllis O'Haver, Jan 6, 1899, in Douglas, Kansas; died Nov 19, 1960, an apparent suicide, in Falls Village, Connecticut; m. William Seeman (NY millionaire), 1929 (div. 1945). ❖ Began career as one of Mack Sennett's bathing beauties; starred in such films as *Up in Mabel's Room, What Price Glory?, The Wise Wife, The Fighting Eagle, Chicago, Tenth Avenue, The Shady Lady, The Way of All Flesh, The Battle of the Sexes* and *Thunder*; retired from screen (1929).

HAVERGAL, Frances Ridley (1836–1879). English-born hymn writer. Born at Astley, Worcestershire, England, Dec 14, 1836; died at Caswell Bay, Swansea, South Wales, June 3, 1879; dau. of Reverend William Henry Havergal (writer of sacred music and rector of Astley) and Jane (Head) Havergal; sister of Maria Vernon Graham Havergal (who wrote *Frances R. Havergal: The Last Week*, 1879, and edited Frances' *Memorials* in 1880, *Poetical Works*, 1884, and *Letters*, 1885), and Jane Havergal Crane (who edited Maria's autobiography, 1887, and published a biography of their father, 1882); studied for a year in Düsseldorf, Germany. ❖ Hymn writer and author of religious poems, tracts, and children's books, wrote the well-known hymn "I Gave My Life for Thee" at 18; also wrote "True-Hearted, Whole-Hearted," "O Savior, Precious Savior" and "Tell It Out Among the Heathen." ❖ See also T.H. Darlow, *Havergal: A Saint of God* (1927); and *Women in World History.*

HAVERS, Elizabeth (1933—). See Butler-Sloss, Elizabeth.

HAVILAND, Laura S. (1808–1898). Canadian-born abolitionist and welfare worker. Born Laura Smith, Dec 20, 1808, in Ontario, Canada; died April 20, 1898, in Grand Rapids, Michigan; dau. of Daniel and Sene (Blancher) Smith, both Quakers; attended public school in Canada and Union Free School in Lockport, NY; m. Charles Haviland Jr., Nov 3, 1825; children: Harvey S., Daniel S., Esther M., Anna C., Joseph, Laura Jane, Almira Ann and Lavina Haviland. ❖ With husband, moved to Quaker settlement in Raisin Township, Lenawee County, Michigan territory (1929), where they joined Elizabeth Margaret Chandler to form the 1st antislavery society in Michigan; after objections from other Quakers regarding abolitionist activities, withdrew from Society of Friends; with husband, opened small school for orphans and indigent county charges (1837), which became River Raisin Institute, a preparatory school that frequently served as a haven for fugitive slaves; by 1844, had become a minister in the Wesleyan Methodist Church; following death of husband (1845), devoted attention to antislavery activities, including riding the Underground Railroad, giving speeches, and teaching in black schools; traveled widely through the South as a paid agent of Michigan Freedmen's Aid Commission (1864). ❖ See also *Women in World History.*

HAVILLAND, Olivia de (b. 1916). See de Havilland, Olivia.

HAVLOVA, Olga (1933–1996). See Havel, Olga.

HAVNÅS, Kristine (1974—). See Duvholt, Kristine.

HAVOC, June (1916—). American actress and writer. Name variations: Baby June. Born Ellen Evangeline Hovick, Nov 8, 1916, in Seattle, WA;

dau. of John Hovick and Anna Thompson Hovick, known as Rose Hovick; sister of Gypsy Rose Lee (1914–1970); married at 13; m. William Spier (director). ❖ Began performing in vaudeville at 8 with sister; left the act (1929); appeared in such films as *My Sister Eileen* (1942), *Brewster's Millions* (1945), *Gentleman's Agreement* (1947), *The Iron Curtain* (1948), *Lady Possessed* (1952), *The Private Files of J. Edgar Hoover* (1977) and *Can't Stop the Music* (1980), but had more success on NY stage in *Pal Joey* (1940) and *Mexican Hayride*, for which she won a Donaldson Award (1944); also wrote and directed *I, Said the Fly* and successful Broadway play *Marathon 33*, starring Julie Harris. ❖ See also memoirs *Early Havoc* (1959) and *More Havoc* (1980); the play and film of *Gypsy*; and *Women in World History.*

HAWAII, princess of.
See Nahienaena (c. 1815–1836).
See Kamamalu, Victoria (1838–1866).
See Kaiulani (1875–1899).

HAWAII, queen of.
See Kamamalu (c. 1803–1824).
See Kinau (c. 1805–1839).
See Kalama (c. 1820–1870).
See Kapiolani (1834–1899).
See Emma (1836–1885).
See Liliuokalani (1838–1917).

HAWAII, queen-regent of. See Kaahumanu (1777–1832).

HAWARDEN, Clementina (1822–1865). Scottish photographer. Name variations: Lady Clementina Hawarden; Clementina Maude. Born Clementina Elphinstone Fleeming at Cumbernauld House, near Glasgow, Scotland, 1822; died in South Kensington, London, England, in 1865; dau. of Admiral Charles Elphinstone Fleeming and Catalina Paulina (Alessandro) Fleeming; m. Cornwallis Maude, later 4th viscount Hawarden and 1st earl de Montalt, 1845; children: 10 (7 daughters and 1 son survived infancy). ❖ Took up photography (1857); with children as subjects, explored the medium in new ways, using mirrors and fabric backgrounds which would strongly influence later photographers; was among the 1st amateur women photographers to be recognized by Photographic Society of London, where she won awards for her work and was elected for membership (1863). ❖ See also *Women in World History.*

HAWCO, Sherry (d. 1991). Canadian gymnast. Born in Cambridge, Ontario, Canada; died Oct 26, 1991. ❖ Placed 2nd at Commonweath Games (1978); at Canadian nationals, won bronze medals for all-around (1978, 1980) and a gold medal (1981); won a gold medal for balance beam at Pan American Games.

HAWES, Elizabeth (1903–1971). American fashion designer, writer and union organizer. Born Elizabeth Hawes, Dec 16, 1903, in Ridgewood, NJ; died Sept 6, 1971, in New York, NY; dau. of John Hawes and Henrietta (Houston) Hawes; m. Ralph Jester (sculptor), Dec 12, 1930 (div. 1935); m. Joseph Losey (film and theater director), July 24, 1937 (div. 1944); children: (1st m.) 1 son (b. 1938). ❖ Designed clothes for Paris couturier Nicole Groult and wrote articles on fashion (1928); with Rosemary Harden, ran own fashion business in NYC, Hawes-Harden (1928–30), renamed Hawes Inc., after Harden withdrew (1930); was 1st American designer to show fashion collection in Paris (1931) and 1st American woman to display collection in USSR since 1917 (1935); wrote *Fashion is Spinach* (1938), *Why Women Cry* (1943), and *Anything But Love* (1948); closed business, certain that custom-made clothing had no future (1940); was columnist for newspaper, *PM* (1940–42); during WWII, worked at Wright Aeronautical Plant in Paterson, NJ, and joined United Auto Workers (UAW, 1943); moved to Detroit and worked at education department of UAW (1944); ran fashion business, Elizabeth Hawes Inc., in NYC (1948–49); unsuccessfully attempted return to fashion designing (1952); had retrospective show of her designs held by Fashion Institute of Technology (1967). Favored pants for women, skirts for men, and child-care centers for working women.

HAWES, Harriet Boyd (1871–1945). American archaeologist. Name variations: Harriet Boyd. Born Harriet Ann Boyd in Boston, Massachusetts, Oct 11, 1871; died in Washington DC, Mar 31, 1945; graduate of Smith College, 1892; studied at American School of Classical Studies in Athens, Greece, 1896; Smith College, MA, 1901; m. Charles H. Hawes (British anthropologist), Mar 1906. ❖ Set off on her own expedition to island of Crete (1896); while in Kavousi, discovered some Iron Age tombs (1900); at Gournia, was 1st to discover and excavate a

Minoan town from Early Bronze Age (1901, 1903, 1904), and the 1st woman to direct a major field project, bringing her worldwide attention; lectured on pre-Christian art at Wellesley College (1920–36). ❖ See also *Women in World History.*

HAWISE. *Variant of Hadwig or Hedwig.*

HAWISE (d. after 1135). Countess of Penthievre. Died after 1135; m. Stephen, count of Penthievre and Lord of Richmond, before 1100 (died 1136); children: Alan III the Black, 1st earl of Richmond (d. 1146), Theophania, Henry, Maud, Olive.

HAWISE OF BRITTANY (d. 1072). Duchess of Brittany. Died 1072; dau. of Alan III, duke of Brittany, and Bertha of Chartres (d. 1084); m. Hoel, duke of Brittany; children: Alan IV, duke of Brittany.

HAWISE OF NORMANDY (d. 1034). Duchess of Brittany. Name variations: sometimes mentioned as Hedwig or Hadwisa. Died Feb 21, 1034; dau. of Richard I the Fearless (d. 996), duke of Normandy (r. 942–996), and Gunnor of Denmark (d. 1031); m. Geoffrei or Geoffrey I (d. 1008), duke of Brittany (r. 992–1008), c. 997; children: Alain or Alan III, also known as Alan V (d. 1040), duke of Brittany (r. 1008–1040); Odo de Porhoet, count of Penthievre (d. 1079); Adela of Rennes (d. 1067, abbess of St. Georges Rennes).

HAWISE OF SALISBURY (fl. 12th c.). Countess of Dreux. Name variations: Hawise de Salisbury. Married Rotrou the Great, count of Perche; m. Robert (c. 1123–1188), count of Dreux.

HAWKE, Hazel (1929—). Australian prime-ministerial wife. Born Hazel Masterson, July 20, 1929, in Perth, Western Australia; m. Robert Hawke (prime minister of Australia, 1983–91) Mar 3, 1956 (div. 1995); children: Susan (b. 1957), Stephen (b. 1959), Roslyn (b. 1960), and Robert (b. 1963). ❖ Worked at the Indian High Commission (1956); deeply involved in husband's 5 successful election campaigns; while prime-ministerial wife, actively campaigned for many causes, including welfare, education, arts, and the environment; worked for the Australiana Fund to help restore The Lodge's interior (the official prime-ministerial residence); chair of the New South Wales Heritage Council. Awarded Order of Australia (2001). ❖ See also autobiography *My Own Life* (Text, 1992).

HAWKER, Lilian E. (1908–1991). English mycologist. Born 1908 in UK; died Feb 5, 1991. ❖ Appointed the 1st mycology professor in Britain (University of Bristol, 1965–73) and the 1st woman dean of Faculty (of Science) at University of Bristol (1970–73); studied plant physiology at University of Reading (BS and MS) and University of Manchester; studied mycology at Imperial College, London, on a grant (1932); helped set up Honours School of Microbiology; advocated study of biological sciences as part of BEd degree programs; retired (1973) and appointed emeritus professor. Writings include *Fungi-An Introduction* (1966).

HAWKES, Jacquetta (1910–1996). British archaeologist and writer. Name variations: Jacquetta Hopkins in Cambridge, England, Aug 5, 1910; died Mar 18, 1996; dau. of Sir Frederick Hopkins (Nobel prize-winner); educated at Newnham College, University of Cambridge; took part in many archaeological excavations between 1931 and 1940, in Britain, Ireland, France, and Palestine; m. Christopher Hawkes (archaeologist), in 1933 (div. 1953, died 1992); m. J.B. Priestley (novelist), 1953 (died 1984); children: (1st m.) 1 son. ❖ One of the foremost popularizers of archaeology, worked for British government at Ministry of Education during WWII; was principal and secretary of UN National Commission for UNESCO (1943–49), vice-president of Council for British Archaeology (1949–52), adviser to Festival of Britain (1951), governor of British Film Institute (1950–55), and member of Central Committee of UNESCO (1966–79); writings include *The Archaeology of Jersey* (1939), (with Christopher Hawkes) *Prehistoric Britain* (1944), *Early Britain* (1945), *A Land* (1951), *The World of the Past* (1963), *Atlas of Ancient Archaeology* (1975) and *Shell Guide to British Archaeology* (1986). Named Officer of the British Empire (OBE, 1952). ❖ See also memoir (co-authored with Priestly) *Journey Down a Rainbow* (1955); and *Women in World History.*

HAWKES, Rechelle (1967—). Australian field-hockey player. Born May 30, 1967, in Albany, Western Australia. ❖ Forward/midfielder, won team gold medals at Seoul Olympics (1988), Atlanta Olympics (1996) and Sydney Olympics (2000).

HAWKES, Sharlene (c. 1964—). Miss America. Name variations: Sharlene Wells. Born Sharlene Wells c. 1964 in Asuncion, Paraguay; attended high school in Buenos Aires, Argentina; Brigham Young University, magna

cum laude; married Robert Hawkes; children: 4. ❖ Named Miss America (1985), representing Utah, only foreign-born winner; became one of the 1st women to work on-air for ESPN tv (1987); continues to appear on ESPN; serves as president of Hawkes Communications. Author of *Living In, But Not Of, the World.*

HAWKINS, Charlotte (c. 1883–1961). *See Brown, Charlotte Hawkins.*

HAWKINS, Jamesetta (1938—). *See James, Etta.*

HAWKINS, Laetitia Matilda (1759–1835). British novelist and memoirist. Born Laetitia Matilda Hawkins, 1759 in London, England; died 1835 in Twickenham, Middlesex, England; dau. of Sir John Hawkins and Sidney Storer. ❖ Published *Letters on the Female Mind: Its Powers and Pursuits* (1793), which expresses anti-feminist and pro-slavery sentiments; other writings include *Rosanne, or Father's Labour Lost* (1814), *Anecdotes, Biographical Sketches and Memoirs* (1823), *Annaline, or Motive Hunting* (1824), and *Memoirs* (1978); believed in firm discipline but humanity towards children and servants.

HAWKINS, Lottie (c. 1883–1961). *See Brown, Charlotte Hawkins.*

HAWKINS, Mary (1875–1950). Canadian birth-control clinic founder. Name variations: Mrs. W.C. Hawkins. Born Mary Elizabeth Chambers, July 31, 1875, in New York, NY; died Oct 9, 1950; dau. of Frank Ross Chambers and Mary Elizabeth (Pease) Chambers; graduate of Vassar College, 1897; m. William Clark Hawkins (engineer), 1898 (died 1925); children: Francis Chambers Hawkins and Elizabeth Hawkins (who m. Lester F. Merrick). ❖ Moved to Hamilton, Ontario (1901); during WWI, served as administrator of Canadian Field Comforts Fund; was a founder of Family Service Bureau (1923), Community Chest (1927), and Women's Civic Club; active in Red Cross, also served as president of Infant's Home; founded Hamilton Birth Control Society (later part of Planned Parenthood Society), which opened the 1st birth-control clinic in Canada, serving as its president (1932–50).

HAWKINS, Mary Ann (1919–1993). American surfing pioneer. Born Mar 7, 1919, in Pasadena, CA; died Jan 28, 1993. ❖ Won AAU 500-meter freestyle (1936); won 1st ever all-female paddle-board race (1936); was National Paddleboard champion and Pacific Coast Women's Surfboard champion (1938–40); was the 1st female to enter the Catalina–Manhattan Beach aquaplane race (1939); won women's half-mile swim (1939); was also a Hollywood movie stunt double. ❖ See also "Heart of the Sea" (documentary, PBS).

HAWKINS, Paula Fickes (1927—). American politician. Born Paula Fickes, Jan 24, 1927, in Salt Lake City, Utah; dau. of Paul B. (navy chief warrant officer) and Leoan (Staley) Fickes; attended Utah State University; m. Walter Eugene Hawkins, Sept 5, 1947; children: Ginean, Kevin and Kelley Ann Hawkins. ❖ US Republican Senator (Jan 1, 1981–Jan 3, 1987), served as a Florida co-chair for Nixon's presidential campaigns (1968, 1972); won election to Florida Public Service Commission (1972); after unsuccessful bids for US Senate (1974) and state lieutenant governor (1976), elected to US Senate (1980); during tenure, served on Committee on Agriculture, Nutrition, and Forestry and Committee on Labor and Human Resources; also served on Joint Economic Committee (97th Congress), Committee on Banking, Housing, and Urban Affairs (98th), and Special Committee on Aging (99th); initiated an investigation into problem of missing children, resulting in Missing Children's Act of 1982, through which a central information center was established. ❖ See also *Women in World History.*

HAWKINS, Mrs. W.C. (1875–1950). *See Hawkins, Mary.*

HAWLEY, Christine (1949—). English architect. Born 1949 in Shrewsbury, England; graduate of London's Architectural Association (1975). ❖ Accomplished architect whose London firm has won 5 international awards and whose partnership with Peter Cook yielded many acclaimed designs; practiced with De Soissons Partnership Architects and Yorke Rosenberg & Mardell Architects in London (1972–73); became partner in Cook and Hawley Architects (1975); taught at Architectural Association School of Architecture (1979–87); with Cook, won international competition for Pfaffenberg museum in Austria; served as head of University of East London School of Architecture (1987–93); became member of Royal Institute of British Architects (1982) and fellow of RIBA (1983); practiced with Pearson International Architects (1980s), then established Christine Hawley Architects (1998); places special emphasis on creation of high-quality, low-cost housing.

HAWLEY, Florence (1906–1991). *See Ellis, Florence Hawley.*

HAWLEY, Wanda (1895–1963). American silent-film actress. Name variations: Wanda Petit. Born Selma Wanda Pittack, July 30, 1895, in Scranton, Pennsylvania; died Mar 18, 1963, in Los Angeles, CA; m. Allen Burton Hawley (div. 1922). ❖ One of Cecil B. De Mille's many mistresses, starred in *The Heart of a Lion, Mr. Fix-It, Peg o' My Heart, Miss Hobbs, The Young Rajah* and *Smouldering Fires*; later said to have been a San Francisco call girl.

HAWN, Goldie (1945—). American actress. Born Goldie Jeanne Studlendgehawn, Nov 21, 1945, in Washington, DC; dau. of Edward Rutledge Studlendgehawn; attended American University; m. Gus Trikonis, 1969 (div. 1976); m. Bill Hudson (singer), 1976 (div. 1979); lived with actor Kurt Russell (1984–2004); children: Oliver Hudson, Kate Hudson (actress); (with Kurt Russell) Wyatt Russell. ❖ Versatile actress, best known for comedy, made stage debut at 11, dancing in *The Nutcracker*; made tv debut on short-lived series "Good Morning World" (1967); came to prominence on "Rowan and Martin's Laugh-In" (1968–70); won Academy Award for Best Supporting Actress for performance in *Cactus Flower* (1969); starred in *The Sugarland Express* (1974), *Shampoo* (1975), *Foul Play* (1978), *Private Benjamin* (also producer, 1980), *Swing Shift* (1984), *Bird on a Wire* (1990), *My Blue Heaven* (producer, 1990), *The First Wives Club* (1996), *The Out-of-Towners* (1998), *Town and Country* (2000), and *Banger Sisters* (2002). Nominated for 8 Golden Globes as well as an Oscar for *Private Benjamin* (1980).

HAWORTH, Cheryl (1983—). American weightlifter. Born Cheryl Ann Haworth, April 18, 1983, in Savannah, Georgia. ❖ Won a bronze medal for +75kg at Sydney Olympics (2000); won Jr. World championships (2001, 2002).

HAWTHORNE, Margaret Jane Scott (1869–1958). New Zealand tailor, trade unionist, and factory inspector. Name variations: Margaret Jane Scott, Margaret Jane Smith. Born Margaret Jane Scott, Jan 17, 1869, in Co. Cavan, Ireland; died May 1, 1958, in Auckland, New Zealand; dau. of Henry Scott (farmer) and Anne (Kenny) Scott; m. Mark Henry Hawthorne (boot and shoe importer), 1989 (div. 1915); m. James Smith (farmer), 1916; children: 1 daughter. ❖ Immigrated with family to New Zealand (1880); trained as a tailor and became active in trade union movement; was 1st woman secretary of Christchurch Tailoresses' and Pressers' Union; elected council vice president of Canterbury Trades and Labour Council (1894); appointed to manage Women's Branch of Department of Labour in Wellington, and then appointed as inspector of factories (1895); became one of highest paid women public servants. ❖ See also *Dictionary of New Zealand Biography* (Vol. 2).

HAWTHORNE, Rose (1851–1926). See Lathrop, Rose Hawthorne.

HAWTHORNE, Sophia Peabody (1809–1871). One of the famous Peabody sisters and wife of Nathaniel Hawthorne. Born Sophia Amelia Peabody in Salem, Massachusetts, Sept 21, 1809; died in London, England, of typhoid pneumonia, Feb 1871; dau. of Nathaniel Peabody (dentist) and Elizabeth Palmer Peabody (1778–1853, teacher and writer); sister of Elizabeth Palmer Peabody (1804–1894) and Mary Peabody Mann (1806–1887, wife of Horace Mann); m. Nathaniel Hawthorne (novelist), July 1842 (died 1864); children: Julian Hawthorne (b. 1846); Una Hawthorne (b. 1844); Rose Hawthorne Lathrop (1851–1926). ❖ See also Louise Hall Tharp, *The Peabody Sisters of Salem* (Little, Brown, 1950); and *Women in World History*.

HAWTREY, Marjory (1900–1952). English stage actress. Name variations: Marjory Clark. Born Marjory Clark, Mar 7, 1900, in Surbiton, Surrey, England; died Sept 22, 1952; m. Anthony Hawtrey (actor, died 1954). ❖ Made London debut as Kate in *The Punctual Sex* (1919), followed by *Interference, Fame* (as Lady Myrtle Frampton), *Cold Blood, All God's Chillun, Charlotte Corday, Walk in the Sun, To Kill a Cat, Julius Caesar* (as Calpurnia), *The Two Mrs. Carrolls* (Harriett Carroll), *The Passing of the Third Floor Back, The Old Ladies* and *The Mother* (title role), among others; with husband, co-managed Embassy theater in Hampstead (1939, 1945–54).

HAY, Eliza Monroe (1786–1840). See Monroe, Eliza Kortright.

HAY, Elizabeth Dexter (1927—). American cell biologist. Born Elizabeth Dexter Hay, April 2, 1927, in St. Augustine, Florida; dau. of a physician (father); had twin brother Jack Hay (died 1942); Smith College, AB, 1948; Johns Hopkins University School of Medicine, MD, 1952; never married; no children. ❖ Embryologist and anatomist, who initially studied cancer cells and birth defects (e.g., cleft plate); worked with Dr. S. Meryl Rose at Smith College and, during summers, at Marine Biological Institute at Woods Hole, MA; was assistant anatomy professor at Cornell Medical College (1957–60); was assistant anatomy professor at Harvard Medical School (1960–64), becoming full embryology professor (1969), then chair of Department of Anatomy and Cellular Biology (1975–93), Harvard's 1st woman chair of an academic department; with Jean-Paul Revel at Harvard University, successfully applied auto-radiography to the electron microscope and wrote a monograph on developing avian cornea (considered a classic); studied eye tissues and collagen. Elected to National Academy of Sciences (1984); received Alcon Award for Vision Research (1988) and New York Academy of Sciences' Salute to Contemporary Women Scientists Award (1991).

HAY, Elzey (1840–1931). See Andrews, Eliza Frances.

HAY, Georgina (1916–2003). See Coleridge, Georgina.

HAY, Jean Emily (1903–1984). New Zealand teacher and broadcaster. Born June 17, 1903, at Collie, Western Australia; died Feb 14, 1984, at Christchurch, New Zealand; dau. of William Arthur Hay (cleric) and Emma Jane (Langridge) Hay; Christchurch Training College, 1924–1926. ❖ Moved to New Zealand with family (1911); taught at Somerfield School, New Brighton School, and Normal School before traveling to London to study Dalcroze method of teaching music and movement to young children; was staff member at Normal School (1933–50); gained reputation as innovator in childhood education; following retirement (1960), traveled to Britain and Europe and accepted position as assistant principal at Kindergarten College for 2 years. ❖ See also *Dictionary of New Zealand Biography* (Vol. 4).

HAY, Lucy (1599–1660). Countess of Carlisle. Born 1599; died 1660; dau. of Henry Percy, 9th earl of Northumberland; m. James Hay, 1st earl of Carlisle, 1617. ❖ Exercised influence over Queen Henrietta Maria; was an intimate of Thomas Wentworth (earl of Stafford) and John Pym, and acted as an intermediary between Scottish and English leaders during English Civil War; was imprisoned in Tower of London (1649–50) and died 10 years later; distinguished by beauty and wit, inspired a number of English poets, including Thomas Carew, John Suckling, Robert Herrick, Edmund Waller, and William D'Avenant.

HAY, Mary (1901–1957). American musical-comedy actress and dancer. Born Mary Hay Caldwell, Aug 22, 1901, in Fort Bliss, TX; died June 4, 1957, in Inverness, California; trained at Denishawn school in Los Angeles, then studied with Ned Wayburn; m. Richard Barthelmess (actor), 1920 (div. 1927); m. David Bath. ❖ Made NY debut in chorus of *Ziegfeld Midnight Frolics of 1918*; played title role in musical *Mary Jane McKane* (1922) and appeared in vaudeville with Clifton Webb; silent films include *Way Down East* and *No Toys*; co-wrote *Greater Love* and *She's No Lady*.

HAY, Mary Garrett (1857–1928). American suffragist and temperance reformer. Born Aug 29, 1857, in Charlestown, Indiana; died Aug 29, 1928, in New Rochelle, NY; dau. of Andrew Jennings Hay (physician and Republican politician) and Rebecca H. (Garrett) Hay; attended Western College for Women, 1873–74; lived with Carrie Chapman Catt. ❖ Formed close association with Carrie Chapman Catt and assisted her with formation of Organization Committee of National American Woman Suffrage Association (1895); with Catt, traveled 13,000 miles, visiting 20 states to organize women's groups (1899); a dedicated Republican, was chair of the Republican National Convention's strategic platform committee (1918)—an unprecedented appointment for a woman—and obtained a plank that endorsed the federal suffrage amendment; once the women's suffrage amendment passed in Congress (June 1919), threw energies into campaigning for its ratification in state legislatures; was chair of Republican Women's National Executive Committee (1919–20) and chair of NYC League of Women Voters (1918–23); also served as chair of Women's Committee for Law Enforcement in fight to enforce prohibition. ❖ See also *Women in World History*.

HAY, Timothy (1910–1952). See Brown, Margaret Wise.

HAY, Vanessa Briscoe (1955—). American singer. Name variations: Vanessa Briscoe, Vanessa Ellison; Pylon. Born Vanessa Briscoe, Oct 18, 1955, in Atlanta, Georgia; m. Bob Hay (guitarist for band, Squalls). ❖ As vocalist for funk-rock band Pylon (formed in Athens, GA, 1979), released successful 1st single, "Cool," backed by "Dub," and went on to release *Gyrate* (1980) and *Chomp* (1983); after Pylon disbanded (1984), reunited for a tour (1988) and the record *Chain* (1990); said to now be registered nurse.

HAYA, Maria Eugenia (1944–1991). See Marucha.

HAYAKAWA, Mrs. Sessue (1892–1961). *See Aoki, Tsuru.*

HAYAKAWA, Tsuru Aoki (1892–1961). *See Aoki, Tsuru.*

HAYASHI, Fumiko (1903–1951). Japanese writer. Pronunciation: HAH-yah-SHE FOO-me-KOE. Born in Yamaguchi Prefecture, Japan, 1903; died 1951; 4th illeg. child of Hayashi Kiku (mother) and Miyata Asataro (father), itinerant peddlers; graduate of Onomichi Higher Girls' School in Hiroshima Prefecture, Japan; m. Tezuka Ryokubin (a painter), 1926. ❖ The 1st woman fiction writer in modern Japan, enjoyed both popular success and critical recognition during a 20-year career; lived in and wrote about the margins of Japanese life, having worked as a maid and as a factory worker on a night shift; published 1st book, *Vagabond's Song* (1930); masterpiece novel, *Ukigumo* (*The Floating Cloud*, 1950), was based on her travels to Southeast Asia. ❖ See also *Women in World History.*

HAYASHI, Kyoko (1930—). Japanese novelist. Born 1930 in Nagasaki, Japan. ❖ Lived in Shanghai, China (1931–45), but returned to Nagasaki just before the dropping of atomic bomb; writings, which describe devastation of radiation sickness and dangers of nuclear power, include *The Ritual of Death, Round Dance,* and *Home in This World.* Received Gunzo Prize for a New Writer and Akutagawa Prize (1975).

HAYCRAFT, Alice (1932—). *See Haycraft, Anna Margaret.*

HAYCRAFT, Anna Margaret (1932–2005). British novelist. Name variations: Anna Margaret Haycraft; (pseudonyms) Alice Haycraft; Alice Thomas Ellis. Born Anna Margaret Lindholm, Sept 9, 1932, in Liverpool, England; died Mar 8, 2005; dau. of John and Alexandra Lindholm; grew up in Penmaenmawr, North Wales; attended Liverpool School of Art; m. Colin Haycraft (owner of Duckworth publishing), 1956; children: 7 (2 of whom died young). ❖ Served as fiction editor at Gerald Duckworth & Co.; published novels under pseudonym Alice Thomas Ellis; works, which are often set in Wales and combine realism and satire with supernatural and mystical elements, include *The Sin Eater* (1977), *The Birds of the Air* (1980), *The 27th Kingdom* (1982), *The Other Side of the Fire* (1985), *Unexplained Laughter* (1985), *Home Life* (1986), *Pillars of Gold* (1992), and *Fairy Tale* (1996); her trilogy, *The Clothes in the Wardrobe* (1987), *The Skeleton in the Cupboard* (1988), and *The Fly in the Ointment* (1989), was filmed for tv as "The Summerhouse," starring Jeanne Moreau; worked as journalist for *The Universe* (1989–91), *Catholic Herald,* and *Oldie*; wrote "Home Life" column for *The Spectator* (1985–89). ❖ See also memoir *A Welsh Childhood.*

HAYDÉE, Marcia (1939—). Brazilian dancer and director. Name variations: Marcia Haydee. Born Marcia Pereira da Silva in Niteroi, Brazil, April 18, 1939; studied with Yvonne Gama e Silva, Yucco Lindberg, and Vaslav Veltchek, as well as at Sadler's Wells Ballet (1954–55). ❖ One of the greatest ballerinas of her day, made professional debut with Ballet Madeleine Rosay in Quitandinha, Petropolis, and danced with Rio de Janeiro Teatro Municipal (1953); joined Grand Ballet of Marquis de Cuevas (1957), soon becoming a soloist; moved to Stuttgart Opera Ballet (1961), where, under direction of John Cranko, created roles in *Romeo and Juliet* (1962), *Onegin* (1965), *Carmen* (1971), and *Initials R.B.M.E.* (1972); appointed artistic director of Stuttgart Ballet (1976), set about expanding the repertoire; retired from the Stuttgart (1996), after 35 years.

HAYDEN, Anna Tompson (1648–after 1720). American poet. Born 1648 in Braintree, Massachusetts; died after 1720; sister of Benjamin Tompson. ❖ Only poem extant is "Verses on Benjamin Tompson."

HAYDEN, Esther Allen (c. 1713–1758). American poet. Born c. 1713 in Braintree, MA; died 1758; dau. of Samuel Allen; m. Samuel Hayden; children: 9. ❖ Composed poem on deathbed (1759), which was published posthumously in *A Short Account of the Life, Death and Character of Esther Hayden* as "Composed About Six Weeks Before Her Death, When Under Distressing Circumstances."

HAYDEN, Mary (1862–1942). Irish historian, senator, and campaigner for women's educational rights. Born Mary Teresa Hayden in Dublin, Ireland, May 19, 1862; died in Dublin, July 12, 1942; dau. of Thomas Hayden (professor of anatomy at Catholic University) and Mary Anne (Ryan) Hayden; educated at Alexandra College, Dublin; Royal University of Ireland, BA (1st class honors), 1885, and MA (1st class honors), 1887; never married. ❖ Elected to a senior fellowship in History and English at Royal University (1895), was forced to accept a demotion to junior fellowship because, as a woman, she could not deliver senior fellowship lectures at University College Dublin (UCD); elected vice-president of newly formed Association of Women Graduates (1902); when National University of Ireland was established (1908), was 1st woman member of its senate, then appointed Professor of Modern Irish History at UCD (1911), now a constituent college of the new university, a post she held until 1938; was active in the cause of women's suffrage and also involved in Irish language movement with Patrick Pearse; in middle of Irish war of independence, published, with George A. Moonan, *A Short History of the Irish People from the Earliest Times to 1920* (1921) which became the most widely used school and college text in Irish history. ❖ See also *Women in World History.*

HAYDEN, Mother Mary Bridget (1814–1890). Irish-born American missionary. Name variations: Sister Mary Bridget. Born Margaret Bridget Hayden, Aug 26, 1814, in Kilkenny, Ireland; died Jan 23, 1890, at Osage Mission, Kansas (later Oklahoma); dau. of Thomas Hayden (died 1830) and Bridget (Hart) Hayden. ❖ Received habit from Sisters of Loretto order (1841) and served under name Sister Mary Bridget at Ste. Genevieve, Missouri, and Loretto, Kentucky (1840s); journeyed by boat and lumber wagon to Osage Mission (later Saint Paul), Kansas, to instruct Indian girls (1847); became superior of Osage Mission (1859) and acted as mother and nurse in addition to teacher; known as "Medicine Woman" for compassionate care of those afflicted by rugged mission life. Also served as superior of St. Vincent's Academy in Cape Girardeau for 4 years (1863–67). ❖ See also William W. Craves, *Life and Times of Mother Bridget Hayden* (1938).

HAYDEN, Melissa (1923—). Canadian-born ballerina. Born Mildred Herman, April 25, 1923, in Toronto, Canada; dau. of Jacob and Kate Herman; attended Lansdowne Street elementary school; studied ballet with Boris Volkoff, Anatole Vilzak and Ludmila Schollar; m. Donald Hugh Coleman Jr., Feb 1954; children: Stuart. ❖ Became a member of Radio City Music Hall corps de ballet (1945), then joined Ballet Theatre (later American Ballet Theatre) corps de ballet and rose swiftly to rank of soloist; made triumphant debut with Balanchine's New York City Ballet in *The Duel* (1950); went on to perform in numerous ballets, including *The Miraculous Mandarin* (1951), *The Pied Piper* (1951), *Caracole* (1952), and *The Cage* (1952); aside from a brief return to American Ballet Theatre, and various guest appearances with Chicago Opera Ballet, spent career at New York City Ballet; appeared in Chaplin's film *Limelight* (1952), doubling for Claire Bloom in the dance sequence; also appeared on "Kate Smith Show," one of the earliest performances of classical ballet on tv (1952); made acclaimed appearances in *Ivesiana* (1955), *Still Point* (1956), and in premiere of Balanchine's *Divertimento No. 15* (1956); also danced in *Agon* (1957), *Stars and Stripes* (1958), *A Midsummer Night's Dream* (1962), and *In the Night* (1970) and frequently guest starred with other ballet companies, including National Ballet of Canada, Royal Ballet of London and Cullberg Ballet of Stockholm; retired (1973). Received Albert Einstein Award (1962). ❖ See also *Melissa Hayden—Off Stage and On* (1963); and *Women in World History.*

HAYDEN, Sophia (1868–1953). American architect. Born in Santiago, Chile, Oct 17, 1868; died of pneumonia, Feb 3, 1953; dau. of Dr. George Henry Hayden (New England dentist) and his Spanish wife (name unknown); graduated with honors from Massachusetts Institute of Technology, 1890; m. William Blackstone Bennett (artist), by 1900 (died 1913); children: (stepdaughter) Jennie Bennett (b. 1890). ❖ The 1st woman to graduate from the 4-year course in architecture at MIT, was also the 1st prizewinner in the contest to design the Woman's Building of the World's Columbian Exposition (1893). ❖ See also *Women in World History.*

HAYDOCK, Mary (1777–1855). *See Reibey, Mary.*

HAYDON, Ann (1938—). *See Jones, Ann Haydon.*

HAYDON, Ethel (1878–1954). Australian actress and singer. Born June 13, 1878, in Melbourne, Australia; died Jan 1954; dau. of Thomas Haydon (secretary of Victorian Club); m. George Robey. ❖ Made stage debut in Melbourne in *In Honor Bound* (1893), followed by *Jo, On Change, The Morals of Mayfair, The Grasshopper* and *Friends,* among others; made London debut as Alice in *Dandy Dick Whittington* (1895), then appeared as Bessie Brent in *The Shop Girl*; performed in several pantomimes and at various music halls; retired (1902).

HAYDON, Julie (1910–1994). American actress. Born Donella Lightfoot Donaldson, June 10, 1910, in Oak Park, Illinois; died of abdominal cancer, Dec 24, 1994, in La Crosse, Wisconsin; dau. of Orren Madison (editor and publisher) and Ella Marguerite (Horton) Donaldson (musician and music critic); attended Gordon School for Girls, Hollywood;

m. George Jean Nathan (drama critic), June 19, 1955 (died April 8, 1958); no children. ❖ Made stage debut as the maid in West Coast production of *Mrs. Bumpstead-Leigh* (1929), and played minor roles in films during 1930s; made NY stage debut as Hope Blake in *Bright Star* (1935); appeared in *Shadow and Substance* (1938) and *The Time of Your Life* (1939), but is best remembered as the original Laura in *The Glass Menagerie* (1945). ❖ See also *Women in World History.*

HAYE, Charlotte de la (1737–1805). *See Montesson, Charlotte Jeanne Béraud de la Haye de Riou, marquise de.*

HAYE, Helen (1874–1957). English stage and screen actress. Born Aug 28, 1874, in Assam, India; died Sept 1, 1957, in London, England; m. Ernest Attenborough. ❖ Had over 130 roles in a long, illustrious career; debuted on West End as Mrs. Holroyd in *The Way the Money Goes* (1910); other plays include *Hedda Gabler, Above Suspicion, Caesar's Wife* and *Command Performance*; toured Canada with Marie Löhr; appeared on Broadway in *The Last of Mrs. Cheyney, John Gabriel Borkman* and *After All*; last portrayal was the Dowager Empress in *Anastasia*; appeared in over 50 films, including *Masks and Faces, Bleak House, The 39 Steps, Drake of England, Richard III, Sidewalks of London* and *Anna Karenina.*

HAYE, Nicolaa de la (1160–1218). Sheriff of Lincolnshire. Born 1160 in Lincolnshire, England; died 1218 in Lincolnshire; heiress of the de la Haye barony and hereditary castellan of Lincoln; lived during reigns of Richard I and King John; m. Gerard de Camville. ❖ Inherited substantial wealth and property from father, including the post of castellan (constable of a castle) of Lincoln; several times, had to defend her castle and estates against enemies, most notably when the castle was placed under siege during rebellion of English barons against King John (1216); despite a breach in the walls, her forces captured half the knights in the rebel army and won a virtually bloodless victory. ❖ See also *Women in World History.*

HAYEK, Salma (1966—). Mexican actress. Born Salma Hayek-Jimenez, Sept 2, 1966, in Coatzacoalcos, Veracruz, Mexico; dau. of Lebanese father and Mexican-born mother; attended Universidad Iberoamericana. ❖ Appeared in title role of Mexican tv-series "Teresa" (1989); moved to Los Angeles (1990); had 1st decent role, opposite Antonio Banderas, in *Desperado*; won ALMA award as Best Actress for tv-movie "In the Time of the Butterflies" (2001); produced and starred in *Frida* (2002), for which she was nominated for an Academy Award for Best Actress; directed *The Maldonado Miracle* (2003); other films include *From Dusk Till Dawn, Fools Rush In, Breaking Up, Dogma, Wild Wild West, Once Upon a Time in Mexico, After the Sunset* and *Ask the Dust.*

HAYES, Allison (1930–1977). American actress. Born Mary Jane Haynes, Mar 6, 1930, in Charleston, WV; died Feb 27, 1977, in La Jolla, California, from blood poisoning. ❖ Began career as concert pianist; films include *Francis Joins the Wacs, So This Is Paris, Double Jeopardy, Mohawk, Steel Jungle, Counterplot, Who's Been Sleeping in My Bed?, Tickle Me* and *Attack of the 50-Foot Woman*, a cult favorite; was a regular on tv series "General Hospital."

HAYES, Catherine (1690–1726). English murderer. Born Catherine Hall near Birmingham, England, 1690; burned alive at stake at Tyburn, 1726; m. John Hayes (carpenter and merchant), 1713. ❖ Ran away from home at 15; secretly married John Hayes (1713); complained that her prosperous husband was miserly and beat her; when Thomas Billings, a young tailor, appeared at the door seeking lodging, convinced husband to rent him a room; became involved with Billings, as well as another lodger, Thomas Wood; convinced both to help kill husband, offering them part of his fortune; was arrested for the particularly grisly murder, a case that created a sensation; became the subject of many pamphlets and broadsheets. ❖ See also *Women in World History.*

HAYES, Catherine (1825–1861). Irish soprano. Name variations: Mrs. Bushnell. Born in Limerick, Ireland, Oct 29, 1825; died at Sydenham, Kent, England, Aug 11, 1861; studied in Dublin with Antonio Sapio and in Milan with Felici Ronconi; m. William Avery Bushnell (electioneering agent who became her manager), 1856 (died 1858). ❖ Made debut at Milan's La Scala (1845), then toured Vienna and Venice; made 1st appearance at London's Covent Garden (1849), performing in *Linda di Chamouni*; made triumphant tour of US (1851), followed by an extensive world tour, singing in South America, India, Polynesia, and Australia; returned to England (1856) where she enjoyed popularity as a ballad singer until her premature death at 36. ❖ See also *Women in World History.*

HAYES, Evelyn (1874–1945). *See Bethell, Mary Ursula.*

HAYES, Helen (1900–1993). American actress. Born Helen Hayes Brown, Oct 10, 1900, in Washington, DC; died Mar 17, 1993, in Nyack, NY; dau. of Catherine (Hayes) Brown and Francis Van Arnum Brown; graduate of Washington's Sacred Heart Academy, 1917; m. Charles MacArthur (playwright), 1928 (died 1956); children: Mary MacArthur (1930–1949); (adopted) James MacArthur (actor). ❖ Known as the first lady of the American stage, made Broadway debut at 9 in musical, *Old Dutch* (1909); came to prominence in *Dear Brutus* (1918); appeared to good reviews in *What Every Woman Knows* (1926) and *Coquette* (1927); won Academy Award for Best Actress for *The Sin of Madelon Claudet* (1932), before returning triumphantly to Broadway as Mary Stuart in Anderson's *Mary, Queen of Scotland* (1933), followed by what is considered her finest role in *Victoria Regina* (1935); further triumphs included *Harriet* (1943), *Happy Birthday* (1947), for which she won her 1st Tony, and *The Wisteria Trees* (1950); appeared as the Grand Duchess in film of *Anastasia* (1956), then won 2nd Tony for *Time Remembered* (1958); ventured into tv, appearing with son James on an episode of "Hawaii Five-O" and with Mildred Natwick in mystery series, "The Snoop Sisters"; retired from the stage (1971); continued to work sporadically in films and tv for next 20 years, as well as publishing 6 volumes of memoirs and co-writing a novel. Won Academy Award as Best Supporting Actress for work as Ada Quonset in *Airport* (1971); received National Medal of the Arts from Ronald Reagan (1988). ❖ See also (with Katherine Hatch) *My Life in Three Acts* (Harcourt, 1990); and *Women in World History.*

HAYES, Joanna (1976—). American hurdler. Born Dec 23, 1976, in Williamsport, Pennsylvania; attended University of California, Los Angeles. ❖ Won gold medal at Pan Am 400-meter hurdles (2003); won a gold medal for 100-meter hurdles at Athens Olympics (2004), the 2nd American to win that event in history.

HAYES, Lucy Webb (1831–1889). American first lady. Born Lucy Ware Webb, Aug 28, 1831, in Chillicothe, Ohio; died June 25, 1889; dau. of Dr. James Webb and Maria (Cook) Webb; graduated with honors from Ohio Wesleyan Female College, 1852; m. Rutherford Birchard Hayes (19th president of US), Dec 30, 1852; children: Birchard Austin Hayes (1853–1926); Webb Cook Hayes (1856–1935, who became 1st presidential son to win Congressional Medal of Honor); Rutherford Platt Hayes (1858–1927); Frances, known as Fanny Hayes (1867–1950); Scott Russell Hayes (1871–1923); and 3 who died in infancy. ❖ When husband was governor of Ohio, traveled through state visiting prisons and mental hospitals; during his presidential campaign (1876), was lauded for her ability to talk astutely about politics; dubbed "Lemonade Lucy," for her pro-temperance stand, but never officially joined Women's Christian Temperance Union (WCTU), possibly because she had slightly more tolerance for the opposition than husband; though known to favor women's suffrage, opted for a less controversial role in White House, aligning herself with such social issues as Native American welfare, veterans' benefits, and rehabilitation of the defeated South. ❖ See also *Women in World History.*

HAYES, Maggie (1916–1977). American stage, tv and screen actress. Name variations: Margaret Hayes, Dana Dale. Born Florette Regina Ottenheimer, Dec 5, 1916, in Baltimore, MD; died Jan 26, 1977, in Miami Beach, FL; m. Leif Erickson (actor), 1942 (div. 1942); m. Herbert Bayard Swope Jr., 1947 (div. 1973); children: 3, including Tracy Brooks Swope (actress). ❖ Broadway credits include *Many Happy Returns, Little Women, Step on a Crack* and *Fair Game for Lovers*; films include *Sullivan's Travels, The Glass Key, Omar Khayyam, Fraulein, The Beat Generation* and *House of Women*; before acting career, was a fashion model, fashion editor for *Life* magazine, director of special events for Bergdorf Goodman, designer of jewelry and owner of a boutique. Nominated for Academy Award for *Blackboard Jungle.*

HAYES, Margaret (1916–1977). *See Hayes, Maggie.*

HAYES, Mary (1754–1832). *See McCauley, Mary Hays Ludwig.*

HAYES, Nevada (1885–1941). Duchess of Oporto. Born Nevada Stoody, Oct 21, 1885, in Ohio; died Jan 11, 1941; m. Lee Agnew; m. William Henry Chapman; m. Philip van Volkenburgh; m. Alfonso (1865–1920), duke of Oporto, on Sept 26, 1917.

HAYES, Patricia (1909–1998). English stage, tv and screen actress. Born Patricia Lawlor Hayes, Dec 22, 1909, in Camberwell, London, England; died Sept 19, 1998, in London; m. Valentine Rooke, 1939 (div. 1951); children: 3, including actor Richard O'Callaghan. ❖ As a child, made

London stage debut in *The Great Big World* (1921), followed by *Eileen, The White Devil* and *The Blue Bird*; attended RADA, winning the Bancroft gold medal (1928); as an adult, appeared in *The Glory of the Sun, Jean de la Lune, The Tidings Brought to Mary* and *Night Must Fall* (as Dora Parkoe); created role of Frankie in *George and Margaret* (1937) and was highly successful as Ruby Birtle in *When We Are Married* on stage and in film (1938); on tv, appeared regularly on "Benny Hill," as Min on "Till Death," and starred in "The Trouble with Lilian" and "The Last of the Baskets" (both 1971); headed the Catholic Actors Guild in Britain for many years. Named Officer of the British Empire (OBE, 1987).

HAYES, Patty (1955—). American golfer. Born Jan 22, 1955, in Hoboken, NJ. ❖ Won Sun City Classic (1981); played on LPGA tour (1974–96).

HAYES, Rosa (c. 1843–1864). *See Buckingham, Rosetta.*

HAYGOOD, Laura Askew (1845–1900). American educator and missionary. Born Laura Askew Haygood, Oct 14, 1845, in Watkinsville, Georgia; died April 29, 1900, in Shanghai, China; dau. of Greene B. Haygood (lawyer, died 1862) and Martha Ann (Askew) Haygood (schoolteacher); sister of Atticus Green Haygood; graduate of Wesleyan Female College, 1864. ❖ Served as principal of Atlanta Girls' High School (1877–84); placed in charge of missionary work in Shanghai by Woman's Board of Foreign Missions of the Methodist Church, South (1844); in Shanghai, supervised several schools; helped found McTyeire Home and School (1892), which became a top-ranking private girls' high school in Shanghai until it was closed by Communist government (1949).

HAYLES, Alice (d. after 1326). Countess of Norfolk. Name variations: Alice Italys. Died after May 8, 1326; dau. of Roger Hayles; m. Thomas of Brotherton, earl of Norfolk (son of King Edward I and Margaret of France [1282–1318]), around 1316; children: Edward Plantagenet (c. 1319–c. 1332); Margaret, duchess of Norfolk (c. 1320–1400); Alice Plantagenet (d. 1351).

HAYMAN, Lillian (1922–1994). African-American stage, tv, and screen actress and singer. Born July 17, 1922, in Baltimore, MD; died Oct 25, 1994, in Hollis, NY. ❖ Made stage debut in NY as Momma in *Dream about Tomorrow* (1947), followed by *Kiss Me Kate, Show Boat, Kwamina, 70 Girls 70, No No Nanette* and *Along Came a Spider*; also toured internationally with *Porgy and Bess* for over 3 years; films include *The Night They Raided Minsky's, Mandingo* and *Drum*. Won a Tony Award as Best Actress in a Musical for *Hallelujah Baby* (1968).

HAYNAU, Edith von (1894–1978). *See von Haynau, Edith.*

HAYNE, Julia Dean (1830–1868). *See Dean, Julia.*

HAYNES, Elizabeth Ross (1883–1953). African-American social worker, sociologist, author. Born Elizabeth Ross, July 30, 1883, in Lowndes Co., Alabama; died Oct 26, 1953, in New York, NY; dau. of Henry and Mary (Carnes) Ross (former slaves); Fisk University, AB, 1903; Columbia University, AM in sociology, 1923; m. George Edmund Haynes (sociologist and a founder of National Urban League), Dec 14, 1910; children: George Edmund Haynes Jr. (b. 1912). ❖ Began longstanding association with Young Women's Christian Association (YWCA) when she became its 1st black national secretary (1908); published watershed study on black women and employment, "Two Million Negro Women at Work" (1922); as 1st black woman elected to national board of YWCA, served 1924–34; elected co-leader of NY's 21st Assembly District (1935), tackling unemployment, assistance to elderly, soldiers' and widows' pensions, delinquency and legislation; was a member of the Colored Division of National Democratic Speakers Bureau (1936); appointed to NY State Temporary Commission on the Condition of the Urban Colored Population (1937); wrote *Unsung Heroes* (1921) and *The Black Boy of Atlanta* (1952). ❖ See also *Women in World History.*

HAYNES, Margery (fl. 15th c.). English businesswoman. Fl. in Wiltshire, England. ❖ Widow and entrepreneur of Wiltshire, was left with 3 grain mills when husband died; expanded the business, reinvesting wisely and eventually building a small shop with profits. ❖ See also *Women in World History.*

HAYNIE, Sandra B. (1943—). American golfer. Born Sandra Jane Haynie, June 4, 1943, in Fort Worth, TX; daughter of Jim Haynie (golfer). ❖ Entered 1st golf tournament at 11 (1954); captured 1st of 5 consecutive Austin City Women's golf titles (1956); turned pro (1961); won Texas State Publinx (1957, 1958), Texas Amateur (1958, 1959), Austin Civitan Open and Cosmopolitan Open (1962), Phoenix

Thunderbird Open (1963), Baton Rouge Open and Las Cruces Open (1964), Cosmopolitan Open and LPGA championship (1965), Buckeye Savings Invitational, Glass City Classic, Alamo Open, and Pensacola Invitational (1966), Amarillo Open and Mickey Wright Invitational (1967), Pacific Open (1968), St. Louis Invitational, Supertest Open, and Shreveport Kiwanis Invitational (1969), Raleigh Invitational and Shreveport Kiwanis Invitational (1970), Burdines Invitational, Dallas Civitan Open, San Antonio Alamo Open, and Lem Immke Buick Open (1971), National Jewish Hospital Open, Quality First Classic, and Lincoln-Mercury Open (1972), Orange Blossom Classic, Lincoln-Mercury Open, Charity Golf Classic (1973), Lawson's Open, George Washington Classic, National Jewish Hospital Open, Charity Golf Classic, LPGA championship, and US Women's Open (1974), Naples-Lely Classic, Charity Golf Classic, Jacksonville Open, and Ft. Myers Classic (1975), Henredon Classic (1981), Rochester International and Peter Jackson Classic (1982). Inducted into LPGA Hall of Fame (1977) and Texas Golf Hall of Fame (1984). ❖ See also *Women in World History.*

HAYS, Cherie Currie (1959—). *See Currie, Cherie.*

HAYS, Mary (1754–1832). *See McCauley, Mary Hays Ludwig.*

HAYS, Mary (1760–1843). English novelist and feminist. Name variations: (pseudonym) Eusebia. Born in Southwark, London, England, 1760; died in London, 1843; never married; no children. ❖ Member of a Dissenting family, gained notoriety with her defense of public worship, *Cursory Remarks* (1792), published under pseudonym Eusebia, which brought her to the attention of some of the eminent radicals of the day, including Mary Wollstonecraft, who became her friend and mentor; subsequent writings include *Memoirs of Emma Courtney* (1796), *The Victim of Prejudice* (1799), *Female Biography* (1803), a 6-volume work on significant women, and 2 collections of morality tales, *The Brothers; or Consequences* (1815) and *Family Annals; or The Sisters* (1817). ❖ See also *Women in World History.*

HAYSOM, Esther (1900–1990). *See James, Esther Marion Pretoria.*

HAYWARD, Lillie (1891–1978). American screenwriter. Born Sept 12, 1891, in St. Paul, Minnesota; died June 29, 1977, in Hollywood, CA; m. Jerry Sackheim. ❖ Began career as script editor; as screenwriter, spent many years under contract with Warner Bros., specializing in action films; later worked for Paramount, RKO, and Disney; films include *Janice Meredith, Driftwood, Front Page Woman, The Walking Dead, Penrod and Sam, Sons of the Legion, Aloma of the South Seas, My Friend Flicka, Black Beauty, Cattle Drive, Tarzan and the Lost Safari, The Shaggy Dog, Tonka, Toby Tyler* and *Lad: A Dog.*

HAYWARD, Susan (1917–1975). American actress. Born Edythe Marrener in Brooklyn, NY, June 30, 1917; died in Los Angeles, CA, Mar 14, 1975; dau. Walter (transit worker) and Ellen (Pearson) Marrener; m. Jeffrey (Jess) Thomas Barker (actor), July 23, 1944 (div. 1956); m. Eaton Chalkley (lawyer and businessman), Feb 8, 1957 (died 1966); children: (1st m.) twins, Timothy and Gregory (b. 1955). ❖ Made film debut in *Beau Geste* (1939), followed by 16 other movies, only 3 of which—*Adam Had Four Sons* (1941), *Reap the Wild Wind* (1942), and *The Hairy Ape* (1944)—are noteworthy; beginning 1945, made a series of pictures with independent producer Walter Wanger, including *The Lost Moment* (1947) and *Smash-Up: The Story of a Woman* (1947), the 1st film to showcase her talent in what would become her trademark role as the feisty woman who triumphs over adversity and for which she received the 1st of her 5 Academy Award nominations; received 2nd Academy Award nomination for *My Foolish Heart* (1950); earned 3 subsequent Oscar nominations, all for roles based on actual women: *With a Song in My Heart* (1952) recounts the life of Jane Froman, *I'll Cry Tomorrow* (1956) recalls the downfall of Lillian Roth, and *I Want to Live!* (1958) details the death of Barbara Graham; won an Academy Award for *I Want to Live!*; other films include *David and Bathsheba* (1951), *The Snows of Kilimanjaro* (1952), *The President's Lady* (1953), *Soldier of Fortune* (1955), *The Conqueror* (1956), *The Marriage-Go-Round* (1961), *Back Street* (1961), *Valley of the Dolls* (1967) and *The Revengers* (1972). ❖ See also Beverly Linet, *Susan Hayward: Portrait of a Survivor* (Atheneum, 1980) and LaGuardia and Arceri, *Red: The Tempestuous Life of Susan Hayward* (Macmillan, 1985); and *Women in World History.*

HAYWOOD, Claire (c. 1916–1978). American ballet teacher. Born c. 1916, in Atlanta, Georgia; died Sept 23, 1978, in Washington, DC; attended Spellman College and Howard University. ❖ With Doris

Jones, co-founded Jones-Haywood School of Ballet (1941) and Capitol Ballet, both in Washington, DC (1961), where their students included a generation of black dancers.

HAYWOOD, Eliza (c. 1693–1756). English novelist and playwright. Name variations: Eliza Heywood. Born Eliza Fowler in London, England, c. 1693; died Feb 25, 1756; dau. of London tradesman named Fowler; m. Reverend Valentine Haywood, 1717 (sep. 1721); children: 2. ❧ Surfaced on stage as an actress in Dublin (1714), then moved to London; wrote 1st original play, *A Wife to be Lett,* which opened at Drury Lane (1723); also collaborated on adaptation of Henry Fielding's *Tom Thumb*; published *Love in Excess, or the Fatal Enquiry* (1719–1720), which met with substantial commercial success, then wrote nearly 40 sensational and sizable novels, many based on social scandals of the day, including *Letters from a Lady of Quality to a Chevalier* (1720), *British Recluse* (1722), *The Injur'd Husband* (1722) and *Eovaai* (1736). ❧ See also G.F. Whicher, *The Life and Romances of Eliza Haywood* (1915); and *Women in World History.*

HAYWORTH, Rita (1918–1987). American actress. Name variations: Rita Cansino. Born Margarita Carmen Cansino, Oct 17, 1918, in New York, NY; stricken with Alzheimer's, 1981, lived under care of 2nd daughter until her death, May 14, 1987, in New York, NY; dau. of Eduardo Cansino and Volga (Haworth) Cansino (both Spanish dancers); attended high school to 9th grade in Los Angeles; m. Edward C. Judson, 1936 (div. 1942); m. Orson Welles (actor-director), Sept 7, 1943 (div.); m. Ali Shah Khan, 1949 (div. 1953); m. Dick Haymes (singer), 1953 (div. 1955); m. James Hill, Feb 2, 1958 (div. 1961); children: (with Welles) Rebecca Welles; (with Ali Shah Khan) Princess Yasmin Aga Khan. ❧ One of the most enduring of Hollywood legends, began career dancing with father as the Dancing Cansinos; made film debut as Rita Cansino in supporting role in *Dante's Inferno* (1935); signed 7-year contract with Columbia and appeared in *Girls Can Play* (1937); came to prominence as the adulterous wife in Hawks' *Only Angels Have Wings* (1939), followed by *The Strawberry Blonde* (1941) and *Blood and Sand* (1941); after *Life* published a photo of her clad in a negligee that many US soldiers carried with them during WWII, was elevated to status of "cultural icon" (1941); starred in *You'll Never Get Rich* (1941), *You Were Never Lovelier* (1942), *Cover Girl* (1944), and *Gilda* (1946), for which she is best remembered for her striptease with elbow-length gloves while singing "Put the Blame on Mame"; other films include *Tonight and Every Night* (1945), *The Lady from Shanghai* (1948), *Salome* (1953), *Miss Sadie Thompson* (1953), *Fire Down Below* (1957), *Pal Joey* (1957), *Separate Tables* (1958), *They Came to Cordura* (1959) and *The Story on Page One* (1960). ❧ See also Barbara Leaming, *If This Was Happiness: A Biography of Rita Hayworth* (Viking, 1989); and *Women in World History.*

HAZA, Ofra (1957–2001). Israeli pop singer. Born Nov 19, 1957, to Yemenite Jewish Parents in Tel Aviv ghetto, Israel; died of AIDS-related pneumonia, Feb 23, 2000, in Tel Aviv; m. Doron Ashkenazi, 1997. ❧ At 12, joined Hatikva theater troupe; won Israeli music awards for albums recorded with troupe; served compulsory years in Israeli army (1977–78); became popular singer in Israel and surrounding Arab nations (1980s); won 2nd prize in annual Eurovision song contest (1983); recorded a collection of ancient melodies on album *Yemenite Songs* (1985); had worldwide hit with "Im nin alu" (1988); released 1st US album, *Shaday* (1989), followed by *Desert Wind* (1989), *Kirya* (1992), and *Ofra Haza* (1997); recorded single "Temple of Love" with Sisters of Mercy (1992); sang at Nobel Prize Ceremony (1994); sang on soundtrack to Disney's *Prince of Egypt* (1998); at death, eulogized by Israeli Prime Minister Enud Barak.

HAZAN, Adeline (1956—). French judge and politician. Born Jan 21, 1956, in Paris, France. ❧ Nominated to the National College for Judicial Officials (1980); judge for juvenile cases, Nanterre High Court (1983) and Paris High Court (1995); served as president of the Association of Judicial Officers (1986–89) and as Socialist Party national secretary responsible for social issues (1995—); elected to 5th European Parliament (1999–2004).

HAZARD, Caroline (1856–1945). American author and educator. Born June 10, 1856, in Peace Dale, Rhode Island; died Mar 19, 1945, in Santa Barbara, California; dau. of Rowland Hazard (owner of Peace Dale Woolen Mills) and Margaret Anna (Rood) Hazard; attended Miss Mary A. Shaw's School, Providence, Rhode Island, and private study abroad; never married; no children. ❧ The 5th president of Wellesley College, published volume of poetry *Narragansett Ballads* (1894); also became an authority on history of Rhode Island and wrote a bi-weekly

column in *Providence Evening Bulletin*; elected president of Wellesley College (1899), embarked on a development campaign and, over next 11 years, raised enough money for 5 dormitories, 5 academic buildings, library, gymnasium, observatory, botany building, music hall, and several residence halls; resigned (1910); continued publishing poetry and other books. ❧ See also *Women in World History.*

HAZELTINE, Mary (1868–1949). American librarian. Born Mary Emogene Hazeltine, May 5, 1868, in Jamestown, NY; died June 16, 1949, in Jamestown, NY; dau. of Abner Hazeltine (lawyer) and Olivia A. (Brown) Hazeltine; graduate of Wellesley College (1891). ❧ Worked 2 years as high school principal in Danielsville, Connecticut (early 1890s); became librarian of James Prendergast Free Library in Jamestown, NY (1893); helped Melvin Dewey organize Summer School for Library Training at Chautauqua, NY (1901), where she served as resident director for 4 years; elected president of NY State Library Association (1902); served as head of new Wisconsin Library School in Madison (1906–37), which was designated "school of library science" of University of Wisconsin (1909). Over 1,000 students graduated from Library School during her tenure as principal. Wrote *Anniversaries and Holidays* (1909) and *One Hundred Years of Wisconsin Authorship, 1836–1937* (1937), one of the earliest regional bibliographies.

HAZEN, Elizabeth Lee (1883–1975). American scientist. Name variations: Lee Hazen. Born Elizabeth Lee Hazen, Aug 24, 1883, in Coahoma County, Mississippi; died June 24, 1975, at Mount St. Vincent Hospital, Seattle; dau. of William Edgar Hazen (cotton farmer) and Maggie (Harper) Hazen, both of whom died before she was 3; raised by Uncle Robert Hazen and Aunt Laura (Crawford) Hazen; Columbia University, MA in biology, 1923, PhD in microbiology, 1929; never married; no children. ❧ Served as technician in Army diagnostic lab at Camp Sheridan, Alabama (1918–19); was assistant director of Clinical and Bacteriology Laboratory of Cook Hospital, Fairmont, WV (1919–23); appointed resident bacteriologist at Presbyterian Hospital (1928); was a member of teaching staff at College of Physicians and Surgeons, Columbia University (1929); took charge of bacterial diagnosis lab at NY State Department of Health, Division of Laboratories and Research (1931); paired with chemist Rachel Fuller Brown to find antifungal agents (1948); with Brown, discovered nystatin (1950), the 1st highly active antifungal agent to be found safe and effective for use in humans; with Brown, applied for patent and assigned rights and royalties of nystatin to establish the Brown-Hazen Fund (1951); with Brown, discovered the antibacterial agent phalamycin (1953) and antifungal agent capacidin (1959). Received Squibb Award in Chemotherapy (1955), Rhoda Benham Award of Medical Mycology Society of the Americas (1972), and Chemical Pioneer Award (1975). ❧ See also Richard S. Baldwin, *The Fungus Fighters* (Cornell University, 1981); and *Women in World History.*

HAZLETT, Olive C. (1890–1974). American mathematician. Born Olive Clio Hazlett in Cincinnati, Ohio, 1890; died 1974; Radcliffe College, BA, 1912; University of Chicago, SM, 1913, PhD, 1915. ❧ One of the most notable American women in the field of mathematics, wrote master's thesis and doctoral dissertation on linear associative algebras; began academic career at Harvard (1915–16) as an Alice Freeman Palmer Fellow of Wellesley College; taught at Bryn Mawr (1916–18); was assistant professor at Mount Holyoke, where she shifted attention to modular invariants and covariants (1918–25); moved to University of Illinois (1925); was a cooperating editor of *Transactions of the American Mathematical Society* (1923–35) and also served on their council for 2 years. ❧ See also *Women in World History.*

HAZRAT MAHAL (c. 1820–1879). Begum of Oudh and Muslim queen-mother. Name variations: surname reportedly Iftikarun-nisa; took name Hazrat Mahal, Begum ("honored lady") of Oudh, when raised to status of King's Wife after birth of son. Born c. 1820 in Faizabad, Oudh (or Oudhad), India (modern-day Awadh); died 1879 while in exile in Nepal; m. Wajid Ali Shah (king of Oudh, deposed by British for incompetence, 1857); children: Mohd Ramzan Ali Bahadur Birgis Qadr (b. around 1845 and crowned king of Oudh in July 1857). ❧ In the name of underage son, led local resistance against the British East India Company during the Indian Mutiny, or Sepoy War as Victorians often called it (1857–58); born into a poor family (c. 1820), trained as a dancing girl; entered harem of Wajid Ali Shah some time before 1845; gave birth to son Birgis Qadr, possibly after a liaison with Mammu Khan (c. 1845); led resistance in Oudh after arrest of husband (1857–59); driven into exile in Nepal and died there (1879). ❧ See also *Women in World History.*

HAZZARD, Shirley (1931—). Australian novelist and short-story writer. Born Jan 30, 1931, in Sydney, Australia; dau. of Reginald (government official) and Catherine (Stein) Hazzard; attended Queenswood College; m. Francis Steegmuller (writer), 1963 (died 1994). ❖ Worked for British Intelligence in Hong Kong (1947–48) and for British High Commissioner's Office, Wellington, New Zealand (1940–50); was general service category assistant, Technical Assistance to Underdeveloped Countries, at United Nations in NY (1952–62), serving in Italy (1957); became US citizen; wrote *Defeat of an Ideal: A Study of the Self-destruction of the United Nations* (1973); won National Book Award for *The Great Fire* (2003); other novels include *The Evening of the Holiday* (1966), *People in Glass Houses* (1967), *The Bay of Noon* (1970), and *The Transit of Venus* (1980); short-story collections include *Cliffs of Fall* (1963); nonfiction includes *Coming of Age in Australia* (1985), and *Countenance of Truth* (1990).

H.D. (1886–1961). *See Doolittle, Hilda.*

HE JIANPING (1963—). Chinese handball player. Born May 5, 1963, in China. ❖ At Los Angeles Olympics, won a bronze medal in team competition (1984).

HE JUN (1969—). Chinese basketball player. Born in China. ❖ At Barcelona Olympics, won a silver medal in team competition (1992).

HE LIPING. Chinese softball player. Born in China. ❖ Won a silver medal at Atlanta Olympics (1996).

HE QI (1973—). Chinese volleyball player. Born Aug 24, 1973, in China. ❖ Setter, joined the national team (1995); won a team silver medal at Atlanta Olympics (1996).

HE XIANGNING (1879–1972). Chinese revolutionary and feminist. Name variations: Ho Hsiang-ning. Born 1879 in Nanhai, Kwangtung, China; died 1972; dau. of a famous merchant; m. Liao Zhongkai (Liao Shung Kai or Liao Chung-k'ai), 1897 (killed 1925). ❖ Studied with husband in Japan where both joined a group led by Sun Yat-sen (1905); became one of 3 women in Guomindang Congress (1923) and was active in feminist politics; was one of the 1st to bob her hair as a gesture of independence; after assassination of husband, left job as head of women's department of Guomindang and went to Hong Kong with Song Qingling (Madame Sun Yat-sen); returned to Beijing (Peking) after the Revolution (1949) and became head of Overseas Chinese Affairs Commission until 1959 and honorary chair of the China Women's Federation (1960).

HE YANWEN (1966—). Chinese rower. Born Sept 29, 1966, in China. ❖ At Seoul Olympics, won a bronze medal in coxed eights (1988).

HE YING (1977—). Chinese archer. Born April 17, 1977, in Jilin, China; attended Jilin Institute of Physical Education. ❖ Won a silver medal for indiv. FITA round at Atlanta Olympics (1996); placed 1st for team at World championships (1999, 2001); won a silver medal for team at Athens Olympics (2004).

HE ZIZHEN (fl. 1930s). Chinese Communist and 3rd wife of Mao Zedong. Name variations: Ho Tzu-chen. Fl. in 1930s; m. Mao Zedong (1893–1976, founder of People's Republic of China), c. 1931 (div. 1937); children: 5. ❖ Was with Mao on the "Long March" (1934–35); is said to have suffered 20 shrapnel wounds but survived. ❖ See also *Women in World History.*

HEABURG (d. 751). *See Edburga.*

HEAD, Bessie (1937–1986). South African author. Born Bessie Amelia Emery, July 6, 1937, in Pietermaritzburg, South Africa; died in Botswana of hepatitis, April 17, 1986; dau. of Bessie Amelia "Toby" Birch (classified white) and unknown father (classified black under apartheid legislation); classified as "coloured"; raised by foster-parents Nellie and George Heathcote and in orphanages; affected by death of foster father and biological mother at age 7; educated at Umbilo Road High School; trained as primary teacher; m. Harold Head (journalist), Sept 1, 1961 (sep. soon after and later div.); children: Howard Head. ❖ Internationally recognized South African author who lived as an exile in Botswana for 15 years before being granted citizenship; taught primary school in South Africa and Botswana for 3 years; worked as journalist at Drum Publications in Johannesburg for 2 years; fled to Botswana (1964) and joined a refugee community at Bamangwato Development Farm; granted Botswanan citizenship (1979); worked as writer and unpaid agricultural worker in Botswana; published 1st novel, *When Rain Clouds Gather* (1969); nominated for Jock Campbell Award for literature for *The Collector of Treasures*

and Other Botswana Village Tales (1978); published 6 full-length works, about 25 short stories, and 1 poem. A number of her unpublished stories and letters appeared posthumously, including 1 long work of fiction, *The Cardinals*; writings include the novels *Maru* (1971) and *A Question of Power* (1973) and historical chronicles *Serowe: Village of the Rain Wind* (1981) and *A Bewitched Crossroad: An African Saga* (1984). ❖ See also autobiography *A Woman Alone* (1993) and *A Gesture of Belonging: Letters from Bessie Head, 1965–1979* (1991); Gillian S. Eilersen, *Bessie Head: Thunder Behind Her Ears* (Heinemann, 1996); Virginia Uzoma Ola, *The Life and Works of Bessie Head* (Mellen, 1994); and *Women in World History.*

HEAD, Edith (1897–1981). American costume designer. Name variations: Edith Spare. Born Edith Claire Posener in San Bernardino, California, Oct 28, 1897; died Oct 24, 1981; dau. of Max and Anna (Levy) Posener; following parents' divorce, adopted stepfather's surname Spare; graduate of University of California, Berkeley; Stanford University, MA; m. Charles Head, early 1920s (div. 1938); m. Bill (Wiard Boppo) Ihnen, Sept 8, 1940 (died 1979). ❖ Designer who greatly influenced fashion trends during 58-year career in film and won a record 8 Academy Awards while being nominated for 35; hired as sketch artist at Paramount (1923); became assistant designer (1929), then chief designer (1938); moved to Universal (1967); also worked at MGM, Warner Bros., Columbia and Fox; served as fashion editor of *Holiday* magazine; made many radio and tv appearances; won Academy Awards for costume design in black-and-white and color film (sometimes with associates as indicated): (with Gile Steele) *The Heiress* (1949), (with Charles LeMaire) *All About Eve* (1950), (with others) *Samson & Delilah* (1950), *A Place in the Sun* (1951), *Roman Holiday* (1953), *Sabrina* (1954), (with Edward Stevenson) *The Facts of Life* (1960) and *The Sting* (1973); nominations for Academy Awards for costume design in black-and-white and color include: *The Emperor Waltz* (1948), *Carrie* (1952), (with others) *The Greatest Show on Earth* (1955), *The Rose Tattoo* (1955), *To Catch a Thief* (1955), *The Proud and the Profane* (1956), (with others) *The Ten Commandments* (1956), (with Hubert de Givenchy) *Funny Face* (1957), (with others) *The Buccaneer* (1958), *Career* (1959), *The Five Pennies* (1959), *Pepe* (1960), *Pocketful of Miracles* (1961), *The Man Who Shot Liberty Valance* (1962), *My Geisha* (1962), *Love with the Proper Stranger* (1963), *A New Kind of Love* (1963), *Wives and Lovers* (1963), *A House Is Not a Home* (1964), (with Moss Mabry) *What a Way to Go* (1964), *The Slender Thread* (1965), (with Bill Thomas) *Inside Daisy Clover* (1965), *The Oscar* (1966), *Sweet Charity* (1969), *Airport* (1970) and *The Man Who Would Be King* (1975). ❖ See also (with Paddy Calistro) *Edith Head's Hollywood* (Dutton, 1983); and *Women in World History.*

HEAD, Pat (1952—). *See Summitt, Pat.*

HEADLEY, Lady (1857–1929). *See Baynton, Barbara.*

HEADY, Bonnie (1912–1953). American kidnapper. Name variations: Bonnie B. Heady. Born 1912; executed at State Penitentiary, Jefferson City, Missouri, Dec 18, 1953. ❖ Posing as aunt of 6-year-old Robert Greenlease Jr. (son of a wealthy Kansas City automobile dealer), kidnapped the boy (Sept 28, 1953); after her boyfriend Carl Austin Hall murdered the boy and buried him in her yard in St. Joseph, demanded and received $600,000 ransom; was deserted by Hall, who left her only $2,000 (Oct 5); with Hall, taken into custody (Oct 6), found guilty and received death penalty (Nov 19); executed with him in gas chamber. More than half of the $600,000 ransom was never located.

HEAL, Sylvia (1942—). Welsh politician and member of Parliament. Born Sylvia Fox, July 20, 1942; sister of Ann Keen (MP); m. Keith Heal, 1965. ❖ Representing Labour, lost bid to House of Commons for Mid Staffordshire (1992); elected to House of Commons for Halesowen and Rowley Regis (1997, 2001, 2005); named first deputy chair of Ways and Means committee (2000).

HEALEY, Eunice (c. 1920—). American tap dancer. Born c. 1920, in San Francisco, CA. ❖ Appeared in Fanchon and Marco West Coast units early in career; moved to NYC where she performed as tap dancer in *Girl Crazy* (1930); danced in many Broadway shows including *The Laugh Parade* (1931), *Two for the Show* (1940), *Hold Onto Your Hats* (1940) *and Beat the Band* (1942); toured with Benny Goodman, Glen Miller, and Artie Shaw orchestras; appeared in film *Follow Your Heart* (1936).

HEALY, Pamela (1963—). American yacht racer. Born June 24, 1963, in US. ❖ At Barcelona Olympics, won a bronze medal in 470 class (1992).

HEANEY, Geraldine (1967—). Irish-born Canadian ice-hockey player. Born Oct 1, 1967, in Ireland; lives in North York, Ontario. ❖ Won a team silver medal at Nagano (1998), the 1st Olympics to feature women's ice hockey; won team gold medals at World championships (1990, 1992, 1994, 1997, 2001); won a team gold medal at Salt Lake City Olympics (2002).

HEAP, Jane (1887–1964). American philanthropist and publisher. Name variations: jane heap. Born 1887; died 1964. ❖ Though Margaret Carolyn Anderson founded the *Little Review*, doubled as cook and editor in their office in Chicago as well as Greenwich Village; as a confirmed modernist, also exerted a profound influence on contents of journal. ❖ See also *Women in World History.*

HEAP, Marguerite (1871–1948). *See Moreno, Marguerite.*

HEAP, Sarah (1870–1960). New Zealand teacher. Name variations: Sarah Miller. Born Sarah Miller, Nov 27, 1870, in Ashton-under-Lyne, Lancashire, England; died on July 14, 1960; dau. of Henry Miller and Elizabeth Ann (Dixon) Miller; m. Henry Heap (master sadler), 1893 (died 1940). ❖ Immigrated with husband to New Zealand (c. 1904); considered New Zealand's preeminent expert on physical training of young women, administered physical training at Diocesan High School for Girls, Auckland (1908); gave classes for girls at Young Women's Christian Association (YWCA) and instructed physical culture and swimming to women students at Auckland Training College (1910). ❖ See also *Dictionary of New Zealand Biography* (Vol. 3).

HEARN, Mary Anne or Marianne (1834–1909). *See Farningham, Marianne.*

HEARNSHAW, Susan (1961—). English track-and-field athlete. Born May 26, 1961, in UK. ❖ At Los Angeles Olympics, won a bronze medal in the long jump (1984).

HEARST, Catherine Campbell (1917–1998). American philanthropist, socialite, and mother of prominent kidnap victim Patty Hearst. Born Catherine Wood Campbell, July 5, 1917, in Kentucky; died Dec 30, 1998, in Los Angeles, CA; graduate of Washington Seminary, 1930s; m. Randolph Hearst (president of the *San Francisco Examiner*), 1938 (div.); children: Catherine, Virginia, Anne, Victoria and Patricia Campbell Hearst (b. 1954). ❖ Lived life of a socialite and philanthropist, organizing events on behalf of several charities; a conservative Republican, was appointed to a 2-year replacement term on University of California board of regents (1956), where she remained for 20 years; supported restrictions forbidding Communists to speak on campus and was an advocate for removal of radical activist Angela Davis from teaching position; when the Symbionese Liberation Army kidnapped her daughter (1974), waited helplessly as daughter began to identify with captors and denounced her parents as "pigs" of wealth. ❖ See also *Women in World History.*

HEARST, Millicent (1882–1974). American socialite. Name variations: Millicent Willson; Mrs. William Randolph Hearst. Born 1882; died at home in New York, NY, Dec 1974; dau. of George H. Willson (popular vaudeville performer); younger sister of dancer Anita Willson; m. William Randolph Hearst (newspaper publisher), April 28, 1903; children: 5 sons, including George Hearst, John Randolph Hearst, and twins Elbert Willson Hearst and Randolph Apperson Hearst (b. 1915); grandmother of Patricia Campbell Hearst. ❖ At 16, met William Randolph Hearst while dancing with sister in *The Girl from Paris* at Herald Square Theater; when husband publicly pursued another chorine, Marion Davies, continued to hold head high; was a devoted war worker during WWI, heading women's division of Mayor's Committee on National Defense in NY; even though she would not grant husband a divorce, remained on friendly terms with him. ❖ See also *Women in World History.*

HEARST, Patricia Campbell (1954—). American kidnap victim turned bank robber. Name variations: Patty Hearst; Tania. Born Patricia Campbell Hearst, 1954, in San Francisco, CA; dau. of Randolph Apperson Hearst and Catherine (Campbell) Hearst (1917–1998); attended University of California at Berkeley; m. Bernard Shaw (her former bodyguard), 1979; children: daughter. ❖ Born into wealthy Hearst family, was kidnapped by Symbionese Liberation Army (SLA), an obscure terrorist group (Feb 1974); kept in a closet and brainwashed for 2 months while captors demanded a ransom of $2 million in food to be distributed to the poor, pledged allegiance to the SLA, calling herself "Tania"; participated in a robbery of Hibernia Bank in San Francisco; captured (Sept 18, 1975); after lengthy trial, received sentence of 7 years for armed robbery; had sentence commuted by President Jimmy Carter (Feb 1979). ❖ See also autobiography (with Alvin Moscow) *Every Secret Thing* (Doubleday, 1982); and *Women in World History.*

HEARST, Phoebe A. (1842–1919). American philanthropist. Born Phebe Apperson (given name was spelled Phebe until later years) in Franklin County, Missouri, Dec 3, 1842; died of influenza at home near Pleasanton, California, April 13, 1919; dau. of Randolph Walker Apperson and Drucilla (Whitmire) Apperson; m. George F. Hearst (US senator from California), June 15, 1861 (died 1891); children: William Randolph Hearst (b. 1863). ❖ Was active in charitable and philanthropic enterprises and gave extensively, especially to educational institutions; in San Francisco, established kindergarten classes for children of the poor, as well as a manual training school, and organized a number of working girls' clubs; built National Cathedral (Episcopal) School for Girls in Washington, DC; was a major contributor to restoration of Mount Vernon; turned attention to University of California at Berkeley, where she erected and equipped the mining building and was responsible for Hearst Hall; became a regent at the university (1897); also contributed to causes of archaeology and anthropology, financing expeditions to Italy, Mexico, Russia, and Egypt; distributed about $20 million to causes. ❖ See also *Women in World History.*

HEARST, Mrs. William Randolph (1882–1974). *See Hearst, Millicent.*

HEATH, Clarita (c. 1916–2003). American skier. Name variations: Clarita Heath Bright. Born Clarita Heath, c. 1916; died Oct 13, 2003 in Brookline, MA; m. William W. Reiter (Navy pilot killed in WWII); Alexander H. Bright (Olympic skier, died 1980); children: (1st m.) Candy Reiter Midkiff; (2nd m.) Cameron Bright and Sierra Heath Bright. ❖ Pioneer skier, was on 1st US Women's Olympic Ski Team (1936); placed 2nd in downhill at World championships (1937); taught skiing at Sun Valley. Inducted into US Ski Hall of Fame (1968).

HEATH, Mary (1896–1939). *See Heath, Sophie.*

HEATH, Sophie (1896–1939). Irish aviator. Name variations: Mary Peirce; Sophie Peirce; Sophie C. Elliott-Lynn or Sophie C. Elliott Lynn (wrongly seen as Elliot-Lynn and Eliott-Lynn); Lady Sophie Heath or Lady Mary Heath; Sophie Williams. Born Mary Sophie Catherine Teresa Peirce Evans, Nov 10, 1896, at Knockaderry House, near Newcastlewest, Co. Limerick, Ireland; died from shock of injuries after falling from the steps of a public bus, May 1939 (other sources cite Nov 27, 1939); studied at Dublin's University College, 1920–21, and University of Aberdeen; m. Major William Davies Elliott-Lynn, 1919 (died 1927); Sir James Heath, Oct 12, 1927 (div. 1932); George Anthony Reginald Williams (aviator), 1932 (div. 1936). ❖ Aviation pioneer who was the 1st woman to earn a B aviator's license, the 1st woman to loop-the-loop and the 1st woman to make a parachute jump from 15,000 ft, served as vice president of Women's Amateur Athletic Association (1922); as an International Athletics Federation representative, presented arguments to International Olympic Council in Prague (1926) about why women should be allowed to compete in Olympics (subsequently, committee opened 3 events to women in 1928 games); influenced International Commission for Air Navigation's (ICAN) decision to permit women to become commercial pilots after successfully flying newspapers to Paris during British general strike (May 1926); broke an aviation height record at 19,000 feet (Oct 1927); flew from Pretoria, South Africa, to London in her plane, the *Avian* (Feb 25–May 17, 1928); worked as a KLM pilot (1929–33); was 1st woman instructor at Dublin's Kildonan Aerodrome, which she later purchased. Writings include *East African Nights and Other Verses* (1925) and *Athletics for Women and Girls–How to Be an Athlete and Why* (1925), 1st book of its kind.

HEATHCOTE-AMORY, Lady (1901–1997). *See Wethered, Joyce.*

HEATON, Anne (1930—). English ballet dancer. Born Nov 19, 1930, in Rawalpindi, India; grew up in England. ❖ Trained at Sadler's Wells school; performed with Sadler's Wells and Royal Ballets in classical as well as newer repertory works; created roles in many pieces by Ninette de Valois, including *Promenade* and *The Gods Go A-Begging* (1946), and in works by Andrée Howard, such as *Assembly Ball* and *Mardi Gras* (1946); also danced featured roles in Frederick Ashton's *Valses Nobles et Sentimentales* (1947) and *Don Juan* (1948), as well as in works by Kenneth Macmillan; retired from performance career (1962) and taught.

HEATON, Hannah Cook (1721–1794). American religious writer. Born 1721 in Long Island, NY; died 1794. ❖ Joined Great Awakening revival and wrote accounts of her experiences; autobiographical writings excerpted in *The World of Hannah Heaton* (1988).

HEATON, Lucy (1898–1980). *See Morton, Lucy.*

HEAVENLY SUNBEAMS, The.
See Hutchinson, Jeanette.
See Hutchinson, Sheila.
See Hutchinson, Wanda.

HEBARD, Grace Raymond (1861–1936). American educator, author, and suffragist. Born Grace Raymond Hebard, July 2, 1861, in Clinton, Iowa; died Oct 11, 1936, in Laramie, Wyoming; dau. of Reverend George Diah Alonzo Hebard and Margaret E. Dominick (Marven) Hebard; State University of Iowa, BS, 1882, MA, 1885; earned doctorate at Illinois Wesleyan University, 1893. ❖ Became associate professor of political economy at University of Wyoming (1906), then head of department, and served as university librarian (1894–1919); was 1st woman admitted to Wyoming bar (1898), though she never practiced law; admitted to practice before Supreme Court of Wyoming (1914); supported many causes, including child-labor reform, woman suffrage, and immigration restriction; was a leader at Cheyenne women's convention of 1889; interested in history of American West, particularly Wyoming, wrote 7 books, including *The Bozeman Trail* (1922), *Washakie* (1930), and *Sacajawea* (1933); adopted into Shoshoni tribe; retired (1931); was also Wyoming state tennis champion, both singles and doubles, and state golf champion. ❖ See also *Women in World History*.

HEBDEN, Mary Jane (c. 1823–1895). See Bennett, Mary Jane.

HEBERLE, Thérèse (1806–1840). Austrian ballet dancer. Name variations: Therese Heberle. Born 1806 in Vienna, Austria; died Feb 5, 1840, in Naples, Italy. ❖ Performed in Kinderballet (children's ballet) of Frederick Horschelt at Theater an der Wein (c. 1816–21); danced 1 season with Royal Italian Opera, a company based in London; performed at Teatro alla Scala in Milan (starting 1820s) where she appeared in works by Jean Aumer, Filippo Taglioni, and Louis Henry, among others; remained at La Scala until end of her short career.

HÉBERT, Anne (1916–2000). French-Canadian poet and prose writer. Name variations: Anne Hebert. Pronunciation: Hay-BARE. Born Aug 1, 1916, at Sainte-Catherine-de-Fossambault, Quebec, Canada; died in Montreal, Jan 22, 2000; dau. of Maurice Hébert (writer and government official) and Marguerite Marie Taché; attended Collège Notre-Dame-de Bellevue and Collège Mérici in Quebec. ❖ One of French-Canada's most distinguished writers, who has been praised for her psychological insight as well as her expression of growing discontent of Quebec's French-speaking population under English rule, published 1st poems and stories (1939); endured death of cousin, poet Hector de Saint-Denys Garneau (1943); published short stories *Le Torrent* (1950), her most significant early work of prose; began work as scriptwriter for Canadian National Film Board (1953); published poems, *Le Tombeau des Rois* (1953), considered to be her crowning achievement as a writer of verse; began residence in Paris (1954); published 1st novel *Les Chambres de bois* (*The Silent Rooms*, 1958); her early prose works dealt at 1st gingerly, then more specifically, with a critique of French-Canadian society, notably prevailing attitudes among upper-middle class in her native Quebec; published poems, *Mystère de la parole* (*Mystery of the Verb*, 1960); elected to Royal Society of Canada (1960); settled permanently in Paris (1965). Won Molson Prize (1967); received *Prix des Libraires de France* for her novel *Kamouraska* (1970); won *Académie française* prize for novel *Les Enfants du sabbat* (1976); received *Prix Fémina* (1982). ❖ See also Delbert W. Russell, *Anne Hébert* (Twayne, 1983); and *Women in World History*.

HÉBERT, Madame (d. 1794). French revolutionary. Died on the guillotine in Paris, April 13, 1794; m. Jacques René Hébert (1757–1794).

HECHER, Traudl (1943—). Austrian Alpine skier. Born July 28, 1943, in Austria. ❖ Won bronze medals for downhill at Squaw Valley Olympics (1960) and Innsbruck Olympics (1964).

HECK, Barbara Ruckle (1734–1804). German religious pioneer. Born Barbara Ruckle, 1734, at Ruckle Hill in Balligarane, Ireland; died Aug 17, 1804, near Auga, Canada; dau. of Sebastian Ruckle; m. Paul Heck, 1760 (died 1792 or 1795); children: 2 daughters, 3 sons. ❖ Organizer of the 1st Methodist society in New York City, now regarded as the beginning of Wesleyan movement in US, immigrated to America with husband and others from a German Methodist colony in Co. Limerick, Ireland, settling in NYC (1760); discouraged by the community's lack of belief, encouraged Philip Embury, who had been an itinerant Methodist preacher in Ireland, to begin preaching to their community (1766), then opened (Oct 30, 1768), the 1st official Methodist Chapel in America on John Street; with husband and other members of the community, moved upriver to farmland near Salem in Washington Co., NY (1770); for political reasons, moved with family to Montreal (1774); when husband received a grant of land for his military service in Maitland, near August in Upper Canada, moved there with family and remained there for rest of life (1785). ❖ See also G. Lincoln Caddell, *Barbara Heck: Pioneer Methodist* (Pathway, 1961); William Henry Withrow, *Barbara Heck: A Tale of Early Methodism* (Briggs, 1895); Abel Stevens, *The Women of Methodism; Its Three Foundresses, Susanna Wesley, the Countess of Huntingdon, and Barbara Heck* (Carlton & Porter, 1866); and *Women in World History*.

HECKART, Eileen (1919–2001). American stage, tv and screen actress. Born Anna Eckart Herbert, Mar 29, 1919, in Columbus, Ohio; died Dec 31, 2001, in Norwalk, Connecticut; m. John Harrison Yankee Jr., 1944 (died 1997); children: 3. ❖ Made NY debut in *Tinker's Dam* (1943), followed by *Hilda Crane, In Any Language, A View from the Bridge, A Memory of Two Mondays, Invitation to a March*, the title role in *Everybody Loves Opal*, and one-woman show *Eleanor*, in which she portrayed Eleanor Roosevelt; made film debut in *Miracle in the Rain* (1955); other films include *Bus Stop, Hot Spell, Heller in Pink Tights, Up the Down Staircase, The Hiding Place* and *The First Wives Club*; on tv, played the aunt on "The Mary Tyler Moore Show," among others. Won Outer Circle Award for *Picnic* (1953), Donaldson Award for *The Bad Seed* (1954), NY Drama Critics Award for *The Dark at the Top of the Stairs* (1957), and was granted a special Tony for lifetime achievement (2000); won Emmy for "Save Me a Place at Forest Lawn" (1967), an Oscar as Best Supporting Actress for *Butterflies Are Free* (1972); nominated for an Oscar for *The Bad Seed* (1956) and nominated for 3 other Tony awards.

HECKENDORF, Sylvia (1962—). See Albrecht, Sylvia.

HECKER, Genevieve (1884–1960). American golfer. Name variations: Mrs. C.T. Stout. Born 1884; lived in West Orange, NJ; died July 29, 1960, in New York, NY; m. C.T. Stout. ❖ Early golf great, won USGA Women's Amateur (1901, 1902); won the Metropolitan (1900, 1901, 1905, 1906). Author of *Golf for Women* (1904, the 2002 replica ed. has a preface by Peggy Kirk Bell).

HECKLER, Margaret M. (1931—). American politician. Name variations: Mrs. John M. Heckler. Born Margaret Mary O'Shaughnessy, June 21, 1931, in Flushing, NY; dau. of John and Bridget (McKeown) O'Shaughnessy; Albertus Magnus College, BA, 1953; postgraduate work at University of Leiden, 1953; Boston College Law School, LLB, 1956; m. John M. Heckler, Aug 29, 1952; children: Belinda West Heckler; Alison Anne Heckler; John M. Heckler. ❖ Republican Congressional representative from Massachusetts (1967–83), was admitted to Massachusetts bar (1956); elected to Massachusetts Governor's Council (1962 and 1964); was a member of Republican town committee of Wellesley, MA (1958–66); elected to US House of Representatives (1966), became the 2nd-ranking Republican member of Veterans' Affairs Committee; as an advocate of childcare, was critical of Nixon's veto of a comprehensive child-development program (1971); worked for Equal Rights Amendment (ERA) and co-sponsored 1977 joint resolution to extend the deadline for its ratification; also drafted Equal Credit Opportunity Act of 1974 and worked with Elizabeth Holtzman to organize Congressional Caucus for Women's Issues (1977); served as secretary of Department of Health and Human Services for Ronald Reagan (1983–85), establishing new guidelines for Social Security disability program and campaigning to increase federal funding for research and care for patients with Alzheimer's and AIDS; was ambassador to Ireland (1985–89).

HECKSCHER, Grete (1901–1987). Danish fencer. Born Nov 8, 1901, in Denmark; died Oct 6, 1987. ❖ At Paris Olympics, won a bronze medal in individual foil (1924).

HECTOR, Annie French (1825–1902). Irish-born novelist. Name variations: Mrs. Hector; (pseudonym) Mrs. Alexander. Born Annie French in Dublin, Ireland, June 23, 1825; died in London, England, July 10, 1902; educated by governesses; m. Alexander Hector (merchant), 1858 (died 1875). ❖ Widowed at 50, turned to writing novels, producing over 40 titles, including the extremely successful *The Wooing O't* (1873), as well as *Ralph Wilton's Weird* (1875), *Her Dearest Foe* (1876), *The Frères* (1882), *At Bay* (1885), *Mona's Choice* (1887) and the semi-autobiographical *Kitty Costello* (1902).

HEDBERG, Doris (1936—). Swedish gymnast. Born Feb 18, 1936, in Sweden. ❖ At Melbourne Olympics, won a silver medal in teams all-around, portable apparatus (1956).

HEDDLE, Kathleen (1965—). Canadian rower. Born Nov 27, 1965, in Trail, British Columbia, Canada; grew up in Vancouver; attended University of British Columbia. ❖ Won a gold medal at Pan American Games (1987); along with Marnie McBean, won gold medals for coxless pairs and coxed eights at World championships (1991), gold medals in coxed eights and coxless pairs at Barcelona Olympics (1992), and a gold medal for double sculls and bronze medal for quadruple sculls at Atlanta Olympics (1996). Received Thomas Keller Award (1999); inducted into Canadian Sports Hall of Fame (1997).

HEDERMAN, Carmencita (1939—). Irish politician. Born Carmencita Cruess-Callaghan, Oct 23, 1939, in Dublin, Ireland; m. William Hederman (surgeon). ❖ Served as Lord Mayor of Dublin (1987–88); as an independent, elected to the Seanad from University of Dublin (1989–93). Received the People of the Year award and Spirit of Dublin award (both 1988); nominated for the European of the Year award (1989).

HEDGEPETH, Whitney L. (1971—). American swimmer. Born Mar 19, 1971, in Colonial Heights, Virginia; attended University of Texas, 1990–94. ❖ Won silver medals for 100- and 200-meter backstroke at Atlanta Olympics (1996).

HEDKVIST PETERSEN, Ewa (1952—). Swedish politician. Born Jan 15, 1952, in Arvidsjaur, Sweden. ❖ Member of the Riksdag (1985–94) and 2nd vice-chair of the Social Democratic group in the Riksdag (1991–94); named chair of the State Committee on Child Abuse (1999—); as a European Socialist (PSE), elected to 5th European Parliament (1999–2004).

HEDMAN, Martha (1883–1974). Swedish stage actress. Born Aug 12, 1883, in Ostersund, Sweden; died June 20, 1974, in DeLand, Florida; studied for stage with Siri von Essen; m. Henry Arthur House. ❖ Made stage debut in Helsingfors, Finland, in a Hans Christian Andersen fairy tale (1905); appeared with Emile von der Osten as Desdemona in *Othello* and Katusha in *Resurrection*; other plays include Hauptmann's *Elga* (title role) and *Life's Masquerade*; had 3-year engagement under Albert Ranft at Vasa Theater, Stockholm, starring in *Quality Street, You Never Can Tell, Catherine* and *L'Autre Danger*; under management of Charles Frohman, made NY debut as Renée de Rould in *The Attack* (1912), followed by *Liberty Hall* and *Indian Summer*; appeared in London in *The Attack* (1914) but returned to US, appearing in *The Heart of a Thief, The Trap, The Boomerang* and *Three for Diana*; with husband, wrote the play *What's the Big Idea* (1926).

HEDREN, Tippi (1931—). American actress and activist. Born Nathalie Kay Hedren, Jan 19, 1931, in New Ulm, Minnesota; m. Peter Griffith, 1952 (div. 1961); m. Noel Marshall, 1964 (div. 1982); m. Luis Barrenecha, 1985 (div. 1995); m. Martin Dinnes, 2002; children: Melanie Griffith (b. 1957, actress). ❖ Began career as fashion model; made film debut in bit part in *The Petty Girl* (1950); after over 10-year absence, returned to Hollywood with lead in Hitchcock's *The Birds* (1963), followed by *Marnie* (1964); other films include *A Countess from Hong Kong, The Harrad Experiment, Mr. Kingstreet's War, Roar, Pacific Heights, Shadow of a Doubt* and *Citizen Ruth*; became actively involved in humanitarian causes, including animal rights, as founder and director of the Roar Foundation. Received Presidential Medal for her work in film at Hofstra University.

HEDRICK, Heather (c. 1972—). American triathlete and duathlete. Born c. 1972, possibly in Indiana; University of Illinois, Urbana-Champaign, BS in dietetics, MS in exercise physiology. ❖ Among the top triathletes and duathletes in US, ran 1st race at Champaign Urbana Mayor's Duathlon; serves as assistant director of Center for Educational Services at National Institute for Fitness and Sport; became ISF Triathlete of the Year (1998), named Female Triathlete of the Year by Master's Swim Team, and awarded All-American status for duathlon by USA Triathlon (2000).

HEDVIG (d. 1436). Countess of Oldenburg. Name variations: Hedwig; Hedwig von Holstein. Died 1436; dau. of Gerhard VI, duke of Holstein (r. 1386–1404), and Elizabeth of Brunswick; m. Balthasar, prince of Mecklenburg, in 1417 (died 1421); m. Didrik also known as Diedrich or Dietrich (c. 1390–1440), count of Oldenburg, in 1423; children: (2nd m.) Christian I (1426–1481), king of Denmark, Norway and Sweden (r. 1448–1481). Dietrich 1st m. Adelheid von Delmenhorst, c. 1401.

HEDVIGIS (1374–1399). *See Jadwiga.*

HEDWIG. *Variant of Jadwiga.*

HEDWIG (d. 903). Duchess of Saxony. Name variations: Hedwige. Died Dec 24, 903; dau. of Henry (d. 886), margrave of Mark (some sources claim that Hedwig was the dau. of Oda of Bavaria and Arnulf of Carinthia, king of Germany, but dates do not correspond); m. Otto (c. 836–912), duke of Saxony, around 869; children: Liudolf; Thangmar (d. 938); Henry I the Fowler (c. 876–936), Holy Roman emperor (r. 919–936); Oda (who m. Zwentibold, king of Lorraine).

HEDWIG (c. 915–965). Duchess of France, countess of Paris, and duchess of Burgundy. Name variations: Hadwig, Hedwige, or Avoie. Born in duchy of Saxony c. 915 (some sources cite 922); died Mar 10, 965, in Aix-la-Chapelle (Aachen); dau. of Henry I the Fowler (c. 876–936), king of Germany, Holy Roman emperor (r. 919–936), and Matilda of Saxony (c. 892–968); sister of Otto I the Great (912–973), king of Germany (r. 936–973), Holy Roman emperor (r. 962–973); m. Hugh the Great also known as Hugh the White (c. 895–956), count of Paris and duke of Burgundy, in 938; children: Beatrice (b. 938, who m. Frederick, count of Bar); Hugh Capet (939–996), duke of France (r. 956–996), king of France (r. 987–996, first of the Capetian kings, who m. Adelaide of Poitou); Emma of Paris (d. 968), duchess of Normandy; Odo or Otto (b. around 945), duke of Burgundy; Otto Henry the Great (b. around 948), duke of Burgundy; Herbert, bishop of Auxerre. Hugh the Great's 1st wife was Edhild (d. 946).

HEDWIG (1374–1399). *See Jadwiga.*

HEDWIG, Saint (1174–1243). *See Hedwig of Silesia.*

HEDWIG OF DENMARK (1581–1641). Electress of Saxony. Born Aug 5, 1581; died Nov 26, 1641; dau. of Frederick II (1534–1588), king of Denmark and Norway (r. 1559–1588), and Sophia of Mecklenburg (1557–1631); sister of Anne of Denmark (1574–1619); m. Christian II (1583–1611), elector of Saxony (r. 1591–1611), Sept 12, 1602.

HEDWIG OF EBERHARD (930–992). Countess of Ardennes. Born in Germany, 930; died 992; m. Siegfried of Luxemburg (c. 922–998), count of Ardenne (r. 963–998), around 950; children: possibly Henry I of Luxemburg (d. 1026); Frederick I of Luxemburg (born around 965), count of Salm or Solm; Cunigunde (d. 1040?, who m. Henry II, Holy Roman emperor). Henry I was possibly a son from a previous marriage of Siegfried's.

HEDWIG OF HABSBURG (d. 1286). Margravine of Brandenburg. Birth date unknown; died before Oct 27, 1286; dau. of Anna of Hohenberg (c. 1230–1281) and Rudolph or Rudolf I of Habsburg (1218–1291), king of Germany (r. 1273), Holy Roman emperor (r. 1273–1291); m. Otto, margrave of Brandenburg.

HEDWIG OF HOLSTEIN (d. 1325). Queen of Sweden. Name variations: Hedwig von Holstein. Died c. 1325; dau. of Gerhard I, count of Holstein, and Elizabeth of Mecklenburg; m. Magnus I Ladulas, king of Sweden (r. 1275–1290), Nov 11, 1276; children: Eric; Berger, king of Sweden (r. 1290–1318); Erik, duke of Sudermannland; Richiza Magnusdottir (abbess of St. Klara); Ingeborg (d. 1319); Valdemar or Waldemar, duke of Finland.

HEDWIG OF HOLSTEIN-GOTTORP (1636–1715). Queen of Sweden. Name variations: Hedvig. Born Hedwig Eleanor, Oct 23, 1636; died Nov 24, 1715; m. Karl X also known as Charles X Gustavus (1622–1660), king of Sweden (r. 1654–1660), Oct 24, 1654; children: Charles XI (1655–1697), king of Sweden (r. 1660–1697).

HEDWIG OF OLDENBURG (1759–1818). *See Charlotte of Oldenburg.*

HEDWIG OF POLAND (1513–1573). Electress of Brandenburg. Name variations: Jadwiga. Born Mar 25, 1513; died Feb 7, 1573; dau. of Barbara Zapolya and Sigismund I, king of Poland (r. 1506–1548); became 2nd wife of Joachim II (1505–1571), elector of Brandenburg (r. 1535–1571), on Sept 1, 1535. Joachim's 1st wife was Magdalene of Saxony (1507–1534).

HEDWIG OF SILESIA (1174–1243). Duchess of Silesia, German noble, and saint. Name variations: Saint Hedwig; Jadwiga of Silesia. Pronunciation: Hate-vik. Born in Andrechs castle, Bavaria, 1174; died in Silesia, 1243; dau. of Count Berthold III of Andrechs (marquis of Meran, count of Tirol, and duke of Carinthia and Istria) and Agnes of Dedo (dau. of count of Rotletchs); sister of Agnes of Meran (queen of France) and Gertrude of Andrechs-Meran (queen of Hungary); aunt of

Elizabeth of Hungary (1207–1231); m. Duke Henry I of Silesia also known as Henry the Bearded, duke of Cracow (r. 1228–1229, 1232–1238), 1186 (died 1238); children: Henry II the Pious, duke of Cracow (r. 1238–1241); Conrad; Boleslas; Agnes; Sophia; and Gertrude. ❖ Renowned holy woman, spent early years at convent of Franken; at 13, married Duke Henry I of Silesia and eventually had large family; was distressed at husband's refusal to become a Christian and worked for years to convert him to the faith, eventually succeeding; used substantial resources to establish numerous hospitals, especially for lepers; worked in hospitals, as did most of her children; also founded and endowed many monasteries and convents, of which the most famous is Cistercian convent at Treibnitz, near Breslau; when husband died (1238), retired to convent at Treibnitz, where she lived her remaining years in austerity; canonized (1266 or 1267), became the patron saint of Silesia. Feast day is Oct 17. ❖ See also *Women in World History*.

HEDWIG SOPHIA (1681–1708). Princess of Sweden and duchess of Holstein-Gottorp. Name variations: Hedwig Sophie of Sweden; Hedwig von Simmern. Born June 26, 1681; died Dec 22, 1708; dau. of Ulrica Eleanora of Denmark (1656–1693) and Charles XI (1655–1697), king of Sweden (r. 1660–1697); m. Frederick IV (1671–1702), duke of Holstein-Gottorp (r. 1695–1702), on June 12, 1698; children: Charles Frederick (1700–1739), duke of Holstein-Gottorp (r. 1702–1739, who m. Anne Petrovna [1708–1728], dau. of Peter the Great and Catherine I of Russia).

HEDWIG WITTELSBACH (fl. late 1600s). Daughter of the Elector Palatine. Name variations: Hedwig Elizabeth Amelia of Pfalz-Neuburg. Fl. in late 1600s; born Hedwig Elizabeth; dau. of Philip William, Elector Palatine, and possibly Elizabeth Amalia of Hesse (1635–1709) or, more likely, Anna Constancia (1619–1651); m. James Sobieski (son of John III Sobieski and Marie Casimir); children: 5, including Clementina Sobieski (1702–1735).

HEDWIGE. *Variant of Hedwig and Jadwiga.*

HEDYLE (fl. 3rd century BCE). Greek poet. Name variations: Hydele of Athens. Dau. of Moschine; children: Hydelus (male epigrammatist). ❖ Athenaeus (2nd century) mentions Hedyle and her mother Moschine; 1 quotation survives from the mythological poem *Scylla*.

HEEMSKERK, Marianne (1944—). Dutch swimmer. Born Aug 28, 1944, in Netherlands. ❖ At Rome Olympics, won a silver medal in 100-meter butterfly (1960).

HEEMSTRA, Ella van (1900–1984). Dutch aristocrat. Born 1900; died 1984; dau. of Baron Aarnoud Van Heemstra (burgomeister of Arnhem and lawyer at court of Queen Wilhelmina) and Elbrig Van Asbeck (baroness); m. Jan Hendrik Gustaaf Quarles van Ufford of House of Orange-Nassau (aristocrat), 1920; m. Joseph Victor Anthony Hepburn-Ruston (English-Irish banker), Sept 1926; children: (1st m.) Alexander and Jan (Ian); (2nd m.) Audrey Hepburn (1929–1993, actress). ❖ Grew up in a sizeable castle at Doorn in Utrecht, until estate was sold to Kaiser Wilhelm II (1918) as his last refuge when he fled Germany; worked in the Resistance. ❖ See also *Women in World History*.

HEENAN, Frances (1910–1956). Subject of a 1926 scandal. Name variations: Peaches Browning. Born Frances Belle Heenan, June 23, 1910; died Aug 23, 1956; m. Edward West Browning (real-estate magnate), April 10, 1926 (div. 1927, died 1934). ❖ While attending Textile High School in NY City, met Edward Browning, a tycoon who was called Daddy because he was generous with his money; with his help, got a chorus-line job in Earl Carroll's *Vanities*; at 15, when the Society for the Prevention of Cruelty to Children began legal action in children's court against Heenan's mother for neglect, married Browning who was 51; with mother's prompting, sued for divorce after 7 months, making headlines with her lurid accusations against him; awarded his entire estate (1934).

HEENAN, Katie (1985—). American gymnast. Born Nov 26, 1985, in Indianapolis, Indiana. ❖ Won bronze medals in team all-around and uneven bars at World championships (2001).

HEER, Anna (1863–1918). Swiss physician. Born in Olten, Switzerland, Mar 22, 1863; died in Zurich, Switzerland, Dec 19, 1918; University of Zurich, MD, 1888. ❖ One of Switzerland's 1st woman physicians, began working with 2 other physicians, Ida Schneider and Marie Vögtlin, to create the 1st professional nursing school in Zurich (1896); opened the Swiss Nurse's School (1901), a training academy with attached women's

hospital, which soon gained an international reputation; was depicted on a postage stamp issued June 1, 1963. ❖ See also *Women in World History*.

HEFFERNAN, Fallon (1986—). American inline skater. Born Aug 29, 1986, in Jacksonville, Florida. ❖ Won silver (2001) and bronze (2002) in Park at X Games; other finishes include 2nd in Park at EXPN Invitational, Grand Prairie, TX (2002), and 1st in Street at Niss Core Tour, Venice Beach, CA (2003).

HEFFORD, Jayna (1977—). Canadian ice-hockey player. Born May 14, 1977, in Kingston, Ontario, Canada. ❖ Played for Brampton Thunder; won a team silver medal at Nagano (1998), the 1st Olympics to feature women's ice hockey; won a team gold medal at World championships (2001); won a team gold medal at Salt Lake City Olympics (2002) and a team gold at Torino Olympics (2006). Was the OWIAA Rookie of the Year with the University of Toronto.

HEFFORD, Muriel Emma (1898–1974). *See Bell, Muriel Emma.*

HEFLIN, Alma (fl. 1930s). American pilot. Name variations: Alma Heflin McCormick. Born in Lock Haven, Pennsylvania; flourished in 1930s. ❖ Began flying lessons in Spokane, Washington (1934); became 1st woman to lead annual light plane cavalcade to Florida (1938); served as publicity director for Piper Aircraft Corporation and edited Piper's *Cub Flier*; became 1st woman test pilot for a commercial aircraft company, for Piper (1941); bush piloted in Alaska (1942); hired by US Army to test planes used for "Grasshopper Squadron." ❖ See also memoir *Adventure Was the Compass* (1942).

HEGAMIN, Lucille (1894–1970). African-American jazz singer. Born Lucille Nelson in Macon, Georgia, Nov 29, 1894; died in New York, NY, Mar 1, 1970; m. William "Bill" Hegamin (pianist), 1914 (div. 1923). ❖ Left home at 15 to tour with Leonard Harper Revue; performed in clubs in Chicago with sidemen Tony Jackson, Jelly Roll Morton, and pianist Bill Hegamin; moved West with her own band; went to NY (1919) to sing lead and record with Blue Flame Syncopators, a group that included Charlie Irvis; soloed at The Shuffle Inn and fronted her own Dixie Daisies (1921); sang with Sunnyland Cottonpickers, accompanied by pianist Cyril J. Fullerton (1926–27); appeared in several Broadway shows (1920s), earning sobriquet "The Cameo Girl"; also worked with George "Doc" Hyder's Southernaires; after brief appearances at the Paradise in Atlantic City (1933–34), became a registered nurse (1938); made renowned recordings, including "Everybody's Blues" (1920), "Some Early Morning" (1923) and "Number 12," which was featured on her album *Basket of Blues* (1962). ❖ See also *Women in World History*.

HEGAN, Alice (1870–1942). *See Rice, Alice Hegan.*

HEGAN, Eliza Parks (1861–1917). Canadian nurse. Born Eliza Parks Hegan, 1861, probably in Saint John, New Brunswick, Canada; died Feb 18, 1917, in Canada; dau. of Eliza (Black) Hegan and John Hegan. ❖ Pioneering nurse in New Brunswick, was 1 of 10 women selected to study nursing at, and 6th student to graduate from, Saint John General Public Hospital (1890); as matron, worked at Victoria Public Hospital, then at Saint John General Public Hospital (1892–95, 1898); created and ran a private hospital in New Brunswick; contributed to the creation (1903) and served as 5th president of the 1st local nursing association, the Graduate Nurses' Society of Saint John General Public Hospital, later called Saint John Graduate Nurses Association (from 1909); helped create the bylaws of the New Brunswick Association of Graduate Nurses (1916).

HEGGTVEIT, Anne (1939—). Canadian alpine skier. Name variations: Anne Heggtveit Hamilton; Anne Heggtveit-Hamilton. Born Jan 11, 1939, in Ottawa, Ontario, Canada; dau. of Dr. Halvor Heggtveit (qualifier for Canada's 1932 Olympic ski team but did not compete); m. Ross Hamilton. ❖ At 15, won the Holmenkollen giant slalom in Norway (1954), youngest winner in event's 50-year history; won the combined title at Aalberg-Kandahar championship in Garmisch, West Germany (1959), 1st non-European to do so; at Squaw Valley, won a gold medal for slalom (1960), the 1st Canadian skier to win an Olympic medal; won gold medals in combined and slalom at Fédération Internationale du Ski World championship (1960); retired (1960). ❖ See also *Women in World History*.

HEGH, Hanne (1960—). Norwegian handball player. Born April 27, 1960, in Norway. ❖ At Seoul Olympics, won a silver medal in team competition (1988).

HEI, Agnes (1877/78?–1910). *See Hei, Akenehi.*

HEI, Akenehi (1877/78?–1910). New Zealand tribal leader, nurse, and midwife. Name variations: Agnes Hei. Born probably in 1877 or 1878 at Te Kaha, Bay of Plenty, New Zealand; died on Nov 28, 1910, in Gisborne, New Zealand; dau. of Heemi Hei and Maria Nikora; sister of Hamiora Hei (lawyer); attended Hukarere Girls' School in Hawkes Bay. ❖ Trained as nurse and midwife, entered private nursing in Gisborne (c. 1909); hired briefly by Department of Public Health during typhoid epidemic (1909); worked to improve health standards among Maori. ❖ See also *Dictionary of New Zealand Biography* (Vol. 3).

HEIBERG, Johanne Luise (1812–1890). Danish writer, director, and actress. Born Johanne Luise Pätges in Copenhagen, Denmark, 1812; died 1890; dau. of Christian Pätges and Henriette Hartvig Pätges; father was Catholic, mother of Jewish heritage (both of German descent); m. Johan Ludvig Heiberg (writer and critic), 1831; daughter-in-law of Thomasine Gyllembourg-Ehrensvärd (writer); no children. ❖ Brilliant comedian who achieved prominence as a tragedian toward end of career in *Macbeth* and Schiller's *Maria Stuart*; started her training at ballet school of Danish Royal Theater and continued career there as an actress; from age 14 until retirement (1864), performed lead roles in plays written for her by prominent Danish playwrights of the time, including those of her husband, as well as in dramas by Molière, Scribe, Calderon, and Sheridan; after husband's death (1831), adopted 3 motherless girls from West Indies; was the Danish Royal Theater's primary director (1867–74); spent remainder of life writing her memoirs. ❖ See also Annalisa Forssberger (in Danish), *Johanne Luise Heiberg* (Nordisk, 1973); Bodil Wamberg (in Danish), *Johanne Luise Heiberg* (G.E.C. Gad, 1989); and *Women in World History.*

HEIBERG, Marianne (1945–2004). Norwegian social researcher and peace broker. Born Dec 7, 1945; died Dec 26, 2004; attended Harvard University and London School of Economics; graduate of University of Oslo, 1971; m. Johan Jorgen Holst (Norwegian foreign minister, died 1994); children: 2 sons. ❖ Commissioned to survey Palestinian living conditions in Gaza and West Bank for Norwegian Trade Union Centre for Social Science and Research (FAFO), formed close relations with PLO and Rabin's Labour Party; helped instigate the secret talks that led to the Oslo Accords (1993); was senior researcher at Norwegian Institute of International Affairs (1983–2004).

HEIDEMANN, Britta (1982—). German fencer. Born Dec 22, 1982, in Cologne, Germany. ❖ Won a silver medal for épée team at Athens Olympics (2004); at World championships, placed 2nd for team épée (2003) and 3rd for indiv. épée (2002); had 2nd overall World Cup ranking for indiv. épée (2003–04).

HEIDEN, Beth (1959—). American speedskater and cyclist. Name variations: Beth Heiden Reid. Born Elizabeth Lee Heiden, Sept 27, 1959, in West Allis, Wisconsin; sister of Eric Heiden (Olympic speedskater). ❖ Placed 11th at Innsbruck Olympics (1976); placed 1st at World Jr. championships all-around (1978, 1979); won silver medals at World sprint championships (1978, 1979) and a bronze (1980); at World championships, won a gold medal for small allround (1979) and a silver (1980); won a bronze medal for 3,000 meters at Lake Placid Olympics (1980); won the NCAA Cross Country Ski championship in Bozeman, Montana (1983); also won the World championship in bicycling in Sallanches, France (1980).

HEIDENREICH, Charlotte (1788–1859). *See Siebold, Charlotte Heidenreich von.*

HEIFETZ, Mrs. Jascha (1895–1977). *See Vidor, Florence.*

HEIGHT, Dorothy (1912—). American activist. Born Dorothy Irene Height in Richmond, Virginia, Mar 24, 1912; dau. of James Edward (building contractor) and Fannie (Burroughs) Height; New York University, BA, then MA in educational psychology, 1933; attended New York School of Social Work; never married; no children. ❖ Organization official who worked on behalf of civil and women's rights, serving over 3 decades as president of National Council of Negro Women (NCNW); spent most of professional career with Young Women's Christian Association (YWCA), where she rose to post of associate director of leadership training services and director of Office for Racial Justice; was also president of Delta Sigma Theta Sorority (1944–53); became president of NCNW (1957), where she became a driving force in a variety of economic, political, and social issues affecting black women; a major leader during civil-rights movement (1960s), held voter registration drives in South and voter education drives in North; was largely responsible for erection of Bethune Memorial statue, the 1st monument of an African-American placed in a public park in Washington, DC. Received Presidential Medal of Freedom (1994). ❖ See also *Women in World History.*

HEIJTING-SCHUHMACHER, Irma (1925—). Dutch swimmer. Born Feb 24, 1925, in Netherlands. ❖ Won a bronze medal at the London Olympics (1948) and a silver medal at the Helsinki Olympics (1952), both in the 4x100-meter freestyle relay.

HEIKEL, Karin Alice (1901–1944). Finnish poet. Name variations: (pseudonyms) Katri Vala; Pecka. Born Karin Alice Wadenström, 1901, in Muonio, Finland; died of TB, April 28, 1944, in Eksjö sanatorium, Sweden; dau. of Robert Waldemar Wadenström (forest officer) and Alexandra Frederika "Maki" Wadenström; sister of Erkki Vala (writer and journalist); attended teacher's training school in Heinola; m. Armas Heikel (chemist and leftist radical), 1930; children: Mauri Henrik Heikel (b. 1934). ❖ One of the foremost poets in Finland (1920s–30s), was the central member of literary group Tulenkantajat (The Fire Bearers) and introduced free verse to the nation; published 1st collection *Kaukainen Puutarha* (1924), followed by *Sininen Ovi* (1926); wrote for magazine *Tulenkantajat*, publishing reviews under pseudonym Pecka; translated Swedish poets into Finnish; was a passionate pacifist during the Winter War with the Soviet Union (1941–44), though she had sympathized with anti-Franco fighters during Spanish civil war; last collection published as *Pesapuu Palaa* (1942).

HEILBRON, Rose (1914–2005). English lawyer. Name variations: Dame Rose Heilbron. Born Aug 19, 1914, in Liverpool, England; died Dec 8, 2005; graduate of Liverpool University, 1935; Gray's Inn, LLM, 1937; m. Dr. Nathaniel Burstein, 1945; children: 1 daughter. ❖ Called to the bar (1939); a Queen's Counsel, was appointed recorder of Burnley (1956), a post she held until 1974; was appointed second High Court Judge (1974), on the Northern Circuit in the Family Division; advanced to Presiding Judge of Northern Circuit (1979); served as chair of Home Secretary's Advisory Group on Rape (1975); was the first woman to sit as judge at the Old Bailey. Made DBE (1974).

HEILBRUN, Carolyn Gold (1926–2003). American feminist, novelist and literary critic. Name variations: (pseudonym) Amanda Cross. Born Carolyn Gold, Jan 13, 1926, in East Orange, NJ; committed suicide, Oct 9, 2003, in New York, NY; Columbia University, MA, 1951, and PhD, 1959; m. James Heilbrun (economist and professor), 1945; children: 2 daughters, 1 son. ❖ Feminist literary scholar, taught at Columbia (1960–93) and wrote the pioneering studies *Toward a Recognition of Androgyny: Aspects of Male and Female Literature* (1973), *Reinventing Womanhood* (1979), and *Writing a Woman's Life* (1988); also wrote *The Garnett Family* (1961), *Christopher Isherwood* (1970), *Lady Ottoline's Album* (1976), *Hamlet's Mother and Other Women* (1990), *The Education of a Woman: The Life of Gloria Steinem* (1995), *The Last Gift of Time: Life Beyond Sixty* (1997) and *When Men Were the Only Models We Had* (2002); edited with Nancy K. Miller, Columbia University Press's Gender and Culture series; as Amanda Cross, wrote 10 detective novels around the character Kate Fansler, including *In the Last Analysis* (1960), *The Question of Max* (1976), *Death in a Tenured Position* (1981), and *The Players Come Again* (1990); was president of the Modern Language Association (1984) and a trustee.

HEILL, Claudia (1982—). Austrian judoka. Born Jan 24, 1982, in Austria. ❖ Placed 5th at World championships (2001) and 1st at Super A (2002), both for 63kg; won a silver medal for 63kg at Athens Olympics (2004).

HEILLY, Anne d'. *See Étampes, Anne de Pisseleu d'Heilly, Duchesse d' (1508–c. 1580).*

HEIM, Andrea (1961—). East German volleyball player. Born Feb 11, 1961, in East Germany. ❖ At Moscow Olympics, won a silver medal in team competition (1980).

HEIM-VÖGTLIN, Marie (1845–1916). *See Vögtlin, Marie.*

HEINE, Jutta (1940—). West German runner. Born Sept 16, 1940, in Germany. ❖ At Rome Olympics, won silver medals in the 4x100-meter relay and the 200 meters (1960).

HEINECKE, Birgit (1957—). East German handball player. Born April 10, 1957, in East Germany. ❖ At Moscow Olympics, won a bronze medal in team competition (1980).

HEINECKE, Iraida (c. 1895–1990). *See Odoevtseva, Irina.*

HEINEL, Anna (1753–1808). German ballerina. Born in Bayreuth, Bavaria, Germany, Oct 4, 1753; died Mar 17, 1808, in Paris;

m. Gaëtan Vestris (dancer and choreographer), c. 1792; children: Adolphe-Apoline-Marie-Angiolo Vestris (b. May 1791); (stepchild) Auguste Vestris. ❖ Renowned for introducing the *pirouette à la seconde* (multiple pirouette), began dancing at 14 at the opera house in Stuttgart (1753); debuted at Paris Opéra in *danse noble* (1768), impressing critics with her tall, stately figure; dubbed *La Belle Statue*, became extremely popular at the Opéra, even eclipsing renowned dancer and choreographer Gaëtan Vestris, who was reputedly so jealous that he used his position as ballet master to discredit her; took refuge in England, where she contracted at the King's Opera House (1771); returned to Paris (1776) and appeared as Roxane in *Apelles et Campaspe*; eventually married Vestris. ❖ See also *Women in World History*.

HEINEMANN, Barbara (1795–1883). American religious leader. Name variations: Barbara Heynemann; Barbara Landmann. Born Jan 11, 1795, in Leitersweiler, Alsace, France; died May 21, 1883, at Amana, Iowa; dau. of Peter and Anna Heinemann; m. George Landmann, 1823 (died 1880). ❖ Member of the Pietist sect, Community of True Inspiration, which was revived by Christian Metz, served as *Werkzeug* (instrument of God) in the society and with Metz acted as spiritual leader to Amana Society, network of settlements in Iowa County, IA; after Metz's death, led Amana alone with assistance from the Great Council of Brethen. ❖ See also Bertha M.H. Shambaugh, *Amana That Was and Amana That Is* (1932).

HEINK, Ernestine Schumann- (1861–1936). See *Schumann-Heink, Ernestine*.

HEINRICH, Christina (1949—). East German runner. Born July 8, 1949, in East Germany. ❖ At Munich Olympics, won a silver medal in the 4x100-meter relay (1972).

HEINRICHS, April (1964—). American soccer player. Born Feb 27, 1964, in Denver, Colorado; graduate of University of North Carolina. ❖ Pioneer of US Women's national team program, captained the US team that won the World Cup (1991); named head coach at Princeton (1990), University of Maryland (1991), University of Virginia (1996), and US national team (2000). Named US Soccer Female Athlete of the Year (1986, 1989); was the 1st woman inducted into US Soccer Hall of Fame (1998).

HEISE, Charlotte (1834–1907). See *Führer, Charlotte*.

HEISS-JENKINS, Carol (1940—). American figure skater. Name variations: Carol Heiss; Carol Heiss Jenkins. Born Carol Elizabeth Heiss, Jan 20, 1940, in New York, NY; sister of skater Nancy Heiss; attended New York University; married Hayes Alan Jenkins (figure-skating champion), 1960. ❖ Won National Novice title (1951); took National Junior championship (1952); at World championship, finished 4th (1953) and 2nd (1955); won silver medal at Cortina Olympics (1956); won 4 straight US National titles (1957–60), 4 consecutive World titles (1956–59), and 2 North American crowns (1958, 1959); won a gold medal at Squaw Valley Olympics (1960); turned to coaching. ❖ See also Robert Parker, *Carol Heiss: Olympic Queen* (Doubleday, 1961).

HEITER, Amalie (1794–1870). See *Amalie of Saxony*.

HEITZER, Regine (fl. 1960s). Austrian figure skater. Name variations: Régine Heitzer. Born in Austria. ❖ Won a silver medal at Innsbruck Olympics (1964); at World championships, won a bronze medal (1962) and silver medals (1963–66); won European championships (1965, 1966).

HEJMADI, Padma. See *Perera, Padma*.

HELAKH, Natallia (1978—). Belarusian rower. Name variations: Natalia Helakh. Born May 30, 1978, in Brest, USSR. ❖ At World championships, placed 2nd for coxless pair (2003); won a bronze medal for coxless pair at Athens Olympics (2004).

HELARIA (fl. 6th c.). Deaconess of the early Frankish church. Fl. in 6th century France; dau. of Remy, bishop of Rheims (who was eventually canonized); never married; no children. ❖ Highly educated woman, was consecrated as a deaconess after she was widowed, possibly because of father's influence. ❖ See also *Women in World History*.

HELBING, Ulla (1958—). See *Salzgeber, Ulla*.

HELBURN, Theresa (1887–1959). American theatrical producer, director, and playwright. Name variations: Terry Helburn. Born Jan 12, 1887, in New York, NY; died Aug 18, 1959, in Weston, Connecticut; dau. of Julius Helburn (businessman) and Hannah (Peyser) Helburn;

Bryn Mawr College, BA, 1908; attended Sorbonne, 1913; m. John Baker Opdycke (teacher and author), 1919 (died 1956); no children. ❖ During 30-year tenure as co-director of Theatre Guild in NY, was a leading force in the development of American theater, helping to bring to attention numerous playwrights, actors, and designers; began career as playwright, then served as drama critic for *The Nation* (1918); became executive secretary of Theater Guild (1919); instrumental in producing plays of S.N. Behrman, Eugene O'Neill, Elmer Rice, Sidney Howard, Maxwell Anderson, Robert E. Sherwood, and Philip Barry; also produced *Oklahoma!* (1943) and *Carousel* (1945). ❖ See also memoir, *A Wayward Quest* (1960); and *Women in World History*.

HELD, Anna (c. 1865–1918). Polish-born musical entertainer. Born in Warsaw, Poland, Mar 18, c. 1865; died in New York, NY, Aug 12, 1918; dau. of Maurice (glove-maker) and Yvonne (Pierre) Held; m. Maximo Carrera (tobacco planter), 1894 (div. c. 1896); m. Florenz Ziegfeld (theatrical producer), 1897 (div. 1913); children: (1st m.) Liane. ❖ Cultivating a "naughty" French stage persona, became one of the most popular stars in US and Europe; moved to Paris with family (c. 1871), then London (1875), where she was a member of Jacob Adler's Yiddish Theatre (1875–80); found niche as music-hall comedian, capitalizing on her considerable endowments and laced 18-inch waist; made successful Paris debut (1894); made NY debut at Herald Square Theater (1896), in a Ziegfeld revival of *A Parlor Match*, charming audiences with a song that became something of a trademark, "Won't You Come and Play Wiz Me?"; subsequently starred in a series of light musical farces, including *The French Maid* (1898), *Papa's Wife* (1899), in which she also toured, *The Little Duchess* (1901), *Mlle. Napoleon* (1903), and *Higgledy-Piggledy* (1904); created a sensation with the song, "I Just Can't Make My Eyes Behave" in *Parisian Model* (1906), then triumphed in *Follies of 1907*; continued to perform in US and abroad and made her only movie, *Madame la Présidente* (1915). ❖ See also *Women in World History*.

HELDMAN, Gladys (1922–2003). American sports magazine editor. Born Gladys Medalie, May 13, 1922, in New York, NY; died from self-inflicted gunshot wound, June 22, 2003, in Santa Fe, New Mexico; Stanford, BA, 1942; University of California at Berkeley, MA, 1943; m. Julius D. Heldman (tennis player), June 15, 1942; children: Carrie Medalie Heldman and Julie Medalie Heldman (both tennis players). ❖ Major force behind women's tennis, was an amateur tennis player (1945–54), ranking #2 in the southwest and #1 in Texas, competing in 4 US Opens; played doubles with Althea Gibson (1953–54) and won a berth on Wimbledon team; launched, published, and began to edit *World Tennis* magazine (1953), which would become the most successful tennis magazine in the world; underwrote US Lawn Tennis Association's National Indoor championship (1959); often documenting the inequities in prize money for men and women, decided the only way women would be treated decently at a tournament was to have one of their own; helped create the Virginia Slims professional tour (1970). With Pancho Gonzales, also wrote *The Book of Tennis*. Inducted into International Tennis Hall of Fame (1979).

HELDMAN, Julie (1945—). American tennis player. Born Julie Medalie Heldman, Dec 8, 1945 in Berkeley, CA; daughter of Gladys (Medalie) Heldman (1922–2003, publisher) and Julius Heldman (tennis player who also worked on the Manhattan Project); graduated Stanford University, 1966; married Bernard Weiss (businessman), 1978. ❖ Won Italian Open, Maccabiah Games, and played for US in Wightman Cup competition (1969); graduate of UCLA Law School, became an attorney after retiring from professional tennis because of injuries (1975); as a tv commentator, was the 1st woman to give color analysis at a men's tennis tournament (1976).

HELDY, Fanny (1888–1973). Belgian soprano. Born Marguerite Virginia Emma Clementine Deceuninck, Feb 29, 1888, in Ath, near Liège, Belgium; died Dec 13, 1973, in Passy, France; studied at Liège Conservatory. ❖ Debuted at Théatre de la Monnaie in Brussels (1910); was acknowledged star of the Opéra-Comique and the Paris Opéra (1917–37); appeared at Teatro alla Scala and Covent Garden (1926). ❖ See also *Women in World History*.

HELEN. Variant of *Yelena*.

HELEN (fl. 1100s). Queen of Sweden. Fl. in 1100s; m. Inge I the Elder, king of Sweden (r. 1080–1110, 1112–1125); children: Katerina Ingesdottir (who m. Bjorn, prince of Denmark); Christina of Sweden (d. 1122); Margaret Frithpoll (d. 1130); Rognvald of Sweden. Inge I was also married to Maer.

HELEN (fl. 1275). Countess of Mar. Became countess of Mar, 1291; more than likely a dau. of Llywelyn the Great (1173–1240), prince of Wales; m. Malcolm (MacDuff), earl of Fife (r. 1228–1266); m. Donald, 6th (some say 10th) earl of Mar (died c. 1292); children: (1st m.) Colbran, earl of Fife; (2nd m.) Gratney or Gartnait, 7th earl of Mar (d. before Sept 1305); Margaret of Mar (who m. John of Strathbogie, earl of Atholl); Isabella of Mar (d. 1296).

HELEN (b. 1950). Romanian princess. Name variations: Princess Helen; Helen Hohenzollern; Helen Medforth-Mills. Born Nov 15, 1950, in Lausanne, Switzerland; dau. of Michael, king of Romania, and Anne of Bourbon-Parma (b. 1923); m. Robin Medforth-Mills, July 20, 1983; children: Nicholas (b. 1985).

HELEN ASEN OF BULGARIA (d. 1255?). Nicaean empress. Name variations: Helena. Died c. 1255; dau. of Asen II also known as Ivan Asen II, ruler of Bulgaria (r. 1218–1241); m. Theodore II Lascaris, Nicaean emperor (r. 1254–1258); children: Irene Lascaris (d. around 1270, who m. Constantine Tich, tsar of Bulgaria); Maria (who m. Nicephorus I of Epirus); John IV Lascaris, Nicaean emperor (b. 1251, r. 1258–1261). ❖ A Bulgarian princess, was brought to Nicaean court as a child where she grew up as Theodore II Lascaris' intended bride.

HELEN OF DENMARK (d. 1233). Duchess of Brunswick-Luneburg. Died Nov 22, 1233; dau. of Sophie of Russia (c. 1140–1198) and Valdemar also known as Waldemar I the Great (1131–1182), king of Denmark (r. 1157–1182); m. William of Winchester (1184–1213), duke of Brunswick-Luneburg, in July 1202; children: Otto I Puer also known as Otto the Child (1204–1252), duke of Brunswick-Luneburg (r. 1235–1252).

HELEN OF GNESEN (d. 1299). See Yolanda of Gnesen.

HELEN OF GREECE (1896–1982). Princess of Greece. Name variations: Helen Oldenburg; Helen of Greece; Helen of Romania; Helen of Rumania. Born May 2 or 3, 1896, in Athens, Greece; died Nov 28, 1982, in Lausanne, Switzerland; eldest dau. of Constantine I, king of Greece (r. 1913–1917, 1920–1922), and Sophie of Prussia (1870–1932); sister of George II, king of the Hellenes; m. Carol II (1893–1953), crown prince, then king of Romania (r. 1930–1940), Mar 10, 1921 (div., June 21, 1928); children: Michael (b. Oct 25, 1921), king of Romania (r. 1927–1930, 1940–1947).

HELEN OF HUNGARY (fl. mid-1000s). Queen of Croatia. Born c. 1040; dau. of Richesa of Poland (fl. 1030–1040) and Bela I, king of Hungary (r. 1060–1063); sister of St. Ladislas I (1040–1095), king of Hungary (r. 1077–1095) and Geza I, king of Hungary (r. 1074–1077); m. Zwoinimir, king of Croatia.

HELEN OF NASSAU (1831–1888). Duchess of Waldeck and Pyrmont. Name variations: Helene or Hélène Henrietta von Nassau. Born Helen Wilhelmina Henrietta Pauline Marianne, Aug 12, 1831; died Oct 27, 1888; dau. of William (b. 1792), duke of Nassau, and Pauline of Wurttemberg (1810–1856); m. George II Victor, prince of Waldeck and Pyrmont, on Sept 26, 1853; children: Sophie Nicoline (1854–1869); Pauline Emma (1855–1925, who m. Alexis, 4th prince of Bentheim and Steinfurt); Maria of Waldeck (1857–1882); Emma of Waldeck (1858–1898, queen and regent of the Netherlands); Helen of Waldeck and Pyrmont (1861–1922); Frederick, prince of Waldeck and Pyrmont (1865–1946); Elizabeth (b. 1873, who m. Alexander, prince of Erbach-Schönberg).

HELEN OF RUMANIA (1896–1982). See Helen of Greece.

HELEN OF SCHLESWIG-HOLSTEIN (1888–1962). Princess of Schleswig-Holstein-Sonderburg-Glücksburg. Name variations: Helene of Schleswig-Holstein. Born June 1, 1888; died 1962; dau. of Frederick Ferdinand (1855–1934), duke of Schleswig-Holstein (r. 1885–1934), and Caroline Matilda of Schleswig-Holstein (1860–1932); m. Harald (son of Louise of Sweden and Frederick VIII, king of Denmark); children: Feodora Caroline-Mathilde (1910–1975, who m. Prince Christian Nicholas of Schaumburg-Lippe); Caroline Matilda of Denmark (1912—); Alexandrine-Louise (1914–1962, who m. Luitpold Alfred, count of Castell-Castell); Gorm Christian (b. 1919); Oluf (b. 1923), count of Rosenburg.

HELEN OF WALDECK AND PYRMONT (1861–1922). Duchess of Albany. Name variations: Helene Friederike Auguste, princess of the small German principality of Waldeck-Pyrmont, in Arolsen, Hesse, Germany, Feb 17, 1861; died in Hinterris, Tyrol, Austria, Sept 1, 1922; dau. of George Victor, prince of Waldeck and Pyrmont, and Helen of Nassau (1831–1888); sister of Emma of Waldeck (1858–1898, queen and regent of the Netherlands); m. Leopold Saxe-Coburg (1853–1884), duke of Albany, in 1882; children: Alice of Athlone (1883–1981); Charles Edward Saxe-Coburg, 2nd duke of Albany (1884–1954).

HELEN OF WALDECK AND PYRMONT (1899–1948). Grand duchess of Oldenburg. Name variations: Princess Helene or Hélène Bathildis Charlotte zu Waldeck. Born Helen Bathildis Charlotte Mary Fredericka, Dec 22, 1899; died Feb 18, 1948; dau. of Frederick, prince of Waldeck and Pyrmont (1865–1946), and Bathildis of Schaumburg-Lippe (1873–1962); m. Nicholas (b. 1897), grand duke of Oldenburg, Oct 26, 1921; children: Anton (b. 1923); Rixa Elizabeth (1924–1939, who died after she fell from a horse); Peter (b. 1926); Eilika of Oldenburg (b. 1928); Egilmar (b. 1934); Frederick Augustus (b. 1936), duke of Oldenburg; Altburg Elizabeth (b. 1938); Hans-Frederick (b. 1940) and Huno-Frederick (b. 1940). ❖ Two years after Helen's death, Grand Duke Nicholas married Anne-Marie von Schutzbar.

HELEN PALEOLOGINA (c. 1415–1458). Queen of Cyprus. Name variations: Helen Paleologa; Helen Palaeologa. Born in Greece c. 1415; died April 1458 at a Dominican monastery and was interred there; dau. of Theodore II Paleologus, despot of Morea and duke of Sparta (and 2nd son of Byzantine emperor Manuel II); m. John II, the Lusignan king of Cyprus (r. 1432–1458), 1442 (whose 1st wife Medea died in 1440, after only a few months of marriage); children: Cleopatra (died in infancy); Charlotte of Lusignan (1442–1487). John II also had an illeg. son, James II the Bastard, king of Cyprus (r. 1460–1473), with Marietta. ❖ As a child, grew up in the court at Mistra, one of the last bastions of Byzantine culture; married John II, the Lusignan king of Cyprus (1442); was extremely hostile to the Latin religious rite and to the Westerness which then dominated what had for so long been a Byzantine possession; set out to re-Hellenize her adopted home with help of foster-brother Thomas of Morea; though she met much opposition, became a force to be reckoned with because husband had little interest in ruling; won recognition as John's regent and took over rule of Cyprus; effectively dominated politics of the island for 16 years. ❖ See also Women in World History.

HELENA. Variant of Elena; (French) Heléna, Hélène; (German) Helene; (Italian) Elena, Eleonora and Leonora.

HELENA (fl. after 333 BCE). Ancient Greek painter. Name variations: Helen or Helene. Fl. after 333 BCE; dau. of an otherwise unknown Timon from Egypt. ❖ Painted a famous picture of the battle of Issus. ❖ See also Women in World History.

HELENA (c. 255–329). Roman empress and mother of Constantine the Great. Name variations: Saint Helena; Helena of Constantinople. Born c. 255, of lowly origins, probably in northwestern Asia Minor; died c. 329; buried in Rome, where remains were long sought out by Christians pilgrims; became consort, or possibly wife, of Constantius I Chlorus (Western Roman emperor with Galerius, r. 305–306), probably in 270s (died 306); children: Flavius Valerius Aurelius Constantinus Magnus, known as Constantine I the Great (c. 285–337), Roman emperor (r. 306–337). ❖ Made a famous pilgrimage through the Holy Land in search of relics and sites associated with life of Jesus, thereby helping to set a trend in religious piety which would help to define the Middle Ages; rose to top of Roman imperial society when she became companion of Constantius I Chlorus (probably 270s); had son Constantine (c. 285) but was dismissed by Constantius when he married the daughter of 1 of the 2 Roman senior emperors in order to assure his (and Constantine's) political future; when Constantius called Constantine to the West (306), followed in his train, to be established in German city of Trier; became a devout Christian and may have influenced Constantine increasingly towards Christianity (which he was the 1st to legalize); when Constantine defeated several rivals to control the Western Empire (312), seems to have left Trier for Rome, where she probably remained until 326, acting as her son's liaison in the West and dispensing imperial largesse; probably called East (326) to play some role in the tragedy which saw Constantine 1st (unjustly) execute his oldest son for treason, and then his wife; named by her son an Augusta (324), was thereafter without peer in his life until she died; to atone for the family murders and to help overcome the contemporary tendency for the Church to disintegrate into different theological factions, made a famous pilgrimage to the Holy Land, where she again dispensed largesse in name of son, built churches, and perhaps sought religious relics (this early excursus helped to establish the Medieval passion for pilgrimage, especially to the Holy Land). ❖ See also Women in World History.

HELENA (c. 320–?). Byzantine and Roman empress. Born c. 320; dau. of Constantius also known as Constantine I the Great, Roman emperor (r. 306–337), and Fausta (d. 324); granddau. of Helena (c. 255–329); m. Julian, Roman emperor and Byzantine emperor (r. 361–363). ❖ See also *Women in World History.*

HELENA (1846–1923). Duchess of Schleswig-Holstein-Sonderburg-Augustenberg. Name variations: Helena of Saxe-Coburg; Princess Christian of Schleswig-Holstein. Born Helena Augusta Victoria, May 25, 1846, in Buckingham Palace, London, England; died June 9, 1923, in London, England; 3rd dau. of Queen Victoria (1819–1901) and Prince Albert Saxe-Coburg; sister of King Edward VII of England; m. Christian of Schleswig-Holstein-Sonderburg-Augustenberg, July 5, 1866; children: Christian; Albert, duke of Schleswig-Holstein-Sonderburg-Augustenberg; Helena Victoria (1870–1948); Marie-Louise (1872–1956); Harold. ❖ See also *Women in World History.*

HELENA CANTACUZENE (fl. 1340s). Byzantine empress. Fl. in 1340s; dau. of Irene Asen and John VI Cantacuzene, emperor of Nicaea (r. 1347–1354); m. John V Paleologus (d. 1391), emperor of Nicaea (r. 1341–1347, 1355–1391); children: Andronicus IV Paleologus (d. 1385), emperor of Nicaea (r. 1376–1379); Manuel II Paleologus, emperor of Nicaea (r. 1391–1425); Theodore I, despot of Morea.

HELENA DRAGAS (fl. 1400). Byzantine empress. Name variations: Dragases. Born in Serbia; fl. in 1400; m. Manuel II Paleologus, emperor of Nicaea (r. 1391–1425); children: John VIII Paleologus (1391–1448), emperor of Nicaea (r. 1425–1448); Theodore II; Andronicus; Constantine XI Paleologus, emperor of Nicaea (r. 1448–1453); Demetrius; Thomas.

HELENA LEKAPENA (c. 920–961). Byzantine empress. Name variations: Helen Lecapena or Lecapenus. Born c. 920 in Constantinople; died Sept 19, 961 (some sources cite 960); dau. of Romanos I Lekapenos also known as Romanus I Lecapenus (r. 919–944, who reigned as co-emperor with Constantine VII), and Theodora (fl. early 900s); sister of Theophylaktos, patriarch of Constantinople; m. Constantine VII Porphyrogenitus (c. 906–959), Byzantine emperor (r. 913–959), on April 27, 919; children: Romanos or Romanus II, Byzantine emperor (r. 959–963); and 5 daughters, including Agatha and Theodora (late 900s, who m. John I Tzimiskes, emperor of Byzantium [r. 969–976]). ❖ As a young girl, was married off to 13-year-old Constantine (VII Porphyrogenitus), so her father could reign as senior co-emperor (919–944); when her son ascended the throne as Romanus II, was banished from court by his wife, Theophano (c. 940–?), and died some months later. ❖ See also *Women in World History.*

HELENA OF ALYPIA (fl. 980s). Byzantine empress. Name variations: Helena of Alypius. Fl. in 980s CE; born into a noble family of Constantinople; m. Constantine VIII, Byzantine emperor (r. 1025–1028); children: Eudocia (b. 978); Zoë Porphyrogenita (980–1050); Theodora Porphyrogenita (c. 989–1056); possibly Irene of Byzantium (d. 1067).

HELENA OF CONSTANTINOPLE (c. 255–329). *See Helena.*

HELENA OF EPIRUS (fl. 1250s). Queen of Sicily. Fl. in 1250s; 2nd wife of Manfred, king of Naples and Sicily (r. 1258–1266, illeg. son of Frederick II, Holy Roman emperor [r. 1215–1250]). Manfred's 1st wife was Beatrice of Savoy.

HELENA OF ITALY (1873–1952). *See Elena of Montenegro.*

HELENA OF MONTENEGRO (1873–1952). *See Elena of Montenegro.*

HELENA OF RUSSIA (1882–1957). Grand duchess of the imperial court in St. Petersburg. Name variations: Helen, Helene, Hélène Romanov, Helen Vladimirovna; Princess Nicholas of Greece. Born Helen Vladimirovna, Jan 17, 1882; died Mar 13, 1957; dau. of Maria of Mecklenburg-Schwerin (1854–1920) and Grand Duke Vladimir Alexandrovitch (son of Alexander II, tsar of Russia); m. Prince Nicholas (Oldenburg) of Greece (uncle of England's Prince Philip), Aug 29, 1902; children: Olga Oldenburg (1903–1981); Elizabeth Oldenburg (1904–1955); Marina of Greece (1906–1968).

HELENA OF SAXE-COBURG (1846–1923). *See Helena.*

HELENA OF SERBIA (fl. 1100s). Queen of Hungary. Fl. in 1100s; m. Bela II, king of Hungary (r. 1131–1141); children: Jolanta (who m. Boleslas of Kalisz); Geza II (1130–1161), king of Hungary (r. 1141–1161); Ladislas II, king of Hungary (r. 1162); Stephen IV, king of Hungary (r. 1162–1163).

HELENA PAVLOVNA (1784–1803). Russian princess. Name variations: Helene or Hélène Romanov. Born Dec 24, 1784; died Sept 24, 1803; dau. of Sophia Dorothea of Wurttemberg (1759–1828) and Paul I (1754–1801), tsar of Russia (r. 1796–1801); sister of Anna Pavlovna (1795–1865), Marie Pavlovna (1786–1859), and Catherine of Russia (1788–1819); became 1st wife of Frederick Louis (1778–1819), duke of Mecklenburg-Schwerin, Oct 23, 1799; children: Paul Frederick, grand duke of Mecklenburg-Schwerin (b. 1800). Frederick Louis' 2nd wife was Caroline Louise of Saxe-Weimar (1786–1816).

HELENA VICTORIA (1870–1948). Princess of Great Britain. Born Victoria Louise Sophia Augusta Amelia Helena, May 3, 1870, in Windsor, Berkshire, England; died Mar 13, 1948, in London; dau. of Helena (1846–1923), duchess of Schleswig-Holstein-Sonderburg-Augustenberg, and Christian of Schleswig-Holstein-Sonderburg-Augustenberg.

HELENE. *Variant of Helena.*

HELENE (1903–1924). Duchess of Wurttemberg. Born Oct 30, 1903, in Linz; died Sept 8, 1924, in Tubingen; dau. of Maria Cristina of Sicily (1877–1947) and Archduke Peter Ferdinand (1874–1948).

HELENE LOUISE OF MECKLENBURG-SCHWERIN (1814–1858). Duchess of Chartres and Orléans. Name variations: Hélène Louise of Mecklenburg-Schwerin; Helen of Mecklenburg-Schwerin; Helene Louise Elisabeth d' Orleans. Born Jan 24, 1814; died May 18, 1858; dau. of Frederick Louis, grand duke of Mecklenburg-Schwerin, and Caroline Louise of Saxe-Weimar (1786–1816); m. Ferdinand Philippe (1810–1842), duke of Chartres and Orléans (r. 1830–1842), May 30, 1837 (killed in carriage accident, July 13, 1842); children: Louis Philippe (1838–1894), count of Paris; Robert (1840–1910), duke of Chartres.

HELENE OF BAVARIA (1834–1890). Princess of Thurn and Taxis. Born April 4, 1834; died May 16, 1890; dau. of Ludovica (1808–1892) and Maximilian Joseph (1808–1888), duke of Bavaria; m. Maximilian Anton Lamoral, prince of Thurn and Taxis; children: Elizabeth Maria of Thurn and Taxis (1860–1881).

HELENE OF BRUNSWICK-LUNEBURG (d. 1273). Duchess of Saxony. Died Sept 6, 1273; dau. of Matilda of Brandenburg (d. 1261) and Otto I Puer also known as Otto the Child (1204–1252), duke of Brunswick-Luneburg (r. 1235–1252); became second wife of Albrecht also known as Albert I, duke of Saxony (r. 1212–1261), in 1247. Albert I was previously married to Agnes of Thuringia.

HELENE OF MOLDAVIA (d. 1505). Princess of Moscow. Died Jan 18, 1505; dau. of Stephen III, hospodar of Moldavia; m. Ivan the Younger (1456–1490), prince of Moscow (r. 1471–1490), Jan 6, 1482; children: Dimitri of Moscow (b. 1485).

HELENE OF MOSCOW (1474–1513). Queen of Poland. Born May 19, 1474 (some sources cite 1476); died Jan 24, 1513; dau. of Sophia of Byzantium (1448–1503) and Ivan III (1440–1505), grand prince of Moscow (r. 1462–1505); m. Alexander (1461–1506), king of Poland (r. 1501–1506), Feb 15, 1495.

HELENE OF SCHLESWIG-HOLSTEIN (1888–1962). *See Helen of Schleswig-Holstein.*

HELENE OF WURTTEMBERG (1807–1873). Grand duchess of Russia. Name variations: Charlotte; Helene von Württemberg. Born Jan 9, 1807; died Feb 2, 1873; dau. of Catherine Charlotte of Hildburghausen (1787–1847) and Paul Charles Frederick (1785–1852), duke of Wurttemberg; m. Grand Duke Michael of Russia (1798–1849), on Feb 20, 1824; children: Marie Michailovna Romanov (1825–1846); Elizabeth Romanov (1826–1845); Catherine Romanov (1827–1894); Alexandra (1831–1832); Anna (1834–1836).

HELFER, Gail (1953—). *See Ricketson, Gail.*

HELFMAN or HELFMANN, Guessia (d. 1882). *See Gelfman, Gesia.*

HELGA. *Variant of Olga.*

HELIA DE SEMUR (fl. 1020–1046). Duchess of Burgundy. Name variations: Helie de Semur-en-Brionnais. Fl. between 1020 and 1046; dau. of Damas I de Semur-en-Brionnais and Aremburge de Bourgogne; m. Robert I (1011–1076), duke of Burgundy (r. 1032–1076), c. 1033 (div. 1046); children: Hugh (b. 1034); Henry (1035–1066), duke of Burgundy; Robert (b. 1040); Simon; Constance of Burgundy (1046–c. 1093, who m. Alphonso VI, king of Castile & Leon). Robert I was also m. to Ermengarde of Anjou (1018–1076).

HELLA, Eeva (1921–2004). *See Joenpelto, Eeva.*

HELLABY, Amy Maria (1864–1955). New Zealand entrepreneur. Name variations: Amy Maria Briscoe. Born on Feb 3, 1864, in Birkenhead, Cheshire, England; died on April 7, 1955, in Epsom, New Zealand; dau. of John Briscoe (cabinet-maker) and Elizabeth (Bishop) Briscoe; m. Richard Hellaby (butcher), 1885 (died 1902); children: 3 daughters, 3 sons. ❖ Immigrated to New Zealand with father (1872); after death of husband, managed large business in meat industry (1902); employed more than 250 people at R&W Hellaby Ltd, which exported frozen meat to Great Britain and tinned corned beef to Pacific Island and was New Zealand's largest privately owned company. ❖ See also *Dictionary of New Zealand Biography* (Vol. 3).

HELLEMANS, Greet (1959—). Dutch rower. Born May 25, 1959, in Denmark. ❖ At Los Angeles Olympics, won a bronze medal in coxed eights and a silver medal in double sculls (1984).

HELLEMANS, Nicolette (1961—). Dutch rower. Born Nov 30, 1961, in Denmark. ❖ At Los Angeles Olympics, won a bronze medal in coxed eights and a silver medal in double sculls (1984).

HELLENES, queen of.
See Amalie (1818–1875).
See Olga Constantinovna (1851–1926).
See Sophie of Prussia (1870–1932).
See Elisabeth (1894–1956).
See Manos, Aspasia (1896–1972).
See Fredericka (1917–1981).
See Anne-Marie Oldenburg (b. 1946).

HELLIWELL, Ethel (c. 1905—). English theater and film dance director. Born c. 1905 in UK; sister of Dorothy Helliwell. ❖ Performed with sister Dorothy in ballet act as children; worked as dance director of Lew Mangam's Plaza theatre and head of production of his cine-variety circuit, the equivalent of US Prologs; created numerous precision lines and adagio pieces for Plaza-Tiller and Mangam-Tiller Girls; worked on many musical films, including *Avec l'assurance* (1931), *Louise* (1931), *L'Amour chante* (1932), and *Il est charmant* (1932).

HELLMAN, Ilse (1908–1998). *See Noach, Ilse.*

HELLMAN, Lillian (1905–1984). American playwriter, screenwriter, and memoirist. Name variations: Lily; Lillian Kober. Born Lillian Hellman, June 20, 1905, in New Orleans, Louisiana; died at Martha's Vineyard, June 30, 1984; dau. of Max Hellman (salesman) and Julia (Newhouse) Hellman; attended New York University for 2 years; m. Arthur Kober (press agent), 1925 (div. 1933); lived with Dashiell Hammett; no children. ❖ Major American playwright, distinguished for her unprecedented success for a woman on Broadway and for her literary career, including screenwriting and memoirs, which spanned nearly 50 years; with family moved back and forth between New Orleans and New York City before she settled in NY at 16; at 19, worked for Liveright Publishing Co. as clerk-reader until she married (1925); moved to Paris, then Hollywood with husband; landed job as a script reader for MGM; met Dashiell Hammett (1930); wrote *The Children's Hour*, her 1st hit play (1934); became a screenwriter for MGM but continued theater work; known for her political and social activism (1930s–40s), supported anti-fascist cause in Spain by financing and collaborating on film documentary on Spanish Civil War; was one of the chief sponsors of Waldorf Peace Conference (1949); called to testify before House Un-American Activities Committee (1952), where she narrowly avoided being cited for contempt for refusal to "name names"; blacklisted from Hollywood (late 1940s–early 1950s); after 12 original plays and 3 adaptations, illustrious career in theater was over by 1963; collaborated on final screenplay, *The Chase* (1966); in her 60s, embarked on literary career with her critically acclaimed memoirs; organized and chaired Committee for Public Justice (1970s); plays include *The Little Foxes* (1939), *Watch on the Rhine* (1941), *Another Part of the Forest* (1946), *The Autumn Garden* (1951) and *Toys in the Attic* (1960); books include *An Unfinished Woman* (1969), *Pentimento* (1973), *Scoundrel Time* (1976) and *Maybe* (1980). Received Drama Critics Circle Award for *Watch on the Rhine* (1941) and *Toys in the Attic* (1960); National Book Award for Arts and Letters for *An Unfinished Woman* (1969). ❖ See also William Wright, *Lillian Hellman: The Image, The Woman* (Simon & Schuster, 1986); Joan Mellen, *Hellman and Hammett* (HarperCollins, 1996); and *Women in World History*.

HELLMANN, Angelika (1954—). East German gymnast. Born April 10, 1954, in Halle, East Germany; dau. of Rudi Hellmann (sports official). ❖ At World championships, won a team silver in all-around (1970) and a bronze all-around (1974); at European championships, won bronze medal for uneven bars (1971) and gold medal for vault and silver for uneven bars (1973); won silver medal at Munich Olympics (1972) and bronze medal at Montreal Olympics (1976), both in team all-around; placed 2nd all-around at Chunichi Cup (1973), 1st all-around at Milk Meet (1974); coaches in Germany.

HELLMANN, Ilse (1908–1998). *See Noach, Ilse.*

HELLMANN-OPITZ, Martina (1960—). East German track-and-field athlete. Name variations: Martina Opitz. Born 1960 in East Germany. ❖ At Seoul Olympics, won gold medal in discus throw (1988).

HELLMUTH, Hermine Hug (1871–1924). *See Hug-Hellmuth, Hermine.*

HELM, Brigitte (1908–1996). German actress. Born Eva Gisela Schittenhelm (also seen as Gisele Eve Schittenhelm) in Berlin, Germany, Mar 17, 1908 (some sources cite 1906); died in Ancona, Switzerland, June 11, 1996; m. Hugh Kunheim (industrialist). ❖ At 16, was given the lead in Fritz Lang's *Metropolis*, an allegory of totalitarianism written by Thea von Harbou (1926); became an international star; appeared in 2 important early films directed by G.W. Pabst: *Die Liebe der Jeanne Ney* (1927) and *Crisis* (1928); starred in over 35 movies during German film industry's golden age, then retired to marry (1933). ❖ See also *Women in World History*.

HELM, June (1924—). American sociocultural anthropologist. Name variations: June Helm MacNeish; June King. Born June Helm, Sept 1924 in Twin Falls, Idaho; only child of Julia Frances (Dixon) Helm and William Jennings Helm; University of Chicago, PhB, AM, and PhD; m. Richard "Scotty" MacNeish (archaeologist), 1945 (div. 1958); m. Pierce E. King (architect), 1968. ❖ Served as teacher (1951) in village of Slavey Indians (part of Dene/Athapaskan peoples) in Canada; conducted additional research among the Slave (1952, 1954, 1955) which became basis of *The Lynx Point People* (1961); began association with Athapaskan Dogrib Indians of Northwestern Canadian subarctic (1959) and began to study Dogrib at Rae (1962); served as assistant professor (beginning 1960) and professor (beginning 1966) of anthropology at University of Iowa; served as president of American Anthropological Association (1985–87); known primarily for ethnographic studies of Dene Indians.

HELMBOLDT, Margitte (1941—). *See Gummel-Helmboldt, Margitte.*

HELMER, Bessie Bradwell (1858–1927). American lawyer and editor. Born in Chicago, Illinois, Oct 20, 1858; died in Battle Creek, Michigan, Jan 10, 1927; dau. of Myra (Colby) Bradwell (legal reformer and entrepreneur) and James Bolesworth Bradwell; graduated 1st in class, Chicago High School, 1876, and 1st in class, Union College of Law (later Northwestern University Law School), 1882; m. Frank A. Helmer (lawyer), 1885. ❖ Following mother's death (1894), became assistant editor of *Chicago Legal News*; was editor-in-chief and president of the company (1907–27). ❖ See also *Women in World History*.

HELMOND, Katherine (1934—). American stage, tv, and screen actress and director. Born July 5, 1934, in Galveston, TX; m. David Christian, 1962. ❖ Came to prominence as Jessica Tate on tv's "Soap" (1977–81); directed the film *Bankrupt* and episodes for tv's "Benson" and "Who's the Boss?"; films include *The Hospital, Believe in Me, The Hindenburg, Family Plot, Time Bandits, Brazil, Shadey, Overboard, Lady in White* and *Big Paw: Beethoven 5.*

HELMRICH, Dorothy (1889–1984). Australian singer. Born Dorothy Jane Adele Hellmrich (later changed to Helmrich), in Woollahra, New South Wales, July 25, 1889; died in Strathfield, Australia, Sept 1, 1984; studied singing at New South Wales State Conservatorium and at Royal College of Music, London; never married. ❖ Began musical career with Mosman Musical Society; made London debut at Wigmore Hall, followed by engagements throughout the provinces as well as radio broadcasts; built an international reputation, touring widely in Britain, Europe, and US; held a teaching post at New South Wales State Conservatorium (1941–74); founded Australian Council for the Encouragement of Music and the Arts (CEMA, 1943), which evolved into Arts Council of Australia (1946), of which she served as vice president and later president of NSW division for 20 years. ❖ See also *Women in World History*.

HELOISE. *Variant of Lois.*

HELOISE (c. 1100–1163). French nun and paramour. Born c. 1100; died May 16, 1163 (some sources cite 1164); educated at convent of Argenteuil; tutored by Peter Abelard, around 1117, in Paris; m. Peter

Abelard, around 1118 (died 1142); children: Astrolabe. ❖ Highly educated French abbess of the 12th century who was the mistress and wife of the medieval philosopher Peter Abelard; attracted the attention of her contemporaries in 3 periods of her life: as a young girl (when her reputation for learning was known to many 12th-century scholars and clergy), as a young woman (when her passionate affair with the towering intellectual Peter Abelard resulted in love songs immortalizing the relationship), and as a maturing woman (when she went on to become the abbess of her own convent); gave birth to her only child Astrolabe and subsequently married Abelard (c. 1118); became a nun at Argenteuil (1118); installed as abbess of the Paraclete (1129); corresponded with Abelard (early 1130s). ❖ See also Betty Radice, trans., *The Letters of Abelard and Heloise* (Penguin, 1974); Etienne Gilson, *Heloise and Abelard* (University of Michigan Press, 1960); and *Women in World History*.

HELSER, Brenda (1926—). American swimmer. Name variations: Brenda Helser DeMorelos (also seen as DeMoreles). Born May 26, 1926; trained under Jack Cody in Portland, Oregon; graduate of Stanford University, 1946. ❖ At London Olympics, won a gold medal in the 4x100-meter freestyle relay (1948).

HELTEN, Inge (1950—). West German runner. Born Dec 31, 1950, in Germany. ❖ At Montreal Olympics, won a bronze medal in 100 meters and a silver medal in 4x100-meter relay (1976).

HELUIDIS. *Variant of Helvidis.*

HELVÉTIUS, Madame (1719–1800). French salonnière. Name variations: Anne-Catherine Helvetius; Anne-Catherine de Ligniville d'Autricourt; Anne Catherine "Minette" de Ligniville. Born Anne-Catherine de Ligniville d'Autricourt, 1719, in France; died 1800; m. Claude-Adrien Helvétius (1715–1771, philosopher and father of utilitarianism); children: Marie Adelaide Genevieve, countess d'Andlau (1754–1817). ❖ Renowned, well-connected beauty, reigned over a salon of Enlightenment philosophes on her estate near the Bois de Boulogne; was the object of Benjamin Franklin's amorous attentions.

HELVIDIS (fl. 1136). French physician. Name variations: Heluidis. Fl. in 1136 in Lille, France. ❖ Physician and lay healer, was the 1st woman doctor of northern Europe listed as such in contemporary records.

HELVIG. *Variant of Helwig.*

HELVIG OF DENMARK (fl. 1350s). Queen of Denmark. Name variations: Heilwig Ericsdottir; Helvig of Slesvig or Schleswig. Fl. in 1350s; died c. 1374; dau. of Erik, duke of Schleswig, and Adelheid of Holstein; sister of Valdemar or Waldemar III, duke of Schleswig; married Valdemar IV also known as Waldemar IV Atterdag, king of Denmark (r. 1340–1375), June 1340; children: Margaret I (1353–1412), queen of Denmark, Norway, and Sweden; Ingeborg (1347–1370, who m. Henry of Mecklenburg); Christof (1344–1363), duke of Laaland; Margaret (1345–1350); Katherina Valdemarsdottir (b. 1349); Waldemar (b. 1350).

HELVIG OF SLESVIG (fl. 1350s). *See Helvig of Denmark.*

HELWIG. *Variant of Helwig.*

HELWIG OF PRAGUE (fl. 14th c.). Leader of Beguines in Germany. Fl. in 14th century in Prague; never married; no children. ❖ A German member of the Beguine religious order, was an acknowledged leader of the sect when it was condemned by Pope John XXII (1332). ❖ See also *Women in World History*.

HEMANS, Felicia D. (1793–1835). English poet and dramatist. Name variations: Felicia Browne. Born Felicia Dorothea Browne in Duke Street, Liverpool, England, Sept 25, 1793; died at Redesdale, near Dublin, May 16, 1835; dau. of George Browne (merchant of Irish extraction) and Felicity (Wagner) Browne (dau. of Austrian and Tuscan consul at Liverpool); educated by mother; m. Captain Alfred Hemans (Irish soldier), 1812 (sep. 1818); children: 5 sons. ❖ At 7, moved with family to Wales; extremely popular in her day, published *The Domestic Affections and Other Poems* (1812), *The Restoration of Works of Art to Italy* (1816), *Modern Greece* (1817) and *Translations from Camoens and other Poets* (1818); when husband abandoned family (1818), devoted her time to educating her children and writing, generating income to add to meager finances; published *Tales and Historic Scenes in Verse* and *The Meeting of Wallace and Bruce on the Banks of the Carron* (1819); issued *The Sceptic* and *Stanzas to the Memory of the late King* (1820); won Royal Society of Literature award for poem "Dartmoor" (1821) and published the poems, "Sieve of Valencia," "Last Constantine," and "Belshazzar's

Feats" (1823); published the *Records of Woman* (1828); received many awards for poetry which was found in many school collections, though now considered sentimental. ❖ See also *Women in World History*.

HEMENWAY, Abby (1828–1890). American historian. Born Abby Maria Hemenway, Oct 7, 1828, in Ludlow, Vermont; died Feb 24, 1890, in Chicago, Illinois; dau. of Daniel Sheffield Hemenway (farmer) and Abigail (Barton) Hemenway. ❖ Taught school in Michigan (mid-1850s), wrote sentimental poetry, and published 1st work, *Poets and Poetry of Vermont* (1858); began anthologizing history of VT with 6 issues of *Vermont Quarterly Gazetteer* (1860–63) until work had to be suspended for lack of financial support; published poetry anthology *Songs of the War* (1863) and 3 volumes of religious verse (1865–73) after converting to Roman Catholic faith (1864); republished fragments from gazetteer with additional materials as 1st volume of *The Vermont Historical Gazetteer* (1867), which was followed by subsequent volumes, the 5th of which was partially destroyed in fire (1886) and completed after her death by sister Carrie E. H. Page (1891). Her over 6,000 pages of work have been relied upon heavily by subsequent historians of VT.

HEMENWAY, Mary Porter Tileston (1820–1894). American philanthropist. Born Mary Porter Tileston in New York, NY, Dec 20, 1820; died in Boston, Massachusetts, Mar 6, 1894; dau. of Thomas (shipping merchant) and Mary (Porter) Tileston; attended private schools in NY; m. Augustus Hemenway (wealthy Boston merchant), June 25, 1840 (died 1876); children: Charlotte Augusta (b. 1841), Alice (1845–1847), Amy (b. 1848), Edith (b. 1851) and Augustus Hemenway (b. 1853). ❖ Embarked on long career in philanthropy (1860), primarily revolving around education; established Boston Normal School of Cookery to train more teachers (1887); donated funds to establish Tileston Normal School in Wilmington, NC, for poor whites (1871); contributed to Tuskegee and Hampton Institutes; purchased land for Brambleton School in Norfolk, VA (1880); also commissioned the Hemenway Southwestern Archaeological Expedition to carry out archaeological and ethnological field studies among the Zuñi and Hopi tribes (1886) and underwrote a report of the work, which appeared in 5 volumes of the *Journal of American Ethnology and Archaeology* (1891–1908). ❖ See also *Women in World History*.

HEMESSEN, Caterina van (c. 1528–c. 1587). Flemish painter. Name variations: Catherina. Born in Antwerp, Belgium, c. 1528; died in Spain, c. 1587; dau. of Jan van Hemessen (notable painter); m. Chrétien de Morien (musician), 1554; no children. ❖ One of the 1st Flemish women artists ever documented, is known to have rendered 10 paintings (1548–52), 8 small portraits of women and 2 religious works probably based on prints. ❖ See also *Women in World History*.

HEMING, Violet (1895–1981). English-born actress. Born Violet Hemming, Jan 27, 1895, in Leeds, Yorkshire, England; died July 4, 1981, in New York, NY; dau. of Alfred Hemming (actor); m. Grant Mills (div.); m. Bennett Champ Clark (judge, died 1954). ❖ Made 1st stage appearance in US (1908) in *Peter Pan*; on Broadway, appeared in numerous productions including *Sonya, The Rubicon, The Rivals, Trelawny of the Wells, Loose Ends, Within the Law, Ladies All, Yes My Darling Daughter, Love for Love* and *Dear Barbarians*; made several films, including *The Man Who Played God*; retired (1945).

HEMINGS, Sally (1773–1835). African-American slave. Name variations: Sally Hemmings; Black Sally. Born Sally Hemings in 1773, on one of the Virginia plantations belonging to John Wayles; died 1835 (some sources cite 1836), in Albemarle Co., Virginia; dau. of John Wayles (wealthy planter and slave trader) and his mulatto slave Elizabeth (Betty) Hemings; half-sister of Martha Jefferson; no legal marriage noted; children: Thomas (whose actual existence is questionable but may have been Thomas Woodson [1790–1879]); Edy (b. 1796, died in infancy); Harriett (1795–1797); Beverly (1798–?); Harriett (1801–?); Madison (1805–1877); Eston (1808–1852). ❖ Slave who for years was the subject of speculation regarding her relationship with Thomas Jefferson (now thought to be the father of at least one of her children), arrived at Monticello as an infant (1774); was among the slaves inherited by her half-sister Martha Jefferson, wife of Thomas Jefferson; lived in Paris as a personal servant to the Jefferson daughters (1787–89), and upon return to Monticello resumed duties as a housemaid; freed by Jefferson's daughter, Martha Jefferson Randolph, not long after Jefferson's death, went to live with her two freed sons, Madison and Eston, for the remainder of her life. DNA tests proved that at least one son, Eston, is of the Jefferson blood-line (1999). ❖ See also Annette Gordon-Reed, *Thomas Jefferson and Sally Hemings: An American*

Controversy (U. Press of Virginia, 1997); Barbara Chase-Riboud, *Sally Hemings* (Viking, 1979); and *Women in World History.*

HEMINGWAY, Margaux (1955–1996). American model and actress. Born Feb 16, 1955, in Portland, Oregon; committed suicide, July 1, 1996, in Santa Monica, CA; dau. of Jack Hemingway; granddau. of Ernest Hemingway; sister of Mariel Hemingway (actress); m. Erroll Weston, 1977 (div. 1978); m. Bernard Foucher, 1979 (div.). ❖ Began career as a model; films include *Lipstick, Killer Fish, They Call Me Bruce, Over the Brooklyn Bridge,* and *Inner Sanctum.*

HEMINGWAY, Marie (c. 1893–1939). English actress. Born c. 1893 in Yorkshire, England; died June 11, 1939; m. Claude Rains (actor), 1920 (div. 1920). ❖ Made stage debut as Nahasi in *False Gods* (1909), followed by *Playing with Fire, Dad, The Great John Ganton, Quality Street, Seven Days, Pen, The Passing of the Third Floor Back, The Liars, Up in Mabel's Room, In Nelson's Days,* and *No No Nanette,* among others; appeared as Ellean Tanqueray in the film *The Second Mrs. Tanqueray* (1916).

HEMINGWAY, Mariel (1961—). American actress. Born Hadley Mariel Hemingway, Nov 22, 1961, in Mill Valley, California; dau. of Jack Hemingway; granddau. of Ernest Hemingway; sister of Margaux Hemingway (actress); m. Stephen Crisman (filmmaker), 1984; children: daughters Dree and Langley. ❖ Came to prominence in Woody Allen's *Manhattan* (1979), for which she was nominated for an Academy Award; other films include *Lipstick* (1976), *Personal Best* (1982) and *Star 80* (1983); on tv, appeared in "Civil Wars" (1991–93).

HEMINILDE. *Variant of Emnilde.*

HEMMA OF BOHEMIA (c. 930–c. 1005). Duchess of Bohemia. Born c. 930 in Prague, Czechoslovakia; died c. 1005; 2nd wife of Boleslaw also known as Boleslav II the Pious (c. 920–999), duke of Bohemia (r. 972–999); children: possibly Boleslav III, duke of Bohemia; Jaromir Premysl, duke of Bohemia; Ulrich (b. around 966), duke of Bohemia. Boleslav's 1st wife was possibly Elfgifu (c. 914–?).

HEMMINGS, Deon (1968—). Jamaican runner. Name variations: Deon Marie Hemmings. Born Oct 9, 1968, in St. Ann, Jamaica. ❖ Won a gold medal for the 400-meter hurdles at Atlanta Olympics (1996); won a silver medal for 400-meter hurdles and a silver for 4x400-meter relay at Sydney Olympics (2000); at World championships, won a bronze medal (1997, 1999) and silver medal (1997), all for 400-meter hurdles.

HEMPEL, Claudia (1958—). East German swimmer. Born Sept 25, 1958, in East Germany. ❖ At Montreal Olympics, won a silver medal in 4x100-meter freestyle relay (1976).

HEMPEL, Frieda (1885–1955). German-born American coloratura soprano. Born Freda Hemple in Leipzig, Germany, June 26, 1885; died in West Berlin, Oct 7, 1955; studied voice with Selma Nicklass-Kempner at Stern Conservatory; m. William B. Kahn (div. 1926). ❖ Made debut as Mrs. Ford in *Die lustigen Weiber von Windsor* at Berlin's Royal Opera House (1905); while based at Schwerin Opera House during next several years, saw reputation spread throughout Germany; sang at London's Covent Garden opera, starring in both a Mozart role and in Humperdinck's *Hansel und Gretel* (1907); starred in Berlin revival of Meyerbeer's *Les Huguenots* (1908); sang Marschallin in Berlin premiere of *Der Rosenkavalier* (1911); debuted at NY's Metropolitan Opera (1912) as Marguerite de Valois (Margaret of Valois [1553–1615]) in *Les Huguenots*; during next 7 seasons, was one of Met's leading sopranos, giving performances as Rosina in *The Barber of Seville,* Queen of the Night in *The Magic Flute,* Olympia in *The Tales of Hoffmann,* Violeta in *La Traviata,* Gilda in *Rigoletto,* and title role in *Lucia di Lammermoor,* other outstanding performances include portrayal of the Marschallin in US premiere of *Der Rosenkavalier* (1913), the numerous times she sang opposite Enrico Caruso in *Elisir d'amore* and her appearance in US premiere of *Euryanthe* (1914); with advent of WWI and hatred for all things German, saw career flounder in US; appeared at Carnegie Hall (1920) in a duplicate of the concert given by Jenny Lind; went on to give more than 300 Jenny Lind concerts, then concentrated on Lieder recitals for more than 3 decades; gave last recital (1951). Received title of *Kammersängerin* (Court Singer). ❖ See also autobiography (with Johnston and Moran) *My Golden Age of Singing* (Amadeus, 1998); and *Women in World History.*

HEMPSTEAD, Mary (1782–1869). *See Lisa, Mary Manuel.*

HEMSLEY, Estelle (1887–1968). African-American stage and screen actress. Born May 5, 1887, in Boston, MA; died Nov 5, 1968, in Hollywood, CA. ❖ Began career as a dancer at Luna Park in Coney Island; toured with successful black companies, including Sisseretta Jones' *Black Patti's Troubadours* and Sid Archer's *Chocolate Drops*; on Broadway, appeared in *Darktown Follies, Harvey, Take a Giant Step, Tobacco Road* and *Mrs. Patterson*; films include *Harvey, Tobacco Road, Traveling Lady, America, America!* and *Baby, the Rain Must Fall*; had a long stint on radio on "Pretty Kitty Kelly." Nominated for Academy Award for Best Supporting Actress for *Take a Giant Step* (1960).

HENDEL, Henriette (1772–1849). German Greek revivalist actress and mime. Born Johanne Henrietta Schüler, Feb 13, 1772, in Döbeln, Sachsen, Germany; died Mar 4, 1849, in Köslin, Germany. ❖ Made performance debut in private showing, before touring Mainz, Bonn, and Amsterdam (1790s); portrayed title role in *Joan of Arc* for 10 years; studied archaeology and Greek mythology, from which she developed mime-like performance style she called "Mimischeplastik"; toured with repertory of tableaux including *Cassandra, Agrippina,* and *Ariadne* (until 1820).

HENDEL, Yehudit (1926—). Israeli novelist and short-story writer. Born 1926 in Warsaw, Poland; studied in Haifa. ❖ Major writer of the 1950s whose works include *Anashim Acherim* (1950), *Rechob Ha'Madregot* (1956), *The Yard of Momo the Great* (1969, reissued as *The Last Hamsin,* 1993), and *They are Different* (1951, 2000). Received Israeli Prize for Literature (2003).

HENDERLITE, Rachel (1905–1991). American Presbyterian minister and theologian. Born Dec 30, 1905, in Henderson, North Carolina; died of a heart attack, Nov 6, 1991, in Austin, TX; dau. of Rev. James H. and Nelle (Crow) Henderlite; attended Mary Baldwin College; Agnes Scott College, BA, 1928; New York University, MA in Christian education, 1936; Yale University, PhD in Christian ethics, 1947. ❖ The 1st woman to be ordained as Presbyterian minister in US, began career as a dean and professor of Bible at Mississippi Synodical College (1936–38), then Montreat College, near Black Mountain, NC (1938–41); studied ethics at Yale Divinity School under Niebuhr (1942–44); began 16-year professorship in applied Christianity and Christian nurture at Presbyterian School of Christian Education, a graduate program especially for women, in Richmond, VA; helped found Richmond's 1st predominantly black Presbyterian church; ordained as minister of All Souls Presbyterian Church in Richmond (1965), the 1st woman of her denomination to receive ordination; became 1st woman professor of Christian education at Austin Theological Seminary, TX (1966); served as 1st woman president of Presbyterian Council of Church Union (1977–82); writings include *A Call to Faith* (1955) and *Paul, Christian and World Traveler* (1957).

HENDERSON, Alice Corbin (1881–1949). American poet and editor. Name variations: Alice Corbin. Born Alice Corbin in St. Louis, Missouri, 1881; died 1949; dau. of Fillmore Mallory Corbin and Lula Hebe (Carradine) Corbin; m. William Penhallow Henderson (artist), 1905; children: Alice Henderson Evans. ❖ An associate editor of *Poetry* (1912–16), also wrote *Adam's Dream and Two Others Miracle Plays for Children* (1907), *The Spinning Woman of the Sky* (verse, 1912), *Red Earth* (verse, 1920), *The Sun Turns West* (verse, 1933), and *Brothers of Light, the Penitentes of the Southwest* (prose, 1937); co-edited, with Harriet Monroe, *The New Poetry: An Anthology* (1917); compiled *The Turquoise Trail,* an anthology of New Mexico poetry (1928). ❖ See also *Women in World History.*

HENDERSON, Annie Heloise Abel (1873–1947). *See Abel, Annie Heloise.*

HENDERSON, Catherine (1895–1977). *See Taylor, Eva.*

HENDERSON, Christina Kirk (1861–1953). New Zealand educator and suffragist. Born Christina Kirk Henderson, Aug 15, 1861, at Emerald Hill, Melbourne, Australia; died Sept 27, 1953, in Christchurch, NZ; 2nd of 9 children of Alice Connolly Henderson and Daniel Henderson (storekeeper); sister of Alice Henderson (missionary), Elizabeth McCombs (1873–1935, politician), and Stella Henderson (journalist); University of New Zealand, BA, 1891. ❖ Taught at Christchurch Girls' High School (1886–1912); helped found Association of Women Teachers (1901) and was its 1st president; was a founder member of National Council of Women (NCW) and its secretary (1902–05); president of Christchurch branch of Women's Christian Temperance Union (WCTU) for 20 years (1926–46); with Kate Sheppard and Jessie Mackay, helped revive NCW (1916). ❖ See also *Dictionary of New Zealand Biography* (Vol. 2).

HENDERSON, Danielle (1977—). *American softball player.* Born Jan 29, 1977, in Commack, NY; graduate of University of Massachusetts, 1999. ❖ Won a team gold medal at Sydney Olympics (2000). Won Honda award (1999); inducted into New England Women's Sports Hall of Fame (2002).

HENDERSON, Elizabeth May (1899–1963). *See Knox, Elizabeth.*

HENDERSON, Elizabeth Reid (1873–1935). *See McCombs, Elizabeth Reid.*

HENDERSON, Helen (1909–2001). *See Dickens, Helen Octavia.*

HENDERSON, Jo (1934–1988). *American stage, tv, and screen actress.* Born May 10, 1934, in Buffalo, NY; died Aug 6, 1988, in auto accident near Chinle, Arizona. ❖ Off-Broadway, appeared in *Camille, The Little Foxes, A Scent of Flowers, Dandelion Wine, Fallen Angels, Threads* and *Little Footsteps*; on Broadway, was seen in *Rose* and *84 Charing Cross Road*; films include *Lianna, Matewan* and *Hostile Witness*. Received Obie for *Ladyhouse Blues* and Tony nomination for *Play Memory*.

HENDERSON, Mary (1919–2004). *Greek-born journalist and host.* Name variations: Lady Henderson; Mary Barber. Born Mary Xenia Cawadias, Mar 29, 1919, in Athens, Greece; died Jan 22, 2004, dau. of Professor A.P. Cawadias (physician to King George of the Hellenes); m. Stephen Barber (journalist); m. Sir Nicholas Henderson (British diplomat), 1951; children: Alexandra, countess of Drogheda. ❖ Moved to London with family with the fall of the Greek monarchy (1924); during WWII, was a Red Cross nurse in Albania and sentenced to death by SS for assisting the allies; released on liberation; as Mary Barber, was the only woman correspondent covering the Greek civil war (1946–49); as wife of the British ambassador to Warsaw, Bonn, Paris and Washington, was a legendary hostess during Reagan years; was also an advisor on the British Fashion Council and received its Hall of Fame Award. Appointed OBE (1988). ❖ See also *Xenia: A Memoir* (1988).

HENDERSON, Monique (1983—). *American runner.* Born Feb 18, 1983, in San Diego, CA. ❖ Won a gold medal for 4x400-meter relay at Athens Olympics (2004).

HENDERSON, Paul (1913–1968). *See France, Ruth.*

HENDERSON, Stella (1871–1962). *New Zealand-born Australian journalist and feminist.* Name variations: Stella May Allan; Vesta. Born Stella May Henderson, Oct 25, 1871, at Kaiapoi, South Island, New Zealand; died Mar 1, 1962, in Melbourne, Australia; dau. of Alice (Connolly) Henderson and Daniel Henderson (clerk); sister of Elizabeth McCombs; Canterbury University College, BA, 1892, MA, 1893, LLB, 1896; m. Edwin Frank Allan (leader-writer for the Wellington *Evening Post*), 1900 (died 1922); children: 4 daughters. ❖ Despite laws prohibiting women from practicing law in New Zealand, entered law school (1893); completed degree (1896), when the New Zealand legislature relaxed the ban; became Wellington parliamentary correspondent and political writer for *Lyttelton Times* (1898); moved to Melbourne with husband, where she worked as a freelance journalist, authoring a column, "Women to Women," under name Vesta for the *Argus*; wrote about women's issues, such as child care and "domestic feminism"; was a founding member of National Council of Women of New Zealand (1896), and of Australian National Council of Women; appointed substitute Australian delegate to assembly of League of Nations in Geneva (1924). ❖ See also *Dictionary of New Zealand Biography* (Vol. 2).

HENDERSON, Virginia (1897–1996). *American nurse.* Born Virginia Avenel Henderson, Nov 30, 1897, in Kansas City, Missouri; died Mar 19, 1996, in Branford, Connecticut; dau. of Lucy Minor Abbot Henderson and Daniel Brosius Henderson (attorney); graduate of Army School of Nursing, 1921; Columbia University Teachers College, BS, 1932, MA, 1934. ❖ Referred to as "first lady of nursing," created a standard definition of nursing as well as textbooks and an index to literature about nursing; worked at Lillian Wald's Henry Street Visiting Nurse Service in NYC and later at Visiting Nurse Association in DC; began teaching at Norfolk Protestant Hospital School in VA (1924), the 1st full-time nursing teacher there, and in the state of VA; researched nursing with Yale University sociologist Leo Simmons (from 1953) and appointed director of the Nursing Studies Index Project (1959); was a Yale University research associate emerita (from 1972); embarked on an international speaking tour (1972). Wrote the popular *Textbook of the Principles and Practice of Nursing* (1939), *Basic Principles of Nursing Care* (1960, trans. into 25 languages), *The Nature of Nursing* (1966) and the multivolumed *Nursing Studies Index* (1963–72).

HENDERSON, Zenna (1917–1983). *American science-fiction writer.* Born Zenna Chlarson, Nov 1, 1917, in Tucson, Arizona; died May 11, 1983, in Tucson; Arizona State University, MA 1955. ❖ Worked as teacher in Japanese Relocation Camp, Sacatona, Arizona, in Laon sur Marne, France, and at Seaside Children's Hospital, Waterford, Connecticut; writings, which focus on spiritual themes and religious tolerance, include *Pilgrimage: The Book of the People* (1962), *The People: No Different Flesh* (1966), *The Anything Box* (1966) and *Holding Wonder* (1971).

HENDL, Susan (1949—). *American ballet dancer.* Born Sept 18, 1949, in Wilkes-Barre, Pennsylvania. ❖ Made debut with New York City Ballet where she performed throughout dance career; danced solos in numerous works by Balanchine, including *Divertimento No. 15, Agon, Liebeslieder*, and *Slaughter on Tenth Avenue*; created roles in Balanchine's *Who Cares?* (1970) and Robbins' *Goldberg Variations* (1971); performed in many company premieres including Robbins' *Requiem Canticles II*, Danilova's restaging of *Chopiniana* (1972) and Bolender's *Serenade in A*; staged *Themes and Variations* for Miami City Ballet; served as vice president of George Balanchine Foundation.

HENDRAWATI, Agung (1975—). *Indonesian climber.* Born May 11, 1975, in Yogyakarta, Indonesia; m. Nur Rosyid (speed climber). ❖ Won bronze at X Games in Speed Climbing (1999); became 1st Muslim woman to win a gold medal at X Games (speed climbing, 2000); received 1st-place year-end ranking in Indonesian Federation for Speed (2000); other 1st-place finishes in Speed include Asian X Games (1999 and 2000) and UIAA Asian Cup (2001).

HENDRICKS, Wanda (1928–1981). *See Hendrix, Wanda.*

HENDRIKS, Irene (1958—). *Dutch field-hockey player.* Born April 13, 1958, in Netherlands. ❖ At Los Angeles Olympics, won a gold medal in team competition (1984).

HENDRIX, Brunhilde (1938—). *West German runner.* Born Aug 2, 1938, in Germany. ❖ At Rome Olympics, won a silver medal in the 4 x 100-meter relay (1960).

HENDRIX, Wanda (1928–1981). *American actress.* Name variations: Wanda Hendricks. Born Dixie Wanda Hendrix, Nov 3, 1928, in Jacksonville, Florida; died Feb 1, 1981, in Burbank, California; m. Audie Murphy (actor), 1949 (div. 1950); m. James Stack (brother of actor Robert Stack), 1954 (div. 1958); m. Steve LaMonte, 1969 (div. 1979). ❖ Made film debut as an ingenue in *Confidential Agent* (1945); starred in *Prince of Foxes, Capt. Carey, U.S.A., Sierra, The Admiral was a Lady, My Outlaw Brother, Ride the Pink Horse, Miss Tatlock's Millions, Sierra, The Highwayman, Black Dakota, Johnny Cool* and *Stage to Thunder Rock*.

HENDRYX, Nona (1945—). *African-American singer and songwriter.* Born Aug 18, 1945, in Trenton, NJ. ❖ Multitalented singer-composer, sang with Patti LaBelle and the Bluebelles (1962–77); established rock credentials with solo debut *Nona Hendryx* (1977); collaborated with Talking Heads on album *Remain in Light* (1981); released dance-funk album *Nona* (1983), which featured R&B hits "Keep It Confidential" and "Transformation"; released albums *Female Trouble* (1987), *SkinDiver* (1989), *You Have to Cry Sometime* (1992), and *Transformation: The Best of Nona Hendryx* (1999); wrote music and lyrics for Charles Randolph-Wright's comedy *Blue* (2000); composed for Alvin Ailey and Dance Theatre Workshop; acclaimed for mastery of various musical genres, including girl-group pop, glam funk, hard rock, new wave, and New Age.

HENGLER, Flora (c. 1887–1965). *American tandem dancer.* Born c. 1887 in Brooklyn, NY; died Sept 7, 1965, in New York, NY; sister of May Hengler. ❖ As a child, performed with sister May in Hengler and Delehanty troupe; made tandem act debut with May in spectacle *1492* (1893); performed specialty tandem dances in ballet and Spanish technique throughout Europe billed as The American Beauty Sisters; returned to NYC where they performed as the Sisters Hengler in *The Sleeping Beauty and the Beast* (1901), *Tommy Rot* (1902), *The Runaways* (1903), and *The Cingalee* (1904); worked with Weber and Field shows and with Charles Frohman; retired (early 1920s).

HENGLER, May (c. 1884–1952). *American tandem dancer.* Born c. 1884 in Brooklyn, NY; died Mar 15, 1952, in New York, NY; sister of Flora Hengler. ❖ Performed as a child with sister Flora in Hengler and

Delehanty troupe; performed with Flora as the Sisters Hengler into the 1920s; made film *The Sisters Hengler Speciality Dancers* (1896).

HENIE, Sonja (1912–1969). Norwegian figure skater and actress. Name variations: Sonia Henje. Born April 8, 1912 (some sources erroneously cite 1910), in Oslo, Norway; died of leukemia on board an ambulance plane traveling from Paris to Oslo, Oct 12, 1969; dau. of Selma (Nilsen) Henie and Wilhelm Henie (fur merchant and former champion cyclist); m. Dan Topping, 1940; m. Winthrop Gardner, 1949; m. Niels Onstad, 1956. ❖ In addition to 3 Olympic gold medals (1928, 1932 and 1936), won 10 consecutive World titles (1927–36) and 6 European championships (1931–36); starred in films (1927–58), including *Sun Valley Serenade* (1941), *Wintertime* (1943), *The Countess of Monte Cristo* (1948) and *Hello London* (*London Calling*, 1958); along with Niels Onstad, acquired an important art collection, the major part of which was donated to Norway where it found a home in a new art museum the Ostads erected outside Oslo (1968). Awarded Norwegian Government's Medal for Versatility and Achievement in Sport (1931) and Order of St. Olav (1938). ❖ See also autobiography *Wings on My Feet* (Prentice-Hall, 1940) and documentary *Sonja Henie: Queen of the Ice* (60 min.), which 1st aired on PBS (1995).

HENIN-HARDENNE, Justine (1982—). Belgian tennis player. Name variations: Justine Henin. Pronunciation: Zhoo-STEEN EN-ah ar-DEN. Born Justine Henin, June 1, 1982, in Liège, Belgium. ❖ Turned pro (1999); was runner-up at Wimbledon (2001); in singles, won French Open (2003 and 2005), US Open (2003) and Australian Open (2004); won a gold medal for singles at Athens Olympics (2004).

HENJE, Sonja (1912–1969). See *Henie, Sonja.*

HENKE, Jana (1973—). German swimmer. Born Oct 1, 1973, in Germany. ❖ At Barcelona Olympics, won a bronze medal in 800-meter freestyle (1992).

HENKEL, Andrea (1977—). German biathlete. Born Dec 10, 1977, in Ilmenau, Germany; sister of Manuela Henkel (cross-country skier). ❖ Won gold medals for the 4x7.5km relay and 15km indiv. and a silver medal for 10km pursuit at Salt Lake City (2002); won a team silver medal for the 4x6 km relay at Torino Olympics (2006).

HENKEL, Manuela (1974—). German cross-country skier. Born Dec 4, 1974, in Grossbreitenbach, Germany. ❖ Won a gold medal for the 4 x 5km relay at Salt Lake City Olympics (2002).

HENKEL-REDETZKY, Heike (1964—). German track-and-field athlete. Name variations: Heike Redetzky. Born May 5, 1964, in Germany. ❖ At Barcelona Olympics, won a gold medal in the high jump (1992).

HENLEY, Beth (1952—). American actress, playwright and screenwriter. Born Elizabeth Becker Henley, May 8, 1952, in Jackson, Mississippi; dau. of a lawyer and actress; Southern Methodist University, BFA (1974); attended University of Illinois (1975–76); children: Patrick Henley. ❖ Performed with Dallas Minority Repertory Theater, as well as Salem State Park Theater (1976); began writing plays with one-act *Am I Blue*, produced at SMU's Margo Jones Theater (1973); lived with and collaborated with actor-director Stephen Tobolowsky on screenplay *True Stories*, which was made into 1986 movie starring David Byrne; wrote *Crimes of the Heart* (1978) which won New York Drama Critics Circle Award (1981), Pulitzer Prize (1981) and Tony Award nomination; took play to Broadway's John Golden Theater (1981); also wrote the screenplay (1986), which was nominated for an Academy Award; other plays include *The Wake of Jamey Foster* (1983), *The Miss Firecracker Contest* (1985), *The Lucky Spot* (1987), *Abundance* (1991), *The Debutante Ball* (1991), *Impossible Marriage* (1998), *Family Week* (2000), *Signature* (2003) and *Revelers* (2003).

HENLEY, Rosalind (1907–1990). See *Pitt-Rivers, Rosalind.*

HENMYER, Annie W. (1827–1900). American temperance reformer. Born 1827 in Sandy Spring, Ohio; died 1900. ❖ Became 1st president of US Woman's Christian Temperance Union (WCTU, 1874); nursed wounded during Civil War and opened a public kitchen in Nashville, TN, for wounded patients; was among organizers of Ladies' and Pastors' Christian Union (1868); served as president of Iowa State Sanitary Commission (1863); published successful periodical *Christian Woman* (1871–82); became president of Woman's Relief Corps (1889–90).

HENNAGAN, Monique (1976—). African-American runner. Born May 26, 1976, in Columbia, SC; attended University of North Carolina. ❖ Won gold medals for 4x400-meter relay at Sydney

Olympics (2000) and Athens Olympics (2004); won US Indoor championship in the 400 meters (2002, 2003).

HENNE, Jan (1947—). American swimmer. Born Aug 11, 1947, in Oakland, California; attended Arizona State University. ❖ At Mexico City Olympics, won a bronze medal in 200-meter individual medley, a silver medal in 100-meter freestyle, and gold medals in 100-meter freestyle and 4x100-meter freestyle relay (1968); won 9 Amateur Athletic Union titles and set 8 US records; was also an outstanding water polo player.

HENNEBERG, Jill. American equestrian. Lives in Voorhees, NJ. ❖ Won a team silver medal for eventing at Atlanta Olympics (1996), on Nirvana.

HENNEBERGER, Barbi (d. 1964). German Alpine skier. Name variations: Barbara Henneberger. Born in Germany; killed in an avalanche while shooting a ski film in Switzerland, April 12, 1964, along with skier Bud Werner. ❖ Won a bronze medal for slalom at Squaw Valley Olympics (1960).

HENNEKEN, Thamar (1979—). Dutch swimmer. Born Aug 20, 1979, in Netherlands. ❖ Won a silver medal for 4x100-meter freestyle relay at Sydney Olympics (2000).

HENNING, Anne (1955—). American speedskater. Born Sept 6, 1955, in Raleigh, North Carolina; grew up in Northbrook, Illinois. ❖ Won a gold medal for the 500 meters at World championships and a gold medal for the 500 meters at World Sprint championships (1971); set a new world record in both the 500- and 1000-meter events in Davos, Switzerland (1972); won a gold medal in the 500 meters and a bronze medal in the 1,000 meters at Sapporo Olympics (1972). ❖ See also *Women in World History.*

HENNING, Eva (1920—). American-born actress. Born May 10, 1920, in New York, NY; dau. of a Norwegian father and Swedish mother; stepdaughter of Uno Henning (actor); graduated from Royal Dramatic Theatre in Stockholm; m. Hasse Ekman (director), 1946 (div.); m. Toralv Maurstad (Norwegian actor), 1954 (div.). ❖ Popular film star in Sweden whose breakthrough came with title role in *Elvira Madigan* (1943); also appeared in 2 Ingmar Bergman movies, *Fängelse* (*The Devil's Wanton*) and *Törst* (*Three Strange Loves*); following 2nd marriage, moved to Norway (1958) and appeared mostly on stage; films include *Gentleman for Hire, The Royal Rabble, One Swallow Doesn't Make a Summer, Banketten* (*The Banquet*), *Flicka och hyacinter* (*Girl with Hyacinths*), *The White Cat, Gabrielle* and *Black Palm Trees.*

HENNING, Rachel (1826–1914). Australian letter writer. Born 1826 in England; died 1914 in Australia. ❖ Visited Australia twice before settling there (1861); lived on brother's station in Bowen, Queensland, and married her overseer; wrote letters to sisters about colonial life in Queensland outback; letters, edited by David Adams and illustrated by Norman Lindsay, published as *The Letters of Rachel Henning* (1962).

HENNING-JENSEN, Astrid (1914–2002). Danish film director and screenwriter. Born Astrid Smahl, Dec 10, 1914, in Frederiksberg, Denmark; died Jan 5, 2002, in Copenhagen; m. Bjarne Henning-Jensen (1908–1995, film director), Aug 10, 1938; children: Lars. ❖ Celebrated in Denmark, began career as an actor in the Copenhagen theater where she met fellow-actor Bjarne Henning-Jensen; at first, was his assistant director at Nordisk Films Kompagni; with him, worked on several undistinguished films before their breakthrough *Ditte Menneskebarn* (1943) which established them as the most promising co-directorial team in Danish cinema; collaborated with husband on many documentaries, most notably *Dansk politi I Sverige* (*The Danish Brigade in Sweden*, 1945), using sophisticated technology; made 1st solo film (1945), then continued to work either alone or in collaboration with husband until his retirement in 1974; subsequently, made a number of documentaries and features in Denmark, Norway, and Geneva, Switzerland, where she worked for UNESCO; found an international audience with *Palle, Alone in the World* (1949); appeared as herself in the Danish film *Danske piger user alt* (*Danish Girls Show Everything*, 1996). Received Catholic Film Office Award, Cannes Festival for *Paw* (1960); named Best Director at Berlin Film Festival for *Winter Children* (1979); won Berlinale Camera at Berlin for *Bella min Bella* (*Bella, My Bella*, 1996). ❖ See also *Women in World History.*

HENNINGS, Betty (1850–1939). Danish actress. Name variations: Betty Schnell. Born Betty Schnell, Oct 26, 1850, in Copenhagen, Denmark; died 1939. ❖ The 1st great Ibsen actress, began career as a ballet star, dancing lead roles for August Bournonville; starred opposite Emil Poulsen as the 1st Nora in *A Doll's House* which opened at Royal

Theatre, Copenhagen (Dec 21, 1879); also created roles of Hedwig in *The Wild Duck* and Mrs. Alving in *Ghosts*.

HENNINGS, Emmy (1885–1948). German poet and actress. Born 1885 in Germany; died 1948; m. Hugo Ball (died 1927). ❖ Traveled with itinerant theater group and often did poetic recitals; joined cabaret *Simplicissimus* in Munich; later participated in Dada movement in Zurich; published collection of poems *Die letzte Freude* (1913); also edited work of husband and wrote fairytales, legends, and autobiographies.

HENNINGSEN, Agnes (1868–1962). Danish memoirist. Born Nov 18, 1868, on island of Fyn, Denmark; died April 21, 1962; children: 4. ❖ Raised 4 children after husband immigrated to US; lived and wrote about lifestyle of sexually liberated woman; became noted in Danish literature for leftist politics and exploration of female sexuality; works include *Polens Døtre* (1901), *Kærlighedens Aarstider* (1927–30) and *Let Gang paa Jorden* (8 vols., 1941–55).

HENNOCK, Frieda B. (1904–1960). American lawyer, politician, and tv pioneer. Name variations: Frieda Barkin Hennock Simons. Born Sept 27, 1904, in Kovel, Poland; died June 20, 1960, following surgery for a brain tumor; dau. of Boris Hennock (businessman in banking and real estate) and Sarah (Barkin) Hennock; Brooklyn Law School, LLB, 1924; m. William H. Simons, Mar 1956; no children. ❖ The 1st woman to serve as a Federal Communications Commissioner, is also credited with establishing educational tv in US; emigrated with family from Poland (1910); obtained US citizenship through father's naturalization (1916); worked as law clerk during law school for Thomas & Friedman, for Miller, Boardman & Ruskay, and for John D. Flynn; admitted to state bar in New York, age 22, and entered private practice (1926); joined in law partnership, Silver & Hennock (1927); dissolved firm and resumed private practice (1934); served as assistant counsel to Mortgage Commission of State of New York (1935–39); was associated with law firm of Choate, Mitchell and Ely (1941–48); was an active member of Democratic Party; served as member of executive committee of National Health Assembly (1948); served as Federal Communications Commissioner (1948–55), and, as a result of her efforts, the 1st educational tv station, KUHT-TV in Houston, began broadcasting (June 1953), followed by 12 more during her term; resumed law practice in Washington, DC (1955). ❖ See also *Women in World History.*

HENRI, Florence (1895–1982). American avant-garde photographer. Born in New York, NY, 1895; died in Compiègne, France, 1982; studied music in Paris, Italy, and Berlin; studied art in Berlin; attended Académie Moderne, Paris, 1924; attended Bauhaus in Dessau, Germany, 1927; m. Karl Anton Koster, 1924 (div. 1954); no children. ❖ Identified with European avant-garde movement (1920s–1930s), pursued an early interest in music, studying piano in Paris, Italy and Berlin, then embarked on a brief concert career; concurrently, began art studies; explored photography at Bauhaus in Dessau; published experimental portraits, combining Bauhaus and Purist elements, in Dutch journal *110* (1928); opened studio in Paris (1929), where she specialized in portraits and also worked on fashion and advertising projects; was represented in important exhibitions: *Photografie der Gegenwart* in Essen and *Film and Foto* in Stuttgart (1929), followed by one-woman show in Paris (1930); became well-known for her portraits, which included likenesses of many of the avant-garde artists of her day, such as Hans Arp, Wassily Kandinsky, and Alberto Giacometti; photographs, paintings, and collages were exhibited, including a show at Museum of Modern Art in NY (1970–72) and a retrospective at San Francisco Museum of Modern Art (1990). ❖ See also *Women in World History.*

HENRICH, Christy (1973–1994). American gymnast. Born 1973 in Independence, Missouri; died of bulimia and anorexia nervosa, July 26, 1994. ❖ Promising gymnast, placed 5th in all-around at National Junior championships (1986) and 10th at Senior nationals (1988); warned by a US judge to lose weight for Olympic hopes, became anorexic; died of multiple organ failure after weight plummeted to 47 pounds. ❖ See also *Women in World History.*

HENRIETTA. *Variant of Harriet or Henriette.*

HENRIETTA ADRIENNE (1792–1864). Married the ex-king of the Netherlands. Born Henrietta Adrienne Ludovica Flora in Maastricht in 1792; died Oct 26, 1864, in Schloss Rahr, near Aachen; became 2nd wife of William I (1772–1843), king of the Netherlands (r. 1813–1840, abdicated in 1840), Feb 17, 1841. William's 1st wife was Frederica Wilhelmina of Prussia (1774–1837).

HENRIETTA ANNE (1644–1670). Duchess of Orléans. Name variations: Henrietta Stuart; Henrietta of England; Henrietta-Anne, Duchesse d'Orleans or Orléans; Henriette of England or Henriette d'Angleterre; (nickname) Minette. Born at Bedford House, Exeter, England, June 16, 1644; died June 30, 1670, at St. Cloud Palace, Paris; 5th dau. of Charles I, king of England (r. 1625–1649), and Henrietta Maria (1609–1669); m. Philip (1640–1701), duke of Orléans (r. 1660–1701), Mar 30 or 31, 1661; children: Marie Louise d'Orleans (1662–1689), who m. Charles II of Spain); Philip Charles (1664–1666), duke of Valois; Anne-Marie d'Bourbon-Orleans (1669–1728), who m. Victor Amadeus II of Savoy); also had 4 miscarriages. ❖ Born in the midst of the English Civil War, was placed in the care of governess Lady Dalkeith, who pulled off a daring escape with her and sailed for France; quickly became a favorite ornament of French court, where she was raised a Roman Catholic; returned to England with mother (1660) and became equally popular in court of brother Charles II, recently restored to their father's throne; was married to Philip, first duke of Orléans and brother of Louis XIV (1661); felt no attraction for husband, who returned the feelings, and began to dabble in court politics; became known as patron of the arts and underwrote works by Racine, Corneille and Molière; used family connections to act as a mediator in diplomacy between English and French courts; became close confidante of Louis XIV, arousing increasing ire in a jealous husband; traveled to Dover (1670), where she negotiated a treaty between Charles II and Louis XIV, in which Louis promised Charles a substantial subsidy in return for Charles' promise to work toward the restoration of the Catholic Church and of absolute royal power in England; died suddenly. Though a quick post-mortem attributed her end to natural causes, suspicions of foul play were heard throughout Europe. ❖ See also Henrietta Haynes, *Henrietta Maria* (Putnam, 1912); Erica Veevers, *Images of Love and Religion: Queen Henrietta Maria and Court Entertainments* (Cambridge University Press, 1989); and *Women in World History.*

HENRIETTA CATHERINE OF NASSAU (1637–1708). Princess of Anhalt-Dessau. Name variations: Henrietta Catherine Orange-Nassau. Born Jan 31, 1637; died Nov 4, 1708; dau. of Amelia of Solms (1602–1675) and Frederick Henry (b. 1584), prince of Orange (r. 1625–1647); sister of Louisa Henrietta (1627–1667), electress of Brandenburg; m. John George II, prince of Anhalt-Dessau, on July 9, 1659; children: Leopold I (b. 1676), prince of Anhalt; Amelia of Anhalt-Dessau (1666–1726).

HENRIETTE D'ANGLETERRE (1644–1670). *See Henrietta Anne.*

HENRIETTA MARIA (1609–1669). French-born queen of Charles I of England. Name variations: Henrietta Marie. Born in Paris, France, Nov 25, 1609; died at Château St. Colombes, near Paris, Aug 31, 1669; buried in Church of St. Denis, near Paris; dau. of Henry IV the Great (1553–1610), king of France (r. 1589–1610), and Marie de Medici (c. 1573–1642); sister of Elizabeth Valois (1602–1644, who m. Philip IV, king of Spain), Christine of France (1606–1663), and Louis XIII, king of France (r. 1610–1643); m. Charles I (1600–1649), king of England (r. 1626–1649), on May 11 (some sources cite June 13), 1625; children: Charles II (b. 1630), king of England (r. 1649–1685); Mary of Orange (1631–1660), princess of Orange; James II (b. 1633), king of England (r. 1685–1688); Elizabeth Stuart (1635–1650); Anne Stuart (1637–1640, died of consumption at age three); Catherine (1639–1639); Henry (1640–1660), duke of Gloucester; Henrietta Anne (1644–1670), duchess of Orléans. ❖ During England's Civil War, played an integral part, using all her influence to try to aid husband's cause; moved from France to England at time of marriage (1625); acted frequently in plays in the English royal court; conspired with Catholic monarchs and the pope for aid to husband during English Civil War (1642–49); lived in exile in France until her eldest son was invited to restore the Stuart dynasty to the English throne as Charles II (1660); moved to England (1662); returned to France to the Château at Colombes (1665) and died there (1669). ❖ See also Henrietta Haynes, *Henrietta Maria* (Putnam, 1912); Erica Veevers, *Images of Love and Religion: Queen Henrietta Maria and Court Entertainments* (Cambridge University Press, 1989); and *Women in World History.*

HENRIETTA MARIA (1626–1651). Princess Palatine. Name variations: Henrietta Mary Simmern. Born July 17, 1626, at The Hague, Netherlands; died Sept 18, 1651, in Fogaras, Hungary; dau. of Elizabeth of Bohemia (1596–1662) and Frederick V, Elector Palatine and titular king of Bohemia; sister of Elizabeth of Bohemia (1618–1680) and Sophia (1630–1714), electress of Hanover; m. Sigismund Rakoczy also known as Sigismund Ragotski, prince of Transylvania, or Prince Sigismund of Siebenburgen, April 4, 1651 (some sources cite June 26).

HENRIETTA OF BELGIUM (1870–1948). Duchess of Vendôme. Name variations: Henriette of Belgium. Born Nov 30, 1870; died in 1948; dau. of Marie of Hohenzollern-Sigmaringen (1845–1912) and Philip (1837–1905), count of Flanders; m. Emanuel or Emmanuel of Orleans, duke of Vendôme, Feb 12, 1896. ❖ See also *Women in World History.*

HENRIETTA OF CLEVES (r. 1564–1601). Duchess and ruler of Nevers. Name variations: Henriette de Cleves; Henriette Gonzaga. Reigned 1564 to 1601; dau. of François or Francis II, duke of Nevers, and Margaret of Vendôme; m. Luigi or Louis de Gonzague also known as Ludovico Gonzaga of Mantua (1539–1585), duke of Nevers, count of Rethel; children: Carlo also known as Charles II (1580–1637), duke of Nevers (r. 1601–1637), and at least one daughter. ❖ Spent a large part of her life foundering in a sea of inherited debt. ❖ See also *Women in World History.*

HENRIETTA OF NASSAU-WEILBURG (1780–1857). Duchess of Wurttemberg. Name variations: Henriette of Nassau-Weilburg. Born April 22, 1780 (some sources cite 1770); died Jan 2, 1857; dau. of Charles Christian, prince of Nassau-Weilburg, and Caroline of Orange (1743–1787); m. Louis Frederick Alexander (1756–1817), duke of Wurttemberg (1806–1817), brother of Frederick I of Wurttemberg), on Jan 28, 1797; children: Maria of Wurttemberg (1797–1855); Amelia of Wurttemberg (1799–1848); Elizabeth of Wurttemberg (1802–1864); Pauline of Wurttemberg (1800–1873); Alexander of Wurttemburg (1804–1883).

HENRIETTA OF SAVOY (c. 1630–?). Electress of Bavaria. Born c. 1630; dau. of Christine of France (1606–1663) and Victor Amadeus I (1587–1637), duke of Savoy (r. 1630–1637); m. Ferdinand Maria, elector of Bavaria (r. 1651–1679); children: Maximilian II Emmanuel (1662–1726), elector of Bavaria (r. 1679–1726).

HENRIETTE. *Variant of Henrietta.*

HENRIETTE (1727–1752). French princess. Name variations: Anne Henriette. Born 1727; died 1752; dau. of Louis XV (1710–1774), king of France (r. 1715–1774), and Marie Leczinska (1703–1768); twin sister of Louise Elizabeth, duchess of Parma (1727–1759).

HENRIETTE OF ENGLAND (1644–1670). *See Henrietta Anne.*

HENRIKSEN, Henriette (1970—). Norwegian handball player. Born June 12, 1970, in Norway. ❖ At Barcelona Olympics, won a silver medal in team competition (1992).

HENRION, Daphne Hardy (1917–2003). English sculptor. Name variations: Daphne Hardy. Born Daphne Hardy, Oct 20, 1917, in Amersham, Buckinghamshire, England; died Oct 31, 2003, in England; dau. of Major Clive Hardy, diplomat and translator at the International Court of Justice, The Hague; studied at Royal Academy Schools in London, 1934–37; m. F.H.K. (Henri) Henrion (German-born graphic designer), 1947 (died 1990); children: Max, Paul and Emma. ❖ Grew up in The Hague; was fluent in French, Dutch and German; shared a house in Provence with Arthur Koestler and appears under the initial G in his *Scum of the Earth,* an account of their escape from the Germans; trans. and titled his *Darkness at Noon* for English publication (1941); her portraits, which were influenced by Roman and Italian traditions, include Koestler, Laurie Lee, Enzo Sereni (*The Parachutisst*) and victims of Belsen in *Belsen I* and *Belsen II*; also known for terracotta busts of children.

HENRIOT-SCHWEITZER, Nicole (1925–2001). French pianist, concert artist, and teacher. Name variations: Nicole Henriot. Born Nov 23, 1925, in Paris, France; died Feb 2, 2001, in Louveciennes, France; studied with Marguerite Long in Paris. ❖ Toured Europe as well as North and South America on concert tours; made US debut (1948), with Charles Munch conducting the New York Philharmonic-Symphony Orchestra; also made recordings with Munch and Boston Symphony Orchestra; specializing in French repertoire, taught at Liége Conservatory (1970–73) and served on faculty of Brussels Conservatory.

HENROTIN, Ellen Martin (1847–1922). American society leader and social reformer. Name variations: Mrs. Charles Henrotin. Born Ellen Martin, July 6, 1847, in Portland, Maine; died June 29, 1922, in Cherryplain, Rensselaer Co., NY; dau. of Edward Byam Martin and Sarah Ellen (Norris) Martin; m. Charles Henrotin (banker), Sept 2, 1869 (died 1914); children: 3 sons. ❖ Chicago socialite, joined Chicago Woman's Club (early 1880s), a public-spirited club involved in reformist projects; with sister Kate Byam Martin, wrote *The Social Status of European and American Women* (1887); co-founded Friday Club (1887); as vice president of Woman's Branch of Congress Auxiliary (organizing body for conferences held in conjunction with World's Columbian Exposition), made 1893 fair a national site for feminist activity; served as president of General Federation of Women's Clubs (1894–98), Chicago Woman's Club (1903–04), Fortnightly Club (1904–06) and National Women's Trade Union League (1904–07); headed committee which organized Chicago Industrial Exhibit (1907); appointed by Chicago mayor to Chicago Vice Commission, helped prepare report on white slavery, *The Social Evil in Chicago* (1911); served as director of private Chicago antivice organization known as Committee of Fifteen; served as president of Park Ridge School for dependent girls and on executive committee of Amanda Smith School, similar school for African-American girls in Harvey, Illinois; elected trustee of University of Illinois (1912).

HENRY, Alice (1857–1943). Australian-American journalist and labor leader. Born in Richmond, Australia, Mar 21, 1857; died in Melbourne, Australia, Feb 14, 1943; dau. of Charles Ferguson Henry and Margaret (Walker) Henry; privately educated; never married; no children. ❖ Wrote for *Melbourne Argus* (1884–1904); immigrated to America (1906), settling in Chicago; was editor of the women's section, *Union Labor Advocate* (1908–11); served as editor of *Life and Labor* (1911–15) and as national WTUL organizer (1918–20); was director of WTUL education department (1920–22); retired (1928) and returned to Australia (1933); devoted life to social reform, especially the cause of working women. ❖ See also *Memoirs of Alice Henry* (1944); Diane Kirkby, *Alice Henry: The Power of Pen and Voice* (Cambridge University Press, 1991); and *Women in World History.*

HENRY, Annie (1879–1971). New Zealand missionary. Born on July 25, 1879, at Riverton, Southland, New Zealand; died on July 29, 1971, at Whakatane, New Zealand; dau. of Francis Henry (sawmiller) and Catherine (McKillop) Henry; children: adopted 2 sons. ❖ Appointed first matron of Manunui Maori Boys' Agricultural College (1913); ordained deaconess at St John's Church, Wellington, and joined Maori Mission Committee of Presbyterian Church of New Zealand (1916); built strong relationship with Tuhoe people, establishing successful school for children and adults; made justice of peace (1929). Received King George VI Coronation Medal (1937); Member British Empire (1951). ❖ See also *Dictionary of New Zealand Biography* (Vol. 3).

HENRY, Charlotte (1913–1980). American actress. Name variations: Charlotte V. Henry. Born Charlotte Virginia Henry, Mar 3, 1913, in Brooklyn, NY; died April 11, 1980, in La Jolla, CA; m. James J. Dempsey (physician). ❖ At 5, made stage debut; at 17, made film debut in *Courage,* reprising her Broadway role (1930); other films include *Huckleberry Finn, Arrowsmith, Rebecca of Sunnybrook Farm, Alice in Wonderland* (title role), *Babes in Toyland, Laddie, Bowery Blitzkreig, Stand and Deliver* and *She's in the Army*; retired (1942).

HENRY, Gale (1893–1972). American comedic actress. Born April 15, 1893, in Bear Valley, California; died June 17, 1972, in Palmdale, CA. ❖ Began career in shorts at Universal (1914); started own production company (1919); films include *Lady Baffles and Detective Duck, A Wild Woman, Quincy Adams Lawyer, Merton of the Movies* and *Stranded.*

HENRY, Heather (1974—). *See French, Heather.*

HENRY, Jodie (1983—). Australian swimmer. Born Nov 17, 1983, in Brisbane, Australia. ❖ At World championships, placed 2nd in 100-meter freestyle (2003); won gold medals for 100-meter freestyle, 4 x 100-meter freestyle relay (with world record time of 54.75) and 4 x 100-meter medley relay at Athens Olympics (2004).

HENRY, Lea (1961—). American basketball player. Born Nov 22, 1961, in Albany, Georgia; attended University of Tennessee, 1980–83. ❖ At Los Angeles Olympics (as starting guard), won a gold medal in team competition (1984); was a member of 10 USA basketball squads (1978–84); coached at University of Florida, Mercer University and Georgia State.

HENRY, Marguerite (1902–1997). American children's author. Born 1902 in Milwaukee, Wisconsin; died Nov 26, 1997, in Rancho Santa Fe, California; attended University of Wisconsin at Milwaukee. ❖ Won Newbery Honor Award for *Justin Morgan Had a Horse* (1948) and *Misty of Chincoteague* (1949); won Newbery Medal for *King of the Wind* (1949), William Allen White Award for *Brighty of the Grand Canyon* (1956) and Sequoyah Children's Book Award for *Black Gold* (1959) and *Mustang,*

Wild Spirit of the West (1969); also wrote *Stormy, Misty's Foal* (1963), *Gaudenzia: Pride of the Palio* (1973) and *San Domingo: The Medicine Hat Stallion,* among others; received Kerlan Award from University of Minnesota (1975).

HENRY, Mary E.F. (1940—). Irish politician. Born May 11, 1940, in Blackrock, Cork, Ireland; m. John McEntagart. ❖ As an Independent, elected to the Seanad from the University of Dublin (1993–97, 1997–2002, 2002).

HENRY-GRÉVILLE, Alice (1842–1903). *See Gréville, Alice.*

HENRY OF BATTENBURG, Princess (1857–1944). *See Beatrice.*

HENRYS, Catherine (c. 1805–1855). Irish-born Australian convict. Name variations: Jemmy the Rover. Born Catherine Henrys in Co. Sligo, Ireland, c. 1805; died in Melbourne Hospital, 1855. ❖ In Derby, was convicted of pickpocketing and sentenced to transportation for life (1835); sent to Australia aboard the *Arab,* arriving in Hobart, Tasmania (1836); over next few years, was assigned to 7 masters throughout the colony, though her behavior was such that she stayed with some only a matter of weeks; escaped authorities (1841) but apprehended (1842); convicted for assault and confined to a female factory (1848); within weeks, escaped; continued the arrest-conviction-escape pattern until 1850, when she was granted a conditional pardon and left Tasmania. ❖ See also *Women in World History.*

HENSEL, Fanny Mendelssohn (1805–1847). *See Mendelssohn-Hensel, Fanny.*

HENSEL, Luise (1798–1876). German religious poet. Born Mar 30, 1798, in Linum, Brandenburg, Germany; died in Paderborn on Dec 18, 1876; sister of Wilhelm Hensel; sister-in-law of Fanny Mendelssohn-Hensel. ❖ Poet of devotional verse, is best known for her evening hymn, *Müde Bin Ich, Geh' zur Ruh* ("I am weary and go to rest"), considered one of the best pieces of religious verse in German language; her poetry was collected into a volume of *Songs.*

HENSON, Lisa (1960—). American business executive and film producer. Born Elizabeth Henson, May 9, 1960, in Greenwich, Connecticut; dau. of Jim Henson (creator of the Muppets) and Jane Anne Nebel; sister of Brian, Cheryl, John and Heather Henson; attended Harvard University; m. James Otis. ❖ Became the 1st woman president of the Harvard Lampoon; when father died, took over Jim Henson Productions with siblings; worked at Warner Bros., overseeing works of Tim Burton, *Free Willy* and "Lethal Weapon" series; named president of Columbia Pictures (1994), the youngest studio head in Hollywood.

HENTSCHEL, Franziska (1970—). German field-hockey player. Born June 29, 1970, in Germany. ❖ At Barcelona Olympics, won a silver medal in team competition (1992).

HENTZ, Caroline Lee (1800–1856). American author. Born Caroline Lee Whiting in Lancaster, Massachusetts, June 1, 1800; died in Marianna, Florida, Feb 11, 1856; dau. of John (businessman) and Orpah (Danforth) Whiting; m. Nicholas Marcellus Hentz (entomologist of note), Sept 30, 1824; children: Marcellus (1825–1827), Charles (b. 1827), Julia (b. 1828) and Thaddeus Hentz (b. 1830). ❖ Wrote play *DeLara; or The Moorish Bride* (1831), followed by *Constance of Werdenberg,* produced in NY (1832), and *Lamorah, or The Western Wilds,* produced in Cincinnati (1832); also published several short stories in *Western Monthly;* after husband became disabled (1849), published 7 short-story collections and 8 novels within 6 years, becoming, at 50, one of the most prolific writers of the period; wrote popular novels, often of domesticity, for 30 years, including *Eoline* (1852), *The Planter's Northern Bride* (1854) and *Ernest Linwood, or The Inner Life of the Author,* which was published posthumously (1856) and presented an almost autobiographical account of her own difficult marriage; like other antebellum writers, also helped create and popularize an idealized view of slavery and plantation life. ❖ See also *Women in World History.*

HENZE, Leni (1914—). *See Lohmar, Leni.*

HEPBURN, Audrey (1929–1993). Dutch theater, film, and tv actress. Born Edda Kathleen van Heemstra Hepburn-Ruston, May 4, 1929, in Brussels, Belgium; died Jan 27, 1993, in Tolochenaz, Switzerland; dau. of Baroness Ella van Heemstra (in Dutch resistance) and Joseph Victor Anthony Hepburn-Ruston (English-Irish banker); studied ballet with Marie Rambert and Olga Tarassova; m. Mel Ferrer (actor), Sept 25, 1954 (div. 1968); m. Andrea Mario Dotti (psychiatrist), Jan 18, 1969 (div. 1983); lived with Robert Wolders; children: (1st m.) Sean Hepburn

Ferrer (b. 1960); (2nd m.) Luca (b. 1970). ❖ Elegant actress, nominated for 4 Best Actress awards, who became an advocate for starving children worldwide; during WWII, grew up in occupied Belgium and worked as a child for Dutch resistance; began career as a dancer, appearing in chorus of *High Button Shoes* in London; landed bit part in film *Lavender Hill Mob,* then played a sister to Valentina Cortesa in *The Secret People,* a movie about the Resistance; made NY stage debut starring in *Gigi* (1951) and American film debut in *Roman Holiday* (1953); other films include *War and Peace* (1956), *Funny Face* (1957), *Love in the Afternoon* (1957), *Green Mansions* (1959), *The Unforgiven* (1960), *The Children's Hour* (1962), *Charade* (1963), *My Fair Lady* (1964), *Two for the Road* (1967), *Wait Until Dark* (1967), *Robin and Marian* (1976) and *Always* (1989); on tv, played Marie Vetsera in "Mayerling" (1958) and appeared in "Love Among Thieves" (1987); filmed 6-part PBS series, "Gardens of the World"; worked with UNICEF for years, publicizing the plight of starving children. Won Academy Award for Best Actress in *Roman Holiday* and Tony Award for Best Actress in *Ondine* (both 1954); nominated for Academy Awards for Best Actress for *Sabrina* (1955), *The Nun's Story* (1959) and *Breakfast at Tiffany's* (1961); granted Presidential Medal of Freedom (1991); Jean Hersholt Humanitarian award given posthumously (1993). ❖ See also Robyn Karney, *A Star Danced: The Life of Audrey Hepburn* (1993); Diana Maychick, *Audrey Hepburn* (1993); Warren G. Harris, *Audrey Hepburn* (1994); and *Women in World History.*

HEPBURN, Edith (1883–1947). *See Wickham, Anna.*

HEPBURN, Katharine (1907–2003). American theater, film, and tv actress. Born Katharine Houghton Hepburn, May 12, 1907, in Hartford, Connecticut; died June 29, 2003, in Old Saybrook, Connecticut; dau. of Dr. Thomas Norval Hepburn (a surgeon) and Katharine Martha (Houghton) Hepburn (suffragist and pioneer for women's rights); Bryn Mawr College, BA, 1928; m. Ludlow Ogden Smith, Dec 12, 1928 (div. 1934); no children. ❖ Actress who enjoyed one of the longest stage and screen careers of 20th century, due not only to her talent but her feisty nature, excelled in both comic and dramatic roles and won an unprecedented 4 Academy Awards; made Broadway debut in *These Days* (1928); claimed public's attention as the Amazon queen Antiope in *The Warrior's Husband* (1932); other stage roles include Tracy Lord in *The Philadelphia Story* (1939), The Lady in *The Millionairess* (1952), Mrs. Basil in *A Matter of Gravity* (1976), and Margaret Mary Elderdice in *The West Side Waltz* (1981); made screen debut in *A Bill of Divorcement* (1932); won 1st Academy Award for Best Actress for *Morning Glory* (1934); met Spencer Tracy (1941), sharing a relationship with him that spanned 27 years and included 9 films; awarded 2 consecutive Oscars, for *Guess Who's Coming to Dinner?* (1968) and *The Lion in Winter* (1969); other films include *Christopher Strong* (1933), *Little Women* (1933), *The Little Minister* (1934), *Alice Adams* (1935), *Sylvia Scarlett* (1936), *Stage Door* (1937), *Bringing Up Baby* (1938), *Holiday* (1938), *Woman of the Year* (1942), *State of the Union* (1948), *Adam's Rib* (1949), *The African Queen* (1951), *Pat and Mike* (1952), *Summertime* (1955), *The Rainmaker* (1956), *Desk Set* (1957), *Suddenly Last Summer* (1959), *Long Day's Journey into Night* (1962), *The Madwoman of Chaillot* (1969), *Rooster Cogburn* (1975) and *On Golden Pond* (1981); made a much celebrated return to stage in *Coco,* her 1st and only musical (1969); received an Emmy Award for Best Actress in *Love Among the Ruins* (1975); awarded 4th Oscar for *On Golden Pond* (1982); during a professional career that spanned almost 7 decades, performed in 43 films, 33 stage plays, and 7 tv movies. ❖ See also memoirs *Me: Stories of My Life* (Knopf, 1991) and *The Making of "The African Queen"* (Knopf, 1987); Anne Edwards, *A Remarkable Woman: A Biography of Katharine Hepburn* (1985); Barbara Leaming, *Katharine Hepburn* (1995); A. Scott Berg, *Kate Remembered* (2003); and *Women in World History.*

HEPWORTH, Barbara (1903–1975). English sculptor. Name variations: Dame Barbara Hepworth. Born Barbara Hepworth in Wakefield, Yorkshire, Jan 10, 1903; died at her studio at St. Ives, Cornwall, of injuries sustained in a fire, May 20, 1975; dau. of Herbert Raikes Hepworth (surveyor and civil engineer) and Gertrude Allison (Johnson) Hepworth; attended Leeds School of Art, 1920–21 and Royal College of Art, 1921–24; m. John Skeaping, May 13, 1925 (div. 1933); m. Ben Nicholson, 1932, some sources cite 1936 (div. 1951); children: (1st m.) Paul (d. 1953); (2nd m.) triplets, Simon, Rachel, and Sarah. ❖ One of the leading artists of the 20th century, accomplished her greatest works using the tools of abstract, geometric forms; gave 1st exhibition (1927); had 1st solo exhibition (1928); joined Abstraction-Creation group in Paris (1933); began to work exclusively with abstract forms (1934);

moved to Cornwall (1939); moved to Trewyn studio (1949); represented Britain at Venice Biennale and received commissions for statues at Festival of Britain (1950); designed theatrical set for *The Midsummer Marriage* (1955); unveiled UN building sculpture, a spectacular bronze entitled *Single form* (1964); producing over 600 pieces, became famous for a style that featured piercing the solid form to create new possibilities of light, air, and shadow; major works include *Pierced form* (1931), *Two heads* (1932), *Mother and child* (1934), *Forms in echelon* (1938), *Sculpture with color (deep blue and red)* (1940), *Sculpture with color (oval form) pale blue and red* (1943), *Pelagos* (1946), *Head (elegy)* (1952) and *The Family of Man* (1970), as well as *Winged figure* which decorates the front of a prominent building in London's Bond Street, and *Squares with two circles* which stands outside Churchill College at Cambridge University. Won grand prize at Sao Paolo competition (1959); made Dame Commander of the Order of the British Empire (1965); elected to American Academy of Arts and Letters (1973). ❖ See also *Barbara Hepworth: A Pictorial Autobiography* (1985); Sally Festing, *Barbara Hepworth: A Life of Forms* (1995); Margaret Gardiner, *Barbara Hepworth: A Memoir* (1982); and *Women in World History.*

HERANGI, Te Kirihaehae Te Puea (1883–1952). New Zealand tribal leader. Name variations: Princess Te Puea. Born Nov 9, 1883, at Whatiwhatihoe, near Pirongia, New Zealand; died on Oct 12, 1952; dau. of Te Tahuna Herangi and Tiahuia; m. Rawiri Tumokai Katipa, 1922; children: adopted several. ❖ Influential tribal leader who played crucial role in re-establishing King movement among Tainui people, and in bridging cultural differences between Maori and Pakeha, and working to establish economic and political strength for her people; led opposition to government's conscription policy during World Wars I and II; purchased confiscated land on bank of Waikato River and moved people there (1921); strengthened community by struggling for years to drain swampy land and raise funds to erect buildings; sought to improve economic condition of her people through land development and dairy farming and, by mid-1930s, Turangawaewae community was well-established; agreed to accept prime minister's offer of £5,000 annually in perpetuity as vindication for resettlement of people (1946); traveled throughout Polynesia working toward unity among all tribes (1950s); elected as patron of Maori Women's Welfare League (1951). Made Commander of the Order of the British Empire (1950). ❖ See also *Dictionary of New Zealand Biography* (Vol. 3).

HERBELIN, Jeanne Mathilde (1820–1904). French painter of miniatures. Name variations: Jeanne-Mathilde Herbelin. Born Jeanne Mathilde Habert in Seine-et-Oise, France, Aug 24, 1820; died 1904. ❖ Painted the 1st miniature admitted to the Louvre.

HERBER, Maxi (1920—). German pairs skater. Name variations: Maxi Herber Baier. Born Oct 8, 1920, in Germany; m. Ernst Baier. ❖ With Ernst Baier, won 4 World championships (1936–39), 5 European championships (1935–39) and a gold medal at Garmisch-Partenkirchen Olympics (1936); with Baier, created "shadow skating" (performing the same moves without touching).

HERBERT, Anne (1590–1676). *See Clifford, Anne.*

HERBERT, Hilda Beatrice (1864–1943). *See Hewlett, Hilda.*

HERBERT, Jocelyn (1917–2003). British stage designer. Born Feb 22, 1917, in London, England; died May 6, 2003, in Odiham, Hampshire, England; dau. of Gwendolen and Sir Alan P. Herbert (humorist and MP); attended Slade School of Art; m. Anthony B. Lousada, 1937 (div. 1960); children: 1 son, 3 daughters. ❖ Known for austere but evocative sets, began career designing at Royal Court for such productions as Ionesco's *The Chairs* (1958), Wesker's *Roots* (1959), Beckett's *Krapp's Last Tape* (1959) and Arden's *Serjeant Musgrave's Dance* (1959); also designed sets for Osborne's *Luther* (1963) and Olivier's *Othello* (1964) at the National; as well, designed for opera, most notably for *Lulu* at the Metropolitan (1977), and films, including *Isadora, Hamlet, The Hotel New Hampshire* and *The Whales of August.*

HERBERT, Katherine (c. 1471–?). Countess of Pembroke. Name variations: Katherine or Catherine Plantagenet. Born c. 1471; ill. dau. of Richard III (1452–1485), king of England (r. 1483–1485); m. William Herbert (1455–1491), 2nd earl of Pembroke, in Mar 1484. William Herbert's 1st wife was Mary Woodville (sister of Queen Elizabeth Woodville).

HERBERT, Lucy (1669–1744). British devotional writer. Name variations: Lady Lucy Herbert. Born 1669; died 1744; dau. of William Herbert (1617–1696), 3rd baron Powis, 1st marquis of Powis, and

Lady Elizabeth Somerset. ❖ Her father was imprisoned in connection with the Popish plot and his estates in England were confiscated; was the prioress of the English convent at Bruges (1709–44). Her *Devotions,* edited by Reverend John Morris, S.J., were published (1873).

HERBERT, Magdalene (1561–1627). *See Danvers, Magdalene.*

HERBERT, Mary (1561–1621). Countess of Pembroke, English aristocrat and scholar. Name variations: Mary Sidney. Born Mary Sidney in Worcestershire, England, 1561; died of smallpox in London, Sept 25, 1621; 3rd dau. of Sir Henry Sidney (president of The Marches of Wales) and Mary Dudley (d. 1586, dau. of Jane Guildford and John Dudley, duke of Northumberland); sister of poet and diplomat Sir Philip Sidney (1554–1586); aunt of poet Mary Wroth; became 3rd wife of Henry Herbert, 2nd earl of Pembroke, 1577 (died 1601); children: 4. ❖ Respected literary figure, joined the court of Queen Elizabeth I (1575); married Henry Herbert (1577), who had been briefly married to Lady Catherine Grey; collaborated on many of brother Philip's writings, most notably his famous *Arcadia* (1560), which she both revised and added to, and a metrical version of the Psalms; after his death (1586), edited his works; also translated Plessis du Mornay's *Discourses of Life and Death* (1593) and Garnier's *Antonie* (1592); took over as patron of brother's literary circle, which included poets Samuel Daniel, Nicholas Breton, and Ben Jonson; upon husband's death (1601), received a small inheritance and moved to London; built Houghton House on land granted to her by James I (1615).

HERBERT, Winifred (1672–1749). *See Maxwell, Winifred.*

HERBST, Christine (1957—). East German swimmer. Born July 19, 1957, in East Germany. ❖ At Munich Olympics, won a silver medal in the 4x100-meter medley relay (1972).

HERBST, Josephine (1892–1969). American writer and journalist. Born Mar 5, 1892, in Sioux City, Iowa; died of cancer, Jan 28, 1969, in New York, NY; dau. of William Benton Herbst (salesman) and Mary (Frey) Herbst; University of California at Berkeley, BS, 1918; m. John Herrmann (writer), Sept 2, 1926 (div. 1940); no children. ❖ Writer who figured prominently in both the literature and the political radicalism of 1920s–30s, published widely acclaimed 1st novel, *Nothing is Sacred* (1928); on release of *Pity Is Not Enough* (1933), was hailed as a major literary figure; later added 2 more volumes for a trilogy: *The Executioner Waits* (1934) and *Rope of Gold* (1939); contributed reports from crisis spots throughout world to *New York Post* and *Nation,* among others; covered Hitler's regime in Germany, farmers' strike in Iowa (1932), general strike in Cuba (1935), automobile strike in Flint (1937) and Spain's civil war (1937); last published works included *New Green World* (1954), about botanists John and William Bartram, and some shorter critical essays. ❖ See also Elinor Lange, *Josephine Herbst: The Story She Could Never Tell* (1984); and *Women in World History.*

HERCUS, Ann (1942—). New Zealand politician. Born Ann Sayers, Feb 24, 1942, in Wellington, NZ; m. John Hercus. ❖ Served as Labour Party MP for Lyttelton (1978–87); became one of two women ministers in Labour Cabinet (1984); handled three important portfolios: Social Welfare, Police, and Women's Affairs; resigned (1987); became 1st woman to be New Zealand's permanent representative at the UN (1988–90). Made Dame Commander of the Order of St. Michael and St. George.

HEREDIA, Isabel (1963—). Peruvian volleyball player. Born April 23, 1963, in Peru. ❖ At Seoul Olympics, won a silver medal in team competition (1988).

HEREFORD, countess of.
See Margaret of Huntingdon (c. 1140–1201).
See Maud of Lusignan (d. 1241).
See Bohun, Maud (fl. 1275).
See Joan de Quinci (d. 1283).
See Elizabeth Plantagenet (1282–1316).
See Bohun, Alianore (d. 1313).
See Fitzalan, Joan (fl. 1325).
See Fitzalan, Joan (d. 1419).

HEREMBURGE (d. 1126). *See Ermentrude.*

HERESWITHA (d. around 690). Saint and queen of East Anglia. Name variations: Heruswith. Died c. 690; dau. of Hereric (a nephew of Edwin, king of the Northumbria kingdom of Deira), and Berguswida (Breguswith), origin unknown; sister of Hilda of Whitby; m. St. Ethelbert; m. Anna, king of East Anglia; children: 1 son who was the king of East Anglia; daughter Ethelburga (d. 665); stepmother of Sexburga (d. 699?) and Elthelthrith (630–679). ❧ With consent of 2nd husband, the king of East Anglia, journeyed to France accompanied by daughter Ethelburga and granddaughter Ercongata (c. 646), and took the veil at Chelles. Feast day is Sept 23.

HERFORD, Beatrice (c. 1868–1952). British monologist and actress. Born in Manchester, England, c. 1868; died at Little Compton, RI, July 18, 1952; sister of Oliver Herford (1863–1935, writer and illustrator); m. Sidney Willard Hayward, 1897. ❧ Noted British monologist, most famous sketches were *The Shop Girl* and *The Sociable Seamstress*; also appeared on Broadway in *Two by Two, Cock Robin, See Naples and Die* and *Run, Sheep, Run.*

HÉRICOURT, Jenny Poinsard (1809–1875). French philosopher, medical practitioner, Communist, and feminist. Name variations: Jenny d'Hericourt; Jeanne Marie; Mme Marie; (pseudonyms) Félix Lamb; Jeanne Marie; and Poinsard d'Héricourt. Born Jeanne-Marie-Fabienne Poinsard in Besançon, Sept 10, 1809; died Jan 1875; dau. of Jean-Pierre Poinsard (clockmaker) and Marguerite-Baptiste-Alexandrine Brenet; received Instructrice diploma at 18; diploma from Medical Homeopathic Institute of Buenos Ayres (Paris); diploma of maitresse sage femme; m. Michel-Gabriel-Joseph Marie, Aug 1832. ❧ Serialized a novel about working-class misery in Étienne Cabet's journal *Le Populaire*; worked for the women's revolutionary press and signed the published manifesto of Society for Women's Emancipation (1840s–50s); wrote under name "Jeanne Marie" for *Voix des Femmes (Women's Voice)*; also worked as a medical practitioner and midwife; published extensively in *Revue Philosophique et réligieuse (Review of Philosophy and Religion)* and in the liberal Italian journal *La Ragione (Reason)*; in response to male intellectuals who wrote of women's inferiority, published *La Femme affranchie: réponse à M.M. Michelet, P.-J. Proudhon, E. de Girardin, A. Comte et aux autres novateurs modernes* (1860), which was abridged in English trans. as *A Woman's Philosophy of Woman or Woman Affranchised* (1864); moved to US (mid-1860s), settling in Chicago, becoming a facilitator between American and French feminists; returned to France (1873) and became involved in the intellectual circle surrounding periodical *L'Avenir des femmes (Women's Future)*. ❧ See also *Women in World History.*

HERING, Genevieve (1926–1991). See *Southern, Jeri.*

HERITAGE, Doris Brown (1942—). American runner. Name variations: Doris Brown. Born Sept 17, 1942 in Tacoma, Washington. ❧ Was a 5-time World Cross Country champion (1967–71); competed with 2 US Olympic teams; held 14 national titles and once held the World record for the 3,000 meters; joined coaching staff at Seattle Pacific University (1975), became head coach (1980); was the 1st woman elected to IAAF Cross Country and Road Race committee (1988). Inducted into USA Track & Field Hall of Fame (1990) and National Distance Running Hall of Fame (2002).

HERKER, Centa (b. 1909). See *Beimler-Herker, Centa.*

HERLEVA or HERLEVE (fl. c. 1010). See *Arlette.*

HERLIE, Eileen (1919—). Scottish actress. Born Eileen O'Herlihy in Glasgow, Scotland, Mar 8, 1919; dau. of Patrick and Isobel (Cowden) O'Herlihy; attended Shawland's Academy, Glasgow; m. Philip Barrett (producer), Aug 12, 1942 (div. 1947); m. Witold Kuncewicz, 1950 (div. 1960). ❧ Made stage debut in *Sweet Aloes* in Glasgow (1938) and London debut as Mrs. de Winter in *Rebecca* (1942); came to prominence in Jean Cocteau's *The Eagle Has Two Heads* (1946); appeared in title role in *Medea* (1948); made Broadway debut as Mrs. Molloy in *The Matchmaker* (1955), which ran for 488 performances; appeared at Shakespeare Festival in Stratford, Ontario, as Paulina in *The Winter's Tale* and Beatrice in *Much Ado About Nothing* (1958); on NY stage, was also seen as Ruth Gray in *Epitaph for George Dillon*, Lily in *Take Me Along* (1959), Gertrude in Gielgud's *Hamlet* (1964), and Queen Mary in *Crown Matrimonial* (1973); made a number of films, among them *Isn't Life Wonderful?* (1953), *Freud* (1962) and *The Sea Gull* (1968). ❧ See also *Women in World History.*

HERLIND OF MAASRYCK (fl. 8th c.). Nun and artist of Belgium. Fl. in 8th century in Maasryck, in the Low Countries. ❧ A famous nun and artist whose life is preserved in a biography written a century after her death, entered convent of Maasryck in the Low Countries to obey devout parents, who wanted to show their love for God by dedicating one of their children to the religious life; was well-educated by nuns; highly literate

and a good singer, copied and illuminated manuscripts in the convent's scriptoria, spun and wove cloth, and embroidered beautifully.

HERMAN, Barbara (c. 1952—). American cantor. Born c. 1952; married to a cantor. ❧ Had investiture at Hebrew Union College–Jewish Institute of Religion; became 1st woman cantor in US Reform Judaism (1975), as cantor for Beth Sholom Temple in Clifton-Passaic, NJ.

HERMAN, Robin (c. 1952—). American reporter. Born c. 1952; grew up on Long Island; attended Princeton University; married an editor; children: 2. ❧ As the 1st female sports reporter for *The New York Times*, covered a hockey game in Canada between NY Islanders and Montreal Canadiens where she was one of the 1st two women reporters (with Marcelle St. Cyr of Canadian radio) to enter a male professional sports locker room (1975); became a political reporter for the *Times*, then a health and medical writer for *The Washington Post.*

HERMANGE, Marie-Thérèse (1947—). French politician. Name variations: Marie-Therese Hermange. Born Sept 17, 1947, in Algeria. ❧ Served as deputy mayor of Paris (1989—) and vice-president of the National Council of Frenchwomen; as a member of the European People's Party (Christian Democrats) and European Democrats, elected to 4th and 5th European Parliament (1994–99, 1999–2004); named vice-chair of Committee on Employment and Social Affairs.

HERMES, Gertrude (1901–1983). British wood engraver and sculptor. Born Gertrude Anna Bertha Hermes in Bromley, Kent, England, Aug 18, 1901; died 1983; dau. of L.A. Hermes; studied at Beckenham School of Art, then at Leon Underwood's School of Painting and Sculpture, 1922–26; m. Blair Rowlands Hughes-Stanton (engraver), 1926 (div. 1932); children: son and daughter. ❧ Produced distinctive pieces which have found their way into major collections in Europe and North America; with husband, worked as an engraver at Gregynog Press (1926); following divorce (1932), moved to London, where she produced a variety of sculptures, prints (linocuts), and decorative pieces, including a stone foundation for Shakespeare Memorial Theater in Stratford; during WWII, worked in tank factories and shipyards in US and Montreal, producing working drawings; returned to London (1945), resuming work in printmaking and sculpture, including bronze portrait heads; also taught at several London art schools and at Royal Academy School of Arts. Became a fellow of Royal Society of Painters, Etchers, and Engravers (1951); received Jean Masson Davidson Prize for portrait sculpture (1967); made OBE (1982).

HERMINE OF REUSS (1887–1947). Princess of Reuss. Born Sept 17, 1887, in Greiz, Germany; died Aug 7, 1947, in Frankfurt-am-Oder, Germany; dau. of Henry XXII (1846–1902), prince of Reuss, and Ida of Schaumburg-Lippe (1852–1891); m. Johann Georg (1873–1920), prince of Schönaich-Carolath, on Jan 7, 1907; became 2nd wife of Wilhelm II, emperor of Germany (r. 1888–1918), Nov 5, 1922; children: (1st m.) Henrietta of Schönaich-Carolath (1918–1972, who m. Charles Francis Joseph, prince of Prussia.

HERMINE OF WALDECK AND PYRMONT (1827–1910). Princess of Schaumburg-Lippe. Name variations: Hermine of Waldeck-Pyrmont. Born 1827; died 1910; dau. of Prince George II; m. Adolphus I Georg, prince of Schaumburg-Lippe, Oct 25, 1844; children: 8, including Ida of Schaumburg-Lippe (1852–1891); Adolphus (1859–1916), prince of Schaumburg-Lippe.

HERMODSSON, Elisabet Hermine (1927—). Swedish poet and illustrator. Born 1927 in Göteburg, Sweden; attended art school and University of Stockholm. ❧ Multimedia artist, trained as visual artist and studied philosophy; composed music for and illustrated own works, which include *Dikt=ting* (Poem=Thing, 1966) and *Disa Nilssons visor* (Disa Nilsson's Ballads, 1974).

HERMON, Sylvia (1955—). Northern Ireland politician and member of Parliament. Name variations: Lady Hermon; Sylvia Paisley. Born Sylvia Paisley, Aug 11, 1955, in Co. Tyrone, Northern Ireland; no relation to Ian Paisley; dau. of Robert and Mary Paisley; m. Sir Jack Hermon (Royal Ulster Constabulary chief constable); children: 2 sons. ❧ Was a law lecturer, Queen's University of Belfast (1978–88); representing UUP, elected to House of Commons at Westminster (2001, 2005) for North Down.

HERNANDEZ, Amelia (c. 1930—). Mexican dancer and choreographer. Born c. 1930 in Mexico City, Mexico. ❧ Trained in German-influenced modern-dance techniques in Mexico City; taught at National Institute of

Fine Arts; founded own folklore company, Ballet Folklórico de México, the most renowned company of its kind there.

HERNANDEZ, Angela (c. 1949—). Spanish bullfighter. Name variations: Angelita Hernandez. Born c. 1949 in Spain. ❖ Caused controversy by insisting on women's right to enter bull ring on foot like male bullfighters (1973), despite law limiting women to bullfighting on horseback; was refused license by Ministry of Interior.

HERNÁNDEZ, Luisa Josefina (1928—). Mexican playwright and novelist. Name variations: Luisa Josefina Hernandez. Born 1928 in Mexico City, Mexico; earned MA in dramatic arts, 1955; attended Columbia University. ❖ Prolific writer whose plays include *Aguardente de caña* (1951), *Los surdomudos* (1953), and *Popol Vuh* (1966); novels include *El lugar donde crece la hierba* (1959), *La Plaza de Puerto Santo* (1961), *Los palacios desertos* (1963), *Lo noche exquisita* (1965) and *El valle que elegimos* (1965).

HERNÁNDEZ, Maria (1896–1986). Chicana civil-rights advocate. Name variations: Maria Hernandez. Born in Mexico, 1896; died 1986. ❖ Prominent Mexican-American activist, was a co-founder of the Orden Caballeros of America, a civil-rights organization established in 1929, and instrumental in the formation of the Raza Unida Party (1970).

HERNANDEZ, Maria de la Paz (1977—). Argentinean field-hockey player. Born Jan 11, 1977, in Buenos Aires, Argentina; sister of Rocio and Juan Martin Hernandez (both athletes). ❖ Forward, won a team silver medal at Sydney Olympics (2000) and a team bronze medal at Athens Olympics (2004); won Champions Trophy (2001), World Cup (2002), and Pan American Games (2003).

HERNE, Chrystal (1882–1950). American actress. Name variations: Chrystal Katharine Herne. Born June 17, 1882, in Dorchester, Massachusetts; died Sept 19, 1950, in Boston, MA; dau. of James A. Herne (actor and playwright) and Katharine Corcoran Herne; m. Harold Stanley Pollard (chief editorial writer of the New York *Evening World*), Aug 31, 1914. ❖ Made stage debut in father's play *The Reverend Griffith Davenport* (Washington, DC, 1899) and NY debut in same play (1899); had 1st leading role in *Major André* (1903); performed opposite Arnold Daly in series of plays by George Bernard Shaw (1905–06); made London debut in *The Jury of Fate* (1906); had greatest success in title role of Pulitzer Prize-winning *Craig's Wife* (1925); gave last performance in *A Room in Red and White* (1936).

HERNE, Mrs. James A. (1857–1943). *See Herne, Katharine Corcoran.*

HERNE, Katharine Corcoran (1857–1943). American stage actress. Name variations: Katharine Corcoran; Mrs. James A. Herne; Katherine Corcoran Herne. Born 1857 in Abbeyleix, Ireland; died Feb 8, 1943, in Astoria, NY; m. James A. Herne (actor and playwright), 1878 (died 1901); children: Julie Herne, Dorothy Herne, and Chrystal Herne (actress). ❖ Came to US as a child; grew up in San Francisco; on stage, gained reputation as an advocate of the new realism; appeared in husband's play *Hearts of Oak* (1879); also appeared in David Belasco's *Chums* (1879).

HERODIAS (c. 14 BCE–after 40 CE). Jewish princess and ruler. Born c. 14 BCE; died after 40 CE; dau. of Aristobulus I and Berenice (c. 35 BCE–?); granddau. of Herod the Great; m. paternal half-uncle Herod Philip I (son of Herod the Great and Mariamne II), c. 4 CE; m. half-uncle Herod Antipas (son of Malthace and Herod the Great); children: (1st m.) Salome III (c. 15 CE–?), of 7 veils fame. ❖ Jewish princess who ruled with husband; was actively involved in the politics of her home region and a major force behind Herod Antipas' reign and rivalries, particularly the rivalry with her brother Herod Agrippa I; initially, urged husband to help brother with money and status, but soon quarreled with brother who fled to Rome and was granted title of king by Caligula; urged husband to request elevation to royal status also, which led both to Herod Antipas' exile in Gaul and to his realm being turned over to her brother (40 CE); joined husband in exile, there to die at an unknown date. ❖ See also *Women in World History.*

HERON, Matilda (1830–1877). Irish-American actress. Born Matilda Agnes Heron in Londonderry, Ireland, Dec 1, 1830; died at home in New York, NY, Mar 7, 1877; dau. of John Heron (Irish farmholder) and Mary (Laughlin) Heron; secretly m. Henry Herbert Byrne (San Francisco lawyer), June 1854 (sep. 1 month later); m. Robert Stoepel (orchestra leader and composer), Dec 24, 1857 (sep. 1869); children: (2nd m.) Hélène Stoepel (known by stage name, Bijou Heron). ❖ Immigrated to America with parents (1842), settling in Philadelphia; appeared at

Bowery Theater, NY, as Lady Macbeth, Juliet, Parthenia (1852); played Camille, based on life of Alphonsine Plessis (1885), a role with which her name would be identified. ❖ See also *Women in World History.*

HEROPHILE. Greek poet. Name variations: Herophyle. Possibly lived before Trojan War. ❖ Wrote *Hymn to Apollo* and is associated with several places such as Marpessus, Erythrae, Samos, and Delphi.

HEROPHYLE. *See Herophile.*

HERRAD OF HOHENBERG (c. 1130–1195). German abbess, philosopher, artist, and writer. Name variations: Herrad von Hohenbourg or Hohenburg; Herrad of Landsberg; Herrad von Landsberg; Herrad of Landsburg; Herrade of Landsburg. Born c. 1130; died July 25, 1195, at convent of Hohenburg, Germany; possibly educated at abbey of Hohenberg, Alsace; never married; no children. ❖ Entered the convent of Hohenburg as a child, and rose to become its abbess; may have been educated at Hohenberg (previously known as Mt. Ste. Odile) in Alsace by her predecessor, Rilinda (Relinda or Relindis); continued Rilinda's reform work with great success when she took over (c. 1176); is famous for her production of the *Hortus Deliciarum* or *Garden of Delights,* the 1st encyclopedia written for women, a work on which Rilinda probably assisted. ❖ See also *Women in World History.*

HERRAD or HERRADE OF LANDSBURG (c. 1130–1195). *See Herrad of Hohenberg.*

HERRANZ GARCÍA, Maria Esther (1969—). Spanish politician. Name variations: Maria Herranz Garcia. Born July 3, 1969, in Logroño, Spain. ❖ Served as chair of the Environment Committee of the La Rioja branch of the People's Party (1996–2000); as a member of the European People's Party (Christian Democrats) and European Democrats, elected to 5th European Parliament (1999–2004).

HERRERA GARRIDO, Francisca (1869–1950). Spanish novelist and poet. Name variations: Francisca Herrara. Born 1869 in La Coruña, Spain; died Nov 4, 1950, in La Coruña. ❖ Wrote in Castilian and Galician; works include *Néveda* (1920), *Pepiña* (1922), *A ialma de Mingos* (1922), *Marted de antroido* (1925), *Réproba* (1926), and *Familia de lobos* (1928).

HERRICK, Christine Terhune (1859–1944). American writer. Born Christine Terhune, June 13, 1859, in Newark, NJ; died Dec 2, 1944, in Washington, DC; dau. of Reverend Edward Payson Terhune and Mary Virginia (Hawes) Terhune (1830–1922, writer); m. James Frederick Herrick (newspaper editor), April 23, 1884 (died 1893); children: Horace and James. ❖ Specializing in domestic science, published 1st article, "The Wastes of the Household," in maiden issue of *Good Housekeeping* (May 1885), followed by contributions to *Ladies' Home Journal* and *Harper's Bazaar;* published 1st book, *Housekeeping Made Easy* (1888); edited woman's page of the Baptist *New York Recorder* (1888–93); collaborated on series of cookbooks with mother: *The Cottage Kitchen* (1895), *The National Cook Book* (1896), and *The Helping Hand Cook Book* (1912); also edited *Consolidated Library of Modern Cooking and Household Recipes,* a 5-volume set of cookbooks (1904). ❖ See also *Women in World History.*

HERRICK, Elinore Morehouse (1895–1964). American labor-relations specialist. Born in NY, June 15, 1895; died in North Carolina, 1964; dau. of Daniel W. (Unitarian minister) and Martha Adelaide (Bird) Morehouse (teacher and educational administrator); attended Barnard College, 1913–15; Antioch College, BA, 1929; m. H. Terhune Herrick (chemical engineer and son of Christine Herrick), 1916 (div. 1921); children: Snowden Terhune (1919), and Horace Terhune Jr. (1920). ❖ Worked as executive secretary of NY Consumers League, campaigning for passage of NY State minimum wage law and overseeing studies of the canning, candy, and laundry industries which resulted in *Women in Canneries* (1932) and *Cut Rate Wages* (1933); with formation of National Recovery Act (1933), was only woman appointed to head a regional office of National Labor Relations Board (ran NY office for 7 years during Depression); became head of personnel department of New York *Herald Tribune* (1945) with occasional editorial assignments; used columns to defend democratic procedures and individual rights; contributed articles to *New Republic, Nation, Independent Woman* and *The New York Times Magazine,* among others. ❖ See also *Women in World History.*

HERRICK, Genevieve Forbes (1894–1962). American newspaper reporter. Name variations: Mrs. John Origen Herrick. Born in Chicago, Illinois, May 21, 1894; died in New Mexico, 1962; dau. of Frank G. Forbes and Carolyn D. (Gee) Forbes; Northwestern, BA, 1916;

University of Chicago, MA, 1917; m. John Origen Herrick, Sept 6, 1924; no children. ❖ Joined *Chicago Tribune* (1918) and 1st gained national recognition with a story about immigrant women, which she wrote while traveling incognito in steerage (1921); her later testimony before Congress led to an investigation of the practices of immigration officials on Ellis Island. ❖ See also *Women in World History.*

HERRICK, Hermione Ruth (1889–1983). New Zealand Girl Guide leader and naval administrator. Born on Jan 19, 1889, at Forest Gate, Ruataniwha, New Zealand; died on Jan 21, 1983, in Wellington; dau. of Jasper Lucas Herrick (sheepfarmer) and Emily Martha (Duncan) Herrick; attended Queen's College, London. ❖ Became provincial commissioner for girl guides in Hawke's Bay (1929); traveled to England for further study in Girl Guide movement (1931); appointed deputy chief commissioner for girl guides in New Zealand (1932) and served as chief commissioner (1934–61); became director of Women's Royal New Zealand Naval Service (1942). Made CBE (1962). ❖ See also *Dictionary of New Zealand Biography* (Vol. 4).

HERRING, Geilles.
See Martin, Violet.
See Somerville, Edith.

HERRMANN, Liselotte (1909–1938). German anti-Nazi activist. Name variations: Lilo Herrmann. Born in Berlin, Germany, June 23, 1909; executed in Berlin, June 20, 1938; dau. of Richard Herrmann and Elise Fänger Herrmann; never married; children: Walter (b. May 15, 1934). ❖ While attending University of Berlin, joined Communist Party of Germany (KPD, 1931); expelled, along with 111 other students, on political or religious grounds (July 1933); worked as secretary of central KPD organization and was responsible for maintaining contact with allied Communist cells in Switzerland and ferreting out information on secret German rearmament plans; arrested by Gestapo (Dec 7, 1935), went on trial in closed session for treason (June 8, 1937) and was sentenced to death; despite major European protests, was decapitated at Berlin's Plötzensee penitentiary (June 20, 1938). In addition to streets and schools named in her honor in German Democratic Republic, major works of art, including a musical melodrama by composer Paul Dessau and a biographical poem by Friedrich Wolf, were created. ❖ See also *Women in World History.*

HERRON, Carrie Rand (1867–1914). American political patron. Name variations: Caroline Rand Herron. Born Caroline Rand, Mar 17, 1867, in Burlington, Iowa; died Jan 11, 1914, in Florence, Italy; dau. of Elbridge Dexter Rand (businessman) and Caroline Amanda Rand (1828–1905, philanthropist); m. George Davis Herron (minister), May 25, 1901; children: 2 sons. ❖ Served as instructor in social and physical culture (1893–99) and principal for women (1894) at Iowa College in Grinnell (later Grinnell College); helped fund E.D. Rand Gymnasium for women at Iowa College (1897); campaigned with husband for socialist causes, including presidential candidacy of Eugene Debs; was secretary of Social Apostolate in Chicago, IL; served as delegate to Indianapolis convention which created new Socialist Party of America (1901); with mother's bequest, established Rand School of Social Science in NY (1906).

HERRON, Cindy (1965—). American singer. Name variations: En Vogue; Vogue. Born Sept 26, 1965, in San Francisco, CA. ❖ Member of En Vogue, R&B girl group known for 4-part harmonies, which enjoyed great success (1990s). En Vogue hits include "Hold On" (1990), "My Lovin' (You're Never Gonna Get It)" (1992), "Free Your Mind" (1992), "Don't Let Go (Love)" (1996), "Whatever" (1997) and "Too Gone, Too Long" (1997); albums include *Born to Sing* (1990), *Remix to Sing* (1991), *Funky Divas* (1992, multiplatinum), *Runaway Love* (1993), *EV3* (1997) and *Best of En Vogue* (1999).

HERSCH, Jeanne (1910–2000). Swiss philosopher. Name variations: Jeanne Hersche. Born in Geneva, Switzerland, July 13, 1910; died in 2000; degree in literary history from University of Geneva, 1931; University of Basel, PhD, 1946. ❖ Leading Swiss philosopher and follower of German existentialist Karl Jaspers, whose work dealt with the nature of freedom; taught at École Internationale in Geneva (1933–55); received Montaigne Prize; was professor of philosophy, University of Geneva (1956–77); served as director of Department of Philosophy, UNESCO, Paris (1966–68); was Swiss representative on executive council of UNESCO (1970–72); was president of Karl Jaspers Foundation in Basel; served as guest scholar for Karl Jaspers Lectures, University of Oldenburg (c. 1995); wrote *The Right to be a Man.* ❖ See also *Women in World History.*

HERSCHEL, Caroline (1750–1848). German-born astronomer. Name variations: Lina. Born Caroline Lucretia Herschel, Mar 16, 1750, in Gartengemeinde, Hanover, Germany; died Jan 9, 1848, in Hanover; dau. of Isaac (musician) and Anna Ilse Herschel; sister of Sir William Herschel and aunt of Sir John Herschel (both astronomers); tutored by father; never married; no children. ❖ Pioneer in the field of astronomy, assisted brother Sir William Herschel in discovery of the planet Uranus, was the 1st woman to discover a comet, and is credited with identifying 8 comets and some 2,500 nebulae; moved from Hanover to Bath, England, to live with brother (Aug 1772); had singing career there (1773–82); served as assistant to William in astronomy (1782–1822); discovered 1st comet (Aug 1, 1786); completed Index of stars in "British Catalogue" (1798); completed list of errata with 561 omitted stars, published by Royal Society (1798); retired to Hanover (1822–48). Received gold medal of Royal Astronomical Society (1828); made honorary member of Royal Astronomical Society (1835) and Royal Irish Academy (1838); granted gold medal of science from king of Prussia (1846). ❖ See also Agnes Mary Clerke, *The Herschels and Modern Astronomy* (1895); Mrs. John Herschel, *Mrs. John Herschel's Memoir and Correspondence of Caroline Herschel* (1876); and *Women in World History.*

HERSCHER, Sylvia (1913–2004). American theatrical producer, agent and general manager. Born Sylvia Kossovsky, 1913, in New York, NY; died Dec 29, 2004, in NY, NY; m. Seymour Herscher (producer, died 1994); children: 2 sons, 2 daughters. ❖ During 50-year career in theater, served as longtime aide-de-camp for composer Jule Styne, oversaw such shows as *Hazel Flagg* (1953), *Mr. Wonderful* (1956), *A Visit to a Small Planet* (1957) and *Say, Darling* (1958); was associate producer for *Will Success Spoil Rock Hunter?* (1955); was an agent at William Morris (1960–66), then headed the theater department at Edwin H. Morris, music publishers (1966–75). Received a special Tony Award (2000).

HERSCHMANN, Nicole (1975—). German bobsledder and track-and-field athlete. Born Oct 27, 1975, in Rudolstadt, Germany. ❖ With Susi-Lisa Erdmann, won a bronze medal for the two-man bobsleigh at Salt Lake City Olympics (2002), the 1st women's bobsleigh competition in Winter Games history; also competes in the long jump.

HERSENDE OF CHAMPAGNE (fl. 12th c.). French abbess and healer. Name variations: Hersende of Fontevrault. Fl. in early 12th century in southern France. ❖ Religious founder from a noble family, became a supporter of reformer Robert d'Arbrissel who preached many changes, chief among them to build religious establishments with a convent and monastery together, with authority for both given to an abbess; planned several such double monasteries and endowed them with her own money; became abbess at the large monastery of Fontevrault, and also acted as a healer. ❖ See also *Women in World History.*

HERSENDE OF FONTEVRAULT (fl. 12th c.). *See Hersende of Champagne.*

HERSENDE OF FRANCE (fl. 1250). French physician. Fl. in 1250 in Paris; married Jacques, apothecary to the king, c. 1250. ❖ One of the most notable of medieval women doctors, rose to renown in northern France for her great healing abilities and thorough knowledge of medicine as well as midwifery; was chosen royal surgeon by King Louis IX (Saint Louis) and his queen, Margaret of Provence (1221–1295); while serving in this position, met and married the king's apothecary; accompanied Louis and Margaret on 8th Crusade to Palestine (1248). ❖ See also *Women in World History.*

HERSENT, Madame (1784–1862). *See Mauduit, Louise.*

HERTFORD, countess of.
See Fitzrobert, Amicia (d. 1225).
Marshall, Isabel (1200–1240).
See Lacey, Maud (fl. 1230–1250).
See Matilda de Burgh (d. 1315).
See Grey, Catherine (c. 1540–1568).
See Seymour, Frances (1669–1754).

HERTFORD, duchess of. *See Joan of Acre (1272–1307).*

HERTFORD, marquise of. *See Fitzroy, Isabel (1726–1782).*

HERTHA OF YSENBURG AND BUDINGEN (1883–1972). Princess of Schleswig-Holstein-Sonderburg-Glucksburg. Born Dec 27, 1883; died May 30, 1972; dau. of Bruno, 3rd prince of Ysenburg and Budingen; m. Albert, prince of Schleswig-Holstein-Sonderburg-Glucksburg, Sept 15, 1920; children: Ortrud of Schleswig-Holstein-Sonderburg-Glucksburg (b. 1925).

HERUSWITH (d. c. 690). *See Hereswitha.*

HERVÉ, Geneviève (c. 1622–1675). *See Bejart, Geneviève.*

HERVEY, Elizabeth (c. 1748–c. 1820). **British novelist.** Born c. 1748 in UK; died c. 1820; half-sister of William Beckford (1759–1844, writer); m. Colonel William Hervey, 1774 (died 1778). ❖ Writings include *Melissa and Marcia* (1788), *Julia* (1803), and *Amabel* (1813).

HERVEY, Irene (1910–1998). **American actress.** Born Irene Herwick, July 11, 1909, in Venice, CA; died Dec 20, 1998, in Woodland Hills, CA; m. 2nd husband Allan Jones (singer-actor), 1936 (div. 1957); children: Gail Christensen and Jack Jones (b. 1938, singer). ❖ Starred in *Destry Rides Again, The Boys from Syracuse, Bombay Clipper, Mr. Peabody and the Mermaid*; was also featured in *Cactus Flower* and *Play Misty for Me*; on Broadway, starred in *State of the Union* (1940s); on tv, appeared as Aunt Meg on "Honey West."

HERVEY, Mary (1700–1768). **Baroness of Ickworth.** Name variations: Mary Lepel or Lepell; Lady Mary Hervey. Born Mary Lepel or Lepell in 1700; died 1768; dau. of Brigadier-General Lepel or Lepell; m. John Hervey, Baron Hervey of Ickworth, 1720. ❖ Known for her beauty, was lauded in the writings of Alexander Pope, John Gay, Philip Stanhope, 4th earl of Chesterfield, and Voltaire; epitaph was written by Horace Walpole. Her correspondence to Reverend Edmund Morris (1742–68) was published (1821); other correspondence was published in the letters of Henrietta Howard, countess of Suffolk (1824).

HERVORDEN, abbess of. *See Elizabeth of Bohemia (1618–1680).*

HERWEGH, Emma (1817–1904). **German memoirist.** Born May 10, 1817, in Berlin, Germany; died Mar 24, 1904, in Paris, France; m. Georg Herwegh (1817–1875, poet and revolutionary), 1843. ❖ Wrote account of experiences on husband's campaign for support of Revolution in Germany (1848), *Zur Geschichte der deutschen demokratischen Legion aus Paris. Von einer Hochverrätherin* (On the History of the German Democratic Legion from Paris, by a Woman Accused of High Treason, 1849).

HERZ, Henriette (1764–1847). **German writer and Berlin society leader.** Name variations: Henrietta Herz. Born Henriette de Lemos in 1764; died 1847; m. Markus or Marcus Herz (1747–1803, Jewish physician and philosopher); studied many languages. ❖ Childhood friend of Dorothea Mendelssohn, went on to become a well-known woman of culture and beauty; as a famous Jewish leader in Berlin society, was the center of a brilliant salon for the greatest intellectuals of her day. Her memoirs and letters were published as *Henriette Herz in Erinnerungen, Briefen und Zeugnissen* (Henriette Herz: Memoirs, Letters and Testimonies, 1984).

HERZBERG, Judith (1934—). **Dutch poet and playwright.** Name variations: (pen names) Christine de Hondt; Eva de Vries; Marta de Vries. Born Nov 4, 1934, in Amsterdam, Netherlands; dau. of Abel Herzberg. ❖ Leading contemporary poet in Netherlands whose works include *Zeepost* (1963), *Beemdgras* (1968), *Vliegen* (1970), *Strijklicht* (1971), *Botshol* (1980), *Dagrest* (1984), *Zoals* (1992), and *Bijvangst* (1999); also wrote such plays as *Leedvermaak* (1982) and *Een goed hoofd* (1991); published work in several magazines and collections, including *Nine Dutch Poets* (1982) and *Dutch Interiors* (1984); wrote plays for tv and musical theater, opera libretti, and film scripts.

HERZELEIDE (1918–1989). **Princess of Prussia.** Born Herzeleide Ina Marie Sophie Hohenzollern, Dec 25, 1918, in Bristow, Mecklenburg; died Mar 22, 1989, in Munich, Germany; dau. of Ina Maria of Bassewitz-Levitzow (1888–1973) and Karl Heinrich, count von Bassewitz-Levetzow; m. Charles Peter Francis Andrew, prince Biron von Curland, Aug 16, 1938, in Potsdam; children: Victoria Benigna Ina Marie, princess von Curland (b. 1939); Ernest-John Charles Oscar, prince von Curland (b. 1940); Michael Charles Augustus, prince von Curland (b. 1944).

HESELTINE, Mary J. (1910–2002). **Australian pathologist.** Born 1910 in Australia; died 2002 in Australia; Melbourne University, MD, 1934; studied cytology with Papanecolaou at Cornell University, 1955. ❖ An early and forceful proponent of the use of the Pap smear for detecting cervical cancer, was a resident clinical pathologist at Royal Melbourne Hospital (1936) and Royal Hospital for Women in Sydney (1937–43); served as staff specialist pathologist at King George V Hospital (1943–75), where she established the 1st gynecological cytology unit in Australia.

HESLOP, Mary Kingdon (1885–1955). **Egyptian geologist, geographer and teacher.** Born 1885 in Egypt; died 1955; studied physics and geology at Armstrong College, Newcastle-upon-Tyne (University of Durham, 1901–06); Oxford University School of Geography, diploma, 1916. ❖ One of the Geological Society's 1st woman fellows (1919), worked as a demonstrator both at Armstrong College's Geology Department and at Bedford College for Women in London (1909–15); began teaching geography at Church High School in Newcastle-upon-Tyne (1916); worked as a University of Leeds geography lecturer; lectured at Kenton Lodge Teacher Training College in Newcastle-upon-Tyne (1923–50).

HESS, Erika (1962—). **Swiss Alpine skier.** Born Mar 6, 1962, in Grafenort, Switzerland. ❖ Won a bronze medal for slalom at Lake Placid Olympics (1980); at World championships, won gold medals for giant slalom, combined, and slalom (1982), combined (1985), and slalom and combined (1987); won World Cup titles for slalom (1981, 1982, 1983, 1985, 1986), giant slalom (1984), and overall (1982, 1984); placed 5th for slalom at Sarajevo Olympics (1984).

HESS, Myra (1890–1965). **English concert pianist.** Name variations: Dame Myra Hess. Born Julia Myra Hess, Feb 25, 1890, in London, England; died in London, Nov 25, 1965; dau. of Frederick Solomon (textile merchant) and Lizzie (Jacobs) Hess; attended Royal Academy of Music from age 13; never married; no children. ❖ Revered in England, organized daily concerts at National Gallery during WWII, which became an inspiration to the people of the British Isles; started music lessons at age 5 (1895); won Ada Lewis scholarship at Royal Academy of Music (1903); made official debut (1907); had 1st major success with a performance of the Schumann piano concerto in Amsterdam (1912); made NY recital debut (1922); made 1st recordings for Columbia USA, including her famous arrangement of Bach's "Jesu, Joy of Man's Desiring" (1928); founded and organized daily chamber music concerts in wartime London at National Gallery with assistance of Sir Kenneth Clark (Oct 1, 1940); appeared in the 1,000th concert of the National Gallery series (1943) and gave last of National Gallery concerts (April 10, 1946); resumed career with successful annual tours in UK, Europe and US (1950–60); gave last public concert, Royal Festival Hall, London (Oct 31, 1961). Awarded rank of Commander, Order of the British Empire (OBE), the 1st instrumentalist to have received this distinction (1936); received rank of Dame Commander, Order of the British Empire (CBE, 1941); was 2nd woman pianist to receive the gold medal of Royal Philharmonic Society (1942); appointed Commander of the Order of Orange-Nassau by Queen Wilhelmina of the Netherlands (1943). ❖ See also Marian C. McKenna, *Myra Hess: A Portrait* (Hamish Hamilton, 1976); and *Women in World History*.

HESS, Sabine (1958—). **East German rower.** Born Oct 1958 in East Germany. ❖ At Montreal Olympics, won a gold medal in coxed fours (1976).

HESS, Sonya (1924—). *See Dorman, Sonya.*

HESSE, Angelina (1850–1934). *See Hesse, Fanny Angelina.*

HESSE, electress of. *See Wilhelmine (1747–1820).*

HESSE, Eva (1936–1970). **German-American sculptor.** Born in Hamburg, Germany, Jan 11, 1936; died of a brain tumor in New York, NY, May 29, 1970; dau. of Wilhelm Hesse (lawyer) and Ruth (Marcus) Hesse (committed suicide, 1946); graduate of School of Industrial Arts, 1952; studied at Pratt Institute, 1952–53, Art Students League, 1953, and Cooper Union, 1954–57; Yale University, BFA, 1959; m. Tom Doyle (artist), Nov 21, 1961 (sep. 1966); no children. ❖ At 3, immigrated to NY with family, fleeing Nazi Germany (1936); had 1st one-woman show at Allan Stone Gallery (1963); began to create abstract collages and reliefs (1964), then refined technique into the organically curving abstract sculptures for which she became known (1965); created more imposing pieces using latex, rubber, fiberglass, rope, cloth; had a one-woman sculpture show at Fischback Gallery (1968); sold *Repetition Nineteen* to Museum of Modern Art (1969); died, age 33, of cancer. ❖ See also *Women in World History*.

HESSE, Fanny Angelina (1850–1934). **American medical illustrator and laboratory technician.** Name variations: Lina Hesse or Angelina Hesse. Born Fanny Angelina Eilshemius, June 22, 1850, in NY; died Dec 1, 1934; m. Dr. Walther Hesse (practiced medicine in Germany), May 16, 1874, in Geneva, Switzerland (died 1911); children. ❖ Promoted the use of agar jelly in lieu of standard gelatin for bacteria cultivation, because of its ability to remain solid in different temperatures, to be sterilized, and to be preserved for long periods (1881); worked as husband's unpaid lab technician and illustrator in Robert Koch's laboratory (1881–82); influenced Koch to use agar jelly to study bacterial causes of tuberculosis; created drawings for husband's publications; though born in New York State, remained predominately in Germany and Europe after marriage (1874); moved with family to a Dresden suburb in Germany (1900).

HESSE, grand duchess of. See Elizabeth Hohenzollern (1815–1885).

HESSE, landgravine of.
See Sophia of Thuringia (1224–1284).
See Anna of Saxony (1420–1462).
See Jolanthe of Lorraine (d. 1500).
See Christine of Saxony (1505–1549).
See Mafalda of Hesse (1902–1944).

HESSE, Lina (1850–1934). See Hesse, Fanny Angelina.

HESSE, princess of.
See Mary of Hesse-Cassel (1723–1772).
See Christine of Hesse-Cassel (b. 1933).

HESSE, Veronika. See Schmidt, Veronika.

HESSE-BUKOWSKA, Barbara (1930—). Polish pianist. Born in Lodz, Poland, June 1, 1930; studied at Warsaw Conservatory with Margherita Trombini-Kazuro. ❖ Won 2nd prize at Chopin Competition (1949); received Chopin prize at Long-Thibaud Competition (1953); began teaching at Warsaw Academy of Music (1973); lauded for her Chopin interpretations, recorded for both Polish and American recording firms; also known for performances of contemporary Polish composers, whose works she championed.

HESSE-CASSEL, duchess of. See Louise of Denmark (1750–1831).

HESSE-CASSEL, landgravine of.
See Charlotte of Hesse (1627–1687).
See Louise Dorothea of Brandenburg (1680–1705).
See Mary of Hesse-Cassel (1723–1772).
See Caroline of Nassau-Usingen (1762–1823).
See Charlotte Oldenburg (1789–1864).
See Alexandra Nikolaevna (1825–1844).
See Margaret Beatrice (1872–1954).

HESSE-DARMSTADT, grand duchess of.
See Wilhelmine of Baden (1788–1836).
See Princess Matilda (1813–1862).
See Alice Maud Mary (1843–1878).
See Eleanor of Solms-Hohensolms-Lich (1871–1937).
See Victoria Melita of Saxe-Coburg (1876–1936).

HESSE-DARMSTADT, landgravine of.
See Magdalene of Brandenburg (1582–1616).
See Caroline of Birkenfeld-Zweibrucken (1721–1774).

HESSE-DARMSTADT, princess of.
See Victoria of Hesse-Darmstadt (1863–1950).
See Ella (1864–1918).
See Alexandra Feodorovna (1872–1918).

HESSE-HOMBURG, landgravine of.
See Caroline of Hesse-Darmstadt (1746–1821).
See Elizabeth (1770–1840).

HESSELGREN, Kerstin (1872–1962). Swedish social worker and champion of women's rights. Born in Sweden, April 1, 1872; died Aug 19, 1962; attended Cassel Women Teachers Training College and Bedford College, London. ❖ Sometimes called the "Jane Addams of Sweden," taught domestic science for several years during early career; was appointed inspector of housing in Stockholm (1906), the 1st woman to hold this position; during WWI, functioned as a councilor of the government food commission; a liberal, was the 1st woman member of the Swedish Parliament (1921–34, 1936–44); chaired an international society, the Human Relations in Industry (1926–29); joined 4 experts on a League of Nations committee on the Legal Status of Women (1937). ❖ See also Women in World History.

HESSLING, Catherine (1899–1979). Alsatian actress and model. Name variations: Catherine Renoir. Born Andrée Madeleine Heuchling, 1899, in Morionvilliers, Alsace; died Oct 4, 1979; m. Jean Renoir (director), 1920 (div. 1935); children: Alain Renoir (actor and cinematographer). ❖ Modeled for painter Auguste Renoir (1917–19); married his son Jean and starred in his early films; appeared in Une vie sans joie, La fille de l'eau,

Nana, Sur un air de Charleston, La petite marchande d'allumettes, En rade, Le petit chaperon rouge, Du haut en bas, Coralie et Cie and Crime et châtiment.

HESTER. Variant of Esther.

HETEPHERES I (fl. c. 2630 BCE). Egyptian queen. Name variations: "God's Daughter of his body, Mother of the King of Upper and Lower Egypt." Fl. around 2630 BCE; dau. of Huni, last king of the Third Dynasty; m. King Snefru, probably her brother, who is responsible for 3 pyramids built at Dahshur and Meidum; children: Cheops (Greek) also known as Khufu, an Egyptian king. ❖ As mother of the mighty Khufu, would have been highly honored in life and was provided, by her son, with a spectacular suite of furniture, covered in gold, for her tomb, which was found at Giza by Harvard archaeologist George Andrew Reisner (1925). The cult of this queen was maintained for generations after her death.

HETHA (fl. 10th c.). Queen of Zealand and Danish sea captain. Fl. in 10th century in Scandinavia. ❖ As a naval commander, fought for the Danes against Swedish forces at Battle of Bravalla, leading her crew into the battle which was taking place on the shore, where she fought ferociously along with 2 other Danish women captains, Wisna and Webiorg; became queen of Zealand.

HETHERINGTON, Jessie Isabel (1882–1971). New Zealand teacher, lecturer, school administrator, school inspector, and writer. Born on Jan 2, 1882, at Thames, New Zealand; died on Feb 28, 1971, in Auckland; dau. of Samuel Hetherington (draper) and Rebecca (Brown) Hetherington; Auckland University College, BA, 1902; Girton College, University of Cambridge, 1904 (MA awarded by Trinity College, Dublin, for work at Cambridge), c. 1906; St Mary's College, London, c. 1909. ❖ Appointed head mistress of Burwood Ladies' College, Sydney, Australia (1906); assumed assistant lectureship at Cambridge Secondary Training College for Women (1913–14); became tutor and librarian at Wellington Teachers' Training College, New Zealand (1914), named vice principal (1923); also lectured at Victoria University College (1919–23); became 1st woman inspector of secondary schools in New Zealand (1926); published New Zealand: Its Political Connection with Great Britain (1926–27). ❖ See also Dictionary of New Zealand Biography (Vol. 3).

HETHERINGTON, Rachel (1972—). See Teske, Rachel.

HETLEY, Georgina Burne (1832–1898). New Zealand artist. Name variations: Georgina Burne McKellar. Born Georgina Burne McKellar, on May 27, 1832, at Battersea, London, England; died on Aug 29, 1898, at Auckland, New Zealand; dau. of Dugald McKellar (doctor) and Annette (Clarke) McKellar; m. Charles Hetley, 1856 (died 1857); children: 1 son. ❖ Prolific painter of New Zealand's indigenous flora; award-winning work widely exhibited; published The Native Flowers of New Zealand (1888). ❖ See also Dictionary of New Zealand Biography (Vol. 2).

HETTY. Variant of Harriet, Harriot, and Henrietta.

HEWETT, Dorothy (1923–2002). Australian poet and novelist. Born Dorothy Coarde Hewett, May 21, 1923, in Wickepin, Western Australia; died Aug 25, 2002; attended University of Western Australia; m. Les Flood; m. Merv Lilley. ❖ Joined Communist Party at 19 and worked for advertising agency and in factory; plays include This Old Man Comes Rolling Home (1967), The Chapel Perilous (1972), Bon-bons and Roses for Dolly (1972), The Man from Mukinupin (1979), The Raising of Pete Marsh (1988), and Nowhere (2001); novels include Bobbin Up (1959) and Neap Tide (1999); poetry includes Rapunzel in Suburbia (1975), Peninsula (1994), and Collected Poems 1940–1995 (1995); also wrote memoir Wild Card (1990) as well as short stories. Received ABC National Prize for Poetry (1945, 1965), Australian Poetry Prize (1986), and Order of Australia.

HEWETT, Ellen Anne (1843–1926). New Zealand writer. Name variations: Ellen Anne Baker. Born Ellen Anne Baker, on July 15, 1843, in Jersey, Channel Islands; died Feb 14, 1926, in Auckland, New Zealand; dau. of George Baker and Hannah (Hough) Baker; m. James Duff Hewett, 1858; children: 4. ❖ Immigrated with family to New Zealand (1855); husband murdered in raid on family farm at Kai Iwi (1865); returned to England with children (1880s); published book about her domestic life and evangelical and temperance work with Maori during stay in New Zealand, Looking Back (1911). ❖ See also Dictionary of New Zealand Biography (Vol. 1).

HEWETT, Mary Elizabeth Grenside (1857–1892). New Zealand school principal. Born on May 24, 1857, in Leicestershire, England; died on April 8, 1892, at Napier, New Zealand; dau. of John William Hewett (cleric) and Elizabeth (Grenside) Hewett. ❖ Immigrated to New Zealand (1880s); after briefly holding position of substitute principal at Otago Girls' High School (1883), was appointed principal of Napier Girls' High School (1884). ❖ See also *Dictionary of New Zealand Biography* (Vol. 2).

HEWINS, Caroline Maria (1846–1926). American librarian. Born in Roxbury, Massachusetts, Oct 10, 1846; died 1926; studied library science at Athenaeum, Boston; never married; no children. ❖ After training under Dr. William F. Poole, took a job as librarian of Hartford Young Men's Institute (1875), which would become Hartford Public Library in 1893; spent next 50 years in Hartford, where she expanded and improved adult library facilities and established the 1st children's library in the city; helped form Connecticut Library Association (1891), serving as its 1st secretary and, later, as its president. ❖ See also *Women in World History*.

HEWITT, Patricia (1948—). English politician and member of Parliament. Name variations: Rt. Hon. Patricia Hewitt. Born Dec 2, 1948; dau. of Lady Hope Hewitt and Sir Lenox Hewitt (OBE); m. William Jack Birtles, 1981. ❖ Served as press secretary, then policy co-ordinator for Neil Kinnock as Leader of the Opposition (1983–89); representing Labour, elected to House of Commons for Leicester West (1997, 2001, 2005); named secretary of state for Trade and Industry, minister for Women, and e-minister in Cabinet; became secretary of state for Health (2005).

HEWLETT, Hilda Beatrice (1864–1943). New Zealand aviator and aircraft manufacturer. Name variations: Hilda Beatrice Herbert, Grace Bird. Born on Feb 17, 1864, in Vauxhall, London, England; died on Aug 21, 1943, in Tauranga, New Zealand; dau. of George William Herbert (Anglican vicar) and Louisa (Hopgood) Herbert; m. Maurice Henry Hewlett, 1888; children: 1 son, 1 daughter. ❖ Adopted pseudonym Grace Bird and went to Mourmelon-le-Grand aerodome in France to study aeronautics (1909); opened flying school with Gustave Blondeau at Brooklands, Surrey (1910); became 1st British woman to obtain pilot's certificate (1911); formed Hewlett & Blondeau Ltd to manufacture airplanes (1914), and employed 700 workers producing 10 different types of planes. (during WWI, Hewlett & Blondeau supplied more than 800 aircraft); following the war and closure of the company, settled in New Zealand (1920). ❖ See also *Dictionary of New Zealand Biography* (Vol. 4).

HEY, Betty (1915–1989). *See Farrally, Betty.*

HEYER, Georgette (1902–1974). British novelist. Name variations: (pseudonym) Stella Martin. Born Georgette Heyer, Aug 16, 1902, in London, England; died July 4, 1974, in London, England; dau. of George Heyer and Sylvia (Watkins) Heyer; attended Westminster College, London; m. George Ronald Rougier, 1925. ❖ Began writing to support family; wrote mystery novels and novels of the Regency period for which she became an authority; works include *The Black Moth* (1921), *Helen* (1926), *The Barren Corn* (1930), *The Unfinished Clue* (1934), *Royal Escape* (1938), *Friday's Child* (1944) *Arabella* (1949), *Detection Unlimited* (1953), *Venetia* (1958), *Frederica* (1965), and *My Lord John* (1975).

HEYGENDORF, Frau von (1777–1848). *See Jagemann, Karoline.*

HEYHOE-FLINT, Rachael (1939—). British cricketer. Name variations: (also seen as Rachel). Born Rachael Heyhoe, June 11, 1939, in Wolverhampton, Staffordshire, England; received diploma in physical education at Dartford, Kent; m. Derrick Flint (cricketer). ❖ Coached field hockey, worked as journalist and sports reporter for newspaper and tv; right-handed batsman, was a member of England women's cricket team (1960s–70s) and captained side for 11 years; represented England at hockey and played county squash; served as vice-chair of Women's Cricket Association (1981–86) and worked as promoter of various clubs and organizations. Was 1st woman to receive an MBE for services to cricket.

HEYKING, Elisabeth von (1861–1925). German novelist and painter. Born Elisabeth von Arnim, Dec 10, 1861; died 1925; dau. of Armgard von Arnim (1821–1880); grandau. of Bettina von Arnim; m. Edmund von Heyking. ❖ Lived 20 years in Beijing, Valparaiso, Cairo, NY, and Calcutta; anonymously published 1st novel *Briefe, die ihn nicht erreichten* (Letters Which Never Reached Him, 1903), which was a bestseller; also wrote *Tschun: Eine Geschichte aus dem Vorfrühling Chinas* (1914) and *Tagebücher aus vier Weltteilen* (1926).

HEYLEN, Ilse (1977—). Belgian judoka. Born Mar 21, 1977, in Belgium. ❖ At A Tournament, placed 1st for 48kg (2001) and 52kg (2003, 2004); at Super A Tournament, placed 1st at 52kg (2004); won a bronze medal for 52kg at Athens Olympics (2004).

HEYMAIR, Magdalena (c. 1545–after 1586). German writer and educator. Born c. 1545 in Germany; died after 1586. ❖ Wrote popular text books for schools: *Die Sonteglich Epistel* (1566), *Jesus Sirach* (1571), *Die Apostel Geschicht* (1573), and *Das Buch Tobiae* (1580).

HEYMAN, Katherine Ruth (1877–1944). American pianist. Born in Sacramento, CA, 1877; died in Sharon, Connecticut, Sept 28, 1944. ❖ An early proponent of Scriabin, made successful debut in Boston (1899); played a great deal of American music in Europe, and in US was a staunch believer in Scriabin when his work was seldom heard there; toured US and Europe with Ernestine Schumann-Heink, Marcella Sembrich and other noted singers (1905–15); in Paris, founded an organization advocating the cause of modern music (1928); also composed and wrote on musical topics.

HEYMANN, Lida (1867–1943). German feminist. Born Lida Gustava Heymann, Mar 15, 1867, in Hamburg, Germany; died July 31, 1943, in Zurich, Switzerland; dau. of Gustav Christian Heymann (merchant and investor) and Adele von Hennig; educated at private schools; spent 1 semester at University of Berlin and 5 at University of Munich; never married; no children; lived with Anita Augspurg. ❖ Major leader of the German women's movement during early 20th century, combined feminism with pacifism, insisting that Europe would be spared future wars only when women had the right to vote; inherited multimillion dollars (1896); founded a progressive kindergarten, a club for single women, and an association of women office workers, and participated in German abolitionist movement at Munich (1896–98); met Anita Augspurg at a women's meeting in Berlin (1896); with Augspurg, was among 13 co-founders of the German Union for Women's Suffrage (1902), participated in the German Women's Suffrage League (1907), worked in International Women's Suffrage Alliance (1904–09), attended a women's meeting at The Hague which established the Women's International League for Peace and Freedom (1915); went into hiding after being exiled from Bavaria for her criticisms of German government and German war policy (1916); became vice president of the Women's International League for Peace and Freedom (1919); with Augspurg, edited the journal *Woman in the State* (1918–33) and moved to Zurich (1933). ❖ See also *Women in World History*.

HEYMANS, Emilie (1981—). Canadian-Belgian diver. Born Dec 14, 1981, in Brussels, Belgium. ❖ Won a gold medal for 10-meter platform at Pan American Games (1999); won a silver medal for synchronized platform diving at Sydney Olympics (2000); at World championships, won 10-meter platform (2003), Canada's 1st world title in a tower event; with Blythe Hartley, won a bronze medal for 10-meter synchronized platform at Athens Olympics (2004). Named Diving Canada's Athlete of the Year (2002).

HEYNE, Theresa (1764–1829). *See Huber, Therese.*

HEYNEMANN, Barbara (1795–1883). *See Heinemann, Barbara.*

HEYNS, Penny (1974—). South African swimmer. Born Penelope Heyns, Nov 8, 1974, in Springs-Gauteng, South Africa. ❖ Won a gold medal in 100-meter breaststroke at Atlanta Olympics (1996), the 1st South African gold medalist in any sport in 44 years, then won a gold medal in the 200-meter breaststroke with a time of 2.25.41, the only woman in the history of Olympic games to win both the 100m and 200m; set 14 world records; won the bronze medal in the 100-meter breaststroke at Sydney Olympics (2000); retired (Sept 20, 2000).

HEYWARD, Dorothy (1890–1961). American playwright. Born Dorothy Hartzell Kuhns in Wooster, Ohio, on June 6, 1890; died Nov 19, 1961; attended National Cathedral School in Washington, DC; studied playwriting with George Pierce Baker at Harvard University; m. (Edwin) DuBose Heyward (1885–1940, author and playwright), Sept 22, 1923; children: Jenifer DuBose Heyward. ❖ With husband, co-authored the folk dramas *Porgy* (1927) and *Mamba's Daughter* (1939); also collaborated with Moss Hart on *Jonica* (1930). Won Harvard Prize for 1st play, *Nancy Ann* (1924). ❖ See also *Women in World History*.

HEYWOOD, Anne (1932—). English actress. Name variations: Violet Pretty. Born Violet Pretty, Dec 11, 1932, in Handsworth, England;

m. Raymond Stross (producer), 1979 (died 1988). ❖ Named Miss Great Britain (1949); made film debut in *Lady Godiva Rides Again* (1951), followed by *Checkpoint, Doctor at Large, Upstairs and Downstairs, Carthage in Flames, A Terrible Beauty, The Brain, 90 Degrees in the Shade, The Fox, Midas Run, La Monaca di Monza, Trader Horn, Love Under the Elms, I Want What I Want, Good Luck Miss Wyckoff* and *What Waits Below*, among others.

HEYWOOD, Eliza (c. 1693–1756). *See Haywood, Eliza.*

HEYWOOD, Joan (1923—). English wireless operator and cryptanalyst. Born 1923 in India; m. Stuart Heywood (Royal Air Force telegraphist), Jan 10, 1942; children. ❖ A telecommunications specialist, was a Radio Society of Great Britain (RSGB) member; trained as a wireless operator and as a cryptanalyst at Women's Auxiliary Air Force (WAAF) and worked as WAAF ground-to-air wireless operator (1941–44); employed as a Government Communications Headquarters (GCHQ) cryptanalyst and executive officer in Cheltenham (1966–83); served as an RSGB Morse code examiner in Gloucestershire (nearly 8 years). Received G2LR Memorial Trophy (1992) and lifetime membership to Royal Air Force Amateur Radio Society (RAFARS).

H.H. (1830–1885). *See Jackson, Helen Hunt.*

HIBBARD, Edna (c. 1895–1942). American comedic actress. Born c. 1895 in California; died Dec 26, 1942, in New York, NY; m. Lester Bryant. ❖ As a child, made stage debut in Milwaukee in *The Kreutzer Sonata* with Bertha Kalish (1907); appeared in vaudeville with Lynne Overman in "The Highest Bidder" (1915–16); came to prominence in NY as Zoie Hardy in *Rock-a-Bye Baby* (1918), followed by *Tumble In, The Poppy God, The French Doll, Gringo, Possession* and *Sisters of the Chorus*, among others; scored another success as Dot Miller in *Ladies of the Evening* (1924) and as Dorothy Shaw in *Gentleman Prefer Blondes* (1926).

HIBBARD, Hope (1893–1988). American zoologist. Born 1893 in Altoona, Pennsylvania; died May 12, 1988; dau. of Mary (Scofield) Hibbard and Herbert Wade Hibbard (mechanical engineering professor); University of Missouri, BA, 1916, MA, 1918; Bryn Mawr College, PhD, 1921. ❖ Researcher on the Golgi apparatus and the only woman faculty member at Oberlin College's Zoology department for 32 of her 33 years there, studied oogenesis in frog eggs at the Sorbonne's Laboratory of Anatomy and Comparative Histology, where she earned a 2nd doctorate (1925–26, 1927–28); researched histology at Oberlin College, where she worked as assistant professor (1928–30), associate professor (1930–33), professor (1933–61), Zoology department chair (1954–58) and professor emerita (1961–88); created Oberlin Chapter of League of Women Voters. Honors include Oberlin College's Adelia A. Field Johnson Professorship (1952) and stars in the *American Men of Science* (4th–11th editions).

HIBBARD, Kylene (c. 1956—). *See Barker, Kylene.*

HIBBERT, Eleanor (1906–1993). British novelist. Name variations: (pseudonyms) Jean Plaidy; Victoria Holt; Philippa Carr; Ellalice Tate; Elbur Ford; Kathleen Kellow. Born Eleanor Alice Burford, Sept 1, 1906, in London, England; died Jan 8, 1993; dau. of Joe Burford and Alice Louise Tate; m. George Percival Hibbert, 1935. ❖ Known as the Queen of Romantic Suspense, wrote over 200 historical, romance, and gothic novels under own name and pseudonyms, including *Daughter of Anna* (1941), *Not in Our Stars* (1945), *Together They Ride* (1945), *Mistress of Mellyn* (1960) and *Midsummer's Eve* (1986).

HICKEY, Eileen (1886–1960). Northern Ireland politician. Born Eileen Mary Hickey in 1886; died Feb 3, 1960, in Belfast, Northern Ireland; never m. ❖ As an Independent for Queen's University, sat in the Northern Ireland House of Commons (1949–58); was president of the Ulster Medical Society and a fellow of the Royal College of Physicians. Awarded a gold medal of Medicine from Queen's University.

HICKEY, Emily Henrietta (1845–1924). Irish poet and essayist. Born Emily Henrietta Hickey, April 12, 1845, in Co. Wexford, Ireland; died Sept 9, 1924, in London, England; dau. of Canon John Stewart Hickey. ❖ Moved to London from Ireland and worked as secretary and governess; became involved with charity work, then took teacher's certificate through Cambridge University correspondence course; taught at Collegiate School for Girls for 18 years; converted to Catholicism (1901); published poetry, critical and biographical essays, and work on the influence of Catholicism in English literature; also translated Victor Hugo's poetry; works include *A Sculptor and Other Poems* (1881), *Our*

Lady of May and Other Poems (1902), *Thoughts for Creedless Women* (1905), *The Catholic Church and Labour* (1908), *George Leicester, Priest* (1910) and *Jesukin and Other Christmastide Poems* (1924).

HICKEY, Mary Margaret (1882–1958). *See Hickey, Mary St Domitille.*

HICKEY, Mary St. Domitille (1882–1958). New Zealand nun, school principal, historian, writer. Name variations: Mary Margaret Hickey. Born Mary Margaret Hickey, April 13, 1882, at Opunake, Taranaki, New Zealand; died on June 20, 1958, in Christchurch; dau. of John Cornelius Hickey (constable) and Hannah (Stack) Hickey; Canterbury College, BA, 1914, MA, 1916, PhD, 1925. ❖ Joined Sisters of Our Lady of the Missions in Christchurch (1905); served as principal of Sacred Heart Girls' College (1916–39), prioress (1939–43), and provincial (1943–45); helped establish Catholic Women's Conferences in Christchurch (1923); visited England as delegate to congregation's chapter, met Maria Montessori and established Montessori school in Christchurch (c. 1925); wrote textbook, *A Graphic Outline of the Great War* (1921); contributed articles to *New Zealand Catholic Schools Journal*, from 1932; was the 1st woman in New Zealand to be awarded doctorate in literature. ❖ See also *Dictionary of New Zealand Biography* (Vol. 3).

HICKLING, Grace (1908–1986). English ornithologist. Name variations: Grace Watt. Born Grace Watt, Aug 10, 1908; died Dec 30, 1986; Newnham College, Cambridge, MA, 1934; m. Henry George Albert Hickling (geology professor), 1954 (died a few weeks after wedding). ❖ A Farne Islands wildlife expert in Northumberland, began career as a teacher (1932–36); during WWII, worked as a Ministry of Home Security war room intelligence officer and regional intelligence officer, based in Newcastle (1939–45); met Hancock Museum curator, Russell Goddard; after Goddard's death (1948), combined his notes with hers to create a 22-volume series on Farne Island birds; served as Natural History Society of Northumbria's honorary secretary (1948–86); served on Farne Islands local committee of National Trust (from 1949); led annual Farne Islands bird tagging which eventually tagged 187,600 birds. Wrote *The Farne Islands: Their History and Wildlife* (1951) and *Grey Seals and the Farne Islands* (1962); made Member of the Order of the British Empire (1974).

HICKMAN, Libbie (1965—). American marathon runner. Born Elizabeth Johnson, Feb 17, 1965, in Billings, Montana; Colorado State University, BS; m. Walter Hickman. ❖ Won US 5,000 meters (1997) and 10,000 meters (1999); was a 3-time World championship team member.

HICKOK, Lorena A. (1893–1968). American journalist. Born in East Troy, Wisconsin, Mar 7, 1893; died in Rhinebeck, NY, May 1, 1968; dau. of Addison J. Hickok (buttermaker) and Anna (Waite) Hickok; attended Lawrence College and University of Minnesota; never married; no children. ❖ Began journalism career at *Battle Creek Evening News* (1913); moved on to *Milwaukee Sentinel* as a society reporter; took position with *Minneapolis Tribune* (1917), becoming its star reporter; moved to NY, worked for a year at *Daily Mirror*, then transferred to Associated Press; during presidential campaign (1932), covered Eleanor Roosevelt and became a close friend; made several trips together, and when separated, kept up a lively and loving correspondence; realizing that her friendship with the first lady impaired her objectivity as a reporter, left Associated Press (1933); served as investigative reporter for Federal Emergency Relief Administration (1933–36); worked as publicist for NY World's Fair (1937–40); returned to Washington to replace Molly Dewson as executive director of Women's Division of Democratic Party (1940); on retirement, continued to write, producing books on history, and biographies of Franklin D. Roosevelt, Eleanor Roosevelt, Helen Keller and Anne Sullivan Macy. ❖ See also Doris Faber, *The Life of Lorena Hickok* (1980); and *Women in World History*.

HICKS, Adelaide (1845–1930). New Zealand stewardess, midwife, and nurse. Name variations: Adelaide Martens. Born Adelaide Martens, on Mar 6, 1845, in London, England; died on May 20, 1930, at Factory Road, Mosgiel, New Zealand; dau. of George Martens (baker) and Elizabeth Ann (Joyner) Martens; m. Henry Hicks (publican), 1864 (died 1884); children: 9. ❖ Immigrated to New Zealand from Australia (1862); worked on wind-jammers and steamers as stewardess; established maternity home at Factory Road, Mosgiel (1886); served as midwife to local community; recognized for volunteer nursing service during influenza pandemic of 1918. ❖ See also *Dictionary of New Zealand Biography* (Vol. 2).

HICKS, Amie (c. 1839–1917). British labor activist. Name variations: Amelia Jane Hicks. Born c. 1839 in England; died 1917 in England; dau. of a Chartist. ❖ Moved to New Zealand with husband but returned to England (1880s); with husband, joined Hyndman's Social Democratic Federation (1883); lectured and participated in labor demonstrations; worked as midwife and campaigned against regulation of prostitution; helped form Women's Trade union Association, served as secretary of East London Ropemaker's Union (1889–99), and was founder member of Women's Industrial Council; was president of Clubs Industrial Association, encouraging education of girls and helping to reform labor conditions.

HICKS, Betty (1920—). American golfer. Name variations: Elizabeth Hicks. Born Nov 16, 1920, in Long Beach, CA; San Jose State, degree in journalism, 1974. ❖ Won USGA Women's Amateur (1941) and was named Associated Press Woman Athlete of the Year; turned pro, was instrumental in the founding and development of WPGA and served as its 1st president (1941); won All-American Open (1944); became a flight instructor and golf coach; wrote *Patty Sheehan on Golf* (1996) and other books and magazine articles. Inducted into Women's Sports Foundation Hall of Fame (1996); received Ellen Griffin Rolex Award (1999).

HICKS, Betty Seymour (1904—). English actress. Born Jan 16, 1904, in London, England; dau. of Sir Seymour Hicks (actor, writer, and impresario) and Ellaline Terriss (actress). ❖ Made stage debut with parents in Melbourne in *The Man in Dress Clothes* (1924); made London debut in *The Guardsmen* (1925), followed by *Scrooge, Broadway Jones, The Ringer* and *Asleep*; appeared in the film *Glamour* (1931).

HICKS, Elizabeth (1705–1716). English girl accused of witchcraft. Born 1705; hanged at Huntingdon, July 28, 1716; dau. of Mary Hicks. ❖ After mother told authorities that they had sold their souls to the devil, was hanged with her for witchcraft, at age 9.

HICKS, Elizabeth (1920—). *See Hicks, Betty.*

HICKS, Helen (1911–1974). American golfer. Name variations: Helen Hicks Harb. Born Helen B. Harb, Feb 11, 1911, in Cedarhurst, NY; died Dec 16, 1974. ❖ A founding member of LPGA, won US Amateur championship (1931) and Metropolitan (1931, 1933); was a member of the 1st US Curtis Cup team (1932); signed with Wilson Sporting Goods, the 1st woman hired by a sporting goods company for publicity; was also the 1st US Women's Amateur champion to turn pro (1934).

HICKS, Lady (1871–1971). *See Terriss, Ellaline.*

HICKS, Louise Day (1916–2003). American politician. Born Anna Louise Day, Oct 16, 1916, in Boston, MA; died in South Boston, Oct 21, 2003; dau. of William J. (lawyer) and Anna McCarron Day; graduate of Wheelock Teacher's College, 1938; Boston University, BS, 1952, law degree, 1955; m. John Hicks (engineer), 1942 (died 1968); children: William and John. ❖ Admitted to Massachusetts bar (1959); became counsel for Boston Juvenile Court (1960); elected to Boston school committee (1961); during turbulent years of the civil-rights movement, garnered national attention when, in opposition to Washington's effort to desegregate schools, became a staunch foe of integration by busing (1963); as chair of school committee (1965), held fast to her position even when faced with a Massachusetts law that deprived local jurisdictions of state funds if they did not implement desegregation plans; served in US House of Representatives (Jan 3, 1971–Jan 3, 1973) on Committee on Education and Labor where she proposed a system of tax credits for parents of children in private schools and sought a federal ban on busing; also sat on Committee on Veterans' Affairs and called for withdrawal of American troops from Southeast Asia; though a Democrat, supported Nixon on a majority of House votes; lost bid for a 2nd term (1972). ❖ See also *Women in World History.*

HICKS, Mary (d. 1716). English woman hanged for witchcraft. Hanged at Huntingdon, July 28, 1716; children: Elizabeth Hicks. ❖ Told authorities that she and her 9-year-old daughter Elizabeth had sold their souls to devil; was hanged with daughter for witchcraft.

HICKS, Mary Dana (1836–1927). *See Prang, Mary D. Hicks.*

HICKS, Pamela (b. 1929). *See Mountbatten, Pamela.*

HICKS, Peggy Glanville (1912–1990). *See Glanville-Hicks, Peggy.*

HICKS, Sheila (1934—). American weaver. Born 1934 in Hastings, Nebraska; studied at Syracuse University and Yale University; m. Henrik Schlubach, 1959; m. Enrique Zanartu, 1965; children: 2. ❖ Traveled on Fulbright Scholarship to South America; taught in UK and US and then set up studio in Paris; founded workshop at Wuppertal factory, Germany (1964), making large-scale, innovative works; advised weavers of Kozhikode, India, on designs favored by westerners (1966), organized weaving workshop in Huagen, Chile (1968) and advised Moroccan rug industry (1970); worked with architect Luis Barragan in Mexico (1972); often commissioned to do works for new buildings. Works hang in many major museums.

HICKSON, Joan (1906–1998). British actress. Born Aug 5, 1906, in Kingsthorpe, Northampton, England; died Oct 17, 1998, in Colchester, England; studied at Royal Academy of Dramatic Art, London; m. Eric Butler, physician (died 1967); children: 2. ❖ Worked on stage, screen, and tv for more than a half century before "overnight" success on BBC-TV series, "Miss Marple" (1986–89); made London stage debut in *The Tragic Muse* (1928), then spent several years with Oxford Rep; won critical acclaim for performance in *A Day in the Death of Joe Egg* (1967), which she reprised in 1972 film; made Broadway debut in *Bedroom Farce* (1977); appeared in over 100 films, beginning 1927 with *Love From a Stranger* and including the "Carry On . . ." comedy series; also pioneered in tv, appearing in one of BBC's earliest shows, the mystery *Busman's Honeymoon* (1947); was later seen as the receptionist in dramatic series *The Royalty* and played the housekeeper to the vicar in 1960s comedy series *Our Man at St. Mark's.* Received Order of the British Empire (1987).

HIDALGO, Elvira de (1892–1980). Spanish soprano. Born Dec 27, 1892, in Aragò>n, Spain; died Jan 21, 1980, in Milan, Italy; studied with Concetta Bordalba and Melchiorre Vidal. ❖ Debuted in Naples (1908); went on to great success at Sarah Bernhardt Theater in Paris, Khedive in Cairo, and Metropolitan Opera (1910); 1st appeared at Covent Garden (1924); retired (1932); as a teacher at Athens Conservatory, was best known for her famous pupil, Maria Callas. ❖ See also *Women in World History.*

HIDARI, Sachiko (1930–2001). Japanese actress and filmmaker. Born June 29, 1930, in Toyama, Japan; died Nov 7, 2001, in Tokyo; m. Susumu Hani (b. 1928, film director); children: daughter Miyo. ❖ One of the few Japanese women to have worked as an actress, director and producer, is best known in the international film community as one of Japan's leading actresses; began acting career with an independent film company, Sogo Geijutsu (1952); gained recognition from performances in *An Inn at Osaka* and *The Cock Crows Again*; came to international attention with *She and He* and *The Bride of the Andes* (1963), both directed by husband; produced, directed and starred in *The Far Road* (1977); was an outspoken advocate of women's rights (early 1960s), long before others of her generation. ❖ See also *Women in World History.*

HIDEKO, Fukuda (1865–1927). *See Fukuda, Hideko.*

HIDEKO, Maehata (b. 1914). *See Maehata, Hideko.*

HIDEKO, Takamine (b. 1924). *See Takamine, Hideko.*

HIEDEN-SOMMER, Helga (1934—). Austrian politician. Name variations: Dr. Hieden-Sommer. Born Mar 11, 1934, in Villach, Austria. ❖ Sociologist and member of the SPO, was presiding officer of the Austrian Parliament (July 1, 1987–Dec 31, 1987).

HIER, Ethel Glenn (1889–1971). American composer, pianist, and teacher. Born in Cincinnati, Ohio, June 25, 1889; died in Winter Park, Florida, Jan 14, 1971; graduate of Cincinnati Conservatory, 1911, where she studied composition under Stillman-Kelly and Percy Goetschius and piano under Marcian Thalberg; studied at Institute of Musical Art in NY; studied privately with Hugo Kaun in Berlin, Gian-Francesco Malipiero in Italy and Ernest Bloch. ❖ Was 1 of only 2 women awarded a Guggenheim fellowship (1930–31); wrote many vocal pieces as well as for the piano and orchestra.

HIERONYMI, Ruth (1947—). German politician. Born Nov 8, 1947, in Bonn, Germany. ❖ Member of Bonn council (1975–90) and North Rhine–Westphalia Landtag (1985–99); as a member of the European People's Party (Christian Democrats) and European Democrats, elected to 5th European Parliament (1999–2004).

HIETAMIES, Mirja. Finnish cross-country skier. Name variations: Mirja Hietamies-Eteläpää. Born in Finland. ❖ Won a silver medal for 10km at Oslo Olympics (1952); won a gold medal for 3x5km relay at Cortina Olympics (1956).

HIGGINS, Alice Louise (1870–1920). *See Lothrop, Alice.*

HIGGINS, Marguerite (1920–1966). American war correspondent and author. Born Marguerite Higgins, Sept 3, 1920, in Hong Kong; died in Washington, DC, Jan 3, 1966; dau. of Lawrence Daniel Higgins (businessman) and Marguerite de Godard Higgins (teacher); University of California, BS, 1941; Columbia University School of Journalism, MS; m. Stanley Moore (philosophy professor), July 12, 1942 (div. 1948); m. William E. Hall (lieutenant general, US Army), Oct 7, 1952; children: (2nd m.) Sharon Lee (died 5 days after birth), Lawrence O'Higgins, Linda Marguerite. ❖ The most famous journalist in the world in 1950s, served as reporter for *New York Herald Tribune* (1942–44); became war and foreign correspondent for the *Trib* (1944–47), serving in London, then Paris, then at the front, covering the Allied invasion of Germany, filing more front-page stories than any other reporter, providing accounts of the capture of Munich, the American entry into Buchenwald concentration camps, and life at Hitler's lair at Berchtesgaden; for her story on Dachau, won New York Newspaper Women's Club Award for best foreign correspondent of 1945; was chief of the *Tribune*'s Berlin bureau (1947–50), then chief of Tokyo bureau (1950–51), able to cover the initial engagements of Korean War firsthand; was 1st American correspondent allowed in Soviet Union after death of Joseph Stalin (1954); served as staffer (1951–58) and diplomatic correspondent in Washington (1958–63); was a columnist for *Newsday* (1963–65); writings include *War in Korea: Report of a Woman Combat Correspondent* (1951), *Red Plush and Black Bread* (1955), (with Peter Lisagor) *Overtime in Heaven: Adventures in the Foreign Service* (1964), and *Our Vietnamese Nightmare* (1965). Along with 5 fellow war correspondents, won Pulitzer Prize for international reporting (1951); also received George Polk Memorial Award of Overseas Press Club. ❖ See also autobiography *News Is a Singular Thing* (1955); Antoine May, *Witness to War: A Biography of Marguerite Higgins* (1983); and *Women in World History*.

HIGGINS, Pam (1945—). American golfer. Name variations: Pamela Sue Higgins. Born Dec 5, 1945, in Groveport, Ohio. ❖ Won 3 Ohio state championships (1965–67); joined pro tour; won Lincoln-Mercury (1971); had 3 victories in 14 years on the LPGA tour.

HIGGINS, Rosalyn (1937—). English lawyer and judge. Name variations: Rosalyn Inberg, Dame Rosalyn Higgins. Born Rosalyn Inberg, June 2, 1937, in London, England; Cambridge University, BA, 1959, LLB, 1962; Yale University, JD, 1962; m. Lord Terrence Higgins (professor, economist, Conservative MP, 1964–97), 1961; children: 1 daughter, 1 son. ❖ The 1st woman judge to be appointed to International Court of Justice in The Hague, interned with Office of Legal Affairs at UN (1958); served as visiting fellow at Brookings Institution (1960); was junior fellow in international studies at London School of Economics (1961–63, 1974–78); served as staff specialist in international law at Royal Institute of International Affairs (1963–74); was professor of International Law at University of Kent, Canterbury (1978–81), then London (1981–95); became Queen's Counsel (1986) and Bencher of Inner Temple (1989), specializing in public international law and petroleum law; practiced at various international tribunals, including European Court of Human Rights, Court of European Communities and International Court of Justice; served as president of Tribunal of International Center for Settlement of Investment Disputes and as British representative to UN Committee on Human Rights (1984–95) as well as special rapporteur for new cases (1989–91); became associate of Institut de Droit International (1987), then member (1991); served as chair of Public International Law Advisory Board for British Institute for International and Comparative Law (since 1992); appointed judge in International Court of Justice (1995); writings include *Problems and Process* (1995), *Terrorism and International Law* (1997) and *The Role of the International Court of Justice at the Turn of the Century* (1999). Named Dame Commander of British Empire (DBE, 1995).

HIGGINS, Sarah (1830–1923). New Zealand writer and midwife. Name variations: Sarah Sharp. Born Sarah Sharp, Jan 30, 1830, in Kent, England; died Sept 23, 1923, at Belgrove, Waimea South, New Zealand; dau. of Stephen Sharp (laborer) and Mary Ann (Emery) Sharp; m. Sydney Higgins (sawyer), 1849; children: 11. ❖ Immigrated with family to New Zealand (1842); worked as domestic servant; served as nurse, 1st with local physician and then on own, and as midwife to more than 350 births; learned to write in her 70s and wrote history of her life at 83. ❖ See also *Dictionary of New Zealand Biography* (Vol. 1).

HIGGINS, Yvette (1978—). Australian water-polo player. Born Yvette Donna Higgins, Jan 5, 1978, in Australia; attended University of Sydney. ❖ Won a team gold medal at Sydney Olympics (2000).

HIGHSMITH, Patricia (1921–1995). American-born writer. Name variations: (pseudonym) Claire Morgan. Born in Fort Worth, Texas, Jan 19, 1921; died in Locarno, Switzerland, Feb 5, 1995; only child of Jay and Mary (Coates) Plangman (both commercial artists); graduate of Barnard College, 1942; never married; no children. ❖ Specializing in psychological crime thrillers, wrote some 30 books; gained recognition with 1st novel *Strangers on a Train* (1950); best remembered, however, for 5-book series centering on Tom Ripley, the amoral gentleman-murderer who made his debut in *The Talented Mr. Ripley* (1955) and whose final escapade, *Ripley Under Water* (1991), was written when she was 70; other writings include *The Cry of the Owl* (1962), *The Two Faces of January* (1964), *The Tremor of Forgery* (1969), *The Snail Watcher and Other Stories* (1970), *Ripley Under Ground* (1971), *Ripley's Game* (1974), *Slowly, Slowly in the Wind* (1979), *The Boy Who Followed Ripley* (1980), *People Who Knock on the Door* (1982) and *Found in the Street* (1986). ❖ See also *Women in World History*.

HIGHTOWER, Rosella (1920—). American ballet dancer and teacher. Born Jan 30, 1920, in Ardmore, Oklahoma. ❖ Performed with rival companies in US, switching around frequently; danced with Ballets Russe de Monte Carlo (1938–41), where she was featured in Massine's *The New Yorker* and *Rouge et Noir*; joined Ballet Theater (1941) and danced in *Swan Lake*, *Petrouchka*, and *Princess Aurora*; toured with Massine's Ballet Russe Highlights (1945); became principal dancer with Grand Ballet du Marquis de Cuevas (c. 1947–61), her longest engagement with any company, appearing in *Persephone* and *Piège de Lumière*, and creating the ballets *Henry VIII* (1949), *Pleasuredome* (1949), *Salome* (1950) and *Scaramouche* (1951); formed the Centre de Danse Classique in Cannes, France (1960), where she served as director for over 40 years; also served as artistic director of Marseille Opera Ballet (1969–72) and was appointed director of Paris Opéra (1980).

HIGSON, Allison (1973—). Canadian swimmer. Born Mar 13, 1973, in Brampton, Ontario, Canada. ❖ At Seoul Olympics, won a bronze medal in 4x100-meter medley relay (1988); won a bronze medal for 200-meter breaststroke at World championship (1986); was the youngest world-class swimmer in Canadian history.

HIGUCHI, Chako (1945—). Japanese golfer. Born Hisako Matsui Higuchi, Oct 13, 1945, in Tokyo, Japan. ❖ Began playing golf (1963) and quickly became the top woman player in Japan, winning the Japanese Open 8 times and the Japanese LPGA championship 9 times; began competing in America (1970); won Colgate European Open (1976) and LPGA championship (1977). Inducted into the World Golf Hall of Fame (2003).

HIGUCHI, Ichiyo (1872–1896). Japanese feminist, novelist, poet and short-story writer. Name variations: Higuchi Natsuko; Higuchi Natsu. Born Higuchi Natsuko, May 2, 1872, in Tokyo, Japan, in the Meiji Period; died of TB, age 24, Nov 23, 1896, in Tokyo; buried in Yanaka Cemetery; dau. of a minor bureaucrat; forced to end her education in grammar school. ❖ One of most important writers in Japanese literary history, adopted pen name of Ichiyō at 20 and wrote of the unhappy and restricted lives of women; published 1st major work, *Ohtugomori* (1894), followed by *Takekurabe*, *Nigorie, Wakareachi*, and *Jusanya*, all to critical and popular success. Honored with her kimono-clad likeness on the 5,000 yen bill, the 1st woman to grace the front of modern Japanese banknotes (2004). ❖ See also Robert Lyons Danly, *In the Shade of Spring Leaves: The Life and Writings of Higuchi Ichiyo* (1981).

HIGUCHI, Natsu or Natsuko (1872–1896). See Higuchi, Ichiyo.

HIKAGE, Atsuko (1954—). Japanese golfer. Born April 23, 1954, in Iwate, Japan. ❖ Won Japanese Open (1982).

HIKAPUHI (1860/71?–1934). New Zealand tribal prophet and healer. Name variations: Te Hikapuhi. Born between 1860 and 1871, at Rotorua, New Zealand; died on June 13, 1913, at Rotorua; dau. of Wiremu Poihipi and Harete Ngaputo (Harete Manuhuia); m. Alfred Clayton (surveyor), 1906 (died 1913); children: at least 8 daughters, 3 sons. ❖ Nursed Maori by administering doses of strong brandy, which launched official campaign against her (1907–13); credited with various miracles, was also accused of causing several deaths; her methods lost favor as professional nursing became more available to Maori. ❖ See also *Dictionary of New Zealand Biography* (Vol. 3).

HILARIA (fl. 304). German saint. Fl. in 304; died in Augsburg; possibly the mother of St. Afra. ❖ According to legend, when Afra was martyred during reign of Diocletian, was also martyred at her tomb. Feast day is Aug 12. ❖ See also *Women in World History*.

HILD (614–680). *See Hilda of Whitby.*

HILDA, Saint (614–680). *See Hilda of Whitby.*

HILDA OF HARTLEPOOL (fl. 8th c.). English abbess. Fl. in 8th century at Hartlepool, England. ❖ As a young English noblewoman, entered Benedictine abbey of Hartlepool, a double monastery where monks and nuns lived communally under an abbess' direction; eventually became its abbess; highly educated in Latin and the classical liberal arts, continued the tradition of early abbeys as learning centers. ❖ See also *Women in World History.*

HILDA OF WHITBY (614–680). Abbess of Whitby. Name variations: Hild; Saint Hilda. Born 614 in kingdom of Deira, Northumbria; died at Whitby (Streaneshalch or Streonaeshalch), Nov 17, 680; dau. of Hereric (nephew of Edwin, king of the Northumbria kingdom of Deira), and Berguswida (Breguswith), origin unknown; never married; no children. ❖ Founding abbess of the noted double monastery of Whitby in the ancient British kingdom of Northumbria, a center of learning where 5 future English bishops were educated, who was described by the Venerable Bede as "the blaze of light which filled all England with its splendor"; baptized at York on Easter Sunday (April 2, 627); became abbess at Whitby (657); hosted the Council of Whitby (664), an occasion crucial to the development of the English church as an institution; sponsored Caedmon, the illiterate cowherd who 1st retold the stories of the Bible in Old English verse and became known as the Father of English Poetry; founded monastery of Hackness (680); protected and furthered the growth of her church during a crucial, war-torn period of English history. ❖ See also Venerabilis Bede, *Ecclesiastical History of the English Nation* (rep., Dent, 1954); and *Women in World History.*

HILDEBRAND, Sara (1979–). American diver. Name variations: Sara Riley. Born Sara Riley, Sept 18, 1979, in St. Paul, Minnesota; attended Indiana University. ❖ Placed 1st for springboard, synchronized springboard, and synchronized platform at US nationals (2003).

HILDEGARD. *Variant of Hildegar or Hildegarde.*

HILDEGARD (c. 802–841). Countess of Auvergne. Born c. 802; died 841; dau. of Ermengarde (c. 778–818) and Louis I the Pious (778–840), king of Aquitaine (r. 781–814), king of France (r. 814–840), and Holy Roman Emperor (r. 814–840); m. Gerard (c. 795–841), count of Auvergne; children: Ramnulf I (b. around 820), count of Poitou.

HILDEGARD OF BINGEN (1098–1179). Benedictine abbess and visionary. Name variations: Saint Hildegard, Hildegarde, or Hildegarda; Hildegard von Bingen; Hildegarde of Rupertsberg. Born 1098 in Bermersheim near Alzey (Rheinhessen), Germany; died in Rupertsberg near Bingen, Sept 17, 1179; dau. of nobles, Hildebert and Mechthild. ❖ Raised a strong voice of spiritual vision that found an outlet in numerous prose works (visionary, scientific, and hagiographic), public preaching, liturgical poetry, musical composition, and a voluminous correspondence that brought popes and monarchs within her sphere; had 1st illuminative vision (c. 1101); was offered to God as a tithe (10th child of her parents) and placed in the care of anchorite Jutta at monastery of Disibodenberg (c. 1106); made monastic profession in the community that had formed around Jutta (c. 1113); at death of Jutta, succeeded her as *magistra* of community (1136); in response to divine command, reluctantly began to record her visions in what would become *Scivias* (1141); her visionary writing was blessed by Pope Eugenius III (1147–48); moved community to Rupertsberg (1147–50); established daughter house at Eibingen (c. 1165); saw Rupertsberg community placed under interdict (1178). Writings include *Symphonia armonie celestium revelationum* (1150s), *Lingua ignota* (1150s), *Ordo virtutum* (perf. 1152?), *Liber vitae meritorum* (1158–63), *Physica* (1150s), *Causae et curae* (1150s) and *Liber divinorum operum* (1163–70). ❖ See also Barbara Lachman, *The Journal of Hildegard of Bingen* (Crown, 1993); Barbara Newman, ed. *Voice of the Living Light: Hildegard of Bingen and Her World* (University of California, 1998); and *Women in World History.*

HILDEGARD OF BURGUNDY (1050–after 1104). Duchess of Aquitaine. Born 1050; died after 1104; dau. of Ermengarde of Anjou (1018–1076) and Robert I (1011–1076), duke of Burgundy (r. 1031–1076); m. William VIII (c. 1026–1086), duke of Aquitaine (r. 1058–1086), c. 1069; children: Agnes of Aquitaine (d. 1097); William IX the Troubador (b. 1071), duke of Aquitaine.

HILDEGARDE, Saint.
See Hildegarde of Swabia (c. 757–783).
See Hildegard of Bingen (1098–1179).

HILDEGARDE DE BEAUGENCY (fl. 1080). Countess of Anjou. Fl. around 1080; m. Fulk IV the Rude, count of Anjou (r. 1068–1106); children: Ermengarde de Gatinais (d. around 1146). Fulk IV was also m. to Bertrada of Montfort (d. after 1117).

HILDEGARDE OF BAVARIA (c. 840–?). German princess. Born c. 840; death date unknown; dau. of Emma of Bavaria (d. 876) and Louis II the German (804–876), king of the Germans (r. 843–876); 1st wife of Liutpold, margrave of Bavaria (r. 895–907). Liutpold's 2nd wife was Cunigunde of Swabia.

HILDEGARDE OF BAVARIA (1825–1864). Archduchess of Austria. Name variations: Hildegarde Wittelsbach. Born June 10, 1825; died April 2, 1864; dau. of Theresa of Saxony (1792–1854) and Louis I Augustus also known as Ludwig I (1786–1868), king of Bavaria (r. 1825–1848, abdicated); m. Albrecht of Austria also known as Albert (1817–1895), archduke of Austria, May 1, 1844 (d. 1895).

HILDEGARDE OF RUPERTSBERG (1098–1179). *See Hildegard of Bingen.*

HILDEGARDE OF SWABIA (c. 757–783). Queen of the Franks. Name variations: Hildigard; Ildegarde; Saint Hildegarde; Hildegarde of Vinzgau. Born c. 757 or 758; died April 30, 783; dau. of Hildebrand, count of Souave; became 3rd wife of Charles I also known as Charlemagne (742–814), king of the Franks (r. 768–814), Holy Roman emperor (r. 800–814), 771; children: Adelaide (773–774); Bertha (779–after 823); Rotrude (c. 778–after 839); Gisela of Chelles (781–814); Charles (772–811), king of Neustria; Pepin I (773–810), king of Italy (r. 781–810); Louis I the Pious (778–840), king of Aquitaine (r. 781–814), king of France (r. 814–840), and Holy Roman emperor as Louis le Debonaire (r. 814–840); Lothar (778–780). ❖ As legend has it, was falsely accused of infidelity by a servant named Taland and subsequently divorced by Charlemagne; retired to Rome, where she led a life of piety, devoting herself to tending the sick; met Taland, now blind, and restored his sight; was led back to Charlemagne by a remorseful Taland. ❖ See also *Women in World History.*

HILDEGARDE OF SWABIA (fl. 1050). Duchess of Swabia. Name variations: Hildegarde van Buren or van Büren. Fl. around 1050; dau. of Otto II, duke of Swabia; m. Frederick van Büren (d. 1094); children: Frederick I (c. 1050–1105), duke of Swabia; Otto, baron von Strassburg (born around 1050); Ludwig (born around 1055), pfalzgraf of Rhein; Walter; Conrad; Adelheid.

HILDEGARDE OF VINZGAU (c. 757–783). *See Hildegarde of Swabia.*

HILDEGUND (d. 1188). German saint. Died 1188. ❖ Lived as a nun under the name Brother Joseph in Cistercian monastery of Schönau, near Heidelberg. Feast day is April 20.

HILDELETHA (fl. 700). Saint and abbess of Barking. Name variations: Saint Hildilid. Fl. around 700; born in France. ❖ Succeeded Saint Ethelburga (d. 676?) as abbess of Barking (c. 676).

HILGERTOVA, Stepanka (1968–). Czech kayaker. Born April 10, 1968, in Praha, Czech Republic. ❖ Won gold medals for K1 slalom at Atlanta Olympics (1996) and Sydney Olympics (2000); won the World Cup, Olympic, World and European championships within 4 years.

HILL, Abigail (1670–1734). *See Masham, Abigail.*

HILL, Anita (1956—). American lawyer, educator, author and activist. Born Anita Faye Hill, July 30, 1956, in Lone Tree, Oklahoma; youngest of 13 children; Oklahoma State University, BA (1977); Yale University, JD (1980). ❖ Lawyer who became a focal point for growing awareness about sexual harassment in the workplace, began practicing law with Washington, DC, firm of Ward, Hardraker and Ross; became assistant to Clarence Thomas at US Department of Education (1981), then joined his legal staff upon his appointment as chair of Equal Employment Opportunity Commission (EEOC); became law professor at Oral Roberts University (1983), then at University of Oklahoma College of Law; intensely private, was catapulted into public spotlight when her allegations of sexual harassment against Supreme Court nominee Clarence Thomas were leaked during Senate confirmation hearings; called to testify before congress, alleged that Thomas had made unwelcome sexual overtures and crudely explicit remarks while supervising her at EEOC, allegations which were denied by Thomas (1991); delivered compelling testimony which was ignored; went on to prominence as speaker, researcher and writer on race and gender issues in workplace environments; joined faculty of Heller School for Social Policy and

Management at Brandeis University (1997); with Emma Coleman Jordan, edited *Race, Gender and Power in America* (1995). ❖ See also memoir, *Speaking Truth to Power* (Anchor, 1998).

HILL, Betty (1919–2004). American social worker. Born Eunice Elizabeth Barrett, June 28, 1919, in Newton, New Hampshire; died Oct 17, 2004, in Portsmouth, NH; graduate of University of New Hampshire; m. Barney Hill (died 1969). ❖ Social worker who inspired a national obsession, when she reluctantly went public with the claim that she was abducted with husband by aliens from outer space on a moonlit night (Sept 19, 1961); later became a celebrity on the UFO circuit. Experts, including Carl Sagan, felt that the Hills were telling the truth as they knew it. ❖ See also John G. Fuller *The Interrupted Journey: Two Lost Hours Aboard a Flying Saucer* (Dial, 1966); tv movie "The UFO Incident" (1975).

HILL, Cindy (1948—). American golfer. Name variations: Cynthia Hill. Born Feb 12, 1948, in South Haven, Michigan. ❖ Won the Broadmoor (1973); won the USGA Women's Amateur (1974); member of Curtis Cup and World Cup teams (1974); won the North and South, South Atlantic, Doherty Cup (1975), and Rail (1984).

HILL, Cynthia (1948—). *See Hill, Cindy.*

HILL, Debra (1950–2005). American film producer. Born Oct 11, 1950, in Haddonfield, NJ; died of cancer, Mar 7, 2005, in Los Angeles, CA; dau. of Jilda and Frank Hill. ❖ With John Carpenter, co-wrote and co-produced the classic horror film *Halloween* (1978); formed Hill/Obst Productions with Lynda Obst (1985), then Debra Hill Productions (1988); also produced *The Fog* (1980), *Escape from New York* (1981), *The Dead Zone* (1983), *Gross Anatomy* (1989), *The Fisher King* (1991), *Escape from L.A.* (1996) and *Crazy in Alabama* (1999), among others.

HILL, Denean (1964—). *See Howard, Denean.*

HILL, Dorothy (1907–1997). Australian geologist and paleontologist. Born Sept 10, 1907, in Brisbane, Australia; died April 23, 1997; University of Queensland, BS, 1928; earned doctorate at Newnham College, Cambridge. ❖ Australian geology expert, was the 1st Australian woman fellow of Royal Society of London (1965), 1st woman fellow of Australian Academy of Science (1956), as well as its 1st woman president (1970), and the 1st woman president of Royal Society of Queensland (1949); at University of Queensland, worked as research fellow (1937–42), geology department lecturer (1946–52), reader (1955–59), research professor (1959–72) and emeritus professor of geology (1973–97); edited Geological Society of Australia's journal (1958–64); helped establish Queensland Palaeontographical Society (1962). Named Commander of the Order of the British Empire (1971) and Commander of the Order of Australia (1993).

HILL, Dorothy Poynton (1915—). *See Poynton, Dorothy.*

HILL, Emily (1847–1930). New Zealand teacher, temperance worker, suffragist, and social reformer. Name variations: Emily Knowles. Born Emily Knowles, Sept 5, 1847, at Lye, Worcestershire, England; died Aug 27, 1930, at Napier, New Zealand; dau. of John (shoemaker) and Charlotte (Round) Knowles; m. Henry Thomas Hill (teacher), 1873; children: 4 daughters, 3 sons. ❖ Immigrated with husband to New Zealand (1873); managed infants' department of large primary school in east Christchurch (1875–78); held office in New Zealand Women's Christian Temperance Union (WCTU), and was president of Napier Women's Franchise League (1893); also held executive positions in several organizations that worked for social-welfare reform and other issues affecting women and children; active in National Council of Women of New Zealand. ❖ See also *Dictionary of New Zealand Biography* (Vol. 3).

HILL, Ernestine (1899–1972). Australian novelist and travel writer. Born 1899 in Rockhampton, Queensland, Australia; died in Brisbane, 1972; children: 1 son. ❖ Following husband's death (1933), wandered almost continuously, then published *The Great Australian Loneliness* (1937), detailing 5 years of travel in Australian outback; only novel *My Love Must Wait* (1941), based on explorer Matthew Flinders, sold 10,000 copies during wartime; published *Flying Doctor Calling* (1947) and *The Territory* (1951), considered by many to be her best; claimed responsibility, in large part, for the writing of Daisy Bates' *Passing of the Aborigines* (1938), in her *Kabbarli: A Personal Memoir of Daisy Bates* (1973), which was published posthumously. ❖ See also *Women in World History.*

HILL, Frances Mulligan (1799–1884). American missionary. Born Frances Maria Mulligan, July 10, 1799, in New York, NY; died Aug 5,

1884, in Athens, Greece; dau. of John W. (lawyer) and Elizabeth (Winter) Mulligan; m. John Henry Hill (Episcopal leader), April 26, 1821. ❖ Opened school for the poor with husband in Athens (1831), as part of 1st foreign mission to be sent out by Protestant Episcopal Church of US; opened boarding school (1837), which attracted pupils from influential families throughout Greece; in Athens, organized private school for upper-class girls, the Hill Institute (1869), which—as Hill Memorial School—remains a leading educational institution.

HILL, Grace Livingston (1865–1947). American author. Name variations: Grace Livingston Hill-Lutz; (pseudonym) Marcia Macdonald. Born April 16, 1865, in Wellsville, NY; died Feb 23, 1947, in Swarthmore, PA; dau. of Reverend Charles Montgomery (Presbyterian cleric) and Marcia (Macdonald) Livingston (composed religious literature for children); attended Cincinnati Art School and Elmira College; m. Rev. Thomas Franklin Hill (Presbyterian minister), 1892 (died 1899); niece of Isabella Alden (1841–1930); m. Flavius J. Lutz, 1904 (sep.); children (1st m.) Margaret Livingston Hill (b. 1893), Ruth Glover Hill (b. 1898). ❖ Writer of moral stories that incorporated issues of the day, published 1st book, *Chautauqua Idyl*, at 22; following husband's death (1899), began to write novels to support daughters, averaging 2-to-3 books per year; published 79 books, with sales over 3 million; most popular titles include *The Witness* (1917), *The Enchanted Barn* (1918), *Beauty for Ashes* (1935), *April Gold* (1936) and *Matched Pearls* (1933), considered by some to be her best work. ❖ See also *Women in World History.*

HILL, Hannah, Jr. (1703–1714). American religious writer. Born 1703 in Philadelphia, PA; died 1714. ❖ Devout 11-year-old Quaker, who gave moral advice to family as she was dying, resulting in *A Legacy for Children: Being some of the Last Expressions and Dying Sayings of Hannah Hill, Jr.* (1717).

HILL, Jo (1963—). Australian basketball player. Name variations: Joanne Hill. Born Joanne Kay Hill, June 19, 1963, in Murreay Bridge, Australia. ❖ Won a team silver medal at Sydney Olympics (2000); played for Adelaide Lightning in the WNBL (1999–2000).

HILL, Joan (fl. 1460). English mistress. Mistress of Henry Beaufort (1436–1464), 3rd duke of Somerset (r. 1455–1464); children: Charles Somerset (c. 1460–1526), 1st earl of Worcester (r. 1514–1526). ❖ Her son was an emissary for Henry VII.

HILL, Joanne (1963—). *See Hill, Jo.*

HILL, Kathryn (1899–1947). *See Carver, Kathryn.*

HILL, Lauryn (1975—). African-American pop singer. Born May 26, 1975, in South Orange, NJ; dau. of Mal and Valerie Hill; children: (with Rohan Marley) Zion (b. 1996), Selah (b. 1998), Joshua (b. 2002) and John (b. 2003). ❖ Appeared on "As the World Turns" (1991); formed rap group Tranzlator Crew with Pras Michel and Wyclef Jean, then renamed it The Fugees; sang vocals on group's debut album, *Blunted on Reality* (1994); achieved success with band's next effort *The Score* (1996), which sold 17 million copies and featured the single "Killing Me Softly"; topped charts with solo debut *The Miseducation of Lauryn Hill* (1999), which earned 5 Grammy awards; released hits "Doo Wop (That Thing)" (1998), "Nothing Even Matters" (1999), and "Everything is Everything" (1999); films include *Sister Act 2* (1993), *Hav Plenty* (1997) and *Restaurant* (1998); released second solo CD *MTV Unplugged 2.0* (2002).

HILL, Lillie Rosa Minoka (1876–1952). *See Minoka-Hill, Rosa.*

HILL, Lynn (1961—). American rock climber. Born Jan 2, 1961, in Detroit, MI; grew up in California. ❖ Legendary rock climber, was an accomplished gymnast by 14; made 1st climb at 14; made 1st ascent (1979) of Ophir Broke which was then considered the hardest climb ever attempted by a woman; became 1st woman to climb Masse Critique in Cimai, France; placed in, or won, every competition she entered in 1980s, including a win at World Cup (1989); became 1st person, woman or man, to complete free ascent of The Nose on El Capitan in Yosemite National Park (1992); retired from competitive climbing (1992); repeated free ascent of The Nose (1993), this time in less than 24 hours, an unequaled achievement which has been referred to as "mythical." ❖ See also autobiography (with Greg Child) *Climbing Free: My Life in the Vertical World* (2002).

HILL, Mabel (1872–1956). New Zealand painter and art teacher. Name variations: Mabel McIndoe. Born Mar 3 (1872, in Auckland, New Zealand; died Nov 18, 1956, in East Grinstead, Sussex, England; dau. of Charles Hill (hatter) and Eliza Ann (Hulbert) Hill; m. John McIndoe (printer), 1898 (died 1916); children: 1 daughter, 3 sons. ❖ Studied and taught at Wellington School of Design (1886–97); joined Otago Art Society (late 1890s); produced portraits, still lifes, and flower paintings; contributed illustrations to Barbara Douglas' *Pictures in a New Zealand Garden* (1921); opened Barn Studio with A.H. O'Keeffe (early 1920s); taught painting privately and at Archerfield College (1922–25); traveled extensively throughout South Pacific, US, and Europe and lived primarily in London (1926–34), Dunedin (1934–38); moved to England (mid-1940s). Received King George VI's Coronation Medal (1937). ❖ See also *Dictionary of New Zealand Biography* (Vol. 3).

HILL, Martha (1900–1995). American modern dancer and teacher. Name variations: Martha H. Davies. Born Dec 1, 1900, in East Palestine, Ohio; died Nov 19, 1995, in Brooklyn, NY; Columbia University Teachers College, BA; New York University, MA; m. Thurston "Lefty" Davies (director of NY's Town Hall), 1952 (died 1961). ❖ Pioneeer in American dance education, performed with dance troupe of Martha Graham (1929–31); taught at Kansas State Teachers' College, where she organized and trained dancers for a dance festival; worked in similar capacity for other institutions, including University of Chicago and University of Oregon, before being employed as director of Bennington School of the Dance (1934–39) where modern dance was 1st considered a separate art form; was founding director of American Dance Festival (1948–c. 1965) and founding chair and 1st director of dance division at Juilliard School in NY (1951); oversaw the institution's inclusion of both modern and ballet techniques in equal degree in dance instruction; became artistic director emeritus (1985) and remained in that position until her death.

HILL, May (1884–1969). *See Arbuthnot, May Hill.*

HILL, Octavia (1838–1912). British reformer and social worker. Born Octavia Hill, Dec 3, 1838, at Wisbech near Peterborough, England; died Aug 13, 1912, in London; dau. of James Hill (banker and corn merchant) and Caroline Southwood (Smith) Hill (teacher and manager of Ladies Co-operative Guild); had no formal education; never married; no children. ❖ Widely recognized as one of her nation's leading authorities on housing for the poor, became involved in the Christian Socialist movement; shocked at the miserable conditions in which the poor lived because tenants countered their landlords' indifference with their own, decided to become a landlord herself and to institute and encourage new principles of responsibility; with help of John Ruskin, acquired a number of properties (1865–66), then insisted on a "perfect strictness" between herself and her tenants that was tempered by a "perfect respectfulness" in their reciprocal duties; organized an informal bank that encouraged her tenants to save, found work for the unemployed, initiated sewing and dressmaking classes, and established a garden and playground to encourage healthy exercise; asked to take over management of several properties which the London Association for the Prevention of Pauperization and Crime (COS) had acquired in London borough of Marylebone (1869); expanded work throughout Marylebone and surrounding boroughs; began writing annual reports in *Letters to my Fellow-Workers* (1871), which had a significant impact on public opinion and largely facilitated a further extension of her work to the slums of other major English cities; concerned with open spaces, was elected to executive committee of Commons Preservation Society (later National Trust) which sought to preserve the countryside and historic buildings. ❖ See also C. Moberly Bell, *Octavia Hill* (1942); William Thomson Hill, *Octavia Hill: Pioneer of the National Trust and Housing Reformer* (1956); and *Women in World History.*

HILL, Opal S. (1892–1981). American golfer. Born June 2, 1892, in Newport, Nebraska; died June 1981 in Kansas City, Missouri; husband died in 1942. ❖ Won the North and South (1928); selected for the Curtis Cup team (1932, 1934, 1936); reached semifinals of USGA 3 times and the quarterfinals twice; won the Western 5 times, Trans-Mississippi 4 times, Western Open twice, Missouri Valley twice, and Missouri State 3 times; set world record in women's golf with a blazing 66 (1937), then turned pro (Oct 18, 1938), only the 2nd to do so; was a founding member of the LPGA.

HILL, Patty Smith (1868–1946). American educator and reformer in kindergarten schooling. Born in Anchorage, Kentucky, Mar 27, 1868; died in New York, NY, May 25, 1946; dau. of Will Wallace Hill (Presbyterian minister and educator) and Martha Jane (Smith) Hill; sister of Mildred J. Hill (1859–1916), musician; graduate of Louisville Collegiate Institute, 1887; never married; no children. ❖ Became head of Louisville Free Kindergarten Association and Louisville Training

School for Kindergarten and Primary Teachers (1893); as a leader in burgeoning kindergarten movement, participated in series of lectures at Columbia University Teachers College (1904–05); appointed to full-time faculty position at Teachers College (1906) and elected president of International Kindergarten Union (1908); became head of new kindergarten department at Columbia (1910), which also ran the experimental Horace Mann Kindergarten; was instrumental in organizing the Institute of Child Welfare Research at Teachers College; founded the National Association for Nursery Education (1925); retired from Teachers College (1935), after which she established and directed the Hilltop Community Center for underprivileged children; also credited with the song "Happy Birthday," which she wrote with her sister. ❖ See also *Women in World History.*

HILL, Rosa Minoka (1876–1952). *See Minoka-Hill, Rosa.*

HILL, Susan (1942—). British novelist and short-story writer. Name variations: Susan Elizabeth Hill. Born 1942 in Scarborough, Yorkshire, England; studied English at London University; m. Stanley Wells, 1975. ❖ Published 1st novel *The Enclosure* (1961); became book review editor at *Evening Telegraph*; other novels include *I'm the King of the Castle* (1970), *In the Springtime of the Year* (1974) and *The Woman in Black* (1983); short-story collections include *The Albatross* (1971) and *The Custodian* (1972); nonfiction includes *The Magic Apple Tree: A Country Year* (1982), *Lanterns Across the Snow* (1987) and *The Lighting of the Lamps* (1987).

HILL, Thelma (1925–1977). American ballet and modern dancer. Born 1925 in New York, NY; died Nov 21, 1977, in New York, NY. ❖ Performed with the Negro Ballet—or Ballet Americana—in NY; collaborated with Alvin Ailey and was featured in his *Revelations* (1960); was a founding member of Clark Center for Performing Arts; also taught at City College and Lehman College of City University of New York; honored with the naming of the Thelma Hill Performing Arts Center, in Brooklyn.

HILL, Virginia (1907–1967). American badminton player. Name variations: Mrs. Mosdale; Virginia Mosdale. Born Virginia Deignan, April 17, 1907, in Los Angeles, CA; died June 8, 1967. ❖ With Wynn Rogers, won the US mixed doubles (1947); served as administrative secretary and treas. of American Badminton Assoc. (1960–67); received Players' Appreciation Cup (1967).

HILL, Virginia (1916–1966). American Mafia associate and drug peddler. Born Onie Virginia Hill, Aug 26, 1916, in Lipscomb, Alabama; died Mar 24, 1966, in Koppl, Austria, near Salzburg; dau. of W.M. "Mack" Hill (livery-stable operator) and Margaret Hill; possibly m. George Rogers/Randell, c. 1931 (died); m. Ossie Griffin (college football player), Jan 13, 1939 (annulled June 1939); m. Carlos Gonzales Valdez (rhumba dancer), Jan 20, 1940 (div.); m. Hans Hauser (ski instructor), Mar 1950; children: (last m.) Peter (b. Nov 20, 1950). ❖ The only woman ever identified as a Mafia associate, captured attention of Joe Epstein, who headed up Chicago's gambling concerns for Al Capone; was employed as a "bag girl," transporting cash across state lines; was asked to infiltrate inner circle of NY family led by Lucky Luciano; initially, became mistress of Luciano henchman Joe Adonis, teaming up with him in gambling rackets and money laundering, but recorded her activities in a secret diary; headed to Los Angeles, where she became involved with Hollywood elite, as well as gangster Bugsy Siegel of the Luciano gang; when Siegel's Flamingo Casino in Las Vegas failed, deserted him; continued to work for Luciano, transporting money and goods throughout US and European capitals; summoned to appear before Estes Kefauver hearings on organized crime (Mar 15, 1951), was arrested for tax fraud; jumped bail and fled the country. ❖ See also Andy Edmonds, *Bugsy's Baby: The Secret Life of Mob Queen Virginia Hill* (1993); film *Bugsy,* starring Annette Bening and Warren Beatty (1991); and *Women in World History.*

HILL-LOWE, Beatrice. English archer. Name variations: Beatrice Hill Lowe. Born in UK. ❖ At London Olympics, won a bronze medal in national round (1948).

HILLARD, Martha (1856–1947). *See MacLeish, Martha Hillard.*

HILLAS, Lorraine (1961—). Australian field-hockey player. Born Dec 11, 1961, in Australia. ❖ At Seoul Olympics, won a gold medal in team competition (1988).

HILLEN, Francisca (1959—). Dutch field-hockey player. Born Sept 30, 1959, in Denmark. ❖ At Los Angeles Olympics, won a gold medal in team competition (1984).

HILLER, Wendy (1912–2003). British actress. Name variations: Dame Wendy Hiller. Born Wendy Margaret Hiller, Aug 15, 1912, in Bramhall, Cheshire, England; died May 14, 2003, in Beaconsfield; dau. of Frank Watkin Hiller (mill director) and Elizabeth (Stone) Hiller; m. Ronald Gow (playwright), Feb 25, 1937 (died 1993); children: 1 son, 1 daughter. ❖ Acclaimed for her portrayal of Mary of Teck in *Crown Matrimonial* (1972), began career at Manchester Rep, where she worked her way up from apprentice to actor-manager and made stage debut as the Maid in *The Ware Case* (1930); made London debut as Sally Hardcastle in *Love on the Dole* (1935) and was an instant success (made NY debut in same role, 1936); launched film career in *Lancashire Luck* (1937), adapted from *Love on the Dole*, followed by *Pygmalion* (1938) with Leslie Howard, which brought her an Academy Award; captured another Academy Award (1958) for portrayal of Miss Cooper in *Separate Tables*; other films include *Major Barbara* (1941), *Something of Value* (1957), *Sons and Lovers* (1960), *Toys in the Attic* (1963), *A Man for All Seasons* (1966), *David Copperfield* (1970), *Murder on the Orient Express* (1974), *Voyage of the Damned* (1976), *The Cat and the Canary* (1978), *The Elephant Man* (1980) and *The Lonely Passion of Judith Hearne* (1987); appeared in several plays by husband, notably Tess in his adaptation of *Tess of the D'Urbervilles* (1946), and title role in his adaptation of *Ann Veronica* (1949); was also memorable as Catherine Sloper in *The Heiress* (1947), Josie Hogan in *A Moon for the Misbegotten* (1937), Tina in *The Aspern Papers* (1962) and Gunhild in *John Gabriel Borkman* (1975). Named a Dame of the British Empire (1975). ❖ See also *Women in World History*.

HILLERN, Wilhelmine von (1836–1916). German novelist. Born in Munich, Germany, Mar 11, 1836; dau. of Charlotte Birch-Pfeiffer and C.A. Birch; m. Baron von Hillern, 1857 (died 1882). ❖ Began career as an actress but retired from the stage upon marriage; lived in Oberammergau and won fame as a novelist. Her most popular works are *Ein Arzt der Seele* (1869), and *Die Geier-Wally* (1883), which was dramatized and translated into English as *The Vulture Maiden* (1876).

HILLESUM, Etty (1914–1943). Dutch intellectual and diarist. Name variations: Esther Hillesum. Born Esther Hillesum in Middelburg, Holland, Jan 15, 1914; died in Auschwitz, Nov 30, 1943; dau. of Dr. Louis Hillesum (teacher of classical languages) and Rebecca (Bernstein) Hillesum (Russian emigre to Netherlands after a Russian pogrom); graduated from municipal gymnasium, 1932; University of Amsterdam, law degree; attended Faculty of Slavonic Languages; began study of psychology. ❖ Dutch diarist who strove for goodness, praying for an inner freedom, clarity, and peace of mind, even through the worst days of the Holocaust; her diaries, published as *An Interrupted Life*, have become a vademecum for readers around the world. Writings include *Het Verstoorde leven: Dagboek van Etty Hillesum, 1941–1943* (De Haan/Unieboek, 1981, published in America as *An Interrupted Life*, 1983); *Het denkende hart van de barak* (*The Thinking Heart of the Barracks*, De Haan/Unieboek, 1982, published in America as *Etty Hillesum: Letters from Westerbork*, 1986). ❖ See also *Women in World History*.

HILLIARD, Harriet (1909–1994). American actress and singer. Name variations: Harriet Nelson. Born Peggy Lou Snyder in Des Moines, Iowa, July 18, 1909; died in Laguna Beach, CA, Oct 2, 1994; dau. of Roy Snyder (director of a stock theater company whose stage name was Roy Hilliard) and Hazel (McNutt) Snyder (actress as Hazel Hilliard); m. Oswald George "Ozzie" Nelson, 1935 (died 1975); children: Eric "Rick" Nelson (1940–1985), David Nelson (b. 1936, producer-director); grandchildren: Tracy Nelson (actress), and twins Gunnar and Matthew Nelson (pop rock singers who call themselves The Nelsons). ❖ Gave up budding career as bandsinger and movie actress to marry bandleader Ozzie Nelson; worked with him on radio shows of comedians Joe Penner and Red Skelton; with husband and sons, starred on "The Adventures of Ozzie and Harriet" on CBS radio (1944–49), ABC radio (1949–54), and ABC-TV (1952–66); appeared in such films as *Follow the Fleet* (1936), *New Faces of 1937* (1937), *Coconut Grove* (1938), *The Letter* (1940), *Confessions of Boston Blackie* (1941), *The Falcon Strikes Back* (1943) and *Here Come the Nelsons* (1952). ❖ See also *Women in World History*.

HILLIARD, Patricia (1916–2001). English actress. Born Patricia Maud Penn-Gaskell, Mar 14, 1916, in Quetta, India; died June 14, 2001, in Sussex, England; dau. of Stafford Hilliard and Ann Codrington (both actors); m. William Fox, 1938. ❖ Made stage debut as Estelle in *The*

Copy and came to prominence as Catherine Hilton in *Call It a Day* (both 1935); other plays include *Family Group, A Family Man, Up the Garden Path, Under Suspicion, Too True to be Good, Candida, No Medals, Noose* and *Mandragola*; joined BBC Rep (1952); films include *Full Circle, Night Journey* and *The Missing Million*.

HILLIER, Hope (d. 1980). See Topham, Mirabel.

HILLIS, Margaret (1921—). American conductor. Born Oct 1, 1921, in Kokomo, Indiana; dau. of Bernice (Haynes) Hillis and Elwood Hillis; studied at Indiana University; received Master's in choral conducting, Juilliard School of Music, 1949. ❖ Was a naval flight instructor for 2 years during WWII; founded American Concert Choir and American Concert Orchestra (1950) which made many international tours for the State Department; conducted the Kenosha Symphony in Wisconsin (1961–68); also conducted the Cleveland Orchestra, Minnesota Orchestra, Akron Orchestra, National Symphony Orchestra, Milwaukee Symphony Orchestra and Chicago Symphony Orchestra, among others. ❖ See also *Women in World History*.

HILLMAN, Bessie (1889–1970). Russian-born American labor leader. Born Bashe Abramowitz in Russia, 1889; died 1970; educated at home by tutors; m. Sidney Hillman (labor leader), May 1, 1916 (died 1946); children: Philomine (b. 1917) and Selma Hillman (b. 1921). ❖ Immigrated to US (1905), settling in Chicago, and took a job as a button-sewer in a sweatshop managed by Hart Schaffner & Marx; protesting the lowering of her piece rate from 4 cents to 3.75 cents (1910), eventually brought about a strike which spread from company to company and involved 30,000 workers; with husband, founded Amalgamated Clothing Workers of America, the 1st union to represent unskilled immigrant workers (1914); also served on UN Commission on the Status of Women and was on a subcommittee of the President's Commission on the Status of Women. ❖ See also *Women in World History*.

HILLS, Carla (1934—). American lawyer and public official. Born Carla Helen Anderson in Los Angeles, California, Jan 3, 1934; dau. of Carl Anderson (building supplies executive) and Edith (Hume) Anderson; graduated cum laude from Stanford University, 1955; Yale University Law School, LLB, 1958; m. Roderick M. Hills (politician), Sept 27, 1958; children: 4. ❖ The 1st woman secretary of the Department of Housing and Urban Development and 3rd woman to hold a US Cabinet seat, passed the California Bar (1959), then worked for 2 years as assistant district attorney in Los Angeles; with husband and other partners, formed law firm of Munger, Tolles, Hills & Rickershauser (1962); specializing in antitrust and securities cases, gained prominence as a trial lawyer; served on advisory board of California Council on Criminal Justice (1969–71) and on standing committee on discipline for US District Court for Central California (1970–73); was adjunct professor at UCLA School of Law (1972) and on board of councillors of University of Southern California Law Center (1972–74); appointed assistant attorney general in civil division of US Department of Justice (1974); served as secretary of Department of Housing and Urban Development (1975–77); served as US trade representative (1989–93), under administration of George Bush. ❖ See also *Women in World History*.

HILLS, Tina S. (1921—). Italian-American publisher and business executive. Name variations: Tina S. Ramos. Born Argentina Schifano, Oct 4, 1921, in Pola, Istria Province, Italy; attended New York University; m. Angel Ramos (newspaper publisher, died 1960); m. Lee Hill (editor). ❖ At 14, immigrated with parents to US; after death of husband, became head of El Mundo enterprises (which included the newspaper *El Mundo*, 2 radio stations, and the highest-rated tv station in San Juan, Puerto Rico, 1960); served as editor and publisher of *El Mundo* (1961–1987); served as director of Red Cross in San Juan; built Angel Ramos Foundation (Puerto Rico's largest private philanthropic foundation); elected 1st woman president of Inter American Press Association (IPA, 1977); received the Maria Moors Cabot Prize from Columbia University and Americas Foundation Award.

HILLYARD, Blanche Bingley (1864–1938). English tennis player. Name variations: Blanche Bingley; Mrs. George Whiteside Hillyard. Born Blanche Bingley in England in 1864; died 1938; married Commander George Hillyard (secretary of the All England (tennis) Club, 1907–24). ❖ As Blanche Bingley, competed in the 1st women's championship at Wimbledon (1884), then won the singles championship (1886); as Blanche Bingley Hillyard, won 5 more singles titles at Wimbledon (1889, 1894, 1897, 1899, 1900). ❖ See also *Women in World History*.

HILMO, Elisabeth (1976—). Norwegian handball player. Born Nov 29, 1976, in Trondheim, Norway. ❖ Won a team bronze medal at Sydney Olympics (2000).

HILO HATTIE (1901–1979). *See Nelson, Clara.*

HILST, Hilda (1930—). Brazilian poet and short-story writer. Born April 4, 1930, in São Paulo, Brazil. ❖ Works include *Balada do festival* (1955), *Poesia 1959/1967* (1967), *Qadós* (1973), *A obscena Senhora D* (1982), *Com meus olhos de cã e outras novelas* (1986), *Bufólicas* (1992) and *Do amor* (1999).

HILSZ, Maryse (1903–1946). French aviator. Name variations: name often misspelled Hiltz or Hilz. Born in Levallois-Perret, France, 1903; died in airplane accident at Moulin-des-Ponts, Jan 31, 1946. ❖ One of the most admired women flyers, made a series of spectacular flights to the Far East and Africa (1930s) and held the women's world altitude record; received the Harmon International Aviation Trophy for women fliers for 1933. ❖ *See also Women in World History.*

HILTRUDE (fl. 800s). Frankish princess. Born between 783 and 794; dau. of Fastrada (d. 794) and Charles I also known as Charlemagne (742–814), king of the Franks (r. 768–814), Holy Roman emperor (r. 800–814); sister of Theodrada, abbess of Argenteuil.

HILTRUDE OF LIESSIES (d. late 700s). French saint. Died in late 700s; dau. of a Poitevin noble from Hainaut. ❖ Resolved to remain a virgin, fled father's house when presented with a suitor; returned when she learned that the suitor had married her sister; took the veil and lived as a recluse in a cell attached to the church of Liessies until her death.

HIMIKO (fl. 3rd c.). Chinese shaman. Name variations: Pimiko; Pimiku; Pimiho; Pimisho; Yamato-hime-mikoto; Yametsu-hime. Pronunciation: He-ME-koe. Ruled around 190–247. ❖ Ruled Japan in the 3rd century; was responsible for opening trade and diplomatic relations with China. ❖ *See also Women in World History.*

HIMILTRUDE (fl. 700s). Queen of the Franks and wife of Charlemagne. Name variations: Hamiltrude; Himiltude. Fl. in the 700s; became 1st wife of Charles I also known as Charlemagne, emperor of the West, king of the Franks (r. 768–814), Holy Roman emperor (r. 800–814), around 768; children: several, including Pepin the Hunchback (c. 769–810). ❖ A poor Frenchwoman, was the 1st of Charlemagne's 9 wives.

HIMNECHILDIS (r. 662–675). Queen and regent of Austrasia. Name variations: Hymnegilde or Hymnégilde; Chimnechild. Reigned as regent from 662 to 675; m. Sigibert III (630–656), king of eastern Frankish kingdom of Austrasia (r. 632–656), in 633; children: at least one son, Saint Dagobert II (652–678/79), king of Austrasia (r. 674–678); at least one daughter Bilchilde (d. 675). ❖ Upon death of husband (656), named co-regent for her nephew Childeric II (her son Dagobert II had been spirited off to an Irish monastery by Grimoald, mayor of Austrasia, who had tried to install his own son Childebert on the throne but was killed in the process); before Childeric II was assassinated (675), had Dagobert restored to his proper place on the throne (r. 674–678). ❖ *See also Women in World History.*

HIND, Cora (1861–1942). Canadian journalist. Name variations: E. Cora Hind. Born Ella Cora Hind in Toronto, Ontario, Canada, 1861; died in 1942. ❖ Served as a wheat inspector for 3 years before turning to writing for the *Manitoba Free Press* (1901); her judgment of crops and possible yield were so accurate that for the next 25 years her estimates influenced the advance price of Canadian wheat. ❖ *See also Kenneth Haig, Brave Harvest: The Life Story of E. Cora Hind.*

HIND BINT 'UTBA (d. 610). Arabian singer. Name variations: Hind Bint 'Utba. Birth date unknown; died in 610 CE. ❖ Poet and musician, led women in singing war songs and laments for those killed at Badr (605); was considered representative of women performers of the *jahiliyya*, or days of ignorance, that is a period before harems and confinement. ❖ *See also Women in World History.*

HINDE, Barbara (1917–2004). *See Jefferis, Barbara.*

HINDERAS, Natalie (1927–1987). African-American concert pianist. Born Natalie Leota Henderson, June 15, 1927, in Oberlin, Ohio; died of cancer, Aug 1987, in Philadelphia, PA; dau. of a jazz musician and Leota Palmer (conservatory teacher); Oberlin School of Music, bachelor degree in music, 1945; studied with Olga Samaroff at Juilliard and Edward Steuermann at Philadelphia Conservatory; m. Lionel Monagas (tv producer); children: Michele Monagas. ❖ One of the 1st black artists to gain recognition in the field of classical music, made NY debut at Town Hall, playing a program that included Chopin's Ballade in F minor (1954); despite favorable reviews, as an African-American in the white-dominated field of classical music, had trouble launching career; fared better abroad and spent much of 1950s and 1960s touring in Europe, Asia and Africa; joined faculty of Temple University (1960s), where she would be professor of music until her death; finally achieved recognition in US, making stunning debuts with Philadelphia Orchestra and NY Philharmonic (1972); went on to perform with all major orchestras in the country and record with leading labels; best-known for Rachmaninoff's Concerto No. 2 in C Minor, Schumann's Piano Concerto, and *Rhapsody in Blue* by George Gershwin; recorded *Natalie Hinderas plays Music by Black Composers* (1971), one of the 1st anthologies of the work of African-Americans; commissioned George Walker's Piano Concerto No. 1, which she 1st performed with National Symphony Orchestra (1976). ❖ *See also Women in World History.*

HINDLEY, Myra (1942–2002). British serial killer. Born July 1942; died in Bury St. Edmunds, England, Nov 15, 2002; had liaison with Ian Brady. ❖ With boyfriend, killed 2 children and a young man and buried them on England's Saddleworth Moor (1963–65), causing them to be dubbed the Moors Murderers (1966); led authorities to 2 other graves (1986); died in prison. ❖ *See also Emlyn Williams, Beyond Belief; and Women in World History.*

HINDMARCH, Gladys (1940—). Canadian short-story writer. Born 1940 in Ladysmith, British Columbia, Canada. ❖ Works include *Sketches* (1970), *A Birth Account* (1976), *The Peter Stories* (1976), and *The Watery Part of the World* (1988).

HINDMARSH, Mary (1921–2000). Australian botanist. Name variations: Mary Maclean Hindmarsh. Born July 21, 1921; died April 10, 2000; New England University College in Armidale, Australia, BS, 1943; Sydney University, PhD, 1953. ❖ Celebrated botanist, conducted postgraduate research at Chester Beatty Research Institute at Royal Cancer Hospital in London (1953–54); worked as botany lecturer (1954–59), senior lecturer (1959–72), and associate professor (1972–78) at New South Wales University of Technology in Ultimo (later University of New South Wales, Kensington, Sydney); served as a Linnean Society of New South Wales council member (1970–74); began to study rainforest species south of the Macleay River watershed, but the death of colleague John Waterhouse (1983) halted the project.

HINDORFF, Silvia (1961—). East German gymnast. Born June 27, 1961, in Sebnitz, East Germany. ❖ Placed 1st in floor exercises and uneven bars at GDR nationals (1978); won bronze team medals at World championships (1978, 1979) and came in 2nd in all-around at the World Cup (1978); at Moscow Olympics, won a bronze medal in team all-around (1980).

HINE-I-PAKETIA (fl. 1850–1870). New Zealand tribal leader. Born Hine-i-paketia, fl. 1850–1870, in Heretaunga (Hawke's Bay), New Zealand; dau. of Hihipa-ki-te-rangi and his wife, Te Huhuti. ❖ Descended from several groups, claimed ownership of vast lands, which she later sold to the Crown despite much controversy. ❖ *See also Dictionary of New Zealand Biography* (Vol. 1).

HINEIRA, Arapera (1932—). New Zealand poet and short-story writer. Name variations: Arapera Blank; Ngati Porou; Ngati Kahungunu; Rongowhakaata; Te Aitanga-a-Mahaki. Born 1932 in New Zealand. ❖ Stories and poetry, in Maori and English, appeared in journals such as *Te Ao Hou.* Work focuses on race, culture, and family relationships.

HINE-I-TURAMA (c. 1818–1864). New Zealand tribal leader. Name variations: Hineaturama, Hineaturama Tapsell. Born c. 1818 in Te Arawa, Rotorua, New Zealand; died April 2, 1864; dau. of Kahanatokowai and his wife, Te Koeka; m. Phillip Tapsell (trader), c. 1830s (recognized by Catholic bishop, 1841); children: 6. ❖ Her tribal kinship provided security for husband's ventures; during district wars, avoided enslavement and took refuge with family on Mokoia Island before settling in Whakatane; after becoming involved in struggle between government and King's forces, was killed by British soldiers during a siege (1864). ❖ *See also Dictionary of New Zealand Biography* (Vol. 1).

HINEMATIORO (d. 1823). New Zealand tribal leader. Born Hinematioro on East Coast of New Zealand; died in 1823; dau. of Tane-toko-rangi and his wife, Ngunguru-te-rangi; m. Te Hoatiki; children: 4. ❖ Was leader among East Coast peoples at time Captain James Cook made his 1st trip to New Zealand (1769); ruled a large district with many subjects. ❖ *See also Dictionary of New Zealand Biography* (Vol. 1).

HINERANGI, Sophia (c. 1830–1911). New Zealand tribal leader and tourist guide. Name variations: Te Paea (Tepaea), Mary Sophia Gray. Born Te Paea between 1830 and 1834 (baptized Mary Sophia Gray, Aug 4, 1839), in Kororareka (Russell), New Zealand; died Dec 4, 1911, at Whakarewarewa; dau. of Alexander Grey (Gray) and Kotiro Hinerangi; m. Koroneho (Colenso) Tehakiroe, 1851; m. Hori Taiawhio, 1870; children: (1st m.) 14; (2nd m.) 3. ❖ Worked as guide to Pink and White Terraces at Lake Rotomahana before eruption of Mt. Tarawera (1886); relocated to Whakarewarewa and resumed work as tourist guide; joined George Leitch's Land of the Moa Dramatic Company in which she played herself (1895); became president of New Zealand Women's Christian Temperance Union (1896). ❖ See also *Dictionary of New Zealand Biography* (Vol. 2).

HINES, Elizabeth (1899–1971). American actress and dancer. Born Jan 8, 1899, in New York, NY; died Feb 10 or 19, 1971, in Lake Forest, Illinois; m. Frank R. Wharton (Quaker Foods exec), 1927. ❖ Musical-comedy star, made NY stage debut in *See-Saw* (1919); protégé of George M. Cohan, had initial success in his *The O'Brien Girl* (1921) and *Little Nellie Kelly* (1922); as an ingenue, also starred in *The Love Birds, Marjorie, Peg O' My Heart, Show Boat, Manhattan Mary* and *June Days*; retired from stage (1927).

HINGIS, Martina (1980—). Czech-born Swiss tennis player. Born Sept 30, 1980, in Kosice, Czechoslovakia (now Slovakia); dau. of Karol Hingis and Melanie (Molitor) Hingis (tennis player later known as Melanie Molitor). ❖ At 7, moved with mother and new stepfather Andreas Zogg to Trubbach, Switzerland; at 12, won Jr. French Open; turned pro (1994); played on Swiss Olympic team (1966); ranked #1 in the world for 1st time (1997); at 16, won singles title at Australian Open (1997), then won again (1998, 1999); won 37 straight matches and 75 total matches (1997), including singles championships at Wimbledon and US Open; won 40 career titles; retired (2003).

HINGST, Ariane (1979—). German soccer player. Born July 25, 1979, in Berlin, Germany. ❖ Defender; won a team bronze medal at Sydney Olympics (2000) and Athens Olympics (2004); won team European championships (1997, 2001); won FIFA World Cup (2003).

HINKLE, Beatrice M. (1874–1953). American psychiatrist. Born Beatrice M. Van Giesen, Oct 10, 1874, in San Francisco, California; died Feb 28, 1953, in New York, NY; dau. of B. Frederick Mores Van Giesen and Elizabeth (Benchley) Van Giesen; graduate of Cooper Medical School (later medical department, Stanford University), 1899; m. Walter Scott Hinkle (lawyer), 1892 (died 1899); children: Walter Mills Hinkle; Consuelo Andoga Shepard. ❖ One of the earliest US proponents of Carl Jung, was appointed San Francisco's city physician, the 1st woman doctor in US to hold a public-health position (1899); moved to NY (1905); with Dr. Charles R. Dana, established 1st psychotherapeutic clinic at Cornell Medical College (1908); studied in Europe (1905–15), 1st with Sigmund Freud in Vienna, later with Carl Jung; joined faculties of Cornell Medical College and New York Post Graduate Medical school (1915), where she became one of the earliest practitioners of Jungian analysis and also made valuable contributions to the framework of his theories; writings include a translation of Jung's *The Psychology of the Unconscious* (1915) and her major work, *The Recreation of the Individual* (1923).

HINKSON, Katharine (1861–1931). See Tynan, Katharine.

HINKSON, Mary (1930—). American modern dancer and choreographer. Born 1930 in Philadelphia, PA. ❖ Trained with Martha Graham in NY, then joined her company (1951); created roles for Graham in *Ardent Song* (1955), *Samson Agonistes* (1962), *Phaedra* (1969) and *Circe* (1963), her most acclaimed, among others; danced in Pearl Lang's *Chosen One* (1952), Balanchine's *Figure in the Carpet* (1960), and Anna Sokolow's *Seven Deadly Sins* (1975); taught at Martha Graham School, Juilliard and Dance Theater of Harlem. Choreographed *Make the Heart Show* (1951).

HINSON, Lois E. (1926—). American veterinarian. Born 1926 in Hazlehurst, Georgia. ❖ Became the 1st woman graduate from the University of Georgia College of Veterinary Medicine (1950); served as 1st woman president of National Association of Federal Veterinarians (NAFV, 1973–74) and 1st woman in charge of USDA Federal Meat Inspection Division (beginning 1973).

HINZMANN, Gabriele (1947—). East German track-and-field athlete. Born May 31, 1947, in East Germany. ❖ At Montreal Olympics, won a bronze medal in discus throw (1976).

HIPP, Jutta (1925–2003). German-American jazz pianist. Born Feb 4, 1925, in Leipzig, Germany; died April 7, 2003, in Queens, NY. ❖ Pianist with short but celebrated career, performed with saxophonist Hans Koller's band in Germany (1950s); formed own band in Munich (1953) and recorded album, *New Faces–New Sounds From Germany*; moved to US (1955); played at Hickory House jazz club for 6 months in NY (1956); through Blue Note Records, released albums: *Jutta Hipp With Zoot Sims* and 2 vols. of *Jutta Hipp at the Hickory House* (1956); performed at Newport Jazz Festival (1956); retired from performing (1958); worked as painter and eventually dressmaker.

HIPPARCHIA (fl. 300s BCE). Greek philosopher and wife of Crates. Name variations: Hipparchia the Cynic. Pronunciation: HIP-ark-EE-ah. Born in Maroneia; fl. in the 300s BCE; sister of Metrocles (also a Cynic); m. Crates, a Cynic philosopher (368–288 BCE). ❖ Fell in love with Cynic philosopher Crates, who was originally a Theban and a pupil of Athenian philosopher Diogenes; threatened parents with suicide unless she was allowed to marry him; at his insistence, agreed to follow his teachings, that one should live "according to nature" by renouncing wealth and living without possessions; adopted his manner of dress and accompanied him everywhere, even to those places which were considered indecent for women. ❖ See also *Women in World History.*

HIPPISLEY, E. (fl. 1741–1766). English actress. Name variations: Mrs. Fitzmaurice. Dau. of John Hippisley (actor and dramatist, died 1748); sister of Jane Hippisley (died 1791) and John Hippisley (actor and author, died 1767). ❖ The daughter of well-known comedian John Hippisley, acted under name Mrs. Fitzmaurice.

HIPPISLEY, Jane (d. 1791). English actress. Name variations: Mrs. Green. Died 1791; dau. of John Hippisley (actor and dramatist, died 1748); sister of E. Hippisley and John Hippisley (actor and author, died 1767). ❖ Played Ophelia opposite David Garrick's Hamlet at Goodman's Fields; was also the original Mrs. Malaprop in Sheridan's *The Rivals.*

HIPPIUS (1869–1945). See Gippius, Zinaida.

HIPPOLYTA. Variant of Ippolita.

HIRATSUKA, Raichō (1886–1971). Japanese feminist, pacifist, and consumer advocate. Name variations: Hiratuska Haruko; Hiratsuka Raichō. Pronunciation: HE-rah-TSU-kah Ray-CHOE. Born Hiratuska Haruko in Tokyo, Japan, 1886; died in Tokyo, 1971; dau. of a government official who had studied constitutional law in Europe; graduate of Japan Women's University, 1906; lived with the painter Okumura Hiroshi; children: son and daughter. ❖ Was a founder of Seitōsha (Bluestockings) (1911) and the 1st editor of its publication, *Seitō*; was one of the founders of the Shin Fujin Kyokai (New Women's Association), which campaigned for an extension of women's legal rights, higher education, and welfare benefits (1919); became active in the organization of consumer unions (1930s); after WWII, was often a participant in women's international peace initiatives. ❖ See also *Women in World History.*

HIRD, Judith (c. 1946—). American Lutheran pastor. Born c. 1946; graduate of Thiel College and Lutheran Theological Seminary. ❖ At 26, became pastor of Holy Cross Lutheran Church, Toms River, NJ (1972), the 1st woman parish pastor in the Lutheran Church in America.

HIRD, Thora (1911–2003). English stage and screen actress and patron of the arts. Name variations: Dame Thora Hird. Born May 28, 1911, in Morecambe, England; died Mar 15, 2003, in Brinsworth House, Twickenham, Middlesex, England; dau. of the manager of the Royalty Teatre in Morecambe; m. James Scott, May 3, 1937 (died 1994); children: Janette Scott (actress). ❖ In a career that spanned 8 decades, made stage debut as a child and London debut as Mrs. Gaye in *No Medals* (1944); made film debut in *The Big Blockade* (1942), followed by *Go to Blazes, 2,000 Women, The Courtneys of Curzon Street, Maytime in Mayfair, The Magic Box, Time Gentleman Please!, Simon and Laura, Sailor Beware!, The Entertainer, Rattle of a Simple Man* and *Consuming Passions*, among many others; on tv, had recurring roles on "Ours is a Nice House," "Meet the Wife," "Flesh and Blood," "In Loving Memory," "Hallelujah!" and "Last of the Summer Wine"; presenter of the BBC1 religious program "Your Songs of Praise Choice" (later titled "Praise Be!"); subject of BBC1's "This Is Your Life" (1996). Named Officer of the British Empire (OBE, 1983) and Dame Commander of the Order of the British Empire (DBE, 1993); won BAFTA award for Best Television Actress for "Talking Heads" (1987) and an honorary BAFTA (1993).

HIRO, Norie (1965—). Japanese volleyball player. Born July 26, 1965, in Japan. ❖ At Los Angeles Olympics, won a bronze medal in team competition (1984).

HIROSE, Miyoko (1959—). Japanese volleyball player. Born Mar 5, 1959, in Japan. ❖ At Los Angeles Olympics, won a bronze medal in team competition (1984).

HIRSCH, Mary (c. 1913—). American owner and trainer of thoroughbreds. Name variations: Mary McLennan. Born c. 1913; dau. of Max Hirsch (thoroughbred trainer who won the Kentucky Derby with Bold Venture, Assault, and Middleground), 1940. ❖ Served as assistant trainer with father for 3 years; became 1st woman licensed to train thoroughbred horses (Illinois, 1934); received trainer's license in state of NY (1936); as a pioneering woman trainer, became 1st woman to train a horse ("No Sir") which ran in Kentucky Derby (1937).

HIRSCH, Rachel (1870–1953). German-Jewish physician, medical researcher, and professor. Name variations: Rahel Hirsch. Born in Frankfurt am Main, Germany, Sept 15, 1870; died in London, England, Oct 6, 1953; dau. of Mendel Hirsch (1833–1900, school principal); paternal granddau. of Rabbi Samson Raphael Hirsch (1808–1888, foremost exponent of Orthodox Judaism); attended University of Zurich, 1898; University of Strassburg, MD, 1903; never married. ❖ Researcher who was the 1st to discover the mechanism whereby corpuscular elements, after having 1st passed through the lymphatic vessel system, are then finally eliminated from the blood through the renal capillaries; her theory, published in a scientific paper (1906), was ignored in her day but found to be scientifically valid almost 2 generations later and then named the "Rachel Hirsch Effect"; was 1st woman in Prussia to receive title of Professor of Medicine (1913); fled Germany (1938). ❖ See also *Women in World History*.

HIRSCHFELD, Dolly (1910–1994). See Haas, Dolly.

HIRST, Grace (1805–1901). New Zealand merchant, farmer, nurse, and midwife. Name variations: Grace Bracken. Born Grace Bracken, June 1805, in Yorkshire, England; died Sept 8, 1901, at New Plymouth, New Zealand; dau. of Jonathan Bracken (paper manufacturer) and Grace Appleyard; m. Thomas Hirst (wool classer and buyer), 1829 (died 1883); children: 11. ❖ Immigrated to New Zealand (1851); established business selling imported goods from England (1850s); farmed small holding at Bell Block, producing butter, cheese, and other domestic products for market; served community as nurse and midwife; later invested in land and mortgages. ❖ See also *Dictionary of New Zealand Biography* (Vol. 1).

HISCOCK, Eileen (1909—). English runner. Name variations: Eileen Hiscock Wilson. Born Aug 25, 1909, in UK. ❖ Won a bronze medal at Los Angeles Olympics (1932) and a silver medal at Berlin Olympics (1936), both in the 4x100-meter relay.

HITCHCOCK, Alma (1899–1982). See Reville, Alma.

HITCHCOCK, Catharine (1921—). See McClellan, Catharine.

HITE, Shere (1943—). American feminist writer. Born Shirley Diana Gregory, Nov 2, 1942, in St. Joseph, Missouri; dau. of Paul Gregory and Shirley Gregory; stepdau. of Raymond Hite; University of Florida, BA, 1960; University of Florida, MA; attended Columbia University; m. Friedrich Horicke, 1985. ❖ Researcher on psychosexual behavior and gender relations, best known for groundbreaking *The Hite Report: A Study of Female Sexuality*, directed feminist sexuality project at National Organization for Women in NY (1972–78); founded Hite Research International (1978); conducted 5 years of research before publishing the bestselling *Hite Report* (1976), followed by *The Hite Report on Male Sexuality* (1981), *The Hite Report of Women and Love* (1987) and *The Hite Report on the Family* (1994); taught female sexuality at New York University and served as visiting professor on gender and sexuality at Nihon University in Japan; renounced US citizenship (1996); published *The Shere Hite Reader* (2003).

HITOMI, Kinue (1908–1931). Japanese runner. Born Jan 1, 1908, in Okayama, Japan; died of TB, Aug 2, 1931, age 24. ❖ Won a silver medal for 800 meters at Amsterdam Olympics (1928), the 1st woman allowed to join a Japanese Olympic contingent; won 2 gold medals, 1 silver, and 1 bronze, as well as 1 gold medal as all-around athlete at Women's Games at Prague (1930). ❖ See also *Women in World History*.

HLADGERD (b. around 665). See Lathgertha.

HLOTECHILDE or HLUODHILD (470–545). See Clotilda.

HO HSIANG-NING (1879–1972). See He Xiangning.

HO TZU-CHEN. See He Zizhen.

HO XUAN HUONG (fl. late 18th c.). Vietnamese poet. Name variations: Huo Xuan Huong; Hô Xuân Huong. Born at the end of the 2nd Le Dynasty (1592–1788); possibly born in Quynh Luu district of Nghe An province; possibly dau. of Ho Phi Dien; said to be a concubine or a wife of 2nd rank; married twice, then widowed. ❖ One of the most important and most controversial of Vietnamese poets, depicted everyday life with simple and elegant verse; managed to circumvent the censors with her frank eroticism, relying on cleverness, allusions, double entendres and metaphors; dared to revolt against Confucian taboos to liberate women, and questioned the order of things, specifically male authority. The number of poems attributed to her have grown with time. ❖ See also *Spring Essence: The Poetry of Ho Xuan Huong* (Copper Canyon, 2001).

HOBAN, Lillian (1925–1998). American author and illustrator. Born May 18, 1925 in Philadelphia, PA; died July 17, 1998; attended Philadelphia Museum School of Art; Hanya Holm School of Dance; and studied dance with Martha Graham; m. Russell Hoban (author and artist), Jan 31, 1944 (div. 1975); children: Phoebe, Abrom, Esme, Julia. ❖ Probably best known for illustrating husband's "Frances" stories, began career as a dancer; illustrated over 100 books, collaborating with Meindert DeJong, Miriam Cohen, Johanna Hurwitz and Tony Johnston; wrote and illustrated the "Arthur" series which included *Arthur's Christmas Cookies* (1972).

HOBART, Henrietta (1688–1767). See Howard, Henrietta.

HOBART, Rose (1906–2000). American stage and screen actress. Born Rose Kéfer (also seen as Keefer), May 1, 1906, in New York, NY; died Aug 29, 2000, in Woodland Hills, CA; dau. of Paul Kéfer (cellist) and Marguerite Buss Kéfer (vocalist); m. William M. Grosvenor Jr.; m. Barton H. Bosworth; m. Benjamin Winter. ❖ Made NY stage debut in *Lullaby* (1923); on heels of stage success, made film debut reprising female lead in *Liliom* (1930); other films include *Dr. Jekyll and Mr. Hyde, Tower of London, Susan and God, Ziegfeld Girl, The Brighton Strangler, The Cat Creeps, Mr. & Mrs. North, Farmer's Daughter* and *Cass Timberlane*. ❖ See also autobiography *A Steady Digression to a Fixed Point* (1994).

HOBBES, John Oliver (1867–1906). See Craigie, Pearl Mary Teresa.

HOBBS, Lucy (1833–1910). See Taylor, Lucy Hobbs.

HOBBS, Marianne (1830–1908). See Gittos, Marianne.

HOBBY, Gladys Lounsbury (1910–1993). American microbiologist. Born Gladys Lounsbury Hobby in New York, NY, Nov 19, 1910; died in Kennett Square, Pennsylvania, July 6, 1993; dau. of Theodore Y. Hobby and Flora Lounsbury Hobby; graduate of Vassar College, 1931; Columbia University, MA, then PhD in bacteriology, 1935; never married. ❖ Played an important role in making penicillin a mass-produced antibiotic; was a research scientist with Presbyterian Hospital and College of Physicians and Surgeons at Columbia University (1934–43); began working for Pfizer as a senior bacteriologist (1944) and carried on significant research that was linked to the large-scale production of penicillin; became scientific director of Veterans Administration Infectious Disease Research Institute in East Orange, NJ (1959) where she specialized in studying chronic infectious diseases; wrote *Penicillin: Meeting the Challenge* (1985) and served as editor of the journal, *Antimicrobial Agents and Chemotherapy* (1965–80). ❖ See also *Women in World History*.

HOBBY, Oveta Culp (1905–1995). American military leader, government official, and publisher. Born Oveta Culp, Jan 19, 1905, in Killeen, TX; died in Houston, TX, Aug 16, 1995, after a stroke; dau. of Isaac William Culp (lawyer and state legislator) and Emma Hoover Culp; attended Mary Hardin Baylor College; m. William Pettus Hobby (governor of TX, newspaper publisher), Feb 23, 1931; children: William Pettus Hobby Jr. (b. 1932); Jessica Oveta Hobby (b. 1937). ❖ The 1st director of US Women's Army Corps, whose influence grew out of politics and newspaper ownership in Texas, served as parliamentarian in Texas House of Representatives (1926–31); was a newspaper columnist and editor for *The Houston Post* (1931–41); was chief of Women's Interest Section of War Department's Bureau of Public Relations (1941); served as director of Women's Auxiliary Army Corps (later WACs) and was 1st woman to hold rank of colonel (1942–45); served as 1st secretary of Department of Health, Education and Welfare and 2nd female Cabinet member in US (1953–55); was sequentially editor, publisher, and chair of the board of *The Houston Post* (1955–83); served as chair of executive committee of H&C Communications Inc. (starting 1983). Writings include *Around the World in 13 Days with Oveta Culp Hobby* (1947), *Addresses by Oveta Culp Hobby* (1953), and syndicated newspaper column "Mr. Chairman" (1930s). ❖ See also *Women in World History*.

HOBHOUSE, Emily (1860–1926). British humanitarian. Born Emily Hobhouse, April 9, 1860, in St. Ive, Cornwall, England; died June 8, 1926, in London; dau. of Reginald (Anglican cleric) and Caroline (Trelawny) Hobhouse; never married; no children. ❖ Antiwar activist who tried to help the women and children held in concentration camps by the British during the Boer War in South Africa, 1st became involved with the South African Conciliation Committee (1899) and created the South African Women and Children Distress Fund; went to South Africa (1900) to help Boers held in concentration camps; as the death rate in these camps mounted, returned to England to convince officials to change the system (1901); spoke at assemblies, met with politicians, and raised England's consciousness; denied permission to revisit the camps, nevertheless sailed back for South Africa (1901); on arrival, was forcibly placed on another ship for the return voyage (deaths in the camps alone would range from 18,000 to 28,000, most of which were children); developed home industries for women and girls in South Africa after the war; actively opposed WWI; journeyed behind enemy lines, hoping to develop plans to alleviate the suffering of non-combatants and to find an alternative for POW camps; wrote *The Brunt of the War and Where It Fell*. ❖ See also John Fisher, *That Miss Hobhouse* (Secker & Warburg, 1971); A. Ruth Fry, *Emily Hobhouse* (Cape, 1929); and *Women in World History*.

HOBHOUSE, Violet (1864–1902). Irish nationalist. Born Violet McNeill in Co. Antrim, Ireland (now Northern Ireland), 1864; died 1902. ❖ A Unionist, toured England speaking out against Home Rule; was also keen on Irish folklore and culture and fluent in Irish; books include *An Unknown Quantity* (1898) and *Warp and Weft* (1899).

HOBSON, Elizabeth Christophers (1831–1912). American social-welfare worker. Born Elizabeth Christophers Kimball, Nov 22, 1831, on Long Island farm outside Brooklyn, NY; died June 11, 1912, in Bar Harbor, Maine; dau. of Elijah Huntington Kimball (lawyer) and Sarah (Wetmore) Kimball; m. Joseph Hobson (banker), Dec 4, 1850 (died 1881). ❖ Became chair of committee that inspected Bellevue Hospital, NY (1872), and out of which later grew the State Charities Aid Association; wrote report on hospital conditions which led to founding of Bellevue Training School for Nurses (1873), 1st institution in US to use Nightingale plan to train nurses; became chair of State Charities Aid Association's pioneering committee on first aid to the injured (1882); co-conducted study on condition of black women in the South (mid-1880s) which was integral in founding of Southern Industrial Classes, a pilot program in Norfolk, VA, for introducing practical education into black schools and of which she remained president throughout its existence (until 1912); published *Recollections of a Happy Life* (1916).

HOBSON, Laura Z. (1900–1986). Jewish-American writer. Name variations: (joint pseudonym with Thayer Hobson) Peter Field. Born Laura Kean Zametkin in New York, NY, June 19, 1900; died Feb 28, 1986; dau. of Adella (Kean) Zametkin and Michael Zametkin (editor of Yiddish newspaper and labor organizer); Cornell University, AB; m. Thayer Hobson (publisher), 1930 (div. 1935); children: (with Eric Hodgins of *Time* magazine) Christopher Z. Hobson (b. 1941); (adopted) Michael Hobson (b. 1937). ❖ An advocate of tolerance, is best known for novel *Gentleman's Agreement* which topped the bestseller list and was filmed by Elia Kazan (1947); worked as consultant and promotion director for such journals as *Time, Life, Fortune, Sports Illustrated* and *Saturday Review*; spent 1 year as reporter for *New York Evening Post*; had short stories published in *Collier's, Ladies' Home Journal, McCall's,* and *Cosmopolitan*; collaborated with Thayer Hobson on 2 Westerns; also wrote 2 works of juvenile fiction and 9 novels for adults. ❖ See also autobiography, *Laura Z.* (1983); and *Women in World History*.

HOBSON, Valerie (1917–1998). English actress. Born Valerie Babette Louise Hobson in Larne, Co. Antrim, Ireland (now Larne District, Northern Ireland), April 14, 1917; died from a heart attack, Nov 13, 1998; m. Anthony Havelock-Allan (film producer), 1939 (div. 1952); m. John Profumo (politician), 1954; children: (1st m.) 2 sons; (2nd m.) 1 son. ❖ Made London stage debut as a teen; made screen debut in *Eyes*

of Fate (1934); invited to Hollywood (1934), starred in a number of thriller films, including *The Man Who Reclaimed His Head* (1934), *The Werewolf of London* (1935) and *The Bride of Frankenstein* (1935); disenchanted with roles, returned to England (1936); developed into a leading actress, playing mostly refined, elegant, upper-class women in such films as *No Escape* (1936), *Q Planes* (*Clouds over Europe*, 1939), *The Years Between* (1946), *Great Expectations* (1946), *Kind Hearts and Coronets* (1949), *The Rocking Horse Winner* (1950), *Meet Me Tonight* (*Tonight at 8:30*, 1952) and *Monsieur Ripois* (*Knave of Hearts,* 1954); abandoned acting career following marriage to John Profumo, then a junior minister in Churchill government (1954); never wavered in support of husband during Christine Keeler scandal (1963) that brought down the Conservatives and toppled Profumo from office. ❖ See also *Women in World History*.

HOBY, Elizabeth (1540–1609). *See Russell, Elizabeth.*

HOBY, Margaret (1571–1633). British diarist. Name variations: Margaret Devereux, Margaret Sidney, and Lady Margaret Hoby. Born 1571 in Linton, East Riding, Yorkshire, England; died 1633 in Hackness, Yorkshire; dau. of Arthur Dakins and Thomasine Guy; m. Walter Devereux (younger brother of Robert Devereux, earl of Essex), 1589 (died in a skirmish in France); m. Thomas Sidney (brother of Philip Sidney and Mary Herbert, countess of Pembroke), 1591 (died 1595); m. Thomas Posthumous Hoby (son of the writer Elizabeth Russell), 1596. ❖ Wrote *The Diary of Lady Margaret Hoby*, which details the devotional acts of a Puritan believer and recounts her search for salvation.

HÖCH, Hannah (1889–1978). German artist. Name variations: Hannah Hoch. Born Johanne Höch, Nov 1, 1889, in Gotha, Thuringia, Germany; died in Berlin-Heiligensee, May 31, 1978; dau. of Friedrich Höch and Rosa Sachs Höch; studied at Berlin's State Museum School and with graphic artist Emil Orlik; lived with Til Brugman, 1929–35; m. Kurt Matthies. ❖ In a career that spanned more than 6 decades, created bold and often controversial graphics, paintings, collages, photographs, and even puppets, but is probably best known for her photomontages; by end of 20th century, was recognized as an important artist in the history of modern art; starting in 1916, worked for a decade for Ullstein Verlag, creating needlework patterns and lace tablecloth designs; early photomontage, *Cut with the Dada Kitchen Knife through the Last Era of the Weimar Beer-Belly Culture* (1919–20), was exhibited at 1st International Dada Fair (1920); was the only woman member of the Berlin Dada circle; produced witty and subtle photomontages which commented on the major issues of the day, including the growing Nazi threat, using materials gleaned from exhibition catalogues, paper of various colors and textures, typography, fabrics, delicate transparent patterns, as well as fragments from postcards, magazines and newspapers; among her few open acts of defiance was her rescue of the papers and art works of the Berlin Dada circle from destruction by the Nazi-controlled Reichskulturkammer (Reich Chamber of Culture); after WWII, stayed in Berlin, employing a pluralism of styles, in which some of the most telling influences are Expressionism, constructivism, *Neue Sachlichkeit* (New Objectivity), and the work of several Symbolist painters, including Odilon Redon. ❖ See also Adriani Götz, ed., *Hannah Höch, 1889–1978: Collages* (1985); and *Women in World History*.

HOCH, Tisha (1973—). *See Venturini, Tisha.*

HOCHLEITNER, Dorothea. Austrian Alpine skier. Born in Austria. ❖ Won a bronze medal for giant slalom at Cortina Olympics (1956).

HOCKABY, Stephen (1901–1983). *See Mitchell, Gladys.*

HOCKADAY, Margaret (1907–1992). American advertising executive. Name variations: Maggie or Mig; Margaret Hockaday La Farge. Born Margaret Elizabeth Hockaday, Jan 8, 1907, in Wichita, Kansas; died in New York, NY, Dec 18, 1992; dau. of Bird Pixlee (Bohart) Hockaday (publisher's representative) and Isaac Newton Hockaday; graduated Vassar College, 1929; m. Reinhardt Bischoff (German architect), late 1940s (div. mid-1950s); m. Louis Bancel La Farge (architect), 1962; no children; aunt of artist Susan Hockaday Jones. ❖ Pioneer in the last wave of print advertising, started career as copywriter for Marshall Field in Chicago; moved to NY and spent 2 years as fashion editor at *Vogue*; moved to *Harper's Bazaar* (1936); worked briefly at J. Walter Thompson; became fashion editor for Curtis' *Holiday* travel magazine; launched own advertising agency, Hockaday Associates, whose campaigns created such catchphrases as "Just wear a smile and a Jantzen" and "As long as you're up, get me a Grant's" (1949); retired (1970). ❖ See also *Women in World History*.

HOCKFIELD, Susan (1951—). American neuroscientist. Born 1951 in Chicago, Illinois; dau. of Fayetta and Robert Hockfield (electrical engineer); education: University of Rochester, BS, 1973; Georgetown University School of Medicine, PhD; m. Thomas N. Byrne (neuro-oncologist); children: Elizabeth. ❖ Joined faculty of Yale University (1985), named full professor (1994), served as dean of its Graduate School of Arts and Sciences (1889–2002), then provost (2002); became president of Massachusetts Institute of Technology (2004), the 1st woman and 1st life scientist to hold that post.

HOCTOR, Harriet (1905–1977). American dancer and choreographer. Born Sept 25, 1905, in Hoosick Falls, NY; died June 9, 1977, in Arlington, Virginia. ❖ Began career in vaudeville, later appearing regularly at the Palace and in London; made Broadway debut in its *Sally* (1920) and was subsequently featured in *Topsy and Eva* with the Duncan Sisters, *A La Carte, Show Girl, Simple Simon, Earl Carroll Vanities, Ziegfeld Follies* and *The Three Musketeers*; films include *The Great Ziegfeld* and *Shall We Dance?*; known for her acrobatic ballet, ran a school of ballet in Boston.

HODDER, Jessie Donaldson (1867–1931). American prison reformer. Born Mar 30, 1867, in Cincinnati, Ohio; died Nov 19, 1931, in Framingham, Massachusetts; dau. of William and Mary (Hall) Hodder; entered into common-law marriage with Alfred LeRoy Hodder (author and journalist), 1890 (died 1907); children: Olive (b. 1893); J. Alan (b. 1897). ❖ Appointed superintendent of Massachusetts Prison and Reformatory for Women in Framingham (1910), transformed the reformatory into a model institution; was involved with the National Conference of Social Work and the National Prison Association; served as sole woman delegate to International Prison Congress in London (1925); appointed to the National Crime Commission (1927) and to a committee of the Wickersham Commission on Law Observance and Enforcement (1929). ❖ See also *Women in World History.*

HODGE, Annie Mabel (1862–1938). New Zealand teacher and headmistress. Born Feb 5, 1862, at Cheltenham, Gloucestershire, England; died Oct 15, 1938, at Te Awanga, near Havelock North, New Zealand; dau. of George Hodge (master brewer) and Annie (Bellamy) Hodge. ❖ Immigrated to New Zealand (1893); established successful boarding school, Woodford House, which provided academic education augmented by sports, arts and crafts, and practical subjects (1894). ❖ See also *Dictionary of New Zealand Biography* (Vol. 2).

HODGE, Margaret (1944—). English politician and member of Parliament. Born Margaret Oppenheimer, Sept 8, 1944; m. Andrew Watson, 1968 (div. 1978); m. Henry Hodge (OBE), 1978. ❖ Served as senior consultant, Price Waterhouse (1992–94); representing Labour, elected to House of Commons for Barking (1994, 1997, 2001, 2005); named chair, Education and Employment (1997); named minister of State, Department for Work and Pensions (2005).

HODGES, Faustina Hasse (1822–1895). English-born American composer and organist. Born in Malmesbury (some sources cite Bristol), England, Aug 7, 1822; arrived in US, 1841; died in Philadelphia, PA, Feb 4, 1895; dau. of Edward Hodges (1796–1867, English organist, composer and writer). ❖ Appointed professor of organ, singing and piano at Troy Female Seminary (1852); composed mostly sentimental ballads before the Civil War and more sophisticated art songs starting in 1870s. A number of her songs, including *Dreams* (1859) and *The Rose-Bush* (1859), were popular favorites of the day. ❖ See also *Women in World History.*

HODGES, Joy (1914–2003). American singer and dancer. Born Jan 29, 1914, in Des Moines, Iowa; died Jan 19, 2003, in Palm Desert, California. ❖ Appeared in Broadway in *I'd Rather Be Right, Best Foot Forward* and in title role of *Have You Met Miss Jones?*; also sang for such bandleaders as Ozzie Nelson and Glenn Miller; films include *To Beat the Band, Follow the Fleet, Personal Secretary, Boy Meets Joy, Margie* and *I Used to be in Pictures*; while singing on Des Moines' radio station WHO, met Ronald Reagan and later helped launch his acting career.

HODGKIN, Dorothy (1910–1994). English biochemist, Nobel laureate, and peace activist. Name variations: Dorothy Mary Crowfoot, May 12, 1910, in Cairo, Egypt; died July 29, 1994, at home in Shipston-on-Stour, Warwickshire, England, after a stroke; dau. of John Winter (classics scholar and archaeologist) and Grace Mary (Hood) Crowfoot (weaver and amateur botanist); graduate of Sir John Lehman School, Beccles, 1928; Somerville College, BA, 1931; Cambridge University, PhD, 1936; m. Thomas Lionel Hodgkin, Dec 16, 1937; children: Luke (b. 1938), Elizabeth (b. 1941) and Tobias Hodgkin (b. 1946). ❖ Best known for her discovery of the structures of penicillin and vitamin B-12, became

fellow of Somerville College, Oxford (1936); discovered crystalline structure of penicillin (1946); appointed university lecturer and demonstrator at Oxford (1946); discovered structure of vitamin B-12 (1954); became university reader at Oxford (1957); served as Wolfson Research Professor of Chemistry, Royal Society (1960–77); discovered structure of insulin (1969); served as president of Pugwash Conference on Science and World Affairs (1975); served as president of International Union of Crystallography (1972–75) and as president of British Association for the Advancement of Science (1977–78); was chancellor of Bristol University (1970–88); was a fellow of Wolfson College, Oxford (1977–82). Received Nobel Prize in chemistry (1964). ❖ See also *Women in World History.*

HODGKINS, Frances (1869–1947). New Zealand painter. Born Frances Mary Hodgkins in Dunedin, New Zealand, April 28, 1869; died near Dorchester, Dorset, England, May 13, 1947; dau. of William Mathew Hodgkins (attorney, artist, and founder of Otago Society of Artists [c.1833–1898]) and Rachel Owen Parker (Australian); younger sister of Isabel Hodgkins Field (artist); studied oil painting with G.P. Nerli and Pierre Marcel-Béronneau; attended Dunedin School of Art and Design, 1895–96; never married; no children. ❖ One of the most important artists of her era and the 1st New Zealand artist to gain such prominence, initially painted a handful of landscapes of New Zealand and a large number of paintings of Maori women and began exhibiting at Christchurch and Dunedin (1886); work accepted by Royal Academy in England (1903–05); settled in Paris (1908), where she became the 1st woman to teach at Académie Colarossi; established her own watercolor academy in Paris (1910), catering predominantly to women students; at onset of WWI, moved to England; exhibited with London Group and became a member of Calico Printers Association and Manchester Society of Painters (1928); joined the progressive Seven and Five Society (1929); had a studio in Dorset; had retrospective exhibition of 64 paintings and 17 drawings (1902–46) at Lefevre Gallery (1946); worked with landscapes, still lifes, and portraits; paintings include *Loveday and Ann: two women with a basket of flowers* (1915), *The Edwardians* (c. 1918), *Double Portrait* (c. 1922), *Spanish Shrine* (c. 1933), *Flatford Mill* (1930, London, Tate Gallery), *Seated Woman* (1925–30, London, Tate Gallery) and *The Courtyard in Wartime* (1944). ❖ See also M. Evans, ed. *Francis Hodgkins* (1948); E.H. McCormick, *Portrait of Frances Hodgkins* (1981) and *The Expatriate* (1954); and *Women in World History.*

HODGKINS, Sarah Perkins (c. 1750–1803). American letter writer. Born c. 1750; lived in Ipswich, Massachusetts; died 1803; m. Joseph Hodgkins. ❖ Wrote letters to husband in Continental Army during Revolution, published as "The Hodgkins Letters" in *This Glorious Cause* (1958).

HODGSKIN, Natalie (1976—). Australian softball player. Born May 24, 1976, in Brisbane, Australia; attended University of Queensland. ❖ Outfielder and third base, won a team silver medal at Athens Olympics (2004).

HODGSON, Elizabeth (1814–1877). English botanist and geologist. Born Elizabeth Hodgson, 1814; lived in Ulverston, Cumbria, England; died Dec 26, 1877; dau. of Captain James Hodgson (Royal Navy). ❖ Self-educated geologist and botanist, investigated the botany and geology of the Furness area (later part of Cumbria); studied movement and flow of granite fragments in Ulverston, Cumbria; corresponded with British Museum geologists, including Adam Sedgwick; collected Furness area mosses; studied glacial drifts; wrote theories on the weathering of the carboniferous limestone (Furness area, later part of Cumbria).

HODGSON, Tasha (1974—). New Zealander inline skater. Name variations: Natasha or Tash Hodgson. Born c. 1972 in Otaki, New Zealand. ❖ Won gold (1995) and bronze (1996) in Women's Vert at X Games.

HODGSON-BURNETT, Frances (1849–1924). *See Burnett, Frances Hodgson.*

HODIERNA (fl. 1100s). Scottish princess. Name variations: Hodierna Dunkeld. Fl. in 1100s; dau. of David I (b. around 1084), king of Scots (r. 1124–1153), and Matilda (d. 1130?).

HODIERNA OF JERUSALEM (c. 1115–after 1162). Countess and regent of Tripoli. Name variations: Hodierne. Born c. 1115 in the Frankish principality of Jerusalem; died after 1162 in Tripoli; dau. of Baldwin II, count of Edessa, later king of Jerusalem, and Morphia of Melitene; sister of Alice of Jerusalem (b. 1106), Melisande (1105–1160), and Joveta of Jerusalem (1120–?); m. Raymond II, count of Tripoli,

c. 1136; children: Raymond III of Tripoli (b. 1140); Melisande (c. 1143–1161). ❖ The 3rd daughter of the powerful king Baldwin II, was raised with her 3 sisters in Jerusalem, then the capital city of the Frankish kingdom; married Raymond II, count of Tripoli; when husband was murdered (1152), assumed the regency in the name of son Raymond III, then only 12 years old; retained the regency until Raymond came of age, when she seems to have been content to retire from an active political life; was very close to sister Melisande who was queen of Jerusalem. ❖ See also *Women in World History*.

HODIERNE. *Variant of Hodierna.*

HODROVA, Daniela (1946—). Czech novelist and literary critic. Born 1946 in Prague, Czechoslovakia; m. Karel Milota. ❖ One of most important interpreters in Czechoslovakia of the development of the Russian and European novel, 1st worked as publisher's editor, then researcher at Academy Institute of Literature; her novels, which were not published until 1991, include *Kukly* (1991) and *Podobojí* (1991); her criticism, which was heavily edited by authorities, includes *Hledání románu* (1989); also translated criticism by Mikhail Bakhtin and others.

HODSON, Henrietta (1841–1910). English actress. Name variations: Henrietta Labouchere. Born 1841; died 1910; m. 2nd husband Henry Labouchere Du Pré (1831–1912, journalist and politician), 1868. ❖ Popular comedic actress, made theatrical debut (1858) and appeared in Manchester with Sir Henry Irving (1862); made London debut (1866) and joined Queen's Theatre Company (1867); married Henry Labouchere (1868), later one of the most powerful radicals in the House of Commons, who became sole owner of the Queen's (1870); appeared there as Imogen in *Cymbeline* (1871), then took over the management of the Royalty Theatre where she created the system of the unseen orchestra, revived *Wild Oats*, was praised for her portrayal of Peg Woffington, and introduced Lillie Langtry to the English public; retired to Florence with husband (1903). ❖ See also *Women in World History*.

HOEFLY, Ethel Ann (1919–2003). American military nurse. Born Mar 8, 1919; died Aug 3, 2003, in Summerfield, Florida. ❖ Served with US Army Nurse Corps during WWII; transferred to US Air Force Nurse Corps (USAFNC, 1949); named chief of USAFNC (1968); was the 1st air force nurse to become brigadier general (1972); retired (1974).

HOERNER, Silke (1965—). See Hörner, Silke.

HOEY, Iris (1885–1979). English actress and dancer. Born July 17, 1885, in London, England; died May 13, 1979, in London; m. Max Leeds (div.); m. Cyril Raymond (div.). ❖ Popular musical-comedy ingenue, made stage debut as a walk-on in *The Darling of the Gods* (1903), then scored a hit as Ariel in *The Tempest* (1905); other plays include *The Geisha, Butterflies, Madame X, Cinderella, Princess Caprice, Julius Caesar* (as Lucius), *Oh Oh Delphine* (title role), *The Pearl Girl, Baby Mine, The Belle of New York, Just Like Judy* (title role), *The Man from Toronto, Collusion, Sylvia* (title role), *The Country Wife* and *The Damask Cheek*; made NY debut in *Tonight's the Night* (1914); managed Duke of York's Theater (1920–21); films include *East Lynne, The Perfect Crime, The Midas Touch* and *The Girl Who Couldn't Quite.*

HOEY, Jane M. (1892–1968). American government official. Name variations: Jane Margueretta Hoey. Born Jane Margueretta Hoey, Jan 15, 1892, in Greenley County, Nebraska; died Oct 6, 1968, in New York, NY; dau. of John and Catherine (Mullen) Hoey; sister of James J. Hoey, member of NY State Assembly (1907–11). ❖ Was assistant secretary of NYC Board of Child Welfare (1916–17); worked at Home Service of American Red Cross (1918–21); led Bronx unit of NY Tuberculosis and Health Association and helped found Welfare Council of NYC (1923–26); was assistant director and secretary of Welfare Council Health Division (1926–36); appointed to NY State Crime and Correction Commissions (1926); served on Commission of Education of Inmates of Penal Institutions (1933–36); was director of Bureau of Public Assistance, Social Security Board, later Social Security Administration (1936–53); was president of National Conference of Social Work (1940–41) and director of social research for National Tuberculosis Association (1954–57). Was 1st recipient of Florina Lasker Social Work Award (1955); received René Sand Award (1966) and James J. Hoey award by Catholic Interracial Council of NY.

HOEY, Kate (1946—). Irish politician and member of Parliament. Born Catharine Letitia Hoey, June 21, 1946; attended Ulster College of Physical Education and Belfast Royal Academy. ❖ Was a senior lecturer at Kingsway College (1975–85); representing Labour, elected to House of Commons for Vauxhall (1992, 1997, 2001, 2005); served as parliamentary undersecretary of State at the Home Office (1998–99) and minister of Sport (1998–2001).

HOFER, Evelyn (1922—). German-born photographer. Born in Marburg an der Lahn, Germany, Jan 21, 1922; attended Salem School, in southern Germany; studied piano in Madrid, Switzerland and at Paris Conservatory; m. Humphrey Sutton. ❖ Specialist in portraits, architectural documentation and book illustrations, fled Germany for Spain after Nazis came to power (1933), settling in Madrid; served apprenticeships at 2 commercial photographic studios in Zurich, then moved with family to Mexico City, where she freelanced; moved to NY (1946) and became fashion photographer for *Harper's Bazaar*; shot photographs for Mary McCarthy's *The Stones of Florence* (1959); subsequently collaborated on 5 more books: *London Perceived, New York Proclaimed, The Evidence of Washington* and *Dublin: A Portrait* (all with V.S. Pritchett), and *The Presence of Spain* (with James Morris); was a regular contibutor to *Life* and created essays for Time-Life Books, *Life* Special Reports series, and *The New York Times Magazine*. ❖ See also *Women in World History*.

HOFF, Karen (1921—). Danish kayaker. Born May 29, 1921, in Denmark. ❖ At London Olympics, won a gold medal in K1 500 meters (1948).

HOFF, Magdalene (1940—). German politician. Born Dec 29, 1940, in Hagen, Germany. ❖ As a European Socialist, elected to 4th and 5th European Parliament (EP, 1994–99, 1999–2004); served as vice-president of EP (1997–99).

HOFF, Ursula (1909–2005). German-Australian art historian. Born Ursula Hoff, 1909, in London, England; grew up in Germany; died Jan 2005 in Melbourne, Australia; dau. of Hans and Thusnelde Hoff (Jewish Germans); University of Hamburg, PhD; also attended Oxford and the Courtauld Institute of Art; had longtime friendship with classics scholar Greta Hort (died 1967). ❖ Respected scholar in the art academies and museums, moved to London with rise of Hitler (1933); moved to Melbourne on urging of Hort who had become the 1st principal of Women's College (now University College) at University of Melbourne (1939); spent 35 years at the National Gallery of Victoria, making its collection of prints and drawings one of the finest in the world; lectured on European art history at University of Melbourne. Awarded OBE and was made officer of the Order of Australia.

HOFF, Vanda (b. around 1900). American theatrical and interpretive dancer. Name variations: Mrs. Paul Whiteman. Born c. 1900; 3rd wife of Paul Whiteman (bandleader, sep. Feb 1931); children: Paul Whiteman Jr. ❖ Began appearing as specialty dancer (c. 1917), performing dance forms ranging from vaudeville to interpretive to exotic to Broadway; performed with Whiteman Orchestra for many years, as Mrs. Paul Whiteman; appeared in Ned Wayburn's *Two Little Girls in Blue* (1921) as well as the *Ziegfeld Follies of 1922*; danced with husband's band in London, Chicago and NYC nightclubs until end of marriage.

HOFFLEIT, E. Dorrit (1907—). American astronomer. Name variations: Dorrit Hoffleit; Ellen Dorrit Hoffleit. Born Ellen Dorrit Hoffleit, Mar 12, 1907, in Florence, Alabama; dau. of Fred Hoffleit and Kate (Sanio) Hoffleit; Radcliffe College, AB, 1928, MA, 1932, PhD, 1938; never married; no children. ❖ Best known for *The Bright Star Catalogue*, often defined as "the bible of virtually every stellar astronomer," which documents and maps some 9,110 stars visible to the naked eye; worked as a mathematician, Ballistic Research Lab, Aberdeen Proving Ground (1943–48), then consultant (1948–62); was a lecturer, Wellesley College (1955–56); worked as researcher, Harvard College Observatory (1929–56); was a research associate, Yale University Observatory (1956 on); served as director of the Maria Mitchell Observatory, Nantucket, Massachusetts (1957 on); with a career that spanned over 70 years, was one of the most intriguing women in astronomy as well as one of the most visible. ❖ See also *Women in World History*.

HOFFMAN, Abby (1947—). Canadian runner. Name variations: Abigail Hoffman. Born Feb 11, 1947, in Toronto, Ontario, Canada. ❖ Won a gold medal in the 800 meters at the Pan American games (1963, 1971) and a gold medal at the Commonwealth games (1966); carried the flag at the Montreal Olympics (1976).

HOFFMAN, Alice (1952—). American novelist. Born Mar 16, 1952, in New York, NY; Adelphi University, BA; Stanford University Creative Writing Center, MA, 1974; m. Tom Martin (screenwriter); children: 2 sons, including Wolfe Martin (writer). ❖ One of the leading American novelists of her generation, who is known for braiding fantastic elements with every-day events, published 1st novel, *Property Of* (1977); wrote such bestsellers as *Here on Earth*, *The River King* and *Blue Diary*; also wrote several screenplays with husband, including original script for *Independence Day* (1996), while novel *Practical Magic* (1995) was filmed with Sandra Bullock and Nicole Kidman (1998); other works include (novels) *The Drowning Season* (1979), *Angel Landing* (1980), *White Horses* (1982), *Fortune's Daughter* (1985), *Illumination Night* (1987), *At Risk* (1988), *Seventh Heaven* (1990), *Turtle Moon* (1992) and *Second Nature* (1994); (young adult books) *Local Girls* (1999), *Aquamarine* (2001), *Horsefly* (2000), *Fireflies* (1997), *Green Angel* (2003) and *Moondog* (with son Wolfe Martin, 2004); and (short-fiction) *Blackbird House* (2004).

HOFFMAN, Anette (1971—). Danish handball player. Name variations: Anette Hoffman Moberg or Møberg. Born May 5, 1971, in Denmark. ❖ Won a team gold medal at Atlanta Olympics (1996) and at Sydney Olympics (2000); won team European championships (1994, 1996) and World championships (1997).

HOFFMAN, Claire Giannini (1904–1997). American business executive. Born Claire Giannini in San Francisco, California, Dec 30, 1904; died Dec 20, 1997, in San Mateo, CA; dau. of Amadeo Peter Giannini (founder of Bank of America); graduate of Mills College, Oakland; m. Clifford P. Hoffman (investment banker). ❖ Following father's death (1949), succeeded him as a director of Bank of America, the 1st woman to hold such an office; retained this position for 36 years, resigning in 1985; also became the 1st woman to serve on board of trustees of Employees' Profit Sharing Pension Fund of Sears, Roebuck (1962) and the 1st woman to serve as director of Sears (1963). ❖ See also *Women in World History*.

HOFFMAN, Gertrude (1871–1966). See *Hoffmann, Gertrude*.

HOFFMAN, Joyce (c. 1948—). American surfer. Born c. 1948 in San Juan Capistrano, CA; dau. of Walter Hoffman (#1 surfer in the world in 1964); sister of Marty Hoffman (surfer); niece of Phil "Flippy" Hoffman (surfer); sister of Dibi Fletcher (mother of Nathan and Christian Fletcher, both champion surfers). ❖ Won US Surfboard championships (1965); was World champion (1966–67). Included among the 8 original inductees in the International Surfing Hall of Fame. ❖ See also Andrea Gabbard, *Girl in the Curl* (Seal Press).

HOFFMAN, Malvina (1885–1966). American sculptor. Name variations: Mrs. Samuel Bonaries Grimson. Born Malvina Cornell Hoffman, June 15, 1885, in New York, NY; died July 10, 1966, in New York, NY; dau. of Richard Hoffman (concert pianist) and Fidelia Lamson Hoffman; sister of Helen Draper (1871–1951); attended Women's School of Applied Design and Art Students League; studied painting with John W. Alexander, modeling with Herbert Adams and George Grey Barnard, and sculpture with Gutzon Borglum; studied in Paris with Auguste Rodin and others; m. Samuel Bonaries Grimson, 1924 (div. 1936); no children. ❖ Prolific artist, much admired for her classic-style portrait busts and heroic sculpture, was an internationally recognized sculptor; influenced by the Ballet Russe, won 1st honorable mention at Paris Salon for *Russian Dancers* (1911), and her *Bacchanale Russe* was awarded Shaw memorial prize by National Academy of Design (1917); captured the lightness of Anna Pavlova's movements in *La Gavotte* (1915); commissioned to create *The Sacrifice*, a war memorial for Harvard students killed in WWI (1922) and to execute a composition representing Anglo-American friendship, resulting in the colossal, carved-limestone figures representing England and America on the facade of Bush House in London (1924); created 2 powerful African heads, *Martinique Woman* and *Senegalese Soldier* (1928); held 1st extensive exhibition, at Grand Central Art Gallery in NY (1929); gained international recognition for collection of over 100 heads and figures of men and women from Africa, Asia, Europe, Pacific Islands and North America for Chicago World's Fair (1933), the largest sculptural commission ever given to a woman, and possibly the largest ever created by one sculptor anywhere; for 1939 New York's World's Fair, created *International Dance Fountain*; also modeled such diverse personalities as Wendell L. Willkie (1944), Teilhard de Chardin (1948), and Katharine Cornell (1961) and completed 3 busts of Ignace Paderewski (1922–23); had a retrospective exhibit at Virginia Museum of Fine Arts at Richmond (1937). ❖ See also memoirs *Heads and Tales* (1936) and *Yesterday is Tomorrow: A Personal History* (1965); and *Women in World History*.

HOFFMAN, Sylvia (1908–2003). See *Regan, Sylvia*.

HOFFMANN, Beata. Hungarian handball player. Born in Hungary. ❖ Won a team bronze medal at Atlanta Olympics (1996).

HOFFMANN, Gertrude (1871–1966). German-born dancer and choreographer. Name variations: Gertrude Hoffman, Gertrude V. Hoffman, Gertrude W. Hoffman, and Trude Hoffmann. Born May 17, 1871, in Heidelberg, Germany; died Oct 21, 1966, in Hollywood, CA; m. Max Hoffmann (Viennese conductor); children: Max Hoffmann Jr. (dancer, musician). ❖ Popular dancer (1930s) who toured in vaudeville and played in concert halls with her own company; made NY performance début in George Ade's *The Night of the Fourth* (1901); was among 1st women—perhaps the 1st—to direct vaudeville acts for NYC's roof garden theaters and cabarets, including the stages of Oscar and William Hammerstein; danced in Olga Nethersole's *Sappho* and Eddie Foy's *Topsy Turvey*; created precision-line team, The Gertrude Hoffmann Girls, in which she included trapeze work, floor acrobatics, tap and toe dancing, and many other styles; appeared in over 30 films, including *Hell and High Water*, *Foreign Correspondent* and *North of the Rockies*.

HOFFMANN, Melanie (1974—). German soccer player. Born Nov 29, 1974, in Dusseldorf, Germany. ❖ Forward and midfielder; debuted with German national team (1995); won a team bronze medal at Sydney Olympics (2000); played for FCR Duisberg; signed with WUSA's Philadelphia Charge (2003).

HOFFMEISTER, Gunhild (1944—). East German runner. Born July 6, 1944, in Germany. ❖ Won a bronze medal in the 800 meters and a silver medal in the 1,500 meters at Munich Olympics (1972) and a silver medal in the 1,500 meters at Montreal Olympics (1976).

HOFMANN, Adele (d. 2001). American pediatrician. Born Adele Dellenbaugh in Boston, MA; died June 15, 2001, age 74, in Newport Beach, California; granddau. of Frederick Samuel Dellenbaugh (artist, writer and explorer); graduate of Smith College, 1948, and University of Rochester Medical School, 1952; m. Frederick G. Hofmann (div.); children: Peter Hofmann and Annie Gardiner. ❖ Trained at Babies Hospital of Columbia Presbyterian Medical Center; was a National Foundation Fellow in Endocrinology at Presbyterian Hospital; directed pediatric and adolescent programs at New York University, Bellevue, St. Luke's and Beth Israel hospitals; a leader in the movement to redefine how health professionals treated minors, founded Society for Adolescent Medicine and served as its president (1976–77); wrote *Adolescent Medicine* (1986), among others.

HOFMANN, Elise (1889–1955). Austrian geologist and paleobotanist. Born Feb 5, 1889, in Vienna, Austria; graduate of University of Vienna, 1920; died Mar 14, 1955. ❖ Studied fossils in Austrian lignite; at University of Vienna, served as a professor and lecturer, then became professor emeritus (1950); selected to be correspondent for the Austrian State Geological Institution (1931); appointed a Niederoestreichischen Landesmuseum correspondent (1933); wrote *Palaeohistologie der Pflanze* (Paleohistology of the Plant, 1934).

HOFMANN, Hella (1913–1985). See *Shaw, Helen*.

HOFMO, Gunvor (1921–1995). Norwegian poet. Born June 30, 1921, in Oslo, Norway; died Oct 17, 1995. ❖ Works include *Jeg vil hjem til menneskene* (1946), *Fra en annen virkelighet* (1948), *Blinde nattergaler* (1951), *Testamente til en evighet* (1955) and *Gjest på jorden* (1971). Received Kritikerprisen (1971) and Doblougprisen (1982).

HOGAN, Aileen I. (1899–1981). Canadian nurse-midwife. Born Aileen I. Hogan, Nov 10, 1899, in Ottawa, Ontario; died of cardiopulmonary disorder, Jan 7, 1981, in Whiting, NJ; dau. of Christina (McMaster) Hogan and James Hogan; studied at Columbia Presbyterian School of Nursing (late 1930s); Columbia University Teachers College, MA, 1948; received a nurse-midwifery certificate from Maternity Center Association (MCA). ❖ Childbirth education and nurse-midwifery expert, immigrated to NY (1920); worked as a rotating staff nurse and later as a labor and delivery service head nurse (from 1942) at Sloane Hospital of the Presbyterian Medical Center; during WWII, traveled with Presbyterian Hospital Unit to France, England and Ireland; helped create and was the 1st executive secretary of American College of Nurse-Midwifery (ACNM), the 1st organization dedicated solely to support nurse-midwives; retired from MCA (1965).

HOGAN, Brigid (1932—). Irish politician. Name variations: Brigid Hogan-O'Higgins. Born Mar 1932, in Dublin, Ireland; dau. of Patrick Hogan (TD, Galway, 1921–36); m. Michael O'Higgins (TD, Dublin South West/Wicklow, 1948–69, later senator), 1958; children: 4 daughters, 4 sons. ❖ Representing Fine Gael, elected to 16th Dáil for South Galway (1957–61), the 1st woman to represent Galway; returned to 17th and 18th Dáil for East Galway (1961–69) and 19th and 20th Dáil for Clare/South Galway (1969–77); was the Fine Gael front-bench spokesperson on Posts and Telegraphs (1969–72); defeated in newly formed constituency of Galway East (1977).

HOGAN, Linda (1947—). Chickasaw poet, novelist, activist and playwright. Born July 17, 1947, in Denver, Colorado; dau. of Charles Henderson (Chickasaw) and Cleona Bower Henderson; University of Colorado, BA, MA, 1978; children: (adopted, 1979) Sandra Dawn Protector and Tanya Thunder Horse (both of Oglaga Lakota heritage). ❖ Prolific writer, among the most influential and provocative Native American figures on the contemporary US literary scene, experienced rapid success, winning Five Civilized Tribes Playwriting Award for *A Piece of Moon* and appointed writer-in-residence for states of Colorado and Oklahoma (1980); became assistant professor in TRIBES program at Colorado College (1982); was associate professor of American Indian Studies at University of Minnesota, then of English at University of Colorado; poetry collections include *Calling Myself Home* (1979), *Daughters, I Love You* (1981), *Eclipse* (1983), *Seeing Through the Sun* (1985), *Savings* (1991) and *The Book of Medicines* (winner of Colorado Book Award, 1993); novels include *Mean Spirit* (1990) *Solar Storms* (winner of Colorado Book Award, 1995) and *Power* (1998); essay collections include *Dwellings: Reflections on the Natural World* (1995); nonfiction includes *From Women's Experience to Feminist Theology* (1995), *The Sweet Breathing of Plants* (2000) and *Sightings* (2002); short story collections include *That Horse* (1985) and *Aunt Moon's Young Man* (1989). Received Pushcart Prize (1991), Lannan Literary Award for Poetry (1994), Native Writer's Circle of Americas Lifetime Achievement Award (1998) and Wordcraft Circle Writer of the Year Award (2002). ❖ See also memoir, *The Woman Who Watches Over the World: A Native Memoir* (Norton, 2001).

HOGE, Mrs. A.H. (1811–1890). *See Hoge, Jane.*

HOGE, Jane (1811–1890). American reformer and nurse. Name variations: Mrs. A.H. Hoge. Born Jane Currie Blaikie, July 31, 1811, in Philadelphia, PA; died in Chicago, IL, Aug 26, 1890; dau. of George Dundas (trader) and Mary (Monroe) Blaikie; graduate of Young Ladies' College in Philadelphia; m. Abraham Holmes Hoge, June 2, 1831; children: 13, 8 of whom lived to maturity. ❖ Best known for her work during the Civil War, moved from Pittsburgh to Chicago (1848); was founder and president of Home for the Friendless (1858) with Mary Livermore, directed Chicago (later Northwestern) Sanitary Commission (1862–65), a remarkably successful volunteer organization for fundraising and for collecting and distributing medical supplies and food to northern Civil War soldiers; was a fund raiser and Board of Trustees member for Evanston College for Ladies (1871–74), when it merged with Northwestern University; headed Woman's Presbyterian Board of Foreign Missions in the Northwest (1872–85); published *The Boys in Blue* (1867). ❖ See also *Women in World History.*

HOGG, Ima (1882–1975). American philanthropist. Born July 10, 1882, in Mineola, TX; died in London, England, Aug 19, 1975; dau. of James Stephen Hogg (lawyer and governor of Texas) and Sallie (Stinson) Hogg; attended University of Texas, 1899–1901; studied piano at National Conservatory in NY and Germany; never married; no children. ❖ Inherited several parcels of real estate in West Columbia (TX) bubbling with oil; with profits, undertook a major role in establishing a symphony orchestra in Houston, which eventually became one of the nation's finest orchestras; served as president of the Symphony Society for a number of years, bringing in world-famous conductors; began collecting antique furniture (1920), then commissioned Houston architect John Staub to build Bayou Bend, a house that would provide an adequate backdrop for the collection and also serve as the family home (1927); gave the mansion and the collection (which included rare Duncan Phyfe and Chippendale furniture, as well as paintings by John Singleton Copley, Charles Willson Peale, and Edward Hicks) to Houston Museum of Fine Arts (1966); was instrumental in founding Houston Child Guidance Center, a pioneering institution in child psychiatry; established Hogg Foundation at University of Texas (1940), to improve quality of life with new approaches to mental health. ❖ See also Louise Kosches Iscoe, *Ima Hogg: 1st Lady of Texas* (Hogg Foundation for Mental Health, 1976); and *Women in World History.*

HOGG, Sarah (1946—). English economist, journalist and politician. Name variations: Sarah Boyd-Carpenter; Dame Sarah Hogg; Baroness Hogg. Born Sarah Elizabeth Mary Boyd-Carpenter, May 14, 1946, in England; dau. of John Boyd-Carpenter (minister of transport); graduate

of Lady Margaret Hall, Oxford University, 1967; m. Douglas Hogg (lawyer and politician), 1968; children: 1 son, 1 daughter. ❖ The 1st female chair of an FTSE 100 Company, began journalistic career at the *Economist*; was also an economist for *Sunday Times, Independent, Telegraph, Sunday Telegraph* and *Channel 4 News*; served as governor of Centre for Economic Policy Research (1985–92); as deputy head of the Prime Minister Policy Unit for John Major (1990–95), was closely involved in conservative programs of privatization and private finance, performance measurement in public services and international economic issues; became chair of 3i, Europe's leading venture capital company; served as a BBC governor (2000–04); created a life peer (1995). Awarded Dame of British Empire (DBE, 1995).

HOGG, Wendy (1956—). Canadian swimmer. Name variations: Wendy Cook Hogg. Born Sept 5, 1956, in British Columbia, Canada. ❖ Won gold medals at British Nationals for 100 and 200-meter butterfly (1974) and a gold medal at US Nationals for 200-meter backstroke (1974); at Montreal Olympics, won a bronze medal in the 4x100-meter medley relay (1976); set 28 Canadian records. Inducted into Canadian Aquatic Hall of Fame (1983) and British Columbia Sports Hall of Fame (1990).

HOGNESS, Hanne (1967—). Norwegian handball player. Born Feb 16, 1967, in Norway. ❖ Won a silver medal at Seoul Olympics (1988) and a silver medal at Barcelona Olympics (1992), both in team competition.

HOGSHEAD, Nancy (1962—). American swimmer. Name variations: Nancy Hogshead-Makar. Born April 17, 1962, in Iowa City, Iowa; attended Duke University. ❖ Overcame asthma to win gold medals in the 100-meter freestyle (tying with Carrie Steinseifer), 4x100-meter medley relay, and 4x100-meter freestyle, and a silver medal in the 200-meter individual medley at Los Angeles Olympics (1984); served as president of the Women's Sport's Foundation (1993–94). Inducted into International Swimming Hall of Fame (1994). ❖ See also *Women in World History.*

HOGUE, Micki (b. 1944). *See King, Micki.*

HOHENBERG, duchess of (1868–1914). *See Chotek, Sophie.*

HOHENHAUSEN, Elizabeth (1789–1857). German poet, dramatist, and novelist. Name variations: Baroness von Hohenhausen. Born Elizabeth Philippine Amalie von Ochs in Waldau, near Cassel, Germany, Nov 4, 1789; died at Frankfort-on-the-Oder, Germany, Dec 2, 1857; dau. of General Adam Ludwig von Ochs; m. Baron Leopold von Hohenhausen (died 1848). ❖ Published a book of poetry, *Flowers of Spring* (1817); also wrote a historical drama, *John and Cornelius de Witt*, which was well-received. ❖ See also recollections *Nature, Art, and Life.*

HOHENLOHE, princess of. *See Anna Maria Theresa (1879–1961).*

HOHENLOHE-LANGENBURG, princess of.
See Feodore of Leiningen (1807–1872).
See Adelaide of Hohenlohe-Langenburg (1835–1900).
See Leopoldine (1837–1903).
See Alexandra Saxe-Coburg (1878–1942).

HOHN, Annette (1966—). German rower. Born Nov 22, 1966, in Germany. ❖ At Barcelona Olympics, won a bronze medal in coxless fours (1992).

HŌJO MASAKO (1157–1225). Japanese regent. Name variations: Hojo Masako; popularly known as "the nun-general." Pronunciation: HOE-joe mah-SAH-koe. Born in Izu Province, Japan, 1157; died in Kamakura, Japan, 1225; eldest dau. of Hōjō Tokimasa (warrior); m. Minamoto no Yoritomo (1147–1199), shōgun, founder of Kamakura Shōgunate; children: (sons) Yoriie and Sanetomo; (daughters) Ohime and one other. ❖ One of the most powerful and influential women in medieval Japan, significantly strengthened the rule of the Kamakura Shōgunate, the warrior government in which a military general (*shōgun*) governed on behalf of the emperor, established by husband Minamoto no Yoritomo, the 1st *shōgun*; after Yoritomo's death (1199), became regent for her elder son then deposed him for his incompetence, earning her a reputation for treachery; repeated this act with younger son; exiled father when he attempted to conspire against her; rallied warriors to defeat the emperor, who tried to regain the political authority lost to the shōgunate (Jokyu Disturbance, 1221). ❖ See also *Women in World History.*

HOKINSON, Helen E. (1893–1949). American cartoonist. Born Helen Elna Hokinson, June 29, 1893, in Mendota, Illinois; died Nov 1, 1949, in a plane crash near Washington, DC; only child of Adolph Hokinson (salesman) and Mary (Wilcox) Hokinson; attended Chicago Academy of Fine Arts, 1913–18; never married; no children. ❖ Known for her cartoons for *The New Yorker*, of buxom, upper-middle-class women, somewhat out of touch and perpetually bewildered by life's trials, a regular feature of the magazine (1920s–30s); published many cartoon collections. ❖ See also *Women in World History.*

HOLBROOK, Eliza Jane Poitevent (1849–1896). *See Nicholson, Eliza Jane Poitevent.*

HOLDEN, Edith B. (1871–1920). English artist, illustrator and writer. Name variations: Edith Blackwell Smith. Born Edith Blackwell Holden at Holly Green, Moseley, near Birmingham, England, Sept 26, 1871; drowned in the Thames, Mar 15, 1920; 4th child of Arthur Holden (industrialist) and Emma Wearing Holden; sister of Effie M. Holden (b. 1867), Violet Holden (b. 1873), and Evelyn Holden (1877–c. 1969); m. Alfred Ernest Smith (sculptor), June 1, 1911 (died 1938). ❖ A specialist in animals and plants, whose "nature notes" of 1905–06, found years after her death, were released as *Country Diary of an Edwardian Lady* (1977) and *Nature Notes of an Edwardian Lady* (1989), becoming literary sensations; also illustrated children's books, including Margaret Gatty's *Daily Bread* (1910). ❖ See also Ina Taylor, *The Edwardian Lady: The Story of Edith Holden* (Webb & Bower, 1980, rev., 1990); 12-part tv series, "The Country Diary of an Edwardian Lady," starring Pippa Guard, CIT (1984); and *Women in World History.*

HOLDEN, Effie M. (b. 1867). English poet. Name variations: E.M. Holden; Effie Margaret Heath. Born Effie Margaret Holden, 1867; 1st child of Arthur Holden (industrialist) and Emma Wearing Holden; sister of Edith Holden (1871–1920), Evelyn Holden, and Violet Holden; m. Carl Heath (artist), 1900. ❖ Published 11 volumes of poetry under the name E.M. Holden, and wrote a short book about Lucy Stone. ❖ See also *Women in World History.*

HOLDEN, Evelyn (1877–c. 1969). English artist and book illustrator. Born 1877; died c. 1969; dau. of Arthur Holden (industrialist) and Emma Wearing Holden; sister of Edith Holden (1871–1920), Effie Holden, and Violet Holden; attended Birmingham Art School; m. Frank Matthews, 1904. ❖ A successful book illustrator, also exhibited with the Royal Birmingham Society of Artists, specializing in watercolors and pen and ink. ❖ See also *Women in World History.*

HOLDEN, Fay (1893–1973). English actress. Name variations: Gaby Fay. Born Dorothy Fay Hammerton, Sept 26, 1893, in Birmingham, England; died June 23, 1973, in Los Angeles, CA; m. David Clyde (actor), 1914 (died 1945). ❖ Had 30-year career on stage as Gaby Fay; as Fay Holden, had character roles in films, including *Florence Nightingale, I Married a Doctor, You're Only Young Once, Guns of the Pecos* and *Test Pilot*,; portrayed Mickey Rooney's mother in 15 "Andy Hardy" films.

HOLDEN, Gloria (1908–1991). English actress and model. Born Sept 5, 1908, in London, England; died Mar 22, 1991, in Redlands, CA; m. William Hoyt, 1944; grandmother of actress Laurie Holden. ❖ Appeared in title role in *Dracula's Daughter* (1936); other films include *The Life of Emile Zola* (Mme Zola), *Test Pilot, Dodge City, The Corsican Brothers, Miss Annie Rooney, The Hucksters, Killer McCoy, A Kiss for Corliss, The Eddy Duchin Story* and *This Happy Feeling.*

HOLDEN, Helene (1935—). Canadian novelist. Born 1935 in Montreal, Quebec, Canada; of Greek-French descent. ❖ Works include *The Chain* (1969), *Goodbye, Muffin Lady* (1974) and *After the Fact* (1986).

HOLDEN, Joan (1939—). American theatrical producer and playwright. Born Jan 18, 1939, in Berkeley, CA; Reed College, BA; University of California at Berkeley, MA; m. Arthur Holden (principal player in mime troupe, div.); m. David Chumley; children: 3 daughters. ❖ Worked for 2 years as a copywriter for the Librairie Larousse in Paris (1964–66); worked as a research assistant at UofC Berkeley (1966–67); was one of principal members of Tony award-winning San Francisco Mime Troupe when the company formed as a collective (1967), serving as its principal playwright (1967–2000); has written and collaborated on over 23 left-wing political shows, including *L'Amant Militaire, The Independent Female or a Man Has His Pride, The Hotel Universe, Factwino Trilogy, Damaged Care, Electrobucks, Hotel Universe, Steeltown, Back to Normal, Off Shore, City for Sale,* and *Seeing Double*; taught playwrighting at University of California, Davis; adapted Barbara Ehrenreich's *Nickel and Dimed* for stage (2003). Won Obie for co-writing *The Dragon Lady's Revenge* (1973).

HOLDEN, Mari (1971—). American cyclist. Born Mar 30, 1971, Ventura, California. ❖ Won a silver medal for indiv. time trial at Sydney Olympics (2000); won a World team trial championship (2000).

HOLDEN, Molly (1927–1981). British poet and novelist. Born Sept 7, 1927, in London, England; died Aug 5, 1981, in Bromsgrove, Worcestershire, England; dau. of Conor Henry Gilbert and Winifred (Farrant) Gilbert; m. Alan W. Holden, 1949. ❖ Best known for poetry which is influenced by Thomas Hardy and John Clare, also wrote novels and children's books; writings include *The Bright Cloud* (1964), *To Make Me Grieve* (1968), *The Unfinished Feud* (1971), *Air and Chill Earth* (1971), *A Tenancy of Flint* (1972), *White Rose and Wanderer* (1972), *Reiver's Weather* (1973), *The Speckled Bush* (1974), *The Country Over* (1975) and *Selected Poems, with a memoir by A. Holden* (1988).

HOLDEN, Violet (b. 1873). English artist and book illustrator. Born 1873; dau. of Arthur Holden (industrialist) and Emma Wearing Holden; sister of Edith Holden (1871–1920), Effie M. Holden (b. 1867), and Evelyn Holden (1877–c. 1969); attended Birmingham Art School. ❖ Together with sister Evelyn Holden, illustrated *The Real Princess,* a fairy story by Blanche Atkinson (1894), and published a book of nursery rhymes (1895); joined teaching staff of Birmingham Art School (1904); specialized in writing and illumination. ❖ See also *Women in World History.*

HOLDERNESS, countess of (1259–1274). *See Avelina de Forz.*

HOLDMANN, Anni (1900–1960). German runner. Born Jan 28, 1900; died Nov 2, 1960. ❖ At Amsterdam Olympics, won a bronze medal in 4x100-meter relay (1928).

HOLDSCLAW, Chamique (1977—). African-American basketball player. Name variations: (nicknames) Meke; the Claw. Born Aug 9, 1977, in Astoria, Queens, NY; graduate of University of Tennessee, 1999, with a major in political science. ❖ Forward; as the all-time leading scorer and rebounder in Tennessee basketball history, led Tennessee Lady Vols to 3 NCAA championships (1996–98) and placed 3rd on NCAA all-time women's basketball scoring list; selected by Washington Mystics of WNBA as 1st overall pick (1999); won a team gold medal at Sydney Olympics (2000). Was the 1st woman college athlete to win the James E. Sullivan Award; was 4-time All-American, 2-time ESPY award winner, 2-time Associated Press Women's Basketball Player of the Year, and 2-time Naismith award winner; named WNBA Rookie of the Year (1999).

HOLFORD, Alice Hannah (1867–1966). New Zealand nurse, midwife, and hospital matron. Born Nov 12, 1867, in New Plymouth, New Zealand; died Dec 22, 1966, in New Plymouth; dau. of John Henry Holford (mariner) and Annie (Brooking) Holford. ❖ Trained at New Plymouth Hospital (1901), and at Crown Street Women's Hospital, Sydney (1902); began private nursing upon return to New Zealand and was appointed matron of Dunedin St. Helens Hospital (1905); helped found trained nurses' association in Dunedin (1907); was matron of Hanmer Convalescent Home for Soldiers (1916); active in New Zealand Nurses' Memorial Fund (1920s) and National Council of Women in New Zealand; founding member of Otago Women's Club. ❖ See also *Dictionary of New Zealand Biography* (Vol. 3).

HOLFORD, Ingrid (1920—). English meteorologist, writer and teacher. Born Ingrid Bianchi, Jan 10, 1920; University College, London, BS in economics, 1941; m. Garth Holford (yacht racer), 1948; children. ❖ During WWII, worked as an officer-weather forecaster for Women's Auxiliary Air Force (1942–46); presented talks on BBC Radio; was a Royal Meteorological Society fellow for almost 50 years and council member for 3; wrote books and articles on the weather for the general public, including *Interpreting the Weather* (1973), *The Yachtsman's Weather Guide* (1979), *The Air Pilot's Weather Guide* (1988), *British Weather Disasters* (1976), and *The Guinness Book of Weather Facts and Feats* (1977).

HOLGATE, Virginia (1955—). *See Leng, Virginia.*

HOLIDAY, Billie (c. 1915–1959). African-American jazz and blues singer. Name variations: Lady Day. Born Eleanora Fagan, April 7, c. 1915 in Baltimore, MD; died of addiction-related illness, July 17, 1959, in NY; m. Jimmy Monroe (jazz trumpeter), 1941 (div.); m. Louis McKay, 1951. ❖ One of the great American female vocalists of all time, whose recordings are considered classics, was plagued by poverty, racism and drugs; built a following at such places as Yeah Man, Hotcha, and Alhambra Grill; teamed with pianist Teddy Wilson to record for

Columbia' Brunswick label, churning out more than 80 records (1933–38); joined forces with sax player Lester Young on some of the most treasured jazz performances ever recorded, such as "This Year's Kisses," "If Dreams Come True" and "I'll Never Be The Same"; sang for the 1st time at Harlem's Apollo Theater, appearing with a small jazz combo; in her signature white dress and white gardenia, played 1st club date outside Harlem, at Café Society Downtown (1935), where she introduced the protest song "Strange Fruit"; went on tour with Count Basie's band, then joined Artie Shaw's band (both 1938); as the 1st black singer to appear with a white band, was not allowed to sleep in the same hotel with other band members; finally quit Shaw's band when she had to use the frieght elevator in a NY hotel (1940); sang with Lionel Hampton's band in Chicago; became addicted to heroin; embarked on a series of dates at most of NY's 52nd Street jazz clubs, such as Onyx and Famous Door; repeatedly arrested on drug possession charges, causing contracts to be canceled; appeared with Louis Armstrong in film *New Orleans* (1946); checked herself into a Manhattan clinic to shake addiction; 3 weeks after release, was arrested in Philadelphia on drug possession charges and sentenced to 1 year at Federal Women's Reformatory in Alderston, WV; after serving 9 months, released on parole, returning to NY for triumphant concert at Carnegie Hall; began using heroin once more; signed with Verve records (1951) and went on 1st European tour, giving famous performance at Royal Albert Hall in London (1954); made last public appearance (May 25, 1959) at Phoenix Theater in Greenwich Village; 6 days later, collapsed and was admitted to a hospital for cirrhosis of the liver; while hospitalized, her apartment was raided by Federal agents who claimed to have found a packet of heroin and filed charges against her; died in the hospital. ❖ See also autobiography (with William Dufty) *Lady Sings the Blues* (1956); Stuart Nicholson, *Billie Holiday* (1995); John White, *Billie Holiday* (1987); Donald Clarke, *Wishing on the Moon* (1994); Angela Y. Davis, *Blues Legacies and Black Feminism: Gertrude "Ma" Rainey, Bessie Smith, and Billie Holiday* (1998); film *Lady Sings the Blues* (1972); and *Women in World History*.

HOLIFIELD, Ruthie (1967—). See *Bolton, Ruthie*.

HOLLADAY, Wilhelmina Cole (1922—). American museum founder. Born Wilhelmina Cole, Oct 10, 1922, in Elmira, NY; m. Wallace F. Holladay. ❖ While working for Chinese nationalist government (1945–48), served as social secretary to Song Meiling (Madame Chiang Kai-shek); toured galleries and museums in Europe and noted lack of recognition for women artists; with assistance from husband, began 1st major collection of works by women artists (later the nucleus of The National Museum of Women in the Arts collection); led fund-raising drive and promotion for the museum (1982–87), which formally opened in 1987. Inducted into National Women's Hall of Fame (1996).

HOLLAND (1920–2003). See *Gray, Oriel*.

HOLLAND, Agnieszka (1948—). Polish film director. Name variations: Agnieska Holland. Born Nov 28, 1948, in Warsaw, Poland; m. Laco Adamik (Slovak director, div.); children: 1 daughter. ❖ In the top rank of filmmakers, studied at Film Academy, Prague, and returned to Poland to work as assistant to Krzystof Zannussi; wrote some scripts with Andrzej Wajda before directing own films, which include *Provincial Actors* (1978), *The Fever* (1980), *A Woman Alone* (1981), *Angry Harvest* (1988), *Europa Europa* (1991), *Olivier Olivier* (1992), *The Secret Garden* (1993), *Red Wind* (1994), *Total Eclipse* (1995), *Washington Square* (1996), *Golden Dreams* (2001) and *Copying Beethoven* (2005).

HOLLAND, Alianor (c. 1373–1405). Countess of March. Name variations: Alianor Mortimer. Born c. 1373; died Oct 23, 1405; dau. of Thomas Holland, 2nd earl of Kent, and Alice Fitzalan (1352–1416); m. Roger Mortimer, 4th earl of March, c. Oct 1388; children: 6, including Anne Mortimer (1390–1411); Edmund Mortimer (5th earl of March); Roger Mortimer; and Eleanor Mortimer (c. 1395–1418).

HOLLAND, Anne (d. 1432). See *Stafford, Anne*.

HOLLAND, Anne (d. 1457). See *Montacute, Anne*.

HOLLAND, Anne (d. 1474). Marquise of Dorset. Name variations: Anne Grey. Died 1474; dau. of Henry Holland, 2nd duke of Exeter, and Anne Plantagenet (1439–1476), sister of Edward IV and Richard III); m. Thomas Grey, 1st Marquis of Dorset.

HOLLAND, Anne (fl. 1440–1462). Countess of Douglas. Name variations: Anne Douglas, Anne Neville. Fl. 1440 to 1462; died Dec 26, 1486; dau. of John Holland (1395–1447), duke of Huntington (r. 1416–1447), and Anne Stafford (c. 1400–1432); m. John Neville (great-

grandson of 1st earl of Westmoreland), before Feb 18, 1440; m. John Neville (grandson of 1st earl of Westmoreland); m. James Douglas, 9th earl of Douglas, after 1461; children: (2nd m.) Ralph Neville, 3rd earl of Westmoreland (1456–1499). ❖ *The Complete Peerage* (Vol. V, p. 215), makes it clear that Anne Holland is the dau. of Anne Stafford and not Anne Montacute as shown in other sources.

HOLLAND, Annie (1965—). English singer. Name variations: Elastica. Born Aug 26, 1965, in London, England. ❖ Founding member of punk-influenced pop band Elastica (1992), served as bass player; with band, released self-titled debut album which reached #1 in UK (1995) and had hit singles in US, including "Connection" and "Stutter"; quit the band (1995) but returned several years later (1999); released 2nd Elastica album *The Menace* (2000).

HOLLAND, Caroline (1723–1774). See *Lennox, Caroline*.

HOLLAND, Catherine (1637–1720). British religious writer. Born Catherine Holland, 1637, in Norfolk, England; died Jan 6, 1720, in Bruges, Flanders; dau. of Sir John Holland and Alethea (Sandys) Holland. ❖ Aristocratic daughter of Catholic mother who was prohibited by Puritan father from practicing Catholicism; made secret contact with prioress of Nazareth Monastery in Bruges and traveled there alone to join order (1662); trans. religious works from Dutch and French. Autobiography is included in C.S.A. Durrant, ed., *Link Between the Flemish Mystics and English Martyrs* (1925).

HOLLAND, Cecelia (1943—). American science-fiction writer. Name variations: (pseudonym) Elizabeth Eliot Carter. Born Cecelia Anastasia Holland, Dec 31, 1943, in Henderson, Nevada; dau. of William Dean (executive) and Katharine (Schenck) Holland; Connecticut College, BA, 1965. ❖ Became visiting professor of English at Connecticut College (1979); works include *The Firedrake* (1966), *The Kings in Winter* (1968), *Ghost on the Steppe* (1969), *Antichrist* (1970), *The Death of Attila* (1974), *Floating Worlds* (1976), *Two Ravens* (1977), *City of God* (1979), *The Sea Beggars* (1982) and *Pillar of the Sky* (1985).

HOLLAND, Constance (1387–1437). Countess of Norfolk. Born 1387; died 1437; dau. of Elizabeth of Lancaster (1364–1425) and John Holland (c. 1358–1399), 1st duke of Exeter (r. 1397–1399); m. Thomas Mowbray (1387–1405), earl of Norfolk (executed, 1405); m. Sir John Grey.

HOLLAND, countess of.
See *Dunkeld, Ada (c. 1145–1206)*.
See *Philippine of Luxemburg (d. 1311)*.
See *Jeanne of Valois (c. 1294–1342)*.
See *Joanna of Brabant (1322–1406)*.
See *Margaret of Holland (d. 1356)*.
See *Maud Plantagenet (1335–1362)*.
See *Margaret of Burgundy (c. 1376–1441)*.
See *Jacqueline of Hainault (1401–1436)*.

HOLLAND, Dulcie Sybil (1913—). Australian composer, cellist, pianist, and radio broadcaster. Born in Sydney, Australia, Jan 5, 1913; studied at Royal College of Music in London; studied composition with Alfred Hill, piano with Frank Hutchens and cello under Gladstone Bell at Sydney Conservatorium; studied privately with Roy Agnew. ❖ At Royal College of Music, while studying with John Ireland, won Blumenthal Scholarship and Cobbett Prize for chamber composition (1938); became an examiner for Australian music board; performed as concert pianist; won Warringah and Henry Lawson Festival award (1965); received many composition awards from Australian Broadcasting Co. and gave many broadcasts on ABC network; throughout career, composed extensively, writing over 100 works for orchestra, chamber orchestra, piano and vocal groups.

HOLLAND, Eleanor (c. 1385–?). Countess of Salisbury. Name variations: Eleanor Montacute. Born c. 1385; dau. of Thomas Holland, 2nd earl of Kent, and Alice Fitzalan; sister of Elizabeth Holland (c. 1383–?), Alianor Holland (c. 1373–1405), Margaret Holland (1385–1429), and Joan Holland (c. 1380–1434); m. Thomas Montacute, 4th earl of Salisbury; children: Alice Montacute (c. 1406–1463).

HOLLAND, Elizabeth (1364–1425). See *Elizabeth of Lancaster*.

HOLLAND, Elizabeth (c. 1383–?). English noblewoman. Name variations: Elizabeth Neville. Born c. 1383; dau. of Thomas Holland, 2nd earl of Kent, and Alice Fitzalan; sister of Eleanor Holland (c. 1385–?), Alianor Holland (c. 1373–1405), Margaret Holland (1385–1429), and Joan Holland (c. 1380–1434); m. John Neville, before 1404; children:

Ralph Neville, earl of Westmoreland (c. 1404–1484); John Neville (d. 1461).

HOLLAND, Joan (c. 1356–1384). Duchess of Brittany. Name variations: Jane. Born c. 1356; died 1384; dau. of Joan of Kent (1328–1385) and Thomas Holland, 1st earl of Kent; half-sister of Richard II, king of England; 2nd wife of John IV, 5th duke of Brittany.

HOLLAND, Joan (c. 1380–1434). Duchess of York. Born c. 1380; died April 12, 1434; dau. of Thomas Holland, 2nd earl of Kent, and Alice Fitzalan (1352–1416); sister of Eleanor Holland (c. 1385–?), Elizabeth Holland (c. 1383–?), Alianor Holland (c. 1373–1405), and Margaret Holland (1385–1429); became 2nd wife of Edmund of Langley (c. 1380–1434), duke of York, in 1393 (his 1st wife was Isabel of Castile [1355–1392]). ❖ Appears in Shakespeare's *Richard II*.

HOLLAND, Lady.
See Lennox, Caroline (1723–1774).
See Fox, Elizabeth Vassall (1770–1845).
See Fox, Mary (b. 1817).

HOLLAND, Margaret (1385–1429). Countess of Somerset. Name variations: Lady Somerset; Margaret de Holand. Born 1385; died Dec 30, 1429 (some sources cite 1439) at St. Saviours Abbey, Bermondsey, London; buried at Canterbury Cathedral, Kent, England; dau. of Thomas Holland, 2nd earl of Kent, and Alice Fitzalan (1352–1416); m. John Beaufort, earl of Somerset (1373–1410, son of John of Gaunt and Catherine Swynford, Sept 28, 1397; m. Thomas, duke of Clarence, in 1411 or 1412; children: (1st m.) Henry, earl of Somerset (1401–1418); John Beaufort, duke of Somerset (1404–1444); Thomas, earl of Perche (1405–1432); Edmund, duke of Somerset (1406–1455); Margaret Beaufort, Countess of Devon (c. 1407); Joan Beaufort (c. 1410–1445).

HOLLAND, Mary (1935–2004). English journalist and broadcaster. Born June 19, 1935, in Dover, England; died of scleroderma, June 7, 2004; dau. of an engineer who worked in Malaysia (both parents were Irish); attended King's College, London; m. Ronald Higgins (British diplomat, div.); m. Eamonn McCann (revolutionary); children: (2nd m.) Kitty and Luke. ❖ One of the outstanding journalists of her time, joined the staff of the *Observer* (1964) and rose to fashion editor; after begging for "real" reporting, was sent to cover the political violence in Northern Ireland (1968); became known for her fairness and honesty, giving authentic coverage to the problems in Ulster, principally for the *Observer*; campaigned for the next 30 years for a new order in Ireland; also wrote a column for the *Irish Times*; was one of the 3 founding presenters of the LWT current affairs program "Weekend World" (1972–88); also often campaigned to liberalize Ireland's abortion laws.

HOLLAND, Oriel (1920–2003). See Gray, Oriel.

HOLLAND, queen of. See Hortense de Beauharnais (1783–1837).

HOLLAND, Tara Dawn (c. 1972—). Miss America. Name variations: Tara Dawn Christensen. Born c. 1972 in Overland Park, Kansas; University of Missouri-Kansas City, MA in music education; m. Jon Christensen (former US congressional rep.). ❖ Named Miss America (1997), representing Kansas; advocate for literacy campaign; was a featured vocalist with Kansas City Symphony; with husband, founded Cross & Crown Ministries.

HOLLAR, Constance (1881–1945). Jamaican poet. Born 1881 in Jamaica; died 1945. ❖ Works include *Flaming June* (1941); contributed to collections *Independence Anthology of Jamaican Literature* (1962) and *Caribbean Voices* (1966).

HOLLES, Henrietta (d. 1755). See Cavendish, Henrietta.

HOLLEY, Marietta (1836–1926). American author and humorist. Name variations: (pseudonyms) "Jemyma," "Josiah Allen's Wife," and "Samantha Allen." Born in Jefferson Co., NY, near Pierrepont Manor, July 16, 1836; died near Pierrepont Manor, Mar 1, 1926; dau. of John Milton and Mary (Taber) Holley; never married; no children. ❖ Under pseudonym "Josiah Allen's Wife," published 1st of humorous dialect sketches, "Deacon Slimpsey's Mournful Forebodings," in *Peterson's Magazine* (1871); published 1st book *My Opinions and Betsy Bobbet's* (1873), followed by 20 similar volumes, the last of which, *Josiah Allen on the Woman Question*, appeared in 1914. The popular books pitted the practical, wifely Samantha Allen, an advocate of woman's rights, against her counterpart, Betsy Bobbet, a staunch defender of the status quo. ❖ See also *Women in World History*.

HOLLEY, Mary Austin (1784–1846). American writer and land speculator. Born Mary Phelps Austin in New Haven, Connecticut, Aug 30, 1784; died in New Orleans, Louisiana, Aug 2, 1846; dau. of Elijah Austin (merchant) and Esther (Phelps) Austin; m. Horace Holley (Congregational minister), Jan 1, 1805 (died 1827); children: Harriette Williman Holley (b. 1808); Horace Austin Holley (b. 1818). ❖ Made 1st visit to Texas (1831), gathering material for *Texas: Observations Historical, Geographical and Descriptive* (1933), which not only proved to be a valuable source of information on the politics and social conditions within the State, but was written with such style and wit that it stimulated immigration to the territory. ❖ See also *Women in World History.*

HOLLEY, Sallie (1818–1893). American abolitionist and educator. Born Feb 17, 1818, in Canandaigua, NY; died Jan 12, 1893, in New York, NY; dau. of Myron Holley (lawyer) and Sally (House) Holley; lifelong companion was Caroline F. Putnam. ❖ After attending lecture by abolitionist Abby Kelley Foster, became agent of American Anti-Slavery Society (1851); lectured frequently throughout "free states" on emancipation of slaves and negro suffrage; with companion Caroline F. Putnam, devoted remainder of life to Holley School, school for freedmen in Lottsburg, Northumberland County, VA (1870–93). ❖ See also John White Chadwick, *A Life for Liberty* (1899).

HOLLIDAY, Jennifer (1960—). African-American singer. Name variations: Jennifer Linsley; Jennifer-Yvette Holliday. Born Oct 19, 1960, in Houston, TX; m. Billy Meadows, 1991 (div. 1991); m. Andre Woods, 1993 (div. 1995). ❖ Gifted belter, won lead in Broadway musical *Your Arms Too Short to Box With God* (1980); won Tony award for performance in hit musical *Dreamgirls* (1991) and a Grammy for Dreamgirls' showstopper "And I Am Telling You I'm Not Going" (1991); won 2nd Grammy for interpretation of Duke Ellington standard "Come Sunday" (1985); released albums *Feel My Soul* (1983), *Say You Love Me* (1985), *Get Close to My Love* (1987), *I'm on Your Side* (1991), *On & On* (1994) and *The Best of Jennifer Holliday* (1996); appeared in *Grease* (1995) and *Chicago*; portrayed gospel singer on tv series "Ally McBeal" (1997); films include *The Rising Place* (2001).

HOLLIDAY, Jenny (1964—). Australian softball player. Name variations: Jennifer Lisle Holliday. Born Jennifer Lisle, Jan 18, 1964, in Victoria, Australia. ❖ Pitcher, won a bronze medal at Atlanta Olympics (1996). Inducted into International Softball Hall of Fame (2001).

HOLLIDAY, Judy (1921–1965). American actress. Born Judith Tuvim in New York, NY, June 21, 1921; died of breast cancer, June 7, 1965, in New York, NY; only child of Abraham Tuvim (fund raiser for Jewish and socialist causes) and Helen (Gollomb) Tuvim (piano teacher); m. David Oppenheim, Jan 4, 1948 (div. 1957); children: Jonathan (b. 1952). ❖ Actress, generally typecast as a "dumb blonde," who endowed her roles with heart, intelligence, and an awareness of the characters' predicaments; made film debut in *Greenwich Village* (1944), then stage debut in *Kiss Them for Me* (1945); starred in *Born Yesterday* on Broadway (1946–50); appeared in Tracy-Hepburn film *Adam's Rib* (1946); costarred with Broderick Crawford in *Born Yesterday* at Columbia, for which she won Academy Award for Best Actress; because of a brush with McCarthyism, was blacklisted and effectively banned from appearing on tv (early 1950s); made musical-comedy debut in *Bells Are Ringing* (1956); other films include *Something for the Boys* (1944), *The Marrying Kind* (1952), *It Should Happen to You* (1954), *Phffft* (1954), *The Solid Gold Cadillac* (1956), *Full of Life* (1957) and *Bells Are Ringing* (1960). Won Clarence Derwent and Theatre World Award (1945) for performance in *Kiss Them for Me*; won Tony Award (1956) for Outstanding Lead for musical *Bells Are Ringing*. ❖ See also Gary Carey, *Judy Holliday* (1982); Will Holtzman, *Judy Holliday* (1982); and *Women in World History.*

HOLLINGSWORTH, Margaret (1940—). Canadian playwright. Born 1940 in London, England. ❖ Immigrated to Canada (1968) and studied at University of British Columbia; plays, produced in Canada and UK, include *Alli Alli Oh* (1979), *Bushed* (1981), *Operators* (1981), *Mother Country* (1981), and *Smiling Under Water* (1989).

HOLLINGWORTH, Leta Stetter (1886–1939). American psychologist. Born Leta Anna Stetter near Chadron, Nebraska, May 25, 1886; died in New York, NY, Nov 27, 1939; dau. of Margaret Elinor (Danley) Stetter and John G. Stetter; University of Nebraska, AB, 1906; Columbia University, AM, 1913, PhD, 1916; m. Harry L. Hollingworth, Dec 31, 1906. ❖ One of the leading psychologists in US, specializing in women, education, and gifted children, statistically took on erroneous gender assumptions and wrote the highly regarded *Psychology of the Adolescent*; joined staff of New York Clearing-House for Mental Defectives (1913); took position with the New York City Civil Service (1914); studied infants at New York Infirmary for Women and Children (1914); studied effects of menstruation on women (1915); became instructor, Columbia University Teachers College (1916); studied gifted children in association with NY school board (1920); published *The Psychology of the Adolescent* (1928), a standard text in the field for many years; appointed professor of education, Columbia University (1930); served as research director of Speyer School (1936); was instrumental in founding American Association of Clinical Psychologists; spoke frequently on topic of women's suffrage and was a member of the Woman's Suffrage Party. ❖ See also Harry L. Hollingworth, *Leta Stetter Hollingworth* (U. of Nebraska Press, 1943); and *Women in World History*.

HOLLINS, Marion B. (1892–1944). American golfer. Born 1892, in East Islip, NY; died Aug 27, 1944, in Pacific Grove, California. ❖ Won the Women's Metropolitan (1913, 1919, 1921) and the USGA Women's Amateur (1921); was instrumental in building the Women's National Course at Glen Head, Long Island; also helped plan and promote courses at Cypress Point and Santa Cruz, California.

HOLLINSHEAD, Ariel (1929—). American cancer researcher and pharmacologist. Born Ariel Cahill, Aug 24, 1929, in Pennsylvania; mother was a Barnard College valedictorian and president; father was a Quaker with an engineering degree from Lehigh; Ohio University, AB, 1951; George Washington University, MA, 1955, PhD in pharmacology, 1957; m. Montgomery Hollinshead (lawyer), 1958; children: 2. ❖ The 1st to identify human and animal antigens in cancerous tumors, worked with Dr. Joseph Melnick as a Baylor University Medical Center assistant virology and epidemiology professor (1958–59); at George Washington University, served as assistant pharmacology professor (1959–61) and associate pharmacology professor (1961–73); became medical professor at George Washington Medical Center (1974); created the Laboratory for Virus and Cancer Research, serving as head, then director, then president (1964–89). Honors include the Star of Europe Medal (1980), Society for Experimental Biology and Medicine's Distinguished Science Award (1985) and Italy's Scholar Speciale Medicina's Silver Medal (1990).

HOLLISTER, Gloria (1903–1988). See Anable, Gloria Hollister.

HOLLOWAY, Sue (1955—). Canadian kayaker and cross-country skier. Born May 19, 1955, in Halifax, Nova Scotia, Canada. ❖ At Winter Olympics in Innsbruck, came in 7th in cross-country ski relay (1976); at Los Angeles Olympics, won a bronze medal in K4 500 meters and a silver medal in K2 500 meters (1984); won 14 Canadian kayaking championships.

HOLLY, J. Hunter (1932–1982). American science-fiction writer. Name variations: Joan Carol Holly; Joan C. Holly. Born Sept 25, 1932, in Lansing, Michigan; died 1982. ❖ Writings include *Encounter* (1959), *The Green Planet* (1960), *The Flying Eyes* (1962), *The Time Twisters* (1964), *The Man from U.N.C.L.E. 10: The Assassination Affair* (1976) and *Shepherd* (1977); short stories included in Roger Ellwood collections, *And Walk Now Gently Through the Fire* (1972), *Demon Kind* (1973), and *Long Night of Waiting and Other Stories* (1974).

HOLLY, Joan Carol (1932–1982). See Holly, J. Hunter.

HOLM, Celeste (1919—). American actress and singer. Born April 29, 1919, in NYC; dau. of Theodor Holm (insurance executive) and Jean (Parke) Holm (author and artist); attended 14 schools, including Lycée Victor Durée, Paris; studied drama at University of Chicago, 1932–34; m. Ralph Nelson (director, div.); m. Francis Davies, Jan 1940 (div.); m. Wesley Addy (actor). ❖ Made NY debut as Lady Mary in *Gloriana* (1938), followed by *The Time of Your Life* (1939); had breakthrough role as Ado Annie in *Oklahoma!* (1943), drawing raves for rendition of "I Cain't Say No"; made film debut in *Three Little Girls in Blue* (1946), followed by *The Snake Pit* (1948), *Chicken Every Sunday* (1949), *Come to the Stable* (1949), *All About Eve* (1950) and *High Society* (1956), among others; made tv debut on "Chevrolet Show" (CBS, 1949) and was seen regularly as the grandmother on "Promised Land"; as an activist, was a member of the governing boards of World Federation of Mental Health and National Association for Mental Health; was appointed by President Reagan to the National Council for the Arts (1982) and served as chair of the New Jersey Motion Picture and Television Commission (1983). Won Academy Award for Best Supporting Actress for *Gentleman's Agreement*

(1947); earned 2 subsequent Best Supporting Actress nominations, for *Come to the Stable* (1949) and *All About Eve* (1950); received Sarah Siddons Award for performance in title role in national tour of *Mame* (1969); knighted by King Olav V of Norway (1979). ❖ See also *Women in World History*.

HOLM, Dörthe (c. 1973—). Danish curler. Name variations: Dorthe Holm. Born c. 1973 in Denmark. ❖ Won a silver medal for curling at Nagano Olympics (1998), the 1st-ever Danish medal in any sport at Winter Olympics.

HOLM, Eleanor (1913–2004). American swimmer. Name variations: Eleanor Holm Jarrett; Eleanor Holm Whalen. Born Eleanor Grace Holm, Dec 6, 1913, in Brooklyn, NY; died Jan 31, 2004, at home in Miami, Florida; attended Erasmus School; m. Art Jarrett (band leader and singer), 1933 (div. 1938); m. Billy Rose (r.n. William Rosenberg, entertainment mogul), 1939 (div. 1954); m. Tommy Whalen (former football player and oil executive), 1974 (died 1986). ❖ Won the National Indoor Junior championships in 3 different categories; won Outdoor Junior Medley championship; won National Women's Indoor championships in 5 different categories; in all, won 35 US championships and set numerous world records (1927–35); won a gold medal in the 100-meter backstroke at Los Angeles Olympics (1932); probably most remembered for being booted off the US Olympic team on way to the Berlin Olympics by Avery Brundage, pres. of US Olympic Committee (1936); gained fame from the incident while Brundage was disparaged; appeared with the Cleveland Aquacade and at World's Fair (1939–40). Elected to International Swimming Hall of Fame (1966). ❖ See also *Women in World History*.

HOLM, Hanya (1888–1992). German-born dancer, teacher, and choreographer. Born Johanna Eckert in Worms-am-Rhine, Germany, Mar 3, 1888; died of pneumonia in New York, NY, Nov 5, 1992; dau. of Valentin Eckert and Maria (Mörtschel or Moerschel) Eckert; m. Reinhold Martin Kuntze (div.); children: Klaus Holm (noted specialist in theatrical lighting). ❖ One of the founders of the American Dance Festival and choreographer for 13 Broadway musicals, including *Kiss Me Kate* and *My Fair Lady*, had a great influence on dancers and choreographers; joined Mary Wigman Institute in Dresden (1921); choreographed and directed at Ommen, Netherlands, Euripides' *Bacchae* (1928) and *Plato's Farewell to his Friends* (1929); choreographed *L'Histoire d'un Soldat* (Dresden, 1929); was associate director and co-dancer with Wigman in *Das Totenmal* (Munich, 1930); immigrated to US (1931); opened Mary Wigman School of the Dance in NY (1932), reopened as Hanya Holm School of the Dance (1936); choreographed the ballets *Trend* (1937), *Etudes* (1938), *Metropolitan Daily* and *Tragic Exodus* (1939), *They Too Are Exiles* (1940), *The Golden Fleece* (1941), *Parable* and *Suite of Four Dances* (1943), *L'Histoire d'un Soldat* (1954) and *Ozark Suite* (1956); choreographed at Colorado College Summer Sessions (1941–67); choreographed for such Broadway musicals as *The Liar* (1950), *Out of This World* (1951), *The Golden Apple* (1954), *Where's Charley?* (1958) and *Camelot* (1960); choreographed and directed operas *The Ballad of Baby Doe* and *Orpheus and Euridice*; choreographed for film *The Vagabond King* (1956). Won NY Drama Critics award for choreography for *Kiss Me Kate* (1948); received Samuel H. Scripps Award and American Dance Festival Award (1984), and Astaire Award (1987). ❖ See also Walter Sorell, *Hanya Holm: Biography of an Artist* (Wesleyan U. Press, 1969); and *Women in World History*.

HOLM, Jeanne (1921—). American military leader. Born Jeanne Marjorie Holm in Portland, Oregon, June 23, 1921; dau. of John E. Holm and Marjorie (Hammond) Holm; graduate of Air Command and Staff College (1952); Lewis and Clark College, BA (1957). ❖ American Air Force officer, joined Women's Army Auxiliary Corps (1942); commissioned second lieutenant (1943), was captain of women's training regiment by end of WWII; rejoined service (1948) and transferred to Air Force; became major-general, highest rank achieved by any woman in American armed forces at that time (1973); served as director of women in Air Force (1965–73); retired from service (1975); named special assistant to President Gerald Ford (1976); published *Women in the Military: An Unfinished Revolution* (1982). Awarded DSM with oak leaf cluster, Legion of Merit, Human Action medal; inducted into Women's Hall of Fame at Seneca Falls (2000). ❖ See also *Women in World History*.

HOLM, Saxe (1830–1885). See Jackson, Helen Hunt.

HOLMAN, Dorothy (1883—). English tennis player. Born July 18, 1883, in UK. ❖ At Antwerp Olympics, won a silver medal in doubles and a silver in singles (1920).

HOLMAN, Libby (1904–1971). American actress and singer. Born Elizabeth Lloyd Holzman (legally changed to Holman), May 23, 1904, in Cincinnati, Ohio; died June 23, 1971, in Stamford, Connecticut; University of Cincinnati, BA, 1923; attended Columbia University; m. (Zachary) Smith Reynolds (pilot and adventurer), Sept 16, 1931 (died 1932); m. Ralph Holmes (actor), 1939 (died 1945); m. Louis Schanker (artist), late 1960s; children: (1st m.) Christopher Smith "Topper" Reynolds (died mountain climbing, 1950); (adopted) Timmy and Tony. ❖ Torch singer, had major success portraying a prostitute in *The Little Show* (1929), singing "Moanin' Low," a song that would be associated with her from that time on; in *Three's a Crowd* (1930), stopped the show with "Give Me Something to Remember You By" and "Body and Soul"; at height of fame, partied nightly with NY's elite and married millionaire Smith Reynolds, son of tobacco magnate R.J. Reynolds, and heir to a fortune (1931); following a wild party at their home, her husband was found dead in his bedroom (July 1932), a bullet wound in his head; was indicted for murder, along with Reynolds' best friend Albert Walker; though she never went to trial, saw career effectively ended by the scandal. MGM released *Reckless*, based on the tragedy and starring Jean Harlow as Holman (1935). ❖ See also Jon Bradshaw, *Dreams That Money Can Buy* (Morrow, 1985); and *Women in World History*.

HOLMER, Ulrike (1967—). West German shooter. Born Oct 6, 1967, in Germany. ❖ At Los Angeles Olympics, won a silver medal in smallbore rifle 3 positions (1984).

HOLMES, Anna-Marie (1943—). Canadian ballet dancer. Name variations: Anna-Marie Ellerbeck. Born 1943 in Mission City, British Columbia, Canada. ❖ Trained with Lydia Korpova and Heino Heiden at British Columbia School of Dancing, and later with teachers in London, England, and Leningrad; danced with Royal Winnipeg Ballet in Brian MacDonald's *Prothalamium,* among others; performed with Kirov Ballet in Leningrad where she danced in *Romeo and Juliet, Flames of Paris,* and *Taras Bulba*; as guest artist with husband David Holmes, performed Lavrosky's pas de deux with London Festival Ballet, Het Nationale Balett of Holland and Les Grands Ballets Canadiens (c. 1960–70).

HOLMÈS, Augusta (1847–1903). French composer. Name variations: Augusta Holmes; Mary Anne Holmes. Born Augusta Mary Anne Holmès in Paris, France, Dec 16, 1847; died in Paris, Jan 28, 1903; only child of an Irish officer who settled in France (or Alfred de Vigny) and a mother of mixed Scottish and Irish origins; studied with Henri Lambert and César Franck; took instrumentation from Klosé; corresponded with Franz Liszt; mistress of Catulle Mendès; children: (with Mendès) 3 daughters. ❖ Though a brilliant pianist, attained distinction entirely through compositions; wrote opera *Hèro et Lèandre* (1875), including her own librettos; followed this with *Astarté* and *Lancelot du lac* and 4-act lyric opera *La montagne noire*, produced at Grand Opera (1895), one of the few operas written by a woman to be performed in 19th century; influenced by Wagner and Franck, preferred epic themes on classical or mythological subjects for a large orchestra; also liked dramatic symphonies and symphonic poems, but greatest success was with choral works, such as *Les Argonautes* (1881), *Ludus pro patria* (1888), and *Ode triomphale* (1889); wrote over 130 songs; was a dominant figure in French musical circles and literary salons.

HOLMES, Helen (1892–1950). American stage and film actress and stuntwoman. Born June 19, 1892, in Chicago, Illinois (some sources cite Louisville, Kentucky, some San Francisco); died July 8, 1950, in Burbank, California; m. J.P. McGowan (director, div. 1925); m. Lloyd A. Saunders (movie stuntman, died 1946). ❖ Made NY stage debut in *The Virginian* (1904), followed by *The Aviator, Caste, The Confession, The Natural Law, Kick-In* and *Dorian Grey*; came to prominence as a serial queen with daredevil stunts in 1st 65 episodes of *The Hazards of Helen* (1914–15, a series that continued with other actresses to total 119); other films include *The Railroad Raiders, The Lost Express, The Diamond Runners, The Girl and the Game* (serial) and *A Lass of the Lumberlands* (15-part serial).

HOLMES, Julia Archibald (1838–1887). American feminist and mountain climber. Born Julia Archibald in Nova Scotia, Canada, Feb 15, 1838; died 1887; married James Holmes (abolitionist), 1857 (div. 1870); children: 4. ❖ The 1st woman to climb Pike's Peak, was dressed in bloomers, moccasins and a hat, and carrying a 17-pound pack of supplies on her back, when she accompanied husband and 2 other men on the trek (1858); with husband, settled in Taos, New Mexico, where she worked as a news correspondent for *New York Tribune*; after divorce, settled in Washington, DC, where she was one of the 1st women to be promoted in the civil-service system.

HOLMES, Kelly (1970—). English runner. Born April 19, 1970, in Pembury, Kent, England. ❖ Won a bronze medal for the 800 meters at Sydney Olympics (2000); at Commonwealth Games, won a gold medal for 1,500 meters (1994, 2002); at World championships, placed 2nd for 1,500 meters (1995) and 800 meters (2003); won 3 Super Grand Prix 1,500-meter events (2003–04); won gold medals for 800 meters and 1,500 meters at Athens Olympics (2004); was the 1st British-born woman to break 4 minutes for the 1,500 meters. Awarded an MBE (1998).

HOLMES, Mary Jane (1825–1907). American popular novelist. Born Mary Jane Hawes, April 5, 1825, in Brookfield, Massachusetts; died Oct 6, 1907, in Brockport, NY; dau. of Preston Hawes and Fanny (Olds) Hawes; m. Daniel Holmes, Aug 9, 1849. ❖ Published 1st novel, *Tempest and Sunshine; or, Life in Kentucky* (1854); went on to write nearly 40 novels, approximately 1 a year (1855–1905), including best-known work, *Lena Rivers* (1856), but most are now considered conventional; sold over 2 million books. ❖ See also *Women in World History.*

HOLMSEN, Hanna (1873–1943). See Resvoll-Holmsen, Hanna.

HOLMSEN, Thekla (1871–1948). See Resvoll, Thekla.

HOLSBOER, Noor (1967—). Dutch field-hockey player. Name variations: Eleonoor Wendeline Holsboer. Born Eleonoor Wendeline Holsboer, July 12, 1967, in Netherlands. ❖ Won team bronze medals at Seoul Olympics (1988) and Atlanta Olympics (1996).

HOLST, Clara (1868–1935). Norwegian linguist. Born June 4, 1868, in Oslo, Norway; died Nov 15, 1935; granddau. of Fredrik Holst (medical professor); studied at Oslo University, 1889–96, University of Cambridge, 1892–93, and Sorbonne, 1893–94; also studied in Leipzig, 1897–98, and in Berlin, 1902–03, for PhD. ❖ Distinguished linguist and Middle-Low German language expert, taught at Wellesley College in MA (1906–07) and at Kansas University (1907–08); returned to Norway (1908) at age 40 and disappeared from world of academia; was the 1st Norwegian woman to defend a doctoral dissertation (Dec 10, 1903) and the 1st Norwegian woman graduate in philology (University of Oslo, 1895, 1896). A lecture hall at U. of Oslo campus in Kristiansand bears her name.

HOLST, Henriëtte Roland (1869–1952). See Roland Holst, Henriëtte.

HOLST, Imogen (1907–1984). English pianist, conductor, and teacher. Born Imogen Clare Holst in Richmond, Surrey, England, April 12, 1907; died at Aldeburgh, Mar 9, 1984; dau. of Gustav Holst (renowned composer); attended Royal College of Music. ❖ Wrote extensively about music, including a biography of her father (1938); was a member of the Royal Music Association and Society of Women Musicians; composed orchestral, chamber, and vocal pieces throughout career; became interested in folk music and was known for her arrangements of old tunes; for 10 years, collaborated with Benjamin Britten; her work at Britten's Aldeburgh Festival played a crucial role in making his music world renowned.

HOLSTEIN-GOTTORP, duchess of.
See Christine of Hesse (1543–1604).
See Amelia of Denmark (1580–1639).
See Marie Elizabeth of Saxony (1610–1684).
See Frederica Amalie (1649–1704).
See Hedwig Sophia (1681–1708).
See Albertina of Baden-Durlach (1682–1755).
See Anne Petrovna (1708–1728).
See Louise Augusta (1771–1843).

HOLSTON, Isabelle Daniels (1937—). *See Daniels, Isabelle Frances.*

HOLT, Jacqueline (1920–1997). *See Holt, Jennifer.*

HOLT, Jane (fl. 17th c.). *See Wiseman, Jane.*

HOLT, Jennifer (1920–1997). American actress. Name variations: Jacqueline Holt. Born Elizabeth Marshall Holt, Nov 10, 1920, in Hollywood, CA; died Sept 21 (also seen as Sept 28), 1997, in Dorset, England; dau. of Margaret Woods Holt and Jack Holt (star of silent screen); sister of David and Tim Holt (cowboy star); m. William

Bakewell (div.). ❖ Played lead roles in low-budget westerns opposite such cowboy stars as Johnny Mack Brown and Rod Cameron; films include *The Old Chisholm Trail, Cowboy in Manhattan, Lone Star Trail, Raiders of Sunset Pass, Riders of the Santa Fe, Song of Old Wyoming, Moon over Montana, Hop Harrigan, Buffalo Bill Rides Again* and *The Tioga Kid.*

HOLT, Marjorie Sewell (1920—). American politician. Born Marjorie Sewell, Sept 17, 1920, in Birmingham, Alabama; dau. of Edward Roland Sewell and Alice Juanita (Felts) Sewell; Jacksonville (Florida) University, BA, 1945; University of Florida College of Law, JD, 1949; m. Duncan McKay Holt, Dec 26, 1946; children: Rachel Holt Tschantre; Edward Holt; Victoria Holt Stauffer. ❖ Member of US House of Representatives (1973–87), practiced law in Florida for 13 years, then moved to Maryland, where she was admitted to the bar (1962); served as clerk of circuit court in Anne Arundel County (1965–71); was a member of Maryland Governor's Commission on Law Enforcement and Administration of Justice (1970–72); served as legal counsel for Maryland State Federation of Republican Women (1971–72); was delegate to 4 Republican National Conventions (1968, 1976, 1980, 1984); elected to 93rd Congress for Maryland's 4th District (1972), served through the 99th Congress (1987); as a Cold-War politician, concentrated on national defense and armed forces, and consistently advocated increases in defense spending and enhanced benefits for those in military; pushed for reductions in non-military spending while serving 2 terms on Budget Committee; served on Committee on Armed Services during each of 13 years in the House, becoming the ranking Republican on Subcommittee on Procurement and Military Nuclear Systems in last term in office; was actively opposed to busing of schoolchildren to effect racial integration; chose not to run for reelection (1987); writings include *The Case Against the Reckless Congress* (1976) and *Can You Afford This House* (1978). ❖ See also *Women in World History.*

HOLT, Maud (1858–1937). *See Tree, Maud Holt.*

HOLT, Stella (d. 1967). American theatrical producer. Died Aug 28, 1968, age 50, in New York, NY. ❖ Produced 38 off-Broadway plays, mostly at Greenwich Mews with Frances Drucker, including *Orpheus Descending, Simply Heavenly, The Long Gallery, All in Love, Jerico-Jim Crow, The Ox Cart* and *Carricknabauna.*

HOLT, Victoria (1906–1993). *See Hibbert, Eleanor.*

HOLT, Winifred (1870–1945). American sculptor, writer, and philanthropist. Name variations: Winifred Holt Mather; Mrs. Rufus Graves Mather. Born Winifred Holt in New York, NY, Nov 17, 1870; died in Pittsfield, Massachusetts, June 14, 1945; dau. of Henry Holt (publisher) and Mary Florence (West) Holt; sister of Edith Holt (philanthropist); educated at Brearley School, NY; studied anatomy and sculpture in Florence, and with Augustus Saint-Gaudens; m. Rufus G. Mather (researcher and lecturer on art), Nov 16, 1922; no children. ❖ Best known as the founder (along with sister Edith) of the NY Association for the Blind (1912), renamed the Lighthouse (1913); organized 1st Lighthouse for the Blind (1915), in France (eventually, the international Lighthouse movement would spread to over 30 nations); also created *Searchlight,* the 1st Braille magazine for children, and was instrumental in mainstreaming blind children into regular public-school classrooms. Awarded Chevalier of French Legion of Honor (1921). ❖ See also autobiographies *The Light Which Cannot Fail* (1922) and *First Lady of the Lighthouse* (1952); and *Women in World History.*

HOLT, Zara (1909–1989). Australian prime-ministerial wife. Born Zara Kate Dickens, Mar 10, 1909, in Kew, Melbourne, Australia; died June 14, 1989, in Surfers Paradise, Queensland; m. Harold E. Holt (prime minister of Australia, 1966–67), Oct 8, 1946 (died 1967); m. Jefferson Bate, 1969; children: Nicholas (b. 1937), Sam and Andrew (b. 1939). ❖ As co-owner of the boutique Magg in Melbourne's tony suburb of Toorak, actively oversaw renovations to The Lodge (the official prime-ministerial residence); was a major player in developing networks, especially in the area of arts and fashion; husband died in office. Named Dame of the Order of the British Empire (DBE, 1968). ❖ See also autobiography *My Life and Harry* (Herald, 1968).

HOLTBY, Winifred (1898–1935). English journalist, novelist, dramatist, and social reformer. Born Winifred Holtby in Rudstone in Yorkshire, England, June 23, 1898; died of kidney failure, at 37, in London, Sept 25, 1935; dau. of Alice (Winn) Holtby (1st woman alderman elected by East Riding County Council) and David Holtby (farmer); attended Somerville College, Oxford, 1917–21, interrupted during

WWI by her activity in London as a Voluntary Auxiliary Nurse (VAD), 1916–17, and in France as a hostel-forewoman in Signal Unit of Women's Auxiliary Army Corps (WAAC), 1918–19; never married; no children. ❖ Writer who campaigned for women's rights and pacifism and was a major orator for the unionization of black workers in South Africa; wrote extensively for English newspapers and periodicals; served as director of feminist periodical *Time and Tide* (1926–35); was a public speaker for equal-rights feminism, pacifism, and against imperialist exploitation of native races in South Africa; best known for her novels, especially *South Riding* (1937) for which she was awarded James Tait Black Memorial Prize; celebrated in Vera Brittain's *A Testament of Friendship: The Story of Winifred Holtby* (1940); other writings include (juvenilia) *My Garden and Other Poems* (1911), *Anderby Wold* (1923), *The Crowded Street* (1924), *The Land of Green Ginger* (1927), *Eutychus, or The Future of the Pulpit* (1928), *Poor Caroline* (1931), *Virginia Woolf: A Critical Memoir* (1932), *Mandoa, Mandoa!* (1933), *The Astonishing Island* (1933), *Women and a Changing Civilization* (1934), *Truth Is Not Sober and Other Stories* (1934), (poetry) *The Frozen Earth* (1935), *Letters to a Friend* (1937), and (short stories) *Pavements at Anderby* (1937). ❖ See also *Women in World History.*

HOLTER, Harriet (1922–1997). Norwegian social scientist. Name variations: Harriet Bog (1945–49), Harriet Gullvåg (1951–56), and Harriet Holter (1958 on). Born Harriet Bog, 1922; died Dec 18, 1997; University of Oslo, degree in social economy, 1946, then doctorate in social psychology; m. Ingemund Gullvåg; married once more; children: (1st m.) 1 son. ❖ Pioneer of women's studies, was a professor of social psychology at University of Oslo (1972–92); was also professor emeritus at the Center for Women's Studies, which she had established, as well as a member of the Norwegian Academy of Sciences and of numerous academic committees and commissions, including the Norwegian Research Council; later research focused on sexual violence and child abuse; writings include *Sex Roles and Social Structure* (1970) and *Patriarchy in a Welfare State* (1984). ❖ See also *Women in World History.*

HOLTROP-VAN GELDER, Betty (1866–1962). Dutch actress. Name variations: Betty Holtrop Van Gelder. Born Elisabeth Jacoba Philippine Beatrix van Gelder, Dec 16, 1866, in Amsterdam, Holland, Netherlands; died Oct 20, 1962, in Haarlem, Netherlands; studied for the stage at Vienna Conservatoire; m. Jan Arend Holtrop (1862–1917). ❖ Joined Nederlandsch Tooneel (1889), appearing in numerous parts from Joan of Arc, to Suzanne in *Le Monde on l'on s'ennuie,* to Nora in *A Doll's House,* Mrs. Elvsted in *Hedda Gabler,* Ella Rentheim in *John Gabriel Borkman,* Gina Ekdal in *The Wild Duck,* to Ismene, Lady Teazle, Portia, Ophelia, Juliet, Rosalind and Beatrice; appeared in Paris at Comédie Française with the Dutch company (1901).

HOLTZER, Minerva (1894–1966). *See Urecal, Minerva.*

HOLTZMAN, Elizabeth (1941—). American politician. Born Aug 11, 1941, in Brooklyn, NY; dau. of Sidney Holtzman and Filia (Ravitz) Holtzman; Radcliffe College, BA, magna cum laude, 1962; Harvard Law School, JD, 1965. ❖ Member of US House of Representatives (1973–81), began career as assistant to NYC Mayor John Lindsay (1967); served as a Democratic state committeewoman and district leader (1970–72), in addition to founding the Brooklyn Women's Political Caucus; challenged 50-year veteran Emanuel Celler for Democratic nomination to US House of Representatives (1972); at 31, won primary and election, the youngest woman elected to Congress; served 4 consecutive terms in House of Representatives, distinguishing herself during impeachment hearings of Richard Nixon with investigative work as member of House Judiciary; sought to revise immigration laws and contributed to creation of new rules concerning how evidence is presented in federal courts; ran unsuccessfully for a US Senate seat (1980 and 1992); served as district attorney for Kings County in Brooklyn (1981–90) and as comptroller of NYC (1989–93); resumed practicing law in Brooklyn (1994). ❖ See also autobiography (with Cynthia L. Cooper) *Who Said It Would Be Easy?: One Woman's Life in the Political Arena* (1996).

HOLTZMANN, Fanny (1895–1980). American lawyer. Born Fanny Ellen Holtzmann in Brooklyn, NY, Oct 17, 1895; died of cancer, Feb 7, 1980, in New York, NY; dau. of Henry Holtzmann (scholar and tutor) and Theresa Holtzmann; Fordham Law School, LLB, 1922; never married; no children. ❖ Considered one of America's most brilliant legal strategists, made her way into the high echelons of entertainment law, then to England's "castle circuit," and finally into international politics; successfully represented Russian royal family in libel suit against MGM (1934), which involved the misrepresentation of Princess Irina (1895–1970) as mistress and sponsor of Rasputin; her roster of famous clients included Noel Coward, Clifton Webb, Fred Astaire, George Bernard Shaw, Dwight D. Eisenhower, Darryl F. Zanuck and Gertrude Lawrence; with rise of Nazism, convinced US Immigration Service to permit more Jews into the country; was principal US counsel to Republic of China and assisted China in becoming one of 5 countries with veto power at founding session of UN in San Francisco (1945); also used influence to marshal votes from a number of smaller non-aligned nations for admission of Israel into UN (1947). ❖ See also Edward O. Berkman, *The Lady and the Law: The Remarkable Story of Fanny Holtzmann* (1976); and *Women in World History.*

HOLUM, Dianne (1951—). American speedskater. Born May 19, 1951, in Chicago, IL; children: Kirstin Holum (speedskater). ❖ Won silver medal (3-way tie with Jennifer Fish and Mary Meyers) for the 500 meters and bronze medal for the 1,000 meters at Grenoble Olympics (1968); won a gold medal for the 1,000 meters at World championships (1971) and a gold for the 500 meters (1972); won a gold medal for the 1,500 meters, the 1st American woman to win an Olympic gold medal in that event, and a silver medal for the 3,000 meters at Sapporo (1972); retired from competition to coach (1973). Inducted into Women's Sports Hall of Fame (1996); named by US Speedskating Association as National and Developmental Coach of the Year (1997). ❖ See also *Women in World History.*

HOLUM, Kirsten (c. 1981—). American speedskater. Born c. 1981 in Waukesha, Wisconsin; dau. of Dianne Holum (speedskater). ❖ Came in 7th in the 5,000 at Nagano Olympics (1998), the top American finisher, with a personal best time of 7:14.20; retired to attend art school.

HOLY MAID OF KENT (c. 1506–1534). See Barton, Elizabeth.

HOLYOKE, Mary Vial (1737–1802). American diarist. Born 1737 in Salem, Massachusetts; died 1802; m. Edward Augustus Holyoke; children: 12. ❖ Wrote 40-year diary which gives details of marriage and life in wealthy Salem society, published as *The Holyoke Diaries, 1709–1856* (1911).

HOLY ROMAN EMPRESS.
See Ermengarde (c. 778–818).
See Irmengard (c. 800–851).
See Judith of Bavaria (802–843).
See Engelberga (c. 840–890).
See Matilda of Saxony (c. 892–968).
See Oda of Bavaria (fl. 890s).
See Richilde (d. 894).
See Anna of Byzantium (fl. 901).
See Cunigunde of Swabia (fl. 900s).
See Adelaide of Burgundy (931–999).
See Theophano of Byzantium (c. 955–991).
See Agnes of Poitou (1024–1077).
See Cunigunde (d. 1040?).
See Gisela of Swabia (d. 1043).
See Bertha of Savoy (1051–1087).
See Adelaide of Kiev (c. 1070–1109).
See Richensia of Nordheim (1095–1141).
See Matilda, Empress (1102–1167).
See Beatrice of Upper Burgundy (1145–1184).
See Gertrude of Sulzbach (d. 1146).
See Constance of Sicily (1154–1198).
See Irene Angela of Byzantium (d. 1208).
See Mary of Brabant (c. 1191–c. 1260).
See Beatrice of Swabia (1198–1235).
See Constance of Aragon (d. 1222).
See Yolande of Brienne (1212–1228).
See Isabella of England (1214–1241).
See Anna of Hohenberg (c. 1230–1281).
See Beatrice of Silesia (fl. 1300s).
See Isabella of Aragon (c. 1300–1330).
See Margaret of Brabant (d. 1311).
See Blanche of Valois (c. 1316–?).
See Anna of Schweidnitz (c. 1340–?).
See Margaret of Holland (d. 1356).
See Anna of the Palatinate.
See Elizabeth of Pomerania (1347–1393).
See Sophia of Bavaria (fl. 1390s–1400s).
See Eleanor of Portugal (1434–1467).
See Sforza, Bianca Maria (1472–1510).

See Isabella of Portugal (1503–1539).
See Anna of Bohemia and Hungary (1503–1547).
See Marie of Austria (1528–1603).
See Gonzaga, Anna (1585–1618).
See Gonzaga, Eleonora I (1598–1655).
See Maria Anna of Spain (1606–1646).
See Gonzaga, Eleonora II (1628–1686).
See Maria Leopoldine (1632–1649).
See Margaret Theresa of Spain (1651–1673).
See Claudia Felicitas.
See Eleanor of Pfalz-Neuburg (1655–1720).
See Wilhelmina of Brunswick (1673–1742).
See Elizabeth Christina of Brunswick-Wolfenbuttel (1691–1750).
See Maria Theresa of Austria (1717–1780).
See Maria Louisa of Spain (1745–1792).
See Maria Teresa of Naples (1772–1807).

HOLZER, Ashley Nicoll- (1963—). See Nicoll, Ashley.

HOLZNER, Monika (1954—). See Pflug, Monika.

HOLZNER, Ulrike. German bobsledder. Born in Germany. ❖ With Sandra Prokoff, won a gold medal for the two-man bobsleigh at the World Cup (2002) and a silver medal for the two-man bobsleigh at Salt Lake City Olympics (2002), the 1st women's bobsleigh competition in Winter Games history.

HOMAIRA (1916–2002). Queen of Afghanistan. Name variations: Homaira Shah; Homaira Shah Khanoum. Born July 24, 1916, in Kabul, Afghanistan; died June 26, 2002, in Rome, Italy; m. Mohammad Zahir Shah (king of Afghanistan), 1931; children: 9, including princes Nadir Zahir, Ahmed Shah, Mir Wais Zahir and Shah Mahmoud. ❖ Married at 16; as leader of a movement to liberate modern Afghan women, threw off her veil to the horror of the mullahs (1959); independent-minded, led the way for women to be admitted to universities; lived with husband in Rome after he was ousted from power in a coup (1973); intended to return to Afghanistan with husband after US invasion, but died of a heart attack; her body was returned to Kabul.

HOMAN, Gertrude (1880–1951). American actress. Name variations: Gertrude Thanhouser. Born April 23, 1880, in Beauvoir, Mississippi; died May 29, 1951, in Glen Cove, LI, NY; m. Edwin Thanhouser (pioneer film producer). ❖ Began career as a child; created the role of Editha in Frances Hodgson Burnett's *Editha's Burglar* (1886) and starred in *Bootie's Baby*; wrote scenarios for *The Winter's Tale* and *The Price of Her Silence.*

HOMBELINA (1092–1141). French saint. Born in Fontaines les Dijon, France, 1092; died a nun at Jully-les-Nonnains in 1141; dau. of Tescelin Sor (Dijon knight) and Aleth of Montbard; sister of St. Bernard of Clairvaux (1090–1153). ❖ Feast day is Aug 21.

HOME, Cecil (1837–1894). See Webster, Augusta.

HOMEGHI, Olga (1958—). See Bularda-Homeghi, Olga.

HOMER, Louise (1871–1947). American contralto. Born Louise Dilworth Beatty in Shadyside, rural section of Pittsburgh, PA, April 30, 1871; died May 6, 1947, in Winter Park, Florida; studied voice with Fidèle Koenig and acting with Paul Lhérie; m. Sidney Homer (composer), 1895; children: 6, including daughter Louise Homer Stires (1896–1970, who was also an operatic soprano). ❖ Made debut at Vichy in Donizetti's *La Favorita* (June 15, 1898); debuted at Covent Garden (1899); made Metropolitan Opera debut as Amneris in *Aïda* (1900); was one of the Met's greatest stars, appearing there for 20 years, assuming the leading Wagnerian contralto and mezzo-soprano roles (1900–19); appeared with Chicago Grand Opera, and San Francisco and Los Angeles operas, before returning to NY for last performance (1929); made many recordings with Caruso, Martinelli, and Gigli, among others. ❖ See also A. Homer, *Louise Homer and the Golden Age of Opera* (1974); Sidney Homer, *My Wife and I*; and *Women in World History.*

HOMMES, Nienke (1977—). Dutch rower. Born Feb 20, 1977, in the Netherlands. ❖ Won a bronze medal for coxed eights at Athens Olympics (2004).

HOMMOLA, Ute (1952—). East German track-and-field athlete. Born Jan 20, 1952, in East Germany. ❖ At Moscow Olympics, won a bronze medal in javelin throw (1980).

HONAN, Cathy (1951—). Irish politician. Name variations: Catherine Honan. Born Catherine O'Brien, Sept 16, 1951, in Clonmel, Co.

Tipperary, Ireland; m. Adrian Honan. ❖ Elected to the Seanad by the Industrial and Commercial Panel (1993–97).

HONAN, Tras (1930—). Irish politician. Born Tras Barlow, Jan 4, 1930, in Tipperary, Ireland; dau. of Matt Barlow; sister of Carrie Acheson (TD); m. Derry Honan (senator). ❖ Joined Fianna Fáil (1948); nominated to the Seanad by the Administrative Panel: Nominating Bodies Sub-Panel (1977), the only woman nominated from the 5 vocational panels; served until 1993.

HONCHAROVA, Iryna (1974—). Ukrainian handball player. Born Dec 19, 1974, in Ukraine. ❖ Won a team bronze medal at Athens Olympics (2004).

HONE, Evie (1894–1955). Irish artist. Born Evie Sydney Hone, April 22, 1894 in Dublin, Ireland; died Mar 13, 1955, in Dublin; dau. of Joseph Hone and Eva (Robinson) Hone; educated at Byam Shaw School of Art, Central School of Arts and Crafts and Westminster School of Art; studied in France, 1920–23, with André Lhote and Albert Gleizes. ❖ One of the foremost stained-glass designers of the 20th century, contracted infantile paralysis at 12, which affected one of her hands and also left her lame; met Mainie Jellett while studying with Walter Sickert at Westminster Art School (1917); with Jellett, would help champion the cause of modernism in Irish art; after studies in Paris, returned to Ireland with Jellett where they played a seminal role in disseminating the theories and discoveries of Cubism, though met with dirision; spent 2 years in an Anglican convent (1925–27); returned to France and exhibited in Paris at Salons des Indépendants, Salon des Surindépendants, and Salon d'Automne; became increasingly interested in stained glass and joined An Túr Gloine (Tower of Glass, 1934), remaining there until 1943; did windows for St. Naithi's Church in Dundrum, Dublin (1934); commissioned by Irish government to create stained glass for Irish Pavilion at NY World's Fair (1939), for which she designed *My Four Green Fields*; other principal works include armorial windows and *Pentecost* (Blackrock College Chapel, 1937–41), *Saint Brigid* (Loughrea Cathedral, 1942), windows for St. Stanislaus College, Tullabeg, Co. Offaly (1942), windows for Church of the Immaculate Conception, Kingscourt, Co. Cavan (1947–48), Eton College Chapel, Berkshire, England (1949–52) and St. Michael's Church, Highgate, London (1954). ❖ See also *Women in World History.*

HONECKER, Edith (1909–1973). See Baumann, Edith.

HONECKER, Margot (1927—). East German cabinet official. Name variations: Margot Feist. Born Margot Feist in Halle an der Saale, April 17, 1927; dau. of Gotthard Feist; became 2nd wife of Erich Honecker (1912–1994, head of GDR party and state), 1953; children: Sonja Honecker Yanez. Erich Honecker's 1st wife was Edith Baumann (1909–1973), who had daughter Erika Honecker. ❖ Minister of public education (1963–89), whose 26-year tenure reflected the ideology of the GDR's hard-line Communist regime; was known to many East Germans simply as "die Hexe" (the witch); after fall of the GDR, was accused of having forced political dissidents to surrender their children for adoption, as well as of presiding over a reform school known as "Margot's concentration camp" where truant minors were mistreated to the point that some committed suicide (1992); found refuge in Chile with daughter's family (1992). ❖ See also *Women in World History.*

HONEYBALL, Mary (1952—). English politician. Born Nov 12, 1952, in Weymouth, England. ❖ Member of Barnet London Borough Council (1978–86) and Labour Party National Policy Forum (1995–97); as a European Socialist, elected to 5th European Parliament (1999–2004) from UK.

HONEYMAN, Nan Wood (1881–1970). American politician. Born Nan Wood, July 15, 1881, in West Point, NY; died Dec 10, 1970, in Woodacre, California; m. David T. Honeyman (hardware company executive), 1907. ❖ Member of US House of Representatives (1937–39), moved to Portland with family (1883); served as president of Oregon State Constitutional Convention that ratified 21st Amendment (1933), repealing Prohibition; became a member of Oregon House of Representatives (1935); also served as delegate to Democratic National Conventions (1936, 1940); elected US House of Representatives for Oregon's 3rd District (1936); during term in office, served on Committee on Indian Affairs, Committee on Irrigation and Reclamation, and Committee on Rivers and Harbors; ran unsuccessfully for reelection (1938); appointed collector of customs for 29th District in Portland (1942), a post she retained until 1953. ❖ See also *Women in World History.*

HONEYMAN, Susie. English violinist. Name variations: The Mekons. ❖ Classically trained violinist who joined English group, the Mekons, becoming part of core of band; worked on celebrated album, *Fear and Whiskey* (1985), released in US as *Original Sin* (1989); with group, released moderately successful albums, *The Edge of the World* (1986), *Honky Tonkin'* (1987) and *So Good It Hurts* (1988), and critically acclaimed album, *The Mekons Rock'n'Roll* (1989); with group, worked with author Kathy Acker to create *Pussy, King of the Pirates* (1996), which toured and was released on CD; also released album, *Journey to the End of the Night* (2000).

HONG CH-OK (1970—). Korean table-tennis player. Born Mar 10, 1970, in South Korea. ❖ At Barcelona Olympics, won a bronze medal in doubles (1992).

HONG JEONG-HO (1974—). South Korean handball player. Born May 21 (some sources cite May 6), 1974, in South Korea. ❖ Won a team gold medal at Barcelona Olympics (1992) and a team silver at Atlanta Olympics (1996).

HONG, Lady (1735–1850). Korean queen of the Yi dynasty. Born Aug 6, 1735, in Kop'yong-dong, Pangsongbang, Korea; died 1850; dau. of Hong Pong-han (president of the state council) and Lady Yi; m. Crown Prince Sado (1735–1762), Feb 23, 1744 (died 1762); children: son Uiso (1750–1752), son Chongjo (b. 1752, later king of Korea), and daughters, Ch'ongyon (b. 1754) and Ch'ongson (b. 1756). ❖ In her *Memoirs of a Korean Queen,* chronicled court life in 18th-century Korea and the demise of her demented husband at the hand of his father in what came to be known as the Imo Incident (1762). Her story was the subject of a highly popular tv drama in South Korea (1985). ❖ See also *Women in World History.*

HONG QIAO (b. 1968). See Qiao Hong.

HONNER, Maria (1812–1870). Irish actress. Born Maria McCarthy in Enniskillen, County Fermanagh, Ireland, 1812; died 1870; m. Robert William Honner (1809–1852, actor-manager of Sadler's Wells [1835–40] and Surrey Theater [1835–38, 1842–46]), 1836. ❖ Excelled in tragedy; appeared opposite Edmund Kean and as Julia in *The Hunchback* (1835).

HONNINGEN, Mette (1944—). Danish ballet dancer. Name variations: Inge Mette Hønningen; Mette Hønningen or Hoenningen. Born Oct 3, 1944, in Copenhagen, Denmark. ❖ Trained at Royal Danish Ballet before joining its professional company; remained with Danish Ballet throughout most of her career, performing in Roland Petit's *Carmen*, Flemming Flindt's *Dreamland* (1974), Murray Louis' *Cléopâtre* (1976), among others; appeared in film *Ballerina* (1966).

HONOR. *Variant of Nora.*

HONORIA (c. 420–?). Roman princess. Name variations: Honoria Augusta; Justa Grata Honoria. Born c. 420; dau. of Constantius III, emperor of Rome, and Galla Placidia (c. 390–450); sister of Valentinian III. ❖ Caused two scandals in the Roman palace; had an affair with her steward Eugenius who was executed, while she was banished to a convent in Constantinople (434); sent her ring to Attila the Hun, reputedly seeking marriage, and he used the message as an excuse to invade Italy (452), while demanding his "marriage portion" of the Roman empire.

HONSOVA, Zdeka (1927–1994). Czech gymnast. Born July 1927, in Czechoslovakia; died May 1994. ❖ At London Olympics, won a gold medal in team all-around (1948).

HOO, Anne (c. 1425–1484). English noblewoman. Name variations: Anne Boleyn. Born c. 1425; died 1484; dau. of Thomas Hoo, Lord Hoo and Hastings, and Elizabeth Wychingham; m. Geoffrey Boleyn (Lord Mayor of London in 1458); children: William Boleyn (c. 1451–1505, grandfather of Anne Boleyn).

HOOBLER, Icie Macy (1892–1984). American biochemist. Name variations: Icie Gertrude Macy-Hoobler. Born Icie Gertrude Macy, July 23, 1892, near Gallatin, Missouri; died Jan 1984 in Gallatin; University of Chicago, BS, 1916; University of Colorado, MS, 1918; became 4th woman to receive PhD from Department of Physiological Chemistry of Sheffield Scientific School at Yale University, 1920; m. B. Raymond Hoobler (chief of staff at Children's Hospital), 1938; children: reared her late sister Ina's daughters, Christine and Helen Wynne. ❖ Once described as "one of the best physiological chemists of the first half of the 20th century," was a pioneer in the study of infant, child and adolescent growth and nutrition; was instrumental in determing the appropriate amount of Vitamin D to add to milk to prevent rickets; served as director of chemical and biological research at Nutrition Research Laboratory of Merrill-Palmer Institute and the Children's Hospital of Michigan (1923–30); served as director of Children's Fund of Michigan Research Laboratory (1930–54); was the 1st woman president of the American Chemical Society.

HOOD, Darla (1931–1979). American child actress. Born Darla Jean Hood, Nov 4, 1931, in Leedey, Oklahoma; died June 13, 1979, in Canoga Park, California; m. Jose Granson, 1957. ❖ Brown-eyed child star of over 150 "Our Gang" comedies (1935–45); other films include *The Bohemian Girl, Born to Sing, The Calypso Heat, The Bat* and *The Helen Morgan Story*; with husband, formed the vocal group "Darla Hood and the Enchanters," providing background music for such films as *A Letter to Three Wives.*

HOOD, Lady (1783–1862). *See Stewart-Mackenzie, Maria.*

HOOD, Mary (c. 1822–1902). New Zealand merchant. Name variations: Mary Lye, Mary Hoskin. Born Mary Lye, c. 1822 (baptized, Dec 25, 1822) in Martock, Somersetshire, England; died on Nov 4, 1902, in New Plymouth, New Zealand; dau. of John Lye (farmhand) and Grace (Rodd) Lye; m. Peter Facey Hoskin (blacksmith), 1842 (died 1860); m. Archibald Hood (soldier), 1862; children: (1st m.) 10; (2nd m.) 2. ❖ Immigrated to New Zealand with family (1841); managed 1st husband's general store, providing groceries, haberdashery, and fancy goods before and after his death. ❖ See also *Dictionary of New Zealand Biography* (Vol. 2).

HOOD, Sarah (1942—). *See Killough, Lee.*

HOODLESS, Adelaide (1857–1910). Canadian welfare reformer. Born Adelaide Sophia Hunter in Brantford, Ontario, Canada, Feb 27, 1857; died in Toronto, Ontario, Feb 26, 1910; m. John Hoodless (businessman), 1881; children: 4 (perhaps more). ❖ Following death of son from drinking contaminated milk (1889), began a campaign for improved home conditions and education for expectant mothers in nutrition, sanitation and housekeeping; taught classes at Young Women's Christian Association (YWCA) in Hamilton, becoming president (1892), and started a school of domestic science; unable to secure government funding, raised money to build Macdonald Institute, which became part of Ontario Agricultural Institute at Guelph (1904); was responsible for formation of women's department of Farmers' Institute (later named The Women's Institute of Stoney Creek, 1897), which served as a model for similar rural societies which sprang up throughout the world. Her birthplace became a historic site (1967).

HOOKER, Evelyn (1907–1996). American psychologist. Born Evelyn Gentry in North Platt, Nebraska, 1907; died in Santa Monica, California, Nov 18, 1996; University of Colorado, MA; Johns Hopkins University, PhD, 1932; m. 2nd husband Edward Niles Hooker (died 1957); no children. ❖ Pioneering researcher on homosexuality during 1950s, joined faculty of University of California, Los Angeles (1932) and remained there for 30 years; conducted early studies on homosexuality and delivered findings to American Psychological Association (APA, 1956); published results as "The Adjustment of the Male Overt Homosexual" in *Journal of Projective Techniques* (1957), studies which eventually led the APA to remove homosexuality as a psychological disorder from its *Diagnostic and Statistical Manual*; headed a study group on homosexuality for National Institute of Mental Health (1967), which recommended a repeal of sodomy laws and better public education about homosexuality; after retiring from UCLA (1970), went into private practice and also established the Placek Fund of the American Psychological Foundation, which provides money for research into homosexuality.

HOOKER, Isabella Beecher (1822–1907). American suffragist. Name variations: Isabella Beecher. Born Isabella Beecher in Litchfield, Connecticut, Feb 22, 1822; died in Hartford, CT, Jan 25, 1907; dau. of Reverend Lyman Beecher and his 2nd wife Harriet (Porter) Beecher; half-sister of Catharine Beecher and Harriet Beecher Stowe; educated mainly in schools founded by half-sister Catharine; m. John Hooker (lawyer and real-estate entrepreneur), Aug 1841. ❖ Influenced by husband's studies and the essays of John Stuart Mill, became interested in the law as it related to women; joined forces with Susan B. Anthony, Elizabeth Cady Stanton, and Paulina Wright Davis to help found New England Woman Suffrage Association (1868); organized Connecticut Woman Suffrage Association (1869), remaining president until 1905;

lobbied the state legislature for a married women's property act; was a main speaker at National Woman Suffrage Association convention in Washington, DC (1870); spent next few years lobbying in Washington, along with friend Victoria Woodhull. ❖ See also *Women in World History.*

HOOPER, Challis (1894–1982). *See Hooper, Kate Challis Excelsa.*

HOOPER, Ellen Sturgis (1812–1848). American poet. Born Feb 17, 1812; died of TB, Nov 3 or 4, 1848; dau. of William Sturgis (1782–1863, sea captain and merchant) and Elizabeth M. Davis (dau. of Judge John Davis); sister of Caroline Sturgis Tappan; m. Robert William Hooper (1810–1885), doctor): children: Nella Hooper Gurney (1838–1887); Edward William Hooper (who m. Fanny Hudson Chapin, 1844–1881); (Marian) Clover Adams (1843–1885). ❖ Author of hymns and lyrical verse, including *Beauty and Duty.* ❖ See also *Women in World History.*

HOOPER, Jessie Jack (1865–1935). American suffragist and antiwar activist. Name variations: Jessie Annette Hooper. Born Jessie Annette Jack, Nov 8, 1865, in Winneshiek County, Iowa; died May 8, 1935, in Oshkosh, Wisconsin; dau. of David A. Jack Jr. and Mary Elizabeth (Nelings) Jack; m. Ben C. Hooper (attorney), May 30, 1888; children: 1 daughter. ❖ Served as legislative chair and 1st vice president, among other positions, of Wisconsin Woman Suffrage Association (1915–19); became director of National American Woman Suffrage Association (1919); elected 1st president of Wisconsin League of Women Voters (1920); ran unsuccessfully as Democratic candidate for US Senate (1922); stumped for Democratic presidential candidate John W. Davis (1924); campaigned for 1928 Kellogg-Briand Pact; helped present peace petition, with more than 8 million signatures, to League of Nations disarmament conference in Geneva, Switzerland (1932).

HOOPER, Kate. Australian water-polo player. Born in Western Australia. ❖ Won a team gold medal at Sydney Olympics (2000).

HOOPER, Kate Challis (1894–1982). New Zealand nurse, nursing administrator, community worker, and feminist. Name variations: Challis Hooper. Born Kate Challis Excelsa Hooper, June 25, 1894, at Davenport, Auckland, New Zealand; died Nov 29, 1982, at Lower Hutt, New Zealand; dau. of Richard Henry Hooper (farmer and journalist) and Sophia Francis (Hould) Hooper. ❖ Served as general nurse in Wellington (c. 1921); became involved in Plunket Society and was assistant matron of Karitane Hospital in Wanganui (1932); appointed matron of Wellington Clinic and Training School for Dental Nurses in Wellington (1937); active in New Zealand Trained Nurses' Association and council member of Wellington branch of New Zealand Registered Nurses' Association; contributed significantly to New Zealand Federation of Business and Professional Women's Clubs and served as president of Council for Equal Pay and Opportunity (1957); member of New Zealand National Commission for UNESCO (1954–56); founding member of Joint Committee on Women and Employment (1964–68). Awarded OBE (1969). ❖ See also *Dictionary of New Zealand Biography.*

HOOPER, Marian "Clover" (1843–1885). *See Adams, Clover.*

HOOVER, H.M. (1935—). American science-fiction writer. Name variations: Helen Mary Hoover. Born April 5, 1935, in Stark County, Ohio; dau. of Edward Lehr (teacher) and Sadie (Schandel) Hoover; attended Mount Union College and Los Angeles County School of Nursing. ❖ Works of science fiction for children and young adults include *Children of Morrow* (1973), *The Delikon* (1977), *The Lost Star* (1980), *This Time of Darkness* (1982), *The Shepherd Moon* (1984), *Orvis* (1987), *Away is a Strange Place to Be* (1989), and *The Winds of Mars* (1995).

HOOVER, Mrs. Herbert (1874–1944). *See Hoover, Lou Henry.*

HOOVER, Katherine (1937—). American composer, flautist, and lecturer. Born in Elkins, WV, Dec 2, 1937; studied flute at Eastman School of Music under Joseph Mariano and with William Kincaid in Philadelphia; Manhattan School of Music, MA. ❖ Had active concert career with leading orchestras and appeared frequently on tv; taught theory and flute at Manhattan School of Music; an important figure in musical world, both as a composer and activist, originated the concept of a women's musical festival which featured works that had been overlooked; composed many pieces for orchestra, chamber orchestra, piano and voice, as well as sacred music. ❖ See also *Women in World History.*

HOOVER, Lou Henry (1874–1944). American first lady. Born Mar 28, 1874, in Waterloo, Iowa; died Jan 7, 1944, in New York, NY; dau. of

Florence (Weed) Henry and Charles Delano Henry (banker); graduate of San Jose Normal School, 1893; degree in geology from Stanford, 1898; m. Herbert Hoover (president of US), Feb 10, 1899; children: Herbert Hoover Jr. (b. 1903); Allan Henry Hoover (b. 1907). ❖ One of the most neglected and forgotten first ladies of the 20th century, was the 1st to give speeches on the radio, and used her connections with the Girl Scouts to fight the hard times that accompanied the Depression; lived with husband in Tientsin (Tianjin) during Boxer Rebellion (1900); learned to read Chinese during their stay and studied the culture extensively; during next 15 years, followed husband's mining career around the world, circling the globe 5 times; trapped in London at start of WWI (1914), served as president of Society of American Women in London, proving herself to be an efficient organizer on behalf of relief activities in England, France and Belgium; as acting commissioner for Girl Scouts in Washington, DC, rose steadily in the organization, serving as national president (1922–25) and then chairing the national board of directors (1925–28); convinced of the importance of sports for women, was vice president of Women's Division of the National Amateur Athletic Federation (1920s); served as first lady of US (1929–33); was denounced by Texas Legislature and several other legislatures in the South for abusing her position as first lady, when she invited the wife of a congressional representative to the White House who was African-American (1929); during Depression, stressed volunteer service to help destitute Americans. ❖ See also Dale C. Mayer, ed. *Lou Henry Hoover: Essays on a Busy Life* (1993); Helen B. Pryor, *Lou Henry Hoover: Gallant First Lady* (1969); and *Women in World History*.

HOPE, Eva (1834–1909). See Farningham, Marianne.

HOPE, Lady Francis (1869–1938). See Yohé, May.

HOPE, Laura Lee (c. 1893–1982). See Adams, Harriet Stratemeyer.

HOPE, Laurence (1865–1904). See Nicolson, Adela Florence.

HOPE, May (1869–1938). See Yohé, May.

HOPEKIRK, Helen (1856–1945). Scottish pianist. Born Edinburgh, Scotland, May 20, 1856; died in Cambridge, Massachusetts, of a cerebral thrombosis, Nov 19, 1945; dau. of Adam Hopekirk (music-shop proprietor) and Helen (Croall) Hopekirk; studied piano with George Lichtenstein; received lessons in harmony, counterpoint, and composition with A.C. Mackenzie; studied with Carl Reinecke and Salomon Jadassohn (composition), Louis Maas (piano) and E.F. Richter (counterpoint) in Leipzig, 1876–78; studied under Theodor Leschetizky in Vienna; studied composition with Karel Navrátil in Vienna, and composition and orchestration under Richard Mandl in Paris; m. William A. Wilson (Edinburgh merchant and music critic), Aug 4, 1882 (died 1926); along with husband, became US citizen (1918). ❖ Made debut with the Leipzig Gewandhaus Orchestra (1878); after moving to America, became a champion of the music of Edward MacDowell; often performed music of the contemporary French school (Debussy and Fauré); taught for many years at New England Conservatory of Music in Boston; as a composer, best-known works were a Concert Piece as well as a Concerto for Piano and Orchestra; also arranged and edited Scottish folk songs for piano. ❖ See also Hall and Hall, *Helen Hopekirk, 1856–1945* (1954); and *Women in World History*.

HOPF, Alice L. (1904–1988). See Lightner, A.M.

HOPKINS, Ellice (1836–1904). English social reformer. Born Ellice Jane Hopkins in Cambridge, England, Oct 1836; died May 1904; mother was a talented musician; father was a distinguished mathematics tutor at Cambridge University. ❖ An Evangelical feminist, taught in Sunday schools; lectured on Christian morals to working-class men; involved in rescue and reform work, began Ladies Associations for the Care of Friendless Girls, to tackle underlying causes of prostitution (1876); at a time when suspected prostitutes were detained under the Contagious Diseases Acts and incarcerated by the Church of England, was convinced they should be offered love and forgiveness, not punishment; helped pass an amendment to Industrial Schools Act (1880), making it a criminal offense for children under age 16 to live with parents who worked in brothels; convinced that men must also change, founded a men's social purity organization, White Cross Army (1883); helped found National Vigilance Association (1885); wrote numerous pamphlets on social purity, including "The Visitation of Dens" (1874), "Notes on Penitentiary Work" (1879), "Village Morality" (1882), "How to Start Preventive Work" (1884), "Homely Talk on the New Law for the Protection of Girls" (1886) and "The National Purity Crusade" (1904). ❖ See also

Rosa M. Barrett, *Ellice Hopkins: A Memoir* (Wells Gardner, 1907); and *Women in World History*.

HOPKINS, Emma Curtis (1853–1925). American leader of New Thought movement. Born Sept 2, 1853, in Killingly, Connecticut; died April 25, 1925, in New York, NY; dau. of Rufus D. and Lydia (Phillips) Hopkins; attended Woodstock Academy in CT; m. George I. Hopkins (teacher), July 19, 1874 (div.); children: John (died 1905). ❖ Student of Mary Baker Eddy, served on editorial staff of *Christian Science Journal* (1884–85); established Christian Science Theological Seminary which met in her home (1887); published magazine *Christian Metaphysician* (1887–97); established successful Emma Hopkins College of Metaphysical Science, which helped impact influence of women in field; known as "Teacher of Teachers" in New Thought movement, taught many of movement's prominent teachers and leaders, including Charles and Myrtle Page Fillmore; published *High Mysticism* (12 vols, 1920–22).

HOPKINS, Juliet (1818–1890). Confederate hospital administrator. Born Juliet Ann Opie, May 7, 1818, in Jefferson Co., Virginia; died Mar 9, 1890, in Washington, DC; buried with military honors in Arlington National Cemetery; dau. of Hierome Lindsay Opie and Margaret (Muse) Opie; attended Miss Ritchie's school, Richmond; m. Alexander George Gordon (lieutenant in US Navy), May 1837 (died 1849); m. Arthur Francis Hopkins (president of Mobile and Ohio Railroad and justice of Alabama supreme court), Nov 7, 1854; children: (adopted niece) Juliet Opie. ❖ During Civil War, volunteered as superintendent of Alabama section of Chimborazo Hospital in Richmond, Virginia; when Alabama legislature named her husband state hospital agent (1861), took over actual duties of the appointment, administering the staffing and managing the field and base hospitals; undertook battlefield rescue missions herself and, at battle of Seven Pines, suffered a bullet wound in hip that left her with a limp. ❖ See also *Women in World History*.

HOPKINS, Miriam (1902–1972). American actress. Born Ellen Miriam Hopkins, Oct 18, 1902, in Bainbridge, Georgia; died of heart attack, New York, NY, Oct 9, 1972; attended Goddard Seminary and Syracuse University; m. Brandon Peters (actor), 1926 (div. 1931); m. Austin Parker, 1931 (div. 1932), m. Anatole Litvak (director), 1937 (div. 1939); m. Raymond B. Brock, 1945 (div. 1951). ❖ Made Broadway debut in *The Music Box Revue* (1921), then successfully switched to plays, such as *An American Tragedy* (1926), *Excess Baggage* (1927), *Lysistrata* (1930) and *Anatol* (1931); made auspicious screen debut in *Fast and Loose* (1930), followed by *The Smiling Lieutenant* (1931), *Dr. Jekyll and Mr. Hyde* (1932) and *Design for Living* (1933), which established her as a star; turned to comic performance in *Trouble in Paradise* (1932) and was considered effectively brittle in title role in *Becky Sharp* (1935); other films include *Barbary Coast* (1935), *These Three* (1936), *The Old Maid* (1939), *Old Acquaintance* (1943), *The Heiress* (1949), *Outcasts of Poker Flat* (1952), *Carrie* (1952), *The Children's Hour* (1962), *Fanny Hill* (1964) and *The Chase* (1966). ❖ See also *Women in World History*.

HOPKINS, Pauline E. (1859–1930). African-American writer, editor, and playwright. Name variations: (pseudonym) Sarah A. Allen. Born in Portland, Maine, 1859; died in Cambridge, Massachusetts, Aug 13, 1930; never married; no children. ❖ Prolific 19th-century African-American writer, was overlooked until 4 of her novels, including best-known *Contending Forces: A Romance Illustrative of Negro Life North and South*, were reprinted as part of Schomburg Library's "Nineteenth Century Black Women Writers" series; wrote short stories, biographical sketches, and the novels *Hagar's Daughter*, *Winona* and *Of One Blood*; also served as editor of *The Colored American*, the 1st black magazine established in 20th century and the main forum for her work; was also an actress and singer of note. ❖ See also *Women in World History*.

HOPKINS, Peggy (1893–1957). See Joyce, Peggy Hopkins.

HOPKINS, Priscilla (1756–1845). See Kemble, Priscilla.

HOPKINS, Sarah Winnemucca (c. 1844–1891). See Winnemucca, Sarah.

HOPKINS, Shirley Knight (1936—). See Knight, Shirley.

HOPKINS, Thelma (1936—). Irish track-and-field athlete. Born Mar 16, 1936, in Ireland. ❖ Representing Great Britain, tied with Mariya Pisareva for the silver medal in the high jump at Melbourne Olympics (1956).

HOPPE, Marianne (1909–2002). German actress of stage and screen. Born in Rostock, Germany, April 26, 1909; died Oct 23, 2002, in Siegsdorf, Bavaria; attended Königin Luise Academy; studied acting at

Deutsches Theater; m. Gustav Gründgens (actor-director), June 22, 1926 (div. 1946); children: Benedikt. ❖ Made debut at Bühne der Jugend, or Young People's Theatre Group, in Berlin (1928); joined Max Reinhardt's Deutsches Theater, where she often played masculine roles; known for her modern acting style, worked in Frankfurt am Main (1930–32), after which she joined the Kammerspiele in Munich, where for several years she acted under director Otto Falckenberg; made screen debut in *Judas von Tirol* (Judas of the Tyrol, 1933), then appeared in *Heideschulmeister Uwe Karsten* (Schoolmaster Uwe Karsten, 1933); became one of Germany's leading film actresses after appearing as Elke in *Der Schimmelreiter* (The Rider of the White Steed); best known for her serious roles, notably in the melodramas *Auf Wiedersehen, Franziska!* (1941) and *Romanze in Moll* (Romance in a Minor Key, 1943), and appearances in such Americanized films as *Capriolen* (Caprices, 1938) and *Kongo-Express* (1939); also praised for her performance as Effi Briest in *Der Schritt vom Wege* (The False Step, 1939), directed by husband; made tv debut in long-running detective series "Der Komissar" (The Commissioner, 1961); last memorable stage performances was as the mother in Tankred Dorst's *Chimborazo* in Berlin (1975). Named a permanent member of West Germany's Akademie der Künste (1965). ❖ See also *Women in World History.*

HOPPER, Mrs. DeWolf (1873–1919). *See Bergen, Nella.*

HOPPER, Edna Wallace (1864–1959). American comedic actress and singer. Born Jan 17, 1864, in San Francisco, CA; died Dec 12 (some sources cite Dec 14), 1959, in New York, NY; m. (William) DeWolf Hopper (actor who would later marry Hedda Hopper, div.); m. A. O. Brown, 1908. ❖ Made NY stage debut in *The Club Friend* (1891); also appeared in *Lend Me Your Wife, Yankee Doodle Dandy, About Town, Floradora, The Silver Slipper, Fifty Miles from Boston* and *Jumping Jupiter.*

HOPPER, Grace Murray (1906–1992). American computer engineer. Born Grace Brewster Murray in New York, NY, Dec 9, 1906; died Jan 1, 1992, in Arlington, Virginia; dau. of Walter Fletcher Murray (insurance broker) and Mary Campbell (Van Horne) Murray; Vassar College, BA in mathematics and physics, 1928; Yale University, MA in mathematics, 1930, PhD in mathematics, 1934; m. Vincent Foster Hopper, 1930 (div. 1945); no children. ❖ Rear admiral, US Naval Reserve, who pioneered computer technology for military and business applications and was a primary inventor of the standard computer language COBOL; became teacher of mathematics at Vassar (1931); enlisted in US Naval Reserve (Dec 1943); commissioned as a lieutenant (junior grade, June 1944); assigned to Bureau of Ordnance Computation Project at Harvard University to work on the Mark I Automatic Sequence Controlled Calculator (1944); while working in private industry, developed COBOL computer language (1960); achieved rank of rear admiral (1985); retired from navy (1986). Was 1st recipient of the Computer Science "Man-of-the-Year" award from Data Processing Management Association (1969); was 1st American to become a Distinguished Fellow of British Computer Society (1973); inducted into Engineering and Science Hall of Fame (1984). ❖ See also Charlene W. Billings, *Grace Hopper: Navy Admiral and Computer Pioneer* (Enslow, 1989); and *Women in World History.*

HOPPER, Hedda (1885–1966). American actress and gossip columnist. Name variations: Elda Curry; Elda or Ella Furry; Elda Millar. Born Elda Furry, May 2, 1885, in Hollidaysburg, Pennsylvania; died Feb 1, 1966; dau. of David Furry (butcher) and Margaret (Miller) Furry; studied at Carter Conservatory of Music, Pittsburgh, c. 1903; m. William DeWolf Hopper, May 8, 1913 (div. 1922); children: William DeWolf Hopper Jr. (b. 1915, actor). ❖ Wielding considerable power, wrote syndicated gossip column (1938–66) and hosted radio gossip program (1936); appeared in more than 100 films, including *Sherlock Holmes* (1922), *The Women* (1939), *Breakfast in Hollywood* (1946), *Sunset Boulevard* (1950) and *The Oscar* (1966). ❖ See also autobiographies *From Under My Hat* (1952) and *The Whole Truth and Nothing But* (1963); George Eells, *Hedda and Louella* (Putnam, 1972); and *Women in World History.*

HOPPER, Victoria (1909—). Canadian-born actress and singer. Born May 24, 1909, in Vancouver, British Columbia, Canada; m. Basil Dean (actor, div.); m. Peter Walter. ❖ Made highly successful London debut in title role of *Martine* (1933), followed by *The Shop at Sly Corner, Vanity Fair* and *. . . Said the Spider!,* among others; became a popular leading lady of British stage and films in 1930s and toured for troops in France, North Africa and Middle East during WWII; films include *The Constant Nymph, Lorna Doone, Laburnum Grove, Whom the Gods Love, The Lonely Road, The Mill on the Floss* and *Escape from Broadmoor.*

HOPTON, Susanna Harvey (1627–1708). British devotional writer. Born Susanna Harvey, 1627, in England; died July 12, 1702, in Herefordshire, England; m. Richard Hopton (died 1696). ❖ Converted to Roman Catholicism but reverted to Anglicanism; undertook works of charity and, despite lack of formal education, wrote erudite devotional works, including *Daily Devotions Consisting of Thanksgivings, Confessions, and Prayers* (1673), *Devotions in the Ancient Way of Offices* (1700), *Letter to Father Turbeville* in *Second Collection of Controversial Letters* (ed. G. Hickes, 1710), and *Hexaemeron, or Meditations on the Six Days of the Creation and Meditations and Devotions on the Life of Christ* in *Meditations and Devotions, in Three Parts* (ed. N. Spinckes, 1717).

HORE, Kerry (1981—). Australian rower. Born July 3, 1981, in Australia; attended University of Tasmania. ❖ Won World championship for quadruple sculls (2003); won a bronze medal for quadruple sculls at Athens Olympics (2004).

HORN, Camilla (1903–1996). German-born actress. Born April 25, 1903, in Frankfurt am Main, Germany; died Aug 14, 1996, in Gilching, Germany; m. Rudolf Mühlfenzl; m. Robert Schnyder; m. Kurt Kurfis; m. Klaus Geerz. ❖ Made film debut as Gretchen in F.W. Murnau's *Faust* (1926); in US, starred in *Tempest, Eternal Love* and *The Royal Box*; later appeared in many British and Italian productions.

HORN, Catherine (1932—). *See Horne, Katharyn.*

HORN, Miriam Burns (1904–1951). American golfer. Name variations: Miriam Burns, Miriam Tyson. Born Miriam Burns, Feb 3, 1904, in Kansas City, Missouri; died Mar 19, 1951; m. (c. 1926). ❖ Won the Western Amateur (1923, 1930); won the USGA Women's Amateur and Trans-Mississippi Amateur (1927).

HORNA, Kati (1912–2000). Hungarian-born photographer. Born May 19, 1912, in Budapest, Hungary, of Spanish descent; died in Oct 19, 2000, in Mexico City, Mexico; m. José Horna (painter and sculptor), 1938. ❖ Spanish Civil War photographer, studied photography in Hungary; began career in Paris (1933); arrived in Spain shortly after Civil War began (1936) and worked for Propaganda Committee of the anarchist trade union, Confederación Nacional de Trabajo; worked as a photographer and graphics editor for leftist journals (1937–38)—including anarchist publications *Tierra y Libertad* (*Land and Liberty*), *Tiempos Nuevos* (*New Times*) and *Mujeres Libres* (*Free Women*)—portraying the war's effects on civilians within territory held by the Republic; with outbreak of WWII, went to Veracruz, Mexico (1939), where she and husband provided a hub for exiled and Mexican surrealists. The Spanish Ministry of Culture purchased her negatives for the National Historical Archives collection on the Civil War (1979).

HORNBY, Lesley (b. 1946). *See Twiggy.*

HORNE, Alice Merrill (1868–1948). American educator, legislator, social and political activist. Born in Fillmore, Utah, Jan 2, 1868; died Oct 7, 1948; dau. of Clarence Merrill (telegraph operator and farmer) and Bathsheba (Smith) Merrill (thespian); granddau. of Bathsheba Bigler Smith; graduate of University of Deseret (later University of Utah), 1887; m. George H. Horne (banker), Feb 20, 1890; children: Mary (b. 1890), Lyman (b. 1896, who m. Myrtle Horne), Virginia (b. 1899), George Jr. (1902–1903), Zorah (b. 1905) and Albert (b. 1910). ❖ As chair of Utah Liberal Arts Committee for World's Columbian Exposition (1893), published a book of poems written by Utah women poets and illustrated by Utah women artists; as a Democrat, became state representative (1899), the 2nd woman in Utah to be elected to a state office; as a legislator, sponsored a bill to establish an umbrella state agency for the arts; as chair of the University Land-Site Bill, placed the University of Utah in its present location; represented National Women's Relief Society and US at International Congress of Women in Berlin (1904), and gave invited addresses on Utah art movement; established art galleries (1921) and sold 474 paintings from more than 40 exhibiting artists within 10 years. ❖ See also *Women in World History.*

HORNE, Janet (d. 1727). Scot accused of being a witch. Executed by burning in a barrel of tar, 1727. ❖ The last to be executed as a witch before the 1736 repeal of Scotland's Witchcraft Act, had a daughter whose hands and feet were deformed; was charged with casting a spell to put horseshoes on her daughter so that she could be ridden like a pony and used for transportation; in 17th-century Scotland, it is estimated that 4,500 women were executed by stoning, crushing, drowning and burning at the stake.

HORNE, Katharyn (1932—). American ballet dancer. Name variations: Catherine Horn. Born Catherine Horn, June 20, 1932, in Fort Worth, TX; dau. of Catherine Collie Horn and William Sullivan Horn. ❖ Performed locally with Fort Worth Civic Ballet early on in career; moved to NY where she continued her training with Margaret Craske and Antony Tudor; as Catherine Horn, danced with Ballet Theater (1951–56), where she appeared in featured roles in John Taras' *Designs with Strings,* Balanchine's *Theme and Variations,* David Lichine's *Helen of Troy,* and other works; received great acclaim for her performances in Agnes de Mille's *Rodeo* and *Fall River Legend*; danced with Metropolitan Opera Ballet (1957–65) and in numerous works by James Waring, Anton Dolin, and Ron Sequoio for Manhattan Festival Ballet; taught with Craske at Manhattan School of Dance upon retirement; served as artistic director of Omaha Ballet.

HORNE, Lena (1917—). African-American singer and actress. Born Lena Horne, June 30, 1917, in Brooklyn, NY; m. Louis Jones, 1937 (div. 1940); m. Lennie Hayton (musician, composer), 1947 (died Feb 1971); children: (1st m.) Gail Lumet Buckley (b. 1937); Teddy Jones (1940–1971). ❖ Spent most of childhood on the road with mother, an actress; dropped out of high school at 16 to join chorus line at Harlem's Cotton Club (1933); toured with Noble Sissle's Society Orchestra, then Charlie Barnet's band (it was Barnet who taught her emotional phrasing and dramatic overtones which would become trademarks of her style); released 1st album for RCA, *The Birth of the Blues,* and made 1st appearance at NY's Café Society Downtown; signed 7-year contract with MGM (1941), though film roles were mainly limited to cameo singing appearances, including *The Duke Is Tops* (1938), *Panama Hattie* (1942), *As Thousands Cheer* (1943), *Broadway Rhythm* (1944), *Ziegfeld Follies* (1946); *Till the Clouds Roll By* (1946) and *Words and Music* (1948); starred in 2 film adaptations of Broadway musicals featuring top black entertainers, *Cabin in the Sky* and *Stormy Weather,* the film that gave Horne her signature song; blacklisted from film and tv industry during McCarthy era (1950s); active in Civil-Rights campaign (1960s); returned to screen (1969) in 1st non-musical role *Death of a Gunfighter*; made *The Wiz* (1978); career spanned over 6 decades. Won a Tony, Grammy, and Drama Desk award for record-breaking one-woman show, *Lena Horne: The Lady and Her Music* (1982); received Kennedy Center's Lifetime Achievement Award (1984). ❖ See also autobiography (with Richard Schickel) *Lena* (Doubleday, 1965); Brett Howard, *Lena* (Holloway, 1981); Gail Lumet Buckley, *The Hornes: An American Family* (Knopf, 1986); and *Women in World History.*

HORNE, Marilyn (1929—). American mezzo-soprano. Born Marilyn Bernice Horne in Bradford, PA, Jan 16, 1929; studied with father and with William Vennard, Lotte Lehmann and Gwengolyn Koldofsky; attended University of Southern California; Rutgers University, MusD, 1970; Jersey City State College, DLitt; attended St. Peter's College; m. Henry Lewis (composer). ❖ Made debut as Háta in Smetana's *The Bartered Bride,* Los Angeles Guild Opera (1954); appeared at Venice Festival by invitation of Igor Stravinsky (1956); appeared as Marie in Berg's *Wozzeck* at San Francisco Opera (1960) and Covent Garden (1964); made debut at La Scala in *Oedipus Rex* (1969) and at Metropolitan Opera as Adalgisa in Bellini's *Norma* (1970); other roles include Rosina in *Barber of Seville* and Neocle in *The Siege of Corinth,* both at La Scala (1969), and Isabella in *L'Italiana in Algiere* and title role in *Carmen,* both at Metropolitan Opera (1972–73); also appeared with American Opera Society of NY for several seasons which included roles in *Iphigenie en Tauride* and *Semiramide*; appeared with Vancouver Opera (Adalgisa in *Norma*) and at Philharmonic Hall, NY; appeared as Italiana at La Scala (1975), as Rosina at Vienna Opera (1978); recorded for London (often with Joan Sutherland), Columbia, and RCA records; received several Grammy awards. ❖ See also autobiography *My Life* (1984); and *Women in World History.*

HORNE, Myrtle (1892–1969). Utah nurse. Name variations: Myrtle Clara; Myrtle Carolyn. Born Myrtle Clara Swainston, Mar 24, 1892, in Cottonwood, Wyoming; died in Salt Lake City, Utah, Dec 3, 1969; Hospital School of Nursing, Salt Lake City, LDS, 1918; m. Lyman Merrill Horne, MD, Jan 3, 1923. ❖ Was superintendent of the Kapi'olani Hospital in Honolulu (1918–22) and president of Utah State Nurses Association (1927–30); gave frequent lectures. ❖ See also *Women in World History.*

HORNEBER, Petra (1965—). German shooter. Born April 21, 1965, in Floss, Germany. ❖ Won World championship (1994); won a silver medal for 10m air rifle at Atlanta Olympics (1996).

HÖRNER, Silke (1965—). East German swimmer. Name variations: Silke Hoerner. Born Sept 12, 1965, in East Germany. ❖ At Seoul Olympics, won a bronze medal in 100-meter breaststroke and gold medals in 4 x 100-meter medley relay and 200-meter breaststroke (1988).

HORNEY, Brigitte (1911–1988). German actress. Pronunciation: HORN-eye. Born in Berlin, Germany, Mar 29, 1911; died of heart failure in Hamburg, Germany, July 27, 1988; dau. of Oscar Horney and Karen Horney (1885–1952), prominent psychoanalyst); studied at Berlin's Academy of Dramatic Arts; m. Konstantin Irmen-Tschet; m. Hanns Swarzenski (curator for Decorative Arts at Boston Museum for Fine Arts), c. 1953. ❖ Major film star who also enjoyed a considerable following abroad, made film debut in *Abschied* (Farewell, 1930), then appeared on stage at Berlin's Volksbühne (People's Theater) for next 4 years; starred on screen in *Ein Mann will nach Deutschland* (A Man Wants to Go to Germany, 1934); made a number of films which were immensely popular with Germans, especially *Savoy-Hotel 217* (1936), *Befreite Hände* (Unfettered Hands, 1939), *Das Mädchen von Fanö* (The Girl from Fanö, 1941), and *Münchhausen* (1943); when her film, *Am Ende der Welt* (At the End of the World, 1944), was banned by Goebbels, fled to Switzerland (1945); began appearing on Zurich stage, including starring roles in plays by such playwrights as Max Frisch and Jean-Paul Sartre; moved to US and eventually received dual West German–US citizenship; returned to West Germany on regular basis to appear in tv dramas and starred in highly popular West German tv series, "Das Erbe der Guldenburgs" (Legacy of the Guldenburgs), in which she portrayed the matriarch of a German brewing dynasty. ❖ See also *Women in World History.*

HORNEY, Karen (1885–1952). German-American psychoanalyst. Pronunciation: HORN-eye. Name variations: Karen Danielsen. Born Karen Clementine Danielsen, Sept 15, 1885, in Eilbek, Germany; died Dec 4, 1952, in NY; dau. of Berndt Wackels Danielsen (sea captain) and Clotilde (von Ronzelen) Danielsen; m. Oskar Horney (economist), 1909 (sep. 1920); lived with Gertrude Lederer-Eckardt (physical therapist); children: Brigitte Horney (1911–1988, actress); Marianne Horney Lederer Von Eckardt (b. 1913, psychiatrist); Renate Horney (b. 1915). ❖ Theorist and author on psychoanalysis and human psychology, was among the most influential of 20th-century psychologists through her critiques and revisions of Freudian theory, arguing that women's development had to be viewed on its own terms, not seen as a derivative of male development; studied medicine at University of Berlin (1909–13); entered analysis (1911); received medical degree (1913); trained at Lankwitz Sanitarium (1914–18); taught at Berlin Psychoanalytic Institute (1920–32); served as assistant director of Institute for Psychoanalysis in Chicago (1932–34); taught at NY Institute for Psychoanalysis (1934–41); founded American Institute for Psychoanalysis and Association for the Advancement of Psychoanalysis (1941); writings include *The Neurotic Personality of Our Time* (1927), *New Ways in Psychoanalysis* (1939), *Self-Analysis* (1942), *Our Inner Conflicts* (1945) and *Neurosis and Human Growth* (1950). Karen Horney Clinic founded in NY (1952). ❖ See also Susan Quinn, *A Mind of Her Own: The Life of Karen Horney* (Simon & Schuster, 1987); Jack Rubins, *Karen Horney: Gentle Rebel of Psychoanalysis* (Dial, 1978); and *Women in World History.*

HORNIBROOK, Ettie Annie (1877–1936). *See Rout, Ettie Annie.*

HORNIG-MISELER, Carola (1962—). East German rower. Name variations: Carola Miseler. Born April 30, 1962, in East Germany. ❖ At Seoul Olympics, won a gold medal in coxed fours (1988).

HORNIMAN, Annie (1860–1937). English theater patron and manager. Name variations: Miss Horniman; Miss A.E.F. Horniman. Born Annie Elizabeth Fredericka Horniman, Oct 3, 1860, in Manchester, England (some sources cite Forest Hill, London); died Aug 6, 1937; dau. of Rebecca (Emslie) Horniman and F.J. Horniman (tea merchant); studied at Slade Art School. ❖ A major influence in early 20th-century theater in England and Ireland, who pioneered the modern repertory movement, served as William Butler Yeats secretary for 5 years; funded a rep season at London's Avenue Theater (later the Playhouse), which included the 1st commercial presentation of Yeats' play *The Land of Heart's Desire* (1894); turned attention to Irish National Theater (later Irish National Dramatic Society), pet project of Yeats and Lady Augusta Gregory, then purchased 2 adjacent buildings in Dublin (1904) and transformed them into the Abbey Theatre; purchased and refurbished Gaiety Theater (1908), Manchester, making it England's 1st repertory theater and producing more than 200 plays, most of them directed by Lewis Casson (husband of

Sybil Thorndike, a member of the company, 1908–17); major support of George Bernard Shaw. Awarded rank of Companion of Honour. ❖ See also Rogers, W.G. *Ladies Bountiful* (Harcourt, 1968).

HORNY, Katherine (1969—). Peruvian volleyball player. Born in Peru. ❖ At Seoul Olympics, won a silver medal in team competition (1988).

HOROVITZ, Frances (1938–1983). British poet. Born 1938 in London, England; died of cancer, Oct 2, 1983, at 45; dau. of F.E. Hooker; attended Bristol University and Royal Academy of Dramatic Art; m. Michael Horovitz (poet), 1964; m. Roger Garfitt (poet), 1983; children: (1st m.) son (b. 1971). ❖ Began career as actress; published 1st poems in magazine *New Departures*; poetry collections include *Poems* (1967), *The High Tower* (1970), *Snow Light, Water Light* (1983), *Collected Poems* (1985) and *Water Over Stone* (1980), which contained a powerful elegy about her father; a celebrated poetry reader, often made recordings, and was involved with 3 programs for the BBC, reading the work of Russian women poets.

HORRELL, Elizabeth (1826–1913). New Zealand teacher. Name variations: Elizabeth Moore. Born Elizabeth Moore, April 21, 1826, in Devon, England; died on Jan 18, 1913, at Morrinsville, New Zealand; dau. of John Moore (farm bailiff); m. John Horrell (carpenter), 1849 (died 1897); children: 12. ❖ Immigrated to New Zealand (1830); performed teaching duties during voyage and was appointed assistant schoolmistress in Lyttelton upon arrival, becoming Canterbury's 1st woman schoolteacher. ❖ See also *Dictionary of New Zealand Biography* (Vol. 1).

HORSBRUGH, Florence (1889–1969). British politician. Name variations: Baroness Horsbrugh. Born Florence Gertrude Horsbrugh in Edinburgh, Scotland, 1889; died in Edinburgh, Dec 6, 1969; dau. of Henry Moncrieff Horsbrugh (chartered accountant) and Mary Harriet Stark (Christie) Horsbrugh; attended Lansdowne House, Edinburgh, and St. Hilda's, Folkestone, Kent; never married. ❖ Served as a member of Parliament, representing Dundee, the 1st Conservative from that district in 100 years (1931–45); was parliamentary secretary for Ministry of Health (1939–45); was parliamentary secretary for Ministry of Food (1945); appointed minister of education by Winston Churchill (Nov 2, 1951), becoming the 1st woman to hold a post of Cabinet rank in a Conservative government; served in that position until 1954; played an important role in the preparatory stage of creating a national health system for entire UK and did much to advance the cause of women. Named Commander of British Empire (CBE, 1929); made a life peer (1959). ❖ See also *Women in World History.*

HORSLEY, Alice Woodward (1871–1957). New Zealand physician, bacteriologist, pathologist, and anaesthetist. Name variations: Alice Woodward. Born Alice Woodward, on Feb 3, 1871, near Auckland, New Zealand; died on Nov 7, 1957, at Papatoetoe, New Zealand; dau. of William Woodward (farmer and schoolteacher) and Laura (Young) Woodward (schoolteacher); University of Otago Medical School, 1900; m. Arthur John Horsley (pharmacist), 1903; children: 3 daughters, 1 son. ❖ First woman doctor to register in Auckland (1900), established private practice there (1902); at Auckland Hospital, served as honorary bacteriologist and pathologist (1902–03), then honorary anaesthetist (1915–30s); was on anaesthetics staff at Mater Misericordiae Hospital (1936–46); served as primary doctor for Dock Street Mission medical clinic, from early 1930s. Order of British Empire (1939). ❖ See also *Dictionary of New Zealand Biography* (Vol. 3).

HORSTMANN, Dorothy M. (1911–2001). American epidemiologist and virologist. Born Dorothy Millicent Horstmann, July 2, 1911, in Spokane, WA; died Jan 11, 2001, in New Haven, CT; attended University of California at Berkeley; University of California at San Francisco, MD, 1940; never married. ❖ Polio pioneer, showed that the polio virus reached the brain by way of the blood, a finding that upended previous thinking and helped make polio vaccines possible; was the 1st woman appointed a professor at Yale School of Medicine (1961) and the 1st woman to receive an endowed chair there (1969), which was in epidemiology and pediatrics; elected to National Academy of Sciences; served as president of Infectiouis Diseases Society of America.

HORTA, Maria Teresa (1937—). Portuguese writer and feminist. Name variations: The Three Marias. Born in Lisbon, May 20, 1937; studied at Lisbon Arts Faculty; married with children. ❖ Published 1st volume of poetry, *Espelho Inicial* (1960), followed by 1st novel, *Ambas as Mãos sobre o Corpo* (1970); published *Minha Senhora de Mim* (Milady of Me), a collection of poems, confiscated by censors, that celebrated the female body (1971); with Maria Velho da Costa and Maria Isabel Barreno, wrote and published *Novas Cartas Portuguesas* (*The New Portuguese Letters*, 1972), which led the modern feminist literary movement in Portugal and achieved notoriety because of the government's attempt to suppress the work; became national figure, defended by prominent writers and international feminist organizations; continued to explore feminist themes in later poetry and novels: *Os Anjos* (1983), *Ema* (1984), *Cristina* (1985), *Minha Mãe, Meu Amor* (1986), *Rosa Sangrenta* (1987) and *Paixão Segundo Constança H* (1994); co-authored a work on abortion rights, *Aborto: Direito ao Nosso Corpo* (1975). ❖ See also *The Three Marias: New Portuguese Letters* (trans. by Helen R. Lane, Doubleday, 1975); and *Women in World History.*

HORTENCIA (1959—). See Marcari Oliva, Hortencia.

HORTENSE, Queen (1783–1837). See Hortense de Beauharnais.

HORTENSE DE BEAUHARNAIS (1783–1837). French composer, artist, queen and regent of Holland, and mother of Napoleon III. Name variations: Hortense, Queen of Holland; Hortense Beauharnais; Hortense Bonaparte; Eugenie Hortense de Beauharnais. Born Eugénie Hortense de Beauharnais in Paris, France, April 10, 1783; died in Arenenberg, Switzerland, Oct 5, 1837; dau. of Alexander (d. 1794), vicomte de Beauharnais, and Empress Josephine (1763–1814), Joséphine Tascher de la Pagerie, later Bonaparte); sister of Eugene de Beauharnais (1781–1824, viceroy); stepdau. and sister-in-law of Napoleon I; dau.-in-law of Letizia Bonaparte (1750–1836); m. Louis Napoleon (Napoleon's brother who would become king of Holland), 1802; children: Charles Napoleon (1802–1807); Napoleon Louis (1804–1831); Louis Napoleon (1808–1873), later Napoleon III, king of France (r. 1852–1870). ❖ Spent early years on island of Martinique; after father's death by guillotine during Reign of Terror (July 1794), became stepdaughter of Napoleon I (1796); at 18, was married to Napoleon's brother Louis (1802), a marriage doomed from the start; when husband was made king of Holland after French troops conquered that country, became queen; composed many romantic songs in both French and German (her *Partant pour la Syrie* became the national song of France when son Napoleon III reigned); when husband abdicated throne in favor of son Napoleon Louis, was made regent; with Napoleon I's fall from power (1815), fled to Switzerland. ❖ See also *Women in World History.*

HORTENSIA (fl. 1st c. BCE). Roman orator. Fl. in 1st century BCE; dau. of Quintus Hortensius Hortalus (114–50 BCE), a Roman orator known as Hortensius, who, as a leader of the aristocratic party, often clashed with or worked with the orator Cicero. ❖ Protested a proposed law that would allow women's possessions to be taxed to fund a civil war (42 BCE), arguing that women should not be required to fund men's follies when women were not legally involved in the decision making.

HORTON, Ann (1743–1808). Duchess of Cumberland and Strathearn. Name variations: Ann or Anne Luttrell. Born Jan 24, 1743 (some sources cite 1742), in St. Marylebone, London, England; died Dec 28, 1808, in Trieste, Italy; dau. of Simon Luttrell, Lord Irnham, 1st earl of Carhampton, and Judith Maria Lawes; m. Christopher Horton, Aug 4, 1765 (died); m. Henry Frederick (1745–1790), duke of Cumberland and Strathearn, Oct 2, 1771; children: (1st m.) one son. ❖ Was a widow when she married Henry Frederick, brother to King George III (1771), without the king's consent (it was announced from the palace that any who paid court to the duke and duchess would not be received by the king and queen). ❖ See also *Women in World History.*

HORTON, Christiana (c. 1696–c. 1756). English actress. Born c. 1696; died c. 1756. ❖ Discovered by actor-manager Barton Booth at Southwark Fair; 1st appeared in London at Drury Lane as Melinda in *The Recruiting Officer* (1714), and remained there for next 20 years, followed by 15 years at Covent Garden, cast in all the leading tragedy and comedy parts; was the original Mariana in Fielding's *Miser* (1733); also appeared as Mrs. Millamant in *Way of the World* and as Belinda in *Old Bachelor.*

HORTON, Ellen (1840–1910). See Foster, J. Ellen.

HORTON, Gladys (1944—). African-American pop singer. Name variations: Marvelettes. Born in 1944 in Inkster, Michigan. ❖ Was founder and member of the Marvelettes, a popular Motown group whose songs "Don't Mess With Bill," "Please Mr. Postman," "I Keep Holding On" and "Beachwood 4–5789" reached the top of the charts (early 1960s); other members included Georgia Dobbins, Katherine Anderson, Juanita Cowart. ❖ See also *Women in World History.*

HORTON, Judith Ellen (1840–1910). *See Foster, J. Ellen.*

HORTON, Lillias Stirling (1851–1921). *See Underwood, Lillias.*

HORTON, Mildred McAfee (1900–1994). **American college president and military leader.** Name variations: Mildred McAfee. Born Mildred Helen McAfee in Parkville, Missouri, May 12, 1900; died in Randolph, New Hampshire, Sept 2, 1994; dau. of Dr. Cleland Boyd (minister) and Harriet (Brown) McAfee; Vassar College, BA, 1920; attended Columbia University; University of Chicago, MA, 1928; m. Douglas Horton (minister and the 1st world leader of the Congregational Christian Churches), 1945. ❖ Seventh president of Wellesley College and director of US Navy's WAVES during WWII, served as dean of women and professor of sociology at Centre College, Kentucky (1927–32); served as dean of the college of women at Oberlin (1934–36); chosen president of Wellesley College (1936); appointed director of women's reserve of US Naval Reserve (1942), with rank of lieutenant commander; held rank of captain (1943–46); resigned as president of Wellesley College (1949) to join husband in church and educational work in NYC; became 1st female president of American Board of Commissioners for Foreign Missions of the Congregational Christian Churches (1959). ❖ See also *Women in World History.*

HORTON, Stirling (1851–1921). *See Underwood, Lillias.*

HORVAT-FLOREA, Elena (1958—). **Romanian rower.** Name variations: Elena Florea. Born July 4, 1958, in Romania. ❖ At Los Angeles Olympics, won a gold medal in coxless pairs (1984).

HORVATH, Julia (1924–1947). **American ballet dancer.** Born 1924 in Cleveland, Ohio; died in plane crash, May 30, 1947, in Maryland. ❖ Trained at School of American Ballet in NY; performed as soloist with Ballet Russe de Monte Carlo (1940s), where she danced featured roles in *Les Sylphides, Raymonda, Gaité Parisienne,* and others; performed on Broadway for Balanchine's *Song of Norway* (1944) and as principal dancer for Teatro Municipal of Rio de Janeiro; partnering with George Starett, was bound for an engagement in Rio de Janeiro when their plane crashed.

HORVATHNE, Gyongyi. *See Szalay Horvathne, Gyongyi.*

HORWICH, Frances (1908–2001). **American educator.** Name variations: Frances Rappaport Horwich. Born Frances Rappaport on July 16, 1908, in Ottawa, Ohio; died on July 22, 2001, of heart failure in Scottsdale, Arizona; graduate of University of Chicago, 1929; Columbia University, MA, 1933; m. Harvey L. Horwich, June 1931. ❖ Supervised Chicago nursery schools for Works Progress Administration (until 1935); worked in various administrative and counseling positions in Chicago schools; for NBC, developed, wrote, and hosted the 1st educational tv show for preschoolers, "Ding Dong School" (beginning 1952); published series of Ding Dong School Books (beginning 1954); served as supervisor of children's tv for NBC (1955–56); also wrote *Miss Frances' All-Day-Long Book* (1954), *Stories and Poems to Enjoy* (1962) and *The Magic of Bringing Up Your Child* (1959).

HOSAIN, Attia (1913–1998). **Indian actress, journalist, novelist and short-story writer.** Born 1913 in Lucknow, India; died Jan 25, 1998. ❖ After Partition in India (1947), moved to England and worked for BBC's Eastern Service; also acted on stage and tv; published *Phoenix Fled* (1953) and *Sunlight on a Broken Column* (1961).

HOSKENS, Jane Fenn (1694–c. 1750). **American memoirist.** Born 1694 in London, England; died c. 1750. ❖ Wrote about childhood illness, conversion to Quakerism, and travels through North America as preacher in autobiography, *The Life and Spiritual Sufferings of That Faithful Servant of Christ, Jane Hoskens* (1771).

HOSKIN, Mary (c. 1822–1902). *See Hood, Mary.*

HOSKINS, Olive (1882–1975). **American US Army warrant officer.** Born in Pasadena, CA, possibly Dec 2, 1882; died possibly Oct 1975 in Los Altos, CA. ❖ Became civilian-grade headquarters clerk in US Army (1907); appointed army field clerk (1916); became (1st woman) army warrant officer (1926); in charge of personnel at Judge Advocate's Office, San Francisco, CA (during WWI); served in Philippines (1919–22, 1933–36), in Omaha, NE (1922–33) and in San Francisco, CA (until retirement, 1937).

HOSMER, Harriet (1830–1908). **American sculptor.** Name variations: Hatty. Born Harriet Goodhue Hosmer, Oct 9, 1830, in Watertown, Massachusetts; died Feb 21, 1908, in Watertown; dau. of Hiram Hosmer (physician), and Sarah (Grant) Hosmer; studied sculpture with Paul Stephenson in Boston. ❖ The 1st American woman to achieve an international reputation as a neoclassical sculptor, was denied admittance to Boston Medical School's anatomy course; moved to St. Louis, studied anatomy at Missouri Medical College; created 1st major sculpture, *Hesper, the Evening Star* (1852); traveled to Rome (1852); studied with John Gibson; established reputation in Rome (1853) with marble busts of *Daphne* and *Medusa,* followed by full-length *Oenone* (1855); completed 2 popular sculptures, *Puck* and *Will o' the Wisp,* followed by critically acclaimed *Beatrice Cenci* (1857); her 7-foot marble, *Zenobia* (1859) brought international praise; rendered last full-scale sculpture *Queen Isabella* for World's Columbian Exposition in Chicago (1893); her statues grace the Metropolitan Museum of Art, National Gallery of Art, London Academy, and other venues of distinction. ❖ See also Cornelia Carr, ed. *Harriet Hosmer: Letters and Memories* (1912); Dolly Sherwood, *Harriet Hosmer: American Sculptor; 1830–1908* (U. of Missouri Press, 1991); and *Women in World History.*

HOSPITAL, Janette Turner (1942—). **Canadian novelist and short-story writer.** Born 1942 in Australia; Queen's University, MA in literature. ❖ Worked as librarian at Harvard University; immigrated to Canada (1971); writings, which often deal with alienation and cultural dislocation, include *The Ivory Swing* (1982), *The Tiger in the Tiger Pit* (1983), *Borderline* (1985), *Dislocations* (1986), *Charades* (1989), *Isobars* (1990) and *Oyster* (1998).

HOSSAIN, Rokeya Sakhawat (1880–1932). **Bengal Muslim emancipator and educator.** Name variations: Begum Rokeya Sakhawat Hossain. Born Rokeya Saber in rural Rangpur (present-day Bangladesh), 1880; died 1932; sister of Karimunnessa Saber (poet); m. Sakhawat Hossain (deputy magistrate of Bhagalpur); no children. ❖ Managed to receive an education from eldest brother, Ibrihim Saber; started a school with a handful of local girls, personally conducting them to school in a specially designed *purdahnasheen* carriage; established the successful Sakhawat Memorial Girls' School in Calcutta (1911); simultaneously campaigned for emancipation of *purdahnasheen* women by establishing the Bengal branch of Anjuman-e-Khawatin Islam (1916); was also a noted writer, producing a novel, several plays, poems, and short stories; published best-known work, *Sultana's Dream,* in *Indian Ladies Magazine* (1905). ❖ See also *Women in World History.*

HOTCHKISS, Avis (fl. 1915). **American motorcyclist.** Lived in Brooklyn, NY; children: Effie Hotchkiss. ❖ With daughter Effie, embarked on 5,000-mile motorcycle journey to San Francisco, CA (1915), riding in the sidecar of the Harley-Davidson, then returned to NY; considered by some as the 1st motorcycle tourer.

HOTCHKISS, Effie (fl. 1915). **American motorcyclist.** Lived in Brooklyn, NY; dau. of Avis Hotchkiss. ❖ Unsatisfied with working on Wall Street, embarked on 5,000-mile motorcycle journey to see Panama-Pacific International Exposition in San Francisco, CA, with mother Avis in the sidecar (1915), then rode rig back to NY, becoming the 1st known women to make round-trip transcontinental trip on motorcycle alone.

HOTCHKISS, Hazel (1886–1974). *See Wightman, Hazel Hotchkiss.*

HOTOT, Agnes (fl. 14th c.). **English noblewoman.** Fl. 14th century in England; dau. of the earl of Dudley. ❖ When father was too sick to participate in a jousting tournament to settle a dispute against another earl, went in his place; easily hid her identity from opponent with helmet and armor, then proceeded to win the tournament. ❖ See also *Women in World History.*

HOU YUZHU (1963—). **Chinese volleyball player.** Born Feb 7, 1963, in China. ❖ Won a gold medal at Los Angeles Olympics (1984) and a bronze medal at Seoul Olympics (1988), both in team competition.

HOUDETOT, Sophie, Comtesse d' (1730–1813). **French poet.** Name variations: Countess d'Houdetot; Mme Houdetot. Name variations: Sophie de Bellegarde. Born Élisabeth Françoise Sophie de la Livé de Bellegardé in Paris, France, 1730; died Jan 22, 1813; dau. of Louis-Denis de la Livé de Bellegardé (rich fermier-général) and Madame de Bellegarde (d. 1743, sister of Florence-Angelique Prouveur de Preux, who was the mother of Madame d'Épinay); sister of Alexis Janvier de La Live de La Briche (1735–1785, secretair honoraire des commandements to Marie Antoinette); sister-in-law and cousin of Mme d'Epinay (1726–1783); m. the comte de Houdetot, 1748; children: son César Louis Marie François Ange (b. 1749) was governor of Martinique. ❖ A sometime poet known more for her charm than beauty, had a relationship with Marquis de Saint Lambert which lasted until his death (1753); met Jean-Jacques Rousseau while staying with her cousin Mme d'Épinay at Montmorency; received a great deal of notoriety as the subject of Rousseau's *Confessions* in which he describes his unrequited passion for her. Her poetry was included in a volume of the work of Saint-John Crèvecour (1833).

HOUGHTON, Edith (1912—). American baseball player. Born Feb 12, 1912, in Philadelphia, PA. ❖ At 10, began playing shortstop for Philadelphia Bobbies; joined other teams, including Passaic (NJ) Bloomer Girls and Hollywood Bloomer Girls, often playing against minor league teams; tried out and was accepted by the Fisher A.A.'s, a men's semipro team (1933), playing first base; played for Roverettes; hired by the Philadelphia Phillies (1946), the 1st woman to work as a major league scout. ❖ See also *Women in World History.*

HOUGHTON, Frances (1980—). English rower. Born Sept 19, 1980, in Oxford, England; attended Kings College, London. ❖ Won a silver medal for quadruple sculls at Athens Olympics (2004).

HOULD-MARCHAND, Valérie (1980—). Canadian synchronized swimmer. Name variations: Valerie Marchand. Born May 29, 1980, in Riviere-Du-Loup, Quebec, Canada. ❖ Won a team silver medal at Atlanta Olympics (1996).

HOULT, Norah (1898–1984). Irish novelist, journalist and short-story writer. Born Sept 20, 1898, in Dublin, Ireland, of Anglo-Irish parentage; died April 1984. ❖ Accepted a position on editorial staff of Sheffield *Daily Telegraph,* where she worked for 2 years; subsequently worked for Pearson's Magazines in London, wrote book reviews for Yorkshire *Evening Post,* became active as a freelance journalist, and wrote fiction; 1st book, a collection of short stories titled *Poor Women,* was well-received; novels include *Holy Ireland, Father and Daughter, Husband and Wife, There Were No Windows, Only Fools and Horses Work* and *Not for Our Sins Alone.*

HOUSDEN, Jane (d. 1714). English coiner. Executed Sept 19, 1714 (some sources cite 1712). ❖ While in dock awaiting sentence for coining at Old Bailey, encouraged her lover William Johnson to shoot a turnkey named Spurling in court; was tried, convicted, and condemned to death with Johnson for the murder, with Spurling's body lying in front of the bench.

HOUSDEN, Nina (1916—). American murderer. Born in Kentucky, 1916; m. Charles Housden. ❖ Lived in Highland Park, Michigan, with husband until her pathological jealousy caused him to file for divorce and move out (1947); invited him over for a drink, strangled him and dismembered the body (Dec 18, 1947); enroute to Kentucky, had car trouble in Toledo, Ohio, where a mechanic discovered husband's leg wrapped in one of many packages in back seat; sentenced to life imprisonment.

HOUSTON, Cissy (1933—). African-American gospel singer. Name variations: Emily Houston. Born Emily Drinkard, Sept 30, 1933, in Newark, NJ; dau. of Nitch and Delia Drinkard; sister of Anne, Nicky and Larry Drinkard of the Drinkard Singers; aunt of Dionne Warwick (singer); married, c. 1953 (div. c. 1955); m. John Houston, 1959 (sep. 1980, div. 1993); children: Gary, Michael, and Whitney Houston (singer). ❖ Sang 1st with family's gospel group, the Drinkards; formed the Gospelaires trio with Dee and Dionne Warwick; was a member of 1960s soul group the Sweet Inspirations, which scored a few pop hits and sang backup for Aretha Franklin, Elvis Presley, Neil Diamond and Dusty Springfield; released solo album *Cissy Houston* and was 1st to record "Midnight Train to Georgia" (1971); sang back up for Chaka Khan, Luther Vandross and others (1980s); hosted weekly radio show from Newark's New Hope Baptist Church (1980s); performed NY club dates with daughter (1980s); won Grammys for Gospel albums *Face to Face* (1996) and *He Leadeth Me* (1997). ❖ See also autobiography, *How Sweet the Sound: My Life with God and Gospel* (1998).

HOUSTON, Lucy (1858–1936). English philanthropist. Name variations: Lady Houston; Dame Fanny Houston. Born Fanny Lucy Radmall, 1858 (some sources cite 1857) in St. Margarets, Twickenham, England; died Dec 29, 1936; m. Theodore Brinckman (future baronet), 1883 (div. 1895); m. George Gordon, 9th Lord Byron, 1901 (died 1917); m. Sir Robert Paterson Houston, 1924 (died 1926). ❖ When last husband died (1926), was bequeathed most of his fortune and moved to island of Jersey to avoid income tax; by then, her politics had veered to extreme right; bought weekly *Saturday Review* and catered to fascist-minded readers, but when it came to aviation, was ahead of her time; financed the struggling Schneider Trophy (1931), wherein seaplanes competed over water, and financed Clydesdale's flight over Mt. Everest to great fanfare in 1933. Without her involvement, there might never have been a fighter plane dubbed a Spitfire, and Spitfires

would win the Battle of Britain, earning her the titles "Fairy Godmother of the RAF" and "The Woman who Won the War." Made Dame of the British Empire (DBE, 1917), for founding a rest home for nurses during WWI. ❖ See also *Women in World History.*

HOUSTON, Margaret Lea (1819–1867). First lady of Texas. Born Margaret Moffette Lea, April 11, 1819, near Marion, Alabama; died during yellow fever epidemic, 1867, in Independence, Texas; dau. of Temple Lea and Nancy (Moffette) Lea; attended Judson Female Institute; became 3rd wife of Sam Houston (1793–1863, who was instrumental in earning Texas its independence and statehood), May 9, 1840; children: 4 sons, 4 daughters; grandmother of Margaret Bell Houston (d. 1966, American novelist and poet). ❖ Sam Houston was married for only 1 year to 1st wife Eliza Allen; he then married Tiana Rogers, a Cherokee, in 1830. ❖ See also Madge Thornall Roberts, *Star of Destiny: The Private Life of Sam and Margaret Houston* (1998); and *Women in World History.*

HOUSTON, Thelma (1946—). African-American pop singer. Born May 7, 1946, in Leland, Mississippi; thrice married; thrice div.; children: Kimberlynn and Rodney. ❖ Disco diva with gospel-tinged delivery, sang in Mississippi churches; scored 1st hit with cover of Laura Nyro's "Save the Country" (1970); received critical praise for debut album *Sunshower* (1971); acted in films *Death Scream* (1975) and *Norman . . . Is That You?* (1976); hit #1 with disco classic "Don't Leave Me This Way"; scored lesser hits with "Saturday Night, Sunday Morning" (1979) and "You Used to Hold Me So Tight" (1984); recorded music for soundtrack of film *Lean on Me* (1989); performed on tv's "It's Showtime at the Apollo" (2004).

HOUSTON, Whitney (1963—). African-American pop singer. Born Whitney Elizabeth Houston, Aug 9, 1963, in East Orange, NJ; dau. of John and Cissy Houston (gospel singer); m. Bobby Brown (musician), 1992; children: Bobbi Kristina. ❖ Began performing in mother's night-club act at 15; appeared on cover of *Vogue* before signing recording contract; signed with Arista records and released debut album *Whitney Houston* (1985); had hits "You Give Good Love" (1985), "How Will I Know" (1985) and "Greatest Love of All" (1986); from next album, *Whitney* (1987), scored more hits with "I Wanna Dance With Somebody," "So Emotional" and "Love Will Save the Day" (1987); made successful transition to film acting, starring in *Waiting to Exhale* (1995) and *The Bodyguard* (1992), with a soundtrack that included hit covers of Dolly Parton's "I Will Always Love You" and Chaka Khan's "I'm Every Woman"; pursued a more urban image with album *Your Love is My Love* (1998), which included the hits "Heartbreak Hotel" (1999) and "It's Not Right But It's Okay" (1999); exacerbated pre-existing diva image with erratic behavior (early 2000s).

HOUTER, Marleen (1961—). Dutch gymnast and tv commentator. Born Dec 11, 1961, in Hoorn, Netherlands. ❖ Was the Dutch national champion on vault and a member of the Dutch team (1976–80); has her own tv sports program and serves as news anchor in the Netherlands.

HOVICK, Rose Louise (1914–1970). *See Lee, Gypsy Rose.*

HOVING, Jane (1908–1992). *See Pickens, Jane.*

HOVLAND, Ingeborg (1969—). Norwegian soccer player. Born Oct 3, 1969, in Norway. ❖ Won a team gold medal at Sydney Olympics (2000).

HOW-MARTYN, Edith (1875–1954). English reformer. Born Edith How in Cheltenham, England, 1875; died in Sydney, Australia, Feb 4, 1954; degree from University College, Aberystwyth; London University, DSc in economics; m. Herbert Martyn, 1899. ❖ An early recruit to Women's Social and Political Union (WSPU), was arrested for attempting to make a speech in lobby of House of Commons (1906); critical of leadership of WSPU, helped found Women's Freedom League (WFL, 1907), and was its secretary until 1911, when she began heading the political and militant department; stood unsuccessfully as an Independent Feminist candidate in General Election (1918); had more success when she stood for Middlesex County Council, becoming its 1st woman member; also lent energy to birth-control movement led by Marie Stopes; founded Birth Control International Information Centre (BCIIC) with Margaret Sanger (1929); also wrote *The Birth Control Movement in England* (1931) and accompanied Sanger on travels through India (1935–36); with war approaching, moved to Australia (1939). ❖ See also *Women in World History.*

HOWARD, Ada Lydia (1829–1907). American educator. Name variations: Mrs. A.L. Howard. Born Dec 19, 1829, in Temple, New

Hampshire; died Mar 3, 1907, in Brooklyn, NY; graduate of Mount Holyoke Seminary (now Mount Holyoke College), 1853; never married; no children. ❖ Began teaching at Mount Holyoke Seminary (1858); took a teaching post at Western College for Women (now Western College) in Oxford, Ohio, and also served as principal of women's department at Knox College in Galesburg, Illinois (1866–69); opened her own school, Ivy Hall, in Bridgeton, NJ (1869); named 1st president of Wellesley College (1875); retired due to illness (1881). ❖ See also *Women in World History*.

HOWARD, Agnes (1476–1545). *See Tylney, Agnes.*

HOWARD, Anne (1475–1511). English princess and duchess of Norfolk. Name variations: Lady Anne Howard; Lady Anne Plantagenet. Born Nov 2, 1475, at Westminster Palace, London, England; died Nov 23, 1511 (some sources cite 1513); interred at Framlingham, Suffolk, England; dau. of Edward IV (b. 1442), king of England (r. 1461–1483), and Elizabeth Woodville (1437–1492); became 1st wife of Thomas Howard (1473–1554), 3rd duke of Norfolk (r. 1524–1554), Feb 4, 1494 or 1495; children: 2 sons and 2 daughters (all died young). ❖ Following her death, Thomas Howard married Elizabeth Stafford (1494–1558).

HOWARD, Anne (d. 1559). Countess of Oxford. Name variations: Anne de Vere. Died in 1559 (some sources claim she died before Feb 22, 1558); interred at Lambeth Parish Church; dau. of Thomas Howard (1443–1524), earl of Surrey and 2nd duke of Norfolk (r. 1514–1524), and Agnes Tylney (1476–1545); m. John de Vere, 14th earl of Oxford.

HOWARD, Anne (1557–1630). *See Arundel, Ann.*

HOWARD, Anne (d. 1662). *See Somerset, Anne.*

HOWARD, Blanche Willis (1847–1898). American author. Name variations: Countess von Teuffel. Born Blanche Willis Howard, July 21, 1847, in Bangor, Maine; died Oct 7, 1898, in Munich, Germany; dau. of Daniel Mosely Howard (insurance broker) and Eliza Anne (Hudson) Howard; m. Julius von Teuffel (court physician to King of Würtemburg), 1890 (died 1896); no children. ❖ Published 1st novel *One Summer* (1875), which sold over 50,000 copies; settled in Stuttgart, Germany, and wrote romantic novels with European settings; also wrote *Seven on the Highway* (1897), *Dionysius the Weaver's Heart's Dearest* (1899), usually regarded as her best work, and *The Garden of Eden* (published posthumously, 1900); an accomplished pianist, was a friend of Wagner and Liszt.

HOWARD, Caroline (1794–1888). *See Gilman, Caroline Howard.*

HOWARD, Caroline Cadette (1821–?). New Zealand employment agent, immigration officer, lecturer, and journalist. Name variations: Caroline Cadette Bollin, Caroline Cadette Alpenny, Caroline Cadette Blanchard; (pseudonym) Carina. Born Caroline Cadette Bollin, Aug 3, 1821, probably in London, England; dau. of Charles (plumber) and Ann Bollin; m. William Morris Alpenny (artist), 1843; m. George Richard Howard, 1867 (died 1872); m. Edward Litt Laman Blanchard (playwright and critic), 1874 (died 1889); children: (1st m.) perhaps 1 daughter. ❖ Established flax farm in Ireland to provide work for women and children (1850s); sailed to New Zealand in charge of a group of women and assisted matron of immigrants' barracks (1862); lectured to promote educational and cultural pursuits in colony; established servants' registry office (1863); returned to England after 2nd husband's death; traveled between London and Ireland seeking Irish women for New Zealand immigration scheme; became recruiting agent for Queensland government (1875); under pseudonym Carina, published articles on immigration and colonial life for periodicals; claimed to have sent more than 12,000 people to Australia and New Zealand. ❖ See also *Dictionary of New Zealand Biography* (Vol. 1).

HOWARD, Caroline Sarah (1876–1934). *See Low, Caroline Sarah.*

HOWARD, Catherine (fl. 1450). Baroness Berners. Name variations: Lady Berners; Katherine. Fl. around 1450; dau. of John Howard (1420–1485), 1st duke of Norfolk (r. 1483–1485), and Margaret Howard (fl. 1450); m. John Bourchier, 1st baron Berners; children: Henry Bourchier, 2nd baron Berners (d. 1471); Joan Neville (fl. 1468, who m. Henry Neville).

HOWARD, Catherine (d. 1452). English noblewoman. Name variations: Catherine or Katherine Hungerford; Catherine Molines or Catherine Moleyns. Died 1452; dau. of William Hungerford, Lord Moleyns, and Margery Hungerford; 1st wife of John Howard (1420–1485), 1st duke of

Norfolk (r. 1483–1485); children: Thomas Howard (1443–1524), earl of Surrey and 2nd duke of Norfolk (r. 1514–1524); Anne Howard (who m. Sir Edmund Gorges); Isabel Howard; Jane Howard; Margaret Howard.

HOWARD, Catherine (d. after 1478). Baroness Abergavenny. Name variations: Katherine. Died after 1478; dau. of Sir Robert Howard and Margaret Mowbray; became 2nd wife of Edward Neville, baron Abergavenny (r. 1438–1476), Oct 15, 1448. Edward's 1st wife was Elizabeth Beauchamp.

HOWARD, Catherine (1520/22–1542). Queen of England. Born between 1520 and 1522 in Lambeth, England; beheaded for adultery and treason, Feb 13, 1542, in the Tower of London; interred at Chapel Royal, Tower of London; dau. of Lord Edmund Howard and Joyce Culpeper; 1st cousin of Anne Boleyn (1507–1536); m. Henry VIII (1491–1547), king of England (r. 1509–1547), July 28, 1540. ❖ Young, headstrong woman who captured the heart of the aging Henry VIII and became his 5th wife; grew up in household of step-grandmother Agnes Tylney, duchess of Norfolk; came to court to serve in Anne of Cleves' household and fell in love with one of the king's courtiers, Thomas Culpeper; caught the attention of the king and was married to him (1540); began adulterous relationship with Culpeper (1541); her fall was swift; arrested (Nov 12, 1541), was condemned to die (Feb 11, 1542), under an Act of Attainder; not yet 21, was executed on the same block and in the same place as her cousin Anne Boleyn.

HOWARD, Catherine (d. 1548). English noblewoman. Died April 12, 1548; interred May 11, 1554; dau. of Thomas Howard (1443–1524), earl of Surrey and 2nd duke of Norfolk (r. 1514–1524), and Agnes Tylney (1476–1545); m. Rhys ap Gruffydd FitzUryan; children: Agnes FitzUryan; Griffith ap Rice FitzUryan.

HOWARD, Catherine (d. 1596). English noblewoman. Name variations: Lady Berkeley. Died 1596; dau. of Henry Howard (1517–1547), earl of Surrey, and Frances de Vere (d. 1577); m. Lord Henry Berkeley, in 1554. Lord Henry's 2nd wife was Jane Stanhope.

HOWARD, Catherine (d. 1633). *See Knyvett, Catherine.*

HOWARD, Catherine (d. 1672). Countess of Salisbury. Name variations: Catherine Cecil. Died Jan 27, 1672; dau. of Thomas Howard (1561–1626), 1st earl of Suffolk (r. 1603–1626), and Catherine Knyvett (d. 1633); m. William Cecil, 2nd earl of Salisbury; children: Elizabeth Cecil (1619–1689, who m. William Cavendish, 3rd earl of Devonshire); Anne Cecil (who m. Algernon Percy, 10th earl of Northumberland).

HOWARD, Catherine (d. 1874). English noblewoman. Died Jan 27, 1874; dau. of Henry Howard (1757–1842), High Sheriff Cumberland, and Catherine Mary Neave (d. 1849); m. Honorable Philip Stourton, July 28, 1829.

HOWARD, Cordelia (1848–1941). American actress. Name variations: Cordelia Howard Macdonald. Born Feb 1, 1848, in Providence, Rhode Island; died Aug 8, 1941, in Bourne, Massachusetts; dau. of George C. Howard (actor) and Caroline Emily Fox Howard (actress); m. Edmund Jesse Macdonald (businessman), June 21, 1871. ❖ Debuted at 2½ in *The Mountain Sylph* at Odeon Theatre in Boston, MA (June 15, 1850); best known for portrayal of Little Eva in *Uncle Tom's Cabin,* debuted in the role at Troy Museum in Troy, NY (Sept 27, 1852), then played the part in NY and on national tour until age 13; retired shortly thereafter (Dec 1861). Other roles include Little Dick (*Oliver Twist*), Katy (*Little Katy, or the Hot Corn Girl*), and Pearl (*The Scarlet Letter*).

HOWARD, Denean (1964—). African-American runner. Name variations: Denean Howard-Hill. Born Oct 5, 1964, in Sherman, TX; sister of Artra, Tina and Sherri Howard. ❖ In the 400 meters, took 1st place at World University Games (1987) and 3 consecutive 1sts at TAC championships (1981–83); won a gold medal at Los Angeles Olympics (1984), a silver medal at Seoul Olympics (1988) and a silver medal at Barcelona Olympics (1992), all in 4x400-meter relay.

HOWARD, Dorothy (fl. 1500). Countess of Derby. Dau. of Thomas Howard (1443–1524), earl of Surrey and 2nd duke of Norfolk (r. 1514–1524), and Agnes Tylney (1476–1545); m. Edward Stanley, 3rd earl of Derby, Feb 21, 1530; children: Maria Stanley; Henry Stanley, 4th earl of Derby.

HOWARD, Elizabeth (c. 1410–1475). Countess of Oxford. Name variations: Elizabeth de Vere. Born c. 1410; died in 1475 at Stratford Nunnery; interred at Austin Friars Church, London; dau. of John

Howard and Joan Walton; m. John de Vere, 12th earl of Oxford, in 1425; children: Aubrey de Vere; John de Vere (b. 1442), 13th earl of Oxford; Sir George de Vere.

HOWARD, Elizabeth (d. 1497). *See Tylney, Elizabeth.*

HOWARD, Elizabeth (1494–1558). Duchess of Norfolk. Born Elizabeth Stafford in 1494; died in 1558; dau. of Edward Stafford, 3rd duke of Buckingham (1478–1521, executed by order of Henry VIII); 2nd wife of Thomas Howard, 4th duke of Norfolk.

HOWARD, Elizabeth (d. 1534). Countess of Sussex. Name variations: Lady Fitzwalter. Died Sept 18, 1534; interred at Boreham; dau. of Thomas Howard (1443–1524), 2nd duke of Norfolk (r. 1514–1524), and Agnes Tylney (1476–1545); m. Henry Ratcliffe also known as Henry Radcliffe (c. 1506–1556), 2nd earl of Sussex, and 8th baron Fitzwalter, before May 21, 1524; children: Thomas Radcliffe (b. around 1525), 3rd earl of Sussex; Henry Radcliffe (b. around 1532), 4th earl of Sussex. Following Elizabeth Howard's death, Henry Radcliffe married Anne Calthorp.

HOWARD, Elizabeth (?–1538). Countess of Wiltshire. Birth date unknown; died April 3, 1538, at Barnard Castle, Durham, England; buried at Lambeth Church, London; dau. of Thomas Howard (1473–1554), earl of Surrey and 2nd duke of Norfolk, and Elizabeth Tylney (d. 1497); m. Thomas Boleyn, earl of Wiltshire, before 1507; children: George Boleyn, 2nd viscount Rochford (d. 1536); Mary Boleyn (d. 1543); Anne Boleyn (c. 1507–1536); Thomas and Henry (both died young).

HOWARD, Elizabeth (b. before 1566). *See Dacre, Elizabeth.*

HOWARD, Elizabeth (d. 1567). *See Leyburne, Elizabeth.*

HOWARD, Elizabeth (c. 1586–1658). *See Knollys, Elizabeth.*

HOWARD, Elizabeth (c. 1599–1633). *See Hume, Elizabeth.*

HOWARD, Elizabeth (d. 1704). *See Percy, Elizabeth.*

HOWARD, Elizabeth Ann (1823–1865). Countess of Beauregard and mistress of Napoleon III. Name variations: Miss Howard; Harriet Howard. Born Elizabeth Ann Haryatt in England in 1823; died 1865; m. Charles Trelawney, May 1854; children: (with a Major Martyn) son Martin (b. 1842). ❖ Ran off to London at age 16 with well-known jockey Jem Mason; passed off to a Major Martyn who treated her handsomely; met 39-year-old Louis Napoleon Bonaparte (soon to be Napoleon III, 1846); accompanied him to France when he became president; when Napoleon turned his attentions to Empress Eugénie, threatened scandal and was paid off; eventually, purchased the Château de Beauregard, near Paris, and was granted the title countess of Beauregard (1852). ❖ See also *Women in World History.*

HOWARD, Elizabeth Jane (1923—). British novelist. Born Mar 26, 1923, in London, England; dau. of David Liddon Howard and Katharine Margaret (Somervell) Howard; m. Peter Scott, 1942; m. James Douglas-Henry, 1960; m. Kingsley Amis (writer), 1965. ❖ Began career as an actress; writings, which often revolve around relationship conflicts among the middle class, include *The Beautiful Visit* (1950), *The Long View* (1956), *The Sea Change* (1959), *The Odd Girl Out* (1972), *Getting it Right* (1982), *Casting Off* (1995) and *Falling* (1999); also wrote *The Cazelet Chronicles: Light Years* (1990), *Marking Time* (1992) and *Confusion* (1994). ❖ See also *Slipstream: A Memoir* (2002).

HOWARD, Esther (1892–1965). American character actress of stage and screen. Born April 4, 1892, in Montana; died Mar 8, 1965, in Hollywood, CA. ❖ Began career on Broadway; films include *Vice Squad, Murder, My Sweet, Champion* and *All That I Have.*

HOWARD, Frances (d. 1577). *See Vere, Frances de.*

HOWARD, Frances (1593–1632). English murderer and countess of Somerset. Name variations: Lady Frances Howard; Lady Somerset. Born in England, May 31, 1593 (some sources cite 1590); died in Chiswick, Middlesex, England, Aug 23, 1632; dau. of Thomas Howard (1561–1626), 1st earl of Suffolk (r. 1603–1626), and Catherine Knyvett; sister of Elizabeth Knollys; m. Robert Devereux, 3rd/20th earl of Essex, Jan 5, 1605 (annulled 1613); m. Robert Carr (c. 1587–1645), later earl of Somerset, Dec 26, 1613; children: Anne Carr (1615–1684, who m. William Russell, 1st duke of Bedford, in 1637, and had 10 children). ❖ Something of a femme fatale, 1st appeared at court at 15 and immediately captured the attention of Robert Carr, a page and one of James I's male favorites; though married at 12 to Robert Devereux, earl of

Essex, entered into a love affair with Carr, keeping husband at bay by dosing his food with "debilitation powders" that rendered him impotent; after 2 years, petitioned James for an annulment of her marriage, which the king agreed to; when Sir Thomas Overbury criticized the annulment and was ordered by James I to Tower of London, sent Overbury food rations laced with exotic poisons which killed him (1613); received her annulment and married Carr; privileged life ended when one of the apothecaries involved in the murder plot made a deathbed confession; prosecuted at trial by Sir Francis Bacon (1616), was convicted and condemned to death, then pardoned by the king and banished with husband to a cloistered but comfortable life in the Tower; released (1622). ❖ See also David Lindley, *The Trial of Frances Howard* (Routledge, 1993); and *Women in World History.*

HOWARD, Frances (c. 1633–1677). *See Villiers, Frances.*

HOWARD, Frances (1903–1976). American actress. Name variations: Frances Goldwyn. Born June 4, 1903, in Omaha, Nebraska; died July 2, 1976, in Beverly Hills, CA; m. Robert Stevenson (director); m. Samuel Goldwyn (film producer), 1925; children: Samuel Goldwyn Jr. ❖ As an actress, films include *The Swan, Too Many Kisses* and *The Shock Punch;* collaborated with husband in producing many notable films.

HOWARD, Harriet (1823–1865). *See Howard, Elizabeth Ann.*

HOWARD, Henrietta (1669–1715). *See Somerset, Henrietta.*

HOWARD, Henrietta (1688–1767). English patron and paramour. Name variations: Countess of Suffolk; Lady Suffolk; Henrietta Hobart. Born Henrietta Hobart in Norfolk, England, in 1688 (some sources cite 1681); died July 26, 1767, in Marble Hill, Twickenham, Middlesex; dau. of Sir John Hobart and Elizabeth Maynard (d. 1701); m. Charles Howard (b. 1675), 9th earl of Suffolk, Mar 2, 1705 or 1706 (died 1733); m. Honorable George Berkeley, June 26, 1735 (died 1746); children: (1st m.) Henry Howard (1706–1745), 10th earl of Suffolk. ❖ One of England's most notable royal mistresses, also made her mark as a patron of letters and the arts; secured a position as Lady of the Bedchamber to Princess Caroline of Ansbach (1714), wife of Prince of Wales, future George II; became his lover (1720), in a relationship that would last for 13 years; began construction of a magnificent Palladian country house, called Marble Hill, on her lands in Middlesex (1724); became known as a patron of artists and writers, including 3 of the great English literary figures of the period: John Gay, Alexander Pope, and Jonathan Swift; also exchanged letters on philosophical issues with other aristocrats of her circle. ❖ See also Lewis Benjamin, *Lady Suffolk and Her Circle* (1924); Julius Bryant, *Mrs. Howard: A Woman of Reason* (1988); and *Women in World History.*

HOWARD, Isabel (fl. 1500s). English noblewoman. Fl. in the 1500s; dau. of Lord Edmund Howard (d. 1513) and Joyce Culpeper; sister of Catherine Howard (1520/22–1542, 5th wife of Henry VIII).

HOWARD, Jane (d. 1593). Countess of Westmoreland. Name variations: Jane Nevill; Jane Neville. Died in 1593; dau. of Henry Howard (1517–1547), earl of Surrey, and Frances de Vere (d. 1577); m. Charles Neville, earl of Westmoreland.

HOWARD, Jane (1934–1996). American biographer. Name variations: Jane T. Condon. Born Jane T. Condon, June 20, 1934, in Winnetka, Illinois; died June 28, 1996, in New York, NY; dau. of a political reporter for *Chicago Tribune;* graduate of University of Michigan. ❖ Began career doing profiles at *Life* magazine; best known for *A Different Woman* (1973), an account of the feminist movement, and her acclaimed biography of Margaret Mead (1984); also wrote *Families* (1978); taught writing at Yale, Columbia and University of Georgia.

HOWARD, Janette (1944—). Australian prime-ministerial wife. Born Janette Parker, 1944; m. John Howard (became 25th prime minister of Australia, 1996), 1971; children: Melanie (b. 1974), Tim (b. 1977), and Richard (b. 1980). ❖ Though an active member of the Liberal Party, preferred to fulfill public duties, writes one biographer, "out of the public gaze."

HOWARD, Jean (1910–2000). American photographer and actress. Name variations: Ernestine Mahoney. Born Ernestine Hill, Oct 10, 1910, in TX; died Mar 20, 2000, in Beverly Hills, CA; m. Charles K. Feldman (producer), 1934 (div. 1948). ❖ Noted Hollywood photographer, began career as an actress in such films as *Dancing Lady* and *The Final Hour;* published *Jean Howard's Hollywood* (1989).

HOWARD, Jessica (1984—). American rhythmic gymnast. Born Feb 4, 1984, in Jacksonville, Florida. ❖ Won Rhythmic Senior nationals (1999, 2000, 2001); won a team gold medal and silver medals for all-around, clubs, and hoops at Pacific Alliance championships (2002).

HOWARD, Joyce (fl. 1500s). English noblewoman. Fl. in the 1500s; dau. of Lord Edmund Howard (d. 1513) and Joyce Culpeper; sister of Catherine Howard (1520/22–1542, 5th wife of Henry VIII).

HOWARD, Katherine (1520/22–1542). *See Howard, Catherine.*

HOWARD, Kathleen (1879–1956). Canadian-born opera singer. Born July 27, 1879, in Clifton, Ontario, Canada; died Aug 15, 1956, in Hollywood, CA. ❖ Sang with the Metropolitan Opera (1916–28); became a fashion editor for *Harper's Bazaar* (1928); films include *Born to be Bad, The Bride Goes Wild,* and *Laura*; best remembered for role as W.C. Fields' wife in *It's a Gift* (1934) and *The Man on the Flying Trapeze* (1935).

HOWARD, Kathy (c. 1961—). American gymnast. Born c. 1961 in Oklahoma. ❖ Won Antibes International and a silver medal in floor exercises at Pan American Games (1975); won a silver medal in all-around at American Cup (1976).

HOWARD, Leslie (1956—). *See Burr, Leslie.*

HOWARD, Mabel (1893–1972). New Zealand politician and Cabinet official. Born April 18, 1893 (some sources cite 1894), in Australia; died June 23, 1972; dau. of Ted Howard (MP for Sydenham). ❖ Had a long, distinguished political career, which included 26 years in Parliament (1943–69) marked by a number of 1sts: was elected secretary of the New Zealand Federated Laborers Union (1942), the 1st woman to hold such a post; appointed minister of Health and Minister of Mental Hospitals (1947), the 1st woman to hold full Cabinet status; crafted and promoted New Zealand's 1st animal protection act. Championed women's and children's rights and campaigned for social security, housing provisions, and consumers' rights.

HOWARD, Margaret (fl. 1400). *See Mowbray, Margaret.*

HOWARD, Margaret (fl. 1450). Duchess of Norfolk. Name variations: Margaret Chedworth. Born Margaret Chedworth; dau. of Sir John Chedworth; 2nd wife of John Howard (1420–1485), 1st duke of Norfolk (r. 1483–1485); children: Catherine Howard (fl. 1450).

HOWARD, Margaret (fl. 1500s). English noblewoman. Fl. in the 1500s; dau. of Lord Edmund Howard (d. 1513) and Joyce Culpeper; sister of Catherine Howard (1520/22–1542, 5th wife of Henry VIII).

HOWARD, Margaret (d. 1564). *See Audley, Margaret.*

HOWARD, Marie (1563–1578). *See Dacre, Marie.*

HOWARD, Mary (c. 1519–1557). *See Fitzroy, Mary.*

HOWARD, Mary (fl. 1500s). English noblewoman. Dau. of Lord Edmund Howard (d. 1513) and Joyce Culpeper; sister of Catherine Howard (1520/22–1542, 5th wife of Henry VIII).

HOWARD, Muriel (d. 1512). Viscountess L'Isle. Died in childbirth, Dec 14, 1512, in Lambeth, England; dau. of Thomas Howard (1443–1524), earl of Surrey and 2nd duke of Norfolk (r. 1514–1524), and Elizabeth Tylney (d. 1497); sister of Elizabeth Howard (d. 1538) and aunt of Anne Boleyn (1507–1536); m. John Grey, 2nd viscount L'Isle or Lisle, also seen as 4th viscount Lisle (died 1512); m. Sir Thomas Knyvett, before July 1506; children: (1st m.) Elizabeth Grey (1505–1526).

HOWARD, Rosalind Frances (1845–1921). English reformer and Countess of Carlisle. Name variations: Rosalind Stanley. Born Rosalind Frances Stanley in England, 1845; died Aug 12, 1921; dau. of Edward John (1802–1868), 2nd Baron Stanley of Alderley, and Henrietta Maria Dillon (d. 1895); sister of Henrietta Blanche Stanley (d. 1921, who m. David Ogilvy); m. George Howard (1843–1911), 9th earl of Carlisle, Oct 4, 1864; children: Charles James Howard (b. 1867), 10th earl of Carlisle; Hubert George Howard (b. 1871); Lt. Christopher Edward Howard (b. 1873); Lt. Oliver Howard (b. 1875); Geoffrey William Howard (b. 1877); Michael Francis Howard (b. 1880); Mary Henrietta Howard (who m. George Gilbert Aimé Murray, professor of Greek); Cecilia Maude Howard (d. 1947, who m. Charles Henry Roberts); Dorothy Georgiana Howard (who m. Francis Robert Eden, 6th baron Henley); Elizabeth Dacre Howard (died young); Aurea Fredeswyde Howard (who m. Denyss Wace and Major Thomas MacLeod). ❖ Champion of women's rights and temperance reform,

possessed an astute business sense which she put to use on the political front; served as president of National British Women's Temperance Association (1903), as well as the Women's Liberal Federation (1891–1901, 1906–14).

HOWARD, Sherri (1962—). African-American runner. Born June 1, 1962, in Sherman, TX; sister of Artra, Tina and Denean Howard. ❖ Won a gold medal at Los Angeles Olympics (1984) and a silver medal at Seoul Olympics (1988), both in the 4x400-meter relay.

HOWATCH, Susan (1940—). British novelist. Born July 14, 1940, in Leatherhead, Surrey, England; dau. of George Sturt and Ann Watney Sturt; received law degree from King's College, London (1961); m. Joseph Howatch, 1964. ❖ Moved to NY to begin writing career (1964), then lived in Ireland (1976–80) before returning to England (1980); converted to Christianity and began writing novels dealing with Anglican church history and spiritual themes; works include *The Dark Shore* (1965), *The Shrouded Walls* (1968), *The Devil on Lammas Night* (1970), *The Rich Are Different* (1977), *Sins of the Fathers* (1980), *Glittering Images* (1987), *Scandalous Risks* (1990), *Mystical Paths* (1992) and *Wonder Worker* (1997).

HOWE, Constance Beresford (1922—). *See Beresford-Howe, Constance.*

HOWE, Fanny (1942—). American poet and novelist. Born 1942; dau. of Mark DeWolfe Howe Jr. and Mary Manning (Howe), Irish dramatist (1906–1999); sister of Susan Howe (poet and literary critic) and Helen Howe. ❖ Novels include *First Marriage* (1974), *In the Deep North* (1988), and *Indivisible*; poetry collections include *Poems From a Single Pallet* (1980), *Alsace-Lorraine* (1982), *Robeson Street* (1985), *Introduction to the World* (1986), *The Lives of a Spirit* (1987), *The Vineyard* (1988), *In the Deep North* (1988) and *Selected Poems* (2001).

HOWE, Julia Ward (1819–1910). American poet, author, social reformer and women's suffrage leader. Born Julia Ward, May 27, 1819, in New York, NY; died Oct 17, 1910, in Newport, Rhode Island; dau. of Samuel Ward (Wall Street banker) and Julia Rush (Cutler) Ward (amateur poet); m. Samuel Gridley Howe (Boston educator and reformer who pioneered with the blind), 1843; children: Julia Rowana Anagnos (1844–1886), Florence Howe, Henry Marion Howe, Laura E. Richards (1850–1943), Maud Howe Elliott (1854–1948), Samuel Howe (b. 1861, died of diphtheria in childhood); all 4 daughters pursued careers as writers and educators. ❖ Best known for writing the Civil War anthem, "The Battle Hymn of the Republic," published 1st book of poems, *Passion Flowers,* anonymously (1854); an outspoken abolitionist (1850s), helped husband publish a newspaper supporting the anti-slavery Free Soil Party, and was friends with Boston's leading abolitionists; founded one of the nation's 1st woman's clubs (1868); was 1st president of New England Woman Suffrage Association; helped create Woman's International Peace Association (1870s); for 50 years, wrote and lectured on women's suffrage, social reform, literature and liberal Christianity; treated as an honored guest on podiums around the country; writings include *Words for the Hour* (1857), *At Sunset* (1910), (travel literature) *From the Oak to the Olive: A Plain Record of a Pleasant Journey* (1868), *Trip to Cuba* (1860), (social commentary) *Modern Society* (1881), *Is Polite Society Polite?* (1895), (biography) *Memoir of Dr. Samuel Gridley Howe* (1876) and *Margaret Fuller* (1883). Was 1st woman elected to American Academy of Arts and Letters. ❖ See also (autobiography) *Reminiscences* (1899); Deborah P. Clifford, *Mine Eyes Have Seen the Glory: A Biography of Julia Ward Howe* (1978); Laura E. Richards and Maud Howe Elliott, *Julia Ward Howe, 1819–1910* (2 vols., 1916); Maud Howe Elliott, *Three Generations* (1923); Louise Hall Tharp, *Three Saints and a Sinner: Julia Ward Howe, Louisa, Annie and Sam Ward* (1956); and *Women in World History.*

HOWE, Lady (1621–after 1684). *See King, Anne.*

HOWE, Lois (c. 1864–1964). American architect. Born c. 1864; died 1964; graduated from 2-year course in architecture at Massachusetts Institute of Technology, 1890. ❖ Primarily a designer and renovator of private homes, served as architect for buildings scattered throughout Boston suburbs of Arlington, Cambridge, Concord and Wellesley; in partnership with Eleanor Manning (1913–37), ran one of the most successful women's architectural firms in the country. Became a member of American Institute of Architects (1901) and was made a fellow (1931). ❖ See also *Women in World History.*

HOWE, Mary Manning (1906–1999). *See Manning, Mary.*

HOWE, Maud (1854–1948). *See Elliott, Maud Howe.*

HOWE, Susan (1937—). American poet and literary critic. Born 1937 in Boston, MA; dau. of Mark DeWolfe Howe and Mary Manning Howe (Irish dramatist under Mary Manning); sister of Fanny Howe (writer) and Helen Howe; children: 2. ❖ Became professor of English at State University of New York at Buffalo (1989); was distinguished fellow at Stanford Institute of the Humanities (1998); elected chancellor of Academy of American Poets (2000); works include *My Emily Dickinson* (1985), *The Europe of Trusts: Selected Poems* (1990), *Singularities* (1990), *The Nonconformist's Memorial* (1993), *Pierce-Arrow* (1999) and *The Midnight* (2003); also wrote books on literary history, including *The Birth-Mark: Unsettling the Wilderness in American Literary History* (1993), which was chosen as *Times Literary Supplement*'s International Book of the Year.

HOWE, Tina (1937—). American playwright. Born 1937 in New York, NY; dau. of Quincy Howe (historian and radio-tv journalist) and Mary Post Howe (painter); studied at Bucknell College, Sarah Lawrence, Sorbonne, and Columbia University; m. Norman Levy. ❖ Worked as secondary schoolteacher and university professor; received Guggenheim fellowship (1990); plays, which are absurdist and demonstrate the influence of Beckett and Ionesco, include *The Nest* (1969), *Birth and After Birth* (1974), *The Art of Dining* (1974), *Painting Churches* (1983), *Approaching Zanzibar and Other Plays* (1995), and *Pride's Crossing* (1998). Nominated for a Tony award for *Coastal Disturbances* (1987); won an Obie for Distinguished Playwriting.

HOWELL, Alice (1888–1961). American comedic actress. Born Alice Clark, May 5, 1888, in New York, NY; died April 12, 1961, in Los Angeles, CA; m. 2nd husband Richard Smith (film director); children: Yvonne Stevens (b. 1905, who m. director George Stevens). ❖ Had a vaudeville act with husband Dick Smith, as Howell and Howell; cited by Stan Laurel as one of the greatest comedic actresses, starred in dozens of little-known two-reel comedies.

HOWELL, Lida (1859–1939). American archer. Name variations: Lida Scott. Born Lida Scott, Aug 28, 1859; died Dec 20, 1939; attended Ohio State University; m. Millard C. Howell, 1883. ❖ At St. Louis Olympics, won gold medals in double national round and double Columbia round (1904); competed for 25 years (1883–1907), winning 17 US national championships.

HOWELL, Mary (1932–1998). American physician. Name variations: Mary Raugust Howell; Mary Raugust Jordan; (pseudonym) Margaret A. Campbell. Born Mary Catherine Raugust, Sept 2, 1932, in Grand Forks, North Dakota; died of breast cancer, Feb 5, 1998, in Watertown, MA; Radcliffe College, AB, 1954, University of Minnesota, MA, 1958, PhD in psychology, 1962, and MD; Harvard Law School, law degree, 1991; m. Robert Jordan (div.); Dr. A. Ervin Howell; children: (1st m.) Nicholas Jordan; (2nd m.) Eve, Sarah, Samuel, Aaron and Eli Howell. ❖ Feminist physician who advocated women's rights and improved health care, began working as a pediatrics instructor at Harvard University Medical School (1969), then as associate dean for Student Affairs (1972), the 1st woman to become an associate dean there, then as a member of the Medical School's Division of Medical Ethics (1992–94); practiced pediatrics in York, Maine (from 1975); served as an adoption agency executive director in Watertown, MA; wrote a column for *Working Mother* magazine (1977–87); also wrote (as Margaret Campbell) *Why Would a Girl Go into Medicine?* (1973) and *Healing at Home* (1978).

HOWES, Barbara (1914–1996). American poet, editor, and author. Born May 1, 1914, in New York, NY; died in Bennington, Vermont, Feb 24, 1996; dau. of Osborne Howes and Mildred (Cox) Howes; Bennington College, BA, 1937; m. William Jay Smith (poet), 1947 (div. 1965); children: Gregory and David. ❖ Was an editor of the literary quarterly *Chimera* (1943–47); in addition to writing poetry, edited 2 highly regarded anthologies of Latin American writers, and also published several collections of short stories, including 1 for children, *The Sea-Green Horse*; was nominated for the National Book Award, for her *Collected Poems, 1940–1990.* ❖ See also *Women in World History.*

HOWES, Dulcie (1908–1993). South African ballet dancer and teacher. Born Dulcie Joyce Lind Howes, 1908 in near Mossel Bay, Cape Province, South Africa; died 1993; dau. of Justice Reed Howes and Muriel (Lind) Howes; m. Guy Cronwright, 1937; children: Amelia and Victoria. ❖ One of great influences upon ballet in South Africa, 1st trained with Margaret Craske, Tamara Karsavina, and Ella Brunelleschi in London; performed with Anna Pavlova's company there for 1 season; returned to South Africa where she founded University of Cape Town

(UCT) Ballet School (1932); choreographed 30 original ballets such as *La Famille, Vlei Legend, Bach Suite and The Enchanted Well* (1932–52); appointed director of the Little Theatre (the 1st woman to hold that position) and established the UTC Ballet Company (1935), later renamed CAPAB (Cape Performing Arts Board, 1965), where she was artistic director until 1972. ❖ See also Richard Glasstone, *Dulcie Howes* (1997).

HOWES, Edith Annie (1872–1954). New Zealand children's writer. Born Aug 29, 1872, in London, England; died July 9, 1954, in Dunedin, New Zealand; dau. of Cecilia Brown Howes and William Howes (post office clerk); never married. ❖ Moved to New Zealand as child; became teacher and writer; wrote books to help in development of Montessori teaching methods; wrote *Tales Out of School* (1919), in which she criticized the state of New Zealand schools; also wrote about 30 books for children, including *The Cradle Ship* (1916) and the oft-reprinted *Fairy Rings* (1911). Received MBE (1935) and George VI Coronation Medal (1937).

HOWES, Mary (1941—). Canadian poet and nurse. Born 1941 in Edmonton, Canada. ❖ Works include *Lying in Bed* (1981) and *Vanity Shades* (1990).

HOWES, Sally Ann (1930—). English stage, tv and screen actress and singer. Born July 20, 1930, in London, England; dau. of Patricia Malone Clark and Bobby Howes (1885–1972); m. Maxwell Coker (div.); m. Richard Adler (div.). ❖ Made London debut in the revue *Fancy Free* (1951), followed by *Paint Your Wagon, Romance in Candlelight, Summer Song* and *A Hatful of Rain*; made Broadway debut replacing Julie Andrews in *My Fair Lady* (1958), followed by *Brigadoon, What Makes Sammy Run?* and *Lover*; films include *Thursday's Child, Halfway House, Nicholas Nickleby, Anna Karenina, My Sister and I, Fools Rush In, Honeymoon Deferred, The Admirable Crichton, Chitty Chitty Bang Bang* and *Death Ship*.

HOWEY, Kate Louise (1973—). English judoka. Born May 31, 1973, in Andover, Hampshire, England; graduate of Bath University. ❖ Won World championship (1997); won a bronze medal at Barcelona Olympics (1992) and a silver medal at Sydney Olympics (2000), both for middleweight. Awarded MBE.

HOWIE, Fanny Rose (1868–1916). New Zealand Maori singer and composer. Name variations: Fanny Rose Porter, Fanny Rose Poata; (stage name) Te Rangi Pai. Born Fanny Rose Porter, Jan 11, 1868, at Tokomaru Bay, New Zealand; died on May 20, 1916, at Opotiki, New Zealand; dau. of Thomas William Porter and Herewaka Porourangi Potae (Te Rangi-i-paea); m. John Howie, 1891. ❖ Studied singing in Australia and toured there (1898); performed in New Zealand under stage name Te Rangi Pai (early 1900s); traveled to England for concert, oratorio, and ballad training with baritone Charles Santley (1901); enjoyed successful tour in England, performing frequently at Royal Albert Hall; returned to New Zealand and toured throughout country (1906–07). ❖ See also *Dictionary of New Zealand Biography* (Vol. 3).

HOWITT, Mary (1799–1888). English poet, essayist, translator, and historian. Born Mary Botham in Coleford, Gloucestershire, England, Mar 12, 1799; died in Rome, Italy, Jan 30, 1888; dau. of Samuel Botham and Annie (Wood) Botham, both Quakers; educated in Quaker schools; m. William Howitt (writer), 1821; children: 5, including Alfred William Howitt (English explorer and anthropologist in Australia) and Margaret Howitt (novelist who edited *Mary Howitt: An Autobiography*, [1889]). ❖ With husband, published 1st collection of poetry, *The Forest Minstrel* (1823), and wrote many other works in collaboration; on her own, wrote a series of successful children's books; translated the novels of Fredrika Bremer from the Swedish (1842–63); wrote many poems, hymns, ballads and some novels, numbering 110 distinct works, including *Literature and Romance of Northern Europe* (1852) and *Ruined Abbeys and Castles of Britain* (1862, 1864). Honored by Literary Academy of Stockholm. ❖ See also autobiographies *My Own Story* (1845) and *An Autobiography* (1889); and *Women in World History.*

HOWLAND, Emily (1827–1929). American educator, reformer, and philanthropist. Born Nov 20, 1827, in Cayuga Co., NY; died June 29, 1929, in Cayuga Co.; dau. of Slocum Howland (merchant) and Hannah (Tallcot) Howland; attended Poplar Ridge Seminary, NY; never married; no children. ❖ Raised in a devout Quaker family, moved to Washington, DC, to fill in for the ailing Myrtilla Miner as principal of Washington School for Colored Girls (1857); when it became apparent that the government would not grant land to each freed slave as promised (1867), persuaded father to buy 400 acres in Heathville, VA, where she relocated former slave families and established a school which she would fund for over 50 years; financed an enlargement of the local Sherwood Select School (1882), a Quaker institution which she supported until 1927; subsidized an additional 30 educational institutions for blacks in the South and took a particular interest in Tuskegee Institute, founded by Booker T. Washington, who was a friend; also championed the women's-rights movement; was a regular delegate at conventions of National American Woman Suffrage Association, and supported temperance and peace movements as well. ❖ See also *Women in World History.*

HOWLAND, Jobyna (1880–1936). American actress and dancer. Born Mar 31, 1880, in Indianapolis, Indiana; raised in Denver, Colorado; died June 7, 1936, in Los Angeles, CA; sister of Olin Howlin (actor); m. Arthur Stringer (div.). ❖ Began career as a model for Charles Dana Gibson; appeared as a dancer early in career; made NY stage debut as Princess Flavia in *Rupert of Hentzau* (1899), followed by appearances in *Miss Print, The Whirl of Society, The Passing Show of 1912, The Painted Woman, Ourselves, The Third Party, Ruggles of Red Gap, Kid Boots, Papa, The Gold Diggers* and *Dinner at 8,* among others; films include *The Cuckoos, Stepping Sisters, Once in a Lifetime, The Cohens and Kellys in Trouble* and *The Story of Temple Drake.*

HOWLEY, Bridget (1848–1933). *See Howley, Calasanctius.*

HOWLEY, Calasanctius (1848–1933). New Zealand nun and teacher. Name variations: Bridget Howley. Born Bridget Howley on June 17, 1848, in County Clare, Ireland; died on Dec 13, 1933, at Kensington, South Australia; dau. of Timothy Howley and Catherine (Meehan) Howley. ❖ Joined Sisters of St Joseph of the Sacred Heart, which was founded in 1866 to educate poor (1869); moved to Temuka, the Josephites' 1st New Zealand foundation (1883); established school in Kerrytown (1883); returned to Australia (1884). ❖ See also *Dictionary of New Zealand Biography* (Vol. 2).

HOXHA, Nexhmije (1920—). Albanian politician. Born 1920; m. Enver Hodja also seen as Enver Hoxha (1908–1985), prime minister of Albania, 1945–1953. ❖ For many years, held a series of posts alongside husband in Albania's Communist Party of Labour (PPSh) as well as affiliated organizations; removed from posts because of her strong opposition to reform (1990); expelled from the Party of Labour and arrested on corruption charges (1991); convicted of misuse of public funds (Jan 1993) and was sentenced to 11 years' imprisonment.

HOXIE, Vinnie Ream (1847–1914). *See Ream, Vinnie.*

HOY, Bettina (1962—). West German equestrian. Name variations: Bettina Overesch. Born Nov 7, 1962, in Rheine, Germany; dau. of Eduard Overesch (her trainer); married Andrew Hoy (equestrian). ❖ Won a gold medal at European championships (1997); at Los Angeles Olympics, won a bronze medal in team 3-day event on Peacetime (1984); on Ringwood Cockatoo, won a gold medal for indiv. eventing and a gold medal for team eventing at Athens Olympics (2004).

HOYA, Katherina von (d. around 1470). German composer. Died c. 1470; was 15th-century abbess of the Cistercian convent of Wienhausen (1420–70). ❖ For 50 years, was abbess of the Cistercian convent of Wienhausen, near Celle, a powerful position in the Middle Ages; helped compile the *Wienhausen Liederbuch* which contained many German and Latin songs.

HOYER, Dore (1911–1967). German concert dancer and choreographer. Born Dec 12, 1911, in Dresden, Germany; died Dec 1967 in Berlin, Germany. ❖ Created numerous solo pieces as well as group performances for recital concerts (1930s), most of which reflected the dark underpinnings of Nazi Germany; was engaged as director of Dresden Wigman school; directed numerous productions at Hamburg Staatsoper (late 1940s); toured throughout Western Europe and also South America, dancing and creating works of her own. Choreographed works include *Masks* (c. 1938), *Demon Machine* (c. 1938), *Dances for Käthe Kollwitz* (1945), *Bible Works* (1949), *Bolero* (1953), *South American Journey* (1957) and *On a Black Background* (c. 1958).

HOYERS, Anna Ovena (1584–1655). German poet. Born Anna Ovena, 1584, in Koldenbüttel, Schleswig; died Sept 27, 1655, in Gut Sittwik, near Stockholm, Sweden; dau. of astronomer Johann Oven; m. Hermann Hoyer (died 1622); children: 9. ❖ Knew Latin, Greek, and Hebrew;

after husband's death, began participating in public religious debates and was exiled to Sweden by Protestants for heresy; wrote religious pamphlets, songs, and poems; published *Geistliche un Weltliche Poemata* (1650).

HOYOS, Angela de (1940—). *See de Hoyos, Angela.*

HOYT, Beatrix (1880–1963). American golfer. Born July 5, 1880, in Westchester Co., NY; died Aug 14, 1963, in Thomasville, Georgia; daughter of William Sprague Hoyt and Janet Ralston (Chase) Hoyt; sister of Franklin Chase Hoyt (judge); granddau. of Salmon P. Chase, chief justice of US Supreme Court (1864–73). ❖ At 16, won the 2nd USGA Women's Amateur ever held and went on to win the Women's Amateur qualifying medal for 5 consecutive years and the championship for 3; retired from competition at 20.

HOYT, Julia (c. 1897–1955). American actress and socialite. Born c. 1897 in New York, NY; died Oct 31, 1955, in NY, NY; m. Lydig Hoyt (div.); m. Louis Calhern (actor, div.); m. Aquila Giles. ❖ Broadway appearances include *The Squaw Man* (revival), *The Virgin of Bethulia, The Rhapsody, Anatomy of Love* and *Hay Fever.*

HOYT, Mary F. (1858–1958). American Civil Service appointee. Born June 17, 1858, in Southport, Connecticut; died Oct 20, 1958, in New York, NY. ❖ Received the highest score on 1st Civil Service examination administered and became 1st woman appointed to a federal position under provisions of Civil Service Act (1883); served clerkship in Bank Redemption Agency of Treasury Department for 5 years; worked for US Census Bureau; received letter from President Eisenhower on 100th birthday which said, "A door was opened to a new world of careers for women in our land and you were the first to enter it."

HOYTE, Joslyn (1954—). *See Hoyte-Smith, Joslyn Y.*

HOYTE-SMITH, Joslyn Y. (1954—). English runner. Name variations: Joslyn Hoyte; Joslyn Smith. Born Dec 16, 1954, in Barbados. ❖ Won a team gold in the 1,600-meter relay at the Commonwealth Games (1978) and a gold medal in the 400 meters at the United Kingdom championships (1979); at Moscow Olympics, won a bronze medal in the 4 x 400-meter relay (1980).

HREBRINOVA, Anna (1908—). Czech gymnast. Born Nov 11, 1908. ❖ At Berlin Olympics, won a silver medal in team all-around (1936).

HROSTWITHA, Hroswitha or Hrosvitha (c. 935–1001). *See Hrotsvitha of Gandersheim.*

HROTRUD or HROTRUDE (c. 778-after 839). *See Rotrude.*

HROTSVITHA OF GANDERSHEIM (c. 935–1001). German nun, poet, and historian. Name variations: Hrosvitha; Hroswitha; Hrotsuit; Hrotsuitha; Hrotsvit; Hrotsvith von Gandersheim; Hrotswitha; Roswitha. Pronunciation: Ros-VI-thuh (name derived from the old Saxon word "hrodsuind," meaning strong voice). Born c. 935 in Saxony; died in 1001 at Gandersheim monastery; educated at St. Benedict monastery in Gandersheim. ❖ Resided in the monastery in Gandersheim and was the 1st woman playwright of the West; stands as the sole figure connecting the rich theatrical tradition of classical Greece and Rome with the medieval religious drama staged throughout Europe; wrote 6 plays, *Gallicanus* (Parts I and II), *Dulcitius, Callimachus, Abraham, Paphnutius,* and *Sapientia*; 8 narrative religious poems concerned with the Nativity of the Virgin, the Ascension, and a series of legends of saints (Gandolph, Pelagius, Theophilus, Basil, Denis, Agnes); 2 versified histories *Carmen de gestis Oddonis,* detailing the deeds of Otto I; and *De primordiis et fundatoribus coenobii Gandersheimensis,* a history of the foundation of Gandersheim monastery. ❖ See also Larissa Bonfante, trans., *The Plays of Hrotsvitha of Gandersheim* (Golchazy-Carducci, 1986); and *Women in World History.*

HROTSWITHA (c. 935–1001). *See Hrotsvitha of Gandersheim.*

HRUBA, Berta (1946—). Czech field-hockey player. Born April 1946. ❖ At Moscow Olympics, won a silver medal in team competition (1980).

HRUBA, Vera (1921–2003). *See Ralston, Vera Hruba.*

HSIANG CHING-YU or CHIN-YU (1895–1928). *See Xiang Jingyü.*

HSIAO FU-JEH (1902–1970). *See Aylward, Gladys.*

HSIAO HUNG (1911–1942). *See Xiao Hong.*

HSIEH HSI-TEH (1921–2000). *See Xie Xide.*

HSIEH WAN-YING (1900–1999). *See Xie Wanying.*

HSUEH T'AO (760–832). *See Xue Tao.*

HU DIE (1908–1989). Chinese film star. Name variations: Hu Tieh; Hu Baojuan; Butterfly Wu; Miss Butterfly; Pan Baojuan. Pronunciation: Hu TiEh. Born Hu Baojuan, 1908, in Shanghai, China; died in Vancouver, Canada, April 23, 1989; dau. of Hu Shaogong (railroad inspector); attended Zhonghua Film School, 1924; m. Eugene Penn (Pan Yousheng), a Shanghai manufacturer, 1936 (died 1958); children: son Jiarong; daughter Jiali. ❖ One of China's early film stars, whose achievements in many ways encouraged other women to pursue careers in the performing arts, made 1st silent film, *Changong* (War Achievement, 1925); made 1st sound film, *Genu hongmudan* (Singing Peony, 1931); starred in about 70 films, including *Qiushan yuan* (Autumn Fan's Sorrow, 1926), *Bai she zhuan* (Legend of the White Snake, 1927), *Baiyun ta* (White Pagoda, 1927), *Genu hongmudan* (Singing Peony, 1931), *Kuang lu* (Torrents, 1933), *Zimui hua* (Two Sisters, 1935), *Yongyuan di weixiao* (Smile Forever, 1937), *Jianguo zhilu* (The Way of a Nation, 1944), *Jinshou tiantang* (Beautiful Paradise, 1949), *Kuer liulangji* (Adventure of a Poor Orphan, 1963), *Mingyue jishi yuan* (When Will the Moon be Round Again?, 1966) retired (1966); moved to Taiwan (1967); moved to Vancouver (1975); published memoirs (1986). Won Best Actress award for *Houmen* (Back Door, 1960); won Special Achievement award at Taiwan Golden Horse Film Festival (1986). ❖ See also *Women in World History.*

HU TIEH (1908–1989). *See Hu Die.*

HU YADONG (1968—). Chinese rower. Born Oct 3, 1968, in China. ❖ At Seoul Olympics, won a silver medal in coxed fours and a bronze medal in coxed eights (1988).

HUA MU-IAN (fl. 5th c.). *See Hua Mu-Lan.*

HUA MU-LAN (fl. 5th c.). Chinese soldier. Name variations: Hua Mu-Ian; Hua Mulan; Hwa Mu-Lan; Mu-Ian, Mu-Lan or Mulan. Lived between 386 and 618. ❖ China's most famous woman warrior, possibly legendary, who lived during the Wei dynasty of the Tartars (386–557); when father was conscripted to go to war but was too sick to fight, offered to go in his place to protect the family honor; renowned for courage and leadership, joined the emperor's troops and fought for 12 years disguised as a man. Appears as a character in many Chinese operas and plays; was the basis for Disney film *Mulan* (1998).

HUANG HUA (1969—). Chinese badminton player. Born Nov 16, 1969, in China. ❖ At Barcelona Olympics, won a bronze medal in singles (1992).

HUANG MANDAN (1983—). Chinese gymnast. Born Feb 17, 1983, in Shantou (Guangdong Province), China. ❖ At World championships, won a bronze medal for team all-around and a medal for uneven bars (1999); at Sydney Olympics, won a bronze medal for team all-around (2000).

HUANG NANYAN (1977—). Chinese badminton player. Born April 11, 1977, in Guangsi, China. ❖ Won a silver medal for doubles at Sydney Olympics (2000).

HUANG QINGYUN (1920—). Chinese children's writer. Born 1920 in China. ❖ Wrote children's stories influenced by Hans Christian Andersen and edited children's magazine; published "Annals of a Fossil" (1980, trans. by Perry Link in *Roses and Thorns*).

HUANG QUN (1969—). Chinese gymnast. Born Mar 18, 1969, in China. ❖ At Los Angeles Olympics, won a bronze medal in team all-around (1984).

HUANG SHANSHAN (1986—). Chinese trampolinist. Born Jan 18, 1986, in China; attended York University. ❖ Won a bronze medal for indiv. at Athens Olympics (2004).

HUANG SUI (1982—). Chinese badminton player. Born Jan 8, 1982, in Hunan Province, China. ❖ At World championships, won doubles (2001, 2003); won a silver medal for doubles at Athens Olympics (2004).

HUANG XIAOMIN (1970—). Chinese swimmer. Born April 6, 1970, in China. ❖ At Seoul Olympics, won a silver medal in the 200-meter breaststroke (1988).

HUANG ZHIHONG (1965—). Chinese track-and-field athlete. Born May 7, 1965, in China. ❖ At Barcelona Olympics, won a silver medal in shot put (1992).

HUANG ZONGYING (1925—). Chinese actress, journalist and short-story writer. Born July 13, 1925, in Beijing, China; m. Zhao Dan (actor and activist). ❖ Works include *The Flight of the Wild Geese* (1978) and *The Little Wooden Cabin*; appeared in the films *Wuya yu maque* (1949), *Wei hai zi men zhu fu* (1953), *Nie Er* (1959) and *Mikan no taikyoku* (1982).

HUBACKOVA, Ida (1954—). Czech field-hockey player. Born Oct 1954. ❖ At Moscow Olympics, won a silver medal in team competition (1980).

HUBBARD, Mabel (1857–1923). *See Bell, Mabel Hubbard.*

HUBBARD, Mina (1870–1956). *See Ellis, Mina A.*

HUBBARD, Ruth (1924—). American biologist. Name variations: Ruth Wald. Born Mar 3, 1924, in Vienna, Austria; dau. of physicians; Radcliffe College, AB, 1944, PhD, 1950; m. Frank Hubbard (pioneered a harpsichord revival), 1941; George Wald (scientist); children: (2nd m.) Elijah Wald (b. 1959), Deborah Hannah Wald (b. 1961). ❖ Activist, scientist, educator and women's health advocate and Harvard University's 1st tenured woman biology professor, fled Nazism as a teenager; developed a reputation for challenging proponents of sociobiology; was a Guggenheim fellow at Carlsberg Laboratory in Copenhagen (1952–53); at Harvard University, served as a research fellow (1950–52, 1954–58), research associate (1958–74), biology professor (1974–90) and professor emerita (from 1990); served on board of directors for Council for Responsible Genetics' (from 1982); worked as a Boston Women's Healthbook Collective consultant; believed that the male-gendered language of science affects women's thoughts, beliefs and health; wrote *The Politics of Women's Biology* (1990) and *Profitable Promises: Essays on Women, Science and Health* (1994), among others. Received University of Zürich's Paul Karrer Medal (with George Wald, 1967) and Women's International League for Peace and Freedom's Peace and Freedom Award (1985).

HUBBELL, Helen Johnson (1906–1995). *See Johnson, Helene.*

HUBER, Andrea (1975—). Swiss cross-country skier. Born May 9, 1975, in La Punt, Switzerland. ❖ Won a bronze medal for the 4 x 5km relay at Salt Lake City Olympics (2002).

HUBER, Brigitte (1967—). *See McMahon, Brigitte.*

HUBER, Gusti (1914–1993). Viennese stage and screen actress. Born Auguste Huber, July 27, 1914, in Vienna, Austria; died July 12, 1993, in Mt. Kisco, NY; m. Joseph G. Besch; children: 3 daughters, including Bibi Besch (actress, d. 1996); granddau.: Samantha Mathis (actress). ❖ Famed actress, made stage debut at the Deutsches Volkstheater, Vienna (1929); appeared in over 160 roles at the Schauspielhaus, Zurich (1930–35); made NY debut in *Flight in Egypt* (1952); played Anne Frank's mother in *Diary of Anne Frank* on Broadway and in film; retired (1961).

HUBER, Marie (1695–1753). Swiss-born essayist. Born 1695 in Geneva, Switzerland; lived in France; died 1753; great aunt of François Huer, the naturalist. ❖ Swiss deist who wrote on religious and theological subjects; her works, which reflect opposition to dogma and anticipate Jean-Jacques Rousseau's deist philosophy, include *Le Monde fou préféré au monde sage* (1731, trans. as *The World Unmask'd; or, the Philosopher the greatest Cheat; in Twenty-Four Dialogues between Crito a Philosopher, Philo a Lawyer, and Erastus a Merchant,* 1736), *Le Système des anciens et des modernes concilié* (1738, 1739), *Lettres sur la religion essentielle* (1738, 1754) and *Réduction du 'Spectateur anglais'* (1753); was also a translator and editor.

HUBER, Therese (1764–1829). German writer of novels and short stories. Name variations: Theresa Heyne. Born Therese or Theresa Heyne in Göttingen, Germany, 1764; died in Augsburg, 1829; dau. of Professor D.C.G. Heyne; m. Georg Forster (1754–1794), son of naturalist Johann Reinhold Forster; m. Ludwig Ferdinand Huber, Saxon diplomat (died 1804). ❖ One of the most prolific writers of late 18th- and early 19th-century Germany, wrote more than 60 stories, 6 novels, 3,800 letters, and translated several works from French and English into German; also edited the popular German newspaper, *Morgenblatt für gebildete Stände* (Morning Daily for the Cultured Classes, 1816–23); published 1st novel *Die Familie Seldorf* (1795–96), with the French Revolution as its central theme; also wrote 1st novel set in an Australian penal settlement, *Adventures on a Journey to New Holland* (1801), followed by its sequel *The Lonely Deathbed* (1810). ❖ See also *Women in World History.*

HÜBLER, Anna (1885–1976). See Huebler, Anna.

HUCH, Ricarda (1864–1947). German poet, novelist and short-story writer. Name variations: (pseudonym) Richard Hugo. Born Ricarda Octavia Huch, Aug 18, 1864, in Braunschweig, Germany; died Nov 17, 1947, in Frankfurt am Main; dau. of Richard Huch (merchant) and Emilie Huch; sister of Rudolf Huch, novelist, and Lilly Huch; bachelor and doctor of philosophy degrees from University of Zurich; m. Ermanno Ceconi, July 9, 1898 (div. 1906); m. Richard Huch (cousin and former husband of her sister Lilly), July 6, 1907 (div. 1911); children: (1st m.) Marietta Ceconi (b. 1899). ❖ Often considered the outstanding German woman author of the 20th century, moved to Zurich (1887); was 1st woman to earn a doctorate from University of Zurich (1891) and chronicled experiences as a graduate student in *Spring in Switzerland* (*Frühling in der Schweiz*, 1938); published initial book of poetry, *Gedichte* (1891), followed by *Neue Gedichte* (1907); published 1st novel, *Memories of Ludolf Ursleu the Younger* (*Erinnerungen von Ludolf Ursleu dem Jüngeren*, 1893); moved to Trieste with 1st husband (1898); published novel *From Triumph Street* (*Aus der Triumphgasse*, 1902); took up residence in Munich (1907); published a trilogy of German history, *The Great War in Germany* (*Der grosse Krieg in Deutschland*, 1912–14); published best prose work, the psychological detective thriller *The Deruga Trial* (*Der Fall Deruga*, 1917); elected to membership in Academy of Prussian Writers (1931), resigned from Academy (1933), protesting expulsion of Jewish writers; published a 3-part *German History* (*Deutsche Geschichte*, 1934, 1937, and posthumously in 1949); published "Open Letter to the German People" (1947); in a career spanning nearly 60 years, produced more than 50 books and an even larger number of articles, some under pseudonym Richard Hugo. Made honorary senator of University of Munich (1924) and awarded Goethe Prize of Frankfurt (1931). ❖ See also *Women in World History.*

HUCK, Winnifred Sprague Mason (1882–1936). American politician, writer and lecturer. Born Winnifred Sprague Mason, Sept 14, 1882 in Chicago, Illinois; died Aug 24, 1936, in Chicago; dau. of William E. Mason (US congressional representative) and Edith Julia (White) Mason; m. Robert Wardlow Huck, June 29, 1904; children: Wallace, Donald, Edith and Robert Wardlow Huck Jr. ❖ Member of US House of Representatives (1922–23); when father died while serving in Congress (1921), replaced him, becoming the 3rd woman elected to US Congress (2 years after the 19th Amendment established women's right to vote); during 5-month tenure, served on Committee on Woman Suffrage, Committee on Expenditures in Department of Commerce, and Committee on Reform in the Civil Service; best-known proposal was Resolution 423, calling for a "war plebiscite" whereby the power to declare war on another country would rest solely with American public by way of a popular vote; unsuccessfully sought Republican Party's nomination to a seat in 68th Congress; joined National Woman's Party's political council, which encouraged women to seek public office; became a lecturer and writer, and was a staff writer for *Chicago Evening Post* (1928–29). ❖ See also *Women in World History.*

HUCLES, Angela (1978—). American soccer player. Born July 5, 1978, in Virginia Beach, Virginia; attended University of Virginia. ❖ Midfielder, was University of Virginia's all-time scorer with 59 goals; played for the San Diego Spirit; won a team gold medal at Athens Olympics (2004).

HUDA SHAARAWI (1879–1947). See Shaarawi, Huda.

HUDDLESTON, Deserie (1960—). See Baynes, Deserie.

HUDSON, Caroline Harriet (1809–1877). See Abraham, Caroline Harriet.

HUDSON, Johari (1935—). See Amini-Hudson, Johari.

HUDSON, Martha (1939—). African-American track-and-field athlete. Name variations: Peewee Hudson. Born Mar 21, 1939, in Eastman, Georgia. ❖ One of the famed Tigerbelles of Tennessee State University, won a gold medal in the 4x100-meter relay at Rome Olympics (1960). ❖ See also *Women in World History.*

HUDSON, Mrs. (1831–1884). See Ames, Mary Clemmer.

HUDSON, Nikki (1976—). Australian field-hockey player. Name variations: Nikki Mott. Born Nicole Mott, July 6, 1976, in Rockhampton, Queensland, Australia. ❖ Forward, won a team gold medal at Sydney Olympics (2000).

HUDSON, Peewee (1939—). See Hudson, Martha.

HUDSON, Rochelle (1916–1972). American actress. Born Rochelle Elizabeth Hudson in Oklahoma City, Oklahoma, Mar 6, 1916; died of liver ailment in Palm Desert, California, Jan 17, 1972; only child of Ollie Lee Hudson (head of State Employment Bureau in Oklahoma) and Mae (Goddard) Hudson; m. Harold Thompson (story editor and naval reserve officer), 1939 (div. 1947); m. Richard Hyler (*Los Angeles Times* sportswriter), 1948 (div. 1950); m. Charles Brust (Kansas businessman, div.); m. Robert Mindell (hotel executive), 1963 (div. c. 1971). ❖ Signed with RKO and appeared in *Laugh and Get Rich*, followed by 1st lead in *Are These Our Children?* (both 1931); made 3 movies at Fox with Will Rogers, *Doctor Bull, Mr. Skitch* and *Judge Priest*; appeared in *Harold Teen, Imitation of Life, The Mighty Barnum, Way Down East* and as Cosette in *Les Miserables*; played Shirley Temple (Black)'s sister in *Curly Top* and sang "The Simple Things in Life"; loaned to Paramount to play W.C. Fields' daughter in *Poppy* (1935); consigned mostly to B movies (1930s–40s), had final role for Fox in *Mr. Moto Takes a Chance* (1938); during WWII (1942–45), worked with 1st husband for Naval Intelligence, making "fishing" trips to Mexico and other Central American countries to engage in espionage; appeared on stage in *Burlesque* (1948) with Bert Lahr, was seen in tv series "Racket Squad" (1951), and was a regular on "That's My Boy" (1954–55); also appeared in films *Rebel Without a Cause* (1955) and *Strait-Jacket* (1964). ❖ See also *Women in World History.*

HUDSON, Winson (1916–2004). African-American civil-rights activist. Born Anger Winson Gates, Nov 17, 1916, in Harmony, Mississippi; died April 24, 2004, in Jackson, Mississippi; dau. of John Wesley Gates and Emma Kirland; sister of Dovie Hudson; m. Cleo Hudson (landowner), 1936; children: Annie Maude Horton. ❖ With sister Dovie, began the habit of trying to register to vote (1937) and finally succeeded (1962); with sister, brought the 1st suit to desegregate schools in a rural Mississippi county (1963) and won the case (1964); was chair of the country chapter of the NAACP for 38 years. ❖ See also memoir (written with Constance Curry), *Mississippi Harmony, Memoirs of a Freedom Fighter* (2002).

HUEBLER, Anna (1885–1976). German pairs skater. Name variations: Anna Hübler or Hubler. Born Jan 1885 in Germany; died July 1976. ❖ With Heinrich Burger, won the World championships (1908, 1910) and placed 1st at London Olympics (1908), winning the 1st gold medal in pairs competition.

HUEBNER, Robin (1961—). American gymnast and tv journalist. Born Oct 9, 1961; grew up in Minnetonka, Minnesota. ❖ Won US nationals (1976); became a news anchor for KVLY-TV in Fargo, North Dakota.

HUELSENBECK, Sarina (1962—). East German swimmer. Name variations: Sarina Hülsenbeck. Born July 1962 in East Germany. ❖ At Moscow Olympics, won a gold medal in 4x100-meter freestyle relay (1980).

HUERTA, Dolores (1930—). American Chicana labor organizer. Born in Dawson, New Mexico, April 10, 1930; dau. of Juan Fernández (miner, union leader and member of New Mexico state legislature) and Alicia Chávez Fernández (hotelier and restaurant owner); graduated from college; m. Ralph Head (div.); m. Ventura Huerta (div.); companion, Richard Chávez; children: 11. ❖ Major personality in world of American unionism and co-founder with Cesar Chávez of United Farm Workers of America, joined the Community Service Organization (CSO), a Mexican-American self-help association (1955); became a prominent CSO member, working as a lobbyist in the state capital; also became active with Agricultural Workers Association (AWA), a northern California group committed to improved labor conditions; with Chávez, intent on organizing a union for California's farmworkers, co-founded the National Farm Workers Association (NFWA), later United Farm Workers of America (UFW), and was one of the organization's vice presidents (1962); during grape pickers' strike (1965–70), which drew national media attention, was arrested numerous times and placed under FBI surveillance; by 1967, was chief negotiator of UFWOC and successfully hammered out several contracts with wine-grape growers; as a non-violent tactic in the strike, was sent to NYC to coordinate a national boycott of all California table grapes (1968), one of the most successful boycotts in US history; has appeared at rallies coast to coast and served on boards of numerous organizations including California Labor Federation, Fund for the Feminist Majority and National Farm Workers Service Center; has also served as vice president of Coalition of Labor Union Women. ❖ See also *Women in World History.*

HUIE, Margaret Gordon (1825–1918). See Burn, Margaret Gordon.

HUFF, Louise (1895–1973). American stage and silent-film actress. Born Nov 4, 1895, in Columbus, Georgia; died Aug 22, 1973, in New York, NY; m. Edwin Stillman. ❖ Known as the "Kate Greenaway Girl of the Screen," made film debut (1914) and came to prominence with the Lubin Company; films include *Seventeen, Great Expectations, Tom Sawyer, What Women Want* and *Disraeli.*

HUFSTEDLER, Shirley Mount (1925—). American judge. Name variations: Mrs. Seth M. Hufstedler. Born Shirley Mount, Aug 24, 1925, in Denver, Colorado; dau. of Earl Stanley Mount and Eva (Von Behren) Mount; University of New Mexico, BBA, 1945; Stanford Law School, LLB, 1949; m. Seth Martin Hufstedler, 1949; children: Steven. ❖ Served as member of law firm Beardsley, Hufstedler & Kemble (Los Angeles, CA, 1949–59); served on Los Angeles County Superior Court and California Court of Appeals; appointed to US Court of Appeals by Lyndon Johnson (1968) and served until appointed secretary of US Office of Education by Jimmy Carter (1979); returned to private life (1981); taught and practiced law; served on board of trustees of Carnegie Endowment for International Peace and numerous other organizations; served on governing boards or visiting committees of numerous organizations including US Military Academy, Harvard Law School, and the American Law Institute; serves on board of directors of John D. and Catherine T. MacArthur Foundation; became 1st woman to receive Lewis F. Powell Jr. Award for Professionalism and Ethics (2001).

HUG-HELLMUTH, Hermine (1871–1924). Austrian psychoanalyst. Born Hermine Hug von Hugenstein in Vienna, Austria, Aug 31, 1871; University of Vienna, doctoral degree, 1909; murdered in Vienna by nephew Rudolph Otto Hug, Sept 8–9, 1924; dau. of Hugo Ritter Hug von Hugenstein; sister of Antonie Hug (professor, died 1915); never married. ❖ As the world's 1st practicing child psychoanalyst, developed a technique of observing children at play which preceded research later carried out by Helene Deutsch, Anna Freud and Melanie Klein; passed *Matura* examinations (1897) and was one of 1st Austrian women to enroll at University of Vienna; became an independent scholar in psychoanalysis (1901); published 1st of many psychoanalytic papers (1912), followed by 1st book, *Aus dem Seelenleben des Kindes* (On the Spiritual and Mental Life of the Child, 1913); admitted to Vienna Psychoanalytic Society (1913); within a few years, became the foremost expert in child analysis and education and was often invited to lecture on her work, including before 6th International Psychoanalytic Congress at The Hague (1920), where she presented the paper, "On the Technique of Child Analysis" a seminal work, generally considered to have been a major influence on later theories of Melanie Klein; published *Tagebuch eines halbwüchsigen Mädchens* (The Diary of a Young Girl), purported to be her edited version of the diary of a young Austrian upper-middle-class girl, which created a firestorm of controversy as to its authenticity (1919); was murdered by her sister's son who lived with her. A fictionalized version of the troubled relationship between Hug-Hellmuth and her nephew appeared in Arthur Schnitzler's novel *Therese: Chronik eines Fraunlebens* (Therese: Chronicle of a Woman's Life). ❖ See also George MacLean and Ulrich Rappen, *Hermine Hug-Hellmuth: Her Life and Work* (Routledge, 1991); and *Women in World History.*

HUGEBERC or HUGEBURC (fl. 8th c.). See Hygeburg.

HUGGETT, Helen Kemp (1899–1987). See Porter, Helen Kemp.

HUGGETT, Susan (1954—). Zimbabwean field-hockey player. Born June 29, 1954. ❖ At Moscow Olympics, won a gold medal in team competition (1980).

HUGGINS, Margaret (1848–1915). Irish astrophysicist. Name variations: Lady Margaret Lindsay Huggins; Lady Margaret Murray Huggins. Born Margaret Lindsay Murray, 1848; died Mar 24, 1915; dau. of a solicitor in Monkstown, Dublin, Ireland; attended school in Brighton; m. Sir William Huggins (astrophysicist), Sept 8, 1875 (died May 12, 1910). ❖ An astrophysics pioneer and research partner of her husband, assisted him for over 30 years at their home observatory at Tulse Hill in London; for astronomy, pioneered the use of the dry gelatin photographic plate with him; studied the spectra of calcium and magnesium and methods to study radiation spectroscopically; donated scientific treasures to Wellesley College in MA (in part due to acquaintance with Wellesley's Sarah Whiting, its observatory director, 1900–16); was a founding member of the British Astronomical Association. With husband, wrote *Atlas of Representative Stellar Spectra* (1899) and edited *The Scientific Papers of William Huggins* (1909); honors include a Royal Astronomical Society honorary membership (1903) and the Order of Merit (1902).

HUGHAN, Jessie (1875–1955). American educator, socialist, and pacifist. Name variations: Jessie Wallace Hughan. Born Jessie Wallace Hughan, Dec 25, 1875, in Brooklyn, NY; died April 10, 1955, in New York, NY; dau. of Samuel Hughan and Margaret (West) Hughan. ❖ Taught at schools in NY, serving as chair of Textile High School English department and head of Cooperative Annex (1900–45); became socialist (1907) and served on executive committee of Socialist Party; published doctoral thesis, *The Present Status of Socialism in America* (1911) as well as *A Study of International Government* (1923) and a collection of poetry, *The Challenge of Mars and Other Verses* (1932); as a Socialist, ran unsuccessfully for alderman in NY (1915), secretary of state (1918), lieutenant governor (1920) and US senator (1924); organized Anti-Enlistment League (1915); became charter member of Fellowship of Reconciliation (FOR); created Committee for Enrollment Against War (1922); founded War Resisters League (WRL), serving as secretary (1923–45); helped found United Pacifist Committee (1938) and Pacifist Teachers League (1940); honored with establishment of Jessie Wallace Hughan Memorial Fund (Dec 1955).

HUGHES, Adelaide (1884–1960). American dancer. Name variations: Adelaide and Hughes. Born Mary Adelaide Dickey, 1884, in NY; died 1960 in NY; m. Johnny "JJ" Hughes (dancer, died 1942). ❖ With husband, formed the popular dance team of Adelaide and Hughes; appeared on Broadway in *The Passing Show of 1912* and other Shubert revues, and played 17 consecutive weeks at the Palace, then a record.

HUGHES, Adella (1869–1950). American orchestra manager. Name variations: Adella Prentiss. Born Adella Prentiss, Nov 29, 1869, in Cleveland, Ohio; died Aug 23, 1950, in Cleveland Heights, Ohio; dau. of Loren Prentiss (lawyer) and Ellen (Rouse) Prentiss; Vassar College, AB, 1890; m. Felix Hughes (singer), Oct 5, 1904 (div. 1923); no children. ❖ Served as professional accompanist and organized concert series and major performances; contributed to establishment of regular concert series in Cleveland, Ohio (1901) and sponsored a Musical Arts Association; served as manager of the Cleveland Orchestra for 15 years (1918–33), the 1st woman manager of a major symphony orchestra. ❖ See also Adella Prentiss Hughes, *Music Is My Life* (World, 1947).

HUGHES, Annie (1869–1954). English stage actress. Born Oct 10, 1869, in Southampton, England; died Jan 7, 1954; m. Nicholas Devereux (div.); m. Edmund Maurice (div.); m. Lt. Mayne Lynton (div.). ❖ Made London debut succeeding Maude Millett as Eva Webster in *The Private Secretary* (1885); came to prominence as Susan McCreery in *Held by the Enemy* (1887), followed by *Mamma, The Weaker Sex, Sweet Nancy* (title role), *Betsy* (title role), *Oh Susannah!, A Bit of Old Chelsea, Dandy Dick, Outward Bound, A Country Mouse* and *Mr. Hopkinson,* among others; appeared often in NY and in Australia (where she eventually turned to broadcasting).

HUGHES, Beverley (1950—). English politician and member of Parliament. Born Beverley Hughes, Mar 30, 1950; m. Thomas McDonald, 1973. ❖ Representing Labour, elected to House of Commons for Stretford and Urmston (1997, 2001, 2005); named minister of State, Home Office; named minister of State, Department for Education and Skills (2005).

HUGHES, Clara (1972—). Canadian cyclist and speedskater. Born Sept 27, 1972, in Winnipeg, Manitoba, Canada. ❖ Began career as a speedskater, then added competitive cycling (1990); won bronze cycling medals in indiv. road race and indiv. time trial at Atlanta Summer Olympics (1996); won a bronze medal for 5000-meter speedskating at Salt Lake City Winter Olympics (2002), the 2nd speedskater to win medals in Winter and Summer games; won a gold medal for 5000 meters at Torino Olympics (2006).

HUGHES, Edna (1916—). English swimmer. Born Aug 1916 in UK. ❖ At Los Angeles Olympics, won a bronze medal in 4 x 100-meter freestyle relay (1932).

HUGHES, Janis (1958—). Scottish politician. Born 1958 in Scotland. ❖ Began career as a nurse; serves as Labour member of the Scottish Parliament for Glasgow Rutherglen.

HUGHES, Joanna (1977—). Australian gymnast. Born Dec 22, 1977, in Sandringham, Australia. ❖ At Australian national championships, placed 1st in vault, 2nd in floor exercises, 3rd in balance beam and all-around (1991), 2nd all-around, 3rd in vault, 1st in uneven bars and floor exercises (1993), 1st all-around (1994), and 2nd in balance beam and floor exercises and 3rd all-around (1995); won a team bronze at the Commonwealth Games (1994).

HUGHES, Karen (1956—). American journalist and presidential advisor. Born Karen Parfitt, Dec 27, 1956, in Paris, France; dau. of Patricia Scully Parfitt and Harold R. Parfitt (US army general, Panama Canal governor, 1975–79); Southern Methodist University, BA in journalism, 1977; m. Jerry Hughes (lawyer); children: Robert. ❖ One of the most powerful women to serve as a White House adviser, began career as a tv reporter for KXAS-TV; became Texas press coordinator for Reagan-Bush campaign (1984), then executive director of Texas Republican Party (1991–93); helped George W. Bush launch his political career as a Texas governor (1994); was director of Communications for his presidential campaign (2000), then served as his adviser (2000–02). ❖ See also memoir *Ten Minutes from Normal* (2004).

HUGHES, Kathleen (1928—). American actress. Born Betty Von Gerkan, Nov 14, 1928, in Hollywood, CA; m. Stanley Rubin, 1954; children: 4, including Michael Hughes (actor). ❖ Lead actress of low-budget films (1950s), appeared in *Mother Is a Freshman, It Came from Outer Space, The Golden Blade, The Glass Web, Dawn at Socorro, Cult of the Cobra, Three Bad Sisters, Unwed Mother* and *The President's Analyst*, among others.

HUGHES, Mary (1874–1958). Australian prime-ministerial wife. Name variations: Dame Mary Hughes. Born Mary Ethel Campbell, June 6, 1874, in Burrandong, New South Wales, Australia; died April 2, 1958, in Double Bay, Sydney; m. 2nd wife of William Morris Hughes (prime minister of Australia, 1915–23), June 26, 1911; children: Helen (b. 1915). ❖ Was a trained nurse and served in that capacity on husband's overseas tours because of his frail health; active in war work in Australia and England, especially for Australian troops during WWI. Was the 2nd Australian (the 1st was Florence Reid) awarded the Dame Grand Cross of the Order of the British Empire (GBE), the highest British award for women (1922).

HUGHES, Mary Beth (1919–1995). American actress. Born Nov 13, 1919, in Alton, Illinois; died Aug 27, 1995, in Los Angeles, CA; m. David Street (div.); m. Ted North, 1943 (div.); m. Nick Stewart, 1973 (div.); m. twice more. ❖ Made film debut in *Broadway Serenade* (1939); often played a tough blonde in over 50 low-budget films; has become a cult favorite.

HUGHES, Monica (1925–2003). Canadian children's and science-fiction writer. Born Monica Ince, Nov 3, 1925, in Liverpool, England; died Mar 7, 2003, in Edmonton, Alberta, Canada; dau. of E.L. Ince; m. Glen Hughes, 1957; children: 4. ❖ Served in Women's Royal Naval Service (1943–46) and as dress designer in London and Zimbabwe; moved to Canada (1952); novels include *Crisis on Conshelf Ten* (1975), *The Tomorrow City* (1978), *The Keeper of the Isis Light* (1980), *Hunter in the Dark* (1982), *Space Trap* (1984), *Sandwriter* (1985), *The Promise* (1989), *The Crystal Drop* (1992), *The Faces of Fear* (1997), *Storm Warning* (2000), and *Don't Forget Remembrance Day* (2002). Received Vicky Metcalf Award (1981), Canada Council Prize (1982, 1983), Order of Canada, and Queen's Golden Jubilee medal.

HUGHES, Russell Meriwether (b. 1898). See La Meri.

HUGHES, Ruth (1918–1980). See Aarons, Ruth Hughes.

HUGHES, Sarah (1985—). American figure skater. Born Sarah Elizabeth Hughes, May 2, 1985, in Manhasset, NY; dau. of Amy and John Hughes (Canadian hockey player); sister of Emily Hughes (skater). ❖ Won US Jr. championship (1998); at US nationals, placed 3rd (2000, 2002) and 2nd (2001, 2003); placed 2nd at Nations Cup and Skate America (2001) and 1st at Skate Canada (2001); at World championships, won a bronze medal (2001); at Salt Lake City Olympics, won a gold medal (2002), marking the 1st time a skater jumped from 4th in the short program to win the title since compulsories were eliminated. Won Sullivan Award (2003).

HUGHES, Sarah T. (1896–1985). American jurist. Born Sarah Tilghman in Baltimore, Maryland, Aug 2, 1896; died April 23, 1985, in Dallas, Texas; dau. of James Cooke Tilghman and Elizabeth (Haughton) Tilghman; Goucher College, BS in Biology, 1917; George Washington University, LLB, 1922; m. George E. Hughes, Mar 13, 1922 (died June 1, 1964); no children. ❖ Texas jurist, state legislator, and feminist who handed down the decision in *Roe* v. *Wade* (1971), based on the right to privacy; admitted to bar, Washington, DC, and Dallas (1922); joined Priest, Herndon, & Ledbetter law firm (1923); elected to Texas House of Representatives (1930, 1932, 1934); appointed to 14th District Court of Texas (1935), then elected (1936) and reelected (1940, 1944, 1948, 1952, 1956, 1960); admitted to practice before US Supreme Court (1937); lost congressional primary election (1946); elected national president, Business and Professional Women's Clubs (1950); nominated for US vice president at Democratic National Convention (1952); lost primary race for Texas Supreme Court (1958); appointed Federal district judge (1961); became senior judge (1979); effectively retired (1982). Best known for being the 1st and only woman to swear in a president of US (Lyndon B. Johnson), but was more important as a women's rights advocate and precedent-setting jurist. ❖ See also *Women in World History*.

HUGHES, Valerie (1935—). See Taylor, Valerie.

HUGHES, Wendy (1950—). Australian actress. Born July 29, 1950, in Melbourne, Victoria, Australia; studied at National Institute of Dramatic Art; m. Sean Scully, 1971 (div. 1973); children: Charlotte and Jay. ❖ Award-winning actress, appeared in *My Brilliant Career* (1979), title role in *Lucinda Brayford* (1980), *Lonely Hearts* (1982), *Careful, He Might Hear You* (1983), *An Indecent Obsession* (1985), *Wild Orchid II* (1992), *Princess Caraboo* (1994), *Paradise Road* (1997) and *The Man Who Sued God* (2001); on tv, appeared on such series as "Return to Eden" (1983), "Amerika" (1987), "A Woman Named Jackie" (1991), "Snowy River: The McGregor Saga" (1993–95) and "State Coroner" (1997–98).

HUGO, Adèle (1830–1915). Daughter of Victor Hugo. Name variations: Adele Hugo. Born Adèle Hugo in Paris, France, July 27, 1830; died in France, 1915; 2nd daughter and youngest child of Victor and Adèle (Foucher) Hugo (1806–1868); sister of Léopoldine Hugo (1824–1843), Charles Hugo (b. 1826) and François-Victor Hugo (b. 1927). ❖ François Truffaut's film *The Story of Adele H* (1975), starring Isabelle Adjani, was based on *Le Journal d'Adele Hugo* by Frances V. Guille, who discovered her coded diaries in 1955; the film traces her obsession with Albert Pinson, an English lieutenant, as she followed him to his garrison assignment in Halifax, Nova Scotia, hoping to rekindle his affections; over time, she became more and more delusional. ❖ See also *Women in World History*.

HUGONNAI, Vilma (1847–1922). See Hugonnay, Vilma.

HUGONNAY, Vilma (1847–1922). Hungarian physician. Name variations: Vilma Hugonnai; Vilma Hugonnai-Wartha or Hugonnay-Wartha; Vilma Wartha. Born 1847 in the Castle Nagytétény in Budapest, Hungary; died 1922; dau. of Count Hugonnay; m. György Szillassy, 1865; m. Vince Wartha (1844–1914, Hungarian chemist). ❖ The 1st qualified woman doctor in Hungary, began studying medicine in Zurich after death of her 6-year-old child; published papers on tracheotomy in diphtheria and burn treatment; permitted only midwife certificate; after degree was finally recognized by Ministry of Culture (1897), began vigorous practice; contributed important research to Hungarian medicine and helped improve status of women in medicine.

HUH SOON-YOUNG (1975—). South Korean handball player. Born Sept 28, 1975, in South Korea. ❖ Won a team silver medal at Atlanta Olympics (1996), team gold medal at Asian Games (2002), and a team silver at Athens Olympics (2004).

HUH YOUNG-SOOK (1975—). South Korean handball player. Born July 2, 1975, in Chongup, South Korea. ❖ Won a team silver at Athens Olympics (2004).

HULDA (1881–1946). See Bjarklind, Unnur Benediktsdóttir.

HULDAH. Prophet. Name variations: Hulda. The wife of Shallum (Josiah's wardrobe keeper). ❖ One of only 3 women in Bible who are called prophets or prophetesses (the other 2 being Miriam the Prophet and Deborah), lived in the part of Jerusalem known as the Mishneh (college), thought by some to be located between the inner and outer wall of the city; held in high esteem, was consulted by Josiah when the lost Book of the Law was found in the temple; prophesied the destruction of Jerusalem but added that it would not occur before the death of Josiah.

HULETTE, Gladys (1896–1991). American silent-film actress. Born July 21, 1896, in Arcade, NY; died Aug 8, 1991, in Montebello, California. ❖ Starred in two major silent films, *Princess Nicotine* (1909) and *Tol'able David* (1921); other films include *The Iron Horse, Lena Rivers* and *A Bowery Cinderella*.

HULL, Eleanor (fl. 15th c.). British translator. Name variations: Dame Eleanor Hull; fl. early 15th century in England; born Eleanor Malet, the only child of Sir John Malet of Enmore in Somerset. ❖ Was connected with the royal court and probably also with the Bridgettine house at Twickenham, Sion Abbey; translated commentary on 7 penitential psalms and daily meditations from French into English.

HULL, Eleanor Henrietta (1860–1935). British journalist and literary scholar. Born 1860 in England; died in Wimbledon, 1935; dau. of a family from Co. Down; attended Alexandra College, Dublin; studied under Kuno Meyer and Standish Hayes O'Grady. ❖ Co-founded the Irish Texts Society (1899); writings include *The Cuchulain Saga in Irish Literature* (1898), *Pagan Ireland* (1904), *Early Christian Ireland* (1904), *A Textbook of Irish Literature* (2 vols., 1906–08), *The Poem-Book of the Gael* (1912) and *A History of Ireland* (2 vols., 1931).

HULL, Hannah (1872–1958). American pacifist and suffragist. Name variations: Hannah Clothier or Hannah Hallowell Clothier; Hannah Clothier Hull. Born Hannah Hallowell Clothier, July 21, 1872, in Sharon Hill, Pennsylvania; died July 4, 1958, in Swarthmore, PA; dau. of Isaac Hallowell Clothier and Mary Clapp (Jackson) Clothier; m. William Isaac Hull, Dec 27, 1898 (died 1939); children: 2 daughters (b. 1900, 1904). ❖ Attended 2nd Hague Conference for International Peace (1907); was vice president of PA Woman Suffrage Association (1913–14) and chair of PA branch of Woman's Peace Party (1917–20); worked with Women's International League for Peace and Freedom (WILPF), serving as delegate to emergency International Conference of Women (1922), national chair of US section (1924–28), chair of national board (1929–38), president of US section (1933–39), and honorary national president (1939–58); was vice chair of American Friends Service Committee (AFSC) board (1928–47), and member of peace committee and of executive committee of foreign service section; was member of board of directors of Pendle Hill (Quaker social and religious study center) (1929–55).

HULL, Helen Rose (1888–1971). American novelist and short-story writer. Born 1888 in Albion, Michigan; died 1971; dau. of Warren C. and Louise (McGill) Hull (both teachers); University of Chicago, PhD; lived with partner Mabel Louise Robinson. ❖ Active feminist, taught at Wellesley College (1912–15), then joined the staff of Columbia University (1916); writings, which are critical of attitudes toward women in US, include *Quest* (1922), *Labyrinth* (1923), *The Surry Family* (1925), *Islanders* (1927) and *Last September* (1988).

HULL, Josephine (1886–1957). American character actress. Name variations: Josephine Sherwood. Born Josephine Sherwood in Newtonville, Massachusetts, Jan 3, 1886; died Mar 12, 1957; dau. of William Henry (importer) and Mary (Tewksbury) Sherwood (board of education executive); graduate of Radcliffe College; m. Shelley Vaughn Hull (actor), 1910 (died 1919). ❖ Best known for portrayals of eccentric old ladies, joined Castle Square Stock Co. in Boston, making stage debut under name Sherwood (1905); on marriage (1910), retired; after husband's death (1919), returned to theater as a director for Jessie Bonstelle's stock company in Detroit; went to NY to become the director of Equity Players (1921) but, more often than not, found herself back on stage; attracted attention as Mrs. Hicks in *Neighbors* (1923); also scored a hit as Mrs. Frazier in *Craig's Wife* (1926); after a string of unsuccessful plays, appeared as Penelope Sycamore in *You Can't Take It With You* (1937), followed by *Arsenic and Old Lace* (1941), *Harvey* (1944), and *The Solid Gold Cadillac* (1954), appearing in all 3 film versions. Won Academy Award as Best Supporting Actress for *Harvey* (1951). ❖ See also William G.B. Carson, *Dear Josephine* (1963); and *Women in World History*.

HULL, Melanie Skillman (1954—). *See Skillman, Melanie.*

HULL, Peggy (1889–1967). American journalist. Born Henrietta Eleanor Goodnough, Dec 30, 1889, near Bennington, Kansas; died 1967 in Carmel Valley, California; m. George Hull (reporter), c. 1910 (div. 1914); m. John Kinley (British captain), 1921 (sep. 1925, div. 1932); m. Harvey Deuell (newspaper editor), c. 1932 (died 1939). ❖ Began career as a typesetter for *Junction City* (Kansas) *Sentinel*; with husband, moved to Hawaii, where she was a feature writer and women's page editor for *Pacific Commercial Advertiser* (1910); left husband (1914) and took a job with *Cleveland Plain Dealer*, writing advertising copy; during WWI, while working for *Chicago Tribune*, made history as 1st woman correspondent accredited by US War Department to cover a war zone, writing of the war from France and signing articles simply "Peggy"; obtained endorsement of Newspaper Enterprise Association to cover an American

military expedition to Siberia to guard the Trans-Siberian Railroad (1918); landing in Vladivostok, began a 9-month, 1,000-mile inspection tour of the Siberian Railroad and reported on the suffering of refugees trying to escape both Red and White armies; during WWII, at 53, traveled with fighting forces to Pacific Islands, documenting experiences of GIs in articles that were likened to those of Ernie Pyle. ❖ See also *Women in World History*.

HULL, Rachel (1866–1941). *See Don, Rachel.*

HULME, Juliet Marion (1938—). British mystery writer and murderer. Name variations: (pseudonym) Anne Perry. Born Juliet Marion Hulme, Oct 28, 1938, in Greenwich, London, England; dau. of Henry Rainsford Hulme (chief assistant at Royal Observatory, then rector of Canterbury College in Christchurch, NZ) and Hilda Marion (Reavley) Hulme, later known as H. Marion Perry on remarriage; never married. ❖ Moved to New Zealand with family; at 15, with friend Pauline Parker, murdered Parker's mother Honora (events are depicted in the film *Heavenly Creatures*, 1994); served out a 5½-year prison term at Mount Eden prison in Christchurch; left New Zealand for England (1959) and took mother's 2nd-marriage surname, becoming Anne Perry; moved to San Francisco, CA (1967), then Los Angeles; returned to England (early 1970s); published 1st novel *The Cater Street Hangman* (1979); wrote other Victorian mysteries, including *Rutland Place* (1983), *Silence in Hanover Close* (1988), *Highgate Rise* (1991), *The Sins of the Wolf* (1994), *Weighed in the Balance* (1996), *The Silent Cry* (1997), and *Tathea* (1999).

HULME, Kathryn (1900–1981). American author. Born Jan 6, 1900, in San Francisco, CA; died Aug 25, 1981, in Lihue, Hawaii; dau. of Edwin Page and Julia Frances (Cavarly) Hulme; attended University of California, 1918–21, Columbia University, 1922, and Hunter College, 1923; never married; lived with Marie-Louise Habets (1905–1986); no children. ❖ Best remembered for book *The Nun's Story*, the biography of her companion Marie-Louise Habets (characterized as Gabrielle Van der Mal, or Sister Luke, in the book), got 1st job as a reporter for *Daily Californian*; lived as an expatriate in Paris (1930s) but returned to US at outbreak of war; served as a deputy director of United Nations Relief and Rehabilitation Administration (UNRRA) in a US Occupied Zone in Germany (1945–47); wrote *Arab Interlude* (1930), (fictional autobiography) *We Lived as Children* (1938), (nonfiction) *The Wild Place* (1953) and (fiction) *Annie's Captain* (1961); later works are marked by a deep spirituality, the result of her relationship with mystic-philosopher Gurdjieff. ❖ See also autobiography *Undiscovered Country: A Spiritual Adventure* (1966); and *Women in World History*.

HULME, Keri (1947—). New Zealand novelist and poet. Born Keri Ann Ruhi Hulme, Mar 9, 1947, in Otautahi, Christchurch, New Zealand, of mixed Maori, Orkney and English descent; dau. of John W. (carpenter) and Mere Hulme; attended University of Canterbury. ❖ Influenced by Maori legends, her stories and poems focus on questions of race, gender, and environment; co-founded Wellington Women's Gallery and served as writer-in-residence at Otago University (1978) and University of Canterbury (1985); writings include *The Silences Between* (1982), *The Bone People* (1983), which won the Booker Prize (1985), *Lost Possessions* (1985), (stories) *Te Kaihu/The Windeater* (1986), *Homeplaces: Three Coasts of the South Island of New Zealand* (1989), *Strands* (1992) and *Bait* (1999).

HÜLSENBECK, Sarina (1962—). *See Huelsenbeck, Sarina.*

HÜLSHOFF, Annette von Droste (1797–1848). *See Droste-Hülshoff, Annette von.*

HULTEN, Vivi-Anne (1911–2003). Swedish figure skater. Name variations: Hultén. Born Aug 25, 1911, in Stockholm, Sweden; died Jan 15, 2003, in Corona de Mar, California; m. Gene Theslof (skating partner), 1942 (died 1983); children: Gene Theslof (adagio skater). ❖ Won 1st of 10 Swedish national figure-skating championships (1927); at European championships, won bronze medals (1930, 1932); at World championships, won a silver medal (1933) and bronze medals (1935–37); won a bronze medal at Garmisch-Partenkirchen, Germany, Olympics (1936), but refused to salute Adolf Hitler; turned professional (1938), skated with the Ice Follies and served as show director for Ice Capades.

HUMBLE, Joan (1951—). English politician and member of Parliament. Born Joan Piplica, Mar 3, 1951; m. Paul Humble, 1972. ❖ Representing Labour, elected to House of Commons for Blackpool North and Fleetwood (1997, 2001, 2005).

HUME, Anna (fl. 1644). Scottish poet and translator. Flourished in Scotland c. 1644; dau. of David Hume of Godscroft (c. 1560–c. 1630). ❖ Translated *The Triumph of Love: Chastitie: Death: Translated out of Petrarch by Mrs. Anne Hume* (1644), which contains explanatory notes that display her wide reading and learning; edited father's work *The History of the Houses of Douglas and Angus* (1644).

HUME, Benita (1906–1967). English actress. Born Oct 14, 1906, in London, England; died Nov 1, 1967, in Egerton, England; sister of Cyril Hume; attended RADA; m. Eric Siepman (div.); m. Ronald Colman (actor), 1938 (died 1958); m. George Sanders (actor), 1959; children: (2nd m.) daughter. ❖ Made London stage debut in *London Life* (1924), British film debut in *The Happy Ending* (1925), and NY stage debut in *Symphony in Two Flats* (1930); starred in such films as *Only Yesterday, Looking Forward, The Private Life of Don Juan, Reserved for Ladies, High Treason, The Lady of the Lake, The Gay Deception, The Moonlight Murder, Tarzan Escapes, Rainbow on the River, The Constant Nymph* and *The Last of Mrs. Cheyney*; appeared on radio and tv in "The Halls of Ivy."

HUME, Elizabeth (c. 1599–1633). Countess of Suffolk. Name variations: Elizabeth Howard. Born c. 1599; died Aug 19, 1633, at Greenwich Park Tower; dau. of George Hume, earl of Dunbar, and Elizabeth Gordon; m. Theophilus Howard (1584–1640), 2nd earl of Suffolk (r. 1626–1640), also known as 2nd Lord Howard of Walden, Mar 1612; children: James Howard (b. 1619), 3rd earl of Suffolk; Honorable Thomas Howard; George Howard (b. 1625), 4th earl of Suffolk; Henry Howard (b. 1627), 5th earl of Suffolk; Frances Villiers (c. 1633–1677); Katherine Howard (d. 1650, who m. George Stuart, Seigneur d'Aubigny and James Livingston, 1st earl of Newburgh); Elizabeth Percy (d. 1704); Margaret Howard (who m. Roger Boyle, 1st earl of Orrery); Anne Howard (who m. Thomas Walsingham).

HUME, Grizel (1665–1746). See Baillie, Grizel.

HUME, Marilyn (1916–2001). See Meseke, Marilyn.

HUME, Sophia Wigington (1702–1774). American Quaker minister and writer. Born Sophia Wigington, 1702, in Charleston, SC; died Jan 26, 1774, presumably in London, England; dau. of Henry and Susanna (Bayley) Wigington; m. Robert Hume, 1721 (died c. 1737); children: 1 daughter, 1 son. ❖ Experienced religious conversion and abandoned life of comfort in favor of Quaker simplicity (c. 1740); preached to public meetings in SC and PA; published *An Exhortation to the Inhabitants of South-Carolina* (1748); recognized as minister by monthly meeting in London (c. 1763); published *A Caution to Such as Observe Days and Times* (c. 1763).

HUMILITAS OF FAENZA (1226–1310). Italian saint and abbess. Name variations: Humility; Rosana; Umilita; Umilta. Born 1226 in Italy; died 1310 in Faenza; m. Hugolotto. ❖ Italian religious founder, lived as a recluse for several years but eventually emerged as head of a Benedictine convent at Faenza; founded Order of Vallumbrosian Sisters, a religious establishment over which she presided. Feast day is May 22. ❖ See also *Women in World History.*

HUMILITY (1226–1310). See Humilitas of Faenza.

HUMISHUMA (c. 1882–1936). See Mourning Dove.

HUMMEL, Barbara W. (1926–2000). See Walker, Barbara Jo.

HUMMEL, Berta (1909–1946). German illustrator and Roman Catholic nun. Name variations: Sister Maria Innocentia. Born in Massing, Lower Bavaria, Germany, May 21, 1909; died Nov 6, 1946, in Convent Siessen bei Saulgau, Württemberg, Germany; dau. of Adolf Hummel and Viktoria (Anglsperger) Hummel. ❖ Artist whose drawings of children became the models for Hummel figurines, completed art studies (1931); entered a convent, where she drew pictures of children that were sold 1st as greeting cards, then as figurines, by W. Goebel porcelain factory, the sales of which provided major financial support for her convent; her images of childhood innocence, captured in porcelain, continue to be much beloved throughout the world and many of the figurines have become collectors' items. ❖ See also *Women in World History.*

HUMMERT, Anne (1905–1996). American writer. Born Jan 19, 1905; died July 5, 1996, in New York, NY; graduated magna cum laude from Goucher College, 1925; m. a journalist (div.); m. Frank Hummert, 1934 (died 1966): children: (1st m.) 1 son. ❖ With husband Frank, created 1st daytime soap opera, "Just Plain Bill," which premiered on radio (1933) and immediately caught the imagination of radio listeners throughout nation; churned out a total of 18 popular daytime serials, 90 15-minute episodes a week (1930s–40s). ❖ See also *Women in World History.*

HUMPHREY, Doris (1895–1958). American dancer and choreographer. Born Doris Batcheller Humphrey, Oct 17, 1895, in Oak Park, Illinois; died Dec 29, 1958, in New York, NY, of cancer; dau. of Horace Buckingham Humphrey (journalist and hotel manager) and Julia Ellen (Wells) Humphrey (musician); m. Charles F. Woodford, June 10, 1932; children: Charles Humphrey Woodford (b. 1933). ❖ Dance pioneer, was known for articulating the meaning of dance and the process of choreography; began dancing at 8; trained and performed with Denishawn (1917–27), creating a popular solo, "Soaring" (1920); with Charles Weidman, co-founded the Humphrey-Weidman Group (1927); gave 1st independent concert in NY (1928); helped found short-lived Dance Repertory Theater (1930–31); created a number of masterpieces that solidified her position as the consummate choreographer of modern dance, including a triumvirate of works celebrating human relationships: "New Dance" (1935), "Theater Piece" (1936) and "With My Red Fires" (1936); with Weidman, founded Studio Theater (1940); offered 1st dance composition class (1945); was artistic director of José Limon dance company (1945–50) and official director of Dance Center at 92nd St. YMHA (1952); was artistic director of Juilliard Dance Theater (1954); wrote *The Art of Making Dances*, published posthumously (1959); along with Martha Graham, invented the new American art form of modern dance. Received Choreographic Award of the year from *Dance Magazine* (1937); received Capezio Award (1954). ❖ See also Marcia Siegel, *Days on Earth: The Dance of Doris Humphrey* (Yale U. Press, 1987); and *Women in World History.*

HUMPHREY, Edith (1875–1977). English chemist. Name variations: Edith Ellen Humphrey. Born Sept 1875 in UK; died 1977; studied physical chemistry at Bedford College, London, 1893–97, and cobalt salt crystals at University of Zurich, PhD, 1901. ❖ A crystal expert, worked as a chemical laboratory assistant to professor Alfred Werner; researched the polarization of light in opposite directions by pairs of crystals with the same chemical makeup (after her death, her crystals were rediscovered in the 1980s); as a chief chemist at Arthur Sanderson and Sons (wallpaper manufacturers) in London, created a company research laboratory.

HUMPHREY, Muriel (1912–1998). American politician. Name variations: Muriel Humphrey Brown. Born Muriel Fay Buck on Feb 20, 1912, in Huron, South Dakota; died Sept 20, 1998, in Minneapolis, Minnesota; dau. of Andrew E. and Jessie May Buck; educated at Huron College; m. Hubert Horatio Humphrey (former vice president and US senator) 1936 (died 1977); remarried; children: (1st m.) Nancy Humphrey; Hubert H. Humphrey, 3rd; Robert Andrew Humphrey; Douglas Sannes Humphrey. ❖ US Democratic senator, was active in husband's 1st campaign at a time when few politicians' wives were, and continued to assist him throughout his career; appointed to fill the Senate seat left vacant by his death (Jan 25, 1978); during 9-month tenure, as the only woman in the 100-member Senate, served on the Committee on Foreign Relations and Committee on Governmental Operations and helped to pass legislation that dealt with women's issues, including providing child-care and flexible work schedules for working mothers, lowering female unemployment, and extending ratification deadline for Equal Rights Amendment (ERA); was also active in work dealing with mental retardation. ❖ See also *Women in World History.*

HUMPHREY, Terin (1986—). American gymnast. Born Terin Maria Humphrey, Aug 14, 1986, in St. Joseph, Missouri. ❖ Won team World championship (2003); won silver medals for uneven bars and team all-around at Athens Olympics (2004).

HUMPHRIES, Carmel (1909–1986). Irish freshwater biologist. Born Carmel Frances Humphries, June 3, 1909, in Dublin, Ireland; died Mar 7, 1986, in Rathmines, Dublin; dau. of William Humphries (died 1941) and Anne Palmer Humphries (died 1956); University College, Dublin, BS in botany and zoology, 1932, MS, 1933, PhD, 1938. ❖ Expert on chironomids (nonbiting midges), studied in Germany under August Thienemann; held a zoology assistantship (1938–39) and senior demonstrator position (1939–41) at University College, Galway; was assistant lecturer (1942–47), lecturer (1947–57), and professor (1956–79) at University College, Dublin; helped design the marine field station and established a Limnology Unit within the zoology department at University College; researched Irish chironomidae; served as International Limnological Association's Irish representative; was a member of Royal Irish Academy of Science (1950) and Royal Dublin Society.

HUNDVIN, Mia (1977—). Norwegian handball player. Born Mar 7, 1977, in Bergen, Norway. ❖ Won a team bronze medal at Sydney Olympics (2000).

HUNEBERC or HUNEBURC (fl. 8th c.). See Hygeburg.

HUNGARY, duchess of. See Sarolta (fl. 900s).

HUNGARY, queen of.
See Gisela of Bavaria (c. 975–1033).
See Anastasia of Russia (c. 1023-after 1074).
See Richesa of Poland (fl. 1030–1040).
See Synadene of Byzantium (c. 1050–?).
See Adelaide of Rheinfelden (c. 1065–?).
See Helena of Serbia (fl. 1100s).
See Preslava of Russia (fl. 1100).
See Euphrosyne of Kiev (fl. 1130–1180).
See Euphemia of Kiev (d. 1139).
See Anne of Chatillon-Antioche (c. 1155–c. 1185).
See Margaret of France (1158–1198).
See Gertrude of Andrechs-Meran (c. 1185–1213).
See Yolande of Courtenay (fl. 1200s).
See Elizabeth of Sicily (fl. 1200s).
See Salome of Hungary (1201–c. 1270).
See Maria Lascaris (fl. 1234–1242).
See Elizabeth of Kumania (c. 1242–?).
See Este, Beatrice d' (d. 1245).
See Agnes of Austria (1281–1364).
See Elizabeth of Poland (1305–1380).
See Elizabeth of Bosnia (c. 1345–1387).
See Maria of Hungary (1371–1395).
See Barbara of Cilli (fl. 1390–1410).
See Elizabeth of Luxemburg (1409–1442).
See Madeleine of France (1443–1486).
See Beatrice of Naples (1457–1508).
See Foix, Anne de (fl. 1480–1500).
See Mary of Hungary (1505–1558).
See Isabella of Poland (1519–1559).
See Zita of Parma (1892–1989).

HUNGER, Daniela (1972—). East German swimmer. Born Mar 20, 1972, in East Germany. ❖ At Seoul Olympics, won a bronze medal in the 400-meter indiv. medley and a gold medal in the 200-meter indiv. medley and the 4x100-meter freestyle relay (1988); at Barcelona Olympics, won a bronze medal in the 4x100-meter freestyle relay and the 200-meter indiv. medley and a silver medal in the 4x100-meter medley relay (1992).

HUNGERFORD, Agnes (d. 1524). English noblewoman. Name variations: Lady Agnes Hungerford. Executed in 1524; m. John Cotell; 2nd wife of Sir Edward Hungerford (died 1522). ❖ Executed for the murder of 1st husband, John Cotell.

HUNGERFORD, Catherine (d. 1452). See Howard, Catherine.

HUNGERFORD, Margaret Wolfe (c. 1855–1897). Irish novelist. Name variations: Margaret Hamilton Wolfe Hungerford; Mrs. Hungerford; (pseudonyms) The Author of Phyllis, The Duchess. Born Margaret Hamilton, c. 1855, in Cork, Ireland; died Jan 24, 1897, in Bandon, Ireland; dau. of Canon Fitzjohn Stannus Hamilton (vicar-choral of St. Faughnan's Cathedral and rector of Ross Co., Ireland); m. Edward Argles, 1872; m. Thomas Henry Hungerford, 1882. ❖ Novels, which are lighthearted and sentimental, include Phyllis: A Novel (1877), Beauty's Daughters (1880), Monica (1883), O Tender Dolores (1885), A Modern Circe (1887), A Born Coquette (1890), The Hoyden (1894) and Nora Creina (1903); best known for Molly Bawn (1878).

HUNT, Eva (1934–1980). American cultural anthropologist. Name variations: Eva Verbitsky Hunt. Born Eva Verbitsky, April 12, 1934, in Buenos Aires, Argentina; raised in Mexico City; died of cancer, 1980; dau. of Alejandro Verbitsky and Josefa Plotkin Verbitsky; Universidad Femina in Mexico City, BS; attended Escuela Nacional de Anthropologia, 1953–57; University of Chicago, MA, 1959, Ph.D. in anthropology, 1962; m. Robert Hunt (anthropologist), 1960; children: Melissa Hunt. ❖ Studied in Mexico and US; served as research associate for Paul Bohannan in anthropology program of Northwestern University; with husband, lived with Cuicatec in Mexico (c. 1964) and performed ground-breaking regional work there by studying an entire district (as opposed to a village) in Oaxaca (1960s); joined staff of University of Chicago (1965); studied kinship systems; published best-known work The Transformation of the Hummingbird: Cultural Roots of a Zinacantecan Mythical Poem (1977); served as associate professor at Boston University (until 1980).

HUNT, Frances Irwin (1890–1981). New Zealand artist. Born on July 26, 1890, in Cambridge, New Zealand; died on Aug 25, 1981, in Auckland; dau. of Nicholas Irwin Hunt (farmer) and Annie Lilian (Souter) Hunt; Elam School of Art, 1932. ❖ Studied watercolor at Frank Wright's academy in Auckland (1920s); working member of Auckland Society of Arts (1924); elected to National Art Association of New Zealand (1925); prominent member of Rutland Group of former Elam School of Art students; produced landscapes, still-lifes and portraits; work included in 2 national centennial exhibitions (1940); retrospective of her work exhibited at Auckland Society of Art (1975). ❖ See also Dictionary of New Zealand Biography (Vol. 4).

HUNT, Harriot Kezia (1805–1875). American medical practitioner and feminist. Born Harriot Kezia Hunt, Nov 9, 1805, in Boston, Massachusetts; died in Boston of Bright's disease, Jan 2, 1875; dau. of Joab Hunt (ship's joiner) and Kezia (Wentworth) Hunt; studied alternative medicine for 2 years; never married; no children. ❖ Alternative healer, sometimes called the 1st woman doctor in US, who sought to expand the legitimacy of women in male-dominated professions and traced mental and physical illness in women to limitations imposed on their lives, opened a school in her home (1827); began 2-year study of alternative medicine (1833), then opened a practice (1835); organized the Ladies Physiological Society in Charlestown, Massachusetts (1843); turned to Swedenborgian religion (1843); applied to Harvard Medical School and denied entry (1847); attended 1st National Women's Rights Conference (1850); reapplied to Harvard and admitted but was too ill to take advantage of the opportunity (1850); was 1st woman to make public protest in Massachusetts against "taxation without representation" (1852); received honorary MD from Female Medical College of Philadelphia (1853); hosted founding meeting of the New England Women's Club (1868). ❖ See also autobiography Glances and Glimpses or Fifty Years Social, Including Twenty Years Professional Life (1856); and Women in World History.

HUNT, Helen (1963—). American actress. Born Helen Elizbeth Hunt, June 15, 1963, in Los Angeles, CA; dau. of Gordon Hunt (director and acting coach); m. Hank Azaria (actor), July 1999 (div. 2000); children: Makena'lei Gordon Carnahan (b. 2004). ❖ Made professional debut at age 9; appeared on tv series "Amy Prentiss" (1974), "Swiss Family Robinson" (1975), "It Takes Two" (1982), "St. Elsewhere" (1984–86), and, with Paul Reiser, starred in "Mad About You" (1992–99); won an Academy Award for Best Actress for performance in As Good As It Gets (1997); other films include Peggy Sue Got Married (1986), Bob Roberts (1992), Mr. Saturday Night (1992), Twister (1996), Pay It Forward (2000), Cast Away (2000) and A Good Woman (2000).

HUNT, Helen Fiske (1830–1885). See Jackson, Helen Hunt.

HUNT, Marsha (1917—). American actress. Born Marcia Virginia Hunt, Oct 17, 1917, in Chicago, Illinois; studied acting at Theodora Irvine School of Dramatics; m. Jerry Hopper (editor, then director), in 1938 (div. 1943); m. Robert Presnell (screenwriter), 1946. ❖ Paid for acting lessons by modeling for John Robert Powers; made screen debut in The Virginia Judge (1935); signed with MGM, where she made a name playing leads in B pictures and supporting roles in major productions, including Irene (1940), Pride and Prejudice (1940), Blossoms in the Dust (1941), Panama Hattie (1942), The Human Comedy (1943), Thousands Cheer (1943), Cry Havoc (1943), The Valley of Decision (1945), Smash-up (1947), and The Happy Time (1952); career suffered a serious setback (1950s), when 2nd husband, Robert Presnell, was accused of sympathizing with Hollywood Ten, a group who refused to testify at House Un-American Activities Committee (HUAC) hearings; a political innocent, protested the committee's methods and was subsequently blacklisted in film, radio and tv; returned to stage, appearing on Broadway in The Devil's Disciple (1950); continued to work in theater for years; later appeared on numerous tv shows, including "Marcus Welby, M.D."; founded Valley Mayors Fund for the Homeless and served as its president for 6 years. ❖ See also Women in World History.

HUNT, Martita (1900–1969). English stage and screen actress. Born Jan 30, 1900, in Buenos Aires, Argentina; died June 13, 1969, in London, England. ❖ At 10, moved to England; made stage debut with Liverpool

Rep (1921); made London debut in *The Machine Wreckers* (1923); other plays include *A Doll's House, Rasputin, Let's Leave It at That, Hamlet, Topaze, Autumn Crocus, All's Well That Ends Well, Fresh Fields, Bitter Harvest, The White Devil* and *Hotel Paridiso*; made film debut in *I Was a Spy* (1933); probably best remembered for portrayal of Miss Havisham in film adaptation of *Great Expectations* (1946). Won Tony award as Best Actress for *The Madwoman of Chaillot* (1948).

HUNT, Mary Hanchett (1830–1906). American temperance leader. Born Mary Hannah Hanchett, June 4, 1830, in South Canaan, Connecticut; died April 24, 1906, in Dorchester, MA; dau. of Ephraim Hanchett and Nancy (Swift) Hanchett; attended Amenia Seminary in NY; attended Patapsco Female Institute, near Baltimore; m. Leander B. Hunt, Oct 1852; children: Alfred E. Hunt (chemist and engineer). ❖ Promoted temperance on scientific grounds; became national superintendent of Department of Scientific Temperance Instruction of WCTU (1880); worked successfully toward goal of mandatory temperance instruction in public schools; held position with World's WCTU comparable to her local position (from 1890); served as editor of *Scientific Temperance Monthly Advices* (from 1892). Writings include *A History of the First Decade of the Department of Scientific Temperance Instruction in Schools and Colleges* (1891) and *An Epoch of the Nineteenth Century* (1897).

HUNT, Pearlie (1904–1993). *See Burton, Pearlie.*

HUNT, Violet (1866–1942). British novelist and biographer. Born Isobel Violet Hunt, 1866, in Durham, England; died Jan 16, 1942, in London; dau. of Alfred William Hunt (pre-Raphaelite painter) and Margaret Raine Hunt (novelist, sometimes used pseudonym Averil Beaumont); educated at Notting Hill High School (1 of 1st girls' high schools) and South Kensington Art School; married (not legally) Ford Madox Hueffer (later known as Ford Madox Ford), 1911. ❖ Wrote sexually frank novels, such as *Unkissed, Unkind* (1897) and *The White Rose of Weary Leaf* (1908, considered her best); published collections of short stories, such as *Tales of the Uneasy* (1911) and *The Tiger Skin* (1924), and a biography of Elizabeth Siddal, *The Wife of Rossetti* (1932); drew on autobiographical details for much of her work, including *The Celebrity at Home* (1904) and *The Celebrity's Daughter* (1913); also wrote for *Black and White* and had weekly column in *Pall Mall Gazette*; worked for women's suffrage, organizing the Women Writers' Suffrage League, and supported Radclyffe Hall as she fought to keep *The Well of Loneliness* from being banned. ❖ See also autobiography *The Flurried Years* (1926, published in US as *I Have This to Say*); Barbara Belford, *Violet* (Simon & Schuster); Joan Hardwick, *An Immodest Violet: The Life of Violet Hunt* (Deutsch, 1993); and *Women in World History.*

HUNTE, Heather (1959—). English runner. Name variations: Heather Oakes; Heather Hunte-Oakes. Born Aug 14, 1959, in England, of Guyanese parentage; m. Gary Oakes (Olympian). ❖ At United Kingdom championships, won a gold medal for 200 meters (1979); won a bronze medal at Moscow Olympics (1980) and a bronze medal at Los Angeles Olympics (1984), both in the 4x100-meter relay; won the 100 meters at the Commonwealth Games (1986).

HUNTER, Alberta (1895–1984). African-American blues singer. Name variations: Alberta Prime; Josephine Beatty. Born in Memphis, TN, April 1, 1895; died Oct 17, 1984 in New York, NY; m. Willard Saxby Townsend, 1919 (div. 1923). ❖ Bridging the gap between classic blues and cabaret pop, performed for over 40 years; at 16, ran away from home to Chicago, making 1st appearances singing in saloons; went to NY to launch recording career on Black Swan label (1921), then signed with Paramount (1922); wrote many songs, such as "Down Hearted Blues," a hit for Bessie Smith; also sang "Your Jelly Roll is Good," "Sugar," "Beale Street Blues" and "Take that Thing Away"; played the Cotton Club in Harlem; continued to record on Biltmore label as Alberta Prime, on Gennett label as Josephine Beatty, and on Okeh, Victor and Columbia under own name; during WWII, traveled with USO to China, Burma, India, Korea and Europe; with star fading, quit performing at 62 and enrolled in YWCA's nursing program (1956); was a practicing nurse (1957–77); made a comeback at the Cookery in Greenwich Village (1977) and was an enormous hit, negotiating a recording contract with Columbia, making debut at Carnegie Hall and singing at Kennedy Center. ❖ See also Frank C. Taylor, with Gerald Cook *Alberta Hunter: A Celebration in Blues* (1987) and *Alberta Hunter: Jazz at the Smithsonian* (video, 1982); and *Women in World History.*

HUNTER, Clementine (1886–1988). African-American folk artist. Born Clementine Reuben near Cloutierville, Louisiana, in Dec 1886; died near Natchitoches, Louisiana, Jan 1, 1988; dau. of Janvier (John) Reuben and Antoinette (Adams) Reuben; m. Charles Dupree (died 1914); m. Emanuel Hunter, 1924 (died 1944); children: (1st m.) 2; (2nd m.) 5. ❖ Often referred to as the "black Grandma Moses," was self-taught and began painting late in life; illiterate, lived in a small cabin in Natchitoches, far removed from urban galleries that sold her paintings for hundreds of dollars; labeled a primitive, had earliest solo exhibitions (1955), at Delgado Museum (now New Orleans Museum of Art), and at Northwestern State College, where she was not allowed to view the exhibit with the white patrons; during lifetime, had over 25 solo exhibitions at galleries and museums throughout US; work now resides in permanent collections of Birmingham Museum of Art, Dallas Museum of Fine Art, High Museum in Atlanta, and Louisiana State Museum, among others. The African House Murals, depicting plantation life along the Cane River, are considered some of her most important works. ❖ See also *Women in World History.*

HUNTER, Holly (1958—). American actress. Born Mar 20, 1958, in Conyers, Georgia; graduate of Carnegie Mellon University, 1980; m. Janusz Kaminski (cinematographer), 1995 (div. 2001). ❖ Came to prominence in the plays of Beth Henley: *Crimes of the Heart* (1982) and *The Miss Firecracker Contest*; had 1st starring film role in *Raising Arizona* (1987), followed by *Broadcast News* (1987); won Academy Award for Best Actress for *The Piano* (1993) and Emmy for "The Positively True Adventures of the Alleged Texas Cheerleader-Murdering Mom" (1993); other films include *Always* (1989), *The Firm* (1993), *Home for the Holidays* (1995), *O Brother, Where Art Thou?* (2000), (voice) *The Incredibles* (2004) and *The Big White* (2005).

HUNTER, Kim (1922–2002). American actress. Born Janet Cole, Nov 12, 1922, in Detroit, Michigan; died Sept 11, 2002, in New York, NY; dau. of Donald Cole (engineer) and Grace (Lind) Cole (concert pianist); studied acting with Charmine Lantaff, 1938–40; was a member of Actors Studio from 1948; m. William A. Baldwin, Feb 11, 1944 (div. 1946); m. Robert Emmett (writer), Dec 20, 1951; children: (1st m.) Kathryn Baldwin; (2nd m.) 1 son. ❖ Made stage debut in title role of *Penny Wise* in Miami (1939); appeared in *Arsenic and Old Lace* at Pasadena Playhouse which brought her to attention of David O. Selznick, who signed her and changed her name; made screen debut in *The Seventh Victim* (1943), then appeared in a number of mediocre movies, until English film *A Matter of Life and Death,* released in US as *Stairway to Heaven* (1946); on Broadway, originated part of Stella Kowalski in *A Streetcar Named Desire* (1947), followed by film version (1952); fell victim to McCarthy hysteria (1950s) and was blacklisted for several years; on Broadway, was particularly notable as Luba in *Darkness at Noon* (1951) and Karen Wright in *The Children's Hour* (1952); on tv, appeared on "Gunsmoke," "Columbo," "Marcus Welby, M.D." and "Ironside"; once blacklist was lifted, appeared in *Planet of the Apes* (1968), *Beneath the Planet of the Apes* (1970) and *Escape From the Planet of the Apes* (1971). Won Donaldson Award (1948) and Critics Circle Award (1948) and Academy Award for Best Supporting Actress (1952), all for *A Streetcar Named Desire.* ❖ See also autobiographical cookbook, *Loose in the Kitchen* (1975); and *Women in World History.*

HUNTER, Kristin (1931—). African-American novelist and short-story writer. Name variations: Kristin Hunter Lattany. Born Kristin Hunter, Sept 9, 1931, in Philadelphia, PA; dau. of George Lorenzo Hunter and Mabel Hunter; m. John I. Lattany, 1968. ❖ Taught creative writing at University of Pennsylvania until 1995; wrote *God Bless the Child* (1964), *The Landlord* (1966), *The Soul Brother and Sister Lou* (1968), *Boss Cat* (1971), *Guest in the Promised Land* (1973), *The Survivors* (1975), *The Lakestown Rebellion* (1978), *Lou in the Limelight* (1981), *Kinfolks* (1996) and *Do Unto Others* (2000); also wrote screenplay for *The Landlord.* Awards include Pennsylvania State Council on Arts Literature Fellowship (1983) and Moonstone Black Writing Celebration Lifetime Achievement Award (1996).

HUNTER, Mollie (1922—). Scottish writer. Born Maureen Mollie Hunter McVeigh, June 30, 1922, in Longniddry, East Lothian, Scotland; m. Thomas McIlwraith, 1940. ❖ Hailed as Scotland's most gifted storyteller, writes in a variety of genres including fantasy, historical fiction and contemporary realism, all set in native Scotland and frequently rooted in Scottish folklore; received *New York Times'* Outstanding Books of the Year award for *The Haunted Mountain* and *A Sound of Chariots* (1972) and Carnegie Medal for *The Stronghold* (1975); young-adult fiction includes *Hi Johnny* (1963), *Thomas and the Warlock* (1970), *A Stranger Came Ashore* (1975), *The Kelpie's Pearls* (1976), *The Third Eye* (1979), *You Never Knew Her As I Did* (1981), and *The Knight of the Golden Plain* (1983); also wrote essays *The Pied*

Piper Syndrome (1992) and *Talent Is Not Enough: Mollie Hunter on Writing for Children* (1990).

HUNTER, Rita (1933–2001). English dramatic soprano. Born Rita Nellie Hunter, Aug 15, 1933, in Wallasey, England; died April 29, 2001, in Sydney, Australia; studied with Olive Lloyd, Harry Burgon, Edwin Francis, Edward Renton, Eva Turner and Redvers Llewellyn; m. John Darnley-Thomas (baritone), c. 1957 (died 1994); children: Mairwyn (b. 1968). ❖ Joined chorus of Sadler's Wells Opera (1954), then Carl Rosa Opera (1957); when the 2 operas merged, began to get featured roles, including Senta in *The Flying Dutchman* (1964); sang Brünnhilde in the acclaimed production of *Ring*, under baton of Reginald Goodall (1970–73); sang title role in *Norma* at the Met in NY (1976); also appeared as Abigaille in *Nabucco* (1978) and Leonora in *Il Trovatore* (1980); sang with the Australian Opera (1981–85); remained in Australia. Made a Commander of the British Empire (1980). ❖ See also autobiography *Wait Till the Sun Shines, Nellie* (1986).

HUNTER-GAULT, Charlayne (1942—). African-American journalist. Born Charlayne Hunter, Feb 27, 1942, in Due West, South Carolina; dau. of Charles S.H. Hunter Jr. (Methodist chaplin in US army) and Althea Hunter; University of Georgia, BA in journalism, 1963; m. Walter Stovall (div.); m. Ronald Gault, 1971; children: (1st m.) Susan Stavall; (2nd m.) Chuma Hunter-Gault (actor). ❖ Was one of two black students who desegregated the University of Georgia (1961); served as "Talk of the Town" reporter for *The New Yorker;* anchored the evening news for WRC-TV in Washington, DC; joined *New York Times* (1968); was national correspondent for the "MacNeil-Lehrer NewsHour" (1978–97); moved to Johannesburg, South Africa. Won 2 Emmys and a Peabody award. ❖ See also autobiography, *In My Place* (Farrar, 1992).

HUNTINGDON, countess of.
See Judith of Normandy (c. 1054-after 1086).
See Adelicia de Warrenne (d. 1178).
See Maude of Chester (1171–1233).
See Margaret (d. 1228).
See Ellen of Wales (d. 1253).
See Hastings, Selina (1707–1791).

HUNTINGTON, Anna Hyatt (1876–1973). American sculptor and philanthropist. Name variations: Anna Vaughn Hyatt; Mrs. Archer M. Huntington. Born Anna Vaughn Hyatt, Mar 10, 1876, in Cambridge, Massachusetts; died Oct 4, 1973, in Redding Ridge, Connecticut; dau. of Audella Beebe Hyatt (painter) and Alpheus Hyatt II (zoologist and paleontologist); sister of Harriet Hyatt Mayor (sculptor); studied with Herman A. MacNeill and Gutzon Borglum at Art Students League, 1903; m. Archer Milton Huntington (scholar, poet, and philanthropist), 1923 (died 1955); no children. ❖ Much admired for her animal, garden, fountain and equestrian statuary, collaborated with Abastenia Eberle on a bronze, *Men and Bull* (1903), which won a bronze medal at Louisiana Purchase Exposition of 1904; with her vast knowledge of animal anatomy, especially horses, became a world-renowned animalier; studied and worked in France and Italy (1906–10); won honorable mention at Paris Salon (1908), with *Reaching Jaguar* (1906) and *Jaguar* (1907); became a part of the new thrust in sculpture due to her rhythmic expressive animal groups, such as *Cranes Rising* (bronze, 1934) and *Peacocks Fighting* (bronze, 1935–36), which showed a decorative art-nouveau quality; executed Joan of Arc astride a horse in bronze for Riverside Drive in NYC (1915), a landmark in the history of women sculptors, for which she won the Saltus Medal for Merit from National Academy of Design (1920); earned highest honors from governments of US, Cuba, and Spain for *Joan of Arc,* as well as for *El Cid Campeador* (bronze, 1927); other notable works of this period are *Diana of the Chase,* which won a 2nd Saltus gold medal (1922), and *Youth Taming the Wild* (1933); with husband, purchased a 6,700-acre tract of land on South Carolina coast near Charleston (1930); laid out a large formal garden, keeping rest of land as a nature preserve of indigenous flora and fauna, then presented this outdoor museum, called Brookgreen Gardens, to state of South Carolina (1932); for entrance, sculpted *Fighting Stallions,* a huge 17′ x 14′ x 7′ statue, representative of the work she pioneered using aluminum; awarded gold medal for distinction by American Academy of Arts and Letters (1930) which also held a retrospective exhibition of 171 of her works (1936); produced 2 major works in bas-relief, *Don Quixote* and *Boabdil,* for Hispanic Society of America (1942–43); with husband, founded 14 museums and established 4 public wildlife preserves; work is represented in the collections of more than 200 museums, parks and gardens of major cities throughout world. Awarded Chevalier of the Legion of Honor from France and named a

corresponding member of the Spanish Academia de Artes de San Fernando, an honor never before given to a woman. ❖ See also Eleanor M. Mellon, *Anna Hyatt Huntington* (Norton, 1947); and *Women in World History.*

HUNTINGTON, Anna Seaton (1964—). *See Seaton, Anna.*

HUNTINGTON, Anne Huntington (d. 1790). American letter writer. Born in Norwich, Connecticut; died 1790. ❖ Letters of Huntington and daughter Rachel, about life in Connecticut, published as *The Huntington Letters* (1905).

HUNTINGTON, Emily (1841–1909). American social-welfare worker. Born Jan 3, 1841, in Lebanon, Connecticut; died Dec 5, 1909, in Windham, CT; dau. of Dan Huntington (merchant) and Emily (Wilson) Huntington. ❖ Became matron of Wilson Industrial School for Girls in New York, NY; published *Little Lessons for Little Housekeepers* (1875); developed "kitchen garden" program to teach poor and urban girls domestic skills, an important piece of the broader movement toward practical or industrial education in US. ❖ See also Emily Huntington, *Children's Kitchen-Garden Book* (1881), *The Cooking Garden* (1885), *How to Teach Kitchen Garden* (1901) and *Introductory Cooking Lessons* (1901).

HUNTINGTON, Helen Gates (d. 1950). *See Granville-Barker, Helen.*

HUNTINGTON, Lady (1707–1791). *See Hastings, Selina.*

HUNTLEY, Frances E. (1865–1941). *See Mayne, Ethel Colburn.*

HUNTLEY, Joni (1956—). American track-and-field athlete. Born Aug 1956 in McMinnville, Oregon; attended Oregon State University. ❖ At Los Angeles Olympics, won a bronze medal in the high jump (1984).

HUNTON, Addie D. Waites (1875–1943). African-American activist. Born Addie Waites in Norfolk, Virginia, July 11, 1875; died in Brooklyn, NY, June 21, 1943; dau. of Jesse Waites (businessman) and Adelina (Lawton) Waites; graduate of Spencerian College of Commerce, Philadelphia, 1889; married William Alphaeus Hunton (official of Young Men's Christian Association for Negroes, 1893), July 19, 1893 (died 1916); children: 4 but only 2, Eunice and William Alphaeus Jr., lived beyond infancy. ❖ Taught at State Normal and Agricultural College (later Alabama Agricultural and Mechanical University); moved to Brooklyn, NY (1906); appointed secretary for projects among black students by National Board of Young Women's Christian Association (YWCA), 1907); during WWI, volunteered for overseas service with YMCA and became 1 of 3 black women assigned to work with the 200,000 segregated black troops stationed in France (1918); along with black troops, assigned to military cemetery at Romagne (1919); after war, served on Council on Colored Work of National Board of YWCA and was president of International Council of the Women of Darker Races and of Empire State Federation of Women's Clubs; an ardent suffragist, joined Brooklyn Equal Suffrage League; was a vice-president and field secretary of National Association for Advancement of Colored People (NAACP) and also remained active in National Association of Colored Women (NACW). ❖ See also memoir (with Kathryn Johnson) *Two Colored Women with the American Expeditionary Forces* (1920); and *Women in World History.*

HUNYADY, Emese (1966—). Hungarian-born speedskater. Name variations: Emese Nemeth-Hunyady. Born Mar 4, 1966, in Budapest, Hungary; m. Thomas Nemeth (Austrian speedskater) to obtain an Austrian passport (div.). ❖ Represented Hungary at Sarajevo Olympics, finishing 13th in the 1,500 meters (1984); defected to Austria (1985); won a bronze medal in the 3,000 meters at Albertville Olympics (1992); won a gold medal at the European championships (1993) and a gold medal at World championships (1994); at Lillehammer, won a silver medal in the 3,000 meters and a gold medal in the 1,500 meters (1994), giving Austria its 1st speedskating gold medal; competed but did not medal at Salt Lake City (2002); after struggling for 2 years with injuries, won gold medals for the downhill and the combined at World championships (2005). ❖ See also *Women in World History.*

HUO XUAN HUONG (fl. late 18th c.). *See Ho Xuan Huong.*

HUPALO, Katherine (1890–1974). Ukrainian-born actress. Born May 1, 1890, in the Ukraine; died Sept 7, 1974, in Ridgewood, NJ. ❖ For over 40 years, was lead dramatic actress in the Ukrainian Art Theatre (US).

HUPPERT, Isabelle (1953—). French actress. Born Isabelle Ann Huppert, Mar 16, 1953, in Paris, France; sister of Elisabeth Huppert; attended

Conservatory of Versailles and Conservatoire d'Art Dramatique; m. Ronald Chammah (film director), 1982; children: Lolita Chammah (actress), Lorenzo Chammah, and Angelo Chammah. ❖ Famed French actress, began career on stage in *A Month in the Country* and title role of *Medea*, among others; made film debut in *Faustine Et Le Bel Été* (1971); won acclaim for performance in *La Dentellière* (1977); often collaborated with Claude Chabrol in his films, including *Violette Nozière* (1978), for which she won Best Actress prize at Cannes, as well as *Une Affaire de Femmes* (1988), *Madame Bovary* (1991), *La Cérémonie* (1995) and *Merci pour le Chocolat* (2000); made US debut in Cimino's disastrous *Heaven's Gate* (1980); recorded album with Jean-Louis Murat, *Madame Deshoulières* (2001); other films include *La Dame aux camélias* (1980), *Coup de foudre* (released in US as *Entre Nous,* 1983), *Sauve Qui Peut* (1979), *Loulou* (1980); *Milan Noir* (1987), *Saint-Cyr* (2000), *Clara* (2000), *La Pianiste* (2001), *8 femmes* (2002) and *I ♥ Huckabees* (2004). ❖ See also (in French) *Isabell Huppert: L'histoire D'une Femme* (Cahiers du Cinema, 1994).

HURD, Dorothy Campbell (1883–1945). Scottish-born golfer. Name variations: Dorothy I. Campbell. Born Dorothy Iona Campbell, May 6, 1883, in North Berwick, Scotland; killed by a train, Mar 20, 1945, in Yemassee, North Carolina; m. J.B. Hurd, 1913. ❖ Won Scottish Ladies' championship (1905, 1906, and 1908), US Women's Amateur championship (1909, 1910), and Canadian Amateur Ladies' Open (1910, 1911, 1912); was 1st woman to win both British and U.S. amateur titles in 1 year (1909), a feat repeated (1911); won the U.S. Women's championship (1924) and the U.S. Women's Senior tournament (1938). Inducted into Golf Hall of Fame, Citizens Savings Hall of Fame Athletic Museum, and Ladies Professional Golfers' Association Hall of Fame. ❖ See also *Women in World History.*

HURD, Edith Thacher (1910–1997). American children's book writer. Name variations: (joint pseudonym with Margaret Wise Brown) Juniper Sage; (nickname) Posey. Born Sept 14, 1910, in Kansas City, Missouri; died Jan 25, 1997; dau. of John Hamilton and Edith (Gilman) Thacher; Radcliffe College, AB, 1933; Bank Street College of Education, additional study, 1934; m. Clement Hurd (artist and illustrator), June 24, 1939 (died 1988); children: John Thacher Hurd (children's book writer and illustrator). ❖ One of the early figures in the development of children's literature in America, taught 4 years at Dalton School, NYC; became a member of Writer's Laboratory at Bank Street College of Education, where she met Lucy Sprague Mitchell, Margaret Wise Brown and Ruth Krauss; wrote 1st book, *Hurry, Hurry,* for Young Scott Books (1938); began working with editor Ursula Nordstrom at Harper (1959); over the years, wrote over 75 books, including *The Wreck of the Wild Wave* (1942), *Jerry, the Jeep* (1945), *The Galleon from Manila* (1949), *Last One Home Is a Green Pig* (1959), *The Golden Hind* (1960), *Stop, Stop* (1961), *Starfish* (1962), *The Day the Sun Danced* (1965), *The White Horse* (1970), *Johnny Lion's Bad Day* (1970), *The Black Dog Who Went into the Woods* (1980), *I Dance in My Red Pajamas* (1982), *Song of the Sea Otter* (1983) and *Dinosaur, My Darling* (1978). ❖ See also *Women in World History.*

HURD, Francine (1947—). *See Barker, Francine.*

HURD, Gale Anne (1955—). American film producer. Born Oct 25, 1955, in Los Angeles, CA; graduate of Stanford University; m. James Cameron (director), 1985 (div. 1989); m. Brian De Palma (director), 1991 (div.); m. Jonathan Hensleigh (screenwriter), 1995; children: (2nd m.) Lolita De Palma. ❖ Began career as executive assistant to Roger Corman at New World Pictures; formed own company, Pacific Western Productions (1982); produced a number of box-office hits, including *The Terminator* (1984), *Aliens* (1986), *The Abyss* (1989), *Terminator 2* (1991), *Raising Cain* (1992) and *Armageddon* (1998); also produced *Virus* (1999) and *Hulk* (2003), among many others.

HURD, Henriette Wyeth (1907–1997). *See Wyeth, Henriette.*

HURD-MEAD, Kate Campbell (1867–1941). American physician. Name variations: Kate Campbell Hurd. Born April 6, 1867, in Danville, Quebec, Canada; died Jan 1, 1941, in Haddam, Connecticut; dau. of Edward Payson and Sarah Elizabeth (Campbell) Hurd; sister of Mabeth Hurd Paige (lawyer and state legislator in Minnesota); Woman's Medical College of Pennsylvania, MD, 1888; also attended New England Hospital for Women and Children (in Boston) and did postgraduate studies in Paris, Stockholm, London, and Vienna; m. William Edward Mead (college professor), June 21, 1893. ❖ Specialized in women's and children's health; participated in and helped found several organizations dedicated to women's and children's health issues; wrote *Medical Women*

of America (1933) and *A History of Women in Medicine from the Earliest Times to the Beginning of the Nineteenth Century* (1938); was organizer of Middletown District Nurses Association (1900), vice-president of State Medical Society of Connecticut (1913–14), organizer of Medical Women's International Association (1919), president of American Medical Women's Association (1922–24), and a financial supporter of American Women's Hospitals, which backed women physicians in undeveloped regions of the world. ❖ See also *Women in World History.*

HURD-WOOD, Kathleen Gertrude (1886–1965). New Zealand advocate for hard of hearing. Name variations: Kathleen Gertrude Chitty. Born on Aug 1, 1886, at Kirikirioa, near Hamilton, New Zealand; died on April 10, 1965, in Hamilton; dau. of Walter Chitty (farmer) and Alicia Wilhelmina de Vere (Hunt) Chitty; m. Gervase Alven Hurd-Wood, 1911 (d. 1924). ❖ During pilgrimage to Rome and Lourdes, decided to devote her life to people who had lost their hearing (1925); trained as lip-reading teacher and held free classes (1926); was instrumental in establishing New Zealand League for the Hard of Hearing (1932). MBE (1961). ❖ See also *Dictionary of New Zealand Biography* (Vol. 4).

HURDON, Elizabeth (1868–1941). English-born gynecologist and pathologist. Born Jan 28, 1868, in Bodmin, Exeter, England; died of liver cancer, Jan 29, 1941, in Exeter; dau. of John Hurdon (linen and woolen draper) and Ann (Coom) Hurdon. ❖ Hired as assistant gynecologist in dispensary of Johns Hopkins Hospital in Baltimore (1897), the 1st woman physician on staff; was assistant in gynecology, instructor, and associate in gynecology at Johns Hopkins Medical School (1898–1916), the 1st woman on the medical faculty; was 1 of roughly 12 women qualified for election to the new American College of Surgeons (1913); volunteered for England's Royal Army Medical Corps (1915) and assigned to active duty in Europe during WWI; assisted in development and was 1st director of Marie Curie Hospital, a women's cancer hospital in London; worked on cancer treatments; retired (1938). Received order of Commander of the British Empire (1938).

HURLOCK, Madeline (1899–1989). American silent-film actress. Name variations: Madeline Sherwood. Born Dec 12, 1899, in Federalsburg, Maryland; died April 4, 1989, in New York, NY; m. Marc Connelly (playwright, div.); m. Robert Sherwood (playwright). ❖ At Mack Sennett and other studios, played a foil to Ben Turpin, Andy Clyde, Harry Langdon, and Laurel and Hardy; films include *The Daredevil, The Prodical Bridegroom* and *Duck Soup.*

HURMUZACHI, Georgeta (1936—). Romanian gymnast. Born Jan 23, 1936. ❖ At Melbourne Olympics, won a bronze medal in team all-around (1956).

HURREM SULTANA (c. 1504–1558). *See Roxelana.*

HURST, Fannie (1889–1968). American novelist and short-story writer. Born in Hamilton, Ohio, Oct 18, 1889; died in New York, NY, Feb 23, 1968; dau. of Samuel Hurst (owner of shoe factory) and Rose (Kopple) Hurst; Washington University, St. Louis, BA, 1909; m. Jacques S. Danielson (pianist), 1915 (died 1952); no children. ❖ One of the most well-known writers of the early and mid-20th century, best remembered for 2 bestselling novels, *Back Street* (1931) and *Imitation of Life* (1933), both of which were made into popular movies; saw a total of 32 films adapted from her fiction and wrote screenplays for several of them; wrote 9 volumes of short stories, 17 novels, 5 plays, a full-length autobiography and autobiographical memoir, and countless nonfiction articles; a social activist and feminist, also supported labor and New Deal policies; chaired the Woman's National Housing Commission and Committee on Workmen's Compensation; was a member of the National Advisory Committee to Works Progress Administration (1940–41) and served on board of directors of NY Urban League; writings include (short stories) *Humoresque* (1919) and (novels) *Star Dust* (1921), *Lummox* (1923), *Mannequin* (1926), *Five and Ten* (1929), *Anitra's Dance* (1934), *Lonely Parade* (1942), *Hallelujah* (1944), *Any Woman* (1950), *The Man with One Head* (1953), *Family!* (1959), *God Must Be Sad* (1961) and *Fool—Be Still* (1964). ❖ See also autobiography *Anatomy of Me* (Doubleday, 1958); Brooke Kroeger, *Fannie: The Talent for Success of Writer Fannie Hurst* (Times, 1999); and *Women in World History.*

HURST, Margery (1913–1989). British entrepreneur. Born Margery Berney in Southsea, Hampshire, England, 1913; died 1989; attended Minerva College and Royal Academy of Dramatic Art; married an army major, 1940 (div.); m. Eric Hurst (attorney), 1948; children: (1st m.)

1 daughter; (2nd m.) 4 daughters. ❖ Founded Brook Street Bureau (1945), the largest international secretarial agency in the world; served on British National Economic Commission (1967–70); became one of the 1st women members of Lloyds Underwriters (1970); retired as managing director of Brook Street (1976). Received the Pimms Cup for Anglo-American business friendship (1962); awarded OBE (1976). ❖ See also memoir *No Glass Slipper* (Crown, 1967); and *Women in World History*.

HURSTON, Zora Neale (c. 1891–1960). African-American anthropologist, novelist, folklorist. Born Zora Neale Hurston, Jan 7, 1891 (according to 1 brother and 1900 census taker) or 1901 (according to her literary biographer and other sources), in Eatonville, Florida; died at St. Lucie County Welfare Home, Jan 28, 1960; dau. of Lucy Ann (Potts) Hurston and John Hurston; Barnard College, BA, 1928; m. Herbert Sheen, May 19, 1927 (div. 1931); m. Albert Price III, June 27 1939 (div. 1943); children: none. ❖ The most prolific as well as the most underrated African-American woman writer (1920–50), who is now considered the spiritual mother of the many successful black women writers from mid-20th century on, saw 1st story published in school literary magazine (1924); won a scholarship to Barnard (1926); undertook periodic folklore expeditions throughout southern US as well as Caribbean, the material of which she incorporated into her literary and stage ventures (1928–60); held teaching posts for brief periods at Rollins College, Bethune-Cookman College and North Carolina College for Negroes (1930s); worked for WPA (1938–39) and, briefly, as staff writer for Paramount Studios; an early black nationalist, her autobiography, 4 novels and 2 books of folklore, together with numerous short stories and critical essays, made her the most prolific if controversial black writer of her time; struggled to keep poverty at bay and the controversies that hounded her in check; spent last years fending off an intestinal illness that plagued her, and worked alternately as a public school teacher, technical librarian, and maid to support herself; died impoverished and in obscurity. Novels include *Jonah's Gourd Vine* (1934), *Mules and Men* (1935), *Their Eyes Were Watching God* (1937), *Tell My Horse* (1938), *Moses, Man of the Mountain* (1939), *Dust Tracks on a Road* (1942) and *Seraph on the Suwanee* (1948). ❖ See also Robert E. Hemenway, *Zora Neale Hurston: A Literary Biography* (U. of Illinois Press, 1977); Lillie P. Howard, *Zora Neale Hurston* (Twayne, 1980); and *Women in World History*.

HURTIS, Muriel (1979—). French runner. Born Mar 25, 1979, in Bondy, France. ❖ At World championships, won a gold medal for 4 x 100-meter relay (2003); placed 1st in 200 meters at Golden League in Saint-Denis, France (2002, 2003) and at World Athletics Final in Monaco (2003); won a bronze medal for the 4x100-meter relay at Athens Olympics (2004).

HUSON, Florence (1857–1915). American physician. Born June 17, 1857, in Ann Arbor, Michigan; died Aug 12, 1915, in Detroit, MI; dau. of Mary L. (Bradley) Huson and Frederick C. Huson; graduate of University of Michigan College of Medicine (1885). ❖ Successful woman physician, who opened doors for future female physicians, had an obstetrical practice in Detroit (1889–1914); established and served as the 1st president of the Woman's Hospital Free Dispensary (1893); worked as vice chief of staff and the 1st woman staff member at Detroit Woman's Hospital; established (1905) and led the Elizabeth Blackwell Medical Society for Women Physicians, the 1st woman's medical society in Detroit; served as the Michigan Medical Society's vice president.

HUSSEIN, Muna (1941—). *See Gardiner, Antoinette.*

HUSSEY, Gemma (1938—). Irish politician. Born Gemma Moran, Nov 1938, in Bray, Co. Wicklow, Ireland; m. Dermot R. Hussey; children: 2 daughters, 1 son. ❖ Was founder director of the English Language Institute, Dublin; entered the Seanad (1977) as in Independent with background in the women's movement; representing Fine Gael, elected to the 23rd Dáil (1982–82) for Wicklow; returned to 24th–25th Dáil (1982–89); served as minister for Education (1982–86) and minister for Social Welfare (1986–87); defeated in the general election (1989) and retired.

HUSSEY, Ruth (1911–2005). American actress. Name variations: from age 17 until she began acting in movies, used stepfather's name O'Rourke. Born Oct 30, 1911, in Providence, Rhode Island; died April 19, 2005, in Newbury Park, CA; dau. of George and Julia Hussey; attended Pembroke Women's College (later Brown University) and University of Michigan; m. Robert Longenecker (talent agent and tv executive), Aug 9, 1942 (died 2002); children: 2 sons, 1 daughter. ❖ Supported herself as a Powers model before landing role of Kay in touring company of *Dead End* (1937); had

small roles in 1st few films, but by 1940s had established herself as a 2nd lead, usually playing sophisticated women; made over 35 films, including *Madame X* (1937), *Judge Hardy's Children* (1938), *Within the Law* (1939), *The Women* (1939), *Another Thin Man* (1939), *Northwest Passage* (1940), *Susan and God* (1940), *H.M. Pulham, Esq.* (1941), *The Great Gatsby* (1949), *Louisa* (1950), *Stars and Stripes Forever* (1952) and *The Facts of Life* (1960); returned to Broadway to star in *State of the Union* (1945) and City Center production of *The Royal Family* (1951); appeared on tv in such shows as "Climax," "Studio One," "Alfred Hitchcock Presents," "Marcus Welby, M.D." and "The New Perry Mason." Nominated for Academy Award for *The Philadelphia Story* (1940) and Emmy for performance in title role of *Craig's Wife* ("Lux Video Theater," 1955). ❖ See also *Women in World History*.

HUSTED, Marjorie Child (c. 1892–1986). American home economist and businesswoman. Born Marjorie Child in Minneapolis, Minnesota, c. 1892; died 1986; dau. of Sampson Reed (lawyer) and Alice Albert (Webber) Child; University of Minnesota, BA, then B.Ed., 1913; m. K. Wallace Husted, Oct 1925. ❖ Secured a job in promotion and marketing with Creamette Co. of Minneapolis (1923); moved to Washburn-Crosby Co., makers of Gold Medal Flour (1924), where she served as home economics field representative; instituted home-service department for Washburn-Crosby (1926); with a staff of advisers answered homemaking inquiries from consumers over signature "Betty Crocker," a name used for that purpose since 1921; when the company merged and consolidated into General Mills (1928) and the home-service department was renamed the Betty Crocker Homemaking Service, served as director of department for next 18 years, helping to transform "Betty Crocker" into potent marketing image. ❖ See also *Women in World History*.

HUSTEDE, Heike (1946—). West German swimmer. Born Jan 16, 1946, in Germany. ❖ At Mexico City Olympics, won a bronze medal in the 4x100-meter medley relay (1968).

HUSTON, Anjelica (1951—). American actress and director. Born July 8, 1951, in Santa Monica, CA; dau. of John Huston (director) and Enrica (Ricki) Soma Huston (Russian ballerina); lived with Jack Nicholson (actor), 1973–89; m. Robert Graham (sculptor), 1992. ❖ Began career as a model; came to prominence in film *Prizzi's Honor* (1985), winning Academy Award for Best Supporting Actress; other films include *Gardens of Stone* (1987), *The Dead* (1987), *Crimes and Misdemeanors* (1989), *The Grifters* (1990), for which she was nominated for an Academy Award for Best Actress, *The Addams Family* (1991), *Manhattan Murder Mystery* (1993), *Ever After* (1998), *The Royal Tenenbaums* (2001); on tv, appeared on "Lonesome Dove" (1989) and "Buffalo Girls" (1995); directed *Bastard Out of Carolina* (1996) and *Agnes Browne* (1999).

HUSTON, Mrs. Walter (1898–1973). *See Sunderland, Nan.*

HUTCHINS, Colleen Kay (c. 1927—). Miss America. Born c. 1927; attended Pasadena City College and Brigham Young University; University of Pennsylvania, MA in drama; m. a physician who was also a member of the New York Knicks; children: four. ❖ Named Miss America (1952), representing Pennsylvania. ❖ See also Frank Deford, *There She Is* (Viking, 1971).

HUTCHINS, Grace (1885–1969). American social reformer. Born Grace Hutchins on Aug 19, 1885, in Boston, MA; died July 15, 1969, in New York, NY; dau. of Edward Webster Hutchins (Boston attorney) and Susan Barnes (Hurd) Hutchins; lived with Anna Rochester (1880–1966, author and social critic). ❖ Worked as teacher and principal at Episcopal St. Hilda's School for Chinese Girls, Wuchang, China (1912–16); joined Socialist Party (late 1910s); worked with pacifist organization, Fellowship of Reconciliation, as contributing editor to *The World Tomorrow* (1922–24), as press secretary (1924–26), and as business executive (1925–26); co-authored with Anna Rochester, *Jesus Christ and the World Today* (1922), and authored *Labor and Silk* (1929) and *Women Who Work* (1933); traveled across Asia and Europe, and met social reformers, including Gandhi (1926–27); joined Communist Party (1927); was correspondent for Federated Press; arrested during demonstration supporting Nicola Sacco and Bartolomeo Vanzetti (1927); co-founded Labor Research Association (LRA, 1927), working as staff member (1929–67), and editing LRA's *Railroad Notes* (1937–62); as a Communist, ran unsuccessfully in NY for alderman (1935), controller (1936), and lieutenant governor (1940); accused of making death threats by Whittaker Chambers during Alger Hiss trial (1948); as trustee of Civil Rights Congress' Bail Bond Fund, was involved in litigation (1951–56).

HUTCHINSON, Abigail (1829–1892). American singer and reformer. Name variations: Abby Hutchinson; Abigail Patton. Born Abigail Jemima Hutchinson, Aug 29, 1829, near Milford, New Hampshire; died Nov 24, 1892, in New York, NY; dau. of Jesse Hutchinson and Mary (Leavitt) Hutchinson; m. Ludlow Patton (stockbroker), Feb 28, 1849; children: raised grandniece Marian Loveridge. ❖ At 10, 1st performed in public; began singing professionally with brothers John, Judson, and Asa as Hutchinson Family singers (1841), performing for such causes as abolition, temperance rallies and woman's rights; retired from public singing career after marriage, but continued to perform in support of favored causes; temporarily rejoined brothers to support Abraham Lincoln's presidential campaign (1860); sang at National Woman's Rights conventions in Rochester, NY (1855) and NY (1857), and at NY convention for American Equal Rights Association (1868).

HUTCHINSON, Amy (1733–1750). English murderer. Born on the British Isle of Ely, 1733; executed Nov 7, 1750; m. John Hutchinson. ❖ At age 12, put to work as servant; at 16, fell in love with a local youth but married elderly John Hutchinson; made husband his ale, after which he died (c. Oct 14, 1748); moved in with lover the next day, provoking suspicions; husband's body exhumed and found to contain arsenic; tried for "petit treason" (crime regarded as more serious than straightforward murder), found guilty, and sentenced to death by burning at the stake.

HUTCHINSON, Amy Hadfield (1874–1971). New Zealand spinner and weaver. Name variations: Amy Hadfield Large. Born on May 20, 1874, in Napier, New Zealand; died on July 20, 1971, in Napier; dau. of James Stanistreet Large (cabinet-maker) and Elizabeth (Ferguson) Large; m. Francis (Frank) Hutchinson (sheepfarmer), 1907 (died 1940). ❖ Organized sewing group and started Rissington branch of Red Cross during WWI; when group became interested in spinning and weaving their own wool, experimented with and wrote articles on plant dyes—*Plant Dyeing*, reprinted until 1981; instrumental in establishing Napier Society of Arts and Crafts and was affiliated with Hawke's Bay Art Gallery and Museum. ❖ See also *Dictionary of New Zealand Biography* (Vol. 4).

HUTCHINSON, Amy May (1888–1985). New Zealand maternity reformer. Name variations: Amy May Scott. Born on July 2, 1888, in Islington, London, England; died on June 11, 1985, in Auckland, New Zealand; dau. of William Scott (salesman) and Clara Rosina Charlotte (Hawkins) Scott; m. Frederick John Hutchinson (merchant), 1912 (died 1948); children: 1 daughter, 1 son. ❖ Immigrated with family to New Zealand (1902); was an advocate for improved maternity services to the disadvantaged and a member of National Council of Women of New Zealand from 1920s; worked for New Zealand Society for the Protection of Women and Children (1930s); appointed justice of peace (1935); elected to Women's War Service Auxiliary during WWII and lobbied government for equity in military allowances to separated women so that they might care for their dependent children; member of Auckland Hospital Board (1956–59). ❖ See also *Dictionary of New Zealand Biography* (Vol. 4).

HUTCHINSON, Anne (1591–1643). English-born religious leader. Name variations: Anne Marbury Hutchinson; Mrs. Hutchinson. Born Anne Marbury c. July 17, 1591, in Alford, Lincolnshire, England; killed at Pelham Bay settlement, Long Island, during Indian raid in Aug or Sept 1643; dau. of Francis Marbury (spiritual divine) and Bridget (Dryden) Marbury; learned reading, writing, and arithmetic at home from father; m. William Hutchinson, Aug 9, 1612; children: Edward (b. 1613), Susanna (b. 1614), Richard (b. 1615), Faith (b. 1617), Bridget (b. 1619), Francis (b. 1620), Elizabeth (b. 1622), William (b. 1623), Samuel (b. 1624), Anne (b. 1626), Mary (b. 1628), Katherine (b. 1630), William (b. 1631), Susanna (b. 1633), Zuriel (b. 1636), and miscarried 16th child in 1637. ❖ Puritan, religious leader and teacher, nurse and midwife, persecuted on religious grounds, who would move with her family from England to Massachusetts Bay Colony, then to Rhode Island and, finally, to Long Island within a span of slightly less than 10 years; moved to London with family when father was appointed to Church of St. Martin in the Vintry, perhaps as rector (1605); as a midwife, began to form her own "rebellious" ideas concerning what she viewed as the inapplicability of the doctrine of original sin to the innocence of newborns; fleeing religious persecution, moved with husband and children to the Massachusetts Bay Colony (1634), voicing her hope that New England would mean the end of what she perceived to be "the onerus dictum that women should be seen but never heard"; was tried for heresy (1637); excommunicated and banished, then publicly recanted her religious views (1638); moved to colony on Rhode Island (1638);

following continued religious persecution and death of husband, moved to Long Island to establish settlement at Pelham Bay (1642). ❖ See also Emery Battis, *Saints and Sectaries: Anne Hutchinson and the Antinomian Controversy in the Massachusetts Bay Colony* (U. of North Carolina Press, 1962); Winnifred King Rugg, *Unafraid: A Life of Anne Hutchinson* (Houghton, 1930); Selma Williams, *Divine Rebel: The Life of Anne Marbury Hutchinson* (Holt, 1981); and *Women in World History*.

HUTCHINSON, Jeanette (1951—). American singer. Name variations: The Emotions; The Heavenly Sunbeams; The Hutchinson Sunbeams; The Three Ribbons and a Bow. Born Feb 1951 in Chicago, IL; dau. of Joe Hutchinson (musician and manager of Emotions); sister of Wanda, Sheila, and Pamela Hutchinson (fellow Emotions members); cousin of Theresa Davis (fellow Emotions member). ❖ With sisters, had R&B successes as the Emotions (primarily 1970s); left group (1970) to marry (replaced by cousin Theresa Davis) but later returned. Albums with Emotions include *So I Can Love You* (1969), *Untouched* (1970), *Flowers* (1976), and *Rejoice* (1977).

HUTCHINSON, Josephine (1903–1998). American actress. Born Oct 12, 1903, in Seattle, WA; died June 4, 1998, in New York, NY; dau. of Leona Roberts (1881–1954, actress); niece of Edith Roberts (1899–1935, actress); m. Robert Bell, 1924 (div. 1930); m. James F. Townsend, 1935 (div.); m. Staats Cotsworth (actor), 1972 (died 1979). ❖ As a child, appeared in Mary Pickford's *The Little Princess*; later joined Eva LeGallienne's Civic Repertory Co. and starred in numerous productions, including *Alice in Wonderland*; films include *Oil for the Lamps of China*, *The Story of Louis Pasteur*, *Tom Brown's School Days* (as Mrs. Arnold), *Ruby Gentry*, *Miracle in the Rain*, *North by Northwest* and *Baby the Rain Must Fall*.

HUTCHINSON, Lucy (1620–post 1675). English author. Born 1620 in London, England; died after 1675; dau. of Sir Allen Apsley, lieutenant of the Tower of London, and Lucy St. John; m. John Hutchinson (colonel during English Civil War and governor of Nottingham Castle), 1638 (died 1664); children: 8. ❖ Known principally for writing *Memoirs of the Life of Colonel Hutchinson*, a biography of her husband, a judge at the trial of Charles I who was imprisoned in the Tower of London, but it was not published until 1806; also wrote *On the Principles of the Christian Religion*, for her daughter, and *On Theology*, both of which were published in 1817. ❖ See also *Women in World History*.

HUTCHINSON, Pamela (1958—). American singer. Name variations: The Emotions. Born 1958 in Chicago, IL; dau. of Joe Hutchinson (musician and manager of Emotions); sister of Wanda, Sheila, and Jeanette Hutchinson (Emotions members); cousin of Theresa Davis (Emotions member). ❖ With sisters and cousin, had R&B successes as the Emotions (primarily 1970s); though not original member of the group, joined mid-1970s and had such hits as "So I Can Love You" (1969), "Show Me How" (1971), "I Don't Wanna Lose Your Love" (1976), and the #1-hit "Best of My Love" (Grammy winner). Emotions albums include *Flowers* (1976), *Sunshine* (1977), *Rejoice* (1977), *Come Into Our World* (1979), *New Affair* (1981), *Sincerely* (1984), *If I Only Knew* (1985), *Best of My Love: Best of the Emotions* (1996).

HUTCHINSON, Sheila (1953—). American singer. Name variations: The Emotions; The Heavenly Sunbeams; The Hutchinson Sunbeams; The Three Ribbons and a Bow. Born Jan 17, 1953, in Chicago, IL; dau. of Joe Hutchinson (musician and manager of Emotions); sister of Wanda, Jeanette, and Pamela Hutchinson (Emotions members); cousin of Theresa Davis (Emotions member). ❖ With sisters and cousin, had R&B successes as the Emotions (primarily 1970s); with group, released hits including "So I Can Love You" (1969), "Show Me How" (1971), "I Don't Wanna Lose Your Love" (1976), and the #1-hit "Best of My Love" (Grammy winner); toured with artists including Jackson 5, Sly and the Family Stone, B.B. King, Stevie Wonder, and Bobby "Blue" Bland. Albums with Emotions include *So I Can Love You* (1969), *Untouched* (1970), *Flowers* (1976), *Sunshine* (1977), *Rejoice* (1977), *Come Into Our World* (1979), *New Affair* (1981), *Sincerely* (1984), *If I Only Knew* (1985), *Best of My Love: Best of the Emotions* (1996).

HUTCHINSON, Wanda (1951—). American singer. Name variations: The Emotions; The Heavenly Sunbeams; The Hutchinson Sunbeams; The Three Ribbons and a Bow. Born Dec 17, 1951, in Chicago, IL; dau. of Joe Hutchinson (musician and manager of Emotions); sister of Sheila, Jeanette, and Pamela Hutchinson (Emotions members); cousin of Theresa Davis (Emotions member). ❖ With sisters and cousin, had R&B successes as the Emotions (primarily 1970s); with group, released hits including "So I Can Love You" (1969), "Show Me How" (1971),

"I Don't Wanna Lose Your Love" (1976), and the #1-hit "Best of My Love" (Grammy winner). Albums with Emotions include *So I Can Love You* (1969), *Untouched* (1970), *Flowers* (1976), *Sunshine* (1977), *Rejoice* (1977), *Come Into Our World* (1979), *New Affair* (1981), *Sincerely* (1984), *If I Only Knew* (1985), *Best of My Love: Best of the Emotions* (1996).

HUTCHINSON SUNBEAMS, The.
See Hutchinson, Jeanette.
See Hutchinson, Sheila.
See Hutchinson, Wanda.

HUTCHISON, Isobel Wylie (1899–1982). Scottish botanist. Born May 30, 1899, in Scotland; died Feb 20, 1982. ❖ Collected plants and traveled solo in Alaska; collected plants on the 1st expedition to Greenland for 5 months (1927); with 2 guides, climbed Kilertinguit (6,250 ft.) and left a Union Jack in a bottle in honor of Edward Whymper (who had climbed the mountain in 1873); lived in an Inuit village (from Sept 1928); traveled through Alaska on a coastal steamer (1934); embarked on a 120-mile trip to Canada via dog sledge; collected plants from the Aleutian Islands (1936). Writings include *North to the Rime-Ringed Sun* (1934), *Stepping Stones from Alaska to Asia* (1937, reprinted as *The Aleutian Islands,* 1943), and articles for journals, including the *National Geographic.* ❖ See also Gwyneth Hoyle, *Flowers in the Snow: The Life of Isobel Wylie Hutchison.*

HUTCHISON, Kay Bailey (1943—). American politician. Born Kathryn Ann Bailey, July 22, 1943, in Galveston, TX; University of Texas, BA, then JD, 1967; m. Ray Hutchison (politician); children: 4. ❖ Republican, was twice elected to Texas House of Representatives (1972–76); served as Texas State treasurer (1990–93); elected to US Senate to replace Lloyd Bentsen (1993), the 1st woman to represent Texas in the Senate; reelected (1994 and 2000); joined the Senate Appropriations Committee; also sits on the Senate Commerce, Science and Transportation Committee; sponsored the federal anti-stalking bill and Homemaker IRA legislation; served as deputy majority whip.

HUTCHISON, Muriel (1915–1975). American stage and screen actress. Born Feb 10, 1915, in New York, NY; died Mar 24, 1975, in NY, NY; m. John Nicholson (art dealer), 1953 (died 1962). ❖ Made NY stage debut in *The Sap Runs High* (1936); other plays include *The Amazing Dr. Clitterhouse, The Man Who Came to Dinner* and *The Vigil*; made such films as *One Third of a Nation, The Women* and *Another Thin Man*; retired to operate an art gallery with husband.

HUTSON, Jean (1914–1998). American library administrator and curator. Born Jean Blackwell, Sept 4, 1914, in Sommerfield, Florida; died Feb 4, 1998, in New York, NY; only child of Paul O. (farmer) and Sarah (Myers) Blackwell (schoolteacher); attended University of Michigan; Barnard College, BA, 1935; Columbia University School of Library Science, MA, 1936; m. Andy Razaf (lyricist), 1939 (div. 1947); m. John Hutson (librarian), 1950 (died 1957); children: (2nd m.) Jean Frances (d. 1992). ❖ The 2nd black woman to graduate from Barnard (1935), the 1st being Zora Neale Hurston, was denied a job at the public library in Baltimore, because there were no more positions for blacks; went to NY, where she was hired as a librarian in NYC Public Branch Library system; became curator of Schomburg Collection (1948); after Schomburg Collection was renamed Schomburg Center for Research in Black Culture (1972), became chief, a position she held until 1980. ❖ See also *Women in World History.*

HUTTON, Barbara (1912–1979). American heiress. Born Barbara Woolworth Hutton, Nov 14, 1912, in New York, NY; died May 11, 1979, in Los Angeles, California; dau. of Franklyn Hutton (vice president and partner, E.F. Hutton) and Edna (Woolworth) Hutton (dau. of dimestore magnet Frank Woolworth); graduated of Miss Porter's School for Girls, 1929; m. Prince Alexis Mdivani, June 22, 1933 (div. 1935); m. Count Haugwitz-Reventlow, 1935 (div. 1941); m. Cary Grant (actor), July 8, 1942 (div. 1945); m. Prince Igor Troubetzkoy, Mar 1, 1947 (div. 1950); m. Porfirio Rubirosa (diplomat), Dec 30, 1953 (div. 1955); m. Baron Gottfried von Cramm (German tennis ace), Nov 8, 1955 (div. 1960); m. Raymond Doan (artist), April 7, 1964 (permanently sep. 1971); children: (with Count Reventlow) Lance Reventlow (d. 1973). ❖ Well-known heiress, endured a rugged childhood, including mother's suicide when she was 5; made auspicious society debut (1930) and gained access to Woolworth fortune estimated at well over $28 million; was dogged by the media and often fodder for jokes, especially since her fortune came from the "Five and Ten Cent Store"; in truth, was frequently generous, though her philanthropy was haphazard; began to lose grasp on reality as she grew older. ❖ See also C. David Heymann, *Poor Little Rich Girl: The Life and Legend of Barbara Hutton* (Lyle Stuart, 1983); Dean Jennings, *Barbara Hutton: A Candid Biography* (Fell, 1968); and *Women in World History.*

HUTTON, Betty (1921—). American actress and singer. Born Betty June Thornburg, Feb 26, 1921, in Battle Creek, Michigan; sister of singer Marion Hutton (b. 1919); m. Theodore Briskin (camera manufacturer), Sept 2, 1945 (div. 1950); m. Charles O'Curran (choreographer), 1952 (div. 1955); m. Alan W. Livingston (Capital Records executive), 1955 (div. 1960); m. Peter Candoli (musician), Dec 24, 1960 (div. 1971); children: (1st m.) Lindsay Diane Briskin (b. 1946) and Candice Briskin; (4th m.) Carolyn Candoli. ❖ At one time Paramount's most valuable star, possessed true comedic talent; at 13, won a contest to sing with Vincent Lopez band; stayed with band for several years, perfecting her "whoop-and-holler" style; made Broadway debut in revue *Two for the Show,* followed by *Panama Hattie* (both 1940); made film debut in *The Fleet's In* (1942), in which her mile-a-minute rendition of "Arthur Murray Taught Me Dancing in a Hurry" brought her immediate visibility; had 1st non-singing role in comedy *The Miracle of Morgan's Creek*; portrayed Texas Guinan in *Incendiary Blonde* (1945), introducing 2 songs, "Ragtime Cowboy Joe" and "It Had To Be You"; portrayed serial star Pearl White in *The Perils of Pauline* (1947); signed with Capitol Records (1943) and made numerous hit recordings; during WWII, traveled with a USO in Pacific (1945); appeared as Annie Oakley in blockbuster film of *Annie Get Your Gun* (1949); followed that with *The Greatest Show on Earth* (1952); walked out on Paramount contract and career came to a halt; starred in ill-fated tv series "Goldie" (1959); addicted to pills and alcohol, filed for bankruptcy (1967); took a job as housekeeper for a priest in Portsmouth, RI (1974); returned to Broadway for a successful 3-week replacement stint as Miss Hartigan in *Annie* (1980); joined faculty at Salve Regina College in Newport, teaching film and tv; other films include *And the Angels Sing* (1944), *Here Come the Waves* (1944) and *Spring Reunion* (1957). ❖ See also *Women in World History.*

HUTTON, Ina Ray (1916–1984). Amerian bandleader. Name variations: Ina Rae Hutton; Ina Ray. Born Odessa Cowan, Mar 13, 1916, in Chicago, IL; died of complications from diabetes, Feb 19, 1984, in Ventura, California; dau. of pianist Marvel Ray; half-sister of June Hutton (1923–1973, singer); m. Lou Parris (saxophonist), 1944 (div.); m. Randy Brooks (bandleader), 1949 (div. 1957); m. 4th husband Jack Curtis (businessman, div. 1981). ❖ The only woman to lead a prominent Big Band in her day, sang and danced in stage revues from age 8; appeared in *Ziegfeld Follies of 1934*; organized all-female band, The Melodears (1934), featuring hot swing; starred with her band in several Paramount musical shorts (1935–37); appeared as herself in several full-length films and starred in film *Ever Since Venus* (1944); after the Melodears broke up (1939), led an all-male band until 1950; led another all-woman band for "The Ina Ray Hutton Show," show locally on California tv (1951–56); also appeared in shows with such bandleaders as Artie Shaw and Harry James; retired (1968).

HUTTON, Lauren (1943—). American fashion model, activist and actress. Born Mary Laurence Hutton, Nov 17, 1943, in Charleston, SC; never married. ❖ With the trademark gap between her two front teeth, became a top fashion model for Ford Modeling Agency, appearing on cover of *Vogue* 28 times; was the 1st to negotiate a major cosmetics deal, with Revlon; appeared in such films as *Paper Lion* (1968) and *American Gigolo* (1980); also appeared on tv's "Falcon Crest" (1981); hosted tv talk show "Lauren Hutton and . . ." (1996–97); outspoken activist, works for women's health issues and environmental and wildlife foundations.

HUTTUNEN, Eevi (1922—). Finnish speedskater. Name variations: Eeva Huttunen. Born Aug 23, 1922, in Finland. ❖ Won World championship allround (1951); won a bronze medal for the 3,000 meters at Squaw Valley Olympics (1960).

HUXLEY, Elspeth (1907–1997). English writer. Born Elspeth Josceline Grant, July 23, 1907, in London, England; died in Tetbury, England, Jan 1997; dau. of Josceline Grant (army major and farmer) and Eleanor Lillian (Grosvenor) Grant (entrepreneur); Reading University, Diploma in Agriculture, 1927; attended Cornell University, 1927–28; m. Gervas Huxley (tea commissioner, writer, grandson of Thomas Henry Huxley and 1st cousin of Julian and Aldous Huxley), Dec 12, 1931 (died 1971); children: Charles Grant Huxley (b. Feb 1944). ❖ Prolific writer of nonfiction and fiction who is especially noted for her widely acclaimed books about her experiences in, and the history of, East Africa during 20th century; joined parents in Kenya (1913); returned to England (1915), sent away to boarding school at Aldeburgh in Suffolk; returned to Kenya (1919); worked as assistant press officer for Empire Marketing board, London (1929–32); worked for BBC in new department (1941–43), member of its general advisory council (1952–59), broadcaster of BBC's "The Critics" program, and on African matters; was justice of the peace for Wiltshire (1946–77); served as member, Monckton Advisory Commission on Central Africa (1959–60); writings include *White Man's Country: Lord Delamere and the Making of Kenya* (1935), *Murder on Safari* (1938), *Red Strangers* (1939), *Atlantic Ordeal: The Story of Mary Cornish* (1942), *English Women* (1942), *Settlers of Kenya* (1948), *The Sorcerer's Apprentice: A Journey through East Africa* (1948), *The Walled City* (1949), *Four Guineas* (1954), *On the Edge of the Rift: Memories of Kenya* (1962), *Love Among the Daughters* (1968), *Livingstone and His African Journeys* (1974), *Florence Nightingale* (1975), *Scott of the Antarctic* (1977) and *Nine Faces of Kenya* (1990). Awarded Commander, Order of the British Empire (1960). ❖ See also autobiographies *The Flame Trees of Thika: Memories of an African Childhood* (1959) *Mottled Lizard* (1926) and *Out in the Midday Sun: My Kenya* (1985); *Nellie: Letters from Africa*; and *Women in World History.*

HUXLEY, Julia Arnold (1862–1908). English educator. Name variations: Mrs. Leonard Huxley, Judy Arnold. Born Julia Frances Arnold, 1862; died of cancer, Nov 30, 1908; granddau. of Thomas Arnold of Rugby (1795–1842, English educator and headmaster); dau. of Thomas Arnold (1823–1900, professor of English literature) and Julia Sorrell (1826–1888); sister of Mrs. Humphry Ward (1851–1920); niece of Matthew Arnold (1822–1888, English poet and critic); earned first-class degree in English literature from Somerville College, Oxford; m. Leonard Huxley (1860–1933, editor and author); children: (Noel) Trevenen Huxley (1890–1914); Julian Huxley (1887–1975, biologist and writer who m. Juliette Huxley; Aldous Huxley (1894–1963, novelist and critic who m. Maria Nuys Huxley, then Laura Archera Huxley); Margaret Arnold Huxley (1896–1979). ❖ Founded Prior's Field, a small but significant experimental girls' school in Godalming, Surrey, England, where she was its headmistress.

HUXLEY, Juliette (1896–1994). Swiss-born sculptor and writer. Name variations: Lady Huxley. Born Marie Juliette Baillot, Dec 6, 1896, in Auvernier, Switzerland; died 1994; dau. of Alphonse (building solicitor) and Mélanie Antonia (Ortlieb) Baillot; attended École Supérieure des Jeunes Filles; m. Julian Sorrell Huxley (1887–1975, biologist and writer), Mar 29, 1919; children: Anthony and Francis. ❖ At 19, left for England; served as a companion for Lady Ottoline Morrell's daughter Julian and was soon a member of Bloomsbury set; traveled extensively with and without husband, journeying to Africa on several occasions (resulting in *Wild Lives of Africa*) and to India, Java, Bali, Thailand, Persia, Syria, Lebanon and Israel; took up clay modeling, then served an apprenticeship at Central School under John Skeaping and began sculpting in wood. ❖ See also memoir *Leaves of the Tulip Tree* (Salem, 1963); Susan Sherman, ed. *Letters of May Sarton to Juliette Huxley* (1999); and *Women in World History.*

HUXLEY, Mrs. Leonard (1862–1908). *See Huxley, Julia Arnold.*

HUXTABLE, Ada Louise (1921—). American architectural critic. Born Ada Louise Landman, Mar 14, 1921, in New York, NY; only child of Michael Louis Landman (physician) and Leah (Rosenthal) Landman; Hunter College BA (magna cum laude); attended Institute of Fine Arts at NYU, 1945–1950; m. L. Garth Huxtable (industrial designer), 1940. ❖ Architectural critic for *The New York Times* (1963–81) who won Pulitzer Prize for distinguished criticism, was assistant curator of department of architecture and design of Museum of Modern Art (1946–50); organized a touring exhibit on architect Pier Luigi Nervi for the museum (1952) and published 1st article on Nervi for *Progressive Architecture* (of which she was a contributing editor, 1952–63); wrote *Four Walking Tours of Modern Architecture in NYC* (1961) and *Classic NY: Georgian Gentility to Greek Elegance* (1964); joined *New York Times* as a full-time architectural critic (1963), a 1st-of-its-kind position, and remained there for 18 years, advancing to editorial board (1973); published *Will They Ever Finish Bruckner Boulevard?*, a collection of her *Times* articles (1970); was instrumental in creation of a Landmarks Preservation Commission for NYC (1965) and also had a hand in saving architectural treasures in other American cities; other books include *Kicked a Building Lately?* (1976), *The Tall Building Artistically Reconsidered: The Search for a Skyscraper Style* (1985) and *Architecture Anyone?* (1985). ❖ See also *Women in World History.*

HVEGER, Ragnhild (1920—). Danish swimmer. Born Dec 10, 1920, in Denmark. ❖ Broke 42 world records at various distances (1936–42); held world records in the 200-, 400-, 800- and 1,500-meters which stood for 15 years; won a silver medal in the 400-meter freestyle at Berlin Olympics (1936). Elected to International Swimming Hall of Fame (1966). ❖ See also *Women in World History.*

HWA MU-LAN (fl. 5th c.). *See Hua Mu-Lan.*

HWANG HAE-YOUNG (1966—). South Korean badminton player. Born July 16, 1966, in South Korea. ❖ At Barcelona Olympics, won a gold medal in doubles (1992).

HWANG HE-SUK (1945—). North Korean volleyball player. Born Dec 9, 1945, in North Korea. ❖ At Munich Olympics, won a bronze medal in team competition (1972).

HWANG KEUM-SOOK (1963—). South Korean field-hockey player. Born Aug 27, 1963, in South Korea. ❖ At Seoul Olympics, won a silver medal in team competition (1988).

HWANG KYUNG-SUN (1978—). South Korean taekwondo player. Born May 21, 1986, in South Korea. ❖ Won a bronze medal in 67 kg at Athens Olympics (2004).

HWANG OK-SIL (c. 1972—). North Korean short-track speedskater. Name variations: Hwang Ok Sil. Born c. 1972 in North Korea. ❖ Won a bronze medal for the 500 meters at Albertville Olympics (1992); competed at Nagano Olympics (1998), but did not medal.

HYAMS, Leila (1905–1977). American screen actress. Born May 1, 1905, in New York, NY; died Dec 4, 1977, in Bel-Air, California; dau. of John Hyams (actor) and Leila McIntyre (1882–1953, actress); m. Phil Berg (agent), 1927. ❖ As a blonde ingenue, appeared in 34 films (1924–36), including *Dancing Mothers, Alias Jimmy Valentine, Hurricane, The Big House, The Bishop Murder Case, The 13th Chair, Island of Lost Souls, Freaks, Phantom of Paris, The Big Broadcast, Red-Headed Woman, Ruggles of Red Gap* and *People Will Talk.*

HYATT, Anna Vaughn (1876–1973). *See Huntington, Anna Hyatt.*

HYCINTHA MARISCOTTI (d. 1640). *See Mariscotti, Hycintha.*

HYDE, Anne (1638–1671). Duchess of York. Born Mar 12, 1638 (some sources cite 1637), at Cranbourne Lodge in Windsor, Berkshire, England; died Mar 31, 1671, at St. James's Palace, London; eldest dau. of Sir Edward Hyde (1609–1674), 1st earl of Clarendon, and Frances Aylesbury (1617–1667); m. James, duke of York, later James II, king of England (r. 1685–1688), in 1660; children: Charles Stuart (1638–1671); Mary II (1662–1694), queen of England (r. 1689–1694), queen of Scots (r. 1689–1694); James Stuart (1663–1667); Anne (1665–1714), queen of England (r. 1702–1707), queen of Scotland (r. 1702–1707), queen of Britain (r. 1707–1714); Charles (b. 1666, died in infancy); Edgar (b. 1667, died in infancy); Henrietta (1669–1669); Catherine (1671–1671). ❖ Mother of two English queens, was maid of honor to Mary of Orange (1631–1660); as a commoner, scandalized the court when she secretly married James, duke of York, heir to the throne and brother of Charles II (1660); gave birth to 2 girls who were swiftly dispatched to the royal nursery; though daughters were brought up Protestant, converted to Catholicism with husband (1669). ❖ See also *Women in World History.*

HYDE, Catherine (1701–1777). Duchess of Queensberry. Name variations: Catherine Douglas. Born 1701; died 1777; interred at Durisdeer; dau. of Henry Hyde, 4th earl of Clarendon and earl of Rochester, and Jane Leveson-Gower (though some think she was the natural dau. of Jane and Lord Carleton); m. Charles Douglas, 3rd duke of Queensbury, Mar 10, 1720; children: Henry Douglas (b. 1722), earl of Drumlanrig; Charles Douglas (b. 1726). ❖ Was a correspondent with Jonathan Swift and a friend to William Congreve, Alexander Pope, James Thomson, Matthew Prior, and William Whitehead.

HYDE, Ida (1857–1945). American physiologist. Born in Davenport, Iowa, Sept 8, 1857; died in Berkeley, California, Aug 22, 1945; dau. of Meyer Heidenheimer (merchant) and Babette (Loewenthal) Heidenheimer; attended Chicago Athenaeum; attended University of Illinois, 1881–82; Cornell University, BS, 1891; studied under zoologist Thomas Hunt Morgan and physiologist Jacques Loeb at Bryn Mawr; attended University of Strassburg, 1893–95; was the 1st woman to receive a PhD from University of Heidelberg, 1896; never married; no children. ❖ After receiving degree, did research at Heidelberg Table of the Zoological Station, a marine biological lab in Naples; returning to US (1896), spent a year as a research fellow at Radcliffe, working with physiologist William Townsend Porter at Harvard Medical School, the 1st woman to do research at that institution; joined faculty of University of Kansas as associate professor of physiology (1898) and promoted to full professor when a separate department of physiology was established (1905); in over 20 years there, gained an outstanding reputation as a teacher and researcher; wrote textbook *Outlines of Experimental Physiology* (1905) and laboratory manual *Laboratory Outlines of Physiology* (1910); retiring from the university (1922), returned to University of Heidelberg for a year to conduct research on the effects of radium; developed microtechniques by which a single cell could be investigated; was 1st woman elected to membership in American Physiological Association. ❖ See also *Women in World History.*

HYDE, Jane (d. 1725). Countess of Clarendon and Rochester. Died 1725; m. Henry Hyde, 2nd earl of Rochester, 1693; children: Henry Hyde (1710–1753), Viscount Cornbury and Baron Hyde, Jacobite MP for Oxford University. ❖ Celebrated beauty, was the inspiration for Myra in Matthew Prior's *Judgement of Venus.*

HYDE, Mary (1912–2003). *See Eccles, Mary Hyde.*

HYDE, Miriam Beatrice (1913–2005). Australian composer, pianist, and teacher. Born in Adelaide, Australia, Jan 15, 1913; died Jan 11, 2005; studied at Royal College of Music as an Elder Scholar (1932–35); studied piano with Howard Hadley and Sir Arthur Benjamin and composition with R.O. Morris and Gordon Jacob. ❖ Won the Sullivan, Farrar and Cobbett prizes for composition at Royal College of Music; won Anzac Song prize 3 times; performed 2 of her Piano Concertos with London Philharmonic conducted by Leslie Heward and London Symphony conducted by Constant Lambert; in Australia, her *Adelaide Overture* was conducted by Sir Malcolm Sargent (1936); composed over 160 works, including a dozen major orchestral pieces. Awarded OBE (1981).

HYDE, Morna (1932—). *See Pearce, Morna.*

HYDE, Robin (1906–1939). *See Wilkinson, Iris.*

HYDE, Shelley (1932—). *See Reed, Kit.*

HYDELE OF ATHENS (fl. 3rd century BCE). *See Hedyle.*

HYDER, Qurratulain (1927—). Indian novelist and journalist. Born 1927 in Aligarh, Uttar Pradesh, India; dau. of S.H. Yildarim (Urdu novelist). ❖ Worked as radio and magazine journalist and was managing editor of *Imprint* (1964–78); taught at universities in India and US; became leading authority in India on Urdu literature; writings, which are preoccupied with cultural interactions of Northern India, include *Mere bhi sanamkhane* (1948), *Ag ka darya* (1959), *Sitaharan* (1968), *Akhir-i shab ke hamsafar* (1979), *Chandni Begam* (1990), *Fireflies in the Mist* (1994), *The Street Singers of Lucknow and Other Stories* (1997), and *River of Fire* (1999). Received Soviet Land Nehru Award (1969), Ghalib Award (1985) and Jhanpith Award (1989).

HYER, Martha (1924—). American actress. Name variations: Martha Hyer Wallis. Born Aug 10, 1924, in Fort Worth, TX; m. C. Ray Stahl, 1951 (div. 1954); m. Hal B. Wallis (producer), 1966 (died 1986). ❖ Made film debut in *The Locket* (1946), followed by *So Big, Sabrina, Cry Vengeance, Francis in the Navy, Kiss of Fire, Battle Hymn, Mister Cory, The Delicate Delinquent, My Man Godfrey, Paris Holiday, Houseboat, The Big Fisherman, The Best of Everything, Ice Palace, Wives and Lovers, The Carpetbaggers, The Sons of Katie Elder, The Chase, The Night of the Grizzly, The Happening* and *Day of the Wolves*, among others; reportedly, under name Martin Julien, wrote screenplay for *Rooster Cogburn.* Nominated for Oscar for Best Supporting Actress for *Some Came Running* (1959). ❖ See also autobiography *Finding My Way* (1990).

HYGEBURG (fl. 8th c.). British religious writer. Name variations: Hugeberc or Hugeburc; Huneberc of Heidenheim; Huneburc. Born in England sometime after 761; fl. 778 to 786. ❖ Joined a Benedictine monastery at Heidenheim, Germany, founded by her relatives, Willibald (701–786), Winibald (702–761), and Walpurgis (c. 710–777); began her life there under the direction of Walpurgis, who was abbess of the women; wrote *The Life of Saints Willibald and Wynnebald* in Latin, describing Willibald's journey to Holy Land and Mediterranean (723–29); work is only surviving 8th-century account of pilgrimage to Holy Land.

HYKOVA, Lenka (1985—). Czech shooter. Born Feb 2, 1985, in Pizen, Czechoslovakia. ❖ Won a silver medal for 25m pistol at Athens Olympics (2004).

HYLAND, Diana (1936–1977). American actress. Name variations: Diane Gentner. Born Diana Gentner, Jan 25, 1936, in Cleveland Heights, Ohio; died Mar 27, 1977, in Los Angeles, CA; lived with John Travolta. ❖ Appeared as Heavenly Finney in original production of *Sweet Bird of Youth* on Broadway (1959); film credits include *One Man's Way, The Chase* and *Smoky*; on tv, had recurring roles on "Young Dr. Malone," "Peyton Place," and as Joan Bradford on "Eight is Enough." Won Emmy for performance in "Boy in the Plastic Bubble" (1976).

HYLAND, Frances (1927–2004). Canadian actress and director. Born April 25, 1927, in Shaunavon, Saskatchewan, Canada; died July 11, 2004, in Toronto, Ontario, Canada; dau. of Thomas and Jessie Worden Hyland; graduate of University of Saskatchewan; attended Royal Academy of Dramatic Art, London; m. George McCowan (stage director, div.); children: 1 son. ❖ Considered the first lady of Canadian theater, began career in London, in the Vivien Leigh starrer *A Streetcar Named Desire*; starred in *The Same Sky* (1952); joined Tyrone Guthrie at Stratford Festival in Ontario for such Shakespearean roles as Bianca, Portia, Desdemona, Olivia, Ophelia and Isabella; also frequently appeared at Niagara-on-the-Lake and at the Crest Theatre in Toronto; on tv, portrayed Louisa Banks on the series "Road to Avonlea." Appointed officer of the Order of Canada (1971).

HYLTON, Jane (1927–1979). English actress. Born Gwendoline Clark, July 16, 1927, in London, England; died Feb 28, 1979, in Glasgow, Scotland; m. Euan Lloyd (producer, div.); m. Peter Dyneley (actor, died 1977). ❖ Leading lady of British B features, including *The Upturned Glass, Dear Murderer, My Brother's Keeper, Daybreak, Passport to Pimlico, It Started in Paradise, House of Mystery* and *Circus of Horrors.*

HYMAN, Dorothy (1941—). English runner. Born May 9, 1941, in UK. ❖ Won a silver medal in the 100 meters and a bronze in the 200 meters at Rome Olympics (1960); won a bronze medal at the Tokyo Olympics in the 4 x 100-meter relay (1964).

HYMAN, Flo (1954–1986). African-American volleyball player. Name variations: Flora Jo Hyman. Born Flora Hyman, July 29 (some sources cite July 31), 1954, in Inglewood, California; died Jan 24, 1986, of a ruptured aorta due to Marfan's syndrome, while on the court in Matsue, Japan. ❖ Helped popularize American volleyball; led the American volleyball team to an Olympic silver medal at Los Angeles (1984). Honored by Women's Sports Association with the creation of the annual Flo Hyman Award (1987). ❖ See also *Women in World History.*

HYMAN, Libbie Henrietta (1888–1969). American zoologist. Born Dec 6, 1888, in Des Moines, Iowa; died Aug 3, 1969, in New York, NY; dau. of Joseph (tailor) and Sabina (Neumann) Hyman; University of Chicago, BS, 1910, PhD, 1915; never married. ❖ An authority on the physiology and morphology of lower invertebrates, did graduate work under direction of Charles Manning Child and, after receiving PhD, stayed on as his research assistant and as a laboratory instructor in vertebrate anatomy and elementary zoology; over next 15 years, published a number of articles in conjunction with Child's projects, as well as her own *Laboratory Manual for Elementary Zoology* (1919) and *Laboratory Manual for Comparative Vertebrate Anatomy* (1922), both of which became widely used texts; became a research associate at American Museum of Natural History (1937), where her expertise on the taxonomy and anatomy of unexplored lower invertebrates gained her respect of scientists in US and Europe, who often sent her specimens to identify; published comprehensive 6-volume encyclopedic survey *The Invertebrates* (1940–67). Received British Royal Society's Gold Medal of Linnean Society (1960). ❖ See also *Women in World History.*

HYMAN, Misty (1979—). American swimmer. Born Mar 23, 1979, in Mesa, Arizona. ❖ Won a gold medal for 200-meter butterfly at Sydney Olympics (2000). Named NCAA Swimmer of the Year (1999).

HYMAN, Phyllis (1949–1995). African-American rhythm and blues singer. Born July 6, 1949, in Philadelphia, PA; died June 30, 1995, by her own hand, in New York, NY; m. Larry Alexander (div.). ❖ Began professional career with the singing group New Direction; formed own band, Phyllis Hyman and the PH Factor; made Broadway debut in *Sophisticated Ladies*, followed by *Dreamgirls*; recorded such singles as "Loving You, Losing You" and "You Know How to Love Me." Nominated for a Tony Award for *Sophisticated Ladies* (1981).

HYMAN, Prudence (1914–1995). English ballet dancer. Born 1914 in London, England; died June 1, 1995, in London. ❖ As a member of Ballet Club and Camargo Society, contributed to development in English ballet (1930s); created roles in numerous works by Frederick Ashton, and for Antony Tudor in his *Cross-Garter'd* (1931), *Adam and Eve* (1932), *Lysistrata* (1932), and others; performed in premieres of Ashton's, including *The Fairy Queen* (1927), *Capriol Suite* (1930), *The Lord of Burleigh* (1931) and *The Lady of Shallott* (1931); performed in London season of Les Ballets '33 in works by George Balanchine; danced for short period in John Maynard Keynes' Arts Theater Ballet.

HYMAN, Trina Schart (1939–2004). American book illustrator and children's writer. Born Trina Schart, April 8, 1939, in Philadelphia, PA; died Nov 19, 2004, in Lebanon, New Hampshire; dau. of Albert H. (salesman) and Margaret Doris (Bruck) Schart; studied at Philadelphia Museum College of Art, 1956–59, Boston Museum School of Arts, 1959–60, and Konstfackskolan (Swedish State Art School), Stockholm, 1960–61; m. Harris Hyman (mathematician), 1959 (div. 1968); lived with partner Jean Aull; children: Katrin Tchana. ❖ Won the Caldecott Medal for illustrations for Margaret Hodges' *St. George and the Dragon* (1984), and Caldecott honors for John Updike's *Little Red Riding Hood* and Eric Kimmel's *Hershel and the Hanukkah Goblins*; was art director of *Cricket* magazine, 1972–79; illustrated more than 150 books; also wrote and illustrated her own.

HYNDE, Chrissie (1951—). American rock musician and leader of the rock band The Pretenders. Born Sept 7, 1951 in Akron, Ohio; dau. of Bud Hynde (telephone company employee) and Dee Hynde; attended Kent State University, 1960s; m. Jim Kerr (rock musician), 1984 (div. 1989); m. Lucho Brieva (sculptor), 1997; children: (with Kinks frontman, Ray Davies) Natalie Rae (b. 1983); (with Kerr) Yasmine (b. 1985). ❖ Began career as rhythm guitarist when she took up the baritone ukulele at 16; moved to London to break into music business (1973); bounced between England, US and France, performing with a variety of bands (mid-1970s); formed group The Pretenders (1978), with British musicians Pete Farndon, James Honeyman-Scott, and Martin Chambers; released self-titled debut album to enormous critical acclaim (1980), earning much of the praise for her cutting lyrics and hard-edged guitar riffs; after Honeyman-Scott and Farndon died from drug overdoses (1982 and 1983, respectively), managed to hold things together by adding 2 members, and released 3rd album, *Learning to Crawl* (1984); remained the center of the group despite more staff changes; released album *Get Close* (1986), embarked on world tour (1987), and made 3 more albums: *Packed!* (1991), *Isle of View* (1995) and *¡Viva El Amor!* (1999); was an animal-rights activist long before it became a celebrity cause. ❖ See also *Women in World History*.

HYPATIA (c. 375–415). Alexandrian scholar. Born c. 375 CE; died 415; dau. of Theon (mathematician and astronomer associated with the Museum of Alexandria, a think tank where famous artists and intellectuals came to ply their expertise). ❖ One of the most famous intellectuals in history, began schooling with father; while still in her 20s, developed such a reputation as a mathematician, astronomer and philosopher that she began to draw students to Alexandria from all over the Roman Empire; established her reputation with a commentary on Diophantus' *Arithmeticorum* (a work dedicated to algebraic theorems), a revision of *Almagest*, the 3rd book of Ptolemy the astronomer (not to be confused with the kings of Egypt), and a commentary on *Conic Sections*; became equally intrigued with cosmogony, and the philosophical questions concerning the origins of the universe; began a serious inquiry into the nature of humanity, its purpose, and its relative position in the cosmic hierarchy; as a result, was drawn to philosophy, especially to Plotinian neo-Platonism which in her time was the prominent philosophy of the Museum; became head of the neo-Platonic school in Alexandria at young age (c. 400), the most influential academic of her world; drew a civic salary, an unusual situation at the time, because she was a woman and because she was a staunch pagan in a city of Christians, ruled by a Christian administration; maintained a high profile throughout Alexandria—so high in fact that her detractors suggested that she was a

brazen woman of loose morals; was consulted about a range of practical issues, some of which were socially volatile, including when Orestes, a prefect of Alexandria, questioned the ethics of Cyril, bishop of Alexandria, and his bid to cleanse the city of all unorthodox thinking and rid it of Jews; when Cyril lost face, became his scapegoat; was pulled from her chariot by a group of monks, led into the Caesarium Church, stripped of her clothes, and skinned alive by shells specially honed to a razor-sharpness (Cyril went on to become recognized, both in the Latin and Greek Orthodox Churches, as a saint). ❖ See also Maria Dzielska, *Hypatia of Alexandria* (trans. by F. Lyra, Harvard U. Press, 1995); and *Women in World History*.

HYSLOP, Beatrice Fry (1899–1973). American historian. Born Beatrice Fry Hyslop on April 10, 1899, in New York, NY; died July 23, 1973, in Rochester, NY; dau. of James Hervey Hyslop and Mary Fry (Hall) Hyslop; Columbia University, PhD in history, 1934. ❖ Taught at Mount Holyoke College (1926–28) and at Kingswood School for Girls, Bloomfield, Michigan (1934–36); researching *cahiers de doléances* of 1789 for doctoral studies, was commissioned by French government to verify and catalog them (1931), publishing work as *Répertoire critique des cahiers de doléances pour les États-généreaux de 1789* (1933) and *Supplément* (1952); published doctoral thesis *French Nationalism in 1789 According to the General Cahiers* (1934), *L'Apanage de Philippe-Égalité, duc d'Orléans, 1785–1791* (1965), and co-wrote *The Napoleonic Era in Europe* (1970); taught at Hunter College (NY), becoming history instructor (1936), assistant professor (1941), associate professor (1949) and professor (1954); edited "France" section of "Recently Published Articles" for *American Historical Review* (1947–68); helped found Society for French Historical Studies (1955), serving as 3rd president; was member of graduate faculty at City University of New York (1964–69); was visiting scholar at University of Kentucky (1969) and Winthrop College (1970). Made Chevalier des Palmes académiques (1931) and Chevalier de la Légion d'Honneur (1952) by French government.

HYSLOP, Fiona (1964—). Scottish politician. Born Aug 1, 1964, in Scotland; Glasgow University, MA in economic history and sociology; married. ❖ Joined SNP (1986), becoming a member of its National Executive; stood as candidate for Edinburgh Leith in general election (1992) and Edinburgh Central in general election (1997); serves as SNP member of the Scottish Parliament for Lothians.

HYSON, Dorothy (1914–1996). American-born stage and screen actress. Born Dorothy Wardell Heisen, Dec 24, 1914, in Chicago, IL; died May 23, 1996, in London, England; dau. of Carl Heisen and Dorothy Dickson (1883–1995, actress); attended RADA; m. Robert Douglas, 1936 (div. 1945); m. Anthony Quayle (actor), 1947 (died 1989). ❖ As a child, made stage debut in London in *Quality Street* (1927), followed by *The Young Visiters, Flies in the Sun, Saturday's Children, Touch Wood, Pride and Prejudice, To Have and to Hold, Three Blind Mice, Only Yesterday,* and the title role in *Lady Windermere's Fan* (which ran over a year); made NY debut in *Most of the Game* (1935); films include *A Cup of Kindness, You Will Remember* and *Spare a Copper*.

HYUN JUNG-HWA (1969—). Korean table-tennis player. Born Oct 6, 1969, in South Korea. ❖ At Seoul Olympics, won a gold medal in doubles (1988); at Barcelona Olympics, won a bronze medal in doubles and a bronze medal in singles (1992).

HYUN SOOK-HEE. South Korean judoka. Born in South Korea. ❖ Won a silver medal for 48–52kg half-lightweight at Atlanta Olympics (1996).

HYYTIANEN, Eija. Finnish cross-country skier. Name variations: Hyytiäinen. Born in Finland. ❖ Won a silver medal for 4 x 5km relay for 5km at Sarajevo Olympics (1984).

I

IAIA (fl. c. 100 BCE). **Ancient Greek painter.** Name variations: Laia; Lala; Laya; Maia; Marcia; Martia. Pronunciation: ee-EYE-ah. Born at an unknown date in Cyzicus (near present-day Erdek in Turkey, on Sea of Marmara); never married. ❖ Was active in Rome; painted mostly portraits of women, obtaining prices that outdid the most celebrated portrait painters of the same period, Sopolis and Dionysius; was skilled in the use of the brush and the cestrum. ❖ See also *Women in World History.*

IAMS, Lucy (1855–1924). **American social-welfare worker and reformer.** Name variations: Lucy Dorsey. Born Lucy Virginia Dorsey, Nov 13, 1855, in Oakland, MD; died Oct 26, 1924, in Pittsburgh, PA; dau. of James Francis Dorsey (minister) and Charlotte (Hook) Dorsey; m. Franklin Pierce Iams (lawyer), Aug 12, 1877; children: 2 sons. ❖ Served as vice president (1902–24), chair, and head of legislative committee of Civic Club of Allegheny County, through which she worked for such causes as housing, woman and child welfare, health, and correctional institutions; sat on legislative committees for State Federation of Pennsylvania Women (1903–23), Consumers' League of Western Pennsylvania, Pennsylvania and Allegheny County Child Labor Association, and Associated Charities of Pennsylvania; ran unsuccessfully for Pittsburgh City Council (1921); was instrumental in drafting and passage of state tenement house law (1903) and appropriation of money from Pittsburgh for inspectors to enforce legislation.

IAN, Janis (1951—). **American folksinger and songwriter.** Born Janis Eddy Fink, April 7, 1951, in New York, NY; m. Peter Cunningham (photojournalist), late 1960s; m. Tino Sargo (Portuguese writer), 1978 (sep. 1983, div. 1988); m. Patricia Snyder, 2003. ❖ Known for forthright lyrics dealing with difficult topics, began composing songs as a student; scored 1st hit at 15 with single "Society's Child" (1967), a tale of interracial love that caused a furor; dropped out of high school during senior year; retired before she was 20; reemerged with albums *Present Company* (1971) and *Stars* (1974); had best career year in 1975, releasing album *Between the Lines*, which included the Grammy-winning single "At Seventeen"; returned from 12-year hiatus with album *Breaking Silence* (1993); released albums *Revenge* (1995), *Hunger* (1997), and *God & the FBI* (2000), which featured collaborations with Willie Nelson and Chet Akins.

IATTCHENKO, Irina (1965—). *See Yatchenko, Irina.*

IBÁÑEZ, Sara de (1909–1971). *See de Ibáñez, Sara.*

IBARBOUROU, Juana de (1895–1979). **Uruguayan poet.** Name variations: Juana Fernández de Morales; Jeanette de Ibar. Pronunciation: HWA-na day EE-bar-BOO-roo. Born Juana Fernández de Morales, Mar 8, 1895, in Melo, Cerro Largo, Uruguay; died July 1979; dau. of Vicente Fernández (Spaniard from Galicia) and Valentina Morales (dau. of a noted Uruguayan politician); m. Captain Lucas Ibarbourou, June 28, 1914; children: Julio César. ❖ Prizewinning poet, noted for her erotic work, who broke conventions to give expression to her most intimate thoughts and dared to come to terms with the position of a woman in a patriarchal society; achieved immediate fame with publication of 1st volume of poetry, *Las lenguas de diamante* (Tongues of Diamond, 1919); a passionate, irreverent writer, followed that with *El cántaro fresco* (The Cool Pitcher, 1920) and *Raíz salvaje* (Wild Root, 1922); also wrote *La rosa de los vientos* (The Compass Rose, 1930) and *Perdida* (Loss, 1950); later works assumed a religious tone as she sought answers to the vexing problems of mortality. Honored as "Juana de América" (1929); awarded the Grand National Literature Prize of Uruguay (1959). ❖ See also autobiographical novel, *Chico-Carlo;* and *Women in World History.*

IBARRA, Rosario (1927—). *See Ibarra de Piedra, Rosario.*

IBARRA DE PIEDRA, Rosario (1927—). **Mexican political activist.** Name variations: Rosario Ibarra. Born Feb 24, 1927, in Saltillo, Coahuila, Mexico; m. Jesús Piedra Rosales; children: 4. ❖ Became human-rights activist after disappearance of son Jesús, who had joined urban guerrilla group to fight for dispossessed (1975); with other mothers (1977), formed Committee for Defense of Political Prisoners, Exiles, Fugitives and Disappeared Persons of Mexico, the nation's 1st human rights organization; held demonstrations and hunger strikes; achieved return of 148 of 481 of the missing as well as a public inquiry (1978); appeared at UN (1978) to denounce disappearances; formed National Front Against Repression (1979), umbrella group of more than 50 other Mexican organizations, to pressure government which resulted in more liberations; was 1st woman candidate for president of Mexico (1982), representing Partido Revolucionario de Trabajo (Revolutionary Workers' Party, PRT); ran again (1988); elected federal deputy for PRT (1985 and 1994); served as advisor on human rights to mayor of Mexico City, worked in solidarity with Chiapas uprising, and served as director of Rosario Ibarra Foundation (founded 1998). Nominated for Nobel Peace Prize (1986, 1987, 1989).

IBÁRRURI, Dolores (1895–1989). **Spanish revolutionary.** Name variations: Dolores Ibarruri; Dolores Ibárruri Gómez; La Pasionaria. Pronunciation: ee-BAR-ru-ree. Born Dec 9, 1895, in Gallarta, Spain; died Nov 12, 1989, in Madrid, Spain; dau. of Antonio Ibárruri and Dolores Gómez; married Julián Ruíz, in Gallarta, 1916: children—6, including 1 set of triplets: Rubén (1921–1942); daughters Esther (1917–1922); Amaya (b. 1923); Amagoya (1923, died young); Azucena (1923–1925); Eva (1928, died young). ❖ Early Communist activist and propagandist known as La Pasionaria who, during the Spanish Civil War, became an internationally recognized speaker for the loyalist cause; was a socialist activist in Vizcaya (1918); elected to provincial committee of Spanish Communist Party (1920); became editor, Communist newspaper *Mundo Obrero* (Madrid, 1931); elected to Parliament (1936); fled Spain for exile in Soviet Union (1939); became secretary-general of Spanish Communist Party (1944); returned to Spain after 38 years in exile (1977). Received Order of Lenin (1965). ❖ See also autobiographies *Memorias de Pasionaria, 1939–1977: Me faltaba España* (Barcelona: Planeta, 1984) and *They Shall Not Pass: The Autobiography of La Pasionaria* (International, 1966); and *Women in World History.*

ICAZA, Carmen de (1899–1979). **Spanish novelist.** Born May 17, 1899, in Madrid, Spain; died Mar 16, 1979; dau. of Francisco de Icaza. ❖ Wrote sentimental romances, including *La boda* (1916), *Cristina de Guzmán, profesora de idiomas* (1936) and *La casa de enfrente* (1945).

ICENI, queen of. *See Boudica (26/30–60 CE).*

ICHIKAWA, Fusae (1893–1981). **Japanese suffragist, feminist, and politician.** Name variations: Ichikawa Fusaye. Pronunciation: ITCH-EE-ka-wa FOO-sa-ae. Born Ichikawa Fusae, May 15, 1893, in Asahi Village, Aichi Prefecture, Japan; died in Tokyo, Japan, 1981; dau. of Ichikawa Fujikurō (farmer) and Ichikawa Tatsu; briefly attended Joshi Gakuin (Girls' Academy) in Tokyo, and graduated from Aichi Prefectural Women's Normal School in 1913; never married; no children. ❖ One of the most outstanding women in 20th-century Japan, taught elementary school (1913–16); was 1st woman newspaper reporter in Nagoya (1917–19); moved to Tokyo to become secretary of the women's section of the Yūaikai (Friendly Society), Japan's 1st labor organization (1919); founded Shin Fujin Kyōkai (New Woman's Association, 1919–21); networked with women's rights leaders in US (1921–23); returned to Tokyo, where she worked for International Labor Organizations (1924–27); founded Fusen Kakutoku Dōmei (Women's Suffrage League, 1924–40); appointed to advisory board of the government's organization, Dai Nihon Fujinkai (Greater Japan Women's Association, 1942–44); organized Sengo Taisaku Fujin Iinkai (Women's Committee on Postwar Countermeasures) to work for women's suffrage (1945); was purged by American occupation (1947–50); served in House of Councillors (upper house of national legislature, 1953–71 and 1974–81). ❖ See also (in Japanese) *Ichikawa Fusawa no jiden—senzen hen* (The Autobiography of Ichikawa Fusae—The Prewar Period, 1974); and *Women in World History.*

ICHINO, Yoko (c. 1954—). American ballet dancer. Name variations: Nancy Ichino. Born c. 1954 in Los Angeles, CA; trained with Mia Slavenska an Margery Mussmann. ❖ Danced with Stuttgart Ballet; performed with City Center Joffrey Ballet (1970s), mainly as Nancy Ichino, in a range of modern as well as classical works, including Arpino's *Sacred Grove on Mount Tamalpais* and *Viva Vivaldi,* Robbins' *New York Export: Opus Jazz,* Tharp's *As Time Goes By;* danced with American Ballet Theater, primarily in company's revival of such classics as *The Sleeping Beauty* and *Don Quixote;* danced solos by Mussmann including *Rondo* and *Episodes;* won the international ballet competition in Moscow (1977).

ICHIYO HIGUCHI (1872–1896). *See Higuchi, Ichiyo.*

ICHMOURATOVA, Svetlana (1972—). *See Ishmouratova, Svetlana.*

ICHO, Chiharu (1981—). Japanese wrestler. Born Oct 6, 1981, in Aomori, Japan. ❖ Won World championships for 51kg freestyle (2003); won Asian championships for 51kg (2001) and 48kg (2004); won a silver medal for 48kg freestyle at Athens Olympics (2004).

ICHO, Kaori (1984—). Japanese wrestler. Born June 13, 1984, in Aomori, Japan. ❖ Won World championships (2002, 2003) and Asian championships (2004), all for 63kg freestyle; won a gold medal for 63kg freestyle at Athens Olympics (2004).

ICHTCHENKO, Natalia (1986—). Russian synchronized swimmer. Born April 8, 1986, in USSR. ❖ Won a team gold medal at Athens Olympics (2004).

ICKES, Anna Thompson (1873–1935). American politician and reformer. Name variations: Anna Wilmarth Ickes. Born Anna Wilmarth, Jan 27, 1873, in Chicago, IL; killed in auto accident, Aug 31, 1935, in Velarde, NM; dau. of Henry Martin Wilmarth (manufacturer and organizer of First National Bank) and Mary Jane (Hawes) Wilmarth (1837–1919, civic and reform leader); educated at University of Chicago; m. James Westfall Thompson (historian), 1879 (div. 1909); m. Harold LeClaire Ickes (Secretary of the Interior), Sept 16, 1911; children: (1st m.) Wilmarth Thompson and (adopted) Frances Thompson; (2nd m.): Raymond Wilmarth Ickes and (adopted) Robert Ickes. ❖ Became involved with Women's Trade Union League; with 2nd husband Harold, helped form Progressive Party in Illinois (1912); served on board of trustees for University of Illinois (1924–29); also served on boards for Chicago Home for the Friendless and Chicago Regional Planning Association (1920s); successfully ran for state legislature as a Republican (1928) and was reelected handily (1930 and 1932); during time in office, sat on several committees in the lower house, including those on civil service, education, charities and corrections, and industrial affairs; with husband in Washington, did not run for reelection (1934), instead, focused attention on the culture, archaeology, and welfare of Native Americans, issues which had long held her interest, having published *Mesa Land* (1933). ❖ See also *Women in World History.*

IDA. *Variant of Ita and Edith.*

IDABERGA (d. 751). *See Edburga.*

IDA DE MACON (d. 1224). Duchess of Lorraine. Name variations: Ida of Macon. Died 1224; dau. of Gerard I, count of Macon and Vienne, and Maurette de Salins, heiress of Salins; m. Humbert II de Coligny, around 1170; m. Simon II, duke of Lorraine, after 1190.

IDA OF ALSACE (c. 1161–1216). *See Ide d'Alsace.*

IDA OF AUSTRIA (d. 1101?). Margravine of Austria. Possibly died in 1101; m. Leopold II, margrave of Austria (r. 1075–1096); children: Leopold III the Pious of Austria, margrave of Austria (r. 1096–1136, who m. Agnes of Germany and was canonized in 1485). ❖ With the duke of Aquitaine and duke of Bavaria, led an army on crusade; was surrounded by the Turks (Sept 15, 1101) but remained on the field of battle. Though no one knows what became of her, there is some speculation that she was taken prisoner, added to the harem of Aqsonqor and had a son Imad ed-din Zengi, a military hero and atabeg of Mosul and Aleppo. ❖ See also *Women in World History.*

IDA OF BOULOGNE (c. 1161–1216). *See Ide d'Alsace.*

IDA OF BRABANT (1040–1113). *See Ida of Lorraine.*

IDA OF IRELAND (d. 570). *See Ita of Ireland.*

IDA OF LORRAINE (1040–1113). Saint and countess of Boulogne. Name variations: Ida of Lower Lorraine; Ida of Brabant. Born 1040; died 1113 and was buried at the abbey of Vasconvilliers, near Boulogne; dau. of Doda and Godfrey II the Bearded, duke of Lower Lorraine (r. 1065–1069); sister of Godfrey III the Hunchback (d. 1076); was the 2nd wife of Eustace II (d. 1093), count of Boulogne (r. around 1057); children: many, including Godfrey, duke of Bouillon and king of Jerusalem (r. 1099–1100); Baldwin I, count of Edessa and king of Jerusalem (r. 1100–1118); Eustace III of Boulogne (who m. Mary of Atholl [d. 1116]); and possibly a daughter who m. Henry IV, king of Germany (though she would not be either of his known wives, Bertha of Savoy and Adelaide of Kiev). Eustace II's 1st wife was Godgifu (c. 1010–c. 1049). ❖ Extremely pious, was often visited by spiritual counselor St. Anselm, then abbot of Bec in Normandy; gave much of her considerable wealth to charity and enjoyed making fine ornaments for altars; following death of husband (1093), sold all her disposable goods to found and endow religious institutions. Feast day is April 13.

IDA OF LORRAINE (c. 1161–1216). *See Ide d'Alsace.*

IDA OF LOUVAIN (d. 1260). Cistercian nun and saint. Born in Louvain, France; died at the abbey of Ramiège in 1260. ❖ Feast day is April 13.

IDA OF LOWER LORRAINE (1040–1113). *See Ida of Lorraine.*

IDA OF LOWER LORRAINE (d. 1162). Noblewoman of Lower Lorraine. Died July 27, 1162; dau. of Godfrey I, duke of Brabant or Lower Lorraine (r. 1106–1139) and Ida of Namur; sister of Godfrey II of Brabant or Lower Lorraine (d. 1142) and Adelicia of Louvain (c. 1102–1151, queen of England).

IDA OF NAMUR (fl. 12th c.). Duchess of Lower Lorraine. Probably died between 1117 and 1121; dau. of Albert III, count of Namur; 1st wife of Godfrey I, duke of Brabant or Lower Lorraine also known as Louvain (r. 1106–1139); children: Godfrey II of Brabant or Lower Lorraine (d. 1142); Adelicia of Louvain (c. 1102–1151, queen of England); Ida of Lower Lorraine (d. 1162). Godfrey I's 2nd wife was Clementia.

IDA OF NIJVEL (597–652). *See Ida of Nivelles.*

IDA OF NIVELLES (597–652). Cistercian nun and queen of the Franks. Name variations: Blessed Ita, Itta, or Iduberga; Ida of Nijvel; Ida de Nivelles. Born 597; died 652; m. Pepin I of Landen, mayor of Austrasia (king of the Franks, d. 640); aunt of Saint Modesta of Trier (d. about 680); children: Gertrude of Nivelles (626–659); Begga (613–698); Grimoald, mayor of Austrasia (d. 656). ❖ Following death of husband Pepin I, became a nun at abbey of Nivelles (Belgium) where daughter Gertrude of Nivelles was abbess. Feast day is May 8.

IDA OF NIVELLES (d. 1232). Belgian abbess. Died 1232 (some sources cite 1231) at convent of La Ramée, Belgium; never married; no children. ❖ Given by parents to Cistercian convent of La Ramée as a little girl, remained there entire life; was exceptionally well educated and grew up a devout woman who was dedicated to writing and preserving holy works; eventually became closely identified with the large *scriptorium* (book-production center) of La Ramée, supervising the writing and illustration of manuscripts and performing these functions as well; was a spiritual guide of Beatrice of Nazareth (c. 1200–1268).

IDA OF SAXE-COBURG-MEININGEN (1794–1852). Princess of Saxe-Coburg-Meiningen. Born June 25, 1794; died April 4, 1852; dau. of Louise of Hohenlohe-Langenburg (1763–1837) and George I (b. 1761), duke of Saxe-Meiningen; m. Charles Bernard of Saxe-Weimar (1792–1862); children: Louise Wilhelmina of Saxe-Weimar (1817–1832); William Charles of Saxe-Weimar (b. 1819); Amelia Augusta (1822–1822); Edward (b. 1823); Hermann Henry (b. 1825), prince of Saxe-Weimar; Gustav of Saxe-Weimar (b. 1827); Anne Amelia of Saxe-Weimar (1828–1864); Amelia Maria da Gloria of Saxe-Weimar (1830–1872, who m. Henry von Nassau of the Netherlands).

IDA OF SCHAUMBURG-LIPPE (1852–1891). Princess of Reuss. Name variations: Ida Mathilde Adelheid, princess of Schaumburg-Lippe. Born Ida Matilda Adelaide, July 28, 1852; died Sept 28, 1891; dau. of Hermine of Waldeck and Pyrmont (1827–1910) and Adolphus I Georg, Prince of Schaumburg-Lippe; m. Henry 22nd, prince of Reuss, Oct 8, 1872; children: 6, including Hermine of Reuss (1887–1947, who m. Kaiser Wilhelm II).

IDA OF SWABIA (d. 986). Duchess of Swabia. Died 986; dau. of Herman I, duke of Swabia; m. Liudolf also known as Ludolf (980–957), duke of

Swabia (r. 948–957), in 948; children: Otto I (b. 954), duke of Bavaria; Matilda of Essen (949–1011); and one other daughter.

IDA PLANTAGENET (fl. 1175). Countess of Norfolk. Name variations: Isabel Plantagenet. Fl. around 1175; dau. of Isabel de Warrenne (c. 1137–1203) and Hamelin de Warrenne (c. 1129–1202, illeg. son of Geoffrey of Anjou), 5th earl of Surrey; m. Roger Bigod, 2nd earl of Norfolk, one of the 25 sureties of the Magna Carta, and steward of the household of Richard I, king of England; m. Robert de Lascy; m. Gilbert de Laigle, Lord of Pevensey; children: (1st m.) Hugh Bigod, 3rd earl of Norfolk (r. c. 1200–1225) and earl marshall of England; Margaret Bigod (who m. Sir John Jeremy); Margery Bigod (who m. William Hastings, steward to Henry II, king of England); Alice Bigod (who m. Aubrey IV, 2nd earl of Oxford).

IDAR, Jovita (1885–1946). Mexican-American journalist, organizer, and educator. Name variations: Idár. Born Jovita Idar de Juarez, 1885, in TX; died 1946; dau. of a Mexican-American newspaper publisher. ❖ As a journalist, took active interest in poverty and racism facing her people; helped her father organize the First Mexican Congress, an educational and cultural conference which brought together Mexican-American leaders (1911); became president of Mexican Feminist League (1911), which actively opposed lynching, promoted equal rights for women, and fostered education for Mexican-American children; co-founded the White Cross (1913), a group of women who provided medical care for civilians and soldiers from both sides of the Texas-Mexico border; moved to San Antonio (1917), where she opened a free kindergarten and edited a Methodist Spanish-language newspaper. ❖ See also *Women in World History.*

IDE, Letitia (1909–1993). American modern dancer. Name variations: Letitia Ide Ratner. Born June 2, 1909, in Springfield, IL; died Aug 29, 1993, in Hastings On Hudson, NY; graduate of University of Chicago; trained at Humphrey-Weidman studio in NY; m. Victor M. Ratner. ❖ With Humphrey-Weidman Concert Group, appeared in works by Doris Humphrey, including *Water Study* (1928), *La Valse* (1930) and *New Dance* (1935), and works by Charles Weidman, including *Farandole* (1932), *Memorials* (1935) and *Petite Suite* (1936); performed on Broadway in *As Thousands Cheer* (1932) and *Candide* (1933), among others; appeared in Limón's *The Exiles* (1950), *The Visitation* (1952) and *The Queen's Epicedium* (1952).

IDE D'ALSACE (c. 1161–1216). Countess of Boulogne. Name variations: Ida of Alsace; Ida of Boulogne; Ida of Lorraine; Ide de Lorraine. Born c. 1161; died 1216; reigned 1173–1216; dau. of Marie of Boulogne (d. 1182) and Matthew I (Mattheu d'Alsace), count of Boulogne; sister of Maude of Alsace (1163–c. 1210); m. Matthew of Tulli; m. Erchard also known as Gerard III of Guelders, count of Guelders; m. Berthold, duke of Zarengen; m. Reinaldo, count of Dammartin; children: Matilda de Dammartin (d. 1258). ❖ Succeeded her mother as countess of Boulogne (1173) and ruled until 1216; was succeeded by daughter Matilda de Dammartin.

IDEHEN, Faith (1973—). Nigerian runner. Born Feb 5, 1973, in Nigeria. ❖ At Barcelona Olympics, won a bronze medal in the 4 x 100-meter relay (1992).

IDEM, Josefa (1964—). German-Italian kayaker. Name variations: Josefa Idem-Eichin, then Josefa Idem Guerrini or Idem-Guerrini. Born Josefa Idem, Sept 23, 1964, in Goch, Germany; m. Gugliemo Guerrini (her trainer), 1990. ❖ Representing West Germany, won a bronze medal in K2 500 meters at Los Angeles Olympics (1984); moved to Italy (1988); became an Italian citizen (1992); representing Italy, won a bronze medal at Atlanta Olympics (1996), a gold medal at Sydney Olympics (2000), and a silver medal at Athens Olympics (2004), all for K1 500 meters; won World Cup (1999); won 6 gold medals at World championships and 8 at European championships.

IDLIBI, 'Ulfah al- (1912—). Syrian teacher and author. Name variations: Ulfa al-Idlibi; Ulfat Idlibi. Born 1912 in Damascus, Syria; children: son (died 1947). ❖ One of the most prominent female writers in Syria, devoted the bulk of her writing to short stories, many of which explore the lives of Arab women, particularly in Damascus; wrote more than 100 stories and 4 books, including *Shamian Stories* (1954), *Farewell, Damascus* (1963), *Damascus, Smile of Sorrow* (released in US as *Sabriya: A Novel,* 1980).

IDUBERGA (597–652). See Ida of Nivelles.

IENCIC, Ecaterina (1946—). See Stahl-Iencic, Ecaterina.

IFFAT (1916–2000). Saudi queen. Name variations: 'Iffat; Iffat al Thunayan; Iffat bint Ahmad al-Saud. Born Iffat bint Ahmad al-Saud in 1916 (some sources cite 1910) in Istanbul, Turkey, a descendant of Saudi notables who had been exiled there during Turkish domination of the peninsula; died Feb 18, 2000; dau. of Ahmad ibn Abdallah al-Saud; sister of Sheikh Kamal Ahmad; m. Crown Prince Feisal or Faisal (1905–1975), son of Abd Al-Aziz Ibn-Saud (founder of Saudi Arabia), who was later king of Saudi Arabia (r. 1964–75); children: 9, including Muhammad (b. 1937), Latifah, Sara, Saud (b. 1940), Abdalrahman, Bandar (b. 1943), and Turki (b. 1945). ❖ Grew up in Turkey but was taken back to Saudi Arabia by her father's cousin Crown Prince Feisal whom she then married; became husband's partner as they modernized and oversaw the development of the kingdom; her influence was recognized both inside and outside the palaces of Riyadh; started government boys' school (1942) and girls' school (1956); after husband became king (1964), pushed for education for girls, then unknown in the Arab world; later helped plan adult-education centers and Institute of Management and Administration for Women; started girls' College of Education (1967); husband was assassinated (Mar 26, 1975), ending a remarkable reign.

IFFAT AL THUNAYAN (1916–2000). See Iffat.

IFFAT BINT AHMAD AL-SAUD (1916–2000). See Iffat.

IFILL, Gwen (1955—). African-American journalist and newscaster. Born Sept 29, 1955, in Queens, NY; dau. of a preacher; graduate of Simmons College. ❖ Was a *New York Times* reporter before joining the NBC Washington bureau; became correspondent on "Today" (1994); began serving as moderator of "Washington Week in Review" on PBS (1999); was co-host of "Flashpoints USA with Bryant Gumble and Gwen Ifill" (2003) and senior correspondent on "The NewsHour with Jim Lehrer."

IGALY, Diana (1965—). Hungarian shooter. Name variations: Díana Igaly. Born May (some sources cite Jan) 31, 1965, in Budapest, Hungary; divorced. ❖ Won a bronze medal at Sydney Olympics (2000) and a gold medal at Athens Olympics (2004), both for skeet shooting; at World championships, placed 1st (2002).

IGHODARO, Irene (1916–1995). Nigerian physician and social reformer. Born Irene Elizabeth Beatrice Wellesley-Cole in Sierra Leone, Africa, May 16, 1916; died Nov 29, 1995; dau. of Robert Wellesley-Cole (engineer); graduate of Annie Walsh Memorial School, Freetown; University of Durham, England, MBBS; m. Samuel Ighodaro (judge of High Court of Midwestern Nigeria); children: 5. ❖ One of Nigeria's foremost physicians, served as chair of board of management of University of Benin Teaching Hospital in Benin City, Nigeria, and was a consultant in maternal and child health to World Health Organization; wrote *Baby's First Year,* as well as many articles; was active in both the national and international YWCA, serving also as a member of the YWCA World Executive Committee. Made Member of the British Empire (MBE, 1958). ❖ See also *Women in World History.*

IGNAT, Doina (1968—). Romanian rower. Born Dec 20, 1968, in Radauti, Romania. ❖ At Barcelona Olympics, won a silver medal in quadruple sculls without coxswain (1992); won a gold medal for coxed eights at Atlanta Olympics (1996) and gold medals for coxed eights and coxless pair at Sydney Olympics (2000); at World championships, won gold medals for coxed eights (1993, 1997, 1998, 1999); won a gold medal for coxed eights at Athens Olympics (2004).

IGNATOVA, Lilia (1965—). Bulgarian rhythmic gymnast. Born May 17, 1965, in Sofia, Bulgaria. ❖ At European championships, placed 2nd in all-around (1981) and 1st (1986); at World championships, placed 2nd (1981, 1983, 1985); won two World Cups and 6-consecutive Julieta Shishmanova Cups (1981–86). Starred in Gueorgui Duylguerov's musical film *Akatamus;* inducted into FIG Hall of Fame (1999).

IHLE, Kristin (1961—). See Midthun, Kristin.

IHRER, Emma (1857–1911). German labor leader and feminist. Born Emma Rother-Faber, Jan 3, 1857, in Glatz, Silesia, Germany (now Klodzko, Poland); died in Berlin, Jan 8, 1911. ❖ One of the 1st women to head a Social Democratic union in Germany, served as editor of the journal *Die Gleichheit;* wrote *The Female Worker in the Class Struggle* (*Die Arbeiterin im Klassenkampf,* 1898). Depicted on postage stamp in the "Women of German History" definitive series (1989). ❖ See also *Women in World History.*

IIDA, Takako (1946—). Japanese volleyball player. Born Feb 1946 in Japan. ❖ Won a silver medal at Munich Olympics (1972) and a gold medal at Montreal Olympics (1976), both in team competition.

IIVARI, Ulpu (1948—). Finnish politician. Born Mar 20, 1948, in Salla, Finland. ❖ Journalist (1968–71), agent and editor (1971–74); SDP press secretary (1974–76), then party secretary (1987–91); served as member of Parliament and vice-chair of the Committee on Agriculture and Forestry (1991–95); as a European Socialist, elected to 5th European Parliament (1999–2004).

IKEDA, Hiroko. Japanese gymnast. Born in Japan. ❖ Won Japanese nationals (1951, 1952, 1956); placed 6th team all-around at Melbourne Olympics (1956).

IKEDA, Keiko (1933—). Japanese gymnast. Name variations: Keiko Tanaka. Born Nov 11, 1933, in Hiroshima, Japan. ❖ Won Japan nationals (1959–61, 1964–65, 1967); at World championships, won bronze medals in team all-around, all-around and balance beam (1962) and bronze medals in team all-around and all-around and a silver in uneven bars (1966); at Tokyo Olympics, won a bronze medal in team all-around (1964).

IKO, Momoko (1940—). Japanese-American playwright. Born 1940 in Wapato, Washington. ❖ During WWII, interned with family at Hart Mountain, Wyoming; recounted internment experience in *Gold Watch* (1970), which won East West Players contest; other writings include *Old Man* (1972), *When We Were Young* (1973), *Flowers and Household Gods* (1975), *Second City Flat* (1976–77), *Hollywood Mirrors* (1978) and *Boutique Living and Disposable Icons* (1987–88).

ILDEGARDE. *Variant of Hildegarde.*

ILDICO (fl. 453). Teutonic princess. Fl. around 453; m. Attila (c. 370/400–453), leader of the Huns, in 453. Attila also m. Princess Honoria in 450. ❖ A young Hun, was married to an aging Attila (453) who died on their wedding night. ❖ See also *Women in World History.*

ILEANA (1909–1991). Archduchess of Austria. Name variations: Ileana Hohenzollern; Mother Alexandra. Born Jan 5, 1909, in Bucharest, Romania; died Jan 21, 1991, at St. Elizabeth's Hospital, Youngstown, Ohio; dau. of Ferdinand I, king of Romania, and Marie of Rumania (1875–1938); m. Anthony, archduke of Austria, July 26, 1931 (div. 1954); m. Dr. Stephen Virgil Issarescu, June 19, 1954 (div. 1965); children: (1st m.) Stephen (b. 1932); Marie-Ileana (1933–1959); Alexandra (b. 1935); Dominic (b. 1937); Maria Magdelena (b. 1939); Elizabeth (b. 1942). ❖ Following 2nd divorce, became a nun in the Orthodox faith at Monastery of the Transfiguration in Ellwood City, Pennsylvania, and took the name Mother Alexandra.

ILES, Katica (1946—). Yugoslavian handball player. Born Mar 30, 1946. ❖ At Moscow Olympics, won a silver medal in team competition (1980).

ILIENKO, Natalia (1967—). Russian gymnast. Name variations: Natalia Ilienko-Jarvis. Born Mar 26, 1967, in Alma Ata, Kazakhstan; m. Gary Jarvis (British coach). ❖ Won a gold medal for floor exercises (1981) and team gold medals at World championships (1981, 1983); won a team silver medal for balance beam at Europeans (1981); coaches in England; was British Women's aerobics champion (1997, 1998).

ILIENKOVA, Irina (1980—). *See Ilyenkova, Irina.*

ILIEVA, Valentina (1962—). Bulgarian volleyball player. Born Mar 12, 1962, in Bulgaria. ❖ At Moscow Olympics, won a bronze medal in team competition (1980).

ILIEVA, Zhaneta (1984—). Bulgarian rhythmic gymnast. Born Oct 3, 1984, in Veliko Tanovo, Bulgaria. ❖ Won team all-around bronze medal at Athens Olympics (2004).

ILINA, Vera (1974—). *See Ilyina, Vera.*

ILIUTA, Ana (1958—). Romanian rower. Born Jan 10, 1958, in Romania. ❖ At Moscow Olympics, won a bronze medal in coxed eights (1980).

ILLINGTON, Margaret (1881–1934). American actress. Name variations: Margaret Frohman. Born July 23, 1881, in Bloomington, IL; died Mar 11, 1934, in Miami Beach, FL; dau. of Mary Ellen Light and I.H. Light; m. Daniel Frohman (producer), 1903 (div. 1909); m. Edward J. Bowes. ❖ Made NY debut under the management of Daniel Frohman in *The Pride of Jennico* (1900), followed by *Frocks and Frills* and *If I Were King* (with E.H. Sothern); came to prominence as Yuki in *A Japanese Nightingale* (1903); other plays include *Yvette* (title role), *Mrs. Leffingwell's Boots* (title role), *A Maker of Men, His House in Order* and *Kindling;* also appeared as Marie Loise Voysin in *The Thief* which ran for 14 months (1907–08).

ILLINGTON, Marie (d. 1927). Scottish actress. Born in Scotland; died Feb 3, 1927; dau. of Edward Frederick Inman; m. Gordon Maddick. ❖ Made prominent stage debut in Edinburgh (1874); made London debut in *Red Tape* (1875), followed by *Jane Shore, The World, Mrs. Dane's Defence, The Duke of Killicrankie, The Bondman, Mrs. Bill, Mrs. Gorringe's Necklace, Are You a Mason?* and *Tilly of Bloomsbury,* among others; made NY debut in *The Whip* (1912).

ILLYRIA, queen of. *See Teuta.*

ILY, Nicole (1932—). French girl who conspired to murder. Born 1932 in France. ❖ While a 16-year-old schoolgirl in Paris, encouraged 2 classmates (Claude Panconi and Bernard Petit) to shoot their schoolmate Alain Guyader (Dec 1948); police needed more than 2 years to solve the murder; received 3-year sentence, as did Petit, while Panconi (the shooter) was sentenced to 10.

ILYENKOVA, Irina (1980—). Belarusian rhythmic gymnast. Name variations: Ilienkova. Born April 10, 1980, in Belarus. ❖ Won a silver medal for team all-around at Sydney Olympics (2000).

ILYINA, Vera (1974—). Russian diver. Name variations: Vera Ilina. Born Feb 20, 1974, in Moscow, Russia; attended University of Texas. ❖ Won European championship (1995); with Yulia Pakhalina, won a gold medal for 3-meter synchronized springboard diving at Sydney Olympics (2000); with Yulia Pakhalina, won a silver medal for 3-meter synchronized springboard at Athens Olympics (2004).

ILYINA-KOLESNIKOVA, Nadezhda (1949—). Soviet runner. Name variations: Nadezhdav Kolesnikova. Born Jan 14, 1949, in USSR. ❖ At Montreal Olympics, won a bronze medal in the 4x400-meter relay (1976).

IMAGI OF LUXEMBURG (c. 1000–1057). Countess of Altdorf. Born c. 1000; died Aug 21, 1057; dau. of Frederick (c. 965–1019), count of Luxemburg; sister of Ogive of Luxemburg (d. 1030); m. Guelph also known as Welf or Wolfard, count of Altdorf and duke of Nether Bavaria, around 1015 (died 1030, some sources cite 1036); children: Guelph or Welf, duke of Carinthia; Cunegunda d'Este (c. 1020–1055).

IMALEYENE, Fatime-Zohra (1936—). Algerian novelist and film director. Name variations: Assia Djebar or Assia Djebbar. Born 1936 in Cherchell, Algeria; m. Ahmed Ould-Rouïs, 1958; m. Malek Alloula. ❖ First Algerian woman accepted at L'École Normale Supérieure de Sèvres, joined Algerian student strike (1965) and later collaborated with FLN newspaper *Moudjahid* during independence struggle; taught North African history and worked for radio and press (1960s); appointed director of Center for French and Francophone Studies at Louisiana State University and Silver Chair Professor of French and Francophone Studies at New York University (2001); works often explore difficulties of altering patriarchal society and tensions between Western and Arabic cultures; novels include *La Soif* (1957), *Les Impatients* (1958), *Les Enfants du nouveau monde* (1962), *Les Alouettes naïves* (1967), *Les Femmes d'Alger dans leur apartements* (1980), *L'Amour, la fantasia* (1985), *Ombre Sultanes* (1987), *Vaste est la prison* (1995), *Les nuits de Strasbourg* (1997), and *La Femme sans sepulture* (2002); films include *La Nouba* (1979) and *La Zerda ou les chantes de l'oubli* (1982).

IMES, Nella (1891–1964). *See Larsen, Nella.*

IMISON, Rachel (1978—). Australian field-hockey player. Born Dec 16, 1978, in Palmerston North, New Zealand. ❖ Goalkeeper, won a team gold medal at Sydney Olympics (2000).

IMLAY, Fanny (1794–1816). Daughter of Mary Wollstonecraft. Name variations: Fanny Imlay Godwin. Born in Le Havre, France, May 1794; committed suicide, Sept 1816; illeg. dau. of Mary Wollstonecraft (1759–1797) and Gilbert Imlay; half-sister of Mary Shelley (1797–1851). ❖ Seven of her letters, written the year of her death, are included in *The Clairmont Correspondence,* published by Johns Hopkins (1996).

IMLAY, Mary (1759–1797). *See Wollstonecraft, Mary.*

IMMA or IMME. *Variant of Emma.*

IMMERWAHR, Clara (1870–1915). German chemist. Born in Breslau, Germany (now Wrocław, Poland), June 21, 1870; died May 2, 1915; awarded doctorate in physical chemistry, her dissertation being a study of the solubility of metal salts, from University of Breslau, magna cum laude (1900); m. Fritz Haber (noted chemist); children: Hermann. ❖ The 1st woman to be awarded a doctorate in chemistry at a German university, committed suicide to protest husband's involvement in military use of poison gas; was the subject of Tony Harrison's play *Square Rounds* (1992). The German Section of International Physicians for the Prevention of Nuclear War designated its most prestigious award, the Clara Immerwahr Prize. ❖ See also (in German) Gerit von Leitner, *Der Fall Clara Immerwahr: Leben für eine humane Wissenschaft* (Verlag C.H. Beck, 1993); and *Women in World History.*

IMPEKOVEN, Niddy (1904–2002). German dancer. Born Luise Antonie Crescentia Impekoven in Berlin, Germany, Nov 2, 1904; died Nov 20, 2002; dau. of Toni Impekoven (actor and playwright) and Frida (Kobler) Impekoven; studied with Heinrich Kröller; children: one daughter. ❖ German dancer of Weimar epoch, famed in her day, who combined several styles to become one of the most renowned artists on the periphery of expressionist dance; made stage debut in Berlin at 10 at charity performance (1910); moved to Munich (1917), where she studied classical gymnastics at Bieberstein Castle School; presented 1st solo program at Berlin's Theater unter den Linden (1918); was one of the most creative as well as popular dancers in German-speaking Central Europe (1920s), at home on stages of Berlin, Munich, Vienna and Prague; became international celebrity, performing in Far East, France and UK; praised for her interpretation of 2nd movement of Beethoven's "Moonlight Sonata"; with rise of Nazism, gave farewell appearances in Germany (1933–34). ❖ See also *Women in World History.*

INA MARIA OF BASSEWITZ-LEVITZOW (1888–1973). Countess of Prussia and countess von Ruppin. Name variations: Ina-Maria. Born Jan 27, 1888, in Bristow, Mecklenburg; died Sept 17, 1973, in Munich, Germany; dau. of Karl Heinrich, count von Bassewitz-Levetzow, and Margarete Cacilie, countess von der Schulenburg; m. Oscar Charles, prince of Prussia, July 31, 1914; children: Oscar William (b. 1915); Burchard (b. 19170; Herzeleide (1918–1989); William Charles (b. 1922).

INAN (fl. c. 800). Arabian singer. Born and raised in Yamama, Arabia. ❖ Purchased by Al-Natifi who taught her music; bought for over 30,000 pieces of gold by Harun al-Rashid, caliph of Baghdad; dominated the court with her songs. ❖ See also *Women in World History.*

INANNA (fl. c. 3000 BCE). Sumerian composer. Lived in Sumer. ❖ Was said to have composed *The Song of Life and Marriage* as well as other Sumerian hymns; venerated as the goddess of the date palm and eventually as the mother of all creation. ❖ See also *Women in World History.*

INAYAT-KHAN, Noor (1914–1944). See Khan, Noor Inayat.

INBER, Vera (1890–1972). Russian poet, writer, and journalist. Born Vera Mikhaylovna Inber, 1890, in Odessa, Russia; died 1972; dau. of publisher and teacher. ❖ Published 1st work of poetry in Paris; early in career, wrote light verse and was influenced by Anna Akhmatova; became part of constructivist movement and applied technological symbolism and utilitarian theory to poetry (1920s); wrote short stories that depicted the clash between old and new Soviet life, as shown in "Nightingale and Rose" (1924); also wrote for the theater, including verse comedy *Mother's Union* (1938), and opera librettos; during WWII, joined Communist Party and began producing the patriotic works that would bring her renown, including poem "Pulkovo Meridian" (1941), detailing daily life in Leningrad during the siege.

INBERG, Rosalyn (1937—). See Higgins, Rosalyn.

INCHBALD, Elizabeth (1753–1821). English novelist, playwright and actress. Born Elizabeth Simpson, Oct 15, 1753, near Bury St. Edmunds in Suffolk, England; died at Kensington House, a home for Roman Catholic women, Aug 1, 1821; dau. of John Simpson (Roman Catholic farmer at Stanningfield) and Mary (Rushbrook) Simpson; m. Joseph Inchbald (actor), June 9, 1772 (died 1779). ❖ Left home to seek fortune in London (1772); to avoid male advances, impulsively married an actor more than twice her age, and made debut in Bristol, as Cordelia to his Lear (1772); for several years, acted with husband in provinces; following his death (1779), made London debut at Covent Garden as Bellario in *Philaster* (1780); remained there for 9 years, but a speech impediment prevented her from enjoying more than moderate success; wrote or adapted 19 plays, and some of them, especially *Wives as They Were and Maids as They Are* (1797), were highly successful; gained fame chiefly for 2 novels: *A Simple Story* (1791) and *Nature and Art* (1796). Her *Memoirs,* compiled by J. Boaden from her private journal, appeared in 2 volumes (1833). ❖ See also *Women in World History.*

INDIA, empress of.
See Nur Jahan (1577–1645).
See Mumtaz Mahal (c. 1592–1631).

INDIA, prime minister of. See Gandhi, Indira (1917–1984).

INDIA, queen of.
See Razia (1211–1240).
See Jodha Bai (d. 1613).
See Manmati (d. 1613).

INDIA, vicereine of. See Curzon, Mary Leiter (1870–1906).

INES or INÉS. Variant of Agnes.

INESCORT, Elaine (c. 1877–1964). English actress. Name variations: Elaine Inescourt. Born Charlotte Elizabeth Ihle, c. 1877, in London, England; died July 7, 1964, in Brighton, East Sussex, England; m. John Wightman (journalist, div.); m. Capt. Harry de Windt; children: Frieda Inescort (actress). ❖ Made professional stage debut on tour with George Edwardes's Co.; made London debut with H. Beerbohm Tree (1903), appearing in such plays as *Richard II, The Last of the Dandies, The Man Who Was, Merry Wives of Windsor* and *Julius Caesar;* replaced Lena Ashwell in title role of *Leah Kleschna* (1905), then joined company of H.B. Irving, touring English provinces and US (1906–07); other plays include *Raffles, The Mollusc, Lanval, Into the Light, Mavourneen, Bitter Sweet* and *Vile Bodies.*

INESCORT, Frieda (1900–1976). Scottish-born actress. Born Frieda Wightman, June 29, 1900, in Edinburgh, Scotland; died of multiple sclerosis, Feb 21, 1976, in the Motion Picture Country Hospital where she had been a patient since 1969; dau. of John Wightman (journalist) and Elaine Inescort (actress); m. Ben Ray Redman (critic and poet), 1926 (died 1961). ❖ Was private secretary to Lady Nancy Astor before making stage debut in Colchester in *The Mollusc* (1917), where she also understudied her mother; made Broadway debut in *The Truth about Blayds* (1922), followed by *You and I* (1923), *Hay Fever* (1925), *Escape* (1927) and *Springtime for Henry* (1931); made film debut in *Dark Angel* (1935) and appeared regularly (1950s) in mostly dignified character roles, notably in *Pride and Prejudice* (1940) and *A Place in the Sun* (1951); other films include *The Dark Angel, Mary of Scotland, The Letter, The Trial of Mary Dugan, You'll Never Get Rich, Remember the Day, The Courtship of Andy Hardy, The Return of the Vampire, Never Wave at a WAC, Casanova's Big Night* and *The Eddy Duchin Story.*

INES DE CASTRO (c. 1320–1355). See Castro, Inez de.

INES DE LA CRUZ, Juana (1651–1695). See Juana Inés de la Cruz.

INES OF POITOU.
See Agnes of Poitou (1024–1077).
See Agnes of Poitou (1052–1078).

INEZ. Variant of Agnes.

INEZ DE CASTRO (c. 1320–1355). See Castro, Inez de.

INGA (fl. 1204). Queen of Norway. Fl. around 1204; m. Haakon III, king of Norway (r. 1202–1204, killed); children: Haakon IV the Elder (1204–1263), king of Norway (r. 1217–1263).

INGALLS, Laura H. (c. 1900–c. 1988). American aviator and Nazi spy. Born, possibly 1900, in New York, NY; died possibly in 1988. ❖ Learned to fly (1928), becoming a highly successful woman pilot by 1930s; set women's record for consecutive loops (1930) and record for most barrel rolls by a man or woman (1930); made numerous record-breaking flights, including flight from NY to CA (30 hrs, 27 mins) and return flight from CA to NY (25 hrs, 35 mins, 1930); made most well-known flights in 1934, becoming 1st American woman to fly over the Andes, 1st person to make solo flight around South America in a landplane, and 1st woman to fly from North America to South America; became 1st woman to fly nonstop east to west across North America (1935); broke Amelia Earhart's record by flying nonstop from LA to NY in 13 hrs, 34 mins (1935); dropped pamphlets over White House from air to support Women's National Committee to Keep the United States Out of the War (1939) and consequently had license suspended for violating 2 Civil Aeronautic Board regulations; was a member of America First; arrested by FBI (1941) for failure to register as a German agent; convicted as Nazi espionage agent (1942) and sentenced to 2 years and 8 months in prison; released (1943).

INGEBIORGE (fl. 1045–1068). Queen of Scotland. Name variations: Ingibiorg Finnsdottir. Died before 1070; dau. of Finn Arnasson, jarl of Halland, and Bergliot Halfdansdottir; m. Thorfinn the Black, earl of Orkney, before 1038; became 1st wife of Malcolm III Canmore, king of Scots, c. 1059 (some sources cite 1066); children: (1st m.) Paul I, earl of Orkney; Erlend II, earl of Orkney; (2nd m.) Duncan II (1060–1095), king of Scots; Malcolm (d. after 1094); Donald (d. 1085).

INGEBORD. *Variant of Ingeborg.*

INGEBORG (c. 1176–1237/38). Queen of France. Name variations: Ingeborg of Denmark; Ingeborg Valdemarsdottir; Ingeburge or Ingelburge (French); Ingelborg, Isemburge, Ingibjörg (Danish). Born in Denmark c. 1176; died July 29, c. 1237 or 1238 (some sources cite 1236); dau. of Valdemar aka Waldemar I the Great (1131–1182), king of Denmark (r. 1157–1182) and Sophie of Russia (c. 1140–1198); sister of Canute VI (1163–1202), king of Denmark (r. 1182–1202), Waldemar II the Victorious (1170–1241), king of Denmark (r. 1202–1241), Richizza of Denmark (d. 1220) and Helen of Denmark (d. 1233); m. Philip II Augustus (1165–1223), king of France (r. 1180–1223), Aug 14, 1193 (div. in eyes of the council of Compiègne in 1193; marriage reinstated in 1213). ❖ Charming and good-natured, was married at 18 to Philip II Augustus, king of France (1193); the following day, was repudiated by him, claiming she had bewitched him; for next 20 years, watched as husband used every avenue to obtain a declaration of nullity from Catholic Church; when council of Compiègne, a conclave of French bishops, acceded to his wish (Nov 5, 1193), was packed off to a monastery near Paris; appealed her case to popes Celestine III and Innocent III successively, who declared the dissolution of the marriage had no validity; thrown into prison in the château of Étampes; was eventually reconciled with husband for political considerations, though they never resumed marital relations; survived him by more than 14 years, passing the greater part of the time in priory of St. Jean at Corbeil, which she founded; on good terms with ensuing French kings, lived peacefully, gaining a reputation for kindness; died highly esteemed.

INGEBORG (d. 1254). Swedish princess. Name variations: Ingeborg Ericsdottir. Died in 1254; dau. of Richizza of Denmark (d. 1220) and Eric X, king of Sweden (r. 1208–1216); m. Birger of Bjälbo, regent of Sweden, around 1240; children: Waldemar (b. 1243), king of Sweden; Magnus I Ladulas, king of Sweden; Richiza (who m. Haakon the Younger, king of Norway); Eric; Christine Birgersdottir (who m. Sigge Guttormson); Katherina Birgersdottir (who m. Siegfried, prince of Anhalt-Zerbst); Bengt (b. 1254), duke of Finland.

INGEBORG (d. 1319). Queen of Denmark. Name variations: Ingeborg Magnusdottir. Died Aug 15, 1319; dau. of Hedwig of Holstein (d. 1325) and Magnus I Ladulas, king of Sweden (r. 1275–1290); m. Erik or Eric VI Menved (1274–1319), king of Denmark (r. 1286–1319), June 1296; children: Valdemar or Waldemar; twins Eric and Magnus; and one other son.

INGEBORG (c. 1300–c. 1360). Duchess of Südermannland. Name variations: Ingebjorg, Ingeburga; Ingeborg Haakonsdottir, duchess of Sudermannland. Born c. 1300; died after 1360; dau. of Haakon V (b. 1270), king of Norway (r. 1299–1319), and Euphemia of Rugen (d. 1312); m. Eric Magnusson (son of Magnus I, king of Sweden), duke of Südermannland (r. 1303–1318), Sept 29, 1312; m. Knud, duke of South Holland, on June 21, 1327; children: (1st m.) Magnus VII (II) Eriksson (1316–1374), king of Norway (r. 1319–1343), king of Sweden (r. 1319–1365); Euphemia (1317–c. 1336, who m. Albert II, duke of Mecklenburg). ❖ Exerted great influence over affairs of son Magnus Eriksson; planned to enlarge the combined kingdom of Norway and Sweden with Denmark; provoked a war with the Danes that proved to be so costly that a popular noble, Erling Vidkunnsson, was made viceroy and ruled Norway until Magnus Eriksson came of age in 1332. ❖ See also *Women in World History.*

INGEBORG (1347–1370). Danish princess. Name variations: Ingeburga. Born April 1, 1347; died before June 16, 1370; dau. of Waldemar IV Atterdag, king of Denmark, and Helvig of Denmark; sister of Margaret I of Denmark (1353–1412); m. Heinrich also known as Hendrik or Henry, duke of Mecklenburg (r. 1379–1383), in 1361; children: Marie of Mecklenburg (who m. Vratislas of Pomerania).

INGEBORG LORENTZEN (b. 1957). *See Lorentzen, Ingeborg.*

INGEBORG OF DENMARK (c. 1176–1237/38). *See Ingeborg.*

INGEBORG OF DENMARK (d. 1287). Queen of Norway. Name variations: Ingeborg Ericsdottir or Eriksdottir. Died 1287; dau. of Jutta of Saxony (d. around 1267) and Erik or Eric IV Ploughpenny (1216–1250), king of Dennmark (r. 1241–1250); m. Magnus VI the Law-mender (1238–1280), king of Norway (r. 1263–1280), Sept 11, 1261; children: Eric II (b. 1268), king of Norway (r. 1280–1299); Haakon V Longlegs (1270–1319), king of Norway (r. 1299–1319); Olaf (b. 1262); Magnus (b. 1264).

INGEBORG OF DENMARK (1878–1958). Princess of Sweden. Name variations: Ingeborg Oldenburg; Ingeborg Bernadotte; Ingeborg Charlotte of Denmark. Born Aug 21, 1878; died Mar 11, 1958; dau. of Frederick VIII, king of Denmark (r. 1906–1212), and Louise of Sweden (1851–1926); m. Charles of Sweden (1861–1951, son of Oscar II, king of Sweden, and Sophia of Nassau, Aug 27, 1897; children: Margaretha of Sweden (1899–1977); Martha of Sweden (1901–1954, who m. the future Olav V, king of Norway); Astrid of Sweden (1905–1935, who m. Leopold III, king of the Belgians); Carl Gustaf (b. 1911, who renounced the right of succession, July 6, 1937).

INGEBORG OF NOVGOROD (fl. 1118–1131). *See Ingeborg of Russia.*

INGEBORG OF RUSSIA (fl. 1118–1131). Duchess of South Jutland. Name variations: Ingeborg of Novgorod. Fl. between 1118 and 1131; dau. of Christina of Sweden (d. 1122) and Mstislav I (b. 1076), grand prince of Kiev (r. 1125–1132); m. Knud or Canute Lavard, duke of South Jutland, around 1118; children: Valedmar also known as Waldemar I the Great (1131–1182), king of Denmark (r. 1157–1182); Margaret Knutsdottir (who m. Stig Whiteleather); Kristin of Denmark (who m. Magnus IV the Blind, king of Norway, in 1332; he repudiated the marriage in 1133); Katrin Knutsdottir (who m. Prizlaw of Obotriten).

INGEBORG OF SWEDEN (fl. 1070). Swedish noblewoman. Fl. around 1070; m. Almos, son of Geza I and Synadene of Byzantium (c. 1050–?).

INGEBORG OLDENBURG (1878–1958). *See Ingeborg of Denmark.*

INGEBURGE. *Variant of Ingeborg.*

INGELBERG or INGELBURGE. *Variant of Engelberg, Engelberga, or Ingeborg.*

INGELOW, Jean (1820–1897). English poet and novelist. Name variations: (pseudonym) Orris. Born in Boston, Lincolnshire, England, Mar 17, 1820; died in Kensington, England, July 20, 1897; dau. of William Ingelow (banker) and Jean (Kilgour) Ingelow; never married; no children. ❖ Contributed verses and tales to magazines under pseudonym "Orris," but her 1st (anonymous) volume, *A Rhyming Chronicle of Incidents and Feelings,* did not appear until she was 30 (1850); achieved popularity with collected *Poems* (1863), which included "Divided," her most acclaimed work, as well as "Song of Seven," "Supper at the Mill" and "High Tide on the Coast of Lincolnshire, 1571"; turned to novels and short stories, many of the latter intended for children, including *Mopsa the Fairy* (1869). ❖ See also autobiographical novels *Off the Skelligs* (1872) and *Fated to be Free* (1873); and *Women in World History.*

INGERINA. *See Eudocia Ingerina.*

INGHAM, Mary Hall (1866–1937). American reformer and suffragist. Born Nov 24, 1866, in Philadelphia, PA; died Jan 1, 1937, in Bryn Mawr, PA; dau. of William Armstrong Ingham and Catherine Keppele (Hall) Ingham; granddau. of Samuel Delucenna Ingham (secretary of treasury under Andrew Jackson). ❖ Supported Philadelphia garment workers' strike (1910); served as reform-minded director of Bureau of Municipal Research of Philadelphia; worked in presidential campaign for Theodore Roosevelt as vice-chair of Women of the Washington Party (1912); formed Progressive League of Philadelphia, composed of many of Roosevelt's supporters; headed woman's department of investment firm William P. Bonbright & Co. (1915–19); co-founded Equal Franchise Society of Philadelphia (1909); became PA state chair of Alice Paul's National Woman's Party (1917); 1 of 16 women arrested for picketing in front of White House, served 3 days before being pardoned by Woodrow Wilson (July 1917); helped win ratification of 19th Amendment in PA legislature (1919).

INGIBIORG. *See Ingebiorg.*

INGIGERD HARALDSDOTTIR (fl. 1075). Norwegian noblewoman. Fl. around 1075; dau. of Elizabeth of Kiev and Harald III Haardrada or Haardraada also known as Harald III Hardrade (1015–1066), king of Norway; m. Olaf I Hunger, king of Denmark (r. 1086–1095); m. Philip, king of Sweden (r. 1112–1118); children: (1st m.) Ulfhild of Denmark (died before 1070).

INGIGERD OLAFSDOTTIR (c. 1001–1050). Princess of Kiev. Born c. 1001 in Sweden; died Feb 10, 1050, in Kiev, Ukraine; dau. of Olof or Olaf Skötkonung or Skötkonung, king of Sweden (r. 994–1022), and Astrid of the Obotrites (c. 979–?); sister of Anund Jakob, king of Sweden (r. 1022–1050); m. Jaroslav also known as Yaroslav I the Wise (978–1054), prince of Kiev (r. 1019–1054), c. 1019; children: Vladimir; Izyaslav also known as Yziaslav I (1025–1078), prince of Kiev (r. 1054–1078); Sviatoslav; Vyacheslav; Igor; Vsevelod I (r. 1078–1093); Anne of Kiev (1024–1066, who m. Henry I, king of France); Anastasia of Russia (c. 1023–died after 1074, who m. Andrew I, king of Hungary); Elizabeth of Kiev (who m. Harald Hardraade); Maria of Kiev (d. 1087).

INGIRID (fl. 1067). Queen of Norway. Name variations: Ingirid Svendsdottir. Fl. in 1067; illeg. dau. of Thora Johnsdottir and Svend II Estridsen (d. 1076), king of Denmark (r. 1047–1074); m. Olav the Gentle also known as Olaf III Kyrri (the Peaceful), king of Norway (r. 1066–1093), in 1067.

INGLESBY, Mona (1918—). English dancer, choreographer, and founder. Born Mona Vredenburg, May 3, 1918, in London, England; trained with Marie Rambert; m. E.G. Derrington. ❖ At age 5, made stage debut at the Scala Theatre as Silver Bell; danced in the early works of Ashton and Andrée Howard at the Ballet Club (1932–35); choreographed *Endymion* (1938) and *Amoras* (1939); appeared as the star and choreographer of her own company, International Ballet, dancing the great classic roles on tour for 12 years, bringing full-scale ballet to the English provinces and throughout Europe (1941–53).

INGLEWOOD, Kathleen (b. 1876). See Isitt, Kathleen.

INGLIS, Elsie Maud (1864–1917). British physician and surgeon. Born in Naini Tal, India, Aug 16, 1864; died at Newcastle Upon Tyne, England, Nov 26, 1917; studied medicine at Edinburgh School of Medicine for Women, Edinburgh Medical College, and Glasgow Royal Infirmary. ❖ After qualifying as a doctor, was appointed to teaching post at New Hospital for Women in London; returned to Edinburgh and began practice; was associated with Edinburgh Bruntsfield Hospital and Dispensary and also saw private patients; a staunch supporter of women's causes, established a free maternity hospital for women and children in the city's slums (1901), staffed entirely by women, and also founded Scottish Women's Suffrage Federation (1906); at onset of WWI, established Scottish Field Hospital, which she staffed entirely with women; was responsible for 14 medical units serving in France, Serbia, Corsica, Salonika, Romania, Russia and Malta; during German and Austrian invasion (1915–16), was captured by Austrians and imprisoned for a time; along with 80 other women, was financed by the London Suffrage Society to support Serbian soldiers fighting in Russia; while there, was taken ill and forced to travel back to England; died the following day. ❖ See also *Women in World History*.

INGLIS, Esther (1571–1624). British calligrapher. Name variations: Hester or Esther Kello. Born Esther or Hester Langlois, 1571, in France; died 1624; dau. of Marie Prissott Langlois and Nicholas Langlois (name later changed to Inglis or Inglish); m. Bartholomew Kello (parson of Willingale Spayne, Essex), 1596; children: Esther, Elizabeth, Mary and Barbara. ❖ Fled with family to England after St. Bartholomew massacre of French Protestants; learned calligraphy at early age from her mother and worked as scribe for husband; produced hand-illuminated manuscripts for wealthy patrons of which over 40 are extant.

INGLIS, Helen Clyde (1867–1945). New Zealand nurse, midwife, teacher, hospital matron, and political activist. Born Nov 15, 1867, in Christchurch, New Zealand; died Feb 12, 1945, in Eastbourne, New Zealand; dau. of John Inglis (merchant) and Jane Anne (Eames) Inglis. ❖ After teaching at Christchurch Girls' High School, trained as nurse in Edinburgh Royal Infirmary (1900) and as midwife in Glasgow Maternity Hospital (1904); became assistant matron at St Helens Hospital, Wellington (1906) and matron (1913–23); was 1st matron of St Helens Hospital, Christchurch (1907–10); appointed matron of Te Waikato Sanatorium near Hamilton (1910); helped form Canterbury Trained Nurses' Association (1908); active in New Zealand Trained Nurses' Association (NZTNA), from 1909; based on fear that proposed legislation would lead to refusal of other countries to recognize qualifications of New Zealand nurses, led unsuccessful opposition to Nurses and Midwives Registration Amendment Act, but managed to secure

safeguards in bill (1930). ❖ See also *Dictionary of New Zealand Biography* (Vol. 3).

INGOBERGE (519–589). Queen of Paris. Born 591; died 589; m. Caribert also spelled Charibert I (521–567), king of Paris (r. 561–567), in 561; children: possibly Bertha of Kent (c. 565–c. 616).

INGOLDSTHORP, Isabel (fl. 15th c.). Countess of Northumberland. Name variations: Isabel Neville. Dau. of Edmund Ingoldsthorp; m. John Neville, marquess of Montagu, earl of Northumberland (r. 1461–1471); children: George Neville, duke of Bedford; Elizabeth Neville (Lady Scrope of Masham); Margaret Neville (b. 1466); Lucy Neville.

INGRAHAM, Mary Shotwell (1887–1981). American founder. Born in Brooklyn, NY, Jan 5, 1887; died in Huntington, Long Island, NY, April 16, 1981; dau. of Henry Titus Shotwell and Alice Wyman (Gardner) Shotwell; Vassar College, AB, 1908; Wesleyan University, LHD, 1958; Columbia University, LHD, 1961; m. Henry Andrews Ingraham, Oct 28, 1908; children: Mary Ingraham Bunting (1910–1998, 1st woman to serve on Atomic Energy Commission); Henry Gardner Ingraham; Winifred Andrews Ingraham (who m. Harold L. Warner Jr.); David Ingraham. ❖ Founder of United Service Organizations (USO), spent early career with Brooklyn's Young Women's Christian Association (YWCA), serving as its president (1922–39), then president of national board (1940–45); along with Dorothy Height and others, was instrumental in bringing about the endorsement of the "Interracial Charter," mandating desegregation, at YWCA National Convention (1946); founded USO (1940), which supplied social, recreational and welfare services to armed services during WWII. Awarded Medal for Merit by President Harry S. Truman (1946), the 1st woman so honored. ❖ See also *Women in World History*.

INGRAM, Sheila Rena (1957—). African-American runner. Born Mar 23, 1957, in Washington, DC. ❖ At Montreal Olympics, won a silver medal in the 4x400-meter relay (1976).

INGRID OF SWEDEN (1910–2000). Queen of Denmark. Name variations: Ingrid Bernadotte; Ingrid Victoria of Sweden. Born Ingrid Victoria Sophia Louise Margaret, Mar 28, 1910, at Royal Palace, Stockholm, Sweden; died Nov 8, 2000; only dau. of Gustavus VI Adolphus (1882–1973), king of Sweden (r. 1950–1973), and Margaret of Connaught (1882–1920); m. Frederick IX (1899–1972), king of Denmark (r. 1947–1972), on May 24, 1935, at Storkyrkan Cathedral, Stockholm; children: Margrethe II (b. 1940), queen of Denmark (r. 1972—); Benedikte (b. 1944, who m. Prince Richard of Sayn-Wittgenstein); Anne-Marie Oldenburg (b. 1946, who m. Constantine II, king of Greece). ❖ During WWII and occupation of Denmark, earned affection of her people by breaking through the isolation of the royal court; known for her common touch, could often be seen pushing a baby carriage along the sidewalks of Copenhagen, biking, walking daughters to school; when husband died (1972), stepped out of limelight and daughter Margrethe II became queen; as dowager queen, remained active well into her late 80s, serving as a patron to dozens of charitable funds. ❖ See also *Women in World History*.

INGROVA, Dana (1922—). See Zatopek, Dana.

INGSTAD, Anne-Stine (c. 1918–1997). Norwegian archaeologist. Name variations: Anne Stine Ingstad. Born Anne-Stine Moe in Lillehammer, Norway, c. 1918; died in Oslo, Norway, Nov 6, 1997; attended University of Oslo, Norway; m. Helge Ingstad (explorer), 1941; children: Benedicta Ingstad. ❖ Following marriage, became husband's companion in adventure and scientific collaborator, retracking a Viking voyage along northern tip of Newfoundland and, on a site known as L'anse aux Meadows, finding conclusive evidence that Vikings had preceded Columbus to North America by 500 years (1961); supervised the excavation to uncover the remains of the 1,000-year-old Viking outpost; wrote *The Norse Discovery of America* (vols. 1 and 2). ❖ See also *Women in World History*.

INGUNDE (fl. 517). Queen of the Franks. Name variations: Ingunda. Sister of Aregunde; became 3rd wife of Chlothar also known as Clothaire, Clotar, or Lothair I (497–561), king of Soissons and the Franks, c. 517; children: Caribert also known as Charibert I (d. 567), king of Paris (r. 561–567); Gontrand also known as Guntram or Gunthram (c. 545–593), king of Orléans and Burgundy (r. 561–593); Sigebert or Sigibert I (535–575), king of Metz (Austrasia, r. 561–575); Clotsinda (who m. a Lombard king). ❖ Lothair I's 1st wife was Guntheuca; his 2nd wife was Chunsina; his 4th wife was Aregunde (sister of Ingunde and mother of

Chilperic I [523–584], king of Soissons); his 5th wife was Radegund (518–587); his 7th wife was Vuldetrade.

INKSTER, Juli (1960—). American golfer. Born Juli Simpson, June 24, 1960, in Santa Cruz, CA; attended San Jose State University; m. Brian Inkster (golfer); children: Hayley (b. 1990), Cori (b. 1994). ❖ The 2nd woman to win all 4 of women's Grand Slam tournaments, began career as the 1st woman since 1934 to win 3 consecutive US Women's Amateur titles (1980–82); went pro and was named LPGA Rookie of the Year (1983); won the Du Maurier Classic (1984), Dinah Shore (1984, 1989), US Open (1999, 2002) and LPGA championship (1999, 2000); also won Samsung World championship (1997–98, 2000), SAFECO Classic (1983, 1988), Lady Keystone Open (1985–86), Crestar Classic (1988–89) and Atlantic City Classic (1986, 1988), among others; played on winning team for Solheim Cup (2002); won Corning Classic (2003), shooting a 10-under-par 62, tying the lowest final-round score by a winner in the history of the LPGA Tour. Won ESPY award (2000); inducted into LPGA Hall of Fame (2000).

INMAN, Elizabeth Murray (c. 1724–1785). Scottish-American letter writer. Born Elizabeth Murray, c. 1724, in Scotland; died May 25, 1785; sister of James Murray; m. Thomas Campbell, 1755; m. James Smith, 1760 (died 1769); m. Ralph Inman, 1771. ❖ Ran millinery in Boston; left Boston for Scotland but returned after 2 years and lived in Cambridge, MA; saw family property confiscated for Loyalist alliances during American Revolution. ❖ See also diary and letters collected in *The Letters of James Murray, Loyalist* (1901).

INMAN, Florence (1890–1986). Canadian politician. Born Dec 3, 1890, at West River, Prince Edwards Island, Canada; died 1986 in Ottawa, Canada. ❖ Appeared before provincial legislature to fight for suffrage (1916); won nomination as candidate (1920s), but defeated, since women were still "non-persons"; appointed to PEI Senate (July 28, 1955); served for over 30 years.

INO-ANASTASIA (fl. 575–582). Byzantine empress. Fl. around 575 to 582; m. Tiberius II Constantine, Byzantine emperor (r. 578–582); children: Constantina (who m. Maurice Tiberius [Mauritius], Byzantine emperor [r. 582–602]); another daughter. ❖ See also *Women in World History.*

INOUE, Setsuko (1946—). Japanese volleyball player. Born Sept 16, 1946, in Japan. ❖ At Mexico City Olympics, won a silver medal in team competition (1968).

INNES, Annabella (1826–1916). See Boswell, Annabella.

INNES, Catherine Lucy (1839/40–1900). New Zealand writer. Name variations: Catherine Lucy Williams, Pilgrim (pseudonym). Born Catherine Lucy Williams, c. 1839 or 1840, in England; dau. of Theodore Williams and Mary Ann Williams; m. David Innes (sheep farmer), 1860 (died 1865); children: 1. ❖ Immigrated with family to New Zealand (1850); under pseudonym of Pilgrim, wrote weekly articles for newspapers, which were revised and expanded as *Canterbury Sketches; or, Life from the Early Days* (1879). ❖ See also *Dictionary of New Zealand Biography* (Vol. 1).

INNES, Mary Jane (1852–1941). New Zealand brewery manager. Name variations: Mary Jane Lewis. Born Mary Jane Lewis, April 18, 1852, at Llanvaches, Monmouthshire, Wales; died Nov 14, 1941, at Auckland, New Zealand; dau. of Thomas Lewis and Hannah (Morgan) Lewis; m. Charles Innes, 1874 (died 1899); children: 10. ❖ Immigrated to New Zealand (1870); acquired ownership of husband's Te Awamuru Brewery (1888), and management of Waikato Brewery (1889); after husband's death, repaid his debts and assumed ownership of Waikato Brewery (1899). ❖ See also *Dictionary of New Zealand Biography* (Vol. 2).

INNES, Shane (b. 1956). See Gould, Shane.

INNESS, Jean (1900–1978). American actress. Born Dec 18, 1900, in Cleveland, Ohio; died Dec 27, 1978, in Santa Monica, CA; m. Victor Jory (actor), 1928; children: Jon Jory (producer-director) and Jean Jory (actress). ❖ Films include *Mrs. Mike, The Gunfighter, Edge of Doom* and *I'd Climb the Highest Mountain;* on tv, appeared as Nurse Fain on "Dr. Kildare" series (1965–66).

INSHTATHEAMBA (1854–1902). See La Flesche, Susette.

INSULL, Carolina Ada (1874–1955). See Seville, Carolina Ada.

INTROPODI, Ethel (d. 1946). American actress. Died Dec 18, 1946, in New York, NY. ❖ First appeared on stage at age 14; appeared in the film

Madonna of the Slums (1919); plays include *East is West, The Trial of Mary Dugan, Dinner at Eight* and *Doctors Disagree.*

INUI, Emi (1983—). Japanese softball player. Born Oct 26, 1983, in Japan. ❖ Catcher, won a team bronze at Athens Olympics (2004).

INVERNIZIO, Carolina (1858–1916). Italian novelist. Name variations: Carolina Maria Margaritta Invernizio. Born 1858 (some sources cite 1851) in Voghera, Pavia, Italy; lived in Florence; died Nov 27, 1916. ❖ Enjoyed popularity during lifetime but later scorned; feminist critics revived interest in her Gothic settings and depictions of female suffering; writings include *Le figlie della duchessa* (1889), *La bastarda* (1892), *Cuor di donna* (1894), *Dora la figlia dell'assassino* (1895), *I drammi dell'adulterio* (1898), and *I disperati* (1904); works collected as *Romanzi del peccato, della perdizione e del delitto* (1970).

INYAMA, Rosemary (b. 1903). Nigerian educator, politician, business tycoon, and community developer. Name variations: Mrs. Inyama. Born Rosemary Ike, Nov 11, 1903, in Arochukwu, Igboland, Nigeria; incapacitated since 1996 due to age and sickness; dau. of Mazi Okoronkwo Ike (soldier, WWI) and Madam Otonahu Ike (who played an instrumental role in relocation and "cleansing" of famous *Ibiniukpabi* oracle after the 1901–02 attack on it); m. P.K. Inyama (grade 11 teacher), 1934; children: Hycientha Inyama Nwauba (consul-general of Nigeria in NY); Nnenna Inyama; Jennifer Inyama; Okoro Inyama. ❖ Champion of the cause of women in Igboland, taught in primary schools (1923–35); established a Domestic Science Business Training Center at Ikot Ekpene; dealings in the gold business took her on several business trips to Ghana (1940s–50s); went into trading partnership with 19 women and men across the country, buying and selling foodstuffs; active in Nigeria's politics (1940s–50s); played a key role in community development at Arochukwu; started motherless babies home; honored several times by women's organizations such as the National Council of Women Societies, Nigeria, Imo state branch. ❖ See also *Women in World History.*

INZHUVATOVA, Galina (1952—). Soviet field-hockey player. Born Feb 28, 1952, in USSR. ❖ At Moscow Olympics, won a bronze medal in team competition (1980).

IOAHNE (b. 1907). See Giovanna of Italy.

IOLA (1862–1931). See Wells-Barnett, Ida.

IOLANDE. Variant of Yolande.

IOLANDE MARGHERITA OF ITALY (b. 1901). See Yolanda Margherita of Italy.

IOLANDE OF HUNGARY (1215–1251). Queen of Aragon. Name variations: Iolande Arpad; Violante of Hungary; Yolande of Hungary. Born 1215; died 1251 (some sources cite 1271); dau. of Andrew II, king of Hungary (r. 1205–1235), and his second wife Yolande de Courtenay (d. 1233); became 2nd wife of James I (1208–1276), king of Aragon (r. 1213–1276), also known as Jaime the Conqueror of Aragon, 1235; children: Peter III (d. 1285), king of Aragon (r. 1276–1285); Yolande of Aragon (d. 1300, who m. Alphonso X, king of Castile and Leon); Isabella of Aragon (1243–1271, who m. Philip III, king of France); James II, king of Majorca; Constance of Aragon (d. 1283, who m. Manuel of Castile, senor de Villena); Ferran. James I's 1st wife was Eleanor of Castile (1202–1244).

IONESCU, Atanasia (1935—). Romanian gymnast. Born Mar 19, 1935, in Romania. ❖ At Rome Olympics, won a bronze medal in team all-around (1960).

IONESCU, Nastasia (1954—). Romanian kayaker. Born Mar 5, 1954, in Romania. ❖ At Los Angeles Olympics, won a gold medal in K4 500 meters (1984).

IONESCU, Valeria (1960—). Romanian track-and-field athlete. Born Aug 2, 1960, in Romania. ❖ At Los Angeles Olympics, won a silver medal in the long jump (1984).

IONITA, Raluca (1976—). Romanian kayaker. Born 1976 in Romania. ❖ Won a bronze medal for K4 500 meters at Sydney Olympics (2000).

IORDACHE, Maricica Titie (1962—). See Taran-Iordache, Maricica Titie.

IORDANIDOU, Maria (1897–1989). Greek novelist. Name variations: Maria Iordanidu. Born 1897 in Constantinople (Istanbul); died 1989. ❖ Lived in Stavropol, Russia, before moving to Athens; did not begin writing until age 65; had success with 1st novel, the autobiographical *Loxandra* (1960), based on her experiences in Constantinople; writings, based on historial events, include *Like Crazy Birds* (1978), *The Circle's Turnings* (1982) and *Vocations in the Caucasus* (1985).

IOTA (1853–1926). *See Caffyn, Kathleen.*

IOTTI, Nilde (1920–1999). Italian lawmaker. Born in Reggio Emilia, Italy, 1920; died Dec 3, 1999, in Rome; attended University of Milan; dau. of railway worker; lived with Palmiro Togliatti (Communist Party leader), c. 1948–64 (died 1964); children: (adopted 1950) Marisa Malagoli Togliatti. ❖ The 1st woman to become president of the lower house of Parliament in Italy, served as a Partisan during WWII, before moving to Rome; representing the Communist Party, was elected to the constitutional assembly (1946) and took part in the "Committee of the 75," a delegation that wrote the 1st draft for Italy's postwar constitution; during many years in Parliament, campaigned to legalize divorce and abortion; was 2nd in line to succeed the presidency (1979–92), while serving as Italy's president of the lower house; known as a faithful member of the central committee of the Communist Party, softened views with the collapse of Berlin Wall; was among the 1st to propose abandoning the hammer and sickle and renaming the party "Democrats of the Left"; resigned (Nov 1999) and died of heart failure the following month; given a state funeral.

IOUCHKOVA, Angelina. Russian rhythmic gymnast. Born in USSR. ❖ Won a team bronze medal at Atlanta Olympics (1996).

IOVAN, Sonia (1935—). Romanian gymnast. Born Sept 29, 1935, in Romania. ❖ Won a bronze medal at Melbourne Olympics (1956) and a bronze medal at Rome Olympics (1960), both in team all-around.

IOWA, Marie (c. 1790–1850). *See Dorion, Marie.*

IPATESCU, Ana (1805–1855). Romanian revolutionary. Name variations: Anna Ipatescu. Born 1805 in Romania; died 1855. ❖ Romanian heroine of the rising of 1848 against Russian and Turkish domination, a movement that was partly nationalist and partly social in character; led mobilized forces.

IPP (b. 1909). *See Breslauer, Marianne.*

IPPOLITA (1446–1484). Queen of Naples. Name variations: Hippolyta Sforza; Ippolita Sforza. Born 1446; died Aug 20, 1484; dau. of Bianca Maria Visconti (1423–1470) and Francesco Sforza (1401–1466), 4th duke of Milan (r. 1450–1466); m. Alfonso of Aragon (1448–1495), duke of Calabria, later known as Alphonso II, king of Naples (r. 1494–1495), Oct 10, 1465; children: Isabella of Naples (1470–1524, who m. Gian Galeazzo Sforza, duke of Milan); Ferdinand also known as Ferrante II (1469–1496), king of Naples (r. 1495–1496); Piero, prince of Rossano (b. 1472). Alphonso II had a mistress Trogia Gazzela with whom he had 2 children: Alfonso, prince of Salerno (b. 1481) and Sancha of Aragon (1478–1506). ❖ One of the accomplished women of Renaissance Italy, once astonished Pope Pius II while he was visiting her father's court by reciting a Latin oration she had composed (she was 12 at the time).

IPPOLITA (1503–1570). *See Gonzaga, Ippolita.*

IPPOLITA (1535–1563). *See Gonzaga, Ippolita.*

IRAIA, Maikara (1863–1937). *See Te Whaiti, Kaihau Te Rangikakapi Maikara.*

IRAN, queen of. *See Esmat (d. 1995).*

IRELAND, Jill (1936–1990). English actress and dancer. Born April 24, 1936, in London, England; died May 18, 1990, in Malibu, CA; m. David McCallum (actor), 1957 (div. 1967); m. Charles Bronson (actor), 1968; children: 6. ❖ First appeared with Monte Carlo Ballet; starred opposite husband Charles Bronson in 15 films, including *The Valachi Papers, Hard Times, Breakout, Love and Bullets, Death Wish II* and *Assassination;* other films include *Oh Rosalinda!, Three Men in a Boat, Hell Drivers, Carry On Nurse* and *So Evil So Young.* ❖ See also Ireland's *Life Wish* (1987) and *Life Lines* (1989); tv movie "Reason for Living: The Jill Ireland Story" (1992).

IRELAND, Patricia (1945—). American lawyer and social activist. Born in Oak Park, IL, Oct 19, 1945; dau. of James Ireland (metallurgical engineer) and Joan (Filipak) Ireland; attended DePauw University; graduated from University of Tennessee, 1966; attended Florida State University, 1972; received law degree from University of Miami, 1975; m. Donald Anderson (college student), in 1962 (div. 1963); m. James Humble (artist and businessman), 1968; no children. ❖ Worked in corporate law for 12 years, during which time she also did pro-bono work for National Organization of Women (NOW) and assisted corporate clients in establishing affirmative-action programs; succeeded Molly Yard as the 9th president of NOW (1991); became a driving force in transforming it into the largest and most prominent feminist group in US; was reelected to the office several times. ❖ See also *Women in World History.*

IREMONGER, Lucille (c. 1916–1989?). Jamaican novelist and historian. Name variations: Mrs. Thomas Lascelles. Born Lucille d'Oyen Parks, c. 1916, in Jamaica; died possibly in 1989; studied in UK; m. Thomas Lascelles Iremonger (1916–1998, Conservative MP for Ilford). ❖ West Indian author and collector of folktales, who often wrote books with a Caribbean theme, moved to England and married there; works include novel *Creole* (1951) and *The Ghosts of Versailles;* also published books for children.

IRENE. *Variant of Irina.*

IRENE (fl. 200 BCE?). Ancient Greek painter. Name variations: Eirene, Yrenes. Pronunciation: ee-RAY-nay. Date and place of birth uncertain; daughter and pupil of the painter Cratinus. ❖ The 2nd female painter mentioned by Pliny the Elder in his *Natural History,* executed a portrait of a young maiden at Ephesus. ❖ See also *Women in World History.*

IRENE (d. 304). Saint. Name variations: Irena. Born in Roman Empire; died 304; sister of Agape of Thessalonica and Chionia (saints). ❖ With sisters, accused of being in possession of the Holy Scriptures, a crime punishable by death, and burned alive. Feast day is April 3. ❖ See also *Women in World History.*

IRENE (fl. 700s). Byzantine empress. Fl. in 700s; m. Anastasius II Artemius, emperor of Byzantium (r. 713–715).

IRENE (c. 1085–1133). *See Priska-Irene of Hungary.*

IRENE (fl. late 1100s). Byzantine princess. Fl. in late 1100s; dau. of Alexius III Angelus, Byzantine emperor (r. 1195–1203) and Euphrosyne (d. 1203); sister of Anna Angelina (d. 1210?) and Eudocia Angelina; m. Alexius Paleologus; children: Theodora Paleologina (who m. Andronicus Paleologus).

IRENE (fl. 1310). Queen of Thessaly. Dau. of Andronicus II (1259–1332), Byzantine emperor (r. 1282–1328) and possibly Irene of Montferrat (fl. 1300) or possibly illeg.; m. John II, king of Thessaly (r. 1303–1318).

IRENE (1901–1962). Hollywood costume designer and entrepreneur. Name variations: Irene Lentz. Born Irene Lentz, Dec 8, 1901 (also seen as 1908), in Brookings, SD; died Nov 15, 1962; dau. of Emil Lentz (rancher) and Maude (Watters) Lentz; attended University of Southern California; graduate of Wolfe School of Design; m. Richard Jones (movie director, died c. 1930); m. Eliot Gibbons (screenwriter), 1936. ❖ Opened a dress shop in Los Angeles, gaining a number of Hollywood celebrities for clients; headed custom-design salon at Bullock's Wilshire department store; signed with MGM as executive designer (1942) and remained there throughout 1940s, dressing Hedy Lamarr, Greer Garson, Judy Garland and Irene Dunne; won praise for naturalness and originality of designs, particularly her dressmaker suits and figure-revealing gowns; designed all-white outfits for Lana Turner in *The Postman Always Rings Twice* (1946); nominated for Academy Awards for designs for Barbara Stanwyck in *B.F.'s Daughter* and for Doris Day in *Midnight Lace* (1960). ❖ See also *Women in World History.*

IRENE (1904–1974). Greek princess and duchess of Aosta. Name variations: Princess Irene; Irene von Schleswig-Holstein-Sonderburg-Glücksburg. Born Feb 13, 1904 in Greece; died April 15, 1974; dau. of Constantine I, king of the Hellenes, and Sophie of Prussia (1870–1932); sister of George II (1890–1947), king of Greece (r. 1922–1923, 1935–1947), and Helen of Greece (1896–1982), who m. Carol II of Romania); m. Aimoe di Savoia-Aoste, duke of Aosta, 1939; children: Amadeo di Savoia-Aoste (b. 1943), prince of Savoy.

IRENE (1942—). Greek princess. Born May 11, 1942 in Cape Town; dau. of Fredericka (1917–1981), queen of the Hellenes, and Paul I, king of the Hellenes; sister of Sophia of Greece (b. 1938, queen of Spain) and Constantine II, king of Greece (b. 1940; r. 1964–1973).

IRENE (1953—). Romanian princess. Name variations: Irene Hohenzollern. Born Feb 28, 1953, in Lausanne, Switzerland; dau. of Michael, king of Romania (r. 1927–1930, 1940–1942), and Anne of Bourbon-Parma (b. 1923); m. John Krueger, Dec 10, 1983; children: 2, including Michael Krueger.

IRENE, Saint.
See *Irene of Spain (fl. 300)*.
See *Irene of Santarem (fl. 7th c.)*.
See *Irene of Constantinople (d. around 921)*.

IRENE, Sister (1823–1896). English-born nun and founder. Name variations: Sister Irene Fitzgibbon. Born Catherine Fitzgibbon in Kensington, London, England, May 11, 1823; died in New York, NY, Aug 14, 1896; attended parish schools in Brooklyn, NY. ❖ Roman Catholic Sister of Charity who established the 1st foundling home in NYC; came to US as a child; at 27, entered novitiate of Sisters of Charity (1850), serving as a teacher at St. Peter's Academy in NY until 1858, when she became mother superior of St. Peter's Convent; with staff of 4 sisters, opened the Foundling Asylum (1869), which later became NY Foundling Hospital; established 3 allied institutions: St. Ann's Maternity Hospital (1880), Hospital of St. John for Children (1881) and Nazareth Hospital for convalescent children at Spuyten Duyvil, NY (1881). ❖ See also *Women in World History*.

IRENE ANGELA OF BYZANTIUM (d. 1208). Holy Roman empress. Name variations: Irene of Byzantium. Died Aug 27, 1208; dau. of Margaret-Mary of Hungary (c. 1177–?) and Isaac II Angelus, Eastern Roman Emperor (r. 1185–95 and 1203–04); sister of Alexius IV Angelus, Byzantine emperor (r. 1203–1204); m. Philip of Swabia (c. 1176–1208), Holy Roman emperor (r. 1198–1208), on May 25, 1197; children: Marie of Swabia (c. 1201–1235); Beatrice of Swabia (1198–1235, who m. Otto IV, Holy Roman emperor, and Ferdinand III, king of Castile and Leon); probably Cunigunde of Hohenstaufen (fl. 1215–1230). Philip of Swabia was also m. to a dau. of Waldemar I the Great and Sophie of Russia.

IRENE ASEN (fl. 1300s). Empress of Nicaea. Name variations: Sister Eugenia. Fl. in 1300s; dau. of Andronicus; m. John VI Cantacuzene, emperor of Nicaea (r. 1347–1354); children: Mathew; Manuel; Maria Cantacuzene (who m. Nicephorus II of Epirus); Theodora Cantacuzene (who m. Orchan); Helena Cantacuzene (who m. John V Paleologus). ❖ In later years, entered a convent as Sister Eugenia.

IRENE DUCAS (c. 1066–1133). Byzantine empress. Name variations: Irene Doukas; Irene Doukaina or Ducaena. Born c. 1066; died Feb 19, 1133; dau. of Marie of Bulgaria (b. 1046) and Andronicus Ducas (general, known as the traitor of Manzikert); granddau. of Caesar John Ducas; 2nd wife of Alexius I Comnenus (1048–1118), emperor of Byzantium (r. 1081–1118); children: 7, including Anna Comnena (1083–1153/55); John II Comnenus or Kalojoannes (1088–1143), emperor of Byzantium (r. 1118–1143); Andronicus (killed in battle against the Turks, 1129); Theodora Comnena (fl. 1080s, who m. Constantine Angelus); Maria Comnena; Eudocia Comnena. ❖ Often accompanied husband on campaign and was alert to plots against him; on several occasions, saved him from danger; when he began to suffer from severe respiratory complaint, would sit up all night with him propped in her arms, attempting to ease his breathing; unsuccessfully endeavored to divert the succession from son John II Comnenus to Nicephorus Bryennius, husband of her 1st-born daughter Anna Comnena; following husband's death (1118), retired to the convent of Kecharitomene, which she had founded. ❖ See also *Women in World History*.

IRENE EMMA (1939—). Dutch princess. Born Irene Emma Elizabeth, Aug 5, 1939; dau. of Juliana (b. 1909), queen of the Netherlands (r. 1948–1980), and Prince Bernard of Lippe-Biesterfeld; sister of Beatrix (b. 1938), queen of the Netherlands (r. 1980—); m. Carlos Hugo, prince of Bourbon-Parma.

IRENE GODUNOV (d. 1603). See *Godunov, Irene*.

IRENE LASCARIS (fl. 1222–1235). Nicaean empress. Name variations: Irene Laskaris. Fl. around 1222–1235; dau. of Anna Angelina (d. 1210?) and Theodore I Lascaris, emperor of Nicaea (r. 1204–1222); m. John III Ducas Vatatzes, Nicaean (Byzantine) emperor (r. 1222–1254); children: one son, Theodore II Lascaris, Nicaean emperor (r. 1254–1258). ❖ Was a young widow when she married John III Vatatzes and shared with him the Byzantine throne, then a government in exile; was injured in a horseback-riding incident soon after birth of only child and remained an invalid all her life; with husband, was an exemplary ruler, turning the Byzantine court into a center of learning and culture. ❖ See also *Women in World History*.

IRENE LASCARIS (d. around 1270). Tsarina of Bulgaria. Name variations: Irene Laskaris. Died c. 1270; dau. of Helen Asen of Bulgaria (d. 1255?) and Theodore II Lascaris, emperor of Nicaea (r. 1254–1258);

1st wife of Constantine Tich, tsar of Bulgaria (r. 1257–1277). Maria Paleologina was also m. to Constantine Tich.

IRENE OF ATHENS (c. 752–803). Byzantine empress. Name variations: Irene the Great; Eirene. Pronunciation: EYE-REE-nee. Born in Athens c. 752; died Aug 9, 803, on Lesbos; parents unknown, probably noble; grew up an Athenian orphan; m. Leo IV the Khazar, Byzantine emperor (r. 775–780), Dec 769; children: Constantine VI (b. 771), emperor of Byzantium (r. 780–797). ❖ The 1st woman to be sole ruler of the Byzantine empire, ruled for 10 years, displaying firmness and intelligence, and summoned the council at Nicaea in 787, which formally revived the adoration of images and reunited the Eastern church with that of Rome; served as regent and co-emperor with Constantine VI (780–790); organized Seventh Ecumenical Council (Second Council of Nicaea, 787); deposed (790–792); reinstated as co-emperor with Constantine VI (792–797); having deposed son, was sole emperor (797–802); was sought as wife by Charlemagne (800), dealings that almost united the Eastern and Western empires and might have had a profound effect on the subsequent history of East and West relations; overthrown and exiled (802). ❖ See also *Women in World History*.

IRENE OF BRUNSWICK (fl. 1300s). Byzantine (Nicaean) empress. Name variations: Adelheid of Brunswick; Adelheid-Irene of Brunswick. Fl. in 1300s; 1st wife of Andronikos also spelled Andronicus III Paleologus, Byzantine (Nicaean) emperor (r. 1328–1341). Andronicus' 2nd wife was Anne of Savoy (c. 1320–1353).

IRENE OF BYZANTIUM (d. 1067). Byzantine princess. Died in 1067; dau. of Constantine VIII, Byzantine emperor (r. 1025–1028), and possibly Helena of Alypia; became 1st wife of Vsevolod I (1030–1093), grand prince of Kiev (r. 1078–1093), in 1046; children: Vladimir II Monomakh (b. 1053), grand prince of Kiev.

IRENE OF BYZANTIUM (fl. 1200s). See *Eulogia Paleologina*.

IRENE OF CONSTANTINOPLE (d. around 921). Saint. Name variations: Irene of Chyrsobalanton. Died around 921. ❖ A Cappadocian, became a nun rather than marry Michael III (the Drunkard), emperor of Byzantium; became abbess of the great Chrysobalanton convent in Constantinople, and an important cult flourished around her; was famous for her prophecies, levitations, and miracles.

IRENE OF HESSE-DARMSTADT (1866–1953). Princess of Hesse-Darmstadt. Born Irene Louise Mary Anne, July 11, 1866, at Neues Palais, in Darmstadt, Hesse, Germany; died Nov 11, 1953, in Hemmelmark, near Eckenford, Schleswig-Holstein, Germany; dau. of Alice Maud Mary (1843–1878), dau. of Queen Victoria) and Louis IV, grand duke of Hesse-Darmstadt; sister of Alexandra Feodorovna (1872–1918); m. Henry of Prussia (brother of Kaiser Wilhelm II), May 24 1888; children: Waldemar (1889–1945); Sigismund (1896–1978); Henry Victor (b. 1900).

IRENE OF HUNGARY (c. 1085–1133). See *Priska-Irene of Hungary*.

IRENE OF KIEV (fl. 1122). Princess of Kiev. Dau. of Mstislav I (b. 1076), grand prince of Kiev (r. 1125–1132), and Christina of Sweden (d. 1122); m. Andronicus (d. 1129), brother of Anna Comnena, in 1122.

IRENE OF MONTFERRAT (fl. 1300). Byzantine empress. Name variations: Yolande-Irene; Yolande of Montferrat; Violante of Montferat or Violante of Montferrat. Born Violante or Yolande; fl. c. 1300; dau. of William V the Great, marquis of Montferrat, and Isabelle of Cornwall; became 2nd wife of Andronicus II Paleologus (1259–1332), emperor of Nicaea and Byzantine emperor (r. 1282–1328), c. 1305; children: John; Teodoro also known as Theodore I (b. 1292), margrave of Montferrat; Demetrius; possibly Irene (who m. John II of Thessaly); possibly Simonis (who m. Milutin). ❖ An Italian princess, married Andronicus II Paleologus, following the death of his wife Anna of Hungary; said to be hotheaded, became discontented with the fact that Anna of Hungary's son, Michael IX, was heir to the throne while her sons were considered only private citizens; turned against husband and moved to Thessalonica. ❖ See also *Women in World History*.

IRENE OF SANTAREM (fl. 7th c.). Spanish saint. Name variations: Irene of Santárem. Lived at Tomar in Estremadura. ❖ Much revered in Spain and Portugal, was born of nobility, raised for the most part in a convent, and received her later education from a monk; living a sequestered life, ventured out only once a year to pray in church; on one such outing, was spotted by the noble Britald who was smitten but knew that his love would be unrequited; when his health gave way because of despair, visited his bedside, telling him that she had vowed to remain a virgin; was eventually murdered by an assassin hired by a jealous Britald and dumped into the Tagus river, where she was later recovered by the Benedictines near the town of Scalabis. ❖ See also *Women in World History.*

IRENE OF SPAIN (fl. 300s). Spanish saint. Born in Rome in early days of 4th century; dau. of Laurentia and a father who later became a priest of the church and was known as S. Lorenzo; sister of pope, St. Damasus I (c. 305–384). ❖ Feast day is Feb 21.

IRENE OF SULZBACH (d. 1161). *See Bertha-Irene of Sulzbach.*

IRENE OF THE KHAZARS (d. 750?). Byzantine empress. Born a princess of the Khazar tribe in the Russian steppes; died c. 750; 1st wife of Constantine V Kopronymus, Byzantine emperor (r. 741–775); children: Leo IV the Khazar, Byzantine emperor (r. 775–780), who m. Irene of Athens). ❖ Died young while giving birth to Leo IV, heir to the throne.

IRENE PALEOLOGINA (fl. 1200s). *See Eulogia Paleologina.*

IRENE PALEOLOGINA (fl. 1279–1280). Tsarina of Bulgaria. Dau. of Michael VIII Paleologus (1224–1282), emperor of Nicaea (r. 1261–1282), and Theodora Ducas; sister of Andronicus II (1259–1332), emperor of Nicaea (r. 1282–1328); m. Asen III also known as Ivan Asen III, tsar of Bulgaria (r. 1279–1280); children: Andronicus; Maria Asen (who m. Roger de Flor).

IRENE THE GREAT (c. 752–803). *See Irene of Athens.*

IREYS, Alice (1911–2000). American landscape designer. Born Alice Recknagel, April 24, 1911, in Brooklyn, NY; died Dec 12, 2000, in New York, NY; attended Cambridge School of Architecture; m. Henry T. Ireys, 1943 (died 1963); children: Henry Ireys, Catherine Gandel and Anne Lennon. ❖ One of the most prominent landscape architects of latter half 20th century, completed over 1,000 public and private projects; her Fragrance Garden at Brooklyn Botanic Garden became an international prototype for gardens used by people with disabilities; wrote 4 books, including *Small Gardens for City and Country;* elected fellow of American Society of Landscape Architects (1978). ❖ See also (documentary) "The Living Landscapes of Alice Recknagel Ireys" (2000).

IRFAN (fl. mid-800s). Arabian singer. Fl. in 9th century. ❖ Representing the Persian romantic school of music, performed at the court of Caliph al-Mutawakki (r. 847–861). ❖ See also *Women in World History.*

IRIGARAY, Luce (1930—). French philosopher, feminist and psychoanalyst. Born 1930 in Belgium; University of Louvain, MA, 1955; University of Paris, MA in psychology, 1961, diploma in psychopathology, 1962, doctorate in linguistics, 1968. ❖ Worked for the Fondation Nationale de la Recherche Scientifique in Belgium (1960); became director of Research in Philosophy at National Centre for Scientific Research, Paris; participated in Jacques Lacan's psychoanalytic seminars; beame an analyst; taught at University of Paris VIII–Vincennes (1968–74); was a member of the École Freudienne de Paris (EFP), a school directed by Lacan; because of her 2nd doctoral thesis, *Speculum de l'autre femme (Speculum of the Other Woman),* which argues that history and culture are written in patriarchal language, lost job at Vincennes; interpreted Freud in light of Jacques Derrida's deconstruction; challenged Lacan's notions of feminine psycho-sexual development and idea of *parler femme;* works include *Le Langage des déments* (The Language of the Demented, 1973), *This Sex Which is Not One* (1977), *Amante marine: de Friedrich Nietzsche* (1983), *L'Oubli d l'air: Chez Martin Heidegger* (1983), *L'Ethique de la différence sexuelle* (An Ethics of Sexual Differences, 1984), *Parler n'est jamais neutre* (Speaking is Never Neutral, 1985) and *Sexes et Parentés* (1987).

IRINA. *Variant of Irene.*

IRINA (1895–1970). Russian princess. Name variations: Irene Yusupov; Irina Alexandrovna Youssoupoff or Yussoupov; Irina Alexandrovna Romanov or Romanova. Born Irina Alexandrovna Romanova, July 3, 1895; died 1970; m. Felix Yussoupov (1887–1967), count Soumarokov-Elston, 1914; dau. of Xenia Alexandrovna (1876–1960) and Grand Duke Alexander Michaelovitch (grandson of Nicholas I of Russia). ❖ Niece of Tsar Nicholas II, was the sponsor of the notorious Rasputin, a Siberian peasant and self-proclaimed holy man who entered the circle surrounding the Russian imperial family sometime after 1905; married Felix Yussoupov (1914), who was among the nobles who poisoned, shot, clubbed and drowned Rasputin in Petrograd in (1916); sued MGM over depiction of her as an intimate of Rasputin in *Rasputin and the Empress* (1933). ❖ See also *Women in World History.*

IRINA ROMANOV. *See Romanov, Irina.*

IRINE. *Variant of Irina.*

IRISH QUEEN (1857–1934). *See Cline, Maggie.*

IRMA OF HOHENLOHE-LANGENBURG (1902–1986). German royal. Born Irma Helen, July 4, 1902, in Langenburg, Germany; died Mar 8, 1986, in Heilbronn, Baden-Wurttemberg, Germany; dau. of Alexandra Saxe-Coburg (1878–1942) and Ernest, 7th prince of Hohenlohe-Langenburg.

IRMENGARD (c. 800–851). Holy Roman empress. Born c. 800; died Mar 20, 851; dau. of Hugh, count of Tours; m. Lothair also known as Lothar I (795–855), Holy Roman emperor (r. 840–855), in 821; children: Louis II le Jeune also known as Louis II the Child (c. 822–875), Holy Roman emperor (r. 855–875); Lothair or Lothar II (c. 826–869), king of Lorraine; Bertha of Avenay (c. 830–c. 852); Charles the Child (c. 845–863), king of Provence; Rothilde; another daughter (name unknown) m. Giselbert, count of Maasgau.

IRMENGARD OF HESBAIN (c. 778–818). *See Ermengarde.*

IRMENGARD OF OETTINGEN (fl. 14th c.). Countess Palatine. Married Adolph the Simple (1300–1327), count Palatine (r. 1319–1327); children: Rupert II (1335–1398), count Palatine (r. 1390–1398).

IRMENTRUDE (d. 820). Countess of Altdorf and founder of the Welf line. Name variations: Irmentrudis. Died in 820; dau. of Bertha (719–783) and Pepin III the Short, king of the Franks (r. 747–768), mayor of Neustria (r. 741); sister of Charlemagne, king of the Franks (r. 768–814), Holy Roman emperor (r. 800–814); m. Isembert, count of Altdorf; children: Welf I. ❖ As the mother of Welf I, founded both the Italian (Guelf or Guelph) and German branches of that famous family. The younger branch of Welf established itself in Germany and became dukes and duchesses of Brunswick; the British house of Windsor, through the German house of Hanover, descended from this line; hence, Irmentrude was the direct ancestor of Queen Victoria.

IRMINA (d. 716). Frankish saint. Died c. 716; dau. of St. Dagobert II, Merovingian king of Austrasia (r. 674–678), and Matilda (Anglo-Saxon princess); sister of Saint Adela (d. 735). ❖ Founded a convent under Benedictine rule in Horren at Trier; when her religious community was threatened by an epidemic, sought help from St. Williborord, whose prayers, it was thought, ended the danger; in gratitude, offered Willibrord the land of Echternach, where he established his abbey; canonized as saint. ❖ See also *Women in World History.*

IRMINGARD OF ZELLE (c. 1200–1260). Margravine of Baden. Born c. 1200; died Feb 24, 1260; dau. of Agnes of Hohenstaufen (d. 1204) and Henry, count Palatine of Rhine; m. Herman V, margrave of Baden (r. 1190–1243), around 1220; children: Herman VI, margrave of Baden (r. 1243–1250); Rudolf I, margrave of Baden (r. 1243–1288).

IRMTRUDE. *Variant of Ermentrude.*

IRVIN, Mrs. K. E. (1927—). *See Fry, Shirley.*

IRVIN, Shirley Fry (1927—). *See Fry, Shirley.*

IRVINE, Jean Kennedy (c. 1877–1962). Scottish pharmacist. Born Jean Kennedy, c. 1877, in Hawick, Scotland; died Mar 3, 1962; m. Peter Irvine (pharmacist). ❖ The Royal Pharmaceutical Society's 1st woman president (1947–48) and the Insurance Officers' Association for England and Wales' 1st woman president (1932), trained as a pharmaceutical apprentice in Hawick, Scotland (qualified, 1900); worked as a Glasgow Hospital pharmacist (1900–04); employed as an assistant and later as chief pharmacist for Glasgow Apothecaries Co.; helped husband manage 2 Glasgow pharmacies (1904–14); worked as retail pharmacist (1914–16); was a superintendent of South-Eastern Pricing Bureau which oversaw prescription pricing in region (1916–46); served as a Royal Pharmaceutical Society council member (1937–52). Made Member of the Order of the British Empire (1928).

IRVINE-SMITH, Fanny Louise (1878–1948). New Zealand teacher, lecturer, and writer. Name variations: Fanny Louise Smith. Born on Sept 10, 1878, at Napier, New Zealand; died Dec 20, 1948, in Wellington; dau. of Thomas Smith (master mariner) and Margaret Isabella (Sproule) Smith; Victoria College, BA, 1908; MA, 1921. ❖ Taught at New Plymouth and Kaimiro schools in Taranaki, and at Waipawa school in Hawke's Bay; founding editor of Victoria College magazine, *Style* (1902); lectured in New Zealand history and Maori culture at Teachers' Training College, Wellington, beginning 1932; published history of Wellington,

The Streets of My City (1948). ❖ See also *Dictionary of New Zealand Biography* (Vol. 4).

IRVING, Birdie (1869–1963). *See Irving, Ethel.*

IRVING, Dorothea (1875–1933). *See Baird, Dorothea.*

IRVING, Ethel (1869–1963). English actress. Name variations: Birdie Irving; Ethelyn Irving. Born Frances Emily Irving, Sept 5, 1869, in England; died May 3, 1963, in Bexhill-on-Sea, East Sussex, England; dau. of Joseph Irving (stage actor, died 1870); m. Gilbert Porteous (actor, died 1928). ❖ Made stage debut in London under name Birdie Irving as a peasant in *The Vicar of Wideawakefield* (1885); made NY debut in *The Red Hussar* (1890), then remained there for 6 years; returned to London, appearing in *The Babes in the Wood, San Toy, The Cherry Orchard, La Tosca,* and most successfully as Winnie Harborough in *The Girl from Kay's* (1902), Mrs. Millament in *The Way of the World* (1904), Julie in *The Three Daughters of M. Dupont* (1905) and title role in *Lady Frederick* (1907); briefly managed the Criterion, then the Globe.

IRVING, Isabel (1871–1944). American stage actress. Born Feb 28, 1871, in Bridgeport, CT; died Sept 1, 1944, in Nantucket, MA; dau. of Charles and Isabella Irving; m. William H. Thompson, 1899. ❖ Member of Augustin Daly's company (1888–94); as leading lady, appeared opposite John Drew in *Rosemary, A Marriage of Convenience, Smith* and *Tyranny of Tears,* and with Helen Hayes and Katharine Cornell in several productions; last appeared opposite William Gillette in *Three Wise Fools.*

IRVING, Lady (1875–1933). *See Baird, Dorothea.*

IRVING, Margaret (1898–1988). American theatrical dancer and actress. Name variations: Margaret Irving-James. Born Jan 18, 1898, in Pittsburgh, PA; died Mar 5, 1988. ❖ Studied with Ned Wayburn in NYC and debuted in his *Girlies' Gambols* (1916) where she danced a ballet-hula on point; performed specialty dances in many productions, including *Jack O'Lantern* (1917), *Ziegfeld Follies* (1919, 1920, 1923), *Manhattan Mary* (1927), *As Thousands Cheer* (1933) and *Hold Onto Your Hats* (1940), but best remembered for exotic dances in *The Desert Song* (1927) and *Animal Crackers* (1928); had small parts in over 30 films, including *Charlie Chan at the Opera* (1936), *Follow Your Heart* (1936), *Three Men on a Horse* (1936) and *Mr. Moto's Last Warning* (1939).

IRWIN, Agnes (1841–1914). American educator. Born in Washington, DC, Dec 30, 1841; died in Philadelphia, PA, Oct 16, 1914; dau. of William Wallace Irwin (Whig lawyer and congressman from PA) and Sophia Arabella Dallas (Bache) Irwin (granddau. of Sarah Bache); never married; no children. ❖ The 1st dean of Radcliffe College was the great-great-granddau. of Benjamin Franklin and Deborah Read; assumed principalship of Penn Square Seminary of Philadelphia (1869) and remained there for 25 years, earning a reputation for high educational standards (school was renamed the Agnes Irwin School shortly after her appointment); recommended for post of dean of newly chartered Radcliffe College (1894); spent early years of her tenure there expanding its curriculum, which, by 1902, was offering a doctoral program; raised money for gymnasium, library, and administration building, and worked for establishment of college-owned residences (1894–1909); served as president of Woman's Education Association of Boston (1901–07) and Head Mistresses' Association of Private Schools (1911–14). ❖ See also *Women in World History.*

IRWIN, Elisabeth (1880–1942). American progressive educator. Born Elisabeth Antoinette Irwin, Aug 29, 1880, in Brooklyn, NY; died Oct 16, 1942, in New York, NY; dau. of William Henry Irwin and Josephine Augusta (Easton) Irwin; children: adopted several informally and one legally, Elizabeth Westwood (Mrs. Howard Gresens). ❖ Became field worker and psychologist for Public Education Association of New York City (from 1910); developed experimental program initially housed in and named Little Red School House (1921); after city Board of Education withdrew support, opened private school of same name (1932); added high school department (1941), now named Elisabeth Irwin High School; served as school's director for remainder of life; her school was a focus for progressive school movement, and many of her practices were adopted by NY public elementary-school system.

IRWIN, Estelle Mae (1923—). American bankrobber. Name variations: Stella Irwin; Estelle Dickson. Born 1923 in Topeka, Kansas; m. Bennie Dickson. ❖ At 15, ran away from home to be with bankrobber Bennie Dickson in Los Angeles (1937); married Dickson, who taught her tricks of trade; in SD, robbed Corn Exchange Bank (Aug 25, 1938) and Northwest Security National Bank of Brookings with husband (Oct 31);

evaded arrest for many months, until FBI caught up with them in St. Louis, and husband was shot when he reached for his guns (April 6, 1939); escaped but was apprehended in Kansas City the next day; convicted in SD for bank robbery, received 10-year sentence.

IRWIN, Flo (born c. 1860). Canadian-born American performer. Name variations: Ada Campbell. Born Ada Campbell in Whitby, Ontario, Canada; 1st of two daughters of Robert E. and Jane (Draper) Campbell; sister of May Irwin (entertainer); attended St. Cecilia Convent, Mount Hope, Ontario. ❖ Appeared with sister May in vaudeville.

IRWIN, Inez Haynes (1873–1970). American suffragist, novelist and short-story writer. Name variations: Inez Gillmore. Born Inez Leonore Haynes in Rio de Janeiro, Brazil, Mar 2, 1873; died in Norwell, MA, Sept 25, 1970; dau. of Gideon Haynes and his 2nd wife Emma Jane (Hopkins) Haynes; graduate of Boston Normal School, 1892; attended Radcliffe College as special student, 1897–1900; m. Rufus Hamilton Gillmore (newspaper reporter), Aug 30, 1897 (div. c. 1913); m. William Henry Irwin (political journalist and biographer of Herbert Hoover), Feb 1, 1916. ❖ With Maud Wood Park, founded Massachusetts College Equal Suffrage Association (1900), which later expanded into National College Equal Suffrage League; published 1st novel, *June Jeopardy* (1908); became fiction editor of Max Eastman's *The Masses;* became involved with the more radical National Woman's Party (1918), serving on its advisory council and providing an account of its activities with *The Story of the Woman's Party* (1921); other writings include *Angels and Amazons: A Hundred Years of American Women* (1933), the novels *The Lady of the Kingdoms* (1917), *Gertrude Haviland's Divorce* (1925) and *Gideon* (1927), and children's books, including the popular "Maida" series, based on her own childhood; served as president of Authors Guild (1925–28) and Authors' League of America (1931–33); was vice president of NY chapter of PEN (1941–44). ❖ See also *Women in World History.*

IRWIN, Juno (1928—). *See Stover-Irwin, Juno.*

IRWIN, Kelly (1961—). *See Kryczka, Kelly.*

IRWIN, May (1862–1938). Canadian-born American actress and singer. Name variations: May Campbell. Born Georgia Campbell, June 27, 1862, in Whitby, Ontario, Canada; died Oct 22, 1938, in New York, NY; 2nd of 2 daughters of Robert E. and Jane (Draper) Campbell; sister of Flo Irwin (entertainer); attended St. Cecilia Convent, Mount Hope, Ontario; m. Frederick W. Keller (businessman), 1878 (died 1886); m. Kurt Eisfeldt (her agent), May 26, 1907; children: (1st m.) Walter and Harry. ❖ With sister Ada (known as Flo Irwin), made 1st professional appearance as Irwin Sisters in Buffalo (1875); with sister, debuted in NY at London Theatre (1877) and performed vaudeville and burlesque with Tony Pastor's co. (NY); launching a solo career, joined Augustin Daly's stock co. (1883); made London debut in *Dollars and Sense* (1884); had greatest successes in full-length farces including *A Country Sport* (1893) and *The Widow Jones;* known for introducing such songs as "After the Ball," "I'm Looking for de Bully" (published as "May Irwin's Bully Song"), "A Hot Time in the Old Town" and "The Opera Rag."

IRWIN, P. K. (b. 1916). *See Page, P. K.*

IRYNA. *See Variant of Irena or Irene.*

ISAAC, Jane (1907–1998). *See West, Dorothy.*

ISAAC, Joan (fl. 1300s). Lady of Lorn. Name variations: Joan de Ergadia. Dau. of Thomas Isaac and Matilda Bruce (d. 1353, dau. of Robert the Bruce); m. Ewen de Ergadia, Lord of Lorn; children: Janet de Ergadia.

ISAACS, Edith (1878–1956). American magazine editor and critic. Name variations: Edith Rich or Edith Juliet Rich; Edith J. Isaacs or Edith J.R. Isaacs or Edith Juliet Rich Isaacs. Born Edith Juliet Rich, Mar 27, 1878, in Milwaukee, WI; died Jan 10, 1956, in White Plains, NY; dau. of Adolph Walter Rich and Rosa (Sidenberg) Rich; m. Lewis Montefiore Isaacs, Nov 28, 1904 (died 1944); children: 2 daughters (b. 1906, 1915), 1 son (b. 1908). ❖ Was reporter for *Milwaukee Sentinel* (c. 1897–1902), becoming literary editor (1903); was drama critic for *Ainslee's Magazine* (1913) and wrote articles for *The Delineator* and *Ladies' Home Journal;* joined editorial board of quarterly magazine, *Theatre Arts* (1918), becoming editor (1922); organized exhibition of Blondiau-Theater Arts Collection of Primitive African Art, 1st such large show in NY (1920s); helped create National Theater Conference (1925) and American National Theater and Academy (1935); worked with Federal Theater Project (1930s); wrote *The American Theater in Social* and Educational Life: A Survey of Its Needs and Opportunities (1932) and The Negro in the American Theater (1947); had Theater Arts Project named for her at James Weldon Johnson Community Center (1958); discovered several subsequently famous performers, including dramatist Eugene O'Neill and dancer Martha Graham.

ISAACS, Stella (1894–1971). English government official. Name variations: Stella Reading; the Marchioness of Reading; Baroness Swanborough. Born 1894 in Constantinople (now Istanbul), Turkey; died 1971; dau. of Charles Charn (one source says Charnaud); m. Rufus Isaacs, earl of Reading (later marquess of Reading), 1931. ❖ Influential aid worker in WWII England, who organized and ran the women's branch of civil-defense service, 1st served as Red Cross worker during WWI; traveled to India (1925) to serve as secretary to Lady Reading, wife of the viceroy of India (1930); appointed founding chair of Women's Volunteer Service for Civil Defense (WVS, 1938); helped WVS grow into an organization of a million women by 1942; named a governor of BBC (1946) and served as vice-chair (1947–51). Made Dame of the British Empire (1941); became the 1st woman life peer (1958). ❖ See also Women in World History.

ISAACS, Susan (1885–1948). English child psychologist and primary schoolteacher. Name variations: Susan Sutherland Isaacs; Susan Sutherland Brierley; (pseudonym) Ursula Wise. Born Susan Sutherland Fairhurst, May 24, 1885, at Bromley Cross, near Bolton, Lancashire, England; died Oct 12, 1948; University of Manchester, BA, 1912; University of Cambridge's psychological laboratory, MA, 1913; m. W. B. Brierley (plant pathologist), 1914 (div.); Nathan Isaacs (psychologist), 1922. ❖ A child psychologist expert who advocated observation and recording of children at play, lectured in infant schoolteaching at Darlington Training College (1913–14); lectured in logic at University of Manchester (1914–15); tutored psychology tutorial classes at University of London (1916–33); employed as a Malting School House principal in Cambridge (1924–27); served as head of the Institute of Education's Child Development Unit at University of London (1933–43); worked as assistant editor of British Journal of Psychology (1921–48); chaired British Psychological Society's Education Section (1923–39). Writings include Intellectual Growth in Young Children (1930), Social Development in Young Children (1933), Introduction to Psychology (1921) and The Nursery Years (1929); as Ursula Wise, wrote a question-and-answer column for Nursery World (1929–36). Named Commander of the Order of the British Empire (1948).

ISABEAU DE LORRAINE (1410–1453). See Isabelle of Lorraine.

ISABEAU OF BAVARIA (1371–1435). Queen of France. Name variations: Elizabeth of Bavaria; Isabeau of France; Isabel, Isabelle, Isabella. Born c. 1371 (some sources cite 1369) in Bavaria; died Sept 29 (or 24), 1435, in Paris, France; dau. of Stephen III, duke of Bavaria (r. 1375–1413), and Thaddaea Visconti (d. 1381); m. Charles VI (1368–1422), king of France (r. 1380–1422), July 17, 1385; children: Charles (d. 1386 in infancy); Joan (1388–1390); Isabella of Valois (c. 1389–c. 1410, who m. Richard II of England); Joan Valois (1391–1433); Charles (d. 1401); Marie (1393–1438, prioress of Poissy); Michelle Valois (1394–1422); Louis, duke of Guienne (d. 1415); John, duke of Touraine (1398–1417, who m. Jacqueline of Hainault); Catherine of Valois (1401–1437, later queen of England m. to Henry V); Charles VII (1403–1461), king of France (r. 1422–1461); Philip (1407–1407). ❖ A German princess and one of France's most despised queens, married Charles VI as part of a political alliance between Bavaria and France; provided heirs to the throne by having 12 children, but had misfortune of marrying the king called "Charles the Mad," who suffered long bouts of insanity for several decades; contributed to power struggles by allegedly having an affair with one of the contenders, Duke Louis of Orleans; with husband disabled, attempted to administer the government in his name but was largely unsuccessful; as regent, signed the notorious Treaty of Troyes with the invading English which proved unpopular with the French (it dispossessed her son Charles, agreed that Henry V of England would succeed Charles as king of France, and provided for the marriage of her daughter Catherine of Valois to King Henry); recognized as an important patron of artists and writers, among them the celebrated Christine de Pizan. ❖ See also Women in World History.

ISABEL. Variant of Isabella.

ISABEL (fl. 1183). Lady Annandale. Name variations: Isabel Bruce; Isabel Roos. Fl. around 1183; illeg. dau. of William I the Lion, king of Scots (r. 11665–1214), and a mistress; m. Robert Bruce, 3rd Lord of Annandale, in 1183; m. Robert Roos; children: (2nd m.) William Roos.

ISABEL (fl. 1225). Scottish princess and countess of Norfolk. Name variations: Isabel Dunkeld; Isabel Bigod; Isabella. Fl. around 1225; interred at Church of the Black Friars, London; dau. of William I the Lion (b. 1143), king of Scots, and Ermengarde of Beaumont (d. 1234); m. Roger Bigod (c. 1212–1270), 4th earl of Norfolk, May 1225, in Alnwick, Northumberland.

ISABEL (1386–1402). English noblewoman. Name variations: Isabel Plantagenet. Born Mar 12, 1386; died c. April 1402; dau. of Thomas Woodstock, 1st duke of Gloucester, and Eleanor de Bohun (1366–1399). ❖ Was a nun at Aldgate.

ISABEL (d. around 1410). See Stewart, Isabel.

ISABEL (1409–1484). Countess of Essex. Name variations: Isabel Plantagenet. Born 1409; died Oct 2, 1484; interred at Little Easton Church, Essex; dau. of Richard of Conisbrough (c. 1375–1415), 2nd earl of Cambridge (r. 1414–1415), and Anne Mortimer (1390–1411); aunt of Edward IV and Richard III, kings of England; m. Sir Thomas Grey of Heton, after Feb 1413 (annulled 1426); m. Henry Bourchier (c. 1404–1483), 1st/14th earl of Essex (r. 1461–1483), before April 25, 1426; children: (2nd m.) William Bourchier, viscount Bourchier (d. 1483); Henry Bourchier; Humphrey Bourchier, Lord Cornwall; John Bourchier; Thomas Bourchier; Edward Bourchier; Fulke Bourchier; Isabel Bourchier (died young); Hugh Bourchier; Florence Bourchier (d. 1525).

ISABEL (d. 1457?). Countess of Lennox and duchess of Albany. Died c. 1457; dau. of Duncan, 8th earl of Lennox; m. Murdoch Stewart, 2nd duke of Albany, on Feb 17, 1392; children: Robert Stewart, master of Fife (d. 1421); Walter Stewart of Lennox (d. 1425); Alexander (d. 1425); James (d. 1451); Isabel (who m. Walter Buchanan).

ISABEL (1772–1827). Countess of Sayn-Hachenburg. Born April 19, 1772; died Jan 6, 1827; m. Frederick William, prince of Nassau-Weilburg; children: 4, including William, duke of Nassau (1792–1839).

ISABEL, Doña (d. 1551). See Tecuichpo.

ISABEL, Princess.
See Isabel of Brazil (1846–1921).
See Maria Isabel Francisca (1851–1931).

ISABEL, Queen of Portugal (1432–1455). See Isabel la Paloma.

ISABEL, Saint (1207–1231). See Elizabeth of Hungary.

ISABEL, the infanta (1851–1931). See María Isabel Francisca.

ISABEL I (1451–1504). See Isabella I.

ISABEL II (1830–1904). See Isabella II.

ISABEL BEAUMONT (d. 1368). See Beaumont, Isabel.

ISABEL BRUCE (c. 1278–1358). See Bruce, Isabel.

ISABEL DE BORBON (1602–1644). See Elizabeth Valois.

ISABEL DE BRAOSE (d. 1248?). See Braose, Isabel de.

ISABEL DE CLARE (c. 1174–1220). See Clare, Isabel de.

ISABEL DE CLERMONT (d. 1465). Queen of Naples. Died 1465; dau. of Caterina Orsini and Tristan, count of Capertino; became 1st wife of Ferdinand or Ferrante I (1423–1494), king of Naples (r. 1458–1494), in 1444; children: Alfonso or Alphonso II (1448–1495), king of Naples (r. 1494, abdicated in 1495); Leonora of Aragon (1450–1493); Frederick IV (1452–1504), king of Naples (r. 1496–1501, deposed); Giovanni of Naples (1456–1485), cardinal of Tarento; Francesco (1461–1486), duke of Sant'Angelo; Beatrice of Naples (1457–1508).

ISABEL DE FARNESE. See Farnese, Elizabeth.

ISABEL DE GATINAIS. See Matilda of Anjou.

ISABEL DE LIMOGES (1283–1328). Duchess of Brittany. Name variations: Isabel of Limoges. Born 1283 in Toro; died July 24, 1328; dau. of Sancho IV, king of Castile and Leon (r. 1284–1296), and Maria de Molina (d. 1321); m. Jaime also known as James II the Just, king of Aragon and Sicily, Dec 1, 1291 (annulled in 1295); m. John III (1276–1341), duke of Brittany (r. 1312–1341), 1310.

ISABEL DE WARRENNE (d. before 1147). See Isabel of Vermandois.

ISABEL DE WARRENNE (c. 1137–1203). Countess of Surrey. Name variations: Isabel de Warenne. Born c. 1137; died c. July 12 or 13, 1203 (some sources cite 1199); buried at Chapter House, Lewes, East Sussex, England; only daughter and heiress of William de Warrenne (1119–1148), 3rd earl of Warrenne and Surrey (r. 1138–1148), and Adela Talvace (d. 1174); m. William of Boulogne also known as William de Blois, 4th earl of Warrenne and Surrey (2nd son of King Stephen), in 1148 (died 1159); m. Hamelin de Warrenne (c. 1129–1202, illeg. son of Geoffrey of Anjou), 5th earl of Surrey, April 1164; children: (2nd m.) William de Warrenne (d. 1240), 6th earl of Warrenne and Surrey (r. 1202–1240); Ela Plantagenet (who m. Robert Newburn and William FitzWilliam of Sprotborough); Ida Plantagenet (who m. Roger Bigod, 2nd earl of Norfolk); Maud Plantagenet (d. around 1212, who m. Henry Hastings, Lord Hastings, count of Eu, and Henry d'Estouteville, Lord of Valmont and Rames); Mary de Warrenne (d. after 1208); another daughter (name unknown) associated with John I Lackland, king of England, and gave birth to Richard of Dover, baron of Chilham.

ISABEL DE WARRENNE (b. 1253). Queen of Scots. Name variations: Isabel Balliol; Isabel of Warenne; Isabel de Warren. Born 1253; death date unknown; dau. of John de Warrenne or Warenne (c. 1231–1304), 7th earl of Warenne and Surrey, and Alice le Brun (d. 1255); m. John Balliol (1249–1315), king of the Scots (r. 1292–1296), before Feb 7, 1280; children: Edward Balliol (c. 1283–1364), briefly king of Scots (r. 1332–1338); Henry Balliol (d. 1332); Margaret Balliol.

ISABEL DE WARRENNE (d. 1282). Countess of Arundel. Name variations: Isabel de Warren; Isabel of Warenne. Died in 1282; dau. of Maud Marshall (d. 1248) and William de Warrenne, 6th earl of Warenne and Surrey (r. 1202–1240); m. Hugh de Albini, earl of Arundel. ❖ Patron of the arts.

ISABEL FARNESE. See Farnese, Elizabeth.

ISABEL FRANCISCA, Princess (1851–1931). See Maria Isabel Francisca.

ISABEL LA PALOMA (1432–1455). Queen of Portugal. Born 1432; died Dec 2, 1455, at Evora; interred at Batalla; dau. of Pedro or Peter of Coimbra, regent of Portugal, and Isabel of Aragon (1409–1443); m. Afonso or Alphonso V, king of Portugal (r. 1438–1481), on May 6, 1448; sister of Pedro the Constable also known as Peter the Constable (1429–1466); children: Joao (1451–1455); Joanna (1452–1490), regent of Portugal; Juan also known as John II (1455–1495), king of Portugal (r. 1481–1495). ❖ Had strong interests in religion, history and literature; commissioned translations of Ludolph von Sachen's *Vita Christi* and Christine de Pizan's 1405 *Livre de Trois Vertues* (*The Book of the Three Virtues*). Her brother Peter the Constable wrote *Tragédia de la Insigne Reyna Dona Isabel*, a biography of her life.

ISABEL MARIA (1801–1876). Regent of Portugal. Born July 4, 1801, in Lisbon, Portugal; died April 22, 1876, in Benfica, Lisbon; dau. of Carlota Joaquina (1775–1830) and John VI (1767–1826), king of Portugal. ❖ Was regent of Portugal (1826–28). ❖ See also *Women in World History*.

ISABEL NEVILLE (1451–1476). See Neville, Isabel.

ISABEL OF ANGOULÊME (1186–1246). See Isabella of Angoulême.

ISABEL OF ARAGON (1271–1336). See Elizabeth of Portugal.

ISABEL OF ARAGON (1409–1443). Duchess of Coimbra. Name variations: Isabel de Aragon; Isabel de Aragón. Born in 1409; died 1443; dau. of Jaime, count of Urgel; m. Pedro or Peter (b. 1392), duke of Coimbra (r. 1439–1549), regent of Portugal, on Sept 13, 1428; children: Pedro or Peter the Constable (b. 1429) who tried to seize the Aragonese throne in the right of his mother in 1465; John of Coimbra (b. 1431); Isabella la Paloma (1432–1455); Jaime or Jaimes, cardinal of Lisbon (b. 1434); Beatriz (1435–1462, who m. Adolf of Cleves); Filippa (1437–1497).

ISABEL OF BAR (1410–1453). See Isabelle of Lorraine.

ISABEL OF BEAUMONT (fl. 1150). English royal. Name variations: Isabel Beaumont; Isabel de Beaumont. Fl. c. 1150; dau. of Waleran of Meulan also known as Waleran de Beaumont (1104–1166), earl of Worcester; m. Maurice de Craon.

ISABEL OF BRAGANZA (1846–1921). See Isabel of Brazil.

ISABEL OF BRAZIL (1846–1921). Regent of Brazil. Name variations: Isabel of Braganza and Orleans (Isabel de Bragança e Orléans); Isabella of Brazil; Princess Royal; Princess Isabel; Condessa or Countess d'Eu; The Redeemer. Born Isabel Cristina Leopoldina Augusta de Bragança, July 29, 1846, in Rio de Janeiro, Brazil; died Nov 14, 1921, in the Castle d'Eu, northern France; dau. of Pedro II of Braganza, emperor of Brazil,

and Empress Teresa Cristina of Bourbon (1822–1889); m. Gastao de Orléans aka Gaston of Orleans, Conde or Count d'Eu, in Rio de Janeiro, Oct 15, 1864; children: Pedro de Alcantara, prince of Grao Pará (b. Oct 15, 1875); Luis (b. Jan 26, 1878); Antonio (b. Aug 9, 1881). ❖ Heiress to throne of Brazil, was the only woman to have served as chief of state in Latin America in 19th century and the only woman to have held immense political power; was regent of the Brazilian Empire (1871–72, 1876–77, 1887–88); as regent, signed the Free Womb Law (Sept 28, 1871); a staunch abolitionist, abolished slavery with the Lei Aurea (May 13, 1888), the most momentous piece of legislation ever to be implemented in Brazil. ❖ See also Lourenço Luiz Lacombe, *Isabel, A Princesa Redentora* (Petrópolis: Instituto Histórico de Petrópolis, 1989); and *Women in World History*.

ISABEL OF BUCHAN.
See Isabella of Buchan (fl. 1290–1310).
See Isabella of France (1296–1358).

ISABEL OF CASTILE (1355–1392). Duchess of York. Name variations: Isabella. Born in Morales, Spain, in 1355; died Nov 23, 1392; dau. of Pedro el Cruel also known as Peter I the Cruel, king of Castile and Leon (r. 1350–1369), and Marie de Padilla (1335–1365); sister of Constance of Castile (1354–1394); m. Edmund of Langley (1341–1402), duke of York, in 1372; children: Edward, 2nd duke of York (1372–1415); Richard of York, also known as Richard of Conisbrough, 2nd earl of Cambridge (1376–1415, who m. Anne Mortimer); Constance (c. 1374–1416).

ISABEL OF FIFE (c. 1332–1389). Countess of Fife. Name variations: Isabel Fife; Isabel Macduff; Elizabeth. Acceded as countess of Fife in 1359. Born before 1332; died after Aug 12, 1389; dau. of Duncan Fife (1285–1353), 10th earl of Fife (r. 1288–1353), and Mary de Monthermer (1298–after 1371); m. William Ramsey of Colluthie; m. Walter Stewart (d. 1363), after July 22, 1360; m. Thomas Bisset of Upsetlington, in 1363; m. John de Dunbar.

ISABEL OF FRANCE (1545–1568). See Elizabeth of Valois.

ISABEL OF GLOUCESTER (c. 1167–1217). See Avisa of Gloucester.

ISABEL OF PORTUGAL (1397–1471). See Isabella of Portugal.

ISABEL OF PORTUGAL (1428–1496). Queen-consort of John II of Castile. Name variations: Isabella. Born 1428; died Aug 15, 1496, in Arévalo; dau. of Isabella of Braganza (1402–1465) and John of Portugal, grand master of Santiago; became 2nd wife of Juan also known as John II (1404–1454), king of Castile and Leon (r. 1406–1454), July 22, 1447; children: Isabella I (1451–1504), queen of Castile; Alfonso or Alphonso (1453–1468). ❖ Wed John II of Castile, a marriage arranged by his chief minister, Alvaro de Luna, who saw it as a political match; quickly became a rival to Alvaro's power rather than a pawn through which he could continue to control John II; eventually, persuaded husband to strip the minister of his power and send him to the scaffold (1453); when John died (1454), had to leave the court; with son and daughter, took up residence at Arévalo; became deeply depressed which degenerated into a form of madness, a prolonged insanity that made her irrelevant to the unfolding political struggle over succession. ❖ See also *Women in World History*.

ISABEL OF SPAIN (1501–1526). See Elisabeth of Habsburg.

ISABEL OF URGEL (fl. 1065). Queen of Aragon. Dau. of Armengol III, count of Urgel, and Sancha of Aragon (d. 1073); m. Sancho Ramirez, king of Aragon (1063–1094) and Navarre (1076–1094), c. 1065 (div. in 1071); children: Peter I (1069–1104), king of Aragon and Navarre (r. 1094–1104); possibly Alphonso I (1073–1134), king of Aragon and Navarre (r. 1104–1134); possibly Ramiro II (c. 1075–1157), king of Aragon (r. 1134–1157).

ISABEL OF VERMANDOIS (d. before 1147). Countess of Warrenne and Surrey. Name variations: Elizabeth of Vermandois; Elizabeth de Crepi or de Crépi; Isabel de Warenne; Isabel de Warrenne. Died before July 1147; dau. of Hugh the Great (b. 1057), count of Vermandois, and Adelaide of Vermandois (d. 1123); m. Robert of Meulan, 1st earl of Leicester; m. William de Warenne, 2nd earl of Warenne and Surrey (1088–1138); children: (1st m.) Waleran of Meulan also known as Waleran de Beaumont (1104–1166), earl of Worcester; Isabel Beaumont (c. 1104–d. after 1172); Robert Beaumont, 2nd earl of Leicester; (2nd m.) William de Warrenne (1119–1148), 3rd earl of Warrenne and Surrey (r. 1138–1148), a crusader who died in the Holy Land; Adelicia de Warrenne (d. 1178); Gundred de Warrenne (d. after

1166, who m. Robert de Newburgh, 2nd earl of Warwick, and William de Lancaster, Lord of Kendal); Ralph de Warrenne; Rainald de Warrenne.

ISABEL PLANTAGENET (c. 1317–c. 1347). English noblewoman. Born c. 1317; died c. 1347; dau. of Henry, earl of Lancaster (r. 1281–1345) and Maud Chaworth (1282–c. 1322). ❖ Entered a convent (1337), eventually becoming the abbess of Amesbury.

ISABEL STEWART (d. 1494). *See Stewart, Isabel.*

ISABELLA.
Spanish for Elizabeth.
Variant of Isabel.

ISABELLA (b. 1180). French noblewoman and poet. Born in 1180 in southern France. ❖ Wrote troubadour poetry during the height of the troubadour period; probably met the troubadour and smith Elias Cairel, with whom she composed tensons, in Italy (c. 1220). Only one of her poems has survived, a tenson with Elias, in which the 2 discuss the love they once had. ❖ See also *Women in World History.*

ISABELLA (1206–1251). Lady Annandale. Name variations: Isabel or Isobel; Isabel Dunkeld; Isobella le Scot. Born 1206; died 1251; interred at Saltre Abbey, Stilton, Gloucester; dau. of Maude of Chester (1171–1233) and David Dunkeld, 1st earl of Huntingdon; sister of Margaret, countess of Huntingdon (d. 1228) and Ada Dunkeld; m. Robert Bruce (d. 1245), 5th Lord of Annandale, 1209; children: Robert Bruce of Annandale, known as The Competitor (1210–1295); Beatrice Bruce (d. 1276, who m. Hugo Neville).

ISABELLA (fl. 1219–1269). *See Zabel.*

ISABELLA (d. 1282). Queen of Beirut. Died in 1282; eldest dau. of John II of Beirut (d. 1264) and Alice de la Roche of Athens; m. Hugh II (d. 1267), child-king of Cyprus (r. 1253–1267); m. Hamo L'Étranger (Edmund the Foreigner) of England (soon died); m. Nicholas L'Aleman; m. William Barlais. ❖ Reigned (1264–82).

ISABELLA (1332–1382). English princess and countess of Bedford. Name variations: Isabel Plantagenet; Isabella de Coucy. Born in Woodstock, Oxfordshire, England, June 16, 1332; died before Oct 7, 1382; dau. of Philippa of Hainault (1314–1369) and Edward III (1312–1377), king of England (r. 1327–1377); m. Enguerrand VII (1340–1397), lord of Coucy and earl of Bedford, July 27, 1365; children: Mary de Coucy; Philippa de Coucy.

ISABELLA (r. 1398–1412). Countess of Foix. Name variations: Isabel or Isabella of Foix. Reigned from 1398 to 1412; dau. of Gaston III Phebus (Febus or Fébus), count of Foix (r. 1343–1391); sister of Matthieu de Castelbon, count of Foix (1391–1398); m. Archambaud de Graille; children: at least one son, Jean de Graille, count of Foix. ❖ Following death of brother Matthieu de Castelbon (1398), ruled Foix for next 14 years, until her own death.

ISABELLA, Queen of Spain (1602–1644). *See Elizabeth Valois.*

ISABELLA, Saint (1225–1270). *See Isabelle.*

ISABELLA I (1451–1504). Queen of Castile. Name variations: Isabel I; Isabella of Spain; Isabella I of Castile; Isabella the Catholic or Isabel la Católica. Born April 22, 1451, at Madrigal de las Altas Torres, Spain; died Nov 26, 1504, at Medina del Campo, Spain; dau. of Juan also known as John II (1405–1454), king of Castile (r. 1406–1454), and his 2nd wife Isabel of Portugal (1428–1496); m. Fernando also known as Ferdinand II, king of Aragon (r. 1479–1516), Oct 19, 1469, at Valladolid; children: Isabella of Asturias (1471–1498); Juana la Loca (1479–1555); Maria of Castile (1482–1517); Catherine of Aragon (1485–1536); Juan or John (1478–1497, who m. Margaret of Austria [1480–1530]). ❖ Prominent figure in history, sponsor of Christopher Columbus' voyages of discovery, who is credited, along with husband King Ferdinand II of Aragon, with the creation of modern unified Spain; was recognized as heir to throne of Castile (1468); proclaimed queen (1474); with husband, enjoyed a remarkable partnership, successful both as a domestic arrangement and as a political alliance, but was fiercely protective of her royal prerogatives, and it was she, not Ferdinand, who dictated the terms under which the partners shared authority at all; established Spanish Inquisition (1480); conquered Granada, expelled Jews, and sponsored Columbus' 1st voyage (1492). ❖ See also Felipe Fernández-Armesto, *Ferdinand and Isabella* (Taplinger, 1975); Peggy K. Liss, *Isabel the Queen: Life and Times* (Oxford University Press, 1992); and *Women in World History.*

ISABELLA II (1830–1904). Queen of Spain. Name variations: Isabel II or Maria Isabella Louisa. Born Oct 10, 1830, in Madrid, Spain; died April 9, 1904, in Paris, France; eldest surviving daughter born to Ferdinand VII, king of Spain (r. 1813–1833), and his 4th wife, Maria Cristina I of Naples (1806–1878); m. Francisco de Asís or Asiz, Oct 10, 1846 (died April 17, 1902); children: Ferdinand or Fernando (1850–1850); Maria Isabel Francisca (b. 1851); Maria Cristina (1854–1854); Alfonso or Alphonso XII (1857–1885), king of Spain (r. 1875–1885); Pilar (b. 1861); Maria de la Paz (1862–1946); Eulalia (b. 1864, who m. Anthony Bourbon, 5th duke of Galliera). ❖ Reigned 1833 to 1868, during the nation's difficult transition from absolutism to constitutional monarchy; proclaimed monarch with Maria Cristina as regent (Oct 24, 1833); endured 1st Carlist War against her monarchy (1833–39); declared of age to rule (Nov 10, 1843), but had little preparation for governing; achieved some popularity for her generosity; nearly assassinated twice (May 1847 and Feb 2, 1852); as a ruler attempting to moderate the partisan disputes of Spanish politics, remained too partial to the conservatives, refusing to admit the Progressives to power; in the "September Revolution," her loyalists were defeated at the battle of Alcolea (Sept 28, 1868); left for France and exile (Sept 30, 1868); abdicated in favor of son Alphonso (June 25, 1870). ❖ See also Peter de Polnay, *A Queen of Spain: Isabel II* (Hollis & Carter, 1962); and *Women in World History.*

ISABELLA I OF JERUSALEM (d. 1205). Queen of Jerusalem. Name variations: Isabel I. Reigned 1192–1205; died 1205; dau. of Amalric I, king of Jerusalem (r. 1162–1174), and Maria Comnena; half-sister of Sibylla (1160–1190); m. Humfred of Turon also known as Humphrey IV, lord of Torun; m. Conrad of Montferrat, margrave of Montferrat and king of Jerusalem (r. 1190–1192); m. Henry II of Champagne, king of Jerusalem (r. 1192–1197); m. Aimery de Lusignan (brother of Guy de Lusignan) also known as Amalric II, king of Jerusalem (r. 1197–1205), king of Cyprus, in 1197; children: (2nd m.) Marie of Montferrat (d. 1212); (3rd m.) Alice of Champagne (who m. her stepbrother Hugh I, king of Cyprus); Isabella of Cyprus (fl. 1230s, who m. Henry of Antioch); (4th m.) Melisande (who m. Bohemund IV of Antioch).

ISABELLA II OF JERUSALEM (1212–1228). *See Yolande of Brienne.*

ISABELLA CAPET (fl. 1250). Queen of Navarre. Fl. around 1250; dau. of Margaret of Provence (1221–1295) and Louis IX, king of France (r. 1226–1270); sister of Philip III the Bold (1245–1285), king of France (r. 1270–1285); m. Teobaldo also known as Theobald II, king of Navarre (r. 1253–1270).

ISABELLA CLARA EUGENIA OF AUSTRIA (1566–1633). Spanish ruler of the Netherlands and archduchess of Austria. Name variations: Infanta Isabella, Archduchess Isabella, Isabella d'Autriche; Isabella Clara of Spain. Born Isabella Clara Eugenia in 1566; died in Brussels in 1633; dau. of Philip II (1527–1598), king of Spain (r. 1556–1598), and king of Portugal as Philip I (r. 1580–1598), and Elizabeth of Valois (1545–1568); m. Albrecht also known as Albert the Pious, archduke of Austria (governor of the Spanish Netherlands), in 1599. ❖ Received the low countries from father for her dowry (1598); with husband, was co-ruler of the Spanish Netherlands (1598–1621); after his death (1621), was sole governor; remained ruler of the Netherlands, as regent for nephew Philip IV, until her death. Her skill in archery was celebrated in paintings and poems.

ISABELLA DE FORTIBUS (1237–1293). *See Isabella de Redvers.*

ISABELLA DE FORZ (1237–1293). *See Isabella de Redvers.*

ISABELLA DEL BALZO (d. 1533). Queen of Naples. Died 1533; m. Frederick IV (1452–1504), king of Naples (r. 1496–1501, deposed and died while in prison), in 1487; children: Fernando (b. 1488), duke of Calabria; Alfonso of Naples; Cesare of Naples; Charlotte of Naples (d. 1506, who m. Gui XV, count of Laval); Isabel of Naples (d. 1550); Julia of Naples (d. 1542, who m. Gian Giorgio, margrave of Montferrat). Frederick's 1st wife was Anna of Savoy (1455–1480).

ISABELLA DE LORRAINE (1410–1453). *See Isabelle of Lorraine.*

ISABELLA DE REDVERS (1237–1293). Countess of Devon and Aumale. Name variations: Isabella de Fortibus; Isabella de Forz. Born 1237 in England; died 1293 in England; dau. of Baldwin de Redvers, 7th earl of Devon, and Amice de Clare; m. Count William de Forz of Aumale, c. 1249 (died 1260); children: Avelina de Forz (1259–1274), countess of Holderness; and one son. ❖ English heiress of great wealth, married a powerful landholder of Yorkshire at age 12; was left extensive properties at time of his death (1260); on death of only brother, inherited even more wealth and became countess of Devon (1262); refused to remarry; was actively involved in political tensions of her time, a period in which England's barons were planning rebellions against King Henry III, under leadership of Simon de Montfort; probably sided with fellow nobles, but played role of royal supporter on occasions when it would help preserve her estates; also spent much time in court, suing and being sued over various issues relating to her rights as an overlord and property holder; sold Isle of Wight to the king (1293). ❖ See also *Women in World History.*

ISABELLA D'ESTE (1474–1539). *See Este, Isabella d'.*

ISABELLA GONZAGA (1474–1539). *See Este, Isabella d'.*

ISABELLA LEONARDA (1620–1704). *See Leonarda, Isabella.*

ISABELLA OF ANGOULÊME (1186–1246). Queen of England. Name variations: Isabelle d'Angoulême or Angouleme; Isabel of Angoulême. Born 1186 (some sources cite 1187) in Angoulême; died 1246 at abbey of Fontevrault, France; dau. of Aymer Taillefer, count of Angoulême, and Alice de Courtenay (d. 1211); m. John I Lackland (1166–1216), king of England (r. 1199–1216), in 1200; m. Hugh X, count of Lusignan, about 1218; children: (1st marriage) Henry III (1206–1272), king of England (r. 1216–1272); Richard (1209–1272), earl of Cornwall, king of the Romans; Joan, queen of Scotland (1210–1238, who m. Alexander II of Scotland); Isabella of England (1214–1241, who m. Frederick II, Holy Roman emperor); Eleanor of Montfort, countess of Leicester (1215–1275, who m. the earl of Pembroke and then Simon de Montfort, founder of the English Parliament); (2nd m.) Alice le Brun (d. 1255); Margaret le Brun (d. 1283); Guy Lusignan; William de Valence, 1st earl of Pembroke (d. 1296). ❖ At 14, married King John I Lackland, even though she had been betrothed to nobleman Hugh de Lusignan; like husband, was ambitious and power-hungry; aided John with his various struggles to maintain English lands on the Continent and with his own rebellious barons during his troubled reign; when John died (1216), saw to it that young son Henry was put on the throne safely and was surrounded by capable advisors, then returned to her native France and married Hugh, her fiancé of childhood; during last years, was caught up in several scandals involving conspiracy against the French king, including allegations that she had paid two cooks to try to poison him; fled to the abbey of Fontevrault, where she remained until her death. ❖ See also *Women in World History.*

ISABELLA OF ARAGON (1243–1271). Queen of France. Name variations: Isabel or Isabelle. Born 1243 (some sources cite 1247); died 1271; dau. of James I, king of Aragon (r. 1213–1276), and Iolande of Hungary (1215–1251); became 1st wife of Philip III the Bold (1245–1285), king of France (r. 1270–1285), in 1262; children: Blanche of France (c. 1266–1305, who m. Rudolf III, king of Bohemia); Philip IV (1268–1214), king of France (r. 1285–1314); Charles I (1270–1325), count of Valois. Philip's 2nd wife was Marie of Brabant (c. 1260–1321).

ISABELLA OF ARAGON (c. 1300–1330). Holy Roman empress. Name variations: Elisabeth or Elizabeth of Aragon, queen of Germany. Born c. 1300 or 1302; died July 2, 1330; m. Friedrich also known as Frederick I (III) the Fair of Austria (1289–1330), king of Germany (r. 1314–1322), (co-regent) Holy Roman emperor (r. 1314–1325).

ISABELLA OF ASTURIAS (1471–1498). Queen of Portugal. Name variations: Isabel Trastamara, princess of Asturias. Born May 31, 1471 (some sources cite 1470), in Duenas; died in childbirth, Aug 23 or 25, 1498, in Saragosa; dau. of Isabella I of Castile (1451–1504) and Ferdinand II, king of Aragon (r. 1479–1516); m. Prince Afonso also known as Alphonso (1475–1491), heir to the Portuguese throne, April 18, 1490 (he died from a riding accident shortly thereafter); m. Miguel also known as Manuel I the Fortunate (1469–1521), king of Portugal (r. 1495–1521), Sept or Oct 1497; children: surviving infant son Miguel (1498–1500) died 2 years after his mother.

ISABELLA OF AUSTRIA (1503–1539). *See Isabella of Portugal.*

ISABELLA OF AUSTRIA (1566–1633). *See Isabella Clara Eugenia.*

ISABELLA OF BRAGANZA (1402–1465). Princess of Braganza. Name variations: Isabel de Barcelos. Born Oct 1402; died Oct 26, 1465, in Arévalo; dau. of Alphonso, duke of Braganza, and Beatriz Pereira (c. 1380–1412), countess of Barcellos; m. Joao or John of Portugal, grand master of Santiago, Nov 11, 1424; children: Diego (b. 1426); Isabel of Portugal (1428–1496); Beatrice of Beja (1430–1506); Filippa (b. 1432).

ISABELLA OF BRAGANZA (1459–1521). Duchess of Braganza. Name variations: Isabella of Beja. Born in 1459; died in April 1521; dau. of Beatrice of Beja (1430–1506) and Fernando also known as Ferdinand, duke of Beja and Viseu; m. Fernando also known as Ferdinand, duke of Braganza, on Sept 14, 1472; children: Filippe or Philip (b. 1475), duke of Guimaraes; Jaime or James (1479–1532), duke of Braganza (who m. Eleonore de Guzman); Diniz or Denis (b. 1481); Alfonso or Alphonso (b. around 1482); Margarida (1477–1483); Caterina (1483, died young).

ISABELLA OF BRAGANZA (c. 1512–1576). Duchess of Guimaraes. Name variations: Isabel of Braganza. Born c. 1512; died Sept 16, 1576, at Villa Vicosa, Evora; m. Edward also known as Duarte (1515–1540, son of Manuel I of Portugal and Maria of Castile), duke of Guimaraes, April 23, 1537; children: Maria of Portugal (1538–1577), duchess of Parma; Catherine of Portugal (1540–1614); Duarte (1541–1576), duke of Guimaraes.

ISABELLA OF BRIENNE (1212–1228). *See Yolande of Brienne.*

ISABELLA OF BUCHAN (fl. 1290–1310). Scottish royal and countess of Buchan. Name variations: Isabel. Fl. between 1290 and 1310; dau. of Duncan Fife (1262–1288), 9th earl of Fife (r. 1270–1288), and Joan de Clare (c. 1268–after 1322); sister of Duncan Fife (1285–1351), 10th earl of Fife; m. John Comyn, 3rd earl of Buchan (d. 1313?, constable of Scotland). ❖ Was a staunch supporter of Robert the Bruce of Scotland, in direct opposition to husband; standing in for brother, the earl of Fife (who was being held prisoner by the British), bravely volunteered to crown Robert king of Scotland as Robert I (1306); to atone for this crime, was besieged in the castle of Berwick by the English under leadership of Edward I; when the castle was taken, was imprisoned for 4 years in the castle of Roxburgh in a suspended iron and wooden cage; husband was later killed by Robert the Bruce.

ISABELLA OF CAPUA (d. 1559). *See Gonzaga, Isabella.*

ISABELLA OF CROY-DULMEN (1856–1931). Archduchess. Born in Dulmen, Feb 27, 1856; died in Budapest, Hungary, Sept 5, 1931; m. Archduke Friedrich (1856–1936); children: Maria Christina (1879–1962); Maria Anna (1882–1940); Gabriele (1887–1954); Isabella (1888–1973); Maria Alice (1893–1962); Albrecht also known as Albert (1897–1955).

ISABELLA OF CYPRUS (fl. 1230s). Princess of Jerusalem. Name variations: Isabel. Fl. in 1230s; dau. of Henry II of Champagne, king of Jerusalem (r. 1192–1197), and Isabella I of Jerusalem (d. 1205); m. Henry of Antioch (son of Bohemond IV, prince of Antioch); children: Hugh III (1267–1284), king of Cyprus (r. 1267–1284), king of Jerusalem (r. 1268–1284); Margaret of Antioch-Lusignan (fl. 1283–1291).

ISABELLA OF CYPRUS (fl. 1250s). Queen of Jerusalem and Cyprus. Fl. in 1250s; dau. of Henry I, king of Cyprus (r. 1218–1253) and Plaisance of Antioch (d. 1261); sister of Hugh II, king of Cyprus (r. 1253–1267); m. Hugh III, king of Cyprus (r. 1267–1284), king of Jerusalem (r. 1268–1284); children: John I, king of Cyprus (r. 1284–1285); Henry II, king of Cyprus (r. 1285–1324); Amalric of Tyre (d. 1310), governor of Cyprus.

ISABELLA OF ENGLAND (1214–1241). Holy Roman empress. Name variations: Isabel Plantagenet; Elizabeth, empress of France. Born 1214 in Gloucester, Gloucestershire, England; died Dec 1, 1241, in Foggia, Italy; buried in Andria, Sicily; dau. of John I Lackland (1166–1216), king of England (r. 1199–1216), and Isabella of Angoulême (1186–1246); became 3rd wife of Frederick II (b. 1194–1250), Holy Roman emperor (r. 1215–1250), July 15, 1235 (some sources cite July 20); children: Jordan of Germany (b. 1236); Margaret of Germany (1237–1270, who m. Albert of Thuringia); Agnes (1237–1237); Henry of Germany (1238–1253), king of Jerusalem. Frederick II's 1st wife was Constance of Aragon (d. 1222); his 2nd wife was Yolande of Brienne (1212–1228). ❖ See also *Women in World History.*

ISABELLA OF FRANCE (1296–1358). Queen consort of England. Name variations: Isabel of Buchan; Isabella the Fair; She-Wolf of France. Born in 1296 (some sources erroneously cite 1292), in Paris, France; died at Hertford castle and thought to be buried at Christ Church, Newgate, London, Aug 22, 1358; dau. of Philip IV the Fair (1268–1314), king of France (r. 1285–1314) and Joan I of Navarre (1273–1305); sister of Charles IV, king of France (r. 1322–1328); m. Edward II (1284–1327), king of England (r. 1307–1327), on Jan 25 or 28, 1308; children: Edward of Windsor (1312–1377, later Edward III, king of England, r. 1327–1377, who m. Philippa of Hainault); John of Eltham (1316–1336, became earl of Cornwall, 1328); Eleanor of

Woodstock (1318–1355), duchess of Guelders; Joan of the Tower (1321–1362), queen of Scotland. ❖ Married Edward II of England (1308); granted the counties of Montreuil and Ponthieu as her dower; quickly began to confront realities of husband's court politics and personal behavior, especially his relationship with dominating boyhood friend, Piers Gaveston; as with the rest of the court, detested the control Gaveston wielded over husband (Gaveston was soon beheaded); gained influence with husband as she matured, but relationship soured noticeably when he acquired a new favorite, Hugh Despenser the Younger (1322); saw her estates sequestered by the king at urging of Despenser; with negotiations between England and France in tatters, sailed for France and brought the 2 sides together in agreement (1325); when Despenser convinced the king to send son Edward to sign agreement in his place, took full advantage of Despenser's mistake by pledging not to return to England with son as long as Despenser was there; led a rebellion against husband with disaffected English nobles, including Roger Mortimer (1325–27); enjoyed short period of power (1327–30), when she and Mortimer ruled England in name of her young son, Edward III. ❖ See also *Women in World History.*

ISABELLA OF FRANCE (1389–c. 1410). *See Isabella of Valois.*

ISABELLA OF GLOUCESTER (c. 1167–1217). *See Avisa of Gloucester.*

ISABELLA OF GUISE (1900–1983). Countess of Harcourt. Name variations: Isabella de Guise; Isabella Murat; Princesse Isabelle de France. Born Nov 27, 1900; died Dec 12, 1983; dau. of Isabella of Orleans (b. 1878) and John (1874–1940), duke of Guise; m. Bruno, count of Harcourt, Sept 15, 1923; m. Prince Pierre Murat, July 12, 1934; children: (1st m.) Bernard, Gilone, Isabelle and Monique.

ISABELLA OF HAINAULT (1170–1190). Queen of France. Name variations: Isabel; Elizabeth of Hainault or Hainaut. Born at Lille in 1170; died in childbirth in 1190; dau. of Baldwin V, count of Hainault, and Margaret of Alsace (c. 1135–1194, sister of Philip of Alsace); m. Philip II Augustus (1165–1223), king of France (r. 1180–1223), in 1180; children: Louis VIII (1187–1226), king of France (r. 1223–1226). ❖ The daughter of a count from one of the important Flemish feudal territories, was crowned queen at St. Denis (May 29, 1180); despite receiving praise from certain chroniclers, failed to win the affections of husband, who, while waging a war against Flanders (1184), was angered at seeing her father support the opposing side and called a council at Sens for the purpose of nullifying the marriage. ❖ See also *Women in World History.*

ISABELLA OF MAR (d. 1296). Queen of Scotland. Name variations: Isabel; Isobel of Mar. Died 1296; dau. of Donald, 6th earl of Mar, and Helen (fl. 1275, possibly dau. of Llywelyn the Great); became 1st wife of Robert I the Bruce, king of Scotland (r. 1306–1329), c. 1295; children: Margaret Bruce (1296–1316). Robert I's 2nd wife was Elizabeth de Burgh (d. 1327).

ISABELLA OF NAPLES (1470–1524). Duchess of Milan. Name variations: Isabella of Aragon; Isabella Sforza; Isabella di Bari; duchesa di Bari. Born Oct 2, 1470; died in Naples in 1524; dau. of Alphonso II (b. 1448), king of Naples, and Ippolita (1446–1484); m. Giangaleazzo or Gian Galeazzo Sforza (1469–1496), 6th duke of Milan; sister-in-law of Caterina Sforza (c. 1462–1509); children: Francesco (d. 1511); Bona Sforza (1493–1557, who m. Sigismund, king of Poland).

ISABELLA OF ORLEANS (1848–1919). *See Maria Isabella.*

ISABELLA OF ORLEANS (1878–1961). Duchess of Guise. Name variations: Isabella d'Orleans. Born May 7, 1878; died April 21, 1961; dau. of Maria Isabella (1848–1919) and Louis Philippe (1838–1894), count of Paris; m. Jean also known as John (1874–1940), duke of Guise, on Oct 30, 1899; children: Isabella of Guise (b. 1900); Françoise of Guise (1902–1953); Anne of Guise (b. 1906, who m. Amadeus, duke of Aosta); Henry (b. 1908), count of Paris.

ISABELLA OF ORLEANS (1911–2003). Countess of Paris. Name variations: Isabelle d'Orléans et Bragance; Isabella d'Eu. Born Isabel Marie Amélie Louise Victoire Thérèse Jeanne d'Orléans-Bragance, Aug 13, 1911, at Chateau d'Eu in Normandy; died July 5, 2003, in Paris; dau. of Pedro de Alcántra, prince of Grao Para, and Elizabeth Dobrzenska (b. 1875); m. her cousin, Henry (b. 1908), count of Paris, April 8, 1931 (died 1999); children: Isabella of Guise (b. 1932); Henry of Clermont (b. 1933, who m. Maria Theresa of Wurttemberg); Helene of Guise (b. 1934); François (1935–1960); Michael and James (b. 1941); Thibaut (b. 1948). ❖ Was married to the pretender to the French throne; lived in exile in Belgium, Brazil, Morocco and Spain; returned

to France (1950); wrote 3 volumes of memoirs and biographies of Marie Antoinette (*Moi*) and Maria Amelia.

ISABELLA OF PARMA (1692–1766). *See Farnese, Elizabeth.*

ISABELLA OF PARMA (1741–1763). Princess of Parma. Born Dec 31, 1741, in Buen Retiro near Madrid, Spain; died Nov 27, 1763, in Vienna; dau. of Louise Elizabeth (1727–1759) and Philip de Bourbon (1720–1765, duke of Parma and son of Elizabeth Farnese); became first wife of Joseph II (1741–1790), emperor of Austria (r. 1780–1790), Holy Roman emperor (r. 1765–1790), on Oct 6, 1760; his 2nd wife was Maria Josepha of Bavaria (1739–1767).

ISABELLA OF POLAND (1519–1559). Queen of Hungary. Name variations: Izabella Szapolyai. Born 1519; died 1559; dau. of Bona Sforza (1493–1557) and Zygmunt I Stary also known as Sigismund I the Elder (1467–1548), king of Poland (r. 1506–1548); m. Jan Zapolya also known as John Zapolya (1457–1540), king of Hungary (r. 1526–1540); children: John (II) Sigismund Zapolya, king of Hungary (r. 1540–1571).

ISABELLA OF PORTUGAL (1271–1336). *See Elizabeth of Portugal.*

ISABELLA OF PORTUGAL (1397–1471). Duchess of Burgundy. Name variations: Isabel of Portugal. Born Feb 21, 1397, in Evora; died Dec 17, 1471 (some sources cite 1472 or 1473), in Nieppe; interred in Dijon; dau. of Joao I also known as John I of Aviz (1357–1433), king of Portugal (sometimes called the Bastard and the Great, r. 1385–1433) and Philippa of Lancaster (1359–1415, who was the dau. of John of Gaunt); sister of Prince Henry the Navigator and Edward I, king of Portugal; became 3rd wife of Philip the Good (1396–1467), duke of Burgundy (r. 1419–1467), on Jan 10, 1430; children: Charles the Bold (1433–1477), duke of Burgundy (r. 1467–1477). Philip the Good's 1st wife was Michelle Valois (1394–1422); his 2nd wife was Bonne of Artois (d. 1425).

ISABELLA OF PORTUGAL (1503–1539). Holy Roman empress. Name variations: Isabel of Portugal; Isabella of Austria. Born Oct 24, 1503, in Lisbon; died May 1, 1539, in Toledo; dau. of Manuel I the Fortunate (1469–1521), king of Portugal (r. 1495–1521), and his second wife Maria of Castile (1482–1517); m. Charles V (1500–1558), king of Spain (r. 1516–1556), king of the Romans (r. 1519–1530), Holy Roman Emperor (r. 1519–1558), on Mar 10, 1526; children: Philip II (b. 1527), king of Spain (r. 1556–1598), king of Portugal as Philip I (r. 1580–1598); Joanna of Austria (1535–1573); Fernando; Marie of Austria (1528–1603). ❖ Governed as regent of Spain during husband's prolonged absences from the peninsula; took an active role in the policy-making process, suggesting her own solutions rather than merely accepting the advisors' recommendations; actively participated in negotiations of marital alliances between the French and Spanish royal families. ❖ See also *Women in World History.*

ISABELLA OF PORTUGAL (1797–1818). *See Maria Isabel of Portugal.*

ISABELLA OF SPAIN.
See Isabella I (1451–1504).
See Isabella II (1830–1904).

ISABELLA OF VALOIS (1389–c. 1410). Queen of England. Name variations: Isabella de France; Isabella of France; Isabel Valois. Born Nov 9, 1389, in Paris, France; died in childbirth, Sept 13, 1410 (some sources cite 1409), in Blois, Anjou, France; buried at the Church of the Celestines, in Paris, c. 1624; 2nd dau. of Charles VI the Mad, king of France (r. 1380–1422), and Isabeau of Bavaria (1371–1435); became 2nd wife of Richard II (1367–1400), king of England (r. 1377–1399), Oct 31, 1396; became 1st wife of Charles Valois (1391–1465), duke of Orléans and count of Angoulême, June 29, 1406; children: (2nd m.) Jeanne de Orléans (c. 1410–1432, who m. Jean II d'Alencon). ❖ Became child bride of king of England (1396), who was deposed and imprisoned 3 years later; led rebel army against husband's foes, but was unsuccessful; was judged too immature, and little actual threat, to be charged with any crime; was finally allowed to return to France; wed her cousin (1406). ❖ See also *Women in World History.*

ISABELLA THE CATHOLIC (1451–1504). *See Isabella I.*

ISABELLE (1225–1270). French princess and saint. Name variations: Isabel; Saint Isabelle; Blessed Isabelle. Born in Mar 1225; died in 1270; dau. of Blanche of Castile (1188–1252) and Louis VIII, king of France (r. 1223–1226); sister of Saint Louis IX (1214–1270), king of France (r. 1226–1270). ❖ Known for her piety, was sickly throughout her life; when Pope Innocent IV championed her marriage to Conrad IV, told the pope that she would rather be last in the ranks of the Lord's virgins than 1st in the world as empress; founded abbey of Longchamp (1258); lived there for the last 10 years of her life without taking vows, repairing clothes for the poor. Feast day is Feb 22.

ISABELLE D'AUTRICHE.
See Elisabeth of Habsburg (1554–1592).
See Isabella Clara Eugenia of Austria (1566–1633).

ISABELLE DE CLARE (c. 1167–1217). *See Avisa of Gloucester.*

ISABELLE D'ORLÉANS ET BRAGANCE (1911–2003). *See Isabella of Orleans.*

ISABELLE OF AUSTRIA (1554–1592). *See Elisabeth of Habsburg.*

ISABELLE OF BAVARIA (1371–1435). *See Isabeau of Bavaria.*

ISABELLE OF BOURBON (d. 1465). Countess of Charolois. Name variations: Isabel or Isabella of Bourbon. Died in 1465 or 1466; dau. of Agnes of Burgundy (d. 1476) and Charles I, duke of Bourbon (r. 1434–1456); 2nd wife of Charles the Bold (1433–1477), duke of Burgundy (r. 1467–1477); children: Mary of Burgundy (1457–1482), who m. Maximilian I, Holy Roman emperor). Charles the Bold's 1st wife was Catherine de France (1428–1446); his 3rd wife was Margaret of York (1446–1503).

ISABELLE OF CORNWALL (fl. 14th c.). Marquise of Montferrat. Married William V the Great, marquis of Montferrat; children: Irene of Montferrat (who m. Andronicus II Paleologus, emperor of Nicaea, r. 1282–1328); possibly Beatrix of Montferrat (who m. Andre [Guigues] VI, dauphin de Viennois).

ISABELLE OF FRANCE (1349–1372). French princess. Name variations: Isabella de France; Isabella or Isabelle of Valois. Born 1349; died 1372; dau. of Jean or John II the Good (1319–1364), king of France (r. 1350–1364), and Bona of Bohemia (1315–1349); sister of Charles V (1337–1380), king of France (r. 1364–1380), and Jane of France (1343–1373), queen of Navarre; m. John Galeas Visconti also known as Giangaleazzo or Gian Galeazzo Visconti (1351–1402), lord of Milan (r. 1378–1402), duke of Milan (r. 1396–1402), in 1364; children: a son who died young; Valentina Visconti (1366–1408); and 2 others. ❖ See also *Women in World History.*

ISABELLE OF GLOUCESTER (c. 1167–1217). *See Avisa of Gloucester.*

ISABELLE OF LORRAINE (1410–1453). Queen of Naples. Name variations: Isabel, Isabella, Isabelle or Isabeau de Lorraine; Isabel of Bar. Born c. 1410 in Lorraine, France; died 1453 in Anjou; dau. of Charles II, duke of Lorraine, and Margaret of Bavaria; m. René I the Good (1408–1480), duke of Lorraine and Bar, duke of Provence, duke of Anjou and Guise, and later king of Naples; children: John II (1424–1470), duke of Calabria; Margaret of Anjou (1429–1482); Yolande of Vaudemont (1428–1483, who m. Frederick of Vaudemont). ❖ Like many educated noblewomen of her age, patronized the arts and helped endow several colleges; when a rival noble kidnapped husband, gathered an army and rode at its head, gaining her husband's release; also served as his regent after he conquered Sicily.

ISABELLE OF SAVOY (d. 1383). Duchess of Bourbon. Name variations: Isabelle of Valois; Isabella de Valois. Died Aug 26, 1383 (some sources cite 1388); dau. of Charles I, count of Valois, and Mahaut de Chatillon (d. 1358); m. Pierre or Peter I (1311–1356), duke of Bourbon (r. 1342–1356), on Jan 25, 1336; children: Jeanne de Bourbon (1338–1378, who m. Charles V, king of France); Blanche of Bourbon (c. 1338–1361, who m. Peter the Cruel, king of Castile and León); Marie de Bourbon (fl. 1350s), prioress of Poissy.

ISABELLE OF VALOIS (d. 1383). *See Isabelle of Savoy.*

ISAIA, Nana (1934—). *See Issaia, Nana.*

ISAKHOVA, Natalya. *See Issakova, Natalia.*

ISAKOVA, Maria (1918—). Russian speedskater. Born Maria Grigorevna Isakova, July 5, 1918, in Kirov, USSR. ❖ Won the World distance championships (1948, 1949, 1950); won 6 Soviet championships. ❖ See also *Women in World History.*

ISAKSEN, Lone (1941—). Danish ballet dancer. Born Nov 30, 1941, in Copenhagen, Denmark; m. Lawrence Rhodes. ❖ Danced with Scandinavian Ballet for 1 season as soloist; joined Joffrey Ballet in NY where she created roles in Joffrey's *Gamelan* (1963), Ailey's *Feast of Ashes* (1962), and Arpino's *Incubus* (1962); joined Harkness Ballet—after the

Joffrey disbanded—where she created roles in Hodes' *The Abyss* (1965), Butler's *After Eden* (1966), Neumeier's *Stages and Reflections* (1968), and others; performed with Dutch National Ballet (1970–71) before retiring.

ISARESCU, Andreea (1984—). Romanian gymnast. Name variations: Andreea Florenta Isarescu. Born July 3, 1984, in Onesti, Romania. ❖ At World championships, won a gold medal in team all-around (1999); at Sydney Olympics, won a gold medal for team all-around (2000).

ISBERGE (c. 753–807). *See Gisela.*

ISCAH. Biblical woman. Dau. of Haran; sister of Milcah and Lot.

ISE (877–940). Japanese poet. Name variations: Lady Ise. Pronunciation: EE-say. Born in 877 (some sources cite 875) in an unknown location; real name is not known (Ise was the Japanese province of which her father was once governor); died 940 (some sources cite 938), most likely in the capital, Kyoto; dau. of Fujiwara no Tsugikage, governor of Ise and, later, Yamamoto; lover of Prince Atsuyoshi; concubine of the Emperor Uda; children: (with Prince Atsuyoshi) daughter Nakatsukasa (a poet); (with Uda) Prince Yuki-Akari. ❖ Court woman, known as Lady Ise, who was considered one of the most accomplished poets of her age; is thought to have entered the service of Empress Onshi, consort of Emperor Uda (c. 892); was one of a larger group of Japanese women writers of this time, whose prominence is said to be unparalleled in world literature. More than 500 of her poems, characterized by wit and passion, were compiled in various anthologies. ❖ See also *Women in World History.*

ISELDA, Lady (fl. 12th c.). Provençal troubadour. Fl. in 12th century in Provence. ❖ Wrote an unusual *tenson*, a humorous anti-marriage poem, with 2 other women—Alais and Carenza. ❖ See also *Women in World History.*

ISEUT DE CAPIO (1140–?). French noblewoman and poet. Born in 1140 in southern France. ❖ A troubadour in southern France during height of troubadour period, was probably from town of Les Chapelins. Only one of her poems still survives, a *tenson*, or dialogue, written with another female troubadour, Almucs de Castelnau.

ISHAHOVA, Natalya. *See Issakova, Natalia.*

ISHIDA, Kyoko (1960—). Japanese volleyball player. Born July 12, 1960, in Japan. ❖ At Los Angeles Olympics, won a bronze medal in team competition (1984).

ISHIGAKI, Rin (1920—). Japanese poet and banker. Born 1920 in Japan. ❖ Began working for bank at 14 and retired 1975; co-founded magazine *Dansō* (1938) and published poems in bank's pamphlets; writings, which reflect daily working life, include *Watakushi no mae ni aru nabe to okama to moeru hi* (1959), *Hyōsatsu* (1968), *The Poetry Collection of Ishigaki Rin* (1971), and *Ryakureki* (1979); published 5-volume collection of poems (1987). Received Tamura Toshiko Prize.

ISHIKAWA, Taeko (c. 1976—). Japanese softball player. Born c. 1976 in Japan. ❖ Pitcher, won a team silver medal at Sydney Olympics (2000).

ISHMOURATOVA, Svetlana (1972—). Russian biathlete. Name variations: Ichmouratova or Ishmuratova. Born April 20, 1972, in Cheljabinsk, Russia. ❖ Won a bronze medal for 4 x 7.5 km relay at Salt Lake City Olympics (2002) and gold medals for 15 km Individual and 4 x 6 km relay at Torino Olympics (2006).

ISHMURATOVA, Svetlana (1972—). *See Ishmouratova, Svetlana.*

ISHOY, Cynthia (1952—). Canadian equestrian. Born June 19, 1952, in Edmonton, Alberta, Canada. ❖ At Seoul Olympics, won a bronze medal in team dressage (1988).

ISINBAYEVA, Yelena (1982—). Russian pole vaulter. Name variations: Elena Isinbayeva. Born June 2, 1982, in Volgograd, Russia. ❖ Won the World junior championship (2000); placed 3rd at World championships and 1st at World Indoor championships (2004); won a gold medal at Athens Olympics (2004), setting an Olympic and world record by clearing 4.89 meters.

ISITT, Adeline Genée (1878–1970). *See Genée, Adeline.*

ISITT, Kathleen (1876—). New Zealand novelist. Name variations: Kate Isitt; (pseudonym) Kathleen Inglewood. Born 1876; dau. of a Methodist minister. ❖ Worked as journalist and wrote novel about prohibition, *Patmos* (1905).

ISLER, Jennifer (1963—). American yacht racer. Name variations: (nickname) JJ Isler. Born Dec 1, 1963, in San Diego, CA; graduate of Yale

University; m. Peter Isler (ESPN sportscaster). ❖ Was 1st female captain of the varsity sailing team at Yale; won 470 World championship (1991); at Barcelona Olympics, with Pam Healy, won a bronze medal in 470 class (1992); crewed on America^3, the 1st all-woman America's Cup Team (1995); with Pease Glaser, won a silver medal for double-handed dinghy (470) at Sydney Olympics (2000). Named Rolex Yachtswoman of the Year (1986, 1991).

ISLER BÉGUIN, Marie Anne (1956—). French politician. Name variations: Marie Anne Isler Beguin. Born June 30, 1956, in Boulay, France. ❖ Member of the French Greens' National Council, then Executive Committee (1986–89), then national spokesperson (1994–99); co-founded Eurorégionale verte (1989); representing Group of the Greens/European Free Alliance, elected to 3rd and 5th European Parliament (EP, 1990–94, 1999–2004); served as vice-president of the EP (1991–94).

ISOBE, Sata (1944—). Japanese volleyball player. Born Dec 19, 1944, in Japan. ❖ At Tokyo Olympics, won a gold medal in team competition (1964).

ISOBEL. *Variant of Isabel.*

ISODA, Yoko. Japanese synchronized swimmer. Born in Japan. ❖ Won a team silver medal at Sydney Olympics (2000).

ISOM, Mary Frances (1865–1920). American librarian. Born Mary Frances Isom, Feb 27, 1865, in Nashville, TN; died April 15, 1920, in Portland, OR; dau. of John Franklin Isom (surgeon) and Frances A. (Walter) Isom; attended Wellesley College and Pratt Institute Library School in Brooklyn, NY; never married; children: (adopted) Berenice Langdon. ❖ Began cataloging John Wilson Collection at the Library Association, then a private library, in Portland, Oregon (1901); became librarian there (1902), and, in accordance with the stipulations of the institution's donor, transformed the library from a private subscription library to a free public one; added registration system, children's department, and larger reference services, and expanded to serve the county as well as city; within 6 years, helped set up 3 branches and 11 reading rooms around the county; played a crucial role in getting legislation passed that established the Oregon State Library Commission (1905). ❖ See also *Women in World History.*

ISRAELS, Belle Lindner (1877–1933). *See Moskowitz, Belle.*

ISSAIA, Nana (1934—). Greek poet and translator. Name variations: Nana Isaia. Born 1934 in Athens, Greece; studied painting at School of Fine Arts, Athens. ❖ Had first solo exhibition (1974); writings include *Poems* (1969), *A Glance* (1974), *Alice in Wonderland* (1977), *Form* (1980), *In the Tactic of Passion* (1982), and *Consciousness of Oblivion* (1982); translated Sylvia Plath (1974) and contributed poems to non-Greek magazines and journals.

ISSAJENKO, Angella (1958—). *See Taylor, Angella.*

ISSAKOVA, Natalia. Russian short-track speedskater. Name variations: Natalya Ishahova or Isakhova. Born in USSR. ❖ Won a bronze medal for 3,000-meter relay at Albertville Olympics (1992).

ISSATCHENKO, Tatiana (1901–1993). *See Gsovsky, Tatiana.*

ISTOMINA, Anna (1925—). Canadian ballet dancer. Born Audrée Thomas, Oct 9, 1925, in Vancouver, British Columbia, Canada; studied with June Roper; m. Serge Ismailoff (dancer); children: Gregory Ismailov (dancer). ❖ Performed 1 season with Opéra Russe à Paris (c. 1939); danced with Ballet Russe de Monte Carlo (1940–44) where she was featured in works by Massine, including *Rouge et Noir, Bacchanale* and *Aleko;* danced for Ballet Russe Highlights in *Polish Festival* and *Première Polka* (1944–46); as guest prima ballerina, danced with Ballet de Teatro Colón in Rio de Janeiro, in *Swan Lake, Giselle,* and *Les Sylphides* (1947–48), and with Ballet Nacional de Venezuela (1957–58); worked at Radio City Music Hall (1950s); ran a ballet school with husband in White Plains, NY.

ISTOMINA, Avdotia (1799–1848). Russian ballet dancer. Born Jan 6, 1799, in St. Petersburg, Russia; died Jan 26, 1848, in St. Petersburg. ❖ Studied in St. Petersburg with Charles-Louis Didelot, with whom she continued to work throughout career; created principal roles in numerous works by Didelot, including his *Acis et Galatée* (1816), *Le Calife de Bagdad* (1818) and *Russlan et Ludmilla* (1824).

ITA. *Variant of Ida.*

ITA OF IRELAND (d. 570). Irish princess and saint. Name variations: Saint Ida of Ireland; Ite; Mida; Mary of Munster. Born near Drum,

County Waterford, birth date unknown; baptized Dorothy or Deirdre; died at Killeedy c. 569 or 570 in Limerick, Ireland; was of royal descent; never married; no children. ❖ The most revered Irish holy woman, 2nd only to Saint Bridget (c. 453–c. 524), was encouraged by parents to pursue a religious life; took the veil as a girl and eventually founded a community of women at Killeedy (Cill Íde) near Newcastle West, Co. Limerick, which was soon established as an abbey; as its leader, was highly regarded as learned and wise, and was often consulted by peasants and nobles alike; was credited with several miracles and corresponded with many of the leaders of early Christian church. Feast Day is Jan 15. ❖ See also *Women in World History.*

ITA OF NIVELLES (597–652). *See Ida of Nivelles.*

ITALY, queen of.
See Bertha of Toulouse (fl. late 700s).
See Cunegunde (fl. 800s).
See Engelberga (c. 840–890).
See Bertha of Swabia (fl. 900s).
See Marie Adelaide of Austria (1822–1855).
See Margaret of Savoy (1851–1926).
See Elena of Montenegro (1873–1952).
See Marie José of Belgium (b. 1906).

ITALYS, Alice (d. after 1326). *See Hayles, Alice.*

ITE. *Variant of Ida.*

ITI (c. 2563–2424 BCE). Egyptian singer. Lived around the time of the reign of Neferefre, 2563–2424 BCE. ❖ Believed to be the 1st chronicled songstress in Egyptian history; her tomb near the Chefren (Khafren) pyramids in the Necropolis of Giza, as well as numerous references to her in writing and in pictures document her celebrity during her lifetime; was also depicted in the Necropolis of Saqqarah which was part of Memphis, the former capital of Ancient Egypt. ❖ See also *Women in World History.*

ITKINA, Maria (1932—). Russian runner. Born Maria Leontyavna Itkina, May 3, 1932, in Smolensk, Russia. ❖ At European championships, won gold medals for 200 meters (1954), 4 x 100-meter relay (1954) and 400 meters (1958, 1962); competed in 3 Olympiads (Melbourne 1956, Rome 1960, and Tokyo 1964) but did not medal; set numerous world records. Inducted into International Jewish Sports Hall of Fame; received USSR's Merited Master of Sports. ❖ See also *Women in World History.*

ITO, Kazue (1977—). Japanese softball player. Born Dec 22, 1977, in Japan. ❖ Infielder, won a team silver medal at Sydney Olympics (2000) and a team bronze at Athens Olympics (2004).

ITO, Midori (1969—). Japanese figure skater. Born Aug 13, 1969, in Nagoya, Aichi, Japan. ❖ At 12, did the triple loop-triple loop combination in competition; won 8 consecutive All-Japan championships (1985–92); placed 5th at Calgary Olympics (1988); won the World championship (1989), the 1st Asian skater to do so; won a silver medal at Albertville Olympics (1992); lit the flame at Nagano Olympics (1998); was the 1st woman to land a triple axel and triple-triple combination in competition.

ITTA. *Variant of Ita or Ida.*

ITURBI, Amparo (1898–1969). Spanish pianist. Born in Valencia, Spain, Mar 12, 1898; died in Beverly Hills, CA, April 21, 1969; dau. of Ricardo Iturbi (piano tuner) and Teresa (Baguena) Iturbi; sister of José Iturbi (1895–1980, pianist). ❖ Distinguished pianist with an international career, gave 1st major concert outside Spain, at Salle Gaveau in Paris (1925); made US debut on CBS radio (May 2, 1937), performing the Haydn Piano Concerto; 2 months later, played the Mozart Concerto for Two Pianos with brother, José Iturbi, at Lewisohn Stadium; as a teacher, trained a number of artists, including Bruce Sutherland.

IULIA. *Variant of Julia.*

IULIA BALBILLA (fl. 130 CE). *See Balbilla.*

IUREVSKAIA, Princess (1847–1922). *See Dolgorukova, Ekaterina.*

IVAN, Paula (1963—). Romanian runner. Born July 20, 1963, in Romania. ❖ At Seoul Olympics, won a silver medal in the 3,000 meters and a gold medal in the 1,500 meters (1988).

IVAN, Rosalind (1880–1959). English actress and writer. Born Nov 27, 1880, in London, England; died April 6, 1959, in NYC. ❖ As a musical prodigy, gave London piano recitals at 10, then often appeared as an actress on London stage; made NY debut (1912); appeared on Broadway with John Barrymore in *Richard III;* other credits include *Once is Enough, The Father, Knights of Song, The Corn is Green* and *A Night's Lodging;* films include *The Suspect* (as the shrewish wife of Charles Laughton), *None but the Lonely Heart, The Corn is Green, Johnny Belinda* and *Elephant Walk;* as a writer, translated *The Brothers Karamazov* for the Lunts' Theater Guild production (1927).

IVANOVA, Borislava (1966—). Bulgarian kayaker. Born Nov 24, 1966, in Bulgaria. ❖ At Seoul Olympics, won a bronze medal in K4 500 meters (1988).

IVANOVA, Ioulia. Russian rhythmic gymnast. Name variations: Julia Ivanova. Born in USSR. ❖ Won a team bronze medal at Atlanta Olympics (1996).

IVANOVA, Julia. *See Ivanova, Ioulia.*

IVANOVA, Kira (c. 1963–2001). Russian figure skater. Born c. 1963 in USSR; found murdered in her apartment on Dec 20, 2001, in Moscow. ❖ Won a bronze medal at Sarajevo Olympics (1984), the 1st female Soviet skater to win a singles Olympic medal; won a silver medal at World championships (1985); coached at Dynamo in Moscow.

IVANOVA, Natalia (c. 1971—). Russian taekwondo player. Born c. 1971 in USSR. ❖ Won a silver medal for + 67kg at Sydney Olympics (2000).

IVANOVA, Natalya (1981—). Russian runner. Born June 25, 1981, in USSR. ❖ Won a silver medal for 4x400-meter relay at Athens Olympics (2004).

IVANOVA, Olimpiada (1970—). Russian track-and-field athlete. Born May 5, 1970, in Mun-Syut, USSR. ❖ At World championships, placed 1st for 20 km road walk (2001); won a silver medal for 20 km road walk at Athens Olympics (2004).

IVANOVA, Svetlana (1974—). Russian gymnast. Born Oct 4, 1974, in Zhdanov, USSR. ❖ Won the Jr. European championship (1988).

IVANOVA-KALININA, Lidiya (1937—). Soviet gymnast. Name variations: Lidiya Kalinina. Born Jan 27, 1937, in USSR. ❖ At Melbourne Olympics, won a bronze medal in teams all-around, portable apparatus, and a gold medal in team all-around (1956); at Rome Olympics, won a gold medal in team all-around (1960).

IVANOVNA, Anna (1693–1740). *See Anna Ivanovna.*

IVANOVSKAIA, Praskovia (1853–1935). Russian revolutionary. Name variations: P.S. Voloshenko; Praskovya Ivanovskaya. Pronunciation: E-van-OFF-sky-ya. Born Praskovia Semenovna Ivanovskaia in 1853 in Sokovnina, Russia; died in USSR, 1935; dau. of Semen Ivanov (village priest); educated at church boarding school in Tula until 1871; attended Alarchin courses in St. Petersburg, 1773–76; m. I.F.(?) Voloshenko; no children. ❖ Revolutionary and terrorist who was involved in 2 of the most sensational political assassinations in Russian history; was active in "to the people" movement and other Populist enterprises (1876–79); helped organize 1st armed demonstration in Russian history in Odessa (1878), and spent 3 months in a tsarist jail; was a member of terrorist group Narodnaia Volia (1880–82), with special responsibility for running the party's illegal printing presses; because of this, was arrested and accused of assisting in assassination of Tsar Alexander II (1882), tried (1883) and sentenced to hard labor for life in Siberia; escaped (1903); resumed terrorist activity as a member of Combat Organization of the Socialist Revolutionary Party in St. Petersburg (1903–05); played a support role in the organization's assassination of V.K. Plehve (1904), the despised minister of the interior; participated in the election campaign to the First State Duma (1906). ❖ See also (in Russian) "Avtobiografiia," in *Entsiklopedicheskii slovar'* (Vol. XL, 1927, pp. 151–163); and *Women in World History.*

IVANTZOVA, Elizabeth (c. 1893–1973). *See Anderson-Ivantzova, Elizabeth.*

IVERS, Alice (1851–1930). *See Tubbs, Alice.*

IVES, Morgan (1930–1999). *See Bradley, Marion Zimmer.*

IVETTA. *Variant of Ivette, Joveta, and Yvette.*

IVETTA OF HUY (1158–1228). Belgian anchoress and saint. Name variations: Ivette of Huy; Jutta of Huy; Yvette of Huy. Born in 1158 in Huy, Belgium; died 1228 in Belgium; dau. of nobles; married; children: 3. ❖ A holy woman of the Low Countries, was forced to wed at 13 and was widowed at 18; longing to pursue a religious life, induced a local bishop to help convince her parents; did penance by serving in a leper

hospital in Huy; received necessary permissions to become a recluse, or anchoress, and had a cell built next to the leper hospital; famed for piety, spent more than 4 decades in her cell, consulting with those seeking guidance, and eventually a community of other religious men and women grew up around her; became the indirect leader of this community. Feast day is Jan 13. ❖ See also *Women in World History.*

IVEY, Jean Eichelberger (1923—). American composer. Born in Washington, DC, July 3, 1923; dau. of Joseph S. Eichelberger (editor of anti-feminist newspaper) and Elizabeth (Pfeffer) Eichelberger; Trinity College, BA, 1944; Peabody Conservatory, MA in music, 1946; Eastman School of Music, MA; University of Toronto, PhD, 1972; studied under Claudio Arrau, Pasquale Tallarico, Katherine Bacon and Herbert Elwell. ❖ Taught at Peabody Conservatory, Trinity College, Catholic University in Washington, and College Misericordia; became a leader in electronic composition and was founder-director of the Peabody Electronic Music Studio. ❖ See also "A Woman Is . . . " (documentary, 1973); and *Women in World History.*

IVINS, Molly (c. 1944—). American political columnist and humorist. Born c. 1944 in Texas; dau. of Jim and Margo Ivins; Smith College, BA; Columbia University, MA; attended Institute of Political Science, Paris. ❖ Liberal newspaper columnist for *Fort Worth Star-Telegram,* came to national prominence with her scathing commentary on Texas politics and George Bush, done in a folksy, irreverent style; became nationally syndicated; wrote *You Got to Dance with Them What Brung You: Politics in the Clinton Years* (1998) and *Nothin' but Good Times Ahead.*

IVINSKAYA, Olga (1912–1995). Russian magazine editor. Name variations: Olga Ivinskaia; Lara. Born in Russia in 1912; died in Moscow, Sept 8, 1995; lived with Boris Pasternak (1890–1960); m. twice; children: 2, including Dmitri Vinogradov. ❖ Inspiration for the character Lara in Pasternak's Nobel Prize-winning *Doctor Zhivago,* played by Julie Christie in the 1965 film; a magazine editor for a Moscow literary journal, was jailed twice, spending more than 8 years in Soviet prison camps because of her anti-Soviet activities related to 14-year affair with Pasternak; wrote about her life with Pasternak in *A Captive of Time* (1978). ❖ See also *Women in World History.*

IVINSKAYA, Tatyana (1958—). Soviet basketball player. Born Mar 27, 1958, in USSR. ❖ At Moscow Olympics, won a gold medal in team competition (1980).

IVOGÜN, Maria (1891–1987). Hungarian coloratura soprano. Name variations: Maria Ivogun. Born Ilse Kempner, Nov 18, 1891, in Budapest, Hungary; died Oct 2, 1987, in Beatenberg, Lake Thun; dau. of singer Ida von Günther; studied with Schlemmer-Ambros in Vienna and with Schöner in Munich; m. Karl Erb (tenor), 1921 (div. 1932); m. Michael Raucheisen (her accompanist), 1933. ❖ Performed at Bavarian Court Opera (1913–25), often under baton of Bruno Walter; followed him to Berlin (1925), eventually appearing at both the Stätische Oper and the Staatsoper and notably portrayed Zerbinetta in *Ariadne auf Naxos;* established an extensive recital career with husband after retiring from opera stage (1932); taught at Vienna Academy of Music and Berlin Hochschule für Musik and had Elisabeth Schwarzkopf as one of her pupils. ❖ See also *Women in World History.*

IVOSEV, Aleksandra (1974—). Yugoslavian shooter. Born Mar 17, 1974, in Nov Sad, Yugoslavia. ❖ Won a gold medal for 50 m rifle 3 positions and a bronze medal for 10 m air rifle (40 shots) at Atlanta Olympics (1996).

IWABUCHI, Yumi (1979—). Japanese softball player. Born Sept 10, 1979, in Saitama, Japan. ❖ Outfielder, won a team bronze at Athens Olympics (2004).

IWAHARA, Toyoko (1945—). Japanese volleyball player. Born May 11, 1945, in Japan. ❖ Won a silver medal at Mexico City Olympics (1968) and a silver medal at Munich Olympics (1972), both in team competition.

IWASAKI, Kyoko (1978—). Japanese swimmer. Born July 21, 1978, in Japan. ❖ At Barcelona Olympics, won a gold medal in 200-meter breaststroke (1992).

IYALL, Debora (1954—). Native-American singer. Name variations: Romeo Void. Born April 29, 1954, in Washington; grew up in Fresno, CA; attended San Francisco Art Institute (1970s). ❖ Cowlitz Indian, sang with pop band, the Mummers and the Poppers, while at San Francisco Art Institute; with Frank Zincavage, Jay Derrah, Peter Woods and Ben Bossi, formed band, Romeo Void (1979), in San

Francisco; with group, released critically acclaimed albums, *It's a Condition* (1981) and *Never Say Never* (1982), but had only 1 hit single, "A Girl in Trouble (Is a Temporary Thing)," from album *Instincts* (1984); pursued solo career after Romeo Void disbanded (1985) and released album *Strange Language* (1986).

IZABEL, Izabela or Izabella. *Variant of Isabel or Isabella.*

IZQUIERDO, Lilia (1967—). Cuban volleyball player. Name variations: Lilia Izquierdo Aguirre or Aguiar. Born Feb 10, 1967, in Havana, Cuba. ❖ At Barcelona Olympics, won a gold medal in team competition (1992); won team gold medal at Atlanta Olympics (1996) and Sydney Olympics (2000), though she did not play in any game at Sydney.

IZQUIERDO ROJO, Maria (1946—). Spanish politician. Born Sept 13, 1946, in Oviedo, Spain. ❖ Served as deputy in the Cortes (1977, 1986), member of the Bureau of the Congress of Deputies (1979), and secretary of state for the Autonomus Communities (1982–87); as a European Socialist, elected to 3rd, 4th and 5th European Parliament (EP, 1990–94, 1994–99, 1999–2004); served as chair of the EP Intergroup on the Mediterranean (1990–95).

IZUMI SHIKIBU (c. 975–c. 1027). Japanese poet. Born c. 975 CE; died, possibly around 1027 CE; m. Tachibana no Michisada (div.); m. Fujiwara no Yasumasa (958–1036); children: (1st m.) daughter Koshikibu no naishi (poet who served Empress Shoshi and died young). ❖ Served Empress Shoshi, like her friend Murasaki Shikibu, and was known for her extramarital affairs with Prince Tametaka and Prince Atsumichi which resulted in the eventual dissolution of her 1st marriage; wrote the fictionalized diary *Izumi shikibu nikki*. 240 of her poems were included in imperial anthologies. ❖ See also *Women in World History*.

IZZARD, Molly (1919–2004). English writer. Born Molly Crutchleigh-Fitzpatrick, Aug 1, 1919, in Cornwall, England; attended schools in Cherbourg, Darjeeling and Genoa; died Feb 4, 2004 in Tunbridge Wells, England; m. Ralph Izzard (foreign correspondent), c. 1946 (died 1992); children: 2 sons, 2 daughters. ❖ During WWII, served in the Political Warfare Executive, an agency of propaganda; spent years living in India, Egypt and Beirut, while husband covered the Middle East for *Daily Mail;* published memoirs, *Smelling the Breezes* (1959) and *A Private Life* (1963); also wrote *The Gulf* (1979) and controversial biography of Freya Stark (1993).

J

JAAPIES, Mieke (1943—). Dutch kayaker. Born Aug 7, 1943, in the Netherlands. ❖ At Munich Olympics, won a silver medal in K1 500 meters (1972).

JAATTEENMAKI, Anneli (1955—). Finnish politician. Name variations: Anneli Tuulikki Jaatteenmaki. Born Feb 11, 1955, in Lapua, Finland. ❖ Became leader of the Centre Party (2000); with her party's narrow victory, became the first woman prime minister of Finland (Mar 16, 2003); was forced to resign (June 2003), because of her role in a leaked-document scandal which gave details of talks on Iraq between her predecessor and President Bush; was acquitted of charges of illegally obtaining secret documents about Iraq war while she was opposition leader (Mar 2004).

JABAVU, Noni (1919—). South African memoirist. Born Helen Nontando "Noni" Jabavu in 1919, Eastern Cape, South Africa; m. Michael Cadbury Crosfield (English film director). ❖ Born into well-educated Xhosa family and educated in England, worked in radio and tv; traveled with film director husband and lived in Uganda; works, which place personal history within context of Xhosa culture and history, include *Drawn in Colour: African Contrasts* (1960) and *The Ochre People: Scenes from a South African Life* (1963).

JABURKOVA, Jozka (d. 1944). Czechoslovakian feminist and patriot. Died 1944. ❖ Journalist and author by trade, edited *The Disseminator* magazine, wrote children's books, and published 3 novels about working women; was also an early leader in the women's progressive movement and a member of Prague City Council; joined Communist Party (1930s), campaigning for employment equity for women; during WWII, was sent to Ravensbrück concentration camp, where she organized a resistance movement; at end of war, was a national hero. Statue was erected to her memory in Prague (1965).

JACCO, Sada (d. 1946). *See Yakko, Sada.*

JACHMANN-WAGNER, Johanna (1826–1894). *See Wagner, Johanna.*

JACK, Mrs. (1840–1924). *See Gardner, Isabella Stewart.*

JACKMAN, Mary (1943—). Irish politician. Born Mary Furlong, April 1943 in Cappawhite, Co. Tipperary, Ireland; dau. of George Furlong (politician); m. Nicholas Jackman. ❖ Representing Fine Gael, elected to the Seanad from the Labour Panel: Nominating Bodies Sub-Panel (1989–93, 1997–2002), the 1st woman senator from Limerick; became the 1st woman Cathaoirleach of Limerick County Council in its 100-year history (1998).

JACKSON, Alice (1887–1974). Australian journalist. Born Alice Archibald, Oct 15, 1887, in Ulmarra, New South Wales; died Oct 28, 1974; dau. of William Archibald (schoolteacher) and Clara Amelia (Baker) Archibald; m. Samuel Henry Jackson (businessman); children: daughter and son. ❖ One of Australia's leading magazine editors, joined the newly established *Australian Women's Weekly* (1933), becoming editor (1939); added heft to the paper's regular mix of food, fashion, beauty, child care, and fiction, as it grew to command Australia's largest readership, with features on distinguished women, including sports figures; also covered the more controversial issues of her day, such as women's problems in marriage and in the workplace, and the refusal of the Chief Protector of Aborigines to permit an Aboriginal woman to marry the man of her choice; started *Woman's Day and Home*, a Melbourne-based paper owned by Keith Murdoch (1950), but resigned after a year and returned to Sydney. ❖ See also *Women in World History.*

JACKSON, Ann Fletcher (1833–1903). New Zealand evangelist. Name variations: Ann Fletcher. Born Ann Fletcher, Feb 27, 1833, at Leigh, Lancashire, England; died Oct 15, 1903, in Auckland, New Zealand; dau. of John Fletcher (clogger) and Mary (Brown) Fletcher; m. Thomas Jackson (cordwainer), 1859 (died 1900); children: 11. ❖ Immigrated to New Zealand with husband and children (1879); settled at Otonga; spoke at church meetings, visited families in community, and assisted local Maori with medical needs (1880s); accompanied visiting Quaker (Society of Friends) evangelist to Auckland (1885); traveled widely and brought members together (1886–1902); helped establish Victoria Hall as public meeting place for Quakers in Avondale (1903). ❖ See also *Dictionary of New Zealand Biography* (Vol. 2).

JACKSON, Anne (1926—). American stage, film, and tv actress. Born Anna Jane Jackson in Millvale, PA, Sept 3, 1926; dau. of John Ivan Jackson (hairdresser) and Stella Germaine (Murray) Jackson; studied drama with Herbert Berghof at New School for Social Research, with Sanford Meisner at Neighborhood Playhouse, 1943–44, and with Lee Strasberg at Actors Studio from 1948; m. Eli Wallach (actor), Mar 5, 1948; children: Roberta Wallach (actress); Katherine Wallach (actress); Peter Wallach (artist and filmmaker). ❖ Launched stage career with road tour as Anya in *The Cherry Orchard* (1944); made Broadway debut in *Signature* (1945), which closed after 2 performances; with future husband, joined Le Gallienne's American Repertory Theater where she had small roles; had 1st solid Broadway hit with *Oh, Men! Oh, Women!* (1953); replaced Glynis Johns in title role of *Major Barbara* (1957); with husband, scored a number of successes, including *Rhinoceros* (1961), *Luv* (1964), *Promenade, All!* (1972) and *The Waltz of the Toreadors* (1973); appeared frequently on live tv dramas, including "Armstrong Circle Theater" and "Philco Playhouse"; appeared in "84 Charing Cross Road" for PBS; other notable stage appearances include *Marco Polo Sings a Solo* (1977) and *Absent Friends* (1977); appeared sporadically in films, including *So Young, So Bad* (1950), *Tall Story* (1960) and *The Secret Life of an American Wife* (1968). Won Obie for Best Actress for *The Typist and the Tiger* (1963). ❖ See also autobiography *Early Stages* (Little, Brown, 1979); and *Women in World History.*

JACKSON, Barbara (1914–1981). *See Ward, Barbara.*

JACKSON, Bessie (1897–1948). *See Bogan, Lucille.*

JACKSON, Caroline F. (1946—). English politician. Born Nov 5, 1946, in Penzance, Cornwall, England. ❖ Worked for the Conservative Group in the European Parliament (1975–84); as a member of the European People's Party (Christian Democrats) and European Democrats, elected to 4th and 5th European Parliament (EP, 1994–99, 1999–2004), from UK; served as deputy chair, Conservative Group in EP (1997–99) and chair of the Committee on the Environment, Public Health, and Consumer Policy.

JACKSON, Cordell (1923–2004). American guitarist and rockabilly star. Born Cordell Miller in Pontotoc, Mississippi, in 1923; died Oct 14, 2004. ❖ As a teenager, performed with father's band, the Pontotoc Ridge Runners; joined Fisher Air Craft Band (1943); launched her own record label, Moon Records, with hit single "Rock 'n' Roll Christmas" (1956); also produced a contemporary Christian radio show, "Let's Keep the Family Together, America"; enjoyed some popularity when she performed a dueling guitar sequence with Brian Setzer of the Stray Cats in a Budweiser beer commercial (1991). ❖ See also *Women in World History.*

JACKSON, Doris Kenner (1941–2000). *See Coley, Doris.*

JACKSON, Elaine (1929—). *See Freeman, Gillian.*

JACKSON, Ethel (1877–1957). American actress and singer. Born Nov 1, 1877, in New York, NY; died Nov 23, 1957, in East Islip, LI, NY; m. J. Fred Zimmerman; m. Benoni Lockwood (div.). ❖ Came to prominence as the original Sonia in *The Merry Widow* in US (1907); also appeared on Broadway in *Little Miss Nobody, Vienna Life, A Wild Goose, The Purple Road, A Pair of Sixes, Dodsworth, So Proudly We Hail, The Women* and *Key Largo.*

JACKSON, Freda (1909–1990). English stage and screen actress. Born Dec 29, 1909, in Nottingham, England; died Oct 20, 1990; m. Henry Bird. ❖ Made London debut in *The Sacred Flame* (1936), followed by *Judgment Day, The Silent Knight, Hamlet, No Room at the End, Tomorrow's Eden, The Father, They Walk Alone,* title role in *Anna Christie, The Old Ladies, Sergeant Musgrave's Dance, John Gabriel Borkman, Naked, The Man on the Stairs, When We Are Married* and *Mother Courage;* films include *Great Expectations, Henry V, No Room at the Inn, Women of Twilight, Bhowani Junction, Boy with a Flute, Tom Jones* and *House at the End of the World.*

JACKSON, Gail Patrick (1911–1980). See *Patrick, Gail.*

JACKSON, Glenda (1936—). British actress and politician. Born in Birkenhead, Cheshire, England, May 9, 1936; dau. of Harry Jackson (building contractor) and Joan Jackson; attended Royal Academy of Dramatic Art; m. Roy Hodges (actor-director), 1958 (div.); children: Daniel. ❖ Distinguished by her flinty personality and intense approach to craft, acted and stage-managed for various repertory companies (1950s); accepted into Royal Shakespeare Company and spent 1st season with the company's experimental Theater of Cruelty (1963); received international acclaim as Charlotte Corday in *Marat/Sade* (1964); appeared as Masha in *The Three Sisters* (1967) and Tamara Fanghorn in *Fanghorn* (1967); on film, appeared in *The Music Lovers* (1971), *Sunday, Bloody Sunday* (1971), and as Elizabeth I in *Mary Queen of Scots* (1971), a role she also played in BBC-TV 6-part biography, "Elizabeth R"; on tv, also starred in "The Patricia Neal Story" (1981) and as Elena Bonner in "Sakharov" (1984); on stage, appeared in *Collaborators, The Maids* and *The White Devil;* had great success in title role of *Stevie* (1977), about poet Stevie Smith, and starred in the film (1978); at RSC, starred in *Antony and Cleopatra* and won acclaim in *Rose* (1980); also portrayed Lady Macbeth (1988) and *Mother Courage* (1990); retired from stage (1990); a Socialist, was a parliamentary candidate for Labour Party (1990) and elected a Labour member of Parliament for Hampstead and Highgate (1992); served 7 years in the House of Commons; was also London's junior transport minister under Prime Minister Tony Blair until 1999. Won Academy Awards for Best Actress for *Women in Love* (1970) and *A Touch of Class* (1973). ❖ See also *Women in World History.*

JACKSON, Grace (1961—). Jamaican-born track-and-field athlete. Born June 14, 1961, in St. Ann, Jamaica. ❖ Won the 200 meters and 400 meters at the International Amateur Athletic Federation Grand Prix (1988); won the silver medal in the 200 meters at Seoul Olympics (1988). ❖ See also *Women in World History.*

JACKSON, Mrs. H. Arnold (1881–1961). See *Harley, Katherine.*

JACKSON, Helen (1939—). English politician. Born Helen Price, May 19, 1939; m. Keith Jackson, 1960 (div. 1998). ❖ Representing Labour, elected to House of Commons for Sheffield and Hillsborough (1992, 1997, 2001); left Parliament (2005).

JACKSON, Helen Fiske (1830–1885). See *Jackson, Helen Hunt.*

JACKSON, Helen Hunt (1830–1885). American poet, novelist, and activist. Name variations: Helen Fiske Jackson; Helen Fiske Hunt; (pseudonyms) H.H., Marah, Rip Van Winkle, Saxe Holm, and No-Name. Born Helen Maria Fiske, Oct 15, 1830, in Amherst, MA; died Aug 12, 1885, in San Francisco, CA; dau. of Nathan Welby Fiske (professor) and Deborah Waterman (Vinal) Fiske; m. Lieutenant Edward Bissell Hunt, Oct 28, 1852 (died 1863); m. William Sharpless Jackson, Oct 22, 1875; children: Murray (1853–1854); Warren "Rennie" (1856–1865). ❖ Prolific writer who documented the conditions of Native Americans in *A Century of Dishonor* (1881), a scathing critique of government policy that went largely ignored, then recast the same material into the novel *Ramona,* which became the most popular romance of late 19th century; after 1st marriage, moved to Washington (1852); husband died in explosion (Oct 1863); moved to Newport and began writing poems that were published in NY *Evening Post,* the *Nation, Atlantic,* and elsewhere (1870–79); became well known as a writer of children's books and poetry, as well as articles that had appeared in most popular magazines; remarried and moved West (1875); attended lecture about the fate of the Ponca Indian tribe that became the turning point for her Indian crusade (1879); other books include *Versus* (1870, 1873, 1879), *Bits of Travel* (1872), *Mercy Philbrick's Choice* (1876), *Hetty's Strange Story* (1877) and *Nelly's Silver Mine* (1878). ❖ See also Evelyn I. Banning, *Helen Hunt Jackson* (Vanguard, 1973); Valerie Sherer

Mathes, *Helen Hunt Jackson and Her Indian Reform Legacy* (U. of Texas, 1990); and *Women in World History.*

JACKSON, Janet (1966—). African-American pop singer. Name variations: Janet Damita Jackson. Born Janet Damita Jackson, May 16, 1966, in Gary, Indiana; sister of Michael Jackson (singer); m. James DeBarge, 1984 (annulled 1985); m. Rene Elizondo, 1991 (div. 2000). ❖ Youngest of the Jackson music family, appeared as regular on tv series "Good Times" (1976); released teen-pop albums *Janet Jackson* (1982) and *Dream Street* (1984) and broke through to stardom with album *Control* (1986), which generated a series of hits, including "What Have You Done for Me Lately," "Nasty," "Control," "Let's Wait Awhile" and "The Pleasure Principle"; released successful follow-up album *Rhythm Nation: 1814* (1989); had hit singles "Miss You Much" (1989), "Escapade" (1990), "Alright" (1990) and "Come Back to Me" (1990); made film debut playing lead in *Poetic Justice* (1993); other hits include "That's the Way Love Goes' (1993), "Again" (1994), "Runaway" (1995), "Doesn't Really Matter" (2000), and "Scream" (1995), a duet with brother Michael; caused a considerable stir for "inadvertently" revealing breast during Super Bowl halftime performance (2004).

JACKSON, Julia (fl. 19th c.). Voodoo woman of New Orleans. Fl. in 19th century. ❖ One of the most notorious practitioners of voodoo, was said to have incredible skills, including the ability to cause unwanted pregnancies or abortions and induce a case of venereal disease that could put a lady of the night out of business.

JACKSON, Katherine Harley (1881–1961). See *Harley, Katherine.*

JACKSON, Lady (1914–1981). See *Ward, Barbara.*

JACKSON, Laura (1901–1991). See *Riding, Laura.*

JACKSON, Lauren (1981—). Australian basketball player. Born May 11, 1981, in Albury, Australia; attended La Trobe University. ❖ Topped the league in averaging 23.4 points per game for Canberra Capitals (1999–2000); won a team silver medal at Sydney Olympics (2000) and a team silver at Athens Olympics (2004); selected by Seattle Storm of WNBA in 1st round (2001), becoming Storm's all-time leading scorer (2002). Won WNBL Rookie of the Year award (1997); was Australia's Women's National Basketball League's MVP (1999, 2000); named Australian International Player of the Year (1999, 2000, 2002); named WNBA MVP (2003), the 1st non-American to win the award.

JACKSON, Louisa (c. 1893–1926). See *Calvert, Louie.*

JACKSON, Mahalia (1911–1972). African-American gospel and spiritual singer. Born in New Orleans, Louisiana, Oct 26, 1911; died of heart failure in Evergreen Park, Illinois, Jan 27, 1972; m. Isaac "Ike" Hockenhull (entrepreneur), 1936 (div.); m. Sigmond Galloway (musician), 1965 (div.). ❖ At 16, moved to Chicago (1927); began touring with Johnson Gospel Singers (mid-1930s); had 1st hit recording (1937), "God's Gonna Separate the Wheat from the Tares"; traveled throughout US with Thomas A. Dorsey, "Father of Gospel Music" (1940s); established herself as Queen of Gospel when "Move On Up a Little Higher" sold 1 million copies (1946); soloed at Carnegie Hall with National Baptist Convention (1950); won prestigious French award with "I Can Put My Trust in Jesus" (1952), then toured Europe; on tv, starred on "The Mahalia Jackson Show" (1954); had such hits as "I Believe," "Precious Lord, Take My Hand," "How Great Thou Art," "It's No Secret What God Can Do," "He's Got the Whole World in His Hands" and "When I Wake Up in Glory"; as a strong supporter of civil-rights movement, was highly visible during bus boycott in Montgomery, Alabama (1956) and delivered her own charged version of "We Shall Overcome"; sang at John F. Kennedy's inauguration (1961); sang "How I Got Over" in front of Lincoln Memorial during "March on Washington" rally led by Martin Luther King Jr. (1963), then sang "Precious Lord" at his funeral (1968). ❖ See also autobiography (with Evan McLeod Wylie) *Movin' On Up* (Hawthorne, 1966); Laurraine Goreau, *Just Mahalia, Baby* (Pelican, 1975); Jules Schwerin, *Got to Tell It: Mahalia Jackson, Queen of Gospel* (Oxford U. Press, 1992); and *Women in World History.*

JACKSON, Mariechen (1906–1992). See *Wehselau, Mariechen.*

JACKSON, Marjorie (1931—). Australian runner. Name variations: Marjorie Nelson; Marjorie Jackson-Nelson. Born Marjorie Jackson, Sept 13, 1931, in Coffs Harbor, New South Wales, Australia; m. Peter Nelson (Olympic cyclist), 1953 (died 1977). ❖ Set four world records (1950); won sprints at the Auckland British Empire games (1950); won gold medals in the 100 meters and 200 meters at Helsinki Olympics

(1952); tied world and Olympic records in the 100 meters with 11.5 second time (1952); improved the 100-meter mark to 11.4 seconds (1952); set and broke the 200-meter world record with 23.6 second and 23.4 second times (1952); broke the world 100-yard mark three times (1950, 1951, 1958); won gold medals in the 100-yard, 220-yard, and 4x110-yard relay at Vancouver Commonwealth Games (1954). ❖ See also *Women in World History.*

JACKSON, Mary Jane (b. 1836). American murderer. Name variations: known as Bricktop. Born in New Orleans, Louisiana, 1836. ❖ Turned to prostitution at 14; became one of toughest women in New Orleans' French Quarter, known for beating and stabbing (sometimes to death) men who angered her; opened her own brothel in Dauphine Street, where she worked with Delia Swift (known as Bridget Fury), Ellen Collins and America Williams; stabbed lover John Miller to death (Dec 5, 1861); released from prison by military governor of Louisiana, General George Shepley, who freed all the felons (1862), then disappeared.

JACKSON, Mary Percy (1904–2000). English physician. Name variations: Mary Percy. Born Mary Percy, 1904, in Dudley, near Birmingham, England; died May 2000 in Edmonton, Alberta, Canada; graduate of Birmingham University, 1927; m. Frank Jackson (Canadian settler), 1931. ❖ One of the 1st physicians recruited to treat early Canadian settlers in northern Alberta, began career as a Children's Hospital house surgeon in Birmingham, England; sailed for Canada (1929) to work as a settler physician in Battle River Prairie (100 miles from nearest hospital in Peace River); educated settlers about health issues; battled typhoid and tuberculosis outbreaks; after marriage (1931), moved to husband's ranch (in Keg River area of Canada); practiced there without salary until health insurance was instituted in 1969; retired (1974).

JACKSON, Mercy B. (1802–1877). American physician. Name variations: Mercy Ruggles Bisbe Jackson. Born Mercy Ruggles on Sept 17, 1802, in Hardwick, MA; died Dec 13, 1877, in Boston, MA; m. Rev. John Bisbe (died 1829), 1823; m. Capt. Daniel Jackson (died 1852), 1835; children: 11. ❖ Began homeopathic-medicine practice; graduated from New England Female Medical College (1860); established medical practice in Boston, MA; due to gender, was rejected annually for membership in American Institute of Homeopathy (beginning 1861) until finally admitted with two other women in 1871; became adjunct professor of diseases of children at Boston University School of Medicine (1873); lectured on behalf of temperance and woman suffrage.

JACKSON, Nell (1929–1988). African-American track champion, coach, and educator. Born July 1, 1929, in Athens, GA; died April 1, 1988, in Vestal, NY; Tuskegee University, BS in physical education; Springfield College, MS in physical education, 1953; University of Iowa, PhD, 1962; never married. ❖ Won US national 200-meter title (1949, 1950); at 1st Pan-American Games, won a silver medal for the 200 meters and a gold for the 4 x 100-meter relay (1951); coached women's track-and-field team at Tuskegee (1954–62); became 1st black woman head coach of an Olympic track-and-field team (1956); chaired both US Women's Track and Field and AAU Women's Track and Field committees and served as a member of board of directors of US Olympic Committee (1968); coached women's track-and-field Olympic team at Munich (1972); hired as director of women's athletics at Michigan State University, becoming the 1st black woman to head athletics at a major university (1973); became director of intercollegiate athletics at State University of New York (SUNY, 1981). ❖ See also *Women in World History.*

JACKSON, Rachel Donelson (1767–1828). Wife of Andrew Jackson. Name variations: Rachel Robards. Born June 17, 1767, in Pittsylvania Co., Virginia; died Dec 22, 1828, in Nashville, Tennessee; dau. of Colonel John Donelson (iron master and surveyor) and Rachel (Stockley) Donelson; m. Lewis Robards, Mar 1, 1785 (div.); m. Andrew Jackson (7th president of US), Aug 18, 1791 (remarried, Jan 17, 1794); children: (adopted) Andrew Jackson Jr. ❖ Frontier woman who died shortly before taking her place as 1st lady of US, victim of a heart attack and the scandal that had punctuated her marriage; mistakenly thinking a divorce from 1st husband had been finalized, married Jackson (1791), only to learn 2 years later that the divorce had only been sanctioned, not granted; quietly remarried (1794); when Jackson beat John Quincy Adams for the presidency (1828), was portrayed as "adulteress" by husband's enemies. ❖ See also *Women in World History.*

JACKSON, Rebecca Cox (1795–1871). African-American mystic. Born Feb 15, 1795, in Hornstown, Pennsylvania; died 1871; dau. of Jane Wisson (or Wilson); m. Samuel S. Jackson; no children. ❖ Free-born African-American, experienced a dramatic religious conversion at 35, after which she claimed to have visions in which she could heal the sick, make the sinful holy, and speak with angels; fled husband's bed so as to live a life of "Christian perfection"; related visionary experiences and conducted prayer meetings in private homes; faced intense criticism from husband, as well as clergy of the African Methodist Episcopal church, who objected to women preaching in general and to Jackson's specific renouncement of "the flesh"; at the height of accusations against her, requested a formal trial for heresy from Methodist and Presbyterian ministers (1837); severing relationship with church and family, traveled through Pennsylvania, Delaware, NJ, New England, and NY, testifying to her powers and preaching; stayed with a Shaker community at Watervliet, near Albany, attracted by the sect's practice of celibacy and their recognition of the motherhood as well as the fatherhood of God (1847–51); in Philadelphia, established a small, predominately black and female, Shaker family around the time of the start of the Civil War; writings were collected in a single volume, *Gifts of Power* (1980). ❖ See also *Women in World History.*

JACKSON, Rowena (1926—). English ballet dancer. Born 1926 in Invercargill, New Zealand; m. Philip Chatfield (dancer), 1958. ❖ Trained on scholarship at Sadler's Wells Ballet (1946), and performed with that company the following year, appearing in *Swan Lake* and *The Sleeping Beauty*; created roles in numerous works by Frederick Ashton, including *Homage to the Queen* (1953), *Variations on a Theme by Purcell* (1955) and *A Birthday Offering* (1956); returned to New Zealand with husband and taught classes at Wellington National School of Ballet.

JACKSON, Sarah Elizabeth (1858–1946). New Zealand teacher, school administrator, and social-welfare reformer. Born on Aug 5, 1858, near Birmingham, Warwickshire, England; died on Nov 9, 1946, in Auckland, New Zealand; dau. of James Jackson (earthenware dealer) and Fanny Brittain (Chapman) Jackson. ❖ Worked as clerk and bookkeeper in father's firm until financial hardship compelled them to immigrate to New Zealand (1892); taught briefly at Beresford Street School; served as matron of Auckland Industrial School (1882–1916); served as district agent inspecting all foster homes and children's institutions in Auckland; active in numerous religious and philanthropic groups that advocated for social reform, including Girls' Friendly Society, Auckland Community Welfare Council, and Mothers' Union of Anglican church; became executive member of New Zealand Society for Protection of Women and Children (1916); helped revitalize National Council of Women of New Zealand in Auckland, becoming 3rd woman to be named life member (1933); was one of the 1st women justices of peace (1926). ❖ See also *Dictionary of New Zealand Biography* (Vol. 3).

JACKSON, Shirley (1916–1965). American novelist and short-story writer. Born Dec 14, 1916, in San Francisco, CA; died Aug 8, 1965, in North Bennington, Vermont; dau. of Leslie Jackson and Geraldine (Bugbee) Jackson; attended Syracuse University; m. Stanley Edgar Hyman (critic), Aug 13, 1940; children: Laurence Hyman (b. 1942); Joanne Hyman (b. 1945); Sarah Hyman (b. 1948); Barry Hyman (b. 1951). ❖ A master of gothic horror and psychological suspense, began writing at an early age, composing poetry and short stories; enrolled as English major at Syracuse University (1937); published nearly 20 pieces in the school humor magazine, became its fiction editor, and established a literary magazine before her graduation (1940); married (1940) and moved with husband to North Bennington (1945), populated by the type of white, middle-class Christians who were the chief characters of Jackson's fiction, inhabiting a world narrowly bound by agricultural cycles, church festivals and a deep suspicion of outsiders; wrote most famous short story, "The Lottery," which was published amid much controversy in *The New Yorker* (1948); published 6 novels and some 45 short stories, including *The Haunting of Hill House* (1959) and *We Have Always Lived in the Castle* (1962). ❖ See also autobiographical *Life Among the Savages* and *Raising Demons*; Judy Oppenheimer, *Private Demons: The Life of Shirley Jackson* (Putnam, 1988); and *Women in World History.*

JACKSON, Shirley Ann (1946—). African-American physicist. Born Aug 5, 1946, in Washington, DC; dau. of George Hiter Jackson and Beatrice (Cosby) Jackson; Massachusetts Institute of Technology, SB in physics, 1968, PhD, 1973, the 1st African-American woman to receive a doctorate at MIT in any subject; m. Morris A. Washington (physicist); children: Alan. ❖ Conducted research in theoretical physics, solid state and quantum physics, and optical physics at AT&T Bell Laboratories (1976–91); was professor of theoretical physics at Rutgers University (1991–95); served as chair of the US Nuclear Regulatory Commission

(1995–99); became president of Rensselaer Polytecnic Institute (1999); was president of American Association for the Advancement of Science (AAAS, 2004). Inducted into Women in Technology International Foundation Hall of Fame (2000).

JACKSON, Sylvia (c. 1951—). Scottish politician. Born c. 1951 in Scotland. ❧ Began career as a chemistry teacher; serves as Labour member of the Scottish Parliament for Stirling.

JACKSON, Tammy (1962—). African-American basketball player. Born Dec 3, 1962, in Gainesville, FL; graduate of University of Florida, 1985. ❧ Center, played 3 seasons for Solna in Sweden (1985–88) and Chanson Cosmetics in Japan (1990–93); also played in Italy; at Barcelona Olympics, won a bronze medal in team competition (1992); played with Houston Comets in WNBA (1997–2002).

JACKSON, Trina (1977—). American swimmer. Born 1977 in Jacksonville, FL; attended University of Arizona. ❧ Won a gold medal for 800-meter freestyle relay at Atlanta Olympics (1996).

JACKSON, Wanda (1937—). American rockabilly singer. Born Wanda Lavonne Jackson in Maud, OK, Oct 20, 1937; m. Wendell Goodman. ❧ Undisputed queen of musical genre known as rockabilly (1950s–60s), learned to play piano and guitar as a youngster and hosted a radio show on Oklahoma's station KLPR at 13; after high school, toured with Hank Thompson and his Brazos Valley Boys and with Elvis Presley, who, along with Gene Vincent of "Be-Bop-A-Lula" fame, influenced her later style; signed with Decca (1954) and had 1st hit, "You Can't Have My Love," a duet with bandleader Billy Gray; switched to Capitol (1956) and had another hit with "Let's Have a Party"; also sang "Mean Mean Man" (one of several songs she wrote), "Right or Wrong" and "In the Middle of a Heartache"; cut versions of some of her hit songs, like the explosive "Fujiyama Mama," in 3 languages; as rockabilly faded, returned to country music and with husband Wendell Goodman and her own band, The Party Timers, had a series of hits (1960s); moved into gospel (1970s). ❧ See also *Women in World History.*

JACKSON, Zina Garrison (b. 1963). See Garrison, Zina.

JACKSON-COPPIN, Fanny (1837–1913). See Coppin, Fanny Jackson.

JACKSON OF LODSWORTH, Baroness (1914–1981). *See Ward, Barbara.*

JACLARD, Anna (1843–1887). Russian writer. Name variations: Anna Korvin-Krukovsky or Corvin-Krukovsky; Anna Krukovskaya or Krukovskaia. Born Anna Vasilevna Korvin-Krukovsky or Korvina-Krukovskaia in late 1843 in Moscow; died Oct 1887; dau. of Vasily Vasilevich Korvin-Krukovsky (1801–1875, noble who served in the army and later managed his provincial estate) and Elizaveta (Schubert) Fedrovna (1820–1879); sister of Sophia Kovalevskaya (1850–1891); received instruction from personal tutors; m. Victor Jaclard (French revolutionary). ❧ See also *Women in World History.*

JACOB, Mary Phelps (1892–1970). *See Crosby, Caresse.*

JACOB, Naomi Ellington (1889–1964). English novelist and actress. Born Naomi Ellington Jacob, July 1, 1889, in Ripon, Yorkshire, England; died Aug 26, 1964; dau. of Nina Ellington Collinson (novelist as Nina Abbott). ❧ Began career teaching in Middlesbrough; made stage debut in Devonshire as Brownie in *Scandal* and London debut as Julia in *The 'Ruined' Lady* (both 1920); also appeared in *The Young Idea, Outward Bound, The Ringer, Excelsior* and *Fame,* among others; published 1st novel, the bestseller *Jacob Ussher* (1926); retired from stage (1929–41) because of ill health (caused by an earlier bout with TB) and lived in Italy until advent of WWII when she joined staff of ENSA; other novels include *Rock and Sand, Roots, Props, Young Emmanuel, Four Generations* and *Founder of the House;* also wrote about Marie Lloyd (*Our Marie*). ❧ See also autobiographical works, *Me, Me Again, More about Me, Me in the Kitchen, Me in Wartime* and *Me in the Mediterranean.*

JACOB, Rosamund (1888–1960). Irish journalist, author, and activist. Name variations: Rose or Rosa Jacob; (pseudonym) F. Winthrop. Born Rosamund Jacob, 1888, in Co. Waterford, Ireland; died in Dublin, Oct 11, 1960; never married; no children. ❧ Campaigner on feminist, nationalist, pacifist and humanitarian issues, became a member of militant Irish Women's Franchise League, contributing regularly to IWFL journal, *The Irish Citizen;* was a prominent member of nationalist women's organization, Cumann na mBan, and of separatist nationalist party, Sinn Fein; as one of the few women delegates to Sinn Fein Convention of Oct 1917, was instrumental in achieving a tacit

commitment to female suffrage; was resolutely opposed to Anglo-Irish Treaty and briefly imprisoned for her republican activities (1923); represented Ireland at 1921 International Congress of Women's International League for Peace and Freedom (WILPF), and, as secretary of the Irish branch, played a leading part in the organization of the 5th International Congress (1926); in addition, maintained a career as a journalist and author, publishing 1st novel, *Callaghan,* under pseudonym F. Winthrop (1920); also wrote *The Rise of the United Irishmen* (1937), *The Rebel's Wife* (1957) and the children's book *The Raven's Glen* (1960). ❧ See also *Women in World History.*

JACOBA. *Variant of Jacqueline.*

JACOBA DI SETTESOLI (d. about 1273). Saint. Name variations: Jacqueline of Settesoli; Saint Jacoba. Died c. 1273; m. Gratian Frangipini; children: 2 sons. ❧ As a loyal friend, was 2nd only to Clare of Assisi in the eyes St. Francis of Assisi; would have undoubtedly entered the religious life following death of husband had she not had been left with 2 sons to care for; entered 3rd order (the lay branch of the religious order); was buried in the Great Umbrian basilica, not far from her dear friend. Feast day is Feb 8. ❧ See also *Women in World History.*

JACOBA FELICIE (fl. 1322). See de Almania, Jacqueline Felicie.

JACOBA OF BAVARIA (1401–1436). See Jacqueline of Hainault.

JACOBA VON BEIJEREN (1401–1436). See Jacqueline of Hainault.

JACOBELLIS, Lindsey (1985—). American snowboarder. Born Aug 19, 1985, in CT. ❧ Wins include US championships, Northstar, CA, in Halfpipe (2002), Junior Worlds, Wanaka, NZ, in both Giant Slalom and Boadercross (2002), and gold medal in Snowboarder X and bronze medal in Slopestyle at X Games (Winter 2003); won Snowboardcross at World championships (2005); won a silver medal for Snowboardcross at Torino Olympics (2006).

JACOBI, Lotte (1896–1990). German-born American photographer. Born Johanna Alexandra Jacobi, Aug 17, 1896, in Thorn, West Prussia, Germany (now Torun, Poland); died in Concord, New Hampshire, May 6, 1990; dau. of Sigismund Jacobi (photographer) and Marie (Mia) Lublinski Jacobi; sister of Ruth Jacobi (photographer); studied at Munich's Bavarian State Academy for Photography; m. Siegbert Fritz Honig; m. Erich Reiss; children: (1st m.) Jochen (known as John Frank Hunter after immigrating to US). ❧ Major figure in history of photography, whose portraits of many of the greatest individuals of 20th century are an archive of the modern age; headed a photography studio in Berlin (1927–35) and photographed leading personalities of Weimar Republic, including Albert Einstein, Käthe Kollwitz, Kurt Weill, Lotte Lenya, Bertolt Brecht, Gerhart Hauptmann, George Grosz, Lion Feuchtwanger, Fritz Lang, Erwin Piscator, Emil Jannings and Peter Lorre; fled Nazism (1935); opened a studio in NY and contributed to *Life, New York Times,* and *New York Herald-Tribune;* also continued shooting photos of luminaries, including Eleanor Roosevelt, Margaret Mead, W.H. Auden, Benjamin Britten, Paul Robeson, Theodore Dreiser, Robert Frost and Billie Holiday. ❧ See also Kelly Wise, ed. *Lotte Jacobi* (Addison, 1978); and *Women in World History.*

JACOBI, Mary Putnam (1842–1906). English-born American physician. Name variations: Mary Putnam, Minnie. Born Mary Corinna Putnam, Aug 31, 1842, in London, England; died in New York, NY, June 10, 1906; dau. of George Palmer Putnam (publisher) and Victorine (Haven) Putnam; graduate of New York College of Pharmacy, 1863, Female Medical College of Pennsylvania, 1864, and École de Médecine in Paris, 1871; m. Dr. Abraham Jacobi, July 22, 1873; children: Ernst (1875–1883); Marjorie Jacobi (b. 1878). ❧ First woman admitted to the renowned École de Médecine in Paris (1868) and foremost woman physician of her era, whose career won the respect of her male colleagues and inspired many women physicians; returned to NY from England with family (1848); had 1st article published in *Atlantic Monthly* (1860); interned at New England Hospital for Women and Children (1864); did clinical, laboratory, and course work in Paris (1866–71); was professor of materia medica and therapeutics at Woman's Medical College of New York Infirmary (1871–89); had private medical practice (1871–1902); served as president of Association for Advancement of Medical Education for Women (1874–1903); was clinical lecturer on children's diseases at Post-Graduate Medical School (1882–85); was president of Alumnae Association of Woman's Medical College of Pennsylvania (1888 and 1894); helped found Consumer's League (1890) and League for Political Education (1894). Was 1st woman elected to membership in New York Academy of Medicine (1880). ❧ See also *Mary Putnam*

Jacobi, M.D.: A Pathfinder in Medicine (Putnam, 1925); Ruth Putnam, ed. *Life and Letters of Mary Putnam Jacobi* (Putnam, 1925); Rhoda Truax, *The Doctors Jacobi* (Little, Brown, 1952); and *Women in World History.*

JACOBINI, Maria (1890–1944). Italian actress. Born in Rome, Italy, Feb 17, 1890; died Nov 20, 1944, in Rome; niece of Cardinal Jacobini, minister of state to Pope Leo XIII; studied at Rome's Academy of Dramatic Arts; sister of actresses Bianca (b. 1888) and Diomira Jacobini (1896–1959). ❖ One of the most revered European stars of her day, made stage and screen debuts (1910) and quickly became one of Italy's leading "divas" of the silent screen; starred mostly in Italian historical spectacles and social dramas; also appeared in German, Austrian, and French productions; performed in Fedor Ozep's Soviet screen adaptation of Leo Tolstoy's *The Living Corpse* (1920); other films include *Lucrezia Borgia, Beatrice Cenci, Vampe di Gelosia, Resurrezione, La Vie de Bohème, Il Carnavale di Venezia, La Scala, Giuseppe Verdi* and *Melodie eterne.* ❖ See also *Women in World History.*

JACOBS, Aletta (1854–1929). Dutch physician. Born Aletta Henriette Jacobs, Feb 9, 1854, in Sappemeer, Holland; died Aug 10, 1929, in Baarn, Holland; dau. of Abraham Jacobs (physician) and Anna (de Jongh) Jacobs; attended University of Groningen; m. Carel Gerritsen (Dutch politician), April 28, 1892; children: son (b. 1893, lived only one day); (foster son) Charles Jacobs (son of her deceased brother Julius). ❖ An international leader in family planning, women's rights and pacifism, received medical degree from University of Amsterdam (1879); established free clinic for poor women and children (1880), which she would operate for 14 years; opened a birth-control clinic (1882), facing condemnation and slander by much of the medical establishment, who opposed contraception on moral and religious grounds despite its legal status in Holland; translated *Women and Economics* by Charlotte Perkins Gilman into Dutch (1900); led Dutch Association for Woman Suffrage (1903–19); organized International Woman Suffrage Alliance conference (1908); translated *Women and Labor* by Olive Schreiner; went on speaking tour of Africa and Asia (1911–12); ran for political office (1918); is still considered a national hero in the Netherlands. ❖ See also autobiography *Memories* (1924); and *Women in World History.*

JACOBS, Frances Wisebart (1843–1892). American welfare worker. Born in Harrodsburg, KY, Mar 29, 1843; died in Denver, CO, Nov 3, 1892; dau. of Leon Henry Wisebart (tailor) and Rosetta (Marx) Wisebart; m. Abraham Jacobs (merchant), Feb 18, 1863; children: 1 daughter, 2 sons. ❖ Known as Colorado's "Mother of the Charities," served as president of Hebrew Benevolent Ladies Aid Society; was a founding officer of non-sectarian Ladies' Relief Society (1874) and became a leading force in establishing the Charity Organization Society (1877), a federation of Denver's charitable groups; was the only woman among 16 Colorado pioneers memorialized in a stained-glass portrait in the state capitol dome. ❖ See also *Women in World History.*

JACOBS, Harriet A. (1813–1897). American abolitionist and writer. Name variations: (pseudonym) Linda Brent. Born Harriet Ann Jacobs into slavery, autumn 1813 (exact date unrecorded), in Edenton, North Carolina; died in Washington, DC, Mar 7, 1897; dau. of slave parents Daniel Jacobs (carpenter, died 1826) and Delilah (died 1819); taught to read and write by 1st owner, then self-educated; never married; children: Joseph (b. 1829); Louisa Matilda (b. 1833). ❖ Born into slavery, was bequeathed to the 3-year-old niece of her 1st owner after he died (1825); after ongoing threats of rape by owner Dr. James Norcom, began a relationship with white neighbor Samuel Sawyer; gave birth to son by Sawyer (1829), then daughter by Sawyer (1833); sent to a plantation and ran away, eventually hiding under roof of grandmother's house where she would remain for 7 years; escaped to the North and worked in New York as nursemaid to Willis family (1842); fleeing slave hunters, went to Boston with daughter and worked as seamstress (1844); worked in Anti-Slavery Reading Room in Rochester, NY (1849); moved to NY and worked for Willis family again (1850); was purchased and freed by Cornelia Grinnell Willis (1852); approached Harriet Beecher Stowe about writing her story and decided to write the book herself (1853); anonymously published *Incidents in the Life of a Slave Girl,* one of the most powerful testimonies of the experiences of a woman under slavery, with white abolitionist Lydia Maria Child as editor (1861); throughout Civil War and aftermath, took part in relief work and efforts to help freed slaves (1862–68). Because she wrote under a pseudonym, and because the lives of slaves are difficult to document, for over 100 years her name was virtually forgotten. ❖ See also *Women in World History.*

JACOBS, Helen Hull (1908–1997). American tennis player. Born Helen Hull Jacobs, Aug 6, 1908, in Globe, AZ; died June 2, 1997, in East Hampton, NY; daughter of Roland Herbert Jacobs and Eula (Hull) Jacobs; attended University of California at Berkeley, 1926–29, and William and Mary College, 1942; never married. ❖ Won US National jr. championships (1924–25); was 1st to win 4 consecutive US women's singles championships (1932, 1933, 1934, 1935); won US doubles championships (1932, 1933, 1934); won Wimbledon singles championship (1936); was a 6-time Wimbledon finalist; was a member of the American Wightman Cup team for 13 successive years; ranked in the world's top 10 (1928–40). Designed sports clothes, NYC; was senior editor, Grolier Book of Knowledge; served on Republican National Committee (1932); served as lieutenant in the US Naval Reserve (1954), becoming Commander USNR, retired. ❖ See also autobiography *Beyond the Game* (1936); and *Women in World History.*

JACOBS, Pattie Ruffner (1875–1935). American suffragist and social reformer. Born Oct 2, 1875, in Malden, WV; died Dec 22, 1935, in Birmingham, Alabama; dau. of Lewis Ruffner and Virginia Louise (West) Ruffner; m. Solon Harold Jacobs, Feb 8, 1898; children: 2 daughters. ❖ Co-founded (1911) and assumed presidency of Birmingham Equal Suffrage Association; served as president (1912–16) and chair (1918–20) of Alabama Equal Suffrage Association; served as 2nd auditor (1916–18) and congressional committee member of National American Woman Suffrage Association; after ratification of 19th Amendment, helped transform state suffrage association into Alabama League of Women Voters; during Franklin D. Roosevelt's administration, worked as head of women's division of Consumers' Advisory Board of National Recovery Administration and as publicity speaker for Tennessee Valley Authority.

JACOBS, Simmone (1966—). English runner. Name variations: Simone Jacobs. Born Sept 5, 1966, in England. ❖ At Los Angeles Olympics, won a bronze medal in 4x100-meter relay (1984).

JACOBS-BOND, Carrie. *See Bond, Carrie Jacobs.*

JACOBSEN, Else (1911–1965). Danish swimmer. Born May 31, 1911, in Denmark; died April 1965. ❖ At Los Angeles Olympics, won a bronze medal in 200-meter breaststroke (1932).

JACOBSEN, Inger Kathrine (1867–1939). New Zealand midwife. Name variations: Inger Kathrine Nielsen. Born Inger Kathrine Nielsen, on Sept 5, 1867, at Tyrsted, near Horsens, Denmark; died on Oct 22, 1939, in Kihikihi, New Zealand; dau. of Søren Nielsen (farmer) and Mette Katharine Mikkelsen; m. Charles Leonard Jacobsen, 1885; children: 12. ❖ Placed into domestic service at age 8, never attended school or learned to read or write; with no formal training, became skilled in nursing and midwifery, delivering hundreds of babies in Maharahara and Kihikihi districts without loss of mother or baby; during influenza pandemic in 1918, successfully nursed patients in local hall, losing none. When Parliament passed Nurses and Midwives Registration Act in 1925, doctors verified a false certificate so that she might continue her work. ❖ See also *Dictionary of New Zealand Biography* (Vol. 3).

JACOBSEN, Josephine (1908–2003). American poet, short-story writer and critic. Born Josephine Winder Boylan, Aug 19, 1908, in Cobourg, Ontario, Canada; died July 9, 2003, in Cockeysville, MD; m. Eric Jacobsen, 1932; children: Erland. ❖ Brought to US at 3 months of age; earned recognition with 1st publication, *Let Each Man Remember,* a collection of 15 love sonnets; also published *The Human Climate: New Poems* (1953), *The Animal Inside* (1966), *Distances* (1991), *In the Crevice of Time* (1995) and *What Goes Without Saying: Collected Stories of Josephine Jacobsen* (2000); was consultant in poetry (title later changed to poet laureate) to Library of Congress (1971–73); inducted into American Academy of Arts and Letters (1994); frequent contributor to *The New Yorker.* Received Robert Frost Medal for Lifetime Achievement in Poetry from Poetry Society of America (1997).

JACOBSOHN, Berta (1878–1967). *See Lask, Berta.*

JACOBSON, Dorothy (1899–1987). *See Hammerstein, Dorothy.*

JACOBSON, Ethel May (1877–1965). New Zealand teacher, newspaper editor and manager, and journalist. Born Sept 6, 1877, at Lyttelton, New Zealand; died June 14, 1965, at Mt. Leinster, New Zealand; dau. of Charles Jacobson (newspaper editor and owner) and Margaret (Dougherty) Jacobson; Canterbury College, BA, 1900, MA, 1901. ❖ Taught at Nelson College for Girls (1901–03); after father died, served as editor and business manager for his paper, *Akaroa Mail, and*

Banks Peninsula Advertiser (1910–52). ❖ See also *Dictionary of New Zealand Biography* (Vol. 3).

JACOBSON, Helen (d. 1974). American producer. Died Nov 17, 1974, age 53, in Los Angeles, CA. ❖ Produced *See the Jaguar, Abraham Cochrane, After the Rain* and *Fly Blackbird*.

JACOBSON, Henrietta (1906–1988). American-born Yiddish actress. Name variations: Henrietta J. Adler. Born Mar 27, 1906, in Chicago, IL; died Oct 9, 1988, in New York, NY; m. Julius Adler (actor); children: Bruce Adler (actor). ❖ Made stage debut as a child and NY debut in *Israel's Hope* (1912); other plays include *It Could Happen to You, The World of Mrs. Solomon, Kosher Widow, Come Blow Your Horn* and *70 Girls 70*.

JACOBSON, Louise (1924–1943). French correspondent. Born in Paris, France, Dec 24, 1924; died in Auschwitz, 1943; dau. of Olga Jacobson (d. 1943). ❖ As a 17-year-old Jew during German Occupation of France, defied the edict to wear the yellow star; was arrested as a political prisoner and taken to Fresnes (1942), then Drancy, then Auschwitz; while imprisoned, wrote often to schoolfriends in a tiny script; left articulate record of her thoughts and experiences which was published by Serge Klarsfeld in France (1989) as *Lettres de Louise Jacobson* and adapted for the theater. ❖ See also *Women in World History*.

JACOBSON, Sada (1983—). American fencer. Born Feb 14, 1983, in Rochester, Minnesota; attended Yale University. ❖ At World championship, won a gold medal for team sabre (2000); placed 1st overall for indiv. sabre World Cup ranking (2002–03 and 2003–04); won a bronze medal for indiv. sabre at Athens Olympics (2004).

JACOBSSON, Ulla (1929–1982). Swedish actress. Born May 23, 1929, in Göteborg, Sweden; died of bone cancer, Aug 20, 1982, in Vienna, Austria; m. an Austrian scientist; no children. ❖ After an early stage career, gained international attention with 2nd film, *One Summer of Happiness* (1951), directed by Arne Mattsson; subsequently appeared in *Smiles of a Summer Night* (1955), the breakthrough film of Ingmar Bergman; starred internationally in such film as *The Sacred Lie* (1955), *Crime et Châtiment* (*Crime and Punishment*, 1956), *Song of the Scarlet Flower* (1956), *Riviera Story* (1961), *Love Is a Ball* (1963), *Zulu* (1964), *The Heroes of Telemark* (1965), *Nightmare* (1965), *The Double Man* (1967) and *The Servant* (1970). ❖ See also *Women in World History*.

JACOBY, Annalee (1916–2002). See Fadiman, Annalee.

JACOT, Michele (1952—). French Alpine skier. Born Jan 5, 1952, in Pont de Beauvoisin, Chamonix Argentiere, France. ❖ Won a World championship for the combined and a World Cup overall (1970), the only French skier to win the cup in the 20th century; retired (1976).

JACQUELINE. *Variant of Jacoba.*

JACQUELINE FELICIE DE ALMANIA (fl. 1322). See de Almania, Jacqueline Felicie.

JACQUELINE OF BAVARIA (1401–1436). See Jacqueline of Hainault.

JACQUELINE OF HAINAULT (1401–1436). Countess of Hainault and Holland. Name variations: Jacqueline of Bavaria; Jacqueline of Holland; Jacoba or Jakobäa of Bavaria; Jacoba von Beijeren; (family name) Wittelsbach. Born July 25, 1401 (some sources cite 1402), in Hainault, a Flemish province; died Oct 9, 1436, in Teylingen, Netherlands; created countess (1417); dau. of William VI, count of Hainault and Holland, and Margaret of Burgundy (c. 1376–1441); m. John (1398–1417), duke of Touraine and dauphin of France, July 1416; m. John IV, duke of Brabant (r. 1415–1427), Mar 10, 1418 (annulled c. 1422); m. Humphrey, duke of Gloucester, 1422 (annulled 1428); m. Francis of Borselen also known as Franz von Borselen or Franz de Borselle, count of Ostrevent, July 1432. ❖ Powerful noblewoman, inherited father's vast estates at 15, becoming countess of Hainault and Holland; embroiled in a war with Philip the Good, duke of Burgundy, who successfully wrenched control of Hainault from her; captured and imprisoned, disguised herself as a pageboy and managed to escape; returning to Holland, again took up the fight for the right to rule her inheritance; eventually had to concede defeat and sign the Treaty of Delft, which made Philip her guardian and guaranteed him the right to her lands upon her death and the right to choose her next husband; married the man of her choice, Franz von Borselen, soon after signing the treaty, and the war for Hainault and Holland continued until Franz was captured; when Philip offered to spare Franz's life if she signed over all of her properties to him, agreed to his conditions. ❖ See also *Women in World History*.

JACQUELINE OF HOLLAND (1401–1436). *See Jacqueline of Hainault.*

JACQUELINE OF SETTESOLI (d. about 1273). *See Jacoba di Settesoli.*

JACQUES, Hattie (1922–1980). English comedic actress. Born Josephine Edwina Jacques, Feb 7, 1922, in Sandgate, Kent, England; died from a heart attack, Oct 6, 1980, in London; m. John Le Mesurier (actor), 1949 (div. 1965); children: sons Robin and Kim Le Mesurier. ❖ Made stage debut (1944); appeared in over 20 films, including *Chance for a Lifetime, The Gay Lady, The Adventures of Sadie, School for Scoundrels, Make Mine Mink, Follow a Star, The Pickwick Papers* and *Oliver Twist*; best known for playing Matron (as in "Ooh, Matron") in 4 "Carry On" films and also made 10 others; was a mainstay on radio and tv. ❖ See also Rebecca Sandiford's "The Unforgettable Hattie Jacques" (documentary, 2000).

JACQUET DE LA GUERRE, Elisabeth-Claude (c. 1666–1729). French composer and musician. Name variations: Elisabeth de la Guerre. Born Elisabeth-Claude Jacquet c. 1666; died June 27, 1729, in Paris, France; dau. of Claude Jacquet (organist and harpsichord maker); m. Marin de la Guerre (Parisian organist), 1684 (died 1704); children: 1 son (died young). ❖ Widely regarded as a prodigy, 1st performed on the harpsichord before Louis XIV when she was 4; won lifelong support and protection of Louis and subsequent admiration of Paris; continued to play frequently at the royal court, where the king placed her under the protection of his mistresses, Madame de Montespan and Madame de Maintenon, and provided her an annual stipend; declined his invitation to move with his court to Versailles (1682), preferring to remain in Paris, where she enjoyed a long, successful career which brought her considerable wealth; composed for the harpsichord and for ballet scores, performed professionally as a singer and musician, mostly in salons of the nobility but also in public recitals; became widely known for improvisational techniques; also wrote at least 1 opera, *Cephale et Procris* (1694), along with sonatas and Biblical cantatas; performed for almost 50 years. ❖ See also *Women in World History*.

JACQUETTA OF LUXEMBURG (c. 1416–1472). Luxemburg princess. Name variations: Duchess of Bedford. Born in Luxemburg c. 1416; died May 30, 1472; dau. of Peter of Luxemburg, count of St. Pol, and Margaret del Balzo; m. John of Lancaster, duke of Bedford (son of Henry IV and Mary de Bohun), April 20, 1433; m. Richard Woodville, 1st earl Rivers, in 1436; children: (2nd m.) Elizabeth Woodville (1437–1492); Anthony Woodville, 2nd earl Rivers (c. 1442–1483); John Woodville (c. 1445–1469); Lionel Woodville, bishop of Salisbury (c. 1453–1484); Richard, 3rd earl Rivers (d. 1491); Edward Woodville (d. 1488); Margaret Woodville (who m. Thomas Fitzalan, 14th earl of Arundel); Anne Woodville (who m. William Bourchier, viscount Bourchier, and George Grey, 2nd earl of Kent); Jacquetta Woodville; Katherine Woodville (c. 1442–1512); Mary Woodville (c. 1443–c. 1480); Eleanor Woodville (who m. Anthony Grey).

JACQUIN, Lisa (1962—). American equestrian. Born Feb 22, 1962; lives in Pennsylvania. ❖ At Seoul Olympics, won a silver medal in team jumping (1988); also on Olympic team in Barcelona (1992); won Valley Classic Grand Prix (2003), on Justice.

JACUBOWSKA, Wanda (b. 1907). See Jakubowska, Wanda.

JACULIN. *Variant of Jacqueline.*

JACZYNOWSKA, Katarzyna (1875–1920). Polish pianist. Born in Stawle, Poland, 1875; died 1920; studied with Anton Rubinstein (1883–94), then for 2 years with Leschetizky in Vienna. ❖ Embarked on successful virtuoso career throughout Central Europe; began teaching a master class at Warsaw Conservatory (1912).

JADWIGA. *Variant of Hedwig or Hedvig.*

JADWIGA (1374–1399). Queen of Poland. Name variations: Hedwig, Hedwiga, Hedvigis; Jadwiga of Anjou. Born in Hungary, Feb 18, 1374; died in Poland from complications of childbirth 3 days after death of only child, July 17, 1399; buried with daughter in cathedral at Wawel Hill, Cracow; youngest dau. of Louis I the Great, king of Hungary (r. 1342–1382) and Poland (r. 1370–1382) and Elizabeth of Bosnia (c. 1345–1387); m. Jagello or Jagiello (1377–1434), grand duke of Lithuania, who became Vladislav also known as Ladislas II (or V) Jagello, king of Poland (r. 1386–1434), Feb 18, 1386; children: Elizabeth Bonifacio (June 22, 1399–July 14, 1399). ❖ One of Poland's great rulers, whose reign is seen as the beginning of the golden age in her nation's history and whose policies and foundations continued to bear fruit after her death; crowned king [sic] of Poland (Oct 15, 1384); exhibited a remarkable strength of character, skilled diplomacy, and inspired political acumen; was a model of Christian virtue in both her public and private life and dedicated to solving her country's problems by peaceful means; gave up her betrothed, William of Austria, in order to marry Jagiello, grand duke of Lithuania, and so united their 2 countries under the banner of Roman Catholicism, pushed forward the frontier of Western civilization and made possible the emergence of that region described as Central East Europe; her concern for the spiritual well-being of her nation and her devotion to the poor and to charitable works earned her the love of her people and the special recognition and continuing support of the Catholic Church; refounded Cracow University; died a queen, venerated as a saint, at age 25. Beatified by Pope John Paul II during his visit to Poland (1979). ❖ See also Oscar Halecki, *Jadwiga of Anjou and the Rise of East Central Europe* (Columbia University, 1991); M.M. Gardner, *Queen Jadwiga of Poland* (London, 1934); C. Kellogg, *Jadwiga, Poland's Great Queen* (1931, rep. 1971); and *Women in World History.*

JADWIGA OF ANJOU (1374–1399). *See Jadwiga.*

JADWIGA OF GLOGOW (fl. late 1300s). Queen of Poland. Fl. in late 1300s; 4th wife of Kazimierz III also known as Casimir III the Great, king of Poland (r. 1333–1370); children: possibly Elizabeth (who m. Boguslaw V of Slupsk); Cunegunde; Anna. Casimir III was 1st m. to Aldona of Lithuania, Adelaide of Hesse, and Krystyna Rokiczanska.

JADWIGA OF SILESIA (1174–1243). *See Hedwig of Silesia.*

JAEL (fl. c. 1125 BCE). Biblical woman. Name variations: Jahel; Yael. Fl. around 1125 BCE; wife of Heber the Kenite (Judg. 4:17–22). ❖ A Kenite woman, welcomed Israel's enemy Sisera into her tent with an offer of milk and a promise to guard against intruders while he slept; when he fell asleep, killed him by driving a tent nail into his temple with a mallet; was later honored in the song of Deborah as "most blessed above women."

JAEL, Mama (1939—). *See Mbogo, Jael.*

JAENISCH, Karolina (1807–1893). *See Pavlova, Karolina.*

JAFFE, Else (1874–1973). *See von Richthofen, Else.*

JAGAN, Janet (1920—). Jewish-American Guyanese politician and president. Born Janet Rosenberg, Oct 20, 1920, in Chicago, IL; attended University of Detroit, Wayne State University, Michigan State College (now University), Cook County School of Nursing; m. Cheddi Jagan (dentist and East Indian from Guyana), 1943 (died Mar 1997); children: Nadira Jagan; Cheddi Jagan Jr. ❖ Known as the "matriarch of Guyanese sovereignty," married Cheddi Jagan and moved to Guyana (1943); co-founded the Women's Political and Economic Organization and the Political Affairs Committee (1946); co-founded the People's Progressive Party (1950); served as general secretary of the PPP (1950–70); served as deputy speaker of the Legislature (1953); jailed for 6 months (1955); served as minister of Labour, Health and Housing (1957), as minister of Home Affairs and Senate (1963–64); served on the Guyana Elections Commission (1967–68); was president, Union of Guyanese Journalists (1970–97); worked as editor of the *Mirror* (1973–97); was first lady of the Republic and acting ambassador to UN (1993); was prime minister and vice-president (1997); elected president of Guyana (Dec 1997); resigned office because of ill health (Aug 1999). Awarded Order of Excellence of Guyana and Gandhi Gold Medal for Peace, Democracy, and Women's Rights. ❖ See also *Women in World History.*

JAGELLO, Catherine (1525–1583). *See Catherine Jagello.*

JAGELLONICA, Catherine (1525–1583). *See Catherine Jagello.*

JAGEMANN, Karoline (1777–1848). German actress and singer. Name variations: Caroline; Frau von Heygendorf; Madame Kegendorf. Born in Weimar, Germany, Jan 5, 1777; died in Dresden, Germany, July 10, 1848; dau. of Christian Joseph Jagemann (1735–1804, German scholar); sister of Ferdinand Jagemann (1780–1820, portrait painter); children: (with Charles Augustus, grand duke) 2 sons. ❖ Noted singer, debuted at Mannheim (1795); was such a sensation when she sang at Weimar (1796), caught the attention of Goethe and Schiller; had another success in Berlin (1801); returned to Goethe's theater in Weimar (1809); became mistress of the grand duke Charles Augustus (1809) and became such a powerful influence that she often hampered Goethe's work, causing the poet to resign from directing in the theater to avoid her (1817); remained at Weimar until death of grand duke, when she retired to Dresden. ❖ See also *Women in World History.*

JAGGER, Amy. English gymnast. Born in UK. ❖ At Amsterdam Olympics, won a bronze medal in team all-around (1928).

JAGIELLO, Appolonia (1825–1866). Polish-Lithuanian hero and fighter. Born 1825 in Poland, a descendant of Poland's royal house; died 1866; m. Gaspard Tochman (1795–1880, Polish patriot, soldier, orator and lawyer), 1851. ❖ Disguised as a soldier, fought in the Cracow Insurrection (1846) and Hungarian Revolution (1848–49); by displaying valor at the battle of Enerzey (1848), was promoted to rank of lieutenant; became superintendent of the military hospital at Komarom Fortress; after Hungarians were defeated, moved to Washington, DC (1849), where her fame preceded her; lived in Virginia.

JAHAN, Nur.
See Nur Jahan (1577–1645).
See Jehan, Noor (1926–2000).

JAHANARA (1614–1681). Indian princess. Name variations: Princess Jahan Ara; Jahanara Begum. Born April 2, 1614, in India; died Sept 6, 1681; eldest dau. of Mumtaz Mahal (c. 1592–1631) and Shah Jahan, Mughal emperor (r. 1628–58); sister of Aurangzeb (1618–1707, Mughal emperor); aunt of Zeb-un-Nissa; never married; no children. ❖ On mother's death (1631), assumed her position as head of the harem; became known to members of the Mughal court as Begum Sahib, her father's uncrowned empress, one of the most powerful women at court; well educated, wrote and commissioned poetry; was involved in the design of the Taj Mahal and commissioned 5 buildings in Shahjahanabad (1650), including Chandni Chowk, the central bazaar; negotiated the weddings of her siblings and was politically active during the War of Succession (1658); tended to her father while he was in captivity; under Aurangzeb's reign, was known as Padisha Begum (Empress of Princesses); wrote a biography of Mu'in al-Din, a Muslim saint (1671); revered in India to this day.

JAHEL (fl. 1125 BCE). *See Jael.*

JAHL, Evelin (1956—). East German track-and-field athlete. Name variations: Evelin Jahl-Schlaak. Born Mar 28, 1956, in East Germany. ❖ Won a gold medal at Montreal Olympics (1976) and a gold medal at Moscow Olympics (1980), both in discus throw.

JAHN, Rita (1947—). *See Wilden, Rita.*

JAHN, Sabine (1953—). East German rower. Born June 27, 1953, in East Germany. ❖ At Montreal Olympics, won a silver medal in double sculls (1976).

JAHNKE, Clara Muller (1860–1905). *See Müller, Clara.*

JAHODA, Marie (1907–2001). Austrian-born social psychologist. Born Jan 26, 1907, in Vienna, Austria; died April 28, 2001; attended University of Vienna; m. Paul F. Lazarsfeld, 1927; Austen Albu, 1958 (died 1994). ❖ An expert in social psychology, was imprisoned by Austrian government because of her antifascist activities (1936–37) and later released to England; during WWII, ran Radio Rotes Wien (secret radio station) at the Ministry of Information in England; worked as a New York University social psychology professor (1949–58), Brunel University psychology professor in Uxbridge, Middlesex (1958–65) and University of Sussex psychology professor (1965–73) and professor emeritus (1983–2001); employed as a Science Policy Research Unit senior research consultant at University of Sussex (1971–83); explored subsistence farming, nursing, and race relations; wrote *Research Methods in Human Relations* (1953), *Current Concepts of Modern Mental Health* (1958), *Freud and the Dilemmas of Psychology* (1977) and *Employment and Unemployment* (1982). Named Commander of the Order of the British Empire (1974).

JAHREN, Anne. Norwegian cross-country skier. Born in Norway. ❖ Won a gold medal for 4 x 5 km relay and a bronze medal at Sarajevo Olympics for 20 km (1984); won a silver medal for 4 x 5 km relay at Calgary Olympics (1988).

JAICH, Minna (1837–1912). *See Kautsky, Minna.*

JAIPUR, maharani of. *See Gayatra Devi (b. 1919).*

JAKOBA or JAKOBÄA. *Variant of Jacoba or Jacqueline.*

JAKOBSDÓTTIR, Svava (1930—). Icelandic playwright, novelist, short-story writer and politician. Name variations: Svava Jakobsdottir. Born 1930 in Neskaupstadur, Iceland; studied in US and England. ❖ As a Socialist, was a member of Icelandic parliament (1971–79); works include *12 konur* (1965), *Veizla undir grjótvegg* (1967), *Gefid* *hvort ödru* (1982), and *Leigjandinn* (1969); was also active in the Icelandic feminist movement.

JAKOBSEN, Nina (1972—). *See Nymark Andersen, Nina.*

JAKOBSSON, Ludowika (1884–1968). Finnish pairs skater. Name variations: Ludovika or Ludowika Eilers or Jakobsson-Eilers. Born Ludowika Eilers, July 25, 1884, in Finland; died Nov 1, 1968; m. Walter Jakobsson (skater, 1882–1957), c. 1911. ❖ With Walter Jakobsson, won 3 World championships (1911, 1914, 1923), as well as a gold medal at Antwerp Olympics (1920) and a silver medal at Chamonix Olympics (1924).

JAKUBOWSKA, Krystyna (1942—). Polish volleyball player. Born Dec 15, 1942, in Poland. ❖ Won a bronze medal at Tokyo Olympics (1964) and bronze medal at Mexico City Olympics (1968), both in team competition.

JAKUBOWSKA, Wanda (1907–1998). Polish film director. Name variations: Jacubowska. Pronunciation: Ya-koo-BOV-ska. Born Nov 10, 1907, in Warsaw, Poland, then a part of the Russian empire; died Feb 25, 1998, in Warsaw; studied art history at University of Warsaw. ❖ One of Poland's most important film directors, whose films were influential in advancement of post-WWII Polish cinema, was a founding member of left-wing START, the "Organization for the Promotion of Artistic Films" (1929); completed 1st documentary, *Report One* (1930); completed 1st feature film, *On the Banks of the Niemen* (1939), but negative was lost during WWII; captured by Nazis in Poland (1942), was sent to Auschwitz (1943); returned to Auschwitz to make the highly successful *The Last Stop* (also known as *The Last Stage* or in Poland *Ostatni etap*), depicting life in that German concentration camp (1945–47); other films include *Report Two* (1931), *Impressions, The Sea* (1932), *We Build* (1934), *The Atlantic Story* (1955), *Soldier of Victory* (1953), *Farewell to the Devil* (1956), *King Matthew I* (1958), *Encounter in the Shadows* (*Encounters in the Dark*, 1960), *It Happened Yesterday* (1960), *The End of Our World* (1964), *The Hot Line* (1965), *At 150 Kilometers Per Hour* (1971), *Ludwik Warynski* (1978), *Dance in Chains* (*The Mazurka Danced at Dawn*, 1979), *Invitation to Dance* (*Invitation*, 1986) and *Colors of Love* (1987). Won International Peace Prize for *The Last Stop* (1951). ❖ See also (in German) Danuta Karcz, *Wanda Jakubowska* (Henschelverlag, 1967); and *Women in World History.*

JALANDONI, Magdalena (1891–1978). Filipino novelist, short-story writer and feminist. Born 1891 in Boilo, Philippines; died 1978. ❖ The 1st Filipino woman novelist, published 66 works, including *Ang Tunuk Sang Isa Ka Bulak* (1907), *Ang Bantay Sa Patio*, and *Ang Dalag sa Tindahan*; also fought for women's suffrage.

JALINTO, A. (1862–1934). *See Almeida, Julia Lopes de.*

JAMBRIŠAK, Marija (1847–1937). Croatian writer, educator, and women's-rights activist. Name variations: Maria Jambrisak. Born 1847 in Karlovac, Croatia; died 1937. ❖ Trained as teacher in Zagreb where she taught at girls' high school (1847–92) and at Girls' Lyceum; wrote articles in books and magazines; co-founded Croatian and Slovenian Ladies' Association for Women's Work and Education.

JAMES, Alice (1848–1892). American diarist. Born Alice James in New York, NY, Aug 7, 1848; died in Campden Hill, Kensington, England, Mar 6, 1892; youngest of 5 children of Henry James, Sr. (1811–1882, writer and lecturer) and Mary Walsh James (1810–1882); sister of William James (1842–1910, philosopher and psychologist) and Henry James (1843–1916, novelist and short story writer); never married; no children. ❖ Chronic invalid whose many brilliant letters and the diary she kept during the last 3 years of her life have been recognized as shrewd commentaries on the famous family, and on the nature of an invalid woman's life in that era. ❖ See also *The Diary of Alice James* (Dodd, 1964); Jean Strouse, *Alice James: A Biography* (Houghton, 1980); Ruth B. Yeazell, *The Death and Letters of Alice James* (U. of California, 1981); and *Women in World History.*

JAMES, Alice Gibbens (1849–1922). American socialite. Born in Weymouth, MA, 1849; died in Cambridge, MA, 1922; dau. of Daniel Lewis Gibbens and Eliza (Putnam) Gibbens; m. William James (1842–1910, psychologist and progressive thinker) in 1878; sister-in-law of Alice James (1848–1892, diarist) and Henry James (1843–1916, novelist and short story writer); children: Henry James (1879–1947); William James (1882–1961); Herman James (1884–1885); Margaret Mary James (Porter) (1887–1950); Alexander James (1890–1946). ❖ Wife of philosopher William James.

JAMES, Annie Isabella (1884–1965). New Zealand missionary. Born April 22, 1884, at Otepopo, North Otago, New Zealand; died Feb 6, 1965, in Auckland, New Zealand; dau. of Joseph James (farmer) and Elizabeth (Morrison) James; children: adopted several Chinese orphans. ❖ Trained as missionary at Presbyterian Women's Training Institute (1910–11); assigned to Canton Villages Mission at Kong Chuen (Jiangcun), China (1912); returned to New Zealand to train in midwifery (1914), then to Melbourne, Australia, to train in child welfare (1929); established branch hospital in Kaai Hau, where she began maternity and dispensary work; compiled Cantonese handbook on principles of infant care (1930s); forced out of China by Communist takeover (1947). Made a Member of British Empire (1942, presented, 1952). ❖ See also *Dictionary of New Zealand Biography* (Vol. 3).

JAMES, Cheryl (1964—). American singer. Name variations: Cheryl "Salt" James; "Salt"; Salt-n-Pepa. Born Mar 8, 1964, in Brooklyn, NY; m. Gavin Wray, Dec 24, 2000; children: 2. ❖ With Sandy "Pepa" Denton, recorded minor hit single, "The Show Stoppa," credited to band, Super Nature; with Denton, formed Salt-n-Pepa (1985) and released platinum debut album, *Hot, Cool and Vicious* (1986), with hit "Push It," which was nominated for Grammy (1988); added Deidre "Dee Dee" Roper as DJ and released gold album, *A Salt With a Deadly Pepa* (1988); with band, produced or co-produced 4 tracks on platinum album, *Blacks' Magic* (1990), from which "Expression" went gold; with group, released hit album, *Very Necessary* (1993), appeared in several films, including *Who's the Man?* (1993) and *Raw Nerve* (1999), and won Grammy for Best Rap Performance (1995) for "None of Your Business."

JAMES, Claire (1920–1986). American actress. Born April 23, 1920, in Minneapolis, Minnesota; died Jan 18, 1986, in Woodland Hills, CA; m. Blake James (actor). ❖ Was 1st runner-up in Miss America pageant (1938); films include *Forty Little Mothers, Gone with the Wind, The Ziegfeld Girl, Road to Singapore, Coney Island, Good Sam, Only the Valiant, Caprice* and *The Sunshine Boys.*

JAMES, Eleanor (c. 1645–1719). *See James, Elinor.*

JAMES, Elinor (c. 1645–1719). British printer and political writer. Name variations: Eleanor James. Born c. 1645 in England; died in 1719; m. Thomas James, London printer. ❖ Wrote and printed over 90 pamphlets and broadsides on political, religious and commercial issues; interviewed Charles II and James II and admonished George I; published *Vindication of the Church of England* (1687); petitioned Parliament about legislation concerning the printer trades, among other matters; was committed to Newgate for "dispersing scandalous and reflective papers" which condemned William III for accepting the crown (1689).

JAMES, Esther Marion Pretoria (1900–1990). New Zealand inventor, fashion model, long-distance walker, and builder. Name variations: Esther Haysom, Esther Julian. Born on Nov 5, 1900, at Pahiatua, New Zealand; died Jan 7, 1990, at Auckland; dau. of Thomas Joseph James (carpenter) and Eliza Jane (Whitmore) James; m. Leslie Harrison Haysom (architect), 1924 (div. 1935); m. Edward Scanlon Julian (sheep farmer), 1937 (div. 1971); children: (1st m.) 1 daughter; (2nd m.) 1 son, 1 daughter. ❖ Patented several inventions for domestic use (1920s); was one of New Zealand's first professional fashion models (1930s); promoted New Zealand-made goods and improved trading through long-distance walk of nearly 1,600 miles in 197 days (1931–32); walked 1,400 miles from Melbourne to Brisbane, Australia (1932–33); purchased land, where she designed and built several houses. ❖ See also autobiography, *Jobbing Along* (1965); *Dictionary of New Zealand Biography* (Vol. 4).

JAMES, Etta (1938—). African-American rhythm-and-blues singer. Name variations: Jamesetta Hawkins. Born Jamesetta Hawkins on Jan 25, 1938, in Los Angeles, CA; married; children: 2 sons. ❖ Discovered by legendary band leader Johnny Otis, who cowrote her 1st hit "Roll With Me, Henry" (1955); joined Chess Records' subsidiary, Argo (1960); released hit singles "All I Could Do Was Cry" (1960), "My Dearest Darling" (1960), "At Last" (1961), "Pushover" (1963), and "Loving You More Every Day" (1964); fought heroin addiction throughout 1960s; played Montreux Jazz Festival (1967); opened for Rolling Stones (1968); released hits "Losers Weepers" (1970) and "I've Found a Love' (1972); won 1st Grammy for tribute album, *Mystery Lady: The Songs of Billie Holiday* (1995). Elected to Rock and Roll Hall of Fame (1993). ❖ See also autobiography (with David Ritz), *Rage to Survive* (1995).

JAMES, Florence (1902–1993). New Zealand-born writer. Born in Gisborne, New Zealand, 1902; died in 1993; graduate of University of Sydney; m. William "Pym" Heyting, 1932 (div. 1948); children: 2 daughters. ❖ Moved to Australia as a child; with co-author Dymphna Cusack, published children's book *Four Winds and a Family* (1947) and novel *Come in Spinner* (1951); an activist Quaker, was briefly imprisoned for activities with Campaign for Nuclear Disarmament.

JAMES, Hilda (b. 1904). British swimmer. Born 1904 in Great Britain. ❖ Won a silver medal for the 4 x 100-meter freestyle at Antwerp Olympics (1920).

JAMES, Mary Walsh (1810–1882). American socialite and mother of the brilliant Jameses. Born in New York, NY, 1810; died in Cambridge, MA, 1882; dau. of James Walsh and Elizabeth (Robertson) Walsh; m. Henry James, Sr., in 1840; sister of Catherine Walsh (b. 1812); children: William James (1842–1910, philosopher and psychologist); Henry James (1843–1916, novelist); Garth Wilkinson James (1845–1883); Robertson James (1846–1910); Alice James (1848–1892, diarist).

JAMES, Naomi (1949—). New Zealand sailor. Born Naomi Power, Mar 2, 1949, in Gisborne, New Zealand; m. Rob James (yachtsman drowned while sailing, 1983); married once more, 1990, and moved to Washington DC; children: (1st m.) daughter (b. 1983). ❖ After 9 months at sea, became the 1st woman to sail solo around the world via Cape Horn, known as the Clipper Route (Sept 9, 1977–June 8, 1978) and broke the round-the-world sailing record of Francis Chichester by 2 days; competed in the single-handed Transatlantic race, setting a record for a female competitor (1979); suffering from seasickness, gave up sailing (1982). Made DBE (1979); inducted into New Zealand Hall of Fame (1990). ❖ See also memoirs *At One with the Sea* (1979) and *At Sea on Land* (1981).

JAMES, P.D. (1920—). British mystery writer. Name variations: Phyllis Dorothy James; Phyllis Dorothy James White; Baroness James of Holland Park. Born Phyllis Dorothy James, Aug 3, 1920, in Oxford, England; dau. of Sidney Victor James (Inland Revenue officer) and Dorothy May (Hone) James; educated at Cambridge Girls' High School, 1931–37; m. Ernest Connor Bantry White, 1941 (died 1964); children: 2 daughters. ❖ Known as the "Queen of Crime," began work for National Health Service (1949); entered the Home Office (1968) and served 1st as a principal in the Police Department and later in the Criminal Policy Department; also served as a magistrate in London; published 1st book, *Cover Her Face* (1962), which featured Inspector Adam Dalgliesh, her most popular character, who also appears in *A Mind to Murder* (1963), *Unnatural Causes* (1967), *Shroud for a Nightingale* (1971), *The Black Tower* (1975), *Death of an Expert Witness* (1977) and *Devices and Desires* (1989); other famous literary creations include private detective Cordelia Gray, featured in *An Unsuitable Job for a Woman* (1972) and *The Skull Beneath the Skin* (1982), and Kate Miskin, detective inspector, who appears in *A Taste for Death* (1986) and *A Certain Justice* (1997); had greatest success with 8th novel, *Innocent Blood* (1980); became a member of House of Lords (Baroness James of Holland Park). Awarded OBE (Officer, Order of the British Empire, 1983); elected a fellow of Royal Society of Arts and associate fellow of Downing College, Cambridge (1985). ❖ See also *Women in World History*.

JAMES, Susan Gail (1953—). Canadian nurse and midwife. Born Susan Gail James, June 21, 1953, in Toronto, Ontario, Canada; dau. of Barbara Joan (Bagsley) James and Alan Leslie James; Women's College Hospital School of Nursing, RN, 1973; University of Toronto, bachelors in nursing, 1979; University of Alberta, midwifery certificate, 1989, MA, 1990, PhD, 1997. ❖ Canadian leader in field of midwifery, was employed as a Women's College Hospital staff nurse in labor and delivery (1973–82); practiced as an obstetrical nurse (1983–87) in Toronto; trained with midwives Sandy Pullin and Noreen Walker in Edmonton, then joined Pullin's practice, With Woman Midwifery Care (1989); was on faculty of University of Toronto's nursing school (1990–92); worked as a John Dossetor Health Ethics Centre research associate (from 1992) and course guest lecturer (1994–99); began serving as director of Laurentian University Midwifery Education Programme in Sudbury (1999).

JAMES, Zerelda (c. 1824–1911). American mother of notorious outlaw Jesse James. Name variations: Mrs. Robert James; Mrs. Zerelda Samuel; Mrs. James-Samuel. Born Zerelda Cole in KY, c. 1824; died in Oklahoma City, OK, Feb 10, 1911; m. Robert James (preacher), Dec 28, 1841 (died Aug 1851); m. Benjamin Simms (farmer), Sept 30, 1852 (died); m. Dr. Reuben Samuel (physician), 1857; children: (1st m.) Frank James (b. 1844); Jesse James (b. 1847); Susan James (b. 1849); (3rd m.) Sallie, Johnnie, and Archie (who died in childhood). ❖ Widowed with 3 young children (1851), wed twice more; a raw-boned, stern-looking woman, bore her difficult life with little complaint; brought up her children strictly, though she somewhat idolized them; when sons turned to crime, provided a safe haven for them when necessary; had her arm blown off below the elbow and saw her young son Archie killed by a Pinkerton bomb that was tossed into her home. ❖ See also *Women in World History*.

JAMESON, Anna Brownell (1794–1860). Irish writer. Name variations: Mrs. Jameson; Anna Bronwell Jameson. Born Anna Brownell Murphy in Dublin, Ireland, May 17, 1794; died in Ealing, London, England, Mar 17, 1860; eldest of 5 daughters of D(enis) Brownell Murphy (Irish patriot and noted miniature-painter-in-ordinary to Princess Charlotte Augusta [1796–1817]) and an English mother; m. Robert Jameson (lawyer), 1825 (sep. Sept 1837; died 1854). ❖ Chiefly known for her works on travel and art, 1st published a journal, *Diary of an Ennuyée*, written in a fictitious narrative, which was an immediate success and brought her a host of intense friendships with the literary great, including Fanny Kemble, Lady Noel Byron, Jane Welsh Carlyle, Elizabeth Barrett Browning, George Eliot (Mary Anne Evans), Elizabeth Gaskell and Mary Russell Mitford; many sojourns in Germany added other friends: Ottilie von Goethe, critic Ludwig Tieck, painter Moritz Retzsch, and Friedrich von Schlegel; writings include *Characteristics of Women* (1832), analyses of Shakespeare's heroines, and a 4-volume series of *Sacred and Legendary Art*; also took a keen interest in questions affecting the education, occupations, and support of women, and her private lectures before friends became well-springs for many later reformers and philanthropists. ❖ See also Clara Thomas, *Love and Work Enough: The Life of Anna Jameson* (1967); and *Women in World History*.

JAMESON, Betty (1919—). American golfer. Born Elizabeth May Jameson in Norman, Oklahoma, May 19, 1919. ❖ Won the Trans-Amateur championships twice, Texas state championship 4 times; won both the Trans-Mississippi and Texas Open twice; won the US Amateur (1939, 1940) and Western Amateur (1940, 1942); took the Western Open and the Western Amateur (1942), the 1st player to win both titles in the same year; turned pro (1945); won US Women's Open (1947) with a 295 total, the 1st woman to score below 300 in a 72-hole event; was a founder and charter member of the LPGA (Ladies Professional Golf Association); conceived of and donated the Vare Trophy (1952), which is awarded to the player with the lowest scoring average in a minimum of 70 official rounds of tournament play. Inducted into LPGA Hall of Fame (1951). ❖ See also *Women in World History*.

JAMESON, Elizabeth (1900–1988). See Mears, Elizabeth.

JAMESON, Helen (1963—). English swimmer. Born Sept 25, 1963, in UK. ❖ At Moscow Olympics, won a silver medal in 4 x 100-meter medley relay (1980).

JAMESON, Joyce (1932–1987). American stage, tv, and screen actress. Born Sept 26, 1932, in Chicago, IL; died Jan 16, 1987, in Burbank, CA; m. Billy Barnes (div.); children: Tyler Barnes (musician). ❖ Began career in stage revues produced by husband Billy Barnes; films include *Showboat, The Balcony, Good Neighbor Sam, Boy Did I Get a Wrong Number, The Apartment, The Outlaw Josey Wales* and *Every Which Way But Loose*.

JAMESON, Margaret (1891–1986). See Jameson, Storm.

JAMESON, Storm (1891–1986). British novelist, playwright, literary critic, editor, and administrator. Name variations: (pseudonyms) James Hill and William Lamb. Born Margaret Storm Jameson, Jan 8, 1891, in Whitby, Yorkshire, England; died in Cambridge, Sept 30, 1986; dau. of Hannah Margaret (Gallilee) Jameson and William Storm Jameson (sea captain); 1st woman graduate in English, Leeds University, BA (1st class honors), 1912; King's College, MA, 1914; m. 2nd husband Guy Patterson Chapman (writer and historian), Feb 1, 1926 (died 1972); children: (1st m.) Charles William Storm Clark. ❖ Worked as a copywriter for London advertising firm (1918–19); edited *New Commonwealth* (1919–21); published 1st novel, *The Pot Boils* (1919), then her master's thesis, *Modern Drama in Europe* (1920), which caused a literary stir; served as English representative and later co-manager for Knopf (1925–28); became an established literary figure (1920s), associating with Rose Macaulay and Naomi Royde-Smith, Walter de la Mare, Frank Swinnerton and Q.D. Leavis; trans. stories of Guy de

Maupassant, wrote literary criticism, and strove for a spare, non-emotional style in such novels as *The Lovely Ship* (1927), *The Voyage Home* (1930), and *A Richer Dust* (1931), collected in a trilogy entitled *The Triumph of Time*; served as 1st woman president of English Center of International PEN (1938–45) and worked to help writers escape from Nazi Germany and Eastern Europe before and during WWII; created body of anti-fascist fiction, including *Europe to Let* (1940), *Cousin Honoré* (1940), *Cloudless May* (1943) and *The Black Laurel* (1947); wrote over 45 books. Several of her novels were reproduced by Virago (1980s), including *Women Against Men* (1933) and *The Mirror in Darkness* trilogy: *Company Parade* (1934), *Love in Winter* (1935), and *None Turn Back* (1936). ❖ See also autobiographies *No Time Like the Present* (1933) and *Journey from the North* (2 vols., 1969–70); and *Women in World History*.

JAMET, Marie (1820–1893). French nun. Name variations: Marie Augustine de la Compassion. Born 1820 in Lambéty, France; died 1893 in La Tour-Saint-Joseph, France. ❖ With Jeanne Jugan and Virginie Trédaniel, founded order of nuns devoted to charitable work, Little Sisters of the Poor (1840); based congregation on Rule of St. Augustine, taking perpetual vows of poverty, chastity and obedience, as well as hospitality; took religious name of Marie Augustine de la Compassion; helped establish refuge for aged men and women who had no other shelter; amid controversy, succeeded Jugan as mother superior (1843); helped spread order and its charitable works throughout world.

JAMIESON, Cathy (1956—). Scottish politician. Born 1956 in Scotland. ❖ Was on Labour's National Executive Committee; serves as Labour member of the Scottish Parliament for Carrick, Cumnock and Doon Valley; is minister for Education and Young People.

JAMIESON, Margaret (1953—). Scottish politician. Born 1953 in Kilmarnock, Scotland. ❖ Became the 1st female full-time officer of the National Union of Public Employees (now UNISON, 1979); serves as Labour member of the Scottish Parliament for Kilmarnock and Loudoun.

JAMIESON, Penny (1942—). New Zealand bishop. Name variations: Penelope Jamieson. Born 1942 in England; graduate in linguistics from University of Edinburgh; m. Ian Jamieson (teacher at University of Otago); children: 3 daughters. ❖ Grew up in England, immigrating to New Zealand when she was 22 (1964); after some years as a cleric, was named bishop of the Diocese of Dunedin (1989), the 1st woman diocesan bishop in the Anglican Communion; retired (2004). ❖ See also Penny Jamieson, *Living at the Edge: Sacrament and Solidarity in Leadership* (Mowbray, 1997).

JAMISON, Cecilia V. (1837–1909). Canadian-American author and painter. Name variations: Cecilia Viets Dakin Hamilton Jamison; Cecilia Hamilton. Born Cecilia Viets Dakin, 1837, in Yarmouth, Nova Scotia, Canada; died April 11, 1909, in Roxbury, MA; educated privately in Boston, NY, and Paris; m. George Hamilton, 1860; m. Samuel Jamison (lawyer), 1878 (died 1902). ❖ Published 1st book *Something To Do: A Novel* (1871); with assistance from Henry Wadsworth Longfellow, published *Woven of Many Threads* (1872); painted portraits of Longfellow (now located at Tulane University) and Louis Agassiz (now located at Boston Society of Natural History), among others; became well known for juvenile literature and adult romances (1880s), including *Ropes of Sand and Other Stories* (1873), *Lady Jane* (1891) and *The Penhallow Family* (1905).

JAMISON, Judith (1943—). African-American dancer and choreographer. Born May 10, 1943, in Philadelphia, PA; dau. of John Jamison (sheet-metal mechanic) and Tessie (Bell) Jamison (part-time teacher); attended Philadelphia Dance Academy and John Kerr's Dance School; m. Miguel Godreau (dancer), Dec 1972 (div.). ❖ Regal in stature, was acclaimed for her impeccable technique and individualistic style, the result of an eclectic training program that included classical ballet and a wide variety of modern-dance disciplines; made NY debut as Mary Seaton in Agnes de Mille's ballet *The Four Marys* (Feb 1965); debuted with Alvin Ailey's Dance Theater in *Conga Tango Palace* (1965), followed by *Revelations*; made mark as a principal dancer with Dance Theater (1967–80), performing in a number of memorable roles, including Voudoun Erzulie in Holder's *The Prodigal Prince*, the Mother in *Knoxville: Summer of 1915*, and the Sun in Hoving's *Icarus*; was also seen in *Panambi*, *Masakela Language*, *Cry*, *Mary Lou's Mass* and *The Lark Ascending*; left Ailey company to perform in Broadway musical *Sophisticated Ladies* (1980); formed own company, the Jamison Project (1988); following Ailey's death (1989), named artistic director of Alvin Ailey American Dance Theater and Alvin Alley American Dance Center,

one of the few women to head up a major dance company. Among the recipients of Kennedy Center Honors (1999). ❖ See also autobiography (with Howard Kaplan) *Dancing Spirit* (Doubleday, 1993); and *Women in World History*.

JANAUSCHEK, Fanny (1829–1904). Czech actress. Name variations: Fanny Janauscheck. Born Francesca or Franziska Magdalena Romana Janauschek in Prague, Bohemia (now Czech Republic), July 20, 1829; died at Brunswick Home in Amityville, Long Island, NY, Nov 28, 1904; m. Frederick J. Pillot (died July 1884). ❖ Celebrated actress, was playing lead roles in Prague by age 16; after a series of successful engagements in European cities, became a European star, touring Germany, Austria and Russia for the next 20 years; though she spoke little English, arrived in US (1867) with her own troupe of actors, playing in NY and elsewhere, in German language; after learning English, gave numerous memorable performances before American public as Lady Macbeth (Gruoch), Medea, Meg Merrilies, Elizabeth I, Mary Stuart and Marie Antoinette; eventually settled in US, where she continued to appear until her retirement (1898). ❖ See also *Women in World History*.

JANE. *Variant of Jean and Joan.*

JANE, countess of Montfort (c. 1310–c. 1376). *See Jeanne de Montfort.*

JANE, queen of Naples. *See Joanna I.*

JANE, queen of Scotland (c. 1410–1445). *See Beaufort, Joan.*

JANE I OF NAPLES. *See Joanna I of Naples.*

JANE II OF NAPLES. *See Joanna II of Naples.*

JANE FRANCIS DE CHANTAL, St. (1572–1641). *See Chantal, Jeanne de.*

JANE GREY, Lady (1537–1554). *See Grey, Jane, Lady.*

JANE OF BOURBON-VENDOME (d. 1511). Countess of Auvergne. Name variations: Jane Bourbon; Jane de Bourbon-Vendôme; Jane de la Tour. Died Jan 22, 1511 (some sources cite 1512); dau. of John II, count of Vendome, and Isabeau, duchess de La Roche-sur-Yon; became 2nd wife of John II (1426–1488), duke of Bourbon (r. 1456–1488), June 1487; m. John II de la Tour, count of Auvergne, Jan 11, 1495; children: (1st m.) Mathieu of Bourbon; Charles of Bourbon; Hector of Bourbon; (2nd m.) Anne de la Tour (c. 1496–1524); Madeline de la Tour d'Auvergne (1501–1519).

JANE OF FLANDERS (c. 1310–c. 1376). *See Jeanne de Montfort.*

JANE OF FRANCE (1343–1373). Queen of Navarre. Name variations: Joanna of France; Jane Valois. Born 1343; died 1373; dau. of John II the Good (1319–1364), king of France (r. 1350–1364), and Bona of Bohemia (1315–1349); sister of Charles V (1337–1380), king of France (r. 1364–1380), and Isabelle of France (1349–1372); m. Charles II (1332–1387), king of Navarre (r. 1349–1387), in 1352; children: Joanna of Navarre (c. 1370–1437, who m. Henry IV, king of England); Charles III, king of Navarre; Pierre.

JANE SEYMOUR (c. 1509–1537). *See Seymour, Jane.*

JANE SHORE (c. 1445–c. 1527). *See Shore, Jane.*

JANÉS, Clara (1940—). Spanish novelist, poet and translator. Name variations: Clara Janes. Born 1940 in Barcelona, Spain. ❖ Works of poetry include *Las estrellas vencidas* (1964), *En busca de Cordelia y Poemas Rumanos* (1975), *Libro de alienaciones* (1980), *Vivir* (1983), *Fósiles* (1984), *Kampa* (1986), and *Lapidario* (1988); novels include *La noche de Abel Micheli* (1965) and *Desintegración* (1969).

JANEWAY, Elizabeth (1913–2005). American author, critic and lecturer. Born Elizabeth Hall, Oct 7, 1913, in Brooklyn, NY; died Jan 15, 2005, in Rye, NY; dau. of Charles H. Hall (naval architect) and Jeanette F. (Searle) Hall; attended Swarthmore College, 1930–31; Barnard College, BA, 1935; m. Eliot Janeway (economist and author), Oct 29, 1938 (died 1993); children: Michael Charles, William Hall. ❖ Won *Story Magazine's* Intercollegiate Short Story Contest (1935); began working on a short story which, on the 3rd attempt, was finished and published as *The Walsh Girls* (1943); turned out several novels, including *Daisy Kenyon* (1945), *The Question of Gregory* (1949), *Leaving Home* (1953) and *The Third Choice* (1958); also penned 2 children's books, *The Vikings* (1951) and *Ivanov VII* (1967); later works include *Man's World-Woman's Place: A Study in Social Mythology* (1971) and *Between Myth and Morning: Women Awakening* (1974); was also a regular contributor to numerous literary and popular journals. ❖ See also *Women in World History*.

JANG HYE-OCK. South Korean badminton player. Born in South Korea. ❖ Won a silver medal for doubles at Atlanta Olympics (1996).

JANG JI-WON (1979—). South Korean taekwondo player. Born Aug 30, 1979, in South Korea. ❖ Placed 1st for featherweight 55–59 kg at World championships (2001); won a gold medal for -57 kg at Athens Olympics (2004).

JANG MI-RAN (1983—). South Korean weightlifter. Born Oct 9, 1983, in South Korea. ❖ At World championships, placed 3rd for +75 kg clean & jerk (2003); won a silver medal for +75 kg at Athens Olympics (2004).

JANG OK-RIM (1948—). North Korean volleyball player. Born Feb 8, 1948, in North Korea. ❖ At Munich Olympics, won a bronze medal in team competition (1972).

JANG RI-RA (1969—). North Korean handball player. Born May 4, 1969, in North Korea. ❖ At Barcelona Olympics, won a gold medal in team competition (1992).

JANG SO-HEE (1978—). South Korean handball player. Born Mar 15, 1978, in Seoul, South Korea. ❖ Won a team silver at Athens Olympics (2004).

JANG YONG-HO. South Korean archer. Born in South Korea. ❖ Won a gold medal for teams at Atlanta Olympics (1996).

JANICKE, Marina (1954—). East German diver. Born June 19, 1954, in East Germany. ❖ At Munich Olympics, won a bronze medal in springboard and a bronze medal in platform (1972).

JANICS, Natasa (1982—). Hungarian kayaker. Born June 24, 1982, in Bacskapalanka, Yugoslavia. ❖ At World championships, placed 1st for K4 1000 (2003) and K4 200 (2002); won a gold medal for K2 500 and a gold medal for K1 500 at Athens Olympics (2004).

JANINE-MARIE DE FOIX (fl. 1377). See *Foix, Janine-Marie de.*

JANIS, Elsie (1889–1956). American actress, musical-comedy star, and author. Born Elsie Bierbower in Columbus, Franklin County, Ohio, Mar 16, 1889; died at home in Beverly Hills, CA, Feb 25, 1956; dau. of John E. Bierbower and Jane Elizabeth (Cockrell) Bierbower; m. Gilbert Wilson (actor), 1931. ❖ Guided firmly by mother, made stage debut in Columbus at 8, as the boy Cain in *The Charity Ball*; appeared in vaudeville in NY as "Little Elsie" (1900); had 1st substantial hit in *When We Were Forty-One* (1905), in which her imitations of popular actors created a furor; starred on Broadway as Dorothy Willetts in *The Vanderbilt Cup* (1906); was again successful as Joan Talbot in *The Hoyden* (1907); also seen as Cynthia Bright in *The Fair Co-Ed* (1908), Princess Kalora in *The Slim Princess* (1909), and Cinderella in *The Lady of the Slipper* (1912); made triumphant London debut (1914), as Kitty O'Hara in *The Passing Show*; during WWI, toured trenches of France, becoming known as the "sweetheart of the American Expeditionary Force"; back in NY, starred in *Miss Information* (1915), *The Century Girl* (1916), *Miss 1917* (1919), *Elsie Janis and her Gang* (1922), *Puzzles of 1925* and *Oh, Kay!* (1925); also took her *La Revue de Elsie Janis* to Apollo in Paris (1921); made farewell stage appearance in Frank Fay's vaudeville *Laugh Time* (1939); also appeared in silent and talkie films, composed over 50 songs, penned screenplay for *Close Harmony,* starred in her own revues and plays *A Star for a Night* (1911) and *It's All Wrong* (1920), for which she was also co-composer, staged *New Faces of 1934,* and wrote several books (*Love Letters of an Actress, If I Know What I Mean,* as well as her autobiography *So Far So Good,* 1932).

JANISZEWSKA, Barbara (1936—). Polish runner. Name variations: Barbara Janiszewska-Sobotta; Barbara Sobotta. Born Barbara Lerczak, Dec 4, 1936, in Poland. ❖ At Rome Olympics, won a bronze medal in 4 x 100-meter relay (1960).

JANITSCHEK, Maria (1859–1927). Austrian poet, novelist and short-story writer. Name variations: (pseudonym) Marius Stone. Born July 22, 1859, in Mödling, Vienna, Austria; died April 28, 1927, in Munich, Germany; illeg. dau. of Anna Tölk (officer's widow); m. Hubert Janitschek (art historian), 1882 (died 1893). ❖ Wrote notorious poem, "Ein modernes Wein," about a disgraced woman who challenges a man to a duel and kills him; published *Irdische und unirdische Träume* (1899), *Im Sommerwind* (1895) and *Gesammelte Gedichte* (1910).

JANKA, Amalia (1899–1932). See *De Putti, Lya.*

JANKO, Eva (1945—). Austrian track-and-field athlete. Born Jan 24, 1945, in Austria. ❖ At Mexico City Olympics, won a bronze medal in the javelin throw (1968).

JANKOVIC, Ljubinka (1958—). Yugoslavian handball player. Born Sept 23, 1958. ❖ At Los Angeles Olympics, won a gold medal in team competition (1984).

JANNSEN, L. (1843–1886). See *Koidula, Lydia.*

JANNY, Amélia (1838–1914). Portuguese poet. Name variations: Amelia Janny. Born 1838 in Portugal; died 1914. ❖ Known as the 'Poetess of the Mondego,' published poems in magazines including *Almanaque de Lembranças*; wrote a poem in praise of Brazilian revolutionary poet Gonzago.

JANOSI, Zsuzsanna (1963—). Hungarian fencer. Born Nov 19, 1963, in Hungary. ❖ At Seoul Olympics, won a bronze medal in team foil (1988).

JANOSINE-DUCZA, Aniko (1942—). Hungarian gymnast. Name variations: Aniko Ducza. Born Aug 1942 in Hungary. ❖ At Tokyo Olympics, won a bronze medal in floor exercises (1964).

JANOTHA, Natalia (1856–1932). Polish pianist and teacher. Name variations: Nathalie Janotha. Born Maria Cecylia Natalia Janotha in Warsaw, Poland, June 8, 1856; died at The Hague, Netherlands, June 9, 1932; father was a professor at Warsaw Conservatorium. ❖ Considered one of Clara Schumann's most gifted pupils, made debut in Leipzig (1874); besides receiving many honors as a pianist, composed piano pieces, including a series of *Mountain Scenes,* which was dedicated to Schumann; also taught (her most famous student being Paderewski); appointed pianist to Prussian court (1885), a post she held until 1916; made 4 recordings, one of which was of Chopin's unpublished fugue (1905); also wrote several books on Chopin as well as translating into English Tarnowski's biography of Chopin. ❖ See also *Women in World History.*

JANOWITZ, Gundula (1937—). German soprano. Born Aug 2, 1937, in Berlin, Germany; studied with Herbert Thöny at Graz Conservatory. ❖ Made debut at Vienna Staatsoper (1959); appeared at Bayreuth (1960–63); was a member of Frankfurt Opera (1963–66); triumphed as Sieglinde for Von Karajan's Salzburg *Ring* (1967); made Metropolitan Opera debut (1976), Paris Opéra (1973), Covent Garden (1976); became a director of the Graz Opera (1990). ❖ See also *Women in World History.*

JANS, Annetje (c. 1605–1663). American Dutch settler. Born in Netherlands c. 1605; died in NY, 1663; m. Roeloef Janssen (died c. 1636); sister of Tryntje Jonas (midwife and nurse); m. Dominie Bogardus (minister), 1638; children: (1st m.) 3 daughters, 2 sons; (2nd m.) 4 sons. ❖ One of the many exceptional Dutch women who came to NY during 17th century, is best remembered for the 200-year dispute over her valuable Manhattan holdings; immigrated to America (1630) and 1st settled with family on a farm in Fort Orange (now Albany); moved to farming village of New Amsterdam (1635), where they acquired 62 acres of land (running along what is now Broadway, between Fulton and Canal streets); following 1st husband's death, kept financial independence at time of 2nd marriage with a prenuptial agreement; when 2nd husband died at sea, added his estate to her considerable holdings; drew up prenuptial agreements for daughters. ❖ See also *Women in World History.*

JANSEN, Elly (1929—). Dutch-born social worker. Born in Holland, 1929. ❖ A leading figure in field of mental health, studied psychology, trained as a nurse, and worked with disturbed children; went to England to train as a missionary (1955), which led her into social work with mentally ill; started 1st therapeutic community, or halfway house, for mental patients (1959); established Richmond Fellowship, through which she promoted re-integration of mental health patients into mainstream society; became international director of the fellowship, which grew to include some 50 houses in Britain, and another 50 scattered throughout world, including Australia, New Zealand, Austria, India, Pakistan, Bangladesh, Nepal and US. Made OBE (1980). ❖ See also *Women in World History.*

JANSEN, Linda. American vocalist. Name variations: The Angels (originally known as the Starlets). Born in Orange, NJ. ❖ With Barbara and Phyllis "Jiggs" Allbut, formed The Angels (1961), one of most successful early 1960s girl groups; left group and was replaced by Peggy Santiglia McCannon (1962).

JANSSON, Tove (1914–2001). Finnish artist, author, and illustrator. Born Aug 9, 1914, in Helsinki, Finland; died in Helsinki, July 2001; dau. of Viktor (sculptor) Jansson and Signe (Hammarsten) Jansson (artist);

studied book design in Stockholm, 1930–33; painting in Helsinki, 1933–36; and at Atelier Adrien Holy, Paris, France, 1938, and in Florence, Italy; never married; no children. ❖ Creator of the "Moomins," wrote and illustrated 1st children's book (1939); published 1st of her "Moomin" books (1945), a series of troll stories set in the bizarre "Moominworld"; won Stockholm Award, Nils Holgersson Plaque, and Selma Lagerlöf Medal, all for *The Book about Moomin, Mymbie and Little My* (1952, 1953); won Hans Christian Andersen Medal for "Moomintroll" books (1966), which over the years have won countless other awards and have been translated into 27 languages; wrote and drew the comic-strip "Moomin," for *The* [London] *Evening News* (1953–60); in later years, published several collections of adult short stories, including *The Listener* (1971) and *The Doll's House* (1978), and a few adult novels. ❖ See also autobiography *Sculptor's Daughter* (1968); and *Women in World History*.

JANUARIA (1822–1901). Princess Imperial of Brazil and countess of Aquila. Name variations: Januária. Born Januária María Joana de Brangança, Mar 11, 1822, in Rio de Janeiro, Brazil; died on Mar 13, 1901, in Nice; dau. of Leopoldina of Austria (1797–1826) and Pedro I (r. 1822–1831), emperor of Brazil (also known as Peter IV, king of Portugal, and Peter I of Brazil); m. Luigi Carlo Maria Giuseppe of Sicily, count of Aquila, April 28, 1844.

JANVIER, Catherine Ann (1841–1922). *See Drinker, Catherine Ann.*

JANZ, Karen (1952—). East German gymnast. Born Feb 17, 1952, in Berlin, East Germany. ❖ At Mexico City Olympics, won a bronze medal in team all-around and a silver medal in uneven bars (1968); at Munich Olympics, won a bronze medal in balance beam, silver medal in team all-around and indiv. all-around, and gold medals in vault and uneven bars (1972); at Europeans, won a gold medal in all-around (1969); at World championships, won a gold medal in uneven bars and silvers in vault and team all-around (1970); won Chunichi Cup (1972); now an orthopedic surgeon.

JAPAN, empress of.
See Jingū (c. 201–269).
See Suiko (554–628).
See Kōgyoku-Saimei (594–661).
See Jitō (645–702).
See Gemmei (c. 661–721).
See Gensho (680–748).
See Kōken-Shōtoku (718–770).
See Onshi (872–907).
See Sadako (r. 976–1001).
See Meisho (1624–1696).
See Go-Sakuramachi (1740–1813).
See Yoshiko.
See Haruko (1850–1914).
See Sadako (1885–1951).
See Nagako (b. 1903).
See Michiko (b. 1934).

JAPHA, Louise (1826–1889). German pianist. Born in Hamburg, Germany, 1826; died 1889; m. Friedrich Langhans (violinist, div. 1874). ❖ Like her lifelong friend Johannes Brahms, was born and studied in Hamburg; later studied with Clara Schumann; on her many European tours, was particularly appreciated in Paris for performances of music of Robert Schumann; participated in the 1st public performance in Paris of the Brahms Piano Quintet in F minor, Op. 34 (1868); following divorce (1874), lived in Wiesbaden as a teacher.

JARBORO, Caterina (1908–1986). African-American soprano. Born July 24, 1908, in Wilmington, NC; died Aug 1986 in New York, NY; trained in Paris and Milan. ❖ Became the 1st African-American to appear with an American opera company when she made her debut with the Chicago Opera (1933), in *Aïda.* ❖ See also *Women in World History*.

JARDIN, Anne (1959—). Canadian swimmer. Born July 26, 1959, in Montreal, Canada. ❖ At Montreal Olympics, won a bronze medal in 4 x 100-meter medley relay and the 4 x 100-meter freestyle relay (1976).

JARMAN, Frances Eleanor (c. 1803–1873). *See Ternan, Frances Eleanor.*

JARMAN, Margaret (1907–1963). *See Hagood, Margaret.*

JARNEVIĆ, Dragojla (1812–1875). Croatian diarist. Name variations: Dragojla Jarnevic. Born 1812 in Karlovac, Croatia; died 1875. ❖ Kept diary which often focused on tensions for women between intellectual and domestic life (1194 pp.); also wrote plays, poems, and novel.

JAROSS-SZABO, Herma (1902–1986). *See Planck-Szabó, Herma.*

JAROSZEWICZ, Antonina (1908–1973). *See Halicka, Antonina.*

JARRATT, Jan (1958—). Australian politician. Name variations: Janice Heather Jarratt. Born Oct 22, 1958. ❖ Teacher; as a member of the Australian Labor Party, elected to the Queensland Parliament for Whitsunday (2001).

JARRELL, Helen Ira (1896–1973). *See Jarrell, Ira.*

JARRELL, Ira (1896–1973). American superintendent of schools. Name variations: Helen Ira Jarrell. Born Helen Ira Jarrell on July 27, 1896, in Meriwether County, Georgia; died Aug 27, 1973, in Little Rock, Arkansas; dau. of William Henry Jarrell and Emma (Hutchison) Jarrell. ❖ Began career as elementary schoolteacher in Atlanta, GA (1916), then senior teacher (1930), then principal (1934); worked with Atlanta Public School Teachers' Association (APSTA), becoming recording secretary (1929), member of executive board, 1st vice president (serving 3 terms), and delegate to Atlanta Federation of Trades; became president of APSTA (1936); became 1st female superintendent of schools in Atlanta (1944), overseeing doubling in number of schools, tripling in number of teachers, increased teachers' salaries, introduction of special programs for handicapped children, and addition of radio and tv stations to school system; accused of resisting desegregation and racial equality in school system, retired during controversy (1960); was director of curriculum development section of GA State Department of Education (c. 1960–67).

JARRETT, Eleanor Holm (b. 1913). *See Holm, Eleanor.*

JARRETT, Mary Cromwell (1877–1961). American medical social worker. Born Mary Cromwell Jarrett, June 21, 1877, in Baltimore, MD; died Aug 4, 1961, in New York, NY; dau. of Frank Asbury Jarrett and Caroline Watkins (Cromwell) Jarrett. ❖ Worked at Boston Children's Aid Society, becoming head of casework department (1903–13); worked at Boston Psychopathic Hospital (1913–19), creating social work education program (1914), and developing social service section; applied social casework techniques to treatment of psychiatric patients, naming method "psychiatric social work" (1916); became director of 1st training program for psychiatric social workers to treat WWI soldiers, at Smith College (1918); helped found Smith College Training School for Social Work, and became associate director (1919–23); established Psychiatric Social Workers Club (1920), later known as American Association of Psychiatric Social Workers; worked for Research Bureau of Welfare Council of NYC (1927–43); became secretary of Committee on Chronic Illness (c. 1933–43); was director of Works Progress Administration project to teach home care for chronically ill (1935–40); began organization of Subcommittee on Arthritis (1939), later NY Rheumatism Association; was consultant on planning long-term health care (1943–49). Wrote *Chronic Illness in New York City* (1933) and (with E.E. Southard) *Kingdom of Evils* (1922).

JARVELA, Satu. Finnish snowboarder. Name variations: Satu Järvelä. Born in Finland. ❖ Placed 1st in Halfpipe at US Open (1995), 1st in Halfpipe at Nippon Open (1997), and 3rd in Halfpipe at World Cup Snowboarding (2001).

JARVIS, Anna M. (1864–1948). American founder of Mother's Day. Born in Grafton, WV, May 1, 1864; died in West Chester, PA, Nov 24, 1948; attended Mary Baldwin College; never married; no children. ❖ Following mother's death (May 10, 1905), campaigned to set aside one day a year to honor mothers everywhere, resulting in Mother's Day. ❖ See also *Women in World History*.

JARVIS, Lilian (1931—). Canadian ballet dancer. Born 1931 in Toronto, Canada. ❖ Performed in London's West End while traveling on study trip to England (1950); danced as charter member of National Ballet of Canada; performed numerous classical roles including Odette/Odile, Swanilda, and Sugar Plum Fairy; appeared in wide range of works including Tudor and Cranko revivals, abstractions by Gwynneth Lloyd and Arnold Spohr, and dramatic works by Grant Strate.

JARVIS, Lucy (1919—). American tv producer. Born Lucile Howard in New York, NY, 1919; dau. of Herman Howard and Sophie (Kirsch) Howard; Cornell University, BS in home economics, 1938; Columbia University Teachers College, MS, 1941; attended New School for Social Research, 1942; m. Serge Jarvis (lawyer), July 18, 1940; children: Barbara Ann Jarvis; Peter Leslie Jarvis. ❖ One of the 1st women to produce for prime-time network tv, became assistant producer for David Susskind's Talent Associates (1955); co-produced "Capitol Close-up," a syndicated radio program (1957), with Martha Rountree; was known for NBC documentaries, including "The Kremlin" (1963), "Museum Without Walls" (1963), "The Louvre" (1964), "Who Shall Live?" (1965), "Mary Martin: Hello Dolly! Around the World" (1965), "Khrushchev in Exile" (1967), "Bravo, Picasso!" (1967) and "Scotland Yard: The Golden Thread" (1971). Received Golden Mike Award from American Women in Radio and Television (1967). ❖ See also *Women in World History.*

JARVIS, Natalia (1967—). *See Ilienko, Natalia.*

JASCHKE, Martina (1960—). East German diver. Born May 1960 in East Germany. ❖ At Moscow Olympics, won a gold medal in platform (1980).

JASNORZEWSKA, Maria Pawlikowska (1891–1945). *See Pawlikowska, Maria.*

JASONTEK, Rebecca (1975—). American synchronized swimmer. Born Feb 26, 1975, in Cincinnati, Ohio; Ohio State University, BA in Communications. ❖ Won a team bronze medal at Athens Olympics (2004). Named Collegiate Athlete of the Year (1996).

JAUNZEME, Ineze (1932—). Soviet track-and-field athlete. Born May 21, 1932, in USSR. ❖ At Melbourne Olympics, won a gold medal in javelin throw (1956).

JAY, Harriett (1863–1932). English playwright and actress. Name variations: (pseudonym) Charles Marlowe. Born 1863 (some sources cite 1857) in London, England; died Dec 21, 1932; dau. of Richard Jay (engineer); sister of Mary Jay (who married writer Robert Buchanan). ❖ Around age 2, adopted by older sister Mary and Robert Buchanan; made stage debut in the provinces (1879) and London debut as Lady Jane Grey in *A Nine Day's Queen* (1880); with Buchanan wrote such plays as *Alone in London, Fascination, The Strange Adventures of Miss Brown, The Romance of a Shopwalker, A Wanderer from Venus, The Mariners of England* and *Two Little Maids from School;* also wrote the play *When Knights Were Bold* (1907) which was revived often; novels include *The Dark Colleen, Madge Dunraven, The Priest's Blessing, My Connaught Cousins, Through the Stage Door* and *The Queen of Connaught* (which she also adapted for the stage); also wrote a biography of Buchanan.

JAY, Isabel (1879–1927). English actress and singer. Name variations: Isabel Cavendish; Isabel Curzon. Born Oct 17, 1879, in Wandsworth, London, England; died Feb 26, 1927, in Monte Carlo; m. H.S.H. "Henry" Cavendish (African explorer), 1902 (div. 1906); m. Frank Curzon (actor-manager), July 28, 1910; children: Cecilia Cavendish (b. 1903); Pamelia Stephanie Curzon (b. 1915). ❖ Made stage debut as Elsie Maynard in 1st London revival of *The Yeomen of the Guard;* became a principal D'Oyly Carte soprano, appearing as Josephine in *H.M.S. Pinafore,* Tessa in *The Gondoliers,* Aloës in *The Lucky Star,* Mabel in *The Pirates of Penzance,* the title role in *Patience* and Phyllis in *Iolanthe;* also created role of Blush-of-Morning in *The Rose of Persia,* then replaced Ellen Beach Yaw as Sultana Zubeydah (Nov 1899); created role of Lady Rose Pippin in *The Emerald Isle* (1901) and Gipsy Woman in *Ib and Little Christina* (1901); starred in other plays, including *A Country Girl, The Cingalee, Véronique, The White Chrysanthemum, The Girl Behind the Counter, The Vicar of Wakefield, Miss Hook of Holland, King of Cadonia* and *The Balkan Princess;* retired (1911); wrote and starred in *The Inevitable* (1923).

JAYAKAR, Pupul (1915–1999). Indian feminist. Born Sept 11, 1915, at Etawah in Uttar Pradesh, India; died of cardiac arrest at home in South Bombay, India; graduate of London School of Economics; m. Manmohan M. Jayakar (lawyer). ❖ Began career as an assistant secretary in National Planning Committee, which was then chaired by prime minister Jawaharlal Nehru; popularized Indian art, culture and heritage by promoting Festivals of India abroad and was soon recognized as the tsarina of Indian culture; also active in elevating Indian handicrafts and served as executive director and later chair of Handicrafts and Handloom Corporation of India; appointed vice-president of Indian Council for Cultural Relations (1982); founded Indian National Trust for Art and Cultural Heritage (INTACH, 1984); served as vice-chair of Indira Gandhi Memorial Trust (1985–90) and was adviser on heritage and cultural resources to the prime minister; was a close friend of Indira Gandhi and a disciple of philosopher Jiddu Krishnamurti, writing biographies of both.

JAYASINGHE, Susanthika (1975—). Sri Lankan runner. Born Dec 17, 1975, in Sri Lanka. ❖ Won a silver medal at World championships (1997) and a bronze medal at Sydney Olympics (2000), both for 200 meters.

JAYROE, Jane (c. 1947—). Miss America and news anchor. Name variations: Jane Jayroe Gamble. Born Jane Anne Jayroe c. 1947 in Laverne, Oklahoma; University of Tulsa, MA; m. Gerald Gamble; children: one son. ❖ Named Miss America (1967), representing Oklahoma; served for 16 years as prime-time news anchor in Oklahoma and on the NBC affiliate in Dallas/Fort Worth; serves as executive director of the Oklahoma Tourism and Recreation Dept. Frequent contributor to magazines. ❖ See also Frank Deford, *There She Is* (Viking, 1971).

JEAKINS, Dorothy (1914–1995). American costume designer. Born Jan 11, 1914 in San Diego, CA; died Nov 21, 1995, in Santa Barbara, CA; attended Otis Art Institute, 1931–34; children: Stephen Sydney Dane; Peter Jeakins Dane. ❖ Designed for stage before arriving in Hollywood; frequently collaborated with Edith Head and Charles LeMaire (1950s); worked as costume designer, alone or in collaboration, on such films as *The Greatest Show on Earth* (1952), *Niagara* (1952), *Titanic* (1952), *Three Coins in the Fountain* (1954), *Friendly Persuasion* (1956), *The Ten Commandments* (1956), *South Pacific* (1958), *Let's Make Love* (1960), *The Children's Hour* (1961), *The Music Man* (1962), *The Sound of Music* (1965), *Finian's Rainbow* (1968), *The Way We Were* (1973), *Young Frankenstein* (1974) and *On Golden Pond* (1981); also designed costumes for network tv. Shared Academy Awards for *Joan of Arc* (1948), *Samson and Delilah* (1950), and *The Night of the Iguana* (1964). ❖ See also *Women in World History.*

JEAN, Gloria (1926—). American actress and singer. Born Gloria Jean Schoonover, in Buffalo, NY, April 14, 1926; married (1962–66). ❖ Made singing debut at 3 (billed as Baby Schoonover) and by 5 had her own radio program in Scranton; signed with Universal and made film debut in *The Under-Pup* (1939), followed by *If I Had My Way* (1940), with Bing Crosby, and *Never Give a Sucker an Even Break* with W.C. Fields (1941); made guest appearances radio shows (1940); with Universal losing interest, was paired with Donald O'Connor in a series of low-budget musicals that began with *What's Cookin'?* (1942) and ended with *Moonlight in Vermont* (1943); made a few tv appearances and starred in low-budget programmer *Air Strike* (1955), then retired from acting. ❖ See also *Women in World History.*

JEAN, Sally Lucas (1878–1971). American nurse. Born Sally Lucas Jean, June 18, 1878, in Towson, MD; died July 5, 1971, in New York, NY; dau. of George and Emilie Watkins (Selby) Jean; graduate of Maryland Homoepathic Training School for Nurses (1898); shared a home with close friend Dorothy Goodwin, her secretary. ❖ Coiner of the term "health education," 1st served as an army nurse in the south during Spanish-American War; became director of Maryland Social Health Service (1914); organized People's Institute Department of Health Service in NY (1917); served on New York Academy of Medicine's Committee on Wartime Problems of Childhood, which led to the establishment of the Child Health Organization (CHO, 1918), and was its 1st director; when American Child Hygiene Association merged with CHO to form American Child Health Association (1923), served as director of its Health Education (1 yr); developed health education programs in China, Japan, Philippines, Virgin Islands and Panama Canal Zone; worked as a health consultant to companies (e.g., Quaker Oats); directed health education work for National Foundation for Infantile Paralysis (1944).

JEANES, Anna Thomas (1822–1907). American Quaker philanthropist. Born April 7, 1822, in Philadelphia, PA; died at Stapeley Hall, in Germantown, PA, Sept 24, 1907; dau. of Isaiah Jeanes (shipping merchant and Quaker) and Anna (Thomas) Jeanes (died 1826); never married; no children. ❖ Inherited over $2 million (1894) and spent remaining years dispersing the funds: $200,000 to the Spring Garden Institute, $100,000 to the Hicksite Friends, and $200,000 to Pennsylvania Home for Aged Friends, a Quaker institution where she lived for the closing years of her own life; at time of death, left $1 million for African-American elementary schools in the South and to develop improved means of education for blacks.

JEANMAIRE, Renée (b. 1924). *See Jeanmaire, Zizi.*

JEANMAIRE, Zizi (1924—). French ballerina and film actress. Name variations: Renée Jeanmaire; Zizi Petit. Born Renée Jeanmaire in Paris, France, April 29, 1924; dau. of Marcel Jeanmaire (owner of a Paris chromium factory) and Olga (Brunus) Jeanmaire; studied ballet at Paris Opera Ballet School under Alexandre Volinine and Boris Kniaseff; m. Roland Petit (dancer and director of Les Ballets des Champs Elysées), Dec 29, 1954; children: Valentine Petit. ❖ Spent several seasons with the de Basil and de Guevas Russian ballets, then joined Les Ballets de Champs-Elysées, a company formed by Roland Petit; joined Petit's Les Ballets de Paris de Roland Petit (1948), a troupe of 15 solo dancers; during company's initial season, danced leading roles in *Que le Diable l'Emporte*, *Études Symphoniques*, and *Carmen*, 3 new ballets choreographed by Petit; at company's NY debut (1949), dazzled US audiences with her unconventional interpretation of Carmen; starred in *Hans Christian Andersen* with Danny Kaye, a film that contains a 17-minute ballet choreographed by Petit; went on to star in several French movies and also appeared on Broadway in *The Girl in Pink Tights* (1953); combined singing and acting with dancing and starred in the stage shows *Revue des Ballets de Paris* (1956), *Le Patron* (1959), and *An Evening with Zizi*, which came to US (1964). ❖ See also *Women in World History*.

JEANNE. *Variant of Joan and Juana.*

JEANNE, Pope (d. 858). *See Joan (d. 858).*

JEANNE I (1273–1305). *See Joan I of Navarre.*

JEANNE I (d. 1346). Countess of Dreux. Born in Dreux, France; died in 1346; dau. of Robert V, count of Dreux (r. 1309–1329); sister of Jean III, count of Dreux (r. 1329–1331); sister of Pierre, count of Dreux (r.1331–1345). ❖ Succeeded deceased brothers, ruling Dreux from 1345 until her death in 1346; replaced by aunt, Jeanne II.

JEANNE II (r. 1346–1355). Countess of Dreux. Born in Dreux, France; reigned (1346–55); 2nd dau. of Jean II, count of Dreux (r. 1282–1309); sister of Robert V, count of Dreux (r. 1309–1329); m. Louis, vicomte de Thouars; children: Simon de Thouars, count of Dreux (r. 1355–1365). ❖ Succeeded niece Jeanne I (1346).

JEANNE I DE NAVARRE (1273–1305). *See Joan I of Navarre.*

JEANNE II DE NAVARRE (1309–1349). *See Joan II of Navarre.*

JEANNE I OF BURGUNDY (c. 1291–1330). Queen of France. Name variations: Jeanne de Bourgogne; Joan I, countess of Artois; Joan of Burgundy. Born c. 1291; died in 1330 (some sources cite 1325); dau. of Count Otto IV of Burgundy, and Mahaut (c. 1270–1329), countess of Artois; m. Philip V the Tall (1294–1322), king of France (r. 1316–1322), in 1306 or 1307; children: Jeanne II of Burgundy (1308–1347); Margaret of Artois (d. 1382, who m. Louis II of Flanders); Isabelle Capet (who m. Guigne VIII of Viennois).

JEANNE II OF BURGUNDY (1308–1347). Countess of Artois. Name variations: Joan II, countess of Artois; Jeanne II of Artois; Jeanne II of Bourgogne. Born May 2, 1308; died Aug 13, 1347; dau. of Jeanne I of Burgundy (c. 1291–1330) and Philip V (c. 1294–1322), king of France (r. 1316–1322); m. Eudes IV, duke of Burgundy, June 18, 1318; children: Philip Capet (d. 1346); and 5 other sons who died in infancy.

JEANNE III D'ALBRET (1528–1572). *See Jeanne d'Albret.*

JEANNE D'ALBRET (1528–1572). French noblewoman. Name variations: Joan III, Queen of Navarre; Jeanne III d'Albret. Born in 1528; died in Paris in 1572; dau. of Henry or Henri II d'Albret, king of Navarre, and Margaret of Angoulême (1492–1549); niece of Francis I, king of France (r. 1515–1547); m. Guillaume de la March also known as William, duke of Cleves, in 1541 (annulled); m. Antoine also known as Anthony (1518–1562), duke of Bourbon and Vendôme, in 1548; children: (2nd m.) Henri or Henry of Navarre (1553–1610, later Henry IV, king of France, r. 1589–1610); Catherine of Bourbon (c. 1555–1604). ❖ One of the 1st members of the French nobility to convert to Protestantism, became a leader of the Huguenot movement; is also credited with seeing that her mother's greatest work, *L'Heptaméron*, was published true to her mother's concept; wed Antoine, duke of Bourbon; inherited her father's estates and gave birth to Henry of Navarre; visited Henry II, king of France, and Catherine de Medici and made an informal agreement to betroth son to their daughter Margaret of Valois (1553–1615), then three-and-a-half; when Henry II died, husband Antoine lost influence; at a time of religious turmoil in France, began openly worshipping as a Huguenot (1561) and became a guiding light to the movement; for this, faced opposition from husband and was banished from court; when husband died in battle, tried to regain custody of son, but Catherine de Medici insisted that he remain at court; called before the Inquisition by Pope Pius V, was unexpectedly

championed by Catherine de Medici; grateful for her intervention, accepted an invitation to join the court; finally allowed to take son from court (1567), joined brother-in-law, Prince of Condé, at the Huguenot stronghold; within months, 15-year-old son was nominal leader of the Huguenot faction; agreed to have son wed Margaret of Valois to secure tranquility; died soon after. Son Henry of Navarre brought peace to France and founded the royal dynasty of Bourbon, which would rule France for almost 2 centuries, until the French Revolution in 1789. ❖ See also Nancy Layman Roelker, *Queen of Navarre: Jeanne d'Albret* (Harvard University, 1968); and *Women in World History*.

JEANNE D'ARC (c. 1412–1431). *See Joan of Arc.*

JEANNE D'AUTRICHE (1535–1573). *See Joanna of Austria.*

JEANNE DE BELLEVILLE (fl. 1343). French noblewoman and pirate. Name variations: Jeanne de Clisson. Fl. in 1343 in France and England; m. Olivier III, lord of Clisson (died 1343); m. Gautier de Bentley, an English courtier; children: at least 3, including Olivier IV, lord of Clisson. ❖ A French noblewoman, whose rebellion against Philip VI, king of France, gained her a reputation for being vicious, bloodthirsty, and vengeful; when husband was executed for treason on king's orders (1343), revolted, gathering other discontented petty nobles and beginning a bloody rampage against the king's followers; found support from Edward III, king of England, who, in his desire to weaken the French king, agreed to loan her some arms and English warships; from the coast of Brittany, conducted skirmishes against French soldiers; later escaped to the protection of the English king and lived at his court.

JEANNE DE BOURBON (1338–1378). Queen of France. Name variations: Joan of Bourbon. Born Feb 3, 1338, in Bourbon (some sources erroneously cite 1326 or 1327); died Feb 6, 1378, in Paris; dau. of Pierre or Peter I, duke of Bourbon, and Isabelle of Savoy (d. 1383); m. Charles V (1338–1380), king of France (r. 1364–1380), in 1350; children: Charles VI the Mad (1368–1422), king of France (r. 1380–1422); Louis (1372–1407), duke of Orléans (assassinated in 1407); Isabelle (1378–1378); Catherine of France (who m. John of Montpensier). ❖ Primarily recognized for her important religious patronage and generosity to convents, founded a Celestine monastery among others; was also a benevolent patron of the arts, commissioning numerous paintings and sculptures, mostly on religious topics; presided over a large and intellectual court; was also noted as an avid book collector and often commissioned works to be copied for her; throughout life, was plagued by bouts of mental instability of unknown origin. ❖ See also *Women in World History*.

JEANNE DE BOURGOGNE (1293–1348). *See Jeanne of Burgundy.*

JEANNE DE CASTILE (r. 1366–1374). Co-ruler of Vendôme. Name variations: Castille; Jeanne of Vendôme or Vendome; Juana of Castile; countess of Vendome. Reigned in Vendôme with her son Bouchard VII from 1366 to 1374; m. Jean VI, count of Vendôme (r. 1336–1366); children: Catherine of Vendôme (r. 1374–1412); Bouchard VII, count of Vendôme (r. 1366–1374).

JEANNE DE CHATILLON (d. 1292). Countess of Blois. Reigned (1279–92); died 1292; dau. of Jean de Chatillon, count of Blois and Chartres (r. 1241–1279); m. Pierre, count d'Alençon.

JEANNE DE CLISSON (fl. 1343). *See Jeanne de Belleville.*

JEANNE DE DAMMARTIN (d. 1279). *See Joanna of Ponthieu.*

JEANNE DE FRANCE (c. 1464–1505). Queen of France and saint. Name variations: Jeanne of France; Jeanne de Valois; Joan de Valois; Joan of France; duchess of Orleans or duchess of Orléans. Born c. 1464; died in 1505; dau. of Charlotte of Savoy (c. 1442–1483) and Louis XI, king of France; sister of Anne of Beaujeu (c. 1460–1522) and Charles VIII, king of France; m. Louis, duke of Orléans (later Louis XII, king of France), on Sept 8, 1476 (annulled 1498). ❖ After Louis XII repudiated his marriage to her in order to marry Anne of Brittany (1499), retired to Bourges and was given a dowry for the rest of her life; considered a saint by contemporaries, has come down through history as deformed; was canonized (1950). ❖ See also *Women in World History*.

JEANNE DE LAVAL (d. 1498). Duchess of Lorraine and Guise. Name variations: Duchess of Lorraine and Bar; duchess of Provence; duchess of Anjou and Guise. Died 1498; became 2nd wife of René I the Good (1408–1480), duke of Lorraine and Bar, duke of Provence, duke of

Anjou and Guise (r. 1431–1480), and king of Naples (r. 1435–1442), in 1454. René's 1st wife was Isabelle of Lorraine (1410–1453).

JEANNE DE LESTONAC (1556–1640). French saint. Name variations: Baroness de Landiras. Born in Bordeaux, France, in 1556; died 1640; niece of Michel de Montaigne; m. the baron de Landiras; children: 7. ❖ Widowed at 41, was a novice for 5 months at the Feuillantines of Toulouse before founding, with help of 2 Jesuits, the Institute of the Daughters of Our Lady. Feast day is Feb 2.

JEANNE DE MONTFORT (c. 1310–c. 1376). Countess of Montfort and duchess of Brittany. Name variations: Jane or Joan of Flanders; Jane, countess of Montfort; Jeanne of Flanders. Born c. 1310 in Flanders; died c. 1376 in England; dau. of Louis de Nevers, count of Flanders; m. Jean de Montfort also known as John III (IV) de Montfort (d. 1345), duke of Brittany (r. 1341–1345); children: Jean also seen as John IV (or V) the Valiant or John IV de Montfort (1339–1399), 5th duke of Brittany (r. 1364–1399). ❖ A woman of valor, capable of leadership that would rival the most experienced general, warred against claimants to husband's estates; throughout married life, fought French king Philip VI of France who sought to annex Brittany and place his nephew, Charles of Blois, on the ducal throne; after husband was captured by the French and imprisoned in Paris (1342), was forced to continue the war to save Brittany from Charles of Blois and his formidable wife, Jeanne de Penthièvre; assembled an army of supporters from neighboring towns to take up arms; from castle of Hennebonne (or Hennobont) on coast of Brittany, led a defense against constant attack from Charles of Blois; when husband escaped from Paris but died during siege of Hennebonne (1345), refused to give up and finally received reinforcements from some English troops; mounted a nighttime attack on Charles of Blois' encampment, dispatched his army, and took him hostage; appears in later chronicles fighting in a naval battles off the coast of Guernsey. ❖ See also *Women in World History.*

JEANNE DE PENTHÌERRE (c. 1320–1384). *See Jeanne de Penthièvre.*

JEANNE DE PENTHIÈVRE (c. 1320–1384). French noblewoman and countess of Blois. Name variations: Jeanne de Penthierre or Penthierre or Penthievre; Joan of Blois. Born c. 1320; died in 1384 in France; dau. of Guy of Brittany and Jeanne of Avaugour; m. Charles of Blois, 1337 (killed 1364). ❖ A French noblewoman, became the primary enemy of Jeanne of Montfort, since both had legitimate claims to the duchy of Brittany; when husband was taken hostage, became commander of his supporters, even leading troops into battle herself; when Charles was slain (1364), was forced to sign a treaty relinquishing her claims to Brittany. ❖ See also *Women in World History.*

JEANNE DE SARMAIZE (fl. 1456). Impersonator of Joan of Arc. Name variations: Jeanne of Sarmaize; Joan, the Maid of Sarmaize. Fl. in 1456 in France; real name unknown. ❖ One of several French women who claimed to be Joan of Arc following the real Joan's death (1431), was a young peasant woman from the small town of Sarmaize; like the real Joan, wore men's clothing. Many French people, including a few who had actually known Joan, believed she was truly the reincarnation of their heroine, and some believers even accompanied Jeanne as she traveled across France.

JEANNE DES ARMOISES (fl. 1438). Captain in the French army. Name variations: Joan of Armoises. Fl. in 1438 in France; married and mother of 2. ❖ A soldier from the peasantry, fought well and was made a captain in the army by the king's marshal; arrested by the king's soldiers as an impostor of Joan of Arc at the urging of a displeased clergy. ❖ See also *Women in World History.*

JEANNE DE VALOIS.
See Jeanne of Valois (c. 1294–1342).
See Jeanne of Valois (c. 1304–?).
See Jeanne de France (c. 1464–1505).

JEANNE HACHETTE (c. 1454–?). *See Hachette, Jeanne.*

JEANNE OF BOULOGNE (1326–1360). *See Blanche of Boulogne.*

JEANNE OF BOURBON (1434–1482). Duchess of Bourbon. Name variations: Jeanne de France or Jeanne of France. Born in 1434; died on May 4, 1482; dau. of Marie of Anjou (1404–1463) and Charles VII (1403–1461), king of France (r. 1422–1461); sister of Louis XI, king of France (r. 1461–1483); became 1st wife of Jean also known as John II (1426–1488), duke of Bourbon (r. 1456–1488), Mar 11, 1447; no children. John II's 2nd wife was Jane of Bourbon-Vendome (d. 1511).

JEANNE OF BOURBON (d. 1493). Princess of Orange. Name variations: Jeanne de Bourbon. Died July 10, 1493; dau. of Agnes of Burgundy (d. 1476) and Charles I, duke of Bourbon (r. 1434–1456); m. John IV the Good, prince of Orange, Oct 21, 1467.

JEANNE OF BURGUNDY (1293–1348). Queen of France. Name variations: Jeanne de Bourgogne; Joan of Burgundy; countess of Valois; called The Lame. Born 1293; died Sept 12, 1348, in Paris, France (some sources cite 1349); dau. of Robert II, duke of Burgundy, and Agnes Capet (1260–1327, dau. of Louis IX of France); sister of Margaret of Burgundy (1290–1315); became 1st wife of Philip VI of Valois (1293–1350), king of France (r. 1328–1350), July 1313; children; Jean also known as John II the Good or Le Bon (1319–1364), king of France (r. 1350–1364); Louis (d. 1328); Louis (d. 1330); Jean or John (d. 1333); Philip (1336–1375), count of Beaumont, count of Valois, duke of Orléans. Philip VI's 2nd wife was Blanche of Navarre (1331–1398).

JEANNE OF BURGUNDY (1344–1360). French princess. Name variations: Joan of Burgundy. Born 1344; died 1360 in Larrey-en-Montagne; dau. of Blanche of Boulogne (1326–1360) and Philip Capet (d. 1346); stepdau. of John II (1319–1364), king of France (r. 1350–1364).

JEANNE OF CHALON (1300–1333). Countess of Tonnerre. Name variations: Jeanne de Chalon. Born in 1300; died Oct 15, 1333; dau. of Eleonore of Savoy (d. 1324) and William, count of Auxerre and Tonnerre; m. Robert of Burgundy (1302–1334), count of Tonnerre, June 8, 1321.

JEANNE OF FLANDERS (c. 1310–c. 1376). *See Jeanne de Montfort.*

JEANNE OF LORRAINE (1458–1480). Countess of Maine and Provence. Name variations: Jeanne of Vaudemont-Lorraine. Born in 1458 (some sources cite 1448); died on Jan 25, 1480; dau. of Yolande of Vaudemont (1428–1483) and Ferrey de Vaudemont also known as Frederick, count of Vaudemont; m. Charles II of Anjou (1436–1481), count of Maine and Provence.

JEANNE OF NAVARRE (1273–1305). *See Joan I of Navarre.*

JEANNE OF NAVARRE (1309–1349). *See Joan II of Navarre.*

JEANNE OF NEMOURS (1644–1724). Duchess and regent of Savoy. Name variations: Giovanna Battista; Jeanne de Nemours; Jeanne-Baptist de Savoie-Nemours; Jean de Savoie-Nemours; Marie-Jeanne-Baptiste; Marie de Savoy-Nemours; Marie of Savoy-Nemours; Madame Royale. Born Marie Jeanne Baptiste de Savoie-Nemours, April 11, 1644; regent (1675–84); died Mar 15, 1724 in Savoy; dau. of Charles Amadeus of Savoy-Nemours also known as Charles Amedeé of Savoy (who was killed in a celebrated duel with his brother-in-law, François de Vendome, duke of Beaufort) and Elizabeth de Bourbon; sister of Marie Françoise of Savoy (1646–1683); became 2nd wife of Charles Emmanuel II (1634–1675), duke of Savoy (r. 1638–1675), in 1664; children: Victor Amadeus II (1666–1732), duke of Savoy (r. 1675–1713), king of Sicily (r. 1713–1718) and Sardinia (r. 1718–1730). Charles Emmanuel's 1st wife was Françoise d'Orleans (fl. 1650). ❖ Became 2nd wife of 4th cousin, Charles Emmanuel, duke of Savoy, who had, with aid of his mother Christine of France, ruled over the politically important state of Savoy since 1638; presided over the court's administration and activities, but took no overt political role until husband's death (1675); became regent for 9-year-old son Victor Amadeus; is credited with maintaining Savoy's independence against its internal and external enemies; ambitious and politically astute, dismissed husband's council and named her own advisors; attempted to appease the nobles, who grew more openly partisan each day, with financial rewards for their loyalty; also attempted to keep her volatile son from being exposed to the politics of the court, which led him to resent her; accepted the financial and military support of King Louis XIV of France, but eventually became convinced that France was more of a threat than an ally. ❖ See also *Women in World History.*

JEANNE OF VALOIS (c. 1294–1342). Countess of Hainault and Holland. Name variations: Jeanne de Valois; Joan Valois; Joan of Valois. Born c. 1294; died Mar 7, 1342; dau. of Charles III (1270–1325, son of Philip III of France), duke of Anjou and count of Valois, and Margaret of Anjou (c. 1272–1299); sister of Philip VI, king of France (r. 1328–1350); m. William III the Good, count of Hainault and Holland, on May 19, 1305; children: William IV, count of Hainault and Holland (d. 1345); Margaret of Holland (d. 1356); Joan of Hainault (c. 1310–?); Philippa of Hainault (1314–1369).

JEANNE OF VALOIS (c. 1304–?). Countess of Beaumont. Name variations: Jeanne de Valois. Born c. 1304; dau. of Catherine de Courtenay (d.

1307) and Charles of Valois also known as Charles I (1270–1325), count of Valois (son of Philip III the Bold, king of France); half-sister of Philip VI of Valois (1293–1350), king of France (r. 1328–1350), and Jeanne of Valois (c. 1294–1342, mother of Philippa of Hainault); m. Robert III of Artois, count of Beaumont.

JEANNE OF VAUDEMONT-LORRAINE (1458–1480). *See Jeanne of Lorraine.*

JEANNE OF VENDÔME (r. 1366–1374). *See Jeanne de Castile.*

JEANNERET, Marie (d. 1884). Swiss poisoner. Died 1884. ❖ Nurse who poisoned her clients, 1st killed a friend named Berthet (1866); used atropine, morphine, and antimony to poison possibly as many as 30 people; arrested after a physician reported his suspicions about her to authorities; convicted of 7 murders but won sympathy of jury and received only 20-year sentence.

JEANS, Constance (b. 1899). English swimmer. Born Aug 23, 1899, in UK. ❖ Won a silver medal at Antwerp Olympics (1920) and a silver medal at Paris Olympics (1924), both in 4 x 100-meter freestyle relay.

JEANS, Isabel (1891–1985). English actress. Born in London, England, Sept 16, 1891; died in London, Sept 4, 1985; dau. of Frederick George Jeans and Esther (Matlock) Jeans; m. Claude Rains (actor), 1913 (div. 1920); m. Gilbert Edward Wakefield (playwright-screenwriter). ❖ In a career that spanned 60 years, was one of England's most versatile actresses; made London stage debut in *Pinkie and the Fairies* (1909); had 1st speaking role as Peggy Bannister in *The Greatest Wish* (1913); toured US with Granville Barker's co. (1915–16); back in London, appeared as Celia in *Volpone* (1921), Cloe in *The Faithful Shepherdess* (1923) and Margery Pinchwife in *The Country Wife*; also performed in modern works, including *The Rat* (1924) and *The Road to Rome* (1928); with gift for high comedy, remained in demand for both classic and modern roles, then made a graceful transition into character parts, including Mrs. Malaprop in *The Rivals* (1967) and Lady Bracknell in *The Importance of Being Earnest* (1968); made last stage appearance as Madame Desmortes in *Ring Round the Moon* (1968); films include *Tilly of Bloomsbury* (1921), *The Triumph of the Rat* (1926), *Easy Virtue* (1928), *Sally Bishop* (1932), *Suspicion* (1941), *Gigi* (1958), *Heavens Above!* (1963) and *The Magic Christian* (1969). ❖ See also *Women in World History.*

JEANS, Ursula (1906–1973). British actress. Born Ursula McMinn, May 5, 1906, in Simla, India; died in a nursing home near London, England, April 21, 1973; dau. of C.H. McMinn and Margaret Ethel (Fisher) McMinn; studied at Royal Academy of Dramatic Art; m. Robin Irvine (died); m. Roger Livesey (actor). ❖ Made stage debut as Sophie Binner in *Cobra* in Nottingham (1925) and London debut as Angela in *The Firebrand* (1926); appeared as Evelyn Seymour in *High Treason* (1928), Cora Wainwright in *The Five O'clock Girl* (1929), Elsie Fraser in *The First Mrs. Fraser* (1929), Flaemmchen in *Grand Hotel* (1931), Alithea in *The Country Wife* (1936), Karen in *The Children's Hour* (1936), and Sally Grosvenor in *They Came by Night* (1937); with Old Vic, played Kate Hardcastle in *She Stoops to Conquer*, Katherine in *The Taming of the Shrew*, Olivia in *Twelfth Night*, Lady Cicely Waynflete in *Captain Brassbound's Conversion*, and Mistress Ford in *The Merry Wives of Windsor*, among others; though primarily a stage actress, also made occasional films beginning in 1922 with *The Gypsy Cavalier*; made only two NY appearances: *Late One Evening* (1933) and *Escapade* (1953); toured Australia and New Zealand with husband Roger Livesey (1956–58,) co-starring in *The Reluctant Debutante* and *The Great Sebastians*. ❖ See also *Women in World History.*

JEBB, Eglantyne (1876–1928). English philanthropist. Born Eglantyne Jebb in Ellesmere, Shropshire, England, 1876; died in Geneva, Switzerland, 1928; sister of Dorothy Buxton; graduate of Lady Margaret Hall, Oxford, 1898; never married; no children. ❖ Founder of Save the Children Fund, went to Macedonia to organize aid for the millions of children left destitute following Balkan wars (1913); during WWI, when Allies blockaded Europe, set up Save the Children and included those of the enemy nations, Austria and Germany; expanded the fund quickly, allowing her to feed and provide for children in Greece, Bulgaria, Romania, Armenia and Poland; at Declaration of Geneva, her Children's Charter was adopted by UN, the 1st Declaration of the Rights of the Child (1924). ❖ See also F.M. Wilson, *Eglantyne Jebb: Rebel Daughter of a Country House* (1967); and *Women in World History.*

JECHOLIAH. Biblical woman. Pronunciation: Jek-uh-LIGH-uh. Married King Amaziah; children: King Azariah (or Uzziah).

JEDIDAH. Biblicalwoman. Pronunciation: juh-DIGH-duh. Married Amon, king of Judah; children: Josiah, who succeeded his father to the throne at age 8.

JEDRZEJCZAK, Otylia (1983—). Polish swimmer. Born Dec 13, 1983, in Ruda Slaska, Poland. ❖ At World championships, won a gold medal for 200-meter butterfly (2003); won silver medals for 400-meter freestyle and 100-meter butterfly and a gold medal for 200-meter butterfly at Athens Olympics (2004).

JEFFERIS, Barbara (1917–2004). Australian writer. Name variations: Barbara Hinde; (pseudonym) Margaret Sydney. Born Barbara Tarlton Jefferis, Mar 25, 1917, in Adelaide, NSW, Australia; died Jan 3, 2004, in Sydney; dau. of Tarlton Jefferis (analytical chemist) and Lucy Ingoldsby (Smythe) Jefferis (died 1917); granddau. of James Jefferis (minister and philosopher); Adelaide University, BA; m. John Hinde (film critic), 1939; children: Rosalind (b. 1944). ❖ Began career as a journalist for *The Daily News* (1939), then the *Telegraph*, *Women's Weekly* and *Pix*; wrote radio plays; wrote 1st novel, *Contango Day* (1953); other works include *Half-Angel* (1959), *One Black Summer* (1967), *Time of the Unicorn* (1974), *The Tall One* (1977), *Three of a Kind* (1982); was 1st woman president of Australian Society of Authors (1973–75). Made a member of Order of Australia (1986); received Emeritus Award of Australia Council (1995).

JEFFERSON, Martha (1748–1782). Wife of Thomas Jefferson. Name variations: Martha Skelton. Born Martha Wayles, Oct 1748 (specific day is in dispute) in Charles City County, Virginia; died Sept 6, 1782, in Monticello, VA; dau. of John Wayles (planter and lawyer) and Martha (Eppes) Wayles; half-sister of Sally Hemings (1773–1835); m. Bathurst Skelton, Nov 20, 1766, in Williamsburg, VA (died 1768); m. Thomas Jefferson (1743–1826, 3rd president of US), Jan 1, 1772, in Williamsburg, VA; children: (1st m.) son who died in infancy; (2nd m.) 5 daughters and 1 son—only 2 daughters, Martha Jefferson Randolph (1775–1836) and Maria Jefferson Eppes (1778–1804), lived to adulthood; both served as White House hostesses during Jefferson's administration, 1801–09. ❖ Though she had been dead 19 years before Thomas Jefferson became president (1801), historians agree that she was a great love of his life and had a lasting influence on him. ❖ See also *Women in World History.*

JEFFERSON AIRPLANE. *See Slick, Grace.*

JEFFERY, Dorothy (1685–1777). *See Pentreath, Dolly.*

JEFFREY, Matilda Alice (1875–1973). *See Williams, Matilda Alice.*

JEFFREY, Mildred (1910–2004). American labor and civil-rights activist. Name variations: Millie Jeffrey. Born Mildred McWilliams, Dec 29, 1910, in Alton, Iowa; died Mar 24, 2004, in Detroit, MI; University of Minnesota, degree in psychology, 1932; Bryn Mawr, MA in social economy, 1932; m. Homer Newman Jeffrey (labor organizer), 1936 (div. 1950s); children: Balfour Jeffrey, Sharon Lehrer. ❖ As the 1st woman to head a department for United Automobile Workers union, became director of its Women's Bureau (1944), ran the union's radio station (1949–54) and the consumer affairs department (1968–76); marched in the South with Martin Luther King Jr.; was a founder of the National Women's Political Caucus (1971); helped propel careers of women into politics; served on board of governors of Wayne State University for 16 years. Awarded Presidential Medal of Freedom by Bill Clinton (2000).

JEFFREY, Rhi (1986—). American swimmer. Born Oct 25, 1986, in Delray Beach, FL. ❖ At World championships, placed 1st for 4 x 100-meter freestyle relay and 4 x 200-meter freestyle relay (2003); won a gold medal for 4 x 200-meter freestyle relay at Athens Olympics (2004).

JEFFREYS, Anne (1923—). American actress and singer. Born Anne Carmichael, Jan 26, 1923, in Goldsboro, NC; m. Joseph R. Serena (div. 1949); m. Robert Sterling (actor), 1951; children: 3 sons. ❖ Began career as a junior model for John Robert Powers, then sang with NY City Opera as Mimi in *La Boheme* and Cio-Cio in *Madame Butterfly* (1940–41); made Broadway debut in musical version of *Street Scene* (1947), followed by *My Romance*, *Kiss Me Kate* and *Bittersweet*, among others; made film debut in *I Married an Angel* (1942), followed by *Step Lively*, *Wagon Tracks West*, *Nevada*, *Zombies on Broadway*, *Dillinger*, *Riff-Raff*, *Return of the Badmen*, *Boys' Night Out*, *Panic in the City*, *Clifford* and as Tess Trueheart in *Dick Tracy*; on tv, starred with husband in series "Topper" (1953–55) and "Love that Jill."

JEFFREYS, Ellen Penelope (1827–1904). New Zealand artist. Name variations: Ellen Valpy. Born Ellen Valpy, Feb 12, 1827, in Hummeripore (Hamirpur), India; died Sept 8, 1904, in Mornington, New Zealand; dau. of William Henry Valpy and Caroline (Jeffreys) Valpy; m. Henry Jeffreys (cousin), 1852 (died 1863); children: several, but none survived. ❖ Immigrated with family to New Zealand (1849); lived with husband in NSW, Australia, until 1860, when they returned to New Zealand. Bulk of her work were watercolors of local scenes and are collected at Otago Early Settlers Museum and Hocken Library. ❖ See also *Dictionary of New Zealand Biography* (Vol. 1).

JEFFREYS, Ellis (1872–1943). English actress. Born Minnie Gertrude Ellis Jeffreys, May 17, 1872, in Colombo, Ceylon; died Jan 21, 1943, in Surrey, England; m. Frederick Graham Curzon (div.); m. Herbert Sleath (Skelton). ❖ Made stage debut at Savoy, London, in chorus of *Yeoman of the Guard* (1889), then sang nearly all female roles in *La Cigale* during its long run (1890); subsequently appeared in *The Prancing Girl, The Bauble Shop, The Two Orphans, The Notorious Mrs. Ebbsmith, My Soldier Boy, Sweet Lavender, The Vagabond King, The Elixor of Youth, A Woman of No Importance, The Prince Consort* and *On the Love Path,* among others; films include *Limelight, Lilies of the Field, Eliza Comes to Stay* and *Sweet Devil.*

JEFFRIES, Elizabeth (d. 1752). English woman convicted of murder. Hanged in Epping Forest, Mar 28, 1752. ❖ In Walthamstow, managed estate of uncle who alternately promised to leave estate to her or exclude her from his will; conspired with one of his employees, John Swan (with whom she may have been intimate), to murder her uncle; with Swan, hired man named Matthews to assist in killing; after Matthews abandoned the plan and Swan killed her uncle (July 3, 1751), was arrested with Swan; convicted, fainted repeatedly on way to gallows.

JEFFS, Doreen (d. 1965). English murderer. Committed suicide by jumping off cliff into English Channel, Jan 1965. ❖ Murdered 1-month-old daughter in Eastbourne (Nov 1960) and subsequently faked the child's kidnapping; after body found, pleaded guilty; successful defense argued that murder had been committed while she was "under the stress of childbirth"; after spending time in mental institution, placed on probation.

JEGADO, Hélène (1803–1851). French poisoner. Name variations: Helene Jegado. Born 1803 in Plouhinec, Morbihan, France; beheaded, 1851. ❖ Illiterate Breton peasant, was orphaned at 7; worked as cook and housekeeper for cleric in France; while many deaths occurred around her, remained above suspicion; employed in Rennes by university professor Théophile Bidard (1850); after deaths of 2 servants in Bidard household, arrested and tried (Dec 1851); found guilty. It has been speculated that she may have poisoned to death more than 60 victims. ❖ See also Victor MacClure, *She Stands Accused* (2002).

JEGGLE, Elisabeth (1947—). German politician. Born July 21, 1947, in Untermarchtal, Germany. ❖ Home economist; as a member of the European People's Party (Christian Democrats) and European Democrats, elected to 5th European Parliament (1999–2004).

JEGOROVA, Lyubov (1966—). See Egorova, Lyubov.

JEHAN, Noor (1926–2000). Pakistani singer and actress. Name variations: Nur Jahan or Nur Jehan; Noorjahan. Born Allah Wasai, 1926, in Kasur, Punjab, India; died of heart failure, Dec 23, 2000, in Karachi, Pakistan; m. Shaukat Hussain Rizvi; m. Ejaz Durrani (div.); married a pilot (div.); m. Yusuf Khan (Pakistani film star, div.); grandmother of actress Sonya Jehan. ❖ Known as "Melody Queen," began career at age 5, performing on stage in Calcutta; as the subcontinent's 1st female child star, appeared in 1st film at age 9, the Punjabi-language *Pind Di Kuri* (1935); went on to star in numerous films; moved to Pakistan after the partition of India (1947); following film career, became Pakistan's most popular singer; recorded thousands of songs over a 5-decade career, singing in Urdu and Punjabi.

JEHAN, Nur (1577–1645). See Nur Jahan.

JEHOSHEBA (fl. 9th c.). Biblical woman. Name variations: Josaba. Fl. in 9th century; sister of Jehoram of Judah; sister-in-law of Athaliah; m. Jehoiada (high priest). ❖ With help of husband, safeguarded the life of nephew Joash when the entire royal family was slain by Athaliah, and later organized a revolution in his favor, causing Athaliah and her followers to be put to death.

JEHUDIJAH. Biblical woman. Pronunciation: jee-huh-DIGH-juh. One of 2 wives of Mered; children: Jered, Heber, and Jekuthiel.

JEKYLL, Gertrude (1843–1932). English garden designer and horticulturist. Pronunciation: JEE-kl. Born Nov 29, 1843, in London; died at Munstead Wood, Surrey, Dec 8, 1932; dau. of Edward Joseph Hill Jekyll (military officer) and Julia (Hammersley) Jekyll (member of prominent banking family); educated at Kensington School of Art, 1861–63; never married; no children. ❖ Distinguished garden designer and expert on plants who has had a profound and continuing influence on English and American horticulture; published 1st article in Robinson's magazine, *The Garden* (1881); forced to give up painting and other artistic activities because of weak eyesight (1891); joined architect Edwin Lutyens, designing gardens to enhance the country houses he was planning and produced 100 such country houses with accompanying gardens; moved into her permanent home of Munstead Wood and was honored by Royal Horticultural Society (1897); became joint editor of *The Garden* (1900); designed garden in Provence, her 1st on foreign soil (1902); working on her own, designed an additional 300 gardens, many of them located in US; also wrote 15 books and 2,000 articles, making her the foremost authority on gardening of her time. Awarded Veitch Memorial Gold Medal (1922); received George Robert White Medal of Honor from Massachusetts Horticultural Society (1929). ❖ See also Jane Brown, *Gardens of a Golden Afternoon: The Story of a Partnership: Edwin Lutyens and Gertrude Jekyll* (Van Nostrand Reinhold, 1982); Sally Festing, *Gertrude Jekyll* (Viking, 1991); Richard Bisgrove, *The Gardens of Gertrude Jekyll* (Little, Brown, 1992); and *Women in World History.*

JELICICH, Dorothy (1928—). New Zealand politician. Born Dorothy Catherine Macdonald, Jan 19, 1928, in Sydney, Australia; m. Paul Jelicich, 1949 (bricklayer); children: 3. ❖ Joined the Labour Party (1950s); served as a trade union official (1970–72); elected Labour MP, for Hamilton East (1972); lost seat (1975).

JELINEK, Elfriede (1946—). Austrian novelist, poet and playwright. Born Oct 20, 1946, in Mürzzuschlag, Austria; dau. of Czech-Jewish father and Austrian mother; studied composition at Vienna Conservatory; attended University of Vienna; m. Gottfried Hüngsberg. ❖ Reclusive writer who depicts "the horrors of reality," published 1st collection of poems, *Lisas Schatten* (1967), followed by 1st novel *Wir sind lockvögel baby!* (*We Are Decoys, Baby!* 1970); her writings, which denounce oppression, sexual violence and right-wing extremism, include *Die Liebhaberinnen* (*Women as Lovers,* 1975), *Die Klavierspielein* (*The Piano Teacher,* 1983), which was filmed in France with Isabelle Huppert, *Die Ausgesperrten* (*Wonderful, Wonderful Times,* 1980) and *Lust* (1989); a fierce opponent of Austria's far-right Freedom Party, was a member of Austrian Communist Party (1974–91); her play *Bambiland* (2003), attacks US invasion of Iraq; awarded the Nobel Prize for literature (2004).

JELISAVETA. *Variant of Elizabeth.*

JELLETT, Mainie (1897–1944). Irish artist. Born in Dublin, Ireland, April 29, 1897; died of pancreatic cancer at St. Vincent's Hospital, Dublin, Feb 16, 1944; dau. of William Morgan Jellett and Janet (Stokes) Jellett; studied art with William Orpen at Dublin Metropolitan School of Art, with Walter Sickert at Westminster School of Art, and with André Lhote and Albert Gleizes in France. ❖ Met with a hostile reaction when she exhibited some of her Cubist paintings in Dublin (1923–24); continued to exhibit regularly in Dublin and also in London and Paris; was a founder member of the Abstraction-Création group, which led the European abstract movement (1930s); gradually spread the gospel of modernism and won acceptance for her work and the work of other modern artists; exhibited at Royal Hibernian Academy (1930), a bastion of conservatism; also designed for the stage, particularly at the Edwards–MacLiammóir Gate Theater in Dublin; finally reaped major recognition when Irish government commissioned her to decorate the Irish Pavilions at Glasgow Exhibition and NY World Fair (1938–39); was a lifelong friend and colleague of Evie Hone. ❖ See also Bruce Arnold, *Mainie Jellett and the Modern Movement in Ireland* (Yale U. Press, 1991); Stella Frost, *A Tribute to Evie Hone and Mainie Jellett* (Browne and Nolan, 1957); and *Women in World History.*

JELLICOE, Ann (1927—). English playwright and director. Born Patricia Ann Jellicoe, July 15, 1927, in Middlesborough, Yorkshire, England; m. C.E. Knight-Clarke, 1950; m. Roger Mayne, 1962. ❖ Began career as an actress and stage manager in repertory, also directing a number of plays; of the "New Drama" generation, wrote *The Sport of My Mad Mother, The Knack, Shelley, The Giveaway, The Rising Generation, You'll Never Guess!, Clever Elsie,* and *A Good Thing or a Bad Thing;* trans. *Rosmersholm, The*

Lady from the Sea, and *The Seagull;* founded the Cockpit Theatre Club to Experiment with the Open Stage (1951); wrote screenplay for *The Knack* (1965) and teleplay for "Det" (1970).

JELLICOE, Anne (1823–1880). Irish educationalist. Born Anne Mullin in Mountmellick, County Laois, 1823; died in Birmingham, Oct 18, 1880; dau. of William Mullin (schoolmaster); mother's name unknown; m. John Jellicoe, 1846 (died 1862); no children. ❖ Heavily involved in movement to improve educational provision for middle-class Irish women, set up embroidery and lace crochet schools in Co. Offaly; moved to Dublin (1858) and ran infant schools for poor children; founded the Irish Society for Promoting the Training and Employment of Educated Women, later known as the Queen's Institute (1861); founded Alexandra College in Dublin (1866), one of the most celebrated and successful schools for women, and held the position of Lady Superintendent until her death. ❖ See also *Women in World History.*

JELSMA, Clara Mitsuko (1931—). Japanese-American essayist and short-story writer. Born 1931 in Glenwood, Hawaii; dau. of Umetaro Kubojiri and Iku (Hayashi) Kubojiri (both Japanese immigrants); m. Dallas Jelsma, 1956. ❖ Stories reflect experiences of Kubojiri family and consider racial tension against a backdrop of Hawaiian history and landscape; works include *Tempest Tales* (1981) and *Mauna Loa Rains* (1991).

JEMIMA. Biblical woman. Name variations: Jemimah (means "handsome as the day" in Hebrew and "dove" in Arabic). Born in the land of Uz; eldest of Job's 3 daughters; sister of Keziah and Kerenhappuch.

JEMISON, Alice Lee (1901–1964). Native American political leader and journalist. Born Alice Mae Lee, Oct 9, 1901, at Silver Creek, New York (just off the Cattaraugus Reservation); died Mar 6, 1964, in Washington, DC; dau. of Daniel A. Lee (Cherokee) and Elnora E. Seneca (Seneca); educated at Silver Creek High School; m. LeVerne Leonard Jemison, Dec 6, 1919 (sep. Dec 1928); children: LeVerne "Jimmy" Lee (b. 1920); Jeanne Marie Jemison (b. 1923). ❖ Concerned about plight of poverty-stricken Seneca Nation, became secretary to Ray Jimerson, president of the Nation; was a syndicated columnist for North American Newspaper Alliance (1932–34); as spokesperson for Joseph Bruner, president of American Indian Federation (1935–39), fought for repeal of Indian Reorganization Act of 1934, disagreed with herd reduction program among Navaho, lobbied against construction of Blue Ridge Parkway through Cherokee land, and advocated abolishment of Bureau of Indian Affairs (BIA). ❖ See also *Women in World History.*

JEMISON, Mae (1956—). African-American astronaut. Born Mae Carol Jemison, Oct 17, 1956, at Decatur, Alabama; dau. of Charlie Jemison (contractor) and Dorothy Jemison (teacher); Stanford University, BS and BA, 1977, Cornell University, MD, 1981; div. ❖ The 1st African-American woman to fly in space, served as a Peace Corps medical officer in Sierra Leone and Liberia (1983–85); selected by NASA (1987); flew aboard the shuttle *Endeavor* on 1st cooperative mission with Japan, focusing on scientific experiments (1992); left NASA to teach a class on space-age technology and developing countries at Dartmouth College; established the Jemison Group in Houston to improve health care in West Africa. ❖ See also *Women in World History.*

JEMISON, Mary (1742–1833). Indian captive. Name variations: Dickewamis (Di-keh-WAH-mes), Dehewamis (Deh-he-WA-mes), Dehgewanus (Deh-ge-WAH-nus). Born Mary Jemison, 1742, aboard the ship *William and Mary* en route to America; died at Buffalo Creek Reservation, near Buffalo, NY, Sept 19, 1833; dau. of Thomas Jemison (Irish-born farmer) and Jane (Erwin) Jemison; m. Delaware warrior Sheninjee, 1760 (died); m. Seneca warrior Hiokatoo, c. 1765; children: (1st m.) Thomas; (2nd m.) John, Nancy, Betsey, Polly, Jane, Jesse. ❖ Captive of the Iroquois Indians in French and Indian War, who, having decided to stay with the Senecas following the war, survived tremendous hardship during American Revolution and became a great, though temporary, landowner in western NY. ❖ See also James Seaver, *A Narrative of the Life of Mrs. Mary Jemison* (1824); and *Women in World History.*

JEMMY THE ROVER (c. 1805–1855). See Henrys, Catherine.

JENCKES, Virginia Ellis (1877–1975). American congressional representative. Born Virginia Ellis, Nov 6, 1877, in Terre Haute, Indiana; died Jan 9, 1975, in Terre Haute; dau. of James Ellis and Mary (Oliver) Somes; m. Ray Greene Jenckes, Feb 22, 1912 (died 1921); children: Virginia Ray Jenckes (died young). ❖ Following marriage, helped husband manage their 1,300-acre farm and continued with farm after his death; was a founder of Wabash and Maumee Valley Improvement

Association and served as its secretary (1926–32); ran successfully for Congress as a Democrat (1932), representing Indiana's 6th District; during 3 terms (73rd–75th congresses), served on both the Committee on Civil Defense and the Committee on the District of Columbia (1933–39); also served on Committee on Mines and Mining in 1st 2 terms; was a US delegate to Interparliamentary Union in Paris (1937); lost 1938 election but remained in Washington for decades, working for Red Cross; helped 5 priests escape from Hungary during the uprising (1956).

JENKIN, Penelope M. (1902–1994). English zoologist. Name variations: P.M. Jenkin. Born 1902 in UK; died 1994; dau. of B.M. Jenkin (engineer and creator of a corer and surface mud sampler); attended Newnham College, Cambridge, 1921–25, 1927–31; University of Glasgow, postgraduate studies, 1925–27. ❖ The 1st to conduct independent research (1931) at the Freshwater Biological Association's laboratory and the 1st person to use 1 algae species to measure daily photosynthetic rates, held a teaching scholarship at University of Birmingham (1927–29); as a Percy Sladen expedition member, measured photosynthesis in Kenya's Lakes Nakuru and Naivasha (1929); employed as a University of Bristol zoology lecturer (1934–62); conducted significant work on the food web of Lake Nakuru germane to the role of the lesser flamingo; was (most likely) the 1st woman to be approved for a postgraduate degree (Cambridge, MS, 1948) via the Board of Research Studies.

JENKINS, Carol Heiss (b. 1940). See Heiss-Jenkins, Carol.

JENKINS, Eileen (1924—). See Radyonska, Tanya.

JENKINS, Helen Hartley (1860–1934). American philanthropist. Born Aug 16, 1860, in New York, NY; died April 24, 1934, in Morristown, NJ; dau. of Marcellus Hartley (firearms manufacturer) and Frances Chester (White) Hartley; m. George Walker Jenkins (lawyer), June 30, 1892; children: 2 daughters. ❖ Soon after inheriting father's fortune (1902), gave dormitory Hartley Hall to Columbia University, with nephew Marcellus Hartley Dodge (1903); donated $350,000 anonymously to Columbia for construction of Philosophy Hall; in memory of daughter Helen (died 1920), gave main-entrance gates of Barnard College; served as trustee of Teachers College of Columbia University (1907–34); was a principal donor of New York Polyclinic Hospital; endowed Marcellus Hartley Chair of Materia Medica of New York University Medical School (1910, 1921); served as president of board of trustees of Hartley House (1926–34), originally established by father (1897); continuing family's work in tenement reform, constructed Hartley Open Stair Tenement (1913) and other small residential model dwellings in NY area; founded Hartley Trust Corporation (1921).

JENNER, Andrea (1891–1985). Australian actress, journalist, and broadcaster. Name variations: Dorothy Gordon; (pseudonym) Andrea. Born Dorothy Gordon, 1891, in Australia; died in Sydney, Mar 24, 1985; dau. of William A. Gordon (stockbroker) and Dora (Fosbery) Gordon; attended Ascham and Sydney Church of England Girls' Grammar School, Sydney; m. Murray Eugene McEwen, 1917 (div.); m. George Onesiphorus Jenner, 1922 (sep.); no children. ❖ Began career in Hollywood, performing bit parts and stunts for Paramount; returned to Sydney, where she starred in *The Hills of Hate* (1926) and was a scriptwriter on *For the Term of His Natural Life* (1927); left for London and, after long illness, began writing highly successful column for *Sydney Sun* under pseudonym "Andrea"; during WWII, served as a correspondent in Pacific and was captured in Hong Kong after Japanese invasion and imprisoned for 4 years; became nationally known for her pioneering "talk-back" radio show, and her famous greeting "Hullo, mums and dads." ❖ See also memoirs, *Darlings, I've Had a Ball* (1975).

JENNER, Ann (1944—). English ballet dancer. Born Mar 8, 1944, in Ewell, Surrey, England. ❖ Joined Royal Ballet in London (1961), where she created numerous roles including in Frederick Ashton's *Jazz Calendar* and Kenneth Macmillan's *Marguerite and Armand* (1963); danced in company productions of *Cinderella, Giselle, Symphonic Variations,* Tudor's *Shadowplay,* and numerous others.

JENNER, Caryl (1917—). English director and theater manager. Born Pamela Penelope Ripman, May 19, 1917, in London, England. ❖ Began career as an actress and assistant stage manager at the Gate (1935); became resident director for Sally Latimer's Amersham Rep, directing over 200 plays (1938–49); launched Caryl Jenner Mobile Theatre (1949), a second company (1951), and a third, for children only (1952); established the Unicorn Children's Theatre (1962).

JENNINGS, Carin (1965—). See Gabarra, Carin.

JENNINGS, Elizabeth Joan (1926–2001). British poet. Born Elizabeth Joan Jennings, July 18, 1926, in Boston, Lincolnshire, England; died Oct 26, 2001, in Bampton, Oxford, England; dau. of Henry Cecil Jennings. ❖ Devout Roman Catholic, read English at St. Anne's College, Oxford; works include *A Way of Looking: Poems* (1955), *Every Changing Shape* (1961), *Recoveries: Poems* (1964), *The Mind Has Mountains* (1966), *The Secret Brother and Other Poems for Children* (1966), *Hurt* (1970), *Growing Points: New Poems* (1975), *Winter Wind* (1979), *Collected Poems, 1953–1985* (1986), and *In the Meantime* (1997); translated *The Sonnets of Michelangelo* (1961) which remains the definitive translation.

JENNINGS, Frances (d. 1730). English aristocrat. Name variations: Frances Hamilton. Died 1730; elder sister of Sarah Jennings Churchill, duchess of Marlborough (1660–1744); dau. of Richard Jennings (Jenyns) and Frances Thornhurst; m. Sir George Hamilton. ❖ Mentioned by Samuel Pepys in his diary and courted by Richard Talbot, earl and titular duke of Tyrconnel.

JENNINGS, Gertrude E. (d. 1958). English playwright. Born in England; died Sept 28, 1958; dau. of Madeleine (Henriques) Jennings and Louis Jennings (editor of *New York Times* and later PM for Stockport). ❖ Began career as an actress; plays include *Between the Soup and the Savory, The Girl Behind the Bar, The Rest Cure, The Bathroom Door, Elegant Edward, Poached Eggs and Pearls, No Servants, The Lady in Red, Money Doesn't Matter, Isabel Edward and Anne, The Voice Outside, Richmond Park, The Bride, Pearly Gates, In the Fog* and *Bubble and Squeak.*

JENNINGS, Lynn (1960—). American distance runner. Born July 1, 1960, in Princeton, NJ; grew up in MA. ❖ At Barcelona Olympics, won a bronze medal in the 10,000 meters (1992); won 9 US National Cross-Country championships; won World Cross-Country championships (1990, 1991, 1992); competed in 2 more Olympics. Inducted into National Distance Running Hall of Fame.

JENNINGS, Margaret (1904–1994). *See Florey, Margaret.*

JENNINGS, Sarah (1660–1744). *See Churchill, Sarah Jennings.*

JENS, Salome (1935—). American actress. Born May 8, 1935, in Milwaukee, WI; m. Ralph Meeker (actor); m. Lee Leonard. ❖ Made NY debut in *Sixth Finger in a Five Finger Glove* (1956), followed by *The Bald Soprano, The Disenchanted, A Far Country, Night Life, Desire Under the Elms, The Winter's Tale, After the Fall, A Moon for the Misbegotten, A Patriot for Me,* and the title role in *Mary Stuart,* among others; films include *The Fool Killer, Me Natalie, Seconds, Harry's War, Just Between Friends* and *Room 101*; frequently appeared on tv in such shows as "Star Trek: Deep Space Nine."

JENSEN, Anne Elisabet (1951—). Danish economist, journalist and politician. Born Aug 17, 1951, in Kalundborg, Denmark. ❖ Served as chief economist, Unibank (1985–94), and editor-in-chief, *Berlingske Tidende* (1996–98); as a member of the European Liberal, Democrat and Reform Party, elected to 5th European Parliament (1999–2004).

JENSEN, Anne Grethe (1951—). Danish equestrian. Born Nov 7, 1951, in Denmark. ❖ At Los Angeles Olympics, won a silver medal in indiv. dressage (1984).

JENSEN, Bjorg Eva (1960—). Norwegian speedskater and cyclist. Name variations: Bjørg Eva Jensen; also seen as Bjørg. Born Feb 15, 1960, in Larvik, Norway. ❖ Won a gold medal for the 3,000 meters speedskating at Lake Placid Olympics (1980), the only gold medal won by Norway at those games; won the World Jr. championships in speedskating (1980); won National championships in speedskating (1979–83, 1986–88); as cyclist, won a team trial at the National championships (1979).

JENSEN, Christine Boe (1975—). Norwegian soccer player. Born June 3, 1975, in Norway. ❖ Won a team gold medal at Sydney Olympics (2000).

JENSEN, Dorte (1972—). Danish sailor. Born Oct 20, 1972, in Nybord, Denmark. ❖ Won a bronze medal for Yngling class at Athens Olympics (2004), a debut event; placed 2nd at World championships in Yngling (2004).

JENSEN, Elise Ottesen (1886–1973). *See Ottesen-Jensen, Elise.*

JENSEN, Johannah (1880–1943). *See Kempfer, Hannah Jensen.*

JENSEN, Thit (1876–1957). Danish novelist and lecturer. Name variations: Thit Jensen Fenger. Born Maria Kirstine Dorothea "Thit" Jensen, Jan 19, 1876, at Farsø in Northern Jutland, Denmark; died May 14, 1957, in Bagsvaerd; had 10 sisters and brothers, including Johannes V.

Jensen (1873–1950, Nobel Prize-winning novelist); m. Gustav Fenger, 1912. ❖ Became renowned lecturer on motherhood and contraception; novels, which often feature female protagonists torn between work and love, include *To Søstre* (1903), *Gerd* (1918), *Aphrodite fra Fuur* (1925) and *Stygge Krumpen* (1936).

JENSEN, Trine (1980—). Danish handball player. Born Oct 16, 1980, in Denmark. ❖ Right back, won a team gold medal at Athens Olympics (2004).

JENSEN, Zoe Ann (1931—). *See Olsen, Zoe Ann.*

JENSEN FENGER, Thit (1876–1957). *See Jensen, Thit.*

JENSSEN, Elois (1922–2004). American costume designer. Name variations: Eloise Jenssen. Born in Palo Alto, CA, Nov 5, 1922; died Feb 14, 2004, in Woodland Hills, CA; attended Parson's School of Design, Paris; graduated from Chouinard Art Institute (now California Institute of the Arts). ❖ Began career as assistant to Natalie Visart; received 1st screen credit for *Dishonored Lady* (1947); shared an Academy Award for work on Cecil B. De Mille's *Samson and Delilah* (1948); did a 3-year stint with 20th Century-Fox before moving into tv, where she designed for "Private Secretary," "I Love Lucy," "My Living Doll," and "Bracken's World"; nominated for Academy Award for work with Rosanna Norton on *Tron* (1982); other films include *Mrs. Mike* (1949), *Phone Call from a Stranger* (1951), and *Forever Darling* (1955). ❖ See also *Women in World History.*

JENTSCH, Martina (1968—). East German gymnast. Born Mar 22, 1968, in Leipzig, East Germany. ❖ Won team bronze medals at World championships (1985, 1987); at Seoul Olympics, won a bronze medal in team all-around (1988).

JENTZER, Emma R.H. (c. 1883–1972). American special agent. Born c. 1883; died May 4, 1972, in Brooklyn, NY; m. Harry R. Jentzer (1st agent appointed at Bureau of Investigation). ❖ Worked as interpreter at Ellis Island immigrant station in NY; served as 1st woman special agent at Bureau of Investigation (later called FBI, 1911–19).

JEON YOUNG-SUN. South Korean field-hockey player. Born in South Korea. ❖ Won a team silver medal at Atlanta Olympics (1996).

JEONG HYOI-SOON (1964—). Korean handball player. Born April 28, 1964, in South Korea. ❖ At Los Angeles Olympics, won a silver medal in team competition (1984).

JEONG MYUNG-HEE (1964—). Korean basketball player. Born May 16, 1964, in South Korea. ❖ At Los Angeles Olympics, won a silver medal in team competition (1984).

JEPSON, Helen (1904–1997). American soprano. Born in Titusville, PA, Nov 28, 1904; died in Bradenton, FL, Sept 16, 1997; studied with Queena Mario at Curtis Institute, graduating with honors, 1928; m. George Roscoe Possell (also seen as Poselle), 1931. ❖ Debuted with Philadelphia Civic Opera Company in *The Marriage of Figaro,* then appeared with the Philadelphia Grand Opera Company, singing the role of Nedda in *Pagliacci* to excellent reviews; sang on radio with Bamberger Little Symphony Orchestra and was hired to sing with Paul Whiteman's orchestra; made Metropolitan debut (1935), as Helene in Seymour's *In the Pasha's Garden*; went on to become a featured singer with the Met, performing roles in French, Italian, and German operas; made numerous recordings of her most popular arias and was the 1st soprano to record the female lead in Gershwin's *Porgy and Bess.* ❖ See also *Women in World History.*

JEREMIC, Slavica (1957—). Yugoslavian handball player. Born May 1957. ❖ At Moscow Olympics, won a silver medal in team competition (1980).

JERGENS, Adele (1917–2002). American actress. Born Nov 28, 1917, in Brooklyn, NY; died Nov 22, 2002, in Camarillo, CA; m. Glenn Langan (actor), 1949 (died 1991). ❖ Worked briefly as a Rockette; played leads and second leads in 47 films, including *A Thousand and One Nights, Ladies of the Chorus, The Fuller Brush Man, The Dark Past, Abbott and Costello Meet the Invisible Man* and *The Day the World Ended.*

JERIOVA, Kvetoslava (1956—). Czech cross-country skier. Name variations: Květoslava Jeriová; Kveta or Kvéta Jeriova; Kveta Jeriova-Peckova. Born 1956 in Czechoslovakia. ❖ Won a bronze medal for 5 km at Lake Placid Olympics (1980); won a silver medal for 4 x 5 km relay and a bronze medal for 5 km at Sarajevo Olympics (1984).

JERITZA, Maria (1887–1982). Czech soprano. Born Marie Jedlitzka or Jedlitska, Oct 6, 1887, in Brünn, Moravia; died July 10, 1982, in Orange,

NJ; studied at Brünn Musikschule and with Auspitzer; m. Baron Leopold von Popper de Podharagn (div. 1935); m. Winfield Sheehan (motion picture executive), 1935 (died 1945). ❖ Debuted at Olmütz as Elsa in *Lohengrin* (1910) and at Vienna Volksoper as Elisabeth in *Tannhäuser* (1912); engaged by Vienna Hofoper (1913), where she became famous for interpretations of roles in operas of Richard Wagner as well as Giacomo Puccini who considered her the greatest of Toscas; was the 1st Ariadne in both versions of Strauss' *Ariadne auf Naxos* in Stuttgart (1912) and Vienna (1916); also created Marietta in 1st Vienna performance of Korngold's *Die tote Stadt* (*The Dead City*) and the Empress in *Die Frau ohne Schatten* in Vienna (1919); debuted at Metropolitan Opera in US premier of Korngold's *The Dead City* (1921); debuted at Covent Garden (1925); remained with Met (1921–32), singing 290 performances in 20 roles, and starred in many US premieres including those of Janáček's *Jenufa*, Puccini's *Turandot*, Korngold's *Violanta*, and Strauss' *Ægyptische Helena*; other roles included Carmen, Santuzza, Thaïs, and Sieglinde. Received Austrian Order of Knighthood, 1st class—one of the highest awards ever bestowed on a civilian by the Austrian government (1935). ❖ See also autobiography *Sunlight and Song* (1924); and *Women in World History*.

JERMOLEWA, Galina. *See Ermolaeva, Galina.*

JERMY, Louie (1864–1934). English literary inspiration. Name variations: The Maid of the Mill. Born in Sidestrand, Norfolk, England, c. 1864; died 1934; dau. of Alfred Jermy (miller); never married; no children. ❖ Country maiden known as "The Maid of the Mill," who was a lifelong resident of Sidestrand, Norfolk, a thriving tourist mecca during mid-1880s; at 19, met Clement Scott, theater critic and travel writer for London's *Daily Telegraph*, who stayed at her family's cottage and dubbed the house "Poppyland" because of the profusion of red poppies that blanketed its hillsides; after other members of the literati stayed there, gained fame through their writings. ❖ See also *Women in World History*.

JEROME, Helen (b. 1883). English playwright. Born May 10, 1883, in London, England; m. George D. Ali. ❖ Contributed short stories to magazines and newspapers in Sydney and was subsequently dramatic critic for Melbourne *Dramatic News*; adapted Austen's *Pride and Prejudice* which was 1st produced at St. James's Theatre (Feb 1936); other adaptations include *Limelight, Jany Eyre, Charlotte Corday* and *All the Comforts of Home*; dramatizations became the basis for two screenplays: *Conquest* (starring Greta Garbo as Marie Walewska, 1937) and *Pride and Prejudice* (starring Greer Garson, 1940); also wrote *Petals in the Wind* and *The Secret of Woman*.

JEROME, Jennie (1854–1921). *See Churchill, Jennie Jerome.*

JEROME, Rowena (1889–?). English actress. Born Rowena Dorothy Jerome, Dec 12, 1889, in England; dau. of Georgina Henrietta (Nesza) Jerome and Jerome K. Jerome (actor and writer). ❖ Made London debut as Mrs. Peekin in *The Master of Mrs. Chilvers* (1911), then appeared in *Esther Castways, Robina in Search of a Husband, A Scrap of Paper*, and her father's *The Passing of the Third Floor Back*, among others.

JEROSCHINA, Radia. *See Yeroshina, Radya.*

JERROLD, Mary (1877–1955). English actress. Born Dec 4, 1877, in London, England; died Mar 3, 1955, in London; great-granddau. of Douglas Jerrold (playwright and journalist); m. Huber Harben; children: Joan Harben (actress). ❖ Made triumphant London debut as Prudence Dering in *Mary Pennington Spinster* (1896); acted with the Kendals for over 3 years (1902–05); other plays include *Dick Hope, A Royal Divorce, Nan, The Sentimentalists, The Pride of Life, Idle Women, Disraeli, Mary Rose, Quality Street, The Sport of Kings, The Lavender Ladies, The Constant Wife, But for the Grace of God* and *We Proudly Present*; appeared as Martha Brewster in *Arsenic and Old Lace* (1942–46) and in over 30 films.

JERSEY, countess of. *See Villiers, Margaret Elizabeth Child- (1849–1945).*

JERSEY LILY (1853–1929). *See Langtry, Lillie.*

JERUSALEM, queen of.
  See Morphia of Melitene (fl. 1085–1120).
  See Maria Comnena (fl. 1100s).
  See Melisande (1105–1161).
  See Adelaide of Savona (d. 1118).
  See Agnes of Courtenay (1136–1186).
  See Sibylla (1160–1190).
  See Berengaria of Castile (b. around 1199).

  See Isabella I of Jerusalem (d. 1205).
  See Marie of Montferrat (d. 1212).
  See Yolande of Brienne (1212–1228).
  See Isabella of Cyprus (fl. 1250s).
  See Charlotte of Lusignan (1442–1487).

JERUSALMI, Myriam (1961—). *See Fox-Jerusalmi, Myriam.*

JERUSHA. Biblical woman. Name variations: Jerushah. M. Uzziah, king of Judah; children: Jotham who succeeded his father.

JERVEY, Caroline Howard (1823–1877). American novelist. Name variations: (pseudonym) Gilman Glover. Born Caroline Howard Gilman in South Carolina, 1823; died 1877; dau. of Caroline Howard Gilman (1794–1888) and Samuel Gilman (Unitarian minister); married; children. ❖ Wrote such novels as *Vernon Grove* and *Helen Courtenay's Promise*.

JESENSKÁ, Milena (1896–1945). Czech journalist and humanist. Name variations: Milena Jesenska; Milena Krějcárova or Milena Krejcarova. Born Milena Jesenská in Prague, Czechoslovakia, 1896; died in Ravensbrück, May 17, 1945; dau. of Jan Jesensky (professor at Charles University in Prague); niece of Marie and Ruzena Jesenská (both writers); m. Ernst Polak (Jewish translator), 1918 (div. 1924); m. Jaromír Krějcár (architect), 1927; children: (2nd m.) Honza Krějcár (b. around 1928). ❖ Became enmeshed in bohemian feminist movement; fell in love with Ernst Polak; when father learned of affair with the Jewish Polak, had her committed to a mental home at Veleslavin (1917–18); on release, married Polak and moved to Vienna, though she was disinherited; began writing articles and became fashion correspondent for Czech daily *Tribuna*; also trans. works of Franz Kafka—*The Stoker, The Judgment, Metamorphosis* and *Contemplation*—from German to Czech; met Kafka and started a love affair "confined to letters" which lasted several years; entrusted by him with his diaries; became an established reporter; published 3 books and co-edited the illus. magazine, *Pestrý Týden* (1926–28); during Nazi occupation of Czechoslovakia, edited liberal democratic journal, *Přítomnost* (*The Present*) and founded underground journal, *Vboj!* (*On with the Struggle!*); when Jews of Czechoslovakia were told to wear Star of David, sewed one on her clothes; told to cease publishing (June 1939), continued to edit until Aug; arrested and sent to Pankrac Prison in Prague, then to women's concentration camp at Ravensbrück where she met Margarete Buber-Neumann (Oct 1940). ❖ See also Margarete Buber-Neumann, *Milena: The Story of a Remarkable Friendship* (Trans. by Ralph Manheim, Seaver, 1988); Mary Hockaday, *Kafka, Love and Courage: The Life of Milena Jesenská* (Overlook, 1997); Franz Kafka, *Letters to Milena* (Schocken, 1965); and *Women in World History*.

JESENSKÁ, Ruzena (1863–1940). Czech writer. Name variations: Ruzena Jesenska. Born 1863; died 1940; sister of Marie Jesenská (writer); aunt of Milena Jesenská. ❖ Wrote more than 50 collections of poetry, volumes of short stories, novels, plays and children's books. ❖ See also *Women in World History*.

JESIONOWSKA, Celina (1933—). Polish runner. Name variations: Celina Gerwin. Born Celina Jesionowska, Nov 3, 1933, in Poland. ❖ At Rome Olympics, won a bronze medal in 4 x 100-meter relay (1960).

JESPERSEN, Helle (1968—). Danish sailor. Born Feb 12, 1968, in Denmark. ❖ Won a bronze medal for Yngling class at Athens Olympics (2004), a debut event; placed 2nd at World championships for Yngling (2004).

JESSE, Fryniwyd Tennyson (1888–1958). English playwright and novelist. Name variations: F. Tennyson Jesse; Fryn Jesse. Born Wynifried Margaret Jesse, Mar 1, 1888, in Chislehurst, Kent, England; died Aug 6, 1958, in London; dau. of Reverend Eustace Tennyson d'Eyncourt and Edith Louisa (James) Jesse; granddau. of Emily Tennyson, sister of Alfred, Lord Tennyson; studied art at Newlyn School, Cornwell; m. Harold Marsh Harwood (playwright), Sept 9, 1918. ❖ During early years, worked as reporter for *The Times* and *Daily Mail* and wrote book reviews for *English Review*, which also published her 1st short story "The Mask," the success of which led to publication of 1st novel *The Milky Way* (1913), and a collaboration with playwright Harwood, on adaptation of "The Mask" for the stage; during WWI, was a war correspondent for *Daily Mail*, one of the 1st women so assigned; was later assigned by Ministry of Information to report on Women's Army, which resulted in *The Sword of Deborah: First Hand Impressions of the British Women's Army in France* (1919); collaborated with husband on several plays, including *The Pelican* (1916), *Billeted* (1917) and *How to be Healthy though Married*

(1930); published novel *The White Riband* (1921) to good reviews, followed by *Tom Fool* (1926), *Moonraker; or The French Pirate and her Friends* (1927) and *The Lacquer Lady* (1929); also wrote crime novels. ❖ See also Joanna Colenbrander, *A Portrait of Fryn: A Biography of F. Tennyson Jesse* (Deutsch, 1984); and *Women in World History*.

JESSEL, Patricia (1929–1968). English actress. Born Oct 15, 1920, in Hong Kong, British Crown Colony, China; died June 8 (some sources cite June 10), 1969, in London, England; great-niece of Lillah McCarthy (English actress, 1875–1960); m. Dr, George Feinberg; children: daughter. ❖ Made stage debut as Wendy in *Peter Pan* at Lyceum in Sheffield (1933); appeared with Shakespeare Memorial Theatre (1943–44) in such parts as Viola, Goneril, Katherine and Lady Macbeth; starred in other plays, including *Forsaking all Others, Heartbreak House, The Love of Four Colonels, Verdict* and *The Sound of Murder*; appeared in numerous films. Won Tony Award as Best Supporting Actress for performance in *Witness for the Prosecution* (1954).

JESSEN, Ruth (1936—). American golfer. Name variations: Mary Ruth Jessen. Born Nov 12, 1936, in Seattle, WA. ❖ As an amateur, won Seattle City title thrice, Pacific Northwest twice, and Washington State once; turned pro (1956); won Tampa Open (1959); won five tournaments (1964), the Zaharias, Flint, Omaha, Santa Barbara, and Phoenix opens; won Sears Classic (1971).

JESSUP, Marion (b. 1897). American tennis player. Name variations: Mrs. M.Z. Jessup; Marion Zinderstein. Born Marion Zinderstein, May 1897. ❖ As Marion Zinderstein, won US Open doubles with Eleanor Goss (1918, 1919, 1920), but lost in singles finals (1919, 1920); as Marion Jessup, won doubles wth Helen Wills at US Open (1922) and a silver medal in mixed doubles–outdoors with Vincent Richards at Paris Olympics (1924).

JESSYE, Eva (1895–1992). African-American composer, musician, and choral director. Born Jan 20, 1895, in Coffeyville, Kansas; died Feb 21, 1992, in Ann Arbor, MI; graduated from Western University, Quindaro, Kansas, 1914; received teaching certificate from Langston University, Langston, OK, 1916; never married. ❖ Often referred to as "the dean of black female musicians," directed music department at Morgan State College in Baltimore and was newspaper reporter before moving to NY (1926); joined and later directed the Dixie Jubilee Singers, which eventually became Eva Jessye Choir and performed regularly at Capitol Theater; with choir, performed in King Vidor's film *Hallelujah*, the 1st African-American musical (1929); served as choral director for experimental opera *Four Saints in Three Acts* (1934) and *Porgy and Bess* (1935); established music collections in her name at University of Michigan and Pittsburg State University in Kansas; best-known compositions include *Chronicle of Job* and *Paradise Lost and Regained*. ❖ See also *Women in World History*.

JESÚS, Carolina Maria de (c. 1913–1977). Brazilian writer. Name variations: Bitita; Carolina de Jesus. Pronunciation: Kah-ro-LEE-nah Mah-REE-ah day HAY-soos. Born Carolina Maria de Jesús in either 1913 or 1914 in Sacramento, Minas Gerais, Brazil; died in Parelheiros of asthma, Feb 13, 1977; dau. of unknown father and mother who was an unmarried farm worker; attended elementary school for 2 years; never married; children: 3 illeg., Joâo (b. around 1947); José Carlos (b. around 1949); Vera Eunice (b. 1953). ❖ Wrote the bestselling *Child of the Dark: The Diary of Carolina Maria de Jesús*, which detailed the misery of life in a Brazilian shanty town (eventually the work was trans. into 13 languages and published in 40 countries); published 2nd book, *Casa de Alvenaria: Diário de uma Ex-Favelada (The Brick House: Diary of an Ex-Slumdweller)* (1961), followed by *Provérbios de Carolina Maria de Jesús* and *Pedaços da Fome (Bits of Hunger*, both 1969). ❖ See also *Women in World History*.

JESUS, Clementina de (1902–1987). Brazilian singer. Born Feb 7, 1902, in Valença, state of Rio de Janeiro, Brazil; died July 1987 in state of Rio de Janeiro; dau. of Amélia de Jesus. ❖ One of the last links in Brazil to native music of 19th-century Africa, was born into rural poverty and grew up singing traditional Afro-Brazilian songs passed on by mother; discovered by Herminio Bello de Carvalho at age 61, became instant success with both public and critics; combined traditional African melodies (sometimes sung in native dialects) with music of Afro-Brazilian spiritualism as well as Catholic hymns and traditional samba music; sang in coarse voice with deep feeling using oratorical delivery style and interaction of body and song; recorded 1st album at 68 and went on to record 9 albums, including samba and popular music, with many of Brazil's most famous composers and musicians; embodied emerging black consciousness in Brazil; died in poverty.

JESUS, Gregoria de (1875–1943). Filipino hero. Name variations: Lakambini. Born May 15, 1875, in Kalookan, Philippines; died Mar 15, 1943; dau. of Nicholas de Jesus (carpenter) and Baltazara Alvarez Francisco; m. Andres Bonifacio (founder of Katipunan & leader of the 19th-century revolution against Spain), 1894 (shot by the Spanish, May 10, 1897); m. Julia Nakpil. ❖ With others, formed the women's chapter of the revolutionary Katipunan (1894) which fought in the uprising for Philippine independence from Spain; made custodian of the Katipunan seal and of the society's valuable papers; to escape capture, often crossed provinces on foot; was caught, tried for sedition by the Spanish, and condemned to death (1897); sentence was commuted to exile, but husband was killed anyway; lived in the mountains of Pasig, where she met Julia Nakpil.

JESUSITA (1908—). *See Aragon, Jesusita.*

JETT, Joan (1958—). American musician, singer and actress. Name variations: The Runaways. Born Joan Marie Larkin, Sept 22, 1958, in Philadelphia, PA; mother's maiden name was Jett. ❖ Rocker credited as mother of Riot Grrrl movement, moved to Southern California at 14 (1974); joined producer Kim Fowley's notorious girl group The Runaways (1975); played guitar and sang vocals on albums *The Runaways* (1976) and *Queens of Noise* (1977), both of which went gold in Japan; collaborated with ex-members of Sex Pistols on 2 singles, released only in Holland (1979); produced debut album by the Germs (1979); released 1st album under title *Joan Jett* in Europe and *Bad Reputation* in US (1981); became surprise success with #1 single "I Love Rock and Roll" (1982), along with "Crimson and Clover"; appeared in film *Light of Day* (1987); enjoyed comeback with album *Up Your Alley* (1988), which included hit singles "I Hate Myself for Loving You" and "Little Liar"; joined Broadway cast of *The Rocky Horror Picture Show* (2000).

JEUNG SOON-BOK (1960—). Korean handball player. Born Aug 9, 1960, in South Korea. ❖ At Los Angeles Olympics, won a silver medal in team competition (1984).

JEWELL, Isabel (1907–1972). American stage and screen actress. Name variations: Isobel Jewell. Born July 19, 1907, in Shoshone, Wyoming; died April 5, 1972, in Hollywood, CA. ❖ Debuted on stage with a Lincoln, Nebraska, stock company; made Broadway debut in *Up Pops the Devil* (1930); film appearances include *Blessed Event, Lost Horizon, A Tale of Two Cities, Manhattan Melodrama, Northwest Passage, Small Town Girl, Here Comes the Groom, Shadow of a Doubt* and as Emmy Slattery in *Gone with the Wind*.

JEWELL, Lynne (1959—). American yacht racer. Name variations: Lynne Jewell Shore. Born Nov 26, 1959; graduate of Boston University, 1981. ❖ At Seoul Olympics, won a gold medal in 470 class with Allison Jolly (1988); placed 2nd at World championships in standard (1980, 1983, 1985); while at BU, was the 1st female to qualify for the men's collegiate single-handed championship.

JEWELL, Wanda (1954—). American shooter. Born June 19, 1954. ❖ Won World championships for 10 m air rifle 40 shots and 50 m standard rifle 3 x 20 shots (1978); at Los Angeles Olympics, won a bronze medal in smallbore rifle 3 positions (1984).

JEWETT, Sarah Orne (1849–1909). American author. Born Theodora Sarah Orne Jewett in South Berwick, Maine, Sept 3, 1849; died June 24, 1909, in South Berwick; dau. of Theodore Herman Jewett (rural doctor) and Caroline Frances (Perry) Jewett; graduate of Berwick Academy, 1865; never married; primary relationship was with Annie Adams Fields for approximately 30 years. ❖ Best known for her depictions of rural life on coast of Maine, created works that still have great significance for modern readers; published 1st short story at 17; in addition to short stories, wrote numerous children's books, several popular histories, and 3 novels; best known for *The Country of the Pointed Firs* (1896), a novel hailed by many critics as one of the finest in American literature; other writings include *Deephaven* (1877), *Country By-Ways* (1881), *A Country Doctor* (1884), *A White Heron and Other Stories* (1886), *The King of Folly Island and Other People* (1888), *Strangers and Wayfarers* (1890), *A Native of Winby and Other Tales* (1893) and *The Tory Lover* (1901). ❖ See also Paula Blanchard, *Sarah Orne Jewett: Her World and Her Work* (Addison, 1994); Francis O. Matthieson, *Sarah Orne Jewett* (Houghton, 1929); Elizabeth Silverthorne, *Sarah Orne Jewett: A Writer's Life* (Overlook, 1993); and *Women in World History*.

JEWSBURY, Geraldine (1812–1880). English novelist. Born Geraldine Endsor Jewsbury in Measham, Derbyshire, England, Aug 22, 1812; died of cancer in London, Sept 23, 1880; dau. of Thomas Jewsbury (Manchester merchant and insurance agent) and Maria (Smith) Jewsbury; sister of Maria Jane Jewsbury (1800–1833); never married; no children. ❖ Published 1st novel *Zoe: The History of Two Lives* (1845), which revealed feminist views; followed that with *The Half Sisters* (1848), *Marian Withers* (1851),*Constance Herbert* (1855), *The Sorrows of Gentility* (1856) and *Right or Wrong* (1859); invited by Charles Dickens to write for *Household Words* (1850), was also a frequent reviewer of fiction for *Athenaeum* and *Westminster Review*, as well as other journals and magazines; was a close friend of Jane Welsh Carlyle. ❖ See also *Women in World History.*

JEWSBURY, Maria Jane (1800–1833). English poet and prose writer. Name variations: Mrs. Fletcher. Born Maria Jane Jewsbury in Measham, Derbyshire, England, Oct 25, 1800; died of cholera in Poona, India, Oct 4, 1833; dau. of Thomas Jewsbury (Manchester merchant and insurance agent) and Maria (Smith) Jewsbury; sister of Geraldine Jewsbury (1812–1880); m. Reverend William Kew Fletcher (chaplain in East India projects), 1832. ❖ Published collection of verse, *Phantasmagoria* (1825), followed by poetry collection, *Lays of Leisure Hours* (1829) and collection of stories, *The Three Histories: The History of an Enthusiast, The History of a Nonchalant, and The History of a Realist* (1830), which made her reputation as a writer. ❖ See also *Women in World History.*

JEX-BLAKE, Sophia (1840–1912). British physician and education reformer. Name variations: Sophia Jex Blake. Born Jan 21, 1840, in Sussex, England; died Jan 7, 1912, in Sussex; dau. of Thomas Jex-Blake and Maria (Cubitts) Jex-Blake; never married; no children. ❖ One of the 1st female physicians in Europe, was a leader in the struggle for higher education for women in UK; entered Queen's College (1858); published *A Visit to Some American Schools* (1867); started medical studies in Edinburgh (1869); along with 6 other women (Edith Pechey-Phipson, Mary Anderson, Isabel Thorne, Matilda Chaplin, Helen Evans, and Emily Bovell), known as "Edinburgh Seven," was subjected to harassment by male students and professors and encountered numerous barriers; published *Medical Women* (1873); helped establish London School of Medicine for Women (1874); obtained medical license (1877); opened private practice (1878); founded Edinburgh School of Medicine for Women (1886); retired (1899). ❖ See also Shirley Roberts, *Sophia Jex-Blake: A Woman Pioneer in Nineteenth-century Medical Reform* (Routledge, 1993); Margaret G. Todd, *The Life of Sophia Jex-Blake* (Macmillan, 1918); and *Women in World History.*

JEZEBEL (d. 884 BCE). Canaanite queen. Name variations: Jezabel. Pronunciation: JEZ-eh-belle. Date of birth unknown, sometime in late 900s BCE, in Sidon, on eastern Mediterranean coast; died 884 BCE in Jezreel, in Israel; dau. of Ethbaal of Sidon (king of Tyre and priest of the goddess Astarte); mother unknown; m. Ahab of Israel, date unknown; children: Ahaziah; Jehoram; Athaliah; perhaps others. ❖ Canaanite princess and queen of nation of Israel, ruling beside husband King Ahab, whose values and beliefs brought her into violent conflict with those of her adopted country; found in I Kings 17–II Kings 10, was raised in Sidon and trained for queenship; given in diplomatic marriage to Ahab of Israel; participated in the rule of Israel with her husband's consent; sponsored Canaanite religion in Israel, while hunting down and persecuting the prophets of the God of Israel, especially Elijah; reigned as queen for ten years after the death of husband, ruling with Ahaziah first, and then with Jehoram; killed in coup d'état by usurper Jehu, to avenge the murder of certain prophets of the God of Israel. ❖ See also *Women in World History.*

JEZEK, Linda (1960—). American swimmer. Born Mar 10, 1960, in Homestead, CA. ❖ At Montreal Olympics, won a silver medal in 4 x 100-meter medley relay (1976).

J.F. (1851–1891). See *Fothergill, Jessie.*

JHABVALA, Ruth Prawer (1927—). German-born British fiction writer and screenwriter. Pronunciation: JAHB-vah-lah. Born Ruth Prawer in Cologne, Germany, May 7, 1927; dau. of Marcus Prawer and Eleonora (Cohn) Prawer; Queen Mary College, MA, 1951; m. Cyrus S.H. Jhabvala, 1951; children: daughters, Renana, Firoza, and Ava Jhabvala. ❖ Writer whose status as a "permanent refugee" gave rise to a unique view of cultural traditions; lived in Germany (1927–39), England (1939–51), India (1951–75), and New York (1975—); published 1st novel *To Whom She Will* (*Amrita*, 1956), followed by *The Nature of Passion* (1957), *The Householder* (1959), *Shakespeare Wallah* (1973), *A Stronger Climate: Nine Stories* (1968), *Travelers* (1973), *Autobiography of a Princess, Also Being the Adventures of an American Film Director in the*

Land of the Maharajas (1975), *Heat and Dust* (1974), *Out of India: Selected Stories* (1987), *Shards of Memory* (1996) and *East into Upper East* (1998), among others; wrote many screenplays for Merchant-Ivory, including *Shakespeare Wallah* (1965), *The Guru* (1969), *Bombay Talkie* (1970), *Autobiography of a Princess* (1975), *Roseland* (1977), *The Europeans* (1979), *Heat and Dust* (1983), *The Bostonians* (1984), *Jefferson in Paris* (1995) and *Surviving Picasso* (1996). Won Booker Prize for *Heat and Dust* (1975); received MacArthur Foundation grant (1984); won Academy Awards for Best Screenplay Adaptation for *A Room With a View* (1986) and *Howards End* (1992); won Best Screenplay Adaptation award for *Mr. and Mrs. Bridge* by NY Film Critics Circle (1990); nominated for Academy Award for Best Screenplay Adaptation for *Remains of the Day* (1993); received Writers Guild of America's Screen Laurel Award, its highest honor (1994). ❖ See also Aruna Chakravarti, *Ruth Prawer Jhabvala: A Study in Empathy and Exile* (B.R., 1998); and *Women in World History.*

JHANSI, rani of. See *Lakshmibai* (c. 1835–1858).

JI LIYA (1981—). Chinese gymnast. Born Oct 20, 1981, in Hunan, China. ❖ At World championships, won a silver medal in team all-around (1995); placed 4th team all-around at Atlanta Olympics (1996).

JIAGGE, Annie (1918–1996). Ghanaian lawyer, national and international women's rights activist. Pronunciation: JHEE-aggie. Born Annie Ruth Baeta, Oct 7, 1918, in Lome, French Togoland; died in Accra, Ghana, June 12, 1996; dau. of Reverend Robert Domingo Baeta (pastor of Presbyterian Church) and Henrietta Baeta (schoolteacher); Achimota College, Teacher's Certificate, 1937; London School of Economics, LLB, 1949; m. Fred Jiagge, Jan 10, 1953; children: Rheinhold (adopted 1959). ❖ Author of the basic draft and introduction to the UN Declaration on Elimination of Discrimination against Women, who was the 1st Ghanaian woman to become a High Court judge and the 1st woman judge of the Commonwealth; started career as schoolteacher; was headmistress of Evangelical Presbyterian Girls School (1940–46); embarked on legal career (1946); admitted to London School of Economics and Lincoln's Inn (1946); called to Bar at Lincoln's Inn (1950); returned to Ghana, then known as the Gold Coast (1950), and went into private practice; became senior magistrate (1956), Circuit Court judge (1959), High Court judge (1961), Appeal Court judge (1969), and president of Court of Appeal (1980–83); retired (1983). Served as president of YWCA Ghana (1958–62), vice chair of World YWCA (1962–72), as president, UN Commission on the Status of Women 21st Session (1968), founder and chair, Ghana National Council on Women and Development (1975–83); awarded the Grand Medal of Ghana (1969). ❖ See also *Women in World History.*

JIANG CUIHUA. Chinese cyclist. Born in Liaoning, China. ❖ Won a bronze medal for 500-meter time trial at Sydney Olympics (2000), China's 1st cycling medal.

JIANG QING (1914–1991). Chinese leader. Name variations: Shumeng (1914–c. 1925); Li Yunhe or Li Yun-ho (c. 1925–1934); Lan Ping or P'ing (1934–c. 1940); Jiang Qing (Chiang Ch'ing, c. 1940–1991); Madame Mao. Pronunciation: JEE-yahng CHING. Born Mar 1914 in Shantung province, China; committed suicide in Beijing, May 14, 1991; dau. of Li Tewen; married a merchant named Fei, 1930 (div. 1931); common-law marriage, Yu Qiwei (Yü ch'i-wei, revolutionary propagandist), 1931; common-law marriage, Dang Na (also called Tang Na; arts critic), 1936 (div. 1937); common-law marriage, Mao Zedong (Mao Tse-tung), 1938 (died Sept 9, 1976); children: (with Mao) daughter Li Na. ❖ One of the most powerful women in China's 4,000-year history, joined a theatrical troupe in Licheng (1928); at 20, made 1st mark as actress with portrayal of Nora in *A Doll's House*; played leading parts in 2 films: *Blood on Wolf Mountain* and *Old Bachelor Wang*; with her promise to abstain from political activity for 30 years, was allowed to marry Mao Zedong (1938); after Mao proclaimed the People's Republic of China (Oct 1949), served on a Film Guidance Committee of Ministry of Culture (1949–51), where she engaged in heavy-handed censorship; headed the secretariat of General Office of the Party's Central Committee but was quickly eased out (1951–52); was turned into a veritable political partner by Mao (1960s); "elected" to the National People's Congress (parliament), representing Shantung (1964); was at forefront of The Great Cultural Revolution (1965–69), a full-scale attack on the party which resulted in closing of schools and factories, fragmentation of army, beating and imprisonment of scholars, and destruction of art treasures; as informal cultural commissar, wrote and promoted an opera, *Spark Among the Reeds*; appointed chief adviser to the army on cultural matters by Lin Biao, a post that put her squarely in mainstream of political power (1966); became 1st woman ever elected to 21-member Politbureau (1969); found close allies in Shanghai Faction of the Cultural Revolution Group, better known as Gang of Four: Zhang Chunqiao, Yao Wenyuan, and Wang Hongwen; as Mao grew weaker, grew stronger; when Mao died (1976), set out with Gang of Four to gain formal control of China; was arrested and indicted for counterrevolution; defended herself and received suspended death sentence. ❖ See also Ross Terrill, *Madame Mao, The White-Boned Demon* (Touchstone, 1992); Roxane Witke, *Comrade Chiang Ch'ing* (Little, Brown, 1977); and *Women in World History.*

JIANG YING (1963—). Chinese volleyball player. Born July 19, 1963, in China. ❖ Won a gold medal at Los Angeles Olympics (1984) and a bronze medal at Seoul Olympics (1988), both in team competition.

JIANG YONGHUA (1973—). Chinese cyclist. Born Sept 7, 1973, in Beijing, China. ❖ Placed 2nd at 500-meter time trial at World championships (2004); won a silver medal for 500-meter time trial at Athens Olympics (2004); set a world record in the 500-meter time trial at the Track World Cup (2002), the 1st time a Chinese cyclist had held a world record in an Olympic event; placed 1st overall in World Cup ranking for 500-meter time trial (2002).

JIANG JIESHI, Madame (1897–2003). *See Song Meiling.*

JIAO ZHIMIN (1963—). Chinese table-tennis player. Born Dec 1, 1963, in China. ❖ At Seoul Olympics, won a bronze medal in singles and a silver medal in doubles (1988).

JILES, Pamela (1955—). African-American runner. Born Pamela Theresa Jiles, July 10, 1955, in New Orleans, LA. ❖ At Montreal Olympics, won a silver medal in 4 x 400-meter relay (1976).

JILLANA (1934—). American ballet dancer. Name variations: Jillana Zimmerman. Born 1934 in Hackensack, NJ; married; children: William and Ana. ❖ Performed with Ballet Society; danced with New York City Ballet throughout most of career, creating roles in numerous works by Balanchine, including *Capriccio Brillante* (1951), *Liebeslieder Walzer* (1960), *Midsummer Night's Dream* (1962), as well as in Jerome Robbins' *The Pied Piper* (1951), *Quartet* (1954), and *Afternoon of the Faun*; danced with Ballet Theater (1957–58), performing in *Les Sylphides* and *Fall River Legend,* among others; created roles in Enrique Martinez' *La Muerte Enamorada* (1957) and in Herbert Ross' *Ovid Metamorphoses* (1958), both produced by Ballet Theater Workshop; served as artistic director for San Diego Ballet; became director of Jillana School in California.

JIMBO, Rei. Japanese synchronized swimmer. Born in Japan. ❖ Won a team bronze medal at Atlanta Olympics (1996) and a team silver medal at Sydney Olympics (2000).

JIMENA MUNOZ (c. 1065–1128). *See Munoz, Jimena.*

JIMÉNEZ, Soledad (1874–1966). Spanish actress. Name variations: Soledad Jimenez. Born Feb 28, 1874, in Santander, Spain; died Oct 17, 1966, in Woodland Hills, CA. ❖ Appeared in such films as *The Mission Play, The Cock-Eyed World, Arizona Kid, Romance of Rio Grande, Captain Thunder, In Caliente* and *The Turning Point.*

JIMENEZ MENDIVIL, Soraya (1977—). Mexican weightlifter. Name variations: Soraya Jiménez Mendivil. Born Aug 5, 1977, in Mexico. ❖ Won a gold medal for 53–58kg at Sydney Olympics (2000); won North-Central American and Caribbean championship (2000).

JIN DEOK SAN. South Korean field-hockey player. Born in South Korea. ❖ Won a team silver medal at Atlanta Olympics (1996).

JIN WON-SIM (1965—). Korean field-hockey player. Born Dec 13, 1965, in South Korea. ❖ At Seoul Olympics, won a silver medal in team competition (1988).

JINGA (c. 1580s–1663). *See Njinga.*

JINGŪ (c. 201–269). Japanese empress. Name variations: Jingo; Jingō; Jingo-kogo; Jingu. Pronunciation: gin-GOO. According to the *Kojiki* and the *Nihongi,* she was born in 201 in western Japan and died in 269; dau. of Prince Okinaga Sukune and Princess Katsuraki Takanuka; m. Emperor Chūai; children: Prince Homuda, later known as Emperor Ōjin. ❖ Legendary empress of Yamato, the ancient kingdom of Japan, who led military campaigns to defeat the Korean kingdoms of Silla and Paekche; ruled as regent between the reigns of Emperor Chūai and the Emperor Ōjin when there was no official sovereign; ruled as a shamaness

with the assistance of divination and acted as a spiritual medium; during regency, led troops in a number of military campaigns to subdue internal resistance in the Yamato kingdom and defeat neighboring kingdoms, most notably, the Korean kingdoms of Silla and Paekche. Her historical existence has not been proven; she may have been a composite of several imperial consorts in ancient Japan who were shamanesses. ❖ See also *Women in World History.*

JINNAH, Fatima (1893–1967). Pakistani politician. Name variations: Mohtarama Fatima Jinnah; Fatimah Jinnah; Madar-i-Millat Mohtarama Fatima Jinnah. Pronunciation: FAH-tee-mah JIN-nah. Born 1893 in Karachi, India; died 1967 in Pakistan; 3rd dau. of Jinnah Poonja (merchant) and Mithibai; sister of Mohammad Ali Jinnah (1st governor-general of Pakistan); attended Bandra Convent school, 1902; enrolled in Dr. Ahmad Dental College, Calcutta, 1919. ❖ Sister of Mohammad Ali Jinnah who helped him realize his goal of an independent nation for Indian Muslims and was a leader in the Pakistani independence movement in her own right; became ward of brother upon death of father (c. 1901–18); opened dental clinic in Bombay (1923); moved in with brother upon death of his wife Ruttenbai (1929); traveled in Europe (1929–35); entered politics (1936), with the express aim of establishing an independent homeland for Indian Muslims; elected delegate to Bombay Provincial Muslim League Council (Mar 1947); served as public speaker and politician (1947–67); supported and nursed brother during his final illness until his death (Sept 11, 1948); worked to establish educational institutions, including Fatima Jinnah Medical College for Girls (c. 1949–51); worked to ease plight of Muslim refugees entering Pakistan by founding Industrial Homes in Karachi, Peshawar and Quetta (c. 1949–51); assisted in funding and maintaining scholarships, schools and hospitals (1958–59); unsuccessfully stood for president of Pakistan (1964), challenging Ayub Khan. ❖ See also *Women in World History.*

JIRICNA, Eva (1939—). Czech architect. Born Mar 3, 1939, in Zlín, Czechoslovakia; graduate of University of Prague (1962); Prague Academy of Fine Arts, MA, 1967; Royal Institute of British Architects, diploma, 1973; married an architect. ❖ Followed husband to London for temporary work (1968); after Soviets invaded Prague and revoked her citizenship, had to remain in England; lived in exile for 22 years; a modernist, worked with Greater London Council (1968–69), De Soissons partnership (1969–80), David Hodges (1982–84) and Richard Rogers Partnership (1984), designing interior for Lloyd's Headquarters building; worked with Jan Kaplicky and Future Systems office, then independently (1982–85), then partnered with Kathy Kerr (1985–87); established Eva Jiricna Architects in London (1987), becoming important figure in interior design; elected fellow of Royal College of Art (1990) and Royal Society of Arts; elected president of Architectural Association (2003). Named Commander of British Empire (CBE, 1994).

JITŌ (645–702). Japanese empress. Name variations: Princess Uno, Sasara, or Hirono; Empress Jito; Jito-tennō or Jitō Tenno. Pronunciation: jhee-TOE. Born in 645 (some sources cite 625) in the capital, Naniwa; died 702 (some sources cite 701) in Fujiwara, Japan; dau. of emperor Tenji (also seen as Tenchi) and Oichi; sister of Gemmei (c. 661–721); m. Prince Oama who later became Emperor Temmu; children: Prince Kusakabe (r. 690–697). ❖ The 41st Japanese sovereign, who completed the centralization of the Japanese state under imperial rule, was politically astute, initially assisting husband in his ascent to the throne by developing military strategies and commanding the troops at Ise; to forestall power struggles following his death, assumed the throne and moved immediately to consolidate central political authority: ordered a national census in order to more effectively collect taxes, and established the army and drafted their training regulations and service codes; established a new national capital in Fujiwara (694); created a government bureaucracy (Taika Reforms), ended the tribal (kingship) system, and placed the Japanese state under a single sovereign (*tennō*) rather than many chieftains; abdicated (697), installing grandson, Emperor Mommu, on throne; was the 1st to use the title *dōjo-tennō* (ex-empress), which enabled her to continue wielding power until her death. ❖ See also *Women in World History.*

JO HEA-JUNG (1953—). Korean volleyball player. Born Mar 5, 1953, in South Korea. ❖ At Montreal Olympics, won a bronze medal in team competition (1976).

JOAN. *Variant of Jane, Jeanne, Joanna, Johanna, and Juana.*

JOAN (d. 858). Possibly real, possibly fictitious, female pope. Name variations: The She-Pope; Pope Jeanne; John VIII. Reputedly born in

Mainz or Ingelheim; sat in the Chair of Peter as pope, 855–58 (some sources cite 853–55); supposedly stoned to death around 858 in Rome; dau. of an Irish father and peasant mother who died soon after her birth. ❖ Until early 17th century, the Catholic Church and the people of Europe believed that Pope John VIII was a woman of English birth (or German birth of English parents) who reigned as pope for 2 years (855–57); she was listed as a historical pope until around 1601, when Pope Clement VIII officially declared her a myth and ordered all mention of her destroyed; in some reference works the popes were even renumbered to eradicate John VIII altogether. Images of Pope Joan can be found in artistic works throughout the Middle Ages and the Renaissance; more than 500 manuscripts between the 13th and 17th centuries address the story, many written by Catholics. ❖ See also Peter Stanford, *The Legend of Pope Joan: In Search of the Truth* (Holt, 1998); and *Women in World History.*

JOAN (1210–1238). Queen of Scotland. Name variations: Joan or Joanna Plantagenet; (nickname) Joan Makepeace. Born in Gloucester, Gloucestershire, England, Dec 1210 (some sources cite July 22, 1213); died Mar 4, 1238, in London, England; eldest dau. of Isabella of Angoulême (1186–1246) and John I Lackland, king of England (r. 1199–1216); became 1st wife of Alexander II (1198–1249), king of Scotland (r. 1214–1249), on June 19, 1221; children: none. ❖ Though betrothed to Hugh of Lusignan the younger, was married at York at age 11 to Alexander II, king of Scotland. Following her death at age 28, Alexander married Mary de Coucy (c. 1220–1260).

JOAN (1384–1400). English noblewoman. Born 1384; died Aug 16, 1400; buried at Walden Priory, Essex, England; dau. of Thomas of Woodstock, 1st duke of Gloucester, and Eleanor de Bohun (1366–1399); betrothed to Gilbert, Lord Talbert.

JOAN, queen of Scotland (c. 1410–1445). See Beaufort, Joan.

JOAN, Pope (d. 858). See Joan.

JOAN I, countess of Artois (c. 1291–1330). See Jeanne I of Burgundy.

JOAN II, countess of Artois (1308–1347). See Jeanne II of Burgundy.

JOAN I OF NAPLES (1326–1382). See Joanna I of Naples.

JOAN II OF NAPLES (1374–1435). See Joanna II of Naples.

JOAN I OF NAVARRE (1273–1305). Queen of France and Navarre. Name variations: Jeanne I of Navarre or Jeanne de Navarre; Joan of Champagne and Navarre; Joan of Navarre; Joan de Blois; Jeanne I, countess of Champagne; Juana I, queen of Navarre. Reigned as queen of Navarre (r. 1274–1305) and countess of Champagne (r. 1274–1305); born Jan 14, 1273 (some sources cite 1271), in Bar-sur-Seine, France; died April 2, 1305, in Vincennes, Paris, France; dau. of Henry I, king of Navarre (r. 1270–1274), and Blanche of Artois (c. 1247–1302, dau. of Robert I, count of Artois); m. Philip IV the Fair (1268–1314), king of France (r. 1285–1314), in 1284; children: Isabella of France (1296–1358, who m. Edward II of England); Louis X (1289–1316), king of France (r. 1314–1316); Philip V (1293–1322), king of France (1316–1322); Charles IV (1294–1328), king of France (r. 1322–1328), and king of Navarre as Charles I (r. 1322–1328). ❖ Came to throne as queen of Navarre on death of father (1274), giving her hegemony over the lands of Navarre, Brie, and Champagne; though her kingdom was annexed to France by her marriage to the powerful king Philip IV the Fair, seems to have been allowed to continue free reign over her lands; when the Count de Bar attacked Champagne, led a small army and forced him to surrender; founded the College of Navarre (1304).

JOAN II OF NAVARRE (1309–1349). Queen of Navarre. Name variations: Jeanne of France, Jeanne of Navarre; Juana II. Born 1309 in France (some sources cite 1312); died 1349 in Navarre; dau. of Louis X (1289–1316), king of France (r. 1314–1316), and Margaret of Burgundy (c. 1290–1315); m. Philip III (Philip d'Evreux), king of Navarre, in 1317; children: Carlos II also known as Charles II the Bad (1332–1387), king of Navarre; Blanche of Navarre (1331–1398); Joanna, Agnes, Marie. ❖ With husband, succeeded to throne of Navarre (1328). Competent and well-liked by their subjects, they eventually left its rule to able governors and returned to their estates in Evreux. ❖ See also *Women in World History.*

JOAN III OF NAVARRE (1528–1572). See Jeanne d'Albret.

JOAN BEAUFORT.
See Beaufort, Joan (c. 1379–1440).
See Beaufort, Joan (c. 1410–1445).

JOAN DE CLARE (c. 1268–after 1322). Duchess of Fife. Born c. 1268; died after 1322; dau. of Gilbert de Clare (1243–1295), 7th earl of Hertford, 3rd earl of Gloucester (r. 1262–1295) and Alice de Lusignan (d. 1290); m. Duncan (1262–1288), 9th earl of Fife (r. 1270–1288), in 1284 (murdered by Sir Patrick Abernethy); m. Gervase Avenel; children: (1st marriage) Isabella of Buchan (fl. 1290–1310); Duncan Fife (1285–1351), 10th earl of Fife. ❖ Was the stepdaughter of Joan of Acre (1272–1307).

JOAN DE QUINCI (d. 1283). Countess of Hereford and Essex. Born 1283; dau. of Ellen of Wales (d. 1253) and Robert de Quinci; granddau. of Llywelyn II the Great, Ruler of All Wales; 2nd wife of Humphrey Bohun (d. 1265), 6th earl of Hereford and Essex; children: John Bohun of Haresfield. Humphrey Bohun's 1st wife was Eleanor de Braose (fl. 1250s).

JOAN DE ROUERGUE (d. 1271). See Joan of Toulouse.

JOAN DE VERE (fl. 1280s). Countess of Warren and Surrey. Dau. of 5th earl of Oxford; m. William de Warrenne (d. 1286), 7th earl of Warren and Surrey, June 1285; children: John de Warrenne (1286–1347), 8th earl of Warren and Surrey (r. 1304–1347); Alice Fitzalan (d. around 1338).

JOAN HOLLAND (c. 1356–1384). See Holland, Joan.

JOAN MAKEPEACE.
See Joan (1210–1238).
See Joan of the Tower (1321–1362).

JOAN OF ACRE (1272–1307). Duchess of Hertford and Gloucester. Name variations: Joanna of Acre; Joan Plantagenet. Born in Acre or Akko, Israel, 1272; died April 23, 1307, in Clare, Suffolk, England; buried at Clare Priory, Suffolk, England; dau. of Edward I Longshanks, king of England (r. 1272–1307), and Eleanor of Castile (1241–1290); m. Gilbert de Clare (1243–1295), 7th earl of Hertford, 3rd of Gloucester, on May 2, 1290, in Westminster Abbey; m. Ralph Monthermer (d. 1325), earl of Gloucester and Hertford, in 1297; children: (1st m.) Gilbert de Clare (1291–1314), 8th earl of Hertford and 4th earl of Gloucester; Eleanor de Clare (1292–1337); Margaret de Clare (c. 1293–1342); Elizabeth de Clare (1295–1360); (2nd m.) Thomas Monthermer (1301–1340), 2nd baron Monthermer (killed in sea battle against the French in 1340); Mary de Monthermer (1298–after 1371); Joan de Monthermer, a nun at Amesbury; Edward de Monthermer (b. 1304), 3rd baron Monthermer. ❖ Was betrothed to Hartmann, son of Rudolf of Habsburg (1279); at 18, wed Gilbert de Clare in Westminster Abbey; following death of Gilbert and without consulting father, secretly married Ralph de Monthermer, a squire of her deceased husband's (1297). ❖ See also *Women in World History.*

JOAN OF ARC (c. 1412–1431). French military leader and saint. Name variations: Jeanne d'Arc; La Pucelle d'Orléans; La Petite Pucelle; The Maid of Orléans or The Maid of Orleans. Born and baptized c. 1412 at Domrémy in duchy of Bar in northern France; burned at stake, May 30, 1431, at Rouen; dau. of Jacques d'Arc and Isabelle (Romée) d'Arc; never married. ❖ French hero, revered as a national saint, whose achievements can now be seen as a turning point in Hundred Years' War; from age 13, reported hearing her "voices," as she called them; at 17, was ordered by "voices" to free France from the stranglehold of the English occupation and to see the dauphin crowned in Rheims Cathedral, where, by tradition, all French kings were consecrated (at the time, Rheims was under the command of the English); commanded the French troops who raised the siege of Orléans (April 1429); led Charles VII to his coronation in Rheims (July 17, 1429); captured by the Burgundians during a skirmish at Compiègne (May 23, 1430) and sold to the English (Jan 3, 1431); was imprisoned and interrogated more than 12 times by canon lawyers either in the castle chapel or in her prison (Feb 21–Mar 24); brought before the Trial of Condemnation (Mar 1341), had to answer to 70 charges which had been drawn up against her, and which were based on the contention that her behavior showed blasphemous presumption; proved to be more than a match for her inquisitors, responding to their questioning with an eloquence unexpected in one so young; was condemned to death by burning as a relapsed heretic; condemnation revoked by the pope (July 1456); beatified (1909); canonized (1920). Her trials and her execution have inspired numerous books, dramas, and poems by authors as diverse as Christine de Pisan and George Bernard Shaw; artists through the centuries have portrayed her as a warrior saint dressed in armor, carrying the banner of God and the standard of France. ❖ See also A. Buchan, *Joan of Arc and the Recovery of France* (1984); Régine Pernoud, *Joan of Arc:*

By Herself and Her Witnesses (1969); G. Hopkins, *Joan of Arc* (Trans. by L. Fabre, 1954); and *Women in World History.*

JOAN OF BEAUFORT.
See Beaufort, Joan (1379–1440).
See Beaufort, Joan (c. 1410–1445).

JOAN OF BLOIS (c. 1320–1384). See Jeanne de Penthièvre.

JOAN OF BOULOGNE (1326–1360). See Blanche of Boulogne.

JOAN OF BOURBON.
See Jeanne de Bourbon (1338–1378).
See Jeanne de Bourbon (d. 1493).

JOAN OF BRITTANY (c. 1370–1437). See Joanna of Navarre.

JOAN OF BURGUNDY.
See Jeanne of Burgundy (1293–1348).
See Jeanne of Burgundy (1344–1360).

JOAN OF CHAMPAGNE (1273–1305). See Joan I of Navarre.

JOAN OF CONSTANTINOPLE (c. 1200–1244). See Johanna of Flanders.

JOAN OF ENGLAND (d. 1237). Princess of North Wales. Name variations: Joanna, Anna, or Janet. Died Feb 2, 1237, in Aber, Gwynedd, Wales; buried at Llanfaes, Gwynedd, Wales (another source maintains that her stone coffin now resides in Baron Hill Park, Beaumaris); illeg. dau. of John I Lackland, king of England (r. 1199–1216), and Agatha Ferrers (others suggest mother was Clemantina, wife of Henry Pinel); m. Llywelyn II the Great (1173–1240), Ruler of All Wales, in 1205 or 1206; children: David II (c. 1208–1246), Ruler of All Wales; possibly Ellen of Wales (d. 1253); possibly Margaret verch Llywelyn (who m. Walter Clifford). Llywelyn II the Great also had offspring with his mistress Tangwystl, and there is some confusion between Joan of England and Tangwystl as to who had which children.

JOAN OF EVREUX (d. 1370). Queen of France. Name variations: Jeanne d'Evreux; Jeanne of Evreux or Évreux. Born c. 1305; died 1370; dau. of Louis, count of Evreux (son of Philip III, king of France); sister of Philip III, king of Navarre (d. 1343); became 3rd wife of Charles IV the Fair (1294–1328), king of France (r. 1322–1328), and king of Navarre (r. 1322–1328), c. 1324 or 1325; children: Blanche of France (1328–1392, who m. Philip of Orleans, the brother of John II, king of France). Charles IV's other wives were Blanche of Burgundy (1296–1326) and Mary of Luxemburg (1305–1323).

JOAN OF FLANDERS (c. 1200–1244). See Johanna of Flanders.

JOAN OF FLANDERS (c. 1310–c. 1376). See Jeanne de Montfort.

JOAN OF HAINAULT (c. 1310–?). Duchess of Juliers. Name variations: Joan de Juliers. Born c. 1310; dau. of Jeanne of Valois (c. 1294–1342) and William III the Good, count of Hainault and Holland; sister of Philippa of Hainault (1314–1369) and Margaret of Holland (d. 1356); m. William de Juliers, duke of Juliers; children: Elizabeth de Juliers (d. 1411, who m. John, 3rd earl of Kent).

JOAN OF KENT (1328–1385). English countess. Name variations: Princess of Wales; Fair Maid of Kent; Joan, countess of Kent; Joan Plantagenet. Born Sept 28, 1328; died Aug 7 (or Aug 14) 1385, of dropsy(?) at Wallingford Castle, Oxfordshire, England; buried in Stamford, Lincolnshire, England; dau. of Edmund of Woodstock (1307–1330), 1st earl of Kent, and Margaret Wake of Liddell (c. 1299–1349); m. Sir Thomas Holland, 1st earl of Kent, c. 1346 (died Dec 28, 1360); m. William de Montacute, 2nd earl of Salisbury, c. 1348 (annulled by pope Clement VI, Nov 13, 1349); m. Edward, prince of Wales (known as the Black Prince), Oct 6, 1361 (died June 8, 1376); children (1st m.) 5, including Thomas Holland, 2nd earl of Kent (1350–1397); John, duke of Exeter (1352?–1400); Matilda Holland (c. 1359–1391, who m. Hugh Courtenay); Joan Holland (who m. John IV, duke of Brittany); (3rd m.) Edward (1365–1372, died of plague at 7); Richard II (1367–1400), king of England (r. 1377–1399). ❧ Famed for her courage and beauty, was the wife of Edward, prince of Wales (the Black Prince), mother of Richard II, king of England, and left her own mark on history; when she was 2, her father was beheaded (1330); married Thomas Holland and then contracted to earl of Salisbury; restored to Holland (1349); became countess of Kent (1352); left England for Normandy with Holland (1358); married Edward, prince of Wales (1361), following Holland's death; lived in Aquitaine where another 2 sons were born (1362–71); following death of husband (1376), 9-year-old son Richard became heir to the throne of England and succeeded his

grandfather (1377); able to reconcile enemies and mediate disputes, guided her son and played a significant role in English politics until her death (1385). Inducted into the Order of the Garter. ❧ See also *Women in World History.*

JOAN OF KENT (d. 1550). See Bocher, Joan.

JOAN OF MONTFERRAT (d. 1127). Countess of Flanders. Died 1127; dau. of Rainer also spelled Reiner, marquess of Montferrat, and Gisela of Burgundy; half-sister of Adelaide of Maurienne (d. 1154); 2nd wife of William III the Clito (1101–1128), count of Flanders (r. 1127–1128). William III's 1st wife was Sybilla of Anjou (1112–1165).

JOAN OF SICILY (1165–1199). See Joanna of Sicily.

JOAN OF THE TOWER (1321–1362). Queen of Scotland. Name variations: Joanna of the Tower; Joan Plantagenet; Joan Makepeace; Johane. Born in the Tower of London, July 5, 1321; died Aug 14, 1362, in Hertford, Hertfordshire, England; youngest child of Isabella of France (1296–1358) and Edward II (1284–1327), king of England (r. 1307–1327); sister of Edward III (1312–1377), king of England (r. 1327–1377); became 1st wife of David Bruce also known as David II (1323–1370), king of Scotland (r. 1329–1370), July 17, 1328; no children. ❧ As a sister of Edward III, was married at 7 to Robert Bruce's 4-year-old son David to cement a treaty between England and Scotland (1328); crowned with David at Scone (1331); when Edward Balliol attempted to claim the throne of Scotland with the covert backing of Edward III (1332), was forced to flee to France with husband; remained in exile (1334–41); following capture of husband in England (1346), repeatedly tried to win his release from prison; was finally successful (1357), after his 11-year captivity in the Tower of London. ❧ See also *Women in World History.*

JOAN OF TOULOUSE (d. 1271). Countess of Toulouse. Name variations: Joan de Rouergue. Died 1271; dau. of Raymond VII, count of Toulouse (r. 1222–1249), and Margaret le Brun (d. 1283); m. Alphonso, count of Poitiers (Poitou) and Toulouse (r. 1249–1271, son of Louis VIII, king of France, and Blanche of Castile).

JOAN OF VALOIS (c. 1294–1342). See Jeanne of Valois.

JOAN PLANTAGENET (c. 1312–c. 1345). Baroness Mowbray. Name variations: Baroness Mowbray. Born c. 1312; died c. 1345; dau. of Henry, earl of Lancaster (r. 1281–1345), and Maud Chaworth (1282–c. 1322); m. John Mowbray, 3rd baron Mowbray, 1327; children: 3, including John Mowbray, 4th baron Mowbray.

JOAN THE MAID OF SARMAIZE (fl. 1456). See Jeanne de Sarmaize.

JOAN VALOIS (1391–1433). Duchess of Brittany. Name variations: Jeanne, duchess of Bretagne; Joan de France; Joan of France. Born in 1391; died in 1433; third dau. of Charles VI, king of France (r. 1380–1422), and Isabeau of Bavaria (1371–1435); 1st wife of John V (1389–1442), duke of Brittany (r. 1339–1442); children: Francis I (b. 1414), duke of Brittany; Peter II, duke of Brittany.

JOANA. Variant of Jeanne, Joan, Joanna, Johanna, or Juana.

JOANA DE MENDOZA (d. 1580). Duchess of Braganza. Died 1580; dau. of Diego de Mendoza; m. Jaime or James (1479–1532), duke of Braganza, 1520; children: Jaime (b. 1523, priest); Constantino (b. 1528, viceroy of India); Fulgencio (b. around 1529, prior of Guimaraes); Teotonio (b. 1530, archbishop of Evora); Isabella of Braganza (c. 1512–1576); Joana of Braganza (1521–1588, who m. Bernardo de Cardenas, marquis of Elche); Eugenia of Braganza (c. 1525–1559, who m. Francesco de Mello); Maria of Braganza (c. 1527–1586, abbess of Cloisters); Vincenca of Braganza (c. 1532–1603, abbess of Cloisters). The duke of Braganza's 1st wife was Eleonore de Guzman (d. 1512).

JOANNA. Variant of Jeanne, Joan, Joanna, Johanna, or Juana.

JOANNA. Biblical woman. Married Chuza, the steward of Herod Antipas, a man of position and wealth. ❧ Along with Mary Magdalene, Susanna, and others, provided for Jesus out of her own funds; was also one of the woman who witnessed the empty tomb and announced the Lord's resurrection to the apostles.

JOANNA (1333–1348). English princess. Name variations: Joan Plantagenet. Born 1333 in Woodstock, Oxfordshire, England; died of the plague on journey to wed Alphonso XI (1311–1350), king of Castile (r. 1312–1350), Sept 2, 1348, in Bordeaux, Aquitaine, France; buried in Bayonne Cathedral, Gascony, France; dau. of Philippa of Hainault

(1314–1369) and Edward III (1312–1377), king of England (r. 1327–1377).

JOANNA (1452–1490). Regent of Portugal. Reigned as regent (1471–81); born Feb 6, 1452, in Lisbon; died May 12, 1490, in Aveiro; dau. of Isabel la Paloma (1432–1455) and Afonso V, king of Portugal (r. 1448–1481).

JOANNA I OF NAPLES (1326–1382). Queen of Naples. Name variations: Giovanna or Giovanni; Giovanna d'Angiò; Joan I; Joanna of Naples; Joanna of Sicily; Joanna of Provence; also known as Jane. Born 1326 in Spain; died 1382 in Naples; dau. of Charles of Calabria and Marie of Valois; sister of Marie of Naples; m. Andrew of Hungary, c. 1333 (died 1345); m. Louis of Taranto; m. Jayme of Majorca; m. Otto of Brunswick; children: none, except for adoption of Louis I, count of Provence and duke of Anjou (1339–1384), as her successor king. ❖ Reigned as queen-regnant of Naples (1343–82); inherited Naples and Provence from Robert the Wise of Anjou, her grandfather (1343); moved to that state, where she reigned for over 40 years, years marked by political disruption, warfare, and general turmoil. ❖ See also *Women in World History.*

JOANNA II OF NAPLES (1374–1435). Queen of Naples. Name variations: Giovanna or Giovanni; Joan II; Joanna II of Naples; Johanna of Durazzo. Born June 25, 1374, in Naples; died Feb 2, 1435, in Naples; dau. of Charles III of Durazzo, king of Naples (r. 1382–1386), also ruled Hungary as Charles II (r. 1385–1386) and Margaret of Naples (dau. of Marie of Naples); sister of Ladislas I, king of Naples (r. 1386–1414); m. Wilhelm also known as William (1370–1406), duke of Austria; m. James of La Marche (French count); children: none. ❖ Was the daughter of Charles III, king of Naples, who had stolen the throne from Joanna I and had her murdered (1382); when brother Ladislas died without heirs (1414), became its queen; reigned (1414–35), governing under the same chaos which had marked the reign of Joanna I of Naples; with Naples suffering under the feudal warring and rivalries of its nobility, did not seem to care much about its people, concentrating instead on her personal enjoyment. ❖ See also *Women in World History.*

JOANNA I OF PROVENCE (1326–1382). *See Joanna I of Naples.*

JOANNA I OF SICILY (1326–1382). *See Joanna I of Naples.*

JOANNA ENRIQUEZ (1425–1468). Queen of Navarre and Aragon. Name variations: Juana Enriquez. Born 1425; died Feb 13, 1468, in Zaragoza; dau. of Fadrique, count of Malgar and Rueda; became 2nd wife of Juan also known as John II (1398–1479), king of Navarre and Aragon (r. 1458–1479), April 1, 1444; children: Ferdinand II of Aragon (1452–1516) also known as Ferdinand V the Catholic, king of Castile and Leon (r. 1474–1504, who m. Isabella I of Spain); Joanna of Aragon (1454–1517, who m. Ferrante I of Naples); Maria of Aragon (b. 1455, died young).

JOANNA OF ARAGON (1454–1517). Queen of Naples. Name variations: Juana; Giovanna. Born 1454 in Barcelona; died Jan 9, 1517, in Naples; dau. of Joanna Enriquez (1425–1468) and Juan also known as John II (1398–1479), king of Navarre and Aragon (r. 1458–1479); became 2nd wife of Ferdinand also known as Ferrante I (1423–1494), king of Naples (r. 1458–1494), on Sept 14, 1476; children: Joanna of Naples (1478–1518); Carlo of Naples (b. 1480). Isabel de Clermont (d. 1465) was the 1st wife of Ferrante I.

JOANNA OF AUSTRIA (1535–1573). Austrian regent and Jesuit. Name variations: Joana or Juana of Austria; Jeanne d'Autriche or Jeanne of Austria; Joanna Hapsburg or Habsburg. Born June 24 or 27, 1535 (some sources cite 1537), in Madrid; died Sept 7, 1573, at Escorial; dau. of Charles V (1500–1558), king of the Romans (r. 1519–1530), Holy Roman emperor (r. 1530–1558) and king of Spain as Charles I (r. 1516–1556), and Isabella of Portugal (1503–1539); sister of Philip II, king of Spain (r. 1556–1598), and king of Portugal as Philip I (r. 1580–1598); sister of Marie of Austria (1528–1603); half-sister of Margaret of Parma (1522–1586); half-sister of John of Austria; m. Portuguese prince Joao or João, the infante, also known as John of Portugal (1537–1554), Jan 11, 1552; children: Sebastiao also known as Sebastian or Sebastián (1554–1578), king of Portugal (r. 1557–1578). ❖ Was nearly 4 when mother, Empress Isabella, died from complications of childbirth (April 30, 1539); wed Prince John, her mother's nephew (Jan 11, 1552); husband died while she was 8 months pregnant (1554); fell into a temporary depression reminiscent of grandmother, Juana la Loca; served as regent of Spain (1554–59) and never saw son again; gave herself over to the political responsibilities of the regency and religious piety; used the Inquisition to defend the kingdom against the protestant heretics;

presided at a large auto-de-fe in Valladolid during which 13 heretics were executed and others were punished (1558); also issued decrees prohibiting the import of foreign books and ruled that Spaniards could not leave the country to study; used her power to compel the Society of Jesus to secretly make her a member; admitted under the alias of "Mateo Sánchez," remained a member of the Society for the rest of her life, the only female Jesuit; founded Las Descalzas convent in Madrid (1557). ❖ See also *Women in World History.*

JOANNA OF AUSTRIA (1546–1578). Grand duchess of Tuscany. Name variations: Giovanna of Austria; Joanna, Archduchess of Austria; Joanna de Medici. Born Jan 1, 1546, in Vienna; died April 11, 1578, in Florence; dau. of Anna of Bohemia and Hungary (1503–1547) and Ferdinand I, Holy Roman emperor (r. 1558–1564); sister of Elizabeth of Habsburg (d. 1545) and Maximilian II, Holy Roman emperor (1527–1576); m. Francesco I also known as Francis I de Medici (1541–1587), grand duke of Tuscany (r. 1574–1587); children: Romola (b. 1566, died young); Eleonora de Medici (1567–1611), duchess of Mantua; Isabella (b. 1567, died young); Caterina also seen as Anna (1569–1584, died young); Marie de Medici (c. 1573–1642); Filippo (b. 1577, died young). ❖ Condemned by the Florentines for her Austrian haughtiness, was never happy in Florence; died at age 30. ❖ See also *Women in World History.*

JOANNA OF BRABANT (1322–1406). Duchess of Brabant and countess of Hainault and Holland. Name variations: Johanna, Joan Louvain; Joan of Brabant. Reigned as duchess of Brabant, 1355–1404; abdicated in 1404. Born June 24, 1322 (some sources cite 1332); died Dec 1, 1406; dau. of John III, duke of Brabant (r. 1312–1355), and Marie of Evreux (d. 1335); sister of Margaret of Brabant (1323–1368) and Marie of Guelders (1325–1399); m. William IV (1307–1345), count of Holland and Hainault, before Nov 1334 (died 1345); m. Wenzel of Bohemia also known as Wenceslas (1337–1383), duke of Luxemburg and Brabant (r. 1353–1383), in 1354; no children. ❖ As duchess of Brabant, succeeded husband upon his death (1355); the following year, offered her subjects a new constitution, known as the *Joyeuse Entrée*, granting much wider liberties. ❖ See also *Women in World History.*

JOANNA OF CASTILE (1339–1381). Queen of Castile and Leon. Name variations: Juana Manuela de Castilla; Juana de la Cerda; Joanna de Castilla. Born 1339; died Mar 27, 1381 (some sources cite 1379), in Salamanca, Leon, Spain; dau. of John Manuel also known as Juan Manuel "el Scritor" and Blanche de la Cerda (c. 1311–1347); m. Enrique also known as Henry II Trastamara (1333–1379), king of Castile and Leon (r. 1369–1379), on July 27, 1350; children: John I (b. 1358), king of Castile and Leon (r. 1379–1390); Eleanor Trastamara (d. 1415); Juana (died young).

JOANNA OF CASTILE (1462–1530). *See Juana la Beltraneja.*

JOANNA OF ENGLAND (1165–1199). *See Joanna of Sicily.*

JOANNA OF FRANCE (1343–1373). *See Jane of France.*

JOANNA OF NAPLES (1326–1382). *See Joanna I of Naples.*

JOANNA OF NAPLES (1478–1518). Queen of Naples. Name variations: Giovanna of Naples. Born 1478; died Aug 27, 1518; dau. of Joanna of Aragon (1454–1517) and Ferdinand also known as Ferrante I (1423–1494), king of Naples (r. 1458–1494); m. her nephew Ferdinand also known as Ferrante II (1469–1496), king of Naples (r. 1495–1496), in 1496.

JOANNA OF NAVARRE (c. 1370–1437). Queen of England. Name variations: Joan of Brittany; Joan of Navarre; Joan, Johanne, Juana; Joanna Evreux. Born Joanna c. 1370 in Pamplona; died July 9, 1437, at Havering-atte-Bower, Essex, England; interred at Canterbury Cathedral, Kent; dau. of Charles II d'Albret also known as Charles II the Bad, king of Navarre (r. 1349–1387), and Jane of France (1343–1373, dau. of King John II of France); m. John IV de Montfort (1339–1399), 5th duke of Brittany (r. 1364–1399, son of Jeanne de Montfort), Sept 11, 1386, at Saillé, near Guerrand, Navarre (died Nov 1, 1399); became 2nd wife of Henry IV (1367–1413), king of England (r. 1399–1413), Feb 7, 1403; children: (1st m.) Joanna (1387–1388); daughter (1388–1388); John V (1389–1442), duke of Brittany (r. 1399–1442); Marie of Dreux (1391–1446); Arthur of Brittany (1393–1458), count of Richmond, duke of Brittany (r. 1457–1458); Gilles or Giles (1394–1412), lord of Chantocé; Richard Montfort (1395–1438), count of Étampes; Blanche of Dreux (c. 1396–c. 1418); Margaret de Rohan (1397–1428); (2nd m.) none. Henry IV's 1st wife was Mary de Bohun

(1369–1394). ❖ Queen of England by her marriage to Henry IV who was later accused of witchcraft and of plotting the death of her stepson Henry V, imprisoned for 3 years, and then restored to her former position as dowager queen; at 10, was betrothed to John, heir of Castille (a betrothal which was later broken off); held as a hostage in Paris with her 2 brothers (1381); became 3rd wife of John IV, duke of Brittany, at age 16; widowed for 4 years, assumed role of regent for eldest son John V (1399–1403); married King Henry IV of England (1403); widowed again after 10 years of marriage; without a trial, imprisoned for treason for 3 years on charges of sorcery and necromancy, solely based on allegations; released and remained in England as dowager queen, with property restored, until her death at age 67. ❖ See also *Women in World History*.

JOANNA OF PONTHIEU (d. 1251). Countess of Ponthieu. Name variations: Marie of Ponthieu. Died 1251; dau. of William II, count of Ponthieu, and Alais of France (b. 1160, dau. of Louis VII of France); married Simon de Dammartin, count of Aumâle; children: Joanna of Ponthieu (d. 1279); Philippe de Dammartin.

JOANNA OF PONTHIEU (d. 1279). Queen of Castile and Leon. Name variations: Joan of Ponthieu; Joan de Ponthieu; Jean de Ponthieu; Jeanne de Dammartin; Jeanne d'Aumale, Countess Aumale; Countess Ponthieu. Birth date unknown; died Mar 16, 1279; dau. of Simon de Dammartin, count of Ponthieu and Aumale, and Joanna of Ponthieu (d. 1251); became 2nd wife of Fernando also known as St. Ferdinand or Ferdinand III (1199–1252), king of Castile (r. 1217–1252) and Leon (r. 1230–1252), in 1237; children: Fernando, count of Aumale; Eleanor of Castile (1241–1290); Luis; Simon; Juan.

JOANNA OF PORTUGAL (1439–1475). Queen of Castile and Leon. Name variations: Joana, Juana of Portugal, Juana de Aviz, Juana de Aviz. Born late Mar 1439 (some sources cite 1438) in Portuguese town of Almada; died June 13, 1475, in Madrid; dau. of Edward also known as Duarte I, king of Portugal (r. 1433–1438), and Leonora of Aragon (1405–1445); sister of Alphonso V, king of Portugal (r. 1438–1481), and Eleanor of Portugal (1434–1467); betrothed to Enrique IV also known as Henry IV of Castile, in 1454; m. Henry IV, king of Castile and Leon (r. 1454–1474), on May 21, 1455; children: Juana la Beltraneja (1462–1530). ❖ At 15, probably because of her famed beauty and certainly because the marriage offered Castile an alliance against the expansionism of John II of Aragon, wed Henry IV of Castile; did not conceive for 7 years, finally giving birth to a daughter, Juana la Beltraneja; when dissidents moved to depose Henry and Henry offered Joanna as a hostage to guarantee that he would recognize his half-brother Alphonso as his heir, was locked in Fonseca's castle at Alaejos; became pregnant as the result of an adulterous relationship with warden's son (1468); when Alphonso died (July 1468) and dissidents championed the rights of his sister Isabella I, was accused of having conceived daughter Juana with a courtier, Beltrán de la Cueva (thus Juana became known to the Isabelline faction as *la Beltraneja*). It remained for Isabella's propagandists and historians to defame the memory of Henry and Joanna of Portugal to help establish the new monarch's legitimacy. ❖ See also *Women in World History*.

JOANNA OF PORTUGAL (1636–1653). Portuguese princess. Name variations: Joana. Born Sept 18, 1636; died Nov 17, 1653; dau. of Luisa de Guzman (1613–1666) and John IV the Fortunate, king of Portugal (r. 1640–1656).

JOANNA OF SICILY (1165–1199). Queen of Sicily. Name variations: Joan or Johanna of Sicily; Joanna of England. Born in Angers, 1165; died in childbirth, 1199; 3rd dau. of Henry II, king of England, and Eleanor of Aquitaine; sister of Richard the Lionheart, king of England, and Matilda of England, among others; m. William II (d. 1189), king of Sicily (whose mother was Margaret of Navarre), 1177; m. Raymond VI (d. 1222), count of Toulouse, 1196. ❖ After death of husband William II of Sicily (1189), accompanied her brother Richard the Lionheart and Berengaria of Navarre to the Holy Land; became a lasting friend of her sister-in-law Berengaria; when Richard suggested to Saladin that in return for Jerusalem he would arrange for a marriage between Joanna and Saladin's brother Saphadin, indignantly refused, unless Saphadin would convert to Christianity (which, of course, he would not). ❖ See also *Women in World History*.

JOANNA THE MAD (1479–1555). See *Juana la Loca*.

JOAQUINA CARLOTA (1775–1830). See *Carlota Joaquina*.

JOBE, Mary Lee (1878–1966). See *Akeley, Mary Jobe*.

JOCELIN, Elizabeth (1596–1622). British writer. Born 1596 in Norton, Chester, England; died Oct 21, 1622, in Cambridgeshire, England; dau. of Sir Richard Brooke and Joan Chaderton Brooke; m. Tourell Jocelin, 1616; children: 1. ❖ Wrote *The Mothers Legacie to Her Unborne Childe* (1624) because she feared death in childbirth; died 9 days after daughter's birth.

JOCELINE. *Variant of Joscelyn or Josselyn.*

JOCHEBED. Biblical woman. Name variations: (Hebrew) Yokebed. Pronunciation: JAH-kuh-bed or JOH-kee-buhd. Dau. of Levi; m. her nephew Amram; children: Miriam the Prophet; Moses; Aaron. ❖ Gave birth to Moses shortly after the pharaoh demanded that every newborn male Hebrew child be killed; hid Moses for 3 months; when his concealment became too difficult, conceived of a plan to bring him to the attention of the daughter of the king (probably Thermuthis), with the hope that she would take pity on the child; constructing a miniature vessel of bulrushes, placed Moses inside and set the boat among the reeds on the bank of the Nile, near the spot where the princess came to bathe; posted daughter Miriam the Prophet as a sentinel to watch over him; when Princess Thermuthis discovered the child, was chosen to nurse him. ❖ See also *Women in World History*.

JOCHMANN, Rosa (1901–1994). Austrian revolutionary and labor activist. Born Rosa Jochmann in Vienna, Austria, July 19, 1901; died 1994; dau. of Karl Jochmann (foundry worker) and Josefine Jochmann (waitress and laundress); self-taught after age 14; never married; no children. ❖ Leading Austrian official of the underground Social Democratic movement, went to work in a factory that produced chocolate and other confections (1914); transferred to a cable factory and injured her finger in an accident; became an official of the Chemical Workers' Union; rising in party leadership in the "Red Vienna" period of socialist reform was concerned with the interests of women, working conditions and environmental hazards to industrial workers (1918–34); arrested and imprisoned by Austro-Fascist regime of Kurt von Schuschnigg (Aug 1934); was a leader in the underground Social Democratic movement (1934–38); remained in Austria after Nazi occupation of Mar 1938; arrested by German Gestapo (Aug 1939); spent more than 5 years in German captivity, mostly in Ravensbrück concentration camp, until liberation (1945); was quickly accepted by new party leadership as a member of the presidium and chair of women's central committee and was soon serving in Parliament; worked to educate young people about Nazi era, appearing on radio and tv, and traveling throughout Austria to spread her message of *Niemals wieder!* (Never again). ❖ See also *Women in World History*.

JOCHUM, Trude (1927—). See *Beiser, Trude*.

JODHA BAI (d. 1613). Rajput princess and queen. Name variations: Jodh Bai; Mariam-Uz-Zamani; Mariam or Maryam Zamani; Princess of Amber. Born Jodha Bai; died Jan 2, 1613; dau. of Shri Bhar Mal, raja of Amber (r. 1548–73); became 3rd wife of Akbar (1542–1605), Mughal emperor (r. 1556–1605), Feb 6, 1562; children: Salim (Jahangir, 1569–1627, Mughal emperor, r. 1605–27), Murad (b. 1570), Daniyal (b. 1572) and daughters Shakrunnissa and Aram Banu. ❖ Considered Akbar's favorite queen, converted to Islam on marriage and received the name Wali Nimat Miriam uz-Zamani Begum; to celebrate the birth of her son Salim, had a magnificent mosque built which still stands and is known as the Mariam Zamani Mosque (or Begum Shahi Masjid) in Lahore.

JODHA BAI (d. 1619). See *Manmati*.

JODIN, Mademoiselle (fl. 18th c.). French lecturer. Name variations: Mlle Jodin. Dau. of a clockmaker from Geneva. ❖ Collaborated on the *Encyclopédie* of Diderot, D'Alembert and others; wrote a speech on divorce addressed to Assemblée Nationale, *Vues législatives pour les femmes* (1790); works published in P. Duhet (ed.), *Cahiers de doléances des femmes et autres textes*.

JOEHNCKE, Louise (1976—). See *Jöhncke, Louise*.

JOEL, Grace Jane (1865–1924). New Zealand painter. Born May 28, 1865, in Dunedin, New Zealand; died Mar 6, 1924, at Kensington, London, England; dau. of Maurice Joel (merchant) and Kate (Woolf) Joel. ❖ Joined Otago Art Society (c. 1886); studied at National Gallery School in Melbourne before settling in London and studying in France and Netherlands (c. 1899); her portraits and figures were widely exhibited in France and Great Britain, gaining moderate success. ❖ See also *Dictionary of New Zealand Biography* (Vol. 2).

JOENPELTO, Eeva (1921–2004). Finnish novelist. Name variations: (pseudonyms) Eeva Antare, Eeva Hella. Born June 17, 1921, in Lohja, Finland; died Jan 28, 2004. ❖ Graduated from College of Social Sciences and became professor of arts (1980); novels, which often contrast urban and rural lifestyles, include *Johannes vain* (1952), *Neito kulkee vetten päällä* (1955), *Kipinöivät vuodet* (1961), *Ritari metsien pimennosta* (1966), and *Kuin kekäle kedessä* (1976).

JOENS, Karin (1953—). German politician. Name variations: Karin Jöns. Born April 29, 1953, in Kiel, Germany. ❖ Became a member of Bremen Social Democratic Party (SPD) Land Executive (1998); as a European Socialist, elected to 4th and 5th European Parliament (EP, 1994–99, 1999–2004).

JOERGENSEN, Rikke Horlykke (1976—). *See Jorgensen, Rikke Horlykke.*

JOHANN, Zita (1904–1993). Hungarian-born stage and film actress. Born July 14, 1904, near Temesvar, Austria-Hungary (now Timisoara, Romania); died Sept 24, 1993, of pneumonia in Nyack, NY; dau. of an officer in emperor's Hussars; m. John Houseman (actor), 1929 (div.); m. twice more. ❖ At 7, moved with family to NY; toured in such productions as *Peer Gynt*, *The Devil's Disciple* and *He Who Gets Slapped*; made Broadway debut in Theater Guild production of *Man and the Masses* (1924), followed by leads in *Machinal*, *The Goat Song*, *Tomorrow and Tomorrow*, *Panic*, *Flight into China*, *The Burning Deck* and *The Broken Journey* (1931), among others; made film debut as Florrie in *The Struggle* (1931), the last movie made by D.W. Griffith; other films include *Tiger Shark*, *Luxury Liner*, *The Sin of Nora Moran* (title role), and, most memorably, *The Mummy*.

JOHANNA. *Variant of Joanna or Joan.*

JOHANNA, queen of Scotland (c. 1410–1445). *See Beaufort, Joan.*

JOHANNA ELIZABETH OF BADEN-DURLACH (1651–1680). Margravine of Ansbach. Name variations: Joanna Elizabeth. Born Nov 16, 1651; died Oct 8, 1680; dau. of Christina Casimir and Frederick VI (b. 1617), margrave of Baden-Durlach; became 2nd wife of John Frederick (1654–1686), margrave of Ansbach (r. 1667–1686), on Feb 5, 1673; children: (stepdaughter) Caroline of Ansbach (1683–1737), queen of England. John Frederick's 1st wife was Eleanor of Saxe-Eisenach (1662–1696).

JOHANNA ELIZABETH OF HOLSTEIN-GOTTORP (1712–1760). Princess of Holstein-Gottorp. Name variations: Joanna Elizabeth. Born Oct 24, 1712; died May 30, 1760; dau. of Albertina of Baden-Durlach (1682–1755) and Christian Augustus, duke of Holstein-Gottorp; m. Christian August, prince of Anhalt-Zerbst, Nov 8, 1727; children: Sophia Augusta Fredericka (1729–1796), princess of Anhalt-Zerbst (who would be known as Catherine II the Great, empress of Russia). ❖ Born into a family that ruled the Duchy of Holstein; was well-connected with some of the great royal families of Europe; received an invitation to visit at the court of Empress Elizabeth Petrovna of Russia (1744) to arrange for a marriage between daughter Sophia and Grand Duke Peter Feodorovich (later Tsar Peter III); when it was discovered that Frederick the Great, King of Prussia, had asked her to intercede secretly on behalf of Prussian interests at the Russian court, was promptly banished from Russia (1745) and never saw daughter again; daughter married Peter and was received into the Orthodox Church as Catherine Alexeievna, later known to the world as Catherine II the Great. ❖ See also *Women in World History.*

JOHANNA OF BAVARIA (c. 1373–1410). Duchess of Austria. Name variations: Johanna Sophia of Bavaria; Johanna Sophia of Bavaria-Straubing. Born c. 1373 in Munich; died Oct 17, 1410, in Vienna; m. Albrecht also known as Albert IV the Patient (1377–1404), duke of Austria (r. 1395–1404); children: Albert V (1397–1439), duke of Austria (r. 1401), king of Hungary (r. 1437), king of Bohemia (r. 1438), and Holy Roman emperor as Albert II (r. 1438–1439); Margaret (1395–1447), duchess of Bavaria.

JOHANNA OF FLANDERS (c. 1200–1244). Countess of Flanders and Hainault. Name variations: Joan of Constantinople; Joan of Flanders; Joanna of Flanders or Jeanne of Flanders; Joanna, Countess of Belgium. Born c. 1200; died Dec 5, 1244 (some sources cite 1245); dau. of Baudouin also known as Baldwin IX, count of Flanders and Hainault (crowned Baldwin I of Constantinople), and Marie of Champagne (c. 1180–1203); sister of Margaret of Flanders (1202–1280); m. Ferdinand of Portugal (1188–1233), Jan 1, 1212; m. Thomas of Savoy; children: (1st m.) Marie (1224–1236). ❖ When father Baldwin IX departed on

4th Crusade (April 1202), was reportedly 2 years old; mother died in Acre (1203); father died a captive of the Bulgars (1205); orphaned with sister Margaret of Flanders (1202–1280), was heir to father's feudal domain, Flanders and Hainault; with sister, was put under protection of Philip II Augustus, king of France (1208); was married to Ferdinand of Portugal because Philip thought it enabled him to control Flanders more easily; when husband joined forces against Philip and fell captive in the battle of Bouvines (1214), was allowed to retain her fiefs, on condition that her fortifications be destroyed; governed an increasingly restive Flanders; when the discontented rallied to the banner of the "False Baldwin," an impostor who claimed to be her father returned from the crusade (1225), fled for refuge to Tournai, appealing to the new king of France, Louis VIII, for assistance; managed to cling to power and was finally reunited with husband after 12 years. ❖ See also *Women in World History.*

JOHANNA OF PFIRT (1300–1351). Duchess of Austria. Name variations: Johanna von Pfirt; Jeannette de Ferette; Johanna of the Palatinate. Born 1300 in Basel; died Nov 15, 1351, in Vienna; m. Albrecht also known as Albert II (1298–1358), duke of Austria (r. 1326–1358), duke of Carinthia (r. 1335); children: Rudolf IV (1339–1365); Albert III (d. 1395), duke of Austria; Catherine (1342–1387); Margaret (1346–1366, who m. Meinhold of Tyrol); Frederick III (1347–1362), duke of Austria; Leopold III (1351–1386), duke of Austria.

JOHANNA OF THE PALATINATE (1300–1351). *See Johanna of Pfirt.*

JOHANNE. *Variant of Joanna or Joanne.*

JOHANSEN, Aud (1930—). Norwegian-born actress, dancer, and singer. Born Jan 17, 1930, in Norway; dau. of Henry Johansen and Asluag (Rage) Johansen; studied ballet in Norway and London; m. Patric Doonan (actor, div.; committed suicide 1958). ❖ As a child, made stage debut in Bergen in a war-time revue (1940); made London debut in revue *Sauce Tartare* (1949), followed by *Music at Midnight*, *Blue for a Boy* (ran for 18 months), *Over the Moon* and *Intimacy at 8:30*, among others; films include *Lilli Marlene* and *Second Fiddle*; also appeared in cabarets in London and on the Continent.

JOHANSEN, Hanna (1939—). German novelist. Born June 17, 1939, in Bremen, Germany. ❖ Works include *Die Stehende Uhr* (1978), *Trocadero* (1980), *Zurück nach Oraibi* (1986), *Der Mann vor der Tür* (1988), and *Lena* (2002).

JOHANSON, Margareta (1895–1978). Swedish diver. Born Jan 9, 1895; died Jan 28, 1978. ❖ At Stockholm Olympics, won a gold medal in platform (1912).

JOHANSSON, Anna (1860–1917). Russian ballet dancer. Born 1860, possibly in St. Petersburg, Russia; died 1917 in St. Petersburg. ❖ Trained at School of Imperial Ballet with father; danced with Maryinsky Ballet for 20 years (1878–98), where she performed principal roles in Ivanov's *La Tulipe d'Haarlem*, *Midsummer Night's Dream*, and Petipa's *Esmeralda*, among others; joined faculty of Imperial Ballet School where her students included Tamara Karsavina and Lyubov Egorova.

JOHANSSON, Elisabet (1964—). *See Gustafson, Elisabet.*

JOHANSSON, Irma. Swedish cross-country skier. Born in Sweden. ❖ Won a silver medal for 3 x 5 km relay at Cortina Olympics (1956); won a gold medal for 3 x 5 km relay at Squaw Valley Olympics (1960).

JOHANSSON, Ronny (b. 1891). Swedish concert dancer. Born 1891 in Riga, Latvia, of Swedish parents. ❖ Began dance studies after returning to Sweden from Latvia (early 1910s); presented solo program of character and folk technique work on tour (1914); made debut in US with touring concert series (1925); taught at Denishawn in New York City; performed in US on numerous occasions thereafter, often with modern dance pioneers including Rosalinde Fuller and Charles Weidman.

JOHN, Eugenie (1825–1887). *See Marlitt, Eugenie.*

JOHN, Gwen (1876–1939). Welsh painter. Born Gwendoline Mary John, June 22, 1876, in Haverfordwest, Wales; died Sept 18, 1939, in Dieppe, France; dau. of Edwin John (solicitor) and Augusta (Smith) John; sister of Augustus John (1878–1961) and Winifred John; attended Miss Wilson's Academy, Tenby, 1890–93, Miss Philpott's Educational Establishment, London, 1893–94, Slade School of Fine Art, London, 1895–98, Académie Carmen, Paris, 1898; never married; no children. ❖ Welsh painter who lived in Paris for most of her working life and produced a small number of paintings and copious drawings and watercolors utilizing a narrow range of subject matter, primarily that of her own passionate but somewhat solitary existence; at 8, moved with family to Tenby following mother's death (1884); awarded Melvill Nettleship Prize for figure composition at Slade (1898); lived in London (1899–1903); exhibited periodically at New English Art Club (1900–11); held joint exhibition with brother Augustus John at Carfax Gallery, London (1903); lived in Paris (1904–11), then lived in suburb of Meudon, retaining Paris flat as studio (1911–18); patronized by John Quinn (1910–24); exhibited *Girl Reading at a Window* in NY Armory show (1918); exhibited frequently at Paris Salons (1919–25); had works included in NY exhibition, Modern English Artists (1922); had retrospective exhibition of work held at New Chenil Galleries, London (1926); output and exhibition of paintings and drawings diminished (1930s); posthumous exhibitions, organized by Matthiesen Ltd., accelerated the growth of her reputation in England and America (1940, 1946). Paintings include *The Artist's Sister Winifred* (c. 1899), *Mrs. Atkinson* (1899–1900), *Self-portrait* (1902), *A Corner of the Artist's Room in Paris* (1907–09), *Mère Poussepin* (1913–21), *Girl in Profile* (c. 1918), *The Convalescent* (c. 1923) and *Young Woman Holding a Black Cat* (c. 1923–28). The largest public collection of her drawings and watercolors is held in the National Museum of Wales, Cardiff. ❧ See also Mary Taubman, *Gwen John* (Scolar, 1985); and *Women in World History.*

JOHN, Rosamund (1913–1998). English stage and screen actress. Name variations: Rosamund Jones; born Nora Rosamund Jones, Oct 19, 1913, in London, England; died Oct 27, 1998, in London; m. Hugh Russell Lloyd (div.); m. John Silkin (Labour MP and Secretary of State for Agriculture), 1950 (died 1997). ❧ British leading lady, made London debut in *Antony and Cleopatra* (1935), followed by *Home and Beauty, Welcome Stranger, The Devil's Disciple, You Never Can Tell, Gaslight, Dragon's Mouth, The Golden Thread* and *Murder on Arrival,* among others; films include *The First of the Few, The Gentle Sex, Tawny Pipit, The Way to the Stars* and *Fame is the Spur.*

JOHN-PAETZ-MOEBIUS, Sabine (1957—). East German heptathlete. Name variations: Sabine John, Sabine Paetz, Sabine Moebius. Born Oct 16, 1957, in East Germany. ❧ At Seoul Olympics, won a silver medal in heptathlon (1988).

JÖHNCKE, Louise (1976—). Swedish swimmer. Name variations: Johncke or Joehncke. Born July 31, 1976, in Stockholm, Sweden. ❧ Won a bronze medal for 4 x 100-meter freestyle relay at Sydney Olympics (2000).

JOHNS, Ethel (1879–1968). Canadian nurse. Born Ethel Mary Incledon Johns, May 13, 1879, in Meonstoke Southampton, England; died Sept 2, 1968, in Vancouver, Canada; dau. of Amy (Robinson) Johns and Rev. Henry Incledon Johns (teacher); graduate of Winnipeg (Manitoba) Hospital Training School for Nurses, 1902; studied at Columbia University Teachers College (from 1914). ❧ One of Canada's pioneer nurses, began working as an instructor and head nurse at Winnipeg General Hospital (1905), then head of its X-ray department (1907); helped found and served as an editor of Winnipeg General Hospital's *Nurses' Alumnae Journal* (1907); served as principal and superintendent of Children's Hospital of Winnipeg's nursing school (1915–19); appointed to Public Welfare Commission of Manitoba (1917); at Vancouver General Hospital, served as director of Nursing Service and Education (1919–21) and became a full-time faculty member (1922); worked as a special member of the Field Staff in Nursing Education for the Rockefeller Foundation in Europe (from 1925); helped reorganize the nursing school in Debrecen, Hungary; was 1st director of The University of British Columbia's School of Nursing; served as editor and business manager of *Canadian Nurse,* the official journal of the Canadian Nurses Association; retired (1944). ❧ See also Margaret Street, *Watch-Fires on the Mountains: The Life and Writings of Ethel Johns* (1973).

JOHNS, Glynis (1923—). English actress. Born Oct 5, 1923, in Durban, South Africa; dau. of Mervyn Johns (actor) and Alys Steele; when father remarried (1976), her stepmother was actress Diana Churchill (b. 1913); m. Anthony Forwood (manager, div., died 1988); m. David Foster (div.); m. Cecil Henderson, 1960 (div. 1962); m. Elliott Arnold, 1964 (div.); children: Gareth. ❧ At 12, made London stage debut (1935); appeared in 1st film, *South Riding* (1938); with her gravel-voice and flair for comedy, won a Tony award for performance in *A Little Night Music* where she introduced "Send in the Clowns"; was also nominated for an Oscar as Best Supporting Actress in *The Sundowners* (1960); other films include *Forty-Ninth Parallel* (1941), *The Halfway House* (1944), *Frieda* (1947), *Miranda* (1948), *The Magic Box* (1951), *The Sword and the Rose* (1953), *Mad About Men* (1954), *Around the World in 80 Days* (1956), *All Mine to Give* (1958), *Shake Hands with the Devil* (1959), *The Cabinet of Caligari* (1962), *Papa's Delicate Condition* (1962), *Mary Poppins* (1964),

Under Milkwood (1972), *Zelly and Me* (1988) and *While You Were Sleeping* (1995); starred on tv in "Glynis" (1963).

JOHNS, Helen (1914—). American swimmer. Name variations: Helen Johns Carroll. Born Sept 25, 1914; graduate of Brown University, 1936. ❧ At Los Angeles Olympics, won a gold medal in the 4 x 100-meter freestyle relay (1932); moved to Sumter, South Carolina.

JOHNSEN, Vibeke (1968—). Norwegian handball player. Born Oct 16, 1968, in Norway. ❧ At Seoul Olympics, won a silver medal in team competition (1988).

JOHNSON, Adelaide (1859–1955). American sculptor and feminist. Born Sarah Adeline Johnson, Sept 26, 1859, in Plymouth, IL; died Nov 10, 1955, in Washington, DC; dau. of Christopher William Johnson (farmer) and Margaret Huff (Hendrickson) Johnson; studied at St. Louis School of Design; m. Alexander Frederick Jenkins (English businessman) Jan 29, 1896 (div. 1908). ❧ Considered the major sculptor of the women's suffrage movement, traveled to Europe to study art, 1st in Dresden, then with Giulio Monteverde in Rome (1883–84); as part of her feminist perspective, exhibited busts of suffragists and a pioneer woman physician at Woman's Pavilion of World's Columbian Exposition in Chicago (1893); differences with Susan B. Anthony prompted her to turn to Alva Belmont, NY suffragist; secured commission for a national monument honoring women's movement (1904); presented *The Woman Movement,* also known as *The Portrait Monument* (her sculpture containing portrait busts of Susan B. Anthony, Lucretia Mott, and Elizabeth Cady Stanton) at the Capitol building (Feb 15, 1921); with career in decline and frustrated over her dream of a studio-museum showcasing the women's movement, mutilated many of her works (1939). Her "Portrait Monument" remained in basement of Capitol until June 1997 when it was rededicated in the rotunda, the only sculpture that is a national monument to the women's movement. ❧ See also *Women in World History.*

JOHNSON, Amy (1903–1941). British aviator. Name variations: Amy Mollison. Born Amy Johnson, July 1, 1903, in Hull, England; died Jan 5, 1941, after parachuting from a plane she was ferrying for Air Ministry over the Thames Estuary; eldest dau. of John William Johnson (herring importer) and Amy (Hodge) Johnson; graduate of Sheffield University, 1925; m. Jim Mollison (pioneer pilot), July 1932 (div. 1938); no children. ❧ The 1st woman to fly solo to Australia and who subsequently broke many records in pioneering flights around the world, joined London Aeroplane Club based at Stag Lane airport (1928); was 1st woman in Britain to qualify as ground engineer as well as pilot; shot to fame after solo flight to Australia (1930); continued to engage in record-breaking flights until outbreak of war (1939); joined Air Transport Auxiliary (1939); killed while on active service with this unit (1941). Pioneering and record flights: soloed to Australia (May 5–24, 1930); co-piloted, with engineer and mentor Jack Humphreys, record-breaking flight from England to Tokyo (July 1931); made record-breaking solo flight to Cape Town and back (Nov 1932); made non-stop flight from London to NY with husband which narrowly failed (July 1933); made record-breaking flight with husband from London to Karachi (Oct 1934); soloed to Cape and back, beating both records (May 1936). ❧ See also autobiography *Skyroads of the World* (Chambers, 1939); Constance Babington-Smith, *Amy Johnson* (Thorosons, 1967); film *They Flew Alone* (released in US as *Wings and the Woman),* starring Anna Neagle as Amy Johnson (1942); and *Women in World History.*

JOHNSON, Mrs. Andrew (1810–1876). *See Johnson, Eliza McCardle.*

JOHNSON, Betsy Ancker (1927—). *See Ancker-Johnson, Betsy.*

JOHNSON, Brandy (1973—). American gymnast. Name variations: Brandy Johnson Scharpf. Born April 30, 1973, in Tallahassee, FL; m. Bill Scharpf (waterskier). ❧ Won Cottbus Cup and American Cup (1989); at World championships, won a silver medal in vault (1989); at US nationals, won a gold medal in all-around (1989) and a bronze medal in all-around and gold medals in vault and floor exercises (1990). Inducted into USA Gymnastics Hall of Fame (2000).

JOHNSON, Celia (1908–1982). English actress. Born Celia Elizabeth Johnson, Dec 18, 1908, in Richmond, Surrey, England; died in Nettlebed, England, April 23, 1982; dau. of Robert Johnson (doctor) and Ethel (Griffiths) Johnson; studied at RADA; m. Peter Fleming (travel writer and brother of Ian Fleming); children: Nicholas (b. Jan 3, 1939); Kate Fleming (b. Mary 24, 1946, writer); Lucy (b. May 15, 1947, actress). ❧ Actress who left behind an enduring reminder of her talent, the movie *Brief Encounter,* a classic of British cinema; made debut as

Sarah Undershaft in *Major Barbara* in Yorkshire (1928); won excellent reviews in 3 flops in a row, bringing her to prominence (1929); played Ophelia to Raymond Massey's Hamlet in NY (1931); back in England, opened in *The Wind and the Rain* (1933), which ran for 2 years; scored one of her greatest triumphs as Elizabeth Bennet in *Pride and Prejudice* (1936); played Mrs. de Winter in *Rebecca* (1940); made 1st full-length film *In Which We Serve* (1942), followed by *Dear Octopus, This Happy Breed, The Holly and the Ivy, A Kid for Two Farthings* and *The Good Companions*; appeared in *Never Too Late* (1954) and *The Reluctant Debutante* (1955); played Madame Ranevskaya in Lindsay Anderson production of *The Cherry Orchard* (1967); had another success in Ayckbourn's *Relatively Speaking* (1967); played Miss Mackay in film *The Prime of Miss Jean Brodie* (1968) and Lady Boothroyde in *Lloyd George Knew My Father* (1972); on tv, appeared in "Mrs. Palfrey at the Claremont," for which she won BAFTA Best Actress (1973); for performance in *Staying On* with Trevor Howard (Mar 1980), was nominated for another Best Actress by BAFTA. Named Commander of the British Empire (CBE, 1958); nominated for Oscar for Best Actress for *Brief Encounter* (1946); created Dame Commander of British Empire (1981). ❖ See also Kate Fleming, *Celia Johnson* (Weidenfeld & Nicholson, 1991); and *Women in World History.*

JOHNSON, Chris (1958—). American golfer. Born April 25, 1958, in Arcata, CA; attended University of Arizona. ❖ Won Samaritan Classic and Tucson Open (1984), GNA/Glendale Classic (1986), Columbia Savings National Pro-Am (1987), Atlantic City Classic (1990), PING/Welch's championship (1991), and Star Bank Classic (1995); won LPGA championship and Safeway (1997); member of Solheim Cup team (1998). Inducted into University of Arizona Sports Hall of Fame (1985).

JOHNSON, Claudia Alta (b. 1912). *See Johnson, Lady Bird.*

JOHNSON, Courtney (1974—). American water-polo player. Born May 7, 1974, Salt Lake City, Utah. ❖ Won a team silver medal at Sydney Olympics (2000).

JOHNSON, E. Pauline (1861–1913). Indigenous poet and writer. Name variations: Tekahionwake; Emily Pauline Johnson; The Mohawk Princess. Born Emily Pauline Johnson, Mar 10, 1861, on Six Nations Indian Reserve near Brantford, Ontario, Canada; died of cancer, Mar 7, 1913, in Vancouver, British Columbia; dau. of George Henry Martin Johnson (Mohawk chief and Canadian government interpreter) and Emily Susanna (Howells) Johnson; attended school in Brantford, 1875–77; never married; no children. ❖ Writer, who emphasized her native Indian heritage to become a popular and acclaimed recitalist throughout Canada and England, published 1st poem (1885) and her gifts as a poet would gain recognition in literary circles; gave 1st public recital (1892); made trip to England and published 1st book *The White Wampum* (1894) which was well received by the critics and had robust sales; also wrote *Canadian Born* (1903), *Legends of Vancouver* (1911), *The Shaganappi* (1913), and *The Mocassin Maker* (1913); poems include "The Song My Paddle Sings," "In the Shadows," "At the Ferry," "Fight On," "Canadian Born," and "Riders of the Plains"; at the peak of her career as an entertainer, toured Canada and England reciting her own poems and other works, wearing the traditional buckskin and beads of a Mohawk and appeared onstage under the names of Tekahionwake and The Mohawk Princess (1892–1909); retired in Vancouver (1909); helped in diminishing the prejudice against native peoples of Canada. ❖ See also Betty Keller, *Pauline: A Biography of Pauline Johnson* (Douglas & McIntyre, 1981); Marcus Van Steen, *Pauline Johnson: Her Life and Work* (Musson, 1965); and *Women in World History.*

JOHNSON, Eleanor Murdoch (1892–1987). American educator and editor. Born in Hagerstown, Maryland, 1892; died 1987; dau. of Richard Potts Johnson and Emma J. (Shuff) Johnson; attended Colorado College, 1911–12; graduate of Central State Teachers College, 1913; University of Chicago, PhB cum laude, 1925; Columbia University, MA, 1932. ❖ Founder of the children's newspaper *My Weekly Reader,* taught in Oklahoma public schools of Lawton (1913–16), Chickasha (1916–17) and Oklahoma City (1917–18); served as superintendent of elementary schools, Drumright, Oklahoma (1918–22), Oklahoma City (1922–26) and York, Pennsylvania (1926–30); was assistant superintendent of schools in Lakewood, Ohio (1930–34); co-founded (1928) and edited *My Weekly Reader* (1934); retired (1965). ❖ See also *Women in World History.*

JOHNSON, Elinor (1902–2000). *See Swinburne, Nora.*

JOHNSON, Eliza McCardle (1810–1876). American first lady. Born Oct 4, 1810, in Leesburg, Kentucky; died Jan 15, 1876, in Greeneville, Tennessee; only dau. of John McCardle also seen as McArdle or McCardell (shoemaker and innkeeper) and Sarah (Phillips) McCardle; m. Andrew Johnson (1808–1875, 17th president of US, 1865–69), May 17, 1827; children: Martha Johnson Patterson (1828–1901); Mary Johnson Stover (1832–1883); Robert Johnson (1834–1869); Charles Johnson (1830–1863); Andrew Johnson Jr., called Frank (1852–1879). ❖ At 17, married and taught husband how to read and write; endured separation and hardship to promote his political career; after he was sworn in as president following assassination of Lincoln, was too ill with TB to function as first lady; appeared at only 2 official functions during her tenure (1865–69): a reception for Queen Emma of Hawaii and for children honoring husband's 60th birthday; daughters Martha Johnson Patterson and Mary Johnson Stover carried out most social duties. ❖ See also *Women in World History.*

JOHNSON, Ella (1923–2004). African-American jazz singer. Born June 22, 1923, in Darlington, SC; died Feb 16, 2004, in Greeneville, SC; sister of bandleader and composer Buddy Johnson (died 1977); m. Odell Day. ❖ Performed in dance bands led by her brother (1940s–50s); had 1st hit "Please, Mr. Johnson" (1940), followed by "Since I Fell for You" (1945), "When My Man Comes Home" (1944) and "That's the Stuff You Gotta Watch" (1945); also recorded "Hittin' on Me," "Did You See Jackie Robinson Hit That Ball?" and "I Don't Want Nobody."

JOHNSON, Ellen Cheney (1829–1899). American prison reformer. Born Ellen Cheney, Dec 20, 1829, in Athol, Massachusetts; died June 28, 1899, in London, England; only child of Nathan Cheney (agent of a cotton mill) and Rhoda (Holbrook) Cheney; attended an academy in Francestown, New Hampshire; m. Jesse Crane Johnson (businessman); no children. ❖ Concerned with plight of women prisoners who were often incarcerated under deplorable conditions, helped establish the Temporary Asylum for Discharged Female Prisoners in Dedham, MA (1874); served as a member of state prison commission (1878–84); was instrumental in establishing Massachusetts Reformatory Prison for Women in Sherborn (1877) and served as its superintendent (1884–99), incorporating some of the most enlightened practices of her day. ❖ See also *Women in World History.*

JOHNSON, Elnora B. (1902–2000). *See Swinburne, Nora.*

JOHNSON, Emma (1980—). Australian swimmer. Born 1980 in Sydney, Australia. ❖ Won a bronze medal for 800-meter freestyle relay at Atlanta Olympics (1996).

JOHNSON, Esther (1681–1728). Irish literary inspiration. Name variations: Hetty Johnson; Stella. Born Mar 13, 1681, near Richmond, Surrey, England; died in Dublin, Ireland, Jan 28, 1728; dau. of Edward Johnson (William Temple's steward) and Bridget Johnson; probably secretly married to Jonathan Swift (satirist), 1716. ❖ Immortalized by Jonathan Swift, was referred to as Stella in his correspondence and in his *Journal to Stella.* ❖ See also *Women in World History.*

JOHNSON, Gail (1954—). *See Buzonas, Gail Johnson.*

JOHNSON, Georgia Douglas (1877–1966). African-American writer. Born Georgia Blanche Douglas Camp, Sept 10, 1877, in Atlanta, Georgia; died in Washington, DC, May 14, 1966; dau. of George Camp and Laura (Jackson) Camp; completed Normal Program at Atlanta University, 1896; studied Oberlin Conservatory, Cleveland College of Music and Howard University; m. Henry Lincoln Johnson (lawyer and politician), 1903 (died 1925); children: Henry Lincoln Jr., and Peter Douglas. ❖ Poet, playwright, educator, and political activist whose work, incorporating many threads of the artistic tapestry of the Harlem Renaissance, explored the duality women of color endure in American society; served as an assistant principal in Atlanta; moved to Washington, DC (1910), where husband established a law firm and their home became a literary salon known as the "Round Table," which drew many of the major figures of the Harlem Renaissance; published 1st poems in *Crisis* (1916); published 1st volume of poetry, *The Heart of a Woman and Other Poems* (1918); explored racial stereotypes in 2nd volume of poetry, *Bronze* (1922); published more than 200 poems (1918–30), and became active in civil-rights issues and in politics, participating in Pan-African movement, Congregational Church meetings, and Republican Party; after death of husband (1925), became commissioner of conciliation at Department of Labor (1927) and began writing plays; won 1st prize in *Opportunity* magazine play contest for *Plumes*

(1927); became involved with Federal Theater Project, part of the New Deal. ❖ See also *Women in World History.*

JOHNSON, Halle (1864–1901). African-American physician. Name variations: Halle Tanner Dillon Johnson; Halle Tanner Dillon. Born Halle Tanner, Oct 17, 1864, in Pittsburgh, PA; died April 26, 1901, in Nashville, TN, from childbirth complications; dau. of Sarah Elizabeth (Miller) Tanner and Benjamin Tucker Tanner (African Methodist Episcopal Church leader); sister of Henry Ossawa Tanner (artist); m. Charles E. Dillon, 1886; John Quincy Johnson (African Methodist Episcopal minister), 1894; children: (1st m.) 1; (2nd m.) 3. ❖ The 1st woman licensed to practice medicine in Alabama, graduated from the Woman's Medical College of Pennsylvania (May 7, 1891), the only African-American student; served as a resident physician of Booker T. Washington's African-American Tuskegee Institute (1891–94), after passing rigorous Alabma state physician exams; established Lafayette Dispensary to treat local Tuskegee residents and to train local nurses.

JOHNSON, Helen Kendrick (1844–1917). American author, editor, and anti-suffragist. Name variations: Mrs. Rossiter Johnson. Born Helen Louise Kendrick, Jan 4, 1844, in Hamilton, NY; died Jan 3, 1917, in New York, NY; dau. of Asabel Kendrick and Anne Elizabeth (Hopkins) Kendrick; attended Oread Institute, Worcester, MA, 1863–64; m. Rossiter Johnson (newspaper editor), May 1869; children: 2 who died young, though she may have had others. ❖ Wrote a series of children's stories, the "Roddy" books, followed by *Tears for the Little Ones, Our Familiar Songs and Those Who Made Them* (1881), and a 6-volume collection of epigrams known as the "Nutshell" series (1884), among others; as editor of *American Woman's Journal* (1894–96), became active in the suffrage movement; changed position and became an outspoken anti-suffragist, publishing *Women and the Republic* (1897). ❖ See also *Women in World History.*

JOHNSON, Helene (1906–1995). African-American writer. Name variations: Helen Johnson Hubbell. Born Helen Johnson, July 7, 1906, in Boston, Massachusetts; died July 6, 1995, in New York, NY; only child of Ella (Benson) Johnson and William Johnson; cousin of Dorothy West (1907–1998); attended Boston University and Columbia University Extension School; m. William Warner Hubbell (motorman), 1930s; children: Abigail Calachaly Hubbell (b. 1940). ❖ Poet, part of the younger generation of writers of the Harlem Renaissance, whose literary career, though brief, had an important impact on American poetry; while still living in Boston, was a member of the literary group, the Saturday Evening Quill Club; also won 1st prize for short-story contest in *Boston Chronicle*; moved to NYC with cousin Dorothy West (1920s); published poems in numerous publications, including *Opportunity, Vanity Fair* and *Fire!*; became active in A'Lelia Walker's literary salon, the Dark Tower, and in Fellowship for Reconciliation, an international organization; won literary awards for poems "My Race" and "Metamorphism" (1926); published one of her best poems, "Bottled," in *Vanity Fair* (1927); probably returned to Boston (c. 1929); disappeared from Harlem literary scene (1929). ❖ See also *Women in World History.*

JOHNSON, Jenna (1967—). American swimmer. Name variations: Jenna Johnson-Younker. Born Sept 11, 1967, in CA; attended Stanford University, 1986–89; m. Joel Younker; children: Baylor. ❖ At Los Angeles Olympics, won a silver medal in the 100 meters and gold medals in the 4 x 100-meter medley relay and the 4 x 100-meter freestyle relay (1984); was 6-time NCAA champion. Won Broderick Award for swimming (1986).

JOHNSON, Josephine Winslow (1910–1990). American writer. Name variations: Josephine J. Cannon. Born June 20, 1910, in St. Louis Co., Missouri; died Feb 27, 1990, in Cincinnati, Ohio; dau. of Benjamin H. (merchant) and Ethel (Franklin) Johnson; Washington University, BA, 1931; m. Grant G. Cannon, 1942 (editor of *Farm Quarterly*, died). ❖ Having spent most of life on a farm, published *Now in November*, at age 24, depicting middle-class, urban family that turns to subsistence farming during Depression, for which she won Pulitzer Prize (1935); also wrote *Wildwood* (1946), *The Dark Traveler* (1963) and *The Inland Island* (1969); involved with organizations that deal with inequality and poverty, including St. Louis Urban League, American Civil Liberties Union, and Cooperative Consumers of St. Louis. ❖ See also Josephine Winslow Johnson, *Seven Houses: A Memoir of Time and Places* (Simon & Schuster, 1973).

JOHNSON, Julie (1903–1973). American exhibition ballroom dancer. Name variations: Juliette Murphy. Born Juliette Henkel in 1903; died 1973 in Los Angeles, CA; m. George Murphy (1902–1992, actor, dancer and politician), 1926; children: Dennis and Melissa. ❖ Trained with Ned Wayburn and danced as chorus girl in his Prologs and vaudeville acts; performed exhibition ballroom acts with partner—later husband—George Murphy; performed as ballroom team at numerous venues, including George Olsen's nightclub circuit, as well as in London at Kit Kat Klub, Café de Paris, and Mayfair Hotel, and on the West End in *Good News*, doing the Varsity Drag; performed at Central Park Casino and in Broadway's *Hold Everything, Shoot the Works* (1931) and *Of Thee I Sing*; retired from performing (c. 1935).

JOHNSON, Kate (1978—). American rower. Born Dec 18, 1978, in Portland, OR; attended University of Michigan. ❖ Won a gold medal for coxed eights at World championships (2002); won a silver medal for coxed eights at Athens Olympics (2004); won 2 World Cups for coxed eights (2003 and 2004).

JOHNSON, Kathryn (1967—). English field-hockey player. Born Jan 21, 1967, in UK. ❖ At Barcelona Olympics, won a bronze medal in team competition (1992).

JOHNSON, Kathy (1959—). American gymnast. Name variations: Kathy Johnson Clarke. Born Sept 13, 1959 in US. ❖ Won American Cup (1977); at US nationals, won silver medal for all-around (1977) and gold for all-around (1978); at World championships, won a bronze medal for floor exercise (1978); at Los Angeles Olympics, won a bronze medal in balance beam and a silver medal in team all-around (1984); does commentary for ABC Sports.

JOHNSON, Katie (1878–1957). English stage and screen actress. Name variations: Katie Jane Johnson. Born Nov 18, 1878, in Clayton, England; died May 4, 1957, in Elham, England. ❖ Appeared in over 30 films, including *A Glimpse of Paradise, Marigold, Freedom Radio* and *Three Steps in the Dark*; best known for performance in *The Lady Killers*.

JOHNSON, Kay (1904–1975). American actress. Born Catherine Townsend, Nov 29, 1904, in Mount Vernon, NY; died Nov 17, 1975, in Waterford, CT; m. John Cromwell, 1928 (div.); children: (adopted) James Cromwell (actor). ❖ Made NY stage debut in *Go West, Young Man* (1923), followed by *Beggar on Horseback, The Morning After, No Trespassing, Crime* and *One of the Family*, among others; films include *Dynamite, The Spoilers, Billy the Kid, The Spy, 13 Women, Of Human Bondage, Jalna, White Banners, Son of Fury* and *Mr. Lucky*.

JOHNSON, Lady Bird (1912—). American first lady. Name variations: Claudia Alta Johnson. Born Claudia Alta Taylor in Karnack, Texas, Dec 12, 1912; dau. of Thomas Jefferson Taylor (merchant and politician) and Minnie Lee (Patillo) Taylor; University of Texas, B.A. in liberal arts (1933), BA in journalism (1934); m. Lyndon Baines Johnson (1908–1973, president of US, 1963–68), Nov 17, 1934; children: Lynda Bird Johnson Robb (b. 1944); Luci Baines Johnson Nugent Turpin (b. 1947). ❖ During WWII, while husband served with navy, purchased a small debt-ridden radio station, KTBC, in Austin (1943); under her full-time management, turned the station into a multimillion-dollar radio and tv enterprise, the Texas Broadcasting Corporation; entered White House following assassination of President John F. Kennedy, having to replace the popular Jacqueline Bouvier Kennedy, but held her own and emerged as a highly respected first lady (1963–69); became a popular Washington host, celebrated for her Southern charm and self-effacing wit; worked in support of War on Poverty, especially in promotion of Head Start program; remembered primarily, however, for her national conservation and beautification campaign; appointed to University of Texas Board of Regents. ❖ See also memoir *A White House Diary* (Holt, 1970); Jan Jarboe Russell, *Lady Bird: A Biography of Mrs. Johnson* (Scribner, 1999); and *Women in World History.*

JOHNSON, Laraine (1917—). See Day, Laraine.

JOHNSON, Luci Baines (1947—). American first daughter. Name variations: Luci Nugent; Luci Turpin. Born Luci Baines Johnson in 1947; youngest dau. of Lady Bird Johnson (b. 1912) and Lyndon Baines Johnson (1908–1973, president of US, 1963–68); m. Patrick Nugent, 1966 (div. 1979); m. Ian Turpin, 1984; children: (1st m.) 5. ❖ Following 1st marriage, had to drop out of Georgetown School of Nursing (undergraduates were not allowed to be married); divorced and remarried, managed the Johnson family radio and real estate concerns in Texas with 2nd husband; enrolled at St. Edward's University in Austin (1994), determined to have her degree; graduated with a 4.0 GPA. ❖ See also *Women in World History.*

JOHNSON, Lynda Bird (1944—). American first daughter. Name variations: Lynda Johnson Robb. Born Lynda Bird Johnson in 1944; dau. of Lady Bird Johnson (b. 1912) and Lyndon Baines Johnson (1908–1973, president of US, 1963–68); m. Charles S. Robb (US senator), 1967; children: 3. ❖ Campaigned with parents during presidential race (1960); married Charles S. Robb in a White House ceremony (1967); became a contributor to the *Ladies' Home Journal*; an activist, campaigned for Reading is Fundamental, a national organization aimed at motivating children to read, and against high infant mortality rates. ❖ See also *Women in World History*.

JOHNSON, Margaret (1884–1955). See Martin, Sara.

JOHNSON, Marjorie (1920–2003). See Fowler, Marjorie.

JOHNSON, Martha (1828–1901). See Patterson, Martha Johnson.

JOHNSON, Melanie (1955—). English politician and member of Parliament. Born Melanie Johnson, Feb 5, 1955; m. William Jordan. ❖ Representing Labour, contested Cambridgeshire (1994) for European Parliament election; elected to House of Commons for Welwyn Hatfield (1997, 2001); named parliamentary under-secretary of State for Competition, Consumers and Markets, Department of Trade and Industry; lost general election (2005).

JOHNSON, Minnie Louie (1909–1984). See Abercrombie, M.L.J.

JOHNSON, Nancy (1935—). American politician. Born Jan 5, 1935, in Chicago, IL; attended University of Chicago; Radcliffe College, BA, 1957; m. Ted Johnson; children: 3. ❖ Ran for CT state senate (1976), becoming 1st Republican elected to New Britain seat in 30 years; held seat for 3 terms (1977–82); elected to US House of Representatives (1982); reelected for 11 more terms, serving longer in House than any US congressional representative in Connecticut history; became a senior member of House Ways and Means Committee and the 1st woman to chair one of its subcommittees (Health); co-authored the law that added prescription drug benefits to Medicare.

JOHNSON, Nancy Napolski (1974—). See Napolski, Nancy.

JOHNSON, Nicole (c. 1974—). Miss America. Born Nicole Johnson c. 1974; Regent University, MA in Journalism (1998). ❖ Named Miss America (1999), representing Virginia; a Type I diabetic, had advocated and lobbied on behalf of diabetes issues; writer. ❖ See also Johnson's *Living with Diabetes*.

JOHNSON, Opha Mae (c. 1899—). American marine. Born c. 1899, possibly in Missouri. ❖ Known as the 1st Lady Leatherneck, became the 1st woman member of US Marine Corps Reserve (Aug 13, 1918); held rank of private; served as clerk in headquarters of Quartermasters Corps in Washington, DC; discharged (1919).

JOHNSON, Osa (1894–1953). American explorer, film producer, author, and big game hunter. Born Osa Helen Leighty, Mar 14, 1894, in Chanute, Kansas; died Jan 7, 1953, in NY; dau. of Ruby (Holman) Leighty and William Leighty; attended Chanute High School; m. Martin Johnson, May 15, 1910 (killed in plane crash, Jan 13, 1937); m. Clark H. Getts, April 29, 1939 (div. 1949); no children. ❖ Well-known explorer and big game hunter, met future husband, adventurer Martin Johnson (1905); journeyed to Solomon Islands and was captured by cannibals (1912); presented 1st motion picture *Captured by Cannibals* to astonished audiences (1912); returned to Solomon Islands (1914); explored Northern Borneo (1917–19); went on 1st expedition to Africa (1921); learned how to hunt and became a crack shot; discovered Lake Paradise (1921); became a licensed pilot (1929); released film *Simba* to popular acclaim (1929); led an expedition through East Africa to obtain footage for film *Stanley and Livingstone* (released, 1939). Writings include *I Married Adventure* (1940) and *Four Years in Paradise* (1941). ❖ See also Imperato & Imperato, *They Married Adventure: The Wandering Lives of Martin and Osa Johnson* (Rutgers U. Press, 1992); and *Women in World History*.

JOHNSON, Pamela Hansford (1912–1981). British novelist, dramatist, and critic. Born Pamela Hansford Johnson, May 29, 1912, in Clapham, London, England; died June 18, 1981, in London; dau. of Reginald Kenneth and Amy Clotilda (Howson) Johnson; granddau. of actor C.E. Howson; educated at Clapham County Secondary School; m. Gordon Neil (Australian journalist), 1936 (div. 1949); m. C.P. Snow (novelist), 1950; children: (1st m.) 1 son, 1 daughter; (2nd m.) 1 son. ❖ Published 1st novel *This Bed thy Centre* (1935), which received both critical acclaim as well as notoriety for its frank sexuality; published *Too Dear for My*

Possessing (1940), 1st of a trilogy that included *An Avenue of Stone* (1947) and *A Summer to Decide* (1949); also wrote 7 plays and 6 radio plays, was a reviewer for *Daily Telegraph* and *Sunday Chronicle*, and published *On Iniquity* (1961), about the infamous Moors Murders; other books include *Catherine Carter* (1952), *An Impossible Marriage* (1954), *The Unspeakable Skipton* (1959), *The Humbler Creation* (1959), *An Error of Judgement* (1962), *Night and Silence—Who is Here?* (1965), *The Honours Board* (1970) and *A Bonfire* (1981). Named Commander of Order of the British Empire (1975). ❖ See also memoirs, *Important to Me* (1974); and *Women in World History*.

JOHNSON, Pauline (1861–1913). See Johnson, E. Pauline.

JOHNSON, Pee-Wee (1974—). See Johnson, Shannon.

JOHNSON, Phyllis (1886–1967). English pairs skater. Name variations: Phyllis Wyatt Johnson. Born Dec 1886 in Great Britain; died Dec 2, 1967. ❖ With James H. Johnson, placed 2nd (1908), then 1st (1909, 1912) and 3rd (1910) at World championships, and won a silver medal at London Olympics (1908); won a bronze medal (1912, 1914) and a silver medal (1913), both for singles, at World championships; with Basil Williams, won a bronze medal at Antwerp Olympics (1920).

JOHNSON, Rebecca (c. 1760–1823). See Franks, Rebecca.

JOHNSON, Rita (1912–1965). American stage and screen actress. Born Rita McSean, Aug 13, 1912, in Worcester, MA; died Oct 31, 1965, in Hollywood, CA; m. Stanley Kahn, 1940 (div. 1943); m. Edwin Hutzler, 1943 (div. 1946). ❖ Appeared on radio and in stock; made Broadway debut (1935); made over 35 films, including *My Friend Flicka*, *Her Comes Mr. Jordan*, *Susan Slept Here*, *General Hospital*, *The Major and the Minor* and *The Big Clock*.

JOHNSON, Shannon (1974—). African-American basketball player. Name variations: Shannon Pee-wee Johnson. Born Aug 18, 1974, in Hartsville, SC; attended University of South Carolina. ❖ Guard, scored 2,230 points in college career; won a team gold medal at Athens Olympics (2004); played for Columbus Quest in ABA; played in WNBA for Orlando Miracle, Connecticut Sun and San Antonio Silver Stars. Inducted into South Carolina Hall of Fame.

JOHNSON, Sheryl (1957—). American field-hockey player. Born Dec 1957 in CA; University of California, BA, 1980; Stanford University, MA, 1981. ❖ At Los Angeles Olympics, won a bronze medal in team competition (1984); was a member of US national team (1978–91); spent 18 seasons at helm of Stanford University field hockey team (1984–2002). Inducted into USFHA Hall of Fame (1994).

JOHNSON, Sunny (1953–1984). American actress. Born Sunny Suzanne Johnson, Sept 21, 1953, in Bakersfield, CA; died of ruptured aneurysm, June 19, 1984, in West Hollywood, CA. ❖ Films include *National Lampoon's Animal House*, *Almost Summer*, *Where the Buffalo Roam*, *Flashdance*, *The Night the Lights Went Out in Georgia*, and *The Immoral Minority Picture Show*.

JOHNSON, Susannah Willard (1729–1810). American writer. Born 1729 in Charlestown, NH; died 1810. ❖ Wrote *A Narrative of the Captivity of Mrs. Johnson* (1796) about 3 years of captivity among Abenakis Indians.

JOHNSON, Tish (1962—). American bowler. Born June 8, 1962, in Oakland, CA. ❖ Named Ladies Professional Bowling Tour Bowler of the Year (1990, 1992, 1995); won Women's Open and Sam's Town Invitational (1992); won 25 tournaments (1982–2002).

JOHNSON, Virginia E. (1925—). American psychologist and sociologist. Name variations: Virginia Johnson Masters; Virginia E. Johnson-Masters. Born Virginia Eshelman in Springfield, Missouri, Feb 11, 1925; dau. of Hershel Eshelman and Edna (Evans) Eshelman; attended Drury College, 1940–42, University of Missouri, 1944–47, and Washington University, St. Louis, 1964; m. George Johnson, June 13, 1950 (div., Sept 1956); m. William Howell Masters (professor of obstetrics and gynecology and author), Jan 7, 1971 (div. 1992); children: (1st m.) Scott Forstall Johnson; Lisa Evans Johnson. ❖ With 2nd husband William Masters, compiled information on human sexuality which documented sexual revolution of 1960s; began career at St. Louis *Daily Record* (1947–50); worked at radio station KMOX, St. Louis (1950–51); joined division of reproductive biology, department of obstetrics and gynecology, Washington University School of Medicine (1957–63) and was research instructor (1962–64); at Masters and Johnson Institute, served as research associate (1964–69), assistant director (1969–73) and co-director (1973–94); became director of Virginia Johnson Masters Learning Center (1994); served on advisory board, Homosexual Community Counseling Center; co-wrote with William H. Masters: *Human Sexual Response* (1966), *Human Sexual Inadequacy* (1970), *The Pleasure Bond* (1975), *Homosexuality in Perspective* (1979) and *Textbook of Sexual Medicine* (1979); co-wrote with Robert Kolodny: *Crisis: Heterosexual Behavior in the Age of AIDS* (1988). ❖ See also *Women in World History.*

JOHNSON-MASTERS, Virginia (b. 1925). *See Johnson, Virginia E.*

JOHNSTON, Amy Isabella (1872–1908). New Zealand dentist. Born on April 5, 1872, at Greymouth, New Zealand; died Sept 17, 1908, at Invercargill, New Zealand; dau. of Robert James Johnston (surveyor) and Marion (Jennings) Johnston. ❖ Trained in dentistry through apprenticeship with J.F. Wilson, with whom she later practiced; was among 5 women registered by government as dentist (1896), and was recognized by New Zealand Dental Association. ❖ See also *Dictionary of New Zealand Biography* (Vol. 2).

JOHNSTON, Anna (1866–1902). *See MacManus, Anna.*

JOHNSTON, Annie Fellows (1863–1931). American writer. Born May 15, 1863, in Evansville, Indiana; died in Pewee Valley, Kentucky, Oct 5, 1931; dau. of Albion Fellows (Methodist minister) and Mary (Erskine) Fellows; sister of Albion Fellows Bacon (1865–1933); attended University of Iowa, 1881–82; m. William L. Johnston, Oct 1888 (died 1892). ❖ A widow with 3 stepchildren to support, published *Big Brother* (1894) and *Joel: A Boy of Galilee* (1895); wrote 1st of her popular 12-volume series of *The Little Colonel* (1896); authored over 50 books, selling over 1 million. ❖ See also *The Land of the Little Colonel: Reminiscence and Autobiography* (1929); and *Women in World History.*

JOHNSTON, Carol (1958—). Canadian gymnast. Born with one arm, Mar 10, 1958, in Calgary, Alberta, Canada. ❖ Was on Canadian Olympic team (1975); at Cal State-Fullerton, placed 2nd on balance beam and floor exercises at NCAA championships (1978). The documentary "Lefty," produced by Disney, chronicles her NCAA (1978–79) season. ❖ See also *Carol Johnston: The One-armed Gymnast* (Children's Press, 1982).

JOHNSTON, Frances Benjamin (1864–1952). American photographer. Born Frances Benjamin Johnston, Jan 15, 1864, in Grafton, West Virginia; died May 16, 1952, in New Orleans, Louisiana; only child of Anderson Dolophon Johnston (bookkeeper at Treasury Department) and Frances Antoinette (Benjamin) Johnston; studied drawing and painting at Julien Academy, Paris, 1884–85; studied at Art Students League; studied photography with Thomas William Smillie at Smithsonian Institution; never married. ❖ Pioneer in photojournalism, and one of only a handful of women in her era to take up photography as a business, published 1st photographs in *Demorest's Family Magazine* (1889); began photographing the White House, publishing her early interior shots in *The White House* (1893); continued photographing the executive mansion and celebrities from Washington's political and social circles for next 15 years, documenting 5 administrations and earning title of "Photographer of the American Court"; created portraits of other distinguished Americans, including Alexander Graham Bell, Mark Twain, Andrew Carnegie, Jane Cowl and Susan B. Anthony; became a champion of women in photography, organizing a traveling exhibition of 142 prints by 26 American women photographers (1900); focused documentary work on industry and education; became associate member of Photo-Secession (1904); received Carnegie grants to photograph Southern architecture (1930s), netting some 7,000 negatives, some of which were published in *The Early Architecture of North Carolina* and *The Early Architecture of Georgia*; donated prints, negatives, and correspondence to Library of Congress, which held an exhibition of her work (1947). Won gold medal at Paris Exposition (1900). ❖ See also Pete Daniel and Raymond Smock. *A Talent for Detail: The Photographs of Miss Frances Benjamin Johnston 1889–1910* (Harmony, 1974); and *Women in World History.*

JOHNSTON, Harriet Lane (1830–1903). *See Lane, Harriet Rebecca.*

JOHNSTON, Henrietta (c. 1670–1728). Irish-born artist. Born Henrietta Deering before 1670, probably in Ireland; died in Charleston, South Carolina, Mar 7, 1728 (some sources cite 1729); m. Gideon Johnston (cleric of Church of England), April 11, 1705; children: several stepchildren. ❖ Possibly the 1st woman artist in America, produced some 40 pastel portraits of distinguished citizens of Charleston, South Carolina, during early 18th century and, in doing so, provided income for her struggling family. ❖ See also *Women in World History.*

JOHNSTON, Jennifer (1930—). Irish novelist. Born Jennifer Prudence Johnston, Jan 12, 1930, in Dublin, Ireland; dau. of Denis Johnston (playwright) and Shelah Richards (1903–1985, actress and director); m. Ian Smyth, 1951; m. David Gilliland, 1976. ❖ Widely admired by critics of Irish literature, explored Irish political and culture tensions in such works as *The Captains and the Kings* (1972), *The Gates* (1973), *How Many Miles to Babylon?* (1974), *The Christmas Tree* (1981), *The Railway Station Man* (1986), *Fool's Sanctuary* (1987), *The Invisible Worm* (1991), *The Illusionist* (1995), *The Desert Lullaby: A Play in Two Acts* (1996), *Two Moons* (1998) and *The Gingerbread Woman* (2000). Received Whitbread Award (1979) for *The Old Jest*; was short-listed for Booker Prize for *Shadows on Our Skin* (1977).

JOHNSTON, Jill (1929—). American journalist. Name variations: F.J. Crowe. Born 1929 in London, England; children: 2. ❖ Began writing column for *Village Voice* (1959) and contributed to *Art News* and *Art in America*; writings include *Marmalade Me* (1971), *Lesbian Nation: The Feminist Solution* (1973), *Gullibles Travels* (1974), *Autobiography in Search of a Father, Volume One: Motherbound* (1983) and *Volume Two: Paper Daughter* (1985).

JOHNSTON, Julanne (1900–1988). American actress and dancer. Name variations: Julianne Johnstone. Born May 1, 1900, in Indianapolis, Indiana; died Dec 26, 1988, in Grosse Pointe, Michigan. ❖ Once a solo dancer with Ruth St. Denis, films include *The Brass Bottle, The Thief of Bagdad, Big Pal, Aloma of the South Seas, Oh Kay!* and *Her Wild Oat.*

JOHNSTON, Katie Jane (1878–1957). *See Johnson, Katie.*

JOHNSTON, Margaret (1866–1951). *See Fraser, Margaret.*

JOHNSTON, Margaret (1917–2002). Australian stage and screen actress. Born Aug 10, 1917, in Coolangatta, NSW, Australia; died June 29, 2002, in England; m. Al Parker (director, died 1974). ❖ Made stage debut in Sydney (1936); made London debut in *Saloon Bar* (1939), followed by *To Fit the Crime, Murder without Crime, The Shouting Dies, The Time of Your Life,* Elizabeth Barrett in *The Barretts of Wimpole Street,* *Always Afternoon,* Alma Winemiller in *Summer and Smoke, The Ring of Truth* and *Masterpiece,* among others; films include *The Prime Minister, The Rake's Progress, A Man about the House, Portrait of Clare, The Magic Box, Knave of Hearts, Touch and Go, Life at the Top* and *Sebastian.*

JOHNSTON, Mary (1870–1936). American novelist. Born Nov 21, 1870, in Buchanan, Virginia; died May 9, 1936, near Warm Springs, Virginia; dau. of John William Johnston (lawyer and major in Confederate Army) and Elizabeth (Alexander) Johnston: never married. ❖ Published 1st novel, *Prisoner of Hope* (1898), to moderate notice, followed by *To Have and To Hold* (1900), about the women of the Jamestown colony, which was a phenomenal success, selling a half-million copies and adapted for the screen several times; also wrote 2 Civil War books, *The Long Roll* (1911) and *Cease Firing* (1912); in other works, explored such diverse subjects as Henry VII's England, 12th-century feudal France, and Christopher Columbus' voyage; also published blank-verse drama, *The Goddess of Reason* (1907), which was produced in NY (1909), starring Julia Marlowe; an ardent feminist, founded Equal Suffrage League in Richmond with Ellen Glasgow (1909). ❖ See also *Women in World History.*

JOHNSTON, Rita Margaret (1935—). Canadian politician. Born Rita Margaret Leichert, April 22, 1935, in Melville, Saskatchewan, Canada; married. ❖ First woman premier in Canada; was elected to British Columbia Legislature in provincial election for Surrey riding (1983), then represented Surrey Newton riding (1986–91); appointed to Cabinet position (1986); served as deputy premier (1990–91); chosen acting premier of British Columbia (April 2, 1991) and elected leader at the Social Credit leadership convention (July 20, 1991); served as premier until her party's defeat in provincial general election (Oct 17, 1991); resigned as Social Credit leader (Jan 11, 1992).

JOHNSTON-FORBES, Cathy (1963—). American golfer. Born Catherine Johnston, Dec 16, 1963, in High Point, NC; attended University of North Carolina; m. Foster Forbes, 1993. ❖ Won du Maurier Classic (1990).

JOHNSTONE, Ann Casey (1921—). American golfer. Born Ann Casey, Feb 14, 1921, in Mason City, Iowa; attended University of Iowa. ❖ Won 6 Iowa state championships; member of Curtis Cup team (1958, 60, 62); played competitively for more than 20 years, winning key events; became a professional teacher (1964); named LPGA Teacher of the Year (1966); staff instructor at National Golf Foundation seminar for teachers (1970–75); taught at Stephens College (MO). Received Ellen Griffin Rolex Award; charter member of National Golf Coaches Hall of Fame.

JOHNSTONE, Anna Hill (1913–1992). American costume designer. Name variations: Anna Hill Johnstone; Anna Johnstone Robinson. Born in Greenville, SC, 1913; died in Lennox, MA, Oct 15, 1992; dau. of Albert Sidney Johnstone (banker) and Anna Hill (Watkins) Johnstone; Barnard College, BA, 1934; m. Curville Jones Robinson (mechanical engineer), May 8, 1937 (died 1989). ❖ Designer in theater, film, and tv, received 1st full credit for Broadway hit *Having Wonderful Time* (1937); other stage productions include *Bell, Book, and Candle, Lost in the Stars, Tea and Sympathy, The Tender Trap* and *A Streetcar Named Desire*; began working for films with *Portrait of Jennie* (1948); designed costumes for over 60 films and some tv, working frequently with directors Elia Kazan and Sidney Lumet; film credits include *Serpico, The Wiz, On the Waterfront, East of Eden, America America, Prince of the City, The Verdict, Running on Empty, Baby Doll, Edge of the City, Dog Day Afternoon, The Group* and *A Face in the Crowd.* Nominated for Academy Awards for *The Godfather* and *Ragtime.* ❖ See also *Women in World History.*

JOHNSTONE, Catherine (1818–1883). *See Mathieson, Catherine.*

JOHNSTONE, Mrs. Christian Isobel (1781–1857). *See Johnstone, Isobel.*

JOHNSTONE, Doris Grahame (1898–1991). *See Zinkeisen, Doris.*

JOHNSTONE, Euphemia (1849/50?–1928). *See Richardson, Effie Newbigging.*

JOHNSTONE, Hilda Lorne (b. 1902). English equestrian. Name variations: Hilda Johnstone. Born in England, 1902. ❖ At age 70, was the oldest athlete to compete in the Olympics, placing 12th as a member of the British riding team at Munich (1972). ❖ See also *Women in World History.*

JOHNSTONE, Isobel (1781–1857). Scottish writer. Name variations: Mrs. Christian Isobel Johnstone; (pseudonym) Mistress Margaret Dods. Born 1781 in Fife, Scotland; died 1857 in Edinburgh; m. John Johnstone (printer and newspaper editor). ❖ Began working for husband's newspaper *Inverness Courier*; published 1st novel *The Saxon and the Gaël* (1814), then wrote *Clan-Albin, A National Tale* (1815) and historical novel *Elizabeth de Bruce* (1827); had great success with collection of short fiction *Edinburgh Tales*; as journalist, wrote for *Schoolmaster, Johnstone's Magazine* and *Tait's Magazine*; perhaps best-known for her immensely popular *The Cook and Housewife's Manual* (also known as *Meg Dod's Cookery*) in which she used characters from Sir Walter Scott's *St. Ronan's Well* to give commentary on preparing national specialties.

JOHNSTONE, Julianne (1900–1988). *See Johnston, Julanne.*

JOHNSTONE, Justine (1895–1982). American actress, dancer, and pathologist. Name variations: Justine Wanger. Born Jan 31, 1895, in Englewood, NJ; died Sept 3, 1982, in Santa Monica, CA; m. Walter Wanger (film producer), 1919 (div. 1938). ❖ Famed for her beauty, was a model for artist Harrison Fisher before making Broadway debut as a show girl in *Folies Bergère* (1911), followed by *Ziegfield Folllies of 1915* and *1916,* and *Stop! Look! Listen!* (1915), *Betty* (1916) and *Oh, Boy* (1917); opened a nightclub with Billie Allen in Shubert Alley; starred in silent films (1920–21), including *The Crucible, Sheltered Daughters,* and *A Heart to Let*; retired from screen (1926), entered medical school and became a noted pathologist and innovator in the treatment of syphilis.

JOKIEL, Dorota (1934–1993). *See Jokielowa, Dorota.*

JOKIELOWA, Dorota (1934–1993). Polish gymnast. Name variations: Dorota Jokiel. Born Dorota Horzonek, Feb 3, 1934, in Poland; died in 1993 (some sources cite 1992). ❖ At Melbourne Olympics, won a bronze medal in teams all-around, portable apparatus (1956).

JOLANDE. *Variant of Yolande.*

JOLANTA. *Variant of Yolande.*

JOLANTA (fl. 1100s). Princess of Hungary. Fl. in 1100s; dau. of Helena of Serbia and Bela II, king of Hungary (r. 1131–1141); m. Boleslas the Pious, of Kalisz.

JOLANTHE. *Variant of Yolande.*

JOLANTHE OF LORRAINE (d. 1500). Landgravine of Hesse. Died May 21, 1500; dau. of Yolande of Vaudemont (1428–1483) and Ferrey de

Vaudemont also known as Frederick, count of Vaudemont; sister of Margaret of Lorraine (1463–1521); m. William II, landgrave of Hesse, Nov 9, 1497.

JOLAS, Betsy (1926—). French-American composer. Born Elizabeth Jolas in Paris, France, Aug 5, 1926; dau. of Maria Jolas (publisher, editor, and journalist) and Eugene Jolas (who founded *transition,* an international literary review, with his wife); sister of Tina Jolas; studied at Bennington College with Karl Weinrich and Hélène Schnabel and at Paris Conservatoire with Darius Milhaud, Olivier Messiaen and Simone Plé Caussade; married a French physician, 1949; children: 3. ❖ One of France's best-known composers, was educated in US and returned there at outbreak of WWII (1940); worked for French radio-tv network editing *Ecouter Aujourd'hui,* a leading musical periodical (1955–65); composition *Quatuor II* was premiered by Pierre Boulez; received French author and composer award (1961); received American Academy of Arts and Letters Award (1973); appointed professor of composition at Paris Conservatoire (1978), replacing Olivier Messiaen; composed numerous orchestral works and made many recordings of them.

JOLAS, Maria (1893–1987). American publisher, editor, translator, critic, and journalist. Born Maria McDonald in Louisville, KY, Jan 1893; died in Paris, France, Mar 4, 1987; studied voice in NY, Berlin and Paris, 1913–25; m. Eugene Jolas, Jan 12, 1926 (died 1952); children: Betsy Jolas (b. 1926, French composer); Maria Christina Jolas known as Tina Jolas (b. 1929). ❖ With husband, co-founded and edited the prestigious review *transition,* in Paris (1927–38), which introduced such writers as Djuna Barnes, Kay Boyle, Laura Riding, Katherine Anne Porter, Ernest Hemingway, Hart Crane, Samuel Beckett and Dylan Thomas; trans. French and German writers, including Franz Kafka; met James Joyce and published fragments of *Finnegans Wake* in *transition* (1926); established the École Bilingue (Franco-American school) in Neuilly (1932); moved school to château near Vichy (1939); left France (Aug 1940); edited *A James Joyce Yearbook* (1949); published "Joyce en France 1939–40" in *Mercure de France* (1950); lived in France most of her adult life. ❖ See also *Women in World History.*

JOLETA. *Variant of Yolande.*

JOLIOT-CURIE, Irène (1897–1956). French physicist. Name variations: Irène or Irene Curie; Irene Joliot-Curie. Born Irène Curie in Paris, France, Sept 12, 1897; died of leukemia, Mar 17, 1956, in Paris; dau. of Pierre Curie and Marie Curie (both famous physicists); sister of Éve Curie (b. 1904); studied at University of Paris and worked under mother's supervision at Radium Institute in Paris; m. Frédéric Joliot, Oct 9, 1926; children: Hélène Joliot-Curie Langevin and Pierre (both physicists). ❖ Nobel-prize winner who was appointed a minister of France before the nation's women were allowed to vote and was dedicated to preserving the use of nuclear energy for peaceful purposes; during WWI, accompanied mother to battlefield X-ray stations (1914–18); granted PhD with a thesis on the alpha rays of polonium (1925); assumed joint last name with husband at time of marriage (1926); took increasing responsibility for the Radium Institute and became director (1932); awarded Nobel Prize for Chemistry with husband for discovery of artificial radium (1935); as undersecretary of scientific research, one of 3 women in Cabinet of Léon Blum, helped to establish the National Center for Scientific Research (1936); driven into hiding in France and Switzerland by husband's active role in the resistance during WWII (1940–45); appointed to the chair of nuclear science at Sorbonne, previously held by both father and mother; appointed to French Atomic Energy Commission (CEA); dismissed with husband from the CEA for Communist sympathies and opposition to use of atomic energy for nuclear weapons (1950); lobbied successfully for a new Institute of Nuclear Physics, constructed in 1950s; given a state funeral, befitting one of the pre-eminent scientists of France (1956). Won Barnard Gold Medal for Meritorious Service to Science, Henri Wilde Prize, and Marquet Prize of Academy of Sciences (1940);. ❖ See also *Women in World History.*

JOLLEY, Elizabeth (1923—). British-born Australian short-story writer and novelist. Born Monica Elizabeth Knight, June 4, 1923, in Gravelly Hill, England; dau. of Charles Wilfred Knight (1890–1977, teacher) and Margarethe Johanna Carolina (von Fehr) Knight (1896–1979); m. Leonard Jolley (1914–1994, librarian); children: Sarah, Richard and Ruth Jolley. ❖ Preeminent in Australia and overseas for her innovative and experimental fiction, immigrated with family to Australia (1959); started writing for publication (1960s); had 1st book published, *Five Acre Virgin and Other Stories* (1976); became a university lecturer in creative writing at Curtin University (1978); produced about a book a year, including *Peabody, Milk and Honey, Palomino, Newspaper, The Sugar Mother, Foxybaby, Cabin Fever, My Father's Moon, Mr. Scobie's Riddle, The Well* and the Vera Wright trilogy. Received New South Wales Prize for Fiction for *Milk and Honey* (1985) and Miles Franklin Award for *The Well* (1987); named Officer of the Order of Australia for Services to the Arts (1988); won Canada-Australia Literary Award (1989); joint winner with Françoise Cartano of the Inaugural France-Australia Literary Award for *The Sugar Mother* (*Tombé du ciel*), a book in French translation (1993). ❖ See also Caroline Lurie, ed. *Central Mischief: Elizabeth Jolley on Writing, Her Past and Herself* (Viking, 1992); and *Women in World History*.

JOLLY, Allison (1956—). America yacht racer. Born Aug 1956; grew up in St. Petersburg, FL. ❖ At Seoul Olympics, won a gold medal in 470 class (1988), with Lynne Jewell.

JOLLY, Doris Clifton (1890–1956). *See Gordon, Doris Clifton.*

JOLY, Andrée (1901–1993). French pairs skater. Name variations: Andree Joly; Andrée Brunet or Andrée Joly Brunet. Born Sept 16, 1901, in Paris, France; died in 1993; m. Pierre Brunet, c. 1926; children: Jean-Pierre Brunet (skater). ❖ With Pierre Brunet, won a bronze medal at Chamonix Olympics (1924); with husband, was the 1st to take consecutive gold medals in 2 Olympics for pairs, the 1st in St. Moritz (1928), the 2nd under married name of Madame Brunet in Lake Placid (1932); also won 4 World championships (1926, 1928, 1930, 1932).

JONAS, Maryla (1911–1959). Polish pianist. Born in Warsaw, Poland, May 31, 1911; died in New York, NY, July 3, 1959; studied with Paderewski, Sauer and Turczynski. ❖ A prodigy, made official debut (1926); had a successful virtuoso career until WWII, when she fled Poland for South America; came to US, where she made NY debut (1946); was one of the 1st pianists to record on LP (long-playing records); career was prematurely terminated by a long illness.

JONAS, Regina (1902–1944). German-Jewish rabbi. Born Regina Jonas in Berlin, Germany, Aug 3, 1902; murdered in Auschwitz, Dec 12, 1944; dau. of Wolf Jonas and Sara (Hess) Jonas; was a rabbinical student at Berlin's Hochschule für die Wissenschaft des Judentums (Academy for the Science of Judaism), a seminary for the training of liberal rabbis and educators. ❖ The 1st woman rabbi in the history of Judaism, who played a key role in maintaining morale at the Theresienstadt-Terezin concentration camp, was controversially ordained (1935); never presiding officially over a congregation, temporarily replaced rabbis in Frankfurt, Bremen and Stolp; lectured at 3 of Berlin's synagogues; was conscripted as a slave laborer by the Nazis (1942); spent next 2 years in Theresienstadt-Terezin near Prague (1942–44); working with Victor Frankl's organization, met new arrivals to the camp to soften the 1st shock for trusting Jews; was transferred to Auschwitz (1944) and murdered there, at age 42. ❖ See also *Women in World History*.

JONE. *Variant of Jane or Joan.*

JONES, Amanda Theodosia (1835–1914). American author and inventor. Born Oct 19, 1835, in East Bloomfield, NY; died of influenza, Mar 31, 1914, in Brooklyn, NY (some sources cite Junction City, Kansas); dau. of Henry Jones (master weaver) and Mary Alma (Mott) Jones; attended East Aurora Academy in NY. ❖ Published works, including *Ulah, and Other Poems* (1861), *Poems* (1867), *A Prairie Idyl* (1882), *Flowers and a Weed* (1899), and *A Psychic Autobiography* (1910); edited periodicals; converted to spiritualism and regarded herself as a medium; held patents for food-preserving process and liquid fuel burner for furnaces and boilers; organized Woman's Canning and Preserving Company to make use of her canning process (1890).

JONES, Anissa (1958–1976). American actress. Born Mary Anissa Jones, Mar 11, 1958, in West Lafayette, Indiana; died Aug 29, 1976, in Oceanside, CA, from overdose of barbiturates. ❖ Played Buffy in tv series "Family Affair"; also appeared in Elvis Presley film *The Trouble with Girls.*

JONES, Ann Haydon (1938—). English tennis player. Name variations: Ann Haydon, Ann Jones-Haydon, and Ann Haydon-Jones; Mrs. P.F. Jones. Born Ann Adrianne Shirley Haydon, Oct 7, 1938, in Birmingham, England; dau. of prominent table tennis players; m. Phillip Jones, 1962 (died 1993). ❖ Took up ping-pong, reaching finals in World Table Tennis championships (1954, 1959); developed into powerful lawn tennis player, twice winning British junior championships (1954, 1955); won 1st title at French Open (1961) and made finals at US

Open (1961), losing to Darlene Hard; won 2nd French Open (1962); was 9-time semifinalist at Wimbledon; as a Wimbledon finalist, lost to Billie Jean King (1967), then beat King (1969), the 1st left-handed woman to win Wimbledon singles title; also won Wimbledon mixed doubles with Fred Stolle (1969) and was voted BBC Sports Personality of the Year; joined King, Françoise Durr and Rosie Casals as 1st professional female touring group (1968); became BBC tennis commentator (1975) and director of Women's Tennis, Lawn Tennis Association (1990). Inducted into International Tennis Hall of Fame (1985). ❖ See also Ann Jones, *Game to Love* (Stanley Paul, 1971).

JONES, Barbara (1937—). African-American track-and-field athlete. Born Barbara Pearl Jones, Mar 26, 1937, in Chicago, IL; m. Marcellus Slater. ❖ Over 8-year career, won 335 medals and 56 trophies; was national AAU indoor champion in 100-yard dash (1954–55) and national AAU outdoor champion in 100 meters (1953–54); won gold medals in Olympics in 4 x 100 meters (1952 and 1960); was a member of Tennessee Tigerbelles. ❖ See also *Women in World History*.

JONES, Beatrix (1872–1959). *See Farrand, Beatrix Jones.*

JONES, Brenda (1936—). Australian runner. Born Nov 17, 1936, in Australia. ❖ At Rome Olympics, won a silver medal in the 800 meters (1960).

JONES, Caroline R. (1942–2001). African-American advertising executive. Born Caroline Robinson, Feb 15, 1942, in Benton Harbor, Michigan; died of cancer, June 28, 2001, in the Bronx, NY; University of Michigan, BS; children: Anthony R. Jones. ❖ One of the most prominent black women among ad agency executives, founded or helped found several agencies that specialized in advertising aimed at blacks or minorities; began career at J. Walter Thompson (1963), where she became creative director; helped form Zebra Associates (1968), then Black Creative Group and Mingo-Jones Advertising, where she was executive vice president and creative director; opened her own agency, Caroline Jones Inc. (1986); was moderator and host of radio and tv programs.

JONES, Carolyn (1929–1983). American actress. Born April 28, 1929, in Amarillo, TX; died Aug 3, 1983, in Los Angeles, CA; studied at Pasadena Playhouse; m. Aaron Spelling (tv producer), 1953 (div. 1964). ❖ Worked as a radio disk jockey; appeared in many films, including *House of Wax, The Big Heat, Shield for Murder, Desiree, The Seven Year Itch, The Tender Trap, Invasion of the Body Snatchers, The Opposite Sex, Marjorie Morningstar, A Hole in the Head, Career, Ice Palace, How the West Was Won* and *A Ticklish Affair*; on tv, portrayed Morticia on "The Addams Family" (1964–66). Nominated for Oscar for Best Supporting role in *The Bachelor Party* (1957).

JONES, Carolyn (1969—). American basketball player. Born July 28, 1969, in Soso, Mississippi; attended Auburn University. ❖ Guard, twice named SEC Player of the Year; played for gold-winning US teams at World championships (1990) and World University Games (1991); at Barcelona Olympics, won a bronze medal in team competition (1992).

JONES, Dawn (1960—). *See Coe, Dawn.*

JONES, E.E. Constance (1848–1922). *See Constance Jones, E.E.*

JONES, Elizabeth (c. 1935—). American sculptor-engraver. Born c. 1935 in Montclair, NJ; Vassar College, BA; attended Art Students League; also earned a diploma at Scuola dell'Arte dolla Medaglia in Rome, 1964. ❖ Spent 2 decades in Rome and designed gold medal in honor of Pope John Paul II for Italian government (1979); became chief sculptor-engraver of US Mint (1981), the 1st woman; designed George Washington commemorative half dollar (1982), presidential medal for President Ronald Reagan, and Olympic silver dollar (1983); designed figure of Greek goddess Nike for obverse of Olympic 5-dollar gold piece, the half eagle (1988).

JONES, Elizabeth Marina (1926—). Welsh murderer. Name variations: (stage name) Georgina Grayson. Born 1926 in Wales. ❖ At 18, worked as striptease artist in London and wanted to do "something exciting"; with Karl Hulten, an American GI, got into cab of cleft-chinned driver, George Edward Heath (Oct 7, 1944), whom Hulten shot in the back; at Old Bailey, found guilty and sentenced to death (Jan 1945); though Hulten was hanged for the crime (Mar 8, 1945), was reprieved; released at age 27 (Jan 1954). Known as the Cleft Chin murder, the case caused a national furor. ❖ See also film *Chicago Joe and the Showgirl* (1990), starring Emily Lloyd.

JONES, Esther (1969—). *American runner.* Born April 7, 1969; attended Louisiana State University; sister of Mark Jones, basketball player. ❖ At Barcelona Olympics, won a gold medal in 4 x 100-meter relay (1992).

JONES, Etta (1928–2001). *African-American jazz and pop singer.* Born Nov 25, 1928, in Aiken, South Carolina; died of cancer, Oct 16, 2001, in New York, NY. ❖ Often confused with Etta James, sang jazz and pop and was a frequent partner of saxist Houston Person (1970s–80s); began career singing with Buddy Johnson band; earned gold record for "Don't Go to Strangers" (1960) and Grammy nomination for "Save Your Love for Me" (1981); albums include *Something Nice* (1960), *Fine and Mellow* (1987), *Sugar* (1989) and *My Buddy–Etta Jones Sings the Songs of Buddy Johnson* (1999). Received Lifetime Achievement Award from International Women in Jazz Foundation. ❖ See also *Women in World History.*

JONES, Grace (1952—). *Jamaican performer.* Born May 19, 1952, in Spanishtown, Jamaica; dau. of a Jamaican cleric; m. Atila Altaunbay, 1996. ❖ Disco diva, moved with family to Syracuse, NY (1964); joined Wilhelmina Modeling Agency (1970s) and became a success in Paris, appearing on *Vogue, Der Stern,* and *Elle*; landed record deal with Island (1977); was a cult favorite of NY gay clubs; recorded disco hits "I Need a Man," "La Vie en Rose" and "Do or Die" (late 1970s); moved into rock genre with album *Warm Leatherette* (1980); scored hits with "Pull Up to the Bumper" (1981), "Slave to the Rhythm" (1985), and "I'm Not Perfect (But I'm Perfect for You)" (1986); acted in films *A View to a Kill* (1985) and *Boomerang* (1992); scored dance hit comeback with single "Sex Drive" from album of same name (1993).

JONES, Gwyneth (1936—). *Welsh soprano.* Name variations: Dame Gwyneth Jones. Born Nov 7, 1936, in Pontnewynydd, Wales; studied with Ruth Parker at Royal College of Music at Accademia Chigiana in Siena, and with Maria Carpi in Geneva; m. Till Haberfeld. ❖ Best known for interpretations of Wagner and Strauss operatic heroines, made professional debut as mezzo-soprano in role of Annina in Strauss opera *Rosenkavalier* in Zurich (1962); performed 1st soprano role as Amelia in *Un Ballo in Maschera,* leading to engagement with Covent Garden to replace an ailing Leontyne Price in *Trovatore* (1964), which led to overnight fame; made frequent appearances at Bayreuth Festival after debut as Sieglinde (1966); debuted at Vienna State Opera (1966); gave highly acclaimed performances as Desdemona, Elisabetta de Valois, Aida, Lady Macbeth, Tosca, Butterfly and Santuzza in world's finest opera houses; established a precedent for sopranos to double as Elisabeth and Venus at Bayreuth (1972); made debut at Metropolitan Opera (1972); specialized in German opera and played nearly all leading Wagner solo roles; performed all 3 Wagner Brünnhildes at Bayreuth in the internationally televised *Ring* cycle (1976); elected president of British Wagner Society. Made Dame of British Empire (DBE, 1986); named Kammersangerin of both Vienna and Bavarian Operas. ❖ See also *Women in World History.*

JONES, Hazel (1896–1974). *English actress.* Born Oct 17, 1896, in Swarraton, Hants, England; died Nov 13, 1974, in New York, NY; m. Harold Dimock Lee, June 1927. ❖ Made London stage debut in *The Two Hunchbacks* (1910), followed by numerous plays, including *Pomander Walk, L'Aiglon, Nurse Benson, Green Pastures and Piccadilly, Too Many Cooks* and *Damaged Goods*; made Broadway debut in *Pygmalion* (1945); other NY plays include *The First Mrs. Frazer, Gayden, The Living Room, The Entertainer* and *Tea Party.*

JONES, Helen (1954—). *English politician and member of Parliament.* Born Helen Jones, Dec 24, 1954; m. Michael Vobe, 1988. ❖ Solicitor; contested Lancashire Central (1994) for European Parliament election; representing Labour, elected to House of Commons for Warrington North (1997, 2001, 2005).

JONES, Helen Loder (1883–1903). *See Elseeta.*

JONES, Jane Elizabeth (1813–1896). *American abolitionist and suffragist.* Born Jane Elizabeth Hitchcock, Mar 13, 1813, in Vernon, Oneida Co., NY; died Jan 13, 1896, in Vernon; dau. of Reuben Hitchcock and Electa (Spaulding) Hitchcock; m. Benjamin Smith Jones, Jan 13, 1846 (died 1862); children: 1 daughter. ❖ An eloquent, forceful speaker, part of 1st generation of militant American women activists, traveled New England and PA on speaking tour with abolitionist Abby Kelley Foster; co-edited with husband *Anti-Slavery Bugle* (1845–49); addressed 1st convention of women in Ohio (1850) and lectured on woman's rights throughout North; published children's tract *The Young Abolitionists* (1848); lectured profitably throughout country on health and hygiene

for women (1850–56); spoke at national woman's rights' conventions (1852, 1856, 1860); testified before joint committee of Ohio legislature.

JONES, Jennifer (1919—). *American actress.* Name variations: Jennifer Jones Simon. Born Phylis Lee Isley, Mar 2, 1919, in Tulsa, OK; only child of Philip (vaudeville performer) and Flora Mae (Suber) Isley; attended Northwestern University, 1936, and American Academy of Dramatic Arts; m. Robert Walker (actor), Jan 2, 1939 (div. 1945, died 1951); m. David O. Selznick (film producer), July 18, 1949 (died 1965); m. Norton Simon (billionaire industrialist and art collector), 1971 (died 1993); children: (1st m.) Michael and Robert; (2nd m.) Mary Jennifer Selznick (died 1976). ❖ A shy, dark-haired beauty, captured an Academy Award for 1st major movie *The Song of Bernadette* (1943), the story of Bernadette Soubirous (Bernadette of Lourdes); career flourished (1940s–50s), controlled largely by producer-husband David O. Selznick; starred in such films as *Since You Went Away* (1944), *Love Letters* (1945), *Cluny Brown* (1946), *Portrait of Jennie* (1949), *Madame Bovary* (1949), *Carrie* (1952), *Ruby Gentry* (1952), *Good Morning, Miss Dove* (1955), *The Barretts of Wimpole Street* (1957), *A Farewell to Arms* (1957) and *Tender Is the Night* (1962); donated $1 million to establish the Jennifer Jones Simon Foundation for Mental Health and Education and served as president of Norton Simon Museum in Pasadena. Nominated as Best Actress for *Duel in the Sun* (1946) and *Love Is a Many-Splendored Thing* (1955). ❖ See also Edward Z. Epstein, *Portrait of Jennifer: A Biography of Jennifer Jones* (Simon & Schuster, 1995); Beverly Linet, *Star-Crossed: The Story of Robert Walker and Jennifer Jones* (Putnam, 1986); and *Women in World History.*

JONES, Kimberly (1975—). *See Lil' Kim.*

JONES, Lady (1889–1981). *See Bagnold, Enid.*

JONES, Leisel (1985—). *Australian swimmer.* Born Aug 30, 1985, in Katherine, Northern Territory, Australia. ❖ Won silver medals for 100-meter breaststroke and 4 x 100-meter medley relay at Sydney Olympics (2000); at World championships, placed 1st for 4 x 100-meter medley relay (2001); won a bronze medal for 100-meter breaststroke, silver medal for 200-meter breaststroke, and gold medal for 4 x 100-meter medley relay at Athens Olympics (2004).

JONES, Linda (1944–1972). *African-American soul singer.* Born Jan 14, 1944, in Newark, NJ; died of diabetes, Mar 17, 1972, backstage at the Apollo. ❖ One of the most dramatic soul singers of all time, saw her recording of "Hypnotized" hit the charts (1967); in later recordings for Turbo, displayed the full range of her talent with such songs as "Let It Be Me" and "Your Precious Love"; collapsed during performance at NY's Apollo Theater (1972). Two albums were released posthumously: *Hypnotized* (1989) and *Your Precious Love* (1991). ❖ See also *Women in World History.*

JONES, Lois M. (1934–2000). *American geochemist.* Born Sept 6, 1934; died Mar 13, 2000, in Westerville, Ohio; Ohio State University, PhD, 1969. ❖ Served as geologist at Ohio State University; led 1st all-women expedition to Antarctica (1969), where research topics included salty lakes fed by freshwater glaciers; opened the door for other women to conduct research in Antarctica.

JONES, Loïs Mailou (1905–1998). *African-American artist and educator.* Name variations: Lois Mailou Jones; Madame Vergniaud Pierre-Noël. Born Nov 3, 1905, in Boston, MA; died June 9, 1998, in Washington, DC; dau. of Thomas Vreeland Jones (lawyer) and Carolyn Dorinda (Adams) Jones (hat designer); attended Boston Normal Art School (now Massachusetts College of Art), 1926; graduate of School of the Museum of Fine Arts, Boston, 1927; attended Designers Art School, Boston, 1927–28; Howard University, AB in art education (magna cum laude), 1945; m. Louis Vergniaud Pierre-Noël (graphic artist), Aug 8, 1954 (died 1982). ❖ Acknowledged by the art world as one of America's premier painters just 2 years before her death at 90, combined painting with a long and distinguished teaching career; began as a designer; taught at Howard University (1930–77), where many of her students would go on to notable careers; received earliest recognition winning honorable mention for charcoal drawing *Negro Youth* (1929); other paintings of this period include *Mememsha by the Sea* (1930), *Portrait of Hudson* (1932) and *Brown Boy* (1935), reflecting the renewed interest in African subjects that sparked the Harlem Renaissance; exhibited breakthrough painting *The Ascent of Ethiopia* with Harmon Foundation (1933); studied at Académie Julian in Paris (1937), where she moved from realism to impressionist landscapes, to Cézannesque portraits and still lifes; won Robert Woods Bliss Prize for *Indian Shops, Gay Head, Massachusetts* (1940) which had been submitted to the Corcoran Gallery of Art by a white friend, since many galleries and museums were then closed to blacks; created numerous character studies of blacks, including *The Janitor* (1939), *Jennie* (1943), and the powerful *Mob Victim* (1944); inspired by Haiti, abandoned the restrained palette for a more aggressive, colorful style in such works as *Cockfight* (1960), *Street Vendors, Haiti* (1978) and *Haiti Demain?* (1987); from 1937 on, exhibited in over 50 shows, including a retrospective at Howard University (1972) and an exhibition at Washington's Corcoran (1995). ❖ See also Tritobia Hayes Benjamin, *The Life and Art of Loïs Mailou Jones* (Pomegranate, 1994); and *Women in World History.*

JONES, Lynne (1951—). English politician. Born Lynne Stockton, April 26, 1951. ❖ Representing Labour, elected to House of Commons for Birmingham Selly Oak (1992, 1997, 2001, 2005).

JONES, Marcia (1941—). American kayaker. Born July 18, 1941, in US. ❖ At Tokyo Olympics, won a bronze medal in K1 500 meters (1964).

JONES, Margo (1911–1955). American theatrical producer and director. Born Margaret Virginia Jones, Dec 12, 1911, in Livingston, Texas; died in Dallas, Texas, July 24, 1955; dau. of Richard Harper (lawyer) and Martha Pearl (Collins) Jones; Texas State College for Women in Denton, BA in speech, 1932, MS in philosophy and education, 1933; never married; no children. ❖ Director and producer who founded one of the nation's earliest professional regional theaters, Theater '47, in Dallas, helping to spawn the nationwide movement that revolutionized theater and cultural life in America; worked as assistant director of Houston Federal Theater Project (1935); founded Houston Community Players (1936); served as faculty member in drama department of University of Texas at Austin (1942–43); founded Theater '47 in Dallas (1947); wrote *Theater-in-the-Round* (1951); directed over 50 plays, including several of Tennessee Williams' early plays, *You Touched Me* (1943), *The Purification* (1944), and the Broadway premieres of *The Glass Menagerie* (1945, co-director) and *Summer and Smoke* (1948); also directed dozens of world premieres, such as *Farther off from Heaven* (1947), *The Coast of Illyria* (1949), and *Inherit the Wind* (1955). The Margo Jones Award was established by playwrights Jerome Lawrence and Robert E. Lee (1961) to recognize those who demonstrate commitment to production of new plays. ❖ See also Helen Sheehy, *Margo: The Life and Theatre of Margo Jones* (Southern Methodist U. Press, 1989); and *Women in World History.*

JONES, Marilyn (1940—). Australian ballet dancer. Born Feb 14, 1940, in Newcastle, New South Wales, Australia. ❖ Trained in London with Royal Ballet School, then briefly danced with Royal Ballet (1957–58); danced with Borovansky Ballet (c. 1959–61); began performing with Australian Ballet (1971), with featured parts in Cranko's *Romeo and Juliet,* Ashton's *The Dream* and *La Fille Mal Gardée,* Nureyev's *Raymonda,* and others; served as artistic director of Australian Ballet.

JONES, Marion (1879–1965). American tennis player. Born Nov 2, 1879; died Mar 14, 1965. ❖ At Paris Olympics, won a bronze medal in singles and a bronze medal in mixed doubles–outdoors (1900).

JONES, Marion (1975—). African-American runner. Born Oct 12, 1975, in Los Angeles, CA; dau. of George and Marion Jones Toler (born in Belize); attended University of North Carolina; m. C.J. Hunter (shot-putter), 1998 (div. 2001); children: (with Tim Montgomery, sprinter) Tim, Jr. (b. 2003). ❖ Began NCAA career as a starting point guard at U. of North Carolina, on a team that won the NCAA women's championship (1994); turned to track and won the 100 meters at US nationals (1997); at World championships, won gold in the 100 meters (1997, 1999) and 200 meters and 4 x 100 meters (2001); won gold medals for the 100 meters, 200 meters, and 4 x 400-meter relay and a bronze medal for the long jump and 4 x 100-meter relay at Sydney Olympics (2000), becoming the 1st woman to win 5 medals in athletics in the same Olympics; competed in Athens Olympics (2004) and finished 5th in the long jump.

JONES, Marion Patrick (1934—). Trinidadian novelist. Born 1934 in Trinidad; educated at St. Joseph's convent in Port of Spain, Trinidad and then obtained scholarship to Imperial College of Agriculture. ❖ Did postgraduate work in London (1959), founding Campaign Against Racial Discrimination; wrote 2 well-known novels, *Pan Beat* (1973) and *J'Ouvert Morning* (1976), both of which deal with middle-class family life in Trinidad's capital city, Port of Spain.

JONES, Mary (1700–1740). See Diver, Jenny.

JONES, Mary Dixon (1828–1908). See Dixon Jones, Mary Amanda.

JONES, Mary Harris (1830–1930). American labor leader. Name variations: Mother Jones. Born Mary Harris, May 1, 1830 in Co. Cork, Ireland; died in Silver Spring, MD, Nov 30, 1930; dau. of Richard and Mary Harris; attended public school in Toronto and 1 year of normal school; m. George Jones (molder), 1861; children: 4. ❖ Organizer for the Knights of Labor and United Mine Workers of America who struggled to obtain better working and living conditions for workers and their families; immigrated to Toronto (1841); became private tutor in Maine (1855); taught at St. Mary's Convent, Monroe, MI (1859); moved to Memphis, TN (1860); lost husband and children to yellow fever epidemic (1867); moved to Chicago and became 1st woman organizer for Knights of Labor (1871); was field organizer for United Mine Workers of America (1900); led march of mill children (1903); helped found Industrial Workers of the World (1905); was sentenced to 20 years in prison by a military court in WV and served 3 months in solitary confinement before she was released (1912); participated in strikes nationwide (1877–1923), including the Baltimore and Ohio strike of railroad workers in Pittsburgh (1877), Pullman railroad strike in Birmingham, Albama (1894), Pennsylvania anthracite coal miners' strike (1902), Ludlow strike in Colorado (1913), and nationwide steel strike (1919); was often imprisoned or escorted out of town. ❖ See also Dale Fetherling, *Mother Jones: The Miners' Angel* (Southern Illinois University, 1974); Mary F. Parton, ed. *The Autobiography of Mother Jones* (Kerr, 1925); Philip S. Foner, ed. *Mother Jones Speaks* (Monad, 1983); and *Women in World History.*

JONES, Mary Katharine (1864–1950). See Bennett, Mary Katharine.

JONES, Matilda (1868–1933). See Jones, Sissieretta.

JONES, Maxine (1966—). American singer. Name variations: En Vogue; Vogue. Born Jan 16, 1966, in Paterson, NJ. ❖ Member of En Vogue, R&B girl group known for 4-part harmonies, which enjoyed great R&B and pop success (1990s). En Vogue hits include "Hold On" (1990), "My Lovin' (You're Never Gonna Get It)" (1992), "Free Your Mind" (1992), "Don't Let Go (Love)" (1996), "Whatever" (1997) and "Too Gone, Too Long" (1997); albums include *Born to Sing* (1990), *Remix to Sing* (1991), *Funky Divas* (1992, multiplatinum), *Runaway Love* (1993), *EV3* (1997) and *Best of En Vogue* (1999).

JONES, Michellie (1969—). Australian triathlete. Born Sept 6, 1969, in Fairfield, Australia; graduate of Wollondong University, 1990. ❖ Won World championship (1992, 1993, 1997); won silver medal at Sydney Olympics (2000). Named Triathlete of the Year (1992, 1993, 1998, 1999, 2000).

JONES, Mother (1830–1930). See Jones, Mary Harris.

JONES, Mrs. P.F. (1938—). See Jones, Ann Haydon.

JONES, Patricia (1930—). Canadian runner. Born Oct 16, 1930, in Canada. ❖ At London Olympics, won a bronze medal in 4 x 100-meter relay (1948).

JONES, Priscilla Coolidge-. See Coolidge, Priscilla.

JONES, Rebecca (1739–1818). American Quaker minister. Born July 8, 1739, in Philadelphia, PA; died April 15, 1818, in Philadelphia; dau. of William Jones (sailor) and Mary Jones (teacher). ❖ Widely known woman minister in Society of Friends in America, began speaking at Friends worship meetings (1758); combined ministry and teaching in mother's school for girls; traveled throughout British Isles to minister and speak to 1,578 worship meetings and 1,120 Friends meetings for servants, apprentices, and laborers (1784–88); upon returning to US, continued to preach, correspond, and perform local charity.

JONES, Rosamund (1913–1998). See John, Rosamund.

JONES, Shirley (1934—). American actress and singer. Born Mar 31, 1934, in Smithton, PA; only child of Paul Jones (brewery owner) and Marjorie (Williams) Jones; studied drama at Pittsburgh Playhouse; m. Jack Cassidy (singer), Aug 5, 1956 (div.); m. Marty Ingels (comedian and actor-agent), 1978 (sep. 1995); children: Shaun Paul Cassidy (singer); stepson David Cassidy (actor-singer). ❖ Made NY debut in chorus of *South Pacific*; cast in a small role in *Me and Juliet,* won starring role when show went on tour; rose to prominence in film versions of musicals *Oklahoma!* (1955) and *Carousel* (1956); also appeared as Marion, small-town librarian, in *The Music Man* (1962); starred on ABC-TV as matriarch of "The Partridge Family" (Sept 25, 1970–Aug 31, 1974); had short run in another tv series, "Shirley" and running role as Kitty Noland in comedy series "The 'Slap' Maxwell Story"; other films include *April*

Love (1957), *Never Steal Anything Small* (1959), *The Courtship of Eddie's Father* (1963), *The Cheyenne Social Club* (1970) and *Beyond the Poseidon Adventure* (1979). Won Academy Award for Best Supporting Actress for performance in *Elmer Gantry* (1960) and Emmy nomination for tv movie *Silent Night, Lonely Night* (1969). ❖ See also *Women in World History.*

JONES, Sissieretta (1869–1933). African-American soprano. Name variations: Matilda Jones; Matilda Joyner. Born Matilda Sissieretta Joyner in Portsmouth, Virginia, Jan 5, 1869; died in Providence, RI, June 24, 1933; studied voice at Providence Academy of Music and New England Conservatory, Boston, MA; m. David Richard Jones (newsdealer and bellman), 1883 (div. 1898). ❖ Made NY debut (1888), followed by 6-month tour of West Indies as a featured performer with Jubilee Singers of Fisk University; toured Europe, sang at White House, gave a command performance for Prince of Wales, and appeared at "Grand African Jubilee" in Madison Square Garden (1888–98); generally performed a program combining operatic arias with popular songs like "Old Folks at Home" and "The Last Rose of Summer," though, as time went on, audiences began to push her toward a more ethnic repertoire; formulated a troupe of jugglers, comedians, dancers, and singers called the Black Patti Troubadours (1896) which enjoyed great success, playing primarily to white audiences in major cities across nation; disbanded troupe (1906). ❖ See also *Women in World History.*

JONES, Steffi (1972—). German soccer player. Born Stephanie Jones, Dec 22, 1972, in Frankfurt am Main, Germany; dau. of an American father and German mother; has dual citizenship. ❖ Won a team bronze medal at Sydney Olympics (2000) and Athens Olympics (2004); with FFC Frankfurt, won German championship (2001); signed with WUSA's Washington Freedom (2002); won FIFA World Cup (2003).

JONES, Susan (1952—). American ballet dancer. Born June 22, 1952, in York, PA; trained at Washington School of Ballet in Washington, DC. ❖ Danced on apprenticeship with City Center Joffrey Ballet; performed with American Ballet Theater in wide range of repertory, including de Mille's *Fall River Legend,* Loring's *Billy the Kid* and works by George Balanchine.

JONES, Sybil (1808–1873). American preacher and missionary. Born Feb 28, 1808, in Brunswick, Maine (then part of Massachusetts); died Dec 4, 1873, in Dirigo, Maine; dau. of Ephraim Jones (farmer) and Susanna (Dudley) Jones (both Quakers); m. 2nd cousin Eli Jones (Quaker preacher), June 1833; children: James Parnell (b. 1835), Sybil Narcissa (b. 1839), Richard Mott (b. 1843), Susan Tabor (b. 1847), and Eli Grellet (b. 1850). ❖ Soon after marriage, became a Quaker minister; with husband, traveled widely on preaching and visiting tours in US and abroad; visited military hospitals during Civil War; helped found Friends Girls School in Ramallah, Palestine.

JONG, Erica (1942—). American novelist and poet. Born Mar 26, 1942, in New York, NY; dau. of Seymour (importer) and Eda (Mirsky) Mann (painter and designer); Barnard College, BA, 1963; Columbia University, MA, 1965; m. Michael Werthman (div.); m. Allan Jong (child psychiatrist), 1966 (div. 1975); m. Jonathan Fast (writer), 1977 (div. 1983); m. Ken Burrows (lawyer), 1989; children: (3rd m.) Molly Jong-Fast. ❖ Came to prominence with the bestselling *Fear of Flying* (1973), a "hymn to one woman's sexual liberation" wrote the *New York Times;* writings include *Fruits and Vegetables* (1971), *Loveroot* (1975), *How to Save Your Own Life* (1977), *At the Edge of the Body* (1979), *Fanny* (1980), *Ordinary Miracles* (1983), *Serenissima* (1989), *Any Woman's Blues* (1990) and *Sappho's Leap* (2003). ❖ See also memoir, *Fear of Fifty.*

JONKER, Ingrid (1933–1965). Afrikaaner poet. Born Sept 19, 1933, in Douglas Cape Province, South Africa; drowned herself in ocean at Green Point, Cape Town, July 19, 1965; dau. of Abraham Jonker (writer and editor) and Beatrice (Cilliers) Jonker; m. Pieter also seen as Peter Venter; children: Simone Venter (b. 1957). ❖ Afrikaaner whose poetry mirrored the horror of apartheid, published 1st collection, *Ontvlugting* (1956); wrote "Die Kind wat doodgeskiet is deuv soldate by Nyanga" (The Child Who Was Shot Dead by Soldiers in Nyanga) which appeared in her 2nd collection *Rook en Oker,* for which she won South Africa's largest literary prize (1963); poems have also been translated into 12 other languages including Zulu and Hindi; traveled through Europe. Her last collection, *Kantelson,* was published from manuscripts after her death, a death regarded by many as a protest against the immorality of the South African government during apartheid; when Nelson Mandela gave his 1st State of the Nation address, he invoked her memory. ❖ See also *Women in World History.*

JONROWE, DeeDee (1953—). American musher. Born Dec 20, 1953, in Frankfurt, Germany, while American soldier father was stationed there; attended school in Ethiopia, Okinawa, Virginia, then Anchorage; m. Mike Jonrowe, 1977. ❖ Worked in predominately Eskimo community of Bethel, Alaska, while employed by Alaska Department of Fish and Game; entered 1st Iditarod (1980); became only musher to compete in both Alpirod and Iditarod for 3 years straight (1992, 1993, 1994); finishes include 2nd at Iditarod (1993 and 1998); wrote *Iditarod Dreams* (with Lew Freedman, 1995).

JÖNS, Karin (1953—). *See Joens, Karin.*

JONSSON, Magdalena (1969—). Swedish skier. Born Sept 26, 1969, in Stockholm, Sweden; married; children: 2. ❖ Won silver in Skier X at X Games (Winter 2001 and 2002); place 1st at US Nationals, Snowbird, UT, in Skiercross (2002), Swiss Army Skiercross, Crested Butte, CO (2002), Saab Crossmax, International Series, Are, Sweden, in Skiercross (2002), and FIS World Cup, Tignes, France, in Skiercross (2002).

JÖNSSON, Sara (1880–1974). *See Sandel, Cora.*

JOO MIN-JIN (1983—). Korean short-track speedskater. Born Aug 1, 1983, in South Korea. ❖ Won a gold medal for the 3,000-meter relay at Salt Lake City Olympics (2002).

JOPLIN, Janis (1943–1970). American rock and blues singer. Name variations: (nickname) Pearl. Born Janis Lyn Joplin, Jan 19, 1943, in Port Arthur, TX; overdosed and died at Landmark Hotel, Los Angeles, CA, Oct 4, 1970. ❖ Sang in coffee houses in San Francisco's Haight-Ashbury district (1963); joined Big Brother and the Holding Company (1966); recorded 1st album with Mainstream Records (1966); broke out at Monterey Pop Festival (1967); signed with Columbia Records and recorded *Cheap Thrills* (1968) which reached #1; left Big Brother and formed Kozmic Blues band (1968); toured Europe (1969); appeared at Woodstock (1969); formed the Full Tilt Boogie Band (1970); died of an overdose of alcohol and heroin while recording *Pearl* (1970), which rose to top of Billboard Charts, while "Me and Bobby McGee" became #1 hit single and *Rolling Stone* declared Joplin the "premier white blues singer of the 1960s"; over course of career, wrote lyrics for such songs as "Intruder," "Turtle Blues," "Oh, Sweet Mary," "One Good Man," "Move Over," (with Sam Andrew) "I Need a Man to Love," (with Peter Albin) "Road Block," (with Nick Gravenites) "Ego Rock," (with Gabriel Mekler) "Kozmic Blues," and (with Michael McClure) "Mercedes Benz." ❖ See also Ellis Amburn, *Pearl* (Warner, 1992); David Dalton, *Piece of My Heart: The Life, Times and Legend of Janis Joplin* (St. Martin's, 1986); Myra Friedman, *Buried Alive: The Biography of Janis Joplin* (Morrow, 1973); Laura Joplin, *Love XX Janis* (Villard, 1992); Alice Echols, *Scars of Sweet Paradise* (1999); and *Women in World History.*

JORDAN, Barbara (1936–1996). African-American lawyer and congressional representative. Born Barbara Charline Jordan, Feb 21, 1936, in Houston, TX; died of pneumonia believed to be a complication of leukemia, Jan 17, 1996; dau. of Benjamin M. Jordan (Baptist minister) and Arlyne Jordan; graduated magna cum laude from Texas Southern University, 1956; Boston University, LL.B., 1959; admitted to bar in both TX and MA; never married; no children. ❖ Noted attorney and legal scholar, spellbinding orator, and 1st Southern African-American woman elected to US House of Representatives, completed law school in Boston, then practiced general civil law in Houston; became active in Democratic Party politics, and worked to turn out the black vote for Kennedy-Johnson presidential ticket (1960); ran for Texas House of Representatives unsuccessfully (1962, 1964); elected to Texas State Senate (1966), the 1st black woman in that body; after a successful career in Texas Senate, ran for US House of Representatives (1972), winning handily; pursued many domestic policies to aid the disadvantaged, and was an outspoken critic of increased military expenditures; served on House Judiciary Committee during impeachment hearings on Richard M. Nixon, during which she 1st came to national prominence for her skilled oratory and fine legal reasoning; was keynote speaker at 1976 Democratic National Convention, the 1st African-American woman so honored; retired from US House (1978), due in part to illness; pursued a distinguished career of public speaking and teaching at Lyndon B. Johnson School of Public Affairs, at University of Texas. Received Presidential Medal of Freedom (1994). ❖ See also autobiography (with Shelby Hearon) *Barbara Jordan: A Self-Portrait* (Doubleday, 1979); Ira B. Bryant, *Barbara Charline Jordan—From the Ghetto to the Capitol* (D. Armstrong, 1977); Mary Beth Rogers, *Barbara Jordan: American Hero* (Bantam, 1998); and *Women in World History.*

JORDAN, Dora (1761–1816). Irish-born actress and paramour. Name variations: Dorothea Bland; Dorothea Ford; Mrs. Jordan; Dorothy Jordan. Born Dorothea Bland near Waterford, Ireland, Nov 22, 1761; died possibly in St. Cloud, near Paris, July 3 (some sources cite Aug 5), 1816; dau. of Francis Bland (stagehand) and Grace Phillips (d. 1789, Welsh actress known as Mrs. Frances); never married; associated with Richard Daly; associated with Richard Ford (lawyer); associated with William IV (1765–1837), king of England (r. 1830–1837); children: (with Daly) Fanny Daly (1782–1821, who m. Thomas Alsop); (with Ford) Dorothea Maria Ford (b. 1787, later Mrs. Frederick March); son (1788–1788); Lucy Hester Ford (1789–1850, later Lady Hawker); (with William IV) 10, including George Fitzclarence (1794–1842), 1st earl of Munster; Sophia Fitzclarence (1795–1837, who would marry Philip Sidney, 1st baron d'Lisle and die in childbirth); Henry Fitzclarence (1797–1817); Mary Fitzclarence (1798–1864, who m. General Charles Richard Fox); Frederick Fitzclarence (1799–1854, a lieutenant general who m. Lady Augusta Boyle); Elizabeth Fitzclarence (1801–1856, who m. William George Hay, 18th earl of Erroll); Adolphus Fitzclarence (1802–1856); Augusta Fitzclarence (1803–1865, who m. John Erskine and Lord John Frederick Gordon); Augustus Fitzclarence (1805–1854, who m. Sarah Gordon), rector of Mapledurham, Oxfordshire; Amelia Fitzclarence (1807–1858, who m. Lucius Bentinck, 10th Viscount Falkland). ❖ At 15, made debut in Dublin as Phoebe in *As You Like It*; experienced various adventures as a provincial actress in Ireland, Leeds, and other Yorkshire towns; appeared at Drury Lane as Peggy in *The Country Girl* (1785) and quickly won great popularity, exhibiting talent in comedy and musical farce; for 25 years, was the favorite comedy actress of her time, 2nd only to Kitty Clive; became mistress of duke of Clarence, the future William IV, king of England (1790); during 20-year connection with him, gave birth to 10 children, all of whom took the name of Fitzclarence and were raised to rank of nobles; died in poverty. ❖ See also *Women in World History*.

JORDAN, Dorothy (1906–1988). American actress. Born Aug 9, 1906, in Clarksville, TN; died Dec 7, 1988, in Los Angeles, CA; m. Merian C. Cooper (film producer), 1933 (died 1973); children: 3. ❖ Appeared in several Broadway musicals, including stage debut in *Garrick Gaieties* (1926), before making film debut in *Black Magic* (1929), followed by *Words and Music, The Taming of the Shrew, In Gay Madrid, Min and Bill, Hell Divers, The Lost Squadron, Cabin in the Cotton, The Seachers* and *The Wings of Eagles*.

JORDAN, Elizabeth Garver (1865–1947). American editor and author. Born Mary Elizabeth Carver Jordan, May 9, 1865, in Milwaukee, Wisconsin; died Feb 24, 1947, in New York, NY; dau. of William Francis Jordan (real-estate broker), and Margaretta (Garver) Jordan; never married. ❖ Became a reporter for *New York World* (1890); a talented interviewer, launched a series of Sunday features, "True Stories of the News"; also worked as a reporter, covering events like the Lizzie Borden trial; published short stories as *Tales of the City Room* (1895); left the *World* (1900), where she had worked her way up to assistant Sunday editor, to become editor of *Harper's Bazaar*, a position she held for next 13 years; continued to write, producing a series of novels (including *May Iverson, Her Book*, the 1st of several featuring the popular heroine), short-story collections, and a play, *The Lady from Oklahoma*, which had a brief run on Broadway (1913); became a literary adviser for Harper & Brothers (1913), where she was instrumental in introducing works of Zona Gale, Eleanor Porter, Dorothy Canfield Fisher and Sinclair Lewis; was a script consultant for Goldwyn Pictures at its Fort Lee, NJ, studio (1918–19); after 1919, produced close to a novel a year for rest of life; also wrote theater column for Catholic weekly, *America* (1922–45). ❖ See also autobiography *Three Rousing Cheers* (1938); and *Women in World History*.

JORDAN, Ellen Violet (d. 1982). See Jordan, Vi.

JORDAN, Emily (1858–1936). See Folger, Emily.

JORDAN, June (1936–2002). African-American essayist and poet. Born July 9, 1936, in Harlem, NY; died June 14, 2002; dau. of Granville Jordan and Mildred Jordan; attended Barnard College and University of Chicago; m. Michael Meyer, 1955 (div. 1965); children: 1. ❖ Taught at Connecticut College, City University of New York, Sarah Lawrence College, State University of New York at Stony Brook, and University of California at Berkeley; author of poetry, plays, essays, short fiction, and novels, including *Who Look at Me* (1969), *His Own Where* (1971), *New Life: New Room* (1975), *Things I Do in the Dark: Selected Poetry* (1977), *Civil Wars* (1981), *Naming Our Destiny* (1989), *Technical Difficulties* (1992), *Haruko Love Poems* (1994), *I Was Looking at the Ceiling and Then I Saw the Sky* (1995), and *Soldier: A Poet's Childhood* (2001). Received Achievement Award for International Reporting from National Association of Black Journalists (1984).

JORDAN, Marian (1896–1961). Radio comedian. Born Marian Driscoll in Peoria, IL, Nov 15, 1896; died April 7, 1961; dau. of Daniel Driscoll and Anna (Carroll) Driscoll; graduate of Academy of Our Lady, Peoria; m. James Edward Jordan (entertainer); children: James Carroll Jordan; Kathryn Jordan. ❖ Co-starred with husband James Jordan on the popular radio series "Fibber McGee and Molly" (1935–1956). ❖ See also *Women in World History*.

JORDAN, Mary Raugust (1932–1998). See Howell, Mary.

JORDAN, Mrs. (1761–1816). See Jordan, Dora.

JORDAN, princess of (1941—). See Gardiner, Antoinette.

JORDAN, queen of.
See Noor al-Hussein (b. 1951).
See Rania (1970—).

JORDAN, Sara Murray (1884–1959). American physician. Born Sara Claudia Murray, Oct 20, 1884, in Newton, Massachusetts; died Nov 21, 1959, in Boston; dau. of Patrick Andrew Murray and Maria (Stuart) Murray; Radcliffe College, AB, 1905; University of Munich, PhD in archaeology and classical philology, 1908; Tufts University, MD, 1921; m. Sebastian Jordan (lawyer), Jan 14, 1913 (div. 1921); m. Penfield Mower (broker), Sept 26, 1935; children: (1st m.) Mary Jordan. ❖ Co-founded Lahey Clinic in Burlington, MA, then one of the few independent clinics in Boston area (1922); was a proponent of noninvasive treatment when dealing with gastrointestinal patients, advocating stress reduction, rest, and a regulated diet; was 1st woman elected to board of directors of Boston Chamber of Commerce; was also 1st woman president of American Gastroenterological Association (1942–44), and was secretary, vice chair, and chair of AMA Section on Gastroenterology (1941–48). ❖ See also *Women in World History*.

JORDAN, Sheila (1928—). American jazz singer. Born Sheila Jeanette Dawson, Nov 18, 1928, in Detroit, Michigan; studied with Lennie Tristano and Charles Mingus; m. Duke Jordan (African-American pianist), 1952 (div. 1962). ❖ In early teens, performed in Detroit clubs; greatly influenced by Charlie Parker, formed vocal trio, Skeeter, Mitch and Jean (taking stage name Jean), and sang versions of Parker's solos; moved to NY (1951), where she became increasingly involved with jazz scene; made 1st recordings (early 60s), gaining popularity for 10-minute version of *You Are My Sunshine* on album *Outer View* with George Russell, and also recording solo album *Portrait of Sheila* (1962); performed on recordings with pianist Steve Kuhn (becoming member of Kuhn's quartet), as well as on album *Home* (Robert Creeley's poems set to music); with bassist Harvie Swartz, recorded *Old Time Feeling* (1982); received critical acclaim for tribute to bebop roots, *Lost and Found* (1989). Recordings include *Songs from Within* (1993), *Hear Strings* (1994), *Jazz Child* (1999), *I've Grown Accustomed to the Bass* (2000) and *Little Song* (2003).

JORDAN, Vi (d. 1982). Australian politician. Name variations: Ellen Violet Jordan. Born June 29, in Ipswich, Queensland, Australia; died May 7, 1982; m. David Jordan, 1932. ❖ Joined Australian Labor Party (ALP, 1946); served as 1st female alderman, Ipswich City Council (1961–67); was a member of the Queensland Parliament for Ipswich West (1966–74); was president of the ALP Women's Executive (1974–76). Awarded Queens Jubilee Medal.

JORDAN LLOYD, Dorothy (1889–1946). See Lloyd, Dorothy Jordan.

JORDI, Rosa de Sant (b. 1910). See Arquimbau, Rosa Maria.

JORGE, Carmen Acedo (1975—). See Acedo, Carmen.

JORGE PÁDUA, Maria Tereza (1943—). Brazilian ecologist. Name variations: Maria Tereza Jorge Padua. Born in São José do Rio Pardo, Brazil, May 8, 1943. ❖ Became a director of Brazil's national park system (1970), assisting in establishment of nearly 20-million acres of parks and reserves in Amazonia; her work to protect the wilderness provoked death threats from those wishing to exploit the environment; in 1986, founded Fundação Pró-Natureza (Foundation for the Protection of Nature) which seeks to expand protected areas while exploring environmentally sound options to develop Brazil's resources.

JORGENSEN, Janel (1971—). American swimmer. Born May 18, 1971, in Ridgefield, CT; attended Stanford University. ❖ At Seoul Olympics, won a silver medal in 4 x 100-meter medley relay (1988).

JORGENSEN, Karin Riis (1952—). See Riis-Jorgensen, Karin.

JORGENSEN, Rikke Horlykke (1976—). Danish handball player. Name variations: Rikke Hoerlykke Joergensen or Rikke Hørlykke Jørgensen. Born May 2, 1976, in Denmark. ❖ Pivot, won a team gold medal at Athens Olympics (2004).

JORGENSEN, Silje (1977—). Norwegian soccer player. Name variations: Silje Jørgensen or Joergensen. Born May 5, 1977, in Norway. ❖ Won a team gold medal at Sydney Olympics (2000).

JOSABA. See Jehosheba.

JOSEFA. Variant of Josepha.

JOSEFA DE AYALA (1630–1684). See de Ayala, Josefa.

JOSEFINE. Variant of Josephine.

JOSEPH, Helen (1905–1992). Anti-apartheid campaigner. Born Helen Beatrice May Fennell in Sussex, England, 1905; died in Johannesburg, South Africa, Dec 25, 1992; King's College of University of London, BA, 1928; University of London, Diploma of Theology, 1975; m. Billie Joseph, 1931 (div. 1948); no children. ❖ Officer of the Federation of South African Women and of the Congress of Democrats, who survived many years of banning and house arrest; in early career, taught at Mahbubia School for Indian girls in Hyderabad (1928–30); moved to South Africa (1931); was a welfare and information officer with South African Air Force (1939–45); supervised National War Memorial Fund community centers for "Coloureds" in Western Cape (late 1940s); became secretary of Medical Aid Fund of Garment Workers' Union in Johannesburg (1951); elected honorary secretary of Transvaal branch of Federation of South African Women (early 1950s); elected to national executive committee of Congress of Democrats, the white branch of the ANC-led anti-apartheid organization called Congress Alliance (1953); helped organize Congress of the People, where the now famous Freedom Charter was read (1955); was a leader of women's march on Union Buildings, Pretoria (Aug 9, 1956); charged with high treason (Dec 1956); banned for 5 years (April 1957); put under house arrest for 5 years (1962); wrote 2nd book, *Tomorrow's Sun*, about the hundreds of black activists who had been banished to remote parts of the country (1966); put under house arrest for another 5 years (1967); made national tour of English-speaking white universities of South Africa as honorary national vice-president of National Union of South African Students (NUSAS, 1972); renounced British nationality (1973); jailed for 4 months for refusing to answer questions which might implicate Winnie Mandela (1977); banned for 2 years (June 1980). ❖ See also memoirs *If This Be Treason* (1963) and *Side by Side* (Zed, 1986); and *Women in World History*.

JOSEPH, Jenefer (1932—). British poet. Name variations: Jenny Joseph. Born Jenefer Ruth Joseph, May 7, 1932, in Birmingham, England; dau. of Louis Joseph and Florence Joseph; m. Tony Coles, 1961. ❖ Worked as journalist after graduating from Oxford (1953) and spent time in South Africa reporting for Drum Publications; collections of poetry include *The Four Elements* (1950), *The Unlooked-For Season* (1960), *Nursery Series* (1966–68), *Rose in the Afternoon* (1974), *Persephone* (1984), *The In-Land Sea* (1989), *Warning* (1990), *Upside Down* (1991), *Ghosts and Other Company* (1995), and *Extended Similes* (1997). Won Cholmondeley Award for *Rose in the Afternoon* and James Tait Black memorial Prize for *Persephone*.

JOSEPH, Mother (1823–1902). Canadian-born American nun and architect. Born Esther Pariseau in Montréal, Québec, Canada, 1823; died 1902. ❖ Referred to by American Institute of Architects as "the Pacific Northwest's 1st architect," was one of 4 Providence Sisters who journeyed from Montréal to Washington Territory (1856); over next 46 years, designed and built hospitals and schools across region, from Oregon to Alaska, using carpentry skills learned from father; her institutions were available to all faiths and were financed by funds she raised in "begging tours" through Army posts and mining camps that dotted the area. Honored with a statue in Capitol's National Statuary Hall in Washington, DC (1977).

JOSEPH, Mother Mary (1882–1955). See Rogers, Mother Mary Joseph.

JOSEPH, Sister (1956–1939). See Dempsey, Sister Mary Joseph.

JOSEPHA. Variant of Josephine.

JOSEPHA OF BAVARIA (1739–1767). See Maria Josepha of Bavaria.

JOSEPHE OR JOSEPHÉ. Variant of Josephine.

JOSEPHINE. Variant of Josepha or Josephé.

JOSEPHINE (1763–1814). French empress. Name variations: Joséphine Beauharnais; Josephine de Beauharnais; Vicomtesse de Beauharnais; called Yeyette, Marie-Rose, or Rose by her family. Born Marie-Josèphe-Rose Tascher de la Pagerie on family's sugar plantation on Martinique, June 23, 1763; died at home at château of Malmaison outside Paris, May 29, 1814, of diphtheria; dau. of Joseph-Gaspard Tascher de la Pagerie and Rose-Claire des Vergers de Sannois Tascher de la Pagerie; attended convent school in Fort-Royal on Martinique, 1773–77; m. Alexandre-François-Marie, vicomte de Beauharnais, 1779; m. Napoleon Bonaparte (1769–1821), emperor of France (r. 1804–1815), in 1796; children: (1st m.) Eugène-Rose de Beauharnais (b. 1781, who m. Amalie Auguste [1788–1851]); Hortense de Beauharnais (1783–1837). ❖ Was the great love of Napoleon's life during the era in which he dominated European history; years before, sailed to France for an arranged marriage with vicomte de Beauharnais (1779); left husband and took up residence in convent (1783); legally separated from husband (1785); returned permanently to France after final visit to Martinique (1790); arrested, then released during the Terror, became mistress to French revolutionary leader, Paul Barras (1794); married the rising young general Napoleon Bonaparte and started love affair with Captain Hippolyte Charles (1796); became empress when Napoleon became emperor (1804); unable to provide the child he required for political purposes, was divorced by Napoleon who then married Princess Marie Louise of Austria (1810); remained a respected figure among the French population. ❖ See also Theo Aronson, *Napoleon and Josephine: A Love Story* (Murray, 1990); Evangeline Bruce, *Napoleon and Josephine: An Improbable Marriage* (Scribner, 1995); Ernest John Knapton, *Empress Josephine* (Harvard U., 1963); Hubert Cole, *Joséphine* (Viking, 1962); and *Women in World History*.

JOSÉPHINE (1807–1876). See Josephine Beauharnais.

JOSÉPHINE BEAUHARNAIS (1763–1814). See Josephine.

JOSEPHINE BEAUHARNAIS (1807–1876). Queen of Sweden. Name variations: Joséphine; Josephine Beauharnais; Josephine de Beauharnais; Josephine Leuchtenburg. Born Mar 14, 1807, in Milan, Italy; died June 7, 1876, in Stockholm, Sweden; dau. of Amalie Auguste (1788–1851) and Eugéne de Beauharnais (1781–1824); niece of Hortense de Beauharnais (1783–1837); granddau. of Josephine (1763–1814); m. Oscar I (1799–1859), king of Sweden (r. 1844–1859), on June 19, 1823; children: Charles XV (1826–1872), king of Sweden (r. 1859–1872); Gustaf (b. 1827); Oscar II (1829–1907), king of Sweden (r. 1872–1907); Eugenie (1830–1889); August (1831–1873).

JOSEPHINE-CHARLOTTE OF BELGIUM (1927—). Grand duchess of Luxemburg. Name variations: Josephine Charlotte Saxe-Coburg. Born Josephine Charlotte Ingeborg Saxe-Coburg, Oct 11, 1927, in Brussels, Belgium; dau. of Astrid of Sweden (1905–1935) and Leopold III (1901–1951), king of the Belgians (r. 1934–1951); sister of Baudouin I and Albert II, both king of the Belgians; m. Jean also known as John (b. 1921), grand duke of Luxemburg (r. 1964—), April 9, 1953; children: Marie Astrid of Luxemburg (b. 1954); Henri (b. 1955); Jean Felix (b. 1957); Margareta of Luxemburg (b. 1957); Guillaume, prince of Nassau (b. 1963).

JOSEPHINE LOUISE OF SAVOY (d. 1810). See Marie Josephine of Savoy.

JOSEPHINE OF BADEN (1813–1900). Queen-mother of Romania. Name variations: Josephine Zahringen. Born Oct 21, 1813; died June 19, 1900; dau. of Charles Ludwig, grand duke of Baden, and Stephanie de Beauharnais (1789–1860); m. Charles Anthony I of Hohenzollern-Sigmaringen (1811–1885), prince of Romania, Oct 21, 1834; children: Leopold, prince of Hohenzollern-Sigmaringen (1835–1905); Stephanie (1837–1859); Carol I (1839–1914), king of Romania (r. 1881–1914), who m. Elizabeth of Wied [1843–1916]); Anthony (1841–1866); Frederick (1843–1904, who m. Louise of Thurn and Taxis); Marie of Hohenzollern-Sigmaringen (1845–1912).

JOSEPHINE OF BELGIUM (1872–1958). Belgian princess. Name variations: Josephine of Hohenzollern-Sigmaringen. Born Oct 18, 1872; died 1958; dau. of Marie of Hohenzollern-Sigmaringen (1845–1912) and Philip, count of Flanders (d. 1905); sister of Albert I, king of Belgium

(r. 1909–1927); m. Charles Anthony II (1868–1919), prince of Hohenzollern-Sigmaringen, May 28, 1894.

JOSEPHINE OF LORRAINE (1753–1757). Princess of Carignan. Name variations: Josepha de Lorraine-Brionne. Born 1753; died 1797; dau. of Louis III, duke of Lorraine-Brionne, and Louise de Rohan (1734–1815); m. Victor Amadeus (d. 1780), prince of Carignan or Carignano; children: Charles Emmanuel (1780–1800), duke of Carignan; possibly daughter Gabriela of Savoy-Carignan (1748–1828).

JOSEPHSON, Karen (1964—). American synchronized swimmer. Name variations: The J's. Born Jan 10, 1964, in Bristol, CT; identical twin sister of Sarah Josephson. ❖ Won a silver medal at Seoul Olympics (1988) and a gold medal at Barcelona Olympics (1992), both in duet; won 16 consecutive championships (1991–92); at World championships, recorded highest overall total score for duet in international swimming history (1991), with 199.762 points.

JOSEPHSON, Sarah (1964—). American synchronized swimmer. Name variations: The J's. Born Jan 10, 1964, in Bristol, CT; identical twin sister of Karen Josephson. ❖ Won a silver medal at Seoul Olympics (1988) and a gold medal at Barcelona Olympics (1992), both in duet; won 16 consecutive championships (1991–92); at World championships, recorded highest overall total score for duet in international swimming history (1991), with 199.762 points.

JOSHEE, Anandibai (1865–1887). See Joshi, Anandibai.

JOSHI, Anandibai (1865–1887). Indian physician. Name variations: Anandi or Anandibai Joshee; Anandi Joshi. Born Yamuna Joshi, Mar 31, 1865, in Poona (now known as Pune), India; died of TB at 22, Feb 26, 1887, in India; dau. of Gungubai Joshi and Ganpatrao Joshi (wealthy landlord family of Pune); distant cousin of Pandita Ramabai; Woman's College of Pennsylvania, MD, 1886; m. Gopal Vinayak Joshi (Sanskrit scholar), Mar 31, 1874. ❖ The 1st Indian woman to receive a doctor of medicine degree, met and married her Sanskrit tutor Gopal Vinayak Joshi, a widower, when she was 9 (1874); at 14, was inspired to study medicine after the loss of her only child; at the Serampore College Hall in Calcutta, gave a famed speech, "The Courage of Her Conviction," about why she felt it was important to study medicine in US, to a crowd of Bengalis (who opposed her decision to travel to America without husband), Christians (who wanted her to "submit to baptism before she went") and Europeans; was supported, in part, by H.E.M. Jones, India's Post Office director-general and creator of the Jones Fund, who offered proceeds to husband for her schooling in America; sailed to America on *City of Calcutta* (1883); after earning MD (1886), was offered position as physician-in-charge of female ward at Albert Edward Hospital in Kolhapur, India, but contracted TB in US and died soon after her return to India. Received a hero's welcome upon her return, and, upon her death, was the subject of many laudatory articles.

JOSHUA, Joan O. (1912–1993). English veterinary surgeon. Name variations: Joan Olive Joshua. Born July 11, 1912, in UK; died Feb 21, 1993. ❖ The Royal College of Veterinary Surgeons' (RCVS) 1st woman fellow (1950) and 1st woman council member (1953–63), founded (with Margaret Bentley) and served as the 1st president of the Society of Women Veterinary Surgeons (1941); studied at Royal Veterinary College in London (1933–38); appointed a Beaumont Hospital house surgeon (1938–39); held a veterinary practice at in Finchley (1939–62); served as a reader for University of Liverpool's Department of Clinical Studies (1962–93); was the sole woman member of British Veterinary Codex Committee (1950–65); established the Society for Women Veterinary Surgeons Trust (1968), to support women's education in the field of veterinary science. Was the 1st woman recipient of RCVS Francis Hogg Prize (1959) and 1st woman recipient of Victory Medal of the Central Veterinary Society (1976–77).

JOSIAH ALLEN'S WIFE (1836–1926). See Holley, Marietta.

JOSLAND, Claudie (1946—). French fencer. Born May 3 1946, in France. ❖ At Montreal Olympics, won a silver medal in team foil (1976).

JOSSELYN. Variant of Joceline or Joscelyn.

JOSSINET, Frederique (1975—). French judoka. Born Dec 16, 1975, in Rosy-sous-Bois, France. ❖ At Super A Tournament, placed 1st at 48kg (2002, 2003); won a silver medal for 48kg at Athens Olympics (2004).

JOTUNI, Maria (1880–1943). Finnish author. Name variations: Maria Haggrén or Maria Haggren; Maria Tarkiainen. Born Maria Gustava

Haggrén in Kuopio, Finland, April 9, 1880; died in Helsinki, Sept 30, 1943; attended University of Helsinki; m. Viljo Tarkiainen (1879–1951, literary scholar). ❖ Writer whose realistic depictions of ordinary people paint a group portrait of her country in 1st decades of 20th century, and whose novel *A Tottering House* remains a powerful statement about the collapse of both a marriage and a civilization; under her pseudonym, published 1st book, *Suhteita* (*Relationships*, 1905), a collection of short stories that pleased readers and critics; followed that with *Rakkautta* (*Love*, 1907), a portrait of Finnish lower-middle class; tended to title books, such as *Kun on tunteet* (*When There Are Feelings*, 1913), with irony, given that her characters exhibit a lack of the traits her titles imply; published 1st novel, *Arkielämää* (*Everyday Life*, 1909), a look at rural life, and 1st play, the tragedy *Vanha koti* (*The Old Home*, 1910); other plays include *Miehen kylkiluu* (*Man's Rib*, 1914), the wartime *Kultaine vasikka* (*The Golden Calf*, 1918) and *Tohvelisankarin rouva* (*Wife of a Henpecked Husband*, 1924); also published a children's book, *Musta Härkä* (*The Black Ox*, 1915). Honored with commemorative postage stamp (April 9, 1980). ❖ See also *Women in World History*.

JOUARRE, abbess of.
See Bertille (d. 705/713).
See Agnes of Jouarre (fl. early 13th c.).

JOUBERT, Elsa (1922—). South African novelist. Born Oct 19, 1922, in Paarl, Western Cape, South Africa; University of Stellenbosch, BA; University of Cape Town, MA; m. Klaas Steytler, 1950 (died 1998); children: 2. ❖ Worked as editor of *Die Huisgenoot* magazine (1946–48); came to prominence with *The Long Journey of Poppie Nongena* (1980); writings, which explore racial tension in South Africa, also include *Ons Wag op die Kaptein* (1963), *Die Wahlerbrug* (1969), *Bonga* (1971), *Melk* (1980), *Die Vier Vriende* (1987), *Dansmaat* (1993), and *Die Reise van Isobelle* (1995); travelogues include *Water en Woestyn* (1957), *Suid van die Wind* (1962), *Die Staf van Monomotapa* (1964), *Die Nuwe Afrikaan* (1974) and *Gordel van Smarag* (1997). Received CNA Prize, W.A. Hofmeyr Prize, Olivier Award and Hertzog Prize.

JOUBERT, Linda (1922—). See Grové, Henriette.

JOUDRY, Patricia (1921–2000). Canadian playright and novelist. Born Oct 18, 1921, in Spirit River, Alberta, Canada; died Oct 28, 2000, in Powell River, British Columbia, Canada. ❖ Wrote plays for radio including adaptations of *Anne of Green Gables*; suffered from acute sensitivity to noise and, with daughter Rafaele Joudry, wrote *Sound Therapy: Music to Recharge Your Brain*; works include *Teach Me How to Cry* (1955), *The Dweller on the Threshold* (1973), *Spirit River to Angels: Religions I Have Loved and Left* (1977) and *The Selena Tree* (1980).

JOVETA OF JERUSALEM (1120–?). Abbess of Bethany. Name variations: Ivetta; Jovette; Juditta; Yvetta. Born in 1120 in Frankish principality of Jerusalem; died after 1162; dau. of Baldwin II, count of Edessa, later king of Jerusalem (r. 1118–1131), and Morphia of Melitene (fl. 1085–1120); sister of Hodierna of Jerusalem (c. 1115–after 1162), Melisande (1105–1161), and Alice of Jerusalem (b. 1106); never married; no children. ❖ At 4, became a political pawn in the conflict between her father and his Muslim enemy Timurtash; joined convent of St. Anne of Jerusalem (c. 1136) and remained there in relative seclusion until 1138; when older sister, Queen Melisande, purchased the village of Bethany and built a magnificent convent there dedicated to Saint Lazarus, was relocated to Bethany to serve as its abbess; returned to royal palaces of her youth to nurse Melisande (1160), who had suffered a stroke; became a well-respected religious figure. ❖ See also *Women in World History*.

JOVETTE. Variant of Joveta.

JOWELL, Tessa (1947—). English politician. Name variations: Rt. Hon. Tessa Jowell. Born Tessa Palmer, Sept 17, 1947; m. Roger Jowell, 1970 (div. 1977); m. David Mills, 1979. ❖ Representing Labour, elected to House of Commons for Dulwich and West Norwood (1992, 1997, 2001, 2005); named secretary of state for Culture, Media and Sport (2001).

JOY, Geneviève (1919—). French pianist. Name variations: Geneviève Joy-Dutilleux. Born in Bernaville, France, Oct 4, 1919; m. Henri Dutilleux (composer). ❖ Studied with Yves Nat and went on to receive the 1st prize of Paris Conservatory (1941); played many contemporary French scores, including the 1948 premiere of husband's Piano Sonata; premiered his *Figures de resonances* for two pianos (1970).

JOY, Leatrice (1893–1985). American actress. Name variations: Mrs. John Gilbert. Born Leatrice Joy Zeidler in New Orleans, LA, Nov 7, 1893; died of acute anemia, May 13, 1985, in Riverdale, NY; m. John Gilbert (actor), 1922 (div. 1924); children: Leatrice Gilbert Fountain (who wrote *Dark Star*, a biography of John Gilbert). ❖ A leading star of 1920s, began career as an extra in a Mary Pickford film (1915); starred in comedies of Oliver Hardy and Billy West (1918); also appeared in many silents directed by Cecil B. De Mille; eloped to Mexico with actor John Gilbert (1924), but the marriage lasted only 2 years; with advent of sound, went into semi-retirement; films include *The Water Lily* (1919), *Smiling All the Way* (1920), *Down Home* (1920), *Manslaughter* (1922), *The Ten Commandments* (1923), *Triumph* (1924), *The Wedding Song* (1925), *The Blue Danube* (1928), *The Bellamy Trial* (1929), *The Love Trader* (1930), *First Love* (1939) and *Love Nest* (1951).

JOYCE, Adrien (1934–2004). See Eastman, Carole.

JOYCE, Alice (1889–1955). American actress. Name variations: The Madonna of the Screen. Born Oct 1, 1889, in Kansas City, Missouri; died Oct 9, 1955, in Hollywood, CA; sister of Frank Coleman Joyce (owned Los Angeles talent agency Joyce-Selznick, partnered with Myron Selznick); m. Tom Moore (actor), 1914 (div. 1920); m. James B. Regan, 1920 (div. 1932); m. Clarence Brown (director), 1933 (div. 1945); children: Alice Moore (1916–1960, actress); Margaret "Peggy" Regan Harris. ❖ Popular early film star, joined Kalem Company (1911), then Vitagraph (1916); films include *The School for Scandal*, *The Green Goddess*, *The Lion and the Mouse*, *Cousin Kate*, *Stella Dallas*, *Beau Geste*, *Mannequin*, *13 Washington Square* and *Song O' My Heart* (talkie); also appeared as Clara Bow's mother in *Dancing Daughters*.

JOYCE, Brenda (1915—). American actress. Born Betty Graffina Leabo, Feb 25, 1915, in Kansas City, Missouri; m. Owen Ward, 1941 (div. 1949); children: 3. ❖ Made film debut in *The Rains Came* (1939); played the 2nd Jane in the "Tarzan" series, following Maureen O'Sullivan; retired (1949).

JOYCE, Eileen (1908–1991). Australian pianist. Born Eileen Alannah Joyce in Zeehan, Tasmania, Nov 12, 1908; died Mar 25, 1991, in Westerham, England. ❖ Popular in UK and the English-speaking world, was brought to the attention of Percy Grainger while still young; went to Europe where she studied with Max Pauer, Tobias Matthay, and Artur Schnabel; gave British premiere performances of Dmitri Shostakovich's 2 piano concertos (1936 and 1958); gave countless concerts for British commonwealth troops during WWII; can be heard on the haunting soundtrack for film *Brief Encounter*, playing Rachmaninoff's Piano Concerto #1; appeared in several films, including one based on her childhood, *Wherever She Goes*. Awarded the rank of Companion to the Order of St. Michael and St. George (1981).

JOYCE, Joan (1940—). American softball player. Born Aug 18, 1940, in Waterbury, CT; attended Chapman College in California. ❖ At 13, joined Raybestos Brakettes, amateur women's fast-pitch softball team in Stratford, CT (1953); launched pitching career during Amateur Softball Association's (ASA) National championships (1958); became a dominant force behind Raybestos Brakettes team with her pitching, hitting and fielding expertise (1970s); led team to World championship, 1st ever won by Americans (1974); helped found International Women's Professional Softball Association (1975); retired from softball (1978); named head coach for women's softball program at Florida Atlantic University (1994). Inducted into National Softball Hall of Fame (1983) and Women's Sports Foundation Hall of Fame (1990). ❖ See also *Women in World History*.

JOYCE, Kara Lynn (1985—). American swimmer. Born Oct 25, 1985, in Brooklyn, NY; attended University of Michigan. ❖ Won silver medals for 4 x 100-meter freestyle relay and 4 x 100-meter medley relay at Athens Olympics (2004).

JOYCE, Lucia (1907–1982). Irish literary inspiration and dancer. Born 1907 in Trieste; died 1982 in an asylum; dau. of Nora Joyce and James Joyce (writer). ❖ Became a dancer; had dead-end relationships with a series of men, including Alexander Calder and Samuel Beckett, which left her despondent; spent last 45 years of her life in institutions; was what scholars call the "Rainbow Girl" (Issy) in *Finnegan's Wake*. ❖ See also Carol Loeb Shloss, *Lucia Joyce* (Farrar, Straus, 2003).

JOYCE, Nora (1884–1951). Wife of Irish novelist James Joyce and inspiration for many of the female characters in his works. Name variations: Nora Joseph Barnacle; Norah Barnacle. Born Mar 22 (or 23), 1884, in Galway, Ireland; died April 10, 1951, in Zurich, Switzerland;

dau. of Thomas Barnacle (baker) and Honoraria "Annie" (Healy) Barnacle (dressmaker); m. James Joyce (writer), 1931 (died 1941); children: Giorgio Joyce (b. 1905); Lucia Joyce (1907–1982). ❖ One of modern literature's most intriguing real-life personalities, sacrificed a great deal for husband's art, fleeing a harsh, repressive Ireland with him (1904) and living for years in poverty on the Continent; seemed to deal effortlessly with his less-than-easygoing personality and became a lifeline to him when his eyesight failed; was the object of husband's devotion, and her voice—which teased, hectored, and assailed him—is clearly echoed in that of his memorable female characters. ❖ See also Brenda Maddox, *Nora: A Biography of Nora Joyce* (Fawcett, 1988); and *Women in World History*.

JOYCE, Peggy Hopkins (1893–1957). American actress and showgirl. Name variations: Peggy Hopkins. Born Marguerite Upton, May 26, 1893, in Berkley, Virginia; died June 12, 1957, in New York, NY; m. Everett Archibald Jr., 1919 (annulled); m. Sherburne Philbrick Hopkins, 1913 (div. 1915); m. J. Stanley Joyce, 1920 (div. 1921); m. Gustave Morner, 1924 (div. 1928); m. Anthony Easton, 1945; m. Andrew Meyer, 1953. ❖ Famed showgirl, who appeared in 2 films, *Skyrocket* (silent) and *International House* (talkie), was thought to be the inspiration for Anita Loos' character Lorelei Lee.

JOYCE, Rebecca. Australian rower. Born in NSW, Australia; dau. of Bob Joyce (Olympian). ❖ Won a bronze medal for lightweight double sculls at Atlanta Olympics (1996).

JOYEUSE, duchess of. See Marguerite of Lorraine (c. 1561–?).

JOYEUX, Odette (1914–2000). French stage and screen actress and screenwriter. Born Dec 5, 1914, in Paris, France; died Aug 26, 2000, in Grimaud, France; m. Pierre Brasseur (actor), 1935; m. Philippe Agostini (cinematographer), 1958; children: Claude Brasseur (b. 1936, actor); grandmother of Alexandre Brasseur (actor). ❖ Made screen debut at 14 but generally worked on the Paris stage until appearing in Marc Allegret film *Entrée des Artistes* (*The Curtain Rises*, 1938); a leading star of the French cinema, appeared in such films as *Jean de la Lune*, *Le chien jaune*, *Grisou*, *Le lit à colonnes*, *Le mariage de Chiffon*, *Lettres d'amour*, *Douce*, *Sylvie et le fantôme*, and *La Ronde*; screenplays include *La Mariée est trop belle*, *L'amour est en jeu*, *Sois belle et tais-toi* and *Rencontres*; has also written for tv.

JOYNER, Florence Griffith (1959–1998). African-American track-and-field athlete. Name variations: Flo-Jo; Florence Griffith-Joyner. Born Delorez Florence Griffith, Dec 21, 1959, in Los Angeles, CA; died of heart seizure, Sept 21, 1998; sister-in-law of Jackie Joyner-Kersee (heptathlete); m. Alfred Joyner (her trainer), Oct 10, 1987. ❖ Won a silver medal in 200-meter sprint at Los Angeles Olympics (1984); medaled at World Outdoor championships, taking 2nd in the 200-meter and 1st with the 4 x 100-relay team; won 3 gold medals at Seoul Olympics (100, 200, 4 x 100) and 1 silver (4 x 400), becoming the most decorated female sprinter in Olympic history (1988); announced retirement from professional track and founded Florence Griffith Joyner Youth Foundation (1989); chosen by President Bill Clinton to co-chair the President's Council on Physical Fitness (1997). Named US Olympic Committee's Sportswoman of the Year, AP Sportswoman of the Year, UPI's Sportswoman of the Year, and Tass News Agency's Sports Personality of the Year (1988); given the Jessie Owens Award as most outstanding track-and-field athlete (1988); won Sullivan Trophy (1988); inducted into USATF Hall of Fame (1995). ❖ See also Nathan Aaseng, *Florence Griffith Joyner: Dazzling Olympian* (Lerner, 1989); April Koral, *Florence Griffith Joyner: Track and Field Star* (Watts, 1992); and *Women in World History*.

JOYNER, Marjorie Stewart (1896–1994). African-American inventor, entrepreneur, political activist, and philanthropist. Born in Mississippi, 1896; died just after Christmas, 1994; granddau. of a slave; mother worked as maid; m. Robert Joyner (podiatrist). ❖ Began career as a beautician; became an inventor and business executive, and dedicated her life to racial and gender equality in Chicago's black community and throughout US; received a patent for the Joyner Permanent Waving Machine, which involved a group of curling irons hanging from above, with each clip capturing a hank of hair, allowing a full head of curls or waves to be set at once (1928); received a patent for a Scalp Protector to make the "curling" process more comfortable (1929); was vice president of a chain of 200 Madame C.J. Walker beauty colleges; founded United Beauty School Owners and Teachers Association (1940s). ❖ See also *Women in World History*.

JOYNER, Matilda Sissieretta (1869–1933). *See Jones, Sissieretta.*

JOYNER-KERSEE, Jackie (1962—). African-American track-and field athlete. Name variations: Jackie Kersee; Jackie Joyner. Born Mar 3, 1962, in East St. Louis, IL; sister-in-law of Florence Griffith Joyner; m. Robert Kersee (her coach), Jan 11, 1986. ❖ Won 1st of 4 AAU Junior Olympics pentathlon titles (1977); became a star performer on UCLA's basketball and track teams; competed at Los Angeles Olympics (1984), winning a silver medal in heptathlon; broke the world high-jump record at Goodwill Games in Moscow, and became the 1st woman to score more than 7,000 points (1986); won gold medals in high jump and heptathlon at Seoul Olympics (1988); won a bronze in long jump and a gold in the heptathlon at Barcelona Olympics (1992), making her the greatest multi-event champion ever, man or woman; won a bronze in the long jump at Atlanta Olympics (1996); won a gold medal in the heptathlon at Goodwill Games in NY (1998); organized and funded the Jackie Joyner-Kersee Community Foundation in East St. Louis. ❖ See also Geri Harrington, *Jackie Joyner-Kersee: Champion Athlete* (Chelsea House, 1995) and autobiography (with Sonja Steptoe) *A Kind of Grace* (Warner, 1997); and *Women in World History.*

JOZWIAKOWSKA, Jaroslawa (1937—). Polish track-and-field athlete. Name variations: Jaroslawa Jozwiakowska-Bieda-Zdunkiewicz. Born Jan 20, 1937, in Poland. ❖ At Rome Olympics, won a silver medal in the high jump (1960).

JUANA. *Variant of Joan or Joanna.*

JUANA, Sor or Sister (1651–1695). *See Juana Inés de la Cruz.*

JUANA I OF NAVARRE (1273–1305). *See Joan I of Navarre.*

JUANA II OF NAVARRE (1309–1349). *See Joan II of Navarre.*

JUANA DE ASBAJE Y RAMIREZ DE SANTILLANA (1651–1695). *See Juana Inés de la Cruz.*

JUANA DE AVIZ (1439–1475). *See Joanna of Portugal.*

JUANA DE LA CERDA (1339–1381). *See Joanna of Castile.*

JUANA INÉS DE LA CRUZ (1651–1695). Mexican poet and playwright. Name variations: Sor (Sister) Juana Ines de la Cruz; the Tenth Muse; the Mexican Nun. Pronunciation: HWAH-na ee-NEYSS they la KROOTH. Born Juana Ramírez de Asuaje, frequently spelled Asbaje, near San Miguel de Nepantla, Mexico, Nov 12, 1651 (some writers, citing plausible but inconclusive evidence, have argued that it was actually 3 years earlier, in 1648); died April 17, 1695, in Mexico City; dau. of Isabel Ramírez de Santillana and Pedro Manuel de Asuaje y Vargas Machuca; never married; no children. ❖ Though recognized in her own time for her genius, nonetheless struggled against great odds to achieve the freedom to devote herself to scholarship and creative activity; entered Hieronymite convent, Mexico City (1668); had earliest known work published in Mexico (1676); had 1st collection of works published in Spain (1689); engaged in polemic on women's rights (1691); withdrew from literary life (1693); defied the limits imposed by Hispanic tradition and the Roman Catholic Church to become one of the most significant writers in the history of Spanish literature; for more than 20 years, maintained a brilliant literary career but, shortly before death, was finally forced into silence. Wrote long poem *Primero sueño* (First Dream), numerous sonnets and *villancicos,* religious and secular plays, and an important autobiographical essay entitled *Respuesta a Sor Filotea* (Reply to Sister Filotea). ❖ See also *A Woman of Genius: The Intellectual Autobiography of Sor Juana Inés de la Cruz* [*Respuesta a Sor Filotea*] (Trans. and ed. by Margaret Sayers Peden, Lime Rock, 1982); Octavio Paz, *Sor Juana: Or, the Traps of Faith* (Trans. by Margaret Sayers Peden, Harvard U. Press, 1988); and *Women in World History.*

JUANA LA BELTRANEJA (1462–1530). Spanish heir to the throne. Born Infanta of Castile; Joanna of Castile. Born in Madrid, Spain, Feb 28, 1462; died in Lisbon, Portugal, in 1530; only child of Enrique also known as Henry IV, king of Castile (r. 1454–1474), and Joanna of Portugal (1439–1475), sister of Afonso also known as Alphonso V of Portugal); never married; no children. ❖ Heir of Henry IV of Castile and rival of Isabella I for the crown of Castile, symbolized the turmoil of late medieval Spain, torn apart by weak monarchs and rapacious, feuding nobles; became known derisively as *la Beltraneja,* because it was rumored she was the bastard offspring of an adulterous relationship between the queen and a royal favorite Beltrán de la Cueva; claims to the throne were disregarded by many nobles who supported her aunt Isabella I, launching a war of succession; over the years, refused to relinquish claim to Castile;

having long outlived Isabella, formally abdicated in favor of John III of Portugal (1522). ❖ See also *Women in World History.*

JUANA LA LOCA (1479–1555). Queen of Castile. Name variations: Juana or Joanna the Mad; Juana of Castile; Juana of Spain; Joanna of Spain. Born Nov 6, 1479, in Toledo, Spain; died in Tordesillas, April 11 or 12, 1555; 2nd daughter and 3rd child of Isabella I (1451–1504), queen of Castile (r. 1474–1504), and Ferdinand II, king of Aragon (r. 1479–1516); sister of Catherine of Aragon (1485–1536); m. Philip I the Fair also known as Philip the Handsome (1478–1506, son of the Holy Roman Emperor Maximilian I), archduke of Austria, king of Castile and Leon (r. 1506), Oct 19, 1496; children: Eleanor of Portugal (1498–1558); Carlos also known as Charles V (1500–1558), king of Spain (r. 1516–1556), Holy Roman Emperor (r. 1519–1558); Elisabeth of Habsburg (1501–1526); Fernando also known as Ferdinand I (1502 or 1503–1564), king of Bohemia (r. 1526–1564), king of Hungary (r. 1526–1564), Holy Roman Emperor (1558–1564); Mary of Hungary (1505–1558); Catherine (1507–1578, who m. John III, king of Portugal). ❖ Queen from 1504 to 1555, during which time Spain became a world power, but never actually ruled due to her own mental instability (suffered from manic depression) and the greed for power of her father, husband, and son; nephew Miguel died, making her heir to the throne (1500); proclaimed queen of Castile upon death of mother (1504); was declared incompetent by father Ferdinand II and the Cortes of Toro recognized his regency (1505); with husband Philip, arrived in Spain from Flanders and was acclaimed monarch of Castile (1506); despite the fact that she showed little inclination to reign, was confined to palace in Tordesillas by Ferdinand, where she spent most of her adult life under forced seclusion, isolated for more than 4 decades within its dreary walls (1509–1555); when Ferdinand died (1516), her son Charles arrived in Spain to rule (1517); during Comunero Revolt, was temporarily freed from seclusion by the rebels (1520), but was isolated again by son; daughter Catherine, who had lived with her, was taken away. ❖ See also Amarie Dennis, *Seek the Darkness: The Story of Juana la Loca* (Madrid: Sucesores de Rivadeneyra, 1956); Michael Prawdin, *The Mad Queen of Spain* (Houghton, 1939); and *Women in World History.*

JUANA OF AUSTRIA (1535–1573). *See Joanna of Austria.*

JUANA OF CASTILE (r. 1366–1374). *See Jeanne de Castile.*

JUANA OF CASTILE (1479–1555). *See Juana la Loca.*

JUANA OF PORTUGAL (1439–1475). *See Joanna of Portugal.*

JUANA OF SPAIN (1479–1555). *See Juana la Loca.*

JUANA THE MAD (1479–1555). *See Juana la Loca.*

JUAREZ, Margarita (1826–1871). First lady of Mexico. Born Margarita Mazas, Mar 29, 1826, in Oaxaca, Mexico; died Jan 2, 1871 in Mexico City, Mexico; dau. of Antonio Maza and Petra Parada; m. Benito Juarez (1806–1872, 4-term president of Mexico, 1861–72), July 1843; children: 12. ❖ Followed husband on the run with her 8 children (eventually had 12); fully supported his federalist efforts against the French and the dictator Santa Anna; while living in exile in NY and Washington DC (1863–67), was important in negotiations with US government; with the revenue cutter *Wilderness* placed at her disposal by President Andrew Johnson, was reunited with husband at Veracruz (July 14, 1867).

JUCH, Emma (1860–1939). American operatic singer. Born Emma Johanna Antonia Juch, July 4, 1860, in Vienna, Austria; died Mar 6, 1939, in New York, NY; dau. of Justin Juch (musician and artist) and Augusta Hahn; m. Francis Lewis Wellman (lawyer), June 25, 1894 (div. 1911). ❖ Made operatic debut in *Mignon* in London (1881); sang 3 seasons at New York Academy of Music (1881–83); was 1st singer to be engaged for American Opera Co. (1886), which was reorganized as National Opera Co. the following season; established Emma Juch Grand English Opera Co. (1889), which toured US, Canada, and Mexico for 2 seasons; was 1 of the 1st singers recorded by Victor Talking Machine Co.; sang as Gilda (*Rigoletto*), Queen of the Night (*The Magic Flute*), Marguerite (*Faust*), Elsa (*Lohengrin*) and Senta (*The Flying Dutchman*).

JUCHACZ, Marie (1879–1956). German Social Democratic leader. Born Marie Gohlke in Landsberg-Warthe, Germany, Mar 15, 1879; died in Bonn, Jan 28, 1956; dau. of Friedrich Theodor Gohlke and Henriette (Heinrich) Gohlke; m. Bernhard Juchacz, 1904; children: 2. ❖ Was chosen to replace Clara Zetkin as women's leader of the Social Democratic Party (SPD) when it split over the issue of WWI and the

Bolshevik Revolution; founded the social welfare organization Arbeiterwohlfahrt (1919) which would provide many kinds of services, including child-care centers, children's camps, care for pregnant women, and household assistance for women who were ill, pregnant or had recently given birth; was among a handful of women elected to German National Assembly, the Reichstag (1920–33) and was the 1st woman in German history to address a national parliamentary body; when the SPD was banned, fled Nazi Germany (1933) and became a member of German Social Democratic Party in exile, organizing resistance groups within Germany; found refuge in US (1941); returned to (West) Germany (1949); wrote *Sie lebten für eine bessere Welt* (*They Lived for a Better World*), a biographical study of 29 women who had fought for social justice. ❖ See also *Women in World History*.

JUDD, Ashley (1968—). American actress and feminist. Born Ashley Tyler Ciminella, April 19, 1968, in Granada Hills, CA; dau. of Naomi Judd (singer) and Michael Ciminella; sister of Wynonna Judd (singer); graduate of University of Kentucky; m. Dario Franchitti (racer), 2001. ❖ Appeared on tv series "Sisters" (1991–94); came to screen prominence in *Double Jeopardy* (1999), followed by *Where the Heart Is* (2000), *Someone Like You* (2001), *High Crimes* (2002), *Divine Secrets of the Ya-Ya Sisterhood* (2002) and *De-Lovely* (2004), among others.

JUDD, Isabel. English gymnast. Born in UK. ❖ At Amsterdam Olympics, won a bronze medal in team all-around (1928).

JUDD, Naomi (1946—). American country-and-western singer. Name variations: Diana Judd. Born Diana Ellen Judd, Jan 11, 1946, in Ashland, KY; completed nursing degree; married Michael Ciminella, 1963 (div. 1972); m. Larry Strickland, 1989; children: Christina Ciminella, later known as Wynonna Judd (b. 1964, singer) and Ashley Judd (actress). ❖ Matriarch of famed mother-daughter singing duo, moved to California (1970s); signed with Wynonna to RCA Records (1979); released series of successful albums, including *The Judds: Wynonna & Naomi* (1984), *Heart Land* (1987), *River of Time* (1989), *Love Can Build a Bridge* (1990); topped country charts with singles "Mama He's Crazy" (1984), "Girls Night Out" (1985), "Grandpa (Tell Me 'Bout the Good Old Days)" (1986), "Turn It Loose" (1988) and "Change of Heart" (1988); performed with daughter in well-publicized farewell tour (1991), then was forced to retire due to chronic hepatitis C; began hosting syndicated radio show "Heart to Heart With Naomi Judd" (1999); reunited with Wynonna for album *The Judds Reunion* (2000). ❖ See also autobiography *Love Can Build a Bridge* (1993).

JUDD, Winnie Ruth (1905–1998). American murderer. Name variations: Marian Lane. Born Winnie Ruth McKinnell, Jan 29, 1905, in Oxford, Indiana; died in Phoenix, Arizona, Oct 1998; dau. of a minister and schoolteacher; m. William C. Judd (physician), April 18, 1924; no children. ❖ In one of the most notorious murder cases of 1930s, was accused of killing 2 women, dismembering one of the bodies, and shipping all the remains (in 2 trunks and a suitcase) to Los Angeles via the Southern Pacific railroad; found guilty, was sentenced to hang, but was spared when her lawyer persuaded her to plead insanity; escaped from prison 7 times. ❖ See also Jana Bommersbach, *The Trunk Murderess: Winnie Ruth Judd* (Simon & Schuster, 1992); and *Women in World History*.

JUDD, Wynonna (1964—). American country singer. Name variations: Hurricane Wyoming; Wynonna. Born Christina Clare Ciminella, May 30, 1964, in Ashland, KY; dau. of Naomi Judd and Charles Jordan; grew up believing father was Michael Ciminella; sister of Ashley Judd (actress); m. Arch Kelly, 1996 (div. 1999); m. D.R. Roach, 2003; children: (1st m.) Elijah (b. 1994) and Grace Pauline (b. 1996). ❖ Known for mastery of both ballads and country rock material, took up guitar as teenager; was musical backbone of mother-daughter duo The Judds (1980s); emerged from mother's shadow with solo debut *Wynonna* (1992); released 3 #1 C&W singles, "She is His Only Need," "I Saw the Light" and "No One Else on Earth" (all 1992); recorded single with Clint Black, "A Bad Goodbye" (1993); released 2nd solo album *Tell Me Why* (1993); began recording album *Revelations* (1996); released 8-minute cover of Lynyrd Skynyrd's rock anthem "Free Bird" (1996); reunited with mother for New Year's Eve concert (1999); covered Joni Mitchell's "Help Me" and the Fabulous Thunderbirds' "Tuff Enuff" on album *New Day Dawning* (2000).

JUDGE, Arline (1912–1974). American actress. Name variations: Bella Grifiths. Born Feb 21, 1912, in Bridgeport, CT; died Feb 7, 1974, in Hollywood, CA; m. Wesley Ruggles (film director), 1931 (div. 1937);

m. Daniel Reid Topping, 1937 (div. 1940); m. James M. Bryant, 1940 (div. 1941); m. James Ramage Adams, 1942 (div. 1945); m. Vincent Morgan Ryan, 1945 (div. 1947); m. Henry J. (Bob) Topping, 1947 (div. 1947); m. George Ross, 1949 (div.); m. Edward Cooper Heard (div. 1960). ❖ Began career as Broadway dancer; made film debut in *Bachelor Apartment* (1931); films include *American Tragedy, Girl Crazy, Age of Consent*, George White's *Scandals, King of Burlesque, Pigskin Parade* and *Two Knights in Brooklyn*.

JUDITH. Biblical woman. Name variations: Aholibamah. Dau. of Beeri (also known as Anah), the Hittite; m. Esau; children: three sons. ❖ Was one of the 6 wives of Esau, whose 3 sons founded the 3 tribes of Edomites.

JUDITH (fl. early 6th c. BCE). Biblical woman. Name variations: Judith of Bethulia; Judith of Bethulin. In the Biblical account, Judith was born in Bethulia (near Jerusalem) after the Jews returned from exile in Babylonia (537 BCE); died in Bethulia at 105 years of age; m. Manasses (died); no children. ❖ Hebrew heroine-slayer and widow of Bethulia who, through insistence on absolute fidelity to Mosaic Law, saved Judea from the Assyrians; lived in devout seclusion until Judea was threatened by an Assyrian army, at which time she saved her people by a feigned defection to the enemy which allowed her the opportunity to decapitate their general, Holofernes. Though the Book of Judith is contained in the Apocrypha, there is no evidence that the incident related in the book of Judith corresponds to a single historical event, and we should not think of Judith as a real person, but as a composite or a symbol of Judaism generally. ❖ See also Carey A. Moore, *Judith* (Doubleday, 1985); Enslin & Zeitlin, *The Book of Judith* (E.J. Brill, 1972); and *Women in World History*.

JUDITH (fl. 10th c.). Queen of the Falashas. Name variations: Esther; Esato; Yehudit. Fl. in Ethiopia in 10th century. ❖ According to tradition, was a Jewish queen of the Falashas, who fought the Christian persecutors of her people. ❖ See also *Women in World History*.

JUDITH (1271–1297). Queen of Bohemia. Name variations: Jutta; Guta or Gutta. Born Mar 13, 1271; died June 18, 1297; dau. of Rudolph or Rudolf I Habsburg, Holy Roman emperor (r. 1273–1291), and Anna of Hohenberg (c. 1230–1281); sister of Albert I, duke of Austria and Holy Roman emperor (r. 1298–1308); 1st wife of Wenceslas II (1271–1305), king of Bohemia (r. 1278–1305). Wenceslas II's 3rd wife was Elizabeth of Poland (fl. 1298–1305); his 2nd was Ryksa of Poland (1288–1335).

JUDITH (1876–1930). *See Zauditu.*

JUDITH MARTEL (c. 844–?). *See Martel, Judith.*

JUDITH OF BAVARIA (802–843). Holy Roman Empress. Born 802 in Bavaria; died 843 in France; dau. of Welf of Bavaria and Heilwig; sister of Emma of Bavaria (d. 876); became 2nd wife of Louis I the Pious (778–840), king of Aquitaine (r. 781–814), king of France (r. 814–840), and Holy Roman emperor (r. 814–840), in 819; children: Charles I the Bald (823–877), king of France (r. 843–877), known also as Charles II, Holy Roman emperor (r. 875–877); Gisela (c. 819–c. 874, who m. Eberhard of Friuli). Louis I the Pious' 1st wife was Ermengarde (c. 778–818). ❖ Born into a powerful family of Germany, became Holy Roman empress on marriage to Louis I the Pious, who had succeeded his father Charlemagne; ruled the expansive Frankish kingdom jointly with Louis; was involved in political negotiations, issued decrees in her own name, and presided over the royal court at Aachen; gave birth to a son (823) whom Louis proclaimed would succeed him, though he had already promised the imperial throne to Lothair, eldest child of his 1st wife, Ermengarde; for remainder of the reign, was in constant struggle with Louis over which son would get the inheritance; was twice banished from court on false charges of adultery and witchcraft, but each time persuaded Louis to take her back and was reinstalled in position of power; died with the issue of succession still unresolved. ❖ See also *Women in World History*.

JUDITH OF BAVARIA (c. 925–987). Duchess of Bavaria. Born c. 925; died June 28, 987; dau. of Arnulf the Bad, duke of Bavaria, and Judith of Fiuli; m. Henry I the Quarrelsome (918–955), duke of Bavaria (r. 947–955), in 938; children: Gerberga, abbess of Hildesheim (r. 959–1001); Henry II (b. 951), duke of Bavaria; Hedwig (d. 994, who m. Burckhardt, duke of Swabia); Brunon I (d. 972), count of Brunswick.

JUDITH OF BAVARIA (fl. 1120s). Duchess of Swabia. Fl. in 1120s; dau. of Henry the Black (d. 1126), duke of Bavaria, and Wolfida of Saxony (c. 1075–1126); sister of Welf also known as Guelph VI (d. 1191) and Henry the Proud (d. 1139), duke of Bavaria and Saxony; m. Frederick II

(c. 1100–1139), duke of Swabia; children: Frederick I Barbarossa (1123–1190), 1st of the Hohenstaufen kings of Germany and Holy Roman emperor (r. 1152–1190). ❖ On marriage, united the Guelph (Welf) and Hohenstaufen families.

JUDITH OF BAVARIA (fl. 1390s–1400). Bavarian princess. Name variations: Joanna of Bavaria. Fl. 1390s to 1400; 1st wife of Wenceslas IV the Drunkard (1361–1419), duke of Luxemburg (r. 1383–1419), king of Bohemia (r. 1378–1419), and Holy Roman emperor (r. 1378–1400) as just Wenceslas.

JUDITH OF BETHULIA OR BETHULIN (fl. early 6th c. BCE). See *Judith.*

JUDITH OF BRITTANY (c. 982–1018). See *Judith of Rennes.*

JUDITH OF FIULI (fl. 910–925). Duchess of Bavaria. Fl. between 910 and 925; dau. of Eberhard, count of Friuli, and Gisela (c. 819–c. 874); sister of Berengar, Holy Roman emperor (r. 905–924); m. Arnulf the Bad, duke of Bavaria (r. 907–937), around 910; children: Eberhard, duke of Bavaria (r. 937–938); Judith of Bavaria (c. 925–987); Arnulf, platzgraf of Bavaria; Hermann; Berthold, margrave of Bavaria; Luitpold, margrave of East Mark; Ludwig.

JUDITH OF FLANDERS (1032–1094). Duchess of Bavaria. Name variations: Fausta. Born 1032 in Flanders; died Mar 5, 1094, at Weingarten Abbey in Bavaria; dau. of Baldwin V, count of Flanders (r. 1035–1067), and Adela Capet (c. 1010–1079); sister of Matilda of Flanders (c. 1031–1083); m. Tostig Godwinson (an English knight and brother of King Harold II), earl of Northumberland, in Oct 1051 (died 1066); m. Guelf or Guelph also known as Welf IV (c. 1035–1101), duke of Bavaria, in 1071; children: (1st marriage) Skuli Tostisson; Ketil Tostisson; (2nd m.) Guelph also known as Welf V the Fat (c. 1073–1120), duke of Bavaria; Henry III the Black (b. around 1074–1126), duke of Bavaria. ❖ At about 18, was married to the Anglo-Saxon knight Tostig Godwinson and moved to England; with husband, went on a pilgrimage to Rome (1061) and returned more devout than ever; spent much of her time patronizing artists of religious works and commissioning numerous books to be copied, including *Book of Gospels;* when husband died (1066) and she wed Welf IV, duke of Bavaria (1071), took books with her when she moved to Germany and is thus credited with bringing the 1st examples of the magnificent Anglo-Saxon illuminated manuscripts to the Continent, where their artistic and calligraphic techniques were studied and emulated by numerous scribes and painters. ❖ See also *Women in World History.*

JUDITH OF HUNGARY (fl. late 900s). Queen of Poland. Fl. in late 900s; dau. of Geza, prince of Hungary (r. 970–997), and Sarolta (fl. 900s); sister of Stephen I, king of Hungary, and Maria, dogaressa of Venice; became 2nd wife of Boleslaw Chobry also known as Boleslaus the Brave (967–1025), king of Poland, in 988 (div.); children: possibly Regelinda; Mieszko II (990–1034), king of Poland (r. 1025–1034).

JUDITH OF NORMANDY (c. 1054–after 1086). Countess of Huntingdon and Northampton. Born c. 1054; died after 1086; dau. of Lambert II, count of Ponthieu, Lenz, and Champagne, and Adelicia (1029–1090, half-sister of William the Conqueror); niece of William the Conqueror; m. Waltheof (d. 1076), earl of Huntingdon and Northampton, in 1070; children: Matilda of Northumberland (c. 1074–1131, who m. David I, king of Scotland); Judith of Huntingdon (who possibly m. Ralph II de Toni); and another daughter who died young.

JUDITH OF RENNES (c. 982–1018). Duchess of Normandy. Name variations: Judith of Brittany. Born c. 982; died 1018; dau. of Conan I the Crooked, duke of Brittany (r. 990–992); m. Richard II the Good (d. 1027), duke of Normandy (r. 996–1027), c. 1000; children: Richard III (c. 1008–1027), duke of Normandy (r. 1027–1028); Robert I the Devil (1010–1035), duke of Normandy (r. 1028–1035); Nicholas of Normandy (d. 1025, also referred to as William), a monk at Féchamp; Alice of Normandy (fl. 1017–1037); Eleanor of Normandy.

JUDITTA. Variant of *Joveta* or *Jovita.*

JUDSON, Ann Hasseltine (1789–1826). American missionary. Name variations: Nancy Judson. Born Nancy Ann Hasseltine, Dec 22, 1789, in Bradford, Massachusetts; died Oct 24, 1826, in Amherst, near Rangoon, Burma (now Myanmar), from jungle fever; dau. of John Hasseltine (deacon in Congregationalist church) and Rebecca Hasseltine; attended Bradford Academy; m. Adoniram Judson (Congregationalist minister), Feb 5, 1812; children: Roger Williams

Hasseltine (1815–1816); Marie Elizabeth Butterworth (1825–1827). ❖ Baptist missionary, arrived in Rangoon, Burma (1813); established a school for Burmese girls and, with husband, trans. the New Testament into Burmese; returned to US weakened from fever (1822) and published *The American Baptist Mission in Burma* (1823); returned to Burma (late 1823), then moved to Ava, Burma, intending to establish a mission there (Feb 1824); husband held prisoner by Burmese nationals during British-Burma war (June 1824–Feb 21, 1826); moved to Amherst in Burma with the British (July 5, 1826); her assistance in the translation of the Bible into Burmese, a work that served as the cornerstone of the Christianization of the East, and her status as the 1st woman missionary to the East, is regarded as incomparable in the history of the Christian mission to the East. ❖ See also Cecil B. Hartley, *The Three Mrs. Judsons, the Celebrated Female Missionaries* (1863); Dawn Langley Simmons, *Golden Boats from Burma: The Life of Ann Hasseltine Judson, The First American Woman in Burma* (Macrae Smith, 1961); and *Women in World History.*

JUDSON, Emily Chubbuck (1817–1854). American writer and missionary. Name variations: (pseudonym) Fanny Forester. Born Aug 22, 1817, in Eaton, NY; died June 1, 1854, in Hamilton, NY; dau. of Charles Chubbuck and Lavinia (Richards) Chubbuck; became 3rd wife of Rev. Adoniram Judson (missionary), June 2, 1846 (died April 12, 1850); children: 1 daughter, 1 son. ❖ Published series of children's books, 1st of which was *Charles Linn, or How to Observe the Golden Rule* (1841); contributed light sketches of village life in upstate NY to *New Mirror* magazine under pseudonym "Fanny Forester"; after marrying Judson, moved to Burma (1846) and Rangoon (1847) for his American Baptist missionary work; published *Memoir of Sarah B. Judson* (1848), about Judson's 2nd wife. Other books include *Trippings in Author-Land* (1845), *Alderbrook* (1847), *An Olio of Domestic Verses* (1852), *The Kathayan Slave, and Other Papers Connected with Missionary Life* (1853), and *My Two Sisters* (1854). ❖ See also Asahel Clark Kendrick, *The Life and Letters of Mrs. Emily C. Judson* (1860).

JUDSON, Nancy (1789–1826). See *Judson, Ann Hasseltine.*

JUDSON, Sarah Boardman (1803–1845). American missionary. Name variations: Sarah Hall Judson; Sarah Hall Boardman. Born Sarah Hall, Nov 4, 1803, in Alstead, NH; died Sept 1, 1845, anchored just off island of St. Helena; dau. of Ralph Hall and Abiah (Hall) Hall; briefly attended local female seminary; m. George Dana Boardman, July 3, 1825 (died 1831); became 2nd wife of Adoniram Judson, April 10, 1834; children: (1st m.) Sarah Ann Boardman (1826–1829); George Dana Boardman (b. 1828, later a well-known Baptist minister); Judson Wade Boardman (1830–1831); (2nd m.) Abigail Ann Judson; Adoniram Brown Judson (later orthopedic surgeon); Elnathan Judson; Henry Hall Judson; Edward Judson (later minister); and 3 others who did not survive infancy. ❖ With husband George Boardman, moved to Burma (now Myanmar) to be a missionary; set up schools and church for the Karen, an indigenous tribe; trans. the New Testament, various religious tracts, and Adoniram Judson's *Life of Christ* into the language of the Peguans; trans. the 1st part of *Pilgrim's Progress* into Burmese and put together a Burmese hymn book. ❖ See also *Women in World History.*

JUDY, Aunt (1809–1873). See *Gatty, Margaret.*

JUELL, Johanne (1867–1950). See *Dybwad, Johanne.*

JUGAN, Jeanne (1792–1879). French nun. Name variations: Sister Mary of the Cross. Born 1792 in Petites-Croix, Brittany; died 1879. ❖ With Marie Jamet and Virginie Trédaniel, founded Little Sisters of the Poor (1840), a pioneer mission for the care of the elderly; took religious name of Mary of the Cross; received little recognition from the church; reappointed superior (1843) but reappointment was overturned by Father Le Pailleur; was allowed no part in further development of the order (1852); beatified (1982). Little Sisters of the Poor have denounced Le Pailleur's decision to push her aside and they recognize her as one of the order's founders.

JUHACZ, Marie (1880–1956). See *Juchacz, Marie.*

JUHASZNE-NAGY, Katalin (1932—). Hungarian fencer. Born Nov 24, 1932, in Hungary. ❖ Won a silver medal at Rome Olympics (1960) and a gold medal at Tokyo Olympics (1964), both in team foil.

JULIA (d. 68 BCE). Roman noblewoman and aunt of Julius Caesar. Died in 68 BCE (some sources cite 69 BCE); dau. of Marcia (fl. 100 BCE) and Gaius Julius Caesar; sister of C. Julius Caesar (praetor, 85 BCE, father of Julius Caesar) and Sextus Julius Caesar (consul, 91 BCE); aunt of

Julius Caesar, Roman emperor; m. Gaius Marius (consul, d. 86 BCE). ❖ It was her marriage to dictator Gaius Marius that propelled the young Caesar into politics; at her death, was glorified by Caesar's funeral oration. ❖ See also *Women in World History.*

JULIA (d. 54 BCE). Daughter of Julius Caesar. Born c. 83 BCE; died in 54 BCE; dau. of Roman emperor Julius Caesar (c. 100–44 BCE) and Cornelia (c. 100–68 BCE); m. Pompey (106–48 BCE), the Roman general, in 59 BCE. ❖ Was married to Pompey to cement the bond between Pompey, Crassus and Julius Caesar, the First Triumvirate. When the marriage bond dissolved with her death in 54 BCE, Pompey refused to negotiate a new one.

JULIA (39 BCE–14 CE). Daughter of Caesar Augustus. Born in Rome in 39 BCE; died in Rhegium near end of 14 CE of malnutrition and despair; dau. of Gaius Julius Caesar Octavianus also known as Octavian or Augustus (63 BCE–14 CE), 1st emperor of Rome, and Scribonia (c. 75 BCE–after 16 CE), a Roman noblewoman; m. Marcus Marcellus (a son of Augustus' sister Octavia, and thus Augustus' nephew), in 25 BCE (died, autumn 23 BCE); m. Marcus Vipsanius Agrippa, in 21 BCE (died 12 BCE); m. Tiberius Claudius Nero (emperor), in 11 BCE; children: (2nd m.) Gaius Caesar (20 BCE–4 CE); Julia (b. 19 or 18 BCE); Lucius Caesar (17 BCE–2 CE); Agrippina the Elder (c. 14 BCE–33 CE); Marcus Vipsanius Agrippa Postumus (born after March, 12 BCE); (3rd m.) one son (b. 10 BCE) who died in infancy. ❖ Only daughter of Augustus, 1st emperor of Rome, who was a favorite and politically useful child—until her love affairs brought him disgrace; prosecuted for adultery and banished from Rome (2 BCE). ❖ See also *Women in World History.*

JULIA (c. 18 BCE–28 CE). Roman noblewoman. Name variations: Vipsania Julia. Born c. 18 or 19 BCE; died in 28 CE; dau. of Julia (39 BCE–14 CE) and Marcus Agrippa; granddau. of Octavian also known as Augustus (Roman emperor); sister of Agrippina the Elder; m. Lucius Aemilius Paullus; children: M. Aemilius Paullus; Aemilia. ❖ At age 26, was banished by Augustus into perpetual exile to island of Tremerus for adultery (8 CE); was kept alive by stepgrandmother Livia Drusilla until 28 CE.

JULIA, Aunt (1828–1909). *See Colman, Julia.*

JÚLIA, Francisca (1871–1920). Brazilian poet. Name variations: Francisca Julia; Francisca Júlia da Silva Munster; (pseudonyms) Caju, Maria Azevedo. Born 1871 in Brazil; died 1920. ❖ Worked as teacher and wrote for Rio and São Paulo newspapers; writings include *Marmores* (1895), *Livro da infância* (1899), *Esfinges* (1903), *Alma infantil* (with Júlio César da Silva, 1912) and *Poesias* (1961).

JULIA, Sister (1827–1901). *See McGroarty, Sister Julia.*

JULIA AGRIPPINA (15–59 CE). *See Agrippina the Younger.*

JULIA BERENICE (28 CE–after 80 CE). *See Berenice (28 CE–after 80 CE).*

JULIA DOMNA (c. 170–217 CE). Empress of Rome. Name variations: Julia Domna Augusta. Born c. 170 CE; died in 217 CE: dau. of Julius Bassianus (high priest of Elagabalus at Emesa); sister of Julia Maesa (c. 170–224 CE); became 2nd wife of Lucius Septimius Severus (who subsequent to their marriage became emperor of Rome), in 187; children: Septimius Bassianus (b. 188), later known as Marcus Aurelius Severus Antoninus or "Caracalla"; Publius Septimius Geta (b. 189). ❖ At 17, married Septimius Severus (187) and established herself as his confidante; when husband became an Augustus (senior emperor), reigned as an official Augusta (empress); was hailed as "Venus Victrix, Venus Genetrix"—titles which helped link Septimius' house to that of Julius Caesar, because the great Caesar had claimed direct descent from Venus (193); was honored with the title "Mater Castrorum" ("Mother of the Camp," 195), which publicly recognized her role in devising the political and military strategy which culminated in Septimius' unrivaled mastery of the Roman Empire; remained at his side when he invaded the Parthian Empire (197–98), Syria (198–99), Egypt (199–200), Syria (200–02), Rome (202), Africa (203), Italy (203–08), and Britain (208–11); when Gaius Fulvius Plautianus briefly undermined her relationship with husband, took solace in the company of sophists and philosophers, including Philostratus and Cassius Dio, and in the process got a reputation for promiscuity, probably as a result of Plautianus' slanders; continued to function as an Augusta, presiding over court ceremonies, religious rituals and sporting contests; following death of husband, held a dying son Geta in her arms after son Caracalla had ambushed him in a power struggle; despite this, served Caracalla for several years, reigning as the most influential woman of the empire; when Macrinus murdered Caracalla,

began plotting Macrinus' overthrow; was ordered into exile, and committed suicide by self-imposed starvation. ❖ See also *Women in World History.*

JULIA LIVILLA (c. 16 CE–after 38 CE). Roman noblewoman. Name variations: Livilla. Born c. 16 CE; dau. of Germanicus Caesar (15 BCE–19 CE) and Agrippina the Elder (c. 14 BCE–33 CE); sister of Agrippina the Younger (15–59), Caligula (12–41), and Drusilla (14–38); exiled in 38.

JULIA MAESA (c. 170–224 CE). Empress of Rome. Name variations: Julia Varia; Julia Maesa Augusta. Born c. 170; died in 224 CE; dau. of Julius Bassianus (high priest of Elagabalus at Emesa); sister of Julia Domna (c. 170–217 CE); m. Gaius Julius Avitus Alexianus also known as Julius Avitus (Roman senator); children: Julia Soaemias and Julia Mamaea, whose respective sons, Elagabalus and Severus Alexander, both became Roman emperors. ❖ Followed sister Julia Domna to Rome and saw husband Gaius Julius Avitus promoted to senatorial rank; following deaths of husband, sister, and sister's son Caracalla, lost the imperial influence she had been able to exert for close to 30 years; having no sons of her own, set out to remain politically prominent through her oldest grandchild, Elagabalus, when it was proposed that the 14-year-old pose as the dead emperor Caracalla's illegitimate son; when the ploy worked and Elagabalus became Rome's emperor, was appointed an "Augusta" in reward for her role in his accession; was undermined by her daughter Julia Soaemias; with other daughter, Julia Mamaea, maneuvered to bring 14-year-old grandson Severus Alexander to the throne (222). ❖ See also *Women in World History.*

JULIA MAIOR (fl. 1 BCE). Sister of Julius Caesar. Name variations: Julia the Elder. Born before 100 BCE; dau. of Gaius Julius Caesar (a patrician who had attained relatively modest political offices) and Aurelia (c. 120–54 BCE, of the Cotta family); sister of Julius Caesar (100–44 BCE) and Julia Minor (c. 100–51 BCE).

JULIA MAMAEA (c. 190–235). Empress of Rome. Name variations: Julia Avita Mamaea; Julia Mammaea; Julia Mamaea Augusta. Born c. 190; died in 235; dau. of Gaius Julius Avitus Alexianus and Julia Maesa (c. 170–224 CE); sister of Julia Soaemias; m. twice, the 1st time to an unknown, the 2nd time to Gessius Marcianus; children: Gessius Bassianus Alexiaus known later as Marcus Aurelius Severus Alexander or Severus Alexander (a Roman emperor); daughter Theocleia. ❖ Rose to prominence with marriage of aunt Julia Domna to Roman emperor Septimius Severus (mother Julia Maesa was sister of Domna); with mother, maneuvered to bring 14-year-old son Severus Alexander to the throne (222); became an "Augusta"; until mother's death (224), collaborated with her in running the Roman Empire, with Alexander as its figurehead; ran an efficient and enlightened regency; won over large segments of the civil administration by extensively seeking counsel before pursuing any public policy, and by seeing to it that Rome's traditional gods were revered; over the years, continued to influence her son, so much so that a substantial civilian opposition rose against her and publicized the "effeminacy" of Alexander, now 19 and still under the rule of his mother; when Rome was militarily threatened, son's competency was questioned; was eventually murdered along with son by their own troops. ❖ See also *Women in World History.*

JULIA MINOR (c. 100–51 BCE). Younger sister of Julius Caesar and grandmother of the emperor Augustus. Name variations: Julia; Julia the Younger. Born in Rome some time after 100 BCE, to date of elder brother Julius Caesar's birth; died in Rome in 51 BCE; dau. of Gaius Julius Caesar (patrician who had attained relatively modest political offices), and Aurelia (c. 120–54 BCE, of the Cotta family); received the education of Roman noble woman; sister of Julia Maior; m. Marcus Atius Balbus; children: two daughters, Atia the Elder (c. 80 BCE–?) and Atia the Younger. ❖ Possible witness in the Bona Dea trial of Publius Clodius Pulcher (61 BCE), an infamous event in the chaotic final years of the Roman Republic; supervised the upbringing and education of her grandson, the future emperor Augustus (c. 58–51 BCE); at time of death, was lauded in a funeral oration by grandson, which is often seen as an important stepping-stone in his advancing public career (51 BCE). ❖ See also *Women in World History.*

JULIA PAULA (fl. 220 CE). Roman empress. Name variations: Julia Cornelia Paula; m. Varius Avitus Bassianus Marcus Aurelius Antoninus, known as Elagabalus, Roman emperor (r. 218–222), in 219 (div. 220/221). ❖ Was the 1st of Roman emperor Elagabalus' 3 wives (he was also married to Aquilia Severa and Annia Faustina).

JULIA SOAEMIAS (d. 222). Empress of Rome. Name variations: Julia Soaemias Bassiana; Julia Soaemias Augusta; Julia Soemias; Julia Symiamira. Birthdate unknown; died in 222; dau. of Julia Maesa (c. 170–224 CE) and Gaius Julius Avitus Alexianus also known as Julius Avitus (a Roman senator); sister of Julia Mamaea; m. Sextus Varius Marcellus; children: Elagabalus (Roman emperor, with whom she was assassinated). ❖ See also *Women in World History.*

JULIA THE ELDER. *See Julia Maior.*

JULIA THE YOUNGER (c. 100–51 BCE). *See Julia Minor.*

JULIAN, Esther (1900–1990). *See James, Esther Marion Pretoria.*

JULIAN OF NORWICH (c. 1342–c. 1416). English Christian mystic and theologian. Name variations: St. Juliane in Norwice. Born c. Dec 1342, probably near Norwich, England; died c. 1416 (though some have speculated as late as 1423), in an anchorhold attached to church of St. Julian in Norwich; parents and education unknown; never married; no children. ❖ Best known for her *Revelations of Divine Love,* wished for 3 gifts from God as a girl, including an illness, which she endured at age 30; received a series of 16 revelations of God's love when thought to be at the point of death; shortly after, wrote an account of her experience; in an expanded version of her recollections, written 20 years later, included her understanding of their meaning; became an anchoress at the church of St. Julian in Conisford at Norwich and adopted the name of the church as her own, which is all we know of her given name; apparently remained in her cell until her death. *Revelations of Divine Love,* also referred to as *Showings* exists in 2 versions, the early account known as the "Short Text" and the longer and later version known as the "Long Text"; the book was published as the 1st volume of the acclaimed series *Classics of Western Spirituality.* ❖ See also Grace Jantzen, *Julian of Norwich: Mystic and Theologian* (Paulist Press, 1988); Joan Nuth, *Wisdom's Daughter: The Theology of Julian of Norwich* (Crossroad, 1991); and *Women in World History.*

JULIANA (1729–1796). *See Maria Juliana of Brunswick.*

JULIANA (1909–2004). Queen of the Netherlands. Name variations: Juliana of the Netherlands, Julia van Bueren. Born Juliana Louise Emma Marie Wilhelmina, princess of Orange-Nassau, duchess of Mecklenburg, in The Hague, the Netherlands, April 30, 1909; died Mar 20, 2004, in the Söstdijk Palace; only child of Wilhelmina (1880–1962), queen of the Netherlands (r. 1898–1948), and Duke Henry of Mecklenburg-Schwerin; studied at University of Leyden, 1927–30; m. Prince Bernard or Bernhard of Lippe-Biesterfeld, on Jan 7, 1937 (died Dec 1, 2004); children—4 daughters: Beatrix (b. 1938), queen of the Netherlands (r. 1980—); Irene Emma (b. 1939, who m. Carlos Hugo of Bourbon-Parma); Margaret or Margriet Francisca (b. 1943, who m. Pieter von Vollenhoven), and Maria Christina of Marijke (b. 1947). ❖ Owing to illness of mother Queen Wilhelmina, temporarily assumed royal power (Oct 14, 1947), ruling as princess regent until Dec 1; became regent for 2nd time (May 14, 1948); took oath as queen of the Netherlands (Sept 6, 1948); a popular ruler, dealt with the postwar rehabilitation of the Netherlands, plight of displaced persons, granting of independence to Indonesia, and often devastating floods that threatened the economic structure of her country; jettisoning formality, discarded a great deal of the pomp and ceremony that went with monarchy, including the curtsy; ruled until 1980, then abdicated in favor of daughter Beatrix. ❖ See also *Women in World History.*

JULIANA (1981—). *See Ribeiro Cabral, Juliana.*

JULIANA FALCONIERI (1270–1341). *See Falconieri, Juliana.*

JULIANA MARIE (1729–1796). *See Maria Juliana of Brunswick.*

JULIANA OF CORNILLON (1192–1258). Saint. Born in Rhétines in 1192; died in Fosses in 1258. ❖ A nun at Liége, was instrumental in establishing the feast of Corpus Christi. Feast day is April 5.

JULIANA OF NICOMEDIA (d. about 305). Saint. Died c. 305; dau. of Africanus. ❖ According to legend, was betrothed by father to a young noble named Evilase (Evilatius); informed her intended that she would not marry him until he became prefect of Nicomedia; when he did, reneged, demanding that he become a Christian; was tortured by father and beheaded by Evilase. Feast day is Feb 16.

JULIANA OF NORWICH (c. 1342–c. 1416). *See Julian of Norwich.*

JULIANE OF NASSAU-DILLENBURG (1546–1588). Countess Rudolstadt. Born Feb 11, 1546; died Aug 31, 1588; dau. of Juliane of Stolberg-Wernigrode (1506–1580) and William (1487–1559), count of Nassau-Dillenburg (r. 1516–1559); sister of William I the Silent (1533–1584), prince of Orange, and stadholder of Holland, Zealand, and Utrecht (r. 1572–1584); m. Albert VII (1537–1605), count Rudolstadt, June 14, 1575; children: Anna Sibylle (1584–1623, who m. Christian Gunther, count Sonderhausen).

JULIANE OF NORWICE (c. 1342–c. 1416). *See Julian of Norwich.*

JULIANE OF STOLBERG-WERNIGRODE (1506–1580). Countess of Nassau-Dillenburg. Name variations: Juliana of Stolberg-Wernigerode; Juliane von Stolberg-Wernigerode. Born Feb 27, 1506; died June 18, 1580; dau. of Botho III, count of Stolberg-Wernigrode, and Anna von Eppenstein; became 2nd wife of William (1487–1559), count of Nassau-Dillenburg (r. 1516–1559), Sept 20, 1531; children: William I the Silent (1533–1584), prince of Orange, and stadholder of Holland, Zealand, and Utrecht (r. 1572–1584); John (b. 1536), count of Nassau-Dillenburg; Juliane of Nassau-Dillenburg (1546–1588). William, count of Nassau-Dillenburg, was 1st m. to Walpurgis von Egmont (1505–1529).

JULIANNA DU GUESDIN (fl. 1370). French nun. Name variations: Julienne du Guesdin. Fl. in 1370 in Brittany; never married; no children. ❖ Played a modest role in protecting France from English aggression during Hundred Years' War; when a small English war troop tried storming over the walls of the Breton convent where she was a cloistered nun (1370), rallied her sisters to stay firm, and eventually the Englishmen were forced to give up in defeat.

JULIANNA OF RUTHENIA (fl. 1377). Grand princess of Lithuania and mother of the king of Poland. Married Olgierd, grand prince of Lithuania (died 1377); children: Jagiello, grand duke of Lithuania (1377–1434, who became Ladislas or Vladislav II [or V] Jagello, king of Poland and m. Jadwiga (1374–1399]).

JULIE (fl. 1770). Marquise de Marigny. Fl. around 1770; eldest dau. of Marie Irène Catherine de Buisson de Longpré (dau. of the seigneur of Longpré, near Falaise) and a wine commissioner and royal secretary named Filleul; sister of Adélaïde Filleul, marquise de Souza-Botelho (1761–1836); m. Abel François Poisson (1727–1781), marquis de Marigny (brother of Madame de Pompadour).

JULIE, Chévalier de Maupin (c. 1670–1707). *See Maupin, d'Aubigny.*

JULIERS, duchess of.
See Joan of Hainault (c. 1310–?).
See Mary of Guelders (d. 1405).
See Mary (1531–1581).

JULIET (d. 1962). *See Delf, Juliet.*

JULIN-MAUROY, Magda (1894–1990). Swedish figure skater. Name variations: Magda Mauroy. Born Magda Mauroy, July 24, 1894, in Sweden; died Dec 21, 1990. ❖ Won a gold medal for singles at Antwerp Olympics (1920), three-months pregnant at the time.

JULITTA OF CAESAREA (d. about 305). Saint. Died c. 305; lived in Caesarea, Cappadocia. ❖ A wealthy widow, was taken advantage of by an unscrupulous townsman who sought to rob her of her property; brought suit against him; in court, was accused of being a Christian; when the tribunal's president had an altar and incense brought in, refused to sacrifice to idols; was condemned to the stake. It was said that at the place of her torture, a spring arose which sometimes healed the sick. Feast day is July 30. ❖ See also *Women in World History.*

JULL, Roberta (1872–1961). Scottish-born Australian physician. Born Roberta Henrietta Margaretta Stewart, Aug 16, 1872, in Glasgow, Lanark, Scotland; died Mar 6, 1961, in Subiaco, Western Australia, Australia; Glasgow University, Doctor of Medicine and Master of Surgery, 1896; m. Martin Edward Jull (Under Secretary for the Public Works Dept., Western Australia), Nov 12, 1898; children: Henrietta Drake-Brockman (writer). ❖ Leader in the infant movement, became local supervisor of public examinations for University of Adelaide; was the 1st woman to establish a medical practice in Perth (1897); became 1st Medical Officer of Schools in Western Australian Public Health Department (1918); was a member of the Senate for University of Western Australia (1915–42); served as founding president of Association of University Women (1926–28); member of Australian delegation to League of Nations (1929).

JUMEL, Eliza Bowen (1775–1865). Second wife of Aaron Burr. Name variations: Betsy Bowen; Eliza Brown. Born in 1775 in Providence,

Rhode Island; died July 16, 1865; dau. of John Bowen (sailor) and Phebe Kelley; m. Stephen Jumel, April 9, 1804 (died 1832); m. former vice-president Aaron Burr, July 1, 1833 (div. 1836); children: (illeg.) George Washington Bowen (b. Oct 9, 1794); (adopted) Mary Eliza (illeg. dau. of Eliza Jumel's half-sister Polly Clarke). ❖ Infamous American beauty and wealthy widow, who, after a scandalous past, married 77-year old Aaron Burr, because of her desire for social acceptance and his desire for money; began divorce proceedings following year; spent next 28 years moving around NY area, chasing after and being rebuffed by society until gradually she grew more reclusive. The Jumel mansion, bought in 1903 by City of New York, is one of Manhattan's historical landmarks. ❖ See also *Women in World History.*

JUMPER, Betty Mae (1923—). Native American nurse. Name variations: Betty Mae Tiger Jumper. Born Betty Mae Tiger, April 27, 1923, in the Everglades, near Lake Okeechobee, FL; dau. of Mae Tiger (full Seminole) and Abe Partan (Euro-French trapper and cane cutter); granddau of Mary Tiger (Seminole midwife); studied nursing at Kiowa Indian Hospital in Lawton, OK; m. Moses Jumper (1 of only 2 Seminole WWII veterans), 1946; children: 3. ❖ The 1st Seminole Indian trained woman nurse, the 1st Seminole (with cousin) high school graduate (1945) and the 1st and only female Seminole tribal council chair (1967–71), began work as a Bureau of Indian Affairs nurse (1946) for Seminole reservations in state of FL; acted as an interpreter for old tribe members (1950s) to support continued official recognition of the Seminole Nation; served as director of operations for Seminole Communications (from 1971); established (1979) and served as editor in chief of official newspaper of the Seminole Nation, the *Seminole Tribune*; writings include *Legends of the Seminoles* (1994). ❖ See also autobiography, *A Seminole Legend: the Life of Betty Mae Tiger Jumper* (2001).

JUNE (1829–1901). See Croly, Jane Cunningham.

JUNE (1901–c. 1984). English theatrical ballet dancer. Name variations: June Howard Tripp. Born June 11, 1901, in Blackpool, England; died c. 1984. ❖ Performed in Anna Pavlova's London production of *Snowflakes* as a child (1911); moved to Paris, where she performed at Folies Bergère; back in London, began performing as specialty dancer in such stage productions as *The Passing Show* (1914), *Watch Your Step* (1915), *London, Paris and New York* (1920); appeared in numerous musical comedies as soubrette and dance lead, including in *Little Nellie Kelly* (1923), *Happy-Go-Lucky* (1926), *Here's How!* (1934) and *The Town Talks* (1936).

JUNG JAE-EUN (c. 1981—). South Korean taekwondo player. Born c. 1981 in South Korea. ❖ Won World championship (1997, 1999, 2001); won Asian Games (1998); won World Cup (2000, 2002); won a gold medal for 49–57kg at Sydney Olympics (2000); won Asian championship (2002).

JUNG, Lovieanne (1980—). American softball player. Born Jan 11, 1980, in Honolulu, Hawaii; attended University of Arizona. ❖ Shortstop, won World championship (2002); won team gold medal at Athens Olympics (2004).

JUNG SOO-NOK (1955—). Korean volleyball player. Born Feb 16, 1955, in South Korea. ❖ At Montreal Olympics, won a bronze medal in team competition (1976).

JUNG SUN YONG. South Korean judoka. Born in South Korea. ❖ Won a silver medal for 52–56kg lightweight at Atlanta Olympics (1996).

JUNG SUNG-SOOK. South Korean judoka. Born in South Korea. ❖ Won World championship (1995); won a bronze medal for 56–61kg half-middleweight at Atlanta Olympics (1996) and a bronze medal for 57–63 kg half-middleweight at Sydney Olympics (2000).

JUNGE, Traudel (1920–2002). German secretary. Born Gertraud Humps, 1920, in Munich, Germany; died of cancer, Feb 10, 2002, in Munich; dau. of Max Humps (early Nazi devotee); m. Hans Junge (Hitler aide), 1943 (killed 1944). ❖ Became one of Adolf Hitler's personal secretaries (Dec 1942); moved with Hitler and staff into underground bunker (Jan 1945); took his last will and testament; claimed she only found out about the Holocaust after the war and spent her years racked with guilt. ❖ See also (documentary) *Blind Spot: Hitler's Secretary* (2002).

JUNGER, Esther (c. 1915—). American dancer and theatrical choreographer. Born c. 1915 in New York, NY. ❖ Trained with Bird Larson at Neighborhood Playhouse in NYC before joining his troupe; performed with New World Players and Senia Gluck-Sandor's Dance Center;

worked at Humphrey-Weidman studio; danced at Radio City Music Hall as soloist in *2036*; choreographed own solo recitals (starting 1930), including *Go Down Death* (1930), *Closed in Cities* (1932), and *Bach Goes To Town*; also choreographed for such Broadway shows as *Tis of Thee* (1940), *Dark of the Moon* (1945) and *Dear Judas* (1947); received one of the 1st Bennington Choreographic fellowships (1937). Further works of choreography include *Bolero* (1930), *Ballad of a Nun* (1930), *Soap Box* (1932), *Dance for the People* (1937), *Ravage* (1937), *Stage Characters* (1940), *Judgment Day* (1940), *Negro Sketches* (1940), *Cinema Ballerinas* (1940) and *Black Narcissus* (1942).

JUNGJOHANN, Caren (1970—). German field-hockey player. Born Mar 8, 1970, in West Germany. ❖ At Barcelona Olympics, won a silver medal in team competition (1992).

JUNGMANN, Elisabeth (d. 1959). German-born author and literary figure. Name variations: Elizabeth Jungmann; Lady Beerbohm. Died in 1959; m. Sir Max Beerbohm (critic and essayist), 1956 (died 1956). ❖ Served as secretary to Gerhart Hauptmann (1922–34); left Germany as a "non-Aryan"; worked with Rudolf Binding; immigrated to England (1938); married Max Beerbohm one month before his death, having looked after him for many years following the death of his first wife, Florence Kahn.

JUNIA I (fl. 1st c. BCE). Roman noblewoman. Fl. in 1st century BCE; dau. of Servilia II (c. 100–after 42 BCE) and D. Junius Silanus (consul); m. M. Aemilius Lepidus.

JUNIA II (fl. 1st c. BCE). Roman noblewoman. Fl. in the 1st century BCE; dau. of Servilia II (c. 100–after 42 BCE) and D. Junius Silanus (consul); m. P. Servilius Isauricus.

JUNIA III (fl. 1st c. BCE). Roman noblewoman. Fl. in 1st century BCE; dau. of Servilia II (c. 100–after 42 BCE) and D. Junius Silanus (consul); m. C. Cassius Longinus, better known as Cassius (an assassin of Julius Caesar).

JUNIA CLAUDILLA (fl. 32 CE). Roman noblewoman. Fl. around 32 CE; 1st wife of Caligula (12–41), Roman emperor (r. 37–41). ❖ Became the 1st wife of Caligula on the island of Capri, at the urging of Tiberius. Following her death, Caligula married Livia Orestilla.

JUNKER, Helen (1905—). German runner. Born Dec 8, 1905, in Germany. ❖ At Amsterdam Olympics, won a bronze medal in the 4 x 100-meter relay (1928).

JUNKER, Karin (1940—). German politician. Born Dec 24, 1940, in Düsseldorf, Germany. ❖ Member of SPD (Social Democratic Party) Bureau and Executive and chair of SPD Women; as a European Socialist, elected to 4th and 5th European Parliament (EP, 1994–99, 1999–2004).

JUNKIN, Margaret (1820–1897). See Preston, Margaret Junkin.

JUNKO TABEI (b. 1939). See Tabei, Junko.

JUNOT, Madame (1784–1838). See Abrantès, Laure d'.

JUPP, Catherine Augusta (1836–1916). See Francis, Catherine Augusta.

JURADO, Alicia (1915—). Argentinean novelist and short-story writer. Born May 22, 1915, in Buenos Aires, Argentina; received PhD from University of Buenos Aires. ❖ Received international scholarships and became member of Argentinean Academy of Letters (1980); works include *La cárcel de los hierros* (1961), *Lenguas de polvo y sueño* (1965), *En soledad vivía* (1967), and *Los rostros del engaño* (1968); also wrote study of Jorge Luis Borges, *Genio y figura de Borges.*

JURADO, Jeanette (1966—). American singer. Name variations: Exposé. Born Nov 14, 1966, in Los Angeles, CA. ❖ Was member of vocal trio Exposé which had great success with Latin-tinged dance songs; with Exposé, released multiplatinum debut album *Exposure* (1987) and had such singles hits as "Come Go With Me" (1987), "Point of No Return" (1987), "Seasons Change" (1987), and "I'll Never Get Over You (Getting Over Me)" (1993).

JURADO, Katy (1924–2002). Mexican actress. Born Maria Cristina Jurado Garcia, Jan 16, 1924, in Guadalajara, Mexico; died July 5, 2002, in Cuernavaca, Morelos, Mexico; m. Victor Velasquez (div.); m. Ernest Borgnine (actor), 1959 (div. 1964); children: 2. ❖ Following a Mexican film career, moved to Los Angeles as a columnist for Mexican publications; was featured in such films as *High Noon* (1952), *Trapeze* (1956), *The Man from Del Rio* (1956), *One-Eyed Jacks* (1961), *Barabbas* (1961), *The Children of Sanchez* (1968) and *Under the Volcano* (1984).

Nominated for an Academy Award for Best Supporting Actress for *Broken Lance* (1954), the 1st Mexican actress so honored.

JURCA, Branca (1914–1999). Slovenian writer. Name variations: Branka Jurca. Born near Sezana, Slovenia, in 1914; died in 1999; educated in Maribor. ❖ Worked as a teacher, editor and freelance author; during WWII, was active in the resistance against the Nazis; was captured and sent to 2 concentration camps, Gonars and Ravensbrück; survived the camps and returned to Yugoslavia (1945); wrote and published several books and articles, eventually becoming a full-time editor and freelance writer who concentrated on books for young readers; best known for autobiography *Rodis se samo enkrat* (*You're Only Born Once,* 1972); also published novel *Ko zorijo jagode* (*When the Berries Bloom,* 1974), which was filmed as *Strawberry Time.* ❖ See also *Women in World History.*

JURIC, Maria (1873–1957). *See Zagorka, Maria.*

JURINAC, Sena (1921—). Bosnian soprano. Born Srebrenka Jurinac, Oct 24, 1921, in Travnik, Yugoslavia; m. Sesto Bruscantini (baritone), 1953 (div. 1957); m. Josef Lederle, 1975; studied with Milka Kostrencic in Zagreb. ❖ Made debut at Zagreb (1942), Vienna Staatsoper (1945), Salzburg (1957), Teatro all Scala (1948), Glyndebourne (1949), and Chicago (1963); one of the fine sopranos championed by Herbert von Karajan, specialized in Mozart and Strauss and was known for her Butterfly, Tosca, and Donna Anna; though excelling in tragedy, also sang a number of comic roles to great success. ❖ See also U. Tamussino, *Sena Jurinac* (Augsburg, 1971); and *Women in World History.*

JURNEY, Dorothy Misener (1909–2002). American reporter and editor. Name variations: Dorothy Misener. Born May 8, 1909, in Michigan City, Indiana; died June 19, 2002, in Saint Petersburg, Florida; dau. of Herbert Roy Misener (newspaper publisher) and Mary Zeola Hershey Misener (politician and suffragist who was 1 of the 1st 3 women elected to Indiana House of Representatives). ❖ Served as reporter for *Michigan City News* (1938), *News Dispatch* (1938–39), and *Post-Tribune* (Gary, IN, 1939–41); served as editor in women's department of *Miami News* (1943–44, 1946–49), women's editor for *Miami Herald* (1949–59), and women's editor for *Detroit Free Press* (1959–72); served as (1st woman) assistant city editor and later acting city editor for *Washington Daily News* (1944–46), assistant managing editor for *Detroit Free Press* (1973), and assistant managing editor for features at *Philadelphia Inquirer* (1973–75); became 1st woman board member of Associated Press Managing Editors association (1972); founded Women's Network (editorial talent search firm) and served as media specialist to Women's Study Program and Policy Center at George Washington University.

JURRILËNS, Henny (1949—). Dutch ballet dancer. Name variations: Henny Jurrilens. Born Feb 21, 1949, in Arnheim, Holland, Netherlands. ❖ Performed with Norwegian National Opera Ballet early on for short period; joined Dutch National Ballet (1973), where she danced featured roles in Toer van Schayk's *Pyrric, Dances,* and *Eight Madrigals,* Rudi van Dantzig's *Ginastera* and *Ramifications,* and in works by Hans van Manen.

JURY, Huhana (Susan/Susanna) (c. 1820–1854). *See Jury, Te Aitu-o-te-rangi.*

JURY, Te Aitu-o-te-rangi (c. 1820–1854). New Zealand landowner and farmer. Name variations: Huhana (Susan/Susanna) Jury. Born Te Aitu-o-te-rangi, c. 1820, in Wairarapa, New Zealand; died 1854; dau. of Te Whatahoronui and his wife, Aromea; m. John Milsome Jury, 1840 (died 1902); children: 4. ❖ Forced off ancestral lands by tribal wars, returned with husband to claim them, building home there on Te Urera (Jury's Island), where they farmed and raised cattle. ❖ See also *Dictionary of New Zealand Biography* (Vol. 1).

JUSTIN, Enid (1894–1990). American boot manufacturer. Name variations: Miss Enid. Born Enid Justin in Nocona, Texas, near the Red River, April 8, 1894; died Oct 14, 1990, in Nocona; dau. of Herman Joseph Justin and Anna (Allen) Justin (pioneer Texas bootmakers); m. Julius L. Stelzer, Aug 6, 1915 (div. 1935); m. Harry Whitman, Nov 9, 1940 (div. 1945); children: (1st m.) Anna Jo (1916–1918). ❖ A leader in the boot industry, left Nocona school at 13 to work in father's boot factory (1907); father died (1918) and brothers moved boot company to Fort Worth (1925); started the Nocona Boot Company, becoming in the process the 1st woman in what was truly the male-dominated world of bootmaking (1925); built larger boot factory and relocated it away from downtown area in Nocona (1948); after several expansions, saw plant reach its greatest size (1981); following controversial legal action, effectively retired when Nocona Boot Company merged with Justin Industries (1981). ❖ See also *Women in World History.*

JUSTINA (d. 64). Saint and patron of Padua. Name variations: Justina of Lombardy. Died c. 64 CE; her martyrdom is placed by most under reign of Nero (54–68). ❖ Her supposed relics, said to have been recovered in 1177, are preserved at Padua in a church which bears her name. Feast day is Oct 7.

JUSTINA (d. 304). Saint. Name variations: Justina of Damascus. Died 304. ❖ Shared her martyrdom with St. Cyprian, under reign of Diocletian (284–305) or Claudius II (268–270). East Roman empress Eudocia (c. 401–460) recorded the story in verse during 5th century; feast day is Sept 26.

JUSTINA (fl. 350–370). Roman empress. Fl. between 350 and 370; 2nd wife of Valentinian I, Roman emperor (r. 364–375); children: Valentinian II, Western emperor of Rome (fl. 375–392); Galla (c. 365–394); Justa; Grata. Valentinian I's 1st wife was Marina Severa.

JUTTA. *Variant of Judith.*

JUTTA (d. 1284). Prioress of Roskilde. Name variations: Jutta Eriksdottir or Ericsdottir. Died in 1284; dau. of Erik or Eric IV Ploughpenny (1216–1250), king of Denmark (r. 1241–1250) and Jutta of Saxony (d. around 1267).

JUTTA OF HUY (1158–1228). *See Ivetta of Huy.*

JUTTA OF MECKLENBURG-STRELITZ (1880–1946). Nominal queen of Montenegro. Name variations: known as Militza following her marriage. Born Augusta Charlotte Jutta Alexandra Georgina Adolpine, Jan 24, 1880; died Feb 17, 1946; dau. of Adolphus Frederick V, grand duke of Mecklenburg-Strelitz, and Elizabeth of Anhalt-Dessau (1857–1933); m. Daniel or Danilo Petrovitch-Njegos (son of Nicholas, king of Montenegro), July 15, 1899.

JUTTA OF SAXONY (d. around 1267). Margravine of Brandenburg. Died before Feb 2, 1267; dau. of Albert I, duke of Saxony, and Agnes of Thuringia; m. Erik or Eric IV Ploughpenny (1216–1250), king of Denmark (r. 1241–1250), Nov 17, 1239; became 2nd wife of John I, margrave of Brandenburg, May 7, 1255; children: (1st m.) Ingeborg of Denmark (d. 1287); Sophie of Denmark (d. 1286); Jutta (d. 1284, prioress of Roskilde); Agnes (nun at Roskilde); Christof; Knut; (2nd m.) Agnes of Brandenburg (d. 1304). John I's 1st wife was Sophia of Denmark.

JUTTA OF SPONHEIM (d. 1136). German mystic. Fl. between 1100–1136; died in 1136 at the convent of Disibodenberg in Germany; sister of Count Meginhard of Sponheim; never married; no children. ❖ A German noble and holy woman, felt a religious calling even as a child; grew up receiving mystical visions; became a recluse at the small establishment of Disibodenberg; within a few years, saw a large community of women establish itself near her cell, which included Hildegard of Bingen whom Jutta raised to understand the calling of the mystic.

JUVONEN, Helvi (1919–1959). Finnish poet. Born Nov 5, 1919, in Iisalmi, Finland; died Oct 1, 1959, in Helsinki; dau. of Juho Petterinpoika Juvonen (owned a clothes shop) and Impi Maria Liimatainen; attended University of Helsinki. ❖ Considered the most important writer of Finnish modernism of 1950s, studied German mystics and wrote lyric poems of spiritual intensity; suffering from depression, was hospitalized a number of times; works include *Kääpiöpuu* (1949), *Pohjajäätä* (1952), and *Päivästä päivään* (1954); also trans. Robinson Jeffers and Emily Dickinson, among others, into Finnish.

JUWAIRIYAH (fl. 627). One of the wives of Muhammad. An Arabian woman taken captive at the campaign against the tribe of the Banu 'l-Mustalik, married Muhammad in 627 CE. ❖ See also *Women in World History.*

K

KAAHUMANU (1777–1832). **Hawaiian queen regent.** Name variations: Ka'ahumanu. Pronunciation: Kah-ah-HEW-mon-ew. Born 1777 (some sources cite 1768) in Hana, Maui, Hawaii; died June 5, 1832, at Manoa, Oahu, Hawaii; dau. of Keeaumoku (chief of the island of Hawaii) and Namahana (dau. of a chief of Maui); at 5, given to Kamehameha I the Great (1758–1819), king of Hawaii (r. 1810–1819), to live in his household until old enough to become his wife, c. 1782; no children. ❖ Chief wife of Kamehameha I and, as co-regent of Kamehameha II and Kamehameha III, was the driving force behind the abolition of the *kapu* system in Hawaiian Islands (Hawaiian women were subject to a system of religious restraints that regulated much of their lives) and was the architect of the 1st code of secular law; took father's place in the chiefs' council (1794); received from Kamehameha the power to be a *puuhonua* or sanctuary (1795); named *kahu* (sacred guardian) of the heir of Kamehameha I (1804); served as *kuhina nui* (reigned as regent, co-ruler, 1819–1832); influenced Kamehameha II to abandon the *kapu* system (1819); adopted Christianity (1824); established a code of law for the Hawaiians based on Christian teachings (1827). ❖ See also Jane L. Silverman, *Kaahumanu, Molder of Change* (1987); and *Women in World History.*

KAARO, Ani (fl. 1885–1901). **New Zealand tribal leader and prophet.** Dau. of Hohaia and Harata; m. Ngakete Hapeta. ❖ Became tribal leader during difficult times when European settlement conflicted with emerging movement for tribal unity and autonomy; made pilgrimage to Parihaka (1885), and converted to faith of visionary Whiti-o-Rongomai, who believed authority of Maori would ultimately be restored; endured rivalry with Remana Hane's religious leadership to become unchallenged leader of Ngati Hao (1889). ❖ See also *Dictionary of New Zealand Biography* (Vol. 2).

KABAEVA, Alina (1983—). **Russian rhythmic gymnast.** Name variations: Alina Kabayeva; (nickname) Lina or Alja. Born Alina Maratovna Kabaeva, May 12, 1983, in Tashkent, Uzbekistan, USSR. ❖ Won Goodwill Games (1998); won World championship in all-around, clubs and ribbon (1999) and all-around, ball and ribbon (2001, 2003); won European championship (1998, 1999); won French International (1999), Grand Prix (1998), Pan American Games (1987); at Sydney Olympics, won a bronze medal for indiv. all-around (2000); won Grand Prix (2000); banned from competition for doping offenses (2002–03) and had to return 2001 World medals; won an indiv. all-around gold medal at Athens Olympics (2004).

KABAYEVA, Alina (1983—). *See Kabaeva, Alina.*

KABERRY, Phyllis (1910–1977). **British social anthropologist.** Born Phyllis Mary Kaberry in 1910 in California; grew up in Sydney, Australia; then moved to London, England; died 1977; dau. of an English architect; Sydney University, BA, 1933, MA, 1935; London School of Economics, PhD, 1939; never married. ❖ Became 1st woman anthropologist to focus full attention on women's roles in Aboriginal Australia; published the classic, *Aboriginal Woman* (1930); served as research assistant at London School of Economics (1936–39); conducted fieldwork among the Abelam of Sepik River in New Guinea (1939–40); taught at Sydney University; conducted research on the Nso (Nsaw) women in the Cameroons (1940s); developed dominant interest in African anthropology; joined department of anthropology at University College London (late 1940s); also wrote *Women of the Grassfields* (1952).

KABLER-SKALA, Carole Jo (1938—). *See Callison, Carole Jo.*

KABOS, Ilona (1893–1973). **Hungarian pianist.** Born in Budapest, Hungary, Dec 7, 1893; died in London, May 28, 1973; m. Louis Kentner. ❖ After teaching at Royal Budapest Academy of Music (1930–36), moved to London; specialized in duo-piano music, often

performing works of Béla Bartok with husband; settling in US (1965), taught for a number of years at Juilliard School of Music.

KACIUSYTE, Lina (1963—). **Soviet swimmer.** Born Jan 1963 in USSR. ❖ At Moscow Olympics, won a gold medal in the 200-meter breast-stroke (1980).

KADARÉ, Elena (1943—). **Albanian short-story writer.** Name variations: Elena Kadare; Elena Gushi-Kadare. Born 1943 in Fier, Albania; m. Ismail Kadaré (writer). ❖ The 1st woman to publish a novel in post-1945 Albania, worked as journalist and editor after graduating from University of Tirana; writings include *Turn off the Light, Vera!* (1965), *A Difficult Birth* (1970), *The Bridge and the State of Siege* (1978), *The Spouses* (1981) and *Një grua nga Tirana* (1994).

KÁDÁRNÉ, Ibolya (1915—). *See Csák, Ibolya.*

KADE-KOUDIJS, Gerda van der (1923—). *See van der Kade-Koudijs, Gerda.*

KADIJAH (c. 555–619 CE). *See Khadijah.*

KADLECOVA, Jirina (1948—). **Czech field-hockey player.** Born June 1948. ❖ At Moscow Olympics, won a silver medal in team competition (1980).

KAEL, Pauline (1919–2001). **American film critic.** Born June 19, 1919, in Petaluma, California; died Sept 3, 2001, in Great Barrington, MA; dau. of Isaac Paul Kael (farmer) and Judith (Friedman) Kael; graduate of University of California at Berkeley, 1940; Georgetown University, LLD, 1972; div. (3 times according to some published sources; 4 according to others); children: Gina James. ❖ One of the most influential movie critics from 1960s to 1980s, wrote 1st piece of film criticism for *City Lights* in San Francisco, followed by articles in *Partisan Review, Sight and Sound, Moviegoing, Kulchur* and *Film Quarterly;* her widely acclaimed collection of articles in book form, *I Lost It at the Movies* (1965), led to assignments from *Life, Holiday* and *Mademoiselle;* was also regular film critic for *McCall's* (1965–66) and *The New Republic* (1966–67); joined *The New Yorker* (1968), reviewing there for 24 years; retired (1991); other books include *Kiss Kiss Bang Bang* (1968), *Going Steady* (1970), *The Citizen Kane Book* (1971), *Reeling* (1976), *When the Lights Go Down* (1980), *Taking It All In* (1984), *State of the Art* (1985), *Hooked* (1989) and *For Keeps* (1994). Received National Book Award for *Deeper into Movies* (1974). ❖ See also memoir *5001 Nights at the Movies* (Holt, 1991); and *Women in World History.*

KAESLING, Dagmar (1947—). **East German runner.** Born Feb 15, 1947, in East Germany. ❖ At Munich Olympics, won a gold medal in the 4 x 400-meter relay (1972).

KAFFKA, Margit (1880–1918). **Hungarian poet and novelist.** Born in Nagykároly, Hungary (now Carei, Romania), June 10, 1880; died of influenza in Budapest, Hungary, Dec 1, 1918; dau. of Gyula Kaffka; earned teaching diploma at Erzsébet Training College for Women, 1902; m. Bruno Fröhlich (forestry engineer), 1905; m. Ervin Bauer, 1914; children: (1st m.) László. ❖ Generally regarded as Hungary's 1st major woman writer, published poems and short stories in journals *Hét, Magyar Geniusz* and *Nyugat* (The West); published 2 volumes of verse, *Tallózó évek* (Years of Search, 1911) and *Utolszor a lyrán* (For the Last Time on the Lyre, 1912), and 1st novel *Szinek és évek* (Colors and Years, 1912); novels include *Mária évei* (The Years of Mária, 1913), *Állomások* (Stations, 1914), *Két nyár* (Two Summers, 1916) and *Hangyaboly* (*The Ant Heap,* 1917); probed 2 pressing issues of her day: the decline of the gentry class and the problems faced by women in an era of major social changes; died of influenza (1918), her son dying the next day. ❖ See also *Women in World History.*

KAFKA, Helene (1894–1943). *See Restituta, Sister.*

KAGABU, Yoko (1960—). Japanese volleyball player. Born Oct 28, 1960, in Japan. ❖ At Los Angeles Olympics, won a bronze medal in team competition (1984).

KAGAN, Elena (1960—). American lawyer and educator. Born April 28, 1960, in New York, NY; Princeton University, AB, 1981; Worcester College, Oxford, MPhil, 1983; Harvard Law School, JD, 1986. ❖ Began career as clerk to Justice Thurgood Marshall; was professor of law, University of Chicago Law School (1995–97); during Clinton administration, was associate counsel to the president (1995–96) and deputy assistant to the president for domestic policy (1997–99); at Harvard, was visiting professor of law (1999–2001), professor (2001), then became the 1st woman dean of Harvard Law School (2003).

KAGAN, Elsa (1896–1970). See Triolet, Elsa.

KAHANA-CARMON, Amalia (1930—). Israeli novelist. Name variations: Amalia Kahana Carmon. Born 1930 on Kibbutz Ein Harod, Israel; raised in Tel Aviv. ❖ Lived in England and Switzerland before returning to live in Tel Aviv; works include *Bichfifa Achat* (1966), *Ve'Yreach Be'Emek Ayalon* (1971), *Sadot Magnetim* (1977), *Lema'alah Be'Montifer* (1984) and *Kan Nagour* (1996). Received Bialik Award (1994).

KAHINA (r. 695–703 CE). Priestess and queen of Carthage. Name variations: Cahina; Dhabba the Kahina; Dahiyah Kahinah; Dahia-al Kahina; Kahiyah. Reigned between 695 and 703. ❖ Powerful and ruthless ruler of the Berber tribes of northern Africa, rallied the normally pastoral Berbers of the Atlas Mountains of North Africa around the time of the capture of Carthage by the Arabs (695); successful in driving the Arabs back to Egypt, remained queen over a large region of North Africa for next 5 years; hoping to ward off another attack, laid waste to her lands, ordering all Berber cities destroyed, gold and silver buried, and even fruit trees cut down, leaving a desert; when Arabs attacked again (c. 705), was either killed in battle or beheaded, and the Berbers ultimately became allies of the Arabs.

KAHLO, Frida (1907–1954). Mexican painter. Name variations: Frida Rivera. Born Magdalena Carmen Frida Kahlo y Calderón in Coyoacan, Mexico, July 6, 1907; died in Coyoacan, July 13, 1954; dau. of Guillermo Kahlo (photographer) and Matilde Calderón; m. Diego Rivera, 1929 (div. 1939, remarried 1940). ❖ Painter whose singular self-images, unconventional in style and startling in content, distinguished her from her peers; at 6, as a result of Polio, was left with an atrophied and shortened right leg; endured horrific injuries in a bus accident (1925); produced 1st serious painting, a self-portrait, the 1st of over 55 works she would make representing her own image (1926); became involved in circle of revolutionaries, artists, and intellectuals which included Diego Rivera (1927); lived in San Francisco (1929–31); painted a portrait of Luther Burbank, a California horticulturalist, in a style marking the advent of a more fantastical Frida Kahlo (1931); traveled to NY and Detroit with husband as he worked on murals; returned to Mexico (1933), where husband began affair with her sister, Cristina Kahlo; became actively involved with politics when she and Diego played hosts to Bolshevik revolutionaries, Leon and Natalia Trotsky, who had been offered asylum in Mexico (1937); held 1st solo exhibition, NY (1938), receiving favorable reviews; selected as a member of Seminario de Cultura Mexicana (1942); held 1st Mexican solo exhibition (1953); lived as an invalid; paintings include *Henry Ford Hospital* (1932), *My Nurse and I* (1937), *The Two Fridas* (1939), *The Little Deer, The Broken Column* and *Without Hope.* ❖ See also Malka Drucker, *Frida Kahlo: Torment and Triumph in her Life and Art* (Bantam, 1991); Hayden Herrera, *Frida* (Harper & Row, 1983); film *Frida,* starring Salma Hayek; and *Women in World History.*

KAHN, Florence (1878–1951). American actress. Name variations: Lady Beerbohm; Mrs. Max Beerbohn. Born Mar 3, 1878, in Memphis, TN; died Jan 13, 1951, in Rapallo, Italy; m. Sir Max Beerbohm (critic and essayist), 1910. ❖ Made stage debut on tour in *The Girl I Left Behind* (1897); became identified with Independent Theatre movement in NY; appeared in such plays as *El Gran Galeoto, Ties, The Three Musketeers, King Henry V* (with Richard Mansfield), *Don Caesar's Return, Rosmersholm, When We Dead Awaken,* and *Hedda Gabler* as Mrs. Elvsted in support of Alla Nazimova's Hedda (1907); made London debut as Rebecca West in *Rosmersholm* (1908); lived in Italy on marriage.

KAHN, Florence Prag (1866–1948). American politician. Born in Salt Lake City, Utah, Nov 9, 1866; died in San Francisco, California, Nov 16, 1948; dau. of Conrad Prag and Mary (Goldsmith) Prag; University of California at Berkeley, AB, 1887; m. Julius Kahn (Republican US congressional rep for almost 25 years), Mar 19, 1899 (died 1924); children: Julius Kahn; Conrad P. Kahn. ❖ Republican from California, was elected to husband's vacated seat in US House of Representatives following his death (1925), then reelected to 5 succeeding Congresses (1925–37); served on Committee on Military Affairs and on Appropriations Committee; credited with securing expanded military installations in her district, was also instrumental in gaining congressional approval for San Francisco Bay Bridge; lost bid for a 6th term during Democratic landslide (1936).

KAHN, Lilly (c. 1898–1978). German-born actress. Name variations: Lily Kahn. Born c. 1898, in Peitz, Spreewald, Germany; died Nov 2, 1978. ❖ At 15, made stage debut at Goethe Festival, Düsseldorf, in *Penthesilea;* appeared at National Theater, Dresden (1923–32) in such parts as Medea, Lady Macbeth, Judith, The Lady in *To Damascus,* Clytemnestra in *The Oresteia,* and Brunhild in *Nibelungen;* played lead roles at the Jewish theater in Berlin (1933–39); fled to England (1939); made London debut in *Awake and Sing* (1942), followed by *Blow Your Own Trumpet, The Cradle Song, Tomorrow the World, Dutch Family, I Remember Mama, The Father* and *The Golden Door,* among others; films include *Escape to Danger, Mrs. Fitzherbert* (as Queen Charlotte), *The Third Man, Betrayed, Foreign Intrigue* and *Cat Girl.*

KAHN, Madeline (1942–1999). American actress and comedian. Born Madeline Gail Kahn, Sept 29, 1942, in Boston, MA; died of ovarian cancer, Dec 3, 1999, in NY; dau. of Bernard B. Wolfson (dress manufacturer) and Paula (Wolfson) Kahn; Hofstra University, BA, 1964; m. John Hansbury (attorney), Oct 6, 1999. ❖ Best known for her ditzy characters in films of Mel Brooks, made Broadway debut in *New Faces of 1968;* other stage appearances include *Two by Two* (1970), *She Loves Me* (1977), *On the Twentieth Century* (1978), *Born Yesterday* (1988) and *The Sisters Rosensweig* (1992); made film debut in *What's Up, Doc?* (1972); reached zenith as the tired saloon singer Lili von Shtupp in *Blazing Saddles* (1974); other films include *Young Frankenstein* (1974), *The Adventure of Sherlock Holmes's Smarter Brother* (1975), *Won Ton Ton— The Dog Who Saved Hollywood* (1976), *High Anxiety* (1977), *The Cheap Detective* (1978), *History of the World: Part I* (1981) and *Clue* (1985); appeared in 3 tv series, "Oh Madeline" (1983–84), "Mr. President" (1989), and "Cosby." Nominated for Tony for *Boom Boom Room* (1973); nominated for Oscars as Best Supporting Actress for *Paper Moon* (1973) and *Blazing Saddles* (1974). ❖ See also *Women in World History.*

KAHUNGUNU, Ngati.
See Bridger, Bub (1924—).
See Hineira, Arapera (1932—).

KAHUTIA, Riparata (c. 1838–1887). See Kahutia, Riperata.

KAHUTIA, Riperata (c. 1838–1887). New Zealand tribal leader. Name variations: Riparata Kahutia. Born probably in 1838 or 1839, at either Makauri or Taruheru, in Poverty Bay, New Zealand; died on June 10, 1887, at Whataupoko, New Zealand; dau. of Kahutia and Uaia (Uwaia); m. Mikaera (died 1886); children: 3. ❖ Well-known tribal leader, who actively pursued land claims for her people; established meeting house ornamented by carved figure representing her ancestor (1884), from whose descent she had claimed Awapuni land for her people. ❖ See also *Dictionary of New Zealand Biography* (Vol. 2).

KAI, Una (1928—). American ballet dancer. Born Mar 7, 1928, in Glenridge, NJ. ❖ Trained with George Balanchine at School of American Ballet; joined Ballet Society (1948); became charter member of New York City Ballet, where she danced featured roles in Robbins' *The Cage,* Ashton's *Picnic at Tintagel,* and Tudor's *La Gloire,* then began serving as ballet master (1956); staged numerous productions of Balanchine works for companies throughout US and also internationally; served as ballet master briefly at Robert Joffrey Ballet (early 1960s) and New Zealand Ballet (1973–76).

KAIN, Karen (1951—). Canadian ballet dancer. Born Mar 28, 1951, in Hamilton, Ontario, Canada. ❖ Trained by Betty Oliphant at school of National Ballet of Canada, then joined company (1969); danced principal roles in Frederick Ashton's *La Fille mal Gardée,* Erik Bruhn's *Swan Lake,* and in productions of *The Sleeping Beauty* and *Giselle;* danced frequently opposite Rudolf Nureyev during season in NY; was guest artist with several companies, including Ballet National de Marseilles in France, Makarova and Company troupe (1980), and others. ❖ See also (documentary) *Karen Kain: Dancing in the Moment* (1997).

KAIRI, Evanthia (1797–1866). Greek educator and feminist. Born 1797 (some sources cite 1799) on island of Andros; died 1866; sister of Theophilos Kairis (well-known philosopher). ❖ For many years headed up a famous girls' school in Kydonies (Greek Asia Minor, now Turkey), where she also taught; during Greek War of Independence against the Turks (1821), solicited help from women's organizations in Europe and influenced the development of a strong philhellenistic movement in Europe and US among women intellectuals; with the fall of the garrison at Missolonghi to the Turks after years of defiance (1826), wrote the play *Nikiratos,* about Greek women who had given their lives during siege; became a leading feminist; spent final years on Andros, where she ran a home for war orphans.

KAISER, Christina (1938—). *See Baas-Kaiser, Christina.*

KAISER, Isabella (1866–1925). Swiss novelist. Born 1866 in Geneva, Switzerland; grew up in German-speaking section of Switzerland; died 1925. ❖ Bilingual writer, published *Gloria victis* (Glory to the Vanquished) in French at 18; other works include (poems) *Ici-bas* (1888), semi-autobiographical novels *Coeur de femme* (1891) and *Die Friedensucherin* (1908), and the collected novellas, *Wenn die Sonne untergeht* (1901).

KAISER, Louisa (c. 1835–1925). *See Dat So La Lee.*

KAISER, Natasha (1967—). American runner. Name variations: Natasha Kaiser-Brown; Natasha Brown. Born May 14, 1967, in Des Moines, Iowa; graduate of University of Missouri; m. Brian Brown; children: Elexandria, Quinton and Kristian. ❖ Was 6-time NCAA All-American at Missouri; at Barcelona Olympics, won a silver medal in 4 x 400-meter relay (1992); became head track coach at Drake University.

KAISER, Ray (1912–1988). *See Eames, Ray.*

KAISER, Stien (1938—). *See Baas-Kaiser, Christina.*

KAISHEVA, Rumyana (1955—). Bulgarian volleyball player. Born Dec 26, 1955, in Bulgaria. ❖ At Moscow Olympics, won a bronze medal in team competition (1980).

KAIULANI (1875–1899). Hawaiian princess. Born Victoria Kawekiu Lunalilo Kalaninuiahilapalapa Kaiulani Cleghorn, Oct 16, 1875, in Honolulu, Hawaii; died Mar 6, 1899; only child of Archibald Scott (businessman) and Princess Miriam Likelike; never married; no children. ❖ On death of mother (1886), was named heir to the throne and sent to England to prepare for royal succession; studied at Great Harrowden Hall in Northamptonshire, and later in Brighton under private tutor; learned that Queen Liliuokalani had been forced to yield her authority to a provisional government (1893); accompanied by guardian, traveled to Washington, DC, where she petitioned President Cleveland to help restore the monarchy, to no avail; returned to Honolulu, heir to a nonexistent throne (1897); died suddenly (1899), age 24. ❖ See also *Women in World History.*

KAJIWARA, Mari (1952—). American modern dancer. Born 1952, in New York, NY. ❖ Danced 1 season with company of Glen Tetley (1969); joined Alvin Ailey Dance Theater (c. 1970), where she created roles in Ailey's *Archipelago* (1971), *Hidden Rites* (1973), *Feast of Ashes* (1974), and in Jennifer Muller's *Crossword* (1977); had featured roles in Ailey's *Revelations* and *Choral Dances,* McKayle's *Blood Memories* and *Rainbow Round My Shoulder,* and in works by John Butler, Joyce Trisler, Rael Lamb, and Talley Beatty, among others.

KAJOSMAA, Marjatta. Finnish cross-country skier. Name variations: Ritva Kajosmaa. Born in Finland. ❖ Won silver medals for the 5 km and the 3 x 5 km relay and a bronze for the 10 km at Sapporo Olympics (1972); won a silver medal for 4 x 5 km relay at Innsbruck Olympics (1976).

KALAMA (c. 1820–1870). Hawaiian queen. Name variations: also known as Hakaleleponi Kapakuhaili. Born at Kaelehuluhulu, near Kailua, Kona, Hawaii, c. 1829; died Sept 20, 1870; dau. of naval officer known as Captain Jack the Pilot; m. Kauikeaouli (1814–1854), later known as Kamehameha III, king of Hawaii (r. 1824–1854), Feb 1837; children: Keaweaweula I and Keaweaweula II, both of whom died in infancy; (adopted son) Alexander Liholiho (1834–1863), later known as Kamehameha IV, king of Hawaii (r. 1855–1863). ❖ The wife of Kamehameha III, came from a humble background; was praised for her beauty, ladylike demeanor and charitable nature; when the king died (1854), retired from court and established a sugar plantation at Kaneohe

and skillfully turned the venture into a successful operation. ❖ See also *Women in World History.*

KALAMA, Thelma (1931–1999). American swimmer. Name variations: Thelma "Keko" Kalama; Thelma Kalama Aiu. Born Mar 24, 1931, in Hawaii; died May 17, 1999, in Honolulu, Hawaii; children: 4 daughters, 4 sons. ❖ At London Olympics, won a gold medal in the 4 x 100-meter freestyle relay (1948).

K'ALANDADZE, Ana (1924—). Georgian poet. Name variations: Ana Kalandadze. Born 1924 in Khidistavi in the Gurian region of western Georgia; dau. of a scientist (father) and a teacher (mother); graduate of the university in Tbilisi, 1946, with a degree in Caucasian languages. ❖ Published 1st poems, melodious and impressionistic (1945), which reflected a people's yearning for peace after many years of war; became active member of Georgian Writers' Union (1946), serving on its organizing committee and the editorial board of the union's journal, *Literary Georgia;* achieved great literary success, publishing 6 volumes of lyrical poetry (1953–85); was also active in political life of Georgia's capital, being elected twice to Tbilisi City Council, and 3 times to Tbilisi Workers' Council. ❖ See also *Women in World History.*

KALEDIENE, Birute (1934—). Soviet javelin thrower. Name variations: Birute Viktorovna Kalediene; Birute Zalogaityte or Zalogaitite (also seen as Zalagaityte or Zalaogaitite). Born Nov 1934 in Lithuania. ❖ At Rome Olympics, won a bronze medal in the javelin throw (1960); was the 1st Lithuanian to break a world record (57.49 m. in 1958).

KALEK, Lucyna (1956—). *See Langer, Lucyna.*

KALELEOKALANI or KALELEONALANI (1836–1885). *See Emma.*

KALICH, Bertha (1874–1939). Famed Yiddish actress. Name variations: also seen as Kalish. Born May 17, 1874 (also cited as 1872) in Lemberg, Galicia (Austrian Poland); died April 18, 1939, in New York, NY; only child of Solomon Kalich (brush manufacturer) and Babette (Halber) Kalich; m. Leopold Spachner, c. 1890; children: Lillian Spachner. ❖ Referred to as the "Jewish Bernhardt" and "Yiddish Duse," took on 125 different roles in 7 languages during career; at 13, made stage debut (1887) in Lemberg; immigrated to US (1894); made NY debut in Yiddish version of *La Belle Hélène,* followed by Goldfaden's *The Ironmaster;* made 1st English-speaking appearance in the title role of Sardou's *Fedora* (1905), then appeared in such plays as *Monna Vanna, Therese Raquin, Marta of the Lowlands, Sappho and Phaon, The Unbroken Road, Cora, Jitta's Atonement, Magda* and *The Soul of a Woman;* also made several movies (1916–18); retired from stage (1931).

KALIMBET, Irina (1968—). Soviet rower. Name variations: Iryna Kalimbet. Born Feb 29, 1968, in USSR. ❖ At Seoul Olympics, won a silver medal in quadruple sculls without coxswain (1988).

KALINCHUK, Yekaterina (1922—). Soviet gymnast. Born Dec 1922 in USSR. ❖ At Helsinki Olympics, won a silver medal in teams all-around, portable apparatus, and gold medals in the vault and team all-around (1952).

KALININA, Ganna (1979—). Ukrainian sailor. Born May 1, 1979, in Ukraine. ❖ Won a silver medal for Yngling class at Athens Olympics (2004), a debut event.

KALININA, Irina (1959—). Soviet diver. Born Feb 1959, in Penza, USSR. ❖ At World championships, won a bronze in platform (1973), gold in springboard and silver in platform (1975) and gold in springboard and platform (1978); at Moscow Olympics, won a gold medal in springboard (1980). Named World Springboard and World Platform Diver of the Year (1978) and World Springboard Diver of the Year (1980); inducted into ISHOF (1990).

KALININA, Lidiya (1937—). *See Ivanova-Kalinina, Lidiya.*

KALININA, Natalia (1973—). Ukrainian gymnast. Born Dec 16, 1973, in Kherson, Ukraine, USSR. ❖ Won Goodwill Games and USSR nationals (1990); at European championships, won a gold medal for uneven bars, silvers for all-around and beam (1990) and bronze for team all-around (1994); at World championships, won a gold medal for team all-around (1991).

KALISH, Bertha (1874–1939). *See Kalich, Bertha.*

KALISKA, Elena (1972—). Slovakian kayaker. Born Jan 19, 1972, in Zvolen, Czechoslovakia. ❖ Won a gold medal in K1 singles at Athens Olympics (2004); placed 1st overall for World Cup K1 ranking (2001, 2003).

KALLEN, Kitty (1922—). *American pop vocalist.* Born in Philadelphia, PA, May 25, 1922 (some sources cite 1923). ❖ A popular singer (1940s–50s), performed on the "Children's Hour" in Philadelphia as a child, then sang on radio with Jan Savitt; joined Jack Teagarden's band (1939); subsequently sang with some of the biggest bands of the era, Jimmy Dorsey, Harry James, and Artie Shaw; was a frequent headliner on popular radio shows (1940s); hit the charts with single "Little Things Mean a Lot" (1954), followed by "In The Chapel in The Moonlight" and "I Want You All To Myself"; retired (1957) but returned with another blockbuster, "If I Give My Heart To You" (1959). ❖ See also *Women in World History.*

KALLEN, Lucille (1922–1999). *American comedy writer.* Born May 28, 1922, in Los Angeles, CA; died Jan 18, 1999, in Ardsley, NY. ❖ Was the only woman writer for "Your Show of Shows," starring Sid Caesar and Imogene Coca; having worked with Carl Reiner, was partly the basis for the character Sally Rogers on "The Dick Van Dyke Show."

KALLIES, Monika (1956—). *East German rower.* Born July 31, 1956, in East Germany. ❖ At Montreal Olympics, won a gold medal in coxed eights (1976).

KALLIR, Lilian (1931–2004). *Austrian pianist.* Born in Prague, Czechoslovakia, May 6, 1931; died Oct 25, 2004, in New York, NY; dau. of Rudolf F. Kallir and Moina M. (Rademacher) Kallir; studied at Mannes College of Music, 1946–49, and Berkshire Music Center, 1947–49; attended Sarah Lawrence College, 1948–50; studied piano with Hermande Grab and Isabelle Vengerova; m. Claude Frank (pianist), Aug 29, 1959; became a naturalized citizen of US (1947); children: violinist Pamela Frank. ❖ With parents, fled Nazism (1939); made NY debut (1949) with Dimitri Mitropoulos conducting NY Philharmonic Orchestra; appeared with husband in duo-piano recitals; lauded for recording of the Mozart Concerto No. 17, K. 453 and her chamber-music recitals.

KALLSTROM, Marjo (1965—). *See Matikainen, Marjo.*

KALMUS, Natalie (1878–1965). *American entrepreneur.* Born Natalie Dunfee, 1878, in Boston, MA; died Nov 15, 1965; graduate of Boston Art School and Curry School of Expression; m. Herbert T. Kalmus (inventor and film pioneer), 1902 (div. 1921). ❖ With husband, perfected the three-color process of Technicolor for movies and was instrumental in marketing the process known as Technicolor; began to serve as color consultant of the Technicolor Motion Picture Corporation (1915); traveled extensively in US and Europe, conducting courses for art directors and technicians; put together the 1st business package designed to "sell" color to Hollywood studios (1932); also developed several techniques to make Technicolor seem more realistic; supervised the Technicolor process on some of the great film classics, including *Robin Hood* (1938), *The Wizard of Oz* (1939) and *Gone With the Wind* (1939). ❖ See also *Women in World History.*

KALMYKOVA, Maria (1978—). *Russian basketball player.* Born Jan 14, 1978, in Ryazan, USSR. ❖ Center, won a team bronze medal at Athens Olympics (2004); placed 2nd at World championships (2002) and 1st at European championships (2003); played for Dynamo Novosibirsk.

KALOCSAI, Margit (b. 1909). *Hungarian gymnast.* Born Dec 27, 1909, in Hungary. ❖ At Berlin Olympics, won a bronze medal in team all-around (1936).

KALP, Uryan (1862–1918). *See Hanim, Nigar.*

KALSOUM, Oum (c. 1898–1975). *See Um Kalthum.*

KALTHUM, Um (c. 1898–1975). *See Um Kalthum.*

KALVAK, Helen (1901–1984). *Canadian Inuit folk artist.* Born 1901 at Tahiryuak Lake, Victoria Island, Northwest Territories, Canada; died May 7, 1984, in Holman, Northwest Territories; dau. of Halukhit and Enataomik; m. Edward Manayok (died 1960); children: Elsie Nilgak, among others; grandmother of Julia Manoyok Ekpakohak (artist). ❖ Lived the traditional migratory existence of the Inuit most of her life; moved into the settlement at Holman Island (1960), where she helped found the Holman Eskimo Cooperative (1961); created drawings depicting lives, beliefs, and traditions of Copper Inuit people of Northwestern Territories until Parkinson's disease limited use of her hands (1961–78); became internationally acclaimed at end of life and elected member of Royal Canadian Academy of Arts (1975). Made a member of the Order of Canada (1979).

KALYPSO (fl. 200 BCE). *See Calypso.*

KAMAL, Sufia (1911–1999). *Bangladeshi poet, political activist and feminist.* Born 1911 in Barisal, Bangladesh; died Nov 20, 1999; only dau. of an eminent lawyer; self-educated; married cousin Syed Nehal Hossai, 1922 (died 1932); m. Kamaluddin Ahmed, 1937; children: (1st m.) daughter, Amena Kahnar; (2nd m.) 2 daughters, Sultana Kamal and Saida Kamal, and 2 sons, Shahed Kamal and Sazid Kamal. ❖ Published 1st story at 14; began activism and involvement in socio-economic issues (1952); during early 1970s, aided women hurt by war of independence between Pakistan and Bangladesh; though deeply religious, denounced fundamentalists' treatment of women, for which an Islamic fundamentalist group called for her execution (1993); was 1st Bangladeshi woman to be buried with full state honors (1999). ❖ See also *Women in World History.*

KAMALI, Norma (1945—). *American fashion designer.* Born Norma Arraez, June 27, 1945, in New York, NY; dau. of Lebanese mother and Basque Spanish father; graduate of Fashion Institute of Technology, 1964; m. Mohammed Houssein Kamali. ❖ Three-time Coty Award winner, whose fashions are often inspired by classic 1930s and 1940s style, 1st opened a basement boutique with husband in their Manhattan East side apartment (1968); eventually moved headquarters to a 5-story townhouse on West 56th Street; invented the sleeping-bag coat, parachute dress, and hot pants; designed costumes for film *The Wiz.*

KAMAMALU (c. 1803–1824). *Hawaiian queen.* Born c. 1803; died in London, England, July 8, 1824; dau. of Kamehameha I the Great (1758–1819), king of Hawaii (r. 1810–1819), and Kaheiheimalie; sister of Kinau (c. 1805–1839); as a teenager, m. half-brother Liholiho known as Kamehameha II (1797–1824), king of Hawaii (r. 1819–1824); no children. ❖ The wife and half-sister of Kamehameha II, was noted for her intelligence and beauty; fluent in both English and Hawaiian, oversaw the vast collection of gifts brought to the king as taxes, and corresponded daily with missionaries and those chiefs who could read and write; known as a gracious host, was particularly solicitous of the queen mother Keopuolani, whom she nursed through her final illness; accompanied husband to England (1823–24); when one of the chiefs in the royal party contracted measles, a disease for which the Hawaiians had no immunity, died along with husband. ❖ See also *Women in World History.*

KAMAMALU, Victoria (1838–1866). *Hawaiian princess.* Born Nov 1, 1838; died May 29, 1866, in Honolulu; only daughter and youngest of 5 children of Kekuanaoa (governor of island of Oahu) and Kinau (*kuhina nui*); sister of Alexander Liholiho (1834–1863), later known as Kamehameha IV, king of Hawaii (r. 1855–1863), and sister of Lot Kamehameha (1830–1872), later known as Kamehameha V, king of Hawaii (r. 1863–1872); granddau. of Kamehameha I the Great (1758–1819), king of Hawaii (r. 1810–1819); never married; no children. ❖ Was *kuhina nui* (co-ruler) of the kingdom and heir to throne; officially elected heir of her aunt Kaahumanu, the 1st *kuhina nui* of the kingdom, and received title to large areas of land throughout islands (1850); took duties as co-ruler seriously and was considered a worthy successor of her aunt and her mother; retained title until 1863, when brother Lot ascended the throne as Kamehameha V and appointed their father as *kuhina nui*; was founder and lifetime president of Kaahumanu Society, an organization concerned with the ill and elderly. ❖ See also *Women in World History.*

KAMEAIM, Wandee (1978—). *Thai weightlifter.* Born Jan 18, 1978, in Thailand. ❖ Won a bronze medal for 58kg at Athens Olympics (2004).

KAMENSHEK, Dorothy (1925—). *American baseball player.* Name variations: Kammie or Dottie Kamenshek. Born Dec 21, 1925, in Cincinnati, Ohio; attended University of Cincinnati; graduate of Marquette University, 1958. ❖ Played first base for Rockford Peaches (1943–52) and had a lifetime batting average of .292, the highest of any longtime league player; was considered the best player in the history of the All-American Girls Baseball League. ❖ See also *Women in World History.*

KAMINSKA, Ida (1899–1980). *Polish actress, producer, and director.* Name variations: Ida Kaminski. Born Ida Kaminska, Sept 4, 1899, in Odessa, Ukraine; died May 21, 1980, in New York, NY; dau. of Abraham Isaac Kaminski (actor, playwright, director, and producer) and Esther Rachel (Halpern) Kaminska (actor); graduate of Gymnasium Francke, Warsaw, 1916; m. Zygmunt Turkow (actor and director), June 16, 1918 (div. 1932); m. Marian Melman (lawyer and journalist), July 1936; children: (1st m.) Ruth Turkow; (2nd m.) Victor Melman. ❖ Best known for performance in *The Shop on Main Street,* made professional debut as Itzik in *Akejdas Itzchok* in Warsaw (1916); performed in Jewish and classical repertory (1916–19); co-founded Warsaw Jewish Art Theater (1922); was founder and producing director of Ida Kaminska Theater (1928–39); toured Russia (1939–45); was founder and artistic director of the Jewish State Theater of Poland (1945–68); made London debut in title role of *Glikl fun Hameln* (1948); made NY debut with Jewish State Theater of Poland in title role of *Mirele Efros,* which she also adapted into Yiddish and directed (1967); adapted, directed and played title role in *Mother Courage* (1967); appeared in such films as *A Vilna Legend* (Pol., 1924), *Without a Home* (Pol., 1936), and *The Angel Levine* (US, 1970); wrote 2 plays, *Once There Was a King* (1928) and *Close the Bunkers* (1964), both of which were successfully produced in Poland. Nominated for Oscar for Best Actress for *The Shop on Main Street* (1966); received Polish National Flag of Labor, First and 2nd Class, the Officer's Cross of Polish Liberation, and the Polish Cross of Merit. ❖ See also *Women in World History.*

KAMINSKAITE, Leonora (1951–1986). Soviet rower. Born Jan 29, 1951, in USSR; died Feb 1986. ❖ At Montreal Olympics, won a bronze medal in double sculls (1976).

KAMMERLING, Anna-Karin (1980—). Swedish swimmer. Born Oct 19, 1980, in Malmö, Sweden. ❖ At LC European championships, won a gold medal for 50-meter butterfly (1999, 2000, 2002); won a bronze medal for 4 x 100-meter freestyle relay at Sydney Olympics (2000); at LC World championships, won a gold medal for 50-meter butterfly (2002).

KANAGA, Consuelo (1894–1978). African-American photographer. Born in Astoria, Oregon, 1894; died in Yorktown Heights, NY, 1978; m. Evans Davidson (mining engineer), 1919 (div. 1926); m. briefly for a 2nd time, early 1930s; m. Wallace Putnam (painter), 1936. ❖ Known for her portraits, especially of children, started out as a writer-reporter for *San Francisco Chronicle,* and newspaper's photographer (1915–22); became involved in portrait photography and joined California Camera Club (1918); worked as a news photographer for *New York American* (1922–24), then opened portrait studio in San Francisco; was included in historic exhibit of Group f/64 (1932), along with photographers Imogen Cunningham and Edward Weston; moved to NY (1935), where she worked on assignment for Index of American Design, a WPA project, and aligned herself with political left, photographing for such publications as *New Masses, Labor Defender* and *Sunday Worker;* work included in 3 important shows at Museum of Modern Art (1948); had last solo exhibition at Brooklyn Museum (1976–77). ❖ See also Millstein and Lowe, *Consuelo Kanaga: An American Photographer* (U. of Washington Press, 1992); and *Women in World History.*

KANAHELE, Helen Lake (1916–1976). American labor leader. Born May 26, 1916, in Kona, Hawaii; died June 12, 1976, in Honolulu; adopted at age 6 by Irene West; educated to 8th grade; m. Alfred Kanahele; children: Mary Jane and Helen Kanahele. ❖ Controversial figure, assembled the workers into a division of United Public Workers (UPW) while employed as a laundry worker at Maluhia Hospital (1948); held several offices in Hawaiian Homesteaders Improvement Club; joined Women's Auxiliary of International Longshoremen and Warehousemen's Union (ILWU, 1949); active in Democratic Party, ran unsuccessfully as a delegate to Constitutional Convention (1950); was elected president of ILWU Women's Auxiliary (1951); from 1954 on, held numerous offices, including Oahu division vice president, territorial secretary-treasurer, and secretary and board member of the political action committee; at a time when women were not involved as leaders in union and other organizational activities, her authority and power were accepted. ❖ See also *Women in World History.*

KANAKAOLE, Edith K. (1913–1979). Hawaiian composer, chanter, dancer, teacher, and entertainer. Name variations: Aunt Edith; Kanaka'ole. Born Edith Ke'kuhikuhi-i-pu'u-one-o-na-ali'i-o-kohala Kenao, Oct 30, 1913, in Honomu, Puna, Hawaii; died Oct 3, 1979; dau. of John Kanaele Kenao and Mary Keliikuewa Ahiena; m. Luka Kanakaole, Jan 23, 1933; children: 6, including daughters Nalani Kanakaole and Pualani Kanakaole, who studied and then danced with her. ❖ Was an instructor at Hawaii Community College (1971–79) and University of Hawaii at Hilo (1973–79); pioneered courses and seminars in ethnobotany, chant, mythology, genealogy, land ownership, and *ohana* (extended Hawaiian family), Polynesian history, and the Hawaiian oral arts; trained in *oli* chanting, choreographed hulas for many of her chants. Her record albums *Haakui Pele I Hawaii* ("Pele Prevails in Hawaii," a selection of traditional and original chants) and *Hiipoi I Ka Aiina Aloha* ("Cherish the Beloved Land") won Na Hoku Hanohano (Stars of

Distinction) award for best traditional albums (1978, 1979). ❖ See also *Women in World History.*

KANDER, Lizzie Black (1858–1940). American welfare worker and author. Born May 28, 1858, in Milwaukee, Wisconsin; died July 24, 1940, in Milwaukee; dau. of John Black (operator of dry goods shop) and Mary (Pereles) Black; sister of Herman Black, publisher of *Chicago American* (1913–33); m. Simon Kander (businessman and politician), May 17, 1881 (died 1931): no children. ❖ Served as president of Milwaukee Jewish Mission (1896–1918), joining with another Jewish charitable group, the Sisterhood of Personal Service, to form the city's 1st social settlement house; published *The Settlement Cook Book: The Way to a Man's Heart* (1901), which was revised and expanded through the years and went through 40 editions, selling over 1 million copies. ❖ See also *Women in World History.*

KANE, Amy Grace (1879–1979). New Zealand journalist. Born on Dec 9, 1879, in Wellington, New Zealand; died on April 9, 1979, in Wellington; dau. of Robert William Kane (bank accountant) and Martha Lydia (Warburton) Kane. ❖ Began career as columnist of "Women's Pages" of *New Zealand Free Lance* (c. 1908); worked for *New Zealand Times* (1914–27), and was appointed lady editor of *Dominion* (1927); involved in relief work for unemployed women during depression (1930s); instrumental in founding several organizations, including Federation of Women's Clubs in New Zealand (1925), New Zealand Federation of Women's Institutes (1933), and Pan-Pacific Women's Association (1940s). ❖ See also *Dictionary of New Zealand Biography* (Vol. 3).

KANE, Babe (1909–1992). *See Kane, Marjorie.*

KANE, Gail (1887–1966). American actress. Born Abigail Kane, July 10, 1887, in Philadelphia, PA; died Feb 17, 1966, in Augusta, Maine; m. Iden Ottmann. ❖ Along with a successful career on Broadway in such plays as *The Affairs of Anatol, Seven Keys to Baldpate, The Hyphen, The Woman in Room 13, Come Seven,* and *The Breaking Point,* appeared in over 35 films, including *Nathan Hale* and *White Sister;* retired (1927).

KANE, Helen (1903–1966). American actress, dancer and singer. Born Helen Schroeder in the Bronx, NY, Aug 4, 1903; died Sept 16, 1966, in Jackson Heights, NY; studied with Ned Wayburn; m. Joseph Kane, 1924 (div. 1928); m. Max Hoffman Jr., 1932 (div. 1933); m. Dan Healy, 1939. ❖ Vaudeville performer from age 17, made Broadway debut in musical *A Night in Spain* (1927); her squeaky "boop-boop-a-doop" rendition of "I Wanna Be Loved by You," in the musical *Good Boy* (1928), catapulted her to a short-lived career in early talkies; films include *Nothing but the Truth* (1929), *Sweetie* (1929), *Paramount on Parade* (1930), *Dangerous Nan McGrew* (1930) and *Heads Up* (1930). Portrayed by Debbie Reynolds in film *Three Little Words* (1950), for which Kane dubbed the singing. ❖ See also *Women in World History.*

KANE, Julia (1897–1985). *See Robins, Denise Naomi.*

KANE, Marjorie (1909–1992). American film dancer. Name variations: Babe Kane, Margie Babe Kane. Born April 28, 1909, in Chicago, IL; died Jan 8, 1992. ❖ Made professional debut with Balaban and Kath theater Prolog; toured West Coast of US with *Good News* as specialty dancer and remained in Los Angeles, CA; appeared in some of earliest sound musicals such as *The Dance of Life* (1929), *The Great Gabbo* (1929), *Border Romance* (1930) and *Be Yourself* (1930).

KANE, Rosetta Lulah (1871–1934). *See Baume, Rosetta Lulah.*

KANE, Sarah (1971–1999). British playwright. Born 1971 in Kelvedon Hatch, Essex, England; died Feb 20, 1999, at King's College Hospital in London, England, of an apparent suicide; dau. of a journalist; Bristol University, honors in drama; Birmingham University, master's degree in playwriting. ❖ Became writer-in-residence at Paines Plough, an experimental company; also ran workshops for Royal Court International in Bulgaria and Spain; at 23, saw 1st play, *Blasted,* performed in London at Royal Court; though quite popular in continental Europe, was the subject of controversy in Britain, criticized for the amount of explicit sexual and violent content in her work; upset by all the negative publicity, used a pseudonym during early run of last play, *Crave;* also wrote *Phaedra's Love* and *Cleansed.* ❖ See also *Women in World History.*

KANESAKA, Katsuko (1954—). Japanese volleyball player. Born Mar 1, 1954, in Japan. ❖ At Montreal Olympics, won a gold medal in team competition (1976).

KANG CHO-HYUN (1982—). South Korean shooter. Born 1982 in South Korea. ❖ Won a silver medal for 10 m air rifle at Sydney Olympics (2000).

KANG JAE-WON (1965—). Korean handball player. Born Nov 30, 1965, in South Korea. ❖ At Seoul Olympics, won a silver medal in team competition (1988).

KANG KE-CHING (1911–1992). *See Kang Keqing.*

KANG KEQING (1911–1992). Chinese revolutionary. Name variations: Kang Ke-ching; K'ang K'o-ching. Pronunciation: KAHNG ke-CHING. Born Kang Guixiu in autumn 1911 (some sources cite 1910 or 1912 but 1911 is documented), in Wanan, Jiangxi, China; died in Beijing, China, April 22, 1992; dau. of Kang Nianxiao (fisherman) and Huang Niangu; attended the Red Military Academy at Ruijin, Jiangxi; attended the Kangda (Anti-Japanese Political and Military Academy) at Yanan, Shaanxi; m. Zhu De (Chu Teh, general), in 1929 (died July 6, 1976); children: (stepson) Zhu Qi; (stepdaughter) Zhu Min. ❖ A survivor of the rigors of the Long March, who participated in the Communist Revolution and emerged as an eminent woman leader in the People's Republic of China; served as chair of the Women's Union at Luotangwan, Jiangxi, and was a member of the Communist Youth (1927); joined Red Army (1928); was a member of the Chinese Communist Party (1931); served as commander of the Women Volunteers, Ruijin (1932); participated in the Long March (1934–36); was vice-chair of the Committee for the Protection of Children in the Liberated Areas (1946); was a member of the Preparatory Committee for the Foundation of the Democratic Women's Federation (1948); was a member of the Standing Committee of the Democratic Women's Federation (1949–55); served as secretary of the Democratic Women's Federation (1955); was a member of the Chinese People's Political Consultative Conference (1949–75); was a deputy for Henan Province to 1st National People's Congress (1954) and reelected to 2nd NPC (1959); was a vice-chair of Federation of Women (1957–77); was deputy for Jiangxi to 3rd NPC (1965); was a member of the Standing Committee of 4th NPC (1975), reelected to 5th NPC (1978), reelected to 6th NPC (1986); was a member of Standing Committee of the Chinese People's Political Consultative Conference (1975–78); was a member of Central Committee of Chinese Communist Party (1977–85); was chair of Federation of Women (1977–88); was a vice-chair of Chinese People's Political Consultative Conference (1978–92); was honorary chair of Federation of Women (1988–92); made important contributions to the women's movement. ❖ See also *Women in World History.*

KANG OK-SUN (1946—). North Korean volleyball player. Born April 14, 1946, in North Korea. ❖ At Munich Olympics, won a bronze medal in team competition (1972).

KANGA (fl. 1220). Queen of Norway. Fl. in 1220; 1st wife of Haakon IV the Elder (1204–1263), king of Norway (r. 1217–1263); children: Sigurd; Cecilie (d. 1248, who m. Gregor Anderson and Harold, king of Man). Haakon's 2nd wife was Margaret (d. 1270).

KANIA-ENKE, Karin (1961—). East German speedskater. Name variations: Karin Enke; Karin Kania; Karin Enke Kania; Karin Busch-Enke. Born Karin Enke, June 20, 1961, in Dresden, East Germany; m. a student named Busch (1981, div.)m. Rudolf Kania (school sports instructor), 1984 (div.); m. a man named Richter. ❖ Placed 9th at European championships for figure skating (1977); switched to speedskating (1978); won 8 Olympic medals: gold for the 500 meters at Lake Placid (1980), gold for the 1,000 and 1,500 meters and silver for the 3,000 and 500 meters at Sarajevo (1984), silver for the 1,000 and 1,500 meters and bronze for the 500 meters at Calgary (1988); held 6 World sprint titles (1980, 1981, 1983, 1984, 1986, 1987) and 5 World all-around championships (1982, 1984, 1986, 1987, 1988); was the 1st to skate a sub 2 minutes in the 1,500 (1986).

KANIN, Fay (1917—). American screenwriter, playwright, and actress. Born Fay Mitchell, May 9, 1917, in New York, NY; dau. of David Mitchell (department store manager) and Bessie (Kaiser) Mitchell; attended Elmira College, 1933–36; University of Southern California, BA, 1937; m. Michael Kanin (screenwriter), April 1940; children: Joel (deceased); Josh. ❖ Began career as script reader at RKO (1937); collaborating with husband, wrote *Rhapsody* (1954) and *Teacher's Pet* (1958), which won an Academy Award, and 2 successful plays, *His and Hers* (1954) and *Rashomon* (1959); had solo success with play *Goodbye My Fancy* (1948), which ran for 2 years on Broadway; wrote tv movies

"Heat of Anger" (1971), "Tell Me Where it Hurts" (1974) and "Friendly Fire" (1979); served as president of Motion Picture Academy of Arts and Science for 4 terms, only the 2nd woman to hold that post; also served a long stint as president of Writers Guild of America and was board member of American Film Institute. Received Writers Guild Award and Emmy nomination for tv movie "Hustling" (1975); nominated for a Tony for book to musical *Grind* (1985). ❖ See also *Women in World History.*

KANKUS, Roberta A. (1953—). American power-plant operator. Born 1953 in Elmira, NY. ❖ Served as assistant mechanical engineer for Philadelphia Electric Co. (PECO); trained at PECO's Peach Bottom Power Plant and became 1st woman licensed to be commercial nuclear power plant operator (1976); became senior strategic planner.

KANN, Edith (1907–1987). Austrian freshwater biologist. Born April 19, 1907, in Vienna, Austria; died Oct 7, 1987; University of Vienna, PhD, 1933. ❖ Noted cyanophyte (blue-green algae) expert, who was a founding member of the International Association of Cyanophyte Research, completed a dissertation on the littoral vegetation of the Lunzer Untersee; studied lakes in Holstein region and lectured on taxonomy and ecology of littoral algae while working at Institute of Hydrobiology in Plon, Austria; studied ecology and taxonomy of cyanophyte genera from alpine aquatic habitats.

KANNER-ROSENTHAL, Hedwig (1882–1959). Hungarian pianist and teacher. Born Hedwig Kanner in Budapest, Hungary, June 3, 1882; died in Asheville, NC, Sept 5, 1959; studied in Vienna with Theodor Leschetizky and Moriz Rosenthal; m. Moriz Rosenthal. ❖ After Vienna debut, taught in that city for 5 years; appeared as a concert artist, accompanist, chamber-music pianist and duo-piano partner, often performing with husband; began working alongside husband at his piano school in New York City (1939), coaching such students as Robert Goldsand and Charles Rosen.

KANTOR, Aniko. Hungarian handball player. Name variations: Anikó Kántor. Born in Hungary. ❖ Won a team bronze medal at Atlanta Olympics (1996) and a team silver medal at Sydney Olympics (2000).

KANTÛRKOVA, Eva (1930—). Czech novelist. Name variations: Eva Kanturkova. Born 1930; dau. of a journalist father and Bohumila Sílová (1908–1957, writer); graduate of Charles University, 1956; m. the head of Czech television. ❖ Worked as journalist; after Soviet invasion, was banned as a dissident (1968); arrested on subversion charges and held without trial for 1 year (1981); was founding member of Civic Forum and served as president of Council of Writers; works include *Jen si tak maličko povyskočit* (Just a Little Leap, 1966), *Pozůstalost pana Ábela* (Mr. Abel's Legacy, 1971), *Černa hvězda* (Black Star, 1981), and *Přitelkyně z domu smutku* (My Companions in the Bleak House, 1987); adapted her mother's fairytales for a tv series.

KANUKA, Lynn (1960—). *See Williams, Lynn.*

KANWAR, Roop (c. 1969–1987). Indian woman. Name variations: Roopwati Kunwar. Pronunciation: Kun-WAR. Born c. 1969 (most sources cite her age upon death as 18) in Jaipur, Rajasthan, India; burned to death on husband's funeral pyre, Sept 4, 1987; passed India's tenth standard; m. Maal Singh, Feb 1987; no children. ❖ Following husband's death after only 8 months of marriage, mounted his funeral pyre and burned to death in its flames; her death incited national controversy over the religious tradition of sati. ❖ See also Sakuntala Narasimhan, *Sati: Widow Burning in India* (Doubleday, 1990); and *Women in World History.*

KAPHEIM, Ramona (1958—). East German rower. Born Jan 8, 1958, in East Germany. ❖ At Moscow Olympics, won a gold medal in coxed fours (1980).

KAPIOLANI (c. 1781–1841). Hawaiian high priestess. Born in Hilo, Hawaii, c. 1781; died May 5, 1841; dau. of Keawemauhili (half-brother of Kalaniopuu), king of the island of Hawaii, and Kekikipaa (former wife of Kamehameha I the Great); tutored by missionaries; discarded all husbands except Naihe (chief, orator, and councilor of King Kamehameha). ❖ Famed for her defiance of the fire goddess Pele and her role in introducing Christianity to the island, was one of the chiefesses who greeted the 1st missionaries upon their arrival (1820); eagerly embraced their teachings and was quick to adopt Western dress and decorum; determined to challenge the hold of the fire goddess Pele on her people, made a 100-mile pilgrimage to the crater of Mount Kilauea, and entered the mouth of the crater, proclaiming that her faith and belief in God would save her from Pele's wrath (1824); on husband's death, succeeded him as magistrate over districts of Ka'u and South Kona on island of Hawaii. Her dramatic act at Mount Kilauea inspired the poem *Kapiolani*, by Alfred, Lord Tennyson, which brought her international attention. ❖ See also *Women in World History*.

KAPIOLANI (1834–1899). Hawaiian queen and philanthropist. Born Dec 31, 1834, in Hilo; died June 24, 1899, at home in Waikiki; dau. of Kuhio (high chief of Hilo) and Kinoiki (dau. of Kaumualii, last king of Kauai); niece and namesake of Kapiolani (c. 1781–1841); sister of Victoria Kalanikuikapooloku Kalaninuiamamao Poomaikelani and Mary Kinoiki Kekaulike; m. Bennett Namakeha, a high chief (died 1860); m. David Kalakaua (1836–1891), a high chief and later king of Hawaii (r. 1874–1891), Dec 19, 1863; no children. ❖ Came to Honolulu and married High Chief Namakeha (c. 1855); 3 years after his death, married High Chief David Kalakaua (1863), who later became king; presided over opening ceremonies of Kapiolani Home for Girls in Kakaako (1885); visited US and also attended Queen Victoria's Silver Jubilee in England (1887); raised funds for and opened maternity home for Hawaiian women (1890). ❖ See also *Women in World History*.

KAPLAN, Fanya (1883–1918). Russian revolutionary. Name variations: Fanny Kaplan. Born 1883 into a Jewish peasant family; shot and killed, Sept 3, 1918. ❖ Joined the Socialist Revolutionaries; having participated in attempted assassination of a tsarist official in Kiev (1906), was arrested and sentenced to life at hard labor in Siberia; during February Revolution, was released (1917); furious when Lenin closed down the Constituent Assembly, shot and wounded him (left shoulder and left lung) at close range (Aug 30, 1918); was shot by Pavel Malkov on orders of Yakov Sverdlov; her act contributed to the launching of the Red Terror.

KAPLAN, Nelly (1931—). Argentinean director, screenwriter, and actress. Name variations: (pseudonym) Belen. Born 1931 in Buenos Aires, Argentina. ❖ Worked in France as a correspondent for Argentine film magazines; became assistant and close collaborator of director Abel Gance; began directing shorts (1961), then feature films; was co-screenwriter and director of, and sometimes appeared in, *Rodolph Bresdin, La fiancée du Pirate, Papa les petits bateaux, Néa, Le satellite de Vénus* and *Carles et Lucie;* has also written books, including a collection of short stories and a collection of erotic poems under pseudonym Belen. Won Golden Lion award in Venice for medium-length film *Le regard Picasso* (*The Picasso Look*, 1967).

KAPLANOVA, Ludmila (1890–1943). See *Slavikova, Ludmila*.

KAPRALOVA, Vitezslava (1915–1940). Czech composer. Born in Brünn, Moravia (later Brno, now Czech Republic), Jan 24, 1915; died in Montpellier, France, June 16, 1940; received 1st musical instruction from father Vaclav Kapral (1889–1947), composer; studied composition and conducting at Brno Conservatory with Zdenek Chalabala, 1930–35; studied at Prague Conservatory with Vitezslav Novakl (composition) and Vaclav Talich (conducting). ❖ At 20, saw her Piano Concerto performed in Brno; saw her *Military Sinfonietta* performed in Prague (1937); received a scholarship for study in France (1937), enabling her to study conducting with Charles Münch and composition with Bohuslav Martinu; appeared as guest conductor of BBC Symphony Orchestra at Festival of the International Society of Contemporary Music in London (1938); returned to France after Nazi occupation of Bohemia and Moravia (1939); fled Paris from advancing German armies; continued to compose, but the stress of evacuation and TB resulted in her death.

KAPTUR, Marcy (1946—). American politician. Born Marcia Carolyn Kaptur, June 17, 1946, in Toledo, Ohio, into a Polish-American family; dau. of Stephen and Anastasia Kaptur; graduate of Ursula Academy, University of Wisconsin, BA, 1968; University of Michigan, MA, 1974; Massachusetts Institute of Technology, PhD in urban planning, 1981. ❖ Trained as a city and regional planner, practiced for 15 years in Toledo; served as urban advisor to Carter White House (1977–79); as a Democrat, ran successfully for US House seat (1982); eventually became the senior Democratic woman on House Appropriations Committee; reelected to 12th term (2004); introduced the legislation for National World War II Memorial (1987).

KAPULE, Deborah (c. 1798–1853). Hawaiian queen. Name variations: also known as Haakulou. Born in Waimea, Kauai, Hawaii, c. 1798; died in Waimea, Aug 26, 1853; dau. of Kahekili, sometimes called Haupu (chief of Waimea, Kauai) and Hawea; m. King Kaumualii, c. 1815 (died 1824); m. Kealiiahonui (son of Kaumualii), c. 1822; m. Simeon Kaiu

(judge), April 1824. ❖ Was the favorite wife of Kaumualii, the last king of Kauai and Niihau; husband was kidnapped by King Kamehameha II and taken to Oahu (1821), where he was forced to marry Kaahumanu, the powerful widow of Kamehameha I; became a leading local personality, married the king's son Kealiiahonui, and maintained a school in Waimea that served 50 students; 2nd husband was also forced to marry Kaahumanu; on death of King Kaumualii (1824), raised her sword to help defend an attack by rebels at a fort near Waimea and swayed many to remain loyal to a united Hawaii; became a Christian, built a church at Wailua and helped raise money for construction of a church at Koloa. ❖ See also *Women in World History*.

KAR, Ida (1908–1970). Russian-born photographer. Born Ida Karamian in Tambov, Russia, 1908; died in London, England, 1970; educated in Paris; m. Edmond Belali (photographer), late 1930s (div.); m. Victor Musgrave, 1944 (sep. 1979); no children. ❖ A surrealist who also did portraits and documentary work, spent early years in Russia, Iran and Egypt, though family eventually settled in Alexandria; went to Paris (1928) where she studied music and mingled with the avant-garde; returned to Alexandria (1933) and worked as assistant in a photography studio; with 1st husband, opened photography studio in Cairo and exhibited in 2 Surrealist displays (1943 and 1944); divorced and remarried, moved to London (1945); photographed artists and writers, including Marc Chagall, T.S. Eliot, Eugene Ionesco, Doris Lessing and Henry Moore; worked as a photojournalist, creating picture stories around London for *Tatler* and *Observer* and taking photographic junkets to Armenia, Moscow, East Germany and Sweden (1950s); worked exclusively for *Animals* magazine (1963–64); photographed the Celebration of the Cuban Revolution (1964).

KARADJORDJEVIC, Helen (1884–1962). Grand duchess of Russia. Born Nov 4, 1884 (some sources cite 1881); died in 1962; dau. of Zorka of Montenegro (1864–1890) and Peter I (1844–1921), king of Serbia (r. 1903–1921); m. Ivan Constantinovich, grand duke and prince of Russia, Sept 3, 1911; children: Vselevod Ivanovich Romanov, prince (b. 1914); Ikaterina or Catherine Ivanovna Romanov, princess (b. July 12, 1915, who m. Rugero Farace di Villaforesta in 1937, div. in 1945).

KARAGIANNI, Eftychia (1973—). Greek water-polo player. Born Oct 10, 1973, in Piraeus, Greece. ❖ Won team silver medal at Athens Olympics (2004).

KARAKA, Kiti (1870–1927). See *Riwai, Kiti Karaka*.

KARALLI, Vera (1889–1972). Soviet ballet dancer and actress. Name variations: Vera Alexeyevna Karalli. Born Aug 8 (some sources cite July 27), 1889, in Moscow, Russia; died Nov 16, 1972, in Baden, Austria. ❖ Trained with Bolshoi Ballet before joining company (1906) where she was featured in Mikhail Fokine's *Le Pavillion d'Armide,* among others; performed with Diaghilev Ballet Russe (1909) and with companies of Anna Pavlova and Mikhail Mordkin on tour (1910s); became one of Russia's 1st film stars, appearing in numerous dance-related silents, including *The Dying Swan* (1917); served as ballet master of State Opera in Bucharest (c. 1930–37).

KARAMANOU, Anna (1947—). Greek politician. Born May 3, 1947, in Pyrgos Ilias, Greece. ❖ Served as official for the Greek Telecommunications Organization (OTE, 1969–91); founder member and secretary-general of the Women's Political Alliance; as a European Socialist, elected to 4th and 5th European Parliament (1994–99, 1999–2004); named chair of the Committee on Women's Rights and Equal Opportunities. Wrote *Greek Women in Education and Work* (1984); awarded Attalos the Philadelphian prize (1997) and Ipekçi prize for promotion of Graeco-Turkish friendship (1999).

KARAN, Donna (1948—). American fashion designer. Born Donna Faske, Oct 2, 1948, in Forest Hills, Queens, NY; dau. of Gabby Faske (tailor) and Helen Faske (model); attended Parsons School of Design, 1968–70; m. Stephan Weiss (sculptor); children: 3. ❖ Called the "Queen of Seventh Avenue," began career designing for Anne Klein, becoming head of Anne Klein design team (1974); launched own company (1984); introduced DKNY collection of modern, moderately-priced young urban styles (1988), embarking on period of rapid growth; launched DKNY jeans (1990) and menswear (1991), then added cosmetics (1992), shoes (1992) and children's line (1993); pioneered comfortable business clothing. Won Coty Award (1977, 1981, and 1984); named Council of Fashion's Designer of the Year (1985).

KARASYOVA, Olga (1949—). Soviet gymnast. Name variations: Olga Kharlova. Born Olga Kharlova, July 27, 1949, in USSR. ❖ At World championships, won a silver for team all-around (1966) and a silver for floor exercise and a gold for team all-around (1970); at Mexico City Olympics, won a gold medal in team all-around (1968); at European championships, won a silver medal for all-around and a gold for floor exercise (1969).

KARATZA, Rallou (1778–1830). Greek theater producer and freedom fighter. Born 1778 in Walachia, Romania (belonging to the Ottoman Empire of which Greece was a part); died 1830; dau. of a Greek prince. ❖ Was the 1st Greek woman to organize her own theater group, recruiting actors to Walachia from the Greek School in Bucharest; became a member of the secret society "Philiki Etaireia" which organized the Greeks to fight against the Turks, and began presenting revolutionary plays espousing freedom, helping to raise the political fervor among the Greeks that led to the uprising of 1821.

KARAVAEVA, Elizaveta (1891–1945). See Skobtsova, Maria.

KARAVAEVA, Irina (1975—). Russian trampolinist. Born May 18, 1975, in USSR. ❖ Won World championship (1994–2000); won European championship (2000); won a gold medal at Sydney Olympics (2000), in the inaugural trampoline event.

KARELLI, Zoe or Zoi (1901–1998). See Argiriadou, Chryssoula.

KARENIN, Vladimir (1862–1942). See Komarova, Varvara.

KARIAMI, Chara (1983—). See Karyami, Zacharoula.

KARINA. Variant of Catherine or Katherine.

KARINA, Anna (1940—). Danish actress. Born Hanne Karin Blarke Bayer, Sept 22, 1940, in Copenhagen, Denmark; m. Jean-Luc Godard (film director), 1961 (div. 1964 or 1967); m. Daniel-Georges Duval (film director), 1978. ❖ Began career as a model before appearing in Danish short that won a prize at Cannes Festival; debuted as lead in French film *Le Petit Soldat*, work of New Wave director and future husband, Jean-Luc Godard (release delayed until 1976); also starred in his *Une Femme est une Femme* (*A Woman is a Woman*, 1961) and *Vivre sa Vie* (*My Life to Live*); wrote, directed and starred in *Vivre Ensemble* (1973); other films include *Ce Soir ou jamais* (1960), *Les Quatre Vérités* (*Three Fables of Love*, 1962), (title role) *Shéherazade* (*Scheherazade*, 1963), *La Ronde* (*Circle of Love*, 1964), *Alphaville* (1965), *La Religieuse* (*The Nun*, 1965), *The Magus* (1968), *Before Winter Comes* (1969), *Justine* (US, 1969), *The Salzburg Connection* (1972), *Pane e Cioccolata* (*Bread and Chocolate*, 1973), *The Story of a Mother* (Denmark, 1979), *L'Ami de Vincent* (1983), *Cayenne Palace* (1987) and *The Man Who Would Be Guilty* (1990). ❖ See also *Women in World History*.

KARIN OF SWEDEN (c. 1330–1381). See Catherine of Sweden.

KARINSKA, Barbara (1886–1983). Ukrainian-born costume designer. Name variations: Madame Karinsky. Born Varvara Zhmoudsky, Sept 9, 1886, in Kharkov, Ukraine, Russia; died Oct 1983 in New York, NY. ❖ Studied law in Moscow but upon immigration to Paris began making costumes for Comédie Française; designed costumes for George Balanchine in Monte Carlo and for Ballet Russe in Paris; moved to New York (1938); noted for flamboyant style and use of bright colors, opened design business in NY, becoming the foremost expert in constructing ballet costumes in US; also designed for opera and film. Shared an Oscar for best costumes for *Joan of Arc* (1948); won Capezio Dance Award (1961).

KARIOKA, Tahiya (c. 1921–1999). Arab actress and belly dancer. Name variations: Taheya Cariocca or Tahia Carioca. Born Badawiya Mohammed Karim, c. 1921, in Cairo, Egypt; died in Cairo, Sept 20, 1999; m. 14 times; children: (adopted) Atiyat Allah. ❖ Acclaimed as "Queen of Oriental Dancing," began performing as a young girl and starred on stage in Cairo (1930s–40s); followed 1st film, *Doctor Farahat* (1935), with some 300 films, plays, and tv soap operas, the most popular film being *Youth of a Woman*, an entry at Cannes Film Festival (1956).

KARK, Nina Bawden (1925—). See Bawden, Nina.

KARLE, Isabella (1921—). American chemist and crystallographer. Born Isabella Helen Lugoski, Dec 2, 1921, in Detroit, Michigan, to Polish immigrant parents; University of Michigan, BS, 1940, MS, PhD in physical chemistry, 1944; m. Jerome Karle (co-winner of Nobel Prize for chemistry, 1985), 1942; children: 3 daughters. ❖ With husband, began work at Naval Research Laboratory in Washington, DC, developing techniques to study electron diffraction; became head of NRL X-ray Diffraction Section for Structure of Matter (1959); with husband,

published landmark paper on Symbolic Addition Procedure for determining molecular structures directly from X-ray diffraction experiments (1966); successfully applied same method to living materials, many of which are important in biochemical and medical research; discovered structures of numerous substances, including naturally occurring analgesic enkephalin, found in human brain; elected president of American Crystallographic Association (1976). Received Garvan Medal (1976) from American Chemical Society and American Institute of Chemists' Chemical Pioneer Award (1985).

KARLEN, Maud (1932—). Swedish gymnast. Born Nov 25, 1932, in Sweden. ❖ At Melbourne Olympics, won a silver medal in teams all-around, portable apparatus (1956).

KARLOVA, Larisa (1958—). Soviet handball player. Born Aug 1958 in USSR. ❖ Won a gold medal at Montreal Olympics (1976), gold medal at Moscow Olympics (1980), and bronze medal at Seoul Olympics (1988), all in team competition.

KARLOVNA, Anna (1718–1746). See Anna Leopoldovna.

KARLSSON, Eva (1961—). Swedish kayaker. Born Sept 21, 1961, in Sweden. ❖ At Los Angeles Olympics, won a silver medal in K4 500 meters (1984).

KARLSTADT, Liesl (1892–1960). German cabaret performer. Name variations: Lisl Karlstadt. Born Dec 12, 1892, in Munich, Germany; died July 27, 1960, in Garmisch-Partenkirchen, Germany. ❖ Along with Karl Valentin, set the tone of popular culture in Munich for a generation; appeared in 70 films. ❖ See also (in German) Monika Dimpfl, *Immer veränderlich: Liesl Karlstadt (1892–1960)* (1996).

KARNILOVA, Maria (1920–2001). American ballet dancer and actress. Born Maria Dovgolenko, Aug 3, 1920, in Hartford, CT; died April 20, 2001, in New York, NY; m. George S. Irving, 1948; children: 2. ❖ Trained with Anton Dolin, Antony Tudor, Mikhail Fokine, Edward Caton, Rosina Galli, and more; performed in children's ballet of Metropolitan Opera in NYC; danced with Victor Dandré's Opera Co. in Caracas; performed in ballet troupes of Mikhail Mordkin and Fokine with American Ballet (1936); was founding member of Ballet Theater and danced there intermittently (1939–59), in works by Tudor, Eugene Loring, Agnes de Mille, and others; performed with Metropolitan Opera (1952–53) and with Jerome Robbins' Ballet USA (1958–61); on Broadway, appeared in *Call Me Mister* (1946), *High Button Shoes* (1948), *Two's Company* (1952), *Gypsy* (1959) and *Bravo Giovanni* (1962). Won Tony Award for Best Supporting Actress in a Musical for creating role of Golde in *Fiddler on the Roof* (1964); nominated for Best Actress Tony for *Zorba* (1968).

KÄRNTEN, Margarete von (1318–1369). See Margaret Maultasch.

KARODIA, Farida (1942—). South African novelist and short-story writer. Born 1942 in Aliwal North, South Africa; graduate of Coronationville Teacher Training College, 1961. ❖ Taught in Johannesburg and Zambia; had passport removed by government and immigrated to Canada (1969); returned to South Africa (1994); writings, which often describe hardships of life under apartheid, include *Daughters of the Twilight* (1986), *Coming Home and Other Stories* (1988), *A Shattering of Silence* (1991) and *Against an African Sky* (1995); also wrote radio plays.

KAROLCHIK, Yanina (1976—). See Korolchik, Yanina.

KAROLINA OR KARLINE. Variant of Carolina or Caroline.

KARPATI-KARCSICS, Iren (1927—). Hungarian gymnast. Born Mar 18, 1927, in Hungary. ❖ At London Olympics, won a silver medal in team all-around (1948); at Helsinki Olympics, won a bronze medal in teams all-around, portable apparatus, and a silver medal in team all-around (1952).

KARPATKIN, Rhoda Hendrick (1930—). American attorney. Born June 7, 1930, in New York, NY. ❖ Maintained private law practice (1954–74); became 1st woman executive director of Consumers Union of the United States, Inc. (1974).

KARPENKO, Viktoria (1984—). Ukrainian gymnast. Born Mar 15, 1984, in Kherson, Ukraine. ❖ Won Bluewater International, Kiev Invitational, and Wild Rose International (1996), Chunichi Cup (1997, 1998), Hungarian International (1997), American Cup (1998) and Ukrainian nationals (1998, 1999); at European championships, won a bronze medal in uneven bars (1998) and silver medals in team all-around, uneven bars, and floor exercises (2000); at World championships, won a silver medal in all-around (1999).

KARPINSKI, Stephanie (1912–2005). Polish aviator. Name variations: Stefania Barbara Wojtulanis-Karpinska; Stephanie Wojtulanis; Barbara Wojtulanis. Born Stefania Barbara Wojtulanis, 1912, in Poland; died Feb 11, 2005, in Los Angeles, CA; studied mechanical engineering at Warsaw Technical University; m. Polish Air Force Gen. Stanislaw Karpinski, c. 1946 (died 1982). ❧ Obtained glider, balloon and motor aircraft pilot licenses and became an instructor in parachute jumping (1939); as a pilot in the Polish army during WWII, was assigned to the Polish general staff, flew missions delivering fuel to the fighter brigade defending Warsaw from the Nazis, worked at Polish Army Headquarters in Paris, then was a ferry pilot in Britain; after the war, immigrated to US.

KARPOVA, Elena (1980—). Russian basketball player. Born June 14, 1980, in Leningrad, USSR. ❧ Forward, won a team bronze medal at Athens Olympics (2004).

KARR, Carme (1865–1943). Spanish short-story writer and feminist. Name variations: Francès Alphonse Karr; Carme Karr i Alfonsetti; Carme Karr de Lasarte; L. Escardot. Born 1865 in Spain; died Dec 29, 1943, in Barcelona. ❧ Catalan writer, served as president of Acció Femenina (Women's Action) and was influential in the successful campaign to secure women's suffrage (1932–33); wrote short-fiction collections Bolves, quadrets (1906) and Clixies, estudis en prosa (1906); also wrote short novel La vida d'en Joan Franch (1912) and tales for children Cuentos a mis nietos (1932) and El libro de Puli (1958).

KARR I ALFONSETTI, Carme (1865–1943). See Karr, Carme.

KARRES, Sylvia (1976—). Dutch field-hockey player. Born Nov 8, 1976, in Netherlands. ❧ Won European championship (2003); forward, won a team silver medal at Athens Olympics (2004).

KARSAVINA, Tamara (1885–1978). Russian ballet dancer. Name variations: Tamara Karsavin; Tata. Born Tamara Platonovna Karsavina in St. Petersburg, Russia, Mar 9, 1885; died in London, England, May 26, 1978; dau. of Platon Karsavin (ballet dancer and instructor); graduate of St. Petersburg Theater School, 1902; m. Vasili Moukhin (div.); m. Henry J. Bruce, 1915 (died 1950); children: (2nd m.) Nikita (b. 1916). ❧ Outstanding dancer of her generation who helped introduce Russian ballet to Western audiences before WWI and, in later years, continued to exercise a major influence on development of European ballet; became a junior member of Marinskii Ballet (1902); promoted to rank of prima ballerina (1912); was leading dancer with Diaghilev's Ballets Russes in Paris and partner to Vaclav Nijinsky (1909–14, 1919–20); returned to Russia at beginning of WWI and resumed dancing career with Marinskii until 1917 revolution; escaped to England (1918), which became her permanent home until her death; continued to dance in Europe and toured US (1924); after retiring from dancing (1933), established herself as a ballet teacher, writer on dance, and choreographic consultant; was vice-president of Royal Academy of Dance in London (1930–55). Beginning in 1902 at Marinskii, danced in Giselle, Nutcracker, La Bayadere, Swan Lake, and other ballets; created leading female roles for many of Diaghilev's Ballets Russes productions such as Fokine's Les Sylphides (1908), Cleopatre (1909), Firebird (1910), Narcisse (1911), Petrushka (1911), Le Dieu Bleu (1912), Tamar (1911), Daphnis and Chloe (1912), Pappillion (1914), as well as Nijinsky's Jeux (1913), and Massine's Le Tricorne and Pulcinella (1920). ❧ See also autobiographical Theatre Street (London, 1930); and Women in World History.

KARSCH, Anna Luise (1722–1791). German poet. Name variations: Anna Louisa Karsch or Karschin. Born Anna Louisa Dürbach in Silesia, Germany, 1722; died 1791; married twice; children: 3, including daughter Karoline Luise von Klencke (1754–1812) who was also a poet. ❧ The 1st woman writer in Germany to live off her writing, had 2 difficult marriages; with family near poverty, began writing poetry to celebrate patriotic and family occasions; soon caught attention of such literary figures as Gotthold, Mendelssohn, Herder, and Goethe, who extolled her as "Sappho Resurrected"; granted audience with Frederick II, king of Prussia, in recognition of her long poem inspired by the Seven Years' War; fell in love with poet Johann Wilhelm Gleim, who arranged for 1st publication of her poetry (1764), but did not return her affection; later moved to Berlin, establishing herself there as a writer of note and a woman of independence; works include Auserlesene Gedichte (Selected Poems, 1764), Einige Oden über verschiedene hohe Gegenstände (Odes on Various Subjects, 1764), Poetische Einfälle, Erste Sammllung (Poetical

Ideas, 1764), Kleinigkeite (Little Nothings, 1765) and Neue Gedichte (New Poems, 1772).

KARSTEN, Ekaterina (1972—). See Khodotovich, Ekaterina.

KARSTENS, Gerda (1903–1988). Danish ballet dancer. Name variations: Gerda Elisabeth Karstens. Born July 9, 1903, in Copenhagen, Denmark; died June 13, 1988; dau. of Johan Emil Karstens and Kirsti Thovaldine Andersen. ❧ Studied at school of Royal Danish Ballet and—on apprenticeship—danced children's character roles in numerous repertory works by August Bournonville; joined the company (1923) where she performed in further works by Bournonville such as Napoli and Far from Denmark, and in works by Gasparo Angiolini, including Loves of a Ballet Master.

KARTINI (1879–1904). Indonesian feminist and nationalist. Name variations: R.A. Kartini; honorary titles "Raden Adjeng or Ajeng" and "Ibu" are sometimes added, though she preferred to use her one name. Born Kartini, April 21, 1879, in Mayong, on island of Java; died Sept 17, 1904, soon after childbirth; dau. of Raden Adipati Sosroningrat (Indonesian civil servant of high rank) and Ngasirah (1 of his 2 wives); educated in Dutch schools; m. Raden Adiati Djojo Adiningrat, Nov 8, 1903; children: son, Raden Mas Singgih (b. 1904). ❧ At 12, as prescribed by Islamic law, was sequestered in preparation for marriage but resisted (1891); reached outside world through letters, corresponding with Marie Ovink-Soer, who contributed to the feminist journal, The Dutch Lily, and J.A. Abendanon, who would collect and publish the letters under title From Darkness into Light (another translation was later published as Letters of a Javanese Princess); began to be referred to as "the well-known Raden Ajeng Kartini" by newspapers; was permitted to enroll in a Dutch school in Japara (1898), one of the 1st Indonesian women ever to attend a European school; founded a school for women (1903). Her letters have exerted a powerful influence in Indonesia and proceeds from their publication have been used to found "Kartini schools" for women throughout nation; regarded as a pioneer for women's liberation and national liberation, her birthday has become a national holiday. ❧ See also Women in World History.

KARYAMI, Zacharoula (1983—). Greek rhythmic gymnast. Name variations: Chara or Hara Kariami. Born April 7, 1983, in Greece. ❧ Won a bronze medal for team all-around at Sydney Olympics (2000).

KASABIAN, Linda (1949—). American member of Manson family. Born Linda Drouin, 1949, in New Hampshire; married twice; children: daughter (b. 1968). ❧ Met Charles Manson (1969) and moved to Manson commune in California (1969); was the getaway driver, during the murders of Abigail Folger, Voytek Frykowski, Jay Sebring, Sharon Tate, and Leno and Rosemary LaBianca; turned state's witness in exchange for immunity; changed her name and moved to Pacific North West.

KASAEVA, Zarema (1987—). Russian weightlifter. Born Feb 25, 1987, in Vladikavkaz, USSR. ❧ Won a bronze medal for 69kg at Athens Olympics (2004).

KASAI, Masae (1933—). Japanese volleyball player. Born July 14, 1933, in Japan. ❧ At Tokyo Olympics, won a gold medal in team competition (1964).

KASATKINA, Natalia (1934—). Soviet ballet dancer and choreographer. Name variations: Natalia Kasatkina. Born July 7, 1934 in USSR; m. Vladimir Vasilyev (choreographer). ❧ Trained with Maria Kazhukova and Sulamith Messerer at Bolshoi Ballet; joined the Bolshoi (1953) and became a well-known character dancer in such roles as Phrygia in Spartacus; with husband, choreographed numerous works for the Kirov, Bolshoi, and Nemirovich-Danchenko Theater. Works of choreography include Vanina Vanini (1962), Heroic Poem, or Geologists (1964), Sacre du Printemps (1965), Preludes and Fugues (1968), Gayané (1970), Creation of the World (1971) and Seeing the Light (1974).

KASCHNITZ, Marie Luise (1901–1974). German poet and writer. Born Marie Luise von Holzing-Berstett, Jan 31, 1901, in Karlsruhe, Germany; died Oct 10, 1974, in Rome, Italy; m. Guido von Kaschnitz-Weinberg (Viennese archaeologist), 1925. ❧ Published a collection of essays, Men and Things (1945), which describes the devastation of wartorn Germany; other writings include Liebe beginnt (Love Begins, novel, 1933), Griechische Mythen (1943), Totentanz und Gedichte zur Zeit (Danse Macabre and Poems for the Times, 1947), Zukunftsmusik (Music of the Future, 1950), Das dicke Kind und andere Erzählungen (The Fat Kid and Other Tales, 1951), Ewige Stadt (Eternal City, 1952), Das Haus der

Kindheit (*The House of Childhood*, 1956), *Lange Schatten* (*Long Shadows*, 1960), *Dein Schweigen—meine Stimme* (*Your Silence—My Voice*, 1962), *Wohin denn ich?* (*Where Am I To Go?*, 1963), *Ein Wort weiter* (*One More Word*, 1965), *Gespräche im All* (*Conversations in Space*, 1971) and *Kein Zauberspruch* (*No Magic Formula*, 1972). ❖ See also *Women in World History*.

KASCHUBE, Ilse (1953—). East German kayaker. Born June 24, 1953, in East Germany. ❖ At Munich Olympics, won a silver medal in K2 500 meters (1972).

KÄSEBIER, Gertrude (1852–1934). American photographer. Name variations: Gertrude Kasebier. Born Gertrude Stanton in Fort Des Moines, Iowa, May 18, 1852; died in New York, NY, Oct 13, 1934; dau. of John W. Stanton (entrepreneur) and Gertrude Muncy (Shaw) Stanton; attended Pratt Institute, 1889–93; m. Eduard Käsebier, May 18, 1874; children: Frederick William (b. 1875); Gertrude Elizabeth O'Malley (b. 1878); Hermine Mathilde Turner (b. 1880). ❖ At turn-of-the-century, gained renown as one of the finest pictorialists in the country; opened a professional portrait studio, Brooklyn (1896); established reputation at 1st Philadelphia Photographic Salon (1898); was 1 of the 1st two women admitted to The Linked Ring (1900); had photographs included in "The New School of American Photography" exhibition at Royal Photographic Society, London (1900); was founding member of Photo-Secession Group (1902); joined Professional Photographers of New York (1906); pioneered portraits of high-profile personalities and well-known artists, such as Auguste Rodin and Alfred Stieglitz, elevating the role of portrait photographer from technician to artist; resigned from Photo-Secession Group (1912); named honorary vice-president of Pictorial Photographers of America (1916); had last major exhibit during lifetime at Brooklyn Institute of Arts and Science (1929). Her allegorical pictorial photographs of women and children remain among the most arresting and recognizable photographs hanging in modern-day museums. ❖ See also Barbara L. Michaels, *Gertrude Käsebier: The Photographer and Her Photographs* (Abrams, 1992); and *Women in World History*.

KASHFI, Anna (1934—). Welsh-born actress. Born Joan O'Callaghan, Sept 30, 1934, in Cardiff, Wales; raised in Calcutta where her father William O'Callaghan was a traffic superintendent for Indian State Railway; m. Marlon Brando (actor), 1957 (div. 1959); m. James Hannaford, 1974 (div.); children: Christian Devi Brando (b. 1958, who murdered his half-sister Cheyenne's boyfriend, 1990). ❖ Films include *The Mountain*, *Battle Hymn*, *Cowboy* and *Night of the Quarter Moon*. ❖ See also memoir *Breakfast with Brando* (1979).

KASIA (c. 800/810–before 867). *See Kassia.*

KASILAG, Lucrecia R. (1918—). Philippine composer, pianist, professor and writer. Born in La Union, Philippines, Aug 31, 1918; Philippine Women's University, BA cum laude, 1936; St. Scholastica College, music teacher's diploma, 1939; Philippine Women's University, BM, 1949; Eastman School of Music, University of Rochester, MA, 1950; Centro Escolar University, PhD in music, 1975; held degrees in law as well. ❖ Served as dean of College of Music and Fine Arts at Philippine Women's University as well as professor of music (1953–77); directed Theater for Performing Arts and presided over National Music Council of the Philippines; headed cultural delegations to UN and presided over international music conferences; was interested in occidental and oriental instruments, a theme reflected in her compositions and writing; served as chair of League of Philippine composers; wrote almost 100 works, including a violin concerto recorded in 1980s.

KASPARKOVA, Sarka (1971—). Czech triple jumper. Born May 20, 1971, in Karvina, Czechoslovakia. ❖ Won a bronze medal at Atlanta Olympics (1996), gold medal at World championship (1997), and silver medal at European championship (1998).

KASSEBAUM, Nancy Landon (1932—). American politician and US senator. Name variations: Nancy Baker. Born Nancy Josephine Landon, July 29, 1932, in Topeka, Kansas; dau. of Alfred Mossman Landon (politician who ran against FDR for presidency, 1936) and Theo (Cobb) Landon; University of Kansas, BA, 1954; University of Michigan, MA, 1956; m. Philip Kassebaum, June 8, 1955 (div. 1979); m. Howard Baker (former US senator from TN), Dec 7, 1996; children: (1st m.) John Philip Kassebaum Jr.; Linda Josephine Kassebaum; Richard Landon Kassebaum; William Alfred Kassebaum. ❖ US senator (R-Kansas), noted for both independence and consensus-building, who worked on legislation in foreign affairs, aviation, labor, welfare and

health-care reform; worked as aide to US senator James Pearson (R-Kansas) and was a member of Executive Committee of Kansas Republican Party (1975); won election to Congress (1976), only the 4th woman in US history to be elected to a full 6-year Senate term and the 1st who had not followed a husband into politics; was assigned to Senate committees on Commerce, Science and Transportation, on Banking Housing and Urban Affairs, on the Budget, and on the Special Committee on Aging, as well as to 6 subcommittees; reelected (1984); won 3rd term in a landslide (1990); served on Foreign Relations Subcommittee on African Affairs, and sponsored legislation to impose economic sanctions on the white-minority government in South Africa, warning Reagan that Congress would act if he would not; parted ways from Republicans to vote in support of economic sanctions against Iraq at a time when US was supporting the regime of Saddam Hussein (1990); became chair of Labor and Human Resources Committee (1994), the 1st woman to chair a full committee; was part of a small coterie of moderate Republicans who often deviated from their party line, especially on social issues; capped career in Senate by authoring health-care legislation guaranteeing that working Americans would have access to health insurance when they changed or lost jobs even if they or family members had preexisting health conditions (1996); announced retirement from Senate (1996). ❖ See also *Women in World History*.

KASSI (1241–?). Empress of Mali. Born 1241; chief wife and paternal cousin of Emperor Suleyman who governed Mali; children: Kassa (emperor). ❖ Was very popular with the Malian royal court, which included some of her relatives; when husband divorced her to marry the commoner Bendjou, assembled the noblewomen of the court who were unwilling to pay reverence to the new empress; was compelled to seek refuge in the mosque; from her sanctuary, influenced the nobles, particularly her cousins, to rebel against Suleyman. ❖ See also *Women in World History*.

KASSIA (c. 800/810–before 867). Byzantine author of liturgical hymns. Name variations: Kasia; Kasiane or Kassiane; Elkasia. Born (probably in Constantinople) between 800 and 810 CE; died before 867 CE, perhaps much before. ❖ Was famous throughout the Byzantine Empire as the author of liturgical hymns, dedicated to the ethical and moral strengths and weaknesses of women; became a nun in a convent in Constantinople at a time when the religious controversy over icons split Byzantium in two; sided with those who thought icons not only acceptable, but beneficial. ❖ See also *Women in World History*.

KASSIANE (c. 800/810–before 867). *See Kassia.*

KASTEN, Barbara (1936—). American experimental photographer. Born 1936 in Chicago, Illinois; University of Arizona, BFA, 1959; California College of Arts and Crafts, MFA, 1970. ❖ Studied for a year with fiber sculptor Magdalena Abakanowicz in Poland; upon returning to California, began to work in photography, making abstract photograms of folded mesh and large-scale Polacolor prints of sculptural arrangements; moved to NY (1982); was involved in a number of varied projects, including designing stage settings for Margaret Jenkins Dance Co. in San Francisco, photographing existing modern architecture for an architectural series, and creating a series of photographs based on the 19th-century (Jackson) Pollock-(Lee) Krasner House and Study Center in East Hampton. ❖ See also *Women in World History*.

KASTL, Sonja (1929—). Yugoslavian ballet dancer and choreographer. Born July 14, 1929, in Zagreb, then Yugoslavia (now Croatia). ❖ Danced with Margaret Frohman's Zagreb State Opera Ballet where she had featured and principal roles in numerous classics, including *Swan Lake* and *Coppélia*, as well as in works by Frohman and Pio and Pina Mlaklar; succeeded Frohman as director.

KASTOR, Deena (1973—). American marathoner. Name variations: Deena Drossin. Born Feb 14, 1973, in Waltham, MA; attended University of Arkansas; married. ❖ Began sports career as a figure skater; won US marathon (2001); was the 1st American to set the 5 km world road mark since 1986 (2002); at World Cross Country championships, placed 2nd in indiv. long distance (2002, 2003); won a bronze medal for marathon at Athens Olympics (2004). Inducted into University of Arkansas Hall of Fame (2001); named US Athlete of the Year (2002).

KATARINA. *Variant of Catharine or Catherine.*

KATARINA OF SAXE-LÜNEBURG (1513–1535). Queen of Sweden. Name variations: Catherine of Saxe-Luneberg, Luneburg, or Lauenburg. Born 1513; died Sept 23, 1535; dau. of Magnus, duke of Saxe-Luneburg, and Catherine of Brunswick-Wolfenbuttel (1488–1563); became 1st wife of Gustavus I Adolphus Vasa (1496–1560), king of Sweden (r. 1523–1560), on Sept 24, 1531; children: Eric XIV (1533–1577), king of Sweden (r. 1560–1568). ❖ According to an unconfirmed rumor, was killed by Gustavus with a hammer.

KATARINA STENBOCK (1536–1621). Queen of Sweden. Born July 22, 1536; died Dec 13, 1621; dau. of Gustav Stenbock; became 3rd wife of Gustavus I Adolphus Vasa (1496–1560), king of Sweden (r. 1523–1560), Aug 22, 1552; no children.

KATARZYNA. *Variant of Catharine or Catherine.*

KATE, Dirty (1751–c. 1800). *See Corbin, Margaret."*

KATERIN. *Variant of Catharine or Catherine.*

KATHARINA VON GEBWEILER (fl. c. 1340). German religious writer. Name variations: Sister Catherine Gebweiler or Catherine von Gebweiler. Flourished between 1330 and 1340; died c. 1340. ❖ Wrote *Vitae sororum* in Latin, about lives of fellow nuns in Dominican Convent of Unterlinden, near Colmar in Alsace, one of the earliest works in what became a common genre in southern German Dominican convents.

KATHARINE OR KATHERINE. *Variant of Catharine or Catherine.*

KATHERINE (fl. 13th c.). English physician. Fl. in 13th century in London; dau. of a London surgeon. ❖ Was a highly skilled physician who lived and worked in London, specializing in surgery and gaining widespread respect for healing abilities.

KATHERINE (c. 1471–?). *See Herbert, Katherine.*

KATHERINE HOWARD (1520/22–1542). *See Howard, Catherine.*

KATHERINE OF ARAGON (1485–1536). *See Catherine of Aragon.*

KATHERINE OF FRANCE (1401–1437). *See Catherine of Valois.*

KATHERINE OF HOLLAND (d. 1401). Countess of Guelders. Died in 1401; dau. of Albert I (b. 1336), count of Hainault and Holland (r. 1353–1404); sister of Margaret of Bavaria (d. 1424); m. Edward, count of Guelders.

KATHERINE OF PORTUGAL (1540–1614). *See Catherine of Portugal.*

KATHERINE OF SUTTON (d. 1376). British playwright and abbess. Name variations: Abbess of Barking. Died 1376. ❖ The 1st known English woman playwright, was abbess of Barking Abbey (1363–76); wrote religious plays in Latin, based on Easter liturgy, which are found in J. B. L. Tolburst (ed.), *The Ordinale and Customary of the Benedictine Nuns of Barking* (1977–78) as well as K. Young's *Transactions of the Wisconsin Academy of Sciences, Arts and Letters* (1910) and *The Drama of the Medieval Church* (1933).

KATHERINE PLANTAGENET (1253–1257). English princess. Born Nov 25, 1253, in Westminster, London, England; died May 3, 1257, in Windsor, Berkshire, England; buried in Westminster Abbey; dau. of Henry III (1206–1272), king of England (r. 1216–1272) and Eleanor of Provence (c. 1222–1291). ❖ Was born deaf and died at age three.

KATHERINE PLANTAGENET (1479–1527). English princess and duchess of Devon. Born c. August 14, 1479, in Eltham, Kent, England; died Nov 15, 1527, in Tiverton, Devon, England; dau. of Edward IV, king of England, and Elizabeth Woodville (1437–1492); m. William Courtenay, earl of Devon, Oct 1495; children: 3, including Henry Courtenay (c. 1498–1539), marquess of Exeter.

KATIA (1977—). Brazilian soccer player. Name variations: Katia Cilene Teixeira da Silva. Born Katia Cilene Teixeira da Silva, Feb 18, 1977, in Rio de Janeiro, Brazil. ❖ As a heptathlete, broke the Brazilian national record 6 times; as a soccer player, played for Vasco da Gama (1992–96), Saad (1996–97), and Sao Paulo (1997–00); scored 158 goals in 5 seasons of Brazilian League matches, ranking #1 goal scorer every season; signed with WUSA's San Jose CyberRays (2000). Voted Offensive Player of the Year by teammates (2002).

KATINKA. *Variant of Catherine or Katherine.*

KATO, Kiyomi (1953—). Japanese volleyball player. Born Mar 9, 1953, in Japan. ❖ At Montreal Olympics, won a gold medal in team competition (1976).

KATREN, Katrein, or Katrin. *Variant of Catherine or Katherine.*

KATUSHEVA, Marita (1938—). Soviet volleyball player. Born April 19, 1938, in USSR. ❖ At Tokyo Olympics, won a silver medal in team competition (1964).

KATZ, Fran (1941—). *See Ventre, Fran.*

KATZ, Lillian (1927—). American entrepreneur. Name variations: Lillian Vernon. Born Lilly Menasche, 1927, in Leipzig, Germany; studied psychology at New York University; m. Sam Hochberg, c. 1950 (div.); m. Robert Katz (div. 1990); m. Paolo M. Martino (hairstylist and interior designer); children: David and Fred Hochberg. ❖ Forced to flee Germany with rise of Nazism, moved with parents to Amsterdam, Holland, then NY (1938); while married and living in Mount Vernon, NY, started her own mail-order business, Lillian Vernon Corp. (c. 1950); became a pioneer in the catalog industry; changed name officially to Lillian Vernon (1990); sold the business and stepped down (2003).

KATZNELSON, Shulamit (1919–1999). Israeli professor. Born in Geneva, Switzerland, 1919; died Aug 6, 1999, of a heart attack at home in Netanya, Israel; dau. of Bat-Sheva Katznelson (legislator in Israel's Parliament); niece of Rachel Katznelson-Shazar (1888–1975); attended teacher's college in Jerusalem and master's program at University of Michigan. ❖ Immigrated to Palestine with family at age 2 (1921); founded Ulpan Akiva, an independent, residential language school in Netanya, Israel (1951); received Israel Prize for Life Achievement for bringing Arabs and Jews together through study of each other's language (1986); nominated for Nobel Peace Prize for helping to reconcile Jews and Arabs (1993); retired as head of Ulpan Akiva (1997). ❖ See also *Women in World History.*

KATZNELSON-RUBASHOV, Rachel (1888–1975). *See Katznelson-Shazar, Rachel.*

KATZNELSON-SHAZAR, Rachel (1888–1975). Russian-born Israeli editor, teacher, labor union activist and first lady. Name variations: Rachel Shazar; Rachel Katznelson-Rubashov; Rachel Katznelson-Rubachov. Born Rachel Katznelson in Bobroisk, Russia, in 1888; died as a Zionist pioneer in Israel, Aug 11, 1975; dau. of Nissan Katznelson and Selde (Rosowski) Katznelson; aunt of Shulamit Katznelson (d. 1999); studied at Academy of Jewish Studies in Berlin; m. Schneor Zalman Rubashov (1889–1974), who, as 3rd president of the Jewish State, was known as Zalman Shazar; children: daughter, Roda Shazar. ❖ First lady of Israel (1963–73), played a part in the foundation and development of the Jewish State; moved to Palestine (1912); was one of the 1st women to join the Mapai Party, eventually serving on its executive committee; was a member of the central cultural committee of the Histadrut, the General Federation of Jewish Labor (1924–27); as a member of presidium of the Zionist Actions Committee, was a delegate to Zionist Congresses for almost 4 decades; founded the labor journal *Dvar Hapoelet* (1934), serving as its editor until 1963, then became chair of journal's editorial board; a respected journalist and editor, won several literary prizes, including an Israel Prize (1958) for book *Masot Urshimot* (Essays and Articles); was also an influential member of Women's Workers Council (1930–63). Won Brenner Prize (1947), Chaim Greenberg Prize, and Prize of the Pioneer Women in US. ❖ See also memoir *The Person as She Was* (1989); and *Women in World History.*

KAUAI, queen of. *See Kapule, Deborah (c. 1798–1853).*

KAUF, Patti (1963—). *See Sherman-Kauf, Patti.*

KAUFER, Evelyn (1953—). East German runner. Born Feb 22, 1953, in East Germany. ❖ At Munich Olympics, won a silver medal in 4 x 100-meter relay (1972).

KAUFFMANN, Angelica (1741–1807). Swiss artist. Name variations: Angelika Kauffman; Maria Angelica Kauffmann; Kauffmann-Zucchi; Kauffman-Z; K.-Z.; A. K. Z. Born Marie Anne Angelica Catherine Kauffmann, Oct 30, 1741, in Chur (or Coire), capital of Graubünden canton, Switzerland; died Nov 5, 1807, in Rome; dau. of Johann Josef Kauffmann (itinerant painter) and Cléofa Lucin (or Lucci, or Luz) Kauffmann; m. "Count Frederick de Horn," in fact an impersonator by the name of Brandt, Nov 22, 1767 (legally sep. Feb 10, 1768); m. Antonio Zucchi, Sept 8, 1781; children: none. ❖ Achieved fame and fortune in portraiture and the hitherto male domain of history painting; began commissioned portraiture in Como, Italy, at age 11 (1752); traveled with father in Italy and France, studying and painting; elected to Academy of Fine Arts, Florence, Academy of St. Clement, Bologna (1762), and Academy of St. Luke, Rome (1765); accompanied Lady Wentworth to England (1765 or 66); selected as a founding member of Royal Academy of

Art, London (1768); left England (1781), traveled in Europe and elected to Academy of Fine Arts, Venice; established last studio in Rome by Dec 1782; was a central figure in neoclassical movement in art which began in mid-18th-century Europe, and it was she who introduced history painting in the neoclassical style to England. Paintings include *The Family of the Earl of Gower* (National Museum of Women in the Arts, Washington, DC, 1772), *Zeuxis choosing his Models for the Painting of Helen of Troy* (Brown University, Providence, RI, late 1770s), *Cornelia, Mother of the Gracchi* (Virginia Museum of Fine Arts, Richmond, 1785), *The Sadness of Telemachus* (Metropolitan Museum of Art, NY, 1788), *Angelica Kauffmann hesitating between the Arts of Music and Painting* (Nostell Priory, Yorkshire, c. 1794–96), and many more; signed work: Angelica Kauffmann (or Kauffman) Pinx. ❖ See also Frances A. Gerard, *Angelica Kauffmann* (1893); Lady Victoria Manners and Dr. G.C. Williamson, *Angelica Kauffmann, R.A.: Her Life and Her Works* (Bodley Head, 1924); and *Women in World History*.

KAUFFMANN, Maria A. (1741–1807). *See Kauffmann, Angelica.*

KAUFMAN, Barrie (1933—). *See Chase, Barrie.*

KAUFMAN, Beatrice (1894–1945). American playwright and editor. Name variations: Bea Kaufman, Mrs. George S. Kaufman. Born Beatrice Bakrow, Jan 20, 1895, in Rochester, NY; died Oct 6, 1945; m. George S. Kaufman (producer, playwright, director), Mar 15, 1917; children: Anne Kaufman. ❖ Wrote the play *Divided by Three* (1934); was East Coast representative for Samuel Goldwyn Productions and the 1st to see the dramatic potential in *Of Mice and Men;* with Joseph Hennessey, edited *The Letters of Alexander Woollcott* (1944). Portrayed in the film *Act One* by actress Ruth Ford.

KAUFMAN, Mrs. George S.
See Kaufman, Beatrice (1894–1945).
See MacGrath, Leueen (1914–1992).

KAUFMANN, Sylvia-Yvonne (1955—). German politician. Born Jan 23, 1955, in Berlin, Germany. ❖ Member of the Volkskammer of the GDR (1990) and the German Bundestag (1990); served as federal vice-chair of the PDS (Partei des Demokratischen Sozialismus, 1993–2000); representing the Confederal Group of the European United Left/Nordic Green Left (GUE/NGL), elected to 5th European Parliament (1999–2004).

KAUN, Elfriede (1914—). German high jumper. Born Oct 5, 1914, in Germany. ❖ At Berlin Olympics, won a bronze medal in the high jump (1936).

KAUPPI, Piia-Noora (1975—). Finnish politician. Born Jan 7, 1975, in Oulu, Finland. ❖ Served as deputy secretary in Finnish Parliament (1997–98) and secretary in Legislation Directorate (1998–99); as a member of the European People's Party (Christian Democrats) and European Democrats (EPP), elected to 5th European Parliament (1999–2004).

KAUR, Amrit (1889–1964). *See Kaur, Rajkumari Amrit.*

KAUR, Rajkumari Amrit (1889–1964). Indian nationalist, politician, and social worker. Name variations: Princess Amrit Kaur. Born Rajkumari Amrit Kaur on Feb 2, 1889, in Lucknow, India; died Feb 6, 1964, in New Delhi, India; dau. of Raja (or King) Sir Harnam Singh. ❖ Indian Christian nationalist who served as secretary to Mahatama Gandhi for 16 years and worked for improvement in status of women; was arrested numerous times for participation in India's freedom struggle; helped found All India Women's Conference (1927), serving as secretary (1930), and as president (1931–33, 1938); helped found All India Women's Education Fund Association (1929); was 1st woman cabinet minister, serving as 1st Health Minister of independent India (1947–57); was 1st woman member of Advisory Board of Education; founded All India Institute of Medical Sciences in New Delhi; was founder and president of Delhi Music Society and of the National Sports Club of India; helped found Indian Council for Child Welfare, National Association for the Prevention of Blindness, and Tuberculosis Association.

KAUS, Gina (1894–1985). Austrian playwright, screenwriter, biographer and novelist. Name variations: Gina Kauss; Andreas Eckbrecht. Born Nov 21, 1894, in Vienna, Austria-Hungary (now Austria); died Dec 23, 1985, in Los Angeles, CA; m. Otto Kaus, 1920 (div. 1926). ❖ Became part of Viennese literary circles after success of 1st play; knew Herman Broch, Robert Musil and Karl Kraus; published journal and ran advisory service for women; banned under Nazis, left Germany for

Switzerland, France, then US; works include *Diebe im Haus* (1917) and *Die Überfahrt* (1932), *Luxury Liner* (1933), and (play) *Prison without Bars* (1938); also wrote biography of Catherine the Great, *Katherine die Große* (1935); had a long and successful career in Hollywood writing screenplays for *The Wife Takes a Flyer* (1942), *The Law Rides Again* (1943), (adaptation) *Julia Misbehaves* (1948), *The Red Danube* (1949) and *All I Desire* (1953), among others.

KAUSCHKE, Katrin (1971—). German field-hockey player. Born Sept 13, 1971, in Germany. ❖ At Barcelona Olympics, won a silver medal in team competition (1992).

KAUSS, Gina (1894–1985). *See Kaus, Gina.*

KAUTSKY, Luise (1864–1944). Austrian Social Democratic activist and author. Born Luise Ronsperger in Vienna, Austria, Aug 11, 1864; died in Auschwitz-Birkenau concentration camp, early Dec 1944; became 2nd wife of Karl Kautsky (1854–1938, Marxist theoretician and son of writer Minna Kautsky [1837–1912]), 1890; children: Benedikt Kautsky (1894–1960, leader of the postwar Austrian Social Democratic Party). ❖ Married to Karl Kautsky, one of the major personalities of the period of European Socialism, was a significant figure in her own right; joined the nascent Socialist movement, where she became an important voice for women's rights; with husband, settled in Vienna (1920), where her articles appeared in many Socialist newspapers and journals; with Nazi annexation of Austria (1938), fled with husband to the Netherlands (son Benedikt had been arrested by the Nazis soon after the Anschluss and was being held in Dachau); arrested in the Netherlands and sent to Auschwitz-Birkenau (1944). ❖ See also *Women in World History*.

KAUTSKY, Minna (1837–1912). Austrian actress, novelist and short-story writer. Name variations: Minna Kautsky-Jaich or Minna Jaich; (pseudonym) Eckert. Born Wilhelmine Eleanore Jaich, June 11, 1837, in Graz, Austria; died Dec 20, 1912, in Berlin Friedenau, Germany; one of 7 children of Anton Jaich (Viennese painter at the Graz national theater); m. Johann Kautsky (Czech landscape painter), 1853 or 1854; children: 4, including Karl Kautsky (1854–1938, Marxist theoretician who m. the socialist Luise Kautsky). ❖ Moved to Prague (1845); read Marx and Engels and began to write about working-class people; became known for progressive, socialist politics; published *Moderne Frauen* (1870); novels include *Stefan vom Grillenhof* (1879), *Herrschen oder Dienen* (1882), *Die Alten und die Neuen* (1885), *Victoria* (1889) and *Im Vaterhause* (1904).

KAVAN, Anna (1901–1968). English-French writer. Name variations: original name Helen Woods changed to Anna Kavan; Helen Ferguson; Helen Woods Edmonds. Born Helen Emily Woods in Cannes, France, April 10, 1901; grew up in California; committed suicide in London, England, Dec 5, 1968; dau. of C.C.E. Woods and Helen (Bright) Woods; m. Donald Ferguson, c. 1920; m. Stuart Edmonds (painter), c. 1930; children: (1st m.) 1 son (deceased). ❖ Initially wrote under name Helen Ferguson; after 1940, wrote under Anna Kavan, borrowed from a central character in her novel, *A Stranger Still* (1935); was 14 when father committed suicide; wrote conventional romantic novels (1920s–30s); following 2nd marriage, entered a Swiss clinic for treatment of acute depression, a mental illness that would plague her for the rest of her life and lead to a dependence on heroin; wrote about her experiences with mental illness in *Asylum Piece* (1940), a collection of short stories and 1st work under Kavan; published *Change the Name* (1941), considered by some to be her best early novel, though it is also something of a transitional work; writings became more surrealistic in form, including *House of Sleep* (1947) and *Ice* (1967); despite addiction and a number of stays in mental institutions, traveled extensively and purchased and renovated several houses at Campden Hill, in England. Her work has received worldwide recognition and has been translated into 7 major European languages. ❖ See also David Callard, *The Case of Anna Kavan* (1994); and *Women in World History*.

KAVANAGH, Julia (1824–1877). British novelist, historian and biographer. Born at Thurles, County Tipperary, Ireland, 1824; died in Nice, France, Oct 28, 1877; dau. of Morgan Peter Kavanagh (1800–1874, writer); educated at home; never married; no children. ❖ Spent early life in Normandy and Paris; began writing magazine stories and a series of children's books, the 1st of which was *Three Paths* (1847); years in France provided inspiration for many subsequent novels, including *Madeleine* (1848) and *Nathalie* (1851); most popular novels were *Adéle* (1857), *Queen Mab* (1863) and *John Dorrien* (1875); was perhaps better known for nonfiction, particularly biographical volumes about women: *Woman in France in the 18th Century* (1850), *Women of Christianity* (1852),

French Women of Letters (1862) and *English Women of Letters* (1863). ❖ See also *Women in World History.*

KAVANAGH, Spencer (d. 1910). *See Cook, Edith Maud.*

KAWABE, Miho (1974—). Japanese synchronized swimmer. Born 1974 in Japan. ❖ Won a team bronze medal at Atlanta Olympics (1996).

KAWAKUBO, Rei (1942—). Japanese fashion designer. Born 1942 in Tokyo, Japan; graduate in fine art, Keio University, 1964. ❖ Modernist, worked at Asahikasei Textile Co.; founded the label, Comme de Garçons (1973); held 1st Paris show (1981), creating shock with her minimalist style, use of asymmetry, austere mood, and rejection of traditional couture methods.

KAWAGUCHI, Yoriko (1941—). Japanese politician. Born Jan 14, 1941, in Tokyo, Japan; Tokyo University, BA in International Relations, 1965; Yale University, MA in philosophy, 1972. ❖ Speaking fluent English, spent several years in Washington, DC, with the Japanese Embassy and the World Bank; began serving as Japanese minister of Environment (2001); appointed minister for Foreign Affairs (2002); reappointed (2003).

KAWAMOTO, Evelyn (1933—). American swimmer. Name variations: Evelyn Kawamoto-Konno. Born Sept 17, 1933, in Honolulu, Hawaii; children: 2 daughters. ❖ At Helsinki Olympics, won a bronze medal in 4 x 100-meter freestyle relay and a bronze medal in 400-meter freestyle (1952).

KAWASAKI, Ayumi (1984—). Japanese skater. Born July 27, 1984, in Osaka, Japan. ❖ Won gold (1999), silver (1998 and 2000), and bronze (1997) at X Games in Vert; other 1st-place finishes in Vert include: NISS championships (1996) and World championships—ASA (1997 and 1998).

KAWASE, Akiko (1971—). Japanese synchronized swimmer. Born 1971 in Japan. ❖ Won a team bronze medal at Atlanta Olympics (1996).

KAWASHIMA, Naoko (1981—). Japanese synchronized swimmer. Born April 7, 1981, in Japan. ❖ At World championships, placed 1st in free routine combination (2003); won a team silver medal at Athens Olympics (2004).

KAWASHIMA, Yoshiko (1906–1947). Chinese-born Japanese spy. Name variations: Eastern Jewel. Born Aisingoro Xianwangyu (Manchu name) in 1906; executed in China in Oct 22, 1947; dau. of Prince Su of Mongolia and his 2nd wife, a concubine; given at birth to Naniwa Kawashima, Prince Su's Japanese military advisor, who named her Yoshiko Kawashima and raised her as his own daughter; educated in Tokyo; m. Kanjurjab (son of a Mongol prince), in 1927 (separated within 4 months). ❖ Took to wearing men's clothing, particularly uniforms with riding breeches and shiny black boots; among a string of lovers, had a liaison with Major Ryukichi Tanaka, head of the Japanese Intelligence Service in Shanghai; when Tanaka was ordered to create disturbances in Shanghai to divert attention from the Japanese takeover of Manchuria (1931), was instructed to hire dozens of Chinese thugs to break into homes and businesses and create general mayhem; was also dispatched to Tientsin, where she successfully "persuaded" the deposed boy emperor Henry Puyi to move to Mukden, where he served as a puppet ruler of the Japanese militarists; was brought before a Chinese tribunal and condemned to death as a traitor (1947). ❖ See also *Women in World History.*

KAY, Beatrice (1907–1986). American radio singer and comedian. Born April 21, 1907, in New York, NY; died Nov 8, 1986, in North Hollywood, CA. ❖ Came to prominence as "The Gay 90's Girl"; Broadway appearances include *Secrets, Sweet Adeline, The Provincetown Follies* and *Tell Me Pretty Maiden.*

KAY, Bernice (1925—). *See Williams, Cara.*

KAYE, Mrs. Danny (1913–1991). *See Fine, Sylvia.*

KAYE, M. M. (1908–2004). English novelist and painter. Name variations: Mollie Kaye; Mollie Hamilton. Born Mary Margaret Kaye, Aug 21, 1908, in Simla, India; died Jan 29, 2004, in Suffolk, England; dau. of a British parents; her father Sir Cecil Kaye was an Indian civil service linguist and cipher agent and titular head of the Indian state of Rajputana; m. Major-General G. J. "Goff" Hamilton (British officer), 1942 (died 1985); children: 2 daughters, Carolyn and Nicky. ❖ Sent back to Britain for schooling at age 10; returned to India (1926–35); moved with husband to various postings; began writing career with detective stories, *Death Walks in Kashmir* (1953), *Berlin* (1955), and *Cyprus*

(1956), among others; spent about 16 years writing *The Far Pavilions*, about her upbringing in the India of the British Raj, which became a bestseller (1978) and was adapted into a 6-hour miniseries (1984); other books included *Shadow of the Moon* (1956) and *Trade Wind* (1963); also wrote stories for younger readers, including the "Potter Pinner" series (1937–41). ❖ See also autobiographies, *The Sun in the Morning* (1990), *Golden Afternoon* (1997), and *Enchanted Evening* (1999).

KAYE, Mollie (1908–2004). *See Kaye, M. M.*

KAYE, Nora (1920–1987). American ballerina. Born Nora Koreff in New York, NY, Jan 17, 1920; died in Los Angeles, California, April 30, 1987; dau. of Gregory Koreff (an actor) and Lisa Koreff; studied at Metropolitan Opera Ballet School and under Michel Fokine; studied at School of American Ballet; m. Michael Van Buren, Jan 2, 1943 (div.); m. Isaac Stern (violinist), Nov 10, 1948 (div.); m. Herbert Ross (director and choreographer), 1959. ❖ At 15, graduated to Metropolitan Opera's corps de ballet; joined American Ballet (1935); abandoned ballet for Broadway, dancing in musical productions *Virginia* (1937), *Great Lady* (1938), and *Stars in Your Eyes* (1939), then spent 9 months in corps de ballet of Radio City Music Hall; joined Ballet Theater (later American Ballet Theater, 1939) and had 1st substantial role in *Gala Performance* (1941); achieved rank of prima ballerina as Hagar in *Pillar of Fire* (1942), a role Anthony Tudor choreographed for her; subsequently danced new and classic roles in a variety of ballets, including Tudor's *Dark Elegies, Lilac Garden* and *Dim Lustre,* Fokine's *Bluebeard* and *Apollo,* Massine's *Mademoiselle Angot* and *Romeo and Juliet,* Balachine's *Waltz Academy* (premiere, 1944), Kidd's *On Stage!* (premiere, 1945), Semenoff's *Gift of the Magi* (premiere, 1945), Taras' *Graziana* (premiere, 1945), and Robbins' *Facsimile* (premiere, 1946); scored great success as the Accused in Agnes de Mille's *Fall River Legend* (1948); danced lead roles in Tudor's *Nimbus* and Dollar's version of *Jeux* (1950); at New York City Ballet, performed in Robbins' *The Cage* (premiere, 1951) and Tudor's *La Gloire* (premiere, 1952), among other works; appeared as principal dancer in *Two's Company* (1952); at Ballet Theater, created role of Blanche in Bettis' *A Streetcar Named Desire* (1954); subsequently danced in *Winter's Eve, Journey* and *Paean;* with husband Herbert Ross, formed Ballet of Two Worlds (1959); retired from performing (1961); was named assistant to director of American Ballet Theater (1964) and associate director (1977); was also executive producer on film *The Turning Point* (1977). ❖ See also *Women in World History.*

KAYE-SMITH, Sheila (1887–1956). English novelist and poet. Name variations: Mrs. Penrose Fry. Born in St. Leonard's-on-Sea, Sussex, England, Feb 4, 1887; died near Rye, Sussex, England, Jan 14, 1956; dau. of Edward Kaye-Smith (physician and surgeon); her mother, whose maiden name was de la Condamine, was his 2nd wife; attended Hastings and St. Leonard's Ladies' College; m. Theodore Penrose Fry, later known as Sir Penrose Fry (minister turned farmer); no children. ❖ Raised in Sussex, which later became the setting of most of her novels; with husband, purchased "Little Doucegrove" in Northiam, Sussex, and combined prolific writing career with duties as a farmer's wife; at 21, published 1st work of fiction, *The Tramping Methodist* (1908); established reputation as a writer with *Sussex Gorse* (1916); made love of the land a dominant theme in all 31 novels that followed, including *Little England* (1918), *Green Apple Harvest* (1920), and *Joanna Godden* (1921), which was later filmed; also known for 2 studies written in collaboration with G.B. Stern: *Talking of Jane Austen* (1943) and *More Talk about Jane Austen* (1950). ❖ See also 3-volume autobiography, *Three Ways Home* (1937), informal cookbook-autobiography, *Kitchen-Fugue* (1945), and memoir, *All the Books of My Life* (1956); and *Women in World History.*

KAYSER, Louisa (c. 1835–1925). *See Dat So La Lee.*

KAZAKOVA, Oksana (1975—). Russian pairs skater. Born April 8, 1975, in St. Petersburg, Russia; m. Alexei Novitski. ❖ With partner Dmitri Sukhonov, placed 15th at World championships (1993); began skating with Artur Dmitriev, who had previously skated with Natalia Mishkutunok (early 1995) and won European championships (1996, 1998) and a gold medal at Nagano Olympics (1998).

KAZAN, Barbara (1932–1980). *See Loden, Barbara.*

KAZAN, Molly (d. 1963). *See Thatcher, Molly Day.*

KAZANKINA, Tatyana (1951—). Russian runner. Name variations: Tatiana Kazankina. Born Dec 17, 1951, in Leningrad (now St. Petersburg), USSR. ❖ Won gold medals for the 800 meters and 1,500 meters at Montreal (1976), the only woman to win double gold in those events in the same Olympics until then; won a gold medal for the

1,500 meters at Moscow Olympics (1980); was the 1st woman to run the 1,500 in 3:52.47, faster than the men's record set by Paavo Nurmi in 1924 (Aug 13, 1980).

KAZANTZAKI, Eleni (1903–2004). Greek journalist and biographer. Born 1903 in Athens, Greece; died Feb 18, 2004, in Athens; became 2nd wife of Nikos Kazantzakis (author), 1945 (died 1957); children: (adopted) Patroklos Stavrou. ❖ Lived with Nikos Kazantzakis for more than 20 years before marrying him; wrote biography *Nikos Kazantzakis, the Uncompromising* (1968).

KAZANTZAKI, Galateia (1886–1962). Greek novelist and poet. Born 1886 in Crete, Greece; died 1962; sister of Elli Alexiou (novelist); was 1st wife of Nikos Kazantzakis (writer); m. Marko Avgeri. ❖ Works include *Ridi Pagliacco* (1909), *Sonetta* (1922), *11 a.m. till 1 p.m.* (1929), *The Sinful One* (1931), *Crucial Moments* (1933), *Men* (1934) and *Men and Supermen* (1957).

KAZANTZIS, Judith (1940—). British poet, short-story writer and feminist. Born 1940 in East Sussex, England; children: 2. ❖ Member of Women's Literature Collective; reviewed works for feminist journal *Spare Rib*; writings include *Minefield* (1977), *The Wicked Queen* (1980), *Let's Pretend* (1984), *The Flame Tree* (1988), *The Rabbit Magician Plate* (1992), and *Swimming Through the Grand Hotel* (1997); wrote poems and stories for collections and anthologies including *Poems on the Underground* (2001); novels include *Of Love and Terror* (2002).

KAZEL, Dorothy (1931—). American nun and martyr. Born June 30, 1939; killed Dec 2, 1980 in El Salvador. ❖ Joined Ursuline Sisters and taught in Cleveland (1960–67); joined the diocese of Cleveland's mission team in El Salvador (1974), where she transported homeless people, especially women and children, to refugee centers, and oversaw Catholic relief aid, among other things; was slain by National Guardsmen in El Salvador, along with Ita Ford, Maura Clarke and Jean Donovan.

KAZEM, Tahia (b. 1923). See Nasser, Tahia.

KCSHESSINSKAYA, Matilde (1872–1971). See Kshesinskaia, Matilda.

KE YAN (1929—). Chinese children's writer and poet. Born 1929 in China. ❖ Staged children's plays, including *Taking Off from Earth* and *The Crystal Cave;* gained national acclaim for poem "Where are you, Premier Zhou?" (1976); novels include *Retrieval of Time Lost.*

KEALL, Judy (1942—). New Zealand politician. Born Judy Dixon, Jan 10, 1942, in Timaru, NZ; m. Graeme Keall (sep. 1992). ❖ Active in the peace movement; served as Labour MP for Glenfield (1984–90), supporting anti-nuclear legislation; lost her seat (1990); elected Labour MP for Horowhenua (1993), later Otaki; served as chair of the health select committee; resigned Parliament (2002).

KEAN, Betty (1915–1986). American actress and comedian. Born Dec 15, 1915, in Hartford, CT; died Sept 28, 1986, in Hollywood, CA; sister of Jane Kean (actress and comedian). ❖ Made Broadway debut in George White's *Scandals,* followed by *It's All Yours, The Girl from Nantucket, Ankles Aweigh* (with her sister), *The Pajama Game, Hit the Deck, Show Boat* and *No No Nanette;* also appeared on tv and in nightclubs, often as the comedy duo of "Betty and Jane Kean."

KEAN, Mrs. Charles (1805–1880). See Kean, Ellen.

KEAN, Ellen (1805–1880). English actress. Name variations: Ellen Tree; Mrs. Kean. Born Ellen Tree in 1805; died in London, England, Aug 21, 1880; sister of singer-actress Maria Bradshaw (Mrs. Bradshaw); sister of a Mrs. Quin, dancer at the Drury Lane; m. Charles John Kean (c. 1811–1868, actor and 2nd son of Edmund Kean), Jan 1842. ❖ Made debut as Ellen Tree at Covent Garden, playing Olivia to sister Maria Bradshaw's Viola in *Twelfth Night* (1822–23); at Drury Lane, appeared in such comedic roles as Lady Teazle and Jane Shore (1826–28); returned to Covent Garden (1829), where she originated several parts until 1836 and appeared as Romeo to Fanny Kemble's Juliet; toured America (1836–39), becoming famous there under name Ellen Tree; married Charles Kean (1842), with whom she played leading parts at Princess Theater in London, and whose success she helped further; had greatest successes in roles of Viola, Rosalind, Gertrude and Mrs. Beverley.

KEAN, Jane (1924—). American actress. Born April 10, 1924, in Hartford, CT; sister of Betty Kean; m. Richard Linkroum, 1962 (div. 1970); m. Joe Hecht, 1970. ❖ Appeared on stage, tv and in nightclubs, often with her sister as comedy duo "Betty and Jane Kean"; replaced Joyce Randolph as Trixie Norton in "The Honeymooners" (1966–70); films include *Pete's Dragon* and *Chatterbox.*

KEANE, Constance (1919–1973). See Lake, Veronica.

KEANE, Doris (1881–1945). American actress. Born Dec 12, 1881, in St. Joseph, Michigan; died Nov 25, 1945, in New York, NY; m. Basil Sydney (div.). ❖ Appeared as Joan Thornton in *The Happy Marriage,* Hope Summers in *Our World,* Sonia in *Arsène Lupin,* Mimi in *The Affairs of Anatol,* Bess Marks in *The Lights o' London,* and title role in *Roxana;* had huge success as Margherita Cavallini in *Romance,* with a long run on Broadway (1913–15) and 3-year run in London; was last seen in *The Pirate* in Los Angeles (1929).

KEANE, Emma Hilda (1873–1970). See Rollett, Hilda.

KEANE, Fiorella (1930–1976). English ballet dancer and teacher. Name variations: Fiorella Brown. Born Dec 8, 1930, in Rome, Italy; died June 9, 1976, in New York, NY. ❖ Trained at Royal Academy of Dancing and Sadler's Wells Ballet school; danced for Sadler's Wells and Royal Ballet, mainly in productions of classical repertory works; toured US with Royal Ballet and moved to US soon after; taught at Juilliard School; collaborated on choreography of *Gradus ad Parnassum* (1962); served as ballet master of Alvin Ailey Dance Theater (c. 1965–74) and later of American Ballet Theater (c. 1974–76).

KEANE, Molly (1904–1996). Irish novelist and playwright. Name variations: Mary Nesta Skrine; (pseudonym) M.J. Farrell. Born Mary Nesta (Molly) Skrine in Co. Kildare, Ireland, July 20, 1904; died at Ardmore, Co. Waterford, April 22, 1996; dau. of Walter Clermont Skrine and Agnes Shakespeare Higginson Skrine (who wrote under pseudonym Moira O'Neill); educated at French School, Bray, Co. Wicklow; m. Robert Lumley Keane, Oct 1938 (died Oct 7, 1946); children: Sally Keane; Virginia Keane. ❖ Writing with wit and intelligence, published 1st novel, *The Knight of Cheerful Countenance,* followed by *Young Entry* (both 1928); often wrote of an Anglo-Irish society insulated within its gracious 18th-century houses, obsessed with horses and hunting and, for the most part, cheerfully philistine; collaborated with John Perry on such plays as *Spring Meeting* (1938), which ran successfully in London and NY, followed by *Ducks and Drakes* (1941), *Guardian Angel* (1944), and *Treasure Hunt* (1949), with most directed by John Gielgud; after late 1930s, wrote few novels of which *Two Days in Aragon* (1941) was the most important; gave up writing (1961), because of hostile reaction to last play with Perry, *Dazzling Prospects;* retired to Ireland; published *Good Behaviour* when she was 77, which won the Booker Prize (1981), followed by *Time After Time* (1983) and *Loving and Giving* (1988). Elected to Aosdána, an affiliation of Irish artists who receive state subsidies (1981). ❖ See also *Women in World History.*

KEARNEY, Belle (1863–1939). American temperance reformer and suffragist. Born Mar 6, 1863, near Flora, Madison Co., Mississippi; died Feb 27, 1939, in Jackson, MS; dau. of Walter Guston Kearney (planter) and Susannah Owens. ❖ Became lecturer and organizer of national Woman's Christian Temperance Union (1891); elected president of state WCTU (1895); toured US and Europe lecturing on temperance and suffrage; served as president of Mississippi Woman Suffrage Association (1906–08); lobbied for WCTU in Washington, DC; had longstanding interest in "social purity movement" and published novel, *Conqueror or Conquered?* (1921), which promoted ideals of feminine sexuality and evils of male lust; ran unsuccessfully for US Senate (1922); won seat in state senate (1924), the 1st woman in South to hold office in state senate, and was reelected to 2nd term.

KEARNEY, Miriam (1959—). Irish politician. Born July 1959 in Cork, Ireland. ❖ Representing Fine Gael, nominated to the Seanad by Taoiseach Garret FitzGerald (1981) and served until 1982, the youngest member of the Upper House.

KEARNS-MacWHINNEY, Linda (1888–1951). Irish politician and nurse. Name variations: Linda Kearns; Linda MacWhinney. Born Linda Kearns, July 1888 in Dromard, Co. Sligo, Ireland; died June 5, 1951, in Howth, Co. Dublin. ❖ Began career as a nurse; joined Cumann na mBan; set up a Red Cross hospital and served as a dispatch carrier for rebels during the Rising (1916); opened a nursing home in Dublin (1919) which was also used as a safe house for Volunteers in peril; imprisoned and escaped (1920–21); imprisoned and released (1922–23); was a founder member of Fianna Fáil (1926) and a member of its national executive; joined with National Council of Women to fight the discriminatory Conditions of Employment Bill (1935); elected to the Seanad from the Industrial and Commercial Panel (1938).

Received the Florence Nightingale medal from the International Red Cross (1951). ❖ See also Annie Smithson, ed. *In Times of Peril: Leaves from the Diary of Nurse Linda Kearns from Easter Week, 1916 to Mountjoy, 1921* (Talbot, 1922).

KEATING, Annita (1949—). Australian prime-ministerial wife. Born Anna Johanna Marie Van Iersel, 1949, in Holland; m. Paul Keating (prime minister of Australia, 1991–96), Jan 17, 1975; children: Patrick (b. 1977), Caroline (b. 1979), Katherine (b. 1983), and Alexandra (b. 1985). ❖ Accompanied husband on many overseas visits; with command of 7 languages, helped bring the 2000 Olympics to Sydney (1993).

KEATON, Diane (1946—). American actress. Born Diane Hall, Jan 5, 1946, in Los Angeles, California; attended Santa Ana College and Neighborhood Playhouse; children: Dexter and Duke. ❖ Scored 1st major stage role on Broadway in rock musical *Hair* (1968); starred opposite Woody Allen in the play *Play It Again, Sam* (1970), as well as the film adaptation; appeared as Kay in *The Godfather,* and in its sequels; won Oscar for Best Actress for *Annie Hall* (1977); received nominations for Academy Award and Golden Globe, for her portrayal of Louise Bryant in *Reds* (1981); turned to directing, receiving high marks for 1st major feature *Unstrung Heroes* (1995); received Emmy nomination for *Amelia Earhart: The Final Flight* (1994), Academy Award nomination for *Marvin's Room* (1996) and Golden Globe award for *Something's Gotta Give* (2004); other films include *Sleeper* (1973), *Looking for Mr. Goodbar* (1977), *Manhattan* (1979), *Shoot the Moon* (1982), *The Little Drummer Girl* (1984), *Crimes of the Heart* (1986), *Father of the Bride* (1991), *Manhattan Murder Mystery* (1993), *The First Wives Club* (1996), *The Other Sister* (1999), *Hating Her* (2005).

KEAVENEY, Cecilia (1968—). Irish politician. Born Nov 1968 in Derry, Ireland; dau. of Paddy Keaveney (TD, 1976–77). ❖ Representing Fianna Fáil, elected to the 27th Dáil in a by-election (1996–97) for Donegal North East, following the death of Neil T. Blaney; returned to 28th Dáil (1997–2002) and 29th Dáil (2002).

KE-CHING KANG (1911–1992). *See Kang Keqing.*

KECKLEY, Elizabeth (c. 1824–1907). African-American writer, dressmaker, and White House modiste. Born Elizabeth Hobbs in Dinwiddie, Virginia, c. 1824; died in Washington, DC, May 26, 1907; dau. of slaves, Agnes and George Pleasant; m. George Keckley (sep.); children: George, who died in battle. ❖ Grew up a slave; with help of patrons, purchased her freedom (1855); settled in Washington, DC, where she began a modest dress-making business; attracting a prominent clientele, expanded the shop, employing 20 young women as seamstresses; began sewing for Mary Todd Lincoln; through her skill as a seamstress and her trustworthiness, developed a close relationship with the first lady and in due course became her personal maid, traveling companion, and confidante; after Lincoln's assassination (1865), remained with the grieving widow, even as she moved back to Chicago; returned to Washington and re-established dressmaking business; with help of a ghost writer, published *Behind the Scenes; or, Thirty Years a Slave, and Four Years in the White House,* hoping to help Mary Lincoln, but it had the opposite effect. ❖ See also *Women in World History.*

KEDROVA, Lila (1918–2000). Russian-born actress. Name variations: Lila Kédrova. Born Oct 9, 1918, in St. Petersburg, Russia; died in Sault Ste. Marie, Ontario, Canada, Feb 16, 2000; m. Richard Howard, 1968. ❖ Flamboyant character actress of European and American films, lived in France from 1928 on, as well as Canada; films include *Weg ohne Umkehr* (*No Way Back,* 1953), *Razzia sur la Chnouff* (*Razzia,* 1955), *Des Gens sans Importance* (1956), Montparnasse 19 (*Modigliani of Montparnasse,* 1958), *A High Wind in Jamaica* (1965), *Torn Curtain* (1966), *Penelope* (1966), *The Kremlin Letter* (1970), *Moi Fleur bleue* (1977), and *Some Girls* (1988). Won Academy Award as Best Supporting Actress for portrayal of Madame Hortense in *Zorba the Greek* (1964), and a Tony for same role (1984); received Golden Mask at Taormina for *Tell Me a Riddle* (1980).

KEE, Elizabeth (1895–1975). American politician. Name variations: Maude Elizabeth Kee. Born Maude Elizabeth Simpkins in Radford, Virginia, June 7, 1895; died in Bluefield, Virginia, Feb 15, 1975; graduate of Roanoke Business College; m. John Kee (attorney and Democratic US congressional representative, 1932–51), Sept 1926 (died May 1951); children: James and Frances Kee. ❖ Democratic congressional representative from West Virginia (82nd–88th Congresses, July 17, 1951–Jan 3, 1965); following death of husband, won a special election to fill his vacant congressional seat; served 6 terms

and was then succeeded by son James Kee; while in Congress, was a member of the Committee on Governmental Operations and chaired a Veterans' Affairs subcommittee on veterans' hospitals; a liberal and ardently pro-labor, was a proponent of many of the domestic policies of the Kennedy and Johnson administrations. ❖ See also *Women in World History.*

KEEBLE, Lillah (1875–1960). *See McCarthy, Lillah.*

KEEBLE, Sally (1951—). English journalist, politician and member of Parliament. Born Oct 13, 1951; dau. of Lady Keeble and Sir Curtis Keeble (GCMG); m. Andrew Hilary Porter, 1990. ❖ Worked as a journalist for *Daily News,* Durban, South Africa (1973–79) and *Birmingham Post* (1978–83); representing Labour, elected to House of Commons for Northampton North (1997, 2001, 2005); named parliamentary under-secretary of state, Department for International Development.

KEECH, Margaret Majella. Australian politician. Married; children: 3. ❖ Lectured at Queensland University of Technology; as a member of the Australian Labor Party, elected to the Queensland Parliament for Albert (2001); became minister for Tourism, Fair Trading and Wine Industry Development (2004).

KEEFE, Zena (1896–1977). American silent-film actress. Born Zena Virginia Keefe, June 26, 1896, in San Francisco, CA; died Nov 16, 1977, in Danvers, MA; m. William M. Brownell. ❖ Worked at Vitagraph (1909–16); became a Selznick star; films include *The Light that Failed, The Cross Roads, The Mill of the Gods, The Tigress, Piccadilly Jim, After Midnight* and *The Broken Violin;* retired (1924).

KEELER, Christine (1942—). British call girl. Born in Uxbridge, Middlesex, England, Feb 2, 1942; raised in Wraysbury; m. James Levermore (div.); remarried; children: (1st m.) son Jimmy. ❖ Was the "tainted woman" involved in the notorious "Profumo Affair," the scandal that brought England's Tory Party to the brink of disaster (1963). ❖ See also autobiography, *The Truth at Last* (2001); and *Women in World History.*

KEELER, Kathryn (1956—). American rower. Name variations: Kathryn Elliott-Keeler. Born Kathryn Elliott, Nov 3, 1956, in Texas; attended Wesleyan University. ❖ At Los Angeles Olympics, won a gold medal in coxed eights (1984); won a silver medal for coxed fours at World championships (1982).

KEELER, Ruby (1909–1993). American actress, dancer, and singer. Name variations: Ruby Keeler Jolson. Born Ethel Hilda Keeler, Aug 25, 1909, in Halifax, Nova Scotia, Canada; died Feb 28, 1993, in Palm Springs, CA; attended Professional Children's School, NY; m. Al Jolson (singer-actor), Sept 21, 1928 (div. 1940); m. John Lowe (real estate broker), Oct 29, 1941 (died 1969); children: (adopted with Jolson) son, Al (name later changed to Peter); (2nd m.) John, Christine, Theresa, and Kathleen Lowe. ❖ Best known for energetic hoofing in films of 1930s, many of which became classics because of dance numbers staged by Busby Berkeley, made early professional appearances in cabaret as a buck-dancer; made theater debut in chorus of *The Rise of Rosie O'Reilly* (1923); appeared as Ruby in *Bye Bye Bonnie* (1927), Mazie Maxwell in *Lucky Knickerbocker* (1927), Mamie and Ruby in *Sidewalks of New York* (1927); also appeared in *Whoopee* (1928) and the revue *Show Girl* (1929); made film debut in a bit part in *Show Girl in Hollywood* (1930), followed by *42nd Street* (1933), *Gold Diggers of 1933* (1933), *Footlight Parade* (1933), *Dames* (1934), *Ready, Willing and Able* (1937) and *Mother Carey's Chickens* (1938), among others; made a phenomenal comeback in Broadway revival of *No, No, Nanette* (1971). ❖ See also *Women in World History.*

KEELEY, Mary Anne (c. 1806–1899). Irish-born English actress. Name variations: Miss Goward. Born Mary Anne Goward in Dublin, Ireland, Nov 22, 1806 (some sources cite 1805); died Mar 12, 1899; dau. of a brazier and tinman; m. Robert Keeley (1793–1869, comedian), 1829. ❖ Moved to London (1825) and became a member of Covent Garden Co.; appeared with husband at Covent Garden, John Buckstone at the Adelphi, Charles Mathews at the Olympic, and William Macready at Drury Lane (1832–42); toured US (1836); had 1st major success as Nydia in *The Last Days of Pompeii* (1838); followed this with equally striking portrayal of Smike in *Nicholas Nickleby;* had another triumph in title role of *Jack Sheppard* (with its glorification of an escaped convict, the Lord Chamberlain ultimately forbade future performances of any plays of a similar nature); with husband, managed the Lyceum (1844–47), where their production of *Cricket on the Hearth* ran for over a year; returned for

5 years to the Adelphi; made last theatrical appearance at the Lyceum (1859). ❖ See also Walter Goodman, *The Keeleys on the Stage and Off* (London, 1895); and *Women in World History.*

KEEN, Ann (1948—). Welsh politician and member of Parliament. Born Ann Fox, Nov 26, 1948; sister of Sylvia Heal (MP); m. Alan Keen (MP), 1980. ❖ Nurse; representing Labour, elected to House of Commons for Brentford and Isleworth (1997, 2001, 2005).

KEEN, Dora (1871–1963). American traveler, mountain climber, and writer. Name variations: Dora Keen Handy. Born in Philadelphia, PA, June 24, 1871; died Jan 1963 in Vermont; dau. of William W. Keen (1837–1932, surgeon and neurologist who performed the 1st successful removal of a brain tumor in US) and Emma Corinna Borden; graduate of Bryn Mawr College, 1896; m. G.W. Handy (climber). ❖ Made 8 ascents of 1st-class peaks in the Alps (1909–10); though an under-equipped expedition failed to make ascent of Mount Blackburn (16,523 feet) in Alaska (1911), returned and battled snowstorms (1912) to accomplish in 33 days the 1st ascent of this peak without Swiss guides, and the 1st by way of the avalanche-prone southeast face via a direct route on Kennicott glacier; journeyed 300 miles on foot and by open camp-built boat over Alaskan wilderness to Yukon River, by way of Skolai Pass, the 1st woman to cross it; with 3 men, made scientific observations of various glaciers in Alaska (1914); contributed numerous articles to popular and geographical magazines, and lectured on experiences; became a fellow of Royal Geographical Society, London.

KEENE, Carolyn.
See Adams, Harriet Stratemeyer (c. 1893–1982).
See Benson, Mildred (b. 1905).

KEENE, Constance (1921–2005). American pianist and teacher. Born in New York, NY, Feb 9, 1921; died Dec 24, 2005, in New York City; m. Abram Chasins, 1949. ❖ Was a student of future husband Abram Chasins; played hundreds of solo recitals and appeared with such orchestras as Boston Symphony and Berlin Philharmonic; had a long career as a teacher and served on faculty of Manhattan School of Music; successful recordings include the 3 Mendelssohn études, Dussek and Hummel sonatas, the Charles Tomlinson Griffes Sonata, Chopin's 24 Preludes, and the 24 Rachmaninoff Preludes. Won Naumburg Award.

KEENE, Laura (c. 1826–1873). British-born American actress and theatrical manager. Born possibly Mary Moss c. 1826 in London, England; died Nov 4, 1873, in Montclair, New Jersey; m. John Taylor, c. 1846 (died c. 1860); m. John Lutz, 1860 (died 1869); children: (1st m.) Emma Taylor; Clara Marie Cecilia Stella Taylor. ❖ Made London debut (1851), playing Pauline in *The Lady of Lyons;* some 6 months later, joined Lucia Vestris' company at Royal Lyceum; made US debut (1852) at Wallack's Lyceum in New York City; took over as theatrical manager for Charles Street Theater in Baltimore (1853), one of the 1st women theatrical managers in America; over next couple years, toured Australia with Edwin Booth and spent a season in San Francisco; opened Laura Keene's Theater in NY (1856) and for next 7 years, produced well-received comedies and extravaganzas, playing all female leads, excelling in high comedy and melodrama; opened most famous production, *Our American Cousin* (1858), which ran an unprecedented 5 months; was appearing in *Our American Cousin* at Ford's Theater in Washington, DC, when Lincoln was assassinated during 3rd act; identified John Wilkes Booth as his killer; managed Chestnut Street Theater in Philadelphia (1869–70). ❖ See also John Creahan, *Life of Laura Keene* (1897); and *Women in World History.*

KEESE, Oline (1827–1881). See Leakey, Caroline Woolmer.

KEESING, Nancy (1923–1993). Australian poet and literary critic. Born Sept 7, 1923, in Sydney, Australia; died Jan 19, 1993; graduate of University of Sydney; m. Mark Keesing. ❖ Writings include *Elsie Carewe* (1965) and *Douglas Stewart* (1965), as well as criticism, poetry, biography and children's works; edited *Australian Post-War Novelists* (1975); with Douglas Stewart, edited the anthologies *Australian Bush Ballads* (1955) and *Old Bush Songs* (1957). ❖ See also memoir, *Garden Island People* (1975).

KEFALA, Antigone (1935—). Australian poet and novelist. Name variations: Antigone Kephala. Born 1935 in Braila, Romania, of Greek parents; graduate of Victoria University, Wellington, 1960. ❖ Moved with family to Australia after WWII and then to New Zealand (1951); taught English in Australia and became member of Literature Board of Australia Council; poetry includes *The Alien* (1973) and *Thirsty Weather* (1978); fiction includes *The First Journey* (1975), *The Island* (1984), and

Alexia (1984); translated John Koutsoleras's *Men for the Rights of Men, Rise: A Poetic Manifesto* (1974).

KEGENDORF, Madame (1777–1848). See Jagemann, Karoline.

KEHAJIA, Kalliopi (1839–1905). Greek educator and feminist. Born in Greece, 1839; died 1905; educated as a teacher in London. ❖ Devoted life to improving the social and intellectual status of women of her country; for many years, was headmistress of Hill School for girls in Athens; also offered innovative series of 80 open lectures on classical literature and social problems, many dealing with women's issues; founded Society for Promoting Women's Education (1872); by invitation, went to Constantinople (now Istanbul) to organize the Zappeion School for Girls (1875), of which she was head mistress for 15 years; traveled to US (1888), visiting schools, orphanages, and women's organizations; upon return, published series of newspaper articles about women in US, hoping to alert people to inferior status of women in Greek society.

KEHEW, Mary Morton (1859–1918). American labor and social reformer. Name variations: Mary Kimball Kehew. Born Mary Morton Kimball in Boston, Massachusetts, Sept 8, 1859; died in Boston of nephritis, Feb 14, 1918; dau. of Susan Tillinghast (Morton) Kimball and Moses Day Kimball; educated privately in Boston and in Europe; m. William Brown Kehew, Jan 8, 1880; no children. ❖ Served as president, Women's Educational and Industrial Union of Boston (WEIU, 1892–1913, 1914–18), transforming WEIU from a charity group to pro-active agency interested in educating and organizing women workers; was trustee, Simmons College (1902); served as president, National Women's Trade Union League (WTUL, 1903); sought to use her social position, her political connections, and even her own economic resources on behalf of the working class. ❖ See also *Women in World History.*

KEHL, Mary Anne (1815–1895). See Stirling, Mary Anne.

KEIKO IKEDA (1933—). See Ikeda, Keiko.

KEIKO TANAKA (1933—). See Ikeda, Keiko.

KEIL, Birgit (1944—). German ballet dancer. Born Sept 22, 1944, in Kowarchen, Sudetenland, Germany; trained at Wurttemberg State Theater Ballet and with Royal Ballet School, London. ❖ Danced with Stuttgart Ballet where she created roles in works by John Cranko, including *Opus I* (1965), *Jeu de Cartes* (1965) and *The Seasons* (1971), and danced in his repertory works, *Swan Lake, Romeo and Juliet, Eugene Onegin, Carmen,* and *Taming of the Shrew;* danced in premieres of Tetley's *Greening* (1975), Kylian's *Return from Strange Land* (1975), and Macmillan's *Lady of the Camelias* (1978); was a guest dancer in Eliot Feld's *Impromptu* in NY (1976).

KÉITA, Aoua (1912–1979). Politician and stateswoman of Mali. Name variations: Aoua Keita. Born Aoua Kéita in Bamako, French Sudan, 1912; died in Bamako, 1979; dau. of a French-educated laboratory worker (member of influential Kéita family) and one of his several wives; educated at École des filles, Orpheliat des Métisses, and School of Midwifery in Dakar; m. M. Diawara (physician), 1935 (div. 1949); m. Mahamane Alassane Haidara (senator representing Sudan in French National Assembly 1942–59); children: none. ❖ Leader in the struggle for independence in the former French Sudan, now Republic of Mali, who established an agenda for women's participation in the political life of her country; began practice of midwifery, one of few professional women in her country (1931); joined USDRA, the main nationalist party, and became politically active after 1st marriage (1935); campaigned in 1st elections in which women were allowed to vote (1946); founded Union of Salaried Women of Bamako (1957); participated in creation of Federation of Black African Workers, or UGTAN (Union Générale de Travailleurs de l'Afrique Noir); served as representative to World Federation of Trade Unions, or FSM (Fédération des Syndicats du Monde); helped draft a constitution for new Mali Federation (1958); was 1st woman elected to Mali National Assembly (1959); retired from politics (1968). ❖ See also autobiography (in French), *Femme d'Afrique* (1975); and *Women in World History.*

KEITH, Agnes Newton (1901–1982). American writer. Born in Oak Park, IL, July 6, 1901; died Mar 1982; dau. of Joseph Gilbert and Grace (Goodwillie) Newton; m. Henry George Keith (in British Commonwealth government service in Asia), July 23, 1934; children: Jean Alison Keith; Henry George Keith. ❖ American writer on Asia and Africa, began career as a reporter for *San Francisco Examiner* (1924);

moved to Borneo with husband and eventually published book about that country, *Land Below the Wind;* during WWII, was interned in the Japanese concentration camp on Berhala Island, North Borneo; wrote a book about her experiences in camp, *Three Came Home,* which was later filmed with Claudette Colbert; left Borneo (1952). ❖ See also *Women in World History.*

KEITH, Marcia (1859–1950). American physicist. Born in Brockton, MA, 1859; died in Braintree, MA, 1950; dau. of Arza Keith and Mary Ann (Cary) Keith; Mount Holyoke, BS, 1882; attended Worcester Polytechnic Institute as a special student, 1887 and 1889; attended University of Berlin, 1897–98, and University of Chicago, 1901. ❖ Noted teacher of physics, was a science instructor at the Michigan Seminary (1885–89); became 1st full-time instructor in physics department at Mount Holyoke (1889) and also chaired the department (1889–1903); along with 1 other woman, was among the 36 founders of American Physical Society (1899); later became an engineer with the firm Herbert Keith in NY.

KEITH, Margaret (fl. 1395). Noblewoman of Scotland. Name variations: Lady Lindsay: Margaret Lindsay. Fl. 1395 in Scotland; possibly m. Sir James Lindsay, 9th Baron Crawford, of Lanarkshire (d. 1396). ❖ Successfully defended her castle-estate from an attack by her own nephew Robert Keith.

KEITH, Marian (1874–1961). *See MacGregor, Esther Miller.*

KEITH, Muriel (d. 1449). Duchess of Albany. Name variations: Muriella Keith; Muriella de Keith; Muriel Stewart. Died June 1, 1449; dau. of William Keith and Margaret Fraser; became 2nd wife of Robert Stewart (c. 1339–1420, son of Elizabeth Muir), 1st duke of Albany (r. 1398–1420), who was prime minister to his brother Robert III, king of Scotland, and regent to James I, after May 4, 1380; children: John Stewart, 3rd earl of Buchan (1380–1424); Andrew Stewart (d. before 1413); Robert Stewart; Marjory Stewart (d. before 1432, who m. Duncan Campbell, 1st Lord Campbell of Lochawe or Lochow); Elizabeth Stewart (who m. Malcolm Fleming).

KEITH, Vicki (1959—). Canadian marathon swimmer. Name variations: Vicki Keith-Munro. Born 1959 in Kingston, Canada; m. John Munro (Toronto police detective). ❖ Was the 1st Canadian, male or female, to swim across all 5 Great Lakes in a 2-month period (summer 1988); completed 5 successful crossings of Lake Ontario (1986–89), a world record; swam the English Channel using the butterfly stroke (1989); also swam Sydney Harbour, Catalina Channel and Juan de Fuca Strait; broke 17 world records; retired (1991). Received Order of Canada (1992).

KEITH, Viscountess.
See Elphinstone, Hester Maria (1764–1857).
See Elphinstone, Margaret Mercer (1788–1867).

KÉKESSY, Andrea. Hungarian pairs skater. Name variations: Andrea Kekessy. Born in Hungary. ❖ With partner Ede Király, won European championships (1948, 1949), World championship (1949), and a silver medal at St. Moritz Olympics (1948). Both were considered the best jumpers in Europe.

KELEMEN, Marta (1954—). Hungarian gymnast. Born Sept 17, 1954, in Hungary. ❖ At Munich Olympics, won a bronze medal in team all-around (1972).

KELESIDOU, Anastasia (1972—). Greek discus thrower. Name variations: Tasia Kelesidou. Born Anastasia Kelesidou, Nov 28, 1972, in Thessaloniki, Greece; attended Thessaloniki University. ❖ Placed 2nd at World championships (1999, 2003); won a silver medal at Sydney Olympics (2000) and a silver medal at Athens Olympics (2004).

KELETI, Ágnes (1921—). Jewish-Hungarian gymnast. Name variations: Agnes Keleti. Born Jan 9, 1921, in Budapest, Hungary. ❖ Won the 1st of 10 Hungarian national all-around titles (1937); went in hiding during WWII (father died in Auschwitz); won bronze medal in all-around, portable apparatus—teams, bronze medal in uneven bars, silver medal in all-around team, gold medal in floor exercises in Helsinki Olympics (1952); defected to the West after Hungarian uprising (1956); won silver medal in all-around team, silver medal in all-around indiv., gold medal in all-around, portable apparatus—teams, gold medal in uneven bars, gold medal in floor exercises, and gold medal in balance beam at the Melbourne Olympics (1956); eventually settled in Israel as a gymnastics coach. ❖ See also *Women in World History.*

KELETY, Julia (d. 1972). Hungarian-born actress and singer. Born in Budapest, Hungary; died Jan 1, 1972, age 85, in New York, NY. ❖ Moved to US (1940); appeared in NY in *The Merry Widow, Joanne of Arkansas, Two Little Girls in Blue, Gingham Girl, Roberta* and *Music in the Air.*

KELLAR, Becky (1975—). Canadian ice-hockey player. Born Jan 1, 1975, in Haldimand, Ontario, Canada; Brown University, BA in psychology, 1997. ❖ Played 4 seasons at Brown University; won a team silver medal at Nagano (1998), the 1st Olympics to feature women's ice hockey; won a team gold medal at World championships (2001); won a team gold medal at Salt Lake City Olympics (2002) and a team gold medal at Torino Olympics (2006).

KELLAS, Eliza (1864–1943). American educator. Born Oct 4, 1864, in Mooers Forks, NY; died April 10, 1943, in Troy, New York; dau. of Alexander Kellas (farmer and lumberman) and Elizabeth Jane (Perry) Kellas; graduate of Potsdam (NY) Normal School, 1889; attended University of Michigan and Sorbonne; Radcliffe College, AB, 1910; never married; no children. ❖ Became principal of Emma Willard School in Troy, NY, which had moved to a new campus (1911); remained there for 31 years, making it one of the leading preparatory schools in the nation; transformed the old campus into Russell Sage College of Practical Arts, a vocational school for girls; while continuing to serve as principal of Emma Willard School, also served as president of Russell Sage, which was authorized to confer the degree of Bachelor of Arts in 1918. ❖ See also *Women in World History.*

KELLER, Evelyn Fox (1936—). American biologist. Born Evelyn Fox, Mar 20, 1936, in New York, NY; dau. of Rachel Fox and Albert Fox (Russian-Jewish immigrants); Brandeis University, BA, 1957; Radcliffe College, MA, 1959; Harvard University, PhD in theoretical physics, 1963; m. Joseph Bishop Keller, 1964. ❖ Biologist who combined work in several fields (molecular biology, theoretical physics, mathematical biology, pattern formation) and offered science a feminist critique (argued, for example, that "masculine science" or traditional science is limited, exclusive and biased), taught at several institutions, including New York University (assistant research scientist, 1963–66, associate mathematical biology professor, 1970–72), Cornell University Medical College (assistant professor, 1963–69), SUNY College, Purchase (associate professor, 1972–82), Northwestern University (visiting professor, 1985), MIT (visiting professor, 1985–86, and Science, Technology, and Society Program professor, from 1993) and University of California, Berkeley (Rhetoric, Women's Studies, and History of Science professor, 1988–93); wrote *A Feeling for the Organism* (biography of Barbara McClintock, 1983), *Reflections on Gender and Science* (1985) and *Secrets of Life, Secrets of Death* (1992). Received MacArthur Foundation fellowship award (1992).

KELLER, Helen (1880–1968). American socialist, writer, and activist. Born June 27, 1880, in Tuscumbria, Alabama; died June 1, 1968, in Westport, Connecticut; dau. of Captain Arthur H. Keller (US marshal) and Kate (Adams) Keller; graduated cum laude from Radcliffe College (1904); never married; no children. ❖ Socialist and advocate for the blind and deaf who was one of the 20th century's most celebrated Americans; was stricken blind and deaf (1882); with help of Annie Sullivan, learned to communicate with the manual alphabet (1887), then learned Braille; studied at Perkins Institute; at 13, had 1st writing published, in *St. Nicholas* (1893); attended Wright-Humason School for deaf children, then Gilman School, a college preparatory school in Cambridge, MA; published autobiography *The Story of My Life* (1903); joined American Socialist Party and advocated women's suffrage (1909); embraced a myriad of causes, including anti-child labor legislation, birth-control advocacy, and anti-capital punishment legislation; participated in filming of her life story as *Deliverance* (1918); began work for American Foundation for the Blind (AFB, 1924); teacher Annie Sullivan died (1936); toured Europe on behalf of AFB (1946); awarded honorary degree by Harvard University (1955); suffered stroke and retired from public life (1961); writings include *Optimism* (1903), *The World I Live In* (1908), *Out of the Dark* (1913), *My Religion* (1927), *Midstream: My Later Life* (1928), *A Journal* (1938) and *Teacher: Anne Sullivan Macy* (1955). ❖ See also Joseph P. Lash, *Helen and Teacher: The Story of Helen Keller and Anne Sullivan Macy* (Delacorte, 1980); Dorothy Herrmann, *Helen Keller: A Life* (Knopf, 1998); William Gibson (play) *The Miracle Worker* (Knopf, 1957); and *Women in World History.*

KELLER, Natascha (1977—). German field-hockey player. Born July 3, 1977, in Berlin, East Germany. ❖ Won bronze medal at World Cup (1998) and European championships (2003); won a team gold medal at

Athens Olympics (2004). Named German Hockey's Player of the Year (1997) and International Hockey Federation's Player of the Year (1999).

KELLER, Nettie Florence (1875–1974). American-born physician, surgeon, professor, and social reformer. Name variations: Nettie Florence Armstrong. Born Nettie Florence Armstrong, Mar 18, 1875, probably in Carthage, Missouri; died Jan 15, 1974, in Los Angeles, California; dau. of James Armstrong (timber merchant) and Frances (Haxton) Armstrong; attended Walla Walla College; studied at Battle Creek Sanitarium, 1890s; American Medical Missionary College, diploma in medicine, 1900; m. Peter Martin Keller (physician), 1901; children: 1 daughter. ❖ Arrived in New Zealand as medical missionary with Seventh-day Adventist church (1901); practiced medicine with husband at Christchurch Medical and Surgical Sanitarium, Papanui (1901); lived briefly in Sydney, Australia, and returned to New Zealand (c. 1904), to practice medicine in North Island (1904); returned US to tour children's hospitals (1915), and for postgraduate course in surgery in Chicago (1917); active on Auckland Hospital and Charitable Aid Board (1913–19); executive member of Auckland branch of National Schools Defense League; returned to US to teach in department of obstetrics and gynecology at College of Medical Evangelists, Linda Loma, California (1919); became surgeon at White Memorial Hospital, Pasadena; elected fellow of American College of Surgeons and International College of Surgeons. ❖ See also *Dictionary of New Zealand Biography* (Vol. 3).

KELLERMAN, Annette (1886–1975). Australian swimmer and actress. Name variations: Annette Kellermann. Born Annette Marie Sarah Kellerman, July 6, 1886, in Sydney, Australia; died in Southport, Queensland, Australia, Nov 6, 1975; m. James R. Sullivan (her manager), 1912. ❖ Went to England as athlete and performer (1904); with brother as manager, came to US and made 1st public appearance (1907); made 1st film (1909); as a champion swimmer, recognized health authority, and exponent of physical culture, was the 1st woman swimmer to achieve acclaim; is said to have devised the idea of formation swimming as an art, is credited with having introduced the single-piece swimsuit, making acceptable the kind of minimal swimwear necessary to allow freedom of movement and speed in the water; retired to Australia (1935); held the world record for the two-, five- and ten-minute swimming championships. As an actress, starred in such films as *Miss Annette Kellerman Fancy Swimming* and *Diving Displays* (both reportage, 1909), *Neptune's Daughter* (1914), *Isle of Love* (1916), *A Daughter of the Gods* (1916), *The Honor System* (1917), *Queen of the Sea* (1918), *What Women Love* (1920) and *Venus of the South Seas* (1924). ❖ See also fictionalized screen biography *Million Dollar Mermaid*, starring Esther Williams (1952); and *Women in World History*.

KELLERMAN, Sally (1936—). American actress. Born June 2, 1936, in Long Beach, CA; m. Rick Edelstein (tv director), 1970 (div.); m. Jonathan Krane (talent agent and movie producer). ❖ Made film debut in *Reform School Girl* (1957), followed by *The Boston Strangler, Brewster McCloud, Slither, The Last of the Red Hot Lovers, Lost Horizon, Rafferty and the Gold Dust Twins, The Big Bus, Verna: USO Girl* (tv), *A Little Romance, That's Life, Boris and Natasha,* and *Open House;* created and nominated for an Oscar for role of Major "Hot Lips" Houlihan in film *M*A*S*H*.*

KELLEY, Abby (1810–1887). American abolitionist and woman's rights lecturer. Name variations: Abigail Kelley; Abigail Kelley Foster. Born Abigail Kelley in Pelham, Massachusetts, Jan 15, 1810; died in Worcester, Massachusetts, Jan 14, 1887; dau. of Wing Kelley (farmer) and Diana (Daniels) Kelley; attended Quaker schools, including several years at Friends School, Providence; m. Stephen Symonds Foster (abolitionist lecturer), Dec 1845 (died 1881); children: Pauline Wright Foster. ❖ While teaching in a Quaker School in Lynn, became a follower of abolitionist William Lloyd Garrison; served as secretary of Lynn Female Anti-Slavery Society (1835–37); joined Garrison in founding New England Non-Resistant Society (1838); also participated in 1st and 2nd woman's national antislavery conventions in NY and Philadelphia, where she made her 1st public speech; resigned teaching job (1839); during convention of American Anti-Slavery Society (1840), was appointed to the business committee (1840), so angering the male delegates that almost half left to form American and Foreign Anti-Slavery Society; continued traveling and lecturing; began to address temperance and feminist meetings, including 4th national woman's rights convention in Cleveland (1853). ❖ See also Dorothy Sterling, *Ahead of Her Time: Abby Kelley and the Politics of Anti-Slavery* (Norton, 1991); and *Women in World History*.

KELLEY, Beverly Gwinn (c. 1952—). American Coast Guard skipper. Born c. 1952 in Bonita Springs, FL. ❖ With Debra Lee Wilson, was one of 1st two women to serve on an armed US military vessel (1977); served as the 1st woman commander of a Coast Guard vessel at sea (1979–81), aboard the 95-foot patrol boat *Cape Newagen;* with crew, rescued 12 people during a Hawaiian storm, earning Coast Guard citation for "professionalism" (1980).

KELLEY, Edith Summers (1884–1956). Canadian-American novelist. Name variations: Edith Updegraff. Born Edith Summers in 1884 in Ontario, Canada; died 1956; m. Allan Updegraff (poet and novelist); had common-law husband, C. Fred Kelley; children: 3. ❖ Moved to NY (1926); served as Upton Sinclair's secretary at experimental community Helicon Hall (1906–07); wrote *Weeds* (1923) and *The Devil's Hand* (1974), about farming life.

KELLEY, Florence (1859–1932). American labor leader. Name variations: Florence Kelley Wischnewetzky. Often confused with Florence Finch Kelly (1858–1939). Born Florence Molthrop Kelley, Sept 12, 1859, in Philadelphia, PA; died in Philadelphia, Feb 17, 1932; dau. of Caroline Bantram (Bonsall) Kelley and William Darrah Kelley (congressional representative); attended Quaker schools in Philadelphia; Cornell University, BS, 1882; received law degree from Northwestern University, 1894; m. Lazare Wischnewetzky, 1884 (div. 1892); children: Nicholas Wischnewetzky (b. 1885); Margaret Wischnewetzky (1886–1905); John Bartram Wischnewetzky (b. 1888). ❖ First factory inspector in Illinois and general secretary of the National Consumers' League, who fought against child labor and promoted safer working conditions for all laborers; following graduation from Cornell, traveled to Europe; returned to US (1886); expelled from Socialist Labor Party (1887); was a resident of Hull House (1891); after suggesting that the Illinois Bureau of Labor Statistics investigate the sweatshops of Chicago, was named as the agent to conduct the investigation (1892); her reports led the state legislature to pass the Factories and Workshops Act, which required a number of reforms; became the 1st woman in US to be appointed a state's chief factory inspector (1893); served as general secretary, National Consumers' League (1899); became an organizer for NY Child Labor Committee (1902), National Child Labor Committee (1904), National Association for the Advancement of Colored People (1909); was a founding member, Women's International League for Peace and Freedom (1919). ❖ See also *Notes of Sixty Years: The Autobiography of Florence Kelley* (Kerr, 1986); Dorothy Rose Blumberg, *Florence Kelley: The Making of a Social Pioneer* (1966); Josephine Goldmark, *Impatient Crusader* (U. of Illinois, 1953); and *Women in World History*.

KELLINO, Pamela (1918–1996). *See Mason, Pamela.*

KELLNER, Rosa (1910—). German runner. Born Jan 21, 1910, in Germany. ❖ At Amsterdam Olympics, won a bronze medal in the 4 x 100-meter relay (1928).

KELLO, Esther or Hester (1571–1624). *See Inglis, Esther.*

KELLOGG, Clara Louise (1842–1916). American soprano and impresario. Born Clara Louise Kellogg in Sumterville (now Sumter), SC, July 9, 1842; died of cancer at her home Elpstone, in New Hartford, CT, May 13, 1916; dau. of George Kellogg (inventor and schoolteacher) and Jane Elizabeth (Crosby) Kellogg (schoolteacher and musician); studied with Achille Errani and Emanuele Muzio; m. Carl Strakosch (nephew of her former manager Max Strakosch), 1887. ❖ America's 1st prima donna and one of the 1st female impresarios, worked to bring opera to the American stage; debuted as Gilda in Verdi's *Rigoletto* at Academy of Music (1861); sang Marguerite in 1st NY performance of Gounod's *Faust* which became the most popular opera in US for next 3 decades (1863); made London debut in same role and sang in the Handel Festival (1867); achieved a solid reputation in Europe; began a successful 4-year tour of US (1868); with Pauline Lucca, formed an opera company (1872); directed the English Opera Company (1873–76); on marriage, retired from the stage (1887), having sung more than 40 roles, including Aïda, Carmen, and Lucia in Donizetti's *Linda de Chamounix.* ❖ See also *Memoirs of an American Prima Donna* (1913, rev. 1978); and *Women in World History*.

KELLOGG, Louise Phelps (1862–1942). American historian. Born Eva Louise Phelps Kellogg in Milwaukee, Wisconsin, May 12, 1862; died in Madison, Wisconsin, July 11, 1942; dau. of Amherst Willoughby Kellogg (insurance executive) and Mary Isabella (Phelps) Kellogg; attended Dearborn Seminary, Chicago; graduate of Milwaukee College, 1882; University of Wisconsin, BL, 1897; attended Sorbonne and

London School of History and Economics, 1898–99; University of Wisconsin, PhD, 1901; never married; no children. ❖ Appointed research and editorial assistant to Reuben Gold Thwaites, executive director of State Historical Society of Wisconsin (1901); assisted him in editing and publishing some 40 volumes of documents from the Society's collection until his death in 1913, then edited 3 volumes on her own: *Frontier Advance on the Upper Ohio* (1916), *Frontier Retreat on the Upper Ohio* (1917) and *Early Narratives of the Northwest, 1634–1699* (1917); also edited a Caxton Club edition of *Charlevoix's Journal of a Voyage to North America* (2 vols. 1923); published highly regarded work, *The French Régime in Wisconsin and the Northwest* (1925) and its companion volume, *The British Régime in Wisconsin and the Northwest* (1935); was 1st woman elected president of Mississippi Valley Historical Association (later Organization of American Historians, 1930). Made a fellow of British Royal Historical Society; received Lapham Medal from Wisconsin Archaeological Society (1935). ❖ See also *Women in World History.*

KELLOR, Frances Alice (1873–1952). American sociologist and activist. Born Oct 20, 1873 in Columbus, Ohio; died Jan 4, 1952, in New York, NY; dau. of Daniel and Mary (Sprau) Kellor; Cornell Law School, LLB, 1897; attended University of Chicago; lived with Mary Elisabeth Dreier (1875–1963). ❖ While associated with Jane Addams' Hull House, met Mary Elizabeth Dreier, and the two moved to New York where they worked together on social causes for the rest of their lives; wrote books, founded the National League for the Protection of Colored Women (1906), and became secretary of NY State Immigration Commission (1908); in the climate of the time, tended toward protectionist legislation for women. ❖ See also *Women in World History.*

KELLOW, Kathleen (1906–1993). *See Hibbert, Eleanor.*

KELLS, Isabella (1861–1938). New Zealand teacher and postmaster. Born Isabella Foster Rogers Kells, April 15, 1861, at East Tamaki, New Zealand; died July 12, 1938, in Lichfield, New Zealand; dau. of George Kells and Eliza (Forbes) Kells. ❖ Appointed head female teacher at Panmure School (1878–88); served as head of Lichfield School (1889–1913) and managed Lichfield post and telegraph office (1897–1926). ❖ See also *Dictionary of New Zealand Biography* (Vol. 3).

KELLY (1985—). *See Pereira da Silva, Kelly.*

KELLY, Annie Elizabeth (1877–1946). New Zealand painter. Name variations: Annie Elizabeth Abbott. Born Annie Elizabeth Abbott, April 12, 1877, at Knightstown, Christchurch, New Zealand; died Oct 4, 1946, at Christchurch; dau. of Thomas George Abbott (nurseryman) and Maud Laura (Mason) Abbott; m. Cecil Fletcher Kelly (artist), 1908. ❖ Studied and taught art at Canterbury School of Art (late 1890s–1904); taught privately from 1905; painted landscapes with husband, and exhibited figurative work, gaining recognition as a portrait painter; traveled to Europe and closely followed English style of portrait painting; returned to New Zealand and gained fame for paintings of fashionable Canterbury society women (1920s); exhibited at Royal Academy of Arts, Royal Society of Portrait Painters, and Royal Scottish Academy in Edinburgh (1931); won silver medal at Paris Salon (1934). Made Commander of the British Empire (1946). ❖ See also *Dictionary of New Zealand Biography* (Vol. 3).

KELLY, Dorothy (1894–1966). American actress. Born Feb 12, 1894, in Philadelphia, PA; died May 31, 1966, in Minneapolis, Minnesota. ❖ Star for Vitagraph (1911–16); films include *Vanity Fair, The Troublesome Stepdaughters, The Flirt, Artie* and *The Maelstrom;* retired (1916).

KELLY, Edna Flannery (1906–1997). American politician. Born Edna Patricia Kathleen Flannery, Aug 20, 1906, in East Hampton, LI, NY; died in Alexandria, Virginia, Dec 14, 1997; dau. of Patrick Joseph Flannery (horticulturist) and Mary Ellen (McCarthy) Flannery; Hunter College, BA, 1928; m. Edward Leo Kelly (lawyer and politician), June 1928 (died 1942); children: William Edward Kelly; Maura Patricia Kelly. ❖ Democratic US congressional representative from NY (1949–69), became active in politics following husband's death (1942); elected to Democratic executive committee of Kings County, NY (1944), serving 3 consecutive terms; served as research director for Democratic Party in NY State legislature (1943–49); was chosen Democratic candidate to fill vacancy (1949), becoming the 4th woman from NY State to serve in House of Representatives; tenure was marked by support of federal social and economic programs and concern for US interests in defense and foreign aid; served on Committee on Foreign Affairs and chaired its Subcommittee on Europe, as well as a special Subcommittee on

Canada–US Inter-Parliamentary group; introduced bills to provide equal pay for women; supported a higher minimum wage and lower retirement age requirements for beneficiaries of old age and survivors' insurance benefits. ❖ See also *Women in World History.*

KELLY, Emily (d. 1922). British mountain and rock climber. Birth date unknown; died 1922, following a fall on Tryfan; m. Harry Kelly (rock climber). ❖ Primarily a solo rock climber, helped found the Pinnacle Club (1921), the earliest rock climbing club founded by and for women, and was its 1st honorary secretary.

KELLY, Ethel (1875–1949). Canadian-born Australian actress and author. Name variations: Ethel Mollison. Born Ethel Knight Mollison on Jan 28, 1875, in St. John, New Brunswick, Canada; died Sept 22, 1949, in Sydney, Australia; elder dau. of William Knight Mollison (merchant) and Margaret (Millen) Mollison; educated in St. John; m. a man named Moore c. 1893 (died c. 1894); m. Thomas Herbert Kelly (metal merchant), Aug 29, 1903; children: 2 sons, 2 daughters. ❖ Made stage debut in St. John, New Brunswick, in *A Mischievous Miss* (1893); married, moved to NY, and widowed (1893–94); acting under maiden name, appeared in such classics as *Cyrano de Bergerac* and *The Taming of the Shrew;* while on tour in Australia (1903), married, retired from stage, and remained there; visited India, then published 1st book, *Frivolous Peeps at India* (1911); served as woman's page editor of *Smith's Weekly* (1922–23); also wrote *Why the Sphinx Smiles* (1925) and *Zara* (1927). ❖ See also memoirs *Twelve Milestones* (1929); and *Women in World History.*

KELLY, Eva Mary (1826–1910). *See O'Doherty, Mary Anne.*

KELLY, Fanny Wiggins (1845–1904). American Indian captive. Born 1845 in Orillia, Ontario, Canada; died Nov 15, 1904, in Washington, DC; dau. of James Wiggins and an Irish-born mother (name unknown); m. Josiah S. Kelly, Nov 1863 (died 1867); William F. Gordon (journalist), May 5, 1880; children: (1st m.) 1 son. ❖ Along with 1 woman and 2 children, taken captive by Ogalala Sioux near Fort Laramie (July 12, 1864); became property and servant of Chief Ottawa and lived with his family; soon fluent in Siouan language, took on role as chief's medicine woman; after 5 months in captivity, recaptured by military at Fort Sully, SD (Dec 12, 1864); awarded $5,000 by Congress (April 1870) and reached deal with Sioux to be paid for loss of property; published *Narrative of My Captivity among the Sioux Indians* (1871).

KELLY, Florence Finch (1858–1939). American journalist and author. Name variations: Often confused with Florence Kelley (1859–1932). Born in Girard, IL, Mar 27, 1858; died in New Hartford, CT, Dec 17, 1939; dau. of James Gardner Finch (farmer) and Mary Ann (Purdom) Finch; graduate of University of Kansas, 1881; m. Allen P. Kelly (newspaper publisher), Dec 9, 1884: children: Sherwin Kelly (geophysicist). ❖ Employed briefly in Chicago before settling in Boston, where she worked as a reporter and columnist for the *Globe* for 3 years; with husband, criss-crossed the nation, working on newspapers in San Francisco, Los Angeles, Philadelphia and in New Mexico; wrote 3 novels (1890s), publishing them anonymously or under a pseudonym; following husband's death, moved to NY and worked at *The New York Times Book Review* for 3 decades beginning 1905, turning out hundreds of reviews a year, mostly of nonfiction; also contributed feature stories, interviews, and syndicated articles to paper, and published another half-dozen books of fiction and nonfiction. ❖ See also autobiography *Flowing Stream* (1939); and *Women in World History.*

KELLY, Gloria (c. 1914–1934). *See Warner, Gloria.*

KELLY, Grace (1928–1982). American actress and princess of Monaco. Name variations: Princess Grace of Monaco; Grace Grimaldi. Born Nov 12, 1928, in Philadelphia, PA; died in automobile crash, Sept 14, 1982; dau. of Jack Kelly (millionaire) and Margaret (Majer) Kelly; attended American Academy of Dramatic Arts and Neighborhood Playhouse; m. Prince Rainier III of Monaco, April 18, 1956; children: Princess Caroline Grimaldi (b. 1957); Prince Albert Grimaldi (b. 1958); Princess Stephanie Grimaldi (b. 1965). ❖ American stage and film actress, who won an Academy Award then walked away from Hollywood to marry the prince of Monaco, attended private schools before moving to NY and studying acting; made Broadway debut in Strindberg's *The Father* (1949), attracting attention with her mannered manner and classic beauty; appeared in some 60 tv roles; was cast in 1st major film, opposite Gary Cooper in *High Noon* (1952); won an Oscar as Best Actress for work in *The Country Girl* (1954); starred in 3 of Hitchcock's most successful films *Dial M for Murder* (1954), *Rear Window* (1954) and *To Catch a Thief* (1955);

announced retirement from acting on marriage to Prince Rainier III of Monaco (1956), becoming known to the world from then on as Her Serene Highness Grace, princess of Monaco; never returned to the screen, though there were persistent rumors that she might until her death in an automobile crash at age 52; other films include *Mogambo* (1953), *The Bridges at Toko-Ri* (1955), *The Swan* (1956) and *High Society* (1956). ❖ See also Robert Lacey, *Grace* (Sidgwick & Jackson, 1994); and *Women in World History*.

KELLY, Gwen (1922—). Australian poet, novelist and short-story writer. Born Gwen Smith, 1922, in Thornleigh, Sydney, Australia; graduate of University of Sydney. ❖ Fiction includes *There is No Refuge* (1961), *The Red Boat* (1968), *The Middle-Aged Maidens* (1976), *Always Afternoon* (1981), and *The Happy People* (1988); poetry published in *Fossils and Stray Cats* (1980); won 4 Henre Lawson prose awards.

KELLY, Isabel (1906–1983). American archaeologist. Born Isabel Truesdell Kelly, Jan 4, 1906, in Santa Cruz, CA; died 1983; dau. of Thomas William Kelly and Alice Gardner Kelly; University of California, Berkeley, BA in anthropology, 1926, MA, 1927, PhD, 1932. ❖ Directed archaeological investigations in Culiacan, Sinaloa, Mexico (1935); returned to Mexico for research (1939) and gained Mexican residency (1940); conducted archaeological work at many sites in Mexico including Colima, Apatzingán, and Guadalajara; began serving as ethnologist-in-charge of Smithsonian's Institute of Social Anthropology office in Mexico City (1946); worked at Institute of Inter-American Affairs and studied health centers in Mexico; in Mexico, served as research consultant in archaeology and ethnography for Arizona State Museum; made significant contributions to Mexican archaeology and anthropology.

KELLY, Jo Ann (1944–1990). English jazz singer and guitarist. Born Jan 5, 1944, in Streatham, London, England; died Oct 21, 1990, in London, England; sister of Dave Kelly (jazz/blues musician). ❖ Blues singer with powerful, emotional voice, made 1st limited edition record with Tony McPhee (1964), later joining forces with Tony McPhee's Groundhogs band; gained recognition with National Blues Federation Convention (1968); became major player on British blues circuit, recording with John Dummer Blues Band, Chilli Willi and the Red Hot Peppers, and Stefan Grossman; recorded album with Woody Mann, John Miller and John Fahey (1972) and then formed group called Spare Rib; was interpreter of works by American blues singer Robert Johnson; helped found The Blues Band (1979), along with brother David Kelly and Bob Brunning, and staged *Ladies and the Blues* which paid tribute to female blues heros (early 1980s); diagnosed with brain tumor (1988); gave final performance at festival in Lancashire (Aug 1990), receiving British Blues Federation's Female Singer of the Year award. Recorded works include *Blues & Gospel* (1964), *Jo-Ann Kelly* (1999), *Jo Ann Kelly with J. Fahey, W. Mann & A. Seidler* (2002) and *Black Rat Swing* (2003).

KELLY, Judy (1913–1991). Australian actress. Born Nov 1, 1913, in Sydney, NSW, Australia; died Oct 1991 in London, England; m. Eric Summer. ❖ Made stage debut in Sydney in *The Rising Generation* (1930); moved to England (1932); made London debut in *Courtship Dance* (1934), later renamed *It Happened to Adam*; other plays include *A Ship Comes Home, Take It Easy, Windfall, Bridge of Sighs, Women Aren't Angels, The Crime of Margaret Foley* (title role), and *Violent Friendship*; made over 40 films including *Charing Cross Road, Queer Cargo, At the Villa Rose, The Midas Touch, Premiere, The Butler's Dilemma* and *Warning to Wantons*.

KELLY, Kate (1862–1898). Australian legend. Born 1862; drowned 1898; dau. of John Kelly (Irish ex-convict) and Ellen (Quinn) Kelly; married 1888; sister of Dan and Ned Kelly; no children. ❖ Sister of bushranger Ned Kelly, gained her place in Australian folklore more by association than deed; did not participate in any criminal activities, but was a staunch defender of the Kelly gang, particularly her brother Ned; was present at the siege of Glenrowan and subsequently pleaded Ned's case before the governor of Victoria and before a theater audience in Melbourne on the night of his execution; toured as an equestrian and worked on a central western station in north South Wales. ❖ See also Frank Hatherley's play *Ned Kelly's Sister's Travelling Circus* (later titled *Kate Kelly's Roadshow*, 1980); Jean Bedford's novel, *Sister Kate* (1982); and *Women in World History*.

KELLY, Kathryn Thorne (1904–1998?). American kidnapper. Name variations: Cleo Brooks; Cleo Coleman; Cleo Frye, Kathryn Frye; Kathryn Thorne. Born Cleo Brooks (some sources cite Cleo Coleman) in Saltillo, Mississippi, 1904; possibly died July 27, 1998, in St. Paul,

Minnesota; dau. of James Emery Brooks and Ora Brooks (who would later marry Robert K.G. "Boss" Shannon and take the name Ora Shannon); m. Lonnie Frye (laborer), 1919 (div. soon after); possibly m. Allie Brewer (briefly); m. Charles Thorne (bootlegger), 1924 (died 1927); m. George Kelly Barnes aka George R. Kelly aka Machine Gun Kelly (1895–1954, bootlegger, robber, and kidnapper), Sept 1930; children: (1st m.) Pauline Frye. ❖ Criminal who allegedly advanced the career of husband, Machine Gun Kelly, 1st gained experience as a bootlegger, shoplifter and robber; was the mastermind behind husband George Kelly's bank robberies in Texas, Oklahoma, and Washington state; was also the one who marketed him to the newspapers; moved into kidnapping, but 2nd attempt backfired (1933); arrested with husband by FBI; was sentenced to life (1933); released from prison (1958). ❖ See also *Women in World History*.

KELLY, Kitty (1902–1968). American stage and screen actress. Born April 27, 1902, in New York, NY; died June 29, 1968, in Hollywood, CA. ❖ Began career as a Ziegfeld girl; appeared in several films, including *Men with Wings, Grand Jury Secrets, All Women Have Secrets* and *The Mad Doctor*.

KELLY, Leontine (1920—). African-American bishop. Born Leontine Turpeau, Mar 5, 1920, in Washington, DC; dau. of David De Witt Turpeau (Methodist minister) and Ila (Marshall) Turpeau; Virginia Union University, BA, 1960; Wesley Theological Seminary, 1976; m. Gloster Bryant Current, 1941 (div. 1950s); m. James David Kelly (Methodist minister), 1956 (died 1969); children: (1st m.) Angella, Gloster and John Current; (2nd m.) adopted Pamela Lynne Kelly. ❖ Ordained (1976); served as pastor of Asbury-Church Hill United Methodist Church in Richmond (1977–83); became assistant general secretary of evangelism for United Methodist General Board of Discipleship in Nashville (1983); became United Methodist's 1st African-American bishop when the Western Jurisdictional Conference elected her to the episcopacy (1984); campaigned for end to nuclear arms, AIDS awareness, and wider acceptance of gays and lesbians in the church; retired (1998). Inducted into the Women's Hall of Fame at Seneca Falls, NY (2000).

KELLY, Maeve (1930—). Irish poet, novelist and short-story writer. Born 1930 in Co. Clare, Ireland. ❖ Worked as administrator of Limerick Centre for Battered Women; fiction includes *A Life of Her Own* (1976), *Necessary Treasons* (1985), *Florrie's Girls* (1989), *Orange Horses* (1990), and *Alice in Thunderland* (1993); poetry includes *Resolution* (1986). Won Hennessy Literary Award (1972).

KELLY, Margaret (1910–2004). Irish-born choreographer and dancer. Name variations: Miss Bluebell. Born Margaret Kelly, June 24, 1910, in Dublin, Ireland; given up for adoption soon after, was taken in by a foster mother, Mary Murphy; grew up in Liverpool; died Sept 11, 2004, in Paris, France; m. Marcel Leibovici (Jewish-Romanian pianist), 1939 (died 1961); children: 3 sons, 1 daughter, including Patrick and Francis Leibovici and Florence Leibovici Shapiro. ❖ Founder and force behind the world-famous Bluebell Girls and a celebrated figure in Parisian nightlife, began dancing professionally at 14, traveling throughout Europe with English ballet troupe; performed with a London Tiller School precision team until 18; organized the 1st line of precision dancers (1932), named The Bluebells, who appeared at Folies Bergère in Paris to great acclaim; during WWII, was interned by Nazis but gained release with help of Irish Embassy; after war, ran equally popular line of male performers, The Kelly Boys; began longterm association with dance director Don Arden at the Lido (1948); toured with Bluebells from Hong Kong to Rio De Janeiro to Las Vegas; retired at 79. Made OBE. ❖ See also BBC miniseries "Bluebell" (1986).

KELLY, Margaret (1956—). English swimmer. Born Sept 22, 1956, in UK. ❖ At Moscow Olympics, won a silver medal in 4 x 100-meter medley relay (1980).

KELLY, Mary (1952—). Irish politician. Born in 1952; m. Séan Kelly. ❖ Representing Labour, elected to the Seanad from the Cultural and Educational Panel: Oireachtas Sub-Panel (1993–97).

KELLY, Mary Anne (1826–1910). See O'Doherty, Mary Anne.

KELLY, Molly (c. 1917–2004). See Craig, Molly.

KELLY, Nancy (1921–1995). American actress. Born Mar 25, 1921, in Lowell, MA; died in Bel Air, CA, Jan 2, 1995; dau. of John A. Kelly (ticket broker) and Ann Mary (Walsh) Kelly (model for James Montgomery Flagg); sister of actor Jack Kelly (1927–1992);

Immaculate Conception Academy, NYC, St. Lawrence Academy, LI, and Bentley School for Girls; m. Edmond O'Brien (actor), 1941 (div. 1942); m. Fred Jackman Jr. (cinematographer, div.); m. Warren Caro (exec. director of Theater Guild), Nov 25, 1955. ❖ Best known for her role as Christine Penmark, the mother of a murderous child in *The Bad Seed*, which won her a Tony Award and Academy Award nomination (1956), began career as a child model; by 8, was a veteran of 50 movies; made Broadway debut in *Give Me Yesterday* (1931); began appearing on such radio programs as "Cavalcade of America," "Gangbusters" and "The Shadow"; lauded for portrayal of Blossom in *Susan and God* (1937); embarked on intense period of movie-making beginning with *Submarine Patrol* (1938), and including *Stanley and Livingstone* (1939), *Jesse James* (1939), *He Married His Wife* (1940) and *To the Shores of Tripoli* (1942); occasionally returned to Broadway, notably in *Season in the Sun* (1950); made frequent tv appearances on such shows as "Climax" and "Alfred Hitchcock Presents." Won an Emmy for "The Pilot," an episode of "Studio One" (1956). ❖ See also *Women in World History*.

KELLY, Patsy (1910–1981). American comedic actress. Born Sarah Kelly, Jan 12, 1910, in Brooklyn, NY; died Sept 24, 1981, following a stroke in Woodland Hills, CA; never married; no children. ❖ Usually cast as a wisecracking maid or friend of the heroine, began career dancing in Broadway musicals of early 1930s; appeared in 21 memorable comedy shorts paired with Thelma Todd, before making 1st feature film *Going Hollywood* (1933), one of several movies with Marion Davies; made 3 memorable feature films (1936): *Every Night at Eight*, *Thanks a Million*, and *Page Miss Glory*; during WWI, had radio show with Barry Wood; returned to films with roles in *Please Don't Eat the Daisies* and *The Crowded Sky*; made stunning comeback on Broadway in hit revival of *No, No, Nanette*, winning a Tony (1970); went on to a featured role in revival of *Irene* (1973); other films include *Rosemary's Baby* (1968) and *North Avenue Irregulars* (1979). ❖ See also *Women in World History*.

KELLY, Paula (1939—). American modern dancer and actress. Born Oct 21, 1943, in Jacksonville, FL; studied at High School of Music and Art and Juilliard School in New York City. ❖ Performed briefly as modern dancer in such works as Pearl Lang's *Tongues of Fire* (1968), Donald McKayle's *District Storyville*, and Anna Sokolow's *The Question, Session, and Time Plus*; performed on Broadway in *Something More!* (1964); appeared as Helene in film of *Sweet Charity* (1969); on tv, appeared on "The Women of Brewster Place" (1989), "Run for the Dream" (1996), among others, and was a regular on "Santa Barbara" (1984–85); other films include *Soylent Green* (1973), *Lost in the Stars* (1974), *Uptown Saturday Night* (1974), *Drum* (1976) and *Jo Jo Dancer* (1986).

KELLY, Pearl (1894–1983). Australian harness driver. Born Pearl O'Brien at Koo-wee-rup, Victoria, 1894; died 1983; m. Charles Kelly. ❖ Pioneered in sport of harness racing from age 16; during WWI, married and moved to Melbourne where she continued career; during early 1920s, in addition to her own horses, drove for leading trainer Percy Shipp and finished 3rd on Melbourne Drivers' Premiership; despite success, had running feud with Victorian Trotting and Racing Association who declared the sport unsafe and banned the issuance of driving permits to women (late 1920s); forced to give up driving, continued to train horses until 1961.

KELLY, Petra (1947–1992). German political activist and feminist. Born Petra Karin Lehmann, Nov 27, 1947, in Günzburg, Bavaria, West Germany; killed by companion at her home in Bonn, Germany, Oct 1992; dau. of Richard Siegfried Lehmann and Margarete-Marianne (Birle) Lehmann (who m. US Army Lt. Col. John Edward Kelly, 1958); half-sister of Grace Patricia Kelly (1959–1970); graduated from Hampton High, Virginia (1966); School of International Service at American University, Washington, DC (1966–70); BA cum laude in International Relations (1970); Diploma in European Integration from Europa Institute, University of Amsterdam (1971); never married; lived with Gert Bastian; no children. ❖ Germany's most influential advocate of peace, environmental protection, human rights, and nonviolence, was a 2-term representative to German Parliament and a founding member of the German Green Party and the European Green Peace movement; moved to Amsterdam (1970); accorded internship with European Commission in Brussels and research grant by Christian Democrat Press and Information Office (1971); transferred to cabinet of Sicco Mansholt, president of European Commission, administrator to the Health and Social Policy Section of the Economic and Social Committee of European Commission (1972–83); in memory of sister, established Grace P. Kelly Foundation (1973); elected to board of Bundesverband Bürgerinitiativen Umweltschutz, an umbrella organization for citizens environmental action groups in Germany (1977); co-founded Sonstige Politische Vereinigung—Die Grünen in Frankfurt (1979); at founding conference of Die Grünen, the German Green Party, elected 1 of 3 speakers (1980); was co-organizer of International War Crimes Tribunal for possession of weapons of mass destruction (1983); elected member of German Bundestag (Parliament), member of Foreign Relations Committee (1983–87); was a representative at Western European Union (1985–87); was re-elected to Parliament (1987); served as chair of German Association for Social Defence (1988–90); organized 1st International and Non-Partisan Hearing on Tibet and Human Rights in Bonn (1989); lost seat in Parliament (1990); wrote *Fighting for Hope* (1984); *Hiroshima* (1986) and *Thinking Green! Essays on Environmentalism, Feminism, and Nonviolence* (1995). Named Peace Woman of the Year (1993). ❖ See also Sara Parkin, *The Life and Death of Petra Kelly* (Pandora, 1994); and *Women in World History*.

KELLY, Ruth (1968—). English economist and politician. Born Ruth Kelly, May 9, 1968; m. Derek John Gadd, 1996. ❖ Was economics writer, *The Guardian* (1990–94); representing Labour, elected to House of Commons for Bolton West (1997, 2001, 2005); named financial secretary, HM Treasury; became secretary of state, Department for Education and Skills (2004).

KELMAN, Peggy (1909–1998). *See McKillop, Peggy.*

KELSALL, Karen (1962—). Canadian gymnast. Born Dec 11, 1962, in Canada. ❖ Won the Canadian Jr. National championships (1976), Ontario Cup (1977), British Columbian championships (1977), and Canadian nationals (1977, 1980); was the youngest competitor at the Montreal Olympics (1976); won a team gold at the Commonwealth Games (1978). ❖ See also *The Making of a Gymnast: The Karen Kelsall Story* (1978).

KELSEY, Corinne (1877–1947). *See Rider-Kelsey, Corinne.*

KELSEY, Frances O. (1914—). Canadian-born physician. Name variations: Frances Oldham Kelsey. Born Frances Kathleen Oldham, July 14, 1914; grew up in Cobble Hill on Vancouver Island, British Columbia, Canada; dau. of Katherine and Frank Oldham; McGill University, BS, 1934, MA, 1935; University of Chicago, PhD, 1938; m. Fremont Ellis Kelsey (pharmacologist), 1943; children: 2 daughters. ❖ Joined the Food and Drug Administration (1960) and assigned to review drug applications; citing the failure of the William S. Merrell Co. to prove the safety of the drug thalidomide, turned down Merrell's application to sell the drug in US (Nov 10, 1960); rejected 2 further attempts by Merrell to receive permission to sell thalidomide, single handedly keeping the drug from entering American market; after thalidomide's use in Europe was found to cause severe birth deformations, received Distinguished Federal Civilian Service Medal from President John F. Kennedy (Aug 7, 1962); continued work for FDA for more than 4 decades. Inducted into the National Women's Hall of Fame at Seneca Falls (2000).

KELSEY, Lavinia Jane (1856–1948). New Zealand kindergarten founder and teacher. Born Feb 23, 1856, in South Hackney, London, England; died June 16, 1948, in Dunedin, New Zealand; dau. of Thomas Kelsey (braid manufacturer) and Lavinia (Owen) Kelsey. ❖ Immigrated with brothers to New Zealand (c. 1877); established private school in her home (early 1800s); traveled to England, where she learned of kindergarten work by Friedrich Froebel (1883); returned to New Zealand and implemented idea in own school and helped to establish Dunedin Free Kindergarten Association (1889); retired from teaching (c. 1916). ❖ See also *Dictionary of New Zealand Biography* (Vol. 3).

KELSEY, Susan Sloan (1958—). *See Sloan, Susan.*

KELSO, Elizabeth (1889–1967). New Zealand journalist, editor, and community leader. Name variations: Elizabeth Cumming. Born May 28, 1889, in Fort William, Argyll, Scotland; died July 7, 1967, at Raumati Beach, New Zealand; dau. of Ewen Cumming (master slater) and Elizabeth (Munro) Cumming; m. Robert Kelso (grocer), 1920 (died 1956); children: 1 daughter. ❖ Lived in South Africa before immigrating to New Zealand (mid-1920s); became inaugural president of Paraparaumu Women's Institute (1929), contributed to its journal, *Home and Country*, and served as its editor (1931–34); joined executive committee of Wellington Provincial Federation of Women's Institutes (1932); sat on joint council of Order of St John and New Zealand Red Cross Society; active in Women's Division of Farmers' Union; instrumental in persuading New Zealand Department of Health to organize women's institutes for Maori women; wrote fiction (1930s–1940s). ❖ See also *Dictionary of New Zealand Biography*.

KELTON, Pert (1907–1968). American stage and screen actress. Born Oct 14, 1907, in Great Falls, Montana; died Oct 30, 1968, in Ridgewood, NJ; m. Ralph Bell (actor); children: 2 sons, including Brian Bell (actor). ❖ Began career in vaudeville with parents; made Broadway debut (1925) in *Sunny;* also appeared in *The DuBarry, The Bad Seed, The Music Man, Come Blow Your Horn* and *Spofford;* made film debut in *Sally* (1929); other films include *Bed of Roses, The Bowery, The Meanest Gal in Town, Mary Burns—Fugitive, Hooray for Love, Annie Oakley* and *The Music Man.* Was the original Alice Kramden in "The Honeymooners" with Jackie Gleason (1950–52), until she was blacklisted during McCarthy era.

KEMBLE, Adelaide (1814–1879). English soprano and author. Name variations: Adelaide Sartoris; Mrs. Edward Sartoris. Born in London, 1814; died at Warsash House, Hampshire, England, Aug 4, 1879; dau. of Charles Kemble (actor) and Maria Theresa (De Camp) Kemble (1774–1838, actress); younger sister of Fanny Kemble (1809–1893); niece of Sarah Siddons; studied in London with Braham, in Italy with Pasta; m. Edward Sartoris (wealthy Italian), 1843; children: Algernon Charles Sartoris (m. Ellen "Nellie" Grant [1855–1922], dau. of Ulysses S. Grant). ❖ Made operatic debut as Norma in Venice (1838); sang Norma in London's Covent Garden (1841), then appeared in *Figaro, Sonnambula,* and *Semiramide;* on marriage, retired to Italy (1843); wrote *A Week in a French Country House.* ❖ See also *Women in World History.*

KEMBLE, Mrs. Charles (1774–1838). *See Kemble, Maria Theresa.*

KEMBLE, Eliza (1761–1836). English actress. Name variations: Mrs. Whitlock. Born Elizabeth Kemble, 1761; died 1836; dau. of Roger Kemble (actor-manager) and Sarah (Ward) Kemble; sister of Sarah Siddons (1755–1831); aunt of Fanny Kemble (1809–1893); m. Charles Edward Whitlock (actor), 1785. ❖ Appeared in *The Merchant of Venice* with sister Sarah Siddons at Drury Lane (1783); following marriage (1785), accompanied husband to America; made 1 other journey to US before she retired (1807), subsequent to her appearance as Elwina in *Percy* at Drury Lane.

KEMBLE, Elizabeth (c. 1763–1841). English actress. Name variations: Elizabeth Satchell; Mrs. Stephen Kemble. Born Elizabeth Satchell c. 1763; died 1841; m. Stephen Kemble (1758–1822, actor manager and brother of Sarah Siddons), 1783; aunt of Fanny Kemble (1809–1893); children: Henry Stephen Kemble (1789–1836, actor who played leading parts at Drury Lane). ❖ As Elizabeth Satchell, performed at Covent Garden as Polly Peachum in *The Beggar's Opera* (1780); the following season, appeared as Juliet in *Romeo and Juliet;* continuing Shakespearean roles, played Desdemona to Stephen Kemble's Othello and married him (1783); career would go on to surpass that of her husband.

KEMBLE, Fanny (1809–1893). English Shakespearean actress and writer. Name variations: Frances Anne Kemble or Fanny Kemble (1809–1834, and in print); Frances Butler (1834–1849); Mrs. Fanny Kemble (1849–1893). Born Frances Anne Kemble in London, England, Nov 27, 1809; died in London, Jan 15, 1893; dau. of Charles Kemble (actor and theatrical impresario) and Maria Theresa (De Camp) Kemble (actress and dancer); sister of Adelaide Kemble (1814–1879, singer); fraternal niece of Sarah Siddons (1755–1831, actress); m. Pierce Butler (American), 1834 (div. 1849); children: Sarah Butler Wister (1835–1908, who m. Owen Wister, author of *The Virginian*); Frances Butler Leigh (1838–1910). ❖ Luminary who divorced a prominent American slave-owner and condemned slavery in her best-known book, *Journal of a Residence on a Georgia Plantation;* made a triumphant debut in London as Juliet (1829); wrote a historical drama, *Francis I,* and played the leading female role; appeared as an actress (1829–34, 1847–49); separated from husband and returned to England (1845); toured as a public dramatic reader (1849–70); was one of the 1st trans-Atlantic celebrities, crossing Atlantic 30 times and remaining popular in British and US high society from almost the beginning to end of her life; other writings include *Journal* (1935), *Year of Consolation* (1847), *Records of a Girlhood* (1878), *Records of a Later Life* (1882), *Further Records* (1884) and *Far Away and Long Ago* (1889). ❖ See also J.C. Furnas, *Fanny Kemble: Leading Lady of the Nineteenth Century Stage* (Dial, 1982); Dorothy Marshall, *Fanny Kemble* (Weidenfeld & Nicolson, 1977); and *Women in World History.*

KEMBLE, Frances Anne (1809–1893). *See Kemble, Fanny.*

KEMBLE, Mrs. John Philip (1756–1845). *See Kemble, Priscilla.*

KEMBLE, Maria Theresa (1774–1838). English actress. Name variations: Marie Thérèse De Camp, Mrs. Charles Kemble, Miss De Camp. Born Maria Theresa De Camp in Vienna, Austria, May 13, 1774; died 1838; dau. of a French captain father and Swiss mother; sister of Adelaide De Camp (Aunt Dall); m. Charles Kemble (1775–1854, actor and theatrical impresario), 1806; children: John Mitchell Campbell (1807–1857, a philologist and historian); Fanny Kemble (1809–1893); Adelaide Kemble Sartoris (1814–1879). ❖ At 12, 1st appeared under maiden name at Drury Lane (1786), the sole support of her family; scored a hit as Macheath in *The Beggar's Opera* (1792); went on to create the roles of Judith in *The Iron Chest,* Caroline Dormer in *The Heir at Law* (1797), and Madge Wildfire in *Heart of the Midlothian;* also portrayed Shakespeare's women: Portia, Desdemona, and Katherine; appeared at Covent Garden (1806–19); wrote and appeared in *First Faults* (1799), *The Day after the Wedding* (1808) and *Smiles and Tears* (1815).

KEMBLE, Priscilla (1756–1845). English actress. Name variations: Mrs. Brereton; Mrs. John Philip Kemble; Priscilla Hopkins. Born Priscilla Hopkins, 1756; died 1845; m. John Philip Kemble (1757–1823, brother of Sarah Siddons), in 1787. ❖ Performed with Garrick company at Drury Lane (1775); went on to create roles of Harriet in *The Runaway,* Eliza in *Spleen, or Islington Spa,* and Maria in Sheridan's *School for Scandal* (1777); continued career in secondary parts as Mrs. Brereton, until she married John Philip Kemble (1787); retired 8 years later and, following death of husband (1823), lived out her days at her country place, Heath Farm, in Hertfordshire, lent to her by Lord Essex.

KEMBLE, Sarah (1755–1831). *See Siddons, Sarah.*

KEMBLE, Mrs. Stephen (c. 1763–1841). *See Kemble, Elizabeth.*

KEMBLE-COOPER, Lillian (1891–1977). *See Cooper, Lillian Kemble.*

KEMBLE-COOPER, Violet (1886–1961). *See Cooper, Violet Kemble.*

KEMMER, Heike (1962—). German equestrian. Born April 24, 1962, in Berlin, Germany. ❖ Placed 2nd in indiv. dressage at World Cup final in Gothenburg (2003); on Bonaparte, won a gold medal for team dressage at Athens Olympics (2004).

KEMNER, Caren (1965—). American volleyball player. Born April 16, 1965, in Quincy, IL; attended University of Arizona. ❖ At Barcelona Olympics, won a bronze medal in team competition (1992); outside hitter, was 6-time recipient of USOC Female Volleyball Athlete of the Year (1986–88, 1990–92) and 5-time winner of USA team MVP award.

KEMP, Charlotte (1790–1860). New Zealand missionary. Name variations: Charlotte Butcher. Born Charlotte Butcher, July 27, 1790, in Norfolk, England; died on June 22, 1860, at Kerikeri, New Zealand; m. James Kemp, 1818 (died 1872); children: 8. ❖ Immigrated with husband as missionary to New Zealand (1819), and was 1 of 1st European women at Kerikeri; taught in the girls' and infants' schools until ill health forced retirement (mid-1830s). ❖ See also *Dictionary of New Zealand Biography* (Vol. 1).

KEMP, Janet (1883–1945). *See Fraser, Janet.*

KEMP, Jennifer (1955—). American swimmer. Name variations: Jenny Kemp. Born May 28, 1955, in US. ❖ At Munich Olympics, won a gold medal in 4 x 100-meter freestyle relay (1972); swam for Cincinnati Marlins waterpolo team (1974).

KEMP-WELCH, Joan (1906–1999). British actress and director. Born Joan Kemp-Welch Green in Wimbledon, England, Sept 23, 1906; died July 5, 1999, in England; dau. of Vincent Green and Helen (Kemp-Welch) Green; attended Roedean; m. Ben H. Wright (div.); m. Peter Moffatt. ❖ Began career as a character actress, making stage debut in *Maya* (Gate Theater, 1927); was director at Buxton Repertory (1944), Colchester Rep (1945–48), Wilson Barrett Co. in Scotland (1948–51), New Theater Bromley (1953–54), Pitlochry Festival (1968–69); directed over 250 plays including *Hedda Gabler, The Cherry Orchard, Winterset, A Streetcar Named Desire, Desire Under the Elms, An Ideal Husband, Miss Hargreaves,* and *Vicious Circle;* for tv (1950s), directed over 200 programs, including features, dramas, and series episodes for "Upstairs, Downstairs" and "Life with the Lyons," among others. Won numerous awards, including a tv Oscar for "Cool for Cats" (1958), *Prix Italia* for "The Lover" (1963), Desmond Davis Award for service to tv (1963), and Wilkie Baird award for creative work on tv. ❖ See also *Women in World History.*

KEMPE, Anna Eliza (1790–1883). *See Bray, Anna Eliza.*

KEMPE, Margery (c. 1373–after 1438). English mystic. Name variations: Margery Burnham Kempe; Margerie Kempe. Pronunciation: Kemp.

Born Margery Burnham c. 1373 at King's Lynn (then Bishop's Lynn) in Norfolk, England; died in King's Lynn sometime after 1438; dau. of John Burnham, or de Brunham (5 times mayor and 6 times member of Parliament); nothing is known of mother; m. John Kempe (tax-collector, miller, and brewer), c. 1393; children: 14, about whom little is known. ❖ Religious pilgrim, mystic, and author of the oldest extant autobiography in the English language, a document known only in a severely excerpted form until the discovery of the full manuscript in 1934 which led to a reassessment of her controversial spiritual life and her position in the Western mystical tradition; wrote with aid of 2 scribes *The Book of Margery Kempe* between 1431 and her death, resulting in a highly personal and detailed account of the spiritual life of a woman of the merchant class living at the end of the Middle Ages, including her religious transformation. ❖ See also Clarissa W. Atkinson, *Mystic and Pilgrim: The Book and World of Margery Kempe* (Cornell U. Press, 1983); Katharine Cholmeley, *Margery Kempe: Genius and Mystic* (Longmans, 1947); Karma Lochrie, *Margery Kempe and Translations of the Flesh* (U. of Pennsylvania Press, 1991); Louise Collis, *Memoirs of a Medieval Woman: The Life and Times of Margery Kempe* (Harper & Row, 1983); and *Women in World History.*

KEMPER, Margaret (1948—). *See Trudeau, Margaret.*

KEMPFER, Hannah Jensen (1880–1943). American state legislator. Name variations: Johannah Jensen. Born Dec 22, 1880, on the North Sea; died Sept 27, 1943, in Fergus Falls, Minnesota; dau. of an unknown sailor and a ship stewardess; left at a foundlings' home in Norway and adopted by Ole Jensen (ship's boilermaker) and Martha Jensen; m. Charles Taylor Kempfer (farmer), May 20, 1903. ❖ Elected to Minnesota State House of Representatives (1922); maintained seat in house (to 1941), except for 1 mid-tenure defeat (1930); assumed chair of Game and Fish Committee, and tackled many measures pertaining to conservation; also backed a bill to improve status of illegitimate children.

KEMPNER, Patty (1942—). American swimmer. Born Aug 24, 1942, in US. ❖ At Rome Olympics, won a gold medal in the 4 x 100-meter medley relay (1960).

KEMPSON, Rachel (1910–2003). British actress. Name variations: Lady Redgrave. Born in Dartmouth, Devon, England, May 28, 1910; died May 24, 2003, at her home in Millbrook, NY; dau. of Eric William Edward (headmaster) and Beatrice Hamilton (Ashwell) Kempson; studied at Royal Academy of Dramatic Art; m. (Sir) Michael Redgrave (actor), 1935 (died 1985); children: Vanessa Redgrave (b. 1937); Corin Redgrave (b. 1939); Lynn Redgrave (b. 1942). ❖ Matriarch of the family Redgrave, made stage debut as Hero in *Much Ado About Nothing* (Stratford, 1933); subsequently played Juliet in *Romeo and Juliet* and Ophelia in *Hamlet;* made London debut as Bianca in *The Lady from Albuquerque* (1933); with husband, joined Old Vic in London, where they appeared together in *Love's Labour's Lost* (1936); joined Shakespeare Memorial Theater Co. (1953), and appeared as Queen Elizabeth in *Richard III,* Octavia in *Antony and Cleopatra,* and Regan in *King Lear;* portrayed Thea Elvsted in *Hedda Gabler* (1954); played numerous supporting roles in major London productions and on tour, but came into her own on tv (1960s), with roles in "Conflict," "Man and Superman," "Howards End," and "Uncle Vanya," among others; films include *The Captive Heart* (1946), *A Woman's Vengeance* (1948), *Georgy Girl* (1966), *Out of Africa* (1985) and *Déjà Vu* (1998). ❖ See also autobiography *Life Among the Redgraves* (Dutton, 1986); and *Women in World History.*

KEN, Olga *See Poliakoff, Olga.*

KENDAL, duchess of. *See Schulenburg, Ehrengard Melusina von der (1667–1743).*

KENDAL, Felicity (1946—). English actress. Born Felicity Ann Kendal, Sept 25, 1946, in Olton, Warwickshire, England; dau. of Geoffrey Kendal and Laura Liddell (both actors); sister of Jennifer Kendal (actress); m. Drewe Henley (actor), 1968 (div. 1979); m. Michael Rudman, 1983 (div. 1990); children: 2. ❖ Best known for role of Barbara Good in tv series "The Good Life" (1975–77), made London debut in *Minor Murder* at Savoy (1967); starred in several Tom Stoppard plays, including *The Real Thing* (1982), *Jumpers* (1985) and *Hapgood* (1988); also appeared as Louise in *Hidden Laughter* (1990) and Ariadne Utterwood in *Heartbreak House* (1992); on tv, starred in comedy series "Solo" (1981), "Honey for Tea" (1994) and "Rosemary and Thyme" (2003). Won London Evening Standard Theatre award for Best Actress for performances in *Much Ado About Nothing* and *Ivanov* (1989); named CBE or Commander of British Empire (1995).

KENDAL, Madge (1849–1935). English actress. Name variations: Dame Madge Kendal; Mrs. Kendal; Margaret Brunton Robertson. Born Margaret Shafto (also seen as Sholto) Robertson, Mar 15, 1849 (some sources cite 1848) in Grimsby, Lincolnshire, England; died Sept 14, 1935, in Hertfordshire, England; 22nd child and last dau. of William Robertson (actor and theatrical manager) and Margherita (also seen as Margaretta) Elisabetta (Marinus) Robertson (actress-comedian); sister of dramatist T(homas) W(illiam) Robertson (1829–71); m. W(illiam) H(unter) Kendal (actor), Aug 7, 1869 (died 1917); children: 4. ❖ Considered the greatest comedian of her generation, made stage debut as Marie in *The Orphan of the Frozen Sea* (1854); made adult London debut as Ophelia in *Hamlet* (1865); with husband, performed with Haymarket Co. until 1874, during which time she played in all the classics as well as new plays; with husband, joined John Hare at Court Theater (1875), where she was 1st seen as Susan Hartley in adaptation of Sardou comedy, *A Scrap of Paper,* a role she would repeat many times; when husband went into partnership with John Hare at St. James's Theater (1879), remained there until 1888, playing lead roles in numerous productions; made NY debut in *A Scrap of Paper* (1889) and would make 4 subsequent tours of US; returned to London stage as Mrs. Armitage in *The Greatest of These* (1896); retired (1908). Awarded DBE (1926) and Grand Cross of the Order (1927). ❖ See also *Women in World History.*

KENDAL, Mrs. (1849–1935). *See Kendal, Madge.*

KENDALL, Barbara Anne (1967—). New Zealand windsurfer. Born Aug 30, 1967, in Papakura, Auckland, New Zealand; m. Shayne Bright, 1993. ❖ At Barcelona Olympics, won a gold medal in Lechner (boardsailing, 1992); won a silver medal at Atlanta Olympics (1996) and a bronze medal at Sydney Olympics (2000), both for board (Mistral); won World championships for Mistral (1998, 1999, 2002).

KENDALL, Kay (1926–1959). English actress. Born Justine Kay Kendall McCarthy, May 21, 1926, in Withernsea, near Hull, England; died in London, of leukemia, age 32, Sept 6, 1959; dau. of professional dancers; m. Rex Harrison (actor), in 1957. ❖ At 13, joined the chorus line at London Palladium, then toured with sister Kim in music-hall act; a sophisticated comedian, played minor roles in film early in career before turning to stage repertory; came to public attention with her drunken trumpet solo in movie comedy *Genevieve* (1953); in 1st US film (1957), teamed with Gene Kelly and Mitzi Gaynor for *Les Girls* and was a rollicking success; played wife to husband Harrison in film *The Reluctant Debutante;* other films include *Doctor in the House* (1954), *The Constant Husband* (1955), *Simon and Laura* (1955), *Quentin Durward* (1955) and *Once More with Feeling* (1960). ❖ See also *Women in World History.*

KENDALL, Margaret Louisa (1895–1974). *See Macpherson, Margaret Louisa.*

KENDALL, Marie Hartig (1854–1943). French-born American photographer. Born in Mulhouse, France, 1854; died in Norfolk, CT, 1943; trained as a nurse at Bellevue Hospital, NY, and Charity Hospital on Blackwell's Island; m. John Kendall (physician), late 1870s; children: 3. ❖ Immigrated to US following France's defeat in Franco-Prussian War; took up photography, shooting portraits of her children; won bronze medal at World's Columbian Exposition in Chicago (1893); exhibited at Louisiana Purchase Exposition in St. Louis (1904); before her death, destroyed some 30,000 of her glass negatives. The remaining 250 images, including shots of the 1888 blizzard, are now held at the Norfolk Connecticut Historical Society.

KENDRICK, Pearl L. (1890–1980). American microbiologist. Name variations: Pearl Luella Kendrick. Born Aug 24, 1890, in Wheaton, IL; died Oct 1980, in Grand Rapids, MI; studied at Syracuse and Johns Hopkins universities. ❖ Served as associate director of laboratories of the Michigan Department of Health (1920–51) and resident lecturer in epidemiology at School of Public Health of University of Michigan; with Grace Eldering, developed whooping cough vaccine; created standard diphtheria, whooping cough, and tetanus immunization (DPT) which greatly reduced major childhood diseases in Western world; served as consultant to WHO and UNICEF, wrote articles on contagious disease, and was fellow and vice-president of American Public Health Association. Refused publicity for PDT vaccine.

KENNARD, Gaby (1944—). Australian aviator. Born in 1944 in East Melbourne, Victoria, Australia; married; children: 1 daughter, 1 son. ❖ Was the 1st Australian woman to fly a single-engine plane solo around the world (1989), a journey that took 99 days. Received Harmon Trophy. ❖ See also autobiography, *Solo Woman* (1990).

KENNARD, Olga (1924—). English crystallographer. Name variations: Olga Weisz; Olga Burgen. Born Olga Weisz, Mar 23, 1924; Cambridge University, MA, 1948, DSc, 1971; m. David William Kennard, 1948 (div. 1961); Sir Arnold Burgen (president of Academia Europaea), 1993. ❖ Worked as a Cavendish Laboratory research assistant at University of Cambridge (1944–48); served on staff of Medical Research Council (MRC) of Vision Research Unit in London (1948–51); worked for MRC National Institute for Medical Research in London (1951–61); created a Crystallography Unit for University Chemical Laboratory; established (1965) and served as the scientific director of Cambridge Crystallographic Data Centre (CCDC, 1965–97); appointed University of London visiting professor (1988–90); developed innovations in X-ray crystallography to study the structure of biologically active (and organic) molecules, including adenosine 5-triphosphate (ATP, 1970); made a fellow of Royal Society (1987). Made Officer of the Order of the British Empire (1988).

KENNEDY, Adrienne (1931—). African-American playwright. Born Sept 15, 1931, in Pittsburgh, PA; grew up in Cleveland; dau. of Cornell Hawkins (exec. secretary of YMCA) and Etta Hawkins (teacher); graduate of Ohio State University, 1953; m. Joseph Kennedy, 1953 (div. 1966); children: Joseph Jr. and Adam. ❖ Won an Obie for *Funnyhouse of a Negro*, which was co-produced off-Broadway by Edward Albee (1964); other works include *The Owl Answers* (1965), *Cities in Benzique* (1965), *A Rat's Mass* (1966), *An Evening with Dead Essay* (1974), *A Movie Star Has to Star in Black and White* (1976), *Lancashire Lad* (1980), *The Alexander Plays* (1992) and *Sleep Deprivation Center* (1996). ❖ See also memoirs, *People Who Led to My Plays* (1987).

KENNEDY, Caroline (b. 1957). *See Schlossberg, Caroline Kennedy.*

KENNEDY, Courtney (1979—). American ice-hockey player. Born Mar 29, 1979, in Woburn, MA. ❖ Played for University of Minnesota; on defense, won a team silver medal at Salt Lake City Olympics (2002) and a team bronze medal at Torino Olympics (2006).

KENNEDY, Ethel (1928—). American philanthropist and wife of Senator Robert F. Kennedy. Born Ethel Skakel in Chicago, IL, April 11, 1928; dau. of George Skakel (coal magnate) and Ann (Brannack) Skakel; Manhattanville College of the Sacred Heart, BA, 1949; m. Robert F. Kennedy (b. 1925, US senator), June 17, 1950 (assassinated June 5, 1968); children: Kathleen Kennedy Townsend (b. 1951); Joseph Patrick Kennedy II (b. 1952); Robert F. Kennedy Jr. (b. 1954); David Kennedy (1955–1984); (Mary) Courtney Kennedy Hill (b. 1956); Michael Kennedy (1958–1998); (Mary) Kerry Kennedy Cuomo (b. 1959); Christopher Kennedy (b. 1963); Matthew Maxwell T. Kennedy known as Max (b. 1965); Douglas Harriman Kennedy (b. 1967); Rory Kennedy (b. 1968). ❖ Good at sports and an excellent equestrian, came into her own as the chic, energetic wife of RFK; with her constantly expanding family, settled into their home at Hickory Hill in McLean, Virginia; when brother-in-law Jack ran for president, turned out to be a 1st-rate campaigner, criss-crossing nation on his behalf and winning admiration of the press corps; when husband was attorney general, became one of the most visible and popular women in Washington, presiding over exuberant parties at Hickory Hill; threw herself into husband's campaign for US senate (1964), then president; was standing near him the night he was assassinated; in later years, devoted more time to charitable causes, which included overseeing the $10 million Robert F. Kennedy Memorial Foundation; also became active in some of husband's causes, including the grape pickers' movement in California and the Bedford-Stuyvesant Restoration Corporation; for years, has also supported the Special Olympics. ❖ See also Jerry Oppenheimer, *The Other Mrs. Kennedy* (St. Martin's, 1994); J. Randy Taraborrelli, *Jackie, Ethel, Joan: Women of Camelot* (Warner, 2000); Laurence Leamer, *The Kennedy Women* (Villard, 1994); and *Women in World History*.

KENNEDY, Eunice (b. 1921). *See Shriver, Eunice Kennedy.*

KENNEDY, Florynce (1916–2000). African-American lawyer and activist. Name variations: Flo Kennedy. Born Feb 11, 1916, in Kansas City, Missouri; died Dec 21, 2000, in New York, NY; dau. of Wiley Kennedy and Zella Kennedy; Columbia University, bachelor's degree; Columbia Law School, law degree, 1951; m. Charles Dudley Dye (writer), 1957 (div.); no children. ❖ Well-known activist, established a private law practice (1954) and represented Billie Holiday, Charlie Parker, and H. Rap Brown, though she grew disenchanted with what she saw as a racist

and bigoted court system; was an active and outspoken leader in civil rights and feminist movements (1960s–70s); founded Media Workshop (1966), designed to deal with racism in media and advertising, and was also an original member of National Organization for Women (NOW); attended all 4 Black Power Conferences (1967–70) and also formed the Feminist Party, which worked to support Shirley Chisholm as a presidential candidate; spoke at numerous colleges and universities and at rallies across the nation; co-authored with Diane Schulter, *Abortion Rap* (1972). ❖ See also autobiography *Color Me Flo: My Hard Life and Good Times* (1976); and *Women in World History*.

KENNEDY, Geraldine (1951—). Irish politician and journalist. Born Sept 1951, in Tramore, Co. Waterford, Ireland; m. David Hegarty. ❖ Was a reporter with the *Cork Examiner* and political correspondent with *Sunday Tribune, Sunday Press* and *Irish Times;* while reporting on challenges to the Fianna Fáil leadership of Charles Haughey, discovered phone being tapped (1982) and was eventually awarded damages by High Court (1987), resulting in Haughey's loss of office (1992); representing Progressive Democrats, elected to the 25th Dáil (1987–89) for Dún Laoghaire; defeated (1989).

KENNEDY, Helena (1950—). Scottish lawyer. Name variations: Lady Helena Kennedy, Baroness Helena Kennedy; Baaroness Kennedy of the Shaws. Born May 12, 1950, in Glasgow, Scotland; m. Dr. Iain Hutchinson (surgeon); children: 1 daughter, 2 sons. ❖ Barrister, broadcaster, feminist and writer of the left, grew up in working-class family; was called to bar (1972); practiced predominantly criminal law, arguing high-profile cases, including Brighton Bombing Trial and Guildford Four Appeal; created BBC tv drama series "Blind Justice" (1987); served as chair of British Council to develop closer cultural relations between UK and other countries (1998–2004); hosted various tv programs, including "Heart of the Matter" (1987), "Raw Deal" (1990), "Time, Gentlemen, Please" (1994) and "After Dark" (2003); co-produced documentary *Mothers Behind Bars* (1990) which helped change penal policy on women's prisons; became Queen's Counsel (1991); wrote *Eve Was Framed* (1992) and *Just Law: The Changing Face of Justice–And Why it Matters to Us All* (2004); chaired constitutional reform group Charter 88 (1992–97); was 1st chancellor of Oxford Brookes University (1993–2001) and later president of School of Oriental and African Studies at London University; appointed chair of Humane Genetics Commission (2000). Received Lifetime Achievement in the Law award from Women Lawyers' Conference (1996); life peerage (1997).

KENNEDY, Jacqueline (1929–1994). American first lady. Name variations: Jacqueline Bouvier; Jacqueline Kennedy Onassis; Jackie O. Born July 28, 1929, in Southampton, NY; died from cancer, May 19, 1994, in New York, NY; dau. of John Bouvier (stockbroker) and Janet (Lee) Bouvier (socialite), later known as Janet Auchincloss; sister of Lee Radziwell; educated at Vassar, Smith College, George Washington University and Sorbonne; m. John Fitzgerald Kennedy (35th president of US), Sept 12, 1953 (assassinated Nov 22, 1963); m. Aristotle Onassis (Greek industrialist), 1968 (died 1975); children: (1st m.) Caroline Kennedy Schlossberg (b. 1957); John F. Kennedy Jr. (1960–1999); Patrick (1963–1963). ❖ One of America's most popular first ladies, much admired for her artistic sensibility, sophisticated beauty, and patronage of the arts, 1st worked as a photographer for *Washington Times-Herald;* met John F. Kennedy when he was beginning his campaign for US senator (1952); married him during his 1st year in Senate (Sept 1953); during his run for presidency, remained in background; on occasions when she did take the stump, seemed to reach audience with a combination of sincerity and wry sense of humor; became first lady (1960); redecorated White House during 3 years there, which was launched by her now-famous live tv tour of executive mansion on CBS; brought a contemporary sensibility to state dinners by lending a more informal atmosphere to even the weightiest occasions; injected cultural excitement by inviting the likes of Leonard Bernstein, Jerome Robbins, and Pablo Casals to perform there; called for creation of a formal government structure to fund the arts, leading to eventual creation of National Endowment for the Arts and National Endowment for the Humanities; helped found the Washington National Cultural Center, now called The Kennedy Center; was riding next to husband in Dallas motorcade when an assassin's bullet took his life (Nov 1963); saw to every detail of the state funeral; married much abroad Greek industrialist Aristotle Onassis (1968), spending much of her time abroad until his death (1975), after which she moved back to NY; became an editor for Doubleday (1978), remaining by choice out of the public eye and living quietly until her death; buried in Arlington National Cemetery next to John F. Kennedy. ❖ See also Christopher Anderson, *Jackie After Jack: Portrait of the Lady*

(Morrow, 1998); John H. Davis, *Jacqueline Bouvier: An Intimate Memoir* (Wiley, 1996); Ellen Ladowsky, *Jacqueline Kennedy Onassis* (Park Lane, 1997); Laurence Leamer, *The Kennedy Women* (Villard, 1994); and *Women in World History.*

KENNEDY, Jane (1958—). British politician and member of Parliament. Born Jane Hodgson, May 4, 1958; m. Malcolm Kennedy, 1977 (div. 1998). ❖ Representing Labour, elected to House of Commons for Liverpool Wavertree (1992); served as Cabinet assistant government whip (1997–98), lord commissioner of the treasury (1998–99), and parliamentary secretary in the lord chancellor's department (1999–2001); named minister of State in the Northern Ireland Office with responsibility for Security, Policing, and Prisons (2001) and Education, Employment, and Learning (2002).

KENNEDY, Jean (b. 1928). *See Smith, Jean Kennedy.*

KENNEDY, Joan (1936—). American socialite. Born Virginia Joan Bennett, Sept 5, 1936, in Riverdale, NY; dau. of Harry Wiggin (advertising executive) and Virginia Joan "Ginny" (Stead) Bennett; graduate of Manhattanville College of the Sacred Heart, 1958; m. Edward "Ted" Kennedy (b. 1932, lawyer and US senator), Nov 29, 1958 (div. 1982); children: Kara Anne Kennedy (b. 1960); Edward "Teddy" Moore Kennedy Jr. (b. 1961); Patrick Joseph Kennedy (b. 1967). Ted Kennedy married 2nd wife, Victoria Reggie. ❖ An accomplished pianist who modeled briefly, was active during husband's 1st run for senate (1962); embarked on a glamorous life as wife of a senator and sister-in-law of the president (1963); began feeling like an outsider among the highly competitive Kennedy clan; struck out on her own to successfully narrate "Peter and the Wolf" with National Symphony Washington and several other orchestras; after a number of Kennedy tragedies (1960s–70s), including assassinations, Chappaquiddick, and son's bout with cancer, showed a growing dependence on alcohol for which she eventually sought help. ❖ See also David Lester, *Joan: The Reluctant Kennedy* (Funk, 1974); J. Randy Taraborrelli, *Jackie, Ethel, Joan: Women of Camelot* (Warner, 2000); and *Women in World History.*

KENNEDY, Karol (1932–2004). American pairs skater. Name variations: Karol Kennedy Kucher. Born Feb 14, 1932, in Olympic, Washington; died June 25, 2004, in Seattle; m. Robert Kucher, 1953; children: 2 sons, 4 daughters. ❖ With brother Peter Kennedy, won 5 US National titles (1948–52), 2 North American championships (1949, 1951), a World championship (1950), and a silver medal at Oslo Olympics (1952).

KENNEDY, Kate (1827–1890). American schoolteacher and reformer. Born May 31, 1827, in Gaskinstown, Co. Meath, Ireland; died Mar 18, 1890, in Oakland, CA; dau. of Thomas Kennedy (gentleman farmer) and Eliza King; sister of Katherine Delmar Burke (founder of Miss Burke's School for Girls). ❖ Named principal of North Cosmopolitan Grammar School in San Francisco, CA (1867); objected to fact that pay was equal to that of principal for lower-level school, therefore beginning struggle for "equal pay for equal work"; ran for position of state superintendent of public instruction as Labor candidate (1886); demoted by board of education to principal position at smaller school, and lower salary (1887); sued board and won decision by state supreme court that served as precedent for teacher tenure (1890). Efforts resulted in passage of CA state law requiring parity in pay for men and women in state public school system (1874).

KENNEDY, Kathleen (1920–1948). American socialite. Name variations: Kick; Marchioness of Hartington. Born Kathleen Agnes Kennedy, 1920; died May 13, 1948; dau. of Joseph P. Kennedy (1888–1969, financier) and Rose Fitzgerald Kennedy (1890–1995); m. William "Billy" Cavendish (1917–1944), marquess of Hartington and future duke of Devonshire, May 1944 (died Sept 9, 1944). ❖ The most lively and vivacious of the Kennedy girls, was particularly close to brothers Joseph Kennedy Jr. and John Fitzgerald Kennedy; after London debut (1938), while father was US ambassador to Great Britain, became popular with WWII English society and married eldest son of duke of Devonshire, heir to an enormous estate, against family wishes (he was Protestant); husband was killed by a German sniper just a month after brother Joe Jr. lost his life in plane crash; took up residence in England where she worked with Red Cross until end of war; eased back into society, turning house in Smith Square into salon for such luminaries as Anthony Eden, George Bernard Shaw, and Evelyn Waugh; fell in love with Peter Fitzwilliam, elegant and wealthy aristocrat who was not only Protestant but married; was killed with Fitzwilliam in a private plane crash over Belgium on their way to a holiday weekend getaway. ❖ See also Lynne McTaggart,

Kathleen Kennedy: Her Life and Times (Dial Press, 1983); and *Women in World History.*

KENNEDY, Kathleen (1954—). American film producer. Born Jan 1, 1954, in California; attended Shasta High School in Redding, California; attended San Diego State University; m. Frank Marshall (producer). ❖ Began career at San Diego TV station, KCST; with husband and Steven Spielberg, formed Amblin Entertainment (1981); made producing debut on *E.T.* (1982); served as executive producer on *Gremlins* (1984), *The Goonies* (1985), *Back to the Future* (1985), *Young Sherlock Holmes* (1985), *Who Framed Roger Rabbit?* (1988), *Cape Fear* (1991), *Schindler's List* (1993), *The Lost World: Jurassic Park* (1997), among others; has produced over 65 films; elected interim president of Producers Guild of America (2001). Nominated for Best Picture for *E.T.* (1982), *The Color Purple* (1985), *The Sixth Sense* (1999) and *Seabiscuit* (2003).

KENNEDY, Louise St. John (1950—). Australian architect. Born 1950 in Perth, Australia; attended University of Western Australia; University of Melbourne, BA in architecture, 1978. ❖ The 1st woman appointed to Architects Board of Western Australia, founded practice in Cottesloe, Australia, designing mostly smaller-scale buildings; won Robyn Boyd Award for most outstanding piece of domestic architecture in Australia (1984); designed 24 houses in 8-year period; caused uproar with 1986 design for tearooms jutting out over Mosman Bay but was vindicated; other notable projects include Cribb Residence, Cottesloe (1985), Riseley Square Shopping Center, Applecross (1988), Ledger Residence Additions, Dalkeith (1989), and City Edge Development Commercial Center with 200 residential units, Northbridge (1989).

KENNEDY, Mrs. Ludovic (b. 1926). *See Shearer, Moira.*

KENNEDY, Madge (1890–1987). American actress. Born in Chicago, IL, 1890; died in Woodland Hills, CA, June 9, 1987; dau. of Gordon Kennedy and Carolyn (Warner) Kennedy; m. Harold Bolster; m. William B. Hanley Jr. (radio producer), 1934 (died 1959); no children. ❖ Made professional stage debut in *The Genius* (1910); succeeded Margaret Lawrence as Elsie Darling in *Over Night* (1911); appeared in title role in *Little Miss Brown* (1912), in dual role in *Cornered* (1920), and, most notably, as Poppy McGargle in *Poppy* (1923), with W.C. Fields; recruited from Broadway by Sam Goldwyn (1917), played mainly in demure women in silent movies through 1920s, including *Baby Mine* (1917), *The Fair Pretender* (1918), *Day Dreams* (1919), *Leave It to Susan* (1919), *Strictly Confidential* (1919), *The Purple Highway* (1923) and *Bad Company* (1925); made a strong comeback as a character actress in such films as *The Marrying Kind* (1952), *The Rains of Ranchipur* (1955), *Lust for Life* (1956), *They Shoot Horses, Don't They?* (1969), *The Day of the Locust* (1975) and *Marathon Man* (1976); also appeared on Broadway in *A Very Rich Woman* (1965). ❖ See also *Women in World History.*

KENNEDY, Margaret L. (b. 1892). Irish politician. Born 1892 in Dublin, Ireland. ❖ Took active part in the Rising (1916); was commandant of Dublin City (1919–21); nominated to the Seanad by Taoiseach Éamon de Valera (1938, 1943, 1944).

KENNEDY, Margaret (1896–1967). British novelist, playwright, and critic. Born Margaret Moore Kennedy in London, England, April 23, 1896; died in Adderbury, Oxfordshire, England, July 31, 1967; dau. of Charles Moore Kennedy (barrister) and Elinor (Marwood) Kennedy; attended Cheltenham Ladies' College; received honors degree from Somerville College, Oxford, 1919; m. David Davies (barrister and county court judge), 1925; children: 1 son, 2 daughters, including Julia Birley (novelist). ❖ Published 1st book, *A Century of Revolution* (1922), followed by 1st novel, *The Ladies of Lyndon* (1923); had huge success with 2nd book, *The Constant Nymph*, loosely based on a bohemian circle that surrounded painter Augustus John (1924); collaborated with Basil Dean (1926) on stage dramatization of *Constant Nymph* (there would be 4 film versions); wrote *Red Sky at Morning* (1927, not to be confused with 1971 movie of same name); also enjoyed enormous success with stage play *Escape Me Never*, starring Elisabeth Bergner (1933); suffered from Bell's palsy from 1939 on, but continued to write; also produced several nonfiction works, including *The Outlaws on Parnassus* (1958) and *The Mechanized Muse* (1942). Novel *Troy Chimneys* won James Tait Black Memorial Prize (1953). ❖ See also autobiography, *Where Stands a Winged Sentry;* and *Women in World History.*

KENNEDY, Merna (1908–1944). American actress and dancer. Born Maude Kahler, Sept 7, 1908, in Kankakee, IL; died Dec 20, 1944, of a heart attack in Los Angeles, CA; trained with Ernest Belcher;

m. Busby Berkeley (director-choreographer), 1934 (div. 1935). ❧ Made stage debut as a child ballerina; starred opposite Charlie Chaplin in *The Circus* (1928); other films include *Barnum was Right, Broadway, Wonderbar, The King of Jazz, Easy Millions,* and *Jimmy the Gent;* retired (1934).

KENNEDY, Patricia (b. 1924). *See Lawford, Patricia Kennedy.*

KENNEDY, Rose Fitzgerald (1890–1995). American matriarch. Born in Boston, MA, July 22, 1890; died in Hyannis Port, MA, Jan 22, 1995; dau. of John Francis "Honey Fitz" (politician) and Mary Josephine (Hannon) Fitzgerald; attended Manhattanville College of the Sacred Heart, NY; attended Blumenthal Academy, Valls, the Netherlands; m. Joseph Patrick Kennedy (1888–1969, financier, diplomat, and head of several government commissions), Oct 7, 1914 (died Nov 18, 1969); children: Joseph Kennedy Jr. (1914–1944); John Fitzgerald Kennedy (1917–1963, 35th president of US); Rosemary Kennedy (b. 1918); Kathleen Kennedy (1920–1948); Eunice Kennedy Shriver (b. 1921); Patricia Kennedy Lawford (b. 1924); Robert Francis Kennedy (1925–1968, US senator); Jean Kennedy Smith (b. 1928); Edward "Ted" Kennedy (b. 1932, US senator). ❧ Matriarch of the Kennedy dynasty, lived through the kind of political triumph and numbing tragedy that is usually reserved for classical drama; witnessed 3 of her 9 children elected to US Senate and 1 become the nation's 1st Catholic president; endured death of 1st-born son Joseph Kennedy Jr. and daughter Kathleen Kennedy in plane crashes and saw sons John F. Kennedy and Robert F. Kennedy gunned down by assassins; possessed with an unshakable faith and an iron will, persevered through it all, living to be 104. ❧ See also autobiography *Times to Remember* (Doubleday, 1974); and *Women in World History.*

KENNEDY, Rosemary (1918–2005). American sister of John Fitzgerald Kennedy. Born Rose Marie Kennedy, Sept 13, 1918; died Jan 7, 2005, in Fort Atkinson, WI; 3rd child and eldest dau. of Joseph P. Kennedy (1888–1969, financier) and Rose Fitzgerald Kennedy (1890–1995); sister of John Fitzgerald Kennedy (US president); briefly attended public school; never married; no children. ❧ Though healthy at birth (1918), was slow in developing and by end of 1st grade was diagnosed as mentally disabled; kept home rather than being sent away, began to display disquieting symptoms (1941), regressing in mental skills and having frequent tantrums and convulsive episodes; at suggestion of medical specialists, was lobotomized, a common procedure at the time, but was left in a childlike state by the operation; never having recovered her ability to function on her own, spent her adult life at St. Coletta School in Jefferson, WI (1949–2005). ❧ See also *Women in World History.*

KENNEDY, Suzanne (c. 1955—). American veterinarian. Born c. 1955. ❧ Became veterinarian for National Zoological Park, Washington, DC (1976), the 1st woman vet at a US national zoo; researched fungal diseases of birds.

KENNEDY-FRASER, Marjorie (1857–1930). Scottish singer. Name variations: Marjorie Kennedy. Born 1857 in Perth, Scotland; died in 1930 in Scotland; dau. of David Kennedy (singer); trained with father; m. A.J. Fraser; children: Patuffa Fraser. ❧ Collector, arranger and singer of Gaelic songs, in particular Hebridean folksongs, started studying Gaelic music (1882); took lessons in Gaelic language and developed keen interest in music of Hebrides, traveling to islands to record and write down songs of declining populations; arranged songs for voice, piano and sometimes harp; published *Songs of the Hebrides* which presents 170 traditional songs in 3 volumes (1907, 1917, 1921) and later a 4th; traveled widely, giving lectures and recitals; helped Sir Granville Ransome Bantock with 2-act opera *The Seal Woman* (1924).

KENNELLY, Barbara (1936—). American politician and congressional representative. Born Barbara Bailey in Hartford, CT, July 10, 1936; dau. of John Bailey (politician) and Barbara (Leary) Bailey; Trinity College, Washington, DC, BA in Economics, 1958; graduate of Harvard-Radcliffe School of Business Administration, 1959; Trinity College, MA, 1973; m. James J. Kennelly (lawyer and CT legislator), Sept 26, 1959; children: Eleanor Bride Kennelly; Barbara Leary Kennelly; Louise Moran Kennelly; John Bailey Kennelly. ❧ Entered political arena (1975), when she became a member of Hartford Court of Common Council; served as secretary of state for Connecticut (1979–81); as a Democrat, elected to Congress (1982); was a congressional representative until 1998, the 3rd woman ever appointed to the prestigious Ways and Means Committee; later became 1st woman to serve on Select Committee on Intelligence, and 1st to be appointed Chief Deputy Majority Whip; early in 105th Congress, was reelected for a 2nd term as

vice chair of Democratic Caucus, making her the highest-ranking woman and the 4th-ranking Democrat in the House; decided to forgo a 9th term in Congress to enter the Connecticut gubernatorial race (1997) but was defeated. ❧ See also *Women in World History.*

KENNELLY, Keala (1978—). American surfer. Born Aug 13, 1978, in Kauai, Hawaii. ❧ Won the ASP speciality event in Indonesia; won the WCT Gallaz Women's Pro (2000) and Billabong Pro Teahupoo (2000, 2003).

KENNER, Doris (1941–2000). *See Coley, Doris.*

KENNETT, Margaret Brett (fl. 1723–1725). British travel writer. Born Margaret Brett in England; dau. of an English cleric; m. a man named Kennett. ❧ Traveled with husband to South Carolina where they attempted to establish business; letters to mother published as *An Account of Charles Town in 1725* (1960).

KENNEY, Annie (1879–1953). English trade unionist and militant suffragist. Born in Springhead, near Oldham, Lancashire, England, Sept 13, 1879; died 1953; dau. of Nelson Horatio Kenney and Anne (Wood) Kenney; sister of Jessie Kenney (militant suffragist); m. James Taylor, 1921. ❧ By 10, was working part-time in the Oldham textile mill; at 13, worked full-time; formed a union and organized other unions in other mills; began speaking for the Women's Social and Political Union (WSPU) (1905) and became a dependable lieutenant to Christabel Pankhurst; was arrested and imprisoned numerous times; retired from activism on marriage. ❧ See also memoirs *Memories of a Militant* (1924); and *Women in World History.*

KENNEY, Mary (1864–1943). *See O'Sullivan, Mary Kenney.*

KENNIBREW, Dee Dee (1945—). American singer. Name variations: Dee Dee Kenniebrew; The Crystals. Born Delores Henry in 1945 in Brooklyn, NY. ❧ Helped form girl-group the Crystals (1961), the 1st act signed to Phil Spector's Philles Records; with Crystals, had such hit singles as "There's No Other (Like My Baby)" (1961), "Uptown" (1962), "Da Doo Ron Ron" (1963), and "Then He Kissed Me" (1964); with group, had #1 hit with "He's a Rebel" but it was recorded by session singers the Blossoms, not the Crystals. Albums include *He's a Rebel* (1963) and *The Best of the Crystals* (1992).

KENNY, Alice Annie (1875–1960). New Zealand poet, short-story writer, novelist. Name variations: (pseudonym) Alan Armitage. Born Aug 31, 1875, at Newcastle, New Zealand; died on May 15, 1960, in Auckland; dau. of Thomas Nepean Edward Kenny and Annie (Edgecumbe) Kenny. ❧ After winning story competitions in *Auckland Star* and *New Zealand Graphic* (1890s), began to contribute poems and stories regularly to New Zealand and Australian periodicals; became regular writer for *Triad* and drew attention of Ezra Pound, who was unsuccessful in soliciting work for *Poetry* (1911); poetry, described as lyrical, was often inspired by Gaelic legends; stories were humorous and dealt with New Zealand topics; produced experimental verse play, *Sheila's Child* and novel, *Alan McBretney,* which were serialized; worked as librarian for Paeroa Public Library (1925), while publishing work in numerous periodicals; work appears in anthologies, including *Child Verses from Punch* (1925), *A Treasury of New Zealand Verse,* 2nd ed (1926), and *Kowhai Gold* (1930); after publishing illustrated story and book of children's verse, was commissioned to write junior novels, some for boys under pseudonym Alan Armitage (1940s); wrote plays while in her 80s; member of New Zealand PEN (1946–60). ❧ See also *Dictionary of New Zealand Biography* (Vol. 3).

KENNY, Elizabeth (1880–1952). Australian-born nurse. Name variations: Sister Kenny. Born Elizabeth Kenny, Sept 20, 1880, in Warialda, northwestern Australia; died in Brisbane, Nov 30, 1952; dau. of Michael Kenny and Mary (Moore) Kenny; never married, no children. ❧ Without formal medical training, became known as "Sister" Kenny in WWI and later made a name for herself through her new therapy for polio victims; completed training course as a certified nurse (1911); volunteered for Australian Nursing Service (1915); promoted, despite lack of formal nursing training, to rank of "sister," the title used for the rest of her life (1916); after a worldwide outbreak of polio, opened a clinic in Brisbane, using her unorthodox form of treatment (1934); moved to US, where she 1st introduced her therapy in Minneapolis (1940); named "Woman of the Year" by a NY City newspaper (1942); ranked 2nd after Eleanor Roosevelt in a Gallup poll for "Most Admired Woman in America," a position she continued to hold for the next 9 years (1943). ❧ See also autobiography (with Martha Ostenso) *And They Shall Walk: The Life Story of Sister Elizabeth Kenny* (Dodd, 1943); Victor Cohn, *Sister Kenny:*

The Woman Who Challenged the Doctors (U. of Minnesota Press, 1975); film *Sister Kenny,* starring Rosalind Russell (1946); and *Women in World History.*

KENSINGTON, Baroness of (1891–1975). *See Stocks, Mary Danvers.*

KENT, Allegra (1937—). American ballerina. Born Iris Margo Cohen in Santa Monica, California, Aug 11, 1937; dau. of Harry Herschel Cohen and Shirley (Weissman) Cohen; attended Professional Children's School, NY; briefly attended University of California, Los Angeles, and University of Utah; studied ballet at School of American Ballet; m. Bert Stern (photographer) Feb 28, 1959 (div. 1975); m. Bob Gurney; children: (1st m.) Trista, Susannah, and Bret. ❖ At 18, achieved ballerina status with Balanchine's New York City Ballet and remained a principal there for 3 decades; studied with a variety of teachers, including Bronislava Nijinska, Carmelita Maracci and Maria Befeke; at 13, moved to NY; became a permanent member of New York City Ballet (1953) and gained 1st public notice with the Viola *pas des deux* in *Fanfare* (1954); danced a leading role in *Divertimento No. 15* in Stratford, CT (1956); gaining status as a full-fledged ballerina, danced solo roles in *Serenade, Souvenirs* and *Western Symphone;* also performed in *Valse Fantasy, Interplay, Concerto Barocco, Symphony in C* and *Pastorale* (1957); appeared in Broadway musical *Shinbone Alley* (1957), then returned to New York Ballet, dancing memorably as the Countess in *The Unicorn, the Dragon and the Manticore,* and *Afternoon of a Faun;* continued to expand repertoire with performances as the Swan Queen in *Swan Lake,* the novice in *The Cage,* leader of the Bacchantes in *Orpheus,* Terpsichore in *Appolo,* and the *pas de deux* in *Agon;* reached zenith of career as Annie II in *The Seven Deadly Sins* (1959); created another memorable portrayal as the Sleepwalker in *La Sonnambula* (1960); won acclaim in *Bugaku, The Chase* (1963), and *Sylvia Divertissement* (1965); retired from New York City Ballet (1982); became director of a ballet school in Stamford, CT; appeared as Cousin Ophelia in film *The Addams Family.* ❖ See also autobiography *Once a Dancer. . . .* (St. Martin, 1997); and *Women in World History.*

KENT, Barbara (b. 1906). Canadian-born screen actress. Born Barbara Klowtman, Dec 16, 1906, in Gadsby, Alberta, Canada. ❖ Starred in late silents and early talkies, including *Prowlers of the Night, Flesh and the Devil, The Lone Eagle, Modern Mothers, The Shakedown, Night Ride, What Men Want, Feet First, Indiscreet, Emma, Vanity Fair, Oliver Twist, Marriage on Approval* and *Under Age.*

KENT, Constance (1844–?). English murderer. Born 1844; dau. of Samuel Kent (carpet manufacturer) and Mary Ann (Windus) Kent (died 1852). ❖ Involved in one of the most shocking murders of the Victorian era (1860); was an intelligent, demure schoolgirl of 16 when she killed her 3-year-old half-brother; covered up crime for a period of 4 years, then confessed; was condemned to death (1865), though the sentence was commuted to life imprisonment and she served 20 years; immigrated to Canada, where she was believed to have become a nurse. ❖ See also *Women in World History.*

KENT, countess of.
See Gytha (fl. 1022–1042).
See Joan of Kent (1328–1385).
See Fitzalan, Alice (1352–1416).
See Percy, Katherine (b. 1423).
See Grey, Elizabeth (1581–1651).

KENT, duchess of.
See Margaret de Burgh (c. 1193–1259).
See Margaret Wake of Liddell (c. 1299–1349).
See Constance (c. 1374–1416).
See Victoria of Coburg (1786–1861).
See Marina of Greece (1906–1968).
See Worsley, Katherine (b. 1933).

KENT, Fair Maid of. *See Joan of Kent (1328–1385).*

KENT, Jean (1921—). English stage and screen actress. Name variations: Jean Carr, Joan Kent. Born Joan Summerfield, June 21, 1921, in London, England; m. Josef Ramart (actor), 1946 (died 1989). ❖ At 11, made stage debut as a dancer; made film debut in *Rock of Valpre* (1935), followed by *Hullo Fame, Fanny by Gaslight, 2000 Women, Champagne Charlie, Madonna of the Seven Moons, Waterloo Road, Carnival, Bond Street, The Browning Version, The Prince and the Showgirl, Bonjour Tristesse* and *Shout at the Devil,* among others.

KENT, Joan (1921—). *See Kent, Jean.*

KENT, Leslie (1981—). American wakeboarder. Born Sept 4, 1981, in Winter Park, FL. ❖ Won bronze in Wakeboarding at X Games (Summer 2002) and bronze in Wakeboarding at Gravity Games (2003); other finishes include 4th in Wakeboarding at X Games (Summer 2001); year-end rankings include 4th at World Cup in Freeride (2000), 4th at Pro Wakeboard Tour in Freeride (2000), and 5th at Vans Triple Crown in Freeride (2001).

KENT, Linda (1946—). American modern dancer. Born Sept 21, 1946, in Buffalo, NY; trained at Jacob's Pillow (1963) and at Juilliard School with José Limón and Thelma Hill. ❖ Joined Alvin Ailey Dance Theater (1968), where she created roles in his *Quintet* (1968), *Threnodies* (1969), *The Lark Ascending* (1972), and performed in his *Blues Suite, Revelations,* and *Choral Dancers,* as well as in works by Pearl Primus, Talley Beatty, and Pauline Kroner; joined Paul Taylor Dance Co. (1975), where she danced in *Three Epitaphs, Private Domain, Esplanades,* among others.

KENT, maid of.
See Joan of Kent (1328–1385).
See Barton, Elizabeth (c. 1506–1534).
See Marchant, Bessie (1862–1941).

KENT, nun of. *See Barton, Elizabeth (c. 1506–1534).*

KENT, queen of.
See Bertha of Kent (c. 565–c. 616).
See Redburga (fl. 825).
See Sexburga, Saint (d. 699?).

KENT, Thelma Rene (1899–1946). New Zealand photographer. Born Oct 21, 1899, in Christchurch, New Zealand; died June 23, 1945, in Christchurch; dau. of John Robert Kent (bootmaker) and Catherine Maude (Hales) Kent. ❖ Recognized for her award-winning photographs of New Zealand landscape, which were exhibited and published internationally; contributed articles and illustrations in *Auckland Weekly News* and *New Zealand Railways Magazine;* member of Christchurch Photographic Society and made associate member of Royal Photographic Society of Great Britain; elected fellow of Royal Society of Arts, London (1939). ❖ See also *Dictionary of New Zealand Biography* (Vol. 4).

KENT, Victoria (1898–1987). Spanish lawyer and politician. Name variations: Victoria Kent y Siano. Born in Málaga, Spain, in 1898; died in New York, NY, Sept 27, 1987; studied law at University of Madrid. ❖ Gained national prominence when she acted as defense lawyer for one of the accused officers who had led the Jaca military uprising against Spanish monarchy (late 1930), the 1st woman to argue before Spanish Royal Tribunal of Law; following abdication of Alphonso XIII and proclamation of 2nd Republic (1931), stood as a candidate of Radical Socialist Party and was elected to Cortes to represent Madrid; introduced several initiatives to make Spanish prisons more humane; when Spanish Civil War erupted (1936), sided with Republicans against Nationalists and Francisco Franco; spent part of war in Paris, aiding Republican refugees who fled Spain; at war's end, moved to Mexico and taught law there; immigrated to US (1950); worked for UN and founded anti-Franco political journal, *Ibérica,* which she edited for 2 decades. Awarded Grand Cross of the Order of San Raimundo of Peñafort by King Juan Carlos. ❖ See also memoir (in Spanish) *Cuatro años de mi vida* (Barcelona: Bruguera, 1978).

KENWORTHY, Marion E. (c. 1891–1980). American psychiatrist. Born c. 1891 in Hampden, MA; died June 26, 1980, in NY, NY. ❖ Known as "mother of psychiatric social work," was the 1st woman physician at Gardner State Colony for Chronic Mental Patients (MA); became 1st director of the initial mental hygiene clinic of YWCA (1919); became the 1st woman professor of psychiatry at Columbia University (NY, 1930); was the 1st woman elected president of American Psychoanalytic Association (1958). The Marion E. Kenworthy Chair in Psychiatry at Columbia's School of Social Work was established by friends, colleagues and former students.

KENYATTA, Margaret (1928—). Kenyan activist and politician. Born Margaret Wambui Kenyatta in Nairobi, Kenya, 1928; only daughter of Jomo Kenyatta (1891–1978, nationalist, politician, and 1st president of Kenya) and his 1st wife, Nyokabi; attended Church of Scotland Mission School, Kikuyu, and Alliance High School; never married; no children. ❖ While father served a 7-year prison term for involvement with the Mau Mau, became active in Peoples Congress Party, which worked for African rights and release of political prisoners; also joined social welfare leagues, including Maendeleo ya Wanawake, one of Kenya's most important women's organizations; when father was released and became head of Kenya African National Union (KANU, 1959), served as assistant secretary of party and later as secretary of KANU branch at Kiambu; when father became prime minister, then president, joined his efforts to build a unified nation, working particularly to interest women in political activism; was elected a councilor for Dagoretti in city council of Nairobi (1963); reelected for 4 subsequent terms, continued efforts to unify women in a quest for equality, utilizing contacts with international movements; became president of National Council of Women of Kenya (1964) and began to travel widely, addressing conferences throughout world on women's roles in nation-building; elected deputy mayor of Nairobi (1969), then mayor (1971), the 1st African woman to become mayor of Kenya's capital city and 2nd African woman mayor in nation; her tenure was marked by many developmental programs, including expansion of subways, building of low-cost housing and sewerage, and expansion of public health facilities. Awarded Order of Queen of Sheba by Emperor Haile Selassie of Ethiopia (1964).

KENYON, Doris (1897–1979). American actress. Born in Syracuse, NY, Sept 5, 1897; died Sept 1, 1979, in Beverly Hills, CA; dau. of a cleric-poet; spent 2 years in Europe studying with Yvette Guilbert; m. Milton Sills (actor), 1926 (died 1930); m. Arthur Hopkins, 1933 (annulled 1934), m. Albert David Lasker, 1938 (div. 1939); m. Bronislaw Mylnarski (music expert) 1947 (died 1971); children: (1st m.) Kenyon Sills (1927–1971). ❖ At 18, made stage debut; moved on to silent films, starring as a flighty ingenue, then made successful transition to more mature parts in talkies; also continued Broadway career; films include *The Rack* (1915), *The Bandbox* (1919), *Shadows of the Sea* (1922), *Bright Lights of Broadway* (1923), *Men of Steel* (1925), *The Valley of the Giants* (1927), *Road to Singapore* (1931), *Whom the God's Destroy* (1934), and *Monsieur Beaucaire*; with cultured voice and aristocratic demeanor, also took on biographical roles, appearing as Betsey Hamilton (Elizabeth Schuyler Hamilton) in *Alexander Hamilton* (1931), Madame Pompadour in *Voltaire* (1933) and Queen Anne in *The Man in the Iron Mask* (1939); following retirement from films, sang and toured for USO during WWII.

KENYON, Dorothy (1888–1972). American lawyer, feminist, judge, and civil libertarian. Born Feb 17, 1888, in New York, NY; died Feb 11, 1972 (some sources erroneously cite Feb 12), in New York, NY; dau. of William Houston Kenyon (patent lawyer) and Maria Wellington (Stanwood) Kenyon; Smith College, AB in economics, 1908; graduate of New York University Law School, 1917. ❖ Passed NY Bar (1917) and spent majority of 54-year career in independent practice; was 1 of 1st women admitted to NYC Bar Association (1937); an ardent advocate of liberal causes, supported suffragist and birth-control movements, and sat on national board of directors of American Civil Liberties Union; active in NYC politics as well, served on committees for American Labor Party, worked against Tammany Hall political machine, and was appointed 1st deputy commissioner of licenses (1936) and a municipal court judge (1939); served on several public commissions, including ones that dealt with issues of relief, minimum wage, public housing, and court procedures for women, as well as being a founder and director of numerous consumer corporations and serving as legal counsel for Cooperative League of US; appointed by council of League of Nations to be 1 of 7 jurists forming a committee to study legal status of women throughout world (1938); was US delegate to UN Commission on the Status of Women (1946–50); career was derailed when she was accused by Senator Joseph McCarthy of membership in Communist-front organizations (1950), though she vehemently refuted the charge; was active in feminist movement and civil-rights movement (1960s). ❖ See also *Women in World History.*

KENYON, Kathleen (1906–1978). British archaeologist. Name variations: Dame Kathleen Kenyon. Born Kathleen Mary Kenyon, Jan 5, 1906, in London, England; died Aug 24, 1978, in Erbistock, Wales; dau. of Sir Frederic George Kenyon (director of British Museum) and Amy (Hunt) Kenyon; graduate of Somerville College, Oxford, 1928; awarded MA, DLitt, DLit, LHD; never married; no children. ❖ One of the most productive and controversial British archaeologists of the 20th-century, pioneered modern field methodology and contributed to understanding of the role of the city in the growth of civilization; began career as an archaeologist by joining the British Association's expedition to Southern Rhodesia (1929); excavated at Verulamium as part of Sir Mortimer and Tessa Wheeler's team (1930–35); participated in the Crowfoot expedition to Samaria (1931–34); helped found University of London Institute of Archaeology (1937); was acting director of same

(1942–46); served as secretary of Council for British Archaeology (1944–49); excavated Roman town of Sabratha (1948, 1949, 1951); was director of British School of Archaeology in Jerusalem (1951–66); excavated at Jericho (1952–58), then Jerusalem (1961–67); served as principal of St. Hugh's College, Oxford (1962–73); served as chair of Council of the British School of Archaeology in Jerusalem (1967–78). Created CBE (1954); created Dame of the British Empire (1973); was a fellow of British Academy and fellow of Society of Antiquaries. ❖ See also memoir *Digging Up Jericho* (Benn, 1957); and *Women in World History.*

KEOGH, Helen (1951—). Irish politician. Born June 1951 in Dublin, Ireland; m. Paddy Hayes. ❖ Served in the Seanad (1989–92); representing Progressive Democrats, elected to the 27th Dáil (1992–97) for Dún Laoghaire; was one of the Taoiseach's nominees to the Seanad (1997); left the Progressive Democrats to join Fine Gael (2000).

KEOGH, Lesbia (1891–1927). *See Harford, Lesbia.*

KEOHANE, Nannerl (1940—). American political scientist and educator. Born Nannerl Overholser, Sept 18, 1940, in Blytheville, Arkansas; dau. of James Arthur and Grace (McSpadden) Overholser; Wellesley College, BA, 1961; Yale University, PhD, 1967; m. Patrick Henry III, 1962 (div. 1969); m. Robert Owen Keohane, 1970; children: (1st m.) Stephan; (2nd m.) Sarah, Jonathan and Nathaniel. ❖ Was on faculty at Swarthmore College (1967–73) and Stanford U. (1973–81); was a fellow at Center for Advanced Study in the Behavioral Sciences (1978–79, 1987–88); served as president and professor of political science at Wellesley (1981–83), then Duke University (1993–2005); became a fellow of Harvard College (2005); wrote *Philosophy and the State in France* (1980); co-edited *Feminist Theory: A Critique of Ideology* (1982). Inducted into National Women;s Hall of Fame (1995).

KEOPUOLANI (c. 1778–1823). Sacred chiefess of Hawaii. Name variations: Keopulani. Born to parents who were half brother and sister of high rank c. 1778; died Sept 16, 1823; raised by grandmother Kalola; became 1st wife of Kamehameha I the Great (1758–1819), king of Hawaii (r. 1810–1819), c. 1795; children: Liholiho (1797–1824), later known as Kamehameha II, king of Hawaii (r. 1819–1824); Kauikeaouli (1814–1854), later known as Kamehameha III, king of Hawaii (r. 1824–1854); Princess Nahienaena (c. 1815–1836). ❖ The mother of kings, was born of high rank, making her a prime bridal candidate for Kamehameha I when still a teen; a woman of power, like Kamehameha's chief wife Kaahumanu, also rebelled against the old ways; when daughter was born, kept her near, rather than hand her over to another chief to raise, as was the custom; on day after husband's death (1819), broke another taboo by sitting down with the chiefs for a meal; approved of the work of the missionaries and had her 2 younger children learn to read and write; began to don Western clothes and study Christianity.

KEPHALA, Antigone (1935—). *See Kefala, Antigone.*

KEPHALIA, Niki (1925—). *See Goulandris, Niki.*

KEPPEL, Alice (1869–1947). English aristocrat and paramour. Name variations: Alice Edmonstone; Mrs. George Keppel. Born Alice Frederica Edmonstone, 1869, in Stirlingshire, Scotland; died Sept 11, 1947, in Florence, Italy; youngest dau. of Admiral William Edmonstone and Mary (Parsons) Edmonstone (d. 1902); great-grandmother of Camilla Parker-Bowles (b. 1949); m. George Keppel (1865–1947, army officer and brother of earl of Albemarle), June 1, 1891; paramour of Charles Windsor, prince of Wales, the future King Edward VII; children: (paternity uncertain) Violet Keppel Trefusis (1894–1972), Sonia Rosemary Keppel (1900–1986); and others. ❖ Was best known for being the mistress of Edward VII, king of England; described as humorous and charming, but with a shrewd intelligence and a keen grasp of British politics and economic events, met the Prince of Wales in 1898 (he was 57, she 29); began a romantic relationship which lasted beyond his accession (1901) until his death (1910); attended social functions with him while the queen, Alexandra of Denmark, welcomed the arrangement, preferring a quiet home life to the constant parties, social engagements, and outdoor activities enjoyed by her husband; a kind woman, became a friend and ally of Alexandra and had a positive influence over Edward; was known to have smoothed over 1 or 2 diplomatic matters and to have acted as an intermediary between the king and the Liberal regime of Prime Minister Sir Herbert Asquith. ❖ See also Diana Souhami, *Mrs. Keppel and Her Daughter* (St. Martin, 1996); and *Women in World History.*

KEPPEL, Mrs. George (1869–1947). *See Keppel, Alice.*

KEPPEL, Violet (1894–1972). See Trefusis, Violet.

KEPPELHOFF-WIECHERT, Hedwig (1939—). German politician. Born May 31, 1939, in Südlohn, Germany. ❖ Member of Christian Democrat Union (CDU) district executive (1981—) and land executive (1989–96); served as president of the German Rural Women's Association (1987–98); as a member of the European People's Party (Christian Democrats) and European Democrats, elected to 4th and 5th European Parliament (1994–99, 1999–2004). Awarded Federal Cross of Merit.

KEPPLER-ELLIOTT, Mme (1811–1882). See Celeste, Madame.

KEQING KANG (1911–1992). See Kang Keqing.

KER-SEYMER, Barbara (b. 1905). British photographer. Born 1905, probably in England; studied painting at Royal College of Art and Slade School of Art, London, mid-1920s. ❖ One of a number of innovative British women photographers, apprenticed with Olivia Wyndham; was contracted by *Harper's Bazaar* to photograph celebrities as well as people in the news (1931), and later moved on to do fashion work with the Colman-Prentice agency; strongly influenced by German cinema and book *Köpfe des Alltags* (*Everyday Faces*) by Helmar Lerski, was known for her experimentation with poses and lighting; her style is most clearly defined by portraits she did of friends Nancy Cunard, Frederick Ashton, Raymond Mortimer, Nancy Moore, David Garnett, and Eddie Sackville-West, among others; at outbreak of WWII, abandoned photography and joined Larkin and Co. to make instructional films for the armed services. ❖ See also *Women in World History*.

KÉRALIO, Louise Félicité de (1758–1821). See Robert-Kéralio, Louise.

KERCKHOVEN, Catherine (d. 1667). See Kirkhoven, Catherine.

KERENHAPPUCH (fl. 2000 BCE). Biblical woman. Name variations: Keren-Happuch. Youngest of Job's 3 daughters; sister of Jemima and Keziah. ❖ Was probably born after Job's restoration to health and prosperity.

KERIMA (1925—). Algerian actress. Born in Algiers, Algeria, Feb 10, 1925. ❖ Exotic actress, played leads and supporting roles in international films (1950s–60s); made screen debut in British film *An Outcast of the Islands* (1951), directed by Sir Carol Reed, which is now considered her most memorable role; other films include *La Lupa* (*The She Wolf*, 1952), *La Nave delle Donne Maledette* (*The Ship of Condemned Women*, 1953), *Cavalleria Rusticana* (1953), *Tam Tam Mayumbe* (1955), *Land of the Pharaohs* (1955), *Fuga nel Sole* (1956), *The Quiet American* (1958), *Il Mondo dei Miracoli* (1959) and *Jessica* (1962).

KERMER, Romy (1956—). East German pairs skater. Born June 28, 1956 in Chemnitz. ❖ With partner Rolf Österreich, won silver medals at World championships (1975, 1976); won a silver medal at Innsbruck Olympics (1976).

KERNOHAN, Liz (1939–2004). Australian politician. Born Elizabeth Anne Kernohan, June 24, 1939, in Glebe, Australia; died Nov 2004; dau. of John and Betty Kernohan; University of Sydney, BSc, 1960, MSc in Agriculture, 1970, PhD, 1978; never married. ❖ As an agricultural scientist, served as director of University of Sydney Farms; held public office for more than 30 years; elected alderman of Camden Municipal Council (1973), became deputy mayor (1974), and mayor (1980); served as mayor for 7 terms (1980–91); as a Liberal, won election to the State Parliament (1991), representing Camden, and served until 2003. Made a Member of the Order of Australia (2004).

KERNS, Daniel R. (1942—). See Lichtenberg, Jacqueline.

KÉROÜALLE, Louise de (1649–1734). Duchess of Portsmouth and Aubigny and mistress of Charles II. Name variations: Louise de Keroualle or Kerouaille, Duchess of Portsmouth; Louise de Querouille or Louise de Querouaille; (in France) variously spelled Queroul, Kéroual and Kéroël. Born Louise Renné in 1649 (some sources cite 1650) in Brittany; died 1734; dau. of Guillaume de Penancourt and Marie de Plaeuc de Timeur; mistress of Charles II, king of England (r. 1649–1685); children: (with Charles II) Charles Lennox (1672–1723), duke of Richmond. ❖ Early in life, was placed in the household of Henrietta Anne, duchess of Orléans, who was the sister of England's king Charles II and sister-in-law of France's king Louis XIV; accompanied the duchess on a visit to Charles II at Dover (1670); when the duchess died suddenly, was placed by the king among the ladies-in-waiting of his queen Catherine of Braganza; established a strong hold on the king's affections; having concealed her wit and strong will under an appearance of weakness, showed her true colors and began to dominate Charles; unpopular with the populace, returned to France following his death and lived beleaguered by debt. ❖ See also H. Forneron, *Louise de Kéroualle* (Paris, 1886); and *Women in World History*.

KERR, Anita (1927—). American singer, pianist, and musical arranger. Born Anita Jean Grilli, Oct 31, 1927, in Memphis, TN; m. 2nd husband, Alex Grob. ❖ Major contributor to Nashville country-pop sound (1960s), performed on mother's Memphis radio show as a child; formed Anita Kerr Singers (1949), which debuted on Red Foley recording "Our Lady of Fatima" (1950) and made later appearances at Grand Ole Opry; provided arrangements and back-up for such country-pop singers as Jim Reeves ("He'll Have to Go" and "Welcome to My World"), Skeeter Davis ("End of the World"), and Bobby Bare ("Detroit City"); led Anita Kerr Quartet, including Gil Wright (tenor), Dottie Dillard (alto), and Louis Nunley (baritone); did orchestral arrangement for RCA; made charts with LPs *The Anita Kerr Singers Reflect on the Music of Burt Bacharach and Hal David* and *Velvet Voices and Bold Brass;* also wrote instrumental music for several poetry albums by Rod McKuen; formed another singing group, Mexicali Singers. ❖ See also *Women in World History*.

KERR, Deborah (1921—). English actress. Born Deborah Jane Kerr-Trimmer in Helensburgh, Scotland, Sept 30, 1921; grew up in England; only dau. of Arthur Kerr-Trimmer (civil engineer and architect); granted scholarship to Sadler's Wells ballet school (1938); m. Anthony Charles Bartley (aviator), Nov 28, 1945 (div. 1959); m. Peter Viertel (writer), 1959; children: (1st m.) Melanie Jane Bartley and Francesca Bartley. ❖ Made London stage debut (1939), and West End debut (1940) in *Heartbreak House*; during WWII, won small film role in *Major Barbara* (1941), followed by *Love on the Dole, Hatter's Castle* and *The Life and Death of Colonel Blimp*; by war's end, was fully established as a major figure in British film and theater; performance in *Black Narcissus* brought her to attention of Hollywood; made US film debut in *The Hucksters* (1947), followed by *If Winter Comes* (1948) and *Edward, My Son* (1949); adorned a long succession of historical epics, including *Quo Vadis* (1951), *Young Bess* (1952), and *Julius Caesar* (1953); fought against demure roles, landing part of adulterous officer's wife in *From Here to Eternity* (1953); appeared on Broadway in *Tea and Sympathy* (1953); other films include *The End of the Affair* (1955), the classic *An Affair to Remember* (1957), *The Innocents* (1961), *Night of the Iguana* (1964) and *The Arrangement* (1969); took 15-year hiatus from film; returned to stage in England and US and enjoyed a long series of acclaimed performances, including a 9-month London run with *The Day After the Fair* (1972) and a run in *Seascape* on Broadway; returned to sporadic filming (1984). Nominated for Academy Award as Best Actress a record-breaking 6 times (without winning), for *Edward My Son, The King and I, Heaven Knows Mr. Allison, From Here to Eternity, Separate Tables* and *The Sundowners;* received honorary Academy Award (1994). ❖ See also Eric Braun, *Deborah Kerr* (1977); and *Women in World History*.

KERR, Jane (1968—). Canadian swimmer. Born May 12, 1968, in Canada. ❖ At Seoul Olympics, won a bronze medal in 4 x 100-meter medley relay (1988).

KERR, Jean (1923–2003). American playwright and humorist. Born Jean Collins, July 10, 1923, in Scranton, Pennsylvania; died Jan 5, 2003, in White Plains, NY; dau. of Thomas J. Collins (construction engineer) and Kitty (O'Neill) Collins; Marywood College, BA, 1943; Catholic University of America, MFA, 1945; m. Walter Kerr (drama critic of *New York Herald Tribune*), Aug 9, 1943; children: Christopher; (twins) Colin and John; Gilbert, Gregory and Katharine Kerr. ❖ With husband, adapted 1st play from Franz Werfel's *The Song of Bernadette* which ran for 3 performances (1946); wrote 1st solo comedy, *Jenny Kissed Me* (1948), which ran for 20; collaborated with husband on revue *Touch and Go* (1949) and with Eleanor Brooke for *King of Hearts* (1954); published 1st book *Please Don't Eat the Daisies* (1957), an autobiographical collection of comic sketches on domestic life, which topped nonfiction bestseller list for 20 weeks (the book would spawn a movie with Doris Day [1960], and tv series); had biggest stage hit with *Mary, Mary* (1961), followed by *Finishing Touches* (1973) and *Lunch Hour* (1980); other books include *The Snake Has All the Lines* (1960), *Penny Candy* (1970) and *How I Got to Be Perfect* (1978). ❖ See also *Women in World History*.

KERR, M.E. (1927—). See Meaker, Marijane.

KERR, Sophie (1880–1965). American novelist, short-story writer, and editor. Name variations: Mrs. Sophie Kerr Underwood. Born in Denton,

MD, Aug 23, 1880; died 1965; dau. of Jonathan Williams Kerr and Amanda Catherine (Sisk) Kerr; Hood College, BA, 1898; University of Vermont, MA, 1901; m. John D. Underwood, Sept 6, 1904 (div. 1908). ❖ Was women's editor of Pittsburgh *Chronicle-Telegraph* and *Gazette Times* and managing editor of *Woman's Home Companion* for several years; writings include *Love at Large* (1916), *The Blue Envelope* (1917), *Painted Meadows* (1920), *Confetti* (1927), *Mareea-Maria* (1929), *Stay Out of My Life* (1933), (play, with A.S. Richardson) *Big-Hearted Herbert* (1934), *Miss J. Looks On* (1935), *Curtain Going Up* (1940) and *Michael's Girl* (1942).

KERR-FISHER, Dehra (1882–1963). *See Parker, Dehra.*

KERRIGAN, Nancy (1969—). American figure skater. Born Oct 13, 1969, in Woburn, MA; m. Jerry Solomon, 1995; children: Matthew. ❖ At US nationals, placed 3rd (1991), 2nd (1992), 1st (1993), but had to withdraw from injury (1994), when henchmen of Tonya Harding clubbed her on the knee; at World championships, won a bronze medal (1991) and a silver medal (1992); won Nations Cup (1991); won a bronze medal at Albertville Olympics (1992) and a silver medal at Lillehammer Olympics (1994); placed 3rd at Goodwill Games (2000).

KERSAINT, Claire (1777–1828). *See Duras, Claire de.*

KERSEE, Jackie Joyner (b. 1962). *See Joyner-Kersee, Jackie.*

KERSHAW, Willette (1890–1960). American actress. Born June 17, 1882, in Clifton Heights, Missouri; died May 4, 1960, in Honolulu, Hawaii; sister of Alice Kershaw (actress, Mrs. Thomas Ince); m. David Sturgis (div.). ❖ Made stage debut as a child in St. Louis (1901); made NY debut as a page in *L'Aiglon*, starring Sarah Bernhardt (1901); replaced Laura Hope Crews in lead in *Brown of Harvard;* other plays include *The Country Boy, Fancy Free, The Unchastened Woman, Hari-Kari, King Henry VIII* and *The Crowded Hour;* had much success in London as well as Paris, where she had her own company and produced *The Well of Loneliness* and *Maya* (1929); films include *The Vortex.*

KERSTEN, Anita (1931—). *See Ekberg, Anita.*

KERSTEN, Dagmar (1970—). East German gymnast. Born Oct 28, 1970, in Cottbus, Germany; m. Peter Heinowski. ❖ Won DTB Cup (1985), GDR nationals (1987, 1988); at European championships, won a bronze medal for vault (1985); at World championships, won a silver medal for uneven bars, and bronze medals for all-around, team all-around and vault (1985); at Seoul Olympics, won a bronze medal in team all-around and a silver medal in uneven bars (1988).

KERTESZ, Aliz (1935—). Hungarian gymnast. Born Nov 17, 1935, in Hungary. ❖ At Melbourne Olympics, won a silver medal in team all-around and a gold medal in teams all-around, portable apparatus (1956).

KERY, Aniko (1956—). Hungarian gymnast. Born Mar 31, 1956, in Hungary. ❖ At Munich Olympics, won a bronze medal in team all-around (1972).

KESHKO, Nathalia (1859–1941). *See Nathalia Keshko.*

KESSLER, Margot (1948—). German politician. Born Sept 8, 1948, in Kehmstedt, Germany. ❖ Served as justice of the peace at the administrative court of Weimar (1994–99); as a European Socialist, elected to 5th European Parliament (1999–2004).

KESSLER, Romi (1963—). Swiss gymnast. Born Feb 20, 1963, in Wald, Switzerland. ❖ Won Coupe de Geneve (1979), Swiss nationals (1980); won a gold medal for uneven bars at Hungarian International (1983); placed 9th all-around at Los Angeles Olympics (1984).

KESTNER, Charlotte (1753–1828). *See Buff, Charlotte.*

KÉTHLY, Anna (1889–1976). Hungarian politician and revolutionary. Name variations: Anna Kethly. Born in Budapest, Hungary, 1889; died in Blankenberg, Belgium, Sept 1976. ❖ Hungarian Social Democratic leader for more than half a century, became an active member of the Social Democratic Party (SDP) early on; drawn to journalism, also became involved in feminist and trade-union activities; by 1920, had become head of the Women's Secretariat of SDP and was elected to Parliament (1922), serving as the only woman in that body until 1937; edited journal *The Female Worker* (1926–38); following WWII, was returned to her old seat in Parliament and within months was elected deputy speaker of Hungarian Legislative Assembly (1945); along with a number of other Social Democrats who had refused to accept the Communist dictatorship, was arrested and sentenced to life imprisonment at hard labor (June 1950), but international protests on her behalf

eventually hastened her release (Nov 1954); was a major force in the Hungarian revolution, serving as minister of state in short-lived government of Imre Nagy that was overthrown by Soviet troops (1956); lived the remainder of her life in exile. ❖ See also *Women in World History.*

KETTLE, Alice (fl. 1324). *See Kyteler, Alice.*

KETURAH (fl. 3rd, 2nd, or 1st c. BCE). Biblical woman. Fl. in 3rd, 2nd, or 1st century BCE; m. Abraham also known as Abrahim ("father of a multitude"), although his original name appears to have been Abram ("exalted father"); children—six sons: Zimran, Jokshan, Medan, Midian, Ishbak, and Shuah. ❖ Married Abraham, the 1st great patriarch of the nation of Israel, after his wife Sarah's death; has also been called Abraham's concubine; had 6 sons, all of whom were the founders of 6 Arabian Tribes in Palestine.

KEULEN, Atje (1938—). *See Deelstra, Atje.*

KEUN, Irmgard (1905–1982). West German novelist. Name variations: (pseudonym) Charlotte Tralow. Born Feb 6, 1905, in Berlin, Germany; died May 5, 1982, in Cologne, Germany; dau. of Eduard Ferdinand Keun. ❖ Published *Gilgi—eine von uns* (*Gilgi—One of Us*, 1931), followed by *Das kuntseidene Mädchen* (*The Artificial Silk Girl*, 1932), which was a bestseller. Wrote of young, petit-bourgeois women searching for independence during the Weimar era and early years of the Nazi movement; after her books were banned by Nazis, went into exile (1936) and published *Nach Mitternacht* (*After Midnight*, 1937) and *D-Zug dritter Klasse* (*On a Railroad to Nowhere*, 1937), among others; though an antifascist, returned to the Third Reich and as a result has remained a controversial figure ever since; after the war, wrote under pseudonym Charlotte Tralow to modest success, until her early works were rediscovered.

KEUR, Dorothy (1904–1989). American cultural anthropologist. Name variations: Dorothy Louise Strouse Keur. Born Dorothy Louise Strouse on Feb 13, 1904, in New York, NY; died Mar 22, 1989; graduate of Hunter College, 1925; Columbia University, AM, 1928, Ph.D., 1941; m. John Y. Keur, 1928. ❖ Studied under Leslie Spier, Edward Sapir, and Franz Boas at Columbia; performed archaeological work at Big Bead Mesa (northeast of Santa Fe, NM) and fieldwork in Gobernador area; became known for Navajo archaeology; appointed assistant professor (1940), associate professor (1947), and professor (1957) at Hunter College; with husband, conducted fieldwork at village of Anderen in the Netherlands (1951–52) and published *The Deeply Rooted* (1955); with husband, studied Dutch Windward Islands of St. Maarten, Saba, and St. Eustatius (beginning 1956), and published *Windward Children* (1960); served as secretary-treasurer (1947–49) and president (1955) of American Ethnological Society; coauthored oral-history project with Ruth Staunton, *Jerkline to Jeep: A Brief History of the Upper Boulder* (1975).

KEVLIAN, Valentina (1980—). Bulgarian rhythmic gymnast. Name variations: Walentina or Valintina Kevliyan. Born Mar 11, 1980, in Bulgaria. ❖ Won a silver medal for team all-around at Atlanta Olympics (1996).

KEY, Dottie Ferguson (1923–2003). *See Ferguson, Dottie.*

KEY, Ellen (1849–1926). Swedish teacher, writer, lecturer, and feminist. Born Ellen Carolina Sophia Key, Dec 11, 1849, at Sundsholm (father's estate), in Småland, southern Sweden; died April 25, 1926, at Strand, Ostergotland; dau. of Emil Key (politician) and Sophie (Posse) Key (dau. of noble family); completed 3 years of study at Jenny Rossander's Teaching Course for Ladies in Stockholm, 1872; never married; no children. ❖ Began contributing to *Tidskrift for Hemmet* (The Home Journal), a magazine which advocated the liberation of women, writing book reviews, translations, and biographical sketches of English writers (1870s); functioned as secretary and housekeeper to father, an Agrarian party member of Swedish Parliament; when family suffered financial reversal, was employed as teacher in Anna Whitlock's private school for girls; also became lecturer on Swedish civilization at People's Institute, where she would spend 20 years speaking to audiences of working-class men and women; retired from teaching to devote herself to writing and lecturing (1903); traveled and lectured abroad, particularly in Germany; a figure of controversy, devoted most of her attention to 3 major issues—the need for a new and free relationship between men and women, the importance of motherhood, and the demand for a new educational system; was a pacifist during WWI; writings include (in English translation) *Love and Ethics, Love and Marriage, The Woman Movement, The Century of the Child, The Renaissance of Motherhood, War, Peace and the*

Future and *Rahel Varnhagen*. ❖ See also Louise Nystrom-Hamilton, *Ellen Key: Her Life and Work* (Putnam, 1913); and *Women in World History*.

KEYES, Evelyn (1919—). American screen actress and writer. Born Nov 20, 1919, in Port Arthur, TX; m. Barton Bainbridge, 1938 (died 1940); m. Charles Vidor (director), 1943 (div. 1945); m. John Huston (director), 1946 (div. 1950); m. Artie Shaw (bandleader), 1957. ❖ Began career as dancer in nightclub choruses; made film debut in *The Buccaneer* (1938), followed by *The Face Behind the Mask, Union Pacific, Slightly Honorable, The Lady in Question, Here Comes Mr. Jordan, Ladies in Retirement, The Jolson Story, Mrs. Mike, The Prowler, 99 River Street, Hell's Half Acre, The Seven Year Itch* and *Return to Salem's Lot*; probably best remembered as Suellen O'Hara, Scarlett's little sister, in *Gone with the Wind*; wrote novel *I Am a Billboard* (1971). ❖ See also autobiographies *Scarlett O'Hara's Younger Sister* (1977) and *I'll Think About That Tomorrow* (1991).

KEYNES, Lady (c. 1892–1981). *See Lopokova, Lydia.*

KEYS, Martha Elizabeth (1930—). American politician and congressional representative. Born Martha Elizabeth Ludwig in Hutchinson, Kansas, Aug 10, 1930; dau. of S.T. Ludwig and Clara (Krey) Ludwig; attended Olivet College, 1946–48; University of Missouri at Kansas City, MusB, 1952; was sister-in-law of Gary Hart, US senator; m. 2nd husband Andrew Jacobs, Jan 3, 1976; children: (previous marriage) Carol, Bryan, Dana, Scott. ❖ As a Democrat, served in US Congress (1974–78); gained early political experience as Kansas state coordinator of George McGovern's presidential campaign (1973); won a vacated congressional seat (1974); was appointed to Ways and Means Committee but spent majority of time drumming up support in her district for a difficult reelection bid; served a 2nd term, then lost seat (1978); was a special adviser to secretary of health, education and welfare (1979–80); served as assistant secretary of education (1980–81); remained in Washington as a political consultant and headed the Center for the New Democracy (1985–86).

KEYS, Mary (1545–1578). *See Grey, Mary.*

KEZHOVA, Eleonora (1985—). Bulgarian rhythmic gymnast. Born Dec 28, 1985, in Bulgaria. ❖ Won team all-around bronze medal at Athens Olympics (2004).

KEZIAH (fl. 2000 BCE). Biblical woman. Second dau. of Job; sister of Kerenhappuch and Jemima. ❖ Was born after Job's restoration to health and prosperity.

KEZINE-PETHOE, Zsuzsanna (1945—). Hungarian handball player. Name variations: Zsuzsanna Kezine Pethoe. Born May 14, 1945, in Hungary. ❖ At Montreal Olympics, won a bronze medal in team competition (1976).

KHABAROVA, Irina (1966—). Russian runner. Born Mar 18, 1966, in Sverdlovsk, USSR. ❖ Won a silver medal for 4 x 100-meter relay at Athens Olympics (2004).

KHADIJAH (c. 555–619). Arabian merchant and religious leader. Name variations: Kadijah or Khadija. Born Khadijah bint Khuwaylid around 555; died in 619; 3rd cousin to Muhammad once removed; m. and widowed twice by age 40; hired Muhammad to manage one of her caravans to Syria in 595, and proposed marriage to the future Prophet shortly thereafter; children: (6 with Muhammad) 2 sons, al-Qasim and Abdallah, who both died as infants; 4 daughters, Zaynab, Ruqaiyah, Umm Kulthum, and Fatimah. ❖ A wealthy merchant of the important Quraysh (or Kuraysh) clan in Arabia, played a critical role in the origin and development of Islam; as Muhammad's 1st wife and the 1st convert to Islam, supported her husband when his revelations began (610), providing him with the material resources to pursue his reflective inclinations, and supporting him emotionally in the early stages of his revelations which gave him the strength and confidence to proclaim his religion's tenets. Her prominent role as Muhammad's beloved wife and supporter suggests that pre-Islamic Arabian women were capable of significantly influencing affairs and events—a point of view that surprises some in the modern West, who hold preconceived notions about the subordinate position of females in Middle Eastern societies and assume that it was always so. ❖ See also *Women in World History*.

KHAIZARAN (d. 790). Arabian queen. Name variations: Khaizuran; al-Khaizurān. Birth date unknown; died in 790; m. al-Mahdi, 3rd Abbasid caliph of Baghdad (present-day Iraq); children: Musa al-Hadi (4th Abbasid caliph, r. 785–786); Harun al-Rashid also seen as Haroun

al-Raschid (763/5–809, 5th Abbasid caliph); and a daughter (name unknown); (stepdaughters) Ulayya and Abassa. ❖ A slave girl from Yemen, was 1st noticed by Abu Jafar (known as al-Mansur), 2nd Abbasid caliph of Baghdad, who brought her to the imperial household of his son, al-Mahdi; when al-Mahdi became caliph on death of al-Mansur (775), was freed by him; became extremely powerful, exerting considerable influence over husband; convinced him to place her favorite son Harun first in line of succession over his elder brother Musa; when plan backfired and Musa became caliph, was confined to quarters; made plans with ladies-in-waiting and was possibly involved with Musa's sudden death (786). ❖ See also *Women in World History*.

KHALIFA, Sahar (1941—). Palestinian novelist. Born 1941 in Nablus, Palestine; Bir Zeit University, BA in English literature; University of North Carolina, MA; Iowa University, PhD in women's studies and American literature. ❖ Studied in US, then returned to Palestine (1988) and founded Women's Affairs Center in Nablus; work, which focuses on lives of Palestinians in Jerusalem and West Bank, has been translated into many languages; writings include *Lasna Jawari Lakum* (1974), *The Cactus* (1976), *Sunflowers* (1980), *Memoirs of an Unrealistic Woman* (1986), *The Door of the Courtyard* (1990), and *The Inheritance* (1997).

KHAM, Alina (1959—). Soviet field-hockey player. Born Jan 16, 1959, in USSR. ❖ At Moscow Olympics, won a bronze medal in team competition (1980).

KHAMBATTA, Persis (1950–1998). India-born actress. Born Oct 2, 1950, in Bombay, Maharashtra, India; died of a massive heart attack, Aug 18, 1998, in Bombay; m. Sean Kassidy; m. Cliff Taylor, 1981. ❖ Named Miss India (1965); appeared as Lieutenant Ilia in *Star Trek: The Motion Picture*; other films include *The Wilby Conspiracy, Conduct Unbecoming, Nighthawks* and *Megaforce*.

KHAMERERNEBTY I (fl. c. 2600 BCE). Egyptian queen. Name variations: Khamerernebti. Fl. around 2600 BCE; dau. of Khufu or Cheops (Greek), king of the 4th dynasty; sister of Merisankh III; m. King Khafre also known as Chephren (Greek), who was probably her half-brother; children: number unknown, including son Menkaure (Menkure or Mykerinos [Greek], who built the 3rd Pyramid at Giza) and daughter Khamerernebty II. ❖ As daughter of the builder of the great pyramid at Giza, was destined to carry on royal line; was married, not to the immediate successor of her father, but to his son King Khafre (builder of 2nd Pyramid of Giza); during her life, fulfilled priestly duties in the cults of major deities, such as the god of wisdom Thoth, and bore queenly titles, such as "Mother of the King of Upper and Lower Egypt, Daughter of the King of Upper and Lower Egypt, Greatly Loved Wife of the King." Her tomb was discovered (1907–08), but indications are that it was not used by her but taken over by eldest daughter, Khamerernebty II. ❖ See also *Women in World History*.

KHAMERERNEBTY II (fl. c. 2600 BCE). Egyptian queen. Name variations: Khamerernebti II. Fl. around 2600 BCE; dau. of Khamerernebty I and King Khafre or Chephren (Greek); m. her brother King Menkaure (Menkure or Mykerinos [Greek], who built the 3rd Pyramid at Giza); children: son Khuenre (died prematurely). ❖ Like her mother, served the cults of important deities and bore the titles of a major queen, such as "God's Daughter of his Body, One Who Sits with Horus, Greatly loved Wife of the King"; either died long before husband or, as seems more likely, fell from his favor before her death, which is suggested by her statement in her tomb that she paid the artisan from her own largess; enlarged the tomb begun by mother and added many statues, among which is one more than twice life-sized, the earliest known colossus of a woman. ❖ See also *Women in World History*.

KHAN, Begum Liaquat Ali (1905–1990). Pakistani diplomat and women's rights activist. Name variations: Begum Raana Liaquat Ali Khan; Rana Liaquat Ali Khan. Born in Almora, India, Feb 13, 1905, as Miss Pant; died in Karachi, Pakistan, June 13, 1990; grew up in a Hindu Brahmin family but converted to Islam when she married; earned a degree in economics from Lucknow University; was 2nd wife of (Zada) Liaquat Ali Khan (1895–1951), 1st prime minister of Pakistan; children: 2 sons. ❖ Diplomat and much-beloved women's rights activist, worked with husband to achieve independence of the Indian subcontinent from British rule; when husband became nation's 1st prime minister, worked to bring assistance to the refugees; played a crucial role in organizing the All Pakistan Women's Association (1949); following husband's assassination (1951), devoted energies to several programs for the poor which included helping set up Pakistani Cottage Industries in Karachi, and

Health and Nutrition Association, as well as sponsoring industrial and health centers for women throughout country; to dramatize her belief that the advancement of women's social, political and economic rights was fully compatible with the tenets of Islam, helped organize and presided over 1st international conference of Muslim women, which was held in Pakistan (1952); appointed delegate to UN (as well as to the International Labor Organization), then only the 2nd Muslim woman to have served in this capacity (1952); served as an ambassador to a number of nations (1954–66), including Italy, the Netherlands, and Tunisia; served as governor of Sind Province (1973–76). Received UN Human Rights Award (1979). ❖ See also *Women in World History.*

KHAN, Chaka (1953—). African-American rhythm-and-blues singer. Born Yvette Marie Stevens, Mar 23, 1953, in Great Lakes, IL; sister of singers Taka Boom (of Undisputed Truth and The Glass Family) and Mark Stevens (of Jamaica Boys); m. Hassan Khan, 1970 (div. 1971); m. Richard Holland, 1974 (div. 1980); m. Doug Rasheed, 2001; children: (2nd m.) Damien Holland; (with Rahsaan Morris) daughter Milini Khan (b. 1973, was a member of group Pretty in Pink). ❖ Formed 1st band, the Crystalettes, at 11 (1964); toured briefly with Mary Wells (late 1960s); took African name Chaka, meaning fire (late 1960s); cofounded band Rufus (1972); sang vocals on several Rufus albums, including *Rags to Rufus* (1974) and *Street Player* (1978); debuted as solo artist with album *Chaka* (1978), which featured the single "I'm Every Woman"; collaborated with Stanley Clarke on album of jazz standards; scored biggest hit to date with cover of Prince song "I Feel For You" (1984); moved to Europe (early 1990s); earned Grammy for duet with Ray Charles, "I'll Be Good to You" (1990); collaborated with Brandy, Tamia, and Gladys Knight on hit single "Missing You" (1996). ❖ See also autobiography, *Chaka! Through the Fire* (2003).

KHAN, Noor Inayat (1914–1944). British spy and hero. Name variations: (code name) Madeleine, as well as Babuly, Nora, Jeanne-Marie Regnier, Rolande, Nora Baker, Marie-Jeanne. Pronunciation: Nur In-AY-at Cawn. Born Pir Zadi Noor-un-Nisa Inayat Khan, Jan 1, 1914, in Moscow, Russia; died in Dachau concentration camp, Sept 13, 1944; dau. of Inayat Khan (Indian mystic and teacher of Sufism) and Ora Ray Baker; sister of Pir Vilayat Inayat-Khan (writer and lecturer on Sufism); attended College Moderne de Filles, France; École Normale de Musique, Paris; Sorbonne Université de Paris, École des Langues Orientales of the University of Paris; never married. ❖ Courageous wireless operator, known as "Madeleine," who worked for British Special Operations Executive in Nazi-occupied France (1943); parents moved from Moscow to London (1916), then to Paris (1920); entered University of Paris (1937); fled wartime France to England (1940); enlisted in British Women's Auxiliary Air Force (WAAF), a branch of Royal Air Force (1940); assigned to Air Ministry, Directorate of Air Intelligence (Feb 1943); dispatched as Special Operations Executive agent into occupied France (June 1943); evaded Nazi pursuers for months before Gestapo captured her in Paris (Oct 1943); despite rigorous interrogations, revealed nothing of use to enemies, and after 2 unsuccessful attempts to escape, the 2nd time with other prisoners, refused to sign a pledge promising to curtail escape efforts; transported and executed at Dachau (Sept 1944); posthumously awarded British George Cross and French Croix de Guerre; designated a saint by Islamic Sufi order. ❖ See also Jean Overton Fuller, *Madeleine: The Story of Noor Inayat Khan* (Gollancz, 1952); and *Women in World History.*

KHANIM, Leyla (d. 1847/48). Turkish poet. Born in Constantinople, Turkey; related to 'Izzat Mollah or Mullah, statesman and man of letters, who tutored her in literature. ❖ Wrote odes in Persian tradition (*ghazels*) and experimented with other classical forms of poetry.

KHANIM, Zubeyda Fitnat (c. 1725–1780). See *Fitnat-Khanim.*

KHANSA (c. 575–c. 645). Arabian poet. Name variations: al-Khansa. Born Tumadir bint Amr ibn al Harith ibn al Sharid in Najd, Arabia, c. 575; died c. 645 or 646; of the tribe Sulaim, a branch of Qais; sister of Sakhr and Mu'awiya (also seen as Moawiya); m. Mirdas ben Abi 'Amir; children: 6, including at least 4 sons and 1 daughter 'Amra who also wrote poetry. ❖ Raised in wealth and privilege, refused to marry Duraid ibn us-Simma, a great poet, warrior, and prince, because he had been chosen for her; instead, married Mirdas; before 632, lost brothers Sakhr and Mu'awiya in battle with warring tribes and wrote elegies about them; became the most famous poet of her time. About 1,000 of her verses are extant; her *dewan* (account book) was edited by L. Cheikho (Beirut 1895) and translated into French by De Coppier (Beirut 1889).

KHARLOVA, Olga (1949—). See *Karasyova, Olga.*

KHASYANOVA, Elvira (1981—). Russian synchronized swimmer. Born 1981 in USSR. ❖ At World championships, won team gold medals (2001, 2003); won a team gold medal at Athens Olympics (2004).

KHENTKAWES (fl. c. 2510 BCE). Egyptian queen. Name variations: Khentkaues. Fl. around 2510 BCE; probably dau. of King Shepseskaf; m. King Userkaf; children: Sahure (Egyptian king) and Neferirkare (Egyptian king). ❖ Queen of the Old Kingdom, who carried the legitimate line from the 4th to the 5th Dynasty as mother of the Two Kings of Upper and Lower Egypt; may have ruled as regent for underage sons because her funerary monument is impressive and has often been called the Fourth Pyramid of Giza (it stands between the causeways of Khafre and Menkaure). ❖ See also *Women in World History.*

KHIEU PONNARY (1920–2003). Cambodian first lady. Born 1920 into a privileged upperclass family in Phnom Penh, Cambodia; died July 1, 2003, in Pailin, Cambodia; dau. of a judge for the French colonial regime; sister of Khieu Thirith, later Ieng Thirith (Minister of Social action and Education of Democratic Kampuchea who married a close friend of Pol Pot, Ieng Sary); studied at the Sorbonne; became 1st wife of Saloth Sar (Cambodian dictator known as Pol Pot), 1956 (died 1998). ❖ A scholar of some distinction, was the 1st Cambodian woman to obtain a baccalaureate; taught literature and linguistics at a college in Takeo, then at Lycée Sisowath; turned to radical politics and with husband was in the hierarchy of the Cambodian Communist Party; traveled with him to Hanoi and China for backing (1965–66); became paranoid, convinced the Vietnamese were out to kill her and husband; possibly in name only, served as president of the Democratic Kampuchea Women's Association (1972–78); was last seen in public (1978); incapacitated by mental illness, spent her last 20 years in exile and seclusion, unaware that her husband took another wife in 1985.

KHIRNIQ (fl. late 6th c.). Iraqi poet. Name variations: al-Khirniq. Fl. in late 6th century; sister of Tarafa (poet); m. Bishir ibn 'Amr. ❖ Largely wrote of love and mourning for husband, who was killed on Mount Qudab by a neighboring tribe.

KHLOPTSEVA, Yelena (1960—). Soviet rower. Born May 21, 1960, in USSR. ❖ At Moscow Olympics, won a gold medal in double sculls (1980); at Barcelona Olympics, won a bronze medal in quadruple sculls without coxswain (1992).

KHNYKINA, Nadezhda (1933–1994). Soviet track-and-field athlete. Born June 24, 1933, in USSR; died 1994. ❖ At Helsinki Olympics, won a bronze medal in the 200 meters (1952); at Melbourne Olympics, won a bronze medal in the long jump (1956).

KHODATOVICH, Yekaterina (1972—). See *Khodotovich, Ekaterina.*

KHODOTOVICH, Ekaterina (1972—). Belarusian rower. Name variations: Yekaterina Khodatovich; Katya Khodotovich; Ekaterina Karsten. Born June 2, 1972, in Belarus. ❖ At Barcelona Olympics, won a bronze medal in quadruple sculls without coxswain (1992); won a gold medal at Atlanta Olympics (1996) and a gold medal at Sydney Olympics (2000), both for single sculls; won a gold medal at World championships for single sculls (1997, 1999); won a silver medal for single sculls at Athens Olympics (2004).

KHOKLOVA, Olga (d. 1955). Russian ballerina. Name variations: Olga Khokhlova. Born in Russia; died in Cannes, France, 1955; m. Pablo Picasso (artist), 1918 (sep. 1935); children: Paulo (b. 1921). ❖ Born into lower echelons of Russian nobility, was a dancer with the Ballets Russes when she met and married Picasso; when he asked for divorce (1935), separated but remained legally married until her death (the dissolution of the marriage was complicated by Spanish law); became obsessed with Picasso, following him around France and taking up residence in hotels not far from his quarters. ❖ See also *Women in World History.*

KHOLODNYA, Vera (1893–1919). Russian actress. Name variations: Kholodnaya; Kholodnaia. Born in Russia in 1893; died in Odessa, Russia, 1919; married a military officer. ❖ One of Russia's most popular pre-revolutionary film actresses, was 1st employed as an extra at Moscow's Alexander Khanzhonkov film studio (1915); caught the attention of director Yevgeni Bauer, who gave her lead role in *Song of Triumphant Love* (1915), which established her as a star; followed this with *Thief* (1916), *A Life for a Life* (1916), *The Woman Who Invented Love* (1918), and *A Living Corpse* (1918); moved to Odessa (1918), where she succumbed to a fatal attack of influenza.

KHOMIAKOVA, Valeriia (d. 1942). **Soviet fighter pilot.** Name variations: Valeria Ivanovna Khomyakova. Died 1942. ❖ Wrongly credited as the 1st woman fighter pilot to shoot down an enemy bomber, her kill occurred Sept 24, 1942, 10 days after Lidiya Litvyak's 1st kill during WWII; was killed 2 weeks later, due to the poor judgment of her commander. ❖ See also *Women in World History.*

KHORANDZEM (c. 320–c. 364). *See Pharandzem.*

KHORKINA, Svetlana (1979—). **Russian gymnast.** Name variations: Svetlana Chorkina. Pronunciation: Horkina. Born Jan 19, 1979, in Belgorod, Russia; sister of Yulia Khorkina (gymnast); attended Belgorod State University. ❖ Won Russian nationals (1993, 1995, 1997), Moscow World Stars (1994, 1995), European Cup (1995), French International (1995, 1999), and Russian Cup (1995, 1997, 1998), Arthur Gander Memorial (1998, 1999); was 5-time European uneven bars champion (1994, 1996, 1998, 2000, 2002) and European all-around champion (1998, 2000, 2002); at Atlantic Olympics, won a gold medal in uneven bars and a silver medal in team all-around (1996); at World championships, won a gold medal for uneven bars (1995, 1996, 1997, 1999, 2001), gold medal for indiv. all-around (1997, 2001, 2003), and gold medal for vault (2001); at Sydney Olympics, won a gold medal for uneven bars and silver medals for team all-around and floor exercises (2000); won a silver medal for indiv. all-around and a bronze medal for team all-around at Athens Olympics (2004).

KHOSTARIA, Anastasia Eristav (1868–1951). *See Eristavi-Xostaria, Anastasia.*

KHOTE, Durga (c. 1905–1991). **Indian actress.** Born Jan 13, 1905, in Bombay, Maharashtra, India; died Sept 22, 1991, in Bombay; mother-in-law of Vijaya Mehta (stage and tv director); grandmother of Tina Khote (who made a film about Durga's life). ❖ One of India's greatest and most highly respected stars, came from a cultured, affluent Brahmin family; her appearance in the early sound film *Ayodhyecha Raja* (1932), opened the doors for other girls from respectable families to become film actresses; appeared in over 200 films, including *Maya Machhindra* (1932), *Rajrani Meera* (1933), *Seeta* (1934), *Amar Jyoti* (1936), *Pratibha* (1937), *Geeta* (1940), *Prithvi Vallabh* (1943), *Phool* (1945), *Maya Bazaar* (1949), *Adil-E-Jahangir* (1955), *Mughal-E-Azam* (1960), *The Householder* (1963), *Kaajal* (1965) and *Daadi Maa* (1966); also appeared on stage often, including as Lady Macbeth in *Rajmukut,* a Marathi adaptation of *Macbeth* (1954).

KHOURI, Callie (1957—). **American screenwriter.** Born Carolyn Ann Khouri, Nov 27, 1957, in San Antonio, TX; attended Purdue University and Strasburg Institute; m. David W. Warfield (writer), 1990. ❖ Wrote the screenplays for *Thelma & Louise* (1991), *Something to Talk About* (1995) and *Divine Secrets of the Ya-Ya Sisterhood* (2002).

KHRISTOVA, Ivanka (1941—). **Bulgarian shot putter.** Born Nov 19, 1941, in Bulgaria. ❖ Won a bronze medal at Munich Olympics (1972) and a gold medal at Montreal Olympics (1976), both in shot put.

KHRISTOVA, Tsvetanka (1962—). **Bulgarian discus thrower.** Born Mar 14, 1962, in Bulgaria. ❖ Won a bronze medal at Seoul Olympics (1988) and a silver medal at Barcelona Olympics (1992), both in discus throw.

KHUDASHOVA, Yelena (1965—). **Soviet basketball player.** Born July 10, 1965, in USSR. ❖ Won a bronze medal at Seoul Olympics (1988) and a gold medal at Barcelona Olympics (1992), both in team competition.

KHUDOROZHKINA, Irina (1968—). **Russian shot putter.** Name variations: Khudoroshkina. Born Oct 13, 1968, in USSR. ❖ Won a bronze medal at Atlanta Olympics (1996).

KHURI, Colette (1937—). **Syrian poet, novelist and short-story writer.** Name variations: Colette al-Khuri; Colette Khoury. Born 1937 in Damascus; received degree in French from University of Damascus. ❖ Published 2 collections of poetry in French, *Twenty Years* (1957) and *Tremors* (1960); works in Arabic include *Days With Him* (1959), *Damascus My Big Home* (1969), and *A Summer Passes* (1975).

KHURREM, sultana (c. 1504–1558). *See Roxelana.*

KHVEDOSYUK, Lyudmila (1936—). *See Pinayeva-Khvedosyuk, Lyudmila.*

KHVOSHCHINSKAIA, Nadezhda (1824–1889). **Russian poet, novelist and literary critic.** Name variations: Nadezhda Dmitrievna Khvoshchínskaia or Khvoshchínskaya; (pseudonym) V. Krestovskii. Born Nadezhda Dmitrievna Khvoshchínskaia, May 20, 1824, in Riazan, Russia; died June 8, 1889, in St. Petersburg; eldest of 4 children; sister of Sofia Khvoshchinskaia and Praskovia Khvoshchinskaia (who wrote under S. Zimarova). ❖ The foremost woman realist of the 19th century, concentrated on the provincial Russian milieu as well as gender inequities in society; poetry includes *Ursa Major* (1870–71); stories include "A Few Summer Days" (1853) and "Brother Dear" (1858); novels include *In Hope of Better Days* (1860) and *Pansionerka* (*The Boarding School Girl,* 1861); also wrote criticism under male pseudonyms and translated works from French and Italian.

KHVOSHCHINSKAIA, Sofia (1828–1865). **Russian short-story writer and painter.** Name variations: Sof'ia or Sofia Dmitrievna Khvoshchínskaia or Khvoshchínskaya; (pseudonyms) Iv. Vesen'ev or Iv. Veseniev; N. Born Sofia Dmitrievna Khvoshchinskaia in 1828 in Riazan, Russia; died 1865; sister of Nadezhda Khvoshchinskaia and Praskovia Khvoshchinskaia (who wrote under S. Zimarova). ❖ Stories reflect life in provincial capital Riazan; wrote the autobiographical, "Reminiscences of Institute Life," about her experiences in a Moscow girls boarding school that offered a harsh, restrictive existence (1861); other writings include "Aunty's Legacy" (1858), "A Provincial's Lament" (1861), "Earthly Joys and Joys of Our Back Street," "A Little About Our Customs" (1862), and "Our Urban Life" (1864).

KI MI-SOOK (1967—). **Korean handball player.** Born Dec 26, 1967, in South Korea. ❖ At Seoul Olympics, won a gold medal in team competition (1988).

KIAERSKOU, Lotte (1975—). **Danish handball player.** Name variations: Kiærskou. Born June 23, 1975, in Frederikshavn, Denmark. ❖ Back and pivot, won a team gold medal at Sydney Olympics (2000) and at Athens Olympics (2004).

KIBBEE, Lois (1922–1993). **American actress.** Born July 13, 1922, in Rhinelander, WI; died Oct 18, 1993, in New York, NY; dau. of actor Milton Kibbee; niece of actor Guy Kibbee. ❖ Appeared on Broadway in *A Man for All Seasons* and *Venus Is;* had recurring role as Geraldine Saxon on "Edge of Night" (1970–71, 1973–84, also wrote for series), as Elizabeth Sanders on "One Life to Live" (1986–88), and as Emily Matson on "Somerset" (1972–73).

KIDD, Margaret Henderson (1900–1989). **Scottish lawyer.** Name variations: Dame Margaret Kidd; Mrs Donald S. Macdonald. Born 1900 in Linlithgow, Scotland; died Mar 22, 1989, in Scotland; dau. of solicitor; m. Donald Somerland Macdonald; children: 1 daughter. ❖ Pioneering lawyer, became 1st woman member of Scottish Bar (1923) as well as 1st woman barrister to appear before House of Lords (1926) and Parliamentary Select Committee (1927); served as Scotland's only female advocate for over 25 years; was 1st woman appointed to Queen's Counsel (1948); held position as keeper of Advocates Library (1956–69); was 1st woman sheriff of Dumfries County (1960–66), going on to serve as sheriff of Perth (1966–74); elected vice president of British Federation of University women; retired after 50-year career (1973). Made Dame of British Empire (DBE, 1975).

KIDDER, Kathryn (1867–1939). **American stage actress.** Born Dec 23, 1867, in Newark, NJ; died Sept 7, 1939; m. Louis Kaufman Anspacher (writer). ❖ Made stage debut in Chicago as Lucy Fairweather in *The Streets of London* and NY debut in *Nordeck* (both 1885); appeared as Mrs. Errol in *Little Lord Fauntleroy* (1888) and came to prominence as Catherine in *Madame Sans-Gêne* (1895).

KIDDER, Margot (1948—). **Canadian actress.** Born Margaret Ruth Kidder, Oct 17, 1848, in Yellowknife, Northwest Territories, Canada; dau. of Kendall Kidder (mining engineer); m. Thomas McGuane (writer), 1975 (div. 1976); m. John Heard (actor), 1979 (div. 1979); m. Philippe de Broca, 1983 (div. 1984); children: (1st m.) Maggie (b. 1976). ❖ Made film debut in *Gaily, Gaily* (1969); starred in *Sisters* (1973), *Black Christmas* (1974), *The Great Waldo Pepper* (1975), *92 in the Shade* (1975), *The Reincarnation of Peter Proud* (1975); came to international renown as Lois Lane in *Superman* (1978) and appeared in its sequels; other films include *The Amityville Horror* (1979) and *Willie and Phil* (1980); suffering from bi-polar disorder, made headlines when she became delusional during a manic episode (1996); worked to get career back on track.

KIDDLE, Margaret (1914–1958). **Australian historian.** Born Margaret Loch Kiddle in South Yarra, Melbourne, Australia, Sept 10, 1914; died May 3, 1958; dau. of John Beacham (solicitor) and Mauna Loa (Burrett) Kiddle; University of Melbourne, BA, 1937, Diploma of Education, 1938, MA, 1947; never married; no children. ❖ Published a series of children's books, beginning with *Moonbeam Stairs* (1945), followed by *West of Sunset* (1949), and *The Candle* (1950); published biography, *Caroline Chisholm* (1950); most acclaimed work, *Men of Yesterday* (1961), traces the history of western district of Victoria in 19th century, from native Aboriginal inhabitants to large-scale immigrations in 1830s and 1840s, and is based largely on records of pioneer families. ❖ See also *Women in World History.*

KIDMAN, Fiona (1940—). New Zealand novelist, playwright and poet. Born 1940 in Hawera, New Zealand. ❖ Worked as radio dramatist, critic, and editor; taught creative writing at Centre for Continuing Education of Victoria University and elsewhere; served as National president of PEN (1981–83); works, which reflect changes in women's lives brought about by women's movement, include *Search for Sister Blue* (1975), *Honey and Bitters* (1975), *On the Tightrope* (1978), *A Breed of Women* (1979), *Mandarin Summer* (1981), *Mrs. Dixon and Friend* (1982), *Paddy's Puzzle* (1983), *Gone North* (1984), *The Book of Secrets* (1987), *Ricochet Baby* (1996), and *New Zealand Stories* (1999). Received New Zealand Book Award for fiction; made OBE.

KIDMAN, Nicole (1967—). Australian actress. Born Nicole Mary Kidman, June 20, 1967, in Honolulu, Hawaii; grew up in Sydney; dau. of Anthony Kidman (biochemist and clinical psychologist) and Janelee Kidman (nurse instructor); sister of Antonia Kidman (tv personality); m. Tom Cruise (actor), 1990 (div. 2001); children: (adopted) Isabella and Connor. ❖ Began career at Philip Street Theater; made film debut in *Bush Christmas* (1983), which led to a starring role in *BMX Bandits* (1983); won Australian Film Institute award for performance in tv-mini series "Vietnam" (1987); made US debut in *Dead Calm* (1989); won Golden Globes for Best Actress for *To Die For* (1995), *Moulin Rouge* (2001), and *The Hours;* other films include *Days of Thunder* (1990), *Billy Bathgate* (1991), *Batman Forever* (1995), *Portrait of a Lady* (1996), *Eyes Wide Shut* (1999), *The Others* (2001), *Cold Mountain* (2003) and *Bewitched* (2005). Nominated for Academy Award for *Moulin Rouge;* won Academy Award for Best Actress for *The Hours* (2002).

KIDSON, Elsa Beatrice (1905–1979). New Zealand soil scientist and sculptor. Born on Mar 18, 1905, in Christchurch, New Zealand; died on July 25, 1979, in Nelson, New Zealand; dau. of Charles Kidson (sculptor) and Kitty Esther (Hounsell) Kidson; Canterbury College, MSc, 1927. ❖ Worked as demonstrator in chemistry at Canterbury College, and chemist at New Zealand Refrigerating Co. (late 1920s), before working at Department of Scientific and Industrial Research and finally the Cawthron Institute (1931–65); internationally recognized for research into magnesium deficiency in apples, vitamin C content of citrus fruits, and link between mineral constituents and nutritional diseases in tomatoes; was 1st woman fellow of New Zealand Institute of Chemistry (1943) and 1st New Zealand woman elected fellow of Royal Institute of Chemistry (1944); fellow of Royal Society of New Zealand; after retirement, studied sculpture at Wimbledon School of Art in London (1965). ❖ See also *Dictionary of New Zealand Biography* (Vol. 4).

KIEHL, Marina (1965—). German Alpine skier. Born Jan 12, 1965, in Munich, Germany. ❖ Won World Cup giant slalom title (1985) and super-G title (1986); won a gold medal for downhill at Calgary Olympics (1988).

KIELAN, Urszula (1960—). Polish track-and-field athlete. Born Oct 10, 1960, in Poland. ❖ At Moscow Olympics, won a silver medal in the high jump (1980).

KIELER, Laura (1849–1932). Norwegian writer and literary inspiration. Born Laura Anna Sofie Müller Petersen von Fyren, Jan 9, 1849, in Tromsø, Norway; died April 21, 1932, in Alsgarde, Hellebaek; dau. of Morten Smith Petersen von Fyren and Anna Hansine Kjerulf Müller (1812–1889); married Victor Kieler (Danish schoolteacher), 1873; children: 5. ❖ Wrote a sequel to one of Henrik Ibsen's plays; met Ibsen who became something of a mentor; served as the basis for Nora in his *A Doll's House* (1879), having lived through similar events. ❖ See also *Women in World History.*

KIELGASS, Kerstin (1969—). German swimmer. Born Dec 6, 1969, in Berlin, Germany. ❖ At Barcelona Olympics, won a bronze medal in 4 x 100-meter freestyle relay and a bronze medal in 200-meter freestyle (1992); at European championships, placed 1st for 200-meter freestyle (1995) and 1st in 800-meter freestyle (1997); won a silver medal for 800-meter freestyle relay at Atlanta Olympics (1996); won a bronze medal for 800-meter freestyle relay at Sydney Olympics (2000).

KIELLAND, Kitty L. (1843–1914). Norwegian painter. Born in Stavanger, Norway, 1843; died 1914; studied at art academies of Karlsruhe and Munich; one of her tutors was Eilif Peterssen; also studied in Paris. ❖ Lived in Paris with artist Harriet Backer (1879–88); spent summers (1886, 1887) in Fleskum, Norway, with a group of Norwegian painters; influenced by Impressionism in her treatment of atmosphere, light, and air, concentrated on plein-air painting. ❖ See also *Women in World History.*

KIELMANSEGGE, Sophia Charlotte von (1673–1725). Countess of Platen, Brentford and Darlington. Name variations: Baroness von Kielmansegge; Countess Leinster; Baroness of Brentford. Born c. 1673; died in 1725; dau. of Ernest Augustus, duke of Brunswick-Luneburg, and Clara Elizabeth Meisenburg; associated with George I (1660–1727), king of England (r. 1714–1727).

KIENGSIRI, Kanha (1911—). Thai novelist and short-story writer. Name variations: K. Surangkhanang; (pseudonyms) Rosamalin; Moruedi; Nakhon Suraphan. Born 1911. ❖ Wrote many short stories, the most famous of which, "Malinee," she wrote at school; edited daily newspaper *Muang Thong,* directed *Narinat* magazine, and owned Rosamalin Press; works, which focus on restrictions placed on Thai women and advocate education and independence for women, include *Ying Khon Chua,Ban Sai Thong,* and *Yai.*

KIENLE, Else (1900–1970). See La Roe, Else K.

KIEPURA, Martha Eggerth (1912—). See Eggerth, Marta.

KIERMAYER, Susanne (1968—). German shooter. Born July 22, 1968, in Kirchberg, Germany. ❖ Won German national championships (1995–99, 2000); won a silver medal for double trap at Atlanta Olympics (1996); won a gold medal at World championships (1999) and European championships (1999, 2000).

KIES, Mary Dixon (fl. 19th c.). American inventor. Born Mary Dixon in South Killingly, Connecticut. ❖ Received the 1st US patent issued to a woman (May 15, 1809), having invented a process for weaving straw with silk or thread.

KIESL, Theresia (1963—). Austrian runner. Name variations: Teresia or Therese Kiesl. Born Oct 26, 1963, in Austria. ❖ Won a bronze medal for the 1,500 meters at Atlanta Olympics (1996).

KIESLER, Hedy (1913–2000). See Lamarr, Hedy.

KIEV, grand princess of.
See Gertrude of Poland (d. 1107).
See Marie of Kiev (d. 1179).
See Barbara of Byzantium (d. 1125).
See Christina of Sweden (d. 1122).

KIGHT-WINGARD, Lenore (1911–2000). American swimmer. Name variations: Lenore Wingard. Born Sept 26, 1911; died Feb 9, 2000, in Cincinnati, Ohio. ❖ Won a silver medal at Los Angeles Olympics (1932) and a bronze medal at Berlin Olympics (1936), both in the 400-meter freestyle.

KIKUCHI, Yuriko (b. 1920). See Yuriko.

KIKUKO, Princess (d. 2004). Japanese princess. Born in Japan; died Dec 18, 2004, age 92, in Tokyo, Japan; granddau. of Yoshinobu Tokugawa (Japan's last shogun); m. Takamatsu (younger brother and advisor to Emperor Hirohito); no children. ❖ Progressive princess, championed cancer research 1930s on and published late husband's diaries (1995), which contained criticism of Japan's wartime military.

KILBORN, Pam (1939—). Australian track-and-field athlete. Name variations: Pam Kilborn Ryan or Kilborn-Ryan; Pam Ryan. Born Aug 12, 1939, in Melbourne, Australia. ❖ Won gold medals at Commonwealth Games for 80-meter hurdles (1962, 1966), long jump (1962), and 4 x 10-meter relay (1966, 1970), 100-meter hurdles (1970); was the 1st woman to win 3 indiv. national titles in same year, winning hurdles, long jump, and pentathlon (1963); won a bronze medal at Tokyo Olympics (1964) and a silver medal at Mexico City Olympics (1968), both for 80-meter hurdles.

KILBOURN, Annelisa (1967–2002). British veterinarian and wildlife expert. Born Annelisa Marcelle Kilbourn, June 27, 1967, in Zurich, Switzerland; was a British citizen; killed in a plane crash in Gabon, Nov 2, 2002; dau. of Hans and Barry Kilbourn; attended University of Connecticut; graduate in veterinary medicine, Tufts University, 1996. ❖ Rescued orangutans in Borneo; while working for the Wildlife

Conservations Society, discovered that the Ebola virus was causing the decline in Africa's gorilla population.

KILBOURNE, Andrea (1980—). American ice-hockey player. Born April 19, 1980, in Saranac Lake, NY; graduate of Princeton University, 2003. ❖ Won a team silver medal at Salt Lake City Olympics (2002).

KILDARE, Lady (1731–1814). *See Lennox Sisters.*

KILDEER, John (1930—). *See Mayhar, Ardath.*

KILGALLEN, Dorothy (1913–1965). American columnist and radio and tv personality. Born Dorothy Mae Kilgallen in Chicago, IL, July 3, 1913; died of a barbiturate overdose in New York, NY, Nov 7, 1965; dau. of James Lawrence Kilgallen (journalist) and Mae (Ahern) Kilgallen; attended College of New Rochelle, NY; m. Richard Kollmar (actor and producer), April 6, 1940: children: Jill-Ellen Kollmar; Richard Kollmar; Kerry Kolmar. ❖ One of the best woman reporters of her era, was hired as a cub reporter at NY *Evening Journal* at 17; by 20, having already covered a myriad of grisly murders and notorious trials, had earned substantial stature; came to national prominence with her "Girl Around the World" series, when she competed against 2 male journalists in a round-the-world race (1936); went to West Coast to report on films for *Journal-American* (1937); wrote autobiographical screenplay *Fly Away Baby*, which starred Glenda Farrell as Torchy Blane; returning to NY, aligned herself with Café Society, covering such events as the wedding of Franklin Delano Roosevelt Jr. and coronation of George VI; officially awarded Broadway beat (1938); her daily column, "Voice of Broadway," was syndicated in 45 newspapers throughout nation; wielded a great deal of power, but never adopted the mean-spirited approach that made Walter Winchell famous; made radio debut on "Voice of Broadway" (1941), then launched daily program with husband, "Breakfast with Dorothy and Dick" (1945); debuted on tv on "Leave It to the Girls" (1949); was a well-known panelist on "What's My Line?" (1949). ❖ See also Lee Israel, *Kilgallen* (Delacorte, 1979); and *Women in World History.*

KILGORE, Anita (1909–1981). *See Frings, Ketti.*

KILGORE, Carrie B. (1838–1908). American lawyer. Born Caroline Burnham in Craftsbury, Vermont, Jan 20, 1838; died in Swarthmore, PA, June 29, 1908; served a medical apprenticeship in Hygeio-Therapeutic College of Bellevue Hospital, NY, and earned a medical degree; 1st woman graduate of Central Pennsylvania Law School (now University of Pennsylvania), 1883; m. Damon Kilgore (lawyer), 1876 (died 1888); children: 2 daughters. ❖ Graduated from law school (1883), inspiring ridicule from the press, bar and bench; was allowed to practice in federal courts (1886) then US Supreme Court (1890); after husband's death (1888), took over and managed his law practice. ❖ See also *Women in World History.*

KILIUS, Marika (1943—). German pairs skater and singer. Born Mar 24, 1943, in Frankfurt am Main, Germany. ❖ With partner Franz Ningel, placed 3rd at European championships (1955–57) and 4th at Cortina Olympics (1956); with partner Hans-Jürgen Bäumler, won 7 European championships (1959–65), 2 World championships (1963, 1964), and silver medals at Squaw Valley Olympics (1960) and Innsbruck Olympics (1964); as a singer, made 5 recordings with Bäumler that reached the German Top 30, including "Honeymoon in St. Tropez."

KILLIGREW, Anne (1660–1685). English poet and painter. Pronunciation: Kill-LI-grew. Born in 1660; died of smallpox, age 25, June 16, 1685; dau. of Judith Killigrew and Henry Killigrew (both royalist supporters of the Stuart kings, closely associated with the court of Charles II, in early years of Restoration); never married; no children. ❖ Celebrated in one of Dryden's odes, "To the pious memory of the accomplished young lady, Mrs. Anne Killigrew," became maid of honor to Mary of Modena, 2nd wife of the duke of York (later King James II); joined an influential circle of women who were to become known for their intellects and accomplishments: Catharine Sedley, Sarah Jennings (Churchill), and Anne Kingsmill (Finch); was valued by her contemporaries as a poet and an artist. One year after her death, *Poems by Mrs. Anne Killigrew* (London: S. Lowndes, 1686) was published by her father; her portrait of James II is now in the possession of Queen Elizabeth II. ❖ See also *Women in World History.*

KILLIGREW, Catherine (c. 1530–1583). English noblewoman. Name variations: Katherine Cooke, Katherine Killigrew; Lady Katherine. Born c. 1530; died in 1583; 4th dau. of Sir Anthony Cooke (1504–1576), politician and tutor to the future Edward VI; m. Sir Henry Killigrew,

1565. ❖ Was said to have been a lady of learning, proficient in Hebrew, Greek, and Latin.

KILLIGREW, Elizabeth (c. 1622–?). Mistress of Charles II. Name variations: Betty Killigrew. Born c. 1622; dau. of Sir Robert Killigrew; sister of the duke of York's chaplin (the duke of York later became James II, king of England); m. Francis Boyle, later 1st Viscount Shannon; mistress of Charles II (1630–1685), king of England (r. 1661–1685); children: (with Charles II) Charlotte Jemima Henrietta Maria Fitzroy or Fitzcharles (1651–1684, who m. James Howard, earl of Suffolk, and William Paston, 2nd earl of Yarmouth).

KILLINGBECK, Molly (1959—). Jamican-born Canadian runner. Born Feb 3, 1959, in Jamaica. ❖ At Los Angeles Olympics, won a silver medal in 4 x 400-meter relay (1984).

KILLOUGH, Karen Lee (1942—). *See Killough, Lee.*

KILLOUGH, Lee (1942—). American science-fiction writer. Name variations: Karen Lee Killough; (pseudonym) Sarah Hood. Born May 5, 1942, in Syracuse, Kansas; m. Howard Patrick Killough, 1966. ❖ Began working as radiologic technologist at Kansas State University Veterinary Hospital (1971); works include *A Voice out of Ramah* (1979), *The Doppelganger Gambit* (1979), *The Monitor, The Miners, and the Shree* (1980), *Deadly Silents* (1981), *Liberty's World* (1985), *Dragon's Teeth* (1990), *Bridling Chaos* (1998), and *Wilding Nights* (2002); also published short-story collection *Aventine* (1982).

KILMURY, Diana (1948—). Canadian union activist. Born 1948; raised in Vancouver, British Columbia, Canada; married and div.; 3. ❖ Joined Local 213 of Teamsters Union, the 1st woman member to work in heavy construction; came to aid of Jack Vlahovic, a dissident British Columbian union representative who had been ousted for whistle-blowing on corruption in union ranks (1977); joined Teamsters for a Democratic Union, crisscrossing Canada, urging union members to get rid of mob-controlled officials and demand democratic elections; elected a Teamsters vice-president and took office (1992), the 1st woman member of the Teamster General Executive Board; was the subject of TNT tv-movie, "Mother Trucker: The Diana Kilmury Story" (1996). ❖ See also *Women in World History.*

KILPI, Eeva (1928—). Finnish novelist, poet and short-story writer. Born Feb 18, 1928 in Hiitola, Karelia (once part of the Soviet Union), Finland; m. Mikko Kilpi, 1949 (div. 1966); children: 3. ❖ Studied literature and languages and served as president of PEN (1970–75); works, which attack puritanism, hypocrisy, and prejudice and insist on right of women to sexual and intellectual independence, include *Noidaulukko* (1959), *Elämä edestakaisin* (1964), *Rokkanden ja kademan pöytä* (1967), *Tamara* (1972), *Ihuisen ääni* (1976), and *Elämän evakonna* (1983); published critically acclaimed trilogy of autobiographical novels about the war years (1989–93).

KILSCH, Claudia (1963—). *See Kohde-Kilsch, Claudia.*

KILSHTÉT, Mariia (1861–1931). *See Veselkóva-Kilshtét, Mariia Grigorevna.*

KIM BO-RAM. South Korean archer. Born in South Korea. ❖ Won a gold medal for teams at Sydney Olympics (2000).

KIM CHA-YOUN (1981—). South Korean handball player. Born Jan 10, 1981, in South Korea. ❖ Won a team silver at Athens Olympics (2004).

KIM CHEONG-SHIM (1976—). South Korean handball player. Born Feb 8, 1976, in South Korea. ❖ Won a team silver medal at Atlanta Olympics (1996).

KIM CHOON-RYE (1966—). Korean handball player. Born June 21, 1966, in South Korea. ❖ Won a silver medal at Los Angeles Olympics (1984) and a gold medal at Seoul Olympics (1988), both in team competition.

KIM EUN-MI (1975—). South Korean handball player. Born Dec 17, 1975, in South Korea. ❖ Won a team silver medal at Atlanta Olympics (1996).

KIM EUN-SOOK (1963—). Korean basketball player. Born Mar 31, 1963, in South Korea. ❖ At Los Angeles Olympics, won a silver medal in team competition (1984).

KIM GWANG SUK (c. 1976—). North Korean gymnast. Born Feb 15, c. 1976 (reputedly North Korean officials falsified her year of birth at several major competitions, claiming she was 15 for 3 years in a row). ❖ At World championships, won a gold medal in uneven bars (1991).

KIM HWA-SOOK (1971—). Korean handball player. Born Mar 2, 1971, in South Korea. ❖ At Barcelona Olympics, won a gold medal in team competition (1992).

KIM HWA-SOON (1962—). Korean basketball player. Born April 12, 1962, in South Korea. ❖ At Los Angeles Olympics, won a silver medal in team competition (1984).

KIM HYANG-MI (1979—). North Korean table tennis player. Born Sept 19, 1979, in North Korea. ❖ At World championships, placed 2nd with team (2001); won the English Open doubles (2001); won a silver medal for table tennis singles at Athens Olympics (2004).

KIM HYUN-MI (1967—). Korean handball player. Born 1967 in South Korea. ❖ At Seoul Olympics, won a gold medal in team competition (1988).

KIM HYUN-OK (1974—). South Korean handball player. Born May 14, 1974, in South Korea. ❖ Won a team silver at Athens Olympics (2004).

KIM JEONG-MI (1975—). South Korean handball player. Born Feb 7, 1975, in South Korea. ❖ Won a team silver medal at Atlanta Olympics (1996).

KIM JIN-HO (1961—). Korean archer. Born Dec 1, 1961, in South Korea. ❖ At Los Angeles Olympics, won a bronze medal in double FITA round (1984).

KIM JO-SUN. South Korean archer. Born in South Korea. ❖ Won a gold medal for teams at Sydney Olympics (2000).

KIM JUM-SOOK (c. 1968—). South Korean climber. Born c. 1968 in Seoul, Korea; m. Seoung Chul Choi (ice climber who died in an avalanche on Mt. Thelay Sagar in the Himalayas, Sept 28, 1998). ❖ Won silver in Ice Climbing (Difficulty) at Winter X Games (1999); won gold medal at the Ice Climbing championship in Seorak, Korea (1997); won silver at Asian Sport Climbing (1993).

KIM KYUNG-AH (1977—). South Korean table tennis player. Born May 25, 1977, in Daejon, South Korea. ❖ Won Japan Open (2002) and Croatian Open for singles (2004); won a bronze medal for table tennis singles at Athens Olympics (2004).

KIM KYUNG-SOON (1965—). Korean handball player. Born Dec 10, 1965, in South Korea. ❖ Won a silver medal at Los Angeles Olympics (1984) and a gold medal at Seoul Olympics (1988), both in team competition.

KIM KYUNG-WOOK. South Korean archer. Born in South Korea. ❖ Won gold medals for indiv. FITA round 70 m and teams at Atlanta Olympics (1996).

KIM MI-HYUN (1977—). South Korean golfer. Born Jan 13, 1977, in Inchon, Korea; attended Sun Gkyun Kwan University. ❖ Turned pro (1996); competed on KLPGA Tour (1996–97); with 2 wins (State Farm Rail Classic and Betsy King Classic), named Rolex Rookie of the Year (1999); won Giant Eagle LPGA Classic and Wendy's Championship for Children (2002).

KIM MI-JUNG (1971—). Korean judoka. Born Mar 29, 1971, in Korea. ❖ At Barcelona Olympics, won a gold medal in half-heavyweight 72kg (1992).

KIM MI-SOOK (1962—). Korean handball player. Born June 10, 1962, in South Korea. ❖ At Los Angeles Olympics, won a silver medal in team competition (1984).

KIM MI-SIM (1970—). South Korean handball player. Born Nov 6, 1970, in South Korea. ❖ Won a team silver medal at Atlanta Olympics (1996).

KIM MI-SUN (1964—). Korean field-hockey player. Born June 6, 1964, in South Korea. ❖ At Seoul Olympics, won a silver medal in team competition (1988).

KIM MOO-KYO. South Korean table tennis player. Name variations: Kim Moo Kyo. Born in South Korea. ❖ Won a bronze medal for doubles at Sydney Olympics (2000).

KIM MYONG-SUK (1947—). North Korean volleyball player. Born April 14, 1947, in North Korea. ❖ At Munich Olympics, won a bronze medal in team competition (1972).

KIM MYONG-SOON (1964—). Korean handball player. Born April 15, 1964, in South Korea. ❖ At Seoul Olympics, won a gold medal in team competition (1988).

KIM MYUNG-OK. South Korean field-hockey player. Born in South Korea. ❖ Won a team silver medal at Atlanta Olympics (1996).

KIM NAM-SOON. South Korean archer. Born in South Korea. ❖ Won a gold medal for team and a silver medal for indiv. FITA round 70 m at Sydney Olympics (2000).

KIM, Nelli (1957—). Russian gymnast. Born July 19, 1957, in central Asian city of Chimkent, Kazakhstan, USSR; dau. of Korean parents. ❖ At European championships, won a silver medal in all-around and beam (1975) and a gold medal in vault (1977); won gold medals in team all-around, vault and floor exercises and a silver medal in indiv. all-around at Montreal Olympics (1976); at World championships, won a gold medal in team all-around (1974), gold medals in team all-around, vault and floor exercises (1978) and gold medal in indiv. all-around (1979); at Moscow Olympics, won a gold medal in team all-around and floor exercises (1980); was the 1st woman to earn a perfect 10 on vault and floor and the 1st to perform a double back salto on floor and a Tsukahara with 360 degree turn on vault in Olympic history. ❖ See also documentary "Nellie" (National Film Board of Canada).

KIM OK-HWA (1958—). Korean handball player. Born Aug 11, 1958, in South Korea. ❖ At Los Angeles Olympics, won a silver medal in team competition (1984).

KIM RANG (1974—). South Korean handball player. Born Oct 9, 1974, in South Korea. ❖ Won a team silver medal at Atlanta Olympics (1996).

KIM, Ronyoung (1926–1987). Korean-American novelist, painter and sculptor. Born Mar 28, 1926, in Los Angeles, CA; died Feb 3, 1987; dau. of Chong-hak Kim and Haeran "Helen" Kim; attended Los Angeles City College; m. Richard Hahn; children: 4. ❖ Helped promote Asian art in San Francisco, aiding in the acquisition of the Avery Brundage Collection at San Francisco Asian Art Museum; wrote *Clay Walls* (1987), one of the 1st Korean-American novels.

KIM RYANG-HEE. South Korean short-track speedskater. Born in South Korea. ❖ Won a gold medal for 3,000 relay at Lillehammer Olympics (1994).

KIM SO-HEE. South Korean short-track speedskater. Born in South Korea. ❖ Won a gold medal for 3,000-meter relay and a bronze medal for 1,000 meters at Lillehammer Olympics (1994).

KIM SOO-NYUNG (1971—). South Korean archery champion. Name variations: Soo-Nyuong Kim. Born April 5, 1971, in Choong Choong Book Province, Korea. ❖ Considered the greatest woman archer of the modern era; at Seoul Olympics, won gold medals in team round and double FITA round (1988); at Barcelona Olympics, won gold medals in team round and double FITA round (1992); at Sydney Olympics, won a gold medal for team round and a bronze medal for indiv. FITA round (2000); was indiv. and team World champion (1989, 1991); through 1990, held every women's world record at all distances, and overall as well.

KIM SOON-DUK (1967—). Korean field-hockey player. Born Nov 20, 1967, in South Korea. ❖ At Seoul Olympics, won a silver medal in team competition (1988).

KIM SU-DAE (1942—). North Korean volleyball player. Born May 13, 1942, in North Korea. ❖ At Munich Olympics, won a bronze medal in team competition (1972).

KIM YEUN-JA (1943—). North Korean volleyball player. Born Feb 10, 1943, in North Korea. ❖ At Munich Olympics, won a bronze medal in team competition (1972).

KIM YOUNG-HEE (1963—). Korean basketball player. Born May 17, 1963, in South Korea. ❖ At Los Angeles Olympics, won a silver medal in team competition (1984).

KIM YOUNG-SOOK (1965—). Korean field-hockey player. Born Feb 17, 1965, in South Korea. ❖ At Seoul Olympics, won a silver medal in team competition (1988).

KIM YUN-MI. South Korean short-track speedskater. Name variations: Yoon-Mi Kim. Born in South Korea. ❖ Won a gold medal for 3,000 relay at Lillehammer Olympics (1994) and a gold medal for 3,000-meter relay at Nagano Olympics (1998).

KIM ZUNG-BOK (1945—). North Korean volleyball player. Born July 27, 1945, in North Korea. ❖ At Munich Olympics, won a bronze medal in team competition (1972).

KIMBALL, Judy (1938—). American golfer. Born June 17, 1938, in Sioux City, Iowa. ❖ Won Iowa state championship (1958); turned pro and won American Open (1961); won LPGA championship (1962); won O'Sullivan Open (1971); served as secretary of the LPGA executive board (1974).

KIMBALL, Martha G. (1840–1894). American philanthropist and war nurse. Born in Portland, Maine, 1840; died in 1894. ❖ Accompanied husband, an appraiser of captured cotton, to the front in the Civil War; acted as a nurse during Sherman's campaign in Georgia and was appointed inspector of hospitals; was the 1st to suggest the observance of Decoration Day. ❖ See also *Women in World History.*

KIMBELL, Maud Winifred (1880–1956). *See Sherwood, Maud Winifred.*

KIMENYE, Barbara (1940—). Ugandan children's writer, novelist and short-story writer. Born 1940 in England; trained as a nurse in London. ❖ Worked as columnist for Kenyan newspaper *Daily Nation;* served on government of the Kabaka of Buganda in Uganda; short fiction collections include *Kalasanda* (1965) and *Kalasanda Revisited* (1966); children's works, which are used widely in East African elementary schools, include *Moses* (1967), *Moses and the Ghost* (1971), *Sarah and the Boy* (1973), *The Money Game* (1992), *Kayo's House* (1996), *The Smugglers* (1997), and *Beauty Queen* (1997).

KIMURA, Saeko (1963—). Japanese synchronized swimmer. Born Jan 28, 1963, in Japan. ❖ At Los Angeles Olympics, won a bronze medal in duet (1984).

KINAU (c. 1805–1839). Hawaiian queen. Name variations: Kaahumanu II. Born in Waikiki c. 1805; died in Honolulu, April 4, 1839; dau. of Kamehameha I the Great (1758–1819), king of Hawaii (r. 1810–1819), and Kaheiheimalie; sister of Kauikeaouli (1814–1854), later known as Kamehameha III, king of Hawaii (r. 1824–1854), and Queen Kamamalu (c. 1803–1824); educated by missionaries; m. Liholiho known as Kamehameha II (1797–1824), king of Hawaii (r. 1819–1824); m. Kahalaia (died); m. Kekuanaoa, Sept 19, 1827; children: (with Kahalaia) one son, Kamehameha; (with Kekuanaoa) David Kamehameha (b. 1828); Moses Kekuaiwa (b. 1829); Lot Kamehameha (1830–1872), later known as Kamehameha V, king of Hawaii (r. 1863–1872); Alexander Liholiho (1834–1863), later known as Kamehameha IV, king of Hawaii (r. 1855–1863); Victoria Kamamalu (1838–1866); (adopted) Bernice Pauahi Bishop (1831–1884), the great-granddau. of Kamehameha I the Great (1758–1819), king of Hawaii (r. 1810–1819). ❖ Hawaiian *kuhina nui* (co-ruler) during reign of half-brother Kamehameha III; learned to speak English and became a devout Christian; at young age, became 1 of 5 primary wives of Liholiho, the future Kamehameha II (1819); following Liholiho's death (1824), was given in marriage to Kahalaia who died of whooping cough shortly thereafter; married Kekuanaoa (1827); succeeded Kaahumanu as *kuhina nui* and regent for the boy king Kamehameha III (Kauikeaouli) (1832); survived a rocky regency with the 19-year-old king who embarked on a 2-year period of revelry, until her relationship with him steadied; undertook many reforms. ❖ See also *Women in World History.*

KINCAID, Jamaica (1949—). American writer. Born Elaine Cynthia Potter Richardson, May 25, 1949, in St. John's, Antigua; dau. of David Drew (stepfather) and Annie Richardson; studied photography at New School for Social Research; attended Franconia College; m. Allen Shawn (composer, professor and son of William Shawn), 1979; children: Annie and Harold. ❖ Was sent to Westchester, NY, to work as au pair at 16 (1965); wrote series of articles published in *Ingenue* magazine; changed name to Jamaica Kincaid to keep parents from knowing she was writing; was a regular contributor and staff writer on *The New Yorker* (1976–95); published 1st collection of short stories *At the Bottom of the River* (1983); published semi-autobiographical novels *Annie John* (1985) and *Lucy* (1991); wrote non-fictional account of home island *A Small Place* (1988); also wrote *My Brother* (1997), nominated for a National Book Award, *The Autobiography of My Mother* (1996), and *Among Flowers: A Walk in the Himalaya* (1995). ❖ See also Frank Birbalsingh, *Jamaica Kincaid: From Antigua to America* (St. Martin, 1996).

KINCAID, Jean (1579–1600). Scottish murderer. Born in Scotland in 1579; beheaded in 1600; dau. of John Livingstone of Dunipace; m. John Kincaid of Warriston. ❖ Having paid to have her husband, a man of some influence in Edinburgh, murdered, was beheaded for her efforts.

KINCH, Myra (1904–1981). American modern dancer and choreographer. Born 1904 in Los Angeles, CA; died Nov 20, 1981, in Bonita Springs, FL. ❖ In California, performed at Coconut Grove and at Fanchon and Marco's West Coast De Luxe Theater Prologs; performed with Max Reinhardt's company in Germany (1932) and throughout Eastern Europe and US; danced in film *The Lives of a Bengal Lancer* (1935); served as dance director of local Federal Theater Project in CA, where she choreographed historical works for Golden Gate International Exposition; worked summers at Jacob's Pillow and taught in and around NY until retirement (1967); choreographed a variety of works, ranging from serious to satirical to comical.

KIND, Marien (1871–1955). *See Handel-Mazzetti, Enrica von.*

KING, Alberta Williams (1903–1974). African-American church organist and mother of Martin Luther King Jr. Name variations: Mama King. Born Alberta Christine Williams in 1903; assassinated in 1974; dau. of Reverend Adam Daniels Williams, pastor of Ebenezer Baptist Church; m. Martin Luther King Sr. (b. 1899, prominent Baptist preacher) in 1926; children: Martin Luther King Jr. (1929–1968). ❖ Was playing "The Lord's Prayer" on the new organ at the morning service in Ebenezer Baptist Church, when she was gunned down by African-American Marcus Wayne Chenault Jr. (June 30, 1974). Chenault was sentenced to life in prison because of doubts about his mental competency. ❖ See also *Women in World History.*

KING, Andrea (1919–2003). French-born actress. Name variations: Georgette McKee. Born Georgette André Barry, Feb 1, 1919, in Paris, France; died April 22, 2003, in Woodland Hills, CA; dau. of Belle Hart (dancer with Isadora Duncan); m. Nat Willis (lawyer), 1940 (died 1970); children: daughter. ❖ Brought to US as an infant; made film debut as Hilda Bensinger in *The Ramparts We Watch* (1940), followed by *The Very Thought of You, Hollywood Canteen, Hotel Berlin, God Is My Co-Pilot, The Beast with Five Fingers, Mr. Peabody and the Mermaid, The Lemon Drop Kid, Darby's Rangers, Blackenstein* and *The Color of Evening,* among others; on tv, appeared frequently on such shows as "Lux Theatre" and "Perry Mason."

KING, Anita (1891–1963). American silent-screen actress. Born Aug 14, 1891, in Indiana; died June 10, 1963, in Hollywood, CA; m. Timothy McKenna. ❖ Made film debut in *The Virginian* (1914); for publicity, became the 1st woman to drive a roadster from LA to NY (1916); best remembered as *The Girl of the Golden West.*

KING, Anne (1621–after 1684). British poet. Name variations: Lady Howe. Born 1621 in England; died after 1684; dau. of John King, bishop of London, and Joan (Freeman) King; sister of Henry King, poet; m. John Dutton, 1648 (died 1657); m. Sir Richard Grobham Howe, before 1671. ❖ Only 2 poems can be attributed to her with certainty, "Under Mr. Hales Picture" (1636) printed in J. Butt, "Izaak Walton's Collections for Fulman's Life of John Hales" in *MLR* (1934) and "Inscription on monument of Dorothy, Lady Hubert at Langley, Buckinghamshire" (1684) in G. Greer et al (eds.), *Kissing the Rod: An Anthology of Seventeenth-Century Women's Verse* (1988).

KING, Annette (b. 1913). *See Reid, Charlotte Thompson.*

KING, Annette (1947—). New Zealand politician. Born Annette Robinson, Sept 13, 1947, in Murchison, NZ; m. Doug King. ❖ Served as Labour MP for Horowhenua (1984–90), becoming Minister of Employment and Youth Affairs; lost seat (1990); elected Labour MP for Miramar (1993), becoming Minister of Health.

KING, Barbara Ann (1928—). *See Scott, Barbara Ann.*

KING, Betsy (1955—). American golfer. Born Aug 13, 1955, in Reading, PA. ❖ Won Women's Kemper Open (1984, 1988, 1989); won Freedom Orlando Classic and Columbia Savings Classic (1984); won Samaritan Turquoise Classic and Ladies' British Open (1985); won Rail Charity (1985, 1986, 1988); won Henredon Classic (1986); won Circle K Tucson Open, McDonald's, Atlantic City, and Nabisco Dinah Shore (1987); won Cellular One-PING (1988); won Jamaica Classic, USX Classic, McDonald's, Nestle, and US Women's Open (1989); won Nabisco Dinah Shore, JAL Big Apple Classic, and US Women's Open (1990); won Corning Classic, JAL Big Apple (1991); won Mazda LPGA championship, Phar-Mor, and Mazda Japan Classic (1992); won Toray Japan Queens Cup (1993); won ShopRite Classic (1995, 2000); won Nabisco Dinah Shore (1997); won Cup Noodles Hawaiian Open, Corning Classic (2000); thrice named Rolex Player of the Year; twice won Vare Trophy; five-time member of the Solheim Cup team. Inducted into LPGA Hall of Fame (1995).

KING, Billie Jean (1943—). American tennis player. Name variations: Billie Jean Moffitt; Mrs. L.W. King. Born Billie Jean Moffitt, Nov 22, 1943, in Long Beach, CA; m. Larry King, Sept 17, 1965 (div.). ❖ Member of the Southern California Junior Wightman Cup team (1959–60); achieved 1st national tennis ranking (1959); turned professional (1968); won Wimbledon singles (1966–68, 1972–73, 1975), doubles (1961–62, 1965, 1967–68, 1970–73), mixed doubles (1967, 1973); won US Open singles (1967, 1971, 1972, 1974), doubles (1965, 1967, 1974, 1980), mixed doubles (1967, 1971, 1973); won French Open singles and doubles (1972), mixed doubles (1967, 1970); won Australian Open singles and mixed doubles (1968); won Italian Open singles and doubles (1970); won US Hard Court singles (1966); won West German Open singles (1971); won South African Open singles (1966, 1967, 1969); won U.S. Indoor singles (1966–68, 1971); played key role in establishing the 1st Virginia Slims tournament (1971); founded the Women's Tennis Association and played Bobby Riggs at the Houston Astrodome (1973); co-founded and published *WomenSports* magazine (1974); named in controversial palimony suit (1981); had international tv sports commentary position for NBC expanded to coverage of male players (1982); wrote, with Cynthia Starr, *We Have Come a Long Way: The Story of Women's Tennis* (McGraw-Hill, 1988). Named Associated Press Women's Athlete of the Year (1967, 1973); named *Sports Illustrated* Sportsperson of the Year (1972); named Top Woman Athlete of the Year (1972) and *Time* magazine Woman of the Year (1976); elected to International Tennis Hall of Fame (1987) and National Women's Hall of Fame (1990). ❖ See also (autobiographies) with Kim Chapin *Billie Jean* (Harper & Row, 1974) and with Frank Deford *Billie Jean* (Viking, 1982); and *Women in World History*.

KING, Carol Weiss (1895–1952). American lawyer and civil libertarian. Born Aug 24, 1895, in New York, NY; died Jan 22, 1952, in NY; dau. of Samuel Weiss (lawyer) and Carrie (Stix) Weiss; graduate of Barnard College, 1916; New York University Law School, JD, 1920; m. Gordon Congdon King (writer), 1917 (died 1930); children: Jonathan. ❖ Specializing in cases involving immigration legislation, was frequently pitted against officials of US Immigration Service; took a job as a research fellow for American Association for Labor Legislation; earned law degree and gained experience in civil liberty and deportation cases; became a head partner at Shorr, Brodsky, and King (1925); when partner Joseph Brodsky helped organize the International Labor Defense, became a member, serving on its legal advisory committee; in that capacity, worked on numerous cases, notably the defense of the "Scottsboro Boys," Harry Bridges, and Communist Party leader William Schneiderman; her frequent defense of Communists led some to brand her a Communist sympathizer, particularly during Cold War hysteria (1950s); was active in a number of civil libertarian organizations; helped found National Lawyers Guild (1936) and was a member of the Joint Anti-Fascist Refugee Committee; founded *International Juridical Association Bulletin* (1932). ❖ See also Ann Fagan Ginger, *Carol Weiss King: Human Rights Lawyer, 1895–1952* (U. Press of Colorado, 1993); and *Women in World History*.

KING, Carole (1942—). American composer and performer. Born Carole Klein, Feb 9, 1942, in Brooklyn, NY; attended Queens College; m. Gerry Goffin, 1960 (div. 1968); m. Charles Larkey (div.); m. Rick Evers (died from drug overdose one year after their marriage); m. Richard Sorenson; children: (1st m.) Louise Goffin and Sherry Goffin-Kondor; (2nd m.) daughter Molly Larkey. ❖ After studying piano as a child, wrote songs and organized her 1st group in high school, a vocal quartet called The Co-Sines, changing last name to King; dropped out of college and worked part-time for a NY music publishing co., composing with lyricist husband the music for a string of Top-40 hits which came to be called "uptown R&B," including 1st #1 song, "Will You Still Love Me Tomorrow?" (1960), followed by "Chains," "One Fine Day," "The Loco-Motion," "Up on the Roof," "Go Away, Little Girl" and (You Make Me Feel Like a) "Natural Woman," written for Aretha Franklin; after a divorce (1968), began to promote herself as a solo performer and wrote "You've Got a Friend"; released album *Tapestry* to great acclaim (1971), winning 4 Grammy awards; released a collection of children's songs based on Sendak's *Really Rosie*, which was later turned into the score for an animated film and, later still, a Broadway play; has continued to write and perform, as well as composing music for film scores and occasionally acting in films and on stage; is also an outspoken environmentalist. Inducted into Songwriters' Hall of Fame and Rock and Roll

Hall of Fame. ❖ See also "Tapestry Revisited: A Tribute to Carole King," Lifetime TV (1st aired, 1995); and *Women in World History*.

KING, Charlotte (c. 1772–1825). *See Dacre, Charlotte.*

KING, Christine (1915–1991). *See Dunbar, Dixie.*

KING, Coretta Scott (1927–2006). African-American civil-rights activist. Name variations: Corrie or Cora; Mrs. Martin Luther King Jr. Born Coretta Scott, April 27, 1927, in Heiberger, Alabama; died Jan 31, 2006, at a hospital in Mexico; dau. of Obidiah "Obie" Scott (farmer, independent truck driver, and small store owner) and Bernice McMurry (also seen as McMurray) Scott; attended Antioch College, 1945–51, and New England Conservatory of Music, 1951–54; m. Martin Luther King Jr., June 18, 1953; children: Yolanda Denise King (b. 1955, actress); Martin Luther King, III (b. 1957); Dexter Scott King (b. 1961); Bernice King (b. 1963). ❖ Wife of civil-rights leader Martin Luther King Jr., who took on an independent role in the civil-rights movement in years following husband's assassination (1968); received Antioch College Race Relations Committee scholarship (1945); received Jesse Smith Noyes fellowship to New England Conservatory of Music (1951); met Martin Luther King Jr. (1952); moved to Montgomery, Alabama (1954); confronted with up to 40 phone-call threats a day during Montgomery bus boycott (1955); was present with baby daughter when King home was bombed (1956); became a featured performer at money-raising concerts to support the cause of civil rights and integration (1956); moved to Atlanta, GA (1960); attended Geneva disarmament talks (1962); began a series of "Freedom Concerts" (1964); following assassination of husband (1968), emerged as a powerful, and sometimes controversial, personality in her own right; spoke at St. Paul's Church in London, the 1st woman in history to have such an opportunity (1969); began planning for Martin Luther King Jr., Memorial (1969); founded Center for Non-Violent Change (1971), serving as founding president and chief executive officer until 1994; toured South Africa (1986), meeting with black civil-rights leaders; worked to preserve husband's legacy. ❖ See also memoirs, *My Life with Martin Luther King, Jr.* (1969, rev. 1993); and *Women in World History*.

KING, Debra Flintoff (b. 1960). *See Flintoff, Debra.*

KING, Dottie (c. 1896–1923). American model and dancer. Name variations: Dot King; Dorothy Keenan. Born Anna Marie Keenan, c. 1896, possibly Rochester, NY; found dead in New York, NY, Mar 15, 1923; possibly sister of Louisa Marshall; married a chauffeur, c. 1914 (sep. c. 1916). ❖ NY model and theatrical ballet dancer, called Broadway Butterfly by tabloid writers, began career in a tandem dancing act with Louisa Marshall; was found dead at 27 in her 57th Street apartment; her killer was never found. SS. Van Dine based his celebrated *Canary Murder Case* in his "Philo Vance" series on her killing (1927).

KING, Eleanor (1906–1991). American modern dancer and choreographer. Born 1906, in Middletown, PA; died 1991. ❖ Charter member of Humphrey/Weidman Concert Group, created roles in numerous early works by both choreographers, including Humphrey's *Water Study* (1929), *The Shakers* (1932) and *Suite in F* (1933); choreographed works for what was known as "The Little Company," a small group of dancers including herself, José Limón, and Letitia Ide; performed with and choreographed further works for Theater Dance Group, where dancers included Sybil Shearer and William Bales; formed own company in Seattle, WA (c. 1948), where she continued to dance and choreograph; taught at Toankust Dansschool in Rotterdam, College of Santa Fe, and University of Arkansas.

KING, Ellen (b. 1909). Scottish swimmer. Born Jan 16, 1909, in Scotland. ❖ At Amsterdam Olympics, won a silver medal in the 100-meter backstroke and a silver medal in the 4 x 100-meter freestyle relay (1928).

KING, Mrs. Frances (1863–1948). *See King, Louisa Yeomans.*

KING, Grace Elizabeth (c. 1852–1932). American novelist, short story writer, and historian. Born in Louisiana, c. 1852; died 1932. ❖ Prominent Southern writer at turn of the century, wrote largely about Southern subjects; published novel *Monsieur Motte* (1888), followed by *Balcony Stories*, considered one of her best works, and *Tales of a Time and Place*; nonfiction books include *New Orleans: The Place and the People*, and a life of Sieur de Bienville, founder of New Orleans.

KING, Helen Dean (1869–1955). American biologist. Born Helen Dean King in Oswego, NY, 1869; died in Philadelphia, PA, in 1955; dau. of George (businessman) and Leonora (Dean) King; graduate of Oswego Free Academy, c. 1877; Vassar College, BA, 1892; Bryn Mawr College,

PhD, 1899; never married; no children. ❖ Known for pioneering research on the breeding of rats, was the subject of much controversy during career; at Bryn Mawr, majored in morphology under Thomas Hunt Morgan and minored in physiology and paleontology under J.W. Warren and Florence Bascom; completing degree (1899), remained at Bryn Mawr for 5 years, serving as an assistant in biology; was an assistant in anatomy at University of Pennsylvania (1906–08), after which she took a teaching post at Philadelphia's Wistar Institute of Anatomy and Biology, remaining there for next 41 years, working her way from assistant to assistant professor and finally to professor of embryology; after studying 25 generations of albino rats to determine the effects of inbreeding, concluded that brother-sister matings produced animals that were superior, causing a furor in the press; devoted herself to research involving domestication of the Norway rat (1919–49), which was considered too wild to breed in the laboratory, and succeeded in producing rats with the specific genetic characteristics required for particular research projects. Awarded Ellen Richards Research Prize of the Association to Aid Scientific Research for Women (1932). ❖ See also *Women in World History.*

KING, Henrietta Chamberlain (1832–1925). American cattle rancher and philanthropist. Born Henrietta Maria Morse Chamberlain in Boonville, Missouri, July 21, 1832; died in Santa Gertrudis, TX, Mar 31, 1925; dau. of Hiram Bingham Chamberlain (preacher) and Maria Chamberlain; attended a female institute in Holly Springs, Mississippi; m. Captain Richard King (steamboat master turned rancher), Dec 1854 (died April 1885); children: 5, including Alice King Kleberg. ❖ At time of husband's death (1885), inherited 500,000 acres of Texas land and $500,000 of debt; at her death (1925), left an estate of nearly 1 million acres and almost 95,000 head of cattle; built one of the largest ranching enterprises in US; also helped foster the use of scientific techniques in cattle breeding, thus producing a safer, more abundant beef supply. ❖ See also *Women in World History.*

KING, Isabel Grace Mackenzie (1843–1917). Canadian mother of a prime minister. Born Feb 6, 1843, in New York; died Dec 18, 1917; dau. of William Lyon Mackenzie (known as the "Rebel of Upper Canada" who took part in the unsuccessful Rebellion of 1837) and Isabel Baxter Mackenzie; m. John King (lawyer), 1872 (died 1916); children: Isabel Christina Grace (Bella, 1873–1915), William Lyon Mackenzie King (1874–1950, prime minister of Canada, 1921–26, 1926–30, 1935–48), Janet Lindsey (Jennie, b. 1876), Dougall Macdougall (Max, b. 1878). ❖ Had an enormous impact on the thinking and political views of her son, the prime minister, and was the only woman who ever occupied a place of any real significance in his life.

KING, Isabella (1886–1953). *See Greenway, Isabella Selmes.*

KING, Jane (d. 1971). American vaudevillian and musical-comedy performer. Name variations: King Sisters. Died May 23, 1971, age 75, in Arlington, Virginia; sister of Mary King; m. Leslie H. Baker (Washington broker), 1924. ❖ With sister Mary, appeared as the King Sisters in vaudeville and on Broadway in several shows, including *Irene, Jim Jam Jems,* and *I'll Say She Is;* retired (1924).

KING, Jessie Marion (1875–1949). Scottish artist and graphic designer. Born in New Kilpatrick, Scotland, 1875; died in Kirkcudbright, Scotland, in 1949; attended the Glasgow School of Art; married E.A. Taylor (artist). ❖ Associated with the British version of Art Nouveau, developed a style strongly influenced by Charles Rennie Mackintosh, a Scottish designer at the forefront of modernism; produced watercolors, wallpaper, jewelry, and tile and textile designs which she actively exhibited at Royal Scottish Academy, Glasgow Institute of Fine Arts, and Bruton Galleries (1897–1940); won a gold medal for drawings and watercolors at Turin International Exhibition of Modern Decorative Art (1902); authored several books and produced book illustrations and jacket designs.

KING, Joyce (1921—). Australian runner. Born Sept 1, 1921, in Sydney, NSW, Australia; twin sister of Bruce King (sprint champion). ❖ Won NSW State titles (1943, 1946); won a silver medal for 4 x 100-meter relay at London Olympics (1948); set national records for 100 and 220 yards; also played softball and netball and won a silver medal at state swimming championships.

KING, Julie Rivé (1854–1937). *See Rivé-King, Julie.*

KING, June (1924—). *See Helm, June.*

KING, Katie (1975—). American ice-hockey player. Born May 24, 1975, in Salem, NH. ❖ Won a team gold medal at Nagano (1998), the 1st Olympics to feature women's ice hockey; won team silver medals at World championships (1997, 1999, 2000, 2001); won a team silver medal at Salt Lake City Olympics (2002) and a team bronze medal at Torino Olympics (2006). ❖ See also Mary Turco, *Crashing the Net: The U.S. Women's Olympic Ice Hockey Team and the Road to Gold* (HarperCollins, 1999); and *Women in World History.*

KING, Lida Shaw (1868–1932). American scholar. Born Sept 15, 1868, in Boston, MA; died Jan 10, 1932, in Providence, RI; dau. of Henry Melville King (cleric) and Susan Ellen (Fogg) King. ❖ Held teaching fellowship in Latin and instructorship in Latin and Greek at Vassar College (1894–97); focused on archaeology at American School of Classical Studies in Athens, Greece (1899–1901); participated in excavation of Nymph's Cave at Vari on Mount Hymettus in Attica, Greece; was director of Latin and Greek department at Packer Collegiate Institute (1901–02); served as dean of Women's College (now Pembroke College) in Brown University (1905–22); taught in addition to administrative responsibilities, 1st as professor of classical philology (from 1905) and then as professor of classical literature and archaeology (from 1909).

KING, Louisa Yeomans (1863–1948). American gardener. Born Louisa Boyd Yeomans in Washington, NJ, Oct 17, 1863; died in Milton, MA, Jan 16, 1948; dau. of Alfred Yeomans (Presbyterian cleric) and Elizabeth Blythe (Ramsay) Yeomans; m. Francis King, June 12, 1890; children: Elizabeth, Henry and Frances King. ❖ Planted 1st garden (1902); was a founding member of Garden Club of America (1913) and served as president of Woman's National Farm and Garden Association (1914–21); wrote magazine articles on gardening and published 1st of 9 books, *The Well-Considered Garden* (1915); advocated artistry over practicality, particularly when it came to groupings and color considerations; became 1st woman to receive George White Medal of Massachusetts Horticultural Society, the highest gardening award in America (1921); was a fellow of Royal Horticultural Society of Great Britain.

KING, Mrs. L.W. (b. 1943). *See King, Billie Jean.*

KING, Louise Augarde (1863–1909). *See Augarde, Louise.*

KING, Mabel (1932–1999). African-American actress and singer. Born Donnie Mabel Elizabeth Washington, Dec 25, 1932, in Charleston, SC; died Nov 9, 1999, in Woodland Hills, CA; m. Melvin King (div.). ❖ Best remembered as the Wicked Witch of the West in *The Wiz,* on stage and in film; other films include *The Bingo Long Traveling All-Stars and Motor Kings, The Jerk, The Gong Show Movie* and *Scrooged;* starred in tv series "What's Happening!" (1976–78); battled diabetes for many years, losing her legs to the disease.

KING, Martha (1802/03–1897). New Zealand schoolteacher, gardener, and botanical artist. Born Martha King, c. 1802 or 1803, in Ireland; died May 31, 1897, in New Plymouth, New Zealand; sister of Maria King and Samuel Popham King. ❖ Immigrated with brother and sister to New Zealand (1840); settled in Wanganui and opened 1st dame school there (1841), and in New Plymouth (1848); commissioned to prepare drawings of indigenous botanical specimens, which were published as plates in Edward Wakefield's *Illustrations to "Adventure in New Zealand"* (1845); donated her garden to New Plymouth Recreation Grounds Board; work held in Alexander Turnbull Library. ❖ See also *Dictionary of New Zealand Biography* (Vol. 1).

KING, Mrs. Martin Luther Jr. (b. 1927). *See King, Coretta Scott.*

KING, Mary (1961—). British equestrian. Born June 8, 1961, in Newark, Nottinghamshire, England. ❖ Placed 1st for 3-day event (team) at World Equestrian Games (1994); on King Solomon III, won a silver medal for team eventing at Athens Olympics (2004). ❖ See also *Pippa Funnell: Road to the Top.*

KING, Mary Bea (1949—). *See Porter, Mary Bea.*

KING, Maxine (b. 1944). *See King, Micki.*

KING, Mazie (b. around 1880). American innovative toe dancer. Born c. 1880; m. John Leonard (died 1908). ❖ Began career at young age; made NY debut in Leonard and Gilmore's *Hogan's Alley* (1896) as principal specialty dancer; performed toe dances at NY's roof gardens; performed in revue *The Mimic World* (1908), where she imitated Bessie Clayton; appeared in numerous vaudeville and Broadway productions including Lew Fields' *The Hen-Pecks* and *The Midnight Sons;* walked down 1,000 steps of NY's Metropolitan Tower on point, for which she received so much publicity that she had to repeat the feat in high buildings in the many cities she toured; performed ballet and exhibition ballroom dances known as *The Spirit of Spring* and appeared with Mazie King's Terpsichorean Beauties, one of the most popular dance acts in vaudeville.

KING, Micki (1944—). American diver. Name variations: Captain Maxine King; team manager under name Micki Hogue for US Olympic divers (1988). Born Maxine J. King on July 26, 1944, in Pontiac, Michigan; graduated from University of Michigan, 1966; enlisted in U.S. Air Force, 1966; graduate of University of Michigan, 1966. ❖ Enlisted in US Air Force (1966); competed against men at World Military Games (1969), placing 4th in platform and 3rd in springboard; at Mexico City Olympics, broke left forearm in next-to-last dive off springboard but performed final dive, finishing 4th (1968); won a gold medal at Munich Olympics (1972); won 10 national springboard and platform diving championships (1969–72); appointed diving coach at Air Force Academy (1973), the 1st woman to hold a faculty position at a US military academy; retired with rank of colonel (1992); served as president of US Diving (1990–94). Inducted into International Swimming Hall of Fame.

KING, Mollie (1885–1981). American theatrical dancer. Born April 16, 1885, in New York, NY; died Dec 28, 1981, in Fort Lauderdale, FL; sister of Nellie King (1895–1935) and Charles King (1889–1944). ❖ Made stage debut as a child with brother and sister, as The Three Kings, and toured until 1905; played Maxine Elliott's daughter in a number of plays, including *Her Own Way*; returned to Broadway musicals in *A Winsome Widow* (1911), *The Passing Show of 1913*, *The Bell of Bond Street* (1914), and *Blue Eyes* (1921); appeared in film serials, including *The Seven Pearls* (1917), *Mystery of the Double Cross* (1917), and *Women Men Forget* (1919); retired at 29 (1924).

KING, Nellie (1895–1935). American theatrical dancer. Born 1895 in New York, NY; died July 1, 1935, in West Palm Beach, FL; sister of Mollie King (1885–1981) and Charles King (1889–1944). ❖ Made stage debut as a child in The Three Kings, with brother and sister, touring extensively; continued working with brother in vaudeville acts and in *Mimic World of 1909*; retired early due to illness.

KING, Oona (1967—). English politician and member of Parliament. Born Oona King, Oct 22, 1967; m. Tiberio Santomarco, 1994. ❖ Representing Labour, elected to House of Commons for Bethnal Green and Bow (1997); named PPS to Stephen Timms as minister of State, Dept. of Trade and Industry.

KING, Rebecca (c. 1950—). Miss America. Name variations: Rebecca Dreman. Born Rebecca Ann King c. 1950; attended Colorado Women's College; m. George Dreman; children: two daughters. ❖ Named Miss America (1974), representing Colorado; a practicing attorney, specializes in family law.

KING, Sophia (1849–1926). See Anstice, Sophia.

KING SISTERS. See King, Jane.

KINGA. Variant of Cunegunde.

KINGSBURY, Susan (1870–1949). American social investigator and educator. Born Susan Myra Kingsbury, Oct 18, 1870, in San Pablo, CA; died Nov 28, 1949, in Bryn Mawr, PA; dau. of Willard Belmont Kingsbury (physician) and Helen Shuler (De Lamater) Kingsbury (college dean); Stanford University, MA in history, 1899; Columbia University, PhD in American colonial history, 1905. ❖ While teaching economics at Simmons College in Boston, also served as director of research department of Women's Educational and Industrial Union of Boston (from 1907); was professor of social economy and director of Carola Woerishoffer Graduate Department of Social Economy and Social Research (later Graduate School of Social Work) at Bryn Mawr (1915–36); helped found American Association of Schools of Social Work (later Council on Social Work Education, 1919); toured China and India (1921–22) and Soviet Union (1929–30, 1932, 1936) to observe conditions for women and children. Wrote *Licensed Workers in Industrial Homework in Massachusetts* (1915), *Newspapers and the News* (1937) and *Factory, Family and Woman in the Soviet Union* (with Mildred Fairchild, 1935).

KINGSFORD, Anna (1846–1888). British physician and religious writer. Born Anna Bonus in 1846; died 1888; studied medicine in Paris; awarded MD, 1880; m. Algernon Godfrey Kingsford (vicar of Atcham, Shropshire), 1867. ❖ Established herself as a writer before taking up the study and practice of medicine; began publishing miscellaneous works

(1863) and contributed stories to the *Penny Post* (1868–72); converted to Roman Catholicism (1870); purchased the *Lady's Own Paper* (1872), which she edited for a year; began medical studies in Paris (1874); practiced in London for only 8 years before her death; was also president of the Theosophical Society (1883) and founded the Hermetic Society (1884).

KINGSLEY, Dorothy (1909–1997). American screenwriter. Born Dorothy Kingsley, Oct 14, 1909, in New York, NY; died of a heart ailment, Sept 26, 1997, in Carmel, CA; dau. of Alma Hanlon (silent-screen actress) and Walter Kingsley (Broadway press agent); 1st marriage ended in divorce; m. William Durney (died 1989); children: (1st m.) 3 sons. ❖ Was hired as a gag writer for Edgar Bergen; became staff writer at MGM (1943); wrote scripts for over 25 films, including *A Date with Judy, Dangerous When Wet, Valley of the Dolls, Half a Sixpence* and *Green Mansions;* created tv series "Bracken's World," (1969); with husband, founded Durney Vineyards in Carmel. Nominated for Academy Award for *Seven Brides for Seven Brothers;* received Best Script nominations from Writers Guild for *On an Island with You, Angels in the Outfield, Kiss Me, Kate, Don't Go Near the Water, Pal Joey* and *Can-Can.* ❖ See also *Women in World History.*

KINGSLEY, Elizabeth (1871–1957). American double-crostic-puzzle creator. Born 1871 in Brooklyn, NY; died 1957 in Brooklyn. ❖ Created the 1st double-crostic puzzle to appear in print (1934); published weekly puzzle in *Saturday Review of Literature.*

KINGSLEY, Madge (1909–1981). See Evans, Madge.

KINGSLEY, Mary H. (1862–1900). English traveler and writer. Born Mary Henrietta Kingsley, Oct 13, 1862, in Islington, England; died June 3, 1900, in South Africa, of typhoid fever; dau. of George Kingsley (physician) and Mary (Bailey) Kingsley; educated mostly through father's travel books; never married; no children. ❖ Victorian Englishwoman and daring adventurer, famed for her exploits in West Africa, who wrote several books detailing her trips and caused considerable controversy with her ideas about how West Africa should be governed; following death of parents, used inheritance for solo visit to Canary Islands (1892); inspired by previous journey, set sail for Freetown, West Africa (Aug 1893); spent 11 months in West Africa leading an expedition of Africans in exploring the Ogooué River, crossing overland from the Ogooué to the Ramboé River, and becoming the 1st person, along with African assistants, to ascend the southeast side of Mount Cameroon (1895); convinced that the British government was mismanaging its holdings in that part of the continent and would soon ruin it, was against interventionist colonial rule and favored a loose system of government resembling economic imperialism that would allow free trade to continue unfettered; gave lectures throughout United Kingdom on a wide range of topics related to the region she had explored; after 4 years back in England, departed for South Africa, where she nursed military prisoners of the Boer War (1900); came down with typhoid, dying 3 weeks later; writings include *Travels in West Africa, Congo Français, Corisco and Cameroons* (1897), *West African Studies* (1899), *The Story of West Africa* (1900). ❖ See also Dea Birkett, *Mary Kingsley: Imperial Adventuress* (Macmillan, 1992); and *Women in World History.*

KINGSLEY, Mary St. Leger (1852–1931). British writer. Name variations: Mary St. Leger Kingsley Harrison; (pseudonym) Lucas Malet. Born June 4, 1852, in Eversley, England; died Oct 27, 1931, in Tenby, Wales; dau. of novelist Charles Kingsley (1819–75) and Frances Grenfell; niece of writer Henry Kingsley; attended Slade School of Fine Art, London; m. Reverend William Harrison (sep., died 1887); children: (adopted dau.) Gabrielle Vallings. ❖ Wrote more than 20 novels, many featuring themes of unhappy marriages, grotesque characters and macabre plots; adopted pseudonym of Lucas Malet in order to disassociate herself from her literary family; published 1st novel, *Mrs Lorimer: A Sketch in Black and White* (1882), but made her reputation with *Colonel Enderby's Wife* (1885); was a well-known member of literary circles in her day, friends with Henry James, among others; also wrote *The Wages of Sin* (1891), *The Gateless Barrier* (1900), *Sir Richard Calmady* (1901), *The Far Horizon* (1906), *Deadham Hard* (1919), *The Survivors* (1923) and *The Dogs of Want* (1924).

KINGSLEY, Mrs. Sidney (1909–1981). See Evans, Madge.

KINGSLEY, Susan (1946–1984). American stage actress. Born May 1, 1946, in Middlesboro, KY; died Feb 6, 1984, of injuries sustained in an auto accident in Commerce, GA; m. David Hurt. ❖ Lead actress at the Actors Theatre of Louisville for many years; made auspicious off-

Broadway debut in *Getting Out* and Broadway debut in *The Wake of Jamey Foster* (1982); films include *Reckless* and *Old Enough*.

KINGSMILL, Anne (1661–1720). *See Finch, Anne.*

KINGSOLVER, Barbara (1955—). American journalist, essayist and novelist. Born April 8, 1955, in Kentucky; graduate of DePauw University, 1977; University of Arizona, MS; m. Steven Hopp (chemist), 1985; children: Camille and Lily. ❖ Published 1st novel *The Bean Trees* (1988), followed by an oral history, *Holding the Line: Women in the Great Arizona Mine Strike of 1983* (1989); other novels include *Animal Dreams* (1990), *Pigs in Heaven* (1993) and *Prodigal Summer* (2000); also wrote (short stories) *Homeland*, (poems) *Another America/Otra America* (1992) and the bestselling (essays) *High Tide in Tucson* (1998). Awarded National Humanities medal (2000).

KINGSTON, duchess of. *See Chudleigh, Elizabeth (1720–1788).*

KINGSTON, Elizabeth (1720–1788). *See Chudleigh, Elizabeth.*

KINGSTON, Maxine Hong (1940—). American memoirist and novelist. Born Oct 27, 1940, in Stockton, CA; dau. of Tom Hong and Ying Lan Chew; m. Earl Kingston, 1962; children: 1. ❖ Lived with husband in Hawaii for 17 years before returning to mainland US; taught creative writing at University of California, Berkeley; wrote *The Woman Warrior: Memoirs of a Girlhood Among Ghosts* (1976), *China Men* (1980), *Hawaii One Summer* (1987), *Tripmaster Monkey: His Fake Book* (1989), *Conversations With Maxine Hong Kingston* (1998), *To Be The Poet* (2002) and *The Fifth Book of Peace* (2003); edited *The Literature of California: Native American Beginnings to 1945, Volume 1* (2000). Won National Book Critics Circle Award for *The Woman Warrior* and PEN West award for *Tripmaster Monkey*.

KINGSTON, Winifred (1894–1967). English-born silent-film actress. Born Nov 11, 1894, in England; died Feb 3, 1967, in La Jolla, CA; m. Dustin Farnum (actor), 1924 (died 1929); children: daughter. ❖ Appeared opposite her husband in several films, including *The Squaw Man* and *Corsican Brothers*.

KINIGI, Sylvie (1953—). Burundi politician. Born in 1953 in Burundi; graduate in economic management of Burundi Univerity; married to a Hutu (died 1993); children: 5. ❖ A moderate member of Tutsi-based National Party for Unity and Progress (UPRONA), served as prime minister of Burundi (July 10, 1993–Feb 11, 1994), during which time democratically elected president Melchior Ndadaye, a Hutu, was killed by renegade Tutsi troops (Oct 21, 1993); managed to hold the government together; was president of Federation of African Creators (1993–94).

KINKEL, Johanna (1810–1858). German choral conductor, pianist, composer, poet, and writer. Born Johanna Mockel in Bonn, Germany, July 8, 1810; committed suicide in London, England, Nov 15, 1858; dau. of Peter Joseph Mockel (singing teacher at Royal Bonn Gymnasium); m. Johann Paul Matthieux (bookseller), 1832 (marriage annulled after a few days); m. Gottfried Kinkel (poet and revolutionary), 1843; children: 4. ❖ Became involved with chamber and vocal ensembles; during Revolution of 1848, 2nd husband was arrested for political activities and condemned to death; when he escaped from Spandau Prison and went to London, followed him there and supported family as a choir director and composer; also wrote essays on music.

KINNAIRD, Mrs. Arthur (1816–1888). *See Kinnaird, Mary Jane.*

KINNAIRD, Mary Jane (1816–1888). English philanthropist and baroness. Name variations: Lady Kinnaird; Mrs. Arthur Kinnaird. Born Mary Jane Hoare, 1816, at Northwick Park, Northamptonshire; died 1888; m. Arthur Fitzgerald Kinnaird, 10th baron Kinnaird (1814–1887), philanthropist). ❖ Edited *Servants Prayers* (1849); along with Lady Canning, sent aid to the wounded in the Crimea; with Emma Robarts and others, was one of the founders of Young Women's Christian Association.

KINNAN, Marjorie (1896–1953). *See Rawlings, Marjorie Kinnan.*

KINNAN, Mary (1763–1848). American memoirist. Born 1763 in Virginia; died Mar 12, 1848, in NJ. ❖ Captured by Shawnees (1791) and held for 3 years; after being freed, settled in New Jersey and wrote account of survival, *True Narrative of the Sufferings of Mary Kinnan, Who Was Taken Prisoner by the Shawanee Nation of Indians* (1795).

KINNEY, Dita Hopkins (1854–1921). American nurse. Born Dita Hopkins, Sept 13, 1854, in New York, NY; died April 16, 1921, in

Bangor, Maine; dau. of Myra (Burtnett) Hopkins and C.T. Hopkins; graduate of Massachusetts General Hospital Training School for Nurses, 1892; m. Mark Kinney, 1874 (died 1878); children: 1. ❖ Served as a superintendent of Long Island Almshouse (1892–96), City and County Hospital, St. Paul, MN (1897) and, much later, Addison Gilbert Hospital in Gloucester, MA; cared for Spanish-American War veterans as a US Army contact nurse (1898); worked at General Hospital (San Francisco, CA), French Hospital (San Francisco, CA), Red Cross Society's convalescent home (Oakland, CA) and Fort Bayard Army Hospital (NM); appointed the 1st superintendent of the US Army Nurse Corps (c. 1905).

KINNOCK, Glenys (1944—). Welsh politician. Born July 7, 1944, in Roade, Northamptonshire, England. ❖ Teacher (1967–94); as a European Socialist, elected to 4th and 5th European Parliament (1994–99, 1999–2004) from UK; named co-president of members from the EP to the Joint Parliamentary Assembly of the Agreement between the African, Caribbean, and Pacific States and the European Union (ACP-EU). Wrote *Eritrea: Images of War and Peace* (1988), *Namibia: Birth of a Nation* (1990), and *By Faith and Daring* (1993).

KINOSHITA, Alicia (1967—). Japanese sailor. Born Feb 4, 1967, in Copenhagen, Denmark. ❖ Won a silver medal for double-handed dinghy (470) at Atlanta Olympics (1996).

KINSELLA, Kathleen (d. 1961). English-born actress. Born in England; died Mar 25, 1961, age 83, in Washington, DC. ❖ Came to Canada as a child, making debut in Montreal with Robert B. Mantrell; had featured roles on Broadway and with touring companies.

KINSHOFER, Christa (1961—). German Alpine skier. Name variations: Christa Kinshofer Guethlien or Güthlein. Born Jan 24, 1961, in Rosenheim, Germany. ❖ Won giant slalom World Cup title (1979); won a silver medal for slalom at Lake Placid Olympics (1980); won a silver medal for giant slalom and a bronze medal for slalom at Calgary Olympics (1988).

KINSKY, Countess (1843–1914). *See Suttner, Bertha von.*

KINT, Cor (d. 2002). Dutch swimmer. Born Cornelia Kint in Holland, Netherlands; died July 10, 2002 in Nambucca Heads, Australia. ❖ Set world records for backstroke in 100 meters (1:10.9 on Sept 22, 1939, which stood for 21 years), 100 yards, 200 meters (stood for 11 years), and 150 yards (stood for 11 years); unfortunately, could not test her dominance in an Olympics event because of WWII; moved to Australia (1960). Inducted into International Swimming Hall of Fame (1971).

KINUE or KINUYE HITOMI (1908–1931). *See Hitomi Kinue.*

KINUYO TANAKA (1907–1977). *See Tanaka, Kinuyo.*

KINZIE, Juliette Magill (1806–1870). American pioneer and author. Born Juliette Augusta Magill, Sept 11, 1806, in Middletown, CT; died Sept 15, 1870, in Amagansett, NY; dau. of Frances (Wolcott) Magill (dau. of Alexander Wolcott, leader of Republican Party in CT) and Arthur William Magill; dau.-in-law of John Kinzie (Chicago pioneer); attended Troy Female Seminary; m. John H. Kinzie (Indian agent at Fort Winnebago in WI), Aug 9, 1830; children: Eleanor Kinzie Gordon. ❖ Moved to the newly incorporated town of Chicago (1834) where she became a social and cultural leader; published works include *A Narrative of the Massacre at Chicago* (anonymous, 1844) and the successful *Waubun: The "Early Days" in the North-west* (1856) which helped establish the reputation of her father-in-law John Kinzie as Chicago's founding father; also wrote novels *Walter Ogilby* (1869) and *Mark Logan, the Bourgeois* (published posthumously, 1887).

KIPLAGAT, Lornah (1974—). Kenyan long-distance runner. Born Lorah Simba Kiplagat, May 1, 1974, in Kabiemit, Kenya; m. Pieter Langerhorst. ❖ Won Los Angeles marathon (1997, 1998), Amsterdam marathon (1999), Osaka marathon (2002); placed 3rd in NY marathon (2003); became a Dutch citizen (2003) and runs for the Netherlands.

KIPLING, Charlotte (1919–1992). English fish biologist and statistician. Name variations: Charlotte Harrison Kipling. Born Charlotte Harrison, June 7, 1919, in UK; died Aug 9, 1992; dau. of a ship broker; Newnham College, Cambridge, MA, 1948; attended University College, London, 1946–47. ❖ Worked as a Freshwater Biological Association (FBA) biologist and statistician (1947–83) at Ferry House, Windermere, where she conducted calculations for FBA staff and introduced computers (1960s); served as a Women's Royal Navy Service cipher officer

(1940–46); researched the history of Windermere fisheries; was a fellow of Statistical Society and member of Institute of Biology; wrote a series of papers (many with Winifred Frost) on the perch, pike, and char populations in Windermere (1941–82).

KIPPIN, Vicky (1942—). Australian politician. Born Sept 7, 1942, in Ayr. ❖ Served in the Queensland Parliament for Mourilyan (1974–1980), the 1st woman to be elected to any parliament in Australia for the National (Country) Party.

KIRALY PICOT, Hajnalka (1971—). Hungarian-born French fencer. Born Mar 2, 1971, in Veszprem, Hungary; m. Patrick Picot (her French coach). ❖ Was a member of the Hungarian World champion épée team (1993, 1995, 1997, and 2002); moved to France (2000), married, and took out French citizenship; representing France, won a bronze medal for team épée at Athens Olympics (2004).

KIRA OF LEININGEN (b. 1930). Princess of Leiningen. Born Kira Melita Feodore Mary Victoria Alexandra, July 18, 1930, in Coburg, Bavaria, Germany; dau. of Charles, 6th prince of Leiningen, and Marie of Russia (1907–1951); m. Andrei Karadjordjevic (son of Alexander I, king of Yugoslavia), Sept 18, 1963 (div. 1972, died in Irvine, California, 1990, as a result of carbon monoxide poisoning); children: Lavinia Maria (b. 1961); Vladimir (b. 1964); Dmitri (b. 1965). Andrei Karadjordjevic's 1st wife was Christine of Hesse-Cassel (b. 1933); his 3rd was Eva Maria Andjelkovich, known as Mitsi.

KIRA OF RUSSIA (1909–1967). Princess of Prussia. Name variations: Kira Cyrillovna. Born May 9, 1909, in Paris, France; died Sept 8, 1967, at St. Briac-sur-Mer, France; buried in Hechingen, Germany; dau. of Cyril Vladimirovitch (grandson of Tsar Alexander II of Russia) and Victoria Melita of Saxe-Coburg (1876–1936); niece of Marie of Rumania (1875–1938); m. Louis Ferdinand Hohenzollern (1907–1994), prince of Prussia, on May 2, 1938; children: Frederick (b. 1939); Michael (b. 1940); Marie-Cecile Hohenzollern (b. 1942, who m. Frederick Augustus of Oldenburg); Kira Hohenzollern (b. 1943); Louis (1944–1977); Christian (b. 1946); Xenia Hohenzollern (b. 1949).

KIRBY, Dorothy (1920—). American golfer. Born Mary Dorothy Kirby, Jan 15, 1920, in West Point, GA. ❖ Won the Georgia state championship five times; won the USGA Women's Amateur (1951); member of Curtis Cup team (1948, 1950, 1952, 1954). Inducted into Georgia Golf Hall of Fame (1989).

KIRBY, Kate (1863–1952). See Kirby, Mary Kostka.

KIRBY, Mary Kostka (1863–1952). New Zealand nun. Name variations: Kate Kirby. Born on July 9, 1863, in Limerick, County Limerick, Ireland; died on Aug 18, 1952, in Dunedin, New Zealand; dau. of John Kirby (clerk) and Kate (Synan) Kirby. ❖ Joined Sisters of Mercy at Ennis, Co. Clare, Ireland (1881), became nun (1884); managed orphanage at Singleton, NSW, Australia (1882); started new mission in Dunedin (1897); served as mother superior (1897–1909, 1912–18); served as mistress of novices (1918–24); founded St Patrick's Orphanage (1897); opened home for boys at Waverley, Dunedin (1920); helped to establish convents and mission schools throughout New Zealand. ❖ See also Dictionary of New Zealand Biography (Vol. 3).

KIRBY, Sarah (1741–1810). See Trimmer, Sarah.

KIRCH, Margarethe (1670–1720). See Kirch, Maria Winkelmann.

KIRCH, Maria Winkelmann (1670–1720). German astronomer. Name variations: Maria Winkelmann. Born Maria Margarethe Winkelmann, Feb 25, 1670, in Panitzsch, Germany; died of fever, Dec 29, 1720, in Berlin; m. Gottfried Kirch (Berlin Academy astronomer), 1692; children: 4, including Christfried Kirch (who occupied the observer's position at Berlin Academy until his death, 1740), Christine Kirch (who assisted brother and was calculator of Silesia's calendar), and Margaretha Kirch. ❖ Noted for calculating calendars and ephemerides, became an advanced student of Christoph Arnold and later Gottfried Kirch, whom she married; as unofficial assistant to husband, spent most of her time calculating calendars and ephemerides; gained fame in her own right through discovery of a comet (1702) and publication of astrological pamphlets (1709–12); following husband's death (1710), petitioned Berlin Academy of Sciences for appointment as assistant astronomer and calendar maker (the academy, fearful of setting a precedent by hiring a woman for such an important position, refused); moved family to Baron von Krosigk's private observatory in Berlin and produced calendars as well as daily observations of planets, eclipses and sunspots with aid of 2 students; when son Christfried was appointed 1 of 2 observers for Berlin

Academy (1716), became his unofficial assistant; was reprimanded by academy for being too "visible" and warned to stay in background (1717); when she refused, was removed from the observatory and, lacking her own equipment, was forced to end her observations; died 2 years later. ❖ See also Women in World History.

KIRCHGESSNER, Marianne (1769–1808). German musician. Born 1769 in Germany; died 1808. ❖ Blinded by illness in childhood, studied glass harmonica (also known as a glass armonica) with J.A. Schmittbauer in Karslruhe; a virtuoso, began to tour widely; (after hearing her play, Mozart wrote two pieces for the glass harmonica: Adagio in C and the Adagio and Rondo for Armonica, Flute, Oboe, Viola and Cello, 1791); received new instrument from Fröschel in London (1794); befriended Goethe shortly before her death.

KIRCHWEY, Freda (1893–1976). American political activist, editor and publisher. Born in Lake Placid, NY, Sept 26, 1893; died in St. Petersburg, FL, Jan 3, 1976; dau. of George Washington Kirchwey (1855–1942, lawyer, criminologist, and dean of law school, Columbia University) and Dora Child (Wendell) Kirchwey; Barnard College, AB, 1915; LittD, Rollins College, 1944; m. Evans Clark, Nov 9, 1915; children: Brewster Kirchwey (died young); Michael Kirchwey; Jeffrey Kirchwey (died young). ❖ Began working for *The Nation*, the oldest liberal journal in US (1918); became managing editor (1922), chief editor (1936), and publisher and owner (1937); a radical feminist (1920s) as well as a champion of social justice domestically, emerged as one of the 1st major public figures in US to warn of threat posed by international fascism, and was a supporter of collective security and the cause of the Spanish Republic; after 1945, fought successfully to maintain *The Nation* as a forum for Americans who challenged many of the basic assumptions of the Cold War. ❖ See also Sara Alpern, *Freda Kirchwey: A Woman of "The Nation"* (Harvard U. Press, 1987); and *Women in World History*.

KIRIASIS, Sandra (1975—). See Prokoff, Sandra.

KIRICHENKO, Olga (1976—). Soviet swimmer. Born Jan 27, 1976, in USSR. ❖ At Barcelona Olympics, won a bronze medal in the 4 x 100-meter medley relay (1992).

KIRK, Cybele Ethel (1870–1957). New Zealand teacher, temperance reformer, and welfare worker. Born Oct 1, 1870, in Auckland, New Zealand; died May 19, 1957, in Wellington; dau. of Thomas Kirk (secretary) and Sarah Jane (Mattocks) Kirk. ❖ Became primary teacher first in country schools and then private denominational schools in Wellington; helped to establish Richmond Free Kindergarten Union (1905); taught at Tory Street Free Kindergarten, and at schools near Hokitika and in Marlborough Sounds; taught at Otaki Maori College (1917); after 1920, became increasingly involved in social work; served as secretary of New Zealand Society for Protection of Women and Children (1924–37); appointed justice of peace (1926); served in executive capacity in local, district, and dominion branches of Women's Christian Temperance Union (1923–46). King George V Silver Jubilee Medal (1935). ❖ See also *Dictionary of New Zealand Biography* (Vol. 3).

KIRK, Eleanor (1830–1908). See Ames, Eleanor Maria.

KIRK, Jenny (1945—). New Zealand politician. Born Jenny Kirk, Feb 18, 1945, in Auckland, NZ; m. Theo Sala, 1966 (div.); children: two. ❖ Served as Labour MP for Birkenhead (1987–90); critical of the economic approach of Finance Minister Roger Douglas; lost seat (1990).

KIRK, Lily (1866–1921). Atkinson, Lily May.

KIRK, Margaret Anne (1921—). See Bell, Peggy Kirk.

KIRK, Phyllis (1926—). American actress. Born Phyllis Kirkegaard, Sept 18, 1926, in Syracuse, NY; m. Warren Bush. ❖ Made film debut in *Our Very Own* (1950), followed by *Two Weeks with Love, About Face, The Iron Mistress, Thunder Over the Plains, Johnny Concho, Back from Eternity,* and *The Sad Sack,* among others; probably best remembered for star turns as Sue Allen in *The House of Wax* (1953) and Nora Charles opposite Peter Lawford in tv's "The Thin Man" (1957–59).

KIRKALDY, Jane Willis (c. 1869–1932). English zoologist. Born c. 1869 in UK; died June 19, 1932; Somerville College, Oxford, BS, 1891, MA, 1920. ❖ Tutor at Somerville College, Oxford, for 36 years, was one of its 1st two women to graduate with first-class honors in the natural sciences; worked as a visiting teacher and a science lecturer in London; employed as a private tutor in Yorkshire; served as a tutor for Association for the Education of Women at Oxford's School of Natural Sciences

(1894–30); lectured and tutored for Oxford Women's Societies; coauthored *An Introduction to the Study of Biology* (with I.M. Drummond, 1909); (trans. with E. Pollard, 1896) *Textbook of Zoology*, a book by J.E.V. Boas.

KIRKBRIDE, Eliza (1801–1881). *See Gurney, Eliza.*

KIRKBRIDE, Julie (1960—). English producer, journalist, and politician. Born June 5, 1960; m. Andrew Mackay (MP), 1997. ❖ Served as producer, BBC News and Current Affairs (1986–89), ITN (1989–92); was political correspondent, *Daily Telegraph* (1992–96), and social affairs editor, *Sunday Telegraph* (1996); as a Conservative, elected to House of Commons for Bromsgrove (1997).

KIRKEBY, Elizabeth (fl. 1482). English goldsmith and merchant. Fl. around 1482 in London; m. John Kirkeby, a goldsmith (died 1482). ❖ Following husband's death (1482), carried on their goldsmith business and expanded it as well; created and sold gold pieces, and subsequently used profits to open a shipping firm and a mercantile shop; was one of London's wealthiest women when she died.

KIRKHOVEN, Catherine (d. 1667). English aristocrat. Name variations: Katherine or Catherine Kerckhoven or Kerchhoven; Lady Stanhope; Countess of Chesterfield. Born Catherine Wotton (also seen as Katherine Wooton), before 1612; died Mar 7, 1667; dau. of Thomas Wotton, 2nd Baron Wotton, and Mary Throckmorton; m. Henry Stanhope, Lord Stanhope, Dec 4, 1628 (died 1634); m. Jan van der Kerchhoven (also seen as John Polyander à Kerckhoven, Lord of Henvliet); m. Daniel O'Neill (died 1664); children: (1st m.) Catherine Stanhope (b. before 1634–1662); Philip Stanhope, 2nd earl of Chesterfield (1634–c. 1714); (2nd m.) Charles Henry Kirkhoven, 1st and last earl of Bellomont, and possibly Helena Dorothea Kirkhoven (d. 1703, who m. Charles Stanley, 8th earl of Derby). ❖ Was governess to Mary of Orange (1631–1660), princess royal, daughter of Charles I; married Jan van der Kerchhoven, one of the ambassadors from the States-General who negotiated the marriage between Mary and the prince of Orange, William II (1641); was a confidential advisor to the princess; arrested in England for being privy to Royalist plots (1651), was acquitted and returned to Holland (1652); gained title countess of Chesterfield (1660); following Mary's death (1660), entered service of duchess of York (Mary II), becoming lady of the bedchamber (1663).

KIRKLAND, Caroline Matilda (1801–1864). American author. Name variations: (pseudonym) Mrs. Mary Clavers. Born Caroline Matilda Stansbury, Jan 11, 1801, in New York, NY; died April 6, 1864, in NY; dau. of Samuel Stansbury (bookseller and inventor) and Eliza (Alexander) Stansbury; attended Quaker girls' schools; m. William Kirkland (educator and editor), Jan 10, 1828; children: 7 (3 of whom died in childhood). ❖ Considered the 1st author to write about the American frontier in realistic terms, moved with family to tiny village of Pinckney, Michigan (1836), enduring primitive conditions; wrote amusing letters to friends back East, recounting new life, letters which grew into the extended narrative *A New Home—Who'll Follow? or Glimpses of Western Life*, which was published under pseudonym "Mrs. Mary Clavers" (1839); followed that with *Forest Life* (1842); returned to NY (1843) and produced a 2nd collection of stories on frontier theme, *Western Clearings* (1845); following husband's death (Oct 1846), succeeded him as editor of *Christian Inquirer*, and began 18-month tenure as editor of *Union Magazine of Literature and Art* (1847); became a central figure in NY literary community; served on executive committee of Home for Discharged Female Convicts and wrote *The Helping Hand* on its behalf (1853). ❖ See also *Women in World History*.

KIRKLAND, Gelsey (1952—). American ballet dancer. Born Dec 29, 1952, in Bethlehem, PA; dau. of Jack Kirkland (playwright) and Nancy (Hoadley) Kirkland (actress); sister of Johnna Kirkland, dancer; attended Professional Children's School, NY; studied ballet at New York City Ballet's School of American Ballet; m. Greg Lawrence (writer), on May 13, 1985. ❖ Known for her legendary partnership with Mikhail Baryshnikov, had a meteoric rise as a soloist; joined New York City Ballet's corps de ballet, becoming its youngest member at 15; danced 1st solo role as Butterfly in *A Midsummer Night's Dream* and went on to perform leads in Clifford's *Reveries* and Balanchine's *Monumentum Pro Gesualdo* (1969); won accolades for appearance as Sugar Plum Fairy in *The Nutcracker* (1970); promoted to rank of soloist and selected by Balanchine to dance title role in *Firebird* (1970); became darling of the media, dancing the lead in Robbins' *The Goldberg Variations*, Clifford's *Tchaikovsky Suite*, and Tanner's *Concerto for Two Pianos* (1970–71); further expanded repertory to include *Brahms Schoenbert Quartet*,

Symphony in C, Theme and Variations and *Harlequinade;* delighted audiences in d'Amboise's *Irish Fantasy;* promoted to principal dancer (1972), took on additional roles, but began to rebel against Balanchine's demands; split with New York City Ballet to partner Baryshnikov at American Ballet Theatre, performing the grand *pas de deux* from *Don Quixote* (1974); won particular acclaim as Lise in *La Fille Mal Gardée* (1974); made spectacular debut in *La Sylphide*, partnered with Ivan Nagy (1975); reached zenith in *Giselle*, partnered with Baryshnikov (1975); appeared in 2 works by Tudor: *Shadowplay* and *The Leaves Are Fading* (1975); dealt with anorexia and bulimia throughout career and resigned from American Ballet Theatre to confront an addiction to cocaine (1984); danced *Romeo and Juliet* with Royal Ballet (1986). ❖ See also autobiography *Dancing On My Grave* (Doubleday, 1986); and *Women in World History.*

KIRKLAND, Johnna (1950—). American ballet dancer. Born Feb 14, 1950, in Bethlehem, PA; dau. of Jack Kirkland (playwright) and Nancy (Hoadley) Kirkland (actress); sister of Gelsey Kirkland, dancer. ❖ Trained at School of American Ballet; performed child roles for New York City Ballet in *The Nutcracker* and *A Midsummer Night's Dream* (1962); joined its professional company (1965) and was featured in Balanchine's *Raymonda Variations, Four Temperaments,* and *Tchaikovsky Suite #3,* and Robbins' *Goldberg Variations;* created roles in Clifford's ballets, *Fantasies* (1969) and *Sarabande and Danse I* (1970), Tanner's *Octandre* (1971), and Massine's *Four Last Songs* (1971); founded Los Angeles Ballet with John Clifford (1974); created roles in over 15 further ballets by Clifford including his *The Red Back Book* (1974), *Serenade in A* (Stravinsky), *Sitar Concerto, Das Hammlische Leben* (1977) and *Transcended Etudes* (1978).

KIRKLAND, Muriel (1903–1971). American stage and screen actress. Born Aug 19, 1903, in New York, NY; died Sept 26, 1971, in New York, NY; m. Staats Cotsworth (actor). ❖ Made NY stage debut in *The Knave of Hearts* (1923); starred or was featured in *School for Scandal, Brass Buttons, Cock Robin, Strictly Dishonorable, The Greeks Had a Word For It, Abe Lincoln in Illinois, Inherit the Wind* and *Life with Father,* among others; films include *Fast Workers, Little Man, What Now?, Hold Your Man, Cocktail Hour* and *Nana.*

KIRKLAND-CASGRAIN, Marie-Claire (1924—). Canadian politician. Name variations: Claire Kirkland-Casgrain. Born Sept 8, 1924, in Palmer, Massachusetts; dau. of Dr. Charles-Aimé Kirkland (politician). ❖ The 1st woman elected to the Legislative Assembly of Quebec and the 1st woman appointed as a Cabinet minister in Quebec, was 1st elected to Quebec Legislature as a Liberal member for the Jacques-Cartier riding (1961), serving until 1973; was Cabinet minister without portfolio (1962–64), minister of Transportation and Communications (1964–66), minister of Tourism (1970–72) and minister of Cultural Affairs (1972–73); was also the 1st woman appointed as interim premier of a provincial government (1972); served as a judge in the Montreal judicial district (1980–91); wrote for *Châtelaine.*

KIRKPATRICK, Helen (1909–1997). American journalist. Name variations: Helen Milbank. Born Helen Paull Kirkpatrick, Oct 18, 1909, in Rochester, NY; died Dec 30, 1997; dau. of Lyman Bickford Kirkpatrick (real estate broker) and Lyde (Paull) Kirkpatrick; graduate of Smith College, 1931; attended Zimmern School, Geneva, 1931, and Geneva Institute of International Relations, 1932; m. Victor Polachek, 1934 (div. 1937); m. Robbins Milbank, 1954; no children. ❖ Began journalism career writing for leading British newspapers and magazines and acting as Geneva correspondent for *New York Herald Tribune;* published 1st book, *This Terrible Peace* (1939); co-edited *Whitehall Letter,* a weekly London digest that warned of Hitler's takeover; joined Chicago *Daily News'* London bureau (1939) and immediately became known for her "exclusives"; like most wire service reporters during war, covered "headquarters" stories, including communiqués and briefings, but also wrote articles on military strategy, diplomacy, and eyewitness accounts of fighting; spent 6 months in Algiers (1943), covering North African campaign, and was present during surrender of Italian forces in North Africa; also covered surrender of Italian Fleet in Malta, then reported from a field hospital a mile from the front in Naples (1943); chosen to represent all newspapers on a committee assigned to cover the landings in Normandy (1944), though US War Department had ruled that no women correspondents would be allowed to accompany the invasion (June 6, 1944); was one of the 1st correspondents to enter Paris on Liberation Day (Aug 25, 1944); after war, covered the 1st war crimes trial in Nuremberg; concluded career by serving as chief of information for the French mission, Economic Cooperation Administration, Paris, where she worked to help implement the Marshall Plan. Awarded French Legion of Honor, French Medaille de la Reconnaissance, and US Medal of Freedom. ❖ See also *Women in World History.*

KIRKPATRICK, Jeane (1926—). American diplomat, political scientist and scholar. Name variations: Mrs. Evron M. Kirkpatrick. Born Jeane Duane Jordan in Duncan, Oklahoma, Nov 19, 1926; dau. of Welcher F. Jordan (oil contractor) and Leona (Kile) Jordan; Stephens College, AA, 1946; Barnard College, AB, 1948; Columbia University, MA, 1950; attended Institut de Science Politique of University of Paris, 1952–53; Columbia University, PhD, 1967; m. Dr. Evron M. Kirkpatrick (political science professor), Feb 20, 1955 (died 1995); children: Douglas Jordan; John Evron; Stuart Alan. ❖ The 1st woman US ambassador to UN, began career as assistant professor of political science at Trinity College (1962); joined faculty at Georgetown University (1967), becoming full professor (1973); also served intermittently as consultant to American Council of Learned Societies and to departments of State, Defense, and Health, Education, and Welfare (1955–72); contributed to a number of journals and edited *The Strategy of Deception: A Study in World-Wide Communist Tactics* (1963); also wrote *Political Woman* (1974) and *The New Presidential Elite* (1976); though then a Democrat, became politically active during antiwar movement (1960s), helping to found the Coalition for a Democratic Majority (1972), whose members, mostly writers and scholars, became known as "neoconservatives"; became a resident scholar of American Enterprise Institute for Public Policy (1977), a conservative think tank; wanting a stronger anti-Soviet stance, supported Reagan's presidential campaign (1980) and served on his interim foreign policy advisory board following his election; served as US Permanent Representative to UN (1980–85), while also a member of the Cabinet and National Security Council; was a member of President's Foreign Intelligence Advisory Board (1985–90) and Defense Policy Review Board (1985–93). Awarded Medal of Freedom. ❖ See also *Women in World History.*

KIRKUS, Virginia (1893–1980). American critic and entrepreneur. Born in Meadville, Pennsylvania, Dec 7, 1893; died in Danbury, Connecticut, Sept 10, 1980; dau. of the Reverend Frederick Maurice Kirkus and Isabella (Clark) Kirkus; graduate of Vassar College, 1916; attended Columbia University Teachers College; m. Frank Glick (personnel executive). ❖ Headed children's book department of Harper & Brothers (1925–32); launched Virginia Kirkus Bookshop Service, a bimonthly bulletin that contained brief critical evaluations of new books (1933); by the time she retired (1962), her reviewers were previewing books for some 4,000 subscribers. ❖ See also *Women in World History.*

KIRKWHITE, Iris (c. 1900–1975). English theatrical ballet dancer. Name variations: possibly Iris Fenwick. Born c. 1900, in London, England; died Oct 22, 1975, in London, England; sister of Sylvia Fenwick (dancer). ❖ Performed specialty dance act—toe tapping waltz dance—in London theaters in *The Blue Mazurka* (1925), *Sunny* (1926) and *André Charlot 1928 Revue;* performed in Albertina Rasch's *Rio Rita* with Errol Addison (1930); opened dance school with sister, where she served as co-director for years; began staging yearly Bertram Montague Christmas pantomimes (1942).

KIRKWOOD, Julieta (1936–1985). Chilean sociologist, feminist and educator. Name variations: María Julieta Kirkwood Bañados; Adela H. Born María Julieta Kirkwood Bañados, April 5, 1936, in Santiago de Chile, Chile; died of breast cancer, April 8, 1985, in Santiago de Chile; dau. of Johnny Kirkwood (accountant) and Julieta Bañados; m. Rodrigo Baños, 1970; children: 2. ❖ Central figure in contemporary Latin American feminism, began work as teacher and researcher at non-governmental organization, FLACSO (1972); became more politicized under repressive regime of Pinochet; with others, formed Círculo de Estudios de la Mujer (Women's Studies Circle, 1979) to promote dialogue and action among women of diverse backgrounds; was initially supported in Círculo work by Academy of Christian Humanism, umbrella organization of Catholic Church; contributed to Círculo presentation *El Trabajo de la Mujer* (Women's Work, 1979); organized workshops and gave talks around Santiago de Chile, with special emphasis on working with poor and working women; diagnosed with breast cancer (1979) and given 5 years to live; created *Boletín del Círculo de Estudios de la Mujer* (Women's Studies Circle Bulletin, 1980); created journal *Furia* (Fury) as member of Federation of Socialist Women (1981); offended Church hierarchy with views on divorce, prompting *Círculo* to split from Academy of Christian Humanism (1983); with others, established 2 independent centers for feminist research and action, La Morada Women's House (for political

and research activity) and Center for the Study of Women (to develop theoretical material derived from La Morada); led formation of Movimiento Pro Emancipación de la Mujer Chilena (Movement for the Emancipation of Chilean Women or MEMCH83, 1983), which coordinated activities of both feminist and nonfeminist groups; traveled to Peru for Second Latin American and Caribbean Feminist Conference (1983). Writings include (essays) *Knots of Feminist Knowledge* (1983); (compilations of articles) *Tejiendo rebeldías* (Weaving Rebellions, 1987) and *Feminarios* (1987); (book) *Ser política en Chile: Las feministas y los partidos* (Being Female and Political in Chile: Feminists and Political Parties, 1986). ❖ See also Patricia Crispi, ed., *Tejiendo rebeldías. Escritos feministas de Julieta Kirkwood Hilvanados por Patricia Crispi* (Centro de Estudios de la mujer and Casa de la Mujer La Morada, 1987).

KIRKWOOD, Pat (1921—). English actress and singer. Name variations: Patricia Kirkwood. Born Feb 24, 1921, in Pendleton, Manchester, England; m. John Lister (theater manager, div.); m. Spiro de Spero Gabriele, 1952 (died 1954); m. Hubert Gregg (producer, writer, composer), 1956 (div. c. 1977); m. Peter Knight (lawyer), 1981. ❖ Considered the queen of West End musicals, was the highest-paid English musical star of 1940s–50s; made London stage debut as Dandini in *Cinderella* (1937), followed by *Black Velvet* (singing "My Heart Belongs to Daddy" and "Oh Johnny" for 2-year run), *Top of the World, Lady Behave, Let's Face It, Starlight Roof, Ace of Clubs, Wonderful Town, Chrysantheum* and *Noel/Cole,* among others; on tv, appeared in "Our Marie" (as Marie Lloyd, 1953), "The Pat Kirkwood Show" (1954), "The Great Little Tilley" (as Vesta Tilley, 1956), and the series "Pat" (1968); films include *Save a Little Sunshine, Come on George, Me and My Gal, The Band Wagon* and *After the Ball.* ❖ See also autobiography *The Time of My Life.*

KIRNER, Joan (1938—). Australian politician. Name variations: Joan Elizabeth Kirner. Born June 20, 1938, in Melbourne, Australia; graduate of University of Melbourne; m. Ray Kirner, 1960; children: 2 sons, 1 daughter. ❖ The 1st woman to head the Victorian government, was elected to Victorian Parliament (1982), as a MLC (ALP) for the province of Melbourne West; was MP for 12 years (1982–94), heading ministries of Conservation, Forests and Lands, Education, and Women's Affairs; served as deputy premier (1989–90), premier (1990–92), and Opposition Leader (1992–94); resigned (1994); with Moira Rayner, wrote *The Women's Power Handbook* (1999); became co-convenor of EMILY's List Australia (1996).

KIROUAC, Martha Wilkinson (1948—). American golfer. Name variations: Martha Wilkinson. Born Martha Wilkinson, Sept 24, 1948, in Los Angeles, CA. ❖ Won USGA Women's Amateur, the Trans-Mississippi, Doherty Challenge Cup, and Harder Hall Invitation (1970); member of Curtis Cup (1970, 1972) and World Cup team (1970).

KIRPISHCHIKOVA, Anna (1848–1927). Russian short-story writer. Name variations: Anna Aleksandrovna Kirpíshchikova; A.A. Kirpíshchikova; A.A. Vydarina. Born Anna Aleksandrovna Vydarina in 1848 in Russia; died 1927. ❖ Wrote short works that draw on life in Urals and reflect reformist spirit of Russian realism; writings include "The Past" (1876), "Not Long Ago" (1877), "Petrushka Rudometov: Sketches from Life at the Mines" (1878) and "Twenty Years Ago" (1889).

KIRSCH, Sarah (1935—). German poet and short-story writer. Born Ingrid Bernstein, April 16, 1935, Limlingerode, Harz, Germany; attended Johannes R. Becher Institute to Literature in Leipzig; m. Rainer Kirsch (poet), 1958 (div. 1968). ❖ Grew up in East Germany; after protesting the expulsion of Wolf Biermann (1976), was excluded from the SED and the writer federation of the GDR; moved to West Berlin (1977); writings include *Landaufenthalt* (1967), *Zaubersprüche* (1973), *Rückenwind* (1976), *La Pagerie* (1980), *Erdreich* (1982), *Katzenleben* (1984), *Schneewärme* (1989), *Schwingrasen* (1991), and *Erlkönigs Tochter* (1992). Received Literature Prize of City of Mainz (1988) and Peter Huchel Prize (1993).

KIRSCHNER, Lola (1854–1934). Czech-born novelist. Name variations: Aloisia or Aloiysia Kirschner; (pseudonym) Ossip Schubin. Born June 17, 1854, in Lochkov, Prague, Czechoslovakia; died Feb 10, 1934, at Schloss Kosatek, Czechoslovakia; dau. of a Jewish Bohemian landowner; sister of Marie Kirschner (1852–1931, painter). ❖ Traveled widely with mother and mixed in literary circles that included George Sand and Ivan Turgenev; her novellas reflect European salon culture.

KIRSOVA, Helene (1910–1962). Danish ballet dancer. Born Ellen Wittrup Hansen, 1910, in Copenhagen, Denmark; died Feb 22, 1962, in London, England; trained with Lyubov Egorova; m. Erik Fischer (Danish vice-consul in Sydney), 1938. ❖ As a founding member of Ballet Russe de Monte Carlo, created a role in Fokine's *Don Juan* and performed in Fokine's Diaghilev revivals of *Les Sylphides, Le Carnaval,* and *Petrouchka,* among others (1932–36); moved to Sydney, Australia (1938), where she founded the Kirsova Ballet (1940), the 1st professional ballet company in Australia; choreographed numerous works for her company until her retirement (1947), including *Faust* (1941), *Vieux Paris* (1942), *Harlequin* (1944), *Waltzing Mathilda* (1946) and *A Dream and a Fairy Tale* (1947).

KIRST, Jutta (1954—). East German track-and-field athlete. Born Nov 10, 1954, in East Germany. ❖ At Moscow Olympics, won a bronze medal in the high jump (1980).

KIRSTEN, Dorothy (1910–1992). American lyric soprano. Born July 6, 1910, in Montclair, NJ; died Nov 18, 1992, in Los Angeles, CA; grandniece of singer Catherine Hayes; studied voice at Juilliard in NY and in Rome with Astolfo Pescia; m. Edward MacKaye Oates (broadcasting production expert), 1943 (div.); m. John Douglas French (physician), 1955. ❖ Made concert debut at NY World's Fair (1939), followed by operatic debut with Chicago Civic Opera (1940), as Pousette in *Manon;* joined San Carlo Opera Company (1942) and made NY debut with the troupe as Micaela in *Carmen;* had her own radio show, "Keepsake" (1943–44), and also appeared frequently as guest artist on other programs; debuted with NY Metropolitan Opera (1945), as Mimi in *La Bohème,* winning acclaim, if not raves; sang with Met for next 30 years, distinguishing herself in lyric roles of Verdi and Puccini, and performed in such productions as *Madama Butterfly, Roméo et Juliette, La Traviata, Tosca, Faust,* and in Charpentier's *Louise,* a role she prepared with the help of the composer; continued to appear with San Francisco, New Orleans, and Chicago opera companies and was a frequent guest at City Center; was 1st US soprano to sing grand opera in Soviet Union (1962); retired from Met (1975), after farewell performance in *Tosca;* retired (1982). ❖ See also autobiography *A Time to Sing* (1982); and *Women in World History.*

KIRSZENSTEIN-SZEWINSKA, Irena (b. 1946). *See Szewinska, Irena.*

KIRVESNIEMI, Marja-Liisa (1955—). Finnish cross-country skier. Name variations: Marja-Liisa Hamalainen, Haemaelaeinan, Haemaelainen, Hamalajnen, or Hämäläinen. Born Marja-Liisa Hämäläinen, Sept 10, 1955, in Simpele, Finland; dau. of Kalevi Hämäläinen (an Olympic gold medalist); m. Harri Kirvesniemi (champion skier). ❖ Competed in 6 Winter Olympics (1976–94); won gold medals for 20 km, 5 km, and 10 km and a bronze for 4 x 5 km relay at Sarajevo Olympics (1984); won a bronze medal for 4 x 5 km relay at Calgary Olympics (1988); won bronze medals for the 30 km and 5 km at Lillehammer Olympics (1994).

KISABAKA, Linda (1969—). German runner. Name variations: Linda Rohlander, Rohländer or Rohlaender. Born April 4, 1969, in Wuppertal, Germany. ❖ Won a bronze medal for the 4 x 400-meter relay at Atlanta Olympics (1996).

KISCHE, Marion (1958—). East German gymnast. Born Mar 30, 1958, in Dresden, East Germany. ❖ Placed 3rd all-around at East German championships (1975); at Montreal Olympics, won a bronze medal in team all-around (1976).

KISELEVA, Maria (1974—). *See Kisseleva, Maria.*

KISELYOVA, Larisa (1970—). Soviet handball player. Born Nov 3, 1970, in USSR. ❖ At Barcelona Olympics, won a bronze medal in team competition (1992).

KISHAK-COHEN, Shula. *See Cohen, Shula.*

KISHIDA, Toshiko (1863–1901). Japanese writer, orator, and political activist. Name variations: also known as Nakajima Toshiko; (pseudonym) Nakajima Shoen. Pronunciation: Key-SHE-dah Toe-SHE-koe. Born in Kyoto, Japan, 1863, into a family of cloth merchants; died 1901; mother was Kishida Taka; m. Nakajima Nobuyuki (political activist), 1884. ❖ Japan's 1st woman orator, served Empress Haruko as lady-in-waiting, the 1st commoner to hold that post; abruptly left court to embark on a national lecture tour (1882), sponsored by the Jiyuto (Liberal Party); drew standing-room-only crowds of mostly women and gained national fame, as she criticized the marriage system (in which women had no right to divorce), the concubine system (in which men could have multiple wives), and the lack of educational opportunities for girls. ❖ See also *Women in World History.*

KISSELEVA, Maria (1974—). Russian synchronized swimmer. Name variations: Maria Kiseleva. Born Sept 28, 1974 in USSR. ❖ At World championships, won team gold medals (1998, 2003); won team and duet gold medals at Sydney Olympics (2000); won a team gold medal at Athens Olympics (2004).

KISSLING, Margaret (1808–1891). New Zealand teacher and missionary. Name variations: Margaret Moxon. Born Margaret Moxon, Aug 18, 1808, in Yorkshire, England; died Sept 20, 1891, in Parnell, New Zealand; dau. of John Moxon (banker) and Margaret (Heaton) Moxon; m. George Adam Kissling, 1837 (died 1865); children: 6. ❖ Returned with husband to teach at missionary station in Sierra Leone, West Africa (1837); helped husband with station at Te Kawakawa (Te Araroa) on East Coast of New Zealand (1843); established boarding school for Maori girls, renamed St. Stephen's School for Native Girls, where she taught, beginning 1846. ❖ See also *Dictionary of New Zealand Biography* (Vol. 1).

KITAO, Kanako (1982—). Japanese synchronized swimmer. Born Feb 6, 1982, in Japan. ❖ At World championships, placed 1st in free routine combination (2003); won a team silver medal at Athens Olympics (2004).

KITCHELL, Iva (1908–1983). American concert dancer and dance satirist. Born Emma Baugh, Mar 31, 1908, in Junction City, Kansas; died 1983 in Flagler Beach, FL; took name of adoptive parents; m. Stokely Webster (painter and aeronautical engineer), 1933. ❖ Began career performing with Andreas Pavley and Serge Oukrainsky at Chicago Opera Ballet; was a concert dancer for 20 years, often appearing with Fritz Kreisler, Arthur Rubinstein, Ballet Theater, and Don Cossack Chorus, parodying classical and modern-dance styles; on Broadway, had solo dance acts in *The Broken Appointment* (1940), *Salesman* (1941), and *Maisie at the Movies* (1943), among others; retired (1957).

KITE, Jessie. English gymnast. Born in UK. ❖ At Amsterdam Olympics, won a bronze medal in team all-around (1928).

KITIC, Svetlana (1960—). *See Dasic-Kitic, Svetlana.*

KITSON, Theo A.R. (1871–1932). American sculptor. Name variations: Theo Alice Ruggles Kitson. Born Theo Alice Ruggles in 1871, in Brookline, MA; studied with painter Pascal and sculptor Dagnan-Bouveret in Paris and with future husband; became 1st wife of Henry Hudson Kitson (English sculptor), 1893. ❖ One of the few women members of the National Sculpture Society; received honors at Paris salon, the only American woman to have gained such distinction at the time. Among the best of her monumental statues are the Massachusetts State Monument at Vicksburg, The Minute Man of '76 in Framingham, MA, the statue of Tadeusz Kosciuszko on Boston Common, an equestrian statue of victory in Hingham, MA, and various soldiers' monuments.

KITT, Eartha (1928—). African-American singer, dancer, and actress. Name variations: (nickname) Kitty Charles. Born Eartha Mae Kitt, Jan 26, 1928, in NC; educated at New York School for Performing Arts; m. William McDonald, 1960 (div. 1965); children: daughter Kitt McDonald. ❖ Versatile entertainer who created an international career which was almost derailed by her views on Vietnam War; toured US, Mexico, South America, England and France as singer and dancer (1944–49); made European nightclub debut in Paris (1949); played in Orson Welles' production of *Faust,* Paris (1951); had 1st American nightclub and Broadway successes (1952); recorded albums and singles, including "Santa, Baby" and "Let's Do It"; made tv appearances on "The Ed Sullivan Show," "Colgate Comedy Hour," "I Spy" and as Catwoman in "Batman" (1953–59); appeared in such films as *New Faces* (1954), *Anna Lucasta* (1959) and *Synanon* (1965); appeared on Broadway in such plays as *Mrs. Patterson* and *Shinbone Alley* (1954–59); attended White House luncheon and denounced Vietnam War (Jan 1968); became *persona non grata* in US, forcing her to work mostly overseas (1968–74); attended White House reception by invitation of President Jimmy Carter and returned to Broadway (1978); appeared at Carnegie Hall (1985). Given Golden Rose First Place Award for best special of the year (*This is Eartha*) from Montreux Film Festival (1962); received Woman of Year Award from National Association of Black Musicians (1968). ❖ See also autobiographies *Thursday's Child* (Duell, 1956) and *Alone With Me* (Regnery, 1976); and *Women in World History.*

KITTELSEN, Grete Prytz (1917—). Norwegian artist. Name variations: Grete Korsmo. Born Grete Prytz, June 28, 1917, in Oslo, Norway; dau. of Jacob Prytz (goldsmith); trained at Norwegian State School of Arts and Crafts and Institute of Design, Chicago; m. Arne Korsmo; remarried. ❖ Joined Oslo firm of goldsmiths, J. Tostrup (1945), where she pioneered new methods of decorating silver with enamel; was a design consultant with husband for Cathrineholm firm in Halden, which collaborated with Hadeland Glass Factory in production of stainless-steel articles with transparent enamel, unique at the time; over several decades, work was exhibited in Scandinavian and European countries and in US and Canada; served as president of Norwegian Society of Arts and Crafts (1975–78). Received Lunning Prize (1952), Grand Prix at the Milan Triennale (1954), gold medal at Munich Applied Art Fair (1960), and Jacob Prize from the Norwegian Society of Arts and Crafts (1972). ❖ See also *Women in World History*.

KITTRELL, Flemmie (1904–1980). African-American educator and nutritionist. Born Flemmie Pansy Kittrell, Dec 25, 1904, in Henderson, North Carolina; died Oct 3, 1980, in Washington, DC; dau. of James Lee Kittrell and Alice (Mills) Kittrell; Hampton Institute, BS, 1928; Cornell University, MA, 1930, PhD, 1938; never married. ❖ Headed up home economics department at Howard University for nearly 30 years, during which time she also conducted studies of nutrition problems in Liberia and India and established training programs in nutrition and child care for women in India and Zaire (now Republic of Congo). ❖ See also *Women in World History*.

KITZINGER, Sheila (1929—). British pregnancy and childbirth expert. Born Sheila Helena Elizabeth Webster in Somerset, England, 1929; St. Hugh's College, B.Litt. in social anthropology; m. Uwe Kitzinger (economist), 1952; children: 5 daughters. ❖ Appointed to advisory board of National Childbirth Trust (1958); lectured throughout world and produced a number of books, beginning with *The Experience of Childbirth* (1962), and including *Education and Counselling for Childbirth* (1977), *Women as Mothers* (1978), *Giving Birth* (1979), *Pregnancy and Childbirth* (1980), *The Year After Childbirth* (1992) and *Ourselves as Mother;* also serves on Board of Consultants of International Childbirth Education Association of US. ❖ See also *Women in World History*.

KIZER, Carolyn (1925—). American poet. Born Carolyn Ashley Kizer, 1925, in Spokane, WA; attended Columbia University and University of Seattle; m. Charles Bullitt, 1948 (div. 1954); m. John Marshall Woodbridge, 1975; children: 3. ❖ Founded the journal, *Poetry Northwest* (1959); worked in Pakistan for State Department (1964–65); directed literary programs for National Endowment for the Arts and taught at several universities; served as chancellor of American Academy of Poetry (1995); works include *The Ungrateful Garden* (1961), *Knock Upon Silence* (1965), *Yin: New Poems* (1984), *Mermaids in the Basement: Poems for Women* (1984), and *The Nearness of You* (1986); also published collection of essays, *Proses: On Poems and Poets* (1993). Won Pulitzer Prize for *Yin*, Borrestone Award, Pushcart Prize and Theodore Roethke Poetry Prize.

KJAERGAARD, Tonje (1975—). Danish handball player. Name variations: Kjärgaard. Born June 11, 1975, in Denmark; attended Aarhus University. ❖ Won a team gold medal at Atlanta Olympics (1996) and at Sydney Olympics (2000); won team European championships (1994, 1996) and World championships (1997). Twice named Danish Handball Player of the Year.

KJÄRGAARD, Tonje (1975—). *See Kjaergaard, Tonje.*

KJELDAAS, Stine Brun (1975—). Norwegian snowboarder. Name variations: S. Brun Kjeldaas; also seen as Kjelldaas. Born April 23, 1975, in Fornebu, Oslo, Norway. ❖ At Nagano, won the 1st silver medal ever awarded for women's half-pipe snowboarding at Winter Olympics (1998); won gold in Women's Halfpipe at X Games (2000). Other 1st-place finishes in Halfpipe include: Vans Triple Crown, Sierra-at-Tahoe, CA (2000); Motorola ISF World championship, Kokanee, Canada (2000); ISF World Cup Finals, Davos, Switzerland (2000); ISF Season End Ranking Overall (2000); FIS World Cup, Whistler, British Columbia (2000); Nippon Open, Ishiuchimaruyama, Japan (2001); and ISF World Ranking, Season End (2001).

KLAFSKY, Katharina (1855–1896). Hungarian opera singer. Name variations: Katharina Lohse-Klafsky. Born at Mosonszentjános (St. Johann), Wieselburg, Hungary, 1855; died in Hamburg, Germany, Sept 29, 1896; studied in Vienna with Mathilde Marchesi, then Leipzig with Sucher; m. 3rd husband, Otto Lohse (conductor). ❖ Made debut as a mezzo-soprano in Salzburg (1875); graduated from small roles and became well known in Wagnerian roles at Leipzig theater (1882); appeared in London and enjoyed a huge success in Wagner's operas (1892), notably as

Brünnhilde and Isolde; toured US (1895); returned to Hamburg (1896), where she died suddenly of a brain tumor at 41. ❖ See also L. Ordemann, *Aus dem Leben und Wirken von Katharina Klafsky (A Life)*, 1903); and *Women in World History*.

KLAGSBRUNN, Elizabeth M. (1906–1993). *See Ramsey, Elizabeth M.*

KLAMT, Ewa (1950—). German politician. Born May 26, 1950, in Straubing, Germany; attended high school and college in Sacramento, California, and the Munich campus of the University of Maryland. ❖ Served as deputy mayor of Gifhorn (1991–99); as a member of the European People's Party (Christian Democrats) and European Democrats, elected to 5th European Parliament (1999–2004).

KLAPEZYNSKI, Ulrike (1953—). East German runner. Born Nov 17, 1953, in East Germany. ❖ At Montreal Olympics, won a bronze medal in the 1,500 meters (1976).

KLARSFELD, Beate (1939—). German-born French Nazi-hunter. Born Beate Auguste Künzel in Berlin, Germany, Feb 13, 1939; dau. of Kurt Künzel and Helene (Scholz) Künzel; m. Jewish Holocaust survivor Serge Klarsfeld, 1963; children: Lida Klarsfeld; Arno Klarsfeld. ❖ With husband, exposed former Nazis, including the infamous Klaus Barbie; began career in Paris with French-German Youth Service; incensed that a former Nazi occupied the highest political post in West Germany, provoked several incidents against Kurt Georg Kiesinger (1968) and penned a series of articles on his Nazi links in Paris newspaper *Combat;* because of this, was fired from job at French-German Youth Service (1967); confronted Kiesinger from visitors' gallery of West Germany's Parliament, the Bundestag (1968), then slapped him on another occasion, a slap heard around the world (Kiesinger was defeated at the polls the following year); with husband, sought justice in the cases of over 1,000 Nazi bureaucrats who had been tried, but not punished, for crimes they committed in France during WWII; after many years of agitation, saw West Germany and France ratify an extradition treaty making it possible for the French to punish Nazi war criminals (1975). ❖ See also Beate Klarsfeld, *Wherever They May Be!* (Trans. by Monroe Stearns and Natalie Gerardi, Vanguard, 1975); and *Women in World History*.

KLASS, Christa (1951—). German politician. Name variations: Christa Klaß. Born Nov 7, 19451, in Osann, Germany. ❖ Named vice-chair of the Christian Democrats Union (CDU) district association (1993) and a member of the Federal executive of the women's union (1997); as a member of the European People's Party (Christian Democrats) and European Democrats, elected to 4th and 5th European Parliament (1994–99, 1999–2004).

KLASSEN, Cindy (1979—). Canadian speedskater. Born Aug 12, 1979, in Winnipeg, Manitoba, Canada. ❖ Began career as a hockey player; at the World Distance championships, won bronze medals for the 1,500 meters (2001) and the 1,000 meters (2003); won a bronze medal for the 3,000 meters at Salt Lake City Olympics (2002); won silver medals for allround at World championships (2002) and sprint at World Sprint championships (2003); won a gold medal for 1,500 meters, silver medals for 1,000 meters and Team Pursuit, and bronze medals for 3,000 meters and 5,000 meters at Torino Olympics (2006).

KLATA, Katarzyna (1972—). Polish archer. Born Katarzyna Kowalska, 1972, in Poland. ❖ Won a bronze medal for teams at Atlanta Olympics (1996).

KLEBER, Ina (1964—). East German swimmer. Born Sept 29, 1964, in East Germany. ❖ At Moscow Olympics, won a silver medal in 100-meter backstroke (1980).

KLECKER, Denise (1972—). German field-hockey player. Born Jan 26, 1972, in Mainz, Germany; attended Johannes Gutenburg University. ❖ Won bronze medal at World Cup (1998) and European championships (2003); won a team gold medal at Athens Olympics (2004).

KLEEBERG, Clotilde (1866–1909). French pianist. Born in France, 1866; died 1909; studied with Louise Aglae Massart at Paris Conservatoire. ❖ A successful concert artist, was one of the 1st to revive the old French clavecinist (harpsichord) composers.

KLEEGMAN, Sophia (1901–1971). Russian-born gynecologist and obstetrician. Born Sophia Josephine Kleegman in Kiev, Russia, July 8, 1901; died in New York, NY, Sept 26, 1971; dau. of Israel Kleegman (Talmudic scholar) and Elka (Siergutz) Kleegman; sister of Anna, Mary, and Rae Kleegman; University of Bellevue Hospital Medical College, MD, 1924; m. Dr. John H. Sillman (orthodontist), Dec 31, 1932;

children: Frederick (b. 1937); Anne Marice Sillman (b. 1942). ❖ Pioneer in study of infertility, came to US (1906); became naturalized citizen (1923); joined staff of Bellevue Hospital and became 1st woman appointed to NY University College of Medicine faculty of obstetrics and gynecology (1929); began research on conception and infertility, including diagnosis and treatment of sterility in both men and women; was one of the few physicians to incorporate psychological issues into gynecological practice; an outspoken advocate of birth control, toured nation lecturing on subject before it was acceptable; supported the early clinic established in NY by Margaret Sanger and served as medical director of NY State Planned Parenthood Association (1936–61), after which she became a medical consultant to Eastern Planned Parenthood League; fought for improved sex education and convinced New York University Medical Center to include sex education in its medical curriculum after a 12-year battle; served as president of Women's Medical Association of NY (1942–44) and American Association of Marriage Counselors; elected president of NYU Medical Alumni Association (1965), the 1st woman to hold that post.

KLEEMANN, Gunda (1966—). *See Niemann, Gunda.*

KLEIBERNE-KONTSEK, Jolan (1939—). Hungarian track-and-field athlete. Name variations: Jolan Kontsek. Born Aug 29, 1939, in Hungary. ❖ At Mexico City Olympics, won a bronze medal in discus throw (1968).

KLEIN, Anne (1923–1974). American fashion designer. Name variations: Hannah Golofski or Golofsky. Born Hannah Golofsky (also seen as Golofski), Aug 3, 1923, in Brooklyn, NY; died Mar 19, 1974; dau. of Morris Golofsky (owner of fleet of cabs) and Esther Golofsky; m. Ben Klein (div.); m. Matthew Rubinstein (businessman), 1963; no children. ❖ Known as the mother of contemporary American style, reinvented the sportswear popularized by early designers and brought it into the ranks of high fashion by creating a simple "programmed wardrobe," consisting of blazers, skirts, pants, blouses, and sweaters that could be combined in a variety of outfits; at 15, began working as a freelance sketcher on 7th Avenue in NY; with 1st husband, started a firm called Junior Sophisticates, which specialized in updated, sleek styles for smaller women (1948); opened Anne Klein Studio on West 57th St. (1965); with 3 others, formed Anne Klein & Co. (1968), which began as a sportswear house but gradually expanded to include perfume, scarves, jewelry, handbags and belts, sleepwear, perfume, and menswear; went international (1973). ❖ See also *Women in World History.*

KLEIN, Catherine (1910–1985). *See Klein, Kit.*

KLEIN, Helga (1931—). West German runner. Born Aug 15, 1931, in Germany. ❖ At Helsinki Olympics, won a silver medal in the 4 x 100-meter relay (1952).

KLEIN, Kit (1910–1985). American speedskater. Name variations: Catherine Klein; Kit Klein-Outland. Born Catherine Klein, Mar 28, 1910, in Buffalo, NY; died April 13, 1985, in Holmes Beach, Fl; dau. of Adam Klein; m. George Nichols (boxer), 1933 (annulled); m. Dr. Thomas Outland, 1936. ❖ Won the 1st women's overall World championship in speedskating (1936), one of only 2 Americans to win that title in the 20th century; won demonstration gold (1,500 meters) and bronze medals (500 meters) at Lake Placid Olympics (1932); was the 2nd woman to grace a Wheaties box.

KLEIN, Melanie (1882–1960). Austrian-born psychoanalyst. Born Melanie Reizes in Vienna, Austria, Mar 30, 1882; died in London, England, Sept 22, 1960; dau. of Moriz Reizes (medical doctor) and Libussa (Deutsch) Reizes (shopkeeper); m. Arthur Klein, 1903 (div. 1923); children: Melitta Klein; Hans Klein; Eric Klein. ❖ Controversial psychoanalyst whose revolutionary technique of "play analysis" and insights into early childhood development made an important and lasting contribution to the practice of psychoanalysis; began analyzing children in Budapest (1919); moved to Berlin (1921); elected a full member of Berlin Psychoanalytic Society (1923); developed technique of "play analysis" (1921–23); moved to London (1926); became 1st European analyst elected to British Psycho-Analytical Society (1927); analyzed last child patient (late 1940s); for more than 40 years, wrote, taught and conducted research in field of child psychology; writings include *The Psycho-Analysis of Children* (1932), *Contributions to Psycho-Analysis, 1921–1945* (1948), *Envy and Gratitude* (1957) and (published posthumously) *Narrative of a Child Psycho-Analysis* (1961). ❖ See also Phyllis Gross-Kurth, *Melanie Klein: Her World and Her Work* (Knopf, 1986);

Hanna Segal, *Melanie Klein* (Viking, 1979); *Mrs. Klein,* play by Nicholas Wright, starred Uta Hagen (1995); and *Women in World History.*

KLEIN, Robin (1936—). Australian children's writer. Born Feb 28, 1936, in Kempsey, Australia; dau. of Leslie Macquarie (farmer) and Mary (Cleaver) McMaugh; m. Karl Klein, 1956 (div. 1978); children: Michael, Peter, Ingrid, Rosalind. ❖ Worked as teacher, nurse, and librarian assistant before beginning to write full time (1981); wrote several works with Max Dann; writings include *The Giraffe in Pepperell Street* (1978), *Sprung* (1982), *Hating Alison Ashley* (1984), *Penny Pollard's Diary* (1984), *Penny Pollard in Print* (1986), *The Lonely Hearts Club* (1987), *Against the Odds* (1989), *Came Back to Show You I Could Fly* (1990), *Amy's Bed* (1992) and *The Sky in Silver Lace* (1995). Received Children's Book of the Year Award for *Boris and Borsch* (1990) and Dromkeen Medal (1991).

KLEINE, Megan (1974—). American swimmer. Born Dec 22, 1974; grew up in Lexington, Kentucky; attended University of Texas, 1993–97. ❖ At Barcelona Olympics, won a gold medal in 4 x 100-meter medley relay (1992).

KLEINERT, Nadine (1975—). German shot putter. Name variations: Nadine Kleinert-Schmitt. Born Oct 20, 1975, in Magdeburg, Germany. ❖ Won a silver medal at Athens Olympics (2004).

KLEMENCIA. *Variant of Clementia.*

KLEPFISZ, Irena (1941—). American poet and feminist. Born 1941 in Warsaw, Poland; dau. of Michal and Rose Klepfisz; educated at City College, NY. ❖ Immigrated to US with family (1949); taught English, Yiddish, and women's studies; was founding editor of feminist journal *Conditions* and contributor to various feminist and lesbian journals, including *Sinister Wisdom;* works include *Keeper of Accounts* (1982), *Dreams of an Insomniac* (1990), and *A Few Words in the Mother Tongue* (1990); writings collected in *Different Enclosures: Poetry and Prose of Irena Klepfisz* (1985).

KLIER, Cornelia (1957—). East German rower. Born Mar 19, 1957, in East Germany. ❖ At Moscow Olympics, won a gold medal in coxless pairs (1980).

KLIER-SCHALLER, Johanna (1952—). East German runner. Name variations: Johanna Klier; Johanna Schaller. Born Johanna Schaller, Sept 13, 1952, in Erfurt, Germany. ❖ Won a gold medal for 100-meter hurdles at European championships (1978); won a gold medal at Montreal Olympics (1976) and a silver medal at Moscow Olympics (1980), both for 100-meter hurdles.

KLIMEK, Tillie (1865–1936). Polish-American serial killer. Born 1865; died at Illinois Women's Prison, 1936; m. John Mitkiewitz (died c. 1914); m. John Ruskowsi (died within 3 months of marriage); m. Joseph Guszkowski (died 1916); m. Frank Kupszyk (died 1920); m. Anton Klimek, 1921. ❖ Because she had a habit of accurately predicting deaths of her husbands from which she benefited financially, came under suspicion when she picked out a funeral dress for 5th husband who had not yet died (he survived); suspected in arsenic poisoning deaths of 4 husbands and a neighbor (Rose Chudzinski), was tried and sentenced to life imprisonment.

KLIMOVA, Marina (1966—). Russian ice dancer. Born July 22, 1966, in USSR; m. Sergei Ponomarenko. ❖ With Sergei Ponomarenko, won a bronze medal at Sarajevo Olympics (1984), silver medal at Calgary Olympics (1988) and gold at Albertville Olympics (1992); won gold medals at World championships (1989, 1990, 1992) and European championships (1989–92).

KLIMOVA, Natalya (1951—). Soviet basketball player. Born May 31, 1951, in USSR. ❖ At Montreal Olympics, won a gold medal in team competition (1976).

KLIMOVA, Rita (1931–1993). Czech revolutionary and ambassador. Name variations: Rita Budin. Born in Jasi, Romania, Dec 10, 1931; died in Prague, Dec 30, 1993; dau. of Stanislav Budin (journalist whose real name was Batya Bat) and Hana Coifman Budin (journalist); m. Zdenek Mlynar (div.); m. Zdenek Klima, 1978; children: (1st m.) Milena (Michaela Barlova); Vladimir (Vladya). ❖ Czech political dissident, who coined the term "Velvet Revolution" to describe the bloodless collapse of Marxism in Czechoslovakia (1989); grew up in US during WWII; returned to Prague with parents (1946); joined Communist Party (1948); earned master's and doctorate at Prague School of Economics; appointed instructor in history of economic thought at Charles

University; was shocked by Soviet invasion of Czechoslovakia (Aug 1968), which ended "Prague Spring"; expelled from the party and lost teaching job (1970); hosted regular meetings of Czech dissident movement when son Vladya became part of a clandestine courier network; became a member of Czechoslovak Helsinki Committee, reporting human-rights abuses (1986); worked closely with emerging circle of non-Marxist economists, the most important of whom was Václav Klaus; emerged as important contact for foreign journalists and Western human-rights activists; wrote numerous articles on social and economic themes for underground *samizdat* press; served occasionally as an interpreter for leading dissident Václav Havel; after fall of hardline Czechoslovak regime (1989), served as ambassador to US (1990–92). ❖ See also *Women in World History*.

KLIMOVICA-DREVINA, Inta (1951—). Soviet runner. Born Dec 14, 1951, in USSR. ❖ At Montreal Olympics, won a bronze medal in 4 x 400-meter relay (1976).

KLINE, T.F. (1920–1995). *See Harwood, Gwen.*

KLINK, Gertrud Scholtz- (b. 1902). *See Scholtz-Klink, Gertrud.*

KLOBUKOWSKA, Ewa (1946—). Polish runner. Born Oct 1, 1946, in Poland. ❖ At Tokyo Olympics, won a bronze medal in 100 meters and a gold medal in the 4 x 100-meter relay (1964); failed a sex-determination test and a *Times* magazine article reported she had "one chromosome too many" (1967).

KLOCHKOVA, Yana (1982—). Ukrainian swimmer. Born Aug 7, 1982, in Simferopol, Romania; dau. of former track-and-field athletes. ❖ At LC European championships, won gold medals for 200- and 400-meter indiv. medley (1999, 2000, 2002) and 400-meter freestyle (2000, 2002); at SC World championships, won gold medal for 400-meter indiv. medley (1999, 2000, 2002), 200-meter indiv. medley (2000–02), 400-meter freestyle (2002); at SC Europeans, won gold medals for 400- and 800-meter freestyle (1999) and 200-meter indiv. medley (1999–2001) and 400-meter indiv. medley (1999, 2000); won a gold medal for 200- and 400-meter indiv. medley and a silver medal for 800-meter freestyle at Sydney Olympics (2000); at LC World championships, won a gold medal for 400-meter freestyle and 400-meter indiv. medley (2001); won a gold medal for 200-meter indiv. medley and a gold medal for 400-meter indiv. medley at Athens Olympics (2004). Voted Ukraine's Athlete of the Year (2000).

KLOCHNEVA, Olga (1968—). Russian sharpshooter. Name variations: Olga Kuznetsova. Born Nov 17, 1968, in Samara, Russia; m. Vladimir Kuznetsov, 1995. ❖ Won a gold medal for 10 m air pistol (40 shots) at Atlanta Olympics (1996).

KLOOT, Lea (1903–1943). *See Nordheim, Helena.*

KLOPFER, Sonya. *See Dunfield, Sonya Klopfer.*

KLOTHILDE. *Variant of Clotilde.*

KLOTZ, Ulrike (1970—). East German gymnast. Born Nov 15, 1970, in East Germany. ❖ At Seoul Olympics, won a bronze medal in team all-around (1988).

KLUFT, Carolina (1983—). Swedish heptathlete and track-and-field athlete. Born Feb 2, 1983, in Boras, Sweden. ❖ Placed 1st in the heptathlon at World championships (2003); at World Indoor championships, won a gold medal for pentathlon (2003); won a gold medal for heptathlon at Athens Olympics (2004); for heptathlon, ranked 1st overall in World Combined Events Challenge (2003); at Super Grand Prix, placed 1sat in long jump (2003, 2004). Named European Athlete Association Athlete of the Year (2003) and Swedish Sports Foundation Sportswoman of the Year.

KLUG, Annette (1969—). West German fencer. Born Jan 8, 1969, in Germany. ❖ At Seoul Olympics, won a gold medal in team foil (1988).

KLUGE, Anja (1964—). East German rower. Born Nov 9, 1964, in East Germany. ❖ At Seoul Olympics, won a gold medal in coxed eights (1988).

KLUMPKE, Anna Elizabeth (1856–1942). American painter. Born Anna Elizabeth Klumpke in 1856; died 1942; dau. of Dorothea Tolle Klumpke and John Gerard Klumpke (San Francisco real-estate magnate); attended Académie Julian, 1883–84; studied with Tony Robert-Fleury and Jules Lefebvre in Paris; sister of Augusta Klumpke (1859–1927), Dorothea Klumpke (1861–1942), and Matilda and Julia Klumpke. ❖ Won many prizes for her portraits and landscapes; became a companion of mentor

Rosa Bonheur (1898); after Bonheur's death the following year, inherited Bonheur's studio-estate at By and wrote a biography, *Rosa Bonheur, sa vie, son oeuvre* (1908); also painted portraits of Bonheur and Elizabeth Cady Stanton. ❖ See also autobiography *Memoirs of an Artist* (1940); and *Women in World History*.

KLUMPKE, Augusta (1859–1927). American doctor. Name variations: Augusta Dejerine or Déjerine. Born Augusta Klumpke in 1859; died 1927; dau. of John Gerard Klumpke and Dorothea Matilda (Tolle) Klumpke; sister of Anna Elizabeth Klumpke (1856–1942) and Dorothea Klumpke (1861–1942); m. Joseph Jules Dejerine. ❖ Studied in Switzerland and Paris because, as a woman, could not gain admittance to medical school in America; granted a prize from Academy of Medicine for discovery of Klumpke palsy, a partial paralysis of the arm, caused by injury to the lower brachial plexus nerve. ❖ See also *Women in World History*.

KLUMPKE, Dorothea (1861–1942). American astronomer. Name variations: Dorothea Klumpke Roberts. Born Dorothea Klumpke, Aug 9, 1861, in San Francisco, CA; died Oct 5, 1942, in San Francisco; dau. of John Gerard Klumpke and Dorothea Matilda (Tolle) Klumpke; sister of Anna Elizabeth Klumpke (1856–1942), Augusta Klumpke (1859–1927), and Matilda and Julia Klumpke; attended public and private schools in San Francisco and Europe; University of Paris, BS, 1886, PhD, 1893; m. Isaac Roberts (1829–1904, famed Welsh amateur astronomer and nebular astrophotography pioneer), Oct 17, 1901; no children. ❖ Studied mathematics and mathematical astronomy at University of Paris and received PhD (1893), the 1st awarded to a woman at that institution, and the 1st PhD awarded to an American woman on an astronomical topic (the rings of Saturn); served as an attachée at Paris Observatory (1887–1901) and became involved with International Congress of Astronomers' Carte du Ciel, a photographic star chart project; appointed head of Special Bureau of Measurements at Observatory (1891), and was responsible for charting and cataloguing stars down to 14th magnitude; became widely known for her selection as observer for a balloon flight for the Perseid meteor shower (1889); assisted husband at his observatory in Sussex, England (1901–04); following his sudden death (1904), lived with sister Anna in France while continuing his work on charting and cataloguing nebulae; published *Isaac Roberts Atlas of 52 Regions: A Guide to William Herschel's Fields of Nebulosity* (1929), with a supplement (1932), for which she received the Helene-Paul Helbronner prize of French Academy of Science (1932); later returned to San Francisco and endowed prizes for astronomers at Paris Observatory and students at University of California. Given Prix des Dames, Societe Astronomique de France (1889); named Officer of the Paris Academy of Sciences (1893); elected Chevalier of the Legion of Honor (1934); presented with Cross of the Legion by Albert Lebrun, president of France, for her 48 years of service to French astronomy. ❖ See also *Women in World History*.

KNAB, Ursula (1929–1989). West German runner. Born Nov 22, 1929, in Germany; died May 23, 1989. ❖ At Helsinki Olympics, won a silver medal in the 4 x 100-meter relay (1952).

KNACKE, Christiane (1962—). East German swimmer. Born April 17, 1962, in East Germany. ❖ At Moscow Olympics, won a bronze medal in the 100-meter butterfly (1980).

KNAPE, Ulrika (1955—). Swedish diver. Name variations: Ulrika Knape. Born April 26, 1955, in Göteborg, Sweden. ❖ Won a silver medal for springboard and gold medal for platform at Munich Olympics (1972), the youngest gold medalist ever at the Games; won a gold for platform and a silver for springboard at World championships (1973); won 2 gold medals at European championships (1974); won a silver medal for platform at Montreal Olympics (1976).

KNAPP, Evalyn (1908–1981). American actress. Born Pauline Evelyn Knapp, June 17, 1908, in Kansas City, Missouri; died June 12, 1981, in Los Angeles, CA; sister of Orville Knapp (orchestra leader); m. Dr. George A. Snyder, 1934. ❖ Began career with brother Orville in a dancing vaudeville act; made film debut in Pathé Checkers Comedies (1929), followed by *Sinners' Holiday, 50 Million Frenchmen, The Millionaire, Side Show, Fireman Save My Child, This Sporting Age, His Private Secretary, Dance Girl Dance, The Perils of Pauline* (serial), *Confidential, The Lone Wolf Takes a Chance* and *Two Weeks to Live*, among others.

KNATCHBULL, Patricia (b. 1924). *See Mountbatten, Patricia.*

KNEEBONE, Nova (1971—). *See Peris-Kneebone, Nova.*

KNEF, Hildegard (1925–2002). German-born actress, author, and singer. Name variations: name spelled "Neff" during film career. Born Hildegard Frieda Albertina Knef, Dec 28, 1925, in Ulm, Germany; died Feb 1, 2002, in Berlin; trained at German Film Studio UFA; m. Kurt Hirsch (div.); m. David Cameron; m. Peter Rudolph Schell, 1977; children: (2nd m.) Christina Cameron. ❖ Appeared in German propaganda films (1945); acted on stage in 1st German postwar stage productions at the Schlossparktheater, Berlin (1945); appeared in 1st German postwar film, *The Murderers among Us* (1946); auditioned in Hollywood (1947) and began to build an international stage and film career; became major German film star with role in *The Sinner* (1950); played the female lead on Broadway in Cole Porter's *Silk Stockings* (1955–56); sang role of Jenny in German film of *The Three Penny Opera* (1962); began new career as a nightclub singer (1963); wrote the celebrated *The Gift Horse: Report on a Life* (1971); also wrote *The Verdict* (1975). Won Bundesfilmpreis (1959, 1977); given Edison Prize (1972); won Karlsbad Film Festival prize for Best Actress (1976) and the Golden Tulip award at Amsterdam Film Festival (1981). ❖ See also *Women in World History*.

KNEP, Mrs. (fl. 1670). *See Knipp, Mrs.*

KNETSCH, Christiane (1956—). *See Koepke-Knetsch, Christiane.*

KNIGHT, Mrs. Damon (1928—). *See Wilhelm, Kate.*

KNIGHT, Ellis Cornelia (1758–1837). British novelist and scholar. Born Ellis Cornelia Knight, Mar 27, 1758, in Westminster, London, England; died Dec 18, 1837, in Paris, France; dau. of Sir Joseph Knight (rear admiral of the White) and Lady Philippina (Deane) Knight. ❖ Known chiefly for association with Samuel Johnson and members of his circle, was also a companion to Charlotte of Mecklenburg-Strelitz, queen of England; works include *Dinarbus, A Tale: being a Continuation of Rasselas, Prince of Abyssinia* (1790), *Marcus Flaminius, or a View of the Military, Political, and Social Life of the Romans* (1793), *Chronological Abridgement of the History of Spain* (1809), *Chronological Abridgement of the History of France* (1811), *Translations from the German in Prose and Verse* (1812) and *Sir Guy de Lusignan: A Tale of Italy* (1933).

KNIGHT, Gladys (1944—). African-American rhythm-and-blues singer. Born Gladys Maria Knight, May 28, 1944, in Atlanta, GA; m. James Newman, 1960 (div. 1964); m. Barry Hankerson, 1974 (div. 1979); Les Brown, 1995 (div. 1997); m. William McDowell, 2001; children: (1st m.) 2; (2nd m.) 1. ❖ Toured with Morris Brown choir before she was 5; won 1st prize on *Ted Mack Amateur Hour* at 7; formed The Pips with siblings Merald and Brenda, and cousins William and Eleanor Guest (1952); released unsuccessful debut album (1957); sang lead vocals on group's 1st hit "Every Beat of My Heart" (1961); joined Motown (mid-1960s) and began scoring hits, beginning with "I Heard it Through the Grapevine" (1967) and ending with "Neither One of Us" (1973); moved with Pips to Buddah records, singing vocals on "Midnight Train to Georgia" (1973), "I've Got to Use My Imagination" (1974), and "Best Thing That Ever Happened to Me" (1974); collaborated with Curtis Mayfield on soundtrack to film *Claudine* (1974); made acting debut in film *Pipe Dreams* (1976) and co-starred on tv series "Charlie and Co." (1985); had more hits with "Landlord" (1980), "Save the Overtime (for Me)" (1983), and "Love Overboard" (1987); became a Mormon (late 1990s). ❖ See also autobiography *Between Each Line of Pain and Glory: My Life Story* (1997).

KNIGHT, June (1913–1987). American stage and screen dancer and actress. Born Margaret Rose Valliquietto, Jan 22, 1913, in Los Angeles, CA; died June 16, 1987, in Los Angeles; m. Paul S. Ames (div.); m. Arthur Arden Cameron (div.); m. Harry Packer; m. Jack Buhler. ❖ Made Broadway debut in *50 Million Frenchmen* (1929), followed by *Girl Crazy, The 9 O'Clock Revue, Take a Chance, Jubilee,* and *Sweethearts,* among others; films include *Take a Chance, Ladies Must Love, Gift of Gab, Wake Up and Dream, Broadway Melody of 1935* and *The House Across the Bay;* retired (1949).

KNIGHT, Laura (1877–1970). English painter. Name variations: Dame Laura Knight. Born Laura Johnson, Aug 4, 1877, in Long Eaton, Derbyshire, England; died in London, July 7, 1970; 3rd dau. of Charles Johnson (deserted family before her birth) and Charlotte Bates Johnson (art teacher); attended Nottingham School of Art, 1890–94; m. Harold Knight (artist), June 3, 1903 (died 1961); no children. ❖ One of the 1st prominent English women artists of 20th century, was a prolific painter whose work stressed realistic portrayals of women, Gypsies, and circus performers, as well as scenes of Britain during WWII; studied art in France (1889); won Princess of Wales scholarship (1894); lived in Staithes (1895–1903), concentrating on painting the seafarers and other villagers; exhibited painting *Mother and Child* at Royal Academy (1903); moved to artists' colony of Newlyn in Cornwall (1907); moved to London and began studies of backstage life at the ballet (1919); made extended trip to US (1926); named an associate of Royal Academy (1927), only the 2nd woman to receive such recognition in 20th century; toured with circus and painted her memorable *Three Clowns* (1930); made full member of Royal Academy (1936); during WWII, was commissioned by War Artists' Advisory Commission, becoming a familiar sight at Britain's factories and military bases (her most famous wartime painting showed factory worker Ruby Loftus using her machinist's skill at Royal Ordnance Factory); witnessed Nuremberg War Crimes Trial (1946); honored with retrospective exhibit at Royal Academy (1965); paintings include *The Beach, The Boys, On the Cliff, Two Girls on the Cliff, Flying a Kite, The Green Feather, Blue and Gold, A Cottage Bedroom* and *Susie and the Wash-basin.* Named Dame Commander of the British Empire (1929). ❖ See also autobiographies *Oil Paint and Grease Paint* (Nicholson & Watson, 1936) and *The Magic of a Line* (Kimber, 1965); Janet Dunbar, *Laura Knight* (Collins, 1971); Caroline Fox, *Dame Laura Knight* (Phaidon, 1988); and *Women in World History*.

KNIGHT, Margaret (1838–1914). American industrial inventor. Name variations: Mattie Knight. Born Feb 14, 1838, in York, Maine; died Oct 12, 1914, in Framingham, MA; dau. of James Knight and Hannah (Teal) Knight; raised in Manchester, NH, but lived most of adult life in Framingham; mostly self taught; never married. ❖ Industrial inventor with at least 23 patents for diverse products including window frames, improvements in engines, machines for cutting shoe soles, and machinery for folding and gluing square-bottomed paper bags. ❖ See also *Women in World History*.

KNIGHT, Mary (1749–1788). English murderer. Born 1749; hanged at Warwick, Aug 24, 1778; widowed; children: at least 2 sons. ❖ While living in Warwick, beat her younger son Roger with a stick when he failed to bring home enough corn from the fields, then closed him in the pantry where he died; was then seen by her surviving son and neighbors as she dumped son's body into the well.

KNIGHT, Sarah Kemble (1666–1727). Colonial diarist. Born Sarah Kemble on April 19, 1666, in Boston, Massachusetts; died Sept 25, 1727, in New London, Connecticut; dau. of Thomas Kemble (merchant) and Elizabeth (Trerice) Kemble; m. Richard Knight, sometime before 1689; children: Elizabeth Knight (b. 1689). ❖ Remembered for her daring horseback journey from Boston to New York, then back, during fall and winter of 1704–05. The diary of her travels, *The Journal of Madam Knight,* published in 1825, has gone through numerous editions and provides an invaluable account of the early 18th-century southern New England landscape and the customs and manners of the American colonists who lived there. ❖ See also *Women in World History*.

KNIGHT, Shirley (1936—). American stage and screen actress. Name variations: Shirley Knight Hopkins. Born July 5, 1936, in Goessel, Kansas; m. Eugene Persson (producer), 1959 (div. 1969); m. John Hopkins (British dramatist), 1970 (died 1998); children: Sophie Hopkins and Kaitlan Hopkins (b. 1964, actress). ❖ Made NY stage debut in *Journey to the Day* (1963), followed by *The Three Sisters, We Have Always Lived in the Castle* and *The Watering Place;* made film debut in *Five Gates to Hell* (1959); other films include *Ice Palace, House of Women, The Group, Petulia, The Rain People, Secrets, Beyond the Poseidon Adventure* and *Someone is Waiting;* appeared on BBC-TV, mostly in husband John Hopkins' plays. Nominated for Oscar for Best Supporting Actress for *The Dark at the Top of the Stairs* (1960) and *Sweet Bird of Youth* (1962); won Volpi Prize as Best Actress at Venice Film Festival (1967) for performance in husband Gene Persson's *Dutchman;* won Tony award for *Kennedy's Children* (1975) and Emmy for recurring role as Mel Harris' mother on "thirtysomething" (1988).

KNIGHTON, Margaret (1955—). New Zealand equestrian. Born Feb 14, 1955, in New Zealand. ❖ At Seoul Olympics, won a bronze medal in team 3-day event (1988).

KNIP, Henriette Ronner- (1821–1909). *See Ronner-Knip, Henriette.*

KNIPP, Mrs. (fl. 1670). English actress. Name variations: Mrs. Knep. ❖ Probably 1st appeared as Epicene in Ben Jonson's *Silent Woman* (1664); acted in plays by Jacobean and Restoration dramatists and disappeared from the bills by 1678; primarily known from entries in Samuel Pepys' diary.

KNIPPER-CHEKOVA, Olga (1870–1959). Russian actress. Name variations: Olga Chekova; Olga Chekhova; Olga Knipper-Chekhova; Olga Knipper. Born Olga Leonardovna Knipper in Russia in 1870 (some sources cite 1868); died 1959; aunt of composer Lev Knipper (b. 1898); studied drama with Alexander Fedotov and Vladimir Nemirovich-Danchenko; m. Anton Chekhov (1860–1904, dramatist), May 25, 1901; no children. ❖ Member of the 1st company of Moscow Art Theater (founded in 1898), became famous for portrayals of heroines of dramatist Anton Chekhov, whom she married; was 1st seen as Madame Arkadina in Moscow Art Theater's revival of *The Seagull* (1898) and went on to create the roles of Elena Andreyevna in *Uncle Vanya* (1899), Masha in *Three Sisters* (1901), and Madame Ranevskaya in *The Cherry Orchard* (1904); following husband's death (1904), remained with Moscow Art Theater, becoming best known for dramatic roles, including acclaimed performance in revival of Turgenev's *A Month in the Country*, directed by Stanislavski; was also delightful in comedies, including role of Shlestova in *Woe from Wit* (1925); recreated role of Madame Ranevskaya in *The Cherry Orchard* on occasion of 300th performance of play (1943). ❖ See also Jean Benedetti Ecco, ed. and trans. *Dear Writer, Dear Actress: The Love Letters of Anton Chekhov and Olga Knipper* (1997); and *Women in World History*.

KNOL, Monique (1964—). Dutch cyclist. Born Mar 31, 1964, in Netherlands. ❖ Won a gold medal at Seoul Olympics (1988) and a bronze medal at Barcelona Olympics (1992), both in indiv. road race.

KNOLL, Florence Schust (1917—). American furniture and interior designer. Name variations: Florence Knoll Bassett. Born Florence Schust in Saginaw, Michigan, May 24, 1917; dau. of Frederick and M.H. (Hastings) Schust; studied at Architectural Association in London; Illinois Institute of Technology, BA, 1941; m. Hans G. Knoll (producer and distributor of modern furniture and founder of Knoll International), July 1, 1946 (died Oct 1955); m. Harry Hood Bassett, June 22, 1958. ❖ One of America's leading designers of furniture and interiors, trained at Michigan's Cranbrook Academy under Eliel and Eero Saarinen and studied architecture in London and at Illinois Institute of Technology under Ludwig Mies van der Rohe; after working for both Marcel Breuer and Walter Gropius, was employed by Knoll International in NY (1943), a leading producer and distributor of modern furniture; added to product line with her own designs and was put in charge of Planning Unit, an interior design service that the firm offered; following husband's death (1955), took over as owner and chief designer of Knoll, and the firm continued to prosper. Received Medal of Arts (2002). ❖ See also *Women in World History*.

KNOLLYS, Catherine (1529–1569). See Carey, Catherine.

KNOLLYS, Elizabeth (c. 1586–1658). English noblewoman. Name variations: Lady Knollys; Elizabeth Howard. Born Elizabeth Howard c. 1586 in Saffron, Walden, Essex, England; died April 17, 1658, in Dorking, Surrey; dau. of Thomas Howard (1561–1626), 1st earl of Suffolk (r. 1603–1626), and Catherine Knyvett; m. William Knollys (1547–1632), later earl of Banbury, Lord Vaux, comptroller of Queen Elizabeth I's household; sister-in-law of Lettice Knollys (c. 1541–1634); children: 2 sons (widely thought to have been the children of Edward Vaux, not William Knollys).

KNOLLYS, Lettice (c. 1541–1634). Countess of Leicester and Essex. Name variations: Lettice Dudley; Lettice Knollys Devereux. Born c. 1541 (some sources cite 1539); died in 1634; eldest dau. of Catherine Carey (1529–1569) and Francis Knollys (c. 1514–1596, diplomat); sister of William Knollys (1547–1632), comptroller of Queen Elizabeth I's household; sister-in-law of Elizabeth Knollys; m. Walter Devereux, 1st earl of Essex, c. 1562; became 2nd wife of Robert Dudley, earl of Leicester (c. 1532–1588, a favorite of Queen Elizabeth), in 1578 or 1579; m. Sir Christopher Blount, in 1589; children: Penelope Rich (c. 1562–1607); Robert Devereux, 2nd earl of Essex; Dorothy Devereux. Some accused Robert Dudley of bringing about the murder of his 1st wife, Lady Amy Robsart.

KNOPF, Blanche (1894–1966). American publisher. Pronunciation: KUH-noff. Born Blanche Wolf, July 30, 1894, in New York, NY; died June 4, 1966, in NY; dau. of Julius W. Wolf (jeweler) and Berta Wolf (both immigrants from Vienna); attended Columbia University; m. Alfred A. Knopf (publisher), April 4, 1916; children: Patrick Knopf. ❖ Full partner with husband in one of the world's most successful publishing firms, who wielded power in an era when few women served as executives and brought authors of the stature of Albert Camus, Jean-Paul Sartre, and Simone de Beauvoir to America's attention; helped husband to found Alfred A. Knopf publishing company (1915); traveled with husband to acquire European writing talent (1921); was vice-president of the firm (1921–56); was the 1st American talent scout to seek literary talent in South America (1943); served as president of Alfred A. Knopf (1957–66), merging with Random House (1960). Named a Chevalier of Legion of Honor in France (1949); made a Cavaliero of Brazilian National Order of the Southern Cross (1950); decorated 2nd time in Brazil, receiving the rank of Oficial in recognition of her literary contributions (1964). ❖ See also *Women in World History*.

KNOPF, Eleanora Bliss (1883–1974). American geologist. Name variations: Eleanora Frances Bliss; Eleanora Knopf or Eleanora Frances Bliss Knopf. Born Eleanora Frances Bliss, July 15, 1883, in Rosemont, PA; died Jan 21, 1974, in Menlo Park, CA; dau. of Tasker Howard Bliss and Eleanora Emma (Anderson) Bliss; m. Adolph Knopf (geologist), 1920 (died 1966). ❖ Was assistant curator at Bryn Mawr College's Geological Museum and demonstrator at geological laboratory (1904–09); joined US Geological Survey (USGS) as geologic aide in Washington, DC (1912), being promoted to assistant geologist (1917), and working as geologist on important assignments (1920–55); announced discovery of 1st American sighting of mineral glaucophane east of Pacific coast, in PA (1913); worked for USGS on metamorphic rocks in NY and CT and on Stissing Mountain (beginning 1925); was visiting lecturer at Yale and Harvard universities (1930s); wrote *Structural Petrology* (1938); held appointments at Geological Society of America; at National Research Council, was chair of committee on experimental deformation of rocks (1945–49) and on glossary on structural petrology (1951–53); was research associate at Stanford University's geology department (beginning 1951).

KNORR, Frances (1868–1894). English-born Australian murderer. Name variations: Minnie Thwaites. Born Minnie Thwaites in London, England, 1868; hanged, Jan 15, 1894, in Australia. ❖ Immigrated to Australia (1887); worked in Melbourne, finding homes for unwanted children; after she moved to Sydney and 2 bodies of children were found buried in her Melbourne garden, was arrested and put on trial (April 1893); found guilty, received death sentence; confessed to both murders before she was hanged.

KNOWLES, Ann O'Connor (1842–1915). See Alabaster, Ann O'Connor.

KNOWLES, Beyoncé (1981—). African-American singer and actress. Name variations: Beyonce or Beyoncé; Destiny's Child. Born Beyoncé Giselle Knowles, Sept 4, 1981, in Houston, TX; dau. of Matthew Knowles (music manager) and Tina Knowles (stylist); sister of Solange Knowles (singer). ❖ As lead singer of Destiny's Child (formed 1989), had hit singles "No, No, No," "The Writing's on the Wall," "Bills, Bills, Bills," "Say My Name," "Jumpin', Jumpin'," and "Independent Women, Part 1" (from film *Charlie's Angels* soundtrack); was the 1st African-American woman to win the ASCAP Pop Songwriter of the Year award (2001); appeared in films *Austin Powers in Goldmember* (2002), and *Dreamgirls* (2006), among others.

KNOWLES, Emily (1847–1930). See Hill, Emily.

KNOWLTON, Helen Mary (1832–1918). American painter, art teacher, and writer. Born Aug 16, 1832, in Littleton, MA; died May 5, 1918, in Needham, MA; dau. of John Stocker Coffin Knowlton (editor and publisher) and Annie Wheeler (Hartwell) Knowlton. ❖ Opened own studio in Boston, MA (1867); took over art class for William Morris Hunt (1871–75); exhibited paintings in Boston Museum of Fine Arts, National Academy in NY, and Pennsylvania Academy in Philadelphia; her major contribution to art world was defending and preserving record of Hunt, an experimental and frequently misunderstood painter. Books included *Talks on Art* (1875), *Hints for Pupils in Drawing and Painting* (1879) and *Art-Life of William Morris Hunt* (1899).

KNOX, Debbie (1968—). Scottish curler. Born Sept 26, 1968, in Dunfermline, Scotland. ❖ Competed at Albertville (1992), when curling was a demonstration sport; won gold medals at the Scottish Ladies events (1992, 1999); (as 3rd player and deputy skip) won a team gold medal for curling at Salt Lake City Olympics (2002).

KNOX, Elizabeth (1899–1963). Scottish paleobotanist and palynologist. Name variations: Elizabeth May Henderson; Elizabeth May Knox. Born Elizabeth May Henderson, Mar 26, 1899, in Edinburgh, Scotland; died Dec 14, 1963; dau. of Andrew Henderson (prominent Edinburgh biscuit manufacturer); University of Edinburgh, BS, 1922, MA, 1923, and DSc, 1949; married a geologist named Knox. ❖ Published (1938–59) a series of papers on coal deposit spores in *Transactions of the*

Botanical Society of Edinburgh, Transactions of the Institute of Mining Engineers, and *Transactions of the Edinburgh Geological Society;* studied husband's coal samples in search of fragments fractured by faulting; served as president of Botanical Society of Edinburgh (1949–50).

KNOX, Elyse (1917—). American actress. Born Dec 14, 1917, in Hartford, CT; dau. of William Franklin Knox (Naval Secretary under FDR during WWII); m. Tom Harmon (football player), 1944 (died 1990); children: actors Mark Harmon (b. 1951), Kristin Harmon (b. 1945) and Kelly Harmon (b. 1948). ❖ Began career as a designer for *Vogue;* made film debut in *Wake Up and Live* (1937), followed by leads and second leads in *Lillian Russell, The Mummy's Tomb, Hit the Ice, Army Wives, Joe Palooka—Champ, Sweetheart of Sigma Chi, Winner Take All* and *There's a Girl in My Heart,* among others.

KNOX, Isa (1831–1903). Scottish writer. Name variations: Isa Craig; Mrs. Knox. Born Isa Craig in Edinburgh, Scotland, 1831; died 1903; m. cousin John Knox (iron merchant), 1866. ❖ Employed on staff of *Scotsman* for some time, contributing material under name Isa, before moving to London (1857); was secretary to National Association for the Promotion of Social Science until marriage; wrote prize poem for the Burns festival at Crystal Palace celebration (1859); went on to publish several novels, as well as *Tales on the Parables* (1872), *The Little Folks' History of England* (1872), and *In Duty Bound* (1881).

KNOX, Mary (1909–2000). See Shepard, Mary.

KNOX, Penelope (1916–2000). See Fitzgerald, Penelope.

KNOX, Rose Markward (1857–1950). American businesswoman. Born Rose Markward, Nov 18, 1857, in Mansfield, Ohio; died Sept 27, 1950, in Johnstown, NY; dau. of David Markward (druggist) and Amanda (Foreman) Markward; m. Charles Briggs Knox (glove salesman), Feb 15, 1883 (died 1908); children: Charles, James and Helen (died in infancy). ❖ Was one of the nation's outstanding businesswomen; with husband, invested savings in a gelatin business in Johnstown, NY (1890) and set out to bring the product into the mainstream by selling it to the American housewife; when husband died (1908), took over the business; instituted a 5-day work week for employees and later provided a 2-week paid vacation and sick-leave policies (1913); invested heavily in research, conducted in her own experimental kitchen and at laboratories of Melon Institute; began a newspaper column of recipes and household hints, "Mrs. Knox Says"; became nation's top producer and distributor of gelatin; remained head of firm until she was 90. ❖ See also *Women in World History.*

KNUDSEN, Monica (1975—). Norwegian soccer player. Born Mar 25, 1975, in Norway. ❖ Won a team gold medal at Sydney Olympics (2000).

KNUDSEN, Peggy (1923–1980). American actress. Born April 27, 1923, in Duluth, Minnesota; died July 11, 1980, in Encino, CA; children: 3 daughters. ❖ Had Broadway success in *My Sister Eileen* (1940–43); films include *The Big Sleep, Never Say Goodbye, Midnight, Unchained, Good Morning, Miss Dove* and *Hilda Crane;* retired (1960); later crippled by arthritis.

KNUTH, Maria (d. 1954). Russian spy. Born in Germany; died in prison from cancer, 1954. ❖ Out of work as an actress after WWII, was recruited as Soviet spy working for Kolberg Ring; entertained US and British officers at villa outside of Cologne while gathering information for Moscow about West German military strategy and other secret information; caught collecting coded letters in central Post Office in Cologne (c. 1953), was convicted.

KNUTSON, Coya Gjesdal (1912–1996). American politician. Born Cornelia Genevive Gjesdal, Aug 22, 1912, in Edmore, Ramsey County, ND; died Oct 10, 1996; dau. of Christian Gjesdal (farmer) and Christine (Anderson) Gjesdal; Concordia College, Moorhead, Minnesota, AB, 1934; postgraduate work in library science at Moorhead State Teachers College and in music at Juilliard School; m. Andrew Knutson (hotel owner), 1940 (div.); children: Terrance. ❖ Known as "the farm woman's Congresswoman," was the 1st woman to represent Minnesota in US Congress, though she did not enter politics until after successful career in education, public relations, and social welfare; embarked on 16-year high school-teaching career (1934); elected to Minnesota House of Representatives (1950), serving 2 terms; elected as Democratic-Farmer Labor candidate from 9th District to US House of Representative (1954); in Congress, was 1st woman to serve on House Committee on Agriculture; called for increased price supports for farm production, an extended food-stamp program for the distribution of farm surpluses, and a federally supported school-lunch program; lost election (1958) when husband published what came to be known as the "Coya, Come Home" letter, claiming her career had devastated their marriage (he later claimed that his wife's political opponents had convinced him to write it); made 2 more unsuccessful bids for reelection; under Kennedy administration, served as congressional liaison for Office of Civilian Defense. ❖ See also Gretchen Urnes Beito, *Coya Come Home: A Congresswoman's Journey* (Pomegranate, 1990); and *Women in World History.*

KNYAZEVA, Olga (1954—). Soviet fencer. Born Aug 1954, in USSR. ❖ At Montreal Olympics, won a gold medal in team foil (1976).

KNYVETT, Catherine (d. 1633). Countess of Suffolk. Name variations: Catherine Howard. Died Sept 1633; dau. of Sir Henry Knyvett and Elizabeth Stumpe; m. the Honorable Richard Rich; m. Thomas Howard (1561–1626), 1st earl of Suffolk (r. 1603–1626), c. 1583; children: (2nd m.) Theophilus Howard (1584–1640), 2nd earl of Suffolk (r. 1626–1640); Thomas Howard, 1st earl of Berkshire; Henry Howard; Sir Charles Howard; Sir Robert Howard; Sir William Howard; Edward, Baron Howard; Elizabeth Knollys; Frances Howard (1593–1632); Catherine Howard (d. 1672).

KO GI-HYUN (1986—). Korean short-track speedskater. Born May 11, 1986, in South Korea. ❖ Won a gold medal for the 1,500 meters and a silver medal for the 1,000 meters at Salt Lake City Olympics (2002).

KOBALSKAYA, Elizaveta (1851–1943). See Kovalskaia, Elizaveta.

KOBAN, Rita (1965—). Hungarian kayaker. Name variations: Rita Köbán; Rita Koeban. Born April 10, 1965, in Hungary. ❖ At Seoul Olympics, won a silver medal in K4 500 meters (1988); at Barcelona Olympics, won a gold medal in K4 500 meters, a bronze medal in K2 500 meters, and a silver medal in K1 500 meters (1992); at Atlanta Olympics, won a gold medal for K1 500 meters (1996); at Sydney Olympics, won a silver medal for K4 500 meters; won 6 World championships.

KOBART, Ruth (1924–2002). American stage, tv, and screen actress. Born Ruth Maxine Finkelstein, April 24, 1924, in Des Moines, Iowa; died Dec 14, 2002, in San Francisco, CA. ❖ Before acting, pursued a career in opera; appeared as Madame Pernelle in *Tartuffe* in American Conservatory Theater's premiere production in San Francisco (1967) and remained with the company, off and on, until 1994. Nominated for Tony Award for *A Funny Thing Happened on the Way to the Forum* (1963).

KOBAYASHI, Yoshimi (c. 1968—). Japanese softball player. Born c. 1968 in Japan. ❖ Won a team silver medal at Sydney Olympics (2000).

KOBER, Alice Elizabeth (1906–1950). American classical scholar. Born Dec 23, 1906, in New York, NY; died May 16, 1950, in Brooklyn, NY; dau. of Franz Kober (weaver) and Katharina (Gruber) Kober. ❖ Joined original faculty of Brooklyn College (1930) and was promoted to assistant professor (1935); began to devote research time to translation of so-called "Linear B" tablets of Minoan writing (1935), which eventually led to successful decipherment of tablets by Michael Ventris and identification of language used. ❖ See also John Chadwick, *The Decipherment of Linear B* (Cambridge U. Press, 1958).

KOBIAKOVA, Aleksandra (1823–1892). Russian novelist and short-story writer. Name variations: Aleksandra Petrovna Kobiaková. Born 1823 in Russia; died 1892. ❖ Born into wealthy family but became concerned with poverty and social conditions; writings include *The Podoshvin Household* (1860); autobiography appeared in journal *Russian Word* (1860).

KOBRYNSKA, Natalia Ivanovna (1855–1920). Ukrainian writer and feminist. Name variations: N.I. Kobrinskaia; Natal'ia Kobrynskaia; Natalia Kobryns'ka. Born in Belelui, Ukraine, June 8, 1855; died Jan 22, 1920, in Stanislav (now Ivano-Frankivs'k), Ukraine. ❖ Writer and organizer of the feminist movement in Galicia, depicted the poverty and backwardness of Ukrainian peasant life, condemning the caste system and patriarchy which kept women ignorant and superstitious; was the central figure of Ukrainian feminist movement for almost 4 decades; demanded equal rights for Ukrainian women in short story "Dukh chasu" ("The Spirit of the Times," 1887); founded Society of Ruthenian Women in city of Stanislav (1884); with Olena Pchilka, published almanac *Pershyi vinok (The First Wreath,* 1887), which contained essays and articles by women to watch on the intellectual landscape, including the young Lesya Ukrainka, Olena Pchilka's daughter; published 3 additional almanacs (1893–96), collectively entitled *Our Fate,;* played a key role in persuading a number of young authors, the most important being Olha Kobylianska, to write in Ukrainian rather than German; best known short stories are "For a Piece of Bread" (1884) and "The Elector" (1889), while novella *Iadzia and Katrusia* (1890) was a landmark in development of Ukrainian realist literature. ❖ See also *Women in World History.*

KOBYLIANSKA, Olha (1863–1942). Ukrainian writer. Name variations: Olga Kobilyanska; Olha Yulianovna Kobylianska; Ol'ga Iulianovna Kobylianskaia. Born in Gura Humorului, Bukovina, Austria-Hungary, Nov 27, 1863; died in Chernvitsi (Chernovitsy), Romania, Mar 21, 1942; grew up in southern part of Bukovina, then a province of Austro-Hungary. ❖ Modernist, whose writings are celebrated for their lyrical descriptions and psychological portraits which struck a blow against prevailing populist myths about peasant life, was influenced by the idealism in German literature; wrote 1st *novellen* in German (1880s), along with 1st drafts of novels *Liudyna* (*A Person*, 1891) and *Tsarivna* (*The Princess*, 1895); wrote of the Ukrainian peasantry in such novels as *Zemlia* (*The Land*, 1902) and *V nedilu rano zillia kopala* (*On Sunday Morn She Gathered Herbs*, 1909). ❖ See also *Women in World History.*

KOCH, Beate (1967—). East German javelin thrower. Born Aug 18, 1967, in East Germany. ❖ At Seoul Olympics, won a bronze medal in javelin throw (1988).

KOCH, Ilse (1906–1967). German war criminal. Born Margarete Ilse Köhler in Dresden, Germany, Sept 22, 1906; committed suicide at Aichach prison, Bavaria, Sept 2, 1967; m. Karl Otto Koch (1897–1945, member of SS and concentration camp commandant), May 1937; children: 2 daughters (one of whom died in infancy); 2 sons. ❖ German concentration camp overseer whose name has become a universal byword for sadism; known to the world as the "Witch of Buchenwald," was arrested by Allied forces (1945); placed on trial, received a sentence of life imprisonment at hard labor (1947), which was commuted to 4 years for political reasons, setting off a hue-and-cry in US; upon release from American custody (1949), was rearrested by West German state; went on trial in Augsburg, for 135 cases of murder (1950); sentenced to life imprisonment. ❖ See also *Women in World History.*

KOCH, Marianne (1925—). *See Makaryeva, Nadiezhda.*

KOCH, Marianne (1930—). German screen actress and physician. Name variations: Often billed in US and England as Marianne Cook. Born Aug 19, 1931, in Munich, Germany. ❖ Leading lady of German films, made debut in *Der Mann der zweimal leben wollte* (1950), followed by *Czardas der Herzen, Dr. Holl, Geheimnis einer Ehe, Night People, Der Keusche Lebemann, Wetterleuchten am Dachstein, Die Grosse Schuld, Ludwig II, Königswalzer, Interlude, Four Girls in Town, Napoleon III, Die Fledermaus, Frozen Alive, A Fistful of Dollars, Coast of Skeletons, La Balada de Johnny Ringo* and *Clint il Solitario*, among many others; returned to university to study medicine (1973–77), then practiced medicine (1985–97).

KOCH, Marita (1957—). East German runner. Born Feb 18, 1957, in Wismar, East Germany. ❖ Won a gold medal for the 400 meters and a silver for the 4 x 400 meters at Moscow Olympics (1980); at World championships, won gold medals for 200 meters, 4 x 100 meters and 4 x 400 meters and a silver medal for 100 meters (1983); placed 1st for 400 meters at European games in Athens, Greece, with a time of 48.16 (1982); once held world records in both the 200 meters and 400 meters and was the 1st woman to better 49 seconds in the 400.

KOCH, Martina (1959—). West German field-hockey player. Born May 20, 1959, in Germany. ❖ At Los Angeles Olympics, won a silver medal in team competition (1984).

KOCHANSKA, Marcella (1858–1935). *See Sembrich, Marcella.*

KOCHERGINA-MAKARETS, Tatyana (1956—). Soviet handball player. Born Mar 26, 1956, in USSR. ❖ Won a gold medal at Montreal Olympics (1976) and a gold medal at Moscow Olympics (1980), both in team competition.

KOCHETKOVA, Dina (1977—). Russian gymnast. Born July 27, 1977, in Moscow, USSR. ❖ At European championships, won silver medals in all-around, team all-around, and a bronze in floor exercise (1994), a silver in floor (1995) and a silver in team all-around and bronze in floor (1996); won Goodwill Games and Russian nationals (1994); at World championships, won a gold medal in floor exercises and bronze medals in all-around and uneven bars (1994) and a gold in balance beam (1996); at Atlanta Olympics, won a silver medal in team all-around (1996); underwent knee surgery (1997).

KO-CHING KANG (1911–1992). *See Kang Keqing.*

KÖCK, Brigitte. *See Koeck, Brigitte.*

KOCK, Karin (1891–1976). Swedish economist and politician. Name variations: Karin Kock-Lindberg. Born in Stockholm, Sweden, July 2, 1891; died 1976; dau. of Ernst Kock (chief supervisor in the Swedish Customs Office) and Anna (Aslund) Kock; graduate of Whitlockska Samskolan, in Stockholm, 1910; University of Stockholm, BA, 1918, MA, 1925, PhD, 1929; m. Hugo Lindberg (lawyer), 1936. ❖ One of Europe's foremost economists and the 1st woman Cabinet member in Sweden's history, was a professor of economics at University of Stockholm; was involved in a number of economic surveys for Swedish government, one of which explored the economic and social trends of the period and proposed certain reforms in the compilation of statistics (1934–35); appointed consultative minister in Social Democratic Labor Cabinet of Tage Erlander, the 1st time a woman was seated at the King's council table (1947); served as minister of Supply (1948–49); was Sweden's delegate to International Labor Organization Conference in Paris (1947) and served for several years as Swedish delegate to conferences of Economic Commission for Europe. ❖ See also *Women in World History.*

KOCSIS, Erzsebet. Hungarian handball player. Born in Hungary. ❖ Won a team bronze medal at Atlanta Olympics (1996).

KOEA, Shonagh (1939—). New Zealand journalist, novelist and short-story writer. Born 1939 in Taranaki, New Zealand; grew up in Hawkes Bay; married a journalist (died 1987). ❖ Began career as a journalist; won Air New Zealand Short Story Competition (1981); works include *The Women Who Never Went Home and Other Stories* (1987) and novels, *The Grandiflora Tree* (1989), *The Wedding at Bueno-Vista* (1996), *The Lonely Margins of the Sea* (1998) and *Time for Killing* (2001).

KOEBAN, Rita (1965—). *See Koban, Rita.*

KOECHLIN-SMYTHE, Pat (1928–1996). *See Smythe, Pat.*

KOECK, Brigitte. Austrian giant-slalom snowboarder. Name variations: Brigitte Köck. Born in Austria. ❖ At Nagano, won the 1st bronze medal ever awarded for women's giant-slalom snowboarding at Winter Olympics (1998).

KOEFOED, Charlotte (1957—). Danish rower. Name variations: Charlotte Köföd. Born Sept 17, 1957, in Denmark. ❖ At Los Angeles Olympics, won a bronze medal in quadruple sculls with coxswain (1984).

KOEHLER, Christa (1951—). East German diver. Name variations: Christa Köhler. Born Aug 18, 1951, in East Germany. ❖ At Montreal Olympics, won a silver medal in springboard (1976).

KOEHLER, Gisela (1931—). East German runner. Name variations: Gisela Köhler. Born Dec 22, 1931, in Germany. ❖ Won a silver medal at Melbourne Olympics (1956) and a bronze medal at Rome Olympics (1960), both in 80-meter hurdles.

KOEHLER, Kathe (1913—). German diver. Name variations: Kathe Köhler. Born Nov 10, 1913, in Germany. ❖ At Berlin Olympics, won a bronze medal in platform (1936).

KOEN, Fanny Blankers (b. 1918). *See Blankers-Koen, Fanny.*

KOENIG, Alma Johanna (1887–c. 1942). *See König, Alma Johanna.*

KOENIG, Rita. German fencer. Name variations: Rita König. Born in Germany. ❖ Won a silver medal for indiv. foil and a bronze for team foil at Sydney Olympics (2000).

KOENIGSDORF, Helga (1938—). *See Königsdorf, Helga.*

KOEPKE-KNETSCH, Christiane (1956—). East German rower. Name variations: Christiane Köpke-Knetsch. Born Aug 24, 1956, in East Germany. ❖ Won a gold medal at Montreal Olympics (1976) and a gold medal at Moscow Olympics (1980), both in coxed eights.

KOEPPEN, Kerstin (1967—). German rower. Name variations: Kerstin Köppen or Koppen. Born Nov 24, 1967, in Germany. ❖ Won a gold medal for double sculls at Barcelona Olympics (1992) and a gold medal for quadruple sculls at Atlanta Olympics (1996).

KOERING, Dorothea (1880–1945). German tennis player. Born July 11, 1880, in Germany; died Feb 13, 1945. ❖ At Stockholm Olympics, won a silver medal in singles and a gold medal in mixed doubles–outdoors (1912).

KOERT-KRONOLD, Selma (1861–1920). *See Kronold, Selma.*

KOESEM (1589–1651). *See Kösem.*

KOESTLER, Marie (1879–1965). *See Köstler, Marie.*

KOESTLIN, Josephine Lang (1815–1880). *See Lang, Josephine.*

KOESUN, Ruth Ann (1928—). **American ballet dancer.** Born May 15, 1928, in Chicago, IL; trained with Vechslav Swoboda. ❖ Danced with Chicago Opera Ballet and San Carlo Opera; joined Ballet Theater (1945), where she created roles in de Mille's *Fall River Legend* (1948), Tudor's *Shadow of the Wind* (1948) and Ross' *Paean* (1957), and appeared in *Les Sylphides, Caprichos* (1950) and *This Property is Condemned* (1957); best-remembered for performance as the Mexican Sweetheart with John Kriza in *Billy the Kid;* appeared on tv in "Omnibus" (1953).

KOETELES, Erzsebet (1924—). *See Gulyasne-Koeteles, Erzsebet.*

KOETHER, Rosemarie (1956—). *See Gabriel-Koether, Rosemarie.*

KOFFLER, Camilla or Ylla (1911–1955). *See Ylla.*

KOFORD, Helen (1929—). *See Moore, Terry.*

KOGAN, Claude (1919–1959). **French mountaineer.** Born 1919; killed in avalanche while attacking Cho Oyu, Oct 1959; m. Georges Kogan (mountaineer), 1945 (died 1951). ❖ Ascended North Face of the Dru (1946); was 1st female lead of South Ridge of Aiguille Noire de Peuterey (1949); made 2nd ascent of Quitaraju (1951); made 1st ascent of Salcantay (1952); made 1st ascent of Nun Kun (23,400 ft.) in Kashmir (1953); made 1st ascent of Ganesh Himal in Nepal, with Raymond Lambert (1955). ❖ See also *Women in World History.*

KOGAWA, Joy (1935—). **Canadian poet, novelist and children's writer.** Born 1935 in Vancouver, British Columbia, Canada; studied at University of Alberta, Toronto Conservatory of Music, and University of Saskatchewan. ❖ Having been placed in an internment camp with family during WWII, wrote the award-winning *Obasan* (1981), about internment of Japanese in Canada, which she then rewrote for children as *Naomi's Road* (1986); other writings include *The Splintered Moon* (1967), *A Choice of Dreams* (1974), *Woman in the Woods* (1985), *Itsuka* (1993), and *The Rain Ascends* (1995).

KŌGYOKU-SAIMEI (594–661). **Japanese empress.** Name variations: Princess Takaru; (1st reign) Empress Kōgyoku; (2nd reign) Empress Saimei; Kogyoku-tennō. Pronunciation: KOE-gyoe-koo Sigh-may. Reigned 642–45, 655–61. Born 594; died in Kyushu, Japan, 661, while seeing off her forces to defend the Paekche kingdom from Chinese invasion; grandmother of Empress Jitō (645–702); m. Emperor Jomei; children: Emperor Tenji; Emperor Oama; and the consort of Emperor Kotoku. ❖ The 35th and 37th sovereign of Japan; during power struggles after death of husband, was installed as sovereign by imperial counselors; stunned when son Prince Naka (later Emperor Tenji) murdered an ambitious minister before her eyes; abdicated two days later; upon death of successor, Emperor Kotoku, 9 years later, was again called upon to take the throne and served until her death; during 2nd reign, frequently sent military expeditions to the northern part of Japan to subdue the aboriginal people there. ❖ See also *Women in World History.*

KOHARY, Antoinette (1797–1862). **German royal.** Name variations: Antonia. Born July 2, 1797; died Sept 25, 1862; m. Ferdinand of Saxe-Coburg (uncle of Queen Victoria), Jan 2, 1816; children: Ferdinand of Saxe-Coburg (1816–1885), who m. Maria II da Gloria, queen of Portugal); Augustus of Saxe-Coburg (1818–1881); Victoria of Saxe-Coburg (1822–1857); Leopold Saxe-Coburg (1824–1884). ❖ Was aunt by marriage to Queen Victoria.

KOHDE-KILSCH, Claudia (1963—). **West German tennis player.** Name variations: Claudia Kilsch. Born Dec 11, 1963, in Germany. ❖ At Seoul Olympics, won a bronze medal in doubles (1988).

KOHL, Hannelore (1933–2001). **German first lady.** Born Mar 7, 1933, in Berlin, Germany; grew up in Leipzig; committed suicide, July 5, 2001, in Ludwigshafen, Germany; dau. of an engineer from Rhineland-Palatinate; m. Helmut Kohl (chancellor of Germany, 1982–98), 1960; children: 2 sons. ❖ Was often by husband's side during his long political career, but worked to keep herself and sons out of the spotlight; led a charity for helping accident victims, the Hannelore Kohl Foundation; having suffered from a painful sunlight allergy for 7 years, only leaving the house in darkness, took her own life when it grew worse.

KÖHLER, Christa (1951—). *See Koehler, Christa.*

KÖHLER, Gisela (1931—). *See Koehler, Gisela.*

KÖHLER, Kathe (1913—). *See Koehler, Kathe.*

KÖHLER-RICHTER, Emmy (1918—). **German ballet dancer and choreographer.** Name variations: Koehler-Richter. Born Feb 9, 1918, in Gera, Germany. ❖ Trained with Mary Wigman and Tatiana Gsovsky in Berlin; danced with German opera ballets in Bonn, Berlin, and Leipzig, among others; after WWII, served as ballet master at state operas in Cologne, Weimar and Basel, Switzerland; became choreographer-in-residence for Leipzig Opera Ballet (c. 1955) where she created numerous works, including popular *Sklaven,* based on story of Spartacus (1961); also choreographed *The Daughter of Castille* (1960), *Dornroeschen* (1960), *Legend of Love* (1961), *Till Eulenspiegel* (1965) and *Der Rowdy und Das Maedchen* (1972).

KOHNER, Kathy (1941—). **American surfer.** Name variations: Gidget Kohner; Kathy Kohner Zuckerman. Born 1941 in Brentwood, CA; dau. of Frederick Kohner (writer and screenwriter). ❖ Gutsy teenager who crashed the all-male surfer scene at Malibu Beach (1957), was dubbed Gidget (Girl Midget); became the basis for her father's book *Gidget,* as well as 8 film spinoffs, including *Gidget* (starring Sandra Dee), *Gidget Goes Hawaiian* and *Gidget Gets Married,* and the tv series of the same name starring Sally Field.

KOHNER, Susan (1936—). **American actress.** Born Nov 11, 1936, in Los Angeles, CA; dau. of Paul Kohner (Hollywood agent) and Lupita Tovar (b. 1911, Mexican-born actress); sister of Pancho Kohner (producer); m. John Weitz (fashion designer), 1964 (died 2002). ❖ Made film debut in *To Hell and Back* (1955), followed by *The Last Wagon, Dino, Trooper Hook, The Big Fisherman, The Gene Krupa Story, All the Fine Young Cannibals, By Love Possessed* and *Freud;* retired from acting (1964). Nominated for Oscar for Best Supporting Actress for performance in *Imitation of Life* (1959).

KOHUT, Rebekah (1864–1951). **American social welfare leader and educator.** Born Rebekah Bettelheim in Kaschau, Hungary, Sept 9, 1864; died in New York, NY, Aug 11, 1951; dau. of Albert Siegfried Bettelheim (rabbi and physician) and Henrietta (Wientraub) Bettelheim (teacher); immigrated to US with family (1867); attended University of California, San Francisco; m. Alexander Kohut (rabbi), Feb 14, 1887 (died 1895); stepchildren: 8. ❖ After husband died (1894), founded Kohut School for Girls (1899), which she ran for 5 years; became a driving force behind NY branch of National Council of Jewish Women and served as president (1894–98); established Employment Bureau of Young Women's Hebrew Association (1914); during WWI, worked for US Employment Service and was a member of Woodrow Wilson's Federal Employment Committee; also served as industrial chair of National League for Women's Service; elected president of World Congress of Jewish Women (1923); appointed to NY State Advisory Council on Employment and to Joint Legislative Commission on Unemployment (1931); returned to school administration (1934), serving for several years as head of Columbia Grammar School. ❖ See also autobiographies *My Portion* (1925) and *More Yesterdays* (1950); and *Women in World History.*

KOIDULA, Lydia (1843–1886). **Estonian poet and playwright.** Born Lydia Emilie Florentine Jannsen in Vändra (Pärnu), Estonia, Dec 24, 1843; died in Kronstadt, Russia, Aug 11, 1886; dau. of Johann Voldemar Jannsen (1819–1890, teacher); m. Eduard Michelson. ❖ A major figure in the Estonian national awakening of the 19th century, assisted father in editing the country's 1st weekly newspaper, *The Postman of Pärnu,* later named *The Estonian Postman;* changed name from Swedish-sounding Jannsen to the more Estonian Koidula; published 1st volume of verse, *Meadow Flowers* (1866), and a volume of original verse in Estonian, *The Nightingale of Emajõgi* (1867); over next decade, published large number of verse attacking feudal oppression and national apathy; wrote several plays (1870–72), including *The Cousin from Saaremaa, The Wooing Birches, or Maret and Miina* and *Such a Mulk, or a Hundred Barrels of Coarse Salt;* many of her poems were adapted into beloved popular songs; remains a revered Estonian author. During Soviet occupation (1940–41, 1944–91), Estonian nationalists drew inspiration from Koidula's poem "My Fatherland is Dear to Me," an unofficial anthem set to music by Gustav Ernesaks, while her father's "My Native Land" is the official national anthem of post-Soviet Estonia. ❖ See also Madli Puhvel, *Symbol of Dawn: The Life and Times of the 19th-Century Estonian Poet*

Lydia Koidula (Tartu University Press, 1995); and *Women in World History.*

KOJEVNIKOVA, Elizaveta. Russian freestyle skier. Name variations: Elisabeta Koyevnikova; Kojewnikow; Yelizaveta Kozhevnikova. Born in USSR. ❖ Won a silver medal at Albertville Olympics (1992) and a bronze medal at Lillehammer Olympics (1994), both for moguls.

KOJEWNIKOW, Elisabeta. *See Kojevnikova, Elizaveta.*

KOJIMA, Yukiyo (1945—). Japanese volleyball player. Born Dec 10, 1945, in Japan. ❖ At Mexico City Olympics, won a silver medal in team competition (1968).

KOK, Aagje (1947—). *See Kok, Ada.*

KOK, Ada (1947—). Dutch swimmer. Name variations: Aagje Kok. Born June 1947 in Netherlands. ❖ At Tokyo Olympics, won silver medals in the 4 x 100-meter medley relay and the 100-meter butterfly (1964); at Mexico City Olympics, won a gold medal in the 200-meter butterfly (1968).

KOK, Irene de (1963—). *See de Kok, Irene.*

KŌKEN-SHŌTOKU (718–770). Japanese empress. Name variations: (1st reign) Empress Kōken or Koken; (2nd reign) Empress Shōtoku or Shotoku. Pronunciation: KOE-ken SHOW-toe-ku. Reigned 749–58 and 764–70. Born 718 in Nara, Japan; died 770 in Nara; dau. of Emperor Shomu and Empress Komyo; never married; no children. ❖ One of only 8 empresses of Japan to have been officially designated as heir apparent, ascended the throne twice; played a significant role in popularizing Buddhism, which flourished as the national religion for centuries. ❖ See also *Women in World History.*

KOKENY, Beatrix. Hungarian handball player. Name variations: Kökény. Born in Hungary. ❖ Won a team bronze medal at Atlanta Olympics (1996) and a team silver medal at Sydney Olympics (2000).

KOKHANOVSKAIA (1823–1884). *See Sokhánskaia, Nadezhda.*

KOKORO-BARRETT, Hiria (1870–1943). New Zealand tribal leader and artisan. Name variations: Hiria Kokoro-Gray. Born on June 3, 1870, possibly at Tuahiwi in Canterbury, New Zealand; died on Sept 4, 1943, at Niagara, New Zealand; dau. of Henare Kokoro Tiratahi and Mere Pukuwaitai Kahaki; m. William Gray (laborer), 1890 (died 1895); m. Francis George Te Hau Barrett (Pareti), 1902 or 1903; children: (1st m.) 3 daughters; (2nd m.) 5 daughters and 4 sons. ❖ Learned arts and skills of mother, including making flax and ribbonwood baskets, cloaks, headbands, and sandals; also made flax traps to catch fish; fished and hunted for birds, fish, and seal; in later years, became reclusive and lived alone in improvised shelter at Niagara. ❖ See also *Dictionary of New Zealand Biography* (Vol. 3).

KOKORO-GRAY, Hiria (1870–1943). *See Kokoro-Barrett, Hiria.*

KOLA, Pamela. Kenyan short-story writer. Born in Kenya; University of Leeds, Diploma in Education. ❖ Runs a nursery in Nairobi; contributed stories to *East Africa When, How and Why Stories,* including "The Wise Little Girl," "How the Leopard Got His Spots," and "Why Hyena Laughs."

KOLAR-MERDAN, Jasna (1956—). Yugoslavian handball player. Name variations: Jasna Merdan. Born Oct 19, 1956. ❖ Won a silver medal at Moscow Olympics (1980) and a gold medal at Los Angeles Olympics (1984), both in team competition.

KOLASHNIKOVA, Vera (1933—). *See Krepkina, Vera.*

KOLB, Annette (1870–1967). German novelist and essayist. Born Anna Mathilde Kolb, Feb 3, 1870, in Munich, Germany; died Dec 3, 1967, in Munich; dau. of Sophie Danvin Kolb (Parisian concert pianist) and Max Kolb (Munich landscape architect). ❖ German-French writer and translator, who ardently advocated pacifism during and after World War I and campaigned for Franco-German reconciliation, fled Germany with rise of Nazis (Feb 21, 1933) for Luxembourg; at 71, traveled by way of Lisbon to NY (1941); returned to Europe (1945), settling in Paris (1945–61); shifted her allegiance to Catholicism during her later years and was a passionate believer in a united Europe; works include *Das Exemplar* (1913), *Daphne Herbst* (1926), and *Die Schaukel* (1934). Received Fontane Prize for *Das Exemplar.*

KOLB, Barbara (1939—). American composer. Born Barbara Anne Kolb in Hartford, CT, Feb 10, 1939; dau. of Helen (Lily) Kolb and Harold Judson Kolb (music conductor); University of Hartford, BM, 1961, MA, 1965; studied with Lukas Foss, Gunther Schuller, and Arnold Franchetti. ❖ Composer of numerous contemporary pieces for chamber groups, ensembles, and orchestra, was a professor of composition at Brooklyn College during a time when there were less than 100 women teaching composition in US; was 1st American woman to win Prix de Rome (1969) and 1st woman to be commissioned to compose for concerts at Tanglewood (1970); received commissions from Koussevitzky Foundation, NY State Council for the Arts, and Washington Performing Arts Society, among others; specialized in composing non-traditional chamber orchestras which often combined prerecorded non-electronic sounds with various instruments; composed *Soundings,* for 3 orchestras, *Spring River Flowers Moon Night* and *Trobar Clubs.*

KOLB, Claudia (1949—). American swimmer. Born Dec 19, 1949, in Hayward, CA. ❖ Won AAU outdoor 100- and 200-meter breaststroke championships (1964, 1965), 200-meter indiv. medley (1966, 1967, 1968) and 400 meters (1966, 1967); won AAU indoor 100-yard breaststroke (1964), 200-yard (1967, 1968) and 400-yard (1968), among others; at Tokyo Olympics, won a silver medal in the 200-meter breaststroke (1964); at Mexico City Olympics, won a gold medal in 400-meter indiv. medley and a gold medal in the 200-meter indiv. medley (1968).

KOLB, Thérèse (1856–1935). French actress. Name variations: Therese Kolb. Born Jan 19, 1856, in Altkirch, France; died Aug 19, 1935, in Levallois-Perret, France. ❖ Made stage debut at Comédie Française as Dorine in *Tartuffe* (1898), then appeared there in *Cabotins, Blanchette, La plus faible, Claudie, Monsieur Alphonse, L'Ame des Héros, L'Amour Veille, Simone, Sapho, Debureau, La robe rouge, Sire, Les affaires sont les affaires* and *Turcaret,* among others; elected a sociétaire of Comédie Française (1904); films include *Enfants de Paris, Blanchette, Dans l'ombre du harem, Le crime de Sylvestre Bonnard* and *Ces dames aux chapeaux verts.*

KOLCHINA, Alevtina (1930—). *See Olunina, Alevtina.*

KOLESNIKOVA, Anastasia (1984—). Russian gymnast. Name variations: Anastassia. Born Mar 6, 1984, in St. Petersburg, Russia. ❖ At Sydney Olympics, won a silver medal for all-around team (2000).

KOLESNIKOVA, Nadezhda (1949—). *See Ilyina-Kolesnikova, Nadezhda.*

KOLESNIKOVA, Vera (1968—). Russian gymnast. Born Oct 7, 1968, in Perlevka, Voronezh, Russia. ❖ Placed 2nd all-around at the Catania Cup (1983, 1984) and Jr. USSR championships (1984); won Moscow News (1984), Australian Games (1985), and Goodwill Games (1986).

KOLEVA, Elizabeth (1972—). Bulgarian rhythmic gymnast. Born Nov 11, 1972, in Sofia, Bulgaria; m. Martin Stoev (volleyball player). ❖ Won Jr. European championship (1987); at World championships, tied Adriana Dunavska for the silver medal for all-around (1987); at European championships, tied Dunavska and Alexandra Timochenko for a gold medal in all-around (1988); retired (1988).

KOLEVA, Maria. Bulgarian rhythmic gymnast. Born in Bulgaria. ❖ Won a silver medal for team all-around at Atlanta Olympics (1996).

KOLISKO, Agnes (1911–1991). *See Ruttner-Kolisko, Agnes.*

KOLKOVA, Olga (1955—). Soviet rower. Born May 29, 1955, in USSR. ❖ At Montreal Olympics, won a silver medal in coxed eights (1976).

KOLLING, Janne (1968—). Danish handball player. Born July 12, 1968, in Denmark. ❖ Debuted on national team (1988); won a team gold medal at Atlanta Olympics (1996) and at Sydney Olympics (2000); won team European championships (1994, 1996) and World championships (1997).

KOLLONTAI, Alexandra (1872–1952). Russian revolutionary and feminist. Name variations: Aleksandra Kollontay; (nickname) Shura. Pronunciation: KOLL-lon-TIE. Born Alexandra or Aleksandra Mikhailovna Domontovich in St. Petersburg, Russia, Mar 19, 1872; died in Moscow, Mar 9, 1952; dau. of Mikhail Domontovich (cavalry officer) and Aleksandra Masalina (dau. of a Finnish lumber merchant); tutored at home, leading to certificate, 1888; auditor, University of Zurich, 1898–99; m. Vladimir Kollontai, 1893 (div.); m. Pavel Dybenko, in 1918; children: (1st m.) Mikhail. ❖ The 1st woman to be a member of the Bolshevik Central Committee and the Council of People's Commissars as well as the world's 1st female ambassador, joined Russian Social Democratic Labor Party (1899); wrote and lectured on Marxism and social issues (1900–05); promoted Marxist organization of Russian factory women (1906–08); fled abroad (Dec 1908), where she served as Russian representative to International Women's Secretariat

(1910–15), lectured at Bologna Party School (1910–11), and wrote extensively on issues relating to maternity, sexuality and pacifism; returned to Russia and called for overthrow of new Provisional Government (Mar 1917); elected to Executive Committee of the Petrograd Soviet and to Central Committee of the Bolshevik Party and arrested (July 1917); served as commissar of Social Welfare (1917–18); never subservient to party discipline, was a member of Left Communist opposition (1918) and Workers' Opposition (1921–22); served as director, Women's Section (*Zhenotdel*) of Central Committee of the Russian Communist Party (1920–22); performed diplomatic work in Norway (1922–25, ambassador 1927–30), Mexico (ambassador 1926–27) and Sweden (ambassador 1930–45); is now recognized for what she was: a revolutionary sufficiently important to be a member of the Bolshevik Central Committee, the leading feminist in the early Soviet state, a surprisingly successful and durable diplomat, and a person whose writing on the psychological and sexual liberation of women is a significant contribution to the mainstream of 20th-century European feminism. Wrote over 230 newspaper and journal articles many of which have been reproduced in A.M. Kollontai, *Izbrannye stat'i i rechi* (*Collected Articles and Speeches*, Moscow, 1972); wrote 30 pamphlets, novellas and books. ❖ See also *The Autobiography of a Sexually Emancipated Woman* (ed. by Irving Fetscher, Schocken, 1971); Barbara Evans Clements, *Bolshevik Feminist: The Life of Aleksandra Kollontai* (Indiana U. Press, 1979); Beatrice Farnsworth, *Aleksandra Kollontai: Socialism, Feminism and the Bolshevik Revolution* (Stanford U. Press, 1980); and *Women in World History*.

KOLLWITZ, Käthe (1867–1945). German artist. Pronunciation: KAY-tee KOHL-witz. Born Käthe Schmidt on July 8, 1867, in Königsberg, Germany; died at Moritzburg, April 22, 1945; dau. of Karl Schmidt (lawyer) and Katherina (Rupp) Schmidt; attended art schools in Berlin and Munich; m. Karl Kollwitz (physician), June 13, 1891; children: Hans and Peter. ❖ Artist whose Expressionist etchings, lithographs, woodcuts, and sculpture sympathetically and dramatically portrayed the German working class and victims of violence, making her the best-known German woman artist of 1st half of 20th century; began art studies with Rudolf Mauer, an engraver (1881); arrived in Berlin to study at Women's School of Art (1885); took up residence, with husband, in slum area of North Berlin (1891); attended premiere of Hauptmann's play *The Weavers* and was inspired to do a series of prints (1893); received gold medal for "Revolt of the Weavers" (1899); won Villa Romana prize (1907); became 1st woman elected to Prussian Academy of Arts (1919); was co-founder of Society for Women Artists and Friends of Art (1926); visited Soviet Union as a guest of the government (1927); was forced to resign from Prussian Academy by the National Socialist government, the beginning of the period when her works were condemned by the Nazis as "degenerate art" (1933); evacuated to Nordhausen because of bombing of Berlin (1943); moved to Moritzburg, located near Dresden, after that home was bombed (1944); died the following year; major works include *Self Portrait of a Young Couple* (1893), *The Downtrodden* (1900), *The Peasant Wars* (1908), *Run Over* (1910), *From the Living to the Dead* (1919), *Tower of Mothers* (1938) and *Seed for the Planting Must Not Be Ground* (1942). ❖ See also *The Diary and Letters of Käthe Kollwitz* (ed. by Hans Kollwitz, trans. by Richard and Clara Winston, Regnery, 1955); Martha Kearns, *Kathe Kollwitz: Woman and Artist* (Feminist Press, 1976); Mina and H. Arthur Klein, *Käthe Kollwitz: Life in Art* (Holt, 1972); and *Women in World History*.

KOLMAR, Gertrud (1894–1943). German poet. Name variations: Gertrud Chodziesner. Born Gertrud Chodziesner, Dec 10, 1894, in Berlin; died in Auschwitz (her date of death unrecorded); dau. of a prominent attorney in a wealthy German-Jewish family; sister of Hilde Chodziesner; studied linguistics after completion of high school; never married; no children. ❖ "Poet of women and animals," gifted linguist, and writer whose works, mostly unknown at the time of her death, now identify her as one of the best German poets of 20th century; worked as translator for the Foreign Office during WWI and published *Gedichte*, a volume of poetry (1917); published 2nd book of poems, *Preussisch Wappen* (Prussian Arms), at end of war; tutored sick and handicapped children while continuing to write poetry (1920s–30s); removed to Berlin ghetto (1939); was sent to Auschwitz (Feb 1943); writings include *Dark Soliloquy: The Selected Poems of Gertrud Kolmar* (trans. by Henry A. Smith, 1975). ❖ See also *Women in World History*.

KOLOKOLTSEVA, Berta (1937—). Russian speedskater. Born Albertina Kolokoltseva, Oct 29, 1937, in USSR. ❖ Won a bronze medal for the 1,500 meters at Innsbruck (1964).

KOLPAKOVA, Irina (1933—). Soviet ballet dancer. Born May 22, 1933, in Leningrad, Russia. ❖ Trained at Leningrad Choreographic Institute; performed as member of Kirov Ballet in traditional works, including *The Sleeping Beauty* and *Cinderella*, and newer works, such as Grigorovich's *The Stone Flower* (1957), Belsky's *Coast of Hope* (1959), and Kasatkina and Vasilov's *Creation of the World* (1971).

KOLPAKOVA, Tatyana (1959—). Soviet track-and-field athlete. Born Oct 18, 1959, in USSR. ❖ At Moscow Olympics, won a gold medal in the long jump (1980).

KOLSTAD, Eva (1918–1998). Norwegian politician. Born Eva Lundegaard in Halder, Norway, 1918; died Mar 26, 1998; qualified as an independent chartered accountant, 1944. ❖ Worked as a bookkeeping teacher before becoming active in the cause of women's rights; began political career with International Alliance of Women and was a member of the board (1949–58, 1961–68, 1973); served as president of Norwegian Association for the Rights of Women (1956–68) and was a member of UN Committee on the Status of Women (1969–75); was also a member of Oslo City Council (1960–75); served 2 terms as a member of Parliament (1958–61 and 1966–69), with last term marked by leadership on Government Council on Equal Status of Men and Women; served as Ombudsman (1977–88).

KOLTSCHINA, Koltshina, or Koltsjina, or Alevtina (1930—). *See Olunina, Alevtina.*

KOLTUNOVA, Julia (1989—). Russian diver. Born May 4, 1989, in USSR. ❖ With Natalia Goncharova, won a silver medal for 10-meter synchronized platform at Athens Olympics (2004).

KOMAROVA, Stanislava (1986—). Russian swimmer. Born June 12, 1986, in USSR. ❖ Placed 2nd at World championships for 200-meter backstroke (2001); won a silver medal for 200-meter backstroke at Athens Olympics (2004).

KOMAROVA, Varvara (1862–1942). Russian biographer and novelist. Name variations: Varvara Dmitrievna Komaróva; (pseudonym) Vladimir Karenin. Born 1862 in St. Petersburg, Russia; died 1942. ❖ Wrote 4-volume biography of George Sand, *George Sand, sa vie et ses oeuvres;* also wrote short stories and novel *Musia* (1888).

KOMAROVSKY, Mirra (1906–1999). Russian-born educator and feminist. Born Mirra Komarovsky in Baku, Russia, Feb 4, 1906; died at home in New York, NY, Jan 30, 1999; dau. of Mendel Komarovsky (Jewish banker and writer) and Anna (Steinberg) Komarovsky; Barnard College, AB, 1926; Columbia University, MA, 1927, PhD, 1940; married, 1926 (div. 1928); m. Marcus A. Heyman, 1940 (died 1970). ❖ Immigrated with parents and younger sister to US (1921); studied under Franz Boas and Ruth Benedict; appointed assistant professor at Skidmore College; was later research assistant at the Institute of Human Relations, Yale University (1930–31), and research associate at Columbia University's Council for Research in the Social Sciences (1931–35); was hired as an instructor in sociology at Barnard (1938), where she rose rapidly to assistant professor, associate, and then chair of the department (1947); retired (1970), then returned to Barnard to chair its women's studies program; writings include *The Unemployed Man and His Family* (1940), *Women in the Modern World* (1953), and *Women in College: Shaping New Feminine Identities* (1985). Received Distinguished Career Award of the American Sociological Association (1991). ❖ See also *Women in World History*.

KOMEI EMPRESS. *See Yoshiko.*

KOMEN, Susan G. (1944–1980). American breast cancer victim. Born 1944 or 1945 in Peoria, IL; died 1980, age 36; sister of Nancy G. Brinker. ❖ Died of breast cancer at age 36 and became inspiration for Susan G. Komen Breast Cancer Foundation, considered the world's leading catalyst in fight against breast cancer, which was founded by her sister.

KOMISARJEVSKAYA, Vera (1864–1910). *See Komissarzhevskaya, Vera.*

KOMISARZ, Rachel (1976—). American swimmer. Born Dec 5, 1976, in Warren, Michigan; attended University of Kentucky. ❖ At World championship, placed 1st for 4 x 200-meter freestyle relay (2003); won a gold medal for 4 x 200-meter freestyle relay at Athens Olympics (2004); won 4 World Cup events (2001–02).

KOMISOVA, Vera (1953—). Soviet runner. Born June 11, 1953, in USSR. ❖ At Moscow Olympics, won a gold medal in the 100-meter hurdles and a silver medal in the 4 x 100-meter relay (1980).

KOMISSARZHEVSKAYA, Vera (1864–1910). Russian actress and theater manager. Name variations: Vera Fyodrovna Komissarzhevskaya; Vera Federovna Komisarjevskaya or Kommisarjevskaya, Countess Muravyova. Born Nov 8, 1864, in St. Petersburg, Russia; died Feb 23, 1910, in Tashkent, Uzbekistan; dau. of Fyodor Komissarzhevskaya (opera star and teacher); sister of Theodore Komissarzhevskaya (producer and director); trained with father. ❖ Appeared as Betsy in 1st Russian production of Tolstoy's *Fruits of Enlightenment* under direction of Stanislavsky (1891); was a member of the Alexandrinsky Imperial Theatre in St. Petersburg (1896–1902), appearing as Rosy in Sudermann's *The Battle of the Butterflies* and Larisa in Ostrovsky's *The Dowerless Girl,* among others; was the leading Russian actress of her day, particularly esteemed by Anton Chekhov and Russian symbolist writers; opened her own theater in St. Petersburg (1904), engaging producer Vsevolod Meyerhold and mounting productions of works by Gorky, Ibsen, Maeterlinck and Blok; unable to turn profit with theater or unsuccessful tour of US (1908), was forced to close (1909); returned to touring provinces to raise money to cover debts but died of smallpox in Tashkent.

KOMNENA, Anna (1083–1153/55). *See Anna Comnena.*

KOMNENOVIC, Jelica (1960—). Yugoslavian basketball player. Born April 20, 1960. ❖ At Moscow Olympics, won a bronze medal in team competition (1980).

KONDAKOVA, Yelena (c. 1955—). Soviet cosmonaut. Name variations: Elena Kondakova. Born c. 1955; m. Valeri Ryumin (cosmonaut and director of Russia's end of the Mir-shuttle program who went on 3 space flights). ❖ With her 169-day Mir mission (1995), held the record for the longest spaceflight by a woman until Shannon Lucid topped it (1996); became 1st Russian woman to fly on a US spaceship (1997).

KONDO, Masako (1941—). Japanese volleyball player. Born Mar 27, 1941, in Japan. ❖ At Tokyo Olympics, won a gold medal in team competition (1964).

KONDRASHINA, Anna (1955—). Soviet rower. Born Dec 23, 1955, in USSR. ❖ At Montreal Olympics, won a silver medal in quadruple sculls with coxswain (1976).

KONDRATEEVA, Ludmila (1958—). *See Kondratyeva, Lyudmila.*

KONDRATIEVA, Marina (1934—). Soviet ballet dancer. Name variations: Marina Kondratyeva. Born Feb 1, 1934, in Leningrad, Russia; studied at Moscow Choreographic School under Galina Petrova. ❖ Trained at school of Bolshoi Ballet and performed with its professional company throughout career (1952), in such productions as *Cinderella, The Sleeping Beauty, Chippolino, The Stone Flower,* and Maya Plisetskaya's *Anna Karenina,* among others; also danced *Giselle* and *Romeo and Juliet* with Maris Liepa; retired from dancing (1980), to teach at the Bolshoi.

KONDRATYEVA, Lyudmila (1958—). Russian runner. Name variations: Ludmila Kondrateeva. Born April 11, 1958, in Shakhty, USSR. ❖ At European championships, won gold medals for the 200 meters and 4 x 100-meter relay (1978); won a gold medal for the 100 meters at Moscow Olympics (1980), beating East German Marlies Göhr by 100th of a second; won a team bronze for the 4 x 100-meter relay at Seoul Olympics (1988).

KONER, Pauline (1912–2001). American concert dancer and choreographer. Name variations: Pauline Mahler. Born Pauline Koner, 1912, in New York, NY; died Feb 8, 2001, in New York, NY; dau. of Samuel Koner (lawyer); m. Fritz Mahler (conductor), 1939 (died 1973). ❖ Danced with the Fokine Ballet (mid-1920s); performed on tour with Michio Ito; created many solo works which she performed in recitals, among them *Upheaval* (1931), *Two Laments: For the Living, for the Dead* (1931), *Spanish Impressions* (1931), and *Jitterbug Sketches* (1945); choreographer noted for powerful solos, became permanent guest-artist for company of José Limón (1949), where she created roles in such major works as Limón's *Moor's Pavane* (1949) and Doris Humphrey's *Ruins and Visions* (1953); also was involved with *La Malinche* (1949), *The Visitation* (1953), *The Exiles* (1953) and premieres of Humphrey's *The Story of Mankind* (1949), *Lament for Ignácio Sánchez Mejías* (1949), and *Ritmo Jondo* (1953); honored Humphrey with her best-known piece of choreography, an elegiac 30-minute solo "The Farewell" (1962); headed the Pauline Koner Dance Consort (1976–82). Also choreographed *Allegretto* (1930), *Visions* (1930), *Spanish Impressions* (1931), *Dances of Longing* (1934), *Three Soviet Songs* (1939), *Love Song* (1945), *Cassandra* (1953), *The Shining Dark* (1958), *Elements of Performing* (1963), and

Solitary Song (1975). ❖ See also autobiography *Solitary Song* (Duke U. Press, 1989).

KONETZNI, Anny (1902–1968). Austrian soprano. Born Anny Konerczny in Ungarisch-Weisskirchen, Austria, Feb 12, 1902; died Sept 6, 1968, in Vienna; sister of soprano Hilde Konetzni (1905–1980); studied with Erik Schmedes in Vienna and Jacques Stückgold in Berlin. ❖ Debuted as contralto soloist in Wagner's *Rienzi* at Vienna Volksoper (1925); was a member of Berlin State Opera (1931–34) and sang the 1st performance at that theater of Verdi's *I vespri Siciliani* (1932); began long association with Vienna State Opera (1933) and was soon one of its best-known artists; performed throughout Europe and North America, debuting at Metropolitan Opera (1935); appeared frequently at Salzburg (1934–36, 1941); after WWII, worked to revive opera in Vienna; sang premiere of Lenore under baton of Josef Krips at Theater an der Wien (1945); was an honored guest at a gala reopening of Vienna Staatsoper (1955); retired (1955); taught at Viennese Music Academy until 1957. ❖ See also *Women in World History.*

KONETZNI, Hilde (1905–1980). Austrian soprano. Born Hilde Konerczny, Mar 21, 1905, in Vienna; died April 20, 1980, in Vienna; sister of soprano Anny Konetzni (1902–1968); studied at Vienna Conservatory; m. Mirko Urbanic, 1940. ❖ Debuted at Vienna Staatsoper (1935) and joined the company; lost everything in WWII, but recouped her fortunes as she was in great demand after the war; after retirement (1974), continued to teach. ❖ See also *Women in World History.*

KONG, Madame H.H. (1890–1973). *See Song Ailing.*

KONGA, Pauline (c. 1971—). Kenyan runner. Born c. 1971 in the Nandi district of Kenya; m. Paul Bitok (runner). ❖ Won a silver medal for the 5,000 meters at Atlanta Olympics (1996), the 1st Kenyan woman to win an Olympic medal.

KONIE, Gwendoline (1938—). Zambian diplomat. Name variations: Gwendoline Chomba Konie. Born 1938 in Lusaka, Zambia; studied at University College, Cardiff, Wales, and at American University, Washington DC. ❖ Worked in Ministry of Local Government and Social Welfare and became member of Legislative Council; worked in Ministry of Foreign Affairs (1964) and in Presidential Office (1972); was Zambian ambassador to Sweden, Norway, Denmark, and Finland (1974–77); represented Zambia at UN, chairing UN Council for Namibia, and from 1979 worked as permanent secretary in Zambian Civil Service; started Social Democratic Party (SDF); was one of two women who made history as presidential candidates (2001).

KÖNIG, Alma Johanna (1887–c. 1942). German-Jewish novelist. Name variations: Alma Johanna Konig or Koenig. Born Aug 18, 1887, in Prague, Czechoslovakia; lived in Vienna; died c. 1942. ❖ Persecuted and deported by Nazis, later disappeared in Minsk Ghetto (May 1942); works include *Der heilige Palast* (The Holy Palace, 1922), *Die Geschichte von Half, dem Weibe* (The Story of Half, A Woman, 1924), and the autobiographical novel, *Leidenschaft in Algier* (Passion in Algiers, 1932).

KÖNIG, Rita. *See Koenig, Rita.*

KÖNIGSDORF, Helga (1938—). East German novelist. Name variations: Helga Konigsdorf or Koenigsdorf. Born 1938 in Germany. ❖ Was a professor of physics and mathematics before Parkinson's disease curtailed scientific career; works include *Meine ungehörigen Träume* (1978), *Lauf der Dinge* (1982), *Lichtverhältnisse* (1988), *Die geschlossenen Türen am Abend* (1989) and *Fission* (trans. by Susan Gillespie, 2000).

KÖNIGSMARK, Aurora von (1662–1728). Countess of Königsmark, paramour, and abbess. Name variations: Maria Aurora von Konigsmark. Born Maria Aurora von Königsmark, May 8, 1662 (some sources cite 1668 or 1669), in Worms, Estonia, Russia; died at Quedlinburg, Prussia, Feb 16, 1728; dau. of Swedish nobles; sister of Count Philipp Christoph von Königsmark (1665–c. 1694); had liaison with Augustus II the Strong ("Mocny"), elector of Saxony (r. 1670–1733) and king of Poland (r. 1697–1706 and 1709–1733); children: (with Augustus II) Count Maurice de Saxe, generally called Marshal de Saxe or Marshal Saxe (1696–1750), who served under Marlborough in the War of the Spanish Succession). ❖ Described by Voltaire as "the most famous woman of two centuries," went to Dresden to look into circumstances surrounding mysterious disappearance of brother, Philipp Christoph, count of Königsmark (1694); caught the attention of Augustus, then elector of Saxony (and future king of Poland), and became his mistress; secured position of abbess of Quedlinburg; was made coadjutor abbess and lady-provost (*Pröpstin*) of Quedlinburg but lived mainly in Berlin, Dresden, and Hamburg; went on a diplomatic errand to Charles XII, king of Sweden, on behalf of Augustus (1702), but adventurous journey ended in failure. ❖ See also *Women in World History.*

KONIHOWSKI, Diane Jones (1951—). Canadian pentathlete. Born Diane Jones, Mar 7, 1951, in Vancouver, British Columbia, Canada; m. John Konihowski (athlete), 1977. ❖ At Pan American Games, won a gold medal (1975 and 1979); at Commonwealth Games, won a gold medal (1978).

KONNO, Evelyn (b. 1933). See *Kawamoto, Evelyn.*

KONO, Taeko (1926—). Japanese novelist. Born 1926 in Osaka, Japan. ❖ Served as director of Japan Association for Writers and of Museum of Modern Japanese Literature; works include *Hunting for Children* (1961), *Crabs* (1963), *Unexpected Voice* (1968), and *Bizarre Story of a Husband and Wife during Wartime* (1990). Won several awards, including Shincho Prize and Yomiuri Prize for Literature.

KONOPACKA, Halina (1900–1989). Polish track-and-field athlete. Name variations: Halina Konopacka-Matuszewska-Szczerbinska. Born Nov 11, 1900, in Poland; died Jan 28, 1989. ❖ At Amsterdam Olympics, won a gold medal in discus throw (1928).

KONOPNICKA, Maria (1842–1910). Polish poet, writer, and nationalist activist. Name variations: Marja Konopnicka; Marii Konopnickiej; (pseudonyms) Marko, Jan Sawa, and Jan Warez. Born Maria Wasilowska, May 23, 1842, in Suwalki; died Oct 8, 1910, in Lemberg (Lvov), Austrian Galicia (now Lviv, Ukraine); dau. of Józef Wasilowski; married a landowner; children: 6. ❖ One of the leading exponents of the realistic school of literature, was strongly influenced by Polish Positivist school, which embraced the progressive social, political and economic ideals of the West; debuted as a poet (1870); published cycle of poems "In the Mountains" (1876) in *Tygodnik Ilustrowany* (Illustrated Weekly); separated from husband and moved to Warsaw with children (1877); as a Polish nationalist, blamed some but not all of Poland's problems on the Russian and German empires which occupied much of the nation's territory; since she also blamed the plight of the poor on the landowning *szlachta* (gentry) class and Roman Catholic Church, often found herself in trouble with Russian tsarist censors and Polish conservatives; raged against the exploitation of the working class in her cycle *Obrazki* (Tableaux); wrote short stories and children's books and published 3 collections of poems (1881–86); was also a critic, publicist, and translator; an outspoken feminist, edited the women's magazine *Swit* (Dawn, 1884–86); lived in Western Europe (1890–1902); on her return, gained recognition as a major poet and writer, and her short stories "Niemczaki" (German Boys), "Nasza szkapa" (Our Jade), "Dym" (Smoke), "Urbanowa" and "Milosierdzie gminy" (Township Charity), published between 1888 and 1897, are considered to be among the best in Polish literature. ❖ See also *Women in World History.*

KONOUKH, Sofia (1980—). Russian water-polo player. Born Mar 9, 1980, in Chelyabinsk, Russia; attended University of Southern California. ❖ Won a team bronze medal at Sydney Olympics (2000).

KONRADS, Ilsa (1944—). Australian-Latvian swimmer. Born Mar 29, 1944, in Riga, Latvia; dau. of Elza (Grasmanis) Konrads and Janis (John) Konrads; sister of Eve Konrads (b. 1940) and John Konrads (b. 1942, swimmer and Olympic gold medalist). ❖ Immigrated to Australia with family (1949); won a gold medal at Commonwealth Games (1958); won a silver medal at Rome Olympics in the 4 x 100-meter freestyle relay (1960); broke 12 indiv. world records in 800 and 1,500 meters, 880 and 1,650 yards during career.

KONSTAM, Phyllis (1907–1976). English actress. Born Phyllis Kohnstamm, April 14, 1907, in London, England; died Aug 20, 1976, in Somerset, England; sister of Anna Konstam (actress, b. 1914); m. H.W. Austin. ❖ Made stage debut in London as Abigail in *The Jew of Malta* (1925), followed by *The Shingling of Jupiter, Enchantress, Escape, The Beaux' Stratagem, Living Together, The Fanatics, The Matriarch, Magnolia Street* and *If I Were King,* among others; made NY debut in *Murder on the Second Floor* (1929); films include *Escape, Tilly of Bloomsbury* and *Voice of the Hurricane.*

KONSTANZ. Variant of *Constance.*

KONTSEK, Jolan Kleiberne- (1939—). See *Kleiberne-Kontsek, Jolan.*

KOŃWATSI'TSIAIÉŃNI (c. 1736–1796). See *Brant, Molly.*

KONYAYEVA, Nadezhda (1931—). Soviet track-and-field athlete. Name variations: Nadezhda Konyaeva. Born Oct 1931 in USSR. ❖ At Melbourne Olympics, won a bronze medal in the javelin throw (1956).

KONZETT, Ursula (1959—). Liechtenstein Alpine skier. Born Nov 15, 1969, in Triesen, Liechtenstein. ❖ Won a bronze medal for giant slalom at World championships (1982) and a bronze medal for slalom at Sarajevo Olympics (1984).

KOOLEN, Nicole (1972—). Dutch field-hockey player. Name variations: Nicole Tellier-Koolen. Born Dec 1, 1972, in the Netherlands. ❖ Won a team bronze medal at Atlanta Olympics (1996).

KOONTZ, Elizabeth (1919–1989). African-American educator. Born Elizabeth Duncan, June 3, 1919, in Salisbury, NC; died Jan 6, 1989, in Salisbury; dau. of Samuel E. Duncan and Lena Bell (Jordan) Duncan (both educators); Livingstone College, BA, 1938; Atlanta University, MA, 1941; graduate work at Columbia University, Indiana University, and North Carolina College (now North Carolina Central University); m. Harry L. Koontz (educator), Nov 26, 1947; no children. ❖ The 1st African-American to become president of National Education Association (NEA), took a position at Harnett County Training School in Dunn, NC, teaching special education classes (1938); was fired for protesting against high rents teachers were forced to pay at a school-owned boarding house (1940); joined North Carolina chapter of NEA (1952) and became an outspoken leader in the organization, working for improved teaching conditions and higher wages; was president of NEA's Department of Classroom Teachers (1965); elected president of the organization (1967), the 1st of her race and gender; appointed head of Women's Bureau of Department of Labor by Richard Nixon (his 1st appointment of an African-American); used this position to speak out for black women's rights, and was particularly instrumental in helping to improve working conditions for domestic workers; served as assistant state superintendent for teacher education in North Carolina Department of Public Instruction; was a member of the North Carolina Council on the Status of Women (1977–79). ❖ See also *Women in World History.*

KÖPKE-KNETSCH, Christiane (1956—). See *Koepke-Knetsch, Christiane.*

KOPLAN, Rosemary (1923–1979). See *LaPlanche, Rosemary.*

KÖPPEN, Kerstin (1967—). See *Koeppen, Kerstin.*

KOPSKY, Doris. American cyclist. Name variations: Doris Kopsky Muller. Born in US; dau. of Joseph Kopsky (won gold medal as New York City Cycling Olympian, 1912). ❖ At a tournament in Buffalo, NY, became the 1st woman champion of the National Amateur Bicycle Association (Sept 4, 1937).

KOPTAGEL, Yuksel (1931—). Turkish composer and concert pianist. Born in Istanbul, Turkey, Oct 27, 1931; granddau. of General Osman Koptagel, famous commander from Turkish War of Independence; studied piano, theory, and composition with Turkish composer Cemal Resit; journeyed to Madrid and Paris for further work with Joaquin Rodrigo, José Cubiles, Lazare Lévy, Tony Aubin, and Alexandre Tansman. ❖ Known for compositions of French and Spanish interpretation, gave 1st concert at age 6; at Paris Conservatory, won several 1st prizes both for composing and for piano; became a concert artist and performed with many international orchestras as a piano soloist; a member of the Istanbul State Symphony Orchestra, also served on jury of Schola Cantorium and École Superieur de Musique.

KORBUT, Olga (1955—). Soviet gymnast. Name variations: Olga Corbut, Olya Korbuta. Born Olga Valentinovna Korbut, May 16, 1955, in Grodno, Belarus; sister of Ludmilla Korbut (gymnast); m. Leonid Bortkevich (Soviet pop singer), Jan 7, 1978 (div.); remarried. ❖ Placed 4th at Soviet nationals (1970); won Riga Cup (1972), University Games (1973); won Olympic gold medals for balance beam, floor exercises, and all-around team competition, and a silver medal for asymmetrical bars in Munich (1972); awarded the "Master of Sport" (1972); at World championships, won gold medals in vault and team all-around and silvers in all-around, uneven bars, beam and floor (1974); won a silver medal for balance beam and a gold medal for all-around team competition in Montreal Olympics (1976); retired from competition (1977); exposed to radiation following nuclear accident at Chernobyl (1986); moved to US (1989); tested for radiation sickness (1991). Named "Woman of the Year" by United Nations (1975); inducted in International Women's Sports Hall of Fame (1982); was 1st inductee into International Gymnastics Hall of Fame (1988). ❖ See also Justin Beecham, *Olga* (Paddington, 1974); and *Women in World History.*

KORCHINSKA, Maria (1895–1979). Russian-born British harpist. Born in Moscow, Russia, Feb 16, 1895; died in London, England, April 17, 1979; m. Count Konstantin Benkendorff; children: son and daughter. ❖ Was the 1st harp of the Bolshoi Theater as well as a professor of harps at Moscow Conservatory (1918–24); while at the conservatory, won the 1st gold medal awarded to a harpist; left Russia (1926) and established herself in Great Britain and on the Continent as 1st harp in many orchestras; also played contemporary chamber music with the Harp Ensemble and the Wigmore Ensemble; gave 1st performance of Arnold Bax's *Fantasy Sonata* for viola and harp; also took part in 1st performance of Britten's *Ceremony of Carols* in which the harp is prominently featured; founded Harp Society of United Kingdom; with Dutch harpist Phia Berghout, organized 1st annual international harp week in the Netherlands (1960); concertized widely.

KORD, Mira (1894–1973). *See Vorlova, Slavka.*

KORDACZUKOWNA, Danuta (1939–1988). Polish volleyball player. Born Sept 1939 in Poland; died April 10, 1988. ❖ At Tokyo Olympics, won a bronze medal in team competition (1964).

KOREA, queen of.
See Hong, Lady (1735–1815).
See Min (c. 1840–1895).

KOREN, Katja (1975—). Slovenian Alpine skier. Born Aug 6, 1975, in Maribor, Slovenia. ❖ Won a bronze medal for slalom at Lillehammer Olympics (1994).

KORHOLA, Eija-Riitta Anneli (1959—). Finnish politician. Born June 15, 1959, in Lahti, Finland. ❖ As a member of the European People's Party (Christian Democrats) and European Democrats (EPP), elected to 5th European Parliament (1999–2004).

KORHOLZ, Laurel (1970—). American rower. Born June 10, 1970, in New York, NY; attended Wesleyan University. ❖ Won a gold medal for coxed eights at World championships (1995); won a silver medal for coxed eights at Athens Olympics (2004); won 2 World Cups for coxed eights (2004).

KORINNA (fl. 5th or 3rd c. BCE). *See Corinna.*

KORJUS, Miliza (1900–1980). Polish singer and actress. Name variations: The Berlin Nightingale. Born Miliza Elizabeth Korjus, Aug 18, 1900, in Warsaw, Poland; died Aug 26, 1980, in Culver City, CA; dau. of Arthur Korjus (lt. col. in Russian imperial army and later chief of staff to war minister in Estonia) and Anna Gintowt; m. Dr. Kuno Foelsch (physicist), 1929; m. Dr. Walter E. Shector, 1952; children: 3. ❖ Coloratura soprano, made operatic debut with Vienna State Opera singing the lead in *The Magic Flute,* with Richard Strauss conducting; starred with many opera companies in Europe, including the Berlin Opera; portrayed Johann Strauss' mistress in *The Great Waltz* (1938) and was nominated for an Academy Award for Best Supporting Actress; involved in serious auto accident (1940), effectively ending film career; made many concert appearances.

KORMLOD (fl. 980–1015). *See Gormflaith of Ireland.*

KORN, Alison (1970—). Canadian rower. Born Nov 22, 1970, in Ottawa, Ontario, Canada. ❖ Won a silver medal at Atlanta Olympics (1996) and a bronze medal at Sydney Olympics (2000), both for coxed eights.

KORNMAN, Mary (1915–1973). American actress. Born Dec 27, 1915, in Idaho Falls, Idaho; died June 1, 1973, in Glendale, CA. ❖ Appeared as female lead in "Our Gang" comedies for 7 years; other films include *The Boy Friends, Picture Brides, Strictly Dynamite, Youth on Parole, I Am a Criminal* and *On the Spot.*

KOROLCHIK, Yanina (1976—). Belarusian shot putter. Name variations: Yanina Karolchik. Born Dec 26, 1976, in Belarus. ❖ Won a gold medal at Sydney Olympics (2000); at World championships, won a gold medal (2001).

KOROLEVA, Maria (1974—). Russian water-polo player. Born Oct 16, 1974, in USSR. ❖ Won a team bronze medal at Sydney Olympics (2000).

KOROLEWICZ-WAYDOWA, Janina (1875–1955). Polish soprano and opera director. Name variations: Janina Korolewicz-Wayda, Korolewicz-Waydova or Korolewicz-Wajdowa. Born Jan 3, 1875 (some

sources cite 1876), in Warsaw, Poland; trained by Walery Wysocki; died June 20, 1955, in Warsaw, Poland. ❖ Made debut at 17 as Hanna in *The Haunted Manor;* sang at Warsaw Opera (1898–1902), then Berlin Opera; joined the San Carol Royal Opera in Lisbon for a season, then Royal Opera in Madrid, followed by Venice, Bucharest, Odessa, Kiev, St. Petersburg Kharkov, London, New York, Chicago; ofen performed with Shalyapin, as well as Caruso; performed internationally for 11 years; returned to Warsaw (1913), where she became probably the world's 1st female director of an opera house, managing the Warsaw opera (1917–19 and 1934–36); was also noted for recordings of arias from *Halka* and *La Juive.*

KORONDI, Margit (1932—). *See Plachyne-Korondi, Margit.*

KOROTKOVA, Kira (1934—). *See Muratova, Kira.*

KORPUS, Lilly (1901–1976). *See Becher, Lilly.*

KORSHUNOVA, Tatyana (1956—). Soviet kayaker. Born Mar 1956 in USSR. ❖ At Montreal Olympics, won a silver medal in K1 500 meters (1976).

KORSMO, Grete Prytz (b. 1917). *See Kittelsen, Grete Prytz.*

KORSMO, Lisbeth (1948—). Norwegian speedskater. Name variations: Lisbeth Korsmo-Berg; Lisbeth Berg. Born Jan 14, 1948, in Norway. ❖ Won a bronze medal for the 3,000 meters at Innsbruck Olympics (1976).

KORSTIN, Ilona (1980—). Russian basketball player. Born May 30, 1980, in Leningrad, USSR. ❖ Guard, won a team bronze medal at Athens Olympics (2004); placed 2nd at World championships (2002) and 1st at European championships (2003).

KORTEN, Maria (1904–1987). *See Dronke, Minnie Maria.*

KORTY, Sonia (1892–1955). Russian ballet dancer and teacher. Born Sophia Ippar, Oct 25, 1892, in St. Petersburg, Russia; died Dec 1, 1955, in Salzburg, Austria. ❖ Performed with Diaghilev Ballet Russe during its final season; performed as specialty dancer with Opéra Comique in Paris; was highly successful in portrayal of Fenella in *Dumb Girl of Portici;* staged productions for German ballet companies in Baden-Baden and Goettingen (late 1930s); served as ballet master for Royal Opera of Flanders in Antwerp; retired from dance career to pursue acting in Austrian operetta theaters; taught at Mozartium conservatory in Salzburg until her death (1955).

KORUKOVETS, Alexandra (1976—). Russian volleyball player. Born Oct 1, 1976, in USSR. ❖ Won a team silver medal at Athens Olympics (2004).

KORWIN-PIOTROWSKA, Gabriela (1857–1921). *See Zapolska, Gabriela.*

KORYTOVA, Svetlana (1968—). Soviet volleyball player. Born Mar 24, 1968, in USSR. ❖ Won a gold medal at Seoul Olympics (1988) and a silver medal at Barcelona Olympics (1992), both in team competition.

KOSACH, Laryssa (1871–1913). *See Ukrainka, Lesya.*

KOSCHAK, Marie Pachler- (1792–1855). *See Pachler-Koschak, Marie.*

KOSCIANSKA, Czeslawa (1959—). Polish rower. Name variations: Czessawa or Czeslawa Koscianska-Szczepinska. Born May 22, 1959, in Poland. ❖ At Moscow Olympics, won a silver medal in coxless pairs (1980).

KOSCINA, Sylva (1933–1994). Yugoslavian actress. Born Aug 22, 1933, in Zagreb, Yugoslavia; died after a long illness complicated by heart problems, Dec 26, 1994, in Rome, Italy. ❖ Began career as leading lady in Italian films, but was soon in demand internationally; spent early years decorating costume spectaculars, but later work included romantic comedies and dramas; is best remembered for supporting role as sister of the hapless Juliet in Fellini's *Giulietta degli Spiriti (Juliet of the Spirits,* 1965); other films include *Il Ferroviere (The Railroad Man,* 1955), *Michel Strogoff* (1956), *Le Fatiche di Ercole (Hercules,* 1957), *Ercole e la Regina di Lidia (Hercules Unchained,* 1958), *Erode il Grande* (1959), *Jessica* (1962), *Deadlier Than the Male* (1966), *Three Bites of the Apple* (1967), *The Secret War of Harry Frigg* (1978), *A Lovely Way to Die* (1968), *Battle of Neretva* (1970), *Clara and Nora* (Spanish, 1975), *Sunday Lovers* (1980), *Cinderella '80* (1984) and *C'e Kim Novak al telefono* (1994). ❖ See also *Women in World History.*

KÖSEM (1589–1651). Ottoman sultana. Name variations: Kosem Sultan or Sultana; Koesem; Kösem Mahpeyker. Probably born in Greece in 1589; assassinated in Constantinople in 1651; 3rd wife of Ahmed I, Ottoman sultan (r. 1603–1617); children: daughters Ayse, Fatma, Hanzade, and perhaps Gevherhan (1609–1640); sons Murad IV (1609–1640), Ottoman sultan (r. 1623–1640), and Ibrahim, Ottoman sultan (r. 1640–1648); grandson: Mohammed IV (1641–1691, also seen as Mahomet, Mehmet, Mehmed, Mehemmed, Mohammed, and Muhammed), Ottoman sultan (r. 1648–1687). ❖ Became valide sultan when son Murad IV ascended the throne (1623); remained valide sultan when 2nd son Ibrahim became sultan (1640); continued her political role under reign of grandson Mehmed IV (r. 1648–1687) until she was strangled by Hadice Turhan Sultan, consort of Ibrahim. ❖ See also *Women in World History.*

KOSEKI, Shiori (c. 1972—). Japanese softball player. Born c. 1972 in Japan. ❖ Won a team silver medal at Sydney Olympics (2000).

KOSENKOVA, Klavdiya (1949—). Soviet rower. Born Mar 22, 1949, in USSR. ❖ At Montreal Olympics, won a silver medal in coxed eights (1976).

KOSHEL, Antonina (1954—). Soviet gymnast. Born Nov 20, 1954, in USSR. ❖ At Munich Olympics, won a gold medal in team all-around (1972).

KOSHEVAYA, Marina (1960—). Soviet swimmer. Born April 1960, in USSR. ❖ At Montreal Olympics, won a bronze medal in 100-meter breaststroke and a gold medal in 200-meter breaststroke (1976).

KOSMODEMYANSKAYA, Zoya (1923–1941). Soviet partisan. Name variations: Tanya; Kosmodemjamskaja; Kosmodemianskia. Pronunciation: Kos-MO-dem-YAHN-sky-ah. Born Zoya Kosmodemyanskaya, Sept 13, 1923, in Osinovye Gai, Tambov Oblast, near Moscow; executed by hanging, Nov 29, 1941, in Petrishchevo, Moscow Oblast; dau. of an office worker and a mother widowed early; educated at Moscow's School No. 201; never married. ❖ Became a symbol of heroism in Soviet Union's war against Nazi Germany after her capture and execution by German troops; joined the Labor Front and worked in a factory; at 18, joined a sabotage unit engaged in guerrilla activities (autumn 1941); captured within a few weeks by the Germans, was tortured but refused to reveal her name and identities of comrades; hanged the next day in village square, where her body was left for a month, in warning to all who dared defy the Nazi occupation; when word of her courage and martyrdom spread throughout Soviet Union, helping to sustain the nation, was proclaimed a Hero of the Soviet Union (Feb 16, 1942). ❖ See also *Women in World History.*

KOSSAK, Maria (1891–1945). *See Pawlikowska, Maria.*

KOSSAK, Zofia (1890–1968). Polish writer. Name variations: Zofia Kossak-Szczucka; Zofia Kossak-Szatkowska; Zofia Kossak-Szczucka-Szatkowska; Zofdja de Szatkowska. Born in Kosmin, Volhynia, Polish Ukraine (then part of Russia), Aug 8, 1890; died in Górki Wielkie, April 9, 1968; dau. of Tadeusz Kossak (officer); granddau. of painter Juliusz Kossak; cousin of poet Maria Pawlikowska and writer Magdalena Samozwaniec; m. Stefan Szczucki; m. Zygmunt Szatkowski; children: 2 sons. ❖ Polish Roman Catholic writer of historical novels, which were popular both in Poland and the English-speaking world, who created the underground organization Zegota to save Jewish lives in German-occupied Poland during the Holocaust; published 1st story "Bulli zaginal" (Bulli Disappeared) in journal *Wies Polska* (Polish Village, 1913); published 1st novel, *Pozoga* (*The Conflagration,* 1922), followed by a number of historical novels, including *Beatum scelus* (1924), *Golden Freedom* (1928), *The Great and the Small* (1928), *God's Madmen* (1929), *The Battlefield of Legnica* (1930), *The Unknown Country* (1932) and *From the History of Silesia* (1933); published epic *The Crusaders* in 4 vols. in Poznan (1935); crowned with "golden laurel" of Polish Academy of Literature (1936); from 1st days of German occupation (1940), was active in the underground, writing, teaching, and acting as a liaison; headed Roman Catholic underground organization Front Odrozenia Polski (Polish Resistance Front); with onset of Nazi assault on Poland's Jewish population, wrote *Protest!,* which received wide circulation in underground circles; founded Tymczasowy Komitet Pomocy Zydom (1942), later renamed Rada Pomocy Zydom (Council for Aid to Jews), generally known as Zegota, which was supported by a broad political spectrum of the underground movement; arrested by Germans (Sept 1943), but her forged papers were excellent and her real name was never discovered; released from Auschwitz by the Germans before their defeat and left Poland (1945), settling with husband in UK; returned to Poland

(1956); during last years, wrote a number of short stories for young people as well as several more historical novels, including an epic in 3 volumes, *Dziedzictwo* (*Heredity,* 1961–67). ❖ See also memoir *Z otchlani: Wspomnienaia z lagru* (*From the Abyss: Memoirs from the Camp,* 1946); and *Women in World History.*

KOSSAMAK (1904–1975). Queen of Cambodia. Name variations: Sisowat or Sisowath Kossamak Nearireath; Kossamak Nearirath also seen as Nearyreath, Nearrireak, or Nearirat. Born April 9, 1904, in Phnom Penh, Cambodia; did April 27, 1975; dau. of Sisowath Monivong, king of Cambodia (1875–1941, r. 1927–41, died April 23, 1941) and Norodom Kanviman Norleak Tevi (dau. of Norodom Hassakan, 1876–1912); m. Prince Norodom Suramarit (1896–1960), 1920, king of Cambodia (r. 1955–60); children: one son, Prince Norodom Sihanouk (b. 1922), king of Cambodia (r. 1941–55, 1993–2004), prime minister (1952–53, 1955–63) and head of state 1960–70, 1975–76, 1992–93). ❖ Ruled jointly with husband (1955–60), having survived a bomb attack with him in an enclosure in the Royal Palace blamed on the Khmer Serei; when son was overthrown with the rise of the Khmer Rouge (1970), fled to Beijing (Peking) with the royal family (Nov 5, 1973). ❖ See also *Women in World History.*

KOSTA, Tessa (1893–1981). American musical star. Born 1893 in Chicago, IL; died Aug 23, 1981, in New York, NY; m. Richard Madden (died). ❖ Made NY debut as Anna Budd in *The Beauty Shop* (1914), subsequently starred in *Stop Look and Listen!, Chu Chin Chow, The Royal Vagabond, Lassie, The Chocolate Soldier, Caroline, Rose of Stamboul, Princess April, Fioretta* and *The Fortune Teller,* among others; retired (1929).

KOSTADINOVA, Stefka (1965—). Bulgarian high jumper. Born Mar 25, 1965, in Bulgaria. ❖ Won the World championship at Rome with a jump of 2.09 meters (Aug 30, 1987) and won again (1995); won a silver medal at Seoul Olympics (1988) and a gold medal at Atlanta Olympics (1996).

KOSTELIC, Janica (1982—). Croatian Alpine skier. Born Jan 5, 1982, in Zagreb, Croatia; sister of Ivica Kostelic (skier). ❖ At Nagano Olympics, placed 8th in the combined event (1998), the best result by a Croatian athlete in the history of the Winter Games; won the World Cup overall title (2001, 2003); at Salt Lake City (2002), won a silver medal in the super giant slalom and gold medals in the slalom, combined, and giant slalom, becoming the 1st skier to ever win 4 Alpine medals at an Olympics and the only Croatian to win a Winter Olympics medal; won gold medals for combined and slalom at World championships (2003) and gold medals for combined, slalom and downhill (2005); won a gold medal for combined and silver medal for super-G at Torino Olympics (2006).

KOSTELLOW, Rowena (1900–1988). *See Reed, Rowena.*

KOSTER, Barbel (1957—). East German kayaker. Born May 26, 1957, in East Germany. ❖ At Montreal Olympics, won a bronze medal in K2 500 meters (1976).

KOSTEVYCH, Olena (1985—). Ukrainian shooter. Born April 14, 1985, in Khabarovsk, Ukraine. ❖ Won a gold medal at World championships for 10 m air pistol (2002); won a gold medal for 10 m air pistol at Athens Olympics (2004).

KOSTINA, Oksana (1972–1993). Russian rhythmic gymnast. Born April 15, 1972, in Irkutsk, Siberia, Russia; died Feb 11, 1993, in an auto accident while driving with fiancé Eduard Zenovka (pentathlete). ❖ At World championships, won silver medals for ball and team (1989) and swept all events with 5 gold medals (1992); placed 3rd at European championships (1992); won CIS nationals (1992).

KÖSTLER, Marie (1879–1965). Austrian politician. Born Marie Kostler; Marie Koestler. Born 1879; died in Austria, 1965. ❖ Austrian Social Democrat whose 40 years in public life included a turbulent period of exile politics in London during WWII, was a nurse by profession; became one of the 1st women to be elected to Austrian National Assembly (1920s); when Nazi Germany absorbed independent Austria in the *Anschluss* (Mar 1938), fled to London; was one of the most active members of Austrian emigres in UK; convinced a working coalition with Austrian Communist exiles was necessary, was excluded from the Socialist Democratic Party (1941); with Annie Hatschek, co-founded the League of Austrian Socialists which was later absorbed by Free Austrian Movement (FAM); returned to Austria (1945), but was denied readmittance to Social Democratic Party; joined Austrian Communist Party

(KPÖ); was much admired as the Grand Old Lady of Austrian Communism until her death. ❧ See also *Women in World History.*

KÖSTLIN, Josephine Lang (1815–1880). *See Lang, Josephine.*

KOSTNER, Isolde (1975—). Italian Alpine skier. Born Mar 20, 1975, in Bolzano, Italy. ❧ Won 1st World Cup race (1994); won a bronze medal in both the downhill and super-G at Lillehammer Olympics (1994); at World championships, won gold medals (1996, 1997) and a silver (2001), all for super-G; won World Cup downhill title (2001); won a silver in the downhill at Salt Lake City Olympics (2002).

KOSTRZEWA, Ute (1961—). East German volleyball player. Born Dec 27, 1961, in East Germany. ❧ At Moscow Olympics, won a silver medal in team competition (1980).

KOSTRZEWA, Wera (1876–1939). *See Koszutska, Maria.*

KOSUGE, Mari (1975—). Japanese gymnast. Born Dec 16, 1975, in Tokyo, Japan. ❧ Won All-Japan championships (1988, 1989, 1991), Japanese nationals (1990, 1992), NHK Cup (1990, 1993), International Jr. championships (1991); won a gold medal for vault at Asian Games (1990) and World Sports Fair (1991).

KOSYRYEVA, Lyubov. *See Baranova, Lyubov.*

KOSYTIYEVA, Lyubov. *See Baranova, Lyubov.*

KOSZUTSKA, Maria (1876–1939). Polish politician and revolutionary. Name variations: (party names) Wera Kostrzewa; Vera Kostrzewa; Vera Kocheva; Vera Kostisheva; M. Zboinska; M.Z. Born Maria Koszutska in Glowczyn near Kalisz, Russian Poland, Feb 2, 1876; died 1939; dau. of a landowner. ❧ Polish Socialist and Communist leader who was the most politically prominent non-Soviet woman killed during the Soviet purges of 1930s; a professional revolutionary, was one of the founders and leaders of the Communist Party of Poland; when Joseph Stalin attacked her views (1924), defended them as a delegate to a Congress of the Communist International; like most of the Polish Communist leaders residing in Soviet Union (1930s), was secretly arrested (1937) and killed (1939). ❧ See also *Women in World History.*

KOT, Natalia (1938—). *See Kotowna-Walowa, Natalia.*

KOT-WALA, Natalia (1938—). *See Kotowna-Walowa, Natalia.*

KOTANI, Mikako (1966—). Japanese synchronized swimmer. Born Aug 30, 1966, in Japan. ❧ At Seoul Olympics, won a bronze medal in duet and a bronze medal in solo (1988).

KOTANNER, Helene (fl. 1440). *See Kottanner, Helene.*

KOTERBA, Pamela (c. 1949—). *See Chelgren, Pamela.*

KÖTH, Erika (1925–1989). German soprano. Born Sept 15, 1925, in Darmstadt, Germany; died Feb 20, 1989; studied with Elsa Blank in Darmstadt. ❧ One of Germany's important coloratura sopranos after WWII, debuted in Kaiserslautern (1948); sang with City Theater in Karlsruhe (1950–53); joined Munich State Opera (1954), then appeared with Vienna State Opera (1955–65), singing Constanze in *Die Entführung aus dem Serial* (1955–57, 1962–63) to great success; also sang the Queen of the Night (1955–60); appeared at Bayreuth (1965–68) and at Teatro alla Scala and Covent Garden; toured Russia (1961); performed role of the Waldvogel in *Siegfried* (1965–68); made many recordings and appeared frequently on tv; became a professor at the Hochschule für Musik (1973). Made a Bavarian Kammersängerin (1956) and a Berlin Kammersängerin (1970). ❧ See also *Women in World History.*

KÖTHER, Rosemarie (1956—). *See Gabriel-Koether, Rosemarie.*

KOTLYAROVA, Olga (1976—). Russian runner. Born April 12, 1976, in Sverdlovsk, Russia. ❧ Won a bronze medal for 4 x 400-meter relay at Sydney Olympics (2000).

KOTOPOÚLI, Maríka (1887–1954). Greek actress. Name variations: María Kotopoúli; Marika Kotopouli or Kotopuli. Born 1887 in Tsepelovo in Ioannina, Greece, to theatrical family; died Mar 24, 1953, in Syro, Greece. ❧ One of the top Greek actresses of early 20th century, began career in her youth, touring the Greek-speaking East with parents' acting troupe; debuted as Puck at Royal Greek Theater (1903); able to switch from vaudeville and low comedy to classical drama and tragedy, enjoyed 1st successes in Royal Theater playing Athena in *Orestia,* Margarita in *Faust,* and Ifigenia and Viola; founded Kotopoúli Theater company in Athens (1908), which she ran for 30 years, devoting later

years to revival of ancient Greek drama; best remembered for productions of Euripides' *Hecouba* (1927), *Eleftheri Skini* (1929–30) and for US tour (1930–31); received critical acclaim for such productions as *As You Like It, Don Juan,* and *Sixth Floor;* made films as well, including *Kakos dromos* (1933). Maríka Kotopoúli Museum opened (1990).

KOTOVA, Tatyana (1976—). Russian long jumper. Name variations: Tatiana. Born Dec 11, 1976, in Kokand, Uzbekistan. ❧ Won gold medals for long jump at World Indoor championships (1999, 2003); won a bronze medal for long jump at Athens Olympics (2004).

KOTOWNA-WALOWA, Natalia (1938—). Polish gymnast. Name variations: Natalia Kot; Natalia Kot-Wala. Born June 29, 1938. ❧ At Melbourne Olympics, won a bronze medal in teams all-around, portable apparatus (1956).

KOTTANERIN, Helene (fl. 1440). *See Kottanner, Helene.*

KOTTANNER, Helene (fl. 1440). Austrian courtier and writer. Name variations: Helen Kottannerin. Born in Odenburg, Germany; lived in Hungary; died in Hungary after 1440; m. Peter Szekeles (German merchant, died 1438); m. Kotanner or Kottanner (valet of Vienna). ❧ Following death of 1st husband (1438), became lady-in-waiting to Queen Elizabeth of Luxemburg (1409–1442), wife of Habsburg ruler of Germany and Hungary, Albert II; as the queen's primary aide and confidante, was involved in intrigues which followed Albert's death (1439); when Germanic nobility did not support the succession of Elizabeth's 3-month-old son Ladislav (V), was asked by Elizabeth to steal the royal insignia, to keep this symbol of the throne out of hands of enemies and thus weaken their political position; did as requested and secured the throne for Ladislav for a few months; when Elizabeth died soon after, lost her privileged position and Ladislav was deposed; wrote an autobiography in retirement.

KOTUKUTUKU, Mihi (1870–1956). *See Stirling, Mihi Kotukutuku.*

KOUDIJS, Gerda (1923—). *See van der Kade-Koudijs, Gerda.*

KOUJELA, Olga (1985—). Russian synchronized swimmer. Born Aug 29, 1985, in USSR. ❧ Won a team gold medal at Athens Olympics (2004).

KOUKLEVA, Galina (1972—). Russian biathlete. Name variations: Galina Kukleva or Kuklewa. Born Nov 21, 1972, in Tjumen, Russia. ❧ Won a gold medal for 7.5 km and a silver medal for 4 x 7.5 km relay at Nagano Olympics (1998); won a bronze medal for 4 x 7.5 km relay at Salt Lake City Olympics (2002); won a gold medal for 7.5 km sprint and a silver for pursuit at World championships (2003).

KOULAKOVA, Galina (1942—). *See Kulakova, Galina.*

KOURNIKOVA, Anna (1981—). Russian tennis player. Born June 7, 1981, in Moscow, Russia; dau. of Sergei Kournikov and Alla Kournikova. ❧ Turned pro (1995) and won the Fed Cup competition at 14; reached the top ten (1998); won doubles title at Australian Open (1999); photogenic, earned $11 million on endorsements (1999).

KOUTOUZOVA, Natalia (1975—). Russian water-polo player. Born Mar 18, 1975, in USSR. ❧ Won a team bronze medal at Sydney Olympics (2000).

KOUZA, Loujaya M. Papua New Guinean poet. Born in Papua New Guinea. ❧ Worked as journalist; poetry, which was widely praised by critics, was published in journals, including *Ondobondo 6.*

KOUZINA, Svetlana (1975—). Russian water-polo player. Born June 8, 1975, in USSR. ❧ Won a team bronze medal at Sydney Olympics (2000).

KOUZNETZOVA, Maria (1880–1966). *See Kuznetsova, Maria.*

KOVACH, Nora (1931—). Hungarian ballet dancer. Born 1931 in Satoraljaujhely, Hungary; trained with Agrippina Vaganova; m. István Rabovsky (ballet dancer). ❧ Danced for Budapest State Opera in Hungary until 1953; with husband, defected to the West (1953); performed with husband with London Festival Ballet for 1 season, then came to US on the *Andrea Doria* (1956); appeared on tour in US with chamber ballet company, performing in concert halls and nightclubs; taught in NY state with husband.

KOVACS, Agnes (1981—). Hungarian swimmer. Name variations: Ágnes Kovács. Born July 13, 1981, in Budapest, Hungary. ❧ Won a bronze medal at Atlanta Olympics (1996) and a gold medal in Sydney Olympics (2000), both in the 200-meter breaststroke; won gold medals for all breaststroke events (50 m, 100 m, and 200 m) at the European championships (1999); came in 1st in the 200-meter breaststroke in the World championship (2001).

KOVACS, Annamaria (1945—). *See Tothne-Kovacs, Annamaria.*

KOVACS, Edie (1927—). *See Adams, Edie.*

KOVACS, Edit (1954—). Hungarian fencer. Born June 1954 in Hungary. ❖ Won a bronze medal at Montreal Olympics (1976), bronze medal at Moscow Olympics (1980), and bronze medal at Seoul Olympics (1988), all in team foil.

KOVACS, Katalin (1976—). Hungarian kayaker. Name variations: Katalin Kovács. Born Feb 29, 1976, in Budapest, Hungary. ❖ Won silver medals for K2 500 meters and K4 500 meters at Sydney Olympics (2000); at World championships, placed 1st for K4 200 and 500 (1999, 2001), K1 500 and 1000 and K4 500 (2002) and K1 500 and 1000 and K4 200 and 500 (2003); won a silver medal for K4 500 and a gold medal for K2 500 at Athens Olympics (2004).

KOVACSNE-NYARI, Magdolna (1921—). Hungarian fencer. Born July 1921 in Hungary. ❖ At Rome Olympics, won a silver medal in team foil (1960).

KOVALEVSKAIA, Sonia (1850–1891). *See Kovalevskaya, Sophia.*

KOVALEVSKAYA, Sophia (1850–1891). Russian mathematician. Name variations: Kovalevskaya (or Kovalevskaia) is the feminized version of her married name; is also referred to as Sonya, Sofya, or Sofia Kovalevsky or Kovalevski, or Sophia Korvin-Krukovsky or Corvin-Krukovsky. Born Sophia Vasilevna Korvin-Krukovsky, Jan 15, 1850, in Moscow; died in Stockholm, Feb 10, 1891, of pneumonia; dau. of Vasily Vasilevich Korvin-Krukovsky, or Corvin-Krukovsky (1801–1875, noble who served in army and later managed his provincial estate) and Elizaveta (Schubert) Fedrovna (1820–1879); sister of Anna Vasilevna (Jaclard); education began at age 8; m. Vladimir Onufrievich Kovalevsky (1842–1883), 1868; children: Sophia Vladimirovich Kovalevskaya (b. Oct 17, 1878). ❖ Renowned mathematician, teacher, writer, occasional nihilist sympathizer and 1st modern woman to receive a doctorate in mathematics, went to Germany to continue her higher education, specializing in mathematics (1869); was a minor participant in Paris Commune of 1871, and an occasional supporter of Russia's nihilists, though she was never fully committed to their radical cause; earned PhD from University of Göttingen (1874) with her dissertation on partial differential equations, a simplification of Augustin Cauchy's 1842 solution to a problem involving the conduction of heat (the solution is now known as the "Cauchy-Kovalevsky Theorum"); became a lecturer at University of Stockholm (1883), the 1st modern woman to receive a post at a European university; became a professor (1884); worked as an editor of mathematical journal *Acta Mathematica;* awarded permanent professorship at University of Stockholm (1889). Received a number of accolades, including Paris Academy's Prix Borodin (a 1st for a woman) for her work on the rotation of a solid body around a fixed point (1888); became 1st woman elected as a corresponding member to Russian Academy of Sciences. ❖ See also memoir *Recollections of Childhood* (1889); Don H. Kennedy, *Little Sparrow: A Portrait of Sophia Kovalevsky* (Ohio U. Press, 1983); Ann Hibner Koblitz, *A Convergence of Lives: Sofia Kovalevskaia, Scientist, Writer, Revolutionary* (Birkhäuser, 1983); and *Women in World History.*

KOVALOVA, Marie (1927—). Czech gymnast. Born May 11, 1927. ❖ At London Olympics, won a gold medal in team all-around (1948).

KOVALSKAIA, Elizaveta (1851–1943). Russian feminist and revolutionary. Name variations: Elizabeth Koval'skaia or Kovalskaya; Kobalskaya. Pronunciation: Ko-VAL-sky-ya. Born Elizaveta Nikolaevna Solntseva, July 17, 1851 (o.s.) in Solntsevka, Russia; died in Soviet Union, 1943; illeg. dau. of Colonel Nikolai Solntsev (landowner) and a female serf on his estate; attended girls' gymnasium in Kharkov, 1862–67, and Alarchin courses in St. Petersburg, 1869–71; m. Iakov I.Kovalskii, late 1860s; m. M. Mankovskii, c. 1900; children: none. ❖ Active in the Populist movement, was a serf until 1858 when she was adopted by her father and brought up as a noble's daughter (1858); conducted women's courses in Kharkov (1867–69); was a member of female study circles in St. Petersburg (1869–71); lived in Zurich and became a follower of Bakunin (1872–73); was an active participant in the Russian Populist movement (1874–80); was a member of Chernyi Peredel (1879); was co-founder of the illegal South Russian Workers Union (1880); arrested (1880), tried (1881), and sentenced to a life of hard labor in Siberia exile;

was confined there (1881–1903); immigrated to Switzerland (1903–07) and France (1907–17) where she was active in the maximalist wing of the Russian Socialist Revolutionary Party; returned to Russia after Oct Revolution; was a researcher in the State Historical Archives in Petrograd (1918–23); was a member of the editorial board of *Katorga i ssylka* in Moscow (1923–35). ❖ See also *Women in World History.*

KOVALYOVA, Anna (1983—). Russian gymnast. Born Jan 18, 1983, in Novgorod, Russia; half-sister of Dmitry Lvov (gymnast). ❖ Won Jr. European championships, Russian championships, and World Stars (1998).

KOVPAN, Valentina (1950—). Soviet archer. Born Feb 28, 1950, in USSR. ❖ At Montreal Olympics, won a silver medal in double FITA round (1976).

KOWAL, Kristy (1978—). American swimmer. Born Oct 9, 1978, in Reading, PA; attended University of Georgia. ❖ At LC World championships, won a gold medal for 100-meter breaststroke (1998); won a silver medal for 200-meter breaststroke at Sydney Olympics (2000).

KOWALSKI, Kerstin (1976—). German rower. Name variations: Kerstin El Qalqili. Born Kerstin Kowalski, Jan 25, 1976, in Potsdam, Germany; twin sister of Manja Kowalski (rower). ❖ At World championships, won a gold medal for quadruple sculls (1999, 2002) and double sculls (2001); won a gold medal for quadruple sculls at Sydney Olympics (2000) and at Athens Olympics (2004).

KOWALSKI, Manja (1976—). German rower. Born Manja Kowalski, Jan 25, 1976, in Potsdam, Germany; twin sister of Kerstin Kowalski (rower). ❖ At World championships, won a gold medal for quadruple sculls (2001); won a gold medal for quadruple sculls at Sydney Olympics (2000).

KOWIN, Barbara (1933—). *See Shelley, Barbara.*

KOWN SOO-HYUN. South Korean field-hockey player. Born in South Korea. ❖ Won a team silver medal at Atlanta Olympics (1996).

KOYEVNIKOVA, Elisabeta. *See Kojevnikova, Elizaveta.*

KOZAKOVA, Olga (1951—). Soviet volleyball player. Born Mar 14, 1951, in USSR. ❖ At Montreal Olympics, won a silver medal in team competition (1976).

KOZHEVNIKOVA, Yelizaveta. *See Kojevnikova, Elizaveta.*

KOZLOVA, Anna (1972—). Russian-American synchronized swimmer. Born Dec 30, 1972, in Leningrad (now St. Petersburg), USSR. ❖ Competed on the Russian national team (1989–93); moved to US; became a US citizen (Oct 1999); with Alison Bartosik, won a bronze medal for duet at Athens Olympics (2004), as well as a bronze medal for team. Named US Synchronized Swimming Athlete of the Year (1997, 2003, 2003); US Olympic Committee Athlete of the Year (2002).

KOZMINSKA, Maria (1913—). *See Kwadzniewska, Maria.*

KOZNICK, Kristina (1975—). American Alpine skier. Born Nov 24, 1975, in Burnsville, Minnesota. ❖ Was US National Slalom champion (1995–98 and 2003); competed in Nagano and Salt Lake City Olympics.

KOZOMPOLI, Stavroula (1974—). Greek water-polo player. Born Jan 14, 1974, in Athens, Greece. ❖ Won team silver medal at Athens Olympics (2004).

KOZYR, Valentina (1950—). Soviet track-and-field athlete. Born April 25, 1950, in USSR. ❖ At Mexico City Olympics, won a bronze medal in the high jump (1968).

KOZYREVA, Lyubov. *See Baranova, Lyubov.*

KOZYREVA, Lyubov (1956—). Soviet volleyball player. Born Dec 12, 1956, in USSR. ❖ At Moscow Olympics, won a gold medal in team competition (1980).

KRACHEVSKAYA-DOLZHENKO, Svetlana (1944—). Soviet track-and-field athlete. Born Nov 23, 1944, in USSR. ❖ At Moscow Olympics, won a silver medal in shot put (1980).

KRAEKER, Steffi (1960—). *See Kraker, Steffi.*

KRAFT, Karen (1969—). American rower. Born May 3, 1969, in San Mateo, CA. ❖ Won a silver medal for coxless pair at Atlanta Olympics (1996) and a bronze medal for coxed eight at Sydney Olympics (2000).

KRAHWINKEL, Hilde (b. 1908). *See Sperling, Hilde.*

KRAINIK, Ardis (1929–1997). American opera administrator. Born in Manitowoc, WI, Mar 8, 1929; died in Chicago, IL, Jan 18, 1997; dau. of Arthur Krainik and Clara (Bracken) Krainik; Northwestern University, BS in drama, 1951, PhD, 1954; never married. ❖ Was general director of Lyric Opera of Chicago (1981–96), which under her leadership, became one of the most important companies in US and a major force in world opera; as a singer, made professional stage debut as the mother in Menotti's *Amahl and the Night Visitors;* took a job as a clerk-typist at Lyric Opera of Chicago (1954); a lyric mezzo, began to appear in a number of small operatic roles, then supporting roles; became assistant manager of Lyric Opera (1960), then artistic administrator (1975); with the company near financial ruin, accepted position of general director (1981) and immediately turned things around. ❖ See also *Women in World History.*

KRAJCIROVA, Maria (1948—). Czech gymnast. Born June 1948 in Czechoslovakia. ❖ Won a silver medal at Tokyo Olympics (1964) and a silver medal at Mexico City Olympics (1968), both in team all-around.

KRAKER, Steffi (1960—). East German gymnast. Name variations: Steffi Kräker or Kraeker. Born April 21, 1960, in Leipzig, East Germany. ❖ At Montreal Olympics, won a bronze medal in team all-around (1976); at World Cup, won gold medals in uneven bars (1978, 1979); at Chunichi Cup, placed 1st all-around (1979) and 1st on bars (1980, 1981); at Moscow Olympics, won bronze medals in uneven bars and team all-around and a silver medal in vault (1980).

KRALICKOVA, Jarmila (1944—). Czech field-hockey player. Born May 11, 1944, in Czechoslovakia. ❖ At Moscow Olympics, won a silver medal in team competition (1980).

KRALL, Diana (1964—). Canadian jazz singer and pianist. Born Diana Jean Krall, Nov 16, 1964, in Nanaimo, British Columbia, Canada; grew up on Vancouver Island; m. Elvis Costello (pop rocker) Dec 2003. ❖ Was playing jazz in a local restaurant by age 15, but didn't start singing until age 26; earned a scholarship to Berklee College of Music in Boston (1981); moved to Los Angeles where she studied with Jimmy Rowles; released 1st album, *Stepping Out,* while living in Toronto (1993); also recorded such albums as *Only Trust Your Heart* (1995), *All for You* (1996), *Love Scenes* (1997), *The Look of Love* (2001), and *The Girl in the Other Room* (2004); appeared in film *De-Lovely.* Won Grammys for Jazz Vocal Album of the Year for *When I Look in Your Eyes* (1999) and *Live in Paris* (2003), and for Best Jazz Vocal Performance (2000); received Order of British Columbia (2000).

KRALL, Hanna (1937—). Polish-Jewish novelist and journalist. Name variations: Hanny or Hannie Krall. Born 1937 in Warsaw, Poland. ❖ Began career as a journalist writing for *Zycie Warszawy* and *Polityka;* published *Shielding the Flame* which arose from an interview with Merek Edelman, the last survivor of the Warsaw Ghetto uprising (1977), and was issued in English (1986); other writings include *What Happened to Our Fairy Tale* (1994) and *So You Are Daniel* (2001). Won the Solidarity Culture Prize for *The Subtenant: To Outwit God,* a semi-autobiographical account of a childhood hiding from the Nazis (1986).

KRAMER, Ingrid (b. 1943). *See Engel-Kramer, Ingrid.*

KRAMER, Leonie (1924—). Australian educator and writer. Name variations: Dame Leonie Kramer. Born in Melbourne, Australia, in 1924; educated at universities of Melbourne and Oxford. ❖ An expert on works of Henry Handel Richardson, became a professor at University of Sydney (1968); writings on Richardson include *Henry Handel Richardson and Some of Her Sources* (1954), *A Companion to Australia Felix* (1962), and *Myself When Laura* (1966), concerning Richardson's novel *The Getting of Wisdom;* with R.D. Eagleson, wrote *Language and Literature: A Synthesis* (1976) and *A Guide to Language and Literature* (1978); also edited a number of scholarly volumes, including *Australian Poetry* (1961), *Coast to Coast* (1962), *Henry Kendall* (with A.D. Hope, 1972), and *The Oxford History of Australian Literature* (1981). Made OBE (1976) and DBE (1981).

KRANDIEVSKAYA, Anastasiia (1865–1938). Russian novelist and short-story writer. Name variations: Anastasiia Romanovna Krandiévskaia or Krandievskaia. Born 1865 in Russia; died 1938; children: Natalia Krandievskaya (poet); great-grandchildren: Tatyana Tolstaya (short-story writer). ❖ Worked as journalist before first story appeared (1896); works include *That Happened in Early Spring* (1900) and *The Secret of Joy* (1916).

KRANDIEVSKAYA, Natalia (1888–1963). Russian poet and memoirist. Name variations: Natalia or N.V. Krandievskaia; Nataliia Vasilevna Krandiévskaia; Nataliia, Nataliya or Natal'ia Vasil'evna Krandievskaia-Tolstaia; Natalia Vasilyevna Krandievskaya-Tolstaya; Natalia Tolstaya. Born Natalia Vasilyevna Krandievskaya in 1888 in Moscow, Russia; died 1965; dau. of Vasiliy Afanasievich Krandievsky (writer) and Anastasiia Romanovna Krandievskaya (writer); m. 2nd husband Aleksei Nikolaevich Tolstoi (A.N. Tolstoy, 1883–1945, prominent writer distantly related to Leo Tolstoy), 1914 (sep. 1935); children: Nikita Tolstoy (1923–1996, physicist); grandchildren: Tatyana Tolstaya and Natalia Tolstaya (both writers). ❖ Began writing poetry at 7; published 1st work at 14; did not write during marriage (1914–35); created a libretto opera in verse, "Decembrists" (1934); published several collections of lyric poetry, including *Diary of a Heart.* ❖ See also memoirs *I Remember* (1959, 2nd ed. titled *Memoirs,* 1977).

KRANDIEVSKAYA, Natalia (1923—). Russian painter. Name variations: Natalia Krandievskaia; Natalia Navashina-Krandievskaia. Born in 1923 in Moscow, USSR; dau. of an artist and an architect; studied at Moscow secondary art school; graduated with honors from Moscow V.I. Surikov State art institute, 1947. ❖ Painter of landscapes, portraits, and still-lifes, began participating in many art exhibitions (1948); held solo shows in Moscow (1975 and 1984). ❖ See also *Women in World History.*

KRANTZ, Judith (1928—). American novelist. Born Jan 9, 1928, in New York, NY; graduate of Wellesley College, 1948; m. Steve Krantz; children: 2. ❖ Worked as magazine publicist and journalist; was fashion editor at *Good Housekeeping* (1949–56); at 50, published 1st novel, *Scruples* (1978), which was a bestseller; other works of romance fiction include *Princess Daisy* (1980), *I'll Take Manhattan* (1986), *Till We Meet Again* (1988), *Mistral's Daughter* (1990), *Secrets* (1992), and *Dazzle* (1995); adapted many of her novels into miniseries for tv.

KRASNER, Lee (1908–1984). American painter. Name variations: Leonore Krassner. Born Lena Krassner, Oct 27, 1908, in Brooklyn, NY; died June 19 (sometimes seen as June 20), 1984, in New York, NY; dau. of Joseph Krassner and Anna (Weiss) Krassner; attended Women's Art School of Cooper Union, 1925–28, Art Students League, 1928, National Academy of Design, 1929–32; m. Jackson Pollock (artist), Oct 25, 1945 (died Aug 1956). ❖ Leading 20th-century American painter and one of the founders of Abstract Expressionism, produced more than 600 works which both reflected and helped to shape many of the most important artistic trends in US (1930s–60s); worked as an artist for Works Progress Administration (1935–43); began study with Hans Hofmann (1937); 1st exhibited paintings (1940); began to live with Jackson Pollock (1942); painted Little Image paintings (1946–49); presented 1st solo exhibition (1951); painted Green Earth series (1956–57); held exhibition at Martha Jackson Gallery (1958); had 1st retrospective exhibition of her work at Whitechapel Gallery, London (1965); picketed Museum of Modern Art to protest the museum's lack of interest in women artists (1972); major works include *Self-Portrait* (1930), *Red, White, Blue, Yellow, Black* (1939), *Image Surfacing* (1945), *Composition* (1949), *The City* (1953), *Bird Talk* (1955), *Triple Goddess* (1960), and *Gaea* (1966). Was awarded Augustus St. Gaudens Medal by Cooper Union Alumni Association (1974); received Ordre des Arts et des Letters from French government. ❖ See also Robert Carleton Hobbs, *Lee Krasner* (Abbeville, 1993); and *Women in World History.*

KRASNIKOVA, Natella (1953—). Soviet field-hockey player. Born Oct 14, 1953, in USSR. ❖ At Moscow Olympics, won a bronze medal in team competition (1980).

KRASNOHORSKA, Eliska (1847–1926). Czech poet, editor and librettist. Name variations: (pseudonym) Solimna Retkvicka. Born Nov 18, 1847, in Prague, Czechoslovakia; died Nov 26, 1926, in Prague; dau. of Dorota Vodvarkova and Pech Krasnohorski; never married. ❖ Wrote many works of lyric poetry, books for children (especially *Her Stubborn Head*), and social literary criticism; wrote libretto for the opera *Leila* by composer Bendl; also wrote 4 librettos for Smetana: *Hubicka* (*Kiss*), *Tajemstvi* (*Sacred*), *Certova stena* (*The Devil's Wall*) and the unfinished *Viola;* edited the 1st Czech women's journal (Women's Letter) and helped found the 1st girls' gymnasium in Prague; trans. the works of Pushkin and Byron, among others. ❖ See also autobiographies *From My Life* and *What the Years Bring.*

KRASNOMOVETS, Olesya (1979—). Russian runner. Born July 8, 1979, in Nizhny Tagil, USSR. ❖ Placed 1st for 4 x 400-meter relay and 2nd for 400 meters at World Indoor championships (2004); won a silver medal for 4 x 400-meter relay at Athens Olympics (2004).

KRASNOVA, Vera (1950—). Russian speedskater. Born April 3, 1950, in USSR. ❖ Won a silver medal for the 500 meters at Sapporo Olympics (1972); placed 5th for the 500 meters at Innsbruck Olympics (1976).

KRASOVSKA, Olena (1976—). Ukrainian hurdler. Born Aug 17, 1976, in Ukraine. ❖ Won a silver medal in the 100-meter hurdles at Athens Olympics (2004).

KRASOVSKAYA, Vera (d. 1999). Russian ballet historian and critic. Died Aug 15, 1999, age 83, in St. Petersburg, Russia; trained at Leningrad Choreographic School with Agrippina Vagonova; m. David Zolotnitsky; children: Yuri. ❖ Performed with Kirov Ballet (1933–41); studied at Leningrad Ostrovsky Institute of Theater (1946), then joined its faculty (1951); wrote about the ballet world for Soviet and foreign periodicals; wrote 2 4-volume histories, *Ballet Theater in Russia* (1958–72) and *Western European Ballet Theater* (1996); also wrote biographies of Pavlova, Nijinsky and Vagonova, among others.

KRASSOVSKA, Nathalie (1918–2005). Soviet ballet dancer. Name variations: Nathalie Leslie. Born Nathalie Leslie, June 1, 1918, in Petrograd, Russia; died Feb 8, 2005, in Dallas, Texas; father was Scottish; trained by Russian mother, Lydia Krassovska Egorov (ballerina); granddau. of Eugenie Krassovska (ballerina); became US citizen (1964). ❖ Performed with Ballets Russe de Paris; danced in Réné Blum's Ballet Russe (1936–37), where she appeared in numerous works by Fokine, including *Les Sylphides, Scheherezade, Spectre de la Rose, Carnaval,* and *L'Epreuve d'Amour;* appeared as principal dancer on US tour with Ballet Russe de Monte Carlo (1938), starring in works by Massine, including *Vienna–1814* (1938), *Le Tricorne,* and *Le Beau Danube,* and such classical works as *Swan Lake* and *Giselle,* for which she was best known; was a ballerina with London Festival (1950–55); after retiring from performance career, formed own company, Ballet Jeunesse, in Dallas (1963) and taught and created numerous works for that company.

KRATOCHVILOVA, Jarmila (1951—). Czech runner. Born Jan 26, 1951, in Czechoslovakia. ❖ At Moscow Olympics, won a silver medal in 400 meters (1980).

KRATSA-TSAGAROPOULOU, Rodi (1953—). Greek politician. Born April 15, 1953, in Zakynthos, Greece. ❖ Sociologist; worked for service preparing Greek accession to the EC and the social affairs department of the Ministry of Coordination (1979–89); was founder and president of the European Centre for Communication and Information; as a member of the European People's Party (Christian Democrats) and European Democrats, elected to 5th European Parliament (1999–2004).

KRAUS, Alanna (1977—). Canadian short-track speedskater. Born June 30, 1977, in Abbotsford, British Columbia, Canada. ❖ At World Team championships, placed 1st in the 500 and 1,000 meters (2001); placed 3rd at World championships and 2nd at Goodwill Games (2000), both in relay; won a bronze medal for the 3,000-meter relay at Salt Lake City Olympics (2002) and a silver medal for the 3,000 meter relay at Torino Olympics (2006).

KRAUS, Angelika (1950—). West German swimmer. Born May 9, 1950, in Germany. ❖ At Mexico City Olympics, won a bronze medal in 4 x 100-meter medley relay (1968).

KRAUS, Greta (1907–1998). Austrian-born Canadian pianist and harpsichordist. Born Aug 3, 1907, in Vienna, Austria; died Mar 30, 1998, in Toronto, Ontario, Canada; became Canadian citizen (1944); studied at Vienna Academy of Music; m. Erwin Dentay (chemist). ❖ Made debut as a harpsichord soloist in Vienna (1935) and as an ensemble player (1936); moved to Ontario (1938); appeared as soloist and duo-harpsichordist over the CBC; founded and played with the Toronto Baroque Ensemble (1958–63); with flutist Robert Aitken, formed and performed as the Aitken-Kraus Duo (1965–86); was director of the Collegium Musicum (1963–76); also taught at University of Toronto (1963–76) and privately. Appointed a member of the Order of Canada (1992).

KRAUS, Lili (1903–1986). Hungarian pianist. Born in Budapest, Hungary, Mar 4, 1903; died in Asheville, NC, Nov 6, 1986; studied at Royal Academy in Budapest with Béla Bartok and Edward Steuermann and Artur Schnabel. ❖ By early 1930s, had made dozens of records; captured and interned by Japanese during WWII; became a British subject (1948); lived and taught in US in later years; made American debut (1949); re-recorded many of the works she had put on disc decades earlier (1950s), including the complete Mozart concerti, many solo sonatas, much of the Schubert repertoire, as well as some Bartok.

Awarded Austria's Cross of Honor for Science and Art (1978). ❖ See also *Women in World History.*

KRAUS-BOELTÉ, Maria (1836–1918). German-American educator. Name variations: Maria Kraus-Boelte; Maria Boelté. Born Maria Boelté on Nov 8, 1836, in Hagenow, Mecklenburg-Schwerin, Germany; died Nov 1, 1918, in Atlantic City, NJ; dau. of Johann Ludwig Ernst Boelté and Louise (Ehlers) Boelté; trained with Luise Froebel, widow of Friedrich Froebel; m. John Kraus (German-born educator), 1873 (died 1896). ❖ Studied methods of Friedrich Froebel in Hamburg; taught at Froebel Union training school (Hamburg) and worked in kindergartens in London and Lübeck; came to US on request of Elizabeth Peabody (1872); with husband, opened New York Seminary for Kindergartners (1873), one of the most significant centers for kindergarten work in US; with husband, published *The Kindergarten Guide* (2 vols, 1877); served as president of Kindergarten Department of National Education Association (1899–1900).

KRAUS-MAAS, Annelies. *See Maas, Annelies.*

KRAUSE, Barbara (1959—). East German swimmer. Born July 7, 1959, in East Germany. ❖ At Moscow Olympics, won a gold medal in the 4 x 100-meter freestyle relay, the 200-meter freestyle, and the 100-meter freestyle (1980).

KRAUSE, Christiane (1950—). West German runner. Born Dec 14, 1950, in West Germany. ❖ Won a gold medal in the 4 x 100-meter relay at Munich Olympics (1972).

KRAUSE, Roswitha (1949—). East German swimmer and handball player. Born Nov 3, 1949, in East Germany. ❖ Won a silver medal at Mexico City Olympics in the 4 x 100-meter freestyle relay swim (1968); won a silver medal at Montreal Olympics (1976) and a bronze medal at Moscow Olympics (1980), both in handball team competition.

KRAUSE, Sigrun. East German cross-country skier. Name variations: Sigrun Filbrich-Krause. Married Wolfgang Filbrich (Olympian); children: sons Raik and Jens Filbrich (Olympian). ❖ Won a bronze medal for the 4 x 5 km relay at Innsbruck Olympics (1976).

KRAUSHAAR, Silke (1970—). German luge athlete. Born Oct 10, 1970 in Germany. ❖ Won a gold medal for singles luge at Nagano Olympics by two-thousandths of a second (1998), the closest luge race in Olympic history; won a bronze medal for singles luge at Salt Lake City Olympics (2002) and a silver medal for singles luge at Torino Olympics (2006); won the singles World championship (2004) and European championships (1998, 2004, 2006).

KRAUSS, Alison (1971—). American bluegrass fiddler and singer. Born July 23, 1971, in Decatur, IL; m. Pat Bergeson, 1997 (div. Aug 2001); children: 1. ❖ Was Illinois state fiddling champion at age 12; at 14, joined Union Station, a local bluegrass band; released 1st solo effort, *Too Late to Cry,* followed by *Two Highways* with Union Station; won 1st Grammy with solo album *I've Got That Old Feeling* (1990); was the 1st bluegrass artist in 29 years to join the Grand Old Opry (1992); named Female Vocalist of the Year by International Bluegrass Music Association (1992); had single hit, "When You Say Nothing at All" (1995); has received 18 Grammy Awards, more than any other female in history of the Grammys; other albums include *Every Time You Say Goodbye* (1992), *Now That I've Found You* (1995), *So Long So Wrong* (1997) and *Forget About It* (1999).

KRAUSS, Gertrud (1903–1977). Austrian concert dancer. Born May 6, 1903, in Vienna, Austria; died Nov 23, 1977, in Tel Aviv, Israel. ❖ Considered one of the founders of Israeli modern dance, trained 1st as pianist before studying dance at Vienna State Academy where she performed as staff accompanist for concert dancer Eleanore Tordis; began performing as solo concert dancer and creating works for other companies (1920), including *The Last Days of Mankind* (1932), *Songs of the Ghetto,* and *The City Waits* (1930–32); toured Palestine and immigrated there (1935); choreographed works for own group, Gertrud Krauss Dancers, in Israel; worked with Habima Theater on such productions as *Sabbatai Zvi, Peer Gynt,* and *A Midsummer Night's Dream;* taught classes in modern dance throughout Israel.

KRAUSS, Kathe (1906–1970). German runner. Born Nov 29, 1906, in Germany; died Jan 1970. ❖ At Berlin Olympics, won a bronze medal in the 100 meters (1936).

KRAVETS, Inessa (1966—). Ukrainian track-and-field athlete. Born Oct 5, 1966, in Dnipropetrovsk, Ukraine. ❖ At Barcelona Olympics, representing the Soviet Union, won a silver medal in the long jump (1992); at World championships, won a gold medal for triple jump (1995); at European championships, won a silver for long jump and bronze for triple jump (1994); at Atlanta Olympics, representing the Ukraine, won a gold medal for triple jump (1996).

KRAYNOVA, Tatyana (1967—). Soviet volleyball player. Born June 7, 1967, in USSR. ❖ At Seoul Olympics, won a gold medal in team competition (1988).

KREBS, Nathalie (1895–1978). Danish ceramist. Born Johanne Nathalie Krebs, Aug 5, 1895, in Arhus, Denmark; died Jan 5, 1978, in Copenhagen; dau. of Frederick Christian Krebs and Johanne Margrethe Busch; m. Henry Goldmann, 1950. ❖ A chemist and glaze specialist, started Saxbo Pottery (1930), one of the finest independent ceramic workshops in Scandinavia; working with Edith Sonne-Bruun and Eva Staehr-Nielsen, among others, continued to produce high quality art pottery until her retirement (1968), when she destroyed all the molds, designs and glaze formulas.

KREBS-BRENNING, Marie (1851–1900). German pianist. Born Marie Krebs in Dresden, Germany, Dec 5, 1851; died 1900; dau. of Karl Krebs (music critic and philosopher). ❖ Toured Europe at early age; was particularly well-liked in London, and had no fear of including the large-scale concertos in her repertoire, including Beethoven's *Emperor*; toured US as accompanist to violin virtuoso Henri Vieuxtemps (1870). ❖ See also *Women in World History*.

KREFT, Galina (1950—). See *Alekseyeva-Kreft, Galina*.

KREHL, Constanze Angela (1956—). German politician. Born Oct 14, 1956, in Stuttgart, Germany. ❖ Elected to the Volkskammer and vice-chair of SPD (Social Democratic Party) Group (1990); as a European Socialist, elected to 4th and 5th European Parliament (1994–99, 1999–2004).

KREINER, Kathy (1954—). Canadian Alpine skier. Name variations: Cathy Kreiner. Born June 30, 1954, in Timmins, Ontario, Canada. ❖ Won a gold medal for giant slalom at Innsbruck Olympics (1976); placed 5th for downhill at Lake Placid Olympics (1980).

KRÉJCÁROVÁ, Milena (1896–1945). See *Jesenská, Milena*.

KREMER, Mitzi (1968—). American swimmer. Born Mar 18, 1968, in Titusville, FL; attended Clemson University. ❖ Won US nationals for 500- and 200-yard freestyle (1987); at Seoul Olympics, won a bronze medal in the 4 x 100-meter freestyle relay (1988); was a 16-time All-American.

KREMNITZ, Marie (1852–1916). German writer. Name variations: Marie von Kremnitz; Mite Kremnitz; (pseudonym) George Allan. Born Marie von Bardeleben in Greifswald, Germany, 1852; died 1916; m. Dr Kremnitz of Bucharest. ❖ Was lady-in-waiting to Elizabeth of Wied; collaborated with Elizabeth under pseudonym "Dito Und Idem" to indicate their joint authorship of several works, including *Aus zwei Welten* (1884), a novel, *Anna Boleyn* (1886), a tragedy, *Inderlrre* (1888), a collection of short stories, *Edleen Vaughan; or Paths of Peril* (1894), another novel, and *Sweet Hours* (1904), a collection of poems written in English. ❖ See also *Women in World History*.

KRENWINKEL, Patricia (1947—). American murderer (accused). Born Patricia Diane Krenwinkel, Dec 3, 1947, in Los Angeles, CA. ❖ Met Charles Manson in San Francisco and moved to Manson commune in Los Angeles; with other Manson gang members, committed murders of Gary Hinman, Sharon Tate, Jay Sebring, Abigail Folger, Voytek Frykowski, and Leno and Rosemary LaBianca; arrested with others of the Manson family for auto theft (1969), charged with murders, and sentenced to death (1971); sentence commuted to life.

KREPKINA, Vera (1933—). Soviet long jumper. Name variations: Vera Krepkina-Kolashnikova. Born April 16, 1933, in USSR. ❖ At Rome Olympics, won a gold medal in the long jump (1960).

KREPS, Juanita (1921—). American economist and educator. Born Juanita Morris on Jan 11, 1921, in Lynch, KY; dau. of Elmer Morris and Cenia (Blair) Morris; Berea College, AB, 1942; Duke University, MA, 1944, PhD, 1948; m. Clifton H. Kreps (economist), Aug 11, 1944; children: Sarah Blair Kreps; Laura Ann Kreps; Clifton H. Kreps. ❖ Expert in labor economics, had a distinguished career in education, private industry, and public service; taught at Hofstra University until 1954; taught and performed research at Duke University for over 20 years, becoming nationally recognized as an authority on economics of labor in

US, focusing on race and gender equity and aging workers; promoted to full professor at Duke (1967) and served as dean of the women's college (1969–72); named 1st female director of NY Stock Exchange; became 1st female vice-president of Duke (1973); served on boards of numerous large corporations; named secretary of commerce by Jimmy Carter (1977), the 1st woman to hold that office, as well as the 1st professional economist; was also only the 5th woman to hold any Cabinet post; as secretary, focused on US trade issues and development of poor regions of US; led a delegation to Beijing, the 1st secretary of commerce to visit China, and helped bring about an important trade agreement; resigned Cabinet post and returned to Duke (1979); became James B. Duke Professor of Economics, Emeritus. ❖ See also *Women in World History*.

KRESTOVSKAYA, Maria V. (1862–1910). Russian novelist and actress. Name variations: Mariia Vsevolodovna Krestóvskaia or Krestovskaya. Born Mariia Vsevolodovna Krestovskaya in 1862; died 1910; dau. of Vsevolod Krestovskii (historical novelist). ❖ Works include *Early Storms* (1886), *The Actress* (1891), and *Discord* (1887); published diary entries and travel notes in *To the Sunshine!* (1905).

KRESTOVSKII, V. (1824–1889). See *Khvoshchinskaia, Nadezhda*.

KRETSCHMAN, Kelly (1979—). American softball player. Born Aug 26, 1979, in Indian Harbor Beach, Fl; attended University of Alabama. ❖ Outfielder, won team gold medal at Athens Olympics (2004).

KRETZSCHMAR, Waltraud (1948—). East German handball player. Born Feb 1, 1948, in East Germany. ❖ Won a silver medal at Montreal Olympics (1976) and a bronze medal at Moscow Olympics (1980), both in team competition.

KREY, Ursula (1926—). See *Happe-Krey, Ursula*.

KRIEGER, Victorina (b. 1896). Soviet ballet dancer and critic. Name variations: Viktorina Krieger. Born April 9, 1896, in St. Petersburg, Russia; dau. of Vladimir Krieger and Nadezhda Bogdanovskaya-Krieger (both in theater). ❖ Trained at school of Bolshoi Ballet, then joined the company (c. 1910), where she danced in numerous productions of 19th-century classics to great success; danced with Laurent Novikoff with Anna Pavlova's Co. in US (1921); remained in US and worked with Mihkail Mordkin on dance acts for East Coast Prologs and Criterion Theater, including *The Doll Shop* (1921) and Mordkin's *Bacchanalia*; returned to Soviet Union where she rejoined Bolshoi Ballet (1925); influenced by Stanislavski, formed Moscow Arts Theater of Ballet (1929), dedicated to creating a repertory of more naturalistic ballets; worked as writer and dance critic and served as director of Bolshoi Theater Museum. ❖ See also memoirs (in Russian), *Moil Zapiski* (My Notes, 1930).

KRIEL, Marianne. South African swimmer. Born in Bellville, Cape Town, South Africa. ❖ Won a bronze medal for 100-meter backstroke at Atlanta Olympics (1996).

KRIENKE, Nadine (1974—). See *Ernsting-Krienke, Nadine*.

KRIM, Mathilde (1926—). American research biologist and virologist. Born Mathilde Galland, July 9, 1926, in Como, Italy; dau. of Italian-speaking Swiss agronomist and a German-speaking Czech mother; University of Geneva, BS, 1948, PhD, 1953; m. Jewish medical student (div. 1958); m. Arthur B. Krim (chair of Orion Pictures). ❖ Health educator, best known for her work in combating AIDS and HIV through research and education, 1st worked on biomedical research at Weizmann Institute of Science in Rehovot, Israel (1953–59), during 1st marriage; remarried and moved to US; worked at Cornell Medical College (1959–62); became researcher at Sloan-Kettering Cancer Center in NYC (1962), then head of interferon laboratory (1981–85); worked in department of pediatrics at St. Luke's Roosevelt Hospital and at Columbia University (1986–90); became adjunct professor of public health and management at Columbia (1990); established the AIDS Medical Foundation (1983), which later merged to form the American Foundation for AIDS Research (AmFAR). Awarded Presidential Medal of Freedom by Bill Clinton (2000).

KRINGEN, Goril (1972—). Norwegian soccer player. Name variations: Gøril or Goeril Kringen. Born Feb 28, 1972, in Norway. ❖ Defender; won a team gold medal at Sydney Olympics (2000).

KRIPALANI, Sucheta (1908–1974). Indian nationalist and politician. Name variations: Sucheta Mazumdar. Born Sucheta Mazumdar on June 25, 1908, in Ambala, India; died 1974 in New Delhi; dau. of S.N. Mazumdar (doctor); Government Woman's College, Lahore, Pakistan, BA; University of Delhi, MA; m. Jiwatram Bhagwandas Kripalani (politician), April 1936 (died 1982). ❖ India's 1st woman chief minister, taught at Benares Hindu University; established Women's Section of Indian National Congress (INC) and became secretary (1939); was head of Foreign Department of INC; was imprisoned by British authorities for participation in India's freedom struggle (1940–42, 1944–45); elected to Constituent Assembly of India from state of Uttar Pradesh (UP, 1946); was a member of Lok Sabha (lower house of Indian Parliament) (1952–56, 1957–62, 1967–71); became UP Cabinet minister for Labor, for Community Development, and for Industry (1962); was chief minister of UP (1963–67); helped found Tibetan Relief Committee and the social welfare organization, Lok Kalyan Samiti.

KRISAN, Asokesin (1931—). See Yanaranop, Sukanya.

KRISHNA, Bal (1868–1952). See Cory, Annie Sophie.

KRISTEVA, Julia (1941—). French linguist and literary critic. Born 1941 in Bulgaria; m. Philippe Sollers. ❖ Moved to France at 23 and studied Freudian and Lacanian psychoanalysis; was active member of leftist intellectual group *Tel Quel* and published articles on language in *Critique* and other journals; became chair of Linguistics at University of Paris and guest lecturer at Columbia University, NY; works, which address themes of feminine identity, motherhood, abjection, foreignness, and madness, include *Language: A Semiotic Approach to Literature and Art* (1980), *Powers of Horror* (1980), *Revolution in Poetic Language* (1984), *Tales of Love* (1987), *Soleil noir: dépression et mélancholie* (1987), and *Strangers to Ourselves* (1991), winner of the Prix Henri Hertz. ❖ See also Toril Moi, ed., *The Kristeva Reader* (Columbia U. Press, 1986); Kelly Oliver, *Reading Kristeva: Unraveling the Double-bind* (Indiana U. Press, 1993).

KRISTIANSEN, Ingrid (1956—). Norwegian long-distance runner. Born Ingrid Christensen, Mar 21, 1956, in Trondheim, Norway. ❖ Won European championship (1986) and World championship (1987), for 10,000 meters; won cross-country World championship (1987); placed 1st in London Marathon (1984, 1985, 1987), Boston Marathon (1986, 1989), Houston Marathon (1983, 1984), and Stockholm Marathon (1980, 1981, 1982); held world records in 5,000 and 10,000 meters, marathon and half-marathon (1987); also participated in world and European ski events (late 1970s).

KRISTINA. Variant of Christina.

KRISTINA (fl. 1150). Swedish royal. Name variations: Kristina Bjornsdottir. Fl. around 1150; dau. of Bjorn, prince of Denmark, and Katerina Ingesdottir; m. Erik or St. Eric IX, king of Sweden (r. 1156–1160); children: Knut Ericsson, king of Sweden (r. 1167–1195); Philipp; Margaret (d. 1209); Katharina Ericsdottir (who m. Nils Blaka).

KRISTINA, Queen (1626–1689). See Christina of Sweden.

KRISTOLOVA, Anka (1955—). Bulgarian volleyball player. Born Jan 12, 1955, in Bulgaria. ❖ At Moscow Olympics, won a bronze medal in team competition (1980).

KRIVELYOVA, Svetlana (1969—). Soviet track-and-field athlete. Born June 13, 1969, in Bryansk, USSR. ❖ At Barcelona Olympics, won a gold medal in the shot put (1992); won a bronze medal at Athens Olympics (2004); at World championships, placed 1st (2003); at World Indoor championships, placed 1st (1993, 1999, 2004).

KRIVOCHEI, Elena. Russian rhythmic gymnast. Born in USSR. ❖ Won a team bronze medal at Atlanta Olympics (1996).

KRIVOSHEYEVA, Olga (1961—). Soviet volleyball player. Born May 15, 1961, in USSR. ❖ At Seoul Olympics, won a gold medal in team competition (1988).

KRIZOVA, Jirina (1948—). Czech field-hockey player. Born Feb 21, 1948, in Czechoslovakia. ❖ At Moscow Olympics, won a silver medal in team competition (1980).

KRIZOVA, Olga (1962—). See Charvatova, Olga.

KROC, Joan (1928–2003). American philanthropist. Name variations: Joan Dobbins. Born Joan Beverly Mansfield, Aug 27, 1928, in St. Paul, Minnesota; died Oct 12, 2003, in Rancho Santa Fe, CA; the dau. of a railroad telegrapher and a concert violinist; m. and div.; became 2nd wife of Raymond Kroc (owner of McDonald's fast-food chain), Mar 8, 1969 (died 1984); children: Linda Kliber. ❖ Avoided the spotlight, but made national headlines when she was identified as the anonymous donor of $15 million to aid the flood victims of Grand Forks, North Dakota (1997); donated millions to causes ranging from local theater to medical

research; reportedly gave $33 million to institutions, including the Betty Ford Center and University of San Diego (1996); also contributed over $100 million to various Ronald McDonald charities and $80 million to the Salvation Army; in her will, bequeathed $200 million to National Public Radio (NPR).

KROEBER, Theodora (1897–1979). American writer and anthropologist. Born Theodora Kracaw (also seen as Krakow) on Mar 24, 1897, in Denver, CO; died July 1979 in Berkeley, CA; dau. of Phebe Johnston Kracaw and Charles Kracaw (general-store owners in Telluride, CO); University of California, Berkeley, BA, 1919, MA, 1920; m. Clifton Spencer Brown (died Oct 1923); m. Alfred Kroeber (anthropologist), 1926; m. John H. Quinn (artist and psychotherapist), 1969; children: (1st m.) Clifton Jr., and Theodore Brown; (2nd m.) Karl Kroeber and Ursula K. Le Guin (b. 1929, fiction writer). ❖ With Alfred Kroeber, made trip to Peru and dug primarily in Nazca Valley (1926); conducted extensive research about Ishi, who was the sole survivor of the Yahi group (Northern California tribe); established her reputation with *Ishi in Two Worlds* (1961) which is considered a modern classic. Other works include *The Inland Whale* (1959), *Almost Ancestors* (with Robert F. Heizer, 1968), *Alfred Kroeber: A Personal Configuration* (1970), and *Drawn from Life* (with Heizer, 1976).

KROEGER, Alice (1864–1909). American librarian and library school director. Born Alice Bertha Kroeger, May 2, 1864, in St. Louis, Missouri; died Oct 31, 1909, in Philadelphia, PA; dau. of Adolph Ernst Kroeger (journalist) and Eliza Bertha (Curren) Kroeger; graduate of New York State Library School at Albany, 1891. ❖ Worked as assistant in issue department of St. Louis Public Library (1882–89); hired to organize school of library science at Drexel Institute in Philadelphia (1891) which opened as 3rd such school in US (1892). Books include *Aids in Book Selection* (1908) and *Guide to the Study and Use of Reference Books* (1902), which has become standard guide for reference materials.

KROG, Cecilie (1858–1911). See Thoresen, Cecilie.

KROG, Gina (1847–1916). Norwegian women's-rights activist. Born Jørgine Anna Sverdrup, June 20, 1847, in Flakstad, Lofoten, Northern Norway; died April 14, 1916; dau. of a Lutheran pastor; never married. ❖ After some years as a schoolteacher, resigned in order to lead the women's movement in Norway and to argue the cause in newspaper and magazine articles; helped found Norsk Kvinnesaksforening (Norwegian Association for Women's Rights, 1884); established Kvinnestemmerettsforening (Association for Women's Suffrage, 1885), remaining its chair until 1897, when she resigned over the issue of giving voting rights to middle-class women only; edited magazine *Nylaende* (New Land, [1887–1916]); established the National Council of Norwegian Women and remained its lifelong chair; supported Venstre (Liberal Party) in politics, and was elected deputy member of its national committee (1909). ❖ See also *Women in World History*.

KROGER, Helen (1913–1993). See Cohen, Lona.

KROKHINA, Lyudmila (1954—). Soviet rower. Born Jan 10, 1954, in USSR. ❖ At Montreal Olympics, won a bronze medal in coxed fours (1976).

KROL, Lidia (1935—). See Szczerbinska-Krolowa, Lidia.

KROLOWA, Lidia (1935—). See Szczerbinska-Krolowa, Lidia.

KROMAN, Anne (1895–1985). See Forrest, Ann.

KRONAUER, Brigitte (1940—). German novelist and essayist. Born Dec 29, 1940, in Essen, Germany. ❖ Came to prominence with 1st novel *Frau Mühlenbeck im Gehäus* (Mrs. Mühlenbeck in Her Shell, 1980); subsequent works also praised by critics for their innovation and sophistication, including *Der unvermeidliche Gang der Dinge* (1974), *Die Revolution der Nachahmung* (1975), *Rita Münster* (1983), *Berittene Bogenschütze* (1986), *Die Frau in den Kissen* (1990), *Schnurrer* (1992), and *Die Wiese* (1996); short stories collected in *Die gemusterte Nacht* (1981). Received Berliner Literature Prize (1994) and Fontane Prize (1996).

KRONBERGER, Lily. Hungarian figure skater. Name variations: Lilly Kronberger. Born in Budapest, Hungary, of Jewish parents. ❖ Won the World Championships (1908, 1909, 1910, 1911).

KRONBERGER, Petra (1969—). Austrian Alpine skier. Born Feb 21, 1969, in Pfarrwerfen, Austria. ❖ Won 3 consecutive World Cup overall titles (1990–92); won the World championship for downhill (1991); won gold medals in slalom and combined at Albertville Olympics (1992).

KRONE, Julie (1963—). American jockey. Born Julieann Louise Krone, July 24, 1963, in Benton Harbor, Michigan; m. Matthew Muzikar (tv sports producer), Aug 26, 1995. ❖ Winningest female jockey, and one of the top jockeys—male or female—of all time; had $81 million in purse earnings and more than 3,500 wins; was the 1st woman to win a Triple Crown race (1993), taking the Belmont Stakes aboard Colonial Affair; was the 1st female jockey to win the Breeder's Cup (2003), riding Halfbridled. Became 1st woman elected to racing's Hall of Fame (2000). ❖ See also Dorothy M. Callahan, *Julie Krone: A Winning Jockey* (Dillon, 1990), Christina Lessa, *Women Who Win* (Universe, 1998); and *Women in World History*.

KRONFELD, Minnie (1904–1987). *See Dronke, Minnie Maria.*

KRONIGER, Annegret (1952—). West German runner. Born Sept 24, 1952, in Germany. ❖ At Montreal Olympics, won a silver medal in the 4 x 100-meter relay (1976).

KRONOLD, Selma (1861–1920). Polish-born opera singer. Name variations: Selma Koert-Kronold. Born Aug 18, 1861, in Kraków, Poland; died Oct 9, 1920, in New York, NY; dau. of Adolph Kronold and Louise (Hirschberg) Kronold; sister of Hans Kronold (cellist-composer); cousin of Moritz Moszkowski (pianist-composer); m. Jan Koert (violinist), c. 1890 (div.). ❖ Debuted as Agathe in *Der Freischütz*, at Royal Conservatory in Leipzig; reputedly made NY debut in *Der Freischütz* at Thalia Theatre (1885); sang in 1st US performance of *I Pagliacci* at Grand Opera House in NY (June 15, 1893); sang with Metropolitan Opera, Angelo Neumann Wagner Opera, Gustav Hinrichs Co., Italian Opera Co., and Royal Opera House in Berlin; founded Catholic Oratorio School to train aspiring singers. Repertoire included more than 40 operas, such as *Die Walküre, Das Rheingold, Faust, La Gioconda, Cavalleria Rusticana, William Tell, Il Trovatore,* and *Tannhäuser.*

KRÜDENER, Julie de (1764–1824). Russian writer, traveler, evangelist, and mystic. Name variations: Juliana de Krudener; Madame de Krüdener; Baroness von Krüdener. Pronunciation: CREW-de-ner. Born Barbara Juliana von Vietinghof, Nov 22, 1764, in Riga, Livonia, a Baltic province of Russian Empire; died, probably of cancer, in Karasu-Bazar, Crimea, Dec 24, 1824; dau. of Otto Hermann, Baron von Vietinghof (landed noble and government official), and Countess Anna Ulrica von Münnich Vietinghof (granddau. of a distinguished Russian military leader); m. Burchhard Alexis Constantine, Baron von Krüdener, 1782; children: Paul (b. 1784); Juliette (b. 1787); (stepdaughter) Sophie. ❖ Writer whose career included a crucial encounter with Tsar Alexander I at the close of the Napoleonic wars, which may have contributed to the formation of the postwar Holy Alliance; made 1st trip to Central and Western Europe (1777); made 1st trip to St. Petersburg, and accompanied husband to increasingly important diplomatic posts: 1st Venice (1784), then Copenhagen (1786); began extended visit to France (1789); began love affair with the Marquis de Frégeville (1790); separated from husband, returned to Livonia (1792); began travels in Germany, Switzerland, and France, and met Jean Paul Richter (1796); produced a small work, *Pensées d'une dame étrangère* (*Thoughts of a Foreign Lady*), that appeared in the *Mercure de France* (1802); published *Valérie* in Paris (1804) to substantial commercial success and a measure of praise from critics; had religious conversion in Livonia (1805); took on missionary work after battle of Eylau and visited Moravian Brethren (1807); met with Tsar Alexander I of Russia (1815); was occupied with missionary activities in Switzerland and Germany as her religious enthusiasm deepened into full-fledged mysticism with a tinge of social radicalism (1816–17); made final return to Riga (1818); journeyed to the Crimea (1824). ❖ See also Ernest John Knapton, *The Lady of the Holy Alliance: The Life of Julie de Krüdener* (1939); and *Women in World History*.

KRUEGER, Katrin (1959—). East German handball player. Name variations: Katrin Krüger. Born April 10, 1959, in East Germany. ❖ At Moscow Olympics, won a bronze medal in team competition (1980).

KRUEGER, Luise (1915—). German track-and-field athlete. Name variations: Luise Krüger. Born Jan 11, 1915, in Germany. ❖ At Berlin Olympics, won a silver medal in the javelin throw (1936).

KRUG, Barbara (1956—). East German runner. Born May 6, 1956, in East Germany. ❖ At Moscow Olympics, won a silver medal in 4 x 400-meter relay (1980).

KRUGER, Alma (1868–1960). American actress. Born Sept 13, 1868, in Pittsburgh, PA; died April 5, 1960, in Seattle, WA. ❖ On stage from early childhood, appeared in Shakespearean repertory with Julia Marlowe and E.H. Sothern (1907, 1909–12, 1920s); Broadway credits include *Daisy Mayme, John Gabriel Borkman, Julius Caesar, Twelfth Night, Pride and Prejudice* and *John Brown;* appeared with Eva Le Gallienne's Civic Rep in revivals of *Camille, Hedda Gabler, The Would-Be Gentleman* and *Alison's House* (1927–31); on screen, played character roles in over 50 movies, most memorably as the grandmother in *These Three* (1936) and as the head nurse in "Dr. Kildare" series.

KRUGER, Barbara (1945—). American artist. Born Jan 26, 1945, in Newark, NJ; attended Syracuse University and Parsons School of Design. ❖ Began career as a Condé Nast graphic designer; started working in soft sculpture, turned to painting and photography; working often in black, white and red, uses photo-collage with a caption overlay to create political and feminist works; also created public-service ads for such issues as abortion rights and AIDS; work appears in permanent collections of the Whitney Museum and MoMA.

KRÜGER, Katrin (1959—). *See Krueger, Katrin.*

KRÜGER, Luise (1915—). *See Krueger, Luise.*

KRUGLOVA, Larisa (1972—). Russian runner. Born Oct 27, 1972, in Murmansk, USSR. ❖ Won a silver medal for 4 x 100-meter relay at Athens Olympics (2004).

KRUGLOVA, Yelena (1962—). Soviet swimmer. Born Mar 22, 1962, in USSR. ❖ At Moscow Olympics, won a bronze medal in 4 x 100-meter medley relay (1980).

KRULL, Germaine (1897–1985). Polish-born photographer. Born in Wilda-Poznan, Poland, 1897; died in Wetzlar, West Germany, 1985; dau. of German parents; educated in Paris; studied photography at Bayerische Staatslehranstalt für Lichtbildwesen, Munich, 1916–18; m. Joris Ivens (filmmaker); no children. ❖ Began career as a portrait photographer in Munich and Berlin; freelanced in Netherlands (1921–24), photographing architecture and industry; moved to Paris, where she worked for such major magazines as *Vu, Arts et métiers graphiques, Marianne* and *Voilà;* was the only photographer to exhibit in Salon D'Automne in Paris (1926), and her industrial photographs appeared in *Métal* (1927); was represented in influential *Film and Foto* exhibition in Stuttgart (1929); during WWII, was accredited as a war correspondent and photographed for Free French publications in Africa, Germany and Italy; after the war, opened an Oriental Hotel in Bangkok, but continued to work on a freelance basis, making trips to Thailand, Burma, Nepal, India and Tibet; lived with Tibetan refugees in northern India (1965–80s), and became a friend of the Dalai Lama. ❖ See also *Women in World History*.

KRUPOWA, Krystyna (1939—). Polish volleyball player. Born Jan 15, 1939, in Poland. ❖ Won a bronze medal at Tokyo Olympics (1964) and a bronze medal at Mexico City Olympics (1968), both in team competition.

KRUPP, Bertha (1886–1957). German industrialist. Name variations: Bertha von Krupp; Bertha Krupp von Bohlen und Halbach. Pronunciation: Krupp rhymes with loop. Born Bertha Krupp, Mar 1886, in Essen, Germany; died in Essen of a heart attack, Sept 21, 1957; dau. of Friedrich (Fritz) Krupp (leading German industrialist) and Margarethe (von Ende) Krupp (Prussian civil servant's daughter); m. Gustav von Bohlen und Halbach, 1906 (died 1950): children: Alfried von Bohlen und Halbach (1907–1967, who m. Anneliese Bahr and Vera Hossenfeldt); Berthold von Bohlen und Halbach (b. 1913, who m. Edith von Maltzan); Arnold von Bohlen und Halbach (1908–1909); Claus von Bohlen und Halbach (1910–1940); Irmgard von Bohlen und Halbach (b. 1912, who m. Hanno Raitz von Frenz); Harald von Bohlen und Halbach (b. 1916, who m. Doerte Hillringhaus); Waldtraut von Bohlen und Halbach (b. 1920); Eckbert von Bohlen und Halbach (1922–1945). ❖ German heiress to the Krupp armaments fortune and one of the richest individuals in Europe, who played a significant, if discreet, role in directing her family's enterprises during much of 20th century; became heiress to Krupp fortune (1902); saw 1st use of "Big Bertha" cannon (named for her) in attack on Belgium during WWI (1914); had a significant role in determining the direction of the great industrial enterprise of which she was the legal owner; disliked Hitler and opposed husband's conversion to Nazism (1933), but her personal feelings did not disrupt the close links between the Krupp enterprises and the German government; her firm granted special status by Hitler with the *Lex Krupp* (Krupp Law, 1943); fled to Austrian Alps during bombing of Essen, while her sister was arrested following failed plot on Hitler's life (1944); during war, 2 sons were killed, another was captured by Soviet army and spent 11 years in a prison camp, and a 4th was arrested by American authorities and convicted of war crimes; at war's end, once again helped to direct the family fortune and the vast influence that came with it. ❖ See also Peter Batty, *The House of Krupp* (Stein & Day, 1967); William Manchester, *The Arms of Krupp, 1587–1968* (Little, Brown); and *Women in World History.*

KRUPSKAYA, Nadezhda (1869–1939). Russian educator, writer, and Marxist revolutionary. Name variations: N.K. Krupskaya; Nadya Krupskaia; Nadya Lenin. Pronunciation: NA-de-AH KROOP-skay-yah. Born Nadezhda Konstantinovna Krupskaya, Feb 26, 1869, in St. Petersburg, Russia; died Feb 27, 1939, in Moscow; dau. of Konstantin Ignatevich Krupsky and Elizaveta Tistrova Krupskaya; attended University of St. Petersburg; m. Vladimir Ilyich Ulianov or Ulyanov, later known as Vladimir Ilyich Lenin (Russian revolutionary), 1899 (died 1924); no children. ❖ Wife of Lenin, who took on Stalin but was powerless to stop him, left University of St. Petersburg (1890) and became involved in radical politics; met Lenin (1894); arrested for recruiting members for the revolution, disseminating propaganda, and assisting in the organization of strikes (1895); sentenced to 3 years' internal exile (1898); published 1st Marxist work on the emancipation of women (1899); endured foreign exile (1901–05); served as editorial secretary of *Iska* (1901–03), and of *Vpered* and *The Proletarian* (1903–05); returned to Russia (1905); lived in exile once more (1907–17); headed Commission for Aid of Russian Prisoners of War (1915); returned to Russia and was elected to local soviet of Vyborg, a suburb of Petrograd (1917); in Moscow, became commissar for Adult Education (1918); husband was shot (1918), had his 1st stroke (1922) and died (Jan 21, 1924); signed manifesto against Stalin's agricultural policy (1925); urged greater democracy and intellectual freedom within the party, both of which Stalin's autocratic methods precluded; forced to support Stalin (1927); was a member of the Central Committee (1927); served as deputy commissar of education (1929); was a member of the Soviet Academy of Sciences (1931); served as deputy of the Supreme Soviet (1937); became the maternal symbol of Communism. ❖ See also memoir *Memories of Lenin* (International, 1930); Robert H. McNeal, *Bride of the Revolution: Krupskaya and Lenin* (U. of Michigan Press, 1972); and *Women in World History.*

KRUSCENISKI, Salomea (1873–1952). Ukrainian soprano. Name variations: Krushelnytska. Born in Bilavyntsy, Ukraine, Sept 23, 1873; died in Lvov, Nov 16, 1952; studied in Lvov with Wysocki and in Milan with Crespi. ❖ A Ruthenian dramatic soprano, made debut in Lvov (1893) as Léonore in *Favorite;* was an admired Isolde and Elektra; her singing at Brescia (1904) was largely responsible for the early popularity of Puccini's *Madama Butterfly;* retired (1920). ❖ See also *Women in World History.*

KRUSE, Pamela (1950—). American swimmer. Born June 1950 in Pompano Beach, FL. ❖ At Mexico City Olympics, won a silver medal in 800-meter freestyle (1968); held the World record in the 400-meter freestyle.

KRUSENSTJERNA, Agnes von (1894–1940). Swedish novelist. Name variations: Agnes Julie Fredrika von Krusenstjerna. Born Agnes Julie Fredrika von Krusenstjerna, Oct 9, 1894 in Växjö, Sweden; died Mar 10, 1940, in Stockholm; dau. of Eva and Ernst von Krusenstjerna; m. David Sprengel, 1921. ❖ Known as the "Swedish Proust," suffered several mental breakdowns; writings, which address female sexuality and madness, stirred up heated debate in 1930s because of sexual content; work includes *Ninas dagbok* (1917), *Tony* (trilogy, 1922–26), 7 books about *Misses von Pahlen* (1930–35), and 4 volumes of *Fattigadel* (1935–38).

KRUSHELNYTSKA, Salomea (1873–1952). See *Krusceniski, Salomea.*

KRUTOVA, Ninel (1926—). Soviet diver. Born Nov 11, 1926, in USSR. ❖ At Rome Olympics, won a bronze medal in platform (1960).

KRUTZLER, Eszter (1981—). Hungarian weightlifter. Born Mar 4, 1981, in Szombathely, Hungary. ❖ Placed 2nd for 69kg and 69kg clean & jerk at World championships (2003); won a silver medal for 69kg at Athens Olympics (2004).

KRYCZKA, Kelly (1961—). Canadian synchronized swimmer. Name variations: Kelly Kryczka Irwin. Born July 1961 in Alberta, Canada. ❖ At Los Angeles Olympics, won a silver medal in duet (1984). Canadian Female Aquatic Athlete of the Year (1982).

KRYLOVA, Anjelika (1973—). Russian ice dancer. Born July 4, 1973, in Moscow, Russia. ❖ With Vladimir Fedorov, placed 3rd at World championships (1994); with Oleg Ovsyannikov, won Russian nationals (1994, 1997–99), Skate America (1997), Goodwill Games (1998), Cup of Russia (1997–99), World championships (1998–99), ISU Grand Prix (1999), European championship (1999), and a silver medal at Nagano Olympics (1998).

KRYLOVA, Lidiya (1951—). Soviet rower. Born Mar 12, 1951, in USSR. ❖ At Montreal Olympics, won a bronze medal in coxed fours (1976).

KRYSTYNA ROKICZANSKA (fl. 1300s). Queen of Poland. Name variations: Rokiczańska. Fl. in 1300s; 3rd wife of Kazimierz also known as Casimir III the Great, king of Poland (r. 1333–1370); children: possibly Elizabeth (who m. Boguslaw V of Slupsk); Cunegunde; Anna. Casimir III was 1st m. to Aldona of Lithuania and Adelaide of Hesse; Jadwiga of Glogow was his 4th wife.

KRYSZAK, Mary Olszewski (1875–1945). Polish-American leader and state legislator. Name variations: changed spelling of married name from Kryshak to Kryszak after divorce. Born July 27, 1875, in Milwaukee, WI; died July 16, 1945, in Milwaukee; dau. of Constantine Olszewski (railroad worker) and Rozalia (Martyn) Olszewski; m. Anton L. Kryshak (cigar manufacturer), May 23, 1900 (div.); children: 2 daughters, 1 son. ❖ The 1st woman legislator from Milwaukee County, worked as an assistant manager and bookkeeper for Milwaukee Polish-language daily *Nowiny Polskie* (1908–22); founded (1912) and served as president (until 1945) of St. Catherine Society, local lodge of Zwiazek Polek w Ameryce (Polish Women's Alliance of America); held seat in Assembly of WI state legislature (1928–45).

KRYUCHKOVA, Maria (1988—). Russian gymnast. Born July 7, 1988, in Rostov-on-Don, Russia. ❖ Won a bronze medal for team all-around at Athens Olympics (2004).

KRYZHANOVSKAIA, Vera Ivanovna (1861–1924). Russian novelist and short-story writer. Name variations: Vera Kryzhanovskaya or Kryjanovskaya; (pseudonym) J.W. Rochester. Born 1861 in Russia; died of TB, 1924, in Latvia; m. Sergei Semënov. ❖ With husband, attended spiritualist salons and claimed to receive communications from English poet John Wilmot (1647–80); novels, influenced by spiritualist beliefs, were extremely popular and trans. into several languages; wrote over 50 occult and historical novels and novel cycles, including *L'élixir de la vie* (1901) and *Les mages* (1902).

KRZESINSKA, Elzbieta (1934—). Polish track-and-field athlete. Name variations: Elzbieta Krzesinska-Dunska or Dunska-Krzesinska; Ella Krzesinska. Born Nov 11, 1934, in Poland. ❖ Won a gold medal at Melbourne Olympics (1956), setting a world record at 20′10, and a silver medal at Rome Olympics (1960), both in the long jump.

KSCHESSINSKA, Mathilde (1872–1971). See *Kshesinskaia, Matilda.*

KSENIA, Ksenya or Ksenija. *Variant of Xenia.*

KSHESINSKAIA, Matilda (1872–1971). Russian ballerina. Name variations: many transliterations from the Russian, the most common being Mathilde or Matilde Kchessinska or Kchesshinskaya, Kscheschinska or Kcsheschinskaya, Ksheshinskaya; Kshesinskaia or Ksheshinskaia, Kshessinskaya or Kshessinskaia; Princess Romanovsky-Krassinsky (after 1935). Pronunciation: Ke-SHES-in-sky-ya. Born Matilda Feliksovna Kshesinskaia, Aug 19, 1872 (o.s.) in Ligovo, Russia; died Dec 6, 1971, in Paris, France; dau. of Feliks Ivanovich Kshesinskii (Krzhesinskii-Nechui), a ballet dancer, and Julia Kshesinskaia; attended Imperial Ballet School, 1880–90; m. Grand Duke Andrei Vladimirovich, 1921; children: Vladimir (b. 1902). ❖ One of the foremost classical Russian ballerinas between 1890 and 1917, was a member of the Maryinsky Theater (1890–1917), as ballerina (1892–93), as prima ballerina (1893–95), as prima ballerina assoluta (1895–1904), as guest artist (1905–17); was mistress of the future tsar of Russia, Nicholas II (1892–94); danced in Vienna (1903), Monte Carlo (1895, 1912), Paris (1908, 1909), London (1911, 1912) and Budapest (1912); lived abroad near Monte Carlo (1920–28) and in Paris (1929–71); taught ballet (1929–64). Her best known and favorite roles were in *La fille mal gardée, La fille du Pharaon, Esmeralda, La Bayadere, Le Talisman* and *Swan Lake.* ❖ See also (under name Princess Romanovsky-Krassinsky) *Dancing in Petersburg: The Memoirs of Kschessinska* (1960); and *Women in World History.*

KSIAZKIEWICZ, Malgorzata (1967—). Polish shooter. Name variations: Malgorzata Ksiazkiewicz-Kubka. Born May 1967 in Poland.

❖ At Barcelona Olympics, won a bronze medal in smallbore rifle 3 positions (1992).

KUAN, Lady (1262–1319). *See Guan Daosheng.*

KUAN FU-JEN (1262–1319). *See Guan Daosheng.*

KUAN TAO-SHENG (1262–1319). *See Guan Daosheng.*

KUBICKOVA-POSNEROVA, Jana (1945—). Czech gymnast. Name variations: Jana Posnerova. Born Jan 1945. ❖ Won a silver medal at Tokyo Olympics (1964) and a silver medal at Mexico City Olympics (1968), both in team all-around.

KUBKA, Malgorzata (1967—). *See Ksiazkiewicz, Malgorzata.*

KÜBLER-ROSS, Elisabeth (1926–2004). Swiss psychiatrist and thanatologist. Born Elisabeth Kübler in Zurich, Switzerland, July 8, 1926; died Aug 24, 2004, in Scottsdale, Arizona; dau. of Ernest Kübler (businessman) and Emma (Villager) Kübler; University of Zurich Medical School, MD, 1957; m. Emanuel Ross, 1958 (div.); children: Kenneth; Barbara. ❖ Pioneer in field of thanatology, whose groundbreaking work with dying patients transformed Western medicine's approach toward the terminally ill, affected public policy and scholarly research, and radically altered Western society's attitudes toward death and dying; moved to US (1958); worked as rotating intern at Community Hospital, Glen Cove, NY (1958–59); became US citizen (1961); was a research fellow at Manhattan State Hospital (1959–61), resident at Montefiore Hospital, the Bronx (1961–62) and fellow in psychiatry, Psychopathic Hospital, University of Colorado Medical School (1962–65); was an assistant professor in psychiatry, Billings Hospital, University of Chicago (1965–70); published *On Death and Dying* in which she identified the 5 "stages" of dying: denial, anger, bargaining, depression, and acceptance (1969); served as medical director of Family Service and Mental Health Center of South Cook Co., Chicago Heights, IL (1970–73); was president and chair of board of Shanti Nilaya Growth and Health Center, Escondido, CA (1977–83); focused efforts on AIDS (1980s); moved to Virginia (1983), then Scottsdale, AZ (1994). Writings include *Death: The Final Stages of Growth* (1975), *To Live Until We Say Goodbye* (1978), *Working It Through* (1981), *Living With Death and Dying* (1981), *Remember the Secret* (1981), *On Children and Death* (1985), *AIDS: The Ultimate Challenge* (1988) and *On Life After Death* (1991). ❖ See also Derek Gill, *Quest: The Life of Elisabeth Kübler-Ross* (Harper & Row, 1980); and *Women in World History.*

KUBRICK, Ruth Sobotka (1925–1967). *See Sobotka, Ruth.*

KUCHER, Karol (1932–2004). *See Kennedy, Karol.*

KUCHINSKAYA, Natalia (1949—). Soviet gymnast. Name variations: Natalya. Born Mar 1949 in USSR. ❖ Won USSR championships (1965, 1968), Tiflis Invitational and USSR Cup (1966), and USSR Spartakiade (1967); at World championships, won gold medals for bars, beam, and floor, silver medals for team and indiv. all-around, and a bronze for vault (1966); at European championships, won silver medals for beam and floor (1967); at Mexico City Olympics, won gold medals for beam and team all-around and bronze medals for floor and all-around indiv. (1968).

KUCKHOFF, Greta (1902–1981). German resistance leader and politician. Born Greta Lorke, Dec 14, 1902, in Frankfurt an der Oder, Germany; died 1981; studied economics in Berlin and Würzburg (1924–27); attended University of Wisconsin, Madison (1927–29); m. Adam Kuckhoff (1887–1943, writer and leader of Red Orchestra), 1937. ❖ Member of anti-Nazi resistance organization "Red Orchestra" (crucial military information radioed to Moscow by the Red Orchestra network may well have saved the Soviet Union and changed the course of WWII); arrested with husband (Sept 12, 1942), received death sentence, but while his was carried out (Aug 5, 1943), hers was reduced to 10 years' hard labor; liberated from Waldheim penitentiary (May 1945); joined German Communist Party (1945), which became the Socialist Unity Party (1946); appointed to German Economic Commission in Soviet Occupation Zone of Germany (1948); became a division chief of newly created Foreign Ministry of German Democratic Republic (GDR or East Germany, 1949); elected to People's Chamber (1949), holding seat until 1958; was president of the German Bank of Issue, a post that entitled her to a vote in Council of Ministers of the GDR (1950–58); became a vice president of German Peace Council (1958); appointed president of German-British Society (1963); published memoirs (1972). ❖ See also *Women in World History.*

KUCMANOVA, Eva (1946—). *See Suranova-Kucmanova, Eva.*

KUCZINSKI, Ruth (1907–2000). Communist spy. Name variations: Ruth Kuczinsky or Kuczynski; Ruth Beurton; Ruth Werner; (code name) Sonja or Red Sonia, Red Sonja, or Red Sonya. Born Ursula Ruth Kuczinski in Berlin, Germany, May 15, 1907; died in Berlin, July 7, 2000; dau. of Dr. Robert René Kuczinski (well-known economist); sister of Juergen Kuczinski, also a spy; m. Rudolf Hamburger, 1930 (div.); m. Leon (Len) Beurton (British Communist), 1938; children: 2. ❖ Captain in the Soviet army and spy known as Red Sonya, one of the most successful in the history of espionage, who transmitted the secret of the atomic bomb to the Soviet Union; joined the Communist Party (1924); married Rudolf Hamburger and went with him to China (1930); recruited by Richard Sorge and sent to Moscow for training; worked in Peking and Poland; became a captain in Red Army; sent to Switzerland (1938) where she married Leon Beurton, a British Communist, after an earlier divorce from Hamburger; went to England with her children as a German refugee and began transmitting information to Moscow (spring 1941); sent large amounts of information including vital facts from Dr. Klaus Fuchs which allowed the Soviet Union to construct an atomic bomb after WWII; left Great Britain (1950) after serving as a spy for 20 years; retired in East Germany where she was joined by husband; as Ruth Werner, wrote a book about her life, *Sonja's Rapport,* which sold over half a million copies. Awarded Order of the Red Banner for meritorious service to the Soviet Union (1937). ❖ See also *Women in World History.*

KUDERIKOVA, Marie (1921–1943). Czech resistance leader. Born Mar 24, 1921, in Vnorovy-Hodonin, Czechoslovakia; executed in Breslau, Mar 26, 1943. ❖ Anti-Nazi activist and factory worker, was leader of the illegal youth organization of Czechoslovak Communist Party; arrested in Brno (Dec 5, 1941), was transferred to Breslau (now Wroclaw, Poland) and sentenced to death by Nazi People's Court. ❖ See also *Women in World History.*

KUDREVA, Natalya (1942—). Soviet volleyball player. Born June 1942 in USSR. ❖ At Munich Olympics, won a gold medal in team competition (1972).

KUDRUN. *Variant of Gudrun.*

KUEHN, Anke (1981—). German field-hockey player. Name variations: Anke Kühn. Born Feb 28, 1981, in Germany. ❖ Won a team gold medal at Athens Olympics (2004).

KUEHN-LOHS, Gabriele (1957—). East German rower. Name variations: Gabriele Kühn-Lohs. Born Mar 11, 1957, in East Germany. ❖ At Montreal Olympics, won a gold medal in coxed fours (1976); at Moscow Olympics, won a gold medal in coxed eights (1980).

KUEHNE, Kelli (1977—). American golfer. Born May 11, 1977, in Dallas, TX; attended University of Texas; m. Jay Thomas Humphrey (football player), 2000. ❖ Was one of only two players in USGA history to win the US Jr. Girls championship (1994) and US Women's Amateur in successive years (1995); also won US Women's Amateur (1996) and British Amateur (1996), only golfer in history to win those 2 championships in same year; won LPGA Corning Classic and tied for 2nd at Jamie Farr Kroger Classic (1999).

KUEHNE, Rita (1947—). East German runner. Name variations: Rita Kühne. Born Jan 1947 in East Germany. ❖ At Munich Olympics, won a gold medal in 4 x 400-meter relay (1972).

KUEHNEMUND, Jan (1961—). American musician. Name variations: Vixen. Born Jan Lynn Kuehnemund on Nov 11, 1961, in St. Paul, MN. ❖ Founding member, lead guitarist and backup singer for all-girl pop-metal band Vixen, helped formed band in Los Angeles (1980); with Vixen, appeared in film *Hardbodies* (1984); saw numerous personnel changes before forming solid lineup (1987); with group, signed contract with EMI (1988) and released debut album, *Vixen* (1988), which went gold and included Top-40 hits, "Cryin'" and "Edge of a Broken Heart"; released *Rev It Up* (1990), which included hit, "How Much Love"; after Vixen split up (early 1990s), regrouped with minor changes to release *Tangerine* (1998), then disbanded again, joined Janet Gardner and Roxy Petrucci to reform Vixen with original lineup (2001).

KUENZEL, Claudia (1978—). German cross-country skier. Name variations: Claudia Künzel. Born Jan 2, 1978, in Oberwiesenthal, Germany; m. Trond Nystad. ❖ Won a gold medal for the 4 x 5 km relay at Salt Lake City Olympics (2002) and silver medals for sprint and 4 x 5 km relay at Torino Olympic (2006).

KUEPER, Ursula (1937—). East German swimmer. Name variations: Ursula Küper. Born Nov 28, 1937, in Germany. ❖ At Rome Olympics, won a bronze medal in 4 x 100-meter medley relay (1960).

KUEPPERS, Anneliese (1929—). See Küppers, Anneliese.

KUESKA, Beata (1974—). See Sokolowska, Beata.

KUFFNER, Baroness (1898–1980). See Lempicka, Tamara de.

KUGLER, Anna Sarah (1856–1930). American medical missionary. Born April 19, 1856, in Ardmore, PA; died July 26, 1930, in Guntur, South India; dau. of Charles Kugler and Harriet (Sheaff) Kugler. ❖ Served as assistant physician at State Hospital for Insane in Norristown, PA (1880–83); intent on being a medical missionary in India, arrived at Guntur Mission as only woman physician in Madras Presidency (Nov 29, 1883); appointed by Lutheran Women's Missionary Convention as medical missionary (1885), opened dispensary (1886) and 50-bed hospital (1898); oversaw openings of maternity and surgical sections, children's ward, chapel, and nurses' home; published memoir *Guntur Mission Hospital* (1928).

KUHLMAN, Kathryn (1907–1976). American evangelist. Born May 9, 1907, in Concordia, Missouri; died Feb 20, 1976, in Tulsa, OK; dau. of Joseph Kuhlman and Emma (Walkenhorst) Kuhlman; m. Burroughs Waltrip (evangelical preacher), Oct 1938 (div. 1948); no children. ❖ Nationally known evangelical preacher whose ministry across US spanned 5 decades, underwent a religious conversion at a Baptist revival meeting at 14; in Oregon, helped evangelist sister and brother-in-law lead revival meetings (1923–28); popularity led to a 5-year evangelist tour of western US; settled briefly in Pueblo, CO (1933), then moved to Denver where she converted a warehouse into a center for worship services, called the Kuhlman Revival Tabernacle, and became a household name; married an evangelist (1938), but lost popularity when her congregation learned that he had abandoned his wife and children before his divorce; toured nationwide with husband for several years, but the scandal hindered success; separated (1944) and struggled to reestablish herself; hosted weekly radio prayer program in Franklin, PA (1946), which was soon picked up across Pennsylvania; began to include a healing service (1947); though she did not claim to actually perform healing miracles, saw herself as a vessel through which God acted to cure the ill; established a following strong enough to open a temple of her own in Pittsburgh, and preached and performed healing sessions; steadily built a national following while defending herself against growing criticism from other leading evangelists (1950s); brought her revival sessions to Los Angeles, CA, where she preached regularly until 1975; began own weekly program on CBS-TV (1975); an increasingly visible figure, appeared on talk shows and was profiled in mainstream magazines; ordained by the Evangelical Church Alliance (1968). ❖ See also Jamie Buckingham, *Daughter of Destiny: Kathryn Kuhlman . . . her story* (Logos, 1976); Wayne Warner, *Kathryn Kuhlman: The Woman Behind the Miracles* (Servant, 1993); and *Women in World History*.

KÜHN, Anke (1981—). See Kuehn, Anke.

KUHN, Irene Corbally (1898–1995). American journalist. Born Irene Corbally, Jan 15, 1898, in NY City; died in Concord, MA, Dec 30, 1995; dau. of Patrick J. Corbally and Josephine (Connor) Corbally; attended Packard Business School, Marymount College (Tarrytown-on-the-Hudson), and Extension Division, Columbia University; m. Bert L. Kuhn, June 11, 1922 (died 1926); children: Rene Leilani (b. 1923). ❖ Foreign correspondent and feature writer (1920s–30s), started out as reporter on *Syracuse Herald* (1920); wrote for *New York Daily News* (1920), *Chicago Tribune* (European edition, Paris, 1921–22), *Evening Star* (Shanghai, 1922–26); served as a foreign correspondent for Hearst Wire Service and International News Service, Honolulu and Shanghai (1923–26); worked as broadcaster, station KRC Shanghai (1924); wrote for *New York Daily Mirror* (1926), *New York Daily News* (1927–28, 1930), *Honolulu Star-Bulletin* (1929–30); was a scriptwriter for 20th Century-Fox (1931–32), MGM (1932–33), Paramount (1939); worked as feature writer, *New York World-Telegram* (1933–35); was an executive and commentator, NBC (1940–49); was a columnist for King Features Syndicate (1953–69), then Columbia Features (1970). Gathered a number of "1sts": the 1st woman to broadcast in the Orient, probably the 1st female announcer in radio, the 1st woman vice-president of Overseas Press Club, the 1st individual to broadcast from a US Navy vessel, the 1st person to broadcast from liberated Shanghai, the 1st woman reporter sent to Manila, and the 1st woman to write for the *Stars and Stripes*. ❖ See also memoirs *Assigned to Adventure* (Grosset, 1938); and *Women in World History*.

KUHN, Maggie (1905–1995). American political activist. Born Margaret Eliza Kuhn in Buffalo, NY, Aug 31, 1905; died April 22, 1995, in Philadelphia, PA; dau. of Samuel Kuhn (businessman) and Minnie (Kooman) Kuhn; Flora Stone Mather College, BA, 1927; never married. ❖ Founder of Gray Panthers, was an outspoken pacifist, political activist, and advocate of rights of older Americans; served as assistant business and professional secretary, YWCA-Cleveland (1928–30) and YWCA-Philadelphia (1930–41); served as program coordinator for YWCA's USO Division (1941–48); joined staff of National Alliance of Unitarian Women (1948–50); became member of Department of Social Education and Action of Presbyterian Church in USA (1950–65); worked as program executive for the (Presbyterian) Church's Council on Church and Race (1969); formed ad-hoc activist organization, Consultation of Older Persons (1970); founded political action group, Gray Panthers (1971); held 1st Gray Panthers National Convention (1975); served on President Jimmy Carter's Commission on Mental Health (1978–80). ❖ See also autobiography *No Stone Unturned: The Life and Times of Maggie Kuhn* (1991); and *Women in World History*.

KÜHN-LOHS, Gabriele (1957—). See Kuehn-Lohs, Gabriele.

KÜHNE, Rita (1947—). See Kuehne, Rita.

KUHNT, Irina (1968—). German field-hockey player. Born Jan 18, 1968, in Germany. ❖ At Barcelona Olympics, won a silver medal in team competition (1992).

KUI YUANYUAN (1981—). Chinese gymnast. Born June 23, 1981, in Beijing, China. ❖ At World championships, won a gold medal in floor exercises (1996), and bronze medals for balance bar and team all-around (1997); won a silver medal for balance bar at World Cup (1998); at Sydney Olympics, won a bronze medal for team all-around (2000).

KUIPERS, Ellen. Dutch field-hockey player. Born in Netherlands. ❖ Won a team bronze medal at Atlanta Olympics (1996).

KUKLEVA, Galina (1972—). See Koukleva, Galina.

KUKUCK, Felicitas (1914–2001). German composer and teacher. Born Nov 2, 1914, in Hamburg, Germany; died in 2001; taught at home by mother who was a singer; studied at Hochschule für Musik in Berlin, 1935–39; studied composition with Paul Hindemith. ❖ A German Christian of partially Jewish ancestry, lost her teaching position and freedom during Nazi years; following war, went on to become one of Germany's most respected composers of music for Protestant church services; influenced by the choral traditions of German musical history, wrote a Christmas Mass and a Reformation Cantata; conducted world premiere of her church opera, *The Man Moses* (1986).

KULAKOVA, Galina (1942—). Russian cross-country skier. Name variations: Galina Kulakowa or Koulakova. Born April 29, 1942, in Votkinsk, Russia; m. Alexander Tikhonov (biathlete). ❖ One of the best women skiers in history, won a bronze medal for 3 x 5 km relay and a silver medal for 5 km at Grenoble Olympics (1968); won gold medals for 10 km, 5 km and 3 x 5 km at Sapporo Olympics (1972); won a gold medal for 4 x 5 km relay and a bronze for 10 km at Innsbruck Olympics (1976); won a silver medal for 4 x 5 km relay at Lake Placid Olympics (1980); at World championships, won gold medals (1970, 1974), silver medals (1978, 1982), and bronze medals (1970, 1978).

KULCHUNOVA, Mariya (1958—). See Pinigina-Kulchunova, Mariya.

KULCSAR, Anita (1976—). Hungarian handball player. Name variations: Kulcsár. Born Oct 2, 1976, in Hungary. ❖ Won a team silver medal at Sydney Olympics (2000).

KULCSAR, Ilse (1902–1973). Austrian resistance leader and writer. Name variations: Ilse Barea. Born Ilse Pollak in Vienna, Austria, 1902; died 1973; m. Leopold Kulcsar; m. Arturo Barea. ❖ With husband Leopold, was a leading member of the small but influential Gruppe Funke ("Spark Group"), a splinter organization that, with rise of Fascism, hoped to inject a more militant spirit into a seemingly paralyzed Social Democratic movement. ❖ See also memoir *Vienna: Legend and Reality* (1966); and *Women in World History*.

KULESZA, Beata (1974—). See Sokolowska, Beata.

KULESZA, Kasia (1976—). Polish-Canadian synchronized swimmer. Born Aug 29, 1976, in Warsaw, Poland. ❖ Moved to Canada at age 7; won a team silver medal at Atlanta Olympics (1996).

KULICHKOVA, Natalya (1949—). See Sokolova-Kulichkova, Natalya.

KULIKOWSKI, Theresa (1980—). American gymnast. Born Jan 23, 1980, in Tacoma, WA. ❖ Won a bronze medal for team all-around at World championships (1995).

KULISCIOFF, Anna (c. 1854–1925). Ukrainian-born political activist. Name variations: Anja Kulisciov. Pronunciation: KOO-lee-SHOF. Born Anja Moiseevna Rozenstein in Moskaja, southern Ukraine, Jan 9, c. 1854 (the most reliable date, though some sources cite 1853 and 1857); died in Milan, Italy, Dec 29, 1925; dau. of Moisej Rozenstein (merchant); mother unknown; became 1st woman admitted to Exact Science Department of Zurich Polytechnic (1871); enrolled with Faculty of Medicine in Bern (1882), and moved 2 years later to University of Naples; studied in Turin, Pavia, and Padua (1885–88); m. Petr Makarevich, 1873; lived with Andrea Costa, then Filippo Turati (1857–1932), her companion for more than 30 years; children: (with Costa) daughter Andreina (b. Dec 8, 1881). ❖ Renowned in Italy for her tenacious battle for the emancipation of Italian women, was also important in founding the Italian Socialist Party; began as an anarchist before turning to socialism; left Russia for Zurich (1871); returned to Russia (1873); immigrated to Switzerland (1877); moved with Andrea Costa to Paris (1877); arrested and expelled from France (1878); arrested again in Florence (Oct 1878) and expelled from Italy; returned to Lugano (1880); expelled again by police authorities and returned to Switzerland (1881); lived in Naples (1884); with Turati, joined the Socialist League of Milan (1889); co-founded and contributed to the fledgling magazine *Critica Sociale* and founded the Female Section of the Chamber of Work in Milan (1891); lectured at Geneva Congress, where the Socialist Party of Italian Workers was born (1892); promoted a bill for women and children's working conditions (1897–1900); arrested again in Milan (1898); lectured to the Rome Congress (1900); promoted a campaign for "great institutional reforms" at Florence Congress (1908); fought within Socialist Party for women's right to vote (1910); founded magazine *La difesa delle lavoratrici* and National Union of Socialist Women (1912). ❖ See also (in Italian) Maria Casalini, *La Signora del Socialismo italiano: Vita di Anna Kulisciof* (Roma: Editori Riuniti, 1987); and *Women in World History.*

KULMAN, Elisabeth (1808–1825). Russian poet and translator. Name variations: Elisaveta Borisovna Kúl'man or Kúlman; Elizabeth Kulman; Elisabeth Kulmann. Born Elisaveta Borisovna Kúlman in July 5, 1808, in St. Petersburg, Russia; died of consumption, Nov 19, 1825, at 17, in St. Petersburg; dau. of a Russian officer and a German mother; tutored by Karl Friedrich von Grossheinrich. ❖ Received tutoring despite family poverty and learned German, French, Italian, Latin, Church Slavonic, classical and modern Greek, English, Spanish, and Portuguese; translated Russian poems into these languages and 18th-Century Russian tragedies into German; rewrote Kievan folk epics in modern Russian and composed series of poems in spirit of lost Greek poet Corinna; praised by Goethe.

KULMANN, Elisabeth (1808–1825). See Kulman, Elisabeth.

KULP, Nancy (1921–1991). American actress. Born Nancy Jane Kulp, Aug 28, 1921, in Harrisburg, PA; died Feb 3, 1991, in Palm Desert, CA; m. Charles Dacus, 1951 (div.). ❖ Best known for her role as Jane Hathaway on "The Beverly Hillbillies"; films include *The Model and the Marriage Broker, Shane, Sabrina, Forever Darling, The Three Faces of Eve, The Parent Trap, Who's Minding the Store?* and *The Night of the Grizzly;* ran unsuccessfully for Congress in PA's 9th District as a Democrat (1984).

KULTHUM, Umm (c. 1898–1975). See Um Kalthum.

KUM, Matilda (c. 1854–1915). See Lo Keong, Matilda.

KUMARATUNGA, Chandrika Bandaranaike (1945—). President of the Democratic Socialist Republic of Sri Lanka. Name variations: Chandra Bandaranaike. Born June 29, 1945, in Colombo, Sri Lanka; dau. of S.W.R.D. Bandaranaike (founder of Sri Lanka Freedom Party and prime minister of Sri Lanka from 1956 until his assassination, Sept 26, 1959) and Sirimavo Bandaranaike (b. 1916, 1st elected woman prime minister in the world); studied for LLB; awarded PhD in development economics and degree in political science at University of Paris; m. Vijaya Kumaratunga (leading opposition figure and film idol), Feb 20, 1978 (assassinated Feb 16, 1988); children: daughter, Yasodara Kumaratunga; son, Vimukti Kumaratunga. ❖ Both father and husband assassinated; after serving as president of Sri Lanka Mahajana Party (SLMP), emerged as a leader of People's Alliance (early 1990s); was elected Sri Lanka's prime minister (Aug 1994) and a few months later (Nov), became the 1st female president of Sri Lanka, having campaigned with a promise to stop the ethnic civil war between the Sinhalese, who are a majority of the population, and the Tamils (minority); though wounded in an explosion during a suicide bombing attack at a campaign rally, won a 2nd term as president (1999–2005), but fighting continued in a war that has claimed thousands of lives. ❖ See also *Women in World History.*

KUMBERNUSS, Astrid (1970—). German shot putter. Born Feb 5, 1970, in Grevesmuhlen, Germany. ❖ Won a gold medal at Atlanta Olympics (1996) and a bronze medal at Sydney Olympics (2000); won gold medals at World championships (1995, 1997, 1999) and a gold medal at European championships (1990).

KUMIN, Maxine (1925—). American poet and children's writer. Born June 6, 1925, in Germantown, PA; attended Radcliffe College; m. Victor Kumin (engineering consultant), 1946; children: 2 daughters, 1 son. ❖ Taught at several universities and served as poetry consultant to Library of Congress; wrote poetry, novels, children's books, and essays; poetry includes *Halfway* (1961), *The Nightmare Factory* (1970), *Up Country: Poems of New England* (1972), *House, Bridge, Fountain, Gate* (1975), *The Long Approach* (1985), and *Looking for Luck* (1992); short fiction includes *Why Can't We Live Together Like Civilized Human Beings?* (1982); novels include *Through Doom of Love* (1965), *The Passions of Uxport* (1968), *The Abduction* (1971) and *The Designated Heir* (1974); was a close friend of Anne Sexton (1957–74). Awarded Pulitzer Prize for *Up Country* (1973).

KUMMER, Clare (1873–1958). American playwright. Born Clare Rodman Beecher, Jan 9, 1873, in NYC; died April 21, 1958, in Carmel, CA; cousin of William Gillette (actor); m. Frederic Arnold Kummer (playwright, div.); m. Arthur Henry. ❖ Came to prominence as a songwriter with "Dearie" (1906); plays include *The Opera Ball* (with Sydney Rosenfeld), *Good Gracious Annabelle!* (adapted for film as *The Affairs of Annabelle*), *A Successful Calamity, The Rescuing Angel, Be Calm Camilla, Bridges, The Choir Rehearsal, Roxie, The Light of Duxbury, The Mountain Man, One Kiss* (from the French), *Annie Dear, Madame Pompadour, Amourette, Her Master's Voice, Three Waltzes* (with Rowland Leigh), *Spring Thaw* and *Many Happy Returns.*

KUMYSH, Marina (1964—). Soviet volleyball player. Born Dec 27, 1964, in USSR. ❖ At Seoul Olympics, won a gold medal in team competition (1988).

KUNCEWICZ, Maria (1899–1989). Polish writer. Name variations: Maria Kuncewiczowa or Kuncewicowa. Born Maria Szczepanska, Oct 30, 1899 (some sources state 1897), in Samara, Russia; died 1989; dau. of Róza Szczepanska (headmaster); studied French philology at University of Nancy, Polish philology at University of Warsaw and Cracow's Jagiellonian University, and voice at Paris and Warsaw conservatories; m. Jerzy Kuncewicz (1893–1984, author and lawyer); 1 son. ❖ One of interwar Poland's most respected writers, whose essentially autobiographical works, particularly the novel *Cudzoziemka (The Stranger),* are studies of alienation and otherness, published 1st story in journal *Pro Arte et Studio* (1918); by mid-1920s, was a well-known writer and vice-president of Polish section of PEN; published stories which appeared in the collection *Przymierze z dzieckiem (An Alliance with a Child,* 1927) as well as 1st novel, *Twarz mezczyzny (The Face of a Man,* 1928); published *Cudzoziemka* (1935); created Poland's 1st radio serial (1938), *Dni powszednie panstwa Kowalskich* (The Ordinary Days of the Kowalskis), followed by *Kowalscy sie odnalezli* (The Kowalskis Have Returned); other writings include *Serce kraju* (The Heart of the Country), *W domu i w Polsce* (At Home and in Poland), and *Miasto Heroda: Notatki Palestynskie* (The City of Herod: Palestinian Notes); fled German-occupied Poland for Paris (1939), then England; published anthology, *Modern Polish Prose* (1945); remained in England when Communists ruled Poland (1945–48); moved to US (1956); published anthology *The Modern Polish Mind* (1962); taught Polish literature at University of Chicago (1963–71). Received Literary Award of City of Warsaw (1936), "golden laurel" of Polish Academy of Literature (1937), Wlodzimierz Pietrzak Award (1969) and National Award (1st Class, 1974 and 1978); awarded Medal of Kosciuszko Foundation (1971). ❖ See also autobiographies *Fantomy* (Phantoms, 1971) and *Natura* (Nature, 1975); and *Women in World History.*

KUNEGUNDA. See Cunegunde or Cunigunde.

KUNEGUNDE. Variant of Cunigunde.

KUNEHILDA (d. 741). See Sunnichild.

KUNG, Madame H.H. (1890–1973). *See Song Ailing.*

KUNIGK, Gretchen (1919–1994). *See Fraser, Gretchen.*

KUNIGUNDE. *Variant of Cunigunde.*

KUNIN, Madeleine (1933—). American politician. Born Madeleine May, Sept 28, 1933, in Zurich, Switzerland; dau. of Ferdinand May (Grman-Jewish shoe importer) and Renee Bloch May; University of Massachusetts, BA in history; University of Vermont, MA in English literature; Columbia University, MA in journalism; m. Dr. Arthur Kunin, 1961 (div. 1995); children: 4. ❖ With mother and brother, fled the Nazi threat and moved to NY (1940); grew up in Pittsfield, MA; moved to Vermont and was a reporter for *Burlington Free Press;* as a Democrat, was elected lieutenant governor (1978, 1980); became the 1st woman governor of Vermont, serving for 3-terms (1984–91); served as US deputy US secretary of education (1993–96) and ambassador to Switzerland (1996–99). ❖ See also memoir *Living a Political Life* (1994).

KUNISCH, Kornelia (1959—). East German handball player. Born Oct 17, 1959, in East Germany. ❖ At Moscow Olympics, won a bronze medal in team competition (1980).

KUNKE, Steffi (1908–1942). Austrian educator and resistance leader. Born Stefanie Jellinek in Vienna, Austria, Dec 26, 1908; died of typhus in Auschwitz, Dec 1942; dau. of Marie (Ourednik) Jellinek and Ignaz Jellinek; m. Hans Kunke (1906–1940, Socialist activist). ❖ Teacher who, with husband, was involved in anti-fascist underground work in Vienna during Nazi occupation; with husband, became increasingly active in educational work of Young Socialist movement (early 1930s); also led the youth department of the Revolutionary Socialist underground; by 1938, headed a well-organized underground Socialist youth movement in Vienna and surrounding province of Lower Austria with husband; arrested (May 1938) and sent to Lichtenburg concentration camp while husband was transported to Buchenwald where he would commit suicide (Oct 1940); transferred to women's camp of Ravensbrück, then Auschwitz. ❖ See also *Women in World History.*

KUNTOLA, Hilkka. *See Riihivuori, Hilkka.*

KUNTSCH, Margaretha Susanna von (1651–1716). German poet. Born 1651 in Germany; died 1716; children: 14 (but only 1 daughter survived). ❖ Wrote laments on deaths of children which were published posthumously by grandson.

KUNTZ, Florence (1969—). French lawyer and politician. Born June 9, 1969, in Epinal, France. ❖ Elected to Rhône–Alpes Regional Council (1998); representing Group for a Europe of Democracies and Diversities (EDD), elected to 5th European Parliament (1999–2004).

KUO YI-HANG (1975—). Taiwanese weightlifter. Name variations: Kuo Yi-hang. Born 1975 in Pingtung, Taiwan. ❖ Representing Chinese Taipei, won a bronze medal for 69–75kg at Sydney Olympics (2000).

KUPER, Hilda B. (1911–1992). Social anthropologist. Name variations: Hilda Beemer. Born Hilda Beemer, Aug 23, 1911, in Bulawayo, Rhodesia (now known as Zimbabwe); died 1992; dau. of Joseph Beemer from Lithuania and Antoinette Renner Beemer from Vienna, both Jewish immigrants; Witwatersrand University, BA in anthropology; London School of Economics, MA and PhD in social anthropology; m. Leo Kuper (lawyer and sociologist), 1936; children: 2 daughters. ❖ Known particularly for work on the Swazi, began association with Swaziland and the country's royal family (1934) and published 1st books about the Swazi (*An African Aristocracy* and *The Uniform of Colour,* both 1947); a friend of King Sobhuza II of Swaziland for about 50 years, was appointed his official biographer (1972) and published *Sobhuza II, Ngwenyama and King of Swaziland* (1978); served academic career at universities of Witwatersrand (1940–45), Natal (1959–62), and California in Los Angeles (1963–78). Other works include *The Swazi* (1952), *The Shona* (1955), *Indian People of Natal* (1960) and *A South African Kingdom* (1986).

KÜPER, Ursula (1937—). *See Kueper, Ursula.*

KUPERNIK, Tatiana (1874–1952). *See Shchepkina-Kupernik, Tatiana.*

KUPETS, Courtney (1986—). American gymnast. Born July 27, 1986, in Bedford, TX; sister of Ashley Kupets (gymnast). ❖ Won gold medal for uneven bars at World championships (2002); won US nationals all-around (2003); tore left Achille's tendon and had to withdraw from World championship competition (2003); won a bronze medal for uneven bars and a silver medal for team all-around at Athens Olympics (2004).

KUPFERNAGEL, Hanka (1964—). German cyclist. Born Mar 19, 1964, in Gera, Thüringen, Germany. ❖ Won World Cups (1999, 2000); won a silver medal for indiv. road race at Sydney Olympics (2000); won World championships for road racing (2000, 2001).

KÜPPERS, Anneliese (1929—). West German equestrian. Name variations: Anneliese Küppers-Schaurte; Anneliese Kueppers-Schaurte. Born Aug 1929 in Germany. ❖ At Melbourne Olympics, won a silver medal in team dressage (1956).

KURAGINA, Olga (1959—). Soviet pentathlete. Born April 21, 1959, in USSR. ❖ At Moscow Olympics, won a bronze medal in pentathlon (1980).

KURAHASHI, Yumiko (1935—). Japanese novelist and short-story writer. Born 1935 in Shikoku, Japan; received degree in French from Meiji University. ❖ Writings, which range from realism to satire and surrealism and draw on Japanese folk tales, Greek myth, and Noh tradition, include *Partei* (1960), *A Dark Travel* (1963), *The Adventures of Sumiyakist Q* (1969), *The Floating Bridge of Dreams* (1971), *A Castle Among Castles* (1980), *Exchange* (1989) and *The Woman with the Flying Head and Other Stories* (1997).

KURBAKOVA, Tatiana (1986—). Russian rhythmic gymnast. Born Aug 7, 1986, in USSR. ❖ Won 3 group competition events at World championships (2003); won team all-around gold medal at Athens Olympics (2004).

KURBATOVA-GRUYCHEVA, Stoyanka (1955—). Bulgarian rower. Name variations: Stoyanka Gruycheva. Born Mar 18, 1955, in Bulgaria. ❖ Won a gold medal at Montreal Olympics (1976) and a bronze medal at Moscow Olympics (1980), both in coxless pairs.

KURGAPKINA, Ninel (1929—). Soviet ballet dancer. Name variations: Ninel Alexandrovna Kurgapkina. Born Feb 13, 1929, in Leningrad, Russia; studied with Agrippina Vaganova. ❖ A leading prima ballerina with the Kirov Ballet for 25 years, joined the Kirov (1947), where she was noted for performances in Russian classics as well as Western European classics, including *Giselle* and *Swan Lake;* appointed director of the Vaganova School (1972).

KURI, Rosa Guraieb (b. 1931). *See Guraieb Kuri, Rosa.*

KURISHIMA, Sumiko (1902–1987). Japanese actress and dancer. Born Mar 15, 1902, in Shibuya, Tokyo, Japan; died Aug 16, 1987, in Japan; m. Yoshinobu Ikeda (her longtime leading man). ❖ The 1st female Japanese film star, joined Shochiku Kamata Studios (1921); appeared in *Hototogisu* (1922), *Reijin* (1930), *Ojosan* (1930), *Yogoto no yume* (1933), *Shukujo wa nani o wasueta ka* (1937) and *Nagareru* (1956), among others; retired from films but was active as head of the Mizuki school of dance.

KURKOVA, Katerina (1983—). Czech shooter. Born Nov 17, 1983, in Pizen, Czechoslovakia. ❖ Won a gold medal at World championships for 10 m air rifle (2002); won a bronze medal for 10 m air rifle at Athens Olympics (2004).

KURODA, Chika (1884–1968). Japanese chemist. Born Mar 24, 1884, in Matsubara, Saga City, Japan; died Nov 8, 1968, in Fukuoka, Japan; Tohoku Imperial University, BS, 1916. ❖ The 1st woman recipient of BS degree in Japan (1916), the 1st woman to gain a place in Japan's Tohoku Imperial University's chemistry department, the 1st woman to present a paper to Chemical Society of Japan (1918) and the 2nd woman in Japan to earn a doctorate (1929); studied natural pigments with Majima Toshiyuki; served as assistant professor at Tohoku (1916–18); studied with W.H. Perkin at Oxford University (1921–23); appointed a Tokyo Joshi Koto Shihan Gakko professor (1918–21); at Majima Laboratory, worked as a researcher for Institute of Physical and Chemical Research (RIKEN, 1924–49); served as professor (1949–52), as honorary professor (from 1952) and as part-time lecturer (1952–63) at Ochanomizu Women's University; studied onion skin pigment which led to creation of Keruchin C, a drug for high blood pressure. Received Chemical Society of Japan's Majima Prize (1936), a Medal with Purple Ribbon (1959), an Order of the Precious Crown, Butterfly (1965) and a Third Grade Junior of the Court Rank (posthumously).

KUROYANAGI, Tetsuko (1933—). Japanese talk-show host. Born Aug 9, 1933, in Tokyo, Japan; dau. of a celebrated violinist. ❖ Famed tv talk-show host of "Tetsuko no heya" (Tetsuko's room) in Japan, also began serving as goodwill ambassador for UNICEF (1984); wrote the novel *Totto Channel* (1987).

KURSINSKI, Anne (1959—). American equestrian. Name variations: Anne Kindig Kursinski. Born April 16, 1959, in Flemington, NJ. ❖ Won an indiv. gold medal at Pan American Games (1982); was 1st American to win Grand Prix of Rome (1983); won a team silver medal for jumping at Seoul Olympics (1988); won Grand Prix of Aachen (1991); won indiv. American Gold Cup 4 times; won team silver for jumping at Atlanta Olympics, on Eros (1996); became 1st American and 1st woman to win the Pulsar Crown Grand Prix in Mexico (1998). Named USOC Female Equestrian Athlete of the Year (1991).

KURTH, Andrea (1957—). East German rower. Born Sept 30, 1957, in East Germany. ❖ At Montreal Olympics, won a gold medal in coxed fours (1976).

KURTZ, Carmen (1911–1999). Spanish children's writer. Name variations: Carmen de Rafael y Marés Kurtz. Born Carmen de Rafael y Marés in Barcelona, Spain, Sept 18, 1911; died 1999; m. Pedro Kurtz Klein, in 1935; children: one daughter. ❖ Award-winning author, married and moved to France (1935), on eve of Spanish Civil War; returned to Spain (1943), during WWII; published 9 novels, using husband's surname (1954–64); turned to children's literature (1960s), often featuring the protagonist Oscar, who experienced a great variety of adventures, including espionage, space travel, and exploring the Himalayas. Won Lazarillo Prize (1964) and Children's Literature Prize of the Spanish Catholic Commission (1964, 1967).

KURVYAKOVA, Raisa (1945—). Soviet basketball player. Born Sept 15, 1945, in USSR. ❖ At Montreal Olympics, won a gold medal in team competition (1976).

KURYS, Diane (1948—). French director and screenwriter. Born Dec 3, 1948, in Lyons, France; dau. of Russian-Jewish immigrants; educated in Paris; married Alexandre Arcady (a director-producer). ❖ Began career as an actress, spending some time with Jean-Louis Barrault's theater group, and also appearing in a series of films, including Pirès' *Elle court, elle court la banlieu*, Fellini's *Casanova*, and Dugowson's *F . . . comme Fairbanks;* started to write screenplays, finding a wealth of material in her own background; wrote autobiographical debut film, *Diabolo Menthe* (1978, *Peppermint Soda*), story of a rebellious schoolgirl, which won the Prix Louis Delluc as France's film of the year and was an international box-office hit; followed that with *Cocktail Molatov* (1980), drawn from experiences in Paris during May 1968 student revolt; her next film, the autobiographical *Coup de Foudre* (1983), retitled *Entre Nous* in US, was nominated for an Academy Award as Best Foreign Picture; also wrote and directed *Un Homme Amoureaux* (1987, *A Man in Love*), *La-Baule-les-Pins* (1990, *C'est la Vie* in US), *Les Enfants du siÒcle* (1999, *The Children of the Century*).

KURYS, Sophie (1925—). American baseball player. Born Sophie Mary Kurys, May 14, 1925, in Flint, Michigan. ❖ Played second base for 8 seasons for Racine Belles of the All-American Girls Baseball League (AAGBL); stole 201 bases in 203 attempts, a league record that was never broken (1946). ❖ See also *Women in World History.*

KURYSHKO-NAGIRNAYA, Yekatarina (1949—). Soviet kayaker. Name variations: Yekatarina Nagirnaya. Born April 12, 1949, in USSR. ❖ At Munich Olympics, won a gold medal in K2 500 meters (1972).

KURZ, Isolde (1853–1944). German poet, novelist and short-story writer. Born Dec 21, 1853, in Stuttgart, Germany; died April 5, 1944, in Tübingen, Germany; dau. of Hermann Kurz (writer) and Marie (von Brunnow) Kurz. ❖ Was taught several languages by mother; moved to Florence (1880) to escape conservatism of Germany; writings, which reflect interest in Italian Renaissance but also evoke images of contemporary life in Italy and Germany, include *Gedichte* (1888), *Florentiner Novellen* (1890) and *Vanadis* (1930).

KURZ, Selma (1874–1933). Austrian soprano. Born Nov 15, 1874, in Bielitz, Silesia; died May 10, 1933, in Vienna, Austria; studied with Johannes Ress in Vienna and Mathilde Marchesi in Paris; m. Josef Halban (gynecologist), 1910; children: Desirée Halban (b. 1911). ❖ Debuted in Hamburg as Mignon (1895) and at Frankfurt Opera as Elisabeth in *Tannhäuser,* followed by such roles as Marguerite in *Faust* and Queen of the Night in *Die Zauberflöte* (*The Magic Flute*); had a brief affair with composer Gustav Mahler who arranged for her to be coached by Anna Bahr-Mildenburg; gave a successful performance of Mahler's

songs (1901) and became a member of his Vienna Opera ensemble where she remained until 1927, giving almost 1,000 performances; often appeared at Covent Garden as well as in Paris and Monte Carlo; debuted in US (1921); with a repertoire that included some 60 roles, made a number of recordings (1900–25). ❖ See also H. Goldmann, *Selma Kurz* (Bielitz, 1933); and *Women in World History.*

KUSAKABE, Kie. Japanese judoka. Born in Japan. ❖ Won bronze medal for 52–57kg lightweight at Sydney Olympics (2000).

KUSCIK, Nina (c. 1940—). *See Kuscsik, Nina.*

KUSCSIK, Nina (c. 1940—). American marathon runner. Name variations: frequently misspelled Kuscik. Born c. 1940 in South Huntington, LI, NY. ❖ Was a New York State cycling champion; became the 1st sanctioned women's winner in Boston marathon (1972); won NY City Marathon (1972), the 1st woman to run, then won again (1973); influential in getting the women's marathon event in the Olympics. Inducted into National Distance Running Hall of Fame.

KUSHIDA FUKI (1899–2001). Japanese feminist, peace and antinuclear activist. Born Feb 17, 1899, in Yamaguchi Prefecture, Japan; died Feb 5, 2001, age 101, in Tokyo; attended Women's University in Tokyo; m. Tamizo Kushida (Marxist economist who died c. 1939); children: 2. ❖ Pioneer campaigner for women's rights, joined the feminist movement after WWII; worked with Yuriko Miyamoto and became the 1st secretary general of the Women's Democratic Club; elected 3rd president of Federation of Japanese Women's Organizations (1958), a group opposed to nuclear weapons.

KUSHNER, Natalya (1954—). Soviet volleyball player. Born May 1954 in USSR. ❖ At Montreal Olympics, won a silver medal in team competition (1976).

KUSNER, Kathy (1940—). American equestrian. Born Kathryn H. Kusner, Mar 21, 1940, in Gainesville, FL. ❖ As a leading international dressage rider, won the President's Cup, NY championships, and Prix des Amazones; was the 1st woman in 10 years to join US equestrian team (1961); rode on American gold medal team in Pan-American games (1963) and again in Olympics (1964); on Untouchable, won International Grand Prix in Dublin for 2 competitions in a row (1964, 1966); filed a sexual discrimination suit against Maryland Racing Commission for refusing to give her a license as a jockey (1967), a case which she won, becoming the 1st licensed female jockey though not the 1st to race professionally (she was sidelined with a broken leg when Diane Crump rode into the history books at Hialeah, Feb 7, 1969); was victorious at Pocono Downs (Sept 1969); continuing to compete as a dressage rider, won a silver medal at Munich Olympics (1972). ❖ See also *Women in World History.*

KUTI, Funmilayo Ransom- (1900–1978). *See Ransome-Kuti, Funmilayo.*

KUTKAITE, Dalia (1965—). Lithuanian rhythmic gymnast. Born Feb 11, 1965, in Vilius, Lithania. ❖ Won European championship (1982) and tied for a bronze medal with clubs at World championships (1983).

KUTTY, Madhavi (1934—). *See Das, Kamala.*

KUZENKOVA, Olga (1970—). Russian hammer thrower. Born Oct 4, 1970, in Smolensk, Russia. ❖ Was the 1st woman to throw the hammer more than 70 meters (1997); won a silver medal at Sydney Olympics (2000); won silver medals at World championships (1999, 2001); won a silver medal (1998) and a gold medal (2002) at European championships; won a gold medal at Athens Olympics (2004), with a throw of 240:8.19.

KUZMINA-KARAVAEVA, Elizaveta (1891–1945). *See Skobtsova, Maria.*

KUZNETSOVA, Evgenia (1980—). Russian gymnast. Name variations: Yevgeniya or Eugenia Kuznetsova. Born Dec 18, 1980, in Puschkin (Zarkoje Selo), St. Petersburg, Russia. ❖ At Atlanta Olympics, won a silver medal for team all-around (1996); won a silver medal at World championships for team all-around (1997, 1999); at European championships, won a gold medal for balance beam and silver medal for team all-around (1998) and a gold medal for team all-around (2000); won Siska International (1999).

KUZNETSOVA, Maria (1880–1966). Russian soprano and dancer. Name variations: Mariya Nikolayevna Kuznetsov; Marija Nikolaevna Kuznecova; Maria Kouznetzova. Born Maria Nikolaievna Kuznetsova in Odessa, Russia, 1880; died in Paris, April 26, 1966; dau. of Nikolai Kuznetsov (painter); married to a son of Jules Massenet. ❖ With a vast repertoire, expressive voice, and powerful acting, was in the highest rank of singers in early 20th century; made ballet debut at St. Petersburg's Court Opera, then studied as a singer with Joakim Tartakov; made triumphant operatic debut at Mariinsky Theater as Marguerite in *Faust* (1905); took part in several premieres, including that of Rimsky-Korsakov's *The Legend of the Invisible City of Kitezh* (1907); also appeared as Tatiana in *Eugene Onegin*, Traviata, Madame Butterfly, and Juliette in Gounod opera *Roméo et Juliette;* performed in Berlin and Paris (1906); appeared in various French roles at Grand Opéra and Opéra-Comique, including Chabrier's *Gwendoline* (1910) and Massenet's *Roma* (1912), as well as Aïda and Norma; debuted at Covent Garden and NYC's Manhattan Opera House (1909); returned temporarily to dancing (1914), appearing with great success in Paris and London, where she created role of Potiphar's wife in Richard Strauss ballet *Josephs-Legende;* also sang role of Yaroslavna in 1st British performance of Borodin's *Prince Igor*, under baton of Beecham; returned to Russia at start of WWI; during Russian Revolution (1917), fled to Sweden; invited to sing major roles at Copenhagen and Stockholm opera houses (1919); settled in Paris (1920), appearing in opera, operettas, and film; was impresario of Opéra Russe (1927–33); on retirement, became artistic advisor of Russian operatic repertoire at Barcelona's Teatro Lirico; made 36 recordings (1905–28) for Pathé and Odeon labels. ❖ See also *Women in World History.*

KUZNETSOVA, Olga (1968—). *See Klochneva, Olga.*

KUZNETSOVA, Svetlana (1985—). Russian tennis player. Born June 27, 1985, in Moscow, Russia; dau. of cyclists. ❖ At 19, won singles title at US Open (2004); with Martina Navratilova, won 5 doubles titles and was runner-up at US Open (2003).

KUZWAYO, Ellen (1914–2006). South African teacher, social worker, activist, and writer. Name variations: Kuswayo; Mama Soweto. Pronunciation: koo-ZWY-o. Born Ellen Kate Merafe, June 29, 1914, in Thaba'Nchu District, Orange Free State, South Africa; died April 19, 2006, in Johannesburg, South Africa; only dau. of Phillip Serasengwe (civic leader in Johannesburg) and Emma Mutsi Makgothi Tsimatsima Merafe (farmer); certified by Adams College in Durban as lower primary teacher, 1933, and later as higher primary teacher (highest certification that could be attained by a black at a teacher training college), 1935; additional education at Lovedale College in Cape Province, 1936; trained in social work at Jan Hofmeyr School of Social Work in Johannesburg, 1953–55; University of Witwatersrand, Diploma in Advanced Social Work Practice, 1980, Higher Diploma in Advanced Social Work Practice, 1982; m. Dr. Ernest Moloto, 1941 (div. 1947); m. Godfrey Kuzwayo, 1950 (died 1965); children: (1st m.) Matshwene Everington (b. 1942); Bakone Justice (b. 1944); (2nd m.) Ndabezitha Godfrey (b. 1951). ❖ Civil-rights activist who published *Call Me Woman*, the 1st autobiography of a black South African woman, began career teaching at Inanda Seminary in Natal (1937); taught at St. Paul's School in Thaba'Nchu (1938); appointed secretary of Youth League of African National Congress (ANC, 1946); taught at Orlando East in Soweto (1947–53); became a social worker with Johannesburg City Council (1956); worked with Southern African Association of Youth Clubs in Johannesburg (1957–62); served as general secretary of YWCA in Transvaal region, assisting Tsonga-speaking women and children who had been uprooted and resettled by South African government (1964–76); made 1st trip to NY as representative of YWCA congress (1969); saw family farm at Thaba'Nchu dispossessed under Group Areas legislation (1974); appointed to faculty of School of Social Work, University of Witswatersrand (1976); elected only founding female member of Committee of Ten (community leaders elected during martial law of 1976) and founding board member of Urban Foundation (1976); jailed for 5 months at Johannesburg Fort under Terrorism Act but released without being charged (1977–78); appointed consultant to Zamani Soweto Sisters Council (1978); appointed chair of Maggie Magaba Trust (1979); subject of documentary films, *Awake From Mourning* (1981) and *Tsiamelo: A Place of Goodness* (1985); appointed 1st president of Black Consumer Union (1984); at 80, won a seat in South African Parliament as an ANC representative for Soweto (1994); appointed to Truth and Reconciliation Commission (TRC, 1995). Named Woman of the Year by Johannesburg newspaper *The Star* (1979); was 1st black writer to win Central News Agency (CNA) Prize for literary achievement in English-language work, for *Call Me Woman* (1985); received Soweto Milestones Award (2004). ❖ See also *Women in World History.*

KVAPILOVA, Hana (1860–1907). Czech actress. Name variations: Hana Kubesova-Kvapilova. Born Nov 29, 1860, in Prague; died April 8, 1907; m. Jaroslav Kvapil (poet and dramatist), May 26, 1894. ❖ The leading female star of the Prague theater at the turn of the century, joined the Prague National Theater (1888); because of the unconventional women she created in plays by Ibsen and in Czech modern dramas, became a symbol of women's emancipation; was also a nationalist; appeared as Marguerite in *Faust*, Ophelia in *Hamlet*, Masha in *The Three Sisters* and Ellida Wangel in *The Lady from the Sea*, among others; often starred opposite Eduard Vojan.

KVELLO, Berit. *See Aunli, Berit.*

KVESIC, Kornelija (1964—). Yugoslavian basketball player. Born Aug 25, 1963. ❖ At Seoul Olympics, won a silver medal in team competition (1988).

KVITKA, Larysa (1871–1913). *See Ukrainka, Lesya.*

KVITLAND, Bente (1974—). Norwegian soccer player. Born June 23, 1974, in Norway. ❖ Won a team gold medal at Sydney Olympics (2000).

KVRIVICHVILI, Khatuna (1974—). Soviet archer. Born Jan 1, 1974, in USSR. ❖ At Barcelona Olympics, won a bronze medal in team round (1992).

KWADZNIEWSKA, Maria (1913—). Polish track-and-field athlete. Name variations: Maria Kwasniewska Maleszewska; Maria Kwasniewska-Trytko-Kozminska-Maleszewska. Born Aug 15, 1913, in Lodz. ❖ At Berlin Olympics, won a bronze medal in the javelin throw (1936).

KWAG HYE-JEONG (1975—). South Korean handball player. Born May 16, 1975, in South Korea. ❖ Won a team silver medal at Atlanta Olympics (1996).

KWAN, Michelle (1980—). American figure skater. Born July 7, 1980, in Torrance, CA; sister of Karen Kwan (b. 1978, figure skater). ❖ Was Jr. World champion (1994); placed 1st at World championships (1996, 1998, 2000, 2001, 2003) and 2nd (1997, 1999, 2002), the 1st to win back-to-back titles since Kristi Yamaguchi and the 1st to win 4 titles since Katarina Witt; placed 1st at US National championships (1996, 1998, 1999–2005) and 2nd (1997); won Skate America (1995, 1997, 1999, 2000, 2001, 2002), Goodwill Games and World Pros (1998); won a silver medal at Nagano Olympics (1998) and a bronze medal at Salt Lake City Olympics (2002); was a member of Olympic squad at Torino Olympics but had to withdraw because of injuries (2006).

KWAN, Nancy (1939—). Eurasian actress. Born May 19, 1939, in Hong Kong. ❖ Trained with British Royal Ballet before entering films; made Hollywood debut starring as Hong Kong prostitute in *The World of Suzie Wong* (1960), then starred in film version of *Flower Drum Song* (1961); other films include *The Main Attraction* (1962), *Fate Is the Hunter* (1964), *Lt. Robin Crusoe USN* (1966), *Drop Dead Darling (Arrivederci Baby!*, 1966), *The Girl Who Knew Too Much* (1969), *Wonder Women* (1973), *Streets of Hong Kong* (1979), *Angkor* (1981), *Walking the Edge* (1983), *Night of Children* (1989) and *Dragon: The Bruce Lee Story* (1993). ❖ See also *Women in World History.*

KWASNIEWSKA, Maria (1913—). *See Kwadzniewska, Maria.*

KWAST, Frieda Hodapp (1880–1949). German pianist. Name variations: Frieda Kwast-Hoddap. Born Aug 13, 1880, in Bargen, Germany; died in Bad Wiessee, Germany, Sept 14, 1949. ❖ Made a number of recordings at the turn of the century.

KWON CHANG SOOK. South Korean field-hockey player. Born in South Korea. ❖ Won a team silver medal at Atlanta Olympics (1996).

KYASHT, Lydia (1885–1959). Russian ballet dancer. Born Lydia Kyashkt, Mar 25, 1885, in St. Petersburg, Russia; died Jan 11, 1959, in London, England; dau. of Agaffia (Poubiloff) Kyashkt and George Kyashkt; m. Alexis A. Rogosin. ❖ Made stage debut at Imperial Opera House, St. Petersburg, dancing a *pas de deux* in *The Magic Flute* (1902) and remained at Opera House for some time; made London debut in a *divertissement* with Adolf Bolm (1908); selected to succeed Adeline Genée as *première danseuse* of the Empire, appearing there (1909–13) in *A Day in Paris, Round the World, The Fawn, Ship Ahoy!, Sylvia, New York, The Water Nymph, First Love* and *Titania;* made NY debut in *The Whirl of the World* (1914); also appeared in *Javotte, Cythera, La Fille Mal Gardée* and *Ballerina;* opened Lydia Kyasht Dancing Academy (1935); founded Ballet de la Jeunesse Anglaise (1939). ❖ See also reminiscences *Romantic Recollections* (1929).

KYBURZ, Rosemary (1944—). Australian politician. Born Rosemary Annette Kyburz, April 16, 1944, in Sydney, Australia; m. Rob Akers (member of Queenland Legislative Assembly). ❖ Served as a Liberal Party member of the Queensland Parliament for Salisbury (1974–83).

KYE SUN-HI (1979—). *See Kye Sun-Hui.*

KYE SUN-HUI (1979—). North Korean judoka. Name variations: also seen as Sun-Hi Kye. Born Aug 2, 1979, in North Korea. ❖ At 16, won a gold medal for -48kg extra-lightweight at Atlanta Olympics (1996), the youngest jodoka to win an Olympic title; won a bronze medal for 48 half-lightweight at Sydney Olympics (2000) and a silver medal for 57kg at Athens Olympics (2004); at World championships, placed 1st for 52kg (2001) and 1st for 57kg (2003).

KYI, Aung San Suu (b. 1945). *See Aung San Suu Kyi.*

KYME, Anne (c. 1521–1546). *See Askew, Anne.*

KYNISKA (fl. 396–392 BCE). *See Cynisca.*

KYO, Machiko (1924—). Japanese actress. Name variations: Machiko Kyô; real name, Yano Motoko. Born in Osaka, Japan, Mar 25, 1924. ❖ A veteran of over 90 films, began career as a dancer; displayed surprising dramatic skill as vulnerable wife of a samurai in *Rashomon,* the Kurosawa masterpiece (1950); was subsequently featured in a string of movies in a wide variety of roles (1950s–60s); worked with some of Japan's most notable directors, including Kenji Mizoguchi (*Ugetsu, Street of Shame,* and *Princess Yang Kwei Fei*), Kon Ichikawa (*Odd Obsession*), Yasujiro Ozu (*Floating Weeds*), and Shiro Toyoda (*Sweet Sweat*); appeared in US film *The Teahouse of the August Moon* (1956) with Marlon Brando.

KYRK, Hazel (1886–1957). American consumer economist. Born Hazel Kyrk, Nov 19, 1886, in Ashley, Ohio; died Aug 6, 1957, in West Dover, Vermont; dau. of Elmer and Jane (Benedict) Kyrk; University of Chicago, PhD in economics, 1920. ❖ During WWI, worked as statistician for American Division of Allied Maritime Transport Council in London (1918–19); wrote doctoral thesis (1920), which was published as *A Theory of Consumption,* 1923, as well as *The Economic Problems of the Family* (1929) and *The Family in the American Economy* (1953); taught at Bryn Mawr Summer School for Women Workers (1922–25); worked at Food Research Institute at Stanford University (1923–24); was professor at Iowa State College (1924–25); taught economics and home economics at University of Chicago (1925–52), becoming full professor (1941); served as principal economist at Department of Agriculture's Bureau of Home Economics, participating in landmark project, Consumer Purchases Study (1938–41); appointed chair of Consumer Advisory Committee to Office of Price Administration (1943); was chair of Technical Advisory Committee for Bureau of Labor Statistics (1945–46); helped organize, and was board member of, consumer cooperative in Chicago and of Chicago Women's Trade Union League.

KYSELICOVA, Alena (1957—). Czech field-hockey player. Born Nov 14, 1957. ❖ At Moscow Olympics, won a silver medal in team competition (1980).

KYTELER, Alice (fl. 1324). Irish noblewoman tried for witchcraft. Name variations: Alice Kettle. Fl. in 1324 in Kilkenny; m. William Outlawe (died); m. Adam le Blund (died); m. Richard de Valle (died); m. Sir John le Poer (died). ❖ One of the earliest women prosecuted for witchcraft in Europe, was a practitioner of the ancient Celtic pagan religion; when 4th husband died and her stepchildren contested the will, refused to settle; was accused of witchcraft by them to discredit her; excommunicated by Bishop of Ossory, was then indicted on charges ranging from animal sacrifice to prophecy; mounted a spirited defense, having her guards capture the bishop and imprison him in her castle; eventually fled to England for refuge. Her house, the oldest in Kilkenny, has been restored and now serves as the Kyteler's Inn.

KYUNG-WHA CHUNG (1948—). *See Chung Kyung-Wha.*

L

LAAGE, Barbara (1920–1988). French stage and screen actress. Born Claire Colombat, July 30, 1920, in Menthon-Saint-Bernard, France; died 1988. ❖ Began career on stage and in nightclubs; made film debut in *B.F.'s Daughter* (1948), followed by *La rose rouge, Fille d'amour, L'Esclave, Quai des blondes, Act of Love, Crime passionel, Gil Blas, Every Second Counts, The Happy Road, Miss Pigalle, Una Parigina a Roma, Paris Blues, Vacances portugaises, Therese and Isabelle* and *Bed and Board*, among others; came to prominence in *La putain respectueuse* (*The Respectful Prostitute*, 1952).

LA ARGENTINA (c. 1886–1936). *See Mercé, Antonia.*

LA BADIE, Florence (1888–1917). American silent-film actress. Name variations: Florence LaBadie. Born Florence Russ, April 27, 1888, in New York, NY; died Oct 13, 1917, in Ossining, NY, from injuries sustained in earlier auto accident. ❖ Began career as a fashion model; was the top actress for Thanhouser Co. (1911–17); films include *In the Chorus, Dr. Jekyll and Mr. Hyde, The Million Dollar Mystery* (serial), *Monsieu Lecoq, The Fugitive* and *The Man Without a Country.*

LABAKOVA, Jana (1966—). Czech gymnast. Born Jan 26, 1966, in Prague, Czechoslovakia. ❖ Won Kosice International (1980, 1981, 1983) and Antibes International (1981); at World Cup, won a gold medal for vault (1980); won a bronze medal for uneven bars at European championships (1983).

LA BALTEIRA (fl. 13th c.). *See Perez, Maria.*

LA BARBARA, Joan (1947—). American vocalist and composer. Born Joan Linda Lotz, June 8, 1947, in Philadelphia, Pennsylvania; attended Syracuse University (1965–68); New York University, BS in Music Education (1970); Master Classes at Tanglewood with Phyllis Curtin (1967, 1968); also studied voice with Helen Boatwright and Marian Szekely-Freschl; m. Morton Subotnick (composer of electronic music), 1979. ❖ Pioneer in the field of contemporary classical music and "soundart," sang in ensembles of composers Steve Reich (1971–74) and Phillip Glass (1973–76), before specializing in extended techniques such as circular breathing and multiphonics; had pieces written for her by John Cage, Morton Feldman, Phillip Glass, Rhys Chatham and others; founded Wizard Records (1976); recorded numerous albums, including *Voice Is the Original Instrument* (1976), *October Music: Star Showers and Extraterrestrials* (1980), *As Lightning Comes, In Flashes* (1983), *In the Dreamtime* (1990), *Sound Paintings/Joan La Barbara* (1991) and *Awakenings: For Chamber Ensemble* (1994); wrote such compositions as *Winds of the Canyon* (1986), *Events in the Elsewhere* (1990) and *Dragons on the Wall* (2001); featured on soundtracks of such films as *Alien: Resurrection* (1997) and *I Still Know What You Did Last Summer* (1998), as well as independent films of Richard Blau, Amy Kravitz and others; produced and co-hosted radio program "Other Voices, Other Sounds"; taught at Hochschule der Kunst in Berlin (1979–80), Cité des Arts in Paris (1980–81), California Institute of Arts (1981–86), University of New Mexico (1999–2001) and College of Santa Fe (1996–2002); appeared in concert with Los Angeles Philharmonic, San Francisco Symphony, New York Philharmonic, New World Symphony, Women's Philharmonic, among others.

LA BARGY, Simone (1877–1985). *See Simone, Madame.*

LABBÉ, Denise (1926—). French murderer. Name variations: Denise Labbe. Born 1926. ❖ Met officer cadet Jacques Algarron at Saint-Cyr School (May 1954), who essentially treated her as his slave; told by Algarron to prove her love for him by taking life of her 2½-year-old daughter Catherine (Nov 8, 1954); tried for murder at Blois (May 1955), found guilty with extenuating circumstances and received life imprisonment (Algarron received 20-year sentence for having provoked the murder).

LABÉ, Louise (c. 1523–1566). French poet. Name variations: Louise Labe; Loise or Louize Labé; Charlin, also seen as Charlieu, de Charlieu, Charliu, Charly, Charlie, Cheylieu, Charrieu; Labé also seen as Labbé, L'Abbé, Labe, Labbyt; La Belle Cordière or La Belle Cordiere (The Beautiful Ropemaker); La Dame au Luth (The Lady with the Lute). Pronunciation: LAH-bay. Born Louise Charlin between 1515 and 1526 in Lyons, France; died in Feb 1566 in Lyons; dau. of Pierre Charlie also seen as Pierre Charlin (ropemaker or, more probably, rope merchant) and 2nd wife Etiennette Roybert also seen as Etiennette, veuve (widow) Deschamps; m. Ennemond Perrin, before 1545; no children. ❖ Renaissance poet (considered scandalous by some of her contemporaries), who is remembered for her sonnets celebrating the pain and delight of love; was at the center of the literary and cultural society of Lyons, with a salon open to poets, scholars, and knights, as well as other women who lived in Lyons; involved as co-conspirator in an attempted murder trial (1552); was permitted to publish her works (1554); began a love affair with poet Olivier de Magny (1554); wrote letter to Mademoiselle Clémence de Bourges, a feminist manifesto, urging women to further their educations (1555); saw 1st publication of her works by Jean de Tournes (1555); cited by Calvin as an example of a bad woman (1561); wrote testament (1565). Her poems, which include 24 sonnets, 3 elegies, and a "Debate Between Folly and Love," continue to speak to those who love truth and beauty and to those who fight for equality and recognition. ❖ See also Keith Cameron, *Louise Labé: Renaissance Poet and Feminist* (Berg, 1990); and *Women in World History.*

LABELLE, Patti (1944—). African-American singer. Name variations: Labelle, The Ordettes, Patti LaBelle and the Blue Belles (aka BlueBelles). Born Patricia Louise Holt, Oct 4, 1944 (some sources cite May 24), in Philadelphia, PA; m. Armstead Edwards; children: 1 son, 2 adopted sons, and raising son and daughter of her deceased sister Jackie. ❖ Sang with girl group The Ordettes as a teenager; formed Patti LaBelle and the Blue Belles with Nona Hendryx, Sarah Dash, and Cindy Birdsong (1961), one of the foremost groups of the day; when Birdsong departed (1967), changed name of trio to LaBelle and recorded *Nightbirds* (1974), which included hit "Lady Marmalade" (Voulez-vous chouchez avec moi ce soir?); embarked on solo career with album *Patti LaBelle* (1976), followed by *Tasty* (1978), *I'm in Love Again* (1983) and *Gems* (1994); costarred with Al Green in Broadway revival of *Your Arms Too Short to Box With God* (1982), played a blues singer in film *A Soldier's Story*, starred in musical *House of Flowers*, and appeared in sitcoms "A Different World" and "Out All Night"; became particularly known for her duets, including "On My Own" with Michael McDonald (1986); received Grammy (1992) for Best Female R&B Vocal Performance for *Burnin'*; wrote *Patti's Pearls: Lessons in Living Genuinely, Joyfully, Generously* (2001); worked on behalf of AIDS awareness and cancer research. ❖ See also autobiography, *Don't Block the Blessings: Revelations of a Lifetime* (1996).

LA BELLE MARIE (c. 1882–1935). American vaudeville dancer. Name variations: Marie Gilliam; Marie Hart. Born c. 1882, in Ashtabula, Ohio; died Aug 21, 1935, in Clementon, NJ; dau. of trapeze artists. ❖ Toured with parents in numerous circuses as a child (until 1908); performed range of specialty numbers including on horseback on point and on parents' trapeze setups; joined Philadelphia-based troupe, The Crackerjacks, as specialty dancer, where her acts included a popular Salome solo and duet with comedian Billy Hart; appeared with Hart as Marie and Billy Hart (1910–17); continued to perform as specialty dancer after Hart's retirement (1917), but soon moved into music, choir and band performances.

LABELLE OCEANA (c. 1835—). Russian ballet dancer. Name variations: Oceana Smith. Born c. 1835, possibly in Kansas; death date unknown; granddau. of W.H. Bennie, well-known pantomimist. ❖ Made debut as child performer in Fanny Elssler imitation work in Fort Leavenworth, KS (1844); continued to perform with family troupe in numerous

Romantic ballets, taking on roles of increasing importance; performed on Mississippi circuit (1850s) and replaced Emilie Baron at Thomas Placide's Theater Varietés; was last thought to have toured with her horse Black Bess in *Mazeppa*.

LA BELLE OTERO (1868–1965). *See Otero, Caroline.*

LABILLE-GUIARD, Adelaide (1749–1803). French artist. Name variations: Adélaïde Labille-Guiard. Born in Paris, France, 1749; died 1803; dau. of Claude Edmé Labille (haberdasher) and Marie Anne (Saint-Martin) Labille; studied with miniaturist François Elie Vincent; studied oil painting with François Andre; was also one of a select group of artists to study with Maurice Quenton de la Tour (1769–74); m. Louis Nicolas Guiard (financial clerk), in 1769 (legally sep. 1779); no children. ❖ Considered by some to be the greatest woman pastel portraitist after Rosalba Carriera, was a teacher as well as a working artist, serving as both a role model and an advocate for her female students, the most famous being Gabrielle Capet; was frequently compared to her contemporary, Elisabeth Vigée-Le Brun (both were royal artists, both shared many of the same patrons and both were accepted into Académie Royale on same day, May 31, 1783); exhibited a miniature and a pastel at the last exhibition sponsored by Académie de Saint-Luc before it closed (1774); displayed a self-portrait executed in pastels at Salon de la Correspondance (1781); also exhibited several pastels (1782), including a portrait of sculptor Augustin Pajou at work; as a supporter of French Revolution, remained in Paris during that time, though her commissions were limited and she was forced to destroy her huge painting *The Reception of a Knight of St. Lazare by Monsieur, Grand Master of the Order*, because of its glorification of the monarchy (1793); having worked on the canvas for 2½ years, never recovered from the loss. One of her last surviving works is an oil painting of Madame de Genlis. ❖ See also *Women in World History*.

LABORDE DUANES, Yurisel (1979—). Cuban judoka. Born Aug 18, 1979, in Cuba. ❖ Placed 2nd at World championships for 78kg (2003); won a bronze medal for 78kg at Athens Olympics (2004).

LABOTSIBENI GWAMILE LAMDLULI (c. 1858–1925). Ruler in Swaziland. Name variations: laMvelasi; Mgwamie. Born Labotsibeni laMdluli around 1858, at Luhlekweni homestead in Hhohho region in northern Swaziland; died Dec 5, 1925, at Embekelweni, then Swazi national capital; dau. of Matsanjana Mdluli and a mother of Mabuza clan; became chief wife of Prince Mbandzeni, 1875; children: sons Bhunu, Malunge and Lomvazi, and daughter, Tongotongo. ❖ Queen-mother and regent who transcended the usual powers allowed women in her society, grasped the benefits of Western influence, and helped lay the foundations for her country as a nation state; husband died (1889); brought to power as queen-mother upon appointment of son Bhunu as royal heir (1890); became regent to grandson Mona, thus becoming the longest-reigning of all Swazi rulers before her, including its kings (1899); rallied Swazi people against systematic allotment by British of most of country's land to white settlers (1906); organized a deputation to London but failed to reclaim the land; formed a Lifa Fund to which her people contributed money for buying back the land; oversaw grandson's education; relinquished rule with Mona's coronation as Sobhuza II (1921), a man with more formal education than several African heads of state would have at the end of the colonial era in the 1960s. ❖ See also *Women in World History*.

LABOUCHERE, Henrietta (1841–1910). *See Hodson, Henrietta.*

LABOUISSE, Éve (b. 1904). *See Curie, Éve.*

LABOURÉ, Catherine (1806–1875). French saint. Name variations: Catherine Laboure. Born 1806; died 1875; grew up in Yonne, France. ❖ Spent life caring for the sick in environs of Paris; claimed that Mary the Virgin appeared to her 3 times in the chapel of her convent on Rue du Bac in Paris, commanding her to have a medal struck in commemoration (1832). This is the origin of the "Miraculous Medal" of the Roman Catholic faith. Feast day is Dec 31.

LABRADA DIAZ, Yanelis Yuliet (1981—). Cuban taekwondo player. Born Oct 8, 1981, in Cuba. ❖ Won a silver medal in -49kg at Athens Olympics (2004).

LABRINA, Joanna (1898–1953). *See Lambrino, Jeanne.*

LABY, Jean (1915—). Australian atmospheric physicist. Born 1915 in Melbourne, Australia; dau. of Thomas Howell Laby (natural philosophy professor); University of Melbourne, BS, 1939, MSc, 1951, PhD, 1959. ❖ Atmospheric physicist who researched cosmic rays, the stratosphere's

composition and the wind, worked as a demonstrator, senior demonstrator (from mid-1940s) and lecturer (from 1959) at University of Melbourne; employed as a senior lecturer at Royal Australian Air Force Academy at Point Cook (1961–82); worked with University of Wyoming scientists to measure atmospheric aerosols, water vapor in the stratosphere and ozone for the Climate Impact Assessment Program.

LACEY, Janet (1903–1988). English aid worker. Born 1903 in England; grew up in Sunderland; died 1988 in England. ❖ The 1st director of Christian Aid, worked for YWCA in Kendal, Dagenham, and with the British Army in Rhine, Germany, at end of WWII; joined British Council of Churches as youth secretary (1947), moving to inter-church aid and refugee department and becoming director (1952); held hugely successful Christian Aid Week to encourage wider public awareness (1957); continued in role as director, creating "Freedom from Hunger" campaign (1960–64) and changing organization's name to Christian Aid (1964); helped redirect Christian Aid focus to global poverty, funding development projects in 40 countries; became involved in Family Welfare Association and Churches' Council for Health and Healing; was 1st woman to preach in St. Paul's Cathedral; wrote *A Cup of Water* (1970).

LACEY, Maud (fl. 1230–1250). Countess of Hertford and Gloucester. Name variations: Maud de Clare. Fl. around 1230 to 1250; m. Richard de Clare, 6th earl of Hertford, 2nd earl of Gloucester; children: Gilbert de Clare (1243–1295), 7th earl of Hertford, 3rd earl of Gloucester; Margaret de Clare (1249–1313).

LACEY, Venus (1967—). African-American basketball player. Born Feb 9, 1967, in Chattanooga, TN; attended Louisiana Tech. ❖ Center; played for Lady Techsters; won a team gold medal at Atlanta Olympics (1996); played professionally in Japan (1990–92), Italy (1992–95), and Greece (1995–96); played for Long Beach Sting Rays (1997–98) and Nashville Noise of the ABL. Named US Basketball Writers Association Player of the Year (1990).

LACHAPELLE, Marie (1769–1821). French obstetrician. Born Marie Louise Dugés in France, 1769; died 1821; both mother and grandmother were influential midwives; married M Lachapelle (surgeon), 1792 (died 1795). ❖ Upon death of mother, was appointed head of maternity at the oldest hospital in Paris, the Hôtel Dieu, where Jean Louis Baudelocque was teaching obstetrics; respected him but disagreed on some points: believed in restricted use of instruments and reduced his 94 fetus position classifications to 22; published her most important work, the 3-volume *Pratique des accouchements* (1821–25), covering 40,000 cases; established a maternity and children's hospital at Port Royal where she trained many midwives, including Marie Anne Boivin.

LA CHENETTE, Madame (1667–c. 1750). *See Montour, Isabelle.*

LACHMAN, Thérèse (1819–1884). French courtesan. Name variations: Therese Lachman; La Païva or La Paiva; Mme Villoing; Mme la Marquise de Païva; Countess Henckle von Donnersmarck. Born 1819 in Moscow ghetto; died Jan 21, 1884, in husband's castle, Neudeck, Germany; dau. of a weaver; m. Antoine Villoing (tailor), Aug 11, 1836 (died 1849); m. Albino Francesco de Païva-Araujo, a Portuguese marquis, June 5, 1851 (committed suicide 1872); m. Guido Henckel von Donnersmarck (wealthy Prussian and count); children: (1st m.) 1 son; (with Herz) daughter. ❖ Abandoned husband and son and moved to Paris; met pianist Henri Herz and became his mistress (1841); held a salon for the likes of Richard Wagner, Hans von Bülow and Théophile Gautier; journeyed to London, where she had an affair with Lord Stanley; also said to be mistress of Napoleon III; married 2nd husband and became known as La Païva; abandoned him and married once more; a canny businesswoman, amassed a fortune; built the hotel Païva in the Champs-Elysees; exiled with Prussian husband under suspicion of being spies (c. 1878).

LACHMANN, Karen (1916–1962). Danish fencer. Born May 30, 1916, in Denmark; died Sept 30, 1962. ❖ Won a silver medal at London Olympics (1948) and a bronze medal at Helsinki Olympics (1952), both in indiv. foil.

LACIS, Asja (1891–1979). Latvian stage director, actress and author. Name variations: Anna Lacis; Asja Lazis. Born Anna Ernestovna Lacis in Ligatne, Riga District, Russia, Oct 19, 1891; died in Riga, Latvia, Nov 21, 1979; m. Julij Lacis; studied for 2 years at Institute of Psychoneurology in St. Petersburg; m. Bernhard Reich; children: (2nd m.) daughter, Daga Reich. ❖ Theater director who introduced the work of Bertolt Brecht to Soviet stage, wrote the 1st history of the theater of Weimar Republic, and was a major influence on literary critic Walter

Benjamin, moved to Moscow to study at Kommisarshevski Institute of Theater Sciences (1914); sympathetic with the Bolsheviks (1917), established an experimental theater for children in Orel; returned to Latvia (1920), where she directed an innovative theater studio that was part of Communist-oriented People's University in Riga; met and worked with Brecht in Munich (1923); met Benjamin (1924); worked in Soviet trade mission in Berlin (1928), promoting Soviet films in Germany and the West; back in Soviet Union (1931), completed filming of Erwin Piscator's version of a novel by Anna Seghers, *Der Aufstand der Fischer von St. Barbara* (*The Revolt of the Fishermen of Santa Barbara*); directed a Latvian-language version of Friedrich Wolf's play *Baur Baetz* at Moscow's Latvian State Theater (1934); published *The Revolutionary Theater in Germany* (1935); arrested at height of the Great Purges in Soviet Union (1938), sent to a labor camp in Kazakhstan and not released until 1948; returned to Latvia, where she became director of a theater in Valmiera and slowly built up a theatrical ensemble which became widely known; retired (1957). ❖ See also *Women in World History.*

LACKIE, Ethel (1907–1979). American swimmer. Name variations: Mrs. Watkins. Born Feb 10, 1907, in Chicago, IL; died Dec 1979 in Newbury Park, CA. ❖ Won gold medals for the 100-meter freestyle and 4 x 100-meter relay at Paris Olympics (1924); was the 1st woman to swim the 100-yard freestyle in less than 1 minute and the 1st to break the 1 min. 10 sec. barrier in the 100-meter freestyle; won US National outdoor 100-yard freestyle (1924) and 100 meters (1926); was the indoor 100-yard freestyle US champion (1925, 1926, 1928). Inducted into International Swimming Hall of Fame (1969).

LACOCK, abbess of (d. after 1280). *See Beatrice of Kent.*

LACOMBE, Claire (1765–?). French actress and women's-rights activist. Name variations: Rosa Lacombe. Born in Pamiers in southern France on Aug 4, 1765; date and place of death unknown, though it was after 1795. ❖ French actress who became a vocal champion of women's rights during French Revolution only to discover that most men, revolutionary or not, were unwilling to concede the political equality of the sexes; toured southern provinces as a tragic actress in plays of Corneille and Racine and attained a minor reputation in theaters of Lyons and Marseilles; came to Paris during French Revolution (1792), just before her 27th birthday, and took a prominent part in the popular attack on the royal palace, the Tuileries (Aug 10, 1792); organized Women's Republican Revolutionary Society in Paris (spring 1793) to agitate for female political rights, and associated with proto-socialist faction known as the *Enragés;* denounced by Jacobin faction and arrested on orders of the Committee of Public Safety (April 1794); detained in prison until 1795 after which she disappeared from public view. ❖ See also *Women in World History.*

LACORE, Suzanne (1875–1975). French teacher, socialist, and cabinet official. Name variations: (pseudonym) Suzon. Pronunciation: soo-ZAHN la-COR. Born Marie Lacore in Glandier (Corrèze), May 30, 1875; died in Milhac d'Auberoche (Dordogne), Nov 6, 1975; dau. of André Lacore (1839–82) and Marie Malaure Lacore (b. 1845); educated at Dordogne Normal School for Young Women; never married. ❖ Rural schoolteacher and socialist militant who was one of the 1st twelve women in France to be a member of the Cabinet, an anomaly because, until 1944, women still could not vote; certified as a teacher (1894); began teaching at Ajat (1903); converted to socialism and joined Unified Socialist Party, beginning a lifelong activity as a party militant (1906); signed Chambéry Manifesto calling for teachers to join the General Confederation of Labor (1912); helped found Groupe des femmes socialistes (1913); published important articles on women and socialism (1913–14); defended socialism against the communists (1920s); retired from teaching (1930); helped found Comité nationale des femmes socialistes and made a major speech at the Tours party congress (1931); reported on women in agriculture (1935); served as undersecretary of state for child protection (1936–37), bringing children's issues to the fore; served as vice-president of the Superior Council for the Protection of Children (1937–38); opposed the CNFS policy on women in the party (1944–46); published *Enfance d'abord* (1960). Inducted into the Legion of Honor (1956); promoted to officer in the Legion of Honor (1975). ❖ See also *Women in World History.*

LACOSTE, Catherine (1945—). French golfer. Name variations: Mme De Prado. Born June 27, 1945, in Chantaco, France; dau. of Simone Thion de la Chaume (professional golfer who won the British Amateur) and René Lacoste (French tennis champion and manufacturer of Lacoste sport shirt); married, Aug 1969. ❖ Won the 1st Women's World

Amateur Team championships; won the French Closed championship twice and French Open three times; won US Women's Open (1967), the 1st foreign player and 1st amateur to win the event; won the French, British, and US amateur titles (1969); retired from competition (1972), age 27. ❖ See also *Women in World History.*

LACOSTE, Euphémie (1819—). French murderer (accused). Name variations: Euphemie Lacoste. Born Euphémie Vergès, 1819; m. Henri Lacoste, May 1841 (died 1843); lived near village of Riguepeu in Chateau Philibert. ❖ Born into family of small landowners, was wed at 22 to 68-year-old great-uncle Henri Lacoste, a marriage arranged by parents (1841); husband died suddenly under suspicious circumstances and his body was found to contain arsenic (1843); was arrested and tried for his murder with 70-year-old schoolmaster Joseph Meilhan, to whom she had given a minor pension; acquitted because of insufficient evidence (some reports suggested traces of arsenic in Lacoste's blood were due to treatment for syphilis and not poisoning).

LACROSIL, Michèle (1915—). Guadeloupean novelist. Name variations: Michele Lacrosil. Born 1915 in Guadeloupe. ❖ Writings, which focus on race and alienation, include *Sapotille et le Serein d'argile* (1960), *Cajou* (1961) and *Demain Jab-Herma* (1967).

LACUESTA, Natalie (1981—). American rhythmic gymnast. Born Nov 15, 1981, in Chicago, IL. ❖ Won Rhythmic Senior nationals (1994, 1995, 1997, 1998).

LACY, Alice (1281–1348). Countess of Lincoln. Born 1281; died Oct 2, 1348; buried at Birling, Kent, England; dau. of Henry Lacy, earl of Lincoln; m. Thomas Plantagenet, 2nd earl of Lancaster, c. 1311 (div. 1318).

LACY, Harriette Deborah (1807–1874). English actress. Name variations: Harriette Deborah Taylor. Born in London, 1807; died 1874; dau. of tradesman named Taylor; m. Walter Lacy (1809–1898, actor), 1839. ❖ Made 1st stage appearance at Bath as Julia in *The Rivals* (1827); was then cast in leading parts in both comedy and tragedy; made London debut as Nina in *Carnival of Naples* (1830); confirmed popularity with her Aspatia to William Macready's Melantius in *The Bridal* and her Lady Teazle to Walter Lacy's Charles Surface; was the original Helen in *The Hunchback* (1832); also originated role of Nell Gwynn in Jerrold's play of that name, and role of the heroine in his *Housekeeper;* considered the finest Ophelia of her day, retired (1848).

LADD, Anna Coleman (1878–1939). American sculptor and author. Name variations: Mrs. Maynard Ladd. Born Anna Coleman Watts in Philadelphia, PA, July 15, 1878; died 1939; dau. of John S. Watts and Mary (Peace) Watts; studied privately in Paris and Rome with Ferrari and Gallori; m. Maynard Ladd (physician), 1905; children: Gabriella May Ladd May; Vernon Abbott Ladd. ❖ Held 1st special exhibition of 40 bronze sculptures at Gorham's in NY (1913); bronzes now reside in Boston Museum of Fine Arts, NY City's Cathedral of Saint John the Divine, and the Palazzo Bhorghese in Rome; also did 4 war memorials in Massachusetts and portrait busts of Eleonora Duse, Ethel Barrymore, Raquel Meller and Anna Pavlova; wrote several novels, including *Hyeronymus Rides* and *The Candid Adventure* (both 1912).

LADD, Diane (1932—). American actress. Born Rose Diane Lanier, Nov 29, 1932, in Meridian, Mississippi; dau. of Mary Lanier (1912–2002, actress); 1st cousin of Tennessee Williams; m. Bruce Dern, 1960 (div. 1969); m. William A. Shea Jr., 1969 (div. 1977); m. Robert Charles Hunter, 1999; children: Laura Dern (b. 1967, actress). ❖ Began career in the chorus at the Copacabana; came to prominence in NY Equity Library production of *Orpheus Descending* (1959–60); made film debut in *Something Wild* (1961), followed by *The Reivers, WUSA, White Lightning, Chinatown, All Night Long, Something Wicked This Way Comes, A Kiss Before Dying, Shadow of a Doubt, Rambling Rose* and *Raging Angels,* among others. Nominated for Best Supporting Actress for performance as Flo in *Alice Doesn't Live Here Anymore* (1975) and as Marietta Pace Fortune in *Wild at Heart* (1990).

LADD, Kate Macy (1863–1945). American philanthropist. Born Catherine Everit Macy, April 6, 1863, in New York, NY; died Aug 27, 1945, in Far Hills, NJ; dau. of Josiah Macy Jr. and Caroline Louise (Everit) Macy; m. Walter Graeme Ladd (lawyer), Dec 5, 1883. ❖ Continued family tradition of philanthropy, with particular interest in medical field; created Maple Cottage, convalescent home for women in Peapack, NJ (1908); donated infirmary to New Jersey College for Women at New Brunswick (later Douglass College); regularly supported Berry School in GA, YWCA, visiting-nurse service of Henry Street

Settlement, and Maine Seacoast Missionary Society; created medical research-oriented Josiah Macy Jr. Foundation (1930).

LADD-FRANKLIN, Christine (1847–1930). American logician and psychologist. Name variations: Christine Franklin. Born in Windsor, CT, Dec 1, 1847; died of pneumonia in New York, NY, Mar 5, 1930; dau. of Eliphalet Ladd and Augusta (Niles) Ladd (d. 1860); sister of Henry Ladd and Jane Augusta Ladd McCordia; half-sister of Kathanne Ladd and George B. Ladd; graduate of Wesleyan Academy; Vassar College, BA, 1869; studied at Harvard University, 1872; attended Johns Hopkins University, 1878–82, completing requirements for PhD in 1883 which was not awarded until 1926 because women were not officially admitted into the program; m. Fabian Franklin (mathematician and editor of *New York Evening Post*), 1882; children: Margaret Ladd Franklin (b. 1884). ❖ Advocate of greater academic opportunities for women, taught secondary school; was lecturer in psychology and logic, Columbia University (1910–30); became interested in theories of color perception, particularly color-blindness (1890s); published over 100 articles on logic and color vision; is particularly known for contributing to the development of symbolic logic, a system of using mathematical formulas to express the forms of reasoning and argument.

LADDE, Cornelia (1915—). Dutch swimmer. Born Oct 27, 1915, in the Netherlands. ❖ At Los Angeles Olympics, won a silver medal in 4 x 100-meter freestyle relay (1932).

LADEWIG, Marion (1914—). American bowler. Born Marion Van Oosten, Oct 30, 1914, in Grand Rapids, Michigan; married in 1930 (div. 1940). ❖ One of bowling's greats, won the 1st National All-Star Match Games open to women (1949); won numerous Women's International Bowling Congress (WIBC) tournaments; was the 1st woman to win the Bowling Proprietors Association of American Women's All-Star title (1949); won 7 more All-Star tournaments (1949–53, 1957, 1959, and 1963); held World Invitational titles (1957, 1960, 1962–64); was Women's International Bowling Congress All-Events champion (1950, 1955); helped organize Professional Women's Bowling Association (PWBA); retired from tournament play (1965); helped raise professional bowling to new competitive heights and wrote syndicated column on bowling tips. Named Woman Bowler of Year 9 times (1950–54, 1957–59, 1963); inducted into International Bowling Museum Hall of Fame (1991). ❖ See also *Women in World History*.

LADIES OF GREGYNOG, The.
See Davies, Gwendoline (1882–1951).
See Davies, Margaret (1884–1963).

LADIES OF LLANGOLLEN, The.
See Butler, Eleanor (c. 1738–1829)
See Ponsonby, Sarah (1755–1831).

LADIES OF THE VALE.
See Butler, Eleanor (c. 1738–1829)
See Ponsonby, Sarah (1755–1831).

LADUKE, Winona (1959—). Native American environmental activist. Name variations: Winona La Duke. Born 1959 in East Los Angeles, CA; dau. of an Anishinabekwe father and Jewish mother; graduate of Harvard University; children: 3, including Waseyabin and Ajuawak. ❖ Activist, writer and international voice for indigenus environmental concerns, founded the White Earth Recovery Land Project to recover lost lands; helped to defeat a proposed hydroelectric project on James Bay in northern Canada; ran for vice president on Green Party ticket with Ralph Nader (1996 and 2000); an enrolled member of the Mississippi Band of Anishinabeg (also known as the Ojibwe or Chippewa), lives and works on the White Earth reservation in northern Minnesota; wrote (fiction) *Last Standing Woman* (1997), (nonfiction) *All Our Relations* (2000) and *Winona LaDuke Reader*, and (children's book) *In the Sugarbush*.

LADY ELEANOR, The (1590–1652). See Davies, Eleanor.

LADYNINA, Marina (1908–2003). Russian comedic actress. Born Marina Alekseyevna Ladynina, June 24, 1908, in Achinsk (some sources cite Tyombino), Siberia, Russia; died Mar 8, 2003, in Moscow; m. Ivan Pyryev or Pyriev (director), 1901 (died 1968); children: Andrei Ladynin (director). ❖ Appeared for several years with Moscow Theater; made film debut in *Dangerous Paths* (1935); with husband, made a string of highly successful musicals, including *Tractor Drivers* (1939), *The Rich Bride, Cossacks of the Kuban, Battle of Siberia,* and *Swineherd and Shepherd* (1941), which earned the Stalin Prize; a personal favorite of Joseph Stalin,

remained highly popular in Russia long after retirement from the screen (1953). Received 5 state prizes, including People's Artist of the Soviet Union; received a lifetime achievement award at the Nikas (Russian equivalent of Oscars, 1998). ❖ See also *East Side Story*, a documentary on Soviet musicals.

LADY OF THE CAMELLIAS (1824–1847). See Plessis, Alphonsine.

LADY OF THE MERCIANS (869–918). See Ethelflaed, Lady of the Mercians.

LADY OF WINCHESTER (c. 985–1052). See Emma of Normandy.

LAELIA (fl. 2nd c. BCE). Roman orator. Name variations: (nickname) "Sapiens" (the Wise). Fl. in 2nd century BCE; eldest of 2 daughters of Gaius Laelius (Roman orator who was a Roman consul in 140 BCE). ❖ Was nicknamed "Sapiens" (the Wise), since she had inherited the powers of her orator father. The purity of her Latin was admired by Cicero.

LAEMMLE, Beth (b. 1909). See Laemmle, Carla.

LAEMMLE, Carla (b. 1909). American film ballet dancer. Name variations: Beth Laemmle; Carla Leonard. Born Rebecca Isabelle Laemmle, Oct 20, 1909, in Chicago, IL; niece of Carl Laemmle (founder of Universal Studios in Hollywood). ❖ Trained in Chicago, and with Ernest Belcher in Los Angeles; performed briefly in operettas in Los Angeles, before dancing as Beth Laemmle in such films as *The Gate Crasher* (1928) and *King of Jazz* (1930).

LAERKESEN, Anna (1942—). Danish ballet dancer. Name variations: Anna Lärkesen. Born Mar 2, 1942, in Copenhagen, Denmark. ❖ At 17, began studies at school of Royal Danish Ballet, then joined the company (1960); performed in such classics as *La Sylphide, Swan Lake,* and *Giselle,* as well as in new works, including Ashton's *Romeo and Juliet,* Flindt's *The Three Musketeers,* and Cullberg's *Moon Reindeer;* was guest artist with Eliot Feld's American Ballet Company, performing in *Romance, Intermezzo,* and *Early Songs.*

LAETZSCH, Heike (1973—). See Latzsch, Heike.

LAFANU. See Lefanu.

LA FARGE, Margaret Hockaday (1907–1992). See Hockaday, Margaret.

LAFARGE, Marie (1816–1852). French murderer. Born Marie Fortunée Cappelle in Paris, France, 1816; died in Ussat, France, 1852; dau. of Colonel Cappelle (artillery officer in Napoleon's army); on mother's side, lineage could be traced to the reigning royal family, her grandmother being the dau. of the king's father Philippe-Egalité and his mistress Comtesse Stéphanie-Félicité de Genlis; attended convent school of Saint-Denis; m. Charles Lafarge (iron manufacturer), 1839 (died Jan 1840); no children. ❖ The central figure in one of France's most notorious murder cases, was convicted at age 24 of slowly poisoning husband to death with arsenic (1840). ❖ See also Mary S. Hartman, *Victorian Murderesses* (Schocken, 1977); and *Women in World History*.

LAFARGUE, Laura (1845–1911). See Marx, Laura.

LA FAYE, Steffi (1910–1992). See Duna, Steffi.

LAFAYETTE, Adrienne de (1760–1807). See Lafayette, Marie Adrienne de.

LAFAYETTE, Marie Adrienne de (1760–1807). French marquise. Name variations: Adrienne de Noailles; Dame Marie Adrienne de Lafayette; Madame de Lafayette or La Fayette. Born Marie-Adrienne-Françoise de Noailles, in Paris, France, 1760; died in Paris, Dec 24, 1807; 2nd of 5 daughters of Duke and Duchess d'Ayen; m. Gilbert du Motier (1757–1834), marquis de Lafayette (French aristocrat and major general), April 11, 1774; children: Henriette de Lafayette (who died in infancy); Anastasie de Lafayette; Virginie de Lafayette; George Washington de Lafayette. ❖ As wife of American revolutionary hero, marquis de Lafayette, raised 4 children alone in France while husband fought in America or split his French stays with her and his mistress Aglaé de Hunolstein; during French Revolution, when husband was forced to flee Paris and languished in an Austrian prison, attempted to win freedom for him; during Reign of Terror, was jailed in Le Pessis in Paris (1794), while her grandmother, mother, and sister were incarcerated at Luxembourg Palace and later executed by guillotine; finally released (1795), was given permission to live with husband in his primitive prison barracks in Austria; with daughters, set up housekeeping in a barren 2-room suite that would be home for several years; after husband was freed

(1797), returned to France (1799). ❖ See also Constance Wright, *Madame de Lafayette* (Henry Holt, 1959); and *Women in World History.*

LA FAYETTE, Marie-Madeleine de (1634–1693). French writer and memorialist. Name variations: Marie-Madeleine Pioche de la Vergne; Madame de La Fayette; Comtesse de La Fayette; Lafayette. Born Marie-Madeleine Pioche de la Vergne in Paris, Mar 18, 1634; died in Paris, May 25, 1693; eldest dau. of Marc Pioche, sieur de la Vergne, and Isabelle (Péna) Pioche de la Vergne; m. François de Motier, count or comte de La Fayette, 1655 (died 1683); children: Louis (b. 1658); Renaud-Armand (b. 1659). ❖ Author of *La Princesse de Clèves* (1678), which is now considered to be a landmark in the history of the novel, spent early childhood in Paris and French countryside; appointed lady-in-waiting to queen-regent Anne of Austria (1650); developed close friendships with Marie de Sévigné and poet Giles Ménage (1652); joined exiled stepfather in Anjou (1653); lived in Auvergne (1655–61); returned to Paris and spent the rest of her life there (1661–93); befriended Henrietta Anne, wife of Louis XIV's brother (1661); ran her own salon and visited the royal court frequently; published 1st novel *La Princesse de Montpensier* anonymously (1662); formed a close relationship with the Duc de La Rochefoucauld (1660s); other writings include *Zaide* (1670), *Histoire de Madame Henriette d'Angleterre* (1720), *La Comtesse de Tende* (1724), *Memoires de la cour de France* (written 1688–89, published 1731). Several of her works were published posthumously. ❖ See also Stirling Haig, *Madame de Lafayette* (Twayne, 1970); Janet Raitt, *Madame de Lafayette and "La Princesse de Clèves"* (Harrap, 1971); and *Women in World History.*

LAFFITE, Maria (1902–1986). See Laffitte, María.

LAFFITTE, María (1902–1986). Spanish novelist. Name variations: Maria Laffite; Maria de los Reyes Lafitte y Perez del Pulgar; countess of Campo Alange. Born Aug 15, 1902, in Seville, Spain; died 1986. ❖ Works include *La guerra secreta de los sexos* (1948) and *La flecha y la esponja* (1959).

LAFITE, Marie-Elisabeth Bouée de (c. 1750–1794). French translator and short-story writer. Name variations: Madame Lafite. Born c. 1750 in France; died 1794; m. a Protestant preacher. ❖ Collaborated with husband on periodical *Bibliothèque des sciences et des beaux arts;* published educational fiction, including *Entriens, drames et contes moraux* (1778) and *Eugénie et ses élèves* (1787); also wrote *Lettres sur divers sujets* (1775) and trans. Lavater's *Essays on Physiognomy* (1787) and Sophie von la Roche's novel *Miss Lony* (1792).

LA FLESCHE, Susan (1865–1915). Native American physician. Born Susan La Flesche Picotte. Born Susan La Flesche on the Omaha Reservation in what is now Nebraska, June 17, 1865; died in Walthill, Nebraska, Sept 18, 1915; dau. of last recognized Chief of the Omahas, Joseph La Flesche (also called Inshta'maza) of Omaha-French descent, and Mary Gale, also called Hinnuaganun, of Iowa-English descent; sister of Susette La Flesche (1854–1902), Marguerite La Flesche, and Francis La Flesche (1857–1932); attended missionary school (1870–79), Elizabeth Institute of Young Ladies in Elizabeth, NJ (1879–84), and Hampton Normal and Agriculture Institute (1884–86); graduate of Women's Medical College of Pennsylvania, 1889; interned as assistant to resident physician at Women's Hospital, Philadelphia, Mar–Aug 1889; m. Henry Picotte (mixed-blood Sioux), 1894 (died 1905); children: Pierre Picotte; Caryl Picotte. ❖ First Native American woman physician, had tenure as government physician assigned to Omaha Reservation (1889–93) but was forced to resign due to illness; began public health reform as chair of State Health Committee of Nebraska Women's Clubs, lobbied on behalf of Omaha people for public health legislation at Nebraska State Legislature, and was active as a prohibitionist and legislative reformer (1897–1915); following husband's death (1905), returned to small private medical practice, funded by Blackbird Hills Presbyterian Church, and held her position there until her death. ❖ See also Norma Kidd Green, *Iron Eye's Family: The Children of Joseph La Flesche* (Johnson, 1969); and *Women in World History.*

LA FLESCHE, Susette (1854–1902). Native American writer and political activist. Name variations: Inshtatheamba or Inshtatheumba (means Bright Eyes); Susette LaFlesche; Susette La Flesche Tibbles. Born Inshtatheamba also called Susette La Flesche in 1854, on Omaha tribal lands south of the settlement that became Omaha, Nebraska; died in Bancroft, NE, May 1902; dau. of Joseph La Flesche, also called Inshta'maza, of Omaha-French descent and the last chief of the Omaha Nation, and Mary Gale, also called Hinnuaganun, of Iowa-English descent; sister of Susan La Flesche (1865–1915), Marguerite La Flesche, and Francis La Flesche (1857–1932); attended missionary school (1860–69), and Elizabeth Institute of Young Ladies, Elizabeth, NJ (1871–75); m. Thomas Tibbles, July 23, 1881; no children. ❖ An eloquent speaker, famed for her work on behalf of her nation, began teaching on Omaha reservation (1877); went on 1st East Coast lecture and fund-raising tour and was the 1st woman to speak at Faneuil Hall in Boston (1879); criss-crossed the country, gave hundreds of speeches, raised money for the Ponca-Omaha Committee, and lobbied before US Congress at every opportunity; testified before Senate subcommittee (1880); published *Nedawi*, 1st children's story, and helped to petition Congress on behalf of Omaha nation regarding land grants (1883–84); made lecture tour to England (1887–88); moved with husband to Washington, DC, became a correspondent for *The Non-Conformist*, and published additional children's stories (1893); moved with husband to Lincoln, NE, wrote articles and editorials for *Weekly Independent* (1894–99); illus. *Oo-mah-ha Ta-wa-tha*, stories of the Omahas, written by Fannie Reed Griffen, believed to be the 1st published illustrations by a Native American. ❖ See also Norma Kidd Green, *Iron Eye's Family: The Children of Joseph La Flesche* (Johnson, 1969); Dorothy Clarke Wilson, *Bright Eyes: The Story of Susette La Flesche* (McGraw, 1974); and *Women in World History.*

LA FLEUR, Annie (1969—). See Burgess, Annie.

LA FOLLETTE, Belle Case (1859–1931). American social reformer. Name variations: Belle Case; Belle Case LaFollette. Born Belle Case in Summit, WI, April 21, 1859; died in Washington, DC, Aug 18, 1931; dau. of Anton T. Case and Mary (Nesbit) Case; graduate of University of Wisconsin, 1879, and University of Wisconsin Law School, 1885; m. Robert Marion La Follette, Sr. (1855–1925, senator and presidential candidate), Dec 31, 1881; children: Fola La Follette (b. 1882); Robert Marion La Follette Jr. (1895–1953, who served as a senator for 22 years); Philip Fox La Follette (b. 1897); Mary La Follette (b. 1899). ❖ One of the most influential American women of her day, became the 1st to receive a law degree (1885) and was subsequently admitted to the bar and Wisconsin supreme court; used expertise to assist husband during his 3 terms in US House of Representatives (1885–91) and played an unusually active role in his public life; when husband was defeated in 4th congressional run, took up her own political causes (1890–1900): suffrage and protective legislation for women and children; with husband governor (1900), joined him in shaping a series of reforms which became nationally recognized as the "Wisconsin Idea" or "progressivism"; returned to Washington after husband was elected to US Senate (1906); with him, created *La Follette's Weekly Magazine* (1909); also wrote a column for North American Press Syndicate (1911–12); was instrumental in organizing Congressional Club of Washington, and became active in final push for women's suffrage; was one of the organizers of the Women's International League for Peace and Freedom; helped found National Council for the Prevention of War (1921) and was also a leader in the Women's Committee for World Disarmament; following husband's death (1925), assumed associate editorship of *La Follette's Magazine* and prepared husband's biography, a project that was ultimately completed by her daughter. ❖ See also *Women in World History.*

LA FOLLETTE, Fola (1882–1970). American actress and women's rights activist. Name variations: LaFollette. Born in 1882; died Feb 17, 1970, in Arlington, Virginia; dau. of Robert M. La Follette (US senator) and Belle Case La Follette (1859–1931, social reformer); m. George Middleton (playwright, died). ❖ Stage credits include *The Scarecrow* and *Tradition;* following mother's death, took over and finished biography of her father, *La Follette* (Macmillan, 1953).

LAFON, Madeleine (1924–1967). French ballet dancer. Born 1924, in Paris, France; died April 6, 1967, in Paris; trained with Boris Kniaseff, Alexander Volinine, Lyubov Egorova, and at Paris Opéra. ❖ Began performing Paris Opéra company (late 1940s), where she created lead roles in 4th movement of Balanchine's *Le Palais de Crystal* (1947), Gsovsky's *La Dame aux Camilias*, and Lifar's *Mirages* (1947); performed to great acclaim in other works by Lifar, including his *Suite en Blanc,* and in Juan Corelli's *Le Combat de Tancrède et Clorinde;* taught at Paris Opéra's school after 1963.

LAFONT, Bernadette (1938—). French actress. Born in Nimes, France, Oct 26, 1938; children: Pauline Lafont (d. 1988, actress). ❖ Originally a dancer, made film debut in the short *Les Mistons* (*The Mischief-Makers,* 1958); became associated with French New Wave, particularly films of Claude Chabrol; films include *Le Beau Serge* (1958), *Les Bonnes Femmes* (1960), *Compartiment Tueurs* (*The Sleeping Car Murder,* 1965), *Le Voleur*

(*The Thief,* 1967), *Piège* (1969), *Valparaiso Valparaiso* (1970), *La Maman et la Putain* (*The Mother and the Whore,* 1973), *Tendre Dracula* (1974), *Zig Zig* (1975), *Vincent mit l'Ane dans un Pré* (1975), *Noroit* (1977), *Violette Nozière* (1978), *Certaines Nouvelles* (1979), *La Gueule de L'autre* (1979), *Le Roi des Cons* (1981), *La Bête Noire* (1983), *Gwendoline* (1984), *Inspecteur Lavardin* (1986), *Masques* (1987), *Waiting for the Moon* (1987), *Les Saisons du Plaisir* (*The Seasons of Pleasure,* 1988), and *Prisonnières* (1988). ❖ See also *Women in World History.*

LA FORCE, Charlotte-Rose de Caumont de (1650–1724). French novelist. Name variations: Mademoiselle de La Force; Charlotte de Caumont de La Force; (pseudonym) Mademoiselle de X. Born Charlotte-Rose de Caumont de La Force, 1650, in France; died 1724; dau. of Jacques Nompar de Caumont, duc de la Force (1559–1652), maréchal of France and friend of Henry IV of France); m. M de Briou, 1684. ❖ Enjoyed liberated youth but after marriage to younger man her family intervened and had marriage annulled; implicated in publication of satirical verses, was made to choose between exile and convent; chose convent and began writing stories and novels; fairy tales published as *Les Contes des contes* (1697) under pseudonym Mlle de X; wrote secret histories of Mary of Burgundy, Margaret of Valois, Catherine of Bourbon and Enrique IV, king of Castile.

LAFORET, Carmen (1921–2004). Spanish writer. Name variations: Carmen Laforet Diaz. Born in Barcelona, Spain, Sept 26, 1921, in Barcelona, Spain; died Feb 28, 2004; studied philosophy and law at University of Barcelona; m. Manuel González Cerezales, 1946 (sep. 1970); children: Marta, Cristina, Silvia, Manuel and Agustín Cerezales. ❖ Writer whose novels depict the quest for self-fulfillment following Spanish Civil War; when young, moved to Las Palmas, in the Canary Islands, where father worked as an architect; with family, returned to Spain (1939); moved to Madrid (1942); published 1st novel, *Nada* (*Nothing,* 1944), which helped establish *tremendismo* as a Spanish literary movement, portraying an exaggerated realism emphasizing both psychological and physical violence; later books include *La isla y los demonios* (*The Island and Its Devils,* 1952), *La llamada* (*The Vocation,* 1954), *La mujer nueva* (*The New Woman,* 1955), *La insolación* (*Sunstroke,* 1963), *Mis páginas mejores* (1967), and *Paralelo 35* (1967). Won Nadal Prize, Menorca Prize and National Literature Prize. ❖ See also Roberta Johnson, *Carmen Laforet* (Twayne, 1981); and *Women in World History.*

LAFORGE, Margaret Getchell (1841–1880). American businesswoman. Born Margaret Getchell, July 16, 1841, on Nantucket Island, MA; died Jan 25, 1880, in New York, NY; dau. of Barzillai (or Barzilla) Getchell and Phebe Ann (Pinkham) Getchell; m. Abiel LaForge (buyer), Mar 27, 1869 (died 1878); children: 6. ❖ Manager of Macy's during department store's early years, began career as a teacher in Lansingburgh, NY, and at Lawrenceville Female Seminary in NJ; after starting work for a distant relative, Rowland Macy, in his NY dry goods store, was promoted to bookkeeper; became superintendent of the growing enterprise (1866). ❖ See also Ralph M. Hower, *History of Macy's of N.Y., 1858–1919* (1943); and *Women in World History.*

LAGERBERG, Catherina (1941—). Dutch swimmer. Born Jan 13, 1941, in Netherlands. ❖ At Rome Olympics, won a bronze medal in 400-meter freestyle (1960).

LAGERLÖF, Selma (1858–1940). Swedish author. Name variations: Selma Lagerlof. Born Selma Ottilia Lovisa Lagerlöf, Nov 20, 1858, at Maarbacka in Värmland, in Sweden; died at Maarbacka, Mar 16, 1940; dau. of Erik Gustav Lagerlöf and Lovisa (Wallroth) Lagerlöf; attended Royal Women's Superior Training College, Stockholm; never married. ❖ Author of numerous novels, short stories and tales, 1st taught in the southern Swedish town of Landscrona, where she started her writing career as well; following success of *The Story of Gösta Berling* (1891), resigned her post and became a full-time writer; with revenues from that novel and subsequent works, bought back her childhood home, Maarbacka, which had been auctioned off (1889); received honorary doctorate from University of Uppsala (1907), followed by Nobel Prize (1909), the 1st Swede and 1st woman to be honored thus; purchased the property surrounding Maarbacka that had been in the family for generations and resumed the position of landed gentry; was keynote speaker at International Congress of Women (1911); accepted into the Swedish Academy (1914), the 1st and only female member; writings include *Invisible Links* (1894), *The Miracles of Antichrist* (1897), *The Queens of Kungahalla and Other Sketches* (1897), *The Tale of a Manor* (1899), *Jerusalem* (1901–02), *Herr Arne's Hoard* (1903), *Christ Legends* (1904), *The Wonderful Adventures of Nils* (1906–07), *A Saga about a Saga* (1908),

Liljekrona's Home (1911), *Thy Soul Shall Bear Witness* (1912), *The Emperor of Portugalia* (1914), *Trolls and Men* (2 vols., 1916, 1921), *The Outcast* (1918), *Zachris Topelius* (1920), *Maarbacka* (1922), *The Ring of the Lövenskolds* (1925–28), *Memories of My Childhood* (1930), *The Diary of Selma Lagerlöf* (1932), *Autumn* (1933) and *Writings and Re-writings* (1933). ❖ See also Walter A. Berendsohn, *Selma Lagerlöf: Her Life and Work* (Kennikat, 1931); Vivi Edstrom, *Selma Lagerlöf* (Twayne, 1984); and *Women in World History.*

LAGORIO, Gina (1930—). Italian novelist, short-story writer and politician. Born 1930 in Piemonte, Brà, near Cuneo, Italy; received degree in literature from University of Turin. ❖ Elected member of Italian Parliament (1987); writings include *Le novelle di Simonetta* (1960), *Il polline* (1966), *Un ciclone chiamato Titti* (1969), *Tosca dei gatti* (Tosca and Her Cats, 1983), *Il golfo del paradiso* (Paradise Bay, 1987) and *Tra le mure stellate* (1991); probably best known for *Approssimato per difetto* (By Default, 1971), about her life as well as her husband's death.

LA GRANGE, Anna de (1825–1905). Countess of Stankowitch and a coloratura soprano. Name variations: Lagrange. Born Anna Caroline de Lagrange in Paris, France, July 24, 1825; died April 1905; studied with Bordogni and Lamperti; m. Count Stankowitch also seen as Stankowich. ❖ Made debut in Varese, Italy (1842), and sang with success throughout Europe and US; married a wealthy Russian count and retired (1848).

LA GRATIOSA (d. 1659). Italian poisoner. Born in Italy; hanged 1659 in Rome. ❖ Apparently chief accomplice to Hieronyma Spara (La Spara) who sold poison to young wives looking to do away with their husbands; arrested with La Spara and other companions, reportedly confessed under torture; hanged with La Spara and 3 other women.

LAGRAVE, Comtesse de (1770–1820). French novelist. Born 1770 in France; died 1820. ❖ Known for sentimental novels, including *Minuit, ou les aventures de Paul de Mirebon* (1798), *Sophie de Beauregard, ou le véritable amour* (1798), *Zabeth, ou la victime de l'ambition* (1798), *La Chaumière incendiée* (1802), *M. Ménard ou l'homme comme il y en a peu* (1802), *Hector de Romagny, ou l'erreur d'une bonne mére* (1803), *Paulina* (1804), and *La Méprise de diligence* (1820); also wrote Gothic novel *Le Château d'Alvarino, ou les effets de la vengeance* (1799).

LA GUESNERIE, Charlotte Charbonnier de (1710–1785). French novelist. Name variations: Charlotte-Marie-Anne Charbonnière de la Guesnerie. Born 1710 in France; died 1785. ❖ Published popular sentimental works *Mémoires de Milady B* (1760), *Iphis et Aglae* (1768), *Mémoires de Milady Varmonti* (1778), and *Les Resources de la vertu* (1782).

LA GUETTE, Madame de (1613–1676). See Guette, Catherine de la.

LAGUILLER, Arlette (1940—). French politician. Born Mar 18, 1940, in Paris, France. ❖ Longtime militant for Communist Party, ran as 1st woman candidate for the French presidency (1974); elected to French Parliament (1981); was a member of the national leadership of Lutte Ouvrière and its spokesperson; representing the Confederal Group of the European United Left/Nordic Green Left (GUE/NGL), elected to 5th European Parliament (1999–2004). ❖ See also autobiography (in French) *Moi, une militante* (My Life as a Militant).

L'AGUIVOISE, Marie (c. 1790–1850). See Dorion, Marie.

LAGUNA, Frederica de (1906–2004). See de Laguna, Frederica.

LAGUNA, Grace Mead Andrus de (1878–1978). See de Laguna, Grace.

LAHODOVA, Jana (1957—). Czech field-hockey player. Born June 1957. ❖ At Moscow Olympics, won a silver medal in team competition (1980).

LA HYE, Louise (1810–1838). French composer, organist, pianist, singer, and lecturer. Name variations: often published under the masculine name Monsieur Leon Saint-Amans Fils. Born in Charenton, France, Mar 8, 1810; died Nov 17, 1838, age 28, in Paris; dau. of Charles Louis Rousseau; grandniece of Jean-Jacques Rousseau; studied under her father Charles Louis Rousseau and then under Leon Saint-Amans. ❖ At 11, entered Paris Conservatoire to study organ, piano and singing; received 2nd place for organ (1826) and 1st place at the Conservatoire (1828); taught composition and played her *Fantasia* at Sociéte des Concerts (1831); introduced her dramatic opera *Le songe de la religieuse* at the Hôtel de Ville (1835). ❖ See also *Women in World History.*

LAI YAWEN (1970—). Chinese volleyball player. Born Sept 9, 1970, in Liaoning Province, China. ❖ Joined the national team (1989); named team captain (1993); won a team silver medal at Atlanta Olympics (1996). Named MVP at Grand Prix (1993).

LAIA (fl. c. 100 BCE). *See Iaia.*

LAIDLAW, Harriet Burton (1873–1949). American suffragist. Born Harriet Davenport Wright Burton, Dec 16, 1873, in Albany, NY; died Jan 25, 1949, in New York, NY; dau. of George Davidson Burton (bank cashier) and Alice Davenport (Wright) Burton; Albany Normal School (later New York State College for Teachers), Master of Pedagogy, 1896; m. James Lees Laidlaw (banker), Oct 25, 1905 (died 1932); children: 1 daughter. ❖ Served as Manhattan borough chair (1909–16) and vice-chair of New York Woman Suffrage Party; traveled on speaking tours of Far West with husband (1911, 1914); was 2nd auditor (1911–13) and director (from 1917) of National American Woman Suffrage Association; after ratification of 19th Amendment, channeled energy into host of other causes, including international peace, political reform in NY, and reciprocal-trade legislation.

LAILA BINT AL-AKHYAL (fl. 650–660). *See Layla al-Akhyaliyya.*

LAINE, Cleo (1927—). British jazz musician. Name variations: Dame Cleo Laine. Born Clementina Dinah Campbell, Oct 28, 1927, in Middlesex, England; m. George Langridge, 1947 (div.); m. John Dankworth (bandleader), 1958; children: (1st m.) 1 son; (2nd m.) 2, including Jacqui Dankworth (actress-singer). ❖ Renowned for extraordinary vocal range, command of phrasing, and vocal versatility, joined Dankworth Orchestra (1953) and achieved success in recordings and on tv; appeared on stage in, among others, Dankworth's *Lady in Waiting,* Sondheim's *Into the Woods,* and the BBC Prom's production of Britten's *Noyes Fludde;* was 1st British artist to win Grammy (1983). Nominated for a Tony Award as Best Actress for *The Mystery of Edwin Drood* (1986).

LAINE, Doris (1959—). Finnish ballet dancer. Born Feb 15, 1931, in Helsinki, Finland; trained with Anna Sevenskaya and Anna Northcote in London and at Finnish National Ballet. ❖ Danced with Finnish National Ballet (1950s–60s), appearing in *Esmeralda, Swan Lake, Giselle, Don Quixote,* and *The Sleeping Beauty;* performed in numerous ballets of Birgit Cullberg; appeared on tours to US, through Western Europe.

LAINÉ, Jeanne (c. 1454–?). *See Hachette, Jeanne.*

LAING, Eleanor (1958—). English politician and member of Parliament. Born Eleanor Pritchard, Feb 1, 1958; m. Alan Laing, 1983. ❖ As a Conservative, elected to House of Commons for Epping Forest (1997, 2001, 2005); named opposition spokesperson for Education and Skills.

LAING, Elizabeth (1959—). American ballet dancer. Born 1959 in New York, NY; dau. of Kelly Brown (1928–1981) and Isabel Mirrow (both dancers with American Ballet Theatre); sister of Kevin Kelly Brown (producer), Ethan Brown (dancer) and Leslie Browne (dancer). ❖ Trained at American Ballet Theatre, then joined the company (1977); often featured in revivals of 19th-century ballets with Natalia Makarova and Mikhail Baryshnikov; also danced the contemporary works of Agnes de Mille and Antony Tudor.

LAIR, Clara (1895–1973). *See Negron Muñoz, Mercedes.*

LAIRD, Carobeth (1895–1983). American ethnographer and linguist. Name variations: Carobeth Tucker Laird. Born Carobeth Tucker, July 20, 1895, in Coleman, TX; died Aug 5, 1983, in Poway, CA; dau. of Emma (Chaddock) Tucker and James Tucker (newspaper editor); attended San Diego Normal School; m. John Peabody Harrington (linguist), 1916 (div.); m. George Laird (died 1940); children: (1st m.) 2 daughters; (2nd m.) 5, including Georgia Laird Culp (Chemehuevi leader). ❖ Known particularly for work in preserving Chemehuevi language and mythology, worked in the field in CA and Southwest with 1st husband, then published account of her life with him, *Encounter with an Angry God* (1975); married George Laird, a Chemehuevi Indian, who served as primary consultant for *The Chemehuevis* (1976), which established her as a leading authority on Chemehuevi people, and for *Mirror and Pattern* (1984); published account of her experiences in a nursing home, *Limbo* (1979).

LAIS (fl. 425 BCE). Greek hetaerae. Name variations: Laïs; Lais the Elder. Pronunciation: LAY-is. Born probably in Corinth; fl. around 425 BCE. ❖ Noted for her beauty and vices, lived in Corinth during Peloponnesian war (431–404 BCE); following her death at Corinth, a monument was erected to her of a lioness tearing a ram. German painter

Hans Holbein the Younger titled his portrait of a beautiful young girl in elegant dress, *Lais Corinthiaca* (The Corinthian Lais).

LAIS (fl. 385 BCE). Greek hetaerae. Name variations: Laïs; Lais the Younger. Born probably in Hyccara, in Sicily, c. 365 BCE. ❖ Brought to Corinth as a child, sat as a model for the court painter Apelles, who, it is said, induced her to live the life of a courtesan; stunningly attractive, became a rival of Phryne; was reputedly stoned to death in Thessaly by some women whose jealousy she had aroused.

LAIS (fl. 1st c. BCE). Greek midwife and physician. Name variations: Laïs. Fl. in 1st century BCE. ❖ Mentioned by Pliny the Elder in *Historia Naturalis,* was a midwife often at odds with another midwife Elephantis over the administering of drugs; with Salpe, a midwife from Lemnos, came up with a treatment for rabies and intermittent fevers.

LAISNE, Jeanne (c. 1454–?). *See Hachette, Jeanne.*

LAISSE, Madame de (fl. 18th c.). French short-story writer. Fl. in France. ❖ Published collections of tales and songs, including *Receuil d'anecdotes* (1773), *Nouveaux Contes Moraux* (1774), *Ouvrage sans titre* (1775), *Proverbes dramatiques* (1777) and *Nouveau Genre de Proverbes dramatiques* (1778).

LAIS THE ELDER. *See Lais (fl. 425 BCE).*

LAIS THE YOUNGER. *See Lais (fl. 385 BCE).*

LAIT, Jacqui (1947—). Scottish politician and member of Parliament. Born Dec 16, 1947; m. Peter Jones, 1974. ❖ Contested Strathclyde West (1984) for European Parliament election; as a Conservative, elected to House of Commons for Hastings and Rye (1992), then lost election for Hastings and Rye (1997); won by-election for Beckenham (1997); named shadow secretary of state for Scotland; reelected for Beckenham (2001, 2005); was the 1st woman MP to join the Tory whips' office.

LAJOIE, Marie Gérin (1867–1945). *See Gérin-Lajoie, Marie.*

LAKAMBINI (1875–1943). *See Jesus, Gregoria de.*

LAKE, Alice (1895–1967). American stage and silent-screen actress. Born Sept 12, 1895, in Brooklyn, NY; died Nov 15, 1967, in Hollywood, CA. ❖ After a successful stage career, moved to Hollywood and performed in several Mack Sennett shorts with Fatty Arbuckle; appeared in other films, including *Playing Dead, Circumstantial Evidence, The Moonstone, Body and Soul, Dining Out, Glamour, The Mighty Barnum* and *Frisco Kid;* often starred opposite Bert Lytell.

LAKE, Claude (1841–1896). *See Blind, Mathilde.*

LAKE, Florence (1904–1980). American actress. Born Florence Silverlake, Nov 27, 1924, in Charleston, SC; died April 11, 1980, in Woodland Hills, CA; sister of Arthur Lake (actor). ❖ Films include *Thru Different Eyes, The Rogue Song, Ladies of the Jury, Sweetheart of Sigma Chi, Quality Street, Stage Coach, Crash Dive* and *San Diego, I Love You.*

LAKE, Harriette (1909–2000). *See Sothern, Ann.*

LAKE, Leonora Marie (1849–1930). *See Barry, Leonora M.*

LAKE, Marion Turpie (d. 1967). *Turpie, Marion.*

LAKE, Mother (1849–1930). *See Barry, Leonora M.*

LAKE, Veronica (1919–1973). American actress. Name variations: Constance Keane. Born Constance Ockleman, Nov 14, 1919, in Brooklyn, NY; died July 7, 1973, in Burlington, Vermont; m. John Detlie (studio art director), 1940 (div. 1943); m. Andre DeToth (film director), 1944 (div. 1952); m. Joe McCarthy (songwriter), 1955 (div. 1959); m. Robert Carlton-Munro (naval captain), 1972; children: (1st m.) Elaine Detlie; (2nd m.) Andre Anthony Michael DeToth III (known as Mike); Diana DeToth. ❖ Launched a national craze in 1st major film, *I Wanted Wings* (1941), by wearing long blonde hair seductively cascading over one eye; had 2 more successes, co-starring with Joel McCrea in *Sullivan's Travels* (1942) and Alan Ladd in *This Gun for Hire* (1942); co-starred with Ladd in 3 subsequent films: *The Glass Key* (1942), *The Blue Dahlia* (1946), and *Saigon* (1948); was then teamed in a series of bland comedies with Eddie Bracken; other films include *I Married a Witch* (1942) and *So Proudly We Hail* (1943); left Hollywood and settled in NY (1953), where she appeared on tv and in summer stock; appeared in off-Broadway revival of *Best Foot Forward* to good reviews, and made a few low-budget movies, but a real comeback never materialized. ❖ See also *Women in World History.*

LAKEMAN, Hedda (1897–1951). *See Dyson, Elizabeth Geertruida Agatha.*

LAKEY, Alice (1857–1935). American "pure food" leader. Born Oct 14, 1857, in Shanesville, Ohio; died June 18, 1935, in Cranford, NJ; dau. of Charles D. Lakey and Ruth (Jaques) Lakey. ❖ Singing career was derailed by poor health, which drew interest in "pure food movement"; chaired food investigation committee of National Consumers' League (1905–12); lobbied Congress for federal pure-food legislation, resulting in Federal Food and Drug Act of 1906; was charter member of NY Milk Committee (from 1906); helped launch (1914) and served as executive secretary of American Pure Food League; appointed member of First National Conference on Street and Highway Safety by Secretary of Commerce Herbert Hoover (1924).

LAKIC, Mara (1963—). Yugoslavian basketball player. Born Aug 18, 1963. ❖ At Seoul Olympics, won a silver medal in team competition (1988).

LAKINE-TOTH HARSANYI, Katalin (1948—). Hungarian handball player. Born April 1948 in Hungary. ❖ At Montreal Olympics, won a bronze medal in team competition (1976).

LAKSHMIBAI (c. 1835–1858). Indian rani. Name variations: Rani, Maharanee or Maharani of Jhansi; Rani Lakshmibai; Lakshmi Bai; Laksmi; Manikarnika. Pronunciation: RAH-nee Luck-SHMEE-baa-ee. Born Manikarnika, nicknamed Manu, c. 1835 in Varanasi, India; died 1858 (also cited as 1857) on battlefield in Gwalior, near Jhansi; dau. of Moropant Tambe (court advisor) and Bhagirathi; studied literature, military strategy, and equestrian training; m. Gangadhar Rao (a raja), May 1842 (died 1853); children: son (b. 1851, died at 3 months). ❖ Legendary Indian rani (queen), revered for her bravery and leadership, who became a symbol of sacrifice in India's fight for freedom; adopted with dying husband a young male relative as future heir to the throne, because the British-imposed doctrine of "lapse" allowed them to assume control of states whose rulers died without natural heirs; following husband's death (1853), became ruler of the state of Jhansi at age 18; began rigorous training as a soldier and equestrian and also trained a women's military unit; when Lord Dalhousie proclaimed the doctrine of lapse for Jhansi, sent appeals to the governor-general's office asking for recognition of her adopted son and employing well-formulated arguments in lengthy, legalistic dispatches, but an unimpressed Dalhousie claimed that Jhansi had lapsed to the British and she was removed from her fort (May 1854); challenged British authority once more when they held her responsible for the state's debts; when Upper India rebelled against British rule (May 10, 1857), reassumed control of the administration of her state; enlisted troops, cast cannon, commenced manufacture of other weapons, and personally trained her women's military unit in equestrian and military skills; confident of her military strength, now openly challenged British authority, moving from her palace back to her fort and ordering that the Jhansi flag be flown from the wall (1858); fought at the head of her troops, rendering severe losses to the British, pushing them further back each day; but with British reinforcements arriving in large numbers, soon saw her forces decimated; outside of Gwalior, rode out in full battle dress with a meager band of soldiers and clashed with the powerful British Hussars (June 17, 1858) and was fatally wounded, the 1st female hero of India's First War of Independence. Her bravery has sustained itself in the oral tradition of storytelling, as well as ballads, poems, and the cinema. ❖ See also Joyce Lebra-Chapman, *The Rani of Jhansi: A Study in Female Heroism in India* (U. of Hawaii Press, 1992); Shyam Narain Sinha, *Rani Lakshmi Bai of Jhansi* (Chugh, 1980); and *Women in World History.*

LAKWENA, Alice (1960—). Ugandan rebel. Name variations: Alice Auma. Born 1960 in northern Uganda; dau. of Severino Lukoya, an Anglican catechist. ❖ As a young Acholi woman in northern Uganda, claimed she was under orders of a Christian spirit named Lakwena (means "sent" or "messenger" in Acholi) in the guise of a Christian Italian who had died in WWII (1985); raised an army called the Holy Spirit Mobile Forces (HSMF); waged war against the forces of witchcraft and led the very nearly successful Uganda uprisings against the government of Museveni (1986–88), coming close to overthrowing it; fled to a refugee camp in Kenya, where she remained; reportedly received invitation from president of Uganda to return to there (2003). ❖ See also Heike Behrend, *Alice Lakwena and the Holy Spirits.*

LALA (fl. c. 100 BCE). See Iaia.

LALANDE, Amélie Lefrançais de (fl. 1790). French astronomer. Name variations: Mme Lefrançais de Lalande. Born Marie Jeanne Amélie Harlay; m. Michel Jean Jérôme Lefrançais de Lalande (1776–1839, astronomer); children: Caroline Lefrançais de Lalande (b. 1790); Isaac Lefrançais de Lalande. ❖ Worked as assistant to husband and his cousin

Joseph Jérôme Lefrançais de Lalande (1772–1807), who served as husband's mentor; has been credited with calculating the astronomical tables for several publications; constructed the tables appended to Jérôme's *Abrégé de navigation* (1793), which were designed to assist navigators in calculating time at sea, and performed the calculations and reductions included in an astronomical almanac he edited, *Connaissance des temps.* ❖ See also *Women in World History.*

LALAURIE, Delphine (c. 1790–?). American murderer (accused). Name variations: Madame Delphine Lalaurie. Born Marie Delphine, c. 1790; died possibly in 1836; dau. of Louis Barthelemy Chevalier de Maccarthy (name later simplified to Mccarty); m. Don Ramon de Lopez y Angulo, June 11, 1800 (died Mar 26, 1804); m. Jean Blanque, 1808 (died 1816); m. Dr. Leonard Louis Lalaurie, June 12, 1825; children: (1st m.) (Marie Francoise) Delphine de Borgia y Angulo De La Candelaria y Lopez (b. c. 1792). ❖ As a member of Louisiana's high society, kept numerous slaves at her mansion at 1140 Royal Street; following a fire there (April 10, 1834), fled when newspapers reported that authorities had found a torture chamber in her home, where slaves had been subjected to unimaginable cruelties, resulting in some deaths; her subsequent fate is unknown. Some maintain she was not the sadist she was made out to be, but rather the victim of yellow journalism.

LAL DED (b. 1355). Kashmiri mystic and poet. Name variations: Lal-Ded; Lallyogeshwari or Lalla Yogeshwari; Lalla the Mystic; Mother Lalla; Lalleshwari. Born in 1355 in Pandrenthan, near Srinagar, to a Kashmiri Pandit family in the time of Sultan Ala-ud-din; though exact date of death is unknown, died in Bijbehara; married at 12 and was given the name Padmavati by cruel in-laws who nearly starved her. ❖ Wise woman of Kashmir, renounced her husband's family at age 26 and became a disciple of Sidh Srikanth; began to write verse in Kashmiri; preached in countryside, often dancing naked and singing; lived to an old age as a respected hermit and mystic at Bijbehara; considered by some a saint, by others a sufi or a yoga or a devotee of Shiva; her sayings, which are frequently quoted, number around 200.

LALIVE, Caroline (1979—). American Alpine skier. Born Aug 10, 1979, in Truckee, CA. ❖ Placed 7th in combined event at Nagano Olympics (1998); won US championship in slalom and combined events (2000).

LALLA ROOKH (fl. 1600s). Indian princess. Lalla Rookh means Tulip Cheek; fl. in 1600s; supposed dau. of Aurangzeb (1618–1707), Mughul emperor (r. 1658–1707). ❖ As presented in the 1817 poem *Lalla Rookh* by Thomas Moore, was betrothed to Aliris, sultan of lesser Bulcharia; on her journey from Delhi to Cashmere, was entertained by Feramorz, a young Persian poet, with whom she fell in love; was delighted when she learned that the young poet was the sultan to whom she was betrothed. ❖ See also *Women in World History.*

LALLA THE MYSTIC (b. 1355). See Lal Ded.

LALLESHWARI (b. 1355). See Lal Ded.

LALLYOGESHWARI or LALLA YOGESHWARI (b. 1355). See Lal Ded.

LA LOCA, Juana (1479–1555). See Juana la Loca.

LALUMIERE, Catherine (1935—). French lawyer and politician. Name variations: Catherine Lalumière. Born Aug 3, 1935, in Rennes, France. ❖ Served as state secretary for the Civil Service (1981), minister for Consumer Affairs (1981–84), state secretary for European Affairs (1984–86), member of the National Assembly (1986–89), and secretary-general of the Council of Europe (1989–94); as a European Socialist, elected to 4th and 5th European Parliament (EP, 1994–99, 1999–2004); elected vice-president of EP.

LA LUPE (1939–1992). Cuban singer. Name variations: Lupe Victoria Yoli. Born Lupe Victoria Yoli in Santiago, Cuba, 1939; died in the Bronx, Feb 28, 1992; m. twice. ❖ Known as the Queen of Latin Soul, starred in Havana's nightclubs (late 1950s); in aftermath of Cuban Revolution (1959), lost all her property; immigrated to US (1962); began singing with Mongo Santamaria, recording a number of hit singles; became one of Latin music's most popular performers (1960s); moved to Puerto Rico to do concerts and tv shows (1970s); after numerous setbacks, began singing Christian music and recorded a series of albums. ❖ See also *Women in World History.*

LAMA, Giulia (c. 1685–c. 1753). Italian artist. Born c. 1685 in Venice, Italy; died c. 1753; possibly dau. of Agostino Lama (painter); may have studied with Giovanni Battista Piazzetta; never married. ❖ What little is known about her life and work has been pieced together from a Venetian guidebook (1733), which mentions 3 of her altarpieces in Venetian churches, 2 of which survive (*Crucifixion with Saints* in San Vitale and *Madonna in Glory with Two Saints* in Santa Maria Formosa); a self-portrait and another portrait painted by her contemporary Piazzetta; and a letter written by Abbot Luigi Conti (1728); on the basis of 4 identified works, scholars eventually attributed to Lama 26 paintings previously assigned to other well-known artists, including *The Martyrdom of St. Eurosia*, 1st ascribed to Piazzetta, as well as some 200 drawings. ❖ See also *Women in World History.*

LA MARA (1837–1927). *See Lipsius, Marie.*

LAMARCA, Tania (1980—). Spanish rhythmic gymnast. Name variations: Tania Lamarca Celeda. Born April 30, 1980, in Vitoria, Spain. ❖ Won a team gold medal at Atlanta Olympics (1996).

LAMARQUE, Libertad (1908–2000). Argentinean actress and singer. Name variations: Libertad Lamarque Bouza. Born Nov 24, 1908, in Rosario, Santa Fe, Argentina; died Dec 12, 2000, in Mexico City, Mexico; dau. of Gaudencio Lamarque (tinsmith) and Josefa Bouza (Spanish immigrant); m. Emilio Romero, 1926 (div. 1945); m. Alfredo Malerba, 1945 (died 1994); children: (1st m.) Mirtha. ❖ Made stage debut at age 8; moved to Buenos Aires to continue work in theater (1922); came to prominence with 1st recording of tangos (1926); made film debut in silent movie *Adios, Argentina* (1930), followed by *Tango* (1933), the 1st sound movie made in Argentina; for next 3 decades, was the most popular screen star in Latin America; because of an incident with Eva Duarte (later Eva Perón) while filming *La cabalgata del circo*, suffered an unofficial blacklisting and eventually moved to Mexico where she appeared in 43 films (21 in Argentina); recorded over 800 songs.

LA MARR, Barbara (c. 1896–1926). American actress and screenwriter. Name variations: Barbara LaMarr; also billed as Barbara Deely and Barbara La Marr Deely. Born Rheatha Watson, July 28, 1896 (also seen as Sept 3, 1898), in Richmond, Virginia; died Jan 30, 1926, in Hollywood, CA; m. Jack Daugherty. ❖ Former dancer and musical-comedy star, had a brief career in silent movies in "vamp" roles before death from a drug overdose at 29; rose to screen stardom with portrayal of Milady de Winter in *The Three Musketeers* (1921), opposite Douglas Fairbanks Sr.; other notable films include *The Prisoner of Zenda* (1922) and *The Eternal City* (1924); also wrote stories for several screenplays. ❖ See also *Women in World History.*

LAMARR, Hedy (1913–2000). Austrian-born actress. Name variations: H.K. Markey; Hedwig Kiesler. Born Hedwig Eva Maria Kiesler in Vienna, Austria, Nov 9, 1913; found dead at home in Orlando, FL, Jan 19, 2000; dau. of Emil Kiesler and Gertrud (Lichtwitz) Kiesler; m. Friedrich (Fritz) Mandl (proprietor of 1 of Central Europe's leading munitions manufacturing plants, Hirtenberger Patronen Fabrik); m. Gene Markey (Hollywood writer and producer); m. John Loder (British actor), 1943 (div. 1946); m. Ted Stauffer (ex-bandleader); m. W. Howard Lee (Texas oil refiner); m. Lewis Boies (lawyer); children: (2nd m.) James Markey (adopted); (3rd m.) Denise Hedwig Loder; Anthony John Loder. ❖ Though internationally famous as a Hollywood femme fatale, was also an inventor whose work with composer George Antheil laid the groundwork for both military communications systems and the mobile telephone systems now in use around the world; studied with Max Reinhardt in Berlin; had 1st lead in the film *Wir brauchen kein Geld* (We Don't Need Money), then starred in *Die Koffer des Herrn O.F.* (Mr. O.F.'s Suitcases), which was both a critical and box-office success; had breakthrough role in *Extase* (Ecstasy, 1933), which became a worldwide sensation for its nude scenes; signed a 7-year contract with MGM (1937); was an instant hit, co-starring with Charles Boyer in *Algiers* (1938); other successful films followed: *Comrade X* and *Boom Town* (both with Clark Gable), *I Take This Woman, Ziegfeld Girl*, and *Tortilla Flat* (with Spencer Tracy); played a seductress in *White Cargo* (1942), with the line "I am Tondelayo"; had one of her best roles, as Delilah in De Mille's *Samson and Delilah* (1949); gave a well-received performance in *The Female Animal* (1957). Received a Pioneer Award from Electronic Frontier Foundation. ❖ See also autobiography, *Ecstasy and Me*; and *Women in World History.*

LAMAS, Maria (1893–1983). Portuguese essayist. Born 1893 in Torres Novas, Portugal; died 1983. ❖ Served as editor of women's magazine *Modas e Bordados* for 20 years and as leader of National Council of Portuguese Women which she opened to working-class women; lost magazine job when she objected to government closure of council (1946); before going into exile, wrote book about working women,

Mulheres do Meu País (1948), and sociological work, *A Mulher no Mundo* (1952).

LAMB, Caroline (1785–1828). English aristocrat, poet and novelist. Name variations: Caroline Ponsonby; Lady Melbourne; Lady Caroline Lamb; (nickname) Caro. Born Caroline Ponsonby in England, 1785; died Jan 1828 at Brocket Hall, Hertfordshire; only dau. of Frederick Ponsonby, 3rd earl of Bessborough, and Lady Henrietta Frances Spencer, countess of Bessborough; m. William Lamb (1779–1848), later 2nd Lord Melbourne as well as prime minister (1834, 1835–41), in 1805; children: son Augustus (1807–1836); daughter (b. 1809, died at birth). ❖ Best known for her affair with the poet Lord Byron, was born into a wealthy and aristocratic English family; spent several years in Europe as a child, absorbing European culture; as a young girl, was a member of "Devonshire House set," a group of rich, intelligent aristocrats based at London home of her aunt, the duchess of Devonshire; married William Lamb, future prime minister of England (1805); embarked on tempestuous affair, which lasted only a few months but defined the rest of her life, with the young Lord Byron, then at height of his fame and popularity (1812); as well as poetry, wrote 3 novels of which only the 1st, *Glenarvon*, based on her romance with Byron, was successful; spent last decade of life in isolation at her country house because of the scandal provoked by her affair and by the novel; died there at age 42. ❖ See also Henry Blyth, *Caro, The Fatal Passion: The Life of Caroline Lamb* (Coward, 1972); and *Women in World History.*

LAMB, Elizabeth (d. 1818). *See Melbourne, Elizabeth.*

LAMB, Emily (d. 1869). Countess of Cowper and Shaftesbury. Name variations: Emily Lamb; Lady Palmerston; Viscountess Palmerston; Emily Cowper. Born Emily Lamb; died 1869; dau. of Peniston Lamb, 1st viscount Melbourne, and Lady Elizabeth Melbourne (d. 1818); sister of William Lamb, 2nd Lord Melbourne (1777–1848), and George Lamb (1784–1834, politician and writer); sister-in-law of Caroline Lamb; m. Lord Cowper of Althorps, 5th earl of Cowper, July 20, 1805 (died June 21, 1837); m. Henry John Temple, 3rd Viscount Palmerston (British prime minister), Dec 16, 1839 (died 1865); children: (with Cowper) Emily Cowper; Fanny Cowper; Fordwich Cowper. ❖ One of the foremost political hostesses of her day, was privy to intrigues of the inner circle of Whig Party; her correspondence, edited and published by Tresham Lever (*The Letters of Lady Palmerston*, 1957), provides a vivid account of English life and politics from the time of George IV through the middle years of Victoria's reign. ❖ See also *Women in World History.*

LAMB, Félix (1809–1875). *See Héricourt, Jenny Poinsard d'.*

LAMB, Martha J.R. (1826–1893). American historian. Born Martha Joanna Reade Nash in Plainfield, MA, Aug 13, 1826; died in New York, NY, Jan 2, 1893; m. Charles A. Lamb, Sept 1852 (possibly div. 1866). ❖ After marriage, moved to Chicago with husband; became friends with Jane Hoge and Mary A. Livermore and helped found Home for the Friendless and Half-Orphan Society; possibly after divorce, moved to NY (1866) where she became secretary of the 1st Sanitary Fair and held membership in many learned societies; edited *Magazine of American History* (1883–93) and published chief book, *The History of the City of New York* (2 vols., 1877–81), the result of about 15 years labor and research; also wrote *The Homes of America* and *Wall Street History.*

LAMB, Mary Anne (1764–1847). English author. Born in London, England, Dec 3, 1764; died at St. John's Wood, London, May 20, 1847; dau. of John Lamb (servant and clerk) and Elizabeth (Field) Lamb; sister of Charles Lamb (1775–1834, author); children: (with brother Charles) adopted orphan girl named Emma Isola, dau. of an official at Cambridge University (1823). ❖ Resided with brother until his death, except when fits of insanity caused her removal to an asylum, which, through the years, increased in frequency; during a manic phase (1796), wounded her father and killed her invalid mother by stabbing her in the heart; declared insane at an inquest, was removed to Hoxton under restraints; became ward of her brother (1797); wrote a few slight poems, but her principal work, the immensely popular *Tales from Shakespeare* (1807), was written in conjunction with brother; also collaborated on poetry for children; when she was well, was said to be remarkably placid with a sweet disposition. ❖ See also Edwin W. Marrs Jr. *The Letters of Charles and Mary Anne Lamb: Vol. I, Letters of Charles Lamb, 1796–1801* (Cornell U. Press, 1975); and *Women in World History.*

LAMB, Mary Montgomerie (1843–1905). *See Currie, Mary Montgomerie.*

LAMBALLE, Marie Thérèse Louise of Savoy-Carignano, Princesse de (1749–1792). French royal. Name variations: Marie Thérèse Louise de

Savoie-Carignan. Born Marie Thérèse Louise of Savoy-Carignano in Turin, Sept 8, 1749; died in massacre at La Force, Sept 3, 1792; 4th dau. of Louis Victor of Carignano (d. 1774, great-grandfather of King Charles Albert of Sardinia) and Christine Henriette of Hesse-Rheinfels-Rothenburg; m. Louis Alexandre Stanislaus de Bourbon, Prince de Lamballe (son of duke of Penthièvre, a grandson of Louis XIV's illeg. son, the count of Toulouse), in 1766 (died 1767). ❖ A widow at 18 (1767), retired with father-in-law to Rambouillet, where she lived until the marriage of the dauphin and Marie Antoinette (1770), then returned to court; became a companion to Marie Antoinette, a relationship so close that it fueled damaging gossip; was made superintendent of the royal household (1774), the year the dauphin was crowned Louis XVI; lived outside of court (1780–85), possibly because she had been replaced as confidante by Yolande Martine Gabrielle de Polignac; became Marie Antoinette's closest friend once more (1785) and accompanied her to the Tuileries in Paris (Oct 1789), when a mob of women marched on Versailles; when the royal family was caught trying to flee, was thought to be behind the intrigue; visited England to appeal for help for royal family; wrote last will and testament (Oct 1791) and returned to support the queen and to set an example for other emigres; was imprisoned in the Temple along with the queen (Aug 10, 1792); transferred to La Force (Aug 19); after refusing to take the oath against the monarchy, was torn to pieces by the mob as she left the courthouse (Sept 3). ❖ See also George Bertin, *Madame de Lamballe* (Paris, 1888); B.C. Hardy, *Princesse de Lamballe* (1908); and *Women in World History*.

LAMBELLE, Edith. *See La Sylphe.*

LAMBER, Juliette (1836–1936). *See Adam, Juliette.*

LAMBERT, Adelaide (1907–1996). American swimmer. Born Oct 27, 1907; died April 17, 1996. ❖ At Amsterdam Olympics, won a gold medal in 4x100-meter freestyle relay (1928).

LAMBERT, Anne Thérèse de Marguenat de Courcelles, Marquise de (1647–1733). French salonnière. Name variations: Marquise de Lambert. Born in Paris, France, 1647; died 1733; stepdau. of Bachaumont. ❖ A rich widow, opened her salon (1710), which was called the "antechamber of the Academy" since she personally selected half of the Academy's members (though her writings, chiefly on education, were produced for her children, they were read by a much larger audience); was also responsible for the substitution of French scientific formulas for Latin ones: Fontenelle facilitated this change in order that Lambert might be able to read his scientific treatises. Her salon in the Palais Mazarin was considered the bridge between 17th-century and 18th-century institutions. ❖ See also *Women in World History*.

LAMBERT, Betty (1933–1983). Canadian novelist and playwright. Born Betty Lee, Aug 23, 1933, in Calgary, Alberta, Canada; died 1983; m. Frank Lambert; children: 1. ❖ Studied at University of British Columbia and then traveled widely; was associate professor of English at Simon Fraser University until death; wrote radio, stage, and children's plays; writings include *The Visitor* (1970), *The Popcorn Man* (1973), *The Riddle Machine* (1974), *Sqrieux-de-Dieu* (1976), *Jennie's Story* (1981), and *Under the Skin* (1985); also wrote novel *Crossings* (1979). Won ACTRA Award for Best Radio Play (1980) and Governor General's Award for *Jennie's Story*.

LAMBERT, Jean (1950—). English politician. Born June 1, 1950, in Orsett, Essex, England. ❖ Served as political liaison with the Green Group in the European Parliament (1989–92), chair of Green Party Executive (1993–94), and its principal speaker (1998–99); representing Group of the Greens/European Free Alliance, elected to 5th European Parliament (1999–2004) from UK. Wrote *No Change? No Chance!* (1996).

LAMBERT, Juliette (1836–1936). *See Adam, Juliette.*

LAMBERT, Madame de (1647–1733). *See Lambert, Anne Thérèse de Marguenat de Courcelles, Marquise de.*

LAMBERT, Margaret Bergmann (1914—). German-Jewish track-and-field champion. Name variations: Gretel Bergmann. Born Margarethe Gretel Bergmann in Laupheim, Germany, 1914; m. Bruno Lambert (doctor), 1939. ❖ Joined Ulm's athletic club (1930) and began winning events in track and field; despite many medals, was notified by the UFV club (Ulm Soccer club) that she was no longer welcome because she was a Jew (1933); as discrimination intensified, moved to UK and enrolled at London Polytechnic to study English; won British high-jump championship (1934); received notification to return to Germany and compete for

the Nazis at Berlin Olympics or members of her extended family, as well as all Jewish athletes, would suffer; was the only Jewish athlete besides Hélène Mayer invited to represent the German team for 1936 Berlin Olympics, though the Nazis eventually refused to let her participate; left Germany for America (1937); won US high-jump and shot-put championships (1937, 1938). Inducted into Jewish Sports Hall of Fame (1980). ❖ See also *Women in World History*.

LAMBERT, Nathalie (1963—). Canadian short-track speedskater. Born Dec 1, 1963, in Montreal, Canada. ❖ Won a gold medal for the 3,000-meter relay at Albertville Olympics (1992); won silver medals for the 1,000 meters and 3,000-meter relay at Lillehammer Olympics (1994); was 3-time overall World champion.

LAMBERT-CHAMBERS, Dorothea (1878–1960). *See Chambers, Dorothea.*

LAMBERTINI, Imelda (1320–1333). Italian religious. Name variations: Blessed Imelda Lambertini. Born in 1320; died near Bologna in 1333. ❖ Died at 13 at the Dominican house of Val di Petra, near Bologna. Feast day is May 12.

LAMBINE, Janna (c. 1951—). American Coast Guard pilot. Born c. 1951. ❖ Graduated from naval aviation training school at Naval Air Station, Whiting Field, Milton, Florida, and became 1st woman US Coast Guard pilot (1977); assigned as helicopter pilot at Air Station Astoria, Oregon.

LAMBRINO, Jeanne (1898–1953). Romanian royal. Name variations: Joanna Labrina; (nickname) Zizi. Born Joanna Mary Valentina Lambrino, Oct 3, 1898, in Roman, Romania; died Mar 11, 1953, in Paris, France; dau. of Constantin Lambrino and Euphrosine (Alcaz) Lambrino; m. Carol II (1893–1953), crown prince, then king of Romania (r. 1930–1940), Aug 31, 1918 (marriage annulled 1919); children: son, Mircea Carol Hohenzollern (b. Jan 8, 1920).

LAMBURN, Richmal Crompton (1890–1969). English author. Name variations: (pseudonym) Richmal Crompton. Born Richmal Crompton Lamburn, Nov 15, 1890, in Bury, Lancashire, England; died Jan 11, 1969, in Borough Green, Kent; dau. of Edward John Sewall Lamburn (cleric and schoolmaster) and Clara (Crompton) Lamburn; sister of Gwen Lamburn Disher and author Jack Lamburn (also known as Jack Lambourne, John Crompton); Royal Holloway College, University of London, BA (honors), 1914; never married. ❖ Created William, the legendary scamp of British children's literature, who was featured in many of her books; taught classics at St. Elphins (1914–17), and at Bromley (Kent) High School, a private girls' day school in suburban London (1917–23); published "Rice-Mould," in *Home Magazine* (Feb 1919), the 1st story containing the character of William (illus. by Thomas Henry); stricken with polio which left her without use of right leg (1923), was forced to give up full-time teaching; produced 38 William titles (1922–69), which were subsequently adapted into 4 films, 1 radio series and 2 tv series; produced some 40 other titles, many of them love stories which she turned out at rate of one a year, but none had appeal of William books; early novels include autobiographical *The Innermost Room* (1923) and *Anne Morrison* (1925). ❖ See also Mary Cadogan, *Richmal Crompton: The Woman Behind William* (Unwin, 1986); Kay Williams, *Just Richmal: The Life and Work of Richmal Crompton Lamburn* (1986); and *Women in World History*.

LAMDLULI, Labotsibeni (c. 1858–1925). *See Labotsibeni Gwamile laMdluli.*

LA MERI (1899–1988). American dancer, author, and instructor. Name variations: Russell Meriwether Hughes. Born Russell Meriwether Hughes in Louisville, KY, May 13, 1899; died Jan 1988 in San Antonio, TX; grew up in San Antonio, TX; educated at Texas Woman's University, Denton University, and Columbia University; studied ballet with Aaron Tomaroff and Ivan Tarasoff, and modern dance with Michio Ito, 1925; also studied dance in Mexico, South America, Spain, Africa, India, Ceylon, the Philippines, and Japan, 1926–39. ❖ America's leading authority on ethnic dance, made professional debut with a Texas tour (1923); continued to tour world until advent of WWII (1939); returning to NY, helped found the School of Natya (May 1940) with Ruth St. Denis; 2 years later, combined Natya with her Ethnologic Dance Center, which offered study of dance from nations throughout world; toured while creating many ethnic dances, including *El Amor Brujo*, a Bharata Natyam interpretation of *Swan Lake*; books include *Principles of the Dance Art* (1933), *Dance as an Art Form* (1933), *Gesture Language of the*

Hindu (1941), *Spanish Dancing* (1948) and *The Basic Elements of Dance Competition* (1965); also taught at Jacob's Pillow summer dance school.

LAMERS, Annegret Strauch- (1968—). *See Strauch, Annegret.*

LA MESSINE (1836–1936). *See Adam, Juliette.*

LAMMEDAL, Berit. *See Mørdre, Berit.*

LAMON, Sophie (1985—). Swiss fencer. Born Feb 8, 1985, in Sion, Switzerland. ❖ At age 15, won a silver medal for team épée at Sydney Olympics (2000).

LAMONT, Johann (1957—). Scottish politician. Born 1957 in Glasgow, Scotland. ❖ Serves as Labour member of the Scottish Parliament for Glasgow Pollok.

LA MONTAGNE-BEAUREGARD, Blanche (1899–1960). French-Canadian poet. Name variations: Blanche Lamontagne. Born 1899; died 1960. ❖ A regionalist, generally wrote pastorals, dealing affectionately with the simpler ways of early times; works include *Visions Gaspésiennes* (1913) and *Ma Gaspésie* (1928).

LAMORLIÈRE, Rosalie (fl. 1793–1837). French servant. Name variations: Lamorliere. Fl. between 1793 and 1837; a native of Breteuil in Picardy, France. ❖ During Marie Antoinette's 76-day imprisonment at the Conciergerie, the last stop on way to the guillotine (1793), became her servant and was held in high affection by the queen; over 40 years later (1837), dictated a sympathetic, 17-page account of the queen's last days to Abbot Lafont d'Aussonne; was later given an annual pension of 200 francs by Marie Therese Charlotte, daughter of Marie Antoinette. ❖ See also *Women in World History.*

LA MOTTE, Jeanne de Valois, countess de (1756–1791). French adventurer. Name variations: Madame La Motte; Jeanne Lamotte; Jeanne de Valois, countess de la Motte; Countess de La Motte. Born Jeanne de Saint-Rémy de Valois in 1756; died 1791; m. Nicolas de La Motte (soldier). ❖ Daughter of a poor farmer in Champagne who was one of the last of the Valois (a direct descendant of French king, Henry II); after father died and left her penniless, was granted an annual pension of 800 livres by Louis XVI; spent next few years petitioning the court for more; with husband, set out to recoup Valois estates, involving Marie Antoinette in the Affair of the Diamond Necklace (1783–84); when the elaborate plot was revealed (1786), was branded and imprisoned; escaped from jail (1787) and joined husband in England; autobiography published (1793), 2 years after her death. Alexander Dumas pére wrote novel, *Le Collier de la Reine* (1849–50), based on her scam. ❖ See also *Women in World History.*

LAMOUR, Dorothy (1914–1996). American actress. Born Mary Leta Dorothy Kaumeyer, Dec 10, 1914, in New Orleans, LA; died Sept 22, 1996, in Los Angeles, CA; m. Herbie Kaye (orchestra leader), May 10, 1935 (div. 1939); m. William Ross Howard II (businessman), April 7, 1943 (died 1978); children: Ridgely and Richard Howard. ❖ Began performing as a child and won beauty contests in teens, culminating in Miss New Orleans (1931); toured as vocalist, then had her own NBC radio show in Los Angeles, "The Dreamer of Songs"; had immediate success as a sarong-clad beauty in 1st major film, *The Jungle Princess* (1936), introducing song "Moonlight and Shadows"; was typecast in a string of island theme movies that followed; introduced song, "The Moon of Manakoora," in the South Seas romance *The Hurricane* (1937); began 2-year stint on NBC radio's "The Chase and Sanborn Hour"; became sultry foil to Bob Hope and Bing Crosby in zany series of "Road" movies: *Road to Singapore* (1940), *Road to Zanzibar* (1941), *Road to Morocco* (1942), *Road to Bali* (1953) and *Road to Hong Kong* (1962), among others; also appeared in high-budget musical comedies, including *The Fleet's In* (1942), *Dixie* (1943) and *Riding High* (1943); starred on radio in "The Dorothy Lamour Show" (1948–49). ❖ See also autobiography, *The Other Side of the Road* (1980); and *Women in World History.*

LAMPE, Mrs. (d. 1795). *See Young, Isabella.*

LAMPERT, Rachel (1948—). American modern dancer and choreographer. Born Dec 4, 1948, in Morristown, NJ. ❖ Trained with Jean Erdman, Gladys Bailin, and Stuart Hodes; formed own company with fellow dancers and choreographers from New York University's School of Arts, including Clarice Marshall and Holly Harbinger (1975); choreographed for own company, including *Issue* (1975), *Home* (1976), and *Doing the Dance* (1977), and for San Antonio Ballet and Connecticut Ballet, among others. Choreographed *Going Nowhere* (1971), *Brahms*

Variations on a Theme by Handel (1976), *Bloody Mary Sunday* (1976), *In Memory of the Lonesome Pine* (1978), *Prelude at the End of a Day* (1979), *Cliff Walking* (1980) and *Me and Beethoven* (1980).

LAMPERT, Zohra (1937—). American stage, tv, and screen actress. Born May 13, 1937, in NY; m. Bill Alton (div.). ❖ Appeared with Lincoln Center Repertory Theatre, then on Broaday; made film debut in *Pay or Die* (1961), followed by *Splendor in the Grass, A Find Madness, Bye Bye Braverman, Some Kind of a Nut, Let's Scare Jessica to Death, Opening Night, Stanley and Iris* and *Alan and Naomi,* among others. Nominated for Tony awards for *Look We've Come Through* and *Mother Courage and Her Children;* won Emmy for Best Supporting Actress for episode of "Kojak" (1975).

LAMPKIN, Daisy (1883–1965). African-American civil-rights activist and suffragist. Born Daisy Elizabeth Adams, Aug 9, 1883, in Washington, DC; died Mar 10, 1965, in Reading, PA; dau. of George S. Adams and Rosa Anne (Proctor) Adams; m. William Lampkin (restaurateur), June 18, 1912; no children. ❖ For over 50 years, used formidable fund-raising skills to advance civil rights for African-Americans; was president of Lucy Stone Woman Suffrage League (1915–56); served National Association of Colored Women (NACW) as national organizer, vice-president, and chair of the executive board; became vice-president of influential black weekly *Pittsburgh Courier* (1929), a position she would hold throughout life; with Mary McLeod Bethune, founded National Council of Negro Women (1935); was chair of Negro Women's Republican League of Allegheny County, PA, vice-chair of Negro Voters League of Pennsylvania, chair of Colored Voters' Division of Republican National Committee, and the 1st African-American woman elected as an alternate delegate-at-large to Republican National Convention (1928 or 1933, sources differ); joined Pittsburgh branch of National Association for Advancement of Colored People (NAACP) and soon headed a campaign that added 2,000 members (1929); became regional field secretary (1930), then national field secretary (1935) and was instrumental in fund-raising for organization's national anti-lynching campaign. Received 1st Eleanor Roosevelt–Mary McLeod Bethune World Citizenship Award from NCNW (1964); became 1st black woman in Pennsylvania whose house was designated a historical landmark (1983). ❖ See also *Women in World History.*

LAMY, Jennifer (1949—). Australian runner. Name variations: Jenny Lamy. Born Feb 28, 1949, in Australia. ❖ At Mexico City Olympics, won a bronze medal in 200 meters (1968); as a member of 4 x 100-meter relay teams, won gold medals at Commonwealth Games (1970, 1974).

LAN PING (1914–1991). *See Jiang Qing.*

LANAHAN, Frances Scott (1921–1986). *See Fitzgerald, Frances Scott.*

LANCASTER, countess of.
See Blanche of Artois (c. 1247–1302).
See Chaworth, Maud (1282–c. 1322).
See Alice de Joinville.

LANCASTER, duchess of.
See Blanche of Lancaster (1341–1369).
See Beaumont, Isabel (d. 1368).
See Swynford, Catherine (c. 1350–1403).
See Constance of Castile (1354–1394).

LANCASTER, G.B. (1873–1945). *See Lyttelton, Edith Joan.*

LANCASTER, Isabel of (d. 1368). *See Beaumont, Isabel.*

LANCASTER, Nancy (1897–1994). American-born socialite and interior decorator. Name variations: Nancy Tree. Born Nancy Perkins in Albemarle Co., Virginia, 1897; died in Oxfordshire, England, 1994; dau. of Lizzie Langhorne and T. Moncure Perkins (meat-packing executive); niece of Irene Langhorne Gibson (1873–1956) and Nancy Witcher Astor (1879–1964); m. Henry Field (grandson of department-store magnate Marshall Field), 1917 (died 1918); m. Ronald Lambert Tree (later Conservative member of Parliament), 1920 (div. 1947); m. Claud G. Lancaster (British politician), 1947 (div.); children: (2nd m.) Michael and Jeremy. ❖ Socialite whose talent for cultivating the beauty of her stately homes and gardens into an appearance of "pleasing decay" which gave rise to the popular English-country style of decorating, moved to England (1926); credited with inspiring generations of European and American designers, including Mario Buatta and Sister Parish; a world-class hostess, could count among her guests Winston Churchill, John Singer Sargent, Cecil Beaton, and George VI and Elizabeth Bowes-Lyon; became co-owner of the design firm Colefax & Fowler in London (1944), which decorated the homes of elite clients, and continued working there into 1980s. ❖ See also Robert Becker, *Nancy Lancaster: Her Life, Her World, Her Art* (Knopf, 1996); and *Women in World History*.

LANCASTER-WALLIS, Ellen (1856—). English stage actress and playwright. Name variations: Ellen Lancaster Wallis. Born Ellen Wallis, Aug 17, 1856, in England; dau. of Charles Wallis (actor); m. John Lancaster (proprietor of Shaftesbury Theater); m. Walter Reynolds (actor-manager); children: Nora Lancaster (b. 1882, actress). ❖ Made stage debut as Pauline in *The Lady of Lyons* (1872), followed by *Montcalm, Amos Clark* and *Cromwell*, among others; spent many years at Drury Lane in such roles as Cleopatra, Juliet, Amy Robsart, Hermione, Desdemona, and the Abbess in *Dante* with Sir Henry Irving; also appeared in title roles in *Ninon* and *Adrienne Lecouvreur*; wrote *Wife and State* (with J.W. Boulding), *The Pharisee* (with Malcolm Watson), and such 1-act comedies (comediettas) as "Cissy's Engagement," "Cupid in Ermine," "Little Miss Muffet" and "A Sudden Squall."

LANCEFIELD, Rebecca Craighill (1895–1981). American immunologist and microbiologist. Born Rebecca Craighill in Fort Wadsworth, Staten Island, NY, Jan 5, 1895; died Mar 1981 in Little Neck, Queens, NY; dau. of William Edward Craighill and Mary Wortley Montague (Byram) Craighill; Wellesley College, BA, 1916; Columbia University Teachers College, MA, 1918; Columbia University, PhD, 1925; m. Donald Elwood Lancefield (scientist), May 27, 1918; children: Jane Maddox Lancefield (who m. George Leonard Hersey). ❖ Began work on streptococci at Rockefeller Institute (1922); doctoral work, which centered on developing a system for classifying an elusive strain of streptococcus, was published in *Journal of Experimental Medicine*; continued to investigate other strains of streptococci and found that isolated substances from her samples could be used to group the streptococci into 5 different types; findings became the basis of the method of classifying streptococci adopted by International Congress of Microbiology (1940); elected president of Society of American Bacteriologists (1943); continued to classify strains of streptococci throughout career; elected 1st woman president of American Association of Immunologists (1960); also elected to National Academy of Science (1970). ❖ See also *Women in World History*.

LANCHESTER, Elsa (1902–1986). British-born actress. Born Oct 28, 1902, in Lewisham, England; died Dec 26, 1986, in Woodland Hills, CA; dau. of Edith Lanchester and James Sullivan (laborer); attended Mr. Kettle's School, London; m. Charles Laughton (actor), 1929 (died 1962); no children. ❖ Though often remembered for dual performance in *Bride of Frankenstein*, a cult classic, played a wide range of character parts on stage and screen, sometimes teaming with husband; at 17, began performing obscure songs that eventually became her specialty, such as "Please Sell No More Drink to My Father" (Temperance song); won raves in professional stage debut as The Larva in *The Insect Play*; starred in revue *Riverside Nights*; made film debut in *One of the Best* (1927), followed by *The Constant Nymph* (1928); appeared with husband in London run of *Payment Deferred*, which also came to NY (1931) and in film *The Private Life of Henry VIII*, in which she played Anne of Cleves to much acclaim (1933); frequently appeared with husband at Old Vic, most notably as Ariel opposite his Prospero; settled in California and became US citizen (1950); appeared regularly at Turnabout Theater (1941–51) and in concert show, *Elsa Lanchester's Private Music Hall*, and autobiographical revue *Elsa Lanchester—Herself*, which opened in NY (1961); other films include *Ladies in Retirement* (1941), *The Spiral Staircase* (1946), *The Razor's Edge* (1946), *The Bishop's Wife* (1947), *Androcles and the Lion* (1953), *Bell Book and Candle* (1958), *Mary Poppins* (1964), *That Darn Cat* (1965), *Willard* (1971) and *Murder by Death* (1976). Nominated for Academy Awards for *Come to the Stable* (1949) and *Witness for the Prosecution* (1958). ❖ See also autobiographies *Charles Laughton and I* (1937) and *Elsa Lanchester—Herself* (1983); and *Women in World History*.

LANCIEN, Nathalie (1970—). French cyclist. Name variations: Nathalie Even-Lancien or Lancien-Even. Born Mar 7, 1970, in Paimpol, France. ❖ Won a gold medal for points race at Atlanta Olympics (1996).

LANCLOS, Anne de (1623–1705). See Lenclos, Ninon de.

LANCLOS, Ninon de (1623–1705). See Lenclos, Ninon de.

LANDAU, Klavdia Gustavovna (1922–1990). Russian novelist and short-story writer. Name variations: (pseudonym) Inna Varlámova or Varlamova. Born 1922 in USSR; died 1990. ❖ Traveled widely in Urals, Siberia, and throughout Soviet Union; worked as journalist;

writings, which reflect her life of wandering, include short stories and the novel *A Counterfeit Life* (1975).

LANDELLS, Suzanne (1964—). Australian swimmer. Born Dec 12, 1964. ❖ At Los Angeles Olympics, won a silver medal in 400-meter indiv. medley (1984).

LANDER, Louisa (1826–1923). American marble sculptor. Born in Salem, MA, 1826; died in Washington, DC, 1923. ❖ Drawn to sculpting at early age, received a fair number of commissions before traveling to Rome to become a student-assistant to Thomas Crawford (1856); did a bust of Nathaniel Hawthorne, who later modeled the independent women artist in his novel *The Marble Faun* after her; for reasons unknown, so scandalized fellow artists that commissions dried up; forced to finance continuing work, embarked on a major sculpture of Virginia Dare, the 1st English child born in the New World (1860), which was later housed in North Carolina's Hall of History in Raleigh (1926–38) and now occupies a place of honor in Elizabethan Gardens on Roanoke Island; lived out remainder of life in relative obscurity. ❖ See also *Women in World History*.

LANDER, Margot (1910–1961). Danish ballet dancer. Born Aug 2, 1910, in Copenhagen, Denmark; died July 18, 1961, in Copenhagen; m. Harald Lander (dancer and choreographer), 1932 (div. 1950). ❖ Trained with Vera Volkova at Royal Danish Ballet, then joined the company where she performed for next 25 years (1925–50); danced in numerous Fokine revivals, including *Spectre de la Rose* and *Les Sylphides*, in Bournonville's *Napoli*, Harald Lander's *Swan Lake*, and most notably as Swanilda in *Coppélia*; created roles in husband's *l'Apprenti Sorcier* (1940), *Qarrtsiluni* (1942), *Printemps* (1942) and *Etudes* (1948).

LANDER, Toni (1931–1985). Danish ballet dancer. Born Toni Pihi Petersen, June 19, 1931, in Copenhagen, Denmark; died May 1985; trained at Royal Danis Ballet and with Olga Preobrazhenska and Lyubov Egorova in Paris; m. Harald Lander (dancer and choreographer), 1950 (div. 1965); m. Bruce Marks (artistic director). ❖ With Danish Ballet, was featured in future husband's *Etudes* (1948); with him, moved to Paris Opéra where she danced in his *Pas de Deux Romantiques, Printemps*, and *Valse Triste*; also performed in Taras' ballet *Les Rendez-vous manqués* (1958); was a member of American Ballet Theater (1965–70s); taught with 2nd husband in Salt Lake City.

LANDERS, Ann (1918–2002). See Friedman, Esther Pauline.

LANDES, Bertha Knight (1868–1943). American politician. Born Bertha Ethel Knight in Ware, MA, Oct 19, 1868; died in Ann Arbor, Michigan, Nov 29, 1943; dau. of Charles Sanford Knight (painter and real estate agent) and Cordelia (Cutter) Knight; graduate of Indiana University, 1891; m. Henry Landes (college professor), Jan 2, 1894; children: Katherine Landes (b. 1896); Kenneth Landes (b. 1899); (adopted) Viola Landes. ❖ The 1st woman elected to lead a major American city, settled in Seattle, Washington, with husband (1895); elected to Seattle city council (1922); reelected to 2nd term, rose to become president of council (1924); acting as mayor during absence of elected mayor, fired chief of police in effort to draw attention to illegal gambling and other vices ignored by police force; ran vigorous campaign against incumbent mayor and was elected (1926); during 2-year term, attempted to rescue Seattle from patronage system that allowed gambling and vice to flourish, but was only marginally successful and not elected to 2nd term; was president of the state's League of Women Voters and American Federation of Soroptimist Clubs. ❖ See also Sandra Haarsager, *Bertha Knight Landes of Seattle: Big-City Mayor* (U. of Oklahoma Press, 1994); and *Women in World History*.

LANDES, Ruth (1908–1991). American social and cultural anthropologist. Name variations: Ruth Schlossberg Landes. Born Ruth Schlossberg in 1908 in New York, NY; dau. of Joseph Schlossberg (NY labor leader) and Anna Grossman Schlossberg; New York University, BS, 1927; Columbia University, PhD, 1935. ❖ Known largely for work on Ojibwa, Potawatomi, and Sioux Indians, studied with Ruth Benedict and Franz Boas at Columbia; focused on social organization and religious life of Native North Americans; worked in Brazil on African-Brazilian cults that were led by women and homosexuals (1938–39); received permanent position at McMaster University, Ontario (1965). Works include *Ojibwa Sociology* (1937), *The Ojibwa Woman* (1938) and *The City of Women* (1947).

LANDETA, Matilde (1910–1999). Mexican filmmaker. Born Matilde Landeta, Sept 20, 1910, in Mexico City, Mexico; died Jan 26, 1999, in Mexico City; sister of Eduardo Landeta (actor). ❖ Intent on directing, took a job as a script supervisor (1933); after 12 years and with considerable opposition from the Directors' Association, was finally allowed to serve as an assistant director (1944); worked with some of Mexico's best filmmakers, Emilio Fernandez, Julio Bracho, and Roberto Gavaldon (1944–47); with brother and several colleagues, formed Tecnicos y Actores Cinematograficos Associados (TACMA, 1947); directed 1st feature, *Lola Casanova* (1948), based on novel by Francisco Rojas Gonzalez, then directed her own adaptation of another Gonzalez novel, *La Negra Augustus*, to great success; released most controversial film, *Trotacalles* (*Streetwalkers*, 1951); after a confrontation with director of National Cinematographic Bank, was barred from working for Mexican film industry (1956–62); at age 78, directed the feature *Nocturna a Rosario* (1991); subject of Patricia Martínez de Velasco documentary, *Matilde Landeta* (1992). Awarded Ariel Award (Mexican equivalent of Academy Award) for screenplay *Tribunal para menores.* ❖ See also *Women in World History.*

LANDGRAF, Monika (1952—). *See Zehrt, Monika.*

LANDGRAF, Sigrid (1959—). West German field-hockey player. Born May 7, 1959, in Germany. ❖ At Los Angeles Olympics, won a silver medal in team competition (1984).

LANDI, Elissa (1904–1948). Austrian-Italian actress and novelist. Born Elizabeth Marie Christine Kühnelt, Dec 6, 1904, in Venice, Italy; died of cancer in Kingston, NY, Oct 21, 1948; descendant of Emperor Francis Joseph of Austria on mother's side, and stepdau. of an Italian noble, Count Carlo Zanardi-Landi; m. John Cecil Lawrence, 1928 (div. 1936); m. Curtiss Thomas, 1943; children: (2nd m.) daughter (b. 1944). ❖ Made London stage debut in *Dandy Dick* (1923); appeared in *Storm* (1924), *The Painted Swan* (1925), *Lavender Ladies* (1925), and *The Constant Nymph* (1926); made film debut in *London* (1926), with Dorothy Gish, followed by *Bolibar* and *Underground* (both 1928) which brought her a degree of stardom in Britain; also made films in Sweden and France; signed to a longterm contract with Fox, starred in a series of films, the most memorable of which were *The Yellow Jacket* (1931), De Mille's *The Sign of the Cross* (1932) and *The Count of Monte Cristo* (1934); failed to become a box-office draw; also wrote several novels. ❖ See also *Women in World History.*

LANDIN, Hope (1893–1973). American stage and screen actress. Born May 3, 1893, in Minneapolis, MN; died Feb 28, 1973, in Hollywood, CA. ❖ Films include *I Remember Mama, Bridge of San Luis Rey, Reap the Wild Wind, How to Marry a Millionaire* and *The Greatest Story Ever Told.*

LANDIRAS, Baroness de (1556–1640). *See Jeanne de Lestonac.*

LANDIRAS, Jeanne de (1556–1640). *See Jeanne de Lestonac.*

LANDIS, Carole (1919–1948). American actress. Born Frances Lillian Mary Ridste, Jan 1, 1919, in Fairchild, WI; committed suicide, July 4, 1948, in Pacific Palisades, CA; dau. of a railroad switchman; m. Irving Wheeler, 1934 (div. 1939); m. Willis Hunt Jr., 1940 (div. 1940); m. Thomas C. Wallace, 1943 (div. 1945); m. W. Horace Schmidlapp, 1945. ❖ By age 12, was entering beauty contests; by 15, had eloped with a policeman then separated 3 weeks later; at 16, migrated to San Francisco and took a job as singer-hula dancer; came to Hollywood at 18 and appeared with little notice in 17 films; 1st caught audience's attention in *One Million B.C.;* one of the 1st to entertain the troops during WWII, contracted malaria; as career flattened out after war, tried to revive it with NY stage appearance in *A Lady Says Yes* (1945); found dead of an overdose of sleeping pills the night after termination of an affair with the married Rex Harrison (she was 29). Films include *Topper Returns* (1941), *Moon Over Miami* (1941), *It Happened in Flat Bush* (1942), *My Gal Sal* (1942), *Manila Calling* (1942), *Orchestra Wives* (1942), *It Shouldn't Happen to a Dog* (1946), *A Scandal in Paris* (1946), *Out of the Blue* (1947) and *The Brass Monkey* (1948). ❖ See also film *Four Jills in a Jeep* which recounted her experiences overseas, and those of fellow performers Kay Francis, Mitzi Mayfair, and Martha Raye; and *Women in World History.*

LANDIS, Jessie Royce (1904–1972). American stage, tv and screen actress. Born Jessie Royce Medbury, Nov 25, 1904, in Chicago, IL; died Feb 2, 1972, in Danbury, CT; m. Perry Lester Landis, 1923 (div. 1935); m. Rex Smith, 1937 (div. 1944); m. J.F.R. Seitz (major general), 1956. ❖ Initially a successful stage actress, made NY debut in *The Honor of the Family* (1926), followed by over 45 plays in NY and London, including *The Furies, Command Performance, Merrily We Roll Along, Love from a Stranger, Richard II, Little Women, Winter's Tale* and *Richard III;* made film debut in *Mr. Belvedere Goes to College* (1949); other film appearances include *It Happens Every Spring, My Foolish Heart, Tonight at 8:30, North by Northwest, The Swan, Bon Voyage, Boys Night Out* and as Grace Kelly's mother in *To Catch a Thief.* ❖ See also autobiography *You Won't Be So Pretty* (1954).

LANDMANN, Barbara (1795–1883). *See Heinemann, Barbara.*

LANDON, Letitia Elizabeth (1802–1838). English poet and novelist. Name variations: (pen name) better known by initials L.E.L.; Letitia Elizabeth Maclean. Born Letitia Elizabeth Landon in Chelsea, England, Aug 14, 1802; died of poison, Oct 15, 1838; dau. of John Landon (army agent) and Catharine Jane (Bishop) Landon; granddau. of Reverend John Landon (famed for his cause against dissenters); attended school in Chelsea where she studied under Miss Rowden (poet and also teacher of Mary Russell Mitford and Caroline Lamb); m. George Maclean (governor of Gold Coast, Africa), June 1838. ❖ Began contributions to *Literary Gazette* and to various Christmas annuals under initial "L," and finally "L.E.L."; published volumes of verse, which soon won her literary fame; was joint editor of *Literary Gazette;* published 1st volume of poetry as *The Fate of Adelaide* (1820), followed by other collections, including *The Improvisatrice* (1824), *The Troubadour* (1825), *The Golden Violet* (1827) and *The Venetian Bracelet* (1829); also wrote several novels, of which the best is said to be *Ethel Churchill* (1837), along with tragedy *Castruccio Castracani* (1837); secretly married governor of the Gold Coast, and set sail for a 3-year stay in Africa (1838); after arriving there, was found dead in her room with a bottle of prussic acid in her hand. *The Life and Literary Remains of Letitia Elizabeth Landon,* by Laman Blanchard appeared 1841, followed by 2nd edition, 1855. ❖ See also *Women in World History.*

LANDON, Margaret (1903–1993). American author. Born Margaret Dorothea Mortenson, Sept 7, 1903, in Somers, Wisconsin; died Dec 4, 1993, in Alexandria, Virginia; dau. of Annenus Duabus Mortenson and Adelle Johanne (Estburg) Mortenson; Wheaton College, BA, 1925; studied journalism at Northwestern University, 1937–38; m. Kenneth Perry Landon (missionary who became associate dean at US Dept. of State Foreign Service Institute), 1926; children: Margaret Dorothea Landon (who m. Charles W. Schoenherr); William Bradley II; Carol Elizabeth Landon (who m. Lennart Pearson); Kenneth Perry Jr. ❖ Taught English and Latin in Bear Lake, WI (1925–26); lived in Siam, now Thailand (1927–37), working there as principal of Trang Girls' School for 5 years; encountered works of Anna Leonowens, a young English widow employed in 1860s as governess to court of Mongkut, 4th king of Siam; published *Anna and the King of Siam,* based on Leonowens' memoirs, to enormous success (1944) and its many subsequent adaptations, including the Broadway hit *The King and I;* published novel *Never Dies the Dream* (1949). ❖ See also *Women in World History.*

LANDOWSKA, Wanda (1877–1959). Poilish pianist and harpsichordist. Name variations: Alexandra Landowska. Pronunciation: VAHN-da Lan-DOFF-skah. Born in Warsaw, Poland, July 5, 1877; died in Lakeville, CT, Aug 16, 1959; dau. of Marjan Landowski (lawyer and amateur musician) and Eve Landowska (linguist); m. Henry Lew (folklorist), 1900 (died in auto accident, 1919); children: none; naturalized French citizen. ❖ Polish virtuoso, known as the "High Priestess of the Harpsichord," who became an authority on music of 17th and 18th centuries and was responsible for revival of the harpsichord, began to play piano (1883); studied at Warsaw Conservatory of Music under Alexander Michalowski and Moritz Moszkowski; sent to Berlin to study composition and counterpoint with Heinrich Urban (1895); 1st played harpsichord publicly (1903); toured Russia (1909); performed for Count Leo Tolstoy at Yasnaya Polnaya (1909); co-authored *La Musique ancienne* with husband (1909); presented 1st Pleyel harpsichord publicly (1912); appointed head of harpsichord class, Berlin (1913); interned in Germany (1914–18); made North American debut as soloist with Philadelphia Orchestra under Leopold Stokowski, playing 3 concertos: 2 by Handel and Bach on harpsichord and 1 by Mozart on piano (1923); made 1st recording (1923); founded École de Musique Ancienne (1925); commissioned Manuel de Falla to compose a chamber concerto for harpsichord (1926) and Francis Poulenc to compose Concert Champêtre for Harpsichord (1929); gave 1st public performance of Bach's *Goldberg Variations* (1933); awarded Grand Prix of Paris Exposition (1937); of Jewish ancestry, had to flee Paris (1940); lived in NY City (1941–47); moved to Lakeville, CT (1947); devoted herself to teaching, writing and recording. Compositions included *Rhapsodie Orientale,* as well as numerous lieder. ❖ See also Bernard Gavoty, *Wanda Landowska* (Kister, 1957); and *Women in World History.*

LANDRIANI, Lucrezia (fl. 1450s). Italian noblewoman. Married Giampietro Landriani; mistress of Galeazzo Maria Sforza, 5th duke of Milan (r. 1466–1476); children: (with Sforza) Carlo (b. 1461); Caterina Sforza (c. 1462–1509); Chiara Sforza (b. around 1464); and Alessandro.

LANDRY, Jackie (1940–1997). American singer. Name variations: The Chantels. Born 1940; died of breast cancer, Dec 23, 1997. ❖ Sang with Arlene Smith, Lois Harris, Sonia Goring and Rene Minus in their Bronx, NY, parochial school choir and became 2nd soprano for their doo-wop group, The Chantels (1956), one of 1st and most well-received girl groups; with group, released album *We Are the Chantels* (1958) and had such hits as "Maybe" (1958), "Look in My Eyes" (1961) and "Well, I Told You" (1961); appeared with original group in reunion performances (1990s).

LANDSEER, Jessica (1810–1880). British landscape painter. Born 1810; died 1880; dau. of John Landseer (1769–1852, engraver); sister of Sir Edwin Landseer (1802–1873, painter) and Charles A. Landseer (1799–1879, painter). ❖ Though overshadowed by brother Edwin, for whom she kept house most of her life, was a painter, etcher, and miniaturist in her own right; exhibited at Royal Academy and British Institution for many years.

LANDSFELD, countess of (1818–1861). *See Montez, Lola.*

LANDY, Kathryn (1903–1978). *See McGuire, Kathryn.*

LANE, Elizabeth (1905–1988). English lawyer. Name variations: Dame Elizabeth Lane. Born Elizabeth Kathleen Coulbourn, 1905, in England; died 1988; educated privately and attended Malvern Girls College; m. Henry Lane (barrister), 1926 (died 1975); children: 1 son (died young). ❖ Became a barrister at Inner Temple (1940) and member of Home Office Committee on Depositions in Criminal Cases (1948); was assistant recorder of Birmingham (1953–61), recorder for Derby (1961–62), and commissioner of the Crown Courts at Manchester and a Circuit Court judge (1962–65); became the 1st female High Court judge in England, attached to the Family Division, and was also chair of Committee on the Abortion Acts (1971–73); was the 1st woman barrister to appear in the House of Lords on a murder case and the 1st judge to work part-time; remained on High Court until retirement (1979). Created DBE (1965). ❖ See also *Hear the Other Side, Audi ad Alteram Partem: The Autobiography of England's First Woman Judge* (Butterworths, 1985).

LANE, Gertrude B. (1874–1941). American editor. Born Gertrude Battles Lane, Dec 21, 1874, in Saco, Maine; died Sept 25, 1941, in New York, NY; dau. of Eustace Lane (organist) and Ella (Battles) Lane; attended Simmons College. ❖ Became managing editor (1909) and editor in chief (1912) of *Woman's Home Companion,* which was the leading US women's magazine by 1937; during approximately 3 decades there, shaped the magazine to meet needs of mothers and homemakers and had such contributors as Eleanor Roosevelt, Willa Cather, Pearl Buck, and Sinclair Lewis.

LANE, Grace (1876–1956). English actress. Born Jan 13, 1876, in England; died Jan 14, 1956, in Hove, East Sussex, England; dau. of Rosina Grace (Lilley) Lane and Pierrepont G. Lane; sister of Dorothy Lane (actress, b. 1890); m. Kenneth Douglas (actor, real name Savory). ❖ Made London debut in *Parallel Attacks* (1894), followed by *Our Flat;* came to prominence as Lady Babbie in *The Little Minister* (1898), as Joy in *The Secret Orchard* (1901), and as Lady Mary Carlyle in *Monsieur Beaucaire* (1902); other plays include *The Rise of Silas Lapham, If Winter Comes, Ariadne in Naxos, The Queen's Husband* and *The Skin Game;* films include *The Honeypot, The Feather* and *The Mad Hatters.*

LANE, Harriet (1830–1903). American political hostess. Name variations: Harriet Lane Johnston; (nickname) "Hal." Born May 9, 1830, in Mercersburg, PA; died of cancer at Narragansett Pier, RI, July 3, 1903; dau. of Elliott Tole Lane and Jane (Buchanan) Lane (sister of James Buchanan, president of US); graduated from Academy of Visitation in Georgetown, 1848; m. Henry Elliott Johnston (banker), Jan 11, 1866 (died 1884); children: James Buchanan Johnston (1866–1881); Henry Elliott Johnston (1868–1882). ❖ Orphaned at 10, came under guardianship of bachelor uncle, James Buchanan; became hostess of Wheatland, his estate in PA; accompanied him to England when he was ambassador to Court of St. James; during Buchanan's term in White House (1857–61), refurbished the neglected interior with American furniture and had a conservatory built; entertained often, with ease and tact; with a growing rift between North and South, became known as the "Democratic Queen," skillfully warding off sectional

rivalries with judicious seating arrangements; immensely popular, was given title "Great Mother of the Indians" for work in improving Native American living conditions; widowed (1884), spent rest of life in Washington, active in philanthropic work and collecting art; organized Choir School of Cathedral of Saints Peter and Paul in Washington, and founded Harriet Lane Home for Invalid Children at Johns Hopkins. At time of her death, half her art collection went to Johns Hopkins and remainder to Smithsonian Institution, where it provided the basis for National Gallery of Art. ❖ See also *Women in World History.*

LANE, Jane (d. 1689). English heroine. Name variations: Lady Fisher. Died 1689; dau. of Thomas Lane; sister of Colonel John Lane; m. Sir Clement Fisher, baronet of Packington Magna, Warwickshire. ❖ After battle of Worcester (1651), helped Charles II escape his enemies by having him ride with her from Bentley, in Staffordshire, to house of her cousin, near Bristol, disguised as her manservant; fled to France and eventually entered the service of Mary of Orange (1631–1660); for her act of loyalty, was rewarded with a pension by the king during Restoration and granted a family coat of arms.

LANE, Lola (1909–1981). American actress. Born Dorothy Mullican, May 21, 1909, in Macy, IN; died in Santa Barbara, CA, June 22, 1981, after long illness; older sister of Priscilla Lane (1917–1995), Rosemary Lane (1914–1974), and Leota Lane; m. Lew Ayres (actor); m. Alexander Hall (director); m. Henry Dunham; m. Roland West (director); m. Robert Hanlon (lawyer); no children. ❖ At 12, began playing piano for silent films; joined sister Leota in NY, where they appeared together in Gus Edwards' vaudeville revue and made Broadway debut in *Greenwich Village Follies;* landed a lead in *War Song* (1928), with George Jessell, which led to contract at Fox; played mostly small roles at Fox and on loan until 1930s, when she joined Warner Bros. and co-starred in "Four Daughters" series with sisters; retired from screen (1946); went into real estate. ❖ See also *Women in World History.*

LANE, Louisa (1820–1897). *See Drew, Louisa Lane.*

LANE, Lucy (1846–1929). *See Clifford, Mrs. W.K.*

LANE, Maryon (1931—). South African ballet dancer. Born Feb 15, 1931, in Melmouth, South Africa; attended Sadler's Wells Ballet school in England. ❖ Performed with Sadler's Wells, and its successor, the Royal Ballet, for entire performing career; appeared in numerous works by Kenneth Macmillan, including *Laiderette* (1954), *Danses Concertantes* (1955), *House of Birds* (1955) and *Solitaire* (1956); created roles for Ashton in *Les Rendez-vous* (1947) and *Valses Nobles et Sentimentales* (1947); appeared in premieres of Cranko's *Children's Corner* (1948) and *Pineapple Poll* (1951); taught at Royal Ballet school and London Ballet Centre.

LANE, Pinkie Gordon (1925—). African-American poet. Name variations: Pinkie Gordon. Born 1923 in Philadelphia, PA; dau. of William Alexander Gordon and Innez Addie West Gordon; Atlanta University, MA; was the 1st black woman to receive a PhD from Louisana State University (1967); m. Ulysses Simpson Lane; children: 1. ❖ Served as poet laureate to Louisiana (1989); works include *Wind Thoughts* (1972), *The Mystic Female* (1978), *I Never Scream: New and Selected Poems* (1985), and *Girl at the Window* (1991). Inducted into Louisiana Black Hall of Fame (1991).

LANE, Priscilla (1917–1995). American actress. Name variations: Priscilla Howard. Born Priscilla Mullican, June 12, 1917, in Iowa City, IA; died April 4, 1995, in Andover, MA; younger sister of Lola Lane (1909–1981), Rosemary Lane (1914–1974), and Leota Lane; attended Simpson College; m. Oren Haglund (screenwriter), 1940 (annulled); m. Joseph A. Howard (pilot turned building contractor), 1943; children: Larry, Hannah, Judith, and James Howard. ❖ One of the Lane sisters, had the most successful career; with sister Rosemary, began performing as a child, then joined Fred Waring's orchestra, The Pennsylvanians (1931) and, after years of touring, appeared with Waring in film *Varsity Show* (1937); joined sisters Lola and Rosemary in series of popular films about a family with 4 girls, the 4th played by Gale Page, which included *Four Daughters* (1938), *Four Wives* (1939), and *Four Mothers* (1941); on her own, appeared in such films as *Brother Rat* (1938), *The Roaring Twenties* (1939), *Saboteur* (1942), *Arsenic and Old Lace* (1944), *Fun on a Weekend* (1947) and *Bodyguard* (1948). ❖ See also *Women in World History.*

LANE, Rose Wilder (1886–1968). American writer. Born Rose Wilder, Dec 5, 1886, in De Smet, Dakota Territory; died in Danbury, CT, Oct 29, 1968; dau. of Almanzo James Wilder (farmer) and Laura Ingalls Wilder (farmer and author); m. (Claire) Gillette Lane (journalist and merchant), 1909 (div. 1917). ❖ Journalist, fiction writer, and libertarian, who secretly collaborated with mother on "Little House" series, moved with family to Rocky Ridge Farm in Mansfield, MO (1894); after schooling, left Mansfield to work at a series of jobs around the country (1904); was reporter and feature writer for *San Francisco Bulletin* (1915–18); published 1st novel *Diverging Roads* (1918); sailed to Europe to write on behalf of Red Cross (1920); remained overseas until late 1923, traveling in remote corners of Europe and parts of Middle East; published *Peaks of Shala*, travel book about Albania (1923); returned to live with parents, helping mother with article writing while 2 books of her own were published; lived in Tirana, Albania (1926–28); lived at Rocky Ridge Farm (1928–36), where she helped mother write the "Little House" books and published many magazine articles and 2 books of her own; wrote final work of fiction, *Free Land*, a bestseller (1938); settled in Danbury, CT (1938); opposed American entry into WWII; wrote her most extensive political treatise, *The Discovery of Freedom* (1943); became public opponent of social security and income tax; edited *National Economic Council Review of Books* (1945–50); was influential among other individualist thinkers (1950s–1960s); traveled to Vietnam for *Woman's Day* magazine (1965). ❖ See also William Holtz, *The Ghost in the Little House: A Life of Rose Wilder Lane* (U. of Missouri Press, 1993); and *Women in World History*.

LANE, Rosemary (1914–1974). American actress. Born Rosemary Mullican, April 4, 1914, in Indianola, IA; died in Woodland Hills, CA, Nov 25, 1974; sister of Priscilla Lane (1917–1995), Lola Lane (1909–1981) and Leota Lane; attended Simpson College; married; 1 daughter. ❖ With sister Priscilla, joined Fred Waring's orchestra, The Pennsylvanians (1931) and, after years of touring, appeared with Waring in film *Varsity Show* (1937); aside from the "Four Daughters" film series made with sisters, had a brief film career; greatest solo success came when she starred in Broadway musical *Best Foot Forward* (1941); retired (1945). ❖ See also *Women in World History*.

LANEY, Lucy Craft (1854–1933). African-American educator. Born in Macon, GA, April 1854; died in Augusta, GA, Oct 23, 1933; dau. of David Laney and Louisa Laney (both former slaves); graduated in 1st class of Atlanta University, 1873; took graduate courses at University of Chicago; never married; no children. ❖ One of the South's foremost educators, spent 12 years teaching public school in Savannah, Augusta, Macon, and Milledgeville (1873–85); accepted invitation from Presbyterian Board of Missions for Freedmen to begin a private school for black youths in Augusta (1885); with aggressive fundraising, eventually expanded the school (Haines Normal and Industrial Institute) to cover a city block; with progressive curriculum, ensured its reputation as one of the best schools of its kind; established the city's 1st kindergarten and a nurses' training department which evolved into the school of nursing at University Hospital at Augusta (early 1890s). Her portrait hangs in the Georgia State House in Atlanta. ❖ See also *Women in World History*.

LANG, Mrs. Andrew (1851–1933). *See Lang, Leonora.*

LANG, Frances (1911–1983). *See Mantle, Winifred Langford.*

LANG, Ivana (1912–1983). *See Lang-Beck, Ivana.*

LANG, Josephine (1815–1880). German composer. Name variations: Lang-Köstlin, Lang-Kostlin, or Lang-Koestlin. Born Josephine Carolin Lang in Munich, Germany, Mar 14, 1815; died in Tübingen, 1880; father was a court musician; mother an opera singer; taught by mother and Fräulein Berlinghof; m. Christian Reinhold Koestlin or Köstlin (professor of law at Tübingen University), 1842 (died 1856). ❖ One of the most published women composers of Romantic period, composed 1st songs (1828); became professional singer at the Munich court (1836); moved to Tübingen (1842); continued to compose and enjoyed encouragement of composers Felix Mendelssohn, Robert Schumann, and Clara Schumann; following husband's death, began teaching voice and piano to support children (1856); as a composer of over 150 songs and many pieces for piano, established a reputation as a progressive composer during lifetime and was especially popular in German-speaking world. ❖ See also *Women in World History*.

LANG, June (1915—). American actress. Name variations: also acted as June Vlasek. Born Winifred June Vlasek, May 5, 1915, in Minneapolis, MN; m. Vic Orsatti (agent), 1937 (div. 1938); m. John Roselli (mobster), 1939 (div.); m. a businessman named Morgan, 1944 (div. 1954); m. Joss Ambler (British actor, div.); children: (last marriage) Patricia Morgan. ❖ Striking blue-eyed blonde, was professional dancer before

breaking into films as extra in *Young Sinners* (1931); after several other small movie roles, was placed under contract at Fox and groomed for stardom; did not click with public, however, and went on to a series of unremarkable roles in mostly small pictures, the last of which was *Lighthouse* (1947). ❖ See also *Women in World History*.

LANG, K.D. (1961—). Canadian pop and country-music singer. Born Kathryn Dawn Lang on Nov 2, 1961, in Edmonton, Alberta, Canada; dau. of Adam Frederick Lang (pharmacist) and Audrey Lang (teacher); attended Red Deer College. ❖ Known for outspoken political views and androgynous aesthetic, 1st toured with band The Reclines throughout Canada (1982–84); released largely ignored 1st album *A Truly Western Experience* (1984) on local label; signed with Sire Records and came to prominence covering Roy Orbison's "Crying" (1987); recorded *Shadowlands* (1988), paying homage to country's leading women and featuring guest appearances by Loretta Lynn, Kitty Wells and Brenda Lee; won Best Female Country Vocal Performance Grammy for *Absolute Torch and Twang* (1989); made acting debut with Percy Adlon film *Salmonberries* (1991); expanded into other musical genres, recording double platinum pop-inspired album *Ingenue* (1992), which earned a Grammy; came out as a lesbian in interview with *The Advocate* (1992), one of the 1st openly gay pop icons; continued creating sultry dance-pop music with *All You Can Eat* (1995), as well as ballads for album *Drag* and romantic Brazilian surf-pop music in *Invincible Summer* (2000). ❖ See also Victoria Starr, *K.D. Lang: All You Get Is Me* (1994).

LANG, Leonora (1851–1933). British translator and editor. Name variations: Mrs. Andrew Lang. Born Leonora Blanche Alleyne, July 12, 1851, in Clifton, Bristol, England; died July 10, 1933, in London; dau. of Charles Thomas Alleyne; m. Andrew Lang (well-known folklorist, poet and editor of children's books), 1875 (died 1912). ❖ Trans. works from Russian, Polish, and French and provided husband with translations and research for collections and anthologies of children's stories and fairytales; translations include A.N. Rambaud, *The History of Russia from the Earliest Times to 1877* (1879) and Count M. Tyszkiewicz, *Memoirs of an Old Collector* (1898); works for children include *The Gateway to Shakespear for Children, Containing a Life of Shakespeare by Mrs. Andrew Lang, a Selection from the Plays, and from Lamb's "Tales"* (1908) and *All Sort of Stories Book* (1912).

LANG, Lois (1911–1985). *See Delander, Lois.*

LANG, Margaret Ruthven (1867–1972). American composer. Born Margaret Ruthven Lang in Boston, MA, Nov 27, 1867; died in Boston, May 30, 1972; dau. of Benjamin Johnson Lang (who conducted Boston's Cecilia and Apollo Clubs) and Frances Morse (Burrage) Lang; studied piano and composition with father; studied violin under Louis Schmidt in Boston and Drechsler and Abel in Munich; studied composition with Victor Gluth in Munich; studied orchestration under G.W. Chadwick and E.A. MacDowell; never married. ❖ Had 1st works—5 songs—included in a Boston recital and reviewed favorably (Dec 14, 1887); had 1 of her songs performed in Paris during World's Exposition (1889) and at inaugural of Lincoln Concert Hall in Washington, DC (1890); in time, enjoyed the inclusion of her songs in repertoire of leading concert singers, including Ernestine Schumann-Heink; was 1st American woman composer to have a composition played by a major orchestra when the Boston Symphony Orchestra performed her Dramatic Overture, *Opus 12* (1893); had another orchestral composition performed 3 times at World's Columbian Exposition in Chicago (1893); ceased composing (1917). ❖ See also *Women in World History*.

LANG, Maria (1948—). Swedish ballet dancer. Born Mar 21, 1948, in Stockholm, Sweden. ❖ Performed with Royal Swedish Ballet (1965–74), most notably in *The Firebird*; danced with Royal Winnipeg Ballet for 1 season; joined Australian Ballet (1974), where she was featured in Cranko's *Romeo and Juliet*, Helpmann's *The Merry Widow*, and revivals of Ashton: *Les Deux Pigeons* and *Monotones*.

LANG, Marie (1858–1934). Austrian feminist. Born Marie Wisgrill, Mar 8, 1858, in Vienna, Austria; died Oct 14, 1934, in Altmünster; dau. of K. Wisgrill and Emilie Scholz (actress); m. Th. Koechert; m. Edmund Lang (1860–1918, attorney); children: Erwin Lang (painter who m. the dancer Grete Wiesenthal) and Lilith Lang von Foerster (artist and favorite model of Oskar Kokoschka). ❖ One of the founders of the feminist movement in Austria, represented its radical wing; with Rosa Mayreder and Auguste Fickert, founded the progressive journal *Dokumente der Frauen* (1899); was cofounder and member of the board of Allgemeinen Österreichischen Frauenvereines; was the center of a vibrant salon and a theosophist.

LANG PING (1960—). Chinese volleyball player. Born Dec 10, 1960, in China. ❖ At Los Angeles Olympics, won a gold medal in team competition (1984).

LANG, Raven (1942—). American midwife. Born Patricia Lang, Dec 17, 1942, in San Francisco, CA; dau. of Emma Parenti Lang; graduate of San Francisco City College, 1962; attended Tokyo College of Oriental Medicine; m. Ken Kinzie, 1966; children: 2. ❖ Pioneer who reestablished the legitimacy of lay midwifery in US, opened the Santa Cruz (CA) Birth Center which offered prenatal care (1971); questioned the "medicalization" of childbirth and served as a childbirth educator; faced widespread opposition from Santa Cruz physicians who opposed midwifery births; demonstrated competency of trained midwives at symposium (1972); served as a midwife in Vancouver, British Columbia (1973–76); directed Institute of Feminine Arts, a CA state-certified college for midwifery (1978–84); practiced traditional Chinese medicine and acupuncture in Santa Cruz; wrote the immensely popular *Birth Book* (1972).

LANG-BECK, Ivana (1912–1983). Yugoslavian pianist. Name variations: Ivana Lang. Born in Zagreb, Yugoslavia, Nov 15, 1912; died 1983. ❖ Studied at Music Academy of Zagreb and later became a professor there; taught at teachers' academy in Zagreb (1940–43), then taught piano at Vatroslav Lisinski Music Academy; had some of her compositions performed in Salzburg at the Mozarteum, as well as in Hamburg, Strasbourg, Trieste, and Soviet Union; wrote over 50 compositions, many for piano, and composed a full-length opera and several ballet scores; saw work also performed on Yugoslav radio and tv.

LANGBEIN, Martha (1941—). West German runner. Born May 22, 1941, in Germany. ❖ At Rome Olympics, won a silver medal in 4 x 100-meter relay (1960).

LANGDON, Mary (1824–1908). *See Pike, Mary.*

LANGE, Aloysia (c. 1761–1839). German soprano. Name variations: Aloysia Weber. Born Maria Aloysia Louise Antonia Weber in Zell or Mannheim, Germany, between 1759 and 1761; died in Salzburg, Austria, June 8, 1839; dau. of Fridolin Weber (1733–1779, musician and uncle of Carl Maria von Weber) and Cecilia Weber; studied with Mozart in Mannheim; sister of Constanze Weber Mozart (who m. Mozart), Josepha Weber Hofer (c. 1758–1819, soprano), and Sophie Weber (1763–1846, who m. composer Jakob Haibel); m. Joseph Lange (1751–1831, painter), 1780. ❖ Best remembered for her close association with Mozart (though he proposed to her, he married her sister Constanze); studied with Mozart and Vogler in Mannheim, where the young composer wrote 7 concert arias and a role in *Der Schauspieldirektor* for her; went to Munich (1788) before moving on to Vienna, where she was engaged for the National Singspiel; was made a lead singer of Italian troupe in Vienna (1782), but because of a salary dispute was transferred to less prestigious Kärntnertortheater; retained by Emperor Leopold II for his opera seria (1790); undertook a concert tour with sister Constanze (1795). ❖ See also *Women in World History.*

LANGE, Anne Françoise Elizabeth (1772–1816). French actress. Born in Genoa, Italy, Sept 17, 1772; died May 25, 1816; dau. of a musician and an actress at Comédie Italienne; m. the son of a rich Belgian named Simons. ❖ Made successful début at Tours (1781); had successful début at Comédie Française in *L'Écossaise* and *L'Oracle* (1788); when a dispute between patriots and royalists broke out between members of company (1792), followed patriots to help found Théâtre de la République Rue Richelieu, but returned after a few months to Comédie Française; had enormous success in Neuchâteau's *Paméla*, but the play, deemed counterrevolutionary, brought down the wrath of the Committee of Safety and the theater was closed (Sept 3, 1793); with author and other members of the cast, was arrested and imprisoned; after 9th Thermidor (July 27, 1794), rejoined her comrades at the Feydeau, but retired (Dec 16, 1797), reappearing only for a few performances (1807).

LANGE, Dorothea (1895–1965). American documentary photographer. Name variations: Dorothea Lange (in professional life); Dorothea Nutzhorn (1895–1925); Dorothea Dixon (1920–1935); Dorothea Taylor (1935–1965). Born Dorothea Margaretta Nutzhorn in Hoboken, NJ, May 15, 1895; died in San Francisco, CA, Oct 11, 1965; dau. of Joan (Lange) Nutzhorn (librarian) and Henry Nutzhorn; m. Maynard Dixon (artist), 1920 (div. 1935); m. Paul Schuster Taylor (b. 1895, economist), Dec 6, 1935; children: (1st m.) Daniel Dixon (b. 1925); John Dixon (b. 1928). ❖ One of the premier American photographers of 20th century, working exclusively in black and white with large format cameras, made many of the most enduring pictures of the American countryside during the Great Depression, and of the human damage caused by unemployment, migration, and war; owned a photography studio in San Francisco (1919–35), starting with portraiture, then shot some of her most famous work which depicted lines of unemployed, humiliated men seeking food and relief; served as government photographer for Farm Security Administration (1935–45), shooting much of the work upon which her fame now rests, tracing the exit of Southern and Midwestern farmers from their land, "tractored out" by the spread of farm machinery, or forced away when their land was ruined in the vast "dust bowl" storms of 1930s; after Japanese attack on Pearl Harbor, was recruited by War Relocation Administration (WRA) to make a pictorial record of deportation of Japanese-Americans to Manzanar; worked as freelance photographer (1945–64), primarily for *Fortune* and *Life* magazines; helped create a new photography magazine, *Aperture.* ❖ See also Milton Meltzer, *Dorothea Lange: A Photographer's Life* (Farrar, 1978); and *Women in World History.*

LANGE, Elizabeth Clovis (1784–1882). African-American religious founder. Name variations: Mother Mary Elizabeth Lange; Mother Mary Elizabeth. Born in French colony of St. Domingue in 1784; died 1882 in Baltimore, MD; dau. of Clovis Lange and Annette ("Dede") Lange; never married. ❖ Immigrated to US (1817); founded school for black Catholic children in Baltimore (1820s); with support of Father James Hector Joubert, founded Oblate Sisters of Providence, the 1st black Roman Catholic order in US (1829); ran schools and supervised teacher training; began the order's 1st mission school in St. Louis, Missouri (1880s). ❖ See also *Women in World History.*

LANGE, Helene (1848–1930). German reformer. Born April 9, 1848, in Oldenburg, Germany; died in Berlin, May 23, 1930; dau. of Carl Theodor Lange (merchant) and Sophia Elisabeth (Niemeyer) Lange; attended Women's High School of Oldenburg and began private instruction for teacher's examination, 1872; lived with Gertrud Bäumer; never married; no children. ❖ Intellectual leader of League of German Women's Associations for 1st 30 years of 20th century, is still celebrated in Germany for her work in establishing schools for women; was employed in a pastor's house in southern Germany (1864); accepted position in secondary school in Berlin (1876); was signatory to "Yellow Brochure" asking Prussian government to establish schools to help prepare women for high school and university study (1887); was co-founder and 1st president of German General Teachers' organization (1889); began a "practical" curriculum of study for women (1889); transformed the "practical" curriculum into a high school curriculum (1893); founded *Die Frau* (1893); was a co-founder of League of German Women's Associations (1894); became president of the League (1901); engineered election of Gertrud Bäumer to presidency of the League (1910); served in upper house of Hamburg legislature (1919–20); awarded a medal by Prussian government for patriotic service to the state (1928). ❖ See also *Women in World History.*

LANGE, Hope (1931–2003). American stage, tv, and screen actress. Born Nov 28, 1931, in Redding Ridge, CT; died Dec 19, 2003, in Santa Monica, CA; dau. of an actress and a music arranger for Flo Zeigfeld; m. Don Murray (actor), 1956 (div. 1961); m. Alan J. Pakula (producer), 1963 (div. 1971); m. Charles Hollerith Jr., 1986; children: Christopher Murray (actor). ❖ At 12, made Broadway debut in *The Patriots* (1943); made film debut as Emma in *Bus Stop* (1956), followed by *The Young Lions, The Best of Everything, Wild in the Country, Pocketful of Miracles, Jigsaw, Death Wish, The Prodigal, A Nightmare on Elm Street Part 2, Blue Velvet* and *Just Cause,* among others; starred in tv series "The Ghost and Mrs. Muir" (1968–70) and "The New Dick Van Dyke Show" (1971–74). Nominated for Oscar for Best Supporting Actress for *Peyton Place;* won Emmys as Best Actress in a Comedy for "The Ghost and Mrs. Muir" (1969 and 1970).

LANGE, Jessica (1949—). American actress and model. Born Jessica Phyllis Lange on April 20, 1949, in Cloquet, Minnesota; dau. of Al Lange and Dorothy Lange; attended University of Minnesota, 1967–68; studied mime at Opéra Comique, 1971–73; m. Paco Grande (photography professor and filmmaker), 1970; lived with Mikhail Baryshnikov and Sam Shepard; children: (with Baryshnikov) Alexandra Baryshnikov; (with Shepard) Hannah Jane Shepard, Samuel Walker Shepard. ❖ Began career studying mime in Paris with Etienne Decroux, then worked as model with Wilhelmina Agency; made film debut in *King Kong* (1976), and did not work much for a few years thereafter; came to prominence and gained acting credentials in remake of *The Postman Always Rings Twice* (1981); followed that with drama *Frances* (1982), for which she was Oscar-nominated for Best Actress, and comedy *Tootsie*

(1982), for which she won an Oscar for Best Supporting Actress; also nominated for Academy Awards for portrayal of Patsy Cline in *Sweet Dreams* (1985) and for role as Ann Talbot in *Music Box* (1990); appeared on Broadway as Blanche Du Bois in *A Streetcar Named Desire* (1992); won 2nd Academy Award for *Blue Sky* (1995); won Olivier Award for performance in Eugene O'Neill's *Long Day's Journey Into Night* (2000), taking play to Broadway (2001); politically outspoken, has been active on issues of environment and human rights; also appeared in *Country* (1984), *Crimes of the Heart* (1986), *Cape Fear* (1991), *Losing Isaiah* (1995), *Titus* (1999), *Prozac Nation* (2001) and *Big Fish* (2003).

LANGE, Marita (1943—). East German track-and-field athlete. Born June 22, 1943, in Germany. ❖ At Mexico City Olympics, won a silver medal in shot put (1968).

LANGE, Mary Elizabeth (1784–1882). *See Lange, Elizabeth Clovis.*

LANGE, Norah (1906–1972). Argentinean poet and novelist. Name variations: Norah Langue De Girondo. Born 1906 in Buenos Aires, Argentina, on Norwegian descent; died 1973 in Buenos Aires; m. Oliverio Girondo. ❖ Belonged to *Martín Fierro* Group of poets and to leading Buenos Aires intellectual circles, published avant-garde magazines such as *Prisma,Proa,* and *Martín Fierro;* works include *La calle de la tarde* (1924), *Los días y las novelas* (1926), *El rumbo de la rosa* (1930), *45 días y 30 marineros* (1930), *Personas en la sala* (1950), and *Los dos retratos* (1956); published speeches to *Martín Fierro* Group as *Discursos* (1942).

LANGENHAGEN, Brigitte (1939—). German politician. Born Dec 8, 1939, in Hamburg, Germany. ❖ As a member of the European People's Party (Christian Democrats) and European Democrats, elected to 4th and 5th European Parliament (1994–99, 1999–2004); named vice-chair of Committee on Fisheries; founder and member of the board of AMRIE (Alliance of Maritime Regional Interests in Europe). Awarded Federal Cross of Merit.

LANGER, Lucyna (1956—). Polish runner. Name variations: Lucyna Kalek or Langer-Kalek. Born Jan 9, 1956, in Poland. ❖ At Moscow Olympics, won a bronze medal in 100-meter hurdles (1980).

LANGER, Susanne Knauth (1895–1985). American philosopher, writer, and educator. Born Susanne Katerina Knauth, Dec 20, 1895, New York, NY; died July 17, 1985, in New London, CT; dau. of Antonio Knauth (lawyer) and Else (Uhlich) Knauth; Radcliffe College, AB, 1920, AM, 1924, PhD, 1926; graduate study at University of Vienna, 1921–22; m. William Leonard Langer (professor), Sept 3, 1921 (div. 1942); children: Leonard C.R. and Bertrand W. ❖ Implemented her own prescription for better approaches to the most profound problems, arguing that philosophy would be revolutionized in 20th century by the burgeoning knowledge of symbols and how we use them, and that philosophy passes through cycles in which a particular approach becomes exhausted and is succeeded by another; following marriage (1921), did graduate work in logic at Radcliffe; published children's stories, *The Cruise of the Little Dipper and Other Fairy Tales* (1923); published *The Practice of Philosophy* (1930) which stressed importance of mathematics and logic to philosophy; followed this with highly successful *Philosophy in a New Key* (1942); starting in 1942, spent 5 years teaching at Columbia and 8 years at Connecticut College; published *Feeling and Form,* one of her best-known works, which develops the philosophy of art posited in *Philosophy in a New Key* into a comprehensive theory of aesthetics (1953); proceeded to work out a philosophy to address the reasoning processes of the sciences in her final and largest work, *Mind: An Essay on Human Feeling,* published in 3 vols. (1967, 1972 and 1982). ❖ See also *Women in World History.*

LANGFORD, Bonnie (1964—). English tap dancer. Born Bonita Melody Lysette Langford, July 22, 1964, in Twickenham, England; m. Paul Grunert (actor), 1995. ❖ Performed as a child in mother's children's precision pantomime troupe; trained at Arts Educational School and Royal Ballet School's children's division; made debut as ballet performer in Nureyev's *Don Quixote;* danced in Joe Layton musical of *Gone with the Wind* and in Angela Lansbury revival of *Gypsy* (1977); appeared frequently on British tv, including in "Doctor Who" (1963), "Just William" (1977), "The Hot Shoe Show" (1983), and "Through the Keyhole" (1983).

LANGFORD, Frances (1914–2005). American singer and actress. Born April 4, 1914, in Lakeland, Florida; died July 11, 2005, in Jensen Beach, Florida; dau. of Annie Newbern (concert pianist); attended Southern College; m. Jon Hall (actor), 1938 (div. 1955); m. Ralph Evinrude (marine motor company magnate), 1955 (died 1986); m. Harold

Stuart, 1994. ❖ Aspired to a career as an opera singer until a tonsillectomy turned her from soprano into contralto (1930); offered a guest spot on Rudy Vallee's radio show, which led to small role in stage musical *Here Goes the Bride* (1933); made screen debut in *Every Night at Eight* (1935), introducing her 1st hit, "I'm in the Mood for Love"; followed that with "I've Got You Under My Skin" from *Born to Dance* (1936), originally sung in the film by Virginia Bruce but recorded by Langford; other films include *Broadway Melody of 1936* (1935), *Yankee Doodle Dandy* (1942), *This Is the Army* (1943), *Follow the Band* (1943) and *Radio Stars on Parade* (1945); appeared as herself in *The Glenn Miller Story* (1954); was a frequent guest on popular radio show "Hollywood Hotel"; joined "The Texaco Star Theater" (1939); became regular on "The Bob Hope Pepsodent Show" (1941) and during WWII, joined Hope on many USO tours to entertain troops, logging over 250,000 miles and frequently putting herself in harm's way; following war, displayed considerable comedic skills in popular radio show "The Bickersons" with Don Ameche (1946–48); entertained troops in Korea (1952). ❖ See also *Women in World History.*

LANGFORD, Jane (1911–1983). *See Mantle, Winifred Langford.*

LANGGÄSSER, Elisabeth (1899–1950). German author. Name variations: Elisabeth Langgasser; Elisabeth Langgaesser. Born Feb 23, 1899, in Alzey; died in Karlsruhe, July 25, 1950; dau. of Eduard Langgässer and Eugenie (Dienst) Langgässer; m. Wilhelm Hoffmann (1899–1967), 1935; children: (with Herman Heller) Cordelia Edvardson (writer); (with Wilhelm Hoffmann) Annette and Franziska. ❖ Writer whose posthumously published novel *Märkische Argonautenfahrt* (*The Quest,* 1950) is regarded by many as one of the finest German works dealing with the moral burden of Nazi inhumanity; moved to Berlin (1929), where she wrote and produced a successful series of dramatic scripts for Berlin Radio; received Deutsche Staatsbürgerinnenpreis (German Citizen's Prize) for novella *Triptychon des Teufels* (The Devil's Triptych, 1932); published 1st novel, the finely crafted *Proserpina, Welt eines Kindes* (Proserpina, A Child's World, 1933); published *Der Gang durch das Ried* (The Path Through the Marsh, 1936) which was banned by the Nazis; with Aryan mother and Jewish father, was legally defined as a 1st-degree *Mischling* and no longer allowed to publish in Nazi Germany (1936); wrote in secret the book that would be published as *Der unauslöschliche Siegel* (The Indelible Seal, 1946); as one of the few writers of quality to have remained in Nazi Germany, enjoyed considerable fame in 1st years after the war; at First Congress of German Writers (1947), was celebrated as one of the "triumvirate of great contemporary women novelists." Posthumously awarded the Georg Büchner Prize, West Germany's most prestigious literary award (1951). ❖ See also *Women in World History.*

LANG-KÖSTLIN, Josephine (1815–1880). *See Lang, Josephine.*

LANGLEY, Eve (1908–1974). Australian writer. Born on a cattle station near Forbes, NSW, Australia, Sept 1, 1908 (some sources cite 1904); died in her bush hut at Katoomba sometime between 1st and 13th of June 1974; dau. of Arthur Alexander Langley (itinerant laborer and violinist) and Mira Davidson; m. Hilary Clark (artist and art teacher), 1938 (div.); children: 3; sister of June Langley. ❖ Moved to New Zealand with family (1932); after marriage failed (1940s), spent some time in Auckland Psychiatric Hospital, then returned to Australia (1956) where she led a seemingly conventional life and was active in Sydney's literary circles; in later life, turned reclusive, moving to the deserted bush near Katoomba in Blue Mountains and residing in a shack dubbed "Iona-Lympus"; dressed as a man, wore a white topi, carried a knife in her belt, and became obsessed with guns; is best remembered for her sequential semi-autobiographical novels, *The Pea Pickers* (1942) and *White Topee* (1954). ❖ See also Joy Thwaite, *The Importance of Being Eve Langley* (Angus & Robertson, 1987).

LANGLEY, Katherine (1888–1948). American politician. Born Katherine Gudger, Feb 14, 1888, near Marshall, in Madison County, NC; died Aug 15, 1948, in Pikeville, KY; dau. of James Madison Gudger Jr. (US congressional representative); graduate of Woman's College, Richmond, Virginia; attended Emerson College, Boston, MA; m. John Langley (politician), 1903 (died 1932). ❖ When husband was elected to Congress (1906), worked as his secretary and became active in Kentucky Republican Party; succeeded to his seat in US House of Representatives following his bootlegging conviction (1924); successfully ran for House seat from Kentucky's 10th District (1926); appointed to several committees and became the 1st woman to serve on Republican Committee on Committees (1930); was also successful in her petition to Calvin

Coolidge to grant husband clemency provided he informally agree to forfeit the right to stand for public office; when husband declared his intention to run for his old House seat, betraying her and the president (1930), refused to have her name removed from ballot, but the public outcry cost her votes and she lost the election; served as railroad commissioner of 3rd Kentucky district (1939–42).

LANGLEY, Neva (c. 1934—). Miss America. Name variations: Neva Langley Fickling. Born Neva Jane Langley c. 1934; Wesleyan Conservatory, BM, 1955; m. William Fickling. ❖ Named Miss America (1953), representing Georgia. Recipient of the Lady Bird Johnson Award and Woman of the Year Award. ❖ See also Frank Deford, *There She Is* (Viking, 1971).

LANGMANN, Adelheid (d. 1375). German nun and writer. Name variations: Adelaide Langmann. Died Nov 22, 1375, in Engelthal, Germany; dau. of Mechtilde (of Nuremberg) Langmann and Otto Langmann; sister of Sophia Langmann (nun at Engelthal); aunt of Gerhaus and Margarete Sachsen (both nuns at Engelthal); m. Gottfried Teufel. ❖ Wealthy widow, entered cloistered Dominican Convent of Engelthal after death of husband (c. 1330); visions collected as *Offenbarungen.*

LANGNER, Ilse (1899–1987). German poet, playwright and novelist. Born May 21, 1899, in Breslau, Germany; died 1987 in Darmstadt. ❖ Works, which often focus on the devastation of war, include *Frau Emma kämpf im Hinterland* (1929), the 1st antiwar play by German woman, *Die purpurne Stadt* (1937), *Zwischen Trümmern* (1948), *Trümmerstücke, Heimkehr* (1949), *Métro* (1952), and *Die Zyklopen* (1960); opposed German militarism and social injustice throughout her life.

LANGSTRETH, Christina (c. 1814–1882). See Gregg, Christina.

LANGTON, Jane (fl. 15th c.). English silk merchant. Fl. in 15th century in London. ❖ A citizen of London, established and managed her own business, importing and marketing silk cloth; was a well-respected entrepreneur and earned substantial profits from her wealthy noble and bourgeois customers.

LANGTRY, Lillie (1853–1929). British courtesan and actress. Name variations: Lily; The Jersey Lily; Lady de Bathe. Born Emilie Charlotte Le Breton, Oct 13, 1853, on Isle of Jersey; died in Monaco, Feb 12, 1929; dau. of William Le Breton (Anglican dean of Jersey) and Emilie Martin (Londoner); m. Edward Langtry, Mar 9, 1874 (div. 1885); m. Hugo de Bathe, 1899; children: (with Louis Battenberg) Jeanne-Marie Langtry (b. Mar 8, 1881, in Paris). ❖ Rose from an obscure life on the Isle of Jersey to become celebrated as the most beautiful woman of her era; became known as "The Jersey Lily," after 2 paintings Millais did of her (1877); began affair with Edward, prince of Wales (future king Edward VII); became infatuated with Louis Battenberg, the prince's nephew, and soon found she was pregnant by him; made stage debut in supporting role in *She Stoops to Conquer* in London (Dec 15, 1881); was enough of a success that the prince persuaded actor-manager Squire Bancroft to hire her at a handsome salary; organized her own troupe, which was managed by Henrietta Hobson, her business manager; after touring the provinces, traveled with company to US; stopped traffic in NY after American debut in *Unequal Match* (1882); remained in States and invested in real estate on Fifth Avenue; became US citizen, which enabled her to divorce husband on grounds other than adultery (1885); resettled in Britain. ❖ See also memoirs *The Days I Knew* (1925); James Brough, *The Prince and the Lily: The Story of Lillie Langtry* (Coward, 1975); *Lillie*, 7-part tv series starring Francesca Annis; and *Women in World History.*

LANNAMAN, Sonia M. (1956—). English runner. Born Mar 24, 1956, in England; dau. of Jamaican parents. ❖ Won the European Indoor championship for the 60 meters (1976); at the United Kingdom championships, won the 100 meters and 200 meters (1977, 1978); won a gold medal for 100 meters at the Commonwealth Games (1978); at Moscow Olympics, won a bronze medal in 4x100-meter relay (1980).

LANNER, Katti (1829–1908). Austrian ballet dancer. Born Sept 14, 1829, in Vienna, Austria; died Nov 15, 1908, in London, England. ❖ Trained at Court Opera School of Ballet in Vienna, where she made professional debut in Guerra's *Angelica* (1845); performed at Court Opera in *La Muette de Portici* (1847), *Giselle* (1852), and was featured in Bournonville's *The Toreodor*; performed throughout Germany; had 2-year engagement at Hamburg State Theater, where she choreographed *Uriella, der Daemon der Nacht* (1862) and *Die Rose von Sevilla* (1862), among others; retired from performance career (c. 1875), after which she served as ballet master at Her Majesty's Theatre, London, and as director

of the Theatre's National Training School; choreographed and staged numerous productions for Majesty's Theatre, as well as 36 productions for Empire Theatre.

LANNOY, Micheline. Belgian pairs skater. Born in Belgium. ❖ With partner Pierre Baugniet, won European championship (1947), World championships (1947, 1948) and a gold medal at St. Moritz Olympics (1948).

LANPHIER, Fay (1906–1959). Miss America. Name variations: Fay Daniels. Born Fay Lanphier in 1906; died 1959 of viral pneumonia in Orinda, CA; married (div.); m. Winfield Daniels, 1931; children: 2 daughters. ❖ Named Miss Santa Cruz (1924); finished 3rd at Miss America pageant in Atlantic City (1924); named Miss California (1925); named Miss America, the 1st to represent a state at national finals (1925); appeared in film *The American Venus,* starring Louise Brooks. ❖ See also Frank Deford, *There She Is* (Viking, 1971).

LANSBURY, Angela (1925—). English-born stage, tv, and screen actress. Born Oct 16, 1925, in London, England; dau. of Edgar Lansbury (lumber merchant) and Moyna MacGill (actress); granddau. of George Lansbury (British Labour Party leader); sister of twin brothers, Edgar and Bruce Lansbury (both producers); m. Richard Cromwell (actor), 1945 (div. 1946); m. Peter Shaw, 1949 (died 2003); children: Anthony Pullen Shaw. ❖ Began stage career in childhood; evacuated to America during London blitz (1940); moved to Hollywood with mother where both were put under contract with MGM; made film debut in *Gaslight* (1944), followed by *National Velvet, Till the Clouds Roll By, The Harvey Girls, Stage of the Union, The Three Musketeers, Samson and Delilah, The Long Hot Summer, The Dark at the Top of the Stairs, Blue Hawaii, The World of Henry Orient, Bedknobs and Broomsticks* and *The Mirror Crack'd,* among others, and was voice of Mrs. Potts in Disney's *Beauty and the Beast;* made NY stage debut in *Hotel Paradiso* (1957) and London debut in *All Over* (1972); on tv, starred as Jessica Fletcher on "Murder, She Wrote" (1984–96). Nominated for Oscar for Best Supporting Actress in *Gaslight* (1944), *The Picture of Dorian Gray* (1945), and *The Manchurian Candidate* (1962); won Tony awards for *Mame* (1966), *Dear World* (1969), *Gypsy* (1975), and *Sweeney Todd* (1979); named Commander of British Empire (CBE); recipient of Kennedy Center Honors (2000).

LANSING, Joi (1928–1972). American actress. Born Joyce Wassmansdoff, April 6, 1928, in Salt Lake City, Utah; died Aug 7, 1972, in Hollywood, CA; m. Lance Fuller (actor), 1951 (div. 1953); m. Stan Todd. ❖ Supporting actress in primarily buxom roles; films include *The Brave One, A Hole in the Head, Who Was That Lady?, Marriage on the Rocks* and *Klondike;* had recurring role on tv series "Love That Bob" (1955–59).

LANSING, Sherry (1944—). American film-studio executive. Born Sherry Lee Heimann, July 31, 1944, in Chicago, IL; graduate of Northwestern University, 1966; m. William Friedkin (film director), 1991. ❖ The 1st woman to serve as president of a major film studio in US, began career as an actress; worked as executive story editor for Warner International and MGM; became vice-president of creative affairs at MGM (1975); moved to Columbia in charge of production and worked on several successful films, including *The China Syndrome* and *Kramer v. Kramer,* before becoming president of feature-film division at 20th Century-Fox (1980); with Stanley Jaffe, formed Jaffe-Lansing (1984) and produced films, including *Fatal Attraction* (1987); became president of Paramount Pictures (1990), then served as CEO (1993–2005).

LANTRATOV, Vera (1947—). Soviet volleyball player. Born May 11, 1947, in USSR. ❖ At Mexico City Olympics, won a gold medal in team competition (1968).

LANVIN, Jeanne (1867–1946). French fashion designer and perfumer. Born 1867; died July 6, 1946; children: Marguerite (b. 1887), later known as Countess Marie-Blanche de Polignac (who took over the house of Lanvin until 1958). ❖ One of the foremost names in couture (1920s), was trained as a seamstress and began career in a milliner's house on Rue du Faubourg Saint-Honoré; opened her own workroom, La Maison de Couture, in a studio apartment in Paris (1885); was credited with the 1st mother-daughter outfits, though she later became known for her wedding gowns and *robes de style* as well; opened a men's boutique, the 1st of its kind (1926); created the perfume Arpege (1927) and enlisted Art Nouveau artist Paul Tribe to help design the packaging; was renowned for her sense of color, and found inspiration in her own art collection, which contained paintings by Vuillard, Renoir, Fantin-Latour, and Odilon Redon. ❖ See also *Women in World History.*

LANY, Louise-Madeleine (1733–1777). French ballet dancer. Born 1733 in Paris, France; died 1777 in Paris; dau. of Jean Lany; sister of Jean-Barthélemy Lany (ballet dancer and choreographer). ❖ Trained at Paris Opéra's ballet school and later at Académie Royale de Musique; performed with Paris Opéra throughout career (1744–67), except for brief engagement in Kassel working for brother; was featured in numerous Opéra and court productions, including *Les Amours de Tempé* (1752), *La Coquette trompée* (1752), *Anacréon* (1754), and *Amneris* (1762).

LAO FUOYE (1835–1908). *See Cixi.*

LAO LISHI (1987—). Chinese diver. Born Dec 12, 1987, in Zhanjiang, China. ❖ Placed 3rd in Grand Prix ranking (2002); at World championships, won gold medal for synchronized platform and silver for 10-meter platform (2003); placed 1st in 10-meter platform and synchronized platform at Grand Prix Super Final (2004); won silver medal for 10-meter platform and gold medal for 10-meter synchronized platform at Athens Olympics (2004).

LAODICE (fl. 129 BCE). Queen of Parthia. Fl. around 129 BCE; dau. of Cleopatra Thea (c. 165–121 BCE) and Demetrius II Nicator, Seleucid king (r. 145–138); sister of Antiochus VIII Philometor Grypus and Seleucus V; m. Phraates II, king of Parthia.

LAODICE I (c. 285–c. 236 BCE). Queen of Syria. Born c. 285 BCE; died c. 236 BCE; dau. of Achaeus, a Seleucid prince, and an unknown mother; m. Antiochus II, 3rd Seleucid (that is, Macedonian) king of Asia; children: daughters, Stratonice III, Laodice II, and perhaps an unnamed 3rd daughter; sons, Seleucus II and Antiochus Hierax (the Hawk). ❖ Fought fiercely to ensure that sons of her line would rule over Seleucid Asia. ❖ See also *Women in World History*.

LAODICE II (fl. 250 BCE). Queen of Pontus. Born c. 260 BCE; dau. of Laodice I (c. 285–c. 236 BCE) and Antiochus II, Seleucid king (r. 261–246 BCE); sister of Seleucus II and Stratonice III; m. Mithridates II of Pontus (a sub-kingdom in modern Turkey).

LAODICE III (fl. 200 BCE). Syrian queen. Fl. around 200 BCE; m. her cousin, the Seleucid king Antiochus III (r. 223–287); children: Cleopatra I (c. 210–176 BCE); Seleucus IV (r. 187–176 BCE); Antiochus IV Epiphanes (r. 175–164 BCE). ❖ See also *Women in World History*.

LA PALME, Béatrice (1878–1921). Canadian soprano and violinist. Born Marie Alice Béatrix Beloeil near Montreal, Quebec, July 27, 1878; died in Montreal, Jan 8, 1921; studied violin with Frantz Jehin-Prume and voice with Gustave Garcia; m. Salvator Issauerl (French tenor), 1908. ❖ Was 1st winner of Lord Strathcona scholarship to Royal College of Music in London (1895); made debut at Covent Garden, replacing Fritzi Scheff as Musetta in *La Bohème* (1903); debuted at Opéra-Comique in Paris (1905) and Montreal Opera Co. (1911); made NY debut at Century Opera House (1913), singing 56 performances of 15 operas (1913); was the 1st Quebec singer to star in great opera houses after Emma Albani; retired to teach (1914); gave last public performance (1919). ❖ See also *Women in World History*.

LA PASIONARIA (1895–1989). *See Ibárruri, Dolores.*

LAPAUZE, Jeanne (1860–1920). French novelist, playwright and poet. Name variations: Jeanne Loiseau; Jeanne Loiseau Lapauze; Mme Henri Lapauze; (pseudonym) Daniel Lesueur. Born Jeanne Loiseau, 1860, in France; died 1920 (some sources cite 1921); m. Henri Lapauze, 1904. ❖ Was the 1st woman awarded Légion d'honneur for literature (1910); writings include *Fleurs d'Avril* (1882), *Névrosée* (1890), *Justice de femme* (1893), *Théâtre féministe* (1899), *L'Honneur d'une femme* (1901) and *Le Masque d'Amour* (1904).

LAPHAM, Susan (1836–1880). *See Wood, Susan.*

LAPID, Shulamit (1934—). Israeli novelist, playwright and short-story writer. Born 1934 in Tel Aviv, Israel; attended Hebrew University; children: 3. ❖ Best known for novel *Gai Oni* (1982), also wrote *Ka 'Cheres Ha 'Nishbar* (1984), *Iton Mekomi* (1989), *Akavishim Smechim* (1990), *Mif'al Hayav* (1992), *Etzel Babou* (1998) and *Ha-Safsal* (2000); served as chair of Hebrew Writers' Association. Awards include Newman Prize.

LAPIERE, Cher Sarkisian (1946—). *See Cher.*

LAPITSKAYA, Natalya (1962—). Soviet handball player. Born Aug 12, 1962, in USSR. ❖ At Seoul Olympics, won a bronze medal in team competition (1988).

LAPLANCHE, Rosemary (1923–1979). American actress and Miss America. Name variations: Rosemary Koplan. Born Oct 11, 1923 in Los Angeles, CA; died May 1979 in Sherman Oaks, CA; sister of Louise LaPlanche (actress); m. Harry Koplan (TV producer), 1947 (died 1974); children: 2. ❖ Named Miss California (1940, 1941); named 1st runner-up to Miss America (1940), then Miss America (1941); highly popular during WWII, sold war bonds and traveled with USO; signed with RKO and appeared in 84 films; had her own radio show; with husband Harry Koplan, hosted tv's "Meet the Misses" and was a regular on "The Lawrence Welk Show." ❖ See also Frank Deford, *There She Is* (Viking, 1971).

LA PLANTE, Laura (1904–1996). American actress. Name variations: Laura La Plante Asher. Born in St. Louis, MO, Nov 1, 1904; died Oct 14, 1996, at Woodland Hills, CA; m. William Seiter (director at Warner Bros.), 1926 (div. 1932); m. Irving Asher (producer), June 19, 1934; children: (2nd m.) Jill Asher; Tony Asher. ❖ One of the top silent stars of 1920s, began film career at 15, playing bit part in one of the popular comedy shorts made by director-producer Albert Christie; gained notice in *The Old Swimmin' Hole* (1921) and subsequently signed a long-term contract with Universal; was initially cast as the heroine in Westerns and adventure films, but found her niche as girl-next-door in social comedies, though she departed from those vehicles with the spooky melodrama *The Cat and the Canary* (1927) and the original version of Ferber's *Show Boat* (1929), in which she played Magnolia and became the 1st woman to sing onscreen; on marriage to Asher, retired from films to live in London, where she appeared on stage; returned to Hollywood (1940), but was not seen on screen again until 1946, when she took a small role in *Little Mister Jim*; starred in a CBS tv drama (1956) and appeared as Betty Hutton's mother in film *Spring Reunion* (1957). ❖ See also *Women in World History*.

LA PLANTE, Lynda (1946—). English actress and writer. Name variations: Lynda Marchal. Born Lynda Marchal, Mar 15, 1946, in Formby, Liverpool, England; trained at Royal Academy of Dramatic Arts; m. Richard La Plante, 1978 (div. 1996). ❖ Television dramatist, best known for "Prime Suspect" series starring Helen Mirren, began career as an actress (1972), touring with Brian Rix and then working at the National and with Royal Shakespeare Co; starred in tv series' "The Sweeney" (1974–78) and "Minder" (1979–86); turned to writing novels and tv scripts, experiencing great success with *Widows* (1982); wrote several bestselling novels including *Royal Flush* (2002); won BAFTA award for "Prime Suspect" (1991) and "Prime Suspect II" (1992) and "Civvies" (1992); won Emmy for "Prime Suspect III"; had less success with series "The Lifeboat" (1994); also wrote and produced "Trial & Retribution" series (1997–2004) and "Mothers and Daughters" (2004).

LA POLA (1795–1817). *See Salavarrieta, Pola.*

LAPORSKA, Zoya (1918–1996). *See Leporska, Zoya.*

LAPP, Bernice (1917—). American swimmer. Born Sept 11, 1917. ❖ At Berlin Olympics, won a bronze medal in 4x100-meter freestyle relay (1936).

LAPPO-DANILEVSKAIA, N.A. (c. 1875–1951). Russian novelist and short-story writer. Name variations: Nadezhda Aleksandrova Láppo-Danilévskaia or Danilevskaya. Born c. 1875 in Russia; died 1951. ❖ Achieved immense popularity for stories about upper class heroines, female villains, and romance; had several novels reissued multiple times but dropped off in popularity after immigrating to Western Europe; works include *In the Mist of Life* (1911), *The Minister's Wife* (1913), *Michail or The Heart of a Russian* (1914), and *Barren Flowers* (1928).

LARA (1912–1995). *See Ivinskaya, Olga.*

LARA, Adelina de (1872–1961). *See de Lara, Adelina.*

LARA, Contessa (1849–1896). *See Mancini, Evalina.*

LARA, Georgia (1980—). Greek water-polo player. Born May 31, 1980, in Athens, Greece. ❖ Won team silver medal at Athens Olympics (2004).

LA RAMEÉ, Louise (1839–1908). *See Ramée, Louise de la.*

LARCOM, Lucy (1824–1893). American author and educator. Born May 5, 1824, in Beverly, MA; died April 17, 1893, in Boston; dau. of Benjamin Larcom (sea captain) and Lois (Barrett) Larcom; graduated of Monticello Seminary, 1852; never married. ❖ Following death of father (1835), moved with family to Lowell, MA, where mother supervised a dormitory at a textile co. to house its female workers, called "mill girls";

with family in need of income, quit school at 11 to become a mill girl herself; though she became a fairly popular writer in her day, is now known primarily for autobiographical *A New England Girlhood, Outline from Memory,* part of which describes the life she and others lived as factory workers in Lowell mills; was an editor of a children's magazine, *Our Young Folks* (1865–73), and published in other magazines, including *St. Nicholas, Youth's Companion* and *Atlantic Monthly;* taught English literature and rhetoric at Wheaton Seminary (now Wheaton College), where she revolutionized school's teaching methods by using lectures and discussions rather than standard approach of reciting from textbooks (1854–62). ❖ See also *Women in World History.*

LAREDO, Ruth (1937–2005). American pianist. Born Ruth Meckler in Detroit, Michigan, Nov 20, 1937; died of cancer, May 25, 2005, in New York, NY; dau. of Ben Meckler and Miriam (Horowitz) Meckler; studied with Rudolf Serkin at Curtis Institute; m. Jaime Laredo (Bolivian violin virtuoso), 1960 (div. 1974); children: Jennifer Laredo (who married the cellist Paul Watkins). ❖ Debuted in NY with Leopold Stokowski and his American Symphony Orchestra (1962); toured Europe with Serkin and his son Peter (1965), receiving fine reviews; following marriage, appeared in numerous recitals with husband; known and respected as a specialist in Russian music, was widely praised for her performances and recordings of the solo piano compositions of Rachmaninoff and Scriabin.

LARENTIA, Acca (fl. 9th, 8th, or 7th c. BCE). Roman woman. Name variations: Larentina, Laurentia, Fabula. Pronunciation: AK-kah Lar-EN-tia. As stepmother of Romulus and Remus, her floruit would fall before any one of several dates in 9th and 8th centuries BCE that the Romans claimed as the foundation date of their city; as the prostitute and lover of Hercules, her floruit would fall within dates of the reign of King Ancus: 642–617 BCE; was married to herdsman Faustulus according to the former story; was married to Carrutius or Tarrutius according to the latter. ❖ Legendary personage or minor goddess honored on a special Feast day in Rome and the subject of 2 traditions: one associates her with the stepmother of Romulus and Remus, the other depicts her as a prostitute during reign of King Marcius Ancus. Honored by Roman festival day, the Larentalia or Larentinalia, on Dec 23. ❖ See also *Women in World History.*

LARENTINA (fl. 9th, 8th, or 7th c. BCE). See *Larentia, Acca.*

LARGE, Amy Hadfield (1874–1971). See *Hutchinson, Amy Hadfield.*

LARK ELLEN (1868–1947). See *Yaw, Ellen Beach.*

LARKIN, Delia (1878–1949). Irish labor leader. Born Brigid Larkin in Toxteth, Liverpool, England, Feb 22, 1878; died in Dublin, Ireland, Oct 26, 1949; dau. of James Larkin and Mary Ann (McNulty) Larkin; sister of James (Big Jim) Larkin (labor leader) and Peter Larkin (pacifist); m. Peter Colgan, Feb 8, 1921. ❖ An organizer of Irish women workers, 1st worked as nurse and teacher in Liverpool; after brother Jim moved to Ireland where he founded the Irish Transport and General Workers Union (ITGWU), joined him in Dublin (1911); helped form Irish Women Workers Union (IWWU), as part of ITGWU, building a united organization with strong loyalties, with branches in other Irish cities and towns; won 2 small strikes (1912); became involved in the great lock-out of workers which followed the tramway strike (1913), but nearly 400 IWWU members were sacked; left Dublin for London, where she helped nurse wounded soldiers (1915); returned to Dublin and worked for insurance section of ITGWU (1918) but was excluded from membership of IWWU; following marriage, hosted young left-wing writers such as Liam O'Flaherty, Sean O'Casey, and Peadar O'Donnell. ❖ See also *Women in World History.*

LARKIN, Joan (1960—). See *Jett, Joan.*

LAROCHE, Baroness de (1886–1919). See *Deroche, Elise-Raymonde.*

LA ROCHE, Guilhem (1644–1710). French novelist. Born 1644 in France; died 1710. ❖ As a Protestant, fled to England after revocation of Edict of Nantes (1685); works include *Almanzaïde* (1674), *Arioviste, histoire romaine* (1674), *Rare en tout* (1677), and *Singis, histoire tartare* (1692).

LAROCHE, Raymonde de (1886–1919). See *Deroche, Elise-Raymonde.*

LA ROCHE, Sophie von (1730–1807). German novelist and publisher. Name variations: Sophie La Roche. Pronunciation: Roche rhymes with posh. Born Sophie Gutermann in Kaufbeuren, Germany, Dec 6, 1730; died in Offenbach, Germany, Feb 18, 1807; dau. of Georg Friedrich Gutermann (dean of medical faculty at university in Augsburg) and

Regina Barbara (Unold) Gutermann; m. Georg Michael Frank von La Roche, Dec 27, 1753; children: out of 8 only 5 survived infancy, Maximiliane von La Roche Brentano (1756–1793, mother of Bettine von Arnim); Fritz von La Roche (b. 1757); Luise von La Roche (b. 1759); Carl von La Roche (b. 1766); Franz Wilhelm von La Roche (b. 1768). ❖ Novelist and publisher of a journal for women whose writings depict morally strong women capable of rising above all misfortune; wrote 1st novel *Geschichte des Fräuleins von Sternheim* (1771, trans. as *Memoirs of Miss Sophy Sternheim,* 1776); wrote *Rosaliens Briefe an ihre Freundin Marianne von St* (Rosalie's Letters to Her Friend Marianne von St, 1779–81); published journal *Pomona für Teutschlands Töchter* (Pomona for Germany's Daughters, 1782–84); wrote the story *Die zwey Schwestern: Eine moralische Erzählung* (1784, trans. as *Two Sisters*); wrote *Briefe an Lina* (Letters to Lina, 1785–87); published novel *Erscheinungen am See Oneida* (Event at Lake Oneida, 1798); in later years, wrote *Mein Schreibtisch* (My Writing Desk, 1799); published travelogues on Switzerland, France, Holland and England; wrote *Schönes Bild der Resignation* (Beautiful Image of Resignation, 1801), the anthology *Herbsttage* (Autumn Days, 1805), and *Melusinens Sommer-Abende* (Melusine's Summer Evenings, 1807); many of her earlier works were published anonymously. ❖ See also *Women in World History.*

LA ROCHEFOUCAULD, Edmée, Duchesse de (1895–1991). French voting-rights activist and writer. Name variations: (pseudonym) Gilbert Mauge. Pronunciation: lah-ROHSH-foo-COH. Born in Paris, France, April 28, 1895; died in Paris, Sept 20, 1991; dau. of Edmund, Comte de Fels, and Comtesse de Fels, who was a founder of the UNVF; m. Jean, Duc de La Rochefoucauld, Dec 27, 1917; children: 2 sons, 2 daughters. ❖ Catholic leader in the struggle to gain French women the right to vote, who was also a leading figure in French literary establishment for more than 60 years; married the heir to La Rochefoucauld ducal title (1917); published 1st book *Fonction de X* (1926); became an officer in Union Nationale pour le Vote des Femmes (UNVF, 1927); was president of UNVF (1930); reported on Spanish Civil War (1938); became a member of jury for Prix Fémina (1944); published studies of Noailles, Fargue, Goll, and Valéry (1950s); assisted brother André de Fels, publisher of *Revue de Paris* (1961–70); elected to Belgian Royal Academy of the French Language and Literature (1962); published a guide to *Cahiers* of Paul Valéry (1964–66); failed to be elected to Académie Française (1983); published last book, at age 94 (1989). Writings include *Nombres* (1926), *Faust et Marguerites* (1927), *La Vie humaine* (1928), *Spanish Women* (1938), *La Femme et ses droits* (1939), *Les Moralistes de l'intelligence* (1945), *La Vie commode aux peuples* (1947), *Vus d'un autre monde* (1950), *Plus loin que Bételgeuse* (1952), *Choix de poèmes* (1955), *Menton* (1962), *La Nature et l'esprit* (1965), *Femmes dramaturges* (1968), *Courts Métrages* (1970), *Spectateurs* (1972), *L'Acquiescement* (1978), *Courts Métrages II* (1980), and *Flashes* (3 vols., 1982–89). ❖ See also *Women in World History.*

LA ROCHEJACQUELEIN, Marie Louise Victoire, marquise de (1772–1857). French royalist and writer. Name variations: LaRochejaquelein; Marquise de La Rochejacquelein. Born Marie Louise Victoire de Donissan or de Donnisson in Versailles, France, Oct 25, 1772; died at Orléans, France, Feb 15, 1857; m. Louis du Vergier or Verger, marquis de La Rochejacquelein (1777–1815). ❖ The 2nd wife of marquis de La Rochejacquelein, the French Vendean leader who was killed in battle at Pontdes-Mathis, near St.-Gilles, France (June 4, 1815), and the sister-in-law of Henri du Vergier, comte de La Rochejacquelein, who had been killed in battle at Nouaille (Mar 1794), published her *Mémoires* of the Napoleonic Wars (1815).

LA ROE, Else K. (1900–1970). German physician. Name variations: Else Kienle; Else La Roe or LaRoe. Born Else Kienle, June 26, 1900, in Heidenheim, Germany; died 1970; eldest dau. of Elisabeth Kienle and Otto Kienle; graduate of University of Heidelberg Medical School, 1923; m. Stephan Jacobowitz (div.); George Henry La Roe (dentist) 1932 (div.); m. Wesley Le Roy Robertson (Native American musician), 1951. ❖ Pioneer in cosmetic surgery, especially breast reconstructive surgery, conducted clinical training at Lexer Clinic in Freiburg; employed as a dermatologist at Catherine's Hospital in Stuttgart; bought a small surgical hospital (c. 1928); involved in the German movement (early 1930s) for legal abortion and improved birth control accessibility; convicted of high treason by Nazis but escaped charges after marriage to George Henry La Roe, an American; move to US (1932); pioneered an operation to graft breast tissue onto an amputated breast; founded American Society for the Reduction of Cancer Casualties (1952).

LA ROY, Rita (1907–1993). Canadian vaudeville dancer. Name variations: Rita La Roy Corbett. Born Ina La Roi Stuart, Oct 2, 1907 in Paris, France (according to La Roy, but numerous sources cite British Columbia); died Feb 17, 1993. ❖ Immigrated to US (mid-1920s) and performed for 2 years on Pantages and Orpheum theater circuits out of Seattle and Tacoma, WA, where dance specialties included a Frog Dance, the vaudeville standard Peacock Dance, and her unique Cobra Dance; appeared in dozens of films, including *The Gay Diplomat* (1931), *Dangerous to Know* (1938), *Come Across* (1938), *Fixer Dugan* (1939), and *You're My Everything* (1949); made featured appearances in musical revues and in De Mille's biblical extravaganzas such as *Song of Songs* (1933).

LARPENT, Anna Margaretta (fl. 1815–1830). British diarist. Born in England; m. John Larpent (Examiner of Plays). ❖ Kept diary from age 15 until 1830, about theatrical and literary events; diaries published as *A Women's View of Drama, 1790–1830: The Diaries of Anna Margaretta Larpent* (1995).

LARRETA DE GANDARA, Carmen Rodriguez (1900–1977). *See Gándara, Carmen.*

LARRIEU, Francie (1952—). American runner. Name variations: Francie Larrieu Smith or Larrieu-Smith. Born Francie Larrieu, Nov 23, 1952, in San Francisco Bay area; sister of Ron Larrieu (Olympian 10,000-meter runner); attended University of California, Los Angeles; m. 2nd husband Jimmy C. Smith (exercise physiologist). ❖ Once considered the greatest middle-distance runner in US history, broke world records in the mile, 2 miles, 100, 1,500, and 3,000 meters; competed in 3 Olympics: Munich 1972 (youngest member of track-and-field squad), Seoul 1988, and Barcelona 1992 (flag bearer for US Olympic Team); in a 30-year career, set 36 US records and 12 World records. Inducted into National Track and Field Hall of Fame and Texas Women's Hall of Fame. ❖ See also *Women in World History.*

LARRIMORE, Francine (1898–1975). French-born stage and screen actress. Born Aug 22, 1898, in Verdun, France; died Mar 7, 1975, in NYC; dau. of J. Louis La Remée and Sarah Adler (sister of actor Jacob P. Adler); cousin of Stella Adler; m. Con Conrad (songwriter, div.); m. Alfred T. Mannon (died 1972). ❖ At young age, moved to NY; made NY acting debut at 10 in *Where There's a Will* (1910), subsequently appearing in numerous productions for over 30 years, including *A Fool There Was, One Night, Here Comes the Bride, Scandal, Nice People, Chicago, Brief Moment* and *Spring Song*; films include *Devil's Darling, The Princess from the Poorhouse* and *John Meade's Woman.*

LARROCHA, Alicia de (1923—). Spanish composer and pianist. Name variations: Alicia de la Rocha. Born Alicia de Larrocha y de la Calle in Barcelona, Spain, May 23, 1923; dau. of Eduardo de Larrocha and Maria Teresa de la Calle (pianist); studied with Frank Marshall (1883–1959) at Granados Academy; m. Juan Torra, June 21, 1950; children: Juan Francisco and Alicia. ❖ One of the greatest pianists of 2nd half of 20th century, and the most famous pianist in Spain and the Hispanic world, began to study piano at Academia Marshall at age 3; gave 1st public performance at 5 (1929); played a Mozart concerto with Madrid Symphony at 11 (1934); made 1st international tour (1947); played in US with Los Angeles Philharmonic Orchestra (1954); made NY debut at Town Hall (1955); performed several concerts with NY Philharmonic to great critical acclaim (1965); played between 100 and 125 engagements per year (1965–80); for a decade, played annually at NY's Mostly Mozart Festival; had a great command of the Spanish repertoire, especially music of Granados, Falla and Albéniz; played all 5 of Beethoven's piano concertos with André Previn and Pittsburgh Symphony (1979); was known for her incisive and unique interpretation of the classical piano repertoire. Awarded Grand Prix du Disque for recording of Isaac Albéniz's *Iberia* (1960); awarded Paderewski Medal (1961); named *Musical America's* Musician of Year (1977); awarded Deutscher Schallplatten Prize (1979); won Spanish Order of Civil Merit and Harriet Cohen Medal. ❖ See also *Women in World History.*

LARS, Claudia (1899–1974). Salvadoran writer. Name variations: Carmen Brannon. Born Margarita del Carmen Brannon Vega on Dec 20, 1899, in San Silvestre Guaymoco (now Armenia), El Salvador; died July 22, 1974, in El Salvador; dau. of Peter Patrick "Don Patricio" Brannon (engineer and theosophist) and Manuela Vega Zelayandía; m. LeRoy Beers, 1923 (div. 1949); m. Salvador Samayoa Chinchilla (Guatemalan writer), 1949; children: 1 son. ❖ A leading voice in 20th-century Salvadoran literature, wrote mostly lyrical, intimate poetry but also some works of political protest; 1st published poems in *Repertorio*

Americano (American Repertoire, 1919) with help of Nicaraguan poet Salomón de Selva; lived in New York and later moved to Costa Rica with 1st husband and young son; published 1st book of poetry *Estrellas en el pozo* (Stars in the Well, 1934); became emotionally involved with priest José Basileo Acuña and wrote romantic poems to him; left husband and moved to El Salvador, US, then Mexico, in search of economic independence; maintained close ties to many Salvadoran intellectuals and artists and dedicated 2nd volume of poetry *Canción redonda* (Round Song, 1937) to painter Salarrué; collaborated with cultural institutions established under government of moderate colonel Oscar Osorio and served as editor of literary journal *Cultura* (Culture) under auspices of Salvadoran Ministry of Education; mentored many emerging Salvadoran writers; published memoir of youth in rural El Salvador, *Memorias de infancia* (Memoirs of Childhood, 1959); also wrote *La casa de vidrio* (The Glass House, 1942), *Ciudad bajo mi voz* (City Beneath My Voice, 1947), *Fábula de una verdad* (Fable of a Truth, 1959), *Sobre el ángel y el hombre* (Of the Angel and Man, 1963) and *Nuestro pulsante mundo* (Our Pulsing World, 1969), among others.

LARSEN, Christine (1967—). Canadian synchronized swimmer. Born Dec 15, 1967, in New Westminster, British Columbia, Canada; sister of Karen Larsen (synchronized swimmer). ❖ Placed 1st at Commonwealth Games for duet (1999); won a team silver medal at Atlanta Olympics (1996).

LARSEN, Gerd (1920–2001). Norwegian ballerina and actress. Born Feb 20, 1920, in Olso, Norway; died Oct 4, 2001, in London, England. ❖ Moved to London to study with Margaret Craske (1938); performed with Antony Tudor in his London Ballet, dancing role of La Fille de Terpsichore in original production of *Gala Performance* and appearing in *Soirée Musicale, Judgement of Paris, Dark Elegies* and *The Planet*; danced with Sadler's Wells in Ashton's *Persephone* (1961), *Les Patineurs* and *Nocturne*; films include *Romeo and Juliet* (1966) and *Stories from a Flying Trunk* (1979); following retirement, served as senior teacher for Royal Ballet.

LARSEN, Lisa (c. 1962—). *See Weidenbach, Lisa Larsen.*

LARSEN, Mette (1975—). *See Vestergaard, Mette.*

LARSEN, Nella (1891–1964). African-American novelist. Name variations: Nellie Larson; Nella Imes; Nellie Walker; (pseudonym) Allen Semi. Born Nellie Walker, April 13, 1891 in Chicago, IL; died in Manhattan apartment a few days before her body was found on Mar 30, 1964; dau. of Peter Walker, cook and laborer, or Peter Larson or Larsen, railway conductor (the two men might be one and the same), and Mary Hanson Walker Larson or Larsen (seamstress); attended Fisk University, 1907–08; Lincoln Hospital and Home Training School for Nurses, NY, diploma, 1915; Library School of New York Public Library, certificate, 1923; m. Elmer Samuel Imes, May 3, 1919 (div. 1933); no children. ❖ Award-winning novelist of Harlem Renaissance, whose fiction exploring themes of gender, race, class, and sexuality heralded the later work of African-American women writers, had 2 short pieces published in *Brownies' Book* (1920); worked as a library assistant, NY Public Library 135th Street Branch (1922); was a librarian at 135th Street Branch (1923–26), which served as a cultural center during Harlem Renaissance; published 1st two short stories (1926); published 1st novel *Quicksand* (1928) and 2nd novel *Passing* (1929), both of which explore the tensions inherent in the lives of middle-class black women who desire freedom from society's racial and gender limits; was 1st African-American woman recipient of Guggenheim fellowship for creative writing (1930); traveled through Spain and France (1930–31); worked as a nurse at Gouverneur Hospital (1944–61) and at Metropolitan Hospital (1961–64). Received Harmon Foundation's Bronze Award for Distinguished Achievement among Negroes in Literature (1929). ❖ See also Thadious M. Davis, *Nella Larsen, Novelist of the Harlem Renaissance: A Woman's Life Unveiled* (Louisiana State U. Press, 1994); and *Women in World History.*

LARSEN, Tonje (1975—). Norwegian handball player. Born Jan 26, 1975, in Tonsberg, Norway. ❖ Won a team bronze medal at Sydney Olympics (2000).

LARSON, Nicolette (1952–1997). American singer. Born July 17, 1952, in Helena, Montana; died Dec 16, 1997, in Los Angeles, CA; m. Russ Kunkel (drummer), 1990; children: Elsie May Larson Kunkel (b. 1990). ❖ Known for her Top-10 hit "Lotta Love," was a back-up and session singer in Los Angeles country-rock scene (mid-1970s); sang on *Tales from the Ozone* by Commander Cody and His Lost Planet Airmen (1975);

performed on dozens of other albums (1970s–80s); was associated with Neil Young, Linda Ronstadt, Michael McDonald, Graham Nash and many other major West Coast artists; recorded 6 albums as solo artist; had a country-music career (1980s). ❖ See also *Women in World History.*

LARSON-MASON, Christine (1956—). American field-hockey player. Name variations: Christine Larson; Christine Mason. Born Christine Larson, May 21, 1956; grew up in Darby, PA; graduate of Penn State, 1978. ❖ At Los Angeles Olympics, won a bronze medal in team competition (1984); became head coach at Williams College.

LARUE, Florence (1944—). American singer. Name variations: Fifth Dimension or The 5th Dimension; Florence LaRue Gordon. Born Feb 4, 1944, in Philadelphia, PA; m. Marc Gordon (manager of Fifth Dimension), 1969 (div.); children: 1. ❖ With LaMonte McLemore, Marilyn McCoo, Ron Townson and Billy Davis Jr., formed Fifth Dimension and had 1st hit with "Go Where You Wanna Go" (1967); with group, had an even bigger hit with "Up, Up and Away" (1967), which earned 4 Grammys, followed by "Stoned Soul Picnic" (1968), "Sweet Blindness" (1968), "Wedding Bell Blues" (1968), the medley from *Hair* ("Aquarius/Let the Sunshine In," 1969) and "(Last Night) I Didn't Get to Sleep at All" (1972); when McCoo and Davis left the group, sang with Townson, McLemore and others in the national tour of *Ain't Misbehavin'.*

LA RUE, Grace (1880–1956). American musical-comedy star. Name variations: LaRue. Born Stella Gray, April 23, 1880, in Kansas City, MO; died Mar 12, 1956, in Burlingame, CA; m. Byron Chandler (div.); m. Hale Hamilton (actor). ❖ Singer, actress and dancer, made stage debut as a child in Julia Marlowe's company; made NY debut to critical acclaim in *The Blue Moon* (1906); other appearances include *Ziegfeld Follies* (1907–08), *The Troubadour, Betsy, Nothing But Love, Hitchy-Koo of 1917, Music Box Revue of 1922, Greenwich Village Follies of 1928* and *Stepping Out;* in London, created a sensation with rendition of song "You Made Me Love You"; was also a headliner in vaudeville for years, at 1st with a partner, as Burke and La Rue.

LA SABLIÈRE, Marguerite de (1640–1693). French patron and salon-nière. Name variations: Mme de la Sabliere. Born Marguerite Hessein in 1640 in Paris; died Jan 5 (some sources cite Jan 8), 1693, in Paris; dau. of Gilbert Hessein and Margaret Menjot; educated by uncle Antoine Menjot and tutors; m. Antoine Rambouillet (1624–1680), also seen as Antoine de Rambouillet, seigneur de la Sablière (Protestant financier entrusted with administration of royal estates), Mar 15, 1654 (died 1679); children: Anne de Rambouillet; Nicolas de Rambouillet; Marguerite de Rambouillet. ❖ French student of science and mathematics who hosted a popular salon frequented by geniuses; was married at 14 (1654); when marriage broke down (1667), sought refuge in a Catholic convent, but husband succeeded in gaining sole custody of their 3 children, whom she recovered only after his death (1679); lived with brother Pierre Hessein, making the home an important salon, a meeting-place for poets, scientists, writers, and brilliant members of the court of Louis XIV; received instruction in mathematics, astronomy, and physics from Giles Persone de Roberval and Joseph Sauveur, both members of French Academy of Sciences; was a friend and sometime patron of such writers as Moliere, Fontanelle, and La Fontaine (who is said to have lived with her for a number of years); for a time, was mistress of poet Charles Auguste, Marquis de La Fare (1676–82); converted to Catholicism (1685) and devoted herself to volunteer work for Hospital for Incurables; also began lengthy correspondence with Abbot de Rance. ❖ See also *Women in World History.*

LASCARIS, Irene (fl. 1222–1235). See *Irene Lascaris.*

LASCELLES, Ann (1745–1789). See *Catley, Ann.*

LASCELLES, Elizabeth (b. 1924). See *Collingwood, Elizabeth.*

LASCELLES, Ernita (1890–1972). English-born actress and playwright. Name variations: Ernita Ranson. Born May 1, 1890, in England; died June 23, 1972, in Buckingham Valley, PA; m. Herbert Walter Ranson (actor). ❖ Was a leading lady on the London stage; came to US (1920s), appearing with Theatre Guild in *Back to Methuselah, From Morn to Night, Madras House* and *The Weavers;* wrote several plays, including *Fire.*

LASCELLES, Patricia (1926—). Countess of Harewood. Name variations: Patricia Tuckwell; (nickname) Bambi. Born Patricia Elizabeth Tuckwell, Nov 24, 1926, in Melbourne, Australia; became 2nd wife of George Lascelles, 7th earl of Harewood, July 31, 1967. ❖ George Lascelles' 1st wife was Marion Stein.

LASCELLES, Mrs. Thomas. See *Iremonger, Lucille.*

LASCELLES, Viscountess (b. 1948). See *Messenger, Margaret.*

LASCENOVA, Natalja (1973—). See *Laschenova, Natalia.*

LASCHENOVA, Natalia (1973—). Soviet gymnast. Name variations: Natalja Lascenova. Born Sept 16, 1973, in Elgava, Latvia, USSR; m. Nikolai Tikhonovich (gymnast, div.); remarried. ❖ Won a gold medal on balance beam, a silver on vault, and a bronze in all-around at Riga (1985); won Belgian Gym Masters (1986); came in 3rd all-around at European Cup and USSR Cup (1988); at Seoul Olympics, won a gold medal in team all-around (1988); won Chunichi Cup, USSR championships, and came in 2nd at World championships (1989); won Moscow News and Arthur Gander Memorial (1990); moved to US (2000).

LASER, Christine (1951—). East German pentathlete. Born Mar 19, 1951, in East Germany. ❖ At Montreal Olympics, won a silver medal in pentathlon (1976).

LASHKO, Irina (1973—). Russian-Australian springboard diver. Born Jan 25, 1973, in Yekaterinburg, USSR; attended Ural State University; married; became an Australian citizen (1999). ❖ Representing Russia, won European championship for 1-meter springboard (1991); won a silver medal at Barcelona Olympics (1992) and a silver at Atlanta Olympics (1996), both for 3-meter springboard; won World championships for 1-meter (1998); won FINA World Cup (2000); moved to Australia; representing Australia, won a gold medal for springboard at World championships (2003) and a bronze medal for 3-meter sychronized springboard with Chantelle Newbury at Athens Olympics (2004).

LASK, Berta (1878–1967). German poet and playwright. Name variations: Berta Jacobsohn-Lask; (pseudonyms) Gerhard Wieland. Born Berta Lask, Nov 17, 1878, in Wadowice, Galicia; died Mar 28, 1967, in Berlin, East Germany; 3rd of 4 children of a Jewish paper manufacturer and a teacher; 2 of her brothers were killed in WWI; her sister was killed by the Nazis; married Ludwig Jacobsohn (neurologist), 1901; children: 4, including Hermann and Ludwig. ❖ Ardent pacifist and feminist, became the most important German socialist writer after Bertolt Brecht; was one of the few German intellectual exiles in Soviet Union to survive the Stalinist terror (1934–53); poetry collections include *Stimmen* (1914) and *Rufe aus dem Dunkeln* (1921); plays include *Leuna* (1921) and *Thomas Münzer* (1925); also wrote stories for children and the autobiographical novel, *Stille un Sturm* (1955).

LASKARIDOU, Aikaterini (1842–1916). Greek educator and feminist. Name variations: Ekatherina Laskaridou. Born 1842; died 1916. ❖ Studied Western educational systems, then attempted to recreate them in Greece, utilizing her considerable wealth to implement programs of study; opened 1st nursery school in Greece and trained teachers to work in them; championed introduction of gymnastics into curriculum of girls' schools and was instrumental in setting up workshops where poor women could receive a rudimentary education; wrote extensively on child rearing and education and also published a few short stories.

LASKER, Mrs. Albert D. (1900–1994). See *Lasker, Mary.*

LASKER, Mary (1900–1994). American philanthropist. Name variations: Mary Reinhardt; Mrs. Albert D. Lasker. Born Mary Woodard in Watertown, WI, Nov 30, 1900; died in Greenwich, CT, Feb 21, 1994; dau. of Frank Elwin Woodard (banker and investor) and Sara (Johnson) Woodard; sister of Alice Woodard; attended University of Wisconsin; Radcliffe College, AB cum laude, 1923; postgraduate work at Oxford University; m. Paul Reinhardt (NY art dealer), 1926 (div. 1933); m. Albert Davis Lasker (president and owner of Lord & Thomas ad agency), June 21, 1940 (died 1952); children: (stepchildren) Francis Brody; Edward Lasker. ❖ Benefactor and champion of biomedical research whose greatest achievement was the National Cancer Act of 1971, a result of her prodding the Nixon administration into a "war on cancer"; with 2nd husband, established Albert and Mary Lasker Foundation to assist and encourage medical research (1942); founded the prestigious Albert Lasker Medical Research Awards given annually (1944); played a key role in setting up a research center authorized by National Mental Health Act (1946); often lobbied Congress; also played a crucial role in convincing Americans it was socially acceptable to discuss the issue of cancer in public; worked to increase research budgets to seek cures for diabetes, growth disorders, and osteoporosis. Received Presidential Medal of Freedom (1969). ❖ See also *Women in World History.*

LASKER-SCHÜLER, Else (1869–1945). German poet. Name variations: Elsa Lasker-Schuler or Schueler. Born Else Schüler, Feb 11, 1869, in

Elberfeld, Germany; died Jan 22, 1945, in Jerusalem; dau. of Aron Schüler (banker) and Jeanette (Kissing) Schüler; m. Berthold Lasker, 1899 (div. 1903); m. Georg Levin also known as Herwarth Walden (art historian, composer, and founder of art society, Verein für Kunst, and the journal *Der Sturm*), 1903 (div. 1912); children: (1st m.) Paul Lasker (1900–1927). ❖ Recognized by many as the finest lyrical voice of 20th-century Germany, was forced by her Jewish heritage into exile during Nazi era; published 1st poems in *Die Gesellschaft* and *Das Magazin für Literatur* (1899); dressed in outlandish clothes, became famous as a poet and bohemian in Berlin cafes; published 2 books of poetry (*Styx* [1902] and *Der Siebente Tag* [1905]), 2 books of prose (*Das Peter Hille Buch* [1906] and *Die Nächte der Tino von Baghdad*), and a play (*Die Wupper* [1909]); won one of Germany's highest literary honors, the Kleist Preis (1932); fled Germany (1933); reached exile in Israel (1939), age 70; never saw Europe again. ❖ See also Hans W. Cohn, *Else Lasker-Schüler: The Broken World* (Cambridge U. Press, 1974); Ruth Schwertfeger, *Else Lasker-Schüler: Inside This Deathly Solitude* (Berg, 1991); and *Women in World History*.

LASKI, Marghanita (1915–1988). British novelist and critic. Name variations: (pseudonym) Sarah Russell. Born Oct 24, 1915, in London, England; died Feb 6, 1988, in Dublin, Ireland; dau. of Neville J. Laski (lawyer) and Phina Gaster Laski; maternal granddau. of Dr. Moses Gaster, chief rabbi of the Portuguese and Spanish Jews in England; niece of Harold Laski (renowned liberal); educated in Manchester; Somerville College, Oxford, BA, 1936; m. John Eldred Howard (publisher), 1937; children: Rebecca Howard; Jonathan Howard. ❖ Journalist, critic, broadcaster and novelist, published 6 novels (1944–53), including *Love on the Supertax* (1944), *The Victorian Chaise-Longue* (1953), and *Little Boy Lost*, a 1949 novel made into a Bing Crosby film 4 years later; a prolific contributor to periodicals, was also an adept lexicographer and editor, writing for *Oxford English Dictionary* and numerous publications on both sides of the Atlantic, including *The Times Literary Supplement*, *The New Yorker*, *Atlantic Monthly*, *New York Times Book Review* and Manchester *Guardian*. Biographical criticism includes *Mrs. Ewing, Mrs. Molesworth, and Mrs. Hodgson Burnett* (1950), *Jane Austen and Her World* (1969), *George Eliot and Her World* (1973), and *From Palm to Pine: Rudyard Kipling Abroad and at Home* (1987). ❖ See also *Women in World History*.

LASKINE, Lily (1893–1988). French harpist. Born Lily Aimée Laskine in Paris, France, Aug 31, 1893; died in Paris, Jan 4, 1988; dau. of a medical doctor and a mother who was a pianist; m. Roland Charmy (violinist, chamber musician and professor at Paris Conservatoire), Aug 30, 1938. ❖ Concertized and recorded widely in a career that spanned over 8 decades; won a 1st prize at Paris Conservatoire (1906); joined Paris Opéra as a harpist (1909), the 1st woman in the orchestra; joined Orchestre Straram, where she began to play classical as well as solo repertoire; performed in première of Ravel's *Boléro* (1930), conducted by the composer; as solo harpist, joined Orchestre National de France (1934); played under the great conductors of the era—Richard Strauss, Arturo Toscanini, Bruno Walter, Paul Paray, and Philippe Gaubert; made recordings with such popular singers as Edith Piaf and Maurice Chevalier, though her most famous recordings may be with flutist Jean Pierre Rampal; also worked on film scores with Delerue, Michel Legrand, and Francis Lai; served as harpist for Comédie Française for more than 30 years; probably best known for interpretations of Mozart. Awarded Cross of the Légion d'Honneur (1936) and a Chevalier (1958). ❖ See also *Women in World History*.

LASOVSKAYA, Inna (1969—). Russian track-and-field athlete. Born Dec 17, 1969, in Moscow, Russia. ❖ Won a silver medal for triple jump at Atlanta Olympics (1996).

LASSER, Louise (1939—). American comedic actress. Born April 11, 1939, in New York, NY; niece of J.K. Lasser (writer of an annual tax guide); m. Woody Allen (actor and director), 1966 (div. 1970). ❖ Made stage debut in Elaine May's revue *The Third Ear* (1964); made film debut in *What's New Pussycat?* (1965), followed by *What's Up Tiger Lily?*, *Bananas, Such Good Friends, Everything You Always Wanted to Know about Sex but Were Afraid to Ask, Slither, In God We Trust* and *Frankenhooker*, among others; on tv, starred on "Mary Hartman, Mary Hartman" (1976–77).

LASSIG, Rosemary (1941—). Australian swimmer. Born Aug 10, 1941. ❖ At Rome Olympics, won a silver medal in 4 x 100-meter medley relay (1960).

LASTHENIA OF MANTINEA (fl. 4 BCE). Greek student of philosophy. Born into a wealthy Peloponnesian family in the Arcadian city of Mantinea in 4th century BCE. ❖ Donned masculine clothes and traveled to Athens to study philosophy under Plato. ❖ See also *Women in World History*.

LA SUZE, comtesse de (1618–1683). *See Coligny, Henriette de.*

LA SYLPHE (c. 1900—). American acrobatic dancer. Name variations: Edith Lambelle. Born c. 1900 in New York, NY. ❖ At 6, made debut in ballet at a London theater because children were prohibited from performing on New York City stages; danced at music halls of European cities including Milan, London, Paris, and Brussels for 4 more years; returned to US where she danced Salome solos as interpretive dancer; appeared in vaudeville theaters; on Broadway, was featured dancer in *George White Scandals of 1919, 1920,* and *1921;* taught ballet, adagio, and acrobatic forms in New York City.

LATAMBLET DAUDINOT, Norka (1962—). Cuban volleyball player. Born Dec 1962 in Cuba. ❖ At Barcelona Olympics, won a gold medal in team competition (1992).

LATHAN-BREHMER, Christina (1958—). East German runner. Name variations: Christina Brehmer. Born Feb 28, 1958, in East Germany. ❖ At Montreal Olympics, won a silver medal in 400 meters and a gold medal in 4x400-meter relay (1976); at Moscow Olympics, won a bronze medal in 400 meters and a silver medal in 4x400-meter relay (1980).

LATHBURY, Kathleen Culhane (1900–1993). English biochemist and illustrator. Born Kathleen Culhane, Jan 14, 1900; died 1993; m. Major G.P. Lathbury, July 1933; studied chemistry at Royal Holloway College, University of London, BS, 1922. ❖ Developer of analytical techniques in medicine and food chemistry, began work for free (and later as a paid chemical adviser and insulin tester) at Dr. Marrack's diabetic clinic at the London Hospital; oversaw manufacture and testing of insulin for British Drug Houses (BDH); on a Messel Travel Fund grant, visited Canada and US; joined League of Nations Health Organization Committee to study crystalline insulin; after WWII, pursued a successful career as a botanical artist and joined the Haslemere and Farnham Art Society; exhibited work at Salon des Nations and in Paris; became a fellow of Institute of Chemistry (1935) and Royal Statistical Society (1943).

LATHGERTHA (b. around 665). Queen of Denmark and Sweden. Name variations: Hladgerd. Born around 665 (other sources claim 800s); became 1st wife of Regner or Ragnar Lothbrok (Leather Breeches, c. 660–715), king of Denmark and Sweden (his 2nd wife was Aslaug, his 3rd was Thora, 4th was Svanloga); children: Fridlef. ❖ Appears in the writings of Saxo Grammaticus as a skilled Viking warrior "who bore a man's temper in a woman's body"; in *Ragnars saga*, she is named Lathgertha; in *Hálfdanar Saga*, she is named Hladgerd.

LATHROP, Julia Clifford (1858–1932). American social worker and reformer. Born in Rockford, IL, June 20, 1858; died in Rockford, June 29, 1932; dau. of William Lathrop (lawyer and politician) and Sarah Adeline (Potter) Lathrop (suffragist); attended Rockford Seminary (later Rockford College); graduate of Vassar College, 1880; never married. ❖ Pioneer in field of child- and public-welfare administration, joined Jane Addams at Hull House (1889), where she remained for the next 20 years; appointed to Illinois Board of Charities (1893); with others, secured legislation to establish 1st juvenile court in the nation (1899); joined Graham Taylor in developing training program which became the Chicago School of Civics and Philanthropy (1908); continued to serve the school as a trustee until it became part of University of Chicago in 1920; appointed director of US Children's Bureau (1912), the 1st woman to head a federal bureau, and embarked on a series of studies, the 1st of which was on infant mortality; campaigned for Sheppard-Towner Act, offering federal grants-in-aid to states for maternity and infant-care programs, which passed (1921); served as president of Illinois League of Women Voters (1922–24) and was also on a presidential commission investigating conditions for immigrants at Ellis Island; served as an assessor on Child Welfare Committee of the League of Nations (1925–31). ❖ See also Jane Addams, *My Friend, Julia Lathrop* (1935); and *Women in World History*.

LATHROP, Mother Mary Alphonsa (1851–1926). See *Lathrop, Rose Hawthorne.*

LATHROP, Rose Hawthorne (1851–1926). American religious founder. Name variations: Mother Alphonsa; Rose Hawthorne. Born in Lenox, Massachusetts, May 20, 1851; died in New York, NY, July 9, 1926;

youngest of 3 children of Nathaniel Hawthorne (novelist) and Sophia Peabody Hawthorne (1809–1871); m. George Parsons Lathrop, 1871 (sep. 1893); children: Francis Lathrop (1876–1881). ❖ Catholic convert and founder of an order of sisters dedicated to caring for terminally ill and destitute cancer patients, moved with family to Europe (1853); returned to US (1860); father died (1864); with husband, converted to Catholicism (1891); moved to Lower East Side of NY and began work with cancer victims (1894); along with Alice Huber, became a Dominican, taking name Sister Alphonsa (1899); founded sisterhood, Servants of Relief for Incurable Cancer; established a charitable home at Rosary Hill in Hawthorne, NY (1901), serving there (1901–26). ❖ See also *Women in World History.*

LATIF, Badri (1977—). German field-hockey player. Born July 2, 1977 in Berlin, East Germany; attended Freie University. ❖ Won a team gold medal at Athens Olympics (2004).

LATIFAH, Queen (1970—). See *Queen Latifah.*

LATIFE HANIM (1898–1975). See *Hanim, Latife.*

LATIMER, Elizabeth (d. 1395). Baroness Latimer. Died Nov 5, 1395; m. John Neville, 3rd baron Neville of Raby, in 1382; children: John Neville, 6th baron Latimer (d. 1430).

LATIMER, Elizabeth W. (1822–1904). English-born author and translator. Name variations: Elizabeth Wormeley; Elizabeth Wormeley Latimer. Born Mary Elizabeth Wormeley in London, England, July 26, 1822; died in Baltimore, MD, Jan 4, 1904; dau. of Ralph Randolph Wormeley (rear admiral in British Navy) and Caroline (Preble) Wormeley; m. Randolph Brandt Latimer, 1856; children: several. ❖ Spent youth traveling extensively and living in London and Paris; grew up with the socially prominent and made debut in the court of Louis Philippe; moved to US with American-born parents, living in Boston and Newport, RI; published 1st book, *Forest Hill: A Tale of Social Life in 1830–31* (1846); followed up with several novels before marriage (1865); returned to literary career (1878), turning out novels, magazine articles, translations, and histories for next 30 years; best remembered for her extremely popular histories. Writings include *Our Cousin Veronica: or, Scenes and Adventures over the Blue Ridge* (1855), (with A.R.W. Curtis) *Recollections of Ralph Randolph Wormeley, Rear Admiral, R.N.; Written Down by His Three Daughters* (1879), *Princess Amelie: A Fragment of Autobiography* (1883), *Men and Cities of Italy* (1901) and *The Prince Incognito* (1902). ❖ See also *Women in World History.*

LATIMER, Marjorie Courtenay- (1907–2004). See *Courtenay-Latimer, Marjorie.*

LATIMER, May (1876–1929). See *Churchill, May.*

LATIMER, Sally (1910—). English actress, director, and manager. Born Dec 17, 1910, in London, England; m. William Bodsworth. ❖ Founded Amersham Repertory Co. (1936), where she played leading parts in the nearly 500 plays produced there; founded the Mobile Theatre (1947); on tv, appeared on the "Inspector Maigret" series.

LA TOUR D'AUVERGNE, Madeleine de (1501–1519). See *Madeleine de la Tour d'Auvergne.*

LA TOUR DU PIN, Henriette de (1770–1853). French writer. Name variations: Henrietta, Marquise de La Tour du Pin. Born Henriette-Lucy Dillon in Paris, France, 1770; died April 2, 1853; dau. of Arthur Dillon (1750–1794) and Lucie de Rothe (1751–1782, lady-in-waiting to Marie Antoinette); m. Frederic-Séraphin, comte de Gouvernet, later Marquise de La Tour du Pin (1759–1837, soldier, prefect, and minister to the court at The Hague), in 1787; children: Humbert (1790–1816); Séraphine (1793–1795); Charlotte, known as Alix (1796–1822, who m. the comte de Liedekerke Beaufort); Cécile de La Tour du Pin (1800–1817); Aylmar (1806–1867); 3 others died in infancy. ❖ In her *Memoirs of Madame de La Tour du Pin,* wrote of the Revolution and Age of Napoleon, because she had experienced both events firsthand; was lady-in-waiting to Marie Antoinette; when revolution broke out (1789), fled with family to Albany, NY; father was executed by Revolutionaries (1794); following a return to France, was lady-in-waiting to Queen Marie Louise of Austria while husband served Napoleon as prefect in Brussels (1801–12), then prefect in Amiens; having fled the Revolution of 1830, lived with husband in Nice and Lausanne; after husband died (1837), settled at Pisa, in Tuscany. ❖ See also *Women in World History.*

LATRILLE, Brigitte (1958—). See *Gaudin-Latrille, Brigitte.*

LATROBE, Mrs. C.A. (1849–1914). See *Addison, Carlotta.*

LATTA, Victoria (1951—). New Zealand equestrian. Name variations: Victoria Jean Latta. Born June 10, 1951, in New Zealand. ❖ At Barcelona Olympics, won a silver medal in team 3-day event (1992); won a team bronze medal for eventing at Atlanta Olympics (1996), on Broadcast News.

LATTANY, Kristin Hunter (1931—). See *Hunter, Kristin.*

LATTIMORE, Jewel (1935—). See *Amini-Hudson, Johari.*

LA TULES (c. 1820–1852). See *Barcelo, Gertrudis.*

LATYNINA, Larissa (1934—). Soviet gymnast. Name variations: Larisa Latynina. Born Larissa Semyonovna Latynina, Dec 27, 1934, in Kherson, Ukraine, USSR. ❖ Won gold medals at World championships in all-around (1958, 1962), balance beam (1958), vault (1958), and floor exercises (1962); won European championships (1957, 1961); at Melbourne Olympics, won gold medals in indiv. all-around, vault, floor exercises, and team al-around, a silver medal for uneven bars and a bronze medal for teams all-around, portable apparatus (1956); at Rome Olympics, won gold medals for indiv. all-around, floor exercises, and team all-around, silver medals for uneven bars and balance beam and a bronze medal for vault (1960); at Tokyo Olympics, won bronze medals for balance beam and uneven bars, silver medals in indiv. all-around and vault, and gold medals in floor exercises and team all-around (1964); became a coach for Soviet national team. Inducted into International Women's Sports Hall of Fame (1985).

LATZSCH, Heike (1973—). German field-hockey player. Name variations: Heike Laetzsch or Lätzsch. Born Dec 19, 1973, in Braunschweig, Germany; attended University of Cologne. ❖ At Barcelona Olympics, won a silver medal in team competition (1992); forward, won a team gold medal at Athens Olympics (2004).

LAU, Jutta (1955—). East German rower. Born Sept 28, 1955, in East Germany. ❖ Won a gold medal at Montreal Olympics (1976) and a gold medal at Moscow Olympics (1980), both in quadruple sculls with coxswain.

LAUBER, Cécile (1887–1981). Swiss novelist, poet and playwright. Name variations: Cecile Lauber. Born July 13, 1887, in Lucerne, Switzerland; died April 16, 1981, in Lucerne. ❖ Works include *Die Wandlung* (1929), *Stumme Natur* (1939), and *Land deiner Mutter* (4 vols, 1946–57).

LAUDER, Estée (1908–2004). American cosmetics entrepreneur. Name variations: Estee Lauder. Born Josephine Esty (changed to Esther on birth certificate) Mentzer, July 1, 1908, in Corona, Queens, NY; died April 24, 2004, in New York, NY; dau. of Max Mentzer (businessman) and Rose (Schotz) Rosenthal Mentzer; m. Joseph Lauter (later changed to Lauder), 1930 (div. 1939, remarried 1943, died 1983); children: Leonard and Ronald Lauder. ❖ Founder of a cosmetics empire, sold her 1st products, a Cleansing Oil, Creme Pack, and Super-Rich All-Purpose Cream, to the House of Ash Blondes, a beauty salon she frequented on West 72nd Street; with 4 products and a substantial order from Saks Fifth Avenue, established an office in NY (1946); introduced Youth Dew (1953), a bath oil that doubled as a skin perfume and was distinguished by its lasting scent, to great success; introduced several product lines, including Clinique (a hypoallergenic line for women with sensitive skins), Prescriptives (a customized makeup line), and the classic Estée Lauder products. ❖ See also autobiography *Estée* (1985); and *Women in World History.*

LAUDERDALE, duchess of (1626–1698). See *Murray, Elizabeth.*

LAUENSTEIN, Countess (c. 1803–1854). See *Sontag, Henriette.*

LAUER, Bonnie (1951—). American golfer. Born Feb 20, 1951, in Detroit, MI; attended Michigan State University. ❖ Won the 1st national women's collegiate golf championship (1973) and named All-America; won Michigan Amateur championship (1970, 1972); joined LPGA tour and named Rookie of the Year (1976); won Patty Berg Classic (1977); served as LPGA president (1988). Inducted into National Collegiate Hall of Fame.

LAUER, Hilde (1943—). Romanian kayaker. Born Mar 24, 1943. ❖ At Tokyo Olympics, won a bronze medal in K2 500 meters and a silver medal in K1 500 meters (1964).

LAUGHLIN, Clara E. (1873–1941). American author and lecturer. Born Clara Elizabeth Laughlin in New York, NY, Aug 3, 1873; died Mar 3, 1941; dau. of Samuel Wilson and Elizabeth (Abbott) Laughlin; never married. ❖ Author of well-known series of travel guides, also founded Clara Laughlin Travel Services in Chicago, NY, Paris, and London; met with instant success on publication of 1st book, *So You're Going to Paris* (1924); followed this with travel guides for other nations, including Italy and England; was a frequent contributor to magazines and newspapers. ❖ See also memoirs *Traveling Through Life* (1934); and *Women in World History.*

LAUGHLIN, Gail (1868–1952). American lawyer, feminist, and politician. Name variations: Abbie Hill Laughlin, Abigail Laughlin. Born Abbie Hill Laughlin, May 7, 1868, in Robbinston, Maine; died Mar 13, 1952, in Portland, Maine; dau. of Robert C. Laughlin (ironworker) and Elizabeth P. (Stuart) Laughlin; Wellesley College, AB, 1894; Cornell University, LLB, 1898. ❖ State legislator who campaigned for Equal Rights Amendment, prohibition, and right for women to serve on juries, was admitted to NY bar and opened law office in NYC (1899); appointed expert agent to US Industrial Commission (1900); campaigned throughout nation for women's suffrage for National American Woman Suffrage Association (1902–06); admitted to Colorado bar, opened law office in Denver (1908); served on CO board of pardons (1911–14) and on (Denver) Mayor's Advisory Council (1912); moved to San Francisco and opened law office (1914); at 1st convention of National Federation of Business and Professional women, was elected 1st president (1919); moved to Portland, Maine, and began law practice (1924); successfully ran for state legislature (1929) and served 3 terms, introducing legislation aimed at furthering women's rights, and helping organize Maine department of health; served on state senate (1935–41) and was 1st woman recorder of court decisions (1941–45); suffered minor stroke and went into semi-retirement (1948).

LAUGHTON, Vera (1888–1959). *See Mathews, Vera Laughton.*

LAUMANN, Daniele (1961—). Canadian rower. Name variations: Danielle Laumann. Born July 1961, in Mississauga, Ontario, Canada; sister of Silken Laumann. ❖ At Los Angeles Olympics, won a bronze medal in double sculls (1984).

LAUMANN, Silken (1964—). Canadian athlete and motivational speaker. Born Silken Suzette Laumann, Nov 14, 1964, in Mississauga, Ontario, Canada; sister of Daniele Laumann (b. 1961); m. John Wallace; children: William. ❖ Won the bronze medal for double sculls with sister Danielle at the Los Angeles Olympics (1984); won two World Cup championships for rowing (1991); won bronze medal for single sculls at Barcelona Olympics (1992) and silver medal for single sculls at Atlanta Olympics (1996). Named Velma Springstead female athlete of year (1991); given Wilma Rudolph Courage Award (1997); inducted into Canadian Sports Hall of Fame (1998). ❖ See also *Women in World History.*

LAUNAY, Marguerite Cordier de, Mme de Staal (1684–1750). *See Staal de Launay, Madame de.*

LAUNAY, Vicomte de (1804–1855). *See Girardin, Delphine.*

LAUPER, Cyndi (1953—). American pop singer. Born Cynthia Anne Stephanie Lauper, June 22, 1953, in Brooklyn, New York; dau. of Fred and Catrine Dominique Lauper (waitress); studied voice with Katherine Agresta; m. David Thornton (actor), 1991; children: Declyn Wallace Thornton Lauper. ❖ Pop star with thrift-store style and urban wild-child image who had enormous success in 1980s; began playing guitar at 11, dropped out of school, and sang and wrote songs for rock band Blue Angel for 4 years; recorded international hit album *She's So Unusual* (1983), which won a Grammy; was also the 1st woman to have 4 songs from same album in Top 3 on charts ("Girls," "All through the Night," "She-Bop" and "Time After Time"); had considerable success with next album *True Colors* (1986), scoring #1 hit with title track; other albums include *A Night to Remember* (1989), *A Hat Full of Stars* (1993), *The 12 Deadly Cyns and Then Some* (1995), *Sisters of Avalon* (1997), *At Last* (2003) and *Shine* (2004). ❖ See also Carl R. Green and William R. Sanford, *Cyndi Lauper* (Crestwood, 1986).

LAURA (fl. 10th c.). Saint and abbess. Fl. when the Saracens held Spain, between the 9th to 11th centuries. ❖ Abbess of convent of St. Mary of Culédor, was arrested by Saracens and thrown into a cauldron of boiling pitch. Feast day is Oct 19. ❖ See also *Women in World History.*

LAURA (1308–1348). *See Noves, Laure de.*

LAURA (1737–1801). *See Ferguson, Elizabeth Graeme.*

LAUREL, Kay (1890–1927). American film and theatrical dancer. Name variations: Kay Laurell. Born 1890 in Erie, PA; died Jan 31, 1927, in London, England; m. Winfield R. Sheehan (film producer), 1922. ❖ Dance specialty performer, appeared at roof gardens in *Midnight Frolics* (1915–18) and *Ziegfeld Follies* (1916–18); appeared in films *The Brand* (1919), *The Valley of the Giants* (1919) and *The Lonely Heart* (1920); performed briefly—and unsuccessfully—as solo ballroom dancer in vaudeville; toured East Coast with stock companies and danced in film serials in New York City.

LAURENCE, Margaret (1926–1987). Canadian writer. Born Jean Margaret Wemyss, July 18, 1926, in Neepawa, Manitoba, Canada; died in Lakefield, Ontario, Canada, Jan 5, 1987; dau. of Robert Wemyss (lawyer) and Verna (Simpson) Wemyss; attended United College in Winnipeg; m. John Laurence, known as Jack, 1947 (div. 1969); children: Jocelyn (b. 1952) and David (b. 1955). ❖ One of the key figures in the development of 20th-century Canadian literature, submitted 1st story to a *Winnipeg Free Press* writing contest (1939); worked as a reporter for the *Winnipeg Citizen* (1947–48); moved to England with husband (1949), and then to British protectorate of Somaliland (1952); began drafting 1st novel, *This Side Jordan* (1955); returned with family to Canada (1957) and began writing; separated from husband (1960) and returned to England with children; published *The Stone Angel* (1964); published *A Jest of God* (1966) which was later adapted for highly acclaimed film *Rachel, Rachel;* returned to Canada (1973); wrote *The Fire-Dwellers,* the Vanessa MacLeod stories, and *The Diviners* (1974); was chancellor of Trent University in Peterborough (1980–83); hometown of Neepawa serves as the model for the fictional town of Manawaka which is the setting for all of her Canadian stories. Made Companion of the Order of Canada (1971); awarded Governor-General's Medal for fiction (1974). ❖ See also Patricia Morley, *Margaret Laurence* (Twayne, 1981); Clara Thomas, *Margaret Laurence* (McClelland & Stewart, 1969) and *The Manawaka World of Margaret Laurence* (McClelland & Stewart, 1976); and *Women in World History.*

LAURENCE, Mary (b. 1928). *See Wells, Mary.*

LAURENCIN, Marie (1883–1956). French artist, poet, book illustrator, and set designer. Born in Paris, France, Oct 31, 1883; died in Paris, June 8, 1956; buried in Père Lachaise cemetery; illeg. dau. of Pauline Laurencin and Alfred Toulet; m. Baron Otto von Waëtjen, June 21, 1914 (div. 1921); no children. ❖ The only female artist associated with the male-dominated avant-garde art movements in early 20th-century Paris, created a soft pastel world that contrasted sharply with the vivid colors and geometric figures emanating from Picasso's flamboyant and daring coterie of male artists; entered Lycée Lamartine (1893); studied porcelain painting at École de Sèvres (1902–03); took drawing classes in Paris from Madeleine Lamaire; attended Académie Humbert (1903–04); met Georges Braque (1903); exhibited at Salon des Indépendants, Paris (1907); began 6-year affair with Guillaume Apollinaire (1907); did her celebrated canvas, *Apollinaire and His Friends* (1908); saw *Portrait of Mme Fernande X* and *Young Girls (Jeunes Filles)* included in Cubist exhibition of 1911; held 1st individual exhibit of her paintings at Galerie Barbazanges, Paris (1912); completed last large canvas, *Society Ball* (1913); lived in Spain (1914–19) where she was influenced by Spanish culture; returned to Paris (1921), producing her most typical and recognizable work, in muted pastels, which reveals her mature style (1921–37); designed sets and costumes for "Les Biches," Ballet Russes (1923). Awarded Legion of Honor (1937); inauguration of Marie Laurencin Museum, Nagano-Ken, Japan (1983). ❖ See also memoirs *Le Carnet des nuits* (1942); Charlotte Gere, *Marie Laurencin* (Rizzoli, 1977); and *Women in World History.*

LAURENTIA (fl. 9th, 8th, or 7th c. BCE). *See Larentia, Acca.*

LAURETIS, Teresa De (1938—). *See De Lauretis, Teresa.*

LAURETTE DE ST. VALERY (fl. 1200). French noblewoman and healer. Fl. in 1200, in Amiens, France; m. Aléaume de Fontaines, of the petty nobility (died 1205). ❖ A woman of the lower nobility, became a doctor. ❖ See also *Women in World History.*

LAURI, May (1880–1945). *See Beatty, May.*

LAURIE, Annie (1863–1936). *See Black, Winifred Sweet.*

LAURIE, Lillian (1874–1961). *See Thomas, Lillian Beynon.*

LAURIE, Piper (1932—). American actress. Born Rosetta Jacobs, Jan 22, 1932, in Detroit, MI; m. Joseph Morgenstern (film critic), 1962 (div. 1981); children: Anne Morgenstern Grace. ❖ Made film debut in

Louisa (1950), followed by *The Milkman, The Prince Who was a Thief, The Mississippi Gambler, Dangerous Mission, Johnny Dark, Ain't Misbehavin', Until They Sail, Ruby, Appointment with Death, Other People's Money,* and *Wrestling Ernest Hemingway,* among others; took 15-year hiatus from screen work; appeared in a recurring role on "Twin Peaks" (1990–91). Nominated for Best Actress for *The Hustler* (1961), and Best Supporting Actress for *Carrie* (1976) and *Children of a Lesser God* (1986); won an Emmy for "Promise" (1986).

LAURIEN, Hanna-Renate (1928—). German politician. Born April 15, 1928, in Danzig. ❖ Joined the CDU (1966) and was culture minister in Rheinland-Pfalz in the Cabinet of Helmut Kohl; served in Berlin senate (1981–89), was vice-chair of CDU (1984–87) and president of the Berlin parliament (1991–95); was a member of the diocesan council of the Archdiocese of Berlin and also of the Central Council of German Catholics.

LAURIER, Zoé (1841–1921). Canadian first lady. Name variations: Zoe Laurier, Lady Laurier. Born Zoé Lafontaine, June 26, 1841 (some sources cite 1842), in Montreal, Quebec, Canada; died Nov 1, 1921, in Ottawa; m. Wilfrid Laurier (prime minister of Canada, 1896–1911), May 13, 1868 (died Feb 17, 1919); children: none. ❖ A lover of music, was at one time a piano teacher; served as one of the vice-presidents of the National Council of Women at its foundation; 2 days before she died, changed will and left Laurier House in Ottawa to incoming prime minister William Lyon Mackenzie King (he then left it to the Canadian people).

LAURIJSEN, Martha (1954—). Dutch rower. Born April 15, 1954, in Netherlands. ❖ At Los Angeles Olympics, won a bronze medal in coxed eights (1984).

LAURISTIN, Marju (1940—). Estonian politician and journalist. Born April 7, 1940, in Tallinn, Estonia; Tartu University, degree in journalism and sociology of mass communication, 1966; Moscow University, PhD in journalism, 1976. ❖ Began career as journalist at Estonian radio in Tallinn; was a researcher and head of Laboratory of Sociology at Tartu University (1970–72), then associate professor of journalism (1972–88), professor of Social Policy (1995–99), and became professor of Social Communication (2003); served as member of Estonian Parliament (1990–95, 1999–2003); was minister of Social Affairs (1992–94) and deputy speaker; writings include *Towards a Civil Society* (1993) and *Return to the Western World* (1997).

LAURITSEN, Susanne (1967—). Danish handball player. Name variations: Susanne Munk Lauritsen; Susanne Munk. Born Oct 12, 1967, in Denmark; m. Ulrik Wilbek (national team trainer), 1994. ❖ Debuted on national team (1987); played for Viborg; won a team gold medal at Atlanta Olympics (1996); won team European championships (1994, 1996) and World championships (1997); retired (2001).

LAUZON, Patricia Noall- (1970—). *See Noall, Patricia.*

LAVAL, Josée (c. 1906—1990). French personage. Name variations: Josee or José Laval; Josée de Chambrun; Mme de Chambrun; Comtesse de Chambrun. Born c. 1906 in France; died Dec 1990; dau. of Pierre Laval (1883–1945, prime minister of France and open collaborator with the Germans) and Eugenie (Claussat) Laval (dau. of Chateldon's mayor); m. Count Réne de Chambrun (French military attaché in Washington at time of the fall of France, summer 1940), in 1935 (died 2002). ❖ Daughter of Pierre Laval, fought for years to restore his reputation; also published and wrote a preface for a collection of documents, *Laval parle.* ❖ See also *Women in World History.*

LAVALLIÈRE, Eve (c. 1866—1929). French stage actress, singer and comedian. Name variations: Eugénie Lavallière; Eva Lavalliere; Eugénie Feneglio. Born Eugénie Pascaline Feneglio c. 1866, in Toulon, France; died July 10, 1929, in Vosges, France; children: (with Fernand Samuel, theater manager) daughter Jeanne. ❖ Popular and versatile entertainer, was raised in Toulon and Perpignan; moving to Paris, found work singing cabaret in Montmartre bars; became singer and actress in Paris at end of 19th century; most closely associated with Variété Theater, made stage debut as Orestes in *La Belle Hélène* (1892), followed by *Le carnet du diable, Le pompier de service, Les Petites Barnett, Le nouveau Jeu, Le Vieux Marcheur, Education de prince, La Veine, Le Faux Pas, Ange, Le roi,* and *La dame de Chez Maxim,* among others; created title role in *Ma Tante d'Honfleur* (1914); retired (1915); entered l'Ordre des Tertiaires Franciscains and became a nun (1920s). ❖ See also Edward F. Murphy, *Mademoiselle Lavallière* (Doubleday, 1949).

LA VALLIÈRE, Louise de (1644–1710). French royal mistress. Name variations: Duchesse de La Vallière; Sister (Soeur) Louise de la Miséricorde. Born Françoise Louise de la Baume Le Blanc in Tours, Touraine, France, Aug 6, 1644; died 1710; dau. of Laurent de la Baume Le Blanc (d. 1651, officer who took name of La Vallière from a small property near Amboise) and a mother (name unknown) who joined the court of Gaston d'Orléans at Blois; children: (with Louis XIV) Charles (Dec 1663–1666); a 2nd child (Jan 1665–1666); daughter Marie Anne, known as Mlle de Blois (b. Oct 1666, who m. Armand de Bourbon, prince of Conti, in 1680, and whose youngest child, the count of Vermandois, died on his 1st campaign at Courtrai in 1683); another son (b. Oct 1667). ❖ Known for her sweet disposition, was the favorite mistress of Louis XIV (1661–67); as maid of honor to Henrietta Anne, duchess of Orléans, refused to gossip about her possible involvement with the Comte de Guiche, causing a serious breach with Louis; fled to an obscure convent at Chaillot, but Louis soon followed; removed from the service of Henrietta, was established in a small building in Palais Royal, where she gave birth to a son Charles (1663); was made a duchess (May 1667) and granted the estate of Vaujours but was compelled to remain at court as the king's official mistress, sharing Mme de Montespan's apartments at the Tuileries; made an attempt at escape (1671), when she fled to the convent of Ste. Marie de Chaillot, but was forced to return; was finally permitted to enter the convent of the Carmelites in the Rue d'Enfer in Paris (1674), taking her final vows as Sister (Soeur) Louise de la Miséricorde (1675); spent 36 years there in penance and prayer. A necklace with pendants was named for her; it is usually spelled *lavaliere.* ❖ See also *Women in World History.*

LAVANT, Christine (1915–1973). Austrian poet. Born Christine Thonhauser, July 4, 1915, near St. Stefan, Lavanttal, Carinthia, Austria; died June 7, 1973, in Wolfsberg, Austria; m. Josef Habernig, 1939. ❖ The 9th child in a miner's family, who suffered from a disfiguring illness and had a brief stay in a mental asylum, often wrote of despair and dark mystical experiences; began writing under the pseudonym Lavant (1945); poetry collections include *Die Bettlerschale* (The Beggar's Bowl, 1956), *Spindel im Mond* (Spindle on the Moon, 1959), and *De Pfauenschrei* (The Cry of the Peacock, 1962). Won Georg Trakl Prize and Anton Wildgans Prize.

LAVARCH, Linda (1958—). Australian politician. Name variations: Linda Denise Lavarch. Born Nov 27, 1958, in Brisbane, Australia. ❖ Solicitor; as a member of the Australian Labor Party, won a by-election to the Queensland Parliament for Kurwongbah (1997); served as chair of the Scrutiny of Legislation Committee (1998–2001).

LAVATER-SLOMAN, Mary (1891–1980). Swiss novelist and biographer. Born Mary Sloman, 1891, in Hamburg, Germany; died 1980; m. Emil Lavater; children: Warja Lavater-Honegger (b. 1913). ❖ Wrote historical, biographical novels about such women as Lucrezia Borgia, Queen Elizabeth I, and Catherine II the Great.

LAVAUR, Guirande de (d. 1211). *See Guirande de Lavaur.*

LAVEAU, Marie (1801–1881). American voodoo priestess. Name variations: Marie Laveau I; Marie Laveaux; Marie Lavieu; Widow Paris. Born a quadroon in 1801 in New Orleans, LA; died June 15, 1881 in New Orleans; illeg. dau. of Charles Laveau and Marguerite Darcantrel; m. Jacques Paris (freeman of color from Haiti), Aug 4, 1819 (died 1824); began living with a white man who she could not legally marry, Louis Christopher Duminy de Glapion, 1826 (died 1855); children: (with Paris) 1; (with Glapion) 5, including Madame Legendre and Marie Philomene Laveau Glapion (aka Marie Laveau, voodoo priestess). ❖ One of the most powerful voodoo priestesses in world history, was a freewoman of African, American Indian and European blood; began career as a hairdresser than nurse; a devout Catholic, healer and spiritualist, was said to hold voodoo rituals behind St. Louis Cathedral in the French Quarter; became enormously influential and powerful, a power that came from her network of spies and informants among slaves and servants; helped the wounded during the Battle of New Orleans. Often featured in novels, folklore and songs, has reemerged at the center of a far-reaching religious movement and her tomb in St. Louis No. 1 Cemetery has become a place of pilgrimage.

LAVEAU, Marie (1827–1897). American voodoo priestess. Name variations: Marie Laveau II; Marie Laveaux or Lavieu. Born Marie Philomene Laveau Glapion, Feb 27, 1827, in New Orleans, LA; died June 11, 1897, in New Orleans; some claimed she drowned in a storm on Lake Pontchartrain; others claimed to have seen her as late as 1918; dau. of Marie Laveau (1801–1881) and Louis Christopher Duminy de Glapion.

❖ Became a voodoo priestess and was almost as powerful as her mother; but, lacking the warmth and compassion of her mother, inspired fear and subservience; ran a bar and brothel on Bourbon Street.

LAVELL, Carol (1943—). American equestrian. Born April 1943; lives in Loxahatchee, FL. ❖ At Barcelona Olympics, won a bronze medal in team dressage on Gifted (1992); won the Heidelberg Cup on Much Ado (2003).

LAVENSON, Alma (1897–1989). American photographer. Name variations: Alma L. Wahrhaftig. Born Alma Ruth Lavenson in San Francisco, CA, May 20, 1897; died in Piedmont, CA, Sept 19, 1989; University of California, Berkeley, BA, 1919; m. Matt Wahrhaftig (lawyer), 1933 (died 1957); children: Albert (b. 1935); Paul (b. 1938). ❖ Took up photography (1919) and continued working until her death at 92, concentrating on still lifes, industrial and architectural photographs; was a frequent contributor to magazines *Photo-Era* and *Camera Club* and represented in Edward Steichen's *Family of Man* exhibition at Museum of Modern Art in NY (1955). ❖ See also Susan Ehrens, *Alma Lavenson Photographs* (Wildwood Arts, 1991); and *Women in World History*.

LAVERICK, Elise (1975—). English rower. Born July 27, 1975, in Rustington, Sussex, England; attended London College of Law. ❖ Won a bronze medal for double sculls at Athens Olympics (2004).

LAVERICK, Elizabeth (1925—). English engineer. Born Nov 25, 1925, in UK. ❖ The University of Durham's 1st woman student to earn a PhD in a scientific subject (1950) and the 1st woman appointed to a top British defense firm management position, served as the Institute of Electrical Engineers' (IEE) 1st woman deputy secretary (1971–85) and its 8th female fellow; was the 1st woman permitted to use the radio research station's laboratory at Ditton Park, Slough, Berkshire (worked as a technical assistant, 1942–43); worked on a microwave antennae design (1950–53) at GEC Stanmore (Marconi Defence Systems); at Elliott Brothers (1954–68), created a security system using an off-the-shelf seismic sensor (a system later employed at a Wales prison and at a British Myanmar military base); was president (1967–69) and honorary secretary (1991–95) of Women's Engineering Society; served as an editor of the *Journal of the Women's Engineering Society* (1983–90). Made an Officer of the Order of the British Empire (1993).

LA VERNE, Lucille (1869–1945). American stage and screen actress. Name variations: Lucille LaVerne. Born Lucille Mitchum, Nov 8 (some sources cite Nov 7), 1869, in Memphis, TN; died Mar 4, 1945, in Culver City, CA. ❖ Began career on stage as a child actress; had 1st NY stage success as Corin in *As You Like It* in an all-woman cast (1894); best remembered as Widow Cagle in *Sun-Up* (1923–27); appeared in numerous films, silent and talking. The La Verne Empire theater in Richmond, Virginia, was named after her.

LAVERTY, Maura (1907–1966). Irish novelist, playwright and broadcaster. Born Mary Kelly in Rathangan, Co. Kildare, May 15, 1907; died July 26, 1966, in Dublin; dau. of Michael Kelly and Mary Ann (Tracey) Kelly; educated at Brigidine Convent, Co. Carlow; m. Seamus Laverty also seen as James Laverty, Nov 3, 1928; children: Maeve Laverty, Barrie Laverty Castle (artist), and James Laverty. ❖ Spent much of childhood with grandmother, who was immortalized as Delia Sally in successful 1st novel *Never No More* (1942), but next 3 novels—*Alone We Embark* (1943), *No More Than Human* (1944), a sequel to *Never No More*, and *Lift Up Your Gates* (1946)—were all banned under Ireland's strict censorship laws, a fate she shared with other leading writers of her generation; adapted *Lift Up Your Gates* into stage play *Liffey Lane*, an enormous commercial and critical success (1951); followed that with 2 other plays which formed a trilogy, *Tolka Row* (1951), and *A Tree in the Crescent* (1952); had a weekly radio program in which she answered letters on variety of topics, especially cookery, since her cookery books, *Kind Cooking* (1946) and *Full and Plenty* (1961), were enormously popular; adapted *Tolka Row* for 1st Irish tv soap opera; when the 1st episode aired (Jan 1964) and the show quickly became one of the most popular on Irish tv, wrote all the episodes until her death in 1966; also wrote children's books, *Cottage in the Bog* (1992) and *The Queen of Aran's Daughter* (1995), which were illustrated by daughter Barrie Castle. ❖ See also *Women in World History*.

LAVI, Daliah (1940—). Israeli actress. Born Daliah Levenbuch, Oct 12, 1940, in Palestine (now Shavei Zion, Israel). ❖ Began career as a dancer, then served with Israeli army; made film debut at 15 in Swedish production *Hemsöborna* (1955), followed by *Un soir sur la plage, The Return of Dr. Mabuse, Candide, Two Weeks in Another Town, La frusta e il corpo, Il*

Demonio, Lord Jim, Ten Little Indians, The Spy with a Cold Nose, Casino Royale and Catlow.

LAVIEU, Marie.
See Laveau, Marie (1801–1881).
See Laveau, Marie (1827–1897).

LAVIN, Mary (1912–1996). Irish novelist and short-story writer. Born in East Walpole, MA, June 11, 1912; died in Dublin, Ireland, Mar 25, 1996; only child of Thomas Lavin and Nora (Mahon) Lavin; University College Dublin, BA (honors), 1934, MA (1st class honors), 1938; m. William Walsh (lawyer), Sept 1942 (died 1954); m. Michael McDonald Scott, 1969 (died 1990); children: (1st m.) Valentine, Elizabeth and Caroline Walsh. ❖ At 10, returned to Ireland, eventually moving to Bective in Meath, which would provide inspiration for her fiction; published 1st short story, "Miss Holland," (1938), followed by 1st collection of short stories, *Tales from Bective Bridge* (1941), which won James Tait Black Prize; continued to write steadily after marriage, publishing short-story collections *The Long Ago* (1944) and *At Sally Gap* (1946), which included the novella *The Becker Wives;* also wrote 2 novels, *The House in Clewe* (1945) and *Mary O'Grady* (1950); a master of the short story, was variously compared to other Irish short-story writers such as Liam O'Flaherty, Sean O'Faolain, and William Trevor. Received American-Irish Foundation Award (1979) and Aosdána award (Irish Government, 1992). ❖ See also Zack Bowen, *Mary Lavin* (Bucknell U. Press, 1975); Angeline A. Kelly, *Mary Lavin, Quiet Rebel* (Barnes & Noble, 1980); Richard F. Peterson, *Mary Lavin* (Twayne, 1978); and *Women in World History*.

LAVINE, Jacqueline (1929—). American swimmer. Born Oct 1929. ❖ At Helsinki Olympics, won a bronze medal in the 4x100-meter freestyle relay (1952).

LAVOE, Spivy (1906–1971). American nightclub entertainer. Name variations: Madame Spivy; Mme. Spivy. Born Spivy LaVoe or LeVoe, Sept 30, 1906, in Brooklyn, NY; died Jan 7, 1971, in Woodland Hills, CA. ❖ International star of nightclubs, operated Spivy's Roof in NYC (1940–51); became a character actress in later years; films include *Requiem for a Heavyweight, The Fugitive Kind* and *Auntie Mame.*

LAVOISIER, Marie (1758–1836). French chemist. Name variations: Marie Anne Pierrette Paulze; comtesse de Rumford; countess of Rumford; Madame de Rumford; Marie Thompson. Born Marie Anne Pierrette (also seen as Pierette) Paulze, 1758; died Feb 10, 1836; dau. of Jacques Paulze and Claudine (Thoynet) Paulze; m. Antoine Laurent Lavoisier (1743–1794, founder of modern chemistry), 1771; m. Benjamin Thompson (1753–1814, physicist), count of Rumford, Oct 1805; children: (stepdau.) Sarah Thompson (1774–1852). ❖ French scientific collaborator with husband Antoine, played an important role in the birth of modern chemistry; was tutored in chemistry by Jean Baptiste Bucquet; learned English, a language husband would never master; trans. many chemical works for him not only from English but also from other languages, the most important being Richard Kirwan's *Essay on Phlogiston*, which appeared in Paris (1788) and includes a few of her notes as well as commentaries by her husband and other French chemists who effectively refuted Kirwan's erroneous theories; studied drawing with Jacques Louis David and made sketches of the Lavoisier laboratory; assisted husband in preparation of the plates for his epoch-making *Elementary Treatise on Chemistry* (1789); often presided over intellectual soirées, to which were invited many of Paris' most brilliant scientists and artists; survived the French Revolution, which cost her husband and father their lives, but was imprisoned for several months at height of the Terror (1794). ❖ See also *Women in World History*.

LA VOISIN (d. 1680). *See Deshayes, Catherine.*

LAVRIC, Florica (1962—). Romanian rower. Born Jan 1962 in Romania. ❖ At Los Angeles Olympics, won a gold medal in coxed fours (1984).

LAVRINENKO, Natalya. Belarusian rower. Born in Belarus. ❖ Won a bronze medal for coxed eights at Atlanta Olympics (1996).

LAVROVA, Natalia (1984—). Russian rhythmic gymnast. Born Aug 4, 1984, in Penza, Russia. ❖ Won a team gold medal at Sydney Olympics (2000); won World team championships (1999, 2002, 2003); won a gold medal for team all-around at Athens Olympics (2004).

LAVRSEN, Helena (c. 1963—). Danish curler. Name variations: Helena Blach-Lavrsen; Helena Lavrsen. Born Helena Blach, c. 1963, in Denmark; m. Lasse Lavrsen (curler). ❖ Was World champion (1982) and European champion (1994); won a silver medal for curling at

Nagano Olympics (1998), the 1st-ever Danish medal in any sport at Winter Olympics; won World silver medal (1998).

LAW, Alice Easton (1870–1942). New Zealand teacher of the blind. Born Oct 23, 1870, in Burntisland, Fife, Scotland; died Aug 28, 1942, in Auckland, New Zealand; dau. of William Law and Catharine (Morton) Law; sister of Mary Blythe Law. ❖ Immigrated with sister to New Zealand (early 1880s); worked as part-time music teacher at Jubilee Institute for the Blind (1902); active in formation of girls' orchestra at Jubilee Institute. ❖ See also *Dictionary of New Zealand Biography* (Vol. 4).

LAW, Kelley (1966—). Canadian curler. Born Jan 11, 1966, in Burnaby, British Columbia, Canada. ❖ As skip, won a Canadian National championship and World championhip (2000) and a team bronze medal at Salt Lake City Olympics (2002).

LAW, Leslie (1965—). British equestrian. Born May 5, 1965, in England. ❖ Won a team silver medal for eventing at Sydney Olympics (2000), on Shear H20.

LAW, Mary Blythe (1873–1955). New Zealand teacher of the blind. Born Aug 13, 1873, in Burntisland, Fife, Scotland; died Dec 26, 1955, in Auckland, New Zealand; dau. of William Law and Catharine (Morton) Law; sister of Alice Easton Law. ❖ Immigrated with sister to New Zealand (early 1880s); worked as assistant teacher, then head teacher at Jubilee Institute for the Blind (1894–1939); helped supervise and expand Braille library at Jubilee Institute. Made MBE (1939). ❖ See also *Dictionary of New Zealand Biography* (Vol. 4).

LAW, Ruth (1887–1970). American aviator. Name variations: Ruth Law Oliver. Born Ruth Bancroft Law, Mar 21, 1887, in Lynn, MA; died Dec 1, 1970, in San Francisco, CA; m. Charles Oliver, 1913. ❖ Received pilot's license (1912); was the 1st woman pilot to perform a loop-the-loop and the 1st to chance flying at night; made headlines when she flew from Chicago to NY City (Nov 19, 1916), an unprecedented 590 miles in 6 hours, setting the American nonstop record; while in the Philippines (1919), became the 1st woman to carry the airmail; spent the latter part of piloting career barnstorming with a flying circus that bore her name. ❖ See also *Women in World History.*

LAW, Sallie Chapman (1805–1894). American nurse. Born Sallie Chapman Gordon, Aug 27, 1805, in Wilkes County, NC; died June 28, 1894, in Memphis, TN; m. John S. Law, June 1825. ❖ At start of Civil War, organized Southern Mother's Hospital in Memphis, TN, which was to become Southern Mother's Association at war's end; after the Union captured Memphis, transported drugs, including opium and quinine, through Union lines; assisted in a hospital in La Grange, GA, which was named for her; distributed clothing and supplies to Gen. Joseph E. Johnston's men in Columbus, GA; served as president of her Southern Mother's Association, which was one of 1st Civil War memorial societies, until 1889.

LAWANSON, Ruth (1963—). American volleyball player. Born Sept 27, 1963; attended Fresno State University. ❖ At Barcelona Olympics, won a bronze medal in team competition (1992); played professional volleyball in Italy (1992–94) and France (1994–95).

LAWFORD, Patricia Kennedy (1924—). American socialite. Born 1924; dau. of Joseph P. Kennedy (1888–1969), financier, diplomat, and head of several government commissions) and Rose Fitzgerald Kennedy (1890–1995); sister of John Fitzgerald Kennedy, Bobby Kennedy, and Ted Kennedy (all politicians); graduate of Manhattanville College of the Sacred Heart, NY; m. Peter Lawford (actor), June 1954 (div. 1966, died 1984); children: Christopher Kennedy Lawford (b. 1955, independent film producer and actor); Sydney Maleia Lawford (b. 1956, former model who m. Peter McKelvy); Victoria Lawford (b. 1958, who m. Robert Beebe Pender); Robin Lawford (b. 1961, marine biologist). ❖ After college, worked for a time for NBC in NY; became a production assistant for "Kate Smith Hour" (1951); following divorce (1966), concentrated much of her energy on charitable organizations. ❖ See also *Women in World History.*

LAWICK-GOODALL, Jane van (b. 1934). *See Goodall, Jane.*

LAWLESS, Emily (1845–1913). Irish novelist and poet. Name variations: Honorable Emily Lawless. Born June 17, 1845, in Co. Kildare, Ireland; died Oct 19, 1913, in Surrey, England; dau. of Lord Edward Lawless, 3rd Baron Cloncurry, and Lady Elizabeth Kirwan; Trinity College, DLitt; never married. ❖ Praised for her accurate depictions of Irish peasant life, published *Hurrish* (1886); later published her most popular novel *Grania*

(1892); also wrote a history of Ireland (1887) and a biography of Irish novelist Maria Edgeworth (1904). ❖ See also *Women in World History.*

LAWLOR, Patsy (1933–1998). Irish politician. Born Mar 1933 in Kill, Co. Kildare, Ireland; died Feb 1998; m. Tom Lawlor. ❖ Representing Fine Gael, unsuccessfully contested the general election for Kildare (1981), losing by less than 50 votes; elected to the Seanad from the Cultural and Educational Panel: Nominating Bodies Sub-Panel (1981–82).

LAWRANCE, Jody (1930–1986). American screen actress. Name variations: Jody Lawrence. Born Josephine Lawrance Goddard, Oct 19, 1930, in Fort Worth, TX; died July 10, 1986, in Ojai, CA. ❖ Made film debut in *Ten Tall Men* (1951), followed by *The Son of Dr. Jekyll, Mask of the Avenger, The Brigand, All Ashore, Captain John Smith and Pocahontas, The Scarlet Hour, Hot Spell* and *The Purple Gang,* among others.

LAWRENCE, Andrea Mead (1932—). American skier. Name variations: Andrea Mead; Andy Mead. Born Andrea Mead, April 19, 1932, in Rutland, Vermont; m. Dave Lawrence (skier), 1951 (div. 1967). ❖ Won all events held at the Federation International de Ski tryouts in Whitefish, Montana (1949); won 10 out of 16 races (1951); at Oslo Olympics (1952), won gold medals in giant slalom and slalom, the 1st American athlete to win two gold medals in a single Winter Olympics. Awarded White Stag Trophy (1949) and Beck International Trophy (1952); inducted into National Ski Hall of Fame (1958) and International Women's Sports Hall of Fame (1983); at 1960 Squaw Valley Olympics, skied the Olympic flame into the stadium. ❖ See also *Women in World History.*

LAWRENCE, Carmen Mary (1948—). Australian politician and psychologist. Born Mar 2, 1948, in Northam, Western Australia, Australia; University of Western Australia, BS and PhD in psychology, 1971. ❖ Politician who experienced meteoric rise in Labor Party to become 1st female state premier; was a tutor at University of Melbourne (1972–73), then lecturer at Univ. of Western Australia (1974–83); helped found Women's Electoral Lobby (1972) and joined Labor Party; worked in research services for Western Australian Department of Health (1983–1986); won election to Western Australian Legislative Assembly (1986), chaired Child Sexual Abuse Task Force (1986–88) and became minister of Education (1988); won re-election to Parliament (1989), then elected premier of Western Australia (1990), the 1st woman to head a state government; in "Penny Easton affair," was accused of lying about knowledge of political manipulation of court case which ultimately contributed to suicide of Easton; became opposition leader (1993); won by-election for federal seat of Fremantle (1994), accepting appointment as Health Minister in Keating government; faced additional damage to reputation when commission was appointed to rehash Easton case (1995); elected opposition frontbench and appointed shadow minister for Environment (1996); forced to resign after being charged with 3 counts of perjury in Easton case (1997); found not guilty (1999); returned to frontbench (2000) and served as shadow minister for Status of Women as well as Industry, Innovation and Technology (2000–01), then shadow minister for Aboriginal and Torres Strait Islander Affairs, Arts and Status of Women (2001–02); resigned from shadow cabinet (2002); elected president of Labor Party (2003).

LAWRENCE, Carol (1932—). American dancer and actress. Born Carolina Maria Laraia, Sept 5, 1932, in Melrose Park, IL; m. Cosmo Allegretti, 1955 (div. 1959); m. Robert Goulet (singer), 1963 (div. 1981); m. Greg Guydus, 1982 (div. 1983); children: (2nd m.) 2. ❖ Worked with Chicago Opera Ballet in Illinois as adolescent; moved to New York City where she made professional debut in *Borscht Capades of 1951;* appeared on Broadway in *New Faces of 1952,* on tour with *Me and Juliet* (1954), in replacement cast of *Plain and Fancy* (1955) and in *Shangri-La* (1956) and *Ziegfeld Follies* (1956); came to prominence as the original Maria in *West Side Story;* also appeared in *Subways Are for Sleeping, Saratoga, I Do! I Do!,* and *Kiss of the Spiderwoman;* appeared frequently on tv variety shows, was a regular on ABC's "General Hospital" and had her own talk show. ❖ See also autobiography, *Carol Lawrence: The Backstage Story.*

LAWRENCE, Chiara (1975—). American skier. Born April 26, 1975, in Reno, NV. ❖ Placed 2nd at Skiercross World championships (1999 and 2000); won gold medal at Gravity Games in Skiercross (2000); won silver (Winter 2000) and bronze (Winter 2001) in Skier X at X Games.

LAWRENCE, Daisy Gordon (c. 1900—). American girl guide. Name variations: Margaret "Daisy" Gordon; Daisy Gordon. Born Margaret

Gordon, c. 1900; grew up in Savannah, Georgia; niece of Juliette Gordon Low (1860–1927, founder of the Girl Scouts). ❖ Niece of Juliette Gordon Low (founder of the Girl Scouts of USA); became 1st registered Girl Guide in US (1912); with Gladys Denny Schultz, wrote *Lady from Savannah: The Life of Juliette Low* (1958).

LAWRENCE, Eleanor (1936–2001). American flutist. Name variations: Eleanor Steindler. Born 1936 in Boston, Massachusetts; died Jan 16, 2001, in New York, NY; dau. of John C. Baker (president of Ohio University); sister of Elizabeth Baker and Anne Baker; Radcliffe College, BA; New England Conservatory, MA; studied with James Pappoutsakis, Marcel Moyse, William Kincaid and Harold Bennett; m. Frank Steindler; children: Catherine and Frederick Steindler. ❖ Soloist, recording artist and teacher, began long career as teacher at Manhattan School of Music (1960s); played with American Symphony Orchestra, New York Philharmonic, Brooklyn Philharmonic, and Metropolitan Opera; performed as soloist with Boston Pops and at Alice Tully Hall and toured US as recitalist; premiered works of Ernst von Dohnanyi, *Passacaglia* for solo flute and *Aria* for flute and piano at Carnegie Recital Hall (1969), which were composed for her, and later recorded them; founded Monomoy Chamber Ensemble (1969), which played in annual summer series at Monomoy Theater in Chatham, Massachusetts, and in later years at Weill Recital Hall; was member of board of National Flute Association (1977–84) and served as editor of *NFA Newsletter,* an important resource for flutists; gave master classes in flute; founded Marcel Moyse Society and served as its president (1993–2001). Recordings include *French Music for Voice and Flute, The Complete Works of Paul Hindemith,* and *Music for Flute and Piano,Flute Favorites and The Best of Marcel Moyse.*

LAWRENCE, Elizabeth (1904–1985). American landscape architect and writer. Born in Marietta, GA, May 27, 1904; died June 11, 1985, in Annapolis, MD; dau. of Samuel Lawrence and Elizabeth (Bradenbaugh) Lawrence; grew up in NC; graduate of Barnard; 1st woman to receive a degree in landscape architecture from North Carolina State College of Design, 1930. ❖ Designer whose legendary gardens in Raleigh and Charlotte, NC, provided a backdrop for her writings, published *A Southern Garden* (1942), which received decent reviews, sold moderately for the next 15 years, quietly went out of print, was reprinted (1957) and has remained in print for over 50 years; took on a weekly gardening column for *Charlotte Observer* (1957) which she would continue for next 14 years; encouraged the preservation of native wildflowers of the region. Received Herbert Medal of American Plant Life Society (1943) for contributions to gardening and gardening literature; honored by American Horticultural Society and National Council of State Garden Clubs for *A Southern Garden.* ❖ See also *Women in World History.*

LAWRENCE, Emmeline Pethick- (1867–1954). *See Pethick-Lawrence, Emmeline.*

LAWRENCE, Florence (1886–1938). Canadian-born actress. Born Florence Annie Bridgewood in Hamilton, Ontario, Canada, Jan 2 (some sources cite Sept 22), 1886; committed suicide in West Hollywood, CA, Dec 28, 1938; interred in an unmarked grave in Hollywood Memorial Cemetery; dau. of George Bridgewood (British actor and impresario) and Charlotte Amelia (Dunn) Bridgewood (American actress known professionally as Lotta Lawrence); m. Harry L. Solter (director), Sept 1908 (died 1920); m. Charles Bryne Woodridge (Denver business broker), May 21, 1921 (sep. 1929, div. 1931); m. Henry Bolton, Nov 1931 (div. 1932); no children. ❖ At 3, debuted in parents' tent show billed as "Baby Florence, the Child Wonder"; with mother, worked for the fledgling Edison Vitascope film co., where she began to build her reputation with a role in *Daniel Boone* (1907); joined D.W. Griffith's Biograph Co. and was promoted simply as "The Biograph Girl" (1908); appeared in a string of successful pictures at Biograph (21 in 1908 alone), many directed by Griffith; starred under own name in *Love's Stratagem* (1910), for Carl Laemmle's Independent Motion Picture Co. of America (IMP), becoming the nation's 1st named movie star; left Laemmle (1911) and for several years worked for producer Sigmund Lubin; seriously burned while performing a scene in a burning building (1915), was eventually forced, for the most part, into retirement. ❖ See also *Women in World History.*

LAWRENCE, Frieda (1879–1956). German baroness and writer. Name variations: Baroness Frieda von Richthofen; Frieda Weekley. Born Emma Maria Frieda Johanna von Richthofen in French city of Metz, in Lorraine, 1879; died in Taos, New Mexico, Aug 11, 1956; dau. of Friedrich von Richthofen (civil engineer) and Anna (Marquier) von

Richthofen; sister of Else von Richthofen and Johanna ("Nusch") von Richthofen; m. Ernest Weekley (English professor), Aug 29, 1899 (div. May 18, 1914); m. D(avid) H(erbert) Lawrence (1885–1930, novelist), July 13, 1914 (died Mar 2, 1930); m. Angelo Ravagli (captain in Italian army), Oct 31, 1950; children: (1st m.) Montague "Monty" Weekley (b. 1900); Elsa Weekley (b. 1902); Barbara "Barby" Weekley (b. 1904). ❖ Abandoned 1st husband and eloped with British writer D.H. Lawrence, who at the time was struggling to get his literary career off the ground (1912); during their tumultuous 18-year relationship, influenced much of his work, not only serving his characterizations and plots, but also functioning as his best critic; had a substantial hand in refining manuscript of *Sons and Lovers;* enjoyed a social life with a wide circle of friends, including Cynthia Asquith, Ottoline Morrell and Mabel Dodge Luhan. ❖ See also autobiography *Not I, but The Wind...* (1934) and *Frieda Lawrence: The Memoirs and Correspondence;* Janet Byrne, *A Genius for Living: The Life of Frieda Lawrence* (HarperCollins, 1995); Martin Green, *The von Richthofen Sisters: The Triumphant and the Tragic Modes of Love* (Basic, 1974); Rosie Jackson, *Frieda Lawrence* (Pandora, 1994); and *Women in World History.*

LAWRENCE, Gertrude (1898–1952). British singer, dancer, and actress. Born Gertrud (Gertie) Alexandra Dagmar Klasen, July 4, 1898, in Clapham, London; died of cancer, Sept 6, 1952, in NY; dau. of Alice Louise (Banks) Klasen and Arthur Klasen (singer, known professionally as Arthur Lawrence); trained at Miss Italia Conti's Stage School; m. Frank Gordon Hawley, 1918 (div. 1927); m. Richard Stoddard Aldrich, 1940; children: (1st m.) Pamela Hawley (b. 1918). ❖ An idol of the interwar generation who starred on both sides of the Atlantic for nearly 30 years, made professional debut as child dancer in *Babes in the Wood* in London (1908); engaged as understudy to Beatrice Lillie in *Andre Charlot's Revues* (1916–19), in which she sang "Poor Little Rich Girl"; scored successes in several musical shows quickly becoming the toast of London's West End (1921–24); made 1st appearance on Broadway in *Andre Charlot's Revue of 1924* (1924); divided professional life between London and NY (1925–37), appearing in such shows as *London Calling!* with Noel Coward, *Oh Kay!* (1926–27), singing "Do, Do, Do" and "Someone to Watch Over Me," *Private Lives* with Noel Coward and Laurence Olivier (1930–31), singing "Someday I'll Find You" and *Susan and God* (1937); transferred to NY with *Tonight at 8:30* (1936) and did not return to British stage until 1944; dubbed "the greatest feminine performer in the American Theater" when *Lady in the Dark* opened at Alvin Theater (1941); hosted a weekly chat show over network radio and also broadcast a condensed version of *Pygmalion;* during WWII, made tour through Europe with ENSA (1944) and USO tour of Pacific (1945); made numerous recordings of songs, medleys and scenes, and appeared in such films as *Lord Camber's Ladies,Rembrandt, Men Are Not Gods* and *The Glass Menagerie.* Won a Tony Award for *The King and I* (1951). ❖ See also autobiography *A Star Danced* (Merritt and Hatcher, 1945); Sheridan Morley, *A Bright Particular Star* (Michael Joseph, 1986); and *Women in World History.*

LAWRENCE, Jackie (1948—). Welsh politician and member of Parliament. Born Aug 9, 1948; dau. of Sidney and Rita Beale; m. David Lawrence. ❖ Representing Labour, elected to House of Commons for Preseli Pembrokeshire (1997, 2001); left Parliament (2005).

LAWRENCE, Janice (1962—). African-American basketball player. Born June 7, 1962, in Lucedale, Mississippi; graduate of Louisiana Tech, 1984. ❖ Won a team gold medal at Pan American Games and World championships (1983); won a team gold medal at Los Angeles Olympics (1984); played professional ball with the Women's American Basketball Association. Won Wade Trophy (1984). ❖ See also *Women in World History.*

LAWRENCE, Jody (1930–1986). *See Lawrance, Jody.*

LAWRENCE, Margaret (1889–1929). American actress. Born Aug 2, 1889, in Trenton, NJ; died June 8, 1929; m. Orson D. Nunn (div.); m. Wallace Eddinger. ❖ Made stage debut in Chicago in *Her Son* (1910); came to prominence in NY debut as Elsie Darling in *Over Night* (1911); married and retired for 7 years; appeared in *Tea for Three* (1918), followed by *Wedding Bells, Transplanting Jean, Lawful Larceny, The Endless Chain* and *In His Arms,* among others.

LAWRENCE, Marjorie (1908–1979). Australian soprano. Born Marjorie Florence Lawrence in Dean's Marsh, Victoria, Australia, Feb 17, 1908; died Jan 10, 1979, in Little Rock, Arkansas; studied with Cécile Gilly in Paris; m. Thomas Michael King, 1941. ❖ Won a vocal competition sponsored by a Melbourne newspaper (1929); made debut at Monte Carlo as Elisabeth in *Tannhäuser* (1932); debuted as Elsa in *Lohengrin* at Paris Opéra (1933) and as Brünnhilde in *Die Walküre* at Metropolitan Opera (1935); sang at the Met (1935–49); was one of the few actresses who could follow Richard Wagner's instructions for Brünnhilde in *Götterdämmerung*, leaping on her horse Grane and galloping to Siegfried's funeral pyre to the delight of audiences (1936); executed *Dance of the Seven Veils* in Strauss' *Salomé* to similar effect; contracted polio at age 31 (1941); spent rest of her life in a wheelchair, though she continued career; gave last performance, as Amneris in *Aïda,* at Paris Opéra (1947); was a professor of voice at Tulane University (1956–60) and became a director of the Southern Illinois University (SIU) opera workshop (1960). The Marjorie Lawrence Opera Theater was established at SIU in her honor. ❖ See also autobiography *Interrupted Melody* (Appleton, 1949) and MGM film based on the book, starring Eleanor Parker (1955); and *Women in World History*.

LAWRENCE, Mary Wells (1928—). American advertising executive. Born Mary Georgene Wells Berg, May 25, 1928, in Youngstown, Ohio; dau. of Waldemar Berg and Violet (Meltz) Berg; attended Carnegie Institute of Technology, 1949; m. Harding Lawrence, Nov 25, 1967; children: James, State, Deborah, Kathryn and Pamela Lawrence. ❖ One of the few women in 1960s to break into the male-dominated corporate ranks, founded the legendary NY advertising agency Wells, Rich, Greene, Inc. (1966) and turned it into a multi-million-dollar enterprise; was the creative force behind such well-known commercial catch-phrases as "I can't believe I ate the whole thing," "Try it; you'll like it," "Plop, plop, fizz, fizz," and "Friends don't let friends drive drunk." ❖ See also *Women in World History*.

LAWRENCE, Pauline (1900–1971). American modern dancer and costume designer. Name variations: Pauline Lawrence Limón or Limon. Born 1900 in Los Angeles, CA; died July 16, 1971, in Stockton, NJ; m. José Limón (dancer and choreographer), 1941 (died 1972). ❖ Worked as musician for Denishawn School in Los Angeles, CA, while also attending dance classes there; served as conductor on vaudeville tour of Doris Humphrey; performed with Denishawn on tour (1923–26), creating roles in Ted Shawn's *The Feather of the Dawn* (1923), *Five American Sketches: Boston Fancy, 1854* (1924), *The Bubble Dance* (1925), *General Wu's Farewell to His Wife* (1926), and also in Humphrey's *Whims* (1926); moved to New York City with Humphrey and Charles Weidman, where she worked as costume designer, pianist, and business manager for NY Denishawn school; continued to work in same capacities for Humphrey/Weidman Concert Group once they separated from Denishawn (1929); created costumes for numerous works by Humphrey including *Water Study* (1928), *Credo* (1934), *Theater Piece* (1936), *Race of Life* (1938), *Four Choral Preludes* (1942), *Day on Earth* (1947), and *Ruins and Visions* (1953); served as designer and manager for José Limón Co. (as of 1945), creating costumes for his *The Moor's Pavanne* (1949), *La Malinche* (1949), *The Visitation* (1952), *There Is a Time* (1966), *The Winged* (1972), and others; with Frances Hawkins, was influential in the organization and unionization of modern dancers (late 1930s).

LAWRENCE, Susan (1871–1947). British politician. Born in London, England, Aug 12, 1871; died Oct 25, 1947; dau. of an eminent lawyer and a judge's daughter; studied at University College, London, and Newnham College, Cambridge. ❖ Was a member of London County Council (1910–28); elected to Popular Borough Council (1919); served as Labour member of Parliament for East Ham (1923–24, 1926–31); served as parliamentary secretary to Ministry of Health (1929–31) and as chair of Labour Party (1929–30); defeated in another parliamentary bid (1931); was primarily interested in welfare issues. ❖ See also *Women in World History*.

LAWRENCE, Tayna (1975—). Jamaican runner. Name variations: seen incorrectly as Tanya Lawrence. Born Sept 17, 1975, in Jamaica; attended Florida International University. ❖ Won a silver medal for 4 x 100-meter relay and a bronze medal for the 100 meters at Sydney Olympics (2000); won a gold medal for 4x100-meter relay at Athens Olympics (2004).

LAWRENCE, Viola (1894–1973). American film editor. Born Viola Mallory, Dec 2, 1894; died Nov 20, 1973, in Hollywood, CA; m. Frank Lawrence (film editor), 1918 (died 1960). ❖ The 1st female film editor, spent most of 30-year career at Columbia; films include *No Greater Glory, The Whole Town's Talking, Craig's Wife, I Am the Law, Only Angels Have Wings, Here Comes Mr. Jordan, Bedtime Story, My Sister Eileen, Cover Girl, Tonight and Every Night, The Lady from Shanghai,*

Knock on Any Door, Miss Sadie Thompson, The Eddy Duchin Story, Jeanne Eagels, Pal Joey and *Pepe.*

LAWRENNY, H. (1844–1901). *See Simcox, Edith.*

LAWRENSON, Helen (1907–1982). American editor and writer. Name variations: Helen Brown; Helen Brown Nordern. Born Helen Brown, Oct 1, 1907, in LaFargeville, NY; died April 6, 1982, in New York, NY; dau. of Lloyd Brown; attended Bradford School and Vassar; m. Heinz Nordern (musician), 1931 (div. 1932); m. a Venezuelan diplomat named López-Méndez, 1935 (div. 1935); m. Jack Lawrenson (co-founder of National Maritime Union), 1940 (died Nov 1957); children: 1 son; daughter Johanna. ❖ Was the managing editor and film critic of *Vanity Fair* (1932–35) and a frequent contributor to *Vogue, Harper's Bazaar, Look, Esquire* and *Town and Country;* also wrote *Latins are Lousy Lovers.* ❖ See also memoir *Stranger at the Party* (1975); and *Women in World History.*

LAWRIE, Jean Grant (1914—). English doctor. Name variations: Jean Eileen Lawrie. Born Jean Eileen Grant, June 7, 1914, in southern Rhodesia; London School of Medicine for Women, MB, BS, 1938; m. Reginald Seymour Lawrie, April 1941; children: 4. ❖ The Medical Society of London's 1st female fellow, advocated training improvements and more flexible training hours for women doctors; contributed as a founding member of both the Association for the Study of Medical Education and of Women's National Cancer Control Campaign; served as Dame Josephine Barnes' clinical assistant at Elizabeth Garrett Hospital (1947–78); served as general physician for the royal women and children of Brunei (from 1978); made a fellow of British Medical Association. Made Commander of the Order of the British Empire.

LAWS, Annie (1855–1927). American educational activist. Born Jan 20, 1855, in Cincinnati, Ohio; died July 1, 1927, in Cincinnati; dau. of James Hedding Laws and Sarah Amelia (Langdon) Laws. ❖ Organized (1889) and served as president of Cincinnati Training School for Nurses (later College of Nursing and Health of the University of Cincinnati); was president of Cincinnati Kindergarten Association (1891–92, 1901–27); was chair of Committee of Nineteen, influential in issues regarding contemporary kindergarten; was 1st female member of Cincinnati Board of Education (1912–16); was a founder (1894) and 1st president of Cincinnati Woman's Club.

LAWSON, Joan (1907–2002). English ballet dancer and writer. Born 1907 in London, England; died Feb 2002. ❖ Performed briefly with Nemtchimova-Dolin Ballet (c. 1933–34), but soon dedicated most of her time to teaching and writing; during WWII, served on advisory council on education for armed services; directed teacher's course at Royal Academy of Dancing (1947–59) and later served as mime and character teacher for Royal Ballet Society (1963–71); worked as editor of *The Dancing Times* (1940–54) and published numerous books and texts on dance, including *Ballet in the U.S.S.R.* (1945), *"Job," and "The Rake's Progress"* (1949), *Mime, The Theory and Practice of Expressing Gesture* (1957) and *A History of Ballet and Its Makers* (1964). ❖ See.

LAWSON, Louisa (1848–1920). Australian feminist, publisher, editor, journalist, and poet. Born Louisa Albury, Feb 17, 1848, near Mudgee, NSW, Australia; died Aug 12, 1920; dau. of Harry Albury (station hand) and Harriet (Wynn) Albury; m. Niels Hertzberg Larsen aka Peter Lawson (Norwegian sailor), July 7, 1866 (sep. 1883); children: 5, including Henry Lawson (writer). ❖ Began editing radical newspaper *Republican* (1887); founded *Dawn,* the 1st Australian feminist journal (1888), which gave rise to the Dawn Club, a suffrage society which prepared women to speak publicly for the cause; established Association of Women, merging her work with that of Rose Scott and Womanhood Suffrage League (1889); joined Council of the Women's Progressive Association and continued to encourage the appointment of women to public office; in later years, supported herself as a freelance writer, producing short stories which appeared in several Sydney newspapers and publishing a collection of poems, *The Lonely Crossing* (1906). ❖ See also Brian Matthews, *Louisa* (1988); and *Women in World History.*

LAWSON, Mary (1910–1941). English actress and singer. Born Aug 30, 1910, in Darlington, Durham, England; died May 4, 1941, in Liverpool, England, during an air-raid attack; m. Francis W.L.C. Darlington. ❖ Made London stage debut in *The London Revue* (1925), followed by *Good News, White Horse Inn, Casanova, Cinderella, Home and Beauty, Going Greek* and *Running Riot*; films include *A Fire Has Been Arranged, House Broken, To Catch a Thief, Cotton Queen, Can You Hear Me*

Mother?, Toilers of the Sea and *Oh Boy;* also appeared in concerts and cabarets.

LAWSON, Priscilla (1914–1958). American actress. Name variations: Priscilla Curtis. Born Priscilla Shortridge, Mar 8, 1914, in Indianapolis, IN; died Aug 27, 1958, in Los Angeles, CA; m. Alan Curtis (actor, div.). ❖ Crowned Miss Miami Beach (1935); appeared as Princess Aura, daughter of Ming the Merciless, in the popular *Flash Gordon* serial (1936), followed by *The Great Impersonation;* career ended after losing a leg in an auto accident during WWII.

LAWSON, Roberta Campbell (1878–1940). Native American (Delaware tribe) club leader. Born Roberta Campbell, Oct 31, 1878, at Alluwe, Cherokee Nation, Indian Territory (now Oklahoma); died Dec 31, 1940, in Tulsa, OK; dau. of John Edward Campbell (caucasian) and Emma (Journeycake) Campbell (Delaware Indian); m. Eugene Beauharnais Lawson, Oct 31, 1901 (died 1931); children: 1 son. ❖ Served as president of both the District and State Federation of Women's Clubs (latter, 1917–19); held numerous positions in General Federation of Women's Clubs, including director (1918–22), vice president (1928–35), and president (1935–38); along with other anti-New Deal Democrats, supported presidential candidacy of Wendell Willkie; collected books, art, and other materials related to Indian heritage. Was lifelong friend of humorist Will Rogers.

LAWSON, Twiggy (1946—). See *Twiggy.*

LAWSON, Winifred (1892–1961). English actress and singer. Born Nov 15, 1892, in Wolverhampton, England; died Nov 30, 1961; dau. of Florence (Thistlewood) Lawson and Alexander Lawson (artist). ❖ Had 1st success as a concert and festival artist; made London stage debut at Old Vic as Countess Almaviva in *The Marriage of Figaro* (1920); appeared with D'Olyly Carte Opera Co. as guest artist in title role in *Princess Ida,* then replaced Helen Gilliland as their leading soprano (1922–28, 1929–31, 1932), appearing as Phyllis in *Iolanthe,* Casilda in *The Gondoliers,* Patience, Yum-Yum in *The Mikado,* and Elsie Maynard in *The Yeomen of the Guard.* ❖ See also autobiography *A Song to Sing-O!* (Michael Joseph, 1955).

LAWYER, April (1975—). American cyclist. Born April 1, 1975, in Big Bear Lake, CA. ❖ Won silver in Snow Mountain Biking (Biker X Women) at X Games (Winter, 1999). Finishes include 2nd at Downhill Mountain Biker World Cup, Telluride, CO (2002).

LAXE, Julia Cortines (1868–1948). See *Cortines, Julia.*

LAY, Marion (1948—). Canadian swimmer. Born Nov 26, 1948, in Vancouver, British Columbia, Canada; grew up in Covina, CA; California State University at Hayward, MA in sociology. ❖ At Mexico City Olympics, won a bronze medal in 4x100-meter freestyle relay (1968); helped create Canadian Association for the Advancement of Women and Sport and Physical Activity (CAAWS) and Canadian Sport Centre Vancouver.

LAYA (fl. c. 100 BCE). See *Iaia.*

LAYBOURNE, Geraldine (1947—). American television executive. Born 1947 in Plainfield, NJ; education: Vassar College, BA in Art History; m. Kit Laybourne; children: Emily and Sam. ❖ Became president of Nickelodeon (1984) and turned the cable channel into a powerhouse, launching shows like "Rugrats," "Ren and Stimpy" and "Nick News" on "Nick at Nite"; also served as vice chair of MTV; became president of Disney/ABC Cable Networks (1996); with others, founded Oxygen Media (1998) and became its CEO (2003).

LAYBOURNE, Roxie (1910–2003). American ornithologist. Born 1910 in Fayetteville, North Carolina; died Aug 7, 2003, in Manassas, Virginia; Meredith College, BA; George Washington University, MA; m. Philip Simpson (div.); m. Edgar G. Laybourne (died 1966); children: Clarence and Robert. ❖ While working as a scientist at the Smithsonian's National Museum of Natural History (1944–88), pioneered forensic ornithology and helped identify thousands of birds involved in collisions with commercial and military aircraft, enabling engineers to develop aircraft capable of withstanding such accidents.

LAYBURN, Shirley Dinsdale (c. 1928–1999). See *Dinsdale, Shirley.*

LAYE, Evelyn (1900–1996). British star of musical comedy. Born Elsie Evelyn Lay, June 10, 1900, in London, England; died Feb 1996 in London; only child of Gilbert Lay (actor and composer) and Evelyn Stuart (singer and actress); m. Sonnie Hale (actor), 1926 (div. 1927); m. Frank Lawton (actor), c. 1934 (died 1969); no children. ❖ Britain's

"Queen of Musical Comedy," graced the London stage for over 70 years, from her debut in an obscure revue, *Honi Soit* (1916), to her appearance in the nostalgic *Glamourous Nights at Drury Lane,* at age 92; came to public attention as 2nd lead in *Going Up* (1918), which ran for 574 performances, then starred in revival of *The Shop Girl* (1920), stopping the show with her rendition of "Here Comes the Guards Brigade"; starred in *The League of Nations* and *Fun of the Fayre* (both 1921); by 1929, was the most prominent musical-comedy star in England and had also made 1st film, *Luck of the Navy;* made NY debut in Coward's *Bitter Sweet* (1929); toured in variety shows during WWII, entertaining soldiers; toured variety halls in provinces (1945–54); scored a comeback in *Wedding in Paris* (1954); enjoyed 2-year run in *The Amorous Prawn* (1959–61), followed by critically acclaimed performance in *The Circle* (1965); films include *The Night is Young* (1934) in which she introduced her signature song, "When I Grow Too Old to Dream." Awarded CBE (1973). ❖ See also autobiography *Boo, To My Friends* (1958); and *Women in World History.*

LAYLA AL-AKHYALIYYA (fl. 650–660). Arabian Muslim poet. Name variations: Laila or Layla bint al-Akhyal. Pronunciation: LAY-la al-ak-ya-LEE-ya. Born in central part of Arabian peninsula sometime before middle of 7th century; date or location of death is uncertain, but it seems most likely that she died shortly after the beginning of 8th century; m. Sawwar Ibn Awfa al-Qushayri. ❖ One of the 1st Muslim women to become famous for her elegiac verse called *ritha',* was an important historical figure; celebrated for her elegies mourning Tawba Ibn Humayyir, a warrior from her tribe who had been killed in battle, reportedly also composed an elegy in memory of the 3rd man to follow Muhammad as leader of the Islamic polity (caliph), 'Uthman Ibn 'Affan, whose death by assassination in 656 is considered a major turning point in Islamic history. Only fragments of her poetry are extant, preserved in encyclopedic texts compiled beginning in 9th century—such as Ibn Qutayba's *al-Shi'r wa-'l-shu'ara' (Poetry and Poets)* and Abu Faraj al-Isfahani's *Kitab al-aghani (Book of Songs).* ❖ See also *Women in World History.*

LAYLA BINT AL-AKHYAL (fl. 650–660). See *Layla al-Akhyaliyya.*

LAZAKOVICH, Tamara (1954—). Soviet gymnast. Born Mar 11, 1954, in Belarus. ❖ Won Chunichi Cup (1970) and European championship and USSR Spartakiade (1971); at World championships, won a gold medal in team all-around (1970); at Munich Olympics, won a bronze medal in floor exercises, bronze medal in indiv. all-around, silver medal in balance beam, and gold medal in team all-around (1972).

LAZAR, Elisabeta (1950—). Romanian rower. Born Aug 22, 1950, in Romania. ❖ At Montreal Olympics, won a bronze medal in quadruple sculls with coxswain (1976).

LAZAR, Reka (1967—). See *Szabo, Reka.*

LAZAREFF, Hélène (1909–1988). See *Gordon-Lazareff, Hélène.*

LAZAROVÁ, Katarina (1914—). Czechoslovakian novelist. Name variations: Katarina Lazarova. Born 1914 in Czechoslovakia. ❖ Realist novels include *Kamaráti* (1949) and *Osie hniezdo* (1953); popular detective fiction includes *Kňazňa z Lemúrie* (1964), *Interview s labutámi* (1966), and *Kavčie pierko* (1967); also wrote semi-autobiographical novel *Vdovské domy* (The Houses of Widows, 1977).

LAZARUS, Emma (1849–1887). American-Jewish poet, writer and scholar. Born July 22, 1849, in New York, NY; died of Hodgkin's disease on Nov 19, 1887, in New York, NY; dau. of Moses Lazarus (sugar refiner and businessman) and Esther Nathan Lazarus; never married. ❖ Wrote the poem "The New Colossus," welcoming immigrants, which would be inscribed on the Statue of Liberty (1903); was part of a prosperous and distinguished family; remained in parents' home throughout life; began writing in her teens; published 1st poetry collection (1866); met Ralph Waldo Emerson, an early mentor (1868); published 2nd book, *Admetus and Other Poems* (1871), which was well received in US and England; published novel *Alide: An Episode of Goethe's Life* (1874); became committed to helping Russian-Jewish immigrants; wrote articles countering anti-Semitic attacks (1882); wrote "The New Colossus" (1883); also translated other poets. ❖ See also Diane Lefer, *Emma Lazarus* (Chelsea House, 1988); Bette Roth Young, *Emma Lazarus in Her World: Life and Letters* (Jewish Publication Society, 1995); and *Women in World History.*

LAZEROWITZ, Alice (1906–2001). See *Ambrose, Alice.*

LAZHUTINA, Larissa (1965—). See *Lazutina, Larissa.*

LAZIS, Asja (1891–1979). *See Lacis, Asja.*

LAZUK, Maria (1983—). Belarusian rhythmic gymnast. Born Oct 15, 1983, in Belarus. ❖ Won a silver medal for team all-around at Sydney Olympics (2000).

LAZUTINA, Larissa (1965—). Russian cross-country skier. Name variations: Larissa Lazhutina. Born Larissa Ptitsina, June 1, 1965, in Kondopoga, USSR; m. Evgeni Lazutin (Russian skier). ❖ Won 11 World titles; won Olympic 4 x 5km relay gold medals at Albertville (1992) and Lillehammer (1994); won a silver medal in the 15 K freestyle, a bronze medal in the 30 K freestyle, and gold medals in the 5 K classical, 10 K freestyle pursuit and 4 x 5 K relay at Nagano Olympics (1998); won silver medals for 15 K freestyle and 5 K pursuit at Salt Lake City Olympics (2002), but was stripped of a gold medal for the 30 K freestyle and disqualified from the 20 K relay for failing a drug test, coming within one medal of tying the women's Olympic winter record; given a 2-year ban by International Ski Federation for the Salt Lake test failure (2002). Awarded Hero of Russia medal (1998).

LAZZARI, Carolina (c. 1889–1946). American actress. Born c. 1889; died Oct 17, 1946, in Stony Creek, CT. ❖ As a contralto, sang with the Metropolitan Opera; also appeared with the Chicago Civic Opera and as a soloist with the St. Louis Philharmonic Orchestra.

LE JINGYI (1975—). Chinese swimmer. Born Mar 19, 1975, in Shanghai, China. ❖ At Barcelona Olympics, won a silver medal in 4 x 100-meter freestyle relay (1992); won a gold medal for 100-meter freestyle and silver medals for 4 x 100-meter relay and 50-meter freestyle at Atlanta Olympics (1996).

LEA (d. about 383). Saint. Died c. 383; a widow. ❖ Following death of husband, gave up her life of privilege and retired to a Roman monastery, where she eventually rose to the position of superior; exchanged her rich attire for a sackcloth. ❖ See also *Women in World History.*

LEACH, Abby (1855–1918). American educator. Born May 28, 1855, in Brockton, MA; died Dec 29, 1918, in Poughkeepsie, NY; dau. of Marcus Leach and Eliza Paris (Bourne) Leach; educated at Brockton High School, Oread Collegiate Institute, the "Harvard Annex" (which later became Radcliffe College), Johns Hopkins University, and University of Leipzig; Vassar College, BA and MA, both 1885. ❖ Taught at Brockton High School before beginning a 5-year stint at Oread (1873); moved to Cambridge to study Greek, Latin, and English with professors at Harvard College (1878); with some difficulty, managed to convince William Watson Goodwin, professor of Greek, to take her on as a private student; because of her impressive skills, was instrumental in opening Harvard's doors to female scholars, which eventually led to the creation of Radcliffe College; teaching Greek and Latin, became an instructor at Vassar College (1883), then associate professor (1886) and full professor and head of Greek department (1889), a post she would hold for 29 years; was president of American Philological Association (1899–1900) and Association of Collegiate Alumnae (later American Association of University Women, 1899–1901). ❖ See also *Women in World History.*

LEACH, Christiana (fl. 1765–1796). American diarist. Lived in Kingsessing, PA. ❖ Kept diary from Feb 1765 to May 1796, which provides details about life of upper-class German woman in early America (*The Diary of Christiana Leach*).

LEACH, Eveline Willert (1849–1916). *See Cunnington, Eveline Willert.*

LEACHMAN, Cloris (1926—). American actress. Born April 30, 1926, in Des Moines, IA; sister of Claiborne Cary (actress); m. George Englund (producer-director), 1953 (div. 1979); children: Adam, Bryan, George, Morgan, and Dinah Englund (all actors). ❖ Was Miss Chicago and runner-up in Miss America pageant (1946); made film debut in *Kiss Me Deadly* (1955), followed by *Butch Cassidy and the Sundance Kid, Lovers and Other Strangers, Crazy Mama, Dillinger, Daisy Miller, The North Avenue Irregulars, Herbie Goes Bananas,* and in 3 films of Mel Brooks: *High Anxiety, History of the World Part 1,* and as Frau Blucher in *Young Frankenstein* (1974); appeared as Phyllis on "The Mary Tyler Moore Show" (1970–77) and in title role of the spinoff "Phyllis" (1975–77). Won Oscar for Best Supporting Actress for *The Last Picture Show* (1971); won 6 Emmys.

LEACOCK, Eleanor Burke (1922–1987). American cultural anthropologist. Name variations: Eleanor Haughton. Born Eleanor Burke on July 2, 1922; grew up in Greenwich Village, NY; died April 2, 1987, in Honolulu, HI; dau. of Kenneth Burke (literary critic and social philosopher) and Lily Mary Batterham (schoolteacher); attended Dalton School and Radcliffe College; graduate of Barnard College, 1944; Columbia University, MA, 1946, PhD, 1952; m. Richard Leacock; m. Jim Haughton (labor organizer); children: several. ❖ Known particularly for ethnohistorical studies of subarctic Innu social and gender relations, work as Marxist feminist, study of racism in US school systems, and reconsideration of work of Lewis Henry Morgan and Frederick Engels; worked at Queens College, City College, Bank Street College of Education Schools and Mental Health project, New York University, and Brooklyn Polytechnic Institute; brought in as chair to rebuild newly overhauled department of anthropology at City College (1972) and remained there until death (1987); wrote 10 books, including *Teaching and Learning in City Schools* (1969) and *Myths of Male Dominance* (1981).

LEAD, Jane Ward (1623–1704). British mystic. Name variations: Jane Ward Leade. Born Jane Ward, Mar 1623 (some sources cite 1624), in Norfolk, England; died Aug 19, 1704, in London; dau. of Schildknap Ward of Norfolk; m. William Lead or Leade, c. 1644 (died 1670). ❖ After husband's death met Dr John Pordage, follower of Jakob Boehme; began to have visions and receive divine messages; with Dr. Francis Lee, established Philadelphian Society (1694); works, which are record of her visions and mystical teachings, include *The Heavenly Cloud Now Breaking, The Lord Christ's Ascension-Ladder sent down* (1681), *The Revelation of Revelations* (1683), *The Laws of Paradise Given Forth by Wisdom to a Translated Spirit* (1695), *A Revelation of the Everlasting Gospel Message* (1697) and *The First Resurrection in Christ* (1704).

LEADBETTER, Mary (1758–1826). Irish-born poet and storywriter. Name variations: Mary Shackleton; Mrs. Leadbetter. Born Mary Shackleton at Ballitore, Co. Kildare, Ireland, Dec 1758; died in Ballitore, June 27, 1826; granddau. of Abraham Shackleton (1697–1771, schoolmaster); m. William Leadbetter, 1791. ❖ A writer of Quaker birth, became a friend and correspondent of Edmund Burke who had been a student of her grandfather's; published *Poems* (1808), *Cottage Dialogues among the Irish Peasantry* (1811), *Cottage Biography* (1822). Her best work, *Annals of Ballitore,* was published as *The Leadbetter Papers* by R.D. Webb (1862).

LEADE, Jane Ward (1623–1704). *See Lead, Jane Ward.*

LEAH (fl. c. 1500 BCE). Matriarch of Israel. Third matriarch of Israel. Name variations: Lea; Lia. Flourished c. 1500 BCE; buried with Jacob in the ancestral cave in Hebron; dau. of Laban; sister of Rachel; 1st wife of Jacob; children: Reuben, Simeon, Levi, Judah, Issachar, and Zebulun—6 of the 12 tribes of Israel. ❖ On the night the marriage between Rachel and Jacob was to be consummated, was sent by father into the bridegroom's darkened tent in place of Rachel and became his wife (Genesis, chapters 29–35). ❖ See also *Women in World History.*

LEAHY, Mary Gonzaga (1870–1958). New Zealand nun and hospital matron. Born June 12, 1870, near Nelson, New Zealand; died Jan 17, 1958, in Mount Eden, New Zealand; dau. of Daniel Leahy (farmer) and Bridget (McNamara) Leahy. ❖ Joined St Mary's Convent, Auckland (1894) and became a nun (1897); trained as nurse at St Vincent's Hospital, Sydney, Australia (1898); returned to New Zealand to become 1st matron of new Coromandel Hospital (1898); purchased property in Mount Eden and converted house into Mater Misericordiae Hospital (1900); was hospital matron (1900–50); embarked on 3-month tour of US and Canadian hospitals and returned to New Zealand with plans for technological improvements for hospital (1929). Order of British Empire (1939). ❖ See also *Dictionary of New Zealand Biography* (Vol. 3).

LEAKEY, Caroline Woolmer (1827–1881). British novelist and poet. Name variations: Oliné Keese or Oline Keese. Born Mar 8, 1827, in Exeter, England; died July 12, 1881, in England; 6th of 11 children of James Leakey (painter) and Eliza (Woolmer) Leakey. ❖ Lived with sister Eliza Medland in Tasmania (1848–53); succumbed to typhoid and other illnesses and returned to England (1853); following death of her sister Mary (1854), took over as head of her school in London; published *Lyra Australis* (1854), a collection of poems on religion, sickness and death; established home for fallen women in Exeter (1861); under pen name Oline Keese published *The Broad Arrow: Being Passages from the History of Maida Gwynnham, a Lifer* (1859), about a woman in a convict settlement; also published Evangelical tracts; her memoir, *Clear Shining Light* was published by her sister Emily (1882).

LEAKEY, Mary Nicol (1913–1996). English archaeologist. Born Mary Douglas Nicol in London, England, Feb 6, 1913; died in Kenya, Dec 9, 1996; dau. of Cecilia (Frere) Nicol and Erskine Nicol (landscape painter); m. Louis Seymour Bazett Leakey (archaeologist), Dec 24, 1936 (sep. 1968, died Oct 11, 1972); children: Jonathan Leakey (b. 1940); Deborah Leakey (b. 1943); Richard Leakey (b. 1944, renowned paleontologist); Philip Leakey (b. 1949). ❖ With her discovery of the Zinj skull and the Laetoli footprints, furthered understanding of the origins of humanity; undertook 1st archaeological field work, Hembury Fort, a Neolithic site in Devon, and published several drawings of the finds (1930); met Louis Leakey and illustrated his book *Adam's Ancestors* (1933); directed 1st dig at Hembury, resulting in her 1st publication (1934); joined Louis in Tanzania (1935); returned to England (Sept 1935); while husband began a 2-year study of Kikuyu tribe (1936), excavated Hyrax Hill in Kenya, discovering a Neolithic settlement and 19 burial sites (1937); excavated the Njoro River Cave, which yielded many Elementeitan artifacts (1937); conducted research at Ngorongoro in northeast Tanzania, and at Olorgesailie in Kenya (1940); excavated Rusinga Island (1948), unearthing the skull, jaws, and teeth of what came to be known as *Proconsul africanus*; recorded Tanzanian rock paintings (1951); excavated the Olduvai Gorge (1951–58); discovered Zinj, a 1.75-million-years-old skull (July 17, 1959); elected member of British Academy (1973); discovered early hominid footprints at Laetoli, one of the most important finds in archaeological history (1976). With Louis, warded Hubbard Medal of National Geographic Society (1962) and Prestwick Medal of Geological Society of London (1969); received Gold Medal of Society of Women Geographers (1975), Linnaeus Gold Medal of Royal Swedish Academy (1978), Elizabeth Blackwell Award (1980) and Bradford Washburn Award (1980). ❖ See also autobiography *Disclosing the Past* (Doubleday, 1984); and *Women in World History.*

LEAN, Mrs. (1837–1899). *See Marryat, Florence.*

LEANDER, Zarah (1907–1981). Swedish actress and singer. Name variations: Sarah Leander. Born Zarah Stina Hedberg in Karlstad, Sweden, Mar 15, 1907; died in Stockholm, Sweden, June 23, 1981; m. Nils Leander; m. Vidar Forsell; m. Arne Hülpers. ❖ The greatest screen idol of the Third Reich, made debut in provincial theaters in Sweden (1929); regularly appeared on stage at Stockholm's Vasa-Theater and Ekmanstheater (1930–32); in Vienna, starred in operetta, *Axel an der Himmelstür* (Axel at Heaven's Gate, 1936); made 1st German-language film, *Premiere* (1936); signed with UFA studio (1936) which began an extensive promotion of her; within weeks, was famous throughout the German Reich; starred in *La Habañera* (1937), followed by *Heimat* (Homeland, 1938), in which she sang an aria from "Orfeo"; also filmed *Es war eine rauschende Ballnacht* (It Was a Wild Night at the Ball, 1939) and her greatest triumph *Die grosse Liebe* (*The Great Love*) (1942); fled to Sweden (1943), at a time when the war was turning against Hitler, but received a cool welcome; reemerged to tour the Western occupation zones of Germany (1949); appeared in a number of West German films throughout 1950s, including *Cuba Cubana* (1952), *Ave Maria* (1953) and *Der blaue Nachtfalter* (The Blue Moth, 1959); began a successful run at Vienna's Raimund-Theater in musical *Madame Scandaleuse* (1958); returned to Vienna to star in *Lady aus Paris* (The Lady from Paris, 1964); also appeared on tv, including "Star unter Sternen" (A Star under the Stars). ❖ See also autobiographies *Es war so wunderbar! Mein Leben* (1983) and *So bin ich und so bleibe ich* (1958); Ulrike Sanders, *Zarah Leander: Kann denn Schlager Sünde sein?* (1988); Paul Seiler, *Ein Mythos lebt: Zarah Leander* (1991); Cornelia Zumkeller, *Zarah Leander: Ihre Filme, ihr Leben* (W. Heyne, 1988); and *Women in World History.*

LEAPOR, Mary (1722–1746). British poet. Born Feb 16, 1722, in Marston St. Lawrence, Northamptonshire, England; died Nov 12, 1746, in Northamptonshire; dau. of Philip (gardener) and Anne Leapor. ❖ A kitchen maid, was able to write poetry with the support of patron Bridget Fremantle. *Poems Upon Several Occasions, I & II* (1748, 1751) and *The Unhappy Father, a Tragedy* (1751) were published after she died of measles.

LEAR, Evelyn (1926—). American soprano. Name variations: Mrs. Thomas Stewart. Born Evelyn Shulman, Jan 8, 1926, in Brooklyn, NY; studied with John Yard, Sergius Kagen, and Maria Ivogün; attended New York University, 1944–45, Hunter College, 1946–48, Juilliard School of Music, 1953–54, and Hochschule für Musik, Berlin, 1957–59; m. Dr. Walter Lear, 1943; m. Thomas Stewart (baritone), 1955. ❖ Made debut in Berlin (1957), Salzburg (1962–64), Covent Garden (1965), Teatro Colon (1965), and Metropolitan Opera (1967); was one of the few singers to have performed Sophie, Octavian, and the Marshallin in *Der Rosenkavalier,* Despina and Fiodiligi in *Cosi fan tutte,* and Cherubino and the Countess in *Figaro;* appeared in Altman's film *Buffalo Bill and the Indians,* gave many performances of lieder, and, as a member of the West Berlin Opera ensemble, made 33 recordings; retired (1985). Received

honorary title of Kammersaengerin, Senate of Berlin (1964); won Grammy award for performance of Marie in *Wozzeck* (1965). ❖ See also *Women in World History.*

LEAR, Frances (1923–1996). American feminist, magazine editor and founder. Born July 14, 1923, in Hudson, NY; died Sept 30, 1996, in New York, NY; adopted dau. of Herbert Adam Loeb (businessman) and Aline (Friedman) Loeb; briefly attended Sarah Lawrence College; m. Norman Lear (tv producer), Dec 7, 1956 (div. 1988); children: Kate Lear and Maggie Lear. ❖ An ardent women's-rights activist, worked with National Organization for Women (NOW) and as a partner in one of the 1st executive-search firms dedicated to the placement of women; founded *Lear's* magazine (1988), the 1st mass-circulated magazine dedicated to women over 40; remained editor-in-chief until it ceased publication (1994). ❖ See also *Women in World History.*

LEASE, Mary Elizabeth (1853–1933). American politician. Name variations: Mary Ellen Lease. Born Mary Elizabeth Clyens, Sept 11, 1853, in Ridgeway, Elk County, PA; died in Callicoon, NY, Oct 29, 1933; dau. of Joseph P. Clyens (farmer of Irish descent) and Mary Elizabeth Murray Clyens; graduate of St. Elizabeth's Academy in Allegany, NY; m. Charles L. Lease (pharmacist), Jan 1873 (div. 1902); children: 4. ❖ Populist orator and politician whose fiery appeals for Kansas farmers to protest their economic condition made her a national figure during early 1890s; moved to Kansas to teach school at an Indian mission (1870); lived in Texas for a decade after marriage; admitted to the bar in Kansas (1885); became a candidate for local offices for Union Labor Party (1888); identified with People's Party (1890), famously telling an audience of farmers that they should "raise less corn and wheat, and more hell"; campaigned for Populist presidential ticket (1892); appointed to Kansas State Board of Charities (1893) but was removed from office the same year; moved to the East by 1896 and campaigned for William Jennings Bryan, the presidential candidate of the Democrats and the Populists; supported William McKinley and the Republicans (1900); pursued career as a lecturer; endorsed Theodore Roosevelt and Progressive Party (1912); spent last years in obscurity. ❖ See also *Women in World History.*

LEATHERWOOD, Lillie (1964—). African-American runner. Born July 6, 1964, in Northport, Alabama. ❖ Won a gold medal at Los Angeles Olympics (1984) and a silver medal at Seoul Olympics (1988), both in 4 x 400-meter relay.

LEAVER, Henrietta (c. 1916–1993). Miss America. Born Henrietta Leaver, c. 1916, in McKeesport, PA; died in Sept 1993; m. and div.; children: 2 daughters. ❖ Named Miss Pittsburgh (1935); named Miss America (1935); had a successful West Coast modeling career. ❖ See also Frank Deford, *There She Is* (Viking, 1971).

LEAVIS, Q.D. (1906–1981). British literary critic. Name variations: Queenie Dorothy Leavis. Born Queenie Dorothy Roth, Dec 7, 1906, in London, England; died Mar 17, 1981, in Cambridge, England; educated at Girton College, Cambridge; m. F.R. Leavis (literary critic), 1929 (died 1978). ❖ With husband, was coeditor of quarterly review *Scrutiny* and wrote *Lectures in America* (1969) and *Dickens the Novelist* (1970); also wrote *Fiction and the Reading Public* (1932) and a collection of essays on women writers, *The Collected Essays,* which were published posthumously (1983). ❖ See also M.B. Kinch, *F.R. Leavis and Q.D. Leavis: An Annotated Bibliography* (1989).

LEAVITT, Henrietta Swan (1868–1921). American astronomer. Born July 4, 1868, in Lancaster, MA; died Dec 12, 1921, in Cambridge, MA; dau. of Rev. George Roswell Leavitt and Henrietta S. (Kendrick) Leavitt; educated at Cambridge public schools and Oberlin College; graduated from Society for the Collegiate Instruction of Women (later Radcliffe College), 1892; never married. ❖ Established a standard by which to chart the magnitude of the stars and discovered the period-luminosity of Cepheid variable stars, knowledge which was later expanded by astronomers such as Edwin Hubble and used to measure the distances between the Earth and distant stars and galaxies; almost completely deaf, volunteered at Harvard Observatory (1895); made a permanent member of the observatory staff (1902); was soon promoted to chief of photographic photometry department and asked to devise a basic sequence of magnitudes, photographically determined, against which other stars could be measured (1907); observed a group of stars near North Pole, resulting in a standard of brightness known as the "North Pole Sequence," standards which were published in 1912 and 1917; before her death, had fully sequenced 108 areas of the sky; during 26-year career, discovered 4 novas and about 2,400 variable stars, which made up more than half of those known until 1930; was also the 1st to notice that the fainter stars in a sequence were generally redder than the brighter stars. ❖ See also *Women in World History.*

LEAVITT, Mary (1830–1912). American missionary. Born Mary Greenleaf Clement on Sept 22, 1830, in Hopkinton, NH; died Feb 5, 1912, in Boston, MA; dau. of Joshua H. Clement (Baptist minister) and Eliza Harvey Clement; graduate of State Normal School in West Newton, MA, 1851; m. Thomas H. Leavitt (Boston land broker), June 1857 (div. 1878); children: Amy Clement (b. 1858), Agnes Munn (b. 1859), and Edith Harvey (b. 1863). ❖ Served as an organizer of Boston Woman's Christian Temperance Union; started lecturing in New England for temperance and woman suffrage (1881); became head of Franchise Department of national WCTU (1882); persuaded by Frances Willard to make 7-year foreign missionary tour on behalf of temperance (1884), visited Sandwich Islands, New Zealand, India, Africa, and Europe; responsible for organizing 86 branches of WCTU and 24 men's temperance societies; made temperance mission to Latin America; became estranged from WCTU and Willard (late 1890s).

LEAVY, Rosetta Lulah (1871–1934). *See Baume, Rosetta Lulah.*

LE BARILLIER, Berthe (1868–1927). *See Roy de Clotte le Barillier, Berthe.*

LE BEAU, Luise Adolpha (1850–1927). German pianist and composer. Born April 25, 1850, in Rastatt, Germany; died July 17, 1927, in Baden-Baden, Germany. ❖ Began composing at 15; made piano debut at 18; performed her compositions for Hans von Bulow, who became a lifelong advocate of her work; briefly studied with Clara Schumann; won international competition in Hamburg for her Op 24 Cello Pieces (1882); wrote some 150 compositions for such genres as opera, choral and other vocal works, orchestral and chamber pieces; also wrote a book about the obstacles confronting a woman composer.

LEBEDEVA, Natalya (1949—). Soviet runner. Born Aug 24, 1949, in USSR. ❖ At Montreal Olympics, won a bronze medal in 100-meter hurdles (1976).

LEBEDEVA, Sarra (1892–1967). Russian sculptor. Born Sarra Dmitrievna Darmolatova, Dec 23, 1892, in St. Petersburg, Russia; died in Moscow, Mar 7, 1967; studied painting and drawing at Mikhail Bernshtein's school in St. Petersburg; studied sculpting with Leonid Shervud; m. Vladimir Vasilevich Lebedev (graphic artist), 1915. ❖ Produced art that was ideologically correct by Soviet standards and a number of works that transcend time and place; after the Bolshevik Revolution (1917), contributed a number of innovative works to the scheme of mass propaganda through art, namely monumental busts of *Danton* and *Alexander Herzen,* as well as a relief depicting *Robespierre;* after executing a bust of *Leonid Krassin* (1924), took on role of sculptor of high officials of Soviet state; though she did portraits of leading Bolsheviks, including Pavel Dybenko, Semyon Budyonny, and Feliks Edmundovich Dzerzhinsky (chief of the Cheka), was too keen eyed to always flatter her subjects; lived in Moscow (1925–67), where she produced striking portraits of political leaders and prominent artists and intellectuals, including Jewish actor Solomon Mikhoels (1939); executed the memorable bronze *Girl With a Butterfly* (1936); other notable busts include *Portrait of Colonel Yusupov* (1942), *Portrait of Vladimir Tatlin* (1943–44) and *Portrait of Boris Leonidovich Pasternak* (1961–63); was a member of USSR Academy of Arts. ❖ See also *Women in World History.*

LEBEDEVA, Tatyana (1976—). Russian jumper. Name variations: Tatiana Lebedeva. Born July 21, 1976, in Sterlitamak Bashkortostan, Russia. ❖ Won a silver medal for triple jump at Sydney Olympics (2000) and a gold medal for triple jump at World championships (2001, 2003); won gold medals for long jump and triple jump at World Indoor championships (2004); won a gold medal for long jump at Athens Olympics (2004); won a bronze medal for triple jump at Athens Olympics (2004).

LEBLANC, Georgette (c. 1875–1941). French actress and operatic singer. Name variations: Georgette Le Blanc or LeBlanc. Born c. 1875 in Rouen, France; died Oct 26, 1941; dau. of Emile Bianchini (Leblanc) and Mdlle de Brohy; sister of Maurice Leblanc (wrote the detective novels of Arsène Lupin); companion of Belgian poet and playwright Maurice Maeterlinck (1895–18); lived with Margaret Carolyn Anderson (1922–41, editor of *Little Review*). ❖ Created the role of Thaïs at Théâtre de la Monnaie, Brussels; inaugurated the Opéra-Comique, appearing as Carmen (1898); appeared as Ariane in *Ariane and Bluebeard* (1907); sang Mélisande in *Pélléas and Mélisande* at Boston Opera (1912); founded Théâtre Maeterlinck, appearing in *Monna Vanna, Joyzelle,* and

La mort de tintagiles, and adapted Maeterlinck's *The Blue Bird* into *The Children's Blue Bird;* held a noted salon for such personages as Octave Mirabeau, Anatole France, Rodin, Judith Gautier, Colette, Oscar Wilde, and Rachilde (pseudonym of Marguerite Vallette). ❖ See also memoirs *Souvenirs: My Life with Maeterlinck* (trans. from French by Janet Flanner).

LE BLOND, Elizabeth (1861–1934). English mountaineer. Name variations: Mrs. Main; Mrs. Aubrey Le Blond. Born Elizabeth Hawkins-Whitshed in 1861; died 1934; grew up in Ireland; m. Fred Burnaby (soldier who died in 1882); m. a man named Main (died); m. Aubrey Le Blond. ❖ Widowed at 21, began mountain climbing for consolation and made some notable 1st ascents in Chamonix and in the Engadine; was the 1st president of Ladies' Alpine Club (1907) and elected for a 2nd term (1932); with Lady Evelyn McDonnell, dispensed with the services of guides and climbed Piz Palu (1900).

LEBOUR, Marie (1877–1971). English marine biologist. Name variations: Marie Victoire Lebour; M.V. Lebour. Born Marie Victoire Lebour, Aug 20, 1877, in Woodburn, Northumberland, England; died Oct 2, 1971; dau. of a professor of geology at Amstrong College, Newcastle-upon-Tyne (died 1931); studied at Armstrong College; University of Durham, BS, 1904, MSc, 1907, DSc, 1917. ❖ An expert on the larval stages of decapods (crabs), worked as a junior demonstrator (1906–08), demonstrator (1908–09) and assistant lecturer and demonstrator (1909–15) in the University of Leeds' Zoology Department; employed as a marine biologist at the Marine Biological Association (MBA) at Plymouth (1915–46); published over 40 papers on planktonic larvae of the decapods; documented and photographed the various stages of 33 of the 37 known larvae species in her area; as a fellow scientist of marine plankton specialists Walter Garstang and Robert Gurney, collected plankton on a trip to Bermuda on the Royal Society ship, *Culver* (1938–39); contributed to the *Journal of the Marine Biological Association, Proceedings of the Zoological Society of London* and *Naturalist* (1900). Her work and research was transferred to London's Natural History Museum (2000). The Marie Lebour Library is in the special collection of Marine Biological Association in Plymouth.

LE BOURSIER DU COUDRAY, Angelique Marguerite (1712–1789). *See du Coudray, Angelique Marguerite.*

LEBRON, Lolita (1919—). Puerto Rican nationalist and terrorist. Born 1919 in Lares, Puerto Rico; children: 2. ❖ Led 3 men into the gallery of US House of Representatives (Mar 1, 1954), unfurled a Puerto Rican flag, then took out a gun and fired randomly into the assembly, as did her companions, wounding 5; along with companions, was sentenced to a 75-year prison term; considered by some in the Hispanic community as a political prisoner and freedom fighter, was freed after sentence was commuted by President Jimmy Carter (Sept 1979); continued to speak at pro-independence rallies in Puerto Rico and US. ❖ See also *Women in World History.*

LEBRUN, Céline (1976—). French judoka. Name variations: Celine Lebrun. Born Aug 25, 1976, in Paris, France. ❖ Won a silver medal for 70–78kg half-heavyweight at Sydney Olympics (2000); won European championships (1999, 2000, 2001); won World championship (2001).

LE BRUN, Elisabeth Vigée (1755–1842). *See Vigée-Le Brun, Elisabeth.*

LEBRUN, Franziska (1756–1791). German composer, singer, and pianist. Name variations: Franziska LeBrun; Francesca LeBrun; Franziska Danzi LeBrun; Franziska Dorothea Danzi. Born Franziska Danzi in Mannheim, Germany, and baptized on Mar 24, 1756; died May 14, 1791, in Berlin; dau. of Innocenzo Danzi (violinist); sister of composer Franz Danzi; sister-in-law of Maria Margarethe Danzi (1768–1800); m. Ludwig August Lebrun (1746–1790, oboist and composer), 1778; children: Sophie Lebrun Dulcken (b. 1781, singer and pianist better known as Mme Dulcken); Rosine Lebrun Stenzsch (1785–1855, singer, pianist, and actress in comedy). ❖ Made debut as Sandrina in *La contadina in corte* in Schwetzingen (1772); became leading soprano at Mannheim Court opera where she created roles in Holzbauer's *Günther von Schwarzburg* (1777) and Schweitzer's *Rosamunde* (1780); as one of the highest paid prima donnas in Europe, made London debut as Ariene in *Cresco* (1777), followed by roles in works by J.C. Bach and Tommaso Giordano; traveled to Paris to appear at Concert Spirituel, then to Milan, where she sang in the 1st season of Teatro alla Scala (1778); sang in London for 2 more seasons (1779–80, 1780–81), adding roles by Sacchini, Bertoni, Grétry and Rauzzini to her repertoire; composed

2 widely published sets of sonatas for piano and violin (1779–81); in Berlin, gave last performance, in Reichardt's *Brenno* (1790); died there at age 35. ❖ See also *Women in World History.*

LE BRUN or LEBRUN, Mme. (1755–1842). *See Vigée-Le Brun, Elisabeth.*

LE CAMUS, Madame (fl. 17th c.). French poet. Born in France. ❖ Published poetry in *Mercure galant* and was praised by its editor Donneau de Visé; also addressed *Madrigal impromptu* to Duc de Saint-Aignan (1677).

LECAVELLA, Mabilia (fl. 1206). German merchant. Fl. in 1206 in Genoa. ❖ Imported fine linen and canvas from Swabia (southern Germany) and other regions, and arranged for its transport to Genoa. ❖ See also *Women in World History.*

LECHEVA, Vesela (1964—). Bulgarian shooter. Born May 20, 1964, in Bulgaria. ❖ At Seoul Olympics, won a silver medal in smallbore rifle 3 positions (1988); at Barcelona Olympics, won a silver medal in air rifle (1992); representing the Socialist Party, became a member of Parliament.

LECHNER, Erica. Italian luge athlete. Fl. 1960s. ❖ Won a gold medal for singles at Grenoble Olympics (1968).

LECLERC, Annie (1940—). French novelist and philosopher. Born 1940 in France. ❖ One of France's leading feminist writers, published 1st novel *Le Pont du nord* (The North Bridge, 1967); best known for her essay "Parole de femme" ("Woman's Word," 1974), also wrote *La Venue à l'écriture* with Hélène Cixous and Madeleine Gagnon (1977) and *Origines.*

LECLERC, Ginette (1912–1992). French actress. Born Geneviève Menut, Feb 9, 1912, in Paris, France; died Jan 1, 1992, in Paris. ❖ Made film debut in *Cette vieille canaille* (1933); probably best remembered for performance in title role in Pagnol's *The Beggar's Wife* and as the crippled girl in Clouzot's *Le Corbeau* (*The Raven*, 1943); starred in many French films (1930s), but after the war, was accused of collaborating with the Nazis (many feel, wrongly) which hurt career. ❖ See also memoirs *Ma Vie Privée.*

LECLERCQ, Agnes (1840–1912). *See Salm-Salm, Princess.*

LECLERCQ, Carlotta (c. 1840–1893). English actress. Born c. 1840; died 1893; sister of Rose Leclercq (c. 1845–1899). ❖ Appeared as Ariel in *The Tempest*, Nerissa in *Merchant of Venice*, and Rosalind in *As You Like It*; also toured England and America with Shakespearean actor Charles Albert Fechter.

LECLERCQ, Rose (c. 1845–1899). English actress. Born c. 1845; died 1899; sister of Carlotta Leclercq (c. 1840–1893). ❖ Known for her broad style of comedy, appeared as Mrs. Page in *Merry Wives of Windsor* and the queen in *Tosca.*

LE CLERCQ, Tanaquil (1929–2000). French-born ballerina. Name variations: LeClercq. Born Oct 2, 1929, in Paris, France; died Dec 31, 2000, in New York, NY; raised in NY; only dau. of Jacques Georges Clemenceau Le Clercq (writer and professor) and Edith (Whittemore) Le Clercq; attended Lycée Français de New York for 3 years; studied dance at King-Coit School in NY; studied with Michael Mordkin; attended School of American Ballet; m. George Balanchine (choreographer and founder of New York City Ballet), Dec 31, 1952 (div. 1969); no children. ❖ Distinguished by her exquisite technique, unique style, and long limbs, had a dazzling career with New York City Ballet (1948–56); at 17, danced 1st professional solo, the lead in choleric section of *The Four Temperaments;* as a principle dancer with Balanchine's New York City Ballet, won acclaim in a number of roles, among them Ariadne in the ballet-cantata *The Triumph of Bacchus and Ariadne;* also danced in *Bourrée Fantasque, Symphony in C, Orpheus, Afternoon of a Fawn,* and *La Valse;* was touring in Copenhagen when she contracted poliomyelitis (1956) and doctors were barely able to save her life, let alone her career; began teaching ballet at Dance Theater of Harlem (1970). ❖ See also *Women in World History.*

LECOMPTE, Eugenie Anna (c. 1798–c. 1850). Belgian ballet dancer. Born Eugenie Martin, c. 1798, in Lille, Belgium; died c. 1850, possibly in Philadelphia, PA; sister of Jules Martin. ❖ Made professional debut at Paris Opéra (1826) and spent following 8 years on tour with company; performed opposite Auguste Bournonville in Anatole's *Hassan et le Calife,* among others, at King's Theatre in London (1828); performed 1 season in Barcelona; appeared at Théâtre de la Monnaie in Hus' *Cendrillon* (1830), before returning to London and dancing at King's and Haymarket theaters; toured US with brother in NY, Boston,

Philadelphia, and on Mississippi circuit (1837–c. 1850); worked with European dancers in US, including Jean Petipa (1839) and Fanny Elssler (1841–42), and performed such Romantic works as D'Auberval's *Fille Mal Gardée* and Taglioni's *La Sylphide;* settled in US.

LECOUVREUR, Adrienne (1690–1730). French actress. Born April 5, 1690 (some sources cite 1692), at Damery, Marne, France; died Mar 20, 1730, in Paris; dau. of Robert Couvreur (hatter); mother's name unknown; mistress of Maurice of Saxony; children: 3 daughters, one of whom was the grandmother of Maurice Dupin de Francueil, father of George Sand. ❖ Celebrated actress whose premature death left many questions; at 14, began touring with theatrical companies; at 16, became engaged to a baron but he died; had 3 more lovers: the noble Philippe le Ray, the actor Clavel, and the soldier Comte de Klinglin; appeared at Comédie Française (1717) in title role of Crébillon's *Electre* and as Angélique in Molière's *George Dandin;* for next 13 years, was the queen of tragedy there, attaining a popularity never before accorded an actress; is said to have played no fewer than 1,184 times in 100 roles, of which she created 22; recognized as the 1st French actress of her day, excelled in both tragedy and comedy; abandoned the stilted style of her predecessors, developing a natural style, revolutionizing acting, diction, and costuming; was on friendly terms with half the court of Philippe the Regent (later Philip V, king of Spain), and her salon was frequented by many notables and artists, among them Voltaire; fell in love and became mistress to the military leader Comte Maurice of Saxony (1721), fomenting the jealousy of another of his paramours, Françoise de Lorraine, duchess of Bouillon, who tried to poison her (July 1729); was suddenly stricken ill (Mar 20, 1730) and died suspiciously. Eugène Scribe and Ernest Legouvé wrote the well-known tragedy, *Adrienne Lecouvreur,* which starred renowned actress Rachel in the title role (1849). ❖ See also *Women in World History.*

LECZINSKA, Maria (1703–1768). *See Marie Leczinska.*

LEDERER, Eppie (1918–2002). *See Friedman, Esther Pauline.*

LEDERER, Esther P.F. (1918–2002). *See Friedman, Esther Pauline.*

LEDERER, Gretchen (1891–1955). German-born actress. Born May 23, 1891, in Cologne, Germany; died Dec 20, 1955, in Anaheim, CA; m. Otto Lederer (actor). ❖ Lead actress for Pathe, Universal, Ince, and Vitagraph (1910–20), made over 60 films, including *The Violin Maker, Two Men of Sandy Bar, The Grasp of Greed, The Way of the World, Black Friday, The Little Orphan* and *After the War.*

LEDERMANN, Alexandra (1969—). French equestrian. Born May 14, 1969, in Evreux, Taille, France. ❖ Won a bronze medal for indiv. jumping at Atlanta Olympics (1996) and European championship (1999), both on Rochet M.

LEDOUX, Jeanne Philiberte (1767–1840). French painter. Born in Paris, 1767; died 1840. ❖ One of several women students of Jean Baptiste Greuze, exhibited in the salons between 1793 and 1819; paintings include *Little Girl Holding a Dove, Young Boy near an Apple with a Fistful of Sticks, Portrait of a Boy* and *Portrait of Greuze.* Since many of her works are not signed or dated, some may have been mistakenly attributed to the better-known Greuze. ❖ See also *Women in World History.*

LEDOVSKAYA, Tatyana (1966—). Soviet runner. Born May 21, 1966, in USSR. ❖ At Seoul Olympics, won a silver medal in 400-meter hurdles and a gold medal in 4x400-meter relay (1988).

LEDUC, Violette (1907–1972). French writer. Born Violette Le Duc. Born April 7, 1907, in Arras, France; died of cancer in Faucon, France, May 28, 1972; illeg. dau. of Berthe Leduc (servant) and Andre Debaralle (son of Berthe Leduc's employer); attended boarding school, 1923–26; m. Gabriel Mercier, 1939. ❖ Noted author, whose candid autobiography *La Bâtarde* was a literary sensation, began writing for women's magazines (1934); met Simone de Beauvoir who gave her career a major boost by publishing portions of *L'Asphyxie* in *Les Temps Modernes* (1945) and encouraged Gallimard to publish *L'Asphyxie* and *L'Affamée;* endured mental breakdown and confinement in psychiatric hospital (1957); published bestseller, *La Bâtarde* (1964), but its frank discussions of her lesbian affairs as well as other facets of her life such as her illegitimate birth and her physical ugliness—topics which earlier female authors had avoided—disturbed critics writing for the conservative press; published *Thérèse et Isabelle* (1966) which became the basis for a film; continued the formal story of her life with 2 more autobiographical volumes—*La Folie en tête* (1970) and *La Chasse à l'Amour* (1973); a significant figure on the French literary scene in the years after WWII, stood apart from trends. ❖ See also Isabelle de Courtivron, *Violette Leduc* (Twayne, 1985); Alex Hughes, *Violette Leduc: Mothers, Lovers, and Language* (Maney, 1994); and *Women in World History.*

LEDWIGOWA, Jozefa (1935—). Polish volleyball player. Born April 18, 1935, in Poland. ❖ Won a bronze medal at Tokyo Olympics (1964) and a bronze medal at Mexico City Olympics (1968), both in team competition.

LEE, Agnes (1841–1873). Daughter of the Lees of Virginia. Born Eleanor Agnes Lee in 1841; died of an intestinal disorder in 1873, age 32; dau. of Robert E. Lee (1807–1870, the Confederate general) and Mary Custis Lee (c. 1808–1873); tutored at home, then attended a female academy; never married; no children. ❖ See also Mary P. Coulling, *The Lee Girls;* and *Women in World History.*

LEE, Alice G. (1827–1863). *See Haven, Emily Bradley Neal.*

LEE, Alice Hathaway (1861–1884). *See Roosevelt, Alice Hathaway Lee.*

LEE, Alma (1912–1990). Australian botanist. Name variations: Alma Theodora Melvaine. Born Alma Theodora Melvaine, April 12, 1912, in Tingha, NSW, Australia; died Oct 20, 1990; University of Sydney, BS, 1936, MSc in botany, 1940; m. David Lee (entomologist), 1941. ❖ Pioneer taxonomist who contributed to the creation of systematic botany standards in Australia, worked as a botanist at the National Herbarium of New South Wales in Sydney (1938–49, 1960s–82); studied soil algae, the taxonomy of legumes, the Fabaceae, *Lupinus* (with J.S. Gladstones) and *Hovea* (with Joy Thompson); served as a National Herbarium honorary research associate (1982–86); publications include a revision of *Swainsona* (1948) and revision work on *Typha.*

LEE, Ann (1736–1784). British-born religious founder. Name variations: Ann Lees; Mother Ann Lee; Ann Lee Standerin; Ann Stanley. Born Ann Lees, Feb 29, 1736, in Manchester, England; died near Watervliet, NY, at the Shaker colony of Niskeyuna, Sept 8, 1784 (*The Albany Gazette*'s obituary mistakenly reports her death on Sept 7); dau. of John Lees (blacksmith and tailor) and Ann (Beswick) Lees; m. Abraham Standerin (later called Stanley), Jan 5, 1761; children: Elizabeth (d. 1766), and 3 who died in childbirth or infancy. ❖ Founder of the United Society of Believers in Christ's Second Appearing, commonly known as the Shakers, who is believed by her followers to be the second, and female, incarnation of Christ; began attending revival meetings led by Quakers Jane and James Wardley (1758); had revelation that she was the second coming of Christ (1770); sailed for the New World (1774); helped establish the 1st Shaker colony at Niskeyuna, NY (1776); took missionary tour through New England (1781–83); left behind a religious movement that lasted for over 100 years after her death, a movement that served as a pattern and example to countless other communities over the course of American history. ❖ See also *Women in World History.*

LEE, Anna (1913–2004). English-born tv and screen actress. Born Joanna Winnifrith, Jan 2, 1913, in Ightham, England; m. George Stafford, 1945 (div. 1964); m. Robert Stevenson (director), 1933 (div. 1964); m. Robert Nathan (novelist, playwright; his 7th wife), 1970 (died 1985); children: Jeffrey Byron (actor) and Venetia Stevenson (actress, producer, b. 1938). ❖ Had brief career on London stage; came to US (1939); appeared in numerous British and American films, including *Ebb Tide, The Passing of the Third Floor Back, King Solomon's Mines, How Green Was My Valley, The Commandos Strike at Dawn, The Ghost and Mrs. Muir, The Last Hurrah, The Man Who Shot Liberty Valance, What Ever Happened to Baby Jane?, The Sound of Music* and *In Like Flint;* had recurring role as wealthy matriarch Lila Quartermaine on tv soap opera "General Hospital" (1978–2003). Named Member of the British Empire (MBE, 1982).

LEE, Anne Carter (1839–1862). Daughter of the Lees of Virginia. Born Anne Carter Lee (named after her father's mother, Ann Carter Hill) in 1839; died of typhoid in 1862, age 23; dau. of Robert E. Lee (1807–1870, the Confederate general) and Mary Custis Lee (c. 1808–1873); tutored at home, then attended a female academy; never married; no children. ❖ See also Mary P. Coulling, *The Lee Girls.*

LEE, Auriol (1880–1941). English actress and producer. Born Sept 13, 1880, in London, England; died July 2, 1941, in Hutchson, KS, in an auto accident; dau. of Robert Lee (physician); related to General Robert E. Lee; m. Frederick W. Lloyd (div.). ❖ Made stage debut at Drury Lane in *The Price of Peace* (1900), followed by *Frocks and Frills, If I Were King, The Axis, His House in Order* (as Nina), *Arms and the Man, Milestones, The Merchant of Venice, The Cat and the Canary* and *The Vortex,* among others; toured with Forbes-Robertson and Beerbohm Tree; produced

plays in London, NY, and Boston, including *Diversion, The Clandestine Marriage, Nine Till Six, Jealousy, Dance with No Music, London Wall, Sea Fever, There's Always Juliet, Pleasure Cruise, Mother of Pearl, The Distaff Side, The Wind and the Rain, The Dark Tower, People at Sea* and *On Borrowed Time.*

LEE, Barbara (1946—). African-American politician. Born July 16, 1946, in El Paso, TX; Mills College, BA; University of California at Berkeley, MSW; div.; children: 2. ❖ Moved to California (1960); served as chief of staff for Congressman Ron Dellums; as a Democrat, served in California State Assembly (1990–96) and State Senate (1996–98); elected to US House of Representatives (1998); was the only lawmaker in the House or Senate to vote against granting President Bush carte-blanche authority to use military force against terrorism (2001); received enough death threats that she had to travel with bodyguards; became a leader in the global fight against HIV/AIDS; during 4th term, served on the House International Relations Committee and the Financial Services Committee; was co-chair of the Congressional Progessive Caucus and whip for the Congressional Black Caucus.

LEE, Barbara (1947–1992). African-American vocalist. Name variations: The Chiffons. Born May 16, 1947, in the Bronx, NY; died May 15, 1992. ❖ With Judy Craig, Patricia Bennett and Sylvia Peterson, sang as member of the Chiffons, all-girl vocal group which had international hits in early 1960s; with Chiffons, had such single hits as "He's So Fine" (1963), "One Fine Day" (with Carole King on piano, 1963), "Nobody Knows What's Going On" (1965), and "Sweet Talkin' Guy" (1966).

LEE, Belinda (1935–1961). English actress. Born June 15, 1935, in Budleigh Salterton, England; died Mar 12, 1961, in auto accident in CA; m. Cornel Lucas (photographer), 1954 (div. 1959). ❖ Star of British, French, German, and Italian films, including *Runaway Bus, Footsteps in the Fog, Miracle in Soho, Man of the Moment, The Belles of St. Trinian's, Eyewitness,* and the title roles in *Messalina* and *The Nights of Lucretia Borgia.*

LEE, Bessie (1860–1950). *See Cowie, Bessie Lee.*

LEE, Beverly (1941—). African-American singer. Name variations: The Shirelles. Born Aug 3, 1941, in Passaic, NJ. ❖ Began singing at school functions with Shirley Owens, Addie "Micki" Harris, and Doris Coley; with them, formed the Shirelles in Passaic, NJ (1958), among the 1st girl groups of rock era, and wrote their 1st hit "I Met Him on a Sunday"; with group, had other hits, including "Tonight's the Night" (1960), "Will You Love Me Tomorrow?" (1961), "Baby It's You" (1963), as well as "Mama Said," "Soldier Boy" and "Foolish Little Girl"; recorded and performed until group split up in late 1960s; sang with group's surviving members, Owens and Coley, at Rhythm and Blues Foundation awards ceremony (1994), and on Dionne Warwick album. Inducted into Rock and Roll Hall of Fame (1996).

LEE BO-NA (1981—). South Korean trapshooter. Born July 22, 1981, in Gwangju, South Korea. ❖ Won a bronze medal for trap and a silver medal for double trap at Athens Olympics (2004).

LEE, Brenda (1944—). American pop and country-music singer. Born Brenda Mae Tarpley, Dec 11, 1944, in Lithonia, GA; graduate of Hollywood Professional School, 1963; m. Charles R. (Ronnie) Shacklett, 1963. ❖ At 6, began singing on radio in Conyers, GA; while still a child, appeared on radio show "Jubilee USA" with Red Foley and on tv with Steve Allen and Perry Como; signed with Decca (1955) and hit the pop and R&B charts with "Sweet Nothin's," which reached #4, and "I'm Sorry," a ballad which was #1 for 3 weeks and sold over 10 million copies (both 1960); reached #1 again 2 months later with "I Want to Be Wanted"; had 4 singles in the top 10 (1961): "You Can Depend On Me," "Emotions," "Fool Number One," and "Dum Dum"; made a successful crossover to country music, scoring with "If This Is Our Last Time" (1971), "Nobody Wins" (1974), and "Broken Trust" (1980), which she recorded with the Oak Ridge Boys; was a guest artist on k.d. lang's *Shadowland* album (1988). Received the National Academy of Recording Arts and Sciences' Governors Award (1984); inducted into Rock and Roll Hall of Fame (2002). ❖ See also autobiography, *Little Miss Dynamite* (2002); and *Women in World History.*

LEE, Dixie (1911–1952). American actress, dancer, and singer. Name variations: Dixie Lee Crosby. Born Wilma Winifred Wyatt, Nov 4, 1911, in Harriman, TN; died Nov 1, 1952, in Holmby Hills, CA; m. Bing Crosby (actor and singer), 1930; children: Gary (1933–1995), Dennis (1935–1991), Philip (b. 1935) and Lindsay Crosby (1938–1989). ❖ Won a Charleston contest in Chicago, then appeared in *Good News* on Broadway (1928); one of the most popular stars of the early musical film era, appeared in most of the Fox musicals, including *Movietone Follies, Happy Days, Cheer Up and Smile, Why Leave Home?, Harmony at Home, Love in Bloom* and *Redheads on Parade;* recorded "A Fine Romance" with Crosby (1936). ❖ See also Gary Crosby's *Going My Own Way;* the film *Smash Up: The Story of a Woman* (1947) said to be based on her life.

LEE, Doris (1902–1984). *See May, Doris.*

LEE EUN-KYUNG (1972—). Korean archer. Born July 15, 1972, in South Korea. ❖ At Barcelona Olympics, won a gold medal in team round (1992).

LEE EUN KYUNG. South Korean field-hockey player. Born in South Korea. ❖ Won a team silver medal at Atlanta Olympics (1996).

LEE EUN-SIL (1976—). South Korean table tennis player. Born Dec 25, 1976, in Daegu, South Korea. ❖ Won a silver medal for table tennis doubles at Athens Olympics (2004); ranked 2nd in doubles on ITTF Pro Tour (2004).

LEE EUN-YOUNG. South Korean field-hockey player. Born in South Korea. ❖ Won a team silver medal at Atlanta Olympics (1996).

LEE, Gaby (1930—). *See Lincoln, Abbey.*

LEE, Gina (1943–2002). English jazz bassist. Born Feb 10, 1943, in Ilford, Essex, England; died Oct 21, 2002, in London, England. ❖ Played with pianist Bernie Bloom at Troubador, Earls Court, and for many years at Langan's Brasserie in Picadilly; worked with clarinettist Dick Laurie's Elastic Band (1988–92); performed with The Mike Peters Band, Geoff Foster's Little Easy Band, New Temperance Seven, Dirty Rats, tenor saxophonist Bill Parslow, and Max Emmond's New Orleans-styled quartet, One More Time.

LEE GONG-JOO (1980—). South Korean handball player. Born Mar 25, 1980, in South Korea. ❖ Won a team silver at Athens Olympics (2004).

LEE, Gwen (1904–1961). American actress. Born Gwendolyn La Pinski, Nov 12, 1904, in Hastings, Nebraska; died Aug 20, 1961, in Reno, NV. ❖ Often portrayed wisecracking sidekicks in such films as *Pretty Ladies, Upstage, Orchids and Ermine, Laugh Clown Laugh* and *Show Girl.*

LEE, Gypsy Rose (1914–1970). American ecdysiast and writer. Born Rose Louise Hovick, but known as Louise Hovick, Feb 9, 1914, in Seattle, WA; died April 26, 1970, in Los Angeles, CA; dau. of John Hovick and Anna Thompson Hovick (known as Rose); sister of June Havoc (b. 1916, actress); m. Arnold Mizzy (div. 1938); m. Alexander Kirkland (div. 1944); m. Julio de Diego (div. 1951); children: (with film director Otto Preminger) Erik Lee Preminger. ❖ Celebrated ecdysiast who turned the striptease into an art form and gained acceptance as a legitimate actress, began career at age 4 (1918); sang and danced with younger sister June throughout Northwest; led a more settled existence during mother's 2 subsequent but short-lived marriages; auditioned for various vaudeville circuits (early 1920s); won a contract with Pantages circuit through West and Midwest, but remained in the chorus line backing up June; after June eloped with one of the chorus boys (1929), mother built a new act around her, but by now vaudeville was being replaced by its bawdier stepchild, burlesque; at mother's urging, got star billing at a burlesque theater in Toledo, Ohio, where she performed her 1st, modest striptease and adopted name Gypsy Rose Lee; took control of her own career, developing a trademark, almost balletic striptease act appreciated in terms of sophistication and entertainment value more than prurience; went on to even wider audiences in feature films and on radio, wrote a play and 2 novels, including *G-String Murders,* and published her memoirs, which were turned into *Gypsy,* one of the most successful Broadway musicals of all time (1959), and later successfully adapted for film and tv; films include *Sally Irene and Mary, Stage Door Canteen, Babes in Baghdad, The Stripper* and *The Trouble With Angels* (1966). ❖ See also *Women in World History.*

LEE, Hannah Farnham (1780–1865). American writer. Born Hannah Farnham Sawyer in Newburyport, MA, 1780; died in Boston, MA, Dec 17, 1865 (also seen as Dec 28); dau. of Micajah Sawyer (physician); m. George Gardner Lee, 1807 (died 1816); children: 3 daughters. ❖ Widowed with daughters to support, turned to writing; early works focused on the difficulties women face in earning their own living, including 1st novel, *Grace Seymour* (1830), which was published when

she was 50; published the popular *Three Experiments of Living* (1837), followed by its sequel *Elinor Fulton* (1837); turned to nonfiction, publishing such books as *Historical Sketches of Old Painters* (1838), *The Life and Times of Martin Luther* (1839), *The Life and Times of Thomas Crammer* (1841), *The Huguenots in France and America* (1843), *Familiar Sketches of Sculpture and Sculptors* (1954) and *Memoir of Pierre Toussaint* (1851). ❖ See also *Women in World History.*

LEE, Harper (1926—). American writer. Name variations: Nelle. Born Nelle Harper Lee, April 28, 1926, in Monroeville, Albama; dau. of Amasa Coleman Lee (lawyer and editor of the local weekly *Monroeville Journal*) and Frances (Finch) Lee (pianist); attended Huntingdon College, 1944–45; studied law at University of Alabama, 1945–49; studied 1 year at Oxford University; never married; no children. ❖ Author of the 1960 Pulitzer Prize-winning novel *To Kill A Mockingbird,* which presented a loving, yet uncompromising, portrait of the morality of the American South where whites ruled by oppressing blacks; grew up in Monroeville where her dear friend Truman Capote spent summers next door; broke off legal studies and moved to NY to become a writer; worked as airline reservations clerk with Eastern Airlines and British Overseas Airlines (1950s); quit job to devote full time to writing; returned to Alabama to help nurse ailing father and wrote short stories that became *To Kill A Mockingbird,* which was published to universal acclaim (1960); never published again. ❖ See also *Women in World History.*

LEE, Harriet (1757–1851). English writer and novelist. Born in London, England, 1757; died at Clifton, near Briston, England, Aug 1, 1851; dau. of John Lee (d. 1781), actor and theatrical manager; mother an actress, name unknown; sister of dramatist Sophia Lee (1750–1824). ❖ Helped sister Sophia setup a girls' school in Bath; published an epistolary novel, *The Errors of Innocence* (1786), followed by *Clara Lennox* (1797); released chief work, *Canterbury Tales* (1797–1805), a series of 12 stories which became quite popular.

LEE, Holme (1828–1900). *See Parr, Harriet.*

LEE HO-YOUN (1971—). Korean handball player. Born May 3, 1971, in South Korea. ❖ At Barcelona Olympics, won a gold medal in team competition (1992).

LEE HYUNG-SOOK (1964—). Korean basketball player. Born Dec 24, 1964, in South Korea. ❖ At Los Angeles Olympics, won a silver medal in team competition (1984).

LEE, Ida (1865–1943). Australian historian. Name variations: Ida Marriott. Born Feb 11, 1865, in Kelso, NSW, Australia; died Oct 3, 1943; dau. of George Lee (grazier) and Emily Louisa (Kite) Lee; m. Charles John Bruce Marriott (secretary of the Rugby Football Union), Oct 14, 1891; children: 1. ❖ On marriage, moved to England; published 1st work, a volume of poetry, *The Bush Fire and Other Verses* (1897); under maiden name, published *The Coming of the British to Australia 1788 to 1829* (1906) and *Commodore Sir John Hayes, His Voyage and Life* (1912); chronicles of other notable ocean voyages include *The Logbooks of the "Lady Nelson"* (1915), *Captain Bligh's Second Voyage to the South Sea* (1920), *Early Explorers in Australia* (1925) and *The Voyage of the Caroline* (1927); elected a fellow of Royal Geographical Society of London (1913) and honorary fellow of Royal Australian Historical Society (1918).

LEE, Jane (c. 1912–1957). Scottish-born actress. Name variations: Little Janey Lee. Born c. 1912 in Glasgow, Scotland; died Mar 17, 1957, in New York, NY; sister of Katherine Lee (child actress). ❖ As a child team with sister Katherine, appeared in vaudeville and starred in over 40 silent films, including *Neptune's Daughter, Two Little Imps* and *The Troublemakers.*

LEE, Jarena (1783–c. 1849). African-American memoirist. Born 1783 in NJ; died c. 1849; m. Joseph Lee, 1811. ❖ Preacher in First African Methodist Episcopal Church who wrote the spiritual autobiography *Religious Experience and Journal of Mrs. Jarena Lee* (1849).

LEE, Jennie (c. 1846–1930). English actress. Born in London, England, c. 1846; died May 3, 1930, age 84; dau. of Edwin George Lee (artist); m. J.P. Burnett (dramatist and actor). ❖ Made stage debut in London as Henry in *Chilperic* (1870); accompanied E.A. Sothern to America to play Mary Meredith in *Our American Cousin;* became a member of the Union Square Theater Co. (1872), then appeared as Jo in *Bleak House* for 2 years in San Francisco, a part that would bring her fame in London and throughout the world.

LEE, Jennie (1848–1925). American silent-screen actress. Name variations: Jennie Lee Courtright; Jenny Lee. Born Sept 4, 1848, in Sacramento, CA; died Aug 5, 1925, in Hollywood, CA. ❖ Appeared in over 30 films, including *The Reformers, Birth of a Nation* (as Mammy), *Her Shattered Idol, A Child of the Paris Streets, A Woman's Awakening, Stage Struck, Riders of Vengeance* and *North of Hudson Bay*.

LEE, Jennie (1904–1988). Scottish politician. Name variations: Jennie Bevan; Mrs. Aneurin Bevan; Baroness Lee of Asheridge. Born Jennie Lee, Nov 3, 1904, in Lochgelly, Fifeshire, Scotland; died Nov 16, 1988, in London, England; dau. of James Lee (coal miner and trade unionist) and Euphemia Grieg; Edinburgh University, MA, 1926, LLB, 1927; m. Aneurin Bevan (politician and Labour party leader), Oct 24, 1934; children: none. ❖ Held several high offices in the British Labour Party and pursued a left-wing socialist program in Parliament for solutions to social problems; elected to British Parliament for North Lanark (1929), becoming the youngest member in House of Commons; defeated (1931); traveled as a lecturer, journalist and author (1931–40); worked in Ministry of Aircraft Production (1940–45); elected to British Parliament for Cannock (1945) and held seat until retirement (1970); served on National Executive Committee of Labour Party (1958–70); held 4-year tenure as minister for the Arts, during which time government spending on arts doubled and the Open University was created (1964–68); appointed parliamentary secretary, Ministry of Public Building and Works (1964–65); appointed parliamentary under-secretary of state for Education and Science (1965–67); was chair of Labour Party (1967–68); appointed minister of state (1967–70); created Baroness Lee of Asheridge (1970). ❖ See also memoirs *My Life With Nye* (Cape, 1980), *This Great Journey* (Farrar, 1942) and *Tomorrow Is A New Day* (Cresset, 1939); and *Women in World History*.

LEE, Jenny (1848–1925). See Lee, Jennie.

LEE JI-YOUNG. South Korean field-hockey player. Born in South Korea. ❖ Won a team silver medal at Atlanta Olympics (1996).

LEE KI-SOON (1966—). Korean handball player. Born Aug 15, 1966, in South Korea. ❖ At Seoul Olympics, won a gold medal in team competition (1988).

LEE KYUNG-WON (1980—). South Korean badminton player. Born Jan 21, 1980, in Changwon, Korea; attended Yongin University. ❖ Won a bronze medal for doubles at Athens Olympics (2004).

LEE LAI-SHAN (1970—). Hong Kong windsurfer. Name variations: Lai Shan Lee. Born Sept 5, 1970, in Hong Kong, China; attended University of Canberra (Australia). ❖ Won World Windsurfing championships (1993, 1997, 2001); won a gold medal for board (Mistral) at Atlanta Olympics (1996); won a gold medal at Asian Games (1998, 2002). Received World Sailor of the Year Award.

LEE, Lila (1901–1973). American stage and screen star. Name variations: Cuddles. Born Augusta Appel, July 25, 1901, in Union Hill, NJ; died Nov 13, 1973, in Saranac Lake, NY; m. John E. Murphy (div.); m. John R. Paine (div.); m. James Kirkwood (actor-producer), 1919 (div. 1931); children: James Kirkwood Jr. (playwright, died 1989). ❖ At 5, began performing in vaudeville as "Cuddles"; over the years, appeared in numerous plays; came to film prominence appearing opposite Valentino in *Blood and Sand*; other films include *Broken Hearts, Million Dollar Mystery, Honky Tonk, War Correspondent, Midsummer Madness, The People's Enemy* and *Two Wise Maids*.

LEE, Lucinda (fl. 1787). American diarist. Name variations: Lucinda Lee Orr. Born Lucinda Lee in Virginia; m. John Dalrymple Orr; dau. of Thomas Ludwell Lee and Mary Aylett. ❖ One of the Lees of Virginia, addressed *Journal of a Young Lady of Virginia 1782* (edited by Emily V. Mason, 1871) to friend Polly Brent in which she spoke of social life among the notables.

LEE, Mary (1821–1909). Irish-born Australian suffragist. Born Mary Walsh on Feb 14, 1821, in Monaghan, Ireland; died Sept 18, 1909, in North Adelaide, Australia; dau. of John Walsh; m. George Lee (organist and vicar-choral of Armagh Cathedral), 1844 (died c. 1879); children: 7, including Adelaide Lee. ❖ Following death of husband, sailed for Australia and became one of its leading proponents of political and social reform; as secretary of Adelaide branch of women's division of the Social Purity Society, directed campaign for women's suffrage; organized a colony-wide suffrage petition which was presented to Parliament (Aug 1894); was the 1st secretary of Working Women's Trade Union (1890), then vice-president (1893) and as such a delegate to Trades and Labor

Council, where she served on Distressed Women's and Children's Committee; awarded a purse of sovereigns by the premier who acknowledged that the passage of women's suffrage was largely due to her advocacy (1896). ❖ See also *Women in World History*.

LEE, Mary Ann (1823–1899). American dancer. Name variations: May Ann Vanhook. Born Mary Ann Lee, July 1823, in Philadelphia, PA; died Jan 25, 1899, in Philadelphia; dau. of theatrical parents, Charles and Wilhelmina Lee; studied under Jean Coralli at Paris Opéra; m. William F. Vanhook (Philadelphia dry goods merchant, later deputy sheriff), Nov 11, 1847 (died 1889); children: Marie (b. 1850), Charles (b. 1851, died in infancy), and Mabel (b. 1854). ❖ Made 1st appearance as dancer in *The Maid of Cashmere* (1837), in which Augusta Maywood also debuted; made NY debut in interlude selection from *The Maid of Cashmere* at Bowery Theatre (1839); was popular favorite by 1844; with G. Washington Smith, formed ballet company (1845) and presented European dance works; was 1st American to dance *Giselle* (1846) at Howard Athenaeum, Boston; appeared in *La Muette de Portici* (1852 and 1853); retired shortly after marriage.

LEE, Mary Custis (c. 1808–1873). American aristocrat. Born c. 1808 in Arlington, Virginia; died in VA, 1873; dau. of George Washington Parke Custis (1781–1857, grandson of Martha Washington by her 1st marriage) and Mary Lee (Fitzhugh) Custis; great-granddau. of Martha Washington (1731–1802); m. Robert E. Lee (1807–1870, Confederate general), in 1831; children: (4 daughters) Mary Custis Lee (1835–1918); Anne Carter Lee (1839–1862); Eleanor Agnes, known as Agnes Lee (1841–1873); and Mildred Childe Lee (1846–1905); (3 sons) Custis Lee; William Henry Fitzhugh ("Rooney") Lee; and Robert E. Lee Jr. ❖ Grew up in her family home, the now-famous Arlington House, on a hillside not far from the Potomac; with mother, conducted classes to help educate ex-slaves to survive as freedmen, though it was against Virginia law to do so; was a gradualist, however, not an outright abolitionist, preferring to go slow and resolve federal issues in order to save the Union; on father's death (1857), inherited Arlington House, soon known as the Lee mansion; when husband resigned from US Army and accepted a commission as general in army of Confederate States of America (1861), had to abandon her house, family heirlooms and papers to accompany husband south; served the wounded in military hospitals; after war (1865), lost house and grounds to federal government which turned it into a burial ground: Arlington National Cemetery. ❖ See also Mary P. Coulling, *The Lee Girls*; and *Women in World History*.

LEE, Mary Custis (1835–1918). Daughter of the Lees of Virginia. Born Mary Custis Lee in 1835; died 1918; dau. of Robert E. Lee (1807–1870, Confederate general) and Mary Custis Lee (c. 1808–1873); tutored at home, then attended a female academy; never married; no children. ❖ Known as the bright, critical, independent daughter, traveled to more than 24 countries, including Australia, Japan, India, Europe, Africa. ❖ See also Mary P. Coulling, *The Lee Girls*; and *Women in World History*.

LEE, Mary Isabella (1871–1939). New Zealand dressmaker and coal miner. Name variations: Mary Isabella Taylor. Born June 18, 1871, in Coatbridge, Lanarkshire, Scotland; died Aug 7, 1939, in Wellington, New Zealand; dau. of Alexander Taylor (railway porter) and Alison/Alice (McDonald) Taylor; children: 5. ❖ Immigrated with parents to Dunedin, New Zealand (1877); due to mother's alcoholism, moved frequently with family; suffered impaired hearing and eyesight from mother's abusive attacks; lived with Alfred (Alfredo) Lee, an indolent laborer (c. late 1880s), but had to work small leased coal mine to support family; forced to return to live with mother; worked as a dressmaker throughout life, but had to depend upon government assistance to raise her children. ❖ See also *Dictionary of New Zealand Biography* (Vol. 2).

LEE MI-JA (1963—). Korean basketball player. Born Sept 6, 1963, in South Korea. ❖ At Los Angeles Olympics, won a silver medal in team competition (1984).

LEE MI-YOUNG (1969—). Korean handball player. Born Jan 28, 1969, in South Korea. ❖ At Barcelona Olympics, won a gold medal in team competition (1992).

LEE, Mildred Childe (1846–1905). Daughter of the Lees of Virginia. Born 1846; died of a stroke in 1905; dau. of Robert E. Lee (1807–1870, Confederate general) and Mary Custis Lee (c. 1808–1873); tutored at home, then attended a female academy; never married; no children. ❖ See also Coulling, Mary P. *The Lee Girls*; and *Women in World History*.

LEE, Muna (1895–1965). American poet, translator and international affairs expert. Name variations: Muna Lee de Muñoz Marín, Mrs. Luis Muñoz Marín; (pseudonym) Newton Gayle. Born Muna Lee on Jan 29, 1895, in Raymond, Mississippi; died April 3, 1965, in San Juan, Puerto Rico; dau. of Benjamin Floyd Lee (druggist) and Mary (McWilliams) Lee; attended Blue Mountain College, 1909–10, and University of Oklahoma, 1911–12; University of Mississippi, BS, 1913; m. Luis Muñoz Marín (poet, journalist, and PR politician), 1919 (div. 1946); children: Muna (b. 1920) and Luis (b. 1921). ❖ An advocate of Pan-Americanism, was confidential Spanish translator for US government in NYC (1918–19); published poems, *Sea-Change* (1923), and children's stories, *Pioneers of Puerto Rico* (1945); trans. several Spanish works, including Jorge Carrera Andrade's *Secret Country* (1946); moved to Puerto Rico with family (1926); became director of bureau of international relations at University of Puerto Rico (1927); was director of national affairs for National Woman's Party (1931–33); as Newton Gayle, co-authored, with Maurice Guinness, several murder mysteries, including *Murder at 28:10* (1936); became specialist in State Department's Division of Cultural Relations in Washington, DC (1941); with Archibald MacLeish, wrote scripts for radio series, "The American Story" (1944); with Ruth McMurry, co-authored *The Cultural Approach: Another Way in International Relations* (1947); became cultural coordinator at Office of Public Affairs (1951); retired from State Department (1965).

LEE, Patty (1820–1871). *See Cary, Alice.*

LEE, Peggy (1920–2002). American jazz stylist, songwriter, and actress. Born Norma Deloris Egstrom in Jamestown, ND, May 26, 1920; died Jan 21, 2002, in Bel Air, CA; m. David Barbour (guitarist), 1943 (div. 1952); m. Brad Dexter (actor), 1955 (div.); m. Dewey Martin (actor), 1956 (div. 1959); children: (1st m.) daughter, Nicki Lee Foster. ❖ Defined by *Down Beat* as the "greatest white female jazz singer since Mildred Bailey," began singing on local radio stations in high school, then in nightclubs in Chicago and California; hired to sing with Benny Goodman's band (1941), and became nationally known after appearances on network radio, in several musical films, and a string of bestselling records, including "Let's Call It a Day," "Why Don't You Do Right," "Fever," "Alright, Okay, You Win," "Hallelujah, I Love Him So," "The Best Is Yet to Come," and "Is That All There Is?"; began writing songs in collaboration with 1st husband, such as "Mañana," "Golden Earrings," "It's A Good Day," "I Don't Know Enough About You"; also wrote partial scores for motion pictures, including *Johnny Guitar, About Mrs. Leslie, Sharkey's Machine, The Time Machine,* and *The Russians Are Coming, The Russians Are Coming;* also wrote "We Are Siamese" and "He's a Tramp" (music and lyrics for movie *Lady and the Tramp*); continued an active nightclub career into mid-1980s; suffered a stroke (Oct 27, 1998). Nominated for Best Actress for performance in *Pete Kelly's Blues* (1955). ❖ See also autobiography *Miss Peggy Lee* (Fine, 1989); and *Women in World History.*

LEE, Roberta (1944—). *See Gentry, Bobbie.*

LEE, Rose Hum (1904–1964). Chinese-American sociologist. Born Rose Hum on Aug 20, 1904, in Butte, Montana; died Mar 25, 1964, in Phoenix, AZ; dau. of Hum Wah-Lung (businessman) and Hum Lin Fong; Carnegie Institute of Technology, BS, 1942; University of Chicago, AM, 1943, PhD, 1947; m. Ku Young Lee, 1920s (div.); m. Glenn Ginn (lawyer), 1951; children: (1st m.) 1 daughter. ❖ Sociologist who believed in pacifism and international understanding, and gained reputation for work on Chinese immigrant society in America; lived in China, working for government agencies and US corporations (1920s–30s); wrote children's plays, including *Little Lee Bo-Bo: Detective for Chinatown* (1940s); joined sociology faculty at Roosevelt University in Chicago (1945), becoming 1st woman of Chinese ancestry to chair a department at a US university (1956); became full professor (1959); authored *The City: Urbanism and Urbanization in Major World Regions* (1955) and *The Chinese in the United States of America* (1960); also taught at Phoenix College (1962–63). Received Woman of Achievement Award from B'nai B'rith (1959).

LEE, Ruth (1895–1975). American screen actress. Born Sept 14, 1895, in Minnesota; died Aug 3, 1975, in Woodland Hills, CA. ❖ Appeared in over 80 films, including *The Trouble with Husbands, Moonlight in Vermont, The Town Went Wild, Sensations of 1945* and *Whirlpool.*

LEE SANG-EUN (1975—). South Korean handball player. Born Mar 5, 1975, in Incheon, Korea. ❖ Won a World championship (1995); won a team silver medal at Atlanta Olympics (1996) and a team silver at Athens

Olympics (2004); at Sydney Olympics (2000), broke an Olympic record by scoring 18 goals against Hungary.

LEE, Sarah (1791–1856). English writer and artist. Name variations: Sarah Bowdich; Mrs. T.E. Bowdich. Born Sarah Wallis in Colchester, England, Sept 10, 1791; died in Erith, Kent, England, Sept 22, 1856; dau. of John Eglintin Wallis; m. Thomas Edward Bowdich (naturalist), 1813 (died 1824); m. Robert Lee, 1829. ❖ On marriage, accompanied husband to Africa (1814, 1815, and 1823); a popularizer of natural science, wrote *Taxidermy* (1820), *Excursions in Madeira and Porto Santo* (1825), *Memoirs of Baron Cuvier* (1833) and *Adventures in Australia* (1851); also wrote and illustrated *The Fresh-water Fishes of Great Britain* (1828).

LEE, Sondra (1930—). American ballet and theater dancer. Born Sept 30, 1930, in Newark, NJ. ❖ Trained at Metropolitan Opera in New York City, as well as with Edward Caton and Nanette Charisse; made Broadway debut in *High Button Shoes* (1947); also appeared as Tiger Lily in *Peter Pan* (1954) and Minnie Fay in *Hello, Dolly!* (1964); danced throughout Europe with Ballet de Paris (1958), John Butler Co. (1959), and at Spoleto Festival in Italy with Herbert Ross' Ballet of Two Worlds and Jerome Robbins' Ballet: U.S.A.; appeared in Fellini's film *La Dolce Vita.*

LEE SOO-NOK (1955—). Korean volleyball player. Born Sept 28, 1955, in South Korea. ❖ At Montreal Olympics, won a bronze medal in team competition (1976).

LEE SOON-BOK (1950—). Korean volleyball player. Born Mar 26, 1950, in South Korea. ❖ At Montreal Olympics, won a bronze medal in team competition (1976).

LEE SOON-EI (1965—). Korean handball player. Born Oct 15, 1965, in South Korea. ❖ At Los Angeles Olympics, won a silver medal in team competition (1984).

LEE, Sophia (1750–1824). English novelist and dramatist. Born in London, England, 1750; died at home near Clifton, Bristol, Mar 13, 1824; dau. of John Lee (d. 1781, actor and theatrical manager); mother was an actress, name unknown; sister of Harriet Lee (1757–1851). ❖ Presented 1st dramatic work, *The Chapter of Accidents,* a 1-act opera based on Diderot's *Père de famille,* at the Haymarket (Aug 5, 1780); used proceeds to establish a school at Bath, where she made a home for her sisters, including novelist Harriet Lee; subsequent productions included *The Recess, or a Tale of other Times* (1785), a historical romance, and *Almeyda, Queen of Grenada* (1796), a tragedy in blank verse which opened at Drury Lane with Sarah Siddons.

LEE SUN-HEE. South Korean taekwondo player. Born in South Korea. ❖ Won a gold medal for 57–67kg at Sydney Olympics (2000).

LEE SUNG-JIN (1985—). South Korean archer. Born Mar 7, 1985, in South Korea. ❖ At Athens Olympics, won a gold medal for team round and a silver medal for indiv. (2004).

LEE, Susan (1966—). Australian rower. Born June 1, 1966. ❖ At Los Angeles Olympics, won a bronze medal in coxed fours (1984).

LEE, Tanith (1947—). British science-fiction writer. Born Sept 19, 1947, in London, England; m. John Kaiine, 1992. ❖ Works include *The Birthgrave* (1975), *The Storm Lord* (1976), *Quest for the White Witch* (1978), *Kill the Dead* (1980), *The Silver Metal Lover* (1982), *The Dragon Hoard* (1984), *Madame Two Swords* (1988), *Reigning Cats and Dogs* (1996), *Law of the Wolf Tower* (1998), *Wolf Queen* (2001), and *Venus Preserved* (2003); also published short-story collections, including *Cyrion* (1982), *The Gorgon and Other Beastly Tales* (1985), *Women as Demons* (1989), and *The Book of the Dead* (1991).

LEE, Vernon (1856–1935). *See Paget, Violet.*

LEE, Virginia (1965—). Australian rower. Born April 6, 1965, in NSW, Australia. ❖ Won a bronze medal for lightweight double sculls at Atlanta Olympics (1996).

LEE YOUNG-JA (1964—). Korean handball player. Born Jan 5, 1964, in South Korea. ❖ At Los Angeles Olympics, won a silver medal in team competition (1984).

LEE-GARTNER, Kerrin (1966—). Canadian Alpine skier. Born Sept 21, 1966, in Trail, British Columbia, Canada; grew up in Rossland, BC. ❖ At Albertville, was the 1st Canadian—male or female—to win an Olympic gold medal in the downhill (1992). Elected to British Columbia

Sports Hall of Fame (1994) and Canadian Sports Hall of Fame (1995). ❖ See also *Women in World History.*

LEE LONG, Rosa. Australian politician. Born in Atherton, Australia; married an Australian of Chinese descent (died 1985); children: 3 daughters. ❖ As a member of the One Nation Party, elected to the Queensland Parliament for Tablelands (2001).

LEE OF ASHERIDGE, Jennie Lee, Baroness (1904–1988). *See Lee, Jennie.*

LEE SMITH, Jenny (1948—). English golfer. Name variations: Jennifer Lee Smith or Lee-Smith. Born Dec 2, 1948, in Newcastle-on-Tyne, Northumberland, England. ❖ Won Willis Match Play (1974); won British Open Stroke Play (1976); won British Women's Open (1976); member of Curtis Cup team (1974, 1976); qualified for American tour during 1st year as a pro; number one money winner in England (1981, 1982).

LEECH, Faith (1941—). Australian swimmer. Born June 18, 1941, in Australia. ❖ Won a bronze medal in the 100-meter freestyle and a gold medal in the 4 x 100-meter freestyle at Melbourne Olympics (1956).

LEECH, Margaret (1893–1974). American historian. Name variations: Mrs. Ralph Pulitzer. Born Margaret Kernochan Leech, Nov 7, 1893, in Newburgh, NY; died Feb 24, 1974, in NY, NY; dau. of William Kernochan Leech and Rebecca (Taggert) Leech; Vassar College, BA, 1915; m. Ralph Pulitzer (newspaper publisher), Aug 1, 1928 (died June 14, 1939); children: Susan Pulitzer Freedberg; Margaretta Pulitzer (died in infancy). ❖ Won Pulitzer Prize for history for *Reveille in Washington* (1941) and for the biography of President William McKinley, *In the Days of McKinley* (1959); worked for various WWI fund-raising organizations and was on the staff of Anne Morgan's American Committee for Devastated France; published 1st novel *The Back of the Book* (1924), followed by *Tin Wedding* (1926) and *The Feather Nest* (1928); collaborated with Heywood Broun on *Anthony Comstock: Roundsman of the Lord* (1928); investigated life in the nation's capital during Civil War (1935–40), resulting in bestseller *Reveille in Washington, 1859–1865,* which was 1st serialized in *Atlantic Monthly* (1941); worked 12 years on 2nd book, *In the Days of McKinley* (1959). Awarded Bancroft Prize by Columbia University. ❖ See also *Women in World History.*

LEEDS, Andrea (1913–1984). American actress. Name variations: Antoinette Lees. Born Antoinette M. Lees, Aug 18, 1913, in Butte, Montana; died May 21, 1984, in Palm Springs, CA; m. Robert Stewart Howard (sportsman), 1939 (died 1962); children: Leann Howard (died 1971) and Robert S. Howard Jr. ❖ Had leading roles in such films as *Letter of Introduction, Come and Get It, The Goldwyn Follies, They Shall Have Music, The Real Glory, Swanee River* and *Earthbound;* following marriage, retired from the screen (1939) and bred race horses; later owned a jewelry store in Palm Springs. Nominated for Academy Award as Best Supporting Actress for *Stage Door* (1937).

LEEDS, Marian (1918–2002). *See Bergeron, Marian.*

LEELINAU (1800–1841). *See Schoolcraft, Jane Johnston.*

LEEMING, Marjorie (1903–1987). Canadian tennis player. Born 1903 in Kamloops, British Columbia, Canada; died 1987; sister of Hope Leeming (tennis player). ❖ Was Canadian singles, doubles, and mixed champion (1925); won two more national singles titles; with sister, won Canadian doubles title (1930, 1932); forced to retire because of a hip injury. Inducted into Canadian Tennis Hall of Fame.

LEENMANS, Margaretha (1909–1998). *See Fortuyn-Leenmans, Margaretha Droogleever.*

LEES, Antoinette (1913–1984). *See Leeds, Andrea.*

LEES, Sue (1941–2003). English academic, writer, feminist and activist. Born June 16, 1941, in India; died of ovarian cancer, Sept 17, 2002; attended Edinburgh University, London School of Economics, and Birkbeck College; m. 3rd husband John Lea (criminologist); children: (2nd m.) son and daughter. ❖ Was a professor of Women's Studies at Polytechnic of North London (1976–93), then director of its center for research in ethnicity and gender (1993–97); while conducting research into murder trials at the Old Bailey (1980s), was horrified at the treatment of the victim in a rape trial, especially when the rapist walked free; became a leading expert on the conduct of rape trials, a fervent campaigner for legal reform, and a writer and broadcaster; successfully influenced a change in the law; writings include *Losing Out* (1986), *Sugar and Spice: Sexuality and Adolescent Girls* (1993), *Carnal*

Knowledge: Rape on Trial (1996) and *Ruling Passions: Policing Sexual Assault* (1997).

LEETE, Harriet L. (c. 1875–1927). American nurse. Born c. 1875 in Cleveland, Ohio; died Nov 9, 1927, in Brooklyn, NY; graduate of Lakeside Training School for Nurses, 1901. ❖ A leader in child health care, was head of men's surgical ward at Lakeside Hospital in Cleveland (1902–06); as a nurse at Infant's Clinic of the Babies Dispensary in Cleveland, created well-baby programs (1906–17); during WWI, worked for Red Cross Bureau of Tuberculosis in Europe and afterwards for Rockefeller Commission for the Prevention of Tuberculosis in conjunction with French hospitals; named chief nurse of Department of Civil Affairs' Children's Bureau for Red Cross Commission in France; served as chief nurse for Balkan Commission in northern Siberia (from early 1919); as field director for American Child Hygiene Association, oversaw adoption and child-care standards; as director for Maternity Center Association in NY (1920s), organized a Mothercraft Club to teach prenatal care and instruction; served as director of a convalescent home for children, Wavecrest, in Far Rockaway, NY.

LEFANU, Alicia (1753–1817). English playwright. Name variations: Le Fanu. Born 1753; died 1817; dau. of Frances Sheridan (1724–1766, novelist and dramatist) and Thomas Sheridan (well-known actor-manager); sister of Richard Brinsley Sheridan (1751–1816) and Elizabeth Lefanu (1758–1837); m. Joseph Lefanu or Le Fanu (1814–1873, novelist, journalist, and brother of Henry and Philip Lefanu, a divine), in 1776. ❖ Wrote *The Flowers: A Fairy Tale* and the comedy *Sons of Erin* which was performed in London (1812).

LEFANU, Alicia (c. 1795–c. 1826). English writer. Name variations: Le Fanu. Born c. 1795; died c. 1826; dau. of Henry Lefanu or Le Fanu (brother of Joseph and Philip Lefanu) and Elizabeth Lefanu (1758–1837). ❖ Published the *Memoirs of Mrs. Frances Sheridan* (1824); also wrote *Rosara's Chains: A Poem* (1812), *The Indian Voyage* (1816), *Strathallan* (1816), and *Helen Monteage* (1818).

LEFANU, Elizabeth (1758–1837). English writer. Name variations: Le Fanu. Born 1758; died 1837; dau. of Frances Sheridan (1724–1766, novelist and dramatist) and Thomas Sheridan (well-known actor-manager); sister of Richard Brinsley Sheridan (1751–1816) and Alicia Lefanu (1753–1817); m. Henry Lefanu (brother of Joseph and Philip Lefanu); children: Alicia Lefanu (c. 1795–c. 1826).

LEFANU, Nicola (1947—). English composer. Born 1947; dau. of Elizabeth Maconchy (1907–1994, composer) and William Lefanu; studied at Oxford University, Royal College of Music, with Maxwell Davies at Dartington, and in Siena. ❖ Lecturer at King's College, London; compositions, including *Antiworld* (1972) and *Dawnpath* (1977), earned many awards, as did her radiophonic operas, *The Story of Mary O'Neill* (1986) and *Wind Among the Pines: Five Images of Norfolk* (1987).

LEFAUCHEUX, Marie-Helene (1904–1964). French feminist, diplomat, and politician. Born Marie-Helene Postel-Vinay in Paris, France, Feb 2, 1904; died in plane crash in US, Feb 25, 1964; dau. of Marcel and Madeleine (Delombre) Postel-Vinay; graduate of École des Sciences Politiques; studied piano at École du Louvre; m. Pierre-Andre Lefaucheux (lawyer, civil engineer, and president of Renault Automobile Works), 1925. ❖ Pianist of distinction, became active in the Resistance during German occupation of France, serving as vice president of Paris Committee of Liberation; orchestrated husband's escape from Weimar prison, for which she was awarded the Croix de Guerre and Rosette de la Resistance; representing Organisation Civile et Militaire, was elected to Consultative Assembly, the 1st interim parliament of provisional French government (1945); was returned to the Constituent Assembly as a deputy (1945); also elected to Municipal Council of Paris, where she served as vice president; was elected to Council of the Fourth French Republic (1946), and later represented metropolitan France in Assembly of the French Union, serving as vice president (1959–60); was the only female member of the French delegation to attend the 1st General Assembly of the UN (1946), and represented France on UN Commission on the Status of Women; was also a founder of Association des Femmes de l'Union Français, an organization concerned with the welfare of Africans and Algerians; served as president of National Council of Women (1954–64) and was elected president of International Council of Women (1957); retired (1964).

LEFEBVRE, Anne (1654–1720). *See Dacier, Anne.*

LEFEBVRE, Catherine (c. 1764–after 1820). French duchess and literary inspiration. Name variations: Lefevre; duchesse de Dantzig or Duchess of Dantzig; Madame Sans-Gêne or Sans-Gene. Born Catherine Hubscher c. 1764; died after 1820; m. François Joseph Lefebvre (1755–1820), duc de Dantzig (French general), in 1783. ❖ Was the basis for the heroine in Victorien Sardou's comedy *Madame Sans-Gêne* (1893). ❖ See also *Women in World History.*

LEFEBVRE, Janou (1945—). *French equestrian.* Born May 14, 1945, in France. ❖ Won a silver medal at Tokyo Olympics (1964) and a silver medal at Mexico City Olympics (1968), both in team jumping.

LEFFLER, Anne Charlotte (1849–1892). *See Edgren, Anne Charlotte.*

LE FORT, Gertrud von (1876–1971). *German novelist.* Name variations: G. von Stark. Born Gertrud Augusta Lina Elsbeth Mathilde Petrea von le Fort, Oct 11, 1876, in Minden, Germany; died Nov 1, 1971, in Oberstdorf, Germany; dau. of Lothar Friedrich (army officer and baron) and Elsbeth Mathilde (von Wedel-Parlow) von le Fort; attended University of Heidelberg, 1910–14, and University of Berlin, 1916. ❖ Studied philosophy and church history at Heidelberg and converted to Catholicism (1926); writings, which reflect philosophical studies and deep commitment to Catholicism, include *Hymnen an die Kirche* (1924, Hymns to Germany), *Das Schweißtuch der Veronika* (1928, The Veil of Veronica), and *Die Letzte am Schafott* (1931, The Song at the Scaffold).

LE GALLIENNE, Eva (1899–1991). *English-born actress, director, and producer.* Name variations: E. Le G. Born Jan 11, 1899, in London, England; died June 3, 1991, in Weston, CT, of heart failure; dau. of Julie Nørregaard (Danish journalist) and Richard Le Gallienne (English poet and novelist); never married; no children. ❖ Actress-producer who attempted to establish a repertory tradition in the American theater and worked nearly continuously throughout her long career; after graduating from London's Academy of Dramatic Arts, made West End stage debut (1914) and soon crossed Atlantic to appear to great acclaim on Broadway, where she came to prominence as Julie in *Liliom* (1921), followed by *The Swan* (1923) and 2 by Ibsen, *The Master Builder* and *John Gabriel Borkman* (1924); became one of the most famous leading ladies of her day; turned to directing and formed the Civic Repertory Theater (1926), presenting 37 productions over 10 years, including *Cradle Song, The Inheritors, Alice in Wonderland* and *The Cherry Orchard;* launched her 2nd acting company, American Repertory Theater (ART, 1946), then National Repertory Co. (1959); appeared as Elizabeth I in Schiller's *Mary Stuart* at Phoenix Theater (1959), her greatest success in years; topped that with role of Fanny Cavendish in revival of *The Royal Family* (1976), for which she would later win an Emmy for performance in tv adaptation; made few film appearances, though nominated for Oscar for *Resurrection* (1980); wrote a novel for children. ❖ See also autobiographies *At 33* and *With a Quiet Heart;* Helen Sheehy, *Eva Le Gallienne* (Knopf, 1996); and *Women in World History.*

LEGANGER, Cecilie (1975—). *Norwegian handball player.* Born Mar 12, 1975, in Bergen, Norway. ❖ Won a team bronze medal at Sydney Olympics (2000).

LE GARREC, Evelyne. *French journalist and feminist.* Born in France. ❖ Nonfiction focuses on lives of contemporary women, gay and straight, in France; works of social documentary include *Un Lit à soi* (1979) and *Des Femmes qui s'aiment* (1984); other works include *Les Messagères* (1976), *La Rive allemande de ma mémoire* (1980), and *Séverine: une rebelle* (1982).

LEGAT, Nadine (c. 1895–?). *Russian ballet dancer and teacher.* Name variations: Nadine De Briger; Nadine Nicolaeva; Nadine Nicolaeva-Legat. Born Nadine De Briger, c. 1895, in St. Petersburg, Russia; m. Nicholai Legat (ballet dancer), late 1910s (died 1937). ❖ One of the most influential ballet teachers in England, wrote numerous texts on the training of dance teachers; 1st performed with Bolshoi and Maryinsky ballets in 19th-century works; danced with husband to great acclaim in *Coppélia* (1925); founded boarding school of dance in Kent, England.

LEGH, Alice (1855–1948). *British archer.* Born Alice Blanche Legh, in 1855, in Cheshire, England; died 1948; dau. of Piers Legh and Mrs. Piers Legh (archer). ❖ The greatest British archer of all time, won 23 British archery championships spanning 41 years (1881–1922), though her mother, Mrs Piers Legh, beat her for the championship from 1882 to 1885; chose not to compete at the Olympic Games (1908), but beat Olympic champion Sybil Newall the same year.

LEGINSKA, Ethel (1886–1970). *English-born pianist, composer, and conductor.* Name variations: Ethel Liggins. Born April 13, 1886, in Hull, England (some sources cite April 12); died in Los Angeles, CA, Feb 26, 1970, of a stroke; dau. of Thomas Liggins and Annie (Peck) Liggins; attended music schools in Frankfurt (Hoch Conservatory), Vienna, and Berlin; m. Roy Emerson Whittern (also known as Emerson Whithorne, American composer), 1907 (div. 1916); children: Cedric. ❖ Had a significant impact on several branches of the world of music; starting as a successful pianist in Europe and US, by late 20s took up composing and, a decade thereafter, rose to prominence as a founder and conductor of symphony orchestras; made London debut as a pianist (1902); had 1st nervous breakdown (1909); made successful NY debut at Aeolian Hall (1913); spent most of her time in US and appeared regularly on NY concert stage; was particularly known for her repertoire of works by great German composers from Bach through Schubert, as well as for her all-Chopin programs; studied composition with Ernest Bloch (1914); began role as speaker for feminist causes (1915); composed *Four Poems* for string quartet, which debuted in London (1921), and a four-movement suite, *Quatre sujects barbares* (1923); when emotional burdens hampered performing career, appeared as a guest conductor in a number of European musical centers (1924), including Munich, Paris, London and Berlin; made American debut as conductor, appearing with NY Symphony Orchestra at Carnegie Hall, the 1st time a woman had conducted there (1925); founded Boston Philharmonic Orchestra (1926), followed by Boston Woman's Symphony, and Boston English Opera Co.; toured Europe as conductor (1930); conducted premier of her opera *Gale* (1935); relocated permanently to Los Angeles (1940); conducted premier of her opera *The Rose and the Ring* (1957). ❖ See also *Women in World History.*

LE GIVRE DE RICHEBOURG, Madame (1710–1780). *French novelist and short-story writer.* Born 1710 in France; died 1780. ❖ Works include *Le Veuve en puissance de mari* (1732), *Aventures de Clamandès et Clarmonde* (1733), *Aventures de Flores et de Blanchefleur* (1735), *Aventures de Zelin et de Damasine* (1735), *Aventures de Dom Ramire de Roxas et de Dona Leonone de Mendoce* (1737), and *Persiles et Sigismond* (1737).

LEGGE-SCHWARZKOPF, Elisabeth (b. 1915). *See Schwarzkopf, Elisabeth.*

LEGNANI, Pierina (1863–1923). *Italian ballerina.* Born in Milan, Italy, 1863; died 1923; studied in Milan; trained by Catarina Beretta at Ballet School of Teatro all Scala. ❖ Made debut at La Scala, Milan, and then appeared with some success in Paris, Madrid and London; found fame while performing in *The Tulip of Haarlem* at Maryinsky Theater in St. Petersburg (1893), when she executed 32 consecutive *fouettés* for the 1st time in the history of the Imperial Ballet, earning her title "Prima Ballerina Assoluta"; remained there for next 8 years, dancing as Odette in *Swan Lake* and appearing in *Caterina, Coppélia, The Talisman, The Halt of Cavalry, Bluebeard, Camargo* and *Raymonda.*

LEGON, Jeni (1916—). *African-American tap dancer and actress.* Name variations: Jeni Le Gon. Born Aug 14, 1916, in Chicago, IL; trained at Mary Bruce's School of Dance; began living with drummer Frank Clavin, 1975. ❖ At 14, danced in chorus with the Whitman Sisters; performed opposite Bill "Bojangles" Robinson in film *Hooray for Love* (1935), the 1st appearance of an African-American woman in a major Hollywood production; appeared in numerous films thereafter, including *Take My Life* (1941), *I Walked with a Zombie* (1943), and *I Shot Jesse James* (1949), but was rarely again in a leading role; performed with Fats Waller in London (1936) and other European cities; received a 2001 Flo-Bert Award honoring outstanding tap dance figures; moved to Vancouver, British Columbia, Canada, where she opened a dancing school (1960). Other films include *Double Deal* (1939), *Sundown* (1941), *Bahama Passage* (1941), *My Son, the Hero* (1943), *Hi-De-Ho* (1947), and *Easter Parade* (1948); also appears in *Bones* (2001). ❖ See also Grant Greschuk's *Jeni LeGon: Living in a Great Big Way* (National Film Board of Canada, 2000).

LEGRAND, Lise (1976—). *French wrestler.* Born Sept 4, 1976, in Boulogne sur Mer, France. ❖ Won World championships for 70 kg freestyle (1995) and 62 kg freestyle (1997); won European championships for 67 kg freestyle (2002, 2003); won a bronze medal for 63 kg freestyle at Athens Olympics (2004).

LE GUIN, Ursula K. (1929—). *American science-fiction writer.* Name variations: Ursula LeGuin. Born Ursula Kroeber, Oct 21, 1929, in Berkeley, CA; dau. of Alfred L. Kroeber and Theodora Kroeber (writer); attended Radcliffe College; m. Charles A. Le Guin, 1953; children: 3. ❖ Taught French and creative writing at several universities in US, England, and Australia; regarded as one of most literary of science-fiction writers, because of her complex narratives and dense poetic language; works have garnered much critical praise while also having wide popular appeal; writings include *Rocannon's World* (1966), *The Left Hand of Darkness* (1969), *The Lathe of Heaven* (1971), *Malafrena* (1979), *The Earthsea Trilogy* (1979), *The Beginning Place* (1980), *Always Coming Home* (1985), *Tehann* (1990), *The Telling* (2000), *Tales from Earthsea* (2001) and *The Other Wind* (2001); story collections include *The Wind's Twelve Quarters* (1975), *The Compass Rose* (1982), *Four Ways to Forgiveness* (1995), and *The Birthday of the World* (2002); poetry and translations include *Wild Angels* (1974), *Hard Words* (1981), *Going out with Peacocks* (1994), *The Twins, The Dream/ Las Gemelas, El Sueno* (with Diana Bellassi, 1997), and *Sixty Odd* (1999); criticism includes *Dancing at the Edge of the World* (1989) and *Steering the Craft* (1998); children's books include *Leese Webster* (1979), *Solomon Leviathan* (1988), *Fish Soup* (1992) and *Tom Mouse* (2002); also edited several anthologies, including *The Norton Book of Science Fiction* (1993). Received Nebula Award, Hugo Award, Gandalf Award, *Locus* Readers Award, and PEN/ Malamud Award; manuscript collection housed at University of Oregon Library, Eugene, OR. ❖ See also Elizabeth Cummings Cogell, *Ursula K. Le Guin: A Primary and Secondary Bibliography* (Hall, 1983), David. S. Bratman, *Ursula K. Le Guin: A Primary Bibliography* (Potlatch 4, 1995), and Donna R. White, *Dancing With Dragons: Ursula K. Le Guin and the Critics* (Camden House, 1998).

LEHANE, Jan (1941—). Australian tennis player. Name variations: Jan O'Neill. Born 1941 in Grenfell, New South Wales, Australia. ❖ For a brief time (1959–60), ranked #1 in senior tennis in Australia, winning hardcourt title (1959).

LE HAY, Mme (1648–1711). See Chéron, Elisabeth-Sophie.

LEHMANN, Adelaide (c. 1830–1851). French dancer. Born c. 1830 in France; died 1851 in New York, NY; sister of Flora, Julia and Mathilde Lehmann (dancers). ❖ Performed with family troupe, The Lehmann Family, on tours in US (mid-1840s), where she was featured in their productions of *Comus* and *The Spirit of the Air* (1848); performed on Mississippi circuit with own family and members of the Ravel family, traveling from St. Louis to New Orleans; appeared on NY stages (1849–51), where she was fatally burned by a gaslight during a performance.

LEHMANN, Beatrix (1903–1979). English actress and author. Born in Bourne End, Buckinghamshire, England, July 1, 1903; died July 31, 1979, in London; dau. of Alice Mary (Davis) Lehmann (an American) and Rudolph Chambers Lehmann (poet, writer, editor of *Punch* until 1919, and member of Parliament, 1906–14); sister of Rosamond Lehmann (1901–1990). ❖ Made stage debut at Lyric, Hammersmith (1924), succeeding Elsa Lanchester in *The Way of the World*, followed by *An American Tragedy, The Adding Machine, Thunder on the Left, Nju, The Silver Tassie, Salome, Wild Decembers, All God's Chillun, Twenty Below* and *The Wandering Jew*, among others; appeared as Hilda Wangel in *The Master Builder* (1934) and in title role of *Charlotte Corday* (1936); became director-producer of Arts Council Midland Theater Co. (1946); joined Shakespeare Memorial Theatre in Stratford-on Avon (1947), appearing as Portia, Isabella, and Viola; was president of British Actors' Equity (1945); appeared with Old Vic in numerous productions, including *Suddenly Last Summer* and as Lady Macbeth; gave other notable performances in *The Human Voice, Ghosts, Desire Under the Elms, Mourning Becomes Electra, Waltz of the Toreadors, The Aspern Papers, Reunion in Vienna, The Storm* and *The Trojan Wars*; also wrote short stories, 2 novels, and appeared on tv and in such films as *The Passing of the Third Floor Back, The Rat, The Key, The Spy Who Came in From the Cold, A Funny Thing Happened on the Way to the Forum* and *The Staircase*.

LEHMANN, Beatrix (1963—). See Schröer-Lehmann, Beatrix.

LEHMANN, Christa (1922—). German murderer. Born 1922; m. Karl Franz Lehmann, 1944. ❖ Using a then new organic phosphorus compound identified as E-605, attempted to poison neighbor Eva Ruh with a laced chocolate truffle but instead killed her own friend Annie Hamann (Ruh's daughter) and the family dog, both of whom partook of the chocolate; confessed to this crime (Feb 23, 1954) and later to the poisoning murders of her husband Karl and her father-in-law; convicted (Sept 20) and received a life sentence.

LEHMANN, Heike (1962—). East German volleyball player. Born Mar 29, 1962, in East Germany. ❖ At Moscow Olympics, won a silver medal in team competition (1980).

LEHMANN, Helma (1953—). East German rower. Born June 23, 1953, in East Germany. ❖ At Montreal Olympics, won a gold medal in coxed eights (1976).

LEHMANN, Inge (1888–1993). Danish geophysicist and mathematician. Born May 13, 1888, at Osterbro by the Lakes, Copenhagen, Denmark; died in Copenhagen, Feb 21, 1993; dau. of Alfred Georg Ludvig Lehmann (professor of psychology) and Ida Sophie (Torsleff) Lehmann; sister of Harriet Lehmann; University of Copenhagen, MA, 1920, MS in geodesy, 1928; also studied at Cambridge University and University of Hamburg. ❖ One of the most innovative scientists of the 20th century, was chief seismologist of the Royal Danish Geodetic Institute (1928–53); by studying the shock waves generated by earthquakes, was able to theorize that the Earth has a solid inner core, a finding that was substantiated by other scientists; retired (1953). Awarded William Bowie Medal of American Geophysical Union (1971). ❖ See also *Women in World History.*

LEHMANN, Karen. See Cashman, Karen.

LEHMANN, Lilli (1848–1929). German soprano. Born in Würzburg, Germany, Nov 24, 1848; died in Berlin, May 17, 1929; daughter and student of Marie Loewe; sister of Marie Lehmann (1851–1931), soprano); m. Paul Kalish (tenor), 1888. ❖ Famed for interpretive skill, made debut in Prague (1865); took part in 1st complete performance of *Der Ring* at Bayreuth (1876); was a member of Royal Opera in Berlin (1870–85); broke contact with Berlin to debut as Carmen at NY's Metropolitan Opera (1885), where she remained for 7 seasons, retiring from there in 1902 after a final American concert tour; while there, sang Brünnhilde from *Die Walküre*, Bertha from *La prophète*, and Venus from *Tannhäuser*; also appeared in US premieres of *Die Königin von Saba* (1885), *Götterdämmerung* (1885), *Tristan and Isolde* (1886), *Merlin* (1887), *Siegfried* (1887), and the complete cycle of the Ring (1889); appeared at, and was artistic director of, the Salzburg Festival (1902–10); became a successful teacher, with Geraldine Farrar and Olive Fremstad among her pupils. ❖ See also autobiography *Mein Weg (My Path through Life)*, 1913; and *Women in World History.*

LEHMANN, Liza (1862–1918). English composer, pianist, singer. Name variations: Fredrika; Mrs. Herbert Bedford. Born Elizabeth Nina Mary Lehmann in London, England, July 11, 1862; died in Pinner, Sept 19, 1918; dau. of Rudolph Lehmann (painter) and Amelia Lehmann (singer); studied voice with mother, then Albert Bandegger and Jenny Lind, and composition under Raumkilde in Rome and Freudenberg in Wiesbaden before returning to London to study with Hamish MacCunn; m. Herbert Bedford (painter and composer), 1894. ❖ Debuted as a singer at Monday Popular Concerts (1884); accompanied in concert with the Philharmonic by Clara Schumann (1888); on marriage, gave up concertizing to concentrate solely on composing (1894); was the 1st woman in England commissioned to write a musical comedy or operetta, resulting in *Sergeant Brue;* taught at Guildhall School of Music (1913); composed many songs and 2 operas and is best remembered for *In a Persian Garden* (1896), a song-cycle for 4 voices based on *Rubyaiyat of Omar Khayyam*, which included the song "Myself When Young." ❖ See also *Women in World History.*

LEHMANN, Lotte (1888–1976). German soprano and writer. Born Feb 27, 1888, in Perleberg, Germany; died Aug 26, 1976, in Santa Barbara, CA; dau. of Carl Lehmann (secretary to the Ritterschaft, a benevolent society) and Marie (Schuster) Lehmann; studied at Berlin Hochschule für Musik with Helene Jordan, Erna Tiedke and Eva Reinhold (1904); studied with Mathilde Mallinger (1908–09); m. Otto Krause (insurance executive), 1926 (died Jan 1939). ❖ One of the greatest voices of the 20th century, learned nearly 100 operatic roles and gave over 1,600 performances; made debut as Second Boy in *Die Zauberflöte (The Magic Flute)* at Hamburg Opera (1910); debuted in London as Sophie in *Der Rosenkavalier*, Drury Lane (1914); sang with Vienna State Opera (1916–37), where she created roles of Young Composer in Strauss' revised *Ariadne auf Naxos*, the Dyer's Wife in *Die Frau Ohne Schatten* (1919) and Christine in *Intermezzo* (1924); made Covent Garden debut as Marschallin in *Der Rosenkavalier* (1924); appeared in Buenos Aires (1922), Paris (1928–34), Chicago (1930–37), Salzburg (1926–37); was acclaimed for her Leonore in *Fidelio* which she 1st presented at Beethoven Festival in Vienna (1927); debuted at Metropolitan Opera as Sieglinde (1934); performed 12 seasons at the Met until 1945, having left Germany because of Hitler; sought US citizenship (1938); taught privately and as director of Music Academy of the West in Santa Barbara; was an honorary member of Vienna State Opera. Also published several books, including verses, the novel *Orplid, mein Land* (1937), 2 books of memoirs, *Anfang und Aufstieg* (pub. in English as *Wings of Song,* 1937) and *My Many Lives* (1948), and a book on the interpretation of song, *More Than Singing* (1945). ❖ See also *Women in World History.*

LEHMANN, Rosamond (1901–1990). British novelist, short-story writer, translator, and editor. Born Rosamond Nina Lehmann, Feb 3, 1901, in Fieldhead, Bourne End, Buckinghamshire, England; died Mar 12, 1990, in London; dau. of Alice Mary (Davis) Lehmann (an American) and Rudolph Chambers Lehmann (poet, writer, editor of *Punch* until 1919, and member of Parliament, 1906–14); sister of Beatrix Lehmann (actress); educated at Girton College, Cambridge, 1919–22; m. Walter Leslie Runciman, 1922 (div. 1927); m. Wogan Philipps (painter and member of House of Lords), 1928 (div. 1942); had intimate friendship with Cecil Day-Lewis (poet and writer), 1941–50; children: (2nd m.) Hugo Philipps (b. 1929); Sally Philipps Kavanagh (1934–1958). ❖ Writer who explored women's sexuality and disparaged the British class system for its impact on gender and identity, had a popular and critical success with 1st novel, *Dusty Answer* (1927); published 2nd novel, *A Note in Music* (1930); her home (Ipsden House) became a center for artists and writers who were among the younger generation of Bloomsbury crowd, including Leonard and Virginia Woolf, Lytton Strachey and Dora Carrington, and Vanessa Bell; published *Invitation to the Waltz* (1932) and its sequel *The Weather in the Streets* (1936), both later adapted for the BBC; had a great success with *The Ballad and the Source* (1944); also wrote *The Echoing Grove* (1953) and *A Sea-Grape Tree* (1976); served as president of English Center and International vice-president of International PEN; was a fellow of the Royal Society of Literature (member of Council of Authors). Named Commander of the British Empire (CBE, 1982). ❖ See also autobiography, *The Swan in the Evening* (Collins, 1967); Judy Simons, *Rosamond Lehmann* (St. Martin's, 1992); and *Women in World History.*

LEHMANN, Sonja (1979—). German field-hockey player. Born Sept 13, 1979, in Germany. ❖ Won a team gold medal at Athens Olympics (2004).

LEHMANN, Walter (1920–1995). See *Harwood, Gwen.*

LEHN, Unni (1977—). Norwegian soccer player. Born June 7, 1977, in Trondheim, Norway. ❖ Midfielder; played with Norwegian National team for 7 years; won a team gold medal at Sydney Olympics (2000); signed with WUSA's Carolina Courage (2002).

LEHNERT, Josefine (1894–1983). See *Pascalina, Sister.*

LEHR, Anna (1890–1974). American silent-screen actress. Name variations: Anne Lehr. Born Nov 17, 1890, in New York, NY; died Jan 22, 1974, in Santa Monica, CA; m. Sam McKim; children: Ann Dvorak (actress). ❖ Appeared in over 40 films, including *The White Scar, The Target, Grafters, Men, The Yellow Ticket, The Darkest Hour, A Child for Sale, The Cradle* and *Ruggles of Red Gap.*

LEHR, Baby Ann (1912–1979). See *Dvorak, Ann.*

LEHTONEN, Mirja (1942—). Finnish cross-country skier. Born Oct 19, 1942, in Kyynämöinen, Finland. ❖ Won a silver medal for 5 km and a bronze medal for 3 x 5 km relay at Innsbruck Olympics (1964).

LEI LI. Chinese softball player. Born in China. ❖ Won a silver medal at Atlanta Olympics (1996).

LEIBOVITZ, Annie (1949—). American photographer. Born Anna-Lou Leibovitz, Oct 2, 1949, in Westbury, CT; dau. of Samuel and Marilyn (Heit) Leibovitz (dance instructor); San Francisco Art Institute, BFA, 1971; also studied with Ralph Gibson; had long-term relationship with writer Susan Sontag; children: Sarah Cameron Leibovitz (b. 2001). ❖ Was principal photographer for *Rolling Stone* (1973–83); became contributing photographer for *Vanity Fair* (1983); became well known for portraits of political figures, musicians and athletes; published *Annie Leibovitz: Photographs* (1983) and *Women* (1999); produced the portraits campaign for American Express (1987), for which she won a Clio Award; founded the Annie Leibovitz Studio in New York City (1990); was 1 of only 2 living photographers to have an exhibition of her work at the Smithsonian National Portrait Gallery in Washington DC (1991).

LEICESTER, countess of.
See *Montfort, Amicia (fl. 1208).*
See *Eleanor of Montfort (1215–1275).*
See *Knollys, Lettice (c. 1541–1634).*

LEICHTER, Käthe (1895–1942). Austrian reformer. Name variations: Kathe Leichter; (pseudonyms) Anna Gärtner; Maria Mahler. Born Marianne Katharina Pick in Vienna, Austria, Aug 20, 1895; died near Magdeburg, Feb 1942; dau. of Josef Pick (prominent attorney); sister of Vally Weigl (1889–1982), composer and music therapist; attended Beamten-Töchter-Lyzeum, University of Vienna (1914); doctorate from University of Heidelberg (1918); m. Otto Leichter (1897–1973), journalist and Socialist politician), 1921; children: Heinz (b. 1924) and Franz (b. 1930). ❖ One of the most gifted women in the Austrian Social Democratic movement, wrote articles for the Social Democratic press and collected materials for large-scale sociological studies of working conditions of Austrian working class; with husband, became a leader of "New Left" faction within Austrian Social Democratic Party (late 1920s); though the party was banned with the rise of the Nazis (1934), remained in Vienna despite being Jewish; assisted husband in underground work of the Socialists and was active in the educational committee of the Revolutionary Socialist leadership group; arrested and regarded by Gestapo as one of their "biggest catches" (May 1938); sentenced to 4 months' imprisonment (Oct 1939) was moved instead to Ravensbrück concentration camp; near Magdeburg, was gassed in a railway train along with 1,500 other Jewish female prisoners. ❖ See also *Women in World History.*

LEIDER, Frida (1888–1975). German soprano. Born April 18, 1888, in Berlin, Germany; died June 4, 1975, in Berlin; studied with Otto Schwarz; m. Rudolf Deman (violinist). ❖ Leading interpreter of Wagnerian roles, made debut in Berlin (1915); was a member of Berlin State Opera (1923–40); appeared at Covent Garden (1924–38); was one of Bayreuth's greatest guest stars (1928–38), giving memorable performances as Brünnhilde and Isolde; appeared with Chicago Opera as a principal (1928), remaining for 4 seasons; debuted as Isolde at Metropolitan Opera (1933); appeared at Paris Opéra (1930–32); because husband was Jewish, left Berlin to join him in Switzerland (1940); after war, returned to Berlin, directing the Berlin State Opera's voice studio, then accepted a professorship at Berlin Hochschule für Musik (1948). ❖ See also autobiography *Playing My Part* (1966); and *Women in World History.*

LEIGH, Adèle (1928–2004). English soprano. Name variations: Adele Leigh. Born June 15, 1928, in London, England; died May 24, 2004; studied at Juilliard with Maggie Teyte; m. James Pease (American baritone, died 1967); m. Kurt Enderl (Austrian ambassador, died); no children. ❖ Principal soprano at Covent Garden for 8 years (1948–56), debuted there as Xenia in *Boris Godunov* (1948); appeared often in the works of Mozart, including as Cherubino in *The Marriage of Figaro,* Pamina in *The Magic Flute;* also sang Marzelline in *Fidelio,* the page Oscar in *Un Ballo in Maschera,* Susanna in *Figaro,* Aennchen in *Der Freischutz,* Sophie in *Der Rosenkavalier* and title role in *Manon;* was principal soprano at Vienna Volksoper (1963–72); often appeared on BBC radio and tv.

LEIGH, Arbor (1845–1895). See *Bevington, L.S.*

LEIGH, Arran (1846–1914). See *Bradley, Katharine Harris.*

LEIGH, Augusta (1784–1851). Influential sister of Lord Byron. Name variations: Augusta Byron; Mrs. George Leigh. Born Augusta Mary Byron in Paris, France, Jan 26, 1784; died of cancer, Nov 27, 1851; dau. of John Byron and Lady Carmarthen (formerly wife of Francis, Marquis of Carmarthen, later 5th duke of Leeds); aunt of Ada Byron, countess of Lovelace; m. her cousin Colonel George Leigh, 1807 (died 1850); children: Georgiana Augusta Leigh (b. Nov 4, 1808); Augusta Charlotte Leigh (b. Feb 9, 1811); George Henry John Leigh (b. June 3, 1812); (Elizabeth) Medora Leigh (b. April 15, 1814); Frederick George Leigh (b. May 9, 1816); Amelia Marianne Leigh (b. Nov 27, 1817); Henry Francis (b. Jan 28, 1820). ❖ The product of a scandalous liaison between John Byron, known as Mad John, and Lady Carmarthen (her mother was 8 months pregnant with her when she married John Byron and fled to Paris, then died in childbirth), was very close to half-brother Lord Byron, so close that there was some speculation that her daughter Medora was their daughter. ❖ See also *Women in World History.*

LEIGH, Carolyn (1926–1983). American lyricist. Born Carolyn Paula Rosenthal in the Bronx, NY, Aug 21, 1926; died in New York, NY, Nov 19, 1983; dau. of Henry Rosenthal and Sylvia Rosenthal; attended Queens College and New York University; m. David Wyn Cunningham Jr. (attorney), 1959 (div.). ❖ Major Broadway lyricist, wrote radio and advertising copy before landing a job as a lyricist for a music publisher (1951); wrote lyrics for "Young at Heart" (1954); collaborated with Mark

Charlap on 9 songs for *Peter Pan*, including "I'm Flying," "I Won't Grow Up" and "I've Got to Crow"; began collaboration with Cy Coleman (1957), turning out "Witchcraft," "Firefly" and "The Best is Yet to Come" (1961); collaborated with Coleman on 1st Broadway musical, *Wildcat*, which introduced "Hey, Look Me Over" and "High Hopes"; followed by that with *Little Me* (1962), which included "I've Got Your Number," "Real Live Girl" and "Here's to Me"; collaborated with Elmer Bernstein on *How Now, Dow Jones* (1967) and with Marvin Hamlisch for *Smiles*. ❖ See also *Women in World History*.

LEIGH, Dorothy Kempe (fl. 1616). British writer. Born Dorothy Kempe or Kemp in Finchingfield, Essex, England; dau. of Robert Kempe and Elizabeth (Higham) Kempe (dau. of Sir Clement Higham of Barrowhall, Suffolk); m. Ralph Leigh or Lee (soldier under the earl of Essex at Cadiz); children: 3 sons. ❖ Wrote book of advice for her sons, *The Mother's Blessing* (1616).

LEIGH, Frances Butler (1838–1910). American entrepreneur. Name variations: Fanny Butler. Born 1838; died 1910; dau. of Pierce Butler (Georgia plantation owner) and Fanny Kemble (English-born actress, author, abolitionist); m. Reverend James Wentworth Leigh, in 1871. ❖ Reconstruction-era plantation manager, worked to convert plantation to pay-basis (1867–71); moved to England with husband (1871); returned to plantation and repaired it to prosperity (1873). ❖ See also *Women in World History*.

LEIGH, Isla (1862–1913). See Cooper, Edith Emma.

LEIGH, Janet (1927–2004). American actress. Born Jeanette Helen Morrison, July 6, 1927, in Merced, CA; died Oct 3, 2004, in Beverly Hills, CA; attended College of the Pacific; m. John Carlyle, 1942 (annulled); m. Stanley Reames, 1946 (div. 1948); m. Tony Curtis (actor), 1951 (div. 1962); m. Robert Brandt (stockbroker), 1962; children: (3rd m.) Kelly Lee Curtis; Jamie Lee Curtis (actress). ❖ With no acting experience, co-starred with Van Johnson in debut film *The Romance of Rosy Ridge* (1947); remained in ingenue roles throughout early career; ranked as one of Hollywood's top stars (1950s), reached top of her form opposite Charlton Heston in Orson Welles' *Touch of Evil* (1968); had a plum supporting role in *Manchurian Candidate* (1962); appeared with daughter Jamie in *The Fog* (1980); other films include *Words and Music* (1948), *Little Women* (1949), *The Forsyte Saga* (1949), *Strictly Dishonorable* (1951), *Angels in the Outfield* (1951), *Houdini* (1953), *Walking My Baby Back Home* (1953), *Prince Valiant* (1954), *The Black Shield of Falworth* (1954), *My Sister Eileen* (1955), *The Vikings* (1958), *Bye Bye Birdie* (1963), *Wives and Lovers* (1963), *Harper* (1966) and *One Is a Lonely Number;* made stage debut with Jack Cassidy on Broadway in *Murder Among Friends* (1975); wrote *There Really Was a Hollywood* (1984), as well as *Psycho: Behind the Scenes of the Classic Thriller* (1995) and the novel *House of Destiny*. Nominated for Academy Award for *Psycho*. ❖ See also *Women in World History*.

LEIGH, Stuart (1827–1886). See Clarke, Mary Bayard.

LEIGH, Vivien (1913–1967). English actress. Name variations: Lady Olivier. Born Vivian [sic] Mary Hartley in Darjeeling, India, Nov 5, 1913; died in London, England, July 7, 1967, of tuberculosis; only child of Gertrude and Ernest Hartley; attended Royal Academy of Dramatic Arts in London; m. Hubert Leigh Holman (barrister), 1932 (div. 1940); m. Laurence Olivier (actor), 1940 (div. 1960); children: (1st m.) Suzanne Holman. ❖ Two-time Academy Award-winning actress who achieved international stardom for her portrayal of Scarlett O'Hara in *Gone With the Wind*, appeared in 1st film *The Village Squire* (1934), followed by *Look Up and Laugh*; made stage debut in *The Green Sash* (1935), gained fame in *The Mask of Virtue*, then appeared in a number of successful light dramas in the West End before achieving international stardom in *Gone With the Wind* (1939), for which she won the Academy Award for Best Actress; won a 2nd Oscar (1951) for her portrayal of Blanche DuBois in film version of *A Streetcar Named Desire;* suffered from mental illness later in career, eventually being diagnosed with bipolar disorder; other films include *Fire Over England* (1937), *Dark Journey* (1937), *A Yank at Oxford* (1938), *Sidewalks of London* (1938), *Waterloo Bridge* (1940), *That Hamilton Woman* (1941), *Caesar and Cleopatra* (1946), *Anna Karenina* (1948), *The Deep Blue Sea* (1955), *The Roman Spring of Mrs. Stone* (1961) and *Ship of Fools* (1965). ❖ See also Hugo Vickers, *Vivien Leigh* (Hamish Hamilton, 1988); and *Women in World History*.

LEIGH-SMITH, Barbara (1827–1891). See Bodichon, Barbara.

LEIGHTON, Clare (1899–1989). British illustrator and wood engraver. Born Clare Veronica Hope Leighton, April 12, 1898, in London,

England; died Nov 4, 1989, in Watertown, CT; dau. of Robert (literary critic and journalist) and Marie (Connor) Leighton (novelist); attended Brighton School of Art, Slade School of Fine Art, University of London, 1921–23, and London County Council Central School of Arts and Crafts; m. Henry Noel Brailsford; lived in Woodbury, Connecticut. ❖ Along with Wanda Gág, was one of the foremost practitioners of wood engraving of her day; won 1st prize at International Exhibition of Engraving at Chicago Art Institute (1930); represented England in wood-engraving at International Exhibition in Venice (1934); awarded DFA, Colby College (1940); immigrated to US (1939); became a naturalized citizen (1945); wrote and illustrated *The Farmer's Year* (1933), *Four Hedges*, a month-by-month journal of her garden in the Chiltern Hills (1935), *Country Matters* (1937), *Sometime, Never* (1939), *Southern Harvest* (1942), along with several books for children; also illustrated Brontë's *Wuthering Heights*, Wilder's *The Bridge of San Luis Rey*, Tomlinson's *The Sea and the Jungle*, and Hardy's *The Return of the Native;* works reside in permanent collection of Victoria and Albert Museum, British Museum, National Galleries of Stockholm and Canada, Boston Fine Arts Museum, Baltimore Museum, and Metropolitan Museum of Art in NY. ❖ See also autobiography *Tempestuous Petticoat* (Reinhart, 1947).

LEIGHTON, Crissy (1970—). See Ahmann-Leighton, Crissy.

LEIGHTON, Dorothea (1908–1989). American medical anthropologist. Name variations: Dorothea Cross Leighton. Born Dorothea Cross on Sept 2, 1908, in Lunenburg, MA; died 1989; dau. of Frederick Cushing Cross and Dorothea Farquhar Cross (graduate of Bryn Mawr); graduate of Bryn Mawr, 1930; Johns Hopkins School of Medicine, MD, 1936; also attended Columbia University; m. Alexander H. Leighton (psychiatrist). ❖ Known particularly for studies of the Navajo, conducted research focused on psychiatric problems among Native American Groups, including Navajo of New Mexico and Inuit of Alaska; became Special Physician for US Office of Indian Affairs (1942); with husband, commissioned by Bureau of Indian Affairs (BIA) to write *The Navaho Door* (published 1944); participated in important psychiatric epidemiological study of rural population in Stirling Country, Nova Scotia, and coauthored final report on study entitled *The Character of Danger* (1963); taught at institutions including Cornell University, University of North Carolina, University of California at San Francisco, and University of California at Berkeley; served as 1st president of Society for Medical Anthropology. Major publications include *The Navaho* (with Clyde Kluckhohn, 1946), *Children of the People* (with Kluckhohn, 1948), and *People of the Middle Place* (with John Adair, 1966).

LEIGHTON, Margaret (1922–1976). British actress. Born Feb 26, 1922, near Birmingham, England; died Jan 13, 1976; dau. of Augustus George Leighton (businessman) and Doris Isobel (Evans) Leighton; attended Church of England College; m. Max Reinhardt (publisher), 1947 (div. 1955); m. Laurence Harvey (actor), 1957 (div. 1961); m. Michael Wilding (actor), 1964. ❖ Made acting debut as Dorothy in *Laugh With Me* at Birmingham Rep (1938); joined Old Vic, making London debut as Troll King's Daughter in *Peer Gynt* (1944); came to prominence as Raina in *Arms and the Man* (1944); went on to a variety of roles, including Queen Elizabeth (Elizabeth Woodville) in *Richard III*, Yolena in *Uncle Vanya*, Roxanne in *Cyrano*, and Sheila Birling in *An Inspector Calls*; made NY debut with Old Vic (1946), playing Lady Percy (Elizabeth Percy [1371–1417]) in *Henry IV* (Part I and II); earned critical acclaim for undertaking 3 roles in a single play, *The Sleeping Clergyman* (1947); made film debut in *Bonnie Prince Charlie* (1947), followed by *The Go-Between* (1971) for which she was nominated for Academy Award for Best Supporting Actress; appeared in successful London revival of *The Three Sisters* (1951); joined Shakespeare Memorial Theater at Stratford-on-Avon (1952), appearing as Lady Macbeth (Gruoch); turned in much-lauded performances in *Separate Tables* (1954), resulting in Tony award; received 2nd Tony for performance as Hannah Jelkes in *The Night of the Iguana* (1961); appeared as Elena in *Reunion in Vienna* to raves (1972); other films include *The Winslow Boy* (1948), *Under Capricorn* (1949), *The Astonished Heart* (1950), *Calling Bull-Dog Drummond* (1951), *The Holly and the Ivy* (1952), *The Constant Husband* (1955), *Waltz of the Toreadors* (1962), *The Madwoman of Chaillot* (1969) and *A Bequest to the Nation* (1973). Named Commander of the British Empire (CBE, 1974). ❖ See also *Women in World History*.

LEIJONHUFVUD, Margareta (1514–1551). See Margareta Leijonhufvud.

LEININGEN, princess of.
See Mary of Baden (1834–1899).
See Feodore of Hohenlohe-Langenburg (1866–1932).
See Marie of Russia (1907–1951).
See Kira of Leiningen (b. 1930).

LEINSTER, countess of. See Kielmansegge, Sophia Charlotte von (1673–1725).

LEINSTER, duchess of. See Lennox, Emily.

LEISTENSCHNEIDER, Nicole (1967—). West German runner. Born May 10, 1967, in Germany. ❖ At Los Angeles Olympics, won a bronze medal in 4x400-meter relay (1984).

LEITCH, Cecil (1891–1977). British golfer. Name variations: Charlotte Leitch. Born Charlotte Cecilia Pitcairn Leitch, April 13, 1891, in Silloth, Cumberland, England; died Sept 16, 1977, at home in London; sister of Edith Guedalla and May Millar (both champion golfers). ❖ Made debut in golf at British Ladies' championship at St. Andrews (1908); defeated Harold Hilton, leading amateur of the day, in the 1st challenge match to test the disparity between men and women players, an upset that received at least as much attention in suffragist circles as in the golfing world (1910); retired from competition (1928), having won the French championship 5 times, English championship twice, and the Canadian championship once. Elected to American Golf Hall of Fame (1967) and published Golf for Girls (1911), Golf (1922) and Golf Simplified (1924).

LEITCH, Charlotte (1891–1977). See Leitch, Cecil.

LEITCH, Moira (fl. late 1300s). Paramour of the king of Scotland. Fl. in late 1300s; paramour of Robert II (1316–1390), king of Scotland (r. 1371–1390); children: (with Robert II) John Stewart, sheriff of Bute.

LEITZEL, Lillian (1892–1931). German aerial gymnast. Name variations: Lillian Pelikan. Born Leopoldina Alitza Pelikan, in 1892 (some sources cite 1891), in Breslau, Germany; died Feb 13, 1931, in Copenhagen, Denmark; dau. of Nellie Pelikan (aerial performer); m. Clyde Ingalls (executive with Ringling Brothers-Barnum & Bailey Circus), 1920 (div. 1924); m. Alfredo Codona (trapeze artist), July 1928. ❖ With mother, performed in NY with Barnum & Bailey Circus (1908); remained in US, performing on vaudeville circuit; featured in Ringling Brothers center ring (1914); when Ringling and Barnum circuses merged, became featured attraction (1919); was fatally injured during a performance in Copenhagen, when the swivel on a ring broke and she fell to the ground. ❖ See also Women in World History.

LEJEUNE, C.A. (1897–1973). British film critic. Born Caroline Alice Lejeune in Didsbury, Manchester, England, Mar 27, 1897; died 1973; dau. of Adam Edward Lejeune and Jane Louisa (MacLaren) Lejeune; graduate of University of Manchester, 1921; m. Edward Roffe Thompson; children: Anthony. ❖ England's 1st full-time film critic, whose writings for The Observer covered more than 3 decades of filmmaking, recognized the importance of newly emerging cinematic styles, including those in films being made in Russia; contributed music reviews to Manchester Guardian, then critiqued films, signing column C.A.L. (1922–28); worked for The Observer (1928–60). ❖ See also memoir Thank You For Having Me (Stacey, 1971); and Women in World History.

LEJEUNE, Elisabeth (1963—). Dutch field-hockey player. Born July 28, 1963, in Netherlands. ❖ At Seoul Olympics, won a bronze medal in team competition (1988).

LEJEUNE, Marie-Henriette (1762–1860). See Ross, Marie-Henriette LeJeune.

LEJEUNE-ROSS, Marie-Henriette (1762–1860). See Ross, Marie-Henriette LeJeune.

LEJONHUFVUD, Margareta (1514–1551). See Margareta Leijonhufvud.

L.E.L. (1802–1838). See Landon, Letitia Elizabeth.

LELAND, Sara (1941—). American ballet dancer. Name variations: Sara Leland Harrington. Born Sara Leland Harrington, Aug 2, 1941, in Melrose, MA. ❖ Made stage debut in Virginia Williams' Don Quixote Pas de Deux with New England Civic Ballet; created role of Juliet for Williams in her Young Loves (1957); joined Robert Joffrey Ballet (1959), where she was featured in Moncion's Pastoral and Balanchine's Pas de Dix; joined New York City Ballet (1960), where she created roles in Balanchine's Jewels (1967), PAMTGG (1971), and Union Jack (1976); was assistant and regisseur to Jerome Robbins and performed in premieres of his Dances at a Gathering (1969), The Goldberg Variations (1971) and Scherzo Fantastique (1972).

LELAS, Zana (1970—). Yugoslavian basketball player. Born May 28, 1970, in Yugoslavia. ❖ At Seoul Olympics, won a silver medal in team competition (1988).

LELKESNE-TOMANN, Rozalia (1950—). Hungarian handball player. Name variations: Rozalia Tomann. Born Aug 14, 1950, in Hungary. ❖ At Montreal Olympics, won a bronze medal in team competition (1976).

LE MAIR, H. Willebeek (1889–1966). Dutch illustrator of children's books. Name variations: adopted name "Saida" after marriage. Born Henriette Willebeek Le Mair in Rotterdam, Netherlands, April 23, 1889; died 1966; m. Baron van Tuyll van Serooskerken, 1920. ❖ At 15, published 1st book, Premières Rondes Enfantines (1904); opened exclusive school in home (c. 1910) and used young students as models, further developing a distinctive style; commissioned to do a series of nursery-rhyme illustrations for Augener, an English music publisher (1911), which included Our Old Nursery Rhymes (1911), Little Songs of Long Ago (1912), and Old Dutch Nursery Rhymes (1917); illustrated A Gallery of Children by Milne (1925), followed by Stevenson's A Child's Garden of Verses, Twenty Jakarta Tales, and Christmas Carols for Young Children; converted to Sufism and supporting various charitable causes. ❖ See also Women in World History.

LEMASS, Eileen (1932—). Irish politician. Born July 1932 in Cork City, Ireland; m. Noel Lemass (TD, Dublin South West, 1956–76, and son of Sean Lemass, Taoiseach, 1959–66). ❖ Following the death of husband, unsuccessfully contested a by-election representing Fianna Fáil for Dublin South West (1976); elected to the 21st–22nd Dáil for Dublin Ballyfermot (1977–82) and 24th Dáil for Dublin West (1982–87).

LE MAY DOAN, Catriona (1970—). Canadian speedskater. Name variations: Catriona Le May-Doan. Born Catriona Le May, Dec 23, 1970, in Saskatoon, Saskatchewan, Canada; m. Bart Doan (rodeo rider). ❖ Was Saskatchewan Female Athlete of the Year (1994); at World Sprint championships, won a gold medal (1996), silver (1976), and gold (1998, 1999, 2001, 2002), all for the 500 meters; at World Single Distance championships, won a gold medal for the 500 and silver for the 1,000 (1998), a gold for the 500 and bronze for the 1,000 (1999), a bronze for 500 (2000), and gold for the 500 and bronze for 1,000 (2001); won a bronze for the 1,000 meters and a gold medal for the 500 meters at Nagano (1998), the 1st Canadian woman to win an Olympic gold medal in speedskating; won World Cup 1st overall for 500 (1997, 1998, 1999, 2001) and for 1,000 (1998); won 9 out of 10 World Cup 500-meter races, placing 1st overall (2002); carried the flag for Canada at Salt Lake City Olympics and won a gold medal in the 500 meters (2002); won the World and World Cup title (2002), with a 20-race victory streak; broke the world record 8 times; retired (2003). Was a 3-time recipient of Canadian Female Athlete of Year award (1998, 20001, 2002); received Lou Marsh Award (2002).

LEMEL, Nathalie (1827–1921). French socialist, anarchist, and Communard. Born 1827; died 1921. ❖ Member of the Socialist International, became involved in radical politics during epidemic of strikes and growing spread of trade-unionism in France (1860s); once a bookbinder, founded a workers' restaurant with another bookbinder during Paris Commune of 1871, but was deported with Louise Michel after fall of the Commune; later returned to France (1880) and continued work with socialist and feminist groups until start of WWI.

LEMHENYINE-TASS, Olga (1929—). Hungarian gymnast. Born Mar 28, 1929, in Hungary. ❖ At London Olympics, won a silver medal in team all-around (1948); at Helsinki Olympics, won a bronze medal in teams all-around, portable apparatus, and a silver medal in team all-around (1952); at Melbourne Olympics, won a bronze medal in vault, a silver medal in team all-around, and a gold medal in teams all-around, portable apparatus (1956).

LEMLICH, Clara (1888–1982). American labor leader. Name variations: Clara Lemlich Shavelson. Born in Ukraine, 1888; died in Resada, CA, July 12, 1982; married; children: 3. ❖ With family, fled Ukraine during a pogrom (1903); at 15, began work in a New York City shirtwaist shop; joined with several other young garment workers to form the International Ladies Garment Workers' Union (ILGWU) Local 25 (1906); led the 1909 "Uprising of the 30,000" strike (1909); organized for the industrial section of NY Woman's Suffrage Party (1910–12); co-founded Communist Party-USA. ❖ See also Women in World History.

LEMMON, Sarah Plummer (1836–1923). American botanist. Born Sarah Plummer in New Gloucester, Maine, 1836; died in Stockton, CA, 1923; attended Female College, Worcester, Massachusetts; attended Cooper Union, NY; m. John Gill Lemmon (botanist), 1880 (died 1909). ❖ Was a hospital nurse during Civil War; became a noted collector and painter of plants after marriage; made a series of 80 sketches of flowers in the field which won a prize at World's Exposition (1884–85); also created a series of watercolor paintings of flora found on the Pacific slope; is credited with several scientific papers, and contributed occasionally to husband's works; discovered a new genus of plants (1882) which were later named *Plummera floribunda*.

LEMNITZ, Tiana (1897–1994). German soprano. Born Tiana Luise Lemnitz in Metz, Germany, Oct 26, 1897; died in 1994; studied with Anton Kohmann. ❖ Appeared at Aachen (1922–28), Hanover (1928–33), and Dresden (1933–34); became a permanent member of Berlin Staatsoper (1934–56); appeared as Arabella in premiere Richard Strauss' opera; appeared as Eva in *Die Meistersinger* and Octavian in *Der Rosenkavalier*, one of her most celebrated roles (1936–38); after war, continued to perform in Europe and America; retired (1960) and became director of Berlin State Opera Studio. ❖ See also *Women in World History*.

LEMOINE, Angélina (1843—). French murderer (accused). Born 1843 in Chinon, France; dau. of Denis Jules Lemoine and Victoire Mingot Lemoine. ❖ Daughter of prominent local lawyer, began affair with hired family servant and became pregnant; upon death of child, was charged with infanticide along with mother; though accused of complicity was acquitted (1859), while mother was convicted and sentenced to 20 years in prison.

LEMOINE, Gennie (b. 1912). *See Lemoine-Luccioni, Eugénie.*

LEMOINE, Marie (1875–1910). *See Weber, Jeanne.*

LEMOINE, Marie Victoire (1754–1820). French painter. Born in France, 1754; died 1820; studied with F.G. Ménageot (1744–1816); never married; no children. ❖ Exhibited some 20 paintings in the Salon de la Correspondance (1779 and 1785), and in the official Academy Salon (1796–1814); best-known painting, *Interior of the Atelier of a Woman Painter*, was initially exhibited in Salon of 1796 and now hangs in Metropolitan Museum of Art in NY. ❖ See also *Women in World History*.

LEMOINE-LUCCIONI, Eugénie (1912—). French translator and literary critic. Name variations: Gennie Lemoine; Gennie Luccioni. Born 1912 in France. ❖ Psychoanalyst, was member of École Freudienne; published short-story collections *Cercles* (1946) and *Marches* (1977); also published psychoanalytic works, including (with Paul Lemoine) *Le Psychodrame* (1968), *Partage de femmes* (1976), *La Robe* (1983), *Psychanalyse pour la vie quotidienne* (1987), and *Une politique de la psychanalyse*.

LEMON, Margaretta Louisa (1860–1953). English ornithologist and conservationist. Born Margaretta Louisa Smith, Nov 22, 1860, in UK; died July 8, 1953; m. Frank E. Lemon, 1892. ❖ Founding member and honorary secretary (1893–1904) of Royal Society for the Protection of Birds (RSPB), played a key role in the successful growth of RSPB.

LEMOND, Barbara (1918–2005). *See Brewster, Barbara.*

LEMOS, countess of (c. 1640–1706). *See Borja, Ana de.*

LEMP, Rebecca (d. 1590). German accused of witchcraft. Burned at the stake as a witch in Nördlingen, Swabia, Germany, 1590; m. Peter Lemp (accountant); children: 6. ❖ Fell victim to 2 ambitious local lawyers and a burgomaster and was one of 32 highly respected women accused of witchcraft in Nördlingen (1590); arrested and jailed while husband was out of town, was certain she had nothing to fear because she had done nothing wrong; was tortured on 5 occasions and eventually confessed. ❖ See also *Women in World History*.

LEMPEREUR, Ingrid (1969—). Belgian swimmer. Born June 26, 1969, in Belgium. ❖ At Los Angeles Olympics, won a bronze medal in 200-meter breaststroke (1984).

LEMPICKA, Tamara de (1898–1980). Polish painter. Name variations: Baroness Kuffner; Baroness Tamara de Lempicka-Kuffner; La Belle Polonaise. Born Tamara Gorska in Warsaw, Poland, 1898; died in Cuernavaca, Mexico, Mar 18, 1980; dau. of Boris Gorski (attorney for a French trading company) and Malvina (Decler) Gorska; m. Tadeusz Lempicki (Petrograd attorney), 1916 (div. 1928); m. Raoul Kuffner

(Hungarian baron), 1933 (died 1962); children: (1st m.) Baroness Kizette de Lempicka-Foxhall. ❖ High-profile artist of post-Cubist 1920s and neo-classicist 1930s and star of Art Deco movement, was rediscovered (1970s); when husband was arrested during "Red Terror," fled to Copenhagen where she eventually helped secured his release; immigrated to postwar Paris; studied painting with post-symbolist Maurice Denis at Académie Ranson and with muted-Cubist André Lhote; sold 1st paintings through Gallerie Colette Weill; met with immediate financial success and began to acquire impressive contacts with Salon des Indépendants, Salon d'Automne, and Salon des Moins de Trente Ans; surrounded herself with the cultural elite, painting portraits of Russian emigres, impoverished nobility, and the *neauveau riche*; established reputation as a leading Art Deco artist at Exposition Internationale des Artes Décoratifs et Industriels Modernes (1925); self-portrait *Autoportrait* (also known as *Tamara in the Green Bugatti*), was celebrated; painting of daughter, *Kizette on the Balcony*, won 1st prize at Exposition Internationale des Beaux-Arts in Bordeaux, while *Kizette's First Communion*, won bronze medal at Exposition Internationale in Poznan, Poland (1927); with the Nazi threat, left France and took a house in Beverly Hills, CA (1939); sponsored her own solo exhibitions at Paul Reinhart Gallery in Los Angeles, at Julian Levy Gallery in NY, Courvoisier Galleries in San Francisco, and Milwaukee Institute of Art; moved to NY (1943), but her production had slowed. The offbeat play *Tamara: a Living Movie* opened in Toronto, Canada (1981); ran in Los Angeles (1984–93) and NY (1987–89). ❖ See also Baroness Kizette de Lempicka-Foxhall and Charles Phillips, *Passion by Design: The Art and Times of Tamara de Lempicka* (Phaidon, 1987); Gilles Néret, *Tamara de Lempicka, 1898–1980* (Köln, Germany: Benedikt Taschen, 1992); and *Women in World History*.

LEMS, Tina Yuan. *See Yuan, Tina.*

LEMSINE, Aicha (1942—). Algerian novelist. Born 1942 in Nemencha, Algeria. ❖ Works, which focus on roles of women in Algeria, include *La Chrysalide* (1976) and *Ciel de Porphyre* (1978).

LENCLOS, Anne de (1623–1705). *See Lenclos, Ninon de.*

L'ENCLOS, Ninon de (1623–1705). *See Lenclos, Ninon de.*

LENCLOS, Ninon de (1623–1705). French courtesan and salonnière. Name variations: true 1st name "Anne" but usually called "Ninon"; last name sometimes given as "L'Enclos" or "Lanclos," the historically correct spelling. Pronunciation: nee-NŌ duh lā-KLO. Born Anne de Lanclos, Jan 9, 1623, in Paris, France (some sources erroneously cite Nov 11, 1620); died in Paris, Oct 17, 1705; dau. of Henri de Lanclos (minor noble) and Marie-Barbe de la Marche; largely self-taught; never married; children: (with Louis de Mornay, marquis de Villarceaux) Louis de Mornay (1652–1730), later chevalier de La Boissière. ❖ Perhaps the most famous of French 17th-century courtesans, who enticed clients and lovers with an irresistible mixture of wit, charm and intellect, struggled throughout to gain financial independence and overcome the social stigmatism attached to her non-conformist lifestyle; was forced by unfortunate circumstances into prostitution; moved from lover to lover until late in life; slowly attained a degree of social acceptance, thanks to a reputable intellect and the ability to maneuver adroitly within the bounds of permissible behavior; voluntarily entered into convents (1643 and 1648); forcibly committed into a refuge-home for "fallen women" (1656); always emerged from these socially cleansing retreats with a slightly increased degree of respectability; attained complete financial independence (1670s); hosted a small but well-known salon during last decades of life, entertaining both the high Parisian nobility and respected men of letters. ❖ See also Cecil Austin, *The Immortal Ninon: A Character-Study of Ninon de l'Enclos* (Routledge, 1927); M. (Antoine) Bret, *Ninon de Lenclos* (Humphreys, 1904); Douxmenil, *The Memoirs of Ninon de Lenclos* (1761); and *Women in World History*.

LENCZYK, Grace (1927—). American golfer. Name variations: Mrs. Robert Cronin; Grace Lenczyk Cronin. Born Sept 12, 1927, in Newington, CT; m. Robert Cronin. ❖ Won USGA Women's Amateur (1948); won Canadian Women's Amateur (1947 & 1948); member of the Curtis Cup team (1948).

LENDE, Karen (1958—). *See O'Connor, Karen.*

LENDER, Marcelle (fl. 1890–1914). French actress. Born Marie Bastien in France. ❖ Famed music-hall artist of 1890s Paris, later appeared at the Gymnase as Gisèle Vaudreuil in *L'Eventail* (1907), at the Variétés as Thérèse in *Le roi* (1908) and Suzy Barsac in *Le Bonheur sous la main* (1912), and at the Comédie-Marigny as Mme Gréhart in *Le mannequin*

(1914); also appeared in *Grand-Père, Les baisers de minuit, Le Vieux Marcheur, Peg de mon coeur,* and *La possession;* was the subject of Toulouse-Lautrec's "Marcelle Lender Dancing the Bolero in 'Chilpéric'" (1895–96), along with 17 related lithographs.

LENDORFF, Gertrud (1900–1986). Swiss novelist. Born May 13, 1900 in Lausen, Switzerland; died July 26, 1986, in Basel, Switzerland; studied in Paris, Munich and Basel. ❖ Works, which often focus on women, include *Die salige Frau* (1935) and *Timdala* (1937); also wrote radio play *Frau Oberst* (1953).

LENEHAN, Leslie (1956—). *See Burr, Leslie.*

LENG, Virginia (1955—). British equestrian. Name variations: Ginny Leng; Virginia Holgate; Virginia Holgate-Leng. Born Virginia Holgate, Feb 1955, in England. ❖ At Los Angeles, won a team silver medal and a bronze indiv. medal on Priceless, becoming the 1st woman to win an indiv. Olympic 3-day event medal (1984); won the gold medal at the European championships for indiv. on Priceless (1985), on Night Cap (1987), on Master Craftsman (1989), as well as team gold (1981, 1985, 1987, 1989); won a gold medal at World championships for indiv. on Priceless (1986), as well as team gold (1982, 1986); won Badminton on Priceless (1985) and on Master Craftsman (1989); won Burghley on Priceless (1983), on Night Cap (1984), on Priceless (EC, 1985), on Murphy Himself (1986), on Master Craftsman (EC, 1989); at Seoul Olympics, won a bronze indiv. medal on Master Craftsman (1988) and a team silver (1988).

L'ENGLE, Madeleine (1918—). American writer. Name variations: Madeleine Camp, Madeleine Camp Franklin L'Engle. Pronunciation: Leng-*el*. Born Madeleine L'Engle Camp, Nov 28, 1918, in New York, NY; dau. of Charles Wadsworth Camp (foreign correspondent and author) and Madeleine Barnett Camp (pianist); Smith College, BA (with honors), 1941; attended New School for Social Research, 1941–42; Columbia University, graduate study, 1960–61; m. Hugh Franklin (actor), Jan 26, 1946 (died Sept 1986); children: Josephine Franklin Jones (who m. Alan W. Jones); (adopted) Maria Rooney; Bion Franklin. ❖ Author of the popular *A Wrinkle in Time* and "Crosswick journals," had active career in theater (1941–47); taught at St. Hilda's and St. Hugh's School, NY (1960–66); became librarian and writer-in-residence, Cathedral of St. John the Divine, New York (1966); was a writer-in-residence, Ohio State University, Columbus (1970) and University of Rochester, NY (1972); writings include *The Small Rain* (1945), *And Both Were Young* (1949), *The Arm of the Starfish* (1965), *A Wind in the Door* (1973), *Dragons in the Waters* (1976), *A Swiftly Tilting Planet* (1978), *Walking on Water* (1980), *A Severed Wasp* (1982), *And It Was Good* (1983), *Many Waters* (1986), *Glimpses of Grace* (1996), *A Live Coal in the Sea* (1996), as well as the "Austin Family" series. Won Newbery Medal (1963) and Lewis Carroll Shelf Award (1965), for *A Wrinkle in Time;* won Austrian State Literary Prize (1969), for *The Moon by Night;* awarded University of Southern Mississippi Silver Medallion (1978) for "an outstanding contribution to the field of children's literature"; given Smith Medal (1980) and Regina Medal (1984). ❖ See also *Women in World History.*

LENGLEN, Suzanne (1899–1938). French tennis player. Born Suzanne Rachel Flore Lenglen, May 24, 1899, in Compiègne, France; died July 4, 1938, in Paris. ❖ French tennis champion, who won Wimbledon title 6 times, is considered the greatest female player in the history of the game; won 1st Wimbledon championship (1919); won gold medals in singles and mixed doubles in Olympic competition (1920); won 6 French titles; won 5 Wimbledon titles (1920, 1921, 1922, 1923, 1925); collected 269 out of 270 match titles (1919–26). ❖ See also Larry Englemann, *The Goddess and the American Girl: The Story of Suzanne Lenglen and Helen Wills* (Oxford U. Press, 1988).

LENIHAN, Winifred (1898–1964). American actress. Born Dec 6, 1898, in NYC; died July 27, 1964, in Sea Cliff, LI, NY; m. Frank Wheeler. ❖ Made stage debut as Belline in *The Betrothal* (1918); was 1st American actress to play title role in Shaw's *St. Joan* (1923); also appeared in *For the Defense, The Dover Road, Major Barbara* and *Black Limelight;* founded and was the 1st director of Theatre Guild's School of Acting (1925); also directed for radio.

LENIN, Nadezhda or Nadya (1869–1939). *See Krupskaya, Nadezhda.*

LENJA, Lotte (1898–1981). *See Lenya, Lotte.*

LENNART, Isobel (1915–1971). American playwright and screenwriter. Born May 18, 1915, in Brooklyn, NY; died in an automobile accident, Jan 25, 1971, in Hemet, CA; m. John Harding (actor); children: 1 son, 1 daughter. ❖ As an MGM staff writer, wrote musicals, such as *Skirts Ahoy!* (1952) and *Merry Andrew* (1958), and romantic comedies, such as *The Girl Next Door* (1953) and *Meet Me in Las Vegas* (1956); adapted comedies like *Please Don't Eat the Daisies* (1960) and *Two For the Seesaw* (1962); also adapted Tennessee Williams' *Period of Adjustment* (1962); wrote the stage musical *Funny Girl* (1963), about comedian Fanny Brice, then adapted the play for the screen; other credits include *The Affairs of Martha* (1942), *Anchors Aweigh* (1945), *It Happened in Brooklyn* (1947) and *The Inn of the Sixth Happiness* (1958). Nominated for Academy Award for screenplay adaptation for *The Sundowners* (1960). ❖ See also *Women in World History.*

LENNGREN, Anna Maria (1754–1817). Swedish poet. Born Anna Malmstedt, June 18, 1754, Uppsala, Sweden; died Mar 8, 1817; dau. of Magnus Brynolf Malmstedt (1724–1798, lecturer at Uppsala University); m. Carl Peter Lenngren (councillor at Royal Board of Commerce and later editor of the radical *Stockholms Posten*), 1780 (died 1827). ❖ Popular poet who often satirized the upper classes, first published in periodicals and contributed anonymously to husband's newspaper; published *The Conseillen* (1777), *Den glada festen* (The Merry Festival, 1796), *Pojkarne* (The Boys, 1797). Many of her poems have been set to music.

LENNON, Yoko Ono (1933—). *See Ono, Yoko.*

LENNOX, Annie (1954—). Scottish pop singer. Name variations: Eurythmics. Born Dec 25, 1954, in Aberdeen, Aberdeenshire, Scotland; attended Royal Academy of Music; had relationship with David A. Stewart (musician and composer), 1977–81; m. Radha Raman, 1984 (div. 1985); m. Uri Fruchtmann, 1988 (div. 2000); children: (2nd m.) 2 daughters, Lola and Taia. ❖ With David A. Stewart, formed The Tourists (1977) and recorded 3 albums before splitting up in 1980; remained with Stewart to form the Eurythmics (1980) and released such albums as *Sweet Dreams* (Are Made of This, 1982), *Touch* (1983), *Be Yourself Tonight* (1985), *Revenge* (1986), *Savage* (1987), *We Too Are One* (1989) and *Peace* (1999); launched solo career with the album *Diva* (1992), followed by *Bare* (2003); sang "Into the West" for film *The Lord of the Rings: The Return of the King* (2003).

LENNOX, Avril (1956—). Scottish gymnast. Born April 26, 1956, in Scotland. ❖ Won Scottish nationals (1972); won British nationals four years in a row (1974–77); won Champions Cup (1973, 1974, 1976), All-England championships (1973–75); retired (1977) due to injury; formed her own gymnastics club and was coach of British team for international competitions. Named Member of the British Empire (MBE, 1978) for services to sport of gymnastics.

LENNOX, Caroline (1723–1774). English baroness. Name variations: Lady Holland; Caroline Fox. Born Mar 1723 in London, England; died July 1774 in London; dau. of Charles Lennox, 2nd duke of Richmond, and Sarah Cadogan (d. 1751); great-granddau. of Charles II, king of England, and Louise de Kéroüaille; m. Henry Fox, in 1741; children: Stephen Fox (b. 1748); Charles Fox (b. 1749); sister of Emily Lennox (1731–1814), Louisa Lennox (1743–1821), Sarah Lennox (1745–1826). ❖ One of four aristocratic daughters of the duke and duchess of Richmond, renowned for their beauty and intelligence; eloped with Henry Fox (1741), a member of Parliament, causing a major scandal. ❖ See also Stella Tillyard, *Aristocrats: Caroline, Emily, Louisa and Sarah Lennox* (Farrar, 1994); and *Women in World History.*

LENNOX, Charlotte (1720–1804). English-American novelist and poet. Name variations: (pseudonym) Perdita. Born Charlotte Ramsay in NY, 1720; died in England, Jan 4, 1804; dau. of Colonel James Ramsey (lieutenant-governor of NY); m. Alexander Lennox, 1748; children: 1 daughter, 1 son. ❖ Moved to London (1735) and began writing; became friends with Samuel Richardson and Samuel Johnson; writings include *The Life of Harriot Stuart* (1751), *The Female Quixote; or the Adventures of Arabella* (1752), and *Shakespear illustrated* (1753–54), in which she maintained that Shakespeare had spoiled his borrowed stories by adding unnecessary intrigues and incidents; wrote the play *The Sister,* edited 11 editions of monthly *Lady's Museum,* and trans. many books from the French, including memoirs of the Duc de Sully, the countess of Berci, and Madame de Maintenon. ❖ See also *Women in World History.*

LENNOX, countess of.
See Montgomery, Margaret (fl. 1438).
See Isabel (d. 1457?).
See Hamilton, Elizabeth (c. 1480–?).

See Stewart, Anne (fl. 1515).
See Douglas, Margaret (1515–1578).
See Stewart, Elizabeth (fl. 1578).
See Cavendish, Elizabeth (d. 1582).

LENNOX, duchess of. *See Stuart, Frances (1647–1702).*

LENNOX, Emily (1731–1814). Duchess of Leinster. Name variations: Lady Kildare; Emily Fitzgerald. Born Emilia Mary Lennox, Oct 1731, in London, England; died Mar 1814 in London; dau. of Charles Lennox, 2nd duke of Richmond, and Sarah Cadogan (d. 1751); sister of Caroline Lennox (1723–1774), Louisa Lennox (1743–1821), and Sarah Lennox (1745–1826); great-granddau. of Charles II, king of England, and Louise de Kéroüaille; m. James Fitzgerald, earl of Kildare and duke of Leinster, 1747; m. William Ogilvie (her children's tutor), 1774; children: (1st m.) George Fitzgerald (b. 1748); William (b. 1749), later duke of Leinster; Emily Fitzgerald (b. 1752); Charles Fitzgerald (b. 1756); Charlotte Fitzgerald (b. 1758); Henry Fitzgerald (b. 1761); Sophia Fitzgerald (b. 1762); Edward Fitzgerald (b. 1763); Robert Fitzgerald (b. 1765); Gerald Fitzgerald (b. 1766); Fanny Fitzgerald (b. 1768); Lucy Fitzgerald (b. 1770); George Fitzgerald (b. 1771); and 5 others who died young; (2nd m.) Cecilia Ogilvie (b. 1775); Mimi Ogilvie (b. 1778). ❖ One of four aristocratic daughters of the duke and duchess of Richmond, renowned for their beauty and intelligence; by marriage, became one of the wealthy Fitzgeralds, Ireland's largest landholders and consequently important players in Irish politics; the most intellectual of the sisters, read widely and had strong interests in British politics, theology, and Enlightenment philosophies. ❖ See also Brian Fitzgerald, *Emily, Duchess of Leinster: A Study of Her Life and Times* (Staples, 1949); Stella Tillyard, *Aristocrats: Caroline, Emily, Louisa and Sarah Lennox* (Farrar, 1994); and *Women in World History*.

LENNOX, Louisa (1743–1821). English peeress. Name variations: Louisa Lennox Conolly. Born Nov 1743 in London; died in 1821 in Castletown, Ireland; dau. of Charles Lennox, 2nd duke of Richmond, and Sarah Cadogan (d. 1751); sister of Emily Lennox (1731–1814), Caroline Lennox (1723–1774), and Sarah Lennox (1745–1826); great-granddau. of Charles II, king of England, and Louise de Kéroüaille; m. Thomas Conolly (member of Parliament and long-time Speaker of the Irish House of Commons), in 1758; children: adopted sister Sarah's daughter Emily Louisa Napier (b. 1783). ❖ One of four aristocratic daughters of the duke and duchess of Richmond, renowned for their beauty and intelligence. ❖ See also Stella Tillyard, *Aristocrats: Caroline, Emily, Louisa and Sarah Lennox* (Farrar, 1994); and *Women in World History*.

LENNOX, Margaret. *See Douglas, Margaret (1515–1578).*

LENNOX, Sarah (1706–1751). *See Cadogan, Sarah.*

LENNOX, Sarah (1745–1826). English baroness. Name variations: Lady Bunbury; Sarah Napier. Born Feb 1745 in London; died Aug 1826 in London; dau. of Charles Lennox, 2nd duke of Richmond, and Sarah Cadogan (d. 1751); sister of Emily Lennox (1731–1814), Louisa Lennox (1743–1821), and Caroline Lennox (1723–1774); great-granddau. of Charles II, king of England, and Louise de Kéroüaille; m. Thomas Charles Bunbury (heir to the baronetcy and member of the House of Commons), in 1762; m. George Napier (British army hero), in 1781; children: (with Lord William Gordon) Louisa Bunbury (b. 1768); (2nd m.) Charles Napier (b. 1782); Emily Louisa Napier (b. 1783); George Napier (b. 1784); William Napier (b. 1785); Richard Napier (b. 1787); Henry Napier (b. 1789); Caroline Napier (b. 1790); Cecilia Napier (b. 1791). ❖ One of four aristocratic daughters of the duke and duchess of Richmond, renowned for their beauty and intelligence; widely regarded as the most handsome of the Lennox women, drew the attention of the prince of Wales, future George III, but did nothing to encourage him; with husband preoccupied with horseracing and gambling, became involved in a brief affair with Armand de Gontaut (1767), duke of Lauzun, then fell in love with a distant cousin, Lord William Gordon; stunned family and acquaintances by leaving husband for Lord Gordon (1769), then left Gordon a few months later and was taken in by brother Charles Lennox, 3rd duke of Richmond; with marriage to Napier, reentered high society and reestablished her good name. ❖ See also Edith R. Curtis, *Lady Sarah Lennox: A Irrepressible Stuart* (Putnam, 1946); Stella Tillyard, *Aristocrats: Caroline, Emily, Louisa and Sarah Lennox* (Farrar, 1994); and *Women in World History*.

LE NOIR, Elizabeth Anne (c. 1755–1841). English poet and novelist. Born Elizabeth Anne Smart c. 1755; died in Caversham, England, May 6, 1841; dau. of Christopher Smart (poet); m. Jean Baptiste le Noir de la Brosse, 1795. ❖ A favorite with Mary Russell Mitford, wrote *Village Annals* (1803), *Village Anecdotes* (1804) and *Miscellaneous Poems* (1825).

LENOIRE, Rosetta (1911–2002). African-American actress and producer. Born Rosetta Olive Burton, Aug 8, 1911, in New York, NY; died Mar 17, 2002, in Teaneck, NJ; goddau. of Bill "Bojangles" Robinson; studied with Eubie Blake; m. William LeNoire, 1929 (div. 1943); m. Egbert Brown, 1948 (died 1974); children: (1st m.) William. ❖ Appeared in Orson Welles all-black version of *Macbeth*; joined Robert Earl Jones Theater Group; made Broadway debut in *The Hot Mikado* (1939); also appeared in *A Streetcar Named Desire*, *The Sunshine Boys*, *Lost in the Stars* and *Cabin in the Sky*; portrayed Stella in *Anna Lucasta* on stage and in film; on tv, appeared as Nell Carter's mother on "Gimme a Break" and was Mother Winslow on "Family Matters"; founded AMAS, a nonprofit musical theatre group (1968), partly to promote interracial casting; with company, produced such hits as *Bubbling Brown Sugar*. Presented the National Medal of the Arts by President Bill Clinton (1999).

LENOR TELLES DE MENEZES (c. 1350–1386). *See Leonora Telles.*

LENORA. *Variant of Leonora.*

LENORE OF SICILY (1289–1341). Queen of Sicily. Name variations: Eleanor of Naples. Born Aug 1289; died Aug 9, 1341; dau. of Marie of Hungary (d. 1323) and Charles II, duke of Anjou (r. 1285–1290), king of Naples (r. 1285–1309); m. Frederick II (1271–1336), king of Sicily (r. 1296–1336), in May 1302; children: Elizabeth of Sicily (d. 1349); Peter II, king of Sicily (r. 1337–1342).

LENORMAND, Marie Anne Adélaïde (1772–1843). French fortuneteller. Name variations: popularly known as La Sibylle du Faubourg Saint-Germain. Born in Alençon, France, May 27, 1772; died in Paris, June 25, 1843. ❖ Became celebrated when she predicted the marriage of Josephine and Napoleon Bonaparte; wrote a number of books on subjects connected with her profession. Clients included Germaine de Staël, the French actor Talma, and Alexander I, tsar of Russia.

LENSHINA, Alice (1924–1978). *See Mulenga, Alice.*

LENSHINA, Anna (1887–1917). *See Brovar, Anna Iakovlevna.*

LENSKI, Lois (1893–1974). American illustrator and author of children's books. Born in Springfield, Ohio, Oct 14, 1893; died in Tarpon Springs, FL, Sept 11, 1974; dau. of Richard Charles Lenski (Lutheran minister) and Marietta (Young) Lenski; Ohio State University, BS, 1915; additional study at Art Students League, NY, and Westminster School of Art, London; m. Arthur S. Covey (artist and mural painter), 1921 (died 1960); children: Stephen; (stepchildren) Margaret and Laird. ❖ Writer and self-illustrator of nursery rhymes, verse, and stories for children, turned out a steady stream of books over several decades, including *The Little Family*, *The Little Auto*, *Blueberry Corners*, *The Little Train*, *Bayou Suzette*, *Cotton in My Sack*, *Houseboat Girl*, *Shoo-Fly Girl* and *Blue Ridge Billy*; also illustrated Grahame's *Dream Days* (1922), Colum's *The Peep-Show Man* (1924), Lofting's *The Twilight of Magic* (1930), Stong's *Edgar, the 7:58* (1938), Thompson's *Once on a Christmas* (1938), Lovelace's "Betsy-Tacy" series, and Piper's *The Little Engine That Could* (1945), among others. Awarded John Newbery Medal for *Strawberry Girl* (1946), University of Southern Mississippi Special Children's Collection Medallion (1969) and Regina Medal (1969). ❖ See also autobiography *Journey into Childhood* (1972); and *Women in World History*.

LENTON, Lisbeth (1985—). Australian swimmer. Name variations: Libby Lenton. Born Lisbeth Lenton, Jan 28, 1925, in Townsville, Australia. ❖ At Athens Olympics (2004), won a silver medal for 50-meter freestyle and a gold medal for 4x100-meter freestyle relay with a world record time of 54.75.

LENTZ, Irene (1901–1962). *See Irene.*

LENYA, Lotte (1898–1981). Austrian-born actress and singer. Name variations: Lotte Lenja. Born Karoline Wilhelmine Charlotte Blamauer, Oct 18, 1898, in Vienna, Austria; died Nov 27, 1981, in NY; m. Kurt Weill (composer), 1926 (died 1950); m. George Davis (magazine ed. and journalist), 1953 (died 1957); m. Russell Detwiler, 1962 (died 1969); m. Richard Siemanowski, 1971 (div. 1973). ❖ Had walk-on role in opera *Orfeo* at Zurich's Stadttheater; joined Stadttheater's repertory co., the Schauspielhaus; worked as extra in a string of theatrical productions, among them *Der Rosenkavalier* (1918); moved to Berlin (1921) and refined the techniques that would mark her later stage presence—the half-talking, half-singing vocal style popular at the time; married Kurt

Weill (1926); appeared as Jessie in Brecht-Weill collaboration *Mahagonny Songspiel,* which later became the full-length opera, *Aufstieg und Fall der Stadt Mahagonny* (*The Rise and Fall of the City of Mahagonny,* 1930); originated role of prostitute Jenny in Brecht-Weill's *Die Dreigroschenoper* (*The Threepenny Opera*) which became such a hit that it was seen throughout Germany and filmed by G.W. Pabst; with rise of Hitler, fled to Paris (1933), where she appeared in a ballet for which Weill and Brecht had composed the scenario, *The Seven Deadly Sins;* sailed with Weill for NY; became US citizen; appeared at Town Hall in *An American Evening in Honor of Kurt Weill;* made Broadway debut in Weill's *Eternal Road* (1936); had highly successful singing engagement at Le Ruban Bleu (1940), introducing "The Right Guy for Me"; appeared in *Candle in the Dark* (1942) to good reviews; nursed husband until his death (1950); came out of seclusion to appear in triumphant version of *The Threepenny Opera* (1954) which ran for 2,700 performances; recorded more of Weill's music and appeared in her 1st film in 30 years, *The Roman Spring of Mrs. Stone,* earning an Oscar nomination for Best Supporting Actress (1961); opened in *Brecht on Brecht* (1961); appeared as Rosa Klebb in *From Russia With Love* (1963); returned to European stage for *Mother Courage* (1965); originated role of Frau Schnieder in *Cabaret* (1966). ❖ See also Donald Spoto, *Lenya* (Little, Brown, 1989); Symonette & Kowalke *Speak Low (When You Speak Love): The Love Letters of Kurt Weill and Lotte Lenya* (U. of California Press, 1996); and *Women in World History.*

LENZ, Consetta (1918–1980). American gymnast. Name variations: Connie Lenz; Consetta Caruccio. Born Consetta Anna Caruccio, Sept 26, 1918, in US; died July 1980 in Cambridge, MD. ❖ Won AAU championships for All-Around (1933, 1934); at London Olympics, won a bronze medal in team all-around (1948).

LÉO, André (1832–1900). French novelist, journalist, and feminist. Name variations: Andre Leo; Léonide or Léonie Béra; Léonie or Léodile Bréa; Léodile Champseix or Champceix. Pronunciation: ON-dray LAY-o. Born Léodile Béra in Lusignan (some sources cite Champagné-Saint-Hilaire) in Vienne, France, 1832; died 1900, possibly in Paris; dau. of the wife of a retired naval officer, who was at the time a notary and justice of the peace; mother's name unknown; well-educated; m. Grégoire Champseix or Champceix (1817–1863), 1852; m. Benoît Malon (1841–1893), 1873; children: (1st m.) twin sons, André and Léo, and possibly a daughter. ❖ Founder of France's 1st general feminist organization, moved with self-exiled family to Switzerland and married; returned to France (1860) and became a successful novelist; founded Society for the Claiming of the Rights of Women (1866); was heavily involved in Franco-Prussian War and Paris Commune in relief efforts and journalism (1870–71); fled to Switzerland (1871) and wrote for socialist papers; returned to France (1880) and continued as a novelist; writings include *Un Mariage scandaleuse* (1862), *Une Vieille Fille* (1864), *Les Deux Filles de M. Plichon* (1864), *Observations d'une mère de famille à M. Duruy* (1865), *Une Divorce* (1866), *L'Idéal au village* (1867), *Double Histoire* (1868), *La Femme et les moeurs: Liberté ou monarchie?* (1869), *Aline-Ali* (1869), *Legendes corréziennes* (1870), *La Guerre sociale: Discours prononcé au Congrès de la Paix à Lausanne 1871* (1871), *Marie* (1877), *L'Épouse du bandit* (1880), *L'Enfant des Rudères* (1881), *La Justice des choses* (1891), *Le Petit Moi* (1891), *La Famille Androit* (1899), and *L'Éducation nouvelle* (1899). ❖ See also *Women in World History.*

LEOBA (700–779). See Lioba.

LEOBGYTH (700–779). See Lioba.

LEOCADIA (d. about 303). Spanish saint. Died c. 303. ❖ Popular Spanish saint, lived in Toledo when Dacian, an agent of Diocletian, arrived to enforce the Roman edicts against Christianity; brought before Dacian, was told to disavow her Christian faith; for refusing, was beaten and thrown into a dungeon; when she heard about the tortures being endured by 13- or 14-year-old Eulalia in Mérida by the same persecutors, prayed for God to take her from a world of such horrors; died while in prison. Feast day is Dec 9.

LEODEGUNDIA (fl. 10th c.). Spanish poet. Fl. in 10th-century Spain. ❖ Accomplished writer and poet, probably spent most of her time at the royal court; her work is identified with a popular group of painters, illuminators, and writers who flourished in 10th-century Spain, reflecting a complex blend of Christian European and Eastern Arabic cultures, images, and traditions.

LÉON, Léonie (1838–1906). French mistress. Name variations: Leonie Leon. Born 1838 in France; part creole and part Jewish; died 1906.

❖ Well-educated and attractive, was mistress of an imperial official with whom she had a son, then mistress of statesman Léon Gambetta (1872–82).

LEÓN, Maria Teresa (1903–1988). Spanish novelist and essayist. Name variations: Maria Teresa de Leon; Maria Teresa León Goyri. Born Oct 31, 1903, in Logrono, Spain; died Dec 13, 1988, in Madrid; dau. of Angel León and Oliva Goyri; niece of Maria Goyri (the 1st woman in Spain to obtain a doctorate in philosophy); MA in philosophy and letters; m. Gonzalo de Sebastián, 1920 (div. 1929); m. Rafael Alberti (writer), 1932; children: (1st m.) Gonzalo and Enrique. ❖ Was active in Spanish Communist Party, secretary of the Alliance of Antifascist Writers, and served as director of Teatro de las Guerrillas during Spanish Civil War; helped to save Spanish art treasures during conflict; with 2nd husband, often collaborated and founded the magazine *Octubre* (1933); lived in exile for 38 years (1939–77); writings include *Cuentos para soñar, Cuentos de la España actual* (1937), *Contra viento y marea* (1941), *Morirás lejos* (1942), *Las peregrinaciones de Teresa* (1950), and *Fábulas del tiempo amargo* (1962); later works focus on social injustice.

LÉON, Pauline (1758–?). French revolutionary and feminist. Born in Paris, France, 1758; death date unknown; dau. of a chocolate manufacturer; m. (Jean) Théophile Leclerc, Nov 1793. ❖ Joined the Jacobin Société des Cordeliers (1791) and was chosen to speak at the National Assembly where she sought approval for a women's militia; was one of the principle founders of Women's Republican Revolutionary Society (Société des Révolutionaries Républicaines), becoming its president (1793). ❖ See also *Women in World History.*

LEON, queen of. See Berengaria of Castile (1180–1246).

LÉON AND CASTILE, queen of.

LEONARD, Carla (b. 1909). See Laemmle, Carla.

LEONARD, Carol L. (1950—). American midwife. Name variations: Carol L. Leonard. Born June 10, 1950, in Bangor, Maine; dau. of Louis and Parker Leonard; m. Kenneth McKinney (obstetrician), 1981 (died 1987). ❖ Cofounded Concord Midwifery Service; successfully campaigned for legal certification of midwives which passed in 1982; served on New Hampshire Director of Health and Welfare Advisory Committee (1981–84); was charter member (1982), vice president (1984) and president (1986) of Midwives' Alliance of North America (MANA); became 1st certified midwife in NH (1985); opened Longmeadow Farm Midwifery Service (Sept 2000), the only freestanding birth center in NH.

LEONARD, Claudie (1924—). See Algeranova, Claudie.

LEONARD, Louise (1885–1968). See McLaren, Louise.

LEONARD, Marion (1881–1956). American silent-film star. Name variations: Lillian Bedford. Born June 9, 1881, in Ohio; died Jan 9, 1956, in Woodland Hills, CA; m. Stanner E.V. Taylor. ❖ Began career with Biograph, featured opposite D.W. Griffith, in *The Crossroads of Life;*

other films include *The Gibson Goddess*, *In Old California*, *The Dragon's Claw* and *Carmen*.

LEONARDA, Isabella (1620–1704). Italian composer. Born Anna Isabella Leonardi, into a noble family, Sept 6, 1620, in Novara, Italy; died in Novara, 1704; entered the Convent of Saint Ursula of Novara in 1636; studied with Gaspare Casati. ❖ Composed 2 motets for 2 voices (1645); became Mother Superior of Saint Ursula Convent, then Madre Vicaria (1693); published a book of motets (1700); also composed litanies, psalm settings, vespers, responses, and 4 masses. Over 200 of her works in 20 volumes survive.

LEONARDI CORTESI, Natascia (1971—). Swiss cross-country skier. Name variations: Natascia Cortesi. Born May 1, 1971, in Italy. ❖ Won a bronze medal for the 4x5km relay at Salt Lake City Olympics (2002).

LEONARDOS, Stela (1923—). Brazilian novelist, poet and short-story writer. Name variations: Stela Leonardos da Silva Lima Cabassa. Born Aug 1, 1923, in Rio de Janeiro, Brazil. ❖ Works, which were influenced by 1945 Generation in Brazil, include *Palmares* (1940), *A grande visão* (1942), *Poesia em três tempos* (1956), *Estátua de sal* (1961), *Cancioneiro catalão* (1971), and *Romanceiro do Bequimão* (1986).

LEONE, Giuseppina (1934—). Italian runner. Born Dec 21, 1934, in Italy. ❖ At Rome Olympics, won a bronze medal in 100 meters (1960).

LEONE, Lucile (1902–1999). See Petry, Lucile.

LEONETTI, Caroline (1918—). See Ahmanson, Caroline.

LEONHARDT, Carolin (1984—). German kayaker. Born Nov 22, 1984, in Mannheim, Germany. ❖ Placed 1st in K2 500 at World Cup in Racice (2004); won a gold medal for K4 500 and a silver medal for K2 500 at Athens Olympics (2004).

LEONIDA (b. 1914). Georgian princess. Name variations: Leonida Kirby. Born Leonida Bagration-Moukhransky, Sept 23, 1914, in Tiflis, Georgia, Russia, into a Georgian royal family; dau. of George XIII, prince Bagration-Mukhranski, and Helen Sigismondovna Zlotnicka; m. Sumner Kirby, Nov 6, 1934 (div. 1937); m. Vladimir Cyrillovitch (1917–1992, great-grandson of Tsar Alexander II of Russia), Aug 13, 1948; children: (2nd m.) Marie Vladimirovna (b. 1953).

LEONIDA, Florica (1987—). Romanian gymnast. Name variations: Floarea Leonida. Born Jan 13, 1987, in Bucharest, Romania. ❖ Won Romanian nationals and Romanian International (2002).

LEONOR. *Variant of Eleanor, Ellen, Helen, or Leonora.*

LEONOR OF ARAGON (1358–1382). See Eleanor of Aragon.

LEONOR OF AUSTRIA (1498–1558). See Eleanor of Portugal.

LEONOR OF CASTILE (d. 1415). See Eleanor Trastamara.

LEONOR OF NAVARRE (1425–1479). See Eleanor of Navarre.

LEONOR OF PORTUGAL.
See Eleanor of Portugal (1328–1348).
See Eleanor of Portugal (1434–1467).
See Eleanor of Portugal (1458–1525).
See Eleanor of Portugal (1498–1558).

LEONOR OF PORTUGAL (1211–1231). Queen of Denmark. Born 1211; died May 28, 1231; dau. of Urraca of Castile (c. 1186–1220) and Alfonso or Alphonso II the Fat (1185–1223), king of Portugal (r. 1211–1223); m. Valdemar or Waldemar the Younger (1209–1231), king of Denmark (r. 1215–1231), June 24, 1229; children: Sophie Valdemarsdottir (d. 1241).

LEONOR TELES DE MENESES (c. 1350–1386). See Leonora Telles.

LEONORA. *Variant of Eleanora, Ellen, Helen or Leonor.*

LEONORA CHRISTINE (1621–1698). See Ulfeldt, Leonora Christina.

LEONORA DE GUZMAN (1310–1351). See Guzman, Leonora de.

LEONORA D'ESTE (1537–1581). See Este, Eleanor d'.

LEONORA OF ARAGON (1405–1445). Queen of Portugal. Name variations: Eleanor of Aragon. Born 1405; died Feb 19, 1445, in Toledo; dau. of Eleanor of Alburquerque (1374–1435) and Ferdinand I, king of Aragon (r. 1412–1416); sister of Maria of Aragon (1403–1445, mother of Henry IV, king of Castile); m. Duarte I also known as Edward I (1391–1438), king of Portugal (r. 1433–1438); children: Joao or John

(1429–1433); Filippa (1430–1439, died of the plague); Afonso also known as Alphonso V (1432–1481), king of Portugal (r. 1438–1481); Maria (1432–1432); Fernando or Ferdinand (1433–1470), duke of Viseu; Duarte (1435–1435); Caterina (1436–1463); Joanna of Portugal (1439–1475); Eleanor of Portugal (1434–1467, who m. Frederick III, Holy Roman emperor).

LEONORA OF ARAGON (1450–1493). Duchess of Ferrara. Name variations: Eleanora of Aragon; Eleanora d'Este; Leonora of Naples. Born June 22, 1450; died of a gastric infection, Oct 11, 1493 (some sources cite 1492); dau. of Ferdinand also known as Ferrante I, king of Naples (r. 1458–1494), and Isabel de Clermont (d. 1465); m. Ercole I d'Este, 2nd duke of Ferrara and Modena (r. 1471–1502), on June 22, 1473; children: Isabella d'Este (1474–1539); Beatrice d'Este (1475–1497); Alfonso I d'Este (1476–1534), 3rd duke of Ferrara and Modena, who m. Lucrezia Borgia (1477–1540); Ferrando (1477–1540); Ippolito I (1479–1520, cardinal); Sigismondo (1480–1524). Ercole I also had 2 illeg. children: Lucrezia d'Este (d. 1516/18) and Giulio (1478–1561).

LEONORA OF SAVOY (fl. 1200). Ferrarese noblewoman. Name variations: Leonora di Savoia; Leonora d'Este. Fl. around 1200; 2nd wife of Azo also known as Azzo VI d'Este (1170–1212), 1st lord of Ferrara (r. 1208–1212); children: Beata Beatrice I d'Este (d. 1226). ❖ Azzo's 1st wife was a woman of the Aldobrandeschi (name unknown) who gave birth to Aldobrandino I d'Este (d. 1215); his 3rd wife was Alisia of Antioch, mother of Azzo VII Novello (d. 1264).

LEONORA TELLES (c. 1350–1386). Queen and regent of Portugal. Name variations: Leonora Teles de Meneses; Lenor Telles de Menezes; Eleanor Tellez de Meneses. Born Leonora Telles de Meneses in Trás os Montes c. 1350; died April 27, 1386, at Cloister Tordesillas, Valladolid; dau. of Martin Afonso Telles de Meneses and Aldonza de Vasconcelhos also spelled Aldonsa de Vasconcelos; m. João Lourenço also known as John Lorenzo da Cunha; m. Fernando also known as Ferdinand I (1345–1383), king of Portugal (r. 1367–1383), 1372 (died Oct 22, 1383); children: (1st m.) Alvaro da Cunha; (2nd m.) Beatrice of Portugal (1372–after 1409, who m. John I of Castile and Leon); Pedro (1380–1380); Alfonso (1382–1382). ❖ Was niece of the count of Barcelos, a dominant figure at the court of Ferdinand I, king of Portugal; though married, became Ferdinand's mistress; after uncle had marriage annulled, became queen despite public outrage (1372); when Castilian forces laid siege to Lisbon because Ferdinand had broken off his engagement to the daughter of Castilian king Henry II, was unprepared to defend the kingdom with husband and had to sign the ignominious peace of Santarém (Mar 19, 1373), that required the Portuguese monarchy to ally itself with Henry II; following Ferdinand's death, appointed herself regent of Portugal (1383–1384); was overthrown in the Revolution of 1383–85. ❖ See also *Women in World History.*

LEONOVA, Aleksandra (1964—). Soviet basketball player. Born Sept 4, 1964, in USSR. ❖ At Seoul Olympics, won a bronze medal in team competition (1988).

LEONOWENS, Anna (c. 1831–1914). English governess. Born either Anna Harriette Edwards, Nov 6, 1831, in India or Anna Harriette Crawford, Nov 5, 1834, in Caernarvon, Wales, depending on account; died 1914; dau. of either a Private Edwards or a Captain Crawford, who died in military service, and a mother who may have been Anglo-Indian; educated in England until she returned to India at 14; m. Thomas Leon Owens, Dec 25, 1849 (died May 1859); children: Selina (b. 1851) and 2nd child, both of whom did not survive; Avis (b. 1854); Louis (b. 1855). ❖ Governess to children of king of Siam (Thailand) during 1860s, who brought many reforms to his kingdom, fought against the oppressiveness of polygamy and the harem system, wrote several books on harem life, and gained international renown; was widowed (1859); traveled to Siam, where she served as governess to children and wives of King Mongkut, particularly Crown Prince Chulalongkorn, who was 9 years old (1862–67); published *The Romance of the Harem* and other books which appeared as *Siamese Harem Life* and *The Romance of Siamese Harem Life;* lectured in later years to support herself; immortalized by publication of *Anna and the King of Siam* by Margaret Landon (1944), which became the basis for Rodgers and Hammerstein musical and movie *The King and I.* ❖ See also *Women in World History.*

LEONTIA (fl. 602–610). Byzantine empress. Fl. between 602 and 610; m. Phocas I (Phokas), Byzantine emperor (r. 602–610). ❖ Practically nothing is known of Phocas' wife Leontia, except that the public considered her as bad as her husband. ❖ See also *Women in World History.*

LEONTIAS, Sappho (1832–1900). Greek writer and educator. Born in Constantinople (now Istanbul), 1832; died 1900. ❖ Spent many years as headmistress of several girls' schools on the Greek islands; viewed education as a means for women to improve their status; published the literary journal *Euridice,* which printed articles by women; published works written in Greek vernacular, or the common language (there were those who advocated the strict use of pure Greek and those who preferred the spoken language of the people); believed strongly that the vernacular should be used in the schools and introduced the Greek classics in modern translation into the curriculum; translated Aeschylus' *The Persians* into modern Greek, as well as Racine's *Esther* from the French.

LEONTIUM (fl. 300–250 BCE). Greek philosopher. Name variations: Leontion. Born in Greece. ❖ A pupil of philosopher Epicurus, some of whose letters to her survive, was later denigrated by Cicero as a courtesan; sources suggest that she denounced Theophrastus' idea that philosophers should not marry; mentioned in *Life of Epicurus* by Diogenes Laertius.

LEONTOVICH, Eugénie (1894–1993). Russian-born actress, director, playwright, and drama coach. Name variations: Eugenie Leontovich. Born in Moscow, Russia, Mar 21, 1894; died April 2, 1993; dau. of Konstantin Leontovich and Ann (Joukovsky) Leontovich; studied at Imperial School of Dramatic Art, Moscow; m. Paul A. Sokolov (div.); m. Gregory Ratoff (actor-director), c. 1923 (div. 1949). ❖ Veteran of the Moscow Art Theater and Russian State Theater, made NY debut in *Revue Russe* (1922), a Paris revue; spent early career performing on Broadway and touring nation in a number of plays, including *And So to Bed* and *Twentieth Century;* made London debut as Tatiana in *Tovarich* (1935); appeared as Natasha in *Dark Eyes,* which she wrote with Elena Miramova (Belasco, NY, 1943); founded Stage Theater in Los Angeles, where she acted and directed (1948); founded Leontovich Workshop in L.A. (1953), where she directed and coached professional actors; joined faculty of Chicago's Goodman School of Drama (1964), where she also directed a number of productions, including *The Three Sisters;* also taught at Smith College and Columbia College in Chicago; directed and starred in *Anna K.* (1972), her own conception of Tolstoy's *Anna Karenina;* founded Eugénie Leontovich Workshop for actors in NYC (1973); films include *Four Sons* (1940), *Anything Can Happen* (1952) and *The World in His Arms* (1953). Won a Tony Award for performance as the Dowager Empress in *Anastasia* (1954). ❖ See also *Women in World History.*

LEONTYEVA, Galina (1941—). Soviet volleyball player. Born Nov 1941 in USSR. ❖ Won a gold medal at Mexico City Olympics (1968) and a gold medal at Munich Olympics (1972), both in team competition.

LEOPOLDINA. *Variant of Leopoldine.*

LEOPOLDINA OF AUSTRIA (1797–1826). Empress of Brazil. Name variations: Marie-Leopoldine; Marie Leopoldina; Leopoldine; Dona Maria Leopoldina; Leopoldina von Habsburg; Leopoldina Habsburg-Lotharingen. Born Marie Leopoldine, Jan 22, 1797; died of septicaemia after a miscarriage, Dec 11, 1826; dau. of Francis II, Holy Roman emperor (r. 1792–1806), emperor of Austria as Francis I (r. 1804–1835), and Maria Teresa of Naples (1772–1807); sister of Marie Louise of Austria (1791–1847, who m. Napoleon); m. Peter IV, king of Portugal (r. 1826), also known as Pedro I, emperor of Brazil (r. 1822–1831), on May 13, 1817; children: Maria II da Gloria (1819–1853), queen of Portugal (r. 1826–1828, 1834–1853); Miguel (1820–1820); João Carlos (1821–1822); Januaria (1822–1901); Paula Mariana (1823–1833); Francisca of Portugal (1824–1898); Pedro II (1825–1891), emperor of Brazil (r. 1831–1839). ❖ Received an excellent education, showing considerable ability as a painter and displaying broad intellectual curiosity throughout life, especially for the natural sciences; married by proxy (1817), left Vienna to join husband, who had fled to Brazil with the Portuguese court when Napoleon's armies invaded in 1807; married life was generally overshadowed by turmoil of Brazilian independence; when husband became emperor of Brazil as Pedro I, became his popular empress; encouraged Austrian immigration to Brazil, including the colony of São Leopoldo (1824) in Rio Grande do Sul. ❖ See also *Women in World History.*

LEOPOLDINE. *Variant of Leopoldina.*

LEOPOLDINE (1776–1848). *See Maria Leopoldina.*

LEOPOLDINE (1837–1903). Princess of Hohenlohe-Langenburg. Born Leopoldine Wilhelmina Pauline Amelia Maximiliana on Feb 22, 1837; died Dec 23, 1903; dau. of William, prince of Baden, and Elizabeth of Wurttemberg (1802–1864); m. Hermann, 6th prince of Hohenlohe-Langenburg, on Sept 24, 1862; children: Ernest, 7th prince of Hohenlohe-Langenburg (1863–1950); Feodore of Hohenlohe-Langenburg (1866–1932).

LEOPOLDOVNA, Anna (1718–1746). *See Anna Leopoldovna.*

LEPADATU, Viorica (1971—). Romanian rower. Born June 12, 1971, in Romania. ❖ At Barcelona Olympics, won a silver medal in coxed eights (1992).

LEPAUTE, Hortense (1723–1788). French astronomer and mathematician. Name variations: Nicole Reine Lepaute; Nicole-Reine Lepaute. Born Nicole Hortense Reine, 1723, in Luxembourg Palace, Paris, France; died 1788; father was attached to the court of queen of Spain; m. Jean André Lepaute (1709–1789, machinist and royal clockmaker), 1748. ❖ One of the most learned women of her time, was the principal author of husband's *Traité d'horlogerie* (1755); assisted Alexis Clairaut and Joseph-Jérôme Lalande in work on planetary theory (1757), calculating the attraction Jupiter and Saturn had on Halley's comet; helped Lalande edit *La Connaissance des Temps* (1760–75), an astronomical annual of Académie des Sciences; rendered calculations for eclipse of 1762 and for annular eclipse of 1764; worked on 7th and 8th volumes of *Ephemeris* (1774–83), containing future calculations for sun, moon, and planets. ❖ See also *Women in World History.*

LEPAUTE, Nicole Reine (1723–1788). *See Lepaute, Hortense.*

LEPEL OR LEPELL, Mary (1700–1768). *See Hervey, Mary.*

LEPENNEC, Emilie (1987—). French gymnast. Born Dec 31, 1987, in La Garenne-Colombes, France. ❖ Won a gold medal for uneven bars at Athens Olympics (2004).

LEPESHINSKAYA, Olga (1916—). Soviet ballerina. Born Sept 28, 1916, in Kiev; graduate of Bolshoi Ballet School (1933). ❖ At 10, danced the part of Cupid in *Don Quixote;* before graduating from Bolshoi School, also danced the principal part of Masha in *The Nutcracker;* created role of Suok the Circus Dancer for *Three Fat Men* (1935) and played title role in *Svetlana* (1939); performed with the Bolshoi (1933–63), appearing as Aurora in *The Sleeping Beauty,* Lise in *La Fille Mal Gardée,* Jeanne in *Flames of Paris,* Kitri in *Don Quixote,* and Tao Hoa in *The Red Poppy,* among others; taught extensively in USSR and East Germany, and graced the stages of Paris, Japan, China, Hungary, Czechoslovakia and Mexico.

LEPOOLE, Alexandra (1959—). Dutch field-hockey player. Born Oct 20, 1959, in Netherlands. ❖ At Los Angeles Olympics, won a gold medal in team competition (1984).

LEPORIN-ERXLEBEN, Dorothea (1715–1762). *See Erxleben, Dorothea.*

LEPORSKA, Zoya (1918–1996). Russian-American ballet dancer and choreographer. Name variations: Zoya Laporska. Born 1918 in Nikolaevsk-on-Amur, Siberia; died Dec 16, 1996. ❖ Immigrated to US as a child (1925) and studied ballet at numerous schools on West Coast, including Cornish School in Seattle and San Francisco Opera ballet; danced with San Francisco Opera ballet, appearing in *Les Sylphides, A Roumanian Wedding,* and others; moved to NY (1942) danced with Ballet Theater, then Balanchine's New Opera Co. (1943), and in Ballet International productions of *Swan Lake* and Caton's *Sebastien;* began performing in pantomime and theatrical productions (c. 1948), including with Charles Weidman's Theater Dance Co. and with Mata and Hari's pantomime co.; as assistant to Bob Fosse, performed in his Broadway productions, *Pajama Game, Damn Yankees* and *New Girl in Town;* began choreographing for summer theaters, national touring shows, and such operas as *Summer and Smoke* and *Before Breakfast.*

LE PRINCE DE BEAUMONT, Marie (1711–1780). French children's writer. Name variations: Jeanne-Marie Leprince de Beaumont. Born 1711 in Rouen, France; died 1789; educated at Convent of Ernemont; m. Thomas Pichon; children: 6. ❖ Worked as governess and teacher in France before leaving for England after annulment of marriage (1745); wrote about 70 volumes of educational and moral tales for children, as well as lessons and handbooks for teaching children; in London, founded magazine *Le Nouveau Magasin français* for women; published works in magazines and in 2 collections of *Contes Moraux* (1744, 1776); rewrote Gabrielle de Villeneuve's *The Beauty and the Beast* and published it in *Magasin des enfants* (later trans. as *The Young Misses Magazine, Containing Dialogues between a Governess and Several Young Ladies of Quality, Her*

Scholars, 1757); stories and educational plans were used by many teachers and her ideas anticipated the work of Jean-Jacques Rousseau.

LEPROHON, Rosanna (1832–1879). Canadian novelist. Born Rosanna Mullins, 1832, in Montreal, Canada; died 1879; m. Jean-Lucien Leprohon (physician); children: 13. ❖ Works, which evoke 19th-century French Canada, include *Antoinette de Mirecourt; or, Secret Marrying and Secret Sorrowing: A Canadian Tale* (1864) and *Armand Durand; or A Promise Fulfilled* (1868); advocated education of women and marriage as equal partnership.

LERMONTOVA, Julia (1846–1919). Russian-German chemist. Name variations: Yulua Vsevolodovna Lermontova. Born 1846; died 1919. ❖ Because Russian universities were closed to women, journeyed to Heidelberg with Sophia Kovalevskaya where they were allowed to attend lectures (1869); moved to Berlin; published an article on her research on diphenene; was awarded a degree from the University of Göttingen *in absentia* with thesis, "The Study of Methylene Compounds"; returned to Russia to work in Moscow University laboratory of V.V. Markownikov, then went to St. Petersburg to work with A.M. Butlerov; published findings, concerning the catalytic synthesis of the dimer and trimer of isobutylene and of 2-butyne (1881); retired to take on family obligations. ❖ See also *Women in World History.*

LERMONTOVA, Nadezhda Vladimirovna (1885–1921). Russian painter. Born in St. Petersburg in 1885; died 1921 in Petrograd (now St. Petersburg); studied at Zvantseva School (1907–10). ❖ Influenced by Cubism, produced a number of impressive works, including her best-known painting, *On the Sofa: Self-Portrait* (1910s); participated in a number of exhibitions, including those of *Soyuz Molodezhi* (Union of Youth, 1912–13); with Petrov-Vodkin, executed paintings in the church at Ovruch, Ukraine; also designed sets for theater productions in St. Petersburg.

LERNER, Dorothy (1889–1970). *See Gordon, Dorothy.*

LERNER, Gerda (1920—). Austrian-born American historian. Born Gerda Kronstein, April 30, 1920, in Vienna, Austria; dau. of Robert Kronstein and Ilona (Neumann) Kronstein; New School for Social Research, BA, 1963; Columbia University, MA, 1965, PhD, 1966; m. Carl Lerner, 1941 (died 1973); children: Stephanie Lerner; Daniel Lerner. ❖ Influential historian, responsible for the establishment of women's history as a recognized academic field, arrived in US (1939); published 1st book *No Farewell* (1955); created 1st women's history department in US (1972); established 1st doctoral program in same field (c. 1980); writings include *The Grimké Sisters from South Carolina: Rebels Against Slavery* (1967), *The Woman in American History* (1971), *Black Women in White America* (1972), *Women Are History* (1975), *Women and History,* Volume 1: *The Creation of Patriarchy* (1986), *Women and History,* Volume 2: *The Creation of Feminist Consciousness* (1993) and *Why History Matters* (1997). ❖ See also memoir *A Death of One's Own* (1978); and *Women in World History.*

LERNER, Marion (1919–1997). *See Bell, Marion.*

LEROUX, Pauline (1809–1891). French ballet dancer. Born Aug 20, 1809, in Paris, France; died 1891 in Paris. ❖ Trained at Paris Opéra's ballet school and remained with that company throughout most of professional career; created roles in Taglioni's *Nathalie, ou la Laitière Suisse* and *La Révolte au Sérail* (1833), and in Coralli's *Le Diable Boiteux* (1836).

LEROUX, Valerie (1969—). *See Barlois, Valerie.*

LERWILL, Sheila (1928—). English track-and-field athlete. Name variations: Sheila Alexander. Born Sheila Alexander, Aug 16, 1928, in UK. ❖ At Helsinki Olympics, won a silver medal in the high jump (1952).

LESBIA.
See Erinna (fl. 7th c. BCE).
See Clodia (c. 94–post 45 BCE).

LESCZINSKA, Maria (1703–1768). *See Marie Leczinska.*

LESHAN, Eda J. (1922–2002). American psychologist and writer. Born Eda Joan Grossman, June 6, 1922, in New York, NY; died Mar 2, 2002, in Riverdale, NY; dau. of Jean Schick Grossman (parent educator) and Max Grossman (lawyer and president of the Ethical Culture Society of NY); graduate of Teachers College at Columbia University; Clark University, MA; m. Lawrence LeShan; children: Wendy. ❖ Wrote 2 dozen books about parenting and aging; provided radio commentaries for CBS, had her own show on PBS, "How Do Your Children Grow" and a regular column for *Newsday* and *Woman's Day;* writings include *The Conspiracy Against Childhood* (1967), *The Wonderful Crisis of Middle Age: Some Personal Reflections* (1973), and the 1-woman play, *The Lobster Reef.*

LESIK, Vera (1910–1975). Ukrainian-Canadian novelist, journalist and historian. Name variations: (pseudonyms) Vera Lysenko, Luba Novak. Born 1910 in Winnipeg, Canada; died 1975; dau. of Ukrainian immigrants; studied at University of Manitoba. ❖ Worked as nurse, schoolteacher, and journalist; writings, which reflect experiences of Ukrainian Canadians, include *Men in Sheepskin Coats: A Study in Assimilation* (1947), *Yellow Boots* (1954) and *Westerly Wild* (1956).

LESKOVA, Tatiana (1922—). French ballet dancer. Born 1922 in Paris, France, of Russian parents; trained with Boris Kniaseff, Anatole Oboukhoff, and Lyubov Egorova. ❖ Performed with Egorova's Ballet de la Jeunesse and in Paris Opéra-Comique (late 1930s); immigrated to US with Original Ballet Russe (1939) and was featured in Balanchine's *Balustrade,* Lichine's *Graduation Ball,* and company production of *Aurora's Wedding* (1939–45); moved to Rio de Janeiro (c. 1945); began serving as director of Teatro Municipale Ballet (1950) and contributed largely to training of local professional ballet dancers for that company.

LESLIE, Amy (1855–1939). American singer and drama critic. Name variations: Lillie West; Lillie West Brown Buck. Born Lillie West, Oct 11, 1855, in West Burlington, IA; died July 3, 1939, in Chicago, IL; dau. of Albert Waring West (merchant) and Kate Content (Webb) West; m. Harry Brown (singer), c. 1880 (div.); Franklyn Howard Buck (famous big-animal trapper known as Frank Buck), 1901 (div. 1916); children: (1st m.) Francis Albert. ❖ Earned fame as light-opera soprano (mid-1880s); death of son (1889) caused her to leave stage and start career in journalism; wrote for *Chicago Daily News* (1890–1930), the only female drama critic in Chicago; published 2 books, *Amy Leslie at the Fair* (1893) and *Some Players* (1899).

LESLIE, Annie (1869–1948). American columnist. Name variations: Nancy Brown. Born Annie Louise Brown, Dec 11, 1869, in Perry, Maine; died Oct 7, 1948, in Detroit, MI; dau. of Levi Prescott Brown (farmer) and Ann Robinson (Lincoln) Brown; m. James Edward Leslie (editor), Sept 19, 1904 (died 1917). ❖ Hired in women's department of *Detroit News* (1918); began writing advice column, "Experience" (1919), which soon grew into daily feature, but did not reveal identity, even to fellow newspaper staffers, until 1940; answered most letters herself and won respect and widespread readership for common-sense philosophy.

LESLIE, Bethel (1929–1999). American actress. Born Aug 3, 1929, in New York, NY; died Nov 28, 1999, in NY, NY; m. Andrew McCullough, 1953 (div. 1964); children: Leslie McCullough Jeffries. ❖ Made Broadway debut at 15, later appearing in *Inherit the Wind* and *Career;* film credits include *Captain Newman M.D., The Rabbit Trap, A Rage to Live, The Molly Maguires, Ironweed* and *Message in a Bottle;* mainstay of early tv showcases, was also a regular on "Richard Boone Show" (1963–64) and "The Doctors"; at one point, was headwriter for "The Secret Storm." Nominated for Tony award for performance as Mary Tyrone in *Long Day's Journey into Night* (1986).

LESLIE, Eliza (1787–1858). American writer. Name variations: Betsey Leslie. Born Elizabeth Leslie, Nov 15, 1787, in Philadelphia, PA; died Jan 1 (or 2), 1858, in Gloucester, NJ; dau. of Robert Leslie (mathematician and watchmaker and friend of Thomas Jefferson and Benjamin Franklin) and Lydia (Baker) Leslie; never married; no children. ❖ Began writing verse when young, but 1st published work was *Seventy-five Receipts for Pastry, Cakes, and Sweetmeats,* one of the earliest American cookbooks; followed that with several collections of children's stories; magazine articles were later collected in 3 volumes as *Pencil Sketches;* produced several more cookbooks and a manual on etiquette, *The Behavior Book,* which enjoyed several editions; only novel-length work was *Amelia; or A Young Lady's Vicissitudes.* ❖ See also *Women in World History.*

LESLIE, Euphemia (d. after 1424). Countess of Ross. Name variations: Euphamia of Ross; Euphemia of Ross. Died after 1424; dau. of Alexander Leslie, 7th (some sources cite 9th) earl of Ross, and Isabel Stewart (fl. 1390–1410). ❖ Renounced her inheritance and became a nun at North Berwick.

LESLIE, Florence (1854–1912). *See St. John, Florence.*

LESLIE, Mrs. Frank (1836–1914). *See Leslie, Miriam Folline Squier.*

LESLIE, Gladys (1899–1976). American actress. Born Mar 5, 1899, in New York, NY; died Oct 2, 1976, in Boynton Beach, FL. ❖ Billed as the "Girl with the Million Dollar Smile," played leads for Vitagraph (1917–20); films include *Betrayed, Wild Primrose, Too Many Crooks, If Winter Comes* and *Enemies of Youth.*

LESLIE, Joan (1925—). American actress. Name variations: Joan Brodel. Born Joan Agnes Theresa Sadie Brodel (also seen as Brodell), Jan 26, 1925, in Detroit, MI; sister of Mary Brodel (briefly an actress); m. Dr. William Caldwell, 1950 (died 2000); children: twin daughters Patrice and Ellen Caldwell (both teaching physicians). ❖ As a child, had a song-and-dance act with 2 sisters as "The Three Brodels"; made film debut in *Camille* under name Joan Brodel (1937), then changed to Joan Leslie (1941); other films include *The Wagons Roll at Night, The Male Animal, Hollywood Canteen, Rhapsody in Blue, Cinderella Jones, High Sierra, Sergeant York, Yankee Doodle Dandy, The Sky's the Limit, Two Guys from Milwaukee, Repeat Performance* and *Born to be Bad.*

LESLIE, Lisa (1972—). African-American basketball player and model. Born Lisa Deshaun Leslie, July 7, 1972, in Los Angeles, CA; daughter of Walter Leslie (semi-professional basketball player) and Christine Leslie-Espinoza (truck driver); attended University of Southern California, 1990–94. ❖ Center and one of the most popular players in the world of sports, was named Pacific-10 Freshman of the Year (1990); won a team gold medal at World University Games (1991), Jones Cup (1992), and Goodwill Games (1994); won a team bronze medal at World championships (1994) and gold medal (2002); led University of Southern California in scoring and rebounding and the Pac-10 in blocked shots (1993–94); named All-Pac-10 all 4 years of college career, the only player in Pac-10 history to do so; played for Sicilgesso in Italy (1994–95); was a member of the undefeated US National team (1995–96); won a team gold medal at Atlanta Olympics, scoring 29 points in final game against Brazil (1996); won a team gold medal at Sydney Olympics (2000) and Athens Olympics (2004); was a founding member of the Los Angeles Sparks (1997); was the 1st WNBA player to dunk (July 30, 2002) and the 1st to score 3,000 points (July 22, 2002). Won Dial Award (1989); named National College Player of the Year (1993). ❖ See also Sara Corbett, *Venus to the Hoop* (Doubleday, 1997); and *Women in World History.*

LESLIE, Madeline (1815–1893). *See Baker, Harriette Newell.*

LESLIE, Mary (d. 1429). Countess of Ross. Name variations: sometimes seen as Margaret; Mary Macdonald. Died in 1429 (some sources say she died c. 1435); sister of Alexander Leslie, 7th earl of Ross; dau. of Andrew Leslie and Euphemia Ross (d. 1394), countess of Ross; m. Donald Macdonald, 2nd lord of Isles (died 1420); children: Alexander Macdonald, 1st earl of Ross (d. 1449); Angus Macdonald, bishop of Isles.

LESLIE, May Sybil (1887–1937). English chemist. Name variations: May Sybil Burr. Born Aug 14, 1887, in Yorkshire, England; died July 3, 1937; University of Leeds, BS, 1908, MSc in chemisty, 1909, DSc, 1918; m. Alfred Hamilton Burr (college chemistry lecturer), 1923 (died 1933). ❖ During WWI, researched the chemical reactions in nitric acid production as well as the best conditions for its manufacture; conducted research at Paris' Institut Curie with Ellen Gleditsch (1909–11) and at Manchester's Victoria University (1911–12); researched nitric acid as a research chemist and laboratory head at Her Majesty's Factory in Litherland, Liverpool (1915–18); worked as research chemist (1918–20) at Her Majesty's Factory in Penrhyndeudraeth, North Wales; at University of Leeds, was a demonstrator, chemistry department assistant lecturer (1920–24), physical chemistry department lecturer (1924–29) and chemistry department researcher (1933–37); made an associate of the Institute of Chemistry (1918) and a Chemical Society fellow (1920). Wrote *Transactions of the Chemistry Society* (with H.M. Dawson, 1909) and *A Textbook of Inorganic Chemistry* (3 vols. ed. by J. Newton Friend, 1925).

LESLIE, Miriam Folline Squier (1836–1914). American editor, essayist, lecturer, socialite, and suffragist. Name variations: Minnie Montez; Miriam Peacock; Miriam Squier; Frank Leslie; Florence M. Wilde; Baroness de Bazus; Florence de Bazus; Baroness Leslie de Bazus; used both "Miriam" and "Florence" as 1st name; "Folline" was later spelled "Follin"; legally changed name to Frank Leslie on June 4, 1881. Born Miriam Florence Folline, June 5, 1836, in New Orleans, LA; died of a heart attack, Sept 18, 1914, in NY, NY; dau. of common-law marriage of Susan Danforth and Charles Folline (Follin, businessman); m. David Charles Peacock, Mar 27, 1854 (annulled, Mar 24, 1856); m. Ephraim George (E.G.) Squier, Oct 22, 1857 (div. May 31, 1874); m. Frank Leslie (born Henry Carter), July 13, 1874 (died Jan 10, 1880); m. William

Charles Kingsbury Wills Wilde, Oct 4, 1891 (div. June 10, 1893); no children. ❖ Editor and strong-willed businesswoman who saved a publishing empire from bankruptcy, building an independent fortune of her own—which she used to help other women succeed—and whose celebrity in US and abroad grew out of both business triumphs and personal scandal; edited *Frank Leslie's Lady's Magazine* (1863–82), *Frank Leslie's Chimney Corner* (1865–84), and *Frank Leslie's Lady's Journal* which began as *Once A Week: The Young Lady's Own Journal* (1871–81); published 1st book *California: A Pleasure Trip from Gotham to the Golden Gate* (1877); edited *Frank Leslie's Illustrated Newspaper* (1880–89) and *Frank Leslie's Popular Monthly* (1880–95, 1898–1900); legally took husband's full name to save his business empire after his death (1881); made US lecture tour (1890); willed $2 million to cause of women's suffrage (1914); wrote more than 2 dozen articles for various Leslie publications (1865–89); also, articles for *Harper's New Monthly Magazine* (1866), *The Ladies' Home Journal* (1890–92), and several newspapers. ❖ See also Madeleine B. Stern, *Purple Passage: The Life of Mrs. Frank Leslie* (U. of Oklahoma Press, 1953); and *Women in World History.*

LESLIE, Nathalie (1918–2005). *See Krassovska, Nathalie.*

LESLIE, Sharon (1925–1990). *See Christy, June.*

LESOVAYA, Tatyana (1956—). Soviet track-and-field athlete. Born Jan 1956 in USSR. ❖ At Moscow Olympics, won a bronze medal in discus throw (1980).

L'ESPERANCE, Elise Strang (c. 1879–1959). American physician. Name variations: Elise Strang L'Esperance; Elise Depew Strang. Born Elise Depew Strang, c. 1879, in Yorktown, NY; died Jan 21, 1959; dau. of Kate (Depew) Strang (died 1930) and Dr. Albert Strang; sister of May Strang; niece of Chauncey Depew, US senator and financier; m. David L'Esperance (lawyer), 1900. ❖ With sister, founded the world's 1st clinic for prevention and detection of cancer, the Kate Depew Strang Tumor Clinic (1933) at New York Infirmary for Women and Children; received diploma from Woman's Medical College of New York Infirmary (1900); at Tuberculosis Research Commission of New York, studied bacteriology for NYC Department of Health; assisted Cornell University Medical College cancer specialist, James Ewing (1910–12); studied pathology in Munich (1914); at Cornell University, was pathology instructor (1912–20), assistant pathology professor (1920–32), the 1st woman to hold such a position there at the time, then assistant professor in Preventative Medicine Department (1942–50) and full professor (1950–59); served as Bellevue Hospital surgical pathology instructor (1919–32) and pathologist and director of laboratories (1917–27, 1929–54) at New York Infirmary for Women and Children; established the Strang Cancer Prevention Clinic at New York's Memorial Hospital for Cancer and Allied Diseases (1940), where a number of advancements developed, including the Pap smear and the protoscope.

LESPINASSE, Julie de (1732–1776). French writer and salonnière. Name variations: L'Espinasse. Born Jeanne Julie Éléonore de Lespinasse in Lyons, France, Nov 9, 1732; died in Paris, May 23, 1776; illeg. dau. of Comtesse d'Albon and (probably) Comte Gaspard de Vichy; brought up as dau. of Claude Lespinasse. ❖ Left penniless following mother's death, was invited to care for the children of Comte Gaspard de Vichy, who had married her half-sister Mme de Vichy; met Marie du Deffand, the salonnière, who employed her as a companion, and brought her to her home in Paris where Lespinasse lived on the floor above (1754–64); as she grew estranged from Deffand, founded her own salon in rue Saint-Dominique, which became the center for the writers of the famous *Encyclopédie*, edited by d'Alembert; her writings include not only her letters but also 2 chapters which were meant as a sequel to *Sentimental Journey* by Laurence Sterne. ❖ See also *Women in World History.*

LESSER, Patricia (1933—). American golfer. Name variations: Mrs. John Harbottle; Patricia Lesser Harbottle. Born Patricia Ann Lesser, Aug 13, 1933, in Fort Totten, NY; m. John F. Harbottle Jr. (golfer); children: John F. Harbottle III (golf architect). ❖ Won USGA Women's Amateur (1955); member of the Curtis Cup team (1955); never turned pro.

LESSING, Doris (1919—). English novelist. Name variations: (pseudonym) Jane Somers. Born Doris May Tayler (sometimes given as Taylor), Oct 22, 1919, in Kermanshah, Persia; dau. of Alfred Cook Tayler (bank clerk) and Emily Maude (McVeagh) Tayler (nurse); attended convent school and Girls' High School, both in Salisbury, Southern Rhodesia, 1926–33; m. Frank Charles Wisdom, April 6, 1939 (div. 1943); m. Gottfried Anton Nicolai Lessing, 1943 (div. 1949); children (1st m.) John Wisdom; Jean Wisdom; (2nd m.) Peter Lessing (b. 1946). ❖ One of the most distinguished and prolific writers of 2nd half of 20th century, combined a concern for such issues as Marxism, colonialism, and feminism with profound investigations of the nature, ailments, and potential of the human personality; settled with family in Southern Rhodesia (1924); left family farm permanently for employment in Salisbury (1938); left Southern Rhodesia for England (1949); starting with publication of 1st book, *The Grass is Singing* (1950), became both a critically acclaimed and popular author; joined British Communist Party (1951); visited Southern Rhodesia and then banned from returning by the white government (1956); left Communist Party over invasion of Hungary (1956); published *The Golden Notebook* (1962); took up the study of Sufism (1964); began to publish under pseudonym Jane Somers (1983); writings include "Children of Violence" series (1952–65), (collection) *The Habit of Loving* (1957), *Briefing for a Descent into Hell* (1971), (as Jane Somers) "Canopus in Argos: Archives" series (1979–83), *The Good Terrorist* (1985), *The Fifth Child* (1988), *African Laughter: Four Visits to Zimbabwe* (1992) and *Love, Again* (1996). ❖ See also autobiographies *Under My Skin* (1994) and *Walking in the Shade* (1997); Margaret Moan Rowe, *Doris Lessing* (St. Martin, 1994); Ruth Whittaker, *Doris Lessing* (Macmillan, 1988); Jeannette King, *Doris Lessing* (Arnold, 1989); and *Women in World History.*

LESSORE, Thérèse (1884–1945). English painter. Name variations: Therese Lessore. Born 1884 in Brighton, England; died 1945 in Bathampton, England; dau. of Jules Lessore (artist and pottery painter); granddau. of Emile Lessore (decorator for Wedgewood Potteries); sister of Louise Powell (artist who m. Alfred Powell, owner of glassworks); attended South Western Polytechnic Art School, then Slade, 1904–09; m. Bernard William Audenay (Slade artist and member of Bloomsbury Group); m. William Sickert (artist), 1926 (died 1942). ❖ Impressionist painter, won Melville-Nettleship prize (1909); painted landscapes and interiors as well as theater and circus subjects; became part of Walter Sickert's London Group and held 1st solo exhibition (1918); formed lifelong professional relationship with Leicester Gallery (1924); married emotionally unstable Sickert after death of his 2nd wife (1926), serving as guardian and companion of aging artist; settled in Bath (1938), then St. George's Hill House in Bathampton; painted many Bath views and became associated with Victoria Art Gallery there.

LESTER, Eileen (1916–2004). *See Darby, Eileen.*

LESTER, Joyce (1958—). Australian softball player. Name variations: Joycelyn Lester. Born Mar 22, 1958, in Queensland, Australia. ❖ Captained Australian softball team (1985–96); catcher, won a bronze medal at Atlanta Olympics (1996). Inducted into International Softball Hall of Fame and awarded Order of Australia (2001).

LESTONAC, Jeanne de (1556–1640). *See Jeanne de Lestonac.*

LESUEUR, Daniel (1860–1920). *See Lapauze, Jeanne.*

LESUEUR, Emily Porter (1972—). American synchronized swimmer. Name variations: Emily LeSueur. Born Nov 7, 1972, in Glendale, CA. ❖ Won a team gold medal at Atlanta Olympics (1996).

LE SUEUR, Frances (1919–1995). English botanist and ornithologist. Name variations: Frances Adams Le Sueur or LeSueur; Frances Adams Ross. Born Frances Adams Ross, Aug 6, 1919, in Carlisle, Cumbria, England; died May 17, 1995; studied math at University of Manchester; m. Dick Le Sueur, 1952. ❖ Important conservationist on the Channel Island of Jersey, taught and later served as Math Department head at Jersey College for Girls (from 1948); appointed Channel Island representative of British Trust for Ornithology; became recorder for Botanical Society of the British Isles (BSBI, 1982); conducted significant study of Frère Louise-Arsène's herbarium; wrote *A Natural History of Jersey* (1976) and *Flora of Jersey* (1985). As a result of her lobbying efforts with 2 other naturalists, the States of Jersey Nature Conservation Advisory Board was established.

LE SUEUR, Meridel (1900–1996). American writer. Pronunciation: L'-Sooer. Born Meridel Wharton, Feb 22, 1900, in Murray, IA; died Nov 1996; dau. of William Wharton (preacher) and Marian (Lucy) Wharton (feminist-socialist educator); stepdau. of Arthur Le Sueur (socialist lawyer and educator); m. Harry Rice (Russian immigrant and Marxist labor organizer), 1926 (div. 1930); children: Rachel and Deborah Rice. ❖ Author who recorded the stories of Midwestern workers, farmers, women, and Native Americans, the subject matter of which delayed publication of much of her best work for 30 years because editors felt that the topics were of no interest; published 1st stories, "Persephone" and "Afternoon" in *Dial* (1927); hailed as a promising and major writer

after "Annunciation" (1935) and *Salute to Spring* (1940); published short stories and many articles for *Daily Worker, American Mercury, Partisan Review, Nation* and *Woman's Home Companion;* also joined WPA Federal Writers' Project (1939); blacklisted during postwar McCarthy hearings (1940s–50s) and published children's books to generate income; rediscovered (1970s); common themes of labor unrest, Great Depression, the poor, the beauty of the land, and regional history are included in such writings as *Worker Writers* (1939), *North Star Country* (1945), *Corn Village* (1970), *The Mound Builders* (1974), *Rites of Ancient Ripening* (1977), *Harvest: Collected Stories* (1977), *Song for My Time* (1977), *Women on the Bread Lines* (1978), *I Hear Men Talking* (1984), *Ripening* (1982), *Winter Prairie Woman* (1990), *The Dread Road* (1991) and *I Speak from the Shuck* (1992). Received Lumen Vitae Award, College of Saint Benedict (1987); honored by founding of Meridel Le Sueur Center for Peace and Justice, Minneapolis (1987); American Book Award for *Harvest Song* (1991). ❖ See also Constance Coiner, *Better Red: The Writing and Resistance of Tillie Olsen and Meridel Le Sueur* (Oxford U. Press, 1995); and *Women in World History.*

LESZCZYNSKA, Marie (1703–1768). *See Marie Leczinska.*

LETHAM, Isobel (1899–1995). Australian pioneer surfer. Born 1899 in Sydney, Australia; died Mar 11, 1995. ❖ Introduced to the sport by Duke Kahanamoku at Sydney's Freshwater Beach, near Manly Beach (1915), became Australia's 1st female board rider; left Australia for US (1918) to become a stunt woman in movies; later taught swimming and water ballet. Inducted into Australian surfing Hall of Fame. ❖ See also "Heart of the Sea" (documentary, PBS).

LETITIA. *Variant of Laetitia or Lettice.*

LETOURNEAU, Fanny (1979—). Canadian synchronized swimmer. Name variations: Létourneau. Born June 24, 1979, in Quebec City, Quebec, Canada. ❖ Won a team bronze medal at Sydney Olympics (2000); 7-time national champion. Won Helen Vanderburg Trophy (1996).

LETTOOF, Shirefie (c. 1864–1950). *See Coory, Shirefie.*

LEU, Evelyne (1976—). Swiss freestyle skier. Born July 7, 1976, in Buderholz Bottmingen, Switzerland. ❖ Won a World Cup for aerials (2001); won a gold medal for freestyle at Torino Olympics (2006).

LEUCHTENBURG, duchess of.
See Amalie Auguste (1788–1851).
See Maria Nikolaevna (1819–1876).

LEUSTEANU, Elena (1935—). Romanian gymnast. Born July 1935. ❖ At Melbourne Olympics, won a bronze medal in team all-around and a bronze medal in floor exercises (1956); at Rome Olympics, won a bronze medal in team all-around (1960).

LEVERSON, Ada (1862–1933). English novelist. Name variations: (pseudonym) Elaine; "the Sphinx." Born Ada Beddington, Oct 10, 1862, in London, England; died Aug 30, 1933, in London; dau. of Samuel Beddington (property investor) and Zillah Simon Beddington (amateur pianist); m. Ernest Leverson (sep. 1900); children: son (died in infancy); Violet Wyndham (writer). ❖ Novelist of manners and marriage, was part of a circle of late-Victorian and Edwardian authors and artists which included Oscar Wilde, Aubrey Beardsley, George Moore, Edith and Osbert Sitwell, and Max Beerbohm; came to Wilde's attention when she published "An Afternoon Party," a parody of his novel *The Picture of Dorian Gray* (1892); other sketches, articles, and parodies were published in *Punch* and *Black and White;* also wrote weekly columns for periodical *Referee* under pen-name Elaine (1903–05); published 1st novel, *The Twelfth Hour* (1907), followed by *Love's Shadow* (1908), *Tenterhooks* (1912) and *Love at Second Sight* (1916), the last 3, a trilogy, republished under title *The Little Ottleys* (1962). ❖ See also memoir *Letters to the Sphinx from Oscar Wilde with Reminiscences of the Author* (1930); Violet Wyndham, *The Sphinx and her Circle: A Biographical Sketch of Ada Leverson 1862–1933* (1963); and *Women in World History.*

LE VERT, Octavia Walton (1811–1877). American author and socialite. Born Octavia Celeste Walton, Aug 11, 1811, near Augusta, GA; died Mar 12, 1877, near Augusta; dau. of George Walton (secretary and acting governor of Florida territory) and Sally Minge (Walker) Walton; granddau. of George Walton, signer of Declaration of Independence; m. Henry Strachey Le Vert (physician), Feb 6, 1836; children: 4 daughters, 1 son. ❖ Prominent host and supporter of arts in Mobile, Alabama, published *Souvenirs of Travel* (1857), an account of 1853 and 1855 trips to Europe, during which she met Queen Victoria, Pope Pius IX, and Napoleon III;

organized French-style salon in Mobile; served as state vice-regent of Mount Vernon Ladies' Association; worked on 2nd book, *Souvenirs of Distinguished People*, that was never published.

LEVERTON, Irene (1924—). American aviator. Born 1924; grew up in Chicago, IL; never married. ❖ A top pilot, was one of 13 women slated for the "Women in Space" program (1961); passed all the tests while in training, until NASA abruptly cancelled the program (the world was not yet ready for women astronauts); spent most of her career as a charter pilot, then flight instructor; logged more than 25,000 flight hours. ❖ See also Stephanie Nolen, *Promised the Moon: The Untold Story of the First Women in the Space Race* (2002); Martha Ackmann, *The Mercury 13* (2003).

LEVERTOV, Denise (1923–1997). English-born poet, essayist, teacher and translator. Pronunciation: Lev-er-TOFF. Born Oct 24, 1923, in Ilford, Essex, England; died in Seattle, WA, Dec 20, 1997; dau. of Phillip Paul Levertoff (Anglican cleric) and Beatrice Adelaide (Spooner-Jones) Levertoff; m. Mitchell Goodman (American novelist), Dec 2, 1947 (div. 1972); children: Nikolai (b. 1949). ❖ Major poet, known for her attention to craft, sense of aesthetic ethics, weaving of a woman's private and public spheres of experience, and political activism, served as a nurse during WWII; published 1st book of poems, *The Double Image* (1946); after brief hiatus in Europe, came to US (1948) and became naturalized citizen (1955); had teaching residencies at City College of City University of New York (1965–66), Vassar (1966–67), University of California, Berkeley (1969), Massachusetts Institute of Technology (1969–70), Tufts (1973–79), Brandeis (1981–83), and Stanford (1981), among others; co-founded Writers and Artists Protest against the War in Vietnam (1965); was active in anti-nuclear and human-rights movements; writings (poetry) include *Here and Now* (1957), *Overland to the Islands* (1958), *With Eyes at the Back of Our Heads* (1959), *The Jacob's Ladder* (1961), *O Taste and See* (1964), *The Sorrow Dance* (1967), *A Tree Telling Orpheus* (1968), *Relearning the Alphabet* (1970), *To Stay Alive* (1971), *Footprints* (1972), *The Freeing of the Dust* (1975), *Life in the Forest* (1978), *Wanderer's Daysong* (1981), *Candles in Babylon* (1982), *Requiem and Invocation* (1984), *Breathing the Water* (1987) and *Sands of the Well* (1996). Received Besshokin Prize from *Poetry* (1959), for poem "With Eyes at the Back of Our Heads," Longview Award (1961), Harriet Monroe Memorial Prize (1964), Lenore Marshall Poetry Prize (1976), Elmer Holmes Bobst Award in poetry (1983), and Shelley Memorial Award from Poetry Society of America (1984). ❖ See also autobiographical prose pieces, *Tesserae* (1995); Linda Wagner, *Denise Levertov* (Twayne, 1967); Audrey T. Rodgers, *Denise Levertov: The Poetry of Engagement*. Fairleigh Dickinson U. Press, 1993); and *Women in World History*.

LEVESON-GOWER, Elizabeth (1765–1839). Countess of Sutherland and painter. Name variations: Elizabeth, Countess of Sutherland; Duchess of Sutherland; Elizabeth Gordon. Born May 24, 1765, in Edinburgh, Scotland; died Jan 29, 1839, in London; dau. of William Gordon, 18th earl of Sutherland, and Mary Maxwell; m. George Granville Leveson-Gower (1758–1833, son of 1st marquess of Stafford), Sept 4, 1785; children: George Granville Sutherland-Leveson-Gower, 2nd duke of Sutherland (1786–1861); Elizabeth Mary Leveson-Gower (1797–1891); Charlotte Sophia Leveson-Gower (1800–1870); Francis Egerton, 1st earl of Ellesmere (1800–1857). ❖ Artist and reformer, contested title on death of father and was successful (Mar 21, 1771); to gain land for the more prosperous sheep farming, husband initiated the Highland Clearances (1780), removing tenants en-masse to the coasts and the islands, where many starved to death or died on overcrowded emigrant ships to the colonies; said to have backed his policies and carried them out with vigor, policies that are still hotly debated.

LEVESON-GOWER, Georgiana Charlotte (1812–1885). *See Fullerton, Georgiana Charlotte.*

LEVESON-GOWER, Harriet (1785–1862). Countess of Granville. Name variations: Lady Granville Leveson-Gower. Born Harriet Cavendish Aug 28, 1785; died 1862; dau. of Georgiana Cavendish (1757–1806) and William Cavendish, 5th duke of Devonshire; m. Lord Granville Leveson-Gower, 1st earl Granville, Dec 24, 1809; children: 5, including Lady Georgiana Charlotte Fullerton (1812–1885), and Granville George Leveson-Gower, 2nd earl Granville (1815–1891), liberal diplomat in charge of foreign office under Gladstone).

LEVESON-GOWER, Harriet Elizabeth Georgiana (1806–1868). Duchess of Sutherland. Born Harriet Elizabeth Georgiana Howard in

1806; died 1868; dau. of George Howard, 6th earl of Carlisle (1773–1848, diplomat); m. George Granville Leveson-Gower, 2nd duke of Sutherland, in 1823. ❖ A close friend of Queen Victoria, was mistress of the robes under Liberal administrations (1837–41, 1846–52, 1853–58, and 1859–61).

LEVESQUE, Louise Cavelier (1703–1743). French novelist, poet and short-story writer. Born 1703 in Rouen, France; died 1743 in Paris; dau. of a public prosecutor. ❖ Celebrated novelist, wrote *Le Prince des Aigues-Marines* (The Prince of the Aqua Marines), the 1st fantastic tale by a French woman; also wrote *Lettres et chansons de Céphise et d'Uranie* (1731), *Célénine* (1732), *Lilia, ou histoire de Carthage* (1736), *La Vie de Job en vers* (1736), *Remarques critiques sur l'histoire de Don Quichotte* (1738), *Augustin, pénitent* (1738), *Minet* (1738), and *Sancho Pança* (1738).

LEVEY, Ethel (1880–1955). American actress and singer. Name variations: Ethel Levey Cohan. Born Nov 22, 1880, in San Francisco, CA; died Feb 27, 1955, in NYC; m. George M. Cohan (actor, playwright, composer, manager), c. 1901 (div. 1907); m. Claude Grahame-White (div.); children: Georgette Cohan (b. 1900, actress). ❖ Made stage debut in San Francisco in *A Milk White Flag* (1897); appeared for several years with Weber and Fields, then with husband George M. Cohan (1901–07), in his productions of *The Governor's Son, Running for Office*, and *Little Johnny Jones*; performed in music halls in US, England and on the Continent and in several Paris revues; had great success in London in *Outcast* (1914), among others.

LEVI, Natalia (1901–1972). Soviet composer and actress. Born Natalia Nikolayevna Smyslova in St. Petersburg, Russia, Sept 10, 1901; died in Leningrad (now St. Petersburg), Jan 3, 1972; graduate of Russian Drama School, then Leningrad Conservatory where she studied composition under P. Pyazanov. ❖ As actress, headed the Mobile Theater (1924–34); moved to Petrozavodsk (1936) where she collected folk songs of the northern people; returned to Leningrad during WWII, where she served as a translator; during Siege of Leningrad, composed war songs and was later awarded 2 medals for works hailing the defense of the city. ❖ See also *Women in World History*.

LEVI-MONTALCINI, Rita (b. 1909). Italian-born medical doctor and neurobiologist. Name variations: Rita Levi Montalcini. Born Rita Levi in Turin, Italy, April 22, 1909; dau. of Adele (Montalcini) Levi (painter) and Adamo Levi (electrical engineer and mathematician); twin sister of Paola Levi-Montalcini (1909–2000, artist); sister of Gino Levi (d. 1974), architect and professor at University of Turin; graduated summa cum laude in Medicine and Surgery, 1936, and granted advanced degree in neurology and psychiatry, 1940, both at Turin School of Medicine; never married; no children; became US citizen, 1956. ❖ Won Nobel Prize for discovery of Nerve Growth Factor, only the 4th woman to be awarded the Nobel for Physiology or Medicine (Oct 13, 1986); was admitted to Turin School of Medicine (1930); began working as Giuseppe Levi's assistant in neurological research (1936); fired from Institute of Anatomy when a government decree expelled all Jews from Italian universities (1938); fled to Belgium (1939); with invasion of Belgium, returned to Italy and secretly resumed research (1939); hid from Nazis in Florence (1943–44); worked in refugee camp (1944–46); was reinstated by Institute of Anatomy (1946); traveled to US (1946); accepted position of research associate, Washington University (1947), then promoted to associate professor (1951); undertook research at Institute of Biophysics, Rio de Janeiro (1952); with biochemist Stanley Cohen, discovered Nerve Growth Factor (1954), which is crucial to our understanding of the factors that control the growth of cells, their development, and their maintenance; promoted to full professor (1958); established research laboratory in Rome (1961); elected to US National Academy of Sciences (1968); appointed head of Cell Biology Laboratory of Italian Council of National Research (1969); retired from Washington University (1977) and Italian Council of National Research (1979). ❖ See also autobiography *In Praise of Imperfection: My Life and Work* (trans. by Luigi Attardi, Basic, 1988); and *Women in World History*.

LEVIEN, Sonya (1888–1960). Russian-American screenwriter. Born near Moscow, Russia, Dec 25, 1888; died Mar 19, 1960, in Hollywood, CA; graduated from New York University with a law degree; m. Carl Hovey, 1917; children: 2, including daughter Tamara Gold Hovey (screenwriter and biographer). ❖ Immigrated to US with parents when young; was staff writer for both *Woman's Journal* and *Metropolitan* magazines; had 1st screen credit with *Who Will Marry Me?* (1919); joined writing staff of 20th Century-Fox (1929); worked on staff at MGM (1941–56); won

Academy Award for *Interrupted Melody* (1955); wrote or co-wrote such films as *Salome of the Tenements* (1926), *The Brat* (1930), *State Fair* (1933), *Berkeley Square* (1933), *Reunion* (1936), *Drums Along the Mohawk* (1939), *The Hunchback of Notre Dame* (1939), *The Green Years* (1946), *The Valley of Decision* (1946), *Ziegfeld Follies* (1946), *Cass Timberlane* (1947), *The Great Caruso* (1951), *The Student Prince* (1954), *Hit the Deck* (1955), *Oklahoma!* (1955), *Bhowani Junction* (1955) and *Jeanne Eagels* (1957). ❖ See also Larry Ceplair, *A Great Lady: A Life of the Screenwriter Sonya Levien* (Scarecrow, 1996); and *Women in World History*.

LEVIN, Rahel (1771–1833). *See Varnhagen, Rahel.*

LEVINA, Ioulia (1973—). Russian rower. Name variations: Yuliya, Yulia, or Julija. Born Jan 2, 1973, in USSR. ❖ Won a bronze medal for quadruple sculls at Sydney Olympics (2000).

LEVINA-ROZENGOLTS, Eva (1898–1975). *See Rozenbolts-Levina, Eva.*

LEVINE, Lena (1903–1965). American gynecologist and psychiatrist. Born Lena Levine in Brooklyn, NY, May 17, 1903; died in NY, NY, Jan 9, 1965; dau. of Morris H. Levine (clothing manufacturer) and Sophie Levine; Hunter College, AB, 1923; University and Bellevue Hospital Medical College, MD, 1927; m. Louis Ferber (physician), 1929 (died 1943); children: Ellen Louise Ferber (b. 1939); Michael Allen Ferber (b. 1942). ❖ Pioneer in field of marriage counseling and activist in birth-control movement, went into private practice as a gynecologist and obstetrician in early years; underwent psychoanalysis at Columbia Psychoanalytic Institute and became a Freudian; launched a small psychiatric practice in Manhattan, while continuing to maintain gynecological practice in Brooklyn; volunteered services to Birth Control Federation of America (later known as Planned Parenthood, 1930s); also served as medical secretary of International Planned Parenthood Federation; worked at Margaret Sanger Research Bureau, one of the major birth-control clinics in NY, and later became its associate director; teamed with Abraham Stone to pioneer a group-counseling program on sex and contraception, the 1st such undertaking in US (1941); in later years, wrote about women's medical and psychological issues, such as frigidity, menopause, sexual relations in marriage, and contraception; also lectured throughout US and abroad. ❖ See also *Women in World History*.

LEVINSON, Luisa Mercedes (1909–1988). Argentinean novelist, playwright and short-story writer. Born Jan 5, 1909, in Buenos Aires, Argentina; died Mar 4, 1988, in Buenos Aires; m. Pablo Francisco Valenzuela (physician); children: Luisa Valenzuela (b. 1938, writer). ❖ Traveled widely and lectured outside of Argentina; appointed Professor *Honoris Causa* at John F. Kennedy University; works include *La casa de los Felipes* (1951), *Concierto en mi* (1956), *La pálida rosa de Soho* (1959), *La isla de los organille* (1965), *Las tejedoras ein hombre* (1967), *L'Ombre du hibou* (1972), and *El último Zelofonte* (1984); collaborated with Jorge Luis Borges on collection of stories. Received French Academy Palms (1982) and Konex Foundation Prize (1984).

LEVINSON, Tamara (1976—). American rhythmic gymnast. Born Nov 17, 1976, in Buenos Aires, Argentina. ❖ Won US nationals (1993, 1994); at Pan American Games, won silver in all-around (1995); turned to dance.

LEVISKA, Helvi Lemmiki (1902–1982). Finnish pianist, critic, teacher, and composer. Born May 25, 1902, in Helsinki, Finland; died Aug 12, 1982, in Helsinki; studied at Sibelius Academy with Erkki Melartin, graduating 1927; studied with L. Madetoja, L. Funtek, and A. Willner in Vienna (1928–36). ❖ One of Finland's most important women composers, wrote almost 20 pieces for symphony orchestra, including 4 symphonies; became librarian at Sibelius Academy (1933); was music critic of *Ilta-Sanomat*, an evening newspaper (1957–61); her works were widely performed in Finland.

LEVISON, Mary (1923—). English Presbyterian minister. Born Mary Irene Lusk, 1923, in Oxford, England; University of Edinburgh, BA and BD; studied philosophy at Oxford University and theology at Universities of Edinburgh, Heidelberg and Basel. ❖ Presbyterian reformer and minister who helped bring about change in Church of Scotland's policy toward ordination of women, began work as deaconess (1954); became assistant chaplain to Edinburgh University; petitioned General Assembly to be ordained to Ministry of Word and Sacrament (1963), setting in motion the debate which culminated in ordination of women (1968), though Catherine McConachie of Aberdeen was the 1st woman ordained; ordained to serve as assistant minister at St. Andrew's and

St. George's Parish Church in Edinburgh (1978); served as 1st woman chaplain to Queen (1991–93) and extra chaplain to Queen in Scotland (from 1993). ❖ See also memoir, *Wrestling with the Church* (1992).

LEVITT, Helen (1913—). American photographer. Born in Bensonhurst, Brooklyn, NY, 1913; dau. of Sam Levitt (businessman) and May (Kane) Levitt; left high school at 17, one semester short of graduation; never married; no children. ❖ Best known for documentary pictures of street life in New York, 1st in the Italian-Jewish neighborhood of Bensonhurst in Brooklyn, where she grew up, and later in environs of East Village, the garment district, and the Lower East Side; at 18, went to work for a photographer of standard portraits in the Bronx (1931); gravitated toward Film Photo League, a group of young, socially conscious photographers and filmmakers whose influence moved her to begin to experiment with unposed shots; purchased small, second-hand Leica and began to prowl neighborhoods (1936), often photographing children at play; shared darkroom with Walker Evans (1938–39); hired by film director Luis Buñuel as an apprentice film cutter for films he was making for Museum of Modern Art; worked as assistant editor in Film Division of Office of War Information (1944–45); with Janice Loeb and James Agee, filmed a documentary on streets of East Harlem, *In the Street* (1952), followed by *The Quiet One* (1948); taught at Pratt Institute in Brooklyn. ❖ See also Phillips and Hambourg, *Helen Levitt* (San Francisco Museum of Modern Art, 1991); and *Women in World History*.

LEVONAS, Audrey (1943—). *See McElmury, Audrey.*

LEVY, Amy (1861–1889). English poet and novelist. Born at Clapham, London, England, Nov 10, 1861; committed suicide, Sept 10, 1889; dau. of Lewis Levin (editor) and Isabelle Levin; educated at Newnham College, Cambridge (1st Jewish woman to matriculate there). ❖ Called the forgotten poet, published *A Minor Poet and Other Verse* (1884), which contained strong feminist views; tried hand at prose fiction in *The Romance of a Shop* (1888), followed by *Reuben Sachs*, a powerful novel of Jewish life that caused controversy in London; published *A London Plane Tree and Other Poems* (1889), in which her despondency was apparent; committed suicide a week after correcting the book's proofs. ❖ See also *Women in World History*.

LEVY, Chandra (1977–2001). American murder victim. Born April 14, 1977; murdered 2001; dau. of Robert Levy and Susan Levy. ❖ Worked as intern at Federal Bureau of Prisons; disappeared after affair with US congressional representative Gary Condit; remains of body found 1 year later and case declared homicide. Though Condit was not charged, case contributed to the loss of his reelection bid.

LEVY, Florence Nightingale (1870–1947). American arts administrator. Born Aug 13, 1870, in New York, NY; died Nov 15, 1947, in NY; dau. of Joseph Arthur Levy and Pauline (Goodheim) Levy. ❖ Founded, edited, and published *American Art Annual* (1898–1918); acted as director of American Federation of Arts (1909–45), which sponsored the art annual (from 1913); organized and prepared catalogs for exhibitions at Metropolitan Museum of Art (1909–17); established and served as secretary of School Art League of New York (1909–45).

LEVY, Jean (1921–1993). *See Eckart, Jean.*

LEVY, Jerre (1938—). American brain researcher. Born April 7, 1938, in Birmingham, Alabama; California Institute of Technology, PhD, 1970; married and div.; children: 2. ❖ A leading authority on the specializations of the left and right cerebral hemispheres (LH and RH), focused research on the links between neurological organization and behavioral processes in humans; was associate professor at University of Pennsylvania (1972–77); joined the staff of University of Chicago (1977), becoming a full professor, then professor emeritus; wrote more than 80 publications in her field.

LEVY, Julia (1934—). Canadian cancer researcher. Born May 15, 1934, in Singapore; dau. of a Dutch banker and an English mother; University of London, PhD in experimental pathology, 1958; children: 3. ❖ As a microbiologist and immunologist, has focused on cancer treatment using photodynamic therapy (drugs which are activated by light); served as professor of microbiology and immunology, University of British Columbia; co-founder (1981) and former CEO of Quadra Logic Technologies (now QLT PhotoTherapeutics), a leading Canadian pharmaceutical company where she pioneered work with photodynamic therapy; appointed chair of the Scientific Advisory Board of GeneMax Corp; later work has also focused on using photodynamic therapy to treat auto-immune diseases like arthritis and multiple sclerosis. Elected to Royal Society of Canada (1981).

LEW, Bird (c. 1966—). American climber. Name variations: Roberta Lew. Born Roberta Lew, c. 1966, Oakland, CA. ❖ In ice climbing, won gold medals in Difficulty and Speed at X Games (Winter 1997); as an acupuncturist, became a licensed practioner in Oriental Medicine (1987).

LEWALD, Fanny (1811–1889). German novelist, essayist, and journalist. Name variations: Fanny Markus; Fanny Lewald-Stahr; Fanny Stahr-Lewald. Born Fanny Markus in Königsberg, East Prussia (now Kaliningrad, Russia), Mar 24, 1811; died in Dresden, Aug 5, 1889; dau. of David Markus (later David Lewald) and Rosa (Assing) Markus; m. Adolf Stahr (historian), 1854. ❖ One of the most popular writers in 19th-century Germany, published a letter about a trial in Königsberg in *Europa,* launching her career; while living in Berlin, entered influential intellectual circles, which included Henriette Herz, Therese von Bacheracht and Heinrich Laube (1839); published 1st novels *Clementine* (1842) and *Jenny* (1843) anonymously (father frowned on a writing career); published *Eine Lebensfrage* (A Vital Question), a novel in which she argued for divorce and the right of women to choose their own husbands (1845); after success persuaded father to relent, began publishing under her own name; traveled to Italy, England, France, and Switzerland, providing commentary in letters, essays, and book-length travel memoirs; published *Erinnerungen aus dem Jahre 1848* (Memories of the Year 1848), recollections of the 1848 revolution in Germany, an important eyewitness account (1850); over next 4 decades, solidified reputation, publishing 27 novels and more than 30 novellas, as well as short stories, more than a dozen travel reports and memoirs, and countless essays in leading journals of the day, which were then collected in book form. ❖ See also 3-vol. autobiography *Meine Lebensgeschichte* (My Life History, 1861–1862); and *Women in World History.*

LEWICKA, Daniela (1935—). See Walkowiak, Daniela.

LEWIN, Jeannette. Dutch field-hockey player. Born in Netherlands. ❖ Won a team bronze medal at Atlanta Olympics (1996).

LEWIS, Abby (1910–1997). American actress. Name variations: Camelia Albon Lewis. Born Camelia Albon Lewis, Nov 4, 1910, in Mesilla Park, NM; died Nov 27, 1997, in New York, NY; m. John D. Seymour (actor), 1951 (died). ❖ Made Broadway debut in *Hamlet* (1934), followed by *You Can't Take It With You,* Maurice Evans' *Macbeth, The Chase, Four Winds, Howie, Life with Father* and *70 Girls 70,* among others; worked often on tv from its infancy.

LEWIS, Agnes Smith (1843–1926). Scottish Orientalist. Born Agnes Smith in Irvine, Ayr, Scotland, 1843; died 1926; dau. of John Smith (Scottish jurist); twin sister of Margaret Dunlop Gibson; m. Reverend Samuel Savage Lewis, 1887 (div. 1891). ❖ Educated in private schools and by tutors, became especially proficient in modern Greek, Arabic, and Syriac; wrote a number of novels and travel accounts; with twin sister, journeyed to Middle and Near East and discovered in the library of the convent of St. Catherine on Mt. Sinai a palimpsest which contained the Four Gospels in Syriac, representing the oldest text then known of any part of the New Testament (1892).

LEWIS, Augusta (c. 1848–1920). See Troup, Augusta Lewis.

LEWIS, Barbara (1926–1998). See Lewis, Bobo.

LEWIS, Bertha (1887–1931). English actress and singer. Born Bertha Amy Lewis, May 12, 1887, in London, England; died May 8, 1931, in Cambridge, of injuries suffered in an auto accident while driving with Henry Lytton; m. Herbert Heyner. ❖ Made stage debut with D'Oyly Carte Principal Repertory Opera as Kate in *The Pirates of Penzance* (1906); replaced Ethel Morrison as principal contralto and appeared in all leading contralto roles (1909–10, 1914–31), including Little Buttercup in *H.M.S. Pinafore,* Ruth in *Pirates of Penzance,* Lady Jane in *Patience,* Queen of the Fairies in *Iolanthe,* Lady Blanche in *Princess Ida,* Katisha in *The Mikado,* Dame Carruthers in *The Yeomen of the Guard,* and Duchess of Plaza-Toro in *The Gondoliers;* is generally regarded as the greatest contralto in D'Oyly Carte history.

LEWIS, Bobo (1926–1998). American stage and screen actress. Name variations: Barbara Lewis. Born May 14, 1926, in Miami, FL; died Nov 6, 1998, in New York, NY. ❖ Appeared on Broadway in *42nd St., Twigs, The Women, Lorelei, On the 20th Century,* and *The Musical Comedy Murders of 1940;* spent 25 years with Circle Rep in such plays as *Him, The Runner Stumbles* and *Diviners;* films include *It's a Mad Mad Mad Mad World, Running on Empty* and *One True Thing.* Received Drama Desk award for *Working.*

LEWIS, Camelia Albon (1910–1997). See Lewis, Abby.

LEWIS, Catherine Panton (1955—). See Panton, Catherine.

LEWIS, Cathy (1916–1968). American actress and singer. Born Dec 27, 1916, in Spokane, WA; died Nov 20, 1968, in Hollywood, CA; m. Elliott Lewis, 1943 (div. 1958). ❖ Began career as a singer with bands of Kay Kyser and Herbie Kay; appeared in such films as *Fury, The Kid Glove Killer, Crime Does Not Pay* (series), and *Devil at 4 O'Clock;* appeared as Deidre Thompson in tv series "Hazel" (1961–65) and as Jane Stacy on "My Friend Irma" (1952–53).

LEWIS, Charlotte (1955—). African-American basketball player. Born Sept 10, 1955, in Chicago, IL. ❖ Was member of US team at Pan American Games (1975); at Montreal Olympics, won a silver medal in team competition (1976); played professional basketball for France. Named to Illinois State Basketball Hall of Fame.

LEWIS, Denise (1972—). English heptathlete. Born Aug 27, 1972, in West Bromwich, England. ❖ Won a bronze medal at Atlanta Olympics (1996) and a gold medal at Sydney Olympics (2000), both for heptathlon; won silver medals at World championships (1997, 1999) and gold medals at Commonwealth Games (1994, 1998).

LEWIS, Edmonia (c. 1845–c. 1909). African-American sculptor. Name variations: Mary Edmonia Lewis; "Wildfire," the Indian name Lewis gave as her childhood name; "Edmonia," as she preferred to be called as an adult. Born probably 1844 or 1845, of a West Indian father, and perhaps of a mother of mixed Mississauga Indian and African-American blood; date and place of death uncertain, last seen in Rome, Italy, in 1909; attended New York Central College, an abolitionist boarding school; enrolled at Oberlin College, 1859–63; left to study art in Boston. ❖ The 1st African-American sculptor to receive international acclaim, began professional career studying sculpture with Edward A. Brackett in Boston; sold 1st sculpted medallions of abolitionist John Brown; with sale of 100 copies of bust of Robert Gould Shaw (1865), helped finance travel to Europe to study art; went 1st to Florence, later moved to Rome; became part of circle of American women sculptors living and working in Rome; became protégé of actress Charlotte Cushman who helped raise funds for Lewis' 1st marble statue, *Wooing of Hiawatha* (1867); had 1st major public exhibition (of statue of *Hagar*) in US at Farwell Hall in Chicago (Aug 1870); had public dedication at Boston of *Forever Free* (1871); had greatest triumph at Centennial Exposition in Philadelphia, where *Death of Cleopatra* became one of the most celebrated works on display (1876); traveled in America (early 1870s), and returned to Rome (1874); last seen there (1909); other works include *The Muse Urania* (1862), *Minnehaha* (1868), *Henry Wadsworth Longfellow* (1871), *The Old Arrowmaker and His Daughter* (1872), and *Asleep* and *Awake,* the former winning a gold medal at Naples Exposition. ❖ See also *Women in World History.*

LEWIS, Edna (1916–2006). African-American chef. Born 1916 in Freetown, Virginia; died Feb 13, 2006, in Decatur, Georgia; granddau. of freed Virginia slaves. ❖ Celebrated cook, ran the kitchen of Café Nicholson in New York City (1940s); wrote 4 cookbooks, including *The Taste of Country Cooking* and *The Gift of Southern Cooking.* Named Grande Dame of Les Dames d'Escoffier International; inducted into James Beard Hall of Fame (2003).

LEWIS, Eileen Hope (1884–1958). See Williams, Eileen Hope.

LEWIS, Eldece (1965—). See Clarke, Eldece.

LEWIS, Elma (1921–2004). African-American choreographer, arts administrator and educator. Born Sept 16, 1921, in Roxbury, MA; died Jan 1, 2004, in Roxbury; dau. of West Indies immigrants, Edwardine Jordan Corbin Lewis (maid) and Clairmont Richard McDonald Lewis (day laborer); Emerson College, BA, Literature Interpretation, 1943; Boston University School of Education, MA, 1944. ❖ Was a fine-arts worker at Harriet Tubman House in Boston's South End; directed and choreographed 21 operas and operettas for Robert Gould Shaw House Chorus (1946–68); founded Elma Lewis School of Fine Arts in Roxbury (1950); was founder and director of National Center of Afro-American Artists (1968); promoted work of black artists, attracting national attention throughout 1990s; directed annual production of Langston Hughes' *Black Nativity,* with a cast of 150, until she was nearly 80. Was one of the 1st recipients of the MacArthur Foundation Fellowships (1981); received more than 100 citations and awards, including the Mayor's Citation from City of Boston (1970), Henry O. Tanner Award from Black Arts Council of

California (1971) and Presidential Medal for the Arts (1983); also had more than 26 honorary degrees bestowed on her. ❖ See also *Women in World History.*

LEWIS, Estelle Anna (1824–1880). American dramatist and poet. Name variations: Stella. Born Estelle Anna Blanche Robinson near Baltimore, MD, 1824; died 1880; dau. of J.N. Robinson; attended Emma Hart Willard's Female Seminary at Troy, NY; m. S.D. Lewis (Brooklyn lawyer), 1841. ❖ Best known for the drama, *Sappho in Lesbos* (1868), which ran through 7 editions, was trans. into modern Greek, and played in Athens; published letters on travel, literature, and art in American journals under name "Stella," and wrote 2 other tragedies, *Helémah, or the Fall of Montezuma* and *The King's Strategem,* as well as several books of poems. ❖ See also *Women in World History.*

LEWIS, Ethelreda (1875–1946). English-born novelist. Name variations: (pseudonym) R. Hernekin Baptist; Mrs. Ethelreda Lewis. Born 1875 in Matlock, England; died Aug 1, 1946, probably in Johannesburg, South Africa. ❖ Author of *Trader Horn,* moved to South Africa (1904); published first 3 novels, *The Harp* (1924), *The Flying Emerald* (1925), and *Mantis* (1926), under married name of Lewis; published 4 others under pseudonym R. Hernekin Baptist: *Four Handsome Negresses: The Record of a Voyage* (1931), *Wild Deer* (1933), *Love at the Mission* (1938), and *A Cargo of Parrots* (1938); edited *The Life and Times of Trader Horn,* a 3-vol. text based on her conversations with an itinerant trader named Alfred Aloysius Horn, which was highly successful; her novels attempted to address the exploitation of black South Africans at the hands of whites. ❖ See also *Women in World History.*

LEWIS, Flora (1922–2002). American correspondent and columnist. Name variations: Flora Gruson. Born July 29, 1922, in Los Angeles, CA; died June 2, 2002, in Paris, France; dau. of Benjamin Lewis (lawyer) and Pauline Kallin (pianist); graduate of University of California, Los Angeles; graduate degree from Columbia University School of Journalism; m. Sydney Gruson (correspondent for *New York Times*), 1945 (sep. 1972, died 1998); children: Lindsey Gruson; daughters Kerry (reporter) and Sheila Gruson (died 1999). ❖ Began career as reporter for Associated Press, working in NY, and Washington DC, before being sent to London (1945); over the years, worked in Jerusalem, Prague, Warsaw, Geneva, Bonn, Paris, Mexico City, and elsewhere; was a frequent contributor to *The Observer, Economist, Financial Times* and *France-Soir;* hired by Washington Post (1956); began writing syndicated column, "Today Abroad," for *Newsday* (1965); joined *New York Times* (1972) and became head of its Paris Bureau; was Foreign Affairs columnist for the *Times* (1980–90); published 4 books, including *Europe* (1992).

LEWIS, Graceanna (1821–1912). American ornithologist and reformer. Born Aug 3, 1821, in West Vincent Township, Chester County, PA; died Feb 25, 1912, in Media, PA; dau. of John Lewis (farmer) and Esther (Fussell) Lewis; attended Kimberton, Quaker boarding school for girls; never married; no children. ❖ Born into a Pennsylvania Quaker farm family, grew up a staunch abolitionist; took 1st job as a teacher of botany and astronomy at small boarding school in York, PA; moved to Philadelphia, where she began to focus on ornithology; over next 7 years, read at Academy of Natural Sciences library and studied the specimens in its museum; lectured at Vassar (1874, 1879); taught for several years at prep schools: 1st at Friends' School in Philadelphia (1870–71), then Foster School for Girls in Clifton Springs, NY (1883–85); produced articles and drawings for journal *The American Naturalist;* wrote and produced illustrations of plants and animals, including a series of 50 large watercolors of leaves of Pennsylvania trees which were exhibited at Columbian Exposition in Chicago (1893), Pan American Exhibition in Buffalo (1901), and Louisiana Purchase Exhibition in St. Louis (1904). ❖ See also Deborah Jean Warner, *Graceanna Lewis: Scientist and Humanitarian* (Smithsonian, 1979); and *Women in World History.*

LEWIS, Hayley (1974—). Australian swimmer. Born Hayley Jane Taylor, Mar 1974, in Brisbane, Australia; children: Jacob. ❖ Won 5 gold medals at Commonwealth Games (1990); won World championship in 200-meter freestyle (1991), along with a silver for 400-meter freestyle and bronze for 200-meter butterfly; at Barcelona Olympics, won a silver medal in 800-meter freestyle and a bronze medal in 400-meter freestyle (1992); became a triathlete.

LEWIS, Ida (1842–1911). American lighthouse keeper and hero. Born Idawalley Zorada (also seen as Zoradia) Lewis in Newport, RI, Feb 25, 1842; died in Lime Rock, RI, Oct 24, 1911; dau. of Captain Hosea Lewis (keeper of Lime Rock Lighthouse in Newport Harbor); attended public school in Newport until family moved to Lime Rock;

m. William H. Wilson (fisherman), Oct 1870 (sep. and resumed maiden name). ❖ Known as America's Grace Darling, took over father's duties at Lime Rock Lighthouse in Newport Harbor, to which the family had moved in 1857, when he became disabled from a stroke (1859); at age 16, single-handedly saved 4 young men who had capsized their boat offshore; performed 18 more rescues, including pulling 2 soldiers from the wreckage of a sailboat that had capsized in a storm (1869); was 1st woman awarded the Congressional Medal of Honor. ❖ See also *Women in World History.*

LEWIS, Jenny (1921–2001). *See Dagmar.*

LEWIS, Loida (c. 1943—). Filipino-American business executive. Name variations: Loida Nicolas Lewis. Born Loida Nicolas, c. 1943, in Philippines; graduate of St. Theresa's College and University of the Philippines College of Law; m. Reginald F. Lewis (African-American CEO, died Jan 1993); children: 2. ❖ Admitted to the bar in Philippines; was the 1st Asian woman to pass New York State bar exam without having studied law in US; established a monthly magazine for the Filipino-American community (1972); served as general attorney with INS (1979–90); served as informal advisor to husband; following his death, became CEO of the nation's biggest black-owned business, TLC Beatrice International Holdings (Beatrice Foods, 1994); wrote *How to Get a Green Card* and other books.

LEWIS, Mabel Terry (1872–1957). *See Terry-Lewis, Mabel.*

LEWIS, Margaret Reed (1881–1970). American anatomist and physiologist. Name variations: Margaret Adaline Reed Lewis; Margaret Adaline Reed. Born Margaret Adaline Reed, Nov 9, 1881, in Kittaning, PA; died July 20, 1970; dau. of Martha Adaline (Walker) Reed and Joseph Cable Reed; Goucher College, AB, 1901; m. Warren Harmon Lewis (anatomist, editor of "Gray's Anatomy," partner and colleague), May 23, 1910; children: Margaret Nast Lewis, Warren Reed Lewis, and Jessica Lewis Myers. ❖ Tissue culture expert and world-renowned authority on tumors, lectured at New York Medical College for Women in physiology (1904–07) and zoology (1905–06); lectured in biology at Barnard College (1907–09); was a biology instructor at Columbia University (1907–09); at Carnegie Institute of Washington in Baltimore, worked as a department of Embryology collaborator (1915–26) and research associate (1927–46); was a Wistar Institute of Anatomy and Biology guest investigator (1940–46), then a member (1946–64) and an emerita member (after 1958); studied regeneration in crayfish, embryology of amphibians, culturing bone marrow and spleen cells (from a guinea pig); credited as the 1st to achieve a successful mammalian tissue culture. With husband, received the Pathological Society of Philadelphia's William Wood Gerhard Gold Medal (1938); received a star in Cattell's *American Men of Science* (6th ed., 1938).

LEWIS, Mary Edmonia (c. 1845–c. 1909). *See Lewis, Edmonia.*

LEWIS, Mary Jane (1852–1941). *See Innes, Mary Jane.*

LEWIS, McArtha (b. 1940). *See Calypso Rose.*

LEWIS, Shari (1933–1998). American puppeteer, ventriloquist, and entertainer. Born Jan 17, 1933, in New York, NY; died in Los Angeles, CA, Aug 2, 1998; dau. of Abraham Hurwitz (college professor) and Ann Hurwitz (school music coordinator); m. Stan Lewis (advertising executive, div.); m. Jeremy Tarcher (publisher), 1958; children: (2nd m.) daughter Mallory Tarcher. ❖ Perhaps best remembered for her sock puppet Lamb Chop, was one of the most respected performers in children's tv; at 13, excelling as a ventriloquist, made 1st appearance on a tv variety show; starred in NBC's "Facts 'n' Fun" at 18; with puppet Lamb Chop, made 1st tv appearance on "Captain Kangaroo," (1956); adding Hush Puppy and Charlie Horse, had her own NBC Saturday morning program, "The Shari Lewis Show" (1960–63); had syndicated half-hour series, "The Shari Show" (1975–76); penned over 60 children's books; returned to tv with "Lamb Chop's Play-Along" on PBS (1992–97), for which she won 5 Emmys. ❖ See also *Women in World History.*

LEWIS, Vera (1873–1956). American actress. Born Vera Mackey, June 10, 1873, in New York, NY; died Feb 8, 1956, in Woodland Hills, CA; m. Ralph Lewis (actor). ❖ Began working with D.W. Griffith (1914), appearing as one of the "Uplifters" in *Intolerance;* other films include *Sunshine Molly, A Bit of Jade, Lombardi, Ltd., Peg o' My Heart, Stella Dallas* and *Ella Cinders.*

LEWISOHN, Alice (1883–1972). American theater founder. Born 1883; died 1972; dau. of Leonard Lewisohn (businessman) and Rosalie (Jacobs) Lewisohn; m. Herbert E. Crowley, c. 1925; sister of Irene

Lewisohn. ❖ With sister, built the landmark Neighborhood Playhouse, which would serve as a center for experimental and avant-garde theater, producing plays by John Galsworthy, George Bernard Shaw, Eugene O'Neill, James Joyce, Sholem Asch, and Leonid Andreyev. ❖ See also *Women in World History.*

LEWISOHN, Irene (1892–1944). American theater and acting-school founder. Born Sept 5, 1892, in New York, NY; died April 1944 in NY; 5th daughter and youngest of 10 children of Leonard Lewisohn (businessman) and Rosalie (Jacobs) Lewisohn; sister of Alice Lewisohn; attended Finch School in NY; never married; no children. ❖ With sister, built the landmark Neighborhood Playhouse; joined Rita Morgenthau in founding the Neighborhood Playhouse School of the Theater (1928), of which she remained co-director for many years; also founded Museum of Costume Art (later Costume Institute which became part of the Metropolitan Museum of Art). ❖ See also *Women in World History.*

LEWITZKY, Bella (1915–2004). American modern dancer and choreographer. Born Jan 13, 1916, in Llano del Rio, a utopian socialist colony in the Mojave desert, in CA; died July 16, 2004, in Pasadena, CA; dau. of Russian-Jewish émigrés; m. Newell Taylor Reynolds (architect), 1940; children: Nora Reynolds Daniel (dancer). ❖ Modern-dance pioneer and outspoken champion of artistic freedom, trained with Lester Horton in Los Angeles during adolescence; performed with the Horton Dance Group for 14 years, creating roles in *Lysistrata* (1936), *Salome* (1937), *Pasaremos* (1938), *A Noble Comedy* (1940), *The Beloved* (1948), and others; taught at University of Southern California and California Institute of Arts after Horton's death; choreographed numerous solo pieces for concert recitals; formed own dance troupe for which she created original works (1966–97); called before House Un-American Activities Committee (1951), refused to identify acquaintances who might have been members of the Communist Party, replying defiantly, "I'm a dancer, not a singer." Works of choreography include *On the Brink of Time* (1969), *Kinaesonata* (1970), *Pietas* (1971), *Bella and Brindle* (1973), *Voltage Controlled Oscillator* (1975), *Greening* (1976), *Recesses* (1979) and *Suite Satie* (1980); received 1st California Governor's Award for Lifetime Achievement.

LEWSLEY, Patricia (1957—). Northern Ireland politician. Born Mar 3, 1957, in Belfast, Northern Ireland. ❖ Representing SDLP, elected to the Northern Ireland Assembly for Lagan Valley (1998).

LEWSON, Jane (c. 1700–1816). English literary inspiration. Name variations: Lady Lewson. Born Jane Vaughan c. 1700 in England; died 1816; married. ❖ Became a recluse after death of husband (1726); her eccentricities are reputed to have been the basis for Miss Havisham in Dickens' *Great Expectations.*

LEYBURNE, Elizabeth (d. 1567). Duchess of Norfolk. Name variations: Lady Dacre of Gilsland; Elizabeth Howard. Died Sept 4, 1567; dau. of Sir James Leyburne; m. Thomas Dacre, 4th lord Dacre of Gilsland (also seen as Gillesland); became 3rd wife of Thomas Howard (1537–1572), 3rd duke of Norfolk (r. 1554–1572, also seen as 4th duke of Norfolk), in 1566; children: (1st m.) Anne Dacre (who m. Philip Howard, 17th earl of Arundel); Mary Dacre (1563–1578, who m. Thomas Howard, 1st earl of Suffolk); Elizabeth Dacre (who m. Lord William Howard); George Dacre, 5th lord Dacre of Gilsland. Thomas Howard was also m. to Margaret Audley (d. 1564) and Mary Fitzalan (d. 1557).

LEYDA, Si-Lan (b. 1909). *See Chen, Si-Lan.*

LEYEL, Hilda (1880–1957). English herbalist. Name variations: Hilda Winifred Ivy Leyel; Mrs C.F. Leyel. Born Hilda Winifred Ivy Wauton, Dec 6, 1880, in London, England; died April 15, 1957; dau. of a French teacher at Uppingham School, Rutland; m. Carl Frederick Leyel (theatrical manager), 1900 (died 1925). ❖ Founded Society of Herbalists in England and generated a renewed interest in herbalism; began career as a London shop proprietor (1927); studied medicine and herbalists, including Nicholas Culpeper; opened the highly successful Culpeper House, an herbal shop in London (1927); edited 2 volumes of M. Grieve's *A Modern Herbal* (1931); advocated the use of pure water, pure food, artificial fertilizers, and herbs for mental and physical well being; with help of influential friends, had a 1941 bill amended to permit members of the Society of Herbalists to be legally treated with herbs; wrote *The Magic of Herbs* (1926), *Herbal Delights* (1937) and *Green Medicine* (1952).

LEYLAND, Louise Mack (1874–1935). *See Mack, Louise.*

LEYMAN, Ann-Britt (1922—). Swedish long jumper. Born June 10, 1922, in Sweden. ❖ At London Olympics, won a bronze medal in the long jump (1948).

LEYSTER, Judith (1609–1660). Dutch painter. Pronunciation: Ly-ster. Born Judith Leyster, 1609, in Haarlem, Netherlands; died in Heemstede, Netherlands, 1660; dau. of Jan Willemssen (Haarlem brewery owner) and Trijn Jaspers; m. Jan Miense Molenaer (painter), 1636; children: Joannes, Jacobus, Helena, Eva, Constantijn. ❖ Painter, mainly of genre scenes, who—due to the misattribution of her works for almost 3 centuries—reaped critical acclaim while remaining unknown; painted 1st authenticated work, *The Jester* (1625); became the 1st woman to join the Haarlem Guild of St. Luke, allowing her to establish her own workshop and to take on students (1633); had 3 male pupils (1635); painted last known work, *Portrait of a Man* (1652); paintings include *Laughing Man with Wine Glass, The Jolly Toper* (1629), *The Jolly Companions* or *Carousing Couple* (misattributed to Frans Hals, 1630), *The Proposition* (1631), *Boy and Girl with Cat and Eel* or *Two Children and a Cat* (misattributed to Hals), *Still Life, Self-Portrait* (National Gallery of Art, Washington, DC, and another *Self-Portrait* is in the Frans Hals Museum, Haarlem) and *Portrait of a Man* (1652). ❖ See also Frima Fox Hofrichter, *Judith Leyster: A Woman Painter in Holland's Golden Age* (Doornspijk: Davaco, 1989); and *Women in World History.*

LÉZARDIÈRE, Pauline de (1754–1835). French historian. Name variations: Marie Charlotte Pauline Lezardiere. Born 1754 in France; died 1835; dau. of French noble. ❖ Wrote *Théories des lois politiques de la monarchie française*, which was published by brother (1844), analyzing 3 historical periods: imperial law before Clovis, legislation by popular consensus from Clovis to Charles I the Bald, king of France (aka Charles II, Holy Roman Emperor), and feudal customs up to 14th century; most copies of work destroyed during French Revolution and 4th part never recovered.

LEZAY MARNEZIA, Charlotte Antoinette de Bressy, Marquise de (c. 1705–1785). French salonnière. Name variations: Marquise de Lezay Marnesia. Born Charlotte Antoinette de Bressey, c. 1705, in France; died 1785 in Conde-sur-Iton, France; m. François Gabriel de Lezay (1699–1778), 2nd marquis of Lezay, seigneur de Marnezia, Feb 6, 1733, in Metz; children: Claude Lezay Marnezia (1735–1800). ❖ Held a literary salon at her home in Nancy; published *Lettres de Julie à Ovide* anonymously (1753), which was attributed to Marmontel but later revealed by her son to be her work.

L'HÉRITIER, Marie-Jeanne (1664–1734). French novelist and short-story writer. Name variations: Mlle L'Heritier de Villandon or Villaudon; also seen as Lhéritier or Lheritier. Born 1664 in Paris, France; died 1734; niece of Charles Perrault (1628–1703, writer of fairy tales); dau. of a historian; sister was a poet; never married. ❖ Championed cause of women in her writing; inherited the literary salon begun by Madeleine de Scudéry; lived life of virtue and high morals; published stories in *Mercure galant;* wrote several stories attributed to uncle, including *L'Adroite Princesse, ou les Aventures de Finette;* wrote 1st version of "Sleeping Beauty" called "La Belle au bois dormant"; other works include *Marmoison ou L'Innocente tromperie* (1695) and *Histoire de la Marquise-Marquis de Banneville* (1723).

LHEVINNE, Rosina (1880–1976). Russian-born pianist. Name variations: Rosina Lhévinne. Pronunciation: Lay-VEEN. Born Rosina Bessie, Mar 29, 1880, in Kiev, Russia; died Nov 9, 1976, in Glendale, CA; dau. of Jacques Bessie (Dutch merchant) and Maria (Katch) Bessie (Russian); attended Imperial Russian Conservatory, 1889–98; m. Josef Lhevinne, June 20, 1898 (died 1944); children: Constantine (renamed Don) Lhevinne; Marianna Lhevinne. ❖ Considered one of the greatest teachers of the 20th century, spent much of her career playing dual-piano works with husband and, after his death, went on to fame as a soloist and teacher of many of America's leading classical pianists; won gold medal upon graduation from Conservatory (1898); began career as dual pianist with husband (1899); moved to Tiflis (1899); interned in Germany during WWI (1914–18); settled in US (1919); began teaching at Juilliard School in conjunction with husband's appointment to Juilliard faculty (1924); appointed to faculty of Austro-American Conservatory in Mondsee, Austria (1930); with husband, performed 40th anniversary concert as dual pianists at Carnegie Hall (1939); appointed to faculty of Juilliard School (1945), then Los Angeles Conservatory (1946); accepted Van Cliburn as her student at Juilliard (1951); joined faculty at Aspen Music Festival (1956); became faculty member of University of California, Berkeley, and appeared with National Orchestral Association

(1961); made debut with New York Philharmonic (1963). ❖ See also Robert A. Wallace, *A Century of Music-Making: The Lives of Josef and Rosina Lhevinne* (Indiana U. Press, 1976); and *Women in World History*.

LI BUN-HUI (1968—). North Korean table-tennis player. Born Dec 29, 1968, in North Korea. ❖ At Barcelona Olympics, won a bronze medal in doubles and a bronze medal in singles (1992).

LI CH'ING-CHAO (1083–c. 1151). *See Li Qingzhao.*

LI CHUNXIU (1969—). Chinese track-and-field athlete. Born Aug 13, 1969, in China. ❖ At Barcelona Olympics, won a bronze medal in the 10-km walk (1992).

LI DONGMEI (1969—). Chinese basketball player. Born Nov 6, 1969, in China. ❖ At Barcelona Olympics, won a silver medal in team competition (1992).

LI DU (1982—). Chinese shooter. Born Mar 5, 1982, in China. ❖ Placed 2nd at World Championships for 10m air rifle (2002); won a gold medal for 10m air rifle at Athens Olympics (2004).

LI DUIHONG (1970—). Chinese shooter. Born Jan 25, 1970, in Daqing, Heilongjiang, China. ❖ At Barcelona Olympics, won a silver medal in sport pistol (1992); won a gold medal for 25m pistol at Atlanta Olympics (1996).

LI FENG-YING (1975—). Taiwanese weightlifter. Name variations: Li Fengying. Born 1975 in Taiwan. ❖ Representing Chinese Taipei, won World championship (1999, 2001); won a silver medal for 48–53kg at Sydney Olympics (2000).

LI, Florence Tim Oi (1907–1992). Hong Kong Anglican priest. Name variations: Li Tim Oi. Born Li Tim-Oi (Much-Beloved), May 5, 1907, in Hong Kong, China; died Feb 26, 1992, in Toronto, Canada; sister of Rita Lee-Chui; attended Canton Theological Seminary. ❖ The 1st Anglican woman priest, was baptized in Anglican church as a student, taking name Florence; took 4-year course at Canton Theological Seminary and was made deacon and given charge of Anglican congregation in Portuguese colony of Macao (1941), which had large refugee population from war-torn China; was given permission to administer Eucharist during the 3-year period when Japanese occupation of Southern China prevented priests from traveling to perform duty; was subsequently ordained by Bishop R.O. Hall (1944), resulting in major Church controversy; surrendered priest's license to save Hall from forced resignation after ordination was disowned by Archbishop of Canterbury, Geoffrey Fisher (1946); suffered persecution by Maoists after Chinese Revolution and practiced religion clandestinely; appointed teacher at Canton Theological Seminary, then reordained when Hong Kong decided independently to ordain women priests (1971); immigrated to Canada (1983), where she ministered to Chinese immigrant population in Toronto; was also reinstated as priest by Anglican Church of Canada (1984) and celebrated 40th anniversary of original ordination in Westminster Abbey; concelebrated the Eucharist at the ceremony that elevated an African-American, Barbara Harris, as the 1st Anglican woman bishop (1989).

LI GUOJUN (1966—). Chinese volleyball player. Born Mar 21, 1966, in China. ❖ At Seoul Olympics, won a bronze medal in team competition (1988).

LI HUIFEN (1963—). Chinese table-tennis player. Born Oct 14, 1963, in China. ❖ At Seoul Olympics, won a silver medal in singles (1988).

LI HUIXIN (1937—). Chinese physician and short-story writer. Born 1937 in China. ❖ Practised medicine but wrote throughout career; during Cultural Revolution (1966–76) traveled through rural north and southwest China with a medical team and based many stories on her experiences; most anthologized story is "The Old Maid" (1980).

LI JI (1986—). Chinese swimmer. Born July 9, 1986, in China. ❖ Won a silver medal for 4x200-meter freestyle relay at Athens Olympics (2004).

LI JU (1976—). Chinese table tennis player. Born Jan 22, 1976, in Jiangsu Province, China. ❖ Won Asian Cup singles (1996); won a gold medal for doubles and a silver for singles at Sydney Olympics (2000); won World Cup (2000); retired from national team (2001).

LI LAN (1961—). Chinese basketball player. Born July 12, 1961, in China. ❖ At Los Angeles Olympics, won a bronze medal in team competition (1984).

LI LINGJUAN (1966—). Chinese archer. Born April 10, 1966, in China. ❖ At Los Angeles Olympics, won a silver medal in double FITA round (1984).

LI MEISU (1959—). Chinese track-and-field athlete. Born April 17, 1959, in China. ❖ At Seoul Olympics, won a bronze medal in the shot put (1988).

LI NA (1984—). Chinese diver. Born May 1, 1984, in Hefei, China. ❖ Won a gold medal for 10-meter platform at Asian Games (1998); won FINA World Cup for synchronized platform (1999); won a gold medal for synchronized diving 10-meter platform and a silver medal for 10-meter platform at Sydney Olympics (2000); won gold medals in platform and synchronized at Sydney World Cup (2000).

LI NA. Chinese fencer. Name variations: Li-na. Born in China. ❖ Won a bronze medal for team épée at Sydney Olympics (2000).

LI QING (1972—). Chinese diver. Born Dec 1, 1972, in China. ❖ At Seoul Olympics, won a silver medal in springboard (1988).

LI QINGZHAO (1083–c. 1151). Chinese poet. Name variations: Li Ch'ing-chao; Li Ch'ing Chao; Li Chiang-chao; Li Qing Zhao. Born Li Qingzhao in 1083; died c. 1151; dau. of Li Gefei also seen as Li Ke-fei or Li Ko-fei (scholar and minister at court) and a mother who was a poet (name unknown); educated at home; m. Zhao Mingcheng (Chao Ming-ch'eng, famous epigraphist who specialized in deciphering old inscriptions), c. 1101 (died 1129); possibly m. Zhang Ruzhou, 1132 (div. after 100 days). ❖ China's greatest female poet, grew up in Chinan, called "The City of Fountains," where her childhood home is now a historical site; lived during Song dynasty and specialized in lyric ci (tz'u) verse; was praised for the originality of her poetic imagery, her emotional language, and the harmony of her verse; produced a body of work including 6 volumes of poetry and 7 volumes of essays, most of which have been lost. ❖ See also James Cryer, *Plum Blossom: Poems of Li Ch'ing-Chao* (Carolina Wren Press, 1984); Kenneth Rexroth and Ling Chung, *Li Ch'ing Chao: Collected Poems* (1979); and *Women in World History*.

LI RONGHUA (1956—). Chinese rower. Born Sept 21, 1956, in China. ❖ At Seoul Olympics, won a bronze medal in coxed eights and a silver medal in coxed fours (1988).

LI SHAN (1980—). Chinese volleyball player. Born May 21, 1980, in Tianjin, China. ❖ Setter, won a team gold medal at Athens Olympics (2004).

LI SHUFANG (1979—). Chinese judoka. Born Aug 1, 1979, in Shangdong Province, China. ❖ Won a silver medal for 56–63kg half-middleweight at Sydney Olympics (2000).

LI SHUXIAN (1924–1997). Chinese nurse. Born 1924; died in Beijing, June 9, 1997; arranged marriage with Pu Yi, later known as Henry Puyi (the last emperor), in 1962 (died 1967). ❖ Was chosen by prime minister Zhou Enlai of the People's Republic of China to be the wife of Henry Puyi (1962), who had been the last emperor of China; following husband's death (1967), was rarely mentioned in the state-controlled media. ❖ See also *Women in World History*.

LI, Tim Oi (1907–1992). *See Li, Florence Tim Oi.*

LI TING (1980—). Chinese tennis player. Born Jan 5, 1980, in Hebei Province, China. ❖ Won a gold medal for doubles at Athens Olympics (2004).

LI TING (1987—). Chinese diver. Born April 1, 1987, in Guilin, China. ❖ Placed 1st in Grand Prix ranking (2001); at World championships, won a gold medal for synchronized platform (2003); placed 1st in 10-meter synchronized platform at Grand Prix Super Final (2004); with Lishi Lao, won a gold medal for 10-meter synchronized platform at Athens Olympics (2004).

LI XIAOQIN (1961—). Chinese basketball player. Born Dec 7, 1961, in China. ❖ At Los Angeles Olympics, won a bronze medal in team competition (1984).

LI XIN (1969—). Chinese basketball player. Born Nov 5, 1969, in China. ❖ At Barcelona Olympics, won a silver medal in team competition (1992).

LI YAN (1976—). Chinese volleyball player. Born May 1, 1976, in Fujian, China. ❖ Spiker, won a team silver medal at Atlanta Olympics (1996).

LI YAN. Chinese short-track speedskater. Born in China. ❖ At Calgary Olympics, where short track was a demonstration sport, won 2 gold medals and set 2 World records (1988); won a silver medal for the 500 meters at Albertville Olympics (1992); became a Slovenian Olympic coach; named US National Short Track Coach for Programs (2003).

LI YANJUN (1963—). Chinese volleyball player. Born Mar 18, 1963, in China. ❖ At Los Angeles Olympics, won a gold medal in team competition (1984).

LI YUEMING (1968—). Chinese volleyball player. Born Jan 24, 1968, in China. ❖ At Seoul Olympics, won a bronze medal in team competition (1988).

LI YUQIN (d. 2001). Chinese wife of the emperor. Name variations: Jade Lute. Born in Shandong province, China; was a member of the Manchu minority; died April 27, 2001, age 73, in Changchun, China; educated at a Japanese school in Manchuria; m. Pu Yi, later known as Henry Puyi (the last emperor), 1943 (div. 1958); m. tv engineer; children: (2nd m.) 1 son. ❖ At 16, became wife number 4 of the last emperor of China (1943), who was then head of the Japanese puppet state, Manchuria; with husband, arrested by the Communist Party (1945); put to work in a wool mill, was told to study the works of Marx and Lenin; became a local government officer, then librarian. ❖ See also (film) *The Last Emperor* (1987).

LI ZHONGYUN (1967—). Chinese judoka. Born 1967 in China. ❖ At Barcelona Olympics, won a bronze medal in half-heavyweight 52 kg (1992).

LI ZHUO (1981—). Chinese weightlifter. Born Dec 4, 1981, in China. ❖ Won a silver medal for 48kg at Athens Olympics (2004).

LIA. *See Leah.*

LIADAN (fl. 7th c.). Poet of Ireland. Fl. in 7th century in Ireland. ❖ Rejected Cuirithir and joined one of the convents of Christianized Ireland; came to regret her haste and sought his love again, only to find that he had joined a monastery and refused to leave it; wrote a lament which names Cuirithir as a lost lover for whom she is grieving.

LIANG DESHENG (1771–1847). Chinese poet. Born in 1771 in Qiantang, Zhejiang Province, China; died in 1847; dau. of a scholar; sister of Liang Yaoshen; studied under Ruan Yuan; m. Xu Zongyan (1768–1818, scholar); children: 2 sons, 3 daughters. ❖ Wrote 2 collections of poetry still extant, *Guchun xuan shichao* and *Guchun xuan ci*; edited husband's works after his death; took up the narrative of an unfinished work of Chen Duansheng's, *Zaishengyuan*, providing an ending for it.

LIANG QIN. Chinese fencer. Born in China. ❖ Won a bronze medal for team épée at Sydney Olympics (2000).

LIANG YAN (1961—). Chinese volleyball player. Born Oct 4, 1961, in China. ❖ At Los Angeles Olympics, won a gold medal in team competition (1984).

LIAPINA, Oksana (1980—). *See Lyapina, Oksana.*

LIAQUAT ALI KHAN, Begum (1905–1990). *See Khan, Begum Liaquat Ali.*

LIBBEY, Laura Jean (1862–1925). American author. Born Mar 12, 1862, in Brooklyn, NY; died Oct 25, 1925, in New York, NY; dau. of Thomas H. Libbey and Elizabeth (Nelson) Libbey; m. Van Mater Stilwell, 1898; no children. ❖ Specializing in the "working-girl" novel, began contributing stories to *New York Ledger* while still in her teens; during 30-year career, produced over 80 romantic novels, most of which were printed serially and then reproduced in paperbound editions. ❖ See also *Women in World History.*

LIBERÁKI, Margaríta (1919—). Greek novelist and dramatist. Name variations: Margaríta Liberaki, Limberaki or Lymberaki; Margaríta Karapanou. Born in Athens, Greece, April 22, 1919 (some sources cite 1910); dau. of Themistuclis Liberáki and Sapho Fexi Liberáki; awarded law degree from University of Athens, 1943; m. Georges Karapanos, 1941 (div.); children: 1 daughter. ❖ Published 1st novel, *The Trees* (1947), followed by *The Straw Hats* and *Three Summers* (1950); after *The Straw Hats* achieved both critical and commercial success, moved to Paris, dividing time between Paris and Athens; published novel *The Other Alexander* (1952); wrote plays for over 20 years, most of which she drafted in both Greek and French versions, including *Kandaules' Wife* (1955), *The Danaïds* (1956), *The Other Alexander* (1957), *Le saint prince* (1959), *La lune a faim* (1961), *Sparagmos* (1965), *Le bain de mer* (1967), *Erotica* (1970) and *Zoe* (1985); published innovative novel *The Mystery*

(1976); also crafted several film scripts, including "Magic City" (1953) and "Phaedra" (1961), and dramatizations of her novels *The Straw Hats* and *Three Summers* were televised on European tv channels (1995 and 1996). ❖ See also *Women in World History.*

LIBUSSA (c. 680–738). Queen of Bohemia. Name variations: Libusa; Princess Libusa or Libuša. Born in Bohemia c. 680; died 738; dau. of Crocus, king of Bohemia; sister of Tetka and Kascha. ❖ Succeeded father Crocus (c. 700); spent much of her reign engaged in battles, with mostly female soldiers, against many neighboring regions in an effort to expand her realm. ❖ See also *Women in World History.*

LICHFIELD, countess of. *See Fitzroy, Charlotte (1664–1717).*

LICHNOWSKY, Mechthilde (1879–1958). German playwright, essayist and travel writer. Name variations: Mechtild, countess von Arco; Mechtild Peto. Born Mar 8, 1879, in Schönburg, Germany; died 1958 in London, England; dau. of Maximilian, count von Arco, and Olga von Werther; great granddau. of Empress Maria Theresa of Austria; m. Karl Max Lichnowsky, 1904; m. Major Ralph Harding Peto, 1937; children: (1st m.) Wilhelm, Leonore, and Michael Lichnowsky. ❖ Traveled widely in Europe and Egypt and recorded impressions; also wrote of decline of aristocrat European culture and had contempt for Nazism; works include *Götter, Könige und Tiere in Ägypten* (1913) and *Gespräche in Sybaris* (1946).

LICHTENAU, Countess von (1753–1820). Mistress of the king of Prussia. Born Wilhelmine Enke in 1753; died 1820; mistress of Frederick William II, king of Prussia (r. 1786–1797); children: (with Frederick William II) five sons. Frederick William II was 1st m. to Elizabeth of Brunswick (1746–1840), then Frederica of Hesse (1751–1805).

LICHTENBERG, Jacqueline (1942—). American science-fiction writer. Name variations: (pseudonym) Daniel R. Kerns. Born Mar 25, 1942, in Flushing, NY; m. Salomon Lichtenberg; children: 2 daughters. ❖ Works include *House of Zeor* (1974), *Star Trek Lives!* (1975), *Mahogany Trinrose* (1981), *RenSime* (1984), *Zelerod's Doom* (1986), *Those of My Blood* (1988), and *Sime Gen* (2003); published nonfiction on *Star Trek* phenomenon.

LICINIA EUDOXIA (422–before 490). Empress of Rome. Name variations: Eudocia; Eudoxia. Born 422; died before 490; dau. of Eudocia (c. 400–460) and Theodosius II, East Roman emperor; m. Valentinian III (born 419), West Roman emperor, in 437 (died 455); daughter-in-law of Galla Placidia (c. 390–450); sister-in-law of Honoria (c. 420–?); married against her will Petronius Maximus, c. 456; children: (1st m.) Eudocia (who m. Huneric around 462) and Placidia. ❖ Was betrothed to Valentinian III, later emperor (424); married Valentinian in Constantinople (437) and was officially elevated to rank of Augusta at Ravenna, Italy (439), a status which she probably held until her death; was considered the most influential woman in the Western Roman Empire (450–55) until husband's assassination; supported the imperial elevation of Maiorianus, but her advocacy was not enough to enthrone her choice (instead, Petronius Maximus, who was only 22 at the time, secured the Western throne and married her against her will). ❖ See also *Women in World History.*

LID, Hilde Synnove. Norwegian freestyle skier. Name variations: Hilde Synnoeve or Synnøve Lid. Born in Norway. ❖ Won a bronze medal for aerials at Lillehammer Olympics (1994).

LIDDELL, Alice (1852–1934). English literary inspiration. Born Alice Pleasance Liddell, May 4, 1852; died 1934 at Westerham, Kent; dau. of Dr. Henry Liddell (former head of Westminster School and dean of Christ Church, Oxford); sister of Lorina Charlotte Liddell and Edith Liddell, known as Tillie; m. Captain Reginald Hargreaves, 1880 (died 1928); children: Violet, Norah and Reginald Hargreaves. ❖ Was the inspiration for Alice, of Alice in Wonderland. ❖ See also *Women in World History.*

LIDDELL, Helen (1950—). Scottish politician and member of Parliament. Name variations: Rt. Hon. Helen Liddell. Born Helen Lawrie Reilly, Dec 6, 1950, in Monklands; attended Strathclyde University; m. Dr. Alistair Liddell, 1972; children: 1 son, 1 daughter. ❖ Began career as journalist with BBC Scotland (1976–77); served as general secretary, Labour Party in Scotland (1977–88); was director of corporate affairs for Scottish Daily Record and Sunday Mail (1986–92); representing Labour, elected to House of Commons for Monklands East (1994) and Airdrie and Shotts (1997, 2001); became 1st deputy secretary of state for Scotland (1998), then 1st woman secretary of state for Scotland (2001); left Parliament (2005); also a novelist.

LIDMAN, Sara (1923–2004). Swedish novelist, dramatist and social commentator. Born Sara Adela Lidman in Missenträsk, Sweden, Dec 30, 1923; died June 17, 2004, in Umea, Sweden; dau. of Andreas Lidman and Jenny (Lundman) Lidman; educated at University of Uppsala. ❖ Homebound because of a bout with TB in early teens, became a voracious reader and began to write, to allay the sense of isolation reinforced by the strict pietism of her Lutheran parents and neighbors; moved to Stockholm (1944); published 1st novel, *Tjärdalen* (The Tar Well or Tar-Boiler, 1953), a critical and popular success; wrote 3 more novels set in the isolated village world of Sweden's Norrland: *Hjortronlandet* (Cloudberry Land, 1955), which became a bestseller and was chosen as Sweden's best novel of the year, *Regnspiran* (*The Rain Bird*, 1958), and *Bära mistel* (Carrying the Mistletoe, 1960); after a trip to South Africa and a brush with the apartheid system (1960), wrote *Jag och min son* (I and My Son, 1961); lived in Kenya and Tanzania (1962–64), basis for novel, *Med fem diamanter* (With Five Diamonds, 1964); abandoning fiction, became a reporter; during Vietnam war, visited North Vietnam (1966) and wrote impressions in a series of articles for Swedish newspapers, which appeared in book form as *Samtal i Hanoi* (Conversations in Hanoi, 1966); published *Gruva* (The Mine, 1968), exploring the working and living conditions among Lapland's hardrock iron miners; resumed writing fiction (late 1970s); published 5-novel suite which returned to Sweden's far north: *Din tjänare hör* (Thy Obedient Servant, 1977), *Vredens barn* (Anger's Child, 1978), *Nabot's sten* (*Naboth's Stone*, 1981), *Den underbare mannen* (The Miracle Man, 1983), and *Järnkronan* (The Iron Crown, 1985); published *Lifsens rot* (The Root of Life) to critical acclaim (1996). ❖ See also *Women in World History*.

LIDOVA, Irene (1907–2002). Russian dance critic and producer. Name variations: Irène Lidova. Born Irina Kaminskaya, Jan 7, 1907, in Moscow, Russia; died May 23, 2002, in Paris, France; attended the Sorbonne; m. Serge Lidov, known as Serge Lido (Russian dance photographer, died 1984); no children. ❖ Immigrated to France when young; began reviewing dance for *Marianne* (1939); played a major role in founding creative ballet companies in postwar France, presenting the 1st ballets of Roland Petit and Janine Charrat (1943–44) and founding Les Ballets des Champs-Elysées (1945); discovered dancers and choreographers and publicized their achievements.

LIDSTONE, Dorothy (1938—). Canadian archer. Name variations: Dorothy Wagar. Born Nov 2, 1938, in Wetaskawin, Alberta, Canada; m. George Lidstone. ❖ Came in 1st in indiv. and 2nd in team at the World championship (1969), the 1st Canadian to win a world archery title; was Canadian champion (1969–71).

LIDWINA OF SCHIEDAM (1380–1433). Dutch mystic and saint. Born in 1380; died in 1433. ❖ Her life has been recounted in the writings of Thomas à Kempis and J.K. Huysmans. Feast day is April 14.

LIEBERMAN-CLINE, Nancy (1958—). American basketball player and coach. Name variations: Nancy Lieberman; Lady Magic. Born July 1, 1958, in Brooklyn, NY; attended Old Dominion University, 1976–80; m. Tim Cline (basketball player), May 18, 1988. ❖ Was a member of Jr. National team (1977) and Jones Cup team (1979); won a team gold medal at Pan Am Games teams (1975) and World championships (1975, 1979); became youngest basketball player in Olympic history to win a medal (silver), at Montreal (1976); named to Olympic squad (1980); named All-America (1978–80); won Broderick Cup (1979, 1980); finished collegiate career with 2,430 points, 1,167 rebounds, 983 assists, and more than 700 steals in 134 games; led Old Dominion to 2 AIAW championships (1979, 1980); began professional career with WBL's Dallas Diamonds (1980) and led team in scoring during successful championship series (1981); was leading scorer for Diamonds (1984); played for Dallas Diamonds of WABA during its brief season (1984); became 1st woman to play in a men's professional league (1986) by joining USBL's Springfield Fame; played in USBL for 2 years (1986, 1987), 2nd season as a member of Long Island Knights; was a member of Washington Generals (1987–88); worked as a basketball analyst for NBC (1988, 1992); served as broadcaster for ESPN, ABC, Fox and NBC; signed with WNBA (1997) and selected by Phoenix Mercury in 2nd round draft; became coach of Detroit Shock (1998). Inducted into Naismith Memorial Basketball Hall of Fame (1996). ❖ See also autobiography (with Debby Jennings) *Lady Magic* (Sagamore, 1991),

Basketball My Way (Scribner, 1982), and Betty Milsaps Jones, *Nancy Lieberman: Basketball's Magic Lady* (Harvey House, 1980).

LIEBES, Dorothy (1897–1972). American weaver, textile designer, and businesswoman. Born Dorothy Katherine Wright in Guerneville, CA, Oct 14, 1897; died in New York, NY, Sept 20, 1972; dau. of Frederick Wright (entrepreneur) and Elizabeth Calderwood Wright (schoolteacher); University of California at Berkeley, AB, 1921; studied weaving and design at Chicago's Hull House, Columbia University, and California School of Fine Arts; m. Leon Liebes (businessman), 1928 (div. 1946); m. Relman Morin (Pulitzer Prize-winning journalist), 1948. ❖ Had a major aesthetic influence in the textile industry's conversion to synthetic fibers and new technologies in dyeing after WWII; held 1st group show at NY's Decorator's Club (1933); established Dorothy Liebes Design Inc. in San Francisco (1934); served as director of Decorative Arts Exhibition of San Francisco World's Fair (1939); was among the 1st American fabric designers to experiment with the use of such colors as fuchsia, tangerine, turquoise, chartreuse, and lacquer red; also introduced the use of other materials, including beads, bamboo strips, cellophane, and metallic threads, into the weaving process; was hired by Goodall Fabrics (1940) to design 12 new fabrics; served as Dobeckmun's design and color consultant in development of Lurex metallic yarns and provided similar services for DuPont in development of acrylic, synthetic straw, and nylon rug yarns; moved base of operations to NY City (1952); often described as "the greatest weaver in the world," is widely credited with elevating the American textile industry to a level of excellence it had not previously enjoyed. ❖ See also *Women in World History*.

LIEBHART, Gertrude (1928—). Austrian kayaker. Born Oct 26, 1928. ❖ At Helsinki Olympics, won a silver medal in K1 500 meters (1952).

LIEBLING, Estelle (1880–1970). American soprano and voice teacher. Born April 21, 1880, in New York, NY; died Sept 25, 1970, in New York; studied with Mathilde Marchesi and Selma Nicklass-Kempner. ❖ Appeared with a number of European and American opera companies, including a stint with the Metropolitan Opera (1903–04); toured with John Philip Sousa's band, performing at over 1,600 concerts; retired to teach and was at one time affiliated with Curtis Institute; was also longtime singing teacher of Beverly Sills. ❖ See also *Women in World History*.

LIEBRECHT, Savyon (1948—). Israeli short-story writer. Born 1948 in Germany; dau. of Holocaust survivors. ❖ Moved to Israel when young; wrote 4 story collections, published in Hebrew, including *Tapuchim Me'Hamidbar* (1986, trans. as *Apples from the Desert*, foreword by Grace Paley, 1998).

LIENCOURT, Dame de (1573–1599). See Estrées, Gabrielle d'.

LIEVEN, Princess de (1785–1857). See Dorothea, Princess of Lieven.

LIGGINS, Ethel (1886–1970). See Leginska, Ethel.

LIGHTFOOT, Hannah (fl. 1768). English Quaker. Dau. of a Wapping shoemaker; possibly m. George III (1738–1820), king of England (r. 1760–1820), April 17, 1759; children: (with George III) possibly 3. ❖ Documents relating to her possible marriage have been impounded since 1866 and remain in the Royal Archives at Windsor.

LIGHTNER, A.M. (1904–1988). American science-fiction and children's writer. Name variations: Alice M. Lightner; Alice L. Hopf. Born Alice Martha Lightner, Oct 11, 1904, in Detroit, MI; died Feb 3, 1988, in Upper Black Eddy, PA; attended Westover School, Middlebury, CT; Vassar College, BA, 1927; m. Ernest Joachim Hopf, 1935; children: 1 son. ❖ Writings include *The Rock of Three Planets* (1963), *The Planet Poachers* (1965), *Doctor to the Galaxy* (1965), *The Space Ark* (1968), *The Day of the Drones* (1969) and *Star Circus* (1977); also wrote many books for children under name Alice L. Hopf, including *Monarch Butterflies* (1965), *Whose House is It?* (1980) and *Hyenas* (1983).

LIGHTNER, Candy (1946—). American activist. Born Candy Doddridge, May 30, 1946, in Pasadena, CA; dau. of Dykes C. Doddridge (career serviceman) and Katherine (Karrib) Doddridge (civilian employee of US Air Force); attended American River College, 1966; m. Steve Lightner (US Air Force officer, div.); children: (twins) Cari Lightner (died 1980) and Serena Lightner; Travis Lightner. ❖ Formed Mothers Against Drunk Driving (MADD) when her 13-year-old daughter Cari died after being hit by a car operated by a drunk driver who had been previously arrested 3 times and convicted twice for driving while intoxicated, yet retained a valid license (1980); after stricter laws against drunk-driving crimes passed in 27 states (1982), began to focus attention on alcohol-related accidents involving youth and founded Students Against Drunk Driving (SADD). ❖ See also NBC-TV movie *Mothers Against Drunk Drivers: The Candy Lightner Story,* starring Mariette Hartley (1983); and *Women in World History.*

LIGHTNER, Winnie (1899–1971). American comedic actress and singer. Born Winifred Josephine Reeves (maiden name also seen as Hanson), Sept 17, 1899, in Greenport, LI, NY; died Mar 5, 1971, in Sherman Oaks, CA; m. George Holtrey; m. Roy Del Ruth (film director), 1941 (died 1961); children: Thomas Del Ruth (cinematographer). ❖ Star of musical comedies, made stage debut in vaudeville in an act titled the Lightner Sisters and Alexander; stage successes include George White's *Scandals of 1923* and *Gay Paree;* films include *Gold Diggers of Broadway, Show of Shows, She Couldn't Say No, Manhattan Parade* and *Dancing Lady.*

LIGNELL, Kristen (c. 1965—). American mountaineer and skier. Name variations: Kristen Lignell-Valdez or Kristen Lignell Valdez. Born c. 1965 in northern Michigan; received RN degree from University of Michigan. ❖ Grew up in northern Michigan; worked as ski model in CA, appeared in Warren Miller movies, and spent summer months as nurse in pediatric ICU; traveled widely to ski including trips to Greece and Kenya; competed in World Extreme championships in Alaska; climbed Denali (2001).

LIGNOT, Myriam (1975—). French synchronized swimmer. Born July 9, 1975, in Lyon, France. ❖ Won a bronze medal for duet at Sydney Olympics (2000); won European championship for duet (2000).

LIHOTZKY, Margaret Schütte (1897–2000). See Schütte-Lihotzky, Margarete.

LIKIMANI, Muthoni (c. 1940—). Kenyan novelist and poet. Born c. 1940 in Maranga District, Kenya; dau. of Levi Gachanja (one of the 1st ministers of the Kenyan Anglican church). ❖ Worked as teacher, nutritionist, social worker, broadcaster and journalist; represented Kenya at several United Nations conferences and received National Council of Women of Kenya Award; writings include *They Shall be Chastised* (1974), *What Does a Man Want?* (1974), *Shangazi na Watoto* and *Passbook Number F47927: Women and Mau Mau in Kenya* (1985).

LILES, Gloria Joan (1921—). See Child, Joan.

LILEY, Tammy (1965—). American volleyball player. Born Mar 6, 1965, in Westminster, CA; attended Arizona State College. ❖ At Barcelona Olympics, won a bronze medal in team competition (1992).

LILIAN. Variant of Celia, Lillian, or Lily.

LILIANE (1916–2002). See Baels, Liliane.

LILIIA. Variant of Lidia or Lidiya.

LILINA, Maria. See Stanislavski, Maria.

LILIUOKALANI (1838–1917). Queen of Hawaii. Name variations: Lili'uokalani or Lili'uokalani; Lili'uokalani Lydia Kamekaha; Mme. Aorena; named Liliu Loloku Walania Kamakaeha at birth, commonly called Liliu, later christened Lydia and known as Lydia Kamakaeha Paki or Lidia Kamakaehaeha Paki; renamed Lili'uokalani by brother Kalakaua; sometimes referred to as Lily of Kilarney by Americans who could not pronounce her name. Pronunciation: Lee-lee-ew-kah-lah-nee. Born Sept 2, 1838, in Honolulu, HI; died of a stroke in Honolulu, Nov 11, 1917; dau. of the high chief Kapaakea and chiefess Keohokalole, a councilor to King Kamehameha III; sister of Kalakaua (1836–1891), king of Hawaii (r. 1874–1891); according to Hawaiian custom of *hanai,* she was adopted at birth by Abner Paki and his wife Konia, granddau. of Kamehameha I; educated at High Chiefs Children's School and Oahu College; m. John Owen Dominis, 1862; children: no natural children; was *hanai* mother to Lydia, John Dominis Aimoku, and Joseph Kaipo Aea. ❖ The last sovereign of the Islands, whose monarchy, despite the support of her people, was illegally overthrown by white settlers prior to Hawaii's annexation by US; named Princess Liliuokalani when brother was elected king (1874); named heir apparent (1877); served as regent while king was abroad (1881); adopted 1st of 3 children (1882); began Liliuokalani Educational Society for young girls (1886); attended Queen Victoria's jubilee (1887); succeeded brother as queen of Hawaiian Islands (1891); overthrown (1893); accused of treason, forced to sign an act of abdication and imprisoned for 8 months (1895); protested annexation of Hawaiian Islands by US (1897); established Liliuokalani Trust for the benefit of orphaned and destitute children of Hawaiian blood (early 1900s).

Wrote over 200 songs, including the Hawaiian National Anthem, "He Mele Lahui Hawaii," "The Queen's Prayer," and the romantic "Aloha Oe." ❖ See also Helen G. Allen, *The Betrayal of Lili'uokalani Last Queen of Hawaii* (Clark, 1982); and *Women in World History.*

LILIYA. Variant of Lidia or Lidiya.

LIL' KIM (1975—). American rap artist. Name variations: Kimberly Denise Jones, Kim Jones, Li'l Kim, Lil Kim. Born Kimberly Denise Jones, July 11, 1975, in Brooklyn, NY; dau. of Linwood Jones and Ruby Mae Jones; sister of Christopher Jones. ❖ Hip-hop star, known for revealing outfits and raunchy raps, was mentored by Notorious B.I.G. (Biggie Smalls); released popular solo album *Hard Core* (1996) which featured a duet with Sean "Puffy" Combs on hit single "No Time"; launched Queen Bee Records and produced 2nd album *The Notorious K.I.M.* (2000); collaborated with Pink, Mya and Christina Aguilera on remake of Patti LaBelle's "Lady Marmalade" for *Moulin Rouge* soundtrack (2001), scoring #1 hit as well as Grammy Award for best pop collaboration; released *La Bella Mafia* (2003) with hit single "Magic Stick"; appeared in such films as *She's All That* (1999) and *Juwanna Man* (2002); convicted of perjury for lying to a grand jury about a 2001 shooting (2005).

LILLAK, Tiina (1961—). Finnish javelin thrower. Name variations: Ilse Kristiina Lillak. Born Ilse Kristiina Lillak, April 15, 1961, in Helsinki, Finland. ❖ Broke world record in javelin with a throw of 72.40 meters (1982); regained world record at the Helsinki World championships with a throw of 74.76 (1983); won Olympic silver medal at Los Angeles Olympics (1984), only the 2nd Finnish woman to win an Olympic medal.

LILLIE, Beatrice (1894–1989). Canadian-born comedian. Name variations: Lady Peel. Born Beatrice Gladys Lillie, May 29, 1894, in Toronto, Ontario, Canada; died Jan 20, 1989, in Henley-on-Thames, England; dau. of John Lillie and Lucy Shaw Lillie; m. Sir Robert Peel, 1920 (died 1933); children: Robert Peel (died 1942). ❖ Popular star of radio, stage and screen, who delighted in poking fun at society's pretensions and hypocrisies, formed a singing trio at age 15 with mother and sister Muriel (1909); made London debut as an "extra turn" in a music-hall revue at Camberwell Empire (1913); followed with appearances in revues of André Charlot, including *Not Likely, 5064 Gerard, Now's the Time, Tabs* and *Up in Mabel's Room;* made Broadway debut in a Charlot revue (1924); had own radio program on NBC (1935); enjoyed a 50-year career as "the funniest woman in the world," while becoming known equally as well for her friendships with royalty and with such entertainment notables as Noel Coward and Charlie Chaplin; elevated by marriage to British peerage (1920), becoming Lady Peel; retired from show business (1977); films include *Exit Smiling* (1926), *The Show of Shows* (1929), *Are You There?* (1930), *Dr. Rhythm* (1938), *On Approval* (1944), *Around the World in Eighty Days* (1956) and *Thoroughly Modern Millie* (1967). ❖ See also autobiography *Every Other Inch a Lady* (Doubleday, 1972); and *Women in World History.*

LILLY, Gweneth (1920–2004). Welsh children's writer. Born Sept 24, 1920, in Liverpool, England, of Welsh parents; died April 5, 2004. ❖ Lecturer of education at St. Mary's College in Bangor (1946–76), had an interest in Celtic mythology; wrote *Y Drudwy Dewr* (The Brave Starling, 1980) and *Gaeaf Y Cerrig* (Winter of Stones, 1981), among many others; won Welsh Book Council award (1981, 1982).

LILLY, Kristine (1971—). American soccer player. Born Kristine Marie Lilly, July 22, 1971, in Wilton, CT; graduate of University of North Carolina. ❖ Forward; won a team gold medal at World Cup (1991, 1999); won a bronze medal at World championships (1995); won a team gold medal at Atlanta Olympics (1996) and a team silver at Sydney Olympics (2000); was a founding member of the Women's United Soccer Association (WUSA); signed with the Boston Breakers (2001); won a team gold medal at Athens Olympics (2004). Won Hermann Trophy (1991); named Female Soccer Athlete of the Year (1993). ❖ See also Jere Longman *The Girls of Summer* (HarperCollins, 2000).

LILY OF THE MOHAWKS (1656–1680). See Tekakwitha, Kateri.

LILYA. Variant of Lidia or Lidiya.

LIM JEONG-SOOK. South Korean field-hockey player. Born in South Korea. ❖ Won a team silver medal at Atlanta Olympics (1996).

LIM KYE-SOOK (1964—). Korean field-hockey player. Born Oct 3, 1964, in South Korea. ❖ At Seoul Olympics, won a silver medal in team competition (1988).

LIM MI-KYUNG (1967—). Korean handball player. Born May 17, 1967, in South Korea. ❖ At Seoul Olympics, won a gold medal in team competition (1988).

LIM O-KYEONG (1971—). See Lim O-Kyung.

LIM O-KYUNG (1971—). South Korean handball player. Name variations: O-Kyeong Lim. Born Dec 11, 1971, in South Korea. ❖ Won World championship (1995); won a team gold medal at Barcelona Olympics (1992), team silver at Atlanta Olympics (1996), and team silver at Athens Olympics (2004). Named IHF World Handball Player of the Year (1996).

LIMA, Clara Rosa de (1923—). See De Lima, Clara Rosa.

LIMA, Daniela (1984—). See Alves Lima, Daniela.

LIMA, Ricarda (1979—). Brazilian volleyball player. Name variations: Ricarda Raquel Barbosa Lima. Born Sept 12, 1979, in Brazil, Brasilia, Brazil. ❖ Won a team bronze medal at Sydney Olympics (2000).

LIMA, Sisleide do Amor (1967—). See Sissi.

LIMBAU, Mariana (1977—). Romanian kayaker. Born 1977 in Romania. ❖ Won a bronze medal for K4 500 meters at Sydney Olympics (2000).

LIMBERAKI, Margaríta (b. 1919). See Liberáki, Margaríta.

LIMERICK, countess of.
See Pery, Angela Olivia (1897–1981).
See Pery, Sylvia (1935—).

LIMÓN, Pauline Lawrence (1900–1971). See Lawrence, Pauline.

LIMPERT, Marianne (1972—). Canadian swimmer. Born Oct 10, 1972, in Matagami, Quebec, Canada. ❖ Won a silver medal for 200-meter indiv. medley at Atlanta Olympics (1996); at Commonwealth Games, placed 1st in 200-meter indiv. medley (1998).

LIN, Anor (1926—). See Lin, Tai-yi.

LIN CHIAO CHIH (1901–1983). See Lin Qiaozhi.

LIN HAIYIN (1918–2001). Chinese essayist and short-story writer. Born Mar 18, 1918, in Osaka, Japan, where her Taiwanese father was a businessman; died Dec 1, 2001, in Taiwan. ❖ At 3, moved back to family home in Taiwan; grew up in Beijing; returned with husband and children to Taiwan (1948); worked as journalist and editor for women's magazines; founded own publishing house; writings include *Green Weeds and Salted Eggs* (1958), her memoir *Chengnan Jiushi* (*Memories of Old Peking*, 1960), which was made into an award-winning film (1983), *The Story of a Marriage* (1963) and *A Stranger in the US* (1966).

LIN, Hazel (1913–1986). Chinese-American novelist and surgeon. Name variations: Hazel Ai Chun Lin. Born 1913 in Foochow, Fukien, China; died of a stroke, 1986, in Jersey City, NJ; Yenjing University, BS, 1932; Beijing Union Medical College, MD, 1935; University of Michigan, MS, 1938; m. Utah Tsao (chemical engineer). ❖ Worked as endocrinologist and surgeon at Jersey City Medical Center; wrote *The Physicians* (1951), *The Moon Vow* (1958), *House of Orchids* (1960), and *Rachel Weeping for Her Children Uncomforted* (1976). ❖ See also memoir, *Weeping May Tarry, My Long Night With Cancer* (1980).

LIN LI (1970—). Chinese swimmer. Born Oct 9, 1970, in Nantong, Jiangsu Province, China. ❖ At Barcelona Olympics, won a silver medal in 400-meter indiv. medley, gold medal in 200-meter indiv. medley, and silver medal in 200-meter breaststroke (1992); won a bronze medal for 200-meter indiv. medley at Atlanta Olympics (1996).

LIN, Maya (1959—). Chinese-American sculptor and architect. Born Oct 5, 1959, in Athens, Ohio; Henry Huan Lin (ceramist and dean of fine arts at Ohio University) and Julia Chang (poet and professor of literature at Ohio University (both were immigrants); Yale University, School of Architecture, BA, 1981, MA, 1986; m. Daniel Wolf; children: 2. ❖ While a senior at Yale (1980), won the design competition for the Vietnam Veterans Memorial to be built in Washington DC; oversaw construction of the then highly controversial monument (1982), which, over the years, has become revered; also designed the Civil Rights Memorial at the Southern Poverty Law Center in Montgomery, Alabama (1989), *Groundswell* at Ohio State University (1993) and *The Wave Field* at University of Michigan (1993–94). ❖ See also (documentary) *Maya Lin: A Strong, Clear Vision* by Freida Lee Mock (1995).

LIN, Nora (b. 1910). See Alonso, Dora.

LIN QIAOZHI (1901–1983). Chinese physician. Name variations: Lin Chiao Chih, or Lin Ch'iao-chih or Lin Chiao-chi; Lim Kh-at'i; Mother Lin. Born Dec 23, 1901, in Gulangyu Islet, China; died April 23, 1983, in China; graduate of Peking Union Medical College (PUMC) School of Medicine, 1929 (later named Anti-Imperialist Hospital, 1966–72, and then Shoutou Hospital of Beijing); studied at London University, then Manchester University, 1932–33, and Chicago University, 1939–40. ❖ Beloved teacher, researcher, obstetrics and gynecology doctor in China, was the 1st female enrolled at Peking Union Medical College (PUMC) and later its 1st woman Chinese doctor; elected head (1948) of PUMC's Department of Obstetrics and Gynecology; advocated public literacy and public health programs (1950s–70s) and worked for the National People's Congress and for Chinese People's Political Consultative Conferences; was vice president of Chinese Medical Association (1957) and Chinese Academy of Medical Sciences' (CAMS, 1964), and vice chair of National Women's Association (1978); was a founding member and vice president of Family Planning Association of China (May 1980).

LIN SANG (1977—). Chinese archer. Born Aug 17, 1977, in Putian, China. ❖ Won a silver medal for team at Athens Olympics (2004).

LIN, Tai-yi (1926—). Chinese-American novelist and editor. Name variations: Lin Taiyi; Anor Lin; Wu-shuang Lin. Born Anor Lin, April 1, 1926, in Beijing, China; dau. of Dr. Lin Yutang (1895–1976, Chinese-American writer) and Tsuifeng (Liau) Lin; sister of Adet Lin (writer) and Hsiangju Lin (wrote cookbook with mother); m. R. Ming Lai (chief information officer for Hong Kong government), 1949; children: Chih-wen (daughter) and Chih-yi (son). ❖ Taught Chinese at Yale University (1945–46) and was editor-in-chief of *Readers Digest International;* with sister, wrote *Our Family* (1939), *Dawn Over Chungking* (1941), and translated diary of Chinese girl soldier, *Girl Rebel* (1940); wrote 5 novels: *War Tide* (1943), *The Golden Coin* (1946), *The Eavesdropper* (1958), *The Lilacs Overgrow* (1960), and *Kampoon Street* (1964); trans. and edited *Flowers in the Mirror* (1965).

LIN WEINING (1979—). Chinese weightlifter. Born Mar 15, 1979, in Shandong Province, China. ❖ Won World championship (1999); won a gold medal for 63–69kg at Sydney Olympics (2000).

LIN, Wu-shuang (1926—). See Lin, Tai-yi.

LIN YANFEN (1971—). Chinese badminton player. Born Jan 4, 1971, in China. ❖ At Barcelona Olympics, won a bronze medal in doubles (1992).

LINCOLN, Abbey (1930—). American jazz singer and actress. Name variations: Gaby Lee, Aminata Moseka. Born Anna Marie Wooldridge, Aug 6, 1930, in Chicago, Illinois, 10th of 12 children; m. Max Roach (jazz drummer), 1962 (div. 1970). ❖ Legendary jazz singer and songwriter with improvisational style, began working in nightclubs under various pseudonyms at young age; at 20, traveled to California with brother Alex and began singing as Gaby Lee at Moulin Rouge; toured with Rampart Streeters; made 1st records with Benny Carter, including *Abbey Lincoln's Affair: A Story of A Girl in Love* (1955); wrote much of own material, stressing racial politics and black history; collaborated with Roach on *Freedom Now Suite* (1960) and *Straight Ahead* (1961); appeared in such films as *Nothing But a Man* (1964), *For Love of Ivy* (1968) and *Mo' Better Blues* (1990); began recording for Inner City (1973), gradually achieving prominence as jazz singer; adopted name Aminata Moseka (mid-70s) after trip to Africa; returned to love songs (1980s) and produced *Tribute to Billie Holiday* (1987); enjoyed renewed popularity with Verve releases (1990s); albums include *Abbey Is Blue* (1959), *Sounds as a Roach* (1968), *People in Me* (1973), *Golden Lady* (1980), *Talking to the Sun* (1983), *World Is Falling Down* (1990), *You Gotta Pay the Band* (with Stan Getz, 1991), *A Turtle's Dream* (1995), *You & I* (1997), *Over the Years* (2000) and *It's Me* (2003). ❖ See also (documentary) *Abbey Lincoln: You Gotta pay the Band* (1993).

LINCOLN, Almira Hart (1793–1884). See Phelps, Almira Lincoln.

LINCOLN, countess of (1281–1348). See Lacy, Alice.

LINCOLN, Mary Johnson (1844–1921). American educator and cookbook writer. Born Mary Johnson Bailey in Attleboro, MA, July 8, 1844; died in Boston, Dec 2, 1921; dau. of Reverend John Milton Burnham Bailey (Congregational minister) and Sarah Morgan (Johnson) Bailey; graduate of Wheaton Female Seminary (later Wheaton College), 1864; m. David A. Lincoln (clerk), June 21, 1865 (died 1894); no children. ❖ Taught at Boston Cooking School (1879–85) and published *Boston Cook Book* (1884); taught cooking at Lasell

Seminary in Auburndale, MA (1885–99) and published *Peerless Cook Book* (1886), *Boston School Kitchen Text-Book* (1887) and *Carving and Serving* (1887); beginning 1894, was associated with *American Kitchen Magazine*, of which she was also part owner and wrote a popular column, "From Day to Day." ❖ See also *Women in World History.*

LINCOLN, Mary Todd (1818–1882). American first lady. Born Mary Ann Todd on Dec 13, 1818, in Lexington, KY; died in Springfield, IL, July 16, 1882, of a stroke; dau. of Robert Smith Todd (state legislator) and Eliza Ann (Parker) Todd; attended Shelby Female Academy, 1827–32, and Madame Mentelle's boarding school, 1832–36; took classes from Dr. John Ward, 1837–39; m. Abraham Lincoln (president of US), Nov 4, 1842; children: Robert Todd Lincoln (b. Aug 1, 1843); Edward Baker Lincoln (b. Mar 10, 1846); William Wallace Lincoln (b. Dec 21, 1850); Thomas Lincoln (b. April 4, 1853). ❖ First lady who served as a leading Washington host during Civil War and endured the deaths of her husband, father, 3 half-brothers, and 3 sons over a 16-year span; mother died (July 1825); moved from Lexington to Springfield, IL (1839); married (1842); lived with family in Washington, DC (1847–48); father died (July 16, 1849); son Edward died (Feb 1, 1850); moved to Washington after Lincoln elected president (1861); refurbished the White House, made frequent public appearances at twice-a-week winter and spring receptions held in East Room, and visited hospitals where wounded Union soldiers were convalescing; son William died (Feb 20, 1862); husband assassinated (April 15, 1865); never fully recovering from that night of horror, moved to Chicago (May 1865); lived in Europe (1868–71); son Thomas died (July 15, 1871); declared insane (May 19, 1875) and placed in mental institution in Batavia, IL; released (Sept 10, 1875) and declared sane (June 15, 1876); lived in Europe (1876–80), then returned to Springfield. ❖ See also Paul M. Angle and Carl Sandburg. *Mary Lincoln, Wife and Widow* (Harcourt, 1932); Jean H. Baker, *Mary Todd Lincoln* (Norton, 1987); Ruth Painter Randall, *Mary Lincoln: Biography of a Marriage* (Little, Brown, 1953); Ishbel Ross, *The President's Wife* (Putnam, 1973); Turner and Turner, *Mary Todd Lincoln: Her Life and Letters* (Knopf, 1972); James Prideaux's play *The Last of Mrs. Lincoln* (1972); and *Women in World History.*

LIND, Jenny (1820–1887). Swedish soprano. Name variations: Madame Goldschmidt; Jenny Lind-Goldschmidt; the "Swedish Nightingale." Born Johanna Maria Lind, Oct 6, 1820, in Stockholm, Sweden; died of cancer at home in Malvern Hills, Shropshire, England, Nov 2, 1887; illeg. dau. of Niclas Jonas Lind (bookkeeper) and Anna Marie Fellborg Lind (schoolmistress); instructed at Swedish Royal Opera School, Stockholm; m. Otto Goldschmidt (pianist), 1852; children: Walter Otto Goldschmidt, Jenny Goldschmidt Maude, Ernst Goldschmidt. ❖ Considered the greatest soprano of her day and one of the most-loved figures of the age, made 1st stage appearance at age 10 in *The Polish Mine;* appeared in 1st operatic role as Alice in Meyerbeer's *Robert le diable* (1838); made formal operatic debut in Sweden as Agathe in Weber's *Der Freischutz* (1838); was a regular member of Swedish Academy of Music (1840); made Berlin debut in title role of *Norma* (1844) and Viennese debut as Norma (1846); made London debut as Alice (1847); retired as opera singer (1849); as concert singer, embarked on the most spectacular concert tour in US history (1850–52); moved to Dresden after marriage (1852), then to London (1858); appeared in oratorio and concert performances throughout Europe (1852–83); was a professor of singing at the Royal College of Music (1883–87). ❖ See also Jenny Maude, *The Life of Jenny Lind by Her Daughter* (Cassell, 1926); Gladys Shultz, *Jenny Lind, the Swedish Nightingale* (Lippincott, 1962); Edward Wagenknecht, *Jenny Lind* (Houghton, 1931); Ware & Lockard, *The Lost Letters of Jenny Lind* (Gollancz, 1966); and *Women in World History.*

LIND, Joan (1952—). American rower. Name variations: Joan Van Blom. Born Sept 26, 1952, in Long Beach, CA; attended Long Beach State University; St. Thomas College, MA; m. John Van Blom (Olympic rower). ❖ Won a silver medal at Montreal Olympics in single sculls (1976) and a silver medal at Los Angeles Olympics in quadruple sculls with coxswain (1984); won 5 national championships.

LIND, Letty (1862–1923). English actress and music-hall dancer. Born Letitia Rudge, Dec 21, 1862, in Birmingham, England; died Aug 27, 1923, in London; sister of Lydia Flopp, Millie Hylton (1968–1920), Adelaide Astor (1873–1951) and Fanny Dango (all actresses); cousin of Millie Lindon (mime and singer). ❖ Made stage debut in Birmingham as Little Eva in *Uncle Tom's Cabin* (1867); also appeared in *Locked Out, Little Miss Muffet, Monte Christo, A Trip to the Moon, Tact, Ruy Blas, Morocco Bound, Go-Bang, A Gaiety Girl, An Artist's Model, A Greek Slave, The Geisha* and *The Girl from Kay's,* among others.

LIND, Nathalie (1918–1999). Danish politician. Born Nathalie Lind, Oct 1, 1918, in Copenhagen, Denmark; died Jan 14, 1999, in Frederiksberg, Denmark; dau. of Aage Lind (1861–1921) and Ane Johanne (Björndahl) Lind (1878–1942); m. Erik Knud Desiré Tfelt-Hansen, Nov 1943 (died 1962); m. Niels Erik Langsted, April 1968; children: (1st m.) Peer Carstan (b. 1945) and Jan (b. 1947). ❖ Was MF for Venstre (Right Wing Liberals) (1964–66 and 1968–81); was vice chair of the Folketing (1973, 1975–78), deputy president of Nordic Council (1975–78, 1978) and vice chair of the Parliamentary group of her party (1977–78); served as minister of Social Affairs (1968–71), minister of Justice and Police and minister for Cultural Affairs (Dec 19, 1973–Feb 13, 1975) and minister of Justice and Police (Aug 30, 1978–Oct 26, 1979).

LINDAHL, Margaretha (c. 1971—). Swedish curler. Born c. 1971 in Sweden. ❖ Won a bronze medal for curling at Nagano Olympics (1998); placed 1st at World Curling championships (1998, 1999).

LINDBERG, Karin (1929—). Swedish gymnast. Born Oct 6, 1929, in Sweden. ❖ Won a gold medal at Helsinki Olympics (1952) and a silver medal at Melbourne Olympics (1956), both in teams all-around, portable apparatus.

LINDBERGH, Anne Morrow (1906–2001). American poet, novelist, and aviator. Born Anne Spencer Morrow, June 22, 1906, in Englewood, NJ; died Feb 7, 2001, in Vermont; dau. of Dwight Whitney Morrow (ambassador to Mexico and US Senator) and Elizabeth Cutter Morrow (later board chair and acting president, Smith College); Smith College, AB, 1928; m. Charles Augustus Lindbergh Jr. (aviation pioneer), May 27, 1929 (died Aug 26, 1974); children: Charles Augustus Lindbergh Jr. (1930–1932, killed in infancy); Jon Lindbergh (b. 1932); Land Lindbergh (b. 1937); Anne Spencer Lindbergh (1940–1993, who wrote novel *Nick of Time*); Scott Lindbergh (b. 1942); Reeve Lindbergh (b. 1945, who wrote the autobiographical novel, *The Names of the Mountains,* and the reminiscence of her youth in Darien, CT, *Under a Wing*). ❖ Known for her sensitive autobiographical observations and philosophical insights, married Charles Lindburgh 4 years after his flight to Paris (1929); an accomplished aviator, made 8 transcontinental survey flights as co-pilot and navigator with husband, and set a transcontinental speed record by flying from Los Angeles to NY in under 15 hours; became 1st American woman to be awarded a 1st-class glider pilot's license (1930); received private pilot's license (1931); with husband, began round-the-world flight (1931) which was terminated by her father's death; built an estate, "Highfields," near Hopewell, NJ (1930), where 2-year-old son was kidnapped (Mar 1, 1932) and later found dead, one of the most publicized crimes in US history; went on 2nd major survey flight (1933) for which she was awarded the Hubbard Gold Medal of National Geographic Society (1934); published 1st book, *North to the Orient* (1935), then *Listen! the Wind* (1938), both bestsellers; lived in Europe (1935–39); produced well-received novella, *The Steep Ascent* (1944); spent week with sister at Captiva Island, Florida, and published her meditations from that time, contained in 8 essays, under title *Gift from the Sea* (1955), which again catapulted her into national prominence; published *The Unicorn and Other Poems* (1956), another bestseller, but after a devastating review from John Ciardi, permanently abandoned poetry; started publishing excerpts from her diaries: *Bring Me a Unicorn: Diaries and Letters, 1922–1928* (1972), *The Flower and the Nettle: Diaries and Letters, 1936–1939* (1976), *Hour of Gold, Hour of Lead: Diaries and Letters, 1929–1932* (1973), *Locked Rooms and Open Doors: Diaries and Letters, 1933–1935* (1974) and *War Within and Without: Diaries and Letters, 1939–1944* (1980). ❖ See also Dorothy Herrmann, *A Gift for Life: Anne Morrow Lindbergh* (Ticknor & Fields, 1993); Susan Hertog, *Anne Morrow Lindbergh* (Doubleday, 1999); and *Women in World History.*

LINDBLOM, Gunnel (1931—). Swedish actress, director, and screenwriter. Born Dec 18, 1931, in Göteborg, Bohuslän, Sweden. ❖ Came to prominence as Rebecka Andersson in Gustaf Molander's film *Kärlek* (1952); joined Ingmar Bergman's theatrical company at Malmö, appearing as Margareta in *Faust,* and in such Bergman films as *The Seventh Seal, Virgin Spring, Scenes from a Marriage* and *Wild Strawberries;* directed film *Paradistorg* (1977), considered by *Time* one of the 4 best foreign films of 1978; appeared often with Royal Dramatic Theater. Awarded Guldbagge for lifetime achievement in film.

LINDFORS, Viveca (1920–1995). Swedish-born actress. Born Elsa Viveka Torstensdotter Lindfors, Dec 29, 1920, in Uppsala, Sweden; died Oct 25, 1995, in Uppsala; dau. of Torsten Lindfors (book publisher) and Karin (Dymling) Lindfors (painter); attended Royal Dramatic

Theater School, 1937–40; m. Harry Hasso (cinematographer), 1941 (div.); m. Folke Rogard (lawyer), 1946 (div. 1949); m. Don Siegel (director), 1949 (div. 1953); m. George Tabori (writer and director), 1954 (div. 1972); children: (1st m.) John Hasso; (2nd m.) Lena Rogard; (3rd m.) Kristoffer Tabori (actor). ❖ Internationally renowned actress, made stage debut in *Anne Sophie Hedvig* (1937); in Sweden, had walk-on in film *The Crazy Family*, which led to starring role in *If I Should Marry the Minister* (1941); made Broadway debut as Inez Cabral in *I've Got Sixpence* (1952) and London debut as Sophia in *The White Countess* (1954); in NY, appeared as Anna in *Anastasia* (1954), Cordelia in *King Lear* (1956), title role in *Miss Julie* and Missy in *The Stronger* (1956); in Stockholm, played in *Brecht on Brecht* (1963); appeared in solo show *I Am a Woman* (1972–73); films include *Appassionata* (1944), *Night Unto Night* (1949), *No Sad Songs for Me* (1950), *This Side of the Law* (1950), *Moonfleet* (1955), *I Accuse!* (1958), *The Story of Ruth* (1960), *King of Kings* (1961), *The Damned* (1961), *Huis Clos (No Exit*, 1962), *Sylvia* (1965), *Brainstorm* (1965), *Coming Apart* (1969), *Cauldron of Blood* (1971), *The Way We Were* (1973), *Voices* (1979), *The Hand* (1981), *Creepshow* (1982) and *The Exorcist III* (1990). ❖ See also autobiography *Viveka . . . Viveca* (Everest House, 1981); and *Women in World History*.

LINDGREN, Astrid (1907–2002). Swedish writer. Born Astrid Ericsson in Vimmerby, Sweden, Nov 14, 1907; died Jan 28, 2002, in Stockholm; dau. of Hanna (Jonsson) Ericsson and Samuel August Ericsson (both farmers); m. Sture Lindgren, April 4, 1931 (died 1952); children: (prior to her marriage) Lars; Karin Lindgren (b. 1934, who m. Carl Olof Nyman). ❖ Published *Pippi Longstocking* (Pippi Laangstrump, 1945), followed by *Pippi Goes on Board* (1946) and the last of the series, *Pippi in the South Seas* (1948); became editor and head of children's book department at Raben & Sjogren (1946), a position she held until 1970; produced books, radio plays and film manuscripts (Pippi was broadcast on Swedish radio in 1946, the 1st feature film was made in 1949), as well as theater adaptations and lectures; wrote a scathing critique against the Social Democratic government in the guise of a satirical fairy tale, attacking the party apparatus whose leaders had ceased to resemble the activists of the early days, causing a debate which brought to an end the 40-year rule of the Social Democrats in Sweden; protested the mistreatment of farm animals (1985), resulting in Lex Lindgren, the Animal Protection Act (1988). Received Nils Holgersson Medal (1950), Hans Christian Andersen Medal; Swedish Academy's Gold Medal (1971), The Dutch Silver Pen Award (1975), Adelaide-Risto Award, International Writer's Prize, Gold Medal awarded by Swedish Government, French Children's Book Award, Karen Blixen Award, Selma Lagerlof Award (1986), and Leo Tolstoy International Gold Medal (1987); prizes honoring her humanitarian activities include the Janusz Korczak Prize (1979), Dag Hammarskjöld Award (1984), and Albert Schweitzer Medal (1989). ❖ See also Eva-Maria Metcalf, *Astrid Lindgren* (Twayne, 1995); and *Women in World History*.

LINDGREN, Marie. Swedish freestyle skier. Born in Sweden. ❖ Won a silver medal for aerials at Lillehammer Olympics (1994).

LINDH, Anna (1957–2003). Swedish politician. Born June 19, 1957, in Enskede, near Stockholm, Sweden; stabbed Sept 10, 2003, in Stockholm; died of her wounds on Sept 11; dau. of Staffan Lindh (artist) and Nancy Lindh (teacher); earned a law degree at Uppsala University, 1982; m. Bo Holmberg (Social Democrat politician), 1991; children: Filip and David. ❖ Hugely popular Swedish foreign minister who was often mentioned as a successor to Prime Minister Göran Persson, was assassinated at age 46; won a seat in Parliament (1982); served as president of the Social Democratic Party's Youth League (1984–90) and became a member of SDP executive committee (1991); was deputy mayor of Stockholm (1991–94); served as minister for the Environment (1994–98), then named foreign minister (1998); as chief envoy during the Swedish presidency of the European Union (2001), attracted international recognition and helped prevent war in Macedonia.

LINDH, Hilary (1969—). American Alpine skier. Born May 10, 1969, in Juneau, Alaska. ❖ Won a silver medal for downhill at Albertville Olympics (1992); placed 7th for downhill at Lillehammer (1994); at World championships, won a bronze medal (1996) and a gold medal (1997), both for downhill; retired (1998).

LINDLEY, Audra (1918–1997). American actress. Born Audra Marie Lindley, Sept 24, 1918, in Los Angeles, CA; died Oct 16, 1997, in Los Angeles; studied with Max Reinhardt; m. Dr. Aaron Hardy Ulm, 1943 (div. 1960); m. James Whitmore (actor), 1972 (div. 1979). ❖ Made stage debut in Los Angeles as the Mother in Max Reinhardt's production

of *Six Characters in Search of an Author* (1940); appeared on Broadway in *Comes the Revolution, Hear that Trumpet, Venus Is, Take Her She's Mine* and *A Case of Libel;* films include *The Heartbreak Kid, When You Comin' Back Red Ryder, Cannery Row, Desert Hearts* and *Troop Beverly Hills;* perhaps best known for recurring roles on tv's "Bridget Loves Bernie" (1972–73), "Three's Company" (1977–79), and "The Ropers" (1979–80).

LINDNER, Dorte. German diver. Name variations: Doerte or Dörte Lindner. Born in Germany; attended University of Southern California, 1995–99. ❖ Won a silver medal at European championships (2000) and a bronze medal for 3-meter springboard at Sydney Olympics (2000).

LINDNER, Helga (1951—). East German swimmer. Born May 5, 1951, in East Germany. ❖ At Mexico City Olympics, won a silver medal in 200-meter butterfly (1968).

LINDNER, Herta (1920–1943). German-Czechoslovakian political activist. Name variations: Hertha Lindner. Born in Mariaschein, Czechoslovakia (now Bohosudov, Czech Republic), Nov 3, 1920; executed at Plötzensee Prison, Berlin, Mar 29, 1943; dau. of Heinrich Josef Lindner. ❖ A Sudeten German in Czechoslovakia, joined Socialist youth organization Rote Falken (Red Falcons) at 9; attended both Czech and German schools and grew up speaking both languages; as a militant anti-Nazi, joined German Youth League (Deutscher Jugendbund), a successor to the banned Communist youth organization, and quickly emerged as a local leader involved with underground activities; moved to Dresden (1939), where she continued her political activities; arrested by Nazis (Nov 1941), was jailed and interrogated in the town of Most for 1 year, then found guilty of high treason and sentenced to death. In German Democratic Republic (GDR), several streets and schools were named in her honor. ❖ See also *Women in World History*.

LINDO, Olga (1899–1968). English actress. Born July 13, 1899, in London, England; died May 7, 1968, in London; dau. of Frank Lindo (actor) and Winnie Louise Lindo (acted under name Marion Wakeford). ❖ Made stage debut at Drury Lane in *The Sleeping Beauty Re-Awakened* (1913); toured in father's company (1919–21); succeeded Moyna MacGill in *If Four Walls Told* (1922); other plays include *Lavender Ladies, R.U.R., Gruach, Rain* (as Sadie Thompson), *The First Years, The Perfect Marriage, The Stranger Within, Rings on Her Fingers, The Skin Game, White Cargo, The Second Mrs. Tanqueray, Beyond the Horizon* and *The Silver Whistle;* films include *Sapphire, Woman in a Dressing Gown* and *An Inspector Calls.*

LINDSAY, Anne (1750–1825). Scottish poet and diarist. Name variations: Lady Anne Lindsay; Lady Anne Barnard. Born Anne Lindsay at Balcarres House, Lindsay, in Fifeshire, Scotland, Dec 12, 1750; died May 6, 1825, in London; eldest dau. of James Lindsay, 5th earl of Balcarres, and Anne Dalrymple; sister of Margaret Lindsay; educated at home; m. Andrew Barnard (son of the bishop of Limerick), 1793; no children. ❖ Author of the popular Scottish ballad "Auld Robin Gray," which was set to music by Reverend William Leeves, and diarist who wrote about colonial life on the Cape of Africa. ❖ See also *Women in World History*.

LINDSAY, Gillian Anne (1973—). Scottish rower. Born Sept 24, 1973, in Paisley, Renfrewshire, Scotland. ❖ Won World championship for double sculls (1998) and a silver medal for quadruple sculls at Sydney Olympics (2000).

LINDSAY, Helen (1838–1914). See Gibb, Helen.

LINDSAY, Lilian (1871–1959). See Murray, Lilian.

LINDSAY, Margaret (1910–1981). American actress. Born Margaret Kies, Sept 9, 1910, in Dubuque, IA; died May 9, 1981, in Hollywood, CA; sister of Jane Gilbert (production manager). ❖ Made over 80 films in leads or supporting roles, including *Cavalcade, Christopher Strong, Baby Face, Voltaire, Jezebel, Hell's Kitchen, House of Seven Gables, Seven Keys to Baldpate, Cass Timberlane, Please Don't Eat the Daisies* and *Tammy and the Doctor;* played the female lead in 7 "Ellery Queen" mysteries.

LINDSAY, Michaela (1914–2003). See Denis, Michaela.

LINDSEY, Estelle Lawton (1868–1955). American acting mayor and reporter. Born Estelle Lawton, 1868, on a cotton plantation in Abbeville, SC; died Nov 27, 1955; attended schools in Nashville and Germany; m. Dudley Lindsey, 1903. ❖ Taught German, then took her 1st newspaper job for the *Nashville American;* moved to Los Angeles with husband (1907) where she reported for *Los Angeles Express;* was also a syndicated advice columnist; elected to Los Angeles city council (1915), the only woman, and served as mayor for a day in 1915, the 1st acting mayor of a major city; worked for *Santa Barbara News-Press.*

LINDSTROM, Murle (1939—). *See Breer, Murle.*

LINDSTROM, Pia (1938—). American newscaster. Born Friedel Pia Lindström, Sept 20, 1938, in Sweden; dau. of Ingrid Bergman (actress) and Petter Lindstrom (dentist); half-sister of Isotta and Isabella Rossellini; m. Fuller E. Greenway III, 1960 (div. 1961); m. Joseph Daly, Dec 1971; m. John Carley, 2001; children: Justin (b. 1973). ❖ Was a broadcast journalist in New York City. ❖ See also *Women in World History.*

LINE, Anne (d. 1601). Catholic Englishwoman condemned as a heretic. Executed at Tyburn, England, in 1601. ❖ During a period of Catholic persecution in England, harbored Catholic priests and allowed them to conduct masses in her home; was captured by authorities, as she was helping a priest to escape, and condemned as a heretic. ❖ See also *Women in World History.*

LING, Ding (1904–1985). *See Ding Ling.*

LING JIE (1982—). Chinese gymnast. Born Oct 22, 1982, in Hunan, China. ❖ At World championships, won a gold medal for balance beam and a bronze medal for uneven bars (1999); at Sydney Olympics, won a silver medal for uneven bars and a bronze medal for team all-around (2000).

LING SHUHUA (1904–1990). Chinese writer. Name variations: Ling Shu-hua; Su Hua Ling Chen. Born 1904 in Kwantung, China; died 1990; Cantonese father was an official; m. writer and critic Chen Yuan (Ch'en Yüan), 1920s; studied English literature, Yanjing (Yenching) University, early 1920s; studied painting in Paris and had several solo exhibitions of her works. ❖ Considered a brilliant and original writer of short stories, specialized in psychological portraits and telling details; was a friend of writer Bing Xin; had stories published in weekly *Contemporary Review* and in 3 collections: *The Temple of Flowers* (1928), *Women* (1930), and *Little Brothers* (1935); was a professor of literature in Beijing; moved to London (1947) when husband became a delegate to UNESCO, after which they split their time between London and Taipei; taught contemporary Chinese literature in Singapore, and later in Canada and UK. ❖ See also *Women in World History.*

LINGENS-REINER, Ella (1908–2002). Austrian political activist and physician. Name variations: Ella Lingens. Born in Vienna, Austria, in 1908; died Dec 31, 2002. ❖ When Dollfuss crushed the Social Democratic Party (1934), joined the resistance circle that formed around Otto and Käthe Leichter, which remained in contact with the Social Democratic leadership that had fled to Czechoslovakia and France; was arrested by the Gestapo (1942); imprisoned at both Dachau and Auschwitz, became an indispensable member of the camp social system as a physician; served for many years as president of the organization of former Auschwitz prisoners (Österreichische Lagergemeinschaft Auschwitz). ❖ See also memoir *Prisoners of Fear* (Gollancz, 1948); and *Women in World History.*

LINGLE, Linda (1953—). American politician. Born 1953 in St. Louis, MO; education: California State, Northridge, degree in journalism. ❖ At 12, moved with family to Southern California; moved to Hawaii (1975), where she founded and began serving as publisher of the Moloka'i Free Press; served 5 terms on the Maui County Council (1980–90); as a Republican, elected mayor of Maui County (1990), the youngest person and 1st woman to hold this office, then reelected (1994); elected governor of Hawaii (2002), the 1st woman to head the state since it achieved statehood in 1959.

LINGNAU, Corinna (1960—). West German field-hockey player. Born Jan 18, 1960, in Germany. ❖ At Los Angeles Olympics, won a silver medal in team competition (1984).

LINGOR, Renate (1975—). German soccer player. Born Oct 11, 1975, in Karlsruhe, Germany; attended Johann Wolfgang Goethe University. ❖ Midfielder; won a team bronze medal at Sydney Olympics (2000) and Athens Olympics (2004); won team European championships (1995, 2001); won FIFA World Cup (2003).

LINICHUK, Natalia. Russian ice dancer. Name variations: Natalya. Born in Russia; m. Gennadi Karponosov. ❖ With partner Gennadi Karponosov, won World championships (1978, 1979), European championship (1980) and a gold medal at Lake Placid Olympics (1980);

coaches at University of Delaware; called an influential force in figure skating by IFS.

LINKS, Mary (1908–1999). *See Lutyens, Mary.*

LINLEY, Elizabeth (1754–1792). English soprano. Name variations: Eliza Ann Linley; Elizabeth Sheridan; Mrs. Richard Brinsley Sheridan. Born in Bath, England, 1754; died in Bristol, England, 1792; dau. of Thomas Linley the Elder (1732–1795, composer); sister of Maria Linley (1763–1784) and Mary Linley (1758–1787) who were also singers; m. Richard Brinsley Sheridan (playwright), 1773 (died 1816); children: son Thomas Sheridan (1775–1817, a poet, who became colonial treasurer at Cape of Good Hope and m. Caroline Henrietta Sheridan nee Callander); grand-daughters Caroline Norton, Helen Selina Blackwood, and Lady Georgiana Seymour. ❖ Sang in public as early as 12 years old; was admired not only for her exceptional voice, but for her delicate beauty which was immortalized by painters Reynolds and Gainsborough. ❖ See also *Women in World History.*

LINLEY, Maria (1763–1784). English singer. Born 1763; died 1784; dau. of Thomas Linley the Elder (1732–1795, composer); sister of Mary Linley (1758–1787) and Elizabeth Linley (1754–1792). ❖ Sang in oratorio and at the Bath concerts. ❖ See also *Women in World History.*

LINLEY, Mary (1758–1787). English singer. Name variations: Mrs. Tickell. Born 1758; died 1787; dau. of Thomas Linley the Elder (1732–1795, composer); sister of Maria Linley (1763–1784) and Elizabeth Linley (1754–1792); m. Richard Tickell (pamphleteer, dramatist, and commissioner of stamps), 1780. ❖ Made singing debut (1771). ❖ See also *Women in World History.*

LINN, Bambi (1926—). American actress and dancer. Born Bambina Linnemeier, April 26, 1926, in Brooklyn, NY; dau. of Henry William Linnemeier and Mimi (Tweer) Linnemeier; studied ballet with Mikhail Mordkin and Agnes De Mille and modern dance at Neighborhood Playhouse; m. Rod Alexander Burke (dancer, div.); m. Joseph de Jesus. ❖ Made stage debut in NY as Aggie in *Oklahoma!* (1943), followed by *Carousel* (as Louise), *Alice in Wonderland, Sally* (title role), *Great to be Alive!* and *I Can Get It for You Wholesale;* danced as a soloist with the American Ballet Co.; partnered with 1st husband Rod Alexander, appeared regularly on tv series "Your Show of Shows" (1952–54); appeared as Dream Laurey in film *Oklahoma* (1955); directed a dance school in Westport, CT.

LINSE, Cornelia (1959—). East German rower. Born Oct 3, 1959, in East Germany. ❖ At Moscow Olympics, won a silver medal in double sculls (1980).

LINSENHOFF, Ann-Kathrin (1960—). West German equestrian. Born Aug 1, 1960, in Germany; dau. of Liselott Linsenhoff. ❖ At Seoul Olympics, won a gold medal in team dressage (1988).

LINSENHOFF, Liselott (1927—). West German equestrian. Name variations: Linsenhoff-Schindling. Born Aug 27, 1927, in Germany; children: Ann-Kathrin Linsenhoff (b. Aug 1, 1960, also a dressage rider). ❖ Won Olympic indiv. bronze medal in dressage, as well as team silver, on Adular in Stockholm (1956); won Aachen Grand Prix on Piaff (1955, 1956, 1959); won a silver medal at 2 World championships; won Olympic team gold in dressage in Mexico City (1968); was European champion in dressage (1969, 1971); won Olympic gold medal in indiv. dressage on Piaff (1st woman to win indiv. gold medal in dressage) and team silver in Munich (1972). ❖ See also *Women in World History.*

LINSKILL, Mary (1840–1891). English novelist. Name variations: (pseudonym) Stephen Yorke. Born in Whitby, Yorkshire, Dec 13, 1840; died in Whitby, April 9, 1891. ❖ Wrote *Tales of the North Riding* which was published in *Good Words* (1871); also wrote short stories and 4 novels, including *Clevedale* (1876) and *The Haven under the Hill* (1886).

LINSLEY, Jennifer (1960—). *See Holliday, Jennifer.*

LINSSEN-VAESSEN, Marie-Louise (1928–1993). Dutch swimmer. Name variations: Marie-Louise Vaessen. Born Mar 19, 1928, in Maastricht, Netherlands; died Mar 15, 1993. ❖ At London Olympics, won a bronze medal in 4 x 100-meter freestyle relay and a bronze medal in 100-meter freestyle (1948); at Helsinki Olympics, won a silver medal in 4 x 100-meter freestyle relay (1952).

LINTON, Eliza Lynn (1822–1898). English novelist. Name variations: also wrote under Eliza Lynn. Born Eliza Lynn at Keswick, England, Feb 10, 1822; died in London, July 14, 1898; dau. of J. Lynn, vicar of

Crosthwaite, in Cumberland; her mother (name unknown) died when she was an infant; granddau. of Samuel Goodenough; m. William James Linton (1812–1898, engraver), 1858. ❖ Arrived in London (c. 1845) to make her way as a journalist; joined staff of *Morning Chronicle*; published 1st novel, *Azeth the Egyptian* (1846), followed by *Amymone*, a romance set in the days of Pericles (1848), and *Realities* (1851); lived in Paris (1851–54), working as a correspondent for London papers; reached stride with *Grasp Your Nettle* (1865), *Lizzie Lorton of Greyrigg* (1866), *Patricia Kemball* (1874) and *The Atonement of Leam Dundas* (1877); also wrote *Joshua Davidson* (1872), a bold but not irreverent adaptation of the story of Jesus of Nazareth to that of the French Commune, and *Christopher Kirkland*, a veiled autobiography (1885); was extremely anti-feminist. ❖ See also memoir *My Literary Life* (1899); G.S. Layard, *Eliza Lynn Linton: Her Life, Letters and Opinions* (1901); Nancy Fix Anderson, *Woman Against Women in Victorian England: A Life of Eliza Lynn Linton* (1996); and *Women in World History*.

LIOBA (700–779). English saint and missionary. Name variations: Leoba, Liobgetha, Leobgyth, Liobgytha, Liofe, Truthgeba. Born Liobgetha in 700 in Wessex, England; died 779 at Bischofscheim also seen as Bischofsheim abbey in Mainz, Germany; educated at nunnery of Minster-in-Thanet and then at Wimborne in Dorset; never married; no children. ❖ Developed a friendship through correspondence with the missionary St. Boniface (c. 748) and was asked to join him in his work in Germany; with Boniface, founded an abbey at Bischofscheim, and became its 1st abbess (c. 753); was also put in indirect charge of several other Benedictine communities for women; served as abbess for about 28 years, while Bischofscheim became noted as a place of great learning and charity for the poor. ❖ See also *Women in World History*.

LIOBGETHA (700–779). *See Lioba.*

LIOFE (700–779). *See Lioba.*

LIONESS OF LISABILAND (1900–1978). *See Ransome-Kuti, Funmilayo.*

LIOSI, Kyriaki (1979—). Greek water-polo player. Born Oct 30, 1979, in Athens, Greece. ❖ Won team silver medal at Athens Olympics (2004).

LIPA, Elisabeta (1964—). Romanian rower. Name variations: Elisabeta Lipa-Oleniuc; Elisabeta Oleniuc. Born Elisabeta Oleniuc, Oct 26, 1964, in Siret, Romania. ❖ At Los Angeles Olympics, won a gold medal in double sculls (1984); at Seoul Olympics, won a bronze medal in quadruple sculls without coxswain and a silver medal in double sculls (1988); at Barcelona Olympics, won a silver medal in double sculls and a gold medal in single sculls (1992); won gold medals for coxed eights at Atlanta Olympics (1996), Sydney Olympics (2000) and Athens Olympics (2004); won more Olympic medals than any rower; at World championships, placed 1st in single sculls (1989). Named Female Rower of the Century by Romanian Federation (2003).

LIPINSKI, Tara (1982—). American figure skater. Born Tara Kristen Lipinski, June 10, 1982, in Sugar Land, TX; dau. of Jack and Pat Lipinski. ❖ At 14, won the figure-skating World title, the youngest ladies' skater in World championship history (1997); won 3 consecutive medals at US nationals (1996–98), winning the gold medal (1997); at 15, won the figure-skating competition at Nagano, the youngest athlete in Olympic Winter Game history to win a gold medal (1998); was the 1st woman to land a triple loop–triple loop combination (1997); retired from competition (1998); began skating professionally. ❖ See also autobiographies, *Triumph on Ice* and *Totally Tara: An Olympic Journey*; Christina Lessa, *Women Who Win* (Universe, 1998).

LIPKA, Juliane (c. 1860–c. 1929). Hungarian serial killer. Born c. 1860 in Hungary; executed c. 1929. ❖ Was member of Mrs. Julius Fazekas' murder ring in small village of Nagyrev, Hungary; stood trial at age 66 and confessed to murdering 7 people with poison, including her husband Paul and at least 4 other family members; found guilty and hanged (c. 1929).

LIPKIN, Jean (1926—). South African poet. Born 1926 in Johannesburg, South Africa. ❖ Moved to England (1960) and lived mostly in London; works, which have been praised for their lyricism and elegant evocation of emotion, include *Among Stones* (1975) and *With Fences Down* (1986).

LIPKOVSKAY, Natalia (1979—). Russian rhythmic gymnast. Born April 26, 1979, in Krasnoyarsk, Russia. ❖ At World championship, won a team gold (1995) and a silver medal in all-around (1997); at the Europeans, won a bronze with clubs (1996); won the International Tournament of Portugal (1996), L.A. Lights Invitational (1997), and the Corbeil and Aeon Cup.

LIPKOWSKA, Lydia (1882–1958). Russian soprano. Born Lydia Marschner, June 6, 1882, in Babino, Bessarabia, Russia; died in Beirut, Lebanon, Mar 22, 1958; m. Georgi Baklanoff. ❖ After studying at St. Petersburg Conservatory, made debut at Imperial Opera (1908); became an audience favorite; sang in Paris and at NY's Metropolitan Opera (1909); made Covent Garden debut (1911); appeared in Monte Carlo in 1st performances of Ponchielli's *I Mori di Valenza* (1914); made 29 recordings, many of which remain highly rated; after Bolshevik Revolution, immigrated to France (1919) and resumed her career with Russian emigré opera troupes throughout Western Europe; made return tour of Soviet Union (1928–29), then lived and taught singing in Romania; returned to France (1945), then settled some years later in Lebanon, living and teaching in Beirut; had large repertory, including Tatiana, Iolanta, Lakmé, Lucia, and Marfa in *The Tsar's Bride*. ❖ See also *Women in World History*.

LIPMAN, Clara (1869–1952). American actress and playwright. Born Dec 6, 1869, in Chicago, IL; died June 22, 1952, in New York, NY; m. Louis Mann (actor). ❖ Began career with A.S. Palmer Co. (1900); starred with husband in such plays as *The Girl from Paris, All on Account of Eliza, The Telephone Girl, The Marriage of a Star* and *That French Lady*; also wrote several successful plays, including *Pepi, Julie Bon-Bon* and *The Italian Girl*.

LIPMAN, Maureen (1946—). English actress. Born Maureen Diane Lipman, May 10, 1946, in Hull, Yorkshire, England; dau. of Zelma Lipman; attended London Academy of Music and Dramatic Art; m. Jack Rosenthal (playwright), 1973 (died 2004); children: Adam and Amy Rosenthal (playwright). ❖ Versatile actress and comedy writer, made film debut in *Up the Junction* (1967) and theatrical debut in *The Knack* (1969); debuted on West End in Shaw's *Candide* (1976); won acclaim for portrayal of Maggie in *Outside Edge* (1978) and received Laurence Olivier Award for Best Comedy Performance for *See How They Run* (1985); appeared in one-woman shows, *Re: Joyce* (1988), about Joyce Grenfell, and *Alive and Kidding* (1997), which was nominated for another Olivier Award (1998); on tv, starred in "All at Number 20" (1986–89) and "Agony Again" (1995); wrote several books, including *How Was It for You?* (1985) and *When's It Coming Out?* (1992), and columns for *Options, She* and *Good Housekeeping*; won BAFTA award for British Telecom commercials; films include *Educating Rita* (1983), *Solomon and Gaenor* (1999) and *The Pianist* (2002); often appeared in husband's plays, including *The Evacuees*, as well daughter's play, *Sitting Pretty* (2001); starred in *Throughly Modern Millie* (2003), for which she was nominated for Laurence Olivier Theater Award. Made Commander of British Empire (CBE, 1999).

LIPONA, countess of. *See Bonaparte, Carolina (1782–1839).*

LIPPERINI, Guendalina (c. 1862–1914). Italian novelist. Name variations: (real name) Guendalina Lipperini; Guendalina Roti; (pseudonyms) Contessa Anna Roti; Regina di Luanto. Born c. 1862 in Italy; died 1914. ❖ Separated from husband and lived unconventional life; works, which focused on and were critical of aristocratic society, include *Salamandra* (1892), *Un martirio* (1894), and *Le virtuose* (1912). Pseudonym Regina di Luanto is an anagram of Guendalina Roti.

LIPPINCOTT, Sara Clarke (1823–1904). American journalist and lecturer. Name variations: Sara Clarke Lippincott; Sara Jane Lippincott; wrote under Sara J. Clarke and Mrs. L.H. Lippincott; (pseudonym) Grace Greenwood. Born Sara Jane Clarke, Sept 23, 1823, in Pompey, NY; died April 20, 1904, in New Rochelle, NY; dau. of Thaddeus Clarke (physician) and Deborah (Baker) Clarke; great-granddau. of Rev. Jonathan Edwards; attended school in Rochester, NY; m. Leander K. Lippincott, 1853; children: Annie Lippincott. ❖ Adopting the pseudonym "Grace Greenwood," published prose and informal letters in *Sartain's, Graham's, Union Magazine*, and other journals of the day; produced a bestselling collection of her magazine pieces, *Greenwood Leaves* (1850), and a sequel 2 years later; also served on staffs of *Godey's Lady's Book, Graham's, Sartain's*, and *The New York Times*; while making solo tour of Europe (1852–53), sent back series of travel pieces and interviews which appeared in *National Era* and *Saturday Evening Post* and were later collected in a popular book, *Haps and Mishaps of a Tour of Europe* (1854); with husband, coedited successful children's magazine, *The Little Pilgrim* (1853–75). ❖ See also *Women in World History*.

LIPSIUS, Marie (1837–1927). German writer. Name variations: (pseudonym) La Mara. Born in Leipzig, Germany, Dec 30, 1837; died near Wurzen, Saxony, Mar 2, 1927; sister of Richard Adelbert Lipsius (1830–1892, German Protestant cleric and co-founder of the Evangelical

Union) and Justus Hermann Lipsius (1834–1920, classical scholar). ❖ Publishing under pseudonym La Mara, was a noted writer on Liszt and Beethoven, and edited letters of Liszt, Berlioz, and others.

LIPSON, Edna (1914–1996). British novelist and short-story writer. Name variations: (pseudonym) Gerda Charles. Born Aug 14, 1914, in Liverpool, England; died Nov 1996; dau. of Gertrude Lipson. ❖ Worked as tv critic for *Jewish Observer* and *Middle East Review* (1978–79); wrote *The True Voice* (1959), *The Crossing Point* (1960), *A Slanting Light* (1963), *A Logical Girl* (1966) and *The Destiny Waltz* (1971); short stories and reviews appeared in various publications, including *Daily Telegraph, Jewish Chronicle,* and *New York Times.*

LIPSON-GRUZEN, Berenice (1925–1998). American pianist. Born Feb 16, 1925, in New York, NY; died Sept 3, 1998, in Bad Wiessee, Germany. ❖ Won acclaim as pianist performing in major concert halls in North America, Europe and Asia; recorded Chopin's Piano Concerto No. 2 with Beijing Central Philharmonic, the 1st Western artist to record with an orchestra from China (1981); taught master classes at the new Central Philharmonic Conservatory; appeared with Peking Central Philharmonic; devoted recordings to works of Debussy and Chopin.

LISA, Mary Manuel (1782–1869). American pioneer. Name variations: Mary Hempstead. Born Mary Hempstead on Oct 25, 1782, in New London, CT; died Sept 3, 1869; dau. of Stephen Hempstead and Mary Lewis Hempstead; m. John Keeny (sea captain), June 2, 1806 (died 1810); m. Manuel Lisa, in 1818 (died Aug 12, 1820); children: (1st m.) 1 son. ❖ Married Manuel Lisa, explorer, fur trader and head of the Missouri Fur Company; accompanied him on a trading expedition up the Missouri River as far as Council Bluffs, making her perhaps the 1st white woman to visit that region; was a leading figure in Protestant circles, and participated in the founding of the 1st Presbyterian congregation in Missouri. ❖ See also Ambrose C. Smith, *Memorials of the Life and Character of Mary Manuel Lisa* (Lippincott, 1870); and *Women in World History.*

LISA DEL GIOCONDO (1474–?). *See del Giocondo, Lisa.*

LISA LISA. *See Velez, Lisa.*

LISBOA, Henriquetta (1904–1985). Brazilian poet and essayist. Born July 15, 1904, in Lambari, Minais Gerais, Brazil; died Oct 9, 1985, in Belo Horizonte, Minas Gerais, Brazil. ❖ Worked as translator and teacher; writing appeared in journals, newspapers, and anthologies; recognized as neo-symbolist, was 1st woman elected to Academy of Letters in state of Minas Gerais (1963); works include *Flor da noite* (1949), *Madrinha lua* (1952), and *Lírica* (1958).

LISBOA, Irene (1892–1958). Portuguese educator and author. Name variations: Irene do Ceu Vieira Lisboa; (pseudonyms) João Falco and Manuel Soares. Born in Murzinheira, Arruda dos Vinhos, Portugal, Dec 25, 1892; died in Lisbon, Nov 25, 1958. ❖ Began teaching at Beato Parish school in Lisbon during WWI; at war's end, joined with Ilda Moreira to lay the foundations of Portuguese pedagogy for young children, emphasizing considerable freedom rather than structure; had a fellowship at University of Geneva's Institute of Educational Science (1929–31), followed by half year at International Montessori Course in Rome, then spent a year studying in Brussels (1931–32); organized and directed an important conference on "The Methods and Ends of Early Childhood Education" (1933); served as director of Early Childhood Education (Inspectora Orientadora do Ensino Infantil) for the National Institute of Education; wrote and published prolifically, both in pedagogy and literature; using pseudonym João Falco, published *13 Contarelos* (1926), a series of children's stories; authored several official reports on early childhood education (1933–35); also wrote *Começa uma Vida* (1940), *Esta Cidade!* (1943), *Uma Mão Cheia de Nada, Outra de Coisa Nenhuma* (1955), and the posthumous *Crónicas da Serra* (1961) and *Solidão II* (1974), as well as poetry, including *Um Dia e Outro Dia* (1936) and *Folhas Volantes* (1940). ❖ See also *Women in World History.*

LISI, Virna (1936—). Italian stage, tv, and screen actress. Born Virna Pieralisi, Sept 8, 1937, in Ancona, Marches, Italy; m. Franco Pesci. ❖ Made film debut at 16 in *La corda d'acciaio* (1953); other appearances include *La donna del giorno* (*The Doll That Took the Town*), *Caterina Sforza, Les bonnes causes* (*Don't Tempt the Devil*), *Romolo e Remo* (*Duel of the Titans*), *How to Murder Your Wife, Casanova '70, Assault on a Queen, The Secret of Santa Vittoria, Bluebeard, The Serpent* and as Catherine de Medici in *Queen Margot* (1996); often appeared on stage, including Strehler's production of *I giacobini* at Piccolo Teatro di Milano.

LI SIAN TSZY (1887–1928). *See Dmitreva, Elizaveta Ivanovna.*

LISIEWSKA, Anna (1721–1782). German artist. Name variations: Liscewska; Lisziewska; Anna Dorothea Lisiewska-Therbusch. Born Anna Dorothea Lisiewska in Berlin, Germany, July 23, 1721; died in Berlin, 1782; dau. of George Lisiewski or Lisziewski, Polish painter who may have been her 1st teacher; sister of Rosina Lisiewska (1716–1783); m. Ernst Therbusch (innkeeper and artist), 1745; children: several. ❖ Commissioned by the courts of Duke Charles Eugene in Stuttgart and Elector Karl Theodor in Mannheim (1761, 1764); moved to Paris (1765) where she was backed by Diderot; elected to the academy (1767) and exhibited a number of paintings in that year's Salon, including *The Drinker;* by 1771, was back in Berlin, where she remained for rest of life, mainly painting portraits; later gained acceptance into Bologna and Vienna academies, the latter of which granted her membership (1776) on the strength of her portrayal of landscape painter Phillip Hackert. ❖ See also *Women in World History.*

LISIEWSKA, Rosina (1716–1783). German artist. Name variations: Anna Rosina Lisiewska, Liscewska or Lisziewska; Rosina Lisiewska-deGasc; Madame Matthieu. Born Anna Rosina Lisiewska in 1716 (some sources cite 1713); died 1783; dau. of George Lisiewski or Lisziewski, Polish painter who may have been her 1st teacher; sister of Anna Lisiewska (1721–1782); married. ❖ Had great success after 1755, following death of husband; as Madame Matthieu, was invited to Brunswick to undertake royal commissions; was also named to Dresden Academy.

LISKIEWICZ, Krystyna Chojnowska (b. 1937). *See Chojnowska-Liskiewicz, Krystyna.*

LISKOVA, Hana (1952—). Czech gymnast. Born June 1952 in Czechoslovakia. ❖ At Mexico City Olympics, won a silver medal in team all-around (1968).

LISLE, Alice (c. 1614–1685). English sympathizer of religious dissenters. Name variations: Lady Alice Lisle; Alicia Lisle. Born Alicia Beckenshaw c. 1614; executed in Winchester marketplace, Sept 2, 1685; dau. of Sir White Beckenshaw, who was descended from an old Hampshire family; m. John Lisle (1610?–1664), who had been one of the judges at the trial of Charles I and was subsequently a member of Cromwell's House of Lords—thus, his wife's courtesy title. ❖ At age 70, agreed to let John Hickes, a Nonconformist minister and fleeing member of the "Protestant duke" of Monmouth's army, pass the night at her house; was charged with harboring traitors; when her case was tried by Judge George Jeffreys, pleaded that she had no knowledge that Hickes' offense was anything more serious than illegal preaching and that she had no sympathy with the rebellion; since the law recognized no distinction between principals and accessories in treason, was sentenced to be burned (James II allowed beheading to be substituted). ❖ See also *Women in World History.*

LISLE, Honora Grenville (c. 1495–1566). English letter writer. Name variations: Honora Grenville Basset Lisle; Honora L'Isle. Born Honora Grenville, c. 1495 in Cornwall, England; died 1566; dau. of Sir Thomas Grenville and Isabella Gilbert Grenville; m. John Bassett, 1515 (died 1528); m. Arthur Plantagenet, 1st Viscount Lisle or L'Isle (son of Edward IV, king of England, and Elizabeth Lucy), 1529 (died Mar 3, 1542, in Tower of London). ❖ Husband Lord Lisle arrested and charged in Catholic plot; during husband's 2-year imprisonment in Tower of London, was kept under surveillance in Calais; letters to husband show loyalty to him, as well as her piety and relationships with such figures as Thomas Cromwell and Anne Boleyn.

LISNIANSKAYA, Inna (1928—). Russian poet. Name variations: Inna Lvovna (or L'vovna) Lisnianskaia. Born 1928 in Baku; m. Semyon Izrailevich Lipkin (poet, died Mar 2003); children: Elena Makarova (writer). ❖ Doyenne of Russian poetry, published 1st poetry collection (1957); moved to Moscow (1960); published 5 vols. of poetry (1957–78), including *At First Hand* (1966); also published poems in *samizdat Metropol;* frequent contributor to leading Russian literary magazines.

LISOVSKAYA, Natalya (1962—). Soviet track-and-field athlete. Born July 16, 1962, in USSR. ❖ At Seoul Olympics, won a gold medal in shot put (1988).

LISPECTOR, Clarice (1920–1977). Brazilian short-story writer, novelist, and journalist. Born in Chechelnick, Ukraine, Dec 19, 1920; died Dec 9, 1977; dau. of Russian Jews; schooled in Recife, Brazil; studied law in Rio de Janeiro (1944); married a diplomat. ❖ One of Brazil's leading writers of the postmodern period, emigrated from the Ukraine to Recife at age 2; as a teenager, moved to Rio de Janeiro, where she studied law and became a journalist; after marriage, lived in Europe and US, then returned to Rio (1959); at 19, published 1st novel, *Close to the Savage Heart* (1944); later work took a decidedly feminist turn; writings include *Family Ties* (1960), *The Foreign Legion* (1964), *The Passion According to G.H.* (1964), *An Apprenticeship or the Book of Delights* (1969), and *The Hour of the Star* (1977), which became a successful film.

LISSAMAN, Elizabeth Hazel (1901–1991). New Zealand potter. Name variations: Elizabeth Hazel Hall. Born on Oct 11, 1901, in Blenheim, New Zealand; died on Feb 18, 1991, in Cambridge, New Zealand; dau. of Henri Lissaman (sheep farmer) and Helen Eva (Bligh) Lissaman; m. Henry Francis Hall, 1930 (died 1980); children: 3 sons. ❖ Raised on father's sheep station near Seddon; learned pottery from library books and other potters in Australia; established studio on parents' farm; produced primarily domestic ware similar to majolica; published *Pottery for Pleasure in Australia and New Zealand* (1969); member of New Zealand Society of Potters. Received OBE (1982). ❖ See also *Dictionary of New Zealand Biography* (Vol. 4).

LISSIARDI, Sibille (fl. 13th c.). Parisian physician. Dau. of Lissiardus, a surgeon of considerable fame. ❖ A townswoman of Paris, was a doctor credited with remarkable healing powers. ❖ See also *Women in World History*.

LISTER, Anne (1791–1840). English diarist. Name variations: Jack. Born April 3, 1791, in Halifax, England; died near K'ut'aisi, Russia, Sept 22, 1840, after being bitten by a fever-carrying tick; dau. of Rebecca (Battle) Lister and Captain Jeremy Lister (veteran of American War of Independence); attended York's Manor School, age 14–15; for majority of life, engaged tutors to assist with strict regimen of self-education in math, rhetoric, classical languages and literature; never married. ❖ Scholar and heir who kept a detailed account of her life in a 27-volume diary which includes coded passages recording her sexual and romantic relationships with women; began diary at 15 and met Eliza Raine, her 1st "wife"; met 2nd "wife," Marianna Belcombe (later Lawson, 1814); took up residence (as heiress to the estate) in Shibden Hall at age 24 (1815); stayed in Paris (1824–25); inherited Shibden Hall (1826); revisited Paris (1826–28); toured Europe (1827); returned to England (1828) and ended relationship with Lawson; met life-partner, Ann Walker (1832), who moved into Shibden Hall (1834); embarked on journey with Walker to Russia, Persia and Turkey (1839); her diaries serve as a witness to her unique life and provides a rich portrayal of life of landed gentry in early 19th-century England. ❖ See also Helena Whitbread, ed. *I Know My Own Heart: The Diaries of Anne Lister 1791–1840* and *No Priest But Love: The Journals of Anne Lister from 1824–1826* (both New York U. Press, 1992); and *Women in World History*.

LISTER, Moira (1923—). South African-born actress. Born Aug 6, 1923, in Cape Town, South Africa; dau. of Major James Martin and Margaret Winifred (Hogan) Lister; attended Parktown Convent, in Johannesburg; studied acting with Dr. Hulbert and Amy Coleridge; m. Vicomte d'Orthez. ❖ At 6, made stage debut as the Prince in *The Vikings of Helgeland* with Johannesburg University Players; 1st appeared on English stage as Jeeby Cashler in *Post Road* at Golders Green Hippodrome (1937); made London debut as Diana in *Six Pairs of Shoes* (1944); appeared as Juliet and Desdemona with Shakespeare Memorial Theater (1945, 1955); made NY debut as Madeleine in *Don't Listen Ladies* (1948); toured Africa and Australia in one-woman show *People in Love* (1958–59); played Nell Nash in *The Gazebo* (1960–61) for over a year in London; launched film career with *The Shipbuilders* (1943); other films include *The Deep Blue Sea* (1955), *The Yellow Rolls-Royce* (1964), *The Double Man* (1967), *Not Now Darling* (1972) and *Ten Little Indians* (1989); on tv, appeared in popular series "The Very Merry Widow." ❖ See also autobiography, *The Very Merry Moira* (1969); and *Women in World History*.

LISTER, Sandra (1961—). English field-hockey player. Born Aug 16, 1961, in UK. ❖ At Barcelona Olympics, won a bronze medal in team competition (1992).

LISTON, Melba (1926—). African-American jazz trombonist and arranger. Name variations: Melba Doretta Liston. Born in Kansas City, MO, Jan 13, 1926. ❖ One of only a handful of African-American female trombonists and a brilliant arranger, had a career that spanned over 40 years; launched career in a theater-pit orchestra led by Bardu Ali (1942); played with Gerald Wilson's band (1943–48), then joined up with Dizzy Gillespie; after a tour with Billie Holiday (1949), gave up playing before rejoining Gillespie in 1956; went out on her own

(1958), forming an all-woman quintet; worked with a series of band leaders (1960s), including Quincy Jones, Johnny Griffin, Milt Jackson, and Randy Weston; also did arrangements for singers and tv commercials; settled in Jamaica (1974), where she established a music program at University of West Indies and headed up the African-American pop and jazz department at Jamaica School of Music; moved to NY (1979) and formed her own septet, Melba Liston and Company. ❖ See also *Women in World History*.

LISZIEWSKA. See *Lisiewska*.

LISZT, Cosima (1837–1930). See *Wagner, Cosima*.

LITA-VATASOIU, Emilia (1933—). Romanian gymnast. Name variations: Emilia Vatasoiu. Born Oct 20, 1933, in Romania. ❖ Won a bronze medal at Melbourne Olympics (1956) and a bronze medal at Rome Olympics (1960), both in team all-around.

LITCHFIELD, Harriett (1777–1854). English actress. Born Harriett Hay in 1777; died 1854; m. John Litchfield of Privy Council Office, 1794 (died 1858). ❖ Known as Mrs. Litchfield, made stage debut (1792); appeared at Covent Garden (1797) and remained there until her retirement in 1812; is best known for her Emilia in *Othello*.

LITCHFIELD, Jessie (1883–1956). Australian writer. Born Jessie Phillips in Sydney, Australia, in 1883; died in Richmond, Australia, Mar 12, 1956; dau. of John Phillips (contractor) and Jean (Sinclair) Phillips; attended Neutral Bay Public School, Sydney; m. Valentine Augustus Litchfield (miner), Jan 21, 1908; children: 4 sons, 3 daughters. ❖ For 10 years, traveled with husband from mine to mine across the Northern Territory, all the while raising 7 children in crude conditions; later recorded her adventures in *Far-North Memories* (1930); became editor of *Northern Territory Times* (1930); entered politics, unsuccessfully contesting the Territory's federal parliamentary seat as an independent candidate (1951); helped establish *North Australian* monthly and served as assistant editor; became the Territory's 1st woman justice of the peace (1955); wrote other books. Awarded coronation medal for outstanding service to the Northern Territory (1953). ❖ See also Janet Dickinson, *Jesse Litchfield—Grand Old Lady of the Territory* (1982); and *Women in World History*.

LITOSHENKO, Mariya (1949—). Soviet handball player. Born Sept 24, 1949, in USSR. ❖ At Montreal Olympics, won a gold medal in team competition (1976).

LITTEN, Irmgard (1879–1953). German political activist and memoirist. Born Irmgard Wüst in Halle/Saale, Germany, Aug 30, 1879; died in East Berlin, June 30, 1953; m. Fritz Julius Litten (1873–1939), noted University of Königsberg law professor; children: Hans Achim Litten (1903–1938, well-known attorney); Heinz Wolfgang Litten (1905–1955); Rainer Litten (1909–1972). ❖ With Nazi seizure of power, son Hans was thrown into Dachau concentration camp as a "Marxist sympathizer"; used all the stratagems at her employ to secure son's release, bringing the case to attention of the foreign press; received word that Hans had "committed suicide" while in Dachau (1938); immigrated to Great Britain, where she wrote *Beyond Tears: A Mother Fights Hitler*; became active in the exile community's anti-Nazi work. ❖ See also *Women in World History*.

LITTLE, Alberta Freeman (1922—). See *Bower, Alberta*.

LITTLE, Ann (1891–1984). American actress. Name variations: Anna Little. Born Feb 7, 1891, in Mount Shasta, CA; died May 21, 1984, in Los Angeles, CA; m. Allan Forrest (actor), 1916 (div. 1918). ❖ Made film debut (1910); signed with Thomas Ince (1911) and was later under contract to Paramount; appeared in westerns with Jack Hoxie, William S. Hart, and Wallace Reid; other films include *The Squaw Man, Cradle of Courage, Chain Lightning, Hair Trigger Casey* and *The Greatest Menace*; retired (1923) and later managed the Chateau Marmont Hotel in West Hollywood.

LITTLE, Dorothy Round (1908–1982). See *Round, Dorothy*.

LITTLE, Mrs. Douglas (1908–1982). See *Round, Dorothy*.

LITTLE, Janet (1759–1813). Scottish poet. Born 1759 in Dumfriesshire, Scotland; died 1813; m. John Richmond, 1792. ❖ Worked as servant to a patron of Robert Burns and later at dairy of Loudun Castle where an employer showed some of her poems to Burns; wrote in Gaelic and English but did not use accepted pronunciations; published *The Poetical Works of Janet Little* (1792).

LITTLE, Jean (1932—). Canadian children's writer. Born Jean Llewellyn, Jan 2, 1932, in Formosa (Taiwan); University of Toronto, BA in English, 1955. ❖ One of Canada's best children's writers, was visually impaired from birth; works, which often focused on disabled children, include *Mine for Keeps* (1962), *Home From Far* (1965), *When the Pie was Opened* (1968), *Kate* (1972), *Stand in the Wind* (1975), *Listen for the Singing* (1975), *Mama's Going to Buy You a Mockingbird* (1984), *Lost and Found* (1985), *His Banner Over Me* (1996), and *Orphan at My Door* (2002). Received Canadian Library Association Book of the Year award and Canadian Council of Children's Literature Award.

LITTLE, Sally (1951—). South African-born golfer. Born Oct 12, 1951, in Cape Town, South Africa. ❖ Won South African MatchPlay and Stroke Play (1971); had 15 professional career wins, including Honda Classic (1978), Bent Tree Classic, Barth Classic, and Columbia Savings Classic (1979), LPGA championship (1980), Elizabeth Arden Classic and Women's International (1981), Dinah Shore (1982), and du Maurier (1988); granted US citizenship (1982). Named LPGA Rookie of the Year (1971); named Comeback Player of the Year by *Golf Digest* (1988). ❖ See also *Women in World History.*

LITTLE, Tawny (c. 1957—). Miss America and TV host. Name variations: Tawny Godin; Tawny Little-Welch. Born Connie Elaine Godin in Saratoga Springs, NY, c. 1957; attended Skidmore College and University of Southern California; m. John Schneider (actor), July 16, 1983 (div. later 1980s); m. Rick Welch, Jan 1, 2000; children: 3. ❖ Named Miss America (1976), representing NY; became general assignment reporter, KABC-TV, Los Angeles; co-host of numerous tv shows in LA, including "Eye on LA," "Hollywood Close-up," and "The Love Report"; co-news-anchor on UPN nightly news, LA. Appeared in films *Money Talks* (1997) and *Rocky II.*

LITTLE BIDDY (c. 1802/27–1899). See *Goodwin, Bridget.*

LITTLEDALE, Clara (1891–1956). American writer and editor. Name variations: Clara Savage, Clara Savage Littledale. Born Clara Savage, Jan 31, 1891, in Belfast, Maine; died Jan 9, 1956, in New York, NY; dau. of John Arthur Savage (Unitarian minister) and Emma (Morrison) Savage; graduate of Smith College, 1913; m. Harold Aylmer Littledale (*New York Times* managing editor), 1920 (div. 1945); children: Rosemary (b. 1923), Harold Jr. (b. 1927). ❖ Writer who encouraged parents to be educators and called attention to social issues, such as child labor legislation, worked for *New York Evening Post* (1913–14), one of the 1st women reporters in the city room of a newspaper; was chair of National American Woman Suffrage Association (1914–15); worked for *Good Housekeeping* as associate editor (1915–18), and war correspondent (1918); acted with Provincetown Players (1917–18); worked as freelance writer (1919–26); was managing editor for *The Magazine for Parents* (1926–56), later renamed *Parents' Magazine;* lectured widely and frequently appeared on radio and tv.

LITTLE DOVE (c. 1491–1517). See *Dyveke.*

LITTLEFIELD, Caroline (c. 1882–1957). American ballet dancer and teacher. Born c. 1882; died May 7, 1957, in Red Bank, NJ; m. James Littlefield; children: Catherine Littlefield and Dorothie Littlefield (both dancers). ❖ Trained with ballet master Romulus Carpenter at Philadelphia Opera before joining the company; founded school in Philadelphia, where she trained students to dance for opera; began serving as director of ballet at Philadelphia Civic Opera (1925).

LITTLEFIELD, Catharine (1755–1814). See *Greene, Catharine Littlefield.*

LITTLEFIELD, Catherine (1904–1951). American ballet dancer and choreographer. Born Sept 16, 1904, in Philadelphia, PA; died Nov 15, 1951, in New York, NY; dau. of Caroline Littlefield (c. 1882–1957, ballet dancer); sister of Dorothie Littlefield (c. 1908–1953, ballet dancer); m. Sterling Noel. ❖ Pioneer in American ballet, made stage debut in NY in Ziegfeld production of *Sally* and subsequently danced in *Kid Boots, Annie Dear* and *Louie the XIV;* was *première danseuse* with Philadelphia Civic Opera (1925) and Philadelphia Grand Opera (1926–33) and produced many of the ballets within the operas presented; founded the Catherine Littlefield Ballet (Oct 1935) which became the Philadelphia Ballet (1936); made London debut with her company in *Barn Dance, Moment Romantique,* and *Termina* (1937); devised choreography for ice shows and more than 20 ballets.

LITTLEFIELD, Dorothie (c. 1908–1953). American ballet dancer. Born c. 1908, in Philadelphia, PA; died Aug 16, 1953, in Evanston, IL; dau. of Caroline Littlefield (c. 1882–1957, ballet dancer); sister of Catherine

Littlefield (1904–1951, dancer). ❖ Trained with mother, then with Lyubov Egorova; danced with Ballet Russe de Monte Carlo in *Aurora's Wedding* and *Schéhérézade;* taught at School of American Ballet during its 1st season; danced in sister's Littlefield Ballet where she created roles in *Bolero* (1936), *The Sleeping Beauty* (1937), and *Classic Suite* (1937), among others.

LITTLEFIELD, Nancy (c. 1929—). American director. Born Nancy Kassel, c. 1929, in the Bronx, NY; dau. of Benjamin George and Mildred Christine (Herndon) Kassel; children: Joshua and Amy Littlefield. ❖ Became 1st woman accepted into Directors Guild of America (DGA, 1952); served as vice president/national board member of DGA; served as NY's Film Commissioner under Mayor Edward I. Koch (1978–83); received 3 Emmy nominations for documentaries and won Emmy for *And Baby Makes Two* (1979); became president of (212) Studios in Long Island City, NY (1983); served as vice president of NY Women in Film; taught at several universities including NYU Film School of the Arts, USC Film School, and Columbia University School of the Arts; served as executive director/executive producer at 4 public-television stations. Wrote *Movies and Television–Getting In.*

LITTLE FLOWER, The (1873–1897). See *Thérèse of Lisieux.*

LITTLE MITZI (1920–1969). See *Green, Mitzi.*

LITTLE ROCK NINE.
See *Brown, Minnijean.*
See *Eckford, Elizabeth.*

LITTLEWOOD, Joan (1914–2002). English actor, founder and director. Born Joan Maudie Littlewood, Oct 6, 1914, in Stockwell, South London; died Sept 20, 2002, in London; dau. of Kate Littlewood (not married); attended Royal Academy of Dramatic Art; m. Jimmie Miller (later known as Ewan MacColl), 1936 (div.); m. Gerry Raffles (died 1975); children: none. ❖ Founder and director of the Theater Workshop, who pioneered original methods of theater training and developed production styles which have had a profound influence on postwar theater and theater practitioners both in Great Britain and throughout the world; left school prematurely on winning scholarship to RADA; left RADA without completing course and moved to Manchester (1934); joined Theater of Action (agitprop street theater) and met Ewan MacColl (writer); founded Theater Union (1936); worked as freelance writer and broadcaster, though banned from BBC for political outspokenness (1939–45); founded Theater Workshop with Gerry Raffles and others (1945); toured devised work and classical plays (mainly as "one-night stands") in England, Germany, Norway, Sweden and Czechoslovakia (1945–53); moved company to Theater Royal, Stratford-atte-Bowe, London, E.15 (1953); invited to Theater of Nations, Paris (1955), then annually, winning Best Production of the Year 3 times; with *Mother Courage,* offered 1st production of Bertolt Brecht in England (1955); ran workshops at Centre Culturel Hammamet, Tunisia (1965–67) and Image India, Calcutta (1968); created children's environments, bubble cities, learn and play areas around Theater Royal, E.15 (1968–75); left England to work in France (1975). Productions include *Uranium 235* (1949), *The Good Soldier Schweik* (1954), *Volpone* (1955), *The Quare Fellow* (1956), *A Taste of Honey* (1958), *The Hostage* (1958), *Fings Ain't What They Used T'Be* (1959), *Sparrers Can't Sing* (1961), and film (1963), *Oh What a Lovely War* (1963) and *Mrs. Wilson's Diary* (1967). ❖ See also autobiography *Joan's Book* (Methuen, 1994); and *Women in World History.*

LITTON, Marie (1847–1884). English actress. Name variations: Mrs. Wybrow Robertson. Born Mary Lowe in Derbyshire, England, 1847; died in London, April 1, 1884; m. W. Robertson. ❖ An English comedic actress respected for her portrayals of Lady Teazle and Lydia Languish, was also a theatrical manager, overseeing the Court Theater (1871–74), Imperial Theater (1878), and Theater Royal, Glasgow (1880); 1st appeared as an actress at the Princess's Theater (Mar 23, 1868).

LITVINOV, Ivy (1889–1977). British novelist and short-story writer. Born Ivy Low, June 4, 1889, in Maidenhead, Berkshire, England; died April 16, 1977, in Hove, Sussex, England; dau. of Walter and Alice Baker Low; m. Maxim Litvinov (diplomat), 1916 (died 1951); children: 2. ❖ After husband was deported for Bolshevik activities (1918), followed him to Soviet Union and later to US where he was ambassador; wrote *Growing Pains* (1913), *The Questing Beast* (1914), *The Moscow Mystery* (1930), and *She Knew She Was Right* (1971). ❖ See also J. Carswell, *The Exile: A Life of Ivy Litvinov* (1983).

LITVYAK, Lidiya (1921–1943). Soviet fighter pilot. Name variations: Liliya or Lilya Litvyak; Liliia Litviak. Pronunciation: Lit-VYAHK. Born Lidiya Vladimirovna Litvyak, Aug 18, 1921, in Moscow, USSR; died Aug 1, 1943, in Dmitreivka, Ukraine, as a result of air combat; dau. of Vladimir Leontovich Litvyak (railway employee) and Anna Vasilevna Khmeleva Litvyak (saleswoman); never married; no children. ❖ Combat pilot during WWII, who was the 1st woman to shoot down an enemy aircraft and the top woman ace in history; became a pilot (1937) and instructor pilot (1939–41); joined Soviet military (1941); was a fighter pilot with 586th Fighter Aviation Regiment (1942), completing 55 combat flights; transferred to 437th Fighter Aviation Regiment at Stalingrad (1942); on 3rd day of combat, brought down 2 German planes during a single flight; transferred to 9th Guards Fighter Aviation Regiment (1942); transferred to 73rd Guards Fighter Aviation Regiment and achieved all subsequent kills (1943); was badly wounded in air combat (Mar 22, 1943); 6 weeks later, was back in action; wounded once more (July 16, 1943); with her plane trailing smoke, disappeared over enemy territory while in combat (Aug 1943); completed 268 combat flights; personal kills included 1 Ju-87 and 3 Ju-88 bombers, 7 Me-109 fighters, and 1 artillery observation balloon; shared kills included 1 FW-190 and 2 Me-109 fighters. Awards: Order of the Red Star; Order of the Red Banner; medal "For the Defense of Stalingrad"; Order of the Patriotic War, 1st degree; Hero of the Soviet Union (awarded posthumously in 1990). ❖ See also *Women in World History*.

LITWINDE (fl. 850). Bavarian princess. Dau. of Count Ernest; m. Carloman (c. 828–880), king of Bavaria (r. 876–880), c. 850; children: Arnulf of Carinthia (b. around 863), king of Germany (r. 887–899), king of the East Franks (r. 896–899), and Holy Roman emperor (r. 896–899).

LITZ, Katharine (c. 1918–1978). American modern dancer. Born c. 1918 in Denver, CO; died Dec 19, 1978, in New York, NY; trained with Doris Humphrey and Charles Weidman. ❖ Performed and created numerous roles for Humphrey/Weidman including for Humphrey's *New Dance* (1935), *Theater Piece* (1936), and *With My Red Fires* (1936), and Weidman's *Opus 51* (1938) and *Flickers* (1941); performed on Broadway in *Oklahoma* (1943) and *Carousel* (1945); began choreographing own works, with 1st public performance at 92nd Street Y (c. 1948). Choreographed works include *Impressions of Things Past* (1948), *Fire in the Snow* (1949), *That's Out of Season* (1951), *The Lure* (1954), *Transitions* (1961), (with Paul Taylor) *Poetry in Motion* (1963), *Sell Out* (1964), *In the Park* (1973), *They All Came Home Save One Because She Never Left* (1974).

LIU AILING (1967—). Chinese soccer player. Born Feb 5, 1967, in Shiyan, Hubei, China. ❖ Midfielder; joined Chinese national team (1987); also played for Beijing; won a team silver medal at Atlanta Olympics (1996); played for WUSA's Philadelphia Charge (2001); retired (2002) to start a soccer school in Beijing.

LIU CHUNHONG (1985—). Chinese weightlifter. Born Jan 29, 1985, in China. ❖ Won a gold medal for 69kg at Athens Olympics (2004), setting an Olympic and World record at 275.0; at World championships, placed 1st at 69kg, 69kg snatch, and 69kg clean & jerk (2003).

LIU JUN (1969—). Chinese basketball player. Born Oct 15, 1969, in China. ❖ At Barcelona Olympics, won a silver medal in team competition (1992).

LIU LIMIN (1976—). Chinese swimmer. Born 1976 in Hubei Province, China; attended University of Nevada. ❖ Won 100- and 200-meter butterfly at Asian Games and World championships (1994); won a silver medal for 100-meter butterfly at Atlanta Olympics (1996); won NCAA titles for 100-meter butterfly (2000) and 200-meter butterfly (1999, 2000).

LIU LIPING (1958—). Chinese handball player. Born June 1, 1958, in China. ❖ At Los Angeles Olympics, won a bronze medal in team competition (1984).

LIU, Nienling (1934—). American novelist and short-story writer. Name variations: (pseudonym) Mulin Chi. Born 1934 in China; attended University of California at Berkeley, Columbia, Harvard, and Cambridge. ❖ Served as editor of Chinese literary magazine *Convergences;* writings include *The Image in the Bamboo Grove* (1983) and *The Marginal Man* (1987).

LIU QING (1964—). Chinese basketball player. Born Aug 6, 1964, in China. ❖ Won a bronze medal at Los Angeles Olympics (1984) and a silver medal at Barcelona Olympics (1992), both in team competition.

LIU WEI. Chinese table tennis player. Born in China; attended Beijing University. ❖ Won doubles World championship (1991, 1993, 1995); won a silver medal for doubles at Atlanta Olympics (1996).

LIU XIA (1979—). Chinese judoka. Born Jan 6, 1979, in China. ❖ Placed 1st at Super A in Wuppertal for 78kg (2002); won a silver medal for 78kg at Athens Olympics (2004).

LIU XIAONING (1975—). Chinese volleyball player. Born July 14, 1975, in China. ❖ Won a team silver medal at Atlanta Olympics (1996).

LIU XUAN (1979—). Chinese gymnast. Born Mar 12, 1979, in Changsha, Hunan Province, China. ❖ At World championships, won a gold medal for balance beam (1996) and a bronze for team all-around (1997); won East Asian Games (1997), Asian Games and CHN nationals (1998); at Sydney Olympics, won a gold medal for balance beam and bronze medals for indiv. and team all-around, the 1st Chinese female to win an indiv. all-around medal at Olympics (2000); was the 1st female to perform a one-arm giant swing on uneven bars; retired (2001).

LIU XUQING (1968—). Chinese softball player. Born 1968 in China. ❖ Won a silver medal at Atlanta Olympics (1996).

LIU YAJU. Chinese softball player. Born in China. ❖ Won a silver medal at Atlanta Olympics (1996).

LIU YANAN (1980—). Chinese volleyball player. Born Sept 29, 1980, in China. ❖ Opposite hitter, won a team gold medal at Athens Olympics (2004).

LIU YING (1974—). Chinese soccer player. Born June 10, 1974, in Beijing, China. ❖ Midfielder; selected to the national team (1993); won a team silver medal at Atlanta Olympics (1996); best scorer in national women's soccer league (1998, 1999); best scorer at Asian Cup (1999) and won Golden Boot Award.

LIU YUMEI (1961—). Chinese handball player. Born July 17, 1961, in China. ❖ At Los Angeles Olympics, won a bronze medal in team competition (1984).

LIU YUXIANG (1975—). Chinese judoka. Born Oct 11, 1975, in Hunan Province, China. ❖ Won a bronze medal for 48 half-lightweight at Sydney Olympics (2000).

LIU ZHEN (1930—). Chinese short-story writer. Born 1930 in China. ❖ After father and brothers were killed for associating with the Communists, joined Communist army (1939), where she learned to read and write; kept diary and wrote stories about experiences; in story "The Black Flag" (1978), criticized policy of 'Great Leap Forward'; also wrote "The Winding Stream" (1962).

LIUBATOVICH, Olga (1853–1917). Russian revolutionary. Pronunciation: Lu-ba-TOE-vich. Born Olga Spiridonovna Liubatovich, 1853, in Moscow; committed suicide in Tbilisi, Georgia, July 27, 1917; dau. of Spiridon Liubatovich (wealthy factory owner); mother was the dau. of a wealthy gold mine owner (name unknown); sister of Vera Liubatovich (1855–1907); attended Second Moscow Women's Gymnasium, c. 1866–71; Medical Faculty, University of Zurich, 1871–73; m. I.S. Dzhabadari; children: (with Nikolai Morozov) daughter. ❖ Active in all phases of the Populist movement, was a member of the Fritschi Circle in Zurich and Bern (1872–74), which provided an introduction to the radical ideas of the French utopian socialists and contemporary Russian revolutionary theorists; was a Populist propagandist in All-Russian Social-Revolutionary Organization (1875); arrested (1875), tried in the "Trial of the Fifty" (1877), sentenced to exile in Siberia, and escaped (1878); was a member of Land and Liberty (1878–79); as a member of Executive Committee of Narodnaia Volia (1879–81), helped lay the groundwork for assassination of Tsar Alexander II; arrested and exiled to Siberia (1882–1905?). ❖ See also *Women in World History*.

LIUBATOVICH, Vera (1855–1907). Russian revolutionary. Pronunciation: Lu-ba-TOE-vich. Born Vera Spiridonovna Liubatovich, July 26, 1855 (o.s.) in Moscow; died in Moscow, Dec 19, 1907; dau. of Spiridon Liubatovich (wealthy factory owner); mother was the dau. of a wealthy gold mine owner (name unknown); sister of Olga Liubatovich (1853–1917); attended 2nd Moscow Women's Gymnasium, 1868–71; attended Medical Faculty, University of Zurich, 1873; m. V.A. Ostashkin, 1880; no children. ❖ Was a member of the Fritschi circle in Zurich and Bern (1872–74), concerned with the appropriate way to change the autocratic tsarist system; was a Populist propagandist and a central figure in the formation of the All-Russian Social Revolutionary Organization (1875), the 1st formal organization of Russian Populists; arrested (1875), tried in "Trial of the Fifty" (1877) and exiled to Siberia until 1890s; lived thereafter in Orel and Moscow. ❖ See also *Women in World History.*

LIUTGARD. *Variant of Luitgard or Luitgarde.*

LIUTGARD (d. 885). Queen of the East Franks. Died Jan 25, 885; dau. of Oda (806–913) and Liudolf (c. 806–866), count of Saxony; sister of Gerberga (d. 896) and Hathumoda (d. 874); m. Louis the Young, king of the East Franks, c. 876 or 877; children: Louise (b. around 877); Hildegard (d. after 895).

LIUTGARD OF SAXONY (d. 953). Duchess of Lorraine. Name variations: Luitgarde. Born c. 927; died Nov 18, 953; dau. of Edgitha (c. 912–946) and Otto I the Great (912–973), king of Germany (r. 936–973), Holy Roman emperor (r. 936–973); sister of Liudolf, duke of Swabia; m. Konrad der Rote also known as Conrad the Red (d. 955), duke of Lorraine, in 947; children: Otto, duke of Carinthia. ❖ Liutgard and Conrad were ancestors to the Salian branch of Holy Roman Emperors. ❖ See also *Women in World History.*

LIUTGARDE. *Variant of Luitgard or Luitgarde.*

LIUZZO, Viola (1925–1965). American civil-rights activist. Born Viola Gregg in Tennessee in 1925; murdered in Alabama, Mar 25, 1965; m. Anthony Liuzzo (Teamster official); children: Penny Liuzzo; Mary Liuzzo; Thomas Liuzzo; Anthony Liuzzo Jr.; Sally Liuzzo. ❖ Gunned down by the KKK, became the object of unsubstantiated innuendo, possibly as a smoke screen to cover up a government conspiracy in the case (an FBI informant had been riding with the Klansmen who murdered Liuzzo; he may even have been the one who shot her); was the only woman killed while participating in the civil-rights movement. ❖ See also Mary Stanton, *From Selma to Sorrow: The Life and Death of Viola Liuzzo* (U. of Georgia Press, 1998); (film) *Home of the Brave* (2004); and *Women in World History.*

LIVBJERG, Signe (1980—). Danish sailor. Born Feb 21, 1980, in Denmark. ❖ Won a bronze medal for single-handed dinghy (Europe) at Athens Olympics (2004).

LIVELY, Penelope (1933—). British novelist and children's writer. Born Penelope Low, Mar 17, 1933, in Cairo, Egypt; dau. of Roger Vincent Low (manager of the Bank of Egypt) and Vera Reckett (Greer) Low; attended Oxford; m. Jack Lively, 1957 (died 1998); children: 2. ❖ Was short-listed for Booker Prize for *The Road to Lichfield* (1977) and *According to Mark* (1984); won Booker Prize for *Moon Tiger* (1987); other works of fiction include *Judgement Day* (1980), *Corruption and Other Stories* (1984), *Cleopatra's Sister* (1993), *Heat Wave* (1996), and *Spiderweb* (1998); children's books include *Astercote* (1970), *The Ghost of Thomas Kempe* (1973), *Fanny's Sister* (1976), *Dragon Trouble* (1984), *Princess by Mistake* (1993), *Two Bears and Joe* (1995) and *Lost Dog* (1996). ❖ See also memoir *Oleander, Jacaranda: A Childhood Perceived* (1994).

LIVERMORE, Harriet (1788–1868). American evangelist. Born April 14, 1788, in Concord, NH; died Mar 30, 1868, in Philadelphia, PA; dau. of Edward St. Loe Livermore (attorney, judge, and member of Congress) and Mehitable (Harris) Livermore; educated at Byfield Seminary and Atkinson Academy, NH; never married; no children. ❖ Self-described "Pilgrim Stranger," was an itinerant minister who in mid-19th century traveled alone through Kansas, New England, and along Eastern Seaboard to deliver her message; wrote several religious tracts, beginning with *Scriptural Evidence in Favor of Female Testimony in Meetings for the Worship of God* (1824); published *A Narration of Religious Experience* and extended travels to NY and Philadelphia (1826); was invited to preach at a Sunday service in US House of Representatives (1827), returning several times; undertook 10 Atlantic crossings to Jerusalem in anticipation of the second coming of Christ (1837–62); also published *A Testimony for the Times* (1843); was committed to Blockley Almshouse in Philadelphia (1846), remaining there until her death. ❖ See also *Women in World History.*

LIVERMORE, Mary A. (1820–1905). American reformer. Name variations: Mrs. D.P. Livermore. Born Mary Ashton Rice, Dec 19, 1820, in Boston, MA; died May 23, 1905, in Melrose, MA; dau. of Timothy Rice (laborer) and Zebiah Vose Glover (Ashton) Rice (sea captain's daughter); attended Miss Martha Whiting's Female Seminary, Charlestown, MA, 1836–38; m. Daniel Parker Livermore, May 6, 1845; children: Mary Livermore (1848–1852); Henrietta White Livermore (b. 1851); Marcia Elizabeth Livermore (b. 1854). ❖ Popular American reformer, best

known for her volunteer work during Civil War and lectures and writing on behalf of women's social, political and educational rights throughout late 19th century, was associate editor, *New Covenant* (1858–69); with Jane Hoge, directed Chicago Sanitary Commission (1862–65); convened 1st woman suffrage convention in Illinois (1868); was editor of *Woman's Journal* (1870–72); served as president of American Woman Suffrage Association (1875–78); was a professional lecturer (1870–95); is particularly noteworthy for her popularity and for her persistence in campaigning for a broad range of reforms to equalize opportunities for women. ❖ See also Livermore's *My Story of the War* (1887) and *The Story of My Life* (1897); and *Women in World History.*

LIVESAY, Dorothy (1909–1996). Canadian poet. Born 1909 in Winnipeg, Manitoba, Canada; died 1996 in Victoria, British Columbia; dau. of John Frederick Bligh Livesay and Florence Randal; attended universities of Toronto, Sorbonne and British Columbia; m. Duncan Macnair, 1937 (died 1959); children: 2. ❖ Joined Communist Party and worked as journalist, teacher, and activist; taught in Zambia (1959–63) and was writer-in-residence at several universities; was founding member of League of Canadian Poets and named Officer of the Order of Canada (1987); works include *Green Pitcher* (1928), *Signpost* (1934), *Poems for People* (1947), *Call My People Home* (1950), *The Unquiet Bed* (1967), *The Documentaries* (1968), *Ice Age* (1975), *The Phases of Love* (1983), *Beginnings* (1988), *The Woman I Am* (1991), and *Archive for Our Times: Previously Uncollected and Unpublished Poems of Dorothy Livesay* (1998); also wrote *Husband: A Novella* (1990) and edited poetry journal *Contemporary Verse 2.*

LIVIA (fl. 100 BCE). Roman noblewoman. Dau. of M. Livius Drusus (consul in 112 BCE); sister M. Livius Drusus; m. Q. Servilius Caepio (div.); m. M. Portius Cato; children: (1st m.) a son, Q. Servilius Caepio; Servilia (who m. L. Licinius Lucullus); Servilia (who m. M. Junius Brutus the Elder); (2nd m.) Cato the Younger (whose daughter Portia [c. 70–43 BCE] m. M. Junius Brutus, one of the assassins of Julius Caesar); daughter, Portia (fl. 80 BCE).

LIVIA (58 BCE–29 CE). *See Livia Drusilla.*

LIVIA DRUSILLA (58 BCE–29 CE). Roman empress. Name variations: usually referred to simply as Livia; after Augustus died, referred to as Julia Augusta. Born Jan 30, 58 BCE; died in 29 CE; dau. of Marcus Livius Drusus Claudianus (senator) and Alfidia; m. Tiberius Claudius Nero, 43 or 44 BCE and div. 39 BCE; m. Octavian (future emperor Augustus), Jan 17, 38 BCE; children: (1st m.) Tiberius (42 BCE–37 CE), emperor of Rome; Drusus. ❖ The 1st empress of the Roman Empire, who was considered a model of womanly decorum and influence, married Octavian (Augustus), 1st emperor of Rome (38 BCE); granted tribunician protections and the freedom to manage her own affairs (35 BCE), an unprecedented honor which came close to associating women with high public office; with her many financial resources, restored temples and shrines, particularly those associated with goddesses and women, including the temples of Fortuna Muliebris, Bona Dea Subsaxana, and Concordia; was also involved in the construction of a provision market called the Macellum Liviae in Rome; was considered her husband's best confidant and counselor; adopted into the Julian family and renamed Julia Augusta at his death; revered in conjunction with her son the new Emperor Tiberius; appointed priestess to the cult of Augustus (14 CE); deified by the emperor Claudius (42 CE); because of her honored position as Octavian's consort and her creative use of the attendant privileges, she became a revered model of correct feminine behavior in her own time and for centuries after her death, though she had gone beyond the traditional norms of conduct associated with women. ❖ See also *Women in World History.*

LIVIA ORESTILLA (fl. 32 CE). Roman noblewoman. Flourished c. 32 CE; 2nd wife of Caligula (12–41), Roman emperor (div.). Caligula's 1st wife was Junia Claudilla; his 3rd was Lollia Paulina; his 4th was Milonia Caesonia.

LIVILLA (c. 14/11 BCE–c. 31 CE). Roman noblewoman. Name variations: Livia Julia. Born between 14 and 11 BCE; died c. 31 CE; dau. of Antonia Minor (36 BCE–37 CE) and Drusus the Elder (also known as Nero Drusus, brother of the future emperor Tiberius); sister of Germanicus and Claudius (10 BCE–54 CE, future emperor); m. Drusus the Younger (Drusus Julius Caesar, who died in 23 BCE); children: possibly a daughter Julia. ❖ Was caught up in the conspiracy to overthrow Tiberius by her lover Sejanus, captain of the Praetorian Guard; was rumored to have poisoned her husband Drusus the Younger, the adopted son of Tiberius

(23 CE); though Tiberius spared her "out of regard" for her mother Antonia, was executed by mother who starved her to death.

LIVILLA (c. 16 CE–after 38 CE). *See Julia Livilla.*

LIVINGSTON, Alida Schuyler (1656–1727). American letter writer. Name variations: Alida Schuyler van Rensselaer Livingston. Born Alida Schuyler 1656 at Fort Orange (near Albany, NY); died May 1727 at Livingston Manor, Albany; 3rd of 10 children of Philip Peterse Schuyler (wealthy fur trader) and Margaretta van Schlechtenhorst Schuyler; m. Nicholas van Rensselaer, 1675 (died 1678); m. Robert Livingston (Scottish immigrant and one of her 1st husband's clerks), 1679 (died 1728); children: 9. ❖ Her letters, published as *Business Letters of Alida Schuyler Livingston, 1680–1726* (1982), record her partnership with 2nd husband over almost 50 years of marriage; letters also record details of life and business of family estate Rensselaerswyck in New Netherland (New York).

LIVINGSTON, Anne Shippen (1763–1841). American diarist. Name variations: Nancy Shippen; Anne Home Shippen Livingston. Born Anne Home Shippen in 1763 in Philadelphia, PA; died 1841 in Philadelphia; dau. of Dr. William Shippen III and Alice Lee Shippen; m. Colonel Henry Beekman Livingston; children: 1. ❖ Wrote account of unhappy marriage in *Nancy Shippen, Her Journal* (ed. by Ethel Armes, 1935).

LIVINGSTON, Margaret (1896–1984). American screen actress. Name variations: Margaret Livingstone, Marguerite Livingston. Born Nov 25, 1896, in Salt Lake City, Utah; died Dec 13, 1984, in Warrington, PA; m. Paul Whiteman (bandleader). ❖ Made film debut in *The Chain Invisible* (1916), followed by *Alimony, Divorce, Wandering Husbands, Havoc, American Beauty, Streets of Shanghai, The Scarlet Dove, Say It with Sables, The Apache, His Private Life, The Bellamy Trial, Acquitted, Seven Keys to Baldpate* and *The Social Register,* among others; probably best remembered as the temptress in Murnau's *Sunrise* (1927).

LIVINGSTON, Marguerite (1896–1984). *See Livingston, Margaret.*

LIVINGSTON, Mollie Parnis (1905–1992). *See Parnis, Mollie.*

LIVINGSTON, Nora G.E. (1848–1927). Canadian nurse. Name variations: Nora Gertude Elizabeth Livingston. Born May 17, 1848, in Sault Ste. Marie, Michigan; died July 24, 1927, in Val Morin, Quebec, Canada; graduate of New York Hospital Training School, 1889. ❖ Nursing education pioneer in Canada, 1st served as superintendent of nurses at New York Hospital; at Montreal General Hospital, served as superintendent of nurses (1890–1919), as director of the newly opened nurse training school, and established a nurses' home (1897); instituted (1906) the 1st preliminary training class in Canada.

LIVINGSTONE, Margaret (1896–1984). *See Livingston, Margaret.*

LIVINGSTONE, Marilyn (1952—). Scottish politician. Born 1952. ❖ Head of Business School, Fife College; serves as Labour member of the Scottish Parliament for Kirkcaldy.

LIVINGSTONE, Mary Moffatt (1820–1862). English missionary wife. Born April 12, 1820, in Griqua Town, South Africa; died in 1862 on Zambesi delta, Africa; dau. of English missionaries Robert Moffat and Mary Smith Moffat (1795–1870); m. David Livingstone (explorer), Jan 1845, in Kuruman, Cape Province, South Africa; children: 6, one of whom died in infancy. ❖ Daughter of missionaries and wife of missionary and explorer David Livingstone, endured innumerable hardships during her marriage; accompanied husband as he moved from place to place, establishing missions and exploring central Africa. ❖ See also *Women in World History.*

LIVRY, Emma (1842–1863). French ballerina. Born Emma-Marie Emarot, Sept 1842 (some sources cite 1841) in Paris, France; died July 26, 1863 (some sources cite 1862), in Neuilly, France; illeg. dau. of Célestine Emarot (had performed minor roles at the Paris Opéra); studied with Mme Dominique-Venettozzo, then Maria Taglioni. ❖ At 16, made debut as *La Sylphide* at the Paris Opera; appeared as Erigone in a *divertissement* in the opera *Herculaneum* (1859); triumphed in *Le Papillion* (1860), staged by Maria Taglioni; while rehearsing for the ballet *La Muette di Portici,* was severely burned when a gas jet mounted on the scenery ignited her ballet skirt; died 8 months later from her injuries (1863).

LIZARS, Kathleen MacFarlane (d. 1931). Canadian novelist. Born Kathleen MacFarlane Lizars in Stratford, Ontario, Canada; died 1931; dau. of Judge Lizars; sister of Robina Lizars Smith (writer, died 1918).

❖ Worked as private secretary to the premier of British Columbia, John Robson; writings include *Humours of '37, Grave, Gay, and Grim* (1897); with Robina Lizars, wrote *In the Days of the Canada Company: The Story of the Settlement of the Huron Tract and a View of the Social Life of the Period* (1896) and *Committed to His Charge: A Canadian Chronicle* (1900); also wrote articles for newspapers.

LIZZIE. *Variant of Elizabeth.*

LJUDMILA or LJUDMILLA. *Variant of Ludmila.*

LJUNGDAHL, Carina (1960—). Swedish swimmer. Born Feb 21, 1960, in Sweden. ❖ At Moscow Olympics, won a silver medal in the 4 x 100-meter freestyle relay (1980).

LLANES, Tara (1976—). American mountain biker. Born Nov 28, 1976, in Brea, CA. ❖ Won gold in Biker X (Winter 1999) and bronze in Speed and Downhill (both Winter 1997) at X Games.

LLANGOLLEN, the Ladies of.
See Butler, Eleanor (c. 1738–1829).
See Ponsonby, Sarah (1755–1831).

LLANOVER, Lady (1802–1896). *See Hall, Augusta.*

LLEWELYN DAVIES, Margaret (1861–1944). *See Davies, Margaret Llewelyn.*

LLINGA (c 1580–1663). *See Njinga.*

LLORET, Maria Isabel (1971—). Spanish rhythmic gymnast. Born 1971 in Villajoyosa (Alicante), Spain. ❖ At Seoul Olympics, placed 5th all-around, the highest all- around ranking for a Spanish gymnast (1988).

LLOYD, Alice (1873–1949). English music-hall singer. Born Alice Wood, Oct 20, 1873, in Hoxton, suburb of London, England; died Nov 17, 1949, in Bandstead, England; dau. of John Wood (waiter) and Matilda Mary (Archer) Wood; sister of Daisey Wood, Grace Lloyd, Rosie Lloyd, and Marie Lloyd (music-hall star, 1870–1922); m. Tom MacNaughton. ❖ With sisters, formed the Fairy Bell Minstrels and toured local missions singing temperance songs; made 1st stage appearance with sister Grace, as the Sisters Lloyd (1888), and entertained with Grace for many years; won fame as a singer in leading London and provincial music halls; made 1st American appearance at Kosters & Bial's (1897) and subsequently joined US vaudeville circuit with great success; in NY, starred in *Little Man Fix-It* and *The Rose Maid* and played the Palace (1919).

LLOYD, Alice (1876–1962). American educator. Name variations: Alice Geddes, Alice Spencer Geddes, Alice Spencer Geddes Lloyd. Born Alice Spencer Geddes on Nov 13, 1876, in Athol, MA; died Sept 4, 1962, in Caney Creek, KY; dau. of William Edwin Geddes (merchant) and Ella Mary (Ainsworth) Geddes; attended Radcliffe College, 1895–86, 1899–1900; m. Arthur Lloyd, Feb 16, 1914. ❖ American educator who devoted life to bringing education to isolated Kentucky communities, despite being partially paralyzed by spinal meningitis, was publisher of newspaper, *The Cambridge Press* (1904); became managing editor of *Wakefield Citizen and Banner* (1905); separated from husband, moved to Knott County, KY, for health reasons (1916); with contributions from friends, began construction of schoolhouse in Caney Creek, and purchased land to build community center (c. 1917); opened high school (1919), which became accredited Knott County High School at Pippa Passes (1924); opened 7 other high schools in area by early 1920s; established tuition-free Caney Junior College (later renamed Alice Lloyd College), which was funded by private contributions (1922); during fund-raising trip to CA, appeared on Ralph Edwards' tv program, "This Is Your Life," and collected over $50,000 in contributions for college (1951).

LLOYD, Andrea (1965—). American basketball player. Name variations: Andrea Lloyd-Curry. Born Sept 1965 in Moscow, Idaho; attended University of Texas, 1983–87, playing on the NCAA championship team, 1985–86. ❖ At Seoul Olympics, won a gold medal in team competition (1988); won US team gold medals in Pan American Games (1987, 1991); a forward, played in Italy for 9 years and for the Columbus Quest in the ABL.

LLOYD, Chris Evert (b. 1954). *See Evert, Chris.*

LLOYD, Doris (1896–1968). English actress. Born Hessy Doris Lloyd, July 3, 1896, in Liverpool, England; died May 21, 1968, in Santa Barbara, CA. ❖ Began stage career with Liverpool Rep (1914); came to US (1924); had featured roles in over 60 films, including *Disraeli, Oliver Twist, Becky Sharp, Of Human Bondage, The Plough and the Stars,*

Waterloo Bridge, The Letter, Journey for Margaret, The Constant Nymph, The Lodger and *The Sound of Music.*

LLOYD, Dorothy Jordan (1889–1946). English biochemist. Born May 1, 1889, in Birmingham, England; died Nov 21, 1946; never married. ❖ Joined the British Leather Manufacturers' Research Association (1920) and served as its director (1927–46); also planned and contributed to all 3 vols. of *Progress in Leather Science, 1920–45* (1946–48).

LLOYD, Gweneth (1901–1993). English ballet choreographer, founder and teacher. Born Sept 15, 1901, in Eccles, Lancashire, England; died Jan 1, 1993 in Kelowna, British Columbia; dau. of Winnifred Mary (Stace) Lloyd and Joseph Charles Lloyd. ❖ Trained in interpretive dance techniques in England; ran the Torch Studio in Leeds (1926–38); immigrated to Canada (1938) where she founded dance school in Winnipeg with Betty Farally; with Farally, founded the Winnipeg Ballet Club (1938), which became the Royal Winnipeg Ballet (1953), the country's 1st ballet company with regular productions; served as artistic director at Royal Winnipeg Ballet and created numerous works for the company, including *Finishing School* (1942), *The Wise Virgins* 91942), *The Shooting of Dan McGrew* (1950) and *Shadow in the Prairie* (1952). Also choreographed *Chapter Thirteen* (1947), *Romance* (1947), *Visages* (1949), *Parable* (1953), *Arabesque* (1953) and *Rondel* (1954).

LLOYD, Manda (1877–1949). *See Mander, Jane.*

LLOYD, Marian (1906–1969). *See Vince, Marian.*

LLOYD, Marie (1870–1922). English actress, singer, and comedian. Name variations: Tillie, and stage names Bella Delmere and Miss Marie Lloyd; Matilda Wood. Born Matilda Victoria Wood in Hoxton, a suburb of London, England, Feb 12, 1870; died in London, Oct 7, 1922; dau. of John Wood (waiter and maker of artificial flowers) and Matilda (Archer) Wood; sister of Alice Lloyd, Daisey Wood, Grace Lloyd, Rosie Lloyd (all entertainers); m. Percy Courtney, 1887; m. Alexander Hurley, 1904; m. Bernard Dillon, 1914; children: (1st m.) Marie Courtney. ❖ One of the most popular and highest paid stars of the late Victorian and Edwardian music halls of England, was especially adored by the working classes; with sisters, formed the Fairy Bell Minstrels and toured local missions, singing such temperance songs as "Throw Down the Bottle and Never Drink Again"; made 1st stage appearance at Grecian Saloon at age 15, and shortly changed stage name to Miss Marie Lloyd (1885); made 1st appearance at the famous Oxford Music Hall in West End (1885), remaining on the bill for a year; rose rapidly to stardom at £100 a week (1886); after she began singing "When You Wink the Other Eye," adopted a wink that became a trademark; led strike for poorer members of her profession (1907); snubbed by exclusion from royal command performance of music-hall stars, rented a hall for the same night and drew an audience of 6,000 (1912); detained by US immigration officials on Ellis Island at beginning of an American tour, for traveling with a man out of wedlock (1913); died while attempting a musical comeback (1922). Popularized such songs as "Oh, Mr. Porter," "Everything in the Garden's Lovely," "Twiddley Wink," "The Boy I Love Is Up in the Gallery," "Piccadilly Trot," "It's a Bit of a Ruin That Cromwell Knocked About a Bit," "A Little of What You Fancy Does You Good," "My Old Man Said Follow the Van (but I Dillied, I Dallied)" and "Every Little Movement." ❖ See also D.N. Farson, *Marie Lloyd and Music Hall* (Stacey, 1972); and *Women in World History.*

LLOYD, Marilyn Laird (1929—). American politician. Name variations: Mrs. Mort Lloyd; Marilyn Lloyd Bouquard. Born Rachel Marilyn Laird, Jan 3, 1929, in Fort Smith, Arkansas; dau. of James Edgar Laird and Iva Mae (Higginbotham) Laird; graduate of Shorter College, Rome, Georgia, 1963; m. Mort Lloyd (businessman); m. Joseph P. Bouquard; children: (1st m.) Nancy Lloyd Smithson; Mort Lloyd II; Deborah Lloyd Riley. ❖ Owned and operated radio station WTTI in Dalton, GA, and Executive Aviation in Winchester, TN; elected as a Democrat representing Tennessee to the 94th and 9 succeeding Congresses (1975–95); during 1st term in office, won a place on the Committee on Science, Space and Technology, an important appointment because of its jurisdiction over legislation related to the atomic energy facilities at Oak Ridge in her district; went on to chair its Subcommittee on Energy Research and Development, beginning with 97th Congress; was appointed chair of Subcommittee on Housing and Consumer Interests (1990). ❖ See also *Women in World History.*

LLOYD, Maude (1908–2004). South African ballet dancer and critic. Name variations: Mrs. Nigel Gosling; (pseudonym) Alexander Bland. Born Aug 16, 1908, in Cape Town, South Africa; died Nov 26, 2004, in London, England; studied with Helen Webb; m. Nigel Gosling (art critic), 1939 (died 1982); children: Nicholas. ❖ Trained with Marie Rambert in London, before joining Rambert Dancers and Ballet Club; remained with Ballet Rambert (1927–40) and performed in numerous premieres of Antony Tudor, including *Cross-Garter'd* (1931), *Mr. Roll's Quadrilles* (1932), *The Descent of Hebe* (1935), and as Caroline in *Jardin aux Lilas* (1936); also created roles for Frederick Ashton's *Dances from the Fairy Queen* (1927), *A Florentine Picture* (1930), *La Péri* (1931), *Mercury* (1931), *The Lady of Shalott* (1931) and *Valentine's Eve* (1935), among others, as well as for Andrée Howard's *La Fête Étrange* (1940); retired from the stage to undertake war work (1940); with husband (under joint name of Alexander Bland), wrote dance critiques for *The Observer* (1955–82), which were collected as *Observer of the Dance* (1985); also collaborated with him on other books, including *A History of Ballet and Dance* (1976) and *The Royal Ballet–The First 50 Years* (1981).

LLOYD, Rosie (b. 1879). English comedian and music-hall performer. Born Rose Wood, June 5, 1879, in Hoxton, England; dau. of John Wood and Matilda (Archer) Wood; sister of Daisey Wood, Grace Lloyd, Alice Lloyd (1873–1949), and Marie Lloyd (music-hall star, 1870–1922). ❖ Appeared successfully at several London halls, most of the leading provincial halls, and in pantomimes.

LLOYD-DAVIES, Vanessa (1960–2005). English soldier, doctor and equestrian. Born Nov 30, 1960, in London, England; committed suicide, Feb 16, 2005; attended Lady Margaret Hall, Oxford; m. Andrew Jacks, 1988 (div. Jan 2005). ❖ The 1st woman medical officer attached to the Household Cavalry, joined Royal Army Medical Corps (1990); was awarded an MBE for gallantry, treating wounded Bosnian children under fire in Sarajevo (1992); later became a general practitioner in the Barbican and competed with her horse Don Giovanni II in the Badminton and Burghley horse trials.

LLOYD GEORGE, countess (1888–1972). *See Lloyd George, Frances Stevenson.*

LLOYD GEORGE, Frances Stevenson (1888–1972). Countess Lloyd George of Dwyfor. Name variations: Frances Louise Lloyd George. Born Frances Louise Stevenson in 1888; died 1972; dau. of John Stevenson; educated at Royal Holloway College, London; m. David Lloyd George (1863–1945, Liberal politician and prime minister), 1943; children: (earlier marriage) Jennifer (b. 1929). ❖ Worked closely with David Lloyd George, as his personal secretary and mistress, throughout his political career; was involved in the research and writing of all 6 vols. of his *War Memoirs* (1933–36); after the death of his 1st wife, married David (1943) and settled into the family estate at Criccieth in Wales. ❖ See also A.J.P. Taylor, ed. *Lloyd George: A Diary by Frances Stevenson* (Harper, 1971); and *Women in World History.*

LLOYD GEORGE, Margaret (1866–1941). Welsh prime-ministerial wife. Name variations: Dame Margaret Lloyd George; Margaret Owen. Born Margaret Owen, 1866, in Mynyddednyfed, Wales; died Jan 1941; dau. of a prosperous Methodist farmer; became 1st wife of David Lloyd George (1863–1945, British prime minister, and one of the most dominant international figures of early 20th century), Jan 24, 1888; children: Richard, Mair Eiluned (died at 17), Olwen, Gwilyn (later Viscount Tenby), Megan Lloyd George (1902–1966, Liberal and later a Labour member of Parliament). ❖ England's "first lady" as wife of the prime minister of England, did not have a happy marriage because of husband's infidelities, including his 30-year affair with his secretary, Frances Stevenson (Lloyd George). ❖ See also *Women in World History.*

LLOYD GEORGE, Megan (1902–1966). Welsh politician. Name variations: Lady Megan Lloyd George. Born Megan Arvon Lloyd George at Criccieth, Caernarfonshire, North Wales, April 22, 1902; died May 14, 1966, at her home Brynawelon in Criccieth; 3rd dau and youngest child of David Lloyd George (1863–1945, Liberal politician and prime minister) and Margaret (Owen) Lloyd George (d. 1941); educated at Garratts' Hall, Banstead, and in Paris. ❖ The 1st woman member of the British Parliament from Wales, grew up in Downing Street during father's residency there (1916–22), 1st as chancellor of the exchequer and later as prime minister; campaigned successfully (in the Welsh language, as she always did) for the Liberal constituency of Anglesey (Ynys Mon, 1929), joining her father and brother in House of Commons; became deputy leader of the Parliamentary Liberal Party (1949); was defeated at General Election of 1951 after 22 years at Westminster; became president of the Parliament for Wales campaign (1952); resigned from Liberal Party and joined Labour (1955), for which she fought for West Wales parliamentary seat of Carmarthen (Caerfyrddin, 1959) and was returned to Commons; championed women's causes and Welsh issues, focusing on equality for the language in broadcasting and in the law courts, thus paving the way for the nationalist revival (1960s–70s). ❖ See also *Women in World History*.

LOAIES, Ionela (1979—). Romanian gymnast. Born Feb 1, 1979, in Onesti, Romania. ❖ At World championships, won a gold medal for team all-around (1994); at Atlanta Olympics, won a bronze medal for team all-around (1996).

LOBACH, Marina (1970—). *See Lobatch, Marina.*

LOBACHEVA, Irina (1973—). Russian ice dancer. Born Feb 8, 1973, in Moscow, Russia; m. Ilia Averbukh (ice dancer), 1994. ❖ With husband and partner Ilia Averbukh, won the Trophée Lalique (1993); placed 5th at Nagano Olympics (1998); won Russian nationals (1997, 2000–02); won a bronze medal at World championships (2001) and a gold medal (2002); won a silver medal at Salt Lake City Olympics (2002); won a gold medal at European championships (2003).

LOBANOVA, Natalya (1947—). Soviet diver. Born May 30, 1947, in USSR. ❖ At Mexico City Olympics, won a silver medal in platform (1968).

LOBATCH, Marina (1970—). Soviet rhythmic gymnast. Name variations: Marina Lobach. Born June 26, 1970, in Smolevicki, USSR; m. Dmitry Bogdanov. ❖ At Seoul Olympics, won a gold medal in rhythmic gymnastics, all-around (1988).

LOBAZNIUK, Ekaterina (1983—). Russian gymnast. Name variations: Yekaterina or Katya Labazniouk. Born July 10, 1983, in Rubzowsk, Russia. ❖ Won Russian nationals (1998); at Sydney Olympics, won silver medals for balance beam and all-around team and a bronze medal for vault (2000).

LOBO, Mara (1910–1962). *See Galvão, Patricia.*

LOBO, Rebecca (1973—). American basketball player. Born Oct 6, 1973, Southwick, MA; daughter of Dennis Lobo and RuthAnn Lobo (school officials in Granby, CT); sister of Rachel Lobo, basketball coach; University of Connecticut, BA in political science, 1995; m. Steve Rushin (columnist for *Sports Illustrated*), 2002. ❖ Center; as a college senior, was University of Connecticut's all-time career leader in rebounds (1,286) and blocks (396) and gained national popularity (1995); was a member of the undefeated USA Basketball Women's National Team that played 52 games around the world (1996); won a team gold medal at Atlanta Olympics (1996); played for New York Liberty of WNBA (1997–2001); drafted by Houston Comets (2002); joined Connecticut Sun (2003); retired from competition (2003). Voted Big East player of the year (1993–95); earned 1st-team academic All-America honors (1994–95); won Naismith award (1995); named national player of the year by Associated Press (1995), the first time the AP awarded that honor to a woman; received Wade Trophy (1995). ❖ See also RuthAnn and Rebecca Lobo, *The Home Team: Of Mothers, Daughters, and American Champions* (Kodansha, 1997); and *Women in World History*.

LOBOVA, Nina (1957—). Soviet handball player. Born July 20, 1957, in USSR. ❖ At Montreal Olympics, won a gold medal in team competition (1976).

LOCHHEAD, Liz (1947—). Scottish poet, performance artist and playwright. Born Dec 26, 1947, in Motherwell, Lanarkshire, Scotland; attended Glasgow School of Art, 1965–70; m. Tom Logan (architect), 1986. ❖ Worked as art teacher in Glasgow and Bristol before publishing poetry collection, *Memo for Spring* (1972), which won Scottish Arts Council Book Award; staged revue *Sugar and Spite* with Marcella Evaristi (1978); published poetry collections, *The Grimm Sisters* (1981), *Dreaming Frankenstein* (1984), *True Confessions and New Clichés* (1985), *Bagpipe Muzak* (1991) and *The Colour of Black and White: Poems 1984–2003* (2003); plays include *Blood and Ice* (1982), about Mary Shelley, *Mary Queen of Scots Got Her Head Chopped Off* (1987) and *Dracula* (1989); was writer in residence at Edinburgh University (1986–87) and Royal Shakespeare Co. (1988); won Saltire Society Scottish Book of the Year Award for adaptation of Euripides' *Medea* (2000); for tv, wrote short film "Latin for a Dark Room" (1994) and "The Story of Frankenstein"; other plays include *The Big Picture* (1988), *Patter Merchants* (1989), *Jock Tamson's Bairns* (1990), *Quelques Fleurs* (1991), *Cuba* (1997), *Perfect Days* (1998), *Britania Rules* (1998), *The Three Sisters* (2000) and *Misery Guts* (based on Molière's *The Misanthrope*, 2002); often performed her own works.

LOCHORE, Dorothy Ida (1899–1987). *See Davies, Dorothy Ida.*

LOCK, Jane (1954—). Australian golfer. Born Jane Melinda Lock, Oct 19, 1954, in Sydney, Australia. ❖ Won 3 successive Australian Jr. championships; won the Australian junior and senior championships (1975); won 3 Australian championships and represented her country in 30 competitions, setting 6 course records; won Espinrito Santo World Amateur Golf championship for Australia (1978); turned pro (1980); won Australian LPGA and Canadian Amateur championship (1981); played on American circuit for 5 years (1981–86); returned to Australia (1986), after fracturing arm at Glendale Open. Received MBE (1975).

LOCKE, Anne Vaughan (c. 1530–c. 1590). British poet and translator. Name variations: Anna Dering, Anne Prowse; (pseudonym) A.L. Born Anne Vaughan, c. 1530, in England; died after 1590; dau. of Stephen Vaughan and Margaret Gwynneth (Guinet) Vaughan; stepdau. of Margery Brinklow; m. Henry Locke or Lok, c. 1552 (died 1571); m. Edward Dering (radical Protestant preacher), c. 1572 (died 1576); m. Richard Prowse or Prouze, before 1583; children: 6. ❖ Important figure in Elizabethan Protestant community, became close friend of John Knox and joined Knox and other exiles in Geneva, Switzerland, for 2 years; continued correspondence with him after returning to England (1559) in which he gave her messages for English Puritan community; had an unpublished treatise by Knox printed in London; trans. Calvin's *Sermons upon the Songe of Ezechias* (1560) to which is attached sequence of 26 sonnets probably by Locke called *A Meditation of a Penitent Sinner*; also trans. John Taffin's *Of the Markes of the Children of God* (1590). ❖ See also S.M. Felch, ed., *Collected Works* (1998).

LOCKE, Bessie (1865–1952). American educator. Born Aug 7, 1865, in West Cambridge (now Arlington), MA; died April 9, 1952, in New York, NY; dau. of a factory owner; took business classes at Columbia University. ❖ Formed East End Kindergarten Union of Brooklyn; served as financial secretary (1896–1923) and later trustee of Brooklyn Free Kindergarten Society and was noted for fund-raising abilities; was leading founder (1909) of National Association for the Promotion of Kindergarten Education (became National Kindergarten Association, 1911) of which she served as director and executive secretary (until 1952); served as chief of kindergarten division of US Bureau of Education (1913–19), chair of kindergarten extension division of National Congress of Parents and Teachers (1913–22), and director of National Council of Women (1921–46). Her efforts are seen as having made possible the opening of 3,260 kindergartens.

LOCKE, Elsie (1912–2001). New Zealand children's writer. Name variations: Elsie Farrelly Locke; Elsie Violet Locke. Born Elsie Violet Farrelly, 1912, in Hamilton, New Zealand; died April 2001; youngest of 4 children of a builder and a women's-rights activist; educated in Waiuku; attended University of Auckland; married Friedrich Engels "Freddie" Freeman, 1938 (div. 1940); m. John Locke (progressive), 1941; children: (1st m.) Don Freeman (philosopher); (2nd m.) Keith Locke (MP), Maire Locke (social worker), Alison Locke (school councilor). ❖ During the Depression and after the Queen Street Riot, joined Communist Party (1933), remaining a member until 1956; worked as editor of progressive magazine, *Woman To-day*; was a key founder, with Lois Suckling and Jean Dawson, of the Sex Hygiene and Birth Regulation Society (1936, later New Zealand Family Planning Association); wrote 1st children's novel, *The Runaway Settlers* (1965); other fiction and histories for children, which often explore relations between the Maori and Europeans, include *The End of the Harbour* (1968), *Moko's Hideout* (1976), *The Gaoler* (1978), *Journey Under Warning* (1983), *The Kauri and the Willow* (1984), *Two Peoples, One Land* (1988), *Mrs Hobson's Album* (1990) and *Peace People* (1991). Won Katherine Mansfield Non-Fiction Award for an article in *Landfall* (1958). ❖ See also autobiographical *Student at the Gates* (1981).

LOCKE, Katherine (1910–1995). American actress. Born June 24, 1910, in Boston, MA; died Sept 12, 1995, in Los Angeles, CA; m. Morris A. Helprin (div.); m. Norman Corwin. ❖ Made stage debut in *The Joy of the Serpents* (1928), followed by *Firebird, Halfway to Hell, Christmas Eve, Fifth Column* and *Clash by Night*; appeared as Ophelia to Maurice Evans' Hamlet; was a huge hit as Teddy Stern in *Having a Wonderful Time* (1937); films include *Straight from the Shoulder*.

LOCKE, Sumner (1881–1917). Australian playwright and novelist. Name variations: Sumner Locke Elliott. Born Helena Sumner Locke in Sandgate, Brisbane, Australia, 1881; died in Sydney, Oct 18, 1917; m. Henry Logan Elliott (journalist), 1916 or 1917; children: Sumner Locke Elliott (actor, novelist, and playwright). ❖ Though she enjoyed some success as a playwright (her *The Vicissitudes of Vivienne* was produced in Melbourne in 1908), was better known for her popular "Mum Dawson" books, *Mum Dawson, Boss* (1911) and *The Dawsons' Uncle George* (1912); last novel, *Samaritan Mary* (1916), was set in US, where she lived during WWI; married journalist Henry Logan Elliott, who went off to war 10 days after their wedding; died in childbirth 9 months later; her son was raised by an impoverished aunt and uncle until a wealthy aunt from England appeared to claim him, provoking a 6-year court battle which he depicted in his 1st novel, *Careful, He Might Hear You* (1963).

LOCKHART, June (1925—). American actress. Born June 25, 1925, in New York, NY; dau. of Gene Lockhart (actor) and Kathleen Lockhart (1894–1978, actress); m. John Lindsay, 1959 (div.); children: 2 daughters, including Anne Lockhart (actress). ❖ Made professional stage debut at 8 as Mimsey in Metropolitan Opera production of *Peter Ibbetson;* made film debut in MGM's *Christmas Carol* (1938), followed by *All This and Heaven Too, Sergeant York, Miss Annie Rooney, The White Cliffs of Dover, Meet Me in St. Louis, Son of Lassie, The She-Wolf of London, The Yearling, Time Limit, Lassie's Great Adventure, Strange Invaders, Troll* and *Sleep with Me,* among others; made Broadway debut with John Loder in *For Love or Money* (1947), earning a Tony, Donaldson and Theatre World award; on tv, co-starred in series "Lassie" (1958–64), "Lost in Space" (1965–68), and "Petticoat Junction" (1968–70).

LOCKHART, Kathleen (1894–1978). English-born actress. Born Kathleen Arthur, Aug 9, 1894, in Southsea, Hampshire, England; died Feb 17, 1978, in Los Angeles, CA; m. Gene Lockhart (actor, died 1957); children: June Lockhart (b. 1925, actress). ❖ With husband, appeared on radio and stage; plays include *Irene, Bitter Sweet, The Children's Hour* and *The Way of the World;* made over 30 films, including *Blondie, A Christmas Carol, Sweethearts, Mission to Moscow, Bewitched, Mother Wore Tights, Gentlemen's Agreement, I'd Climb the Highest Mountain* and *The Glenn Miller Story.*

LOCKREY, Sarah Hunt (1863–1929). American physician. Born Sarah Hunt Lockrey, April 21, 1863, in Philadelphia, PA; died Nov 8, 1929, in Philadelphia; dau. of Charles and Martha Jane (Wisner) Lockrey; graduate of Woman's Medical College of Pennsylvania (later Medical College of Pennsylvania) and Hahnemann University School of Medicine, 1888). ❖ Physician devoted to improving women's health care, 1st interned then served as Dr. Anna Broomall's assistant (from 1895) and was later named chief of gynecological staff at the hospital of the Woman's Medical College of Pennsylvania; specialized in abdominal surgery; was visiting chief at West Philadelphia Hospital for Women; appointed consultant to Elwyn School for the Feeble-Minded; served as a physician at Methodist Deaconess Home for more than 25 years; participated in a 26-women hunger strike and was given a jail sentence (1918) for participating in a Washington, DC, meeting at Lafayette Square.

LOCKWOOD, Annea F. (1939—). New Zealand-born composer. Born July 29, 1939, in Christchurch, New Zealand; dau. of Gladys (Ferguson) Lockwood (history and physical education teacher) and George Lockwood (lawyer); BMus (hons); further study at Royal College of Music, London, with Peter Racine Fricker (1961–63), at Darmstadt Ferienkurs für Neue Musik (1962–63) and with Gottfried Michael Koenig at Musikhochschule, Cologne, Germany, and in Holland (1963–64); lives with Ruth Anderson (composer and flutist). ❖ Freelanced as a composer-performer in Britain and Europe until moving to US (1973), where she continued to freelance and also taught, 1st at City University of New York (CUNY), then Hunter College; was on faculty of Vassar College (1982–2001); collaborated frequently with sound-poets, choreographers, and visual artists and created a number of works which she herself performed, such as *Glass Concert* (1967); turned attention to performance works that focused on environmental sounds and low-tech devices such as her Sound Ball, including *World Rhythms* (1975), which was widely presented in US, Europe, and New Zealand, as well as *Conversations with Ancestors* (1979), *A Sound Map of the Hudson* (1982), *Delta Run* (1982), and *Three Short Stories and an Apotheosis* (1985); began writing for acoustic instruments and voices, sometimes incorporating electronics and visual elements, producing pieces for a variety of ensembles, including *Thousand Year Dreaming* (1991), *Ear-Walking Woman* (1996), *Duende* (1997); much of her music has been recorded on American, English, and New Zealand labels. ❖ See also *Women in World History.*

LOCKWOOD, Belva Ann (1830–1917). American lawyer and women's rights advocate. Name variations: Belva McNall; Belva Bennett Lockwood. Born Belva Ann Bennett, Oct 24, 1830, in Royalton, NY; died May 19, 1917; dau. of Lewis J. Bennett (farmer) and Hannah (Green) Bennett; attended Royalton Academy (1 year), Gasport (NY) Academy, 1853–54, Genesee Wesleyan Seminary and Genesee College at Lima, NY (later Syracuse University), 1854–57, National University Law School, 1871–73; m. Uriah H. McNall, Nov 8, 1848 (died 1853); m. Ezekiel Lockwood, Mar 11, 1868 (died 1877); children: (1st m.) Lura McNall (1848–1894, who m. DeForest Ormes); (2nd m.) Jessie Lockwood (1869–1871). ❖ The 1st woman admitted to the bar of the Supreme Court and the US Court of Claims, as well as the 1st woman to receive votes in a presidential election, taught in district schools (1844–48), while attending college; appointed preceptor, Lockport (NY) Union School (1857–61), and at seminaries in Gainesville, Hornellsville, and Oswego, NY (1861–66); founded McNall's Ladies Seminary in Washington, DC (1867); lobbied to pass laws in Congress granting women equal pay for equal work (1872) and to permit women to be admitted to the bar of US Supreme Court (1879); became 1st woman admitted to practice before the Supreme Court; nominated as presidential candidate of the National Equal Rights Party (1884 and 1888); founded law firm of Belva A. Lockwood & Co. (1887–94); served as a delegate for the Universal Peace Union to International Peace Congresses (1889–1911); served on nominating committee for Nobel Peace Prize. ❖ See also *Women in World History.*

LOCKWOOD, Margaret (1916–1990). British actress. Born Sept 15, 1916, in Karachi, India (now Pakistan); died July 15, 1990, in Kensington, London, England; dau. of Henry Lockwood (British civil servant) and Margaret Evelyn (Waugh) Lockwood; studied acting at Royal Academy of Dramatic Art; m. Rupert W. Leon (steel broker), c. 1937 (div. 1955): children: Julia Lockwood (b. 1941, actress). ❖ Spent most of her childhood in a London suburb where she lived with an aunt while attending school; made stage debut at 12, playing a fairy in *A Midsummer Night's Dream* at Holborn Empire in London; made successful West End debut in *Family Affair* (1934), which led to 1st film role in *Lorna Doone* (1935); rose to "leading lady" status in *The Amateur Gentleman* (1936), *The Beloved Vagabond* (1936) and *The Lady Vanishes* (1938); was particularly successful in unsympathetic roles, especially those opposite actor James Mason in *Alibi* (1942), *The Man in Grey* (1943) and *The Wicked Lady* (1946); on stage, appeared in *Private Lives* (1949), *Spider's Web* (1954), *Subway in the Sky* (1957), *And Suddenly It's Spring* (1959), *An Ideal Husband* (1966), and the suspense thriller *Double Edge* (1975); was also seen as a barrister in the "Justice" tv series and starred in her own series, "The Flying Swan." ❖ See also autobiography *Lucky Star* (1955); and *Women in World History.*

LOCUSTA (fl. 54 CE). Roman poisoner. Name variations: Lucusta. Fl. around 54 CE; executed in 68 or 69 CE; said to be of Gallic origin. ❖ A professional poisoner living in Rome, was employed by Agrippina the Younger to prepare poison for emperor Claudius; also provided Nero with his own supply of poison; was executed under orders of Galba during his reign. ❖ See also *Women in World History.*

LODEN, Barbara (1932–1980). American actress and film director. Name variations: Barbara Loden Kazan. Born Barbara Ann Loden in Marion, NC, July 8, 1932; died of cancer, Sept 5, 1980, in New York, NY; dau. of George T. Loden and Ruth (Nanney) Loden; m. film producer Laurence Joachim (div.); became 2nd wife of Elia Kazan (director), 1967; children: (1st m.) Leo Alexander Joachim; Jon Marco Joachim. ❖ At 16, moved to NY and danced in the chorus at Copacabana nightclub; began playing minor parts in films of Elia Kazan, including *Wild River* (1960) and *Splendor in the Grass* (1961); was a member of Lincoln Center Repertory (1960–64); appeared as Maggie in Miller's *After the Fall* (1964), a character based on Marilyn Monroe, and won a Tony Award; resurfaced from self-imposed retirement as the producer, director, and star of *Wanda* (1971), which won a number of awards, including the International Critics Prize at Venice Film Festival. ❖ See also *Women in World History.*

LODHI, Maleeha (c. 1953—). Pakistani journalist and diplomat. Born Maleeha Lodhi, c. 1953, in Lahore, Pakistan; dau. of an oil executive father and journalist mother; London School of Economics, BSc, 1976, PhD, 1980; (div.); children: 1 son. ❖ Taught politics and sociology at London School of Economics (1980–85); returned to Pakistan; served as editor of *The Muslim,* a leading English-language newspaper; helped launch and was editor of *The News International,* Pakistan's leading English daily; appointed by Benazir Bhutto, served as ambassador to US (1994–97); reappointed by Musharraf, served once more (1999–03); became ambassador to UK (2003); wrote *Pakistan's Encounter with Democracy* and *The External Challenge* (both 1994).

LOEB, Sophie Irene (1876–1929). Russian-born journalist and welfare worker. Born Sophie Irene Simon in Rovno, Russia, July 4, 1876; died in New York, NY, Jan 18, 1929; dau. of Samuel Simon (jeweler) and Mary (Carey) Simon; m. Anselm Loeb (merchant), Mar 10, 1896 (div. 1910); no children. ❖ With family, immigrated to US (1882) and settled in McKeesport, PA; moved to NY City (1910), where she became a reporter and feature writer for *Evening World;* became interested in plight of impoverished widows who were forced to give up their children for adoption because they could no longer support them; appointed to the newly created State Commission of Relief for Widowed Mothers (1913); successfully proposed a bill for a state-supported relief program for widows with children (1914); appointed to child welfare board of NY (1915), became president, a position she held until 1923; served on commission to codify the laws in the field of child welfare (1920); founded and became president of Child Welfare Committee of America (1924); addressed the 1st International Congress on Child Welfare at Geneva (1925), which later accepted her resolution in favor of keeping children with their families and out of institutions. ❖ See also *Women in World History.*

LOEBINGER, Lotte (1905–1999). German actress. Name variations: Charlotte Loebinger; Lotte Wehner-Loebinger (used in USSR and preferred by Loebinger even after her 1952 divorce); Lotte Loebinger-Wehner. Born Oct 10, 1905, in Kattowitz, Upper Silesia, Germany (now Katowice, Poland); died Feb 9, 1999, in Berlin, Germany; dau. of a physician; m. Herbert Wehner, June 1927; children: 1 daughter. ❖ Began acting career in Breslau, Lower Silesia; by 1929, a highly regarded member of Erwin Piscator's ensemble in Berlin; for several years, toured Germany and Switzerland in Carl Crede's play *Paragraph 218* (Women in Distress); often appeared on stage with the non-socialist Spielgemeinschaft Berliner Schauspieler (Performance Collective of Berlin Actors); fled Nazi Germany to Poland (1933); immigrated to Soviet Union, where she 1st found work as a member of Gustav von Wangenheim's German theater troupe "Kolonne Links" (Column Left); collaborated with von Wangenheim to produce anti-fascist film *Kämpfer* (Those Who Struggle, 1936); worked as a German-language announcer in foreign branch of Radio Moscow; returned to war-shattered Berlin (1945) and appeared at Deutsches Theater in several plays (1945–46); was also featured in the 1st post-Nazi films made in occupied Germany; was one of the featured actresses of East Berlin's Maxim Gorki Theater (1952–70s); also served occasionally as a director, mainly producing Soviet plays; appeared in 2 GDR tv films, "Ich will nicht leise sterben" (I Will Not Die Quietly), and "Guten Morgen, du Schöne" (Good Morning, Beautiful Lady). ❖ See also *Women in World History.*

LOEF, Anke (1972—). See Baier, Anke.

LOEWE, Gabriele (1958—). East German runner. Name variations: Gabriele Löwe. Born Dec 12, 1958, in East Germany. ❖ At Moscow Olympics, won a silver medal in the 4 x 400-meter relay (1980).

LOEWENSTEIN, Helga Maria zu (b. 1910). See Löwenstein, Helga Maria zu.

LOEWY, Dora (1977—). See Lowy, Dora.

LÖF, Anke (1972—). See Baier, Anke.

LOFTUS, Cissie (1876–1943). Scottish actress and impersonator. Name variations: Marie Cecilia Loftus; Marie Cecilia McCarthy. Born Marie Cecilia Brown, Oct 22, 1876, in Glasgow, Scotland; died of a heart attack, July 12, 1943, in New York, NY; dau. of Ben Brown (actor) and Marie Loftus (music-hall singer); m. Justin Huntly McCarthy (writer), Aug 29, 1894 (div. 1899); m. Alonzo Higbee Waterman (physician), June 9, 1909 (div.); children: (2nd m.) Peter John Barrie Waterman. ❖ Made stage debut in Belfast (1892), then appeared at Oxford Music Hall in London (1893); known for expert impersonations of other actresses, appeared in vaudeville as well as theater, doing comedy as well as tragedy; made NY debut (1895); from then on, crossed Atlantic many times, alternating appearances in England and US and switching from variety roles to traditional theatrical performances; most significant roles include Viola in *Twelfth Night,* Hero in *Much Ado About Nothing,* Katherine in *If I Were King,* Ophelia in *Hamlet,* the mother in *Three-Cornered Moon,* and title role in Peter Pan; films include *East Lynne* and *The Old Maid;* became addicted to drugs after an illness and all but retired (1915); made 3 successful comebacks (1923, 1933, and 1938).

LOFTUS, Kitty (1867–1927). Scottish actress, singer, and dancer. Born June 16, 1867, in Kenilworth, Scotland; died Mar 17, 1927; sister of Rosie Leyton (performer); m. P. Warren-Smith. ❖ Made stage debut as Puck in *A Midsummer Night's Dream* (1879); subsequently appeared in *Gentleman Joe, Biarritz, The White Silk Dress, The French Maid* and *Her Royal Highness;* made NY debut as Denise in *In Gay Paree* (1899); produced and starred in *Naughty Nancy* (1902) and appeared in music halls, at the Coliseum, and toured the provinces.

LOFTUS, Marie (1857–1940). Scottish comedian, actress, and music-hall star. Born Nov 24, 1857, in Glasgow, Scotland; died Dec 7, 1940; m. Ben Brown (actor in a minstrel show); children: Marie Cecilia Brown (1876–1943, who performed as Cissie Loftus). ❖ Known as the "Sarah Bernhardt of the Halls," made stage debut at Brown's Music Hall, Glasgow (1874) and London debut (1877), then had a successful tour in South Africa and America; was part of the Drury Lane all-star pantomime which included Marie Lloyd, Ada Blanche, and Mabel Love (1892); played all the leading music halls and popularized such songs as "Sister Mary," "And She Lisped When She Said Yes," "One Touch of Nature Makes the Whole World Kin" and "A Thing You Can't Buy with Gold."

LOFTUS, Marie Cecilia (1876–1943). See Loftus, Cissie.

LOGAN, Annabelle (1930—). See Ross, Annie.

LOGAN, Anna Paterson (1858–1931). See Stout, Anna Paterson.

LOGAN, Deborah Norris (1761–1839). American colonial historian. Born Oct 19, 1761, in Philadelphia, PA; died Feb 2, 1839, near Philadelphia; dau. of Charles Norris (merchant) and Mary Parker; m. George Logan (U.S. senator), Sept 6, 1781 (died 1821); children: 3 sons. ❖ In family home, found correspondence between William Penn and husband's grandfather James Logan, early Pennsylvania leaders; began copying entire collection (1814); also wrote *Memoir of Dr. George Logan of Stenton* (published 1899); kept diary (1815–39) including recollections of Continental Congress secretary Charles Thomson; elected 1st female member of Historical Society of Pennsylvania (1827).

LOGAN, Ella (1913–1969). Scottish-born singer-actress. Born Ella Allan, Mar 6, 1913, in Glasgow, Scotland; died May 1, 1969, in Burlingame, CA; m. Fred Finkelhoffe (playwright and producer), 1952 (div. 1956). ❖ Best known for performance as Sharon McLonergan in long-running Broadway show *Finian's Rainbow,* in which she introduced "How Are Things in Gloccamorra?," made debut at age 3 at Grand Theater in Paisley, Scotland, stopping the show with her rendition of "A Perfect Day"; toured European music halls during early career; made London debut in *Darling, I Love You* (1928); arrived in US (1934), appearing on Broadway in *Calling All Stars;* went on to make a series of films, including *Flying Hostess* (1936), *Top of the Town* (1937), *42nd Street* (1937) and *Goldwyn Follies* (1938); began a recording career, vocalizing with bandleader Abe Lyman, among others; returned to Broadway in *George White Scandals* (1939), followed by *Sons O'Fun* (1941) and vaudeville revue *Show Time* (1942); performed in nightclubs and on tv. ❖ See also *Women in World History.*

LOGAN, Jacqueline (1901–1983). American actress. Born Nov 30, 1901, in Corsicana, TX; died April 4, 1983, in Melbourne, FL. ❖ Made stage debut in revival of *Floradora* (1920), then appeared in *Ziegfeld Follies;* made film debut in *A Perfect Crime* (1921); appeared in 57 films, including *Ebb Tide, Salomy Jane, The Light That Failed, Manhattan, Wise Wife, Stocks and Blondes, Midnight Madness,* and as Mary Magdalene in *The King of Kings;* was a popular leading lady in silent films.

LOGAN, Mrs. John A. (1838–1923). See Logan, Mary Cunningham.

LOGAN, Laura R. (1879–1974). Canadian-born nurse. Name variations: Laura Rebekah Logan. Born Sept 15, 1879, at Amherst Point, Nova Scotia, Canada; died July 16, 1974, in Sackville, Novia Scotia; Acadia University in Wolfville, Nova Scotia, BA in English, 1901; graduate of Mount Sinai Hospital School of Nursing in NY; Columbia University, BA in hospital economics, 1908. ❖ Taught and worked as a supervisor at Mt. Sinai Hospital until 1911; served as superintendent of Hope Hospital and principal of its nursing school in Fort Wayne, IN; became director of Cincinnati General Hospital School of Nursing (1914); helped create University of Cincinnati School of Nursing and Health; appointed dean of Illinois Training School for Nurses in Chicago (1924), then dean of Cook County School of Nursing (1929); was director of Cook County Hospital's nursing service (1929–32); appointed principal of Flower-Fifth Avenue Hospital nursing school in NYC (1936); served as director of Nursing at Boston City Hospital's (1937–40); was director of nursing services and nursing school at St. Louis City Hospital; retired (1953).

LOGAN, Martha (1704–1779). American horticulturist. Name variations: Martha Daniell Logan; Martha Daniell. Born Martha Daniell, Dec 29, 1704, in St. Thomas Parish, SC; died June 28, 1779; dau. of Robert Daniell (lieutenant governor of NC) and Martha Daniell; m. George Logan Jr, July 30, 1719 (died July 1, 1764); children: 5 sons, 3 daughters. ❖ Ran boarding school and reputedly managed family plantation; was assumed to be "Lady of this Province" writing "Gardener's Kalendar" in *South Carolina Almanack* (from 1752); contributed calendar to almanacs in SC and GA (to 1780s); ran nursery business after death of son Robert Daniell; writings published posthumously in almanac *The Palladium of Knowledge* (to 1804); corresponded with King George III's appointed botanist John Bartram, sending plant specimens from the New World to England.

LOGAN, Mary Cunningham (1838–1923). American political wife and writer. Name variations: Mrs. John A. Logan; Mary S. Logan. Born Mary Simmerson Cunningham, Aug 15, 1838, in Petersburgh (now Sturgeon), Boone County, MO; died Feb 22, 1923, in Washington, DC; dau. of John M. Cunningham and Elizabeth Hicks (La Fontaine) Cunningham; m. John Alexander Logan, Nov 27, 1855 (died 1886); children: 1 son, 1 daughter; (adopted) daughter. ❖ Accompanied husband on campaigns for Illinois state legislature, US House of Representatives, US Senate, and vice presidency (on ticket with James G. Blaine, 1884); served as his amanuensis after his promotion to general in Army of Tennessee during Civil War; suggested that holiday be declared for those who fought for the Union, which led to his sponsoring legislation for Memorial Day; declined job offer of federal pensions commissioner from President Benjamin Harrison; stepped in as president of Red Cross after resignation of Clara Barton (1904); published *Thirty Years in Washington* (1901) and *Reminiscences of a Soldier's Wife* (1913); edited domestic arts periodical, *Home Magazine* (1888–95), and collection of biographical sketches, *The Part Taken by Women in American History* (1912).

LOGAN, Mary S. (1838–1923). *See Logan, Mary Cunningham.*

LOGAN, Nedda (1899–1989). *See Harrigan, Nedda.*

LOGAN, Olive (1839–1909). American actress and writer. Name variations: Mrs. Sykes; Mrs. Sikes; Mrs. Wirt Sikes. Born April 22, 1839, in Elmira, NY; died April 27, 1909, in Banstead, England; dau. of Cornelius Ambrosius Logan (actor and manager) and Eliza Akeley; sister of Eliza Logan (actress) and Celia Logan (writer); m. Henry A. Delille (chevalier of Legion of Honor), 1857 (div); William Wirt Sikes (American consul in Cardiff, Wales), Dec 19, 1871 (died 1883); James O'Neill, 1892. ❖ Made formal stage debut in *Bobtail and Wagtail* at Arch Street Theatre in Philadelphia (1854); on Broadway, appeared with Frank S. Chanfrau in comedy *Sam* (1865); lectured throughout US on various subjects including theater (from 1868); trans. and adapted French-language plays for Augustin Daly, with several productions staged without success; published several books including *Chateau Frissac* (1862), *Apropos of Women and Theatres* (1869), *Get Thee Behind Me, Satan!* (1872) and *They Met by Chance: A Society Novel* (1873).

LOGAN, Onnie Lee (c. 1910–1995). African-American midwife. Born c. 1910 in Sweet Water, Marengo County, Alabama; died July 9, 1995, in Mobile, AL; dau. of a midwife; m. 3rd husband Roosevelt Logan; children: (1st m.) at least 1. ❖ Midwife who delivered the babies of impoverished black families for over 50 years, received her 1st midwife permit from Alabama Board of Health (1949); as a maid, often delivered house births with physicians; due to excellent reputation, was permitted to legally practice until 1984, even after the state of Alabama had outlawed lay midwifery (1976); after 1984, continued midwifery without permit; with Katherine Clark, wrote the memoir *Motherwit: An Alabama Midwife's Story* (1989), which became a bestselling feminist classic.

LOGHIN, Mihaela (1952—). Romanian track-and-field athlete. Born June 1, 1952 in Romania. ❖ At Los Angeles Olympics, won a silver medal in shot put (1984); won Romanian national titles (1976–88, 1990).

LOGIC, Lora (c. 1961—). English musician. Name variations: X-Ray Spex, Essential Logic. Born Susan Whitby, c. 1961, in London, England. ❖ Helped form punk band, X-Ray Spex, in London (1977) and recorded hit single, "Oh Bondage, Up Yours," before quitting group; formed own band, Essential Logic (1978), and released *Essential Logic EP* (1979) and *Beat Rhythm News* (1979), fronting as vocalist and saxophonist; disbanded group and released solo single, "Wonderful Offer" (1981), and solo album, *Pedigree Charm* (1982); appeared in film, *Crystal Gazing* (1982); joined Hare Krishna movement and dropped

out of music business; rejoined X-Ray Spex (1996); has played with numerous bands, including Red Krayola and The Raincoats.

LOGINOVA, Lidiya (1951—). Soviet volleyball player. Born Feb 27, 1951, in USSR. ❖ At Moscow Olympics, won a gold medal in team competition (1980).

LOGOUNOVA, Tatiana (1980—). Russian fencer. Name variations: Tatjana Logunowa. Born July 3, 1980, in Moscow, USSR. ❖ As the youngest member of the Russian team, won a gold medal for épée team at Sydney Olympics (2000); won a gold medal for épée team at Athens Olympics (2004); at World championships, placed 1st for team épée (2001, 2003).

LOGUE, Jenny (c. 1982—). British inline skater. Born c. 1982 in Guildford, England. ❖ Placed 4th in Street at X Games (Summer 1999); won silver in Park at X Games (Summer 2000 and 2003).

LOGUNOWA, Tatjana (1980—). *See Logounova, Tatiana.*

LOGVINENKO, Marina (1961—). Soviet shooter. Name variations: Marina Logvinenko-Dobrancheva; Marina Dobrancheva. Born Marina Dobrancheva, Sept 1, 1961, in Russia. ❖ At Seoul Olympics, won a bronze medal in air pistol (1988); at Barcelona Olympics, won gold medals in sport pistol and air pistol (1992); at Atlanta Olympics, won a silver medal for 10m air pistol and a bronze medal for 25m pistol (1996).

LOHMAN, Ann Trow (1812–1878). American abortionist. Name variations: Madame Restell. Born 1812 in Painswick, Gloucestershire, England; committed suicide, April 1, 1878, in New York City; m. tailor Henry Summers, 1828 (died 1833); m. newspaper compositor turned quack physician Charles R. Lohman, 1836 (died 1876); children: (1st m.) stepdaughter Caroline Summers. ❖ Abortionist, dispenser of contraceptives, and operator of a clandestine maternity hospital and adoption agency, immigrated to NY with family (1831); with 2nd husband, began selling diverse medications alleged to prevent contraception and unwanted fetuses, advertising in newspapers as "Madame Restell"; tried and convicted for performing an abortion on a woman who later died (1841); tried and acquitted of giving up a baby for adoption against mother's will (1846), but public protest was intense, causing enactment of a new law, declaring that the abortion of a quickened fetus was considered manslaughter; arrested under the new manslaughter law (Sept 1847), was charged with having completed an abortion; was convicted on a lesser misdemeanor charge after conflicting medical testimony, and served a year at Blackwell's Island prison; set to go to trial once more (for selling contraceptives), committed suicide. ❖ See also *Women in World History.*

LOHMAR, Leni (1914—). German swimmer. Name variations: Maria Lohmar; Leni Henze or Leni Henze-Lohmar. Born Maria Magdalena Lohmar, Oct 19, 1914, in Germany; m. Hermann Henze (coach and later head of the swimming federation), 1939 (died 2004). ❖ At Berlin Olympics, won a silver medal in 4 x 100-meter freestyle relay (1936).

LOHMAR, Maria (1914—). *See Lohmar, Leni.*

LÖHR, Marie (1890–1975). Australian-born actress and singer. Name variations: Marie Lohr. Born July 28, 1890, in Sydney, NSW, Australia; died Jan 21, 1975, in London, England; dau. of Lewis J. Löhr (treasurer of Melbourne Opera House) and Kate (Bishop) Löhr; m. Anthony Leyland Val Prinsep (div.). ❖ Made stage debut in Sydney in *The World Against Her* (1894); made London debut in *Shock-Headed Peter* (1901); toured with the Kendals (1902); remained in London, appearing in title role in *Smith* (1909), Yo-You in *The Darling of the Gods* (1914), Lady Babbie in *The Little Minister* (1914), H.M. Queen Charlotte in *Kings and Queens* (1915), title role in *Marie-Odile* (1915), Lady Ware in *The Ware Case* (1915), title role in *Remnant* (1916), Francis in *L'Aiglon* (which she also produced, 1918), Lady Caryll in *The Voice from the Minaret* (1919), Constance in *Birds of a Feather* (1920); made NY debut as Lady Caryll in *A Voice from the Minaret* (1922); back in London, appeared in *The Return* (1922), *Aren't We All?* (1923), *Peter Pan* (1927), *Beau Geste* (1929), *Berkeley Square* (1929), *The Silent Witness* (1930), *Casanova* (1932), *Call It a Day* (1935), *Crest of the Wave* (1938), *Quiet Wedding* (1938), *Somewhere in England* (1939), *Other People's Houses* (1941), *Sense and Sensibility* (1946), *A Harlequinade* (1948), *A Penny For a Song* (1951), *The Ides of March* (1963), and *Man and Superman* (1966); made film debut in *Aren't We All?* (1932), followed by *Pygmalion* (1938), *Major Barbara* (1940), *Anna Karenina* (1948), *The*

Winslow Boy (1948) and *A Town Like Alice* (1956), among others. ❧ See also *Women in World History*.

LÖHR, Kate Bishop (b. 1847). See Bishop, Kate.

LOHS, Gabriele (1957—). See Kuehn-Lohs, Gabriele.

LOHSE-KLAFSKY, Katharina (1855–1896). See Klafsky, Katharina.

LOIS. Variant of Aloisia and Heloise.

LOIS. Biblical woman. Mother of Eunice (who m. a Greek); grandmother of Timothy. ❧ A devout Jew living in Lystra in Asia Minor, instructed daughter Eunice and grandson Timothy in the Old Testament; with daughter, became a Christian and was later credited by the apostle Paul for Timothy's spiritual education (Timothy became an ardent missionary).

LOISE. Variant of Louise.

LOISEAU, Jeanne (1860–1920). See Lapauze, Jeanne.

LOISINGER, Joanna (1865–1951). Bulgarian royal. Born 1865; died July 1951 in Vienna, Austria; dau. of John Loisinger; m. Alexander I, prince of Bulgaria (r. 1879–1886), Feb 6, 1889; children: Arsen, count von Hartenau (1890–1965) and Zwettana, countess von Hartenau (1893–1935). ❧ See also *Women in World History*.

LOITMAN, Jennie (1891–1969). See Barron, Jennie Loitman.

LOKELANI, Princess Lei (c. 1898–1921). American vaudeville dancer. Born Elizabeth Jonica Lei Lokelani-Shaw, c. 1898 in San Francisco, CA; died April 18, 1921, in San Francisco; sister of Wini Shaw (dancer, singer). ❧ Raised in theatrical family of Scottish, Irish, and Hawaiian origin, made performance debut with family troupe—called The Shaw Family, Shaw's Hawaiians, or Jonica's Hawaiians—at Panama Exposition in San Francisco; toured with family for a number of years until she formed own dance troupe (c. 1917); was one of the most accurate performers of Hula and other Hawaiian dance styles.

LO KEONG, Matilda (c. 1854–1915). New Zealand shopkeeper. Name variations: Matilda Kum, Cum Hong. Born between 1854 and 1856, in Baoan County near Hong Kong, China; died on Dec 18, 1915, in Dunedin, New Zealand; m. Joseph Lo Keong (shopkeeper), 1873 (died 1905); children: 6. ❧ Believed to have been 1st Chinese female immigrant to New Zealand; helped husband in his shop and was active in church and civic endeavors. ❧ See also *Dictionary of New Zealand Biography* (Vol. 2).

LOKHVITSKAIA, Mirra (1869–1905). Russian poet and dramatist. Name variations: Mariia; the Russian Sappho. Born Mariia Aleksandrovna Lokhvitskaia, 1869; died from tuberculosis, 1905; dau. of Aleksandr Lokhvitskii, prominent St. Petersburg lawyer; older sister of N.A. Teffi (1872–1952), the writer; sister of writers Varvara Lokhvitskaia and Elena Lokhvitskaia; m. in 1892; children: 5. ❧ Published 5 vols. of verse (1896–1904); had a scandalous affair with Konstantin Bal'mont (1896–98) which added to her popularity, as did her appearances at poetry readings; for her poetry, won coveted Pushkin prize (1896, 1905); also wrote 3 plays, *On the Road to the East, Immortal Love* and *In nomine Domini*. ❧ See also *Women in World History*.

LOKHVITSKAIA, Nadezhda (1872–1952). See Teffi, N.A.

LOLA MONTEZ (1818–1861). See Montez, Lola.

LOLLIA PAULINA (fl. 38–39 CE). Roman empress. Reigned as empress, 38–39 CE; dau. of M. Lollius (consul in 21 BCE); m. Memmius Regulus; m. Caligula (12–41), Roman emperor (div.). ❧ Known for her dazzling beauty, was taken from her husband by Caligula and briefly reigned as his 3rd wife (38–39 CE). ❧ See also *Women in World History*.

LOLLOBRIGIDA, Gina (1927—). Italian actress and photographer. Name variations: modeled as Diana Loris. Born July 4, 1927, in Subiaco, Italy; dau. of Giovanni (furniture manufacturer) and Giuseppina Lollobrigida; attended Academy of Fine Arts, Rome; m. Drago Milko Skofic (physician and her manager), 1950 (div. 1966); children: son Andrea Milko Skofic. ❧ Won title "Miss Rome" (1948); had 1st major film role in *Miss Italy* (1950); by early 1950s, was one of Continental Europe's most famous stars, appearing in such films as *The Wayward Wife* (1953), for which she won the Grolla d'Oro (Italian equivalent of the Oscar), and the highly successful *Bread, Love and Dreams* (1953) and its sequel *Bread, Love and Jealousy* (1954); made 1st European film with a US cast, *Beat the Devil* (1954), followed by 1st major US film *Beautiful but Dangerous* (1955), about soprano Lina

Cavalieri; also appeared in *Trapeze* (1956), *The Hunchback of Notre Dame* (1956), *Solomon and Sheba* (1959), *Come September* (1961), *Strange Bedfellows* (1965) and *Buona Sera, Mrs. Campbell* (1969); retired from films (1977) and became a photographer; published 5 books of photographs, including *The Wonder of Innocence* (1994); directed acclaimed documentary *Rittrato di Fidel* (Portrait of Fidel Castro, 1975) and appeared in US on 2 episodes of "Falcon Crest"; drafted by the splinter centrist Democrat Party, made an unsuccessful bid for a seat in European Parliament (1999). ❧ See also *Women in World History*.

LOMADY, Clara Schroth (b. 1920). See Schroth, Clara.

LOMBA, Marisabel. Belgian judoka. Name variations: Marie-Isabelle Lomba. Born in Belgium. ❧ Won a bronze medal for 52–56kg lightweight at Atlanta Olympics (1996); won European championship (1997).

LOMBARD, Carole (1908–1942). American actress. Born Jane Alice Peters, Oct 6, 1908, in Fort Wayne, IN; killed in plane crash near Las Vegas, NV, Jan 16, 1942; dau. of Elizabeth Knight Peters and Frederic Peters; m. William Powell (actor), 1931 (div. 1933); m. Clark Gable (actor), 1939; no children. ❧ Film actress and mistress of screwball comedy who, before her untimely death, was the highest paid star in Hollywood and one of its best-loved personalities; made film debut in *A Perfect Crime* (1921); signed 1-year contract with Fox (1924), appearing in 2-reel Westerns; worked in Mack Sennett comedies for 2 years; 1st came to public notice in such lightweight films as *Safety in Numbers, Fast and Loose* and *It Pays to Advertise* for Paramount; appeared opposite Clark Gable in *No Man of Her Own* (1932); came to stardom with *Twentieth Century* (1934); starred with William Powell in *Man of the World, Ladies' Man* and *My Man Godfrey*; also appeared in *Nothing Sacred, True Confessions, Made for Each Other, Vigil in the Night, They Knew What They Wanted* and *Mr. and Mrs. Smith*; did best work in Ernst Lubitsch's *To Be or Not to Be*, playing opposite Jack Benny; at age 33, killed with mother in a plane crash while on a war-bond drive, the 1st American women to die in a war-related accident during WWII. ❧ See also Larry Swindell, *Screwball: The Life of Carole Lombard* (Morrow, 1975); and *Women in World History*.

LOMBARDA (b. 1190). Troubadour of Provence. Born 1190 in Toulouse. ❧ Married in her teens, gained a reputation for writing beautiful love poetry; composed at least one *tenson* which still exists, with troubadour-lover Bernart Arnaut; was also a noted proponent of Catharism (also known as Albigensianism), a heretical religious sect then popular in southern France. ❧ See also *Women in World History*.

LOMBARDI, Lella (1941–1992). Italian racing-car driver. Born Maria Grazia Lombardi, Mar 26, 1941, in Frugarolo, Italy; died of cancer, Mar 3, 1992, in Milan. ❧ Internationally famous racer, known as "the Tigress of Turin," who was the 1st woman to compete in US Grand Prix, came up through the ranks in European Formula car racing; started in Formula Italia, the Italian single-seaters which use the Fiat 850 engine, and from there went into Formula Three and finally Formula 5000; quickly developed an international reputation for skill and daring; made 1st Formula One outing at the wheel of a Brabham in the British Grand Prix and just missed qualifying (1974); finished 6th in Spanish Grand Prix (1975), and soon after became the 1st woman to score a point counting toward the world-driving championship; at Watkins Glen, competed in US Grand Prix (1975). ❧ See also *Women in World History*.

LOMBARDS, queen of the.
See Clotsinda.
See Theodelinda (568–628).
See Guntrud of Bavaria (fl. 715).

LOMBARDY, queen of. See Adelaide of Burgundy (931–999).

LONCAREVIC, Annemarie (b. 1919). See Renger, Annemarie.

LONDON, Julie (1926–2000). American singer and actress. Born Julie Peck, Sept 26, 1926, Santa Rosa, CA; died in Los Angeles, California, Oct 18, 2000; dau. of Jack and Josephine (Taylor) Peck (song-and-dance vaudeville performers); m. Jack Webb (actor), 1947 (div. 1953); m. Bobby Troup (jazz musician and songwriter), 1959; children: (1st m.) Stacy and Lisa Webb. ❧ At 3, made radio debut; made film debut in *Jungle Woman* (1944), then appeared in secondary roles in low-budget films, including *Nabonga* (1945), *The Red House* (1947), *Tap Roots* (1948), and *Task Force* (1949); signed by Liberty Records, made 1st album *Julie is Her Name*, which included hit single "Cry Me a River" (1956); other films include *The Great Man* (1956), *The Girl Can't Help It*

(1956), *Saddle the Wind* (1958), *Night of the Quarter Moon* (1959), and *The George Raft Story* (1961); starred as a nightclub owner in tv series, "Maggie Malone," (1960) and as a nurse on hospital drama "Emergency" (1972). ❖ See also *Women in World History.*

LONDONDERRY, marchioness of.
See Vane-Tempest, Frances Anne Emily (d. 1865).
See Vane-Tempest-Stewart, Theresa (1856–1919).
See Vane-Tempest-Stewart, Edith (1878–1949).

LONG, Catherine Small (1924—). American politician. Born Feb 7, 1924, in Dayton, Ohio; m. Gillis W. Long (1923–1985, lawyer and politician); Louisiana State University, Baton Rouge, BA, 1948. ❖ Served as US Navy pharmacist's mate; was staff assistant to Senator Wayne Morse of Oregon and Representative James G. Polk of Ohio; was a delegate to Democratic National Conventions (1980, 1984); was a member of the Louisiana State Democratic Financial Council and State central committee, and Democratic leadership council; when husband died (Jan 20, 1985), after serving 8 terms as representative from Louisiana's 8th District, stood for his seat in a special election; served as Democrat member of the 99th US Congress (Mar 30, 1985–Jan 3, 1987); co-sponsored the Economic Equity Act of 1985, which secured pension and health benefits for women; supported economic sanctions against South Africa and was a proponent of aid for Nicaraguan refugees. ❖ See also *Women in World History.*

LONG, Jill Lynette (1952—). American politician. Born July 15, 1952, in Warsaw, IN; Valparaiso University, BS, 1974; Indiana University, MBA, 1978, and PhD, 1984. ❖ Taught at Indiana University, Bloomington, Valparaiso University and Indiana University/Purdue University-Fort Wayne; was a Democratic member of Congress (1989–95), serving on the Veterans' Affairs Committee, the Committee on Agriculture and the Select Committee on Hunger; was a fellow at Institute of Politics, John F. Kennedy School of Government, Harvard University; served as a member, board of directors, Commodity Credit Corporation; was under-secretary for rural, economic and community development, Department of Agriculture. ❖ See also *Women in World History.*

LONG, Kathleen (1896–1968). English pianist. Born in Brentford, England, July 7, 1896; died in Cambridge, England, Mar 20, 1968. ❖ At 13, began studies at Royal College of Music, winning Hopkinson Gold Medal (1915); received faculty appointment at Royal College; played as solo performer and in chamber-music ensembles; introduced the music of Gabriel Fauré to British public; gave world premiere of Gerald Finzi's *Eclogue* for Piano and String Orchestra (1957); wrote *Nineteenth Century Piano Music.*

LONG, Marguerite (1874–1966). French pianist. Name variations: Marie-Charlotte Long; Marie Charlotte Long. Born Nov 13, 1874, in Nimes, France; died Feb 13, 1966, in Paris; studied piano at Nimes Conservatory (1880s); studied at Paris Conservatory under Tissot and Antoine Marmontel from 1887; m. Joseph de Marliave (musicologist, died 1914). ❖ One of the most important French pianists of 20th century, made public debut (1893), though she did not perform in public again until 1903; taught at Paris Conservatory (1906–40) and was professor of piano from 1920; premiered Maurice Ravel's *Le tombeau de Couperin* (1919) and Concerto in G major (1932); as friend of Claude Debussy and colleague of Gabriel Fauré, performed world premieres of many of their piano works, along with pieces by Satie, Poulenc and Deodat de Séverac; began own school (1920); published the well-regarded *Les Quatuors de Beethoven* (1925); ran École Marguerite Long-Jacques Thibaud with violinist Jacques Thibaud (from 1940); inaugurated Long-Thibaud international piano and violin competition (1943); a favored performer, toured internationally performing classical, romantic and contemporary repertoire; was noted interpreter of and authority on French music. ❖ See also Cecilia Dunoyer, *Marguerite Long: A Life in French Music, 1874–1966* (Indiana U. Press, 1993); and *Women in World History.*

LONG, Naomi (b. 1923). See Madgett, Naomi.

LONG, Tania (1913–1998). German-born journalist and war correspondent. Born Tatiana Long, April 29, 1913, in Berlin, Germany; committed suicide, Sept 4, 1998, in Ottawa, Canada; dau. of Robert Crozier Long and Tatiana Mouraviev; graduate of Malvern Girls College in England (1930); studied at Sorbonne, 1930–31, and Paris École des Sciences Politiques; m. Raymond Daniell (London bureau chief, *The New York Times*), 1941; children: (from previous marriage) Robert M. Gray. ❖ Got 1st journalistic experience at side of her father, who was a

New York Times financial columnist and Berlin correspondent to *The Economist* of London; became a US citizen (1935); began career at New Jersey's *Network Ledger* (1936); returned to Berlin to work for *New York Herald Tribune*'s bureau there (1938), becoming assistant chief correspondent; with outbreak of WWII (1939), transferred to Copenhagen, then Paris, and finally London, where she won an award for her reporting on the bombing of that city (1941); joined *The Times* as a reporter (1941); covered Allied advance through France from just behind the lines and is thought to be the 1st female reporter to follow the Allies into Berlin; with husband, headed *The Times'* bureau in Ottawa, Canada (1952–64). ❖ See also *Women in World History.*

LONGABARBA, Bona (fl. 15th c.). Italian noblewoman and military leader. Fl. in 15th century in Lombardy; married. ❖ A Lombard noblewoman, fought beside husband in several battles, becoming a respected leader of soldiers; was known for her great strategic abilities and her skill at inspiring bravery even when a battle seemed lost; led troops to the castle of an enemy who had taken her husband prisoner; stormed the castle, rescued husband, and killed her enemy and his supporters.

LONGFELLOW, Frances Appleton (1819–1861). American diarist. Name variations: Fanny. Born Frances Elizabeth Appleton in Boston, MA, Oct 6, 1819; died in Cambridge, MA, July 10, 1861; one of two daughters of Nathan Appleton (wealthy merchant); m. Henry Wadsworth Longfellow (1807–1882, poet), July 13, 1843, in Boston; children: 2 sons, 3 daughters. ❖ Second wife of Henry Wadsworth Longfellow (his 1st wife Mary Storer Potter died in 1835); was heating sealing wax to close a packet containing a lock of one of her children's hair when the sleeve of her light cotton dress caught fire (July 9, 1861); died the next day. ❖ See also *Women in World History.*

LONGFIELD, Cynthia (1896–1991). English entomologist and explorer. Born Cynthia Longfield, Aug 16, 1896; died June 27, 1991; dau. of Alice Mason Longfield and Mountifort Longfield (Anglo-Irish landowners). ❖ An expert on damselflies, dragonflies and the Odonata (insects), served as the 1st woman president of the London Natural History Society (1932); collected beetles and butterflies for Cyril Collinette on a scientific expedition in Pacific Islands (1924); as a British Museum entomologist (1927–57), collected plants, archaeological artifacts, and insects; joined Entomological Society of London (1925) and Royal Geographic Society; from a family trust, financed collection trips abroad to Canada, Brazil (with Collinette), British Africa (1934) and South Africa (1937); during WWII, joined the Auxiliary Fire Service and saved the Natural History Museum (April 1941).

LONGFORD, Elizabeth (1906–2002). English historian and countess. Name variations: Countess of Longford, formerly Lady Pakenham; Elizabeth Harman Pakenham. Born in London, England, Aug 30, 1906; died Oct 23, 2002, at home in Hurst Green, East Sussex; dau. of Nathaniel Bishop Harman (ophthalmologist) and Katherine (Chamberlain) Harman; received degree in Literae Humaniores at Oxford; m. Francis Aungier Pakenham, 7th earl of Longford (writer and politician), 1931 (died 2001); children: Thomas Pakenham; Patrick Pakenham; Judith Kazantzis; Rachel Billington; Michael Pakenham; Catherine Pakenham (died 1969); Kevin Pakenham; Antonia Fraser (b. 1932, writer). ❖ A woman of numerous interests and achievements, was twice a Labour candidate for Parliament, Trustee of the National Portrait Gallery and a Member of the Royal Society of Literature; wrote the bestselling books, *Queen Victoria: Born to Succeed, Wellington: The Years of the Sword* and *Victoria, R.I.* ❖ See also autobiography *The Pebbled Shore: The Memoirs of Elizabeth Longford* (1986).

LONGHI, Lucia Lopresti (1895–1985). Italian biographer, translator, novelist and magazine founder. Name variations: (pseudonym) Anna Banti. Born Lucia Lopresti, 1895, in Florence, Italy; died 1985 in Ronchi, Italy; educated at University of Rome; m. art historian Robert Longhi (died 1970). ❖ With husband, was co-founder and editor of *Paragone;* under pseudonym Anna Banti, began writing in her 30s; produced more than 20 books, including *Itinerario di Paolina*, a collection of short stories (1937); also wrote *Artemisia* (1947) and translated William Makepeace Thackeray's *Vanity Fair* and Virginia Woolf's *Jacob's Room;* focused on women's place in Italian society. ❖ See also the autobiographical work *Un grido lacerante (A Piercing Cry);* and *Women in World History.*

LONGMAN, Evelyn Beatrice (1874–1954). American sculptor. Born Mary Evelyn Beatrice Longman near Winchester, Ohio, 1874; died Cape Cod, Mar 1954; dau. of a farmer; studied at Art Institute,

Chicago; m. Nathaniel Horton Batchelder (headmaster of the Loomis School in Windsor, CT), in 1920. ❖ Was assistant to popular sculptor Daniel Chester French; awarded silver medal for 1st important piece, a male statue, *Victory,* shown in Festival Hall at St. Louis Exposition (1904); won $20,000 competition to create the bronze doors of US Naval Academy Chapel of Annapolis (1906); designed a 2nd pair of doors for Wellesley College; produced a number of fine portrait busts, including that of Alice Freeman Palmer, for American Hall of Fame; was the only sculptor that Thomas Edison posed for and the 1st woman sculptor to be elected a full member of the National Academy of Design.

LONGMAN, Irene Maud (1877–1964). Australian politician. Born April 24, 1877, in Franklin, Tasmania; died July 29, 1964; m. Heber Albert Longman (director of Queensland Museum), 1904. ❖ Joined the Country and Progressive National Party; was the 1st woman in Australia elected to the Queensland Parliament (1929); instrumental in establishing the 1st Queensland women police.

LONGO, Jeannie (1958—). French cyclist. Name variations: Jeannie Longo-Ciprelli. Born Oct 31, 1958, in Annecy, France; m. Patrice Ciprello (her coach). ❖ Began cycling and promptly won the French championship (1979); won Tour de France (1987–89); won Colorado Tour (1981, 1985–87); won World championships for road event (1985–87, 1989, 1995, 1996) and against the clock (1995–96); won French Pursuit championship (1980–89, 1992, 1994) and World Pursuit championship (1986, 1988–89); won a silver medal for indiv. road race at Barcelona Olympics (1992); won a gold medal for indiv. road race and a silver medal for indiv. time trial at Atlanta Olympics (1996); won a bronze medal for indiv. road race at Sydney Olympics (2000).

LONGSHORE, Hannah E. (1819–1901). American physician. Name variations: Hannah E. Myers. Born Hannah Myers, May 30, 1819, in Sandy Spring, MD; died in Philadelphia, PA, Oct 18, 1901; dau. of Samuel Myers (teacher) and Paulina (Iden) Myers; half-sister of Mary Myers Thomas; attended Quaker schools in Washington, DC, until age 13 or 14; attended New Lisbon Academy, New Lisbon, Ohio; Female (later Woman's) Medical College of Pennsylvania, MD, Dec 31, 1851; m. Thomas Ellwood Longshore (teacher), Mar 26, 1841; children: Channing Longshore (b. 1842); Lucretia L. Blankenburg (1845–1937, suffragist). ❖ In the climate of prejudice against female physicians, had difficulty building a private practice; taught and gave a series of public lectures starting in spring 1852 which drew so many patients to her Philadelphia practice that she was forced to give up teaching and lecturing; was eventually caring for 300 families, a record that surpassed any of her colleagues, male or female; continued to practice in Philadelphia for 40 years, retiring in 1892. ❖ See also *Women in World History.*

LONGSHORE, Lucretia (1845–1937). See Blankenburg, Lucretia L.

LONGSTAFF, Mary Jane (c. 1855–1935). English paleontologist. Name variations: Mary Jane Donald. Born Mary Jane Donald, c. 1855 in Carlisle, Cumbria, England; died Jan 19, 1935; m. George Blundell Longstaff (entomologist), 1906 (died 1921). ❖ An amateur paleontologist and an expert on Paleozoic Gastropoda, studied at the Carlisle School of Art; researched mollusks and fossil shells; bred large South African snails called *Cochlitoma;* traveled throughout Britain and abroad to study specimens (1885–1933); made a fellow of Geographical Society of London fellow (1919); was the 2nd woman awarded the Geological Society of London's Murchison Fund (1898).

LONGUEVILLE, Anne Geneviève, Duchesse de (1619–1679). French duchess and revolutionary. Name variations: Anne de Bourbon; Anne Geneviève de Bourbon, Duchesse de Longueville; Anne Geneviève de Bourbon-Conde. Born Anne Geneviève de Bourbon-Condé or Conde on Aug 28, 1619, in Bois de Vincennes; died April 15, 1679, at Convent of the Carmelites, Paris; dau. of Charlotte de Montmorency and Henry II de Bourbon, 3rd Prince de Condé; sister of the Great Condé; m. Henry, the Duc de Longueville, June 2, 1642; children: daughter, name unknown (c. 1646–1650), and 2 sons, Jean-Louis-Charles, the Comte de Dunois, Abbé d'Orléans (c. 1647–1694) and Charles-Paris, the Comte de Saint-Paul (c. 1649–1672); stepdaughter Marie d'Orléans, Mlle. de Longueville, who became Duchesse de Nemours (c. 1625–1707). ❖ French princess who, after a life crowded with excitement, romance, and intrigue, turned her back on the ways of the world and lived the life of a penitent for 20 years before her death; was born in prison during father's imprisonment on suspicion of plotting against Louis XIII (1619); though attracted to the religious life as a young girl, made a glittering debut into French society at 14 after her family's position was restored; a captivating beauty, made a politically advantageous marriage

to a much older man (1642); saw an admirer killed in a duel defending her reputation; conducted a notorious affair with the Duc de la Rochfoucauld; became one of the major participants in the *Fronde,* a sporadic civil war against the court (1642–52); deserted and betrayed by de la Rochfoucauld, returned to her family and gradually resumed her earlier religious devotion; became an influential supporter of the nuns and theologians of Port Royal (1660s) and played a primary role in securing the Peace of the Church (1669); lived with the nuns of Port Royal and at the Carmelite house (1672–79). ❖ See also *Women in World History.*

LONGUEVILLE, duchesse de.
See Mary of Guise (1515–1560).
See Longueville, Anne Geneviève, duchesse de (1619–1679).

LONGUEVILLE, Marie de (c. 1625–1707). See Nemours, Marie d'Orleans, duchess de.

LONGWORTH, Alice Roosevelt (1884–1980). American first daughter. Name variations: Alice Roosevelt. Born Alice Lee Roosevelt, Feb 12, 1884, in New York, NY; died in Washington, DC, Feb 20, 1980; dau. of Theodore Roosevelt (1858–1919, 26th president of US) and Alice Hathaway Lee Roosevelt (1861–1884); became stepdaughter of Edith Kermit Carow Roosevelt (Dec 2, 1886); m. Nicholas Longworth III (US congressional representative), Feb 17, 1906 (died April 10, 1931); children: Paulina Longworth Sturm (1925–1957). ❖ Daughter of Theodore Roosevelt, called Princess Alice, who captivated American society throughout much of 20th century with her iconoclasm and witticisms, began enthralling the public while still a teenager (1901); made debut in East Room of the White House (Jan 3, 1903); was front-page news when she wed in the White House (1906); father died (Jan 6, 1919); was a member of the board of counsellors of women's division of Republican National Committee (1932), and served as delegate to the Republican national convention (1936); published the column "Capital Comment," followed by her memoirs *Crowded Hours* (1933); became less partisan; with "influential political connections," reigned nearly 80 years in Washington society; kept a pillow upon which was embroidered her well-known quote, "If you haven't got anything good to say about anyone, come and sit by me." ❖ See also James Brough, *Princess Alice: A Biography of Alice Roosevelt Longworth* (Little, Brown, 1975); Carol Felsenthal, *Alice Roosevelt Longworth* (Putnam, 1988); Howard Teichmann, *Alice: The Life and Times of Alice Roosevelt Longworth* (Prentice-Hall, 1979); and *Women in World History.*

LONGWORTH, Maria Theresa (c. 1832–1881). Irish writer. Born c. 1832 in Ireland; died 1881; m. William Charles Yelverton, later 4th viscount Avonmore, 1857 (marriage repudiated in 1858). ❖ Best remembered as the plaintiff in a long-running British legal case, was married by a Roman Catholic priest in Ireland (1857); when husband repudiated the marriage and wed the widow of a professor (1858), turned to the courts to resolve the matter (an Irish court upheld the validity of her marriage in 1861; a Scottish court granted her husband an annulment in 1862; the Scottish court's ruling was confirmed by the House of Lords in 1864); published a number of novels (1861–75) and recounted the legal battle surrounding the marriage in *The Yelverton Correspondence* (1863).

LONSBROUGH, Anita (1941—). British swimmer. Born Aug 10, 1941, in Huddersfield, Yorkshire, England. ❖ Won 2 gold medals at Commonwealth Games (1958); won a gold medal for the 200-meter breaststroke at Rome Olympics (1960); at Tokyo Olympics, was the 1st woman to carry the flag in the opening ceremonies for the British team (1964); became the swimming correspondent for the *Daily Telegraph.* ❖ See also *Women in World History.*

LONSDALE, Kathleen (1903–1971). Irish-born crystallographer and pacifist. Born Kathleen Yardley, Jan 28, 1903, in Newbridge, County Kildare, Ireland; died in University College Hospital, London, England, April 1, 1971; dau. of Harry Frederick Yardley (postmaster) and Jessie (Cameron) Yardley; attended Bedford College for Women, London University; m. Thomas Jackson Lonsdale, 1927; children: Jane (b. 1929), Nancy (b. 1931) and Stephen Lonsdale (b. 1934). ❖ One of the leading British scientists of her generation, confronted science's potential for evil as well as good and, as a Quaker and a pacifist, sought to convince politicians and the public of the virtues of disarmament, of nonviolent resistance, and of the settlement of disputes on the basis of justice rather than by armed force; had research appointments at University College, London, and the Royal Institution (1922–27); was Amy Lady Tate Scholar at Leeds University (1927–29); became a Quaker (1935); was a Leverhulme Research fellow (1935–37) and a Dewar fellow at the Royal Institution (1944–46); was one of the 1st of 2 women to be elected fellow of Royal Society (1945); named a special fellow of US Federal Health Service (1947); was a professor of chemistry and head of department of crystallography, University College, London (1949–68); was a member of a Quaker delegation to Soviet Union (1951); delivered Swarthmore Lecture, "Removing the Causes of War" (1953); served as president of British section of Women's International League for Peace and Freedom; was vice president (1960–66) and president (1966) of International Union of Crystallography; served as 1st woman president of British Association for the Advancement of Science (1968); writings include *Is Peace Possible?* (1957). Awarded DBE (1956) and Royal Society's Davy medal (1957). ❖ See also *Women in World History.*

LONZI-RAGNO, Antonella (1940—). Italian fencer. Name variations: Antonella Ragno. Born Antonella Ragno, June 6, 1940, in Italy. ❖ Won a bronze medal in team foil at Rome Olympics (1960), a bronze medal in indiv. foil at Tokyo Olympics (1964), and a gold medal in indiv. foil at Munich Olympics (1972).

LOONEY, Shelley (1972—). American ice-hockey player. Born Jan 21, 1972, in Brownstown, Michigan. ❖ Won a team gold medal at Nagano (1998), the 1st Olympics to feature women's ice hockey; won team silver medals at World championships (1992, 1994, 1997, 1999, 2000, 2001) and Salt Lake City Olympics (2002). ❖ See also Mary Turco, *Crashing the Net* (HarperCollins, 1999); and *Women in World History.*

LOOS, Anita (1893–1981). American novelist, playwright and screenwriter. Born Corinne Anita Loos, April 26, 1893, in Sisson, CA; died Aug 18, 1981, in New York, NY; dau. of Richard Beers Loos (newspaper publisher) and Anita "Minnie" (Smith) Loos; m. Frank Pallma (composer), 1915 (div. 1920); m. John Emerson (film director), June 21, 1920; no children. ❖ Writer who gave the world the unflappable Lorelei Lee in *Gentleman Prefer Blondes*, briefly pursued a career on the stage until she sold her 1st "scenario" for a silent film; many of her early efforts were for pioneering director D.W. Griffith, for whom she wrote the subtitles for his landmark silent film, *Intolerance* (1916); though her long and prolific career was closely tied to films, her talent for sharp social and sexual satire came to full prominence with novel *Gentlemen Prefer Blondes* (1925); wrote, alone or in collaboration, some 200 scripts for stage and film, as well as 3 novels and as many volumes of memoirs of her years in Hollywood; screenplays include *The New York Hat* (1912), *Manhattan Madness* (1916), *Come on In* (1918); *Getting Mary Married* (1919), *Two Weeks* (1920), *Polly of the Follies* (1922), *Dulcy* (1923), *San Francisco* (1936), *Saratoga* (1937), *The Women* (1939), *Susan and God* (1940), *Blossoms in the Dust* (1941) and *I Married an Angel* (1942). ❖ See also memoirs (memoir) *A Girl Like I* (1966) and *Cast of Thousands* (1977); Gary Carey, *Anita Loos: A Biography* (Knopf, 1988); and *Women in World History.*

LOOS, Cécile Ines (1883–1959). Swiss novelist. Name variations: Cecile Ines Loos. Born Feb 4, 1883, in Basel, Switzerland; died Jan 21, 1959, in Basel; dau. of a musician; was orphaned when young, living in an orphanage in Berne (1893–99); children: illeg. son. ❖ Came to prominence with *Matka Boska* (1929), but fame faded quickly; other works, which explore motherhood and other roles of women, include *Die Rätsel der Turandot* (1931), *Der Tod und das Püppchen* (1939), and *Hinter dem Mond* (1942); was impoverished for many years.

LOPES, Katia (1973—). Brazilian volleyball player. Name variations: Kátia Caldeira Lopes. Born July 13, 1973, in Brazil. ❖ Setter; won a team bronze medal at Sydney Olympics (2000).

LOPES, Lisa (1971–2002). African-American singer. Name variations: Lisa "Left Eye" Lopes, TLC. Born Lisa Nicole Lopes, May 27, 1971, in Philadelphia, PA; died in car crash, April 25, 2002, in Jutiapa, Honduras; children: (adopted) daughter. ❖ Rhythm-and-blues singer who was member of hugely successful trio, TLC, which was formed in Atlanta, GA (1991); became known for singing rap sections of songs; with group, released debut album, *Oooooooohhh . . . On the TLC Tip* (1992), which went to #3 on R&B charts and included Top-10 hits, "Ain't 2 Proud 2 Beg," "Baby-Baby-Baby" and "What About Your Friends"; appeared in film, *House Party 3* (1994); sentenced to 5-years' probation for burning down house of boyfriend, Atlanta Falcons football player Andre Rison, after argument (1994); with group, released album *CrazySexyCool* (1994), which went 11-times platinum, won 2 Grammy Awards, and included hits, "Creep," "Waterfalls," "Red Light Special" and "Diggin' On You"; filed for bankruptcy (1995); was hostess of MTV show, "The Cut" (1998); with TLC, released enormously popular album, *Fanmail* (1999), which entered charts at #1, and included #1 pop hits, "No

Scrubs" and "Unpretty"; released solo album, *Supernova* (2001), which sank in US but was successful in Europe and Japan.

LOPES DE ALMEIDA, Julia (1862–1934). *See Almeida, Julia Lopes de.*

LOPES DULCE, Maria Rita (b. 1914). *See Pontes, Sister Dulce Lopes.*

LOPEZ, Encarnación (1898–1945). Argentinean dancer. Name variations: Encarnacion Lopez; known professionally as Argentinita. Born Encarnación Lopez, Mar 25, 1898, in Buenos Aires, Argentina; died Sept 24, 1945, in New York, NY; dau. of Felix Lopez and Lominga Lopez; sister of Pilar Lopez (première danseuse of Madrid Ballet). ❖ One of the leading exponents of Spanish dance, was raised in Madrid, where she studied dancing and acting from age 7; by 15, was known throughout Spain as "Queen of the Dance"; after mastering Spanish dance, introduced Flamenco to Madrid audiences, performed by her own troupe of *gitanos* (1927); toured in France, Mexico, Cuba and US (1930), as part of the *International Revue*; collaborated with poet-musician Federico Garcia Lorca to found Madrid Ballet, for which she choreographed dances, utilizing original folk music that she and Lorca collected and recorded; left Spain during Civil War, performing in Paris, Switzerland, Morocco, Algiers and London; returned to US (1938), winning acclaim; in Monte Carlo, collaborated with Léonide Massine and the Ballets Russes in creation of *Capriccio Espagnol*, which had its US premiere at Metropolitan Opera House (1940); often confused with La Argentina (Antonia Mercé). ❖ See also *Women in World History.*

LÓPEZ, Leonor (1362–1412). *See López de Córdoba, Leonor.*

LOPEZ, Nancy (1957—). Mexican-American golfer. Name variations: Nancy Melton; played as Lopez-Melton, 1980–81. Born Nancy Marie Lopez, Jan 6, 1957, in Torrance, CA; attended University of Tulsa on a golf scholarship; m. Tim Melton (tv sportscaster), 1979 (div. 1982); m. Ray Knight (professional baseball player), 1982. ❖ Led otherwise all-male high school golf team to state championship; entered US Women's Open as a senior in high school, finishing in 2nd place (1975); won Association of Intercollegiate Athletics for Women (AIAW) golf championship (1976); in 1st full season in Ladies Professional Golf Association (LPGA), won 8 tournaments—a record 5 in a row—to break the prize money record winning by more than $189,000 (with more than $3.2 million, was 2nd in career earnings); only golfer, male or female, to be named both Rookie of the Year and Player of the Year in the same year (1978); won the LPGA championship (1978, 1985, and 1989); won her last major LPGA win at the Mazda (1993); lost US Open by one stroke (1997), the only major championship that has eluded her. Named All-American and University of Tulsa's female athlete of the year (1976); named LPGA Rookie of the Year (1978); won twin honors of LPGA Player of the Year and Vare Trophy (1978, 1979, and 1985); inducted into the LPGA Hall of Fame (1987). ❖ See also (with Peter Schwed) *The Education of a Woman Golfer* (Simon & Schuster, 1979); and *Women in World History.*

LÓPEZ DE CÓRDOBA, Leonor (1362–1412). Spanish noblewoman and author. Name variations: Leonor López Carrillo; Leonor Lopez of Cordoba. Born 1362 in Córdoba; died 1412; dau. of Martin López, Grand Master of Calatrava, and Sancha Carrillo of Córdoba; m. Ruy Gutiérrez de Henestrosa (son of the high chamberlain to king of Castile), 1369; children: Juan Fernandez. ❖ Daughter of parents closely connected to royal house of Castile, grew up in highly privileged family and married well at 7; at 8, father was executed by order of King Henry II Trastamara, for supporting the late King Peter the Cruel (1370); imprisoned with family for 9 years (1370–79); eventually gained a high position at the royal court of King Henry III, becoming lady-in-waiting to Catherine of Lancaster (1372–1418), queen of Castile; wrote down life story, an important source of information on daily life of 14th-century Spanish nobility. ❖ See also *Women in World History.*

LOPOKOVA, Lydia (c. 1892–1981). Russian-born ballerina. Name variations: Lopukhova or Lopoukhova; Loppy; Lady Keynes. Pronunciation: Lopokova: LOW-poe-KOE-va; Keynes: KAYNES. Born Lydia Vasilievna Lopukhova in St. Petersburg, Russia, Oct 21 in 1891 or 1892; died at Tilton, Sussex, June 8, 1981; dau. of Vasili Lopukhov (St. Petersburg theater attendant) and Constanza Karlovna Douglas Lopukhova; sister of Evgenia Lopukhova (1884–1941); attended Imperial Ballet School, 1901–09; m. Randolfo Barocchi, 1916 (marriage annulled, 1925); m. John Maynard Keynes, Aug 4, 1925 (died 1946); no children. ❖ Prominent ballerina who, as a member of Diaghilev's dance troupe, played an important role in bringing Russian ballet to Western Europe and US; joined Maryinsky Theater (1909); joined Sergei Diaghilev company in Paris (1910) and was promoted immediately from corps de ballet to fill in for star ballerina Tamara Karsavina; at 18, performed to critical acclaim in such ballets as *The Firebird* and *Le Carnaval;* spent next 6 years in US as a dancer and actress (1910–16), also performing in vaudeville and operettas; rejoined Diaghilev's company and danced for 1st time in London (1918); married noted English economist John Maynard Keynes; moved to Bloomsbury and confined most of her dance and stage appearances to England, linking the ballet world with the Bloomsbury group; made final appearance with Diaghilev's company (1927); turned to acting (1928) and appeared in films, including *Dark Red Roses,* possibly the 1st English movie to use sound (1929); helped found the Camargo Society; gave last public performance as a ballerina (1933); made wartime trips to Canada and US (1941–45). ❖ See also Polly Hill and Richard Keynes, *Lydia and Maynard* (Scribner, 1989); Milo Keynes, ed. *Lydia Lopokova* (Weidenfeld & Nicolson, 1983); and *Women in World History.*

LOPOUKHOVA, Lydia (c. 1892–1981). *See Lopokova, Lydia.*

LOPRESTI, Lucia (1895–1985). *See Longhi, Lucia Lopresti.*

LOPUKHOVA, Evgenia (1884–1941). Russian prima ballerina. Name variations: Yevgenia Lopoukhova. Born 1884; died 1941; dau. of Vasili Lopukhov (St. Petersburg theater attendant) and Constanza Karlovna Douglas Lopukhova; sister of Andrei Lopukhov (1898–1947, character dancer and teacher), Fedor Lopukhov (b. 1886, Soviet choreographer), and Lydia Lopokova (c. 1892–1981). ❖ Was a leading ballerina in Soviet Russia. ❖ See also *Women in World History.*

LOPUKHOVA, Lydia (c. 1892–1981). *See Lopokova, Lydia.*

LORAINE, Violet (1886–1956). English actress. Name variations: Violet Mary Loraine. Born July 26, 1886, in London, England; died July 18, 1956, in Newcastle, England; sister of actor Ernest Sefton; m. Edward Raylton Joicey, 1921. ❖ Made stage debut at Drury Lane in the pantomime *Mother Goose* (1902), followed by *The Medal and the Maid, The Duchess of Dantzic, Sergeant Blue* and *Our Flat,* among others; 1st appeared on variety stage at the Palace in *The New Régime* (1905) and on music-hall stage in a solo turn at Oxford; other plays include *Hop o' my Thumb* (lead role), *Business as Usual, Push and Go, The Bing Boys are Here, The Whirligig* and *London Paris and New York;* retired from the stage (1922), reappearing in *Clara Gibbings* (1928); films include *Britannia of Billingsgate* and *Road House.*

LORCIA, Suzanne (1902–1999). French ballet dancer. Born Dec 18, 1902, in Paris, France; died 1999. ❖ Trained at ballet school of Paris Opéra before joining company (1928); was a première for 22 years (1928–50) and performed in range of works by Serge Lifar including *Salade* (1935), *Le Roi Nu* (1936), *Aneus,* and *Bolero;* also appeared in classics restaged by Albert Aveline such as *Sylvia* and *Les Deux Pigeons;* taught at Paris Opéra's school after retirement from stage (c. 1950).

LORD, Bette Bao (1938—). Chinese-American novelist. Born Nov 3, 1938, in Shanghai, China; dau. of Dora and Sandys Bao (British-trained engineer); grew up in New Jersey; Tufts University, BA, and Tuft's Fletcher School of Law, MA; m. Winston Lord (former ambassador to China), 1962. ❖ At 8, came to US, when father was sent by Chinese nationalist government to purchase equipment (1946); with family, was stranded in US when Communists won civil war in China (1949); wrote of her painful childhood experiences as a Chinese immigrant in the autobiographical, *The Year of the Boar and Jackie Robinson* (1984); also wrote *Eighth Moon* (1964), about her sister's escape from Communist China, followed by the bestselling *Spring Moon: A Novel of China* (1981), as well as *Legacies: A Chinese Mosaic* (1989) and *The Middle Heart* (1996); was chair of Freedom House; served as director of Council on Foreign Relations (1998–2003).

LORD, Lucy Takiora (c. 1842–1893). New Zealand guide and interpreter. Name variations: Bloody Mary, Louisa Dalton, Lucy D'Alton, Takihora, Louisa Grey, Takiora Grey, Mrs Blake. Born Lucy Takiora Lord, c. 1842 (baptized Lucy Elizabeth, Oct 9, 1842), in Kororareka (Russell), in northern New Zealand; died Sept 3, 1893, in New Plymouth, New Zealand; dau. of William Lord and Kotiro Hinerangi; m. Te Mahuki, early 1860s (died 1866); m. Joseph Edwin Dalton, 1878. ❖ Together with 1st husband, acted as guide and interpreter for European military forces; lived controversial life by assisting those her family considered enemies; used several names during her lifetime. ❖ See also *Dictionary of New Zealand Biography* (Vol. 1).

LORD, Marjorie (1918—). American stage, tv and screen actress. Born Marjorie Wollenberg, July 26, 1918, in San Francisco, CA; m. John Archer, 1941 (div. 1955); m. Randolph Hale, 1958 (died 1974); m. Harry Volk, 1977; children: Anne Archer (b. 1947, actress). ❖ Appeared on Broadway; made film debut in *Border Cafe* (1937), followed by *Escape from Hong Kong, Sherlock Holmes in Washington, New Orleans, Masked Raiders, Riding High, Chain Gang* and *Boy Did I Get a Wrong Number,* among others; starred opposite Danny Thomas on tv series "Make Room for Daddy" (1957–64).

LORD, Mary Scott (1858–1948). *See Harrison, Mary Scott Dimmick.*

LORD, Pauline (1890–1950). American actress. Born in Hanford, CA, Aug 13, 1890; died in Alamagordo, NM, Oct 11, 1950; dau. of Edward Lord (tinsmith) and Sara (Foster) Lord; studied acting at school of the Alcazar Theater, San Francisco, California; m. Owen B. Winters (ad executive), April 27, 1929 (div. 1931). ❖ One of the leading actresses of the new realism during 1st half of 20th century, made stage debut as the maid in a Belasco Stock Co. production, *Are You a Mason?* in San Francisco (1903); made NY debut as Ruth Lenox in *The Talker* (1912); appeared as Sadie in *The Deluge* (1917); had breakthrough role at 31 as Anna in *Anna Christie* (1921); also appeared as Amy in *They Knew What They Wanted* (1924), Nina in touring company of *Strange Interlude* (1928–29), Abby in *The Late Christopher Bean* (1932), Zenobia in *Ethan Frome* (1936), and Amanda Wingfield in touring company of *The Glass Menagerie* (1946); made film debut in title role in *Mrs. Wiggs of the Cabbage Patch.* ❖ See also *Women in World History.*

LORDE, Athena (1915–1973). American actress. Born Sept 11, 1915, in New York, NY; died May 23, 1973, in Van Nuys, CA; m. Jim Boles (actor); children: Eric Boles and Barbara Boles (both actors). ❖ Stage, radio, tv, and screen actress, films include *Fuzz, Hush, Hush, Sweet Charlotte, Marjorie Morningstar* and *Dr. Death.*

LORDE, Audre (1934–1992). American poet, essayist, and activist, and feminist. Name variations: also published under name Rey Domini, a Latinate version of Audre Lorde; sometimes known by African name, Gamba Adisa. Born Audrey Geraldine Lorde, Feb 18, 1934, in New York, NY; died of cancer in St. Croix, US Virgin Islands, Nov 17, 1992; dau. of Frederick Byron Lorde (real-estate broker) and Linda (Belmar) Lorde; attended National University of Mexico, 1954; Hunter College, BA, 1959; Columbia University, MLS, 1961; m. Edward Ashley Rollins (attorney), Mar 31, 1962 (div.); life partner of Frances Clayton; children: Elizabeth Rollins and Jonathan Rollins (both born mid-1960s). ❖ One of the foremost feminist voices of 20th century, confronted issues of identity, racism, sexism, and heterosexism; worked at Mount Vernon Public Library (1960–62), and St. Claire's School of Nursing as a librarian (1965–66); was head librarian of Towne School library (1966–68); taught her 1st poetry workshop, at Tougaloo (1967); published *The First Cities* (1967); joined faculty of City College of City University of New York as a lecturer in creative writing (1968); was a lecturer at Herbert H. Lehman College (1969–70); was associate professor of English at John Jay College of Criminal Justice (1970–80); read *Love Poem* at a public reading and published it in *Ms.* (1971); published *The Black Unicorn* (1977); delivered essay, "The Translation of Silence into Action," at MLA Convention (1977); diagnosed with breast cancer (1978), published *The Cancer Journals* (1980); became founding member of Kitchen Table Press (1980); became professor of English at Hunter College of CUNY (1980); moved to St. Croix, US Virgin Islands (1987), saying that she needed to be where it was warmer and where being Black was not an anomaly; frequently introduced herself as a "Black, Lesbian, Feminist, warrior, poet, mother doing my work." Poetry collections include *Cables to Rage* (1970), *From a Land Where Other People Live* (1973), *The New York Head Shop and Museum* (1974), *Coal* (1976), *Between Ourselves* (1976), *The Black Unicorn* (1978), *Our Dead Behind Us* (1986), *Undersong* (1992), *The Marvelous Arithmetics of Distance* (1993); also wrote *The Uses of the Erotic: The Erotic as Power* (1978), *Zami: A New Spelling of My Name* (1982), *Sister Outsider* (1984) and *I Am Your Sister* (1985). Received Manhattan Borough President's Award for Excellence in the Arts (1988); won American Book Award for *A Burst of Light* (1989); given Walt Whitman Citation of Merit, making her the Poet Laureate of NY (1991). ❖ See also *Women in World History.*

LOREN, Sophia (1934—). Italian actress. Born Sofia Scicolone in Rome, Italy, Sept 20, 1934; dau. of Romilda Villani and Riccardo Scicolone; sister of Maria Scicolone; m. Carlo Ponti (film producer), 1966; children: Carlo Jr. (b. Dec 29, 1968) and Eduardo (b. Jan 1973). ❖ Internationally renowned film actress who won an Oscar for *Two*

Women, was raised near Naples by her unmarried mother amid great poverty during WWII; appeared as an extra in 1st film *Quo Vadis?* (1949); met producer Carlo Ponti; film career began in earnest with small featured part in his *La Tratta della bianche* (*The White Slave Trade,* 1953); played Aïda in a film version of Verdi's opera (1953); shot the 1st of her many pictures directed by Vittorio De Sica (1954's *L'Oro di Napoli* [*The Gold of Naples*], 1954); appeared onscreen in 1st of 15 films with Marcello Mastroianni in De Sica's *Peccato che sia una canaglia* (*Too Bad She's Bad,* 1955); rivaled only by Gina Lollobrigida as Italy's best-known actress on both sides of Atlantic (1950s); appeared in *Boy on a Dolphin,* the 1st of many Hollywood-made films (1958), but her finest work is still considered to be her portrayal of a mother in war-ravaged Italy in De Sica's *La Ciociara* (*Two Women,* 1960); married Carlo Ponti as a French citizen (1966), after a protracted legal battle with Italian authorities who refused to recognize Ponti's annulment of an earlier marriage. Other films include *The Pride and the Passion* (1957), *Desire under the Elms* (1958), *The Key* (1958), *It Started in Naples* (1960), *The Millionairess* (1960), *El Cid* (1961), *Madame Sans-Gêne* (1961), *Boccacio '70* (1962), *Ieri Oggi e Domani* (*Yesterday, Today, and Tomorrow,* 1963), *The Fall of the Roman Empire* (1964), *Matrimonio all'Italiana* (*Marriage Italian Style,* 1964), *Arabesque* (1966), *A Countess from Hong Kong* (1967), *Man of La Mancha* (1972), *The Cassandra Crossing* (1977), *Grumpier Old Men* (1995), *Messages* (1996), *Soleil* (1997) and *Between Strangers* (2002). ❖ See also A.E. Hotchner, *Sophia: Living and Loving* (Morrow, 1979); Warren G. Harris, *Sophia Loren* (Simon & Schuster, 1998); and *Women in World History.*

LORENGAR, Pilar (1928—). Spanish soprano. Born Pilar Lorenza Garcia, Jan 16, 1928, in Saragossa, Spain; studied with Angeles Ottein, Carl Ebert, and Martha Klust. ❖ Debuted in Madrid (1949), Covent Garden (1955), Glyndebourne (1956–60), and Salzburg (1961–64); appeared at Metropolitan Opera (1966–78); had long operatic career which led her from a youthful Cherubino in Mozart's *Le nozze di Figaro* (*Marriage of Figaro*) to a mature countess; was also successful in light opera and sang in the *zarzuelas* (musical comedies) of Spain. Named Austrian Kammersängerin (1963). ❖ See also *Women in World History.*

LORENTZEN, Ingeborg (1957—). Norwegian royal. Name variations: Ingeborg Ribeiro. Born Feb 27, 1957, in Oslo, Norway; dau. of Erling Lorentzen and Ragnhild Oldenburg (dau. of Olav V, king of Norway); m. Paolo Ribeiro, on June 4, 1982. ❖ Granddaughter of Olav V.

LORENTZEN, Ragnhild (b. 1930). See Oldenburg, Ragnhild.

LORENTZEN, Ragnhild (1968—). Norwegian royal. Born May 8, 1968, in Rio de Janeiro, Brazil; dau. of Erling Lorentzen and Ragnhild Oldenburg (dau. of Olav V, king of Norway). ❖ Granddaughter of Olav V.

LORENZ, Ericka (1981—). American water-polo player. Born Feb 18, 1981, in San Diego, CA. ❖ Driver, won a team silver medal at Sydney Olympics (2000) and a team bronze at Athens Olympics (2004); won World championship (2003).

LORENZO, Teresa (fl. 1358). Mistress of Peter I. Name variations: Teresa Gille Lourenco. Fl. around 1358; mistress of Pedro I also known as Peter I (1320–1367), king of Portugal (r. 1357–1367); children: (with Peter I) John I the False also known as John I of Aviz (1357–1433), master of Aviz, king of Portugal (r. 1385–1433).

LORENZO, Tina di (1872–1930). See di Lorenzo, Tina.

LORETAN, Brigitte (1970—). See Albrecht-Loretan, Brigitte.

LORETTA DE BRAOSE (d. 1266). See Braose, Loretta de.

LORETTA DE BRIOUZE (d. 1266). See Braose, Loretta de.

LORETTA OF LEICESTER (d. 1266). See Braose, Loretta de.

LORIMER, Margaret (1866–1954). New Zealand school principal and mountaineer. Born on June 9, 1866, at Inverness, Scotland; died on Oct 29, 1954, in Wellington, New Zealand; dau. of James Lorimer (plowman) and Jessie (McLennan) Lorimer; University of New Zealand, MA, 1888. ❖ Taught at Christchurch Girls' school (1886, 1889–97); became headmistress of Mount Cook Girls' School, Wellington (1897); assumed position of principal of Nelson College for Girls (1906); climbed Mt. Cook at age 52 (1918); after retirement (1926), returned to mountaineering and was active in New Zealand Alpine Club, and Ladies' Alpine Club, London; also helped to found Wellington branch of Nelson College for Girls Old Girls' Association. ❖ See also *Dictionary of New Zealand Biography* (Vol. 3).

LORINGHOVEN, Baroness von Freytag (1875–1927). See Freytag-Loringhoven, Elsa von.

LORIOD, Yvonne (1924–2001). French pianist. Born in Houilles, Seine-et-Oise, France, Jan 20, 1924; died at Juan-les-Pins, France, Aug 3, 2001; was a student of Lazare-Lévy and Marcel Ciampi at the Paris Conservatoire; m. her teacher Olivier Messiaen (1908–1992). ❖ Closely associated with husband's music, presented his *Turangalila* with Boston Symphony Orchestra at its world premiere (1949); also performed on the Ondes Martenot, an electrical keyboard named after its inventor which produces only one note at a time.

LORME, Marion de (c. 1613–1650). See Delorme, Marion.

LORN, Lady of (fl. 1300s). See Isaac, Joan.

LORNE, Marion (1888–1968). American comedic actress. Born Marion Lorne MacDougall, Aug 12, 1888, in Philadelphia, PA; died May 9, 1968, in New York, NY; m. Walter C. Hackett (British actor-manager and playwright, died 1944). ❖ Made NY debut in *Mrs. Temple's Telegram* (1905); made London debut in *He Didn't Want to Do It* (1915) and often appeared there; with husband, founded Whitehall Theater; NY plays include *Harvey, The Devil, The Florist Shop* and the revue *Dance Me a Song;* films include *Strangers on a Train* and *The Graduate;* best remembered for her stammering, endearing roles in tv's "Mr. Peepers," "The Garry Moore Show" and "Bewitched" (as Aunt Clara). Awarded Emmy posthumously for "Bewitched."

LOROUPE, Tegla (1973—). Kenyan marathon runner. Born Tegla Loroupe, May 9, 1973 in Kapenguria, Kenya. ❖ Won NY City Marathon (1994, 1995), the 1st African woman to win a major marathon; placed 2nd at Boston Marathon (1996); won Rotterdam Marathon (1997, 1998); won Goodwill Games (1998); won Berlin Marathon (1999) with a time of 2:20:43; won London Marathon (2000); won Kenyan nationals for 10,000 meters (2000); won 10k Avon Global championship and Lausanne Marathon (2002).

LORRAINE, duchess of.
See Liutgard of Saxony (d. 953).
See Ida de Macon (d. 1224).
See Margaret of Bavaria (fl. 1390–1410).
See Yolande of Vaudemont (1428–1483).
See Jeanne de Laval (d. 1498).
See Antoinette of Bourbon (1494–1583).
See Renée of Montpensier (fl. 1500s).
See Christina of Denmark (1521–1590).
See Philippa of Guelders (d. 1547).
See Claude de France (1547–1575).
See Gonzaga, Margherita (1591–1632).
See Nicole of Lorraine (d. 1657).
See Elizabeth-Charlotte (1676–1744).

LORRAINE, Emily (c. 1878–1944). English-born actress. Born c. 1878 in England; died July 6, 1944, in New York, NY. ❖ First appeared on American stage (1904); joined James K. Hackett repertory group; appeared with May Robson in *Martha by the Day* (1915) and William Faversham in *Squaw Man* (1922); other appearances include *Mourning Becomes Electra* and *The Skin of Our Teeth.*

LORRAINE, Louise (1901–1981). American actress. Name variations: Louise Fortune. Born Louise Escovar, Oct 1, 1901, in San Francisco, CA; died Feb 2, 1981, in Sacramento, CA; m. Art Acord (cowboy actor) 1928 (div. 1935); m. Chester J. Hubbard (businessman, died 1963); children: daughter. ❖ Began career as a comedic actress in silent films (1910); became a Baby Wampus Star; was the 2nd Jane to Elmo Lincoln's Tarzan (Enid Markey was the 1st); other films included *Rookies, Legionnaires in Paris, Circus Rookies* and such serials as *The Jade Box* and *Fighting Blood,;* retired (1935).

LORRAINE, Marie (1899–1982). See McDonagh, Isobel.

LORRAINE, queen of. See Waldrada (fl. 9th c.).

LORRAYNE, Vyvyan (1939—). South African ballet dancer. Born April 20, 1939, in Pretoria, South Africa. ❖ Joined Royal Ballet in London (1958), where she created roles for Frederick Ashton in *Monotones I* (1965), *Jazz Calendar* (1968), and *Enigma Variations* (1968), among others; also appeared in *Les Sylphides, La Bayadère,* and *The Sleeping Beauty;* was member of Royal Ballet's New Group and created role in a new pas de deux by Ashton, *Siesta* (1972).

LORTEL, Lucille (1902–1999). American theatrical producer. Name variations: Lucille Schweitzer. Born in New York, NY, 1902; died in New York, NY, April 4, 1999; dau. of Harry (garment industry executive) and Anna (Mayo) Lortel; briefly attended Adelphi College (now Adelphi University); attended American Academy of Dramatic Arts, 1920; studied in Germany with Arnold Korf and Max Reinhardt; m. Louis Schweitzer (chemical engineer and cigarette-paper manufacturer), Mar 23, 1931 (died 1971); no children. ❖ Dubbed "Queen of Off-Broadway," produced over 500 plays, including several nominated for Tony Awards; as founder of the White Barn Theater in Westport, CT, and owner of the Theater de Lys in NY's Greenwich Village (rechristened the Lucille Lortel Theater, 1981), provided countless playwrights and actors with an opportunity to showcase their talent away from the pressures of Broadway. Was the 1st recipient of the Margo Jones Award (1952); received Lee Strasberg Lifetime Achievement Award (1984); was inducted into Theater Hall of Fame (1990). ❖ See also *Women in World History*.

LO-RUHAMAH. Biblical woman. Name variations: Not Pitied. The dau. of Gomer (a harlot) and the prophet Hosea.

LORVANO, abbess of.
See Sancha (c. 1178–1229).
See Branca (1259–1321).

LOSABERIDZE, Ketevan (1949—). Soviet archer. Born Aug 1949 in USSR. ❖ At Moscow Olympics, won a gold medal in double FITA round (1980).

LOS ANGELES, Victoria de (1923–2005). Spanish soprano. Born Victoria Gómez Cima, Nov 1, 1923, in Barcelona, Spain; died Jan 15, 2005, in Barcelona; dau. of Bernardo Lopez Gomez; studied with Dolores Frau at Barcelona Conservatory until 1944; m. Enrique Magrina, 1948; children: 2 sons, Juan Enrique and Alejandro. ❖ Debuted as Mimi in Barcelona (1941); won Geneva International Singing Competition (1947); debuted as Marguerite in Paris (1949); made Covent Garden debut as Mimi (1950); became widely popular, especially in Great Britain; made Metropolitan Opera debut as Marguerite (1951), appearing for more than 100 performances until 1961; was widely known for her 22 recorded operas, especially Bizet's *Carmen* made with Sir Thomas Beecham. ❖ See also P. Roberts, *Victoria de Los Angeles* (London, 1982); and *Women in World History*.

LOSCH, Claudia (1960—). West German track-and-field athlete. Born Jan 10, 1960, in Germany. ❖ At Los Angeles Olympics, won a gold medal in shot put (1984).

LOSCH, Tilly (1903–1975). Austrian dancer, actress, and choreographer. Name variations: often wrongly seen as Tillie Losch; countess of Carnarvon. Born Ottilia or Ottilie Ethel Leopoldine Losch in Vienna, Austria, Nov 15, 1903; died of cancer in a New York hospital, Dec 24, 1975; studied at Vienna Opera Ballet School; m. Edward James (poet, architect, and arts patron), 1930 (div. 1934); m. Edward F. Willis James, 6th earl of Carnarvon, 1939 (div. 1947). ❖ Heralded as one of the great beauties of her day, debuted with Vienna Opera (1924), dancing the role of Princess Teaflower in *Schlagobers;* made dramatic acting debut in *Leonce and Lena* at Vienna Burgtheater; had 1st choreography credit for Max Reinhardt's production of *A Midsummer Night's Dream* (1927), in which she also played First Fairy; choreographed and danced with Reinhardt for some time, traveling with him to US (1928) and dancing the role of the Nun in his production of *The Miracle* (1932); while in America, appeared in several films, including *The Garden of Allah* (1936), *The Good Earth* (1937), and *Duel in the Sun* (1945); was also noted for her "hand dances" and appeared in Brecht-Weill collaboration *The Seven Deadly Sins*, with Lotte Lenya; later enjoyed some success as a painter. ❖ See also *Women in World History*.

LOST BIRD (c. 1890–c. 1919). See Zintkala Nuni.

LOTHROP, Alice (1870–1920). American social worker. Born Alice Louise Higgins on Mar 28, 1870, in Boston, MA; died Sept 2, 1920, in Newton, MA; only child of Albert Higgins (merchant) and Adelaide (Everson) Higgins; m. William Howard Lothrop (businessman), May 17, 1913; no children. ❖ Joined Associated Charities of Boston as an agent-in-training; became general secretary of the organization (1903), succeeding Zilpha Drew Smith; over next 10 years, made a significant contribution to the field of social work, both in method and ideology; won acclaim for organizing disaster relief after the great San Francisco fire (1906) and the enormous explosion in Halifax, Nova Scotia (1917); served variously with Massachusetts Child Labor Committee, Massachusetts Commission to Investigate Employment Agencies, Massachusetts Civic League, and was particularly active in the fight against tuberculosis. ❖ See also *Women in World History*.

LOTHROP, Amy (1827–1915). See Warner, Anna Bartlett.

LOTHROP, Harriet (1844–1924). American author. Name variations: (pseudonym) Margaret Sidney. Born Harriet (also seen as Harriett) Mulford Stone, June 22, 1844, in New Haven, CT; died Aug 2, 1924, in San Francisco, CA; dau. of Sidney Mason Stone (architect) and Harriett (Mulford) Stone; graduate of Grove Hall Seminary, New Haven; m. Daniel Lothrop (publisher), Oct 4, 1881 (died 1892); children: Margaret Lothrop. ❖ Best known for her fictional series detailing the adventures of the five Pepper children, the 1st of which, *Five Little Peppers and How They Grew,* always remained the most popular; wrote over 40 other books, including *Little Maid of Concord Town* (1898) and *The Judges' Cave* (1900). Five of the stories were adapted into films by Columbia Pictures (1939–40). ❖ See also *Women in World History*.

LOTSEY, Nancy (c. 1955—). American baseball player. Born c. 1955 in Morristown, NJ. ❖ At 8, joined the New Jersey Small-Fry League, the 1st girl to play in organized baseball games with boys (1963); was the winning pitcher and hit a home run in her 1st game.

LOTT, Elsie S. (fl. 1940s). American Army nurse. Flourished in 1940s. ❖ Served as 2nd lieutenant in Army Nurse Corps; received US Air Medal for meritorious achievement as a nurse (1943), the 1st woman to receive an Air Medal.

LOTTA (1847–1924). See Crabtree, Lotta.

LOTTIE. *Variant of Charlotte.*

LOTZ, Ingrid (1934—). East German track-and-field athlete. Born Mar 11, 1934, in Germany. ❖ At Tokyo Olympics, won a silver medal in the discus throw (1964).

LOTZ, Irmgard Flügge (1903–1974). See Flügge-Lotz, Irmgard.

LOU, Henri (1861–1937). See Andreas-Salomé, Lou.

LOUCHHEIM, Aline B. (1914–1972). See Saarinen, Aline B.

LOUDON, Dorothy (1933–2003). American actress. Born Sept 17, 1933, in Boston, Massachusetts; died of cancer, Nov 15, 2003, in New York, NY; dau. of James and Dorothy Shaw Loudon; attended Syracuse University and American Academy of Dramatic Arts; m. Norman Paris (died 1977). ❖ Began career in cabaret and on tv, becoming a regular on "The Garry Moore Show"; on Broadway, created the role of Miss Hannigan in *Annie* (1977), for which she won a Tony Award; also starred in *Sweeney Todd* (1979), *West Side Waltz* (1981) and *Noises Off* (1983); films include *Garbo Talks* (1984) and *Midnight in the Garden of Good and Evil* (1997). Nominated for Tony awards for *The Fig Leaves Are Falling* (1969) and *Ballroom* (1978).

LOUDON, Jane Webb (1807–1858). British botanist and writer on horticulture. Born near Birmingham, England, Aug 19, 1807; died in London, England, July 13, 1858; dau. of Thomas Webb; m. John Loudon (landscape gardener and horticultural writer), in 1830. ❖ Following marriage, immersed herself in husband's work, learning about plants and serving as his assistant; began to write books on popular botany, the most successful of which was *The Ladies' Companion to the Flower Garden* (1841); also wrote *The Young Naturalist's Journey; or, the Travels of Agnes Merton and Her Mama* (1840) and *Modern Botany; or, a Popular Introduction to the Natural System of Plants, According to the Classification of de Candolle.* ❖ See also *Women in World History*.

LOUDOV, Ivana (1941—). Czech composer. Born Mar 8, 1941, in Chlumec nad Cidlinou, Czechoslovakia; studied with Miloslav Kabelac and Emil Hlobil at Prague Conservatory, 1968–71, and Academy of Dramatic Arts; studied under Olivier Messiaen and Andre Jolivet; m. Milos Haase, 1973. ❖ Won Young Czech Composer competition with *Concerto* (1974); combining traditional compositional styles with New Music techniques, saw many of compositions premiered in US, Switzerland and Italy; won competition Quido d'Arezzo, Italy (1978, 1980, 1984) as well as dozens of prizes for choral works and choral competitions from International Radio in Moscow (1978) and Redletter Days of Songs at Olomouc (1983); began teaching composition at Academy of Music and Dramatic Arts in Prague (1992); founded "Studio N" for contemporary music in Prague (1996); famed internationally for highly unique compositions. Works include *Symphony No. 1* (1964), *Appointment with Love* for 3 male choruses accompanied by flute and piano (1966), Italian *Triptych* (1982), *Songs on the Rose* (1983), *Tango Music* for piano (1984), *Double Concerto* for violin, percussion and strings (1989), *Harmonie du Soir* for chamber choir (1993) and *Echoes* for horn and percussion (1997).

LOUGH, Blanche Edith (1874–1963). *See Thompson, Blanche Edith.*

LOUGHLIN, Anne (1894–1979). British trade unionist. Name variations: Dame Anne Loughlin. Born June 28, 1894, in Leeds, England; died 1979; dau. of a shoe-factory worker; attended elementary school in Leeds until age 12; never married; no children. ❖ To support sisters after parents died, took a job as a machine worker in a local factory; joined National Union of Tailors and Garment Workers, and shortly thereafter led 200 young women workers in a formal strike; became an organizer for 10,000-member union (1914), a job that took her throughout British Isles to negotiate, consult on factory conditions, and settle disputes; was elected to General Council of powerful Trades Union Congress (1929), of which she was selected chair (1943); elected as the 1st woman general secretary of the National Union of Tailors and Garment Workers (1948); was 1 of 2 women on British delegation sent to Free World Labor Conference (1949); retired as general secretary of the Union (1953), due to ill health. Named Dame of the Order of the British Empire (DBE, 1943). ❖ See also *Women in World History.*

LOUGHRAN, Beatrix (1896–1975). American figure skater. Name variations: Beatrix Harvey. Born June 30, 1896, in New York, NY; died Dec 7, 1975, in Long Beach, NY. ❖ Won a silver medal at Chamonix Olympics (1924); won US National singles championships (1925–27) and pairs (1930–32); won a bronze medal at St. Moritz Olympics (1928); with Sherwin Badger, placed 4th for pairs at St. Moritz Olympics and won a silver medal at Lake Placid Olympics (1932).

LOUISA. *Variant of Louise.*

LOUISA (1622–1709). Princess Palatine and abbess of Maubisson. Name variations: Louise Hollandine; Louise Simmern. Born Louisa Hollandine, April 17 or 18, 1622, at The Hague, Netherlands; died Feb 11, 1709, in Maubuisson; dau. of Elizabeth of Bohemia (1596–1662) and Frederick V, Elector Palatine and titular king of Bohemia; sister of Elizabeth of Bohemia (1618–1680) and Sophia (1630–1714), electress of Hanover. ❖ Became abbess of Maubisson.

LOUISA (fl. 1727–1745). *See Boyd, Elizabeth.*

LOUISA, grand duchess of Naples (1773–1802). *See Louisa Amelia.*

LOUISA AMELIA (1773–1802). Grand duchess of Tuscany. Name variations: Ludovica; Luisa of Naples; Luisa of Bourbon-Two Sicilies; Louise de Bourbon or Louise of Bourbon; Marie Louise of Naples and Sicily. Born July 17, 1773, in Naples; died Sept 19, 1802, in Vienna; dau. of Maria Carolina (1752–1814), queen of the Two Sicilies, and Ferdinand I (or IV), king of the Two Sicilies; m. Ferdinando or Ferdinand III (1769–1824), grand duke of Tuscany (r. 1790–1802, 1814–1824) and archduke of Austria, Sept 19, 1790; children: Caroline (1793–1812); Francis (1794–1800); Leopold II (1797–1870), grand duke of Tuscany (r. 1824–1859); Maria Ludovica (1798–1857); Maria Theresa of Tuscany (1801–1855). ❖ Ferdinand's 2nd wife was Maria Anna of Saxony (1795–1865).

LOUISA ANNE (1749–1768). English royal. Name variations: Louise Anne Guelph. Born Mar 8, 1749, in London, England; died May 13, 1768, at Carlton House, Mayfair, London; buried in Westminster Abbey; dau. of Augusta of Saxe-Gotha (1719–1772) and Frederick Louis, prince of Wales; sister of George III, king of England (r. 1760–1820), and Caroline Matilda (1751–1775).

LOUISA CARLOTTA OF NAPLES (1804–1844). Neapolitan princess and duchess of Cadiz. Name variations: Luisa of Sicily. Born Oct 24, 1804; died Jan 29, 1844; dau. of Francis I, king of the Two Sicilies (r. 1825–1830), and Marie Isabella of Spain (1789–1848); sister of Maria Cristina I of Naples (1806–1878), queen of Spain; m. Francisco de Paula (1794–1865), duke of Cadiz (brother of Ferdinand VII, king of Spain), June 11, 1819; children: Francisco de Asís or Asíz (1822–1902, who m. Isabella II, queen of Spain); Amalia de Paula (b. 1834, who m. Adalbert Wittelsbach on Aug 25, 1856); Marie Christine de Paula (1833–1902, who m. Sebastian de Bourbon); Enrique or Henry, duke of Seville. ❖ Francisco de Paula's 2nd wife was Therese Arredondo.

LOUISA CHRISTINA OF BAVARIA (fl. 1726). Duchess of Savoy. Name variations: Louise Christine; Polyxena-Christina of Hesse. Born c. 1700; dau. of Ernest-Leopold of Hesse Rheinfelt; m. Charles

Emmanuel III (1701–1773), duke of Savoy (r. 1730–1773) and king of Sardinia; children: Victor Amadeus III (1726–1796), duke of Savoy (r. 1773–1796). Charles Emmanuel was also m. to Elizabeth of Lorraine (1711–1741).

LOUISA HENRIETTA DE CONTI (1726–1759). Duchess of Orleans. Name variations: Louise-Henrietta von Conty; Louise-Henriette. Born Louise-Henriette de Bourbon-Conti, June 20, 1726; died Feb 9, 1759; dau. of Louis Armand II, prince of Conti or Conty, and Louise-Elisabeth de Bourbon Condé; m. Louis Philippe (1725–1785), 4th duke of Orléans (r. 1752–1785), Dec 17, 1743; children: daughter (born July 12, 1745; died Dec 14, 1745); Louis Philippe "Egalité" (1747–1793), 5th duke of Orléans (r. 1785–1793), Montpensier (r. 1747–1752), and Chartres (r. 1752–1785); Marie Louise d'Orleans (1750–1822), duchess of Bourbon. ❖ Louis Philippe's 2nd wife was the Marquise de Montesson (1737–1805).

LOUISA HENRIETTA OF ORANGE (1627–1667). Electress of Brandenburg. Name variations: Louise Orange-Nassau; Louise Henriette of Nassau-Orange; Louise Henriette of Orange; (Ger.) Luise Henriette. Born in 1627; died 1667; dau. of Frederick Henry, prince of Orange (r. 1625–1647), and Amelia of Solms (1602–1675); m. Frederick William (1620–1688), the Great Elector of Brandenburg (r. 1640–1688), on Dec 7, 1646; children: Frederick III (1657–1713), elector of Brandenburg (r. 1688–1701), later Frederick I, king of Prussia (r. 1701–1713).

LOUISA ISABEL (1709–1750). *See Louise Elizabeth.*

LOUISA JULIANA (1576–1644). Electress Palatine. Name variations: Louise-Juliana of Orange; Luise Juliane of Nassau. Born Mar 31, 1576; died Mar 15, 1644; dau. of William I the Silent (1533–1584), prince of Orange, and stadholder of Holland, Zealand, and Utrecht (r. 1572–1584), and Charlotte of Bourbon (d. 1582); m. Frederick IV the Upright (1574–1610), elector Palatine; children: Frederick V (1596–1632), king of Bohemia (The Winter King).

LOUISA OF HESSE-DARMSTADT (1751–1805). *See Frederica of Hesse.*

LOUISA OF PRUSSIA (1776–1810). *See Louise of Prussia.*

LOUISA ULRICA OF PRUSSIA (1720–1782). Queen of Sweden. Name variations: Luisa Ulrika. Born in Berlin, July 24, 1720; died July 16, 1782; dau. of Frederick William I (1688–1740), king of Prussia (r. 1713–1740), and Sophia Dorothea of Brunswick-Lüneburg-Hanover (1687–1757, dau. of George I of England); sister of Frederick II the Great, king of Prussia (r. 1740–1786); m. Adolphus Frederick (1710–1771), king of Sweden (r. 1751–1771), Aug 29, 1744; children: Gustavus III (1746–1792), king of Sweden (r. 1771–1792, who m. Sophia of Denmark); Charles XIII (1748–1818), king of Sweden (r. 1809–1818); Frederick Adolf (b. 1750); Albertine (1753–1829). ❖ A friend of Linnaeus, was an intelligent and commanding presence in the Swedish court; was a patron of art and science.

LOUISA WILHELMINA OF BAVARIA (1808–1892). *See Ludovica.*

LOUISE (1692–1712). English princess. Name variations: Louise Stuart. Born Louise Mary Theresa, June 18, 1692, in St. Germain-en-Laye, near Paris, France; died of smallpox, April 18, 1712, in St. Germain-en-Laye; dau. of Mary of Modena (1658–1718) and James II (1633–1701), king of England (r. 1685–1688, deposed).

LOUISE (1776–1810). *See Louise of Prussia.*

LOUISE (1808–1870). Prussian princess. Name variations: Louisa of Prussia; Louise Hohenzollern; Louise Augusta Hohenzollern. Born Louise Augusta Wilhelmina Amelia, Feb 1, 1808; died Dec 6, 1870; dau. of Louise of Prussia (1776–1810) and Frederick William III, king of Prussia (r. 1797–1849); m. Frederick Orange-Nassau (son of William I of the Netherlands); children: Louise of the Netherlands (1828–1871), who m. Charles XV, king of Sweden); Frederick William (1833–1834); William Frederick (1836–1846); Marie of Nassau (1841–1910, who m. William, 5th prince of Wied). ❖ See also *Women in World History.*

LOUISE (1848–1939). English princess, sculptor, and duchess of Argyll. Name variations: Princess Louise; Louise Saxe-Coburg. Born Louise Caroline Alberta, Mar 18, 1848, in Buckingham Palace, London, England; died Dec 3, 1939; 4th dau. and 6th child of Queen Victoria (1819–1901) and Prince Albert Saxe-Coburg; sister of King Edward VII of England; m. John Campbell, 9th duke of Argyll (governor-general of Canada and Marquis of Lorne), Mar 21, 1871 (annulled 1900); children: none. ❖ See also Elizabeth Longford, *Darling Loosy: Letters to Princess*

Louise, 1856–1939 (Weidenfeld & Nicolson); and *Women in World History.*

LOUISE, Queen of Denmark (1817–1898). *See Louise of Hesse-Cassel.*

LOUISE-ADELAIDE (1698–1743). Abbess of Chelles. Name variations: Marie-Adelaide d'Orleans. Born Aug 13, 1698; died Feb 19, 1743; dau. of Françoise-Marie de Bourbon (1677–1749) and Philip Bourbon-Orléans (1674–1723), 2nd duke of Orléans (r. 1701–1723); sister of Louise-Diana (1716–1736) and Louise Elizabeth (1709–1750), queen of Spain. ❖ Became abbess (1719).

LOUISE ADELAIDE DE BOURBON (1757–1824). Princesse de Condé. Name variations: Louise Adélaide de Bourbon; Princess of Conde. Born Louise Adélaide de Bourbon in Chantilly, France, Oct 5, 1757; died in Paris, Mar 10, 1824; dau. of Louis Joseph de Bourbon (1736–1818, French general). ❖ Became abbess of Remiremont (1786); emigrated when French Revolution broke out and her father fled to Turin; returned to Paris where her father became grand master of the King's Household (1815); subsequently founded the religious order of "l'adoration perpetuelle."

LOUISE AUGUSTA (1771–1843). Duchess of Schleswig-Holstein. Name variations: Louise Augusta Oldenburg. Born July 7, 1771; died Jan 13, 1843; legitimized dau. of Caroline Matilda (1751–1775) and Johann Struensee; m. Frederick Christian, duke of Schleswig-Holstein, on May 27, 1786; children: Caroline Amelia of Augustenburg (1796–1881); Christian Charles (b. 1798), duke of Schleswig-Holstein; Frederick Emile (b. 1800), prince of Nöer. ❖ See also *Women in World History.*

LOUISE BERNADOTTE (1851–1926). *See Louise of Sweden.*

LOUISE CAROLINE (1875–1906). Princess of Schaumburg-Lippe. Name variations: Louise Caroline Oldenburg. Born Louise Caroline Josephine, Feb 17, 1875; died April 4, 1906; dau. of Louise of Sweden (1851–1926) and Frederick VIII (1843–1912), king of Denmark (r. 1906–1912); m. Frederick, prince of Schaumburg-Lippe, on May 5, 1896; children: Marie Louise (1897–1938, princess of Schaumburg-Lippe, who m. Prince Frederick Sigismund Hohenzollern); Christian Nicholas (b. 1898); Stephanie (1899–1925, who m. Victor Adolf, 5th prince of Bentheim).

LOUISE CHARLOTTE OF MECKLENBURG-SCHWERIN (1779–1801). Duchess of Saxe-Gotha. Born Nov 19, 1779; died Jan 4, 1801; dau. of Louise of Saxe-Gotha (1756–1808) and Frederick Francis (1756–1837), duke of Mecklenburg-Schwerin (r. 1785–1837); m. August, duke of Saxe-Gotha, on Oct 21, 1797; children: Louise of Saxe-Gotha-Altenburg (1800–1831).

LOUISE DE BRÉZÉ (fl. 1555). Duchess of Aumale. Name variations: Louise de Breze. Fl. around 1555; m. Claude II of Lorraine, marquis of Mayenne and duke of Aumale (1526–1573); children: Charles, duke of Aumale (c. 1555–1621 or 1631).

LOUISE DE COLIGNY (1555–1620). *See Coligny, Louise de.*

LOUISE DE GUZMAN (1613–1666). *See Luisa de Guzman.*

LOUISE DE LA MISÉRICORDE, Soeur (1644–1710). *See La Vallière, Louise Françoise de.*

LOUISE DE MARILLAC (1591–1660). *See Marillac, Louise de.*

LOUISE DE MERCOEUR (1554–1601). *See Louise of Lorraine.*

LOUISE DE MONTMORENCY (fl. 1498–1525). French governess. Name variations: Madame de Chatillon or Châtillon. Fl. from 1498 to 1525; m. a former royal chamberlain; m. Gaspard I de Coligny, Maréchal de Châtillon (c. 1440–1522, marshal of France); children—3 sons, known as the Coligny brothers: Odet de Coligny (1517–1571); François de Coligny (1521–1569); Gaspard II de Coligny (1519–1572, an admiral and leader of the Huguenots and father of Louise de Coligny). ❖ Was governess of Margaret of Angoulême. ❖ See also *Women in World History.*

LOUISE DE SAVOIE (1476–1531). *See Louise of Savoy.*

LOUISE-DIANA (1716–1736). Princess of Conti. Name variations: Princess of Conty. Born June 28, 1716; died Sept 26, 1736; dau. of Françoise-Marie de Bourbon (1677–1749) and Philip Bourbon-Orléans (1674–1723), 2nd duke of Orléans (r. 1701–1723); sister of Louise-Adelaide (1698–1743) and Louise Elizabeth (1709–1750, queen of Spain); m. Louis Francis, prince of Conti, Jan 22, 1732.

LOUISE D'ORLÉANS (1812–1850). Queen of the Belgians. Name variations: Louise Bourbon; Louise of France; Louise of Orleans or Orléans; Louise-Marie d'Orleans; Louise Marie d'Orlans. Born Louise-Marie Bourbon-Penthievre, April 3, 1812, in Palermo, Sicily; died Oct 10 (some sources cite the 11th), 1850, in Ostende, Belgium; dau. of Louis Philippe I (1773–1850), citizen king of France (r. 1830–1850), and Maria Amalia (1782–1866); became 3rd wife of Leopold I, king of the Belgians (r. 1831–1865), Aug 9, 1832; children: Leopold (b. 1833); Leopold II (1835–1909), king of the Belgians (r. 1865–1909); Philip (1837–1905), count of Flanders; Carlota (1840–1927), empress of Mexico. ❖ See also *Women in World History.*

LOUISE DOROTHEA OF BRANDENBURG (1680–1705). Prussian princess. Born 1680; died 1705; dau. of Elizabeth Henrietta of Hesse-Cassel (1661–1683) and Frederick III (1657–1713), elector of Brandenburg (r. 1688–1701), later Frederick I, king of Prussia (r. 1701–1713); m. Frederick (1676–1751), landgrave of Hesse-Cassel (r. 1730–1751), who would later be Frederick I, king of Sweden (r. 1720–1751), upon his marriage to Ulrica Eleanora (1688–1741).

LOUISE-ELISABETH DE BOURBON CONDÉ (1693–1775). Princess of Conti. Name variations: Louise Elizabeth de Bourbon-Conde; Mlle de Charolais. Born Nov 22, 1693, in Versailles; died May 27, 1775 in Paris; dau. of Louis Henry de Bourbon (1668–1710), 7th prince of Condé, and Louise Françoise de Bourbon (1673–1743, legitimized dau. of Louis XIV and Madame de Montespan); granddau. of Louis XIV; m. Louis Armand de Bourbon-Conti (1695–1727), prince de Conti, 1713; children: Louis (1715–1717); Louis François I (1717–1776), prince de Conti; Louis Armand (1722–1722); Louisa Henrietta de Conti (1726–1759).

LOUISE ELIZABETH (1709–1750). Queen of Spain. Name variations: Louise Elizabeth Bourbon-Orléans; (Span.) Louisa Isabel. Born Dec 11, 1709; died June 16, 1750 (some sources cite 1742); dau. of Philippe Bourbon-Orléans (1674–1723), 2nd duke of Orléans (r. 1701–1723) and regent of France, and Françoise-Marie de Bourbon (1677–1749); m. Louis I (1707–1724), briefly king of Spain (r. 1724–1724), Aug 18, 1723.

LOUISE ELIZABETH (1727–1759). Duchess of Parma. Name variations: Elizabeth de France or Elizabeth of France; Marie Louise of France; Marie Louise of Parma; (Span.) Louisa Isabel. Born Aug 14, 1727; died Dec 6, 1759; dau. of Louis XV, king of France (r. 1715–1774), and Marie Leczinska (1703–1768); had twin sister Henriette (1727–1752); also sister of Louise Marie (1737–1787); Adelaide (1732–1800); Victoire (1733–1799), and Sophie (1734–1782); m. Philip de Bourbon (1720–1765), duke of Parma (r. 1748–1765, son of Elizabeth Farnese), Oct 25, 1739; children: Maria Luisa Teresa of Parma (1751–1819); Isabella of Parma (1741–1763); Ferdinand (b. 1751), duke of Parma.

LOUISE-HENRIETTE (1726–1759). *See Louisa Henrietta de Conti.*

LOUISE MARGARET OF PRUSSIA (1860–1917). Duchess of Connaught and duchess of Clarence. Name variations: Louise of Prussia. Born Louise Margaret Alexandra Victoria Agnes, June 25, 1860, in Potsdam, Brandenburg, Germany; died Mar 14, 1917, at Clarence House, St. James's Palace, London, England; m. Arthur Saxe-Coburg (1850–1942, son of Queen Victoria), duke of Connaught, Mar 13, 1879; children: Margaret of Connaught (1882–1920, who m. Gustavus VI, king of Sweden); Arthur Windsor (1883–1938); Lady Patricia Ramsay (1886–1974).

LOUISE MARIE (1737–1787). French princess. Born 1737; died 1787; youngest dau. of Louis XV (1710–1774), king of France (r. 1715–1774), and Marie Leczinska (1703–1768); sister of Louise Elizabeth (1727–1759), Henriette (1727–1752), Adelaide (1732–1800), Victoire (1733–1799), and Sophie (1734–1782). ❖ Became a Carmelite nun.

LOUISE MARIE (1752–1824). *See Louise of Stolberg-Gedern.*

LOUISE-MARIE BOURBON-PENTHIEVRE (1812–1850). *See Louise d'Orleans.*

LOUISE MARIE DE GONZAGUE (1611–1667). Queen of Poland. Name variations: Louise Marie e Gonzague; Louise Marie Gonzaga; Marie-Louise Gonzaga or Gonzague; Marie Louise Gonzague-Cleves or Clèves; Marie de Gonzaga; Princess of Nevers. Born Aug 18, 1611; died May 10, 1667; dau. of Charles I, duke of Mantua; m. Wladyslaw also known as Ladislas IV (1595–1648), king of Poland (r. 1632–1648), king of Sweden (r. 1632–1648), tsar of Russia (r. 1610–1634), on Mar 10, 1646; m. his half-brother John II Casimir (1609–1672), also known as

Casimir V, king of Poland (r. 1648–1668), on May 29, 1649; children: (2nd m.) Marie Theresa (1650–1651); and a son (b. 1652). ❖ Became queen of Poland on marriage to Ladislas IV (1646); following his death (1648), married his half-brother and successor John II Casimir; had enormous influence over 2nd husband; convinced him to name his successor in order to avoid the vote of the *Sejm* after his death, but the plan backfired. ❖ See also *Women in World History*.

LOUISE MARIE OF BOURBON (1753–1821). Duchess of Orleans, Montpensier, and Chartres. Name variations: Louise Marie Adelaide de Bourbon-Penthièvre; Louise-Adelaide de Penthièvre or Penthievre; duchesse d'Orléans; Madame d'Orleans. Born Louise Marie Adelaide de Bourbon Penthievre, Mar 13, 1753; died June 23, 1821; buried in Dreaux, France; dau. of Johann, duke of Penthièvre; m. Louis Philippe "Egalité" (1747–1793), 5th duke of Orléans (r. 1785–1793), Montpensier (r. 1747–1752), and Chartres (r. 1752–1785), April 5, 1769 (div. 1792); children: daughter who died at birth (1771–1771); Louis Philippe I (1773–1850), king of France (r. 1830–1848); Anton Philip (1775–1807); Adelaide (1777–1847); Louis Charles (1779–1808).

LOUISE MOUNTBATTEN (1889–1965). Queen of Sweden. Name variations: Queen Louise. Born Louise Alexandra Mary Irene, July 13, 1889, in Jugenheim, near Darmstadt, Hesse, Germany; died Mar 7, 1965, in Stockholm, Sweden; dau. of Louis of Battenberg, 1st marquess of Milford Haven, and Victoria of Hesse-Darmstadt (1863–1950); became 2nd wife of Gustavus VI Adolphus (1882–1973), king of Sweden (r. 1950–1973), Nov 3, 1923; children: 1 daughter died in infancy. ❖ Gustavus' 1st wife was Margaret of Connaught.

LOUISE OF BADEN (1779–1826). *See Elizabeth of Baden.*

LOUISE OF BADEN (1811–1854). Princess of Baden. Born Louise Amelia Stephanie, June 5, 1811; died July 19, 1854; dau. of Karl Ludwig also known as Charles Ludwig, grand duke of Baden, and Stephanie de Beauharnais (1789–1860); m. Gustavus of Sweden, prince of Vasa, on Nov 9, 1830 (div. 1844); children: Caroline of Saxony (1833–1907); and a son born in 1832.

LOUISE OF BADEN (1838–1923). Grand duchess of Baden. Name variations: Louise Hohenzollern. Born Louise Mary Elizabeth, Dec 3, 1838; died April 23, 1923; dau. of William I also known as Wilhelm I (1797–1888), kaiser or king of Prussia (r. 1861–1871), emperor of Germany (r. 1871–1888), and Augusta of Saxe-Weimar (1811–1890); m. Frederick I, grand duke of Baden, Sept 20, 1856; children: 3, including Victoria of Baden (1862–1930), who m. Gustavus V, king of Sweden), and Frederick II, grand duke of Baden (b. 1857).

LOUISE OF BELGIUM (1858–1924). Belgian princess. Name variations: Louise of Saxe-Coburg-Gotha. Born Feb 18, 1858; died Mar 1, 1924; dau. of Leopold II, king of Belgium (r. 1865–1909), and Maria Henrietta of Austria (1836–1902); m. Prince Philip of Saxe-Coburg-Gotha, Feb 4, 1875 (div. 1906); children: Leopold of Saxe-Coburg-Gotha (b. 1878); Dorothy of Saxe-Coburg-Gotha (b. 1881), princess of Saxe-Coburg-Gotha.

LOUISE OF BOURBON-BERRY (1819–1864). Duchess and regent of Parma and Piacenza. Name variations: Louise du Berry; Louise Marie Thérèse d'Artois; Louise of Artois; Luise-Marie. Born Sept 21, 1819; died Feb 1, 1864; dau. of Caroline of Naples (1798–1870) and Charles Ferdinand (1778–1820), duke of Berry (2nd son of Charles X, king of France); sister of Henry V (1820–1883), duke of Bordeaux and count of Chambord; m. Charles III (1823–1854), duke of Parma (1849–1854), on Nov 10, 1845; children: Margaret of Parma (1847–1893); Robert (b. 1848), duke of Bourbon-Parma; Alicia of Parma (1849–1935); Henry (b. 1851), count of Bardi.

LOUISE OF BRUNSWICK-WOLFENBUTTEL (1722–1780). Mother of the king of Prussia. Name variations: Louisa Amalia; Louise Amelia of Brunswick. Born 1722; died Jan 13, 1780; dau. of Antoinetta Amelia (1696–1762) and Ferdinand Albert II, duke of Brunswick-Wolfenbuttel; m. Augustus William (1722–1758, brother of Frederick II the Great, king of Prussia), Jan 6, 1742; children: Frederick William II (1744–1797), king of Prussia (r. 1786–1797); Frederick Henry (1747–1767); Wilhelmina of Prussia (1751–1820); George Charles (1758–1759).

LOUISE OF DENMARK (1750–1831). Duchess of Hesse-Cassel. Name variations: Louise Oldenburg. Born Jan 30, 1750; died Jan 12, 1831; dau. of Frederick V, king of Denmark and Norway, and Louise of England (1724–1751); m. Charles of Hesse-Cassel, regent of Schleswig-Holstein, Aug 30, 1766; children: Marie Sophie of Hesse-Cassel (1767–1852, who m. Frederick VI, king of Denmark); Frederick (b. 1771), governor of Rendesburg; Julie Louise Amelia (1773–1861), abbess of Itzehoe; Christian (b. 1776); Louise of Hesse-Cassel (1789–1867, mother of Christian IX, king of Denmark).

LOUISE OF ENGLAND (1724–1751). Queen of Denmark and Norway. Name variations: Louisa or Louise Guelph; Louisa Hanover. Born Dec 7, 1724, at Leicester House, St. Martin's, London, England; died, age 27, Dec 8, 1751, at Christiansborg Castle, Copenhagen, Denmark; dau. of George II (1683–1760), king of Great Britain and Ireland (r. 1727–1760), and Caroline of Ansbach (1683–1737); became 1st wife of Frederick V, king of Denmark and Norway (r. 1746–1766), Dec 11, 1743, in Altona, Hamburg, Germany; children: Christian VII (b. 1749), king of Denmark and Norway (r. 1766–1808, who m. Caroline Matilda [1751–1775]); Louise of Denmark (1750–1831); Sophia of Denmark (1746–1813, who m. Gustavus III of Sweden); Wilhelmine (1747–1820); and one other. ❖ Following her death, Frederick V married Maria Juliana of Brunswick (1729–1796).

LOUISE OF HESSE-CASSEL (1688–1765). Mother of the prince of Orange. Name variations: Louise of Orange-Nassau. Born Mary Louise, Feb 7, 1688; died April 9, 1765; m. John William Friso of Orange-Nassau (1686–1711), in 1709; children: Anna Charlotte Amalia of Orange (1710–1777, who m. Friedrich of Baden-Durlach); William IV, prince of Orange (1711–1751), stadholder of United Provinces (r. 1748–1751).

LOUISE OF HESSE-CASSEL (1789–1867). Duchess of Schleswig-Holstein-Sonderburg-Glucksberg. Name variations: Princess Louise Caroline von Hessen-Cassel. Born Louise Charlotte in Gottorp, Schleswig, Germany, Sept 28, 1789; died in Ballenstedt, Mar 13, 1867; dau. of Charles of Hesse-Cassel, regent of Schleswig-Holstein, and Louise of Denmark (1750–1831); m. Frederick William, duke of Schleswig-Holstein-Sonderburg-Glucksberg, Jan 26, 1810; children: Frederick, duke of Schleswig-Holstein-Sonderburg-Glucksberg; Christian IX (1818–1906), king of Denmark (r. 1863–1906).

LOUISE OF HESSE-CASSEL (1817–1898). Queen of Denmark. Born Louise Wilhelmina, Sept 7, 1817, in Cassel; died Sept 29, 1898, in Bernstorff; dau. of William, landgrave of Hesse-Cassel, and Charlotte Oldenburg (1789–1864); m. Christian IX (1818–1906), king of Denmark (r. 1863–1906), May 26, 1842; children: Frederick VIII (1843–1912), king of Denmark (r. 1906–1912); Alexandra of Denmark (1844–1925); Dagmar (1847–1928, also known as Marie Feodorovna); Waldemar (b. 1858); Thyra Oldenburg (1853–1933); William of Denmark, who was elected king of Hellenes as George I (r. 1863–1913). ❖ See also *Women in World History*.

LOUISE OF HESSE-DARMSTADT (d. 1830). Duchess of Saxe-Weimar. Died 1830; dau. of Louis IX, landgrave of Hesse-Darmstadt; m. Charles Augustus (b. 1757), duke of Saxe-Weimar and Eis, on Oct 3, 1775; children: Louise Augusta Amelia of Saxe-Weimer (1779–1784); Charles Frederick, grand duke of Saxe-Weimar (b. 1783); Caroline Louise of Saxe-Weimar (1786–1816); Charles Bernard of Saxe-Weimar (b. 1792).

LOUISE OF HOHENLOHE-LANGENBURG (1763–1837). Duchess of Saxe-Meiningen. Born Louise Eleanor, Aug 11, 1763; died April 30, 1837; dau. of Prince Christian; m. George I, duke of Saxe-Meiningen, Nov 27, 1782; children: 4, including Adelaide of Saxe-Meiningen (1792–1849); Ida of Saxe-Coburg-Meiningen (1794–1852); Bernard II, duke of Saxe-Meiningen (b. 1800).

LOUISE OF LORRAINE (1554–1601). Queen of France. Name variations: Louise de Lorraine; Louise de Mercoeur; Louise de Vaudemont; Louise of Vaudemont; the White Lady of Chenonceau. Born in 1554 (some sources cite 1553); died in 1601; dau. of Nicolas de Mercoeur also known as Nicolas of Lorraine, count of Vaudemont, and Marguerite d'Egmont; sister of Marguerite of Lorraine (c. 1561–?) and Philippe-Emmanuel, duc de Mercoeur; m. Henry III (1551–1589), king of France (r. 1574–1589), Feb 15, 1575; daughter-in-law of Catherine de Medici (1519–1589); no children. ❖ Because her mother died when she was one, was brought up by father's 2nd wife, Jeanne de Savoie-Nemours; caught the eye of heir to the French throne, Henry of Valois (1573); wed Henry (III), though many of his advisors and his mother Catherine de Medici opposed the union; was pushed to the background by her powerful mother-in-law; childless, was denied her rightful place: was neither a queen, nor a wife, nor a mother of royal heirs; tolerated her awkward situation with considerable grace; devoutly Catholic, visited hospitals, cared for the sick, patronized charitable foundations, and spent much of her time in prayer; following assassination of husband (1589), spent remaining 11 years of her life traveling between convents and residing with relatives across France, continuing her charitable activities. ❖ See also *Women in World History*.

LOUISE OF MECKLENBURG-GUSTROW (1667–1721). Queen of Denmark and Norway. Name variations: Louise of Mecklenburg-Güstrow. Born Aug 28, 1667; died Mar 15, 1721; dau. of Magdalena Sybilla of Holstein-Gottorp (1631–1719) and Gustav Adolf, duke of Mecklenburg-Gustrow; m. Frederick IV (1671–1730), king of Denmark and Norway (r. 1699–1730), on Dec 5, 1695; children: Christian (b. 1697); Christian VI (1699–1746), king of Denmark and Norway (r. 1730–1746), who m. Sophia of Bayreuth; Frederick Charles (b. 1701); George (b. 1703); Charlotte Amalie (1706–1782). ❖ Frederick IV had 3 wives: Louise of Mecklenburg-Gustrow, Elizabeth Helene Vieregg, and Anne Sophie Reventlow.

LOUISE OF MECKLENBURG-STRELITZ (1776–1810). *See Louise of Prussia.*

LOUISE OF ORANGE-NASSAU.
See Louise of Hesse-Cassel (1688–1765).
See Louise of the Netherlands (1828–1871).

LOUISE OF ORLEANS (1812–1850). *See Louise d'Orléans.*

LOUISE OF ORLEANS (1882–1952). Princess of Orléans. Name variations: Louise de Orléans. Born Feb 24, 1882; died in 1952; dau. of Maria Isabella (1848–1919) and Louis Philippe (1838–1894), count of Paris; m. Carlos, prince of Bourbon-Sicily, also known as Charles (1870–1949), prince of the Two Sicilies, on Nov 16, 1907; children: Karl (b. 1908); Dolores of Bourbon-Sicily (b. 1909); Maria de las Mercedes (b. 1910); Maria de la Esperanza (b. 1914), princess of the Two Sicilies (who m. Pedro de Alcantra, prince of Grao Para, and was the mother of Maria da Gloria, [1946—]).

LOUISE OF PARMA (1802–1857). Duchess of Savoy. Name variations: Luisa. Born Oct 2, 1802; died Mar 18, 1857; dau. of Maria Luisa of Etruria (1782–1824) and Louis de Bourbon, also known as Louis I (1773–1803), duke of Parma (r. 1801–1803); became 2nd wife of Maximilian (1759–1838), duke of Saxony (r. 1830–1838), on Nov 7, 1825; m. Franz, count of Rossi; m. Johann von Vimercati, on Feb 19, 1855. Maximilian's 1st wife was Caroline of Parma (1770–1804).

LOUISE OF PRUSSIA (1776–1810). Queen of Prussia. Name variations: Louise of Mecklenburg-Strelitz; Louisa, Luise von Preussen. Born Princess Luise Auguste Wilhelmine Amalie von Mecklenburg-Strelitz, Mar 10, 1776, in Hanover, Lower Saxony, Germany; died July 19, 1810, in Hohenzieritz (duchy of Mecklenburg, Germany); buried in Charlottenburg, Berlin, Germany; dau. of Charles II Louis Frederick, hereditary prince (later duke) of Mecklenburg-Strelitz (1741–1816), and Frederica of Hesse-Darmstadt (1752–1782), dau. of Landgrave George of Hesse-Darmstadt); her stepmother was Princess Charlotte of Hesse-Darmstadt (1755–1785); sister of Frederica of Mecklenburg-Strelitz (1778–1841); educated at home by a Swiss governess at maternal grandmother's court in Darmstadt; m. the Prussian crown prince, the future Frederick William III (1770–1840), king of Prussia (r. 1797–1840), Dec 24, 1793; children: Frederick William IV (1795–1861), king of Prussia (r. 1840–1861), who m. Elizabeth of Bavaria [1801–1873]); William I also known as Wilhelm I (1797–1888), the future kaiser or emperor of Germany (r. 1871–1888, who m. Augusta of Saxe-Weimar); Frederica (1799–1800); Charlotte of Prussia (1798–1860, who m. Nicholas I, tsar of Russia); Charles (1801–1883, who m. Marie of Saxe-Weimar-Eisenach); Alexandrine of Prussia (1803–1892); Ferdinand (1804–1806); Louise (1808–1870); Albert (1809–1872, who m. Marianne of the Netherlands); and one other who died in infancy. Frederick William III's 2nd wife was Auguste von Harrach, princess of Leignitz (1800–1873). ❖ Was queen of Prussia during a time of profound crisis brought on by Napoleonic expansionism; emerged as a much-revered icon of patriotism, national unity, and steadfastness in adversity; became queen (1797), when husband succeeded to the throne at death of his father, King Frederick William II; best known for her dramatic meeting with Napoleon at Tilsit (1807), where she naively attempted to gain milder terms for her country, which had suffered a crushing defeat at the hands of the French; immortalized in traditional German historiography as the royal paradigm of virtuous, devoted, and patriotic Prussian motherhood. ❖ See also Constance Wright, *Louise, Queen of Prussia* (Frederick

Muller, 1969); Gertrude Kuntze-Dolton Aretz, *Queen Louise of Prussia, 1776–1810* (trans. from German by Ruth Putman, Putnam, 1929); and *Women in World History*.

LOUISE OF SAVOY (1476–1531). Duchess of Angoulême and regent. Name variations: Louise de Savoie. Regent of France (1515–1516, 1525–1526); born Sept 11, 1476, in the Châteaux de Pont-d'Ain in Savoy, now southwest France; died Sept 22, 1531, at Grez-sur-Loing, south of Fontainebleau, France; dau. of Philip II, count of Bresse, later duke of Savoy (d. 1497) and Margaret of Bourbon (d. 1483); niece of Anne of Beaujeu (c. 1460–1522); m. Charles of Orleans (1460–1496), count of Angoulême, Feb 16, 1488, in the Châtelet at Paris; children: Margaret of Angoulême (1492–1549), queen of Navarre (r. 1527–1549); Francis I (1494–1547), king of France (r. 1515–1547). ❖ A major player on the diplomatic stage of the early 16th century, was mother of King Francis I, who had such confidence in her ability and loyalty as to leave his country in her hands while he sought to increase his position and power by fighting in Italy; as regent (June 1515–Jan 1516, Feb 1525–July 1526), gained and retained the confidence of many of the prominent men in France; negotiated, with Margaret of Austria, the Peace of Cambrai, known as the "Ladies Peace" (1529); after the king's return to France, continued to serve as his chief adviser until her death (1531); throughout her life, sought to solve disputes by peaceful means, preferring to compromise and negotiate rather than resort to arms and the weapons of war. ❖ See also D.M. Mayer, *The Great Regent Louise of Savoy 1476–1531* (1966); and *Women in World History*.

LOUISE OF SAXE-GOTHA (1756–1808). Duchess of Mecklenburg-Schwerin. Born Mar 9, 1756; died Jan 1, 1808; dau. of John August of Saxe-Gotha, and Louise Ruess of Schleiz; m. Frederick Francis (1756–1837), duke of Mecklenburg-Schwerin (r. 1785–1837); children: Frederick Louis (b. 1778); Louise Charlotte of Mecklenburg-Schwerin (1779–1801); Charlotte Frederica of Mecklenburg-Schwerin (1784–1840).

LOUISE OF SAXE-GOTHA-ALTENBURG (1800–1831). Duchess of Saxe-Coburg-Gotha. Born Dorothea Louise Pauline Charlotte Fredericka Augusta, Dec 21, 1800, in Gotha, Thuringia, Germany; died Aug 30, 1831, in Paris, France; dau. of Louise Charlotte of Mecklenburg-Schwerin (1779–1801) and August, duke of Saxe-Gotha; m. Ernest I (1784–1844), duke of Saxe-Coburg and Gotha, July 31, 1817 (div. 1826); children: Ernest II, duke of Saxe-Coburg and Gotha (1818–1893); Prince Albert Saxe-Coburg (1819–1861, who m. Queen Victoria). ❖ One year after her death, Ernest I married Mary of Wurttemberg (1799–1860).

LOUISE OF SAXE-HILBURGHAUSEN (1726–1756). Danish princess. Name variations: Louise Oldenburg. Born Oct 19, 1726; died Aug 8, 1756; dau. of Sophia of Bayreuth (1700–1770) and Christian VI, king of Denmark and Norway (r. 1730–1746); m. Ernest Frederick III, duke of Saxe-Hilburghausen.

LOUISE OF SPAIN (1832–1897). *See Luisa Fernanda.*

LOUISE OF STOLBERG-GEDERN (1752–1824). Countess of Albany and princess of Stolberg-Gedern. Name variations: Louise Marie; Louise Maximilienne of Stolbergg-Gedern; Louisa of Stolberg; Louisa Stewart or Stuart; Louisa Maximilienne Caroline, Countess of Albany. Born Louise Maximiliana Caroline Emmanuele, Sept 20, 1752, at Mons, Hainault, Flanders (Belgium); died Jan 29, 1824, in Florence, Italy; dau. of Gustavus Adolphus, prince of Stolberg-Gedern, and Elizabeth Philippine Claudine (dau. of Maximilian Emanuel, prince of Hornes); m. Charles Edward Stuart (d. 1788), also known as Bonnie Prince Charlie, the Young Pretender, or Charles III, April 17, 1772; possibly m. Vittorio (d. 1803), count Alfieri (poet), 1789; possibly m. Francis Xavier Fabre. ❖ Wife of the last of the Stuarts, Bonnie Prince Charlie, was also celebrated for her association with the Italian poet Alfieri. ❖ See also *Women in World History*.

LOUISE OF SWEDEN (1851–1926). Queen of Denmark. Name variations: Louisa of Sweden; Louise Bernadotte; Louise Josephine Eugenie Bernadotte. Born Oct 31, 1851, in Stockholm, Sweden; died Mar 20, 1926, in Amalienborg; dau. of Louise of the Netherlands (1828–1878) and Charles XV (1826–1872), king of Sweden and Norway (r. 1859–1872); m. Frederick VIII (1843–1912), duke of Schleswig-Holstein-Sonderburg-Augustenburg, king of Denmark (r. 1906–1912); children: Christian X (1870–1947), king of Denmark (r. 1912–1947); Charles or Carl (1872–1957), became Haakon VII, king of Norway (r. 1905–1957); Louise Caroline (1875–1906); Harald

(b. 1876); Ingeborg of Denmark (1878–1958); Thyra of Denmark (1880–1945); Dagmar Louise Elizabeth (1890–1961, who m. Jörgen de Castenskiold, chamberlain at court).

LOUISE OF THE NETHERLANDS (1828–1871). Queen of Sweden.
Name variations: Louise of Orange-Nassau; Lovisa; Louise of Nassau or Louise von Nassau. Born Aug 5, 1828, at The Hague, Netherlands; died Mar 30, 1871, in Stockholm, Sweden; dau. of Frederick Orange-Nassau (1797–1881, son of William I of the Netherlands) and Louise (1808–1870, dau. of Louise of Prussia); m. Karl XV also known as Charles XV (1826–1872), king of Sweden (r. 1859–1872), on June 19, 1850; children: Louise of Sweden (1851–1926); Charles Oscar (b. 1852).

LOUISE OF TUSCANY (1870–1947). *See Toselli, Louisa.*

LOUISE OF VAUDEMONT (1554–1601). *See Louise of Lorraine.*

LOUISE VICTORIA (1867–1931). Princess Royal and duchess of Fife.
Name variations: Louise Victoria Alexandra Dagmar. Born Louise Victoria Alexandra Dagmar Saxe-Coburg, Feb 20, 1867, in London, England; died Jan 4, 1931, in London; dau. of Edward VII, king of England (r. 1901–1910), and Alexandra of Denmark (1844–1925); m. Alexander Duff, 1st duke of Fife, in 1889; children: 3, including Alexandra Victoria (1891–1959, Princess Arthur of Connaught) and Maud Duff Carnegie.

LOUISE, Anita (1915–1970). American actress. Name variations: Anita Fremault. Born Anita Louise Fremault, Jan 9, 1915, in New York, NY; died April 25, 1970, in Los Angeles, CA; m. Buddy Adler (producer), 1940 (died 1960); m. Henry Berger (importer), 1962. ❖ At 6, appeared with Walter Hampden on Broadway in *Peter Ibbetson;* at 7, made screen debut (1922), followed by 6 movies, all billed as Anita Fremault (1922–29); as Anita Louise, appeared in over 70 films, including *Madame Du Barry* (as Marie Antoinette), *A Midsummer Night's Dream* (as Titania), *The Story of Louis Pasteur, Anthony Adverse, Tovarich, The Little Princess, Wagons Westward, Harmon of Michigan, Casanova Brown, Love Letters* and *Retreat Hell!;* starred in tv series "My Friend Flicka" (1956–57).

LOUISE, Augusta (1906–1984). *See Gaynor, Janet.*

LOUISE, Ruth Harriet (1906–1944). American photographer. Born Ruth Harriet Louise Sandrich in Brooklyn, NY, in 1906; died in 1944; m. Leigh Jason (film director), in 1930. ❖ Was the 1st woman to manage her own portrait gallery at MGM; photographed such notables as Greta Garbo, Lon Chaney, Marion Davies, Joan Crawford, Ramon Novarro and Anna May Wong. ❖ See also *Women in World History.*

LOUISE, Tina (1934—). American actress. Born Tina Blacker, Feb 11, 1934, in New York, NY; m. Les Crane (radio-tv personality), 1966 (div. 1970). ❖ Began career as model and nightclub singer; came to prominence on Broadway in *Li'l Abner;* made film debut in *God's Little Acre* (1958), followed by *The Hangman, The Warrior Empress, Armored Command, For Those Who Think Young, The Wrecking Crew, Stepford Wives* and *Johnny Suede,* among others; probably best remembered as Ginger on tv series "Gilligan's Island."

LOUIZE. *Variant of Louise.*

LOURENCO, Teresa (fl. 1358). *See Lorenzo, Teresa.*

LOUW, Anna M. (1913–2003). South African novelist, playwright and short-story writer. Born Dec 31, 1913, in Calvinia, Western Cape, South Africa; died June 12, 2003, in Cape Town; m. L.A. Hurst; m. Gerhard Bassel (died 1990); children: 5. ❖ First stories appeared in *Die Huisgenoot* magazine; works, which often focus on relationships in Afrikaner families, include *Goud* (1948), *Agter My 'n Albatros* (1959), *20 Days that Autumn* (1963), *Die Lyfwag* (1964), *'n Geseënde Dag* (1969), *Kroniek van Perdepoort* (1975), *Die Derde Tempel* (1978), *Op die Rug van die Tier* (1981), *Die Loop Van die Rivier* (1986), *Die Donker Kind* (1996), and *Vos* (1999). Won Hertzog Prize, W.A. Hofmeyr Prize for *Kroniek van Perdepoort,* Scheepers Prize, and Olive Schreiner Prize.

LOUYSE. *Variant of Louise.*

LOVE, Barbara (1941—). African-American vocalist. Name variations: The Friends of Distinction. Born July 24, 1941, in Los Angeles, CA; dau. of Reuben Brown (disc jockey). ❖ Joined Harry Elston, Floyd Butler and Jessica Cleaves to form The Friends of Distinction (1967), black vocal group which released such hits as "Grazin' in the Grass" (1969), "Going in Circles" (1969), and "Love or Let Me Be Lonely" (1970); left the group (1970) and was briefly replaced by Charlene Gibson. Albums

with Friends of Distinction include *Grazin'* (1969) and *Highly Distinct* (1969).

LOVE, Bessie (1898–1986). American actress. Born Juanita Horton on Sept 10, 1898, in Midland, TX; died in 1986; dau. of John Cross Horton and Emma Jane (Savage) Horton; attended school in Los Angeles, CA; m. William Ballinger Hawks (director), 1929 (div. 1935); children: Patricia Hawks. ❖ Began appearing in silent films while still in high school; was featured as Bride of Cana in Judean episode of Griffith's *Intolerance* (1916) and also played opposite Douglas Fairbanks in several films, including *Reggie Mixes In* (1916); graduating to leads, made a series of light films, including *The King of Main Street* (1925) in which she introduced the Charleston; had breakthrough in MGM's 1st sound musical *The Broadway Melody* (1929), for which she was nominated for Oscar as Best Actress; was one of the few silent actresses to make smooth transition to talking pictures; made NY stage debut at the Palace (1931); moved to London (1935); following WWII, made London stage debut as Julie in *Say It with Flowers* (1945), then appeared in minor roles in *Born Yesterday* (1947), *Death of a Salesman* (1949), *The Children's Hour* (1956), *The Glass Menagerie* (1966) and *The Homecoming* (1958), which she also wrote; scored a hit as Aunt Pittypat in London stage production of *Gone With the Wind* (1972); was also seen on tv, playing mostly character roles; later films included *Isadora* (1969) and *Sunday Bloody Sunday* (1971). ❖ See also autobiography, *From Hollywood with Love* (1977); and *Women in World History.*

LOVE, Darlene (1938—). American pop and R&B singer. Name variations: The Blossoms. Born Darlene Wright, July 26, 1938, in Los Angeles, California; dau. of Joe Wright (Pentecostal minister) and Ellen Wright; sister of Edna Wright (singer); m. Alton Allison, 1984; children: 3 sons, 1 daughter. ❖ Recorded with Gloria Jones, Fanita Barrett and Nanette Williams as The Blossoms (1958–60) without success; known as the overqualified back-up singer to major stars, worked extensively for Sam Cooke, Sonny and Cher, and others; though not a member of the Crystals, sang lead vocal on hit single "He's a Rebel," which was credited to the Crystals; went on to record 6 singles under own name for Phil Spector, including "Wait Til My Bobby Gets Home" (1963), "(Today I Met) The Boy I'm Going To Marry" (1963) and "A Fine Fine Boy" (1963); sang lead vocals for Bob B. Soxx and the Blue Jeans, recording some of greatest hits of 60s, including "Zip-a-Dee-Doo-Dah" and "He's Sure the Boy I Love" (both 1963); signed with Blossoms for Reprise and recorded "Good Good Lovin'" (1967), among others, and also sang back-up for Sinatra on such hits as "That's Life" (1967); continued to sing with The Blossoms on *Shindig* and on tour with Elvis Presley (1968–69); pursued solo career (early 1970s), and released albums *Darlene Love* (1981), *Live* (1984), and *Paint Another Picture* (1988); sang back-up for Dionne Warwick (1971–81) and later for Aretha Franklin; appeared in "Lethal Weapon" films as Danny Glover's wife and in Tony-nominated Broadway musical *Leader of the Pack* (1985), as well as off-Broadway musical *Nunsense* (2003–04); won Rhythm and Blues Foundation's Pioneer Award (1995) and a lawsuit against Phil Spector for back royalties (1997); released gospel CD *Unconditional Love* (1998). ❖ See also autobiography (with Rob Hoerburger), *My Name is Love* (Morrow, 1998).

LOVE, Mabel (1874–1953). English actress and musical-hall star. Born Mabel Watson, Oct 16, 1874, in England; died May 15, 1953, in Weybridge, Surrey, England; dau. of Kate Love and Lewis Grant Watson; granddau. of William Edward Love (entertainer). ❖ Made stage debut at Prince of Wales as the Rose in *Alice in Wonderland* (1886), followed by *Masks and Faces* (with Kate Vaughan); came to prominence as La Frivolini in *La Cigale* (1890), then appeared as prima ballerina at Covent Garden in *The Light of Asia* and *Orfeo;* other plays and pantomimes include *Little Red Riding Hood, The Magic Ring, Little Christopher Columbus, The Babes in the Wood, Lord Tom Noddy, Miss Cinderella* (title role), and *The Musketeers* (as Constance with Beerbohm Tree); had highly successful NY debut in *His Excellency* (1895); on returning to England, starred in *Bluebell in Fairyland, The Freedom of Suzanne, Lady Frederick* and *A Woman's Way;* appeared in music halls and later taught dance and elocution.

LOVE, Mary Fenn (1824–1886). *See Davis, Mary Fenn.*

LOVE, Nancy (1914–1976). American aviator and military leader. Born Nancy Harkness, Feb 14, 1914, in Houghton, Michigan; died Oct 22, 1976, on Martha's Vineyard, Massachusetts; attended Vassar; m. Robert Maclure Love (pilot). ❖ At 16, learned to fly; awarded pilot's license one month after 1st flight; at 19, received transport rating (1933); worked with husband as a Beechcraft distributor; served as a test pilot for the Gwinn Air Car Co. (1937–38); at onset of WWII, joined 32 male pilots to ferry American planes to Canada for shipment to France; proposed and became director of the Women's Auxiliary Ferry Squadron (WAFS, 1942). ❖ See also *Women in World History.*

LOVE, Ripeka Wharawhara (1882–1953). New Zealand tribal leader. Name variations: Ripeka Matene (Rebecca Martin). Born on June 28, 1882, at Kapiti Island, New Zealand; died on April 6, 1953, at Lower Hutt, New Zealand; dau. of Paati Matene (farmer) and Anihaka Park; m. Wi Hapi Love (farmer), 1897; children: 10. ❖ Her arranged marriage united Te Ati Awa families (1897); provided medical care for her people and advised mothers on maternity and domestic issues; during WWI, active in war and welfare work; became member of welfare organization, Nga Pani o Te Whanganui-a-Tara (orphans of Wellington, late 1920s); established meeting house (1933); elected patroness of Wellington District Council of Maori Women's Welfare League (1951). Made Order of British Empire (OBE, 1919). ❖ See also *Dictionary of New Zealand Biography* (Vol. 3).

LOVE, Susan (1948—). American physician and breast cancer researcher. Name variations: Susan M. Love. Born Feb 9, 1948, in Little Silver, NJ; children: 1. ❖ Noted breast cancer surgeon, began private practice (1980); became director of breast clinic at Beth Israel Hospital (1982), the 1st on-staff female general surgeon; was surgical oncologist at Dana Farber Cancer Institute; co-founded Faulkner Breast Center in Boston (1988); taught at Harvard Medical School as assistant professor of surgery; considered standard cancer treatment inadequate; co-founded the National Breast Cancer Coalition (1990), which increased research funds from $90 million (1990) to over $420 million (1994); served as director of Revlon–UCLA Breast Center (1992) until retirement from surgery (1996); taught at UCLA School of Medicine as adjunct professor (1996) and worked at Santa Barbara Breast Cancer Institute as medical director; writings include *Dr. Susan Love's Breast Book* (1990) and *Dr. Susan Love's Hormone Book: Making Informed Choices about Menopause* (1997).

LØVEID, Cecilie (1951—). Norwegian writer. Name variations: Løveid or Loeveid. Born 1951 in Norway; raised in Bergen; studied at art college. ❖ Internationally recognized poet, novelist and playwright, published poetic novel *Most* (1972); wrote *Alltid Skyer Over Askoy* (Always Clouds Over Askoy, 1976), *Sug* (Sea Swell, 1979), and the Prix Italia-winning radio drama, *Seagull Eaters* (1982); received acclaim for *Osterrike* (Austria, 1998), a play based on Ibsen's dramatic poem *Brand* (1866) which was performed as part of Ibsen Festival at National Theater in Oslo (1998).

LOVEJOY, Esther Pohl (1869–1967). American physician, administrator, feminist, and author. Born Esther Clayson on Nov 16, 1869, in a logging camp near Seabeck, Washington Territory; died Aug 17, 1967, in New York, NY; dau. of Edward Clayson and Annie (Quinton) Clayson; Medical School of the University of Oregon, MD, 1894 (the university's 2nd woman graduate and the 1st to take up the practice of medicine); attended West Side Post-graduate School, Chicago, IL; m. Emil Pohl (surgeon), 1894 (died 1911); m. George A. Lovejoy (businessman), 1913 (div. 1920); children: Frederick Clayson Pohl (1901–1908). ❖ With 1st husband, opened a practice in Portland (1895), then moved to Skagway, Alaska; as the 1st doctors in the area, worked out of a log cabin and visited patients by dog sled; returned to Portland (1899); was also active in woman suffrage movement, combining political activism with her medical practice; during WWI, as a member of the American Medical Women's Association (AMWA), petitioned unsuccessfully for a woman physician's right to serve in the war; instead, worked for the Red Cross in France as an investigator for claims (1917), documenting her experiences in *The House of the Good Neighbor* (1919); became director of American Women's Hospitals (AWH), a position she held for 42 years; wrote *Women Physicians and Surgeons* (1939) and *Women Doctors of the World* (1957). Awarded medal of Legion of Honor (France), Gold Cross of Saint Sava (Yugoslavia), Gold Cross of the Holy Sepulcher (Jerusalem), and Gold Cross of the Order of George I (Greece). ❖ See also memoir, *Certain Samaritans;* and *Women in World History.*

LOVELACE, Ada Byron, Countess of (1815–1852). English mathematician and inventor of computer programming. Name variations: Lady Lovelace; countess of Lovelace; Augusta Ada Byron. Born Augusta Ada Byron, Dec 10, 1815, at Piccadilly Terrace, London, England; died Nov 27, 1852, in England; buried in the Byron vault at Hucknall Torkard church, near Newstead Abbey; dau. of Anne Isabella Milbanke (1792–

1860) and George Gordon Byron, Lord Byron (poet); m. Lord William Noel King, later earl of Lovelace, July 8, 1835; children: Byron Noel (b. May 12, 1836); Anne Isabella Blunt (1837–1917); Ralph Gordon Noel King Milbanke, 2nd earl of Lovelace (July 2, 1839–1906). ❖ Parents separated (Jan 15, 1816); father died at Missolonghi, Greece (April 19, 1824); with mother, undertook a grand tour of Europe (1826–28); unable to walk after a severe attack of the measles (May 1829), recovered only gradually over a period of 4 years; eloped briefly with tutor (1832); was invited to view Charles Babbage's Difference Engine, forerunner of the modern computer (June 5, 1833); came under the influence of Mary Fairfax Somerville, famed mathematician, who became a lifelong friend (1834); with husband's elevation to an earldom, became countess of Lovelace (June 30, 1837); hired Augustus de Morgan, distinguished professor of mathematics, to tutor her in arithmetic and algebra (1840); after Luigi Federigo Menabrea issued a paper on Babbage's Analytical Engine (Oct 1842), published her translation with annotations, producing a manuscript 3 times the original length, inserted several illustrations which outlined the computer programming of the machine, and proposed a program for the computation of Bernoulli numbers (Aug 13, 1843); devised the 1st complex set of instructions for the Analytical Engine, which delineated the function of input, calculation, output, and printing, and her predictions concerning the future of computers were truly visionary. ❖ See also Doris Langley Moore, *Ada, Countess of Lovelace: Byron's Legitimate Daughter* (Murray, 1977); Vladimir Nabokov, *Ada or Ardor: A Family Chronicle* (McGraw-Hill, 1969); Dorothy Stein, *Ada: A Life and a Legacy* (MIT Press, 1985); Joan Baum, *The Calculating Passion of Ada Byron* (Archon, 1986); and *Women in World History.*

LOVELACE, countess of (1815–1852). *See Lovelace, Ada Byron, Countess of.*

LOVELACE, Linda (1952–2002). American actress. Name variations: Linda Boreman. Born Linda Susan Boreman, Jan 10, 1949, in The Bronx, NY; died April 22, 2002, in Denver, CO, from injuries suffered in an April 3rd auto accident; m. Chuck Traynor, 1971 (div. 1974); m. Larry Marchiano, 1974 (div. 1996); children: (2nd m.) 2. ❖ As Linda Lovelace, starred in the pornographic film *Deep Throat* (1972), and at least 7 others; later claimed 1st husband had forced her to appear in the films, once threatening her during a filming at gunpoint. ❖ See also memoirs (with Mike McGrady) *Ordeal* (1980) and *Out of Bondage* (1986).

LOVELACE, Maud Hart (1892–1980). American writer of novels and children's books. Born Maud Hart, April 25, 1892, in Mankato, Minnesota; died Mar 11, 1980, in California; dau. of Thomas Walden Hart (salesman) and Stella (Palmer) Hart; studied at University of Minnesota, 1911–12; m. Delos Wheeler Lovelace (journalist), 1917 (died 1967); children: Merian Lovelace Kirchner (b. 1931). ❖ Best known for her popular "Betsy-Tacy" series (1940–55), 10 books that relied extensively on exploits of her childhood; at 18, sold 1st short story to *Los Angeles Times* for $10; published 1st book, *The Black Angels* (1926), followed by 5 more historical novels, 2 of which she wrote with husband in the years preceding WWII. ❖ See also *Women in World History.*

LOVELESS, Lea (1971—). American swimmer. Name variations: Lea Loveless Maurer. Born April 1, 1971, in Crestwood, NY; Stanford University, BA in American studies, MA in education, 1994; m. Erik Maurer (champion swimmer). ❖ At Barcelona Olympics, won a bronze medal in 100-meter backstroke and a gold medal in 4x100-meter medley relay (1992); won 8 national titles.

LOVELING, Virginie (1836–1923). Belgian poet and novelist. Name variations: (pseudonym) Louis Bonheyden. Born May 17, 1836, in Nevele, Belgium; died Dec 1, 1923, in Ghent; dau. of Herman Anton Loveling and Marie Loveling; sister of Paulina Loveling Buysse and Rosalie Loveling (1834–1875); aunt of Cyriel Buysse (1859–1932), novelist and playwright). ❖ With sister Rosalie, published *Gedichten* (1870), *Novellen* (1874), and *Nieuwe novellen* (1876); after sister's death, wrote *In onze Vlaamsche Gewesten* (1877), *Sophie* (1885), *Een dure eed* (1891), *Een revolverschot* (1911), among others; with nephew Cyriel Buysse (son of Pauline), wrote *Levensleer* (A Philosophy of Life, 1912), under pseudonym Louis Bonheyden.

LOVELL, Ann (1803/11–1869). New Zealand gold courier and shopkeeper. Name variations: Ann Brown. Born Ann Brown, c. 1803–1811, probably in England; died Dec 15, 1869, in Motupipi, New Zealand; m. James Lovell, 1837; children: 3. ❖ Immigrated to New Zealand (1842); operated husband's butchery and bakery shop, making trips from

Golden Bay to Nelson to buy stock and carry gold deposited with husband by local goldminers. ❖ See also *Dictionary of New Zealand Biography* (Vol. 1).

LOVELL, Maria Anne (1803–1877). English actress and dramatist. Name variations: Mrs. Lovell. Born Maria Anne Lacy, 1803; died 1877; m. George William Lovell (1804–1878, dramatist), 1830. ❖ Made stage debut (1818); appeared at Covent Garden (1822); following retirement as actress, wrote *Ingomar the Barbarian*, which was produced at Drury Lane (1851) and would bring success to Mary Anderson (1859–1940) over 30 years later; also wrote *The Beginning of the End* for the Haymarket (1855).

LOVELL-SMITH, Lucy (1861–1936). *See Smith, Lucy Masey.*

LOVELL-SMITH, Rata Alice (1894–1969). New Zealand artist and teacher. Name variations: Rata Alice Bird. Born on Dec 24, 1894, in Christchurch, New Zealand; died on Sept 28, 1969, in Christchurch; dau. of Alfred Louis Bird (engineer) and Alice Emily (Cox) Bird; m. Colin Stuart Lovell-Smith (artist), 1922 (died 1960); children: 2 sons. ❖ With husband, painted and exhibited landscapes that rejected romantic traditions of scenic grandeur and were praised for their modern, poster-like characteristics; taught at New Zealand School of Art (from 1926); active in Canterbury Society of Arts (1920s–50s); was a leading artist of Canterbury regionalist movement. Won Bledsoe Medal for landscape painting (1939). ❖ See also *Dictionary of New Zealand Biography* (Vol. 4).

LOVELY, Louise (1895–1980). Australian actress. Name variations: Louise Carbasse. Born Nellie Louise Carbasse, Feb 28, 1895, in Paddington, Sydney, Australia; died Mar 19, 1980, in Hobart, Australia; illeg. dau. of actress Elise Lehmann; m. Wilton Welch, Feb 1912 (div. 1928); m. Bert Cowan (theater manager), Nov 1928. ❖ At 8, made Sydney stage debut as Eva in *Uncle Tom's Cabin* under name Louise Carbasse; had successful stage career in Australia and New Zealand and appeared in 9 film melodramas (1911–12); worked with husband in vaudeville in Australia and America; in US, renamed Louise Lovely, starred in Universal's *Stronger than Death* (1915); made over 50 films, including *Father and the Boys, The Field of Honor, The Butterfly Man, Life's Greatest Question* and *Shattered Idols;* as well, signed with Fox (1918) and appeared in numerous westerns opposite Bill Farnum; returned to Australia (1924) and co-produced Marie Bjelke-Petersen's *Jeweled Nights* (1925).

LOVEMAN, Amy (1881–1955). American editor and literary critic. Born Amy Loveman on May 16, 1881, in New York, NY; died Dec 11, 1955, in New York, NY; dau. of Adolph P. Loveman (cotton broker) and Adassa (Heilprin) Loveman (columnist); Barnard College, AB, 1901. ❖ Became book reviewer for *New York Evening Post* (1915); co-founded *Post's Literary Review* (1920); was co-founder of *Saturday Review of Literature* (1924), becoming associate editor, then poetry editor (1950); became head of reading department at Book-of-the-Month Club (c. 1926), and member of editorial board (1951–55); wrote *I'm Looking for a Book* (1942); co-edited *Varied Harvest: A Miscellany of Writing by Barnard College Women* (1953). Received Columbia University Medal for Excellence (1945) and Constance Lindsay Skinner Award (1946).

LOVERIDGE, Emily Lemoine (1860–1941). American nurse. Born Emily Lemoine Loveridge, Aug 28, 1860, in Hammondsport, NY; died April 26, 1941, in Portland, OR; dau. of Marie Lemoine (Wolfolk) Loveridge and Reverend Daniel Loveridge; children: raised nephew and niece, and a girl who was orphaned during the 1919 influenza epidemic. ❖ After a brief career teaching, graduated from Bellevue Hospital Training School of Nursing in NYC (1889); moved to Portland, OR, and founded the School of Nursing at Good Samaritan Hospital (1890), the 1st nurse training school in American Northwest, where she served as nursing superintendent until 1905 and superintendent; helped create what is now the Oregon State Board of Nursing (1910); retired from Good Samaritan (1930).

LOVIN, Fita (1951——). Romanian runner. Name variations: Fita Rafira-Lovin. Born Jan 14, 1951, in Romania. ❖ At Los Angeles Olympics, won a bronze medal in the 800 meters (1984).

LOVISA. *Variant of Louisa or Louise.*

LOW, Bet (1924——). Scottish artist. Born 1924 in Gourock, Scotland; attended Glasgow School of Art (1924–25); studied under James Cowie at Hospitalfield; m. Tom Macdonald (artist). ❖ Member of Glasgow Group, held 1st solo exhibition at Athenaeum in Glasgow

(1946) and followed with 1-woman show at 57 Gallery (1961); became co-founder of New Charing Cross Gallery (1963) and held solo shows there (1965–67); exhibited with husband at Blythswood Gallery in Glasgow (1969); elected to Royal Scottish Watercolor Society (1974); held solo show at Harbor Arts Center in Irvine, California (1975); became member of Royal Glasgow Institute of Artists (1980) and gave shows at The Scottish Gallery (1981), Third Eye Center (1985) and Compass Gallery (1988); became associate of Royal Scottish Academy (1988) and is a longstanding member of Society for Scottish Women Artists. Was 1st winner of Betty Davies "Campus" Award at Royal Scottish Watercolor exhibition (1987).

LOW, Caroline Sarah (1876–1934). New Zealand teacher, social reformer, pacifist, and writer. Name variations: Caroline Sarah Howard. Born Caroline Sarah Howard, Mar 23, 1876, at Loburn, Canterbury, New Zealand; died Aug 10, 1934, at Timaru, New Zealand; dau. of Charles Smith Howard (teacher) and Charlotte (Thompson) Howard; Canterbury College, MA, 1898; m. Benjamin Harris Low (teacher), 1907; children: 4 sons and 1 stepdaughter. ❖ Taught at father's school before appointment as assistant to T.R. Cresswell at Rangiora High School (1902); executive member of New Zealand Women's Christian Temperance Union; helped establish local branch of Workers' Educational Association of New Zealand; advocate of peace and disarmament, joined League of Nations Union of New Zealand (1928); wrote peace and arbitration column in *White Ribbon* (1932). ❖ See also *Dictionary of New Zealand Biography* (Vol. 3).

LOW, Elisabeth (1900–1993). *See Draper, Elisabeth.*

LOW, Juliette Gordon (1860–1927). Founder of the Girl Scouts. Name variations: Daisy Low. Born Juliette Magill Gordon, Oct 31, 1860, in Savannah, GA; died of cancer, Jan 17, 1927, in Savannah; dau. of William Washington II (cotton broker and 2nd lieutenant in Confederate army) and Eleanor Kinzie Gordon; attended Mesdemoiselles Charbonniers' School, NY, diploma, 1880; aunt of Daisy Gordon Lawrence (writer); m. William Low, Dec 21, 1886 (died 1905); no children. ❖ Met Robert Baden-Powell and under his tutelage established Girl Guide troops in Scotland and London (1910); created the 1st troop of Girl Guides in US (Mar 12, 1912); elected president of Girl Scouts of America which was incorporated in NY City (1915); resigned as president (1920); devoted rest of life to increasing the membership of, and international involvement in, Girl Scouting (Girl Scouts of America purchased her birthplace in Savannah, 1953); inducted into Women's Hall of Fame in Seneca Falls (1979). A federal building in Savannah was named for her by President Ronald Reagan—only the 2nd federal building ever to be named for a woman. ❖ See also Anne Hyde Choate, and Helen Ferris, eds. *Juliette Low and the Girl Scouts: The Story of an American Woman, 1860–1927* (Doubleday, 1928); Gladys Denny Shultz, and Daisy Gordon Lawrence. *Lady from Savannah: The Life of Juliette Low* (Lippincott, 1958); and *Women in World History.*

LOW, Mary Fairchild (1858–1946). American painter. Name variations: Mary Louise Fairchild MacMonnies. Born Mary Louise Fairchild in New Haven, CT, 1858; died 1946; descendant of Governor William Bradford of the *Mayflower;* attended St. Louis Art Academy; studied at France's Académie Julian and with Carolus-Duran; m. Frederick MacMonnies (sculptor), 1888 (div.); m. Will Hicok Low (mural painter and illustrator), 1909; children: (1st m.) 2 daughters. ❖ With 1st husband, showcased work at Chicago Exposition (her mural *Primitive Woman* was displayed opposite Mary Cassatt's *Modern Woman*, 1893); was awarded several gold medals in European exhibitions. ❖ See also *Women in World History.*

LOW, Nora Wilson (1886–1930). *See Moon, Lorna.*

LOW COUNTRIES, queen of. *See Mary of Burgundy (1457–1482).*

LOWE, Beatrice. *See Hill-Lowe, Beatrice.*

LÖWE, Gabriele (1958——). *See Loewe, Gabriele.*

LOWE, Helen Porter (1876–1963). *See Lowe-Porter, Helen.*

LOWE, R.H. (1921——). *See Lowe-McConnell, Rosemary.*

LOWE, Sara (1984——). American synchronized swimmer. Born April 30, 1984, in Dallas, TX. ❖ Won a team bronze medal at Athens Olympics (2004).

LOWE-MCCONNELL, Rosemary (1921——). English biologist and ichthyologist. Name variations: Rosemary Lowe McConnell; R.H. Lowe. Born Rosemary Helen Lowe, June 24, 1921, in Liverpool,

England; University of Liverpool, BS, MSc and DSc; m. Richard McConnell, Dec 31, 1953. ❖ Pioneer in research in tropical fish ecology and advocate of the importance of maintaining biodiversity, studied the migration of silver eels as a Freshwater Biological Association (FBA) scientific officer in Windermere, Cumbria (1942–45); surveyed (1945–47) 5 species of tilapias and fish in the southern section of Lake Nyasa (later Lake Malawi) in Malawi; worked as research officer at British Overseas Research Service for East African Fisheries Research (1948–53); discovered 4 new tilapias species in Kenya's Pangani River and in Lake Jipe; conducted 1st survey of freshwater fish in the Guyana shelf as a Guyana Department of Agriculture and Fisheries scientist (1957–62); worked as an associate of British Museum's Fish Section (1962–67); served as 1st editor of *Biological Journal of the Linnean Society;* elected a fellow and vice president of Linnean Society of London (1967); served as a coeditor (with W.H. van Dobben) of *Unifying Concepts in Ecology* (1975), a plenary sessions report for First International Congress of Ecology in The Hague (1974); admired by others for her adept synthesis of many scientific themes (including evolution, population dynamics and predation pressure).

LOWE-PORTER, Helen (1876–1963). American writer and translator. Name variations: Helen Tracy Porter, Helen Porter, Helen Tracy Lowe-Porter, Helen T. Porter Lowe, H.T. Lowe-Porter. Born Helen Tracy Porter on June 15, 1876, in Towanda, PA; died April 26, 1963, in Princeton, NJ; dau. of Henry Clinton Porter (pharmacist) and Clara (Holcombe) Porter; graduate of Wells College, 1898; m. Elias Avery Lowe (paleographer), 1911; children: Prudence Holcombe Lowe (b. 1912), Frances Beatrice Lowe (b. 1913), and Patricia Tracy Lowe (b. 1917). ❖ Translated Thomas Mann's novels, short stories, and essays from German to English (1922–51); wrote blank verse drama, *Abdication,* which was performed at Gate Theatre in Dublin (1948), then published (1950); wrote book of poetry, *Casual Verse* (1957); trans. works of such writers as Arthur Schnitzler, Frank Thiess and Hermann Broch, and papers and writings for Albert Einstein; also trans. works from French, Italian, Dutch, and Latin into English; believed in women's rights and international understanding, and opposed nationalism and anti-communism of McCarthy era.

LOWELL, Amy (1874–1925). American poet, critic, and woman of letters. Born Amy Lowell, Feb 9, 1874, at her family's Sevenels Estate in Brookline, MA; died there, May 12, 1925; dau. of Augustus Lowell (businessman) and Katherine Bigelow (Lawrence) Lowell; sister of Abbott Lawrence Lowell, president of Harvard, and Percival Lowell, astronomer; never married; lived with Ada Dwyer. ❖ Powerful leader in the modernist poetry movement known as Imagism, completed formal education at 17 and returned home to help maintain family estate during mother's illness (1891); inherited Sevenels after death of father (1900); was inspired by a performance of actress Eleonora Duse to become a poet (1902); wrote 1st serious poem (1910); met Ada Dwyer, who would become her lifelong companion (1912); discovered Imagist movement in poetry and met Ezra Pound for 1st time (1913); quarreled with Pound in London and published her own Imagist poetry anthology, effectively taking over the leadership of the Imagist movement in America (1914); for next several years, engaged in public debates about the new form of poetry and played the role of patron as well as promoter and practitioner; began work on Chinese poetry with Florence Ayscough (1917); had an abdominal rupture and underwent the 1st of many operations (1918); was the 1st woman to deliver a lecture at Harvard (1919); published biography of Keats (1925); several works published posthumously; poetry includes *Dream Drops or Stories from Fairy Land by a Dreamer* (1887), *A Dome of Many-Colored Glass* (1912), *Sword Blades and Poppy Seeds* (1914), *Men, Women and Ghosts* (1916), *Can Grande's Castle* (1918), *Pictures of the Floating World* (1919), *Legends* (1921), *A Critical Fable* (1922), *East Wind* (1926) and *Ballads for Sale* (1927). Awarded Helen Haire Levinson prize from *Poetry* magazine (1924); awarded (posthumously) Pulitzer Prize for *What's O'Clock* (1926). ❖ See also Richard Benvenuto, *Amy Lowell* (Twayne, 1985); Jean Gould, *Amy: The World of Amy Lowell and the Imagist Movement* (Dodd, 1975); C. David Heymann, *American Aristocracy: The Lives and Times of James Russell, Amy, and Robert Lowell* (Dodd, 1980); and *Women in World History.*

LOWELL, Josephine Shaw (1843–1905). American philanthropist and social reformer. Born Josephine Shaw, Dec 16, 1843, in West Roxbury, MA; died of cancer, Oct 12, 1905; dau. of Francis George Shaw (abolitionist who organized the Freedmen's Bureau) and Sarah Blake (Sturgis) Shaw; sister of Robert Gould Shaw (led 1st black regiment from free states into battle) and Anna Shaw (Curtis); m. Charles Russell Lowell (colonel in 2nd Massachusetts cavalry and nephew of James Russell

Lowell), Oct 31, 1863 (killed in battle of Cedar Creek, VA, during Civil War, 1864); children: Carlotta Russell Lowell. ❖ Following death of husband, immersed herself in philanthropic work for next 40 years, 1st turning her energies to the National Freedman's Relief Association of New York; was appointed 1st woman member of New York State Board of Charities (1876); reappointed by several succeeding governors (1877–89); also founded Charity Organization Society, becoming one of the most influential women in the charity movement, and was active in prison reform. ❖ See also *Women in World History.*

LOWELL, Maria White (1821–1853). American poet. Born Anna Maria White in Watertown, MA, July 8, 1821; died, possibly of TB, at Elmwood, the Lowell home in Cambridge, Oct 27, 1853; dau. of Abijah White (cattle trader in West Indies) and Anna Maria (Howard) White; along with sisters, attended Ursuline Convent School in Charlestown; m. James Russell Lowell (poet), Dec 26, 1844; sister-in-law of Mary Traill Spence Putnam; children: Blanche Lowell (1845–1847); Mabel Lowell (b. 1847); Rose Lowell (1849–1849); Walter Lowell (1850–1852). ❖ Published 20 poems (1855) and collections (1907 and 1936); greatest work is abolitionist poem "Africa"; an ardent liberal, steered husband from his natural conservatism, stimulating his interests in both the abolitionist and Transcendental movements. ❖ See also Hope Vernon, *The Poems of Maria White Lowell with Unpublished Letters and Biography* (1936); and *Women in World History.*

LOWELL, Mary Traill Spence (1810–1898). *See Putnam, Mary Traill Spence.*

LÖWENSTEIN, Helga Maria zu (1910–2004). Norwegian-born political activist, lecturer, and founder. Name variations: Princess Helga Maria of Loewenstein or Lowenstein; Princess Löwenstein. Born Helga Maria Schuylenburg in Loftus, Norway, Aug 27, 1910; died Nov 23, 2004, in Berlin; dau. of Dutch parents; m. anti-Nazi activist Prince Hubertus zu Löwenstein-Wertheim-Freudenberg (whose full name was Hubertus Maximilian Friedrich Leopold Ludwig Prinz zu Löwenstein-Wertheim-Freudenberg), in 1929 (died Nov 28, 1984); children: Elisabeth Maria (b. 1939); Konstanza Maria (b. 1942); Margareta Maria (b. 1948). ❖ When a group of stormtroopers broke into their Berlin apartment (1933), took the next train to Austria where, with husband, continued her anti-Nazi activities; with husband, founded the German Academy of Arts and Sciences in Exile; visited US to alert American public to Nazi threat and raise funds for the American Guild for German Cultural Freedom (1936); spent war years in US, participating in German exile politics; returned to Germany (1946); over next decades, traveled with husband to nations around the world as representatives of the new democracy that had arisen in the Federal Republic of Germany; after husband died, continued work of fostering European reconciliation. ❖ See also *Women in World History.*

LOWER BAVARIA, duchess of. *See Elizabeth of Hungary (fl. 1250s).*

LOWER LORRAINE, duchess of.
See Clementia.
See Doda (fl. 1040).
See Margaret of Limburg (d. 1172).

LOWERY, Ellin Prince (1849–1921). *See Speyer, Ellin Prince.*

LOWERY, Mrs. John A. (1849–1921). *See Speyer, Ellin Prince.*

LOWERY, Phyllis (1915–1961). *See Dewar, Phyllis.*

LOWEY, Nita M. (1937—). American politician. Born Nita Sue Melnikoff, July 5, 1937 in the Bronx, NY; attended Mount Holyoke College; m. Stephen Lowey; children: 2. ❖ Democrat, served as assistant secretary of state for NY; elected to US House of Representatives (1988) for Westchester and Rockland counties; relected (1990–2004); served on House Appropriations Committee and as ranking Democrat on Foreign Operations, Export Financing; chosen to serve on the Select Committee on Homeland Security (2003); was the 1st woman to chair the Democratic Congressional Campaign Committee (2001–02).

LOWISA. *See Variant of Louisa.*

LOWNDES, Mrs. Belloc (1868–1947). *See Belloc-Lowndes, Marie.*

LOWNEY, Shannon (1969–1994). American activist. Born Shannon Elizabeth Lowney, July 7, 1969, in Norwalk, CT; killed Dec 30, 1994; dau. of Joan (Manning) Lowney (elementary school music teacher) and William T. Lowney (middle school history teacher); Boston College, BA in history (Magna Cum Laude), 1991; never married; no children. ❖ Advocate for women's reproductive rights and prevention of child abuse, was murdered in the Planned Parenthood Clinic in Brookline, Massachusetts, by an anti-abortion-rights activist (he had killed Lee Ann Nichols, another receptionist at a different clinic, that same day). ❖ See also *Women in World History.*

LOWRY, Edith (1897–1970). American religious organization executive. Born Edith Elizabeth Lowry, Mar 23, 1897, in Plainfield, NJ; died Mar 11, 1970, in Claremont, NH; dau. of Robert Hanson Lowry Jr. (banker) and Elizabeth (Darling) Lowry; Wellesley College, AB, 1920. ❖ Was migrant program director of Council of Women for Home Missions (1929–62); became executive secretary of Council of Women (1936); authored booklet, *They Starve That We May Eat* (1938), and helped compile *Tales of Americans on Trek* (1940); was 1st woman to occupy National Radio Pulpit (1939); became coexecutive secretary when Council of Women merged with Home Missions Council of North America (1940); established day-care centers for children of migrant workers (1940s), and worked to inform migrants about eligibility for Social Security; became executive secretary of division of home missions when Home Missions Council became National Council of Churches (1950–62); was part-time consultant to National Council on Agricultural Life and Labor in Washington, DC (1962–64); retired to Perkinsville, Vermont (1965).

LOWRY, Judith (1890–1976). American stage, tv, and screen actress. Born Judith Ives, July 27, 1890, in Fort Sill, OK; died Nov 29, 1976, in New York, NY; m. Rudd Lowry (actor); children: nine. ❖ Made Broadway debut in *Romeo and Juliet* (1915); appeared in numerous plays, including *Goat Song, Beyond the Horizon, J.B.* and *The Effect of Gamma Rays on Man-in-the-Moon Marigolds;* films include *The Trouble with Angels, Valley of the Dolls, Popi, The Night They Raided Minsky's, Sweet Charity, On a Clear Day You Can See Forever* and *Anderson Tapes;* probably best remembered as Mother Dexter on tv series "Phyllis."

LOWRY, Lois (1937—). American children's author. Born Mar 20, 1937, in Honolulu, Hawaii; daughter of Robert E. (dentist) and Katharine (Landis) Hammersberg (teacher); attended Brown University, 1954–56; University of Maine, BA, 1972; married Donald Grey Lowry (attorney), June 11, 1956 (div. 1977); children: Alix, Grey, Kristin, Benjamin. ❖ Writings include *A Summer to Die* (1977), *Anastasia Krupnik* (1979), *Autumn Street* (1980), *Anastasia Again!* (1981), *Us and Uncle Fraud* (1984), *Anastasia, Ask Your Analyst* (1984), *All about Sam* (1988) and *Rabble Starkey* (1989); won Newbery Medals for *Number the Stars* (1990) and *The Giver.* ❖ See also *Looking Back: A Book of Memories* (Houghton, 1998).

LOWRY, Margerie Bonner (1905–1988). *See Bonner, Margerie.*

LOWRY-CORRY, Dorothy (1885–1967). Irish historian, genealogist, and archaeologist. Born in Castlecooke, County Fermanagh, Ireland, 1885; died 1967. ❖ Known particularly for her studies of the Early Christian period, served as vice-president of Royal Society of Antiquaries and contributed numerous papers to the Royal Irish Academy, the most important of which was the recording of the Boa Island and Lustymore stone figures; also studied the Monuments of County Fermanagh and discovered the megalithic tomb in County Leitrim; was a frequent contributor to *Ulster Journal of Archaeology.*

LOWTHER, Patricia Louise (1935–1975). Canadian poet. Name variations: Pat Lowther. Born Patricia Tinmuth, July 29, 1935, in Vancouver, British Columbia, Canada; murdered Sept 24, 1975, in Vancouver; m. 2nd husband Roy Lowther (writer); children: 4, including Christina and Beth Lowther. ❖ Lived life of poverty and hardship; published 4 collections of poetry: *This Difficult Flowering* (1968), *The Age of the Bird* (1972), *Milk Stone* (1974), and *A Stone Diary* (1977); served as co-chair of League of Canadian Poets (1974); suffered abuse from 2nd husband for many years then disappeared (Sept 1975); body found in Furry Creek (Oct 1975); husband was later convicted of her murder and sentenced to life imprisonment (1977), where he died (1985). ❖ See also Keith Harrison, *Furry Creek* (Oolichan Books); film *Water Marks* (2002).

LOWY, Dora (1977—). Hungarian handball player. Name variations: Dóra Löwy or Loewy. Born June 28, 1977, in Hungary. ❖ Won a team silver medal at Sydney Olympics (2000).

LOY, Mina (1882–1966). English-born poet, artist, and designer. Born Mina Gertrude Lowy, Dec 27, 1882, in London, England; died Sept 25, 1966, in Aspen, CO; changed surname to Loy, 1903; dau. of Julian (Bryan) Lowy and Sigmund Lowy (tailor); attended school in England until 1899; studied art at Kunstlerrinen Verein, Munich; returned to

London (1901–02) to study art with Augustus John; studied art in Paris (1903); became a member of Salon d'Automne in Paris (1906); m. Stephen Haweis, Dec 31, 1903 (div. 1917); m. Arthur Cravan, Jan 1918; children: (1st m.) Oda (1904–1905); Joella Haweis (b. July 20, 1907); Giles Haweis (Feb 1, 1909–1923); (2nd m.) Fabi Cravan (b. April 5, 1919). ❖ Breaking ground with her erotic love poetry, satires, plays, paintings, and Modernist manifestoes, was highly regarded and influential among her contemporaries in the NY avant-garde of the 1910s and 1920s; moved with husband to Florence (1906), where she produced some of her best poems and paintings; identified herself with Futurism, an experimental movement within the Modernist revolution; exhibited paintings in London (1913); published 1st poems in *Camera Work* and *Trend* (1914); remained in Florence after Aug 3 declaration of war, and became a nurse in a surgical hospital; new poems appeared in *Rogue* and *Others,* avant-garde magazines published in NY; wrote feminist satire of Futurism, with which she became disillusioned; left Florence for NY (1915); modeled, began selling designs for dresses and lampshades, and was guest-editor of *Others;* exhibited a painting at Society of Independent Artists Exhibition in NY (1917); settled in Berlin (1922), then Paris (1923), where she became part of the artistic and expatriate communities; poems appeared in *The Little Review;* published 1st book *Lunar Baedecker* [sic] (1923); design work appeared in Madison Avenue windows; paintings exhibited in a Connecticut gallery (1925); became agent for Julien Levy Gallery (1931); exhibited paintings in Connecticut and Paris galleries (1933); left Paris (1936) and moved to NY; became a naturalized US citizen (1946); moved to the Bowery (1949) and began to create montage and collage works; poems occasionally appeared in little magazines and anthologies (1936–53); published 2nd book *Lunar Baedeker and Time Tables: Selected Poems* (1958); several poems appeared in *Between Worlds* (1961–62); lived an increasingly reclusive existence until her death. Copley Foundation Award (1959). ❖ See also Carolyn Burke, *Becoming Modern: The Life of Mina Loy* (Farrar, 1996); Virginia Kouidis, *Mina Loy: American Modernist Poet* (Louisiana State U. Press, 1980); and *Women in World History.*

LOY, Myrna (1905–1993). American actress. Born Myrna Adele Williams, Aug 2, 1905, in Radersburg, Montana; died Dec 14, 1993, in New York, NY; dau. of Davis and Della Williams; m. Arthur Hornblow Jr., 1936 (div. 1942); m. John Hertz Jr., 1942 (div. 1944); m. Gene Markey, 1946 (div. 1950); m. Howland Sargeant, 1951 (div. 1960); no children. ❖ Star of the popular "Thin Man" series as the sophisticated, quick-witted Nora Charles, moved to Los Angeles after father's death (1918) and began getting bit parts in silent films, eventually working her way up to larger roles; though she successfully made the transition to sound films, seemed destined to a future of studio typecasting as an exotic and often murderous siren before being offered a comedy role in the 1st "Thin Man" film (1934), playing opposite William Powell's Nick Charles; her popularity increased during a series of sequels to such an extent that she was eventually dubbed "Queen of the Movies"; devoted much of her time during WWII to charitable and fundraising activities, but returned to the screen after the war to great acclaim in such films as *The Best Years of Our Lives, Mr. Blandings Builds His Dream House, The Red Pony, Cheaper by the Dozen* and *Lonelyhearts* (1959); remained active in film and tv through 1980s; made Broadway debut in a revival of *The Women* (1971) and was awarded a special Academy Award for Lifetime Achievement (1991). ❖ See also autobiography (with James Kotsilibas-Davis) *Myrna Loy: Being and Becoming* (Knopf, 1987); and *Women in World History.*

LOY, Rosetta (1931—). Italian novelist and short-story writer. Born 1931 in Rome, Italy. ❖ Published 1st novel *La bicicletta* (The Bicycle, 1974), which won the Viareggio Prize; also wrote *L'estate di Letuqué* (1982), *Le strade di polvere* (1987, trans. as *The Dust Roads of Monferrato,* 1990), and *Sogni d'inverno* (1992).

LOYNAZ, Dulce María (1902–1997). Cuban poet. Name variations: María Mercedes Loynaz; Dulce Maria Loynaz. Born María Mercedes Loynaz, Dec 10, 1902, in Havana, Cuba; died April 27, 1997, in Cuba; dau. of José Antonio Loynaz (army general and memoirist) and Ana de Vergara y Miranda; sister of Carlos Manuel Loynaz (poet and composer); m. Enrique Quesada y Loynaz, 1937 (div. 1943); m. Pablo Alvarez de Cañas, 1946 (journalist). ❖ Prize-winning Cuban poet, traveled to Turkey, Syria, Libya, Palestine, US and Mexico, then published *Carta de amor a Tut-Ank-Amon* (Love Letter to Tut-Ank-Amon, 1929); maintained friendships with prominent literary figures, including Gabriela Mistral, Lydia Cabrera and Frederico García Lorca; won numerous awards for poetry, including Alfonso X El Sabio cross from Spanish minister of culture in Madrid (1947), Carlos Manuel Césepedes cross and Mariana Grajales prize (1948), Cuban National Prize for Literature (1987) and Cervantes Prize (1992); elected to National Academy of Arts and Letters of Havana (1956); remained in Cuba after revolution, despite flight of 2nd husband, and was named president of Cuban Academy of Language by Castro government (1968); regular contributor to several major newspapers in Spain, Mexico and Cuba, including *ABC, Social, Revista Cubana* (Cuban Review) and *Orígenes.* Writings include (poetry collections) *Versos* (Verses, 1938), *Juegos de agua* (Water Games, 1947), *poemas sin nombre* (poems without a name, 1955), and *Poemas náufragos* (Castaway Poems, 1993), (essays) *Confesiones de Dulce María Loynaz* (Confessions of Dulce Maria Loynaz, 1993), *Ensayos* (Essays, 1996) and *Cartas que no se extraviaron* (Unlost Letters, 1997). ❖ See also autobiography, *Jardín* (Garden, 1951); Asunción Horno-Delgado, *Margen acuático: Dulce María Loynaz* (Júcar, 1998).

LOYNES, Antoinette de (fl. 16th c.). French poet and salonnière. Name variations: Mme Loynes or Luynes; Madame de Morel. Born Antoinette de Loynes in 1500s; dau. of a humanist and friend of Erasmus; m. Jean de Morel (1511–1581), poet and orator), shortly before 1544; children: 3 daughters, including Camille de Loynes. ❖ With husband, held literary salon in Paris which was frequented by many writers and known as "temple des Muses"; wrote poems and sonnets in Latin and composed epigram on death of poet Joachim Du Bellay. Few works survive.

LOYNES, Camille de (fl. 16th c.). French poet. Dau. of Jean de Morel and Antoinette de Loynes. ❖ Wrote lament in Latin on death of Henri II as well as poetic dialogue with Joachim Du Bellay, *Joachimi Bellaii et Camillae Morellae Dialogismus extemporalis.*

LOYSE. Variant of Louise.

LOZIER, Clemence S. (1813–1888). American physician and reformer. Born Clemence Sophia Harned, Dec 11, 1813, in Plainfield, NJ; died April 26, 1888, in New York, NY; dau. of David Harned (farmer) and Hannah (Walker) Harned; aunt of Anna Manning Comfort; attended Plainfield Academy and Central Medical College of Rochester, NY; graduated with high honors from Syracuse (NY) Medical College; m. Abraham Witton Lozier (carpenter and builder), 1829 or 1830 (died 1837); m. John Baker, possibly in 1844 (div. 1861); children: (1st m.) Abraham Witton Jr. ❖ Set up a practice in obstetrics and general surgery in NY City, eventually specializing in female disorders, particularly the removal of tumors; obtained a state charter for New York Medical College and Hospital for Women, the 1st women's school of medicine in the state, which opened its doors in 1863; reorganized the school (1867), taking title of professor of gynecology and obstetrics and serving as dean for next 20 years; a prominent woman suffragist, served as president of New York City Woman Suffrage Society (1873–86) and president of National Woman Suffrage Association (1877–78); helped finance Susan B. Anthony's suffrage weekly, *Revolution;* also supported such causes as abolition, sanitary and prison reform, and Indian rights; in later years, served as president of Moral Education Society of New York and of local women's Christian Temperance Union. ❖ See also *Women in World History.*

LOZOVAJA, Svetlana (1945—). See Tsirkova, Svetlana.

L7.
See Finch, Jennifer.
See Garner, Suzi.
See Sparks, Donita.

LÜ, Empress (r. 195–180 BCE). See Lü Hou.

LU BIN (1977—). Chinese swimmer. Born Jan 7, 1977, in China. ❖ At Barcelona Olympics, won a silver medal in 4x100-meter freestyle relay (1992); won 3 gold medals and 2 silver medals at World championships (1994), then tested positive for steriods.

LU CHEN (b. 1976). See Chen Lu.

LÜ HOU (r. 195–180 BCE). Chinese empress and regent of China. Name variations: Empress Lu or Lü; Lu Hou of the Han. Reigned 195–180 BCE; murdered in 180 BCE; m. Gao Zu (Kao Tsu) who became the Han emperor Liu Pang (r. 220–195 BCE); children: Hui Ti. ❖ Persuaded husband to seek the throne; began the Chinese tradition that the mother of a son deemed heir apparent be recognized as an empress; following husband's death (195 BCE), waited until son Hui Ti was safely ensconced on the throne, then dismissed husband's relatives, who were in positions of power, to make way for her own family; a few years later, when her son died, grasped even more power, choosing another child as his successor; when the child balked under her authority, had him imprisoned and

designated a 3rd child as emperor of the Han; was put to death by husband's loyal ministers. ❖ See also *Women in World History.*

LU HUALI (1972—). Chinese rower. Born Mar 14, 1972, in China. ❖ At Barcelona Olympics, won a bronze medal in double sculls (1992).

LU LI (1976—). Chinese gymnast. Born Aug 30, 1976, in Hunan, China. ❖ At Barcelona Olympics, won a gold medal in uneven bars and a silver medal in the balance beam (1992); placed 1st all-around at Pacific Alliance championships (1992).

LU YIN (1899–1934). Chinese short-story writer. Born 1899; died in childbirth 1934. ❖ Was involved in May Fourth Movement and worked as teacher and administrator; writings, which aroused considerable attention in her day, include *The Ivory Ring* (1934), *Autobiography* (1931), *The Homecoming Cranes* (1931), and *Heart of Women* (1933).

LUAHINE, Iolani (1915–1978). Hawaiian-American dancer. Born 1915 in Hawaii; died Dec 10, 1978, in Hawaii. ❖ One of the few individuals responsible for the survival of the sacred hula ceremony, danced and taught the chant-accompanied hula throughout life; appeared on several tv programs as well as in the documentary films *Hula Ho'olaule'a* (1960) and *Iolani Luahine: Hawaiian Dancer* (1960).

LUALDI, Antonella (1931—). Italian-Greek actress. Born Antonietta De Pascale, July 6, 1931, in Beirut, Lebanon; dau. of an Italian father and Greek mother; m. Franco Interlenghi (actor), 1953; children: Antonella Interlenghi (b. 1961, actress). ❖ Appeared in lead roles in many French and Italian films (1949–1994), including *Signorinella, Abbiamo vinto!, Pentimento, Il Cappoto, Le rouge et le noir, Casta diva, Giovani mariti, Une vie, Polikuschka, La notte brava, I Delfini, I cento cavalieri, Columna* and *Eden no sono.*

LUAN JUJIE (1958—). Chinese fencer. Born Sept 14, 1958, in China. ❖ At Los Angeles Olympics, won a gold medal in indiv. foil (1984).

LUANTO, Regina di (c. 1862–1914). See Lipperini, Guendalina.

LUBERT, Mlle de (c. 1710–c. 1779). French novelist and short-story writer. Name variations: Mademoiselle de Lubert; Marguerite de Lubert. Born Marguerite de Lubert (also seen as Marie-Madeleine de Lubert) c. 1710 in France; died c. 1779; dau. of a parliamentary president; never married. ❖ Wrote mostly fairytales which were published anonymously; writings include *Le Prince glacé et la princesse étincelante* (1743), *La Princesse camion* (The Waggon Princess, 1743), *La Princesse Coque d'Oeuf et le prince Bonbon* (Princess Eggshell and Prince Bonbon, 1745), *Amadis des Gaules* (1750), *Les hauts faits d'Esplandion* (1751), and *Mourat et Turquia* (1752); also wrote the short novel *Léonille* (1755); described by Voltaire as "Muse et Grâce."

LUBETKIN, Zivia (1914–1978). Polish-Jewish resistance leader. Name variations: Zivia Lubetkin-Zuckerman; Cywia Lubetkin; Ziviah Lubetkin; underground name: "Celina." Born in 1914 in Beten near Slonim, Polesie, Russian Poland; died in Israel in 1978; m. Icchak Cukierman also seen as Yitzhak Zuckerman (1915–1981). ❖ Resistance leader in Warsaw Ghetto Uprising and a founder of the Jewish Fighting Organization (ZOB), was active before WWII in the Jewish Socialist youth movement Dror-Hechaluts (Freedom-the Pioneer); along with husband, was one of the key leaders of both uprisings in the Warsaw Ghetto (Jan and April 1943); participated in the Warsaw Polish uprising (summer 1944); immigrated to Palestine/Israel (1946); was a member of Kibbutz Lohamei ha-Getta'ot. ❖ See also Zvika Dror, *The Dream, the Revolt, and the Vow: The Biography of Zivia Lubetkin-Zuckerman (1914–1978)* (trans. by Bezalel Ianai, 1983); Rebecca Toueg, *Zivia Lubetkin: Heroine of the Warsaw Ghetto* (1988); and *Women in World History.*

LUBIC, Ruth Watson (1927—). American nurse-midwife. Born Ruth Watson, Jan 18, 1927, in Bristol, PA; dau. of Lillian (Kraft) Watson and Russell Watson; graduate of University of Pennsylvania Hospital School of Nursing; attended Hunter College; Columbia University Teachers College, PhD, 1979; m. William James Lubic (attorney). ❖ Leader in the nurse-midwifery field and 1st nurse to win a MacArthur fellowship (1993), worked at Memorial Center for Cancer and Allied Diseases in NYC (1955–58); at Maternity Center Association (MCA), worked as a clinical instructor (1962), parent educator and counselor (1963–67), general director (1970–95) and director of Clinical Projects (1995–97); with Kitty Ernst, opened MCA Childbearing Center in NY (1975); created a self-help education program for expectant mothers (1978); opened a birth center in the Bronx (1988); established and served as president and CEO of the District of Columbia Developing Families Center (DCDFC). Received Lillian D. Wald Award (2003).

LUBIN, Germaine (1890–1979). French soprano. Born in Paris, France, Feb 1, 1890; died in Paris, Oct 27, 1979; studied with F. Litvinne and Lilli Lehmann as well as at Paris Conservatory, 1909–12; m. Paul Géraldy (French poet). ❖ One of France's greatest sopranos of the 20th century, debuted at Opéra-Comique (1912); appeared at Paris Opéra (1914–44); made debut at Covent Garden (1937); transcended the French repertoire to perform many operatic works, including Wagner, singing *Parsifal* with Lauritz Melchoir in Paris (1937); was the 1st French singer to appear at Bayreuth (1938); soon became a favorite of many high-ranking Nazis, including Hitler, then was reviled in her country for continuing to perform during the German occupation in WWII. ❖ See also *Women in World History.*

LUBY, Susan (1951—). *See Corrock, Susan.*

LUCAS, Caroline (1960—). English politician. Born Dec 9, 1960, in Malvern, Worcestershire, England. ❖ Served as press officer (1989–91), communications officer, Asia Desk (1991–94), policy adviser on trade and the environment (1994–97), policy adviser on trade and investment, Dept. for International Development (1997–98), and team leader for trade and investment, Policy Dept. (1998–99), all for Oxfam; representing Group of the Greens/European Free Alliance, elected to 5th European Parliament (1999–2004) from UK. Wrote *Writing Women* (1989), *Reforming World Trade* (1994), and *Watchful in Seattle* (2000).

LUCAS, Eliza (1722–1793). *See Pinckney, Eliza Lucas.*

LUCAS, Gypsy (c. 1975—). *See Tidwell-Lucas, Gypsy.*

LUCAS, Joy (1917—). American ski instructor. Name variations: Lucky Lucas. Born Joy Piles, Feb 15, 1917, in Spokane, WA. ❖ Became 1st women to be certified as professional ski instructor (1941) and served as ski instructor in Pacific Northwest; authored many instructional articles about skiing and ran training clinics for new ski instructors.

LUCAS, Lucky (b. 1917). *See Lucas, Joy.*

LUCAS, Margaret Bright (1818–1890). English reformer. Born 1818; died 1890; dau. of Jacob Bright (bookkeeper and cotton spinner) and Martha (Wood) Bright (tradesman's daughter); sister of John Bright (1811–1889, reformer); m. Samuel Lucas (1811–1865). ❖ Along with brother and husband, fought to benefit the industrial middle class by participating in the Anti-Corn Law League, a pressure group that agitated for the abolition of import tariffs on foreign foodstuffs as the preliminary to complete free trade in all commodities; was also president of the British Women's Temperance Association. ❖ See also *Women in World History.*

LUCAS, Theresa (1965—). *See Zabell, Theresa.*

LUCAS, Victoria. *See Plath, Sylvia.*

LUCCA, duchess of. *See Maria Luisa of Etruria (1782–1824).*

LUCCA, Elisa (1777–1820). *See Bonaparte, Elisa.*

LUCCA, Pauline (1841–1908). Austrian soprano. Born April 25, 1841, in Vienna, Austria; died Feb 28, 1908, in Vienna; trained in Vienna with Uffmann and Levy. ❖ Known more for her two-octave range and her dramatic flair than for her voice, made debut in Vienna (1859), as Second Boy in *Die Zauberflöte*; appeared in Berlin, London, and Paris, as well as Russia (1868–69) and US (1872–74); had a repertory that included Donna Anna, Zerlina, Valentine, Eva, Selika, Lenora (*Trovatore*) and Azucena, none of which were as celebrated as her Carmen. ❖ See also *Women in World History.*

LUCCA, princess of (1777–1820). *See Bonaparte, Elisa.*

LUCCIONI, Eugénie Lemoine- (b. 1912). *See Lemoine-Luccioni, Eugénie.*

LUCE, Claire (1903–1989). American theatrical dancer. Born Oct 15, 1903, in Syracuse, NY; died Aug 31, 1989, in New York, NY; m. Clifford W. Smith. ❖ Made professional debut with Russian Opera Ballet (1921); appeared on Broadway in numerous musicals, including *Little Jesse James* (1923), *Dear Sir* (1924), *The Music Box Revue of 1924, No Foolin'* (1926) and *The Scarlet Page* (1929); was Fred Astaire's 1st dance partner after his sister Adele's retirement, performing with him on Broadway in *The Gay Divorcée* (1932), among others; switched to straight drama, creating the role of Curley's Wife in *Of Mice and Men* (1937); also appeared in Shakespearean roles on stage, tv and film; films include *Up the River* (1930), *Lazybones* (1935), *Vintage Wine* (1935) and *Over She Goes* (1938).

LUCE, Clare Boothe (1903–1987). American editor, playwright, and political activist. Born Clare Snyder Boothe, April 10, 1903, in New York, NY; died Oct 9, 1987; dau. of William F. Boothe (theater violinist) and Anna Clara (Snyder) Boothe (musical "chorus girl"); attended St. Mary's in Garden City, LI, 1915–17; The Castle, Tarrytown, NY, 1917–19; Colby College, Fordham University, LittD, Creighton University, Georgetown University, and Temple University; m. George Tuttle Brokaw (garment-industry heir), Aug 10, 1923 (div., 1929); m. Henry R. Luce II (the *Time* magnate), Nov 23, 1935 (died 1967); children: (1st m.) Ann Clare Brokaw (1924–1944). ❖ Editor, playwright, congresswoman, ambassador, and eminent convert to Catholicism, was one of the earliest supporters of a constitutional Equal Rights Amendment for women, the 1st congresswoman from her home state, and the 1st woman to represent the US as ambassador in a major European capital; was associate editor for *Vogue* (1930); was associate editor for *Vanity Fair* (1931–32) and managing editor (1933–34); became a newspaper columnist (1934), and playwright (1935); wrote play *The Women* (1936), a roaring success that ran for 657 performances; followed this with 2 more, *Kiss the Boys Goodbye* (1938) and the anti-Nazi drama *Margin for Error* (1939); served as war correspondent (1939–40), traveling extensively through the European and Far Eastern theaters of conflict, and published *Europe in the Spring,* which described the "Phoney War"; served as Republican member of 78th and 79th Congresses from 4th Connecticut district (1943–47); served as US ambassador to Italy (1953–57); began to write frequently for *National Review* and was an ardent champion of the anti-abortion movement. ❖ See also Stephen Shadegg, *Clare Boothe Luce* (Simon & Schuster, 1970); Wilfrid Sheed, *Clare Boothe Luce* (Dutton, 1982); Sylvia Jukes Morris, *Rage for Fame: The Ascent of Clare Boothe Luce* (Random, 1997); and *Women in World History.*

LUCE, Lila (1899–1999). American philanthropist. Name variations: Lila Hotz Luce Tyng. Born Lila Ross Hotz, 1899, in Chicago, IL; died April 1999 in Gladstone, NJ; m. Henry R. Luce II (the *Time* magnate), 1925 (div. Oct 5, 1935); children: Peter Luce and Henry Luce III. ❖ Was a philanthropist and volunteer for numerous NY and NJ cultural institutions.

LUCHAIRE, Corinne (1921–1950). French actress. Born Feb 11, 1921, in Paris, France; died of TB, Jan 22, 1950, in Paris; dau. of Jean Luchaire (journalist, shot for collaboration, Feb 1946). ❖ Was a big hit in *Prison sans barreaux* (*Prison Without Bars*, 1938); made 5 other films (1939–40), including *Conflit* and *Le dernier tournant;* after WWII, was convicted as a collaborator with the Nazis, spent months in jail, and died in poverty. ❖ See also autobiography (in French) *Ma drôle de vie* (1949).

LUCIA. *Variant of Lucy.*

LUCIA (r. 1288–1289). Countess of Tripoli. Name variations: Lucy of Antioch; princess of Antioch; dau. of Bohemund VI, prince of Antioch and count of Tripoli (r. 1252–1275), and Sibylla of Armenia; younger sister of Bohemund VII (d. 1287), count of Tripoli (r. 1275–1287); m. Narjot of Toucy (grand admiral). ❖ When brother Bohemund VII died childless (1287), was named heir, but the succession was bitterly opposed by her mother; though she came into power, was soon deposed. ❖ See also *Women in World History.*

LUCIA (1908–2001). Duchess of Ancona. Name variations: Lucia de Bourbon; Lucie di Borbone; Princess Lucia of Two Sicilies. Born July 9, 1908, at Schloss Nymphenburg, Germany; died Nov 3, 2001, in Sao Paulo; dau. of Ferdinand, duke of Calabria, and Maria of Bavaria (b. 1872); m. Eugene of Savoy, duke of Ancona, in 1938; children: Maria Isabella of Savoy-Genoa (b. 1943).

LUCIA, Saint (d. 303). *See Lucy.*

LUCIA, Sister (1907–2005). Portuguese nun. Name variations: Sister Lucia dos Santos; mistakenly Lucia Marto. Born Lucia Abobora dos Santos, Mar 22, 1907, in Aljustrel, near Fatima, Portugal; died Feb 13, 2005, in Coimbra; dau. of Antonio dos Santos and Maria Rosa. ❖ With cousins Francisco and Jacinta Marto, apparently saw a vision of Mary the Virgin near the Portuguese town of Fatima, while tending the family's sheep (May 13, 1917); claimed that there were subsequent apparitions on the 13th of every month between May and October of that year, where the Virgin spoke of their futures and the future of the world (prophecies that were kept secret for years); after Francisco and Jacinta died in the influenza epidemic (1919), fled to a convent school in Oporto because of hostility to her accounts (1923); was ordained a nun, taking the name Maria de los Dolores (1925); moved to a convent at Pontevedra in Spain

(1928); after the Roman Catholic Church declared the Fatima apparitions "worthy of belief," became one of the churches most influential women of the 20th century; transferred to the Carmelite convent in Coimbra and given the name Sister Lucia de Jesus (1948); wrote *Os apelos da mensagem de Fatima* (*Appeals of the Fatima Message*, 2000). Fatima has become a place of pilgrimage.

LUCIA OF NARNI (1476–1544). Dominican nun and political adviser. Name variations: Lucia Broccadelli; Lucia from Narni. Born Lucia Broccadelli, Dec 13, 1476, in Narni, South Umbria; dau. of Bartolomeo Broccadelli and Gentilina (Cassio) Broccadelli; m. Pietro di Alessio, count of Milan. ❖ Following husband's death, entered the Third Order of Penance of St. Dominic, and was received into a nunnery in Viterbo; received stigmata and was considered deserving of the name of saint (1501); served as political and spiritual advisor of Duke Ercole I of Este in Ferrara; following his death, fell into disgrace and spent last years in the cloister, devoting herself to contemplation. ❖ See also *Women in World History.*

LUCIA OF RUGIA (fl. 1220). Queen of Poland. Fl. around 1220; m. Ladislas III Laskonogi (Spindleshanks) of Wielkopolska, king of Poland (r. 1228–1231).

LUCIC, Mirjana (1982—). German tennis player. Born Mar 9, 1982, in Dortmund, Germany; dau. of Angelka and Marinko Lucic (decathlete). ❖ Fled to US with mother and siblings to avoid abusive father (1998); was a semifinalist in singles at Wimbledon (1999).

LUCID, Shannon (1943—). American biochemist and astronaut. Born Shannon Wells in Shanghai, China, Jan 14, 1943; dau. of Joseph Oscar Wells (Baptist preacher) and Myrtle Wells (missionary nurse); settled in Bethany, OK, 1949; University of Oklahoma, BS in chemistry, 1963, PhD in biochemistry, 1973; m. Michael Lucid (chemist), 1968; children: daughters Kawai Dawn Lucid and Shandara Lucid, son Michael Lucid. ❖ Was a member of NASA's 1st class of female astronauts (1978); went on 1st space mission aboard the shuttle *Discovery* (1985), followed by 3 subsequent missions; set the American record in space, spending 188 days aboard the Russian space station *Mir* (1996). ❖ See also *Women in World History.*

LUCIENNE OF SEGNI (r. around 1252–1258). Princess and regent of Tripoli and Antioch. Reigned (c. 1252–58); great-niece of Pope Innocent III; cousin of Pope Gregory IX; 2nd wife of Bohemund V, prince of Antioch and count of Tripoli (r. 1233–1252); children: Bohemund VI, prince of Antioch (r. 1251–1268), count of Tripoli (r. 1275); Plaisance of Antioch (who m. Henry I, king of Cyprus [r. 1218–1253]). ❖ When husband died (1252), assumed the regency for underage son; was deposed when Tripoli came under control of the Embriaco family (1258). ❖ See also *Women in World History.*

LUCILLA (b. 150). Roman noblewoman. Born Annia or Anna Aurelia Galeria Lucilla on Feb 7, 150; dau. of Faustina II (130–175 CE) and Marcus Aurelius, Roman emperor (r. 161–180); m. Lucius Verus; m. Ti. Claudius Pompeianus.

LUCILLE (1862–1935). See Duff Gordon, Lucy.

LUCKETT, LeToya (1981—). American singer. Name variations: Destiny's Child. Born LeToya Nicole Luckett, Mar 11, 1981, in Houston, TX. ❖ With Beyonce Knowles, LaTavia Roberson and Kelly Rowland, formed R&B group Destiny's Child (1989); with group, released hit singles "No, No, No," "The Writing's on the Wall," "Bills, Bills, Bills" and "Say My Name"; replaced along with Roberson by Michelle Williams (early 2000); with Roberson and Nadia, formed group Angel.

LUCKNER, Gertrud (1900–1995). German pacifist and resistance leader. Born of German parents in Liverpool, England, Sept 26, 1900; died in Freiburg im Breisgau, Germany, Aug 31, 1995; University of Frankfurt am Main, degree in political science, 1920; University of Freiburg im Breisgau, PhD. ❖ A Quaker and a Catholic, assisted in the activities of the Raphaelsverein, a Catholic organization that helped Jews and others who were homeless due to Nazi persecution; began working in Freiburg for another Catholic group, the charity organization Caritasverband (1938), helping Jews to flee Germany; was arrested by the Nazis while traveling on a train en route to Berlin (Mar 24, 1943); survived 2 years in the Ravensbrück concentration camp and liberated by Soviet soldiers (May 1945); began publishing the *Freiburger Rundbrief* (Freiburg Circular) to foster interreligious dialogue between Christians

and Jews (1948); worked to increase understanding between Christians and Jews in postwar Germany. ❖ See also *Women in World History.*

LUCRECE. *Variant of Lucretia.*

LUCRETIA (?–510 BCE). Roman noblewoman. Name variations: Lucrece. Born in Rome; date of birth unknown; died in either Collatia or Rome, c. 510 BCE; dau. of Spurius Lucretius Tricipitinus, a prefect of Rome; m. Lucius Tarquinius Collatinus, a 1st consul of Rome. ❖ Roman matron of historic and legendary fame whose rape, plea for vengeance, and consequent suicide led to the overthrow of kings in Rome and the establishment of the Roman Republic; was raped by Sextus Tarquinius, the king's son; was a catalyst for the Roman overthrow of Etruscan kings and has been the subject of elaborate legend throughout Western history; considered a fictional figure by some. ❖ See also *Women in World History.*

LUCRETIA BORGIA (1480–1519). *See Borgia, Lucrezia.*

LUCREZIA. *Variant of Lucretia.*

LUCREZIA BORGIA (1480–1519). *See Borgia, Lucrezia.*

LUCREZIA DE MEDICI. *See Medici, Lucrezia de.*

LUCUSTA (fl. 54 CE). *See Locusta.*

LUCY. *Variant of Lucille, Lucina, Lucinda, Lucretia, or Lucrezia.*

LUCY (d. 303). Saint. Name variations: Lucia. Martyred in Syracuse, 303, during reign of Diocletian. ❖ According to legend, rejected a pagan suitor who denounced her as a Christian; was condemned to a brothel; though she escaped, was burned to death at the pyre, remaining alive in the midst of the flames until an executioner pierced her throat with a dagger; is the patron saint of the blind. Feast day is Dec 13.

LUCY, Mother (1760–1821). *See Wright, Lucy.*

LUCY MAGDALENA, Dame (1619–1650). *See Cary, Lucy.*

LUCY OF SCOTLAND (d. 1090). Saint. Died 1090; dau. of a king of Scotland. ❖ Descended from Scottish royalty; left the court of her father and went to Lorraine, France, where she became a shepherd for a man named Thiébaut; upon his death, inherited his fortune which she used to build a church and an hermitage on the mountain which still bears her name. Feast day is Sept 19. ❖ See also *Women in World History.*

LUCY, Autherine Juanita (1929—). African-American civil-rights activist. Name variations: Autherine Foster. Born Oct 5, 1929, in Shiloh, Alabama; dau. of Minnie Hosea Lucy and Milton Cornelius Lucy (farmer); Miles College, BA, 1952; m. Rev. Hugh Foster; children: 5. ❖ The 1st African-American to attempt to integrate the University of Alabama, eventually won a federal lawsuit that required the university to admit her as a graduate student in library science (1956); on the 3rd day of classes, faced hostile mobs and needed a police escort; was expelled the next day, with the university claiming it was for her safety and that of the other students; returned to the university (1989) and earned an MA in education (1992). ❖ See also *Women in World History.*

LUCY, Elizabeth (fl. 1460s). English royal mistress. Name variations: Elizabeth Waite or Wayte; Elizabeth Shore. Born Elizabeth Waite of humble origins in the Southampton area of London before 1445; dau. of Thomas Waite or Wayte, a minor Hampshire gentleman; m. Sir William Lucy (died 1492); mistress of Edward IV (1442–1483), king of England (r. 1461–1483); children: (with Edward) Arthur Plantagenet (d. 1541), 1st Viscount L'Isle; Elizabeth Plantagenet (b. around 1464 and married Thomas Lumley); Grace Plantagenet (d. 1492). ❖ Had an affair with Edward IV, king of England, from around his accession in 1461 to his marriage to Elizabeth Woodville in 1464.

LUCY DE BLOIS (d. 1120). French princess. Name variations: sometimes referred to as Agnes; Lucy of Blois. Died with her sister in the wreck of the White Ship, Nov 25, 1120, in Barfleur, Normandy, France; dau. of Stephen Henry of Blois, count of Blois, and Adela of Blois (1062–c. 1137); sister of Matilda de Blois (d. 1120) and Stephen of Blois (c. 1096–1154), later king of England (r. 1135–1154).

LÜDERS, Marie-Elizabeth (1888–1966). German politician and feminist. Name variations: Marie-Elisabeth Luders or Lueders. Born 1888 in Berlin, Germany; died 1966; dau. of a civil servant. ❖ Became one of 1st women to be awarded doctorate in political science and economics (1912); founded National Women's Service with Gertrud Bäumer and others; headed war office dealing with women's labor and later joined Democratic Party (1919); became member of National Assembly and then Reichstag; campaigned against Nazi policy and was arrested by Gestapo (1937); went into exile and upon return became member of senate (1947); was senior member of Bundestag (1953) and made honorary president of Federal Democratic Party (1957).

LUDFORD, Sarah (1951—). English politician. Name variations: Baroness Sarah Ludford. Born Mar 14, 1951, in Halesworth, Suffolk, England. ❖ Barrister; served as vice-chair of Liberal Democrats' Federal Policy Committee (1991–98); served as councillor of London Borough of Islington (1991–99); became life peer in House of Lords (1997); as a member of the European Liberal, Democrat and Reform Party, elected to 5th European Parliament (1999–2004) from UK.

LUDGARDA (fl. 1200s). Polish noblewoman. Fl. in the 1200s; dau. of Henry I, duke of Mecklenburg; 1st wife of Przemysl or Przemyslav II, king of Poland (1257–1296, r. 1290–1296).

LUDING, Christa Rothenburger. See Rothenburger-Luding, Christa.

LUDINGTON, Nancy. American pairs skater. Name variations: Nancy Rouillard; Nancy Ludington Graham. Born Nancy Rouillard; m. Ron Ludington (skater). ❖ With partner Ron Ludington, won 4 US National titles (1957–60) and a bronze medal at Squaw Valley Olympics (1960). Inducted into US Figure Skating Hall of Fame (1993).

LUDINGTON, Sybil (1761–1839). American Revolution hero. Born Sybil Ludington, April 5, 1761, in Fredericksburg, NY; died in NY, 1839; dau. of Henry Ludington (1738–1817, mill owner and colonel in NY militia) and Abigail (Luddington) Ludington (1745–1825); m. Edward Ogden, in 1784; children: 4 sons, 2 daughters. ❖ At 16, volunteered to ride 40 miles through the dark countryside of New York State, warning the local militia about a British raid at Danbury, CT (April 26, 1777). ❖ See also Mary Elizabeth Jones, *The Midnight Ride of Sybil Ludington* (Pimpewaug Press, 1976); and *Women in World History.*

LUDLOW, Johnny. See Wood, Ellen Price.

LUDMILA. Variant of Ludmilla.

LUDMILA (859–920). Saint and duchess of Bohemia. Name variations: Saint Ludmila, Ludmilla, Ljudmila. Born at Psov, a place also known as Melnik, c. 859 CE; murdered, Sept 16, 920 (some sources cite 921); dau. of a Lusatian Serb prince named Slavibor; m. Borojov or Borivoj I, count of Bohemia (r. 871–894), in 873; children: 3 daughters and 3 sons, including Spithnjew also known as Spytihnev I (d. 915), king of Bohemia, and Ratislav also known as Vratislav I (887–920), duke of Bohemia (r. 912–920). ❖ Accepted Christianity shortly after husband's conversion (874); after he died (894), had a large hand in influencing eldest son Spytihnev who fostered Christianity in Bohemia by building the churches of saints Peter and Paul at Budec and the Church of Mary the Virgin at Prague Castle; when he died and her 13-year-old grandson Wenceslas became king, had to contend with daughter-in-law Drahomira, a pagan, who was named regent (920); was placed in charge of Wenceslas' education; retired to her castle and attempted to placate Drahomira by assuring her she did not desire undue power in Bohemia; taken prisoner under orders of Drahomira (920), was strangled to death. The people of Bohemia, deeply moved by the circumstances of her death, visited her tomb where they testified miracles were occurring; when Wenceslas ascended the throne (925) at age 18, he banished Drahomira and transferred Ludmila's remains to Prague. Feast day is Sept 16. ❖ See also *Women in World History.*

LUDMILLA. Variant of Ludmila.

LUDMILLA OF BOHEMIA (fl. 1100s). Duchess of Bavaria. Fl. in the 1100s; m. Ludwig also known as Louis I (d. 1231), duke of Bavaria (r. 1183–1231); children: Otto II the Illustrious (1206–1253), count Palatine (r. 1231–1253, who m. Agnes of Saxony).

LUDOVICA. Variant of Louisa or Luisa.

LUDOVICA (1808–1892). Electress and queen of Bavaria. Name variations: Louisa Wilhelmina of Bavaria. Born in 1808; died in 1892; dau. of Maximilian I Joseph of Bavaria (b. 1756), elector of Bavaria (r. 1799–1805) and king of Bavaria (r. 1805–1825), and Caroline of Baden (1776–1841); m. Maximilian Joseph (1808–1888), duke of Bavaria; children: Louis also known as Ludwig (1831–1920); Charles Theodore also known as Karl Theodor "Gackl" (1839–1909), who m. Maria Josepha of Portugal); Helene of Bavaria (1834–1890); Elizabeth of Bavaria (1837–1898); Maria Sophia Amalia (1841–1925, who m. Francis II of Naples); Mathilde of Bavaria (1843–1925); Sophie of Bayern (1847–1897); Maximilian (1849–1893).

LUDWIG, Christa (1924—). German mezzo-soprano. Born in Berlin, Germany, Mar 16, 1924; dau. of Eugenia Besalla and Anton Ludwig (both opera singers); studied with her mother and Hüni-Mihacek in Frankfurt; m. Walter Berry, 1957 (div. 1970); m. Paul-Emile Deiber (actor and stage director), 1972. ❖ Made debut in Frankfurt (1946) and Salzburg (1954); was a member of Vienna Staatsoper (from 1954); made Metropolitan Opera debut (1959), appearing there for 10 seasons; debuted at Bayreuth (1966–67), Covent Garden (1969); was an honorary member of the Vienna Staatsoper (1980); focused on soprano roles before deciding to return to the mezzo-soprano repertoire; as a soprano, was probably the greatest Leonore of her time. ❖ See also *Women in World History.*

LUDWIG, Paula (1900–1974). German poet. Born Jan 5, 1900, in Altendtadt, Germany; died Jan 27, 1974, in Darmstadt, Germany. ❖ Worked as actress and painter's model; during war years and after, lived in exile in Brazil for 13 years (1940–53); had long relationship with poet Ivan Goll (who was then married to Claire Goll); wrote poems that often dealt with nature and women's experiences, especially mothers; writings include *Die selige Spur* (1932) and *Dem dunklen Gott* (1932).

LUEDERS, Marie-Elisabeth (1888–1966). See Lüders, Marie-Elizabeth.

LUETTGE, Johanna (1936—). East German track-and-field athlete. Name variations: Johanna Lüttge. Born Mar 10, 1936, in Germany. ❖ At Rome Olympics, won a silver medal in shot put (1960).

LUFT, Lia (1938—). Brazilian novelist, poet and literary critic. Name variations: Lya Luft. Born Sept 15, 1938, in Santa Cruz do Sul, Brazil; m. Celso Pedro Luft; children: 3. ❖ Works, which often reflect conflict between German and Brazilian cultures in southern Brazil, include *Canções de Limiar* (1964), *Flauta doce* (1972), *Matéria do cotidiano* (1978), *A asa esquerda do anjo* (1981), *O quarto fechado* (1984), *Mulher no palco* (1984), *O Rio do meio* (1996), *O ponto cego* (1999), and *Mar de dentro* (2000). Won Alfonsina Storni Prize.

LUGARD, Lady (1852–1929). See Shaw, Flora.

LUGO, duchess of. See Elena (b. 1963).

LUHAN, Mabel Dodge (1879–1962). American arts patron and salonnière. Name variations: Mabel Dodge. Born Mabel Ganson, Feb 26, 1879, in Buffalo, NY; died in Taos, NM, Aug 13, 1962; dau. of Charles Ganson (banker) and Sara McKay (Cook) Ganson; m. Karl Evans, 1900 (killed 1902); m. Edwin Dodge (architect), 1905 (div. 1914); m. Maurice Sterne (artist), 1916 (div.); m. Antonio (Tony) Luhan (Lujan), 1923 (died 1963); children: (1st m.) John Ganson Evans (writer). ❖ Early 20th-century benefactor of the arts and of the Pueblo Indians of New Mexico, 1st through her salons in Florence and NY, later through her friendship and support of many artists and intellectuals at her home in Taos, ran her Florence salon (1905–12); ran her NY salon (1912–16); published her autobiographies (1933, 1935, 1936, 1937); writings include *Lorenzo in Taos* (1932), *Intimate Memories: Background* (1933), *European Experiences* (1935), *Winter in Taos* (1935), *Movers and Shakers* (1936), *Edge of the Taos Desert* (1937) and *Taos and Its Artists* (1948). ❖ See also Winifred Frazer, *Mabel Dodge Luhan* (Twayne, 1984); Lois Palken Rudnick, *Mabel Dodge Luhan: New Woman, New Worlds* (U. of New Mexico Press, 1984); and *Women in World History.*

LUIS, Agustina Bessa (1922—). See Bessa-Luís, Agustina.

LUIS, Alejandrina (1967—). Cuban volleyball player. Name variations: Alejandrina Luis Hernandez. Born Aug 25, 1967, in Cuba. ❖ At Barcelona Olympics, won a gold medal in team competition (1992); won team gold medals at Atlanta Olympics (1996) and Sydney Olympics (2000).

LUIS HERNANDEZ, Alejandrina (1967—). See Luis, Alejandrina.

LUISA. Variant of Louisa.

LUISA, duchess of Lucca (1782–1824). See Maria Luisa of Etruria.

LUÍSA DE GUSMÃO (1613–1666). See Luisa de Guzman.

LUISA DE GUZMAN (1613–1666). Duchess of Braganza. Name variations: Louise de Guzman; Luísa de Gusmão, Luisa de Gusmao, Luisa Maria de Guzmán. Born Luisa Francisca de Guzman, Oct 13, 1613, in San Lúcar de Barremeda in southern Spain; died Nov 27, 1666, in Lisbon, Portugal; dau. of Juan Manuel Pérez de Guzman, duke of Medina Sidonia, and Juana de Sandoval; m. João or John (1604–

1656), 8th duke of Braganza or Bragança, later John IV the Fortunate, king of Portugal (r. 1640–1656), Jan 12, 1634; children: Joanna of Portugal (1636–1653); Catherine of Braganza (1638–1705); Afonso or Alphonso VI (1643–1683), king of Portugal (r. 1656–1667); Teodósio or Teodosio (1645–1653), 9th duke of Braganza; Pedro or Peter II (1648–1706), king of Portugal (r. 1667–1706). ❖ Played a decisive role in the restoration of Portuguese independence (1640) and became queen of Portugal as a result; following husband's death (1656), governed as regent for 10-year-old son Alphonso VI; with son's ministers, reorganized and strengthened Portugal's armed forces to resist Spanish aggression; completed negotiations for an alliance with the English, including marriage of daughter Catherine to Charles II, king of England; was forced to turn power over to son (June 23, 1662); retired to the Discalced Carmelite convent in Xabregas. ❖ See also *Women in World History*.

LUISA FERNANDA (1832–1897). Spanish princess and duchess of Galliera and Montpensier. Name variations: Louisa Fernanda; Louise Bourbon; Louise of Spain. Born Jan 30, 1832; died Feb 2, 1897; dau. of Ferdinand VII, king of Spain (r. 1813–1833), and his 4th wife, Maria Cristina I of Naples (1806–1878); sister of Isabella II (1830–1904), queen of Spain; m. Anton or Antoine (1824–1890), duke of Montpensier, Oct 10, 1846; children: Amalie (1851–1870); Christine (1852–1879); Marie de Regla (1856–1861); Ferdinand (1859–1873); Anthony or Antoine Bourbon, 4th duke of Galliera and duke of Montpensier; Maria Isabella (1848–1919); Maria de las Mercedes (1860–1878, who m. Alphonso XII, king of Spain); Philipp (1862–1864); Louis (1867–1874).

LUISA OF BADEN (1779–1826). *See Elizabeth of Baden.*

LUISA OF ETRURIA (1782–1824). *See Maria Luisa of Etruria.*

LUISA OF SICILY (1804–1844). *See Louisa Carlotta of Naples.*

LUISE. *Variant of Louise.*

LUISE VON PREUSSEN (1776–1810). *See Louise of Prussia.*

LUITGARDE. *Variant of Liutgard.*

LUITGARDE (d. 800). Queen of the Franks. Name variations: Liutgard; Luitgard. Died in 800; became 5th wife of Charles I also known as Charlemagne (742–814), king of the Franks (r. 768–814), and Holy Roman emperor (r. 800–814), in 794.

LUKANINA, Ninel (1937—). Soviet volleyball player. Born Sept 18, 1937, in USSR. ❖ At Tokyo Olympics, won a silver medal in team competition (1964).

LUKE, Jemima (1813–1906). English hymn writer. Born Jemima Thompson, Aug 19, 1813, in London, England; died 1906; m. Samuel Luke (Congregational minister), 1843; no children. ❖ Wrote most famous hymn, *The Child's Desire*, better known by its 1st line, "I think, when I read that sweet story of old" (1841); spent later years editing missionary magazines for children and writing Sunday School curriculums to teach about missionary work. ❖ See also autobiography *Early Years of My Life* (1900); and *Women in World History*.

LUKE, Theresa (1967—). Canadian rower. Born Feb 20, 1967, in Vancouver, British Columbia, Canada. ❖ Won a silver medal at Atlanta Olympics (1996) and a bronze medal at Sydney Olympics (2000), both for coxed eights.

LUKENS, Rebecca (1794–1854). American industrialist and iron manufacturer. Name variations: Rebecca Pennock Lukens; Rebecca Webb Lukens. Born Rebecca Webb Pennock in Chester County, PA, Jan 6, 1794; died near Coatesville, PA, Dec 10, 1854; dau. of Isaac Pennock (ironmaster) and Martha (Webb) Pennock; attended Hilles Boarding School for Young Ladies, Wilmington, Delaware; m. Dr. Charles Lloyd Lukens (physician who later became an ironmaster), 1813 (died 1825); children: 6, only 3 of whom, Martha, Isabella and Charlesanna, reached maturity. ❖ Following husband's death, took over the Brandywine Iron Works, which was then almost bankrupt; became legal owner of the Brandywine Iron Works (1853); settled all husband's debts and was able to retire from the mill which was renamed Lukens Iron Works (1859); was perhaps the 1st woman in US to engage in heavy industry. Under her direction, the mill manufactured iron for the new steam locomotives, producing such high quality plate that it was shipped to Boston and New Orleans, and was even exported to England. Inducted into National Business Hall of Fame (1994). ❖ See also *Women in World History*.

LUKHMANOVA, N.A. (1840–1907). Russian playwright, essayist and short-story writer. Name variations: Nadezhda Aleksandrovna Lukhmánova. Born 1840 in Russia; died 1907; widowed, 1873. ❖ Traveled widely and lectured on travels, women's issues, and other popular topics; served as volunteer nurse during Russo-Japanese War; wrote children's fiction, adult fiction, short biographies of famous women, including Marie Bashkirtseff and Harriet Beecher Stowe, and educational tracts, including *On the Position of Unmarried Daughters Within the Family* (1896), *On Happiness* (1898) and *A Woman's Guide* (1898); also wrote the autobiographical novel *Twenty Years Ago (From Life in an Institute)* (1893).

LUKKARINEN, Marjut (1966—). Finnish cross-country skier. Name variations: Marjut Lukkarinen-Rolig; Marjut Rolig. Born Feb 4, 1966, in Finland. ❖ Won a gold medal for the 5km and a silver medal for the 15km at Albertville Olympics (1992).

LUKOM, Elena (1891–1968). Russian Soviet ballet dancer. Name variations: Yelena Mikhailovna Lukom. Born May 5, 1891, in St. Petersburg, Russia; died Feb 27, 1968, in St. Petersburg. ❖ Trained at Imperial Ballet school in St. Petersburg under Mikhail Fokine, among others, then danced there for 8 years; danced for over 30 years with Maryinsky/Kirov in imperial- and Soviet-style ballets; best known for her Giselle, was also frequently partnered with Boris Shavroff; taught and directed repertory and rehearsal classes at Kirov Ballet after retirement (1941).

LULLING, Astrid (1929—). Luxembourg politician. Born June 11, 1929, in Schifflange, Luxembourg. ❖ Member of the Social Democratic Party Executive Committee (1972–82) and chair of its parliamentary group (1974–79); served as mayor of Schifflange (1970–85) and as a member of Schifflange Municipal Council (1970–2000); was a member of the Chambre des députés (Luxembourg Parliament, 1965–1989, 1999) and president of the National Federation of Luxembourg Women; as a member of the European People's Party (Christian Democrats) and European Democrats, elected to 4th and 5th European Parliament (1994–99, 1999–2004). Named Commander of the Order of the Republic (Italy), Grand Officer of the Order of Merit of the Grand-Duchy of Luxembourg, and Grand Officer of the Order of the Crown of Oak (Luxembourg).

LULU (1948—). Scottish pop singer and actress. Born Marie McDonald McLaughlin Lawrie, Nov 3, 1948, in Lennox Castle, Lennoxtown, Glasgow, Scotland; m. Maurice Gibb (singer with Bee Gees), 1969 (div. 1974); m. John Frieda (hairdresser), 1974 (div. 1992); children: (2nd m.) Jordan. ❖ Began singing publicly at young age; at 14, joined group Glen Eagles; changed name to Lulu, group's name to The Luvvers, and recorded 1st single (1964), a remake of Isley Brothers' "Shout" which became 1st of many smash hits in next 2 years, including "Here Comes The Night", "Leave A little Love" and "Try To Understand"; made film debut in *Gonks Go Beat* (1964); left The Luvvers (1966), touring as solo artist; made stage acting debut in *Babes in the Wood* (1966), then appeared in the film *To Sir with Love* and performed its hit title song (1967); on tv, starred in series "Three of a Kind," "Lulu's Back in Town" "Happening to Lulu," "It's Lulu" "Lulu's Party" and had recurring role on "Absolutely Fabulous"; returned to top of European charts with "Boom Bang-A-Bang"; hit top of charts with David Bowie collaboration "The Man Who Sold the World" (1974); performed frequently in London's West End in such shows as *Song and Dance* (1983) and *Guys and Dolls* (1985); had #1 hit with "Relight My Fire" from album *Independence* and co-wrote Tina Turner's "I Don't Want to Fight" (1994); released album of own songs, *Where the Poor Boys Dance* (2000); collaborated with Elton John, Paul McCartney and Sting among others on recent album *Together* (2002). Received Order of the British Empire (OBE, 2000). ❖ See also memoir, *I Don't Want to Fight* (2003).

LUMLEY, Jane (c. 1537–1576). *See Lumley, Joanna.*

LUMLEY, Joanna (c. 1537–1576). British translator. Name variations: Lady Jane or Joanna Lumley. Born Joanna (or Jane) Fitzalan, c. 1537, presumably in Sussex, England; died c. 1576, presumably in Fitzalan home on the Strand; dau. of Henry Fitzalan (c. 1512–1580), 12th earl of Arundel (some record it as 16th earl of Arundel) who was Lord Steward to Elizabeth I, and Katherine Grey Fitzalan (b. around 1520), countess of Arundel; sister of Mary Fitzalan, countess of Arundel (d. 1557); m. John, 1st Baron Lumley, of the Second Creation, c. 1549. ❖ The 1st translator of a Greek drama into English, was responsible for an abridged prose version of Euripides *Iphigenia at Aulis* which was later published as "The

Tragedie of Euripedes called Iphigenia translated out of Greke into Englisshe" (H.H. Child ed., 1909).

LUMLEY, Joanna (1946—). English actress. Born Joanna Lamond Lumley, May 1, 1946, in Srinagar, Kashmir, India; dau. of major in Ghurka Rifles; m. Jeremy Lloyd (comedy writer), 1971 (div. 1971); m. Stephen Barlow (conductor), 1986; children: (with photographer Michael Claydon) Jamie (b. 1967). ❖ Spent early years in Asia, attending army schools in Hong Kong and Malaya before moving to England and taking up ballet in adolescence; made stage debut in *Not Now Darling* (1972); starred in tv series "The New Avengers" (1976–78), "Sapphire and Steel" (1979–82), "Cold Comfort Farm" (1996), "Coming Home" (1998) and "Up in Town" (2002), among many others; came to international prominence as Patsy Stone in "Absolutely Fabulous" (1992–94, 2001) for which she won BAFTA award (1993) and Emmy Award (1994); participated in BBC reality show *Girl Friday* (1994); made travel documentary of Bhutan in *Joanna Lumley in the Kingdom of the Thunderdragon* (1997); won BAFTA Special Award for role in *The Avengers* (2000); films include *Games That Lovers Play* (1970), *The Satanic Rites of Dracula* (1973), *Trail of the Pink Panther* (1982), *Curse of the Pink Panther* (1983), *Shirley Valentine* (1989), *James and the Giant Peach* (1996), *Parting Shots* (1998), *Maybe Baby* (1999) and *Cat's Meow* (2000). Awarded Officer of British Empire (OBE, 1995). ❖ See also autobiography, *Stare Back and Smile* (Viking, 1989).

LUMMIS, Elizabeth (c. 1812–1877). See Ellet, Elizabeth.

LUNA, Rosa (1937–1993). Uruguayan dancer. Born Rosa Amelia Luna, June 20, 1937, in Montevideo, Uruguay; died of heart attack at 55 while performing in Canada, June 13, 1993; dau. of Ceferina "La Chunga" Luna; m. Raúl Abirad; children: (adopted) 1 daughter. ❖ A cultural icon of Uruguay, learned Afro-Uruguayan dance *candombe* as child in tenement slums; began performing in street carnivals as *vedette* dancer with a group called Los Zorros Negros (The Black Foxes), then with Fantasía Negra (Black Fantasy); went on to found dance groups, including Comparsa Afro Oriental (Afro-Uruguayan Group); performed at clubs and concerts, becoming celebrated for expressive, sensual, energetic dance style; while working as a prostitute, killed a man who was attacking her, but was pardoned because of circumstances; returned gradually to dancing and increased in popularity, becoming something of a living myth; performed throughout Latin America and in Canada, Australia and US. For her funeral, a crowd of over 300,000 filled the streets of Montevideo. ❖ See also Rosa Luna and Raúl Abirad, *Sin tanga y sin tongo* (Without a G-String and Without Lies, 1988).

LUNA CASTELLANO, Diadenis. Cuban judoka. Born in Cuba. ❖ Won a bronze medal for 66–72kg half-heavyweight at Atlanta Olympics (1996); won World championships (1995, 1998).

LUND, Hilda M. Canter (1922—). See Canter-Lund, Hilda M.

LUNDBERG, Emma (1881–1954). Swedish-American social worker. Name variations: Emma Octavia Lundberg. Born Emma Octavia Lundberg, Oct 26, 1881, in Tranegärdet, Humle Socken, Västergötland, Sweden; died Nov 17, 1954, in Hartsdale, NY; dau. of Frans Vilhelm Lundberg (machine worker) and Anna Kajsa (Johanson) Lundberg; University of Wisconsin at Madison, AB, 1907, AM, 1908; attended Chicago School of Civics and Philanthropy and New York School of Philanthropy. ❖ Advocate of public welfare services for children and destitute mothers who shaped policy, worked with Associated Charities in Madison and Milwaukee, WI (1910–12) and deputy for Wisconsin Industrial Commission; worked with US Children's Bureau, serving as head of social service division (1914–25), as assistant director of child welfare division (beginning 1935), and as consultant on social services for children (1942–44); retired (1944); with Katharine Lenroot, co-authored Children's Bureau publication, *Illegitimacy as a Child-Welfare Problem*, part I (1920) and part II (1922); worked with Child Welfare League of America, as director of institutional care and as director of studies and surveys, in NYC (1925–29); served as research secretary to Section IV of White House Conference on Child Health and Protection (1929–30); worked for New York State Temporary Emergency Relief Administration (1931–34), becoming director of research and statistics; served as assistant secretary of White House Conference on Children in a Democracy (1940).

LUNDE, Vibeke (1921–1962). Norwegian yacht racer. Born Mar 21, 1921, in Norway; died Aug 12, 1962; m. Peder or Peter Lunde; children: Peter Lunde Jr. (Olympian who won gold and silver medals). ❖ At Helsinki Olympics, won a silver medal in 5.5 meter class with husband (1952).

LUNDEBERG, Helen (1908–1999). American artist. Name variations: Helen Feitelson. Born in Chicago, IL, June 24, 1908; died in Los Angeles, CA, April 19, 1999; studied at Stickney Memorial School of Art, Pasadena, 1930–33; m. Lorser Feitelson (artist). ❖ A cofounder of California's Post-surrealist movement, an independent avant-garde trend of the 1930s, evolved over 6 decades as one of America's foremost painters; worked with husband in same studio for 50 years; paintings include *Double Portrait in Time* (1935) and *The Red Planet* (1939), *Desert Coast* (1963), *Waterways* (1962), and *Double View* (1996); worked for the Southern California Federal Art Project (1933–41), executing *The History of Transportation* (1940), a mosaic wall for Centinela Park in Inglewood; had retrospectives at La Jolla Museum of Modern Art (1971), Los Angeles Municipal Art Gallery (1979) and San Francisco Museum of Modern Art (1980). ❖ See also *Women in World History.*

LUNDEQUIST, Gerda (1871–1959). Swedish actress. Name variations: Gerda Lundeqvist; Gerda Lundeqvist Dahlström or Dahlstrom. Born in Stockholm, Sweden, Feb 14, 1871; died oct 23, 1959; graduate of Stockholm Academy of Music. ❖ Called the "Swedish Bernhardt," made debut (1889), in Strindberg's *Mäster Olof;* distinguished herself in such works as Tolstoy's *Resurrection* and Maeterlinck's *Monna Vanna;* was considered one of the country's leading tragic actresses, with a range that included Antigone and Lady Macbeth (Gruoch), as well as more modern characters such as Mrs. Alving in Ibsen's *Ghosts;* also made several films, including the Mauritz Stiller classic *The Gösta Berling Saga* and *Giflas.*

LUNEBURG, duchess of.
See Sophia of Mecklenburg (1508–1541).
See Dorothy of Denmark (1546–1617).

LUNG, Noemi Ildiko (1968—). Romanian swimmer. Name variations: Noemi Lung-Zaharia; Noemi Zaharia. Born May 16, 1968; attended Florida Atlantic University; m. Christian Zaharia (Olympian in handball). ❖ At 11, began swimming for the Romanian national team; won 5 gold and 2 bronze medals in World University Games (1987); won a bronze medal in the 200-meter indiv. medley and a silver medal in the 400-meter indiv. medley at Seoul Olympics (1988); became head coach at Florida International University (2003).

LUNJEVICA-MASHIN, Draga (1867–1903). See Draga.

LUNN, Janet (1928—). Canadian children's writer. Born Janet Louise Swoboda, Dec 28, 1928, in Dallas, TX; became naturalized Canadian citizen, 1963; dau. of Herman (mechanical engineer) and Margaret (Alexander) Swoboda; attended Queen's University of Kingston, 1947–50; m. Richard Lunn (teacher, died 1987); children: 5. ❖ Immigrated to Canada (1946) and worked as children's editor at Clarke Irwin Publishers (1972–75); works include *Double Spell* (1968), *The Twelve Dancing Princesses* (1979), *The Root Cellar* (1981), *Shadow in Hawthorn Bay* (1986), *Amos's Sweater* (1988), *One Hundred Shining Candles* (1990), *The Hollow Tree* (1997), *Charlotte* (1998), and *Laura Secord* (2001). Received Vicki Metcalf Award (1981), Canadian Council Award for Children's Literature (1986), and Governor General's Award (1998).

LUNYEVITZA-MASHIN, Draga (1867–1903). See Draga.

LUO SHU (1903–1938). Chinese short-story writer. Born 1903 in China; died in childbirth 1938; studied literature in France. ❖ Gained attention with short story, "Wife of Another Man" (1936); also wrote "Aunty Liu," "The Oranges" and "Twice-Married Woman," among others; after death, stories collected and published by writer Ba Jin.

LUO WEI (1983—). Chinese taekwondo player. Born May 23, 1983, in China. ❖ At World championships, placed 1st for 67–72kg (2003); won a gold medal in 67kg at Athens Olympics (2004).

LUO XUEJUAN (1984—). Chinese swimmer. Born Jan 26, 1984, in Hangzhou, China. ❖ At World championships, placed 1st at 50- and 100-meter breaststroke (2001, 2003) and 4x100-meter medley relay (2003); won a gold medal for 100-meter breaststroke at Athens Olympics (2004).

LUPESCU, Elena (c. 1896–1977). Romanian paramour. Name variations: Helena; Elenutza; Magda; Madame Lupescu; (nickname) Duduia. Pronunciation: Loo-PES-que. Born Sept 15, possibly in 1896, in Hertza, Moldavia, Romania; died June 28, 1977, at Estorial outside Lisbon, Portugal; dau. of a small-town Jewish druggist named Nicolas Grünberg Wolff, who changed his name to the Romanian equivalent, Lupescu, and Elizei Falk Wolff, later Elizei Lupescu; attended Pitar Mos convent school, 1907–13; m. Ion Tampeanu or Timpeanu, lieutenant in

Romanian army, 1916 (div. 1920); became 3rd wife of exiled Carol II (1893–1953), king of Romania (r. 1930–1940), July 5 (some sources cite June 3), 1947; no children. ❖ Mistress and later wife of the ruler of Romania, widely thought to be the power behind the throne, who heightened political tensions in her country throughout 1930s; began love affair with Prince Carol (1923); during Carol's trip to England, started open relationship with him, which forced him to renounce his right to the Romanian throne in favor of his son Michael (1925); returned with Carol to Romania where he became king (1930) and established a royal dictatorship (1938); under German and Russian pressure, was forced into exile with husband (1940); was one of the most colorful and politically influential figures in Romania during 1st half of 20th century. ❖ See also Alice-Leone Moats, *Lupescu* (Holt, 1955); and *Women in World History*.

LUPESCU, Magda (c. 1896–1977). *See Lupescu, Elena.*

LUPETEY COBAS, Yurieleidys (1981—). Cuban judoka. Born May 6, 1981, in Cuba. ❖ At A Tournament, won 5 events (2000–03); placed 1st at World championships for 57kg (2001); won a bronze medal for 57kg at Athens Olympics (2004).

LUPICINIA-EUPHEMIA (d. 523). Byzantine empress. Name variations: Lupicina-Euphemia. Died in 523; m. Justin I (Flavius Justinus), Byzantine emperor (r. 518–527); children: adopted son Justinian I (a nephew of Justin's), Byzantine emperor (r. 527–565). ❖ Before being purchased as a slave by Justin I, was a prisoner of war and camp cook; was known for her piety. ❖ See also *Women in World History*.

LUPINO, Ida (1914–1995). American film and tv actress, writer, director, and producer. Born Feb 4, 1914, in London, England; died Aug 3, 1995, in Burbank, CA; dau. of Stanley Lupino (British film comedian) and Constance O'Shay (British actress); sister of Rita Lupino (actress); trained at Royal Academy of Dramatic Arts; m. Louis Hayward (actor), 1938 (div. 1945); m. Collier Young, 1948 (div. 1950); m. Howard Duff (actor), 1951 (div. 1983); children: (3rd m.) Bridget Duff; became US citizen (1948). ❖ One of the few female directors in Hollywood during 1950s–60s, made film acting debut in *Her First Affaire* in England, followed by *Money for Speed*, in which she created the "tough broad" character she would portray so often in her career (both 1933); made Hollywood debut in *Search for Beauty* (1934); appeared in more than 60 films (1933–82), including *Peter Ibbetson* (1935), *Artists and Models* (1937), *The Lady and the Mob* (1939), *The Adventures of Sherlock Holmes* (1939), *The Light That Failed* (1940), *They Drive By Night* (1940), *High Sierra* (1941), *The Sea Wolf* (1941), *Ladies in Retirement* (1941), *Devotion* (1946), *Escape Me Never* (1947), *Beware My Lovely* (1952), *The Big Knife* (1955) and *While the City Sleeps* (1956); directed 1st film, *Not Wanted* (1949), followed by *Outrage* (1950), *Hard, Fast and Beautiful* (1950), *The Hitch-Hiker* (1953), *The Bigamist* (1953) and *The Trouble With Angels* (1966); also wrote, directed and produced for such tv shows as "Have Gun, Will Travel," "Twilight Zone," "Bewitched," "The Untouchables" and "Gilligan's Island"; appeared in CBS series "Four Star Playhouse" and starred with husband Howard Duff in sitcom "Mr. Adams and Eve." Won Best Actress award from New York Film Critics for *The Hard Way* (1943). ❖ See also William Donati, *Ida Lupino* (U. of Kentucky Press, 1996); and *Women in World History*.

LUPINO, Natalina (1963—). French judoka. Born June 13, 1963, in Valenciennes, France. ❖ At Barcelona Olympics, won a bronze medal in +72 kg heavyweight (1992).

LUPITA, Madre (1878–1963). Mexican nun and founder. Name variations: Guadalupe Garcia. Born María Guadalupe García Zavala, April 27, 1878, in Zapopan, Jalisco, Mexico; died June 24, 1963; dau. of Fortino Garcia and Refugio Zavala. ❖ At 23, with Father Cipriano Iniguez, helped found the Congregación de las Siervas de Santa Margarita María y de los Pobres (Congregation of the Servants of Santa Margarita and the Poor) to care for the patients of the Santa Margarita Hospital (1901) in Guadalajara; served as general superior of the order for the remainder of her life and oversaw the formation of 11 more foundations in Mexico; was beatified by John Paul II (2004). Her religious order has 22 foundations in Mexico, Peru, Iceland, Greece and Italy.

LURIE, Alison (1926—). American novelist and literary critic. Born Sept 3, 1926, in Chicago, IL; dau. of Harry and Bernice (Stewart) Lurie; Radcliffe College, AB, 1947; m. Jonathan Peale Bishop (professor), 1948 (div,. 1985); m. Edward Hower; children: (1st m.) 3. ❖ At Cornell University, was a lecturer in literature (1969–73), associate professor (1973–76), then became professor of English (1976); fiction

includes *Love and Friendship* (1962), *The War Between the Tates* (1974), *Only Children* (1979), *The Truth about Lorin Jones* (1988), and *Women and Ghosts;* works of non-fiction include *The Language of Clothes* (1982), *Don't Tell the Grownups: Subversive Children's Literature* (1990), and memoir *Familiar Spirits: A Memoir of James Merrill and David Jackson* (2001); edited 3 collections of folktales for children and was co-editor of 73 volume Garland Library of Children's Classics. Won Pulitzer Prize for *Foreign Affairs* (1984).

LURIE, Nancy O. (1924—). American sociocultural anthropologist. Name variations: Nancy Oestreich. Born Nancy Oestreich on Jan 29, 1924, in Milwaukee, WI; dau. of Carl Ralph Oestreich (professor of engineering at University of Wisconsin–Milwaukee) and Rayline (Danielson) Oestreich; University of Wisconsin–Madison, BA, 1945; University of Chicago, MA; Northwestern University, PhD; m. Edward Lurie (div. 1963); no children. ❖ Known particularly for studies of Winnebago Indians of WI, was an expert witness for Indian petitioners before the US Indian Claims Commission (beginning 1954); served in various positions at University of Wisconsin, Milwaukee, including full professor (from 1966) and chair of anthropology department (1967–70); with June Helm, worked with Dogrib in Canadian Northwest Territories (1959, 1962, 1967); became curator and head of anthropology section of Milwaukee Public Museum (1972); elected president of American Anthropological Association (1982); wrote *Mountain Wolf Woman* (1961).

LURZ, Dagmar (1959—). West German figure skater. Name variations: Dagmar Lurz-Prott. Born Jan 18, 1959, in Germany. ❖ Won a bronze medal at Lake Placid (1980).

LUSARRETA, Pilar de (1914–1967). Argentinean playwright and novelist. Born 1914 in Argentina; died 1967. ❖ Her *Casa en venta* (House for Sale) was 1st performed in 1925; other works include *Job el opulento* (1928), *Celimena sin corazón* (1935), *El culto de los héroes* (1939), *El amor a los sesenta* (1942), *Alondra* (1943), *La gesta de Roger de Flor* (1945), *El manto de Noé* (1965), and *Hombres en mi vida* (1971); also translated and wrote art and literary criticism.

LUSH, Sylvia Rosalind (1935—). *See Pery, Sylvia.*

LUSK, Georgia Lee (1893–1971). American educator and politician. Born Georgia Lee Witt, May 12, 1893, in Carlsbad, NM; died Jan 5, 1971, in Albuquerque, NM; dau. of George Witt (surveyor and rancher) and Mary Isabel (Gilreath) Witt; attended Highlands University and Colorado State Teachers College; graduate of New Mexico State Teachers College (later Western New Mexico University), 1914; married Dolph Lusk (rancher and banker), Aug 1915 (died 1919); children: 3 sons, including Eugene Lusk who served in New Mexico state senate. ❖ Often referred to as "the first lady of New Mexico politics," had a career that spanned 35 years and included several terms in state education posts and a term as the 1st congresswoman elected by the voters in her state; served as school superintendent of Lea County (1924–29) and 4 terms as state superintendent (1931–35, 1943–47); as a Democrat, was elected to US Congress (1946); during her tenure, supported federal aid to education, worked for improvement of school programs and creation of a Cabinet-level department of education, and served on Committee on Veterans' Affairs; after losing bid for reelection (1948), served on War Claims Commission (1949–53). ❖ See also *Women in World History*.

LUSK, Grace (1878–1938). American murderer. Born 1878; died 1938; married and div. ❖ Was a high school teacher in Waukesha, WI; began affair with prominent veterinarian David Roberts (1915); shot his wife Mary Newman Roberts twice with .25 caliber automatic, before making unsuccessful suicide attempt (June 21, 1917); her trial was a national media sensation; after being sentenced to 19-years imprisonment for second-degree murder (May 29, 1918), attacked prosecutor in courtroom; pardoned by Governor John Blaine after serving 5 years (1923).

LUSSAC, Elodie (1979—). French gymnast. Born May 7, 1979, in St. Catherine les Arras, France. ❖ Was Jr. French National champion (1989–92); won Avignon International and Grenoble International (1992), Blume Memorial and Jr. European championships (1993); tied with Laetitia Begue for French National championships (1994); forced to retire due to injuries.

LUSSAN, Marguerite de (1682–1758). French novelist and short-story writer. Born 1682 in Paris, France; died May 31, 1758; believed to be the illeg. dau. of Thomas of Savoy, Comte de Soisson, who provided for her education. ❖ Noted for her intellect, wrote 1st novel *L'Histoire de la comtesse de Gondez* (The Life of the Countess de Gondez, 1725), followed by a collection of fairytales, *Les Veillées de Thessalie* (Evenings in Thessaly, 1731); historical works include *Anecdotes de la cour de Childéric* (1736), *Anecdotes de la cour de François Ier* (1748), *Histoire et règne de Charles VI* (1953), *Histoire de la révolution du royaume de Naples* (1757), and *Vie de Louis Bable Bertonde Crillon* (1757); had many famous friends, including Le Huet and Prince Eugene of Savoy.

LUSSAN, Zelie de (1861–1949). *See De Lussan, Zelie.*

LUSSU, Joyce Salvadori (1912–1988). Italian novelist, essayist and poet. Born Joyce Salvadori, 1812, in Florence, Italy; died Nov 4, 1988, in Rome, Italy; dau. of Gugliemo Salvadori and Giacinta Galletti; sister of Max Salvadori; studied at Heidelberg University, Sorbonne, and Lisbon University; m. Emilio Lussu. ❖ With brother, received non-conformist education in Switzerland; with anti-fascist husband, became a leader in the Movimento di Giustizia e Libertà resistance group (1932) and often lived in exile; out of her experiences, wrote *Fronti e frontiere: Collana della liberazione* (Freedom Has No Frontier, 1945); traveled widely and translated avant-garde writers of Africa and Asia; other writings include *Liriche* (1939), *Donne come te* (1957), *Tradurre poesia* (1967), *Padre, Padrone, Padreterno* (1976), *L'uomo che voleva nascere donna* (1978), and *Donne, guerra e società* (1982); translated work of Turkish poet Nazim Hikmèt.

LUTAYEVA-BERZINA, Valentina (1956—). **Soviet handball player.** Name variations: Valentina Berzina. Born June 18, 1956, in USSR. ❖ At Moscow Olympics, won a gold medal in team competition (1980).

LUTGARD (1182–1246). Flemish Cistercian mystic, stigmatic, and saint. Name variations: Saint Lutgard; Saint Lutgardis. Born in Tongres (Belgium) in 1182; died in Aywières (near Brussels), June 16, 1246. ❖ Joined the Benedictines of Saint-Trond (1194) and became prioress (1205); finding the observance of the Benedictines too lax, transferred to Cistercian convent of Aywières (1208), where she engaged in three seven-year fasts in reparation for the heresy of the Albigensians; at 29, received the stigmata; became totally blind (1235). ❖ See also *Women in World History.*

LUTGARDIS (fl. 1139). Duchess of Brabant. Dau. of Berengar of Sulzbach; m. Godfrey II, duke of Brabant (r. 1139–1142), c. 1139 (died 1142).

LUTHER, Katherine (1499–1550). *See Bora, Katharina von.*

LÜTKEN, Hulda (1896–1947). Danish novelist and poet. Name variations: Hilda Lutken or Luetken. Born 1896 in Jylland, Denmark; died 1947. ❖ Regarded as one of the most important Danish modernists, was influenced by surrealism, psychoanalysis, and expressionism; published 9 collections of poems (1927–45); fiction includes *Mennesket paa Lerfødder* (1943).

LÜTTGE, Johanna (1936—). *See Luettge, Johanna.*

LUTTRELL, Anne (1743–1808). *See Ann Horton.*

LUTYENS, Elisabeth (1906–1983). English composer. Name variations: Mrs. Edward Clarke; Dame Elisabeth Lutyens. Pronunciation: LUTCH-ens. Born Agnes Elisabeth Lutyens in London, England, July 9, 1906; died in London, April 14, 1983; dau. of Edwin Lutyens (preeminent British architect); niece of Constance Lytton; studied at Paris Conservatoire and Royal College of Music; m. Ian Herbert Campbell Glennie, 1933 (div. 1940); m. Edward Clarke (conductor), 1942; children: (1st m.) a son and twin daughters; (2nd m.) Conrad. ❖ Pioneer in 20th-century music, who was recognized in her later years as one of Britain's most important modern composers, composed pieces as soon as she started taking music lessons; began to study the violin and attended Paris Conservatoire, where her talent for composition became increasingly evident; studied with Harold Darke at Royal College of Music; with Elizabeth Maconchy, Anne Macnaghten and Iris Lemare, founded Macnaghten-Lemare concerts at Mercury Theater, Notting Hill Gate, for performance of works by modern composers (1931); through the years, despite her commitment to composing modern atonal music, composed over 200 orchestrations for films and documentaries; struggled against the musical establishment's general rejection of 12-tone music, which she refused to abandon; increasingly became a respected figure in musical world; wrote a lyric drama, *Isis and Osiris* (1969), which was followed by an opera *Time Off? Not the Ghost of a Chance* (1972); having composed some 2,000 pieces, laid new groundwork for future serious composers and led music lovers worldwide into hitherto unknown territories of sound. Major symphonic works include *Fantasy for strings* (1937), Chamber concerto No. 2, op. 8 (1941), *Suite galoise* (1944), *Proud city* (1945), *Petite suite* (1946),

Concerto, op. 15 (1947), Chamber concerto No. 4, op. 8 (1947); Chamber concerto No. 5, op. 8 (1947), *The English Seaside Suite* (1951), *The English Theater Suite* (1951), Chorale, op. 36 (*Homage to Stravinsky*, 1956), *Novenaria* (1967), *The Winter of the World*, op. 98 (1974), *Eos* (1975), *Rondel* (1978), Six Bagatelles (1978) and *Echoi* (1980). Named Commander of the British Empire (CBE, 1969). ❖ See also autobiography *A Goldfish Bowl* (Cassell, 1972); Meirion Harries and Susie Harries, *A Pilgrim Soul: The Life and Work of Elisabeth Lutyens* (Michael Joseph, 1989); and *Women in World History.*

LUTYENS, Emily (1874–1964). *See Lytton, Emily.*

LUTYENS, Mary (1908–1999). English biographer and novelist. Name variations: Mary Links; (pseudonym) Esther Wyndham. Pronunciation: LUTCH-ens. Born Mary Lutyens, 1908, in England; died April 9, 1999, in London, England; dau. of Edwin Lutyens (preeminent British architect) and Lady Emily Lytton (1874–1964); niece of Constance Lytton; sister of Elisabeth Lutyens (1906–1983, composer); m. Joe Links; children: (1st m.) Amanda. ❖ Won praise for biographies, which included *Millais and the Ruskins* (1968); also wrote several books on spiritual philosopher Jiddu Krishnamurti, including *Krishnamurti: His Life and Death.*

LUTZ, Berta (1894–1976). Brazilian feminist, writer, and activist. Pronunciation: BEAR-ta LOOHTS. Born Berta María Júlia Lutz, Aug 2, 1894, in São Paulo, Brazil; died Sept 16, 1976, in Rio de Janeiro, Brazil; dau. of Adolfo Lutz (pioneer of tropical medicine in Brazil) and Amy (Fowler) Lutz (volunteer nurse among lepers in Hawaii); attended primary school in Rio de Janeiro, secondary and advanced study in France; attended University of Paris (Sorbonne), 1911–18, earning a Licenciée dès Sciences; earned bachelor's degree in law from University of Rio de Janeiro, 1933. ❖ Committed to the enfranchisement of women, founded many feminist organizations, including the influential Federaçao Brasileira pelo Progresso Feminino (Brazilian Federation for the Advancement of Women), an organization that pushed for the education of women, protective legislation for women and children, and the right of women in Brazil to vote; served as its president (1922–42); represented Brazil at Pan American Conference of Women (1922); elected president of Inter-American Union of Women at the Inter-American Congress (1925); named to a leadership position at 11th Congress of International Woman Suffrage Alliance (1929); invited to serve on drafting committee for the constitution that gave Brazil's women the vote (1934); ran as a candidate of Partido Autonomista (Autonomous Party) for Federal District for the Chamber of Deputies (Lower House, 1934) and was elected as an alternate; when the incumbent died in office, entered the Chamber of Deputies (1936) and helped to create the Commission for the Code for Women; represented Brazil at Inter-American Commission of Women, a group that offered advice with regard to framing of the UN Charter (1945). ❖ See also *Women in World History.*

LUTZE, Manuela (1974—). German rower. Born Mar 20, 1974, in Germany; attended University Otto Von Guericke. ❖ Won gold medal at World championships for quadruple sculls (1997, 1998, 1999, 2001, 2002); won a gold medal for quadruple sculls at Sydney Olympics (2000) and at Athens Olympics (2004).

LUX, Amelie (1977—). German windsurfer. Born April 5, 1977, in Oldenburg, Germany. ❖ Won a silver medal for board (Mistral) at Sydney Olympics (2000).

LUXEMBOURG, duchess of. *See Luxemburg, duchess of.*

LUXEMBURG, countess of. *See Ermesind of Luxemburg (d. 1247).*

LUXEMBURG, duchess of.
See Elizabeth of Gorlitz (c. 1380–c. 1444).
See Mary of Burgundy (1457–1482).
See Boufflers, Madeleine-Angelique, Duchesse de (1707–1787).

LUXEMBURG, grand duchess of.
See Charlotte (1896–1985).
See Marie Adelaide of Luxemburg (1894–1924).
See Josephine-Charlotte of Belgium (b. 1927).

LUXEMBURG, Madeleine-Angelique de Neufville-Villeroi, Duchesse de (1707–1787). *See Boufflers, Madeleine-Angelique, Duchess de.*

LUXEMBURG, Rosa (1870–1919). Polish-German economist, labor activist, and journalist. Name variations: Rozalia or Róża Luxsenburg. Pronunciation: LOOKS-em-boorg. Born Rozalia Luxsenburg, Mar 5,

1870, at Zamosc, Russian Poland; murdered Jan 15, 1919, in Berlin, Germany; 5th child of Line (Loewenstein) Luxsenburg and Elias (or Eduard) Luxsenburg (timber merchant); University of Zurich, Doctor of Philosophy in economics, 1897; m. Gustav Lübeck, 1898 (div.); no children. ❖ Economist and socialist political theoretician whose work contributed significantly to Marxist thought; at 3, had a disease of the hip which left her with a pronounced limp; was one of the co-founders of the Social-Democratic Party of the Kingdom of Poland and Lithuania (SDKPiL, 1898), which would later merge with other left-wing groups to form the Polish Communist Party; became active as a socialist theoretician and served as editor of the influential journal *Sprawa Robotnicza* (The Workers' Cause); also became increasingly involved in activities of German Social-Democratic Party (SPD), becoming a regular contributor to such party newspapers as *Die Neue Zeit;* moved to Germany (1897); to acquire German citizenship (1898), entered marriage of convenience with Gustav Lübeck; launched her famous attack on the "reformist" faction within the party at SPD congress (1898); over next few years, was involved in propaganda work on behalf of SPD, embarking on a series of speaking tours and editing a variety of Polish journals, such as *Gazeta Ludowa* (People's Gazette), *Przeglad Socjaldemokratyczny* (Social-Democratic Review) and *Czerwony Sztandar* (Red Flag); at an international socialist congress, gave a speech attacking the autocratic German emperor, Wilhelm II (1904); arrested by the authorities, sentenced to 3 months in Zwickau prison in Berlin; during imprisonment, wrote *Organizational Questions of Russian Social-Democracy* which criticized the centralizing and authoritarian tendencies of Lenin and the Bolshevik Party; throughout life, consistently rejected Leninist strategy which viewed a minority "vanguard" party as the leader of the revolutionary process; rather, believed that, if socialism were to be achieved, it could only be the result of a spontaneous movement on the part of the vast majority of the working class itself; published what is widely regarded as her most important theoretical work, *The Accumulation of Capital* (1913); denounced militarism and war; as a result, was arrested (1914), tried for sedition, and sentenced to 1 year in prison; published *The Crisis of Social-Democracy* (1916); launched a forceful attack on SPD leadership for its capitulation to militarism; co-founded the International Group (also known as the Spartacus League), hoping to end WWI by fomenting revolution in Germany (1916); designated a "danger to the safety of the Reich," was placed in "protective custody"; returned to Berlin (Nov 10, 1918) and roundly denounced the new SPD government; at a special congress, during which the Spartacus League founded the German Communist Party (KPD), delivered the keynote address in which she laid out the new party's revolutionary manifesto; now perceived as a dangerous enemy to the SPD government, was captured and shot in the head. Her book *The Russian Revolution* was published posthumously (1921). ❖ See also Richard Abraham, *Rosa Luxemburg: A Life for the International* (Berg, 1989); Elzbieta Ettinger, *Rosa Luxemburg* (Beacon, 1986); J.P. Nettl, *Rosa Luxemburg* (2 vols, Oxford U. Press, 1966); Stephen E. Bronner, *Rosa Luxemburg: Revolutionary for Our Times* (1987); *Rosa Luxemburg* (film), directed by Margarethe Von Trotta, starring Barbara Sukowa (1987); and *Women in World History.*

LUXFORD, Nola (1895–1994). New Zealand actress, radio broadcaster, journalist, and literary inspiration. Name variations: Adelaide Minola Pratt, Nola Bauernschmidt, Nola Dolberg. Born on Adelaide Minola Pratt, Dec 23, 1895, at Hunterville, New Zealand; died Oct 10, 1994, in Los Angeles, California; dau. of Ernest Augustus Pratt (draper) and Adelaide Agnes (McGonagle) Pratt (schoolteacher); m. Maurice George Luxford, 1919 (div. 1927); m. William Bauernschmidt, 1927 (div. 1939); m. Glen Russell Dolberg, 1959 (d. 1977). ❖ Traveled to California (early 1920s) and attempted to find work in Hollywood after 2 disastrous marriages; with assistance of Zane Grey, who claimed to have based some of his heroines on Luxford, secured cameo in Harold Lloyd comedy, *Girl Shy* (1924); made successful transition to talkies and worked with Katharine Hepburn, Basil Rathbone, Norma Shearer, Robert Montgomery, George Arliss and Mary Astor; starred in theater group that toured US and Canada; persuaded executives at NBC affiliate in Los Angeles that she do commentary at Olympic Games for New Zealanders and Australians, and her reports were heard throughout North America; wrote popular column for *New Zealand Free Lance* (1929–55); hired by NBC as one of 1st women news announcers (1939); instrumental in establishing ANZAC garden at Rockefeller Center to commemorate Australian and New Zealand war dead; published children's book, *Kerry Kangaroo*. Received OBE and American Award of Merit (1947); Queen's Service Medal (1989). ❖ See also Carole van Grondelle, *Angel of the ANZACs: Life of Nola Luxford* (Victoria University Press); *Dictionary of New Zealand Biography* (Vol. 4).

LUYNES, Antoinette de (fl. 16th c.). *See Loynes, Antoinette de.*

LUYNES, duchess de. *See Rohan-Montbazon, Marie de (1600–1679).*

LUZ, Cintia (1975—). *See dos Santos, Cintia.*

LUZ, Helen (1972—). Brazilian basketball player. Name variations: Helen Cristina Santos Luz. Born Nov 23, 1972, in Araçatuba, Brazil; sister of Cintia Dos Santos and Silvia Luz (both basketball players). ❖ Won a team bronze medal at Sydney Olympics (2000). Awarded MVP of South American championships (2001); joined the WNBA Washington Mystics (2001).

LUZ, Silvia (1975—). Brazilian basketball player. Name variations: Silvia Andrea Santos Luz; Silvia Santos Luz; known as Silvinha. Born Mar 5, 1975, in Araçatuba, Brazil; sister of Cintia Dos Santos and Helen Luz (both basketball players). ❖ Won a team silver medal at Atlanta Olympics (1996) and a team bronze medal at Sydney Olympics (2000).

L.V.F. (1817–1893). *See François, Louise von.*

LWIN, Annabella (1965—). Burmese-born singer. Name variations: Myant Myant Aye; Bow Wow Wow. Born Myant Myant Aye on Oct 31, 1965, in Rangoon, Burma. ❖ Became singer for London group Bow Wow Wow, which included Matthew Ashman, Dave Barbarossa, and Leigh Gorman (1980); recorded solo album *Fever* (1986); with Gorman and 2 new band members, revived Bow Wow Wow (1997), toured US, and released a live-remix album. Albums with Bow Wow Wow include *See Jungle! See Jungle! Go Join Your Gang Yeah! City All Over! Go Ape Crazy!* (1981), *Last of the Mohicans; I Want Candy; 12 Original Recordings* (1982), and *When the Going Gets Tough, the Tough Get Going* (1983).

LYALL, Edna (1857–1903). *See Bayly, Ada Ellen.*

LYALL, Katharine C. (1941—). American economist and educator. Born Katharine Culbert Lyall, April 26, 1941, in Lancaster, PA; dau. of John D. and Eleanor G. Lyall; Cornell University, BA in Economics, 1963, PhD, 1969; New York University, MBA, 1965. ❖ Was an economist at Chase Manhattan Bank in NY (1963–65); was assistant professor of economics at Syracuse University (1969–72); was professor of economics at Johns Hopkins (1972–77), then director of graduate program in pubic policy (1979–81); was deputy assistant secretary for economics at HUD (1977–79); for University of Wisconsin System, Madison, was vice president of academic affairs (1985–86), professor of economics (1982–2004), acting president (1985–86, 1991–92), executive vice president (1986–91), and its 1st woman president (1992–2004).

LYAPINA, Nataliya (1976—). Ukrainian handball player. Born May 14, 1976, in Ukraine. ❖ Won a team bronze medal at Athens Olympics (2004).

LYAPINA, Oksana (1980—). Russian gymnast. Name variations: Oksana Liapina. Born April 28, 1980, in Armavir, Russia. ❖ At Atlanta Olympics, won a silver medal for team all-around (1996); placed 2nd overall at Australian Cup (1996).

LYDIA (fl. 53 CE). Biblical woman. Name variations: Lydia of Thyatira. Born in Thyatira on the border of Lydia in Asia Minor. ❖ A prosperous businesswoman from the city of Thyatira (she sold purple-dyed cloth, for which the city was known), was converted to Christianity by the apostle Paul and is considered the 1st Christian convert in Europe; her story is recorded in Acts. ❖ See also *Women in World History.*

LYE, Mary (c. 1822–1902). *See Hood, Mary.*

LYELL, Lottie (1890–1925). Australian actress, screenwriter, and director. Born Charlotte Edith Cox in Sydney, Australia, Feb 23, 1890; died Dec 21, 1925; dau. of Charlotte Louise (Hancock) Cox and Edward Cox (real-estate agent); m. Raymond Longford, 1925; no children. ❖ Major pioneer in Australia's nascent motion-picture industry, began film career at 21; by the time she died 14 years later, had become Australia's 1st female box-office attraction, having starred in over 20 films; was also Australia's 1st woman screenwriter, and directed, or co-directed, films that are considered classics of the silent era, including *The Fatal Wedding* and *The Romantic Story of Margaret Catchpole* (both 1911), *The Woman Suffers* (1918), *The Sentimental Bloke* (1919), *The Blue Mountains Mystery* (1921) and *The Dinkum Bloke* (1923). ❖ See also *Women in World History.*

LYELL, Mary Horner (1808–1873). British geologist and conchologist. Born Mary Horner in 1808, probably in London, England; died 1873; eldest of 6 daughters of Leonard Horner (geologist); m. Charles Lyell (1797–1875, geologist), in 1832. ❖ Accompanied husband on expeditions in Europe and North America, and, being fluent in German and French, frequently translated scientific papers for him; became an accomplished geologist and conchologist in her own right. ❖ See also *Women in World History*.

LYLES, Anjette (1917–1977). American serial killer. Born 1917; died in Milledgeville, GA, Dec 1977. ❖ Worked as restaurant owner in Cochran, GA, and practiced black magic and voodoo; murdered 4 people with arsenic: her 9-year-old daughter Marcia (1958), 2 husbands (1952 and 1955), and mother-in-law (1957); in highly publicized trial, tried only for death of daughter Marcia and found guilty; though sentenced to death, later found to be insane and sent to State Hospital at Milledgeville, GA, where she died of heart failure at 52.

LYMAN, Mary Ely (1887–1975). American theologian. Name variations: Mary Ely. Born Mary Redington Ely, Nov 24, 1887, in St. Johnsbury, Vermont; died Jan 9, 1975, in Claremont, CA; dau. of Henry Guy Ely (factory manager) and Adelaide (Newell) Ely; Mount Holyoke College (1911); Union Theological Seminary, BD, 1919; attended Cambridge University, 1919–20; University of Chicago, PhD, 1924; m. Eugene W. Lyman (professor, Union Theological Seminary), Feb 13, 1926 (died 1948). ❖ The only woman in her class at Union Theological Seminary, was ranking scholar at graduation; was also the 1st woman to receive a Philadelphia Traveling fellowship (1919); wrote *Paul the Conqueror* (1919), *The Christian Epic* (1936) and *Into All the World* (1956); taught at Vassar College (1920–26), becoming Weyerhauser Professor of Religion (1923); published doctoral dissertation, "The Knowledge of God in the Fourth Gospel," as *Knowledge of God in Johannine Thought* (1925); taught at Barnard College and at Union Theological Seminary (1929–40); was dean and professor of religion at Sweet Briar College, VA (1940–50); worked with World Council of Churches Commission on Life and Work of Women in the Churches (1948–54); ordained as Congregational minister (1949); at Union Theological Seminary, was Morris K. Jessup professor of English Bible and dean of women students (1950–55), the 1st woman to hold faculty chair there, and one of the 1st women to be a full professor at an American seminary; taught at Scripps College (1964–65).

LYMBERAKI, Margaríta (b. 1919). *See Liberáki, Margaríta.*

LYMPANY, Moura (1916–2005). English pianist. Born Mary Gertrude Johnstone in Saltash, Cornwall, England, Aug 18, 1916; died Mar 28, 2005, in Merton, France; studied piano in Belgium and Vienna, and in London with Tobias Matthay and Mathilde Verne; m. Colin Defries, 1944 (div. 1950); m. Bennet Korn (American advertising exec), 1951 (div. 1961). ❖ At 12, debuted with the Mendelssohn G minor Concerto (1938), winning 2nd prize in the Ysaye Competition in Brussels; after WWII, developed an impressive international career; long a champion of contemporary British music, performed Cyril Scott's Piano Concerto on his 90th birthday (1969); her many recordings from the 1950s were re-released as classic performances in the 1990s. Made Commander of the Order of the British Empire (1979).

LYNCH, Anne Charlotte (1815–1891). *See Botta, Anne C.L.*

LYNCH, Caroline (1819–1884). *See Dexter, Caroline.*

LYNCH, Celia (1908–1989). Irish politician. Born Celia Quinn, 1908, in Kinvara, Co. Galway, Ireland; died June 16, 1989; m. Dr. James B. Lynch (TD, Dublin South, 1932–48, senator, 1951–54); children: 2 daughters, 5 sons. ❖ Began career as a teacher in Dublin vocational schools; following death of husband, won a seat as a Fianna Fáil representative to the 15th and 16th Dáil (1954–61) for Dublin South Central; returned to 17th–20th Dáil for Dublin North Central (1961–77); was assistant government whip (1957–73) and assistant Fianna Fáil whip in opposition (1973–77); served on the Consultative Assembly of Council of Europe (1967–69); retired (1977).

LYNCH, Eliza (1835–1886). Irish-born mistress, first lady, and salonnière. Name variations: Elisa; Ella; Eliza Lynch López. Born Eliza Alicia Lynch, possibly in Co. Cork, Ireland, 1835; died in Paris, France, 1886; youngest dau. of John Lynch (medical doctor) and Adelaide (Schnock) Lynch; m. Xavier Quatrefages (French army surgeon), 1850, but sep. shortly before beginning a 17-year liaison with Francisco Solano López, in 1853; children: (with López) 6 sons and 3 daughters, most of whom survived to adulthood, including Juan Francisco (b. 1855); Enrique Venancio (b. 1858); Federico Noel (b. 1860); Carlos Honorio (b. 1861); Leopoldo Antonio (b. 1862); and Miguel Marcial (b. 1866); the daughters' names are not recorded. ❖ Mistress of the dictator Francisco Solano López, who was a major figure in the cultural and

political development of Paraguay; with family, barely survived Irish famine of 1845; married French army doctor (1850), who deserted her in Paris (1853); took a succession of lovers before meeting López several months later; returned with him to Paraguay (1854) to live openly with him as his mistress; though never accepted by elite society in Asunción, as the lover of the son of the Paraguayan president, was nonetheless very influential: introduced the 1st pianos and sewing machines to Paraguayan society, was the leading force behind the construction of many public buildings, and helped improve the educational establishment of the country, especially after López assumed the presidency (1862); as de facto first lady, became the dominant force in Paraguayan cultural matters; as Paraguay entered a disastrous war against Argentina, Brazil, and Uruguay, joined López at the front (1864), and, according to some sources, actually commanded troops; 5 years later, accompanied what remained of the Paraguayan army as it retreated into the northern jungles; witnessed López's death in battle and buried him and their first-born son herself on the banks of the Aquidaban River (1870); at end of war, was deported, losing most of her wealth; spent rest of her life unsuccessfully trying to reclaim her lost properties in Paraguay. ❖ See also Alyn Brodsky, *Madame Lynch and Friend* (Harper & Row, 1975); and *Women in World History*.

LYNCH, Elizabeth (1964—). *See McColgan-Lynch, Elizabeth.*

LYNCH, Gladys (1930–2003). *See Daniels, Maxine.*

LYNCH, Kathleen (1953—). Irish politician. Born 1953 in Cork, Ireland; m. Bernard Lynch. ❖ Joined Worker's Party (1984); was a founding member of the Democratic Left following a split with the Worker's Party; representing Democratic Left, elected to the 27th Dáil in a by-election (1994–97) for Cork North Central; returned to 29th Dáil (2002).

LYNCH, Laura (1958—). American musician. Name variations: Dixie Chicks. Born Nov 18, 1958, in Dell City, TX. ❖ Became original member of country-music group Dixie Chicks (formed 1989 in Dallas, TX); served as vocalist and played bass and guitar; with Dixie Chicks, made Grand Ole Opry debut (1991) and performed at President Bill Clinton's inauguration (1993); left group (1995). Albums with Dixie Chicks include *Thank Heavens for Dale Evans* (1990), *Little Ol' Cowgirl* (1992), and *Shouldn't a Told You That* (1993).

LYNCH, Madame (1835–1886). *See Lynch, Eliza.*

LYNCH, Margaret (fl. 1867–1868). New Zealand domestic servant. Fl. between 1867 and 1868. ❖ Probably sent to New Zealand as part of government scheme to address domestic servant shortage (1860s); employed by Catherine Hale, who dismissed Lynch and falsely charged her with larceny after she demanded unpaid wages; sentenced to 1 month's hard labor until public petition demanded her release, and Hale was charged with assault and ordered to apologize; was issued full pardon (1868). ❖ See also *Dictionary of New Zealand Biography* (Vol. 1).

LYNCH, Marta (1925–1985). *See Frigerio, Marta Lía.*

LYNCH, Susan Akin (c. 1964—). *See Akin, Susan.*

LYNES, Sally (1773–1842). *See Grubb, Sarah Lynes.*

LYNGSTAD, Frida (1945—). Member of Swedish singing group ABBA. Name variations: Anni-Frid Lyngstad-Fredriksson. Born Anni-Frid Synni Lyngstad in Norway, near Narvik, Nov 15, 1945; m. Ragnar Fredriksson (bass player); m. Benny Andersson, 1978 (div. 1981); children: (1st m.) 2. ❖ Sang with Bengt Sandlund's jazz group; formed own band, the Anni-Frid Four (c. 1964); married fellow band member Ragnar Frederiksson; awarded solo recording contract; with Agnetha Fältskog, Benny Andersson, and Björn Ulvaeus, formed singing group ABBA (acronym of their 1st initials); gained international renown with group when "Waterloo" won Eurovision Song Contest (1974); with ABBA, had more than a dozen Top-40 hits in US, including "Dancing Queen," "Knowing Me, Knowing You," and "Fernando," before split up (1982); recorded solo albums *Something's Going On* (1982) and *Shine* (1984). ❖ See also *ABBA—The Movie*, produced in Australia by Stig Anderson and Reg Grundy; and *Women in World History*.

LYNN, Barbara (1942—). American R&B singer, songwriter and guitarist. Born Barbara Lynn Ozen, Jan 16, 1942, in Beaumont, Texas; children: 3, including Bachelor Wise (musician). ❖ Left-handed guitar player, dubbed "Empress of Gulf Coast Soul," began playing piano at young age; took up guitar as teenager and formed all-female band, Bobbie Lynn and the Idols; met producer Huey P. Meaux, who subsequently produced all of her records; moved to Louisiana with Meaux and scored 1st big hit with New Orleans-style standard "You'll Lose a Good Thing" (1962), based on her poem; had continued success with "You're Gonna Need Me" (1963) and "It's Better to Have It" (1965); signed with Meaux's Tribe label (1966), releasing album *The Barbara Lynn Story* (1967); switched to Atlantic Records and had better success with "This Is the Thanks I Get" (1968) and "Until Then I'll Suffer" (1971); wrote "Oh! Baby (We Got a Good Thing Goin')", which was later covered by Rolling Stones; toured with B.B. King, Gladys Knight, Stevie Wonder, Smokey Robinson, Dionne Warwick, Sam Cooke, James Brown, Ike and Tina Turner, among others; retired from music business (mid-1960s); released albums *Good Thing, Good Thing* (1989), *So Good* (1994), *Until Then I'll Suffer* (1996) and *Hot Night Tonight* (2000), featuring Ivan Neville, Bernard Fowler, Daryl Jones and son, Bachelor Wise.

LYNN, Bonnie (1944—). See Bramlett, Bonnie.

LYNN, Diana (1926–1971). American actress and pianist. Name variations: performed briefly as Dolly Loehr. Born Delores Loehr, Oct 7, 1926, in Los Angeles, CA; died in Los Angeles, Dec 18, 1971; only dau. of Louis Loehr (oil co. executive); educated on Paramount Studio lot; m. John C. Lindsay (architect), Jan 5, 1948 (div. 1953); m. Mortimer Hall; children: 4. ❖ A musical prodigy, began playing piano professionally at 10 and performed in 2 films, *They Shall Have Music* (1939) and *There's Magic in Music* (1941), though she was given little dialogue; signed long-term contract with Paramount (1941); made acting debut in *The Major and the Minor* (1942), followed by *The Miracle of Morgan's Creek* (1944), which led to a string of "kid sister" and young adult roles, the best of which was Emily in *Our Hearts Were Young And Gay* (1944); other films include *And the Angels Sing* (1944), *Henry Aldrich Plays Cupid* (1944), *My Friend Irma* (1949), *Peggy* (1950), *Bedtime for Bonzo* (1951) and *Meet Me at the Fair* (1953); as film career waned, turned to the stage, performing in stock and with La Jolla Players; appeared opposite Maurice Evans in NY City Center's production of *The Wild Duck* (1952) and opposite Sir Cedric Hardwicke in *Horses in Midstream* (1953); also made regular tv appearances. ❖ See also *Women in World History.*

LYNN, Eliza (1822–1898). See Linton, Eliza Lynn.

LYNN, Elizabeth A. (1946—). American science-fiction writer. Born June 8, 1946, New York, NY. ❖ Was public school teacher in Chicago and teacher in Women's Studies Program at San Francisco State University; works include *A Different Light* (1978), *Watchtower* (1979), *The Dancers of Arun* (1979), *The Northern Girl* (1981), *The Sardonyx Net* (1981), *The Red Hawk* (1983), *The Silver Horse* (1984), and *Dragon's Winter* (1998); also wrote short-story collection *The Woman Who Loved the Moon* (1981). Won World Fantasy Award (1980) and James Tiptree Jr. Award (1995).

LYNN, Ethel (1827–1879). See Beers, Ethel Lynn.

LYNN, Janet (1953—). American figure skater. Born Janet Lynn Nowicki, April 6, 1953, in Chicago, IL; attended Rockford College, 1972. ❖ At 14, made US Olympic team (1968); won US National championship (1969, 1970, 1971, 1972, 1973); won a bronze medal at Sapporo Olympics (1972); was a silver medalist at the World figure-skating championships (1973); obtained a 3-year contract for $1.4 million with Shipstad and Johnson Ice Follies, becoming the highest paid woman athlete at that time. ❖ See also *Women in World History.*

LYNN, Kathleen (1874–1955). Irish doctor and political activist. Born Kathleen Florence Lynn in Mullafany, Co. Mayo, Ireland, Jan 28, 1874; died in Dublin, Ireland, Sept 14, 1955; dau. of Reverend Robert Young Lynn and Catherine (Wynne) Lynn; educated at Alexandra College, Dublin; studied medicine at Royal University of Ireland and Royal College of Surgeons of Ireland, 1894–99. ❖ The most brilliant student in her class at Royal College of Surgeons, encountered the widespread prejudice against women doctors upon graduation; took up short-term appointments in Dublin at Eye and Ear Hospital, Sir Patrick Dun's, and Rotunda maternity hospital, before commencing private practice; was drawn into politics through suffrage movement and her concern for poverty; during employers' lock-out of Dublin workers (1913), helped Irish Citizen Army which had been set up to defend the workers; became involved in women's section of ICA and in Cumann na mBan, the women's auxiliary of the Irish Volunteers; subsequently became chief medical officer of ICA and was aware of the preparations being made for a rebellion in Dublin; on Easter Monday (1916), tended the wounded at Dublin Castle until the small garrison surrendered; was taken to Kilmainham Jail and then to Mountjoy Jail before being released; elected

to the executive of the Sinn Fein (1917); spoke out strongly on the subject of equality, a message many men in Sinn Fein were reluctant to hear; took part in the campaign opposing the imposition of conscription in Ireland (1918); as a Sinn Fein candidate, was elected to her local council in Dublin (1920); opposed as inadequate the terms of the treaty which gave independence to Ireland and took the republican side in the civil war (1922); was elected Sinn Fein member for Dublin Co. in the new Irish Parliament (1923) but did not take her seat; also co-founded St. Ultan's Children's Hospital (1919). ❖ See also *Women in World History.*

LYNN, Loretta (1935—). American country-music singer. Born Loretta Webb, April 14, 1935, in Butcher Hollow, KY; sister of Crystal Gayle (b. 1951, singer); m. Oliver Vanetta "Mooney" Lynn, 1948 (died 1996); children: 6, including (twins) Patsy and Peggy Lynn, who released their debut album *The Lynns* (1998). ❖ Married at 13, had 4 children by 17; encouraged to sing by husband as a way to earn money, began performing in small clubs and at agricultural fairs; made a demo of her song "Honky-Tonk Girl" (1960), driving cross-country to promote it ("Honky-Tonk Girl" reached #14 on Billboard's national charts); followed that with "You Ain't Woman Enough to Take My Man" and "Don't Come Home A-Drinkin (With Lovin' on Your Mind)"; made 1st appearance at Grand Ol' Opry (1960); signed by Decca Records, for which she recorded "Fool Number One" and her 1st #1 hit "Success" (1962); became the most popular female country star in US with a string of hits that appealed to working-class women; had cross-over hits with "Blue Kentucky Girl," "Somebody, Somewhere" and her signature, "Coal Miner's Daughter," helping to make country music a mass-market phenomenon; became an unlikely heroine of the feminist movement with such songs as "The Pill" and "We've Come a Long Way, Baby"; recorded album "We're Still Honky-Tonking" (1998). Named Billboard's Top Female Vocalist (1964, 1973); became 1st woman to receive the Country Music Association's Entertainer of the Year Award (1972) and won Academy of Country Music's prestigious Entertainer of the Year award (1975); honored at Kennedy Center (2003). ❖ See also autobiography (with George Vecsey) *Coal Miner's Daughter* (Regnery, 1980) and film *Coal Miner's Daughter,* starring Sissy Spacek (Universal, 1980); and *Women in World History.*

LYNN, Sharon (1901–1963). American actress. Born April 9, 1901, in Weatherford, TX; died May 26, 1963, in Hollywood, CA; m. John Sirshen. ❖ Star of 1930s, films include *Clancy's Kosher Wedding, Give and Take, Speakeasy, Fox Movietone Follies of 1929, Sunny Side Up, Lightnin', The Big Broadcast* and *Way Out West.*

LYNN, Vera (1917—). English popular singer. Name variations: Dame Vera Lynn; Mrs. Harry Lewis. Born Vera Margaret Welch, Mar 20, 1917; m. Harry Lewis (clarinetist and tenor saxophonist), 1941; children: Virginia Lewis (b. 1946). ❖ One of the most beloved singers in England during WWII, gave 1st performance at a workingmen's club at age 7 (1924); made 1st radio broadcast, with Joe Loss Band (1935); joined Charlie Kunz's Casani Club Band (1935); signed with Crown Records (1935), which was purchased by Decca (1938); sang with Ambrose Orchestra, the most popular "big band" in Britain (1937–40); had own BBC radio program "Sincerely Yours" (1941–47), in which she played record requests and sang songs of her own, including "It's a Lovely Day Tomorrow," "Wish Me Luck," "Yours," "Smilin' Through," "When They Sound the Last All Clear," "We'll Meet Again" (the most popular song in Britain in 1941), and "The White Cliffs of Dover"; starred in *Applesauce* at London Palladium (1941); filmed *We'll Meet Again* (1942), *Rhythm Serenade* (1943) and *One Exciting Night* (1944); entertained British troops in Burma and elsewhere (1944–45); recording of "You Can't Be True, Dear" made American hit parade (1948); achieved the same success the following year with "Again"; was a regular on Tallulah Bankhead's US radio program *The Big Show* (1951); recorded "Aufwiederseh'n" (1952) which sold over 12 million copies and made her the 1st British artist to top the US hit parade (1952); had 14 gold records. Awarded Order of the British Empire (OBE, 1969) and Dame of the British Empire (DBE, 1975); granted honorary Doctor of Letters from University of Newfoundland, Canada, where she established the Lynn Musical Scholarship (1978); awarded Commander of the Order of Orange-Nassau (1985); awarded Burma Star (1985). ❖ See also autobiographies *Vocal Refrain* (1975) and *We'll Meet Again* (1989); and *Women in World History.*

LYNNE, Elizabeth (1948—). English actess and politician. Born Jan 22, 1948, in Woking, Surrey, England. ❖ Was an actress (1966–89) and speech consultant (1988–92, 1997–99); as a Liberal Democrat, served as Member of Parliament from Rochdale (1992–97); as a member of the

European Liberal, Democrat and Reform Party, elected to 5th European Parliament (1999–2004) from UK.

LYNNE, Gillian (1926—). British singer, actress, choreographer and director. Born Gillian Barbara Pyrke, Feb 20, 1926, in Bromley, Kent, England; m. Patrick Back, 1949 (div.); m. Peter Land (actor-singer), 1980. ❖ Was principal soloist at Royal Ballet (1944–51), where she danced in premieres of Helpmann's *Adam Zero* (1946), and Ashton's *Les Sirènes* (1946), *Don Juan* (1948) and *Daphnis and Chloe* (1951), among others; performed on London's West End in *Can-Can* (1954), *Becky Sharp* (1955) and *New Cranks* (1960); created dance *Collages* for Edinburgh Festival and went on to choreograph shows on Broadway for David Merrick; choreographed and staged many West End shows, including *Cats, Phantom of the Opera, Aspects of Love* and *Cabaret;* for film, choreographed for *Wonderful Life, Mister Ten Per Cent, Half a Sixpence, The Old Curiosity Shop, Man of La Mancha* and *Yentl.* Won BAFTA award for direction for *A Simple Man* (1987); received Laurence Olivier Theatre Award for Outstanding Achievement in Musicals for *Cats* (1982) and nominated for same award for *Dick Whittington* (1999); made CBE (1997).

LYON, Annabelle (c. 1915—). American ballet dancer. Born Jan 8, c. 1915, in New York, NY; trained with Mikhail Fokine and Alexandra Fedorova. ❖ Performed with Fokine Ballet in *Les Sylphides* and *Schéhérézade* (1934); joined Balanchine's 1st US company—American Ballet—and danced in *Serenade* (1934), *Reminiscence* (1935), *The Card Party* (1937), among others; as member of Ballet Caravan danced in premieres of Eugene Loring's *Harlequin for President* (1936), William Dollar's *Promenade* (1936), and Douglas Coudy's *The Soldier and the Gypsy* (1936); danced in Ballet Theater (early 1940s), creating role in Tudor's *Pillar of Fire* (1942); appeared on Broadway in Agnes de Mille's *Allegro* (1947) and *Carousel* (1948), just before retiring.

LYON, Barbara (1940—). *See Mills, Barbara.*

LYON, Bebe (1901–1971). *See Daniels, Bebe.*

LYON, Elizabeth Bowes- (b. 1900). *See Elizabeth Bowes-Lyon.*

LYON, Genevieve (c. 1893–1916). American interpretative ballroom dancer. Born c. 1893 in Chicago, IL; died 1916 in Denver, CO; m. John Murray Anderson (dancer), 1914. ❖ Worked as model for numerous artists throughout Chicago and New York City before becoming an interpretative dancer; made performance debut in *Daughters of Dawn* (1912); performed in *The Count of Luxemburg* (1912) and *Varieties* (1913) on Broadway; toured as ballroom dancer with husband (1914); forced to abandon career after contracting tuberculosis (1914), having to move to Southwest; died at age 23.

LYON, Mary (1797–1849). American founder and educator. Born Mary Mason Lyon in Buckland, MA, Feb 28, 1797; died Mar 5, 1849; buried on the campus of Mt. Holyoke College; dau. of Aaron Lyon (Revolutionary War veteran) and Jemima (Shepard) Lyon; attended Sanderson Academy, Amherst Academy, and Byfield Female Seminary; never married; no children. ❖ The founder of Mt. Holyoke Seminary, an innovation in higher education for women because of its commitment to educating women from all economic circumstances, started teaching in summer schools (1814); attended academies and Emerson's Ladies Seminary interspersed with continued teaching primarily at Sanderson Academy; opened a girls' school in Buckland (1824); taught summers at Ipswich Female Seminary; attended lectures by Amos Eaton at Amherst College; circulated a plan for a female seminary (1834), then raised money; obtained a charter for Mt. Holyoke Seminary (1836); opened it (Nov 1837) and taught chemistry there; of the early American pioneers of women's higher education, was the most imbued with intense religious convictions, and her successful labors on behalf of women's education were virtually a religious crusade. ❖ See also Elizabeth Alden Green, *Mary Lyon and Mount Holyoke: Opening the Gates* (U. Press of New England, 1979); and *Women in World History.*

LYON, Mary Frances (1925—). English geneticist. Born May 15, 1925, in Norwich, England; Girton College, BA, 1946, PhD (1950), ScD (1968). ❖ Noted geneticist, especially for research regarding X-chromosome inactivation in mammals (also known as "the Lyon hypothesis"), served at the Medical Research Council (MRC) as a member of the Institute of Animal Genetics scientific staff in Edinburgh (1950–55), as a member of Radiobiology Unit in Harwell, Oxfordshire (1955–90), as head of the Genetics Division (1962–87) and as MRC deputy director (1982–90); became a Royal Society fellow (1973), US National Academy of Sciences foreign associate (1979), American Academy of Arts and Science foreign

honorary member (1980),. Received Royal Society's Gold Medal (1984), San Remo (Italy) Prize for Genetics (1985), Gairdner Foundation Award (1985), American Society for Human Genetics' Allan Award (1986) and Wolf Prize for Medicine (1996).

LYONS, Beatrice (1930—). Australian swimmer. Born Oct 1930. ❖ At London Olympics, won a silver medal in the 200-meter breaststroke (1948).

LYONS, Delphine C. (1922–2000). *See Smith, Evelyn E.*

LYONS, Enid (1897–1981). Australian politician and newspaper columnist. Name variations: Dame Enid Lyons. Born Enid Muriel Burnell, July 9, 1897, in Tasmania; died Sept 2, 1981; dau. of William Burnell (sawyer) and Eliza (Tagget) Burnell; attended Stowport and Burnie State Schools and Hobart Teachers' College; m. Joseph Aloysius Lyons (1879–1939), politician and prime minister of Australia, 1932–39); children: 12 (one of whom died in infancy). ❖ Was a valued political partner for husband; between confinements, accompanied him to state and federal Labor conferences and even ran for a contested seat in the 1925 election, losing by 60 votes; when husband was prime minister (1932–39), was invaluable in securing support among women constituents; a women's rights advocate and skilled speaker, addressed women's associations and conferences around Australia; when husband died (1939), retired; returned to politics (1943), winning the election for the Tasmanian seat of Darwin which had been vacated by a retirement, becoming the 1st woman member of the federal Parliament, and later the 1st woman to hold ministerial office; retired from politics (1951) for health reasons; chaired the Jubilee Women's Convention (1951) and served as a member of the Australian Broadcasting Commission (1951–62); worked as a columnist for the *Sun* (1951–54) and *Woman's Day* (1951–52), and wrote 3 books: an autobiography, *So We Take Comfort* (1965), a volume of political reminiscences, *Among the Carrion Crows* (1972), and a book of short essays and sketches, *The Old Haggis* (1969). Awarded Order of Australia (1980). ❖ See also *Women in World History.*

LYONS, Sophie (1848–1924). American swindler and society columnist. Name variations: Sophie Lyons Burke. Born Sophie Levy, Dec 24, 1848, in NY City; died of a brain hemorrhage, May 8, 1924, after being beaten by thieves in Detroit, MI; dau. of Sam Levy and Sophie Elkins (alias); m. Maury Harris (pickpocket), 1865; m. Ned Lyons (bank robber, sep. and reunited); m. Billy Burke (thief); children: (2nd m.) George Lyons (b. 1870); Florence Lyons; Esther Lyons; and one other son. ❖ Dubbed the "Queen of Crime" by NY City chief of police (1880s), lived a life that encompassed both sides of the law; was 1st arrested (1859); sent to Sing Sing prison for 5 years for stealing (1871); escaped and fled to Canada with Ned Lyons (1872); caught pickpocketing and returned to Sing Sing (1876); became 1st American society columnist, for the *New York World* (1897); published booklets on criminal reform; established a home for children with imprisoned parents in Detroit. ❖ See also *Women in World History.*

LYRA, Carmen (1888–1949). *See Carvajal, María Isabel.*

LYSANDRA (fl. 300 BCE). Macedonian princess. Dau. of Ptolemy I Soter and Eurydice (fl. 321 BCE); sister of Ptolemais; full sister of Ceraunus; m. Agathocles.

LYSENKO, Tatiana (1975—). Soviet gymnast. Name variations: Tatyana Lysenko. Born June 23, 1975, in Kherson, Ukraine. ❖ Won the World Cup (1990); won a team gold medal at the World championships (1991); at Barcelona Olympics, won a bronze medal in the vault and gold medals in balance beam and team all-around (1992); placed 3rd all-around at World championships, Arthur Gander Memorial, Birmingham Classic, and Soapberry Challenge (1993); moved to US.

LYSENKO, Vera (1910–1975). *See Lesik, Vera.*

LYTLE, Nancy A. (1924–1987). American nurse. Born Oct 14, 1924, in Fredericksburg, Ohio; died from cancer, Aug 24, 1987, in Cleveland, Ohio; dau. of Bertha G. and George B. Lytle; graduate of Fairview Park Hospital School of Nursing in Cleveland, 1945; University of Pittsburgh, degree in nursing, 1948; Columbia University Teachers College, MA, 1954, doctorate in nursing education, 1968. ❖ Maternity nursing specialist and creator of a maternity nursing graduate program with innovative instruction techniques, 1st worked as a Western Pennsylvania Hospital obstetrics supervisor; was assistant obstetrical nursing professor at Ohio State University (1953–57); became a maternity nursing director at University Hospitals and a nursing professor at Case Western Reserve University's Frances Payne Bolton School of Nursing in Cleveland, Ohio, where she formed a program to encourage greater active participation from fathers during the birthing experience (1969); served as professor (1971–87), director (1971–87) and chair (1973–87) of University Hospitals' maternity and gynecological nursing; served as consultant to Department of Health for Virgin Islands and the state of Ohio.

LYTTELTON, Edith (1865–1948). English activist and playwright. Name variations: Dame Edith Lyttelton. Born Edith Balfour, 1865, in England; died Sept 2, 1948; dau. of Archibald Balfour; m. Hon. Alfred Lyttelton, MP, 1892; children: Oliver Lyttelton. ❖ Served on committees for intellectual cooperation, Stratford Memorial Theatre, women's employment, war refugees, and waste reclamation; was president of the Society for Psychical Research (1933–34) and substitute delegate to League of Nations Assembly (1923, 1926–28, 1931); wrote biographies of her husband, as well as *Our Superconscious Mind* and *Some Cases of Prediction* and such plays as *Warp and Woof, The Macleans of Bairness, The Thumbscrew* and *Peter's Chance.* Made Dame Commander of the Order of the British Empire (DBE).

LYTTELTON, Edith Joan (1873–1945). Tasmanian-born novelist and short story writer. Name variations: (pseudonyms) Keron Hale and G.B. Lancaster. Born Edith Joan Lyttelton, Dec 18, 1873, at the family sheep station at Epping, northern Tasmania; died Mar 10, 1945, in a London nursing home; dau. of Emily Wood and Westcote McNab Lyttelton; m. Hon. Alfred Lyttelton. ❖ Immigrated with family to New Zealand (c. 1879); began to publish stories in magazines but, forbidden to use her own name, settled on G.B. Lancaster for all writings; became widely known in Australasia as a prolific writer of short stories; left New Zealand with mother and sister for London (1908); often wrote family sagas, focusing on a particular region; author of *Pageant, The Tracks We Tread, A Spur to Smite, Jim of the Ranges, The Honorable Peggy, The World is Yours, The Law-Bringers, Promenade, Fool Divine* and *Grand Parade;* during WWI and WWII, was deeply involved in soldier support organizations. ❖ See also F.A. de la Mare, *G.B. Lancaster* (Hamilton, 1945).

LYTTLETON, Lucy (1841–1925). See *Cavendish, Lucy Caroline.*

LYTTON, Constance (1869–1923). English militant suffragist. Name variations: Lady Constance Lytton; Constance Bulwer-Lytton. Born Constance Georgina Lytton in Vienna, Austria, Feb 12, 1869; died May 22, 1923; 3rd child of (Edward) Robert Bulwer Lytton, 1st earl of Lytton (1831–1891, author and viceroy of India) and Lady Edith Villiers Lytton; sister of Betty Balfour (1867–1942) and Emily Lytton (1874–1964); granddau. of Rosina Bulwer-Lytton; aunt of Elisabeth Lutyens (1906–1983); never married. ❖ Joined the Women's Social and Political Union (WSPU); though arrested numerous times and imprisoned, was always released because of her health and her family's illustrious history; in an effort to thwart preferred treatment (1911), disguised herself as a seamstress named Jane Wharton, then protested forced feeding at a prison in Liverpool; arrested, was forcibly fed 7 times while in prison, becoming so ill that she eventually had a stroke, becoming a permanent invalid; turned her rebellion to writing, offering *Prisons and Prisoners: Some Personal Experiences by C. Lytton and Jane Wharton, Spinster* (1914). ❖ See also *Women in World History.*

LYTTON, Elizabeth (1867–1942). See *Balfour, Betty.*

LYTTON, Emily (1874–1964). English theosophist. Name variations: Emily Bulwer-Lytton; Lady Emily Lutyens. Born Dec 26, 1874, in England; died 1964; dau. of (Edward) Robert Bulwer Lytton, 1st earl of Lytton (1831–1891, author and viceroy of India) and Lady Edith Villiers Lytton; sister of Betty Balfour (1867–1942) and Constance Lytton (1869–1923); m. Sir Edwin Landseer Lutyens (architect), 1897; children: Barbara Lutyens, Robert Lutyens, Ursula Lutyens, Elisabeth Lutyens (composer, 1906–1983) and Mary Lutyens (novelist and biographer, 1908–1999). ❖ A theosophist, was a disciple of Annie Besant and sponsored spiritual philosopher Jiddu Krishnamurti for 10 years; wrote *Candles in the Sun* (1957). ❖ See also Jane Ridley, *The Architect and His Wife: A Life of Edwin Lutyens.*

LYTTON, Lady Rosina Bulwer- (1802–1882). See *Bulwer-Lytton, Rosina.*

LYUBIMOVA, Nadezhda (1959—). Soviet rower. Born Dec 28, 1959, in USSR. ❖ At Moscow Olympics, won a silver medal in quadruple sculls with coxswain (1980).

LYUDMILLA. *Variant of Ludmila.*

LYUKHINA, Tamara (1939—). Soviet gymnast. Born May 11, 1939, in Russia. ❖ At Rome Olympics, won a bronze medal in uneven bars, bronze medal in floor exercises, and gold medal in team all-around (1960); at Tokyo Olympics, won a gold medal in team all-around (1964).